# The Book of
# 101
# Opera Librettos

# The Book of 101 Opera Librettos

### COMPLETE ORIGINAL LANGUAGE TEXTS
### WITH ENGLISH TRANSLATIONS

Edited by
Jessica M. MacMurray

With plot summaries by
Allison Brewster Franzetti

NEW YORK

Published by

**Black Dog & Leventhal Publishers, Inc.**
151 W. 19th Street
New York, New York 10011

Distributed by

**Workman Publishing Company**
708 Broadway
New York, New York 10003

Typesetting by ATLIS Publishing Services

Printed and bound in the United States of America

ISBN: 1-884822-79-7

h g f e

**Library of Congress Cataloging-in-Publication data**

The book of 101 opera librettos : complete original language texts
  with English translations.
      p.  cm.
   ISBN 1-884822-79-7
   1.  Operas–Librettos.
 ML48.B66  1996 <Case>
 782.1'0268–dc20

96-32543
CIP
MN

The Editor wishes to thank: The Metropolitan Opera, The Clara Damrosch Library at the Mannes School of Music, and EMI records; Janet Bookspan, David Foil, Rob LaPorta and Deborah Davis for their insight and willingness to help; Stephanie Fleischman, Claire Maher, Terri Leager, Ted Goodman, Katharine Chibnik, Joe Arsenault, Natasha Steinhardt & Sarah Vyden for their efforts on this unique and challenging project; and most especially: J.P. Leventhal, Pamela Horn and Tim Stauffer for their wisdom and support.

# FOREWORD

"The poetry is primary, the music should illustrate it and color it and emphasize the meaning without interrupting the action or weakening it by superfluous ornament. It is much the same as the relation of harmonious color, well disposed light and shade to accurate drawing, which should animate the figures without altering the outines."—Cristoph Willibald Gluck, 1767

Even in 1767, it was clear that the relationship between poetry and music in opera is a crucial one: to balance, illuminate and characterize one another. Very often, the literary richness of opera is lost in the genius of its musical content. This volume was compiled to celebrate the poetry, the drama and the history of the operatic genre.

Throughout its long and varied history, opera has played various social, political and artistic roles. The librettos themselves modulate from the sublime to the ridiculous, exploring fantasy, politics, religion, secular life, love and death. Operas have been written for librettos based on Greek mythology, biblical stories, political events and fairy tales. While all of the following operas are currently performed for audiences of similar natures and tastes, with a wide level of social and artistic acceptance, it is important to recognize that the poetry and stories have been performed and received in a variety of contexts. For instance, Beaumarchais' controversial *La Nozze di Figaro,* adapted for the opera by Mozart and Da Ponte, was banned in France in the late 1700's due to the then-scathing criticism of the aristocracy. Whether they follow in the steps of the popular *commedia del arte* Italian style seen in Leoncavallo's *I Pagliacci,* which laid the foundations for the mime tradition in France, or in Monteverdi's courtly and formal manner seen in *L'Incoronazione di Poppea,* part of the first cornerstones of modern operatic form, these librettos serve not only as extraordinary literary and musical accomplishments, but also as instruments in the understanding of history.

The following librettos also serve as a tool to enhance the operatic experience for the student, the historian and the opera buff. The enjoyment of opera as an art form is incomplete without the poetic experience; it is unfulfilled without a deep grasp of the story that is illustrated in the libretto and brought to life in the score. In Wagnerian opera, especially, where the complexities of character and plot are sometimes virtually undecipherable, the ability to clarify the plotlines frees the listener to enjoy the music without confusion.

Never before has such a collection been compiled: it is now possible to explore the beauty and intricacies of the poetic side of opera in a more complete way than ever before. It is the hope that opera lovers may see the outlines and further appreciate the harmony within the rich and historical operatic tradition.

–J.M.M

# Table of Contents

# Fidelio (1805)

### Music by Ludwig Van Beethoven

Libretto by Josef Sonnleithner, based on French libretto by Jean Nicolas Bouilly; Sonnleithner's Libretto was revised by Stefan von Breuning in 1806 & by Georg Friedrich Treitschke in 1814

---

This lyric two-act opera, set to a libretto by Josef Sonnleithner (after Jean-Nicolas Bouilly's *Léonore, ou L'Amour conjugal* for Gaveaux) was first performed at the Theater an der Wien in Vienna on November 20, 1805. The story begins at a state prison near Seville during the eighteenth century. Leonora, disguised as a youth named Fidelio, is working as an assistant to Rocco, the chief jailer, so as to find out where her husband, Florestan, is imprisoned. Florestan disappeared two years' prior - a rumor spread that he died, but he is actually being held by Don Pizarro, the prison governor, which Leonora suspects. Marcellina, the daughter of Don Pizarro, is in love with Fidelio. Don Pizarro, pleased with his assistant, promises that Marcellina and Fidelio will be married. Fidelio asks that "he" be permitted to assist Rocco more; Rocco agrees, stating that Fidelio must not visit the prisoner held in the dungeon for the past two years. Don Pizarro is given anonymous warning that Don Fernando, the Minister of State, plans to make a surprise inspection of the prison on the following day. He plans to murder Florestan, but Rocco will not kill him and will only agree to dig his grave. Fidelio overhears this plot, and when Pizarro departs "he" reminds Rocco that this is the day when the prisoners come out for a brief walk in the fresh air. Rocco tells "him" that Pizarro has agreed to the wedding of Fidelio and Marcellina and that "he" may come with him to the dungeon to dig the grave. Pizarro re-enters and objects to the prisoners being allowed out, but Rocco replies that this was in celebration of the King's birthday. The prisoners return to their cells, and Fidelio and Rocco go down to the dungeon. Florestan, starving and ill, thinks he hears Leonora calling him from heaven. Fidelio and Rocco begin to dig the grave. Leonora resolves not to let the prisoner be killed (she doesn't yet know it is her husband); when she gives him food she recognizes him. Florestan implores Rocco to give a message to his wife that he is alive, which Rocco refuses to do, and Lenora tries to calm him. Pizarro enters, prepared to stab Florestan. Leonora reveals herself and threatens him with a gun. A trumpet announces the arrival of Don Fernando, and Pizarro must greet him. Fernando promises to free all of those unjustly imprisoned and is shocked to discover Florestan, whom he thought to be dead, alive before him. When he is told the truth, Pizarro is arrested, Leonora frees her husband and all celebrate the fortunate outcome.

---

## ◼ ERSTER AKT

### ERSTE SCENE

(Hof eines Staatsgefängnisses. Im Hintergrunde das Hauptlager und eine hohe Mauer, über welche sich Bäume erheben. In dem Thor, welches verschlossen ist, eine kleine Pforte. Links an dem Thore das Wachthaus des Gefängnisswärters. Die Seitencoulissen stellen die Wohnungen der Gefangenen dar. Die Fenster sind vergittert und die mit Nummern versehenen Thüren stark verriegelt. Links die Thüre zur Wohnung des Schliessers. Rechts Thüren, um welche ein eisernes Gitter sich zieht, und welche den Eingang zum Gefängnissgarten sehen lassen. Marcelline bügelt Wäsche nahe der Thür. Rechts eine eiserne Kohlenpfanne, auf welcher sie die Eisen heiss macht. Jacquino in ihrer Nähe, öffnet Personen, welche ihm Packete von Briefen geben, die er in das Wachthäuschen trägt.)

**JACQUINO:** Jetzt, Schätzchen, sind wir allein, wir können vertraulich nun plaudern.

**MARCELLINE:** Es wird ja nichts Wichtiges sein, ich darf bei der Arbeit nicht zaudern.

**JACQUINO:** Ein Wörtchen, du Trotzige! du —

**MARCELLINE:** So sprich nur, ich höre ja zu.

**JACQUINO:** Wenn du mir nicht freundlicher blickest, so bring' ich kein Wörtchen hervor.

**MARCELLINE:** Wenn du dich nicht in mich schickest, verstopf' ich mir vollends das Ohr.

**JACQUINO:** Ein Weilchen nur höre mir zu.

**MARCELLINE:** So hab' ich denn nimmermehr Ruh'.

**JACQUINO:** Dann lass ich dich wieder in Run', ich, ich habe, ich habe zum Weibe dich gewählet, verstehst du?

## ◼ ACT I

### SCENE I

(The Court Yard of a State Prison. In the back ground the principal gate, and a high rampart wall, over which trees are seen branching out. In the gate, which is closed, there is a little door for foot-passengers. At the side of the gate is the gate-keeper's lodge. The side scenes on the left (of the spectators) present the dwelling of the prisoners. All the windows are grated; and the doors, which are marked with numbers, are strongly bolted. At the foremost wing (a side scene) is the door of the residence of the Turnkey. On the right stand trees, inclosed within iron railings; which together with a garden gate, point out the entrance to the castle garden.)
(Marceline is seen ironing linen at her door; near her stands the firepan in which she heats her irons. Jacquino, who keeps closer to the door, opens it to several persons, who present him with parcels, or packets of letters: he carries them into his little room.)

**JACQUINO:** Now, my little treasure, we are alone, now we may chat in confidence.

**MARCELINE:** Surely it cannot be so important, I dare not tarry at my work.

**JACQUINO:** A little word, you cross one, you!

**MARCELINE:** Well, speak; I'm all attention.

**JACQUINO:** If you look so cross, I won't say a word.

**MARCELINE:** If you won't please me, I'll stop my ears altogether.

**JACQUINO:** One moment only listen,—

**MARCELINE:** Never more shall I be at rest.

**JACQUINO:** I will then leave you alone! I have chosen a wife, and you know that it is you.

MARCELLINE: So rede, so rede nur zu.

JACQUINO: Und, und wenn mir dein Jawort nicht fehlet, was meinst du? Wir könnten in wenigen Wochen—Zum Henker das ewige Pochen.

MARCELLINE: Das ist ja doch klar, so sind wir ein Paar. Recht schön, du bestimmst schone die Zeit, so bin ich doch endlich befreit!

JACQUINO: Da war ich so herrlich im Gang, und immer, immer entwischt mir der Fang.

MARCELLINE: Wie macht seine Liebe mir bang, wie werden die Stunden mir lang. Ich weiss, dass der Arme sich quälet, es thut mir so leid auch um ihn! Fidelio, Fidelio hab' ich gewählet, ihn lieben ist süsser Gewinn.

JACQUINO: Wo war ich, sie sieht mich nicht an!

MARCELLINE: Da ist er, er fängt wieder an!

JACQUINO: Wann wirst du das Jawort mir geben? Es könnte ja heute noch sein. Du bist doch wahrhaftig von Stein.

MARCELLINE: O weh! er verbittert mein Leben. Jetzt, morgen und immer und immer nein. Ich muss ja so hart mit ihm sein.

JACQUINO: Kein Wünschen, kein Bitten geht ein.

MARCELLINE: Er hofft bei dem mindesten Schein.

JACQUINO: So, so wirst du dich nimmer, nimmer bekehren? Was meinst du? Wie? Dich anzusehn willst du mir wehren? (*Man hört pochen.*) Auch das noch? Du hast mir so oft doch versprochen. Zum Henker das ewige Pochen.

MARCELLINE: Du könntest nun gehen. So bleibe hier stehn. Versprochen, nein das geht zu weit. So bin ich doch endlich befreit. (*Wiederholts Pochen.*)

JACQUINO: Zum Henker, es ward ihr im Ernste schon bang, wer weiss, ob es mir nicht gelang.

MARCELLINE: Das ist ein willkommener Klang, es wurde zu Tode, zu Tode mir bang.

JACQUINO: Nun habe ich doch diese Thür heute schon 200 Mal geöffnet, so wahr mein Name Caspar Eustach Jacquino ist. (*Zu Marcelline.*) Endlich können wir wieder mit einander sprechen. (*Pochen.*) Potz Kuckuk! Da geht es schon wieder. (*Er geht um zu öffnen.*)

MARCELINE: Chatter away, chatter away.

JACQUINO: And if I got your consent, what mean you? And in a few weeks we might— The deuce, this eternal knocking.

MARCELINE: Surely, that's plain enough. Why we are then a pair. This is charming. You are already settling the time, and I am released at last.

JACQUINO: Oh, I was so happily pleased, but I am always losing the catch.

MARCELINE: How tiresome is his love. My hours last now for ever, I know this wretched one is his own torment; I pity him. But Fidelio is my choice, and to love him my greatest delight!

JACQUINO: Where was I? She does not look at me.

MARCELINE: There he begins again.

JACQUINO: When shall you give your consent, and why not today? You are really as hard as a stone.

MARCELINE: Alas, he embitters my life, now, tomorrow, and always no! I really must be hard with him.

JACQUINO: And all desires, entreaties, are in vain!

MARCELINE: A shadow gives him hope.

JACQUINO: And will you ever be stubborn? What say you? You even forbid me your sight? (*Knocking at the door.*) Also this? You promised me so often. Oh, the deuce! that eternal knocking.

MARCELINE: You may go, or stay here. I promised you? No, not so quick. Well, released at last. (*Knocking at the door.*)

JACQUINO: In truth, she was frightened. And who knows if I did or did not succeed.

MARCELINE: That was a welcome sound. I was frightened to death.

JACQUINO: Now, if I haven't opened this door already two hundred times today, my name is not Casper Eustach Jacquino (*to Marceline*). At last we can chat again (*somebody knocks*). Zounds! There again? (*He goes to open*).

MARCELLINE: Es ist keine Einbildung von mir, das ich ihn nicht mehr so lieben kann wie früher.

JACQUINO: (*Aus der Thür hinauseilend und dieselbe hastig schliessend.*) Ich will es beherzen. Schon gut. (*Zu Marcelline.*) Nun hoffe ich, wird uns Niemand mehr unterbrechen!

ROCCO: (*Hinter der Scene.*) Jacquino! Jacquino!

MARCELLINE: Hörst du? Der Vater ruft!

JACQUINO: Gut! Er kann ein wenig warten. Also um wieder auf unsere Liebe zu kommen.

MARCELLINE: Mache, das du fortkommst. Der Vater wird dich nach Fidelio fragen wollen!

JACQUINO: (*eifersüchtig.*) So? Wirklich? Ja, da muss ich wohl eilen!

ROCCO: (*Hinter der Scene.*) Jacquino! Hörst du nicht?

JACQUINO: (*laut.*) Ich kommen schon! (*Zu Marcelline.*) Bleib hier, meine Liebe. In zwei Minuten bin ich wieder bei dir! (*Ab, in den Garten.*)

## ZWEITE SCENE

MARCELLINE: Armer Jacquino! Er dauert mich fast. Das Mitgefühl, welches ich für ihn habe, beeinträchtigt meine Liebe für Fidelio. Ich glaube wahrhaftig, dass Fidelio mich auch gern hat, und wenn ich wüsste, was mein Vater denkt, so könnte mein Glück bald vollständig sein.
O wär' ich schon mit dir vereint,
Und dürfte Mann dich nennen!
Ein Mädchen darf ja, was es meint,
Zur Hälfte nur bekennen.
Doch wenn ich nicht erröthen muss
Ob einem warmen Herzenskuss,
Wenn nichts uns stört auf Erden.
Die Hoffnung schon erfüllt die Brust
Mit unaussprechlich süsser Lust.
Wie glücklich will ich werden,
Die Hoffnung schon erfüllt die Brust
Mit unaussprechlich süsser Lust,
Wie glücklich, glücklich, ja wie
Glücklich will ich werden,
In Ruhe stiller Häuslichkeit
Erwach' ich jeden Morgen,
Wir grüssen uns mit Zärtlichkeit,
Der Fleiss verscheucht die Sorgen,
Und ist die Arbeit abgethan,
Dann schleicht die holde Nacht heran,
Dann ruh'n wir von Beschwerden.

## DRITTE SCENE

ROCCO: Guten Tag, Marceline. Fidelio ist also noch nicht zurückgekehrt?

MARCELLINE: It is no fancy of mine that I can no longer love him as I used to.

JACQUINO: (*To the person who has been knocking, shutting the door after him hastily*) I'll take care of it. All's right. (*To Marceline.*) Now I hope nobody will interrupt us.

ROCQUO: (*Calls behind.*) Jacquino! Jacquino!

MARCELINE: Do you hear? Father is calling!

JACQUINO: Well, he may wait a little; but to return to our love matters.

MARCELINE: Be gone; father's inquiry will be after Fidelio.

JACQUINO: (with jealousy). Yes, indeed; then all haste is not enough.

ROCQUO: (*behind the wings*). Jacquino, don't you hear?

JACQUINO: (*loudly*). I come quickly; (*to Marceline*) stay here, my love; in two minutes I will be with you again. (*Goes into the garden.*)

## SCENE II

MARCELINE: Poor Jacquino! I almost pity him. The compassion I feel for him still enhances my love for Fidelio. I really believe that Fidelio is very fond of me too; and if I knew my father's mind, my happiness might soon be complete.
Oh, how happy would I be, if in wedlock united with you,
And I would call you my husband.
But silence becomes best a maiden who's in love, they say.
But I need not blush at a kind and heartfelt kiss,
Where nothing on earth disturbs the hope that fills my breast.
Oh what delight! what bliss is mine!
How happy I! each morn fresh joy does bring,
With fond embrace in union blest,
each other's heart we tell
All care we bid fly from our door,
the labor over, fair night approaches,
And brings sweet rest to us.
Oh what delight, etc.

## SCENE III

ROCQUO: Good day, Marceline! So Fidelio has not yet come back.

MARCELLINE: Nein, Vater!

ROCCO: Die Stunde naht, um welche ich die Briefe, welche Fidelio abholen sollte, zu dem Gouverneur tragen muss. Fast werde ich ungeduldig.
(*Man hört pochen.*)

JACQUINO: (*aus Rocco's Hause.*) Ich komme schon! Ich komme schon! (*Läuft an die Thür und öffnet.*)

MARCELLINE: Er hat sicherlich bei dem Schmied warten müssen. (*Erblickt Leonoren.*) Da ist er! Da ist er!

## VIERTE SCENE

DIE VORIGEN: *Leonore trägt auf dem Rücken einen mit Lebensmitteln gefüllten Korb und über dem Arme Ketten, welche sie über das Wachthaus legt. Sei hat eine Blechbüchse an der Seite hängen.*

MARCELLINE: (*zu Leonora eilend.*) Wie beladen er ist! Guter Gott! Seine arme Stirn!
(*Sie wischt Leonoren den Schweiss von der Stirn.*)

ROCCO: Warte! warte!
(*Hilft Leonoren den Korb ablegen.*)

JACQUINO: Wahrhaftig, es war der Mühe werth, den Burschen einzulassen.
(*Ab in das Häuschen; er kommt bald wieder und passt auf die Andern auf.*)

ROCCO: Armer Fidelio! Dieses Mal hast du dich zu sehr beladen!

LEONORE: (*das Gesicht abtrocknend.*) Ich muss gestehen, dass ich ein wenig müde bin.

ROCCO: Wie viel macht es zusammen?

LEONORE: Ungefähr 12 Piaster, — hier ist die genaue Rechnung.

ROCCO: Bravo! Potztausend, da sind ja Dinge darunter, für welche man den doppelten Preis erhalten kann! Du bist ein gescheuter Bursche! Ich begreife kaum, wie du es so Klug anstellst. Du kaufst Alles wohlfeiler als ich. Seit sechs Monaten habe ich dir den Einkauf überlassen, und du hast mehr verdient, als ich in einem ganzen Jahr.
(*Beiseite.*)
Jawohl, der Tausendsassa gibt sich die Mühe nur wegen meiner Marceline.

LEONORE: Ich thue alles in meiner Macht.

MARCELINE: No, father.

ROCQUO: The hour approaches when I must take the letters to the governor, which Fidelio was to call for. I am beginning to grow rather impatient.
(*Knocking at the door.*)

JACQUINO: (*Coming out of Rocquo's house.*) I'm coming directly, coming directly.
(*Runs alertly to unlock the door.*)

MARCELINE: He has surely been detained at the smith's. (*She observes Leonora coming in.*) There he is! there he is!

## SCENE IV

(*The above. Leonora carrying on her back a large basket, with provisions, and on her arms fetters, which on coming in she deposits in the gatekeeper's room. A tin-plate box hangs from her side by a ribbon.*)

MARCELINE: (*Running to Leonora.*) How he is laden! Good heaven! his poor forehead!
(*She takes her handkerchief, and endeavors to wipe Leonora's brow.*)

ROCQUO: Stay, stay!
(*He assists her, together with Marceline to take the basket from her back.*)

JACQUINO: Well, it was worth while to run so fast to let the fellow in.
(*He enters his little room, but returns soon pretending to be busily engaged, when, in reality, he is trying to watch the others.*)

ROCQUO: Poor Fidelio! This time you have indeed burdened yourself too much.

LEONORA: (*Advancing by the side, and wiping her face and brow.*) I must confess I am a little fatigued.

ROCQUO: What's the amount of it altogether?

LEONORA: About twelve piastres;—here is the exact account.

ROCQUO: Well done. Zounds; there are articles amongst it of which twice the prime cost may be got. You are a sharp lad! I scarcely can conceive how you manage matters so cleverly. You buy every thing cheaper than I do. During the six months I have let it over to you to buy the provisions, you have gained more than I have in a whole year! (*Aside.*) Ah! it's evident the rogue gives himself all this trouble for the sake of my Marceline.

LEONORA: I endeavor to do all in my power.

ROCCO: Ja, ja, du bist ein braver Junge. Man kann nicht eifriger oder geschickter sein. Nein, nein, du steigst täglich in meiner Gunst, und die Belohnung wird dir nicht ausbleiben.
(*Blickt abwechselnd Leonora und Marceline bedeutsam an.*)

LEONORE: (*verwirrt.*) O glaubt nicht, das ich meine Pflicht bloss des Lohnes wegen thue.

ROCCO: (*wie worher.*) Still! Denkst du, ich kann nicht in dein Herz blicken.
(*Er lacht über die steigende Verwirrung Leonoren's und geht dann nach dem Hintergrunde. Marcelline hat Leonoren die Zeit über liebevoll angeblickt.*)

MARCELLINE: Mir ist so wunderbar. Es engt das Herz mir ein. Er liebt mich, es ist klar—Ich werde glücklich sein.

LEONORE: Wie gross ist die Gefahr, Wie schwach der Hoffnung Schein! Sie liebt mich, es ist klar, O namenlose Pein!

ROCCO: Sie liebt ihn, es ist klar, Ja, Mädchen, er wird dein, Ein gutes, junges Paar, Sie werden glücklich sein.

JAQUINO: Mir stäubt sich schon das Haar, Der Vater willigt ein, Mir ist so wunderbar, Mir fällt kein Mittel ein.

ROCCO: Höre, Fidelio! Obgleich ich nicht weiss, wo und wann du geboren bist, und ob du überhaupt einen Vater gehabt hast, so weiss ich doch, was ich thue. Ich mache dich zu meinem Schwiegersohn.

MARCELLINE: Wollt Ihr wirklich, Vater?

ROCCO: Heida! Wie eilig! (*Ernsthaft.*)
Wenn der Gouverneur nach Sevilla abgereist ist, haben wir mehr Zeit. Du weisst, dass er dort alle Monate hinreist, um Rechenschaft über Alles zu geben, was in dem Gefängnisse vorgeht. In wenigen Tagen muss er wieder fort. Am Tage nach seiner Abreise heirathet Ihr, darauf könnt Ihr Euch verlassen!

MARCELLINE: Den Tag nach seiner Abreise; das ist sehr klug, Vater.

LEONORE: (*verlegen.*) Den Tag nach seiner Abreise.
(*Bei Seite.*)
O welch neue und grausame Verlegenheit!

ROCCO: Nun Kinder! Ihr liebet einander von Herzen, nicht wahr? Aber das ist nicht Alles, um die Ehe glücklich zu machen. Wir brau-

ROCQUO: Yes, yes, you are a worthy lad. It is impossible to be more zealous or more skillful. Now, you are getting every day more in my favor, and be assured a reward will not be wanted.
(*While speaking the last words, be glances alternately at Leonora and Marceline.*)

LEONORA: (*Confused.*) Oh, don't think I fulfill my duty merely for the sake of reward.

ROCQUO: Hush! (*glancing as before.*) Do you think I could not look into your heart? (*He is pleased with the increasing confusion of Leonora; he then steps aside to look at the fetters. Whilst Rocquo is commending Leonora, Marceline manifests the greatest interest, and gazes on her with continually increasing emotion.*)

MARCELINE: What rapture do I feel, my heart is oppressed! He loves me it's clear, I shall be happy.

LEONORA: Alas, what danger! and hope is but vain! She loves me, what pain!

ROCQUO: She loves him, it's clear; yes, girl, he is yours. A good young couple; they shall be happy.

JACQUINO: My hair stands on end, her father consents; I don't know how I am nor what to do.

ROCQUO: Hark, Fidelio! Though I don't know how and where you were born, and if you haven't had any father at all, yet I know what I am about; I make you my son-in-law.

MARCELINE: Will you, indeed, father?

ROCQUO: Heyday! how quick. (*Seriously.*) As soon as the governor has set out for Seville we have more leisure; you know he goes there every month to give account of all that occurs in the prison. In a few days he must be off again. The day after his departure I give you to each other—you may depend on that.

MARCELINE: The day after his departure; that's acting very prudently, dear father.

LEONORA: (*Before much puzzled, but now assuming a joyful air.*) The day after his departure. (*Aside!*) Oh! what a new and cruel embarrassment is here!

ROCQUO: Now, my children! you love each other dearly, do you not? but that's not all that is required to make marriage happy; there is like-

# Act I, Scene IV

chen leider—
(*Macht die Pantomine des Geld-zählens.*)

**ARIE. ROCCO:** Hat man nicht auch
Geld bei Leben,
Kann man nicht auch glücklich
sein,
Traurig schleppt sich fort das Le-
ben,
Mancher Kummer stellt sich ein.
Doch wenn's in den Taschen fein
klingelt und rollt,
Da hält man das Schicksal gefangen,
Und Macht und Liebe verschafft dir
das Gold,
Und stillet das kühnste Verlangen.
Das Glück dient wie ein Knecht für
Gold.
Es ist ein schönes Ding das Gold,
das Gold,
Es ist ein schönes Ding, das Gold,
Ein goldnes, goldnes Ding, das
Gold, das Gold.
Wenn sich Nichts mit Nichts ver-
bindet,
Ist und bleibt die Summe klein,
Wer bei Tisch nur Liebe findet,
Wird nach Tische hungrig sein.
Drum lächle der Zufall auch gnädig
und hold,
Und segne und lenk' euer Streben,
Das Liebchen im Arm, im Beutel
das Gold,
So mögt Ihr viel Jahre durchleben.
Das Glück dient wie ein Knecht im
Sold,
Es ist ein mächtig Ding, das Gold,
das Gold.

**LEONORE:** Ihr könnt leicht so
sprechen, Vater Rocco; aber es
giebt noch etwas Anderes, was uns
nicht minder werthvoll sein würde,
und das ich, wie ich mit
Bekümmerniss sehe, nicht von
euch erhalten kann!

**ROCCO:** Und was ist das?

**LEONORE:** Euer Zutrauen! Verzeiht den Vorwurf, aber oft sehe ich
euch aus den unterirdischen
Gewölben des Gefängnisses ausser
Athem und ermattet kommen. Warum erlaubt ihr mir nicht, euch
dorthin zu begleiten? Ich würde
glücklich sein, wenn ich euch bei-
stehen und eure Mühe theilen
könnte.

**ROCCO:** Aber du weisst doch, dass
ich den strengsten Befehl habe,
Niemand zu den Staatsgefangenen
zuzulassen.

**MARCELLINE:** Aber es sind hier ja
gar zu viele in diesem Gefängnisse.
Ihr arbeitet euch noch todt, lieber
Vater!

**LEONORE:** Sie hat Recht, Vater
Rocco, ein Mann soll sicherlich
seine Pflicht erfüllen, aber ich
denke, es ist nicht mehr als recht,
sich für diejenigen zu schonen,
welche uns angehören und uns lieben.
(*Sie umarmt ihn.*)

wise needed.
(*mimicking the handling of money*).

**AIR. ROCQUO:** If we have no mon-
ey, love cannot bring comfort,
Sadly life drags on, and sorrow fol-
lows.
But when the coin jingles in the
pockets,
Then fate is our prisoner.
Yes, gold brings love and power,
And fills all our wishes.
Happiness is the slave of gold;
Oh what a precious thing is gold!
Nothing with nothing united, what
remains?
At dinner sweet love, and after din-
ner hunger;
May fate smile upon you and bless
your endeavors.
Arm in arm, plenty of money in the
purse;
Many a year may you thus live.
Yes, happiness is subservient to
gold; oh, what a precious thing is
gold!

**LEONORA:** You can easily say so,
Mr. Rocquo; yet in truth now there
is something else which would not
be less precious to me; but I observe with sorrow that with all my
endeavors I cannot obtain it.

**ROCQUO:** And what is this?

**LEONORA:** Your confidence. Pardon the reproach; but frequently I
see you return from the subterraneous vaults of this castle, quite out
of breath and spent with fatigue.
Why don't you allow me to accompany you there? It would quite delight me if I could assist your duties, and share your toils.

**ROCQUO:** But you know that I have
the strictest order not to admit any
one whatever to the state prisoners.

**MARCELINE:** But there are far too
many in this fortress; you work and
weary yourself to death, dear father.

**LEONORA:** She is in the right, Mr.
Rocquo; a man should certainly fulfill his duty; (*tenderly*) but I think
it is but justice we spare ourselves
for those that belong to us, and love
us. (*She grasps his bosom.*)

**MARCELLINE:** (*Rocco's Hand ergreifend.*) Ein guter Mensch muss
suchen, sich für seine Kinder zu erhalten.

**ROCCO:** (*gerührt.*) Ja, ihr habt
Recht! Die schwere Arbeit würde
zuletzt zu schwer für mich werden.
Der Gouverneur ist zwar sehr
streng, aber er muss mir erlauben,
dich mit mir in die geheimen
Gefängnisse zu nehmen.
(*Leonore zeigt grosse Freude.*)

**ROCCO:** Da ist jedoch ein Kerker,
in welchen ich dich niemals nehmen kann, obgleich ich dir vollständig vertraue.

**MARCELLINE:** Wahrscheinlich in
den, wo der Gefangene sitzt, von
welchem ihr schon mitunter gesprochen habt!

**ROCCO:** Du hast es gerathen!

**LEONORE:** (*forschend.*) Ich
glaube, es ist schon lange her, das
er im Kerker ist.

**ROCCO:** Länger als zwei Jahre.

**LEONORE:** Zwei Jahre, sagt ihr? Er
muss ein grosser Verbrecher sein!

**ROCCO:** Oder er muss mächtige
Feinde haben, das läuft auf dasselbe
hinaus!

**MARCELLINE:** Und habt ihr nie erfahren können, woher er kommt,
und wie er heisst?

**ROCCO:** Oft hat er gewünscht, mit
mir darüber zu sprechen.

**LEONORE:** Aber?

**ROCCO:** Aber für Leute wie wir, ist
es am besten, so wenig Geheim-
nisse zu wissen, wie möglich, und
deshalb habe ich ihm nie zugehört.
Ich hätte mir schaden können,
ohne ihm zu nützen.
(*Geheimnissvoll.*)
Armer Mann! Er wird mich nicht
lange mehr plagen, er kann nicht
lange mehr aushalten.

**LEONORE:** (*für sich.*) Gerechter
Himmel!

**MARCELLINE:** O, lieber Vater,
nehmt Fidelio nicht zu ihm! Er
könnte den Anblick nicht ertragen!

**LEONORE:** Warum nicht? Ich habe
Muth genug!

**ROCCO:** (*sie auf die Schulter klopfend.*) Ach, wenn ich dir erzählen
sollte, wie ich zuerst gegen mein
Gefühl zu kämpfen hatte, und ich
war ein ganz anderer Bursche, als
du mit deiner zarten Haut und dein-
en weissen Händen!
(*Terzett.*)

**MARCELINE:** (*Pressing Rocquo's
other hand to her bosom.*) A good
man must endeavor to preserve
himself for his children's sake.

**ROCQUO:** (*Looks at them both
much affected.*) Yes, you are in the
right. The heavy labor would in the
end become too much for me. The
governor is indeed very severe, but
yet he must permit that I take you
with me into the secret dungeons.
(*Leonora manifests a powerful
feeling of joy.*)

**ROCQUO:** There is, however, one
dungeon, into which I shall never
be able to take you though I am perfectly confident of you.

**MARCELINE:** Probably where the
prisoner is confined of whom you
have already sometimes spoken, father.

**ROCQUO:** You have guessed right.

**LEONORA:** (*Inquiringly.*) I believe it has been a long time since
he was taken.

**ROCQUO:** It has been over two
years.

**LEONORA:** (*Violently.*) Two
years! you say. He must be a great
criminal.

**ROCQUO:** Or he must have great
enemies—that means nearly the
same thing.

**MARCELINE:** And could you never
learn where he comes from and his
name?

**ROCQUO:** Often, indeed, has he
wished to speak with me about all
that.

**LEONORA:** But?

**ROCQUO:** But for folks like us it is
best to know as few secrets as possible, therefore I have never listened
to him. I might have gossiped to my
injury, without doing him any
good. (*Mysteriously.*) Well, poor
fellow, he will not much longer
plague me, he cannot last a very
long while.

**LEONORA:** (*aside*). Great heavens!

**MARCELINE:** Oh, dear father! do
not take Fidelio to him, this sight he
could not bear.

**LEONORA:** Why not? I have courage and nerve enough.

**ROCQUO:** (*Tapping her on the
shoulder.*) Bravo, my son, bravo!
Ah! if I were to tell you how I had to
struggle with my heart at the first,
in my situation; yet I was quite a different fellow, to what you are, with
your fair skin and white hands.
(*Terzetto.—Rocquo, Leonora,
Marceline.*)

ROCCO: Gut, Söhnchen, gut, hab immer Muth,
Dann wird's dir auch gelingen.
Das Herz wird hart durch Gegenwart
Bei fürcherlichen Dingen.

LEONORE: Ich habe Muth, mit kaltem Blut
Will ich hanab mich wagen.
Für hohen Lohn, kann Liebe schon
Auch hohes Leiden tragen.

MARCELLINE: Dein gutes Herz wird manchen Schmerz
In diesen Grüften leiden,
Dann kehrt zurück der Liebe Glück,
Der Liebe Glück und unnennbare Freuden.

ROCCO: Du wirst dein Glück ganz sicher bauen.

LEONORE: Ich hab' auf Gott und Recht Vertrauen.

MARCELLINE: Du darfst mir auch in's Auge schauen,
Der Liebe Macht ist auch nicht klein.

ALL: Ja, ja, wir werden glücklich sein.

ROCCO: Der Gouverneur soll heut erlauben,
Dass du mit mir die Arbeit theilst.

LEONORE: Du wirst mir alle Ruhe rauben,
Wenn du bis morgen nur verweilst.

MARCELLINE: Ja, guter Vater, bitt' ihn heute,
In Kurzem sind wir dann ein Paar.

ROCCO: Ich bin ja bald des Grabes Beute.

LEONORE: Wie lang bin ich des Kummers Beute.

ROCCO: Ich brauche Hülfe, es ist wahr.

LEONORE: Du Hoffnung, reichst mir Labung dar.

MARCELLINE: Ach, lieber Vater, was fällt Euch ein?
Lang' Freund und Rather müsst Ihr uns sein.

ROCCO: Nur auf der Hut; dann geht es gut,
Gestillt, gestillt wird euer Sehnen.

MARCELLINE: O habe Muth, o welke Gluth,
O welch ein tiefes Sehnen!

LEONORE: Ihr seid so gut, ihr macht mir Muth,
Gestillt wird bald mein Sehnen.

ROCCO: Gebt euch die Hand und schliesst das Band.

LEONORE: Ich gab die Hand zum süssen Band.

MARCELLINE: Ein festes Band mit Herz und Hand.

ROCQUO: Good, my son, good! be ever of good cheer,
Then will you succeed. The heart gets hardened
When often in contact with horrible scenes.

LEONORA: I have courage; with calmness
Will I venture down, for high reward.
Love will endure high suffering also.

MARCELINE: Your good heart will suffer
Woefully in those dread vaults; but the joys of love
Await you in return, and happiness will be yours.

ROCQUO: Your fortune is in your own hands, my lad.

LEONORA: I confide in God and in right.

MARCELINE: You may espy in my eyes, that love's power is not small.

ALL: Yes, yes, we shall be happy.

ROCQUO: Today the governor consents that you share my duty.

LEONORA: You destroy my rest if you delay till tomorrow.

MARCELINE: Good father, intreat him today; the sooner is our union.

ROCQUO: I shall soon go down to my grave.

LEONORA: A long time I have been a prey to woe.

ROCQUO: I need help, and it's true.

LEONORA: A ray of hope fills me.

MARCELINE: Ah, good father, what do you think?
Long, long you'll be our friend and consoler.

ROCQUO: Only be prudent, and all goes well;
Your wishes are gratified.

MARCELINE: Oh, have courage; oh, what ardor!
Oh, what a deep feeling!

LEONORA: You are so good, you inspire me with courage,
My desire is fulfilled.

ROCQUO: Shake hands and be united.

LEONORA: I have given my sacred pledge—
Ah! what bitter tears it cost me.

MARCELINE: A lasting tie, with hand and heart—
Oh! sweet and welcome tears.

ROCCO: In süssen Freudenthränen.

LEONORE: Es kostet bittere Thränen.

MARCELLINE: O süsse, süsse Thränen!

ROCCO: Aber nun ist es auch Zeit, dass ich dem Gouverneur die Briefschaften überbringe.
(*Man hört einen Marsch.*)

ROCCO: O, er kommt selbst hierher!
(*Zu Leonoren.*)
Gieb mir die Büchse, Fidelio, und dann entfernt euch!
(*Leonore giebt Rocco die Blechbüchse und geht dann mit Marcelline ab.*)

## FÜNFTE SCENE

*Rocco, Don Pizarro, Offiziere und Wachen.
Während des Marsches öffnet sich das Hauptthor nach Aussen. Offiziere und Soldaten marschiren hinein, darauf Don Pizarro, dann wird das Thor wieder geschlossen.*

DON PIZARRO: (*zu den Offizieren.*) Drei Wachen auf die Wälle! Sechs Tag und Nacht auf die Zugbrücke, eben so viele in den Garten, und wer sich nähert, wird sofort vor mich gebracht.
(*Zu Rocco.*)
Rocquo! Ist etwas Neues vorgefallen?

ROCCO: Nein, Herr!

PIZARRO: Wo sind die Depeschen?

ROCCO: (*Nimmt die Briefe aus der Brieftasche.*) Hier!

PIZARRO: (*die Briefe öffnend und durchfliegend.*) Immer Befehle und Vorwürfe! Ich würde niemals fertig werden, sollte ich auf Alles dies achten! Doch was sehe ich? Ich glaube, ich kenne diese Handschrift! Lasst uns sehen!
(*Tritt vor; Rocquo und die Wache ziehen sich zurück. Er liest:*)
,,Ich benachrichtige Euch, dass der Minister erfahren hat, dass unter den Staatsgefangenen, die Ihr unter Aufsicht habt, mehrere die Opfer Eurer Willkür sind. Er reist morgen ab, um Euch mit einer Untersuchung zu überraschen. Seid auf Eurer Hut und seht, dass Ihr Euch gut haltet!"
(*Unruhig.*)
Ha, wenn er entdeckte, dass dieser Floristan hier in Ketten liegt, den er längst für todt hielt! Eine kühne That muss und kann alle meine Unruhe beseitigen!

Ha! welch' ein Augenblick!
Die Rache werd' ich külen!
Dich, dich rufet dein Geschick!
In seinem Herzen wühlen,
O Wonne! grosses Glück!

ROCQUO: In sweet tears of joy.

LEONORA: It costs bitter tears.

MARCELINE: Oh! sweet, sweet tears.

ROCQUO: But now it's time that I carry the papers to the governor. (*A March is heard.*)

ROCQUO: Oh! he comes here himself; (*to Leonora*) give them to me, Fidelio, and then depart. (*Leonora takes the tinplate box which is suspended by a ribbon, gives it to Rocquo, and goes away with Marceline into the house.*)

## SCENE V

*Rocquo, Pizarro, Officers, Guards.
(During the March the principal gate opens from without; Officers with a detachment enter, then Pizarro. The gate is again closed.)*

PIZZARRO: (*To the officers.*) Three guards on the rampart, six day and night on the drawbridge, the same number on the side of the garden, and whosoever comes near is immediately brought before me. (*To Rocquo.*) Rocquo, has anything fresh occurred?

ROCQUO: No, sir.

PIZZARRO: Where are the dispatches?

ROCQUO: (*Taking the papers out of a box.*) Here they are.

PIZZARRO: (*Opens the papers, and goes through them.*) Every commands and reprimands. I should never be done were I to pay attention to all this. What do I see? I fancy I know this writing; let's see. (*He opens the letter, advancing a step. Rocquo and the guards step back—he reads.*)
"I inform you what the minister has learned; that among the state prisoners there under your charge, several are victims of arbitrary power; he departs tomorrow to surprise you with an examination. Be on your guard, and endeavor to keep yourself right." (*Disturbed.*) Ha! if he should discover that I have this Florestan lying here in chains, whom he has long ago thought to be dead! One bold deed can and must disperse all my anxieties.

Ah what a moment! Yes, I'll be revenged.
Your fate calls! Yes, I'll pierce his heart.
Oh, joy! high delight! Already I was

Schon war ich nah im Staube,
Dem lauten Spott zum Raube,
Dahin gestreckt zu sein.
Nun ist es mir geworden,
Den Mörder selbst zu morden.
In seiner letzten Stunde,
Den Stahl in seiner Wunde,
Im noch in's Ohr zu schreien:
Triumph, Triumph, Triumph!
Der Sieg, der Sieg ist mein!

WACHE: (leise.) Er spricht von
Tod und Wunde,
Non fort auf unsere Runde,
Wie wichtig muss es sein!

PIZARRO: Hauptmann!
(Giebt ihm leise Befehle.)
Steigt mit einem Trompeter aug
den Thurm. Schaut mit der grössten
Aufmerksamkeit nach der Land-
strasse von Sevilla. Sobald ihr einen
Wagen seht, welcher mit Reitern
umringt ist, lasst mich sofort ein
Signal hören! Ihr verstehet? Sofort!
Ich erwarte die grösste
Pünktlichkeit. Ihr steht mit Eurem
Kopfe dafür!
(Hauptmann ab.)

DON PIZARRO: (zu den Wa-
chen.) Fort auf eure Posten.
(Wachen ab.)

DON PIZARRO: (zu Rocco.) Rocco!

ROCCO: Herr?

PIZARRO: (sieht ihn scharf an,
für sich.) Ich muss suchen, ihn zu
gewinnen; ohne seine Hülfe kann
ich meinen Plan nicht ausführen.
Tritt näher!

PIZARRO: Jetzt Altar! Jetzt hat es
Eile, dir wird ein Glück zu Theile;
du wirst ein reicher Mann!
(Ihm eine Börse gebend.)
Das geb' ich nur daran.

ROCCO: So sagt doch nur in Eile,
womit ich dienen kann.

PIZARRO: Du bist von kaltem
Blute, von unverzagtem Muthe
durch langen Dienst geworden.

ROCCO: Wass soll ich? Redet, redet!

PIZARRO: Morden!

ROCCO: (erschrocken.) Wie?

PIZARRO: Höre mich nun an. Du
bebst, du bist ein Mann? Wir dürfen
gar nicht säumen, dem Staate liegt
daran, den bösen Unterthan schnell
aus dem Weg zu räumen.

ROCCO: O Herr!

PIZARRO: Du stehst noch an?
(Für sich.)
Er darf nicht länger leben, Sonst
ist's um mich geschehen. Pizarro
sollte leben? Du fällst, ich werde
stehen!

crouched in dust,
A prey to base mockery stretched to
the ground,
But now it is mine to kill him that
would have killed me.
In his last hour, the steel in his bo-
som.
Yes, I cry aloud in his ear—
Triumph! the victory is mine!

GUARDS: (In an undertone
among thenselves.) He speaks of
death and vengeance. Watch carefully.
And mind well on your rounds—it
must be important.

PIZZARRO: Captain! (He leads the
captain forward and speaks softly
to him.) Ascend the tower together
with a trumpeter. Look with the
greatest attention towards the high
road to Seville.
As soon as you perceive a carriage
surrounded with riders, let me instantly hear a signal. You understand, instantly? I expect the greatest punctuality. With your head
you answer for it.
(Captain exit.)

PIZZARRO: (to the Guards).
Away to your posts.
(The Guards retire.)

PIZZARRO: (to Rocquo). Rocquo.

ROCQUO: Sir!

PIZZARRO: (Looks at him attentively for a short time). (Aside.) I
must endeavor to win him over;
without his help I cannot execute
my design. Come, approach!

PIZZARRO: Now, old friend,
haste! your fortune's made. You're
a man of riches.
(Gives him a purse).
There, this is only to start.

ROCQUO: Oh, quick, ah, say, in
what can I serve you?

PIZZARRO: You are of old blood,
of undaunted courage from long
service.

ROCQUO: Speak! what shall I do?

PIZZARRO: Kill.

ROCQUO: (alarmed). Whom?

PIZZARRO: Listen, You tremble;
are you a man? We must delay no
longer, on account of the state;
quick, a subject so bad must be gotten rid of.

ROCQUO: Oh, Sir!

PIZZARRO: You still hesitate.
(Aside.) He must live no longer, or
I'm undone. Ha! Pizzarro should
live in fears! No! you die. I stand.

ROCCO: O Herr! die Glieder fühl
ich leben, wie könnt' ich das bestehen! Ich nehm' ihm nicht das Leben, mag, was da will, geschehen.
Nein, Herr! das Leben nehmen, das
ist nicht meine Pflicht.

PIZARRO: Ich will mich selbst bequemen, wenn dir's an Muth ge-
bricht. Nun eile rasch und munter
zu jenem Mann hinunter, du weisst!

ROCCO: Der kaum mehr lebt und
wie ein Schatten schwebt?

PIZARRO: Zu dem hinab, ich wart
in kleiner Ferne. Du gräbst in der
Cisterne sehr schnell ein Grab.

ROCCO: Und dann? Und dann?

PIZARRO: Dann werd' ich selbst,
vermummt, mich in den Kerker
schleichen.
(einen Dolch ziehend.)
ein Stoss und er verstummt. Er stirbt
in seinen Ketten, zu kurz war seine
Pein, sein Tod nur kann mich retten!

ROCCO: Verhungernd in den Ketten ertrug er lange Pein, ihn tödten
heisst ihn retten, der Dolch wird
ihn befrei'n.
(Don Pizarro ab nach dem Garten zu, Rocco folgt ihm.)

## SECHSTE SCENE

Leonore stürzt aufgeregt auf die
Bühne und sieht den Abgehenden
nach.

LEONORE: Abscheulicher! Wo
eilst du hin? Was has du vor?
Was hast du vor im wilden
Grimme?
Des Mitleids Ruf, der Menschheit
Stimme
Rührt nicht mehr deinen Tigersinn.
Doch toben auch die Meereswog-
en,
Dir in der Seele Zorn und Wuth,
So leuchte mir ein Farbenbogen,
Der hell auf dunkeln Wolken ruht,
Der Blick so still, so friedlich nied-
er,
Der spiegelt alte Zeiten wieder,
Und neu besänftigt wallt mein Blut.

ARIE: Komm Hoffnung, lass den
letzten Stern der Müden nicht er-
bleichen,
O komm', erhell' mein Ziel, sei's
noch so fern, so fern,
Die Liebe sie wird's erreichen.
Folg' dem innern Triebe,
Ich wanke nicht, mich stärkt die
Pflicht
Der treuen Gattenliebe.
O du, für den ich Alles trug, könnt
ich zur Stelle dringen,
Wo Bosheit dich in Fesseln schlug,
und süssen Trost dir bringen!
(Ab.)

ROCQUO: My frame is trembling!
how could I bear it? No; I'll not take
his life; let happen what may. Sir, I
am not bound in duty to kill.

PIZZARRO: I'll do it myself if your
courage fails. Only quick, haste
down to the man you know.

ROCQUO: Who scarcely lives the
semblance of a shadow?

PIZZARRO: Yes, to him, to him
down. I at short distance wait. And
quickly, prepare a grave for him in
the cistern.

ROCQUO: And then?

PIZZARRO: You give a signal; and
I'll quickly descend into the dungeon. (Draws a dagger.) One
blow, and he is dumb.

ROCQUO: Famishing in chains his
sufferings are great; to kill him is to
save him, and mine is rest.
(Exit Pizzarro towards the garden, Rocquo follows him.)

## SCENE VI

(Leonore appears in great agitation from the opposite side; she
observes those that go away with
increasing anxiety.)

LEONORA: Monster! Where are
you going in such a hurry? what design breeds your rage?
Nor pity's call, nor humanity's
voice,
Nothing moves your tiger mind.
Yet I see the storm of passion rages
within your soul,
But I still perceive a ray of hope on
heaven's face;
It brings me calm, restores my soul;
In fond recollection of past happiness my heart now beats anew.

ARIA: Sweet hope forsake not this
lingering heart!
Oh! let a ray of joy console my sorrowing love.
See, my bosom beats, I hesitate
not—
Yes, a wife devout, I bring—fresh
vigor.
(Exit into the garden.)

## SIEBENTE SCENE

*Marcelline aus dem Hause, Jacquino folgt ihr.*

**JAQUINO:** Aber Marcelline!

**MARCELLINE:** Nicht ein Wort, nicht eine Silbe! Ich will nichts mehr von deinen thörichten Liebesgeschichten wissen, und damit Basta! —

**JAQUINO:** Wer hätte das gedacht, als ich mich zuerst in dich verliebte, damals war ich der theure Jacquino. Jacquino hier, und Jacquino da. Der liebe Jacquino legt die Bügeleisen auf das Feuer, der liebe Jacquino legt die Wäsche zusammen, er bringt den Gefangenen die Packete, kurz er muss Alles thun, was ein Mädchen von einem ehrlichen Burschen verlangen kann; aber seitdem dieser Fidelio—

**MARCELLINE:** (*schnell.*) Ich läugne nicht, dass ich dir gut war, aber sieh, ich bin offenherzig, es war nicht Liebe. Fidelio ist mir theurer. Ich finde zwischen ihm und mir eine grosse Harmonie.

**JAQUINO:** Harmonie mit einem solchen Vagabunden, der, weiss Gott woher, kommt; den dein Vater aus reiner Barmherzigkeit aufgenommen hat, und der—

**MARCELLINE:** (*ärgerlich.*) Der arm und verlassen ist, und den ich doch noch heirathen werde.

**JAQUINO:** Glaubst du, ich werde das zugeben? Es soll nicht in meiner Gegenwart geschehen, oder ich möchte euch einen Possen spielen.

## ACHTE SCENE

*Die Vorigen, Rocco and Leonora aus dem Garten.*

**ROCCO:** Zankt ihr euch schon wieder?

**MARCELLINE:** Ach, Vater, er neckt mich immer.

**ROCCO:** Und warum?

**MARCELLINE:** (*lachend zu Leonora.*) Er will, ich solle ihn heirathen, ihn lieben, und ich—

**ROCCO:** Ruhe! Wahrhaftig, hätte ich meine einzige Tochter bis zu ihrem sechszehnten Jahre mit so viel Sorgfalt erzogen, blos für ein solch feines Herrchen? (*Lächelnd.*) Nein, Freund Jacquino, ich habe meine Pläne!

**MARCELLINE:** Ich verstehe! (*Sanft zu Leonora.*) Fidelio!

**LEONORE:** Beendigen wir diese Unterhaltung. Rocco, ich bat euch so oft, den armen Gefangenen, welche in den oberen

## SCENE VII

*(Marceline, from the house, Jacquino follows her.)*

**JACQUINO:** But Marceline.

**MARCELINE:** Not a word, not a syllable. I will hear nothing more of your silly love tales, and that's enough.

**JAQUINO:** Who would have said this, when I earnestly fell in love with you? Then I was dear Jacquino; dear hear, and dear there. Dear Jacquino puts the irons to the fire, dear Jacquino folds up the linen, he takes the parcels to the prisoners; in short, must do all that a maiden asks of an honorable lad; but since this Fidelio—

**MARCELINE:** (*hastily*). I don't deny I was good to you; but look, I'm open hearted. It was not love. Fidelio is more endearing; I find a great harmony between him and me.

**JACQUINO:** An harmony with such a vagabond, who comes from God knows where; whom your father out of mere charity, received at the gate, and who—

**MARCELINE:** (*angrily*). Who is poor and forsaken, and whom I shall as yet marry.

**JACQUINO:** Believe you I shall suffer that? It will not take place in my presence, or see I might play you a trick.

## SCENE VIII

*(The former, Rocquo, Leonora, from the garden.)*

**ROCQUO:** Are you both quarreling again?

**MARCELINE:** Ah, father, he ever will tease me?

**ROCQUO:** And why?

**MARCELINE:** (*laughingly to Leonora*). He wants me to marry him, to love him, and I—

**ROCQUO:** Silence! Surely, my only daughter, whom I have brought up with such care to her sixteenth year, (*pats Marceline on the cheek*) and all for this fine gentleman? (*looks smilingly upon Jacquino.*) No, friend Jacquino, other thoughts fill my mind.

**MARCELINE:** I understand father (*tenderly and softly*), Fidelio!

**LEONORA:** Now let's end this conversation. Rocquo, I begged of you many times to suffer the poor prisoners, those that dwell above

Gefängnissen wohnen, zu erlauben, im Garten die freie Luft zu geniessen. Ihr verspracht es mir, habt es stets verschoben. Heute ist das Wetter schön; der Gouverneur kann jetzt nicht kommen.

**MARCELLINE:** Ach ja, ich bitte mit ihm.

**ROCCO:** Meine theuren Kinder, ohne die Erlaubniss des Gouverneurs?

**MARCELLINE:** Aber ihr habt euch so lange mit ihm unterhalten. Vielleicht sollt ihr ihm einen Gefallen thun, und da wird er es nicht so genau nehmen.

**ROCCO:** Einen Gefallen? Du hast Recht, Marcelline, darauf hin will ich's wagen. Wohlan denn, Jacquino und Fidelio geht und öffnet die kleineren Zellen, und ich will zu Don Pizarro gehen und ihn aufhalten, zugleich (*zu Marcelline*) will ich mit ihm zu deinen Gunsten sprechen!

**MARCELLINE:** (*küsst ihm die Hand.*) Ich bitte dich, lieber Vater! (*Rocco ab. Leonora und Jacquino öffnen die Gefängnissthüren und ziehen sich mit Marcelline in den Hintergrund zurück und beobachten mit Mitleid die auftretenden Gefangenen.*)

## NEUNTE SCENE

*Die Vorigen. Chor der Gefangenen.*

**GEFANGENE:** O welche Lust! In freier Luft
Den Athem leicht zu heben, nur hier, nur hier ist Leben,
Der kerker eine Gruft.

**EINER:** Wir wollen mit Vertrauen auf Gottes Hülfe bauer,
Die Hoffnung flüstert sanft mir zu:
Wir werden frei, —wir finden Ruh'.

**ALLE:** O Hoffnung! Rettung! welch ein Glück!
O Freiheit, o Freiheit, kehrst du zurück?

**EINER:** Sprecht leise, haltet euch zurück,
Wir sind belauscht mit Ohr und Blick.

**ALLE:** Sprecht leise etc. etc.

## ZEHNTE SCENE

**LEONORE:** Nun sprecht, wie ging's?

**ROCCO:** Recht gut, recht gut; zusammen rafft' ich meinen Muth und trug ihm Alles vor, und sollst du's glauben, was er zur Antwort mir

ground to walk about in the free air of the garden. You promised it me, but continually defer it. Today the weather is fine; the governor does not come here at this time.

**MARCELINE:** Oh, yes; I entreat with him!

**ROCQUO:** My dear children, without the permission of the governor?

**MARCELINE:** But you were speaking to him for a long time; perhaps you are to do him a favor, and then he will not be so particular.

**ROCQUO:** A favor? You are in the right, Marceline! On this risk I may venture it. Well, then, Jacquino and Fidelio, go and open the minor cells, and I will go to Pizarro, and detain him, at the same time (*turning to Marceline*), I'll speak to him for your best!

**MARCELINE:** (*kisses his hand*). Do so, dear father! (*Exit Rocquo. Leonora and Jacquino open the gates of the prison; they retire with Marceline in the background, and observe, with sympathy, the prisoners, who shortly make their appearance.*)

## SCENE IX

*The above: Chorus of Prisoners.*

**PRISONERS:** Oh, what enjoyment to breathe the fresh air of heaven! Here only is to live; the dungeon is a tomb.

**A PRISONER:** Let us trust in heaven with confidence!
Hope softly whispers—"You will be free, you will have peace."

**CHORUS:** O Heaven! Deliverance! what a blessing! Oh, liberty returns?

**ONE:** Speak softly—restrain yourselves! We are watched by eyes and ears.

**ALL:** Speak softly—restrain yourselves! We are watched by eyes and ears.

## SCENE X

**LEONORA:** Now speak, how did you succeed?

**ROCQUO:** Well! very well! I composed my mind and mentioned every thing. And, would you believe it? That he gave the answer? He al-

gab; die Heirath und dass du mir hilfst, will er erlauben. Noch heute führ' ich die Kerker dich hin.

LEONORE: (*erschreckt.*) Noch heute? O welch ein Glück, Welche Wonne!

ROCCO: Ich sehe deine Freude; nur noch einen Augenblick, dann gehen wir schon Beide.

LEONORE: Wohin? Wohin?

ROCCO: Zu jenem Mann hinab, dem ich seit vielen Wochen stets weniger zu essen gab.

LEONORE: Ha! wird er losgesprochen? so sprich, so sprich!

ROCCO: O nein! o nein! (*Geheimnissvol.*) Wir müssen ihn, doch wie?—befrei'n. Er muss in einer Stunde, den Finger auf dem Munde, von uns begraben sein.

LEONORE: So ist er todt?

ROCCO: Noch nicht, noch nicht.

LEONORE: (*bebend.*) Ist ihn zu tödten deine Pflicht?

ROCCO: Nein, guter Jung, zittre nicht; zum Morden dingt sich Rocco nicht. Der Gouverneur kommt selbst hinab, wir Beide graben nur das Grab.

LEONORE: (*bei Seite.*) Vielleicht das Grab des Gatten graben! Was kann fürchterlicher sein!

ROCCO: Ich darf ihn nicht mit Speise laben, ihm wird im Grabe besser sein!
Wir müssen gleich zum Werke schreiten, du must mir helfen, mich begleiten. Hart ist des Kerkermeisters Brod.

LEONORE: Ich folge dir, wär's in den Tod.

ROCCO: In der zerfallenen Cisterne bereiten wir die Grube leicht. Ich thu' es, glaube mir, nicht gerne, auch dir ist schaurig, wie mich deucht.

LEONORE: Ich bin es nur noch nicht gewohnt.

ROCCO: Ich hätte gerne dich verschont, doch wird es mir allein zu schwer, und gar so streng ist unser Herr.

LEONORE: (*für sich.*) O welch' ein Schmerz!

ROCQUO: (*für sich.*) Mir scheint, er weine.
(*Laut.*)
Nein, nein, du bleibst hier, ich geh' alleine.

LEONORE: (*ihn fassend.*) O nein! O nein! ich muss ihn seh'n, den Armen seh'n und müsst' ich selbst zu Grunde geh'n.

BEIDE: O säumen wir nun länger nicht, wir folgen unserer strengen Pflicht.

lows the marriage, and that you assist me. This very day you shall go with me to the dungeons.

LEONORA: (*breaking forth*). To-day! what happiness, what delight!

ROCQUO: I can see your joy. Only another moment and we both will go.

LEONORA: Where?

ROCQUO: Down to that man whom for weeks past I have continually diminished the food.

LEONORA: God, is he also free?

ROCQUO: No, oh no (*mysteriously.*) We—yes, we must free him. In one hour your lips are closed—He must be in his grave.

LEONORA: Then he is dead?

ROCQUO: Not yet! not yet.

LEONORA: (*starting back*). And must you kill him?

ROCQUO: No, no, my fine fellow, never fear—Rocquo is no murderer. The governor himself comes down—we only dig the grave.

LEONORA: (*aside*). Perhaps to dig the grave of the husband, oh! what can be more horrible?

ROCQUO: I dare not nourish him; in the grave he finds rest. We must proceed to work. You must help and accompany me. The goaler's bread is hard.

LEONORA: I follow you, till death.

ROCQUO: In the old cistern, we'll dig the grave with ease, believe me I don't like it, and you seem to shudder too.

LEONORA: I'm quite prepared, confide in me!

ROCQUO: I willingly would have spared you this. But, all alone, the work's too much.

LEONORA: (*aside*). Oh what grief!

ROCQUO: (*aside*). I think he weeps.
(*aloud*).
No, you remain here: I go alone.

LEONORA: (*clinging to him*). I must see him, the wretched man, even on my own peril.

BOTH: Then let's delay no longer; we follow duty's call.

(*Marcelline und Jaquino, hastig auftretend.*)

MARCELLINE: Ach, Vater! Vater, eilt!

ROCCO: Was hast du den?

JAQUINO: Nicht länger weilt.

ROCCO: Was ist geschehen?

MARCELLINE: Voll Zorn folgt mir Pizarro nach, er drohet dir.

ROCCO: Gemach! Gemach!

LEONORE: So eilet fort!

ROCCO: Nur noch ein Wort! Sprich, weiss er schon?

JAQUINO: Ja, er weiss schon!

MARCELLINE: Der Officier sagt ihm, was wir jetzt den Gefangenen gewähren.

ROCCO: Lasst alle schnell zurücke kehren.
(*Jaquino geht ab in den garten.*)

MARCELLINE: Ihr wisst ja, wie er tobet und kennet seine Wuth.

LEONORE: Wie mir's im Innern tobet, empöret ist mein Blut.

ROCCO: Mein Herz hat mich gelobet, sei der Tyrann in Wuth.

Don Pizarro, zwei Offiziere und Wachen.

PIZARRO: Verweg'ner Alter, welche Rechte legst du dir frevelnd selber bei, und ziemt es dem gedung'nen Knechte, zu geben die Gefang'nen frei.

ROCCO: (*zitternd.*) O Herr! O Herr!

PIZARRO: Wohlan! Wohlan!

ROCCO: (*eine Entschuldigung suchend*) Des Frühlings Kommen, das heitere, warme Sonnenlicht, dann (*sich fassend*) habt ihr wohl in Acht genommen, was sonst zu meinem Vortheil spricht? Des Königs Namensfest ist heute, das feiern wir auf solche Art. (*Heimlich zu Don Pizarro.*) Der unten stirbt, doch lasst die Andern jetzt fröhlich hin und wieder wandern; für jenen sei der Zorn gespart.

DON PIZARRO: (*halblaut.*) So eile, ihm sein Grab zu graben, hier will ich die stille Ruhe haben. Schliesst die Gefangenen wieder ein, mögst du nie mehr verwegen sein.

DIE GEFANGENEN: Leb' wohl, du warmes Sonnenlicht, schnell schwindest du uns wieder; schon sinkt die Nacht hernieder, aus der so bald kein Morgen bricht.

(*Marceline, and Jacquino, rushing in out of breath.*)

MARCELINE: Oh father, hurry!

ROCQUO: What's the matter then?

JACQUINO: Tarry no longer!

ROCQUO: What has happened then?

MARCELINE: Filled with rage, Pizzarro follows my steps threatening you.

ROCQUO: Quiet! peace!

LEONORA: Hasten then!

ROCQUO: Another word more! speak! knows he then?

JACQUINO: Yes, he knows already.

MARCELINE: The officer told him of the new indulgence the prisoners have.

ROCQUO: They all must quickly return.
(*Jacquino exits.*)

MARCELINE: You know how he rages, and are aware of his fury.

LEONORA: How my heart beats! my soul is all in arms.

ROCQUO: My heart rejoices, let the tyrant rave.

(*Pizzarro, two officers, Guards: the above.*)

PIZZARRO: Audacious old man! what rights are you criminally assuming?
Does it become the hireling servant to deliver the prisoners?

ROCQUO: (*embarrassed*). Oh Sir!

PIZZARRO: Well, and—

ROCQUO: (*seeking an excuse*). The coming of spring, the serene ray of the sun, besides—consider—(*recovering himself*)—what pleads in my favor—(*taking off his cap*)—Our gracious king's birthday—we celebrate in this manner. (*Secretly to Pizzarro.*) The one below dies; but suffer the others an happy hour in the free air; reserve your fury for him alone.

PIZZARRO: (*softly*) Then hasten to dig his grave; here all must be quiet. Shut up again the prisoners, and never be so daring again.

PIZZARRO: Farewell, warm ray of the sun, soon you'll vanish again. Night breaks upon us, and never to behold again the morn.

**PIZARRO:** Nun, Rocco, zög're länger nicht, steig' in den Kerker nieder. (*Halblaut.*) Nicht eher kehrst du wieder, bis ich vollzogen das Gericht.

**ROCCO:** Nein, Herr, ich zög're länger nicht, ich steige nieder. (*Für sich*) Mir beben meine Glieder, o unglückselig harte Pflicht!

**LEONORE:** (*zu den Gefangenen.*) Ihr hört das Wort, drum zögert nicht, kehrt in den Kerker wieder. Angst rinnt durch meine Glieder, ereilt den Frevler kein Gericht.

**MARCELLINE:** (*die Gefangenen betrachtend.*) Wie eilten sie zum Sonnenlicht, und scheiden traurig wieder; die andern murmeln nieder: Hier wohnt die Lust, die Freude nicht.

**JAQUINO:** (*zu den Gefangenen*) Ihr hört das Wort, drum zögert nicht, kehrt in den Kerker wieder. (*Rocco und Leonorebeobachtend.*) Sie sinnen auf und nieder; könnt ich versteh'n, was jeder spricht.

## ■ ZWEITER AKT

### ERSTE SCENE

*Dunkles, unterirdisches Gefängniss, links eine alte Cisterne mit Steinen und Unkraut bedeckt. Im Hintergrunde eine Mauer mit Eisengitter, durch welche man eine Treppe sieht, rechts einige Stufen und die Thür zum Kerker. Eine Lampe brennt. Florestan, allein, sitzt auf einem Stein, eine Kette um den Leib, deren Ende in die Wand gemauert ist.*

**FLORESTAN:** Gott, welch' Dunkel hier, o grauenvolle Stille, Oed' ist es um mich her, nichts lebet ausser mir. O schwere Prüfung, doch gerecht ist Gottes Wille, Ich murre nicht, das Maass der Leiden steht bei ihm.

In des Lebens Frühlingstagen Ist das Glück von mir gefloh'n, Wahrheit wagt' ich kühn zu sagen, Und die Ketten sind mein Lohn. Willig duld' ich alle Schmerzen, Ende schmählich meine Bahn, Süsser Trost in meinem Herzen, Meine Pflicht hab' ich gethan. (*In einem Zustande der Verzückung, jedoch ruhig.*) Und spür' ich nicht linde, sanft säuselnde Luft, Und ist nicht mein Grab nur erhellet? Ich seh' wie ein Engel in rosigem

**PIZZARRO:** Now, Rocquo, tarry no longer, descend into the dungeon. (*Softly.*) Do not return until my will has been accomplished.

**ROCQUO:** No, Sir, no, I tarry no longer, I hasten down. (*Aside.*) My limbs tremble; oh, severe and dread duty!

**LEONORA:** (*to the prisoners*). You hear the word—then linger here no longer. Return into the prison; fear overpowers me! Does no judgment overtake this wicked man?

**MARCELINE:** (*looking at the prisoners*) We hasten to behold the light of day—But part again in sorrow. Alas, no cheering ray of joy or hope within these melancholy walls does dwell.

**JACQUINO:** (*to the prisoners*). You hear the word, tarry no longer, return into the prison! (*Aside, looking upon Rocquo and Leonora*). Ah, you are meditating; I wish I knew what each does mean.

## ■ ACT II

### SCENE I

*(The Stage represents a dark subterranean dungeon; on the left of the spectators is an old reservoir covered with stones and rubbish. In the background are several openings provided with gratings in the wall, through which a staircase is seen, leading down from above; on the right, the lower steps, and the door in the prison. A lamp is burning, Florestan alone, he is sitting upon a stone, a long chain round his waist, the end of which is fastened to the wall.)*

**FLORESTAN:** Oh, heavens, what dreary gloom! what awful stillness this! All is desert around, naught breathes life but me, Oh! heavy trial! but let the will of God be done. I do not murmur; you know when the cup of sorrow is full.

In the days of my spring, happiness, all happiness has fled. Truth I boldly spoke, and chains are my reward; These sufferings I bear willingly, and die with resignation; Sweet solace feels thus heart, I fulfilled my duty! (*In a state of inspiration but with calmness.*) Do I not hear soft murmurs in the air? Does not a ray of light surround my grave? Yes, I behold, clad in roseate vapor

Duft Sich tröstend zur Seite mir stellet; Ein Engel, Leonoren, der Gattin so gleich, Der Führt mich zur Freiheit, in's himmlische Reich! (*Sinkt zusammen und bedeckt das Gesicht mit den Händen.*)

### ZWEITE SCENE

*Rocco, Leonore, Florestan. Die beiden ersten steigen die Treppe herab mit einer Laterne, einem Kruge und Werkzeugen zum Graben. Die hintere Thür öffnet sich und das Gefängniss wird matt erleuchtet.*

**LEONORE:** (*halblaut.*) Wie kalt es ist in dieser unterirdischen Höhle!

**ROCCO:** Das ist natürlich, es ist so tief.

**LEONORE:** (*sich ängstlich nach allen Seiten umsehend.*) Ich glaubte schon, wir würden den Eingang nicht finden.

**ROCCO:** (*sich nach Florestan umsehend*) Still! da ist der Gefangene!

**LEONORE:** (*halblaut, suchend, den Gefangenen zu erkennen.*) Er scheint ganz ohne Bewegung zu sein.

**ROCCO:** Vielleicht ist er todt!

**LEONORE:** Meint ihr wirklich?

**ROCCO:** Nein, nein! er schläft nur! Lass uns das benützen und mit der Arbeit beginnen. Wir haben keine Zeit zu verlieren.

**LEONORE:** (*bei Seite.*) Es ist unmöglich, seine Gesichtszüge zu erkennen; Himmel, hilf mir, wenn er es ist!

**ROCCO:** Hier unter diesem Gewölb ist die alte Cisterne, von welcher ich dir erzählte. Es wird uns nicht lange nehmen, an die Oeffnung zu gelangen. Gieb mir deine Haue und komme her. Du zitterst? Hast du Furcht?

**LEONORE:** O nein! Es ist nur so kalt!

**ROCCO:** Vorwärts denn! Du wirst bei der Arbeit bald warm werden. (*Sie beginnen zu graben.*) Während des Melodramas benützt Leonore den Augenblick, wenn Rocco sich bückt, um den Gefangenen zu beobachten. Das Duett wird stiller gesungen.

**ROCCO:** (*arbeitend.*) Nur hurtig fort, nur frisch gegraben, Es währt nicht lang', so kommt er her.

**LEONORE:** (*gleichfalls arbeitend.*) Ihr sollt ja nicht zu klagen haben. Ihr sollt gewiss zufrieden sein.

a beauteous angel like my Leonora, Stand by my side, to point me out the way to liberty and to celestial bliss! (*He sinks exhausted by his last agitation, upon the rocky seat; his hands cover his face.*)

### SCENE II

*(Rocquo, Leonora, Florestan. The two former, who are seen through the aperture by the light of a lantern, carry a pitcher and the tools for digging. The back door opens and the stage becomes half lighted.)*

**LEONORA:** (*in an undertone*) How cold it is in this subterraneous cave!

**ROCQUO:** That's natural, it being so deep.

**LEONORA:** (*looking anxiously around on all sides*). I thought already we should not find the entrance.

**ROCQUO:** (*turning towards Florestan.*) Silence, there is the prisoner.

**LEONORA:** (*halfloud, endeavoring to recognize the prisoner*). He seems quite motionless.

**ROCQUO:** Perhaps he is dead.

**LEONORA:** You don't mean it!

**ROCQUO:** No, no, he only sleeps. Let us take advantage of that and proceed to work, we have no time to lose.

**LEONORA:** (*aside*). It is impossible to distinguish his features, but; oh heavens assist if it is him!

**ROCQUO:** Here, below this rubbish is the old cistern, of which I told you. It will not take us long to get at the opening. Give me your pick-ax, and come here. You tremble. Are you afraid?

**LEONORA:** Oh no, it is only so cold.

**ROCQUO:** Well, then, go on; you will soon get warm with your work. (*They begin to dig.*) (*During the symphony, Leonora takes advantage of the moment when Rocquo stoops to observe the prisoner. The Duet is sung throughout in an undertone.*)

**ROCQUO:** (*while at work*). Only get on quickly, and with smart digging; before long he will come down.

**LEONORA:** (*also working*). You shall not have to complain; for to me no labor is too hard.

## Act II, Scene II

ROCCO: (*einen grossen Stein hebend.*) Komm hilf! komm hilf! doch diesen Stein mir heben, Hab' Acht! Hab' Acht! er hat Gewicht!

LEONORE: Ich helfe schon, sorgt euch nicht, Ich will mir alle Mühe geben.

ROCCO: Ein wenig noch.

LEONORE: Geduld!

ROCCO: Er weicht.

LEONORE: Nur etwas noch.

ROCCO: Er ist nicht leicht. (*Sie rollen den Stein auf die Bühne und schöpfen Athem. Rocco gräbt weiter.*) Nur hurtig fort, nur frisch gegraben, Es währt nicht lang', da kommt er her.

LEONORE: (*ebenfalls wieder arbeitend.*) Lasst mich nur wieder Kräfte haben, Wir werden bald zu Ende sein. (*Betrachtet den Gefangenen, während Rocco von ihr abgewandt mit gekrümmtem Rücken arbeitet, leise.*) Wer du auch seist, ich will dich retten; Bei Gott! Du sollst kein Opfer sein. Gewiss, ich löse deine Ketten; Ich will, du Armer, dich befrei'n.

ROCCO: (*sich schnell aufrichtend.*) Was zauderst du in deiner Pflicht?

LEONORE: Nein, Vater! nein, ich zaud're nicht.

ROCCO: Nur hurtig fort, nur frisch gegraben; Es währt nicht lang, so kommt er her.

LEONORE: Ihr sollt ja nicht zu klagen haben, Lasst mich nur wieder Kräfte haben, Denn mir wird keine Arbeit schwer. (*Rocco trinkt. Florestan erhebt den Kopf, ohne sich nach Leonoren umzusehen.*)

LEONORE: Er ist erwacht!

ROCCO: (*mit dem Trinken einhaltend.*) Er ist erwacht, sagst du?

LEONORE: (*Florestan in der grössten Aufregung betrachtend.*) Ja, er hat soeben sein Haupt erhoben!

ROCCO: Ohne Zweifel wird er wieder tausend Fragen an mich stellen. Ich muss mit ihm allein sprechen. (*Kommt aus der Grube.*) Steige du statt meiner hinein und räume, so viel du kannst fort, das wir die Cisterne öffnen können.

LEONORE: (*hinabsteigend, zitternd.*) Was in mir vorgeht, ist unaussprechlich!

ROCQUO: (*lifting up a large stone on the spot where he went down*). Come—Help me to lift this stone. Take care; take care; it is very heavy.

LEONORA: I'll help you directly. Never fear; I'll exert myself to the utmost.

ROCQUO: A little more.

LEONORA: Patience.

ROCQUO: It moves.

LEONORA: A little more.

ROCQUO: It is not light. (*They roll the stone over the rubbish, and take breath. Rocquo sets to work again.*) Only get on quickly, and with good smart digging. He will soon be here.

LEONORA: (*also working again*). Let me only gain breath again. (*Observes the prisoner, whilst Rocquo, turns away from her, works with his back bent.*) (*softly.*) Who ever you are, I will save you. By all that's sacred, you shall not fall a sacrifice. For certain I will loose your chain; I will set you free, you poor wretched man.

ROCQUO: (*starting up quickly*). What, are you at your work?

LEONORA: No, father, no! I do not hesitate.

ROCQUO: Only get on quickly, and with good smart digging. He will soon be here.

LEONORA: You shall not complain; for no toil is hard to me. (*Rocquo drinks.*) (*Florestan recovers himself, and raises his head up, without turning towards Leonora.*)

LEONORA: He wakes!

ROCQUO: (*suddenly stopping, while drinking*). He wakes, you say?

LEONORA: (*still looking towards Florestan, in the greatest agitation*). Yes—he has just raised up his head.

ROCQUO: Doubtless, he will put me again a thousand questions; I must speak alone with him. He will soon, now, have overcome it all. (*He comes out of the grave.*) Do you go down, instead of me; and clear away as much as you can, so that we may open the cistern.

LEONORA: (*She goes a few steps down, tremblingly*). What passes within me is unspeakable.

ROCCO: (*zu Florestan.*) Nun, habt Ihr ein wenig ausgeruht?

FLORESTAN: Wie könnte ich wohl Ruhe finden!

LEONORE: (*für sich.*) Diese Stimme! Wenn ich nur sein Gesicht einen Augenblick sehen könnte!

FLORESTAN: Willst du ewig taub gegen meine Klagen sein, grausamer Mann! (*Er wendet sich bei diesen Worten nach Leonoren.*)

LEONORE: Gott des Himmels! Er ist es! (*Sie fällt besinnungslos am Rande der Grube nieder.*)

ROCCO: Was wollt Ihr von mir? Ich befolge die Befehle, welche mir gegeben werden; das ist mein Amt, meine Pflicht!

FLORESTAN: Sage mir denn nur einmal, wer ist der Gouverneur dieses Gefängnisses?

ROCCO: (*für sich.*) Ich kann es ihm jetzt wohl ohne Gefahr sagen. (*Laut.*) Der Gouverneur dieses Gefängnisses ist Don Pizarro.

LEONORE: (*sich aufrichtend.*) O Barbar! Deine Grausamkeit, ja dein Name giebt mir meine Kraft wieder!

FLORESTAN: O sendet, so schnell ihr könnt, nach Sevilla. Fraget dort nach Leonora Florestan.

LEONORE: Gott des Himmels! Er ahnt nicht, dass sie ihm jetzt sein Grab gräbt!

FLORESTAN: Saget ihr, dass ich in Ketten hier bin.

ROCCO: Es ist unmöglich, sage ich euch! Ich würde mich ruiniren, ohne euch zu helfen.

FLORESTAN: Wemm ich denn bestimmt bin, hier zu schmachten, o, lasst mich nicht so langsam meinem Ende entgegengehen!

LEONORE: (*aufspringend, aber sich fassend.*) O Gott, wer kann dies ertragen?

FLORESTAN: Habt Mitleid und gebet mir nur einen Tropfen Wasser—sicherlich, das ist wenig genug!

ROCCO: (*für sich.*) Es dreht mir das Herz um.

LEONORE: Er scheint ihn zu erweichen.

FLORESTAN: Ihr antwortet nicht?

ROCCO: Ich kann euren Wunsch nicht erfüllen. Alles, was ich euch anbieten kann, ist der Rest Wein, welchen ich im Kruge habe.

LEONORE: (*bringt den Krug.*) Da ist er, da ist er!

FLORESTAN: (*Leonoren betrachtend.*) Wer ist das?

ROCQUO: (*to Florestan*). Now you have reposed again a little?

FLORESTAN: How could I possibly find repose?

LEONORA: (*to herself*). That voice! If I could only see his face for an instant—

FLORESTAN: Will you always be deaf to my complaints? cruel man. (*With the last words, he turns his face towards Leonora.*)

LEONORA: God of Heaven! It is him. (*She falls senseless on the edge of the grave.*)

ROCQUO: What do you require of me, then? I fulfill the orders given to me;—that is my province, my duty.

FLORESTAN: Only tell me then—at once—who is the governor of this prison.

ROCQUO: (*aside*). Now I can tell him well enough, without danger. (*Aloud.*) The governor of this prison is Don Pizzarro.

LEONORA: (*gradually recovering herself*). Oh, barbarian! Your cruelty—your very name restores me to my strength.

FLORESTAN: Oh! send—send as quickly as possible to Seville. Ask there for Leonora Florestan.

LEONORA: Lord of mercy! He does not suspect that she is now digging his grave.

FLORESTAN: Tell her that I am lying here in chains.

ROCQUO: It is impossible, I tell you, I should be ruining myself, without doing you any benefit.

FLORESTAN: If, then, I am condemned to pine away here, Oh! let me not so slowly linger to my end.

LEONORA: (*springs up, and then restrains herself*). Oh God! Who can endure this?

FLORESTAN: For pity's sake, give me only a drop of water;—surely that is little enough.

ROCQUO: (*aside*). It goes against my very heart.

LEONORA: He appears to soften him.

FLORESTAN: You give me no answer.

ROCQUO: I cannot procure you what you request. All that I can offer you is a remnant of wine, which I have in the pitcher.

LEONORA: (*bringing the pitcher with the utmost haste*). There it is; there it is.

FLORESTAN: (*looking at Leonora*). Who is that?

ROCCO: Mein Gehülfe und in wenigen Tagen mein Schwiegersohn. (*Giebt ihm den Krug. Florestan trinkt.*) Es ist nicht viel, aber ich gebe es euch gerne. (*Zu Leonoren.*) Du bist ganz aufgeregt.

LEONORE: (*verwirrt.*) Wer könnte ruhig bleiben? Ihr selbst, Meister Rocco!

ROCCO: Ja, es ist wahr! Der Mann hat so eine Stimme.

LEONORE: Ja, sie dringt bis in das innerste Herz.

FLORESTAN: Euch werde Lohn in bessern Welten,
Der Himmel hat euch mir geschickt;
O Dank, ihr habt mich süss erquickt,
Ich kann die Wohlthat, ich kann sie nie vergelten.

LEONORE: Der Himmel schicke Rettung dir,
Dann wird mir hoher Lohn gewährt.

ROCCO: Mich rührte oft dein Leiden hier,
Doch Hülfe war mir streng verwehrt. (*Leise zu Leonoren, die er bei Seite zicht.*)
Ich labt' ihn gern, den armen Mann.
Es ist ja bald um ihn gethan.
Ich thu' was meine Pflicht gebeut,
Doch hass' ich alle Grausamkeit.

LEONORE: (*für sich.*) Wie heftig pocht dieses Herz,
Es wogt in Freud' und scharfem Schmerz!
Die hehre, bange Stunde winkt.
Die Tod mir oder Rettung bringt.

FLORESTAN: (*für sich.*) Bewegt seh' ich den Jüngling hier.
Und Rührung zeigt auch dieser Mann;
O Gott, o Gott! du sendest Hoffnung mir,
Das ich sie noch gewinnen kann.

LEONORE: (*leise zu Rocco, indem sie ein Stückchen Brod aus der Tasche zieht.*) Dies Stückchen Brod, ja seit zwei Tagen.
Trag' ich es immer schon bei mir.

ROCCO: Ich möchte gern, doch sag ich dir.
Das hiesse wirklich zu viel wagen.

LEONORE: (*schmeichelnd.*) Ach, ihr labtet gern denarmen Mann!

ROCCO: Das geht nicht an. Das geht nicht an.

LEONORE: (*wie vorher.*) Es ist ja bald um ihn gethan!

ROCCO: So sei es, ja so sei's, du kannst es wagen.

LEONORE: (*in grösster Bewegung, Florestan das Brod reichend.*) Da, nimm das Brod.
Du armer, armer Mann!

ROCQUO: My assistant;—and in a few days, my son-in-law. (*Hands the pitcher to Florestan, who drinks.*) There is, truly not much wine; yet I am glad to give it you. (*To Leonora.*) You are quite agitated.

LEONORA: (*in the greatest embarrassment*). Who could help being so? You, yourself, Mr. Rocquo—

ROCQUO: It is true,—the man has such a voice—

LEONORA: Yes;—it penetrates to the inmost recesses of the heart.

FLORESTAN: May you find a reward in the next world. Heaven has sent you to me. Oh, thanks! you have sweetly revived me. I cannot reward thy kindness.

LEONORA: Heaven send you deliverance; then will I be highly rewarded.

ROCQUO: Your sufferings often moved me; but to keep you was strictly forbidden me. (*Softly to Leonora, whom he takes aside.*) I was glad. Heaven knows, to refresh the poor man. But it is already all over with him. I do what my duty imposes, yet I abhor all cruelty.

LEONORA: (*aside*). How my heart is beating; my life fluctuates between joy and grief. The awful hour beckons on, that death or deliverance does bring.

FLORESTAN: (*to himself*). I see this youth here affected; and this man also shows compassion. O God! you send me hope, that I may again find her for whom alone I live.

LEONORA: (*softly to Rocquo, while she draws a small piece of bread out of her pocket*). This piece of bread I have carried about me for the last two days.

ROCQUO: I would most willingly; but I tell you that would indeed be venturing too much.

LEONORA: (*winningly*). You like to refresh the poor man.

ROCQUO: That will not do; that will not do.

LEONORA: (*as before*). It will very soon be all over with him.

ROCQUO: So be it then; you may venture it.

LEONORA: (*in the greatest agitation, handing Florestan the bread*). There, take the bread, poor man.

ROCCO: (*für sich, sehr gerührt.*) Es ist ja bald um ihn gethan!

FLORESTAN: (*Leonorens Hand ergreifend und an sich drückend.*) O Dank dir, euch werde Lohn in bessern Welten!

ROCCO: Armer Mensch!

LEONORE: O, das ist mehr, als ich ertragen kann!

ROCCO: Est ist ja bald um ihn gethan.

FLORESTAN: O, dass ich euch nicht lohnen kann!
(*Err isst das Stück Brod.*)

ROCCO: (*nach kurzem Stillschweigen zu Leonora.*) Alles ist fertig. Ich will jetzt das Zeichen geben.

FLORESTAN: (*zu Leonora, während Rocco geht, um die Thüre zu öffnen.*) Wohin geht er? (*Rocco öffnet die Thür und giebt das Zeichen, indem er laut pfeift.*) Ist dies der Vorbote meines Todes?

LEONORE: (*in äusserster Aufregung.*) Nein, nein, beruhigt euch, lieber Gefangener!

FLORESTAN: O, meine Leonore! Ich werde sie nie wiedersehen!

LEONORE: (*scheint zu Florestan hingezogen zu werden, bezwingt sich aber.*) Mein ganze Herz zicht mich zu ihm hin. (*Zu Florestan.*) Bleibt ruhig! Vergesst nich, was ihr auch hören und sehen möget, dass eine Vorsehung über uns waltet. (*Sie geht von ihm nach der Cisterne su.*)

## DRITTE SCENE

*Don Pizarro, in einen Mantel gehüllt.*

PIZARRO: (*Zu Rocco mit verstellter Stimme.*) Ist Alles fertig?

ROCCO: Ja wohl, die Cisterne braucht blos geöffnet zu werden.

PIZARRO: Gut! der Bursche muss fortgehen.

ROCCO: (*zu Leonoren.*) Gehe! Entferne dich!

LEONORE: (*sehr bestürzt.*) Ich? Und Ihr?

ROCCO: Muss ich nicht dem Gefangenen die Fesseln abnehmen? (*Leonore geht langsam nach dem Hintergrunde, nähert sich aber langsam wieder in der Dunkelheit Florestan, die Augen fortwährend auf Pizarro gerichtet.*)

PIZARRO: (*für sich, Rocco und Leonore betrachtend.*) Ich muss mir noch heute sie beide vom Halse schaffen, damit Alles für immer verschwiegen bleibt.

ROCQUO: (*to himself, much affected*). Yes, it will be very soon all over with him.

FLORESTAN: (*grasping Leonora's hand, and pressing it to himself.*) Oh, thank you! thank you! May heavenly bliss be your reward.

ROCQUO: Poor fellow!

LEONORA: Oh, more than I can endure.

ROCQUO: It will soon be over with him.

FLORESTAN: Oh, that I cannot reward you. (*He eats the piece of bread.*)

ROCQUO: (*after a momentary silence, to Leonora*). All is ready. I am going to give the signal.

FLORESTAN: (*to Leonora, while Rocquo goes to open the door*). Where is he going? (*Rocque opens the door, and gives the signal by a loud whistle.*) Is that the harbinger of my death?

LEONORA: (*in extremest agitation*). No, no, calm yourself, dear prisoner.

FLORESTAN: Oh, my Leonora! shall I never then see you again?

LEONORA: (*She seems to feel herself drawn towards Florestan, and strives to overcome the impulse*). My whole heart draws me to him. (*To Florestan.*) Be composed I tell you. Do not forget whatever you may hear and see—do not forget that there is a Providence above. (*She separates from him, and goes towards the cistern.*)

## SCENE III

(*Enter Pizzarro, disguised in a mantle.*)

PIZZARRO: (*to Rocquo, in a feigned voice*). Is all ready?

ROCQUO: Yes; the cistern has only to be opened.

PIZZARRO: Good. The lad must go away.

ROCQUO: (*to Leonora*). Go! withdraw.

LEONORA: (*in the greatest perplexity*). Who? I and you?

ROCQUO: Must I not take the irons from the prisoner? Go, go! (*Leonora withdraws to the background, and approaches gradually again in the shade towards Florestan, her eyes directed constantly to the person in the disguise.*)

PIZZARRO: (*aside, casting a look at Rocquo and Leonora*). Today I must shake off these two from me, that all may be ever remain in silence.

ROCCO: (zu Don Pizarro.) Soll ich seine Ketten abnehmen?

PIZARRO: Nein!
(Zieht einen Dolch.)
Er sterbe! doch soll er wissen.
Wer ihm sein stolzes Herz zerfleischt.
Der Rache Dunkel sei zerrissen.
Sieh hier, du hast mich nicht getäuscht!
Pizarro, den du stüzen wolltest.
Pizarro, den du fürchten solltest,
Steht nun als Rächer hier!

FLORESTAN: (ruhig.) Ein Mörder steht vor mir!

PIZARRO: Noch einmal ruf' ich dir.
Was du gethan, zurück.
Nur noch ein Augenblick, und dieser Dolch—
(Er will ihn durchbohren.)

LEONORE: (stürzt mit einem durchdringenden Schrei hervor und bedeckt Forestan mit ihrem Körper.) Zurück!

FLORESTAN: O Gott!

ROCCO: Was soll's?

LEONORE: Durchbohren musst du erst diese Brust!
Der Tod sei dir geschworen für deine Mörderlust!

DON PIZARRO: (sie wegstossend.) Wahnsinniger!

ROCCO: (zu Leonoren.) Halt ein! Halt doch ein!

PIZARRO: Wahnsinniger! Er soll bestrafet sein!

LEONORE: (sich vor Florestan stellend.) Tödt' erst sein Weib!

PIZARRO: Sein Weib!

ROCCO: Sein Weib?

FLORESTAN: Mein Weib?

LEONORE: (zu Florestan.) Ja, sieh' hier Leonoren!

FLORESTAN: Leonore!

LEONORE: (zu den Andern.) Ich bin sein Weib!
Geschworen hab' ich ihm Trost, Verderben dir!

DON PIZARRO: (für sich.) Sein Weib!
Welch' unerhörter Muth!

FLORESTAN: (zu Leonoren.) Vor Freude starrt mein Blut!

ROCCO: Mir starrt vor Angst mein Blut!

LEONORE: Ich trotze siener Wuth.

PIZARRO: Haha! soll ich vor einem Weibe beben?
So opf're ich sie beide meinem Grimme!
Getheilt hast du mit ihm das Leben,
So theile nun den Tod mit ihm.
(Er will sich auf sie stürzen. Leonore zieht plötzlich eine Pistole aus dem Busen und hält sie Don Pizarro entgegen.)

ROCQUO: (to Pizarro). Shall I take off his chains?

PIZZARRO: No! (Draws a dagger.)
He dies; but he shall first know who it is that pierces his proud heart. Let the darkness be torn away that veils revenge. Behold! you have not deceived yourself! (He throws off the mantle.) Pizzarro, whom you wished to overthrow!—Pizzarro, whom you should fear to look upon, stands now before you, his own avenger!

FLORESTAN: (collectedly). A murderer stands before me.

PIZZARRO: Yet, for once will I recall you to what you have done; yet one moment, and my dagger—(He tries to stab him.)

LEONORA: (springs forward with a piercing shriek, and covers Florestan with her body.) Hold!

FLORESTAN: Oh, God!

ROCQUO: What is all this?

LEONORA: You must first stab through this breast. Death is sworn to you for your blood-thirstiness!

PIZZARRO: (thrusting her away). Mad creature!

ROCQUO: (to Leonora). Desist, I say.

PIZZARRO: He shall be punished.

LEONORA: (Once more shielding her husband). Kill first his wife!

PIZZARRO: His wife!

ROCQUO: His wife!

FLORESTAN: Ha! my wife!

LEONORA: (to Florestan). Oh, yes, yes, see here your Leonora!

FLORESTAN: Leonora!

LEONORA: (to the others). I am his wife. I have sworn aid to him, destruction to you.

PIZZARRO: (to himself). His wife! What unheard of courage!

FLORESTAN: (to Leonora). My heart will burst with joy!

ROCQUO: My blood runs cold with terror!

LEONORA: I brave his rage!

PIZZARRO: Shall I tremble before a woman?
No! I will sacrifice them both to my rage. You have shared life with him,—now partake his doom in death.
(He is about to assail her, when Leonora suddenly draws a small pistol out of her bosom, and holds it before Pizzarro.)

LEONORE: Noch einen Laut und du bist todt.
(Trompetenfanfare draussen.)

PIZARRO: Ha, ha! der Minister! Hölle und Tod!

ROCCO: O, was ist das! gerechter Gott!
(Don Pizarro steht vernichtet da, ebenso Rocco. Lenore fällt Florestan um den Hals. Die Trompetenfanfare wird wiederholt.)

## VIERTE SCENE

Jaquino, zwei Offiziere, Soldaten mit Fackeln erscheinen oben am Thore.

JAQUINO: (spricht waehrend der angezeigten Musikpause.) Vater Rocco, der Minister kommt eben an. Seine Wache ist schon vor dem Thor.

ROCCO: (für sich, in freudiger Ueberraschung.) Der Himmel sei gelobt! (Zu Jaquino laut.) Wir kommen, ja, wir kommen sogleich, und die Leute mit den Fackeln sollen herabkommen und dem Gouverneur hinauf leuchten.
(Die Soldaten kommen an die Thüre. Offiziere und Jacquino ab.

PIZARRO: Verflucht sei diese böse Stunde! Die Hölle spottet meiner! Verzweiflung tritt zu meiner Rache.

ROCCO: Tödtlicher Aufschub! O welch' neue Betrübniss wartet jetzt meiner? Ich will nicht länger diesem Tyrannen gehorchen; der Augenblick der Rache ist gekommen, du sollst frei sein!

LEONORE UND FLORESTAN: Der Augenblick der Rache ist da, du sollst frei sein. Liebe im Vereine mit Muth werden mich doch befreien.
(Don Pizarro eilt hinweg, indem er Rocco ein Zeichen giebt, ihm zu folgen. Er benutzt den Augenblick, als Pizarro fortgegangen ist, und vereinigt die Hände der Ehegatten, weist gegen Himmel und folgt Don Pizarro.)

## FÜNFTE SCENE

FLORESTAN: Theures Weib! Was hast du für mich gelitten!

LEONORE: Nichts, nichts, mein Florestan!
O namenlose Freude!
Mein Mann an meiner Brust
Nach unnennbaren Leiden
So übergrosse Lust!
Du wieder nun in meinen Armen,
O Dank dir, Gott, für diese Lust!

LEONORA: Another word, and you are dead!
(The trumpet is heard from the tower.)

PIZZARRO: Ha! the minister! Hell and death!

ROCQUO: Oh, what is that? Just heaven!
(Pizzarro stands confounded. Rocquo the same. Leonora hangs on Florestan's neck. The trumpet sounds louder.)

## SCENE IV

(Jacquino, two officers, and soldiers, with torches, appear at the uppermost grated opening of the gates.)

JACQUINO: (speaks during the pause of the music). Father Rocquo, the minister arrives; his guard is already before the castle gate.

ROCQUO: (to himself, delighted and surprised).
Heaven be praised! (To Jacquino, calling aloud.) We are coming! yes, we are coming immediately; and the men with their torches shall come down and accompany the Governor up. (The soldiers come down as far as the door. The Officers and Jacquino go out again.)

PIZZARRO: Curse be this evil hour. Hell mocks me! Despair now leagues itself with my revenge!

ROCQUO: Dread suspense! Oh! what fresh affliction is now in store for me? I will no longer be controlled by this tyrant. The moment of vengeance has come; you shall be free!

LEONORA AND FLORESTAN: The moment of vengeance has come; you shall be free! Love, in league with courage, will still make me free.
(Pizzarro hastens away, giving Rocquo a sign to follow him. He avails himself of the moment when Pizzarro is going and unites the hands of the husband and wife, presses them to his bosom, points toward heaven, and follows him. The soldiers light Pizzarro off.)

## SCENE V

FLORESTAN: Faithful wife! what have you suffered for me!

LEONORA: Nothing, nothing, my Florestan!
Oh, joy unknown! My husband again restored to my fond embrace!

FLORESTAN: O namenlose Freude,
An Leonoren's Brust,
Nach unnennbaren Leiden,
So übergrosse Lust;
O Gott, wie gross ist dein Erbarmen,
O Dank dir, Gott, für diese Lust.

LEONORE: O himmlisches Entzücken, Florestan!

## SECHSTE SCENE

ROCCO: (eilig.) Gute Nachrichten, meine armen Freunde! Der Minister hat ein Verzeichniss aller Gefangenen. Ihr sollt Alle vor ihn gebracht werden. (Zu Florestan.) Ihr allein seid nicht erwähnt. Eure Gefangenschaft ist eine Willkür des Gouverneurs selbst. Kommt, folget mir. (Alle ab.)

## SIEBENTE SCENE

Saal im Schloss. Die Schlosswache marschirt lierein, darauf Don Fernando mit Don Pizarro und Offizieren. Volk. Die Gefangenen kommen mit Jacquino und Marcelline herbei. Alle werfen sich auf die Kniee. Dann Rocco, Florestan und Leonore.

CHOR: (der Gefangenen und des Volkes.) Heil! Heil! Heil sei dem Tag.
Heil sei der Stunde.
Die lang' ersehnt, doch unvermeint,
Gerechtigkeit mit Huld im Bunde,
Vor unsers Grabes Thor erscheint.

DON FERNANDO: Des besten Königs Wink und Wille,
Führt mich zu euch, ihr Armen, her,
Dass ich der Frevel Nacht ethülle,
Die all' umfangen, schwarz u. schwer,
Nicht länger kniet sklavisch nieder,
Tyrannenstrenge sei mir fern,
Es sucht der Bruder seine Brüder,
Und kann er helfen, hilft er gern.

## ACHTE SCENE

(Florestan und Leonore vorführend.)

ROCCO: Wohlan, so helft den Armen.
PIZARRO: Was seh' ich ha!
ROCCO: Bewegt es dich?
PIZARRO: Fort, fort!
DON FERNANDO: Nein, rede!

ROCCO: Aus Erbarmen vereine dieses Paar.
(Florestan vorfuehrend).
Don Florestan.

DON FERNANDO: Der Todtgeglaubte, der Edle,
Der für Wahrheit stritt!

ROCCO: Und Qualen ohne Zahl erlitt.

DON FERNANDO: Mein Freund, der Todtgeglaubte.
Gefesselt, bleich steht er vor mir.

ROCCO UND LEONORE: Ja, Florestan, ihr seht ihn hier!

ROCCO: Und Leonore—(sie vorstellend.)

DON FERNANDO: (bewegt.) Leonore?

ROCCO: Der Frauen Zierde führ' ich vor;
Sie kam hierher—

PIZARRO: Zwei Worte sagen—

DON FERNANDO: (zu Don Pizarro.) Kein Wort. (Zu Rocco.) Sie kam?—

ROCCO: Dort an mein Thor,
Und trat als Knecht in meine Dienste
Und treue Dienste,
Dass ich zum Eidam sie erkor.

MARCELLINE: O weh mir! weh mir!
Was vernimmt mein Ohr!

ROCCO: Der Unmensch wollt' in dieser Stunde
Vollzieh'n an Florestan den Mord.

PIZARRO: Vollzieh'n mit ihm—

ROCCO: (auf sich und Leonoren deutend.) Mit uns im Bunde,
Nur euer Kommen rief ihn fort.

CHOR: Bestrafet sei der Bösewicht,
Der Unschuld unterdrückt.
Gerechtigkeit hält zum Gericht
Der Rache Schwert gezückt.

DON FERNANDO: (zu Rocco.) Du schlossest auf des Edlen Grab,
Jetzt nimm ihm seine Ketten ab,
Doch halt, euch edle Frau allein,
Euch ziemt es, ganz ihn zu befrei'n.

LEONORE: (nimmt die Schlüssel, lässt in grösster Bewegung die Ketten ab; er sinkt in Leonorens Arme.) O Gott, welch' ein Augenblick!

FLORESTAN: O unaussprechlich süsses Glück!

DON FERNANDO: Gerecht, o Gott, gerecht ist dein Gericht.

ROCCO UND MARCELLINE: Du prüfest, du verlässt uns nicht.

---

FLORESTAN: Pressed to my Leonora's breast, after great sufferings! Oh, delight past utterance!

LEONORA: You again—now in my arms!

## SCENE VI

ROCQUO: (springing in). Good news! My poor sufferers! The minister has a list of all the prisoners. You are all to be brought before him. (To Florestan.) You alone are not mentioned. Your detention here is an arbitrary action on the part of the governor himself. Come, follow me! follow me up. (Exeunt.)

## SCENE VII

(Hall in the Castle.)
(The castle guard march up; then the minister Don Fernando, accompanied by Pizzarro and Officers on one side. People assemble as spectators; and on the other side appear, accompanied by Jacquino and Marceline the state prisoners. They all throw themselves on their knees before Don Fernando. Afterwards Rocquo, with Florestan and Leonora, press through the people and through the guard.)

CHORUS: (of Prisoners and People). All hail the day! All hail the hour, long sought for yet unhoped! Justice, united with mercy, appears to us on the shrine of death.

DON FERNANDO: The command and wish of the best of kings brings me to you, poor wearied sufferers! that I unveil crimes and dreary sorrows, which surround you deep and full. No longer kneel down slavishly. (Prisoners rise.) I do not cherish the tyrant's power. I come a brother loving and help where help can be.

## SCENE VIII

(Enter Rocquo, conducting Leonora and Florestan.)

ROCQUO: There, there,—Help here! help the poor captive.
PIZZARRO: What do I see. Ha!
ROCQUO: Does it move you?
PIZZARRO: Away! away!
DON FERNANDO: No,—speak.

ROCQUO: For mercy sake, have pity, and reunite this hapless pair.
(Florestan advances).
Don Florestan.

DON FERNANDO: He that was supposed dead? The hero, who fought for truth and right?

ROCQUO: And who has suffered torments unimaginable.

DON FERNANDO: My friend! supposed dead;—how is this, that chained, pallid, and exhausted, he stands before me?

ROCQUO AND LEONORA: Yes,—it is Florestan! you see him here.

ROCQUO: And Leonora (presenting her).

DON FERNANDO (still more affected). Leonora!

ROCQUO: I present the pride, the ornament of her sex. She came here—

PIZZARRO: Speak but two words—

DON FERNANDO: (to Pizzarro). Not a syllable! (To Rocquo.) She came?—

ROCQUO: There, at my gate;—she entered my service as a hireling boy, and served me so well and faithfully, that I chose her for a son-in-law.

MARCELINE: Oh, woe is me!— What meets my ear!

ROCQUO: Within this very hour, the cruel man would do a deed of murder on Florestan.

PIZZARRO: Murder! on him?

ROCQUO: (pointing to himself and Leonora). Yes, my lord, he wanted us to join in his base design. Your arrival only drove him away.

CHORUS: Punishment be to the villian who oppressed the innocent! Justice hold for judgment the drawn sword of revenge.

DON FERNANDO: (to Rocquo). You lifted the grave that threatened this noble heart,—now take off his chains;—yet stay,—You noble woman! to you alone it becomes completely to set him free!

LEONORA: (takes the keys, loosens the chains from off Florestan, with great agitation. He sinks into Leonora's arms.) Oh, what a moment!

FLORESTAN: Oh, inexpressible happiness!

DON FERNANDO: Just, O heaven, are your judgments!

ROCQUO AND MARCELINE: You tried—but you did not forsake us.

## Act II, Scene VIII

**CHOR:** Wer ein holdes Weib errungen,
Stimm' in unsern Jubel ein,
Nie wird es zu hoch besungen,
Retterin des Gatten sein.

**FLORESTAN:** Deine Treu' erhielt mein Leben.
Tugend schreckt den Bösewicht.

**LEONORE:** Liebe führte mein Bestreben,
Wahre Liebe fürchtet nicht.

**CHOR:** Preist mit hoher Freude Gluth
Leonorens edlen Muth.

**CHORUS:** Whoever has obtained such a partner of his heart, let him join in our jubilee. Who can ever sufficiently praise the wife that frees her husband from his chains!

**FLORESTAN:** Your fidelity restores my life. Virtue is the sinner's dread.

**LEONORA:** Love guided my endeavors; true love knows no fear.

**CHORUS:** Let us sing praises high to the noble strife of Leonora.

**FLORESTAN:** (*vortretend und auf Leonoren deutend.*) Wer ein solches Weib errungen,
Stimm' in unsern Jubel ein!
Nie wird es zu hoch besungen,
Retterin des Gatten sein.

**LEONORE:** (*umarmt ihn.*) Liebend ist es mir gelungen,
Dich aus Ketten zu befreien;
Liebend sei es hoch gesungen,
Florestan ist wieder mein!

**ROCCO UND CHOR:** Wer ein solches Weib errungen,
Stimm' in unsern Jubel ein!
Nie wird es zu hoch besungen,
Retterin des Gatten sein.

*ENDE.*

**FLORESTAN:** (*advancing, and pointing to Leonora.*) Whoever has obtained a wife, etc.

**LEONORA:** (*embracing him*). Guided by love, my success is complete. Your chains are broken! high praise be to love; I embrace my Florestan again.

**ROCQUO AND CHORUS:** Whoever has a wife, etc.

*THE END.*

# Norma (1831)

## Music by Vincenzo Bellini ■ Libretto by Felice Romani

Bellini's two-act tragedia lirica, Alexandre Soumet's tragedy *Norma,* or *L'Infanticide,* set to a libretto by Felice Romani was first performed at the La Scala in Milan on December 26, 1831. In the sacred forest of the druids, in the center of which stands the oak tree of Irminsul, Oroveso and the Druids express their hatred of the Roman conquerors. Pollione, the Roman proconsul, has left Norma, the Druid high priestess who has borne him two sons, and is now in love with Adalgisa, another priestess. He has dreamt that Norma will seek her revenge. The Gauls perform their sacred rites. Norma proclaims that Irminsul has not yet decreed that the Gauls must go to war and that Rome will eventually destroy herself. She prays to the goddess of the moon (the exquisite *Casta Diva*) for peace. Adalgisa comes to the clearing to meet Pollione and he enjoins her to run away with him to Rome. Adalgisa confesses to Norma that she has a lover, and has broken her vow of chastity as a priestess. Norma forgives her until she discovers that Adalgisa's lover is Pollione. She pronounces a curse upon them both. Pollione departs just as temple gong is rounding up the Gauls. Norma, intending to kill her two children, cannot bring herself to do so. She asks Adalgisa to take them into her care. Adalgisa asks Pollione to return to Norma. Though the Gallic warriors are ready to go to battle, Oroveso advises them to be patient. But, Adalgisa is unable to change Pollione's mind and Norma, enraged, gathers her people and declares that it is Irminsul's wish that Rome be exterminated. The people cry out for a victim to be sacrificed; Pollione is captured in the temple, but Norma stops the rite just as the sacrifice is about to begin to be alone with him. She decides to sacrifice herself instead as she, too, has broken her vow of chastity as a priestess. She gives her children to Pollione and climbs onto the sacred pyre. Norma and Pollione reunite after death.

---

## ■ ATTO PRIMO

*Foresta sacra de' Druidi. In mezzo, la Quercia d'Irminsul; al piè della quale vedesi la pietra druidica, che serve d'altare. Colli in disianza sparsi di selve. E notte: lontani fuochi trapelano dai boschi.*

*(Al suono di marcia religiosa difilano le schiere de' Galli; indi, la processione de' Druidi; per ultimo Oroveso, coi Maggiori Sacerdoti.)*

**OROVESO:** Ite sul colle, o Druidi!
Ite a spiar ne' Cieli;
Quando il suo disco argenteo
La nuova luna sveli,
Ed il primier sorriso
Del verginal suo viso,
Tre volte annunzi il mistico
Bronzo sacerdotal.

**DRUIDI:** Il sacro vischio a mietere,
Norma verrà?

**OROVESO:** Sì, Norma.

**OROVESO E DRUIDI:** (*Coro*)

## ■ ACT I

*Sacred forest of the Druids. In the centre, the Oak of Irminsul; at the foot of which is seen a druidical stone, serving as an altar. Hills in the distance, partially covered with trees. It is night: lights are seen among the trees at the back*

*(A religious march is heard. Enter the Gallic Army, followed by a procession of Druids; and, lastly, the Chief Priests, headed by Oroveso.)*

**OROVESO:** On to the hills, oh holy band of Druids!
On, to your duty, watch the heavens;
And when you see her silvery disk up there,
The new moon (omen of success) unveils,
At the first radiant smile that beams from
Her virgin face, charming the sea and shore,
Thrice the glad tidings, spreading all around,
Announce upon the sacerdotal bronze.

**DRUIDS:** Will, then,
The mighty Norma come to cut the sacred mistletoe?

**OROVESO:** Yes, Norma will.

**OROVESO AND DRUIDS:** (*Chorus*)

**DRUIDI:** Dell' aura tua profetica
Terribil Dio l'informa;
Sensi O Irminsul, le inspira,
D'odio ai Romani e d'ira;
Sensi che questa infrangano,
Pace per noi mortal,

**OROVESO:** Sì, parlerà terribile,
Da queste quercie antiche:
Sgombre farà le Gallie
Dall'aqui le nemi che.
E del suo scudo il suono,
Parial fragor del tuono,

**OREVESO E CORO:** Nella città dei Cesari,
Tremendo eccheggerà!

**TUTTI:** Luna, ti affretta a sorger!
Norma all' altar verrà.
*(Si allontanano tutti e si sperdono nella foresta: di quando in quando si odono ancora le loro voci risuonare in lontananza)*
*(Escono quindi da un lato Flavio e Pollione guardinghi e ravvolti nelle lor toghe)*

**POLLIONE:** Svanir le voci.—Dell' orrenda selva
Libero è il varco.

**FLAVIO:** In questa selva è morte.
Norma tel disse.

**POLLIONE:** Profferisti un nome
Che il cor m'agghiaccia.

**DRUIDS:** Oh! with your prophetic power,
Fire her heart, avenging fate;
Dread Irminsul, it is now the hour,
Inspire to Rome eternal hate;
Let resolution be her dower,
Of deadly peace to spurn the weight.

**OROVESO:** Yes, great God, speak in anger,
Your ancient oaks reply from these;
And free this land, wreak, your vengence
Till the Roman eagles fly afar.
Yes, let the sound of your dread shield,
Like the roar of thunder heard,

**OROVESO AND CHORUS:**
Through the Cesarian city pealed,
Re-echo, Victory the word!

**ALL:** Sweet moon, oh, hasten your propitious rise!
Norma will come—she will bless our wishes.
*(The whole disperse, and disappear in the forest at the back: from time to time their voices are heard in the distance)*
*(Flavio and Pollio enter cautiously, enveloped in their togas)*

**POLLIO:** All is hushed and still.—
In this dread wood
Our course is free.

**FLAVIO:** We seek death in this forest
So Norma warned us.

**POLLIO:** You've pronounced a name
That chills my heart.

# Act I

**FLAVIO:** O! che dì tu?—l' amante—
La madre de' tuoi figli!

**FLAVIO:** Heavens! what are you saying? Your loved one—
The mother of your children!

**POLLIONE:** A me non puoi
Far tu rampogna, ch' io mertar son senta;
Ma nel mio core è spenta
La prima fiamma. E un Dio la spense—un Dio,
Nemico al mio riposo. A piè mi veggo
L' abisso aperto, e in lui m' avvento io stesso.

**POLLIO:** No reproach
Can fall from you that I've not deserved;
But in my hapless bosom burns no longer
My heart's first flame. A God so wills—a God,
Foe to my peace, has wrought this falsehood.
I see the abyss before me, nor would I shun it.

**FLAVIO:** Altra ameresti tu?

**FLAVIO:** What! dost you love someone else?

**POLLIONE:** Parla sommesso!
Un' altra!—sì, Adalgisa!
Tu la vedrai, fior d' innocenza e riso
Di candore e di amor! Ministra al tempio
Di questo Iddio di sangue, ella vi appare
Come raggio di stella in Ciel turbato.

**POLLIO:** Hush! speak softly!
Another!—yes, the enchanting Adalgisa!
You shall see this flower of youth and beauty,
Innocence and love! A priestess in the temple
Of these Gauls' blood-stained God, she beams
Like a bright star that cheers the gloomy night.

**FLAVIO:** Misero amico! e amato
Sei tu del pari?

**FLAVIO:** My ill-fated friend! and is your hapless love
Returned?

**POLLIONE:** Io n' ho fiducia.

**POLLIO:** I trust so.

**FLAVIO:** E l'ira
Non temi tu di Norma?

**FLAVIO:** But the jealous wrath,
Do you not dread, of Norma?

**POLLIONE:** Atroce, orrenda;—
Me la presenta il mio rimorso estremo.
Un sogno—

**POLLIO:** Yes, overpowering;—
My deep remorse but too well pictures it.
A dream—

**FLAVIO:** Ah! narra.

**FLAVIO:** Ah! speak.

**POLLIONE:** In rammentarlo io tremo!
Meco all' altar di Venere,
Era Adalgisa in Roma:
Cinta di bende candide,—
Sparsa di fior la chioma.
Udia d' Imene i cantici,
Vedea fumar gl' incensi;
Eran rapiti i sensi—
Di voluttade e amor.
Quando fra noi terribile,
Viene a locarsi un' ombra,
L' ampio mantel Druidico
Come un vapor l' ingombra
Cade su l' ara il folgore,
D' un vel si copre il giorno.
Muto si spande intorno—
Un sepolcrale orror.
Più l' adorata vergine
Io non mi trovo accanto
N' odo da lunge un gemito,
Misto de' figli al pianto,—
Ed una voce orribile,
Echeggia in fondo al tempio:
'Norma così fa scempio
Di amante traditor!'
(*Squilla il sacro bronzo*)

**POLLIO:** Its memory shakes my soul!
With me kneeling to Venus,
In Rome, with Adalgisa;
White robes revealing, her truth—
Pure flowers her hair's sole treasure.
Hearing, the hymns of Hymen
We saw the incense burning;
Rapture endearing both hearts
Thus love with love returning.
When straight, while thus devoted,
Between us rose a shadow,
In Druid robes, that floated
Like mists over morning meadow.
A thunderbolt struck the altar
Day became overclouded.
I falter with fearful doubt—
Sepulchral awe enshrouded.
My bride, sweet maiden! vanished,
I heard, with senses failing,
A groan, all hope that banished,
Mixed with my children's wailing,—
A voice, my bliss that changes.
The temple's depths rolls over:
'Thus Norma well revenges
The treachery of her lover!'
(*The sacred bronze is heard sounding*)

**FLAVIO:** Odi?—I suoi riti a compiere,
Norma dal tempio move.

**FLAVIO:** Do you hear that?—
The Norma you've forsaken comes to perform her rites.

**VOCI:** (*lontano*) Sorta è la luna, o Druidi!
Ite, profani, altrove.

**VOICES:** (*heard in the distance*) The moon appears, oh Druids!
Hence, profane ones, from these scenes.

**FLAVIO:** Vieni!—Fuggiam! sorprendere,
Scoprire alcun ti può.

**FLAVIO:** They come!—Fly! or we may be surpris'd,
Discover'd; let us, then, away.

**POLLIONE:** Traman conguire i barbari!
Ma io li preverrò.

**POLLIO:** Barbarians! they conspire to entrap us,
But I will defeat their schemes.

**POLLIONE:** (*Solo*) Me protegge! me difende
Un poter maggior di loro:
E il pensier di lei che adoro,
E l' amor, è l' amor che m' infiamma!
Di quel Dio chea me con tende—
Quella vergine celeste!
Arderò le rie foreste,
L' empio altare, l' empio altare abbatterò!
L' empio altare abbatterò l' empio altare abbatterò!
(*Partono rapidamente*)
(*Druidi dal fondo, Sacerdotesse, Guerrieri, Bardi, Eubagi, Sacrificatori. E in mezzo, a tutti, Oroveso*)
(*Coro*)
Norma viene!
Le cinge la chioma
La verbena ai misteri sacrata;
In sua man come Luna falcata,
L' aurea falce diffonde splendor.
Ella viene! e la stella di Roma,
Sbigottita si copre d' un velo;
Irminsul corre i campi del Cielo,
Qual cometa, foriera d' oror;
Qual cometa, foriera d' orra, cometa, foriera d' orror! foriera, foriera d' orror, foriera, foriera d' orror.
(*Norma in mezzo alle sue Ministre: ha sciolti i capegli—la fronte circondata, di una corona di verbena—ed armata la mano di una falce d' oro. Si colloca sulla pietra druidica, e volge gli occhi d' intorno come inspirata. Tutti fanno silenzio*)

**POLLIO:** (*Solo*) Love will shield, will protect; yes, a power,
Greater far than they boast, will defend:
The bright thought of my fair, in this hour,
With love's flame will protect, will befriend!
Of the God who'd turn rival—
Turn with me for the maiden divine!
I'll burn, the fell wood's unholy haunts
and lay low in the dust, in the dust, his foul shrine!
(*Exeunt, hastily*)
(*Enter, from the back, Druids, Priestesses, Soldiers, Bards, Sacrificers, etc. In the centre, at their head, Oroveso*)
(*Chorus*)
See, Norma comes!
She wears on her calm brow
A wreath, of vervain formed, crowned with mystery;
In her right hand, like Luna, bears
A gold-wrought sickle, spreading splendor round
Lo! she comes, and declines, Rome's bright star
Fades obscurely in darkness and night.
Irminsul now shines, in the vaulted sky
Horror! horror! a comet, to frighten the souls of men;
(*Enter Norma, in the midst of attendant Priestesses: her hair streaming wildly over her shoulders—her forehead bound by a wreath of the mystic vervain—in her hand a golden sickle. She ascends with a solemn air the druidical stone, and glances around, as one inspired with prophetic power. All maintain a deep silence*)

**NORMA:** Sediziose voci:
Voci di guerra avvi chi alzar si attenta?
Presso all' ara del Dio? v' ha chi presume
Dettar responsi alla vegente Norma?
E di Roma affrettar il fato arcano—
Ei non dipende da poter umano.

**NORMA:** I hear seditious shouts, and cries for war:
Why do they rise at the altar of our Deity!
Who at this altar dares presume to dictate
Dread fate's responses to all-seeing Norma?
Speeding Rome's untimely appointed doom—
Her fate does not depend upon human agency.

**OROVESO:** E fino a quando oppressi
Ne vorrai tu? Contaminate assai
Non fur le patrie selve e i templi aviti

**OROVESO:** When will the burdens that oppress us end?
Devoured, contaminated, we have seen enough
Our country's sacred woods and

Dall' aquile latine. Omai di Brenno!
Oziosa non può starsi la spada?

**TUTTI:** Si brandisca una volta!

**NORMA:** E infranta cada!
Infranta, sì! se alcun di voi snudarla
Anzi tempo pretende: ancor non sono
Della nostra vendetta i dì maturi—
Delle Sicambre scuri
Sono i pili Romani ancor più forti.

**TUTTI:** E che ti annunzia il Dio?
Parla, quai sorti!

**NORMA:** Io nei volumi arcani
Leggo del Cielo, in pagine di morte
Delle superba Roma è scritto il nome:
Ella un giorna morrà—ma non per voi!
Morrà pei vizi suoi,
Qual consunta morrà! L'ora aspettate—
L' ora fatal che compia il gran decreto.
Pace, v' intimo! e il sacro vischio io mieto.
*(Falchia il vischio, le Sacerdotesse lo raccolgono in canestri di vimini. Norma si avanza, e stende le braccia al cielo. La luna splende in tutta la sua luce. Tutti si prostrano)*

**NORMA:** *(Aria)* Casta Diva, casta Diva, che inargenti
Queste sacre queste sacre, queste sacre antiche piante,
A noi volgi il bel sembiante;
A noi volgi, a noi volgi il bel sembiante, il bel sembiante
Senza nube e senza vel!
Tempra tu de' cori ardenti!
Tempra ancor lo zelo andace!
Spargi in terra quella pace,
Che regnar tu fai nel Ciel.

**TUTTI:** A noi volgi il bel sembiante,
Senza nube e senza vel!

**NORMA:** Fine al rito; e il sacro bosco
Sia disgombro dai profani;
Quando, il Nume irato e fosco,
Chiegga il sangue dei Romani,
Dal Druidico delubro
La mia voce tuonerà.

temples
By Rome's fierce eagles. Sword of Brennus!
Shalt you rest ingloriously and idly!

**ALL:** It must again be drawn!

**NORMA:** Drawn to be broken!
Yes, broken, should there any here presume
To draw it forth ere fate's appointed hour:
The day of retribution yet is distant—
The dreaded battle-axe of the Sicambri has not
Yet strength to turn the Roman javelins.

**ALL:** What does our Deity reveal of fate?—speak!

**NORMA:** In the dread pages of the mystic volumes,
In death-fraught characters inscribed,
The name of proud imperial Rome I read,
She'll one day fall—but 'twill not be by you!
Through her own vices 'tis that she will perish,
Consumed to dust! The hour, then, wait—
The fated hour this great decree foretells.
Peace, all! I go the sacred boughs to gather.
*(Norma cuts the sacred branches of the mistletoe, which the Priestesses receive and deposit in their consecrated baskets. She then advances, upraising her arms on high. At this moment the moon breaks forth in full effulgence. All kneel reverently)*

**NORMA:** *(Air)* Stainless Godess, stainless Godess, whose brilliance beaming,
O'er these ancient, o'er these ancient trees, these ancient trees, is steaming,
Oh, on us, with favor gleaming;
Oh, on us, oh, on us with favor gleaming;
Free from clouds propitious, propitious shine!
Oh! calm thou hearts, too ardent burning,
Oh! calm thou zeal, all prudence spurning!
Then, peace on earth again returning,
Speed on through heaven with ray divine.

**ALL:** Oh, on us, with favor gleaming,
Free from clouds, propitious shine!

**NORMA:** The rites are finished; and the sacred wood
Must now be cleared of all profane intruders;
When He, the Deity of wrath and gloom,
Shall decree the ensanguined fall of Rome,

**TUTTI:** Tuoni! e alcun del popol empio
Non isfugga al giusto scempio!
E primier da noi percosso
Il Proconsole cadrà.

**NORMA:** Sì, cadrà, punirlo io posso.
Ma punirlo il cor non sa.

**NORMA:** *(Aria)* Ah! bello a me ritorna,
Del fido amor primiero;
E contro il mondo intiero,
Difesa a te sarò.
Ah! bello a me ritorna,
Del raggio tuo sereno;
E vita nel tuo seno—
E patria, e Cielo avrò, a Cielo avrò.

**CORO:** Sei lento, sì, sei lento,
O giorno di vendetta;
Ma irato il Dio t' affretta
Che il Tebro condannò.
*(Norma parte; e tutte in ordine la seguono)*
*(Entra Adalgisa)*

**ADALGISA:** Sgombra è la sacra selva,—
Compiuto il rito. Sospirar non vista
Alfin poss' io, quì, dove a me s' offerse
La prima volta quel fatal Romano
Che mi rende rubella al tempio, al Dio.
Fosse l' ultima almen!—Vano desio!
Irresistibil forza
Quì mi strascina: di quel caro aspetto
Il cor si pasce; e di sua cara voce
L' aura che spira mi repete il suono.
*(Corre a prostrarsi, sulla pietra d' Irminsul)*
Deh! proteggimi, o Dio! perduta io sono.

**POLLIONE:** Eccola! va! mi lascia—
Ragion non odo.
*(Flavio parte)*

**ADALGISA:** *(veggendolo sbigottita)* O! Pollione!

**POLLIONE:** Che veggo?—Piangevi tu?

**ADALGISA:** Pregava. Ah, t' allontana—
Pregàr mi lascia!

**POLLIONE:** Un Dio tu preghi attroce,
Crudele, avverso al tuo desire e al mio!
O, mia diletta! il Dio
Che invocar devi è Amor!

Then, from the Druids' consecrated altar,
My summoning voice in thunder shall be heard.

**ALL:** Let it be heard! and of the impious race
Not one shall escape our vengeance!
Beneath our retributive weapons
Shall the Proconsul be the first to fall.

**NORMA:** Yes, first to fall! I have power to punish him.
But how, alas! my weak heart knows not.

**NORMA:** *(Air)* Ah! dear one, as true returning,
As when first burning with love;
Norma, spurning, the whole world
Will be your defender
Ah! dear one, returning, to me
With love serenely yearning;
My breast shall find life's dawning—
Heaven, country, all in you, all in you.

**CHORUS:** Lingering and slow-paced,
Oh day of vengeance, you approach
But the angry God shall haste you,
That the Tiber has condemned.
*(Exit Norma; the rest follow in procession)*
*(Enter Analgisa)*

**ADALGISA:** The sacred wood is free from all intruders,
The rites performed. I here may sigh unseen,
Within these shades that treacherous gave
The first recontre with that fatal Roman,
Who made me false alike to vows and God.
Would that time were the last!—Vain desire!
A force irresistible
Impels me here: his seductive looks
Entrance my heart; and
The air I breathe loves to repeat the sound of his dear voice.
*(Prostrates herself at the altar of Irminsul)*
Protect me, oh God, or I am lost!

**POLLIO:** It is she! leave me! vain's remonstrance now—
I'm deaf to reason.
*(Exit Flavio)*

**ADALGISA:** *(disturbed at the sight of Pollio)* Pollio!

**POLLIO:** What see I?—In tears, love?

**ADALGISA:** I was praying. Leave me, leave me—
Leave me to prayer!

**POLLIO:** Prayer to a ruthless God,
Who frowns on the desires of two fond hearts!
Oh, my beloved, my beautiful! the God
You should invoke, is Love!

ADALGISA: Amor! deh! taci!
Ch' io più non t' oda.
(*Si allontana da lui*)

POLLIONE: E vuoi fuggirmi? e dove
Fuggir vuoi tu ch' io non ti segua?

ADALGISA: Al tempio:
Ai sacri altari ch' io sposar giurai!

POLLIONE: Gli altari!—e il nostro amor?

ADALGISA: Io l' obbliai!

POLLIONE: Va, crudele—e al Dio spietato
Offri in dote il sangue mio—
Tutto, ah! tutto ei sia versato;
Ma lasciarti non poss' io.
Sol promessa al Dio tu fosti—
Ma il tuo cuore a me si diè.
Ah! non sai quel che mi costi;
Perch' io mai rinunzi a te.

ADALGISA: E tu pure, ah! tu non sai!
Quanto costi a me dolente!
All' altare che altraggiai,
Lieta andava ed innocente!
Il pensiero al Ciel s' ergea;
Il mio Dio vedeva in Ciel!
Or per me—spergiura e rea—
Cielo e Dio ricopre un vel.

POLLIONE: Ciel più puro, e Dei migliori,
T' offro in Roma, ov' io mi reco.

ADALGISA: (*colpita*) Parti forse!

POLLIONE: Ai nuovi albori.

ADALGISA: Parti!—ed io?

POLLIONE: Tu vieni meco.
De' tuoi riti, è amor più santo:
A lui cedi, ah! cedi a me!

ADALGISA: (*più comosso*) Ah! non dirlo!

POLLIONE: Il dirò tanto,
Che ascoltato io sia da te.

**ADALGISA E POLLIONE:**
(*Duetto*)

POLLIONE: Vieni in Roma, ah! vieni, o cara:
Dov' è amor, dov' è amor, è gioja, è vita,
Inebbriam nostr' alme a gara,—
Del contento, del contento a cui ne invita.
Voce in cor parlar non senti,
Che promette eterno ben;

---

ADALGISA: Love! hush! no more!
I dare not stay to listen.
(*Retreating*)

POLLIO: Would you fly from me?
Where can you fly that I cannot follow?

ADALGISA: Our temple:
Those sacred altars I have sworn to espouse!

POLLIO: The altar!—and our love?

ADALGISA: I have forgotten it!

POLLIO: Go, cruel beauty—go to your fell Deity,
And offer up my blood in sacrifice—
To the last drop!—all, all—let it be shed;
For I cannot leave, whatever the cost.
You were but promised to your tyrant God—
Not so to me: your heart was given to me.
Ah! none can tell what I would suffer for you
No power shall force me to renounce your love.

ADALGISA: And who can say what I have staked for you
What grief your fatal love has cost me!
To the sacred altar I have outraged,
Cheerful and innocent of heart I came!
My every thought I gave to heaven alone!
And I in heaven with joy beheld my God!
But now I—lost, perjured, guilty thing,
Heaven and my Deity see no longer.

POLLIO: Heavens far purer, Gods more just,
To Rome invite you, where now I go.

ADALGISA: (*amazed*) Depart, you said?

POLLIO: Yes, at the dawn of day.

ADALGISA: Depart!—and I?

POLLIO: You must go with me.
Love's are holier far than your fell rites,
Yield to love! and, yielding, yield to me!

ADALGISA: (*much agitated*) Ah! do not urge like this!

POLLIO: Still shall I urge,
Until you, pitying, consent.

**ADALGISA AND POLLIO:** (*Duet*)

POLLIO: Come to Rome with me, my fairest:
Love, and joy, and life, my dearest,
All will there transport, delight us,
Bliss, and sweet content, invite us.
A voice must be speaking in your heart,
Promising eternal bliss;

---

Ah! da fede ai dolci accenti,
Sposo tuo—sposo tuo mi stringi al sen!

ADALGISA: Ciel! cosi parlar l'ascolto,
Sempre, ovunque, al tempio istesso,
Con quegli occhi, con quel volto—
Fin sull'ara fin sull'ara il voggo impresso.
Ei trionfa del mio pianto,
Del mio duol vittoria ottien.
Ciel! mi togli al dolce in canto,
O l'error, o, l'error perdona almen.

POLLIONE: Adalgisa!

ADALGISA: Ah! mi risparmi
Tua pietà maggior cordoglio!

POLLIONE: Adalgisa! e vuoi lasciarmi?

ADALGISA: Nol poss' io!—Seguir ti voglio!

POLLIONE: Quì, domani, all' ora istessa,
Verrai tu?

ADALGISA: Ne fo promessa

POLLIONE: Giura!

ADALGISA: Giuro!

POLLIONE: O! mio contento!
Ti rammenta!

ADALGISA: Ah! mi rammento!
Al mio Dio sarò spergiura,
Ma fedele a te sarò!

POLLIONE: L' amor tuo mi rassicura,
E il tuo Dio sfidar saprò.
(*Partono*)

*Abitazione di Norma. Norma e Clotilde, recano per mano due piccoli fanciulli*

NORMA: Vanne! e li cela entrambi!—oltre l' usato
Io tremo d' abbracciarli.

CLOTILDE: E qual ti turba
Strano timor, che i figli tuoi rigetti?

NORMA: Non so;—diversi affetti
Strazian quest' alma: amo in un punto ed odio
I figli miei—soffro in vederli, e soffro
S' io non li veggo; non provato mai
Sento ud diletto ed un dolore insieme
D' esser lor madre.

CLOTILDE: E madre sei?

NORMA: Nol fossi!

CLOTILDE: Qual rio contrasto!

---

Such sweet accents still seeking there,
Be mine—yield heaven in your kiss!

ADALGISA: Heavens! the words I now hear sounding,
Are our temple's prayers confounding,
Those eyes, that face, are never from me—
Even at the altar they beam on me,
Heavens! the words I now hear sounding,
Do our temple's prayers confound.
Those eyes, that face, are never from me—
Save me from the spell by which I'm bound.

POLLIO: Adalgisa!

ADALGISA: Ah! spare me,
In pity, from a greater sorrow!

POLLIO: Adalgisa, can you leave me?

ADALGISA: No, I cannot!—I will follow you.

POLLIO: Here, then, tomorrow, at this hour,
Say, will you come?

ADALGISA: You have my promise.

POLLIO: But swear!

ADALGISA: I swear!

POLLIO: Oh! height of joy!
Remember!

ADALGISA: Ah! I shall remember!
I shall be perjured to my God,
But I shall be true to you!

POLLIO: I'm cheered by your, love urged onward.
Defying thus your Diety.
(*Exeunt*)

*Norma's dwelling. Enter Norma and Clotilde, leading by the hand two young children*

NORMA: Away! conceal them!—an unusual terror
Thrills me as I embrace them.

CLOTILDE: What is it that moves you,
That you drive your children from you?

NORMA: I cannot tell;—contending feelings rend
My ill-used soul: at once I love and hate
My hapless children—seeing them, I suffer,
Yet in their absence suffering,
I prove alike a pleasure and a pain—
I feel that I'm their mother.

CLOTILDE: Their mother?

NORMA: Would I were not!

CLOTILDE: Heart-rending confict!

**NORMA:** Immaginar non puossi?
O, mia Clotilde! richiamato al Tebro,
È Pollione.

**CLOTILDE:** E teco ei parte?

**NORMA:** Ei tace
Il suo pensier. O! s' ei fuggir tentasse,
E quì lasciarmi—se obbliar potesse
Questi suoi figli!

**CLOTILDE:** E il credi tu?

**NORMA:** Non l' oso!
E troppo tormentoso—
Troppo orrendo un tal dubbio.
Alcun s'avanza: va—li cela.
(*Norma li abbraccia, Clotilde parte coi fanciulli*)

**NORMA:** Adalgisa!

**ADALGISA:** (*da lontano*) Alma, costanza!

**NORMA:** T'inoltra—o giovinetta—
T'inoltra—e perchè tremi?
Udii che grave a me
Segreto palesar tu voglia.

**ADALGISA:** È ver!—Ma, deh! ti spoglia
Della celeste austerità, che splende
Negli occhi tuoi—dammi coraggio, ond'io
Senz' alcun velo ti palesi il core.
(*Si prostra; Norma la solleva*)

**NORMA:** Mi abbraccia—e parla: che t'affligge?

**ADALGISA:** (*dopo un momento d'esitazione*) Amore!
Non t'irritar!—Lunga stagion pugnai
Per soffocarlo—ogni mia forza ei vinse;
Ogni rimorso—Ah! tu non sai pur dianzi
Qual giuramento io fea!—fuggir dal tempio,—
Tradir l' altare a cui son io legata,—
Abbandonar la patria!

**NORMA:** Ahi, sventurata!
Del tuo primier mattino,
Già turbato è il sereno; e come e quando
Nacque tal fiamma in te?

**ADALGISA:** Da un solo sguardo—
Da un sol sospiro, nella sacra selva,
A' piè dell' ara ov' io pregava il Dio.
Tremai, sul labbro mio
Si arrestò la preghiera; e tutta assorta
In quel leggiadro aspetto, un altro Cielo
Mirar credetti!—un altro Cielo in lui!

**NORMA:** Who can picture it?
Oh, my Clotilde! recalled to the Tiber,
Pollio departs.

**CLOTILDE:** With you?

**NORMA:** He has not said so
He hides his thoughts. Oh! should he resolve
To leave me here alone—should he forget
His helpless children!

**CLOTILDE:** You cannot think he'd act so?

**NORMA:** No, I dare not!
Ah! too tormenting to my faithful heart—
Too horrible, I feel this doubt.
Some one advances: go—hide them.
(*Norma embraces, and Clotilde retires with the children*)

**NORMA:** Adalgisa!

**ADALGISA:** (*in the distance*)
Soul, be firm!

**NORMA:** Approach—young virgin, fear not—
Advance—why do you tremble?
I've heard that some grave matter
You would impart to me in secret.

**ADALGISA:** It is true! But, ah! veil awhile
That heavenly austerity that reigns
Within your eyes—inspire, encourage me,
That, unrestrained, I may unfold my heart.
(*Adalgisa kneels lowly; Norma raises her*)

**NORMA:** Embrace me—speak: what afflicts you?

**ADALGISA:** (*after a moment's hesitation*) Love!
Do not be angry!—Long I struggled
To repress it—but in vain, for it conquered!
All my remorse—Ah! you think little of
The oath I've sworn!—to fly our temple,—
Betray the altar to which I'm bound,—
Forsake my country!

**NORMA:** Lost, unhappy one!
Thus, so early in your life's young morning,
Your calm is overcast; but when, and how,
Was this fame born in you?

**ADALGISA:** It was with one look—
A single sigh, within our sacred forest,
As at the altar I implored our God.
Trembling, alas! I felt upon my lips
The prayer arrested—die; and, all absorbed,
In his bright contenance another heaven!
I saw.—Ah, how believe!—another heaven!

**NORMA:** O rimembranza! io fui
Così rapita al sol mirarlo in volto.

**ADALGISA:** Ma non mi ascolti tu?

**NORMA:** Segui—t' ascolto.

**ADALGISA:** Sola, furtiva, al tempio
Io l' aspettai sovente!
Ed ogni dì più fervida
Crebbe la fiamma ardente.

**NORMA:** Io stessa, anch' io
Arsi così—l' incanto suo fu il mio.

**ADALGISA:** Vieni! ei dicea, concedi
Ch' io mi ti prostri ai piedi,
Lascia che l' aura spiri,
De' dolci tuoi sospiri!
Del tuo bel crin le anella
Dammi poter baciar?

**NORMA:** O, cari accenti!
Così li profferia—
Così trovava del mio cor la via.

**ADALGISA:** Dolci qual arpa armonica,
M' eran le sue parole;
Negli occhi suoi sorridere
Vedea più bello un sole.
Io fui perduta e il sono.
D' uopo ho del tuo perdono:
Deh! tu mi reggi e guida,—
Me rassicura, o sgrida,—
Salvami da me stessa,—
Salvami dal mio cor!

**NORMA:** Ah! tergi il pianto:
Alma non trovi di pietade avara.
Te ancor non lega eterno nodo all' ara.

**NORMA E ADALGISA:** (*Duetto*)

**NORMA:** Ah! si, fa core! e abbracciami—
Perdono e ti compiango;
Dai voti tuoi ti libero,
I tuoi legami io frango.
Al caro oggetto unita—
Vivrai felice ancor;
Al caro oggetto unita,
Vivrai felice ancor, vivrai ancor,
vivrai felice ancor!

**NORMA:** Sad reminiscence! It was thus that I
Felt enraptured when I first beheld him.

**ADALGISA:** But do not hear?

**NORMA:** Go on—I listen to you.

**ADALGISA:** Alone and secret, in our temple
I met him oft—remorse and shame!
Each day my passion grew more fervant
Each day my bosom's flame increased.

**NORMA:** It was thus, I in my pride
Was charmed—sighed as she sighed.

**ADALGISA:** Oh, come! he said, permission grant me
Lowly to kneel before your virgin feet,
Leaving the passing zephyrs to enchant me,
As sweetly they repeat your honeyed sighs?
And your celestial brow, best bliss!
Grant me, oh ecstasy of joy! to kiss!

**NORMA:** Dear accents! remembered but too well!
Such words he softly breathed to me—
And found to my poor heart the way!

**ADALGISA:** Sweet as the notes of the harmonious harp,
Flowed the measure of his love-draught words;
His eyes aiding his conquest, brightly smiled,
More beauteous than the noon-day sun.
I became lost, breathing such ardent passion.
Befriend me—grant your gracious pardon!
Oh! in your virtue, be my help, my guide,—
Kindly console me, or as kind reprove,—
Stretch forth your hand, and save me,—
Save me from my heart!

**NORMA:** Ah! dry your tears!
You find in mine a soul not proof to pity.
You're not eternally bound to our altar.

**NORMA AND ADALGISA:** (*Duet*)

**NORMA:** Oh! cheer yourself, do not weep! come to my arms—
I pardon you;
I free your charms, from all your vows & sever
The bonds that bind
Love gently chaining, your dear one embrace
In joy live, in joy live, ever:
Love gently chaining, embrace your dear one
Live in joy, live in joy ever, in joy, in joy, in joy live ever!

# Act II

**ADALGISA:** Ripeti o Ciel, ripetimi!
Sì lusinghieri, accenti;
Per te, per te s'acquetano,
I lunghi miei tormenti,—
Tu rendi a me la vita,
Se non è colpa amor;
Tu rendi a me la vita,
Se non è colpa amor, non e,
Se non, non è colpa amor.

**ADALGISA:** Repeat, repeat, great heavens! yes,
Those accents sweet, and sorrow chase;
Through you, pure calm my hopes will bless,
My heart shall sever from woe,—
Live's early morning, restored through your grace,
If passion be guiltless, ever;
Life's early morning, restored through your grace,
If passion be guiltless, ever,
If passion be guiltless, ever.

**NORMA:** Ma di'—l'amato giovane,
Quale fra noi si noma?

**NORMA:** But tell me—this much-loved youth,
By what name, amongst us, is he called?

**ADALGISA:** Culla ei non ebbe in Gallia:
Roma gli è patria—

**ADALGISA:** He was not born here in Gaul:
Rome is his country—

**NORMA:** Roma!
Ed è?—prosegui!

**NORMA:** Rome!
His name?—speak!

**ADALGISA:** Il mira!

**ADALGISA:** Behold him!

**NORMA:** Ei! Pollione!

**NORMA:** He! Pollio!

**ADALGISA:** Qual ira?

**ADALGISA:** What means this rage?

**NORMA:** Costui, costui dicesti?
Ben io compresi?

**NORMA:** This man, you say?
Have I heard rightly?

**ADALGISA:** Ah sì!

**ADALGISA:** Ah, yes!

**POLLIONE:** (*inoltandosi ad Adalgisa*) Misera te!—che festi?

**POLLIO:** (*approaching Adalgisa*) Oh, miserable!—what rashness!

**ADALGISA:** Io!

**ADALGISA:** I!

**NORMA:** (*a Pollione*) Tremi tu—perchi?
(*Alcuni momenti di silenzio: Pollione è confuso, Adalgisa tremante, e Norma fermente*)
O non tremare! o perfido!
No, non tremar per lei:
Essa non è colpevole
Il malfattor tu sei!
Trema per te—fellone!
Pei figli tuoi, per me.

**NORMA:** (*to Pollio*) You tremble—for whom?
(*Some moments of silence: Pollio is confused, Adalgisa trembling, and Norma enraged*)
Tremble not! perfidious one!
Tremble not with fear for her:
She's not foresworn and guilty,
The criminal, the guilty, is you!
Then tremble for yourself, betrayer!
For your hapless children, and me.

**ADALGISA:** Che ascolto?—Ah, Pollione!
Taci! t' arretri?—Ahimè!
(*Si copre il volto colle mani: Norma l'afferra per un braccio, e la costringe a mirar Pollione, egli la segue*)

**ADALGISA:** What do I hear?—Ah, Pollio!
Silent! not vindicate yourself?—Alas!
(*She covers her face with her hands. Norma seizes her by the arm, and compels her to look on Pollio, who anxiously observes her*)

**NORMA:** O! di qual sei tu vittima!
Crudo e funesto inganno!
Pria che costui conoscere,
T' era il morir men danno,
Fonte d' eterne lagrime,
L' empio a te pure aperse;
D' orribil vel coperse
L' aurora de' tuoi dì.

**NORMA:** Oh! you are the victim of what treachery!
Cruel, unhappy, infamous deception!
Rather than this man you ever had known,
To you death's self had been preferable
A bitter fountain of eternal tears,
This impious one causes to flow;
With horrid clouds he has overshadowed
The morning of your unsuspecting days.

**ADALGISA:** Q! qual traspare orribile
Dal tuo parlar mistero!
Trema il mio cor di chiedere—

**ADALGISA:** Oh! what treachery gleams forth
Too clearly in your dark mysterious words!

Trema d' udire il vero:
Tutta comprendo, o misera!
Tutta la mio sventura—
Essa non ha misura,
Se m' ingannò così.

My trembling heart no more dares ask—
Dares not, though yearning, hear the truth:
I comprehend all my misery,
All my misfortunes, my overwhelming woes—
They are destined never to end,
If thus he has deceived me.

**POLLIONE:** Norma, de' tuoi rimproveri
Segno, non farmi adesso.
Deh! a questa afflitta vergine,
Sia respirar concesso:
Copra a quell' alma ingenua—
Copra nostr' onte un velo.
Guidichi solo il Cielo
Qual più di noi fallì.

**POLLIO:** Norma, of your well-merited reproaches
Make me not now the object.
Oh! pitying this afflicted virgin,
Her hapless sighs, so undeserved, respect:
Let us conceal from her ingenuous soul—
Let us conceal our shame beneath a veil.
To the justice only of offended heaven
Be left to say which of us has erred.

**NORMA:** Perfido!

**NORMA:** Perfidious one!

**POLLIONE:** Or basti!
(*Per allontanarsi*)

**POLLIO:** Enough! enough!
(*Turning to go*)

**NORMA:** Fermati!
E a me sottrarti speri?

**NORMA:** Hold! hold!
Thus do you hope to escape me?

**POLLIONE:** Vieni!
(*Afferra Adalgisa*)

**POLLIO:** Come!
(*Seizing Adalgisa*)

**ADALGISA:** Mi lascia!—scostati!
(*Dividendosi da lui*)
Tu sei di Norma sposo.

**ADALGISA:** Oh, leave me!—away!
(*Getting free from Pollio*)
Begone! you are the spouse of Norma.

**POLLIONE:** Qual io mi fossi obblio:
L' amante tuo son io.
(*Con tutto il fuoco*)
E mio destino amarti,
Destin costei fuggir.

**POLLIO:** What I have been I will forget:
I am your lover only, from now.
(*With fire*)
It is my destiny to love you
As it's my destiny to fly from her.

**NORMA:** Ebben! Lo compi—e parti.
(*Reprimendo il furore*)
(*a Adalgisa*)
Seguilo.

**NORMA:** Infatuated! accomplish your wish—go.
(*Restraining her rage*)
(*To Adalgisa*)
And you, too, follow.

**ADALGISA:** Ah! pria morir!

**ADALGISA:** Ah! rather would I die!

**NORMA:** (*prorompendo*) Vanne,
sì—mi lascia, indegno.
Figli obblia, promesse, onore.
Maledetto dal mio sdegno
Non godrai d' un empio amore:
Te sull' onde, te sui venti,
Seguiran mie furie ardenti;
Mia vendetta, e notte e giorno,
Ruggirà d' intorno a te.

**NORMA:** (*in great rage*) Yes,
fly—leave me, unworthy one!
Forget your children, promises, honor.
The curse of my just vengeance on you,
Never shall you enjoy your impious love:
On the sounding wave, in the howling wind.
You will find my ardent fury following?
My vengeance, night and day unceasingly,
Blasting your peace, shall rage around you.

**POLLIONE:** (*disperatamente*)
Fremi pur, e angoscia eterna.
Pur m' imprechi il tuo furore.
Questo amor che mi governa,
È di te, di me maggiore
Dio non v' ha che mali inventi
De' miei mali più concenti.
Maledetto io fui quel giarno
Che il destin t' offerse a me.

**POLLIO:** (*with desperation*) Still
madly rave, and endless agonies
Upon me imprecate, in your wild fury.
The mighty love of which I own the empire,
Than you, over me possesses greater power.
No god in malice torments can invent,

**ADALGISA:** (*supplichevole a Norma*) Ah! non fia, non fia ch' io costi
Al tuo cor sì rio dolore.
Mari e monti sian frapposti
Fra me sempre e il traditore.
Soffocar saprò i lamenti—
Divorar i miei tormenti,
Morirò, perchè ritorno
Faccia il crudo ai figli e a te.

**C:** (*di dentro*) Norma! all' ara! In suon feroce,
D' Irminsul tuonè la voce!

**NORMA E ADALGISA:** (*a Pollione*) Suon di morte!—a te s' intima.
Fuggi! va! qui pronta ell' e.

**POLLIONE:** Sì! la spezzo—sì; ma prima
Mi cadrà, il tuo nume al piè!
(*Squillano i sacri bronzi del tempio. Norma è chiamata ai riti. Ella rispinge d' un braccio Pollione e gli accenna di uscire. Pollione si allontana furente*)

## ■ ATTO TERZO

*Interno dell' abitazione di Norma. Da una parte un letto Romano, coperto di pelle d' orso. I figli di Norma sono addormentati.*

(*Norma con una lampa e un pugnale alla mano. Siede e posa la lampa sopra una tavola. E pallida, contraffata.*)

**NORMA:** Dormono entrambi! non vedran la mano
Che li percuote;—non pentirti, o core,
Viver non ponno; quì supplizio, e in Roma
Obbrobrio avrian (peggior supplizio assai):
Schiavi d'una matrigna!—Ah no! giammai!
(*Sorge*)
Muoiano!—sì. Non posso
(*Fa un passo, e si ferma*)
Avvicinarmi—un gel mi prende;
E in fronte mi solleva il crin.
I figli uccido! tenero figli
In questo sen concetti!
Da questo sen nutriti—essi, pur dianzi
Delizia mia!—essi, nel cui sorriso
Il perdono del Ciel mirar credei—
Io, io, li svenerò Di che son rei?
Di Pollione son figli:
Ecco il delitto. Essi per me son morti—
Muoia per lui;

Than my own torments more excruciating,
A curse fell upon that fatal day
When destiny presented you to me.

**ADALGISA:** (*supplicating Norma*) Ah! no, it shall not be that thus
I should lacerate your fond heart.
May seats and mountains alike divide
From me for ever this treacherous lover.
I'll stifle all weak lamentations—
Hide each torment I may feel,
And die without reproach, if he
But return to his children and to you.

**CHORUS:** (*from within*) Norma! hasten! With fearful sound
Irminsul in thunder lifts his voice.

**NORMA AND ADALGISA:** (*to Pollio*) The sound of death! a warning to you
Fly! away! it comes prepared!

**POLLIO:** Yes! I defy it—yes; but first
I'll overthrow your Deity at your feet.
(*The sacred bronze is heard sounding from the temple. Norma is summoned to the rites. With one arm she repulses Pollio, and with the other imperatively points for him to retire, which he does in great anger*)

## ■ ACT III

*Interior of Norma's dwelling. On one side, a Roman couch, covered with bearskins, on which the children of Norma are sleeping.*

(*Enter Norma, with a lamp and a dagger in her hand. She seats herself, placing the lamp on a table. She is pale and distracted.*)

**NORMA:** They sleep—they will not see the hand
That strikes the blow; repent not, my heart,
They must die; their fate in Rome would be
Opprobrium (worse than their suffering here):
Slaves to a stepmother!—Ah no! never!
(*She rises*)
Better they should die!—yes. I cannot
(*Advancing, then drawing back*)
Draw nearer—chill seizes me;
On my brow my hair stands erect.
Murder my children! my helpless children—
My own dear offspring!
(*With tenderness*)
Nurtured at this breast—they who once
Were my delight!—in whose fond smile I thought I saw
The pardon of heaven!—
I, I, their murderer! What is their

E non sia pena che la sua somigli!
Feriam!
(*S'incammina verso il letto, alza il pugnale—essa aa un grido inorridita, i Figli si svegliamo*)
Ah, no! son figli miei!—miei figli!
(*Li abbraccia, e piange*)
Clotilde!

**NORMA:** Corri! vola!
Adalgisa a me guida.

**CLOTILDE:** Ella quì presso—
Solitaria si aggira, e prega e plora.

**NORMA:** Va; si emendi il mio fallo, e poi, si mora!
(*Clotilde parte*)

**ADALGISA:** Me chiami, o Norma. Qual ti copre il volto
Tristo pallor?

**NORMA:** Pallor di morte! Io tutta
L' onta mia ti rivelo. Un preghiera sola
Odi, e l' adempi: se pietà pur merta
Il presente mio duolo, e il duol futuro.

**ADALGISA:** Tutto, tutto, io prometto.

**NORMA:** Il giura!

**ADALGISA:** Il giuro!

**NORMA:** Odi:—Purgar quest' aura
Contaminata dalla mia presenza,
Ho risoluto. Nè trar, meco io posso;
Questi infelici!—a te, gli affido!

**ADALGISA:** O, Cielo! A me gli affidi?

**NORMA:** Nel Romano campo
Guidali a lui—che nominar non oso.

**ADALGISA:** Oh! che mai chiedi?

**NORMA:** Sposo
Ti sia men crudo, io gli perdono, e moro.

**ADALGISA:** Sposo!—Ah! non mai!

**NORMA:** Pei figli suoi l' imploro.

**NORMA:** (*aria*) Deh! con te, con te, li prendi,
Li sostieni, li difendi!
Non ti chiedo onori e fasci—
A tuoi figli ei fian serbati:
Prego sol che i miei non lasci,
Schiavi abbietti, abbandonati—
Bastia te che disprezzata,
Che tradita io fui per te!
Adalgisa, deh ti mova, tanto strazio del mio cor;

crime?
They are the children of Pollio: That is their crime? They're dead to me—
They die for him;
May their sacrifice cause him remorse eternal!
Now will I strike!
(*She advances towards the couch, and raises her dagger—then utters a fearful scream, which awakens the children*)
Ah, no! they are my children!—my children!
(*She embraces them, and weeps*)
Clotilde!

**NORMA:** Hasten! fly!
Bring Adalgisa to me.
She is near—

**CLOTILDE:** She wanders, lonely praying and in tears.

**NORMA:** Go; I will atone my crime, then die!
(*Exit Clotilde*)

**ADALGISA:** You called me, Norma. What horrid pallor
Overspreads your features?

**NORMA:** That of death! Now all
My shame will I reveal. One prayer only
Hear, and my wish fulfil, if you can pity
My present grief, my future woe.

**ADALGISA:** All, all, I promise you.

**NORMA:** But swear!

**ADALGISA:** I swear!

**NORMA:** Hear me:—To purify and free the air,
Too long contaminated by my presence,
Is my resolve. Take them with me I cannot,
What misery!—to thee, then, I confide them!

**ADALGISA:** Oh, heaven!
To me confide them?

**NORMA:** To the Roman camp
Take them to him—I dare not utter his name.

**ADALGISA:** Oh! what do you ask of me?

**NORMA:** A husband may he be
To you less faithless; I forgive him, and die.

**ADALGISA:** A husband!—Ah never!

**NORMA:** I ask it for his children.

**NORMA:** (*Air*) Pray! beneath your care befriend them,
And defend them from very ill!
Not for honors I implore you—
These your children's portions you store:
I ask you'll not deceive them,
Nor leave them to abject slavery
For remember that despised, betrayed,
Forsaken, I've been for you!

Adalgisa, deh ti mova, tanto strazio del mio cor.

**ADALGISA:** Norma! ah, Norma! ancora amata!
Madre ancor sarai per me—
Tienti i figli. Non fia mai
Ch' io mi tolga a queste arene.

**NORMA:** Tu giurasti.
**ADALGISA:** Sì, giurai;
Ma il tuo bene—il sol tuo bene—
Vado al campo, ed all' ingrato.
Tutti io reco i tuoi lamenti
La pietà che mi ha destato.
Parlerà sublimi accenti.
Spera,—spera: amor, natura
Ridestarsi in lui vedrai,—
Del suo cor son io secura—
Norma ancor vi regnerà!

**NORMA:** Ch' io lo preghi? ah! no—giammai!
Piu non t' odo—parti, va!

**ADALGISA E NORMA:** (*Duetto*)

**ADALGISA:** Mira, o Norma! ai tuoi ginocchi,
Questi cari tuoi pargoletti;
Ah! pietàde di lor, ti tocchi,
Se non hai, non hai, di te pietà.

**NORMA:** Ah! perchè, perchè, la mia costanza.
Vuoi scemar con molli affetti?
Più lusinghe, ah più speranza,
Presso amorte un cor non ha.

**ADALGISA:** Cedi, deh! cedi!

**NORMA:** Ah! lasciami!
Ei t' ama.

**ADALGISA:** E già sen pente.

**NORMA:** E tu?

**ADALGISA:** Lo amai, quest' anima
Sol l' amistade or sente.

**NORMA:** O giovinetta!—E vuoi?

**ADALGISA:** Renderti i dritti tuoi
O teco, al Cielo e agli uomini,
Giuro celarmi ognor.

**NORMA:** Hai vinto, hai vinto. Abbracciami—
Trovo un' amica ancor.

**NORMA E ADALGISA:** (*Duetto*)

**NORMA:** Sì, fino all' ore, all' ore estreme,
Campagna tuà, compagna m' avrai;

---

Adalgisa, I implore you, grant the prayer of my poor heart;
Adalgisa, I implore you, grant the prayer of my poor heart.

**ADALGISA:** Norma! ah, Norma! still beloved!
A mother shall you be to me—
Still keep your children. Never shall it be
That I will quit these hallowed woods.

**NORMA:** But you have sworn.
**ADALGISA:** Yes, I have sworn;
To seek your hapiness—restore your peace—
I'll go to the camp of the ingrate
And reveal your sad lamentations.
The ardent pity you have kindled in me,
Shall speak to him in inspiration's accents
Hope all—yes, all: love and nature
Shall again be seen, awakened in him—
His heart I will secure once more to you—
Norma again, shall reign triumphant!

**NORMA:** What! I supplicate him? ah! no—never!
I can no longer listen—hence, away!

**ADALGISA AND NORMA:** (*Duet*)

**ADALGISA:** See, oh, Norma! lowly kneeling,
Endearing these your children sweet;
Have some pity for them, uncaring,
Though for yourself, yourself, you feel none.

**NORMA:** Ah! why thus, my courage shaking,
With these words so soft, so tender?
No more can hope render feeling,
Nor more inspire a dying heart like mine.

**ADALGISA:** Yield, oh yield to my entreaties!

**NORMA:** Leave me!
Does he not love you?

**ADALGISA:** He is now repentant.

**NORMA:** And you?

**ADALGISA:** With love my heart was fired,
But friendship now is all I feel.

**NORMA:** Young maiden!—what would'st though?

**ADALGISA:** Restore to you what is justly yours.
Or else with you from heaven and man,
I swear, concealed to live for ever.

**NORMA:** I am vanquished, conquered. Embrace me—
I find a friend is left me yet.

**NORMA AND ADALGISA:** (*Duet*)

**NORMA:** Calmly till closes life's last fleeting moment,
Truly I'll prove to you a companion.

---

**ADALGISA:** Per ricovrarci, per ricovrarci insieme—
Ampia e la terra è la terraassai.
Teco del fato all' onte,
Ferma opporrò la fronte,
Finchè il mio core a battere,
Io senta sul tuo cor;
Senta sul tuo cor, Io senta,
Io senta sul tuo cor,
Io senta sul tuo cor,
Teco del fato all' onte,
Ferma opperrò la fronte,
Finche mi batte il cor senta
Sul tuo cor, sul cor, Io senta,
Io senta sul tuo cor,
Io senta sul tuo cor,
Io senta sul tuo cor.
(*Partono*)

## ATTO QUARTO

### SCENA I

*Luogo solitario presso il bosco dei Druidi, cinto da burroni e da caverne. In fondo un lago, attraversato da un ponte di pietra*

(GUERRIERI E GALLI)

**CORO 1:** Non parti?

**CORO 2:** Finora è al campo—
Tutto il dice: i feri carmi,
Il fragore, il suon del' armi,
Delle insegne il ventilar.

**TUTTI:** Attendiam: un breve inciampo
Non ci turbi,—non ci arresti.
E in silenzio il cor si appresti
La grand' opra a consumar.

**OROVESO:** Guerrieri! a voi venirne
Credea foriero d' avvenir migliore:
Il generoso ardore,
L' ira che in sen vi bolle,
Io credea secondar—ma il Dio nol volle.

**CORO:** Come? E le nostre selve
L' abborrito Proconsole non lascia?—
Non riede al Tebro?

**OROVESO:** Ma più temuto, e fero
Abatino condottiero, Pollione succeed; e di novelle
Clossenti legioni,
Forza il campo che ne tien prigioni.

---

**ADALGISA:** Above us one roof
shall give safety's enjoyment—
This world's wide enough to yield shelter against love.
Together opposing fate,
Rising, braving sorrow,
Reposing on your breast,
Calm my breast will borrow;
Calm my breast, calm my breast will borrow,
My breast will borrow, will borrow,
My breast will borrow,
My breast will borrow.
Together fate opposing,
Rising, braving sorrow,
On your breast reposing.
Calm my breast will borrow,
My breast will borrow, will borrow,
My breast, my breast will borrow,
My breast will borrow.
(*Exeunt*)

## ACT IV

### SCENE I

*A solitary spot near the Druids' wood, surrounded by rocky coverns. In the distance is a lake, over which is a stone bridge*

(Enter Warriors and Gauls)

**1ST CHORUS:** Has he departed?

**2ND CHORUS:** He's still in the camp—
All things bespeak it: the fierce warlike song,
The clang of arms, that ceaseless sound;
Their standards still wave triumphant

**ALL:** Let us be patient: a slight impediment
Must not disturb us,—nor stop our progress.
In silence let us our hearts prepare
The glorious work to consummate.

**OROVESO:** Gallant warriors! I had hoped
To be the messenger of better prospects:
The patriotic zeal, the generous ardor,
The noble rage which burn in your bosoms,
I hoped to second—the God wills differently.

**CHORUS:** How is it that
This abhorred Proconsul does not leave our consecrated woods?—
Returns not to the Tiber?

**OROVESO:** A more fierce
And cruel Roman commander,
To Pollio succeeds; and myriads of new
Overpowering legions, eager to destroy,
Reinforce the camp to keep us in subjection.

CORO: Corri! ma il sa?—Di pace
Adalgisa igliera ancor?

CHORUS: Does Norma know
this?—Does she peace
Still counsel us?

OROVESO: Invan di Norma
La mente investigai.

OROVESO: I in vain of Norma
Have sought the mind.

CORO: E cha far pensi?

CHORUS: How will you act?

OROVESO: Al fato
Piegar la fronte;—separarci, e nullo
Lasciar sospetto del fallito intento.

OROVESO: To fate.
Submissive bow;—separate all,
and nothing
Leave to awake suspicion of intentions.

CORO: E finger sempre?

CHORUS: Dissembling ever?

OROVESO: Amara legge il sento!
Ah! del Tebro al giogo indegno
Fremo io pure–e all' armi anelo;—
Ma nemico è sempre il Cielo;—
Ma consiglio è il simular:
Divoriamo in cor lo sdegno,
Tal che Roma estinto il creda:
Dì verrà, che desto, ei rieda,
Più tremendo a divampar!

OROVESO: I feel it a bitter law!
Ah! at the Tiber's yoke dishonorable
I rage alike—alike for arms I
pant;—
But unfriendly to us still is heaven!—
My counsel, then, is, we dissimulate:
Let's stifle in our hearts our indignation,
That Rome may believe it extinguished:
The day will come, when it shall return,
More terribly to vanquish and destroy!

CORO: Sì, fingiam, se il finger
giovi;
Ma il furore in sen si covi;—
Guai per Roma, allor che il segno
Dia dell' armi il sacro altar!
(Partono)

CHORUS: Yes, let us feign, if feigning help us;
But fury in our bosoms still we'll
shroud;
Woe be to Rome, whenever the fatal signal,
To arms, sounds from our sacred altar!
(Exeunt)

## SCENA II

(Tempio d' Irminsul: Ara da un
lato Norma, indi Clotilde)

## SCENE II

(Temple of Irminsul: Altar on one
side Enter Norma, afterwards Clotilde)

NORMA: Ei tornerà—Sì! mia fidanza è posta
In Adalgisa: ei tornerà pentito—
Supplichevole, amante! O! a tal
pensiero,
Sparisce il nuvol nero
Che mi premea la fronte! e il sol m'
arride,
Come del primo amor nei dì felici.
(Esce Clotilde)
Clotilde!

NORMA: He will return.—Ah, yes!
my faith is firm
In Adalgisa: he'll return repentant—
A supplicating lover! At that
thought,
How disappear the clouds that so
darkly
Oppressed my brow! the bright sun
smiles,
As in my first loved days of happiness.
(Enter Clotilde)
Clotilde!

CLOTILDE: O, Norma! uopo è d' ardir.

CLOTILDE: Oh, Norma! summon
courage.

NORMA: Che dici?

NORMA: Speak?

CLOTILDE: Lassa!

CLOTILDE: Alas!

NORMA: Favella!

NORMA: Tell me all!

CLOTILDE: Indarno
Parlò Adalgisa, e pianse.

CLOTILDE: Vainly
Spoke Adalgisa's tears.

NORMA: Ed io fidarmi
Di lei dovea? di mano uscirmi, e
bella
Del suo dolore, presentarsi all' empio?
Ella tramava!

NORMA: Should I have
Trusted her? let her, so beauteous
In sorrow, seek that impious one?
She has betrayed me!

CLOTILDE: Ella ritorna al tempio
Trista, dolente implora
Di profferir suoi voti.

CLOTILDE: She has resought the
temple,
Sorrow-stricken, earnestly imploring
To offer up her vows.

NORMA: Ed egli?

NORMA: And he?

CLOTILDE: Ed egli.
Rapirla giura anco all' altar del
Nume!

CLOTILDE: And he swears
To force her even from the altar of
her God!

NORMA: Troppo il fellon presume;
Lo previen, mia vendetta, e quì di
sangue—
Sangue Romano—scorreran torrenti!
(Si appressa all' ara, e batte tre
volte lo scudo d' Irminsul)

NORMA: Foul traitor, he presumes
too much;
Forstalled by my vengeance, seas of
blood—
Of Roman blood—shall flow forth
in torrents!
(She approaches the altar, and
thrice strikes the shield of Irminsul)

CORO: (di dentro) Squilla il bronzo del Dio!

CHORUS: (within) The sacred
shield has sounded!

CLOTILDE: Cielo! che tenti?
(Accorono, da varie parti, Oroveso, i Druidi, i Bardi, e le Ministre.
A poco a poco il tempio si riempe
d' armati. Norma si colloca sull'
altare)

CLOTILDE: Heavens! What do you
dare?
(Enter hastily, from various sides,
Oroveso, Druids, Bards, and officiating Priesteses. By little and little the temple becomes filled with
armed men. Norma takes her
place on the altar)

OROVESO: Norma, che fu? Percosso
Lo scudo d' Irminsul, quali alla terra
Decreti, intima?

OROVESO: Norma, why summon
us? That dread sound,
The shield of Irminsul, what, to this
earth
Decreeing, does it intimate?

NORMA: Guerra! strage! sterminio!

NORMA: War! carnage! extermination!

OROVESO: E a noi pur dianzi pace
S' imponea pel tuo labbro?

OROVESO: And yet but lately was
peace
Imposed by your own lips?

NORMA: Ed ira adesso—
Armi, furore, e morti!
Il cantico di guerra alzate, o forti—
Guerra, guerra! Le Galliche selve
Quante han quercie producon guerrier.
Qual sui greggi fameliche belve,
Sui Romani van essi a cader.
Sangue! sangue! le Galliche scuri
Fino al tronco bagnate ne son,
Sovra i flutti del Liguri impuri,
Ei gorgoglia, con funebre, suon.
Strage! strage! sterminio, vendetta!
Già comincia, si compie, s' affretta.
Come biade da falci mietute,
Son di Roma le schiere cadute;
Tronchi i vanni, recisi gli artigli,
Abbattuta ecco l' aquila al suol!
A mirar il trionfo dei figli,
Viene il Dio sovra un raggio di sol.

NORMA: Now I'd wake wrath—
Arms, fury, exterminating death!
Quick, let the song of war rise loudly—
War to the steel! The Gallic forests
Shall, numerous as their oaks, produce warriors.
As on our flocks rush famished
beasts of prey,
So we the Romans will overpower,
destroy.
Blood! blood! the Gallic battle-axes
Shall cut them off for ever,
And the dark waters of the foul Liguri,
Flowing over them, sound their
dirge.
Slaughter! extermination! vengeance!
Commence, and hasten to complete.
Like ripened corn beneath the sickle
Shall the Roman forces fall;
Clipped the proud wings, and cut
the talons,
Overthrown on the earth shall the
eagle lie!

OROVESO: Nè compi il rito, o Norma?
Nè la vittima accenni?

OROVESO: Do you not consummate the rite, oh Norma?
Nor yet point out the victim?

NORMA: Ella fia pronta.
Non mai l' altar tremendo
Di vittime mancò.—Ma quel tumulto?

NORMA: The victim is ready.
Never, did this dread altar
Its victim lack.—But say, why this tumult?

CLOTILDE: Al nostro tempio insulto
Fece un Romano: nella sacra chiostra
Delle vergini alunne egli fu côlto.

CLOTILDE: Our temple has been insulted
By a Roman: in the sacred cloister
Of our novitiate virgins was he surprised.

TUTTI: Un Romano?

ALL: A Roman?

NORMA: Che ascolto?
Se mai foss' egli?

NORMA: What do I hear?
Should it be he?

TUTTI: A noi vien tratto!

ALL: To us he's dragged!

NORMA: E desso!
(*Pollione, fra Soldata e detti*)

NORMA: It is!
(*Enter Pollio, conducted by Soldiers*)

OROVESO: E Pollione!

OROVESO: Pollio!

NORMA: Son vendicata adesso!

NORMA: This moment avenges me!

OROVESO: Sacrilego nemico! e chi ti spinse
A violar queste temute soglie?—
A sfidar l' ira d' Irminsul?

OROVESO: Sacrelegious foe! what demon urged you
To violate our calm secluded shrine?—
Defy the wrath of Irminsul?

POLLIONE: Ferisci!
Ma non interrogarmi.

POLLIO: Strike!
But do not question me.

NORMA: (*svetandosi*) Io ferir deggio!
Scostatevi!

NORMA: (*discovering herself*)
The blow be mine!
Draw back!

POLLIONE: Chi veggio?—
Norma!

POLLIO: Whom do I see?—
Norma!

NORMA: Sì, Norma!

NORMA: Yes, Norma!

TUTTI: Il sacro ferro impugna!
Vendica il tempio e il Dio.

ALL: The sacred weapon wield!
Vindicate at once thy God and temple.

NORMA: (*prende il pugnale dalle mani di Orovese*) Sì, feriamo!—
Ah!
(*Si arresta*)

NORMA: (*taking the sword from Oroveso's hand*) Yes, let me strike!—Ah!
(*She hesitates*)

TUTTI: Tu tremi!

ALL: Thou tremblest!

NORMA: Ah! non poss' io!

NORMA: Ah! I cannot!

OROVESO: Che fia! perche t' arresti?

OROVESO: What means this? what now keeps you?

NORMA: Poss 'io sentir pietà!

NORMA: Can I, then, feel pity

CORO: Ferisci!

CHORUS: Strike!

NORMA: Io deggio
Interrogarlo, investigar qual sia—
L' insidiata, o complice ministra—
Che il profan persuase a fallo estremo.
Ite per poco.

NORMA: I must
Interrogate, find out who aided him—
What deceitful priestess prompted
This most profane one to a crime so dire.
Withdraw awhile.

OROVESO E CORO: Che far pensa?

OROVESO AND CHORUS: What means all this?

POLLIONE: Io tremo!
(*Oroveso e il Coro si ritirano. Il tempio rimane sgombro*)

POLLIO: I tremble!
(*Exeunt Oroveso and Chorus. The temple is cleared*)

To triumph in his children's triumph,
Will come our God, radiant as the sun.

NORMA: In mia mano alfin tu sei;
Niun potria spezzar tuoi nodi:
Io lo posso!

NORMA: To my hands consigned at length
No one is able now to break your bonds:
I only can!

POLLIONE: Tu!—nol dei.

POLLIO: You! but you must not.

NORMA: Io lo voglio.

NORMA: I have the will.

POLLIONE: Come?

POLLIO: How?

NORMA: M' odi:—
Pel tuo Dio, pe' figli tuoi,
Giurar dei, che d' ora in poi,
Adalgisa fuggirai,
All' altar non la torrai:
E la vita ti perdono,
E non più ti rivedro.
Giura!

NORMA: Hear me:—
By your God, and by your helpless children,
Swear, that from this hour, for ever
You will fly from Adalgisa
Nor from our altar bear her off:
Then I will grant your forfeit life,
And never see you more.
Swear!

POLLIONE: No; sì vil non sono.

POLLIO: Never!—No; so vile I am not.

NORMA: Giura! giura!

NORMA: Swear! swear!

POLLIONE: Ah! pria morrò.

POLLIO: Ah! sooner will I die.

NORMA: Non sai tu, che il mio furore
Passa il tuo?

NORMA: Do you not know the fury
of my purpose
Is greater far than yours?

POLLIONE: Ch' ei piombi attendo.

POLLIO: Let it descend.

NORMA: Non sai tu che al figli in core
Questo ferro—

NORMA: And that in your children's hearts
This dagger—

POLLIONE: Q, Dio! che intendo?

POLLIO: Oh Gods! what do I hear?

NORMA: Sì, sovr' essi alzai la punta—
Vedi, vedi, a che son giunta!
Non ferii; ma tosto—adesso,
Consumar poss' io l' eccesso!
Un' istante, e d' esser madre,
Mi poss' io dimenticar.

NORMA: Yes, I've already raised its point over them—
See, see, to what extreme you've driven me!
I struck not then; but soon—instantly,
I'll consummate my fearful, wild excess!
A moment, and that I am a mother,
I will wash out all memory of.

POLLIONE: Ah, crudele!—In sen del padre
Il pugnal tu dei vibrar:
A me il porgi.

POLLIO: Ah, cruel!—In the bosom of the father
More justly should it be plunged:
To me, then, deal it.

NORMA: A te!

NORMA: To you!

POLLIONE: Che spento
Cada io solo.

POLLIO: That I
Alone may perish.

NORMA: Solo! Tutti—
I Romani—a cento a cento—
Fian mietuti, fian distrutti;
E Adalgisa—

NORMA: Alone! Nay, all—
The Romans—hundreds upon hundreds—
Shall fall, in one wide destruction;
And Adalgisa—

POLLIONE: Ahimè!

POLLIO: Ah me, alas!

NORMA: Infedele A' suoi voti!

NORMA: The traitress
To our altar's vows!

POLLIONE: Ebben, crudele!

POLLIO: Passionate cruelty!

NORMA: Adalgisa fia punita;
Nelle fiamme perirà.

NORMA: Adalgisa shall suffer due punishment;
Perish in torturing flames unpitied.

POLLIONE: Oh, ti prendi la mia vita!
Ma di lei, pietà!

POLLIO: Oh, rather take my life!
But upon her, on her have pity!

NORMA: Preghi alfine?—Indegno, è tardi:
Nel suo cor ti vo' ferire!
Già mi pasco ne' tuoi sguardi
Del tuo duol, del sue morire!

NORMA: Base prayers at last?—It is too late:
Through her's I'll strike your heart
My pasturage shall be your guilty soul—

Posso alfine, e voglio farti
Infelice al par di me!

**POLLIONE:** Ah! t' appaghi il mio terrore!
Al tuo piè son io piangente:
In me sfoga il tuo furore,
Ma risparmia un' innocente!
Basti, ah! basti a vendicarti
Ch' io mi sveni innanzi a te.
Dammi quel ferro.

**NORMA:** Sorgi:
Scostati.

**POLLIONE:** Il ferro! il ferro!

**NORMA:** Olà! ministri, sacerdoti, accorrete!
(*Ritornano Oroveso, i Druidi, i Bardi, e i Guerrieri*)

**NORMA:** Al' ira vostra
Nuova vittima io svelo: una spergiura
Sacerdotessa i sacri voti infranse,
Tradì la patria, il Dio degli avi offese.

**TUTTI:** O, delitto! O, furor! ne sia palese.

**NORMA:** Sì, preparate il rogo!

**POLLIONE:** O! ancor, ti prego, Norma, pietà!

**TUTTI:** Ne svela il nome?

**NORMA:** Io, rea,
L' innocente accusar del fallo mio!

**TUTTI:** Parla, chi è dessa?

**POLLIONE:** Ah, non lo dir!

**NORMA:** Son io!

**OROVESO:** Tu, Norma?

**NORMA:** Io, stessa! Il rogo ergete.

**TUTTI:** D' orrore io gelo!

**POLLIONE:** Mi manca il cor!

**TUTTI:** Tu delinquente!

**POLLIONE:** Non le credete!

**NORMA:** Norma non mente.

**OROVESO:** O! mio rossor!

**NORMA E POLLIONE:** (*Duetto*)

**NORMA:** Qual cor tradisti,
Qual cor perdesti,
Quest' ora orrenda,
Ti manifesti;
Da me fuggire,
Tentasti invano,—
Crudel Romano,
Tu sei con me.
Un Nume, un fato
Dite più forte,
Ci vuole uniti
In vita e in morte,
Sul rogo istesso
Che mi divora,
Sotterra ancora,
Sarò con te.

---

Shall be your anguish, her righteous death!
I can at last, and will, make you
As wretched as myself!

**POLLIO:** Ah! Be content with my terror!
At your feet see me weeping:
On me expend the fury of your anger,
But oh, spare the innocent!
Enough, ah! enough in vindication
That I fall lifelessly before you.
Give me the dagger.

**NORMA:** Arise!
Begone.

**POLLIO:** The dagger! the dagger!

**NORMA:** Ho! ministers, priests, come here!
(*Re-enter Oroveso, Druids, Bards, and Warriors*)

**NORMA:** To your righteous wrath
I a new victim will reveal: a perjured
Priestess, who her sacred vows has broken
Betrayed her land, offended her father's God.

**ALL:** Horrible crime! Oh, fury! make her known.

**NORMA:** Yes, prepare the pile!

**POLLIO:** Again I pray you, Norma, have pity!

**ALL:** Her name?

**NORMA:** I, the misdoer,
The innocent accuse, and of my crime?

**ALL:** Speak, who is she?

**POLLIO:** Oh, do not say!

**NORMA:** It is I!

**OROVESO:** You, Norma?

**NORMA:** I, myself! Make ready the pile.

**ALL:** With horror we are chilled!

**POLLIO:** My failing heart!

**ALL:** You are an offender!

**POLLIO:** Oh, do not believe it!

**NORMA:** Norma has never lied.

**OROVESO:** Oh! what agony!

**NORMA AND POLLIO:** (*Duet*)

**NORMA:** The heart you slighted,
The heart you blighted,
Now lost, benighted,
This dread hour shows you—
It were to fly me,
Neglect, defy me,—
False Roman near me,
I claim your love
A God, whose power
You've felt overtower,
Rules this dark hour,
Comes to oppose you,
Decreeing this fate—
That still out being,
In life and death alike,
We share the same.

---

**POLLIONE:** Ah! troppo tardi,
T' ho conosciuta,
Sublime donna.

**NORMA:** Qual cor, qual cor tradisti,
Qual cor,
Qual cor,
Qual cor.
Quest' ora orrenda.
Io t' ho perduta—
Col mio rimorso
E amor rinato,
Più disperato,
Furente egliè.
Moriamo insieme,
Ah, sì, moria mo:
L'estremo, accento
Sarà ch' io t' amo;—
Ma tu morendo,
Non m' abborrire,
Pria di morire,
Perdona a me.

**OROVESO E CORO:** O, in te ritorna, ci rassicura!
Canuto padre te ne scongiura:
Dì che deliri, dì che tu menti,
Che stolti accenti uscir da te.
Il Dio severo che quì t' intende
Se stassi muto, se il tuon sospende,
Indizio è questo, indizio espresso
Che tanto eccesso punir non de'.

**OROVESO:** Norma! deh! Norma! scolpati!
Taci! ne ascolta appena?

**NORMA:** Cielo e i miei figli!

**POLLIONE:** (*scuotendosi con un grido*)
Ahi! miseri!

**NORMA:** (*volgendosi a Pollione*)
I nostri figli!

**POLLIONE:** O pena!

**CORO:** Norma, sei rea?

**NORMA:** (*disperatamente*) Sì, rea!
Oltre ogni umana idea!

**OROVESO E CORO:** Empia!

**NORMA:** Tu m' odi!

**OROVESO:** Scostati!

**NORMA:** Deh m' odi!

**OROVESO:** O, mio dolor!

**NORMA:** (*piano ad Oroveso*) Son madre!

**OROVESO:** Madre!

**NORMA:** Acquetati!
Clotilde ha i figli miei:
Tu li raccogli—e ai barbari
L' invola insiem con lei.

**OROVESO:** Giammai! giammai!
Va—lasciami!

**NORMA:** Ah, padre! un priego ancor!
(*S'inginoc*)

---

**POLLIO:** Too late the plighted,
In love united,
The lost, the slighted,

**NORMA:** The heart, the heart you slighted,
The heart,
The heart,
The heart.
Now lost, benighted.
I find above me:—
Remorse overtaking
A heart that's breaking,
New love awaking,
I feel for you
Together dying,
Life's latest sighing
Shall murmur, dying,
I love, I love but you—
Then when life's waning,
Breathe no complaining,
At my disdaining,
But pardon me.

**OROVESO AND CHORUS:** Oh, return to yourself, and reassure us!
The gray hairs of a father supplicate you:
Say it was delirium, and spoken falsely;
That senseless words fell idly from you.
The God severe, who heard you,
Remaining silent, his thunder suspending,
Indicates clearly, indicates expressly,
That thus he proclaims pardon.

**OROVESO:** Norma! oh Norma! vindicate yourself!
Silent! what does this protend?

**NORMA:** Heaven and my children!

**POLLIO:** (*with great emotion*)
Alas! most miserable!

**NORMA:** (*turning to Pollion*) Our hapless children!

**POLLIO:** Unutterable anguish!

**CHORUS:** Norma, are you guilty?

**NORMA:** (*with desperation*) Yes, guilty!
Beyond all mortal thought!

**OROVESO AND CHORUS:** Impious!

**NORMA:** Oh, hear me!

**OROVESO:** Away!

**NORMA:** Hear me a moment!

**OROVESO:** Oh, endless sorrow!

**NORMA:** (*in a low voice to Oroveso*) I am a mother!

**OROVESO:** A mother!

**NORMA:** Soft, be calm!
Clotilde has my children:
Do you receive them—from barbarians
Protect alike both them and her.

**OROVESO:** Never! never! Leave me—away!

**NORMA:** Ah, father! one prayer more!
(*Kneeling*)

# Act IV, Scene II

**NORMA:** (*Aria*) Deh! non volerli vittime
Del mio fatale errore—
Deh! non troncar sul fiore
Quell' innocente età.
Pensa che son tuo sangue—
Abbi di lor pietade!
Ah! padre! abbi di lor,
Di lor pietà, abbi di lor, di lor pietà
Abbi di lor, di lor pietà.

**NORMA:** (*Air*) Oh! let them not be victims
Of this my fatal error—
Oh! wither not in blossom
Such fair and innocent flowers
Through them your blood is flowing—
Spare it, pity bestowing!
Ah! father! pity bestow, pity bestow, pity bestow, pity bestow,
Spare them, pity bestow.

**OROVESO:** Oppresso è il core.

**OROVESO:** I feel my heart, oppressed

**NORMA:** Piangi, e perdona!

**NORMA:** Weep, and pardon me!

**OROVESO:** Ha vinto amore!

**OROVESO:** You conquered, love!

**NORMA:** Ah! tu perdoni—quel pianto il dice.

**NORMA:** Ah! you pardon me—those tears bespeak it.

**POLLIONE E NORMA:** Io più non chiedo—Io son felice.
Contento il rogo, ascenderò.

**POLIO AND NORMA:** I ask no more—I now am blessed!
Contented, we'll the fatal pile ascend.

**OROVESO:** Ah! consolarmene—mai non potrò.

**OROVESO:** What can console me—what give me rest?

**CORO:** Piange, prega, che mai spera?
Quì respinta è la preghiera.
Le si spogli il crin del serto:
Sia coperto, di squallor!
(*I Druidi coprono d' un velo nero la Sacerdotessa*)
Vanne al rogo! Ed il tuo scempio
Purghi l' ara, e lavi il tempio.
Maledetta all' ultim' ora!
Maledetta estinta ancor!

**CHORUS:** Tears, prayers, what hope can she befriend?
Her prayers shall be rejected here.
Tear off the wreath her brow now wears,
And shroud it with the hue of death!
(*The Druids throw a black veil over Norma*)
Hence to the pile! May her last breath
Pacify our altar, and our temple.
Malediction after life have power!

**OROVESO:** Va, infelice!

**OROVESO:** Go, unhappy one!

**NORMA:** (*incamminandosi*) Padre, addio!

**NORMA:** (*going to the pile*) Father, farewell!

**POLLIONE:** Il tuo rogo, o Norma! è il mio.

**POLLIO:** Your funeral pyre, oh Norma! shall be mine.

**NORMA E POLLIONE:** Là più puro, là più santo,
Incomincia eterno amor!

**NORMA AND POLLIO:** There more pure, more blessed above,
Shall commence eternal love!

**OROVESO:** Sgorga alfin—prorompi, o pianto!
Sei permesso a un genitor.

**OROVESO:** Gush out at last—break forth, oh tears!
Nature permits you to a suffering father.

# La Sonnambula (1831)

## The Somnambulist

MUSIC BY VINCENZO BELLINI ■ LIBRETTO BY FELICE ROMANI

La Sonnambula premiered at the Teatro Carcano in Milan on March 6, 1831. A melodrama in two acts, with a libretto by Felice Romani, it opens on the wedding celebration of Elvino, a wealthy Swiss landowner, and Amina, an orphan who was adopted by Teresa, the mill-owner's wife. Lisa the innkeeper is green with envy. She has always wanted to marry Elvino, and ignores Alessio, who is in love with her. Elvino gives Amina a wedding ring that used to belong to his mother. Their love duet is interrupted by the arrival of Count Rodolfo, the son of the dead lord of the village, who has been away for so many years that no one recognizes him. He showers Amina with attention, paying her countless compliments and making Elvino jealous. He pokes fun at the villagers recount of a ghostly woman who appears on foggy nights. Rodolfo is flirting with Lisa at the inn when Amina enters, sleepwalking. Lisa hides and Rodolfo leaves. The villagers come to pay their respects, only to find Amina asleep on Rodolfo's sofa. Only Teresa believes that her intentions are innocent and Elvino forsakes her inspite of the fact that he can't forget how much he loves her. Lisa and Elvino are about to wed when Teresa, brandishing Lisa's handkerchief, which was found in the Count's room, accuses her of faithlessness. Elvino, betrayed once again, forsakes this marriage as well. Amina appears, sleepwalking down from the edge of the roof, singing about her love for Elvino, and at last he realizes she is telling the truth. He places the wedding ring on her finger and awakens her, and the village celebrates.

## ■ ATTO I

### SCENA I

*Piazza d' un Villaggio. Da un lato, un' Osteria; dall' altro un molino, in fondo colline praticabili. Suoni pastorali e voci lontane che gridano 'Viva Amina,' sono gli Abitanti del villaggio che vengono a festeggiare gli spousali di lei.*

CORO: Viva Amina, la, la, la, la! Amina bella, la, la, la, la! Viva, viva, viva!
*(Entra Lisa.)*

LISA: Tutto è gioja, tuto è festa, Sol per me non v' ha, non v' ha contento, E per colmo di tormento, Son costretta a simular. O beltade a me funesta, Che m'involi il mio tesoro, Mentre io soffro, mentre moro, Pur ti deggio accarezzar, Ah, pur ti deggio accarezzar.

CORO: Viva Amina! viva ancor!
*(Entra Alessio e Paesani.)*

ALES: Lisa, Lisa!

LISA: Oh, l'importuno!

ALES: Tu mi fuggi!

LISA: Fuggo ognuno!

ALES: Ah, non sempre, o bricconcella, Fuggirai da me così: Per te pure, o Lisa bella, Giungerà di nozze il dì.
*(I suoni si sono fatti piu vicini.—*

## ■ ACT I

### SCENE I

*A Village Green. On one side an inn, a Water-Mill in the background; Mountains in the distance. While the curtain is rising, Peasants are heard singing 'Viva Amina,' as they approach the marriage scene.*

CHO: Long live Amina, la, la la, la! Long life to sweet Amina! Long live Amina!
*(Enter Lisa.)*

LISA: Sounds so joyful, revealing bliss, Pleasures over their senses stealing, Gives my heart but bitter feeling, Though I'm doomed to wear a smile, Every tribute they are bringing, All that beauty they are singing, Like an asp stinging my bosom, Yet I must appear delighted, Ah, yet I must appear delighted.

CHO: Long live Amina! beauteous bride!
*(Enter Alessio and Peasants.)*

ALES: Lisa, dearest!

LISA: Don't call me dearest!

ALES: Nay, do not shun me!

LISA: Hence, I say, sir!

ALES: Ah! not always, lovely Lisa, Will you turn away pouting: Time will come when you and I, love, Shall have, too, a wedding-day.
*(Sounds of joy are heard from*

*Villani e Villanelle, tutti vestiti da festa, con stromenti villereci e canestri di fiori.)*

CORO: Viva Amina!

ALES: Viva! ancor!

LISA: (*Aparte.*) Anch' esso! oh, dispetto!

ALES: Qui schierati—più d' appresso.

LISA: (*Aparte.*) Ah! la rabbia mi divora!

ALES: La canzonè preparata;

CORO: Intuonar di quì si può.

LISA: (*Aparte.*) Ogni speme è a me troncata; La rivale trionfò!

**ALLESSIO AND CHORUS.** In Elvezia non v' h rosa Fresca è cara al par d' Amina, E' una stella mattutina, Tutta luce, tutta amor. Ma pudica ma ritrosa, Quanto è vaga, quanto è bella, E' innocente tortorella, E' l' emblema del candor. Te felice e avventurato Più d' un prence e d' un sovrano, Bel garzon, che la sua mano Sei pur giunto a meritar!

LISA: Ah! per me sì lieti canti Destinati un dì credei; Crudo amor, che sian per lei Non ho cor di sopportar!

*without. —Villagers descend from the mountain, bringing baskets of flowers.)*

CHO: Long live Amina! beauteous bride!

ALES: Long live the bride!

LISA: (*Aside*) And he, too, is shouting!

ALES: Here we'll meet her—here, too, greet her!

LISA: (*Aside*) Oh, how vexing! how perplexing!

ALES: Sing the song we've been preparing;

CHO: Let us join the bridal strain.

LISA: (*Aside.*) Nothing is left for me but despairing; I am racked with jealous pain!

**ALESSIO AND CHORUS:** Though Helvetia's mountain bowers Give us fresh and lovely flowers, Yet there's none possess the powers That play around play beauty. Not the glowworm's evening warning, Not the star adorning the night, Nor the blush of early morning, Half your brightness can display. The gallant youth has noblest form, Heart which beats at love's own telling, Thrice-welcome hope his bosom swelling With the thoughts of her he loves!

LISA: Ah! those sounds I fondly cherished, Hoping they might swell for me; But, alas! all hope has perished, And she's my envied rival!

**ALES:** (*Avvicinandosi a Lisa.*) Lisa mia, sì lieti canti
Risonar potran per noi,
Se pietosa alfin tu vuoi
Dare ascolto al mio pregar! (*Ricominciano gli evviva.*)

**CORO:** Tal tesoro amor t' ha dato
Di bellezza e di virtù,
Che quant' oro il mondo chiude,
Che niun re potria comprar.
Viva! viva!
(*Entra Amina e Teresa.*)

**AMI:** (*Alle Donne.*) Care compagne, e voi,
(*Agli Uomini.*)
Teneri amici, che alla gioja mia,
Tanta parte prendete, oh, come
Dolci scendon d' Amina al core
I canti che v' inspira il vostro amore!
A te, diletta,
Tenera madre, chè a sì lieto giorno
Me orfanella serbasti, a te favelli
Questo, dal cor più che dal ciglio espresso
Dolce pianto di gioja,
E quest' amplesso!

**AMINA:** Come per me sereno Oggi rinacque il dì! Come il terren fiori, come, fiori Più . . . . . bello, più bello, e ameno! Mai, mai di più lieto aspetto, Natura, natura, non, . . . . . . . . . . non . . . . brillò, non brillò; Amor, amor la colorò amor del . . . . . mio, del mio diletto, Amor, amor la colorò amor, amor del . . . . . mio diletto.
(*Amina abbraccia Teresa, e prendendole una mano, se l' avvicina al core.*)

Sovra il sen la man mi posa, Palpitar balzar, balzar lo senti, E gli è il cor che i suoi contenti, Non ha forza a sostener! Ah, non ha forza, a sostener . . . . . . . . . . a sostener! ah, . . . . . no, ah, . . . . . . no, ah, . . . . . no, ah, . . . . . . no, a . . . . . sostener! . . . . . . . . Sovra il sen la man mi posa, Palpitar balzar, balzar lo senti, E gli è il cor che i suoi contenti, Non ha forza a sostener!

**CORO:** Di tua sorte avventurosa, Teco esulta il cor materno: Non potea favor superno Riserbarlo a ugual piacer!

**ALES:** (*To Lisa.*) Lisa, list! those wedding sounds, dear,
Soon my love and me shall greet;
Let me see one ray of hope, dear,
That your heart for me may beat! (*Continued shouting.*)

**CHO:** Richer he in love so tender Than the prince in diadem crowned;
Happier far without such splendor,
With devotion, faith, enthroned,
Is Elvino!—Long live Elvino!
(*Enter Amina and Teresa.*)

**AMI:** (*To the Females.*) Dearest companions! (*To the Men.*)
And you, too, good friends and neighbors,
Who ever kindly sympathize with my feelings,
Oh, how delightful to my heart must prove
The voices raised to celebrate our love!
And you, my mother, dearest and kindest,
Who through childhood protected the orphan,
Let the tears that are flowing from my eyes,
Tell all the joy that's glowing in my bosom.
Companions, accept my friendship!
My mother, oh, how happy am I!

**AMINA:** Oh, love, for me your power brighter bids the day . . . . . to shine! And sweeter smells each flower, . . . . . each flower In . . . . . Love's, Love's fairy bower! love can bid each anguish perish; All nature, all nature, all . . . . . nature owns his power divine; Then love, then love for ever, Then . . . . love, then . . . love, yes, let us cherish, Then love, then love for ever, love, . . . . . ah! . . . . . let us cherish.
(*Amina embraces Teresa, and, taking her hand, places it on her heart.*)

While this heart, its joy revealing, Beats, oh, beats with grateful, grateful feeling, Yet my lips, in vain appealing, Cannot speak my heart's . . delight! Ah, cannot, cannot speak . . . my heart's, my heart's . . . . delight! ah, . . . . no, ah, . . . . . . no, ah, . . . . no, ah, . . . . . . no, my . . . . heart's, my . . . . . heart's delight! . . . . . While this heart its joy revealing, Beats, oh, beats with grateful, grateful feeling. Yet my lips, in . . . . vain appealing, Cannot speak my heart's . . . . delight!

**CHO:** Though her cheek's with rapture glowing,
From her eye the tears are flowing;
To her mother's bosom growing,
At the summons to depart.

**ALES:** Io più di tutti, o Amina, Teco mi allegro. Io preparai la festa,
Io feci le canzoni; io radunai
De' vicini villaggi i suonatori.

**AMI:** E grata a' tuoi favori, Buon Alessio, son io.
Fra poco io spero ricambiarteli tutti,
Allor che sposo tu di Lisa sarai,
Se come è voce, essa a farti felice
Ha il cor disposto.

**ALES:** La senti, o Lisa?

**LISA:** Non sarà si tosto.

**ALES:** Sei crudele!

**TER:** E perchè mai?

**LISA:** L' ignori?
Schiva son io d' amore; mia libertà mi piace.

**AMI:** Ah! tu non sai quanta felicità Riposta sia in un tenero amor.

**LISA:** Sovente amore ha soave, Principio e fine amaro.

**TER:** (*Aparte.*) Vedi l' ipocrisia!

**CORO:** Viene il Notaro!
(*Entra Notaro.*)

**AMI:** Il Notaro? ed Elvino non è presente ancor.

**NOT:** Di pochi passi io lo precedo, o Amina;
In capo al bosco io lo mirai da lungi.

**CORO:** Eccolo!
(*Entra Elvino.*)

**AMI:** Caro Elvino! alfin tu giungi!

**ELV:** Perdona, o mia diletta, il breve indugio.
In questa dì solenne
Ad implorar ne andai sui nostri nodi,
D' un angelo il favor
Prostrato al marmo dell' estinta mia madre.
'Oh, benedici la mia sposa, le dissi!
Ella possiede tutte le tue virtuti!
Ella felice, renda il tuo figlio.
Qual rendesti il padre!
Io lo spero, ben mio, m' udì la madre!

**AMI:** Oh, fausto augurio!

**TUTTI:** E vano esso non fia.

**ELV:** Siate voi tutti, o amici, Al contratto presenti,
(*Il Notaro si dispone a stendere il contratto.*)

**NOT:** Elvino, che rechi alla tua sposa in dono?

**ALES:** Yes, it is all my doing, dear Amina:
Music and singing, I prepared it all;
I wrote the songs, invited all the guests,
Who hither come, obedient to my call.

**AMI:** I am grateful for your favors, Good Alessio, kind friend.
I hope to see you requited for all,
When you are married to Lisa,
Who, I am sure,
Will make you happy.

**ALES:** There, listen, dear Lisa!

**LISA:** No, indeed I shall not.

**ALES:** Still cruel, love?

**TER:** And why so, Lisa?

**LISA:** You know not?
I have made up my mind to keep my liberty.

**AMI:** Ah! then you know not what happiness
There is in loving and being loved.

**LISA:** Ay, love begins sweetly,
But often ends bitterly.

**TER:** (*Aside.*) Oh, the young termagant!

**CHO:** Here comes the Notary!
(*Enter Notary.*)

**AMI:** The Notary? and Elvino has not yet arrived.

**NOT:** He's just by; for I passed him, Amina,
At the end of the wood

**CHO:** Here he is!
(*Enter Elvino.*)

**AMI:** Dear Elvino! at last you are here!

**ELV:** Forgive me, oh, my beloved, my brief delay.
On this eventful morning,
I went to ask a blessing of her, my mother!
There, kneeling at the shrine,
I then implored her that you
May you ever be virtuous, as she was.
'Oh, grant your blessing
On my sweet flower, my loved one!
She who inspires me with fondest love!
Oh, make her as you were to my father!
Watch and bless her, my sainted mother!'

**AMI:** Oh, blessed omen!

**ALL:** It shall prove good to you.

**ELV:** Come, friends, and witness the contract
Which we now sign before you.
(*The Notary proceeds to draw up the contract.*)

**NOT:** Elvino, what do you give your bride as dowry?

ELV: I miei poderi—la mia casa, / Il mio nome ogni bene / Di cui son possessore.

NOT: E Amina?

AMI: Il cor soltanto!

ELV: Ah! tutto è il cor! / (*Mentre la Madre sottoscrive e con essa i testimoni, Elvino presenta l'anello ad Amina.*)

ELVINO: Prendi: l'anel ti do . . . . no, Che un dì, che un dì recava all'ara. L'alma beata è cara Che arride al nostro, al nostro amor, al nostro amor! Sacro ti sia, sacro ti sia tal done Come fu sacro alei, Sia de tuoi voti e miei, Fido custode, fido custode, custode ognor! Sposi or noi siamo!

AMI: Sposi—oh, tenera parola!

ELV: Cara nel sen ti posi / Questa gentil viola. / (*Le dà un mazzetto la baccia.*)

AMI: Puro innocente fiore!

ELV: Ei mi rammenti a tè.

AMI: Ah! non ne ha d'uopo il core.

ELV: Sì, mio tutto egli è!

AMI, ELV: Dal dì chè i nostri cori, / Avvicinava un Dio; / Con te rimase il mio, / Il tuo restò con me.

TUTTI: Scritti nel ciel già sono / Come nel vostro cor!

AMI: Ah! vorrei trovar parola / A spiegar com' io t' adoro! / Ma la voce, o mio tesoro, / Non risponde al mio pensier.

ELV: Tutto, ah! tutto in questo istante / Parla a me del foco ond' ardi: / Io lo leggo ne' tuoi sguardi, / Nel tuo riso lusinghier! / L' alma mia, nel tuo sembiante, / Vede appien la tua scolpita, / E a lei vola, è in lei rapita, / Di dolcezza, e di piacer!

CORO: Ah! così negli occhi vostri / Core a core ognor si mostri: / Legga ognor qual legge adesso / L' un nell' altro un sol pensier.

LISA: Il dispetto in sen represso, / Più non valgo a trattener.

ELV: Domani, appena, aggiorni, / Ci recheremo al tempio, e il nostro imene / Sarà compiuto da più santo rito. / A genial convito tutti quanti io vi at-

---

ELV: All I am possessed of—lands and houses; / And, beside these, the good name / Which I ever hope to preserve me.

NOT: You, Amina?

AMI: Nothing but a fond heart!

ELV: It is that which I most prize! / (*While the Witnesses and Teresa are signing the contract, Elvino gives Amina a ring.*)

ELVINO: Take now this ring,—it is, yours . . . . love, It will make you, at the altar, mine, . . . . love. May fortune ever shine, . . . . love, With smiles benignant, with smiles benignant on . . . . our love! Sacred to you, sacred to you this token, Love's soft vows with it spoken, Like my mother's vows unbroken, Sacred sacred pledge, sacred pledge of mutual love! / Now we are united!

AMI: United—oh, joyful word!

ELV: Sweetest, take these flowers, / As emblems of your virtue. / (*Gives her a bunch of violets.*)

AMI: Dear innocent flowers!

ELV: Let them remind you of me.

AMI: No need of them for that purpose.

ELV: Ah, I know, love, your heart is mine!

AMI, ELV: Nothing now can sever our hearts, / Since Heaven has heard our prayer; / In sweet reliance ever / Each other's trust we share.

ALL: Those vows even now are written on high, / As surely as in your hearts!

AMI: Oh, that I had words to tell you / The love which burns in my bosom! / But my tongue for ever spurns / To confess the love I feel.

ELV: In your looks I read your heart, love: / Glances from your eyes are straying, / Smiles around your lips are playing— / More than words these speak your heart! / And upon your maiden cheek, love, / Where the blush of true affection / Greet me, spouse of your election, / Let this kiss seal our plighting!

CHO: May the flowers that blossom so fairly / Spring around their feet for ever: / And may jealous feelings never / Mar the joy, the love, they feel.

LISA: Scarcely can I wish her joy, / Still all my envy I'll conceal.

ELV: Tomorrow, at the rising of the sun, / We'll away to the altar, / Where our union will be made complete.

---

tendo / E a lieta danza nel mio vicin podere. / (*Odesi suon di sferza, e calpestio di cavalli.*) / Qual rumore?

TUTTI: (*Accorendo.*) Cavalli!

AMI: Un forestiere! / (*Entra Rodolfo e due Postiglioni.*)

ROD: Come nojoso e lungo, / Il cammin mi sembrò! (*Avanzandosi.*) / Distanti ancora dal castello siam noi?

LISA: Tre miglia.—E giunti, / Non vi sarete fuor che a notte oscura, / Tanto alpestre è la via. / Fino a domani quì posar vi consiglio.

ROD: E lo desio avvi albergo al villagio.

LISA: Eccovi il mio.

ROD: Quello?

LISA: Quello.

ROD: Ah! lo conosco.

LISA: Voi, signor?

TUTTI: Costui chi fia?

ROD: Il mulino!—il fonte!—il bosco! / E vicin la fattoria!

TUTTI: Del villagio è conscio assai: / Quando mai—costui vi fu?

RODOLPHO: Vi ravviso o luoghi ameni, In cui lieti, in cui sereni, Si, tranquillo, i di passai, Della prima, della prima gioventù! Cari luoghi io vi trovai, Cari luoghi io vi trovai, Ma quei di non trova più. Vi ravviso o luoghi ameni, In cui lieti i di passai, Della prima gioventù, Cari luoghi io vi trovai, Cari luoghi io vi trovai, Ma quel di non trova più, Cari luoghi io vi trovai, ma quei di non trova più, non trova più. Ma fra voi, se non mi inganno, Oggi ha luogo alcuna festa.

TUTTI: Fauste nozze quì si fanno.

ROD: E la sposa? / (*Accenando Lisa.*) / E quella?

TUTTI: (*Accennando Amina.*) E questa.

---

Then a jovial dinner, and to a merry dance / I hope to see you all, at my home. / (*Cracking of whips and trampling of horses heard.*) / What noise is that!

ALL: (*Running to see.*) Horses!

AMI: A stranger, too! / (*Enter Rodolph and two Postilions.*)

ROD: How tedious has the journey / To this place seemed to me! / (*Advancing.*) / What distance, tell me, am I from the castle?

LISA: Three miles, sir.—Believe me, / You cannot reach it before nightfall: / It grows dark, and the roads are uncertain. / Till the morn I advise that you rest here.

ROD: I wish to do so if some fitting place you have.

LISA: This inn is mine, sir.

ROD: That one?

LISA: Yes, sir.

ROD: Ah! I remember.

LISA: You, signor?

ALL: Who can he be?

ROD: There the mill stands!—the fountain!— / The hills!—and close by them the streamlet!

ALL: He seems to know this place: When was he ever here?

RODOLPHO: As I view these scenes so charming, With dear remembrance my heart is warming, Of days long vanished, of days long vanished—Oh, my breast, my breast is filled with pain, Finding objects that yet remain, While those days, while those days, While those days come not again. As I view . . . . these scenes so charming, With dear remembrance my heart is warming, Oh my breast is filled with pain, Finding objects that still remain, While those days come not again, While those days come not again, While those days, while those days come not again, come not again. But they they tell me that, in this village, Sports and feasting take place today.

ALL: Yes, a wedding there's to be, sir.

ROD: Who's the bride, then? / (*Pointing to Lisa.*) / Is that she?

ALL: (*Pointing to Amina.*) No, this, sir.

## Act I, Scene I

ROD: E gentil, leggiadra molto! (*Additando Amina.*) Ch' io ti miri?—Oh, il vago volto!

RODOLPHO: Tu non sai, con quei begli occhi, Come dolce il cor mi tocchi, quai richiami ai pensier miei, A dorabili, adorabili belta. Era dessa, ah quel tu sei Sul mattino, sul mattino dell' eta. Era dessa qual tu sei Sul mattino dell' età, Era dessa qual tu sei, Sul mattino dell' eta dell' eta.

LISA: (*Aparte.*) Ella sola è vagheggiata!

ELV: (*Aparte.*) Da quei detti è lusingata!

CORO: Son cotesi, son galanti, Gli abitanti di città.

ELV: (*A Rodolfo.*) Contezza del paese avete voi, signor? Testè mostraste di questi Luoghi ravvisar l' aspetto.

ROD: Vi fui da giovinetto Col signor del castello.

TER: Oh, il buon signor! È morto or son quattr' anni.

ROD: E ne ho dolore: Egli mi amò qual figlio.

TER: Ed un figlio egli avea; Ma dal castello sparve il giovane un dì, Nè più novella n' ebbe L' afflitto padre.

ROD: A' suoi congiunti nuova io ne reco, e certa. Ei vive.

LISA: E quando alla terra natìa farà ritorno?

CORO: Ciascun lo brama.

ROD: Lo vedrete un giorno. (*Odesi il suono delle cornamusa che riducono gli armenti all' ovile.*)

TER: Ma il sol tramonta: È d' uopo prepararsi partir.

CORO: Partir?

TER: Sapete che l' ora si avvicina In cui si mostra il tremendo fantasma!

CORO: È vero, è vero!

ROD: Qual fantasma?

TUTTI: E un mistero—un oggetio d' orror!

ROD: Follie!

CORO: Che dite?—se sapeste, signor.

ROD: Narrate.

CORO: Udite!

---

ROD: Gentle maid, she seems so graceful! (*Approaching Amina.*) May I see her?—Ah! that face so charming!

RODOLPHO: Maid, those bright eyes, my heart impressing, Fill my breast with thoughts distressing, By recalling an earthly blessing, Long since dead and passed away, passed away. She was like you before death, oppressing, Sank her beauties, sank her beauties in decay. She was like you, before death Sank her beauties in decay, before death, before death, oppressing, Sank her beauties, sank her beauties in decay.

LISA: (*Aside.*) All admire and caress her.

ELV: (*Aside.*) She seems pleased with his attention.

CHO: How courteous, how polite, Are these gallant men from town.

ELV: (*To Rodolph.*) You are not strange in these parts, sir, If I may judge by your manners?

ROD: The early part of my life Was passed with the lord of yon castle.

TER: Ah, he was very good! But he died four years since.

ROD: And much I regret him: He loved me as his son.

TER: He had one; But while still a child he disappeared, And no one has ever been able To learn any tidings of him.

ROD: Those tidings I now bring to his relations: He is alive.

LISA: But when will he return?

ALL: We are all most anxious to see him.

ROD: You will soon have that pleasure. (*The sound of a shepherd's pipe is heard from without, in the distance.*)

TER: See, the sun is setting; And so, friends, let us hasten to go.

CHO: Must we go?

TER: You know that the hour is approaching When the dread phantom comes!

ALL: Yes, truly!

ROD: What dread phantom?

ALL: Oh, a very frightful one it seems to be!

ROD: What folly!

ALL: What say you?—you know not, good signor.

ROD: Then tell me.

ALL: Listen!

---

CHORUS: A fosco cielo, A notte bruno, Al fioco raggio D' incerta luna, al cupo suono Di tuon lontano Da . . . . colle al pian un' ombra appar, un' ombra appar. In bianco volta Lensuol cadente, Col crin disciolto, Con occhi ardente, Qual densa nebbia Dal vento mossa, Avanza, ingrossa immensa par, immensa par.

ROD: Ve la dipinge: Ve la figura la vostra cieca credulità.

CORO: Ah! non è fola—non è paura; Ciascun la vide: è verità. Dovunque inoltra a passo lento Silenzio regna che fa spavento; Non spira fiato, non move stelo; Quasi per gelo, il rio si sta. I cani stessi accovacciati, Abbassan gli occhi, non han latrati: Sol tratto tratto, da valle fonda, La strige immonda, urlando va. È verita!

ROD: S' io qui restassi, o tosto, o tardi, Vorrei vederla, scoprir che fa.

CORO: Dal ricercarla il ciel vi guardi! Saria soverchia temerita.

ROD: Basta cosi, ciascuno si attenga al suo parer: Verrà stagione che di sifatte larve Fia purgato il villaggio.

TER: Il ciel lo voglia! Questo, o signore, è universal desio.

ROD: (*A Lisa.*) Ma dal viaggio, Mio riposarmi vorrei, se mel concede La mia bella e cortese albergatrice.

TUTTI: Buon riposo, signor; notte felice!

ROD: (*Ad Amina.*) Addio, gentil fanciulla: Fino a domani, addio. T' ami il tuo sposo come amarti io saprei.

ELV: Nessun mi vince in professarle amore.

ROD: Felice te se ne possiedi il core! (*Parte con Lisa il Coro si disperde.*)

AMI: Elvino! e me tu lasci Senza un tenero addio?

ELV: Dallo straniero ben tenero l' avesti.

---

CHORUS: When daylight's going, And nightwinds blowing, When sheeted lightning The heavens brightening, When deep-mouthed thunder Strikes us with wonder, On the distant hills a shade appears, a shade appears. While clouds through heaven By winds are driven, With hair loose streaming, And eyes bright beaming, In robes whose whiteness Shine forth in brightness, Oh, then it comes, oh, then it comes upon our fears.

ALL: It is but some fancy: Perhaps the shadow of one of you.

CHORUS: No, it is no fancy—we've not been dreaming: All here have seen it, and shall again. Wherever it passes, deadly silence reigns; The sight so ghastly the vision pains, As slow it passes, like death alive. The watchdogs fear it, and, closely crouching, Their eyelids shut at its approaching. No sounds are heard then, But owlet only, from tower lonely, Its terror screams. It is true, it is true!

ROD: Well, as I shall remain here a short time, I will endeavor to find out what it is.

CHORUS: Heaven guard him! oh, saints, defend him, And shield him from the phantom's power!

ROD: No, no, good folks, quiet your fears: A short time will serve To solve this mystery.

TER: Heaven assist you! May you succeed.

ROD: (*Turning to Lisa.*) If my kind hostess here will allow me, I will now retire to rest.

ALL: Quiet slumbers be yours, sir; good night!

ROD: (*To Amina.*) Adieu, gentle fair one: Till tomorrow, farewell. May he you love cherish you as I would.

ELV: None could love her more than I do.

ROD: To be beloved by her is happiness indeed! (*Exeunt Rodolph, Lisa, and Villagers.*)

AMI: Elvino! and can you leave me Without one word at parting?

ELV: The stranger bade you adieu most tenderly.

AMI: È ver: cortese, grazio ei parlò.
Da quel sembiante
Ottimo cor traspare.

ELV: È cor d' amante!

AMI: Parli tu il vero, o scherzi?
Qual sorge dubbio in te?

ELV: T' infingi invano.
Ei ti stringea la mano,
Ei ti facea carezze?

AMI: Ebben?

ELV: Discare non ti eran esse,
È ad ogni sua parola
S' incontravano i tuoi negli occhi suoi.
Gioja ne avevi.

AMI: Ingrato! e dir mel puoi?
Occhi non ho, nè core; fuor che per te.
Non ti giurai mia fede?
Non ho l' anello tuo?

ELV: Sì.

AMI: Non t' adoro? Il mio ben non sei tu.

ELV: Si—ma—

AMI: Prosegui: saresti tu geloso!

ELV: Ah si, lo sono.

AMI: Di chi?

ELV: Di tutti.

AMI: Ingiusto cor!

ELV: Perdono!
Son geloso del zefiro amante,
Che ti scherza col crine col velo,
Fin del sol che ti mira dal cielo,
Fin del rivo che specchio ti fà.

AMI: Son, mio bene, del zefiro amante,
Perchè ad esso il tuo nome confido;
Amo il sol, perchè teco il divido,
Amo il rio, perchè l' onda ti dà.

ELV: Ah! perdona all' amore il sospetto!

AMI: Ah! per sempre sgombrarlo dei tu.

ELV: Si, per sempre.

AMI: Il prometti?

ELV: Il prometto.

A 2: Mai più dubbi—timori mai più!
Ah, mio bene!
Ah, costante nel tuo, nel mio seno,
Sia la fede che amore avvalora,
E sembiante a mattino sereno,
Per noi sempre la vita sarà.
Mio bene, addio!

ELV: A me pensa!

AMI: E tu ancora?

A 2: Pur nel sonno il mio cor ti verdrà.

---

AMI: He did: his looks bespoke a
generous heart;
His bearing graceful,
And, for a stranger courteous.

ELV: Quite like a lover!

AMI: Ah, do you mean this? you're
jesting?
Whence these dreadful doubts?

ELV: You'll not deceive me.
Did he not press your fingers,
And say how he could love you?

AMI: What then?

ELV: Your eyes, too, spoke you delighted,
While listening to his praises
No more joy can I hope for:
All now is gloomy.

AMI: Ungrateful! how can you
doubt me?
Life, soul, and all I plighted;
What shall I say to prove I love you?
Remember the ring you gave!

ELV: Yes.

AMI: Not adore you? too well you
know I love you.

ELV: Yes—but—

AMI: But what?—The fact is you
are jealous!

ELV: I own it.

AMI: Of whom?

ELV: Of all men.

AMI: Oh, unwise one!

ELV: Ah, forgive!
Yes, I envy the zephyr that fans you,
And woos your luxuriant hair;
The sun which falls on you from
heaven,
The streamlet that mirrors my fair.

AMI: And I love the fresh breeze as
it sighs,
When I call on the name dear to me;
And the river that playfully flows,
Like the heart that is beating for
you.

ELV: Oh! forgive me, never heeding my suspicions.

AMI: Think no more then that I
could be false.

ELV: I'll not doubt you.

AMI: You promise?

ELV: I promise.

BOTH: No more doubting! no more
fears!
Ah, beloved one!
While our souls by fond love are
united,
Nor by demons of jealousy frighted,
And our heart's dearest wish is requited,
Oh, how blessed and how grateful
we'll be.
My love, adieu!

ELV: Oh, think ever of me!

AMI: And you'll think of me?

BOTH: In bright visions your form
will appear!

---

*FINE DELL' ATTO PRIMO.*

■ **ATTO II**

*SCENA I*

*Stanza nell' Osteria; di fronte una grande finestra; da un lato porta d'ingresso, dall' altro un gabinetto; avvi un letto e un tavolino.*

*Entra Rodolfo, indi Lisa.*

ROD: Davver, non mi dispiace
D' essermi qui fermato;
Il luogo è ameno,
L' aria eccellente,
Gli uomini cortesi, amabili
Le done oltre ogni cosa.
Quella giovine sposa è assai leggiadra—
E quella cara ostessa?
E un po' ritrosa, ma mi piace anch' essa.
Eccola; avanti mia bella albergatrice.

LISA: Ad informarmi veniva io stessa se
L' appartamento va a genio, al signor Conte?

ROD: Al signor Conte! Diamin! on conoscinto!

LISA: Perdonate, ma il sindaco lo accerta,
E a farvi festa tutto il villaggio aduna.
Io ringrazio fortuna che a me prima di tutti
Ha conceduto il favor di offerir il mio rispetto.

ROD: Nelle, belle mi piace un altro affetto.
E tui sei beila, o Lisa, bella davvero—

LISA: Oh! il signor Conte scherza.

ROD: No, non ischerzo.
Questi furbi occhietti, questo bocchin ridente,
Quanti, cori ha sorpresi e ammaliati?

LISA: Non conosco finora innamorati.

ROD: Tu menti, o briconcella. Io ne conosco.

LISA: (*Avvicinandosi.*) Ed è!

ROD: Se quel foss' io che diresti, o carina?

LISA: Io—che direi?

ROD: Si; che diresti tu?

LISA: Nol crederei. In me non è beltà
Degna di tanto—un merito ho soltanto:
Quello di un cor sincero.

ROD: E questo è molto.
(*Odesi strepito dalla finestra.*)
Ma qual romore ascolto?

---

■ **ACT II**

*SCENE I*

*A Bed-Room; at the back a window with folding-doors; on one side the entrance-door; the other a bed and a small table.*

*Enter Rodolph, followed by Lisa.*

ROD: I am not sorry to be obliged
To remain here awhile
The village is pretty,
The air is excellent,
The females amiable,
The inhabitants courteous.
The bride elect beautiful,
Mine hostess charming—rather too
shy,
But still I admire her,—and here
she comes.
Well, my pretty hostess!

LISA: I have just come to see
If your apartment is to your lordship's mind?

ROD: Your lordship! Then I am recognized?

LISA: Pardon me, sir;
But, as all the village is assembling
On account of your lordship's visit,
I came first, to offer my respects.

ROD: My lovely Lisa, I am charmed
With your kind attention: it needs
no apology.

LISA: Oh! my lord, you flatter me.

ROD: Nay, I am sincere.
Those eyes, those lips, that tender
heart,
Must often have called forth love's
emotion.

LISA: I am not conscious of any
such power.

ROD: I know one who has been
smitten by them.

LISA: (*Anxiously.*) Tell me, who is
he?

ROD: No other than myself, my
dear!

LISA: No—not yourself?

ROD: Yes, I protest to you—

LISA: I am not vain enough to believe it.
All I can boast is
Sincerity of heart.

ROD: That is sufficient.
(*A noise is heard outside the window.*)
What sounds are those?

# Act II, Scene I

LISA: Mal venga all' importuno!

ROD: Donde provien? (*Si spalanca la finestra.*)

LISA: (*Fugge nel gabinetto.*) Che non mi vegga alcuno.
(*Nella fretta perde il fazzoletto; Rodolfo lo raccoglie, e lo getta sul letto.*)
(*Comparisce Amina; è coperta di una semplice veste bianca; e si vede alla finestra l' estremita della scala per cui e salita.—Ella dorme è sonnambula; e s'avanza lentamente in mezzo alla stanza.*)

ROD: Che veggio?
Saria questo il notturno fantasma?
Ah!—non m' inganno—
Quest è la villanella che dianzi
Agli occhi miei parve si bella.

AMI: Elvino!—Elvino!

ROD: Dorme.

AMI: Non rispondi!

ROD: È sonnambula.

AMI: Geloso saresti ancor
Dello straniero?—Ah! parla!—
Sei tu geloso ancor?

ROD: Degg' io destarla?

AMI: Ingrato! a me t' appressa—
Amo te solo, il sai.

ROD: Destisi!

AMI: Prendi—la man ti stendo—
Un bacio imprimi in essa, pegno di pace.

ROD: Ah! non si desti—
Alcuno a turbarmi non venga.
In tal momento. (*Va a chiudere la finestra.*)

LISA: (*Affacciandosi dal gabinetto.*) Amina! O traditrice!

ROD: Oh, Ciel!—che tento?
(*Per correre ad Amina breve silenzio.—Amina sogna il momento della cerimonia.*)

AMI: Oh! come lieto è il popolo
Che al tempio ne fa scort.

ROD: In sogno ancor quell' anima
È nel suo bene assorta.

AMI: Ardon le sacre tede.

ROD: Essa all' altar si crede.

AMI: O madre mia, m' aita;
Non mi sostiene il piè!

ROD: No, non sarai tradita,
Alma gentil, da me. (*Amina alza la destra come se fosse all' altare.*)

---

LISA: How unfortunate!

ROD: What can this be?
(*The window is opened.*)

LISA: (*Running into the cabinet.*)
I must not be seen.
(*In her haste she drops her shawl, which Rodolph picks up, and places on the bed.*)
(*Amina appears at the window, in a white night-dress, with a lighted candle in her hand.—She enters cautiously, and slowly walks into the center of the room.*)

ROD: Can it be?
This must be the much-dreaded phantom!
To my eyesight it bears a great resemblance
To the fair one whom I just greeted
As bride last evening.

AMI: Elvino! Elvino!

ROD: Sleeping!

AMI: What! no answer!

ROD: In her sleep she walks

AMI: How! jealous again of the stranger
Who kindly greets us!—Speak to me:
Say you're not jealous.

ROD: Shall I disturb her?

AMI: Unkind one—you know, dearest,
That I love none but you!

ROD: Awake!

AMI: Take then the hand I offer;
Impress on it a fond kiss, my peace requires it.

ROD: Ah! still she's sleeping—
Just now I would not have her wakened,—
I'll not disturb her.
(*He closes the window.*)

LISA: (*Slipping out of the cabinet.*)
Amina! Oh, false traitress!

ROD: Oh, Heavens! (*A pause.—Amina dreams of the marriage ceremony.*)

AMI: How happy are all the people
Who stand round the altar!

ROD: She dreams, then! again she thinks
And speaks of him, her well-beloved.

AMI: How bright are the sacred torches!

ROD: She thinks she's at the altar.

AMI: Oh, mother, dear, support me.—
My strength, alas, fails me!

ROD: No, no, beauteous flower,
I will not do you harm. (*Amina lifts up her hands, as in supplication.*)

---

AMI: Cielo, al mio sposo io giuro
Eterna fede e amore!

ROD: Giglio innocente e puro,
Conserva il tuo candore.

AMI: Elvino!—Alfin sei mio.

ROD: Fuggasi!

AMI: Elvino! gia tua son io. Abbracciami—
Oh! contento che non si può spiegar!

ROD: Ah, se più resto, io sento la mia virtù mancar.
(*Va per uscire dalla porta.—Ode romore di gente parte per la finestra donde è venuta Amina e la chiude.—Ella sempre dormendo, si corica sul letto.*)
(*Contadini d' ambo i sessi, sindaci e Alessio.*)

CORO: (*Sotto voce.*) Osservate;
l' uscio è aperto.
Senza strepito inaltriamo.
Tutto tace! ei dorme certo.
Lo destiamo, o nol destiamo?
Perchè no? ci vuol coraggio:
Presentarsi, o uscir di qua.
Dell' ossequio del villaggio
Mal contento ei non sarà.
Avanziam—v' è! v' è! mirate,
A dormir colà si è messo.
Appressiamoci, ah fermate;
Non è desso, non è desso.
Al vestito, alla figura, è una donna,
Sì e bizzara l' avventura.
Come entrò? che mai fà qui?
(*Entra Teresa, Elvino, e Lisa.*)

ELV: (*Da lontano.*) È menzogna.

CORO: Alcun s' appressa.

LISA: (*Additando Amina.*) Mira, e credi agli occhi tuoi.

ELV: Cielo!—Amina!

TER: Amina! dessa! (*Amina si sveglia al ro more.*)

AMI: Dove son? chi siete voi?
Ah! mio bene!

ELV: Traditrice!

AMI: Io!

ELV: Ti scosta.

AMI: Oh! me infelice! che mai feci?

ELV: E ancor lo chiede?

CORO: Dove sei tu ben lo vedi.

AMI: Qui!—perche?—chi mi v' ha spinta?

ELV: Il tuo core ingannator.

AMI: Madre! oh, madre!
(*Corre nelle braccia di sua made.*)

---

AMI: Father, for him I vow to live,
To him I vow eternal faith and love.

ROD: I would not dim such brightness,
Such artless candor.

AMI: Elvino, now you are mine, love.

ROD: I must go!

AMI: Elvino, I now am yours,
love—embrace me!—
Now I'm happy!

ROD: If I stay longer, my resolution will fail me. (*Goes to the door.—A noise of People is heard; Rodolph goes out at the window at which Amina entered.—Amina lies down and sleeps on the Count's bed.*)
(*Enter Villagers, headed by Alessio.*)

CHO: (*Whispering.*) With respect, then, softly enter,
He is sleeping—shall we in?
Forward, neighbors; come, let's venture,—
Should he wake there'll be no sin.
And why not? there's sure no sin in
Rousing him on such pretence,
And the duty of his tenants
Cannot give his grace offense!
Proceed, then—see, he's reposing,—
On his bed he still is dosing.—
Now approach: ah, what fear you?
See, he is not here reposing—no!
By that garment, by that small figure,
It is a woman, it is a woman,—yes!
It is a strange adventure, surely;—
How she came here who can guess?
(*Enter Teresa, Elvino, and Lisa.*)

ELV: (*In a loud voice, outside the door.*) It is a falsehood!

CHO: Some one approaches.

LISA: (*Pointing to Amina.*)
Look, and let your eyes assure you.

ELV: Heavens! Amina!

TER: Amina! It is she. (*Amina awakes at the noise.*)

AMI: Who are these? What means this clamor?
Ah, Elvino!

ELV: Go, heartless traitress!

AMI: Traitress?

ELV: Approach not!

AMI: Oh, most unhappy! whom have I injured?

ELV: Ah! dare you to ask me?

CHO: How she came here, she must be conscious.

AMI: Who? Oh, speak! why come you here?

ELV: Well you play the shameless part.

AMI: Mother! oh, mother!
(*Amina throws herself into her mother's arms.*)

**CORO:** Ah, sei convinta.

**ELV:** Va spergiura!

**AMI:** O, me infelice! Che feci io mai?
O mio dolor! d' un pensiero,
D' un accento rea non son, nè il fui giammai,
Ah! se fede in me non hai,
Mal rispondi a tanto amor.

**ELV:** Voglia il ciel che il duol
Ch' io sento tu provar non debba mai,
Ah! ti dica s' io t' amai
Questo pianto del mio cor.

**CORO:** Il tuo nero tradimento è palese,
E chiaro assai.

**TER:** Deh! l' udite un sol momento;
Il rigore eccede omai.

**ALES, CORO:** In qual cor fidar più mai,
Se quel corfu mentitor!
(*In questo frattempo Teresa ha raccolto sul letto il fazzoletto di Lisa, e lo ha posto al collo di Amina.*)

**ELV:** Non più nozze; al nuovo amante,
Sconoscente, io t' abbandono.

**TUTTI:** Non più nozze.

**AMI:** Oh! crudo istante! deh! m' udite—
Io rea non sono.

**ELV:** Togli a me la tua presenza,
La tua voce orror mi fà.

**AMI:** Nume amico all' innocenza.
Svela tu la verità.

**ELV, AMI:** Non è questa, ingrato core,
Non è questa la mercede
Ch' io sperai per tanto amore,
Che aspettai per tanta fede,
Ah! m' hai tolto in un momento,
Ogni speme di contento.
Ah! penosa rimembranza
Sol di te mi resterà.

**LISA, ALES, CORO:** Non più nozze, non più imene;
Sprezzo, infamia a lei conviene.
Di noi tutti all' odio eterno,
Al rossor la rea vivrà.

**TER:** Ah! se alcun non ti sostiene,
Se favor nessun t' ottiene
Sventurate, il sen materno,
Chiuso a te non resterà.
(*Partono.*)

---

**CHO:** Ah, she's convicted!

**ELV:** Go, I despise you!

**AMI:** Oh, most unhappy! what have I done?
Oh, my poor heart!
Of no thought, or word, or feeling,
Anything but love and truth revealing, am I guilty;
Never deserving such return for so much love.

**ELV:** May you never know the feeling
That my anguished soul's revealing!
Tears now stealing down my cheeks,
Tell you how this heart can love.

**CHO:** Yes, it is plain she has betrayed you;
All must doubt her faith and truth.

**TER:** Oh, believe not she is faithless,
But think in her you'll find the truth.

**CHO, ALES:** All here feel that you are faithless, Where, oh, where shall we find truth?
(*During the previous, Teresa has picked up from the bed Lisa shawl, and placed it round Amina's neck.*)

**ELV:** No marriage now;—I discard you for ever!—Seek your new lover!

**ALL:** No nuptial feast!

**AMI:** Do not spurn me! hear me—I am innocent!

**ELV:** Away! the voice which once Was music to my soul, thrills me with horror!

**AMI:** Oh! if there be truth in heaven,
Let my innocence appear!

**ELV, AMI:** Can it be that thus you slight
All the love this heart ever bore you?
Can it be that thus you blight
The heart which now is bared before you!
A long adieu to hopes once cherished,—
Oh, would this form might be at rest!
Hours all bright, alas, have perished,—
Dead the love which made me blessed.

**LISA, ALES, CHO:** Bridal trains no more shall meet her,
Shame and infamy shall greet her;
Nothing can wipe away the stain,
So long as she shall live,

**TER:** Though all other tongues should blame you,
Though they should abuse and shame you,
Still your mother's arm shall shield you,
Still her voice shall comfort give.
(*Exeunt.*)

---

*SCENA II*

*Ombrosa Valletta, fra il Villaggio e il Castello.*

**CHORUS:** Qui la selva è più folta ed ombrosa, Qui posiamo, vicini al ruscello; Lunga ancora, scoscesa, sassosa, E' la via che conduce al castella: Sempre tempo per giungere avremo, Pria che sorga dal letto il signore. Riflettiam, riflettiam, quando, quando giunti saremo, Che direm per toccare il suo cor. Eccellenza!—direm con corraggio—
'Signor Conte—la povera Amina Era dianzi l' onor del villaggio, Il desio d' ogni villa vicina— In un tratto, è trovata dormente Nella stanza che voi ricettò— Difendetela, s' ella è innocente, Aiutatela s' ella fallò!'
A tai detti, a siffatti argomenti, Ei si mostra commosso, convinto; Noi preghiamo, insistiam riverenti, Ei ci affida, ei promette, abbiam vinto, Consolati al villaggio torniamo; In due passi, in due salti siam quà. Alla prova!—Da bravi! partiamo— La meschina protetta sarà.
(*Entra Amina e Teresa.*)

**AMI:** Reggimi, o buona madre;
A mio sostengo sola rimanti tu.

**TER:** Fa core. Il Conte dalle lagrime
Tue sarà commosso. Andiamo.

**AMI:** Ah! no—non posso; Il cor mi manca e il piè.
Vedi, siam noi presso il poder d' Elvino.
Oh! quante volte sedemmo insiem di questi
Faggi all' ombra, al mormorar del rio!
L' aura che spira de' giuramenti
Nostra ancor risuona—
Gli obliò crudele! ei m' abbandona!

**TER:** Esser non puote, il credi ch' ei più non t' ami,
Afflitto è forse anch' esso, afflitto al par di te,
Miralo; ei viene solitario e pensoso.

**AMI:** (*A Teresa.*) A lui mi ascondi—rimaner non oso.
(*Entra Elvino.*)

---

*SCENE II*

*A shady Valley, between the Castle and the Village.*

**CHORUS:** Here we'll rest in these sweet shady bowers, Where the streamlet is bordered by flowers; Yes, we'll rest in this wood, since we're weary, For the way to the castle is dreary; And we've time, before the sun with its beaming Wakes his lordship this morning from dreaming. Let us think, let us think in what words, what words to address him, Which way will be best to impress him. Without giving him offense: 'Please your lordship to grant us a hearing, Of facts we will state without fearing. Poor Amina, whom once we loved so, And to whom we looked up as our guide,— From the hour when in your room We found her, sweet peace has fled. Joys, which ever should surround her, Are gone, and woe's her bridal bed!' Then, should he smile, and listen to our cause. And pity take on poor Amina's grief, And promise he'll do all he can To clear her of this cruel ban, We'll straight return, nor idly tarry, But take us back, some hope to carry, That the Count may soon reveal A balm, which every heart will heal.
(*Enter Amina, and Teresa.*)

**AMI:** Speak for me—support me, dear mother,
You only are left me now.

**TER:** Take courage—the Count will listen to you;
Let us hasten to him.

**AMI:** Yet stay: I cannot, my heart beats so—
And see there is Elvino's dwelling
How often have we sat together by yon stream,
Sheltered by the friendly linden-trees!
The breeze, too, must still be laden
With our lately-plighted vows.
He has forgotten them!—he forsakes me!

**TER:** Impossible!—Surely, he still loves you!—
He, too, must, I think, be deeply afflicted;—
But see, he comes, the picture of woe.

**AMI:** (*Clinging to her Mother.*)
Hide me: I dare not see him.
(*Enter Elvino.*)

**ELV:** Tutto è sciolto.—Oh, dì funesto!
Piu per mè non v' ha conforto.
Il mio cor per sempre è morto
Alla gioja ed all' amor.

**AMI:** Vedi, o madre—afflitto e mesto—
Forse, ah! forse ei? m' ama ancor.
(*Amina s' avvicina.—Egli si cuote, la vede, e amaramente le dice.*)

**ELV:** Pasci il guardo, e appaga l' alma
Dell' eccesso de' miei mali;
Il più triste de mortali sono cruda!
E il son per tè.

**AMI:** M' odi, Elvino ti calma—
Colpa alcuna in me non è.
(*Voci lontane, 'Viva il Conte.'*)

**ELV:** (*Per uscire.*) Il Conte!

**AMI, TER:** Ah! resta.

**ELV:** No: si fugga.
(*Entrano Paesani.*)

**CORO:** Buone nuove! dice il Conte ch' ella è onesta,
Ch' è innocente; e a noi gia move.

**ELV:** Egli! oh! rabbia.

**TUTTI:** Ah! placa l' ira.

**ELV:** (*Le toglie l' anello.*)
L' ira mia più fren non ha.

**AMI:** (*Li abbandona fra le braccia di Teresa.*) Il mio anello! oh, madre!

**TER, CORO:** (*Ad Elvino.*) Mira! A tal colpo morirà.

**ELV:** (*Si appresso ad Amina.*) Ah! perchè non posso odiarti, Infedel, com' io vorrei, Ah! del tutto ancor non sei Cancellata, cancellata dal mio cor. Possa un altro, ah! possa amarti, Qual t' amò quest' infelice, Altro voto, o traditrice, No, ah, non temer, non temer dal mio dolor. Altro voto non temer, non temer dal mio dolor, Altro voto, ah! non temer, non temer dal mio dolor. Ah, per me non v' ha conforto. No, Il mio cor per sempre è morto. Alla gioja ed all' amor; Ah! per me, non v' ha conforto. Ah! perchè non posso odiarti, Infedel, con io vorrei, Ah! del tuto ancor non sei Concellata, cancellata dal mio cor! Possa un altro ah! possa amarti, Qual t' amo quest' infelice, Altro voto, o traditrice, No, ah, non temer, non temer dal mio dolor; Altro votro non temer, non temer dal mio dolor; Altro voto ah! non temer, non temer dal mio dolor. Ah! perchè non posso odiarti, Infedel, com' io vorrei, Ah! del tuto ancor non sei Cancellata, cancellata dal mio cor. Ah! perchè non posso odiarti, Infedel, com' io vorrei, Infedel com' io vorrei. Cancellata dal

**ELV:** All is lost now: yes, for me,
Love's star is dimmed for ever;
And this heart, so broken, never
More one ray of hope shall see.

**AMI:** Mother, behold! he seems very sad:
May it be he still loves me? (*Amina approaches.—Elvino starts from her in horror, speaking reproachfully.*)

**ELV:** See, false girl, these looks of sadness,
This face, which once bright with gladness;
And this brain, now racked with madness!
Sad reward for loving you!

**AMI:** Hear me, Elvino—
Hear me swear it— (*Voices without shouting, 'The Count, the Count,'*)

**ELV:** (*About to go.*) The Count!

**AMI, TER:** Oh! stay.

**ELV:** I'll away.
(*Enter Peasants.*)

**CHO:** Good news! The Count will prove
That Amina is virtuous—see, he comes!

**ELV:** He, too! oh, madness!

**ALL:** (*Surrounding Elvino.*) No; stay your anger.

**ELV:** (*Goes to Amina, and snatches the ring from her finger.*) My rage I can no more repress.

**AMI:** (*Throwing herself into Teresa's arms.*) My ring, too!—oh, mother!

**TER, CHO:** (*To Elvino.*) Mercy! That last act will kill her.

**ELV:** (*Slowly approaching Amina.*) Still so gently stealing over me, Memory will bring back the feeling, Spite of all my grief, revealing That I love you, that I dearly love you still. Though some other swain may charm me, Ah! no other ever can warm me, Yet never fear, I will not harm you, I, false one, love you, I dearly love you still. Ah! never fear, I will not harm you, never fear, I will not harm you, Yes, false one, yes, I love you, I dearly love you still. All is lost to me for ever. All, Ah! Love's sun is set for ever. All is lost is lost for me; All is lost, all, all is lost, is lost for me. Still stealing so gently over me, Memory will bring back the feeling, Spite of all my grief, revealing That I love you, that I dearly love you still! Though some other swain may charm you, Ah! no other ever can warm you; Yet never fear, I will not harm you, No, false one, no, no, I fondly love you still; Ah! never fear I will not harm you, never fear I will not harm you, No, false one, no, I love you, I love you, false one, still. Still so gently stealing over me,

mio cor, Si dal mio cor, Si dal mio cor, Si dal mio cor, Si, dal mio cor, Si dal mio cor.

**TER, CORO:** Ah! crudel, pria di lasciarla. Vedi il Conte, al Conte parla.
Ei di rendere è capace a te pace—
A lei l' onor.
(*Elvino parte disperato, Teresa tragge seco Amina da un' altro parte.*)

*FINE DELL' ATTO SECONDO.*

Memory will bring back the feeling, Spite of all my grief, revealing That I love you, love you still. Still so gently over me stealing, Memory will bring back the feeling, Spite of all my grief, revealing That I love you, love you still, I love you still, I love you still, I love you still, I love you still, I love you still.

**TER, CHO:** Oh, cruel! do not leave her: See the Count; and speak with him;
He will give peace to you,
And honor to our beloved Amina.
(*Elvino rushes hurriedly away.—Teresa gently draws Amina apart from the rest.*)

*END OF THE SECOND ACT.*

# ■ ATTO III

## SCENA I

*Villaggio. In fonda al Teatro si scorge il mulino di Teresa; un torrente ne fa girare la ruoto.*

*Entra Lisa e Alessio.*

**VOCI DI DENTRO:** Lisa è la sposa.

**A 2:** Che?

**VOCI DI DENTRO:** La sposa è Lisa.
(*Entra Paesani.*)

**CORO:** A rallegrarci con te veniamo,
Dir tua fortuna ci consoliamo.
A te fra poco, d' Amina in loco,
La man di sposo Elvin darà.
(*Entra Elvino.*)

**LISA:** E fia pur vero, Elvino,
Che alfin dell' amor tuo degna mi credi?

**ELV:** Si, Lisa. Si rinnovi il bel nodo di pria—
L' averlo sciolto perdona a un cor
Sedotto da mentita virtù.

**LISA:** Perdono tutto. Ora che a me
Ritorni più non penso al passato;
Altro non veggo che il ridente
Avvenir che alfin mi aspetta.

**ELV:** Vieni; tu, mia diletta, mia compagna sarai.
La sacra pompa già nel tempio
Si appresta, non si ritardi.

**TUTTI:** Andiam.
(*Entra Rodolfo.*)

**ROD:** Elvino, arresta.

**LISA:** (*Aparte.*) Il Conte!

**ALES:** (*Aparte.*) A tempo giunge.

**ROD:** Ove t' affretti?

**ELV:** (*Fieramente.*) Al tempio.

# ■ ACT III

## SCENE I

*The Village Green. Teresa's Mill in the distance, the wheel of which is turning round.*

*Enter Lisa and Alessio.*

**VOICES WITHOUT:** Lisa is chosen bride!

**BOTH:** Who?

**VOICES WITHOUT:** Lisa! Lisa!
(*Enter Villagers.*)

**CHO:** We come now to hail you Elvino's fond bride,—
As once Amina was,
You'll now be his pride.
(*Enter Elvino.*)

**LISA:** And is it true, Elvino, that at length
You deem me worthy your great love?

**ELV:** Yes, dear Lisa; I would renew our former ties.
Which I blush to think were broken for one
Who has proved herself unworthy of my love.

**LISA:** Well, I forgive you,
And will think only of the happiness
Which I feel is now
In store for me.

**ELV:** Come, then, dear one—even now
They are preparing to unite us:
Let us to the temple.

**ALL:** We come, we come!
(*Enter Rodolph.*)

**ROD:** Elvino, stay.

**LISA:** (*Aside.*) The Count!

**ALES:** He's just arrived in time.

**ROD:** Where are you going?

**ELV:** (*Haughtily.*) To yon temple.

ROD: Odimi prima. Degna d' amor.
Di sima è Amina ancor: io della sua virtude,
Come de preggi suoi mallevador esserti voglio.

ELV: Nella stanza a voi serbata
Non la vidi addormentata?

ROD: La vedesti. Amina ell' era—
Ma svegliata non ventrò.

TUTTI: Come dunque? in qual maniera?

ROD: Tutti udite.

CORO: Udiamo un pò.

ROD: V' han certuni che dormendo
Vanno intorno come desti.
Favelando—rispondendo,
Come vengono richiesti.
E chiamati son sonnambuli
Dall' andar e dal dormir.

TUTTI: E fia vero? E fia possibile?

ROD: Un par mio non può mentir.

ELV: No, non fia: di tai pretesti
La cagione appien si vede.

ROD: Sciagurato! e tu potresti
Dubitar della mia fede?

ELV: (Senza badare a Rodolfo.)
Vieni, o Lisa.

LISA: Andiam.

CORO: Andiam.
A tai fole non crediamo
Un che dorme e che cammina!
No, non è; non si può dar.
(Entra Teresa.)

TER: Piano, amici: non gridate:
Dorme alfin la stanca Amina:
Ne ha bisogno, poverina,
Dopo tanto lagrimar.

TUTTI: Si, tacciamo—noi dobbiamo
I suoi sonni rispettar.

TER: Lisa! Elvino! che vegg' io?
Dove andate in questa guisa?

LISA: A sposarci e la sposa—è Lisa!

ELV: E Lisa.

LISA: E lo merto: io non fui colta sola mai,
Di notte, in volta, ne trovata io fui rinchiusa
Nella stanza di un signor.

TER: Menzognera! a questa accusa
Più non freno il mio furor!
Questo vel fu rinvenuto
Nella stanza del signore.

TUTTI: Di chi è mai? chi l' ha perduto?

TER: (Accenando Lisa.) Ve lo dica il suo rossore.

ROD: No, but hear,—she's aggrieved;—
Indeed you wrong her,
You're deceived.

ELV: Did I not see that form extended
On your couch? All, all is ended.

ROD: True, it was your own, your fair one,
But she entered in her sleep.

ALL: How so? which way could she?

ROD: A moment listen.

CHO: Yes, let us hear.

ROD: There are some, who, amidst sleeping,
Still a watch are always keeping:
Slumbering, still are often talking,
And even in their sleep keep walking.
Somnambulist,—yes, such is she,
So light of heart—so spirit-free.

ALL: Do you hear?—We all feel he speaks truly.

ROD: Why? oh, why should I mislead?

ELV: Think not to deceive me,
Though crushed, heartbroken.

ROD: Since you still doubt,
The misery lie on your own head.

ELV: (Not noticing Rodolph.)
Come, Lisa.

LISA: Yes, let us go.

CHO: Yes, let us go.
Such tales we'll not believe.—
He need not think he'll us deceive.
It is false, there's no truth in it.
(Enter Teresa, from the Mill.)

TER: Stealing over her shattered senses,
Slumber, all her dreams revealing,
Her wrongs, alas, but ill concealing,
Creeps a something like to rest.

ALL: Hush! in sleep, at least,
May she be blessed.

TER: What do I see? Lisa! Elvino! am I dreaming?
Whence would they, so cheerful?

LISA: To be married, and I am the bride.

ELV: Ay, Lisa!

LISA: And why not, pray? People never found me
Wandering at night in the chamber of a lord,
Much less sleep there.

TER: Since you speak thus,
I need no longer conceal anything.
Know you anything of this shawl.
Which I found in my lord's chamber?

ALL: Whose can it be? who has lost one?

TER: (Pointing to Lisa.) Let her answer you.

TUTTI: Lisa!
(Elvino lascia la mano di Lisa, mortificato.)

TER: Lisa. Il Signor Conte
Mi smentisca se lo può.

LISA: (Aparte.) Io non oso alzar la fronte!

TUTTI: (Aparte.) Che pensar, che dir non so.

ELV: Signor?—che creder deggio?
Anch' ella mi tradi.

ROD: Quel ch' io ne pensi manifestar non vo.
Sol ti ripeto, sol ti sostengo,
Che innocente è Amina,
Che la stessa virtu offendi in essa!

ELV: Chi fia che il provi?

ROD: Chi mira—ella stessa!
(Vedesi Amina uscire da una finestra del mulino; ella paseggia, dormendo, sull' orlo del tetto; sotto di lei la ruota del mulino, che gira velocemente, minnaccia di frangerla se pone il piede in fallo.—Tutti si volgono a lei spaventati.—Elvino è trattenuto da Rodolfo.)

TUTTI: (Con un grido.) Ah!

ROD: Silenzio; un sol passo, un sol grido l' uccide.

TER: Oh, figlia!

ELV: Oh, Amina!

CORO: Scende—bontá divina,
Guida l' errante piê.
(Amina giunge presso alla ruota, camminando sopra una trave mezzo fracida che piega sotto di lei.)

TUTTI: È salva!

TER: Oh, figlia!

ELV: Oh, Amina! (Amina si avanza in mezzo al teatro.)

AMI: Oh! se una volta sola riverderlo io potessi,
Anzi che all' ara altra sposa ei guidasse!

ROD: (Ad Elvino.) Odi?

TER: A te pensa, parla di te.

AMI: Vanna speranza! Io sento suonar
La sacra squilla al tempio già move—
Io l' ho perduto—e pur—rea non son io.

TUTTI: Tenero cor!

AMI: (Inginocchiandosi.) Gran Dio, non mirar
Il mio pianto; io gliel perdono
quanto infelice
Io sono felice ei sia.
Questa d' oppresso core
E l' ultima preghiera.

TUTTI: Oh, detti! oh, amore!

ALL: Lisa!
(Elvino, as if electrified, lets fall the hand of Lisa.)

TER: I appeal to his lordship,
Whether I have spoken truly.

LISA: (Aside.) I dare not raise my eyes

ALL: What are we to believe now?

ELV: My lord, what am I to believe,
Since she, too, is false.

ROD: I would rather not say anything of Lisa—
I will ever assert Amina is innocent,
That, in doubting her, you doubt
The existence of the attribute. Virtue!

ELV: But who shall prove it?

ROD: Herself—behold! (Amina appears coming out of one of the upper windows of the mill, with a lighted candle in her hand—the wheel is in motion, threatening to crush her, should she make a false step; all gaze in terror and astonishment; Elvino is held back by Rodolph.)

ALL: (With a shriek.) Ah!

ROD: Silence! a step, a sound, may cause her death!

TER: Oh, my child!

ELV: Oh, Amina!

CHO: Merciful providence, she descends—Oh, guide her feet. (As Amina is just over the wheel, the plank, which is partly decayed, cracks under her weight—she lets fall the candle.)

ALL: She's safe!

TER: Oh, my daughter!

ELV: Oh, Amina!
(Amina descends, and walks slowly to the center)

AMI: Ah! if I might see him,
Before he is wedded to another!

ROD: (To Elvino.) Listen.

TER: She speaks of you.

AMI: Vain hope! alas I hear the bridal bells—
They go towards the temple—
He is lost to me for ever—yet I am innocent.

ALL: What faithful love!

AMI: (Kneeling.) Kind heaven! these tears
Are in sorrow, not in anger;—
I forgive him;—and as my woe is deep,
May his happiness be perfect,
Is the last prayer of this breaking heart.

ALL: What truth! what affection!

# Act III, Scene I

**AMI:** (*Si guarda la mano come cercando l' anello d' Elvino.*)
L' anello mio—l' anello—ei me l'
ha tolto—
Ma non può rapirmi l' immagin sua.
Sculta ella è qui—nel petto.
Nè tè, d' eterno affetto.
(*Si toglie dal seno i fiori ricevuti da Elvino.*)
Tenero pegno, o fior—nè te perdei.
Ti bacio ancor—ma—
Imaridito, sei.—Ah!
Non credea mirarti si presto estinto, o fiore,
Passasti al par d' amore,
Che un giorno sol durò.
(*Piange sui fiori.*)
Potria novel vigore il pianto mio donarti;
Ma ravvivar l' amore il pianto mio non può.

**ELV:** Io più non reggo.

**AMI:** E si egli a me tornasse!
Oh, torna, Elvino.

**ROD:** (*Ad Elvino.*) Seconda il suo pensier.

**AMI:** A me t' appressi? oh, gioja!
L' anello mio mi rechi.

**ROD:** (*Ad Elvino.*) A lei lo rendi.
(*Elvino le rimette l' anello.*)

**AMI:** Ancor son tua; tu sempre mio tutt' or.
M' abbraccia, tenera madre—
Io son felice appieno.

**ROD:** De' suoi diletti in seno
Elle si svegli.
(*Teresa l' abbraccia, Elvino si prostra a' suoi piedi e la sostiene.*)

**CORO:** (*Ad alta voce.*) Viva, Amina!

**AMI:** (*Feeling her hand as seeking the ring Elvino had given at the bethrothing.*) My ring—ah, he took it from me,
But be cannot take back
His own dear image!—
I have it here!
Nor you, poor faded flowers! (*She takes the flowers, all dropping to pieces, from her bosom.*)
Still I may kiss you,
Sad emblems of the love
Of her whose happiness fled
More swiftly than your bloom!
(*Weeps over the flowers*)
My tears may, perchance, revive you;
But nothing can bring back his love

**ELV:** Let me embrace her.

**AMI:** Should he ever love me again!
Oh, return to me, Elvino!

**ROD:** (*To Elvino.*) Let her wish be fulfilled.

**AMI:** Ah! do you approach? Oh, joy!
Will you give me back my ring?

**ROD:** (*To Elvino.*) Restore it—quickly!
(*Elvino replaces the ring on her finger.*)

**AMI:** Again I'm yours, love:
Embrace me, dear mother—
Your poor child is now completely happy!

**ROD:** In the midst of this pleasant reverie
Let her awake.
(*Teresa embraces her, while Elvino kneels and supports her.*)

**CHO:** (*With loud voices.*) Long live Amina!

**AMI:** (*Svegliandosi.*) Oh, cielo!
dove son io?
Che veggo! ah! per pieta,
Non mi svegliate voi!
(*Si copre gli occhi colle mani.*)

**TER:** No: tu non dormi.

**ELV:** Il tuo amante—
Il tuo sposo è a te vicino.
(*Amina alla voce di Elvino si scopre gli occhi lo guarda, indi si getta fra le sue braccia.*)

**AMI:** Oh, gioja! oh, gioja!
Io ti ritrovo Elvino!

**CHO:** Innocente, è a me più cara,
Bella più dal soffrire
Vieni al tempio, e a piè dell' ara
Incominci il tuo gioir.

**AMINA:** Ah! non giunge uman pensiero, Al contento ond' io son pienà: A' miei sensi io credo appena; Tu mi affida o mio tesor. Ah! mi abbraccia, e sempre insieme, Sempre uniti in una speme, Della terra in cui viviamo, Ci formiamo un ciel d' amor. Della terra in cui viviamo, Ci formiamo un ciel d' amor, d' amor, d' amor, d' amor. Ah! mio ben! Ah! Oh, gioja! oh, gioja! Oh, quel gioja! Ah, ci formiamo un ciel, Ah! ci formiamo un ciel d' amor, Oh, gioja, oh, gioja, un ciel d' amore.

**CORO:** Innocente è a noi più cara, &c.

*FINE*

**AMI:** (*Waking.*) Oh, mercy! where am I?
Sweet dream? oh, for pity's sake,
Do not recall me to myself.
(*She covers her face with her hands.*)

**TER:** No,—you're not sleeping?

**ELV:** I am your lover—
They are your husband's arms that enfold you
(*At the sound of Elvino's voice, Amina uncovers her eyes, and, with a shriek of joy, throws herself into his extended arms.*)

**AMI:** Oh, transport!—Oh, happiness!—
To be again my Elvino's!

**CHO:** Receive the love of all who know you,
Made more dear to us by your suffering;
May he, too, at the altar show you,
That love like his can never fade.

**AMINA:** Do not mingle one human feeling With these blisses over each stealing. While these tributes to me revealing Elvino faithful to his love. Ah! embrace me, while thus forgiving, Each a pardon thus receiving; On the earth while we are living, We will form . . . . . a heaven of love. On the earth . . . . . while we are living, We will form . . . . . a heaven of love, form . . . . . form . . . . . a heaven of love. Ah! my love! Ah! What rapture! what rapture! Oh, what rapture! Ah, we will form on earth, a heaven of love.

**CHO:** Receive the love of all who know you.

*END*

# I Puritani (1835)

## The Puritans

MUSIC BY VINCENZO BELLINI ■ LIBRETTO BY COUNT CARLO PEPOLI

This three-act melodramma serio, originally titled I Puritani di Scozia (The Puritans of Scotland) and set to a libretto by Count Carlo Pepoli, was first performed at the Théâtre-Italien in Paris on January 25, 1835. The setting: a Puritan fortress in Plymouth during the English Civil War between Cromwell's supporters and the Royalists in the seventeenth century. Elvira, daughter of the commander Lord Gualtiero Valton, is betrothed to the Royalist Lord Arturo Talbo. Sir Riccardo Forth, who loves her too, confesses his unhappiness. Sir Giorgio Valton, Elvira's uncle, tells Elvira that nothing must stop her marriage. Among the wedding gifts, is a billowing white wedding veil. Gualtiero cannot attend the wedding as he has to accompany a mysterious woman to London - she may in fact be a spy for the Stuarts. He gives Arturo a safe-conduct pass and entrusts Elvira to him. Arturo discovers the woman is Enrichetta di Francia, the late king's widow and helps her escape, disguising her in Elvira's billowing wedding veil. Riccardo stops them as they are leaving, but when he realizes that the woman behind the veil is not Elvira, he allows them to depart. Elvira goes mad when she discovers Arturo's supposed treachery. Giorgio realizes that Riccardo, too, has assisted in the escape and Riccardo persuades him not to sentence Arturo to death. Meanwhile, Elvira is slowly driven to madness, and laments the loss of Arturo. Later, Arturo returns during a storm in order to see Elvira, who is singing a love song to herself that he taught her. He steps under her window to join in with her singing, just as a group of angry Puritans passes by. When they embrace, Arturo realizes that she is insane. But, he will not leave her, even though he knows that the Puritans will kill him when they catch him. He is about to be executed when a general pardon is granted to all Cavalier prisoners as a result of Cromwell's victory. Elvira regains her sanity, and the lovers are reunited.

---

## ■ ATTO I.

### SCENA I.

*Spazioso terrapieno nella fortezza. Si veggono alcune cinte, torri ed altre opre di fortificazioni, con ponti levatoj, ec.*

1: All' erta!—

2: Sto all' erta!—

TUTTI: Già l' alba appari!

1: La tromba—

2: Rimbomba!—

TUTTI: E nunzia del dì.
(*Coro di soldati.*)
Quando la tromba squilla,
Ratto il guerrier si desta,
L' armi tremende appresta,
Alla vittoria va!
Pari del ferro al lampo,
Se l' ira in cor sfavilla,
Degli Stuardi il campo
In cenere cadrà.
(*Odesi un preludio di armonia religiosa.*)

BRUNO: O di Cromvèl guerrieri,
Pieghiam la mente e il cor
A' mattutini cantici
Sacri al divin Fattor.
(*I Soldati s' ingginnocchiano.*)
(*Coro di Puritani. La campana suono la preghiera.*)
La Luna, il Sol, le Stelle,
Le tenebre e il fulgor

## ■ ACT I.

### SCENE I.

*A fortress with drawbridges, towers, and other works of fortification. Cliffs and hills in the distance.*

1: Arouse!

2: I am ready.

ALL: The morn is appearing.

1: The trumpet—

2: Is sounding—

ALL: Announcing the day.
(*Bruno and Chorus of Soldiers.*)
Yes; when the trumpet sounds,
The warrier quickly rouses;
His dreaded arms prepares,
And sallies forth to victory.
Quick as the flash of swords,
If rage enflames his heart,
The camp of the proud Stuarts
Will be reduced to ashes.
(*A prelude of sacred music heard.*)

BRUNO: O, warriors of Cromwell,
Let us our minds and hearts
To morning hymns devote,
In praise of our Creator.
(*The soldiers kneel.*)
(*Chorus of Puritans. The bell sounds for prayer.*)
The moon, the sun, the stars,
The darkness and the light,

Dan gloria al Creator
In lor favede!
La terra e i firmamenti
Esaltano il Signor:
A lui dian laudi e onor
Tutte le genti!

SOLD. 1: Udisti?

2: Udii—

INSIEME: Fini!

BRU: Al re che fece il dì
L' inno dei puri cor
Salì sui venti!

### SCENA II.

*Coro di Castellani e Castellane.*

1: A festa!

2: A festa!

TUTTI: A festa!

BRU: Almo gioir s' appresta—!
A tutti rida il cor
Cantate un casto amor.

CORO: Garzon che mira Elvira,
La bella virginella,
L' appella la sua stella—
Regina dell' amor.
E il riso e il caro viso
Beltà di Paradiso;
E rosa in su lo stel,
E un angelo del ciel!
Sincero un cavaliero
In pianto a lei d' accanto,
Ha il vanto altero e santo
D' innamorar quel cor.

Give glory to the Eternal,
According to their language.
The earth and all the firmament
Pay homage to the Lord;
To Him loud praise and honor
Let every nation give.

1ST SOLD: Did you hear?

2ND SOLD: I heard.

ALL: It is over.

BRU: To him who made the day
The hymn of the pure heart
Is wafted on the winds.

### SCENE II.

*Chorus of Villagers.*

1ST: To mirth!

2ND: To mirth!

ALL: To mirth!

BRU: A day of joy is near;
Let every heart be merry!
Sing of some pure love.

CHO: The youth who sees Elvira,
The beautiful young maiden,
Calls her his shining star;
Calls her his queen of love.
Her smile, her lovely face,
Is of celestial beauty,
A rose upon its stem,
An angel from the sky.
A faithful cavalier.
Beside her shedding tears,
The boast can proudly make
To have her heart enflamed.

Elvira allor sospira,
Gli chiede eterna fede:
Ed oggi dà mercede
A un si fidato ardor.

**1:** A festa!—

**2:** A festa!—

**INSIEME:** A festa!—
Almo gioir s' appresta:
A tutti rida il cor,
Se a nozze invita Amor. (*Tutti partono; il solo Bruno*)

## SCENA III.

*Riccardo e Bruno.*

**RIC:** Or dove fuggo io mai?—dove mai celo
Gli orrendi affanni miei? Come quei canti
Rispondono al mio cor funèrei pianti?—
O Elvira, O Elvira! o mio sospir soave,
Per sempre io ti perdei!
Senza speme ed amor—in questa vita,
Or che rimane a me?—

**BRU:** La Patria e il Cielo!

**RIC:** Qual voce?—che dicesti?—E vero!—è vero!

**BUR:** Apri il tuo core intero
All amistà, n' avrai conforto.

**RIC:** E vano;
Ma pur t' appagherò—Sai che d' Elvira
Il genitor m' acconsentia la mano.
Quando il campo volai,
Ieri alla tarda sera—
Quì giunto con mia schiera,
Pien d' amorosa idea—
Vo al padre—

**BRU:** Ed ei dicea?

**RIC:** "Sospira Elvira a Talbo Cavaliero,
"E sovra il cor non v' ha paterno impero.

**BRU:** Ti calma, O amico—

**RIC:** Il duol, che al cor mi piomba.
Sol calma avrè nel sonno della tomba—
Ah per sempre io ti perdei,
Fior d' amore, o mio speranza:
Ah la vita che m' avanza
Sarà vita di dolor—
Sarà esempio di terror!
Quando errai per anni ed anni
Al poter della ventura,
Io sfidal sciagura e affanni
Nella speme del tuo amor—
Oh qual sogno ingannator!

**BRU:** T' appellan le schiere
A lor condottier.

**RIC:** Di gloria il sentiere
M' è chiuso al pensier!

**BRU:** A patria e ad onore
Non arde il tuo cor?—

**RIC:** Io ardo—e il mio ardore
E amore, è furor!

---

Elvira then did sigh,
Demanded his true faith,
And on, this day she gives
The price of his pure love.

**1ST:** To mirth!

**2ND:** To mirth!

**ALL:** To mirth!
A day of joy is near;
Let every heart be gay
When Love to Hymen leads.
(*Exeunt all, except Bruno.*)

## SCENE III.

*Enter Richard.*

**RICH:** To where shall I now fly?
Where can I hide my horrible affliction?
How these songs resound in my heart, like funeral dirges?
O Elvira, Elvira! my sweetest hope! for ever I have lost thee!
Deprived of hope and love what remains to me in this life now?

**BRU:** Heaven and your country.

**RICH:** What voice? What did you say? It is true—it is true!

**BRU:** Open your heart to friendship, and you will find relief.

**RICH:** It is in vain; but still I will comply with your request.
You know that Elvira's father has granted me her hand. I then hastened to the camp
Arriving here late last night, with my troops, my heart burning with love, I went to him.

**BRU:** And did he say?

**RICH:** "Elvira is sighing for the Knight Talbot, and her father has no empire over her heart."

**BRU:** Calm yourself, my friend.

**RICH:** The grief that weighs upon my heart can only rest in the sleep of death.
Ah! for ever I have lost you,
Lovely flower, my dearest hope!
Ah! my future days of life
Will for me be days of sorrow,
And alone by terror marked.
When I strayed from year to year,
Borne along on wings of fate,
Grief and fortune I defied,
Hoping solely in your love.
Oh, delusion! oh, my dreams!

**BRU:** The army calls for you to become their leader.

**RICH:** The path of glory is barred before my steps.

**BRU:** Is your heart not enflamed at the name of country and honor?

**RICH:** I burn; but my flame is of love and fury.

---

**BRU:** Deh poni in oblio
L' età, che fioriva
Nei sogni d' amor.

**RIC:** Mi è in mente ognor viva,
Mi accresce il desio,
M' addoppia il dolor!
Bel sogno beato
D' amore e contento,
O cangia il mio fato,
O cangia il mio cor.
O come è contento
Nei dì del dolore
La dolce memoria
D' un tenero amor.
(*Exeunt.*)

## SCENA IV.

*Stanza di Elvira.*

*Elvira e Sir Giorgio.*

**ELV:** O amato Zio, O mio secondo Padre!

**GIO:** Perchè mesta cosi? m' abbraccia, Elvira!

**ELV:** Deh chiamami tua figlia!

**GIO:** O figlia—oh nome,
Che la vecchiezza mia consola e alletta,
Per dolce tempo ch' io ti veglio accanto,
E pel soave pianto,
Che in questo giorno d' allegrezza pieno,
Piove dal ciglio ad innondarmi il seno—
O figlia mia diletta,
Oggi, sposa sarai!

**ELV:** Sposa? No:—mai!
Sai come arde in petto mio
Beila fiamma onnipossente,
Sai ch' è puro il mio desio,
Che innocente è questo cor.
Se tramante—all' ara innante
Strascinata—un dì sarò—
Forsennato—in quell' istante
Di dolore io morirò!

**GIO:** Scaccia ormai pensier si nero.

**ELV:** Morir sì—Sposa no mai!

**GIO:** Che dirai, se il Cavaliero
Quì vedrai—se tuo sarà?

**ELV:** Ciel!—ripeti, chi verrà?

**GIO:** Egli stesso—

**ELV:** Egli—chi?—

**GIO:** Arturo—

**ELV:** E fia vero?

**GIO:** Oh figlia—il giuro?

**ELV:** Desso?—Arturo?

**GIO:** Arturo.

**ELV:** Oh gioja!

**a 2:** Non è sogno—oh Arturo/oh Elvira,—oh amor?

---

**BRU:** Ah! bury in oblivion that time which bloomed in dreams of love.

**RICH:** It always returns to my mind, it increases my desires, it augments my sorrows.
O, happy dream
Of love and peace!
Change your fate,
Or change my heart.
O, what a torment,
In days of woe,
Is the remembrance
Of vanished love.
(*Exeunt.*)

## SCENE IV.

*Elvira's Apartment.*

*Enter Elvira and Sir George.*

**ELV:** O, dearest uncle! my second father!

**SIR G:** Why so sad! Embrace me, Elvira.

**ELV:** Ah! call me daughter.

**SIR G:** Oh, daughter oh! name which consoles and charms my old age! By that sweet time since I have watched over your life, and by these sweet tears that on this day of rejoicings flow from these eyes upon my bosom—Oh, dear daughter, today you shall be a bride.

**ELV:** Bride!—no, never!
You well know how in my breast
An all-powerful flame is burning;
You well know how pure my mind
And how candid is this heart.
If all-trembling to the altar
They shall ever drag my steps,
Quite distracted, in that moment
I shall die, oppressed with grief.

**SIR G:** Ah! dispel such gloomy thoughts.

**ELV:** I shall die—but never marry!

**SIR G:** Should the Knight you shall see here
Prove your own, what would you say?

**ELV:** Say again who now is coming?

**SIR G:** Himself.

**ELV:** He?—who?

**SIR G:** It is Arthur.

**ELV:** Is this true?

**SIR G:** My child, I swear it.

**ELV:** Himself—Arthur?

**SIR G:** Yes.

**ELV:** Oh, joy!

**BOTH:** It is no dream—Arthur/my child, oh love.

GIO: Piangi, O figlia, sul mio sene,
Piangi, ah piangi di contento.
Ti cancelli ogni tormento
Questa lagrima d' Amor.
E tu mira, O Dio pietoso,
L' innocenza in uman veio;
Benedici tu dal cielo.
Questo giglio di candor!

SIR G: Weep, oh daughter, on my bosom;
Shed, ah! shed warm tears of joy;
Be all torments washed away
By these tokens of affection.
And you see, merciful Heaven,
Candor pure in human form
From on high your blessing send
On this lily, as white as snow.

ELV: Quest' alma al duolo avvezza,
Si vinta è da! gioir,
Che ormai non può capir
Sì gran dolcezza!—
Chi mosse a' miei desir,
Il Genitor?—

ELV: This soul, to grief accustomed,
Is so overcome by joy,
That scarcely can it sustain
This unexpected bliss!
Who has foreseen my wishes?
Was it my father?

GIO: Ascolta.
Sorgea la notte folta,
Tacea le terra e il ciel,
Parea natura avvolta
D' un fosco e mesto vel.
L' ora propizia a' miseri,
Il tuo pregar, tue lagrime,
M' avvaloran sì l anima—
Ch'io corsi al genitor.

SIR G: Listen!
The night was growing dark;
Were silent heaven and earth,
All nature seemed enwrapped,
As in a gloomy veil;
The hour to sadness favorable,
Your prayers and your tears,
Strengthened so much my soul,
That to your father I ran.

ELV: Oh mio consolator!

ELV: O, my consoler dear!

GIO: Incominciai—"Germano,"
Nè più potei parlar;
Allor bagnai sua mano
D' un muto lagrimar;
Poi ripigliai, tra, gemiti:
"L' angelica lua Elvira
Al prode Artur sospira:
Se ad altre nozze andrà—
La misera—morrà."

SIR G: I thus began:—"My brother—"
Nor could I further speak.
And having bathed his hand
In silence with my tears,
I then resumed with sobs:
"Your angel-like Elvira
For valiant Arthur sighs;
Should she another marry,
The unfortunate girl will die."

ELV: O spirto di pietà,
Sceso dal ciel per me!
E il Padre?—
(Con ansies)

ELV: Oh! my angel kind,
Descended to earth for me!
My father then—
(With anxiety.)

GIO: Ognor tacea.

SIR G: Kept silent.

ELV: Poscia?

ELV: And then—

GIO: Sclamò:—"Riccardo
Chiese e ottenea mia fè:
Ei la mia figlia avrà!"

SIR G: Exclaimed, "Richard
Has asked, obtained my promise,
And he shall have my daughter."

ELV: Ciel! Sol a udirti io palpito!
E tu?—

ELV: Alas! You make me tremble.
And you?—

GIO: "La figlia misera,"
Io ripetea, "morrà!"
"Ah viva," Ei mi dice,
E stringemi al cor,
"Sia Elvira felice,
Sia lieta d' amor."

SIR G: "Your child unhappy,"
I repeated, "will die."
"Ah! let her live," said he,
And pressed me to his heart;
"Ah! may she be happy,
May she be blessed in love!"

ELV: Odi—O ciel, qual suon si desta?

ELV: Heavens! listen; what sound is that?

GIO: Ascoltiam: ti rassicura—

SIR G: Let us hear: assure yourself.

ELV: Vien lo suon dalla foresta—

ELV: From the forest comes the sound.

GIO: E il segnal di gente d' arme,
Che dal vallo nelle mura
Chiede forse penetrar.

SIR G: It is the sound of men at arms,
Who, from out the palisade,
Ask for entrance to the fortress.
Here the brave and noble Count

ARMIGERI: Viene il prode e nobil
Conte, Artur Talbo Cavalier!
(Fuori della fortezza)

SOLDIERS OUTSIDE: Arthur Talbot is advancing.

GIO: Non tel dissi?

SIR G: Did I not say so?

ELV: Ah padre mio!
(Abbracciando Vio.)

ELV: My father!
(Embracing him.)

GIO: Pago alfin è li tuo desio.

SIR G: Now your wishes are fulfilled.

CORO: Lord Arturo varchi il ponte,
Fate campo al prò guerrier!

CHO: Let Lord Arthur cross the bridge:
Clear the way for the great warrior.

GIO: A quel suono, al nome amato,
Al tuo core or presta fede;
Questo giorno venturato,
D' ogni gioia è bel forier!

SIR G: On that sound, on that dear name,
In your heart now place thy faith,
This day will, by fortune blessed,
Be forerunner of your joy.

ELV: A quel nome, al mio contento,
Al mio core io credo appena;
Tanta gioia, oh Dio, pavento,
Non ho lena—a sostener!

ELV: In that name, in my content,
In my heart I scarce put faith.
So much joy! Alas! I fear
I have not strength to bear it.

CORO: Ad Arturo de' Cavalieri,
Bel campione in giostra e amor,
Le donzelle ed i guerrieri
Fanno festa e fanno onor!

CHO: To Lord Arthur, of all knights
The most brave in love and battle,
Sing, maidens and warriors,
Songs of praise, and homage pay.

## SCENA V.

Elvira, Valton, Sir Giorgio, e Lord Arturo.

Sala d' arme con logge vaste, ove l' architettura Gotica mostra la intera sua pompa. Dal lato destro esce Lord Arturo con alcuni scudieri e paggi, li quali recano varii doni nuziali. Dal lato sinistro escono Elvira, Valton, Sir Giorgio—Damigelle con Castellani e Castellane che partono festoni di fiori. Dal fondo della scena escono i soldati giudati da Bruno.

## SCENE V.

Elvira, Walton, Sir George, and Lord Arthur.

An Armory of splendid Gothic architecture, with the background quite open. Lord Arthur enters from the right side, with Esquires and Pages carrying nuptial presents. From the left side, enter Elvira, Walton, Sir George, Ladies, and Peasants carrying garlands of flowers. From the back of the scene, enter Soldiers, led by Bruno.

UOMINI: Ad Arturo!

MEN: To Arthur—

DONNE: A Elvira!

WOMEN: To Elvira—

INSIEME: Onor!

TUTTI: Coroniam beltà e valor!

ALL: Honor.
Let us crown beauty and valor.

DAMIGELLE: Ella è fior di verginelle,
Bella al par di primavera,
Come l' astro della sera
Spira all' alma pace e amor!

LADIES: She of maidens is the flower.
She is as beautiful as spring;
Like the star at evening hour,
She inspires the soul with love.

SCUDIERI: Bello egli è tra' Cavalieri,
Com' è il cedro alla foresta:
In battaglia egli è tempesta:
E campione in giostra e amor.

ESQUIRES: He amidst warriors, is distinguished
As the cedar amongst the trees;
When in battle, he is a thunderbolt,
When in tourneys, glory and love.

ART: A te, O cara, Amor talora
Mi guido furtivo e in pianto,
Or mi guida a te d' accanto
Tra le feste e l' esultar!
Al brillar di si bell' ora,
Se rammento il duol passato,
Vo in ebbrezza—e son beato,
M' è celeste il giubilar!

ART: To you, dearest, love sometimes
Led me, in secret and in tears;
Now it brings me to your side,
In the midst of feasts and joy.
At the brilliancy of this hour,
If my past griefs I remember,
I am charmed; I am full of bliss,
Heavenly is the joy I feel.

GIOR, VAL: Senza occaso questa aurora
Mai null' ombra, o duol vi dia:
Santa in voi la fiamma sia:
Pace ognor v' allieti il cor!

SIR G., WAL: May this dawn have no decline,
Nor bring you clouds or grief;
Holy be this flame in you:
May peace ever glad your heart!

ELV: Oh, mio Arturo!—

ELV: Oh, my Arthur!

ART: Ah, Elvira mia!—

ART: Oh, my Elvira!

ELV: Or son tua—

ELV: Now I am yours.

ART: Sì, mai tu sei!—

ART: Yes; you are mine.

**TUTTI:** Cielo arrdi a' voti mici, Benedici a fede e amor!

**ALL:** Heaven, smile upon my vows; Heaven, bless our faith and love.

## SCENA VI.

*Valton, Sir Giorgia, Elvira, poi Bruno, ed Enrichetta.*

**VAL:** (*Dopo avere piano detto un mootto a Bruno, che s'inchina e parte.*)
Tu m'intendesti—Fia mortal delitto
A chi s'attenta escir da queste mura
Se non abbia il nio assenso—O cara figli,
Si compia senza me l' augusto rito—
Mercè di questo scritto
Voi, sino al tempio, aperto passo avrete:
(*Ad Art. cui dà un foglio.*)
Tu gli accompagnerai.
(*a Sir Gior.*)
O Nobil Dama,
(*Bru. giunge con Enr.*)
L'alto Anglican Sovrano Parlamento
Ti chiama al suo cospetto: Io ti son scorta!

**ENR:** (*Ahimè, che sento!*) E che da me sì chiede!

**VAL:** I me solo s' addice
(*Esitando.*)
Obbedir e tacer!—Altro non lice

**ART:** E de' Stuardi amica?
(*a Gior. in disparte*)

**GIO:** E prigioniera
(*Ad Art. in disparte.*)
Da molte lune, e fu da ognun creduta
Amica de' Stuardi e messaggera,
Sotto mentite spoglie.

**ART:** Oh Dio! che ascolto!
E deciso il suo fato: Essa è perduta—
Oh sventurata!—
(*Da sè, ma guardando pietosamente Enr.*)

**ENR:** (*Qual pietà in quel volto!—*)

**VAL:** O figli: al Tempio e alle pompose feste
Accorra ognun—La nuziale veste
Va, o diletta, a indossar: Ite voi seco—
(*Ad Elv.*)
Fuori del vallo i miei destrier sien presti:
(*a Bru.*)
Chè in brevo io qui sarò—La nostra andata
(*Ad Enr*)
Ci è forza d' affrettar! Com' io v' unisca
E a voi sorrida il Cielo, o Coppio amata.
(*Val. unisce nuovamente le destre di Elv. e di Art. li benedice e parte calle guardie.*)

## SCENE VI.

*Walton, Sir George, Elvira, Bruno, and Henrietta.*

**WALTON:** (*After whispering something to Bruno, who bows and retires.*) You understood me well: whoever attempts to quit these walls without my leave, is doomed to death. My dearest children, to the sacred altar you may go without me. In virtue of this writing (*to Art. giving him a paper*), you will have free admittance to the temple. (*to Sir George*) Accompany them. Noble lady (*to Henrietta, who enters, conducted by Bruno,*) you are called before the High Parliament. I shall be your escort.

**HEN:** (*Alas! what do I hear?*) what do they seek from me?

**WAL:** My duty is (*hesitating, then approaching his daughter and looking at the nuptial gifts*) to obey and be silent. I must submit.

**ART:** (*Aside to Sir G.*) Is she a friend to the Stuarts?

**SIR G:** She has been for many months a prisoner, and was thought by every one a friend to the Stuarts, and their messenger in disguise. (*To Art. aside.*)

**ART:** (*Heavens! what do I hear? Her fate is decided. She is lost. Oh, unfortunate woman!*)
(*Aside, but looking with pity on Hen.*)

**HEN:** (*What compassion in that face!*)

**WAL:** Let all hasten to the temple; and you my dearest, go and adorn yourself with your nuptial dress. You go with her (*to the ladies*); and (*to Bruno*) have my horses ready outside the walls. Shortly I shall be back. Our departure we must hasten, (*to Hen.*) As I do now, may Heaven unite and bless this pair beloved.
(*Walton unites again the hands of Elv. and Art., gives them his blessing, and retires with the Guards.*)

## SCENA VII.

*Enrichetta ed Arturo.*

**ENR:** (Pietà e dolore
(*Guardando attentamente Lord Art.*)
Ha in fronte e fanno sicurt del core.)
Cavalier—

**ART:** S' or ti è d' uopo di consiglio,
Di soccorso e d' aita, in me t' affida!

**ENR:** Se mi stesse sul capo aito periglio?

**ART:** Deh, parla; oh Dio!—che temi?

**ENR:** Breve ora—e sarò spenta! Ah tu ne fremi!
(*Art. fa un segno di fremito.*)

**ART:** Sì fremo—io fremo
Per te, per me—per Padre mio, che spento
Cadea fido a' Stuardi!—E tu chi sei?
O chi tu sii, tu vuo' salvar.

**ENR:** E tardi!
Figlia a Enrico, e a Carlo sposa,
Pari ad essi avrò la sorte—

**ART:** Oh - Regina—
(*S' inginnochia.*)

**ENR:** Attendo morte?

**ART:** Taci, ah taci per pietà!
(*Alzandosi*)
Fuor le mura, a tutti ascosa
Ti trarrò pier vie sicure—
Tu n' andrai di qui—

**ENR:** Alla scure!
Scampa e speme O Artur, non v' ha—

**ART:** No, Regina, ancor v' è speme:
O te salva—o spenti insieme.

**ENR:** Cangia, o Arturo, il pio consiglio,
Pensa ai tuo mortal periglio;
Pensa a Elvira, il tuo tesoro,
Che ti attende al sacro altar!

**ART:** Non parlar di lei che adoro;
Di valor non mi spogliar!

**ENR:** Sventurato prigionera,
Il mi fato io seguirò:
Giunse a me l' estrema sera—
Per te l' alba incominciò!

**ART:** Sarai salva, o sventurata,
O la morte incontrerò—
E la vergin mia adorata
Nel morire invocherò!—

## SCENA VIII.

*Elvira, Giorgio, Arturo, e Enrichetta.*

## SCENE VII.

*Henrietta and Arthur.*

**HEN:** Sorrow and compassion are painted on his face, and clearly show the feelings of his heart. Cavalier!

**ART:** If any advice you want, or any assistance, put your trust in me.

**HEN:** If a great danger were pending over my head—

**ART:** Speak—what do you fear?

**HEN:** A few moments—I shall be put to death!
(*Art. shudders.*) Ah! you shudder!

**ART:** Yes, I shudder, I tremble for yourself, for me, for my father, who, faithful to the Stuarts, for them lost his life! But who are you? Whoever you may be, I will save you.

**HEN:** It is too late.
Henry's daughter, wife of Charles—
Like their fate will be my own.

**ART:** Oh, my Queen—
(*He kneels.*)

**HEN:** Death I expect.

**ART:** Speak not thus, for pity's sake!
(*Rising.*)
Behind these walls, from all concealed,
By sure ways I shall lead you;
You from here shall go!

**HEN:** To the axe!
No more hope is left for me.

**ART:** No, my Queen; there still is hope:
I'll save you, or both shall perish.

**HEN:** Arthur, change your kind intention;
Think what danger you will meet;
Think of your dear Elvira,
Who now waits for you at the altar.

**ART:** Name not her who I adore!
Do not deprive my heart of valor.

**HEN:** In misfortune and captivity,
To my fate I will submit.
On my life the sun is setting;
On your own it rises now.

**ART:** Luckless Queen, you shall be saved,
Or my death I will encounter;
With the name of her I love
On my lips, I shall expire.

## SCENE VIII.

*Enter Elvira and Sir George.*

*Elvira ba il capo coronato di rose: ba un bellissimo monile di perle al collo. Entra in iscena avendo nelle mani il magnifico relo bianco regalatole da Arturo.*

ELV: Son vergin vezzosa—in vesta di sposa.
Son bianca ed umil—qual giglio d'April
Ho chiome odorose—cui cinser tue rose;
Ho il seno gentil—del bel tuo montil.

ENR, ART E GIO: Se miro il suo candor
Mi par la luna, allor
Che tra la nubi appar
La notte a consolar.
Se ascolto il suo cantar
Un' angelo mi par,
Che intuoni al primo albor
Inni al superno amor.

ELV: Dama, s' è ver che m' ami—

ENR: Dimmi, o gentil: che brami?

ELV: Qual mattutina stella,
Bella vogl' io brillar;
Del crin le molli annella
Mia giova ad aggraziar.

ENR: Elvira, mia diletta,
Son presta al tuo pregar.

ART E GIO: Fanciulla e semplicetta,
Ognor desia scherzar;
Scusare a te s' aspetta
Suo troppo vezzeggiar.
(*Ad Enr. quasi scusando la preghiera di Elv.*)

ELV: A illegiadrir mia prova
Deh, non aver a vil;
Ill velo in foggia nova
Sui capo tuo gentil.

ENR: Il vezzo tuo m'aletta,
Mi è caro a sacondar.

ELV: O bella, ti celo
Le anella del crin,
Com' io nel bel velo
Mi voglio celar.
Ascosa, O vezzosa,
Nel velo divin,
Or sembri la sposa,
Che vassi all' altar.

ENR: Ascosa in bianca vel,
Or pos o, O Dio, celar
L' affanno, il palpitar,
L' angoscia del mio cor!
(Deh tu, pietoso ciel,
Raccogli con favor
La prece di dolor
Ch' osia a te levar!)

ART: (Oh come da quel vel,
Che la nosconde il crin,
Veggio un splendor divin
Di speme a balenar!
Deh tu, pietoso ciel,
M' avviva il tuo favor,
Mi fa da un reo furor
La vittima salvar!)

*Elvira with a wreath of roses on her head, wearing a pearl necklace. She holds in her hand the veil that Arthur presented her with.*

ELV: I am a fair maiden adorned as a bride;
I am humble and candid as lilies in April;
My hair is quite fragrant with rose's perfume;
My bosom is graced with necklace of pearls.

HEN, ART AND SIR GEORGE:
When I behold her candor,
She appears to me the moon,
That pierces through the clouds,
To gladden the sad night.
And when I heart her voice,
She seems to me an angel,
That raises, at the dawn,
Hymns to the eternal Love.

ELV: Lady, if you love me truly—

HEN: Speak, dear; what do you wish?

ELV: I wish to shine as brightly
As the morning star,
With elegance and taste.

HEN: Oh, my beloved Elvira!
I am ready at your desire.

ART AND SIR G: A simple girl, and innocent,
She always likes to play.
Indulgent you must be
To her excessive liveliness.
(*To Hen. as if excusing Elvira's childish request.*)

ELV: My trial to adorn your hair,
Alas! do not despise;
I will in a new way
This veil place on your head.

HEN: Your sport affords me joy:
I am pleased to second it.

ELV: My dear, your fine ringlets
I hide in this veil,
As I would in it
Be hidden myself,
O charming lady!
In this lovely veil,
You seem to be the bride
That goes to the altar.

HEN: Now, covered with this veil,
Heavens! I can conceal
The cares upon my face,
The anguish in my heart.
(And most gracious Heaven,
Propitiously receive
The prayers which, in my grief
I dared to raise to you.)

ART: (Oh! how, from that white veil
In which her face is hidden,
I see a ray of hope
Shine forth, that glads my heart.
Ah! most gracious Heaven,
Your favors grant to me,
That I may save this victim
From an unjust oppression.)

GIO: (Elvira col cuo vel,
Un zeffiretto appar,
Un iride sul mar,
Un Silfo, in grembo ai fior.)
(*Guardandola con paterna compiacenza*)
T' arrida, O cara il Ciel
Col roseo suo favor,
Tal ch' io ti veggio ognor
Tra vezza a giubilar!

VAL E COR: Elvira—mia/deh Elvira,
Il di l' ore avanza!

ELV: Se il Padre s' adira—
Io volo a mia stanza!
Ma poscia, o fedel,
Tu posami il vel.
(*Con vezzo semplice.*)

ART, GIO E ENR: Si il Padre s' adira—
Ah rieda a tua stanza!
Sarà il tuo fedel,
Che t' orni del vel!
(*Elv. parte colle Damigelle e con Gio.*)

## SCENA IX.

*Enrichetta ed Arturo.*

*Arturo guarda con grande sospetto all' intorno nuovamente, e trae dalla cintura il foglio ovuto da Valton.*

ENR: Sulla verginea testa
D' una felice un bianco vel s' addice—
A me noa già—

ART: T' arresta
(*Correndo a lei e trattenendola*)
E' chiaro don del ciel! così ravvolta,
Deluderia la vigilante scolta—
Tu mia sposa parria—
(*Con risoluzione.*)
Vieni.

ENR: Che dici mai!
Tu corri a tua ruina, a orribil sorte!

ART: Vieni—Ah vieni—T' involo a certa morte.

## SCENA X.

*Riccardo e detti, con spada ignuda.*

RIC: Ferma. Invan rapir pretendi
Ogni ben ch'io aveva in terra;
Qui ti sfido a mortal guerra—
Trema, ah trema del mio acciar!

ART: Sprezzo, O audace, il tuo furore:
La mortal disfida accetto:
Questo fero nel tuo petto
Sino all' elsa io vuò piantar.
(*Per battersi: Enr. si frappone: il velo si scompone, e il suo volti si scuopre.*)

SIR G: Elvira, with her veil,
Appears a gentle zephyr,
A rainbow over the waters,
A sylph among the flowers.
(May Heaven look on you,
My dear, with rosy smiles!
That I may see you ever
In pleasure and in mirth.)

WAL AND CHO: Come dearest Elvira;
The day is advancing.

ELV: If my father is angry,
I run to my room;
But then dearest,
I put on your veil.
(*With naïvete.*)

ART, SIR G AND HEN: If your father is angry,
Return to your room;
Your lover will then
Put the veil on you.
(*Elv., Sir G. and Ladies, exeunt.*)

## SCENE IX.

*Henrietta and Arthur.*

*Arthur, looking around with caution, draws from his belt the paper received from Walton.*

HEN: The head of a happy maiden is well suited to a white veil (*Aside, and about to take off the veil*), but not mine.

ART: Desist! (*Running to prevent her.*) By the will of Heaven this veil is put on you. Wrapped up in it, you will deceive the vigilance of the sentry. You will be thought my bride. (*With resolution.*) Come.

HEN: What do you say? You will run to your destruction—to a dreadful fate!

ART: Come, come; I will save you from certain death.

## SCENE X.

*Enter Richard with drawn sword.*

RICH: Stop. In vain you attempted to steal
The only treasure I had on earth.
Here I challenge you to death!
Tremble—ah! tremble at my sword!

ART: I despise, bold man, your fury!
I accept your mortal challenge;
Up to the hilt within your chest
I will plunge this very sword.
(*When they are on the point of fighting, Hen. interposes; her veil becomes disordered.*)

ENR: Pace pace—ah v'arrestate,
Per ma sangue non versate.

ART: Ah che fai!—

RICH: La Prigioniera?
(*Con stupore.*)

ENR: Desso io son.

ART: Tua voce altera.
(*a Ric.*)
Or col ferro sosterrai—
Vien—

RIC: Con lei, tu illeso andrai.
(*Freddamente.*)

ART: E fia ver?—

ENR: Qual favella?

RIC: Più non vieto a voi l' andar.

ART: (Se il destino a te m' invola,
O mia Elvira, O amor mio santo,
Un sospiro a te sen vola,
E ti dice in suon di pianto;
Ti consola!—Io lungi e in guai
T' amerò com io t'amai!)

RIC: (Parti, O stolto. e prova intanto
Quel dolor che a me serbavi
Tu vivrai deserto e in pianto
Giorni oscuri, eterni e gravi—
Patria e Amor tu perderai—
Fia tua vita un mar di guai!)

ENR: (Sogno—o avrò conforto al
pianto
Avrò tregna a di si gravi?
Sogno, o andrommi al figlio accanto
Tra gli amplessi suoi suovi?
Tanto ben, se, oh Dio, sognia—
Non mi far destar giammai!)
(*Coro dentro le scene.*)
Genti a festa! Al tempio andiamo!

ART ED ENR: Gente appressa?—
Oh ciel fogiamo!

RIC: Si fuggite—il vuole un Dio!

ART: Pria che siam oltre le mura.
(*Per partire poi si testa.*)
Parlerai?—

RIC: No t' assecura—

ART: Tu lo giura.

RIC: I giuro!

TUTTI: Addio—
(*Art. e Enr. partone.*)

## SCENA XI.

*Riccardo, poi Valton, Bruno, Elvira, con Damigelle in pompa di nozze.*

RIC: (*Quasi segue coll' occhio i passi dei fuggiaschi.*) E gia al
ponte—Passa il forte—
E alle porte—Gia n' andiò!—

CORO: Al tempio, al tempio a festa!
(*Escendo.*)

ELV: Dov' è Artur?

RIC: Dianzi fu qui—

ELV: Ove sei, O Artur?—

---

HEN: Peace! ah! peace! put down
your arms;
Do not risk your lives for me.

ART: Ah! what have you done?

RICH: The prisoner!
(*With amazement.*)

HEN: Truly she.

ART: Your lofty language.
Come, maintain now with your
sword.

RICH: (*Coldly.*) You shall go with
her in safety.

ART: Is it true?

HEN: (What words are these?)

RICH: I no longer stop your going.

ART: If my fate takes me from you,
Dear Elvira, my sweet love,
A deep sigh from here I send,
To tell you, in plaintive tone,
Be consoled. I afar, in grief,
Shall love thee as I do now.

RICH: (Go, madman, and now feel
The same grief reserved for me;
You shall live alone in tears,
Days obscure, and sad, and long;
You shall lose both love and country,
Endless grief your life shall be.)

HEN: Do I dream? or shall I have
To my woes at last a truce?
Do I dream? Or shall I still
Enfold my dear son in my arms
If I dream of so much bliss—
Heaven, never break my rest.
(*Chorus behind the scenes.*)
Friends rejoice! Come to the temple.

ART & HEN: People are coming—
let us fly.

RICH: Yes, do fly. So heaven commands.

ART: (*On the point of going, turns back to Rich.*)
Will you speak before we have
Passed the walls?

RICH: No, no; be certain.

ART: Swear it now.

RICH: I swear.

ALL: Farewell.
(*Art. and Hen. exeunt.*)

## SCENE XI.

*Richard, then Walton, Sir George, Bruno, Elvira, with Damsels dressed for the marriage.*

RICH: (*Looking from the balcony after the fugitives.*) He is at the
bridge—he has passed the fort,
Has reached the gates—he is gone.

CHO: Friends, rejoice!—come to
the temple.

ELV: Where is Arthur?

RICH: He was here just now.

ELV: Where are you, dear Arthur?

---

RIC: Parti!—

ELV, RIC, GIO: Già fuor della
mura—
Laggiù alla pianura.

CORO 1: La tua prigioniera.
La rea messaggiera
Col vil cavaliero?
(*a Val.*)

2: Ciascun su un destriero—
Spronando—volando—

TUTTI: Mirate cola!—
(*Quadro generalo. Elv. getta un grido.*)

VAL: Soldati accorrete—cio bronzi tuonate,
All' arme appellate—correte—volate,
Pel crin transcinate i due traditor.
(*La campana del forte suona a stormo: il cannone spara a lenti intervalli.*

TUTTI: All' arme!—

VAL: T' affretta.
(*a Bru.*)

TUTTI DI DENTRO: All' arme!—

VAL E TUTTI: Vendetta!
(*Val. snuda la spada, e parte.*)

RIC: Oh, come si pasce—d' affini e
d' ambasce
L' ardor di vendetta—che m'ange e
m'alletta:
Oh come nel seno—si masce il veleno
Di sdegno e d'amor—di speme e
dolor!

ELV: La dama d'Arturo—è bianco
velata—
La guarda e sospira—Sua sposa la
chiama:
Elvira è la dama!—Non sono più Elvira?

GIO E CORO: Elvira! che dici?—

ELV: Io Elvira? Ah no—No—
No!—

UOMI: La misera è pallida—

DON: E immobile e squallida—

UOMI: Le luce non gira—

DON: Sorride e sospira—

UOMI: Demente si fa—

TUTTI: O cieli, pietà.
(*Elv. nel suo delirio crede vedere Art. e dice questi versi con la più grande mestizia e delirante passione.*)

ELV: Arturo, ah già ritorni?
Dunque sei fido ancor!
Ah vieni al Tempio, fedel Arturo—
Eterna fede, mia ben, ti giuro!
Come oggi è puro sempre avrò il
core
Vivrò d'Amore, morrò d'Amor!

DON: Si crede all' ara—

UOMI: Giura ed Arturo—

DON: Ella sì tenera—

---

RICH: He is gone.

ELV, RICH, SIR. G: Already beyond
the walls—far away over the plain.

1ST CHO: Your lady prisoner—the
guilty emissary,
With the worthless knight?

2ND CHO: Let us go to the horses
And spur and fly.

ALL: Look there!
(*General Tableau. Elv. utters a shriek.*)

WAL: Come, soldiers, hasten; fire
off the cannons;
Call now to arms—run quickly, fly!
And drag both the traitors quickly
here.
(*The alarm bell of the citadel sounds. The cannon is fired at intervals.*

ALL: To arms!

WAL: Hasten.
(*To Bruno.*)

ALL: (*Within.*) To arms!

WAL AND CHORUS: Revenge!
(*Wall. draws his sword and goes out.*)

RICH: Oh!
The fire of vengeance, that grieves
and delights,
How it is fed on torments and woes.
Oh! how in my breast the feelings
are mixed
Of love and disdain, of hope and despair.

ELV: The lover of Arthur has on a
white veil;
He views her and sighs, he calls her
his bride.'
Elvira is the lady! Am I not Elvira?

SIR G AND CHORUS: Elvira, what
did you say?

ELV: I Elvira? Ah! no, no.

MEN: The sad one is pale.

WOMEN: She does not move.

MEN: Her eyes have no life.

WOMEN: She smiles and she sighs.

MEN: She loses all reason.

ALL: Oh, heavens, have pity!
(*Elv. in her delirium thinks she sees Art. and sings the following lines with profound sorrow and frantic passion.*)

ELV: Dear Arthur, you have returned?
You are still true to me!
Come to the temple, my faithful
Arthur,
I swear fidelity to you forever
My heart, as now, will ever be pure:
On love I'll live, on love I'll die.

WOMEN: She thinks she is at
church.

MEN: She swears to Arthur faith.

WOMEN: She is so loving.

**UOMI:** Ei sì spergiuro—
**DON:** Ella sì candida—
**UOMI:** Ei traditor—
**INSI:** Misera vergine, morrà d'amor!

**RIC E CORO:** Oh come ho l'anima trista e dolente,
Udendo i gemiti dell'innocente;
Oh come perfido fu il traditore.
Che in tanti spasimi lasciò quel cor!

**GIO:** Dio di clemenza, t'offro mia vita,
Se all'innocenza giovi d'aita:
Deh, sii clemente a un puro core!
Deh, sii possente sul traditor!

**RIC:** Più la miro, e più doglia profonda,
E più l'alma s'accende in amore!
Ma più innaspra ed avvampa il furore
Contro chi tanto ben m'involò!

**GIO:** La mia prece pietosa e profonda
Che a te vien sui sospir del dolore;
Tu clemente consola, O Signore,
Per la vergin cui l'empio immolò!
(*Elv. quasi tornando a vedere Art. che fugge.*)

**ELV:** Ti veggo—già fuggi—O ingrato, abbandoni
Chi tanto t'amo! Arturo—Oh Dio!—No!—

**CORO:** Ahi dura sciagura, ahi lutto e dolor!
Sì bella, sì pura del ciel creatura
Nel dì del diletto schernita tradita
Andrà maladetto il vil traditor.

**ELV:** Qua! febbre vorace m'uccide—mi sface—
Quai fiamma, qual' ira mi avvampa e martira!
Fantasmi perversi fuggite dispersi!—
O in tanto furur sbranatemi il cor.

**PURI E POI TUTTI:** Maledizione!
Non casa, non spiaggia raccolga i fuggenti!
Io odio del cielo, in odio a'viventi,
Battuti dai venti, da orrende tempeste,
Le odiate lor teste non possan posar!
Erranti, piangenti in orrida guerra
Cor cielo, la terra il mar, gli elementi—
Ognor maladetti in vita ed in morte,
Sia eterna lor sorte eterno il penar!

*FINE DELL'ATTO PRIMO.*

**MEN:** He is so false.
**WOMEN:** She is so candid.
**MEN:** He such a traitor.
**ALL:** Unhappy maiden! She will die of love.

**RICH & CHO:** Oh! how your mind is filled with sorrow!
Hearing the sighs of this poor heart.
Oh! how perfidious was the traitor
That brought on her so much affliction!

**SIR G:** O God of Mercy, my life I offer.
If to the innocent you will give aid.
Ah! be propitious to a heart so pure,
And show thy power against the traitor.

**RICH:** The more I see her, the more I grieve,
And greater love for her I feel;
But more my fury becomes enflamed
Against him who stole this treasure from me.

**SIR G:** My pious prayer, deep and sincere,
Which comes to you on wings of grief,
Receive it kindly, O, Lord of bounty,
For this poor maiden, that traitor's victim.
(*Elv. as if she saw Art. again escaping*)

**ELV:** I see you—you flew. Ungrateful! You left.
Your lover so true. Oh, Arthur! heavens! No.

**CHO:** Oh, bitter misfortune! Oh, mourning and grief!
So handsome, so pure, beloved of Heaven.
Deceived on the morning that promised her joy,
A curse shall pursue this vilest of traitors.

**ELV:** What fever, devouring, now seizes my brain!
What flame and what rage my heart is consuming!
O, phantoms perverse! go, fly, an disperse,
Or madly my heart come tear from my bosom.

**PURI & CHORUS:** Malediction!
Let nor house nor shore the flyers receive!
By Heaven abandoned, disliked by men,
The sport of the winds, oppressed by the storms,
May their heads never find place of repose.
Bewailing, and wandering in horrible contest
With heaven and earth, the sea and the elements,
For ever detested in life and death,
May their fate and their woes be eternal!

*End of the First Act.*

*SCENA I.*

*Gran Sala con porte laterali.*

*Castellani è Castellane, Puritani, e Bruno.*

**TUTTI:** Piangon le ciglia—Si spezza il cor—
L'inferma figlia—morrà d'amor.

**1:** Il duol l'invase?

**2:** La vidi errante Tra folte piante—

**3:** Or per sue case Gridando va—"Pietà—Pietà!"

**TUTTI:** Piangon le ciglia—Si spezza il cor—
L'inferma figlia—morrà d'amor!

*SCENA II.*

*Giorgio dagli appartamenti d'Elvira: poi Riccardo con foglio.*

**DON:** Qual novella?
**GIO:** Or prende posa.
**TUTTI:** Miserella!
**DON:** E ognor dolente?
**GIO:** Mesta e lieta—
**DON:** E senza tregua?
**GIO:** Splende il senno—or si dilegua
All misera innocente.
**TUTTI:** Come mai?
**GIO:** Dir lo poss' io?
Se nel duol che m'ange il seno,
Ogui voce trema e muor!
**CORO:** Deh favella—
**GIO:** Mi lasciate.
**CORO:** Ten preghiamo—
**GIO:** Ah nò—cessate!
**BRU E CORO:** Deh ti muova quell' ambascia
Che ci aggrava al tuo dolor!
**GIO:** Siate paghi—v' appressate!
Cinta di rose e col bel crin disciolto
Talor la cara vergine s'aggira:
E chiede all' aura e ai fior cou mesto volta:
"Ove andò Elvira."
Bianco-vestita, e qual se all' arra innante,
Adempie al rito, e va cantando: il giuro.
Poi grida, per amor tutta tremante—
"Ah vieni, Arturo."

**CORO:** Ahi, figlia misera delira amor!
Quarto fu barbaro il sedduttor!

*SCENE I.*

*A large Room with side doors.*

*Villagers, Puritans, and Bruno.*

**ALL:** All eyes are weeping—all hearts are breaking.
The afflicted girl of love will die.

**1:** Grief has seized her.

**2:** I saw her wandering Amongst the groves.

**3:** Sometimes, at home, She is heard to exclaim, "Ah! pity! pity!"

**ALL:** All eyes are weeping—all hearts are breaking.
The afflicted girl of love will die.

*SCENE II.*

*Enter Sir George from the apartments of Elvira, then Richard, with a paper.*

**WOMEN:** What fresh news?
**SIR G:** She is now reposing.
**ALL:** Ah! poor girl!
**WOMEN:** Is she still weeping?
**SIR G:** Sad and joyful.
**WOMEN:** Takes she rest?
**SIR G:** Now she shows wisdom and now
The poor girl appears insane.
**ALL:** How is this?
**SIR G:** Can I tell it?
When oppressed by so much grief,
All my words die on my lips.
**CHO:** Pray do speak.
**SIR G:** Ah! let me rest.
**CHO:** We bespeech.
**SIR G:** Ah! do desist.
**BRU, CHO:** Be you moved by this affliction
That your grief has raised in us.
**SIR G:** I will grant your wish. Approach.
With roses crowned, and with her hair disheveled,
The maiden dear now wandering is seen,
Demanding of the air and of the flowers, "Where is Elvira?"
Now enrobed, in white, and as before the altar.
The rites performing, she repeats the oath,
Then, trembling, cries, in ecstasy of love,
"Ah! come, dear Arthur."

**CHO:** Ah! unhappy girl! deranged by love.
Cruel indeed was her betrayer.

## Act II, Scene II

**GIO:** Geme talor, qual tortore amorosa,
Or cade vinta da mortal sudore:
Or l' odi al suon dell' arpa lamentosa
Cantar d' amore!
Or scorge Arturo nell' altrui sembiante—
Poi del suo inganno accorta e di sua sorte,
Geme, piange, s' affanna e ognor più ammante,
Invoca morte.

**CORO:** Ahi, figlia misera morrà d' amor!—
Scenda una folgore sul traditor!
(*Alle ultime parole entra Ric. con un foglio.*)

**RIC:** Di sua folgore il ciel non sarà lento!
"A scure infame è Artùr Talbot dannato
"Dall' Anglican sovrano Parlamento."

**CORO:** E giusto fato!

**RIC:** Quaggiù, nel mal che questa valle serra,
A' buoni e a' tristi è memorando esempio.

**CORO:** Se la destra di Dio tremenda afferra
Il crin dell' empio!
(*Ric. scorre coll' occhio il foglio che tiene aperto. Segue a proclamare li decreti del Parlamento.*)

**RIC:** Di Valton l'innocenza a voi proclama
Il Parlamento, e a' primi onor lo chiama—

**CORO:** Qual doglia, Valton, se vedran tua ciglia
Insana ancor la tua diletta figlia!—

**RIC:** Ed essa? infuria ognor?—

**GIO:** Sol quando un suon marzial misera sente
Più ricorda il fuggir del caro amente
E allor fassi furente.

**RIC:** E non v' ha speme Alcuna?

**GIO:** Medic' arte n' assecura
Che una subita gioia, o gran sciagura
Potria sanar la mente sua smarrita.

**CORO:** Qual mai t' attenda, O Artur, pena infinita!

**RIC:** In me duce premier, parla Cromvello.
Il vil, ch'e ognor in fuga,
E di sangue civil macchiò Inghilterra,
Cercate or voi. E se sua rea fortuna,
O malizia lo tragga a questa terra,
Non abbia grazia, è pietade alcuna.
(*Il Coro parte.*)

**SIR G:** At times she sighs like a loving dove;
At times she sinks oppressed by her great woes;
And then she is heard at her lamenting harp,
Singing of love.
At times she takes another face for Arthur's;
Then her mistake perceiving, and her fate,
She sighs and weeps, and, loving more than ever,
She invokes death.

**CHO:** Unhappy girl! love will kill her.
May thunder fall upon the traitor!
(*At the last words, Richard enters with a paper.*)

**RICH:** The thunder is not far from striking Arthur,
"He stands condemned to die a traitor's death
His sentence is decreed by Parliament."

**CHO:** It is but just.

**RICH:** Amongst the woes that this sad world contains,
It is a warning for the good and bad.

**CHO:** When God's right hand avenging falls upon the wicked man.
(*Rich. glances over the paper, and proceeds to proclaim the decree of Parliament.*)

**RICH:** Likewise the Parliament proclaims the innocence of Walton, and gives him back his honors.

**CHO:** What grief for Walton, if he's condemned to see his darling daughter
Still out of mind!

**RICH:** Is she still mad?

**SIR G:** If martial sounds the unhappy girl but hears
They suddenly recall her lover's flight,
And frantic she becomes.

**RICH:** Is there no hope?

**SIR G:** The art of healing still declares, assures,
That an event of sudden joy or woe
Alone could cure again her mind distracted.

**CHO:** What endless pain now, Arthur, waits for you!

**RICH:** I, Colonel of Cromwell, in his name this to you make known.
The traitor, still a fugitive, and who has stained the English ground with civil blood, must be searched for by you. And should he, either by his adverse fortune or his bad designs, be brought back to this land, let him not find grace nor pity.
(*Exit Chorus.*)

## SCENE III.

*Elvira e detti.*

**ELV:** O rendetemi la speme
(*Dentro la Scena.*)
O lasciatemi morir.

**GIO:** Essa qui vien—la senti?
O come è grave il suon de' suoi lamenti!
(*Esce Elv. scapigliata e in veste bianca.*)

**ELV:** Quì la voce sua soave
Mi chiamava—e poi sparì
Quì giurava esser fedele,
Poi crudele—ei mi fuggì!
Ah, mai più qui assorti insieme
Nella gioia dei sospir?—
Ah rendetemi la speme
Oh lasciatemi morir!

**GIO, RIC:** (Qanto amore è mai raccolto
In quel vlto e in quel dolor!)

**ELV:** Chi sei tu?—
(*Dopo una pausa a Gio.*)

**GIO:** Non mi ravvisi?

**ELV:** Padre mio?—mi chiamai al Tempio?
Non è sogno—oh Arturo—oh amor!
A tu sorridi—asciughi il pianto!
A Imen mi guidi—al ballo, al canto!
Ognun s'appresta a nozze, a festa,
E meco in danza esulterà.
Tu pur meco danzerai?
(*Si volta, e vede Ric., lo prende per la mano.*)
Vieni a nozze!

**GIO E RIC:** (Oh Dio!)

**ELV:** Egli piange.
Egli piange! ei forse amò!
(*a Gio. in disparte e sotto voce—poi torna a fissare Ric.: poi gli afferra la mano e tornando ad atteggiarsi dolorosamente.*)

**RIC E GIO:** (Chi frenar il pianto può!)

**ELV:** M'odi e dimmi, amasti mai!
(*a Ric.*)

**RIC:** Gli occhi affisa in sul mio volto,
Ben mi guarde e lo vedrai—

**ELV:** Ah se piangi—Ancor tu sai
Che un cor fido nell' amor,
Sempre vive di dolor!
(*Si abbandona al pianto. Gio. l'abbraccia.*)

**GIO:** Deh! ti acqueta, O mia diletta,
Tregua al duol dal tempo aspetta.

**ELV:** Mai!

**RIC E GIO:** Clemente il Cie! ti fia.

**ELV:** Mai!—

## SCENE III.

*Elvira within.*

**ELV:** Either restore hope to me,
Or let me die in pity.

**SIR G:** (Here she comes—did you hear her?
O, how grievous is the voice of her laments!)
(*Enter Elv. with looks and actions indicating loss of reason.*)

**ELV:** Here his voice, so soft and sweet,
Called on me—then died away;
Here he swore he would be faithful:
Then, cruel man, he fled from me.
Never more shall we together
Feel the rapture of our love!
Either hope restore to me,
Or in pity let me die.

**SIR G, RICH:** How much love is there expressed
In her face and through her grief!

**ELV:** Who are you?
(*To Sir G.*)

**SIR G:** Do you not know me?

**ELV:** Father called me to church?
It is no dream. Arthur! oh, love!
Ah! You smile!—Dry your tears.
We go to the altar, to dance and sing;
Each one prepares for nuptial feasts,
And, full of joy, will dance with me.
You too shall join the dance with me.
(*Perceiving Rich., and taking him by the hand.*)
Come to the wedding.

**SIR G & RICH:** Oh heavens?

**ELV:** He is weeping.
Yes; he weeps: perhaps he loved
(*Aside to Sir G., then, regarding Rich., grasps his hand, and abandons herself again to grief.*)

**RICH & SIR G:** (Who can now refrain from tears!)

**ELV:** (*To Rich.*) Hear me; say, have you once loved?

**RICH:** (*To Elv.*) Cast your eyes upon this face.
And you soon will know the truth.

**ELV:** If you have wept, you must know
That a loving, faithful heart
Is for ever fed with grief. (*Elv. abandons herself to grief. Sir G. embraces her.*)

**SIR G:** Calm yourself my dearest love;
Time will dispel all your pangs.

**ELV:** Never!

**RICH & SIR G:** Heaven will pity you.

**ELV:** Never!

RIC E GIO: L'ingrato ormai oblia.

ELV: Ah! mai più ti rivedrò!

RIC E GIO: (Si fa mia la sua ferita.
Mi dispera e squarcia il cor.)

ELV: O toglietemi la vita,
O rendetemi il mio amor!

RIC E GIO: Tornò il riso in sul suo aspetto,
Qual pensiero a lei brillò?

ELV: Non temer del padre mio!
Co' miei pianti il placherò—
Ogni affanno andrà in oblio,
Tanto amor consolerò!

GIO: (Essa in pene è abbandonata
Sogna il gaudio che perdè!—)

RIC: (Qual bell' alma innamorata
Un rival rapiva a me!)

ELV: Vien, diletto, è in ciel la luna:
Tutto tace intorno intorno:
Fin che spunti in ciel il giorno,
Vien, ti posa sul mio cor!
Deh t' affretta, O Arturo mio,
Riedi, O caro, alla tua Elvira;
Esssa piange, e ti sospira.
Riedi, O caro, al primo amor—

RIC E GIO: Possa un di, bella infelice,
Mercè aver di tanto affetto:
Possa un giorno nel diletto
Obbliare il suo dolor!

GIO: Ricovrarti ormai t'addice.

BRU: Stende notte il cupo orror—

## SCENA IV.

*Giorgio osserva all' intorno; poi afferra pel braccio Riccardo, come uno che parlando mostra sapere un suo grave segreto.*

GIO: Il rival salvar tu devi,
Il rival salvar tu poi.

RIC: Io nol posso—

GIO: Tu non vuoi?

RIC: No!

GIO: Tu il salva!

RIC: Ei perirà—

GIO: Tu quell' ora ben rimembri
Che fuggi la prigioniera?

RIC: Sì—

GIO: D' Arturo fu colpa interna?

RIC: Tua favella ormai—
(*Quasi sdegnandosi.*)

GIO: E vera!

RIC: Parla aperto!—
(*Come sopra.*)

GIO: Ho detto assai!
(*Come sopra.*)

RICH & SIR G: Ah! forget the traitor.

ELV: Never more shall I see you.

RICH, SIR G: All her woes become my own;
She rends my heart to pieces.

ELV: Either take my life away,
Or restore my love to me.

RICH, SIR G: Now her face appears serene.
What sweet thought revives her mind?

ELV: Have no fear of my dear father;
By these he will be appeased;
All our woes will be forgotten;
So much love shall have reward.

SIR G: (By her sorrows she is bewildered,
And she dreams of lost content.)

RICH: (What a sweet and loving creature
Was a rival from me taking!)

ELV: Come, my dear, the moon is shining;
All is mute and calm around;
The day shall rise in heaven,
Come, repose, upon my heart.
Alas! hasten, my dear Arthur;
Quick return to your Elvira;
She now weeps and sighs for you;
Quick return to your first love.

SIR G, RICH: May, one day, unhappy beauty,
Your great love meet its reward.
May, one day, in sweet delights
Your misfortunes be forgotten.

SIR G: Now it is better that you retire.

BRU: Night overspreads her mantle dark.

## SCENE IV.

*Sir George looks around, then takes hold of Richard's arm with the air of one knowing a great secret.*

SIR G: You must save your rival.
You can save your rival.

RICH: I cannot.

SIR G: You will not.

RICH: No.

SIR G: Save him.

RICH: He shall die.

SIR G: Do you remember the hour
When the prisoner escaped?

RICH: Yes.

SIR G: Was it Arthur's fault?

RICH: At last this speech—
(*Becoming indignant.*)

SIR G: Is true.

RICH: Speak freely.

SIR G: I've said enough.

RIC: Fu voler del Parlamento
Se ha colui la pena estrema,
Dei ribelli l' ardimento
In Artur si domera.
Io non l' odio, io nol pavento,
Ma l'indegno perirà—

GIO: Un geloso e reo tormento
Or t'invade e acceca—Ah trema!
Il rimorso e lo spavento
La tua vita strazierà—
Se il rival per te fia spento
Un' altr' alma il seguirà!

RIC: Chi?

GIO: Due vittime farai,
E dovunque tu n' adrai
L' ombra lor ti seguirà!
Se tra il bujo un fantasma vedrai
Bianco lieve—che geme e sospira
Sarà Elvira, che mesta s' aggira,
E ti grida: io son morta per te.
Quando il cielo è in tempesta più scuro
S' odi un' ombra affannosa che freme
Sarà Artur che t' incalza, ti preme,
Ti minaccia de' morti il furor!

RIC: Se d' Elvira il fantasma dolente
M' apparisce e m' incalzi e s' ardiri,
Le mie preci, i singulti, i sospiri
Mi sapranno ottenere mercè.
Se l' odiato fantasma d'Arturo
Sanguinoso surgesse d' Averno,
Ripiombarlo agli abissi in eterno
Lo farebbe il mio immenso furor!

GIO: Il duol che sì mi accora
Vinca la tua bell' anima—

RIC: Han vinto le tue lacrime—
Mira—ho bagnato il ciglio.

a 2: Chi ben la Patria adora
Onoro la pietà.

RIC: Se inerme ed in periglio—
Salvo ei per te sarà.

GIO: Sì; il salva!—

RIC: E dall' esiglio
Contro la Patria libera
Se armato ei qui verrà?—

GIO: Mia man non è ancor gelida,
Con te il combatterà.

RIC: Forse dell' alba al sorgere
(*Con mistero.*)
L' oste ci assalirà—
S' ei vi sarà!—

GIO: Morra!
Sia voce di terror
Patria, vittoria, onor!

RICH: It was the will of Parliament
That sentenced him to die.
The boldness of the rebels
Will be repressed in Arthur.
I hate him not, nor fear him;
But die the traitor must.

SIR G: A jealous, guilty torment
Invades your soul—But tremble!
Remorse and constant fright
Will make your life most wretched.
If your rival is doomed at your hands,
Another death shall follow.

RICH: Whose?

SIR G: You would make fall two victims,
And wherever you should go,
Their shades will pursue you.
If a phantom by night you should see,
Pale and light, that is moaning and sighing,
It's Elvira, who wanders in sorrow,
And cries to you—"You were the cause of my death."
When the storm in the sky is raging,
If you hear a shadow complaining,
It will be Arthur that follows your steps,
And each moment is threatening your death.

RICH: If the shade of the weeping Elvira
Comes to me in complaints and in anger,
My warm prayers, my sobs and my sighs
Will obtain my pardon from her soul.
If the detested phantom of Arthur
Should arise from the regions of woe,
My fury would for ever hurl
Him again to the realms of the wicked.

SIR G: The grief that I now feel
May move your noble soul.

RICH: Your tears have conquered me;
Behold, I also weep.

BOTH: Who truly loves his country,
Knows how to feel compassion.

RICH: If helpless and in danger,
I will save him for you.

SIR G: Yes, save him.

RICH: Should he come
Against his country's freedom
From his exile in arms?

SIR G: My arm is not yet withered;
We both will fight against him.

RICH: Perhaps at break of day
The foe will attack.
If he be there?

SIR G: He dies.
The cry of terror be—
Victory, country, and honor!

a 2: Suoni la tromba, e intrepido
Io pugnerò da forte,
Bello è affrontar la morte
Gridando libertà.
Amor di Patria impavido
Mieta i sanguigni allori
Poi terga i bei sudoni
E i pianti la pietà.

RIC: All' alba!

GIO: All' alba!

a 2: All' alba!
Alba che sorgi a un popolo
Che a libertà s' affidi,
Giuliva a lui sorridi
Nunzia d' eterno Sol.
Alba, che sorgi ai perfidi
Tiranni della terra
Sii nunzia a lor di guerra,
Alba d' eterno duol.

GIO: Il patto è gia fermato,
Se Artur è inerme o vinto?—

RIC: Avra pieta e conforto—

GIO: Se vien ascoso e armato?—

RIC: Ei sara avvinto e morto!–

*Fine Dell' Atto Secondo.*

BOTH: Let trumpets sound, and bravely
And fearless I shall fight.
It is fine to meet our death,
For ever crying "Liberty!"
Intrepid love of country
Let reap the blood-stained laurel;
Then let us be rewarded
By softest hand of pity.

RICH: At dawn.

SIR G: At dawn.

BOTH: At dawn.
O, day! that on a nation,
Which trusts in freedom, rises
Propitious on us shine;
Bring us eternal glory.
To all perfidious tyrants
That live upon this earth,
Be messenger of war,
And of eternal grief.

SIR G: The agreement is concluded.
If Arthur is defenseless—

RICH: He'll find support and pardon.

SIR G: If he returns in arms—

RICH: He shall be doomed to die.

*End of the Second Act.*

# ■ ATTO III.

## SCENA I.

*Loggia in un giardino e boschetto vicino alla casa di Elvira. La casa internamente vedesi da varie lampade illuminata.*

*Arturo, e poi Elvira.*

ART: Son salvo, alfin son salvo. I miei nemici
Falliro il colpo, e mi smarrir di taccia.
Oh patria—oh amore, onnipossenti nomi!
Quanti' io vi sento e adoro! ad ogni passo
Mi balza il cor nel seno e benedico
Ogni tronco, ogni fronda ed ogni sasso—
Oh com' e' dolce a un esule infelice
Dopo il misero errar di riva in riva,
Toccar alfin la terra sua nativa:
Vedere ed abbracciar colei che in core
Gli fu scolpita per la man d' amore!
(*S' intravvede fra i vetri del palazzo Elvira, vestita di bianco. Essa, non vista da Arturo, trapazza sola e cantando.*)

ELV: A una fonte afflitto e solo
S' assiedeva un trovador;
E a sfogar l' immenso duolo,
Sciolse un cantico d' amor—

ART: La mia canzon d' amore? ah Elvira, al Elvira,
Ove t' aggiri tu? Nessun risponde!
A te cos' io contava
Di queste selve tra la dense fronde,

# ■ ACT III.

## SCENE I.

*A garden and a grove near Elvira's house. Elvira's house is lighted up.*

ART: I am saved; at last I am saved. My foes have missed their aim and lost my trace. O, my dear country! O, my beloved! mighty names! How much I feel your power, and how I adore you both! At every step my heart beats stronger: every tree, every leaf, every stone, I bless. Oh! how sweet it is for an unhappy exile, after sadly wandering from shore to shore, to reach once more his native land!—to see and embrace her whom love so strongly has on his heart imprinted!
(*Elvira, dressed in white, and unperceived by Arthur, is seen passing by the windows of her house.*)

ELV: At a fountain, sad and lonely,
A troubadour once was sitting,
And, to solace his deep grief,
Raised on high a song of love.

ART: My own love-song! Oh, Elvira! where are you? No one replies. Thus to you I sung amidst the branches of this shady grove, and then you made the echo to my song.

E tu allor facevi eco al cantar mio!—
Deh! si ascoltasti l' amoroso canto—
Odi un esulo afflito, odi il mio pianto.
A una fonte afflitto e solo
S' assiedeva un trovador,
Toccò l' arpa, e suonò duolo;
Sciolse un canto e fu dolor!
Corre a valle, corre a monte
L' esciliato pellegrin;
Ma il dolor gli è sempre a fronte,
Gli è compagno nel cammin.
Brama il Sole, allorch' è sera:
Brama sera, allorch' è Sol:
Gli par verno primavera:
Ogni riso gli par duol.
(*Sentesi un sordo battere di tamburo entro la scene.*)
Qual suon?—gente s' appressa.

CORO 1: Agli spaldi—
(*Sommessamente entro la scene.*)

2: Alle torri sara.

TUTTI: Si cherchera—non sfuggira.

ART: Ove m' ascondo?
Ah! l' orde di Cromvello
Sono ancor di me in traccia.
(*Art. si ritira.*)
—Ad altro lato
Vanno i furenti, perchè mai non oso
Porre il piè dentro le adorate soglie?—
Dire a Elvira il mio duol, la fede mia?—
Ah no—perder potrei
Me stesso e lei—Tentiani di nuovo il canto!
A me forse verra, se al cuor le suona,
Quasi a richiamo de' bei dì felici
Quando uniti dicemmo: io t' amo, io t' amo
Cerca il sonno a notte scura
L' esiliato pellegrin:
Sogna e il desta la sciagura
Della patria—e il suo destin!
Sempre eguali ha i luoghi e l' ore
L' infelice trovador—
L'esiliato allorchè muore,
Ha sol posa al suo dolor!

Alas! if once my song of love you heard, hear now a sad exile, hear now my woes.
At a fountain, sad and lonely,
A troubadour was sitting;
Strains of grief came from his harp,
Songs of woe came from his lips.
Through the vales, over the mountains
The banished pilgrim goes in haste!
Grief is always by his side,
Sad companion of his journey.
When it is day he longs for night;
When it is night he longs for day.
He mistakes the spring for winter;
Every smile to him seems sorrow.
(*A distant sound of drums is heard.*)
What sound is that? Some one approaches.

1ST CHO: (*Within.*) Near the ramparts—

2ND CHO: Near the tower he must be.

ALL: We will search—he shall not escape.

ART: Where can I hide? Ah! the troops of Cromwell are still in pursuit of me! (*Arthur withdraws.*) My fierce pursuers go that way. Why dare I not set foot within this palace, where my love is, and declare to Elvira my constancy and my sorrows? Ah! no—it might cause my ruin, and her's too. Let me try the song once more. Perhaps she will come to me, should it reach her heart. It may recall those days of bliss when we said to each other, "I love you, I love you."
When the night is wrapped in gloom,
The banished pilgrim seeks sleep;
Dreams, and starts at the misfortune
Of his country and of his fate.
Every place and hour is equal
For the unhappy troubadour
Only when the exile is dead,
Can his sufferings find repose.

## SCENA II.

*Elvira ed Arturo in dis parte. Elvira esce con un andare smarrito, poi si ferma quasi in atto di stare in ascolto.*

ELV: Finì—Me lassa!—Oh come dolce all' alma
Mi scendea quella voce!—O Dio fini!
Mi parve—Ahi rimembranze, ahi vani sogni!
Ah mio Arturo; ove sei!

ART: A piedi tuoi!
Elvira, ah mi perdona!
(*Inginochiandosi.*)

## SCENE II.

*Elvira is seen through the windows approaching, and Arthur, hearing a slight noise, withdraws. She enters with faltering steps, and as if listening.*

ELV: It has ceased! Unhappy me? Oh! how sweetly that voice has touched my heart! Heavens! it has ceased! It seemed—Oh, sweet memory! Oh, vain dreams! Oh, my dear Arthur! where are you?

ART: At your feet. (*Kneeling.*) Elvira, pardon me!

ELV: Arturo? è desso
(*Gettandosi nelle sue braccia.*)
Sei pur tu—Or non m'inganni?

ART: Ingannarti? Ah no giammia.

ELV: Io vacillo—temo affanni.

ART: Non temer—spariro i guai,
Ove a noi sorride amor!

a 2: Nel mirarti un solo instante,
Io sospiro e mi consolo
D'ogni pianto, d' ogni duolo.

ART: Che provai lontan da te.

ELV: Ch' ei provò lontan da me!
Quanto tempo! Lo rammenti!

ART: Fur tre mesi!

ELV: Ah no—tre socoli
(*Con entusiasmo.*)
Fur tre secoli d'orror!
Ti chiamava ad ogni instante:
Riedi, o Arturo—e mi consola,
E rompeva ogni palola
Coi signulti del dolor!

ART: Deh perdona! Ella era misera
Prigioniera—abbandonata;
In periglio.

ELV: E l' hai tu amata?

ART: Io?—Colei?

ELV: Non è tua sposa?

ART: Chi dir l' oso?

ELV: Io il chiedo, O Arturo!

ART: Mi credevi si spergiuro?
Da quel dì ch' io ti mirai
Avvampai d' un solo ardore,
Per te fido insin che muore
Il mio core avvamperà
La mia vita io ti sacrai
Nella la gioia e nel dolore
E la morte per amore
Cara e santa a me sarà.

ELV: Oh parole d' amore—lieta
son io!
Ei non l'amava adunque; oh Arturo
mio!
Da quel dì che a te giurai,
Solo appresi aver il core;
E a te fido infin che muore
Questo cor palpitera.
La mia vita io ti sacrai
Nella gioia e nel dolore—
E la morte per amore
Cara e santa a me sarà.

ART: Tua crudel dubbiezza amara
Deponesti, e paga or sei?

ELV: Dì—se a te non era cara,
A chè mai seguir colei?

ART: Or t'infingi, o ignori ch' ella
Presso a morte.

ELV: Chi favella!

ART: La Regina.

ELV: La Regina?

ELV: Arthur! (*Falling into his arms.*)
Is it you?
Do you deceive me now?

ART: Deceive you! Ah, never!

ELV: I tremble. I fear new sorrows.

ART: Do not fear; the woes are fled,
When on us again Love smiles.

BOTH: In beholding you for one moment,
My heart sighs and feels relief
From all troubles, from all tears,

ART: That I shed afar from you.

ELV: That he shed afar from me.
Is it long? Do you remember?

ART: It is three months.

ELV: Ah? no—three ages
(*With enthusiasm.*)
Of deep sighs, of great horror.
I repeated at each moment,
"Come, dear Arthur—give me comfort;"
And each word remained unfinished,
Interrupted by my sobs.

ART: Alas! pardon—she was wretched,
And a prisoner forsaken,
In great danger.

ELV: (*With eagerness.*) Have you loved her?

ART: I?—her?

ELV: Is she not your wife?

ART: Who said so?

ELV: I ask it, Arthur!

ART: Could you think me so forsworn?
From the day I saw you first,
For your love I only burnt!
To you faithful until death
Will my heart forever burn.
I devoted my life to you.
In my joy and in my grief,
And my death for your dear love
Will be sweet and holy to me.

ELV: O, words of love! I am now happy again.
He then has loved her not! O, my dear Arthur!
From the day I swore to you
Only, I learnt I had no heart:
To you faithful until death
My heart will forever beat.
I devoted my life for you
Whether it be said or joyful:
And to die for your dear love
Will be sweet and holy to me.

ART: Are your bitter doubts removed?
Is your heart at last content?

ELV: If to you she was not dear,
Say why you followed her

ART: Do you feign, or did you not know
That she was doomed to die?

ELV: Who? speak?

ART: Who? the Queen.

ELV: What! the Queen?

ART: Un indugio—e la meschina
Su d' un palco a morte orribile.

ELV: E fia ver? qual lume rapido
Or balena al mio pensier!—
Dunque m' ami?

ART: E puoi temer?

ELV: Dunque vuoi?—

ART: Star teco ognor
Tra gli amplessi dell' amor.
Vieni fra le mie braccia
Amor, delizia e vita,
Non mi sarai rapita
Or che ti stringo al cor.
Ansante, ognor tremante
Si chiamo—e ognor ti bramo—
Vien; mi ripeti: io t' amo
T' amo d' immenso amor.

ELV: Caro, non ho parola
Ch' esprima il mio contento:
L' alma elevar mi sento
In estasi d' amor.
Ansante—ognor tremante
Ti chiamo e te sol bramo
E mille volte, io t' amo,
A te ripete il cor.
(*Odesi ancora il suono del tamburo.*)

ART: Ancor quel suon funesto, i meie nemici!

ELV: Si, quel suon funesto:
Io conosco vuel suonma—tu non sai
Che più nol tempo ormai!—nella mia stanza
Squarciai il vel di che s' ornò sua testa—
Calpestai le sue pompe—ed all' aura—
Con me tu ancora—
Verrai a festa e danza.

ART: Oh Dio, che dici!
(*Art. la guarda con stupore.*)

ELV: Così come tu guardi,
Mi guardan essi, e intender mai son sanno
Il parlar—il mio riso—il duol, l' affanno!

ART: Oh ti scuoti—tu vaneggi!
(*Sentensi da parti opposte dentro il boschetto le voci di varii drappelli d' Armigeri.*

1: Alto là!

2: Fedel drappello—

1: E chi viva?

2: Anglia Cromvello!

1: Viva!

2: Viva!

TUTTI: Vincerà!

ART: Vien, ci è forza ormai partir!

ELV: A tu vuoi fuggirmi ancor?
No colei più non t' avra!
(*Art. prende per mano Elv. che lo guardae in furia delirando.*)

ART: Vien.

ART: But one moment, and the unfortunate
On the scaffold would have perished.

ELV: Is this true? What sudden light
Comes to illumine all my thoughts?
Still you love me?

ART: Can you fear?

ELV: Then you wish—

ART: To remain
Ever faithful to your love.
Unto my arms returns
My love, delight, and life;
No more shall we be parted,
Since now we meet again.
All breathless, ever trembling,
I call and wish for thee;
Come, say you are my love;
I love you past all bounds.

ELV: My dear, I have no words
That can express my joy;
I feel my soul transported
With ecstasies of love.
All breathless, ever trembling,
I call and wish for you?
And you I love, my heart repeats
A thousand times.
(*A drum is heard again.*)

ART: Again this dreaded sound! My enemies!

ELV: That fatal sound! (*She begins to seem again distracted.*)
I know that sound; but you know
that I no longer fear it. In my room,
I tore the veil with which, one day,
her head was adorned—I trampled
upon her finery—and at the
dawn—with me again you shall
come to sport and dance.

ART: Heavens? what do you say?
(*Looking at her with fright.*)

ELV: As you look at me, so do they,
and can never understand my
words, my laughter, and my grief.

ART: Return to your senses. You
are raving.
(*Voices of Soldiers are heard within.*)

1: Who goes there?

2: A faithful band.

1: Give the word.

2: England and Cromwell.

1: Hurrah!

2: Hurrah!

ALL: I will conquer.

ART: Come—we must at last depart.

ELV: You wish to forsake me again,
No; she never shall have you again.
(*Arthur takes Elvira's band. She becomes frantic; falls at his feet, and cries for help.*)

ART: Come.

ELV: T' arresti il mio dolor!

ART: Taci!

ELV: O genti—Ei vuol fuggir!

ART: Taci!

ELV: Aiuto—per pieta!

ART: Ah!

## SCENA III.

*Riccardo, Giorgio, Bruno, Armigeri, con facelle, Castellani, e Castellane.*

GIO: E qui Arturo?

RIC: Arturo!

TUTTI: Arturo!

RIC: Cavalier, ti colse ilanume Punitor de' tradimenti.

ARMI: Pera ucciso fra tormenti Chi tradiva patria e onor!

GIO, DONNE: Oh' infelice! Un destin rio A tal spiaggia or ti guidò!

RIC, ARMI: Talbo Artur, la Patria e Dio Te alla morte condannò!

ELV: Morte!

ARMI: A morte!

LE DONNE: Ahi qual terror!

ARMI: Dio raggiunge i traditor!

ELV: Che ascoltai?—

DONNE: (Si tramutò!—) Si fè smorta—ed avvampò!

GIO, RIC: Se avra il senno?—avra più lacrime Nel mirar chi per lei muor!

ELV: Qual mia funerea Voce funesta Mi scuote e desta Dal mio martir! Io fui sì barbara— Lo trassi a morte!— M' avra consorte Nel suo morir!

RIC: Quel suon funereo Ch' apre una tomba, Cupo rimbomba, M' infonde orror Lor sorte orribile Spense gia l' ira Mi affanna e inspira Pieta e dolor.

ARMI: Quel suon funereo, Ch' apre una tomba, Cupo rimbomba, Infonde orror. E Dio terribile In sua vendetta, Gli empii ei saetta Sterminator!—

---

ELV: Remain—behold my grief.

ART: Silence.

ELV: Friends, he wants to fly.

ART: Silence.

ELV: Help, for pity's sake.

ART: Ah!

## SCENE III.

*Enter Richard, Sir George, Bruno, Soldiers with torches, and Villagers.*

SIR G: Where is Arthur?

RICH: Arthur!

ALL: Arthur!

RICH: Cavalier, the sword of Justice will fall On your traitorous head.

SOLDIERS: Yes; the traitor to his country Must end his life in torments.

SIR G, WOM: Wretched man! a fatal doom To this place have your steps have led.

RICH, SOLD: Arthur Talbot, men and God Have decreed that you shall die.

ELV: To die!

SOLDIERS: Die!

WOMEN: Ah! what terror!

SOLDIERS: God the traitor always reaches.

ELV: What do I hear?

WOMEN: What sudden change! (*Looking at Elv.*) She seemed dead—now she is all fire.

SIR G, RICH: If her reason she recovers, She will shed for him more tears.

ELV: What is this mournful Voice of horror, That wakes my mind From all its woes; So cruel I was, to cause His death But I will share The grave with him.

RICH: That fatal sound, Proclaiming death has filled My heart with dreadful awe Their cruel destiny subdues My rage Inspires my soul With softest pity.

SOLDIERS: That fatal sound, Proclaiming death has filled, Our hearts With dreadful awe Heaven is terrible In its revenge; It strikes the impious, destroys Their works.

---

ART: Credeasi misera Da me tradita! Traea sua vita In tal martir! Or sfido i fulmini Disprezzo il fato— Se a lei d' allato Potrò morir!

GIO: Quel suon funereo Feral rimbomba Nel sen mi piomba M' agghiaccia il cor? Sol posso, ahi, misero, Tremar e fremere: Non ha più lacrime Il mio dolor!

DONNE: Quel suon funereo Feral rimbomba, Al cor ci piomba, Gelar ci fa! Pur fra le lagrime Speme ci affida, Che Dio ci arrida Di sua pieta!

ARMI E BRUNO: Dio comanda a'figli suoi Che giustizia alfin si renda—

RIC, GIO E DONNE: Sol ferocia or parla in voi? La pietade—Idio v'apprenda.

ART: Deh ritorna a sensi tuoi—

ELV: Qual mi cade orribil benda?—

ART: O mia Elvira!—

ELV: E vivi ancora!

ART: Teco io sono—

ELV: Ah il tuo perdono!— Per me a morte, O Arturo mio—

ART: Di tua sorte il reo sou io—

ELV E ART: Un amplesso!

BRU E UOMINI: Avvampo e fremo!

GIO, RIC E DONNE: Io gelo e tremo!

ART E ELV: Un addio!

TUTTI: : L' estremo!

ARMI: Cada alfin—l' ultrice spada Sovra il capo al traditor—

ART: Arrestate—Vi scostate! Paventate il mio furor: Ella è tremante, Ella è spirante, Anime perfide Sorde a pieta! Un solo istante L' ire affrenate, Poi vi saziate, Di crudelta! (*Coro. di Puritani.*)

1: A vendetta sui ribaldi!

---

ART: Elvira thought She was betrayed: She passed her life In tears and woes. I brave the thunder, I challenge the fate If by her side I now can die.

SIR G: That fatal sound, Proclaiming death, Falls on my breast And makes me freeze. Alas I can Just fear and tremble; In vain I try To shed a tear.

CHO. OF WOMEN: That fatal sound, Proclaiming death, Falls on my heart, And makes it freeze. But, amidst our tears, Still shines the hope, That God with mercy Will look on them.

SOLD, BRU: God commands that on the traitor the sword of Justice Should fall.

RICH, SIR G, WOM: Fierceness only speaks in you. To have pity, learn of God.

ART: Ah! resume your force of reason.

ELV: What a dreadful vail has fallen!

ART: O, my Elvira!

ELV: You still lives?

ART: Yes, for you.

ELV: Alas! your pardon. Of your death I am the cause.

ART: And I caused all your misfortunes.

ELV AND ART: One embrace.

BRUNO AND MEN: I burn and rage!

SIR G, RICH AND WOMEN: I freeze, I tremble!

ART AND ELV: One farewell.

ALL: It is the last!

SOLDIERS: Let at last the sword of justice Strike the traitor!

ART: Do not move. Stand aside, or fear my rage. She is all trembling, She is expiring, Inhuman beings, Devoid of pity! For a single moment Restrain your anger, Then gratify Your cruel wish.

1ST SOLDIER: Now vengeance on the traitors!

**2:** A vendetta!

(*All' improvviso tutti si fermano perche odesi èn suono di Corno da caccia: varii Armigeri Puritani escono ad esplorare, e tornano guidando un mesaggiero.*)

**TUTTI:** Suon d' Araldi!
E un messag'gio?

**DONNE:** Un divin raggio!
Esploriam.

**TUTTI:** Che mai sara?

**GIO:** Esultate, ah si esultate.
Gia i Stuardi or vinto sono,
I captivi han gia perdono,
L' Anglia terra ha liberta!

**RIC E PURI:** A Cromvello—Onore e gloria!
La vittoria—il giudera!

**ELV, ART:** Dall' angoscia al gaudio estremo
Par quest' alma al Ciel rapita:
Ben so dir che sia la vita
Or che tuo/tua l'amor mi fa.

**2ND SOLDIER:** Yes; vengeance!

(*A sound of trumpets is heard. Some soldiers go out and return with a messenger, who gives a letter to Sir G. who reads it with Rich.*)

**ALL:** Sound of heralds!
Is it a message?

**WOMEN:** Some new hope!
Let us see.

**ALL:** What can it be?

**SIR G:** Rejoice, all! yes; all, rejoice!
Now the Stuarts are quite defeated;
All the captives have been pardoned;
Freedom now in England reigns.

**RICH, SOLD:** Fame and victory to Cromwell?
Glory will his banners follow.

**ELV, ART:** From deep woes to joys supreme.
Seems this soul to heaven conveyed.
Now the worth of life I know,
Since now love has made me yours.

**CORO:** Siate liete alme amorose,
Qual d'amor foste dolenti:
Lunghi dì per voi ridenti
Quest' istante segnera.

**ELV E ART:** Ah! sento, O mio bell' angelo,
Che poca è intera l' anima,
Per esultar nel giubilo
Che amor ci donera.
Benediro le lacrime
L' ansia, i sospir i gemiti,
Vanneggerò nel palpito
D' un' ebbra volutta—

**CORO:** Amor pietoso e tenero
Coronera di giubilo
L'ansia, i sospiri, i palpiti
Di tanta fedelta.

*FINE.*

**CHORUS:** May your love be now as merry
As it has before been wretched!
Long your days and quite serene,
May this moment for you sign.

**ELV, ART:** I feel, my charming angel,
That powerless is my heart
To exult in the great joy
Which love prepares for us.
I now shall bless my tears,
My sighs, my woes, my fears;
I shall be enraptured
In ecstasies of pleasure!

**CHORUS:** Love, favorable and tender,
Will crown, with great rejoicing
The throbbings and the sighs
Of these two faithful hearts.

*THE END.*

# Les Pêcheurs de Perles (1863)

## The Pearl Fishers

MUSIC BY GEORGES BIZET ■ LIBRETTO BY EUGÈNE CORMON (PIERRE ETIENNE PIESTRE) & MICHEL CARRÉ

This three-act opera, set to a libretto by Eugène Cormon (Pierre Etienne Piestre) and Michel Carré, premiered at the Théâtre-Lyrique in Paris on September 30, 1863. On a beach in Ceylon (now Sri Lanka), Zurga is elected king of the fishermen. He greets his friend, Nadir, whom he has not seen since they both renounced their love for the same woman; they vow eternal friendship. The old villagers escort a priestess to the clifftop while the fishermen are out diving. The heavily veiled priestess, having taken a vow of chastity, is Leïla, the woman who Zurga and Nadir renounced so long ago. She tells Nourabad, the High Priest, about the time she saved the life of a stranger and shows him the necklace she was given in reward. Thinking she is alone, she removes her veil. Nadir overhears her singing. Recognizing her, he declares his love rekindled. She returns his feelings; Nourabad enters and finds them together. Zurga angrily sentences them both to die. A raging storm breaks out, signifying the fury of the gods. Leïla begs Zurga to spare Nadir's life. She gives Zurga her necklace, and asks him to take it to to her mother. Zurga recognizes it as the one he gave to the girl who saved his life when he was a little boy, and decides to help Nadir and Leïla in repayment. He sets the village on fire, which distracts the fishermen, and the lovers flee. Finally, Zurga dies on the pyre for Leila.

---

### ■ ACTE I

*Une plage aride et sauvage de l'île de Ceylan.—A droite et à gauche quelques huttes en bambous et en nattes.—Au fond, sur un rocher qui domine la mer, les ruines d'une ancienne pagode in-doue.—Au loin, la mer.*

#### SCÈNE I

*Au lever du riedau, les pêcheurs de l'île, couvrent le rivage.*

**CHOEUR:** Sur la grève en feu
Où dort le flot bleu,
Nous dressons nos tentes!
Dansez jusqu'au soir,
Filles à l'oeil noir,
Aux tresses flottantes!
Chassez par vos chants
Les esprits méchants!
(*Danses.*)
Voilà notre domaine!
C'est ici que le sort
Tous les ans nous remène,
Prêts à braver la mort!
Sous la vague profonde,
Plongeurs audacieux
A nous la perle blonde
Cechée à tous les yeux!

Sur la grève en feu
Où dort le flot bleu.
(*Danses.*)

**ZURGA:** Amis, interrompez vos danses et vos jeux!
Il est temps de choisir un chef qui nous commande,

### ■ ACT I

*The scene is in the Island of Ceylon. An arid beach. Right and left a few huts made of matting. At rear on a rock that looks down on the sea the ruins of an ancient Indian pagoda. In the distance the ocean.*

#### SCENE I

*At rise of curtain the fishermen of the island cover the shore.*

**CHORUS:** On the fiery shore
Where the blue wave sleeps,
We dress our tents
And dance until night.
Girls of gloomy eyes,
With floating tresses,
Scatter
All evil spirits by your songs.
(*Dances.*)
**CHORUS OF FISHERMEN:** Here is our domain,
Here it is that fate,
Every year recalls us
Ready to brave death.
Under deepest wave,
Audacious divers,
For us the white pearl
Hidden from all eyes.

On the fiery shore,
Where
The blue wave sleeps, etc.
(*Dances.*)

**ZURGA:** Friends, interrupt your dances and games!
It is time to choose a chief who will command us,

Qui nous protège et nous défende,
Un chef aimé de tous, vigilant, courageux!

**LE CHOEUR:** Celui que nous voulons pour maître
Et que nous choisissons pour roi . . . .

**ZURGA:** Quel est-il donc?—Parlez!—
Faites-le-moi connaître!

**LE CHOEUR:** Ami Zurga c'est toi.

**ZURGA:** Qui?—Moi!

**LE CHOEUR:** Oui, oui, sois notre chef! nous acceptons ta loi.

**ZURGA:** Vous me jurez obéissance?

**LE CHOEUR:** Nous te jurons obéissance!
A toi seul la toute-puissance!
Sois notre chef et notre roi!

**ZURGA:** (*leur serrant la main.*)
Eh bien, c'est dit! . . . c'est dit! je serai votre roi!
(*Nadir paraît au fond et descend parmi les rochers.*)

**LE CHOEUR:** Mais qui vient là?

**ZURGA:** (*courant au-devant de Nadir.*) Nadir! ami de ma jeunesse?
Est-ce bien toi que je revois?

**LE CHOEUR:** C'est Nadir, le coureur des bois!

**NADIR:** Nadir, votre ami d'autrefois!
Parmi vous, compagnons, que mon bon temps renaisse!

**COUPLETS:** Des savanes et des forêts
Où les trappeurs tendent leurs rêts
J'ai sondé l'ombre et le mystère!

Who will protect and defend us
A chief beloved of all, vigilant, courageous . . .

**CHORUS:** He whom we wish for master
And whom we choose for King . . .

**ZURGA:** Who then is he?
Speak!
Let me know him!

**CHORUS:** Friend Zurga, it is you.

**ZURGA:** Who?—Me!

**CHORUS:** Yes, yes, be our chief, we accept your law.

**ZURGA:** You swear to obey me?

**CHORUS:** We swear obedience to you,
To you alone all power,
Be our chief and our king!

**ZURGA:** (*shaking hands.*) Well then it is settled—I'll be your king!
(*Nadir appears and descends to the rocks.*)

**CHORUS:** But who comes here?

**ZURGA:** (*running toward Nadir.*)
Nadir, friend of my youth!
Is it you I see again?

**CHORUS:** It is Nadir, runner of the woods.

**NADIR:** Nadir, your friend of other days
Among you, companions, let the good time return.

**SONG:** In savannas and forests
Where the trappers set their traps
I've sounded shadow and mystery!
I've followed dagger in teeth,

J'ai suivi, le poignard aux dents,
Le tigre fauve aux yeux ardents
Et le jaguar et la panthère! . . .
Ce que j'ai fait hier, vous le feriez
demain!
Compagnons, donnons-nous la
main!

LE CHOEUR: Compagnons, donnons-lui la main!

NADIR: Dans le jongles et sur les
monts
Hantés des loups et des démons,
Sur cette rive abandonnée,
Loin des villes et loin du bruit,
J'ai vécu seul, le jour, la nuit,
Durant tout le cours d'une année!
Ce que j'ai fait hier, vous le feriez
demain!
Compagnons, donnons-nous la
main!

LE CHOEUR: Compagnons, donnons-lui la main!

ZURGA: Demeure parmi nous, Nadir, et sois des nôtres.

NADIR: Oui!—Mes voeux
désormmais, mes plaisirs sont les
vôtres!

ZURGA: Prends donc part à nos
jeux!
Ami, bois avec moi, danse et chante
avec eux!
Avant que la pêche commence,
Saluons le soleil, l'air et la mer immense!

REPRISE DU CHOEUR: Sur la
grève en feu
Où dort le flot bleu, etc.
(*Les danses reprennent, puis les
pêcheurs se dispersent Zurga et
Nadir restent seuls en scène.*)

ZURGA: Nadir!

NADIR: Zurga!

ZURGA: C'est toi!—toi qu'enfin je
revois!—
Après tant de longs jours, après de
si longs mois,
Où nous avons vécu séparés l'un de
l'autre,
Brahma nous réunit!—quelle joie
est la nôtre! . . .
Mais parle . . . es-tu resté fidèle
à ton serment?
Est-ce un ami que Dieu m'envoie,
ou bien un traître? . . .

NADIR: Le mal était pro-
fond . . . j'ai su m'en rendre
maître!

ZURGA: Eh bein, le verre en main,
fêtons ce doux moment!
Comme toi, je suis calme et comme
toi j'oublie
Un jour de fièvre et de folie! . . .

NADIR: Non, non, tu mens!—Le
calme est venu pour toi,—mais
L'oubli ne viendra jamais!

ZURGA: Que dis-tu?

The savage tiger of ardent eyes
And the jaguar and the pan-
ther . . . .
What I did yesterday, you would do
tomorrow,
Companions, let us shake hands.

CHORUS: Companions, let us
shake hands.

NADIR: In the jungles and on the
hills
Haunted by wolves and demons,
On that deserted shore,
Far from towns and noise,
I lived alone the day, the night,
During the course of a year!
What I did yesterday, you would do
tomorrow
Companions, let us shake hands!

CHORUS: Companions, let us
shake hands!

ZURGA: Live with us, Nadir, and be
one of us.

NADIR: Yes, my wishes henceforth, my pleasures are yours.

ZURGA: Take then part in our
games.
Friend, drink with me, dance and
sing with them,
Before the fishing begins
Bow to the sun, to the air, to the immense ocean.

REPEAT OF CHORUS: On the fiery
strand,
Where sleeps the blue wave, etc.
(*The dances begin again, then the
fishermen disperse. Zurga and
Nadir remain.*)

ZURGA: Nadir!

NADIR: Zurga!

ZURGA: It is you! At last I see you
again.
After so many long days, after such
long months,
Where we have lived apart from
one another,
Brahma reunites us—what joy is
ours.
But speak, have you remained true
to your oath?

NADIR: The hurt was deep . . . I
have mastered it.

ZURGA: Well then, glass in hand,
let's toast this sweet moment
Like you I am calm and like you I
forget
A day of fever and folly! . . .

NADIR: No, no, you lie. The calm
has come for you, But
Forgetfulness will never
come . . . .

ZURGA: What are you saying?

NADIR: Quand tous deux nous
toucherons à l'âge
Où les rêves des jour passés
De notre âme sont effacés,
Tu te rappelleras notre dernier voy-
age;
Notre dernière halte aux portes de
Candi . . . .

ZURGA: C'était le soir;—dans l'air
par la brise attiédi,
Les bramines, au front inondé de lumière,
Appelaient lentement la foule à la
prière! . . . .

NADIR: (*se levant.*) Au fond du
temple saint paré de fleurs et d'or,
Une femme apparaît!—Je crois la
voir encor.

ZURGA: Un femme apparaît!—Je
crois la voir encor!

NADIR: La foule prosternée
La regarde étonnée,
Et murmure tout bas:
Voyez, c'est la déesse
Qui dans l'ombre se dresse,
Et vers nous tend les bras!

ZURGA: (*se levant.*) Oui, c'est
elle! c'est elle!
Plus charmante et plus belle
Qui descend parmi nous!
Son voile se soulève! . . .
O vision! ô rêve!
La foule est à genoux!

ENSEMBLE: Oui, c'est elle! c'est
elle! etc.

NADIR: Mais à travers la foule elle
s'ouvre un passage!

ZURGA: Son long voile déjà nous
cache son visage!

NADIR: Elle fuit!

ZURGA: Mon regard, hélas! la suit
en vain!

NADIR: Et dans mon âme soudain
Quelle étrange ardeur s'allume!

ZURGA: Quel feu nouveau me consume!

NADIR: Ta main repousse ma main!

ZURGA: Ta main repousse ma
main!

NADIR: De nos coeurs l'amour
s'empare,
Et nous change en ennemis!

ZURGA: Non!—que rien ne nous
sépare,
Jurons de rester amis!

ENSEMBLE: Amitié sainte, unis nos
âmes fraternelles!
Chassons sans retour
Ce fatal amour!
Et la main dans la main, en compag-
nons fidéles,
Jusques à la mort,
Ayons même sort!
Oui, soyons amis jusques à la mort!

NADIR: When both of us shall
reach the age
Where the dreams of days gone by
Are wiped away from our souls
You will remember our last voyage;
Our final halt before the gates of
Candy . . . .

ZURGA: It was night;—in air
warmed by the breeze
The brahmins, their faces suffused
with light,
Slowly called the faithful to
prayer . . . .

NADIR: (*rising.*) In the depth of
the sacred temple paved with flowers and gold,
A woman appeared, I think to see
her yet.

ZURGA: A woman appears, I think
I see her yet

NADIR: The prostrate crowd
Looks at her, astonished,
And murmurs, lowly
Look, it is the goddess
That arises in the gloom,
And stretches toward us her arms!

ZURGA: (*rising.*) Yes, it is she, it is
she!
More charming and beautiful
Who descends among us.
Her veil is raised . . .
Oh vision, oh dream!
The crowd is kneeling.

TOGETHER: Yes, it is she, it is she,
etc.

NADIR: But amid the crowd she
opens a passage!

ZURGA: Her long veil now hides
her face.

NADIR: She flees!

ZURGA: My eyes, alas, follow her
in vain!

NADIR: And suddenly in my soul
What a strange ardor gleams!

ZURGA: What new fire consumes
me!

NADIR: Your hand rejects my
hand . . .

ZURGA: Your hand rejects my
hand . . .

NADIR: Love takes possession of
our hearts,
And changes us to enemies.

ZURGA: No—nothing must part
us,
Let's swear to stay friends.

TOGETHER: Sacred friendship, un-
ite our fraternal souls
Drive away forever
This fatal love
And hand in hand, as faithful com-
panions,
We'll join our fates until our death
Yes, we'll be friends unto death.

# Act I, Scene I

ZURGA: Depuis ce jour, fidéle à ma parole,
J'ai laissé fuir loin d'elle et les jours et les mois!

NADIR: Pour me guérir de cette ivresse folle
J'ai fui parmi les loups et les oiseaux des bois!

ZURGA: Comme le mien, que ton coeur se console,
Soyons frères, soyons amis comme autrefois!

REPRISE DE L'ENSEMBLE: Amitiè sainte, unis nos âmes fraternelles! etc.

LES PECHEURS: O maître, une pirogue aborde prés d'ici.

ZURGA: C'est bien!—je l'attendais!—
O dieu Brahma, merci!

NADIR: Qui donc attendais-tu dans ce désert sauvage?

ZURGA: Une fille inconnue et belle autant que sage,
Que les plus vieux de nous, soumis au vieil usage,
Loin d'ici, chaque année, ont soin d'aller chercher.
Un long voile à nos yeux dérobe son visage;
Et nul ne doit la voir, nul ne doit l'approcher! . . .
Mais pendant nos travaux, debout sur ce rocher,
Elle prie;—et son chant qui plane sur nos têtes,
Ecarte les esprits méchants et les tempêtes! . . .

LE CHOEUR: La voici! la voici!
Elle vient!—On l'amène ici!
(Leila, le front couvert d'une voile, paraît au fond, suivie par quatre fakirs et par Nourabad.—)

LE CHOEUR DES FEMMES: (entourant Leïla et lui offraut des fleurs.) Sois la bienvenue,
Amie inconnue,
Recois nos présents!
Chante et que l'orage
Apaise sa rage,
A tes doux accents!
Que la troupe immonde
Des esprits de l'onde,
Des prés et des bois,
S'envole à ta voix!
Sois la bienvenue, Etc.
Protége-nous! Veille sur nous!

ZURGA: (s'avançant vers Leila.)
Seule au milieu de nous, vierge pure et sans tache,
Promets-tu de garder le voile qui te cache?
De rester jusqu'au bout fidéle à ton serment;
De prier nuit et jour au bord du gouffre sombre,
D'écarter par tes chants les noirs esprits de l'ombre,
De vivre sans ami, sans époux, sans amant!

ZURGA: Since that day, true to my word,
I've let fly, far from her, the days and the months

NADIR: To cure me of this foolish bliss
I fled to the wolves and the birds of the wood.

ZURGA: Like mine, let your heart be consoled
Let's be brothers and friends as before.

TOGETHER: (as before). Sacred friendship, unite our fraternal souls.

THE FISHERMEN: (entering.) Oh master, a boat lands near by.

ZURGA: It is well, I awaited it.
Oh Brahma, I thank you.

NADIR: Who did you await in this wild desert?

ZURGA: An unknown girl, beautiful as she is good
That the oldest of us faithful to custom,
Far from here, each year, are careful to go find.
From our eyes, a long veil hides her face;
And none must see her, none must approach her . . .
But during our work, standing on this rock,
She prays,—and her song that wafts over our heads,
Scatters the evil spirits and the tempests . . .

CHORUS:
She's here, she's here,
She comes . . . Bring her to us.
(Leila, her head covered by a veil, appears at the rear, followed by four fakirs (priests) and by Nourabad.)

CHORUS OF WOMEN: (Offering Leila flowers.) Be welcome
Unknown friend
Receive our gifts
Sing that the storm
Shall cease to rage,
At your soft accents
That the noisome troop
Of the spirits of the sea
Of the fields and the woods
Fly away at the sound
Be welcome, etc.
Protect us, watch over us.

ZURGA: (advancing on Leila.) Alone in our midst, virgin pure without stain,
Do you promise to keep the veil that hides you?
To remain to the end faithful to your oath;
To pray night and day on the brink of the sombre gulf,
To allay by your songs the black spirits of the dark,
To live without friend, without husband or lover?

NOURABAD ET LE CHOEUR: Parle!—Tiendras-tu ton serment?

LEILA: Oui, Brahma reçoit mon serment!

ZURGA: Si tu restes fidèle,
Et soumise à ma loi,
Nous garderons pour toi,
La perle la plus belle!
Et l'humble fille alors sera digne d'un roi!
(Avec menace) Mais si tu nous trahis! . . . si ton âme succombe
Aux pièges maudits de l'amour,
Que la fureur des cieux sur ta tête retombe!
C'en est fait! . . . c'est ton dernier jour!

LE CHOEUR: C'en est fait! c'est ton dernier jour!

ZURGA: Malheur à toi! . . .
Brahma demande une victime!
La mort t'attend! . . . la mort doit expier ton crime!

LE CHOEUR: La mort t'attend! . . . la mort!

LEILA: Dieu? . . . qu'entends'-je? . . . la mort!

NADIR: (s'avançant.) Hélas! funeste sort!

LEILA: (à part, reconnaissant Nadir.) Ah! c'est lui!

ZURGA: (saisissant la main de Leïla.) Qu'as-tu donc? . . . ta main frissonne et tremble!
D'un noir pressentiment ton coeur est agité . . .
Eh bien! . . . fuis ce rivage où le sort nous rassemble,
Renonce à nous servir, reprends ta liberteé! . . .
Il en est temps encor . . .

LE CHOEUR:
Parle! . . . réponds!

LEILA: (les yeux tournés vers Nadir.) Je reste! . . . Que mon sort glorieux ou funeste
S'accomplisse! . . . ma vie est à vous, mes amis!
(A la voix de Leïla, Nadir fait un mouvement pour s'élancer vers elle, mais il s'arrête.)

ZURGA: C'est bien! . . . A tous les yeux tu resteras voilée,
Tu chanteras pour nous sous la nuit étoilée,
Tu l'as juré! . . . tu l'as promis!

NOURABAD ET LE CHOEUR: Tu l'as juré! . . . tu l'as

LEILA: Je l'ai juré!.. je l'ai promis!

LE CHOEUR: Brahma, divin Brahma, que ton bras nous protège,
Des esprits de la nuit qu'il écarte le piège!
O Dieu Brahma, nous sommes tous
A tes genoux!
(Sur un ordre de Zurga, Leïa gravit le sentier qui conduit aux ruines du temple, suivie par Nour-

NOURABAD AND CHORUS: Speak! Will you keep your oath?

LEILA: Yes, Brahma receive my oath!

ZURGA: If you remain faithful,
And submissive to my law,
We'll keep for you,
The most beautiful pearl.
And the humble girl will be worthy of a King.
(Threatening.) But if you betray . . . if your soul succumbs
To the cursed traps of love,
May the fury of heaven fall on your head.
It is done . . . it is your final day!

CHORUS: It is done. It is your final day!

ZURGA: Misfortune to you! Brahma asks a victim
Death awaits you . . . death must expiate your crime!

CHORUS: Death awaits you! . . . death!

LEILA: God? what do I hear? Death!

NADIR: (rising and advancing.) Alas! unhappy fate!

LEILA: (aside, recognizing him.) Ah! it is he.

ZURGA: (seizing Leila's hand.) What ails you . . . your hand shivers and trembles
With a dark presentiment your heart is torn . . .
Well then.....fly from this shore where fate unites us
Renounce to serve us, take back your liberty . . .
There is yet time . . .

CHORUS: Speak . . . answer!

LEILA: (her eyes on Nadir.) I remain . . . That my fate, glorious or deadly
Be accomplished . . . My life is yours, friends,
(At hearing Leila's voice Nadir is about to start forward but restrains himself.)

ZURGA: It is well . . . To all eyes remain veiled
You'll sing for us in the starry night
You have sworn . . . You have promised it.

NOURABAD AND CHORUS: You have sworn . . . you have sworn it.

LEILA: I have sworn . . . I have promised it.

CHORUS: Brahma . . . divine Brahma, let your arm protect us,
From the spirits of night remove the guile
Oh Brahma, we are all
At your knees.
(On direction of Zurga, Leila climbs the path that leads to the ruins of the temple, followed by

*abad et les fakirs; ils disparaissent avec Leïla dans les profondeurs du temple; les femmes et les enfants se dispersent de différents côtes; les hommes desendent sur le rivage. Zurga se rapproche de Nadir, lui tend la main et s'éloigne.—Le jour baisse peu à peu.)*

**NADIR:** (*seul.*) A cette voix quel trouble agitait tout mon être? Quel fol espoir? . . . comment ai-je cru reconnaître? . . . Hélas! devant mes yeux déjà, pauvre insensé, La même vision tant de fois a passé! Non! non! c'est la remords, la fièvre, le délire! Zurga doit tout savoir, J'aurais dû tout lui dire! Parjure à mon serment, j'ai voulu la revoir! J'ai découvert sa trace, Et j'ai suivi ses pas! Et caché dans la nuit et soupirant tout bas, J'écoutais ses doux chantes emportés dans l'espace!

Je crois entendre encore, Caché sous les palmiers, Sa voie tendre et sonore Comme un chant de ramiers! O nuit enchanteresse! O souvenir charmant! Doux rêve! folle ivresse! Divin ravissement! Aux clartés des étoiles, Je crois encor la voir, Entr'ouvrir ses longs voiles Aux vents tièdes du soir! O nuit enchanteresse! O souvenir charmant! Doux rêve! folle ivresse! Divin ravissement! (*Il s'étend sur une natte et s'endort.*)

**LE CHOEUR DES PECHEURS:** (*dans la coulisse*) Le ciel est bleu! . . . la mer est immobile et claire! . . . (*Leïla, amenée par Nourabad et les fakirs, paraît sur le rocher qui domine la mer.*)

**NOURABAD:** Toi, rest là, debout sur ce roc solitaire! . . . (*Les fakirs s'accroupissent aux pieds de Leïla, et allument un bûcher.*) Aux lueurs du brasier en feu, Aux vapeurs de l'encens qui monte jusqu'à Dieu, Chante . . . nous t'écoutons!

**NADIR:** (*a demi endormi*). Adieu, doux rêve! . . . adieu!

**LE CHOEUR DES PECHEURS:** (*dans la Coulisse.*) Le ciel est bleu! . . . la mer est immobile et claire!

**LEILA:** (*debout sur le rocher.*) O Dieu Brahma! O maître souverain du monde!

---

*Nourabad and the priests. They disappear with Leïla inside the temple, the women and children disperse in various directions, the men descend to the shore. Zurga approaches Nadir, takes his hand and goes away. The day declines.)*

**NADIR:** (*alone.*) At that voice, what emotion moved all my being? Vain hope . . . how did I think to recognize? Alas before my poor foolish eyes The same vision has so often passed . . . No, no, it is remorse, fever, madness! Zurga must know all I should have told him everything False to my oath, I desired to see her again, I discovered her trace And I followed her steps Hidden in the night and softly sighing I heard her soft song floating in space.

I think I still hear Hidden amid the palms, Her tender sonorous voice Like a song of doves Oh enchanting night! Oh charming souvenir! Sweet dream, sweet bliss, Divine ravishment! By the light of stars, I think I still see her, Open her long veils To the soft breeze of night Oh enchanting night Oh charming souvenir Sweet dream, sweet bliss Divine ravishment! (*He stretches himself on a mat and sleeps.*)

**CHORUS OF FISHERMEN:** (*outside.*) The sky is blue . . . the sea is clear and still . . . **LEILA:** (*led by Nourabad and the priests appears on the rock that dominates the sea.*)

**NOURABAD:** You, stay here, on this solitary rock . . . (*The priests gathering at Leila's feet light a fire.*) By the light of this brazier afire, And the vapor of the incense that mounts to God, Sing . . . we listen to you!

**NADIR:** (*half asleep.*) Adieu, sweet dream, adieu!

**CHORUS OF FISHERMEN:** (*outside.*) The sky is blue . . . the sea is still and clear.

**LEILA:** (*standing on rock.*) Oh great Brahma Oh sovereign master of the world.

---

**LE CHOEUR:** (*dans la Coulisse.*) O dieu Brahma!

**LEILA:** Blanche Siva! Reine à la chevelure blonde!

**LE CHOEUR:** Blanche Siva!

**LEILA:** Esprits de l'air, esprits de l'onde, Des rochers, des prés et des bois, Ecoutez ma voix!

**NADIR:** (*se reveillant.*) Ciel! . . . encor cette voix!

**LEILA:** Dans le ciel sans voiles, Parsemé d'étoiles, Au sein de l'azur Transparent et pur, Comme dans un rêve, Penché sur la grêve, Mon regard vous suit A travers la nuit! Ma voix vous implore, Mon coeur vous adore, Et mon chant léger, Ainsi qu'un oiseau semble voltiger!

**LES SORCIÈRES ET LE CHOEUR:** (*dans la coulisse.*) Chante, chante encore! Que te voix sonore, Que ton chant léger, Loin de nous, ce soir, chasse tout danger!

**NADIR:** (*à part.*) O voix que j'adore, Je l'entends encore, Rêve mensonger! . . . . Prestige trompeur, charme passager! (*Nadir se glisse au pied du rocher.—Leïla se penche vers lui et écarte son voile un instant.*) Dieu! c'est elle! O Leïla! . . . Leïla! Ne redoute plus rien! . . . me voici! . . . je suis là! Prêt à donner mes jours, mon sang pour te défendre!

**LEILA:** (*à part.*) Il m'écoute! . . . il est là!

**LE CHOEUR:** Chante, chante encore! Que ta voix sonore, Que ton chant léger, Loin de nous, ce soir, chasse tout danger!

**NADIR:** Chante, chante encore! O toi que j'adore, Ne crains nul danger! Je suis là, je viens pour te protéger!

**LEILA:** Pour toi que j'adore, Oui je chante encore! Et mon chant léger, Ainsi qu'un oiseau semble voltiger!

*FIN DE LA ACTE PREMIERE.*

---

**CHORUS:** (*outside.*) Oh great Brahma!

**LEILA:** White Siva. Queen, of the blonde tresses.

**CHORUS:** White Siva.

**LEILA:** Spirits of air, spirits of the wave Of the rocks, the fields and the woods Listen to my voice.

**NADIR:** (*awaking.*) Heaven— again this voice!

**LEILA:** In the cloudless sky Sown with stars, In the heart of the azure Transparent and pure Like in a dream Bending over the shale My looks follow you Throughout the night My voice implores you My heart adores you And my light song Like a bird seems to plane.

**SORCERESSES AND CHORUS:** (*outside.*) Sing, sing, again That your sonorous voice, That your gentle song Far from us, this night, speed all danger.

**NADIR:** (*aside.*) Oh voice I adore, I hear it again, Deceptive dream! Mistaken thought, furtive charm (*Nadir slips to the foot of the rock—Leila bends toward him and lifts her veil for a moment.*) God it is she! Oh Leila . . . Leila! Fear nothing more. Here I am, here Ready to give my life, my blood to defend you!

**LEILA:** (*aside.*) He hears me . . . he is there.

**CHORUS:** Sing, sing again! That your sonorous voice, That your gentle song, Far from us, this night, speed all danger!

**NADIR:** Sing, sing again! Oh I adore you, Fear no danger I am here, come to protect you.

**LEILA:** For I adore you, Yes I sing again! And my soft song, Just like a bird seems to plane.

*END OF FIRST ACT.*

# Act II

## ■ ACTE II

## ■ ACT II

*Les ruines d'un temple indien.—Au fond, une terrasse élevéc de quelques marches et dominant la mer. Le ciel est étoilé; les rayons de lune éclairent vivement la terrassé. Leila, Nourabad, les fakirs au fond.*

*The ruins of an Indian temple—At rear a terrace higher by a few steps dominating the sea. A starry night and the rays of the moon light up the terrace. Leila, Nourabad and the priests are at the rear.*

**CHOEUR:** (*dans la coulisse.*)
L'ombre descend des cieux;
La nuit ouvre ses voiles,
Et les blanches étoiles
Se baignent dans l'azur des flots silencieux! . . .

**CHORUS:** (*outside.*) Shadows descend from the heavens,
The night opens its drapery
And the white stars
Bathe in the azure of the silent wave . . .

**NOURABAD:** (*s'avançant vers Leïla.*) Les barques ont gagné la grève;
Pour cette nuit, Leïla, notre tâche s'achève.
Ici tu peux dormir.

**NOURABAD:** (*advancing to Leila.*) The boats have gained the strand;
For this night, Leila, our task is done
Here you may sleep.

**LEILA:** Allez-vous donc, hélas!
Me laisser seule?

**LEILA:** Will you then, alas, leave me alone?

**NOURABAD:** Oui; mais ne tremble pas,
Sois sans crainte.—
Par là des rocs inaccessibles
Défendus par les flots grondants;
De ce côte, le camp; et là, gardiens terribles,
Le fusil sur l'épaule et le poignard aux dents,
Les Fakirs veilleront!

**NOURABAD:** Yes, but do not tremble,
Be without fear.
That way inaccessible rocks
Defended by the grumbling waves,
On that side, the camp; and there, terrible guardians,
The gun on shoulder, the dagger between their teeth,
the fakirs watch.

**LEILA:** Que Brahma me protège

**LEILA:** May Brahma protect me.

**NOURABAD:** Si ton coeur reste pur, si tu tiens ton serment,
Dors en paix sous ma garde et ne crains aucun piège!

**NOURABAD:** If your heart remains pure, if your oath is kept,
Sleep in peace in my care and fear no trap.

**LEILA:** En face de la mort, j'ai su rester fidèle,
Au serment qu'une fois j'avais fait . . .

**LEILA:** In the face of death I remained true
To an oath I once made . . .

**NOURABAD:** Toi! comment?

**NOURABAD:** You! How?

**LEILA:** J'étais encore enfant . . . un soir . . . je me rappelle . . .
Un homme, un fugitif, implorant mon secours,
Vint chercher un refuge en notre humble chaumière;
Et je promis, le coeur ému par sa prière,
De le cacher à tous, de protéger ses jours.
Bientôt une horde farouche
Accourt, la menace à la bouche;
On m'entoure! . . . un poignard sur mon front est levé . . .
Je me tais.—La nuit vient . . . il fuit . . . il est sauvé!
Mais avant de gagner la savane lointaine:
"O courageuse enfant, dit-il, prends cette chaîne
Et garde-la toujours, en souvenir de moi!
Moi, je me souviendrai!"—J'avais sauvé sa vie,
Et tenu ma promesse! . . .

**LEILA:** I was yet a child . . . one night . . . I remember . . .
A man, a fugitive, imploring my help,
Came seeking a refuge in our humble hut;
And I promised, my heart touched by his prayer,
To hide him from all, to protect his life.
Soon a bloodthirsty band
Rush in, threats in their mouths;
They surround me, a knife on my forehead is raised . . .
I am silent.—Night comes, he escapes, he is saved!
But before gaining the distant savanna;
"Courageous child", said he, "take this chain
And keep it always, in memory of me.
I shall remember" I had saved his life,
And kept my promise! . . .

**NOURABAD:** A nos lois asservie,
Comme en ce jour, si tu gardes ta foi,
La richesse, la gloire et le bonheur pour toi;
Sinon la mort, le malheur ou la honte!
De tous nos maux Zurga peut te demander compte!
Songes-y! . . . songe à Dieu!
Du repos voici
l'heure . . . adieu!
(*Il sort avec les fakirs.*)

**NOURABAD:** To our laws subjected,
As in this day, if you keep faith,
Wealth, glory and happiness for you;
If not death, misfortune and shame!
For all our ills Zurga can demand account from you
Think on it . . . think on God!
It is the hour of repose . . . adieu . . .
(*He goes out with priests*)

**LE REPRISE DU CHOEUR:** (*dans la coulisse*) L'ombre descend des cieux,
La nuit ouvre ses voiles,
Et les blanches étoiles
Se baignent dans l'azur des flots silencieux.

**REPEAT OF CHORUS:** (*outside.*)
The shadow falls from heaven
Night opens her wings,
And the white stars
Bathe in the azure of the silent wave.

**LEILA:** (*seule.*) Me voilà seule dans la nuit,
Seule en ce lieu désert où règne le silence! (*Regardent autour d'elle avec crainte*)
Je frisonne..j'ai peur! . . . et le sommeil me fuit! . . .
(*Regardent du côté de la terrasse.*)
Mais il est là! . . . mon coeur devine sa présence! . . .
Comme autrefois dans la nuit sombre,
Caché sous le feuillage épais,
Il veille près de moi dans l'ombre,
Je puis dormir, rêver en paix! . . .
C'est lui! mes yeux l'ont reconnu!
C'est lui! . . . mon âme est rassurée!
O bonheur! . . . joie inespérée!
Pour me revoir il est venu! . . .
Comme autrefois dans la nuit sombre. etc.
(*Le son d'une guzla se fait entendre dans la coulisse.*)
Mais qu'entends-je?
O chant méladieux! . . . Doux rêve! . . . trouble étrange!
C'est lui! c'est encor lui.
Qui vient calmer ma crainte et charmer mon ennui!

**LEILA:** (*outside.*) Here alone in the night,
Alone in this desert spot where silence reigns.
(*Looking about her with fear.*)
I shiver . . . I fear . . . and sleep flies away . . .
(*Looking toward the terrace.*)
But he is there . . . my heart divines his presence . . .
As in days gone by, in the dark night,
Hidden under the heavy leafage
He watches over me in the shade
I may sleep, dream in peace . . .
It is he, mine eyes do know him,
It is he, my soul is assured.
Oh happiness . . . joy unexpected
To see me he has come
As before in the dark night, etc.
(*The sound of a guzla is heard.*)
What do I hear
Melodious song, sweet dream . . . . . strange feeling
It is he, it is yet he
Who comes to calm my fear and charm my solitude.

**NADIR:** (*dans la coulisse.*) De mon amie,
Fleur endormie
Au fond du lac silencieux,
J'ai vu dans l'onde
Claire et profonde
Étinceler le front joyeux
Et les doux yeux! . . .

**NADIR:** (*outside.*) Of my love,
Sleeping flower
In depth of the silent lake,
I saw in the rill
Clear and profound
Sparkle the joyous face
And the gentle eyes' . . .

**LEILA:** (*se levant.*) Tout dort autour de nous et la nuit est profonde,
Seule j'entends son chant joyeux!

**LEILA:** (*rising.*) All sleeps about us and the night is dark,
Alone I hear his joyous song!

**NADIR:** Ma bien-aimée,
Est enfermée
Dans un palais d'or et d'azure;
Je l'entends rire,
Et je vois luire
Sous le cristal du gouffre obscur
Son regard pur!

**NADIR:** My well beloved
Is shut up
In a palace of azure and gold;
I hear her laugh,
And I see shine
Under the cristal of the gulf obscure
Her pure regard.

LEILA: Dieu! sa voix se rapproche! . . . un doux charme
m'attire!
Son regard brille au fond du temps
obscur!
(*Nadir paraît sur la terrasse.—Il
s'avance avec précaution et descent parmi les ruines.*)

NADIR: Leïla!

LEILA: Qui m'appelle?

NADIR: Leïla!

LEILA: Dieu puissant! . . . le
voilà!

NADIR: Près d'elle me voilà!
(*Il s'élance vers Leïla.*)

LEILA: Par cet étroit sentier qui
borde un sombre abîme,
Comment es-tu venu?

NADIR: Un dieu guidait mes pas,
un tendre espoir m'anime,
Rien ne m'a retenu!

LEILA: Que viens-tu faire
ici! . . .
Fuis! la mort te menace!
La mort est sur tes pas!

NADIR: Apaise ton ef-
froi . . . Pardonne!
Fais-moi grâce!
Ne me repousse pas!

LEILA: J'ai juré! j'ai promis! . . .
Je ne dois pas t'entendre!
Je ne dois pas te voir!

NADIR: Le jour est loin en-
cor! . . .
Nul ne peut nous surprendre!
Souris à mon espoir!

LEILA: Non, non, séparons-
nous! . . . il en est temps encore!

NADIR: Ah! pourquoi repousser un
ami qui t'implore?
Ton coeur n'a pas compris le mien!
Au sein de la nuit parfumée,
Quand j'écoutais, l'âme charmée,
Les accents de ta voix aimée,
Ton coeur n'a pas compris le mien!

LEILA: Ainsi que toi me souvien!
Au sein de la nuit parfumée,
Mon âme alors libre, et charmée,
A l'amour n'était pas fermée!
Ainsi que toi je me souvien!

NADIR: J'avais juré d'éviter ta
présence,
Et de me taire, hélas! à tout jamais;
Mais de l'amour, ô fatale puissance! . . .
Pouvais-je fuir les beaux yeux que
j'aimais?

LEILA: Malgré la nuit, malgré ton
long silence
Mon coeur joyeux avait lu dans ton
coeur!
Je t'attendais, j'espérais ta presence!
Ta douce voix m'apportait le bonheur!

NADIR: Est-il vrai? . . . que dis-
tu? . . .
Doux aveux! . . . ô bonheur!

---

LEILA: God! his voice comes
near—a soft charm attracts me,
His look shines, in the obscure
depths . . .

NADIR: Leila!

LEILA: Who calls me?

NADIR: Leila!

LEILA: Great Heaven . . . he's
here.

NADIR: Here I am by her side.
(*He rushes toward Leila*)

LEILA: By this narrow path that
skirts a dark abyss
How have you come here?

NADIR: A god my steps did guide, a
gentle hope did spring.
Nothing could retain me!

LEILA: What you've come here to
do!
Fly from threatening death
Death is on your track.

NADIR: Quiet your fears . . . .
forgive, have mercy
Do not repulse me.

LEILA: I've sworn, I've promised.
I must not listen,
I must not see you.

NADIR: The day is far away.
None can surprise us
Smile on my hopes.

LEILA: No, no. let's
part . . . there yet is time.

NADIR: Ah why repulse a friend
who implores you?
Your heart comprehends not mine
In the bosom of the perfumed
night,
When I listened, my soul all
charmed,
The accents of your loved voice,
Your heart understands not mine.

LEILA: Just like you, I remember.
In the bosom of the perfumed night
My soul then free, I was charmed,
And was not closed to love,
Just like you, I remember..

NADIR: I had sworn to avoid your
presence,
To be silent, alas, evermore;
But of love, of fatal power!
Could I flee from the eyes I loved?

LEILA: Despite the night, despite
your long silence,
My joyous heart had read in your
heart,
I awaited you, hoped for your presence,
Your gentle voice brought me bliss!

NADIR: Is it true? . . . what did
you say?
Sweet avowal, oh bliss.

---

NADIR: Ton coeur avait compris le
mien!
Au sein de la nuit parfumée, etc.

LEILA: Ainsi que toi je me souvien!
Au sein de la nuit, etc.
(*Se dégageant de ses bras.*)
Mais le temps fuit et l'heure passe!
Songe à la mort qui nous menace!
Par pitié, songe à mon serment!

NADIR: Si tu m'aimes comme je
t'aime
Que nous importe la mort même?
Que nous importe un vain serment?

LEILA: (*se jetant dans ses bras.*)
Ah! comme toi, l'âme ravie,
Je suis prête à donner ma vie
Pour cette heure d'enchantement!

NADIR: Viens donc! . . . Viens,
enivrée, heureuse,
Mourir dans l'étreinte amoureuse
De ton époux, de ton amant!

LEILA: O radieux enchantement!

NADIR: O douce extase! à doux
moment!
(*On entend au loin les premier
grondements de l'orage.*)

LEILA: (*avec crainte.*)
Chut! . . . écoute! . . . l'orage
gronde!

NADIR: Non, non! . . .
(*Écoutant.*)
Non, c'est le bruit de l'onde,
C'est plainte du flot mouvant
Que soulève le vent!

LEILA: L'éclair ouvre la nue
Et déchire les cieux!

NADIR: Non! c'est l'astre des nuits
qui rayonne à tes yeux
Et sourit à ta bienvenue!

LEILA: (*s'abandonnant de nouveau à l'etreinte amoureuse de
Nadir.*)
Ah! je te crois! ma vie est dans tes
yeux!
Ta voix remplit mon coeur d'une
joie inconnue!

ENSEMBLE: Que la foudre éclate et
groude,
Que le ciel s'ouvre à nos yeux,
Nous bravons la terre et l'onde
Et Brahma maître des cieux!
Doux baiser, brûlant délire!
Amour pur, sublime ardeur!
Un pouvoir divin m'attire
Dans tes bras et sur ton coeur!
(*Le bruit de l'orage se rapproche;
Nourabad paraît au fond.*)

NOURABAD: Un homme dans ces
lieux! . . . trahison! trahison!
(*Il disparaît dans l'ombre.*)

LEILA: (*à Nadir.*) Ah! revenez à la
raison!
Fuyez ces lieux! . . . partez! partez vite! . . . je tremble!

NADIR: Que l'amour chaque soir
dans l'ombre nous rassemble!

---

NADIR: Your heart had understood
mine
In the bosom of the perfumed
night.

LEILA: Just like you I remember
In the bosom, etc.
(*Wresting herself from his arms.*)
But time flies and the hour passes,
Think of the death that threatens,
In pity, think of my oath!

NADIR: If you love me as I love
you,
What even matters death,
And what is a vain oath?

LEILA: (*throwing herself in his
arms*) Ah! like you, my ravished
soul,
I am ready to give my life,
For this enchanting hour!

NADIR: Come then, come blissful-
ly happy,
Die in a loving embrace
Of your husband, of your lover.

LEILA: Oh radiant enchantment!

NADIR: Oh sweet ecstacy, oh
sweet moment!
(*The first rumblings of a storm
are heard.*)

LEILA: (*with fear.*)
Sh . . . listen . . . the storm
grumbles

NADIR: No, no . . .
(*Listening.*)
No, it is the sound of the tide,
It is the plaint of the moving wave
Raised by the wind.

LEILA: The lightning breaks the
cloud
And tears the heavens!

NADIR: No, it is the moon whose
rays shine in the eyes
And smiles a welcome.

LEILA: (*abandoning herself to
Nadir*) Ah! I believe my life is in
your eyes
Your voice fills my heart with an
unknown joy.

TOGETHER: Let the thunder crack
and rumble
Let the heavens open too,
We brave both earth and ocean
And Brahma king of heaven,
Sweet kiss, hot delirium,
Pure love, sublime ardor,
A power divine attracts me
In my arms and on my heart!
(*The storm increases.—Noura-
bad appears at rear.*)

NOURABAD: A man in this place
. . . treason! treason!
(*He disappears in the gloom.*)

LEILA: (*to Nadir.*) Ah! return to
reason
Fly from this place . . . go, go
quickly . . . I tremble.

NADIR: May love bring us here
each night in the dark.

**LEILA:** Oui . . . oui! demain je t'attendrai! . . .

**NADIR:** Oui, demain je te reverrai! (*Ils se séparent.—Coup de feu dans la coulisse. Leïla pousse un cri et tombe à genoux.*)

**NOURABAD ET LES FAKIRS:** Malheur sur lui! malheur sur nous! Accourez! . . . venez tous! (*Ils traversent le fond du théâtre à la poursuite de Nadir.*)

**LE CHOEUR:** Quelle voix nous appelle? Quelle sombre nouvelle, Quel présage de mort nous attend en ces lieux? (*L'orage éclate dans toute sa furie.*) O nuit d'épouvante, la mer écumante Soulève en grondant ses flots furieux! (*Nourabad reparaît suivi de fakirs armés de torches.*)

**NOURABAD:** Dans l'asile sacré, dans ces lieux redoutables, Un homme, un étranger profitant de la nuit. A pas furtifs s'est introduit.

**LE CHOEUR:** Que dit-il! (*montrant Nadir qu'on amène au fond.*)

**NOURABAD:** Le voici! voici les deux coupables.

**LE CHOEUR:** Nadir! . . . ô trahison! . . . ô forfait odieux, Qui déchaîne sur nous la colère des cieux! (*Avec rage, les poignards levés sur Nadir et Leïla.*) Ni pitiè, ni grâce, Pour tous deux la mort! Malgré sa menace Qu'ils aient même sort! Esprits des ténèbres Prêts à nous punir, Vos gouffres runèbres Pour eux vont s'ouvrir! . . . Ni pitié ni grâce.

**LEILA:** O sombre menace! O funeste sort! Tout mon sang se glace; Pour nous c'est la mort!

**NADIR:** Leur demander grâce, Non! plutôt la mort! Lour folle menace, Rend mon bras plus fort! (*On va pour las frapper: Nadir se jette devant Leïla pour la défendre au péril de sa vie.*)

**ZURGA:** Arrêtez! . . . c'est à moi d'ordonner de leur sort!

**LE CHOEUR:** La mort pour eux! . . . la mort! la mort!

**ZURGA:** Voux m'avez donné la puissance, Vous me devez obéissance. (*Les pêcheurs s'arrêtent indécis.*)

---

**LEILA:** Yes . . . yes tomorrow I'll see you.

**NADIR:** Yes . . . yes tomorrow I'll see you (*They separate.—Shot heard.—Leila cries out and falls on her knees.*)

**NOURABAD AND THE FAKIRS:** Misfortune for him, for all of us Come, come quickly. (*They cross at rear in pursuit of Nadir.*)

**CHORUS:** What voice calls us? What sombre news, What presage of death awaits us here (*The storm bursts.*) Oh night of awe the stormy sea Rises grumbling in its furious flood!

**NOURABAD:** (*reappears followed by fakirs.*) In the sacred asylum, in these dreaded vaults A man, a stranger, profiting of the night, Came here with furtive steps Came here with furtive steps

**CHORUS:** What says he?

**NOURABAD:** (*showing Nadir whom they bring.*) This is he! Here are both the guilty ones.

**CHORUS:** Nadir! . . . oh treason . . . oh crime most odious, That unchains on us the anger of heaven! (*Daggers lifted over Nadir and Leïla*) No pity, no grace, For both of them death! Despite his threats They deserve the same fate. Spirits of darkness Ready to punish, Your funeral abysses For both shall open . . . No pity or grace, etc.

**LEILA:** Oh sombre threat Oh terrible fate All my blood freezes; For us it is death!

**NADIR:** Ask them for mercy, No, sooner death! Their insolent threat, Makes me defy them!

**ZURGA:** (*entering.*) Stop . . . it is for me to decide their fate.

**CHORUS:** Death for them . . . death, death!

**ZURGA:** You have given me the power, You owe me obedience. (*The fishermen stop undecided.*)

---

**NADIR:** (*à part.*) O généreux ami!

**LEILA:** (*à part.*) O noble défenseur!

**LE CHOEUR:** (*avec soumission, s'adressant à Zurga.*) Qu'il partent donc! . . . nous faisons grâce au traître. Zurga le veut . . . Zurga commande en maître!

**ZURGIA:** (*bas, à Leïla et à Nadir.*) Partez!

**NOURABAD:** (*arrachant le voile de Leïla.*) Avant de fuir au moins fais-toi connaître!

**ZURGIA:** (*reconnaissant Leïla.*) Dieu! qu'ai-je vu? c'était elle ô fureur! Vengez-vous! vengez-moi! . . . malheur sur eux! . . . malheur!

**LE CHOEUR:** Ni pitié, ni grâce, Pour tous deux la mort! Ni pitié ni grâce! Pour tous deux la mort! Etc.

**LEILA:** O sombre menace; Pour nous, c'est la mort! Etc.

**NADIR:** Leur demander grâce, Non, plutôt la mort! Etc. (*L'orage éclate avec fracas.*)

**TOUS LES PECHEURS:** (*tombant à genoux.*) Brahma, divin Brahma! Que ton bras nous protège! Nous jurons de punir leur amour sacrilège! O dieu Brahma, nous sommes tous A tes genoux! (*Sur un geste de Zurga, Nadir est entraîné par les pêcheurs et les fakirs emmèment Leïla.*)

FIN DE LA ACTE DEUXIEME.

---

**NADIR:** (*aside.*) Oh, generous friend!

**LEILA:** (*aside.*) Oh noble defender.

**CHORUS:** (*submissively to Zurga.*) Then let them go, we grant grace to treason. Zurga wills it . . . Zurga is master!

**ZURGA:** (*low to Leila and Nadir.*) Go!

**NOURABAD:** (*tearing the veil from Leila.*) Before your flight at least we shall know you.

**ZURGA:** (*recognizing Leila.*) God what have I seen, it is she, oh fury Revenge yourselves, revenge me, unfortunates No pity, no grace, For both of them death!

**CHORUS:** No pity, no grace For both of them death!

**LEILA:** Oh sombre menace For us, it is death, etc.

**NADIR:** To ask for mercy Death sooner, far. (*The storm breaks with fury.*)

**ALL THE FISHERMEN:** (*falling on their knees.*) Brahma, divine Brahma, your arm protect us We swear to punish their sacrilegeous love Oh great Brahma, we are all at your knees! (*On a gesture of Zurga's Nadir is dragged away by the fishermen.—the priests take Leila.*)

END OF SECOND ACT.

---

## ■ ACTE III

(*Une tente indienne fermée par une draperie.*)

**ZURGA:** (*seul.*) L'orage s'est calmé.— Déjà les vents se taisent, Comme eux les colères s'apaisent! Moi seul j'appelle en vain le calme et le sommeil. La fiévre me dévore, et mon âme oppressée N'a plus qu'une pensée; Nadir doit expirer au lever du soleil! Nadir! . . . ami de mon jeune âge, Lorsqu'à la mort je t'ai livré, Par quelle aveugle et folle rage Mon coeur était-il déchiré! (*Se levant et avec désespoir.*) Non! non! c'est impossible! J'ai fait un songe horrible! Non! tu n'as pas trahi tes serments

## ■ ACT III

*An Indian tent shut in by a drapery.*

**ZURGA:** (*alone.*) The storm has calmed. The winds are silent Like them is anger modified Alone I vainly call for calm and sleep Fever devours me, and my soul oppressed Has but one thought: Nadir must die at sunrise! Nadir . . . friend of my youth, When I deliver you to death By what blind and crazed rage Is my heart torn! (*Rising with despair.*) No it is impossible! I've had a horrid dream. No, you did not betray your oath and faith And the culprit, alas, the culprit is

et ta foi
Et le coupable, hélas! le coupable,
c'est moi!
Nadir! . . . ami de mon jeune
âge,
Et toi, radieuse beauté,
Pardonnez à l'aveugle rage
Aux transports d'un cœur irrité!
Leïla . . . cher Nadir! . . . Ah!
je maudis ma rage,
J'ai honte de ma cruanté!
(*Il retombe accablé; Leila paraît
à l'entrée de la tente.*)

ZURGA: Dieu! . . . qu'ai-je vu?
Leïla!

LEILA: J'ai voulu te parler . . . à
toi seul! . . . me voilà!

ZURGA: (*Aux pêcheurs.*)
C'est bien! Sortez!
(*Les pêcheurs se retirent et laissent retomber la draperie qui
ferme l'entrée de la tente.*)

ZURGA: (*à part.*) Qu'elle est
belle!
Plus belle encore au moment de
mourir!—

LEILA: (*à part.*) Ah! je
frémis . . . je chancelle!
Hélas! comment attendrir
Cette âme sombre et cruelle!

ZURGA: Approche et calme ton effroi!

LEILA: (*se jetant à ses pieds.*) Je
viens demander grâce!
Par le ciel par tes mains que
j'embrasse,
Epargne un innocent et ne frappe
que moi!

ZURGA: Innocent! . . . lui! . . . Nadir! . . . ah! com-
ment? . . . parle vite!
Dans l'asile sacré ne l'attendais-tu
pas?

LEILA: Vers moi le hasard seul avait
guidé ses pas.

ZURGA: Dois-je te croire?

LEILA: Ah! que je sois maudite
Si je te trompe et si je mens!

ZURGA: (*à part.*) Ainsi donc ses
serments
Et notre amitié sainte,
Il n'avait rien trahi! . . .

LEILA: Pour moi je suis sans
crainte,
Mais je tremble pour lui!
Sois sensible à ma plainte,
Et deviens notre appui!
Par ma voix qui supplie
Ah! laisse-toi fléchir!
Accorde-moi sa vie
Pour m'aider à mourir!

ZURGA: (*à part.*) Pour l'aider à
mourir!

LEILA: Il me donna son âme
Il eut tout mon amour;
Ardente et triste flamme
Voici ton dernier jour!
Par ma voie qui supplie.

me
Nadir, friend of my youth
And you, oh radiant beauty,
Forgive a blind rage
The transports of an irritated heart!
Leila..dear Nadir . . . I curse my
rage
I'm ashamed of my cruelty.
(*He falls exhausted.—Leila ap-
pears at entrance of tent.*)

ZURGA: God! What have I seen?
Leila.

LEILA: I wished to speak with
you . . . you alone . . . I'm
here.

ZURGA: (*to fishermen*) It is well,
go.
(*The fishermen retire.*)

ZURGA: How beautiful she is!
And more so at the hour of death.

LEILA: (*aside.*) I tremble . . . I
stagger,
Alas how mollify
This sombre, cruel soul?

ZURGA: Approach and calm your
fears,

LEILA: (*throwing herself at his
feet.*)
I come to ask mercy!
By heaven, by your hands I embrace,
Spare an innocent and strike only
me.

ZURGA: Innocent . . . he, Nadir . . . but how? quickly speak
In the sacred asylum did you not
await him?

LEILA: Toward me chance alone
had guided his steps.

ZURGA: Should I believe?

LEILA: Ah! may I be cursed
If I deceive you and if I lie.

ZURGA: (*aside*) Ah then his oaths,
And our sacred friendship,
He thus betrayed nothing . . .

LEILA: For myself I fear not,
But I tremble for him!
Be sensible of my plaint,
And become our support.
By my voice that implores,
Ah, let yourself soften
Give me his life
To aid me to die.

ZURGA: (*aside.*) To aid her to die.

LEILA: He gave me his soul
He had all my love;
Sad and ardent flame
Here is your last day
By my voice that implores, etc.

ZURGA: (*à Leïla.*) Pour t'aider â
mourir!

LEILA: Sans doute! ici n'est-tu pas
maître?

ZURGA: Nadir! . . . ah j'aurais
pu lui pardonner peut-être! . . .
Et le sauver! . . . car nous étions
amis!
Mais tu l'aimes!

LEILA: (*effrayée.*) Gran Dieu!

ZURGA: Tu l'aimes!

LEILA: Je frémis!

ZURGA: Tu l'aimes! ce mot seul a
réveillé ma haine.
En croyant le sauver tu le perds à jamais!

LEILA: Par grâce, par pitié!

ZURGA: Plus de prière vaine!
Je suis jaloux!

LEILA: Jaloux!

ZURGA: Comme lui je t'aimais!
(*Avec fureur.*)
Tu demandais sa vie,
Mais de ma jalousie,
Ranimant la furie,
Tu le perds pour toujours!
Que l'arrêt s'accomplisse,
Et qu'un même supplice
Me venge et réunisse
Vos coupables amours!

LEILA: De mon amour, Nadir, on
t'ose faire un crime!

ZURGA: Son crime est d'être aimé
quand je ne le suis pas!

LEILA: Ah! du moins dans son sang
ne plonge pas tes bras
Et que de ta fureur, seule, je sois
victime

ZURGA: Tu l'aimes! . . .

LEILA: (*suppliante.*) Par pitié'!

ZURGA: Tu l'aimes!

LEILA: Par leciel!

ZURGA: Il doit mourir!

LEILA: Eh bien, venge-toi donc,
cruel!

LEILA: Va, prends aussi ma vie;
Mais, ta rage assouvie,
Le remords, l'infamie
Te poursuivront toujours!
Que l'arrêt s'accomplisse,
Et qu'un même supplice
Dans les cieux réunisse
A jamais nos amours.

ZURGA: Tu demandais sa vie,
Mais de ma jalousie,
Ranimant la furie,
Tu le pers pour toujur!
Qu l'arrêt s'accomplisse,
Et qu'un même supplice
Me venge et réunisse
Vos coupables amours!

NOURABAD: (*reparaissant au
fond, suivi de quelques pêcheurs.
Cris de joie dans l'éloignement.*)
Entends au loin ce bruit de fête!
L'heure est venue!

LEILA: Et la victime est prête!

ZURGA: To aid her to die

LEILA: No doubt, are you not master here?

ZURGA: Nadir . . . ah perhaps I
might have pardoned him,
And saved him..for we were
friends!
But you love him!

LEILA: (*in fear.*) Great God!

ZURGA: You love him!

LEILA: I tremble!

ZURGA: You love him! at this word
has my hate revived.
In thinking to save him you have
lost him forever.

LEILA: Mercy, pity.

ZURGA: Vain prayers no longer—
I am jealous.

LEILA: Jealous!

ZURGA: Like him, I love you.
(*with fury.*)
You asked for his life,
But
Reviving the fury of my jealousy,
You must lose him forever!
Let the law take its course,
May a single torture
Avenge me and unite
Your culpable loves

LEILA: Of my love Nadir they dare
to make a crime.

ZURGA: His crime is to be loved
while I am not.

LEILA: Ah! at least do not plunge
your hands in his blood
And that of your fury, alone I be victim.

ZURGA: You love him?

LEILA: (*supplicating.*) Have pity!

ZURGA: You love him?

LEILA: By Heaven!

ZURGA: He must die.

LEILA: Well then avenge yourself,
cruel one.

LEILA: Come, also take my life;
But, your rage satisfied,
Remorse and infamy
Shall always follow you.
Let the law take its course,
And the same torture,
In Heaven unite
Forever our loves.

ZURGA: You did ask for his life.
But
Reviving the fury of my jealousy,
You'll lose him forever.
Let the law take its course,
And that the same torture
In Heaven unite
Your culpable loves.

NOURABAD: (*reappearing at
rear followed by fishermen.—
Cries of joy in distance.*) Listen to
this joyful noise
The hour has come.

LEILA: And the victim is ready.

## Act III

**ZURGA:** Partez!

**LEILA:** Le ciel s'ouvre pour moi!
(*A un jeune pêcheur.*)
Ami, prends ce collier, et quand je serai morte,
Qu'à ma mère on le porte
En souvenir de moi!
(*On entraîne Leïla.—Zurga s'approche vivement du pêcheur, lui arrache le collier des mains, le regarde et sort précipitamment.*)

**ZURGA:** Go!

**LEILA:** Heaven opens for me
(*To a young fisherman.*)
Friend take this necklace and when I am dead
Carry it to my mother
In remembrance of me
(*They drag Leila away.—Zurga quickly goes near fisherman, tears the necklace from him, looks at it and goes out quickly.*)

## DEUXIEME TABLEAU

(*Un site sauvage. Au milieu de la scène un bûcher. Des feux, allumés cà et là.*)

**CHOEUR ET DANSE:** Dès que le soleil,
Dans l'azur vermeil,
Versera sa flamme
Nos bras frapperont
Et se plongeront
Dans leur sang infâme!
Ardente liqueur,
Verse en notre coeur
Une sainte extase;
Qu'un sombre transport,
Présage de mort,
Soudain nous embrase,
Dès que le soleil, etc.
(*Leïla et Nadir paraissent précédés de grands prêtres conduits per Nourabad.*)
(*Marche funèbre.*)

**NOURABAD:** Sombres divinités,
Zurga les livre à nos bras irrités!

**CHOEUR:** Zurga les livre à nos bras irrités!
(*Une lueur rouge, qui éclaire tout à coup le fond du théâtre.*)

**CHOEUR:** Le jour enfin perce la nue,
Le soleil luit, l'heure est venue!
(*Au moment où Nadir et Leïla vont gravir la première marche du bûcher, Zurga paraît une hache à la main.*)

**ZURGA:** Non, ce n'est pas le jour, regardez, c'est le feu!
Le feu du ciel tombé sur nous des mains de Dieu!
Le flamme envahit et dévore
Votre camp! Courez tous! il en est temps encore,
Pour arracher vos enfants au trépas!
Courez, courez, que Dieu guide vos pas!
(*Les Indiens sortent en désorde, Nourabad reste seul avec Zurga, Nadir et Leïla.—Puis il se cache pour entendre ce que va dire Zurga.*)

**ZURGA:** (*à Nadir et à Leila.*) Mes mains ont allumé le terrible incendie.
Qui menace leurs jours et vous sauve la vie,
Car je brise vos fers.—Leïla, souveins-toi.

## SCENE II

*A wild place.—In the center a pyre.—Fires lighted here and there.*

**CHORUS AND DANCE:** As soon as the sun
In reddened azure
Shall drip its flame
Our arms shall strike
And shall plunge
In their infamous blood
Ardent liquor
Pour in our heart
A holy ecstacy
May sombre transports
Presage of death
Suddenly seize us
As soon as the sun, etc.
(*Enter Leila and Nadir preceded by high priest led by Nourabad.— Funeral march.*)

**NOURABAD:** Sombre divinities
Zurga delivers them to our angry arms.

**CHORUS:** Zurga delivers them to our angry arms.
(*A red light illuminates the distance.*)

**CHORUS:** The dawn pierces the clouds
The sun shines, the hour has come.
(*At the moment that Leila starts to step on the pyre Zurga appears torch in hand.*)

**ZURGA:** No it is not day, look, it is fire!
The fire of Heaven fallen on us from God's hands!
The flame invades and destroys!
Your camp, run all, there is yet time,
To save your children from death.
Run, run, may God guide your steps.
(*The Indians run out in disorder.—Nourabad remains with Zurga, Nadir and Leila.—Then be hides to bear what Zurga will say.*)

**ZURGA:** (*to Nadir and Leila.*) My hands started the terrible flame.
That threatens their days but saves your lives,
For I break your irons—Leila, remember,
You saved me once, be both saved

by me.
(*He breaks their chains.—Nourabad runs to warn the Indians.*)

**LEILA ET NADIR:** O lumière sainte,
O divine étreinte,
Mon âme est sans crainte,
Car il nous arrache enfin au trépas!
Zurga nous délivre
Et nous fait revivre,
Oui, je veux te suivre;
Rien ne me saurait ravir à tes bras.

**ZURGA:** O lumière sainte,
O divine étreinte,
Je m'en vais sans plainte,
Les sauvant tous deux, courir au trépas.
Ma main les délivre.
Nadir peut la suivre,
Je ne dois plus vivre,
Puisqu'un sort fatal l'arrache à mes bras.

**NADIR:** (*dans l'extase amoureuse.*) Dans l'espace immense
Brille un jour plus pur,
Notre âme s'élance
Au sein de l'azur.

**LEILA:** Un palais splendide
S'entr'ouvre à nos yeux,
Notre essor rapide.
Nous emporte aux cieux!

**ZURGA:** (*à part.*)
O Dieux! comme ils s'aiment! ô Dieux!

**LEILA ET NADIR:** L'ombre nous couvre encor, le jour ne paraît pas!

**ZURGA:** L'ombre les couvre encor, mais le jour naît la-bas!

**LEILA ET NADIR:** Partons!
L'amour soutient notre coeur!

**ZURGA:** O Dieux! comme ils s'aiment! ô Dieux!

(*On entend quelques mesures du premier choeur.*)

**ZURGA:** Ce sont eux, les voici! Fuyez par ce passage!
(*A Nadir.*)
Emporte ton trésor loin de ce bord sauvage!

**NADIR ET LEILA:** Et toi, Zurga?

**ZURGA:** Dieu seul sait l'avenir.

**NADIR ET LEILA:** Ah! nous te reverrons pour t'aimer, te bénir!
(*Nadir et Leïla se sauvent. Nourabad et les Indiens paraissent.*)

**NOURABAD:** (*désignant Zurga.*) C'est lui, le traître! Il a sauvé leur vie!
Ses mains ont allumé le terrible incendie
Qui menace vos jours! Décidez de son sort.
Il faut une victime.

**LEILA AND NADIR:** Oh, holy light,
Divine embrace,
My soul is without fear,
For he saves us, at last from death
Zurga delivers us
And makes us live again,
Yes, I will follow you
Nothing could tear me from your arms.

**ZURGA:** Oh, holy light,
Divine embrace,
I go without complaint,
Saving them both, rushing to death.
My hand delivers them,
Nadir may follow her,
I must not live,
As a fatal will must tear her from my arms.

**NADIR:** In space immense
Shines a purer day,
Our souls now fly
In the midst of the azure.

**LEILA:** A splendid palace
Opens to our eyes,
Our rapid flight,
Takes us to the skies!

**ZURGA:** (*aside.*) Oh gods how they love, oh gods!

**LEILA AND NADIR:** Shadow yet covers us, day does not appear.

**ZURGA:** Shadow yet covers them, but day will soon appear.

**LEILA AND NADIR:** Let us go.
Love sustains our heart.

**ZURGA:** Gods, how they love oh gods!

(*A bit of first chorus is beard.*)

**ZURGA:** It is them, they come. Escape by this passage.
(*To Nadir.*)
Take your treasure far from this savage coast.

**NADIR AND LEILA:** And you, Zurga?

**ZURGA:** God alone knows the future.

**NADIR AND LEILA:** Ah we shall meet again to love and bless you!
(*Nadir and Leila run out.—Nourabad and the Indians appears.*)

**NOURABAD:** (*pointing to Zurga.*) It is he the traitor he saved their lives
His hands started the terrible flames
That threaten your days. Decide on his fate.
We need a victim.

**CHOEUR:** A mort! à mort! à mort!
(*Les Indiens se jettet sur Zurga et le forcent à monter sur le bûcher.*)

**CHOEUR:** Pour le sacrifice
Tout est prêt!
Que la sombre forêt
De nos airs retentisse
Ah! Brahma!

**ZURGA:** Que sur moi seul leur rage enfin soit assouvie,
Adieu, ma Leïla, je te donne ma vie!
(*Le bûcher commence à brûler. Zurga disparaît dans les flammes.*)

**CHORUS:** Death! death! death!
(*The Indians throw themselves on Zurga and force him to mount the pyre.*)

**CHORUS:** For the sacrifice
All is ready
Let the forest sombre.
Resound with our airs.
Oh Brahma!

**ZURGA:** On me may their rage at last be satisfied,
Farewell, my Leila, I give you my life!
(*The pyre begins to burn. — Zurga disappears in the flames.*)

**CHOEUR:** C'est l'arrêt de Dieu
Qui condamne au feu
Le traître et l'infâme!
C'est un juste sort!
Qu'il trouve la mort.
(*On aperçoit la forêt embrasée.*)
Dans l'horrible flamme!
Déjà le soleil,
Dans l'azur vermeil,
Montre et nous éclaire.
Naguère outragés,
Les Dieux sont vengés.
Restons en prière!
(*Ils se prosternent à terre, puis se redressent les bras levés au ciel.*)
Ah! Brahma!

*FIN.*

**CHORUS:** It is God's decision
that condemns to flame
The infamous traitor!
It is a just fate
That he meets death.
(*A burning forest is revealed at rear*)
In the horrible flame
Already the sun,
In reddened azure
Shows and lights us.
Justly outraged
The gods are avenged,
Let us pray.
(*They prostrate themselves, then rise*)
Ah Brahma!

*END.*

# *Carmen* (1875)

MUSIC BY GEORGES BIZET ■ LIBRETTO BY HENRI MEILHAC AND LUDOVIC HALÉVY

This four-act *drama lyrique*, is set to a libretto by Henri Meilhac and Ludovic Halévy (based on Prosper Mérimée's novel). *Carmen* premiered at the Opéra-Comique in Paris on March 3, 1875. In a town square in Seville, with a cigarette factory on one side and solders' barracks directly opposite, the soldiers wait for the cigarette girls to come out from work. Micaela, a young girl from the country, is looking for one of the soldiers, Don José, but doesn't find him, so she departs. Don José arrives, and the cigarette girls return to work at noon. Carmen, a stunning gypsy, is among them. She has her eye on Don José and tosses him a flower, while singing the famous *Habanera*. Micaela brings him tidings of his mother, and he promises to marry her in accordance with his mother's wishes. A quarrel breaks out at the factory; Carmen wounds one of her friends and is arrested. Don José is to be her guard, and she attempts to seduce him with the hypnotic and sexy *Seguedille* aria. Her scheme to win freedom is successful, and he frees her before they reach the prison. While Carmen is dancing with two of her friends at the inn of Lillas Pastia, Escamillo, a bullfighter, enters and tries to seduce Carmen, but she ignores him in expectation of Don José's arrival. He arrives and they spend a brief passionate moment together before Don José must return to his barracks; Carmen asks him to run away with her to the mountains. Captain Zunigo enters and orders Don José to return at once. Don José refuses and has no choice but to leave his regiment and join Carmen. Hiding in the mountains with the smugglers, Don José regrets breaking his promise. Carmen, already tired of him, moons over Escamillo. She foresees death in the tarot cards. Escamillo arrives. He and Don José argue; Carmen separates them. Don José leaves with Micaela, who has come to the hideout to plead with Don José to visit his dying mother, but threatens Carmen that she has not seen the last of him. Carmen is on his way to the bullfight with Escamillo, when she is warned of Don José's presence nearby. He begs her to come back to him, but she rejects him, throwing his ring at his feet. Don José, blinded by jealousy and pain, stabs Carmen to death. The opera ends with Don José being led off to prison.

## ■ ACTE I

### Prelude

## ■ ACT I

### Prelude

*(A square in Seville. On the right, the door of a tobacco factory. At the back, facing the audience, a bridge from one side of the stage to the other, reached from the stage by a winding staircase beyond the factory door. The bridge is open underneath. In front, a guard-house; in front of that, three steps leading to a covered passage. As the curtain rises, a file of soldiers (dragoons of Almanza) are grouped before the guard-house, smoking and looking at the passers-by in the square coming and going from all parts. The scene is full of animation)*

**LES SOLDATS:** Sur la place
chacun passe,
chacun vient, chacun va;
drôles de gens que ces gens-là!

**MORALÈS:** A la porte du corps de garde,
pour tuer le temps,
on fume, on jase, l'on regarde
passer les passants.

**SOLDIERS:** On the square
everyone comes by,
everyone comes and goes;
funny sort of people these!

**MORALÈS:** At the guard-house door,
to kill time,
we smoke gossip, and watch
the passers-by.

**LES SOLDATS AND MORALÈS:** Sur la place, *etc.*

**MORALÈS:** Regardez donc cette petite
qui semble vouloir nous parler.
Voyez, elle tourne, elle hésite.

**LES SOLDATS:** A son secours il faut aller!

**MORALÈS:** (*à Micaëla*) Que cherchez-vous, la belle?

**MICAËLA:** Moi, je cherche un brigadier.

**MORALÈS:** Je suis là, voilà!

**MICAËLA:** Mon brigadier à moi s'appelle
Don José . . . le connaissez-vous?

**MORALÈS:** Don José! Nous le connaissons tous.

**MICAËLA:** Vraiment! Est-il avec vous, je vous prie?

**MORALÈS:** Il n'est pas brigadier dans notre compagnie.

**MICAËLA:** (*désolée*) Alors, il n'est pas là?

**SOLDIERS AND MORALÈS:** On the square, *etc.*
(*Micaëla enters*)

**MORALÈS:** Now look at this little lass
who seems to want to speak to us.
Look, she's turning round, she's hesitating.

**SOLDIERS:** We must go and help her!

**MORALÈS:** (*to Micaëla*) Whom are you looking for, pretty one?

**MICAËLA:** I'm looking for a corporal.

**MORALÈS:** Here I am, look!

**MICAËLA:** My corporal is called Don José . . . do you know him?

**MORALÈS:** Don José? We all know him.

**MICAËLA:** Really! Is he with you, please?

**MORALÈS:** He isn't a corporal in our company.

**MICAËLA:** (*disappointed*) Then he isn't here?

MORALÈS: Mais en attendant qu'il vienne,
voulez-vous, la belle enfant,
voulez-vous prendre la peine
d'entrer chez nous un instant?

MICAËLA: Chez vous?

LES SOLDATS ET MORALÈS: Chez nous.

MICAËLA: Chez vous?

LES SOLDATS ET MORALÈS: Chez nous!

MICAËLA: Non pas, non pas.
Grand merci, messieurs les soldats.

MORALÈS: Entrez sans crainte, mignonne.
je vous promets qu'on aura,
pour votre chère personne,
tous les égards qu'il faudra.

MICAËLA: Je n'en doute pas;
cependant
je reviendrai, c'est plus prudent.
Je reviendrai quand la garde montante
remplacera la guarde descendanta.

LES SOLDATS ET MORALÈS: Il faut rester car la garde montante,
va remplacer la garde descendante.

MORALÈS: Vous resterez!

MICAËLA: Non pas! non pas!

LES SOLDATS ET MORALÈS: Vous resterez!

MICAËLA: Non pas! non pas! non! non! non!
Au revoir, messieurs les soldats!

MORALÈS: L'oiseau s'envole.
on s'en console.
Reprenons notre passe-temps
et regardons passer les gens.

LES SOLDATS: Sur la place
chacun passe, etc.

MORALÈS: Drôles de gens! Drôles de gens!
Drôles de gens!

MORALÈS: Attention! chut! attention! Taisons-nous!
Voici venir un vieil époux,
Oeil soupçonneux, mine jalouse,
Il tient au bras sa jeune épouse;
L'amant sans doute n'est pas loin;
Il va sortir de quelque coin.
(avec les soldats)
L'amant sans doute n'est pas loin;
Il va sortir de quelque coin.
Ah! ah! ah! ah!

MORALÈS: But while you wait for him to come
will you, my pretty child,
take the trouble
to step inside with us for a moment?

MICAËLA: Inside with you?

SOLDIERS AND MORALÈS: Inside with us.

MICAËLA: Inside with you?

SOLDIERS AND MORALÈS: Inside with us!

MICAËLA: No, no.
Many thanks, soldiers.

MORALÈS: Don't be afraid to come in, my dear,
I promise you we shall treat
your dear self
with every due respect.

MICAËLA: I don't doubt it; all the same
I'll come back, that's wiser.
I'll be back when the new guard
comes to relieve the old guard.

SOLDIERS AND MORALÈS: You must stay, because the new guard
is on its way to relieve the old guard.

MORALÈS: You'll stay!

MICAËLA: Indeed I'll not!

SOLDIERS AND MORALÈS: (surrounding Micaëla) You'll stay!

MICAËLA: Indeed I'll not! No, no, no!
Goodbye, soldiers!
(She escapes and runs off.)

MORALÈS: The bird has flown;
we'll console ourselves.
Let's resume our pastime
and watch the folks go by.

SOLDIERS: On the square
everyone comes by, etc.

MORALÈS: Funny sort of people!
(The movement of the passers-by which had stopped during the foregoing scene has now resumed with a certain animation. Among the people coming and going is an old gentleman with a young lady on his arm. . . . The old gentleman would like to continue his walk, but the young lady is doing all she can to detain him on the square. She seems anxious, uneasy. She looks to right and left, She is expecting someone, and this someone does not come. This pantomine must fit in very exactly with the following verse:)

MORALÈS: Stand by! Let's pipe down!
Look, here comes an old husband with a suspicious eye and a jealous look,
he's holding on to his young wife by the arm;
no doubt the lover's not far off;
he'll pop out of some corner.
(With the soldiers)
No doubt the lover's not far off;

Le voilà.

MORALÈS: Ah! le voilà! oui, le voilà! etc.
(avec les soldats)
Voyons comment ce tournera.

MORALÈS: Vous trouver ici, quel bonheur!
Je sius bien votre serviteur!
Il salue, il parle avec grâce.
Le vieux mari fait la grimace;
Mais d'un air très encourageant
La dame accueille le galant.

MORALÈS: Ils font ensemble quelques pas;
Notre amoureux, levant le bras,
Fait voir au mari quelque chose,
Et le mari, toujours morose,
Regarde en l'air . . . Le tour est fait,
Car la dame a pris le billet!
Et voilà! et voilà! ah! ah!
On voit comment ça tournera!
(avec les soldats)
On voit comment ça tournera!
Ah! ah! ah! ah!
On voit comment ça tournera! etc.

he'll pop out of some corner.
(At this moment a young man comes quickly on to the square)
Ha! ha! ha!
There he is.

MORALÈS: Ah, there he is! Yes, there he is!
(With the soldiers)
Let's see how this'll turn out.
(The second verse follows and must be faithfully adapted to the scene mimed by the three characters. The young man approaches the old gentleman and the young lady, bows, and exchanges a few words in a low voice, etc.)

MORALÈS: (imitating the young man's eager greeting) What luck, finding you here!
(assuming the old husband's sour-tempered look)
Your servant!
(putting on the young man's manner again)
He bows, he turns on the charm.
(then the old husband's expression)
The old husband pulls a face;
(imitating the lady's simpering smiles)
but the lady is greeting the lover in a very encouraging manner.
(At this moment the young man draws from his pocket a note which he shows to the lady. The husband, the wife and the young blade all three slowly take a little stroll on the square, the young man endeavouring to slip his love-letter to the lady)

MORALÈS: They walk a few steps together;
our lovebird, raising his arm,
draws the husband's attention to something,
(The young man, with one hand, points out something in the sky to the old gentleman, and with the other passes his note to the lady)
and the husband, still morose, looks up into the air . . . The trick has worked,
for the lady has taken the note.
And that's that! that's that! Ha! Ha!
We see how that'll turn out!
(With the soldiers)
We see how that'll turn out!
Ha! ha! ha! ha!
We see how that'll turn out! etc.

(A military march of bugles and fifes is heard in the distance. The relief guard is arriving. The old gentleman and the young man exchange a cordial handshake, and the young man bows respectfully to the lady. An officer comes out of the guard-house. Soldiers take their muskets and form up in front of the guard-house. The passers-by gather in a group to watch the parade. The military march comes nearer and nearer. At last the relief guard emerges

*and crosses the bridge. First, two bugles and two fifes. Then a band of street urchins. Behind the children, Lieutenant Zuniga and Corporal Don José, then the troopers)*

CHOEUR DES GAMINS: Avec la garde montante,
Nous arrivons, nous voilà.
Sonne, tompette éclatante!
Taratata, taratata!
Nous marchons la tête haute
Comme de petits soldats,
Marquant sans faire de faute,
Une, deux, marquant le pas.
Les épaules en arrière
Et la poitrine en dehors,
Les bras de cette manière
Tombant tout le long du corps.
Avec la garde montante, *etc.*

CHORUS OF STREET BOYS: Right beside the relief guard, here we come, here we are!
Blow out, loud trumpet!
Taratata, taratata!
We march with head erect like little soldiers, keeping time with no mistakes— one two,—keeping step.
Shoulders back and chest well out, arms this way straight down beside the body.
Right beside the relief guard, *etc.*
*(The relief guard halts facing the guard going off duty. The officers salute with their swords and begin to talk in low voices. The sentries are changed)*

MORALÈS: *(à Don José)* Il y a une jolie fille qui est venue to demander. Elle a dit qu'elle reviendrait...

JOSÉ: Une jolie fille?

MORALÈS: Qui, et gentiment habillée, une jupe bleue, des nattes tombant sur les épaules....

JOSÉ: C'est Micaëla. Ce ne peut être que Micaëla.

MORALÈS: Elle n'a pas dit son nom.

REPRISE DU CHOEUR DES GAMINS: Et la garde descendante
Rentre chez elle et s'en va.
Sonne, trompette éclatante,
Taratata, taratata!
Nous marchons la tête haute
Comme de petits soldats, *etc.*

MORALÈS: *(to Don José)* There's a pretty girl been asking for you. She said she'd come back....

JOSÉ: A pretty girl?

MORALÈS: Yes, and nicely dressed, a blue skirt, plaits down over her shoulders....

JOSÉ: It's Micaëla. It can only be Micaëla.

MORALÈS: She didn't give her name.

CHORUS OF STREET BOYS: *(reprise)* And the old guard goes off home to barracks.
Blow out, loud trumpet!
Taratata, taratata!
We march with head erect like little soldiers, *etc.*
*(Soldiers, urchins and idlers go off at the back; the sound of chorus, fifes and bugles grows fainter. The commander of the new guard, during this time, inspects his men silently. When the chorus of street boys can no longer be heard, the soldiers are dismissed and enter the guard-house. Don José and Zuniga remain)*

ZUNIGA: Dites-moi, brigadier? Qu'est-ce que c'est que ce grand bâtiment?

JOSÉ: C'est la manufacture de tabacs...

ZUNIGA: Ce sont des femmes qui travaillent là?

JOSÉ: Oui, mon lieutenant. Elles n'y sont pas maintenant: tout à l'heure, après leur diner, elles vont revenir. Il y aura du monde pour les voir passer.

ZUNIGA: Il y en a de jeunes?

JOSÉ: Mais oui, mon lieutenant.

ZUNIGA: Et de jolies?

JOSÉ: *(en riant)* Je le suppose... je n'ai les ai jamais beaucoup regardées...

ZUNIGA: Tell me, corporal, what's that great building?

JOSÉ: It's the tobacco factory...

ZUNIGA: It's women who work there?...

JOSÉ: Yes, sir. They're not there now: presently, after their dinner, they'll come back. Everyone'll be here to see them go by.

ZUNIGA: There are young ones?

JOSÉ: Why yes, sir.

ZUNIGA: And pretty ones?

JOSÉ: *(laughing)* I suppose so... I've never taken much notice of them...

ZUNIGA: Allons donc!...

JOSÉ: ...ces Andalouses me font peur, toujours à railler... jamais un mot de raison...

ZUNIGA: Et puis nous avons un faible pour les jupes bleues et pour les nattes tombant sur les épaules...

ZUNIGA: *(riant)* Ah! mon lieutenant a entendu ce que disait Moralès?

ZUNIGA: Oui...

JOSÉ: Je ne le nierai pas... la jupe bleu, les nattes, c'est le costume de la Navarre... ça me rappelle le pays...

ZUNIGA: Vous êtes Navarrais?

JOSÉ: Et vieux chrétien. Malheureusement, j'aimais trop jouer à la paume... Un jour, un gars me chercha querelle; j'eus encore l'avantage, mais cela m'obligea de quitter le pays. je me fis soldat! Ma mère me suivit et vint s'établir à dix lieues de Séville... avec la petite Micaëla...

ZUNIGA: Et quel âge a-t-elle, la petite Micaëla?

JOSÉ: Dix-sept ans.

ZUNIGA: Il fallait dire cela tout de suite... Je comprends maintenant pourquoi vous ne pouvez pas me dire si les ouvrières sont jolies ou laides.

JOSÉ: Voici la cloche qui sonne, mon lieutenant, vous allez pouvoir juger pour vous-même.... Quant à moi, je vais faire une chaine pour attacher mon épinglette.

ZUNIGA: Get away with you!...

JOSÉ: ...These Andalusian girls frighten me...always making fun of you...never a word of sense...

ZUNIGA: And then we've got a weakness for blue skirts and for pigtails down over the shoulders...

JOSÉ: *(laughing)* Ah, sir, so you heard what Moralès said?

ZUNIGA: Yes...

JOSÉ: I won't deny it...blue skirt, pigtails, it's the dress of Navarra... that reminds me of home...

ZUNIGA: You're from Navarra?

JOSÉ: And from an old Christian family. Unfortunately I was too fond of playing paume... one day a lad picked a quarrel with me; I came off best again, but this forced me to leave the country. I went for a soldier! My mother followed me and came to settle ten leagues from Seville... with the little Micaëla.

ZUNIGA: And how old is the little Micaëla?

JOSÉ: Seventeen.

ZUNIGA: You should have said that at once.... Now I understand why you can't tell me whether the factory-girls are pretty or ugly.
*(The factory bell is heard)*

JOSÉ: There's the bell ringing, sir, you'll be able to judge for yourself.... As for me, I'm going to make a chain for fixing my priming-pin.

*(The square fills up with young men who have come to intercept the cigarette girls. The soldiers come out of the guard-house. Don José sits down on a seat, and remains quite indifferent to all the comings and goings, working on a little chain for his priming-pin)*

JEUNES GENS: La cloche a sonné; nous, des ouvrières nous venons ici guetter le retour; et nous vous suivrons, brunes cigarières, en vous murmurant des propos d'amour!

LES SOLDATS: Voyez-les! Regards impudents, mines coquettes, fumant toutes du bout des dents la cigarette.

LES CIGARIÈRES: Dans l'air, nous suivons des yeux la fumée, la fumée, qui vers les cieux monte, monte parfumée.
Cela monte gentiment

YOUNG MEN: The bell has rung: we've come here to catch the factory girls on their way back; and we'll follow you, dark-haired cigarette girls, murmuring words of love to you!
*(At this point the girls appear, smoking cigarettes)*

SOLDIERS: Look at them! Impudent glances, saucy airs, all of them puffing away at a cigarette.

CIGARETTE GIRLS: We gaze after the smoke as it rises in the air, sweet-smelling, towards the skies.
Gracefully it mounts

à la tête, à la tête,
toute doucement
cela vous met l'âme en fête!
Le doux parler des amants,
c'est fumée!
Leurs transports et leurs serments,
c'est fumée!
Dans l'air, nous suivons des yeux
la fumée, *etc.*

**LES SOLDATS:** Mais nous ne voyons pas la Carmencita!

**LES CIGARIÈRES ET LES JEUNES GENS:** La voilà!
La voilà
Voilà la Carmencita!

**LES JEUNES GENS:** Carmen! sur tes pas, nous nous pressons tous!
Carmen! sois gentille, au moins réponds-nous
et dis-nous quel jour tu nous aimeras!

**CARMEN:** (*regardent Don José*)
Quand je vous aimerai?
Ma foi, je ne sais pas.
Peut-être jamais, peut-être demain;
mais pas aujourd'hui, c'est certain.

**CARMEN:** L'amour est un oiseau rebelle
que nul ne peut apprivoiser,
et c'est bien en vain qu'on l'appelle,
s'il lui convient de refuser.
Rien n'y fait, menace ou prière,
l'un parle bien, l'autre se tait;
et c'est l'autre que je préfère:
il n'a rien dit, mais il me plaît.
L'amour! *etc.*

**CHOEUR:** L'amour est un oiseau rebelle, *etc.*

**CARMEN:** L'amour est enfant de bohème,
il n'a jamais connu de loi;
Si tu ne m'aimes pas, je t'aime;
si je t'aime, prends garde à toi! *etc.*

**CHOEUR:** Prends garde à toi! *etc.*
L'amour est enfant de bohème, *etc.*

**CARMEN:** L'oiseau que tu croyais surprendre
battit de l'aile et s'envola—
l'amour est loin, tu peux l'attendre;
tu ne l'attends plus, il est là!
Tout autour de toi vite, vite,
il vient, s'en va, puis il revient—
tu crois le tenir, il t'évite,
tu crois l'éviter, il te tient.
L'amour! *etc.*

to your head,
so gently
it exhilarates you!
Lovers' soft talk—
it's smoke!
Their raptures and promises—
smoke!
We gaze after the smoke
as it rises, *etc.*

**SOLDIERS:** But we don't see La Carmencita!
(*Carmen enters*)

**CIGARETTE GIRLS AND YOUNG MEN:** There she is!
There she is!
There's La Carmencita!
(*She has a bunch of cassia flowers at her bodice, and a cassia flower in the corner of her mouth. The young men come in with Carmen. They follow her, surround her, talk to her. She flirts with them in an offhand fashion. Don José looks up. He glances at Carmen and then quietly resumes his work*)

**YOUNG MEN:** Carmen, we all throng after you!
Carmen, be kind, answer us at least, and tell us when you're going to love us!

**CARMEN:** (*with a glance at Don José*) When I'm going to love you?
My word, I don't know.
Perhaps never, perhaps tomorrow;
but not today, that's certain.

**CARMEN:** Love is a rebellious bird that no one can tame.
and it's quite useless to call him if it suits him to refuse.
Nothing moves him, neither threat nor plea,
one man speaks freely, the other keeps mum;
and it's the other one I prefer:
he's said nothing, but I like him.
Love! *etc.*

**CHORUS:** Love is a rebellious bird, *etc.*

**CARMEN:** Love is a gypsy child,
he has never heard of law.
If you don't love me, I love you;
if I love you, look out for yourself! *etc.*

**CHORUS:** Look out for yourself! *etc.*
Love is a gypsy child, *etc.*

**CARMEN:** The bird you thought to catch unawares
beat its wings and away it flew—
love's far away, and you can wait for it;
you wait for it no longer—and there it is.
All around you, quickly, quickly,
it comes, it goes, then it returns—
you think you can hold it, it evades you.
you think to evade it, it holds you fast.
Love! *etc.*

**CHOEUR:** Tout autour de toi, *etc.*

**CARMEN:** L'amour est enfant de bohème,
il n'a jamais connu de loi;
Si tu ne m'aimes pas, je t'aime;
si je t'aime, prends garde à toi!
Si tu ne m'aimes pas, je t'aime, *etc.*

**CHOEUR:** Prends garde à toi! *etc.*
L'amour est enfant de bohème, *etc.*

**LES JEUNES GENS:** Carmen! sur tes pas, nous nous pressons tous!
Carmen! sois gentille, au moins réponds-nous!

**CARMEN:** Qu'est-ce que tu fais là?...

**JOSÉ:** Je fais une chaine pour attacher mon épinglette.

**CARMEN:** Ton épinglette, vraiment! ton épinglette... épinglier de mon âme...

**LES CIGARIERÈS:** L'amour est enfant de bohème, *etc.*

**JOSÉ:** Qu'est-ce cela veut dire, ces façons-là?... Quelle effronterie!
Avec quelle adresses elle me l'a lancée, cette fleur...
S'il y a des sorcières, cette fille-là en est une.

**MICAËLA:** Monsieur le brigadier?

**JOSÉ:** Qu'est-ce que c'est?... Micaëla!... Tu viens de là-bas?...

**MICAËLA:** C'est votre mère qui m'envoie...

**JOSÉ:** Parle-moi de ma mère!

**MICAËLA:** J'apporte de sa part, fidèle messagère,
cette lettre...

**JOSÉ:** Une lettre! *etc.*

**MICAËLA:** Et puis un peu d'argent pour ajouter à votre traitement.
Et puis...

**JOSÉ:** Et puis?

**CHORUS:** All around you, *etc.*

**CARMEN:** Love is a gypsy child,
he has never heard of law.
If you don't love me, I love you;
if I love you, look out for yourself!
If you don't love me, I love you, *etc.*

**CHORUS:** Look out for yourself! *etc.*
Love is a gypsy child, *etc.*

**YOUNG MEN:** Carmen, we all throng after you!
Carmen, be kind, answer us at least!
(*A pause. The young men surround Carmen, who looks at them one by one. Then she breaks through the circle and goes straight to Don José, who is still busied with his little chain.*)

**CARMEN:** What are you up to there?...

**JOSÉ:** I'm making a chain to fix my priming-pin.

**CARMEN:** Your priming-pin, really! your priming-pin....
Pin-maker of my heart...
(*Carmen throws the cassia flower at Don José. He jumps up. The flower has fallen at his feet. Outburst of general laughter*)

**CIGARETTE GIRLS:** (*surrounding Don José*) Love is a gypsy child, *etc.*
(*The factory bell rings again. Carmen and the other cigarette girls run into the factory. Exeunt young men, etc. The soldiers go into the guard-house, followed by the Lieutenant, who had been chatting to two or three of the girls. Don José is left alone*).

**JOSÉ:** What's all that mean?—all those carryings-on?...
What shamelessness!
(*He looks at the cassia flower on the ground at his feet. He picks it up*)
How cleverly she threw it at me, this flower...
(*He smells the flower*)
If there are witches, *that* girl is one.
(*Enter Micaëla*)

**MICAËLA:** Corporal?

**JOSÉ:** (*hurriedly concealing the cassia flower*) What's this?... Micaëla!... You've come from back there?...

**MICAËLA:** It's your mother who sends me...

**JOSÉ:** Tell me about my mother!

**MICAËLA:** A faithful messenger, I bring from her this letter...

**JOSÉ:** A letter! *etc.*

**MICAËLA:** And then a little money to add to your pay.
And then...

**JOSÉ:** And then?

MICAËLA: Et puis . . . vraiment je n'ose,
et puis encore une autre chose
qui vaut mieux que l'argent
et qui pour un bon fils
aura sans doute plus de prix.

JOSÉ: Cette autre chose, quelle est-elle?
Parle donc.

MICAËLA: Oui, je parlerai;
ce que l'on m'a donné
je vous le donnerai.
Votre mère avec moi sortait de la chapelle,
et c'est alors qu'en m'embrassant:
"Tu vas", m'a-t-elle dit, "t'en aller à la ville;
la route n'est pas longue, une fois à Séville,
tu chercheras mon fils, mon José, mon enfant.
Et tu lui diras que sa mère
songe nuit et jour à l'absent,
qu'elle regrette et qu'elle espère,
qu'elle pardonne et qu'elle attend.
Tout cela, n'est-ce pas, mignonne,
de ma part tu le lui diras;
et ce baiser que je te donne
de ma part tu le lui rendras."

JOSÉ: (très ému) Un baiser de ma mère!

MICAËLA: Un baiser pour son fils!
José, je vous le rends,
comme je l'ai promis.

JOSÉ: Ma mère, je la vois!
Oui, je revois mon village!
O souvenirs d'autrefois,
doux souvenirs du pays!
Doux souvenirs du pays!
O souvenirs chéris!
Vous remplissez mon coeur
de force et de courage!
O souvenirs chéris!
Ma mère, je la vois,
je revois mon village!

MICAËLA: Sa mère, il la revoit!
Il revoit sa village!
O souvenirs d'autrefois!
Souvenirs du pays!
Vous remplissez son coeur
de force et de courage!
O souvenirs chéris!
Sa mère, il la revoit,
il revoit son village!

JOSÉ: Qui sait de quel démon
j'allais être la proie!
Même de loin, ma mère me défend,
Et ce baiser qu'elle m'envoie
écarte le péril et sauve son enfant!

MICAËLA: Quel démon? quel péril?
Je ne comprends pas bien.
Que veut dire cela?

MICAËLA: And then . . . really, I dare not,
and then yet another thing
worth more than money
and which a good son
will surely value higher.

JOSÉ: This other thing, what is it?
Tell me, then.

MICAËLA: Yes, I'll tell you;
what was given to me
I'll give to you.
Your mother and I were coming out of the chapel,
and then, as she kissed me,
"You will go to town," she said.
"it's not far; once in Seville
you'll seek out my son, my José, my boy.
And you'll tell him that his mother
thinks night and day of her absent one,
that she grieves and hopes,
that she forgives and waits.
All that, little one,
you'll tell him from me, won't you;
and this kiss that I'm giving you
you'll give him from me.

JOSÉ: (very moved) A kiss from my mother!

MICAËLA: A kiss for her son!
José, I give it to you
as I promised.
(Micaëla raises herself on tiptoe and gives Don José a frank, motherly kiss. José, very moved, lets her. He gazes into her eyes. There is a moment of silence.)

JOSÉ: I see my mother!
Yes, I see my village again!
O memories of bygone days,
sweet memories of home!
Sweet memories of home!
O precious memories!
You put back strength
and courage into my heart!
O precious memories!
I see my mother,
I see my village again!

MICAËLA: He sees his mother again!
He sees his village again!
O memories of bygone days!
Memories of home!
You put back strength
and courage into his heart!
O precious memories!
He sees his mother again,
he sees his village again!

JOSÉ: (his eyes fixed on the factory) Who knows into what demon's clutches
I was about to fall!
Even from afar my mother protects me
and this kiss she sent me
wards off the peril and saves her son!

MICAËLA: What demon? What peril?
I don't quite understand.
What do you mean by that?

JOSÉ: Rien! Rien!
Parlons de toi, la messagère.
Tu vas retourner au pays?

MICAËLA: Oui, ce soir même:
demain je verrai votre mère.

JOSÉ: Tu la verras!
Et vien, tu lui diras:
que son fils l'aime et la vénère
et qu'il se repent aujourd'hui;
il veut que là-bas sa mère
soit contente de lui!
Tout cela, n'est-ce pas, mignonne,
de ma part, tu le lui diras,
et ce baiser que je te donne,
de ma part tu le lui rendras.

MICAËLA: Oui, je vous le promets,
de la part de son fils
José je le rendrai comme je l'ai promis.

JOSÉ: Ma mère, je la vois! etc.

MICAËLA: Sa mère, il la revoit, etc.

JOSÉ: Attends un peu maintenant. . . Je vais lire sa lettre . . .

MICAËLA: Je viens de me rappeler que votre mère m'a chargée de quelques petits achats . . .

JOSÉ: Attends un peu . . .

MICAËLA: Non, non . . . je reviendrai, j'aime mieux cela . . . je reviendrai, je reviendrai . . .

JOSÉ: "Il n'y en a pas qui t'aime davantage . . . et si tu voulais. . . ."
Oui, ma mère, oui, j'épouserai Micaëla.
Quant à cette bohémienne, avec ses fleurs qui ensorcellent . . .

ZUNIGA: Eh bien! eh bien! qu'est-ce qui arrive? . . .

PREMIER GROUPE DE FEMMES: Au secours! Au secours! N'entendez-vous pas?

DEUXIÈME GROUPE DE FEMMES: Au secours! Au secours! Messieurs les soldats!

PREMIER GROUPE DE FEMMES: C'est la Carmencita!

DEUXIÈME GROUPE DE FEMMES: Non, non, ce n'est pas elle! Pas du tout!

PREMIER GROUPE DE FEMMES: C'est elle! Si fait, si fait, c'est elle! Elle a porté les premiers coups!

DEUXIÈME GROUPE DE FEMMES: Ne les écoutez pas!

TOUTES LES FEMMES: Ecoutez-nous, monsieur! Ecoutez-nous! etc.

JOSÉ: Nothing! Nothing!
Let's talk about you, the messenger.
You're going back home?

MICAËLA: Yes, this very evening:
tomorrow I shall see your mother.

JOSÉ: You'll be seeing her!
Well then, you'll tell her—
that her son loves and reveres her
and that today he is repentant;
he wants his mother back there
to be pleased with him!
All this, my sweet,
you'll tell her from me, won't you,
and this kiss that I give you
you'll give her from me.
(He kisses her)

MICAËLA: Yes, I promise you;
from her son
José I shall give it as I have promised.

JOSÉ: I see my mother! etc.

MICAËLA: He sees his mother again! etc.

JOSÉ: Wait a bit now. . . . I'm going to read her letter . . .

MICAËLA: I've just remembered that your mother asked me to make a few small purchases for her . . .

JOSÉ: Wait a little while . . .

MICAËLA: No, no . . . I'll come back, I'd rather do that . . . I'll come back, I'll come back . . .
(She goes out)

JOSÉ: (reading) "There's not one of them who loves you more . . . and if you wanted to . . ." Yes, mother yes, I'll marry Micaëla.
As for that gypsy with her flowers that bewitch . . .
(Just as he is about to tear the flower from his tunic, an uproar begins in the factory. Zuniga comes on stage, followed by soldiers)

ZUNIGA: Well now, well, what's happening? . . .

FIRST GROUP OF GIRLS: Help! Help!
Can't you hear?

SECOND GROUP OF GIRLS: Help! Help!
You soldiers!

FIRST GROUP OF GIRLS: It's Carmencita!

SECOND GROUP OF GIRLS: No, no, it's not her!
Not a bit of it!

FIRST GROUP OF GIRLS: It's her!
It is, it is! It's her!
She started the fighting!

SECOND GROUP OF GIRLS: Don't listen to them!

ALL THE GIRLS: (surrounding Zuniga) Listen to us, sir!
Listen to us! etc.

**DEUXIÈME GROUPE DE FEMMES:** La Manuelita disait, et répétait à voix haute qu'elle achèterait sans faute un âne que lui plaisait.

**PREMIER GROUPE DE FEMMES:** Alors la Carmencita, railleuse à son ordinaire, dit: "Un âne, pourquoi faire? Un balai te suffira."

**DEUXIÈME GROUPE DE FEMMES:** Manuelita riposta et dit à sa camarade: "Pour certaine promenade, mon âne te servira!—"

**PREMIER GROUPE DE FEMMES:** "—Et ce jour-là tu pourras à bon droit faire la fière deux laquais suivront derrière, t'émouchant à tour de bras!"

**TOUTES LES FEMMES:** Là-dessus, toutes les deux se sont prises aux cheveux!

**ZUNIGA:** Au diable tout ce bavardage! Prenez, Josè, deux hommes avec vous et voyez là-dedans qui cause ce tapage.

**PREMIER GROUPE DE FEMMES:** C'est la Carmencita! *etc.*

**DEUXIÈME GROUPE DE FEMMES:** Non, non, ce n'est pas elle! *etc.*

**ZUNIGA:** Holà! Eloignez-moi toutes ces femmes-là!

**TOUTES LES FEMMES:** Monsieur! ne les écoutez pas! *etc.*

**ZUNIGA:** Voyons, brigadier . . . Maintenant que nous avons un peu de silence . . . qu'est-ce que vous avez trouvé là-dedans?

**JOSÉ:** J'ai trouvé trois cents femmes, hurlant, gesticulant. Il y en avait une qui avait sur la figure un X qu'on venait de lui marquer en deux coups de couteau . . . en face de la blessée . . .

**ZUNIGA:** Eh bien?

**JOSÉ:** J'ai vu mademoiselle . . .

**ZUNIGA:** Mademoiselle Carmencita?

**JOSÉ:** Oui, mon lieutenant.

**SECOND GROUP OF GIRLS:** (*pulling the officer to their side*) Manuelita said, and kept saying at the top of her voice, that she'd make sure she bought a donkey that pleased her.

**FIRST GROUP OF GIRLS:** Then Carmencita, in her usual mocking way, said: "A donkey? What for? A broom will do for you."

**SECOND GROUP OF GIRLS:** Manuelita retorted, and said to her friend: "For a certain ride my donkey will be useful to you!—"

**FIRST GROUP OF GIRLS:** "—And on that day you'll be able to play the lady in your own right; two lackeys will follow behind keeping flies off as best they can!"

**ALL THE GIRLS:** Thereupon they both started to pull each other's hair out!

**ZUNIGA:** To the devil with all this chatter! José, take two men in with you and see who's causing all this commotion. (*Don José takes two men with him. The soldiers go into the factory. All this while the girls are pushing and arguing among themselves*)

**FIRST GROUP OF GIRLS:** It's Carmencita! *etc.*

**SECOND GROUP OF GIRLS:** No, no! It's not her! *etc.*

**ZUNIGA:** Stop! Rid me of all these women!

**ALL THE GIRLS:** Sir, don't listen to them! *etc.* (*The soldiers keep the girls back. Carmen appears at the factory door, led by Don José and followed by two dragoons*) (*The factory-girls go out in a disorderly rush*)

**ZUNIGA:** Let's see, corporal . . . now that we've got a moment's silence . . . what did you find inside there?

**JOSÉ:** I found three hundred women, yelling and waving their arms about. There was one who had an X on her face that someone had just carved on her with two knife-slashes. . . . Facing the wounded girl . . . (*On a glance from Carmen he stops*)

**ZUNIGA:** Well?

**JOSÉ:** I saw the señorita . . .

**ZUNIGA:** The señorita Carmencita?

**JOSÉ:** Yes, sir.

**ZUNIGA:** Et que'est-ce qu'elle disait, mademoiselle Carmencita?

**JOSÉ:** Elle ne disait rien, elle serrait les dents et roulait des yeux comme un caméléon.

**JOSÉ:** J'ai prié mademoiselle de me suivre.

**ZUNIGA:** (*à Carmen*) Eh bien! . . . vous avez entendu? . . . Avez-vous quelque chose à répondre? . . . parlez, j'attends . . .

**CARMEN:** Tra la la la, *etc.* Coupe-moi, brûle-moi, je ne te dirai rien. Tra la la la, *etc.* Je brave tout, le feu, le fer et le ciel même.

**ZUNIGA:** Ce ne sont pas des chansons que je te demande, c'est une réponse.

**CARMEN:** Tra la la la, *etc.* Mon secret je le garde et je la garde bien! Tra la la la, *etc.* J'en aime un autre et meurs en disant que je l'aime.

**ZUNIGA:** Ah! ah! nous le prenons sur ce ton-là . . . (*à José*) Ce qui est sûr, n'est-ce pas, c'est qu'il y eu des coups de couteau, et que c-est elle qui les a donnés . . .

**ZUNIGA:** Eh! vous avez la main leste décidément. (*Aux soldats*) Trouvez-moi une corde.

**JOSÉ:** Voilà, mon lieutenant.

**ZUNIGA:** Prenez et attachez-moi ces deux jolies mains. C'est dommage vraiment, car elle est gentilla . . . si gentille que vous soyez, vous n'en irez pas moins faire un tour à la prison. Vous pourrez y chanter vos chansons de Bohémienne. Le porte-clefs vous dira ce qu'il en pense.

**ZUNIGA:** And what was she saying, the señorita Carmencita?

**JOSÉ:** She wasn't saying anything, she was gritting her teeth and rolling her eyes like a chameleon. (*The lieutenant looks at Carmen; she, after a glance at Don José and a slight shrug of her shoulders, has become impassive again*)

**JOSÉ:** I asked the señorita to come with me . . . (*Carmen turns sharply and looks at José once more*)

**ZUNIGA:** (*to Carmen*) Well . . . you heard? Have you anything to answer? . . . Speak, I'm waiting . . . (*Instead of replying, Carmen starts to sing*)

**CARMEN:** Tra la la la, *etc.* Cut me, burn me, I shall tell you nothing. Tra, la la la, *etc.* I defy everything—fire, the sword and heaven itself.

**ZUNIGA:** It's not songs! I'm asking you for, it's a reply.

**CARMEN:** Tra la la la, *etc.* I'm keeping my secret and keeping it close! Tra la la la, *etc.* I love another and I die in saying that I love him.

**ZUNIGA:** Aha! So that's the attitude we're taking . . . (*to José*) What's certain, isn't it, is that there had been a knife attack and that it's she who made it . . . (*At this moment five or six women on the right succeed in breaking the line of sentries and rush on to the stage shouting: Yes, yes, it's her! One of these women finds herself close by Carmen, who raises her hand and attempts to throw herself upon the woman. Don José stops Carmen. The soldiers haul the woman off and this time force them back completely off the stage. A few sentinels remain in sight, guarding the approaches to the square*)

**ZUNIGA:** Eh! decidedly you have a ready hand. (*to the soldiers*) Find me a cord. (*There is a moment of silence during which Carmen begins humming again in the most impertinent fashion as she watches the officer*)

**JOSÉ:** Here it is, sir.

**ZUNIGA:** Take this and tie those two pretty hands together for me. (*Without offering the least resistance, Carmen smilingly holds out her two hands to Don José*) It's a shame, really, for she's pretty . . . But pretty as you may be, you're nonetheless going to take a stroll to the prison. You can sing your gypsy

Je vais écrire l'ordre. (*à Don José*)
C'est vous qui la conduirez . . .

CARMEN: Où me conduirez-vous?

JOSÉ: A la prison, ma pauvre enfant
. . .

CARMEN: Hélas! que deviendrai-
je? Seigneur officier, ayez pitié de
moi . . . Vous êtes si gentil, Laisse-
moi m'échapper, je te donnerai un
morceau de la *bar lachi*, une petite
pierre qui te fera aimer de tours les
femmes.

JOSÉ: Nous ne sommes pas ici pour
dire des balivernes . . .
Il faut aller à la prison. C'est la con-
signe, et il n'y a pas de remède.

CARMEN: Camarade, mon ami, ne
ferez-vous rien pour une payse?

JOSÉ: Vous êtes Navarraise, vous?

CARMEN: Sans doute.

JOSÉ: Allons donc . . . il n'y a pas un
mot de vrai . . . vos yeux seuls, votre
bouche, votre teint . . . Tout vous
dit
Bohémienne . . .

CARMEN: Bohémienne, tu crois?

JOSÉ: J'en suis sûr.

CARMEN: Au fait, je suis bien
bonne de me donner la peine de
mentir . . . Oui, je suis Bohemienne,
mais tu n'en feras pas moins ce que
je te demande . . . Tu le feras parce
que tu m'aimes . . .

JOSÉ: Moi!

CARMEN: Eh! Oui, tu m'aimes.
Cette fleur que tu as gardée—oh!
tu peux la jeter maintenant . . . cela
n'y fera rien. La charme a opéré . . .

JOSÉ: (*avec colère*) Ne me parle
plus, tu entends, je te défends de
me parler.

CARMEN: C'est très bien, siegneur
officier, c'est très bien. Vous
me défendez de parier, je ne parlerai plus . . .

CARMEN: Près des remparts de
Séville,
chez mon ami Lillas Pastia,
j'irai danser le séguedille,
et boire du manzanilla.
J'irai chez mon ami Lillas Pastia!
Oui, mais toute seule on s'ennuie,
et les vrais plasirs sont à deux.
Donc, pour me tenir compagnie.
j'emmènerai mon amoureux!
Mon amoureux . . . il est au diable:

songs there. The turnkey'll tell you
what he thinks of them.
(*Carmen's hands are bound and
she is made to sit down on a stool
in front of the guard-house. She
remains motionless, her eyes cast
down*)
I'm going to write out the order. (*to
Don José*) It's you who will take
her . . .
(*He goes out*)

CARMEN: Where are you taking
me?

JOSÉ: To the jail, my poor child . . .

CARMEN: Alas, what will become
of me? Noble officer, take pity on
me . . . You are so nice. Let me escape and I'll give you a piece of the
*bar lachi,* a little stone which will
make you loved by all women.

JOSÉ: (*moving away*) We're not
here to talk twaddle . . .
We must go to the jail.
Those are my instructions, and
there's no help for it.

CARMEN: Comrade of my heart,
won't you do anything for a
fellow-countrywoman?

JOSÉ: You're from Navarra, *you?*

CARMEN: Certainly.

JOSÉ: Come off it! . . . There's not a
word of truth in it . . . your
eyes alone, your mouth, your coloring . . . everything
proclaims you a gypsy . . .

CARMEN: A gypsy, you think?

JOSÉ: I'm sure of it.

CARMEN: In fact, I am very simple
to go to the trouble of lying . . .
Yes, I'm a gypsy, but you'll do what
I want nonetheless
. . . You'll do it because you love me
. . .

JOSÉ: I!

CARMEN: Ah, yes, you love me.
That flower you kept—oh, you can
throw it away now . . . that makes no
difference. The charm has worked .
. .

JOSÉ: (*angrily*) Don't talk to me
any more, d'you hear, I forbid you
to talk to me.

CARMEN: That's all right, officer
sir, that's all right. You forbid me to
talk, I'll not talk any more . . .
(*She looks at Don José who backs
away*)

CARMEN: By the ramparts of Seville,
at my friend Lillas Pastia's place,
I'm going to dance the seguidilla
and drink manzanilla.
I'm going to my friend Lillas Pastia's!
Yes, but all alone one gets bored,
and real pleasures are for two.
So, to keep me company,
I shall take my lover!

je l'ai mis à la porte hier.
Mon pauvre coeur trés consolable,
mon coeur est libre comme l'air.
J'ai des galants à la douzaine,
mais ils ne sont pas à mon gré.
Voici la fin de la semaine,
qui veut m'aimer? je l'aimerai.
Qui veut mon âme? elle est à pren-
dre!
Vous arrivez au bon moment!
Je n'ai guère le temps d'attendre,
car avec mon nouvel amant . . .
Près des remparts de Séville, *etc.*

JOSÉ: Tais-toi! je t'avais dit de ne
pas me parler!

CARMEN: Je ne te parle pas,
je chante pour moi-même;
et je pense . . . il n'est pas défendu
de penser!
Je pense à certain officier,
qui m'aime, et qu'à mon tour,
oui, à mon tour je pourrais bien
aimer!

JOSÉ: Carmen!

CARMEN: Mon officier n'est pas un
capitaine,
pas même un lieutenant,
il n'est que brigadier;
mais c'est assez pour une
bohémienne,
et je daigne m'en contenter!

JOSÉ: Carmen, je suis comme un
homme ivre,
si je cède, si je me livre.
ta promesse, tu la tiendras,
ah! si je t'aime, Carmen, tu
m'aimeras?

CARMEN: Oui . . .
Nous danserons la séguedille
en buvant du manzanilla.

JOSÉ: Chez Lillas Pastia . . .
Tu le promets!
Carmen . . .
Tu le promets!

CARMEN: Ah! Près des remparts de
Séville, *etc.*

ZUNIGA: (*à José*) Voici l'ordre;
partez.
Et faites bonne garde.

CARMEN: (*bas à José*) En chemin
je te pousserai,
je te pousserai aussi fort que je le
pourrais . . .
Laissez-toi renverser . . .
le reste me regarde.

CARMEN: L'amour est enfant de
bohème,
il n'a jamais connu de loi.
Si tu ne m'aimes pas, je t'aime;
si je t'aime, prends garde à toi!

My lover . . . he's gone to the devil:
I showed him the door yesterday.
My poor heart, so consolable—
my heart is as free as air.
I have suitors by the dozen,
but they are not to my liking.
Here we are at week end;
Who wants to love me! I'll love
him.
Who wants my heart? It's for the tak-
ing!
You've come at the right moment!
I have hardly time to wait,
for with my new lover . . .
By the ramparts of Seville, *etc.*

JOSÉ: Stop! I told you not to talk to
me!

CARMEN: I'm not talking to you,
I'm singing to myself;
and I'm thinking . . . it's not forbidden to think!
I'm thinking about a certain officer
who loves me,
and whom in my turn I might really
love!

JOSÉ: Carmen!

CARMEN: My officer's not a captain,
not even a lieutenant,
he's only a corporal;
but that's enough for a gypsy girl
and I'll deign to content myself
with him!

JOSÉ: (*untying Carmen's hands*)
Carmen, I'm like a drunken man,
if I yield, if I give in.
you'll keep your promise?
Ah! if I love you, Carmen, you'll
love me?

CARMEN: Yes . . .
We'll dance the seguidilla
while we drink manzanilla.

JOSÉ: at Lillas Pastia's . . .
You promise!
Carmen . . .
You promise!

CARMEN: Ah! By the ramparts of
Seville, *etc.*
(*Her hands behind her, Carmen
goes and re-seats herself on her
stool*)
(*Zuniga returns*)

ZUNIGA: (*to José*) Here's the order; off you go now.
And keep a good lookout.

CARMEN: (*aside to José*) On the
way I shall push you,
I shall push you as hard as I can . . .
Let yourself fall over . . .
The rest is up to me.
(*Carmen places herself between
the two dragoons, with José at her
side. The girls and others return
onstage, kept back by the soldiers.
Carmen crosses the stage, moving
towards the bridge*)

CARMEN: Love is a gypsy child,
he has never heard of law.
If you don't love me, I love you;
if I love you, look out for yourself!
(*Arriving at the foot of the bridge,
Carmen pushes José, who falls. In*

*the confusion Carmen takes to her heels. At the middle of the bridge she stops for a moment, sends her cord flying over the parapet of the bridge, and escapes, while the cigarette girls, with great shouts of laughter, surround Zuniga)*

■ **Entr'acte**

■ **ACTE II**

■ **Entr'acte**

■ **ACT II**

*(The tavern of Lillas Pastia. Carmen, Mercédès, Frasquita, Lieutenant Zuniga, Moralès and another lieutenant are there. A meal has just been finished and the table is in disorder. The officers and gypsy girls are smoking. Two gypsies are strumming guitars in a corner of the room; in the middle, two gypsy girls are singing. Carmen, seated, is watching them dance. An officer is talking to her quietly, but she pays him no attention whatsoever. Suddenly she gets up and begins to sing)*

CARMEN: Les tringles des sistres tintaient
avec un éclat métallique,
et sur cette étrange musique
les zingarellas se levaient.
Tambours de basque allaient leur train,
et les guitares forcenées
grinçaient sous des mains obstinées,
même chanson, même refrain.
Tralalala . . .
Les anneaux de cuivre et d'argent
reluisaient sur les peaux bistrées;
d'orange et de rouge zébrées
les étoffes flottaient au vent.
La danse au chant se mariait.
d'abord indécise et timide,
plus vive ensuite et plus rapide,
cella montait, montait, montait!
Tralalalala . . .
Les bohémiens à tour de bras
de leurs instruments faisaient rage,
et cet éblouissant tapage,
ensorcelait les zingaras!
Sous le rythme de la chanson,
ardentes, folles, enfiévrées,
elles se laissaient, enivrées,
emporter par le tourbillon!
Tralalalala . . .

CARMEN: The sistrums' rods were jingling
with a metallic clatter,
and at this strange music
the *zingarellas* leapt to their feet.
Tambourines were keeping time
and the frenzied guitars
ground away under persistent hands,
the same song, the same refrain.
Tralalala . . .
*(During the refrain the gypsy girls dance, and Mercédès and Frasquita join Carmen in singing: Tralalala)*
Copper and silver rings
glittered on dusky skins;
orange- and red-striped dresses floated in the wind.
Dance and song became one—
at first timid and hesitant,
then livelier and faster
it grew and grew and grew!
Tralalalala . . .
The gypsy boys stormed away
on their instruments with all their might,
and this deafening uproar
bewitched the *zingaras!*
Beneath the rhythm of the song,
passionate, wild, fired with excitement,
they let themselves be carried away,
intoxicated, by the whirlwind!
Tralalalala . . .
*(At the conclusion of the dance Carmen sinks breathless on to a bench. Lillas Pastia begins to circulate among the officers: he looks worried)*

ZUNIGA: Vous avez quelque chose à nous dire, maître Lillas Pastia?

ZUNIGA: You've something to tell us, Master Lillas Pastia?

PASTIA: Mon Dieu, messieurs . . .

MORALÈS: Parle, voyons . . .

PASTIA: Il commence à se faire tard . . . et je suis, plus que personne, obligé d'observer les règlements.

MORALÈS: Cela veut dire que tu nous mets à la porte! . . .

PASTIA: Oh! non, messieurs les officers, oh! non non . . . je vous fais seulement observer que mon auberge devrait étre fermée depuis dix minutes . . .

ZUNIGA: Dieu sait ce qu'il s'y passe dans ton auberge, une fois qu'elle est fermée . . .

PASTIA: Oh! mon lieutenant . . .

ZUNIGA: Enfin, nous avons encore, avant l'appel, le temps d'aller passer une heure au théâtre . . . vous y viendrez avec nous, n'est-ce pas, les belles?

FRASQUITA: Non, messieurs les officiers, non, nous restons ici, nous.

ZUNIGA: Comment, vous ne viendrez pas . . .

MERCÉDÈS: C'est impossible.

MORALÈS: Mercédès!

MERCÉDÈS: Je regrette . . .

MORALÈS: Frasquita! . . .

FRASQUITA: Je suis désolée . . .

ZUNIGA: Mais toi, Carmen, je suis bien sûr que tu ne refuseras pas . . .

CARMEN: C'est ce qui vous trompe, mon lieutenant . . . je refuse.

ZUNIGA: Tu m'en veux?

CARMEN: Pourquoi vous en voudrais-je?

ZUNIGA: Parce qu'il y a un mois, j'ai eu la cruauté de t'envoyer à la prison . . .

CARMEN: A la prison . . . je ne me souviens pas d'être allée à la prison . . .

ZUNIGA: Je sais pardieu bien que tu n'y es pas allée . . . le brigadier qui était chargé de te conduire ayant jugé à propos de te laisser échapper . . . et de se faire dégrader et imprisonner pour cela . . .

CARMEN: Dégrader et emprisonner?

ZUNIGA: Il a passé un mois en prison . . .

CARMEN: Mais il en est sorti?

ZUNIGA: Depuis hier seulement!

PASTIA: My God, gentlemen . . .

MORALÈS: Speak, come now . . .

PASTIA: It's beginning to get late and I, more than anyone, am obliged to observe the regulations.

MORALÈS: That means that you're showing us the door!

PASTIA: Oh no. Officers, oh no! . . . I only remind you that my inn should have been closed ten minutes ago . . .

ZUNIGA: God knows what goes on in your inn after closing time . . .

PASTIA: Oh, sir! . . .

ZUNIGA: Anyway, we still have time before roll-call to pass an hour at the theatre . . . You'll come there with us, eh, girls?
*(Pastia signs to the gypsy girls to refuse)*

FRASQUITA: No, officers, no, we're staying here, we are.

ZUNIGA: What, you're not coming?—

MERCÉDÈS: It's impossible.

MORALÈS: Mercédès!

MERCÉDÈS: Sorry . . .

MORALÈS: Frasquita!

FRASQUITA: Ever so sorry . . .

ZUNIGA: But you, Carmen, I'm quite sure you won't refuse . . .

CARMEN: That's where you're wrong. Lieutenant, I do refuse.
*(While the lieutenant is speaking to Carmen, two other lieutenants try to persuade Frasquita and Mercédès)*

ZUNIGA: You've got a grudge against me?

CARMEN: Why should I have?

ZUNIGA: Because, a month ago, I was cruel enough to send you to prison . . .

CARMEN: *(as though she did not remember)* To prison? . . . I don't recall having gone to prison . . .

ZUNIGA: I know jolly well that you didn't go there . . . the corporal who had the job of taking you having opportunely decided to let you escape . . . and to get himself demoted and imprisoned for that . .

CARMEN: *(serious)* Demoted and imprisoned?

ZUNIGA: He's spent a month in prison . . .

CARMEN: But he's out now?

ZUNIGA: Only since yesterday!

# Act II

**CARMEN:** Tour est bien, puisqu'il en est sorti, tout est bien.

**ZUNIGA:** A la bonne heure, tu te consoles vite...

**CARMEN:** Si vous m'en croyez, vous ferez comme moi, vous voulez nous emmener, nous ne voulons pas vous suivre... vous vous consolerez...

**MORALÈS:** Il faudra bien.

**CHOEUR:** Vivat! vivat le toréro! Vivat! vivat Escamillo! *etc.*

**ZUNIGA:** Qu'est-ce que c'est que ça?

**MERCÉDÈS:** Une promenade aux flambeaux...

**FRASQUITA:** C'est Escamillo... un torero qui s'est fait remarquer aux dernières courses de Grenade.

**MERCÉDÈS:** Pardieu, il faut le faire venir... nous boirons en son honneur!

**ZUNIGA:** C'est cela, je vais l'inviter. Monsieur le toréro... voulez-vous faire l'amitié de monter ici? Vous y trouverez des gens qui aiment fort tous ceux qui, comme vous, ont de l'adresse et du courage...

**CHOEUR:** Vivat! vivat le toréro! Vivat! vivat Escamillo! *etc.*

**ZUNIGA:** Nous vous remercions d'avoir accepté notre invitation; nous n'avons pas voulu vous laisser passer sans boire avec vous au grand art de la tauromachie.

**ESCAMILLO:** Messieurs les officiers, je vous remercie.

**ESCAMILLO:** Votre toast, je peux vous le rendre, señors, car avec les soldats, oui, les toréros peuvent s'entendre, pour plaisirs ils ont les combats! Le cirque est plein, c'est jour de fête, le cirque est plein du haut en bas. Les spectateurs perdant la tête, les spectateurs s'interpellent à grand fracas! Apostrophes, cris et tapage poussés jusques à la fureur! Car c'est la fête du courage! c'est la fête des gens de coeur! Allons! en garde! ah! Toréador, en garde! Et songe bien, oui, songe en combattant, qu'un oeil noir te regarde et que l'amour t'attend! Toréador, l'amour t'attend!

**CARMEN:** Everything's all right then, since he is out, everything's all right.

**ZUNIGA:** Well well, you console yourself quickly...

**CARMEN:** If you take my advice you'll do like me: you want to take us out, we don't want to come with you... you will console yourselves...

**MORALÈS:** We'll have to.
(*The scene is interrupted by a chorus sung in the wings*)

**CHORUS:** Hurrah! Hurrah for the torero! Hurrah! Hurrah for Escamillo! *etc.*
(*The dialogue continues during the singing of the above Chorus*)

**ZUNIGA:** What's all that?

**MERCÉDÈS:** A torchlight procession...

**FRASQUITA:** It's Escamillo... a bullfighter who distinguished himself at the last Granada meetings.

**MORALÈS:** By jove, we must get him up here... we'll drink in his honor!

**ZUNIGA:** That's it, I'll invite him. (*He goes over to the window*) Señor torero, will you do us the kindness to step up here? You'll find chaps who are very fond of all those, like yourself, who have skill and courage...

**CHORUS:** Hurrah! Hurrah for the torero! Hurrah! Hurrah for Escamillo! *etc.* (*Enters Escamillo*)

**ZUNIGA:** We thank you for having accepted our invitation; we didn't want to let you go by without drinking with you to the great art of tauromachy.

**ESCAMILLO:** Gentlemen, I thank you.

**ESCAMILLO:** I can return your toast. gentlemen, for soldiers— yes—and bullfighters understand each other; fighting is their game! The ring is packed, it's a holiday, the ring is full from top to bottom. The spectators, losing their wits, yell at each other at the tops of their voices! Exclamations, cries and uproar carried to the pitch of fury! For this is the *fiesta* of courage, this is the *fiesta* of the stouthearted! Let's go! On guard! Ah! Toreador, on guard! And remember, yes, remember as you fight that two dark eyes are watching you, that love awaits you! Toreador, love awaits you!

**TOUT LE MONDE:** Toréador, en garde! *etc.*

**ESCAMILLO:** Tout d'un coup, on fait silence, on fait silence, ah! que se passe-t-il? Plus de cris, c'est l'instant! Le taureau s'élance en bondissant hors du toril! Il s'élance! Il entre, il frappe! Un cheval roule, entraînant un picador! "Ah! bravo Toro!" hurle la foule; le taureau va, il vient, il vient et frappe encore! En secouant ses banderilles, plein de fureur, il court! Le cirque est plein de sang! On se sauve, on franchit les grilles! C'est ton tour maintenant! Allons! en garde! ah! Toréador, en garde! *etc.*

**TOUT LE MONDE:** Toréador, en garde! *etc.* ....l'amour t'attend!

**FRASQUITA:** L'Amour!

**ESCAMILLO:** L'Amour!

**MERCÉDÈS:** L'Amour!

**ESCAMILLO:** L'Amour!

**CARMEN:** L'Amour!

**TOUT LE MONDE:** Toréador, Toréador! L'Amour! t'attend!

**PASTIA:** Messieurs les officiers, je vous en prie.

**ZUNIGA:** C'est bien, c'est bien, nous partons.

**ESCAMILLO:** Dis-moi ton nom, et la première fois que je frapperai le taureau, ce sera ton nom que je prononcerai.

**CARMEN:** Je m'appelle la Carmencita.

**ESCAMILLO:** La Carmencita?

**CARMEN:** Carmen, la Carmencita, comme tu voudras.

**ESCAMILLO:** Eh bien! Carmen ou la Carmencita, si je m'avisais de t'aimer et d'être aimé de toi, qu'est-ce tu me répondrais?

**CARMEN:** Je répondrais que tu peux m'aimer tout à ton aise mais que quant à être aimé de moi pour le moment, il n'y faut pas songer!

**ESCAMILLO:** J'attendrai alors et me contenterai d'espérer...

**CARMEN:** Il n'est pas défendu d'attendre et il est toujours agréable d'espérer.

**ZUNIGA:** Ecoute-moi, Carmen, puisque tu ne veux pas venir avec nous, c'est moi que dans une heure reviendrai ici...

**CHORUS:** Toreador, on guard! *etc.*
(*Carmen refills Escamillo's glass*)

**ESCAMILLO:** Suddenly everyone falls silent; ah—what's happening? No more shouts, this is the moment! The bull comes bounding out of the *toril*! He charges, comes in, strikes! A horse rolls over, dragging down a picador! "Ah! Bravo bull!" roars the crowd; the bull turns, comes back, comes back and strikes again! Shaking his banderillas, maddened with rage, he runs about! The ring is covered with blood! Men jump clear, leap the barriers. It's your turn now! Let's go! On guard! Ah! Toreador, on guard! *etc.*

**CHORUS:** Toreador, on guard! *etc.* ....love awaits you!

**FRASQUITA:** Love!

**ESCAMILLO:** Love!

**MERCÉDÈS:** Love!

**ESCAMILLO:** Love!

**CARMEN:** Love!

**ALL:** Toreador, Toreador, love awaits you! (*They drink and exchange handshakes with the toreador*)

**PASTIA:** Officers, sirs, I beg you.

**ZUNIGA:** All right, all right, we're going. (*The officers start to get ready to leave.—Escamillo finds himself beside Carmen*)

**ESCAMILLO:** Tell me your name, and the first time I kill a bull it will be your name that I utter.

**CARMEN:** I'm called Carmencita.

**ESCAMILLO:** Carmencita?

**CARMEN:** Carmen, Carmencita, as you like.

**ESCAMILLO:** Well then! Carmen or Carmencita, if I took it into my head to love you and be loved by you, what would you answer?

**CARMEN:** I should answer that you can love me just as you please, but as for being loved by me just at present, you mustn't think of it!

**ESCAMILLO:** Then I'll wait, and content myself with hoping...

**CARMEN:** It's not forbidden to wait, and it's always pleasant to hope.

**ZUNIGA:** (*quietly, to Carmen*) Listen to me, Carmen. Since you won't come with us, it's I who'll come back here in an hour ...

CARMEN: Je ne vous conseille pas de revenir . . .

ZUNIGA: Je reviendrai tout de même.
Nous partons avec vous, torero, et nous nous joindrons au cortège qui vous accompagne.

FRASQUITA: (à Pastia) Pourquoi étais-tu si pressé de les faire partir?

PASTIA: Le Dancaire et le Remendado viennent d'arriver . . .

PASTIA: Les voici . . .

FRASQUITA: Eh bien, les nouvelles?

LE DANCAÏRE: Pas trop mauvaises, les nouvelles; nous arrivons de Gibraltar.

LE REMENDADO: Jolie ville, Gibraltar! . . . on y voit des Anglais, beaucoup d'Anglais, de jolis hommes les Anglais, un peu froids, mais distingués.

LE DANCAÏRE: Remendado! . . .

LE REMENDADO: Patron.

LE DANCAÏRE: Taisez-vous. Nous avons arrangé l'embarquement de marchandises anglaises. Nous irons le attendre près de la côte, nous en cacherons une partie dans la montagne et nous ferons passer le reste. Tous nos camarades ont été prévenus . . . mais c'est de vous trois surtout que nous avons besoin . . . vous allez partir avec nous.

CARMEN: (riant) Pourquoi faire? pour vous aider à porter des ballots?

LE REMENDADO: Oh! non . . . faire porter des ballots à des dames . . . cą ne serait pas distingué.

LE DANCAÏRE: (menaçant) Remendado?

LE REMENDADO: Oui, patron.

LE DANCAÏRE: Nous ne vous ferons pas porter de ballots, mais nous avons besoin de vous pour autre chose.

LE DANCAÏRE: Nous avons en tête une affaire.

MERCÉDÈS ET FRASQUITA: Est-elle bonne, dites-nous?

LE DANCAÏRE ET LE REMENDADO: Elle est admirable, ma chère; mais nous avons besoin de vous.

TOUS LE CINQ: De nous? etc. De vous! etc.

LES DEUX HOMMES: Car nous l'avouons humblement, et fort respectueusement: quand il s'agit de tromperie,

CARMEN: I don't advise you to come back . . .

ZUNIGA: (quietly to Carmen) I'll come back all the same.
(Out loud) We'll leave with you, torero, and tack ourselves on to the procession that accompanies you. (Everybody goes out except Carmen, Frasquita, Mercédès and Lillas Pasita)

FRASQUITA: (to Pastia) Why were you so eager to send them away?

PASTIA: Dancaire and Remendado have just arrived . . .

PASTIA: (opening a door and gesturing as he calls out) Here they are . . .
(Enter El Dancaïro and El Remendado. Pastia closes the doors, puts up the shutters, etc., etc.)

FRASQUITA: Well, the news?

EL DANCAÏRO: Not too bad, the news. We've just come from Gibraltar.

EL REMENDADO: Nice town, Gibraltar! . . . you see the English there, lots of English, nice chaps the English, a trifle cold, but gentlemanly.

EL DANCAÏRO: Remendado! . . .

EL REMENDADO: Boss.

EL DANCAÏRO: Shut up. We arranged to take on board some English goods. We're going to wait for it near the coast. We'll hide some of the stuff up the mountain and run the rest.
All our comrades have been warned . . . but it's you three we need principally . . . you'll leave with us.

CARMEN: (laughing) What for? To help you carry the bales?

EL REMENDADO: Oh no!—make the ladies carry the bales . . . that wouldn't be at all the thing.

EL DANCAÏRO: (threateningly) Remendado?

EL REMENDADO: Yes, boss.

EL DANCAÏRO: We're not going to make you carry any bales, but we do need you for something else.

EL DANCAÏRO: We have a scheme in mind.

MERCÉDÈS AND FRASQUITA: Tell us, is it good?

EL DANCAÏRO AND EL REMENDADO: It's admirable, my dear; but we require your services.

QUINTET: Ours? etc. Yours! etc.

THE TWO MEN: For we humbly and most respectfully acknowledge:
when it's a question of trickery,

de duperie, de volerie, il est toujours bon, sur ma foi, d'avoir les femmes avec soi, Et sans elles, mes toutes belles, on ne fait jamais rien de bien!

LES TROIS FEMMES: Quoi! sans nous jamais rien de bien?

LES DEUX HOMMES: N'êtes-vous pas de cet avis?

LES TROIS FEMMES: Si fait, je suis de cet avis. Si fait, vraiment je suis.

TOUS LES CINQ: Quand il s'agit de tromperie, etc.

LE DANCAÏRE: C'est dit alors; vous partirez?

FRASQUITA ET MERCÉDÈS: Quand vous voudrez.

LE DANCAÏRE: Mais tout de suite.

CARMEN: Ah! permettez! S'il vous plait de partir, partez, mais je ne suis pas du voyage. Je ne pars pas, je ne pars pas!

LES DEUX HOMMES: Carmen, mon amour, tu viendras—

CARMEN: Je ne pars pas; je ne pars pas!

LES DEUX HOMMES: Et tu n'auras pas le courage de nous laisser dans l'embarras.

FRASQUITA ET MERCÉDÈS: Ah! ma Carmen, tu viendras.

CARMEN: Je ne pars pas, etc.

LE DANCAÏRE: Mais, au moins la raison. Carmen, tu la diras.

TOUS LES QUATRE: La raison, la raison!

CARMEN: Je la dirai certainement.

TOUS LES QUATRE: Voyons! Voyons!

CARMEN: La raison, c'est qu'en ce moment . . .

TOUS LES QUATRE: Eh bien? Eh bien?

CARMEN: Je suis amoureuse!

LES DEUX HOMMES: (stupéfaits) Qu'a-t-elle dit?

LES DEUX FEMMES: Elle dit qu'elle est amoureuse!

TOUS LES QUATRE: Amoureuse!

CARMEN: Oui, amoureuse!

LE DANCAÏRE: Voyons, Carmen, sois sérieuse!

CARMEN: Amoureuse à perdre l'esprit!

LES DEUS HOMMES: La chose, certes, nous étonne, mais ce n'est pas le premier jour où vous aurez su, ma mignonne, faire marcher de front le devoir et l'amour.

of deception, of thieving, it's always good, I swear, to have women around. And without them, my lovelies, no one ever does any good!

THE THREE GIRLS: What? Without us no one does any good?

THE TWO MEN: Isn't that your opinion?

GIRLS: Indeed, that's my opinion. Yes indeed, really it is.

QUINTET: When it's a question of trickery, etc.

EL DANCAÏRO: It's settled then; you'll go?

FRASQUITA AND MERCÉDÈS: Whenever you like.

EL DANCAÏRO: Why, straight away.

CARMEN: Ah! just a moment! If you want to go, go; but I'm not in on this trip. I won't go! I won't go!

THE MEN: Carmen, my love, you will come—

CARMEN: I won't go! I won't go!

THE MEN: And you won't have the heart to leave us in the lurch.

FRASQUITA AND MERCÉDÈS: Ah! my Carmen, you will come.

CARMEN: I won't go! etc.

EL DANCAÏRO: But the reason, Carmen, at least you'll tell us the reason.

QUARTET: The reason, the reason!

CARMEN: Certainly I'll give it.

QUARTET: Let's have it! Let's have it!

CARMEN: The reason is that at this moment . . .

QUARTET: Well? Well?

CARMEN: I'm in love!

THE MEN: (astonished) What did she say?

THE GIRLS: She says she's in love!

QUARTET: In love!

CARMEN: Yes, in love!

EL DANCAÏRO: See here, Carmen, be serious!

CARMEN: Head over heels in love!

THE MEN: This is certainly astonishing, but it's not the first time, my pet, that you've been able to combine love and duty.

# Act II

CARMEN: Mes amis, je serais fort aise
de partir avec vous ce soir;
mais cette fois ne vous déplaise,
il faudra que l'amour passe avant le devoir.

LE DANCAÏRE: Ce n'est pas là ton dernier mot?

CARMEN: Absolument!

LE REMENDADO: Il faut que tu te laisses attendrir.

TOUS LES QUATRE: Il faut venir, Carmen, il faut venir!
Pour notre affaire,
c'est nécessaire,
car entre nous . . .

CARMEN: Quant à cela, je l'admets avec vous . . .

REPRISE GÉNÉRALE: Quand il s'agit de tromperie, *etc.*

LE DANCAÏRE: En voilà assez; je t'ai dit qu'il fallait venir, et tu viendras . . . je suis le chef.

CARMEN: Comment dis-tu ca?

LE DANCAÏRE: Je te dis que je suis le chef.

CARMEN: Et tu crois que je t'obéirai?

LE DANCAÏRE: (*furieux*) Carmen! . . .

LE REMENDADO: Je vous en prie . . . des personnes si distinguées.

LE DANCAÏRE: Amoureuse . . . ce n'est pas une raison, cela.

CARMEN: Partez sans moi . . . j'irai vous rejoindre demain, mais pour ce soir je reste.

FRASQUITA: Je ne t'ai jamais vue comme cela; qui attends-tu donc?

CARMEN: Un pauvre diable du soldat qui m'a rendu service . . .

MERCÉDÈS: Ce soldat qui était en prison?

CARMEN: Oui.

LE DANCAÏRE: Je parierais qu'il ne viendra pas.

CARMEN: Ne parie pas, tu perdrais . . .
(*José's voice is heard in the distance*)

JOSÉ: Halte là!
Qui va là?
Dragon d'Alcala!
Où t'en vas-tu par là,
Dragon d'Alcala?—
Moi, je m'en vais faire
mordre la poussière
à mon adversaire.—
S'il en est ainsi,
passez, mon ami.
Affaire d'honneur,
affaire de coeur;
pour nous tout est là
Dragons d'Alcala!

CARMEN: My friends, I'd be most happy
to go with you this evening;
but this time—don't be annoyed—
love must come before duty.

EL DANCAÏRO: That's not your final word?

CARMEN: Absolutely!

EL REMENDADO: You must relent.

QUARTET: You must come, Carmen, you must come!
It's necessary
for our scheme,
for between ourselves . . .

CARMEN: As to that, I admit with you that . . .

QUINTET: (*reprise*) When it's a question of trickery, *etc.*

EL DANCAÏRO: Enough of that; I told you you must come, and you will come . . . I am the leader.

CARMEN: What's that you say?

EL DANCAÏRO: I tell you I'm the leader.

CARMEN: And you think I'll obey you?

EL DANCAÏRO: (*furious*) Carmen! . . .

EL REMENDADO: (*throwing himself between Dancairo and Carmen*) I beg you . . . such genteel persons.

EL DANCAÏRO: In love . . . that's not a reason.

CARMEN: Leave without me. I'll come and join you tomorrow, but for this evening I'm staying.

FRASQUITA: I've never seen you like this. Who are you expecting?

CARMEN: A poor devil of a soldier who did me a service . . .

MERCÉDÈS: That soldier who was in prison?

CARMEN: Yes.

EL DANCAÏRO: I'd bet you he won't come.

CARMEN: Don't bet, you would lose . . .
(*José's voice is heard in the distance*)

JOSÉ: (*in the far distance*) Halt!
Who goes there?
Dragoon of Alcala!
Where are you going there,
Dragoon of Alcala?—
Me, I'm going to make
my rival
bite the dust.—
If that's the case,
pass, my friend.
An affair of honor,
an affair of the heart—
that explains everything for us
Dragoons of Alcala!
(*There is no break in the music.*)

---

*Carmen, Dancáiro, Remendado, Mercédès and Frasquita watch the arrival of José through the half-open shutters*)

MERCÉDÈS: C'est un dragon, ma foi.

FRASQUITA: Un beau dragon.

LE DANCAÏRE: (*a Carmen*) Eh bien, Carmen, puisque tu ne veux venir que demain, sais-tu au moins ce que tu devrais faire?

CARMEN: Qu'est-ce que je devrais faire?

LE DANCAÏRE: Tu devrais décider ton dragon à venir avec toi et à se joindre à nous.

CARMEN: Ah! . . . si cela se pouvait! . . . Mais il n'y faut pas penser . . . ce sont des bêtises . . . il est trop niais.

LE DANCAÏRE: Pourquoi l'aimes-tu puisque tu en conviens toi-même?

CARMEN: Parce qu'il est joli garçon donc et qu'il me plaît.

LE REMENDADO: (*avec fatuité*) Le patron ne comprend pas ça, lui . . . qu'il suffise d'être joli garçon pour plaire aux femmes . . .

LE DANCAÏRE: Attends un peu, attends un peu . . .
(*Remendado makes his escape and goes out. Dancáiro pursues him and goes out in his turn, dragging along Mercédès and Frasquita who are trying to calm him down*)

JOSÉ: Halte là!
Qui va là?
Dragon d'Alcala!
Où t'en vas-tu par là,
Dragon d'Alcala?—
Exact et fidèle,
je vais où m'appelle
l'amour de ma belle!—
S'il en est ainsi,
passez, mon ami.
Affaire d'honneur,
affaire de coeur;
pour nous tout est là
Dragons d'Alcala!

CARMEN: Enfin . . . te voilà . . . C'est bien heureux!

JOSÉ: Il y a deux heures seulement que je suis sorti de prison.

CARMEN: Qui t'empêchait de sortir plus tôt? Je t'avais envoyé une lime et une pièce d'or.

JOSÉ: Que veux-tu? j'ai encore mon honneur de soldat, et déserter me semblerait un grand crime . . . Oh! je ne t'en suis pas moins reconnaissant. La lime me servira pour affiler ma lance et je

MERCÉDÈS: Faith, it's a dragoon.

FRASQUITA: A handsome dragoon.

EL DANCAÏRO: (*to Carmen*) Well, Carmen, since you won't come until tomorrow, d'you know at least what you ought to do?

CARMEN: What is it I ought to do?

EL DANCAÏRO: You ought to persuade your dragoon to come with you and join us.

CARMEN: Ah, if that were possible! . . . But you mustn't think of it . . . it's nonsense . . . he's too simple.

EL DANCAÏRO: Why do you love him, since you yourself admit it?

CARMEN: Because he's a nice boy and he pleases me.

EL REMENDADO: (*fatuously*) The boss, he doesn't understand that . . . that it's enough to be a nice boy in order to please the women . .

EL DANCAÏRO: Wait a moment, you, wait a moment . . .
(*Remendado makes his escape and goes out. Dancáiro pursues him and goes out in his turn, dragging along Mercédès and Frasquita who are trying to calm him down*)

JOSÉ: (*the sound of his voice growing closer*) Halt!
Who goes there?
Dragoon of Alcala!
Where are you going there,
Dragoon of Alcala?—
Punctual and faithful,
I go where the love
of my fair lady calls me!—
If that's the case,
pass, friend.
An affair of the heart,
an affair of the heart,
that explains everything for us
Dragoons of Alcala!
(*Don José enters*)

CARMEN: At last . . . so there you are . . . This is a fine thing!

JOSÉ: It's only two hours since I came out of prison.

CARMEN: What prevented you from getting out sooner? I had sent you a file and a gold coin.

JOSÉ: What d'you expect? I still have my soldier's honour, and to desert would seem to me to be a great crime . . . Oh, I'm none the less grateful to you. The file will be useful to me for sharpening my

l'ai gardé comme souvenir de toi. Quant à l'argent . . .

CARMEN: Tiens, il l'a gardé! Holà! . . . Lillas Pastia, holà!

CARMEN: Apporte-nous du Manzanilla . . . apporte-nous de tout ce que tu as, de tout, de tour . . .

PASTIA: Tour de suite, mademoiselle Carmencita.

CARMEN: (à don José) Tu regrettes de t'être fait mettre en prison pour mes beaux yeux?

JOSÉ: Non. On m'a mis en prison, on m'a ôté mon grade, mais ça m'est égal.

CARMEN: Parce que tu m'aimes?

JOSÉ: Oui, parce que je t'aime, parce que je t'adore.

CARMEN: Ton lieutenant était ici tout à l'heure, avec d'autres officiers, ils nous ont fait danser.

JOSÉ: Tu as dansé?

CARMEN: Oui; et ton lieutenant s'est permis de me dire qu'il m'adorait . . .

JOSÉ: Carmen!

CARMEN: Qu'est-ce que tu as? . . . Est-ce que tu serais jaloux, par hasard?

JOSÉ: Mais certainement, je suis jaloux . . .

CARMEN: Eh bien, si tu le veux, je danserai pour toi maintenant, pour toi seul.

JOSÉ: Ah! que je t'aime, Carmen, que je t'aime!

CARMEN: Je l'espère bien.

CARMEN: Je vais danser en votre honneur, et vous verrez, seigneur, comment je sais moi-même accompagner ma danse! Mettez-vous là, Don José, je commence!

JOSÉ: Attendez, Carmen, rien qu'un moment, arrête!

CARMEN: Et pour quoi, s'il te plaît?

JOSÉ: Il me semble, là-bas . . . oui, ce sont nos clairons qui sonnent la retraite! Ne les entends-tu pas?

lance and I've kept it as a memento of you. (holding out the gold coin to her) As for the money . . .

CARMEN: Hullo, he's kept it! (shouting and hammering) Hi there! . . . Lillas Pastia, hi! (enter Pastia)

CARMEN: (tossing him the coin) Bring us some Manzanilla . . . bring us everything you have, everything, the lot . . .

PASTIA: At once, señorita Camencita. (He goes out)

CARMEN: (to Don José) You regret having been put in prison for the sake of my lovely eyes?

JOSÉ: No. They put me in prison, they stripped me of my rank, but it's all one to me.

CARMEN: Because you love me?

JOSÉ: Yes, because I love you, because I adore you.

CARMEN: Your lieutenant was here just now with some other officers. They made us dance.

JOSÉ: You danced?

CARMEN: Yes; and your lieutenant allowed himself to tell me that he adored me . . .

JOSÉ: Carmen!

CARMEN: What's the matter with you? . . . Would you be jealous, by any chance?

JOSÉ: Why, certainly I'm jealous . . .

CARMEN: Well then, if you want me to, I'll dance for you now, for you alone.

JOSÉ: Ah, how I love you, Carmen, how I love you!

CARMEN: So I should hope.

CARMEN: I am going to dance in your honor, and you will see, my lord, how I am able to accompany my dance! Sit down there, Don José, I'll begin! (She makes José sit down in a corner, and starts to dance, humming and accompanying herself with her castanets. José is entranced. Bugles are heard in the distance sounding Retreat. José cocks an ear. He comes over to Carmen and compels her to stop)

JOSÉ: Wait, Carmen, only for a moment, stop!

CARMEN: And why, if you please?

JOSÉ: I think, over there . . . yes, those are our bugles sounding Retreat! Can't you hear them?

CARMEN: Bravo! Bravo! J'avais beau faire; il est mélancholique de danser sans orchestre. Et vive la musique qui nous tombe du ciel!

JOSÉ: Tu ne m'as pas compris, Carmen, c'est la retraite; il faut que moi, je rentre au quartier pour l'appel.

CARMEN: Au quartier! pour l'appel! Ah! j'étais vraiment trop bête! Je me mettais en quatre et je faisais des frais, oui, je faisais des frais pour amuser monsieur! Je chantais! Je dansais! Je crois, Dieu me pardonne, qu'un peu plus, je l'aimais! Taratata! C'est le clarion qui sonne! Taratata! Il part! il est parti! Va-t'en donc, canari! Tiens; prends ton shako, ton sabre, ta giberne; et va-t'en, mon garçon, va-t'en! Retourne à ta caserne!

JOSÉ: C'est mal à toi, Carmen, de te moquer de moi! Je souffre de partir, car jamais, jamais femme, jamais femme avant toi, aussi profondémént n'avait troublé mon âme!

CARMEN: "Taratata, mon Dieu! c'est la retraite! Taratata, je vais être en retard!" Il court, il perd la tête, et voila son amour!

JOSÉ: Ainsi, tu ne crois pas à mon amour?

CARMEN: Mais non!

JOSÉ: Eh bien! tu m'entendras!

CARMEN: Je ne veux rien entendre!

JOSÉ: Tu m'entendras!

CARMEN: Tu vas te faire attendre!

JOSÉ: Tu m'entendras! Carmen!

CARMEN: Non! non! non! non!

JOSÉ: Oui, tu m'entendras! Je le veux! Carmen, tu m'entendras! La fleur que tu m'avais jetée, dans ma prison m'était restée. Flétrie et sèche, cette fleur gardait toujours sa douce odeur; et pendant des heures entières,

CARMEN: Bravo! Bravo! I was trying in vain; it's dismal dancing without an orchestra. And long live music that drops on us out of the skies! (She resumes her song. The bugles sound nearer, pass beneath the windows of the inn, then fade in the distance. José makes a new effort to tear himself from his contemplation of Carmen. He seizes her arm and compels her to stop once more)

JOSÉ: You didn't understand me, Carmen, it's Retreat; I've got to get back to quarters for roll-call.

CARMEN: To quarters! For roll-call! Ah! Really I was too stupid! I went out of my way and took the trouble, yes, I took the trouble to entertain the gentleman! I sang! I danced! I believe, God forgive me, I almost fell in love! Tartata! It's the bugle sounding! Tartata! He's off! He's gone! Go on then, canary!" (angrily throwing his cap at him) Here! take your shako, your sword, your bandolier; and clear off, my son, clear off! Clear off back to your barracks!

JOSÉ: It's cruel of you, Carmen, to make fun of me! It pains me to go, for never, never has a woman, never before you has any woman so deeply stirred my heart!

CARMEN: "Taratata, my God! It's the Retreat! Taratata, I'm going to be late!" He loses his wits, he rushes off, and that's his love!

JOSÉ: So you don't believe in my love?

CARMEN: Of course not!

JOSÉ: Very well! You shall listen to me!

CARMEN: I won't listen to anything!

JOSÉ: You shall hear me!

CARMEN: You're going to be late!

JOSÉ: You shall hear me! Carmen!

CARMEN: No! No! No! No!

JOSÉ: Yes, you shall hear me! I insist! Carmen, you shall hear me! (He reaches inside his tunic and takes out the cassia flower Carmen threw him in Act One) The flower that you threw to me stayed with me in my prison.

sur mes yeux, fermant mes paupières,
de cette odeur je m'enivrais
et dans la nuit je te voyais!
Je me prenais à te maudire,
à te détester, à me dire;
Pourquoi faut-il que le destin
l'ait mise là sur mon chemin?
Puis je m'accusais de blasphème,
et je ne sentais en moi-même,
je ne sentais qu'un seul désir,
un seul désir, un seul espoir:
te revoir, ô Carmen, oui, te revoir!
Car tu n'avais eu qu'à paraître,
qu'à jeter un regard sur moi,
pour t'emparer de tout mon être,
ô ma Carmen!
et j'étais une chose à toi!
Carmen, je t'aime!

**CARMEN:** Non, tu ne m'aimes pas!

**JOSÉ:** Que dis-tu?

**CARMEN:** Non, tu ne m'aimes pas!
non! Car si tu m'aimais,
là-bas, là-bas,
tu me suivrais.

**JOSÉ:** Carmen!

**CARMEN:** Oui!—
Là-bas, là-bas, dans la montagne,

**JOSÉ:** Carmen!

**CARMEN:** là-bas, là-bas, tu me suivrais.
Sur ton cheval tu me prendrais,
et comme un brave à travers la campagne,
en croupe, tu m'emporterais!
Là-bas, là-bas, dans la montagne!

**JOSÉ:** Carmen!

**CARMEN:** Là-bas, là-bas, tu me suivrais,
Si tu m'aimais!
Tu n'y dépendrais de personne;
point d'officier à qui tu doives obéir
et point de retraite qui sonne
pour dire à l'amoureux
qu'il est temps de partir!
Le ciel ouvert, la vie errante,
pour pays l'univers;
et pour loi ta volonté,
et surtout la chose enivrante:
la liberté! la liberté!

**JOSÉ:** Mon Dieu!

**CARMEN:** Là-bas, là-bas, dans la montagne,

**JOSÉ:** Carmen!

**CARMEN:** là-bas, là-bas, si tu m'aimais,

**JOSÉ:** Tais-toi!

Withered and dried up, that flower
always kept its sweet perfume;
and for hours at a time,
with my eyes closed,
I became drunk with its smell
and in the night I used to see you!
I took to cursing you,
detesting you, asking myself
why did destiny
have to throw her across my path?
Then I accused myself of blasphemy,
and felt within myself,
I felt but one desire,
one desire, one hope:
to see you again, Carmen, to see you again!
For you had only to appear,
only to throw a glance my way,
to take possession of my whole being,
O my Carmen,
and I was your chattel!
Carmen, I love you!

**CARMEN:** No, you don't love me!

**JOSÉ:** What are you saying?

**CARMEN:** No, you don't love me,
no! For if you did,
you'd follow me
over there.

**JOSÉ:** Carmen!

**CARMEN:** Yes!—
Away over there into the mountains,

**JOSÉ:** Carmen!

**CARMEN:** away over there you'd follow me.
You'd take me up behind you on your horse
and like a daredevil you'd carry me off
across the country!
Away over there into the mountains!

**JOSÉ:** Carmen!

**CARMEN:** Away over there you'd follow me,
if you loved me!
There you'd not be dependent on anyone;
there'd be no officer you had to obey,
and no Retreat sounding
to tell a lover
that it is time to go!
The open sky, the wandering life,
the whole wide world your domain;
for law your own free will,
and above all, that intoxicating thing:
Freedom! Freedom!

**JOSÉ:** Oh God!

**CARMEN:** Away over there into the mountains,

**JOSÉ:** Carmen!

**CARMEN:** away over there, if you loved me,

**JOSÉ:** Stop it!

**CARMEN:** là-bas, là-bas tu me suivrais!
Sur ton cheval tu me prendrais . . .

**JOSÉ:** Ah! Carmen! hélas! tais-toi! tais-toi! mon Dieu!

**CARMEN:** et comme un brave, à travers la campagne,
oui, tu m'emporterais, si tu m'aimais.

**JOSÉ:** Hélas! hélas!

**CARMEN:** Oui, n'est-ce pas,
là-bas, là-bas tu me suivrais!
tu m'aimes et tu me suivrais!
Là-bas, là-bas emporte-moi!

**JOSÉ:** Pitié! Carmen! pitié!
O mon Dieu, hélas!
Ah! tais-toi! tais-toi!
Non! Je n veux plus t'écouter!
Quitter mon drapeau . . . déserter
. . .
c'est la honte, c'est l'infamie!
Je n'en veux pas!

**CARMEN:** Eh bien, pars!

**JOSÉ:** Carmen, je t'en prie!

**CARMEN:** Non! je ne t'aime plus!

**JOSÉ:** Ecoute!

**CARMEN:** Va! je te hais!
Adieu! mais adieu pour jamais!

**JOSÉ:** Eh bien, soit . . . adieu, adieu pour jamais!

**CARMEN:** Va-t'en!

**JOSÉ:** Carmen! adieu! adieu pour jamais!

**CARMEN:** Adieu!

**ZUNIGA:** (au dehors) Holà Carmen! Holà! Holà!

**JOSÉ:** Qui frappe? qui vient là?

**CARMEN:** Tais-toi! Tais-toi!

**ZUNIGA:** J'ouvre moi-même et j'entre.
Ah! fi, ah! fi, la belle!
Le choix n'est pas heureux; c'est se mésallier
de prendre le soldat quand on a l'officier.
Allons! Décampe!

**JOSÉ:** Non!

**ZUNIGA:** Si fait, tu partiras!

**JOSÉ:** Je ne partirai pas!

**ZUNIGA:** Drôle!

**JOSÉ:** Tonnerre! il va pleuvoir des coups!

**JOSÉ:** Au diable le jaloux! (appelant) A moi! à moi!

**CARMEN:** away over there you'd follow me!
You'd take me up on your horse . . .

**JOSÉ:** Ah, Carmen! alas! stop! stop! Oh God!

**CARMEN:** and like a daredevil
you'd carry me off
across the country, if you loved me.

**JOSÉ:** Alas! alas!

**CARMEN:** Yes, isn't it so,
you will follow me there,
you love me and you'll follow me!
Take me away over there!

**JOSÉ:** Pity, Carmen! Have pity!
Oh, God, alas!
Ah, stop, stop!
No! I won't listen to you!
To abandon my colors . . . to desert .
. .
that's shameful, that's dastardly!
I'll have none of it!

**CARMEN:** All right then, go!

**JOSÉ:** Carmen, I implore you!

**CARMEN:** No, I don't love you any more!

**JOSÉ:** Listen!

**CARMEN:** Go! I hate you!
Goodbye! And goodbye for ever!

**JOSÉ:** All right, so be it . . . goodbye for ever!

**CARMEN:** Get out!

**JOSÉ:** Carmen! Goodbye, goodbye for ever!

**CARMEN:** Goodbye!
(Don José hurries towards the door; just as he reaches it, somebody knocks)

**ZUNIGA:** (outside) Hallo there, Carmen! Hallo! Hallo!

**JOSÉ:** Who's that knocking? Who's there?

**CARMEN:** Keep quiet!

**ZUNIGA:** (forcing the door) I'm opening up myself, and coming in.
(sees Don José—to Carmen)
Ah! fi, fi! My lovely lady!
This isn't a happy choice; it's demeaning
to take the soldier when you've got the officer.
(to Don José)
Off with you, get moving!

**JOSÉ:** No!

**ZUNIGA:** You certainly will go!

**JOSÉ:** I shall not go!

**ZUNIGA:** (striking him) Scoundrel!

**JOSÉ:** (drawing his sword) By thunder! It's going to rain blows!

**CARMEN:** (throwing herself between them) Devil take the jealous!
(calling) Help! Help!
(Gypsies appear from all sides.

**CARMEN:** Bel officier! Bel officier, l'amour
vous joue en ce moment un assez vilain tour.
Vous arrivez fort mal, hélas! et nous sommes
forcés,
ne voulant être dénoncés,
de vous garder au moins . . . pendant une heure.

**LE DANCAÏRE ET LE REMENDADO:** Mon cher monsieur,
nous allons, s'il vous plaît,
quitter cette demeure;
vous viendrez avec nous?

**CARMEN:** C'est une promenade.

**LE DANCAÏRE ET LE REMENDADO:** Consentez-vous?

**TOUS LES BOHÉMIENS:** Répondez, camarade.

**ZUNIGA:** Certainement,
d'autant plus que votre argument
est un de ceux auxquels on ne résiste guère,
mais gare à vous! Gare à vous plus tard!

**LE DANCAÏRE:** La guerre, c'est la guerre!
En attendant, mon officier,
passez devant sans vous faire prier!

**LE REMENDADO ET LES BOHÉMIENS:** Passez devant sans vous faire prier!

**CARMEN:** Es-tu des nôtres maintenant?

**JOSÉ:** Il le faut bien.

**CARMEN:** Ah! le mot n'est pas galant,
mais qu'importe, va, tu t'y feras quand tu verras
comme c'est beau, la vie errante;
pour pays, l'univers,
et pour loi ta volonté,
et surtout, la chose, enivrante:
la liberté! la liberté!

**TOUS:** (à Don José) Suis-nous à travers la campagne,
viens avec nous dans la montagne,
suis-nous et tu t'y feras
quand tu verras, là-bas,
comme c'est beau, la vie errante;
pour pays, l'univers,
et pour loi, ta volonté!
Et surtout, la chose enivrante:
la liberté! la liberté!
Le ciel ouvert, la vie errante,
pour pays tout l'univers;
pour loi ta volonté,
et surtout la chose enivrante:
la liberté! la liberté!

*Carmen points to Zuniga. El Dancaïro and El Remendado hurl themselves upon him and disarm him)*

**CARMEN:** My fine officer! My fine officer, love
at the moment is playing you a rather dirty trick.
Your arrival is most untimely; and alas,
we are compelled,
not wishing to be betrayed,
to detain you . . . for at least an hour.

**EL DANCAÏRO AND EL REMENDADO:** My dear sir,
if you please, we are going
to leave this establishment;
you'll come with us?

**CARMEN:** Just for a stroll.

**EL DANCAÏRO AND EL REMENDADO:** Do you consent?

**ALL THE GYPSIES:** Answer, comrade.

**ZUNIGA:** Certainly.
the more so since your argument
is one of those that can hardly be resisted;
but take care! Look out for yourselves later!

**EL DANCAÏRO:** War is war!
Meantime, my good sir,
carry on without further argument!

**EL REMENDADO AND THE GYPSIES:** Carry on without further argument!
*(The officer is led out by four gypsies armed with pistols)*

**CARMEN:** (to Don José) Are you one of us now?

**JOSÉ:** I have no alternative.

**CARMEN:** Ah! that's not gallantly put,
but no matter, go, you'll take to it there
when you see
how fine is the wandering life;
the whole world your domain,
your own free will for law,
and above all that intoxicating thing:
Freedom! Freedom!

**ALL:** (to Don José) Take to the country with us.
come with us into the mountains,
come with us and you'll take to it there
when you see, away over there,
how fine is the wandering life;
the whole world your domain,
your own free will for law!
And above all that intoxicating thing:
Freedom! Freedom!
The open sky, the wandering life,
the whole wide world your domain;

your own free will for law,
and above all that intoxicating thing:
Freedom! Freedom!

## ■ Entr'acte

## ■ ACTE III

**CHOEUR:** Ecoute, écoute, compagnon, écoute,
la fortune est là-bas, là-bas,
mais prends garde pendant la route,
prends garde de faire un faux pas!

**LE DANCAÏRE, LE REMENDADO, JOSÉ, CARMEN, MERCÉDÈS ET FRASQUITA:**
Notre métier est bon,
mais pour le faire il faut
avoir une âme forte!
Et le péril est en haut, il est en bas,
il est partout, qu'importe!
Nous allons devant nous
sans souci du torrent,
sans souci de l'orage,
sans souci du soldat
qui là-bas nous attend,
et nous guette au passage—
sans souci nous allons en avant!

**TOUS:** Ecoute, compagnon, écoute, *etc.*

**LE DANCAÏRE:** Halte! nous allons nous arrêter ici . . . ceux qui ont sommeil pourront dormir pendant une demi-heure.

**LE REMENDADO:** Ah!

**LE DANCAÏRE:** Je vais, moi, voir s'il y a moyen de faire entrer les marchandises dans la ville . . . une brèche s'est faite dans le mur d'enceinte et nous pourrions passer parlà.
Remendado!

**LE REMENDADO:** Hé?

**LE DANCAÏRE:** Debout, tu vas venir avec moi.

**LE REMENDADO:** Mais, patron . . .

**LE DANCAÏRE:** Qu'est-ce que c'est?

**LE REMENDADO:** Voilà, patron, voilà!

**LE DANCAÏRE:** Allons, passe devant.

## ■ Entr'acte

## ■ ACT III

*(The curtain rises on a wild and rocky scene; the night is dark and the solitude complete. During the musical prelude a smuggler appears at the top of the rocks, then another, then two, more, and finally twenty here and there, climbing and scrambling over the rocks. Some of them are carrying heavy bales on their shoulders)*

**CHORUS:** Listen, friend, listen.
fortune lies over there,
but take care along the way,
and watch your step!

**EL DANCAÏRO, EL REMENDADO, JOSÉ, CARMEN, MERCÉDÈS AND FRASQUITA:** Our calling is a good one,
but to follow it you must
have a stout heart!
There's danger up above, and down below,
it's everywhere—what of it!
We go forward
without worrying about the torrent,
without worrying about the storm,
without worrying about the soldier
who's wanting for us over there,
and keeping a sharp lookout for us—
we go forward without worrying!

**ALL:** Listen, friend, listen, *etc.*

**EL DANCAÏRO:** Halt! We're going to stop here . . . those who feel sleepy can doss down for half an hour.

**EL REMENDADO:** (*stretching himself out voluptuously*) Ah!

**EL DANCAÏRO:** Me, I'm going to see if there's some way of getting the stuff into the town . . . a gap has been made in the outer wall and we could get through that way.
(*calling out*)
Remendado!

**EL REMENDADO:** (*waking up*) Eh?

**EL DANCAÏRO:** Get up, you're coming with me.

**EL REMENDADO:** But, boss . . .

**EL DANCAÏRO:** What's that?

**EL REMENDADO:** (*getting up*) Here we are, boss, here!

**EL DANCAÏRO:** Right, go on ahead.

LE REMENDADO: Et moi qui rêvais que j'allais pouvoir dormir . . . C'était un rêve, hélas! c'était un rêve!

JOSÉ: Voyons, Carmen . . . si je t'ai parlé trop durement, je t'en demande pardon, faisons la paix.

CARMEN: Non.

JOSÉ: Tu es le diable, Carmen?

CARMEN: Oui, qu'est-ce que tu regardes là, à quoi penses-tu?

JOSÉ: Je me dis que là-bas il y a une bonne vieille femme qui croit que je suis encore un honnete homme . . .

CARMEN: Une bonne vieille femme?

JOSÉ: Oui; ma mère.

CARMEN: Ta mère. Eh bien, tu ne ferais pas mai d'aller la retrouver.

JOSÉ: Carmen, si tu me parles encore de nous séparer . . .

CARMEN: Tu me tuerais, peut-être?
A la bonne heure . . . J'ai vu dans les cartes que nous devions finir ensemble.

JOSÉ: Tu es le diable, Carmen?

CARMEN: Mais oui, je te l'ai déja dit . . .

*(She turns her back on José and goes and sits down by Mercédès and Frasquita.—After a moment of indecision, José moves off in his turn and goes and stretches himself out upon the rocks.—During the final exchanges in the foregoing scene, Mercédès and Frasquita have been spreading out playing cards in front of them)*

FRASQUITA ET MERCÉDÈS:
Mêlons! Coupons!
Bien, c'est cela!
Trois cartes ici . . .
Quatre là!
Et maintenant, parlez, mes belles,
de l'avenir, donnez-nous des nouvelles;
dites-nous qui nous trahira,
dites-nous qui nous aimera! Parlez, parlez!

FRASQUITA: Moi, je vois un jeune amoureux,
qui m'aime on ne peut davantage.

MERCÉDÈS: Le mien est très riche et très vieux,
mais il parle de mariage.

---

EL REMENDADO: And I thought I was going to be able to sleep . . . It was a dream, alas, it was a dream!
*(He goes out, followed by Dancairo)*
*(During this scene between Carmen and José, a few gypsy men light a fire, by which Mercédès and Frasquita come and sit down; the others roll themselves up in their cloaks, lie down and go to sleep)*

JOSÉ: Look, Carmen . . . if I spoke to you too harshly, I ask your forgiveness. Let's make up.

CARMEN: No.

JOSÉ: You're worried, Carmen?

CARMEN: Yes, what's that you're looking at there, what are you thinking of?

JOSÉ: I'm telling myself that down there is a good old woman who believes me still to be an honest man . . .

CARMEN: A good old woman?

JOSÉ: Yes, my mother.

CARMEN: Your mother. Well then, you'd do no harm by going to find her.

JOSÉ: Carmen, if you talk to me any more about us separating . . .

CARMEN: You would kill me, perhaps?
*(José does not answer)*
Well and good . . . I've seen in the cards that we are to finish together.

JOSÉ: You're worried, Carmen?

CARMEN: Why yes, I've already told you so . . .

FRASQUITA AND MERCÉDÈS:
Shuffle! Cut!
Good, that's that!
Three cards here . . .
four there!
And now speak, my lovelies,
give us news of the future;
tell us who's going to betray us,
tell us who's going to love us!
Speak! Speak!

FRASQUITA: Me, I see a young suitor,
no one could love me more.

MERCÉDÈS: Mine is very rich and very old,
but he talks of marriage.

---

FRASQUITA: Je me campe sur son cheval,
et dans la montagne il m'entraîne.

MERCÉDÈS: Dans un château presque royal,
le mien m'installe en souveraine!

FRASQUITA: De l'amour à n'en plus finir,
tous les jours, nouvelles folies!

MERCÉDÈS: De l'or tant que j'en puis tenir,
des diamants, des pierreries!

FRASQUITA: Le mien devient un chef fameux,
cent hommes marchent à sa suite!

MERCÉDÈS: Le mien en croirai-je mes yeux?
Oui . . . il meurt!
Ah! je suis veuve et j'hérite!

REPRISE DE L'ENSEMBLE: Parlez encor, parlez, mes belles, *etc.*

MERCÉDÈS: Fortune!

FRASQUITA: Amour!

CARMEN: Voyons, que j'essaie à mon tour.
Carreau, pique . . . la mort!
J'ai bien lu . . . moi d'abord.
Ensuite lui . . . pour tous les deux la mort!
En vain pour éviter les réponses amères,
en vain tu mêleras;
cela ne sert à rien, les cartes sont sincères et ne mentiront pas!
Dans le livre d'en haut
si ta page est heureuse,
mêle et coupe sans peur,
la carte sous tes doigts se tournera joyeuse,
t'annonçant le bonheur.
Mais si tu dois mourir,
si le mot redoutable
est écrit par le sort,
recommence vingt fois, la carte impitoyable
répétera: la mort!
Encor! encor! Toujours la mort!

FRASQUITA ET MERCÉDÈS: Parlez encor, parlez mes belles, *etc.*

CARMEN: Encore! de désespoir!
Toujours la mort!

CARMEN: Eh bien?

LE DANCAÏRE: Eh bien, j'avais raison de ne pas me fier de Lillas Pastia.
Nous avons aperçu trois douaniers qui gardaient la brèche.

CARMEN: (*en riant*) N'ayez pas peur, Dancaïre, nous vous en répondrons de vos trois douaniers . . .

JOSÉ: (*furieux*) Carmen!

---

FRASQUITA: I settle myself firmly on his horse
and he carries me off into the mountains.

MERCÉDÈS: In an almost royal castle
mine installs me in queenly state!

FRASQUITA: Never-ending love,
every day new raptures!

MERCÉDÈS: As much gold as I can take,
diamonds, precious stones!

FRASQUITA: Mine becomes a famous leader,
a hundred men march in his train!

MERCÉDÈS: Mine . . . can I believe my eyes?
Yes . . . he dies!
Ah! I'm a widow and I inherit!

TOGETHER: (*reprise*) Speak again, speak, my lovelies, *etc.*
*(They begin to consult the cards again)*

MERCÉDÈS: Fortune!

FRASQUITA: Love!

CARMEN: Let's see—let me have a try.
*(She starts to turn up the cards)*
Diamond, spade . . . Death!
I read it clearly . . . me first.
Then him . . . for both of us, Death!
*(In a low voice, while continuing to shuffle the cards:)*
In vain to avoid bitter replies,
in vain will you shuffle;
that achieves nothing, the cards are truthful and will not lie!
If your page in the book
up above is a happy one
shuffle and cut without fear,
the card under your fingers will turn up nicely,
foretelling good luck.
But if you are to die,
if the terrible word
has been written by Destiny,
begin twenty times—the pitiless card
will repeat: Death!
*(turning up the cards)*
Again! Always Death!

FRASQUITA AND MERCÉDÈS:
Speak again, my lovelies, speak! *etc.*

CARMEN: Again! Despair! Always Death!
*(El Dancaïro and El Remendado return.)*

CARMEN: Well?

EL DANCAÏRO: Well, I was right not to trust Lillas Pastia. We spotted three customs men guarding the gap.

CARMEN: (*laughing*) Have no fear, Dancairo, we'll take care of your three customs men for you . . .

JOSÉ: (*furious*) Carmen!

LE DANCAÏRE: Ah! tu vas nous laisser tranquilles avec ta jalousie. Tu vas te placer là, sur cette hauteur. Dans le cas où tu apercevrais quelqu'un, passes ta colère sur l'indiscret.
En route alors . . .
Mais vous me répondrez vraiment de ces trois douaniers?

CARMEN: N'ayez pas peur, Dancaïre.

CARMEN, MERCÉDÈS ET FRASQUITA: Quant au douanier, c'est notre affaire,
tout comme un autre il aime à plaire,
il aime à faire le galant;
ah! laissez-nous/les passer en avant!

TOUTES LES FEMMES: Quant au douanier, c'est notre affaire, *etc.*

TOUS: Il aime à plaire!

MERCÉDÈS: Le douanier sera clément!

TOUS: Il est galant!

CARMEN: Le douanier sera charmant!

TOUS: Il aime à plaire!

MERCÉDÈS: Le douanier sera galant!

FRASQUITA: Oui, le douanier sera même entreprenant!

TOUS: Oui, le douanier c'est notre/leur affaire,
tout comme un autre il aime à plaire,
il aime à faire le galant,
laissez-nous/les passer en avant!

CARMEN, MERCÉDÈS ET FRASQUITA: Il ne s'agit plus de bataille,
non, il s'agit tout simplement de se laisser prendre la taille
et d'écouter un compliment.
S'il faut aller jusqu'au sourire,
que voulez-vous, on sourira!

TOUTES LES FEMMES: Et d'avance, je puis le dire,
la contrebande passera!
En avant! marchons! allons!

TOUT LE MONDE: Oui, le douanier c'est notre/leur affaire, *etc.*

LE GUIDE: Nous y sommes.

MICAËLA: C'est ici.

LE GUIDE: Oui, vilain endroit, n'est-ce pas, et pas rassurant du tout?

MICAËLA: Je ne vois personne.

EL DANCAÏRO: Ah, you will give us a rest from your jealousy. You will post yourself there on that height. If you should happen to stop anyone, take your anger out on such an ill-advised person.
On our way, then . . .
(*to the women*)
But you really will answer to me for these three customs men?

CARMEN: Have no fear, Dancairo.

CARMEN, MERCÉDÈS AND FRASQUITA: As for the customs man, he's our affair;
just like the next man he loves to please,
he loves to play the gallant;
ah! leave us to go on ahead!

ALL THE GIRLS: As for the customs man, he's our affair, *etc.*

EVERYONE: He loves to please!

MERCÉDÈS: The customs man will be easy on us!

ALL: He is gallant!

CARMEN: The customs man will be charming!

ALL: He loves to please!

MERCÉDÈS: The customs man will be gallant!

FRASQUITA: Yes, the customs man will even be forward!

ALL: Yes, the customs man is our/their affair;
just like the next man he loves to please,
he loves to play the gallant;
let us/them go on ahead!

CARMEN, MERCÉDÈS AND FRASQUITA: It's no longer a question of battle;
no, it's simply a question of letting ourselves be taken by the waist
and listening to a compliment.
If it's necessary to go as far as a smile,
what of it?—we'll smile!

ALL THE WOMEN: And here and now I can say
the stuff will get through!
Forward! On our way! Let's go!

ALL: Yes, the customs man is our/their affair, *etc.*
(*Everyone leaves. José brings up the rear, examining the priming of his carbine; just before he disappears, a man is seen moving behind a rock. It is Micaëla's guide*)
(*The guide advances cautiously, then signals to Micaëla that the coast is clear*)

THE GUIDE: We're there.

MICAËLA: (*entering*) This is the place.

THE GUIDE: Yes, nasty spot, isn't it, and not at all reassuring?

MICAËLA: I don't see anybody.

LE GUIDE: Ils reviendront bientôt. Ils n'ont pas emporté toutes leurs marchandises . . . prenez garde . . . l'un de leurs doit être en sentinelle et si l'on nous apercevrait . . .

MICAËLA: Je l'espère bien qu'on m'apercevra . . . puisque je suis venue ici justement pour parler à un de ces contrebandiers . . .

LE GUIDE: Eh bien, vous pouvez vous vanter d'avoir du courage . . . venir ainsi affronter ces Bohémiens . . .

MICAËLA: Je n'aurais pas peur, je vous assure.

LE GUIDE: Bien vrai?

MICAËLA: Bien vrai.

LE GUIDE: (*naïvement*) Alors je vous demanderai la permission de m'en aller. Si ça ne vous fait rien, j'irai vous attendre à l'auberge au bas de la montagne.
Vous restez décidément?

MICAËLA: Oui, je reste!

LE GUIDE: Que tous saints du paradis vous soient en aide alors, mais c'est une drôle idée que vous avez là . . .

MICAËLA: Mon guide avait raison . . . l'endroit n'est pas bien rassurant.

MICAËLA: Je dis, que rien ne m'épouvante,
je dis, hélas! que je réponds de moi;
mais j'ai beau faire la vaillante,
au fond du coeur, je meurs d'effroi!
Seule en ce lieu sauvage,
toute seule j'ai peur,
mais j'ai tort d'avoir peur;
vous me donnerez du courage,
vous me protégerez, Seigneur.
Je vais voir de près cette femme dont les artifices maudits
ont fini par faire un infâme de celui que j'aimais jadis;
elle est dangereuse, elle est belle,
mais je ne veux pas avoir, peur,
je parlerai haut devant elle.
Ah! Seigneur,
vous me protégerez!
Ah! je dis, que rien ne m'épouvante, *etc.*
. . . protégez-moi, O Seigneur,
Protégez-moi, Seigneur!
Mais . . . je ne me trompe pas . . . sur ce rocher, c'est don José.
José! José
Mais que fait-il? . . . Il arme sa carabine, il ajuste . . . il fait feu.
Ah! mon Dieu, j'ai trop présumé de mon courage . . .

THE GUIDE: They'll come back soon, for they haven't taken away all their goods . . . take care . . . one of their men must be on sentry-go, and if we were seen . . .

MICAËLA: I sincerely hope someone *will* see me . . . since that's just what I've come here for, to speak to one of these smugglers . . .

THE GUIDE: Well now, you can boast of having courage, to come here like this to face these gypsies . . .

MICAËLA: I shouldn't be afraid, I assure you.

THE GUIDE: Truly?

MICAËLA: Truly.

THE GUIDE: (*naively*) Then I'll ask you permission to take myself off. If it's all the same to you I'll go and wait for you in the inn at the foot of the mountain.
You're determined to stay?

MICAËLA: Yes, I'm staying!

THE GUIDE: May all the saints in paradise come to your aid then, but it's a funny idea you've got there . . .

MICAËLA: (*looking around her*) My guide was right . . . It's not a very reassuring spot.

MICAËLA: I say that nothing frightens me,
I say, alas, that I have only myself to depend on;
but I have tried in vain to be brave,
at heart I'm dying of fright!
Alone in this wild place,
all alone, I'm afraid,
but I do wrong to be afraid;
you will give me courage,
you will protect me, Lord.
I shall get a close look at this woman
whose evil wiles
have finished by making a criminal of the man I once loved:
she is dangerous, she is beautiful,
but I won't be afraid,
I shall speak out in front of her.
Ah! Lord,
you will protect me!
Ah! I say that nothing will frighten me, *etc.*
. . . protect me, O Lord,
protect me, Lord!
But . . . I'm not mistaken . . . on that rock—It's Don José.
(*calling out*)
José! José!
(*terrified*)
But what is he doing? . . . He's cocking his carbine . . . he's aiming . . . he fires.
(*A shot is heard*)
Ah, my God, I overestimated my courage . . .

# Act III

ESCAMILLO: Quelques lignes plus bas, et ce n'est pas moi qui aurais le plaisir de combattre les taureaux que je suis en train de conduire . . .

JOSÉ: Qui êtes-vous? Répondez.

ESCAMILLO: Eh là . . . doucement!

ESCAMILLO: Je suis Escamillo, Torrero de Grenade!

JOSÉ: Escamillo!

ESCAMILLO: C'est moi!

JOSÉ: Je connais votre nom, soyez le bienvenu; mais vraiment, camarade, vous pouviez y rester.

ESCAMILLO: Je ne vous dis pas non, mais je suis amoureux, mon cher, à la folie, et celui-là serait un pauvre compagnon, qui, pour voir ses amours, ne risquerait sa vie!

JOSÉ: Celle que vous aimez est ici?

ESCAMILLO: Justement. C'est une zingara, mon cher.

JOSÉ: Elle s'appelle?

ESCAMILLO: Carmen.

JOSÉ: Carmen!

ESCAMILLO: Carmen! oui, mon cher. Elle avait pour amant un soldat qui a déserté pour elle. Ils s'adoraient, mais c'est fini, je crois. Les amours de Carmen ne durent pas six mois.

JOSÉ: Vous l'aimez cependant!

ESCAMILLO: Je l'aime! Oui, mon cher, je l'aime à la folie!

JOSÉ: Mais pour nous enlever nos filles de bohème, savez-vous bien qu'il faut payer?

ESCAMILLO: Soit! on paiera.

JOSÉ: Et que le prix se paie à coups de navaja!

ESCAMILLO: A coups de navaja!

JOSÉ: Comprenez-vous?

ESCAMILLO: Le discours est très net. Ce déserteur, ce beau soldat qu'elle aime, ou du moins qu'elle aimait— c'est donc vous?

JOSÉ: Oui, c'est moi-même!

(She disappears behind the rocks. At the same moment Escamillo comes in, holding his hat in his hand)

ESCAMILLO: (looking at his hat) A little lower . . . and it isn't I who would have the pleasure of fighting the bulls I'm about to drive . . . (Enter José)

JOSÉ: (carrying his cloak) Who are you? Answer.

ESCAMILLO: (very calm) Eh eh . . . gently!

ESCAMILLO: I'm Escamillo, the Granada matador!

JOSÉ: Escamillo!

ESCAMILLO: That's me!

JOSÉ: (returning his knife to its sheath) I know your name, you're welcome; but truly, comrade, that could have been the end of you.

ESCAMILLO: I'm not denying it, but, my friend, I am madly in love, and he would be a wretched fellow who wouldn't risk his life to see his ladylove!

JOSÉ: The girl you love is here?

ESCAMILLO: Exactly. She's a gypsy girl, my friend.

JOSÉ: Her name?

ESCAMILLO: Carmen.

JOSÉ: Carmen!

ESCAMILLO: Carmen! yes, my friend. She had as a lover a soldier who once deserted on her account. They adored each other, but it's over, I think. Carmen's affairs don't last six months.

JOSÉ: Yet you love her!

ESCAMILLO: I love her! Yes, my friend, I love her to distraction!

JOSÉ: But to take our gypsy girls away from us you know that you have to pay?

ESCAMILLO: All right! I'll pay.

JOSÉ: And that the price is paid with the knife!

ESCAMILLO: With the knife!

JOSÉ: You understand?

ESCAMILLO: You put it very clearly. This deserter, this fine soldier she loves, or rather, used to love— is you, then?

JOSÉ: Yes, myself!

ESCAMILLO: J'en suis ravi, mon cher, et le tour est complet!

JOSÉ: Enfin ma colère trouve à qui parler! Le sang, je l'espère, va bientôt couler, etc.

ESCAMILLO: Quelle maladresse, j'en rirais vraiment! Chercher la maitresse et trouver l'amant! etc.

ENSEMBLE: Mettez-vous en garde, et veillez sur vous! Tant pis pour qui tarde à parer les coups! En garde! allons! veillez sur vous!

ESCAMILLO: Je la connais, ta garde navarraise. Et je te previens en ami, Qu'elle ne vaut rien . . . A ton aise. Je t'aurai du moins averti.

JOSÉ: Tu m'épargnes, maudit.

ESCAMILLO: A ce jeu de couteau Je suis trop fort pour toi.

JOSÉ: Voyons cela.

ESCAMILLO: Tout beau, Ta vie est à moi, mais en somme J'ai pour métier de frapper le taureau, Non de trouer le coeur de l'homme.

JOSÉ: Frappe ou bien meurs . . . Ceci n'est pas un jeu.

ESCAMILLO: Soit, mais au moins respire un peu.

JOSÉ: Enfin ma colère Trouve à qui parler etc.

ESCAMILLO: Quelle maladresse, J'en rirais vraiment! etc.

CARMEN: Holà, holà! José!

ESCAMILLO: Vrai, j'ai l'âme ravie que ce soit vous, Carmen, que me sauviez la vie! Quant à toi, beau soldat, je prendrai ma revanche, et nous jouerons la belle,

ESCAMILLO: I'm delighted, my friend, and the wheel's come full circle! (Both draw their knives and wrap their left arm in their cloaks)

JOSÉ: At last my rage has found an outlet! Blood, I hope, will soon flow, etc.

ESCAMILLO: What a predicament, I could laugh at it, really! To look for the mistress and find the lover! etc.

TOGETHER: Put up your guard, and look out for yourself! So much the worse for the one who's slow at parrying! On guard! come on! look out for yourself! (They take up positions on guard at some distance from each other)

ESCAMILLO: I know it, your Navarrais-style guard, and I warn you, in a friendly way, that it's no good . . . (Without answering, Don José advances upon the matador) As you like. At least I'll have warned you. (Fight,—Incidental music. The matador, very calm, attempts only to defend himself)

JOSÉ: You're not trying, you devil.

ESCAMILLO: At this knife-play I'm too good for you.

JOSÉ: Let's see. (A swift and very lively hand-to-hand engagement. José finds himself at the mercy of the matador, who does not strike)

ESCAMILLO: Steady, your life belongs to me, but in short my job is to kill bulls, not to bore holes in men's hearts.

JOSÉ: Strike, or die . . . This isn't a game.

ESCAMILLO: (disengaging himself) All right, but at least get your breath. (Reprise of ensemble)

JOSÉ: At last my rage has found an outlet, etc.

ESCAMILLO: What a predicament, I could laugh at it, really! etc. (They fight. The matador slips and falls. Enter Carmen and El Dancairo; she rushes forward and stays José hand. The matador gets to his feet; El Remendado, Mercédès, Frasquita and the smugglers have meanwhile come upon the scene)

CARMEN: Stop, stop, José!

ESCAMILLO: Really, I'm overjoyed that it should be you, Carmen, who saved my life! (to Don José) As for you, my fine soldier,

le jour où tu voudras reprendre le combat!

**LE DANCAÏRE:** C'est bon, c'est bon, plus de querelle! Nous, nous allons partir. Et toi, l'ami, bonsoir!

**ESCAMILLO:** Souffrez au moins qu'avant de vous dire au revoir, je vous invite tous aux courses de Séville. Je compte pour ma part y briller de mon mieux et qui m'aime y viendra! L'ami, tiens-roi tranquille, j'ai tout dit et je n'ai plus ici qu'à faire mes adieux!

**JOSÉ:** (*à Carmen*) Prends garde à toi, Carmen, je suis las de souffrir!

**LE DANCAÏRE:** En route, en route, il faut partir!

**TOUS:** En route, en route, il faut partir!

**LE REMENDADO:** Halte! quelqu'un est là cherche à se cacher.

**CARMEN:** Une femme!

**LE DANCAÏRE:** Pardieu, la surprise est heureuse!

**JOSÉ:** Micaëla!

**MICAËLA:** Don José!

**JOSÉ:** Malheureuse! Que viens-tu faire ici?

**MICAËLA:** Moi, je viens te chercher, Là-bas est la chaumière, où sans cesse priant une mère, ta mère, pleure, hélas sur son enfant. Elle pleure et t'appelle, elle pleure et te tend les bras; tu prendras pitié d'elle, José, ah! José, tu me suivras!

**CARMEN:** Va-t'en! Va-t'en! tu feras bien, notre métier ne te vaut rien!

**JOSÉ:** Tu me dis de la suivre?

**CARMEN:** Oui, tu devrais partir!

**JOSÉ:** Tu me dis de la suivre pour que toi, tu puisses courir après ton nouvel amant! Non! non vraiment! Dût-il m'en coûter la vie, non, Carmen, je ne partirai pas, et la chaine qui nous lie

---

I'll take my revenge, and we'll play for two out of three whenever you wish to renew the fight!

**EL DANCAIRO:** Enough, enough, no more quarrelling! We must get going. (*to Escamillo*) And you, my friend, good night!

**ESCAMILLO:** Allow me at least, before I say goodbye, to invite you all to the bullfights at Seville. I expect to be at my most brilliant there, and who loves me will come! (*to José, who makes a threatening gesture*) Friend, keep calm, I've had my say, and I've nothing more to do here but make my farewells! (*Leisurely exit of Escamillo, Don José tries to attack him but is held back by El Dancaïro and El Remendado*)

**JOSÉ:** (*to Carmen*) Take care, Carmen, I'm weary of suffering! (*Carmen answers him with a slight shrug of her shoulders and walks off*)

**EL DANCAIRO:** Let's get going! We must be off!

**ALL:** Let's get going! We must be off!

**EL REMENDADO:** Stop! there's someone there trying to hide! (*He brings in Micaëla*)

**CARMEN:** A woman!

**EL DANCAIRO:** Lord, a pleasant surprise!

**JOSÉ:** Micaela!

**MICAËLA:** Don José!

**JOSÉ:** Poor girl! What are you doing here?

**MICAËLA:** I've come looking for you. Down there is the cottage where, praying unceasingly, a mother, your mother, weeps, alas, for her son. She weeps and calls you, she weeps and holds out her arms to you; you will take pity on her, José, ah José, you will come with me!

**CARMEN:** Go on! Go on! You'll do well to go; our business means nothing to you!

**JOSÉ:** You're telling me to go with her?

**CARMEN:** Yes, you ought to go!

**JOSÉ:** You're telling me to go with her so that you can run after your new lover! No! Not likely! Though it should cost me my life, no, Carmen, I shall not go away,

---

nous liera jusqu'au trépas! Dût-il m'en coûter la vie, *etc.*

**MICAËLA:** Ecoute-moi, je t'en prie, ta mère te tend les bras, cette chaine qui te lie, José, tu la briseras!

**FRASQUITA, MERCÉDÈS, LE RE-MENDADO, LE DANCAÏRE, CHO-EUR:** Il t'en coûtera la vie, José, si tu ne pars pas, et la chaine qui vous lie se rompra par ton trépas.

**JOSÉ:** (*à Micaëla*) Laisse-moi!

**MICAËLA:** Hélas, José!

**JOSÉ:** Car je suis condamné!

**FRASQUITA, MERCÉDÈS, LE RE-MENDADO, LE DANCAÏRE, CHO-EUR:** José! Prends garde!

**JOSÉ:** (*à Carmen*) Ah! je te tiens, fille damnée, je te tiens, et je te forcerai bien à subir la destinée qui rive ton sort au mien! Dût-il m'en coûter la vie, non, non, non, je ne partirai pas!

**CHOEUR:** Ah! prends garde, Don José!

**MICAËLA:** Une parole encor, ce sera la dernière. Hélas! José, ta mère se meurt, et ta mère ne voudrait pas mourir sans t'avoir pardonné.

**JOSÉ:** Ma mère! elle se meurt?

**MICAËLA:** Oui, Don José.

**JOSÉ:** Partons, ah, partons! (*à Carmen*) Sois contente, je pars, mais nous nous reverrons!

**ESCAMILLO:** (*au loin*) Toréador, en garde! *etc.*

■ **Entr'acte**

■ **ACTE IV**

---

and the bond which unites us shall unite us till death! Though it should cost my me life, *etc.*

**MICAËLA:** Listen to me, I implore you, Your mother holds out her arms to you, that bond which unites you, José, you will break it!

**FRASQUITA, MERCÉDÈS, EL RE-MENDADO, EL DANCAÏRO, CHORUS:** It will cost you your life, José, if you don't go. and the bond which unites you will be broken by your death.

**JOSÉ:** (*to Micaëla*) Leave me!

**MICAËLA:** Alas, José!

**JOSÉ:** For I am doomed!

**FRASQUITA, MERCÉDÈS, EL RE-MENDADO, EL DANCAÏRO, CHORUS:** José! take care!

**JOSÉ:** (*to Carmen*) Ah! I've got you, accursed girl, I've got you, and I shall compel you to bow to the destiny that links your fate with mine! Though it should cost me my life, no, no, no, I shall not go!

**CHORUS:** Ah! Take care, take care, Don José!

**MICAËLA:** One word more, this will be the last. Alas! José, your mother is dying, and she doesn't want to die without having forgiven you.

**JOSÉ:** My mother! she's dying?

**MICAËLA:** Yes, Don José.

**JOSÉ:** Let's go, ah, let's go! (*to Carmen*) Be satisfied! I'm going, but we shall meet again! (*He hurries off with Micaëla*)

**ESCAMILLO:** (*in the distance*) Toreador, on guard! *etc.* (*José stops at the back, on the rocks. He hesitates, but, after a moment, goes on his way with Micaëla. Carmen rushes in the direction of the voice. The gypsies take up their bales and prepare to leave*)

■ **Entr'acte**

■ **ACT IV**

(*A square in Seville, with the walls of the old arena in the background. The entrance to the ring is closed by a long curtain. A bullfight is about to take place, and there is great excitement. Hawkers move about offering water, oranges, fans, etc.*)

## Act IV

**CHOEUR:** A deux cuartos! A deux cuartos!
Des éventails pour s'éventer!
Des oranges pour grignotter!
Le programme avec les détails!
Du vin! De l'eau! Des cigarettes!
A deux cuartos! A deux cuartos! *etc.*
Voyez! A deux cuartos!
Señoras et caballeros!

**ZUNIGA:** Des oranges, vite!

**PLUSIEURS MARCHANDS:** En voici,
prenez, prenez, mesdemoiselles.

**UN MARCHAND:** Merci, mon officier, merci.

**LES AUTRES MARCHANDS:**
Celles-ci, Señor, sont plus belles.
Des éventails pour s'éventer, *etc.*

**ZUNIGA:** Holà! des éventails!

**UN BOHÉMIEN:** Voulez-vous aussi des lorgnettes?

**REPRISE DU CHOEUR:** A deux cuartos! A deux cuartos!
Voyez! voyez! à deux cuartos! *etc.*

**ZUNIGA:** Qu'avez-vous donc fait de la Carmencita?

**FRASQUITA:** Escamillo est ici, la Carmencita ne doit pas être loin.

**ZUNIGA:** Ah! c'est Escamillo, maintenant?

**FRASQUITA:** Et son ancien amoureux José, qu'est-il devenu?

**MERCÉDÈS:** Il est libre.

**ZUNIGA:** Pour le moment.

**FRASQUITA:** Je ne serais pas tranquille à la place de Carmen, je ne serais pas tranquille du tout.

**CHOEUR:** Les voice! voici la quidrille!
La quadrille des toréros!
Sur les lances le soleil brille!
En l'air toques et sombreros!
Les voici! voici la quadrille,
la qadrille des toréros!
Voici, débouchant sur la place,
voici d'abord, marchant au pass,
l'alguazil à vilaine face!
A bas! á bas! á bas!
Et puis saluons au passage,
saluons les hardis chulos!
Bravo! viva! gloire au courage!
Voici les hardis chulos!
Voyez les banderilleros!
Voyez quel air de crânerie!
Voyez! voyez! voyez! voyez!
Quel regards, et de quel éclat
étincelle la broderie
de leur costume de combat!
Voici les banderilleros!
Un autre quadrille s'avance!
Voyez les picadors!
Comme ils sont beaux!
Comme ils vont du fer de leur lance,
harceler le flanc des taureaux!

**CHORUS:** Two cuartos! Two cuartos!
Fans to cool yourselves!
Oranges to nibble!
Programme with details!
Wine! Water! Cigarettes!
Two cuartos! Two cuartos! *etc.*
Look! For two cuartos!
Señoras and cabelleros!

**ZUNIGA:** Some oranges, look sharp!

**SEVERAL FRUITSELLERS:** (*running up*) Here you are.
take these, ladies.

**ONE OF THEM:** (*to Zuniga, who pays*) Thank you, officer, thank you.

**THE OTHERS:** These ones here, sir, are better.
Fans to cool yourselves, *etc.*

**ZUNIGA:** Here you! some fans!

**A GYPSY:** (*running forward*)
Want some opera glasses too?

**CHORUS:** (*reprise*) Two cuartos!
Two cuartos!
Look! Look! Two cuartos! *etc.*

**ZUNIGA:** But what have you done with Carmencita?

**FRASQUITA:** Escamillo is here,
Carmencita can't be far off.

**ZUNIGA:** Ah! It's Escamillo now?

**FRASQUITA:** And her former lover Don José, what's become of him?

**MERCÉDÈS:** He's at large.

**ZUNIGA:** For the moment.

**FRASQUITA:** I shouldn't feel easy in Carmen's place. I shouldn't feel easy at all.
(*From outside loud shouts are heard, trumpet calls, etc. etc. The Cuadrilla is arriving*).

**CHORUS:** Here they come! Here's the caudrilla!
The toreadors' cuadrilla!
The sun flashes on their lances!
Up in the air with your caps and hats!
Here they are! Here's the cuadrilla,
the toreadors' cuadrilla!
Here, coming into the square
first of all, marching on foot,
is the constable with his ugly mug!
Down with him! Down with him!
And now as they go by
let's cheer the bold *chulos!*
Bravo! Hurrah! Glory to courage!
Here come the bold *chulos!*
Look at the *banderilleros!*
See what a swaggering air!
See them! See them!
What looks, and how brilliantly
the ornaments glitter
on their fighting dress!
Here are the *banderilleros!*
Another cuadrilla's coming!
Look at the *picadors!*
How handsome they are!
How they'll torment the bull's flanks

L'Espada! Escamillo!
C'est l'Espada, la fine lame,
celui qui vient terminer tout,
qui paraît à la fin du drame
et qui frappe le dernier coup!
Vive Escamillo! ah bravo!
Les voici! voici la quadrille! *etc.*

**ESCAMILLO:** (*à Carmen*). Si tu m'aimes, Carmen, tu pourras, tout à l'heure,
être fière de moi!

**CARMEN:** Ah! je t'aime, escamillo,
je t'aime, et que je meure si j'ai jamais aimé quelqu'un autant que toi!

**TOUS LES DEUX:** Ah! je t'aime!
Oui, je t'aime!

**LES ALGUAZILS:** Place, place!
place au seigneur Alcade!

**FRASQUITA:** Carmen, un bon conseil, ne reste pas ici!

**CARMEN:** Et pourquoi, s'il te plaît?

**MERCÉDÈS:** Il est là!

**CARMEN:** Qui donc?

**MERCÉDÈS:** Lui, Don José!
Dans la foule il se cache; regarde.

**CARMEN:** Oui, je le vois.

**FRASQUITA:** Prends garde!

**CARMEN:** Je ne suis pas femme à trembler devant lui.
Je l'attends, et je vais lui parler.

**MERCÉDÈS:** Carmen, crois-moi, prends garde!

**CARMEN:** Je ne crains rien!

**FRASQUITA:** Prends garde!

**CARMEN:** C'est toi!

**JOSÉ:** C'est moi!

**CARMEN:** L'on m'avait avertie
que tu n'étais pas loin, que tu devais venir;
l'on m'avait même dit de craindre pour ma vie
mais je suis brave et n'ai pas voulu fuir.

with the tips of their lances!
(*At last Escamillo appears, accompanied by a radiant and magnificently dressed Carmen*)
The Matador! Escamillo!
It's the Matador, the skilled swordsman,
he who comes to finish things off,
who appears at the drama's end
and strikes the last blow!
Long live Escamillo! Ah bravo!
Here they are! Here's the cuadrilla!
*etc.*

**ESCAMILLO:** (*to Carmen*). If you love me, carmen, soon
you can be proud of me.

**CARMEN:** Ah! I love you, Escamillo, I love you, and may I die if I have ever loved anyone as much as you!

**TOGETHER:** Ah! I love you!
Yes, I love you!

**ALGUAZILS:** Make way! Make way for his worship the Mayor!
(*During a little orchestral march the Mayor enters and crosses the stage, preceded and followed by an escort of constables. Meanwhile Frasquita and Mercédès draw near to Carmen*)

**FRASQUITA:** Carmen, a word of advice, don't stay here!

**CARMEN:** And why, if you please?

**MERCÉDÈS:** He's there!

**CARMEN:** Who?

**MERCÉDÈS:** Him, Don José!
He's hding among the crowd; look.

**CARMEN:** Yes, I see him.

**FRASQUITA:** Take care!

**CARMEN:** I'm not a woman to tremble in front of him.
I'm expecting him, and I'll speak to him.

**MERCÉDÈS:** Carmen, believe me, take care!

**CARMEN:** I'm not afraid of anything!

**FRASQUITA:** Take care!
(*The mayor's cortège has entered the arean. Behind him, the procession of the cuadrilla resumes its march and goes into the ring. The crowd follows . . . and in withdrawing has revealed Don José, leaving him and Carmen alone downstage.*)

**CARMEN:** It's you!

**JOSÉ:** Yes, me!

**CARMEN:** I'd been warned
that you were about, that you might come here;
I was even told to fear for my life,
but I'm no coward and had no intention of running away.

JOSÉ: Je ne menace pas, j'implore, je supplie;
notre passé, Carmen, je l'oublie,
Oui, nous allons tous deux
commencer une autre vie,
loin d'ici, sous d'autres cieux!

JOSÉ: I'm not threatening, I'm imploring, beseeching;
our past, Carmen—I forget it!
Yes, together we are going
to begin another life,
far from here, under new skies!

CARMEN: Tu demandes l'impossible,
Carmen jamais n'a menti;
son âme reste inflexible.
Entre elle et toi, tout est fini.
Jamais je n'ai menti;
entre nous, tout est fini.

CARMEN: You ask the impossible,
Carmen has never lied;
her mind is made up.
Between her and you everything's finished.
I have never lied;
all's over between us.

JOSÉ: Carmen, il est temps encore,
oui, il est temps encore,
O ma Carmen, laisse-moi
te sauver, toi que j'adore,
et me sauver avec toi!

JOSÉ: Carmen, there is still time,
yes, there is still time,
O my Carmen, let me
save you, you I adore,
and save myself with you!

CARMEN: Non, je sais bien que c'est l'heure,
je sais bien que tu me tueras;
mais que je vive ou que je meure,
non, non, je ne te céderai pas!

CARMEN: No, I'm well aware that the hour has come,
I know that you are going to kill me;
but whether I live or die,
no, no, I shall not give in to you!

JOSÉ: Carmen, il est temps encore,
ô ma Carmen, laisse-moi
te sauver, toi que j'adore;
ah! laisse-moi te sauver
et me sauver avec toi!
O ma Carmen, il est temps encore,
*etc.*

JOSÉ: Carmen, there is still time,
O my Carmen, let me
save you, you whom I adore;
ah! let me save you
and save myself with you!
O my Carmen, there is still time,
*etc.*

CARMEN: Pourquoi t'occuper encore
d'un coeur qui n'est plus à toi?
Non, ce coeur n'est plus à toi!
En vain tu dis: "Je t'adore",
tu n'obtiendras rien, non, rien de moi,
Ah! c'est en vain,
tu n'obtiendras rien, rien de moi!

CARMEN: Why still concern yourself
with a heart that's no longer yours?
No, this heart no longer belongs to you!
In vain you say "I adore you",
you'll get nothing, no nothing, from me.
Ah! it's useless,
you'll get nothing, nothing, from me!

JOSÉ: Tu ne m'aimes donc plus?
Tu ne m'aimes donc plus?

JOSÉ: Then you don't love me any more?
(*Carmen is silent*.)
Then you don't love me any more?

CARMEN: Non, je ne t'aime plus.

CARMEN: No, I don't love you any more.

JOSÉ: Mais moi, Carmen, je t'aime encore;
Carmen, hélas! moi, je t'adore!

JOSÉ: But I, Carmen, I love you still;
Carmen, alas! I adore you!

CARMEN: A quoi bon tout cela?
que de mots superflus!

CARMEN: What's the good of this?
What waste of words!

JOSÉ: Carmen, je t'aime, je t'adore!
Eh bien, s'il le faut, pour te plaire,
je resterai bandit, tout ce que tu voudras—
tout, tu m'endtends? Tout!
mais ne me quitte pas,
ô ma Carmen,
ah! souviens-toi, souviens-toi du passé!
Nous nous aimions naguère! Ah! ne me quitte pas, Carmen,
ah, ne me quitte pas!

JOSÉ: Carmen, I love you, I adore you!
All right, if I must, to please you
I'll stay a bandit, anything you like—
anything, do you hear? Anything!
but do not leave me,
O my Carmen,
ah! remember the past!
We loved each other once!
Ah! do not leave me, Carmen,
ah, do not leave me!

CARMEN: Jamais Carmen ne cédera!
Libre elle est née et libre elle mourra!

CARMEN: Carmen will never yield!
Free she was born and free she will die!

CHOEUR ET FANFARES: (*dans le cirque*) Viva! Viva! la course est belle!
Viva! sur le sable sanglant
le taureau, le taureau s'élance!
Voyez! voyez! voyez!
Le taureau qu'on harcèle
en bondissant s'élance, voyez!
Frappé juste, en plein coeur,
voyez! voyez! voyez!
Victoire!

CHORUS AND FANFARES: (*in the arena*) Hurrah! hurrah! a grand fight!
Hurrah! Across the bloodstained sand
the bull charges!
Look! Look! Look!
The tormented bull
comes bounding to the attack, look!
Struck true, right to the heart,
look! look! look!
Victory!
(*During the chorus, Carmen and José remain silent . . . both are listening . . . Hearing shouts of "Victory!", a cry of delight escapes Carmen . . . José's eyes are fixed upon her . . . The chorus over, she takes a step towards the main entrance of the ring*)

JOSÉ: Où vas-tu?

JOSÉ: (*blocking her way*) Where are you going?

CARMEN: Laisse-moi!

CARMEN: Leave me alone!

JOSÉ: Cet homme qu'on acclame, c'est ton nouvel amant!

JOSÉ: This man they're cheering, he's your new lover!

CARMEN: Laisse-moi! laisse-moi!

CARMEN: Leave me alone! Leave me alone!

JOSÉ: Sur mon âme,
tu ne passeras pas,
Carmen, c'est moi que tu suivras!

JOSÉ: By my soul,
you won't get past,
Carmen, you will come with me!

CARMEN: Laisse-moi, Don José, je ne te suivrai pas.

CARMEN: Let me go, Don José, I'm not going with you.

JOSÉ: Tu bas le retrouver. Dis . . . tu l'aimes donc?

JOSÉ: You're going to him. Tell me . . . you love him, then?

CARMEN: Je l'aime!
Je l'aime, et devant la mort même,
je répéterais que je l'aime!

CARMEN: I love him!
I love him, and in the face of death itself
I would go on saying I love him!
(*shouts and fanfares again from the arena*)

CHOEUR: Viva! la course est belle!
*etc.*

CHORUS: Hurrah! A grand fight!
*etc.*

JOSÉ: Ainsi, le salut de mon âme,
je l'aurai perdu pour que toi,
pour que tu t'en ailles, infâme,
entre ses bras, rire de moi!
Non, par le sang, tu n'iras pas!
Carmen, c'est moi que tu suivras!

JOSÉ: So I am to lose
my heart's salvation so that you
can run to him, infamous creature,
to laugh at me in his arms!
No, by my blood, you shall not go!
Carmen, you're coming with me!

CARMEN: Non! non! jamais!

CARMEN: No! No! Never!

JOSÉ: Je suis las de te menacer!

JOSÉ: I'm tired of threatening you!

CARMEN: Eh bien! frappe-moi donc, ou laisse-moi passer!

CARMEN: All right, stab me then, or let me pass!

CHOEUR: Victoire!

CHORUS: Victory!

JOSÉ: Pour la dernière fois, démon, veux-tu me suivre?

JOSÉ: For the last time, you devil, will you come with me?

CARMEN: Non! non!
Cette bague autrefois,
tu me l'avais donnée,
tiens!

CARMEN: No! No!
This ring that you
once gave me—
here, take it!
(*She throws it away*)

JOSÉ: Eh bien, damnée!

JOSÉ: (*advancing on Carmen, knife in hand*) All right, accursed woman!
(*Carmen draws back, José following, as fanfares sound again in the ring*)

## Act IV

**CHOEUR:** Toréador, en garde!
Et songe bien, oui, songe en combattant,
qu'un oeil noir te regarde,
et que l'amour t'attend!

**CHORUS:** Toreador, on guard!
And remember, yes, remember as you fight
that two dark eyes are watching you,
and that love awaits you!
(*José has stabbed Carmen; she falls dead. The curtains are thrown open and the crowd comes out of the arena*)

**JOSÉ:** Vous pouvez m'arrêter.
C'est moi qui l'ai tuée!
Ah! Carmen! ma Carmen adorée!

*FIN*

**JOSÉ:** You can arrest me.
I was the one who killed her!
(*Escamillo appears on the arena steps. José throws himself upon Carmen's body*)
Ah! Carmen! My adored Carmen!

*THE END*

# Mefistofele (1868)

MUSIC & LIBRETTO BY ARRIGO BOITO

Arrigo Boito wrote the libretto to this four-act opera with both Prologue and Epilogue (based on Goethe's *Faust*), that premiered at the La Scala on March 5, 1868. Mefistofele makes a bet with God that he can win the soul of Faust. Faust and his student, Wagner, watch the Easter Sunday Elector's procession. As twilight descends, Faust notices a grey friar who is following him. Back in his study, Faust open up the Gospel but is frightened when the friar appears, takes off his robes, revealing his true identity: Mefistofele. He offers Faust one moment of perfect pleasure in exchange for his soul, Faust accepts. Now a young man again, Faust, who now calls himself Enrico, is in love with the beautiful Margherita. He urges her to drug her mother with a sleeping potion so that they may meet later that night. Mefistofele and Faust go to the Brocken to observe the witches' sabbath. Faust, however, is in despair; he has had a vision of Margherita imprisoned, in chains. Margherita is indeed in jail and totally insane. She sings about her wrongdoings, poisoning her mother and drowning her baby, Faust's child. Mefistofele agrees to rescue her, but she rejects any assistance from the devil, briefly regains her sanity, begs for God's mercy and dies. A heavenly choir sings of her soul's salvation. Faust suddenly finds himself on the banks of the River Peneios in Greece, wanting to see Elena; she alone can combine the elements of the Classical and the Romantic. She sings of the collapse of Troy and promises to love Faust. He, back in his study, is now old and tired; his death is imminent. He now sees the emptiness of Mefistofele's offer and prays to God to protect him from any further temptations. He dies in true repentance, and Mefistofele sinks into the ground in defeat.

## PROLOGO IN CIELO

*(Nebulosa. Lo squillo delle sette trombe.—I sette tuoni.—Le Falangi Celesti dietro la nebulosa, invisibili.—Chorus Mysticus. I Cherubini. Le Penitenti.—Poi Mefistofele solo nell'ombra.)*

**FALANGE:** Ave, Signor degli angeli e dei santi,
E dei volanti cherubini d'òr,
Dall'eterna armonia dell'Universo
Nel glauco spazio immerso
Emana un verso di supremo amor;
E s'erge a Te per l'aure azzurre
E cave in suon soave.
Ave, Ave, Ave, Ave.
*(Comparisce Mefistofele.)*

**MEFISTOFELE:** (*Coi pie' fermi sul lembo del suo mantello.*) Ave Signor. Perdona se il mio gergo
Si lascia un po' da tergo le superne
Teodie del paradiso;
Perdona se il mio viso non porta il raggio
Che inghirlanda i crini degli alti cherubini;
Perdona se dicendo io corro rischio
Di buscar qualche fischio.
Il Dio piccin . . . della piccina terra
Ognor traligna ed erra,
E, al par di grillo saltellante,
A caso spinge fra gli astri il naso,
Poi con tenace fatuità superba
Fa il suo trillo nell'erba.
Boriosa polve! tracotato atòmo!
Fantasima dell'uomo!
E tale il fa quell'ebbra
Illusione ch'egli chiama:

Ragion, ragion, Ah!
Si, Maestro divino, in bujo fondo
Crolla il padron del mondo,
E non mi dà più il cuor,
Tant'è fiaccato, di tentarlo al mal.

**CHORUS MYSTICUS:** (*interno*)
T'è noto Faust?

**MEFISTOFELE:** Il più bizzarro pazzo
Ch'io mi conosca, in curiosa forma
Ei ti serve da senno.
Inassopita bramosia di saper
Il fa tapino ed anelante;
Egli vorrebbe quasi trasumanar
E nulla scienza al cupo
Suo delirio è confine.
Io mi sobbarco ad adescarlo
Per modo ch'ei si trovi
Nelle mie reti, vuoi tu farne scommessa?

**CHORUS MYSTICUS:** E sia.

**MEFISTOFELE:** Sia! vecchio Padre, a un rude gioco
T'avventurasti. Ei morderà nel dolce
Pomo de' vizi e sovra il Re del ciel
. . .
Avrò vittoria!

**FALANGI CELESTI:** Sanctus! Sanctus! Sanctus!

**MEFISTOFELE:** (Di tratto in tratto m'è piacevol cosa
Vedere il Vecchio e dal guastarmi seco
Molto mi guardo; è bello udir l'Eterno
Col Diavolo parlar si umanamente.)

## PROLOGUE IN HEAVEN

*(Clouds. The sound of seven trumpets. Seven thunderbolts. The celestial phalanxes invisible behind clouds. Mystic Choir. Cherubim. Penitents. Then Mefistofele alone, in the shadow.)*

**PHALANX:** Ave, Lord of the angels and saints,
And of the winged cherubim of gold.
From the eternal harmony of the Universe,
Floating in the emerald space,
Rises a verse of supreme love:
And comes to you through the azure air,
In sounds suave.
Ave, Ave, Ave,

**MEFISTOFELE:** (*With feet at the edge of the mantle*). Ave, O Lord.
Forgive me, if my language
Gives little heed
To the sublime songs of paradise;
Forgive me, if my countenance bears not the beams
Which circle the tresses
Of the high cherubim.
Forgive me if, speaking, I perchance
Should hiss.
The small God of the small earth,
Like unto a grasshopper,
Now lifts his head amongst the stars
And then, with fatuous and enduring pride,
Sounds his trill in the grass.
Vain dust! proud atom!
Fancy of mankind!
Thus is he made by that mad illusion
Which he calls Reason.
Yes, divine Master, in gloomy depths,
Trembles the lord of the world;
So feeble he I scarce have heart
To tempt him into sin.

**MYSTIC CHOIR:** (*within*) Is Faust known to you?

**MEFISTOFELE:** The strangest madman
I ever knew, in curious fashion
He serves there.
A thirst unquenchable for knowledge
Makes him anxious and wretched;
He would go beyond the reach of man;
No science a boundary to his delirium.
I undertake to lure him on,
Until he falls within my net;
Will you lay a wager on it?

**MYSTIC CHOIR:** So be it.

**MEFISTOFELE:** So be it! Father, you have willed
To play a dangerous game. He will bite
In the apple of vice, and
I shall be victorious over the King of Heaven.

**CELESTIAL PHALANXES:** Sanctus! Sanctus! Sanctus!

**MEFISTOFELE:** (*Aside*). Ever and anon I like it much
To see the Heavenly Father; and right careful am I
Not to offend; it is fine to hear the Eternal One
Speak thus humanly with the devil.

I CHERUBINI: (*Dietro la nebulosa*). Siam nimbi volanti dai limbi, Nei santi splendori vaganti, Siam cori di bimbi, d'amori.

MEFISTOFELE: E' lo sciame legger degli angioletti; Come dell'api n'ho ribr ezzo e noia. (*Scompare.*)

I CHERUBINI: (*Coro interno di ragazzi*). Un giorno nel fango mortale, Perdemmo il tripudio dell'ale, L'aureola di luce e di fiori; Ma sciolti dal lugubre bando, Pregando, cantando, danzando, Noi torniamo fra gli angioli ancor. La danza in angelica spira gira, Si gira, si gira, si gira. Fratelli, teniamci per mano, Fin l'ultimo cielo lontano Noi sempre dobbiamo danzar; Fratelli, le morbide penne Non cessino il volo perenne Che intorno al Santissimo Altar.

I CHERUBINI: Siam nimbi volanti dai limbi, Nei santi splendori vaganti, Siam cori di bimbi, d'amori.

LE PENITENTI: (*dalla terra*). Salve Regina! S'innalzi un'eco Dal mondo cieco Alla divina reggia del ciel. Col nostro canto, Col nostro pianto, Domiam l'intenso Foco del senso, Col nostro canto Mite e fedel. Odi la pia Prece serena.

I CHERUBINI: Sugli astri, sui venti, sui mondi, Sui limpidi azzurri profondi, Sui raggi del sol . . . La danza in angelica spira Si gira, si gira, si gira.

FALANGI: Oriam, oriam per quei morienti oriam

PENITENTI: Odi la pia prece serena. Ave Maria gratia plena. Il pentimento lagrime spande. Di queste blande turbe il lamento Accolga il cielo.

FALANGI: Oriam per quelle di morienti ignavo Anime schiave, si per quell'anime schiave preghiam.

I CHERUBINI: Sian, nimbi volanti dai limbi, Nei santi splendori i vaganti.

TUTTI: Odi la pia, la pia prece serena. Ave, Ave, Ave! Ah! Signor degli angeli e dei santi E delle sfere erranti, E dei volanti cherubini d'òr.

CHERUBIM: (*behind the clouds.*) We are showers fleeting from cloud land, Wandering in heavenly splendors. We are choirs of infants, of loves.

MEFISTOFELE: It is the light band of cherubs; They tire and fret me, like bees. (*Vanishes*)

CHERUBIM: (*Chorus of boys in the background*). One day, amid human corruption, We lost our winged glory. Our halos of flowers and light. But released from that gloomiest exile, Praying, singing, dancing, We return midst the angels once more. The dance, in an angelic spiral, Goes on, goes on, goes on. Brethren, clasp each other's hand. Until the most distant heaven nears, We must ever dance. Celestial pinions Must not stop in perennial flight, Save at the Holiest Altar.

CHERUBIM: We are showers fleeting from cloudland, Wandering in heavenly splendors. We are choirs of infants, of loves.

PENITENTS: (*From earth*). Salve Regina! An echo rises From the blind world To the divine kingdom of heaven. With our song. With our tears, We dominate the intense Fire of the sense, With our song Mild and faithful. Hear the serene And pious prayer.

CHERUBIM: Over stars, over winds, over worlds, Over limpid azure depths, Over the warm sunbeams . . . The dance, in an angelical spiral, Goes on, goes on, goes on.

PHALANXES: We pray for the enslaved souls.

PENITENTS: Hear the serene and pious prayer. Ave Maria, gratia plena. You can save from this earth. From the flesh that weeps and strays Cruel dust!

PHALANXES: Pray we for the enslaved souls. Yes, for those enslaved souls we pray

CHERUBIM: We are showers fleeting from cloudland, Wandering in heavenly splendors.

ALL PHALANXES: Hear the serene and pious prayer. Ave, Lord of the Angels and saints, Of the wandering spheres, And of the winged cherubim of gold.

PENITENTI E FALANGI: Dall'eterna armonia dell'Universo Nel glauco spazio immerso Emana un verso di supremo amor; E s'erge a Te per l'aure azzurre E cave in suon soave. Ave, Ave!

CHERUBINI: Ave, Ave, Signor degli Angeli E dei santi, Ave Signor. S'erge a Te per l'aure azzurre E cave in suon soave.

PENITENTS AND PHALANXES: From the eternal harmony of the Universe, Floating in the emerald space, Rises a verse of supreme love; And comes to you through the azure air In sounds suave. Ave, Ave!

CHERUBIM: Ave, Ave, Lord of the angels And saints, Ave Lord Comes to you through the azure air In sounds suave.

# ■ ATTO PRIMO

## SCENA I

La Domenica di Pasqua.

(*Francoforte sul Meno. Porta e bastioni.—Passeggiatori d'ogni sorta ch'escono dalla città a gruppi. Chiacchiere, risate, grida, mormorio di folla, andirivieni. A intervalli campane di festa. Poi Faust e Wagner.*)

TRE STUDENTI, QUATTRO BORGHESI, DUE CACCIATORI: Perchè di là? Volgiamo verso il casin di caccia. E noi verso il mulino.

OTTO FANCIULLE (*Traversando le scene cantando*). Del vago April La traccia brilla e ride D'intorno baldezza e leggiadria. (*La Fanciulle passano.*)

STUDENTI, BORGHESI E CACCIATORI: Che fate voi, compari? —Stiam colla compagnia. Messeri, andiamo a Burgdorf Costà son le più buffe mattie, La miglior birra, Le donne e le baruffe Più dilettose. —Pazzi! pazzi! Vi prude ancor la schiena? (*Due banditori con una scritta in mano e a suon di tromba atirae la folla dei passeggiatori; sta con lui un araldo. Dalla parte opposta un cerretano seguito da Hanswurst. La passeggiata diventa sempre più vivace.*) (*Un gruppo di balestrieri e popolani, avvieinandosi ad un rivenditore di birra.*)

CORO: Qua il biccnier! Vogliam ber! E fare un brindisi . . . Ai folli amor! E alla beltà corriva! Evviva! Beviam, ridiamo, cantiamo. (*Un Frate grigio col cappuccio sul volto cammina tra la folla; alcuni lo inchinano, altri lo sfuggono.*)

# ■ ACT I

## SCENE I

Easter Sunday.

(*Frankfort-on-the-Main. Gate and bastions. People of every condition leaving the city in groups, · Conversations, laughter, cries and the hum of voices heard; festive chimes, at intervals. Later on, enter Faust and Wagner.*)

THREE STUDENTS, FOUR BURGHERS, TWO HUNTERS: —Why in this direction? —We turn toward the hunting-house. —And we toward the mill.

EIGHT CHILDREN: (*Cross the stage, singing*). Follow we the trace of April. —On its path —Glisten merriment and beauty. (*Exeunt.*)

STUDENTS, BURGHERS AND HUNTERS: What do you here, companions? —We are with company. —Friends, let us go to Burgdorf. There pranks are best, As well as beer, And women and brawls, the most attractive. Madman! do you still covet blows? (*Two public criers, with paper in hand and, with trumpet call, engage attention; with them is a herald. Then enters a charlatan. The scene becomes more and more animated.*) (*A group of archers and working-men approach a vendor of beer.*)

CHORUS: A glass here. We would drink! And propose a toast— To our loves! And to credulous beauty! Hurrah! Let us drink, let us laugh, let us sing. (*A Gray Friar, with hood drawn over his head, passes through the crowd. Some bow to him, others avoid him.*)

**LA FOLLA:** (*Traendo verso un lato della scena*) Guarda! quanti focosi destrier scalpitan là!
C'è il buffon, c'è il falconier . . .
Rendiam omaggio al prence!
Largo, largo al suo passaggio!
Che abbarbaglio di gualdane!
Gloria il principe!
Che frastuono di campane!
Vien la folla a onde a onde . . .
S'arrabatta, si confonde . . .
Guarda là! guarda là!
(*Risata, frastuono, la cavalcata passa; Alla sua testa il Principe Elettore, Dame, Dignitari, Paggi, il Buffone, il Falconiere, ecc. Molti passeggiatori seguono curiosamente la cavalcata*).
(*Faust e Wagner discendono da un'altura.*)

**CROWD:** (*Drawing toward one side of the scene*). See yonder! see yonder!
How many horses paw the ground.
There is the fool—there the falconer.
Do we homage to the Prince.
May way for him, make way!
What a dazzling array!
What a clangor of bells!
The crowd surges like the sea,
It ever moves, and mingles its waters.
Make way! make way!
(*Laughter and din. The cavalcade passes by; at its head the Prince Elector, Ladies, Dignitaries, Pages, Buffoons, Falconers, etc. Many lookers-on follow the cavalcade curiously.*)
(*Faust and Wagner descend from an elevation*).

**FAUST:** Al soave raggiar di primavera
Si scoscendono i ghiacci
E già rinverda di speranza la valle;
Il vecchio inverno fugge al monte
E il sol rallegra e avviva forme e color;
Se per anco al piano non isbucciano i fior,
La somma luce fa pullulare in cambio
I bei borghesi azzimati da festa.
(*Entra in scena rumorosamente una frotta di popolani e popolane.*)

**FAUST:** At the gentle beams of spring,
The ice melts, and the valley is green again
With hope; old winter flies to the mountain,
And the earth rejoices and renews its forms and colors;
If all flowers, as yet, are not in bloom,
The cheering light brings forth in swarms
The burghers, in holiday attire.
(*A crowd of people fill the stage, noisily.*)

**WAGNER:** Movere a diporto con voi, Dottor,
È onorevole e saggio,
Pur da me solo,
Qui mi schiferei fra questa gente.
M'è di noia il vulgo.
(*Faust e Wagner si ritirano nei fondo.*)

**WAGNER:** To join you in your sports,
Is honorable and wise, doctor.
Were I alone, I'd be disgusted
Amid these people.
The vulgar offend me.
(*Faust and Wagner retire to back*)

**POPOLANI:** Juhè! Juhè! Juneisa!
Ah! Il bel giovanetto
Sen viene alla festa,
Coi nastri al farsetto,
Coi fior sulla testa.
E sotto ad un pioppo
Fanciulle e compar
Si danno a danzar
Un matto galoppo.
(*Incominciano a dansare l'Obertas.*)
Juhè! Junè! Juhè!
Tutti vanno alla rinfusa
Sulla musica confusa.
Alla rinfusa tutti van, danziamo,
La danza scalpita sul suol,
La danza rotonda sul suol.
Heisa hè! Juhè! Juheisa!
Ah! Eh! Sorridon le donne
Al bel torneamento,
Svolazzan le gonne
Portate dal vento.
Il bruno e la bionda
Son stretti in un vol,
E scalpita al suol
La danza rotonda,
E sotto ad un pioppo
Fanciulle e compare si danno a danzare

**CHORUS OF THE PEOPLE:** Juhe! Juhe! Juheisa!
The handsome youth
Comes to the fête,
With ribbons in his jacket
And flowers on his head.
Now, beneath a poplar
Lads and lassies
Dance together
A wild gallop.
(*They commence dancing the "Obertas".*)
Juhe! Juhe! Juhe!
All rush pell mell,
To confusing music.
In conclusion, they all go, let us dance,
The dance beats on the soil,
The dance goes round on the soil,
The maidens smile
At the tourney fine,
Gowns fly about,
At bidding of the breeze.
Brunettes and blondes
Are whirled along,
And the mad round dance
Tramples the ground.
And beneath a poplar,
Lads and ladies dance together

Un matto galoppo.
(*Le danse cessano.*)
(*Coro c danzatrici s'allontanano.—Il giorno si oscura lentamente.*)

A wild gallop.
(*The dance ceases. Chorus and dancers withdraw. Night comes on.*)

**FAUST:** (*a Wagner*) Sediam sovra quel sasso.
Osserva come fulgoreggian
A vespro le capanne,
Declina il giorno.

**FAUST:** (*To Wagner*). Sit we on this rock.
As night approaches see how the dwellings
Gleam in the distance.
The day is almost spent.

**WAGNER:** È l'ora degli spettri;
Essi sen vanno fra i vapor della sera
Ordendo reti sotto i piedi dell'uom.
Andiam; s'impregna l'orizzonte di nebbia.
A notte bruna torna dolce la casa.
A che sogguardi, nel crepuscolo assorto immobilmente?
(*Ritorna il Frate Grigio e si dirige lento e spettrale alla volta di Faust.*)

**WAGNER:** It is the hour of specters;
Amid the vapors of evening,
They go forth, stretching their snares
Under the feet of man. Let us be off;
The horizon is filled with mist;
At night one's house is welcome.
At what do you gaze,
Thus motionless, in the twilight?
(*The Gray Friar reappears, and slowly and specter-like approaches Faust.*)

**FAUST:** Vedi quel frate grigio
In mezzo i campi vagolante laggiù?

**FAUST:** Do you see yon Gray Friar,
Wandering in the fields?

**WAGNER:** Da lungo tratto, maestro, l'avvisai;
Nulla di strano appare in esso.

**WAGNER:** I've long observed him, Master,
And nothing strange in him appears.

**FAUST:** Aguzza ben lo sguardo.
Per chi tieni quel frate?

**FAUST:** Sharpen well your sight.
For what do you hold that Friar?

**WAGNER:** È un questuante che va alla cerca.

**WAGNER:** For one in quest of alms,
And now upon his rounds.

**FAUST:** Lo contempla.
Ei move in tortuose spire
E s'avvicina lento alla nostra volta.
Oh! se non erro, or me di focco imprime al suol!

**FAUST:** He contemplates him.
He moves in tortuous ways,
And slowly comes toward this spot.
Oh! if I err not,
He fiery traces leaves beneath his feet.

**WAGNER:** Ah! No! Fantasima quest'è,
Quest'è del tuo cervello,
Lo non iscargo che un frate grigio.

**WAGNER:** A fancy, this,
Of your excited brain.
I only see a Gray Friar.

**FAUST:** Par vada filando de' lacci intorno a noi.

**FAUST:** It seems as though
He wove nets about us.

**WAGNER:** Timidamente va per la sua via;
Due sconosciuti noi siam per esso.
Ah! Fantasima quest'è del tuo cervello.

**WAGNER:** He quietly pursues his path;
We are two strangers to him.
Ah! A fancy, this, of your excited brain.

**FAUST:** La spira si stringe.
Ei n'è vicin . . . ah!

**FAUST:** The circle narrows.
He approaches—

**WAGNER:** (*Freddamente*).
L'osserva; è un frate grigio,
Non è uno spettro;
Brontola orazioni rigirando un rosario.
Andiam, Maestro.
(*Il Frate li segue. Faust e Wagner escono.*)

**WAGNER:** (*Coldly*). Watch him well; he is a Gray Friar,
And not a specter; he mumbles orisons.
And counts his beads.
Let us go, Master.
(*The Friar follows them. Exit Faust and Wagner.*)

**CORO:** (*interno lontanissimo*). Il bel giovinetto
Sen viene alla festa . . .
Il bruno e la bionda
Son stretti in un vol.

**CHORUS:** (*in the distance*). The handsome youth
Comes to the fête . . .
Brunettes and blondes
Are whirled along.

## SCENA II

(*Officina di Faust. Alcova. Notte.—Faust entrando. Il Frate Grigio lo segue e si nasconde entro l'alcova.*)

FAUST: Dai campi, dai prati
Che innonda la notte,
Dai queti sentier ritorno
E di pace, di calma profonda
Son pieno, di sacro . . . mister.
Le torve passioni del core
S'assonnano in placido obblio.
Mi ferve soltanto l'amore
dell'uomo!
L'amore di Dio!
Ah! . . . dai campi, dai prati ritorno
E verso l'Evangel mi sento attratto,
M'accingo a meditar.
(*Apre un Vangelo posto su d'un alto leggio. Mentre s'accinge a meditare è scosso dall'urlo del Frate che esce dall'alcova.*)
Olà! chi urla? il frate! che vegg'io?

. . .
Divider la mia cella io t'acconsento,
Frate, se tu non muggi . . .
E che? . . . mi guarda e non fa motto
. . .
Che orribile fantasma
Transcinai dietro di me?
Furia, demonio o spettro, sarai mio!
Sulla tua razza è onnipotente
Il segno di Salomon.
(*All'ultime parole di Faust il Frate si trasforma e appare Mefistofele in abito da cavaliere con un mantello nero sul braccio.*)

MEFISTOFELE: Che baccano! Messer, mi comandate.

FAUST: Questo era dunque il nocciuol del frate?
Un cavalier! Mi fa rider la facezia.
Come ti chiami?

MEFISTOFELE: La domanda è inezia puerile
Per tal che gli argomenti sdegna
Del Verbo e crede solo agli Enti.

FAUST: In voi, messeri, il nome ha tal virtù
Che rivela l'Essenza.
Dimmi or su, chi sei tu dunque?

MEFISTOFELE: Una parte vivente
di quella forza
Che perpetuamente pensa
Il Male e fa il Bene.

FAUST: E che dir vuole codesto gioco di strane parole?

MEFISTOFELE: Son lo Spirito che nega
Sempre tutto; l'astro, il fior.
Il mio ghigno e la mia bega
Turban gli ozi al Creator.
Voglio il Nulla e del Creato
La ruina universal.
È atmosfera mia vital,
Ciò che chiamasi peccato,

Morte e Mal!
Rido e avvento questa sillaba:
"No."
Struggo, tento, ruggo, sibilo.
"No." Mordo, invischio, fishio!
(*Fischia violentemente colle dita fra le labbra.*)
Parte son d'una latèbra
Del gran tutto: Oscurità.
Son figliuol della Tenebra
Che Tenebra tornerà.
S'or la luce usurpa e afferra
Il mio scettro a ribellion,
Poco andrà la sua tenzon,
V'è sul Sole e sulla Terra:
Distruzion!
Rido e avvento questa sillaba:
"No."
Struggo e tento, ruggo e sibilo.

FAUST: Strano figlio del Caos.

MEFISTOFELE: E tu, se brami farti mio socio.
Di buon grado accetto fin da quest'ora
E tuo compar mi chiamo,
O, se ti piace,
Tuo schiavo, tuo servo.

FAUST: E quali patti in ricambio adempier deggio?

MEFISTOFELE: V'è tempo a ciò.

FAUST: No, i patti e parla chiaro.

MEFISTOFELE: Io qui mi lego ai tuoi servigi
E senza tregua accorro
Alle tue voglie; ma laggiù . . .
M'intendi? la vece muterà.

FAUST: Per l'altra vita non mi turba pensier
Se tu mi doni un'ora di riposo
In cui s'acqueti l'alma.
Se sveli al mio bujo pensier
Me stesso e il mondo.
Se avvien ch'io dica all'attimo fuggente:
Arrestati sei bello!
Allor ch'io muoia
E m'inghiotta l'averno.

MEFISTOFELE: Sta ben!

FAUST: Venga il contratto.

MEFISTOFELE: (*Si danne la mano*). Top, è già fatto.
Fin da stanotte
Nell'orgie ghiotte del mio messer
Da cameriere lo servirò.

FAUST: E quando s'incomincia?

MEFISTOFELE: Tosto.

FAUST: Or ben, presto, a noi, dove andiam?

MEFISTOFELE: Dove t'aggrada.

---

## SCENE II

(*Faust's laboratory. An alcove. Night.*)
(*Enter Faust. The Gray Friar follows him and conceals himself in alcove.*)

FAUST: From fields and meadows, peace sleeping,
And quiet paths, I now return
With calmness filled,
And sacred mystery.
The haggard passions of the heart
Slumber in placid oblivion.
The love of man! the love of God!
Alone burn within me.
I long for the Good; toward the Evangels
I feel attracted. I'll open them, and meditate.
(*Opens a Bible placed upon a high desk. As he begins to meditate, he is startled by a cry from the Friar, in the alcove.*)
Who is there? who cries out? the Friar! what do I see?
I consent to have you share my cell, Friar,
If you do not cry like this—
What! He stares at me, and moves not!
What terrible phantom
Have I drawn here?
Fury, demon or specter, you'll be mine!
Over your race the sign of Solomon
Is all-potent.
(*At Faust's last words, the Friar changes into Mefistoffele, attired as a cavalier, and carrying a black cloak on his arm.*)

MEFISTOFELE: What a din! Sir, what are your commands?

FAUST: This then, was the kernel of the Friar!
A cavalier! The jest's a novel one!
Your name?

MEFISTOFELE: The question is absurd,
And childish for him who despises
The arguments of the Word, and believes but in Entities.

FAUST: In you, sir, your name has virtue such
That it reveals the Essence. Tell me, now,
What are you?

MEFISTOFELE: A living part of that force
Which forever wishes Evil and does Good.

FAUST: What means, I ask,
This strange play of words?

MEFISTOFELE: I am the spirit that denies
Ever, all things; the star, the flower.
My smile, and the thought of me,
Disturb the leisure of the Creator.
I long for nothing, and the ruin
Of all things created.
My vital atmosphere
Is what men call Sin.

Death and Evil!
I laugh and launch out this syllable!
"No."
I destroy, I tempt, I roar, I hiss,
"No."
I bite, I seize, I hiss! I hiss! I hiss.
(*Whistles violently through his fingers.*)
I am part of a cavern
Of the great All: Darkness.
I am a son of Gloom
Which Gloom shall reign anew.
If now light usurps and clutches,
Rebellious, my sceptre,
The dispute will shortly end.
In the sun and on earth
Is Destruction!
I laugh and launch forth this syllable:
"No."
I destroy, I tempt, I roar, I hiss.

FAUST: Strange son of Chaos!

MEFISTOFELE: And you, if you desire
To become my companion, I accept you,
From this hour, and call myself your comrade,
Or, if you like, your servant and slave.

FAUST: To what conditions, in exchange, must I subscribe?

MEFISTOFELE: There is time for that.

FAUST: No!
The conditions, and speak plainly.

MEFISTOFELE: I bind myself, here, unto your service.
And will fulfill your wishes
Without restraint; but, below, do understand,
The parts shall be changed.

FAUST: No thought of another life
Now harasses me. If you bring me
On earth one hour of rest
In which my soul shall know calmness;
If you reveal myself and the world
Unto my dark thought;
If it chance that I say to the fleeting atom:
Stay! you're beautiful! then may I die!
Let Hell engulf me!

MEFISTOFELE: It is well.

FAUST: I tender you this contract.
(*They clasp hands.*)

MEFISTOFELE: Done! I'll not forget it.
From to-night
In the wild orgies of my lord,
As a valet I shall wait upon him.

FAUST: And when do we begin?

MEFISTOFELE: At once.

FAUST: Good. And where
Shall we go?

MEFISTOFELE: Wherever you will.

**FAUST:** Come s'esce di qua?
Dove i cavalli, le carrozze, i staffier?

**MEFISTOFELE:** Pur ch'io distenda questo mantel
Noi viaggeremo sull'aria ...

*Fine Dell'Atto Primo*

# ■ ATTO SECONDO

## SCENA I

*Il Giardino.*

*(Un giardino di rustica apparenza. Faust sotto il nome di Enrico, Margherita, Mefistofele, Marta. Passeggiano due a due in lungo e in largo.)*

**MARGHERITA:** *(Con molta grazia e semplicità quasi puerile).* Cavaliero illustre e saggio. Com mai vi può allettar la fanciulla Del villaggio col suo rustico parlar?

**FAUST:** *(Con amorevolessa e calore).* Dalle labbra imporporate Spandi accento sovruman. *(Baciandole la mano.)* Parla, parla ...

**MARGHERITA:** Ah! non baciate Questa ruvida mia man, *(Con risoluzione.)* No, no, cavalier. *(Passano.)*

**MEFISTOFELE:** *(a Marta).* Sta ben al nubile correr giocondo, In traccia d'ilari Venture, il mondo. Ma quando lugubre tempo verrà, Vecchio nel vedova letto morrà. Pur troppo! e trepido vedo quell'ora.

**MARTA:** Baie! pensateci, c'è tempo ancora.

**MEFISTOFELE:** Ah! si! ahimè! *(Mefistofele e Marta escono.)* *(Faust e Margherita ritornano in scena.)*

**FAUST:** Mi perdona l'ardimento Che dal labbro mi sfuggi Quando il magico portento Del tuo viso m'appari.

**MARGHERITA:** Fui dolente, fui turbata, Dubitai nel mio pensier Che fanciulla scostumata Mi credeste, cavalier. Piansi molto, ma rimasemi nel co. Sempre fiso il vostro volto.

**MARTA E MEFISTOFELE:** *(ride).* Ah! Ah!

**FAUST:** Segui, segui, mio tesor. *(Margherita e Faust passano.)*

**FAUST:** How leave this place? Where are the steeds, The coaches, the lackeys?

**MEFISTOFELE:** I need but spread this cloak; we'll travel Through the air.

*End of Act One*

# ■ ACT II

## SCENE I

*The Garden.*

*(A garden of rustic appearance. Faust, under the name of Henry; Margherita, Mefistofele, Martha. They walk to and fro, two by two.)*

**MARGHERITA:** *(With much grace, and almost puerile simplicity)* Illustrious and learned cavalier, How can you enjoy This country girl's company And her rustic language?

**FAUST:** *(Kindly and affectionately).* A celestial voice comes From those ruddy lips! *(Kissing her hand.)* Speak on, speak on.

**MARGHERITA:** Ah! do not kiss This, my coarse hand. *(Resolutely.)* No, no cavalier. *(They go out.)*

**MEFISTOFELE:** *(to Martha).* It is well enough For a young man to go about In search of adventure. But the last sad time will come When old and a widower he shall die. Alas! I look forward Trembling to that hour.

**MARTHA:** It is idle to think of it; You have time enough yet.

**MEFISTOFELE:** Ah! Yes! Alas! *(Exit Mefistofele and Martha.)* *(Faust and Margherita return on the scene.)*

**FAUST:** Forgive the rash utterance Of my lips when I first Beheld the magic of your face.

**MARGHERITA:** I was confused and troubled; I doubted my thought, Afraid you might take me For an abandoned girl. How much I wept! How much I wept! But your face remained Ever imprinted in my heart.

**MARTHA AND MEFISTOFELE:** *(laughing.)* Ah! Ah!

**FAUST:** Speak on, speak on, my treasure. *(Margherita and Faust go out.)*

**MEFISTOFELE:** Da un antichissimo detto s'impara Che moglie saggia è cosa rara

**MARTA:** Davver?

**MEFISTOFELE:** Rara davver.

**MARTA:** Davver! Nè in trappola cadeste ancor?

**MEFISTOFELE:** Non so, credetelo, che sia l'amor.

**MARTA:** Nè mai d'un palpito, Nè mai d'un sogno V'arse bisogno fascinator?

**MEFISTOFELE:** Non so, credetelo, Che sia l'amor.

**MARTA:** Ah, ah! ah, ah! ... *(Passano.)*

**MARGHERITA:** *(Ritorna in scena con Faust.—Con molta semplicità).* Dimmi se credi, Enrico nella religione.

**FAUST:** Non vò turbar le fedi delle coscienze buone. D'altro parliam; darei perchè amo, Fanciulla, sangue e vita.

**MARGHERITA:** *(Con accento di rimprovero).* Non basta. Creder bisogna, E a nulla tu credi, Enrico.

**FAUST:** Ascolta, vezzoso angelo mio. Chi oserebbe affermare tal detto: Credo in Dio? Le parole dei santi son beffe al ver ch'io chiedo, E qual uomo oserebbe tanto da dir: non credo? Colma il tuo cor d'un palpito ineffabile e vero d'amor E chiama poi quell'estasi: Natura! Amor! Mistero! Vita! Dio! non è che fumo e folla In paragon del senso il nome e la parola.

**MARGHERITA:** Convien che vada, addio. *(Per allontanarsi.)*

**FAUST:** Dimmi, in casa sei sola sovente?

**MARGHERITA:** *(semplicemente.)* È piccioletta la nostra famigliola. Io veglio all'orto, al desco ed allo staio, Attendo ad ogni cura, filo sull'arcolaio. *(Sorridendo.)* E assai minuziosa la mamma. Eppur, beate placidamente passo Tutte le mie giornate.

**FAUST:** Di', non potrò giammai dolce un'ora d'amore Viver teco e confondere il mio cuor col tuo cuore?

**MARGHERITA:** Non dormo sola e in lieve sopor mia madre giace; S'ella t'udisse, *(Con agitazione.)* Credo, ne morrei ...

**MEFISTOFELE:** From a very ancient maxim We learn that a good wife Is a rare thing.

**MARTHA:** Indeed?

**MEFISTOFELE:** Rare indeed!

**MARTHA:** Indeed! and did you Not fall into the trap yet?

**MEFISTOFELE:** I assure you, I do not know what love is.

**MARTHA:** And did no sigh, No dream, Ever burn within your heart?

**MEFISTOFELE:** I assure you, I know not what love is.

**MARTHA:** Ah! Ah! Ah! Ah! *(They go out.)*

**MARGHERITA:** *(Returning with Faust.—With simplicity).* Tell me, Henry, if you believe in your religion.

**FAUST:** I do not wish to trouble the faith of pure consciences. Speak we of something else. I would give my blood and life For the maiden I love.

**MARGHERITA:** *(reprovingly).* It is not enough. You must believe, And you believe nothing, Henry.

**FAUST:** Listen, my charming angel. Who dares affirm the words: "I believe in God"? The words of the saints mock the truth I seek. Yet who dares say this much: "I do not believe"? Fill your heart with ineffable and true bliss, And then call this ecstacy; Nature! Love! Mystery! Life! God! It matters little. Smoke and Folly are name and word, Weighed against sense.

**MARGHERITA:** I must depart. Farewell. *(Going.)*

**FAUST:** Tell me—are often home Alone?

**MARGHERITA:** *(simply).* Our family is very small. I see to the garden, the grain, the table, and all else; I spin with the spinning wheel. *(Smiling.)* My mother is very strict, and yet I pass in peace most happy days.

**FAUST:** Shall I never live with you through an hour of love, And press my heart against yours?

**MARGHERITA:** I do not sleep alone, and my mother slumbers lightly; Should she hear you I think I should die!

# Act II, Scene I

**FAUST:** Datti pace.
(*Porgendole un'ampollina.*)
A te; di questo succo tre sole goccie ponno
Addormentare in placido, in letargico sonno.

**MARGHERITA:** Porgi . . . nè può venirne alcun male a mia madre?
(*Marta e Mefistofele rientrano.*)

**FAUST:** Nessuno, angio! soave dalle guancie leggiadre!

**MARGHERITA:** Dio clemente, nuova, ignara
Son del monda, dell'amore;
Sento un'aura areana e cara
Che mi penetra nel core.

**FAUST:** È l'anelito superno,
Il miracolo divino
Della vita! senza freno, senza fine!
È il miracolo d'amor, si!

**MEFISTOFELE:** Non so, credetelo, che sia l'amore.
Moglie saggia è cosa rara davver.

**MARTA:** Ah! Davver? nè in trappola cadeste ancor?

**FAUST E MARGHERITA:** Ah! sento un'aura arcana e cara . . .
(*Margherita si svincola dalle mani di Faust.*)

**MARGHERITA:** Addio! fuggo, fuggo, lesta, lesta.

**FAUST:** (*insegue Margherita*).
Resta, resta, Margherita.
Amor mio, vieni, dove corri?

**MARTA:** Corri, corri, lesto, lesto.

**MEFISTOFELE:** (*insegue Marta*).
Marta! Marta! dove corri?
Tu sei còlta!

**MARTA:** Fuggo, fuggo, corri, corri.

**MARGHERITA E FAUST:** T'amo! T'amo!

**MARTA E MEFISTOFELE:** Ah! T'amo!
(*Tutti si disperdono.*)

## SCENA II

*La Notte del Sabba.*

(*Scena deserta e selvaggi nella vallea di Schirk, costeggiata dagli spaventosi culmini del Brocken (monte delle streghe). I sinistri profili di roccie staccano in nero sul cielo grigio, un'aurora rossiccia di luna illumina stranamente la scena. Una caverna da un lato. Il picco di Rosstrappe a sinistra. Il vento soffia nei burroni; poi la voce di Mefistofele che aizza Faust a salir la montagna.*)

**MEFISTOFELE:** (*Di dentro, assai lontano con voce lunga e sotterranea*). Su cammina, cammina, cammina;
Bujo è il cielo, scoscesa è la china.

**FAUST:** Fear not.
(*Gives her a vial.*)
Three drops of this liquid
Will plunge one into a peaceful lethargy.

**MARGHERITA:** Give it to me. Can it not harm my mother?
(*Martha and Mefistofele reenter.*)

**FAUST:** No, sweet angel with fairest cheeks!

**MARGHERITA:** Merciful Father, ignorant though I am
Of the world and of love,
I feel a sweet and secret influence
Penetrating my heart.

**FAUST:** It is the supreme desire,
The divine miracle
Of life; immense, eternal,
Without restraint, without end.

**MEFISTOFELE:** I assure you, I do not know what love is.
A good wife is a rare thing.

**MARTHA:** Ah! Indeed! Did you not fall into the trap yet?

**FAUST AND MARGHERITA:** Ah! I feel a sweet and sacred influence . . .
(*Margherita frees herself from Faust's embrace.*)

**MARGHERITA:** Farewell! Fly, fly, quick, quick!

**FAUST:** (*Running after Margherita*). Stay, stay, Margherita.
Come, my love, where are you running?

**MARTHA:** Run, run, quick, quick!

**MEFISTOFELE:** (*following Martha*) Martha! Martha! where are you running?
You are caught!

**MARTHA:** Fly, fly, run, run!

**MARGHERITA AND FAUST:** I love you!

**MARTHA AND MEFISTOFELE:** Ah! I love you!
(*All disappear.*)

## SCENE II

*The Sabbath.*

(*The stage represents a wild and deserted spot in the valley of Schirk, bounded by the fearful heights of the Brocken. The sinister profiles of the rocks stand forth black against a black sky, and reddish moonbeams light up, weirdly, the scene. A cavern is on one side; on the left is the peak of Rosstrappe. The wind moans among the precipices. The voice of Mefistofele, helping Faust climb the mountain, is heard.*)

**MEFISTOFELE:** (*In the distance, in deep and sepulchral tones.*) On, on, on,
Black are the heavens, weary the back,

Su cammina, cammina, cammina,
Che lontano s'erge il monte
Del vecchio Satan.
(*Appariscono dei fuochi fatui, uno di questi si dirige alla volta di Faust e di Mefistofele.*)

**FAUST E MEFISTOFELE:** Folletto, veloce, leggier,
Che splendi soletto per l'ermo sentier,
A noi t'avvicina,
Che buia è la china.
(*Mefistofele e Faust appariscono sovra un'alta roccia isolati ed immobili.*)

**MEFISTOFELE:** Ascolta! S'agita il bosco e gli alti pini antichi
Cozzan furenti colle giganti traccia.

**CORO:** Ah! Ah!

**MEFISTOFELE:** Ascolta, ascolta!
(*con accento concitato e sussultante.*)
Ad imo della valle un ululato
Di mille voci odo sonar
S'accosta l'infernale congrega . . .
Oh! meraviglia!
(*Con uno scoppio di gioia infernale.*)
Già i nembi, il monte, le boscaglie, i cieli
Un furioso intuonar magico carme!

**STREGHE:** Rampiamo, rampiamo che il tempo ci gabba,
E il ballo perdiamo di Re Belzebù,
È notte fatale la notte del Sabba;
Il primo che sale ha un premio di più
Su! Su! Su! Su!

**STREGONI:** Su! Su! Su! Su!
È notte tremenda la notte del Sabba.
Su svelti, su forti che il tempo ci gabba,
Le nostri consorti son giunte lassù.
(*Irrompono freneticamente sulla scena.*)

**CORO:** Siam salvi in tutta l'eternità!
Saboè! Saboè! Saboè!

**MEFISTOFELE:** (*Fendendo la folla*). Largo, largo a Mefistofele,
Al vostro Re!
O razza putrida vuota di fè,
Che ognun m'adori
Ed umile si prostri al Re.

**CORO:** (*Inginocchiato in circolo intorno a Mefistofele*). Ci prostriamo a Mefistofele, al nostro Re,
Ognuno atterrasi dinanzi a te.

**MEFISTOFELE:** (*Su di un sasso in forma di trono*). Popoli! e scettro e clamide
Non date al Re sovrano?
La formidabil mano vuota dovrà serrar?

Upward, on, on, on!
For far away, far away,
Rises the mountain of old Satan.
(*Will-o'-the wisps appear, and one of them moves toward Faust and Mefistofele.*)

**FAUST AND MEFISTOFELE:** Will-o'-the-wisp,
Swift and light,
That shines alone,
Over the lonely path,
Come near unto us.,
For the road is dark.
(*Faust and Mefistofele are disclosed, standing still upon a high rock.*)

**MEFISTOFELE:** Hark! hark!
The woods move, and the aged pines
Meet in furious combat
With their gigantic limbs.

**CHORUS:** Ah! Ah!

**MEFISTOFELE:** Hark! hark!
(*With very excited and unsteady accents.*)
In the valley below I hear the howling
Of a thousand voices. The infernal gathering
Approaches. O marvel!
(*With a crash of infernal joy.*)
Clouds, mountains, woods,
Intone a wild, enchanted song.

**WITCHES:** Climb we, climb we, the world despises us,
And we lose the dance of King Beelzebub.
It is a fatal night: the night of the Sabbath;
Whoever arrives first, bears off a prize.
On, on, on, on!

**SORCERERS:** On! On! On! On!
It is a terrible night: the night of the Sabbath.
Be quick and bold, for time presses;
Our wives, already, have climbed the heights.
(*All rush wildly upon the stage.*)

**CHORUS:** We are saved, for all eternity!
Saboè! har Sabbah!

**MEFISTOFELE:** (*Pushing through the crowd*). Make way for Mefistofele,
Make way for your king!
You putrid race, devoid of faith,
Let all worship
And humbly bow to me.

**CHORUS:** (*Kneeling in a circle around Mefistofele*). Make way for Mefistofele,
For our King,
Let all fall prostrate
In your presence.

**MEFISTOFELE:** (*On a rock in the shape of a throne*). You people!
my sceptre and robe of state
Do you not give to your sovereign?
Must I close my formidable hand
Upon emptiness?

CORO: (*Porgendo una clamide a Mefistofele*). Ecco la clamide, non t'adirar,
Or 'ubbidiscono ciel, terra e mar.

CHORUS: (*Giving Mefistofele a robe and sceptre*). Behold the robe; be not wroth.
Now heaven and earth obey you.

MEFISTOFELE: Ho soglio, ho scettro e despota
Son del mio regno fiero.
Ma voglio il mondo intero
Nel pugno mio serrar.

MEFISTOFELE: I have a throne and sceptre, and am ruler
Of my great realm;
But I would hold the world
With my grasp.

CORO: (*Correndo intorno ad una caldaia che sta in fondo alla scena*). Sotto la pentola corri a soffiar,
Entro la pentola corri a mischiar,
Sopra la pentola corri a danzar!
(*Porgendo a Mefistofele un globo di vetro.*)
Eccoti, o principe, il mondo inter.

CHORUS: (*They run around a caldron at back of stage*). Blow over the caldron!
Mix in the caldron!
Dance around the caldron!
(*Giving Mefistofele a glass globe.*)
This, O prince, the universe.

MEFISTOFELE: (*Col globo di vetro in mano*). Ecco il mondo,
Vuoto e tondo,
S'alza, scende,
Balza e splende,
Fa carole
Intorno al sole,
Trema, rugge,
Dà e distrugge
Ora sterile, or fecondo
Ecco il mondo.
Sul suo grosso
Antico dosso
V'e una schiatta
E sozza e matta,
Fiera, vile,
Ria, sottile,
Che ad ogn'ora
Si divora
Dalla cima sino al fondo
Del reo mondo.
Fola vana
È a lei Satana,
Riso e scherno
È a lei l'Inferno,
Scherno e riso
Il Paradiso.
Oh per Dio! Che or rido anch'io
Nel pensar ciò
Che le ascondo . . .
Ah! ah! ah! ah!
Ecco il mondo!
(*Getta con impeto il globo di vetro che si frange.*)

MEFISTOFELE: (*With the globe in his hand*). Here is the world,
Empty and round.
It rises, falls,
Dances, glitters,
Whirls about
Under the sun,
Trembles, roars,
Creates, destroys,
Now barren, now fecund—
Secli is the world.
Upon its huge
And rounded back
Dwells an unclean
And mad race,
Wicked, subtle,
Proud, vile,
Which forever
Devours itself,
From the depths to the heights
Of the guilty world.
Wild vanity,
Satan's you are
Laughter and scorn
Belong to hell,
Scorn and laughter
For paradise!
By Heaven, it makes me merry,
To think over
What is hidden here!
Behold the world.
(*Hurls down the globe, and shatters it.*)

CORO: Riddiamo! Riddiamo!
Che il mondo è caduto!
Che il mondo è perduto!
Sui morti frantumi del globo fatal . . .
S'accenda, s'intrecci la ridda infernal

CHORUS: About! about! the world has fallen!
The world is lost!
Over the dead fragments of the universe
Rises and circles the infernal round.

FAUST: Stupor! stupor! Là nel lontano,
Nel nebuloso ciel una fanciulla
Pallida, mesta, la scerni?
Il piede lento conduce
E di catene avvinto!
Ahi! pietosa vision . . . mi rassomiglia
Quella dolce figura a Margherita.

FAUST: Wonderful! wonderful! yonder,
In the misty skies, a pale and sad child
Do you not see? She slowly moves,
And is bound in irons
Sweet vision! The gentle face
Resembles that of Margherita.

MEFISTOFELE: Torci il guardo, torci il guardo!
Quello è spettro seduttor,
E fantasma maliardo,

MEFISTOFELE: Turn away, turn away!
It is a misleading spectre,
A sorcerer's phantom,

Che a chi il fissa ammorba il cor.
Torci il guarda, anima illusa,
Dalla testa di Medusa!

That sickens the heart.
Turn away, misguided mortal,
From the head of Medusa.

FAUST: Quell'occhio da celeste spalancato cadavericamente!
E il bianco sen che tanti
Ebbe da me baci d'amor!
Si . . . è Margherita, l'angelo mio!

FAUST: Those celestial eyes are open, corpse-like!
It is the white bosom
I have covered often with kisses loving.
It is Margherita, yes, my angel!

MEFISTOFELE: Torci il guardo!
nella fata
Sogna ognun colci che amò.

MEFISTOFELE: Turn away! It is a dream
Such as lovers harbor.

FAUST: Ah! strano vezzo il collo le circonda
D'una riga sanguigna.

FAUST: See the strange collar about her neck;
A bloody thread.

MEFISTOFELE: Ha la testa ditaccata,
Perseo fu che la tagliò.

MEFISTOFELE: Her head has been cut off,
It was Perseus did it.

CORO: Ah! Su! riddiamo, che il tempo cì gabba,
Sui vecchi rottami del globo fatal;
È notte tremneda la notte del Sabba,
Rimbombi sul monte la ridda infernal.
Sabba, Sabba, Saboè!

CHORUS: Ah! Let us laugh, that time is tricking us,
On the old rocks of the globe fatal,
It is a tremendous night, the night of Sabba
It shall resound on the mountain, the infernal dance
Sabba, Sabba, Saboè.

*Fine Dell'Atto Secondo.*

*End of Act Two.*

# ATTO TERZO

## SCENA I

*Morte di Margherita.*

(*Carcere. Margherita stesa a terra su di un giaciglio di paglia, canticchiando e vaneggiando. Notte. Una lampada accesa inchiodata al muro. Un cancello nel fondo.*)

MARGHERITA: L'altra notte in fondo al mare
Il mio bimbo hanno gittato,
Or per farmi delirare
Dicon ch'io l'abbia affogato.
L'aura è fredda, il carcer fosco,
E la mesta anima mia
Come il passero del bosco
Vola via. Ah! pietà di me!
In funerco sopore
È mia madre addormentata,
E per colmo dell'orrore
Dicon ch'io l'abbia attoscata.

FAUST: (*Fuori del cancello*). Salvala!

MEFISTOFELE: (*Fuori del cancello*). E chi la spinse nell'abbisso?
Io? o tu? Ciò che posso farò.
Ecco le chiavi.
Dormono i carcerieri,
I puledri fatati son pronti per la fuga . . .
(*Mefistofele apre il cancello e parte. Faust entra in carcere.*)

MARGHERITA: Dio di pietà! Son essi, eccoli, aita!
Dura cosa è il morir . . .

FAUST: Pace . . . pace . . . Io son un che ti salva.

# ACT III

## SCENE I

*Margherita's Death.*

(*A prison. Margherita lying on the ground on a bed of straw, singing and raving. Night. A lighted lamp is fastened to the wall. A grating at back.*)

MARGHERITA: The other night they threw
My child into the sea,
Now to make me mad,
They say I drowned it.
The air is cold, the prison dark,
And my sad soul,
Like the sparrow of the wood,
Flies away.
In heavy slumber
My mother is sleeping,
And horror of horrors!
They say I poisoned her.

FAUST: (*behind the grating*). Save her!

MEFISTOFELE: (*Behind the grating*). And who pushed her into the abyss?
I or you? We shall have to escape, oh, yes,
Here are the keys. The jailor sleeps,
The witches' horses ready are
For flight.
(*Mefistofele opens grating, and exits. Faust enters the prison*).

MARGHERITA: God of pity!
It is they! they are here! help!
It is hard to die!

Faust: Hush! hush!
I am here to save you.

# Act III, Scene I

MARGHERITA: Un nom . . . tu sei . . . di carità . . .
L'abbi per me . . .

FAUST: Silenzio. (Con effusione). Margherita.

MARCHERITA: Cielo! ah! parla ancora, ah! parla!
Ah! tu mi salvi! ah! m'hai salvata! (Vaneggiando.)
Ecco la strada è questa
Dov'io ti vidi per la prima volta . . .
Ecco il giardin di Marta . . .

FAUST: (Con ansia dolorosa). Ah! vieni, ah! vieni . . .

MARGHERITA: Resta ancor, resta ancor . . .

FAUST: T'affretta o a prezzo
Tremendo pagherem l'indugio.

MARGHERITA: (Con affettuosa angoscia). E non mi baci?
Ah! le tue labbra son gelo . . . (Tragicamente.)
Che festi dell'amor tuo?

FAUST: Cessa.

MARGHERITA: Tu mi togli pietoso alle catene?
E ignori chi tu salvi, o pietoso?
Ho avvelenata . . . la mia povera madre . . .
Ed ho affogato . . . il fantolino mio . . .
(Affannosamente.)
Qua . . . la tua mano . . . vien . . .
Vo' narrarti . . . il tetro ordin di tombe . . .
Che doman scaverai . . . la . . .
Fra le zolle più verdeggianti . . .
Steaderai mia madre
Nel più bel sito del cimiter . . .
Discosto . . . ma pur vicino . . .
Scaverai la mia . . . la mia povera fossa . . .
E il mio bambino poserà sul mio sen

FAUST: Deh! ti scongiuro, fuggiamo.

MARGHERITA: No. Sta l'inferno a quella porta . . .
Ah! perchè fuggi? perchè non t'arresti?
Non ti posso seguir . . .
E poi . . . la vita per me è dolor;
Che fa sulla terra?
Mendicare il mio pane a frusto a frusto
Dovrò colla coscienza paurosa
De' miei delitti.

FAUST: Rivolgi a me lo sguardo! ah! . . .
Odi la voce dell'amor che prega!
Vieni . . . fuggiam.

MARGHERITA: Si fuggiamo . . . già sogno
Un incantato asil di pace,
Dove soavemente uniti ognor vivrem.
(Faust e Margherita avvinti, guardandosi negli occhi e mormorando languidamente insieme.)

MARGHERITA: A man!—you are—
Have mercy on me!

FAUST: Silence! (Effusively.) Margherita.

MARGHERITA: Heaven, speak again, ah, speak!
You saved me! (Raving.)
You have saved me! Behold the street.
Where first I saw you
Behold the garden of Martha!

FAUST: (with painful anxiety). Ah! come, come!

MARGHERITA: Stay! stay!—

FAUST: Hasten, or the delay
A fearful price will cost us.

MARGHERITA: You do not kiss me? Your lips are ice— (Tragically.)
What have you done with your love?

FAUST: Ah! hush, hush!

MARGHERITA: You release me from my chains,
And flee not in horror? You know not
Whom you save merciful one!
My poor mother I have poisoned, and drowned
My little child!
(With anxiety.)
Give me your hand—come,
I will tell you how I'd have
The graves laid out you'll dig tomorrow.
Beneath greenest turf, where the cemetery
Is most beautiful, my mother lay.
Away from her, but near, I'll have
My own poor grave,
My infant sleeping on my breast.

FAUST: I beseech you, let us fly!

MARGHERITA: No. Hell stands at yonder door.
Ah! Wherefore fly? why not stay?
I cannot follow you; moreover
Life is woe to me;
What shall I do on earth?
Shall I beg my bread, morsel by morsel?
With conscience trembling
At thought of my sins?

FAUST: Look at me!
Hear the voice of love entreating!
Come: let us fly.

MARGHERITA: Ah! yes, let us fly! I dream already
Of an enchanted asylum of peace
Where, sweetly united, we shall ever live.

MARGHERITA E FAUST: Lontano, lontano, lontano
Sui flutti d'un ampio oceàno
Fra i roridi effluvi del mar,
Fra l'alghe, fra i fiori, fra le palme,
Il porto dell'intime calme.
L'azzurra isoletta m'appar.
M'appare sul cielo sereno
Ricinta d'un arcobaleno
Specchiante il sorriso del sol.
La fuga dei liberi amanti
Speranti, migranti, raggianti
Dirige a quell'isola il volo.

MEFISTOFELE: (Comparendo dal fondo). Sorge il di!

MARGHERITA: Ah! Satana rugge!

FAUST: (disperatamente). Ah! deh! t'affretta, il tempo fugge!

MARGHERITA: (a Faust.) Ah! no, non lasciarmi in abbandono!

MEFISTOFELE: Squilla già da quelle porte
La fanfara della morte.

MARGHERITA: (Staccandosi da Faust). Ahimè! gran Dio, tu allontana la mia tentazion!
Mi strazian le membra con dur ritorte.
O Dio, tu m'ainta mi guidano a morte,
O ciel! ah! già sul mio capo la scure brillò.

FAUST: Serena, fanciulla, lo spirto sconvolto,
Ch'io vegga tranquillo quel pallido volto
Pon freno alla foga de' vani sospiri,
C'è d'uopo fuggir, ah! si!

MEFISTOFELE: (accanto a Faust). Cessate, cessate le vane parole,
Dal ciel d'oriente già levasi il sole,
De' neri puledri già s'ode il nitrire,
C'è d'uopo fuggir, fuggiam.

FAUST: Ah! non fossi mai nato!

MEFISTOFELE: Ebben?

MARGHERITA: Chi s'erge? chi s'erge dalla terra?
E' il mostro! Misericordia!
In questo santo asilo
Che vuole il maledetto?
Ah! lo discaccia, è forse me ch'ei vuol!

FAUST: Ah! vieni e vivi,
Deh! vivi, Margherita.

MEFISTOFELE: Mi segui, o entrambi v'abbandono alla mannaia.
(Luce d'alba. Mefistofele va ad esplorare nel fondo, sul cancello. Margherita affranta, agonizzando nelle braccia di Faust.)

FAUST AND MARGHERITA: (In each other's arms, looking into each other's eyes and languidly murmuring:) Far, far away,
On the billows of a vast ocean,
Amidst the sounding waves,
Amidst sea-weeds, flowers and palms
The harbor of placid calmness,
The blue islet appears.
It appears in the serene heaven,
Crowned with a rainbow,
Mirroring the smile of the sun.
The flight of the lovers free,
Journeying, hoping, beaming,
Turns toward this islet its step.

MEFISTOFELE: (appears at back). Day is breaking.

MARGHERITA: Satan calls!

FAUST: (in despair). Come hasten, time has wings.

MARGHERITA: (to Faust). Forsake me not!

MEFISTOFELE: From yonder gates, death's trumpet tones
Peal forth already

MARGHERITA: (Tears herself from Faust). O Heaven, avert the temptation!
They break my limbs with harshest bonds.
O God, help me, they lead me to death!
O Heaven! the axe glitters over my head.

FAUST: Fairest child, your mind wanders.
Let your pale cheek calmness recover.
Curb the fury of vain desires.
We must fly! we must fly!

MEFISTOFELE: (aside). A truce to idle words,
The sun is risen in the eastern sky.
I hear the neighing of our coal-black steeds.

FAUST: Would that I had never been born!

MEFISTOFELE: Well?

MARGHERITA: Who rises before me?
Who rises from the earth? It is the monster!
Mercy! in this holy asylum,
What seeks the accursed one? Turn him forth!
Am I perhaps the one he claims?

FAUST: Ah! come and live!
Come and live, Margherita!

MEFISTOFELE: You follow me, or both of you
I'll abandon to the headsman.
(Light of dawn. Mefistofele goes exploring far down at the gate. Margherita, worn, fatigued, agonizing in the arms of Faust.)

**MARGHERITA:** Spunta . . . l'aurora pallida . . .
L'ultimo dì già viene . . .
Esser doveva . . . il fulgido giorno . . .
Del nostro imene . . .
Tutto è finito in vita!

**FAUST:** O strazio crudel!

**MARGHERITA:** Taci . . . ad ognun s'asconda che amasti Margherita
E ch'io ti diedi il cor.
Ah! a questa moribonda
Perdonerai! Signor . . . perdonerai!
Signor.
Padre santo . . . mi salva . . .
E voi celesti proteggete
Questa che a voi si volge . . .
(*Cade.*)
Enrico . . . mi fai ribrezzo!

**MEFISTOFELE:** È giudicata.

**FAUST:** O strazio!

**CORO** (*interno*). È salva!

**MEFISTOFELE:** A me, Faust.
(*Faust e Mefistofele scompaiono Nel fondo il carnefice circondalo da sgherri. Cala il sipario.*)

*Fine Dell'Atto Terzo.*

---

**MARGHERITA:** Pallid dawn appears;
The last day is come;
It was to have been the bright day
Of our marriage!

**FAUST:** O woe!

**MARGHERITA:** Hush! conceal from all
That you did love, Margherita
And that I gave you my heart.
Unto the dying one
Heaven will grant forgiveness.
Heavenly Father, save me, and you,
Celestial angels of pardon,
Protect beneath your divine wings
The sinner who turns to you—Henry! Henry!
(*Falls.*)
You make me shudder!

**MEFISTOFELE:** She is judged!

**FAUST:** O woe!

**VOICES ON HIGH:** She is saved!

**MEFISTOFELE:** Faust, you are mine!
(*Faust and Mefistofele disappear. At back, the headsman and guards are disclosed. The curtain falls.*)

*End of Act Three*

---

## ■ ATTO QUARTO

### SCENA I

*La Notte del Sabba Classico.*

(*Le sponde del fiume Penèjos, nel fondo di Tempe, il monte Pindo. Acque limpide, cespugli fioriti, lauri, oleandri, ninfee. La luna immobile allo Zenit spande sulla scena una luce incantevole. Un tempio dorico a sinistra, a destra zolle verdeggianti sparse di fiori. Elena, Pantalis, Sirene*).

**ELENA:** La luna immobile
Innonda l'etere
D'un raggio pallido.

**PANTALIS:** Calido balsamo
Stilla n le ramora
Dai cespi roridi.

**ELENA:** Doridi e silfidi,
Cigni e nereidi
Vagan sull'alighe.
L'aura è serena,
La luna è piena,
Canta, o sirena,
La serenata!

**PANTALIS:** Canta, canta, o sirena, canta.

**FAUST:** (*di dentro*). Elèna, Elèna, Elèna!

**ELENA:** Viandante languido
T'appressa al margine
Del flutto flebile.

---

## ■ ACT IV

### SCENE I

*The Night of the Classical Sabbath.*

(*The bank of the river Peneus, at the bottom of the valley of Tempe, and the mountain Pindo. Limpid waters, thick bushes, flowers, and foliage. The moon, motionless at the zenith, casts an enchanted light upon the scene. At left, a temple.*)

**ELENA:** The motionless moon
Bathes the ether
In pallid rays.

**PANTALIS:** A warm balsam
Drops from the branches
Of dewy bushes

**ELENA:** Driads and sylphs,
Swans and nereids,
Wander on wings.
The air is serene—the moon full—
The wave enchanted!
Sing, O sirens—the serenade!

**PANTALIS:** Sing, o sirens, sing.

**FAUST:** (*in slumber*). Elena! Elena! Elena!

**ELENA:** Languid traveler,
Approach the bank
Of the purling waters.

---

**PANTALIS:** Debile cantico t'invita,
E'florida la via di mammole.

**ELENA:** Cantan le tenere sirene
Amabili Grazie del mar.
L'aura è serena,
La luna è piena,
Canta, sirena, la serenata!

**FAUST:** (*Sempre dietro la scena*).
Elèna, Elèna, Elèna!

**MEFISTOFELE:** (*Entra in scena con Faust*). Ecco la notte del classico Sabba.
Gran ventura per te che cerchi la vita
Nel regno delle favole tu sei,
Saggio consiglio è di spiar ciascun
Nostra fortuna per opposto sentier.

**FAUST:** Delibo l'aura del suo vago idioma cantatrice!
Son sul suolo di Grecia!
Ogni mia fibra è posseduta dall'amor.
(*Faust esce.*)

**MEFISTOFELE:** Al Bròcken, fra la streghe del Nord
Ben io sapevo farmi obbedir,
Ma qui fra stranie larve
Più me stesso non trovo.
Atri vapori dell'irto Harz,
Aeri catrami e resine!
O prediletti alle mie nari!
Un'orma di voi non futo
In quest'attica terra,
Ma qual s'inoltra volante o danzante
Gajetto sciame femminil? Vediamo.
(*Entrano le Coretidi. Danza in cerchi (Chorèa). Mefistofele annoiato e confuso esce.*)
(*Entra Elena seguita dal Coro.*)

**CORETIDI:** Ah! Trionfi ad Elena, carmini, corone,
Danze patetiche, ludi di cetera.
Circonfusa di sol il magico viso,
Tu irradi l'anime, riverberi il cielo

**ELENA:** (*Assorta in una fatal visione*) Notte cupa, truce, senza fine funèbre
Orrida notte d'Idillio! implacato rimorso!
Nugoli d'arsa polvere al vento surgono e fanno
Più cieca la tenèbra.

**CORETIDI:** Pace!

**ELENA:** Di cozzantisi scudi e di carri stroscianti
E di catapulte sonanti l'etere è scossa!
Si muta il suol in volutàbro di sangue!

**CORETIDI:** Numi! Numi!

---

**PANTALIS:** Softest song invites;
The path is flowered
With fair violets.

**ELENA:** Sing the soft sirens.
Amiable graces of the sea.
The air is serene.
The moon is full.
Sing, sirens, the serenade!

**FAUST:** (*Still behind the scenes*).
Elena! Elena!

**MEFISTOFELE:** (*Enters with Faust*). This is the night of the classical Sabbath.
A great event for you, that seekest life
In the realm of fairydom. You are now
In the domain of fable, indeed!
It were wise counsel for each of us
To seek fortune in opposite directions.

**FAUST:** I drink the air, rich with its beauteous language.
I tread the soil of Greece; my every fiber
Is possessed with love.
(*Exit.*)

**MEFISTOFELE:** On the Brocken,
Midst the witches of the North,
I knew right well
How to make myself obeyed.
Here, amongst stranger shapes.
I am no more the same.
Dark vapors of the rugged Hartz,
Acrid gums an resins sweet to my nostrils!
No breath of you is blown
Over this Attic ground.
But lo! what mirthful female cohort
Flies or dances here: Let us see—
(*Enter the Corytides. A dance follows. Exit Mefistofele, wearied and confused.*)
(*Enter Elena followed by Chorus.*)

**CORYTIDES:** Triumphs for Elena, songs, crowns,
Dances pathetic, sounds of the zither,
Your magic brow is crowned with sunbeams;
You lighten the soul and reflect heaven.

**ELENA:** (*Absorbed in a fatal vision*). Dark and terrible night, funereal, unending!
Horrible night of Ilion! implacable remorse!
Clouds of burned dust rise on the winds,
And make darkness the darker.

**CORYTIDES:** Peace!

**ELENA:** The heavens are filled with din
Of shock of shields, of rushing chariots,
Of sounding catapults! the ground is changed
Into a pool of blood.

**CORYTIDES:** The gods! the gods!

## Act IV, Scene I

**ELENA:** I numi terribili già ruggono,
L'ire inferocendo della pugna;
L'ispide torri ergonsi tragiche,
Negra, fra la caligin densa.

**CORETIDI:** Elena!

**ELENA:** L'incendio già lambre le case,
Veggonsi l'ombre degli Achèi projette,—bui profili giganti—
Vagolar le pareti in mezzo ai roghi.
Ahimè! Alto silenzio regna
Poscia dove fu Troja.
(*Entra Faust splendidamente vestito coll'abito dei Cavalieri del XV secolo; è seguito da Mefistofele, Nereo, Pantalis, da piccoli Fauni e da Sirene.*)

**CORETIDI:** Chi vien? O strana, o mirabile vista!
Un eroe tutto splendidi s'inoltra!
Sul suo viso mestissimo si legge:
Amor!

**CORO:** Volgiti Regina! Regina volgiti e guarda.

**FAUST:** (*Inchinato davanti ad Elena*). Forma ideal purissima
Della belleza eterna!
Un uom ti si prosterna
Innamorato al suolo.
Vo'gi vêr me la cruna
Di tua pupilla bruna,
Vaga come la luna,
Ardente come il sole.

**ELENA:** Dal tuo respiro pendo e me chiamo beata
Ch'unica fra tutte le troadi e le argive ninfe
Spargo i voluttuosi fascini su cotanto amante!

**FAUST:** La tranquilla immagine
Della fanciulla blanda
Ch'amai là fra le nebbie
D'una perduta landa
Già disvani, conquiso
M'ha un più sublime sguardo,
Un più fulgurato viso
E tremo ed ardo!
Conquiso m'ha più subime amor!

**MEFISTOFELE:** O stupore! Prodigio! Quivi l'amor li aduna!
Stupor! stupor! guarda!
Ah qui li aduna l'amor!
(*Alle Coretidi.*)
Zitti lassù!

**PANTALIS:** Ah! quivi l'amor li aduna!
Guarda! coppia del ciel!

**NERÈO:** Prodigio, o prodigio!
Stupor! Celeste coppia!
Qui li aduna l'amor!
Si, quivi l'amor li aduna!

**CORETIDI:** Quivi l'amor li aduna!
O stupor! celeste coppia!
Sembran Endimione e Luna!
La dea delira l'alito
Dell'eroe rapito!
Lo contempla! quasi lo bacia, o stu-

**ELENA:** The terrible gods cry out,
Their wrath increasing;
The castellated towers rise,
Black and tragical, in the thick darkness.

**CORYTIDES:** Elena!

**ELENA:** Flames lick the dwellings.
I see the shadows
Of the Achæans—sombre, gigantic profiles—
Creeping along the walls by the light of the pyres.
Alas!
Then deep silence reigns
Where Troy once stood.
(*Enter Faust, richly attired as a cavalier of the fifteenth century; Mefistofele, Nereo, Pantalis. Small Fauns and Sirens follow him.*)

**CORYTIDES:** Who comes? O strange, O wondrous sight!
A splendid hero is revealed.
Upon his sad brow we read the word "Love."

**CHORUS:** Turn, O queen! Queen, turn and behold.

**FAUST** (*bowing to Elena*). Ideal and purest form
Of eternal beauty! A man, enamored of you,
Is prostrate before you.
Turn toward me
Your brown eyes,
Lovely as moonbeams,
Burning as the sun.

**ELENA:** I hang upon your breath and am happy!
For, alone among the nymphs of the Troad,
I fascinations scatter on such a lover!

**FAUST:** The gentle image
Of the sweet child
I worshipped, amid the gloom
Of a lost land
Has vanished; I am conquered
By a sublimer gaze,
By a brighter face.
I worship, and tremble and burn.

**MEFISTOFELE:** Oh! Marvel, oh, prodigy, here love unites them,
(*To Corytides.*)
Be silent there!

**PANTALIS:** Ah. Here love unites them
Look, a heavenly couplet.

**NEREO:** Prodigy, oh prodigy!
Marvel! celestial couple!
Here love unites them!

**CORYTIDES:** Here, love unites them,
Oh, wonder, celestial couple!
They seem, Endymion, and Luna
The Goddess sighs for the breath
Of the enraptured hero.

por!
(*Mefistofele, Pantalis, Nerèo e il Coro s'allontanano.*)

**ELENA:** O incantesimo! Parla! qual magico soffio
Cotanto bèa la tua dolce loquela d'amore?
Il suon tu inserti al suon quasi alito d'eco
D'estasi piena.
Dimmi, come farò a parlar l'idioma soave?

**FAUST:** Frugo nel cor e ti rispondo: Ave!

**ELENA:** E mi rispondi: Ave.

**FAUST:** Così tu pur come augello a richiamo
Frughi nel core e mi rispondi: T'amo!

**ELENA:** T'amo! T'amo!

**ELENA E FAUST:** Amore! mistero celeste, profondo!
Già il tempo dilegua, cancellasi il mondo!
Già l'ore dai tetri mortali contate
Ramingan serene per plaghe beate!

**ELENA:** Per plaghe beate ramingan serene!

**FAUST:** Amore!

**ELENA:** E brividi ignoti mi cercan le vene.

**ELENA E FAUST:** E un'aura di cantici esala il mio core.
Guardandoci in viso cantiamo l'amore!
Cantiam d'amore! Ah! l'amore delirio! l'amore sorriso!
Ah! amore, visione, l'amore, canzone,
Sia sempre nel tardo futuro sommerso
Sia l'estremo . . . suo verso! amor! mister! amor!

**CORETIDI:** Poesia libera t'alza pe' cieli!
Voli di folgore! impeti d'aquila!
Spinganti all'ultime reggie del sol poesia!
Alle reggie del sol, sì, spinganti a a vol!

**ELENA:** (*mormorato*). Giace in Arcadia una placida valle . . .

**FAUST:** (*mormorato*). Ivi insiem vivrem.

**ELENA:** E avrem per nido le grotte delle ninfe . . .
E per guanciale . . .

**FAUST:** Le tue morbidi chiome . . .

**ELENA:** E i fior del prato . . .
(*Si perdono mormorando fra i cespugli*)

*Fine Dell'Atto Quarto.*

She contemplates him, almost kisses him, oh, wondrous sight.
(*Mefistofele, Pantalis, Nereo and the Chorus move away.*)

**ELENA:** O enchantment! speak! what magic breath
Has thus informed your language of love?
You link sound to sound, as though they were echoes,
Replete with ecstasy
Tell me, how shall I speak the language soft?

**FAUST:** I seek in my heart, and answer you by loving.

**ELENA:** And answer me by loving.

**FAUST:** And you, like to a bird with answering plant—
I seek in my heart and answer you: I love you!

**ELENA:** I love you! I love you!

**TOGETHER:** Love, mysterious, heavenly, profound!
Already time flies and the world vanishes!
Already the hours counted by poor mortals
Flow peacefully on, in a happy region.

**ELENA:** Flow peacefully on, in a happy region.

**FAUST:** Love!

**ELENA:** And unknown feelings course through my veins.

**TOGETHER:** My heart exhales a heaven of song.
Sing we of love, looking into each other's eyes!
Of love, a delirium! Of love, a smile!
Of love, a poem! of love, a song!
Unto the distant future be delayed
Its final song, its final verse!

**CORYTIDES:** Poetry free, soar to the heavens!
Lightning flight! rush of eagles!
Reaching to the farthest confines of the sun.
To the kingdom of the sun, yes, they fly!

**ELENA:** (*murmuring*). In Arcadia lies a quiet vale—.

**FAUST:** (*murmuring*). There we live together.

**ELENA:** And we shall have a nest
The grottos of the nymph, and for pillow . . .

**FAUST:** Their soft tresses—

**ELENA:** And the flowers of the field—
(*They disappear amid the bushes.*)

*End of Act Four.*

## EPILOGO

*La Morte di Faust.*

*(Laboratorio di Faust come nell'atto primo ma qua e là diroccato dal tempo. Voci magiche sparse nell'aria. Faust, seduto sul seggiolone e conturbato medita. Mefistofele gli sta dietro come un incubo. Notte. Una lampada arde languidamente; scena quasi oscura. Il Vangelo aperto, come nel primo atto, sul leggio.)*

**MEFISTOFELE:** *(Sottovoce con un accento sinistro fissando Faust).* (Cammina, cammina, superbo pensier.)

**FAUST:** *(Alzandosi, come assorto in una estatica visione).* O rimembranza!

**MEFISTOFELE:** (La morte è vicina, cammina, cammina, Superbo pensiero.)

**FAUST:** Corsi attraverso il mondo e i suoi miraggi!
Ghermii pel crine il desiderio alato!

**MEFISTOFELE:** (O canti! o memorie d'incanti e di glorie, Guidate a ruina quell'animo altier.)
Hai bramato, gioito e poi bramato novellamente
Nè ancor dicesti all'attimo fuggente:
*(Ironico.)*
Arrestati sei bello!

**FAUST:** Ogni mortal mister gustai,
Il Real, l'Ideale, l'Amore della vergine,
L'Amore della Dea... Si.
Ma il Real fu dolore
E l'Ideal fu sogno...
Giunto sul passo estremeo
Della più estrema età,
In un sogno supremo
Si bea l'anima già:
Re d'un placido mondo,
D'una landa infinita
Un popolo fecondo...
Voglio donar la vita.

**MEFISTOFELE:** *(Spiar voglio il suo cor.)*

**FAUST:** Sotto una savia legge
Vo' che surgano a mille
A mille e genti e gregge
E case e campi e ville.

**MEFISTOFELE:** (Ah! all'erta, tentator.)

**FAUST:** Ah! Voglio che questo sogno
Sia la santa poesia
E l'ultimo bisogno
Dell'esistenza mia!
Ecco... la nuova turba al guardo mio si svela!

## EPILOGUE

*Death of Faust.*

*(The scene represents Faust's laboratory, as in the first act, but touched here and there by the finger of time. Magic voices fill the air. Faust is seated in an armchair, meditating. Mefistofele stands behind him, like an incubus. Night. The scene is dark, only one lamp burning sluggishly. A Bible is open, as in act the first, on the desk.)*

**MEFISTOFELE:** *(In an undertone, darkly looking at Faust).* Keep on,
Proud thought.

**FAUST:** *(Rising, as if overcome by an ecstatic vision).* O memory!

**MEFISTOFELE:** Death is close at hand.
Keep on, keep on, proud thought!

**FAUST:** I have hurried through the world and its visions,
Have seized winged desire by the tresses!

**MEFISTOFELE:** *(aside).* O songs!
O memories
Of enchantments and glories;
Guide unto ruin this vain soul.
You have desired, have enjoyed, and then desired anew,
Nor have yet said unto the fleeting atom:
*(Ironically.)*
Stay, you are beautiful.

**FAUST:** I have sounded
Each mortal mystery, Reality, the Ideal;
Have had the Love of the Virgin, and the Love
Of the Goddess.—Yes, but Reality was grief,
And the Ideal a dream.
Having reached the uttermost confine
Of extreme age,
My soul steeps itself
In a supreme dream.
King of a peaceful realm,
Of an infinite land,
Unto a fecund people
I'd fain give life.

**MEFISTOFELE:** *(aside).* I want to spy on her heart.

**FAUST:** Under wisest laws
I wish that, by thousands,
Nations and herds and cities,
And houses and fields arise.

**MEFISTOFELE:** *(aside).* Be watchful, tempter!

**FAUST:** I'd have this dream
The sacred poesy
And the last need
Of my existence.
The throngs
Are revealed already to my eye.

**MEFISTOFELE:** *(Ah! qual baglior conturba Il muto tenebror?)*

**FAUST:** Ecco... il colle s'inurba e il popolo s'inciela.

**MEFISTOFELE:** Il Bene già gli si rivela!

**FAUST:** S'ode un cantico in ciel.

**MEFISTOFELE:** *(All'erta! tentator!)*

**FAUST:** Già mi bèo nell'augusto
Raggio di tanta aurora!
Già nell'idea pregusto
L'alta ineffabil ora!

**MEFISTOFELE:** *(All'erta! È la battaglia incerta
Fra Satana e il ciel.)*
*(A Faust dispiegando il mantello come nell'atto primo.)*
Vien! io distendo questo mantel
E volerem sull'aria!
Faust! Faust! Faust!

**FAUST:** Cielo!

**FALANGI CELESTI:** Ah! Ave Signor degli angeli,
Dei santi, delle sfere...

**MEFISTOFELE:** *(Esorcizzando verso l'alcova dove appariscono le Sirene in mezzo ad una luce calda).* Odi il canto d'amor!
Che un dì beò il tuo cor!
Vieni a inebbriar le vene
Sul sen delle sirene!
Vieni!

**CHERUBINI:** *(voci sole).* Delle sfere, dei volanti
E dei volanti cherubini d'or!
Ave Signor!

**FAUST:** *(estaticamente).* Arrestati sei bello!

**MEFISTOFELE:** *(Avventandosi verso Faust.)* Torci il guardo, torci il guardo!

**FAUST:** *(Con un gesto possente va ad afferrare il Vangelo).* Baluardo m'è il Vangelo!
*(Cadendo ginocchioni ed appoggiandosi sulla Bibbia prega mormorando; apparisce la visione celestiale).*
Dio clemente m'allontana
Dal demonio mio beffardo,
Non indurmi in tentazione!

**FALANGI:** Dall'eterna armonia emana un verso,
Un verso di supremo amor.

**FAUST:** *(Rapito nell'estasi della visione).* Vola il cantico ardente
Del celestial drappello

**MEFISTOFELE:** *(Sempre più agitato).* Già strilla l'angelico stuolo,
Ghermiamo quell'anima al volo!
Già l'opra del male distrugge
Iddio col suo stolto perdon!

**MEFISTOFELE:** *(aside).* Ah! what light illumes
The dark heavens!

**FAUST:** Now... The hill is darkening, and the people ascend to Heaven.

**MEFISTOFELE:** Ah! Good is disclosed to him!

**FAUST:** A song is sounding from Heaven.

**MEFISTOFELE:** *(aside).* Be watchful, tempter!

**FAUST:** I drink the august beams
Of such a dawn, already.
In this idea I enjoy
An ineffable hour!

**MEFISTOFELE:** *(aside)* Be watchful, tempter!
The struggle is still uncertain
Between Avernus and Heaven.
*(To Faust, opening his cloak as in act the first.)* See, I need but ope my mantle,
And we travel through the air!
Faust! Faust! Faust!

**FAUST:** Heaven!

**CELESTIAL PHALANXES:** Ave,
Lord of the angels and saints,
Of the wandering spheres.

**MEFISTOFELE:** *(Exorcising toward the alcove, where Sirens appear, bathed in a warm light.)* Hark to the song of love!
Come and intoxicate yourself
On the bosom of the sirens!

**CHERUBIM:** Of the wandering spheres
And of the winged cherubim of gold.

**FAUST:** *(in ecstasy).* Halt, you are beautiful.

**MEFISTOFELE:** *(points to Faust).* You draw his gaze.

**FAUST:** *(With a powerful gesture, seizing the Bible).* Dear Heaven!
Evangels, be my shield!
*(Kneels, still grasping the Bible.)*
Our Fathers save me
From the scornful demon;
Lead me not into temptation!

**CELESTIAL PHALANXES:** From the eternal harmony
Rises a verse of supreme love,

**FAUST:** *(His ecstasy increasing, wrapped in the vision).* The city I dreamt of
Opens its gates at last.

**MEFISTOFELE:** *(More and more agitated).* The angelic cohort sings already!
Pluck this soul at once!
The Eternal now destroys
The work of evil! My prey escapes!

# Act IV, Scene I

**FAUST:** Sacro attimo fuggente
Arrestati sei bello!
A me l'eternità!
(*Muore.*)

**CHERUBINI:** (*Scende una pioggia di rose sulla salma di Faust*). Spargiamo un profluvio di rose,
Un nembo di foglie odorose,
Un efluvio di fior.
(*Mefistofele sotto i raggi e sotto la pioggia di rose dibattendosi e irridendo e sprofondandosi nella terra a poco a poco.*)

**MEFISTOFELE:** Diluvian le rose
Sull'arsa mia testa,
Le membra ho corrose
Da raggi e dai fior.

**CHERUBINI:** Oriamo, la povera salma s'invola,
Redenta quell'alma nel mistico amor.

**FAUST:** Holy fleeting atom;
Stay, you are beautiful!
Eternity be mine!
(*Falls dead.*)

**CHERUBIM:** (*A shower of roses falls upon Faust's body*). We rain a shower of roses,
We pour a deluge of flowers.

**MEFISTOFELE:** (*Writhing furiously, under the shower of roses and the beams of light*). Roses are showered
On my burning head.
My limbs are scarred
By the beams and the flowers.

**CHERUBIM:** Listen, that poor body is ascending,
The soul redeemed in mystic love.

**FALANGI:** E s'erge a te, per l'aurore in suon soave.

**MEFISTOFELE:** M'assale la mischia
Di mille angioletti,
Trionfan gli eletti
Ma il reprobo fischia!

**CHERUBINI:** Spargiamo un diluvio di rose sul mostro,
Le gelide e irose sue membra contorca furente
In mezzo alla pioggia rovente
Che spargono i cherubi d'oro.
Siam nimbi volanti dai limbi,
Nei santi splendori vaganti,
Siam cori, siam nimbi volanti dai limbi,
Siam cori di bimbi, d'amori.

**FALANGI CELESTI:** Ave . . . Ave!

*Fine Dell'Opera.*

**PHALANXES:** And come to you through the dawn in sounds suave.

**MEFISTOFELE:** The dispute of a thousand angels
Now besets me;
The chosen few sing,
But the reproved one hisses.

**CHERUBIM:** Rain we a deluge of roses on the monster,
Till his icy and angry lips
He move in wildest fury,
Under the scorching rain
Of the golden cherubim.
We are showers fleeting from cloudland,
Wandering in heavenly splendors,
We are choirs of infants, of loves.

**CELESTIAL PHALANXES:** Ave . . . Ave!

*The End.*

# Prince Igor (1890)

MUSIC BY ALEXANDRE PORFYREVICH BORODIN ■ LIBRETTO BY VLADIMIR VASILEVICH STASOV & THE COMPOSER

NOTE: THIS OPERA WAS COMPLETED AFTER THE COMPOSER'S DEATH BY NIKOLAI ANDREEVICH RIMSKY-KORSAKOV & ALEXANDRE KONSTANTINOVICH GLAZOUNOV & ANATOL KONSTANTINOVICH LYADOV

---

Alexander Borodin wrote both the libretto and the music to this four act opera with prologue, after Vladimir Stasov's play which is based on *The Song of Igor*, an anonymous poem from the ninth century. Completed by Rimsky-Korsakov and Glazounov, it premiered after Borodin's death, at the Maryinsky Theatre in St. Petersburg on November 4, 1890. The year is 1185; Khan Kontchak's Polovtsians are marching against Putivl. Igor Sviatoslavich, the Prince of Seversk, decides to attack them. In spite of an unexpected solar eclipse, which presages bad tidings Igor departs with Vladimir, his son by his first wife. Skula and Eroshka, two good-for-nothings, run away to join Prince Vladimir Galitsky, who is the brother of Igor's current wife, Yaroslavna, and is himself a ne'er-do-well who lives only for pleasure. Galitsky brags that, if he were in power, no one would be bereft of wine or women. Yaroslavna awaits news of Igor and Vladimir. One of her girls has been seized by Galitsky. Yaroslavna intercedes, and Galitsky gives his word that he will release the girl and reform his behavior. Igor's army is defeated and both he and his son are held captive. At the camp, Vladimir falls in love with the daughter of Khan Kontchak. Ouvlar, a Polovtsian soldier and Christian convert, offers to help Igor escape, but Igor will not hear of it. Kontchak admires this and offers to release him in exchange for peace, but Igor insists that he will immediately wage war against the Tartars if he is freed. The enemy conquers Putivl, and during the festivities celebrating the conquest, the Polovtsians finally collapse into an exhausted sleep and Igor escapes. Vladimir, torn between his father and Kontchakovna, follows Igor. The Khan prevents the guards from killing Vladimir and offers him his daughter's hand in marriage. At the city walls of Putivl, Yaroslavna, overcome with joy, sees her husband approaching with Ovlour. Eroshka and Skula, who are afraid that they will be punished for their desertion, climb the bell tower and ring the bells for Igor's return, which the people celebrate. Igor pardons the deserters, and everyone is confident that victory will be theirs soon.

---

## PROLOGO

*Una pubblica piazza della città di Poutivle. Le truppe stanno per partire alla guerra. Il popolo acclama. Allzato il sipario, si vede il principe Igor, accompagnato da alcuni principi e bojardi, uscire in gran pompa dalla cattedrale.*

**CORO DEL POPOLO:** Al fulgente Sol, gloria, gloria!
Ad Igor, signor nostro, vittoria;
Gloria, Gloria!
Russia, a te, gloria e onor!
O Troubetskoy, a te, superbo vincitor, Sia gloria e onor!
E gloria a te, Vsevolad, o guerrier baldo:
Gloria, gloria, a te gloria, gloria!
A l'aurea prol d'Igor, al nobil Vladimir,
A l'alma Russia, leonessa del mondo, Gloria, gloria a te!
Di ritmi e di canzon la steppa echeggia
E dall'azzurro Don correndo al mare,
Va pei commossi ciel l'immensa voce! Gloria, gloria!
O fulgida vision!
O vivo fiammeggiar!
Verso il Danubio van donzelle a
A gara in cor cantando gloria!
Su pe 'l Danubio van donzelle a

## PROLOGUE

*A square in Poutivle. Troops and followers of the nobles prepared to start for the war. The populace. Prince Igor accompanied by the Princess and Boyards come out of the cathedral in a solemn procession.*

**CHORUS OF THE PEOPLE:** To the sun in his glory, all hail!
Glory to us in the heavens!
And glory to Igor!
Glory and fame to our land!
Glory and honor to Prince Troubetskoy,
Glory to Vsievolod, victor!
Hail to you dauntless warrior;
Hail our noble princes!
Glory to Igor's son, hail to Vladimir!
Hail Svyatoslav, hail to you, Prince of Rilsk!
Sing glory to our princes, glory!
Glory, glory to our land!
From mighty Don to distant seas,
Over boundless steppes,
Your fame be spread
And sung in strange and unknown lands,
Glory, glory! To our famous Princes!
Glory to their valiant followers too!
By the Danube river, maidens fair

gara,
Allor cercando e fior pei vincitori
E l'inno sino a Kiew, chiaro s'effonde Gloria, gloria!

**IL PRINCIPE IGOR:** Andiam: di guerra è l'ora già.

**CORO DEL POPOLO:** Che Dio conceda al principe vittoria! Ah!

**IL PRINCIPE IGOR:** Sterminio sia de l'invasore!

**CORO DEL POPOLO:** Vogliam col sangue l'onta vendicare! Si!

**I BOJARDI:** L'infrangi tu, o vincitor d'Oltave!
Il braccio tuo saprà dar la giustizia!
Infranta sia quell'orda maledetta!
Dei Khan selvaggi dissolviam le schiere!
Mite il ciel con noi sarà!
Dio con noi sarà!

**IL PRINCIPE IGOR:** In Dio la speranza ci guidi.
Eroi: per la Russia lottiam.

**CORO:** Mite il ciel sarà!
La spada nostra è Dio!
Per la fè lottiam! Dio c'illumini per la fè!
Dio con noi sarà!
Dio vi conduca, o prodi eroi,
Allo sterminio dei Khans!

Sing your fame and glory,
Their voices ring from sea to great Kiev.
Glory, glory! To our famous Princes;
To their brave warriors too!

**PRINCE IGOR:** We go to conquer Russia's foes!

**THE PEOPLE:** God give you victory of our enemies!

**PRINCE IGOR:** We war against the Khan of the Polovtsy!

**THE PEOPLE:** Victory to Russia, let our foemen bleed! Hoy!

**THE BOYARDS:** Disperse our foes, as once before at Oltava,
May you, victorious, administer justice,
God, in his mercy will protect us.
And let the Khan of the Polovtsy
Be routed utterly, with all his hosts!

**PRINCE IGOR:** We go, with hope in God, for faith,
And for our country.

**THE PEOPLE:** God be with you!
May He lead you to the battle,
Upholding Russia against the foe!

## Prologue

**IL PRINCIPE IGOR:** Io vo con la lancia le steppe sonanti sfidar! Radiante di gloria, la morte Trovar sapro, o tornar vincitor Di nuova conquista!

**CORO:** Per la fede lottiam! Dio con noi sarà! Mite il ciel con noi sarà! Ritornerai, o Igor fulgente di splendor. Gloria! Gloria!

**IL PRINCIPE IGOR:** Guerrieri andiam: che l'ora e già!
(*Il cielo s'adombra. L'ecclissi del sole comincia. Tutti guardano sorpresi in alto*).

**IL PRINCIPE VLADIMIR GALITSKY:** Ma qual prodigio! L'oscurità dissolve il di!

**CORO:** Vè, signor, cosa appare nel ciel!

**VLADIMIR IGOREVITCH:** Lunare falce di mite luce, appare il Sol!

**CORO:** Esser potrà presagio fatal! A mezzo di fulgor di stelle!
(*La scena si oscura completamente*).
E lenta stende la notte il vel! La notte scende Devi ormai ogni sogno lasciar! Attendi ancor: Giova indugiar!
(*A poco a poco il giorno comincia a rischiararsi*).

**IL PRINCIPE IGOR:** Il ciel coprl l'oscuro nembo. Che vale? Stolto è il timor. Per me, ben più de la minaccia cupa, E forte l'Ideal! Lottiam per una causa santa. Dobbiam gloriosi ritornar; Andiam, coraggio: che l'amor di patria, S vincere o morir! Presto in sella! Laggiù verso Il mar drizziam com'aguila il volo!
(*Si fa luce completa sul teatro*).

**IL POPOLO:** Gloria! Gloria! Gloria!
(*Il Principe Igor va in fondo per fare la rivista delle sue truppe. I principi e i bojardi l'accompagnano*).

**SKULA:** Amico: in guerra andar, Non è poi gran piacer!

**EROSCHKA:** Io, davver . . . Ho gran timor . . .

**SKULA:** Mutiam padrona: Il destin proviam.

**EROSCHKA:** Sì, da Galizky, senza scrupoli, Si vivrà beati!

---

**PRINCE IGOR:** I long to break a lance in Russia's cause Upon the distant steppes of the Polovtsy; There I will fall with honor, slain by them, Or else return a victor crowned with glory!

**THE PEOPLE:** You shall return a victor, Prince, Bringing new glory home! Glory, glory! All hail!

**PRINCE IGOR:** Princes, the hour has come.
(*It begins to grow dark. The sun is eclipsed. All gaze at the sky in wonder*).

**PRINCE V. GALITSKY:** What does this portend? See, in the heavens the sun is darkened.

**THE PEOPLE:** It is God's sign in heaven, Prince!

**VLADIMIR IGORIEVICH:** And like the crescent moon The bright sun hangs, A sickle, in the sky.

**THE PEOPLE:** O, it is an evil portent, noble Prince. The stars are twinkling in the midday heavens! The earth is wrapped in awful darkness.
(*The stage grows quite dark*).
Night closes in. O wait a while! Before you march. Do not go yet. O tarry Prince, tarry a while!
(*Gradually daylight returns*).

**PRINCE IGOR:** What God's sign in the heavens forbodes — Or good, or ill, we soon shall know. But since none can elude his fate What have we then to fear? We go forth in a righteous cause, To fight for God, for faith, and home. Could we turn back and never strike a blow To check the advancing foe? My brothers, quick your fiery coursers mount And gallop to the far blue sea?
(*The sun shines out bright and clear*).

**THE PEOPLE:** Glory, glory!
(*Prince Igor goes off to review his troops, accompanied by the Princes and Boyards*).

**SKOULA:** You, friends, may go, But we stay where we are.

**EROSHKA:** I'm with you! I'm not fond of war.

**SKOULA:** Shall we try our fortune elsewhere?

**EROSHKA:** Yes, let's take service with the Prince Galitsky. There we'll be happy.

---

**SKULA:** Bene! Là si gode! Siberia! È meglio andare!
(*Si liberano delle loro armature e si salvano furtivamente*).

**IL PRINCIPE IGOR:** Salutiam le spose; confortiamole, E poi corriam laggiù sui campi di battaglia.

**JAROSLAVNA:** (*correndo verso Igor*). O dolce amico mio: Così mi vuoi lasciar? Deh! non partir . . . L'azzurro non ha più splendor; Presagio è questo di dolor! Rimani ancor vicino a me: Che avverso fato in ciel si manifesta.

**IL PRINCIPE IGOR:** O candida mia sposa, Iascia il pianto: Non velare l'occhio tuo sereno tanto; Confida in me!

**JAROSLAVNO:** In te confido sempre, Ma il cor d'angoscia freme; E temo! Ah! L'orror m'assale! Io so che tu non puoi restar. Ah! destin crudel! Così non mai piega la fede in me! Ah! straziato ho il cor. L'angoscia vince! Ho timor! Mi sembra avverso il ciel! Oimè!

**IL PRINCIPE IGOR:** Perchè languisci tu così? E sacro il mio dovere! Non posso rinunciar. Sii forte, sposa mia: Opponi il senno al tuo dolor. Confida in me! Un folle languor t'invade, Ma pur tu sai che ascolto ancor, Ah! Per te darò a la voce de l'amor Addio, mio solo ben! . . .

**VLADIMIR IGOREVITCH:** Andiam! Andiam! Dobbiam partir! Che l'onor lo vuole!

**IL PRINCIPE VLADIMIR GALITSKY:** È ver: partir dovrà, Per il nostro onor!

**IL PRINCIPE IGOR:** Il ciel saprà vegliar. Tu pregherai per noi!
(*A Galitzky*).
Io la confido a te, mio buon fratello: Serbar dovrai la sua serentià Fa' che 'l timore più non l'abbatta In te speranza ripongo. Su lei sorveglia, buon fratello.

---

**SKULA:** Gladly! There is mead, and ale, And food in plenty.
(*They throw down their arms and sneak away*).

**PRINCE IGOR:** Now comrades, let us take a fond farewell Of wives and sweethearts. One last kiss, And then, to horse!
(*Enter Yaroslavna, who embraces Igor*).

**YAROSLAVNA:** O, husband, my beloved, stay with me! Do not go forth to battle, for the time Is not propitious. O believe me love! Stay with me, hear my prayer. The signs and omens tell of sorrow, They threaten grief and to you and us.

**PRINCE IGOR:** O, wife beloved, do not weep, dry your eyes. Your tears and prayers are vain. I cannot stay, Believe me, duty calls.

**YAROSLAVNA:** I must believe my heart that bids me fear. O love, what anguish and alarm I feel! I tremble . . . my courage fails. Alas I knew how you would answer me. I know too well Your words are right and true; But ah, my heart speaks louder still Of grief and woe to come! Farewell!

**PRINCE IGOR:** Ah, fear not; do not weep, my wife. How often have we been parted in the past And you have never known such fears before. Honor demands that I should take the field Against the foes of Russia. I must go. Believe me, duty calls. Farewell, dear love.

**PRINCE VLADIMIR IGORIEVICH:** Prince, you are right. We must depart, Duty and honor call us; we must go.

**PRINCE V. GALITSKY:** Prince, you are right. There is no turning back. Yes, duty and honor call us, you must go.

**PRINCE IGOR:** God keep you safe from harm. Pray for us, dear one.
(*To Galitsky*).
To you, as to a brother, I trust her. Guard her from danger and from grief, Lighten for her the sorrow of my absence, Speak kindly to her. And now farewell My friend and brother.

**IL PRINCIPE VLADIMIR GALITSKY:** Sia pur: la mia riconoscenza, Igor ritroverai per sempre. Mio padre allor che m'esiliò, Lontan tu sai, del suo dominio, Io qui, presso te, trovai Difesa contro il suo livor. Ed or che perdono, Tornato in libertà, Mi è dato alfin goder Di tutti i suoi tesori . . . E grazia debbo a te.

**IL PRINCIPE IGOR:** E ben, fratello: Or tu mi puoi ricompensar! (*Jaroslavna esce con le principesse e le mogli dei bojardi*). (*Il Principe Igor si avvicina ad un vecchio*).

**IL PRINCIPE IGOR:** Andiam, che l'ora è già! O santo Padre: prega il ciel: L miei guerrieri, benedici tu! Sorrida il cielo ai nostri eroi!

**IL POPOLO:** Benedici tu gran Padre, gli eroi! Guida, Padre, alla guerra gli eroi! L'irradia tu! O rasserena tu i vincitor! I figli tuoi, Signor, proteggi E li guida, o ciel! Ai figli tuoi, Signor, fa cor: Le spade già brillar nel Sol! Protegga il ciel i suoi guerrier! (*Il vecchio benedice l'esercito*). I tuoi campioni, o Parde, han aite le space davanti nel Sol! I tuoi campioni per te vittoria s'avviano: Son alte spade davanti nel Sol! (*Igor e i principi montano su i lora corsieri e vanno davanti all'esercito*).

**I BOJARDI:** L'inno si sciolga di gloria!

**IL POPOLO:** Al fulgente Sol, gloria! gloria! Grande Igor, Signor nostro, vittoria! Gloria, gloria, Russia a te gloria e onor! O cara patria, o santa Russia, terra di splendor: A te sia gloria, gloria ognor! Al superbo campion, al forte Vsewolod, A la prole d'Igor, al giovin Vladimir; Tutti a voi guerrier, gloria! Austeri vincitor! Guerra, guerra, guerra, gloria, gloria! Gloria, Santa Russia a te! Gloria!

**PRINCE V. GALITSKY:** All is well! I am prepared to serve you faithfully, For much I am beholden to you, Prince. When in his wrath my father banished me, And all my brethren did forsake me too, You took up my cause, And like a brother gave me a friendly welcome; You pleaded forgiveness for me, Till my father yielded And took me home once more. All this I owe you.

**PRINCE IGOR:** No more, no more, friend. I rejoice to know I helped you in the hour of need. (*Exit Yaroslavna with the princesses and the wives of the Boyards*).

**PRINCE IGOR:** (*approaching the Elder*). It is time that we were on our way, Revered and honorable father, Before we go. To meet our foemen, give your benediction. O bless the Princes and our warriors all! (*The Elder blesses the army*).

**THE PEOPLE:** God in the battle shield our warriors brave And lead them on to victory. Scatter the cruel heathen horde. Protect your sons, o Lord, and guide them, oh heaven! Give courage to your sons, oh Lord, Their swords glisten in the sun! May heaven protect its warriors! (*Igor and the Princes mount their war-horses and ride at the head of the troops*).

**THE BOYARDS:** (*semi-chorus*). Hail to the Princes, Hail to their followers!

**THE PEOPLE:** To our bright stars be glory, Glory in highest heaven! To our brave Princes be glory, Glory to all Russians! To the highest and the lowest, Alike be glory given. Hail, all hail! Glory to all the Princes of our land Hail to dauntless Vsievolod, Hail to Sviatoslavich, Hail to the Falcon Prince, The young Vladimir, To all the fearless fighters, hail! Glory to our Princes, Glory to our Boyards, Glory to our warriors bold, Glory, glory!

*CALA IL SIPARIO*

# ■ ATTO I

## SCENA I

*Il cortile della casa del Principe Vladimir Galitsky.*

**CORO DEL POPOLO:** Ah! Salve, principe Galitsky; a Te, O nostro buon signor: Salve! Gloria, gloria!

**SKOULA:** Giochiam! Qual fragor di flutti erompe! L'onda par che qui s'avventi, Infrangendo la riviera, E diffonda il suo terror.

**CORO DEL POPOLO:** Quei signori son gaudenti, Che fanfara di conquista: Ah, ah! Che allegrezza! Ah, ah! Che frastuono! . . . Tutta notte fan baldoria. Che frastuon! Canti e delizie son la loro vita: La folle giovinezza affogan nel piacer!

**EROCHKA:** Tutta in pianto al fanciulla, A' suoi pie' plorando cadde. (*Imitando la voce d'una donna*). O signore! Deh, lascia andare! . . .

**EROCHKA E SKOULA:** Ah, verdi qual dolor! Per pietà! Quale angoscia, oimè! O non farmi soffrir.

**CORO:** Ah, ah! che allegrezza! Ah, ah! che frastuono! Tutta notte' fan baldoria. Che frastuon! Canti e delizie son la loro vita: La folle giovinezza, Affogan nel piacer!

**CORO:** Contento sei, signor?

**IL PRINCIPE VLADIMIR GALITSKY:** Non più soffrir: Io vo' tutto goder. Igor s'affanna nel bollor de le conquiste, Mentr'io passar la vita cerco dolcemente. Che bel piacer, cosi lottar! . . . Se di Poutivile principe foss'io! . . . O come si godrebbe! Si . . . Se domani mi toccasse ottener L'onor sognato d'esser lor signor, Ben saprei regnar! Lieto il giorno in gran simposio, Sbrigherei le mie faccende: Sempre a me d'accanto, Consigliere il vino, I castighi e le sentenze Detterei di mia ragione, Per far rispettar La mia volontà! Viva, viva l'allegria! E ben più farei la notte:

*CURTAIN*

# ■ ACT I

## SCENE I

*The courtyard of Prince Vladimir Galitsky's house*

**CHORUS OF THE PEOPLE:** Glory, glory, to Prince Vladimir. Hurrah!

**SKOULA:** Let's sport! But why this noise? Has the stream broken its banks and overflowed the land?

**THE PEOPLE:** See, how some wild young spark has carried off. With his boon friends, a girl or two. Hoy, hoy! Youth will sport and play, Lads must have their way! All night in song they've praised Their noble Prince. Long live Galitsky Who keeps open house!

**EROSHKA:** Then the pretty lass came weeping, To the Prince's footstool creeping. (*Imitates a girl's voice*). "Prince, my Prince, let me go from here."

**CHORUS:** Hoy, hoy! Youth will sport and play, Lads must have their way! All night in song they praised their noble prince, Long live Galitsky, Who keeps open house!

**CHORUS:** (*approaching Galitsky*). Prince, are you satisfied?

**PRINCE GALITSKY:** I hate a dreary life. I could not live Like Igor, ever amid war's alarms. I crave for pleasure, princely luxury, A merry time on earth! Ah, were I chosen Prince of Poutivle, What glad times for you all! How then? Were the throne on me conferred, My rule to Igor's rule preferred, Quickly you would see How joyous life can be; Daily in my hall I'd hold high festival, My judgments would be light, I'd feast you every night, For high and low The wine should flow. With a heigh-ho, Laugh, laugh and quaff! And night would bring new pleasures,

# Act I, Scene I

Presso me vorrei raccolti
Freschi fiori di fanciulle,
Per cantar e per danzar!
De le più belle e gentili,
Vorrei far per me catene.
Punirei chi m'impedisse.
Di onorar così l'amor, l'amor!
Per tal vita di delizie,
Ci vorrebbe gran ricchezza;
Ma la fonte avrei
Dal regal tesor.
E così ben dolcemente
Governando in tal guisa, certo
Potrei dir di saper goder!
O verdremo ben regnando,
Chi di voi potrà lagnarsi,
Chi mi capirà! Ben mi loderà!!
Viva, viva l'allegria!

**CORO:** Ah! Sempre arrida a voi la sorte!

**UNA PARTE DEL CORO:** Ma la principessa?

**IL PRINCIPE VLADIMIR GALITSKY:** Che stolta! . . . E ancor qui che prega.
Una santa ell'è; in un convento chiudasi!
Ognun di noi avrà così perdon per lei!
Ed or, si rida e canti.
Un premio a chi più beve.
Su, ridete, poiché v'offro di vin un baril!
(*Si dirige verso la sua casa*).

**CORO:** Ah! Sempre il ciel vi sia benigno!
(*Un gruppo di fanciulle entra correndo. Vladimir Galitsky si ferma*)

**CORO DI DONZELLE:** Ah! che viltà! Ah! qual dolor!
I fidi tuoi, Signor, non han riguardo alcun!
Di noi la più gentile offeser ne l'onor
Ah! salvala, salvala nostro Signor!
Sì, per pietà!

**IL PRINCIPE VLADIMIR GALITSKY:** Basta, basta perchè piangete?
Vostra sorella non soffre alcun mal,
Poichè mi degno ammirar sue grazie.
Stolte: non è un grandissimo onor,
Se a' miei diletti la voglio serbar?
Pensiero alcuno non la disturba:
Deve sol amar, cantar!
Via, cessate! Vano è il pianto!
La fanciulla mia sarà!

**CORO DI DONZELLE:** Ah! qual viltà! Ah! giusto ciel!
Ascolta noi, Signor.
Non ci straziare il cor,
Pietà, buon Signor.
Non farci soffrir!

**IL PRINCIPE VLADIMIR GALITSKY:** A che insistete? Per me la tengo!
No, non ho colpa di sua gran beltà.
Non voglio più pianto: uscite di qua!
Guai a voi tutte se l'ira mi assal!

When my fairest maidens came;
They should sing in lively measures
Of their Prince's power and fame,
And the freshest, rosiest maiden,
Lovely in her youthful pride,
With my favors I would laden,
Keep her longest by my side.
But to lead a life of pleasure
I should need a princely treasure.
Well, since Igor's purse I hold
I could dip there for the gold.
If his wealth I freely scatter
In wine and revelry, what matter?
State and power are nothing to me
If they do not bring luxury.
So, heigh-ho,
Come laugh and quaff!

**CHORUS:** Ho! To Galitsky long life and glory!

**SEMI-CHORUS:** Yes, but the Princess?

**PRINCE GALITSKY:** My sister?
She's a meek, religiour woman.
Let her retire to a convent.
There to pray for pardon
For my sinful soul; but you friends
Come to my house and taste
My finest mead; and for the people
I will order forth a vat
Of generous wine!
(*He goes towards the house*)

**CHORUS:** To Prince Galitsky, glory!
(*A group of maidens comes running in, Prince Galitsky remains standing there*)

**THE MAIDENS:** O, the miscreants,
The wicked wretches!
Some of your household, Prince,
Have done us wrong and
Carried one of us away by force!
Have pity, give her back to us.

**PRINCE GALITSKY:** Foolish women, cease your wailing,
Your companion's safe with me,
Nothing lacking, nothing ailing,
She is happy as a bride.
And if I shall choose to keep her,
Who shall dare
Touch her there?
You will never see her again.

**THE MAIDENS:** O unhappy, Heaven befriend her!
Prince, have pity, show mercy
To her mother and her father!
Hear our prayers and let her go!

**PRINCE GALITSKY:** Why do you wait?
The maiden with me stays.
Now get you away from here.
Your cries and tears will raise
A fury in me.
Then you'll know

Via di qua!
(*Le fanciulle scappano*). (*Il Principe esce*).

**EROCHKA:** (*motteggiatore*). Già! sempre accade così,
Quando mamma si vuol lasciar!
Bene vista!

**SKOULA:** (*motteggiatore*). Già! sempre accade così,
Quando si è belle!
Arrossirà la piccina inver!

**SKOULA:** Ah! se la signora saprà come'è la cosa
Starem freschi noi davver!
Oh, sì . . .

**CORO DEL POPOLO:** O principessa;
Troppo sei stanca! No i siam possenti!
I fidi suoi lontani son.
Omai dispersi in guerra.
Non v'ha di che temer!
Andiamo!

**SKOULA:** E ben: se poi la dama non
È per noi propensa,
Perchè dobbiam servirla?

**EROCHKA:** Non giova a nulla.

**SKOULA:** È vero; val più servire Vladimir!
Certo! fa doni d'amor, d'ebrezza,
Essa il conto merita.
(*Alcuni servitori portano avanti un barile di vino facendolo rotolare davanti a loro*).

**SKOULA:** (*Con rudezza e gravità comica*). Chi cercasse un buon signore,
Venga qua: volentieri noi la grazia gli farem.
La sua gente e già con lui,
Per cantar, per ballare a tondo
E con noi trincare!
Per cantar, beviam!

**CORO:** Per cantar, beviam!
Questa gente non sa che gavazzar!

**EROCHKA E SKOULA:** Ma col vizio la miseria cominciò!
E talmente in questa plaga
S'inasprì, che ognuno di sostanza
Non ha già più nè manco un solo rublo
Per restare in piedi,
O signor: Sii gentil:
Noi brindiamo a te, Signor.
Un sorso del tuo vino . . .
Dei bevitor la folla
Giuliva qui verrà da te,
A renderti omaggio ancor!
Così per la tua bontà,
Alfin sarai signore,
Se ci darai la libertà
La morte sfiderem per te. Sì!!

**CORO:** Sol bevendo, la morte saprem sfidar.

That I am to be feared in anger. Go!
(*The maidens make their escape. Exit Galitsky*).

**EROSHKA:** (*mockingly*). Yes, that's the way!
Goodbye father, goodby mother!
Off with you, run home quick!

**SKOULA:** (*mockingly*). A fine feast her's will be.
That is always one's lot
When one is handsome!

**SKOULA:** Hush! Listen friend.
What if the Princess finds out we are here and orders us away?

**THE PEOPLE:** Who heeds the Princess?
Who would take her part?
Her followers are few compared to us;
And all her guards are marching to the war.
What have then to fear, good folk? Come on.

**SKOULA:** Well said!
We know the Princess, she is mean,
And careful of her wine.
Why should we serve her?

**EROSHKA:** For certain, friend, we will not serve her.

**SKOULA:** With Prince Galitsky it is a different tale!
He loves us like a father. See there!
Wine comes in plenty!
(*The Prince's servants roll in a barrel of wine*).

**SKOULA:** (*Clownishly, but with comic gravity*). You who seek a generous master, come here,
Take service with the noble Prince Galitsky.
He assembles, all his followers
Bids them eat and drink their fill,
Wine and mead he spares not,
Brim your cups and toss it down.

**CHORUS:** Wine and mead he spares not,
Brim your cups and toss it down.

**SKOULA AND EROSHKA:** Loudly groan the Prince's followers;
We have lapped up every drop;
Now they're howling, loudly howling;
We have drunk your health so often
That the barrel has run dry.
Not a thimbleful remaining,
Prince, we've swallowed every drop.
Prince, our benefactor,
Treat us once again!
Let the strong wine flow for us like a flood!
Let the heady mead be broached vat on vat!
And the generous vintage run red and bright!
Let us drink one more barrel to your health!

**CHORUS:** In drinking we shall laugh at death!

SKOULA: Con parole sagge il liberal Signor nostro principe,
Risponde: Non più voi dovrete ne l'ombra sospirar:
Ne più l'angoscia crudele patir.
Le mie botti son colme ancora
Per chi m'ama e mi vuole allietar:
Goda ognun!

CORO: De le botti l'ambrosia ci ferve in cor!

EROCHKA: Ognor voi faticate
La vita è tanto dura!
Dal nascere del giorno
Al fiume, al bosco andate:
Davver, così, del bove,
Ben più s'affanna l'uomo.
Ma io che il ver conosco
Or v'offro un buon rimedio:
Canti, balli, e donne
Per ritemprar chi lavora!
Tal linguaggio avrà il nostro grande Signor!

CORO: Canti, balli e donne in fiore:
O qual piacer! Non abbia sognato
Mai tal voluttà.
S'ei fosse pur signor del principato!?
È ver! Si può donargli il nostro trono!
Sia pur così.
Igor è scomparso.
Che più indugiar?
Coraggio . . . Non dobbiam temer.
Gli s'offra la corona.
Minaccia non vediam.

EROCHKA E SKOULA: La truppa è via,
I principi alla guerra,
Bisogna agir!
Ben posson ritornar!
Se forti sono ancor.
Se morti son, n'avrò piacer.

EROCHKA, SKOULA E CORO: Andiam! Non più tardiam;
In piazza ci rechiamo,
Che in discussion la folla è convocata.
Igor detronizziam!
Il regno a Vladimiro.
Or noi la forza abbiam!
Al fato Igor disfatto ha soggiaciuto.
In massa andiam che suona la campana.
Il trono a Vladimiro:
Signore lo vogliam.
Sin che duri l'allegria,
Non avremo trepidanza.
Là, là! Se la vita . . . Là, là!
Presto fugge, dolce è l'ansia
Che si avvolge nel piacer!
Non più tardiam, in piazza ci rechiamo,
Che in discussion la folla è convocata.
Non vogliam saper d'Igor.
Galitsky, gloria a te!
Sin che duri l'allegrezza,
Non avremo trepidanza!
Che la gioia sia completa.

SKOULA: Then our gracious Prince will speak and say:
Do not weep and wail, my servants true,
Surely I'll take pity on your lot,
For your lives are hard, and joyless too,
Working all day.

CHORUS: The mead goes to the heart.

EROSHKA: You're at work
From early morn till evening
From midday till the sun goes down,
From twilight to the break of day,
And oh, such heavy work you do,
You labor like the ox or horse,
Your toil it seems is never done,
Now sing and laugh and play
And drink my health today —
That's what our Prince will say!

CHORUS: Songs and dances and women.
What pleasure!
We never dreamt of such joy!
Yes, he's the man we want to rule Poutivle!
What say you?
Shall we set him on the throne?
The army is not here,
And Igor's far away —
Then what have we to fear?
Why hesitate?
We all want him to reign;
And there are plenty of us
To work our will.
Then what have we to fear?

SKOULA AND EROS: The army is not here,
The Princes, too, have gone,
No one can hinder us.
Rebellion will break out.
The army by this time exists no more
And every Prince in battle has been slain.

SKOULA, EROSHKA AND CHORUS: It is true! Come then!
The army is not here,
And none can stop us.
Come on! Come on!
Now gather in the market-place;
Quick, let the Vêche be assembled there!
Let Igor be dethroned.
Vladimir, hail!
What have we now to fear?
Now make merry, drink and revel
Send misgivings to the devil!
Hoy, hoy! Let all be jolly.
Sing the praise of Galitsky,
Drink his health until we see Dawn appear!
Glory to Vladimir!
Glory Prince Galitsky!
Welcome, Welcome! Hoy!
Send misgivings to the devil!
Hoy, hoy! Let's be jolly.
Sing the praise of Galitsky,
Our good lord, hail,
Glory, hoy!
(The crowd move off. Only Skoula and Eroshka, who are already

Sempre noi godrem!
Gloria! Salve! Principe Galitsky a te!
Nostro buon signor, salve! Gloria!
Ah!
(Tutti escono, Skoula e Erochka, già ubriachi restano soli al loro posto).

EROCHKA E SKOULA: (Vacillanti). Oh! qual dolore!
O quale angoscia!
Non farmi soffrir!
Io muoio di timor!
(Escono appoggiati l'uno all'altro e ridendo).

## SCENA II

Una camera sul terem di Jaroslavna. Jaroslavna sola.

JAROSLAVNA: Da lungo tempo Igor,
Mio dolce amor,
Lontano sei da me,
Con Vladimir e il fratel tuo,
Per la guerra fatal:
Ma nulla seppi ancor,
E già dispero!
Io conto tristemente i dì,
E vo' celando il pianto!
Soccorso imploro su dal ciel!
O fai che tra le braccia
Mi ritorni il solo ben che attendo,
Poi che mai non ascolti il mio dolor: piango!
Invano oimè, trascorre l'ora!
E mi s'agghiaccia il cor
Al soffio del destin.
Or più non va, mio desiato Igor,
Amor spirando come un tempo!
Fioriva il cuore ov'eri tu . . .
Ed ora muto e di squallor; Oimè!
Che sol mi dà conforto
Il rievocar di te, mio dolce Igor!
Per te, te sol, mio ben, respiro ancor;
E ancor per te, mio santo amor
Il pianto a ciel s'invola!
Funesto sogno mi recò la cupa notte:
Sfinito Igor la man tendea,
E il nome mio parea chiamar!
Smarrito il cor mi palpitò ne l'ombra . . .
Ma la pia vision si dileguò.
Invan chiamai, oimè!
Ancor m'agghiaccia. Tremo tutta . . .
Su l'albeggiar, al mio dolor m'abbandonai,
Dimmi: ribacerai la sposa tua?
Io soffro a te lontan!
Senza te a vita manca! . . . .
(Ella si copre il viso con le mani e resta assorta nei suoi pensieri).
(Entra la nutrice).

LA NUTRICE: Un gruppo di fanciulle, o signora,
A te piangendo viene e chiede di parlar.
Ti piace dare ascolto?

rather tipsy, remain. They sit on the barrel and continue to drink).

SKOULA AND EROSHKA: Oh, I want my mommy,
Oh, I want my daddy;
Do not vex a poor maid so,
Let me go back to mommy . . .
(Exeunt, propping each other up).

## SCENE II

(A room in the Terem. Yaroslavna is sitting lost in thought.)

YAROSLAVNA: How long a time has passed since my dear lord, my husband Igor, with his son Vladimir, and our brother Vsievolod, led forth his army against the Polovtsy. I know not what to think? So long it sems since I received a message from the Prince. I would that some news of Igor might reach me, even by chance. O, my heart bodes but of sorrow! It aches, and burns with questioning; and whispers always of some coming trouble.
Where have you fled, happier days before Igor rode forth to the fight?
Alone, from dawn to eve I gaze
Across the distant, empty plain.
I spend the sleepless night weeping,
And long for you to come again.
I yearn for news of you: I wait
Long hours at the casement here.
Send me a message, O my mate,
Send me one word, O husband dear,
Some tidings of thy doubtful fate!
So long, so long the nights and days.
Such visions haunt my hours of rest;
I see you every night, in dreams
You came to me, and it seems
You called me and to your breast
You held me closely once again . . .
And then I woke to sharper pain,
And tears more bitter than before
Fell on my pillow like a rain . . .
Alone, alone, for ever more!
Will you not come to me, my love?
Do I not wait for you? Where are you, husband of mine?
(She hides her face in her hands and is lost in thought).

OLD NURSE (entering). Here are some maidens, Princess, asking your protection.
Are they to enter?
Will you see them, Princess?

**JAROSLAVNA:** Oh sì: Le attendo; vengan pur.
(*La nutrice esce; poi rientra con le fanciulle. Le fanciulle si inchinano davanti alla principessa*).

**CORO:** Noi veniam ploranti,
Mite principessa,
Invocando soccorso,
Rendi a noi giustizia,
Ci concedi grazia,
E proteggi il nostro onor!
Questa notte ne la loggia,
S'introdusse un cavalier:
La più gentil di not rapi, Senza pietà.
Noi piangemmo invano,
E pregammo tanto
Ma quel tristo seduttor
Non si commosse.
Gli chiedemmo la sorella:
Ei fremendo di lussuriò,
Brutalmente noi cacciò. O qual dolor!
Vedi il nostro pianto,
Sii clemente e mite:
Imploriamo il tuo buon cuore!
Non abbandonare l'innocente figlia,
Che sol tu la puoi salvar!
Tu lo vedi quanto strazio!
Oh proteggi il mite fior!
Ah! togli ta al disonor; Abbi pietà!

**JAROSLAVNA:** Chi dunque l'ha rapita?!
Ebben parlate pur.
Fidate in me.

**LE FANCIULLE:** (*esitando*). Il nome dite, orsù! Io?
Perchè tacere ancor? Parla?
Non esitiamo più.

**JAROSLAVNA:** Dite: Chi dunque fu?

**LE FANCIULLE:** Non oso. Abbiam timor!
Su via, parliam; perchè tacer? Parliamo alfin.
Principessa, la voce trema nel dire
Il nome di chi ci offese.
È un gran signore, fiero, superbo,
Temuto e forte: E Vladimiro!
Già da gran tempo ferve l'orrore
De' suoi delitti; mentre s'invoca
d'Igor l'amore,
E si rimpiange la sua bontà. Sì, è ver!
Poi che in guerra Igor fu tratto,
Si vide presto la nostra terra priva di leggi,
Grave di angoscie e mai l'asilo non fu più sacro.
Come uragano, la sua ferocia semina morte!
Ei ci tormenta, ei ci dissolve
Con le sue genti, senza pietà! Sì, è ver!
Senza tregua, ebri di strage,
Recan lo strazio nei casolari.
È un'infinita tortura,
Per noi meschine, che ci divora
E soffocato freme lo sdegno;
Langue ogni cuore di trepidanza:
Tutto è rovina, tutto è dolore,
Da quando lunge, nel tristo esilio,

**YAROSLAVNA:** Surely!
Now call them; let them come.
(*The Nurse goes out and returns accompanied by the girls who salute Yaroslavna respectfully*).

**THE MAIDENS:** We come to you, Princess,
We come as to a mother,
To ask that right be done.
Grant us your sheltering care,
Protect us from dishonor.
Last night a wicked man
Entered our home by stealth,
By force he carried off
One of our dear companions,
A maiden all defenseless.
With tears and supplications
We hastened to his master,
And prayed him to release
Our gentle, stainless sister
And punish him who wronged her.
Alas, he would not hear us.
With cruel mocking laughter
He drove us from his presence,
And threatened us with vengeance
O, be just, be gracious,
Hear our prayers, kind Lady,
Save us from dishonor,
Punish her betrayer,
Set our sister free!

**YAROSLAVNA:** And who was the offender?
Who carried off the maiden?
Tell me his name?

**THE MAIDENS:** (*to each other in confusion*). Ah, who shall speak?
You there!
We, girls? We should not dare!
What, make us tell? Unfair!

**YAROSLAVNA:** Why are you frightened?
Speak the truth.

**THE MAIDENS:** We are afraid . . . We dare not . . .
But we must take courage, and tell all.
Princess, be our friend, be not wrath with us
If we speak the truth. He who did us wrong.
Is a mighty Prince. Yes Prince Vladimir!
Many times before he has done us wrong.
Many a burden laid on Poutivle's folk.
When Prince Igor left for the distant field,
Then our lot grew worse, darker things befell
Town and country-side; now Galitsky's men
Helpless folk oppress, work their wicked will
Whenever they please. Never for a day
Are our lives our own.
Princess, hear our plaint!
Wild and wine-inflamed, careless of all good,
Mocking every prayer, wrecking hearts and homes,

Languisce Igor!
Ci salva Tu dal disonor!
Di tanto duol pietà.
(*Entra Vladimiro Galitsky. Le fanciulle danno in un grido di spavento*).
Ah! Ah! Eccolo!
Eccolo! Ci protegga il cielo!

**VLADIMIRO GALITSKY:** (*Minacciando le fanciulle*). Ola, che vedo: via di qua!
(*Queste scappano. La nutrice esce ad un segno di Jaroslavna*).

**JAROSLAVNA:** Ei giunge.
Ebben, perchè fratello . . .
Sei tu, tu che tenti
Così l'onor di queste beltà?!
L'indegno gesto, sei dunque folle tu?
Rispondi alfin e sii sincero.
Come fu? Oh, parla:
Dimmi il nome.
Perchè l'hai tu rapita?

**VLADIMIRO GALITSKY:** Ma cosa importa a te!
Perchè te ne infaccendi?
Trovai quel che m'andò,
E quel che presi tengo
La preda è poca cosa . . .
E non mi basterà.
Il tuo dire m'allieta:
Davver mi fa buon pro!
Or via, sorella, dammi fede:
Mi ricevi degnamente.
Con la coppa, principessa,
Vanno accolti i pari miei,
E schiumeggiar ben dovrà vecchio vino!
O davver poca fidenza poni in me.
Con un villano pensi trattare tu?
Fors'io disturbo qui?

**JAROSLAVNA:** Ah! S'arrossa già per te il volto di vergogna!
Ah! bada, Vladimir: ch'il posso ancor punir!
Se dalla guerra Igor ritornerà,
Giuro al ciel, l'accuserò di questo insulto vil!
E bada: temi ch'ei ti possa castigar.

**VLADIMIRO GALITSKY:** E cosa importa a me se Igor ritornerà
O rimarrà laggiù senza tregua in guerra ancor?
Padrone mio non è:
Siam pari di potenza:
E qui potrò governar, si mi parrà.
A un cenno sol borghesi e schiavi
Lieti sono al mio servizio.
Questa folla lamentosa.

They have spoiled and slain, ruined and undone
Many a helpless maid, laid waste many fields.
Since Prince Igor went, there is none to hold.
Wickedness in check, and defend the poor.
Send him away, dear Princess, we implore!
(*Enter Prince V. Galitsky*).
(*They perceive the Prince and are terrified*).
O Prince, our little father! What have we done!
God help us all!

**PRINCE GALITSKY:** (*threatening the girls*). Now get! Begone, I say!
(*They run away. The nurse goes out at a sign from Yaroslavna*).

**YAROSLAVNA:** Vladimir! With a band of wild young men, its said
that you forced your way at night into a humble dwelling. and bore
away a maiden, against her will; that you keep her even now a prisoner in the Terem. Can this be true?
Tell me? Who is she? I demand that you answer!

**PRINCE GALITSKY:** What if I have? Lord's sake
It is no concern of yours!
For what I want I take,
And hold to what is mine.
How should I know her name?
But are you glad to see me, sister?
Your welcome is not warm, my dear.
Must I remind you, when guests enter.
We offer them the cup of cheer,
And set them in the place of honors
And bring for them our oldest wine—
These are our customs, sister mine.
But in truth I came at an unlucky moment.
Thou did hold counsel with some stinking beggars.
Bah! I have disturbed your charity?

**YAROSLAVNA:** When will it end!
Your shameless way of life
Becomes intolerable. I am still Princess,
And when my husband, Igor, comes again,
I'll tell him all that you have made me suffer;
And you shall answer then for your misdeeds.
And face a day of reckoning—when he comes.

**PRINCE GALITSKY:** Let Igor come, or stay,
It matters not to me.
Do I not reign today,
As much a Prince as he?
Am I not ruler here?
What then have I to fear?
I only need to raise my voice,
And I might dwell in your palace.
I'm the master, by the people's

Mi si prostra quanto voglia!
E diman potrei sicuro comandar su tutti!
Me dunque onori più decorosa accolta.

JAROSLAVNA: Ed osi minacciar?!

VLADIMIRO GALITSKY: No! me ne guardi Iddio!
Ho detto per celiar.
Così, ne l'ira, io vo'
Li sguardi tuoi mirare.
Sovente nel furor,
Si accende la beltà.
Al fulgor di tua fierezza già,
La fiamma delle pupille è superba voluttà!
Amica mia, ma puoi così
Nel tuo languor restare
Soletta in vedovanza?
E via! non un sospir,
Non, un'occhiata mai?
Mi sembri troppo austera.
Confida pure in me:
Non hai passione alcuna!
Ma come puoi restar fedele?
(In tono allegro e motteggiante).
Di te si riderà! Chi crederà?

JAROSLAVNA: Dell'insolenza il colmo è questo.
Signora son per tutti voi.
Sfidarmi vuoi?
Ebben: silenzio!
Condotto a nostro padre sarai.
Trema! Esci! Esci!
Di qua fuggir t'impongo
La pia fanciulla avrà la libertà,
Non più, non più, va' via di qua!

VLADIMIRO GALITSKY: Ebben taci: Sia pur!
Che a te sia resa la gran beltà.
Ne cerco un'altra più vezzosa! Addio!
(Esce)

JAROSLAVNA: Io tremo ancor, e so frenarmi appena!
O dolce Igor, ritorna a mio conforto.
Ridai la luce a me, l'antica fede.
Lottare ogonor . . . La forza m'abbandona!
(Entrano i bojardi del consiglio che s'inchinano davanti alla principessa).

JAROSLAVNA: Buon dì, bojardi miei fedeli.
Su voi poss'io contar,
E tutta a voi m'affiderò.
Ho prove già del vostro senno.
Sereni nel dolore, sereni nel piacer,
Bojardi foste ognor!
Ma dite omai, di grazia,
Che vi conduce a me?
M'assal pungente angoscia.
Parlate, orsù, che già il cor mio nel dubbio freme.

choice,
Poutivle's folk do wish me well,
I may be Prince today and rule over you.
Remember this—and do not anger me.

YAROSLAVNA: You dare to threaten me?

PRINCE GALITSKY: Enough, enough, I do but sport,
But you do take my jokes amiss.
I love to see you furious.
Do you know, O sister of mine,
How well such rage becomes you!
those flashing eyes, those flaming cheeks!
You are still young and fair; afar
Your husband tarries on the field.
If is dreary work to live alone.
I wonder, sister, are you stern,
Cold and censorious to all
As to your erring brother? Say,
Have you in truth no secret lover?
(Mockingly).
I scarce can credit it. It is past belief!

YAROSLAVNA: (in anger). Do you forget that I am still Princess,
That Igor's power is vested in me still?
Take heed, I have the right to send you away.
Well guarded, to our father in Galicia.
His hand is firm; his judgments are severe.
Release the girl at once—and go from me.
Flee from my presence!

PRINCE GALITSKY: Oho! Is this your wish?
Well, let her go!
I'll choose another more amenable.
How then?
(Exit Prince Galitsky).

YAROSLAVNA (alone). I tremble . . . I am unhinged and nervous . . .
Ah, would that Igor might return today . . .
I breathe more freely at the thought of it!
But I am tired. I have not strength to fight.
(Enter the Boyards of the Council who salute Yaroslavna).

YAROSLAVNA: Good morrow, Boyards, I rejoice to see you
My trusty counsellors, who will uphold
The Prince's power. You are faithful friends
In times of gladness, and in sorrow too.
Welcome, thrice welcome, to my presence
But say, what brings you here? Why
This unexpected visit? Ah, my heart

Oimè, mi par morir d'angor!

I BOJARDI: Fa' cuor, principessa:
ti occorre fermezza.
Su noi l'uragan s'addensa.

JAROSLAVNA: Il mugghio è vicin de l'ira divina.
Funesto presagio!

I BOJARDI: Coraggio!

JAROSLAVNA: Che mai dite?!
Qual presagio?!

I BOJARDI: Le schiere selvagge s'abbatton su noi.
S'appressan spargendo terro!

JAROSLAVNA: Io fremo!

I BOJARDI: Sono qua! . . .
Terribil di, Gzak già l'orda fatal
S'avanza spargendo terror!

JAROSLAVNA: La mala sorte non è sazia mai?

I BOJARDI: Sono qua!
L'odiato invasor già tenta assalir
Col fuoco la nostra città!

JAROSLAVNA: A me, o guerrier!
E il nobile Igor?
O dite: Ei vive? Ov'è?

I BOJARDI: Un cupo destin s'abbatte su noi:
Castigo fatal del ciel.

JAROSLAVNA: O ciel! La truppa non è più!
Il nemico vincitor?! E dunque ver?

I BOJARDI: I figli d'Igor l'antica virtù,
Smarrita han dunque così?

JAROSLAVNA: Ah!

I BOJARDI: È il destin!
sorpresa, distrutta, l'armata d'Igor;
E il figlio con lui prigionier!
qual destin! . . .

JAROSLAVNA: Disfatto omai è dunque Igor?
No, no: Io sogno! Menzogna!
No . . . No! . . .
(Cade senza accorgersene). (La rialzano).
Terribil prova! Supremo orror! qual destino!
(Ella s'inchina davanti ai bojardi. Dietro il teatro rimbombano i tocchi della campana d'allarme. I bojardi ascoltano attentamente).

I BOJARDI: Che! L'allarme! Ma sì . . . laggiù! Campane!
Campane d'allarme son!
Sinistro suon!
Fatale annuncio di dolor!
(Dietro il teatro le donne alzano gridi di disperazione).

Is filled with dark forebodings of ill news!
I pray you tell me what has happened.

THE BOYARDS: Take courage, Princess, for we are
The bearers of ill-tidings.

YAROSLAVNA: What has befallen us? Speak, Sirs!

THE BOYARDS: Courage.

YAROSLAVNA: What evil omen?

THE BOYARDS: The hostile forces of the Khan
Have crossed the Russian frontier.
They are at our gates.

YAROSLAVNA: O Heaven!

THE BOYARDS: The threatening hordes
Advance on Poutivle
Led by the Khan Gzak.

YAROSLAVNA: Will our ill fortune never end?

THE BOYARDS: The ruthless Khan.
Terror on terror.
Sorrow on sorrow,
God sends upon Poutivle.

YAROSLAVNA: Where are our troops?
Where is our Prince?
O, Boyards, tell me, where is Igor now?

THE BOYARDS: A dreadful fate has befallen us.
A punishment from heaven.

YAROSLAVNA: O heaven, the army is no more!
The enemy victorious. It is true?

THE BOYARDS: Has the former valor deserted the sons of Igor?

YAROSLAVNA: Ah!

THE BOYARDS: Our Prince was wounded sore,
And with his brother,
And his son Vladimir,
Is in captivity.

YAROSLAVNA: Ah! Wounded and a captive, my dear Lord?
Nay, nay, it cannot be . . .
Say 'tis not true!
(She falls fainting. She is revived).
Then it is true . . .
The Prince is prisoner . . .
And wounded . . .
(She salutes the Boyards, bowing low. The tocsin is heard ringing. The Boyards listen attentively).

THE BOYARDS: The tocsin! Hark!
In truth the tocsin sounds!
Boyards, the tocsin rings a wild alarm!
Princess, it portends some dreadful thing!
(Behind the stage the women shout is despair).

## Act I, Scene II

**CORO DI DONNE:** Oimè! Oimè!
Oimè! Oimè!
Ora fatal, soccorso alcun!?
Funesto dì!
Ah! è un castigo del ciel!
Ah! tristo dì! Ah! Ah!
Pietà di noi, pietà o ciel!
Per noi dal ciel non polo dal disonor!
(*Si vedono dalle finestre barlumi d'incendio*).

**JAROSLAVNA:** Che intendo?
Pietà, Signor!
Noi siamo allor perduti già?
Signor, pietà! Sii giusto!
Oimè: non odi?
O madre santa, ci proteggi tu!
Ancor non sai placar,
O cielo, il tuo furor!?
Ah, qual dolor!
Ne l'ira sua, il ciel non ode!
O signor: di pietà!
Risparmia un pov'e pietà!
Oh! Signor!

**I BOJARDI:** E Gerak che vien: si abbatte già.
Ma v'è! In fiamme è già il sobborgo!
Avanzan già. La fortezza pur s'accende!
La città fiammeggia!
Ah presto, di qua!
Andiam, coraggio!
Corriamo tutti su! bastione!
All'armi, o guerrieri.
Ma accanto a lei dovrà restar qualcun!
Difender la dobbiam! Gran Padre.
(*I bojardi tiran fuori le spade*).
Deh, proteggi il nostro onor!
Di Dio la man su noi si posi
E ci salvi dal destin!
Per noi dal ciel non v'è pietà!
Oh! Signor!

*CALA IL SIPARIO*

---

## CHORUS OF WOMEN: (*off the stage*).
Woe, woe! The foe is close at hand,
What will become of us?
Have mercy, Lord!
The cruel heathen foe is here!
(*Through the window the red glare of a fire is seen*).

**YAROSLAVNA:** Ah, can this be?
Have mercy, God in Heaven!
The cruel heathen swarm around our gates . . .
What will become of us?
Have mercy, Lord!
O blessed Virgin, help us in our need!
This is God's chastisement for all our sin!

**THE BOYARDS:** Fire! The outer city is in flames!
The women shriek and scream, the people flee!
The Polovtsy have laid the country waste,
And now they're pillaging the outskirts,
Burning our suburbs.
See the leaping flames!
Quick, Boyards, to defend the city walls!
But let a portion of us tarry here
To guard the Princess to the very end.
(*Some of the Boyards draw their swords and assume an attitude of defense. The rest go out*).
This is God's chastisement for all our sin!
What God ordains must be;
From this can no man flee!

*CURTAIN*

---

# ■ ATTO II

*Sera nel Campo dei Polovtsy.*

**CORO DI FANCIULLE:** O fior languente, pallido fiore,
Omai reclini sul funereo suolo.
Ah! morta è già la tua corolla;
Non um bacio da la brezza,
Ah! Ma se a notte la rugiada
Scenderà soave ancor,
Il tuo cuore, o dolce rosa,
A' suoi baci s'aprirà:
E l'effluvio de la vita
Ti darà novello ardor!
O fior languente, a te sorella
E l'alma come te ne la tristezza
Chiede il cor la sua carezza.
Ah! Ma la notte azzurra è mite,
Messaggera di dolci amor.
Ti dirà che al novo sole
Il tuo damo tornerà.
Nei roseti canta
Maggio c ripete l'eco

---

# ■ ACT II

*Evening in the Camp of the Polovtsy.*

**CHORUS OF MAIDENS:** The prairie flower pale annd sweet,
Fades in th parching midday heat,
And earthward droops its weary head,
While all its leaves hang withered.
But when the scorching sun has set
And evening dews are glistening wet
Upon the hot and thirsty plain,
The flower lifts its face again,
And pours forth to the silent night
A dreamful fragrance of delight.
And we are the drooping flower
Poor maidens, heart-whole, fancyfree
Who languish here in weariness
Until we know love's sweet caress.
But when the ruthless sun has set
And all the plain with dew is wet,

---

"Amor!"
De la notte ai freschi baci,
L'alma, come fior,
Dolcemente s'aprirà!
Al par di te,
Il cor langue!
Ma la notte spira amor
L'eco ridirà la gioia d'ogni cuor!

**KONTCHAKOVNA:**
Non si canti omai
Nè si giochi più, muore il dì,
E su noi scende il vel della sera.
O diffendi il mister
Del tuo stellato ammanto
O notte virginal!
Già l'incanto dei sogni aleggia.

**CORO DI FANCIULLE:** Sogna pur, mite fior.
Dolce notte d'amor!

**KONTCHADOVNA:** O dolce amor, per l'almo ciel t'invoca
De' miei sospir la più gentil canzone.
Per te sol, dolce amor, mi vo far bella!
Vieni a me: m'odi tu!
Ah, rispondi alfin!
Di voluttà soave incanto!
M'elevo a te..
Io vo', senza fin,
Di te sognar;
Con te vanir
L'immensità del cielo
Tu raccogli il sospir
Dei cuor sognanti,
O notte l'azzurro
Tuo mistero.
O sognar cosi,
O vanir,
(*Entra la pattuglia "Polovtsinese" che fa il giro del campo. Kontchakovna e le fanciulle escono. Verso la fine del coro la scena resta vuota. Code la notte. Non si vede altro che Ovlour di guardia in fondo alla scena*).

**COR DEI SOLDATI:** (*della pattuglia Polovtsinese*). A la sommità del colle il sol vani;
E l'azzurrità s'effonde sideral!
Or veleggia in ciel la bianca luna.
E le stelle intorno fan diaderna,
Lieti noi vegliam, pronti per marciar. Si vegliam.
(*La pattuglia si allontana dietro la scena*).
Oh, notte, dura eternal!

**VLADIMIR IGOREVITCH:** Fugge fra brividi il Sol,
E s'addormenta la selva
L'ombra con blanda promessa,
Desta i lamenti del l'eco:
Eco d'ebbrezza, soffio di vita,
Che ci carezza l'alma sopita!
Ah! notte d'amor, la tua pace
Mi'lenisce l'aspro dolor,
E mi solleva.
Stella di bontà: brilli tu sola?!
Vedi: il tuo raggio mi scende nel cor.
Ah! vien! Ah! vien!

---

When night with stars is luminous,
Our lover's thoughts shall turn to us,
And like the yearning, sun-parched flower,
Our thirsty hearts shall have their hour.

**KONCHAKOVNA:** Now the day light dies,
Cease your songs and dances, it is enough.
Overhead the quiet night
Spreads her wings.
Gentle night, come soon,
Enfold me in your shades,
Wrap your mists around me
Like a robe.

**MAIDENS:** Dream, gentle flower,
Sweet night of love!

**KONCHAKOVNA:** Bring the hour of meeting,
Bring my love.
Will you come, my dearest friend?
Surely your heart must tell you
How slowly move the moments
While I wait.
Where are you, my beloved, Answer me!
I wait for you, my love.
The hour has come at last,
The hour of meeting,
Of tender greeting.
(*The Polovtsy patrol enter and inspect the camp. The stage is empty for a few minutes. Night draws on. Ovlour is on guard.*)

**SOLDIERS:** (*of the Polovtsy patrol*). The stars are shining bright like lamps.
The moon sails like a white vessel;
It is she patrols the heavens clear,
While we do sentry-go down here,
And far away beyond the west,
All night the lazy sun can rest.
(*Enter Prince V. Igorievich*).

**VLADIMIR IGORIEVICH:** Slowly the sunset fires die out
Behind the distant forests dark;
The western glow is fading now;
Night spreads her veil upon the earth
In mystic shadows
Dim and blue
The silent Steppe is lost.
Warm, gentle night of the south,
Waking sweet visions of bliss,
Stirring my pulses to passion,
Leading my feet to my love!
Do you await me, beloved?

Ah rispondi al mio sospir,
O pura luce, dissipa l'ombra
mortal:
Rispondi; col tuo fulgor
Abbatti il dubbio, crudel Sei tu.
Lungamente t'lio atteso.
Sempre vo' l'amor tuo!
M'intendi tu?
Brilla ognor, bell'astro,
Ne! mio ciel.
O pia stella amica!
Lasciati mirar!
Discendi a me dal trono azzurro.
La terra freme già
Al palpitar del ciel!
Ah! vien! Ah! vien!
O mio ben, discendi alfin.
Deh, così non lasciar
Che il dubbio mi sia nel cor!
Ecco, a te m'affido:
Mi lascio abbagliar.
Estiva notte de' tuoi veli
Così m'avvolgi nel mister.
E tutto un palpitar di stelle:
Riversa il ciel sopir d'amor:
La terra pia li accoglierà
Tutto e amor!
Deh vien!

**KONTCHAKOVNA:** Ecco: discen-
do, ti ascolto;
Intendo il tuo grido.
Il cuore si schiude qual bacio
D'Aprile, ai baci del Sol.

**VLADIMIR IGOREVITCH:** M'ami
tu?

**KONTCHADOVNA:** Viorò per te.

**VLADIMIR IGOREVITCH:** O
dimmi il ver . . .

**KONTCHAKOVNA** Per sempre fedel.

**VLADIMIR IGOREVITCH:** Ripeti
ancor! . . .

**KONTCHADOVNA:** Perchè vuoi
dubitar?
Si: io t'adoro!
Quale ardor tu non puoi capir,
Mi dia l'amor di cui vibrai
Per te dal di che ti vidi.
Per volere fatal,
Così pur la legge mia,
Per te, sdegnai.

**VLADIMIR IGOREVITCH:** Ebben,
sarò lo sposo tuo.

**KONTCHAKOVNA:** Soave a me tu
parli inver!

**VLADIMIR IGOREVITCH:** Divino
ardor: il labbro cor.
Labbro divin, o sorridimi ancor!

**KONTCHAKOVNA:** Tuo già
l'incanto riversa.
Mio sposo tu! M'esalto all'incanto
d'amor!

**VLADIMIR IGOREVITCH:** Oh!
Mite notte di languor!

**KONTCHAKOVNA:** Credo in te,
mio solo amor!
Più che nel ciel!

---

Yea, my heart whispers, you're
waiting for me.
Dearest, where are you?
Answer!
Will you soon come to me, sweet?
Answer the cry of your lover!
Think how I suffer and yearn,
How my heart is consumed as by
fire
While I wait for your coming, O
love.
Why do you tarry, my darling?
Ah rise up and come to me here.
Have no fear, for the soldiers are
sleeping,
All the world is enfolded in dreams.
Dearest, where are you?
Answer!
Answer the cry of your lover!
Come, veiled in the warm dusky
shadows,
While the forest and lake slumber;
When only the stars in the heavens
Look down on our rapture of love.
(*Konchakovna emerges from her
tent*).

**KONCHAKOVNA:** O, is it you, Vla-
dimir,
O, is it you, my love?
You whom my heart adores,
My lover, long desired,
I wait and pine for you!

**VLADIMIR IGORIEVICH:** Do you
love me?

**KONCHAKOVNA:** Ever faithful.

**VLADIMIR:** Repeat it!

**KONCHAKOVNA:** Do I love you,
dear?
O you, my bliss!
Yes, I love you with the passion
And the strength that young hearts
know.
Ah, beloved mine, I love you,
Love you with my heart and soul,
And without you, my Vladimir, The
world would be dark and cold.

**VLADIMIR IGORIEVICH:** Well,
I'll be your husband.

**KONCHAKOVNA:** You speak to
me sweetly!

**VLADIMIR IGORIEVICH:** O, say
again those words of love;
Beloved, speak those words once
more!

**KONCHAKOVNA:** When shall I be
yours for ever?
When shall you call me wife, dear
heart?
My love, my joy, O husband mine!

**VLADIMIR IGORIEVICH:** Oh!
gentle night of languor!

**KONCHAKOVNA:** I believe in
you, my only love,
More than in heaven!

---

**VLADIMIR IGOREVITCH:** Mia già
sei tu:
T'avvince omai
D'amor la legge a me.
Ripeti ancora.

**KONTCHAKOVNA:** Quale ardor
non puoi mai saper
Mi dia l'amor di cui vibrai
Per te, dal di che t'ho veduto.
Ud destino fatal mi colpì.
Sino a morte sarà dolcemente a te,
Il cor mio fedel!!

**VLADIMIR IGOREVITCH:** Sii tu
mia sposa.
Io vo' per te languir d'amor.
La legge tua non gioverà.
Mostra legge e amor
Sul tuo sen languir!
Sul tuo cor sognar e poi morir!!
Tu sei l'eterno palpito!

**INSIEME:** Sei l'amor!

**KONTCHAKOVNA:** E ben tuo padre . . . ancor non ascoltò la tua
preghiera.

**VLADIMIR IGOREVITCH:** Oh no!
Ne oso a lui parlar.
Al libero amore nessun comanda.

**KONTCHAKOVNA:** E ver. Ma Igor
se vero sembra.
Il padre mio ben so che assentirà.

**VLADIMIR IGOREVITCH:** Qui
siam spiati. Odi stormir.

**KONTCHAKOVNA:** Resta.
Sommesso parla.

**VLADIMIR IGOREVITCH:** No,
mio padre verrà: ci può scoprir.

**KONTCHADOVNA:** Ti prego:
rimani ancor! . . .

**VLADIMIR IGOREVITCH:** Addio!

**KONTCHADOVNA:** Vuoi
lasciarmi già!?

**VLADIMIR IGOREVITCH:** Addio!
(*Escono, ognuno dalla parte opposta*).
(*fermandosi davanti a la scena*).

**IL PRINCIPE IGOR:** Oimè! Nel cor
mi graverà l'angoscia ognor!
In preda al mio destin crudel, io
veglio;
E dei lontani di nutrisco il sogno, O
luminosi di!
Mi sembra ancor che il ciel minac-
ci:
Ma pur lontano in gran miraggio
Glorioso veggo l'avvenir.
Stellati di risplenderanno
Pur nel ciel di mia felicità.
Non più ne l'ombra brancolar,
Vinto, qui mi vedrò.
Vo sfidarla la morte.
Che più dovrò soffrir?
Perduto ho già gloria, onor e patria.
Disfatto Igor.
Io, nel disonor!
Tutto mi negò il ciel:
Omai non chiedo che morir
Se Iddio mi desse ancor la forza,
Liberator sarei del patrio suol.
Brillare ancor vedrei rossigno

---

**VLADIMIR IGORIEVICH:** You are
already mine:
May love unite me with you.
Speak those words again.

**KONCHAKOVNA:** Yes, I love you
with the passion
And the strength that young hearts
know.
Ah, beloved, I love you —
Love you with my heart and soul.

**VLADIMIR IGORIEVICH:** Love
me, sweet, with all your being,
Heart and soul and body too!
When shall I call you mine for ever?
When shall I call you wife, dear
heart?
My bride, my love, my heart's de-
sire!

**TOGETHER:** You are love.

**KONCHAKOVNA:** What does your
father say?
Will he give consent?

**VLADIMIR IGORIEVICH:** Alas no!
While we both are captives here,
He will not hear me speak of love
and marriage.

**KONCHAKOVNA:** The Khan, my
father, is less stern.
He'd gladly see my wed with you.

**VLADIMIR IGORIEVICH:** Go
away; someone approaches.

**KONCHAKOVNA:** We're safe. I
hear no sound.

**VLADIMIR IGORIEICH:** Footsteps . . . My father comes!

**KONCHAKOVNA:** Stay, love, be
not afraid.

**VLADIMIR IGORIEVICH:** Farewell!

**KONCHAKOVNA:** Ah! Would you
leave me!

**VLADIMIR IGORIEVICH:** Farewell!
(*They go off right and left*).

**PRINCE IGOR:** (*stopping in the
foreground*).
No sleep, no rest, for my afflicted
soul!
Night brings no boon of sweet for-
getfulness.
The past comes back, I live it
through again,
In dark nocturnal silence, all alone.
God's warning — the eclipse —
comes back to me.
And I hear all the sounds of revelry,
When in my halls my warriors feast-
ed high,
And gloried in my victories of old.
Ah, what an end to all my hopes is
this!
Defeated, wounded, and a captive
too!
I stand disgraced before my native
land.
A captive, you a slave — O wretch-
ed lot!
O, give me back my freedom, God

# Act II

Un ciel di gloria al novo Sol!
O mia sposa sventurata,
Sempre a te va il mio pensiero.
Tu la sorte che insidiava,
Mi svelasti un dì.
Dalla vetta del castello
Scruta il guardo tuo lo spazio;
E sol tu del mio sgomento
Sentirai l'orror.
Potrò trovar conforto a tal disfatta?
Or chi potrà fidar nel mio valor?
Oh! maledizion!
Hanno in mano la mia vita, Igor
E qui nell'abbiezion!
O santa libertà perduta,
Mi lascia tu salvar la patria mia,
O da guerrier per lei morir.
E che? Nel cor non rugge più
l'antico ardor?!
In preda al mio, destin crudel, io
veglio,
E dei trascorsi di nutrisco il sogno.
O luminosi dì, per me non raggian
più.
Io soffro! Qual crudel cupo tormen-
to!
O grazia! Qual dolor!
(*Ovlour s'avvicina al Principe
Igor. Il crepuscolo dell'aurora co-
mincia. Verso la fine della scena si
fa chiaro giorno*).

**OVLOUR:** Signor perdona
l'arditezza: Un mio pensier ti fo palese.

**IL PRINCIPE IGOR:** Che vuoi tu?

**OVLOUR:** Quel fiammeggiar ne lo
spazio profondo,
Di glorioso avvenir predice nuovi
dì.
Benigna alfin pe 'l nostro ciel
l'aurora brilla.
Spezzare io vo' le tue catene.

**IL PRINCIPE IGOR:** Tu?

**OVLOUR:** Un buon destrier ne
l'ombra attende:
Ei volerà come baleno.

**IL PRINCIPE IGOR:** Io? Che?! Taci.
Fuggir è indegno.
Non posso. No, No!
Non voglio. Lasciami restar.

**OVLOUR:** Eppure tu non giurasti
mai
Su l'onor tuo non desti fede.

**IL PRINCIPLE IGOR:** Non fuggirò.
Pe 'l tuo servizio grazie.
Giammai potrò fuggir.
(*Ovlour si ritira triste e pensoso*).
(*Entra Kontchak*).

above,
And let me wipe my shame out on
the field!
If I were free, it would not be too
late to save
My name and honor, and my coun-
try too!
You, alone, my dove, my dearest,
Will not blame grieving husband,
And your tender heart will tell
All my bitterness and sorrow;
I shall win your sweet forgiveness.
Seated at the Terem casement
With strained eyes the wide Steppe
searching,
Love, you wait night and morning,
Weeping for your truant husband.
How shall I live thus, counting
useless days,
In close captivity, and know my
foes
Are harrying Russia.
Gracious God.
Grant me my freedom! It is not too
late
To wipe out my dishonor on the
field,
And save my name, and fame, and
Russia too!
Night brings no hopeful dream of
liberty,
Only the past returns, I live it
through
In the nocturnal silence, all alone,
O my helpless state weighs heavily,
Upon my aching conscience night
and day.
(*The first flush of down appears in
the sky. Enter Ovlour*).

**OVLOUR:** Pardon me, Prince, but
may I speak with you?
I long have wished to say a
word . . .

**PRINCE IGOR:** How now? Who are
you?

**OVLOUR:** Prince, behold: the eastern sky glows pink
The dawn-light chases darkness
from the earth;
And day will dawn for you and Russia too . . .
I know a way . . . a way to set you
free?

**PRINCE IGOR:** You?

**OVLOUR:** I'll saddle you the swiftest horse we have.
Mount him, and leave the camp in
secrecy.

**PRINCE IGOR:** What? I, Prince
Igor, I, to break my word, And win
my liberty by secret flight?
I do this thing? . . .
Sir, you are mad, No!

**OVLOUR:** You have not bound
yourself, Prince, by an oath.
Nor kissed the Cross before this Pagan Khan.

**PRINCE IGOR:** Leave me.
I thank you for your loyalty.
Flight is impossible.
(*Ovlour goes out sad and pensive.
Enter Konchak*).

**KONTCHAK:** Salute Igor!
E sempre il ciel ti guidi:
Ti dispensi felicità.
Ma trasognato sei?
Di: dei falconi il vol,
Va male ne le tue lanciate?
I miei ti do.

**IL PRINCIPE IGOR:** Ah no, i miei
son pur di nobil razza.
Ma v'è un falcon che langue
prigioniero.

**KONTCHAK:** Da pari tuo ciascun ti
rende ommaggio:
Non sei tu l'ospite gradito?
Su, coraggio.
A la Kaiala fu provato
De' prodi tuoi il valor:
La causa tua fu vinta;
Igor, lo volle il ciel.
Ma presso me, tu sei signore,
Ne ti manca mai rispetto.
Co' guerrier, col figlio
Accanto ti lasciai;
E puoi star con lor da pari tuo.
Catene non ti danno gravezza.
Certo. Igor per me è il gran guerrier
che adoro.
Prigioniero non sei. No, davver.
Credi, amico: devi veder tu stesso
Quanta stima ho di te,
Del tuo nobile cor.
La morte godi a sfidar, Si!
Ti vidi io stesso lottar. Si;
E vorrò fare con te,
Come si ospita un re.
Apri tutto il tuo cor,
E il pensiero con me.
Che puoi desiderare?
Dillo ch'io t'amo.
Ho per te languide fiere vergini;
Schiave bellissime:
Stelle fulgide d'oltre mare.
Non devi esser timido
Se a' tuoi pie' le vedrai.
E più t'offro, de l'harem beltà rare,
Dal lungo crine,
Dal mesto fatal guardar,
Ove cede a l'amor,
Naufragando il cor!
Scegli pur: e certo dovrai faticar!
Scegli, dunque: languor mite o sel-
vaggio
T'aggrada in amor! Eh! O miei
schiavi, presto qua,
Con ardor ferverà la danza.
Si canti, orsù!
Lasciar dobbiam le tristi cure. (*En-
trano gli schiavi "Polovcesi,"
uomini e donne: alcuni portano
seco tamburelli, ed altri banno di-
versi strumenti musicali, poi ven-
gono le persone di seguito del
Kontchak*).
(*Danza delle fanciulle a movi-
menti ondulanti*).

**CORO:** Va' su l'ale de la brezza,
Canzone, va' su l'ale del pensiero,
E bacia tu la mia diletta terra:
Ti segue l'alitar de l'alma mia.
L'aria è tutta ebbrezze;

**KONCHAK:** Good morrow, Prince!
Why is my guest so sad,
So lost in gloomy thoughts?
Do you lack snares, or arrows,
Have your falcons grown too tame
To swoop upon the quarry?
Take mine — I grudge them not!

**PRINCE IGOR:** My peregrines are
swift and sure;
It is the prisoned falcon frets and
pines.

**KONCHAK:** No prisoner you are
most noble Prince,
But my most honored guest, I trust.
Is it not so?
Sore wounded at the Kayala,
And have your armies taken or cut
down.
I only keep you as a hostage here.
Not as my captive, but my guest,
Respected as my very self.
All that I have is at your service,
Prince.
Your son, your followers, remain
with you,
And as a Chief you'll dwell in our
midst.
Yes even as myself.
Confess, this is no harsh captivity!
How then? Ah no! My Prince, my
friend, you are not my prisoner in
this camp, but my guest, most dear
to me. Hark then, believe me, I have
always cherished respect for your
great courage in the field. I have
honored — yes, have loved — Igor
for this. Therefore do not regard me
as a foe, but rather as a hospitable
host. Then tell me, Prince, what ails
you? What do you lack? Would you
like my fleetest steed? — It is yours.
Should you desire, most noble
Prince, I'll give you a companion
fair; A slave — a girl of rare beauty,
Sent as a present, not long since,
From lands beyond the Caspian Sea.
She shall be yours. Oh, I have many
lovely slaves.
With fragrant dusky hair that waves
Low on smooth brows, above dark
eyes
So bright with passion that no veil
Conceals the light that flashes
there . . .
What, silent, Prince? Can nothing
avail
To rouse you from your despair?
Ho! Bring the slaves here!
Let them dance and sing.
Perchance it will distract you, and
drive forth
These gloomy thoughts.
(*Enter the Khan's slaves, male
and female, some carry tambou-
rines and other musical instru-
ments. They are followed by the
Khan's retinue*).
(*Dance of the Polovtsy girls with
swaying movements*).

**CHORUS:** On the wings of the wind
borne away,
Fly homeward, song of our Motherland,
To the land where we sang in free-

L'eco pur sospira, par che vaghi il monte,
Quasi nube a mezzo mar.
Già del Sole la carezza inonda
Or le vette de' miei colli,
E lieto da le mie foreste vaghe.
Un canto celestial risponde al mio.
Come sospir, la canzon va trasvolando.
Reca, o rosignolo, la pia canzone:
Ti segue l'alitar de l'alma mia
Lieve ai margini del mar.
(Danza degli uomini. Selvaggia).

CORO: (Danza generale). Viva viva fiero spirto, Ah!
Gloria, gloria, sommo duce! Ah! Ah!
(Danza dei prigionieri "polovcesi").
Le genti, lì prigionieri,
Sciolgon canti di dolor, mesti sospir.
Viva, viva fiero spirto!

KHAN KONTCHAK: (a Igor).
Quelle fanciulle ognor soavi cantano.
Son qua per te: non le vuoi?
Basta un cenno sol.
Scegli orsù: vuoi la bionda recata dal mar,
O la bruna che sembra un folletto infernal?
(Danza generale).

CORO: Egli uguaglia i suoi avi In gloria, in valor.
Gloria a te gran guerrier,
Gloria a te.
(Danza di fanciulle a movimenti ondulanti)

CORO: Va' su l'ale de la brezza,
Canzone, va' su l'ale del pensiero,
E bacia tu la mia diletta terra:
Ti segue l'alitar de l'alma mia.
La foresta dice al mare che si lagna l'usignuol.
L'aria è tutta ebrezza,
E su da l'onda sale un canto;
Par che vaghi il monte quasi nube a mezzo mar.
Che ripete il suo languor.
(Danza lenta di fanciulle e danza rapida di ragazzi).
Or l'allegro rosignolo,
S'è desto più sciogliendo le sue note,
Feconda gioire la vallata mia,
Le vite ferve ognor di sacro umore,
Come sospir.
E da l'onda sale un canto,
Che ripete "spera ancor!"
Tutto è un eterno april!
La canzon va trasvolando,
Lieve ai margini del mar.

CORO: Egli uguaglia i suoi avi in gloria, nel valor.
(Danza di ragazzi).
Gloria a te, fean guerrier!
(Danza generale).

dom
Before the days of captivity.
There beneath the ardent sky
Blows a languid, warm-breathed breeze;
There the cloud-capped mountains dream,
Listening to the murmuring sea;
And the emerald slopes are glowing
In the sunshine's golden rays,
There the roses in the valleys
Hang in heavy, fragrant clusters;
There among the young green branches
Nightingales pour forth their lays.
Fly, my song, upon the zephyrs,
Back to home and liberty.
(Dance of the men. Wild dance).

CHORUS: (All dance). Long live, proud spirit, Ah!
Glory, glory to our chief. Ah!
(Dance of the Polovets prisoners).
The people, the prisoners,
Sing songs of sorrow, sad sighs.
Long live proud spirit!

KONCHAK: (to Igor). Do you see these captives from beyond the sea —
The distant Caspian? Do you see these fair maids?
O, tell me, friend, which one pleases you best;
One word, and she is — yours.
(All dance — Boys dance).

CHORUS: (Men dance). Glorious, famous as his fathers,
Terrible our Khan Konchak.
Praise our Khan,
Great Khan Konchak!
(Dance of the girls in swaying movements).

CHORUS: On the wings of the wind borne away,
Fly homeward, song of our Motherland
To the land where we sang in freedom
Before the days of captivity,
There beneath the ardent sky
Blows a languid, warm breathed breeze;
There the cloud-capped mountains dream,
Listening to the murmuring sea.
(Slow dance of girls and quick dance of boys).
O, joyous nightingale,
May your sweet song resound
Over the valleys, like sighs,
And from the wave rises a song
Which says "hope again."
All is eternal spring!
The song goes flying
Out to the sea!

CHORUS: Glorious, famous as his fathers.
(Dance of boys).
Glory to you, bold warrior!
(All dance).

Con i canti e con le danze,
A l'eroe fate onor.
Sia la danza folle, folle;
E l'ebrezza voli; giova rallietare
Il guerrier vincitor.
Ti rallieta, o signor,
E sia gloria a te!

*CALA IL SIPARIO*

# ■ ATTO III

*Trombette sul palcoscenico dietro il sipario.*
*Alzato il sipario si vede una parte del campo "polovtsiese." I "polovscesi" arrivano da diverse parti, e guardano verso la porta in fondo, aspettando l'arrivo dell'esercito del Gzak: l'esercito compare in fondo alla scena. S'avanzano alcuni guerrieri che portano trombe e chiarine e tamburi; altri conducono i prigionieri russi e portano un ricco bottino. I "polovtsiesi" salutano i guerrieri che entrano, facendo gesti selvaggi. Verso la fine della marcia entra a cavallo sulla scena il Khan Gzak, accompagnato dai soldati e della sua guardia. Kontchak gli va incontro per salutarlo. Il Principe Igor, Vladimiro Igorevitcii e i prigionieri russi si fermano da parte, osservando tutto ciò che avviene.*

CORO: I trionfatori cinti son di gloria
E di lor virtù van superbi a gara!
Fiero il vittorioso muove in gran trionfo,
Segue il cupo stuol dei prigionieri.
A te sia gloria!
Viva Gzak, viva Gzak!
Gloria ai suoi soldati ebri di vittoria.
Gzak, viva Gzak,
Gloria all'invincibil,
Gloria a suoi guerrieri!
Già la squilla avverte il suo passar quel felice dì!
Gloria a voi possenti!
Ardon borghi in vostro onor
E consente lieto il ciel!
Gloria, gloria!
E di Russia il sacro suol
Un ossario immenso!
Gloria, gloria, gloria!
Al gran Kans si faccia onore!
Gloria al suo possente
Duce Gzak trionfatore!
Invincibil Gloria a Kontchak!
Viva il gran' Gsak!
Di sangue intriso geme l'almo suol.
Oimè! Si leva tetro palpitar
Dai campi spogli d'ogni fior.
La morte invitta sta sfidando,
Muta di furor!
Gloria, gloria!

KONTCHAK: La clava ancor possente
Ha vinto questi schiavi.
La sorte ci è propizia.

With songs and with dances,
Pay honor to the hero.
With dances regale him.
Cheer our victorious warrior.
May glory be with you, oh prince!

*CURTAIN*

# ■ ACT III

*The Polovtsy. Trumpets behind the scene. At the rising of the curtain is seen one part of the "Polovets" camp. The Polovtsy arrive from different directions, awaiting the arrival of the army of Khan Gzak. The latter begins to appear by degrees at the back of the stage. Some of the soldiers are bearing trumpets, horns and tambourines. Others escort Russian captives and are laden with rich spoils. The Polovtsy welcome Gzak's warriors with savage gestures. At the end of the march Khan Gzak enters on horseback, with a detachment of his followers. Khan-Konchak goes forward to meet him. Prince Igor, his son Vladimir, and the Russian prisoners stand by, watching and listening to all that is taking place.*

CHORUS: Our warriors come back Triumphant and victorious.
Hail, to you, fierce and glorious,
Hail, warriors of Khan Gzak!
Hail to our Chieftain and his braves
Who went forth to victory;
He is fierce and terrible who
Brings us home a host of slaves, who
Brings a splendid booty back.
Hail, warriors of Khan Gzak,
The trumpets sound for victory,
The drums resound today,
For many a town and hamlet burned,
For many a field laid waste,
And strewn with Russian bones.
They bring hosts of fair captives,
Glory to our Khans,
To our ruthless, fearless Khans!
Hail to Gzak the Terrible,
Like a panther fierce he roves
Across the wide, wide Steppes;
Like a whirlwind, sweeps before him
All his foes;
Men and horses, rank on rank,
Fall before his furious onslaught,
Till the plains are whitened
With the bones of Russian foemen!
Hail! Hail!

KONCHAK: Lo, the splendid victory is yours
You have overcome our foe,
And laid his army low,

# Act III

La Russia invan ancor s'illude,
Il valor s'impone sempre più.
La nostra forza raddoppia.
Or le città conquise abbiam
Ricche provincie a noi piegar.
La nostra fede rivela
L'antica gloria ancor.
Il mondo intier ci temerà:
Ne più su noi alcun potrà.

**CORO:** Gloria a Gzak,
Evviva Kontchak!

**KONTCHAK:** Squillate, o trombe!
(*Trombe*).
E ben: or qui, per iniziar la festa,
Dividiamo il bottino.
Che, tra piaceri e feste,
Celebrar dovremo la conquista.
La gloria consacriam
Dal sonno sian svegliate
Omai le fragranti mie beltà;
E diman con riflession,
Concreteremo il pian di guerra.
Attenti ognor i prigionier,
Dobbiam vegliar con sommo ardor.
Andiam!
(*Esce*).

**CORO DEI KHANS:** Al gran consiglio orsù volgiam:
Che giova omai sapere il ver!
Inerti star conviene ancor,
O l'inimico perseguir?
Chi guiderà l'armata nostra?
O verso Kiew o su Poltava repiegar,
Su chi mai possiam fidar?
O verso Kiew dobbiam marciar,
O su Poltava ripiegar?
(*I "Polovcesi" escono. I prigionieri russi entrano nelle loro tende. Si vedono sulla scena i guerrieri "Polovtsienesi" che sono in sentinelle all'entrata delle tende. Dietro le scene squillano le trombe*).

**CORO DI GUARDIE:** Il vittorioso è pari al sol!
Ed a la luna egli è simil!
Ai fochi fulgidi del ciel
Di valor sempre brilla
Sua gloria in ogni cuor scintilla.
Ah! Devesi cantar e sempre ber.
In omaggio del Signor.
Si! A chi tenta di sfuggirle
Nostre freccie giungono.
Son veloci i nostri alfier,
E sanno dal periglio deviar.
Andiam: il canto d'onor,
Leviamo nel Sol pei nostri vincitor.
Si! Noi saremo forti ognor così
Vigilando i prigionier.
(*Le guardie incominciano la danza*).
(*Uno dei ballerini cade. Un altro cade. Il terzo cade*).
(*A la fine della scena si oscura il palcoscenico. Le guardie si addormentano. Ovlour si avvicina furtivamente e con precauzione alla tenda di Igor*).

The land belongs to you and me!
The rumor of our great renown
Spreads day by day;
The whole world is our own,
None bars our way!

**CHORUS:** Hail to Khan Gzak!
Hail to Konchak!

**KONCHAK:** Sound the trumpets!
(*Trumpets*).
Come now! We will divide the captives and share the spoils between us. Come! Hey!
From now til night you all may feast and sing, and divide the spoils, to celebrate the victory.
The fairest of the captives, lead them to my tent, at once. Tomorrow morn, a council will be held to settle our next move against the foe. Watch the prisoners well. Now come!
(*Exit*).

**CHORUS OF KHANS:** Let us go to hold a council.
Shall we stay here awhile and rest,
Or fall tomorrow on the foe?
Shall we push further towards the west?
Whom will our Chieftains take or leave?
Shall we sack Kiev or Poltava?
Konchak awaits us, let us go.
To follow his advice is best.
Either stay here our men to rest,
Or fall tomorrow on the foe,
And march our horde still further west.
(*The Polovtsy go out. The Russians enter their tents. Warriors mount guard over the captives. Sounds of trumpets behind the scenes*).

**THE GUARDS:** Like the sun is Khan Konchak,
Like the moon is Khan Gzak,
Like the stars are all our Khans.
Their glory shines so brightly,
Like the light of heaven at noonday.
To the glory of our chieftans
Let us now drink deep.
Drink makes us blithe and merry,
But we'll watch our captives closely.
Woe to him who tries to flee!
For our arrows fly true and far,
And our horses gallop swiftly,
On the plain we'd soon overtake him.
Now make a song of praise and glory,
In honor of our Khans' great deeds!
(*The guards drink and begin to dance. One of the dancers falls. Another falls, a third falls. As the dance comes to an end twilight draws on. The guards fall into a drunken slumber. Ovlour approaches Prince Igor's tent furtively and with precaution*).

**OVLOUR:** Sei a tempo ancor, se vuoi partir.
Le guardie non han più un'ombra di ragion.
Al fiume, nell'oscuro, e già il destrier,
T'attenderò: La notte è cupa.
(*A voce bassa*).
Udito il mio segnal t'affretta!
Col figlio tuo, sicuro, verso me;
Scavalcando i giunchi correrai.
Pel tuo cammino, senza tregua,
T'involerai sul tuo destriero:
Al par di falco, fenderai lo spazio.
La strada io t'accenno.

**IL PRINCIPE IGOR:** (*nella tenda*).
Orsù: t'affretta omai.
Lo vuole il ciel.
(*Ovlour esce*).
(*Kontchakovna entra correndo e si ferma davanti alla tenda di Vladimiro. Ella è grandemente agitata*).

**KONTCHAKOVNA:** Ascolta! . . . L'amor tuo si dissolve?
Mi vuoi fuggir?
Il tuo segreto io so.
Tu fuggi con tuo padre:
Nè mai ti rivedrò.
Ebben: Coraggio avrai di dar
Tal strazio a un cuore,
Che vive sol per te?!
Non sai che senza
Te mai più la vita
Avrà sorriso alcun?
Rispondi a me.
A te sia incatenato il mio destino
Con te conducimi.
Io sfiderò con te la morte senza orror.
La libertà l l'onor, la vita t'offrirò.
Mi vuoi con te siccome schiava?
Sii mio re, mio re.
Sii tu Dio.

**VLADIMIR IGOREVITCH:** Addio, mio dolce amor;
Di partir m'è forza
Perchè mi vuoi tener?
L'onor mi chiama lontan di qua;
Ma il cor rimane a te:
Fedele a te
Ed ora, addio.
S'accende già di gloria il ciel.
Addio! Addio!
(*Il Principe Igor esce dalla sua tenda*).

**IL PRINCIPE IGOR:** Che intendo?!
Vladimiro indugia?!
L'onor ti chiama già
Che mai t'avvince?
Sei dunque tu lo schiavo di costor?
Vuoi tu tradire i tuoi?

**VLADIMIR IGOREVITCH:** Ah no! . . . Addio!

**OVLOUR:** Prince, make ready soon for your flight. The people all are drunk; the guard is fast asleep. The horses are saddled, and I will wait for you and Prince Vladimir across the river.
(*Softly*).
When all is still I'll whistle, and when you hear me, hasten to the river. Like the swift, stealthy ermine run through the tall reeds, swim across like a duck, and then without delay, spring on your eager horses like leopards, and like falcons cleave the air, hidden by shades of night.

**PRINCE IGOR:** (*from within the tent*). Go, get the horses, we will be ready.
(*Exit Ovlour. Konchakovna rushes in, wildly agitated, and stands outside Prince Vladimir's tent*).

**KONCHAKOVNA:** Vladimir!
Can it be true that you would flee
And leave me here alone?
O I entreat you love!
Your plans are known to me.
You think by midnight to be free,
You, and your father too,
To see your Russian home again
Before the day breaks anew.
But, ah, can it be true
That I have loved you thus in vain?
Beloved, sweetheart, say,
You could not deceive me;
You will not ride away
And leave me broken-hearted?
O take me with you, dear,
For you, I'll brave all risks
Without a qualm of fear.
I give you all—my liberty,
My love, my honor are for you
I will not ask to be your bride,
But take me as your slave,
And I'll be happy, at your side.

**VLADIMIR:** Farewell, farewell, beloved!
The time has come to part,
For fate and duty tear me from here
O breaking heart,
Eyes blinded with salt tears,
O cruel fears!
How can I speak that word:
Farewell, my love, farewell.
O Princess, hold me not.
Farewell for ever more,
Farewell!
(*Prince Igor appears at his tent-door*).

**PRINCE IGOR:** Vladimir, son!
What does this mean?
Princess, what have you done?
A captive, son, have you thrown in your lot
With the Polovtsy, and forgot your land?

**VLADIMIR:** Ah no!—Farewell!

**KONTCHAKOVNA:** O tu crudel, il cor ti manca.
Io: grande, amata e fiera,
Regina di beltà or qua,
Per te straziata
Son tua prigioniera.
Ove la mia virtù?!
O resta me vicin.
Crudel! Ascolta la preghiera!

**VLADIMIR IGOREVITCH:** O quale lotta in me!
Supremo angor!
Mi strazia il cor questa sua voce.
Il suo dolor sconvolge la ragion.

**IL PRINCIPE IGOR:** Su via, partiam.
Lo vuole il ciel.
Fa cor!
Con me dovrai partir.
L'onor lo vuol: fuggiam!
La patria nostra ci chiamò.

**KONTCHAKOVNA:** Oime! No sai com'io t'adoro?

**VLADIMIR IGOREVITCH:** Amore vince nel mio cor!
O qual dolor!

**IL PRINCIPE IGOR:** Ci abbatte il disonor.
Non odi?
Laggiù, ne l'ombra . . .
E già il segnal!
Non più indugiar.
Orsù: Con tutto ardor.
Dover di patria che chiamò.
Su, via, ritorna in te.
Non indugiar!
Ritorna in te.
Orsù: fuggiam.

**KONTCHAKOVNA:** Rimani ancor, se vuoi or fuggiamo insiem.

**VLADIMIR IGOREVITCH:** Soffro oimè troppo sacro è l'amor.
(*Il Principe Igor vent entraner Vladimir*).

**KONTCHAKOVNA:** Io sfiderò per te la morte senza orror!
La libertà, l'onor, la vita t'offrirò!
Qual grazia val per farmi amar
Sempre da te?

**VLADIMIR IGOREVITCH:** Deh! lasciami un po' calmar il pianto suo;
Il suo dolor!
Soave pianto virginal!

**IL PRINCIPE IGOR:** Su, via, no più . . .
Deh vien1 Fuggiam!

**KONTCHAKOVNA:** Ebben . . . or lancerò l'allarme!

**KONCHAKOVNA:** O, do not leave me!
This is my earnest prayer to you!
You know: I am a daughter of the steppes,
Child of the desert and of liberty!
My father is the greatest of the Khans;
In all the world there's none so proud as he;
And I am of his race, yet bend the knee;
And I entreat you at your feet,
Do not leave me!

**VLADIMIR:** I have not strength to part from you;
My soul's consumed with love of you,
And my heart burns like a furnace,
And in my mind an agony.

**PRINCE IGOR:** O tear yourself away,
My son, and come with me!
'Tis duty leads the way,
Our land has need of you.
Would you see Russia fall?

**KONCHAKOVNA:** Do you not know how I adore you?

**VLADIMIR:** Love conquers my heart!
What sorrow!

**PRINCE IGOR:** Do you hear? The signal for our flight!
Ovlour awaits us, we've no time to waste.
Leave him, Princess! Vladimir, do the right.
Come, follow me, our lives depend on haste.
A moment longer and we are undone.
Conquer thy passion, do your duty, son.

**KONCHAKOVNA:** Remain, and if you will, we'll flee together!

**VLADIMIR:** Alas I suffer, for love is too sacred!
(*Prince Igor tries to drag Vladimir away*).

**KONCHAKOVNA:** Beloved, stay with me!
Or let me share your fate!
I do not fear whatever betides .
Will you forget your mate
And drive her from your side?

**VLADIMIR:** O father, let me dry her tears!
One long last kiss, one tender word,
To soothe her grief and calm her fears!

**PRINCE IGOR:** Enough, enough, son! Come . . .
Farewell!

**KONCHAKOVNA:** Well then, I'll give the alarm.

**IL PRINCIPE IGOR:** (*scappando*).
Addio!
(*Ella batte più volte sulla lama di ferro sospesa. I "Polovcesi" accorrono da diverse parti*).

**KONNTCHAKOVNA:** All'armi
Igor fuggi
Da Ovlour traditi siam,
Che il figlio suo rimanga qua.

**UNA PARTE DEL CORO:** (*"I Polovcesi"*). Le vostre freccie, a presto sella.
Seguiam le traccie del fiero Igor!
Presto, presto, presto!
La guerra si raccenda ancor,
E il giovin Vladimir morir dovrà.
Morte a lui! Morte a lui!

**KONTCHAKOVNA:** O no, pietà v'implora!
Pietà per Vladimir!
Io vo' morir per lui.
La vita mia prendete.
Su me ricada tutta l'ira vostra,
Ma lui non fate, oimè, morir!
Per lui sia grazia,
Ei m'appartien.

**I POLOVCESI:** Morte, Russia, morta à tuoi signor!
(*Accorrono i "Polovcesi"*).

**PRIMO GRUPPO:** Schiumeggia irrompe il chiaro Don!
(*Accorrono i "Polovcesi"*).

**SECONDO GRUPPO:** E l'onda invita rugge ancor!

**PRIMO GRUPPO:** Ove il nemico seguirem?
I duci già deciso avran.

**SECONDO GRUPPO:** La volontà sia respettata:
Ecco e qua. Kontchak!
(*Entrano Kontchak e i khans*).

**IL KHAN KONTCHAK:** Che avviene? Che vuol dir?
Piangi tu? E perchè mai?

**CORO DI POLOVCESI:** Gia lunge e il fier Igor!
Fu Ovlour che ci tradì.
A gran galoppo omai,
Ne l'ombra l'inseguiam!

**IL KHAN KONTCHAK:** Grazia a Vladimiro,
Così mio voler!

**CORO DEI KHANS:** È pronto ognun ad obbedir;
Ma periglioso è l'inseguir.
Igor su noi può ripiombar.
L'orgoglio suo punir dobbiam.
E forse il figlio
Suo per qual cammino sfuggirà,
Ma prima deve soggiacer
Ai nostri colpi di staffil.
Su va Kontchak decidi tu;
Col nuovo sol vedrai cader

**PRINCE IGOR:** (*hurries away*).
Farewell!
(*Konchakovna strikes an alarm gong several times. The Polovtsy come running in from every side*).

**KONCHAKOVNA:** Prince Igor has escaped,
Ovlour has betrayed us.
Let his son remain here!

**THE POLOVTSY:** To horse, to horse without delay,
Let fly a rain of arrows sharp!
Pursue them over the steppe.
Haste like the wind:
Bind young Vladimir to the nearest tree
And pierce his heart with arrows.

**KONCHAKOVNA:** Ah, no! You must not touch him,
I will not let him go!
The young Prince must be saved.
But slay me if you will,
Let the first arrow pierce my heart,
For I will gladly die with him,
But never give him up to you!

**THE POLOVTSY:** Death to all the Russian captives!
Show no mercy!
(*Groups of Polovtsy come rushing in*)

**FIRST GROUP:** The river Don is rising fast!
(*Polovtsy come rushing in*).

**SECOND GROUP:** The flood is rising every moment,
We cannot follow them across the river!

**FIRST GROUP:** We will follow the leaders.

**SECOND GROUP:** Call all the Khans in council
That we may hear what they advise.
See, here comes Khan Konchak!
(*Enter Konchak and other Khans*).

**KONCHAK:** What means this noise?
Daughter, why are you here?

**POLOVTSY:** Prince Igor has escaped,
Ovlour has played the traitor,
He saddled two swift steeds,
And has ridden away with the Prince.

**KONCHAK:** Do not harm the Prince.
These are my orders!

**THE KHANS:** Konchak, listen to our words, hear what we think.
In all affairs of warfare we have followed counsels and commands without a protest.
But now that the old falcon has flown home,
This young bird soon will follow. It were wise,
While still we have him, to make sure of him—

# Act III

Dei prigionier l'odiato stuol.
Nessun di lor potrà sfuggir
Al nostro acciar sterminator!

**IL KHAN KONTCHAK:** No! Meglio assai così il falco tener
In pegno d'una pia fanciulla . . .
Ei forse può giovar. (*A Vladimir*).
Vien! Sii tu di mia famiglia,
Ti vo' donar la figlia mia
Ne' vostri sguardi amor scintilla,
E ride il cor.
(*Ai Khans*).
Or noi partiam.
Vittoria avrem.

**I KHANS:** A l'armi, orsù! Vittoria avrem. (*Trombe sulla scena*).

**CORO DI POLOVCESI:** Andiam! Andiam!
Andiam e de la Russa vincerem l'orgoglio.
Andiam!
Gloria a te, Signor!
(*Trombe*).

*CALA IL SIPARIO*

# ■ ATTO IV

*S'alza il sipario e si vedono davanti i muri e la pubblica piazza della città di Poutivl. Comincia a spuntare il giorno. Jaroslavna è sola sulla terrazza alta sul muro.*

**JAROSLAVNA:** Udirà lo sposo diletto il sospir
Che aleggia sul mar?
Del Danubio alle glauche rive,
Come usignol il cor poserà:
Pel sonante sacro flutto,
Navigherà l'amore;
E così ne l'onda pura,
Guariran le sue ferite.
Vento di terror,
Perchè travolgi senza tregua?
Ai gagliardi eroi d' Igor,
Le frecce ancor sospingi!
Non sei sazio, vento fatale,
Di scagliar così.
Il tuo soffio che diffonde morte?
Tu il mar scuoti, e in tenebror
Gli muti il sorriso.
Senza tregua,
T'abbatti ognor sul mostranato petto.
Il pianto mio d'amor
Che al fiorir del sol
Dell'onda vapor l'azzurrita.
Almo sol, fattor di vita,
Tu che effondí e forza e amore,
Divo sol, perenne fiamma:
Muta a te mi prostro,

---

Send one sharp arrow quivering through his heart.
Believe us, it is good counsel that we give.
You know that we in warfare have followed
Your wise advice without demur or protest.
Now do not scorn our opinion: slay this swarm
Of Russian vermin before they all escape.

**KONCHAK:** No! If the old falcon has flown back to his nest,
We'll chain the young one here.
Give him a mate.
(*To Prince Vladimir*).
Vladimir, here behold your chosen wife!
You are no foe, but dear as any son.
(*To the Khans.*)
Tomorrow morning, burnish all your weapons, We'll march on Russia once again!

**THE KHANS:** To Russia! To fight our foes again!
(*Trumpets*).

**THE POLOVTSY:** To Russia we will march,
To fight the foe!
Glory to Khan Konchak!

*CURTAIN*

# ■ ACT IV

*(The city walls and public Square in Poutivl. Daybreak. Yaroslavna is seen standing alone on the terrace of the wall).*

**YAROSLAVNA:** Ah, still I grieve; ah, still my tears flow on,
I send my sorrow forth at dawn upon the breeze,
To him who tarries by the distant seas.
O, could I, like the cuckoo, fly along the banks
Of the blue Don,
Or dip my sleeve in Kayala's cool flood
And wash the blood from his wounded body!
O, breeze, O boisterous breeze,
Why do you blow across the plains?
Do you bear the cruel arrows
Against the Prince's warriors?
O, breeze, O boisterous breeze,
Driving the clouds before you,
Rocking the ships upon the waves,
Why do you blow so long
Across the plains and scatter
My joys like autumn leaves?
Flow on Dneiper, broad and blue,
Beloved, famous river, flow!
Bring my dear one home to me,
Then I'll weep no more at dawn.
Or send my sorrow forth upon the

---

Obliati, ne l'ignavia,
Essi impolorano la morte;
E i tuoi raggi fanno strazio
Fra tanto squallor?!
(*Un gruppo di villici passa cantando. Jaroslavna siede assorta nei suoi pensieri*).

**CORO DI VILLICI:** (*Dietro le scene; poi si avvicina a poco a poco*). Qual fragor selvaggio di rea tempesta
Sembra di lontan minacciar?!
Passa Gzak il gran guerrier!
Sembra di lontan l'uragano?
È il grande guerrier, il gran guerrier, Il vincitor!
(*Compariscono sul palcoscenico*).
Nero corvo fendi l'orizzonte
Morte stride ogni
Ella vien!
No; no: è Gzak che vuol guerra ancor
E un lupo scarno che brama sangue
E va seguendo il corvo al vol?
(*Morendo in lontananza*).
No, è Gzak, il vincitor,
Che vuol guerra ancor!

**JAROSLAVNA:** (*contemplando i dintorni devastati*). Segni ovunque di terror!
Tutto è squallido, tutto qui supplica!
Non più messi biondeggiar vedrem laggiù.
La gioventù più non canterà l'amore.
Non più.
(*Guardando fisso in lontananza*).
Di lontan due cavalier veder mi pare
Par che un d'essi sia guerrier polacco.
Di novella strage hanno sete ancor?
Il crudel flagello chi potrà mai frenar?
Al fin Poutivl s'arrenderà
Ma l'altro nobile, di nostro sangue par.
Sì, sì: un Russo egli è di certo.
Da gran signor è l'armatura;
Auster egli ha l'atteggiamento,
Un principe soccorso offrirmi vuole?
Mi reca libertà?! . . . Sogno ancor?!
Che penso? . . . Che oso? . . .
Il sogno m'esalta . . .
Qual miraggio! Ah!
Illusa io son! Qual follia! . . .
Invan io spero . . . No!
(*Con strascico di voce*).
È lui! Sì: riconoso il buon Igor
È l'eroe diletto, che ritorna.

---

breeze
To him who tarries by the distant seas.
O sun, resplendent sun,
Shining brightly in the heavens,
Warming all things, all caressing,
Making all the world rejoice!
Why upon the burning steppe,
Where no cooling waters flow,
Did you torture them with thirst;
Exhaust them with your ruthless glow?
Tell me sun?
(*A crowd of village folk appears singing. Yaroslavna is absorbed in thought*).

**CHORUS:** (*Behind the scenes; then gradually approaches*). It was not the furious tempest-wind that brought this great calamity;
It was Khan Gzak who wrought all the evil.
It was not a croaking raven, grim and black,
Foretold that this should be;
Our homes were burnt and ravaged by Khan Gzak,
It was not a hungry wolf, so fierce and grey,
That scattered all our flocks;
It was Khan Gzak who bore our herds away.
(*They pass out*).

**YAROSLAVNA:** (*Gazing over the lands laid waste*). How ruinous and sad the land appears! The hamlets burned, the fields are bare and black, the crops down-trodden—wasted by the foe! It has been long since songs of gladness echoed over the land!
(*She gazes over the distant plains*).
Whom do I see in the distance?.. Two horsemen approaching, and one is dressed like the Polovtsy . . . Surely the foe will not return again so soon. God preserve us! What will now become of us! Poutivle will be taken from us too! . . . The other rider is attired like a Russian, and does not seem to be a common soldier; his bearing, his fine steed, his whole appearance bespeak high birth and power. It is some Russian Prince who visits us. Who can it be? Where does he come from? I do not know . . . I cannot guess . . . It is strange . . . mysterious . . . Ah! Impossible! . . . Am I dreaming, or under a spell? . . . No! (*with emotion*). Those are Prince Igor's features . . . the dear familiar face and figure! It is the Prince! My love comes back to me! (*Prince Igor rides in, accompanied by Ovlour. He dismounts and rushes to Yaroslavna. Ovlour leads away the horses*).

Vive ancor! Odo la sua voce.
(*Il Principe Igor compare sulla scena, a cavollo; è accompagnato da Ovlour. Il principe scende dal cavallo e corre verso Jaroslavna. Ovlour s'allontana con i cavalli*).

**JAROSLAVNA:** Ah! Sei tu ch'io recingo!
Ah, risalgo a la vita
Piango, fremo! qual prodigio!

**IL PRINCIPE IGOR:** Il dolor già dilegua.
Ah! sei tu ch'io recingo!
Sul mio cor posa ancor:
Ch'io t'adori.

**JAROSLAVNA:** Ah! Sogno di dolcezza!

**IL PRINCIPE IGOR:** A te grazie, o ciel.

**JAROSLAVNA:** Sognar credei: Sia lode al ciel.
Son io, son io, che vivo ancor!
L'aspetto tuo non mi tradì Igor,
Sei tu che stringo al sen.
Io temo sempre di sognar,
Poi che m'accadde ancor.
Ma no, sei tu; non è illusion:
Il tuo cor sento vibrar col mio.

**IL PRINCIPE IGOR:** È ver, non è illusion la tua. Son io, che sempre a te pensai,
Che sempre udii la voce tua errar
Pel mare di dolor.

**JAROSLAVNA:** A te vicin non temo più.
Alfin tu sei, mio santo amor:
E il cor mi esulta di dolcezza.
Dal ciel sei sceso ancor.

**IL PRINCIPE IGOR:** Dolce sposa, sacrata sei;
In eterno t'amerò
Raggi a noi verserà
Da! ciel l'amor.

**JAROSLAVNA:** Come i dì passai fremendo!
E credeva udirne l'etra palpitar
L'arcana voce che mi dava fede ancor.
Lungamente il cuore mio s'è nutrito
Di speranza; ben fiammeggia
Or più santa la mia fede e l'offro a te.
E a te così fedel resterò.
E vinto hai tu?

**IL PRINCIPE IGOR:** Amata sposa io ben tornai glorioso
E fier di tua virtù.
Omai lontan non più languirò,
Mio dolce amor.

**YAROSLAVNA:** It is he, my homing mate, my love!
My long-desired husband, my life, my all!

**PRINCE IGOR:** Greeting, my joy, my love!
Greeting, light of mine eyes!
Once more we are together, my wife, my own!

**YAROSLAVNA:** Can it be true? O say it is not a dream!

**PRINCE IGOR:** I give thanks to heaven!

**YAROSLAVNA:** Can it be true! It is no misleading gleam
O witchcraft my poor heart deceiving.
You have come back . . . It is sweet beyond believing!
How often in sleep I saw you by my side,
But now I am awake . . .
O swear to me, my senses have not lied,
Or, love, my heart will break!

**PRINCE IGOR:** It is no dream, beloved
You hold my hand, and I grasp yours.
Once more into your eyes I gaze,
And hear your voice as in past days.

**YAROSLAVNA:** My love, my husband, you have come
Back to your people and your home;
With your return my sorrows cease,
You bring happiness and peace.

**PRINCE IGOR:** My wife, my darling, I have come
Back to my people and my home;
The captive's shame, the wounds, the pain,
Vanish at sight of you again.

**YAROSLAVNA:** Once more I see your dear face,
Once more I hear your voice, my Prince,
With your return my sorrows cease,
You bring happiness and peace.
Did you conquer?

**PRINCE IGOR:** No more waiting; no alarms;
Once more I hold you in my arms!
Beloved wife, friend of my choice,
Seeing you, heart and soul rejoice!

**JAROSLAVNA:** Il ciel si placherà di minacciar così.
Sol nostro amato suol,
Benigno un nuovo Sol di gloria raggerà:
Più bella fiorirà la santa libertà.

**IL PRINCIPE IGOR:** Fuggito dal campo son,
E dal furor nemico io vo,
D'assalto cercar di liberar
La patria nostra e te.
In nome del nostro onor,
O prodi guerrier a me;
Che forse ancor saremo vincitor.

**JAROSLAVNA:** Qual suprema gioia sento
Ne l'udir la tua parola!
O conforto sovrumano,
Di sperar tu vinca ancor.
A al fonte della vita,
Come un dì si nutre il core,
A la fonte della vita,
Torna azzurro il nostro ciel.

**IL PRINCIPE IGOR:** Dolce sposa, io t'amerò,
Sin che torni a noi l'april.
Non più timor vincino a me,
Ne tristi sogni di dolor.

**JAROSLAVNA E IL PRINCIPE IGOR:** Passati sono i foschi dì,
Il tuo destin placato s'è.
Or ne l'azzurro brillerà
Un nuovo sol di redenzion,
Io sul tuo petto sognerò
La santa libertà.

**IL PRINCIPE IGOR:** Ancor gli eroi mi ascolteran
Con sacro ardor, combatterem.
Guerrieri a me!
Sterminio sia del fier invasor.

**JAROSLAVNA:** Il ciel d'amor splenderà.
(*Il Principe Igor e Jaroslavna si diriggono lentamente verso la cittadella. Durante la canzone seguente dei giocatori e dei "Goudok" il principe e la principessa stanno davanti alla porta della cittadella, intenti alla loro conversazione. Poi scompariscono dietro la porta*).
(*Entrano Erochak e Skoula, tutti e due quasi ubbriachi. Essi cantano e suonano*).

**EROCHKA:** Or fiammeggia il sole;
Tutto a noi sorride!
Certo chi godrà, sempre vincerà!
Non abbiam pene, non abbiam noie!
Igor non potrà certo ritornar,
Sempre i vincitor l'anno in schiavitù.
Senza libertà presto ei morirà
Ei lasciò, stolto, nel voler guerra,
Tutto il suo tesor e le genti sue.

**YAROSLAVNA:** Husband, by troth long plighted,
Friend and husband, heaven-united,
Long my heart has ached for you
A new sun will shine for us
And liberty will be more sweet.

**PRINCE IGOR:** Secretly I made my escape,
When I learnt that Gzak had been here.
I fled to save my land from ruin,
And send a rallying cry from end to end
Of suffering Russia. I came to raise
Another army, and to rouse the Princes,
That we may drive our foemen back once more.

**YAROSLAVNA:** You did escape at dusk,
Despite the heathen Khan,
You did break from your captivity?
But you were wounded sore,
Say, do you suffer now?
My love, my homing mate,
O let me comfort you!

**PRINCE IGOR:** Beloved wife, friend of my choice,
Seeing you, heart and soul rejoice!
Gone the hours of evil dreams,
Gone the sad and anxious thoughts.

**PRINCE IGOR AND YAROSLAVNA:** Forgotten all the hours of pain,
Forgotten all the weary days,
For now joy floods our lives again,
As when the heavy storm clouds lift
And through a bright and widening rift
The sun pours down his hopeful rays.

**PRINCE IGOR:** I'll a rallying cry abroad,
And raise another valiant host,
I will not let the heathen boast.
This time I'll crush the Tartar horde!

**YAROSLAVNA:** Heaven of love will shine.
(*Prince Igor and Yaroslavna walk slowly towards the Citadel. While the goudok players sing the following song, they stand by the gateway, absorbed in talk, and then disappear within*).
(*Enter Eroshka and Skoula, both rather tipsy*).

**EROSHKA:** Now the sun is shining,
Everything is smiling,
A new Prince has come!
Igor is far away,
He must stay in prison,
Since all his warriors fell,
We need not weep for him
The Khan will treat him well;
But keep all your pity
For those who in the fight
Were butchered by the foe.

Il fiume schiumeggiando, l'ha con se tolto:
E chi piomba giù non può risalir.
E il denar vola, senza far chiasso:
Chi non fingerà non saprà regnar.
A la Kajala il signor si spinse;
Ma con tal dolor, ci lasciò l'onor.
Tutta Russia afferma ch'egli ha mal oprato.
Igor ne l'inganno si trovò sospinto.
Ora ognum piange e non più spera.
La fatal illusion in Igor vanì!
Si leverà dai borghi dai villaggi,
Dalle rive del Danubio la condanna eterna.
S'ei tornasse ancora via di qua si caccerà.
Sia gloria al gran Signor
Che ci lasciò schiacciar!
Quel prodigioso Igor, quel sovrumano Igor.

SKOULA: Che guerrier prode! Che campion raro! Ma veh! chi è là?! Io sogno!
(S'interrompono stupiti, vedendo da lontano Il Principe e Jaroslavna, che entrano nella cittadella).

EROCHKA: Chi? Lui?!

SKOULA: Egli torna?! Che mai vuol dir?

EROCHKA: Ah! fatalità! Ebbri siam noi! Il principe qua! Ed or che avverrà? Facciam eco agli evviva! Ahi! Ahi! Davvero non c'è da ridere! Bel caso! Noi saremo impiccati!

SKOULA: (facendo l'atto di'suonare). Presto, suona . . .

EROCHKA: Per qual ragion suonar tu vuoi?

SKOULA: Presto, suona! Fate festa al possente gran signore. Tutti qui! correran così, Vedrai, d'allarme al suon. (Entrambi afferrano le funi delle campane e si danno a suonore l'allarme).

EROCHKA E SKOULA: Helà, al suon davver ognun verrà! Di qua, di là, di su, di giù, vicin, Lontan, venite or via così: correte qua!

SKOULA: Helà! Presto tutto qua! Ognun di voi godrà, grazia al ciel! (Il popolo accorre in folla da diverse parti).

CORO: O qual fragor! Dite su. Chi ne minaccia? Ah! Che vuol dire ciò. (con enfasi). Via, accorrete per di qua! Indegni, basta, non è tempo di

---

It was Igor who in spite
Of warnings in the sky
Would still go warning.
And on the sandy plain
Where never waters flow
There perished our great host;
The army Igor lost
We shall never see again.
With pots of Russian gold,
This Prince so wise and bold
Built bridges at great cost
That never have been crossed;
For at the Kayala,
That mighty floods did swell,
The troops were left to drown,
And with his men went down
Prince Igor's fame as well.
Therefore all the land,
From Danube to the distant sea,
The Russian people all deride
The Prince who caused their misery.

SKOULA: A better Prince has come!
Igor is far away,
But who goes there? I dream.
(They suddenly break off in terror, having caught sight of the Prince and Princess as they enter the Citadel).

EROSHKA: Look! Look yonder!

SKOULA: The Prince!

EROSHKA: Oh, mercy on us! It is all over for us now! What's to be done? Oh, oh, our heads will be chopped off! We shall be executed, friend! Drawn and quartered!

SKOULA: (making him a sign to pull). Ring the bell! Ring!

EROSHKA: Ring! What for?

SKOULA: Why, to save our lives, our skins, our necks! To fill our bellies, too, with food and wine. Ring, rouse the people, sound the alarm! (They both seize the bell ropes and pull vigorously).

SKOULA and EROSHKA: Come here, good folk! Hurry, Hurry. Run quick to hear the joyous tidings! Assemble all you orthodox, We have good news for you! (Enter the people from every side).

SKOULA: Come, quickly, you shall all have joy!

CHORUS: What a noise! What's the matter? Is the town on fire? What's it all about? Answer . . . quick! (with emphasis).

---

celiar.
Certo: trincato avete voi,
Già sin d'or molto vin;
Zitti, quanto, già bevuto han molto vino
Di buon mattin!
Via dia qua, maledetti briccon.
È ben meglio che andiate a dormire!
A la tana presto, birbe via di qua!
(con enfasi).
Quale prodigio!
Quanto strepito!

SKOULA: No, no! Questa ebbrezza, certo Non ha per causa il vino! Noi salutiamo qui sua grazia.

CORO: Ma che? S'annuncia il principe? Che il ciel maledica!

EROCHKA: È il nostro Igor che inoltrasi. Sì. Egli è qua: grazia al ciel.

SKOULA: Or la gioia è immensa!

CORO: No, vile; tu mentisci ancor.

SKOULA: Guardate laggiù: chi s'inoltra. Volgesi! E il possent Igor. Miratelo ei sale al Kremlin: Egli ha per mano la sua diletta. Parla con gli anziani suoi Bojardi. Ah!

EROCHKA: Viva!

CORO: È pur lui sì! (Suonano nuovamente). Presto: suonate or tutte le nostre campane: Che qui dovrà la folla si raduni. È il nostro eroe: rinascente sol! Ei riscende a noi dal ciel! (La folla aumenta sempre più. Alcuni si avvicinano a Ovlour e lo caricano di domande). Suonate le nostre campane, Che questo è glorioso dì! Ah! Viva Igor! Gran Signor! (Suonano di nuovo).

EROCHKA: Vittoria, vittoria, vittoria! Fiero ci ridona il suo sorriso, Ed irradia il nostro cor! (Entrano i bojardi e i villici).

BOJARDI E VECCHI: Placa alfin la tetra sorte, Dio, che vedi il nostro stato: Il buon Igor è tornato, E ci irradia il nuovo sol!

IL POPOLO: Oda il cielo i nostri voti E ridoni la speranza, Molto abbiam per te sofferto, Santa libertà!

---

It is those drunken players!
No one but those rascals! Come down,
You guzzling swine, cease to plague us . . .
Wait, hear what they have to say!
No, turn them out . . . Send them packing!
Come down! Be off! Get you gone!
What mystery. What noise!

SKOULA: No, no, I am not drunk with wine. We are welcoming the Prince.

CHORUS: What! Your Galitsky, the traitor? Let him be accursed of Heaven!

EROSHKA: Nay! We speak not of perfidious Galitsky, But of our lawful Prince—Igor.

SKOULA: Igor, son of Svietoslav!

CHORUS: You both are raving mad! Nonsense!

SKOULA: You don't believe us? Then look there, By the Citadel. Do you see him now? He passed a moment since, with the Princess. He is going to the Kremlin. See! That's his helmet! There's his horse! And there's the Polovets who brought him home. Look!

EROSHKA: Long live the Prince!

THE CROWD: Prince, Prince, our Prince! Aye, ring the bells! (Ringing of bells). Run quick and ask the Polovets If in truth the Prince is here! (The people crowd in in great numbers. A few go up to Ovlour and question him). He has returned! It is true, the Prince, our father, has come home! . . . Rejoice, give thanks! (Enter the Boyards and Elders).

THE PEOPLE: Suddenly he has returned from captivity, Igor has come to save us!

THE BOYARDS and ELDERS: Now thanks be to God in Heaven, To whom we have not prayed in vain, Who turned our sorrow into joy And brought our good Prince home again.

THE PEOPLE: Our Prince, from out of captivity Has come back to his folk again; Our Prince, our father, long waited, Takes up his happy reign.

**EROCHKA E SKOULA:** Andar dobbiam in folla,
Per evocarlo ancora.
Apparirà di certo a l'alto de la torre.
Tutti in folla andiam plaudenti!
Andiam! Andiam!

**IL POPOLO:** Andiam! Andiam! ancor cantiam, cantiam
Il saluto andiamo a dare
E plaudisci o sacra terra,
Che giulivi in nobil ritmo,
Cantiam viva Igor!

**BOJARDI E VECCHI:** Ah! E da noi che deve udire
De la gioia il primo urrà!?
Tutti incontro noi moviamo:
Passa il principe di qua.
(*I vecchi e i bojardi si diriggono verso la cittadella*).

**IL POPOLO:** Ben dicesti, lo si attenda,
Pure qua.
I costumi de' nostri avi rispettiam.
(*La folla si accrece a poco a poco. Entrano le donne con vesti eleganti. Alcuni escono dalle loro case portando del pane e del sale*).
Si preparin per la festa molli
Al vento veli d'or.
Adorniam le nostre teste!
Inni sciolga il novo sol!
Si preparin per la festa molli
Ai venti veli d'or.

**SKOULA and EROSHKA:** Haste, good folk, to meet him,
Haste to the Citadel,
Waste no time, go forth to greet him,
And wish Prince Igor well.

**THE PEOPLE:** Let all the people go to meet him,
To welcome our Prince home today;
Waste no time, but run to greet him.
Hail Prince Igor! Come away.

**THE ELDERS and BOYARDS:** Stay!
Let us go first, it is our right,
To give the Prince his due welcome,
Wait here, good people, within sight,
Until Prince Igor sends for you.
(*The Elders and the Boyards go towards the citadel*).

**THE PEOPLE:** The Elders are quite right, good friends,
We are not dressed to meet the Prince.
We shall have time before he sends
To deck us in our Sunday best.
(*The crowd gradually grows in numbers. Enter women in holiday dress. Many people come out of their houses bearing the bread and salt—symbols of welcome*).
Let us all look bright and gay,
Poutivile keeps a holiday,
Songs of welcome we must raise,

Adorniam le nostre teste!
Inni sciolga il novo sol!
Andiam tutti: precediam il buon Igor,
E gli s'offra il sacro pan e l'idromel.

**EROCHKA:** Ah! Viva, o Prence!
Viva il grande Igor!

**SKOULA:** Brindiam a te, signore nostro.
Lieti qui si beva ognora,
E di gloria sempre a te sorrida il cielo.

**IL POPOLO:** Placa alfin la tetra sorte,
Dio che vedi il nostro stato:
Il buon prence è tornato
E ci darà un novo sol!
Il saluto gli rechiamo
Che nessuno più paventi:
Igor sempre vittorioso,
Ci proteggerà
Già la speranza arride
Igor vola a la vittoria:
Il suo braccio sa la gloria!
Viva il grande signor nostro Igor!
(*Il principe esce dal "Kremlin" con la principessa. Essi compariscono sulla pubblica piazza accompagnati da bojardi e da vecchi. Il principe saluta il popolo che lo receve con grida e applausi di gioia*). Ei fiammeggia al nuovo sol!
Sia gloria a te, Igor!
A te! A te, Igor!

*FINE*

Make a song to praise our Prince.
The folk must offer bread and salt,
On a salver chased and fine;
We must proffer mead in plenty
And the best of wine.

**EROSHKA:** Hurrah for the Prince!
Hurrah for the great Igor!

**SKOULA:** Drink the Prince's health,
May he have long life and wealth.
The Prince has come!

**THE PEOPLE:** Let all the people greet the Prince,
Escaped from his captivity.
He is our little father kind,
He is our long-desired Prince.
Let all the people meet him,
Let all the people greet him,
Our noble Prince, our honored guest, Loyal people, bring your best!
Happier days begin for us,
Russia's future's glorious,
Now Prince Igor reigns once more!
(*The Prince and Princess appear from the Citadel and move on towards the public Square, accompanied by the Elders and Boyards. The prince salutes the people who receive him with shouts of joy*).
Long live our little father, long live our noble Prince!

*END*

# La Wally (1892)

MUSIC BY ALFREDO CATALANI ■ LIBRETTO BY LUIGI ILLICA

This four-act opera, set to a libretto by Luigi Illica (based on Wihelmine von Hillern's novel, *Die Geyer-Wally*), premiered at La Scala in Milan on January 20, 1892. Stromminger is celebrating his sixtieth birthday in the square of Hochstoff, a Tyrolese village. Among those gathered to honor him is Gellner, who is in love with Stromminger's daughter Wally. Wally's friend Walter, a minstrel, plays and sings. Giuseppe Hagenbach, son of an old rival of Stromminger's, arrives from Sölden and boasts of his hunting skills. Stromminger picks an argument with him, but Wally steps in. She falls in love with Hagenbach (who is promised to Afra); when her father discovers this he commands her to marry Gellner. Protesting, she departs for Sölden, where the people are celebrating a local holiday. Wally appears haughty and cold; Hagenbach wagers that he will kiss her during the dance. Knowing nothing of this, she agrees to dance with him and lets him kiss her; when she learns that she has been the subject of his bet, she vows revenge. She decides to marry Gellner on condition that he murder Hagenbach. Up in the mountains, Gellner pushes Hagenbach over the edge of a cliff; Wally calls for help. She climbs down into the ravine and rescues the injured Hagenbach. Wally relinquishes him to Afra, and disappears into the mountains. Walter follows, pleading with her to return to the valley, but she refuses. Hagenbach realizes that he is in love with Wally and goes to find her. As they embrace and sing of their future life together a snowstorm begins to swirl around them. Suddenly an avalanche thunders down the mountain, burying Giuseppe. Wally throws herself over the precipice.

## ■ ATTO PRIMO

*Il Paesaggio: L'HOCHSTOFF.— Largo piazzale ingombro da tavole.—A sinistra la casa dello Stromminger; a destra l'alpestre paesaggio sparso di case e di pini.—Nel fondo le altre case dell'Hochstoff in mezzo alle quali serpeggiando passa la strada; poi, più alto, un ponte che unisce due rupi gigantesche dominanti l'abisso profondo dove scorre l'Ache.—A capo del ponte un grande Crocifisso dinanzi al quale pende una lampada.—Un sentiero tortuoso, per curve ora dolci, ora aspre, tracciato fra i massi che lo frastagliano, sale alto, ora scomparendo, ora apparendo improvvisamente, e si smarrisce fra le ardite ineguaglianze del paesaggio.—Nell'ultimo fondo le altissime vette del Murzoll e del Similaun coperte di neve.*

*Lo STROMMINGER festeggia il suo settantesimo anno; beve in mezzo ad Alpigiani, Cacciatori, Pastori e Contadini suoi ospiti.—Tavole imbandite, sparse pel piazzale.—Nel fondo un bersaglio; Vincenzo Gellner lo abbatte in onore dello Stromminger con un ardito colpo di carabina.—Nel fondo del piazzale danzano allegramente Fanciulle e Cacciatori.—Gruppi di Contadine stanno loro intorno.—Lo Stromminger, all'alzarsi della tela, è seduto; egli è allegro e un po' alticcio.*

## ■ ACT I

*THE SCENE: HOCHSTOFF.—A large square covered with tables. To the left STROMMINGER'S house; to the right, the Alpine scene with houses and pine trees here and there. In the background, the other houses of Hochstoff, between which the street winds in and out; then, higher up, a bridge which connects two gigantic cliffs overlooking a deep abyss where flows the Ach. At the end of the bridge, a large crucifix, before which hangs a lamp. A winding path, laid out between the rocks which cut it, rises now by gentle and now by abrupt curves, and is lost among the hazardous uneven parts of the landscape. In the furthest background, the very high summits of Mts. Murzoll and Similaun, covered with snow.*

*STROMMINGER is celebrating his 60th year; he is drinking amid the mountaineers, hunters, shepherds and peasants—his guests. Set tables are standing here and there on the square. In the rear, a target; VINCENZO GELLNER shot it off in honor of STROMMINGER, by a bold shot from his carbine. In the rear of the square, girls and hunters are dancing gaily. Groups of peasant women are standing around them. STROMMINGER, at the rising of the curtain, is seated; he is jolly and slightly tipsy.*

**STROMMINGER:** (*all'ardito colpo di Vincenzo Gellner, si leva dalla sua poltrona e corre a lui abbracciandolo.*) Bravo, mio Gellner! . . .

**ALCUNI:** (*sentenziando.*) Bel colpo davvero! . . .

**STROMMINGER:** (*ironico.*) Ho inteso dir che a Sölden v'abbia un tale
Che si vanta il più destro cacciatore
E sdegna alter . . .
(*indica sorridendo il bersaglio atterrato da Gellner.*)
que' facili bersagli! . . .

**GELLNER:** (*cupo.*) Si
l'Hagenbach! . . .

**STROMMINGER:** (*ridendo più fortemente.*) Lui propri-
o! . . . Or mi ricordo
Ch'io ne conobbi il pa-
dre . . . un orgoglioso . . .
(*ma volendo Gellner abbuiarsi in volto, tronca il suo discorso.*)
Al diavol l'Hagenbach e quei di Sölden!
(*trascina Gèllner a bere e beve primo.*)
A te, mio Gellner! . . .

**ALCUNI:** (*attorniandoli e bevendo.*) Bevi! . . .

**ALTRI:** Evviva Gellner! . . .
(*Un giovanetto entra dalla destra. E WALTER, suonatore di cetra, cantore di fole e di leggende.*)

**STROMMINGER:** (*vendendolo.*)
Che cerchi, piccol Walter? . . .

**STROMMINGER:** (*At the bold shot of VINCENZO GELLNER, STROMMINGER rises from his easy chair, runs up and embraces him.*) Bravo, my Gellner! . . .

**SOME:** (*judging.*) Fine shot indeed! . . .

**STROMMINGER:** (*ironically.*) I heard it said that at Sölden there is one who boasts of being the most skilful hunter and haughtily disdains . . .
(*points smilingly at the target shot off by GELLNER.*)
these easy targets! . . .

**GELLNER:** (*thoughtfully.*)
Yes . . . Hagenbach!

**STROMMINGER:** (*laughing louder.*) Precisely he! Now I recollect that I knew his father—a very haughty man . . .
(*but seeing GELLNER'S face grow gloomy, cuts short his conversation.*)
To the devil with Hagenbach and the people of Sölden!
(*drags GELLNER to drink and drinks first.*)
Your health, Gellner!

**SOME:** (*surrounding them and drinking.*) Drink!

**OTHERS:** Long live Gellner!
(*A young boy enters from the right. It is WALTER, a zither-player and singer of tales and legends.*)

**STROMMINGER:** (*catching sight of him.*) What are you looking for, little Walter?

WALTER: (*avanzandosi.*) La tua Wally.

STROMMINGER: (*crollando le spalle.*) E chi può dirti ov'essa si nasconda? . . . Se giù alla valle . . . oppur pe' gli alti greppi Sovra il ramo d'un pino o in una tana? . . . Che brami tu da lei?

WALTER: Cantiamo insieme.

STROMMINGER: È un bel mestiere per seccar la gente! . . . (*alcuni ridono*)

WALTER: (*piccato.*) Eppur, se udiste, una canzon conosco . . . Una canzon sì bella . . .

LE DONNE: (*a Walter, pressandolo da vicino.*) Walter, cantala!

WALTER: (*continuando.*) . . . dell'Edelweiss è la canzone! . . . È un jodler mesto, soave, blando . . . come un bacio.

LE DONNE: Canta!

LE FANCIULLE: (*pregando.*) Canta!

STROMMINGER: Pettegole, tacete! (*a Walter.*) Ebben, udiam codesta maraviglia! (*tutti circondano Walter; chi siede, chi si appoggia alle tavole; alcuni a gruppi; altri in disparte soli; Stromminger seduto nella sua poltrona; Gellner a cavalcioni di una panca.—Walter leva la cetra e canta:*)

WALTER: Un dì, verso il Murzoll, una fanciulla, per un erto sentiero, moveva il piè leggiero; lenta ascendeva la montagna brulla! Giù susurrava il vento; parea un lontano pianto tornava allegro canto e finiva in lamento! . . . Co' raggi intanto l'avvolgeva il sole! . . . ed ella ognor salia la solitaria via Stavano intorno a lei le nubi sole! E poichè giunta fu su l'alto monte presso alla neve bianca la pellegrina stanca Sciolse le trecce e chinò il bianco fronte. E disse: O figlia candida di Dio risplender t'ho veduta giù, da la valle muta, non l'aspro m'atterri lungo pendio, a te qui son venuta, —esser siccome te bella desio! Ed ecco intorno a lei livide e strane figlie apparire, larve sovrumane! . . . Candide gocce la baciaro in fronte e la valanga scosse il vecchio monte! No, non piangete sulla triste sorte della sua morte . . . Là, della neve ascosa nel candor

WALTER: (*approching.*) Your Wally.

STROMMINGER: (*shrugging his shoulders.*) And who can tell where she is hiding? Whether down in the valley, or over the high precipices . . . On the branch of a pine tree, or in a cave? Why are you so eager to find her?

WALTER: We sing together.

STROMMINGER: That is a fine way of boring people! (*Some laugh.*)

WALTER: (*piqued.*) But yet, if you only heard it . . . I know a song, Such a beautiful song!

THE WOMEN: (*to WALTER, crowding in on him.*) Walter, sing it!

WALTER: (*continuing.*) The song is about the Edelweiss! It is a yodler, sad, gentle, mild—as a kiss.

WOMEN: Sing it.

GIRLS: (*entreating.*) Sing!

STROMMINGER: Be quiet, silly creatures! (*to WALTER.*) Well then, let us hear that wonder! (*All surround WALTER, who sits down, leans on a table; some in groups, others singly, apart, STROMMINGER seated in his easy chair. GELLNER astride a bench. WALTER lifts up the zither and sings.*)

WALTER: One day, towards Mount Murzoll, a young girl tripped so lightly Over a steep path. She slowly climbed the ragged mountain! The wind was murmuring, It seemed a distant lamentation, Turned into a joyful strain And ended in weeping! Meanwhile the sun enveloped her in its rays! And she kept on climbing Up the lonely road. The clouds alone Stood all around her! And when she reached the mountain top, Near the white snow, The weary pilgrim Opened her braids And bowed down her snow-white forehead, And said: O white daughter of God, I saw you shining below, From the silent valley. The long, steep precipice Frightened me not. I came here to you. I want to be as beautiful as you. And behold, all around her Appear strange and pale-faced maidens,

vive mutata la fanciulla in fior! . . .

GELLNER: (*con voce soffocata.*) (Nuova questa canzon non torna a me! . . . Ah, un'altra volta il cor per lei battè!)

STROMMINGER: Non c'è che dire! . . . È veramente bella!

TUTTI: Bella è davver!

WALTER: (*a Stromminger.*) Ebben . . . (*ride*) E di Wally!

STROMMINGER: Toh! Di mia figlia (*sorpreso*) Un canto così mesto?! Giammai l'avrei creduta! . . .

WALTER: Eppure è suo!

GELLNER: (Non m'ingannai! . . . Era il suo canto! . . . Ohimè, Freddo è il tuo cuore come neve, o Wally!) (*Dal fondo, oltre il piccolo ponte, echeggiano suoni di corni da caccia e si leva ontano un canto di cacciatori. Ed eccoli apparire pel sentiero, varcare il ponte e avviarsi avvicinandosi alla strada dell'Hochstoff. Alla testa procede un giovane ardito. Come un trofeo costui porta, avvoltolata intorno alla canna della carabina, una pelle di orso ancora gocciante sangue. È GIUSEPPE HAGENBACH di Sölden.*)

I CACCIATORI: (*ne l'alto.*) Su cacciator, ritorna!—Cade il sol all'orizonte;— Le nubi l'aquila fendo col vol e riede al monte;— Di roseo si colora l'alpe d'intorno;— Echeggi il corno! (*squillano i corni.*)

LE DONNE: (*allegre.*) Odi i corni echeggiar!

UOMINI: Son cacciatori che tornano!

STROMMINGER: (*colla voce rauca dell'avvinazzato, sempre seduto.*) Ben vengano! . . .

DONNE: Di Sölden Sono di certo! . . . Allegro è il loro canto! (*i Cacciatori appaiono a capo del ponte.*)

UOMINI: Eccoli là! . . . Vengono qua! . . .

DONNE: Già il ponte varcano! . . .

Superhuman phantoms! White drops kissed her forehead . . . And the avalanche shook the old mountain! No, do not lament The sad fate of her death. There, hidden in the white snows Lives the young girl Transformed into a flower!

GELLNER: (*in a choked voice.*) (I don't care for this new song at all! Ah, again my heart beats for her!)

STROMMINGER: There's no denying it, the song is really beautiful!

ALL: Beautiful, indeed!

WALTER: (*to Stromminger.*) Well . . . (*laughs.*) It is composed by Wally!

STROMMINGER: Nonsense! By my daughter (*surprised.*) So sad a song? I would never have believed it.

WALTER: And yet it is hers!

GELLNER: (I did not deceive myself! It was her song! Your heart is cold as snow, Wally!) (*From the rear, beyond the small bridge, hunting horns resound, and from a distance is heard a hunter's song. And they are seen approaching the street of Hochstoff. At the head, walks a bold youth. He carries, as a trophy, wound around the stick of his carbine, a bear's hide, still dripping blood. It is GIUSEPPE HAGENBACH, of Sölden.*)

THE HUNTERS: (*from above.*) Hunter return! The sun is setting in the horizon, The eagle, in his flight Cuts through the clouds, And returns to the mountain;— The Alps around grow rosy, Let the horn resound! (*The horns resound.*)

THE WOMEN: (*joyfully.*) Listen to the resounding horns!

MEN: They are the returning hunters!

STROMMINGER: (*in a voice hoarse with drink, still seated.*) Well, let them come!

WOMEN: They are surely from Sölden. Their song is joyous! (*The hunters appear at the end of the bridge.*)

MEN: They are coming here!

WOMEN: They already cross the bridge!

**TUTTI:** (*riconoscendoli.*) È l'Hagenbach!

**STROMMINGER:** (*si lascia sfuggire un gesto di disprezzo, ma, volto, il capo e vedendo i Cacciatori venirsene all' Hochstoff, brontola con voce chioccia.*) Colmi i bicchieri! . . .

**I CACCIATORI:** (*varcano il ponte e si avvicinano all'Hochstoff.*) Ritorna, o cacciator!—il camoscio abbandona
già la vallata
e torna al covo;—il corno suona all'impazzata;
e il tramonto colora
l'Alpè rosea d'intorno;
Echeggi il corno! . . .
(*entrano all'Hochstoff dando fiato nei loro corni, quasi trionfalmente.*)

**STROMMINGER:** (*levandosi con sforzo e andando loro incontro.*) Salute, cacciatori! . . .

**CACCIATORI:** E a voi salute! . . .

**STROMMINGER:** E fu buona la caccia? . . .

**CACCIATORI:** Buona assai . . .

**HAGENBACH:** Guardate qua!
(*mostra allo Stromminger la pelle sanguinolente dell'orso.*)

**STROMMINGER:** (*da conoscitore.*) Chi fece si bel colpo?

**CACCIATORI:** (*ridendo.*) Chi? . . . E lo chiedete? . . . L'Hagenbach soltanto può tai colpi menar! . . .

**HAGENBACH:** (*mostrando la pelle.*) Un solo! . . . Al cuore!
(*Stromminger guarda muto e immusonito il segno del colpo, mentre intorno a lui un mormorio di ammirazione erompe da tutti.*)

**TUTTI:** (*all'Hagenbach.*) Degli uccisori d'orsi il premio hai vinto! . . .

**ALTRI:** Son circa venti bei fiorini d'oro! . . .

**HAGENBACH:** (*a questi sorridendo sprezzante, canticchiando un brano di vecchia canzone.*)
Non è l'oro, no, che tenta
ai perigli il cacciator . . .
E la gloria che cimenta
gli ardimenti alti del cor! . . .
(*Egli siede a cavalcioni di una tavola volgendo in parte le spalle senza accorgersene allo Stromminger; e narra.*)
Su per l'erto sentier
lentamente salìa
e me tentava nella lunga vìa
della caccia il pensier! . . .
Quand'ecco un urlo fendere
l'aër nevoso e, ritto, a me dinante
ecco apparir codesto orso gigante!

**ALL:** (*recognizing them.*) It is Hagenbach!

**STROMMINGER:** (*Makes a gesture of contempt, but, turning his head and seeing the hunters come toward Hochstoff, he mutters in a hoarse voice.*) Fill the glasses!

**THE HUNTERS:** (*cross the bridge and approach Hochstoff.*) Return, o hunter! The chamois
Is already leaving the valley
And goes to its den . . .
The horn madly resounds;
And the sunset colors the Alps
With a rosy hue;
Let the horn resound!
(*They enter Hochstoff, blowing their horns triumphantly.*)

**STROMMINGER:** (*getting up with difficulty and going towards them.*) Greetings to you, hunters!

**HUNTERS:** And greetings to you too!

**STROMMINGER:** Well, was the hunt good?

**HUNTERS:** Good indeed!

**HAGENBACH:** Look here!
(*He shows STROMMINGER the bloody hide of the bear.*)

**STROMMINGER:** (*like a connoisseur.*) Who shot so well?

**HUNTERS:** (*laughing.*) Who? You ask it? Who but Hagenbach could shoot so well?

**HAGENBACH:** (*showing the hide.*) One single shot! Straight to the heart!
(*STROMMINGER looks silently and sullenly at the mark made by the shot, while around him break murmurs of admiration from all.*)

**ALL:** (*to Hagenbach.*) You won the prize of bear-killers.

**SOME:** It is about twenty-five gold florins!

**HAGENBACH:** (*smiling disdainfully at them, and humming a snatch of an old song.*) No it is not the gold which tempts
The hunter to all dangers,
glory puts
His boldness and his daring to test.
(*He sits astride a table, turning his back on STROMMINGER, without noticing what he is doing, and goes on.*)
Slowly I climbed up the steep path
And on the long way,
The thought of the hunt was tempting me!
When hear! A howl
Burst through the snow-filled air,
And straight in front of me
Behold, appears this enormous bear!

**ALCUNI:** E allor? . . .

**DONNE:** Spavento!

**ALTRI:** (*interrompendolo.*) Sul sentier?

**TUTTI:** E allora?

**HAGENBACH:** Mi arresto! . . . Guato!
L'abisso ho a manca . . .
ed a destra un fossato
e la montagna bianca! . . .
Dunque forza è lottare per la vita
chè già l'orso s'avanza! . . .
e me rafforza e incìta
la suprema speranza! . . .
Snudo il coltello . . .
m'avvinghio all'irto vello! . . .
Così
(*descrive col gesto e colle parole.*)
In un laccio
d'un lungo abbraccio! . . .
Colle zanne ei m'afferra
ed avido le affonda . . .
e già-il sangue m'inonda
e già quasi m'atterra . . .

**DONNE:** (*impaurite, rabbrividendo.*) O supremo momento! . . .

**UOMINI:** (*imponendo silenzio alle donne.*) E allor? . . .

**TUTTI:** E allora? . . .

**HAGENBACH:** (*rivolgendo le parole alla pelle sanguinosa.*) O bruno re, perchè alla selva oscura rivolgi il guardo quasi a un mesto addio? . . .
Perchè in un lungo ed ultimo desìo
la tua pupilla si scolora e oscura? . . .
(*con immenso orgoglio, trionfante.*)
Va per le valli un urlo di dolor! . . .
Rantola l'orso e ne' l'abisso muor! . . .
(*come prima.*)
Non è l'oro, no, che tenta
ai perigli il cacciator . . .
E la gloria che cimenta
gli ardimenti alti del cor! . . .

**TUTTI:** Evviva l'Hagenbach!
(*agitano i cappelli.*)

**STROMMINGER:** (*provocatore.*) Ma si direbbe che gli orsi son creati sol per voi! !

**HAGENBACH:** (*volgendosi.*) Che dir volete? . . .

**STROMMINGER:** Che v'è un uom che s'ebbe
molte di queste glorie e . . . men iattanza?

**HAGENBACH:** (*calmo.*) E chi è costui? . . .
(*un profondo silenzio si fa intorno ai due.*)

**STROMMINGER:** (*picchiando colla mano sul suo petto.*) Stromminger!
(*l'Hagenbach sorride, sorriso che finisce coll' esasperare completamente lo Stromminger che urla.*)
Sebben vecchio

**SOME:** And then?

**WOMEN:** O horrors!

**OTHERS:** (*interrupting him.*) On the path?

**ALL:** And then?

**HAGENBACH:** I stop! I watch!
The abyss to the left,
To the right, a torrent
And the white mountain!
I must, therefore, struggle for life,
For the bear is already advancing!
And supreme hope
Strengthens and goads me on!
I unsheath my knife.
I clutch the thick hair!
Thus
(*describes with gesture and words.*)
In the tangle of a long embrace!
He grasps me with his clutches
And eagerly sinks them into me
And already blood is covering me,
And he almost drags me down . . .

**WOMEN:** (*frightened, shuddering.*) O, supreme moment!

**MEN:** (*silencing the women.*) And then?

**ALL:** And then?

**HAGENBACH:** (*addressing his words to the bloody hide.*) You brown bear king, why do you turn your gaze To the dark woods as for a sad farewell?
Why does your eye grow colorless and dark
In one long and last desire?
(*with great pride, triumphantly.*)
Let a howl of pain
Resound through the valleys!
Let the bear die in the abyss,
With death's rattle in his throat!
No, it is not the gold which tempts
The hunter to all dangers,
glory puts
His boldness and his daring to test!

**ALL:** Long live Hagenbach!
(*They wave their hands.*)

**STROMMINGER:** (You inciter.) Really one would think That bears are made only for you!

**HAGENBACH:** (*turning around.*) What do you mean?

**STROMMINGER:** That there is a man who had many such glories and boasted less about them!

**HAGENBACH:** (*calmly.*) And who is he?
(*A deep silence grows around them.*)

**STROMMINGER:** (*striking his breast with his hand.*) Stromminger!
(*HAGENBACH shows a smile, which ends in completely exasperating STROMMINGER, who shouts:*)

alla lotta ed alla caccia
polsi e braccia ho forti ancor.
A voi dica la mia faccia
l'ardimento che ho nel cor! . . .
(*l'Hagenbach ride più forte; i Cacciatori lo imitano.—Lo Stromminger gli si avvicina e picchiandogli colla mano sulla spalla.*)
Ho un consiglio da darti . . .

HAGENBACH: E qual? . . .

STROMMINGER: Non ridere!
Potrei farti arrossir! . . . Se avesser labbra
le spalle di tuo padre potrian dirti
di Stromminger qualcosa . . .

HAGENBACH: (*impallidendo.*)
Ah! Voi mentite!

STROMMINGER: (*fuori di sè gli si avventa contro urlando.*) Che Dio mi danni! Niuno ha osato ancora dirmi così! . . .

HAGENBACH: (*afferra lo Stromminger e lo caccia violentemente sotto di sè a terra urlando alla sua volta.*)
Sarò io il primo!
(*quelli dell'Hochstoff con Gellner accorrono in difesa dello Stromminger: i Cacciatori di Sölden si frappongono in soccorso dell'Hagenbach gridando minacciosi.*)

CACCIATORI: Guai
a chi lo tocca! . . . Guia!

LE DONNE: (*impaurite.*) Ciel!
Che avverà?
(*Ad un tratto una strana creatura irrompe violentemente in mezzo a quella folla, urtando gli uni, ricacciando gli altri. È una bizzarra fanciulla, bizzarramente vestita; ha i lunghi capelli disordinati e sciolti e intrecciati di edelweiss; le braccia forti, completamente ignude; gli occhi larghi e profondi pieni di fuoco: è la WALLY! Vedere suo padre a terra presso all'Hagenbach, afferrare costui alle spalle e cacciarlo con forza lontano così da farlo barcollare, è un colpo solo.*)

WALLY: Chi osò levar sul padre mio la mano? . . .

HAGENBACH: (*furioso si volge; ma vedutosi di fronte una fanciulla, resta sorpreso dapprima, poi, quasi vergognoso balbetta.*)
Primo ei m'offese!
(*La Wally ha riconosciuto l'Hagenbach! Una profonda sensazione di dolcezza passa nei suoi sguardi; impallidisce e rimane immobile, muta, sorpresa, gli occhi suoi fissi nel volto di lui.*)

---

Though old
For struggle and for hunt,
I still have arms and pulses strong.
My face shows you
The boldness in my heart!
(*HAGENBACH laughs still louder, the hunters imitate him. STROMMINGER approaches him, and strikes him on the shoulder.*)
I have advice to give you . . .

HAGENBACH: What?

STROMMINGER: Not to laugh!
For I could make you blush!
If they could speak,
Your father's lips
Could tell you something about Stromminger!

HAGENBACH: (*growing pale.*)
Ah! You lie!

STROMMINGER: (*beside himself, rushes upon him shouting.*) May I be damned! No one yet dared to speak to me thus!

HAGENBACH: (*grasps STROMMINGER and with violence throws him down under him, shouting into his face.*)
I will be first!
(*The people of Hochstoff with GELLNER run up in defense of STROMMINGER. The hunters of Sölden put themselves between the combatants in defense of HAGENBACH, shouting threateningly.*)

HUNTERS: Woe!
Woe to him who touches him!
Woe!

WOMEN: (*frightened.*) Heavens!
What will happen?
(*Suddenly a strange creature breaks violently into the midst of the crowd, pushing some, driving back others. A queer girl, oddly dressed, with long hair in disorder, and open, and entwined in it, edelweiss; strong arms, perfectly bare; large eyes, deep and full of fire; she is WALLY. She sees her father on the ground near HAGENBACH, grasps the latter by the shoulder with such force that he reels—and all this with one blow.*)

WALLY: Who dared to raise his hand on my father?

HAGENBACH: (*enraged, turns around; but seeing a girl before him, is first surprised, then stammers abashed:*)
He offended me first!
(*WALLY recognizes HAGENBACH; a deep tenderness shines forth in her eyes; she grows pale and remains immovable, surprised, her eyes fixed on his face.*)

---

STROMMINGER: (*che si è intanto rialzato, furioso dice all'Hagenbach.*) Va via, accatta brighe!
(*e ai Cacciatori di Sölden.*)
Non c'è più vin per voi!

HAGENBACH: (*guardando bieco la Wally.*) Strana creatura!

CACCIATORI: (*all'Hagenbach.*)
Vientene via!

STROMMINGER:
(*all'Hagenbach.*) Tu? . . . Non temer! . . . T'aspetta ben più d'un orso!

HAGENBACH: (*allontanandosi trascinato via dai suoi.*) Maledetto vecchio
che m'hai costretto a un atto così vile! . . .

WALLY: (*con un gesto ferma l'Hagenbach che si volge sorpreso.—La voce della Wally non è più minacciosa, ma trema così che si direbbe un singhiozzo.*)
Non dir così! . . . Sei giovane . . .
La balda giovinezza
più a perdonar che all'odio
e al maledire è avvezza . . .

STROMMINGER: Che nenia è questa? . . . Taci, Wally! . . .
(*la spinge verso case.*)

CACCIATORI: (*trascinano via l'Hagenbach.*) Andiamo! . . .

UOMINI: È fuor di sè lo Stromminger!

DONNE: Torniamo!
Torniam! È sera!
(*e Uomini e Donne se ne vanno, chi da una parte, chi dell'altra.*)
(*La Wally immobile sulla porta di casa ha veduto allontanarsi l'Hagenbach seguendolo cogli occhi,—scomparso, è rapidamente entrata in casa.—Gellner solo è rimasto presso allo Stromminger.*)

STROMMINGER: (*come se rispondesse ad uno sguardo di Gellner.*)
L'Hagenbach? . . . L'abborro!

GELLNER: (*strisciandogli vicino.*) Che val l'odio del padre allor che i figli . . .

STROMMINGER: (*lo guarda, poi ripete.*) I figli? . . .

GELLNER: (*sorride ironico.*) Non vedeste? . . .

STROMMINGER: Non comprendo!

GELLNER: Che vostra figlia è innamorata pazza dell'Hagenbach! . . .

STROMMINGER: (*scosso, livido.*) Tu scherzi? . . .

GELLNER: O non l'udiste? Nella sua voce dianzi v'eran lacrime!

STROMMINGER: È ver! . . . Che così fosse or mi ricordo!

---

STROMMINGER: (*who rose in the meantime, ragingly says to Hagenbach.*) Get out, you quarrelsome man!
(*to the hunters of Sölden.*)
There is no more wine for you!

HAGENBACH: (*looks askance at WALLY.*) Strange creature!

HUNTERS: (*to Hagenbach.*)
Come away from here!

STROMMINGER: (*to Hagenbach.*) You? You needn't be afraid! Something much worse than a bear awaits you!

HAGENBACH: (*going away, dragged by his men.*) Accursed old man, who forced me to do such a vile thing!

WALLY: (*with a firm gesture, stops HAGENBACH who turns around surprised. Her voice is no longer threatening, it trembles as if she were sobbing:*) Don't say that! Young you are . . .
Daring youth is inclined
To pardon rather
Than to hate and curse.

STROMMINGER: What idle talk is this?
Quiet, Wally!

HUNTERS: (*dragging HAGENBACH away.*) Come on!

MEN: Stromminger is beside himself!

WOMEN: Let us go home, let us go home!
It's evening!
(*The men and women go away, some in one direction, some in another.—WALLY, immovable on the doorstep, watches HAGENBACH going away, following him with her eyes. Once out of sight, she quickly enters the house. GELLNER alone remains near STROMMINGER.*)

STROMMINGER: (*as if answering a look from GELLNER.*) Hagenbach? I hate him!

GELLNER: (*coming close up to him.*) What good if the father hates when the children . . .

STROMMINGER: (*looks at him then repeats*) The children?

GELLNER: (*smiles ironically.*)
Didn't you see?

STROMMINGER: I don't understand!

GELLNER: That your daughter is madly in love with Hagenbach!

STROMMINGER: (*shocked, pale.*)
Are you joking?

GELLNER: Didn't you hear her? There were tears in her voice when she spoke!

STROMMINGER: It is true! Now I recall that so it was.

GELLNER: (*con impeto.*) Il sol pensier che vostra figlia sposa esser possa di lui me'è tal martirio che maggiore non v'ha . . .

STROMMINGER: Tu mi fai ridere. Mia figlia? . . . Sposa a lui? . . . Prima ch'ei l'abbia! . . .
(*poscia a un tratto interrompendosi, colpito da nuova e subita idea, si avvicina a Gellner, le fissa in viso e gli dice.*)
Vedo! . . . Comprendo! . . . L'ami! . . .
(*e prima che Gellner abbia potuto dire una parola, il vecchio Stromminger grida verso la sua casa, chiamando.*)
Wally!
(*Wally appare sulla porta.*)
Wally! . . .
Vincenzo Gellner t'ama! . . . Sei sua sposa! . . .
E dentro il mese si faran le nozze.
(*e lentamente si allontana lasciandoli soli.*)

WALLY: (*calma a Gellner.*) Sei tu che domandata hai la mia mano?

GELLNER: (*cogli occhi a terra.*) Ei mi lesse nel cuore il mio desìo . . .

WALLY: (*avvicinandoglisi.*) Gellner ti prego . . .

GELLNER: (*immobile.*) Parla! . . .

WALLY: Tu sei buono e un amico ti credo . . .

GELLNER: Ebben? . . .

WALLY: Rinunzia a me!

GELLNER: Perchè?

WALLY: (*risoluta.*) Non t'amo!

GELLNER: (*con slancio.*) Ebben? . . . Che importa? T'amo ben io! . . . E sei dentro al mio cuore così che tutto tuo è il mio pensiero! . . .
(*quasi piangendo.*)
Mi avvolge come un'onda affannosa l'amore, o Wally! . . . È mor!
A me freme d'intorno una ebbrezza profonda! . . .
A questa voce ardente che ci chiama l'anima tua deh, schiudi, o Wally, ed ama! . . .
Ah, una lunga carezza . . . un'ebbrezza infinita . . . eterna giovinezza sarà la nostra vita!

WALLY: (*lo guardo negli occhi, fredda, altera, spiccando le parole.*) Non t'amerò giammai! . . . giammai, m'intendi? . . .

GELLNER: (*violently.*) The thought alone that your daughter May become his bride Is the greatest torture for me.

STROMMINGER: You make me laugh.
My daughter? His bride? Before he gets her . . .
(*suddenly, struck by a new idea, he approches GELLNER, stares into his eyes, and says:*)
I see it all! I understand! You love her!
(*Before GELLNER is able to say another word, old STROMMINGER cries in the direction of his house, calling.*)
Wally!
(*WALLY appears at the door.*)
Wally,
Vincenzo Gellner loves you! Be his bride!
And the wedding will take place in a month.
(*He slowly walks away, leaving them alone.*)

WALLY: (*calmly to GELLNER.*) Was it you who asked for my hand?

GELLNER: (*looking on the ground.*) He read my desire in my heart . . .

WALLY: (*approaching him.*) Gellner . . . I beg you . . .

GELLNER: (*immovable.*) Speak!

WALLY: You are good And a friend to me, I believe . . .

GELLNER: Well?

WALLY: Give me up!

GELLNER: Why?

WALLY: (*resolutely.*) I don't love you!

GELLNER: (*impetuously.*) Well then? What does it matter? I love you! And you are engraved in my heart That my only thought is of you!
(*almost weeping.*)
Love envelopes me With sadness, like a wave!
O Wally—it is love!
A deep intoxication comes over me!
Open your heart, O Wally, To this soul which fervidly calls you, and love!
Ah, a long caress, Everlasting rapture, Eternal youth Will be our life!

WALLY: (*looks him in the eyes, cold, haughty, sharply pronouncing her words:*) I will never love you; never, do you understand?

GELLNER: (*stendendo le braccia a lei con voce piena di singhiozzi.*) Ascolta, Wally . . . ascolta . . . ancor ti prego . . .

WALLY: Non t'amerò giammai! . . .

GELLNER: Ebben . . . ti voglio! Devi esser mia! . . .

WALLY: (*con accento selvaggio.*) Giammai! Giammai! . . . Son libera come la luce . . . e il vento . . .
Le tue minacce, o Gellner, non mi fanno spavento! . . .
Come la rupe d'Oetz è fermo il mio voler! . . .

STROMMINGER: (*rientra dal fondo e si avanza tranquillamente.*) Ebbene, o mie colombe? . . .

WALLY: (*risoluta.*) Udite, o padre! Non l'amo e non lo voglio!

STROMMINGER: Non lo vuoi? . . .

WALLY: Nol voglio!

STROMMINGER: Wally, bada!

WALLY: Non lo voglio! Sgozzarmi sull'altar più facil cosa a voi sarebbe! . . . Immutabil son io!
No! Non m'avrà giammai!

STROMMINGER: Wally! . . .

WALLY: Giammai!
(*passa fra questi tre personaggi un momento di silenzio, lungo profondo. Il vecchio Stromminger questa volta sa frenarsi. Rivolto alla figlia, le dice*)

STROMMINGER: Vedi? . . . Già cade il dì! Pria che rintocchi l'Avemaria ti accingi ad obbedir . . .
oppur . . . tu te ne andrai! . . . La casa mia si chiuderà per te! . . .
(*a Gellner.*)
Gellner, vien via! . . . — (*entrano in casa. — Suona l'Avemaria.*)

WALLY: (*rimane un po' pensierosa, poi si scuote, si guarda intorno.*) Ebbene? . . . Andrò! . . . Andrò sola e lontana come va l'eco della pia campana . . .
là, fra la neve bianca;! . . .
là fra le nubi d'or;! . . .
laddove appar la terra come una ricordanza! . . .
ove anche la speranza è un rimpianto o un dolor! . . .
O de la madre mia casa gioconda, la Wally se ne va lontana assai, e forse a te più non farà ritorno, nè più la rivedrai!
Ma fermo è il piè! . . . Già la campana pia suona . . . Partiam . . . che

GELLNER: (*extending his arms to her and in a sobbing voice.*) Listen, Wally, listen — I beg you again.—

WALLY: I will never love you!

GELLNER: Well . . . but I want you! You must be mine!

WALLY: (*widly.*) Never! Never! I am free, Free as light and wind . . .
All your threats, O Gellner, Do not frighten me!
My will is as firm As the rock of Oetz!

STROMMINGER: (*reenters from the rear, and comes nearer, calmly.*) Well, my doves?

WALLY: (*resolutely*) Listen, father!
I don't love him, and I don't want him!

STROMMINGER: You don't want him?

WALLY: No, I don't.

STROMMINGER: Take care, Wally!

WALLY: No, I don't want him! It would be much easier To kill me at the altar.
My will is unchangeable!
No, he will never have me!

STROMMINGER: Wally!

WALLY: Never!
(*A moment of silence, long and deep, between them. Old STROMMINGER knows how to control himself this time. He turns to his daughter and says:*)

STROMMINGER: Do you see? Night is coming on!
Before the Ave Maria tolls Make up your mind to obey!
Or else . . . you must go away!
My house will be closed to you!
(*to Gellner.*)
Gellner, come away!
(*They enter the house—the Ave Maria tolls.*)

WALLY: (*remains at first a little serious, then she starts up and looks around.*) Well then? I will go!
I'll go alone and far As the echo from the church-bell . . .
There, amid the white snow, There, amid the clouds of gold, There where earth appears As but a recollection There where even hope Is a sorrow and a regret!
O, Wally's going far away From her mother's joyous home, Maybe she'll never come back to you, You'll never see her again!
But firm is my step!

lunga è la mia via! . . .
(*Dal fondo intanto scendono, avviandosi alla chiesuola dell'Hochstoff, Pastori e Contadini, Vecchi e Vecchie. Con loro e WALTER.—Nell' attraversare il piazzale costoro si imbattono nella WALLY.*)

DONNE: (*sorprese.*) Ad ora così tarda e così sola,
Wally, ove vai? . . .

WALLY: Mio padre m'ha cacciata!

TUTTI: Tuo padre ti ha cacciata?! . . .

WALLY: Vuol ch'io sposi
Vincenzo Gellner.

UOMINI: Dove te ne andrai? . . .

WALLY: (*fieramente, colla fronte alta, e colla mano ferma, additando.*) Lassù! . . . Su l'erte vette andrò lontana,
ome va l'eco della pia campana.

DONNE: Resta con noi stanotte . . .

UOMINI: Partirai col sol domattina . . .

WALLY: Io vuò partire col sole domattina . . .
ne l'ardente agonia
rimpianta dalle squille
di questa Avemmaria . . .
Ho fretta d'arrivar laddove stende
la libertà ver me le braccia! . . . Addio! . . .

WALTER: Sola non partirai! . . . No! . . . Tuo compagno
sarò! . . . Farem la strada insieme!

WALLY: (*commossa.*) Insieme
Farem la strada! . . . E canteremo! . . . Addio!
(*Le campane suonano ancora l'Avemmaria! E la notte! La Wally e Walter s'allontanano pel sentiero. Pel piazzale Pastori e Contadini si inginocchiano a pregare!— La Wally e Walter scompaiono dietro le case dell'Hochstoff. Si sentono le loro voci intuonare la canzone dell'Edelweiss, perdersi a poco a poco pel silenzio della notte. Sui ponte, la lampada del Cristo è accesa e gitta una tremula luce rossastra intorno a sè.*)

*FINE DEL ATTO PRIMO.*

## ■ ATTO SECONDO

*Il Paesaggio: LA PIAZZA DI SÖLDEN.—Nel fondo la Chiesa alla quale si accede per un'ampia gradinata.— Da una parte all'altra traversalmente, corrono strisce di tela colorata che ricoprono la piazza in parte (la parte riservata alle danze pubbliche.)—L'osteria dell'Aquila è a*

---

The church-bell tolls
Let's start, for long is my way!
(*Meanwhile from the rear, going towards the little church of Hochstoff, descend Shepherds, peasants, old men and women. With them is WALTER. In crossing the square, they meet WALLY.*)

WOMEN: (*surprised.*) At so late an hour and alone,
Wally, where are you going?

WALLY: My father drove me out.

ALL: Your father drove you out?

WALLY: He wants me
To marry Vincenzo Gellner.

MEN: Where will you go?

WALLY: (*proudly, haughtily pointing with firm hand.*) Up there! I will go as far up the steep rocks,
As the echo from the church-bell.

WOMEN: Stay with us tonight.

MEN: You will leave in the early morning.

WALLY: I want to go
With the setting sun,
In the fervid agony,
Bewailed by the bells
Of this Ave Maria.
I hasten to reach the place
Where liberty extends
Her hand to me. Farewell!

WALTER: You will not go alone!
No!
I'll be your companion!
Together we'll depart!

WALLY: (*moved.*) Together we'll depart!
And we'll sing! Farewell!
(*The bells keep tolling the Ave Maria. It is night. WALLY and WALTER go away by the path. Shepherds and peasants kneel to pray on the square. WALLY and WALTER disappear behind the houses of Hochstoff. Their voices are heard singing the song of the Edelweiss, then get lost gradually in the silence of the night. On the bridge, the lamp over the crucifix is burning and throws a flickering rosy light around it.*)

*END OF FIRST ACT.*

## ■ ACT II

*THE SCENE: The square of Sölden. In the background a church, to which leads a wide stairway. From one side to the other, crosswise, run strips of colored cloth which partly cover the square. (The part reserved for public dances.) The Eagle Inn is at the right. The windows, doors, tables,*

---

destra.—Le finestre, la porta, le tavole, le panche, tutto vi è coperto ed ornato di rami frondosi e di fiori.—Anche dalle finestre e dai ballatoi pendono drappi a colori, fronde, ghirlande.—E tutto un paese vestito da festa!—È il Corpus Domini.

*La piazza è gremita di gente; chi va e chi viene; chi si dà al discorrere; chi saluta e passa; chi ride; chi si trattiene a crocchi.—Tutti i variopinti e pittoreschi costumi del Tirolo vivono e si muovono nella piccola piazza.*

*Ecco là, il PEDONE DI SCHNALS già seduto davanti ad una enorme tazza bi birra, in mezzo a un crocchio di giovanotti, che beve, ride, discute e qualche volta alla bell'AFRA tutta in faccende (la padrona dell'osteria dell'Aquila) mormora parole che eccitano la facile allegria dei suoi ascoltatori!—Là, in disparte, c'è anche GELLNER, anch'egli vestito a festa, ma triste, sinistro, taciturno. Come egli è cambiato in un anno! (poiché è passato già l'anno dalla sera che, all'Hochstoff, fu respinto dalla Wally e costei dal padre messsa alla porta.)*

ALCUNE FANCIULLE: (*attraversano la piazza c susurrano fra loro.*) Entro alla folla che intorno si aggira,
ne' dì di festa, è bello il passeggiar . . .
(*le loro parole si perdono.*)

ALTRE FANCIULLE: (*si succedono gaiamente ridendo.*) La v'è un garzon che per me sospira! . . .
(*alcune additando.*)
Là ve n'è un altro che mi stà a guardar! . . .
(*al passare delle fanciulle avanti alla tavola dove siede, beve, sogghigna e fuma il pedone di Schnals.*)

GIOVANNOTTI: (*che gli stanno intorno, osservano.*) Ah, inver s'io mi dovessi ora ammogliar,
di queste mogli, affè!, non ne vorrei
Son volubili troppo
nell'amar . . .
e una fraschetta in casa non torrei!

ALCUNE VECCHIE: (*attraversano la piazza e si avviano alla Chiesa, sogguardano brontolando le belle ragazze.*) Già le campane suonano—
—e le preghiere echeggiano . . .
Esse Dio non ascoltano—
—ma ridono e cinguettano . . .
e a nulla . . . a nulla pensano—

---

benches, everything is covered and decorated with leafy branches and with flowers. From the windows and the galleries hang colored banners, leaves, garlands. The whole town is in holiday array. It is the Corpus Domini.

*The square is crowded with people; a continual coming and going; they talk, they greet, and pass; they laugh, they stand chatting. All the many-colored and picturesque costumes of Tyrol move around the little square.*

*There is the SOLDIER of SCHNALS already seated before an enormous jug of beer, in the midst of a group of men who are drinking, laughing and occasionally busily whispering to the beautiful AFRA (the innkeeper of the Eagle) words which excite the jollity of the listeners. There, aside, is GELLNER; he also is in holiday attire, but sad, gloomy, silent. How he has changed in one year! (For a year has already gone by since that evening at Hochstoff when he was refused by WALLY and she was driven out of the house by her father.)*

SOME GIRLS: (*cross the square and whisper to one another.*) How fine it is to walk,
In the midst of the crowd
Which surges about
On a holiday!
(*Their words are lost in the crowd.*)

OTHER GIRLS: (*Come up laughing gaily.*) There is a youth who sighs for me!
(*Others pointing at him.*)
There is another who stands gazing at me.
(*In passing the table where sits, drinks, grins and smokes the SOLDIER of SCHNALS.*)

YOUNG MEN: (*who stand around and watch.*) Ah, really, if I had to get married,
Never one of those would I take, fie!
Too fickle are they in their love . . .
No frivolous woman for me!

SOME OLD WOMEN: (*cross the square, approach the church and muttering, look askance at the pretty girls.*) The bells are already ringing, and the prayers resound.
They don't heed God, but laugh and chatter,
They think of nothing at all, but of pleasure, frivolous girls,
And of clothes and deceivers who

—che al sol piacer, le frivole . . .
ed alle vesti e ai bindoli—
—che intorno a lor svolazzano!

**ALCUNI BORGHESI:** (*sorridendo malignamente.*) O nonne venerate—perchè con tanta furia alla chiese ne andate?
Tanti anni son passati—che le colpe e i peccati di vostra gioventù
perfin lo istesso Iddio—già non ricorda più! . . .

**LE FANCIULLE:** (*frettolose si avviano alla Chiesa.*) Ecco suona la squilla mattutina!
E il dì di festa;
e i bei garzoni veston gai corsetti
e portano berretti—piumati sulla testa!

**IL PEDONE DI SCHNALS:** (*rivolgendosi ai vicini.*) Or, per la via,
me ne ho incontrate assai brigate allegre e giovinette belle! . . .

**GIOVINOTTI:** (*che l'attorniano si levano da sedere.*) Giorne è per noi di festa e d'allegria,
ed è nostro piacere, in compagnia,
ber del buon vin, . . . le belle corteggiar . . .
cantar . . . danzar . . . e amar!

**IL PEDONE:** (*a un tratto si leva, guarda per la piazza e addita Walter che tutto in fronzoli se ne viene occhieggiando, curioso e un po' spavaldo, le donne*) Vedetelo venire il piccol Walter
Tutto vestito a festa.

**VECCHIE E FANCIULLE:** (*scontrandosi con Walter mentre si avviano alla Chiesa.*) Oh! . . . Il bel corsetto . . . !

**I GIOVANOTTI:** (*beffardi.*) Il piccol seduttore! . . .

**IL PEDONE:** (*ironico a Walter.*) O che già fate
l'occhietto moribondo a maritate? . . .

**WALTER:** (*stizzito, al Pedone.*) Ognun fa quel che più gli piace! . . . A voi
il ber? . . . E a me le belle donne e amar! . . .

**IL PEDONE:** Or or la tua padrona io m'ho incontrata
che a Sölden se ne vien . . .

**WALTER:** (*Punto.*) Non ho padrone! . . .

**IL PEDONE:** (*sogghignando.*) Eh, via! . . . Colei, vuò dir, che così ricche
vesti ti diè! . . .

**WALTER:** (*furente.*) La Wally è sol mia amica!
(*e si allontana.*)
*Intanto HAGENBACH si è seduto ad una tavola avanti all'osteria dell' Aquila. AFRA accorre sorri-*

---

flutter about them!

**SOME CITIZENS:** (*smiling malignantly.*) O you old women, why do you go
So zealously to church?
So many years have passed,
That the sins and faults of your youth
Have been forgotten even by God himself!

**THE GIRLS:** (*hurriedly approach the church.*) Hear, the morning bell is ringing!
It is a holiday;
Handsome youths put on their corsets,
And wear feathered caps!

**THE SOLDIERS OF SCHNALS:** (*turning to those near him.*) Along the road, I met so many
Beautiful, jolly girls!

**YOUNG MEN:** (*who surround him, get up.*) It is a day for mirth and laughter,
And oh, how fine it is to drink Good wine in company,
To woo the pretty girls,
To sing, dance and to love!

**THE SOLDIER:** (*gets up suddenly, looks across the square, and points to WALTER, who, covered with trinkets, goes around curiously and rather boldly eyeing the women around him.*) Looks, here comes little Walter
In holiday attire!

**OLD WOMEN AND GIRLS:** (*meeting WALTER on their way to church.*) Oh! What a beautiful corset!

**YOUNG MEN:** (*mocking.*) The little seducer!

**SOLIDER:** (*ironically, to WALTER.*) Are you making eyes at married women already?

**WALTER:** (*irritated, to the soldier.*) Everyone does as he likes!
You like beer?
And I like beautiful women and love!

**SOLDIER:** I just met your mistress coming to Sölden.

**WALTER:** (*hurt.*) I have no mistress!

**SOLDIER:** (*grinning.*) Ah, come now! I mean the one
Who gave you such rich clothes.

**WALTER:** (*furiously.*) Wally is only my friend!
(*He goes away.*)
(*Meanwhile HAGENBACH sits down at the table in front of the Eagle. AFRA runs up to him, smil-*

---

dente, felice . . . Tutti si fanno intorno all'Hagenbach; chi gli stringe la mano, chi lo saluta, chi beve con lui.

**GIOVINOTTI:** (*continuando il discorso col Pedone. —Hagenbach parla con Afra.*) E avrem la Wally?

**IL PEDONE:** Si; ora che il davolo ha via portato seco il vecchio Stromminger
essa corre le feste e si diverte!

**GELLNER:** (*lanciando un'occhiata sinistra all'Hagenbach.*) (La sciagurata! . . . qui ne vien per lui! . . .)
(*gli sfugge un gesto di minaccia, poi a un tratto si leva e si perde nella folla.*)

**IL PEDONE:** (*continua, aizzando i Giovanotti.*) Avanti, giovanotti! . . . È un bel partito? . . .
La mano della Wally è una cuccagna!

**HAGENBACH:** (*con disprezzo.*) No! . . . Una moglie così non la vorrei! . . .
Colei non per l'amor . . . per l'odio è fatta! . . .

**ALCUNI GIOVANOTTI:** (*scimiotteggiando Hagenbach.*) No! Una moglie così non la vorrei! . . .

**IL PEDONE:** (*malizioso, rimbeccandoli.*) L'udii dire e ridir che nessun uomo un bacio sapria torle . . .

**GIOVANOTTI:** L'orgogliosa! . . .

**HAGENBACH:** (*con fatuità.*) Vuò rivederla e . . . vuò con lei danzar!
(*intanto le Vecchie e le Fanciulle sono entrate in Chiesa. Gli Uomini, tornati a sedersi alle tavole dell' osteria bevono e giuocano.*)

**AFRA:** (*facendosi vicina all'Hagenbach con voce carezzevole.*) No! . . . Coll'amore tu non dèi scherzar . . .
Invan resiste a un suo volere il curo! . . .
Il pianto a ogni pupilla sa strappar . . .
No, tu non dèi scherzare coll'amor!

**HAGENBACH:** (*crollando sprezzante le spalle.*) Ah! Ridere mi fate! . . . Io tremar?
E troppo fermo entro il mio petto il cuor!
Colle orgogliose piacemi scherzar ma il cuore ho chiuso a le malìe d'amor!

**WALTER:** (*che è ritornato, udendo parlare della Wally, esclama in atto di sfida.*) Nessun sparà la Wally far piegar
nè al labbro un bacio sol torle d'amor!

---

ing, happy. All surround HAGENBACH; some shake hands with him, others greet him, still others drink with him.)

**YOUNG MEN:** (*continuing their talk with the soldier —HAGENBACH speaks to AFRA.*) And shall we have Wally?

**SOLDIER:** Yes, now that the devil Has taken old Stromminger with him,
She revels and enjoys herself.

**GELLNER:** (*casting a suspicious look at HAGENBACH.*) The wicked one! She is coming here for him!
(*A gesture of threat escapes him, then he suddenly gets up and is lost in the crowd.*)

**SOLDIER:** (*continues, spurring the youths on.*) Come now, is it a good bargain?
Wally's hand is eternal bliss!

**HAGENBACH:** (*with disgust.*) No! I would not want such a woman! She is not made for love—she's made for hatred!

**SOME YOUNG MEN:** (*imitating HAGENBACH.*) No! I would not want such a woman!

**SOLDIER:** (*maliciously, pushing them away.*) I heard it said again and again
That no man can wrest a kiss from her!

**YOUNG MEN:** Proud woman!

**HAGENBACH:** (*fatuitously.*) I would like to see her again,
To dance with her!
(*Meanwhile the old women and girls enter the church. The men, seating themselves again at the tables, drink and play.*)

**AFRA:** (*coming close to HAGENBACH, caressingly.*) No, you must not jest with love . . .
In vain you resist its commands!
It can draw tears from any eyes,
No, you must not jest with love!

**HAGENBACH:** (*shrugging his shoulders disdainfully.*) Ah, you make me laugh! I tremble?
My heart is too firm in my breast!
I like to jest with haughty women,
But my heart is closed
To the wiles of love!

**WALTER:** (*who has returned, hearing WALLY's name mentioned, exclaims, as if challenging.*) No one will be able to make Wally yield!
Nor to wrest from her a kiss of love!

Essa ha vaghezza solo di celiar,
ma a le malìe d'amor chiuso ha il suo cuor!

IL PEDONE: (*facendo della filosofia:*) Ai giovanotti place lo scherzar! ...
Badate, ohimè!, che assai scaltro è l'amor!
Se alle donne la testa fa girar,
l'uomo che inebria impazza di furor!
(*Frattanto, dalle tavole ove ferve il giuoco, scoppiano lunghe e tumultuose risate, troncate bruscamente dalla esclamazione di:*)

WALTER: Eccola qua!
(*infatti è la Wally! A questo grido di sorpresa ne segue un altro di ammirazione.*)

I GIOVANOTTI: (*mormorano.*) La bella creatura! ...

AFRA: (*all'Hagenbach che studiatamente non si volge a guardare.*) E che arie da regina! ... E che bel vezzo di perle intorno al collo!

WALTER: (*muovendole incontro.*) Alfin, sei giunta!
(*La WALLY è superbamente bella e superbamente vestita di una ricca veste di velluto, ed ha uno splendido vezzo di perle al collo. Alcune amiche l'accompagnano.*)

WALLY: (*a Walter.*) Sei tu, mio Walter?

ALCUNI GIOVANOTTI: (*alla Wally.*) Benvenuta, Wally, se per danzar tu vieni ...

WALLY: (*interrompendoli.*) Perchè no?
(*ad un suo cenno, Afra si toglie dallo Hagenbach e rientra portando una tazza alla Wally poi ritorna presso a Guiseppe.—La Wally la segue coll'occhio, si avvede della presenza dell'Hagenbach e depone senza bere la tazza.*)

ALCUNI GIOVANOTTI: (*corteggiando la Wally.*) Dì! ... Danzerai con me?

ALTRI: Poi con me pure?

WALLY: Io danzerò con chi vorrà il capriccio ...
pel piacer di danzar!

IL PEDONE: (*intervenendo.*) Anche la danza del bacio?

WALLY: (*provocante.*) So che le fanciulle vostre nascondono la voglia che han di baci e ne l'uso di tal danza! ... Io, no!
E poi ...

IL PEDONE: E poi? ...

WALLY: Non facil cosa saria forse strapparmi un solo bacio! ...

IL PEDONE: (*insistente.*) E se ciò fosse? ...

---

She only likes to jest,
But her heart is closed
To the wiles of love!

SOLIDER: (*philosophizing.*) Youths like to jest
Alas, take care!
For love is very cunning!
If he makes women's heads reel,
The man who intoxicates them Goes mad!
(*In the meanwhile, from the tables where the game is going on, loud and tumultuous laughter bursts forth, suddenly broken by shouts of:*)

WALTER: Here she is!
(*Indeed it is WALLY! This cry of surprise is followed by another of admiration.*)

YOUNG MEN: (*whispering.*) What a beautiful creature!

AFRA: (*To HAGENBACH, who purposely avoids turning around to look.*) And what queenly ways! And what a necklace of pearls Around her throat!

WALTER: (*going toward her.*) You came at last!
(*WALLY is wonderfully beautiful and magnificently dressed in a rich, velvet gown, and a fine pearl necklace around her throat. Some friends accompany her.*)

WALLY: (*to Walter.*) You are here, my Walter?

SOME YOUNG MEN: (*to Wally.*) Welcome, Wally, If you come to dance ...

WALLY: (*interrupting.*) Why not?
(*At a sign from him, AFRA tears herself away from HAGENBACH, and reenters, carrying a jug to WALLY; then comes back near GIUSEPPE. WALLY follows her with her eyes, notices HAGENBACH'S presence, and puts the cup down without drinking.*)

SOME YOUNG MEN: (*courting Wally.*) Say, will you dance with me?

OTHERS: Then with me, rather?

WALLY: I will dance with whoever will take it into his head, Just for the sake of dancing!

SOLDIER: (*interrupting.*) Even the kiss-dance?

WALLY: (*exciting them.*) I know that your girls
Conceal their desire for kisses, According to the custom of this dance ...
Not I! and then ...

SOLDIER: And then?

WALLY: Yet it would not be an easy matter
To wrest a single kiss from me!

SOLDIER: (*insisting.*) And if this were so?

---

WALLY: Finor non m'han baciata che i rai del sole, il vento,
la rugiada imperlata,
le stelle in firmamento;
m'ebbi il bacio del fiore; ...
m'ebbi il bacio del prato; ...
della neve il candore
il bacio suo m'ha dato;
mi dier baci coll'ali
gli augelli del Signor ...
Solo baci immortali
la Wally ebbe finor ...
(*e la fanciulla accesa nel volto e negli occhi, rimane come assorta; poi, a un tratto, la sua fronte candida si abbuia. Il suo sguardo corre ad Afra e a Giuseppe! Parlano ... non si curano di lei. Un lampo vibra nella sua pupilla, ed è quasi in atto di sfida che ai Giovanotti lancia queste parole così piene di disprezo.*)
così prezioso don qual uomo mai potria rubarsi?

IL PEDONE: E se alcun lo potesse?

WALLY: Quell'uom? ... Sarebbe mio!
(*prende il braccio di Walter e si allontana.*)
(*Passando vicino all'Hagenbach, lo guarda prima con civetteria, poi con uno squardo profondo così che egli ne è scosso.*)

IL PEDONE: Su giovanotti! Coraggio dunque! il bacio de la Wally val la cuccagna!
(*dalle porte aperte della Chiesa si ode la lenta armonia dell'organo.*)

ALCUNI: (*avviandosi.*) È l'ora della Messa!

ALTRI: (*avviandosi.*) In chiesa andiam.

ALTRI: Andiam ... poscia alla danza ci rivedremo!
(*entrano in chiesa.*)
(*Afra e l'Hagenbach si salutano.—Afra rientra nell'osteria.*)

HAGENBACH: (*incamminandosi alla chiesa.*) Ancora quel suo sguardo! ...
(*entra in Chiesa.—Walter e la Wally che si è attardata colle sue amiche per acconciarsi il velo, stanno pure per entrarvi, quando da una viuzza di destra sbuca fuori Gellner il quale impedisce loro il passo. Wally si ferma, fa segno a Walter di voler rimaner sola, e freddamente rivolgendosi a Gellner*)

WALLY: Sei tu?! ...

GELLNER: Son io ...

WALLY: Da che son la padrona tu sol, dei miei, non sei venuto a me.

GELLNER: Io non l'osai.

---

WALLY: Till now, no one has kissed me
But the sun's rays and the wind,
The pearly dew,
The stars in heaven;
I had the flower's kiss;
I had the meadow's kiss;
The whiteness of the snow,
Gave me its kiss;
The birds of the Lord
Kissed me with their wings,
Only immortal kisses
Had Wally, until now!
(*She stands as if absorbed in thought; then suddenly her snow-white face clouds. Her glance runs to AFRA, then to GIUSEPPE! They speak. They pay no attention to her. A flash gleams in her eyes, and it is almost with disdain that she hurls these words, full of disgust, at the young men.*)
What man could ever deprive himself of so precious a gift?

SOLDIER: And if someone could?

WALLY: That man ... he would be mine!
(*She takes WALTER by the arm and goes away. Passing near HAGENBACH, she first looks at him coquettishly, then with so piercing a glance that he is disturbed by it.*)

SOLDIER: Come, boys!
Have courage! Wally's kiss
Is as good as eternal bliss!
(*From the open churchdoor is heard slow organ music.*)

SOME: (*approaching.*) It is time for Mass!

OTHERS: (*approaching.*) Let us enter the church!

OTHERS: Come on, we may see each other again at the dance!
(*They enter the church.*)
(*AFRA and HAGENBACH bid each other goodbye. AFRA enters the inn.*)

HAGENBACH: (*walking to the church.*) Again that look of hers!
(*He enters the church. WALTER and WALLY, who stopped awhile with her friends to fix her veil, are ready to enter, when GELLNER comes out from an alley on the right, and hinders their passage. WALLY stops, motions to WALTER that she wants to remain alone, and turns coldly to GELLNER.*)

WALLY: Is it you?

GELLNER: It's I.

WALLY: Since I am my own mistress
You alone of all my friends, did not come to me.

GELLNER: I did not dare.

WALLY: Non t'ho dimenticato!
Un dì tu fosti sordo a' preghi miei
ed a' miei pianti . . . Io fui per te
cacciata . . .
Orben, oggi io te caccio!
Però . . . ingrata
esser non vuò . . .
(*gli stende una borsa di denaro.*)
Prendi! . . . È danaro! . . . E
vanne!

GELLNER: Nulla voglio da
te . . .
(*con un gesto allontana la borsa
che la Wally gli porge, e poi risoluto*)
Io t'amo ancora
e più di prima ti amo! . . .
Deh! . . . mi guarda
come io per te mi struggo in desiderii.

WALLY: (*torturandolo femminil-
mente.*) Cantava un dì mia nonna
questa canzone strana:
"Fatto è il mondo così:
"Non v'ha più fiera voluttà in
amore
"che odiare l'uomo che vi ha dato il
cuore.
"Piangi, garzone? . . . E tu bel
Cavaliero,
"perchè sì triste e cupo è il tuo pensiero? . . .
"Nerina si rifiuta a la tua brama? . . .
"Ti deride, se soffri, la tua
Dama?
"Fatto il mondo è così:
"Amore al riso sempre il pianto
unì!
(*ride, provocandolo.*)

GELLNER: (*cogli occhi pieni di lacrime e colla voce piena di preghiere.*) Non ridere! . . .

WALLY: Oggi sono allegra assai! . . .

GELLNER: No .. non lo dir! . . .
(*fissandola in viso.*)

WALLY: (*tornando seria e turbata.*) Che ne sai tu? . . .

GELLNER: Rispondi . . . perchè,
così selvaggia un dì ti adorni
ora di perle e per fiere corri! . . .
Dietro all' amor tu corri . . .

WALLY: (*interrompendolo impetuosa*) Non è vero!

GELLNER: (*implacabile, inves-
tendola.*) Menti!! . . . Il tuo cor
per me non ha secreti . . .
(*le si avvicina, ed abbassando la
voce sussurra*)
Sai tu perchè ti ottenni da tuo padre? . . .
Perchè gli dissi che Giuseppe amavi! . . .

WALLY: (*con impeto selvaggio e
feroce, come una imprecazione.*)
Ed è per me un'ebbrezza il tormen-
tarti! . . .

WALLY: I did not forget you!
One day you were deaf to my
prayers
And to my tears. I was driven away
by you.
Well and good, today I drive you
away!
However, I don't want to be ungrateful . . .
(*stretches out a purse with money
to him*)
Take it, it's money . . . and go!

GELLNER: I want nothing from
you . . .
(*pushes away the purse Wally offers him, and then, resolutely*)
I still love you,
And love you more than ever!
See how I waste away in longing for
you!

WALLY: (*torturing him in a
womanly fashion*) My grandmoth-
er once sang to me
This strange melody:
"Thus goes it in this world:
There is no fiercer pleasure in love
Than to hate the man
Who gave you his heart.
Do you weep, my lad?
And you, fine Cavalier,
Why so sad and deep your
thoughts?
Does Nerina refuse your passion,
When you suffer,
Does she mock at you?
Thus goes it in this world.
Love always unites
Laughter with tears!"
(*laughs, irritating him.*)

GELLNER: (*with tearful eyes, and
entreating voice.*) Don't laugh!

WALLY: I am very gay today.

GELLNER: No—don't say that! . . .
(*staring into her face.*)

WALLY: (*growing serious and
disturbed.*) What do you know
about it?

GELLNER: Answer me . . .
Why, formerly you were so wild,
Now you adorn yourself with pearls
And run to all the fairs!
You are running after love!

WALLY: (*impetuously, interrupting him.*) It is not true!

GELLNER: (*implacable, striking
her.*) You lie! Your heart has no secrets for me . . .
(*approaches her, and lowering
his voice, whispers.*)
Do you know why you broke away
from your father?
Because I told him that you loved
Giuseppe!

WALLY: (*savagely and fiercely,
with an imprecation.*) And it is a
delight for me to torture you!

GELLNER: Mi fai pietà . . .
(*la sua voce è grave eppur dolce.*)
Se tu, Wally, sapessi
dimenticare! . . . Ah . . . vivere felici! . . .
(*interrompe il discorso, e con immenso slancio:*)
Schiavo dei tuoi begli occhi
ai piedi ti starei
e, pregando a ginocchi,
come si prega Iddio, ti adorerei! . . .
(*si inginocchia baciandole la
veste, poscia, con immenso tran-
sporto.*)
. . . e una lunga carezza . . .
una ebbrezza infinita . . .
eterna giovinezza
sarà la nostra vita! . . .

WALLY: (*cupa.*) Suvvia . . . Ti
leva! . . . A che pregar? . . . Non
t'amo.
(*dopo un momento di silenzio e
di riflessione.*)
È ver! . . . Giuseppe . . . io
l'amo.

GELLNER: (*levandosi con impeto; fuori di sè.*) Maledetta!
Ma non l'avrai chè già vicino è il
giorno
de le sue nozze! . . .
(*ride quasi in uno spasimo di ferocia*)

WALLY: (*crollando le spalle.*) Ah,
no! Gellner, tu menti . . .
Per torturarmi menti . . .

GELLNER: Alla bella Afra
chiedilo dunque.
(*Wally, colpita, impallidisce, le
forze a un tratto le mancano e si
appoggia barcollando ad una tavola.*)

GELLNER: Ed or? . . . Perchè
non ridi? . . .

WALLY: (*angosciata ripensando.*) Eran poc'anzi là! . . . Stretti
a colloquio
sorridean fra loro, e le lor teste
si toccavan così che (Vergin santa!)
si saria detto che scambiasser
baci!
(*un singhiozzo le strozza la
voce.*)

GELLNER: Cantava un dì mia non-
na
questa canzone strana . . .
"Fatto è il mondo così . . .
"Nerina si rifiuta a la tua brama?
"Ti deride, se soffri, la tua Dama?
"Fatto il mondo è così:
"Amore al riso sempre il pianto
unì!

WALLY: (*minacciando.*) Ma ancor sua moglie Afra non è . . .
Ed io l'amo!
L'amo! . . . e nessun può leger
nel destino.
(*È fuori di sè: acciecata, pazza,
batte sulla tavola dove sta ancora
la tazza che Afra le aveva portata.—Afra accorre.—La Wally è*

GELLNER: Have pity on me!
(*His voice is serious, yet gentle.*)
Wally, if you were able to forget—
Ah—we would live happily!
(*interrupts the conversation, and
with great force.*)
Slave of your beautiful eyes,
I shall be at your feet
And, praying on my knees,
As one prays to God,
I will worship you!
(*kneels down, kissing her gar-
ments. Then, with ecstasy.*)
. . . and a long embrace . . .
An infinite rapture,
Eternal youth will be our life!

WALLY: (*thoughtfully.*) Up, up!
get up! Why to pray?
I don't love you!
(*after a moment's silence and reflection.*)
It is true! . . . I love Giuseppe!

GELLNER: (*getting up, beside
himself.*) Accursed woman!
But you won't have him,
For his wedding day is very soon!
(*laughs as in a spasm of
madness.*)

WALLY: (*shrugging her shoulders.*) Ah, no! Gellner, you
lie . . .
You lie to torture me!

GELLNER: Then ask pretty Afra.
(*Wally, struck, grows pale, her
strength fails her suddenly, and
she leans, tottering, on a table.*)

GELLNER: And now? . . . Why
don't you laugh?

WALLY: (*in anguish, thinking.*)
They were here a short while ago,
Talking and smiling, one near the
other,
And their heads touched so closely
(Holy Virgin)
As if they exchanged kisses!
(*a sob chokes her voice.*)

GELLNER: My grandmother once
sang to me,
This strange melody:
"Thus goes it in this world:
Does Nerina refuse your passion?
When you suffer
Does she mock you?
Thus goes it in this world:
Love always unites
Laughter with tears!"

WALLY: (*threatening.*) But Afra is
not yet his wife . . .
And I love him, I love him!
And no one can read into fate.
(*She is beside herself; blinded,
mad, she strikes the table where
stands the jug AFRA brought her.
AFRA runs up, WALLY is so upset
that she does not notice the people*

così agitata che non si avvede che già dalla Chiesa esce la gente e che la piazza ritorna piena di voci e di moto.)

AFRA: Che brami Wally?

WALLY: (afferrando la tazza la getta violentemente contro terra così da imbrattarle la veste e grida.)
Invero che tal broda solo i tuoi ganzi posson tranguiare!

AFRA: Ahimè! (prorompe in lagrime)

TUTTI: (frapponendosi.) Che avvenne, Wally? . . . Parla! . . .

WALLY: (tornata calma e sorridente.) Nulla! . . .
(ad Afra.)
Ed ora perchè piangi? . . . Non temere!
(ai Giovanotti che si sono intromessi fra lei ed Afra.)
Come si asciughin gli occhi a le fantesche io so!
(e avvicinandosi ad Afra con finta dolcezza, leva dalla borsa una moneta e la lascia cadere ai suoi piedi, dicendole)
Toh! . . . Ridi! . . .
(Uno si avanza lentamente, si avvicina ad Afra, si abbassa e raccoglie la moneta d'oro. È Hagenbach.)

HAGENBACH: (gettando la moneta ad alcuni Suonatori girovaghi) E la ricca padrona de l'Hochstoff che vi paga . . . Orsù! . . .
un landler de' più gai! . . .

TUTTI: Evviva l'Hagenbach! . . .

WALLY: (Povera me! . . . Vincenzo ha detto il vero!)
(ma, calma, altiera, sorridente in viso, essa si avvicina a un crocchio dove sta Walter.)

HAGENBACH: (ad Afra consolandola.) Non piangere, Afra . . . Ti vendicherò!

ALCUNI GIOVANOTTI: (all'Hagenbach.) Vieni a danzare!

HAGENBACH: Si! . . . Danziam . . . Ma prima facciamo una scommessa . . .

GIOVINOTTI: Qual? . . . Sentiamo!

HAGENBACH: Dieci fiorini d'oro che alla Wally un bacio strapperò! . . .

I GIOVANOTTI: (ridendo.) Scommessa strana!

HAGENBACH: Ebben?

GIOVANOTTI: Sia pur! . . . Teniamo!
La piazza, in un batter d'occhi, si è mutata quasi in una immensa sala da ballo. Le tavole riunite servono da palco pei suonatori. Sulle

coming out from the church and that the square is again echoing with voices and motion.)

AFRA: What do you wish, Wally?

WALLY: (grasping the jug, hurls it violently on the ground, so that she soils her clothes and cries.)
Really, only your lovers could swallow down such stuff!

AFRA: Ah!
(bursts into tears.)

ALL: (coming in between them.) What happened, Wally? Speak!!

WALLY: (turns around calm and smiling.) Nothing!
(to AFRA.)
And now, why are you crying? . . . Don't fear!
(to the young men who come between her and AFRA.)
I know how they dry servants' tears!
(and coming up to AFRA, with feigned tenderness, she takes a coin from her purse and lets it fall at her feet, saying.)
Come now! Laugh!
(One comes up slowly, approaches AFRA, bends down and picks up the gold coin. It is HAGENBACH.)

HAGENBACH: (throwing the coin to some roving musicians.) It is the rich mistress Of Hochstoff who pays you. Come on! Come on! Play One of the gayest "landlers."

ALL: Long live Hagenbach!

WALLY: (Poor me! Vincenzo said the truth!)
(but calm, haughty, smiling, she approaches a group among which is WALTER.)

HAGENBACH: (consoling AFRA.) Don't cry, Afra. I will console you!

SOME YOUNG MEN: (to Hagenbach.) Come to dance.

HAGENBACH: Yes, let's dance, but first let us make a bet . . .

YOUNG MEN: What bet? Let us hear!

HAGENBACH: Ten gold florins that I'll Snatch a kiss from Wally!

YOUNG MEN: (laughing.) A strange bet!

HAGENBACH: Well?

YOUNG MEN: All right then! We take it up.
(In the twinkling of an eye, the square is changed into a large ballroom. The tables, put together, serve as a platform for the mu-

panche, disposte a collana, seggono i vecchi, le vecchie e i borghesi. Le fanciulle prendono il braccio del Giovanotto che le invita . . . L'Hagenbach, levatosi il cappello, ne toglie la penna d'aquila e ve la rimette, ma al rovescio, il che significa nei costumi di Sölden che qualunque giuramento, qualunque promessa, qualunque parola, se la penna è al rovescio non ha valore. Nessuno se n'è accorto, eccettuato Gellner che, confuso nella folla, presso al palco dei suonatori, non ha mai staccato lo sguardo dall'Hagenbach.

GELLNER: (vedendo infatti l'Hagenbach attraversare la piazza alla volta della Wally, si avvicina a lei rapidamente, sussurrandole all'orecchio) Bada Wally!

HAGENBACH: (avvicinandosi grazioso alla Wally.) Danzar con te da tempo desiavo . . .

WALLY: (lusingata.) Se il vero dici! . . .

HAGENBACH: (come se giurasse.) E il ver! . . .

WALLY: (guardandolo dubbiosa.) Pure . . . i tuoi occhi mi guardano con foschi e strani sguardi! . . .
(altro gesto di giuramento da parte dell'Hagenbach.)
(La Wally soggiunge con tristezza)
L'ingannarmi crudel saria . . .

HAGENBACH: (trascina dolcemente con sè la Wally) Danziamo! . . .
(comincia il landler. Anche il Pedone e Walter danzano. — Al momento di lanciarsi, l'Hagenbach si ferma; la Wally sorpresa lo guarda.)

HAGENBACH: M'odi, Wally! . . .

WALLY: Che brami ancora?

HAGENBACH: Bramo con te danzare le danza del Bacio! . . .

WALLY: Quale capriccio! . . .

HAGENBACH: Agil tu sei e forte . . .
Bramo con te lottare . . . ed esser vinto.

WALLY: Quale capriccio! . . . Qui! . . .

HAGENBACH: Hai tu paura?
(sorridendo la trascina con sè danzando.)

I CANTI DEL LANDLER: Già il canto fervido — vola per l'aere; come di rondine — leggiero ha il vol, e i trilli modula — dell'usignol . . .
Agili, rapide — le corde fremono . . . cercano il cuor;
i fiori olezzano — fremon ne l'aure

sicians. On the benches, arranged in a circle, sit the old men, the old women, and citizens. Each girl takes the arm of the young man who invites her. HAGENBACH, taking off his hat, takes out of it an eagle feather and puts in on again, but on the wrong side, which means, according to the customs of Sölden that some oath, some promise, some word, if the feather is on the wrong side, is of no account. No one notices it except GELLNER, who, lost in the crowd near the musicians' platform, has not taken his gaze off HAGENBACH.)

GELLNER: (Seeing HAGENBACH cross the square towards WALLY, approaches her quickly, whispering in her ear.) Take care, Wally!

HAGENBACH: (Gracefully coming up to WALLY.) I have long been wanting to dance with you.

WALLY: (flattered.) If you speak the truth!

HAGENBACH: (as if swearing.) It is the truth!

WALLY: (looking dubiously at him.) Yet you look at me with such a dark and strange gaze!
(another gesture of swearing on the part of HAGENBACH.)
(WALLY adds sadly.)
It would be cruel to deceive me . . .

HAGENBACH: (drags WALLY gently along with him)
Let us dance!
(The ländler begins. The soldier and WALTER dance too. When it is time to turn, Hagenbach stops; Wally looks at him surprised.)

HAGENBACH: You hate me, Wally!

WALLY: What else do you want?

HAGENBACH: I am eager to dance The dance of the kiss with you!

WALLY: What a whim!

HAGENBACH: You are quick and strong . . .
I am anxious to wrestle with you and be conquered.

WALLY: What a whim! Here!

HAGENBACH: Are you afraid?
(smiling, he drags her along with him.)

THE SONGS OF THE LANDLER:
Already the fervid song is flying through the air,
Light as the swallows is its flight,
And the melodious trills of the nightingale.
Nimble, quick, the cords vibrate . . . they seek the heart;
The flowers are fra-

inni d'amor.

(*La lotta del bacio ferve ancora accanita nel fondo. Ad un bacio colto, risa, applausi.—Risate lunghe accolgono la vittoria di Walter.—Ogni bacio dato è una coppia di danzatori che scema. Ormai pochissimi continuano. Ma l'attenzione del Pedone e dei Giovanotti che hanno udita la scommessa è per l'Hagenbach e la Wally, attenzione stuzzicata dai due pel loro contegno. Si direbbe che danzino senza accorgersene e spesso cessano di danzare per parlarsi, quasichè l'armonia che li conduce non sia già quella degli istrumenti, ma quella che esce dalle loro labbra.*)

HAGENBACH: (*ad un tratto eccitato da alcune della Wally, cessa di danzare e turbato le dice.*) No! . . . Parla! . . . Parla! . . . Vuò saper! . . . Dicevi . . .

WALLY: (*continuando il discorso quasi suo malgrado.*) . . . posar sovra il tuo petto . . . scordare il mondo e Dio . . . sempre al tuo cor vicina . . . questo era il sogno mio, e la torva miseria de la mia breve vita eternar de' tuoi baci coll'ebbrezza infinita . . .

HAGENBACH: (*sorpreso, commosso.*) Or chi detto m'avria che nel tuo cuor, fanciulla, vi fosse un paradiso? . . . Io vi ho creduto il nulla!

WALLY: (*contiunando.*) . . . poi . . . m'hanno detto un giorno che odiata ero da te . . .

HAGENBACH: (*turbato, con calore, interrompendola*) No . . . Non t'ho odiata mai . . . Lo giuro . . . Credi a me! . . . (*e stringendola a sè ritorna al landler*)

GIOVANOTTI: (*mormorano.*) Arte è malvagia, il bacioadescar colla parola, Vincere al dolce gioco deve la danza sola!

VECCHIE: (*intervengono, sentenziando.*) No, non è ver! Diritto di ognuno è la favella! E l'arma più cortese che fa la lotta bella . . .

HAGENBACH: (*ad un tratto si arresta nuovamente; questa volta egli cerca di sciogliersi dalle braccia della Wally; è pallidissimo.*) No! . . . Non vuò più danzar! . . .

WALLY: (*trattenendolo e continuando a parlargli, scherzosa, eccitandolo.*) Al mio labbro di rosa Non giunge il labbro timido di bocca paurosa . . .

grant . . . hymns of love Tremble in the air.

(*The wrestle of the kiss still glows furiously in the background. At one loud kiss, laughter, applause. Loud bursts of laughter welcome WALTER's victory. Now but few go on. But the attention of the soldier and the young men who heard the bet, is attracted to HAGENBACH and WALLY. One would say that they dance without noticing it and often stop dancing to speak to each other, so that the music which leads them is not that of the instruments, but that which comes from their lips.*)

HAGENBACH: (*suddenly excited by some of Wally's words, stops dancing, and perplexed, says to her*). No! Speak! Speak! I want to know! Did you say!—

WALLY: (*continuing her talk almost in spite of herself.*) To lean against your breast, Forget the world and God, Almost near your heart, And the severe wretchedness Of my short life, To eternize with infinite rapture Of your kisses . . .

HAGENBACH: (*surprised, moved.*) Who could have told me, girl, That there's paradise in your heart? I thought there was nothing in it.

WALLY: Then . . . they once told me That you hated me . . .

HAGENBACH: (*confused, passionately, interrupting her*). No! I never hated you, I swear! Believe me! (*and pressing her to him, returns to the ländler.*)

YOUNG MEN: (*whispering*). Art is wicked; to allure The kiss with a word, To win in a sweet game,— Only dancing must do that!

OLD WOMEN: (*coming in, judging*). No, it is not true! Everyone has the right to speak! It is the most courteous arm Which wrestles gracefully.

HAGENBACH: (*stops again, suddenly; this time he tries to free himself from Wally's arm. He is ghastly pale*). No! I can't dance any more!

WALLY: (*stopping him and keeping on speaking, jesting and urging him on*). The timid lip of a shy mouth Touches not my rosy lip!

HAGENBACH: (*ancora più turbato e tremante.*) Cessiam! . . . Da te son vinto!

WALLY: Perchè allor, m'hai sfidata e la gloria hai bramato d'avermi tu baciata? (*il lander si è fatto affannoso; nel fondo della scena si danza ancora.*)

HAGENBACH: (*con impeto, stringendosi alla Wally*) Perchè? . . . Perchè dimandi? . . . Perchè Wally sei bella . . . Perchè hai profondi sguardi . . . soave la favella . . . Ne' candidi tuoi denti v'è una malia ascosa . . . V'è la vita e l'amor nel tuo labbro di rosa! Ah, Wally, in nodo ferreo l'anima tutta allaccia questa tua treccia morbida, che a te stretto m'abbraccia! . . . (*a questo punto il Pedone si stacca dal gruppo dei Giovanotti, che si interessano alla lotta fra l'Hagenbach e la Wally, e portandosi nel fondo stuzzica anche la curiosità delle donne narrando loro la scommessa. A poco a poco tutti si avvicinano ai due amanti circondandoli*)

WALLY: No! . . . Taci! . . . Taci! . . . Udirti più non voglio . . . Tu menti! . . .

HAGENBACH: (*arrestandesi bruscamente, colle lagrime agli occhi.*) Lo giuro! . . .

WALLY: Non giurare! . . .

HAGENBACH: Lo giuro! . . . È il ver! . . . Senti . . .

WALLY: (*livida in viso.*) Ad un'altra fanciulla il tuo amore hai giurato . . . E giuri? . . . Tutto io so! . . . Sei già il suo fidanzato.

HAGENBACH: Ah, tu, da un'ora, Wally, con tormenti d'inferno mi torturi! . . . m'uccidi! . . . di me ti prendi scherno!

WALLY: (*cogli occhi pieni di pianto.*) Scherno di te? . . . Non vedi che t'amo e in te rapita tutta ne' tuoi accenti vivo una nuova vita . . .

HAGENBACH: (*affascinato, tremante.*) Ma . . . allor . . . perchè mi nieghi d'un bacio tuo l'ebbrezza? (*l'abbraccia con violenza.*)

WALLY: (*con un lamento.*) Ohimè! . . . Tu mi fai male! . . .

HAGENBACH: (*sussurrando con violenza.*) Del tuo bacio m'inebria! . . . così! . . . così . . . ti voglio! . . . Mia Wally! . . . Sempre! . . .

HAGENBACH: (*still more perplexed and trembling*). Let us stop! I am conquered by you!

WALLY: Why then do you defy me, And long for the glory Of having kissed me? (*The ländler becomes tedious; they are still dancing in the background.*)

HAGENBACH: (*impetuously, pressing close to Wally*) Why? Why, you ask? Why are you so beautiful, Wally, Why such deep looks, Such gentle accents . . . In your white teeth Is hidden wickedness . . . There is life and love In your rosy lips! Ah, Wally, the whole soul Binds Your dark hair in an iron knot Which I tightly clasp to my breast! (*At this moment, the soldier gets away from the group of young men who interest themselves in the wrestle between HAGENBACH and WALLY, and going to the rear, spurs on the curiosity of the women, telling them about the bet. Little by little, all draw near the two lovers, surrounding them.*)

WALLY: No! Be quiet! Be quiet! I don't want to hear you! You lie!

HAGENBACH: (*stopping abruptly, with tears in his eyes.*) I swear it!

WALLY: Don't swear!

HAGENBACH: I swear it! It is true! Hear . . .

WALLY: (*pale*). You swore your love To another girl . . . And you swear? I know all! You are already betrothed.

HAGENBACH: Ah, Wally, it's a whole hour That you torture me With tortures of hell! You kill me! You laugh at me!

WALLY: (*with tearful eyes*). Laugh at you? Don't you see That I love you, and all wrapped up In your words, I live a new life?

HAGENBACH: (*fascinated, trembling*). But, then—why deny me The rapture of one of your kisses? (*He embraces her violently.*)

WALLY: (*lamenting*). Alas! You hurt me!

HAGENBACH: (*whispering, violently*) Intoxicate me with your kisses! So, so! I want you! My Wally! Forever!

WALLY: (*con un sospiro si abbandona a lui.*) Prendimi! (*l'Hagenbach la bacia sulla bocca.—Un urlo confuso di applausi, di grida beffarde, di risa scoppiano come un uragano intorno.*)

TUTTI: La Wally fù baciata! . . . Ed Afra è vendicata! . . . (*i Giovanotti circondano l'Hagenbach, che li guarda come trasognato, ricordando la scommessa.*)

WALLY: (*scossa a quelle risa, guarda l'Hagenbach, non comprendendo.*) Che dicono costoro? . . . E perchè ridono? . . . (*i Giovanotti trascinano verso l'osteria dell'Aquila l'Hagenbach.*)

GELLNER: (*accorre con Walter presso alla Wally.*) Disgraziata! Perchè non m'hai creduto? . . .

WALLY: (*ancora dubitando.*) Ah! . . . Fu crudel vendetta? . . . Ei m'ingannò? . . .

GIOVANOTTI: A bere!

IL PEDONE: A bere! . . .

GIOVANOTTI: (*ad Afra.*) Afra, il miglior tuo vino! . . . (*La Wally, gli occhi vitrei, livida, senza lacrime, guarda avanti a sè . . . Gellner e Walter la circondano; ma ella non vede che uno . . . Un uomo che le volge le spalle . . . Quasi speza ancora! . . . Ed ecco invece le Vecchie, le Fanciulle, tutte le Donne di Sölden che la attorniano, beffarde, sogghignando.*)

LE DONNE DI SÖLDEN: Se un marito torrai, tu pure a lui Wally Un bacio porterai che Iddio non benedì! . . .

GELLNER: (*allontanandole; alla Wally.*) Sù! . . . Vieni! . . . Andiam! . . . (*additandogli l'Hagenbach che cerca di stordirsi bevendo.*) Guardalo là! . . . Lo vedi?

WALLY: (*with a sigh, gives herself up to him.*) Take me! (*HAGENBACH kisses her on the mouth. A confused shout of applause, of ridicule, bursts of laughter like a hurricane, all around.*)

ALL: Wally was kissed! And Afra is avenged! (*The young men surround Hagenbach, who looks at them as in a dream, recollecting the bet.*)

WALLY: (*shocked by this laughter, looks at HAGENBACH, without understanding.*) What are they saying? And why do they laugh? (*The young men drag HAGENBACH toward the Eagle.*)

GELLNER: You unfortunate girl, why didn't you believe me?

WALLY: (*still doubting*). Ah! Was it a cruel revenge? Did he deceive me?

YOUNG MEN: To drink!

SOLDIER: To drink!

YOUNG MEN: (*to Afra*). Afra, your best wine! (*WALLY, with glassy eyes, tearless, looks in front of her. GELLNER and WALTER surround her; but she only sees one,—a man who turns his back to her. She still has some hope. And now the old women, girls, all the women of the Sölden surround her, jeering, grinning.*)

THE WOMEN OF SÖLDEN: If a husband you will take, You will give him a kiss Which God did not bless!

GELLNER: (*going away; to WALLY*). Up! Come! Let us go! (*Pointing to Hagenbach, who tries to stun himself by drinking.*) Look there! Do you see him?

IL PEDONE: (*toccando la sua colla tazza dell'Hagenbach.*) Non v'è maggior piacer d'un ben colmo bicchier. Ah sì! credete a me, altro non v'è! (*vuota la tazza, gridando.*) Io bevo all'Hagenbach . . .

GIOVANOTTI: Evviva l'Hagenbach!

WALLY: (*cogli occhi fissi su l'Hagenbach afferra pel braccio Gellner e gli dice*) Mi vuoi tu ancora? . . .

GELLNER: Sì!

WALLY: (*sempre cogli occhi all'Hagenbach e con voce ferma.*) Lo voglio morto!

*FINE DELL'ATTO SECONDO.*

## ■ ATTO TERZO

*Il Paesaggio: L'HOCHSTOFF.—La scena è divisa. A destra la casa dello Stromminger (ora della Wally); sul davanti l'interno della camera da letto della Wally.— Dall'altra parte una via dell'Hochstoff fiancheggiata a sinistra da case. Dalla via si entra nella camera della Wally da una piccola porta. Due finestre stanno ai lati di questa porta.— Nell'estremo orizzonte, come nel primo atto, ma da un diverso punto di vista, il Murzoll, il Similaun. Il ponte rimane assai più vicino agli spettatori, e il sentiero che vi conduce non è che una continuazione della via dell'Hochstoff.—Cade la sera . . . Davanti al Crocifisso la lampada è accesa.*

THE SOLDIER: (*clinking glasses with HAGENBACH.*) There is no greater joy Than an overflowing glass. Ah yes! Believe me, There is no greater joy! (*empties his jug, shouting.*) I drink to the health of Hagenbach . . .

YOUNG MEN: Long live Hagenbach!

WALLY: (*with her eyes fixed on HAGENBACH, gives her arm to GELLNER, and says to him*). Do you still want me?

GELLNER: Yes!

WALLY: (*with her eyes still on HAGENBACH, and in a firm voice.*) I want him dead.

*END OF SECOND ACT.*

## ■ ACT III

*SCENE: Hochstoff.—The stage is divided. To the right, Stromminger's house (now Wally's); in the foreground, the interior of Wally's bedroom. On the other side a road in Hochstoff with houses on the left side. From the road, one enters Wally's room by a small door. Two windows at the sides of this door. In the extreme horizon, as in Act I, but from a different point of view, Mts. Murzoll and Similaun. The bridge is very near the spectators, and the path which leads to it, is but a continuation of the Hochstoff road. Evening is coming on. The lamp in front of the crucifix is burning.*

# Act III

*Nella camera della Wally.*

*(La camera è immersa in una profonda osurità.)*
*(WALTER apre la porta della camera e vi lascia passare la WALLY, seguendola; poi richiude la porta e accende una lampada.—La Wally rimane immobile in mezzo alla stanza.)*

WALTER: Fa core, Wally!

WALLY: *(sempre pensierosa.)* Hai tu veduto Gellner?

WALTER: No! . . . Forse a Sölden passerà la notte.

WALLY: Non l'hai veduto dunque?
*(La Wally si leva il vezzo di perle, e lo guardo sorridendo amaramente; poi con un gesto di disprezzo lo getta sopra una tavola, e siede annodandosi i capelli che disordinatamente le scendono sulle spalle. Walter la guarda addolorato.)*

WALTER: *(con tenerezza.)* Wally!

WALLY: *(interrompendo.)* Taci . . . Che è questo? Ascolta! . . .

*(Walter apre una della finestre e sta ad ascoltare; poi richiude.)*

WALTER: È un ubbriaco che canta . . .

WALLY: *(che si è alzata, agitata, ad ascoltare, ritorna a sedere mormorando.)* E ver! Pareami un lamento.

WALTER: *(con effetto e quasi supplichevole.)* Vuoi che con te rimanga questa sera?

WALLY: No, voglio restar sola . . . te ne prego.
*(Walter bacia la Wally, ed esce per una porta interna a destra.)*

---

*IN WALLY'S ROOM.*

*(The room is in deep darkness. WALTER opens the door of the room and lets WALLY pass in, following her; then closes the door and lights a lamp.—WALLY remains immovable in the middle of the room.)*

WALTER: Be brave, Wally!

WALLY: *(still thoughtful).* Did you see Gellner?

WALTER: No! Maybe he'll spend the night at Sölden.

WALLY: Then you didn't see him yet?
*(WALLY takes off the pearl necklace, looks at it, smiling bitterly. Then with a gesture of disdain, she throws it on the table and sits down and unties her hair, which falls in disorder on her shoulders. WALTER looks at her sadly.)*

WALTER: *(tenderly).* Wally!

WALLY: *(interrupting him).* Quiet! What is it? Listen! . . .

*(WALTER opens one of the windows to listen, and then closes it.)*

WALTER: It is a drunken man singing.

WALLY: *(who got up, excited, to listen, comes back and sits down, muttering).* It is true. It seemed a lamentation.

WALTER: *(affectionately, and almost supplicating).* Do you want me to stay with you tonight?

WALLY: No, I want to be alone—I beg you!
*(WALTER kisses WALLY, and goes out by an inside door, to the right).*

---

*Nella Strada.*

*(Ritonano a gruppi quelli dell'Hockstoff che sono andati alla festa d Sölden. Tornano a coppie di quattro, di sei, Uomini, Donne; se ne vengono lentamente pel ponte, e silenziosi rincasano. Ultima si vede tornare la Wally, accompagnata del piccolo Walter. La Wally è ancora vestita della splendida veste di velluto, ma i fiori che l'adornavano sono tutti strappati. Essa è assorta in pensieri che l'addolorano, e affannosamente cammina, quasi inconscia di sè, seguendo il piccolo Walter.)*

*(VINCENZO GELLNER viene dal fondo, passa lentamente per la via dell'Hochstoff, ed entra in una delle case che la fiancheggiano. La notte è scesa oscurissma.)*

*Dietro il ponte della Ache si ode avvicinarsi poco a poco una canzone. È il PEDONE DI SCHNALS, mezzo ubbriaco, che canta. Egli traversa il ponte, e se ne viene a sghimbescio verso l'Hochstoff.*

IL PEDONE: Non v'è maggior piacer
d'un ben colmo bicchier.
Ah sì! credete a me,
altro non v'è!
*(Gellner, all'udire la voce del Pedone esce dalla casa ove era entrato poc'anzi, ne chiude la porta con gran precauzione, poi, quasi strisciando per la via, va a porsi allo sbocco del sentiero.)*

IL PEDONE: *(scendendo il sentiero)* così sempre giocondo
è questo falso mondo.
Se l'amor t'inganna
garzon, canta e tracanna!
Ah sì! credilo a me,
altro non v'è.
*Allo sbocco del sentiero là dove questo si congiunge alla strada dell'Hochstoff, GELLNER arresta il Pedone, ponendogli una mano sulla spalla.*

---

*ON THE STREET.*

*(Those who went to the festivities at Sölden, return in groups. They come in couples of four, of six, men, women; they slowly cross the bridge and silently enter their homes. Finally WALLY is seen, accompanied by little WALTER. WALLY is still dressed in her gorgeous velvet gown, but the flowers which adorned her are all torn. She is absorbed in the thoughts that grieve her, and walks wearily, as if unconscious of herself, following little WALTER.)*

*(VINCENZO GELLNER comes from the background, slowly crosses the Hochstoff road, and enters one of the houses. The night is very dark.)*

*(Behind the bridge, across the Ach, a song is heard, coming nearer and nearer. It is the SOLDIER OF SCHNALS, half drunk, who sings.)*
*(He crosses the bridge and comes staggering toward Hochstoff.)*

THE SOLDIER: There is no greater joy
Than an overflowing glass.
Ah, yes! Believe me,
There is no greater joy!
*(GELLNER, at the sound of the drunken man's voice, comes out from the house which he entered a short while ago, closes the door very cautiously, then almost crawling along the road, goes to the entrance of the path.)*

THE SOLIDER: *(going up the path.)* Thus always gay
Is this world so false!
If love deceives you,
Lad, go get drunk!
*(At the entrance to the path, there where it joins the street of Hochstoff, GELLNER stops the soldier and puts his hand on his shoulder.)*

*Nella camera della Wally.*

*In Wally's Room.*

*Nella strada.*

*On the Street.*

GELLNER: (*sottovoce, rapidamente*) Ebben . . . dunque?

GELLNER: (*whispering, quickly.*) Well . . . what then?

IL PEDONE: (*lasciando sfuggire un comico gesto di paura.*) Ah! siete voi? Pel ciel, m'avete fatto paura . . .
(*Gellner impaziente lo scuote.*)

SOLDIER: (*making a comical grimace of fear.*) Ah, it's you? Good heavens, how you frightened me!
(*GELLNER shakes him impatiently.*)

*(La Wally è agitatissima, ad ogni istante paurosa tende l'orecchio; vorrebbe pregare, ma non può. Finalmente da in un pianto dirotto, e, la testa tra le mani, si lascia cadere in ginocchio a piè del letto.)*

*(WALLY is very much excited, every minute she listens, with fear; she would like to pray, but cannot. Finally she bursts into a torrent of tears and holding her head in her hands, she falls on her knees at the foot of the bed.)*

Io là . . . rimasi fino a sera, quando ad un tratto l'Hagenbach disparve.

I stayed there till the evening, When suddenly Hagenbach disappeared.

GELLNER: Disparve?

GELLNER: Disappeared?

IL PEDONE: Me ne uscii; era già notte.
Allor decisi di tornare . . . Un uomo
scendeva lento il sentiero dell'Ache . . .

SOLDIER: I went out; it was already night.
Then I decided to go back. A man Slowly climbed up the path of the Ach.

GELLNER: Che!? . . . forse l'Hagenbach?

GELLNER: What? Maybe it was Hagenbach?

IL PEDONE: Egli in persona! . . .

THE SOLDIER: He himself!

GELLNER: Parla sommesso . . . Ebben?

GELLNER: Speak low . . . Well?

*(La Wally a un tratto si scuote! Le sue mani corrono ai suoi occhi incredula del suo dolore, quasi a convincersi che essa ha pianto! . . . )*

*(WALLY suddenly starts up. Her hands seek her eyes, disbelieving her sorrow, as if to convince herself that she wept.)*

IL PEDONE: Lo riconobbi.
(*maliziosamente.*)
Costui è certo un uomo di coraggio . . .

SOLDIER: I recognized him.
(*maliciously*).
He is surely a brave man . . .

GELLNER: Perchè?

GELLNER: Why?

IL PEDONE: Venir qui solo, e a notte tarda! . . .
Per lui già piange Sölden . . . Là si teme
che qui si voglia vendicar la Wally! . . .

SOLDIER: To come here alone, and late at night!
Sölden is already weeping for him. They fear there that we want to avenge Wally!

GELLNER: (*ridendo*) Ohibò! . . . pazzie!
(*dandogli del denaro.*)
Però . . . non si sa mai.
Vanne a dormir lontano. Mala notte è questa per l'Hochstoff . . .

GELLNER: (*laughing*). Nonsense! . . . madness!
(*giving him money.*)
However . . . you never can tell. Go off to sleep far off. This is A bad night for Hochstoff . . .

IL PEDONE: (*strizzando 'occhio.*) Non mi ci piglia!
(*parte dal fondo a sinistra, scomparendo dietro la casa dello Stromminger zuffolando.*)

SOLDIER: (*rubbing his eyes.*) They won't catch me here.
(*He goes away from the rear at left, disappearing behind STROMMINGER's house, whistling.*)

GELLNER: L'Hagenbach qui? Egli all'Hochstoff? Ohibò!
Ubbriaco è il pedon . . . non è possibile! . . .
(*dopo una pausa.*)
E se ciò fosse? Se . . .
(*arrestandosi e guardando d'intorno.*)

GELLNER: Hagenbach here? He at Hochstoff?
Oh, no! the soldier is drunk, it's impossible!
(*after a pause*).
And if this were true? If—
(*stopping to look around*).

# Act III

**Nella camera della Wally.** | **In Wally's Room.**

**Nella strada.** | **On the Street.**

---

*(Con un gesto risoluto si dà a preparare il letto . . . si toglie di dosso il corsetto di velluto! . . . poi si inginocchia, fa il segno di croce e prega! . . . Ma a un tratto si alza esclamando contristata e dispettosa.)*

*(With a resolute gesture, she begins to make her bed—takes off her velvet corset. Then she kneels down, makes a sign of the cross, and prays. But suddenly she gets up, exclaiming sadly and haughtily.)*

**WALLY:** Nè mai dunque avrò pace?
E da pensieri
sempre o feroci o tristi la mia mente
sarà turbata? Ohimè! solo una celia
io fui per lui, e del mio ardente bacio
egli si rise? . . .
*(con accento d'odio)*
Ebben, morrai, crudele!
*(con raccapriccio prima, poi con isconforto.)*
Misera me, che l'amo più di prima!
*(singhiozzando)*
La giovinezza coi suoi sogni ardenti,
or crudeli tormenti,
tutta sola mi lascia;
e già s'accascia
nel triste ricordar la mia persona,
e la speranza fugge e mi abbandona!
In un suo bacio v'era la mia vita,
in un suo bacio la speranza tutta!
e m'ha il suo bacio la vita distrutta! . . .
Pur gli perdono; io non vo' la sua vita
Vuò a Gellner tosto dir che pazza fui

**WALLY:** Will I never have peace again?
Will my mind be always disturbed
By wild and sad thoughts?
Alas I was only a joke for him
And he laughs at my burning kiss?
*(with hatred)*
Well, then, you will die, cruel one!
*(first with dread and then with discouragement).*
Wretched that I am, to love him more than ever!
*(sobbing)*
Youth with its burning dreams, its cruel tortures,
Leaves me all alone;
And now I waken
From sad recollections,
And hope flees and abandons me!
In his single kiss lay my whole life,
In his kiss alone lay all my hopes!
And it was his kiss ruined my whole life—
I would rather tell Gellner that I was mad . . .

La notte è oscura . . . e una sventura può toccare a tutti . . . la lampada lassù . . . potrebbe spegnersi . . .
impetuoso è il vento . . .
*(esitando)*
Perchè tremo?
Ahimè! mi guarda il Crocifisso nero!
*(riavendosi)*
Gellner, su via! si tratta di Wally!

Dark is the night . . .
And disaster can happen to anyone.
The lamp up there could blow out.
The wind is strong . . . *(hesitating).* Why do I tremble?
Alas! the black crucifix is looking at me!
*(bracing himself again).*
Gellner, up, up! Wally is in danger!

*(Gellner si caccia su pel sentiero scrutando nell'osurità, e tendendo le orecchie per ascoltare il più piccolo rumore. Più che camminare, egli striscia su pel sentiero. Arrivato al ponte, si ferma quasi diffidente; guarda ancora intorno a sè, poi lo varca. Si avvicina al Crocifisso, e con grande destrezza ne spegne la lampada. Il vento soffia più che mai impetuoso. Gellner scompare nella oscurità dietro il ponte e aspetta. La scena rimane completamente immersa nel buio.)*

*(GELLNER hurries over the path, gazing into the darkness and strains his ears to hear the slightest sound. He skulks along the path. Coming to the bridge, he stops suspiciously, looks around him, then crosses. He approaches the crucifix and dexterously puts out the lamp. The wind blows stronger than ever. GELLNER appears in the dark behind the bridge, and waits. The stage is entirely dark.)*

---

*(apre la porta per iscendere nella via, ma si arresta sulla soglia spaventata dall'oscurità.)*
Che tetra notte! . . . Come fischia il vento!
*(guardando verso il ponte.)*
Spento è il lume laggiù! . . . Giuseppe, certo,
a Sölden è rimasto . . . per stanotte
nulla ha a temer . . . Doman l'avvertirò!
*(richiude la porta e più tranquilla si accinge a coricarsi)*

*(She opens the door to go out, but stops, frightened by the darkness.)* What a gloomy night, How the wind howls!
*(looking towards the bridge)* The light up there has blown out!
Giuseppe surely remained at Sölden;
Tonight I have nothing to fear.
Tomorrow I will warn him!
*(She closes the door, and more calmly prepares to go to bed.)*

*L'HAGENBACH compare dietro il ponte; egli cammina a tentoni nella oscurità.*

*(Hagenbach appears behind the bridge; he walks, groping in the dark.)*

**HAGENBACH:** Buio è il sentier . . . la lampada s'è spenta . . .
Ebben che importa? Ai piedi di Wally il rimorso e l'amor mi guideranno.
*(sta per passare il ponte, quando Gellner gli è addosso, e lo fa precipitare dal piccolo parapetto. L'Hagenbach getta un urlo terribile. Gellner scende rapidamente, quasi fuggendo. Poi, giunto allo sbocco del sentiero, rallenta il passo e fa per rientrare in casa sua. Ma vedendo la finestra della camera della Wally ancora rischiarata da un lume, vi si avvicina mormorando)*

**HAGENBACH:** The path is dark—the lamp is out . . .
What's the difference? To Wally's feet
Remorse and love will guide me.
*(He is crossing the bridge, when GELLNER comes upon him and hurls him from the small parapet. HAGENBACH gives an awful howl. GELLNER descends rapidly, fleeing. Then, reaching the entrance to the path, slows up, and enters his house. But seeing WALLY's windows still illuminated, approaches murmuring.)*

**WALLY:** *(sobbalzando.)* È strano!
intorno a me solo lamenti odo stanotte. Oh! fosse digià l'alba!
O ciel! chi batte?
*(con spavento.)*

**WALLY:** *(starting up.)* It is strange!
I hear only
Sobs tonight around me.
Oh, I wish it were dawn already!
Heavens, who knocks?
*(frightened).*

È Gellner! . . . Che vorrà?
*(La Wally, atterrita, corre come una pazza alla porta, l'apre ed esce nella via.)*

It's Gellner! What does he want?
*(WALLY, frightened, runs madly to the door, opens it and goes out.)*

**GELLNER:** È desta ancora la selvaggia . . . e aspetta!
*(batte sommessamente ai vetri di una finestra.)*

**GELLNER:** The wild creature is up yet and waits!
*(He knocks softly on the window pane.)*

*Da questo punto l'azione si svolge*

*(At this point, the action turns entirely to the street of Hochstoff.)*

GELLNER: Se vuoi vederlo morto . . . giù nell Ache discendi . . . e lo vedrai.

GELLNER: If you want to see him dead, Go down to the Ach, and you'll see him.

WALLY: No . . . non è vero.

WALLY: No, it is not true.

GELLNER: Oh com'è vero Iddio . . . giù dal ponte or ora l'ho precipitato . . .

GELLNER: As true as God— I just Threw him down from the bridge.

WALLY: *(afferrandolo convulsa per il collo)* Vile!

WALLY: *(clutching his throat convulsively.)* Coward!

GELLNER: Taci . . . che fai?

GELLNER: Be quiet! What are you doing?

WALLY: *(trascinandolo verso il ponte)* Vieni con me.

WALLY: *(dragging him to the bridge).* Come with me.

GELLNER: *(dibattendosi.)* Mi lascia . . .

GELLNER: *(getting himself loose).* Let me go . . .

WALLY: Vieni! . . . Laggiù . . . noi due insieme! In fondo a quell'abisso, e presso al corpo suo, là v'è l'altare delle nostre nozze. *(La Wally ha trascinato Gellner sin presso al ponte, quando dall'abisso sorge un lamento. La Wally ascolta trepidante. Le sue braccia lasciano sfuggire Gellner.—S'ode distintamente un altro lamento.)*

WALLY: Come! down there—we two together! At the bottom of that abyss And near his body, There is the altar of our wedding. *(WALLY drags GELLNER up to the bridge, when a wail rises from the abyss. WALLY listens anxiously. She lets GELLNER escape. Another sob is clearly heard.)*

WALLY: *(con impeto di gioia.)* Dio! vive ancor! *(scende precipitosa nella via, urlando e picchiando a tutte le porte)* A me, soccorso! A me! . . . *(Si schiudono alcune finestre, si aprono le porte delle case; Uomini e Donne compaiono.)*

WALLY: *(with a cry of joy).* O Lord! He is still alive! *(She hurries up the road, shouting and knocking at all the houses.)* Help me! Help me! *(Some windows are opened, the doors of the houses are opened; men and women appear.)*

CORO: Che avvenne?

CHORUS: What happened?

WALLY: Un uom nell'Ache . . .

WALLY: A man in the Ach.

CORO: Morto?

CHORUS: Dead?

WALLY: Presto! . . . È l'Hagenbach . . . ei vive . . . lo salviamo! *La scena è invasa da Uomini, da Donne; chi porta torcie, chi corde e scale. (Gellner è scomparso.)*

WALLY: Quickly! It is Hagenbach—he lives—let us save him! *(The stage is filled with men and women; some carry torches, some rope and ladders.) (GELLNER has disappeared.)*

ALCUNI: Presto alle corde . . .

SOME: Quickly to the ropes.

ALTRI: presto . . .

OTHERS: Quickly!

I. i nodi stretti! . . .

I. Tighten the knots!

II. Ben stretti i nodi . . .

II. Let the knots be very tight!

WALLY: stretti . . .

WALLY: Tight . . .

TUTTI: Ora allacciamo! *Dall'altra parte del ponte intanto si vedono venire a frotte quei di Sölden con armi e torcie; fra essi è AFRA.*

ALL: Now let's bind! *(From the other side of the bridge, meanwhile, the people of Sölden are seen coming in crowds, with arms and torches; among them is AFRA.)*

WALLY: Siam pronti; andiam! *(s'incammina con gli altri verso il ponte; ma allo sbocco del sentiero s'incontra con Afra e con quei di Sölden.)*

WALLY: We are ready; come on. *(She walks with the others towards the bridge, but at the entrance to the path, meets AFRA and those of Sölden.)*

QUEI DI SÖLDEN: *(minacciosi.)* Dell'Hagenbach cerchiamo . . . Dov'è? *(un gran silenzio; nessuno osa rispondere.)* Dove'è? Rispondi! *(nuovo silenzio)*

THOSE OF SÖLDEN: *(threatening).* We look for Hagenbach . . . Where is he? *(A long silence. No one dares to answer.)* Where is he? Answer! *(Again silence.)*

AFRA: *(scoppiando il lacrime.)* Ah! l'hanno ucciso! *(Quei di Sölden stanno per iscagliarsi contro quelli dell'Hochstoff; la Wally s'interpone gridando.)*

AFRA: *(bursting into tears).* Ah, they have killed him! *(The people of Sölden are about to rush on those of Hochstoff. WALLY comes between them, shouting.)*

WALLY: Morto non è! No! *(a Afra)* Spera lo riavrai! *(Rapidamente si apre un passaggio tra la folla, e corre verso il precipizio. Tutti la seguono collo sguardo. La Wally, senza esitare, per un piccolo sentiero scende nell'abissa Merauigliati quasi a erriti del suo forte atto de coraggio, gli uomini, con le torcie alla mano, si affacciano al precipizio. Le donne s'inginocchiano in disparte e pregano.)*

WALLY: He is not dead! No! *(to Afra.)* Hope . . . You'll have him again! *(A passage is quickly made by her between the crowd. Wally, without hesitating, descends into the abyss by a little path. Amazed, frightend by her great act of bravery, the men, with torches in hand, step up to the precipice. The women kneel aside and pray.)*

TUTTI: Oh! quale audacia . . . oh! spavento . . . oh! terror!

ALL: Oh! What boldness! Oh, horror! Oh, terror!

DONNE: Signor, la proteggete! Salva ce la rendete!

WOMEN: Lord protect her! Lord, give her back to us!

ALCUNI: Caliam le corde . . .

SOME: Let us lower the ropes . . .

ALTRI: L'abisso è profondo . . .

OTHERS: The abyss is deep.

ALTRI: Ascoltiamo in silenzio . . .

OTHERS: Let us listen in silence!

TUTTI: *(sbigottiti.)* Nulla s'ode . . .

ALL: *(terrified).* Nothing is to be heard . . .

WALLY: *(dal fondo dell'abisso, con gioia.)* Vive!

WALLY: *(from the depth of the abyss, with joy.)* He lives!

TUTTI: Alle corde . . . All'opera . . . sù! sù! Forza alle corde. ohè . . . Sù, issa! *(Tutti si affannano intorno all'abisso, tirando le corde. Dopo pochi minuti di un'ansia spaventevole, la Wally compare tenendo legato e stretto a sè il corpo dell'Hagenbach, privo di sensi.)*

ALL: To the ropes—to the task— up, up! Your strength to the ropes, up, now! *(All press around the abyss, pulling the ropes. After a few moments of frightful anxiety, WALLY appears, with HAGENACH's unconscious body bound and tied to her.)*

TUTTI: È salvo! *(Gli amici prendono Giuseppe e lo adagiano per terra. La Wally, in uno stato di suprema esaltazione, dall'alto della rupe, additando alla folla che le si accalca attorno il corpo del giovane cacciatore, esclama)*

ALL: He is saved! *(The friends take HAGENACH and lower him to the ground. WALLY, in a state of highest exaltation, from the tops of the cliff, pointing to the crowd which gathers around the body of the young hunter, exclaims.)*

WALLY: Sì, vive ancora! *(ad Afra)* È Dio che te'l ridona, e tuo lo vuole, per mia man salvato. *(sempre ad Afra con grande commozione.)* Così . . . pur la mia casa . . . e i campi . . . e i prati, Afra, son tuoi . . . *(un singhiozzo le tronca la paro-*

WALLY: Yes, he still lives! *(to Afra.)* It is God who gives him back to you, and wishes him to be yours, saved by my hand. *(with great agitation).* So,—even my house—and the field—and the meadows, Afra— are yours. *(A sob cuts short her speech. She*

# Act III

la, scoppia in lagrime, e s'inginocchia presso Giuseppe baciandolo in volto e mormorando.)
Addio!
(poscia si scosta rapidamente da lui, e prendendo nelle sue le mani di Afra le dice a voce alta per modo che tutti possano udire.)
Allor che gli occhi
ei riaprirà alla luce, gli dirai
che il bacio che mi tolse, ora gli ho reso!

**TUTTI:** O pia creatura generosa e santa!

*FINE DELL'ATTO TERZO.*

bursts into tears, and kneels down near GIUSEPPE, kissing his face, and muttering).
Farewell!
(She breaks away quickly from him, and taking AFRA's hand in hers, tells her in a loud voice so all can hear.)
When he shall have opened his eyes
To the light, you will tell him
That I have now returned
The kiss he snatched from me!

**ALL:** O faithful creature, generous and holy!

*END OF THIRD ACT.*

## ■ ATTO QUARTO

*Sul Murzoll.*
"Stanca, non lontana dalla sua capanna stava un giorno Wally seduta sopra una delle più alte cime del Murzoll. La scena che l'attorniava somigliava nel triste e livido decembre un cimitero sparso di tumuli di neve, colle fronde bizzarramente foggiate dal ghiaccio in croci, coi cespugli di fiori alpestri transformati in tombe trasparenti e candide come il marmo. Sotto a' suoi piedi si stendeva il mare di ghiaccio, desolato, infinito, coi suoi riflessi verdastri e con le sue onde irrigidite che si prolungavano sino all'altro versante della montagna.
L'orizzonte colle sue innumerevoli catene di monti era avvolto nei fantastici vapori del meriggio. Il Similaun, accanto a Wally, era accarezzato da una picola nuvola, e la ragazza, appoggiata la testa nelle mani, ne seguiva macchinalmente gli ondeggiamenti."
(Wally dell'Avvoltoio— W. De Hillern.)

Dalla sinistra, per un piccolo ed ascoso sentiero, sale faticosamente WALTER sino alla capanna, e si avvicina a WALLY.

**WALTER:** Luogo sicuro questo non è più!
Le valanghe distruggono i sentieri!
(La Wally si scuote; guarda d'intorno attentamente, poi ritorna a meditare come prima.)
(abbracciandola e costringendola affettuosamente ad alzarsi.)
Wally, torniamo!

**WALLY:** Se è scritto ch'io non debba
più riveder la terra dove ho amato e pianto tanto . . . il mio destin si compia!

**WALTER:** L'inverno è desolato . . .

**WALLY:** Più non soffro pene di questo mondo! . . .

## ■ ACT IV

*(On the Murzoll.)*
"Weary, not far from her but WALLY sat one day on one of the highest peaks of the Murzoll. The view which surrounded her seemed in the sad and pale December like a cemetery spotted with heaps of snow, with the leaves oddly formed into crosses out of ice, with the bushes of Alpine flowers transformed into tombs transparent and white as marble. Under her feet, extended a sea of ice, desolate, infinite, with greenish reflections, and with its stiffened waves which stretched out to the other slope of the mountain. The horizon, with its innumerable chains of mountains, was wrapped in the fantastic vapors of noon. Similaun, at WALLY's side, was caressed by a small cloud, and the girl, leaning her head on her hands, mechanically followed its undulations."
(Wally of the Vulture— W. DE HILLERN.)

(From the right, by a small steep path, WALTER ascends with difficulty to the hut, and approaches WALLY.)

**WALTER:** Surely this is not a safe place!
The avalanches destroy the paths!
(WALLY starts up, looks around attentively, then comes to meditate as before. WALTER embraces her and affectionately compells her to get up.)
Wally, let us return!

**WALLY:** If it is that I
Am never to see again the land that I loved
And mourned so much—my fate is being fulfilled!

**WALTER:** Winter is desolate . . .

**WALLY:** I no longer suffer pains of this world!

**WALTER:** È già il Natale . . .
Wally torniamo!

**WALLY:** Non ho più famiglia.

**WALTER:** Torniamo a riudir le allegre squille
delle campane della chiesa nostra
che cantano la pace . . .

**WALLY:** (con abbandono.) La mia pace?
È perduta per sempre! Tu ritorna . . .
alla tua casa, alla vita, all'amore!
Walter, ritorna ed ama!

**WALTER:** Senza te!

**WALLY:** (traendo dal seno il vezzo di perle che portava il dì della festa di Sölden e porgendolo a Walter, con un sorriso d'amara tristezza.)
Prendi, o fanciullo! . . . Serbala!
questa memoria pia,
questa, che un dì fu orgoglio
de la bellezza mia.
Son queste le mie lagrime
dal duolo irrigidite,
i ricordi soavi
dell'affranto mio cuor,
le parole d'amore
che ho detto e che ho sentite . . .
a te! . . . prendila. Walter!
È tutto il mio tesor!
(poi con immensa rassegnazione)
Ed or, fanciullo vanne. È già il Natale! . . .

**WALTER:** (piangendo.) Torna con me!

**WALLY:** (melanconicamente.)
Riudrai le allegre squille
della campana della chiesa nostra
cantar la pace . . .

**WALTER:** Wally, deh ritorna!

**WALLY:** Fanciullo, no. Soltanto . . . una preghiera.
(soavemente a Walter indicando il ghiacciaio.)
Allor che avrai varcato il periglioso mare di ghiaccio . . . canta, oh canta ancora
la mesta cantilena del mio jodler!
(le lacrime le impediscono di più proseguire. Ella abbraccia con gran tenerezza Walter, e dolcemente lo spinge sul sentiero del ritorno. Walter pangendo si allontana e scompare dal sentiero di sinistra.)

**WALLY:** (sola.) (appena sola, la Wally si accascia presso la sua capanna. Il cielo, dapprima sereno, va lentamente coprendosi di nubi. Essa si guarda intorno.)
Eterne a me l'intorno
piange la neve lacrime!
Qui lagrima da secoli
eterno pianto il giorno!
(esaltandosi.)
Fra la densa caligine
laggiù la terra appar
mugghiante fra le tenebre
un desolato mar.

**WALTER:** It is Christmas now—
Wally, let us return!

**WALLY:** I have no family any more.

**WALTER:** Let us return to hear
The merry peal of the church-bells
Singing peace . . .

**WALLY:** (with resignation.) My peace?
It is lost forever! Return
To your home, to life, to love!
Walter, return and love!

**WALTER:** Without you?

**WALLY:** (taking from her breast the pearl necklace she wore the day of the festivities at Sölden and handing it to Walter, with a bitter smile of sadness).
Take it, boy! Treasure it!
This pious memory,
This, which once was
The pride of my youth!
Those are my tears,
Grown hard with sorrow,
The tender recollections
Of my broken heart,
The words of love
Which I spoke and heard . . .
It is yours, take it, Walter!
It is my whole treasure!
(then, with great resignation).
And now, go, boy, it is Christmas!

**WALTER:** (weeping). Come back with me!

**WALLY:** (sadly). You will hear again
The merry peal of our church-bells
Singing peace!

**WALTER:** Wally, please return!

**WALLY:** No, boy,—Only—a prayer.
(gently, to WALTER, pointing to the ice.)
When you shall have crossed
The perilous sea of ice,
Sing, sing once again,
My jodler's sad strains.
(The tears prevent her from going on. She embraces WALTER very tenderly and gently pushes him on the path leading down. WALTER, weeping, walks away and disappears from the path to the left.)

**WALLY:** (alone.) (She sinks down on the ground near the hut. The sky, at first calm, becomes covered with clouds. She looks around.)
Eternally the snow around me
Weeps bitter tears!
Here the day, for centuries,
Sheds eternal tears!
(exalted).
Amid the thick gloom
The earth below appears
Like a desolate sea
Bellowing in the darkness!

Funesto mare dell'umana vita!
Un giorno sciolte le sue vele al vento
sfidava la mia nave l'onda ardita,
e dentro a la mia nave, alta, orgogliosa
la giovinezza mia cantava forte
canti d'amor sovra flutti di rosa . . .
(capa.)
Quei canti lieti on son nenie di morti!

WALTER: (da lontano.) E il vento iva lontano . . .
Poi le venìa vicino . . .
Quando fu giunta sovra l'alto monte
presso alla neve bianca
la pellegrina stanca
sciolse le treccie e chinò il bianco fronte.
(la voce di Walter va poco a poco perdendosi.)

WALLY: (con esaltazione.) Sì come te, fanciulla del mio canto
l'amore fu dolor, la vita pianto.
Sì, come te morir deve la Wally . . .
(la Wally getta il mantello di pelle, si scioglie le chiome che le inondano le spalle, s'inginocchia, e come assorta in dolcissima estasi canta.)
O neve, o figlia candida di Dio,
risplender t'ho veduta
dalla vallata muta,
nè l'aspro m'atterri lungo pendìo,
e a te sono venuta.
Essere pari a te bella desìo!
(Lo jodler che segue, la Wally to canta, con immensa passione, quasi nel delirio; ed è durante questo suo canto, che ha del dolore fantastico, che da lungi si sente la voce dell'Hagenbach chiamare: "Wally! Wally!" voce che si fa sempre più distinta.)

WALLY: Come sei triste, o vento, tu somigli al mio pianto.

HAGENBACH: (da lontano.) Wally!

WALLY: Sei l'ultimo lamento, sei l'ultimo mio canto.

HAGENBACH: (più distintamente.) Wally!

WALLY: (impaurita.) Una voce mi chiama! Chi mi vuole!
(ascolta, ma tutto è silenzio.)
No m'ingannai
(poco dopo riudendo ancora il suo nome.)
E ancora . . . Chi mi chiama?
(agitata dallo spavento.)
Ah! sono, ohime, le fanciulle beate!
Dei lividi ghiacciai sono le fate!
(coprendosi gli occhi con le mani per non vedere la spaventosa visione.)
Già la lugubre schiera ecco s'avanza,
ed agitan su me l'orribil velo! . . .

O fatal sea of human life!
One day with its sails
Spread out to the wind,
My ship defied the stormy wave,
And within my ship, tall and proud,
My youth sang loud
Songs of youth about waves of roses!
(thoughtfully).
Those joyful songs are now funeral dirges!

WALTER: (from a distance.And the wind came slowly,
Then came nearer to her . . .
And when she reached the mountain-top
Near the white snow,
The weary pilgrim
Opened her braids and bowed down
Her snow-white forehead!
(WALTER's voice becomes fainter and fainter.)

WALLY: (with exultation). O snow, o white daughter of God,
I saw you shining below,
From the silent valley,
The long, steep precipice frightened me not.
I came here to you,
I want to be as beautiful as you!
(The yodler which follows, is sung by WALLY with great passion, almost as in delirium, and it is during this song, that is fantastically sad, that HAGENBACH'S voice is heard from the distance calling, "Wally, Wally"; the voice becomes more distinct.)

WALLY: How sad, o wind, Your resemble my lamentation.

HAGENBACH: (from a distance). Wally!

WALLY: You are my last lament, You, my last song.

HAGENBACH: (clearer). Wally!

WALLY: (frightened). A voice calls me! Who wants me?
(She listens, but all is quiet.)
No, I made a mistake.
(then, hearing her name again).
Again—who calls me?
(shaking with fear).
Ah, they are, alas, the happy children!
They are the creatures of livid ice!
(She covers her eyes with her hands to shut out the frightful visions.)
Now the mournful band approaches,
And wave at me its horrible veil . . .

e intrecciano d'intorno a me la danza,
ver me tendendo le braccia di gelo!
(cade a terra ansante dallo spavento.)
(Dal sentiero di destra appare HAGENBACH che s'inerpica appoggiandosi a un bastone ferrato. Egli si ferma penosamente impressionato a vedere i segni che i patimenti hanno impresso sul volto della Wally, e dolcemente la chiama.)

HAGENBACH: O Wally!

WALLY: (dirizzandosi e vedendo Giuseppe.) Vergin santa! Egli è Giuseppe!
Perchè sei tu venuto?

HAGENBACH: M'hai salvato
hai voluto obliar l'offesa mia
e tu mi chiedi perchè son tornato?
(con trasporto.)
A te ne vengo come a un santo altare!

WALLY: (con emozione.) (È la sua voce!)

HAGENBACH: Oh! come furon lunghi
i dì lontan da te, e come dentro
mi struggeva il desìo di rivederti!
Tu nel tormento dell'ore infinite
a me apparivi bella e innamorata!
Poi, la visione dolce si mutava . . .
e come la Madonna del dolore
ai miei piè ti vedevo addolorata,
mentre, a lavarvi l'oltraggio del bacio,
dagli tuoi sulla tua scarna gota
vi sgorgava un'amara onda di pianto.

WALLY: (con voce appena intelligibile e rotta dalla commozione.)
Ah! l'armonia delle sue parole m'uccide!

HAGENBACH: (continuando con più passione il racconto.)
Poi . . . m'han detto un dì: la Wally
non è più qui . . . Tu più non la vedrai! . . .
Ma la speranza non m'ha mai lasciato,
e t'ho, fanciulla bella, ritrovata.
(rimane in lunga contemplazione davanti alla Wally, tremante, e mormora)
Io t'amo, Wally.

WALLY: (spaventata, agitata, dubbiosa ancora della felicità che viene a lei nel momento appunto che ella la credeva per sempre perduta, e giudicando male dei sentimenti che animano Giuseppe, gli dice con amarezza, allontanandosi.) Ebben . . . se t'ho salvato . . .
perchè mentir? . . . Non s'ama per pietà.
Afra tu amavi ed ami.

And twist in dance around me,
Stretching out their icy arms!
(She falls to the ground, panting with fear.)
(HAGENBACH appears on the path to the left, clattering up, leaning on an iron stick. He stops, struck by the signs of suffering on WALLY's face, and gently calls her.)

HAGENBACH: Wally!

WALLY: (sitting up, and seeing GIUSEPPE.) Holy Virgin! It is Giuseppe!
Why did you come?

HAGENBACH: You saved me,
You wanted to forget my offense,
And you ask why I returned to you?
(passionately).
I come to you as a sacred shrine!

WALLY: (with emotion). It is his voice!

HAGENBACH: Oh, how long
Where the days without you,
And how the desire to see you
Tortured me!
Enamored and beautiful
Seemed you to me,
In the torments of the infinite hours!
Then the vision sweet changed . . .
And the Mater Dolorosa
I saw you, afflicted, at my feet,
While, to wash off the insult
Of the kiss,
From you eyes, on your thin cheeks
Gushed a bitter stream of tears.

WALLY: (with an almost unintelligible voice, broken with excitement). Ah, the harmony
Of his voice kills me!

HAGENBACH: (continuing, with greater passion). Then, one day they told me
Wally is gone.—I'll see her no more!—
But hope did not leave me,
And I found you, beautiful girl!
(He remains in deep contemplation before WALLY trembling and murmurs:)
I love you, Wally.

WALLY: (Frightened, excited, still doubtful of the happiness which comes to her just at the moment when she thought it forever lost, and thinking ill of the feelings with inspire GIUSEPPE tells him with bitterness, walking away). Well—If I saved you
Why to lie? One does not love Through pity!
Afra you loved and love.

HAGENBACH: Afra tu dici?
Mi guarda! E una menzogna! No,
Wally
Credetti odiarti . . . ma il mio
cuor ti amava
(lentamente si avvicina alla Wally, così che le loro teste quasi si toccano.)
Quando a Sölden provocatrice balda
tu m'apparisti, allora io la credei
una sfida crudel! . . . Pur già lottavo contro l'incanto della tua persona
che dolcemente m'attraeva a sè!
(con estrema passione.)
No, credi, o Wally! E inebbriato e pazzo
nel caro abbraccio alle ardenti parole
che vile fui; ma il bacio che ti presi
sulla tua bocca, era bacio
d'amore . . .

HAGENBACH: Afra, you say?
Look at me! It is a lie! No, Wally.
I thought I hated you—but I loved you.
(He slowly comes up to WALLY, so that their heads touch.)
When at Sölden, bold incited
You appeared to me,
Then I believed it a cruel defiance;
But already I struggled
Against the charms of your beauty
Which so gently drew me to you!
(very passionately).
No, believe me, Wally!
I was drunk and mad
In the dear embrace
And the ardent words.
But the kiss I took
From your sweet lips
Was a kiss of love!

WALLY: (fra sè, rapita dall'incanto soave delle parole di Giuseppe.) O dolce incanto! O paradiso nuovo!

WALLY: (Beside herself from the gentle charm of GIUSEPPE's words.) O sweet charm! O new paradise!

HAGENBACH: (continuando.)
. . . e appena a sera, pieno di rimorsi
io volli rivederti e ai piedi tuoi
cadere. Tempestosa era la notte,
e Dio vegliava sulla colpa mia! . . .
Giù nell'abbisso mi perdetti . . .
(La Wally impallidissce. La Memoria del suo delitto le ritorna in tutto il suo orrore.)

HAGENBACH: (continuing). And towards evening, full of remorse,
I wanted to see you again
And fall at your feet,
The night was stormy,
And God watched my sins!
I was lost in the abyss below!
(WALLY grows pale. The memory of her crime returns to her in all its horror.)

WALLY: (con voce rauca, interrompendolo) Dio?! Non
Dio . . . ma un uom! . . . Gli avean detto: uccidilo!
Ei t'attendeva . . .
(non può più continuare.)

WALLY: (in a hoarse voice, interrupting him). God?!
Not God—but a man!
He was told . . . kill him!
He watched for you! . . .
(She cannot go on.)

HAGENBACH: Un uom? . . .

HAGENBACH: A man?

WALLY: (con sforzo supremo.) Questa crudele
gli aveva susurrato: Va e l'uccidi!
(con raccapriccio.)
Amami adunque ancor, se puoi.
(si copre disperatamente il volto colle mani, e rimane così, ritta dinanzi a Giuseppe; questi commosso la guarda, le si avvicina, e dolcemente le dice.)

WALLY: (with great strength). I, cruel one, murmured to him:
Go and kill!
(with dread).
Love me now, if you can.
(She covers her face in desperation, and remains so erect in front of GIUSEPPE. He looks at her, very much moved, and approaches her and says sweetly).

HAGENBACH: Io t'amo!
(La stringe teneramente al suo cuore. Intanto il cielo si è coperto di nubi; una caligine densa sale, sale minacciosa avvolgendo i picchi circostanti del Murzoll; fra poco anche la capanna della Wally sarà avvolta in questa tenebria spaventosa delle Alpi. Comincia a soffiare il vento. Ma i due amanti, felici, strettamente abbracciati, sembrano di nulla accorgersi, e si sussurrano all'orecchio parole d'amore.)

HAGENBACH: I love you!
(He clasps her tenderly to his heart. In the meantime, the sky becomes covered with clouds; a thick mist and darkness rises threateningly, covering the peaks around Murzoll; soon even the hut will be covered up in this frightful darkness of the Alps. The wind begins to blow. But the lovers, happy, tightly embraced, seem to notice nothing and whisper words of love to each other.)

HAGENBACH: Vieni, vieni: una placida vita
noi vivremo in un mondo ignorato!

HAGENBACH: Come, come we shall live
A peaceful life
In an unknown world!

WALLY: (ripete mormorando.)
Noi viviemo in un mondo ignorato!

WALLY: We shall live in an unknown world.

HAGENBACH: Peregrini, a una piaggia fiorita
chiederemo un asilo incantato.

HAGENBACH: Pilgrims, we shall seek
An enchanted retreat
On a flowery hill!

WALLY: Chiederemo un asilo incantato
peregrini, a una piaggia fiorita.

WALLY: Pilgrims, we shall seek
An enchanted retreat
On a flowery hill!

HAGENBACH: Un asilo baciato dal sole
chiederemo a una piaggia fiorita.

HAGENBACH: A retreat kissed by the sun,
We shall seek on a flowery hill.

WALLY: Chiederemo a una piaggia fiorita
un asilo baciato dal sole.

WALLY: We shall seek on a flowery hill,
A retreat kissed by the sun.

HAGENBACH: Là, su prati, fra rose e viole
noi vivremo una placida vita.

HAGENBACH: We shall live a peaceful life!
There, on the meadows,
Midst violets and roses,

WALLY: Noi vivremo una placida vita
là, su prati fra rose e viole.
(Wally si guarda intorno spaventata dalla oscurità densa che li circonda.)
Giuseppe, ove siam noi? . . .

WALLY: We shall live a peaceful life!
There, on the meadows,
Midst violets and roses.
(WALLY looks around, frightened by the thick darkness surrounding them.)
Giuseppe, where are we?

GIUSEPPE: (con amore.) Sei sul mio cuore . . .
(guardandosi egli sbigottito dintorno)
qual cupa oscurità!

GIUSEPPE: (lovingly). You are my heart . . .
(looking frightened, around him).
What deep darkness!

WALLY: Rugge il Murzoll sinistramente . . .

WALLY: Murzoll rumbles sinistrously . . .

GIUSEPPE: La caligin nera ascende per la valle minacciosa.
(scostandosi dalla Wally.)

GIUSEPPE: The black storm
Threatening ascends the valley.
(getting away from WALLY).

WALLY: Amor mio, sola qui non mi lasciare!

WALLY: My love, don't leave me here alone!

GIUSEPPE: (raccogliendo da terra il suo bastone ferrato s'incammina a tentoni fra la incertezza della nebbia e l'imperversare dell'uragano.)
Fra le tenebre dense io vo cercando il desiato sentiero del ritorno.
(Giuseppe scompare giù pel sentiero pel quale è venuto. Si fa più impetuoso il vento—di quando in quando rumori lontani si ripercuotono cupamente per le valli ingigantiti dall'eco.)

GIUSEPPE: (picking up his iron stick, walks groping his way amid the incertitude of the fog and the raging storm.) I am looking among the thick shadows
For the path leading back.
(Giuseppe disappears down the path by which he came. The wind rages more and more—every once in a while distant rumblings resound in the valley, redoubled by the echo.)

WALLY: (sola.) (guardando giù pei sentieri pel quale Giuseppe è disceso.) Ecco, già più nol vedo!
L'Ha sommerso
la densa nebbia come onda del mare,

WALLY: (alone). (Looking down the path which Giuseppe descended.) Now, I no longer see him!
As a wave of the sea.
The thick fog swallowed him.

GIUSEPPE: (dal fondo del sentiero.) Wally!

GIUSEPPE: (from the bottom of the path.)
Wally!

WALLY: (con gioia.) Mi chiama! . . .
(sporgendosi dal sentiero, forte.)
T'odo!

WALLY: (joyfully). He calls me!
(coming out from the path, loudly).
I hate you!

GIUSEPPE: Il sentiero è scomparso . . .

WALLY: Ohimè!

GIUSEPPE: Fa core!
Discendi per le roccie e . . .
(*lontano, di sotto, grida atterrito.*)
La valanga!
(*Odesi lo schianto terribile della valanga.—L'urto è così forte che la Wally è violentemente gittata a terra—in quello spavento un grido straziante esce dal suo petto.—Subito dopo un profondo silenzio.—La Wally si trascina fino al ciglio del precipizio formato dalla valanga.—e un grido nuovo d'orrore viene strappato a lei dallo spettacolo che si offre ai di lei sguardi.—Protesa col busto fuori—essa guarda con occhi vitrei—e colla voce alterata chiama*)

GIUSEPPE: The path has disappeared.

WALLY: Woe is to me!

GIUSEPPE: Be brave!
Descend over the rocks and—
(*far away, from below, cries frightened*).
The avalanche!
(*The terrible crash of the avalanche is heard. The force is so strong that WALLY is violently thrown to the ground—in this fright a piercing cry comes from her breast. Suddenly after a long silence WALLY drags herself to the edge of the precipice formed by the avalanche—and a new cry of horror bursts from her at the sight which comes before her eyes. Stretched out, chest forward,—she looks with glassy eyes, and in changed voice, calls*).

WALLY: Giuseppe!
(*le risponde il silenzio.*)
M'odi? . . . Giuseppe! . . .
Rispondi! . . .
(*con voce piena di lagrime.*)
Cupo silenzio! . . . La morte è laggiù! . . .
(*Nasconde raccapricciata il volto nelle mani, e rimane così come impietrita.—Quando toglie dal volto le mani—il suo volto è livido—gli occhi larghi che guardano stranamente—si leva ritta sul precipizio, e stendendo con esaltazione le braccia:*)
O neve—o candido destino mio, ecco la sposa di Giuseppe!—Il bianco velo nuzial tu sei della Wally. Anima cara, le tue braccia stendimi!
(*e si getta nel precipizio, larghe le braccia come stese ad un supremo abbraccio*)

*FINE DELL'OPERA.*

WALLY: Giuseppe!
(*silence answers her*).
Do you hate me? Giuseppe! Answer!
(*with a voice full of tears.*)
Deep silence! Death is down there!
(*She hides her face in her hands, with terror, and remains as if petrified. When she takes her hands from her face—it is livid—staring eyes with a strange gaze—gets up erect, on the precipice, and stretching out her arms in exultation:*)
O snow—my white destiny,
Here is Giuseppe's bride,
You are the white bridal veil of Wally.
Dear soul, stretch your arms to me!
(*She throws herself over the precipice, with her arms stretched out as for a final embrace*).

*END OF THE OPERA.*

# Louise (1900)

## MUSIC & LIBRETTO BY GUSTAVE CHARPENTIER

This four-act Roman musical with five scenes, set to a libretto by the composer, was first performed in the Salle Favart at the Opéra-Comique in Paris on February 2, 1900. The story is set in Paris. Louise, the daughter of a working-class couple, is in love with Julien, a poor young poet. Louise's mother catches them talking to each other and immediately puts a stop to it. She chides her daughter, telling her that she is in love with a Bohemian who will amount to nothing. Louise's father agrees, although he has more compassion for his daughter's feelings. Louise promises never to see Julien again but burst into tears while reading to her father from a newspaper about the Parisian spring. In Montmartre at dawn, the streets come alive. Julien bumps into Louise as she and her mother are on their way to work at the dressmaker's. Julien rushes after Louise as her mother disappears, begging her to come and live with him. At work, Louise is distracted and unable to participate in the songs and conversations of her co-workers. They tease her; she hears her beloved's voice singing to her from outside. Pretending to be ill, she leaves; her co-workers watch her go with Julien. Louise and Julien live together in Montmarte, calling upon the city of Paris to protect their love and their lifestyle. A group of Bohemians enter and crown Louise as the Muse of Montmarttre. Louise's mother interrupts the festivities; her father is terminally ill, having taken sick when she left home. Louise agrees to go home with her mother, but gives her word to Julien that she will return. Her mother assures that this decision is all right with her. When Louise's father recovers, he and his wife don't let Louise go back to Julien. Desperate to return to the life behind, she argues with her parents, who tell her Julien will never marry her. She refuses to believe them, and insists on keeping her promise to Julien. Her father orders her to leave his house; as she walks away, he shakes his angry fist at the city which has robbed him of his daughter forever.

---

## ▪ ACTE PREMIER.

*(Une chambre mansardée dans un logement d'ouvrier. Au fond, la porte d'entrée; un peu à droite, la cuisine; sur le même côté, à l'avant-scène, une autre porte. A gauche, une porte vitrée, une grande fenêtre ouvrant sur le balcon; des toits, un coin de ciel parisien. Vis-à-vis le balcon, mais un peu plus élevée, une terrasse précédant un petit atelier d'artiste.)*

*(Six heures du soir en avril.)*

*(Au lever du rideau, Louise va à la porte d'entrée où elle écoute, craintive, puis elle revient près du balcon, regarde d'abord derrière les rideaux, ouvre la fenêtre et se montre à Julien.)*

**JULIEN:** *(debout sur le terrasse.)* O coeur ami! ô coeur promis! Helas si loin, si près!
Toi! mon idole, ma joie, mon regret!
Le jour s'envole... Ah! ta parole va-t-elle apprendre à mon amour que ton coeur prend plaisir à guetter mon bonjour?

**LOUISE:** Vous avez tardé à m'envoyer votre bonjour quotidien; je ne l'espérais plus!...
*(Elle va écouter vers la porte d'entrée, puis revient.)*

## ▪ ACT I.

*A garret room in a workmen's lodging-house. At rear the entrance door. A little to the right, the kitchen; on same side, down stage, another door. Left, a glass door and a large window opening on balcony. Roofs, a little bit of Parisian sky. Opposite, but a little higher, a terrace fronting an artist's studio.*

*It is six o'clock, in April.*

*As the curtain rises, Louise goes to entrance where she listens timidly, then she comes back to the balcony, watches first from behind the curtains, opens the window and shows herself to Julien.*

**JULIEN:** *(standing on terrace).* Oh friendly heart, oh promised heart, alas so far, so near!
You! my idol, my joy, my regret!
The day sinks—Ah shall your speech teach my love that your heart finds pleasure in awaiting my "good-day"?

**LOUISE:** You delayed in sending me your usual "good-day." I had ceased to hope for it.
*(She goes to listen at entrance door, then returns.)*

Je vous en remercie et vous envoie le mien du fond de mon coeur!
*(Elle lui envoie un baiser.)*

**JULIEN:** Tu m'as dit dans ta dernière lettre:
"Prenez patience, l'heure est prochaine, écrivez à mon père; s'il refuse irrévocablement, je promets de fuir avec vous."

**LOUISE:** *(agitée, triste.)* Je suis une folle de vous avoir dit cela. Que puis-je faire? Je vous aime tant! ... et j'aime tant mes parents! Si je les écoute, c'est la mort de mon coeur! ... Si je vous suis, Julien quel chagrin pour les miens!

**JULIEN:** *(doucement).* Ame craintive et toujours flottante ... en songeant trop à leur bonheur, ne fais-tu pas notre malheur!

**LOUISE:** *(avec coquetterie).* Malheur réparable!

**JULIEN:** *(avec chaleur).* Irréparable!

**LOUISE:** Légère déception!

**JULIEN:** Infinie souffrance!

**LOUISE:** Vous m'oublierez!

**JULIEN:** Ah! tais-toi! Tes froides railleries me font trop de peine!

**LOUISE:** On ne peut badiner avec vous: vous ne seriez pas le premier à perdre vite la mémoire. Puis, vous parlez d'amour, et, semble-t-il, vous m'adorez; m'avez-vous jamais dit comment naquit cette tendresse? ...

I thank you for it and send you mine from the bottom of my heart.
*(She sends him a kiss.)*

**JULIEN:** You told me in the last letter, "Be patient, the hour is near, write to my father; if he refuses irrevocably, I promise to fly with you."

**LOUISE:** *(moved, sadly).* I am foolish to have told you that. And I love my parents so much. If I listen to them ... the death of my heart! If I follow you, Julien, what a sorrow for my people! What can I do? I love you so much!

**JULIEN:** *(gently).* Fearsome heart and always doubting. In thinking too much of their happiness, do you not cause our misery?

**LOUISE:** *(coquettishly).* Reparable misfortune!

**JULIEN:** *(with arder).* Irreparable!

**LOUISE:** Slight deception.

**JULIEN:** Infinite suffering.

**LOUISE:** You'll forget me.

**JULIEN:** Oh! be quiet. Your cold sarcasms hurt me too much.

**LOUISE:** One can no longer joke with you. You would not be the first to quickly forget. Besides, you speak of love and, it seems, you adore me. Have you ever told me how this love was born? Would it be indiscreet to ask you to

Serais-je indiscrète en vous demandant d'en parler maintenant? Voyons, racontez et dépêchez-vous; maman va bientôt rentrer.

JULIEN: Que voulez-vous dire?

LOUISE: Contez-moi comment vous m'avez aimée. Avez-vous compris?

JULIEN: Prêtez l'oreille. Depuis longtemps j'habitais cette chambre sans me douter, hélas! que j'avais pour voisine une enfant aux grands yeux, une vierge des cieux, que des parents sévères gardaient comme une prisonnière.

LOUISE: La recluse attendait qu'un beau chevalier, ainsi que dans les livres, vint enfin la délivrer.

JULIEN: Comment l'aurais-je appris? Je dissertais le jour dans quelque brasserie, et, la nuit venue, je rimais des folies pour la lointaine Ophélie qu'évoquait mon désir; tandis que là, près moi, sommeillait l'avenir!

LOUISE: La recluse songeait au prince Charmant qui réveilla la Belle au Coeur Dormant! Comment aurait-elle su que son chevalier habitait au premier sous le ciel, et qu'en écoutant au mur, il pouvait surprendre les secrets de . . . mon coeur?

JULIEN: (s'animant). Mais un soir dans l'escalier sombre, où je dégringolais comme d'habitude en chantant (Louise va écouter à la porte, puis revient), je vis passer près de moi, ô surprise! deux ombres inconnues dont la seconde, toute jolie, de forme frêle, indécise, dans l'ombre grise, laissa comme un sillage lumineux et parfumé. Le lendemain, c'était le jour de Pâques; de grand matin, je guettais votre fenêtre . . . Quelle musique dira l'émerveillement de mes yeux quand tu vins à paraitre, dans le soleil, souriante! . . . Une madone de Vinci ne sourit pas ainsi, non! non! ces sourires mutins ne fleurissent qu'à Paris! Je regardai longuement et mon destin m'apparut, lié pour jamais à ton image; tout autour de moi s'agitait la ville immense; tout fêtait l'heureux jour; tout clamait: Espérance! Et mon coeur chantait les matines d'amour! (La porte d'entrée s'ouvre, la mère parait. Elle reste sur le seuil, écoute, puis s'avance vers la fenêtre.)

LOUISE: Moi, je vous avais remarqué biein avant ce jour-là . . . Vous souvient-il qu'une fois à la fête de Montmartre vous nous avez suivies?

speak of it now? Come, tell me and hurry. Mamma will soon return.

JULIEN: What do you mean?

LOUISE: Tell me how you came to love me. Do you understand?

JULIEN: Lend me an ear. For a long time I lived here without suspecting that I had for neighbor a child with big eyes, a virgin from heaven, whom severe parents were guarding like a prisoner.

LOUISE: The recluse waited for a handsome knight, as in the books, to come and deliver her.

JULIEN: How was I to know it? I argued the day long in some brewery and at night I rhymed follies for the distant Ophelia that grew from my desire. While there, near me, lightly slept the future!

LOUISE: The recluse dreamt of the Prince Charming who awakened the Sleeping Beauty. How could she know that her knight lived on the first floor from the sky, and that, listening against the wall he could surprise the secrets of her heart?

JULIEN: (growing animated). But one evening on the sombre stairs, which I was as usual tumbling down while singing (Louise goes to door and listens, then returns) I saw two unknown shadows passing near me, the second of which, pretty, frail of form, uncertain in the gray light, left behind her something like a luminous and perfumed furrow. The next day, it was Easter, from early morning I watched your window. What music can tell the wonder of my eyes when I saw you appear in the sunlight, smiling! A madonna of Vinci does not smile like that; no, no. These cunning smiles only flower in Paris. I watched long and my destiny appeared to me united forever with your image. All about me was the movement of the immense city. Everything resounded. Hope and my heart sang the matins of love! (The entrance door opens, the mother appears. She remains on the sill, then moves toward window.)

LOUISE: As for me, I had noticed you long before that day. Do you remember that once at the feast of Montmartre you followed us?

JULIEN: S'il m'en souvient . . . Vous m'avez souri et vous vous retourniez si fréquemment que votre mère prit la mouche et vous fit une scène . . . l'entêtée jalouse!

LOUISE: Une autre fois dans la cour, tandis que je puisais de l'eau, de votre fenêtre vous m'avez jeté des pétales de roses . . . J'en étais comme couverte et je restais tout étourdie, toute ravie . . .

JULIEN: Mais votre mère de sa fenêtre nous guettait . . .

LOUISE: Sous l'avalanche parfumée, mon coeur battait à se briser . . .

JULIEN: Notre ennemie, furieuse, vous rappela!

LOUISE: Et le doux songe s'envola! . . .

JULIEN: Mais l'amour veillait et dans l'ombre apprêtait d'inespérées, de chastes fiançailles. Or, un soir que je passais devant votre porte.

LA MERE: (à part.) Que vais-je apprendre?

JULIEN: . . . Je la vis s'ouvrir lentement . . . une forme blanche se dressa . . . et s'élança vers moi! C'était toi! C'était Louise!

LOUISE: Elle venait te dire: L'aveu que mes parents out tenté d'étouffer, je viens le proclamer!

LA MERE: (à part, ricanant). Ah! ah! ah! Très bien!

JULIEN: Ah! les douces fiancailles!

LOUISE: Nous ne pouvions pas nous parler . . .

JULIEN: Mes yeux cherchaient en vain tes yeux . . .

ENSEMBLE: Nos deux coeurs, l'un près de l'autre, follement bondissaient! . . . De la maison endormie le souffle grondait . . . et la nuit nous bercait! . . . (Les deux amants restent un moment pensifs, puis Louise veut aller à la porte, elle se retourne et voit sa mère.)

LOUISE: Ah! . . . (La mère la saisu par le bras, l'entraine dans la cuisine, et revient près de la fenêtre.)

JULIEN: (écoute avec inquiétude). Eh bien! vous ne dites plus rien, chère Louise? (mimique furieuse de la mère.) De grâce, répondez avant que votre geôlière tienne nous prendre.

LA MERE: (se moutrant à Julien). Allez-vous bientôt vous taire? ou faut-il que j'aille vous tirer les oreilles? . . . (Stupeur de Julien. La mère entre dans la chambre voisine; Louise sort de la cuisine. Julien reparait sur le balcon; il montre à Louise la

JULIEN: If I remember—you smiled to me and turned your head so frequently that your mother took alarm and made a scene—jealous obstinacy.

LOUISE: Another time, in the courtyard, as I was drawing water, you threw rose petals on me from your window. I was covered with them and I stood astonished, delighted.

JULIEN: But your mother was watching us from a window.

LOUISE: Under the avalanche of flowers my heart was beating, fit to break.

JULIEN: Our enemy, furious, called you away.

LOUISE: And the sweet dream flew off.

JULIEN: But love was watching and, in the dark, was making ready our unexpected and chaste betrothal. Thus one night I was passing by your door—

MOTHER: (aside). What am I about to learn?

JULIEN: I saw it slowly open—a white form appeared—and rushed toward me. It was you—Louise.

LOUISE: She came to say: "The vow my parents tried to stifle, I come to proclaim."

MOTHER: (aside, grinning). Ah, ah, ah; very good.

JULIEN: And the sweet betrothal—

LOUISE: We couldn't speak.

JULIEN: My eyes sought yours in vain.

TOGETHER: Our two hearts, one next to the other, beat madly. From the sleeping house, breaths grumbled—and the night cradled us! (The lovers remain thoughtful a moment. Louise turns to go to the door and sees her mother.)

LOUISE: Ah! (Mother seizes her by the arm, pulls her in the kitchen, and comes back to the window.)

JULIEN: (listening anxiously). Well, you don't talk any more, dear Louise. (Mother is furious.) For pity's sake answer before your jailer surprises us.

MOTHER: (showing herself to Julien). Are you going to stop talking; or shall I come and pull your ears? (Astonishment of Julien. Mother exits into room. Louise comes out of kitchen and Julien reappears on balcony. He shows Louise the letter he has written to the par-

lettre qu'il doit envoyer aux parents, puis il disparait. Louise craintive, regagne la cuisine.)

JULIEN: (à la cantonade). Tra la la la la la la!
(Il rit bruyamment.)
Ha! ha! ha! ha! ha! ha!
(La mère reparaî t. Elle ferme la fenêtre et guette un moment derrière le rideau. Louise, tremblante, sort de la cuisine; elle range sur le buffet, les provisions apportées par la mère; celle-ci s'avance vers elle.)

LA MERE: (imitant Julien.) "C'etait mon adorée!
(Louise, pour l'eviter, tourne autour de la table.)
"Ma douce fiancée! La fidèle promise! Ma Louise!
(La mère, féroce, prend les mains de Louise.)
"Nous ne pouvions pas nous parler! . . . Mes yeux cherchaient en tes yeux! . . . Nos coeurs bondissaient! L'ombre frémissait! Et tout le monde dormait!"
(Louise s'échappe; la mère lui montre le point.—Exaspérée.) . . . Ah! malheureuse enfant! Si ton père l'apprenait! S'il vous avait surpris! Hein! s'il vous avait surpris! dis!
(Louise se cache le visage.)
Lui qui te croit si naïve, si sage, s'il connaissait ta conduite, il en mourrait!

LOUISE: (suppliante). Pouquoi ne roulez-vous pas nous marier? Pourquoi m'obligez-vous à me chacher? Qu'avez-vous à lui reprocher? Ses manières d'artiste, sa gaité, son métier de poète . . .

LA MERE: Un chenapan! un crève-faim! un débauché sans vergogne!

LOUISE: Lui, si bon, si courageux!

LA MERE: . . . Un pilier de cabaret!

LOUISE: S'il avait une femme, il n'irait pas cabaret!

LA MERE: Une femme! Ah! ah! ah! Ce ne sont pas les femmes qui lui manquent!

LOUISE: Ah, je t'en prie, si tu crois m'en détacher, tu te trompes, car tes attaques me le font chérir davantage!
Tu peux nous empêcher d'être heureux . . . Jamais, jamais tu ne briseras notre amour!

LA MERE: Ah! quel aplomb! Au lieu de baisser la tête, tu oses te vanter de ton amant!

LOUISE: Mon amant! . . . Il ne l'est pas encore! . . . mais on dirait vraiment que vous voulez qu'il le devienne!

LA MERE: (s'élance sur Louise qui l'évite en tournant autour de la table.) Petite malheureuse! Tu nous menaces!

---

ents, then disappears. Louise, frightened, goes into kitchen again.)

JULIEN: (outside). Tra, la, la, la, la, la.
(He laughs loudly.)
Ha, ha, ha, ha, ha, ha.
(Mother reappears. She closes window and watches. Louise, trembling, comes out of kitchen. She arranges on the buffet the provisions brought by mother, who advances on her.)

MOTHER: (Imitating Julien). It was my adored one.
(Louise, to avoid her, turns around table.)
'My gentle betrothed! My promised one; my Louise!
(The angry mother takes Louise's hands in hers.)
'We couldn't speak. My eyes sought yours in vain. Our hearts beat together. The shadows trembled. And the world slept.'
(Louise breaks away. The mother shakes her fist exasperated.)
Oh, unhappy child! If your father knew. If he had surprised you. Eh, say, had he surprised you?
(Louise hides her face in her hands.)
He who believed you to be so innocent, so good; if he knew of your goings on, he'd die of it.

LOUISE: (pleading). Why don't you let us marry? Why compel me to hide? What can you reproach him with—his artist's manners, his good humor, his occupation of poet?

MOTHER: A rascal, a starveling, a dissipator.

LOUISE: He! So good, so courageous.

MOTHER: The pillar of a wine shop.

LOUISE: If he had a wife he wouldn't go to the wine shop.

MOTHER: A wife! Ha, ha, ha! It is not women that he seeks!

LOUISE: I beg of you, if you think to turn me, you are mistaken; your running him down only makes me love him more. You may prevent our being happy. Never, never, will you break our love!

MOTHER: What impudence! In place of being ashamed, you dare to boast of your lover.

LOUISE: My lover! He's not that yet, but one would almost think you wish he were.

MOTHER: (jumping at Louise, who avoids her around the table). Little wretch! You threaten us. Take care that I don't explain to your fa-

---

Ah! prends garde que je n'explique tout à ton père! . . .
(Elles entendent des pas dans l'escalier; craintives elles se taisent, écoutent; le père entre. Le père tient une lettre à la main; la mère va vite à la cuisine; Louise, troublée, débarrasse la table pour le repas.)

LE PERE: Bonsoir! La soupe est prête?

LA MERE: (criant de la cuisine.) Oui, de suite.
(Le père s'assied. Louise tisonne le feu. Le père regarde la lettre, la dècachéte et lit. Louise revient portant les assiettes, les verres, les couverts. Le père pose la lettre sur la table et regarde sa fille. Le père lui tend les bras: ils s'embrassent. La mère rentre, portant la soupe; le père sert la soupe. Ils mangent. La mère se lève, va porter les assiettes et la soupière dans la cuisine.)

LE PERE: Ah! quelle journée!

LOUISE: Tu es fatigué?

LE PERE: Je sens que je ne suis plus jeune et les journées sont longues!

LOUISE: Pauvre père, tu ne te reposeras donc jamais?
(La mère revient avec le ragoût.)

LE PERE: Et qui ferait bouillir la marmite si je quittais l'outil?

LA MERE: Depuis trente ans que tu t'échines, tu aurais bien mérité un peu de repos.
(Regardant du côte de la fenêtre de Julien.)
Quand on pense qu'il y a tant de fainéants qui passent leur vie à faire la fête!

LE PERE: Ils ont la chance d'être venus au monde après leurs pères!

LA MERE: (rageuse). Tu trouves que c'est juste? Moi, je dis que tout le monde devrait travailler!

LE PERE: L'égalité, les grands mots, l'impossible! Si on avait le droit de choisir, on choisirait le métier le moins fatigant!

LA MERE: (regardant sa fille). C'est vrai, tout le monde voudrait être artiste!

LE PERE: (riant). Et il ne resterait personne pour faire les gros ouvrages!
Il y a longtemps que j'en ai pris mon parti! . . .
Quand on n'a pas de rentes, il faut se contenter d'en gagner pour les autres . . .
Chacun son lot dans la belle vie!

LA MERE: Tu es bien résigné aujourd'hui: les rentes ne seraient pas à dédaigner.

---

ther!
(They hear steps on the stairs. Frightened, they stop and listen. Father enters. He holds a letter in his hand. Mother goes quickly to kitchen. Louise, anxious, sets the table.)

FATHER: Good evening. Is the soup ready?

MOTHER: (from the kitchen). Yes, right away.
(Father sits down. Louise pokes the fire. Father looks at letter, opens and reads it. Louise returns with the plates, glasses and napkins. Father puts letter down and looks at his daughter. He opens his arms. They embrace. Mother brings in the soup. They eat. Mother carries plates and tureen into kitchen.)

FATHER: Oh, what a day!

LOUISE: You are tired.

FATHER: I feel that I am no longer young and that the days are long.

LOUISE: Poor father, will you never have a rest?
(Mother re-enters with stew.)

FATHER: And who'd keep the pot boiling if I quit work?

MOTHER: For the thirty years you've kept at it, you've certainly earned a bit of rest.
(Looking toward Julien's window.)
And when one thinks of how many loafers there are who pass their lives enjoying themselves.

FATHER: They had the luck to come into the world after their fathers.

MOTHER: (raging). Do you find that just? I say that everybody ought to work.

FATHER: Equality, big words, the impossible. If one had the right to choose, he'd take the occupation that was easiest.

MOTHER: (looking at Louise). True, everybody would want to be an artist.

FATHER: (laughing). And there would remain nobody to do the hard work. For a long time I've made up my mind when one hasn't an income one must work for others to have it. Everyone to his own fate in the great life.

MOTHER: You are too resigned. An income is not to be despised.

LE PERE: Ceux qui en ont sont-ils plus heureux? Le bonheur, vois-tu, c'est d'être comme nous sommes, nous aimant bien, nous portant bien; ce bonheur-là, nul ne peut nous le prendre!
(*La mère dessert.*)
Le bonheur, c'est le foyer où l'on se repose, où on oublie près de ceux qu'on aime, les malechances de la vie!...
(*Il attire sa fille à lui et l'embrasse.*)
Ceux qui ont des rentes aujourd'hui n'en auront peut-être plus demain...
Nous, toujours, nous serons heureux!
(*Il se lève, saisit par ta taille la mere lui fait faire quelques tours de valse lourde. La mère se dégage.*)

LA MERE: Assez! Vas-tu finir! Grand fou!

LE PERE: (*riant*). Ah! ah! ah! je suis heureux!
(*Il cherche sa pipe, la bourre, s'assied près du feu.*)

LA MERE: (*à Louise, durement*). Vas-tu me laisser faire toute la besogne? Allons, remue toi!
(*La mère débarrasse la table. Louise essuie la table, elle apercoit la lettre de Julien; elle y met un baiser furtif, puis s'avance vers le père et la lui donne.*)

LE PERE: Ah! merci...
(*Il regard malignement sa fille. Louise s'éloigne. La mère apporte une lampe allumée. Le père relit la lettre.*)

LA MERE: (*au père*). Une lettre?

LE PERE: Oui, une lettre du voisin...

LA MERE: Une autre lettre?

LE PERE: Il renouvelle sa demande...

LA MERE: Quel toupet! Après ce qui s'est passé!...

LE PERE: Que veux-tu dire?...

LA MERE: (*embarrassée*). Après notre premier refus...

LE PERE: (*avec bienveillance*). Mon Dieu! sa lettre est gentille...
(*Il montre Louise.*) il semble l'aimer, il n'est pas déteste de Louise...
(*Louise se jette dans les bras de son père.*)

LA MERE: (*dont la colère éclate*). C'est trop fort! Il en a de l'aplomb!

LE PERE: Allons! allons! ce n'est pas la peine de se mettre en colère... Tu tournes tout au tragique... Il serait facile de prendre de nouveaux renseignements... savoir s'il est devenu... plus sérieux. Nous ne sommes pas forcés de lui donner Louise dès demain et il ne va pas nous l'enlever, je suppose?

FATHER: Those who have one, are they any happier? Happiness, you see, is to be just as we are, loving one another, in good health. That happiness no one can take from us.
(*Mother clears table.*)
Happiness is the fireside where one rests, where one forgets, close to those one loves, the ill fortunes of life.
(*He draws her to him and kisses her.*)
Those who have the income today, perhaps won't have any tomorrow. As for us, we'll always be happy.
(*He rises, seizes Mother by the waist and makes a few heavy waltz steps. Mother gets away.*)

MOTHER: Enough. Let up. Big fool!

FATHER: (*laughing*). Ha, ha, ha! I'm happy!
(*He gets his pipe, fills it and sits by the fire.*)

MOTHER: (*to Louise, hard*). Are you going to let me do all the work? Come, move about.
(*Mother clears table; Louise wipes it off and sees letter of Julien. She kisses it furtively and gives it to her father.*)

FATHER: Ah, thank you.
(*He looks banteringly at his daughter. Louise moves away. Mother brings lighted lamp. Father reads letter again.*)

MOTHER: (*to Father*). A letter?

FATHER: Yes; a letter from the neighbor.

MOTHER: Another letter?

FATHER: He renews his request.

MOTHER: What a nerve, after all that has taken place!

FATHER: What do you mean?

MOTHER: (*embarrassed*). After our first refusal.

FATHER: (*kindly*). Good Lord! His letter is nice. (*Pointing to Louise.*) He appears to love her, and he is not displeasing to Louise.
(*Louise throws herself in Father's arms.*)

MOTHER: (*whose anger explodes*). This is too much. He has his impudence with him.

FATHER: Come, come; it's nothing to get in a rage about. You make a tragedy of everything. We can easily make new inquiries about him—find out if he has become more settled.
We are not forced to give him Louise tomorrow, and he's not going to abduct her, I suppose. If our

... Si les renseignements ne suffisent pas, eh bien, on l'invitera... lorsque je l'aurai vu, je...

LA MERE: Lui, ici, par exemple! S'il entre ici, moi, j'en sortirai!

LE PERE: (*conciliant*). Allons! allons!

LA MERE: Tu voudrais m'obliger à recevoir ici ce vaurien qui me rit au nez quand il me rencontre...

LE PERE: Des gamineries!

LA MERE: Ce chenapan, ce débauché, ce bohème, ce pilier de cabaret dont l'existence est le scandale da quartier! Et je ne dis pas tout! car j'en sais sur son compte des infamies!...

LOUISE: (*perdant la tête*). Ce n'est pas vrai!
(*La mère lui donne une gifle. Le père s'interpose, très ennuyé. Louise tombe accablée sur une chaise, et pleure... Le père revient vers sa fille.*)

LE PERE: O mon enfant, ma Louise, tu sais combien nous t'aimons! Si nous sommes prudents vis-à-vis de ceux qui te remarquent, c'est qu'arrivés au bout du chemin que tu vas gravir, nous en connaissons toutes les misères!
(*La mère est allée en bougonnant dans la cuisine, et s'est mise à repasser.*)
A ton âge, on voit tout beau, tout rose!... Prendre un mari, c'est choisir une poupée.
(*Geste étonné de Louise.*)
Oui, une poupée! malheureusement, ces poupées-là, ma fille, vous font parfois pleurer bien des larmes!

LOUISE: Oui, quand elles sont méchantes... Mais en la choisissant bonne, gentille, aimante...

LE PERE: Comment veux-tu la choisir, petite fille?

LOUISE: Avec mon coeur!

LE PERE: C'est un bien mauvais juge...

LOUISE: Pourquoi donc?

LE PERE: Qui dit amoureux, toujours dit aveugle!...

LA MERE: (*à part*). S'il veut discuter avec elle, il n'a pas fini!
(*La mère pose son fer sur la table très fort.*)

LOUISE: (*plus hardiment*). Mais avant d'aimer, avant d'être aveugle, ne peut-on découvrir les défauts de celui... qu'on aimera?

LE PERE: Peut-être, s'il ne nous manquait une chose...

LOUISE: Laquelle?

LE PERE: L'expérience!

LOUISE: (*moqueuse*). Alors ceux qui se marient deux fois sont plus heureux la seconde

inquiries don't result well, then we'll have him call. When I shall have seen him, I—

MOTHER: Him, here! Indeed! If he comes, I leave.

FATHER: (*conciliating*). Come, come.

MOTHER: You would force me to receive here this good-for-nothing who laughs in my face when I meet him.

FATHER: Boyishness!

MOTHER: This rascal, debauchee, bohemian! This saloon supporter whose existence is the scandal of the quarter. And I don't say everything. I know a few other dreadful things about him.

LOUISE: (*losing her head*). It is not true.
(*Mother smacks her face. Father interferes, much annoyed. Louise falls on a chair exhausted and weeps. Father goes toward his daughter.*)

FATHER: Oh, my child; my Louise. You know how we love you. If we are prudent toward those who notice you, it is, that having arrived at the end of the road that you begin, we know all the miseries of it.
(*Mother has gone sulkily into kitchen and starts ironing.*)
At your age everything is beautiful, rose colored. Taking a husband is choosing a doll.
(*Louise is astonished.*)
Yes, a doll. Unfortunately, these sorts of dolls, my daughter, often make you shed many tears.

LOUISE: Yes, when they are wicked. But in choosing one that is good, gentle, loving—

FATHER: How would you choose it, little girl?

LOUISE: With my heart.

FATHER: It's a very poor judge.

LOUISE: But why?

FATHER: One who speaks of love always speaks blindly.

MOTHER: (*aside*). If he's going to argue with her he'll not finish.
(*Mother places iron down very hard.*)

LOUISE: (*boldly*). But before loving, before being blind, can one not discover the faults of the person— who will be loved?

FATHER: Perhaps, only that one thing is wanting.

LOUISE: Which?

FATHER: Experience.

LOUISE: (*mockingly*). Then those who marry twice are happier the second time.

LE PERE: (*sérieux*). Ne plaisante pas, Louise! S'il est difficile de déchiffrer les coeurs, on peut toujours lire dans le passé de celui qu'on aime, et par là pressentir l'avenir.
(*La mère, qui s'impatiente, chante un motif du récit de Julien.*)

LA MERE: La! la! la! la! la!

LE PERE: Crois-tu qu'il t'aime?

LOUISE: Oui!

LA MERE: La! la! la! la! la!

LE PERE: Et toi, crois-tu l'aimer?
(*Louise se cache la tête sur la poitrine de son père.*)

LA MERE: (*à mi-voix*). "C'etait mon adorée . . ."

LE PERE: Il ne t'a jamais parlé?

LOUISE: (*avec effort*). Non!
(*Le père la regarde un peu méflant.*)

LA MERE: (*à part, continuant d'imiter Julien*). "Nous ne pouvions pas nous parler!
. . . Nous ne pouvions pas nous regarder! . . . Nos coeurs bondissaient! L'ombre frémissait! Et tout le monde dormait!"
(*Louise très troublée se détourne; le père lui prend les mains.*)

LE PERE: Louise, si je repousse sa demande, me promets-tu de l'oublier?
(*Louise hésite.*)
Promets-tu d'obéir en fille sage à notre volonté?
Ah! si tu devais un jour renier ma tendresse, sache bien que, privé de toi, je ne pourrais vivre . . . ô mon enfant, ma Louise! . . .

LOUISE: (*émue*). Père, toujours, je vous aimerai!
(*Le père la presse sur son coeur, elle éclate en sauglots.*)

LE PERE: (*relève Louise*). Allons, enfant, sèche tes belles mirettes!
Ce gros chagrin passera . . . et plus tard tu nous remercieras de t'avoir préservée du malheur . . . Allons! allons! petite folle!
(*Il prend le journal sur la table, enjoué.*)
Tiens, lis-moi le journal, ca te distraira et ca ménagera mes pauvres yeux . . . Veux-tu!
(*La mère rentre et s'assied près de la table, reprenant du linge.*)

LOUISE: (*avec effort*). Oui . . .
(*Dix heures sonnent. Louise prend le journal, va s'asseoir près de la lampe et commence sa lecture d'une voix étranglée de sanglots.*) (*lisant*). "La saison printanière est des plus brillantes. Paris

---

FATHER: (*seriously*). Do not joke, Louise. If it is difficult to know hearts, one can read in the past of whoever one loves and by that means learn something of the future.
(*Mother, who is growing impatient, sings snatches from the song of Julien.*)

MOTHER: La, la, la, la.

FATHER: Do you believe he loves you?

LOUISE: Yes.

MOTHER: La, la, la, la.

FATHER: And you; do you believe you love him?
(*Louise hides her head in her father's breast.*)

MOTHER: (*in a low voice*). "He was my adored one."

FATHER: And he never spoke to you?

LOUISE: (*with effort*). No.
(*The Father looks at her doubtingly.*)

MOTHER: (*aside, still imitating Julien*). "We could not speak to one another! We could not see each other. Our hearts beat madly. The shadows trembled. And all the world slept."
(*Louise, troubled, turns away. Father takes her hands.*)

FATHER: Louise, should I reject his request, will you promise me to forget him?
(*Louise hesitates.*)
Do you promise, like a good girl, to obey our will?
Ah, if some day you should betray my love, know this, that deprived of you, I could not live. Oh, my child, my Louise.

LOUISE: (*moved*). Father, always I shall love you!
(*Father presses her to his heart. She bursts into tears*).

FATHER: (*raises her*). Come child, dry your pretty eyes. This big grief will pass, and later you will thank us for having saved you from trouble. Come, come, little fool.
(*He takes up paper on table. Gaily.*)
Here, read me the paper. It will make you forget and will save my poor eyes. Will you?
(*Mother enters, sits at table, mending linen.*)

LOUISE: (*with effort*). Yes.
(*Ten o'clock strikes. Louise takes the paper, sits by the lamp and reads with voice full of tears. Reading.*)
"The Spring season is most brilliant. All Paris is in holiday garb—"

---

tout en fête."
(*Elle sanglote.*)
Paris! . . .
(*Le rideau tombe lentement.*)

## ■ ACTE DEUXIEME

### PREMIER TABLEAU.

(*Un carrefour au bas de la butte Montmartre. A gauche, un hangar; à droite une maison et un cabaret. Au fond, à droite, un escalier montant. Au fond, à gauche, un escalier descendant. Au loin, à droite, la Butte; à gauche le faubourg.*)

(*Sous le bangar, Une Laitiere prèpare son étalage et allume son feu; près d'elle Une Fillette plie les journaux du matin.—A droite, Une petite Chiffonniere travaille bâtivement; à côte d'elle une Glaneuse de charbon et, plus loin, un Bricoleur fouillent les ordures. Des Menageres vont aux provisions.*)

(*Cinq beures du matin, en avril.*)

LA PETITE CHIFFONNIERE: (*à la glaneuse*). Dire qu'en c'moment y a des femmes qui dorment dans d'la soie!

LA GLANEUSE: Bah! les draps de soie s'usent plus vite que les autres . . .

LA PETITE CHIFFONNIERE: Oui, parce qu'on y dort plus longtemps!

LA GLANEUSE: Grande bête! . . . ton tour viendra.

LA PETITE CHIFFONNIERE: Mon tour! . . . si c'était vrai!
(*Un noctambule parait.*)

LE NOCTAMBULE: (*à la plieuse*). Si jolie, si matin! . . .
Malice du destin
qui revêt de satin
et de robes d'aurore
les guetteuses de nuit
aux rides inclémentes
et cache au libertin,
sous des voiles de nuit,
les fillettes d'aurore
que le désir tourmente!
Un baiser?

LA PLIEUSE: Passez vot' chemin!

LE NOCTAMBULE: Mon chemin?
Je le cherche . . .
me tendras-tu la perche?
Sans les lanternes de tes jolis yeux,
je risque fort de me perdre? . . . Tu veux? . . .
(*Elle lui tourne le dos.*)

LA GLANEUSE ET LE BRICOLEUR: Ah! . . . (*s'étirant.*) Ah! . . .

LE NOCTAMBULE: (*regardant autour de lui*). En ce froid carrefour où gémit la souffrance, je me sens mal à l'aise et . . .

---

(*She sobs.*)
"Paris—"
(*The curtain falls slowly.*)

## ■ ACT II.

### SCENE I.

(*A meeting of streets below Montmartre. Left, a shed. Right, a house and a drinking shop. Rear, right, stairway going up. Rear, on left, a stairway going down. In distance, the Butte—left, the Faubourg.*)

(*Under the shed a milk woman prepares her layout and lights her fire. Near her a girl folds the morning papers. Right, a little rag picker works quickly. By her side a coal gatherer, and further a scavenger turning over the dirt. Housekeepers pass to market.*)

(*Five in the morning, April.*)

LITTLE RAG PICKER: (*to coal woman*). And to think that, right now, there are women who sleep in silk.

COAL WOMAN: Bah, silk sheets go quicker than others.

LITTLE RAG PICKER: Yes, because they sleep longer in them.

COAL WOMAN: Big fool. Your turn'll come.

LITTLE RAG PICKER: My turn! If it were only true.
(*Night Walker appears.*)

NIGHT WALKER: (*to newspaper girl*). So pretty, so early!
Malice of fate,
That in satin, clothes
With robes of the dawn,
The watchers of night,
Wrinkled and pale,
And hides from the libertine
Under cover of night
The children of dawn
Whom desire torments!
A kiss?

PAPER FOLDER: Go your way.

NIGHT WALKER: My way I now seek.
Will you be my guide?
Without the lights of your pretty eyes
I risk being lost—Will you?
(*She turns her back on him.*)

COAL WOMAN and SCAVENGER: Ah! (*stretching*). Ah!

NIGHT WALKER: (*looking about*) In this cold, wretched street, where suffering reigns, I am not at my ease, and—

*(A la fillette.)*
sans ta jeune chair,
il me semblerait choir au seuil du
sombre enfer
où le Dante écrivit: "Ici point
d'espérance!"
Le son de ma voix
éveille-t-il en toi
une vague souvenance,
que tu restes songeuse?
Peut-être un frais désir
fait tressaillir
ton coeur d'amoureuse?

**LA PLIEUSE:** *(riant).* Vous êtes
fou!

**LA LAITIERE:** *(riant).* Sa folie
n'est pas dangereuse... Qui êtes-
vous?

**LE NOCTAMBULE:** *(Rejetant son
manteau sur l'épaule et apparaissant séduisant.)*
Je suis le Plaisir de Paris.
*(Les deux femmes font un geste
d'étonnement admiratif. La petite
chiffonnière interrompt son travail et s'approche.)*

**LA LAITIERE:** Où allez-vous?

**LE NOCTAMBULE:** Je vais vers les
amantes
que le désir tourmente.
Je vais cherchant les coeurs
qu'oublia le bonheur.
*(Montrant la ville.)*
Là-bas glânant le rire... ici semant
l'envie,
prêchant partout le droit de tous à
la folie.
Je suis le procureur de la grande
cité,
ton humble serviteur!... ou ton
maitre!...

**LA LAITIERE:** *(le menacant).* Ef-
fronté!
*(Il s'enfuit en riant. Au coin de la
rue, il heurte violemment un chiffonnier et disparaît. Le chiffonnier chancelle et tombe.)*

**LE CHIFFONNIER:** Fait' attention
...butor!

**LE NOCTAMBULE:** *(déjà loin).* Je
suis le procureur de la grande cité!

**LE CHIFFONNIER:** *(à part).* Ah!
... je le connais... le misérable! Ce
n'est pas la première fois qu'il se
trouve sur mon chemin...
*(Au bricoleur.)*
Un soir, il y a longtemps, je m'en
souviens comme si c'était hier...
ici, au même endroit... il m'est ap-
paru... Hélas! il n'était pas seul, ce
jour-là! une fillette lui donnait la
main et souriait à sa chanson!
C'était ma fille!
Je l'avais laissée là, au travail... il
est venu, il lui a soufflé à l'oreille
ses tentations mauvaises... et la coquette l'a écouté! Ell'l'a suivi! En
s'enfuyant ell'm'a heurté!...
Comme aujourd'hui... je suis
tombé!... ah!...
*(Il sanglote et se met au travail.)*

*(To the girl)*
Without your young flesh I would
seem to fall on the brink of sombre
hell, where Dante wrote, "Here
give up hope."
The sound of my voice
wakes in you
A vague remembrance
That you dreamt?
Perhaps some fresh desire makes
Your amorous heart palpitate.

**THE PAPER GIRL:** *(laughing).*
You are crazy.

**MILK WOMAN:** *(laughing).* But
it's not dangerous. Who are you?

**NIGHT WALKER:** *(opening cloak
and looking seductive).* I am the
Pleasure of Paris.
*(The two women express sur-
prised admiration. The Rag Picker stops her work to come nearer.)*

**MILK SELLER:** Where are you going?

**NIGHT WALKER:** I go to the lovers
Whom desire torments;
I go looking for hearts
Forgotten by joy.
*(Pointing at the town.)*
There gathering laughter—here
sowing envy—
Preaching broadcast the right of all
to folly.
I am the soul of the great city.
Your humble servant—or your
master!

**MILK WOMAN:** *(threatening
him).* Impudent!
*(He escapes laughing. At the cor-
ner he knocks down a rag picker
and disappears.)*

**RAG PICKER:** Look out—fool!

**NIGHT WALKER:** *(far away).* I
am the soul of the great city.

**RAG PICKER:** *(aside).* Ah! I know
him—the wretch! This is not the
first time I find him in my way.
*(To the Scavenger.)*
One night, long ago—I remember
it as if it were yesterday—here, at
the same place, he appeared to me.
Alas! he was not alone that day, for a
young girl held him by the hand and
smiled at his song. It was my daughter!
I had left her at work. He came and
whispered his bad temptations in
her ear. And the coquette listened
to him. She followed him and, in escaping, knocked against me—like
today. I fell—ah!
*(He sobs and starts working.)*

**LA GLANEUSE:** Pauvre homme!
...

**LE BRICOLEUR:** Bah! dans toutes
les familles, c'est la même chose!
Moi, j'en avais trois... je n'ai pu les
tenir!... Faut pas leur en vouloir si
elles préfèr' à notre vie d'enfer le
paradis qui les appelle làbas!...

**LA PETITE CHIFFONNIERE:** *(à
part).* Est-c'que les bons lits, les
belles robes, comme le soleil, ne
devraient pas être à tout le monde!
*(Elle tend les bras vers le soleil.)*
*(Deux Gardiens de la Paix traver-
sent lentement la scène et
s'approchent de la laitière. Le carrefour s'anime.—Une Balayeuse
apparait.)*

**PREMIER GARDIEN:** *(à la laitière).* Belle journée!

**LA LAITIERE:** Voici le printemps!

**PREMIER GARDIEN:** La saison des
amours...

**LA LAITIERE:** Pour ceux qui ont
vingt ans!...

**DEUXIEME GARDIEN:** Bah! Chacun son tour!

**LA LAITIERE:** J'attends encore le
mien!

**PREMIER GARDIEN:** Vous n'avez
jamais aimé?
*(Un gavroche s'approche et se
chauffe les mains au fourneau.)*

**LA LAITIERE:** *(simplement).* Je
n'ai pas eu le temps.
*(Les gardiens rient.)*

**LE GAVROCHE:** *(à la laitière).* Un
p'tit noir!

**LA BALAYEUSE:** *(fanfaronne).*
Moi, j'ai eu ch'vaux et voiture... Y
a vingt ans... J'étais la reine de
Paris! Quell' dégringolade! hein?
mais je ne regrette rien!... je me
suis tant amusée. Ah! la belle vie! le
joyeux, le tendre, l'inoubliable
paradis!

**LE GAVROCHE:** *(avec une
naïveté feinte.)* Dites; donnez-moi
l'adresse...

**LA BALAYEUSE:** Quelle adresse?

**LE GAVROCHE:** L'adresse... de
vot' "paradis!"

**LA BALAYEUSE:** Mais, mon petit
...
*(Montrant la ville, tendre.)*
C'est Paris!

**LE GAVROCHE:** *(jouant
l'étonnement).* Paris!... C'est
étonnant! depuis que j'suis au
monde j'm'en étais pas encore
apercu!

**PREMIER GARDIEN:** Allons! circule!

**LE GAVROCHE:** De quoi! On
n'peut pas s'instruire?

**PREMIER GARDIEN:** Va travailler!
*(Il le pousse. Le gavroche s'en va.
Il se retourne.)*

**CHARCOAL WOMAN:** Poor man!

**SCAVENGER:** Hah! It's the same
thing in all families. I had three—I
couldn't hold them. Who's to
blame if they prefer to our life of
hell the paradise that awaits them
over there.

**LITTLE RAG PICKER:** *(aside.)*
Ought not good beds, fine dresses,
like the sun, be the property of ev-
eryone?
*(She lifts her arms toward the sun.
Two Peace Officers slowly cross
stage and approach Milk Woman.
Street gets animated. A Street
Sweeper comes on.)*

**FIRST OFFICER:** *(to Milk Woman).* Fine day.

**MILK WOMAN:** Spring is with us.

**OFFICER:** The season of love.

**MILK WOMAN:** For those who are
twenty.

**SECOND OFFICER:** Bah! Each one
in his turn.

**MILK WOMAN:** I'm still waiting
for mine.

**FIRST OFFICER:** You've never
loved?
*(Street urchin enters; warms his
hands.)*

**MILK WOMAN:** I hadn't the time.
*(Officers laugh.)*

**STREET URCHIN:** *(to Milk Woman).* A little black.

**STREET SWEEPER:** *(boastingly).*
I had horses and carriages—twenty
years ago. I was the queen of Paris.
What a fall, eh? But I regret nothing.
I had so much fun. What a fine
life—the joyous, the sweet, the unforgettable paradise.

**URCHIN:** *(with feigned innocence).* Say, give me the address.

**SWEEPER:** What address?

**URCHIN:** Why, of your "paradise."

**SWEEPER:** Look here, young fellow *(pointing at city tenderly).*
It's Paris.

**URCHIN:** *(pretending astonishment.)* Paris! Astonishing! Since I
came into the world, I never suspected it.

**FIRST OFFICER:** Come, move on.

**URCHIN:** What for? Can't one learn
anything?

**FIRST OFFICER:** Go to work.
*(Officer pushes him. Urchin goes,
then turns.)*

LE GAVROCHE: (criant). Y en a donc que pour les femm's, dans vot' "paradis"?
(Geste menaçant des gardiens; le gamin s'enfuit; les gardiens s'éloignent. La petite chiffonnière s'en va courbée sous le poids d'un sac de chiffons. La balayeuse reprend son travail.)

URCHIN: (shouting). There's only room for women—in your paradise.
(Officers threaten him—he flies. Officers depart. The little Rag Picker exits, bending under load. Sweeper resumes work.)

LA PETITE CHIFFONNIERE: (avec amertume.) Y en a qu'pour les femmes!
(Julien paraît au fond de la scène: il fait un signe à ses amis dont les têtes surgissent en haut de l'escalier descendant. Les Bohèmes, s'avancent, comiquement, avec des allures de conspirateurs.)

LITTLE RAG PICKER: (bitterly). There's only room for women.
(Julien appears at rear. Makes sign to friends whose heads appear above stairs. The Bohemians advance comically, like conspirators.)

LE PEINTRE: (à Julien). C'est ici?

PAINTER: (to Julien.) Is it here?

LE SCULPTEUR: C'est là qu'elle travaille?
(Julien indique la maison.)

SCULPTOR: Is it here she works?
(Julien points to house.)

JULIEN: Sa mère l'accompagnera jusqu'à cette porte . . . sitôt disparue, je m'élance . . . je rattrape Louise, et si ses parents refusent . . .

JULIEN: Her mother will bring her to the door. As soon as she disappears I rush in, catch Louise again and if her parents refuse—

LE PEINTRE: Tu l'enlèves!

PAINTER: You abduct her.

TOUS: (entourant Julien). Bravo!

ALL: (surrounding Julien). Bravo!

LE CHANSONNIER: Mais consentira-t-elle?

SONGSTER: But will she consent?

JULIEN: Je la déciderai! . . .
(Ils se répandent sur la place.)

JULIEN: I shall decide for her.
(They spread over the place.)

L'ETUDIANT: (à Julien). Nous en ferons notre Muse!

STUDENT: (to Julien). We'll make her our Muse.

LE SCULPTEUR: Le coin est joli!

SCULPTOR: The corner is pretty.

UN JEUNE POETE: Muse des Bohèmes!

YOUNG POET: Muse of the Bohemians.

LE PEINTRE: Un vrai carrefour à sérénades . . .

PAINTER: A choice spot for serenades.

UN PHILOSOPHE: (avec dédain). Une Muse?

PHILOSOPHER: (disdainfully). A Muse?

LE CHANSONNIER: Nous aurions du nous munir de nos instruments . . .

SONGSTER: We ought to have brought our instruments.

L'ETUDIANT: On la couronnera!
(Des têtes de bonnes paraissent aux fenêtres de la maison.)

STUDENT: We'll crown her.
(Servant girls' heads appear at window.)

LE SCULPTEUR: Nous reviendrons.

SCULPTOR: We'll come back.

LE PHILOSOPHE: Les Muses sont mortes!

PHILOSOPHER: The Muses are dead.

LE POETE: On les ressuscitera!

THE POET: We'll resurrect them.

LE PEINTRE: (lorgnant les fenêtres). Oh! les jolies filles!

PAINTER: (watching windows). Oh, the pretty girls.

LE SCULPTEUR: Mesdemoiselles?

SCULPTOR: Ladies!

LE CHANSONNIER: Elles sont charmantes!

SONGSTER: They are charming!

LE POETE: Ravissantes!
(Les bohèmes envoient des baisers et saluent; d'autres font les clowns. Le chansonnier, grattant sa canne ainsi qu'une guitare.)

POET: Ravishing!
(Some send kisses. Others play the clown.)

LE CHANSONNIER: Enfants de la bohème,
Nous aimons qui nous aime!
Toujours gais et pimpans,
Les femmes nous trouvent séduisants.

SONGSTER: (striking cane like a guitar). Children of Bohemia.
We love who ever loves us;
Always gay and natty,
Women find us seductive.

DEUXIEME PHILOSOPHE: Pourquoi refuseraient-ils?

SECOND PHILOSOPHER: Why should they refuse us?

LE CHANSONNIER: Quoiqu' sans argents!

SONGSTER: Though very short of money.

PREMIER PHILOSOPHE: Ils préfèrent sans doute en faire la femme d'un bourgeois.

FIRST PHILOSOPHER: They prefer, no doubt, to make them wives of tradesmen.

LE CHANSONNIER: Presqu' indigents!

SONGSTER: Almost "broke."

DEUXIEME PHILOSOPHE: Mais l'ouvrier méprise le bourgeois.

SECOND PHILOSOPHER: But the workman despises the tradesman.

PREMIER PHILOSOPHE: Ha! ha! tu crois ça, toi!
Mais nous somm's très intelligents!
(Cris et bravos: des fenêtres on jette des sous. Les bohèmes saluent ironiquement.)

FIRST PHILOSOPHER: Ha, ha; you believe that?
But we are most intelligent.
(Cries and bravos. They throw pennies from the windows. Bohemians salute ironically.)

LES BOHEMES: (saluant). Aimez-vous la peinture?
—La sculpture?
—La musique?
—Je suis un grand poète!

THE BOHEMIANS: (saluting). Do you like painting?
—Sculpture?
—Music?
—I am a great poet!

LE PREMIER PHILOSOPHE: Mon cher, l'idéal des ouvriers, c'est d'être des bourgeois . . . Le désir des bourgeois; être des grands seigneurs; et le rêve des grands seigneurs . . . devenir des artises!

FIRST PHILOSOPHER: (on the side). My dear fellow, the ideal of the workman is to be a tradesman;
The desire of the tradesman to be a lord;
And the dream of the lord—
To become an artist.

LE PEINTRE: Et le rêve des artistes?

PAINTER: And the dream of the artist?

LE PREMIER PHILOSOPHE: Etre des dieux!

FIRST PHILOSOPHER: To be a god.

TOUS: Bravo!

ALL: Bravo!

LE POETE: (avec enthousiasme). Oui, des dieux! . . .

POET: (with enthusiasm). Yes—gods.

L'APPRENTI: (traversant la scène). Allez donc travailler, tas d'feignants!
(Les bohèmes esquissent une poursuite, puis ils descendent l'escalier en chantant.)

APPRENTICE: (with enthusiasm). Go to work, lot of ne'er-do-wells.
(Bohemians chase him, then go down the stairs.)

LES BOHEMES: Enfants de la Bohème
Nous aimons qui nous aime.
Toujours gais et pimpants,
Les femm's nous trouvent séduisants . . .
Quoiqu' sans argents!
(Déjà loin.)
Presqu' indigents.
(Très loin.)
Mais nous somm's très intelligents!
. . .

BOHEMIANS: Children of Bohemia,
We love who ever loves us,
Always gay and natty,
Women find us seductive,
Though very short of money.
(Far away.)
Almost "broke."
(Very far.)
But we are most intelligent.

JULIEN: (à ses amis). Voici l'heure, laissez-moi . . .

JULIEN: (to his friends). This is the hour; leave me.

LE PREMIER PHILOSOPHE: Allons, bonne chance!

FIRST PHILOSOPHER: Good luck!

LE CHANSONNIER: (l'excitant). Enlève la redoute!
(Ils s'éloignent.)

SONGSTER: Carry the fort.
(They exit.)

LE PEINTRE: Sois éloquent.

PAINTER: Be eloquent!

L'ETUDIANT: (*donnant une accolade à Julien*). A tout à l'heure . . .
(*Ils s'éloignent.*)

STUDENT: (*embracing Julien*). See you by and bye.
(*They are gone.*)

JULIEN: (*dans une agitation douloureuse*). Elle va paraitre, ma joie, mon tourment! mia vie! . . . Voudra-t-elle me suivre? Voudra-t-elle qu'aujourd'hui notre amour soit vainqueur? . . .
Que dois-je lui dire? . . . Comment la décider? . . .
Qui viendrait à mon aide? . . .

JULIEN: (*painfully nervous*). She is about to appear, my joy, my torment, my life. Will she follow me? Will she wish that today our love shall conquer?
What shall I tell her? How convince her?
Who will come to my aid?

LA REMPAILLEUSE: (*lointaine*). La caneus', racc'modeus' de chais's!

CHAIR MENDER: (*in distance*). Caning—mending of chairs.

MARCHAND DE CHIFFONS: (*lointaine*). Marchand d'chiffons, ferraill' à vendre!
(*Il écoute avec émoi croissant; les chants se rapprochent.*)
—Artichauts, des gros artichauts . . . à la tendress', la verduress' . . . à un sou, vert et tendre, et à un sou, en v'là des gros, des bien beaux! . . .
—Du mouron pour les p'tits oiseaux!
—V'là d'la carotte, elle est bell', v'là d'la carotte!
(*Etc., etc.*)

JUNK WOMAN: Rags, bottles, pans to sell.
(*Julien listens; cries come nearer.*)
Artichokes, big artichokes, tender and green—one penny; green and tender, one sou. Here you are, fine and big.
Seed for little birds;
Carrots, very fine—carrots.

JULIEN: (*avec enthousiasme*). Ah! chanson de Paris où vibre et palpite mon âme! . . . Naïfs et vieux refrains du faubourg qui s'éveille, aube sonore qui réjouit mon oreille!
Cris de Paris . . . voix de la rue. Etes-vous le chant de victoire de notre amour triomphant? . . .
(*Des ouvrières paraissent au fond. Julien se cache sons le hangar, épiant.*)

JULIEN: (*with enthusiasm*). Oh song of Paris, wherein my soul vibrates. Simple and ancient refrains of the waking street, deep-voiced dawn that delights my ear!
Cries of Paris . . . Voices of the street.
Are you the song of victory of our triumphant love?
(*Workgirls begin to appear. Julien hides under shed, watching.*)

BLANCHE: Bonjour!

BLANCHE: Good morning.

MARGUERITE: Bonjour!

MARGUERITE: Good morning.

BLANCHE: Comment vas-tu?
(*Elles disparaissent à l'entrée de la maison. Une autre paraît et fait un geste à un quantrième.*)

BLANCHE: How are you?
(*They go into house. A third appears and motions to fourth.*)

SUZANNE: Nous sommes en avance?

SUZANNE: We are early.

GERTRUDE: Il est huit heures . . .

GERTRUDE: It's eight o'clock.

SUZANNE: Ah!
(*Elles entrent dans la maison. Deux autres s'avancent en caquetant.*)

SUZANNE: Ah!
(*They enter house. Two others arrive, cackling.*)

IRMA: Eh bien! tu t'es amusée, hier?

IRMA: Well, did you have a good time, yesterday?

CAMILLE: Ah! c'que j'ai ri!

CAMILLE: How I did laugh.

IRMA: Tu sais, i'grand Léon . . .
(*Elle lui parle à l'oreille.*)

IRMA: Do you know big Leon?
(*Whispers in her ear.*)

CAMILLE: Vrai?

CAMILLE: Really?

IRMA: En mariage, ma chère!
(*Elles disparaissent.*)

IRMA: In marriage, my dear.
(*They go in.*)

JULIEN: Viendra-t-elle?
(*Impatient, il sort de sa cachette; trois ouvrières entrent et le regardent gesticuler.*)

JULIEN: Will she come?
(*Impatient, he leaves his hiding place. Three workgirls watch him gesticulate.*)

L'APPRENTIE: (*riant*). Ah! ah! ah!

APPRENTICE: (*laughing*). Ha, ha, ha.

ELISE: Qu'il est beau!

ELISE: Isn't he handsome?

MADELINE: Hé! l'artiste?

MADELINE: Ha—the artist.

L'APPRENTIE: Il attend sa belle! C'te tête!
(*Elles entrent dans la maison.*)
(*La Mère et Louise entrent.*)

APPRENTICE: He's waiting for his sweetheart—what a guy.
(*They go in house.*)
(*Mother and Louise enter.*)

LA MERE: (*bougonnant*). Pourquoi te retourner? Il nous suit, sans doute . . . Suffit! je demanderai à ton père que dorenavant tu travailles chez nous.
(*Louise lève les yeux au ciel. Mimique de Julien qui, se montre à Louise. Louise, voyant Julien, porte la main sur son coeur.*) Ah! t'as beau faire les gros yeux! . . . On changera ta mauvaise tête; il faudra bien que Louise reste une fille honnête! . . .
Allons, au revoir!
(*Louise, froidement, lui tend la joue; la mère l'embrasse. Louise entre dans la maison; la mère s'éloigne. Arrivée près de la rue, elle guette de tous côtés, puis disparaî. Julien se risque timidement, puis s'élance dans la maison.*)

MOTHER: (*crossly*). What are you turning around for? I suppose he's following us. Enough! I'll ask your father to let you work at home hereafter.
(*Louise lifts her eyes to heaven. Julien shows himself to her. She, seeing him, puts her hand on her heart.*)
Oh, you needn't make big eyes. We'll change that wicked head of yours. I'll see that Louise remains a good girl. Come, au revoir.
(*Louise, coldly, offers her cheek. Mother kisses her. Louise goes within. Mother, after watching on all sides, disappears. Julien comes forth timidly, then rushes in house.*)

CRIS DES RUES: (*lointains*). V'là d'la carotte, elle est bell', v'là d'la carotte, d'la carotte! d'la carotte!
. . .
(*Julien reparait, entrainant Louise.*)

STREET CRIES: (*distant*). Here you are. Carrots, fine carrots, carrots, carrots.
(*Julien reappears, dragging Louise*).

LOUISE: (*affolée, se débattant*). Laissez-moi, ah! de grâce!

LOUISE: (*crazed, struggling*). Let me go, in mercy's name!

JULIEN: Alors, ils ont refusé?

JULIEN: Then they have refused?

LOUISE: Je vous en prie! si ma mère revenait . . .

LOUISE: I beg of you—if my mother came back!

JULIEN: Ils ont refusé?

JULIEN: They refused?

LOUISE: Vous me faites mourir de peur!

LOUISE: You'll make me die of fear.

JULIEN: Et tu supportes cette chose! Tu ne te révoltes pas?

JULIEN: And you'll stand that? You don't rebel?

LOUISE: Que puis-je faire?

LOUISE: What can I do?

JULIEN: Tu le demandes?

JULIEN: You ask it?

LOUISE: Ils sont les maîtres!

LOUISE: They are the masters.

JULIEN: Pourquoi, les maîtres? . . . Parce qu'ils t'ont fait naitre, se croient-ils le droit d'emprisonner ta jeunesse adorable? . . .

JULIEN: Why the masters? Because they gave you birth do they think they possess the right to imprison your golden youth?

LOUISE: Julien! . . .

LOUISE: Julien!

JULIEN: . . . d'asservir ta vie . . .

JULIEN: To enslave your life?

LOUISE: Ah! par pitié!

LOUISE: Have pity!

JULIEN: . . . de la murer pour leur plaisir?

JULIEN: To wall it up for their pleasure?

LOUISE: Laissez-moi partir! . . .

LOUISE: Let me go!

JULIEN: Ta volonté, désormais, est celle d'une femme et vaut la leur: tu es femme, tu peux, tu dois vouloir!

JULIEN: Your will, from this time forth, is that of a woman, and is as good as theirs. You are a woman; you can, you must act.

LOUISE: Ah! je vais être en retard! laissez-moi partir! . . .
(*Julien, fâché, la laisse partir. Elle fait quelques pas, puis revient souriante.*)

LOUISE: Oh, I'm going to be late. Let me go!
(*Julian, angry, releases her. She takes a few steps and returns, smiling.*)

JULIEN: Tu ne m'aimes plus!

JULIEN: You don't love me any more.

LOUISE: (*naïvement.*) Ce n'est pas vrai!
(*Les cris de la rue reparaissent, lointains*).

JULIEN: Si tu m'aimais, oublierais-tu ta promesse?
(*Louise, troublée, se détourne*).

VOIX LOINTAINES: Voilà l'cresson d'fontaine, la santé du corps!...

JULIEN: "Ecrivez encore à mon père; s'il refuse votre demande, je promets de fuir avec vous."

VOIX LOINTAINES: Mouron pour les p'tits oiseaux!

LOUISE: Ah! si je pouvais, si mon père...

VOIX LOINTAINES: Pois verts! pois verts!...

JULIEN: Ton père te pardonnerait.

LOUISE: Jamais!

JULIEN: Plus tard, quand ton bonheur...

LOUISE: Mon abandon le tuerait et je l'aime, mon père, autant que je t'aime!

JULIEN: (*la serrant dans ses bras*). Ah! Louise, si tu m'aimes, partons de suite au pays (*montrant la Butte ensoleillée.*) où vivent libres les amants; veins, je te choierai tant, et toute, et toute ta vie!
(*De la rue voisine viennent des cris et des rires*).
Viens vers la joie! le plaisir!
(*En entendant des rires, Louise, troublée, se cache sous le bangar. Quatre ouvrières traversent la scène en riant et entrent dans la maison*). (*plus pressant*) Si tu m'aimes, Louise, viens, fuyons de suite; si tu m'aimes, n'attends pas plus longtemps; tiens ta promesse dès maintenant!... Louise!... Louise!...
(*Il veut l'entrainer*).

LOUISE: (*se dèbattant*). Julien!

JULIEN: Veins!...

LOUISE: Ah! je deviens folle...

JULIEN: ...vers le plaisir!...

LOUISE: (*affolée*). Je ne sais que faire...laissez-moi partir...demain...plus tard...
(*Avec tendresse*).
Je serai ta femme!... Julien!... mon bien-aimé!...
(*Flûte du chevrier lointaine. Louise se jette à son cou, puis se dégage et s'éloigne vers la maison; sur le seuil de la porte, elle envoie un baiser. Julien répond avec tristesse.—Louise disparaît*).

LE MARCHAND D'HABITS: (*descendant l'escalier*). Marchand d'habits! avez-vous des habits à vendre'?
(*Il interroge les fenêtres*).
Marchand d'habits!...

---

LOUISE: (*simply*). That is not true.
(*The cries of the street are heard again, distantly.*)

JULIEN: If you loved me, would you forget your promise?
(*Louise turns her head.*)

VOICES IN DISTANCE: Fresh water-cress, health of the body.

JULIEN: "Write again to my father. If he refuses your request, I promise to fly with you."

VOICES: (*distant*). Seeds for little birds.

LOUISE: If I could—if my father—

VOICES: (*distant*). Green peas, green peas.

JULIEN: Your father would forgive you.

LOUISE: Never.

JULIEN: And later, when your happiness—

LOUISE: My leaving would kill him, and I love my father as much as I love you.

JULIEN: (*pressing her in his arms*). Ah, Louise, if you love me, let us go at once to our country (*pointing to the sunlit Butte*) where lovers live free. Come, I'll pet you so much and all your life.
(*From the next street come cries and laughter.*)
Come to happiness—to pleasure.
(*Hearing the laughter, Louise hides in shed. Four workgirls cross the stage, laughing, and go in house.*) If you love me, Louise, come, let us fly at once. If you love me, do not wait any longer. Keep your promise from now. Louise, Louise!
(*He tries to drag her.*)

LOUISE: (*struggling*). Julien!

JULIEN: Come!

LOUISE: I am going mad!

JULIEN: —To pleasure!

LOUISE: I know not what to do. Let me go—tomorrow—later—
(*Tenderly.*)
I shall be your wife! Julien!—my beloved.
(*Flute of goatherd in distance. Louise throws her arms about him, releases herself and goes toward the house. She sends him a kiss. Julian responds sadly. She disappears.*)

OLD CLO' MAN: (*coming down stairway*). Old clo'! Any clothes to sell?
(*Looks up at windows.*)
Old clo'!
(*Turns about.*)

---

(*Il se tourne*).
Avez-vous des habits à vendr'?
(*Il sort. Julien s'achemine tristement vers la rue*).

LE MARCHAND D'HABITS: (*au loin*). Marchand d'habits! Avez-vous des habits à vendr'?
(*Julien fait un dernier geste de désespoir et disparaît lentement*).

MARCHANDE DE MOURON: (*au loin*). Mouron pour les p'tits oiseaux!

MARCHANDE D'ARTICHAUTS: (*très loin*). A la tendress'! la verduress'!...

## DEUXIÈME TABLEAU.

(*Un atelier de couture; les ouvrières autour des 'tables travaillent en caquetant; quelques-unes chantent; près du mannequin, deux ouvrières plissent une jupe; l'apprentie, couchée à terre, ramasse les épingles; une ouvrière travaille à la machine*).

LES OUVRIERES, LOUISE. (*Elise, Suzanne, Madeleine et l'apprentie*). La! la! la! la!

VIELLES OUVRIERES: La! la! la! la!

BLANCHE: (*près du mannequin, faisant les plis d'une jupe*). C'est énervant! je n'peux pas y arriver...

MARGUERITE: Quell' mauvaise étoffe! les plis n'marquent pas...

ELISE: (*à Gertrude*). Passez-moi vos ciseaux'...

GERTRUDE: Et les tiens?

ELISE: Perdus!...

GERTRUDE: J'en ai assez d'les prêter.

ELISE: Un' minute?

GERTRUDE: Tu a'as qu à t'en payer.
(*Blanche prend la jupe, la montre à la Première, puis va s'asseoir à la première table*).

IRMA: Moi, j'ai vu l'*Pré aux Clercs* et *Mignon*.

CAMILLE: Moi, j'ai vu *Manon*.

IRMA: C'est beau?

CAMILLE: Très beau, surtout quand ell' meurt.

ELISE: (*à Marguerite, à mi-voix*). Voudrais-tu m'montrer à baleiner?

MARGUERITE: Tu prends ton ruban comm' ceci...tu commenc's par en bas, tu l'fais sout'nir très peu...

GERTRUDE: J'peux pas arriver à finir c'corsage! sur l'mann'quin, c'est bien, mais sur la femme!

IRMA: C'est pour qui?

GERTRUDE: Pour la duchesse...

---

Any clothes to sell?
(*Exits. Julien sadly walks away.*)

OLD CLO' MAN: (*distant*). Old clo'! Any old clothes to sell?
(*Julien, in despair, slowly disappears.*)

BIRD DEALER: (*in distance*). Seed for your little birds.

ARTICHOKE DEALER: (*very distant*). Tender and green.

## SCENE II.

(*A sewing establishment. Work-girls around a table sew while gossiping. Close to a form two girls try on a skirt. The apprentice, on the ground, picks up pins. One girl works at machine.*)

ELISE, SUZANNE, MADELINE and APPRENTICE: La, la, la, la.

OLD WORKWOMEN: La, la, la, la.

BLANCHE: (*by the form, setting skirt*). Oh, bother! I can't seem to get it right.

MARGUERITE: Wretched stuff. The folds won't stay in place.

ELISE: (*to Gertrude*). Pass me your scissors.

GERTRUDE: What about your own?

ELISE: Lost.

GERTRUDE: I've had enough of lending.

ELISE: Just a minute.

GERTRUDE: Better buy your own.
(*Blanche shows skirt to forewoman then sits at table.*)

IRMA: I've been to see the "Pré aux Clercs" and "Mignon."

CAMILLE: I've seen "Manon."

IRMA: Is it fine?

CAMILLE: Very fine, especially where she dies.

ELISE: (*to Marguerite, softly*). Will you show me how to whale-bone?

MARGUERITE: You take your ribbon like this—you begin low down, but supporting it a little bit—

GERTRUDE: I can't get hold of the knack of finishing this waist. On the form it is all right, but on the woman—

IRMA: Who is it for?

GERTRUDE: For the duchess.

CAMILLE: En effet, j'vois ca d'ici!

GERTRUDE: Faut lui mett' du crin sous les bras!

CAMILLE: Faut lui fair' des hanches!

IRMA: Un vrai rembourrag' quoi!

L'APPRENTIE: (*gavroche*). C'qu'y a des clientes, tout d'même!

BLANCHE: (*à Marguerite*). Moi, j'vais m'faire une robe pour le Grand Prix...J'ai vu un modèl', ma chère!

LA PREMIÈRE: (*à Gertrude*). N'oubliez pas le sachet d'héliotrope?...

ELISE: (*à Suzanne qui lui donne des conseils*). Ah! laiss'-moi tranquille, tu m'ennuies!

SUZANNE: C'est pas comm' ca qu'on s'y prend!

ELISE: Tu veux toujours en savoir plus qu'les autres!

SUZANNE: P'tite imbécile! tu n'vois pas qu'ca craqu' sous l'aiguille?

ELISE: Oh! la! la! quel cauch'mar!

SUZANNE: T'en as un caractère!

ELISE: Tu n't'es pas r'gardée!

SUZANNE: Va donc! eh! bouffie! (*Elise lance une pelote à la tête de Suzanne; les autres s'interposent. Toutes rient avec éclats. La première se léve*).

LA PREMIÈRE: Mesd'maiselles, un peu d'silence...nous n'sommes pas au marché. (*Silence relatif. La première va causer avec Gertrude*).

CAMILLE: (*bas à ses voisines*). Voyez Louise, quell' drôl' de tête ell' fait aujourd'hui.

BLANCHE: C'est vrai!

IRMA: C'est vrai! on dirait qu'elle a pleuré.

GERTRUDE: Elle a peut-être des ennuis de famille...

CAMILLE: Ses parents' sont très durs pour elle... (*Les ouvrières se groupent et jettent des regards sur Louise qui semble ne rien voir*).

IRMA: Ell' n'a pas la vie belle...

CAMILLE: Sa mèr' la frappe encore...

BLANCHE, MARGUERITE: Ah!

ELISE: Ce n'est pas moi qui m'laisserais battre!

SUZANNE: Moi non plus!

BLANCHE: Et moi, c'que j'les plaquerais!

CAMILLE: Just so; I can see it from here.

GERTRUDE: Got to put horsehair under the arms.

CAMILLE: You'll have to give her hips.

IRMA: A genuine stuffing, say.

APPRENTICE: Funny clients, all the same.

BLANCHE: (*to Marguerite.*) I'm going to make a dress for myself for the Grand Prix—I came across a model, my dear!

FOREWOMAN: (*to Gertrude*). Don't forget the sachet of heliotrope.

ELISE: (*to Suzanne, who is advising her*). Give me a rest—you're a nuisance.

SUZANNE: That's not the way to do it.

ELISE: You always want to know more than anybody else.

SUZANNE: Little fool, don't you see it breaks under the needle?

ELISE: Oh, la, la; what a nightmare.

SUZETTE: You've got a pretty disposition.

ELISE: You haven't watched yourself, have you?

SUZANNE: Get out, eh—fat head! (*Elise throws a spool at Suzanne. Others interpose. All laugh, loudly. The forewoman rises.*)

FOREWOMAN: Young women—a little silence. We are not in the markets. (*Slight silence. Forewoman talks to Gertrude.*)

CAMILLE: (*low, to others*). Look at Louise. Queer way she's got about her today.

BLANCHE: That's so?

IRMA: Yes, that is so. Looks as if she had been crying.

GERTRUDE: Perhaps she has some family troubles.

CAMILLE: Her parents are very hard on her. (*They group together and watch Louise, who doesn't see them.*)

IRMA: Her life's anything but a dream.

CAMILLE: Her mother still beats her.

BLANCHE, MARGUERITE: Ah!

ELISE: I'm not one to let them beat me.

SUZANNE: Nor I.

BLANCHE: Wouldn't I give it back!

L'APPRENTIE: Moi, quand le père veut m' battre, j'lui dis: cogn' sur maman, y a plus d'largeur! (*Rires, Louise, écoute et reprend son attitude indifferente*).

IRMA: (*regardant ironiquement Louise*). Non; je crois que Louise est amoureuse.

GERTRUDE: (*étonnee*). Amoureuse! Louise...

CAMILLE: Pourquoi Louise serait-ell' pas amoureuse?

BLANCHE: Amoureuse, Louise...

L'APPRENTIE: (*à part*). Amoureuse!

SUZANNE et MADELEINE: Amoureuse!

GERTRUDE et ELISE: Amoureuse!

BLANCHE et MARGUERITE: Amoureuse!

IRMA et CAMILLE: Amoureuse!

TOUTES: (*sauf Irma, Camille, l'apprentie et la première.*) Louise, entends tu? Ou dit que tu es amoureuse.

LOUISE: (*troublée*). Moi?

IRMA et CAMILLE: Est-ce vrai?

LOUISE: (*avec colère*). Vous êtes folles...

GERTRUDE: Un amoureux à ton áge, c'n'est pas un péché, et tu peux l'avouer...A moins que tu ne veuilles garder le secret de tes aventures. (*Orgue de barbarie lointain*).

SUZANNE, ELISE: Louise, raconte-nous...

LOUISE: Je n'ai pas d'aventure.

GERTRUDE: (*Derrière elle, l'apprentie mime ironiquement la chanson*). Que c'est charmant une aventure.
Un garcon de jolie figure qui vous aime et vous le prouve à tout moment.
C'est le rêve d'or jeunes filles...rêve auquel on pense tout enfant.
Pour le baiser d'un amant, je donnerais sans regret le restant de ma vie.

CAMILLE: D'où vient ce sentiment qui nous attire constamment vers les hommes?
D'où vient qu'à leur approche nos coeurs chavirent?
On a beau nous dire: "Prenez garde!"
Qu'apparaisse le prédestiné, les scrupules s'envolent!...A son regard, on rougit; à sa parole on sourit; dans l'enthousiasme du baiser, on s'ouvre au dieu malin; c'est un bonnet de plus qu'on accroche au moulin!...
(*Rires étouffés*).

L'APPRENTIE: Louise, raconte-nous tes aventures...

APPRENTICE: Me, when papa wants to beat me, I tell him: "Give to mamma—there's more surface." (*Laughter. Louise listens, but resumes her indifferent air*).

IRMA: (*looking ironically at Louise*). No; I think Louise is in love.

GERTRUDE: (*astonished*). Louise! In love.

CAMILLE: And why shouldn't Louise be in love?

BLANCHE: In love, Louise—

APPRENTICE: (*aside*). In love!

SUZANNE and MADELINE: In love!

GERTRUDE and ELISE: In love!

BLANCHE and MARGUERITE: In love!

IRMA and CAMILLE: In love!

ALL: (*save Irma, Camille, Apprentice and Forewoman*). Louise, do you hear? They say that you're in love.

LOUISE: (*nervous*). Me?

IRMA and CAMILLE: Is it true?

LOUISE: (*angrily*). You are all mad.

GERTRUDE: A lover, at your age; it is no sin, and you can own up to it, unless you would guard the secret of your adventures. (*Street organ in distance.*)

SUZANNE, ELISE: Louise, tell us—

LOUISE: I have no adventure.

GERTRUDE: (*Behind her the apprentice mimics the song, ironically.*) An adventure is most charming;
A handsome young fellow who loves you and proves it every moment.
It is the golden dream of girls—that one dreams when still a child;
For the kiss of a young lover, without regret I'd give the remainder of life.

CAMILLE: From where comes this sentiment that draws us constantly toward the men?
How does it happen that at their approach our hearts are shipwrecked? It is no use telling us "Look out." Let the predestined appear, scruples fly. At his glance one blushes; at his word one smiles; in the enthusiasm of the kiss one is open to the cunning god. It is another victory he can put down to his cunning wiles.
(*Smothered laughter.*)

APPRENTICE: Louise, tell us your adventures.

LOUISE: (*avec impatience*). Je n'ai pas d'aventures (*Peu à peu les ouvrières reprennent leur travail et causant à voix basse*).

IRMA: (*langoureusement*) Oh! moi quand je suis dans la rue, tout mon être prend comme feu; sous les rayons ardents des yeux qui me désirent, je vais radieuse! Les frôlements, les appels, les flatteries m'attisent et me grisent! . . . Il me semble être en voyage, alors que paysages et maisons tourbillonnent en ronde folle autour du wagon.

ELISE: (*à Gertrude*). C'est un beau brun!

GERTRUDE: Tu l'aimes?

ELISE: J'en suis toquée!

GERTRUDE: Grande folle!

LA PREMIERE: (*à Madeleine*). Voyez la longueur des manches . . .

GERTRUDE: Dieu, qu'l fait chaud! ovrez la f'nêtre! (*L'Apprentie va ouvrir une fenêtre.*)

BLANCHE: (*à Elise*). C'est tordant!

SUZANNE: (*à Madeleine*). Tu viens avec moi, ce soir?

MARGUERITE: Louise, chantenous quelque chose.

LA PREMIERE: (*à Marguerite*). Laissez-la donc tranquille!

L'APPRENTIE: (*à Suzanne*). J'ai rendez-vous à huit heures . . .

ELISE: (*à Blanche*). Il t'a fait la cour?

LA PREMIERE: A qui l'corsage?

GERTRUDE: C'est à moi.

LA PREMIERE: Dépêchez-vous, il le faut pour ce soir.

BLANCHE, ELISE et MADELEINE: (*riant bruyamment*). Ah! ah! ah! ah!

CAMILLE et GERTRUDE: Chut! (*La Première va dans la chambre voisine*).

L'APPRENTIE: Ecoutez! (*L'Apprentie, près d'Irma, l'écoute avec admiration*).

IRMA: Une voix mystérieuse, prometteuse de bonheur, parmi les bruissements de la rue amoureuse, me poursuit et m'enjôle. C'est la voix de Paris! C'est l'appel au plaisir, à l'amour! . . . Et peu à peu l'vresse me gagne; dans un frisson délicieux, à tous les yeux je livre mes yeux; et mon cœur bat la campagne et succombe aux désirs de tous les coeurs.

LOUISE: (*impatiently.*) I have no adventures. (*little by little, the workers go back to their work and begin to make low noises.*)

IRMA: (*langourously.*) As for me when I am in the street All my being takes fire. Under the ardent rays Of eyes That desire me I go radiant. The brushings past, the hints The flatteries, fire me and intoxicate.

ELISE: (*to Gertrude*) He is fine and dark.

GERTRUDE: You love him?

ELISE: I'm mad about him.

GERTRUDE: Big fool.

FOREWOMAN: (*to Madeleine.*) See the length of the sleeves.

GERTRUDE: Heaven! it's hot; open the window. (*Apprentice opens it.*)

BLANCHE: (*to Elise*). It's great fun.

SUZANNE: (*to Madeleine.*) You're coming with me tonight?

MARGUERITE: Louise, sing us something.

FOREWOMAN: (*to Marguerite.*) Please let her alone.

APPRENTICE: (*to Suzanne.*) I meet him at eight o'clock.

ELISE: (*to Blanche*). Did he court you?

THE FOREWOMAN: Whose waist is this?

GERTRUDE: It's mine.

FOREWOMAN: Hurry up, it must be ready tonight.

BLANCHE, ELISE, MADELINE: (*loudly laughing.*) Ha, ha, ha, ha.

CAMILLE and GERTRUDE: Chut! (*Forewoman goes in next room.*)

APPRENTICE: Listen. (*She listens to Irma admiringly.*)

IRMA: A mysterious voice, harbinger of happiness amid the sounds of the street, pursues and captivates me. It is the voice of Paris. It is the call to pleasure, to love. And little by little I'm intoxicated; in a delicious shiver to all eyes I give my eyes; and my heart beats madly and succumbs to the desires of all hearts.

LES JEUNES OUVRIERES: (*Elise, Suzanne, Madeleine et l'apprente*). C'est la voix de Paris . . .

GERTRUDE ET LES VIEILLES OUVRIERES: Régalez-vous, mesdam's, voilà l'plaisir! (*Fanfare dans la coulisse*).

TOUTES: (*diversement*). Ah! la musique! *Irma, Camille, Blanche, Elise, Madeleine et L'Apprentie, vont aux fenêtres et regardent curieusement dans la cour.*

UNE VOIX: (*dans la coulisse, en colère*). Un!

BLANCHE: Quell' drôl' de fanfare!

IRMA: Ils accompagn'nt un chanteur! . . .

CAMILLE: Il est bien, c'lui-là.

BLANCHE: (*pouffant*). Tu trouves?

ELISE: On dirait l'artist' de tout à l'heure . . .

L'APPRENTIE: Il nous r'garde . . .

CAMILLE: Louise! viens voir . . . il est très bien! (*Louise semble ne pas entendre. Guitare dans la coulisse. Elise, Madeleine et l'apprentie, se moquent de Camille. Pendant la première partie de la sérénade, elles envoient des baisers au chanteur*).

JULIEN: (*dans la coulisse*). Dans la cité lointaine, Au bleu pays d'espoir, Je sais, loin de la peine, Un joyeux reposoir, Qui, pour fêter ma reine Se fleurit chaque soir.

LES OUVRIERES: Quelle jolie voix! quelle jolie voix! Ah! ma chère, quelle jolie voix!

LOUISE: (*à part*). C'est lui! c'est Julien!

JULIEN: Les fleurs du beau domaine S'avivent chaque soir; Mais l'insensible reine Ne daigne s'emouvoir. Quand viendras-tu, dis-moi, la belle, Au reposoir d'ivresse éternelle?

TOUTES LES OUVRIERES: (*sauf Louise.*) Quelle caresse! Quelle ivresse! Aux accents de sa tendresse, mon âme s'abandonne . . . Ah! quelle jolie voix!

CAMILLE: Comme il nous regarde!

IRMA: On dirait qu'il s'adresse à l'une de nous!

L'APPRENTIE: C'est vrai!

LOUISE: (*à part*). Pauvre Julien!

ELISE: Il n'a pas l'air content . . .

THE WORKGIRLS, ELISE, etc: It is the voice of Paris.

GERTRUDE and OLD WORKWOMEN: Have a good time, ladies, there's the pleasure. (*Sound of trumpets.*)

ALL: (*diversely*) Ah, here's music. (*Irma, Camille, Elise, Madeleine and Apprentice go to windows and look curiously in street.*)

A VOICE OUTSIDE: (*Angry*). One!

BLANCHE: A funny sort of trumpet-call.

IRMA: They accompany a singer.

CAMILLE: He's good looking, isn't he?

BLANCHE: (*bursting with laughter*). You think so!

ELISE: It might be the artist of this morning.

APPRENTICE: He's looking at us.

CAMILLE: Louise, come, look. He's really a fine fellow. (*Louise seems not to hear. Guitar in the wings. Elise, Madeleine and Apprentice laugh at Camille. During first part of serenade they send kisses to the singer.*)

JULIEN: (*in wings*). In the distant city, In the blue land of hope, I know far from pain, A joyous resting place, Which to pleasure my queen Bursts in bloom each night.

WORKGIRLS: What a pretty voice. Ah, my dear, what a pretty voice.

LOUISE: (*aside*). It is he—Julien.

JULIEN: The flowers of the fine domain Revive each night, But the insensitive queen Won't deign to notice; When will you come, tell me, my belle, To the place of eternal delight.

ALL THE WORKING GIRLS: (*except Louise.*) What caress–what bliss. To his accents of tenderness my soul succumbs. Ah, what a pretty voice.

CAMILLE: How he looks at us.

IRMA: One would think he addressed himself to somebody here.

APPRENTICE: That's so.

LOUISE: (*aside*). Poor Julien!

ELISE: He doesn't seem very happy.

BLANCHE: Jetons-lui des sous!

CAMILLE: Et des baisers... (*Elles jettent des sous et envoient des baisers*).

LOUISE: Ah! j'aurais dú partir tout à l'heure!... (*Julien gratte avec rage les cordes de sa guitare*).

BLANCHE: Qu'est-c' qu'il a?

ELISE: Il devient fou! (*Louise se lève, frémissante, puis se rassied. Les ouvrières, trouvant la chanson moins jolie, échangent des gestes de lassitude, de moquerie. Elsie et Madeleine, raillent et sifflent impitoyablement*).

JULIEN: (*avec émotion*). Si ton âme, oubliant les serments d'autrefois, s'est détournée de moi; si tes voeux sont de vivre sans lumière et sans joie...

GERTRUDE: Que chante-t-il?

ELISE: C'est assommant!

JULIEN: ...Coeur infidèle...

MADELEINE: (*riant*). Ah! ah! ah!

JULIEN: ...va plus loin battre de l'aile!

ELISE: (*agacée*). Ah!

JULIEN: Moi, je renonce à vivre!

CAMILLE: Il nous ennuie!

GERTRUDE: Ah!

JULIEN: Car la vie est sans excuse quand l'adorée, la seule aimée, à mes appels se refuse!

ELISE: Dieu, qu'il m'énerve!

SUZANNE et MADELEINE: Que chante-t-il?

GERTRUDE: S'est rasant!

IRMA et CAMILLE: A-t-il bientôt fini?

BLANCHE et MARGUERITE: C'est assommant!

ELISE, SUZANNE et MADELEINE: (*criant*). Une autre!

L'APPRENTIE: Une autre!

TOUTES: Une autre! (*Durant cette dernière strophe, Louise se lève à demi, frémissante*).

JULIEN: Le temps passe et tu ne réponds pas...

ELISE: Ah! quel malheur!

JULIEN: Je ne sais plus que te dire!...

BLANCHE: Pauvre petit!

JULIEN: Faut-il que tu m'aies menti jadis!...

SUZANNE: Quel raseur!...

L'APPRENTIE: Oh! la la! quell' scie!

---

BLANCHE: Let us throw him some pennies.

CAMILLE: And a few kisses. (*They throw pennies and kisses*).

LOUISE: I should have gone away before this. (*Julien strikes his guitar with rage*).

BLANCHE: What's the matter with him?

ELISE: He's gone crazy. (*Louise rises, trembling, then sits down. The workgirls, finding the song not so pretty, exchange gestures of lassitude and mockery. Elise and Madeleine rail and whistle without ceasing.*)

JULIEN: (*with emotion*). If your soul, forgetting vows of the past, has turned from me. If your wish is to live without life, without joy—

GERTRUDE: What is he singing?

ELISE: It's a fearful bore.

JULIEN: Unfaithful heart!

MADELEINE: (*laughing*). Ha, ha, ha!

JULIEN: Go away and beat your wings.

ELISE: (*out of patience*). Ah!

JULIEN: I'll live no longer.

CAMILLE: He's a bore!

GERTRUDE: Ah!

JULIEN: For life has no excuse when the adored one, the only love, to my call is deaf.

ELISE: Heavens, how he gets on my nerves.

SUZANNE and MADELEINE: What is he singing about?

GERTRUDE: It's awful.

IRMA and CAMILLE: Will he ever stop?

BLANCHE and MARGUERITE: It's killing!

ELISE, SUZANNE and MADELEINE: (*shouting*). Some other.

APPRENTICE: Some other.

ALL: Some other. (*During last verse Louise half rises, trembling.*)

JULIEN: Time passes and you do not answer.

ELISE: What a pity!

JULIEN: I no longer know what to say to you.

BLANCHE: Poor little fellow.

JULIEN: Then I was lied to in the past.

SUZANNE: What a bore!

APPRENTICE: Oh, la, la! a terror!

---

ELISE: Va chez l' coiffeur!

JULIEN: Faut-il que tu m'aies menti!...

LES JEUNES OUVRIERES: (*assises*). Menti...i...i...i...! (*L'apprentie court ramasser des chiffons et les jette dans la cour*).

LES VIEILLES OUVRIERES: A-t-il bientôt fini?

JULIEN: Ah! sois maudite!

Toutes: (*riant aux èclats*). Ah! ah! ah! ah!

IRMA et CAMILLE: Assez! Assez!

GERTRUDE: J'en pleure!

BLANCHE et MARGUERITE: C'te tête!

ELISE: Il est fou!

SUZANNE: Il est saoûl!

GERTRUDE: C'est tordant!

BLANCHE et MARGUERITE: Quel type!

MADELEINE: Assez! quell' scie!

L'APPRENTIE: (*criant*). Ta bouche!

LES JEUNES: (*ironiques*). Bravo! bravo!

LES VIEILLES: Assez!...

MADELEINE: Voyez-le donc...

JULIEN: Fille sans coeur!

IRMA, CAMILLE, MARGUERITE, BLANCHE: (*lui répondant par la fenêtre*). Fille sans coeur!

ELISE et SUZANNE: A Charenton! Quel crampon!

L'APPRENTIE et MADELEINE: Is est fou! il est saoûl!

GERTRUDE: Quell' scie!

LES JEUNES OUVRIERES: Fille sans coeur!

LES VIELLES: (*cri plaintif*). Ah!

JULIEN: ...Ame sans foi!...

IRMA, CAMILLE, MARGUERITE, BLANCHE: Ame sans foi!

SUZANNE: Quel cauch'mar! (*Irma et Camille se rasseyent*).

ELISE: Ah! la la!

GERTRUDE: (*criant*). Ferme ca!

LES JEUNES OUVRIERES: Ame sans foi!

L'APPRENTIE: Musique!

LOUISE: (*étourdie, affolée*). Ah! c'est trop!

JULIEN: Sois maudite!

TOUTES LES OUVRIERES: Music! music! music! (*Les musiciens de la cour obéissent et jouent. Charivari. Les*

---

ELISE: Go get your head shaved!

JULIEN: Have you indeed lied to me?

YOUNG GIRLS: Li, li, li, li, lied! (*Apprentice picks up odds and ends and throws them in courtyard.*)

OLD WORKWOMEN: Will he ever have done?

JULIEN: Be cursed—

ALL LAUGHING: Ha, ha, ha, ha!

IRMA and CAMILLE: Enough, enough.

GERTRUDE: I'm weeping over it.

BLANCHE and MARGUERITE: The head he's got.

ELISE: He's crazy.

SUZANNE: He's drunk!

GERTRUDE: I'm bent double.

BLANCHE and MARGARET: A new type.

MADELEINE: Enough! It's a buzz-saw.

APPRENTICE: (*crying out.*) Shut your mouth.

THE GIRLS: Bravo, bravo!

THE OLD ONES: Enough.

MADELEINE: Look at him.

JULIEN: Heartless girl!

IRMA, CAMILLE MARGUERITE, BLANCHE: (*answering him from the window*). Heartless girl!

ELISE and SUZANNE: To the bug house. He's a clinger.

APPRENTICE and MADELEINE: He's mad! he's drunk.

GERTRUDE: What a bore!

YOUNG ONES: Heartless girl!

OLD ONES: (*plaintively*). Ah!

JULIEN: Faithless soul!

IRMA, CAMILLE, MARGUERITE and BLANCHE: Faithless soul!

SUZANNE: What a nightmare! (*Irma and Camille sit down.*)

ELISE: Oh, la, la!

GERTRUDE: (*shouting*). Shut it up.

YOUNG GIRLS: Faithless soul!

APPRENTICE: Music!

LOUISE: (*crazed, beside herself*). Oh, it's too much.

JULIEN: Be cursed.

ALL THE WORKWOMEN: Music, music, music! (*Musicians in street obey and play. Immense din. Work girls*

*ouvrières dansent et chahutent. Louise se lève. Elle hésite un moment, puis elle prend son chapeau et se dirige vers la porte*).

**LES OUVRIERES:** (*chantant*). La! la! la! la! la!

**GERTRUDE:** (*s'apercevant du trouble de Louise*). Louise, qu'avez-vous? Etes-vous souffrante? (*Da'utres ouvrières s'approchent*).

**L'APPRENTIE:** (*à la fenêtre*). Il s'en va . . .

**LOUISE:** (*avec embarras*). Oui . . . je ne suis pas bien . . . j'étouffe . . . je suis tout étourdie . . .
(*Elle se lève, fiévreuse*).
Je ne puis rester!

**CAMILLE:** Tu veux partier? (*Louise, indécise, semble écouter au loin*).

**LOUISE:** (*décidée*). Oui, je préfèr' rentrer chez nous. (*A Gertrude*). Vous direz à Madame que j'ai dû m'en aller . . .
(*Elle va vers la porte. Quelques ouvrières l'entourent*).

**IRMA:** (*affectueusement*). Louise, qu'as-tu?

**CAMILLE:** (*de même*). Tu souffres? (*Louise, embarrasée, ne sait que répondre*).

**IRMA:** Veux-tu que je t'accompagne?

**LOUISE:** Non, laissez-moi . . .
(*Elle ouvre le porte.*)
Adieu!
(*Elle disparait. Les ouvrières, étonnées, se regardent*).

**ELISE:** Qu'est-c' qui lui prend?

**CAMILLE:** Qu'est-c' que ca veut dire?

**IRMA:** (*prenant la défense de Louise*). Elle était malade!

**BLANCHE:** (*tronique*). Comm' vous et moi!

**L'APPRENTIE:** C'est la faute au chanteur.

**TOUTES:** Voyons!
(*Elles se prècipitent aux fenêtres*).

**CAMILLE:** La voici!

**GERTRUDE:** (*restée assise*). Eh bien! que fait-elle?

**ELISE et SUZANNE:** Parfait!

**IRMA et CAMILLE:** C'est bien ca! (*Les ouvrières restées assises, se lèvent et courent aux fenêtres*).

**TOUTES:** (*avec stupéfaction*). Ah! . . .

**L'APPRENTIE:** (*avec transport*). Ils part'nt en prom'nade!
(*Elle se roule à terre*).
(*Toutes rient. Gertrude joint les mains avec épouvante. Les rires continuent*).

*dance and kick up. Louise rises, hesitates a moment, then takes her hat and goes toward door.*)

**WORK GIRLS:** (*singing*). La, la, la, la, la.

**GERTRUDE:** (*noticing Louise's trouble*). Louise, what's the matter? Are you suffering?
(*Others come near.*)

**APPRENTICE:** (*at window*). He's going away.

**LOUISE:** (*awkwardly*). Yes . . . I don't fell well . . . I'm suffocating . . . I'm all giddy.
(*She rises feverishly*).
I can't stay.

**CAMILLE:** You're going away? (*Louise, undecided, seems to listen far off.*)

**LOUISE:** (*decided*). Yes, I prefer to go home. (*to Gertrude*) You'll say to Madame I had to go.
(*She goes toward door. Girls surround her.*)

**IRMA:** (*affectionately*). Louise, what's the matter?

**CAMILLE:** (*same*). You suffer? (*Louise, embarrassed, doesn't answer.*)

**IRMA:** Would you like me to go with you?

**LOUISE:** No, let me go.
(*She opens door.*)
Good-bye.
(*She exits. Workgirls astonished, look at each other.*)

**ELISE:** What's the matter with her?

**CAMILLE:** What does it mean?

**IRMA:** (*defending Louise*). She is ill.

**BLANCHE:** (*ironically*). Just like you and me.

**APPRENTICE:** It's the fault of the singer?

**ALL:** Let us see!
(*They rush to the window.*)

**CAMILLE:** Here she is.

**GERTRUDE:** (*remaining seated*). Well, what is she doing?

**ELISE and SUZANNE:** Perfect.

**IRMA and CAMILLE:** That's it exactly.
(*Those seated run to window.*)

**ALL:** (*amazed*). Ah!

**APPRENTICE:** (*transported*). They're going to take a walk.
(*She rolls on floor.*)
(*All laugh. Gertrude joins her hands in terror. Laughing continues.*)

## ■ ACTE TROISIEME.

(*Un jardinet au faîte de la butte Montmartre. A gauche, une petite maison sans étage, avec perron et vestibule découvert. A côté de la maison, un mur coupé d'une petite porte. A droite, des échafaudages. Au fond, unc haie. Un sentier extérieur côtoie la haie; au delà s'ètagent les toits des maisons voisines. Panorama de Paris. Le crépuscule est imminent*).

(*Au lever du rideau, Julien, assis près de la maison, semble plongé dans une méditation heureuse. Accoudée sur la rampe du perron, Louise, souriante, le regarde amoureu-sement, puis s'approche.*)

**LOUISE:** Depuis le jour où je me suis donnée, toute fleurie semble ma destinée . . . Je crois rêver sous un ciel de féerie, l'âme encore grisée de ton premier baiser.

**JULIEN:** Louise! . . .

**LOUISE:** Quelle belle vie! Mon rêve n'était pas un rêve!
Ah! je suis heureuse! . . .
L'amour étend sur moi ses ailes!
Au jardin de mon coeur chante une joie nouvelle!
Tout vibre, tout se réjouit de mon triomphe!
Autour de moi tout est sourire, lumière et fête
Et je tremble délicieusement
Au sourire charmant
Du premier jour!
D'amour!

**JULIEN:** Louise est heureuse?

**LOUISE:** (*se jetant dans ses bras*). Trop heureuse!

**JULIEN:** (*avec tendresse*). Tu ne regretes rien?

**LOUISE:** Rien! . . . Que puis-je regretter? A l'atelier, parmi mes compagnes, j'étais une étrangère; personne ne me comprenait et personne ne m'aimait.
Chez nous, mon père me traitait toujours en petite fille . . .
Et la mère:—Qui aime bien, châtie bien—ne perdait pas son temps avec moi! C'était à tout moment, à propos de rien, des rebuffades, des attrapades:
Pan! pan!—"Ca t'apprendra!" Pan! pan! "Atrap' celle-là!"
—"Mais ma mère!"
—"Vas-tu te taire?"
—"Je n'ai rien fait!"
—"P'tite effrontée!"
Pan! pan! pan! pan! pan! pan!

**JULIEN:** (*riant*). Ah! ah! ah! ah!

**LOUISE:** Et mon père la laissait faire . . . Il m'aimait bien pourtant, mon pauvre père! Mais il croyait tout ce qu'inventait la jalouse: elle

## ■ ACT III.

(*A small garden at the apex of the Butte Montmartre. On left a little house of one story with entrance and vestibule open. On side of house a wall with small door. Right, scaffoldings. At rear a hedge. A path along the hedge. Beyond, the roofs of nearby houses.*) (*Panorama of Paris.*) (*Twilight is near.*)

(*As curtain rises, Julien seated near house seems plunged in happy meditation. With elbows on balustrade Louise, smiling, looks at him lovingly, then approaches.*)

**LOUISE:** Since the day I gave myself, my destiny seems fluorescent. I seem to be dreaming under a fairy sky, the soul still drunk with your first kiss.

**JULIEN:** Louise!

**LOUISE:** A beautiful life. My dream was not a dream.
Ah, I am happy.
Love extends its wings over me.
In the garden of my heart sings a novel joy,
All vibrates with pleasure at my triumph;
Around me all is laughter, light and festival.
And I tremble deliciously
At the charming smile
Of the first day
Of love!

**JULIEN:** Louise is happy?

**LOUISE:** (*throwing herself in his arms*). Too happy!

**JULIEN:** (*tenderly*). You regret nothing?

**LOUISE:** Nothing. What can I regret? At the workshop, among my companions, I was a stranger. No one understood me and no one liked me.
At home father always treated me as if I were a little girl.
And the mother—who loves well, chastises well—lost none of her time with me. At every moment, about nothing, rebuffs and blows.
"Take that! Biff! That'll teach you."
Biff, biff. "Good for you."
"But mother."
"Shut up."
"I did nothing."
"Piece of impudence."
Biff, biff, biff, biff, biff.

**JULIEN:** (*laughing*). Ha, ha, ha, ha.

**LOUISE:** And my father let her go on. Yet he loved me well, poor papa. But he believed all that she said. She had made such a portrait

avait fait de toi un tel portrait, critiquant ta conduite, ton métier, que mon père ne pouvait croire qu'il me fût possible de t'aimer.

JULIEN: (*moqueur*). La mère la Routine, le père Préjugé devaient bien s'entendre!

LOUISE: (*imitant son père*). —"A ton âge, disait-il, on voit tout beau, tout rose ... prendre un mari ... c'est choisir une poupée ..."

JULIEN: Une poupée?

LOUISE: "Malheureusement, ces poupées-là, ma fille, vous font parfois pleurer bien des larmes! ..."

JULIEN: (*ironique*). Ah! ah! ah! Les parents voudraient qu'on restât le marmot dont la pensée sommeille, à l'ombre de leur volonté! ... Il fallait lui répondre gentiment: "Les poupées d'amour ne sont pas toutes méchantes ..."

LOUISE: "Comment veux-tu la choisir," disait mon père?

JULIEN: Avec mon coeur!

LOUISE: (*continuant l'imitation*). "C'est un bien mauvais juge?"

JULIEN: Pourquoi donc?

LOUISE: (*ironique*.) "Qui dit amoureux, toujours dit aveugle!"

JULIEN: Aveugle lui-même, d'avoir méconnu la souveraineté de l'amour et d'oser réclamer pour lui le droit d'élire le maitre de ta destinée! ...

LOUISE: (*imitant les gestes paternels*). "C'est le droit de la vieillesse ... le droit de la sagesse ... le droit de l'expérience! ..."

JULIEN: L'expérience! ha! ha! ha! L'expérience, c'est-a-dire la Routine, la Tradition, toute l'oppression des préjugés stupides! L'expérience, qui voudrait Dieu lui-même en servage! L'expérience! lâche et tryannique servante de l'Envie, qui se dresse à l'entrée de la vie! Les juvéniles chevauchées des passions, tout l'idéal, tout l'amour, le vouloir, le génie, honnis, traqués, comme on traque l'ignominie! ... Oh! la misérable, ô l'odieuse, l'infâme, l'hypocrite, l'inféconde expérience! ...

LOUISE: Ainsi, tout enfant a le droit de choisir lui-même le chemin du bonheur!

JULIEN: (*avec conviction*). Tout être a le droit d'être libre! Tout coeur a le devoir d'aimer. Aveugle celui qui voudrait garrotter l'originale et fière volonte d'une âme qui s'éveille et qui réclame sa part de soleil, sa part d'amour! (*Le soir tombe*).

of you, criticizing your conduct, your work, that my father didn't believe it possible I could love you.

JULIEN: (*mockingly*). Mother Routine and Father Prejudice understood each other well.

LOUISE: (*imitating her father*) "At your age," he would say, "one sees everything beautiful and rosy. Taking a thousand ... It's choosing a doll ..."

JULIEN: A doll!

LOUISE: "Unfortunately, these dolls, my daughter, often make you weep bitter tears."

JULIEN: (*ironically*). Ah, ah, ah! Parents would wish that one remained the dormouse, the thoughts of which slumber in the shadow of their will. You ought to have answered that "The dolls of love are not all wicked."

LOUISE: "How would you like to choose it?" said my father.

JULIEN: With all my heart.

LOUISE: (*still imitating*). "It's a very poor judge."

JULIEN: Why?

LOUISE: (*ironically*). "One who speaks of love, speaks blindly."

JULIEN: Blind himself, to have failed to recognize the sovereignty of love and to dare to claim for himself the right to elect the master of your destiny.

LOUISE: (*imitating paternal gestures*). "It is the right of old age ... the right of wisdom ... the right of experience! ..."

JULIEN: Experience! Ha, ha, ha! Experience, that is to say, Routine, Tradition, all the oppression of stupid prejudices. Experience which would put God in slavery. Experience, cowardly and tyrannical servant of Envy, which stands at the portals of life. The juvenile leaps of the passions, all ideality, all love, will, genius, disgraced, tracked as we track ignominy. Oh the wretched, odious, infamous, hypocritical, unfecund experience! ...

LOUISE: Thus every child has the right to choose for itself the path of happiness.

JULIEN: Every being has the right to be free. Every heart has the duty of loving. Blind is he who would stifle the first and proud will of a soul that awakes and that claims its part of sun, its part of love! (*Evening falls.*)

LOUISE: (*avec émotion*). Les désirs de nos coeurs peuvent-ils sans remords briser d'autres coeurs?

JULIEN: L'égoïsme appelle l'égoïsme.

JULIEN: L'amour des parents n'est donc que de l'égoïsme?

JULIEN: Rien qu'égoïsme!

LOUISE: Et mon père lui-même?

JULIEN: Un égoïste plus aveugle que les autres! (*Julien, l'entraine doucement vers le fond du jardin*). Jolie! ... Tu regrettes d'être venue! ... (*Il lui montre la ville*) De Paris tout en fête, entends monter la joyeuse, l'attrayante chanson! C'est pour toi, petite Muse, que la ville cette nuit s'amuse! Hors Paris, Louise ne serait pas Louise! Paris, sans toi, ne serait point Paris! Mignon symbole de la grande cité je t'aime en elle, et je l'adore en ta beauté!

LOUISE: Oh! l'attirante, la chère musique de la grande ville! ...

JULIEN: La Ville m'a donné la Fille ...

LOUISE: L'amour de la Fille te donnera la Ville! ...

JULIEN: Oui, tous deux nous marcherons à la conquête de la Cité Merveilleuse! ...

LOUISE: Ta gloire aura mes yeux pour étoiles!

JULIEN: Par ton amour, j'aurai la victoire!

ENSEMBLE: Paris! Ville de force et de lumière! Paris! Paris! Splendeur première! Paris! ô Paris! Cité de joie! cité d'amour, sois douce à nous amours ... (*s'agenouillent*). Protège tes enfants! Garde nous de'fends nous. (*Dans la nuit, Paris peu à peu s'illumine. Les amants, tendent les bras vers la ville*).

LOUISE: Julien!

JULIEN: Louise!

LOUISE: Vois, la ville s'éclaire ...

JULIEN: C'est le firmament sur terre ...

LOUISE: Entends les mille voix? ...

JULIEN: Elles répondent à nos voix ...

LOUISE: Regarde les lumières ...

JULIEN: La ville tout entière se lève à ta prière! ... (*Ils se relèvent lentement*).

LOUISE: (*with emotion*). Can the desires of our heart, without remorse, break other hearts?

JULIEN: Egoism calls egoism.

LOUISE: The love of our parents then is only egoism?

JULIEN: Nothing but egoism.

LOUISE: And even my father?

JULIEN: An egoist blinder than the rest. (*Julien draws her gently toward end of garden.*) Pretty one ... Do you regret having come? (*Shows the town.*) Of Paris in festival, listen, mount up to us the joyous, the attractive song It is for you, little Muse, that the town amuses itself tonight. Outside of Paris, Louise would not be Louise. Paris without you, would not be Paris. Dainty symbol of the great city, I love her and I adore her in your beauty.

LOUISE: Oh, the attractive, the dear music of the great town! ...

JULIEN: The Town has given me the Girl.

LOUISE: The love of the Girl will give you the Town!

JULIEN: Yes, together we'll march to the conquest of the Marvelous City.

LOUISE: Your glory shall have my eyes for stars.

JULIEN: Through you I shall gain the victory.

TOGETHER: Paris, city of force and of light; Paris, Paris, first amidst Splendor. Paris! oh, Paris! City of joy, city of love, be kind to our loves. (*Kneeling*). Protect your children; Guard us, defend us. (*Little by little the lights appear. The lovers stretch their arms toward the city.*)

LOUISE: Julien!

JULIEN: Louise!

LOUISE: Look, the town lights up.

JULIEN: It is the firmament on Earth.

LOUISE: Listen to the thousand voices.

JULIEN: They answer to ours.

LOUISE: Look at the lights.

JULIEN: The whole town rises at your prayer. (*They arise slowly.*)

LOUISE et JOLIEN: "Libres! vous êtes libres," nous crie la ville immense.

VOIX DE LA VILLE: Libres!

LOUISE et JULIEN: Libres! Soyons libres selon notre conscience.

VOIX DE LA VILLE: Libres!

LOUISE: Libres dans l'amour!

JULIEN: Libres dans la vie!

LOUISE: Libres toujours!

JULIEN: Toujours?

LOUISE: Toujours!

JULIEN: (la pressant dans ses bras). Toujours!

LOUISE: Vois la belle nuit!

JULIEN: C'est notre nuit de noces!

LOUISE: Je t'aime!

JULIEN: Tu m'aimes?

LOUISE: Je t'aime! . . .

JULIEN: Oh! le doux miracle! . . . Je ne suis plus Julien! . . Tu n'es plus Louise!

LOUISE: (passionément). Des baisers! Julien! Des baisers!

JULIEN: (se levant). Nous sommes tous les amants fidèles à leurs serments.

LOUISE: (agenouillée devant lui). Oh! le divin roman! . . .

JULIEN: Nous sommes toutes les âmes qui veulent vivre sans maîtres!

LOUISE: En mes bras, sois mon maitre!

JULIEN: Nous sommes toutes les âmes que brûle la sainte flamme du Désir!
(Il la prend dans ses bras).

JULIEN: Depuis le jour où je l'ai prise toute, jamais Louise ne parut si belle!

LOUISE: (pétulante). Ce n'est plus la petite fille?

JULIEN: C'est une femme nouvelle!

LOUISE: . . . enfant timide et craintive?

JULIEN: Non, c'est l'amante éternelle!

LOUISE: C'est une femme, au coeur de flamme, dont l'être clame, dont l'âme crie éperdument.

JULIEN: Au souffle du désir, Louise enfins'éveille!

LOUISE: (passionnée, impatiente). Prends-moi vite, vite, mon bien-aimé, plus beau que les fiers chevaliers des contes bleus de la Légende! . . .
A mon appel hâte-toi d'accourir, Prince Charmant, dont la caresse éveilla la petite Montmartroise au coeur dormant!

LOUISE and JULIEN: Free you are, free; the whole town shouts to us.

VOICES OF THE TOWN: Free!

LOUISE and JULIEN: Free! let us be free according to our conscience.

VOICES OF THE TOWN: Free!

LOUISE: Free in our love!

JULIEN: Free in our life!

LOUISE: Free always!

JULIEN: Always?

LOUISE: Always!

JULIEN: (pressing her in his arms). Always!

LOUISE: Look! The beautiful night.

JULIEN: It is our wedding night.

LOUISE: I love you.

JULIEN: You love me?

LOUISE: I love you.

JULIEN: Oh the sweet miracle. I am no longer Julien. You are no longer Louise.

LOUISE: (passionately). Kisses, Julien, kisses!

JULIEN: (rising). We are all lovers, faithful
To our oaths.

LOUISE: (kneeling by him). In the divine romance.

JULIEN: We are all beings who would live
Without masters.

LOUISE: In my arms, be my master.

JULIEN: We are all souls wherein burns
The holy flame
Of Desire.
(He takes her in his arms.)

JULIEN: From the day that I took you, never has Louise appeared more beautiful.

LOUISE: (petulant). It is no longer the little girl . . .

JULIEN: It is a new woman.

LOUISE: . . . The timid and frightened child.

JULIEN: No. It is the lover eternal.

LOUISE: It is a woman, with heart of flame, whose being cries out, whose soul madly clamors.

JULIEN: At the breath of desire Louise at last awakens.

LOUISE: (passionate, impatient). Take me quickly, my well beloved, more handsome than the proud knights in the blue stories of the Legend.
At my voice, hasten to come, Prince Charming, whose caresses awake the little girl of Montmartre, of the sleeping heart.

Viens dans mes bras, ô mon poète, ne suis-je pas ta conquête? Embrasse-moi . . . fais-moi mourir sous tes baisers! . . .

JULIEN: Ardente ivresse du baiser! ô vertige! ô volupté! La chair de l'amante a parlé! Elle appelle son maitre! . . .

LOUISE: A toi tout mon être! . . .

JULIEN: Ton cher corps me désire?

LOUISE: Je veux du plaisir!

JULIEN: Prends-moi!

LOUISE: Jadis tu pris la vierge aimante, toute naïve en son printemps; mais aujourd'hui, l'amante femme veut à son tour prendre l'amant!

LOUISE: Viens! ô mon poète! Beau chevalier, sois ma conquête! Ah! viens mourir sous mes baisers!

JULIEN: O bien-aimée, emporte ta conquête! Fais-moi mourir sous tes baisers! . . .

LOUISE: C'est le paradis!

JULIEN: Non, c'est la vie!

LOUISE: C'est une féerie!

JULIEN: Non! C'est la vie! l'éternelle, la toute-puissante vie!
. . .
(Louise entraine Julien au maison. Tambours lointains.)
(Un bohème apparaît sur le sentier; il saute la haie, se dirige vers la maison. Un autre bohème surgit de la même manière).

LE DEUXIEME BOHEME: (au premier). Ils sont là?
(Il ouvre la porte à trois camarades porteurs d'un paquet volumineux. Ils en tirent des oriflammes, des draperies, des lanternes vénitiennes, dont ils décorent la facade et le perron de la maison).

GRISETTES et BOHEMES: (lointains). Régalez-vous, mesdam's, voilà l'plaisir!

LA FOULE: (lointaine) N'en mangez pas, jeun's fill's, ca fait grossir!

GRISETTES et BOHEMES: Régalez-vous, mesdam's, voilà l'plaisir!

LA FOULE: N'en mangez pas, messieurs, ca fait mourir!
(Peu à peu, les badauds se massent l'entrée du jardin. Des gueux apparaissent, grimpés sur les échafaudages).

RODEURS et RODEUSES: (à la porte du jardin). Honneur aux bohèmes!
Gloire aux faiseurs de poèmes!
Gloire aux belles qui les aiment!
(Quelques grisettes, accourent sur le perron).

Come in my arms, oh my poet, am I not your conquest? Kiss me . . . make me die in your arms.

JULIEN: Ardent bliss of the kiss; entrancing, voluptuous. The flesh of the loving one has spoken. She calls her master.

LOUISE: My whole being is yours.

JULIEN: Your dear body desires me.

LOUISE: I want pleasure.

JULIEN: Take me.

LOUISE: You took your loving virgin all innocent in her springtime. But today the loving woman in her turn will take her lover.

LOUISE: Come, oh my poet, proud Knight, be my conquest. Ah, come die under my kisses.

JULIEN: Oh, beloved, take your conquest. Make me die under your kisses!

LOUISE: It is paradise.

JULIEN: No, it is life.

LOUISE: It is a fairy dream.

JULIEN: No, it is life! The eternal and powerful life.
(Louise draws Julien toward the house. Distant drums.)
(A bohemian appears on walk, jumps hedge and goes toward house. A second one appears.)

SECOND BOHEMIAN: (to first). They are there.
(He opens door to three carriers of a voluminous package. They draw from it flags, draperies, lanterns and decorate front and entrance of house).

GRISETTES and BOHEMIANS: (distant). Enjoy yourselves, ladies, this is pleasure.

MOB: (distant). Don't eat too much, young girls, or you'll get big.

GRISETTES and BOHEMES: Enjoy yourselves, etc.

MOB: Don't eat that, gentlemen, it is death.
(Little by little people mass in garden. Loafers climb on scaffolding.)

MEN an WOMEN: (at garden gate). Honor to bohemia.
Glory to makers of rhymes.
Glory to girls who love them.
(Some grisettes appear on the steps. People of the Butte.)

MERES et PERES: Que vienn'nt
faire ces gens-là
avec tout leur tralala!
Regardez ces filles, ah!
En ont-ell's des des falbalas!

LES MERES: Oh! ma chère!
Si j'étais leur mère!

LES PERES: Quell' misère!
Si j'étais leur père!

MERES et PERES: Quelle extravagation!
Quelle dépravation!
C'est l'abomination
De la désolation!

FILLETTES et GARCONS: C'est ici
qu'ils vont s'amuser . . .
Ils vont chanter, rire et danser.

LES FILLETTES: Et peut-être nous
embrasser!

LES GARCONS: Et nous montrer
leurs fiancés!

LES GAMINS: (s'appelant). Ohé!
ohé!

LES GAMINS: (entrant). Le bourgeois voudrait les pendr' d'un seul
coup!
La bourgeois' voudrait se pendr' à
leur cou!
Mais la quille
plus maligne
de son oeil tranquille cligne:
"—O chaleur!
"—Quel malheur! . . .
"—Attendez-moi tout à l'heur!"
(Paraissent les porteurs
d'oriflammes et de bannières).

LES PORTEURS: (criant). Place!
Bonn's gens, élargissez-vous!

GRISETTES et BOHEMES: Y a des
êtres qui s'ennuient . . .
y en a d'autr's qui n's'ennuient pas!
Y en a qui ont du génie!
y en a d'autr's qui n'en ont pas . . .

LES GUEUX: Vivent les artistes!
Gloire aux anarchistes!
En l'honneur des étudiants, compagnons, battons un ban!

LES GAMINS: Voyex donc ces
têtes, ces binett's!
Voyez donc ces têt's qui'ils ont!
Conspuez!

LES GENS DE LA BUTTE: Voyez
ces bannières!
Toutes ces lumières!
Quel étrange carnaval!
Quel infernal bacchanal!
Ils sont fous!
Ils sont saouls!
Ils mett'nt tout sens dessus d'ssous.

GRISETTES et BOHEMES: Dans un
royal bachanal
loin du flic et du cipal,
chantons notre hymne triomphal!
(A la porte de l'enclos, apparaît le
cortège du "Plaisir". Sur un char
escorté par les Filles, le Noctambule, entre solennellement).

FATHERS and MOTHERS: Why
come all these people,
With all their tra-la-la?
Just look at these girls.
Aren't they a queer lot?

MOTHERS: Oh, my dear,
If I were their mother!

FATHERS: What misery,
If I were their father!

MOTHERS and FATHERS: What
extravagance!
What depravity!
The abomination
Of desolation!

GIRLS and BOYS: It's here that
they'll amuse themselves.
They will sing and laugh and dance.

GIRLS: And perhaps they will embrace us.

BOYS: And show us their promised
ones.

URCHINS: (calling each other).
Ohe, ohe!

MORE URCHINS: (entering). The
tradesmen would like to hang them
With one stroke.
Tradeswomen would like to hang
on them
Round the neck.
But knowing ones
Much wiser
With their other eye Wink.
Oh, city!
What a pity!
Wait for me a bit later.
(The carriers of flags appear.)

CARRIERS: (Crying out). Make
room, good people, spread out.

GRISETTES and BOHEMS: There
are people who are bored,
And others who are not;
There are some who have genius,
And others who have not a bit.

LOAFERS: Long live artists, glory
to anarchists.
In honor of the students let's clap
our hands.

URCHINS: Look at their heads,
their faces.
What a queer lot they are.
Boo!

PEOPLE of the BUTTE: Look at
these banners
And all these lights.
What a carnival?
What a bacchanal?
They are crazy,
They are drunk.
They put everything upside down.

GRISETTES and BOHEMS: In a
royal bachanal,
Far from work and order,
We'll sing our hymn of triumph.
(At a gate appears the procession
of pleasure. On a chariot escorted
by girls the Night Walker enters.)

CHOEUR GENERAL: Jour
d'allégresse
et jour d'amour
sur la Butte en liesse!
Tout est rose,
tout flamboie!
C'est la joie!
L'apothéose!
Oyex ces cris.
De tous côtés
c'est la joie de Paris,
aux pieds de la Beauté!
Voici venir
les divins gueux
aux longs cheveux!
Les jeunes dieux!
Voici venir
Les fiers élus de l'avenir!
Gloire au génie
des fils de l'harmonie,
riches d'éternité!
quoique vétus de pauvreté!
(Louise paraît sur le perron. Ses
amies s'empressent autour
d'elle).
Gloire à la muse
dont la lèvre fleurie
jamais rien ne refuse
à son poète qui la prie! . . .
Riez, chantez, dansez!
Tout est rose!
Tout flamboie!
C'est la joie!
L'apothéose!
(Bravos prolongés de la foule).

LE PAPE DES FOUS: (se levant).
Par Mercure aux pieds légers,
puisque s'ouvre ici la Cour
d'amour,
m'est avis, messeigneurs,
qu'il vous sied de céder le verbe
au poète superbe
et seul idoine à louanger
que voici!
(Il va vers la foule et s'incline ironiquement; gambade autour des
grisettes, la Dansense, s'avance
vers lui).

LE PAPE DES FOUS: (montrant la
Danseuse). O jolie!
Cette danseuse
est une fleur de vie
faite d'un peu de chacun de nous
tous.
Et cette fleur vivante,
c'est notre âme
(Les grisettes prennent part à la
danse).
Sous la forme d'une fleur
qui serait une femme,
Fleur-femme,
dont la grâce et le parfum
se traduisent en cadences,
afin que tes sens
aussi bien que ton âme
puissent apprécier l'hommage susuprême!

LA FOULE: Bravo! Bravo!
(Les grisettes, en demi-cercle devant Louise, lui envoient la Danseuse).

GENERAL CHORUS: Day of pleasure
And of love
On the Butte in leash.
All is rose
All is flaring
It is our joy,
Apotheose;
Hear these cries
On all sides;
It is the joy of Paris
At the feet of beauty.
Here they come
The divine tramps;
With longish hair
Young gods.
Here come
The proud elect of the future.
Glory to genius
Of the sons of harmony
Rich in eternity
Though clothed in poverty.
(Louise appears in the doorway.
Her friends surround her.)
Glory to the muse
Whose favored lip
Refuses nothing
To her poet who begs.
Laugh, sing and dance;
All is rose
And repose;
It is our joy,
Apotheose.
(Prolonged applause of the mob.)

FATHER OF FOOLS: (rising). By
Mercury, light of foot
Since here is opened the Court of
Love
It is my advice, my lords
That you must cede the verb
To the superb poet
And only one to praise
Right here.
(He goes toward crowd and salutes ironically, dances around
the grisettes. The Dancer advances to him.)

FATHER OF FOOLS: Oh pretty!
This dancer
Is a flower of life
Made up of a bit of us all.
And this living flower
Is our soul.
(The grisettes join in dance.)
Under form of a flower
Who would be a woman
Flower-woman
Whose grace and perfume
Are translated in cadences
So that all your senses
As well as your soul
May appreciate the supreme homage.

CROWD: Bravo!
(The grisettes in half circle
around Louise send her the Dancer.)

**LE PAPE DES FOUS:** O jolie! Soeur choisie! Harmonie et beauté! Poème de clarté! (*La Danseuse cueille des roses aux mains des enfants, s'incline devant Louise, lui offre ses fleurs. Les grisettes drapent sur les épaules de Louise le châle brodé d'argent, emblème de sa royauté*).

**FATHER OF FOOLS:** Oh, pretty Chosen sister; Harmony and beauty, Poem of light. (*The Dancer gathers flowers from the hands of children, bows before Louise and offers her the flowers. The grisettes drape over Louise's shoulders the shawl embroidered with silver, emblem of royalty.*)

**LE PAPE DES FOUS:** Gente fillette de Paris, en qui revivent Juliette, Ophélie. O charmante, Muse clémente, de tes chevaliers recois l'hommage! (*Acclamations*).

**FATHER OF FOOLS:** Gentle little girl of Paris, In whom are revived Juliet, Ophelia. Oh, charming, Merciful muse, Receive the homage of your knights.

**LA FOULE:** Louise!

**CROWD:** Louise!

**LES GRISETTES et les BOHEMES:** (*entourant Louise*). Louise, acceptes-tu d'être reine de la Bohème? Louise, acceptes-tu d'être Muse de la Butte Sacrée? Réponds? (*Louise, souriante, fait un geste d'acquiescement*). (*Julien s'approche*).

**GRISETTES and BOHEMES:** (*surrounding Louise*). Do you accept, Louise, to be queen of Bohemia? Louise, will you be Muse of the sacred Butte? Answer? (*Louise, pointing, makes sign of acquiescence.*) (*Julien approaches.*)

**JULIEN:** O jolie! Soeur choisie! (*Louise prend une rose à son corsage et l'offre à l'amant*). Je t'aime! (*Orgueilleusement, il prend Louise dans ses bras*).

**JULIEN:** Oh pretty Chosen sister. (*Louise takes rose and offers it to Julien.*) I love you. (*Proudly he takes Louise in his arms.*)

**LOUISE:** Je t'aime! . . .

**LOUISE:** I love you!

**LES GRISETTES:** (*enthousiasmées*). Amoureuse beauté, ton chant d'éternité éveille en nous une adorable ivresse un désir de caresses . . .

**GRISETTES:** (*enthusiastically*). Loving beauty, Your song of eternity Awakes in us an adorable bliss, A want of caresses.

**LES GAMINS:** (*ahuris*). C'est renversant! Epastrouillant! Abracadabrant! Regardez-les! C'qu'ils sont chipés!

**URCHINS:** It's astonishing, Wonderful, Marvelous; Look at them; Ain't they got up fine?

**LES BOHEMES:** (*avec ferveur*). Harmonie et beauté! Poème de clarté! . . . Parisienne sculptée dans de l'éternité, O jolie! Tendre reine des amantes! . . .

**BOHEMES:** (*with fervor*). Harmony of beauty, Poem of light. Sculptured Parisian. In eternity, Oh pretty, Tender queen of lovers.

**LES GUEUX:** (*goguenards*). S'ils continuent, y vont la rendre folle! Y a qu'à Montmartre qu'on voit ca! J'en suis bleu, j'en suis baba! C'est plus bath qu'à l'Opéra! Hourrah! Pour la Muse de Montmartre! Tant pis pour elle! Fallait pas qu'elle y aille! Ell' croit qu'la grande vie

**LOAFERS:** If they keep on They'll make her crazy; Only at Montmartre can you see this; I'm struck dumb and foolish; It's better than at the opera; Hurrah For the Muse of Montmartre! It'll be the worst for her! She shouldn't have gone; She thinks a grand life

ca vaut mieux que l'travail! Quell' folie! Tu n'vois donc pas qu'ils te mentent!

Is worth better than work; Don't you see they're lying to you!

**JEUNES FILLES:** (*admiratives*). Adorable beauté, chacune de nous t'envie; car ta félicité ô jolie, c'est le rêve des amantes!

**YOUNG GIRLS:** (*with admiration*). Adorable beauty, Each of us envies you For your felicity; Oh The dream of lovers is pretty.

**GARCONS:** (*charmés*). Quel frisson de volupté sur nos têtes vient de passer!

**YOUNG MEN:** What a spasm of passion Has passed over us.

**MERES:** (*indignés*). Voyez, quelle effrontée! . . . Dans son immoralité, dans son impudicité, elle oublie qu'ses parents, là-bas, s'tourmentent!

**MOTHERS:** (*indignant*). Look at her boldness; In her immorality, In her impudicity, She forgets That her parents are worried.

**PERES:** (*méprisants*). Admirez l'absurdité de cette solennité! La Folie est triomphante!

**FATHERS:** (*with contempt*). Admire the absurdity Of this solemnity; Folly is triumphant.

**LOUISE et JULIEN:** Non, non, jamais rien ne séperera la muse du poète! L'amante de l'amant! Et Julien de Louise! (*Fanfares et tambours. — Apothéose.*) (*Mais une rumeur vient du fond de l'enclos. La foule s'écarte. Un grand silence se fait. Sur le seuil du jardin, la mère de Lousie, hésitant à entrer, apparaît*).

**LOUISE and JULIEN:** No, no nothing shall ever separate The muse from the poet, The lover from the one he loves, Or Julien and Louise. (*Trumpets and drums. Apotheose.*) (*But a rumor comes from the rear. The crowd gives way. A great silence ensues. On the step of the garden the mother of Louise, hesitating to enter, appears.*)

**LA FOULE:** Ah! Regardez . . . Quelle est cette femme? Que veut-elle?

**CROWD:** Look! Look! Who is this woman? What does she want?

**LES GRISETTES et LES BOHEMES:** La mère de Louise! . . . (*Le pape des Fous se sauve en ricanant suivi des filles*).

**GRISETTES and BOHEMES:** The mother of Louise! . . . (*The Father of Fools runs away laughing, followed by girls.*)

**LA FOULE:** La mère de la Muse!

**CROWD:** The mother of the Muse!

**LOUISE:** Ah! (*Les porteurs d'étendards, les musicions et les danseuses disparaissent*).

**LOUISE:** Ah! (*The carriers of banners, musicians and dancers disappear.*)

**JULIEN:** (*se mettant devant elle*). Je te garde! (*La mère s'avance avec timidité. Les grisettes entourent Louise défaillante.*)

**JULIEN:** (*placing himself in front of her.*) I'll guard you. (*The mother advances timidly. The grisettes surround Louise, who is half fainting.*)

**LA FOULE:** Quelle affaire!

**CROWD:** What an affair.

**LES GAMINS:** Allons-nous-en à quatre patt's C'est pas l'moment d'fair' des éspates!

**URCHINS:** Let us go on all fours; It's not the time to make a row.

**LES GUEUX:** Adieu, cochons, vache et couvée . . . Encore un' rein' de dégommée! (*La mère s'approche de la maison. Un groupe de bohèmes lui barre le passage. Mais le regard de la femme, les font reculer*).

**LOAFERS:** Adieu, cow, pigs and litter, Another queen in the gutter. (*Mother nears the house. A group of bohemes block her way. At her glance they fall back.*)

**LA FOULE:** Quelle affaire!

**CROWD:** What an affair.

**LES GAMINS:** (*déjà loin*). Gar' les mornifl'es et les peignées Y va pleuvoir des giroflées! . . .

**URCHINS:** (*far away*). Take care of troubles and beatings, It's going to rain blows! . . .

LES GUEUX: (*descendant des échafandages*). Adieu, chansons, adieu, chimér's!
Ah! quel malheur d'avoir un'mère!
(*Louise se relève, voit sa mère, et s'elance dans les bras de Julien. La foule s'eloigne. Louise, se refugie dans le vestibule. Julien, dans une attitude de défi, barre la route*).

LA MERE: (*humblement, à Julien*). Je ne viens pas en ennemie . . . Je venais dire à Louise que son père est très souffrant et qu'elle seule peut le sauver!

LOUISE: (*à part*). Mon père!

JULIEN: (*à part*). Que vient-elle faire?

LA MERE: (*à Julien, simplement*). Nous avions tout accepté; nous étions las de lutter, de chercher . . . et nous avions fait une croix sur la porte de sa chambre . . .
Elle était morte, bien morte pour nous! . . .
Mais aujourd'hui que son père est au plus mal, je viens vous supplier, monsieur, de permettre à Louise de revenir chez nous; et ce sera la guérison de mon pauvre homme à la maison.

LOUISE: Mon père est trés malade?
(*Julien manifeste sa méfiance*).

LA MERE: (*à Louise*). Il est bien mal depuis hier . . . Le premier jour, il versa mille larmes! Il allait et venait de la porte à la fenêtre, regardant, écoutant, espérant à chaque minute, te voir revenir . . .
La nuit, comme le sommeil ne voulait pas traînait de lui, pendant des heures, il se trainait dans l'ombre, et gémissait . . . et sanglotait . . . Un soir, je le surpris sur le seuil de ta chambre, à genoux et criant: Louise! Louise! mon enfant! m'entends-tu? . . . ne suis-je plus ton père?
Puis il sembla se faire une raison, et reprit sa vie d'autrefois . . . enfin je crus qu'il oubliait, en le voyant parfois sourire à mes larmes.
Hélas! je m'étais trompée; ton père n'avait rien oublié. La douleur le minait, et plus il la cachait, plus il souffrait!
Seule, une joie peut le sauver . . .
Et vous pouvez la lui donner, en conseillant à Louise de revenir chez nous.
Oh! Elle sera libre maintenant!
Ce que nous voulons, c'est l'avoir un peu . . . nous l'aimions depuis plus longtemps que vous . . . Elle connaître nous aimait avant de vous connaitre.
Oh! monsieur! vous ne voudriez pas que son père vous maudisse!
La malédiction d'un mourant vous poursuivrait toute la vie! . . .
(*Le chiffonnier paraît, au fond de la scène. Il fouille le ruisseau en s'éclairant de sa lanterne*).
(*La mère attend avec inquiétude*).

LE CHIFFONNIER: Un père cherche sa fille qui était toute sa famille.
Mais une fille
dans la cité,
c'est une aiguille
dans un champ de blé!
(*Il s'éloigne*).
Pourquoi chercher
et m'obstiner,
La grande ville
a besoin de nos filles . . .
(*Louise et Julien regardent le chiffonnier avec compassion. Leurs hésitations s'envolent*).

JULIEN: (*à la mère*). Promettez-moi de me rendre Louise?

LA MERE: Je le promets.

LE CHIFFONNIER: (*trés loin*). Tra la la la.
Tra la la la.
Elle est partie dans la nuit!

JULIEN: Allons! va, messagère de bonheur!
Et n'oublie pas que dès ce moment je vais compter toutes les heures!
(*Louise ôte le châle dont on l'avait parée et le donne à Julien*).
(*La mère va vers la porte du jardin. Louise la suit, troublée, s'arrêtant à chaque pas. Sur un geste de Julien elle revient vers lui, se dans jette ses bras. Louise s'éloigne a reculons, une main sur les lèvres*).

JULIEN: (*lui tendant les bras*). O Jolie!

## ■ ACTE QUATRIEME.

(*Même décor qu'au premier acte. La maison et la terrasse de Julien ont disparu et l'on voit, au loin, Paris. Neuf heures du soir. Eté*).

(*Le père est assis près de la table. La mère, dans la cuisine, fait la lessive. A travers la porte vitrée, on apercoit Louise dans sa chambre. La mère, s'approche du père, l'invite à boire. Celui-ci les yeux fixés sur Louise ne semble pas la voir*).

LA MERE: (*cherchant à l'égayer*). Tu devrais te rapprocher de la fenêtre, il y fait si bon depuis que les démolisseurs ont balayé le vieux faubourg et ouvert à Paris le chemin de notre chambre.
Ah! on respire maintenant! Vois la belle trouée d'air, de lumière et de vie!

LE PERE: (*après un silence*). Oui! une fameuse trouée où sont disparues bien des choses . . .

LA MERE: Bien des gens!

LOAFERS: (*descending scaffolding*). Adieu to song, to fancies bright;
What a pity to have a mother.
(*Louise rises, sees her mother, and rushes to the arms of Julien. The crowd melts away. Louise takes refuge in the vestibule. Julien, defiant, bars the way.*)

MOTHER: (*humbly to Julien*). I do not come as an enemy . . . I come to tell Louise that her father is suffering and that she alone can save him.

LOUISE: (*aside*). My father!

JULIEN: (*aside*). What brings her here?

MOTHER: (*to Julien, simply*). We had accepted everything; we were tired of struggling and seeking . . . and we had made a cross on the door of her room.
She was dead . . . quite dead for us.
But today her father is much worse, I came to beseech you, sir, to permit Louise to come back home. And it means the getting well of my poor man at the house.

LOUISE: My father is very sick?
(*Julien manifests incredulity.*)

MOTHER: (*to Louise*). He is very bad since yesterday. The first day he shed a thousand tears. He came and went from door to window, looking, listening, hoping each minute to see you return . . .
At night, as sleep would have nothing to do with him, for hours he would drag himself in the dark, groaning and sobbing. One night I surprised him on the floor of your room, on his knees, exclaiming "Louise, Louise, My child, do you hear me . . . am I no longer your father?"
Then he seemed to come to reason and resumed his ordinary life . . . at last I thought he was forgetting as I saw him sometimes smile at my tears.
Alas, I was mistaken. Your father had forgotten nothing. Sorrow was ruining him. The more he hid it the more he suffered.
Only a great joy can save him . . .
And you can give it to him in advising Louise to come back home.
Oh, she shall now be free.
What we want is to have her a little . . . we have loved her longer than you. She loved us before she knew you.
Oh, sir, you would not wish that her father should curse you.
The malediction of a dying man would pursue you all your life.
(*The rag picker appears at rear of scene. He pokes in the gutter lighting himself with lantern. Mother waits with impatience.*)

RAG PICKER: A father seeks his daughter
She was all he had of family
But a girl
in the city
Is a needle
In a field of wheat.
(*He passes on.*)
Why seek
and pester.
The big town
Is in want of our girls.
(*Louise and Julien look at rag picker with compassion. Their hesitations disappear.*)

JULIEN: (*to the mother*). Do you promise to give me back Louise?

MOTHER: I promise.

RAG PICKER: (*in distance*). Tra, la, la,
Tra, la, la, la,
She disappeared in the night.

JULIEN: There, go, messenger of happiness! And don't forget that from this moment, I shall count all the hours.
(*Louise takes off the shawl they had given her and hands it to Julien. The mother goes toward garden gate. Louise, troubled, follows her, stopping at each step. On a gesture of Julien she returns and throws herself in his arms. Louise goes out backward, one hand on her lips.*)

JULIEN: (*spreading his arms to her*). Oh, pretty one!

## ■ ACT IV.

(*Same scene as first act. The house and terrace of Julien have disappeared and one sees Paris in the distance. Nine o'clock in the evening. Summer.*)

(*The father is seated near the table. The mother, in the kitchen, making ready for the wash. Through a glass door Louise is seen in her room. The mother approaches father, invites him to drink. He, his eyes fixed on Louise, seems not to see her.*)

MOTHER: (*trying to cheer him*). You ought to go to the window. It feels so good since the wreckers did away with old faubourg and opened to Paris the road to our room.
Ah! now we can breathe. See the big tunnel of air, light and life.

FATHER: (*after a silence*). Yes, a famous tunnel through which a good many things disappeared.

MOTHER: Many people.

# Act IV

LE PERE: Et quelque peu de bonheur.

LA MERE: (*affectueusement*). Tu as peut-être eu tort de travailler aujourd'hui . . .

LE PERE: Après vingt jours de paresse, j'ai dû faire un effort pour m'y remettre; mais maintenant, c'est fini et je suis d'aplomb . . .
Le coffre est encore solide et peut lutter longtemps!
La fatigue me fait du bien . . . et j'ai pris l'habitude du chagrin . . .
Les pauvres gens peuvent-ils être heureux?
A qui le bon Dieu donnerait-il son ciel s'il n'y avait sur la terre que des gens heureux?
Bête de somme que je suis, que tous nous sommes, sous le joug pesant de la Fatalité!
Tristes serfs d'une besogne qui ne cesse jamais!
Piteux jouets aux mains de l'injustice, dans un monde où tout n'est que misère et déception, où choses et gens sont nos ennemis, où les enfants même, dans l'égoïsme de l'amour, nous martyrisent et nous disent:
(*Aprement*).
—Vous avez assez vécu! Place! Place! nous n'avons plus besoin de vous! . . . nous ne voulons plus de maitres! . . .
(*Douloureusement*).
Et, si l'on veut lutter contre leur folie, ces êtres d'orgueil, narguant notre tendresse, ajoutent leur haine à toutes nos détresses, et silencieux, implacables, impatients, ils attendent que la mort vienne les délivrer de ceux qui voudraient mourir pour eux!
(*Louise se lève lentement, ouvre la fenêtre de sa chambre et regarde dans la nuit. Le père la suit des yeux*).
Voir naître une enfant, la fleurir de caresse, guider ses premiers pas, sourire à son premier sourire . . .
(*Louise pleure; le père la contemple avec une émotion croissante*).
Les fatigues, les tourments, rien ne coûte: c'est pour elle; qu'elle soit toujours plus belle!
L'enfant grandit; c'est maintenant une jolie demoiselle vers laquelle s'empressent les galants.
(*Louise ferme sa fenêtre et se rassied*).
Tout en elle est ravissant; ils sont fiers, les vieux parents, car la fille de leur sang est pour tous un modèle d'honneur et de sagesse!
Puis, un jour, un inconnu qui passe, d'un regard enjôleur séduit la pure fille et chasse le passé de son coeur; s'empare de sa pensée et détruit à jamais notre bonheur!
Ah! soit maudit le voleur d'amour qui, de notre fille, fit pour nous une étrangère; le ravisseur dont le caprice d'un jour nous causa tant de larmes et changes le foyer de calme et de joie en un enfer de discorde et de haine!
(*Silence.*)

LA MERE: (*de la cuisine*). Louise! Louise!

LOUISE: Quoi?

LA MERE: Viens m'aider!
(*Louise se lève, range son ouvrage, éteint sa lampe, puis ouvre la porte; le père se tourne vers elle, lui tend les bras; elle passe sans le voir, se dirige vers la cuisine et disparaît. Les deux femmes, à la cantonade*).

LA MERE: Auras-tu bientôt fini de bouder? Tu n'as donc pas pitié de ton père?
(*Le père écoute avidement*)
Tu supposes peut-être qu'on va te laisser retourner chez ton amoureux?

LOUISE: (*vivement*). Vous l'aviez promis!

LA MERE: Tu sais bien que c'est impossible. On n'peut pas te laisser r'commencer une vie pareille! Tu la connais, maintenant, la vie de bohème; tu sais que c'est: de la misère en chansons. Voyons, sois raisonnable! . . . sois bonne pour nous . . .
Ton pauvre père souffre tant!
(*Père se lève et s'approche de la cuisine*).

LOUISE: (*dont la voix s'élève*) . . . l'amour libre!

LA MERE: (*moqueuse*). L'amour libre, l'amour libre! en prônant aujourd'hui ce qu'il appelle l'amour libre, il n'a qu'un but: esquiver le mariage!
L'amour libre! . . . en voilà une histoire!
(*Elle rit railleusement. Lentement, le père va se rasseoir*).

LOUISE: Rira bien qui rira la dernière!

LA MERE: C'est ce que nous verrons . . . en attendant, va dormir, c'est l'heure; et n'oublie pas de dire bonsoir à ton père.
(*Louise paraît à la porte; elle s'avance lentement, et se dirige vers le père*).

LOUISE: Bonsoir, père.
(*Elle lui présente son front. Le père la saisit avec violence, et l'embrasse longuement. Sans lui rendre son baiser, Louise se dégage et s'éloigne froidement. Le père tend vers elle ses bras, puis s'élance*).

LE PERE: Louise!
(*Suppliant*).
Louise!
(*Il l'attire à lui*).
Regarde-moi!
(*Tendre*).
Ne suis-je plus ton père? N'es-tu plus l'enfant qu'autre fois j'ai

---

FATHER: And some happiness.

MOTHER: (*affectionately*). You were, perhaps, wrong to work so much today . . .

FATHER: After twenty days of laziness, I had to make an effort to get in harness again; but now its over and I'm all right.
The trunk is still solid and can struggle a long time.
Fatigue does me good and I've taken the habit of sorrow . . .
Can poor people be happy?
To whom would the good God give his heaven if there were only happy people on earth?
Beast of burden that I am, that we all are, under the heavy weight of Fatality.
Sorrowful serfs of a task that never ends.
Piteous toys in the hands of injustice, in a world where everything is but misery and deception, where things and people are our enemies, where even the children, in the egoism of love, martyrize us and say to us:
(*Bitterly.*)
You have lived enough. Room! Room! We don't need you any more. We won't have any more masters! . . .
(*Sadly.*)
And, if one would fight against their folly, these proud beings, laughing at our tenderness, adding their hatred to all our distresses, silent, impatient, wait that death shall come to deliver them from those who would die for them!
(*Louise slowly rises, opens her window and looks into the night. The father's eyes follow her.*)
See a child born, flower her with caresses, guide her first steps, smile at her first smile . . .
(*Louise weeps. The father looks at her with growing emotion.*)
Fatigues, torments, nothing matters. It is for her—that she may always be handsome.
The child grows. She is now a pretty demoiselle upon whom gallants begin to press.
(*Louise closes windows. Sits again.*)
Everything about her is ravishing; they are proud, the old parents, for the girl of their blood is a model of honor and wisdom.
(*He rises.*)
Then one day, a passing stranger with a cunning glance seduces the pure girl and chases the past from her heart, takes possession of her thoughts and destroys our happiness forever.
Ah, cursed be the robber of love, who made our daughter a stranger to us; the ravisher whose caprice of a day caused us so many tears and changed the hearth of calm and joy into a hell of discord and hatred.
(*Silence.*)

MOTHER: (*from kitchen*). Louise! Louise!

LOUISE: What?

MOTHER: Come and help me.
(*Louise rises, arranges her sewing, puts out her lamp, then opens the door. The father turns to her with arms outstretched. She passes him without looking and goes to the kitchen and disappears. The two women, off stage.*)

MOTHER: Will you soon stop sulking? Have you no pity on your father?
(*Father listens anxiously.*) Perhaps you think we are going to let you return to your lover?

LOUISE: (*lively*). You promised it.

MOTHER: You know that it's impossible. We can't let begin again such a life as that. You know now what it is, this bohemian life—misery in songs. Come, be reasonable . . . be good to us . . .
Your poor father suffers so much.
(*Father rises and goes toward kitchen.*)

LOUISE: (*loud voice*) . . . love that is free!

MOTHER: (*mockingly*). Free love, free love. In practicing today what is called free love he had only one aim, to slide out of marriage.
Free love . . . that's a fine story.
(*She laughs mockingly. Father sits down again.*)

LOUISE: Laughs best who laughs last.

MOTHER: We'll see about that. In the meantime, go to your sleep—it's time; and don't forget to say goodnight to your father.
(*Louise appears at door, walks slowly and goes toward father.*)

LOUISE: Good night, father.
(*She presents her forehead. Father seizes her violently and embraces her long. Without giving back kiss, Louise moves away coldly. Father strains his arms toward her then springs.*)

FATHER: Louise!
(*Begging.*)
Louise!
(*He draws her to him.*)
Look at me.
(*Tenderly.*)
Am I not your father? Are you no longer the child who used to cradle

bercée dans mes bras? N'es-tu plus la fille de mon sang?
(*Il l'assied sur ses genoux et la berce comme un enfant*).

LE PÈRE: (*la retenant*). Reste . . . repose-toi . . . comme jadis, toute petite . . .
(*Louise cherche à s'évader*).
Reste . . . Ah! souviens-toi des beaux jours d'autrefois! . . .
(*Louise essaie doucement de se dégager*).
Pourquoi veux-tu partir? Est-il donc pour toi un refuge sur la terre plus doux que le coeur de ton père?
(*La berçant*). L'enfant dormira bientôt . . .
L'enfant dormira bientôt . . .
l'enfant dormira bientôt . . .
Comme autrefois, endors-toil
(*S'efforçant de sourire*).
"Si la p'tite enfant est sage . . . elle aura une belle image . . . do-do . . . l'enfant do."

LOUISE: (*lève la tête*). L'enfant serait sage, tout à fait sage, si son père voulait lui faire moins de peine et comprendre que la douleur est mauvaise conseillère . . .

LE PÈRE: Pourquoi parler de peine et parler de douleur, quand un père, une mère t'aiment et ne vivent que pour ton bonheur?

LOUISE: (*avec ironie*). Mon bonheur? . . .
Vous n'avez qu'un signe à faire pour que revienne le bonheur.
(*Gentiment enfantin, mais toujours triste*).
La belle image que l'enfant désire, la grâce qu'ell-vous demande c'est de n'être plus, comme un oiseau mis en cage . . .
(*Elle se lève*).
privée de liberté et emprisonnée par votre aveugle tendresse, qui s'imagine que je puisse être heureuse à vivre ainsi qu'une captive, dans l'âge où, sans la liberté, la vie est pire que la mort.
(*La mère paraît*).

LE PÈRE: Si tu veux être libre, laisse là ton rêve de folie . . .

LOUISE: (*à part*). Mon rêve de folie! . . .
Vous voulez que j'abandonne tout espoir, et que je mente à mes mentîtes serments . . . comme vous mentîtes . . . à vos promesses!

LA MÈRE: Insolente!

LOUISE: (*imitant sa mère*). "Oh! elle sera libre, maintenant; ce que nous demandons, c'est l'avoir un peu, car nous l'aimons depuis plus longtemps que vous; elle nous aimait avant de vous connaître."
(*Se tournant vers sa mère*).
Vous nous reconnaissiez, alors, le droit de nous aimer et de nous le dire!

---

in my arms? Are you no longer the daughter of my blood?
(*He seats her on his knees like a child.*)

FATHER: (*retaining her*). Remain—rest . . . as in other days—long ago.
(*Louise seeks to escape.*)
Remain. Ah, do you remember the fine days of long ago?
(*Louise tries gently to get away.*)
Why do you want to go? Is there for you a refuge safer on earth than your father's heart?
(*Rocking her.*)
Soon the child will be asleep,
Soon the child will be asleep,
Go to sleep as in the old times.
(*Forcing himself to smile.*)
"If the little child is good
She shall have a pretty picture.
Do, do,
Baby, do, do."

LOUISE: (*raising head*). The child would be good, and very, very good, if her father would give her less trouble and understand that grief is a poor counselor . . .

FATHER: Why speak of trouble and grief, when a father and a mother only live for your happiness?

LOUISE: (*ironically.*) My happiness.
You have only to make a sign and happiness will return.
(*Prettily childish, but sadly.*)
The handsome picture the child wants, the mercy that she requests is no longer to be like a bird in a cage,
(*She rises.*)
deprived of liberty and imprisoned by your blind tenderness, which imagines that I can be happy living like a captive, at an age when, without liberty, life is worse than death.
(*The mother appears.*)

FATHER: If you wish to be free abandon your dream of folly . . .

LOUISE: (*aside*). My dream of folly! . . .
You wish me to abandon all hope, That I belie my oaths . . .
As you lied . . .
In your promises.

MOTHER: Insolent.

LOUISE: (*imitating her mother.*)
"Oh now she will be free. What we ask is to have her a little for we have loved her longer than you. She loved us before she knew you."
(*Turning to her mother.*)
You recognized our right then to love one another and to say it.

---

LA MÈRE: Nous vous reconnaissions le droit de vous marier, pas autre chose! Tant pis pour toi,
(*Sarcastique*)
si ton amant satisfait, réclame maintenant l'union libre.
(*Brutale*).
Tu n'as que ce que tu mérites.

LOUISE: (*indignée*). Comment! . . . comment!. . . Tuoseslenier!. . . n'est-il pas vrai que tu m'avais promis de me laisser libre?

LE PÈRE: La liberté que tu demandes, c'est la liberté de courir les rues . . . la liberté de nous déshonorer!
(*Il prend Louise dans ses bras, avec détresse*).
Louise, ô mon enfant! Qui m'aurait dit qu'un jour tu renierais ma tendresse, et que, loin de moi, tu demanderais à vivre?
O Louise, reviens à toi! Comme autrefois, dans mes bras, endors-toi!
. . . (*Il l'assied sur ses genoux*).
N'est-ce plus mon enfant, ma Louise chérie, que ie presse en mes bras tremblants?

LOUISE: (*avec amertume*). Les parents voudraient qu'on restât le marmot dont la pensée sommeille à l'ombre de leur volonté!

LE PÈRE: Les misères, les tourments, tout s'ouble auprès d'elle; elle est si bonne, si aimante, si belle!

LOUISE: Pourquoi serais-je belle . . . si ce n'est pour être aimée? . . .

LE PÈRE: Ah! n'est-ce pas t'aimer que te donner notre vie?

LOUISE: Vous prenez la mienne!

LE PÈRE: N'est-ce pas t'aimer que t'avoir pardonné . . .

LOUISE: Pour m'emprisonner mieux qu'autrefois!

LE PÈRE: N'est-ce pas t'aimer que te supplier . . . quand j'aurais le droit de commander . . .
(*Louise s'éloigne vivement du père. Celui-ci s'avance sur elle, menaçant*).

LOUISE: Tout être a le droit d'être libre!
Tout coeur a le devoir d'aimer!
Aveugle celui qui veut garrotter l'originale et fière volonté d'une âme qui s'éveille et qui réclame sa part de soleil, sa part d'amour!

LE PÈRE: (*découragé*). Ah! ce n'est pas toi qui parles par ta bouche, méchante! Non! ce n'est pas toi! C'est une étrangère, une ennemie impitoyable. Ce n'est plus ma fille! mon seul bien! mon espoir! ma jolie!

VOIX LONTAINES: O Jolie!

LOUISE: Paris! Paris m'appelle!

VOIX LONTAINES: O Jolie! . . .

---

MOTHER: We recognized your right to marry—nothing else. The worse for you.
(*Sarcastic.*)
And if your lover satisfied, now cries, Free love—
(*Brutally.*)
You've only got what you deserve.

LOUISE: (*indignant.*) What . . . what! . . . You dare deny it? Is it not true that you promised to leave me free.

FATHER: The liberty you ask is the liberty to gad the streets—freedom to dishonor yourself.
(*Taking Louise in his arms, distressedly.*)
Louise, oh my child. Who could have told me that one day, you would give up my love and that you would wish to live far from me?
Oh Louise, come back to yourself as in the past, in my arms, go to sleep.
(*He places her on his knees.*)
Is it no longer my child, my darling Louise, whom I press in these trembling arms?

LOUISE: (*bitterly*). Parents would wish that one remained a dormouse, the thought of which slumbers in the shadow of their will.

FATHER: Miseries and torments, all are forgotten now. She is so good, so loving, so pretty.

LOUISE: Why should I be pretty Unless it is to be loved?

FATHER: Is it not loving you to give you our life?

LOUISE: You take mine.

FATHER: Is it not loving you to have forgiven? . . .

LOUISE: So as to imprison me more than ever.

FATHER: Is it not loving you to beseech,
When I should have the right to command?
(*Louise tears herself away from her father. He advances toward her, threateningly.*)

LOUISE: All beings have the right to be free,
Every heart has the right to love. Blind is he who would fetter the first and proud will of a soul that claims its share of sun,
Its share of love.

FATHER: (*discouraged*). Oh, it is not you who speaks by your mouth, wicked one. No it is not you. It is a stranger, an enemy, unforgiving. It is no longer my daughter, my only possession, my hope, my pretty one.

DISTANT VOICES: Oh, pretty one!

LOUISE: Paris, Paris calls me.

DISTANT VOICES: Oh, pretty one!

LOUISE: O la magique, la chère musique de la grande ville! . . .

LE PERE: (*avec haine*). Paris! . . .

LOUISE: O l'attirante promesse! . . .

LE PERE: Paris! . . .

LOUISE: L'inoubliable, l'affolant vertige! . . .
Au secours de la Fille, la Ville viendrait-elle?
(*On apercoit la ville qui peu à peu s'éclaire*).
Paris! Paris! Fête éternelle du plaisir!
Paris! splendeur de mes désirs!
Paris, ô Paris, secours ma détresse.
Ressucite l'ivresse des hymnes d'allégresse!
Que s'écroulent les murs de la triste prison!
Sonne, cloche de joie des libres épousailles!
Fais revivre le charme de l'heure où mon coeur battait contre son coeur!

LE PERE: (*dont la colère augmente*). Ah!

LOUISE: Vers sa demeure, asile des rêves, ville maternelle, porte moi d'un coup d'aile!

LE PERE: Tais-toi.

LOUISE: Encore un jour d'amour! Encore un jour d'amour!
(*Le père ferme la fenêtre*).

LE PERE: Tais-toi! Tais-toi!

LA MERE: Elle devient folle.

LOUISE: (*à toute volée*). Qu'il vienne vite, vite, mon bien-aimé, pareil aux hardis chevaliers des contes bleus de la Légende.

LA MERE: Que dit-elle?

LOUISE: A mon appel va-t-il accourir, le Prince Charmant, dont la caresse éveilla la petite Montmartroise au coeur dormant!

LE PERE: Tu n'as pas honte!

LOUISE: Qu'il vienne donc le poète, dont la tendresse triomphante fit une Muse de la pauvre recluse!

LA MERE: Veux-tu te taire!

LOUISE: Ce n'est plus la petite fille au coeur timide et craintif, c'est une femme, au coeur de flamme, qui veut reprendre son amant!
(*Elle s'élance vers la porte. Le père lui barre le passage*).

LE PERE: Tu ne passeras pas!

LOUISE: (*tournant dans la chambre comme une ballucinée*). La! la! la! la! la! la! Il va venir bientôt! La! la! la! la! la! la! Je vais revoir les yeux du bien-aimé; je vais entendre sa parole; et mes lévres vont pouvoir se griser de son ardent baiser toute l'éternité!
Julien! à moi! Julien, pour toujours, prends-moi! . . .

LE PERE: (*Au paroxysme de la colère, il s'élance sur elle comme pour la frapper; puis se ravise et, furieusement, ouvre la porte*). Ah! misérable! va-t'en! va-t'en le retrouver! Dans la ville, qui t'appelle, va donc t'amuser! C'est plus gai qu'ici, là-bas! . . .
(*Il court vers Louise, lui saisit les mains, la traine vers la porte*).
Allons, dépêche-toi! voici la fête qui s'allume! Ah! ah! ah! Toutes les filles sont là; on les entend crier:
"—Que la danse commence!"
—Et brûlent les lampions! . . . et ronfle la musique!
(*Montrant Paris*).
—"Voilà l'plaisir, mesdam's!"
On danse à crever, on rit à pleurer.
(*Louise s'échappe et se réfugie au bout de la chambre*).
"Voilà l'plaisir, mesdam's!"
On n'atend plus que toi! allons, va, mais va donc!

LA MERE: Pierre!

LOUISE: (*tremblante, apeurée, hésitant à sortir court autour de la chambre*). Ah!

LA MERE: (*s'accrochant au père*). Laisse-la!

LE PERE: Dépêche-toi!

LA MERE: Laisse-la, je t'en prie!

LE PERE: M'entends-tu?

LA MERE: (*s'accrochant au père*). Pierre!

LE PERE: (*presque burlé*). Vas-tu t'en aller? ou je te jette à la porte!
(*Il vent s'élancer. La mère le retient; bors de lui, il écarte la mère avec violence et s'élance*).

LE PERE: (*Cri*). Ah!

LA MERE: (*tombant*). (*Cri*). Ah!

LOUISE: (*affolée, s'enfuit*). (*Cri*). Ah!
(*Louise partie, le père regarde autour de lui . . . Sa colèrc tombe . . . Il regrette et s'élance dans l'escalier. On l'entend appeler*).

LE PERE: Louise! . . . Louise! . . .
(*La mère se relève, le père apparaît. Il reste un moment sur le seuil, comme terrassé par la douleur tendant le poing vers la ville, avec baine*). O Paris!!!

FIN.

---

LOUISE: Oh, the magic, the dear music of the town.

FATHER: (*with hatred*). Paris!

LOUISE: The attractive promise.

FATHER: Paris!

LOUISE: The unforgettable, the delightful craze.
The town will come and help the girl?
(*The city gradually lights up.*)
Paris, Paris, eternal festival of pleasure;
Paris, splendor of my desires.
Paris, oh Paris, aid my distress.
Resurrect the bliss of your hymns of delight!
That the walls of the sad prison may fall,
Ring out, bell of joy of a free union,
Let the charm revive of the hour when his heart beat against mine.

FATHER: (*whose anger grows*). Ah!

LOUISE: Toward his habitation, home of dreams, maternal city, carry me with a stroke of the wing!

FATHER: Be quiet!

LOUISE: One more day of love! One more day of love!
(*Father closes the window.*)

FATHER: Be quiet! be quiet!

MOTHER: She's going mad.

LOUISE: (*loudly*). Let him come quickly, quickly, my well beloved, like the bold knights of the blue stories of the Legend.

MOTHER: What is she saying?

LOUISE: At my call, will he come, the Prince Charming, whose kiss awakened the little Montmartraise of the sleeping heart.

FATHER: You are not ashamed?

LOUISE: Let him come then, the poet whose triumphant tenderness made a Muse of the poor recluse.

MOTHER: Will you shut up?

LOUISE: It is no longer the little girl of the timid heart and afraid, it is a woman, with heart of flame, who wants back her lover.
(*She rushes to door. Father gets in front of her.*)

FATHER: You shall not pass.

LOUISE: (*turning about like a mad woman.*) La, la, la, la, la, la. He will come soon. La, la, la, la, la. I shall once more see the eyes of my beloved. I shall hear him speak and my lips will get drunk under his ardent kiss for all eternity!
Julien, come to me, Julien, forever. take me!

FATHER: (*In a paroxysm of anger, he throws himself upon her as if to strike her. On second thought, furiously he opens the door.*) Ah, wretch! Go, go and find him. In the town that calls you, go then amuse yourself. It's gayer than here, over there!
(*He goes to Louise, seizes her hands and drags her to door*).
Come, hurry, here is the fête lighting up. Ah, ha, ha. All the girls are there. One can hear them cry out "Let the dance begin!"
The lanterns burn—the music sounds.
(*Showing Paris.*)
Here's your pleasure, ladies.
They'll dance till they die, they'll laugh till they cry.
(*Louise escapes to the end of the room*).
There's the pleasure, ladies.
They're only awaiting you, go on, get out.

MOTHER: Pierre!

LOUISE: (*trembling, frightened runs around the room*). Ah!

MOTHER: (*holding on to father*). Leave her alone.

FATHER: Hurry up.

MOTHER: Let her be, I beg.

FATHER: Do you hear me?

MOTHER: (*holding to father*). Pierre!

FATHER: (*almost howling*). Will you get out? or do you want me to throw you through the door?
(*He rushes at her. Mother holds him back. He pushes her away and rushes at Louise*).

FATHER: (*with a cry*). Ah!

MOTHER: (*falling, with a cry*). Ah!

LOUISE: (*crazed, escapes, with a cry*). Ah!
(*Louise gone, the father looks about him. His anger falls. He regrets and runs to staircase. He is beard calling*).

FATHER: Louise! . . . Louise! . . .
(*The mother rises. The father returns, remains a moment on the sill expressing keenest sorrow. The Father shaking his fist with hatred*).
Oh, Paris!!

THE END.

# Julien, A Poet's Life (1913)

MUSIC & LIBRETTO BY GUSTAVE CHARPENTIER

Set to a libretto by the composer, this four-act opera with prologue premiered at the Opéra-Comique in Paris on June 4, 1913. It was written as a sequel to the opera *Louise*, but this work did not equal the success of its predecessor. The story opens at the Villa Medici in Rome. Julien has received the Prix de Rome and is developing into a fine poet. His wife, Louise, is asleep on a sofa as he enters their room. He sits at his table and leafs through the poem he is writing, for which he has high hopes. He falls asleep and Louise wakes up and caresses him. She is happy about his work though she knows that she comes second in his heart—his writing comes first. Julien dreams that he is accompanied by Louise to the Temple of Beauty. He promises to pray to the Beautiful and the True, and he embraces Louise in happiness, knowing of her love for him. Other pilgrims and lovers travel along the same path. Halfway to the tmeple they must pass the Accursed Valley, a place containing mortals disappointed by their lost dreams, lies, and disillusionments. They pray that hope may be restored to them. Julien decides that he must help them and Louise agrees. He is asked if he will sacrifice everything to the high ideals for which he is searching and he pledges to do so. The high priest tells him of the sacrifices he will make and that his efforts will be in vain. Louise is upset by these words and joins the dream maidens. Julien prays in front of the altar, and the Goddess of Beauty appears to him with Louise's face. She tells him to "fear pride and human reason." Julien is now in a Hungarian valley sleeping near a peasant's cottage. He awakens and sees toil and misery all around him and is discouraged that no one listens to his words about love and beauty. An old peasant farmer and his daughter, who looks very much like Louise, watches him. The old peasant speaks to him and the girl tries to cheer him up, offering him love and asking him to give up his dream. The old peasant then speaks to him in the same voice as the high priest from the temple and he turns away from the peasants and continues on his journey, alone. He finds himself on the coast of Brittany, where he sees women going from their gloomy homes to a dark church. He is once again grieved by the unrelieved drudgery around him. His old grandmother, whose face reminds him of Louise's, comes out from a cottage and asks him to stay with her. She reminds him of his childhood and his belief in Christianity and he kneels to pray, but again he experiences feelings of failure. His grandmother asks him about the people that creep by on the road, and he tells her about the poets, hearing them cry and mock their lost dreams. She tells him to be careful of pride, and his faith is stifled by the mockery of the lost poets. In Paris in the Montmartre district, Julien is chased by the Furies on a dark and foggy night. He rejects his pledge to Love and Beauty, sits down, and a street girl brings him wine from the Cabaret of the Muses. He once again sees the face of Louise and begins to weep. He believes the girl to be Louise, but as he attempts to embrace her she goes laughingly back to the cabaret. He sees that everything he has done is the result of pride and that he is now ruined. Suddenly a crowd enters to celebrate Shrove Tuesday, and there is singing and dancing everywhere. The street girl comes to him again and they celebrate together. At the Theater of the Ideal is an old man who sells tickets to view Beauty. He resembles the high priest and Julien sees the dream maidens and all the others in the crowd who were at his consecration. They are now bestial beings and they destroy the theater. Darkness descends and a vision of the holy temple appears. Julien collapses as his hopes burn his soul. The street girl laughs at him as he dies in front of her.

---

## ■ ACTE PREMIER

*(Enthousiasme)*

### ■ Premier Tableau

*LA MONTAGNE SAINTE*
*Un sentier fleuri la gravit en riants lacets, parmi d'augustes vestiges du passé. Au sommet, la masse sombre du Temple de la Beauté dont l'aube commence à dorer les colonnades.*

*SCÈNE PREMIÈRE*

*LES FILLES DU RÊVE.*

## ■ ACT I

*(Enthusiasm)*

### ■ First Tableau

*THE HOLY MOUNT*
*A flowery path winds up the side of the mountain amid imposing ruins.*
*On the summit, the sombre mass of the Temple of Beauty is gilded by the coming sunrise.*

*SCENE I*

*THE DREAM-MAIDENS*

**LES FILLES DU RÊVE:** *(loin.)* Dioné?
Néora?
Noéli?
Philyra?
Euryté?
Séa?
*(Elles apparaissent peu à peu sur le sentier, le descendent en courant, joyeuses, comme si elles allaient à la rencontre d'êtres chers. Dioné, Néora, Noéli, Philyra, Euryté, Séa, demeurées en scène, échangent des gestes avec celles qui sont descendues dans la vallée.)*
Tiralla, tiralli-é-ti-é!
Tiralla, tiralli-é-ti-é!
La-i, la-i-é-là!

**THE DREAM MAIDENS:** *(off.)* Dioné?
Néora?
Noéli?
Philyra?
Euryté?
Séa?
*(They appear gradually on the path, and come running down joyously as if to meet other dear ones. Dioné, Néora, Noéli, Philyra, Euryté and Séa remain on the stage and exchange gestures with others who have gone down into the valley.)*
Tiralla, tiralli-é-ti-é!
La-i, la-i-é-la!

La-i, la-i-é-là!
(*Rires. Elles vont au-devant de leurs soeurs qui reviennent portant des fleurs et des palmes.*)

**LES FILLES DU RÊVE:** (*revenant.*)
Rallahi! . . .
Rallahi! . . .
(*Elles repassent heureuses, turbulentes.*)

**DIONÉ, NÉORA, NOÉLI, PHILYRA, EURYTÉ:** (*déjà loin.*) Rallahi!
Rallahi! . . .
La-é-i-ti!
**SÉA:** (*survenant, jette un appel et remonte vite.*) Noéli! . . .

**DIONÉ:** (*loin.*) Laéité! . . .

**NOÉLI:** (*plus loin.*) Laéti! . . .

(*They run out to meet their sisters and return bearing flowers and palms.*)

**THE DREAM MAIDENS:** (*returning*) Rallahi!—Rallahi!
(*They pass, gay and noisy.*)

**DIONÉ, NÉORA, NOÉLI, PHILYRA, EURYTÉ:** (*already distant*)
Laéiti! Rallahi!—Rallahi!
(*Séa, coming back, gives a call and goes up quickly.*)
Noéli!.

**DIONÉ:** (*off.*)
Laéité!

**NOÉLI:** (*further off.*)
Laéiti!

## SCÈNE II

SERVANTS, SERVANTES, PÈLERINS DU RÊVE, AMANTS, AMANTES, LOUISE, JULIEN.
Bientôt apparaît sur le sentier le cortège des Pèlerins de la Beauté.

**SERVANTS, ET SERVANTES DE LA BEAUTÉ:** (*semant des roses et portant des emblèmes.*) Douce extase du poète élu
Et de l'amant aimé! . . .

**LES PÈLERINS DU RÊVE:** (*religieusement.*) Pure lumière,
Vers toi s'envole ma prière
Dans le mystère
D'un divin jour! . . .

**LES AMANTS et LES AMANTES:**
(*vêtus de printempts, tendrement enlacés. Louise et Julien sont parmi eux.*) Abue d'amour,
Aube première,
Dans ta lumière,
Chante le mystère
De mon amour!

**LOUISE, puis JULIEN:** Brûle, ô mon âme,
Brûle toujours, voluptueuse flamme!
Troublante aurore
De mon désir,
Dans ton amour,
Je sens éclore
L'ardente aurore
De l'avenir!

**LES PÈLERINS DU RÊVE:** Pure lumière,
Vers toi s'envole ma prière
Dans le mystère
D'un divin jour!
(*Louise et Julien demeurent un moment, tandis que passent les derniers groupes du cortège.*)

## SCENE II

WORSHIPPERS, MEN AND WOMEN, DREAM-PILGRIMS, LOVERS, LOUISE, JULIEN.
(*The procession of the pilgrims to Beauty appears on the path.*)

**WORSHIPPERS OF BEAUTY:**
(*strewing roses and waving emblems.*) Sweet ecstasy of the elect
Poet and well beloved!

**DREAM-PILGRIMS:** (*devotedly.*)
Pure radiance,
My prayer shall ever rise toward you
Wrapped in the mystery
Of sacred day!

**THE LOVERS:** (*in springtide garb, fondly entwined; among them Louise and Julien.*) O dawn of love,
O primal dawn,
In your radiance
Sing the mystery
Of my true love!

**LOUISE, then JULIEN:** Burn, oh my soul,
Burn, burn forever, flame of joy!
You troubling dawn
Of my desire,
In your true love
I feel
The ardent dawn
Of future fame unfold!

**THE DREAM-PILGRIMS:** Pure radiance,
My prayer shall ever rise toward you;
Wrapped in the mystery
Of sacred day.
(*Julien and Louise stand aside while the last of the pilgrims pass them.*)

**LOUISE:** (*à Julien, montrant l'horizon merveilleux.*) Ah! tout est beau . . .
On dirait un cortège
De fleurs d'azur, de fleurs de neige,
Naissant dans un décor nouveau!

**JULIEN:** Sous son grand manteau Renaissant
La terre sent courir,
Comme du sang,
Les sèves
Ainsi je sens
En moi monter le flot grandissant
Des rêves! . . .

**LOUISE:** (*s'attardant à admirer le paysage.*) Roses, lys, amoureuses fleurs . . .

**JULIEN:** (*l'entraînant.*) Prémices de bonheur!

**LOUISE:** Leur éclat est doux comme nos tendresses . . .

**JULIEN:** Leur parfum, ardent comme nos caresses . . .
(*Ils gravissent lentement le sentier jonché de roses. Des nuages descendent derrière lesquels se fait le changement du décor.*)

**VOIX LOINTAINES:** Gloire au Poète
Gloire à l'Amant!
Gloire à l'Amante!
(*Les nuages continuant de descendre, découvrant le décor nouveau.*)

**LOUISE:** (*to Julien.*) How fair it is!
It seems a shining file
Of flowers, blue and gold and white,
All rising from the new green-sward.

**JULIEN:** Beneath her wrappings
Of the Spring
The earth can feel the course
Of rising sap
Like blood.
And so I feel
All through my veins the surging flow
Of dreams.

**LOUISE:** (*lingering to admire the landscape.*) Lily and rose, the flowers of love—

**JULIEN:** (*drawing her away.*)
Foretelling happiness!

**LOUISE:** Their splendor sweet as our dear love!

**JULIEN:** Their perfume ardent as our fond embrace!
(*They go slowly up the path overhung with roses. Clouds come down behind them while the scenery is changed.*)

**DISTANT VOICES:** Hail to the Poet!
To the Lover and the Mistress, hail!
(*The clouds continue to come down, disclosing the new scenes.*)

## ■ Deuxième Tableau

*LA VALLÉE MAUDITE*

Sur la Montagne Sainte, à mi-chemin du Temple, près d'une gorge obscure.
Dans l'abîme, le groupe des POÈTES DÉCHUS. Sur un sentier surplombant, les CHIMÈRES semblent tisser des brouillards et de légères nuées multicolores qui descendent, flottant au-dessus des Poètes et leur dérobant la Montagne Sainte.)

### SCÈNE PREMIÈRE

*LES CHIMÈRES, LES POÈTES DÉCHUS, puis JULIEN et LOUISE.*

**VOIS DANS L'ABÎME:** Rêve! Rêve!
O Rêve! doux printemps de l'amour!
Daigne ouvrir tes ailes pour l'essor du retour!
Viens fleurir nos âmes de tes roses caresses . . .
Ah! ne trahis pas tes promesses!

**LES CHIMÈRES:** Filles du rêve, soeurs clémentes,
Pour ceux qui nous ont fuies . . .
Tissons sans bruit

## ■ Second Tableau

*THE DARK VALLEY*

On the Holy Mount, halfway up to the temple, near a gloomy gorge. In the abyss are the Hapless Poets. On the path above, the Chimeras seem to weave mists and fogs of many colors, which float downward, hiding the Holy Mount from the Poets.

### SCENE I

*THE CHIMERAS, THE HAPLESS POETS, then JULIEN and LOUISE.*

**A VOICE FROM THE ABYSS:**
Dreams!
Dreams!
Dreams!
O sweet Maytime of love!
Unfold your wings to waft it back to us!
Bloom again in our souls with rosy kisses,
And to your promise, oh, be true!

**CHIMERAS:** Dream-Maidens, Sisters of Mercy
For those that fall dismayed,
Weave we noiselessly
The kindly dreams that lie!—

Des songes cléments qui mentent . . .
Flots de trames, vols de rêves, dans
la nuit!!!

**LES POÈTES DÉCHUS:** (*tendant
les bras vers la Montagne.*) Viens,
flamme divine!
Viens, chaude clarté! . . .
Jadis tes rayons embrasaient nos
êtres.
A nos yeux charmés feras-tu
renaître
Le pays du rêve et l'orbe enchanté?
Refleuris, ô Verbe! Érigez vos
faîtes,
Temples si beaux que les plus
beaux soirs
Brillent moins dans la pourpre de
leurs fêtes!

**LES CHIMÈRES:** Tissons des rêves
et des mirages
Pour étoiler
L'éternité de ruine et d'esclavage
Que sous des brumes
Nos doigts d'amour ont voilée.
(*Les brumes qu'elles tissent envahissent peu à peu le haut de la
scène. Louise et Julien paraissent
sur un rocher qui domine la gorge
obscure. Immobiles d'effroi, ils
regardent écoutent.*)

**LES POÈTES DÉCHUS:**
(*s'acheminant vers la vallée.*)
Cieux lointains! ô mers! ô larges miroirs,
Pays inconnus à l'âme éblouie!
Ils s'offrent et l'ombre est
évanouie . . .
(*Apercevant Louise et Julien, les
Chimères remontent vers la cime
et disparaissent derrière les
brumes.*)

**LES CHIMÈRES:** (*s'appelant.*) La-
i, la-i-é-là!
(*Julien entraîne Louise jusqu'au
bord de l'abîme. Tous deux se
penchent.*)

**LES POÈTES DÉCHUS:** (*sanglotant au loin.*) Flamme divine! . . .

**JULIEN:** (*frissonnant contre
Louise.*) Quelle épouvante! . . .

**LES POÈTES DÉCHUS:** (*loin.*) Ah!
ah! ah!
(*Le bas de la Montagne disparaît
à son tour derrière les brumes.
Une émotion violente saisit Julien. Il voudrait secourir ses frères
malheureux. En lui s'éveille
l'instinct de sa mission divine.*)

**JULIEN:** (*avec ferveur.*) Soleil du
monde, suprême amour,
En moi tu t'éveilles! . . .
L'âpre douleur qui blessa mes or-
eilles
M'a révélé la raison de ma vie!
Mon coeur d'enfant prédestiné
Va se donner
Au triomphe de la Beauté!
Au triomphe de l'Amour!

Fateful meshes, flights of dreams,
in the night.

**THE HAPLESS POETS:** (*stretching
their arms to the Mount.*) Come,
fire divine!
Come, fervent glow!
That burned within us in the days
long since;
Can you bring again before our
charmed eyes
The land of dreams and the enchanted world?
Give us old hopes, and show your
starry heights,
Glorious temples, where the clearest nights
Shone yet less brightly than their
festal lamps.

**THE CHIMERAS:** We weave illu-
sions, and kind dreams,
To hang with stars
The void of ruin and of slavery
Whose gloomy fogs
Our loving fingers veil.
(*The mists they have woven grad-
ually fill the top of the stage.
Louise and Julien appear on a
rock above the gloomy gorge.
They stand terrified, looking and
listening.*)

**THE HAPLESS POETS:** (*going
towards the Valley.*) Fair skies!
Blue seas!
A wide and smiling land,
A land unknown to our dazzled
souls;
The sun has risen and the shadows
flee.
(*Perceiving Louise and Julien, the
Chimeras go up to the mountain-
top and disappear in the mists.*)

**THE CHIMERAS:** (*calling.*) La-i!
La-i-é-là!
(*Julien draws Louise to the edge of
the abyss. Both lean over.*)

**THE HAPLESS POETS:** (*sobbing
in the distance.*) Fire divine!

**JULIEN:** (*shuddering.*) How terrible!

**THE HAPLESS POETS:** (*far
away.*) Ah! Ah! Ah!
(*The foot of the mountain is now
lost in the mists. Julien is deeply
moved. He wishes to help his unhappy brothers. The sense of his
divine mission is aroused.*)

**JULIEN:** (*fervently.*) Sun of the
world, O Love supreme,
Awake within me!
The bitter sorrow that my ears have
heard
Has shown me a reason for my life,
And as a consecrated child, my
heart
I now will lay
Upon the shrine of Beauty!
Upon the shrine of Love!

**LOUISE:** (*enthousiaste.*)
L'Amour!

**JULIEN:** L'amour!

**LOUISE:** L'amour!
(*Soudain le décor de la Montagne
s'enfonce; les brumes disparaissent, découvrant le décor suivant.*)

## ■ Troisième Tableau

*LE CHOEUR MAGNIFIQUE DU
TEMPLE COLOSSAL DE LA
BEAUTÉ*

### SCÈNE PREMIÈRE

*LOUISE, JULIEN,
L'HIÉROPHANTE, L'OFFICIANT,
LES FILLES DU RÊVE, SERVANTES,
SERVANTS DE LA BEAUTÉ,
LÉVITES, AUGURES, SAGES, AM-
ANTS, AMANTES, POÈTES ÉLUS,
DANSEUSES SACRÉES, LA FOULE.*

**TOUS:** (*avec des gestes d'appel.*)
Flamme!

**LOUISE et JULIEN:** Soleil du
monde, suprême amour,
En moi tu t'éveilles! . . .

**TOUS:** Flamme!

**LOUISE et JULIEN:** O merv-
eilles! . . .
Des baisers d'or enchantent mes oreilles!

**TOUS:** Flamme!

**LOUISE et JULIEN:** Dans ce pre-
mier printemps,
Sous les cieux éclatants,
Mon coeur d'enfant prédestiné
Va se donner
Au triomphe de l'amour,
Sans nul retour!
Ma voix chante pour l'adorer.
Je m'enivre
De sa beauté!
Je veux suivre
Sa volonté!
Et j'abandonne à tout jamais
Le passé que j'aimais!
L'amour qui luit
Commande en roi: je suis à lui!

**LES FILLES DU RÊVE, LES
LÉVITES, LES AUGURES:** Voix de
mon âme!
Splendeur qui m'illumines, ô
Vérité!
Dieu se proclame
En ta beauté!
Pures musiques,
Promesses magnifiques,
Chant d'éternité,
Dans ta volupté,
Se lève
Mon Rêve!

**LA FOULE DU TEMPLE:** O flamme
immense,
Accable-moi de ta puissance!
Bientôt, naissez,
Soleils triomphants des passés!
Ah! le ciel est dans nos êtres;

**LOUISE:** (*enthusiastically.*) Love!

**JULIEN:** Love!

**LOUISE:** Love!
(*The mountain suddenly disappears; the mists vanish and disclose the following scene.*)

## ■ Third Tableau

*THE MAGNIFICENT CHOIR OF
THE VAST TEMPLE OF BEAUTY*

### SCENE I

*LOUISE, JULIEN, the HIGH PRI-
EST, the OFFICIANT, the DREAM-
MAIDENS, WORSHIPPERS OF
BEAUTY, LEVITES, AUGURS,
SAGES, LOVERS, the CHOSEN
POETS, the SACRED DANCERS,
the CROWD.*

**ALL:** (*with beckoning gestures.*)
Fire!

**LOUISE AND JULIEN:** Sun of the
world, O love supreme,
Awake within me!

**ALL:** Fire!

**LOUISE AND JULIEN:** O marvellous!
What golden kisses now enchant
my ears!

**ALL:** Fire!

**LOUISE AND JULIEN:** In this
young springtime,
Under these brilliant skies,
My heart, in utter consecration,
Will here be laid
Upon the shrine of Love
Unfaltering!
I sing Love's adoration.
I will exalt
Love's beauty,
And forever
Do Love's will!
I will abandon for all time
The past I loved so well!
The love that glows
Speaks like a king—and I obey.

**THE DREAM MAIDENS LEVITES
AND AUGURS:** Voice of my soul!
O piercing splendor of the Truth!
God declares Himself
In your beauty!
Pure music,
Glittering promises,
Song of eternity!
In your magnificence
My Dream rises!

**TEMPLE WORSHIPPERS:** O mas-
tering flame!
Overwhelm me with your strength,
And rise again
You mighty suns long set!
Oh, Heaven is in our souls,

Et l'éclair fait apparaître
Les palais merveilleux,
Les grands temples orgueilleux
Du Rythme et du Rêve!

**LES FILLES DU RÊVE, L'HIÉROPHANTE et L'OFFICIANT:** Beauté!
Beauté puissante!
Beauté!
Beauté clémente!
Lumière, Espoir et Vie . . .
Montre-toi!
Donne-toi!
Reine éternelle!

**LA FOULE DU TEMPLE:** (*en mouvement intense et passionne.*) Dans un rayon,
Suprême vision,
Révèle
A ton peuple d'Amants
Le sublime enchantement
De ta grâce éternelle! . . .

**JULIEN:** (*grave, souriant.*) Vous m'accueillez comme on accueille le printemps,
Et dans vos chants de joie il semble que j'entends
Chanter, plus éloquente et plus pure, ma joie!
Vous avez enflammé mon firmament d'Avril,
Et mes pas, délivrés des langes puérils,
Gravirent les sommets où l'azur se déploie!
(*Murmures d'admiration.*)
Me voici, voici mon âme,
Mon coeur, pur comme la flamme!
Je veux aimer infiniment
Tout être obscur et son tourment . . .
Je suis venu, fervent amant,
Te consacrer, Beauté, ma vie entière.
Ah! voudras-tu fleurir pour mes yeux en prière?

## SCÈNE II

*LES PRÉCÉDENTS, LE SONNEUR, L'ACOLYTE, LES POÈTES DÉCHUS.*

*Majestueux, l'Hiérophante s'avance vers Julien qu'il fixe sympathiquement. Silence subit. Julien, descendu des degrés, soutient bravement l'examen. Cependant on le devine troublé. Louise, craintive, s'est réfugiée dans le groupe des Filles du Rêve empressées autour d'elle. En haut du transept, sur une corniche (ou derrière un pillier), apparaissent le Sonneur et l'Acolyte, invisibles pour l'assemblée.*)

**LE SONNEUR:** (*à l'Acolyte.*) Attention! . . . l'Hiérophante va parler . . .
(*Goguenard.*)
Qu'est-ce qu'il va prendre pour son rhume,
Celui qui oublia de verser

And by the lightning's glare
Appear the palaces
And the proud temples
Of Rhythm and of Dreams.

**DREAM MAIDENS, HIGH PRIEST and OFFICIANT:** Beauty!
Beauty all-powerful!
Beauty!
Beauty all-merciful!
You are our Light, our Hope, Our Life!
Show yourself!
Give yourself!
O Queen eternal!

**TEMPLE WORSHIPPERS:** (*agitated by passionate excitement.*) Vision supreme,
In a clear ray
Reveal
To all your folk of Lovers
The sublime enchantment
Of your eternal grace!

**JULIEN:** (*grave and smiling.*) You welcome me as one would welcome Spring,
And in your chanted joy I seem to hear,
More pure and eloquent, my own joy-song!
Your greeting glorifies my April skies,
And now my feet, struck free of youthful gyves,
Will reach the heights where Heaven seems to rest.
(*Murmurs of admiration.*)
I am here—here is my soul,
Here is my heart, as pure as flame!
I am a brother to the humble ones
And feel their sorrow and their griefs!
I come an ardent lover
To give my whole life unto Beauty!
O Goddess! shine before my prayerful eyes!

## SCENE II

*THE PRECEDING, THE BELL-RINGER, THE ACOLYTE, THE HAPLESS POETS.*

*Majestic, the High Priest advances towards Julien, looking at him with sympathy. Sudden silence. Julien, having come down the steps, meets his eye bravely. Nevertheless, he is uneasy. Louise, frightened, has taken refuge with the Dream-Maidens, who surround her. High up in the transept (or behind a pillar) appear the Bell-Ringer and the Acolyte, unseen by the multitude.*)

**BELL-RINGER:** (*to the Acolyte.*)
Attention! The High-Priest is going to speak.
(*Impudently.*)
Whatever will he take now for his cold?
They're clean forgot the customary

En entrant la coutumière thune?
(*Les Augures, les Sages, les Officiants s'assoient autour du choeur, formant un tableau inspiré des fresques de Raphaël. Sur un geste de l'Hiérophante, la foule s'écarte de Julien et se masse sous les arcades.*)

**L'ACOLYTE:** (*qui a une voix de fausset.*) C'est cocasse! . . . A les voir, on pourrait croire que c'est arrivé!

**LE SONNEUR:** (*secouant la tête.*) Ainsi toute l'année . . . toute la vie!

**L'ACOLYTE:** Mais, dans quel but cette comédie?

**LE SONNEUR:** Hum! . . . Faire croire aux autres ce qu'on suppose être la "Splendeur du Vrai . . . "!

**L'ACOLYTE:** (*ricanant.*) Et tous marchent!

**LA FOULE:** (*impatientée.*) Chut! . . .

**LE SONNEUR:** Tu vois!

**L'HIÉROPHANTE:** (*à Julien, avec douceur et autorité.*) Frère! . . .

**L'ACOLYTE:** (*admiratif, montrant Louise qui s'est avancée de quelques pas vers Julien.*) En voilà une que j'aimerais mieux la voir tomber en mon lit que l'tonnerre! . . .
(*Le Sonneur lui impose silence.*)

**L'HIÉROPHANTE:** Présomptueux poète, qui t'en vins
Déchiffrer les secrets des abîmes divins!
Ô toi, qui désertas les humaines cohortes,
Et n'as point redouté nos redoutables portes!
Ô Juvénile croyant! Téméraire vaillant!
Dont l'audacieuse prunelle, Sans émoi, fixe cet autel . . .

**L'ACOLYTE:** (*au Sonneur.*) T'as pas soif?

**L'HIÉROPHANTE:** Frère! doux héros dont l'appel
Osa provoquer la Reine éternelle,
N'interrogeas-tu point les lendemains amers?
Sais-tu qu'il est des deuils plus profonds que les mers?
(*Julien fait un geste d'insouciance. Fanfares lointaines.*)
Ta jeune foi colore d'espérance
La triste vie où tes pas s'en iront . . .
Et tes désirs te masquent la souffrance
Et les nuits vides d'où tes rêves s'enfuiront . . .
(*Brutal.*)
Prends garde qu'ayant connu la

thummim!
(*The Augurs, the Sages and the Officiant sit around the choir, forming a picture similar to the frescoes of Raphael. At a sign from the High Priest the people draw away from Julien and gather under the arches.*)

**ACOLYTE:** (*in falsetto throughout.*) Get on to that! You'd think they really meant it.

**BELL-RINGER:** (*shaking his head.*) Every year the same—and all through life.

**ACOLYTE:** But what's the use of all this farce?

**BELL-RINGER:** To make the people believe in what they think "The Splendor of the True."

**ACOLYTE:** (*sneering.*) And they fall for it?

**THE CROWD:** (*impatiently.*) Hush!

**BELL-RINGER:** You see!

**HIGH PRIEST:** (*with gentle authority.*) Brother!

**ACOLYTE:** (*admiringly pointing to Louise, who has come forward a few steps towards Julien.*) I'd rather be struck by her than lightning!
(*The Bell-Ringer silences him.*)

**HIGH PRIEST:** Presumptuous poet! have you come
To search the secrets that the gods have hid?
O you, who have abjured the haunts of men,
You are not appalled to stand before these doors?
O trusting youth! O dauntless heart!
That can look unafraid
Upon the altar there!

**ACOLYTE:** (*to Bell-Ringer.*) Are you thirsty?

**HIGH PRIEST:** O gentle hero, who has dared
To call upon the omnipotent queen,
Have you never thought upon the bitter morrows?
Nor yet of griefs far deeper than the seas?
(*Julien makes a gesture of indifference.*)
Your youthful fate colors with hope
The sad life where the road will lead your feet;
Your ardor hides the suffering from your eyes,
And the black nights wherein your dreams shall flee.

source vive de Gloire,
La vie où tu marcheras ne te semble
encor plus noire.
(*Même geste de Julien.*)

**L'ACOLYTE:** (*admiratif.*) Il
crâne! . . .

**L'HIÉROPHANTE:** Bien d'autres
sont venus avant toi sans nul
fruit! . . .
(*Pitoyable.*)
Ils agonisent dans la nuit!

**LES POÈTES DÉCHUS:** (*au loin.*)
Rêve!
Rêve!
Rêve!
Doux printemps de
l'amour! . . .
Daigne ouvrir ton aile à l'essor du
retour . . .
Rêve!
Rêve! Pur arc-en-ciel de pro-
messes
Rêve!
Vois tes suppliants qui
s'empressent!
(*Julien reste impassible.*)

**L'HIÉROPHANTE:** Tu ne redoutes
rien, enfant? Pleurs ni vertige?
Tu veux, dis-tu, aimer infiniment?
(*Julien et Louise, souriants, se
tournent doucement l'un vers
l'autre.*)
La femme t'apparaît en robe de
prestige . . .
Tu sembles ignorer les affres de
l'Amant . . .

**JULIEN:** (*résolu.*) Qu'importent
les regrets et la mort elle-
même . . .
Trois fois heureux l'amant qui
pleure, car il aime!

**L'HIÉROPHANTE:** (*plus pres-
sant.*) Ton vouloir généreux pour
d'obscurs malheureux,
Bêtes de somme parmi les hommes,
Ton rêve d'altruisme et de frater-
nité
Au désastre est voué! . . .
Et ceux-là mêmes dont tu crois
Assurer le bonheur te cloueront sur
la Croix.

**JULIEN:** (*exalté.*) Qu'importe la
fureur des hommes? Je les aime!
(*Dans un grand geste.*)
L'ample moisson surgit des douleurs qu'on sème!

**L'HIÉROPHANTE:** (*menaçant.*)
Puisque ton esprit indompté
Ne veut croire à la vanité
De l'amour et du sacrifice,
Penche ton coeur vers l'orifice
De l'abîme où s'effondre et meurt
le monde entier . . .
Un homme est descendu dans le
gouffre des haines;
Ô frère! il en a parcouru chaque
sentier
Apprends la vanité de tes luttes pro-
chaines! . . .

**ACOLYTE:** (*admiringly.*) Hear
him spout!

**HIGH PRIEST:** Many before you
have brought forth no fruit,
For all their nights of agony!

**THE HAPLESS POETS:** Dreams!
Dreams!
Dreams!
O sweet Maytime of life!
Unfold your wings to waft it back to
us!
Dreams!
Dreams!
The mocking rainbow-hopes!
Dreams!
Behold these suppliants who pray!
(*Julien remains unmoved.*)

**HIGH PRIEST:** Do you fear nothing, youth?
Nor tears, nor qualms?
To love infinitely—is that your
wish?
(*Julien and Louise, smiling, turn
toward each other.*)
This woman comes as garmented
with light:
Do you ignore a lover's mortal
pangs?

**JULIEN:** (*resolutely.*) What matters bitterness, or death itself?
Thrice-blessed the lover's tears, because he loves!

**HIGH PRIEST:** (*more insistently.*)
Thy kindly feeling for the humble
folk,
Those who are beasts of burden
among men,—
Thy altruistic dream of brother's
love,—
Is doomed to come to nothing;
And even those that your have
thought to succor,—
Themselves are they who'll nail
you to the cross.

**JULIEN:** (*in exalted mood.*) I care
not for men's rage!
I love them all.
(*With a lofty gesture.*)
From sorrows sown will grow a
mighty harvest.

**HIGH PRIEST:** (*menacingly.*)
Poet, since your undaunted soul
Will not believe the emptiness
That lies in love and sacrifice,
Incline your ear and listen at the
mouth
Of that abyss where the world sinks
and dies.
One man descended to that gulf of
hate:
Brother! he searched each path and
hidden place;
Learn that your struggles will be

"Au seuil du monde de souffrance
Abandonnez toute
espérance! . . . "

**JULIEN:** (*aved ferveur.*) Si tout me
renie, il me reste un coeur
Assez vaste pour que j'y vive et que
j'y chante!
Si la femme est frivole et la foule
méchante,
Des voix en mon âme ourdiront un
choeur
De victoire!
Comme tous ceux qui par les
ciècles ont chanté.
Mon nom resplendirait, soleil
d'humanité!
De mon rêve je veux éterniser la
gloire!

**HIÉROPHANTE:** Avant que de
chanter, tu verseras des pleurs!

**JULIEN:** Je chanterai mes douleurs!

**HIÉROPHANTE:** Tu n'atteindras
pas ton rêve!

**JULIEN:** (*avec énergie.*) Je
l'atteindrai!
(*Tous deux se contemplent longuement.*)

**HIÉROPHANTE:** Soit, que ton attente s'achève! . . .
Voici l'instant sacré . . .
Contemple! . . .
Et que ta force persévère . . .
Car de ce jour, enfant, commence
ton calvaire.
(*Les Lévites viennent procession-
nellement revêtir Julien des attri-
buts de servant de la Beauté.
L'Hiérophante lui donne
l'accolade et disparaît derrière
l'autel, suivi des Augures. La
Foule, respectueuse, s'écoule silencieusement par les côtés, les regards fixés sur Julien.*)

**LE CHOEUR:** (*s'éloignant.*)

**1ER GROUPE:** Le doux vainqueur
Qui triompha des abîmes
Va connaître l'indicible peur
Des attentes divines.

**2E GROUPE:** Son coeur est animé
De volentés sublimes.
Il est le bien-aimé
Qu'ont espéré les cimes!

**TOUS:** Daigne fleurir, ô mère!
Pour ses yeux en prière.
(*Les deux loustics ont reparu sur
la corniche haute.*)

**LE SONNEUR:** (*à l'Acolyte, railleur.*) Tiens! t'essuies une larme?

**L'ACOLYTE:** Est-ce qu'ils se
r'verront? . . .

**LE SONNEUR:** Qui donc?

**L'ACOLYTE:** La môme et son
crâneur . . .

**LE SONNEUR:** (*hausse les
épaules.*) Viens sonner, c'est
l'heure.
(*Il l'entraîne.*)

vanity:
"Abandon hope, all that enter
here!"

**JULIEN:** (*with fervor.*) Though all
deny me, yet remains a heart,
Where I shall live—that I shall
sing!
If a woman is fickle, and the people
false,
The voices in my heart shall be a
choir
Of victory!
As all those who have sung since
time began,
My name will shine upon humani-
ty!
And I'll make eternity of my dream!

**HIGH PRIEST:** You shall shed bitter tears before your song.

**JULIEN:** I'll sing of all my pain.

**HIGH PRIEST:** You'll never realize
your dream!

**JULIEN:** I shall!
I shall!
(*They gaze at each other.*)

**HIGH PRIEST:** So be it!
May you reach your goal!
Now is the sacred moment.—
Think well!—and may your
strength fail not;
To-day, O youth, begins your Calvary.
(*The Levites come in procession to
clothe Julian with the garments of
a servant of Beauty. The High
Priest embraces him and disappears behind the altar, followed
by the Augers. The people withdraw respectfully, their eyes fixed
on Julien.*)

**CHORUS:** (*departing*)

**1ST GROUP:** The gentle victor
Who conquers the abyss,
Will know the misery
Of striving heavenwards.

**2D GROUP:** His heart glows with
the love
Of noble things!
He is the well beloved,
Destined to reach the heights!

**ALL:** Graciously bloom, O mother!
Before his prayerful eyes.
(*The two Jesters reappear on the
cornice.*)

**BELL-RINGER:** (*to the Acolyte.*)
What!
Are you crying?

**ACOLYTE:** (*with emotion.*) Will
they ever meet again?

**BELL-RINGER:** Who?

**ACOLYTE:** The donkey and his
driver.

**BELL-RINGER:** (*with a shrug.*) It's
time to ring.

L'ACOLYTE: (*revenant avec mystère, une main en porte-voix, souffle à Julien qui ne l'entend pas:*) Tiens bon la rampre!
(*Il ricane et se sauve.*)

LE SONNEUR: (*de loin.*)
Hé! . . . t'es pas folle?

## SCÈNE III

JULIEN, L'OFFICIANT, LES LÉVITES, LES AUGURES.

*Julien se met en prière. La nuit descend, lunaire, mystérieuse.*

L'OFFICIANT: (*loin.*) Ô
Beauté! . . .
Daigne fleurir pour ses yeux en prière!

LES LÉVITES et LES AUGURES:
(*loin.*) Ô Beauté!

## SCÈNE IV

LES PRÉCÉDENTS, LES FILLES DU RÊVE, L'HIÉROPHANTE, L'OFFICIANT, LE CHOEUR INVISIBLE.

*Coups de cloche tombant en tonnerre du haut de la nef. Éclair sur l'autel. Bruit de tempête. L'obscurité s'épaissit brusquement.*

LES FILLES DU RÊVE: (*soli, derrière l'autel, accompagnées de célestas et de harpes. Mélopée religieuse.*) Ah! Ah! Ah!
(*Sur l'autel, l'Officiant, l'Hiérophante et les Augures dessinent dans l'ombre des gestes d'incantation.*)

LE CHOEUR: (*invisible, psalmodiant mystérieusement sous la mélopée.*) Beauté puissante,
Éblouissante,
Immaculée,
Voûte étoilée,
Protégez-nous!
Exaucez-nous!

L'HIÉROPHANTE: (*d'un ton de commandement.*) Ahiha!

L'OFFICIANT: O Beauté!
Soleil sans voiles,
Soleil d'étoiles,
Soleil d'amour,
Source de jour,
Protégez-nous!
Exaucez-nous!
Porte d'aurore,
Porte d'or,
Porte de gloire,
Miroir!
Protégez-nous!
Exaucez-nous!
(*Au-dessus de l'autel passent et repassent à intervalles de plus en plus rapprochés des lueurs vives et prolongées.*)

ACOLYTE: (*comes back mysteriously, and making a megaphone of his hand, calls to Julien, who does not hear him:*) Hold on to the railing!
(*He laughs and runs away.*)

BELL-RINGER: (*off.*) Are you crazy?

## SCENE III

JULIEN, the OFFICIANT, the LEVITES, the AUGURS.

*Julien kneels to pray. The night falls, moonlit and mysterious.*

OFFICIANT: O Beauty!
Graciously bloom before his prayerful eyes!

LEVITES AND AUGURS: (*off.*) O Beauty!

## SCENE IV

THE PRECEDING, the DREAM-MAIDENS, the HIGH PRIEST, the OFFICIANT, the INVISIBLE CHORUS.

*The clash of a bell peals suddenly from the nave. Lightning flashes upon the altar. The darkness deepens suddenly.*

DREAM-MAIDENS: (*behind the altar, accompanied by celestas and harps. Religious melody.*) Ah! Ah!
(*Before the altar of the High Priest, the Officiants and the Augurs are seen dimly in attitudes of incantation.*)

CHORUS: (*invisible, intoning mysteriously through the melody.*) Almighty Beauty!
Dazzling,
Immaculate,
Starry vault,
Deliver us!
Hear our prayer.

HIGH PRIEST: (*with authority.*) Aliha!

OFFICIANT: O Beauty!
Sun of our souls,
Sun of the stars,
Sun of our love,
Source of the day,
Deliver us!
Hear our prayer!
Gate of the dawn,
A door of gold,
A door of glory,
And of truth,
Deliver us!
Hear our prayer!
(*Above the altar, at intervals becoming closer and more prolonged, gleam lights.*)

LES FILLES DU RÊVE: (*toujours invisibles.*) Mère et flamme
Des âmes!
Flamme et fête
Des poètes!
Reine et mère
Des mystères! . . .
Montre-toi!
Donne-toi!
Verse la vie!
(*Orgues lointaines dans le silence. Émergeant insensiblement des vapeurs, la Beauté apparaît.*)

## SCÈNE V

LES PRÉCÉDENTS, LA BEAUTÉ.

JULIEN: (*extasié.*) Ah! je t'aime,
Ô suprême!
Ah!
Te chérir!
Et mourir!
(*Il se traîne jusqu'aux marches de l'autel sur lesquelles il s'abîme.*)

L'OFFICIANT, L'HIÉROPHANTE, LÉVITES et AUGURES: (*encensent la Beauté à larges volées.*)
Blanche clarté d'éternité!
Beauté!

LE CHOEUR: (*autour de l'autel et dans les bas côtés.*) Alléluia!
Alléluia! Alléluia!
Heureux les yeux ouverts
Aux grands éclairs
D'amour!

## ■ ACTE DEUXIÈME

(*Doute*)

*Un paysage pittoresque; un pays slovaque: champs, bois aux nombreuses clairières où un ruisseau serpente. À droite, une vieille chaumière; à gauche, un tertre de gazon, une fontaine. Banc rustique près de la maison. La grande route traverse le fond du théâtre. Un sentier va de la maison au bois. 3 heures. Été.*

## SCÈNE PREMIÈRE

JULIEN, UN PAYSAN, SA FEMME, SA FILLE, UN LABOUREUR, UN BÛCHERON, UN CASSEUR DE PIERRES, TERRASSIERS, BÛCHERONS BOHÉMIENNES, MOISSONNEURS et GLANEUSES, VOIX DANS LA CAMPAGNE.

*Près de la chaumière Julien repose dans un grand accablement. La Jeune Fille le regarde avec pitié et amour. Assis devant la porte, Le Père guette tendrement sa fille. La Mère étend du linge, plus loin, sur les buissons qui séparent la maison de la route.*

DREAM MAIDENS: (*still unseen.*)
Mother and fire
Of souls!
Fire and joy
Of poets!
Queen and mother
Of mysteries!
Show yourself!
Give yourself!
Give us life!
(*Distant organ music amid the silence. Disclosed little by little through the mists, Beauty appears.*)

## SCENE V

THE PRECEDING, BEAUTY.

JULIEN: (*in ecstasy.*) I love you,
Supreme one!
Ah!
To embrace you!
And then to die!
(*He drags himself to the steps of the altar and sinks upon them.*)

THE OFFICIANT, HIGH PRIEST, LEVITES AND AUGURS: (*waving censers before Beauty.*) Clear light of eternity!
Beauty!

CHORUS: (*around the altar and down-stage.*) Alleluia! Alleluia! Alleluia!
Happy the eyes that see
The lightning-flash
Of love!

## ■ ACT II

(*Doubt*)

*A picturesque countryside; fields, a wood with numerous clearings through which a brook winds. To the right an old cottage, to the left a grassy billock and a fountain. A rustic bench near the house. The highway crosses back of stage. A path goes from the house into the wood. Three o'clock. Summer.*

## SCENE I

JULIEN, a PEASANT, his WIFE, his DAUGHTER, a LABORER, a WOODCUTTER, a STONE-BREAKER, DITCHERS, WOODCUTTERS, GYPSIES, HARVESTERS and GLEANERS, VOICES in the Countryside.

*Near the cottage Julien is sleeping as if exhausted. The Young Girl looks at him with love and sympathy. Sitting before the door, her father watches her tenderly. In the distance her mother spreads linen on the bushes that separate the house from the road.*

LES TERRASSIERS: (farouches.)
Hou! Hou!
Creuse vit' ton trou!
La terre gémit sous la pelle,
L'entends-tu qui t'appelle?

LES BÛCHERONS: (goguenards.)
Hein! Hein!
Prépare ta bière
De demain.
Dans le bois qui geint
Sous ta main
Pleure ta dernière
Prière!

LA PAYSANNE: (à son homme qui est venu sur le seuil.) Il dort encore . . .
(Une voiture de Bohémiennes passe sur la route. Des fillettes déguenillées l'escortent.)

BOHÉMIENNES: (en voiture.) Eho!

PAYSANS: (loin.) Eho!

TERRASSIERS: (loin.) Eho!

LES BÛCHERONS: (loin, tirant avec des cordes les troncs d'arbres.) O-hisse! . . . O-hisse! . . .

LE PAYSAN: Depuis son arrivé au pays c'est son premier repos.

LA PAYSANNE: Son âme souffre d'un rêve que nous ne pouvons comprendre.

LE PAYSAN: D'où vient-il? On l'ignore . . .
Où ira-t-il?
Lui-même ne le sait . . .

LA JEUNE FILLE: Il fut très malheureux sans doute?

UN CASSEUR DE PIERRES: (sur la route.) Trimez, les bons ouvriers!
Faut que vous trimiez!
Nul repos, ni trêve pour les amours!
Trimez . . . toujours!

UNE VOIX: (lointaine, en écho.) Toujours! . . .

JULIEN: (s'éveillant.) Une chanson de souffrance plane sur la terre . . .
Quelle est cette plainte?
Est-ce la terre elle-même qui se plaint?

UNE VOIX: (lointaine.) Toujours! . . .

AUTRE VOIX: (plus lointaine.) Toujours!

JULIEN: De partout monte un long cri de misère
Comme la rumeur éternelle de la vie.
L'instant où chacun naît . . .
L'instant où chacun meurt . . .

LE CASSEUR DE PIERRES: Trimer toujours!

VOIX LOINTAINES: Toujours.

JULIEN: Parmi les peuples éplorés
Dont je rêvais la délivrance
Naguère j'ai connu cette désespérance! . . .

---

DITCHERS: (savagely.) Hou! Hou!
Dig the ditch quick!
The earth groans under the spade,
Do you hear her calling?

WOODCUTTERS: (jeeringly.)
Hein! Hein!
Make ready your bier
For tomorrow;
In the wood that moans
Beneath our hand,
Weep your last
Sorrow!

PEASANT WOMAN: (to her husband, who has come to the door.)
He's still asleep.
(A Gypsy wagon passes, escorted by little ragged girls.)

GYPSIES: (in wagon.) Eho!

PEASANTS: (off.) Eho!

DITCHERS: (off.) Eho!

WOODCUTTERS: (drawing tree-trunks with ropes.) Yo-ho!—Yo-ho!

PEASANT: This is his first sleep since he came here!

PEASANT WOMAN: A dream we cannot guess, vexes his soul!

PEASANT: We don't know where he came from,
Nor can we tell where he will go!

YOUNG GIRL: Do you think he was unhappy?

STONE-BREAKER: (on the road.)
Up and down, good workmen!
Up and down all day!
No repose nor time for courting,
On the go forever!

A VOICE: (in the distance, like an echo.) For aye!

JULIEN: (awaking.) A song of suffering pervades the world;
What is this song?
Is it the Earth herself that murmurs?

A VOICE: (off.) Forever!

ANOTHER VOICE: (further off.) Forever!

JULIEN: From everywhere there comes a cry of pain,
Like the eternal muttering of life—
The moment one is born—
The moment that one dies—

STONE-BREAKER: On the go forever!

DISTANT VOICES: Forever!

JULIEN: I knew that hopelessness Among the people as they wept:
My dream, to free them from their pain and tears!

---

Les tristes cités pleines de sanglots!
Là, je m'étais penché sur des êtres de souffrance,
Voulant combler le gouffre
D'où la douleur se répandait à flots! . . .
(Des ouvriers des forges passent, las, sur la route.)

LES TERRASSIERS:
Hou! . . . Hou! . . .

LES BÛCHERONS: O-hisse! . . . O-hisse! . . .

LES PAYSANS: Trimer toujours!
(Les cris et les appels continuent jusqu'à la fin de la tirade de Julien.)

JULIEN: (avec amertume.) A mon chant d'amour
Ils ont jeté des sarcasmes, des cris de haine.
(Farouche.)
Laisse-nous, va-t'en!
Tes paroles sont vaines!
Nos pères furent des gueux,
Nos enfants seront comme eux!
Va prêcher ailleurs ton inutile espoir!
A t'entendre chanter tes rêves illusoires
Notre infernale vie apparaîtrait plus noire!
(Il mime des gestes désespérés et menaçants.)
Malheur sur toi! Poète maudit!
Malheur et mort au prometteur de paradis!
Malheur! . . .

LA JEUNE FILLE: (apitoyée.) Ah!
(Les voix rudes se perdent peu à peu dans la campagne.)

JULIEN: . . . Tristement, je suis reparti . . .
Cherchant un horizon derrière l'horizon,
Où ne gronderaient plus la haine et l'égoïsme.
(Coucher de soleil or et rose.)
Et je suis venu près de cette humble chaumière
Croyant trouver la paix, l'oubli, un coin de terre
Béni des dieux, d'où la douleur serait absente.
(Des voix nouvelles surgissent de l'autre côté de la plaine chantant la gloire de la terre.)

MOISSONNEURS et GLANEUSES: (comme un cantique.) Terre, Terre!
Doux printemps de l'amour!
Donne-nous des ailes pour l'essor du retour!
Terre promise!
Terre conquise!
Protège le joyeux labeur des jours!
(Durant ce choeur le paysan apitoyé s'avance vers Julien que la jeune fille regarde avec une naïve et amoureuse compassion.)

---

O, the sad cities full of misery!
There I have stood beside the suffering creatures,
And tried to bridge the gulf
Whence grief and pain rose like a tide.
(The Blacksmiths pass, wearied, along the road.)

DITCHERS: Hou!—Hou!

WOODCUTTERS: Yo-ho!—Yo-ho!

PEASANTS: On the go forever!
(The cries and calls continue till the end of Julien's speech.)

JULIEN: (bitterly.) My song of love
They mocked with gibes and cries of rage:
(Savagely.)
Leave us!
Get hence!
Your words are vain!
Our fathers begged their bread,
Our children will do the same!
Go preach elsewhere your hopes of Paradise!
If we should hear you sing your rosy dreams,
Our wretches lives would seem but blacker still!
(He mimics their desperate and threatening gestures.)
Curses upon you!
Damned Poet!
Curses and death, singer of Paradise!
Curses!

YOUNG GIRL: (pityingly.) Ah!
(The rough voices are gradually lost in the distance.)

JULIEN: Sadly I went my way,
Seeking the heights that lie behind the heights,
Beyond the grumbling selfishness and hate!
(Sunset of gold and rose-color.)
And then I came to this poor humble cot,
Thinking to find here peace, a bit of earth
Blessed by the gods, where suffering would not be!
(New voices rise on the other side of the plain, singing the glory of the earth.)

REAPERS AND GLEANERS: (like a canticle.) Earth!
Earth!
O, sweet springtime of love!
Give us the wings to bring it back to us!
O promised land!
O conquered land!
Bless the happy labor of our days!
(During this chorus the kindly Peasant goes to Julien; the Young Girl looks at him with loving and naïve compassion.

LE PAYSAN: L'universel bonheur . . . ah! . . . la belle chimère!
N'aie pas l'orgueil de vouloir accomplir
Ce qu'un fils de Dieu n'a pu réussir! . . .
Détourneras-tu le soleil de sa course?
Feras-tu remonter le fleuve à sa source?
(*Pressant.*)
Ah! écoute-moi . . . ami!
Reste avec nous!
(*Les Moissonneurs, les Glaneuses, les Paysans, passent sur la route graves et souriants. Et c'est comme un cortège du travail heureux de la Terre: ni Julien, ni le groupe qui l'entoure ne semblent l'apercevoir. Avec autorité.*)
Reste! . . .
Près de la bonne terre
Ton coeur se guérira de toutes ses folies!
Et le repos, l'oubli viendront . . .
(*Regardant sa fille.*)
Peut-être aussi . . . le bonheur.
(*Le cortège a passé, suivi de groupes dansant au son du tambourin. C'est la fin du coucher du soleil. Le crépuscule va tomber lentement, préparant une nuit claire d'été.*)

JULIEN: Puis-je être heureux . . . loin de ceux que j'aime?
Puis-je être heureux . . . quand je doute de moi-même?

LES MOISSONNEURS: (*au loin.*)
Chasse l'hiver de détresse! . . .
Ne trahis pas tes promesses! . . .

JULIEN: (*agité, nerveux.*) Tandis que je suscitais l'espoir et chantais
Pour calmer la détresse humaine,
Naissait en moi, pire qu'une démence,
Une mortelle angoisse où mon esprit sombrait!
(*Plus calme.*)
A toute heure attristé des trahisons, des haines,
Chaque jour effrayé de mon oeuvre incertaine,
J'errais le coeur transi, sanglotant!
Fantôme en peine de mon esprit flottant,
J'ai fui, ne cherchant qu'à me fuir, qu'à disparaître!
Mais j'emporte avec moi ce qui ronge mon être,
Tenaille ma chair et brûle mon sang:
Le Doute implacable!
Le Doute qui m'accable!
(*Se tournant vers l'horizon assombri.*)
Toutes mes illusions de Vie
N'on pu vivre! . . .
L'illusion de Rêve
Pourra-t-elle survivre?
(*Il cherche à se rappeler son rêve . . . Le Paysan hoche la*

PEASANT: A universal happiness—a lovely dream!
Don't have the pride to think that you can do
What God's own Son could not achieve!
Can you deflect the sun from his set path?
Can you turn back the river to its source?
(*Earnestly.*)
Now, listen to me, friend—
Stay here with us!
(*The Reapers, Gleaners and Peasants pass along the road, grave and smiling. It is like a procession of the happy labor of the Earth. Neither Julien nor the group about him seem to notice it.*)
Stay here—close to the good Earth,
Your heart will heal itself of all its griefs,
And rest will come, and then forgetfulness,
And maybe—happiness.
(*The procession is followed by groups dancing to tambourines. The sunset is fading, and twilight falling before a clear summer night.*)

JULIEN: Can I be happy, far from those I love?
Can I be happy, when I doubt myself?

REAPERS: (*off.*) Drive away distressful winter!
Do not deny your promises!

JULIEN: (*distressed and nervous.*) While I was borne up with hope
To ease the misery of humanity,
Was born in me, but deadlier than madness
A mortal anguish that has wrecked my soul!
(*More quietly.*)
Saddened always by treachery and hate,
And terrified by my uncertain work,
I wandered, weeping, with my heart benumbed,
A tortured phantom of my faltering will!
I fled, and only prayed to disappear.
But I took with me that which gnaws my flesh—
Shackles my body—burns within my blood:
Doubt! Doubt implacable!
Doubt, that rends my soul!
(*He turns to the darkening horizon.*)
All the illusions of life
Have died for me!
And the illusion of my Dream,
Will that survive?

*tête fait signe aux siens et rentre dans la maison. Les deux femmes le suivent, s'arrêtent sur le seuil, écoutent encore.*)

JULIEN: (*avidement.*) Oh! l'ardent souvenir du Mont inaccessible!
Pourquoi fleurissiez-vous, sublimes vision? . . .

LA PAYSANNE: (*à sa fille, en une maternelle complicité de sympathie pour l'inconnu.*)
Son rêve est plus joli que notre vie . . .
(*Railleuse.*)
Ses regrets sont plus forts . . . que ton envie!
(*Elle pousse sa fille doucement vers l'intérieur et ferme al porte. Julien interroge longtemps l'horizon vide . . . puis il s'assied avec accablement, près du tertre, les yeux toujours fixés sur le couchant assombri. Dans l'air flotte l'écho des fanfares féeriques. Un coucou salue la nuit qui monte.*)

## SCÈNE II

JULIEN, LA JEUNE FILLE, LES VOIX DE LA NUIT.

*La lune se lève. La Jeune Fille paraît sur le seuil de la maison, une cruche d'eau à la main. Elle va lentement à la fontaine, s'y accoude, regarde Julien. Subitement décidée, elle s'approche de lui.*

LES VOIX DE LA NUIT: (*choeur invisible.*) Entends-tu la nuit, la nuit calme
Qui te parle?
Un frisson profond d'amour vient des cimes.
Perçois-tu ce bruit étrange et sublime?
L'univers entier frémit de tendresse
Pour ton coeur blessé que l'espoir caresse.
(*Julien lève la tête, aperçoit la Jeune Fille qui lui sourit.*)

LA JEUNE FILLE: Ami, votre souffrance est-elle donc si grande
Que personne ne puisse la partager?
contre votre douleur ne peut-on vous défendre?
Vous parlez de fuir . . . où le destin vous mène . . .
(*Gentiment pressante.*)
Si vous saviez combien nous en souffririons tous! . . .
Pourquoi ne pas rester avec nous?
La solitude rend si dure toute peine.

JULIEN: (*souriant.*) Enfant de tendresse!
Ta voix limpide et douce
En vain berce et caresse

(*He tries to recall his dream. The Peasant nods his head, makes a sign to the women, and goes into the house. They follow him, but pause at the door, listening.*)

JULIEN: (*eagerly.*) O glowing memory of that far Mount;
O wondrous visions that can never die!

PEASANT WOMAN: (*with maternal sympathy for the stranger.*)
His dreams are brighter than our life.
(*Teasingly.*)
His regrets are stronger—than your wish!
(*Gently pushes her daughter before her and closes the door.—Julien gazes long at the empty horizon; then, overcome, he sits on the billock, his eyes always fixed on the fading sunset. In the air floats an echo of fairy music. A cuckoo greets the nightfall.*)

## SCENE II

JULIEN, the YOUNG GIRL, the VOICES OF THE NIGHT.

*The moon rises. The Young Girl appears at the door of the house, a jug in her hand. She goes slowly to the fountain, and leans upon it watching Julien. Suddenly making up her mind, she goes towards him.*

VOICES OF THE NIGHT: (*Invisible Chorus*). Do you hear the Night—the Night that is so still,
That speaks to you?
A quiver of deep love comes from the heights,
Do you perceive this murmur strange and sweet?
The Universe that yearns with tenderness
For your sore heart, that pity seeks to heal.
(*Julien raises his head and sees the Young Girl, who smiles.*)

YOUNG GIRL: And is your suffering so great, my friend,
That it cannot be shared by any one?
And may one not protect you 'gainst your grief?
You say you'll flee as destiny directs.—
(*With sweet insistence.*)
Ah, if you knew how much we suffer here!
Why not stay here with us?—
It is loneliness that makes your grief so hard.

JULIEN: (*smiling.*) Ah, child, so pitiful,
In vain, your tender voice
Will strive to lull and soothe

Mon pauvre coeur meurtri!
Hélas! ce n'est qu'un baume, endormant ma détresse . . .
Le mal est trop profond, rien ne
peut le guérir.

LA JEUNE FILLE: (*ingénument.*)
Si pourtant vous aviez près de vous
une amie
Qui vous aime . . .
A qui vous puissiez vous confi-
er . . .
Qui parvienne à vous faire oublier
L'injustice des hommes et le triste
passé!
(*Plus tendrement.*)
Pour trouver le bonheur n'est-il
d'autre chemin
Que la route sans fin? . . .
Est-ce là vraiment tout sagesse?
(*Persuasive.*)
Le silence a peut-être une voix qui
caresse . . .
Mais sur les monts déserts, qui vous
tendra la main?
(*Julien attendri la regarde un in-
stant, puis détourne la tête.*)

LES VOIX DE LA NUIT: Vois, c'est
la nuit, la nuit calme et belle
Qui t'appelle! . . .

JULIEN: Oh! l'arden souvenir de
mon premier amour! . . .
Louise . . .
(*Sombre.*)
Elle est loin ma Louise . . . que
m'a ravie le destin!

LA JEUNE FILLE: (*humble.*) Je me
nomme aussi . . .
(*Hésitante.*)
Louise . . .

JULIEN: (*supris.*) Louise?

LA JEUNE FILLE: (*timide.*) Vou-
dras-tu m'aimer comme elle?
Je serai pour toi le reflet de celle
(*Grave.*)
Qui fut ton désir.

JULIEN: Tout désir est
mort . . . avec la morte . . .

LA JEUNE FILLE: (*craintive, avec
amour.*) Je serai celle qui guérit la
peine et console . . .
Ah! d'un pur baiser pour ton coeur
blessé
Accepte l'offrande!

LES VOIX DE LA NUIT: (*en murmure.*) Miracles réels . . .
Réelles féeries! . . .

JULIEN: (*pensif, en lui-même.*)
Louise?

LA JEUNE FILLE: (*penchée sur
lui, avec affirmation.*)
Louise! . . .
(*Julien la contemple et la repousse doucement.*)

LES VOIX DE LA NUIT: Des rêves
plus beaux fleurissent sur
terre
Ils ont leur douceur, ils ont leur
mystère! . . .

My weary, broken heart.
Alas! It is but a balm, easing my
pain,
But the real hurt lies deep, and
nothing can heal it.

YOUNG GIRL: (*ingenuously.*)
Still, if you had near you a friend
Who loved you,
In whom you could confide—
Who might at last, perhaps, make
you forget
Both man's ingratitude and the sad
past!
(*More tenderly.*)
Is there no other way to happiness
Than the long road?
Is that indeed the only wisdom?
(*Persuasively.*)
Silence, we know, speaks with a
soothing voice.
But who holds out a hand on desert
hills?
(*Julien looks at her sadly for a
moment and then turns away his
head.*)

VOICES OF THE NIGHT: Behold
the night, the night so fair and still,
That calls to you!

JULIEN: Ah, glowing memory of
my first love!
Louise!
(*Gloomily.*)
She's far from here, ravished from
me by fate.

YOUNG GIRL: That's my name
too—
(*Hesitating.*)
Louise!

JULIEN: (*surprised.*) Louise?

YOUNG GIRL: (*timidly.*) Could
you not love me as you once loved
her?
I might be, to your eyes, as the reflection
(*Seriously.*)
Of her who was your heart's desire.

JULIEN: Desire is dead—with
death.

YOUNG GIRL: (*timidly but lovingly.*) Let me then be the one to
comfort you,
And take the offering of a tender
kiss
For your sick heart.

VOICES OF THE NIGHT: (*murmuring.*) Real miracles—true
fairy tales—

JULIEN: (*aside, pensively.*)
Louise?

YOUNG GIRL: (*bending over
him, positively.*) Louise!
(*Julien looks at her and pushes
her gently away.*)

VOICES OF THE NIGHT: Yet
brighter dreams bloom here upon
the Earth,
That have their softness and their
mystery.

JULIEN: Fol espoir! . . .
Ton amour que j'envie,
Dont s'illuminerait ma sombre
vie . . .
Cette aventure que tu m'offres, Jo-
lie!
Ne serait pour moi qu'amertume,
inutiles regrets!
(*Se levant.*)
Ne crée pas à mon coeur trahi
d'autres remords! . . .
(*Plus brutal.*)
Laisse-moi poursuivre mon che-
min . . .
(*Déchirant.*)
Eloigne-toi, enfant, laisse-moi!
(*Il recule comme pour suivre le
sentier qui va au bois. La porte de
la chaumière s'ouvre. Le paysan
paraît sur le seuil. D'un geste bref,
il indique sa demeure à Julien.*)

## SCÈNE III

*LES MÊMES, LE PAYSAN.*

LE PAYSAN: (*dont la voix et les
gestes évoquent le souvenir de
l'Hiérophante, gardien de l'idéal
sanctuaire.*) Ami, la maison est ouverte . . . si tu veux entrer;
Mais . . . je ne veux pas
d'amourettes . . . à ma porte.
(*La Jeune Fille s'achemine vers la
maison, lentement, comme à regret.*)

JULIEN: (*immobile, sombre.*) La
même voix qui prophétisait là-bas:
"Conter fleurette à la beauté ne suf-
fit pas!"
(*Plus déclamé, un peu railleur.*)
Ici, la menace est plus brève:
"Entre! . . . ou va-t'en!"
(*Avec ferveur, presque parlé.*)
Héros d'un rêve de clarté! . . .
(*Avec amertume et dédain.*)
Ou d'une aventure de banalité!
(*La porte se ferme.*)

## SCÈNE IV

*JULIEN, LES VOIX DE LA NUIT.*

JULIEN: (*se dressant.*) J'ai franchi
le seuil du temple!
J'ai proféré les paroles sacrées! . . .
(*Avec défi, sans colère ni ran-
cune, presque joyeusement.*)
Et je nargue la vie . . . sans prestige et sans beauté!
(*Les voix de la nuit murmurent. Il
va vers la route, s'arrête, écoute,
surpris, la protestation de
l'ombre.*)

JULIEN: (*tendant les bras vers la
nuit.*) Que me réserves-tu, Nuit
Mystérieuse et troublante?
Où ma frêle étoile fuit,
Blanche dans l'ombre flottante?
Où vogues-tu dans la nuit

JULIEN: An empty hope! Your love
might be for me
A pleasant light upon my sombre
life.
The amorous chance you offer,
pretty one,
Would mean regret for me and bitterness!
(*He rises.*)
Don't bring a fresh remorse to my
sad heart.
(*More harshly.*)
Leave me alone to follow my own
road—
(*In agony.*)
Leave me, my child, and go!
(*He draws back as if to follow the
path into the woods. The cottage-
door opens. The Peasant, on the
threshold, with a quick gesture indicates his house to Julien.*)

## SCENE III

*THE SAME, THE PEASANT.*

PEASANT: (*whose voice and
manner recall the High Priest,
guardian of the ideal sanctuary.*)
My door is open, friend, if you'll
come in.
But—if you please—no love-af-
fairs outside here.
(*The Young Girl goes slowly and
regretfully towards the house.*)

JULIEN: (*motionless and
gloomy.*) The same voice prophe-
sied to me, before,
"It will not do to make light love to
Beauty!"
(*In a derisive, more declamatory
tone.*)
Here, the menace is more brief:
"Come in—or get you gone!"
(*With fervor, almost spoken.*)
The hero of a dream of light?
(*Bitterly and disdainfully.*)
Or of a commonplace adventure!
(*The door shuts.*)

## SCENE IV

*JULIEN, the VOICES OF THE
NIGHT.*

JULIEN: (*straightening up.*) I
have crossed the Temple's threshold!
I have taken the sacred vows!
(*Defiantly, but without anger or
bitterness, almost joyfully.*)
And I defy life—that has not charm
or beauty!
(*The Voices of the Night murmur.
Going towards the road, he listens, surprised at the plaint of the
shadows.*

JULIEN: (*extending his arms to
the night.*) What are you holding
back for me,
Uneasy and mysterious night?
There where my faint star floats
White in the shadowy mist?

## Act II, Scene IV

Mystérieuse et troublante,
Stella du Futur qui fuit,
Blanche dans l'ombre flottante?

**LES VOIX DE LA NUIT:** Que veux-tu, toi dont j'entends
L'appel triste en mon silence?

**JULIEN:** Ô Nuit! où mon coeur s'élance,
J'ai peur de toi, peur du temps!
Enveloppé d'ombre dense,
Je tâche de percevoir
Ce que dérobe ton silence:
Triomphe ou mort de mon espoir!
(*Le chant du rossignol fait écho à la plainte du poète. La lune reparaît. Le ruisseau fait à l'horizon un fin collier d'argent. A la fenêtre de la chaumière, le rideau se soulève, la Jeune Fille se penche, regarde Julien s'éloigner.*)

RIDEAU.

---

Where are you sailing in the night,
Uneasy and mysterious,
Star of the Future, drifting away
White in the shadowy mist?

**VOICES OF THE NIGHT:** What will you, whom I hear
Calling me sadly through my silence?

**JULIEN:** O night, where my soul soars,
I am afraid of you—of time!
I am wrapped up in heavy gloom,
I strive to pierce the mystery
That broods upon your silence:
Success—or death to all my hopes!
(*The song of the nightingale echoes the complaint of the poet. The moon reappears. The brook makes a line of silver against the horizon. The curtain is lifted at the cottage-window and the Young Girl leans out, watching Julien depart.*)

CURTAIN

---

# ■ ACTE TROISIÈME

(*Impuissance*)
Un site sauvage, en Bretagne, non loin de la mer. A gauche une maison familiale, délabrée, avec une large terrasse couverte et un perron. A droite, une église pauvre. Plus loin, un calvaire. Une route serpente venant de la vellée abrupte. Aube glaciale. Des nuages obscurs galopent dans le ciel. Automne.

## SCÈNE PREMIÈRE

L'AÏEULE, JULIEN, LES BRETONNES,

VOIX DANS LA TEMPÊTE.
*Au lever du rideau, tempête, tous les éléments déchaînés. Julien sur la terrasse, comme pétrifié par le malheur, confie à la nature tumultueuse son immense désespoir. L'Aïeule le couve d'un regard désolé. Devant le calvaire, des Bretonne récitent des litanies. Une atmosphère de tragique mystère planera sur tout l'acte.*

**LES BRETONNES:** (*devant le calvaire.*) Vierge puissante,
Éblouissante,
Immaculée . . .
Vierge Marie,
Priez pour nous!
Soleil sans voiles,
Soleil d'étoiles,
Soleil d'amour . . .
Protégez-nous,
Exaucez-nous!
Porte d'aurore,
Porte d'or!
Priez pour nous!
Porte de gloire,

---

# ■ ACT III

(*Impotence*)
A wild spot in Brittany near the sea. At the left, a ruined manor-house with a large covered terrace and porch. To the right, a poor church. Further on, a wayside crucifix. The road winds upward from a deep valley. Chill daybreak. Dark clouds scud across the sky. Autumn.

## SCENE I

The GRANDMOTHER, JULIEN, BRETON WOMEN, VOICES IN THE STORM.

*As the curtain rises, a furious tempest is raging. Julien on the terrace, stands as if petrified by grief, confiding his deep despair to the stormy elements. The Grandmother watches him with a brooding look of sadness. Before the crucifix Breton Women are reciting litanies. An atmosphere of tragic mystery pervades the entire act.*

**BRETON WOMEN:** (*before the crucifix.*) Virgin omnipotent,
Dazzling,
Immaculate,
Mary the Virgin,
Pray for us!
Sun of our souls,
Sun of the stars,
Sun of our love,
Deliver us,
Hear our prayer!
Gate of the dawn,
O door of gold,
Pray for us!
O door of glory

---

Pur miroir!
Priez pour nous!
Reine charitable
Et secourable!
Protégez-nous!
(*Les Bretonnes se relèvent et vont vers l'église où elles disparaissent.*)

**JULIEN:** (*tendant les bras avec angoisse.*) Ciel sans pitié! De ma lutte dernière
N'entends-tu pas gémir la suprême prière?
(*Il écoute les bruits de la tempête, insensible à éblouissement des éclairs.*)

**VOIX DANS LA TEMPÊTE:** Ho! ho!

**JULIEN:** Voix de revenants
Ressuscitant . . .
Voix d'ancêtres,
Créateurs de mon être . . .
Venez-vous à mon secours? . . .

**VOIX DANS LA TEMPÊTE:** Ho! ho!

**JULIEN:** Messagers du Néant d'où je vins . . . où je cours?
(*L'Aïeule va s'asseoir dans un coin sombre d'où elle surveille avidement les gestes de Julien, tout en disant son rosaire. Elle se signe à chaque éclair.*)
Mon coeur battu par la tourmente,
Comme vous, hurle et se lamente,
Jouet du fatal tourbillon!
(*Perdu dans ses pensées, les yeux fixés sur les cimes lointaines où la lueur d'un phare tournoie, affolée.*)
Jadis, dans un splendide songe,
Pourquoi m'appelais-tu, pur et divin rayon? . . .
Oh! l'odieux mensonge! . . .
(*L'Aïeule se lève, va vers Julien.*)
Mystérieux tumulte où je suis entraîne . . .
Ah! pourquoi suis-je né? . . .
(*L'Aïeule, qui s'est approchée, lui ferme la bouche d'une main tremblante. Elle le prend dans ses bras comme une mère son enfant, le cajole tendrement, puis l'entraîne vers le perron. Orgues lointaines.*)

## SCÈNE II

L'AÏEULE, JULIEN, puis LES POÈTES DÉCHUS.
*Les sons de l'orgue évoquent en l'esprit de Julien le souvenir de l'ineffable apparition. Les larmes jaillissent de ses yeux. Il se cache la tête sur l'épaule de l'Aïeule frissonnante.*)

**L'AÏEULE:** Ô mon fils bien-aimé, pour ton coeur désolé, la prière, seule, est salutaire! . . .
Te souviens-tu . . . mon fils . . . de celle que jadis tu récitais avect ta bonne mère . . . au coin de l'âtre . . . de la vieille mai-

---

And the truth,
Pray for us!
Queen of mercy
And charity,
Deliver us!
(*The Breton Women rise, go towards the church, and disappear.*)

**JULIEN:** (*stretching out his arms in agony.*) Pitiless sky—do you not hear the groan
Of final agony in my last prayer?
(*He bears the noise of the storm, indifferent to the glare of the lightning.*)

**VOICES IN THE STORM:** Ho! ho!

**JULIEN:** Voices of ghosts
Come back again—
Ancestral voices,
Creators of my being—
Come you to help me now?

**VOICES IN THE STORM:** Ho! ho!

**JULIEN:** Envoys of nothingness from where I've come—and where I go!
(*The Grandmother goes to sit in a dark corner, whence she watches Julien closely while telling her beads. At each lightning flash she crosses herself.*)
My heart, tossed and tormented,
Shrieks and laments like you,
Toy of the whirlwind's wrath!
(*Lost in thought, his eyes fixed on the distant hilltops where the lamp from a lighthouse flashes fitfully.*)
Why did you call me in a splendid dream,
Once, long ago, O clear and shining gleam,
To prove a hideous lie?
(*The Grandmother rises and approaches Julien.*)
The mysterious vortex drew me in:—
Why was I ever born?
(*The Grandmother covers his mouth with a trembling band; she takes him in her arms like a child and caresses him tenderly, then draws him back towards the porch. Distant organ music.*)

## SCENE II

The GRANDMOTHER, JULIEN, later the HAPLESS POETS.
*The tones of the organ awaken in Julien's soul a memory of the ineffable vision. Tears start from his eyes; he buries his face on the shoulder of the trembling Grandmother.*

**GRANDMOTHER:** O well-beloved son! for your broken heart there is only prayer!
Do you recall, my son, the prayer recited to your dear mother in the inglenook of the old house?
The old house that she left forever, to go up there, to pray—to pray for

son? . . .

La vieille maison qu'elle a quittée à jamais! . . . s'en allant là-haut, prier . . . prier pour son fils . . . pour qu'il ne soit pas damné! . . .

(Au loin dans la clarté blafarde du matin, un lugubre cortège s'avance lentement.)

**VOIX LOINTAINES:** Si l'esprit dans le vide
Tourne et crie, éperdu,
Sois maudit, Dieu perfide!
C'est toi qui l'as voulu.

**L'AÏEULE:** (inquiète.) Quel est ce long troupeau qui rôde dans le soir? . . .

**JULIEN:** (reconnaissant les malheureux Pèlerins du Rêve.) Tous ceux dont un espoir, frère de mon espoir,
Égara vers l'azur les âmes inquiètes:
Mes frères, les Poètes!

**LES POÈTES DÉCHUS:**
(s'avançant sur la route.) Si l'esprit dans le vide, etc.

(L'Aïeule, terrifiée, se cache la tête dans les mains. Julien a descendu le perron, s'est avancé vers la route; son visage exprime tour à tour l'enthousiasme et la terreur.)

**L'AÏEULE:** (s'élançant vers Julien qu'elle entraîne derrière la terrasse, hors du regard des Déchus.) Mon fils! . . . Ne m'abandonne pas! . . .

**JULIEN:** (avec ferveur.) Tous ceux qui, comme moi, ravagés par le doute
Et voyant chaque jour avorter leur effort,
Sont tombés sur la route
En maudissant le sort!

**PREMIER GROUPE:** Si tout être agonise
A chaque heure du jour! . . .

(Suivent les Poètes Déchus, sombres, agressifs, appuyés sur les Muses en deuil.)

**DEUXIÈME GROUPE:** Si le deuil s'éternise
Aux baisers de l'amour! . . .

(Puis de groupes d'Éphèbes et d'Amantes éplorées.)

**TROISIÈME GROUPE:** Si la douce espérance
Passe, rit et s'enfuit! . . .

**L'AÏEULE:** (s'accrochant à Julien qui semble vouloir les suivre.) Julien! . . .

**JULIEN:** (dans la plus vive émotion.) Laisse-moi! . . . Pitié!

**PREMIER GROUPE:** Éternel recommencement de l'existence
Qui naît et meurt à tout moment! . . .
C'est le Temps qui mène la danse.
Tout vient en se tenant la main,
S'en va, revient, jadis, aujourd'hui, demain.
Tout s'assemble et tout se ressemble,
Tout meurt et tout refleurit, danse et rit,
Et soudain s'enfuit!

**DEUXIÈME et TROISIÈMES GROUPES:** Si la pire souffrance
Nous brise sans répit! . . .
Si l'envie et la haine
Dans leur malignité
A jamais souveraines
Te raillent, Charité!
Si l'âme dont le songe
Est d'exprimer le ciel
S'épuise au vain mensonge
Qui l'abreuve de fiel! . . .

(Tous se tournent vers la croix avec des gestes de blasphème.)

**L'AÏEULE:** (Ad libitum.)
Blasphémateurs!
Diaboliques menteurs!
Lucifer vous inspire! . . .
Oui! comme le sien, votre orgueil délire!
Dignes servants de son empire! . . .

(Elle les menace de gestes forcenés et tremblants.)

**LE CHOEUR:** Vérité! Beauté! Rêve!
Si tout l'homme est trahi . . .
Sois maudit! oh! sans trêve!
Dieu trompeur! Dieu haï!

(Tous reprennent leur marche vers la grève, groupe par groupe, indifférents.)

**JULIEN:** (tendant les bras vers le calvaire. (Ad libitum.)) O Créateur!
O Rédempteur!
Surhumaine figure!
Et toi, nature!
Mère en qui j'avais foi!
Ton obscur devenir
N'est-il donc qu'un cercle étroit
Où tout passe et tournoie?
Trop incertaine voie . . .
Trop sinueux détours . . .
Dans l'éternel retour
Des deuils et des fêtes
Des victoires et des défaites!

(L'Aïeule suit du regard la disparition du sombre cortège. Trottinant menu elle s'avance vers Julien calmé.)

**L'AÏEULE:** (en confidence grave à Julien.) De Satan s'écroula le rêve ambitieux . . .
Ainsi sont-ils tombés du haut de leur folie
En maudissant la Vie
Et le doute éternel!

(Peu à peu prophétique et plus directement à Julien qui l'écoute étonné.)

Crains l'orgueil . . .
C'est l'écueil! . . .

**JULIEN:** (se souvenant, douloureusement.) Crains l'orgueil? . . .

**L'AÏEULE:** La raison:
Du poison!

---

her son, that he might not be lost!

(Far off, in the chilly morning light, a dismal procession advances slowly.)

**DISTANT VOICES:** If the soul in the void
Turns and cries, dismayed:
Curses on you perfidious God!
It is so your will is done.

**GRANDMOTHER:** (fearfully.) Who are those people trailing through the gloom?

**JULIEN:** (recognizing the unhappy Dream-Pilgrims.) All those a hope—the brother to my hope—Has lured into the blue of restless souls!
They are my kin—the Poets!

**HAPLESS POETS:** (drawing nearer.) If the soul in the void, etc.

(The Grandmother, terrified, hides her face in her hands, Julien comes down from the porch to the road. His face expresses alternately enthusiasm and terror.)

**GRANDMOTHER:** (running to Julien and drawing him behind the terrace out of sight of the unfortunates.) My son—do not abandon me!

**JULIEN:** (earnestly.) Those who, like me, have been destroyed by doubt,
And, seeing every effort come to nothing,
Have fallen by the way
And cursed their destiny!

**FIRST GROUP:** If every soul sweats agony,
At every day and hour!

(The Hapless Poets follow, gloomy and defiant, leaning on the Muses draped in mourning.)

**SECOND GROUP:** And if our woe perpetuates
The kisses of our loves!

(Then come groups of young men and weeping true-loves.)

**THIRD GROUP:** If every pleasant hope
Draws near, and mocks, and flies!

**GRANDMOTHER:** (clinging to Julien, who would follow them.) Julien!

**JULIEN:** (deeply moved.) Leave me!
Have pity!

**FIRST GROUP:** Eternal recommencement of existence,
That dies each moment, and is born again,
For it is Time itself that leads the dance.
All come to us, and all hold out the hand,
Then go, return, past, present and to come.
All dies, and grows again, dances and laughs,
And suddenly is gone!

**SECOND AND THIRD GROUPS:** If the worst suffering
Breaks us remorselessly!—
If envy and hate,
Forever sovereign,
In their malignity
Mock you, O Charity!
If the dream of the soul
Is Heaven to express,
And pours itself in lies,
And slakes its thirst with gall!

(All turn to the crucifix with blasphemous gestures.)

**GRANDMOTHER:** Blasphemers!
And devilish liars!
Lucifer prompts you!
Even as his, your presumptuous pride
Worthy servants of his empire!

**CHORUS:** Truth!
Beauty!
Dreams!
If all men be betrayed—
Curses upon you forever,
God, the traitor! God we hate!

(Group by group they go slowly and listlessly toward the shore.)

**JULIEN:** (stretching his arms towards the crucifix. (Ad libitum)) O Creator!
O Redeemer!
Figure divine!
And you, O nature,
In whom I put my trust!
Is your veiled path
Only a narrow round
Where all men must pass and turn?
A too uncertain road—
Too many winding paths—
An everlasting round
Of mourning and rejoicing,
Of victory and defeat!

(The Grandmother watches the gloomy procession disappear, and goes, tottering, to Julien, who is now more calm.)

**GRANDMOTHER:** (to Julien, with grave faith.) It was for ambition, too, that Satan fell,
As these have fallen from their heights of madness
While cursing life
And the eternal doubt!

(Growing prophetic and speaking directly to Julien, who listens, amazed.)

Beware of Pride!
That is the reef!

**JULIEN:** (sadly reminiscent.) Beware of Pride?

**GRANDMOTHER:** Your reason: It is poison!

## Act III, Scene II

**JULIEN:** (*frémissant.*)
Grand'mère! . . . qui t'a dit?
Comment peux-tu savoir?
Qui t'inspire? . . .
Toi, qui ne sais pas même lire . . .

**L'AÏEULE:** (*grave, montrant le Christ du calvaire.*) Celui dont tu ne veux pas voir
Le pitoyable sourire!

**JULIEN:** (*avec reproche mais sans conviction.*) Grand'mère! . . .
(*Les Bretonnes sortent de l'office et s'éloignent. L'orgue élève de nouveau sa voix plaintive. Lentement l'Aïeule va sur le calvaire, s'agenouille et prie. Julien écoute les voix lointaines des Déchus, regarde l'Aïeule.*)

**JULIEN:** Maudire? . . . Prier?
(*Il secoue la tête, s'assied, médite douloureusement. Au loin, un pâle arc-en-ciel se dessine sur le ciel de cuivre et de suie.*)

**LES POÈTES DÉCHUS:** (*très loin.*)
Si tout l'homme est trahi
Sois maudit! oh! sans trêve
Dieu trompeur, Dieu haï!

**JULIEN:** (*sombre, fatal, fixant l'Aïeule, de plus en plus courbée sur les marches du calvaire.*)
Vainement à travers les cieux,
Sans écho dans l'ombre infinie,
Se perdent nos cris et notre agonie,
Dans l'abîme silencieux
Vainement l'homme souffre et pleure . . .
Tout rayon divin n'est qu'un leurre!
(*Dans un geste désespéré, tendant le poing vers l'horizon.*) Sois maudit!
(*Au pied de la croix l'Aïeule tombe comme morte, silencieusement.*)

*RIDEAU.*

---

**JULIEN:** (*trembling.*) Grandmother!
Who told you that?
How can you know?
Who prompted you?
You cannot even read.

**GRANDMOTHER:** (*gravely pointing to the crucifix.*) He, whose pitying smile
You will not see!

**JULIEN:** (*reproachfully, but unconvinced.*) Grandmother!
(*The Breton Women come out from Mass. The organ peals plaintively. The Grandmother goes slowly to the crucifix, kneels and prays. Julien listens to the distant voices of the unfortunates while watching her.*)

**JULIEN:** To curse?
Or pray?
(*He shakes his head sadly. Overhead a pale rainbow is seen against the coppery, murky sky.*)

**THE HAPLESS POETS:** (*far off.*) If all men be betrayed,
Curses upon you—yes, forever!
God the Traitor!—God we hate!

**JULIEN:** (*Gloomy, watching the Grandmother bent lower and lower over the steps beneath the crucifix.*) Vainly, across the skies
Silent in infinite gloom,
Are lost our agonized cries!
And in the deep abyss,
Vainly man suffers and dies,
The heavenly light is a lure!
(*Shaking his fist towards the sky; despairingly.*)
Be accursed!
(*The Grandmother falls, as if dead, at the foot of the crucifix.*)

*CURTAIN*

---

# ACTE QUATRIÈME

## Premier Tableau

(*Ivresse*)

*Un coin désert près du boulevard extérieur en fête. A gauche, "entrée des artistes" d'un théâtre forain. A droite, terrasse de guinguette. Nuit d'hiver.*

### SCÈNE PREMIÈRE

*JULIEN, CHOEUR INVISIBLE.*

---

# ACT IV

## First Tableau

(*Intoxication*)

*A deserted corner in one of the outer boulevards, decorated for a holiday. At the left, "Stage Entrance" of a traveling show. At the right, the terrace of a public-house.*

### SCENE I

*JULIEN, the INVISIBLE CHORUS.*

---

*Julien entre, égaré, comme poursuivi par les voix fatales. Il a vieilli, sa barbe et ses cheveux sont grisonnants et sa démarche, ses gestes, le désordre de son costume témoignent d'un commencement de déchéance morale et physique.*

**JULIEN:** (*à lui-même.*) Des maudits la plainte obsédante
Harcèle ma douleur ardente! . . .
Devant elle, sans cesse, je fuis . . .
M'enfonçant plus avant dans la nuit!
(*Il lève la tête vers le ciel fleuri d'étoiles. En lui chantent les souvenirs des jours enfuis.*)

**CHOEUR INVISIBLE:** Vois, c'est la nuit, la nuit calme . . .

**JULIEN:** (*mélancolique.*) Et toi, nuit malicieuse et fausse!
Que me dit ton mystère? . . .
M'announces-tu la fin de mon triste calvaire?
(*Des bruits de fête glissent dans l'aire. Railleur:*)
Là-bas, dans Paris, on s'amuse.
La joie grouille, confuse . . .
(*Une Fille sort de la guinguette.*)
Tout brille, et tout rit, et tout chante! . . .
Ces hommes sont heureux! . . .
Suis-je un homme comme eux?
(*Il s'assied.*)
Moi seul, ne puis rien oublier!
(*La Fille l'écoute. Elle s'approche.*)
Sous ma douleur . . . je reste brisé!

### SCÈNE II

*LA FILLE, JULIEN, LES CHIMÈRES, UN GARÇON DE CAFÉ.*

**LA FILLE:** (*à l'oreille de Julien.*)
Pour tuer le chagrin
Faut la chaleur du vin.
(*S'offrant.*)
Pour oublier l'amour
Il faut aimer toujours.

**LES CHIMÈRES:** (*dans l'ombre.*)
Tissons des songes . . .

**LA FILLE:** (*fait signe à un garçon qui paraît sur le seuil.*) Moi je connais un philtre
Qui dans la peau s'infiltre (1)
Et guérit tous les maux . . .

**LES CHIMÈRES:** Tissons des brumes d'oubli . . .
((1) *Variante: Qui dans le sang s'infiltre.*)

**LA FILLE:** (*orgueilleuse.*) C'est une science
Toute en nuances . . .
C'est un métier divin
Comme le tien,
Poète malchanceux,
Que rendre un homme heureux.

---

*Julien enters, wildly, as if pursued by haunting voices. He has aged, his hair and beard are gray, and his walk, his movement, his untidy clothes, bear witness to the beginning of a moral and physical decline.*

**JULIEN:** (*to himself.*) The haunting song of the accursed
Harasses my consuming grief!
From that refrain I strive to flee
And hide myself within the night.
(*He raises his eyes to the starry sky. The memories of other days sing within him.*)

**INVISIBLE CHORUS:** Behold the night!—the night so still.

**JULIEN:** (*gloomily.*) And you, O mocking and deceitful night,
What is it that your mystery tells?
Is my sad Calvary to end at last?
(*The noise of merrymaking is heard.—Derisively:*)
Down there, in Paris, all is gay,
And joy is murmuring, confused.
(*A Grisette comes from the public-house.*)
All glitters there, they laugh and sing;
Those men are happy there!—
Am I a man like them?
(*He sits.*)
I, who alone cannot forget!
(*The Grisette listens and comes towards him.*)
Under my grief—I am a broken thing!

### SCENE II

*The GRISETTE, JULIEN, the CHIMERAS, a WAITER from the cabaret.*

**GRISETTE:** (*in Julien's ear.*)
There's nothing like red wine
To drive away your pain!
(*Offering herself.*)
And to forget your love.
You needs must love again!

**THE CHIMERAS:** (*in the dark.*)
We weave the dreams.

**GRISETTE:** (*signaling a Waiter in the door of the public-house.*) I know a famous philtre,
That runs through all your veins
And makes you young again.

**THE CHIMERAS:** We weave the mists of sweet oblivion.

**GRISETTE:** (*boastfully.*) It is a science
Made all of tones!
It is a noble trade,
A bit like yours,
Unlucky Poet,
That makes a man feel glad.

**LES CHIMÈRES:** Tissons des voiles, des mirages dans la nuit! . . .
(*Le garçon apporte deux verres qu'il remplit.*)

**LA FILLE:** (*se méprenant à un geste de Julien.*) Qui je suis? . . .
(*Se drapant avec mystère.*)
Une muse
Qui s'use (1)
A souffler de tendres sons
Dans les cornemuses
Des coeurs polissons.
(*Crânant.*)
Je suis la Belle
(*Humble.*)
A qui fait la Bête
(*Gamine, tendant la main.*)
Pour avoir du son!
(*Curieuse, familièrement.*)
Es-tu riche . . .
Ou chiche
De pognon?
(*Effarée.*)
Tu pleures! . . .
Tes illusions? . . .
(*L'invitant à trinquer.*)
Elle peut t'en vendre de plus belles
((1) *Variante: Qui s'amuse.*)
Celle qu'on appelle
Casque d'Ognon! . . .
Pourquoi?
Je vais te le dire . . .
(*Elle prend une chaise et s'assied près de Julien qui l'écarte d'un geste las, presque brutal. Avec reproche.*)
Décidément, je te fais peur?
(*Avec toute sa séduction.*)
On trouve pire
Pourtant
Sur le chemin du bonheur.
(*Julien se détourne.*)
Sois indulgent . . .
(*Humble, avec une exagération plaisante.*)
Si le feu de mes châsses
N'es plus aussi joyeux,
C'est que, vois-tu, j'ai fait la chasse
A tant d'yeux!
(*Julien ne l'entend plus. Il compare le magnifique passé à la hideuse réalité.*)
Si mes dents ont des brèches . . .
Sois généreux,
C'est qu'elles ont trop mordu dans la dèche!
Si je suis . . . démolie,
C'est d'avoir, si lasse . . .
Dormi sur des lits
Sans paillasse.
(*Délurée, le verre en main.*)
Mais ceci n'est rien
Quand on s'aime bien!
Et ce soir, je suis l'amoureuse,
Et c'est toi, le vaurien,
(*Elle vide son verre d'un trait et le repose sur la table.*)
Qui va la rendre heureuse!
(*Comme inspirée.*)
Oui, je veux me payer
Avec toi le loyer
D'une nuit à la belle étoile . . .
(*Julien tend l'oreille, dans l'air vi-

**THE CHIMERAS:** We weave in clouds, a mirage of the night.
(*The Waiter brings out two glasses, which he fills.*)

**GRISETTE:** (*misunderstanding Julien's movement.*) Who am I?
I'm a Muse,
Who can breathe
A sentimental tune
Through the bagpipes
Of rascal's hearts!
(*Boastfully.*)
I am Beauty!
(*Humbly.*)
Who makes the Beast.
(*Holding out her hand.*)
To have his cash!
(*With familiar curiousity.*)
Are you rich?
Are you stingy
Of the ready?
(*Disconcerted.*)
You're crying!
Your illusions?
(*Inviting him to drink.*)
They will sell you the finest ever;
They call the drink
The Onion Head!
Why's that?
I'll tell you why.—
(*She takes a chair and sits near Julien, who draws away with a weary movement, almost brutal. Reproachfully.*)
O, really, do I frighten you?
(*Seductively.*)
You can find worse,
You know,
Upon the road of joy!
(*Julien turns away.*)
Won't you be kind?
(*Humbly, with comical exaggeration.*)
If these old bones of mine,
Are not so gay as once,
It is because I've made my hunt
Before so many eyes!
(*Julien does not heed. He compares the magnificent past with the hideous reality.*)
And if some teeth are gone—
Forget it!
They've bitten deep in poverty!
If I am—broken up,
It is because I've slept
Dog-tired on a bed
Without a quilt!
(*Briskly, waving her glass.*)
But all this doesn't count
When one's in love!
And tonight I am in love
With good-for-nothing you!
(*She empties her glass at a gulp, and puts it on the table.*)
Who means to make me happy?
(*As if inspired.*)
Yes, yes, tonight
I'll lodge with you
Under the open sky.
(*Julien listens; the air quivers with the memories of his dead love. He looks with growing emotion at her whose voice evokes these radiant recollections.*)

brent les réminiscences de ses amours defuntes. Il contemple avec une émotion croissante celle dont la voix évoque de radieux souvenirs.)

**JULIEN:** Spectre infernal! Que veux-tu?

**LA FILLE:** (*se découvrant le visage.*) Je veux pour ciel de lit
Ces toiles d'araignées . . .
Et pour oreiller
(*Grandiloquente.*)
Ta puissante poitrine! . . .

**JULIEN:** (*effrayé, croyant revoir l'adorée disparue.*) D'où reviens-tu?

**LA FILLE:** . . . Tout imprégnée
De choses divines!

**LES CHIMÈRES:** (*comme un écho plaintif.*) Soeur clémente!
(*Julien semble se débattre dans un cauchemar. Il contemple, frissonnant, la Fille qui maintenant esquisse une dans qu'elle voudrait lascive.*)

**JULIEN:** (*se détournant.*) Quelle épouvante!

**LA FILLE:** (*s'éloigne en dansant, tournée vers lui, comme pour l'inviter à la suivre.*) C'est un métier divin
Comme le tien,
Poète malchanceux! . . .
(*L'appelant du doigt.*)
Que savoir rendre un homme heureux!
(*Un groupe de masques sort de la guinguette vers la fête.*)

## SCÈNE III

*JULIEN, seul.*

**JULIEN:** (*sombre.*) Mystère de la destinée!
Quel est ce doute dont mon âme s'épouvante? . . .
J'ai vu
Devant moi se lever le fantôme éperdu
De mes jeunes années!
Si je n'étais certain que Louise n'est plus,
Je croirais que c'est elle,
Cette femme damnée!
J'étais halluciné!
(*Avec remords.*)
Louise! . . .
(*En un appel lointain.*)
Louise! . . .
Ah! me consume le remords,
D'avoir sacrifié à la chimère insaisissable
Plus d'amoureux bonheur
Que n'en auront connu les plus heureux des hommes.
(*Il se rassied.*)
Mystère des destinées! . . .
(*Creusant ses souvenirs.*)
Je me vois tout enfant
Dévoré d'un orgueil immense . . .

**JULIEN:** Infernal spectre!
What is it that you want?

**GRISETTE:** (*uncovering her face.*) I want my bed-curtains
To be these spider-webs!
And for my pillow
(*Grandiloquently.*)
Your mighty breast—

**JULIEN:** (*startled, thinking he sees again his lost love.*)
From where have you come back again?

**GRISETTE:** —that is all filled
With lofty fancies!

**THE CHIMERAS:** (*like a plaintive echo.*) Sister of Mercy!
(*Julien seems to struggle with a nightmare. He gazes, shuddering, at the Grisette, who is attempting a would-be lascivious dance.*)

**JULIEN:** (*turning away.*) How terrible!

**GRISETTE:** (*dancing away, turns as if inviting him to follow.*) It is a noble trade,
A bit like yours,
Unlucky poet!
(*Beckoning.*)
That can make a man feel glad!
(*Some Maskers come from the public-house and drag her with them to the merrymaking.*)

## SCENE III

*JULIEN, alone.*

**JULIEN:** (*gloomily.*) O mystery of fate!
What is this doubt that shakes my very soul?
I've seen
Rise up the sad forlorn ghost
Of my lost youth!
Were I not certain that Louise is dead,
I'd think that it was she,
This outcast courtesan.
I was bewitched!
(*Remorsefully.*)
Louise!
(*Like a distant call.*)
Louise!
I am consumed by remorse;
I've sacrificed, all for an empty dream,
More amorous happiness
Than often is the lot of lucky men!
(*Sits.*)
O, mystery of fate!
I see myself a child,
Devoured by growing pride!
More than my love, I loved my hopes!
I loved love, too!
(*Ardently.*)

Plus que l'amour, j'aimais mon espérance!
J'aimais aussi l'amour . . .
(*Ardent.*)
J'aimais la vie!
J'aimais les êtres qu'elle offense!
J'aimais toute peine et toute beauté! . . .
(*Avec une fierté un peu gavroche.*)
Et Paris et la France . . .
Et l'Humanité!
(*Il se dresse, esquisse un grand geste d'enthousiasme, puis retombe.*)
Si m'attirait la souffrance,
Si je cherchais tant d'amour,
C'était que mon orgueil avide de victoires
Précipitait mon être à l'assaut des émotions:
Duperie inconsciente dont mon âme agonise
Je ne peux plus aimer
Depuis que mon espoir a sombré!
Depuis qui ma raison
A compris le néant
De l'immortalité!
(*Répondant à une voix intérieure.*)
Mourir? . . .
(*Comme inspiré.*)
Finir . . .
(*Souriant à l'idée qui l'illumine.*)
En beauté!
(*Musique de bal dans la guinguette.*)

And I loved life!
I loved the creatures that it hurts;
I loved distress, as well as I loved beauty!
And Paris, yes, and France,
And all humanity!
(*He rises with a gesture of enthusiasm and then falls back.*)
If I were drawn by suffering,
And if I sought love everywhere,
It was my pride, hungry for victory,
That tossed me as a sop to my emotions.
Unconscious trickery of my tortured soul!
I can no longer love,
Since my fond hopes were wrecked;
Nor since my understanding
Has grasped the nothingness
Of immortality!
(*Answering an inner voice.*)
To die?
(*With an idea.*)
To end—
(*Smiling at an inspiring thought.*)
In beauty!
(*Dance-music in the public-house.*)

## SCÈNE IV

*JULIEN, UNE BANDE JOYEUSE.*

*Précédés d'une bande de gavroches et de fillettes en liesse, des Modèles et des Rapins, déguisés sous leurs manteaux d'hiver, débouchent de la rue voisine et se dirigent vers la fête. Une fanfare les précède. Des couples attirés par le bruit paraissent sur le seuil de la guinguette, encore essoufflés d'avoir dansé. Les Modèles et les Rapins chantent une scie du quartier latin en gambadant follement.*)

**MODÈLES ET RAPINS:**
(*s'éloignant vers la fête.*) Nina, la pauvre fille est morte, etc.

**GAVROCHES et FILLETTES:** (*les entourant.*) Gais et contents
Nous allions triomphants, etc.
(*Cris, rumeurs, Julien regarde avidement la foule turbulente.*)

## SCÈNE V

*JULIEN, LE CHOEUR INVISIBLE.*

**LE CHOEUR:** (*plaintif.*)
Ah! . . . Ah! . . .

## SCENE IV

*JULIEN, a MERRY GROUP.*

*Preceded by a merry group of Street Boys and Girls, the Models and Rowdies, muffled in winter cloaks, come from a neighboring street and go towards the merrymaking. They are preceded by horns. Other couples, attracted by the noise, come to the door of the public-house. They are out of breath from dancing. The Models and Rowdies sing a song of the Latin Quarter, as they gambol madly.*

**MODELS AND ROWDIES:** (*as they go.*) Nina, poor girl, is dead, etc.

**STREET BOYS AND GIRLS:** (*surrounding them.*) Gay and content,
We go triumphantly, etc.
(*Cries, noise. Julien looks longingly at the turbulent crowd.*)

## SCENE V

*JULIEN, the INVISIBLE CHORUS.*

**CHORUS:** Ah!—Ah!

---

**L'ACOLYTE:** (*avec envie.*) Les chouettes pourboires!
(*Rageur.*)
Même pour deux sous . . .
(*Montrant le poing à la ville.*)
Ils n'en veulent point!

**LE SONNEUR:** (*sarcastique.*) Ils ont aut' chose à penser!

**L'ACOLYTE:** (*plaintif, approuvant.*) Y a trop d'misère! . . .

**LE SONNEUR:** (*goguenard.*)
Penses-tu
Y z'aim'nt mieux rigoler!
(*Sentencieux.*)
L'humanité . . . c'est une . . .

**L'ACOLYTE:** (*l'interrompant joyeux.*) Tiens! . . . V'là nos déesses!
(*Trois Filles du Rêve, déguisées en fées, débouchent d'une rue voisine et s'empressent vers les deux compères.*)

**LA PREMIÈRE:** (*à l'Acolyte.*) C't'autre! Bonjour! . . .

**LA DEUXIÈME:** (*se recoiffant.*) Mince de bousculade!

**LA TROISIÈME:** (*remontant sa jupe.*) Va-t'on z'arriver enfin?

**L'ACOLYTE:** (*saluant d'autres Fées et Sirènes qui accourent essouflées.*) Pas de presse! . . .
La baraque est encore vide . . .
(*Tous s'éloignent vivement. Obscurité subite, durant laquelle le décor change. Lumière aussitôt.*)

**ACOLYTE:** (*regretfully.*) The nice little tips!
(*Furiously.*)
Even a penny or two!
(*Shaking his fist towards the town.*)
But they won't have it!

**BELL-RINGER:** (*sarcastically.*) They've other things to think of!

**ACOLYTE:** (*agreeing sadly.*) There's too much misery!

**BELL-RINGER:** (*jeering.*) Do you think
That makes them like to lark?
(*Sententiously.*)
Humanity—is a—

**ACOLYTE:** (*cheerfully interrupting.*) Look—Here come our Goddesses!
(*Three Dream-Maidens, dressed like Fairies, come from the neighboring street.*)

**THE FIRST:** (*to the Acolyte.*) Hello you!
Howdy!

**THE SECOND:** (*pinning her hair.*) Where's the push?

**THE THIRD:** (*gathering up her skirt.*) Will they ever get here?

**ACOLYTE:** (*greeting other Fairies and Sirens who have come up breathlessly.*) No hurry!
The booth is empty.
(*All go off quickly. Sudden darkness, during which the scene is changed.*)

## ■ Deuxième Tableau

*La Place Blanche à Paris, un soir de Carnaval et de fête foraine.
A droite, premier plan, cabaret avec terrasse débordant sur la chaussée, fenêtre au premier étage, lampions; second plan, un toboggan.
A gauche, à l'avant-scène, le coin d'une baraque.
Au centre, le "Théâtre de l'Idéal" au décor défraichi de féerie.
Sur les côtés, on aperçoit, en enfilade, les façades merveilleuses des cabarets montmartrois. Au fond, très loin, bal populaire (rue Lepic). Les ailes du Moulin-Rouge dominent la scène de leurs lumières en tournoiement intermittent.
Foule de fête et de Carnaval. Il est dix heures du soir.*

## ■ Second Tableau

*The Place Blanche in Paris, the evening of the Carnival. At right, down-stage, a cabaret, with a terrace reaching the sidewalk. A window in the first story. High lamps. Further up-stage a toboggan slide. At left, the corner of a booth. In the centre, "Theatre of the Ideal," with shabby pantomime scenery. At the sides are seen in a long line the wonderful façades of the cabarets of Montmarte. At the back in the distance a public hall. The sails of the Moulin-Rouge dominate the scene with their lights that revolve intermittently. Holiday crowd, Carnival maskers. Ten o'clock, evening.*

## SCÈNE PREMIÈRE

*LE MAGE, LES FÉES et SIRÈNES, LE SONNEUR, L'ACOLYTE, LA FOULE, puis LA FILLE, et JULIEN.*

## SCENE I

*The SHOWMAN, the FAIRIES and SIRENS, the BELL-RINGER, the ACOLYTE, the CROWD, then the GRISETTE and JULIEN.*

*Au lever du rideau, la foule déambule, grouillante et chantante. Des curieux sont massés devant le théâtre où paradent des Danseuses Sacrées, rappelant piteusement les Danseuses du Temple, dont elles imitent le geste en lançant au-dessus des têtes une nuée de légers serpentins, tandis qu'un Mage, grotesque Hiérophante, montre à la foule l'énorme tableau-réclame du spectacle du jour. Les terrasses regorgent de buveurs en perpétuel mouvement, exubérants et familiers. La fanfare du Toboggan, par instants, domine le tumulte. Une compagnie de cors sur les marches d'une estrade, attend, d'un air noble, le moment de jouer. Bruits de fête foraine, cloches, trompes, coups de feu, tambours, sirènes . . .*

*As the curtain rises, the Crowd moves about shouting and singing. Some sightseers are massed in front of the theatre where the Sacred Dancers are parading. They are a wretched travesty of the Dancers of the Temple, whose gestures they imitate as they throw out over the heads of the crowd light serpentines, while the Showman, like a grotesque High Priest, shows the Crowd a huge picture poster of the performance. The terraces are choked with people who drink and move on continually, gay and saucy. The noise of the toboggan is heard from time to time above the tumult. A brass band on the steps of the platform waits, with a lofty air, the time for it to play. Noise of the fair, bells, horns, fireworks, drums, whistles.*

LE MAGE: Miracle inconcevable! Prodige avéré! La Splendeur du Vrai Est visible à toute heure! Ceci n'est pas pour les bêtes . . . Seuls sont invités moyennant dix centimes. Les serviteurs de l'Idéal, Hors duquel, pour l'humanité, Il n'est point de salut!

SHOWMAN: Wonderful miracle! Genuine prodigy! The Splendor of the True On view every hour! It is not a show for dunces! No one invited under ten centimes To worship the Ideal! Without the price, mankind Can't get salvation!

COMMIS (1) et GAVROCHES (2): (*soufflant dans des mirlitons, etc.*) Ta, ta, ta, taratata, ta, ta, Etc.

CLERKS (1) AND STREET-URCHINS, (2): (*blowing whistles, etc.*) Ta, ta, ta, taratata, ta, ta, etc.

MODÈLES, RAPINS: (*encore loin.*) Nina, la pauvre fille, est morte, Etc.

MODELS AND ROWDIES: (*off.*) Nina, poor girl, is dead, etc.

LORETTES et ÉTUDIANTS: (*apparaissent au bout de la place, en monôme, comiquement lugubre.*) Aux larmes, citoyens!

LORETTES AND STUDENTS: (*appearing in single file, with mock solemnity.*) To tears, O citizens!

(*Des Danseuses allant au bal sont entourées par des Commis qui font autour d'elles une ronde endiablée.*)

(*The Women going to the ball are surrounded by the Clerks, who dance around them furiously.*)

LE MAGE: (*bonimentant.*) Entrez, entrez, vous verrex la Beauté! Authentique! . . . sans rivale! . . . Dépêchez-vous! C'est si beau qu'on en pleure! C'est si grand qu'on en meurt! Messieurs et dames! (*Il salue cérémonieusement.*) Entrez! Entrez! (*Les Fées et Sirènes, venant de l'intérieur, font irruption sur l'estrade, suivies du Sonneur et de l'Acolyte.*)

SHOWMAN: (*grandiloquently.*) Come in! Come in! Behold our Beauty! Positively genuine! Unrivalled! Make haste! It is so beautiful, that you will weep! It is so noble that you will want to die! (*Bowing.*) Ladies and Gentlemen, Come in! Come in! (*The Fairies and Sirens, coming from within, burst out on the platform, followed by the Acolyte and the Bell-Ringer.*)

LES FÉES, LES SIRÈNES: Jadis les Sirènes et les Fées Changeaient en Dieux et en Orphées De simples hommes. Leur pouvoir

FAIRIES AND SIRENS: In former times the Sirens and the Nymphs Changed into gods and into Orpheus Your everyday plain men. Their

Est toujours le même . . . Il suffit d'y croire pour avoir A l'instant tout ce qu'on aime!

power Remains the same today. You've only to believe, to have All that you wish for on the minute!

LES GARÇONS: (*criant.*) Voyez terrasse! Versez! Boum! Voilà! . . . ((1) *Les Commis en cache-poussière.* (2) *Les Gavroches en chienlits amusants, quelques pierrots.*)

BOYS: (*shrieking.*) Get on to that! Fill up! Boum! Hello there! ((1) *The Clerks in dust-coats.*) ((2) *The Street-urchins in motley garb, some as Pierrots.*)

LE SONNEUR: (*sur l'estrade.*) Deux sous! Deux sous!

BELL-RINGER: (*on the platform.*) Tuppence! Tuppence!

L'ACOLYTE: Prenez vos places!

ACOLYTE: Take your places!

LORETTES, ÉTUDIANTS, MODÈLES, RAPINS: (*soudainement délirant de gaîté.*) Cloum, catacloum, catacloum, Cloum! Cloum! Ohé! Louisette! Lève ta liquette! Boum, Baïboum, Baïboum, Boum! Boum! Lève ta liquette Bien plus haut que ça! Aussi haut que le font les Pierrettes De Willette! Pas autant que l'osa la Phrynette. De Donnay! Mais aussi gaîment que Marcel Legay Sortant d'un banquet!

LORETTES, STUDENTS, MODELS, ROWDIES: (*wild with mirth.*) Cloum! Catacloum! Catacloum! Cloum! Cloum! Ah there, Louisette! Lift up your leg! Boum! Baïboum! Baïboum! Boum! Boum! Lift up your leg! As high as you can reach! As high as do all the Pierrettes Of Willette! Not so high as dared the Phrynette Of Donnay! But be as jolly as Marcel Legay When he comes from a spread!

JULIEN: (*au bout de la place, encore invisible.*) Hallali! . . . Hallili! . . .

JULIEN: (*at the end of the square, but unseen.*) Hallali! Hallali!

LES FÉES, LES SIRÈNES, LE MAGE: Venez voir la Beauté!

FAIRIES, SIRENS, THE SHOWMAN: Come in! Come see Beauty!

LORETTES et ÉTUDIANTS: (*s'éloignant vers le toboggan.*) Lève ta liquette! (*En scie populaire répétée aux quatre coins de la place. L'attention du public se partage. Des groupes se portent vers Julien, qui s'avance entouré de noceurs du faubourg, beau de gaîté trépidante et farouche. Le plus grand nombre écoute la parade du Théâtre de l'Idéal, où les danseuses ébauchent des danses sacrées, où des cors romantiques semblent saluer l'arrivée de Julien d'un ballali rappelant les fanfares féeriques.*)

LORETTES AND STUDENTS: (*going towards the toboggan-slide.*) Lift up your leg! (*The popular song is repeated from every side. The attention of the crowd is divided. Some go towards Julien, who is surrounded by merrymakers from the neighborhood full of wild and headlong gayety. Most of the Crowd listens to the address before the Theatre of the Ideal, where the dancers perform the sacred dances, where the horns seem to greet Julien with a ballali that recalls the flourishes of the fairy trumpets.*)

JULIEN: (*s'avançant comme triomphalement.*) Hallali! Le vin crapuleux Devient miraculeux! La généreuse absinthe Devient sainte!

JULIEN: (*advancing triumphantly.*) Hallali! The crapulous wine Becomes miraculous! And generous absinthe Becomes a holy thing!

**LES FÉES, LES SIRÈNES, LE MAGE, LE SONNEUR, L'ACOLYTE:** Pour deux sous: la Splendeur du Vrai!
Pour deux ronds: l'Éternité!

**MODÈLES, RAPINS, COMMIS, GAVROCHES:** (*à la Fille qu'ils portent en triomphe.*) Ohé! Louisette!
Lève ta liquette!

**LA FOULE:** (*hilare.*) Y a qu'à Montmartre qu'on rigole comme ca!
C'est inimaginable!
Même les gens les plus minables
S'amusent comme des pachas!
Et sans galette
S'offrent des lippettes
De gala!
(*Apogée du tumulte . . . Julien et sa bande s'assoientt à la terrasse du cabaret. Ils toastent en cadence.*)

**LES NOCEURS:** Hip! Hip! Hourrah!
(*Ils boivent.*)

**LA FOULE:** (*applaudissant.*) Bravo! . . .

**LE MAGE:** (*continuant son boniment, le regard fixé sur Julien.*) Venez à la Beauté!
Mortels infortunés!
La Beauté, pour vos yeux,
Va sa faire plus belle
Que pour des dieux!
(*Bonhomme.*) "Si qu'on" vous la réserve
Cette soeur de Minerve
Qui se rit de Pluton
Et sourit à Platon!
C'est parce que vous êtes
Le contraire des bêtes! . . .

**LA FILLE:** (*dans un groupe, loin de Julien.*) C'est moi la Beauté,
Un peu désenchantée!
(*En confidence, mais de façon à être entendue de Julien.*)
Et c'est lui mon Orphée!
Il ressemble à mon premier
Qu'était un sage . . .
Car il s'en est allé
A la fleur de l'âge!
(*Agressive pour le Mage.*)
Plus sage
Que ce mage,
Il sourit à Pluton
Et se rit de Platon!
(*Elle s'avance vers Julien et rôde autour de lui avec ostentation.*)

**LE MAGE:** Venez à la Beauté!
D'un éternel été
Elle parera vos
Juvéniles cerveaux.

**JULIEN:** (*à ses voisins de table ou plutôt à lui-même, lointain.*) J'ai connu la Beauté
Moins qu'une éternité . . .
(*Rageur.*)
La Beauté n'est qu'un mot

**FAIRIES, SIRENS, THE SHOWMAN, BELL-RINGER, ACOLYTE:** For tuppence: The Splendor of the True!
For tuppence: Eternity!

**MODELS, ROWDIES, CLERKS, STREET-URCHINS:** (*to the Grisette, whom they carry in triumph.*)
Ah there!
Louisette!
Lift up your leg!

**THE CROWD:** (*hilariously.*) It's only in Montmartre we lark like this!
You'd never guess how much!
Even the very proper ones
Amuse themselves like pachas!
Without a penny
They stand a gala treat
To every one!
(*Height of the tumult. Julien and his crowd sit on the terrace of the cabaret and toast the Crowd in cadence.*)

**MERRYMAKERS:** Hip! Hip! Hurrah!
(*They drink.*)

**CROWD:** (*applauding.*) Bravo!

**THE SHOWMAN:** (*Continuing his gabble, his eyes fixed on Julien.*) Come to Beauty!
Unfortunate mortals!
Beauty, for your eyes,
Will make herself more fair
Than for the gods.
(*Ingratiatingly.*)
If "they" reserve for you
That sister of Minerva
Who laughed at Pluto
And smiled at Plato,
It is because you are
The opposite of dull!

**GRISETTE:** (*in a group at a distance from Julien.*) I am your Beauty,
Somewhat disenchanted!
(*In confidence, but so that Julien may hear her.*)
And there's my Orpheus!
He looks like my first love,
Who had good sense—
Because he went
While he was young!
(*Defiantly, to the Showman.*)
And wiser
Than this guy,
He smiled on Pluto
And laughed at Plato!
(*She goes towards Julien and prowls about him ostentatiously.*)

**THE SHOWMAN:** Come to Beauty!
She will adorn
Your youthful wits
With lasting summer!

**JULIEN:** (*to his table-companions, or rather to himself, absently.*) I once met Beauty
Less than an eternity ago—
(*Angrily.*)
Beauty is just a word,—

Et ce mot c'est: mensonge!
(*Le regard de la Fille ne quitte pas Julien dont la curiosité demeure attachée aux gens de la parade.*)

**LE MAGE:** (*aux Étudiants, montrant les cabarets.*)
Fuyex ces gynécées
Déprimants, infertiles,
Qu'ont bâtis vos aînés
Pour que devienne un jour
Ce triomphant faubourg,
Le fabourg des ratés!
(*Approbation.*)

**UN RAPIN:** (*au Mage.*) Raté toi-même!

**UN ÉTUDIANT:** (*La Beauté! C'est un mythe!*)

**UN BOHÈME:** Elle est mangée aux mites!

**UN OUVRIER:** La Beauté! c'est l'amour!

**UNE FILLE:** L'amour? . . .

**LA FILLE:** (*lançant un baiser à Julien.*) Je t'aime!

**LE MAGE:** (*lyrique, tourné vers Julien, joyeux presque.*) Venez à la Beauté,
Mortels infortunés!
La Beauté, pour vos yeux,
Va se faire plus belle
Que pour des dieux!
(*Sa voix éveille en Julien des échos de voix anciennes. Peu à peu celui-ci s'énerve de sentir dans le discours du bateleur un reproche direct à sa déchéance. Brusquement, il se lève, s'adresse à la foule, surprise, puis amusée.*)

**JULIEN:** (*railleur, avec défi, provoquant du regard le Mage.*) O foule,
Sublime et hargneuse foule!
Dont l'énorme gaîté
S'écoule et se déroule . . .
Toi! dont j'entendis s'enfler
Comme une houle
Le rire moqueur . . .
O foule,
Qui déchaînais contre mon coeur
Ton outrage inexorable!
Foule, je viens à toi, faire amende honorable!
(*Applaudissements ironiques et rires.*)
Mes paroles, jadis, n'étaient point de saison!
La vérité réside en ta gaîté bruyante,
Foule grouillante!
Ta folie est pure raison!
(*Le Mage et sa troupe, comme pour lui répondre, frappent sur des gongs et agitent les cloches.*)

**LE MAGE, LES FÉES:** Deux sous: la Splendeur du Vrai!
Deux ronds: l'Éternité!

**JULIEN:** (*narguant la parade, frénétique.*) Bêtes
De somme
Que vous êtes,
Les hommes!
Bêtes de somme que je suis, que

And the word's name is—lie!
(*The Grisette keeps her eyes on Julien, who continues to gaze curiously on the passing show.*)

**THE SHOWMAN:** (*to students, indicating the cabarets.*)
Avoid these female haunts,
Blighting and barren, too!
Your elders built them here,
That one day they might be
This glorious neighborhood
Of down-and-outers!
(*Applause.*)

**ROWDY:** (*to the Showman.*)
Down-and-out yourself!

**A STUDENT:** Beauty!
That's a myth!

**A BOHEMIAN:** She's gnawed by maggots!

**A WORKMAN:** Beauty is Love!

**A GIRL:** Love?

**GRISETTE:** (*throwing a kiss to Julien.*) I love you!

**THE SHOWMAN:** (*in lyric vein, to Julien, almost happy.*) Come to Beauty.
Unfortunate mortals!
Beauty, for your eyes,
Will make herself more fair
Than for the gods!
(*His voice awakes in Julien the echo of former voices. Little by little he is overcome to feel in the mountebank's address a reproach of his decline. Suddenly he rises and addresses the Crowd, that is surprised and then amused.*)

**JULIEN:** (*mocking, defiant; attracting the Showman's attention.*) O Crowd!
Sublime and surly Crowd,
Whose mighty gaiety,
Flows and expands.
O Crowd, that I've seen fill
And rise and swell
With mocking laughs!
O Crowd!
That loosed against my heart
Your deadly outrage!
I come to ask your pardon, Crowd!
(*Ironical applause and laughter.*)
But formerly my words were not in season:
The truth indeed lives in your noisy glee!
O swarming Crowd!
You madness is pure reason!
(*As if in answer, the Showman and his troupe strike their gongs and ring their bells.*)

**SHOWMAN AND FAIRIES:** Tuppence: The Splendor of the True!
Two coins: For Eternity!

**JULIEN:** (*frenziedly.*) Beasts
Of burden
That you are,
You men!
Beast of burden that I am! That we all are!

tous nous sommes!
(*Approbations qui se continuent durant la tirade.*)
Bêtes, vivons comme des bêtes!
Sans évangile!
Et sans remords, lâchons la bride
Aux appétits
Grands et petits,
Qui fermentent dans notre argile!
La vertu, c'est trop fragile!
Le songe,
C'est du mensonge!
Rions,
Crions
A tue-tête.
Partout où le plaisir appelle
Galopons pêle-mêle . . .
Il n'y a plus ni Bien, ni Mal!
L'Homme est mort! Vive l'Animal!
(*La Fille enthousiasmée se jette dans les bras de Julien.*)

**LA FOULE:** Bravo! Bravo!

**LA FILLE:** (*avec une sincérité gouailleuse.*) Bêtes
De somme
Que vous êtes,
Les hommes!
Bêtes de somme
Que je suis, que tous nous sommes . . .
Bêtes,
Vivons comme des bêtes:
Sans évangile . . .
Lâchons la bride
Aux appétits
Qui fermentent dans notre argile!
(*Faisant la nique au Mage.*)
Il n'y a plus ni Bein, ni Mal!
L'Homme est mort: Vive l'Animal!
(*Rumeurs et bravos. Elle entraîne Julien dans le cabaret.*)
Hop! . . . Hop! . . .

## SCÈNE II

*LES PRÉCÉDENTS, sauf JULIEN et LA FILLE, puis D'AUTRES GROUPES DE LA FÊTE, DANSEUSES DU MOULIN-ROUGE.*

*Sortie du Toboggan et du Moulin-Rouge. La Foule de tout à l'heure, de plus en plus agitée, reparaît, faisant cortège aux danseuses du Moulin-Rouge qui s'avancent comme à la parade, saluant de la jambe le public qui s'écarte et applaudit.*)

**GROUPES:** (*riant.*) Hi! Hi!

**GROUPES:** (*gambadant.*) Ho! Ho!

**CHŒUR GÉNÉRAL:** (*en canon.*)
Bêtes de somme
Que nous sommes . . .
Les hommes.
Bêtes, vivons comme des bêtes, etc.
(*Le Mage contemple avec dédain l'orgie populaire. Il salue le mot Bêtes de gestes approbatifs. On le hue.*)

(*Continuous plaudits.*)
Beasts, we'll live like beasts!
Without a gospel
And without remorse, let free the rein
Of appetites
Both great and small,
That ferment in this clay of ours!
Virtue is far too frail,
And dreams
Are only lies!
Let's laugh,
Let's cry,
To split our throats!
Wherever pleasure calls to us,
Let's rush pell-mell!
There is no Good nor Evil!
And Man is dead! Long live the Beast!
(*The Grisette, carried away, throws herself into Julien's arms.*)

**THE CROWD:** Bravo! Bravo!

**GRISETTE:** (*with jesting sincerity.*) Beasts
Of burden
That you are,
You men!
Beast of burden that I am! That we all are!
Beasts!
We'll live like beasts!
Without a gospel
Let free the rein
Of appetites
That ferment in this clay of ours!
(*Making a face at the Showman.*)
There's no more Good or Evil!
And Man is dead!
Long live the Beast!
(*Noise and applause. She drags Julien into the cabaret.*)
Hop!—Hop!

## SCENE II

*THE PRECEDING (except JULIEN and the GRISETTE), then OTHER CARNIVAL GROUPS, DANCERS FROM THE MOULIN-ROUGE.*

*The toboggan-slide and the Moulin-Rouge let out their patrons. The Crowd becomes more and more lively and makes a procession with the dancers from the Moulin-Rouge, who come forward, saluting with their legs the crowd that makes way and applauds.*

**GROUPS:** (*laughing.*) Hi! Hi!

**GROUPS:** (*prancing.*) Ho! Ho!

**GENERAL CHORUS:** Beasts of burden
That we are,
We men!
Beasts, let us live like beasts, etc.
(*The Showman looks disdainfully at this orgy of the people. He bows at the word 'Beasts' with appropriate gestures. He is hissed.*)

**LE MAGE:** (*haussant les épaules.*) Turpitude!
Servitude!
(*Des Noceurs embrassent les Fées de la parade.*)
(*Repoussant les Noceurs.*)
L'âme des bouteilles est leur âme!
Et la flamme des verres, leur flamme!

**LES NOCEURS:** (*le narguant.*) Il n'est rien de vrai,
De sacré
Sur la terre
Que l'ivresse salutaire!
(*Un gavroche va effacer quelques lettres au tableau de façon qu'on lise: Ceci est pour les Bêtes.*)

**UN GROUPE:** A la vie, il n'est aucun lendemain,
Aucun refuge!

**AUTRE GROUPE:** Rions, buvons, la main dans la main!

**TOUS:** (*menaçant la baraque et sa parade.*) Mort à l'Idéal! . . .
A bas les Mages! . . .
(*Ils bombardent le tableau d'oranges et d'ordures.*)

**LE MAGE:** (*les menaçant.*) Barbares!
Bipèdes!

**LES FÉES, LES SIRÈNES:** (*épeurées.*) Ah! voyez! . . . leur imbécile rage . . .

**LA FOULE:** (*en émeute.*) A bas! A bas!
(*Les Commis reparaissent dans le costume des Poètes Déchus du troisième acte. Ils montent à l'assaut de la baraque. Les cafés et les établissements voisins ferment hâtivement.*)

**LES FÉES, LES SIRÈNES:** Bornés! Ratés!
Sauvages!
(*Elles se sauvent à l'intérieur ainsi que les Danseuses. Le Mage essaie furieusement de repousser les assaillants. Il est débordé et doit battre en retraite.*)

**LA FOULE:** (*démolissant.*) Pan! Pan! Pan! Pan!
(*Sous la poussée des énergumènes, la façade du théâtre s'ébranle et s'écroule avec fracas. La foule épouvantée fuit dans tous les sens. Obscurité subite.*)

## SCÈNE III

**LA FILLE:** (*dans le cabaret, riant.*) Ah! Ah! Ah!
La, la, la, la, la,
Hop!! Hop!!
Ah!
Hop! Hop!
Ah!
(*Elle apparaît, suivie de Julien, sur le seuil du cabaret.*)

**THE SHOWMAN:** (*shrugging his shoulders.*) Turpitude!
Servitude!
(*The Merrymakers kiss the Fairies. He pushes them away.*)
The soul of bottles is their soul!
The fire of goblets is their flame!

**MERRYMAKERS:** (*scoffing.*)
There's nothing that's true,
Or sacred
On earth
But wholesome drunkenness!
(*A Street-urchin rubs some letters from the picture on the wall, making it read: "It is a show for dunces.)"*

**A GROUP:** In life there is no morning after,
And no appeal!

**ANOTHER GROUP:** Hand in hand, let's laugh and drink!

**ALL:** (*threatening the theatre and its show.*) Death to the Ideal!
Down with the mountebanks!
(*They bombard the picture with oranges and rubbish!*)

**SHOWMAN:** (*threateningly.*) Barbarians!
Loafers!

**FAIRIES AND SIRENS:** (*scared.*) O look there!—Their silly rage!

**THE CROWD:** (*infuriated.*) Down with him!
Down with him!
(*The Clerks reappear, dressed as the Hapless Poets of Act III. They climb up to attack the booth. The cabaret and other establishments shut up hastily.*)

**FAIRIES AND SIRENS:** Donkeys! Has-beens!
Swine!
(*They escape inside, as do the dancers. The Showman tries desperately to drive back his assailants. He is overcome and beats a retreat.*)

**THE CROWD:** (*demolishing.*)
Bang! bang! Go hang!
(*The front of the theatre totters and falls with a crash. The Crowd takes to its heels in all directions. Sudden darkness.*)

## SCENE III

*The GRISETTE.*

**THE GRISETTE:** (*laughing in the cabaret.*) Ha! Ha! Ha!
La, la, la la!
Hop! Hop!
Ah!
Hop! Hop!
Ah!
(*She comes to the door of the cabaret, followed by Julien.*)

## SCÈNE IV

*JULIEN, LA FILLE, LA FOULE DU TEMPLE.*

*Julien et la Fille, ivres, sortent du cabaret. Ils regardent d'un oeil vague le désordre de la place. Soudain, Julien sursaute . . . Il lui semble que dans l'ombre du théâtre écroulé des voix chantent, comme jadis chantaient les Pèlerins du Rêve . . . Une lueur mystérieuse envahit tout le fond. Le Temple apparaît peu à peu.*

**JULIEN:** (*avec stupeur.*) Là-bas . . . on dirait . . . des choses . . . déjà vues . . . dans ma jeunesse . . .
Je rêve encore . . . Ces chants? . . . (*Les reconnaissant, il crie*) Oui!
(*Comme brûlé par le souvenir.*) Ah!
(*Pressant sa poitrine à mains crispées.*) Ça fait mal!
(*Il sanglote.*)

**VOIX LOINTAINES D'AUTREFOIS:** Douce lumière, Vers toi s'envole ma prière . . . etc.
(*La vision grandit. Le temple du Rêve se dresse tout vibrant de chants et de chants et de lumières.*)

**JULIEN:** (*à la Fille, se raccrochant à la rélité comme à une épave.*) Trille, O Fille! . . . Chante, Bacchante! . . .

## SCENE IV

*JULIEN, the GRISETTE, the THRONG of the TEMPLE.*

*Julien and the Grisette, both intoxicated, come out of the cabaret. They look about vacantly at the disorder of the place. Suddenly Julien starts—it seems to him that in the shadow of the ruined theatre voices are singing, as in other days the Dream-Pilgrims sang. A mysterious light fills the back of the stage. The Temple is gradually discovered.*

**JULIEN:** (*dazed.*) Out there—I see the—things—I've seen—when I was young!
Do I dream now—Those songs?—
(*He recognizes them and cries:*) Yes!
(*As if stabbed by a memory.*) Ah!
(*Pressing his breast with his clenched hands.*) It hurts!
(*He sobs.*)

**DISTANT VOICES OF OTHER DAYS:** O tender radiance, My prayer will ever rise to you, etc.
(*The vision grows clearer. The Temple of Dreams rises, alive with music and lights.*)

**JULIEN:** (*to the Grisette, clinging to reality as to a spar.*) O sing You thing! And chant, Bacchante!

**LES VOIX DU TEMPLE:** (*formidables.*) O flamme immense, Accable-moi de ta puissance! . . . etc.

**LA FILLE:** (*riant de la tête que fait Julien.*) Ha! Ha! Ha!
(*Elle s'affale sur un banc . . .* )

**JULIEN:** (*délirant.*) Trille, O Fille En guenille (1) Ton rire fou.
(*La vision disparaît. Nuit épaisse.*)
Chante, Bacchante, Délirante, Que je suis saoul! . . . Rogne, Besogne, Ma charogne! . . . (2) Gentil démon! Vide, Avide Et livide, Jusques au fond! . . .
(*Trébuchant.*)
Sèves Et rêves, Coeurs Et pleurs! . . .

**LA FILLE:** (*sur le banc.*) Ha! Ha! Ha!

**JULIEN:** Pleurs . . .
(*Il s'écroule aux pieds de la Fille.*)

**VOIX LOINTAINES:** Ah!
(*Plaintivement.*)
Ah!
Ah!

*RIDEAU.*

((1) Variante: *Éparpille.*)
((2) Variante: *Sans vergogne.*)

**VOICES OF THE TEMPLE:** O Fire Divine!
Overwhelm me with your power—etc.

**GRISETTE:** (*laughing at Julien's expression.*) Ha, ha, ha!
(*Throws herself on a bench.*)

**JULIEN:** (*deliriously.*) O sing You thing And throw like chaff Your silly laugh!
(*The vision vanishes. Dark night.*)
O chant Bacchante! In a funk! Oh, but I'm drunk! Defame, O shame! My corpse! Kind devil, I'm needy, You're greedy, Be speedy—Until I am gone!
(*Stumbling.*)
Screams And dreams! Fears And tears!

**GRISETTE:** (*from the bench.*) Ha! Ha! Ha!

**JULIEN:** Tears!
(*He collapses at her feet.*)

**DISTANT VOICES:** Ah!
(*Wailing.*)
Ah! Ah!

*CURTAIN*

# Il Maestro di Cappella (1790)

## The Choir-Leader

MUSIC BY DOMENICO CIMAROSA

This short work, in one movement, was intended possibly as an intermezzo giocoso, humorous cantata, or aria buffa to be performed between acts of an opera seria. It follows in a tradition of parodies of music professors, music directors, presenters/impresarios and prima donnas to be found in works of the 18th century. It is scored for solo baritone, flute, oboes, bassoons, horns and strings. The Music Director states that he is singing an aria for everyone to hear, and he is also directing the orchestra in a rehearsal. But the musicians show a distinct lack of discipline, starting with the oboes entering at the wrong time, followed by the basses doing the same thing. He shows that the violins must play their passage in a certain manner and begs that they do it right. Then the violas and flutes are the next ones to mess up the works. He loses patience with everyone, and he pleads with them to pay attention to what he is saying. He demonstrates each line, imitating the melodies of each instrument, until at last he succeeds in getting them to play together correctly. He commends each section and is finally consoled by their beautiful playing. He repeats this same exercise in a different piece, an Allegro. At the end, he thanks them and promises to present them in the next season with an Andante, Allego e Presto "that a first-rate talent could never imitate".

---

## ◼ Atto Unico

*Un appartamento ammobigliato modestamente.—Nel fondo un caminetto con orologio.—Due usci, uno di prospetto, l'altro di fianco.—Una tavola a sinistra.—Un cembalo a destra, nel fondo.*

### Scena Prima

*GELTRUDE sola, in atto di preparare la tavola.*

**GELTRUDE:** Ah! quel maestro! gli è venuto in mente
D'invitar suo nipote a desinare . . .
Quel noioso Benetto, e per di più
Vuol che gli canti un certo suo duetto . . .
Io che so appena canticchiar il *Credo*!
È matto! . . . da una parte far *Cleopatra*,
È da quell'altra far andar lo spiedo!

### Scena II

*BARNABA, BENETTO e GELTRUDE.*

**BARNABA:** Ma ti par, cara mia?
Lasciar la casa
Aperta, a questi lumi
Di luna? Se mi rubano *Cleopatra*!

**GELTRUDE:** Piove che Dio la manda!

**BARNABA:** Eh! ma mon conti
I francesi?

## ◼ Act I

*A modestly furnished apartment. — In the rear, a mantel with a clock. — Two doors, one in the front view and the other at the side. — A table to the left. — To the right, a cymbal, in the background.*

### Scene I

*GELTRUDE, alone, setting the table.*

**GELTRUDE:** Oh, that teacher! he has taken into his head
To invite his neighbor to dinner—
That boresome Benetto, and what's more,
He wants me to sing one of his duets—
I, who can hardly hum through the *Credo*!
He is mad! On the one hand to sing the *Cleopatra*.
And on the other to turn the spit!

### Scene II

*BARNABA, BENETTO and GELTRUDE.*

**BARNABA:** Do you think it's right, my dear, to leave the house
Open to the light
Of the moon? If they should steal my Cleopatra!

**GELTRUDE:** It's raining cats and dogs!

**BARNABA:** What! Don't you count the Frenchmen?

---

**BENETTO:** I francesi? Ah ci scommetto,
Zio, che a voi fan paura!

**BARNABA:** E a te?

**BENETTO:** Chi ha visto . . .

**BARNABA:** Che cosa?

**BENETTO:** Faccia a faccia . . . corpo a corpo . . .

**BARNABA:** Ma che cosa?

**BENETTO:** Il Vesuvio!

**BARNABA:** Bella bravura! Io . . . come tu mi vedi . . . Senza ombrello . . . sfidato ho . . . Giove Pluvio!

**GELTRUDE:** Udite quel rumor?

**BARNABA e BENETTO:** Zitti! che mai sarà?

**GELTRUDE:** Ma nol sentite ancor?
Son Francesi che fan chiasso . . .
Nelle case penetrar
E d'ogni erba un fascio far,
Quando è notte, è il loro spasso!
Quando è notte, è il loro spasso!

**GLI ALTRI DUE:** (*guardandosi l'un l'altro*). Son Francesi che fan chiasso . . .
Nelle case penetrar
E d'ogni erba un fascio far,
Quandro è notte, è il loro spasso!

**GELTRUDE:** Non sentite là il cannon? Pon, pon, pon!

**I DUE:** Questo è il rombo del cannon! Pon, pon, pon!

---

**BENETTO:** The Frenchmen? I can wager
That they frighten you!

**BARNABA:** And you?

**BENETTO:** He who has seen—

**BARNABA:** What?

**BENETTO:** Face to face, body to body—

**BARNABA:** But what?

**BENETTO:** Vesuvius!

**BARNABA:** Fine bravery! I, as you see me—
Without an umbrella—have defied Rainy Jupiter!

**GELTRUDE:** Do you hear that noise?

**BARNABA and BENETTO:** What can it be?

**GELTRUDE:** But don't you hear it?
They are Frenchmen who are making an uproar—
To penetrate the houses
And to make a bundle of all the grass,
At night, it's their pastime!

**THE OTHER TWO:** (*looking at each other*). They are Frenchmen who are making an uproar—
To penetrate the houses
And to make a bundle of all the grass,
At night, it's their pastime!

**GELTRUDE:** Don't you hear the cannon?
Bang, bang, bang!

**THE TWO:** It's the roar of the cannon!
Bang, bang, bang!

# Act I, Scene II

GELTRUDE: E quest'altra è proprio tromba!
Una squilla e l'altro romba!

I DUE: All'inferno anche la tromba!

GELTRUDE: (*imitando la tromba*). Tara ta ta, tara ta!
Or vedremo il mio padrone
Come esponga il petto ignudo,
In sì orribil occasione!

BARNABA: In cantina io mi richiudo . . .

BENETTO: L'orme vostre io seguirò . . .
Di lasciarvi il cor non ho!

BARNABA: Tremi troppo! io non ti vo'!
Siamo andati! a ognun in volto
Vedo nascere il pallor;
E quantunque io valga, e molto,
Sento in core un gran terror!

BENETTO: Persi siam! a ognuno in volto
Vedo nascer il pallor!
E, benchè sia prode e molto,
Sento in petto un gran terror!

GELTRUDE: (*additando BENETTO*). Al veder su quella faccia
La tristezza ed il pallor,
Il coraggio che ei minaccia,
Mi fa rider di gran cor!
(*Mettendosi a ridere allegramente.*)
Ah! riuscita è la burletta!
Voi mi fate sgansaciar!

BARNABA e BENETTO: Che pretendi dir, fraschetta?
Ci hai tu presi a canzonar?

GELTRUDE: Perchè dir dovrei di no?

BARNABA e BENETTO: (*alternandosi*) Che? lo squillo del claron . . .
Come? il rombo del cannon . . .
La pesante artiglieria?

GELTRUDE: Tutto vol di fantasia!

BENETTO: M'hai voluto spaventar,
Ma hai perduto il tuo sapone . . .

GELTRUDE: Anche un miglio da lontano
L'ardimento vostro appar!

BENETTO: Se si tratta di pugnar
Ho un coraggio da leone!

BARNABA: Grazie al cielo, pel momento
È passata l'occasione!

BENETTO e BARNABA: La non può finir così!
Della burla, o rea fraschetta,
Pria che vada a monte il dì,
Voglio trar crudel vendetta!

---

GELTRUDE: And that other is the trumpet!
The one roars and the other rumbles!

THE TWO: To the devil with the trumpet!

GELTRUDE: (*imitates the trumpet*). Tara ta ta, tara ta!
Now let us see my master,
How he bears his breast,
On such a terrible occasion!

BARNABA: I'll lock myself in the cellar—

BENETTO: I'll follow your footsteps—
I haven't the heart to leave you!

BARNABA: You tremble too much! I don't want you!
Let us go! I see every one's face grow pale;
And however much I try,
And more, still I feel awful terror in my breast.

BENETTO: We are lost! I see every one's face
Grow pale! And, though I am brave,
I feel awful terror in my heart!

GELTRUDE: (*pointing to BENETTO*). In seeing that face
Sad and pale,
The courage which he musters up
Makes me laugh!
(*Beginning to laugh joyfully.*)
Ah, the joke worked well!
You make me burst with laughter!

BARNABA and BENETTO: What do you mean, you fool?
Have you taken to jesting?

GELTRUDE: Why should I say no?

BARNABA and BENETTO: (*in turn*). What? The sound of the horns—
What? The war of cannon—
The heavy artillery?

GELTRUDE: All flights of fancy!

BENETTO: You wanted to frighten us,
But your trick failed—

GELTRUDE: One could see your excitement
A mile off!

BENETTO: When it comes to fighting,
I have the courage of a lion!

BARNABA: Thank heaven that for the
Moment, the opportunity has passed!

BENETTO and BARNABA: One can't let her off so easily!
For this jest, oh, wicked rogue,
Before the day goes behind the mountain
I'll take cruel vengeance on you!

---

GELTRUDE: Perdonare, miei signor.
Non vi spiaccia la burletta!
Una celia, se ha sapor,
Non è degna di vendetta!

BARNABA: Ma il nostro pranzo?

GELTRUDE: È pronto.

BARNABA: E la tacchina . . .
E il duetto?

GELTRUDE: Allo spiedo!

BARNABA: Ah! malandrina!
Anche Cleopatra arrosto!

GELTRUDE: Eh! nossignore!

BARNABA: Meno mal! . . . Vieni qua . . . Senti, Benetto,
Val dal curato a chiedergli
Una di quelle sue certe bottiglie . . .
Fra una mezz'ora, al più tardi, ti aspetto!
(*BENETTO esce dall'uscio di prospetto: GELTRUDE da quello di fianco.*)

## Scena III

*BARNABA, solo.*

BARNABA: Approfittiam di questo quarto d'ora
Per ripassar le pagine sublimi
Dell'opera e del salmo . . .
Ma incominciam da quella . . .
Mi par già di vedermi
Incipriato e in abito di gala
Chiamato alla ribalta della Scala!
Oh! qual piacer di pregustar la gloria!
Fra il nuovo De-profundis,
E l'opera che fo,
Insediato io m'ho
Fra i Dei con la Vittoria!
L'orchestra udir mi par
Gli accordi modular!
Con un *Tutti* maestoso
La sinfonia comincia . . .
Ivi i fagotti gemono
(*imita il fagotto*).
Là sospirano i corni . . .
(*li imita*).
D'una regina in lagrime
La mesta melodia
Annuncia la presenza!
Ad imitar l'incanto seduttor,
Ispirami, Cleopatra, alma Sirena!
Del labbro tuo mi distilla l'ardor,
Ed otterò le palme della scena!
Ella compar . . . un superbo larghetto
Pinge lo stato del trepido core . . .
Poche battute ancora e l'allegretto
Ne scolpisce l'amore!
Ogni palpito di lei
E dal timpano imitato . . .
Pan . . . pan . . . pan . . . pan . . .
Ella vede il suo bello arrivar?
Ed in flauto vel fa divinar!
(*Imita il flauto.*)
Esprimo i lor sospir,
I fervidi desir,

---

GELTRUDE: Pardon me, sirs,
Let this jest not anger you!
A joke, if there is a point to it,
Does not deserve vengeance!

BARNABA: But our meal?

GELTRUDE: It is ready.

BARNABA: And the turkey—
And the duet?

GELTRUDE: To the spit!

BARNABA: Ah! you rogue!
And Cleopatra roasted, too?

GELTRUDE: Oh! No, sir!

BARNABA: That's good. Come here. Listen, Benetto,
Go to the curate and ask him
For one of those bottles of his—
I'll expect you in a half an hour, at the latest!
(*BENETTO goes out of the front door: GELTRUDE out of the side.*)

## Scene III

*BARNABA, alone.*

BARNABA: Let us profit by this quarter of an hour
In going over the sublime pages
Of the opera and of the psalm—
But let us begin by that—
I can already see myself
In holiday attire
Called to the foot-lights of the Scala!
Oh! what pleasure to taste glory!
Between the new De-profundis
And the work which was before,
I have placed myself
Between the gods with Victory!
I seem to hear the harmonies
Of the orchestra.
With a sad *Tutti*
The symphony begins—
Then the bassoons sob
(*imitates the bassoons*).
There the horns sigh—
(*imitates them*).
The sad melody
Announces the presence
Of a queen in tears!
Inspire me, Cleopatra, benign Siren,
To imitate the seducing charm!
Distil for me the passion of your lips,
And I shall obtain the palm of the stage!
She appears—a proud *larghetto*
Depicts the state of her trembling heart—
A few more beats and the *allegretto*
Will pronounce her love!
Every trembling of hers
Is imitated by the tabour—
Pan—pan—pan—pan.
Does she see her loved one coming?
The flute makes her guess it!
(*Imitates the flute.*)
I express their sighs,

|  |  |
|---|---|
| Nel mentre degli amor<br>La leggera coorte<br>Danza intorne di lor!<br>(*Si mette a ballare.*)<br>Ma . . . rea fatalità,<br>Quasi peggior di monte!<br>Marc' Antonio soccombe<br>Al tetro suo destin<br>Ed il tam-tam re annuncia l'atra fin!<br>Cleopatra allor delira<br>E sul suo corpo si dispera e spira!<br>Ed il pubblico, commosso<br>A spettacolo sì grande,<br>Mi applaudisce a più nn posso,<br>Mi tempesta di ghirlande,<br>E trottar a vol mi fa<br>Per la gran posterità!<br>(*Si odono dei fischi.*)<br>Ma . . . chi sibila . . . chi la-tra?<br>Questo strepito che è?<br>Forse fischi contro me?<br>No — è il serpente di Cleopatra.<br>Ma invano, invan si vuol dai vili ar-mar<br>Avverso ai grandi l'aspide invidio-so!<br>Di fischi e d'urli in mezzo al tempestar,<br>Sa il vero genio uscir vittorioso!<br>(*Chiamando.*)<br>Geltrude, Geltrude! | Their fervid desires,<br>In the midst of their love<br>The light cohort<br>Dances around them!<br>(*Begins to dance.*)<br>But—evil fate,<br>Almost worse than death!<br>Marc Antony succumbs<br>To his bitter destiny<br>And the tam-tam announces the dreadful end!<br>Then Cleopatra raves<br>And on his body she despairs and expires!<br>And the public, moved<br>At so great a spectacle,<br>Applauds me to its utmost,<br>Showers garlands upon me<br>And sets my fame flying<br>Through posterity!<br>(*Hisses are heard.*)<br>But—who whistles, who barks?<br>What noise is that?<br>Are those hisses for me?<br>No—it is Cleopatra's serpent.<br>But in vain, in vain does the jealous snake<br>Want to arm itself with the evil ones against me.<br>The true genius is able to come great and victorious<br>Out of the hisses and cries in the midst of the tempest!<br>(*Calling.*)<br>Geltrude, Geltrude! |

## Scena IV / Scene IV

|  |  |
|---|---|
| *GELTRUDE e detto.* | *GELTRUDE and above.* |
| **BARNABA:** Stavi forse studiando i tuoi francesi? | **BARNABA:** Were you studying your Frenchmen? |
| **GELTRUDE:** E perchè no? son pur miei patrioti! . . . | **GELTRUDE:** Why not? They are my compatriots! |
| **BARNABA:** Come sarebbe a dir? | **BARNABA:** And how is that? |
| **GELTRUDE:** Son Savojarda! | **GELTRUDE:** I am a Savoyarde. |
| **BARNABA:** (*con sussiego*). La tua patria, mia cara, è . . . la leccar-da. | **BARNABA:** (*seriously*). Your country, my dear, is—the dripping pan. |
| **GELTRUDE:** (*erigendosi*). Grazie davvero! | **GELTRUDE:** (*straightening up*). Many thanks! |
| **BARNABA:** Ah! fra i piccanti intin-goli<br>El il velluto della tua vocina,<br>Vorrei . . . vorrei . . . | **BARNABA:** Ah! You are such a dear,<br>That, twixt the piquant stews<br>And the velvet of your little voice,<br>I should like—I should like— |
| **GELTRUDE:** Sentiamo! . . . | **GELTRUDE:** Listen! |
| **BARNABA:** Intenderti e mangiarti notte e giorno! . . .<br>(*Fa atto di morderla.*) | **BARNABA:** To hear you and eat you night and day!<br>(*Pretends to bite her.*) |
| **GELTRUDE:** Padron, le gira! | **GELTRUDE:** Master, look out! |
| **BARNABA:** Non lo sai che t'amo!<br>Vieni al cembalo, vien! cara e pro-viamo. | **BARNABA:** Don't you know that I love you!<br>Go to the cymbal, go, dear, and let us try. |
| **GELTRUDE:** Cantar? Invero, che questa è bella!<br>In italiano? . . . se non lo so! | **GELTRUDE:** To sing? Indeed, that's fine!<br>In Italian—and if I don't know it! |
| **BARNABA:** Tel vo' insegnar, o cattivella,<br>Sol devi fare com'io farò! | **BARNABA:** I'll teach you, little rascal,<br>But you must do as I tell you! |
| **GELTRUDE:** Ebben! proviamolo questo duetto . . .<br>Lo zelo mio vi vo' mostrar!<br>(*Comincia a cantare.*) | **GELTRUDE:** Well then, let's try this duet:<br>My ardor will teach you!<br>(*Begins to sing.*) |
| **BARNABA:** C'è il ritornello e poi l'aspetto<br>L'a solo tuo pria d'attaccar!<br>(*Canta il ritornello.*) | **BARNABA:** There is the refrain and then the pause—<br>You a *solo* before beginning!<br>(*Sings the refrain.*) |
| **GELTRUDE:** Ma . . . padron, che mai farà<br>Quella povera regina,<br>Sin che il lungo ritornello<br>La cadenza non combina? | **GELTRUDE:** But, master, what will<br>That poor queen do,<br>Until the long refrain<br>Will combine with the cadence? |
| **BARNABA:** Eh! anche lei passegg-erà,<br>Ruminando nel cervello,<br>Come all'Opera si fa!<br>(*Cammina maestosamente agi-tando il fazzoletto che tiene in mano.*) | **BARNABA:** Ah! She'll pace up and down,<br>Thinking it over,<br>As they do at the opera!<br>(*Walks sadly pulling at a band-kerchief which he holds in his hand.*) |
| **GELTRUDE:** Sta ben! sta ben! | **GELTRUDE:** That's good! That's fine! |
| **BARNABA:** Comincia! il tempo stringe! | **BARNABA:** Begin! It's high time. |
| **GERTRUDE:** (*storpiando gli ac-centi*).<br>"Perchè crudel, o Dio,<br>Rapirmi il caro ben?" | **GERTRUDE:** (*accents incorrect-ly*). "Why, O cruel God,<br>To deprive me of my beloved?" |
| **BARNABA:** Ahimè! no — no — così non va<br>Tu dèi badar — com'io pronunzio! | **BARNABA:** Alas,—no, that's not right,<br>You must listen to how I pro-nounce! |
| **GELTRUDE:** Ma se lo so che non mi sta! . . .<br>A proseguire omai rinunzio! | **GELTRUDE:** But if I know that it's not for me!<br>I refuse to go on! |
| **BARNABA:** Non t'inquietare! vien dietro a me<br>E senza sforzo vedrai che canti!<br>"Perchè crudel, o Dio,<br>Rapirmi il caro ben?" | **BARNABA:** Don't get confused!<br>Come behind me<br>And you'll see that you'll sing with-out effort.<br>"Why, cruel God<br>To deprive me of my beloved?" |
| **GELTRUDE:** (*senza sbagliare gli accenti*).<br>"Perchè crudel, o Dio,<br>Rapirmi il caro ben?" | **GELTRUDE:** (*accenting correct-ly*). "Why, cruel God<br>To deprive me of my beloved?" |
| **BARNABA:** Bene! benissimo! in fede mia<br>Hai bene espresso il sentimento,<br>Ma . . . un pò di spasimo, dell'energia,<br>Quasi il delirio! | **BARNABA:** Good! Fine! By my faith<br>You have well expressed my feel-ings,<br>But a little more sobbing, more en-ergy,<br>As if in a delirium! |
| **GELTRUDE:** Ah! vi comprendo . . .<br>Espresso meglio il gran tormento!<br>"In quel funesto addio<br>Voglio morir almen!"<br>(*Torna a sbagliare gli accenti.*) | **GELTRUDE:** Ah! I understand you—<br>I express great torments!<br>"In this fatal farewell<br>I at least want to die!"<br>(*Accents incorrectly.*) |
| **BARNABA:** Ma Geltrude, me Gel-trude,<br>Siamo fuor di careggiata! | **BARNABA:** But Geltrude, my Gel-trude,<br>You are all wrong! |
| **GELTRUDE:** Son parole troppo crude,<br>È una frase indiavolata! | **GELTRUDE:** Your words are too cruel,<br>It is a fiendish phrase! |
| **BARNABA:** La imparerai — ten do mia fè . . .<br>La imparerai — vien dietro a me! | **BARNABA:** You'll learn it—by my faith<br>You'll learn it—come behind me. |
| **A DUE:** "In quel funesto addio<br>Voglio morire insiem!" | **BOTH:** "In this fatal farewell<br>Let us die together." |

## Act I, Scene IV

**BARNABA:** Non si può aver, in fede,
Più spirito di te!
E, a ringraziarti, lascia ch'io t'abbracci!

**GELTRUDE:** Padron, no, no, di grazia . . .
E troppo onor per me!
Non siamo qui per coniugar l' "io t'amo!"

**BARNABA:** One can't have more Spirit than you!
And to thank you, let me embrace you.

**GELTRUDE:** Master, no, please don't—
It's too much honor for me!
We're not here to conjugate "I love."

**BARNABA:** Insieme, a due, mia cara, allor cantiamo!

**BARNABA e GELTRUDE:** "O barbaro momento!
Nell'anima mi sento
Furiosa una tempesta
Che mi solleva il cor!
Pietà, stella funesta,
Pietà di tanto amor!"

*FINE.*

**BARNABA:** Together, my dear, let us sing!

**BARNABA and GELTRUDE:** "O barbarous moment!
I feel
A furious tempest in my breast.
Excites my heart.
Pity, O fatal star,
Pity so much love!"

*END.*

# Pelléas et Mélisande (1902)

## Pelleas and Melisande

MUSIC BY CLAUDE DEBUSSY ■ LIBRETTO BY MAURICE MAETERLINCK

*Pelléas et Mélisande*, set to a libretto based on Maurice Maeterlinck's play, premiered at the Opéra-Comique in Paris on April 30, 1902. In Allemonde, an imaginary kingdom, during an imaginary time. Golaud, grandson of King Arkel, comes upon a beautiful, crying young girl in the forest. She doesn't recall anything about herself except her name, Mélisande. He writes to his blind father, King Arkel, asking for permission to bring home his new bride, Mélisande. He will arrive in three days and will look for a lit lamp up in the tower as a sign that he may come. Arkel gives his consent- Golaud's first wife has died and left him with a young son, Yniold, who needs a mother. On a stormy night, Pelléas escorts Mélisande on the castle, while Golaud goes to find his son. At the edge of an old fountain whose waters supposedly cure blindness Mélisande toys with her wedding band, which slips off her finger into the water. While tending to Golaud's hunting injuries Mèlisande has a premonition. Taking her hand in his to comfort her, Golaud sees that her ring is missing; she tells him that she lost it in a seaside cave. He insists that she look for it immediately, accompanied by Pelléas, for it is already dark. In the castle tower Mélisande lets down her hair à la Rapunzel and sings at her window. Pelléas is spellbound. She leans out to give him her hand and he is completely surrounded by her hair. Golaud, who witnessed this event, tells Pelléas that he must not see Mélisande any longer. Goland asks his son about how Pelléas and Mélisande act with each other and lifts up Yniold so he can watch through a window. Yniold says that they are doing and saying nothing, and he begins to cry in fright. Pelléas, who has decided to leave, begs his beloved to meet him one final time at the fountain. Golaud comes upon them and drags his wife off by the hair. Yniold is looking for a golden ball he has dropped by the fountain, and Pelléas and Mélisande appear as if pre-ordained. They swear their love for each other and embrace for the first and only time. Watching from behind the scenes, Golaud confronts the lovers, first killing his brother, then chasing his petrified wife. Poor Mèlisande, who has just given birth to a baby daughter, is dying. Golaud, in total despair, demands to know whether she has been faithful to him. She dies without saying a word.

---

## ■ ACTE I.

### SCENE I.

*(Un forêt. On découvre Mélisande au bord d'une fontaine.—Entre Golaud).*

**GOLAUD:** Je ne pourrai plus sortir de cette forêt.—
Dieu sait jusqu'où cette bête m'a mené.
Je croyais cependant l'avoir blessée à mort; et voici des traces de sang.
Mais maintenant, je l'ai perdue de vue; je crois que je me suis perdu moi-même—et mes chiens ne me retrouvent plus—je vais revenir sur mes pas . . . —
J'entends pleurer . . .
Oh! oh! qu'y a-t-il là au bord de l'eau?
Une petite fille qui pleure au bord de l'eau?
*(Il tousse.)*—
Elle ne m'entend pas.
Je ne vois pas son visage.
*(Il s'approche et touche Mélisande à l'épaule.)*
Pour-quoi pleures-tu?
*(Mélisande tressaille, se dresse et veut fuir.)*—
N'ayez pas peur.
Vous n'avez rien à craindre. Pour-quoi pleurez-vous ici toute seule?

**MÉLISANDE:** Ne me touchez pas! ne me touchez pas!

**GOLAUD:** N'ayez pas peur . . .
Je ne vous ferai pas . . .
Oh! vous êtes belle!

**MÉLISANDE:** Ne me touchez pas! Ne me touchez pas! ou je me jette à l'eau! . . .

**GOLAUD:** Je ne vous touches pas . . .
Voyez, je resterai ici, contre l'arbre.
N'ayez pas peur.
Quelqu'un vous a-t-il fait du mal?

**MÉLISANDE:** Oh! oui! oui, oui! . . .
*(Elle sanglote profondément).*

**GOLAUD:** Qui est-ce qui vous a fait du mal?

**MÉLISANDE:** Tous! tous!

**GOLAUD:** Quel mal vous a-t-on fait?

**MÉLISANDE:** Je ne veux pas le dire! je ne peux pas le dire! . . .

**GOLAUD:** Voyons; ne pleurez pas ainsi. D'où venez-vous?

## ■ ACT I.

### SCENE I.

*Melisande discovered on the edge of a fountain.—Enter Golaud.*

**Golaud:** I shall not be able to leave this forest again.
God knows how far this beast has led me.
Yet I thought I had wounded it to death; and here are traces of blood.
But now, I have lost sight of it.
I fear that I am lost myself—and my dogs no longer find me.
I shall retrace my steps . . .
I hear weeping . . .
Oh, oh, what is it there by the water? . . .
A little girl who weeps near the water?
*(He coughs.)*
She does not hear me.
I do not see her face.
*(He goes near and touches Melisande on the shoulder.)*
Why do you weep?
*(Melisande rises, trembles and wants to fly.)*
Do not fear.
You have nothing to be afraid of.
Why do you weep here all alone?

**MÉLISANDE:** Do not touch me! do not touch me!

**GOLAUD:** Have no fear
I will do you no . . .
Oh, you are beautiful!

**MÉLISANDE:** Do not touch me!
Do not touch me! or I shall throw myself in the water . . .

**GOLAUD:** I do not touch you . . .
See, I'll stay here, against the tree.
Have no fear.
Has any one hurt you?

**MÉLISANDE:** Oh, yes, yes, yes!
*(She weeps profoundly.)*

**GOLAUD:** Who has done you harm?

**MÉLISANDE:** All, all!

**GOLAUD:** What harm has been done to you?

**MÉLISANDE:** I will not say it.
I cannot say it.

**GOLAUD:** Come; do not weep thus.
Where do you come from?

**MÉLISANDE:** Je me suis enfuie . . . enfuie, enfuie!

**GOLAUD:** Oui; mais d'où vous êtes-vous enfuie?

**MÉLISANDE:** Je suis perdue! . . . perdue ici . . .
Je ne suis pas d'ici . . .
Je ne suis pas née là . . .

**GOLAUD:** D'où êtes-vous?
Où êtes-vous née?

**MÉLISANDE:** Oh! oh! loin d'ici . . . loin . . . loin

**GOLAUD:** Qu'est-ce qui brille ainsi au fond de l'eau?

**MÉLISANDE:** Où donc?—
Ah! c'est la couronne qu'il m'a donnée.
Elle est tombée en pleurant.

**GOLAUD:** Une couronne?—
Qui est-ce qui vous a donné une couronne?
Je vais essayer de la prendre . . .

**MÉLISANDE:** Non, non; je n'en veux plus!
Je n'en veux plus!
Je préfère mourir tout de suite . . .

**GOLAUD:** Je pourrais la retirer facilement.
L'eau n'est pas très profonde.

**MÉLISANDE:** Je n'en veux plus!
Si vous la retirez, je me jette à sa place! . . .

**GOLAUD:** Non, non; je la laisserai là; on pourrait la prendre sans peine cependant.
Elle semble très belle.
Y a-t-il longtemps que vous avez fui?

**MÉLISANDE:** Qui, oui . . . qui êtes-vous?

**GOLAUD:** Je suis le prince Golaud—le petit-fils d'Arkël, le vieux roi d'Allemonde . . .

**MÉLISANDE:** Oh! vous avez déjà les cheveux gris . . .

**GOLAUD:** Oui; quelques-uns, ici, près des tempes . . .

**MÉLISANDE:** Et la barbe aussi . . .
Pourquoi me regardez-vous ainsi?

**GOLAUD:** Je regarde vos yeux.—
Vous ne ferme jamais les yeux?

**MÉLISANDE:** Si, si; je les ferme la nuit . . .

**GOLAUD:** Pourquoi avez-vous l'air si étonné?

**MÉLISANDE:** Vous êtes un géant?

**GOLAUD:** Je suis un homme comme les autres . . .

**MÉLISANDE:** Pourquoi êtes-vous venu ici?

**MELISANDE:** I escaped, escaped, escaped!

**GOLAUD:** Yes; but from where did you escape?

**MELISANDE:** I am lost . . . lost here.
I am not from here . . .
I was not born there . . .

**GOLAUD:** Where are you from? Where were you born?

**MELISANDE:** Oh, oh! far from here . . far . . . far

**GOLAUD:** What sparkles at the bottom of the water?

**MELISANDE:** Why, where?
Oh, it is the crown that he gave me.
It fell because of my weeping.

**GOLAUD:** A crown?
Who gave you a crown?
I will try to get it . . .

**MELISANDE:** No, no; I do not want it any more.
I do not want it.
I prefer to die at once . . .

**GOLAUD:** I could recover it easily.
The water is not very deep.

**MELISANDE:** I do not want it any more.
If you recover it, I shall throw myself in its place! . . .

**GOLAUD:** No, no; I shall leave it there.
Yet one could get it very easily.
It appears very handsome.—Has it been long since you fled?

**MELISANDE:** Yes, yes . . . who are you?

**GOLAUD:** I am Prince Golaud—grandson of King Arkel, the old King of Allemond.

**MELISANDE:** Oh! you already have grey hair.

**GOLAUD:** Yes, a few, here, by the temples.

**MELISANDE:** And the beard too . . .
Why do you look at me in that way?

**GOLAUD:** I look at your eyes.
You never close your eyes?

**MELISANDE:** Yes, I do.
I close them at night.

**GOLAUD:** Why do you wear such a look of surprise?

**MELISANDE:** You are a giant.

**GOLAUD:** I am a man like any other . . .

**MELISANDE:** Why did you come here?

**GOLAUD:** Je n'en sais rien moi-même.
Je chassais dans la forêt.
Je poursuivais un sanglier.
Je me suis trompe de chemin.—
Vous avez l'air très jeune.
Quel âge avez-vous?

**MÉLISANDE:** Je commence à avoir froid . . .

**GOLAUD:** Voulez-vous venir avec moi?

**MÉLISANDE:** Non, non;! je reste ici . . .

**GOLAUD:** Vous ne pouvez pas restez seule.
Vous ne pouvez pas rester ici toute la nuit . . .
Comment vous nommez-vous?

**MÉLISANDE:** Mélisande.

**GOLAUD:** Vous ne pouvez pas rester ici, Mélisande.
Venez avec moi.

**MÉLISANDE:** Je reste ici . . .

**GOLAUD:** Vous aurez peur, toute seule.
On ne sait pas ce qu'il y a ici . . .
Toute la nuit . . . toute seule, ce n'est pas possible.
Mélisande, venez, donnez-moi la main . . .

**MÉLISANDE:** Oh! ne me touchez pas! . . .

**GOLAUD:** Ne criez pas . . .
Je ne vous toucherai plus.
Mais venez avec moi.
La nuit sera très noire et très froide.
Venez avec moi . . .

**MÉLISANDE:** Où allez-vous?

**GOLAUD:** Je ne sais pas . . .
Je suis perdu aussi . . .
(Ils sortent.)

## SCENE II.

(Une salle dans le château. On découvre Arkel et Geneviève.)

**GENEVIEVE:** Voici ce qu'il a écrit à son frère Pelléas:
"Un soir, je l'ai trouvée tout en pleurs au bord d'une fontaine, dans la forêt où je m'étais perdu.
Je ne sais ni son âge, ni qui elle est, ni d'où elle vient et je n'ose pas l'interroger, car elle doit avoir eu une grande épouvant, et quant on lui demande ce qui lui est arrivé, elle pleure tout à coup comme un enfant et sanglote si profondément qu'on a peur.
Il y a maintenant six mois que je l'ai épousée et je n'en sais pas plus qu'au jour de notre rencontre.
En attendant, mon cher Pelléas, toi que j'aime plus qu'un frère, bien que nous ne soyons pas nés du même père; en attendant, prépare mon retoure . . .
Je sais que ma mère me pardonnera

**GOLAUD:** I do not know, myself.
I was hunting in the forest.
I followed a boar.
I missed my way.
You look very young.
How old are you?

**MELISANDE:** I am beginning to feel cold . . .

**GOLAUD:** Will you come with me?

**MELISANDE:** No, no; I remain here . . .

**GOLAUD:** You cannot remain alone.
You cannot remain here all night . . .
What is your name?

**MELISANDE:** Melisande.

**GOLAUD:** You cannot remain here, Melisande.
Come with me

**MELISANDE:** I stay here . . .

**GOLAUD:** You will be afriad, all alone.
One does not know what there is here . . . all night . . . all alone, it is not possible.
Melisande, come, give me your hand . . .

**MELISANDE:** Oh! do not touch me . . .

**GOLAUD:** Do not cry out
I will not touch you.
But come with me.
The night is very dark and very cold.
Come with me . . .

**MELISANDE:** Where are you going?

**GOLAUD:** I do not know . . .
I am lost also.
(They depart.)

## SCENE II.

(A Room in the Castle. Arkel and Genevieve discovered).

**GENEVIEVE:** Here is what he has written to his brother, Pelléas:
'One evening, I found her all in tears on the rim of a fountain, in the forest where I had gotten lost.
I know not her age, nor whom she is, nor where she comes from and I do not dare question her, for she must have had a great fright, and when I ask her what had happened to her, she weeps all at once like a child and sobs so deeply that one is afraid.
It is now six months since I married her and I know no more than the day of our meeting.
In the meantime, my dear Pelléas, you, that I love more than a brother, even though we were not born of the same father; in the meantime, prepare my return.
I know that my mother will willing-

volontiers.
Mais j'ai peur d'Arkël, malgré toute sa bonté, car j'ai déçu, par ce mariage étrange, tous ses projets politiques, et je crains que la beauté de Mélisande n'excuse pas à ses yeux, si sages, ma folie.
S'il consent néanmoins à l'accueillir comme il accueillerait sa propre fille, le troisième soir que suivra cette lettre, allume une lampe au sommet de la tour que regarde la mer.
Je l'apercevrai du pont de notre navire; sinon j'irai plus loin et ne reviendrai plus . . .
Qu'en dites-vous!

ARKEL: Je n'en dis rien.
Cela peut nous paraître étrange, parce que nous ne voyons jamais que l'envers des destinées . . .
Il avait toujours suivi mes conseils jusqu'ici; j'avais cru le rendre heureux en l'envoyant demander la main de la princesse Ursule.
Il ne pouvait pas rester seul, et depuis la mort de sa femme il était triste d'être seul; et ce mariage allait mettre fin à de longues guerres et à de vieilles haines . . .
Il ne l'a pas voulu ainsi.
Qu'il en soit comme il l'a voulu: je ne me suis jamais mis en travers d'une destinée: et il sait mieux que moi son avenir.
Il n'arrive peut-être pas d'événements inutiles . . .

GENEVIEVE: Il a toujours été si prudent, si grave et si ferme..
Depuis la mort de sa femme il ne vivait plus que pour son fils, le petit Yniold.
Il a tout oublié . . .
—Qu'allons-nous faire? . . .
(Entre Pelléas.)

ARKEL: Qui est-ce qui entre là?

GENEVIEVE: C'est Pelléas.
Il a pleuré.

ARKEL: Est-ce toi, Pelléas?—
Viens un peu plus près, que je te voie dans la lumière . . .

PELLÉAS: Grand-père, j'air reçu, en même temps que la lettre de mon frère, une autre lettre; une lettre de mon ami Marcellus . . .
Il va mourir et il m'appelle.
Il dit qu'il sait exactement le jour où la mort doit venir . . .
Il me dit que je puis arriver avant elle si je veux, mais qu'il n'y a plus de temps à perdre.

ARKEL: Il faudrait attendre quelque temps cependant . . .
Nous ne savons pas ce que le retour de ton frère nous prépare.
Et d'ailleurs ton père n'est-il pas ici, au-dessus de nous, plus malade peut-être que ton ami?
Pourras-tu choisir entre le père et l'ami? . . .
(Il sort.)

ly forgive me.
But I fear Arkel, in spite of all his goodness, for I deceived, by this strange marriage, all his political projects, and I fear that the beauty of Melisande will not excuse in his eyes, so wise, my folly.
If, nevertheless, he consents to receive her as he would receive his own daughter, the third evening that follows this letter, light a lamp at the summit of the tower that looks on the sea.
I shall perceive it from the bridge of our ship; if not, I shall go farther and shall never return' . . .
What do you say of it?

ARKEL: I say nothing of it.
It may appear strange to us, for we never see but the reverse of destinies . . .
He had always followed my advice until this; I had thought to make him happy in sending him to ask for the hand of the Princess Ursula . . .
He could not remain alone, and since the death of his wife he was sad in being alone; and this marriage was to put an end to long wars and to some ugly hatreds . . .
He would not have it so: Let it be as he wishes.
I have never put myself at cross purposes with a destiny; and he knows his future better than me.
There, perhaps, happen no useless events . . .

GENEVIEVE: He has always been so prudent, so serious and so firm.
Since the death of his wife he only lived for his son, the little Yniold.
He has forgotten everthing.
What shall we do?
(Enter Pelléas.)

ARKEL: Who enters there?

GENEVIEVE: It is Pelléas. He has wept.

ARKEL: Is it you, Pelléas?
Come a little nearer, that I may see you in the light . . .

PELLÉAS: Grandfather, I received, at the same time as the letter from my brother, another letter; a letter from my friend Marcellus.
He is about to die and he calls me.
He says he knows exactly the day that death must come.
He tells me that I can arrive before it if I please, but that there is no more time to lose.

ARKEL: And yet it is needful to wait awhile.
We do not know what the return of your brother prepares for us.
And besides is not your father here, just above us, sicker, perhaps, than your friend?
Could you choose between the father and the friend?
(He leaves).

GENEVIEVE: Aie soin d'allumer la lampe dès ce soir, Pelléas . . .
(Ils sortent séparément).

## SCENE III.

(Devant le château. Entrent Genevieve et Mélisande.)

MÉLISANDE: Il fait sombre dans les jardins.
Et quelles forêts, quelles forêts autour des palais! . . .

GENEVIEVE: Oui; cela m'étonnait aussi quand je suis arrivée ici, et cela étonne tout le monde.
Il y a des endroits où l'on ne voit jamais le soleil.
Mais l'on s'y fait si vite . . .
Il y a longtemps, il y a longtemps . . .
Il y a près de quarante ans que je vis ici . . .
Regardez de l'autre côté, vous aurez la clarté de la mer . . .

MÉLISANDE: J'entends du bruit au-dessous de nous . . .

GENEVIEVE: Oui; c'est quelqu'un qui monte vers nous . . .
Ah! c'est Pelléas . . .
Il semble encore fatigué de vous avoir attendue si longtemps . . .

MÉLISANDE: Il ne nous a pas vues.

GENEVIEVE: Je crois qu'il nous a vues, mais il ne sait ce qu'il doit faire . . .
Pelléas, Pelléas, est-ce toi?

PELLÉAS: Oui! . . .
Je venais du côté de la mer . . .

GENEVIEVE: Nous aussi; nous cherchions la clarté.
Icic, il fait un peu plus clair qu'ailleurs! et cependant la mer est sombre.

PELLÉAS: Nous aurons un tempête cette nuit: il y en a toutes les nuits depuis quelque temps . . . et cependant elle est si calme ce soir . . .
On s'embarquerait sans le savoir et l'on ne reviendrait plus.

MÉLISANDE: Quelque chose sort du port . . .

PELLÉAS: Il faut que ce soit un grand navire . . .
Les lumières sont très hautes, nous le verrons tout à l'heure quand il entrera dans la bande de clarté . . .

GENEVIEVE: Je ne sais si nous pourrons le voir . . .
il y a encore une brume sur la mer . . .

PELLÉAS: On dirait que la brume s'élève lentement . . .

MÉLISANDE: Oui; j'aperçois, là-bas, une petite lumière que je n'avais pas vue . . .

GENEVIEVE: Be careful to light the lamp from tonight on, Pelléas.
(They go out separately.)

## SCENE III.

(In front of the Castle. Enter Genevieve and Melisande.)

MELISANDE: It is dark in the gardens.
And what forests, what forests around the palaces! . . .

GENEVIEVE: Yes; it astonished me too when I came here, and it astonishes everybody.
There are places where one never sees the sun.
But one is soon used to it.
It is a long time, it is a long time . . .
It is nearly forty years that I live here . . .
Look on the other side and you will have the light of the sea . . .

MELISANDE: I hear a noise beneath us . . .

GENEVIEVE: Yes; it is someone coming up to us . . .
Ah! it is Pelléas . . .
He seems still tired from having waited for you so long . . .

MELISANDE: He has not seen us.

GENEVIEVE: I think he has seen us, but he does not know what he should do . . .
Pelléas, Pelléas, is it you?

PELLÉAS: Yes.
I was coming from the side of the sea . . .

GENEVIEVE: We also; we were looking for light.
Here, it is a little clearer than elsewhere.
And yet the sea is dark.

PELLÉAS: We shall have a storm tonight.
There is one every night since some time . . . and yet it is so calm this evening . . .
One would embark without knowing it and never come back.

MELISANDE: Something leaves the port.

PELLÉAS: It must be a large ship.
The lights are very high, we will see it by and by, when it enters the ray of light.

GENEVIEVE: I do not know if we will see it, there is still a mist on the sea.

PELLÉAS: It looks as if the mist were slowly rising.

MELISANDE: Yes; I perceive, over there, a little light I had not seen.

PELLÉAS: C'est un phare; il y en a d'autres que nous ne voyons pas encore.

MÉLISANDE: Le navire est dans la lumière . . .
Il est déjà bien loin . . .

PELLÉAS: Il s'éloigne à toutes voiles . . .

MÉLISANDE: C'est le navire qui m'a menée ici. Il a de grandes voiles
Je le reconnais à ses voiles . . .

PELLÉAS: Il aura mauvaise mer cette nuit . . .

MÉLISANDE: Pourquoi s'en va-t-il cette nuit?
On ne le voit presque plus . . .
Il fera peut-être naufrage . . .

PELLÉAS: La nuit tombe très vite . . . (Un silence.)

GENEVIÈVE: Il est temps de rentrer.
Pelléas, montre la route à Mélisande.
Il faut que j'aille voir, un instant, le petit Yniold.
(Elle sort.)

PELLÉAS: On ne voit plus rien sur la mer.

MÉLISANDE: Je vois d'autres lumières.

PELLÉAS: Ce sont les autres phares.
Entendez-vous la mer? . . .
C'est le vent qui s'élève . . .
Descendons par ici.
Voulez-vous me donner la main?

MÉLISANDE: Voyez, voyez, j'ai les mains pleines de fleurs.

PELLÉAS: Je vous soutiendrai par le bras, le chemin est escarpé et il fait très sombre . . .
Je pars peut-être demain . . .

MÉLISANDE: Oh! . . . pourquoi partez-vous?
(Ils sortent.)

# ACTE II.

## SCENE I.

(Une fontaine dans le parc. Entrent Pelléas et Mélisande).

PELLÉAS: Vous ne savez pas où je vous ai menée?—
Je viens souvent m'asseoir ici, vers midi, lorsqu'il fait trop chaud dans les jardins.
On étouffe, aujourd'hui, même à l'ombre des arbres.

MÉLISANDE: Oh! l'eau est claire . . .

PELLÉAS: Elle est fraîche comme l'hiver.
C'est une vieille fontaine abandonnée.
Il paraît que c'était une fontaine

PELLÉAS: It is a beacon; there are others that we do not yet see.

MELISANDE: The vessel is in the light.
It is already very far . . .

PELLÉAS: It is going away with all sails set.

MELISANDE: It is the ship that brought me here. It has great sails.
I recognize it by its sails.

PELLÉAS: There will be a bad sea tonight.

MELISANDE: Why does it go away tonight?
One hardly sees it any more.
It will perhaps be wrecked.

PELLÉAS: Night is falling very fast . . .
(A silence.)

GENEVIEVE: It is time to go within.
Pelléas, show the way to Melisande.
I must go and see, for a moment, the little Yniold.
(She leaves.)

PELLÉAS: One no longer sees anything on the sea . . .

MELISANDE: I see other lights.

PELLÉAS: It is the other beacons.
Do you hear the sea?
It is the wind that is rising.
Let us get down this way.
Will you give me your hand?

MELISANDE: See, see, I have my hands full of flowers.

PELLÉAS: I will support you by your arm, the way is steep and it is very dark,
I go away perhaps tomorrow.

MELISANDE: Oh! . . .
Why do you go away?
(They leave.)

# ACT II.

## SCENE I.

(A Fountain in the Park. Enter Pelleas and Melisande.)

PELLÉAS: You do not know where I have brought you—
I come often to sit here, toward noon, when it is too hot in the gardens.
It is suffocating today, even in the shade of the trees.

MELISANDE: Oh! the water is clear . . .

PELLÉAS: It is as fresh as in winter.
It is an old abandoned fountain.
It seems that it was a miraculous fountain,—it made the blind to see.

miraculeuse,—elle ouvrait les yeux des aveugles.—
On l'appelle encore la "fontaine des aveugles."

MÉLISANDE: Elle n'ouvre plus les yeux des aveugles?

PELLÉAS: Depuis que le roi est presque aveugle lui même, on n'y vient plus . . .

MÉLISANDE: Comme on est seul ici . . .
On n'entend rien.

PELLÉAS: Il y a toujours un silence extraordinaire
On entendrait dormir l'eau.
Voulez-vous vous asseoir au bord du bassin de marbre?
Il y a un tilleul où le soleil n'entre jamais . . .

MÉLISANDE: Je vais me coucher sur le marbre.
Je voudrais voir le fond de l'eau . . .

PELLÉAS: On ne l'a jamais vu.—
Elle est peut-être aussi profonde que la mer.

MÉLISANDE: Si quelque chose brillait au fond, on le verrait peut-être . . .

PELLÉAS: Ne vous penchez pas ainsi . . .

MÉLISANDE: Je voudrais toucher l'eau . . .

PELLÉAS: Prenz garde de glisser . . .
Je vais vous tenir la main . . .

MÉLISANDE: Non, non, je voudrais y plonger mes deux mains . . . on dirait que mes mains sont malades aujourd'hui . . .

PELLÉAS: Oh! oh! prenez garde! prenez garde!
Mélisande!
Mélisande!—
Oh! votre chevelure! . . .

MÉLISANDE: (se redressant). Je ne peux pas, je ne peux pas l'atteindre.

PELLÉAS: Vos cheveux on plongé dans l'eau . . .

MÉLISANDE: Oui, ils sont plus longs que mes bras.
Ils sont plus longs que moi . . .
(Un silence.)

PELLÉAS: C'est au bord d'une fontaine aussi, qu'il vous a trouvée?

MÉLISANDE: Oui . . .

PELLÉAS: Que vous a-t-il dit?

MÉLISANDE: Rien;—je ne me rappelle plus . . .

PELLÉAS: Etait-il tout près de vous?

MÉLISANDE: Oui; il voulait m'embrasser . . .

PELLÉAS: Et vous ne vouliez pas?

MÉLISANDE: Non.

It is still called the "Fountain of the Blind."

MELISANDE: It no longer opens the eyes of the blind?

PELLÉAS: Since the King is nearly blind himself, no one comes to it any more . . .

MELISANDE: How lonely it is here . . . one hears nothing.

PELLÉAS: There is always an extraordinary silence.
One might hear the water sleep.
Will you sit on the edge of the marble basin?
There is an elm which the sun never penetrates . . .

MELISANDE: I will lie on the marble.
I should like to see the depth of the water . . .

PELLÉAS: No one has ever seen it
It is, perhaps, as deep as the sea.

MELISANDE: If something sparkled at the bottom, perhaps one could see it.

PELLÉAS: Do not lean over so . . .

MELISANDE: I would like to touch the water . . .

PELLÉAS: Take care of slipping.
I will hold your hand . . .

MELISANDE: No, no, I should like to plunge in my two hands . . . it seems as if my hands were sickly today . . .

PELLÉAS: Oh, oh, take care, take care.
Melisande!
Melisande?
Oh, your hair . . .

MELISANDE: (drawing herself back). I cannot, I cannot reach it.

PELLÉAS: Your hair is soaked with water.

MELISANDE: Yes, it is longer than my arms . . .
It is longer than myself.
(A silence.)

PELLÉAS: It is on the brink of a fountain, also, that he found you.

MELISANDE: Yes

PELLÉAS: What did he say to you?

MELISANDE: Nothing;—I no longer remember . . .

PELLÉAS: Was he quite close to you?

MELISANDE: Yes; he wanted to embrace me . . .

PELLÉAS: And you did not wish to?

MELISANDE: No.

**PELLÉAS:** Pourquoi ne vouliez-vous pas?

**MÉLISANDE:** Oh! oh! j'ai vu passer quelque chose au fond de l'eau . . .

**PELLÉAS:** Prenez garde! prenez garde!— Vous allez tomber!— Avec quoi jouez-vous?

**MÉLISANDE:** Avec l'anneau qu'il m'a donné . . .

**PELLÉAS:** Ne jouez pas ainsi, au-dessus d'une eau si profone . . .

**MÉLISANDE:** Mes mains ne tremblent pas.

**PELLÉAS:** Comme il brille au soleil!— Ne le jetez pas si haut vers le ciel . . .

**MÉLISANDE:** Oh! . . .

**PELLÉAS:** Il est tombé?

**MÉLISANDE:** Il est tombé dans l'eau! . . .

**PELLÉAS:** Où est il? Où est-il?

**MÉLISANDE:** Je ne le vois pas descendre . . .

**PELLÉAS:** Je crois que je le vois briller . . .

**MÉLISANDE:** Ma bague?

**PELLÉAS:** Oui, oui, . . . là-bas . . .

**MÉLISANDE:** Oh! Oh! elle est si loin de nous! . . . non, non, ce n'est pas elle . . . ce n'est plus elle . . . Elle est perdue . . . perdue . . . Il n'y a plus qu'un grand cercle sur l'eau . . . Qu'allons-nous faire maintenant? . . .

**PELLÉAS:** Il ne faut pas s'inquiéter pour une bague. Ce n'est rien . . . nous la retrouverons peut-être. Ou-bien nous en retrouverons une autre.

**MÉLISANDE:** Non, non; nous ne la retrouverons plus, nous n'en trouverons pas d'autres non plus . . . Je croyais l'avoir dans les mains cependant . . . J'avais déjà fermé les mains, et elle est tombée malgre tout . . . Je l'ai jetée trop haut, du côté du soleil . . .

**PELLÉAS:** Venez, nous reviendrons un autre jour . . . venez, il est temps. On irait à notre rencontre . . . Midi sonnait au moment où l'anneau est tombé . . .

**MÉLISANDE:** Qu'allons-nous dire à Golaud s'il demande où il est?

**PELLÉAS:** La vérité, la vérité, la vérité . . .
*(Ils sortent.)*

**PELLÉAS:** Why did you not wish to?

**MELISANDE:** Oh, oh! I saw something pass at the bottom of the water . . .

**PELLÉAS:** Take care, take care! You will fall! What are you playing with?

**MELISANDE:** With the ring he gave me . . .

**PELLÉAS:** Do not play like that, above water so deep.

**MELISANDE:** My hands do not tremble.

**PELLÉAS:** How it shines in the sun! Do not throw it so high toward the sky . . .

**MELISANDE:** Oh!

**PELLÉAS:** It has fallen?

**MELISANDE:** It has fallen in the water! . . .

**PELLÉAS:** Where is it, where is it?

**MELISANDE:** I do not see it sinking . . .

**PELLÉAS:** I think that I see it sparkle . . .

**MELISANDE:** My ring?

**PELLÉAS:** Yes, yes, . . . over there . . .

**MELISANDE:** Oh, oh, it is so far from us . . . no, no, that is not it . . . that is no longer it . . . It is lost . . . lost . . . There is no longer anything but a great circle on the water . . . What shall we do now?

**PELLÉAS:** There is no need to be anxious over a ring. It is nothing, we will find it again, perhaps. Or else we will find another.

**MELISANDE:** No, no; we shall never find it again, nor shall we find others either. Still I thought I had it in my hands. I had already closed my hands, and it fell in spite of all . . . I threw it too high, on the sunny side . . .

**PELLÉAS:** Come, we will return another day . . . come, it is time. They would come out to meet us. Noon sounded at the moment the ring was lost.

**MELISANDE:** What shall we say to Golaud if he asks where it is?

**PELLÉAS:** The truth, the truth, the truth . . .
*(They go out.)*

## SCENE II.

*(Un appartement dans le château. On découvre Golaud étendu sur son lit; Mélisande est à son chevet.)*

**GOLAUD:** Ah! ah! tout va bien, cela ne sera rien. Mais je ne puis m'expliquer comment cela s'est passé. Je chassais tranquillement dans la forêt. Mon cheval s'est emporté tout à coup, sans raison. A-t-il vu quelque chose d'extraordinaire? . . . Je venais d'entendre sonner les douze coups de midi. Au douzième coup, il s'effraie subitement, et court, comme un aveugle fou, contre un arbre. Je ne sais plus ce qui est arrivé. Je suis tombé, et lui doit être tombé sur moi. Je croyais avoir toute la forêt sur la poitrine; je croyais que mon coeur était déchiré. Mais mon coeur est solide. Il parait que ce n'est rien . . .

**MÉLISANDE:** Voulez-vous boire un peu d'eau?

**GOLAUD:** Merci; je n'ai pas soif.

**MÉLISANDE:** Voulez-vous un autre oreiller? . . . Il y a une petite tache de sang sur celui-ci.

**GOLAUD:** Non, non; ce n'est pas le peine.

**MÉLISANDE:** Est-ce bien sûr? . . . Vous ne souffrez pas trop?

**GOLAUD:** Non, non, j'en ai vu bien d'autres. Je suis fait au fer et au sang . . .

**MÉLISANDE:** Fermez les yeux et tâchez de dormir. Je resterai ici toute la nuit . . .

**GOLAUD:** Non, non; je ne veux pas que tu te fatigues ainsi. Je n'ai besoin de rien; je dormirai comme un enfant . . . Qu'y a-t-il, Mélisande? Pourquoi pleures-tu tout à coup? . . .

**MÉLISANDE:** *(fondant en larmes)*. Je suis . . . Je suis malade ici . . .

**GOLAUD:** Tu es malade? . . . Qu'as-tu donc, qu'as-tu donc, Mélisande? . . .

**MÉLISANDE:** Je ne sais pas . . . Je suis malade ici . . . Je préfère vous le dire aujourd'hui; seigneur, je ne suis pas heureuse ici . . .

**GOLAUD:** Qu'est-il donc arrivé? . . . Quelqu'un t'a fait du mal? . . . Quelqu'un t'aurait-il offensée?

## SCENE II.

*(An apartment in the Castle. Golaud is discovered extended on his bed. Melisande is at the head.)*

**GOLAUD:** Ah, ah! All goes well. It will be nothing. But I cannot explain to myself how it took place. I was hunting quietly in the forest. My horse suddenly ran away, without reason. Did he see something extraordinary? I had just heard ring the twelve strokes of noon. At the twelfth stroke, he is suddenly frightened, and runs like a blind fool, against a tree. I know no longer what happened. I fell and he must have fallen on me. I thought I had the whole forest on my chest; I thought that my heart was torn apart. But my heart is solid. It appears that it is nothing . . .

**MELISANDE:** Would you like to drink a little water?

**GOLAUD:** Thanks; I am not thirsty.

**MELISANDE:** Will you have another pillow? . . . There is a little stain of blood on this one.

**GOLAUD:** No, no; it is not worth the trouble.

**MELISANDE:** Are you sure? . . . You do not suffer too much?

**GOLAUD:** No, no, I have seen much worse. I am inured to iron and blood.

**MELISANDE:** Shut your eyes and try to sleep. I will remain here all night . . .

**GOLAUD:** No, no; I will not let you tire yourself thus. I am in want of nothing; I will sleep like a child . . . What is it, Melisande? Why do you weep all of a sudden?

**MELISANDE:** *(breaking into tears)*. I am . . . I am sick here.

**GOLAUD:** You are sick? What ails you, what ails you, Melisande? . . .

**MELISANDE:** I do not know . . . I am sick here. I prefer to tell you today; lord, I am not happy here.

**GOLAUD:** What has happened? Someone has done you harm? Has some one offended you?

## Act II, Scene II

MÉLISANDE: Non, non; personne ne m'a fait le moindre mal . . . Ce n'est pas cela . . .

GOLAUD: Mais tu dois me cacher, quelque chose? . . . Dis moi tout la vérité, Mélisande Est-ce le roi? . . . Est-ce ma mère? . . . Est-ce Pelléas? . . .

MÉLISANDE: Non, non; ce n'est pas Pelléas. Ce n'est personne . . . Vous ne pouvez pas me comprendre . . . C'est quelque chose qui est plus fort que moi.

GOLAUD: Voyons; sois raisonnable, Mélisande.— Que veux-tu que je fasse? Tu n'es plus une enfant.— Est-ce moi que tu voudrais quitter?

MÉLISANDE: Oh! non; ce n'est pas cela . . . Je voudrais m'en aller avec vous . . . C'est ici, que je ne peux plus vivre . . . Je sens que je ne vivrais plus longtemps . . .

GOLAUD: Mais il faut une raison cependant. On va te croire folle. On va croire à des rêves d'enfant.— Voyons, est-ce Pelléas, peut-être?— Je crois qu'il ne te parle pas souvent . . .

MÉLISANDE: Si, si; il me parle parfois. Il ne m'aime pas, je crois; je l'ai vu dans ses yeux . . . Mais il me parle quand il me rencontre . . .

GOLAUD: Il ne faut pas lui en vouloir. Il a toujours été ainsi. Il est un peu étrange. Il changera, tu verras; il est jeune.

MÉLISANDE: Mais ce n'est pas cela . . . ce n'est pas cela . . .

GOLAUD: Qu'est-ce donc?— Ne peux-tu pas te faire à la vie qu'on mène ici? Fait-il trop triste ici? Il est vrai que ce château est très vieux et très sombre . . . Il est très froid et très profond. Et tous ceux qui l'habitent sont déjà vieux. Et la campagne peut sembler bien triste aussi, avec toutes ses forêts, toutes ses vieilles forêts sans lumière. Mais on peut égayer tout cela si l'on veut. Et puis, la joie, la joie, on n'en a pas tous les jours; il faut prendre les

MELISANDE: No, no; no one has done me the least harm . . . It is not that . . .

GOLAUD: But you must be hiding something from me? Tell me the whole truth, Melisande . . . Is it the King? Is it my mother? Is it Pelléas? . . .

MELISANDE: No, no; it is not Pelléas. It is nobody . . . You cannot understand me . . . It is something that is stronger than myself . . .

GOLAUD: Come; be reasonable, Melisande. What would you have me do? You are no longer a child. Is it me that you would leave?

MELISANDE: Oh no! it is not that . . . I would like to go away with you . . . It is here that I cannot longer live . . . I feel that I should not live long.

GOLAUD: But there still needs a reason. They will think you mad. They will think you have childish dreams. Come, is it Pelléas, perhaps? I think he does not speak to you often . . .

MELISANDE: Yes. yes; he speaks to me at times. He does not like me, I think; I have seen it in his eyes . . . But he speaks to me when he meets me . . .

GOLAUD: You must not mind him. He has always been that way. He is a little singular. He will change, you will see; he is young . . .

MELISANDE: But it is not that . . . it is not that.

GOLAUD: What is it then? Can you not fit yourself to the life we lead here? Is it too sad here? It is true that this castle is very old and very sombre. It is very cold and very deep. And all those who live in it are already old. And the country side may seem very sad also, with all its forests, all its old forests without light. But we can make all that gayer if we want to. And after that joy, joy. One does not taste it every day; one must take things as they are. But tell me something; no matter

choses comme elles sont. Mais dis-moi quelque chose; n'importe quoi; je ferai tout ce que tu voudras . . .

MÉLISANDE: Qui, c'est vrai . . . on ne voit jamais le ciel clair . . . Je l'ai vu pour la première fois ce matin . . .

GOLAUD: C'est donc cela qui te fait pleurer, ma pauvre Mélisande?— Ce n'est donc que cela?— Tu pleures de ne pas voir le ciel?— Voyons, tu n'es plus à l'âge où l'on peut pleurer pour ces choses . . . Et puis l'été n'est-il pas là? Tu vas voir le ciel tous les jours.— Et puis l'année prochaine . . . Voyons, donne-moi ta main; donne-moi tes deux petites mains. (Il lui prénd les mains.) Oh! ces petites mains que je pourrais écraser comme des fleurs . . . — Tiens, où est l'anneau que je t'avais donné?

MÉLISANDE: L'anneau?

GOLAUD: Oui; la bague de nos noces, où est-elle?

MÉLISANDE: Je crois . . . Je crois qu'elle est tombée . . .

GOLAUD: Tombée?— Où est-elle tombée . . . Tu ne l'as pas perdue.

MÉLISANDE: Non, elle est tombée . . . elle doit être tombée . . . mais je sais où elle est . . .

GOLAUD: Où est-elle?

MÉLISANDE: Vous savez bien . . . vous savez bien . . . la grotte au bord de la mer?

GOLAUD: Oui.

MÉLISANDE: Eh bien, c'est là . . . Il faut que ce soit là . . . Oui, oui; je me rappelle . . . J'y suis allée ce matin, ramasser des coquillages pour le petit Yniold . . . Il y en a de très beaux . . . Elle a glissé de mon doigt . . . puis la mer est entrée; et j'ai dû sortir avant de l'avoir retrouvée.

GOLAUD: Es-tu sûre que ce soit là?

MÉLISANDE: Oui, oui; tout à fait sûre . . . Je l'ai sentie glisser . . .

GOLAUD: Il faut aller la chercher tout de suite.

MÉLISANDE: Maintenant?—tout de suite?—dans l'obscurité?

what, I will do all that you wish.

MELISANDE: Yes, it is true . . . one never sees the clear sky . . . I saw it for the first time this morning.

GOLAUD: So it is that which makes you weep, my poor Melisande? Then it is only that. You weep to have not seen the sky. Come you are no longer at the age when one weeps for these things . . . And then, is not summer here? You will see the sky every day. And then next year. Come, give me your hand; give me your two little hands. (He takes her hands.) Oh, these little hands that I could crush like flowers . . . Eh, where is the ring that I gave to you?

MELISANDE: The ring?

GOLAUD: Yes; our nuptial ring, where is it?

MELISANDE: I think . . . I think it fell . . .

GOLAUD: Fell! Where did it fall? You have not lost it?

MELISANDE: No, it fell . . . it must have fallen . . . but I do not know where it is.

GOLAUD: Where is it?

MELISANDE: You know very well . . . you know . . . the grotto on the seashore?

GOLAUD: Yes.

MELISANDE: Very well, it is there . . . it must be there . . . Yes, yes; I remember . . . I went there this morning, to gather shells for little Yniold . . . there are some beautiful ones . . . it slipped from my finger . . . and then the sea came in; and I had to go before having found it.

GOLAUD: Are you sure that it was there?

MELISANDE: Yes, yes; entirely sure . . . I felt it slip . . .

GOLAUD: You must go and look for it at once.

MELISANDE: Now!—at once—in the dark?

GOLAUD: Maintenant, tout de suite, dans l'obscurité. J'aimerais mieux avoir perdu tout ce que j'ai plutôt que d'avoir perdu cette bague. Tu ne sais pas ce que c'est. Tu ne sais pas d'où elle vient. La mer sera très haute cette nuit. La mer viendra la prendre avant toi . . . dépêche-toi.

MÉLISANDE: Je n'ose pas . . . Je n'ose pas aller seule . . .

GOLAUD: Vas-y, vas-y avec n'importe qui. Mais il faut y aller tout de suite, entends-tu?—Dépêche-toi; demande à Pelléas d'y aller avec toi.

MÉLISANDE: Pelléas?—Avec Pelléas?—Mais Pelléas ne voudra pas . . .

GOLAUD: Pelléas fera tout ce que tu lui demandes. Je connais Pelléas mieux que toi. Vas-y, hâte-toi. Je ne dormirai pas avant d'avoir la bague.

MÉLISANDE: Oh! oh! Je ne suis pas heureuse! . . . Je ne suis pas heureuse! . . . (*Elle sort en pleurant.*)

---

GOLAUD: Now, at once, in the dark. I would sooner have lost all I have than to have lost this ring. You do not know what it is. You do not know where it comes from. The sea will be very high tonight. The sea will come to take it before you . . . You must hurry.

MELISANDE: I dare not . . . I dare not go alone . . .

GOLAUD: Go there, go there, it matters not with whom. But you must go at once, do you hear? Hurry; ask Pelléas to go with you.

MELISANDE: With Pelléas? But Pelléas would not like . . .

GOLAUD: Pelléas will do whatever you ask him. I know Pelléas better than you. Go, hasten. I will not sleep until I have the ring.

MELISANDE: Oh, oh! I am not happy . . . I am not happy! (*She goes out weeping.*)

## SCENE III.

(*Devant une grotte. Entrent Pelléas et Mélisande.*)

PELLÉAS: (*parlant avec une grande agitation*). Oui; c'est ici, nous y sommes. Il fait si noir que l'entrée de la grotte ne se distingue pas du reste de la nuit. Il n'y a pas d'étoiles de ce côté. Attendons que la lune ait déchiré ce gran nuage; elle éclairera toute la grotte et alors nous pourrons y entrer sans danger. Il y a des endroits dangereux et le sentier est très étroit, entre deux lacs dont on n'a pas encore trouvé le fond. Je n'ai pas songé à emporter une torche ou une lanterne, mais je pense que la clarté du ciel nous suffira.— Vous n'avez jamais pénétré dans cette grotte?

MÉLISANDE: Non . . .

PELLÉAS: Entrons-y . . . Il faut pouvoir décrire l'endroit où vous avez perdu la bague, s'il vous interroge . . . Elle est très grande et très belle. Elle est pleine de ténèbres bleues. Quand on y allume une petite lampe, on dirait que la voûte est couverte d'étoiles, comme le ciel. Donnez-moi la main, ne tremblez pas, ne tremblez pas ainsi. Il n'y a pas de danger: nous nous arrêterons au moment que nous n'apercevrons plus la clarté de la

---

## SCENE III

(*Before a Grotto. Enter Pelléas and Melisande.*)

PELLÉAS: (*speaking with great excitement*). Yes, it is here, we have arrived. It is so black that the entrance to the grotto cannot be distinguished from the rest of the night. There are no stars on this side . . . Let us wait until the moon has torn apart this great cloud; it will light up the whole grotto and then we can enter without danger. There are dangerous places and the path is very narrow, between two lakes of which they have not found the bottom. I had not thought of bringing a torch or a lantern, but I think that the light of heaven will suffice us. You have penetrated into this grotto?

MELISANDE: No . . .

PELLÉAS: Let us enter . . . You must be able to describe the place where you lost the ring, if he questions you. It is very large and very beautiful. It is full of blue darkness. When one lights a little lamp, it is as if the vault were covered with stars, like the heavens. Give me your hand, do not tremble, do not tremble so. There is no danger: we will stop at the moment when we longer see the light of the sea . . .

---

mer . . . Est-ce le bruit de la grotte qui vous effraie? Entendez-vous la mer derrière nous? —Elle ne semble pas heureuse cette nuit. Ah! voici la clarté! (*La lune éclaire largement l'entrée et une partie des ténèbres de la grotte; et l'on aperçoit, à une certaine profondeur, trois vieux pauvres à cheveux blancs, assis côte à côte, se soutenant l'un à l'autre, et endormis contre un quartier de roc.*)

MÉLISANDE: Ah!

PELLÉAS: Qu'y a-t-il?

MÉLISANDE: Il y a . . . Il y a . . . (*Elle montre les trois pauvres.*)

PELLÉAS: Oui, oui; je les ai vus aussi . . .

MÉLISANDE: Allons-nous-en! Allons-nous-en! . . .

PELLÉAS: Ce sont trois vieux pauvres qui se sont endormis . . . Pourquoi sont-ils venus dormir ici? . . . Il y aura une famine dans le pays.

MÉLISANDE: Allons-nous-en! . . . Venez . . . Allons-nous-en! . . .

PELLÉAS: Prenez garde, ne parlez pas si fort . . . Ne les éveillons pas . . . Ils dorment encore profondement . . . Venez.

MÉLISANDE: Laissez-moi; je préfère marcher seule . . .

PELLÉAS: Nous reviendrons un autre jour . . . (*Ils sortent.*)

---

Is it the noise of the grotto that frightens you? Do you hear the sea behind us? It does not seem happy tonight . . . Ah! here comes the light. (*The moon clearly illuminates the entrance and a part of the darkness of the grotto; and one perceives, at a certain depth, three old, poor, men with white hair, seated side by side, supporting each other and asleep against a boulder.*)

MELISANDE: Ah!

PELLÉAS: What is it?

MELISANDE: It is . . . it is . . . (*She points at the three poor men.*)

PELLÉAS: Yes, yes; I saw them also . . .

MELISANDE: Let us go! Let us go! . . .

PELLÉAS: It is three old poor men who have fallen asleep Why have they come to sleep here? There will be a famine in the country.

MELISANDE: Let us go . . . Come . . . Let us go! . . .

PELLÉAS: Take care, do not speak so loud . . . Let us not awaken them . . . They still sleep profoundly . . . Come.

MELISANDE: Let me be; I prefer to walk alone . . .

PELLÉAS: We will return another day . . . (*They go out.*)

## ■ ACTE III

### SCENE I

(*Une des tours du château.—Un chemin de ronde passe sous une fenêtre de la tour.*)

MÉLISANDE: (*à la fenêtre, pendant qu'elle peigne ses cheveux dénoués*) Mes longs cheveux descendent jusqu'au seuil de la tour! Mes cheveux vous attendent tout le long de la tour! Et tout le long du jour! Et tout le long du jour. Saint Daniel et Saint Michel, Saint Michel et Saint Raphaël,

---

## ■ ACT III

### SCENE I

(*One of the towers of the Castle.—A watchman's path passes under one of the windows of the tower.*)

MELISANDE: (*at the window combing her unbound hair*) My long, long hair it reaches to the foot of the tower! My hair is waiting for you down the tower all the way! And waiting all the day! And waiting all the day! Saint Daniel and Saint Michel, Saint Michel and Saint Raphael,

## Act III, Scene I

Je suis née un Dimanche!
Un Dimanche à midi!
(*Entre Pelléas par le chemin de ronde*)

**PELLÉAS:** Holà! Holà! ho!

**MÉLISANDE:** Qui est là?

**PELLÉAS:** Moi, moi, et moi! . . . Que fais-tu là à la fenêtre en chantant comme un oiseau qui n'est pas d'ici?

**MÉLISANDE:** J'arrange mes cheveux pour la nuit . . .

**PELLÉAS:** C'est là ce que je vois sur le mur! . . . Je croyais que c'était un rayon de lumière . . .

**MÉLISANDE:** J'ai ouvert la fenêtre. Il fait trop chaud dans la tour, il fait beau cette nuit.

**PELLÉAS:** Il y a d'innombrables étoiles; je n'en ai jamais autant vu que ce soir; . . . mais la lune est encore sur la mer . . . Ne reste pas dans l'ombre, Mélisande, penche-toi un peu, que je voie tes cheveux dénoûes. (*Mélisande se penche à la fenêtre.*)

**MÉLISANDE:** Je suis affreuse ainsi.

**PELLÉAS:** Oh! Mélisande! . . . oh! tu se belle! . . . tu es belle ainsi! . . . penche-toi! penche-toi! . . . laisse-moi venir plus près de toi . . .

**MÉLISANDE:** Je ne puis pas venir plus prés de toi . . . je me penche tant que je peux . . .

**PELLÉAS:** Je ne puis pas monter plus haut . . . donne-moi du moins ta main ce soir . . . avant que je m'en aille . . . Je pars demain . . .

**MÉLISANDE:** Non, non, non . . .

**PELLÉAS:** Si, si; je pars, je partirai demain . . . donne-moi ta main, ta main, ta petite main sur mes lèvres . . .

**MÉLISANDE:** Je vois une rose dans les ténèbres

**PELLÉAS:** Où donc? Je ne vois que les branches du saule qui dépasse le mur . . .

**MÉLISANDE:** Plus bas, plus bas, dans le jardin; là-bas, dans le vert sombre.

**PELLÉAS:** Ce n'est pas une rose . . . J'irai voir tout à l'heure, mais donne-moi ta main d'abord; d'abord ta main . . .

**MÉLISANDE:** Voilà, voilà; . . . je ne puis me pencher davantage . . .

**PELLÉAS:** Mes lèvres ne peuvent pas atteindre ta main

---

I was born on a Sunday!
On a Sunday at noon!
(*Pelléas enters by the path*)

**PELLÉAS:** Hey ho! Hey ho! there!

**MELISANDE:** Who is there?

**PELLÉAS:** I, I and I! . . . What are you doing up at the window, singing so like a bird that comes from afar?

**MELISANDE:** I'm arranging my hair for the night.

**PELLÉAS:** Is that what I see there on the wall? . . . Why, I thought you had a light there in the window.

**MELISANDE:** I have opened the window. It was too warm in the tower; it is lovely tonight.

**PELLÉAS:** There's no end to the stars that are shining; I never saw so many of them before; . . . but the moon is still over the sea . . . Keep not within the shadow, Mélisande, but bend down more; let me look at your hair all unbound. (*Mélisande leans out of the window.*)

**MELISANDE:** I'm very ugly so.

**PELLÉAS:** Oh! oh! Mélisande! . . . oh! you are lovely . . . you are lovely so! . . . But lean out! but lean out, so that I'll not be so far away.

**MELAISANDE:** This is as near to you as I can come . . . I'm leaning as far as I can.

**PELLÉAS:** And I can come no higher up . . . Let me touch your hand at least tonight . . . before I go away . . . I leave in the morning.

**MELISANDE:** No, no, no . . .

**PELLÉAS:** Yes, yes, I must; tomorrow I must go . . . Let me have your hand, your hand, put your little hand on my lips now—

**MELISANDE:** I see a rose in the darkness

**PELLÉAS:** Where? I only see the branches of the willow which surmount the wall . . .

**MELISANDE:** Lower down, lower down, in the garden; over there in the dark greenery.

**PELLÉAS:** It is not a rose. I will go and see by and bye, but give me your hand first; first your hand . . .

**MELISANDE:** There, there; . . . I cannot bend over farther

**PELLÉAS:** My lips cannot reach your hand . . .

---

**MÉLISANDE:** Je ne puis pas me pencher davantage . . . Je suis sur le point de tomber . . .
—Oh! oh! mes cheveux descendent de la tour!
(*Sa chevelure se révulse tout à coup, tandis qu'elle se penche ainsi et inonde Pelléas*).

**PELLÉAS:** Oh! oh! qu'est-ce que c'est? Tes cheveux, tes cheveux descendent vers moi! . . . Toute ta chevelure, Mélisande, toute ta chevelure est tombée de la tour! Je les tiens dans les mains, je les tiens dans ma bouche, Je les tiens dans les bras, je les mets autour de mon cou . . . Je n'ouvrirai plus les mains cette nuit . . .

**MÉLISANDE:** Laisse-moi! laisse-moi! . . . Tu vas me faire tomber! . . .

**PELLÉAS:** Non, non, non; . . . je n'ai jamais vu de cheveux comme les tiens, Mélisande! . . . Vois, vois, vois, ils viennent de si haut et ils m'inondent jusqu'au coeur . . . Ils m'indondent encore jusqu'aux genoux . . . Et ils sont doux, ils sont doux comme s'ils tombaient du ciel! . . . Je ne vois plus le ciel à travers tes cheveux. Tu vois, tu vois, mes mains ne peuvent plus les tenir . . . Il y en a jusque sur les branches du saule . . . Ils vivent comme des oiseaux dans mes mains . . . et ils m'aiment, ils m'aiment mille fois mieux que toi!

**MÉLISANDE:** Liasse-moi . . . laisse-moi . . . quelqu'un pourait venir . . .

**PELLÉAS:** Non, non, non; je ne te délivre pas cette nuit . . . Tu es ma prisonnière cette nuit; toute la nuit, tout la nuit . . .

**MÉLISANDE:** Pelléas! Pelléas!

**PELLÉAS:** Tu ne t'en iras plus . . . Je les noue, je les noue aux branches du saule, tes cheveux. Je ne souffre plus au milieu de tes cheveux. Tu entends mes baisers le long de tes cheveux? Ils montent le long de tes cheveux. Il faut que chacun t'en apporte. Tu vois, tu vois, je puis ouvrir les mains . . . Tu vois, j'ai les mains libres et tu ne peux m'abandonner
(*Des colombes sortent de la tour et volent autour d'eux dans la nuit.*)

---

**MELISANDE:** I cannot bend over farther . . . I am on the point of falling. Oh, oh, my hair descends from the tower! . . . (*Her hair suddenly revolutes, as she bends over thus, and covers Pelléas.*)

**PELLÉAS:** Oh, oh, what is it? . . . Your hair, your hair comes down toward me! . . . All you hair, Melisande, all your hair is fallen from the tower . . . I hold it in my hands, I hold it in my mouth . . . I hold it in my arms, and I put it around my neck. I shall not open my hands again tonight . . .

**MELISANDE:** Let me go, let me go! You will make me fall! . . .

**PELLÉAS:** No, no, no; I have never seen hair like yours, Melisande . . . Look, look, look, it comes from so high and it inundates me to the very heart. It inundates me more, even to the knees . . . It is so soft, it is soft as if it fell from heaven! I no longer see the sky through your hair. You see, you see, my hands can no longer hold it. It even reaches to the branches of the willow. It lives as a bird in my hands, and it loves me, it loves me a thousand times more than you!

**MELISANDE:** Let me go . . . let me go . . . someone might come . . .

**PELLÉAS:** No, no, no; I will not deliver you tonight. You are my prisoner this night; all the night, all the night.

**MELISANDE:** Pelléas! Pelléas!

**PELLÉAS:** You shall not go away any more . . . I tie it, I tie it to the branches of the willow, your hair. I suffer no longer in the midst of your hair. You hear my kisses through the length of your hair. They go up through your hair. Each particular one must carry some. You see, you see, I can open my hands . . . You see, I have my hands free and you cannot abandon me (*Two doves come out of the tower and fly about them in the night.*)

MÉLISANDE: Oh! oh! tu m'as fait mal . . .
Qu'y-a-t-il, Pelléas?—
Qu'est-ce qui vole autour de moi?

PELLÉAS: Ce sont les colombes qui sortent de la tour.
Je les ai effrayées; elles s'envolent.

MÉLISANDE: Ce sont mes colombes, Pelléas.—
Allons-nous en, laisse-moi; elles ne reviendraient plus . . .

PELLÉAS: Pourquoi ne reviendraient-elles plus?

MÉLISANDE: Elles se perdront dans l'obscurité . . .
Laisse-moi relever la tête . . .
J'entends un bruit de pas . . .
Laisse-moi!—
C'est Golaud! . . .
Je crois que c'est Golaud! . . .
Il nous a entendus . . .

PELLÉAS: Attends!
Attends! . . .
Tes cheveux sont autour des branches . . .
Ils se sont accrochés dans l'obscurité.
Attends, attends! . . .
Il fait noir . . .
(Entre Golaud par le chemin de ronde.)

GOLAUD: Que faites-vous ici?

PELLÉAS: Ce que ja fais ici? . . .
Je . . .

GOLAUD: Vous êtes des enfants . . .
Mélisande, ne te penche pas ainsi à la fenêtre, tu vas tomber . . .
Vous ne savez pas qu'il est tard?—
Il est près de minuit.—
Ne jouez pas ainsi dans l'obscurité.—
Vous êtes des enfants . . .
(Riandt nerveusement.)
Quels enfants!
Quels enfants!
(Il sort avec Pelléas.)

## SCENE II.

(Les souterraines du château. Entrant Golaud et Pelléas0.)

GOLAUD: Prenez garde: par ici, par ici.—
Vous n'avez jamais pénétré dans ces souterrains?

PELLÉAS: Si, une fois, dans le temps; mais il y a longtemps.

GOLAUD: Eh bien, voici l'eau stagnante dont je vous parlais . . .
Sentez-vous l'odeur de mort qui monte!—
Allons jusqu'au bout de ce rocher qui surplombe et penchez-vous un peu.
Elle viendra vous frappe au visage.
Penchez-vous; n'ayez pas peur . . . je vous tien-

MELISANDE: Oh, oh! you hurt me.
What is it, Pelléas?
What is it that flies around me?

PELLÉAS: It is the doves that come out of the tower.
I frightened them.
They fly away.

MELISANDE: They are my doves, Pelléas.
Let us go, leave me; they would not return . . .

PELLÉAS: Why would they not return?

MELISANDE: They will be lost in the obscurity . . .
Let me lift my head . . .
I hear a noise of footsteps . . .
Leave me!
It is Golaud . . .
I think it is Golaud . . .
He has heard us . . .

PELLÉAS: Wait, wait! . . .
Your hair is around the branches . . .
It has got caught in the darkness.
Wait, wait!
It is black . . .
(Golaud enters by the watch path)

GOLAUD: What are you doing here?

PELLÉAS: What I am doing here? . . .
I . . .

GOLAUD: You are like a child
Melisande, do not lean that way from the window, you will fall . . .
You do not know it is late?
It is nearly midnight.
Do not play thus in the dark.
You are like a child
(Laughing nervously.)
What children, what children!
(He goes out with Pelléas.)

## SCENE II.

(The Vaults of the Castle. Enter Golaud and Pelléas.)

GOLAUD: Take care: this way, this way.
You have never been in these vaults?

PELLÉAS: Yes, once, a while ago; but it is a long time.

GOLAUD: Well, then, here is the stagnant water of which I spoke to you . . .
Do you smell the odor of death that rises?
Let us go to the end of this rock that overlooks it and lean over a little.
It will come and strike you in the face.
Lean over; do not be afraid . . .

drai . . . donnez-moi . . . non, non, pas la main . . . elle pourrait glisser . . . le bras . . .
Voyez-vous le gouffre? . . .
Pelléas? Pelléas?

PELLÉAS: Oui, je crois que je vois le fond du gouffre . . . Est-ce la lumière qui tremble ainsi? . . .
Vous . . .

GOLAUD: Oui; c'est la lanterne . . .
Voyez, je l'agitais pour éclairer les parois.

PELLÉAS: J'étouffe ici . . . sortons.

GOLAUD: Oui, sortons . . .
(Ils sortent en silence.)

## SCENE III.

(Une terrasse au sortir des souterrains.)

PELLÉAS: Ah! je respire enfin!
J'ai cru un instant que j'allais me trouver mal dans ces énormes grottes; j'ai été sur le point de tomber . . .
Il y a là un air humide et lourd comme un rosée de plomb, et des ténèbres épaisses comme une pâte empoisonnée.
Et maintenant tout l'air de toute la mer!
Il y a un vent frais, voyez; frais comme un feuille qui vient de s'ouvrir, sur les petites lames vertes.
Tiens!
On vient d'arroser les fleurs au pied de la terrasse et l'odeur de la verdure et des rose mouillées monte jusqu'ici.
Ild doit être près de midi, elles sont déjà dans l'ombre de la tour.
Il est midi; j'entends sonner les cloches et les enfants descendent sur la plage pour se baigner.
Tiens, voilà notre mère et Mélisande à une fenêtre de la tour.

GOLAUD: Oui, elles se sont réfugiées du côté de l'ombre.
A propos de Mélisande, j'ai entendu ce qui s'est passé et ce qui s'est dit hier au soir.
Je le sais bien, ce sont là jeux d'enfant; mais il ne faut pas que cela se répète.
Elle est très délicate et il faut qu'on la ménage, d'autant plus qu'elle sera peut-être bientôt mère et la moindre émotion pourrait amener un malheur.
Ce n'est pas la première fois que je remarque qu'il pourrait y avoir quelque chose entre vous.
Vous êtes plus âgé qu'elle; il suffira de vous l'avoir dit.
Evitez-la autant que possible; mais sans affectation d'ailleurs; sans affectation.
(Ils sortent.)

I will hold you . . . give me . . . no, no, not your hand . . . it might slip . . . your arm.
Do you see the abyss?
Pelléas, Pelléas? . . .

PELLÉAS: Yes, I think I see the bottom of the abyss.
Is it the light that trembles in that way? . . .
You . . .

GOLAUD: Yes; it is the lantern . . .
See, I was swinging it to light up the walls.

PELLÉAS: I suffocate here . . .
Let us go out.

GOLAUD: Yes, let us go out . . .
(They leave in silence.)

## SCENE III.

(A Terrace at the exit of the Vaults.)

PELLÉAS: Ah, at last I breath!
I believed for a moment that I was going to be faint in these enormous vaults; I was on the point of falling . . .
There is there a damp and heavy atmosphere like a dew of lead and a thick darkness like a poisoned paste.
And now all the air of all the sea!
There is a fresh wind, see; fresh as a leaf that has just opened, on the little green blades.
Ah! they have just watered the flowers at the foot of the terrace and the smell of the verdure and of wetted roses rises this far . . .
It must be nearly noon, they are already in the shadow of the tower.
It is noon; I hear the bells ring and the children descend to the shore to bathe.
Ah, there are our mother and Melisande at a window of the tower.

GOLAUD: Yes, they have taken refuge in the shade.
On the subject of Melisande, I heard what took place and what was said last night.
I know it well, those are children's games; but it must not be repeated.
She is very delicate and we must be careful about her, all the more that she may perhaps soon be a mother and that the least emotion might bring about a misfortune.
It is not the first time I notice that there might be something between you.
You are older than she; it will suffice to have told you . . . avoid her as much as possible; but besides, without affectation; without affectation.
(They go out.)

## SCENE IV.

*(Devant le château. Entrent Golaud et le petit Yniold.)*

GOLAUD: Viens, nous allons nous asseoir ici, Yniold; viens sur mes genoux: nous verrons d'ici ce qui se passe dans la forêt.
Je ne te vois plus du tout depuis quelque temps.
Tu m'abandonnes aussi; tu es toujours chez petite-mère.
Tiens, nous sommes tout juste assis sous les fenêtres de petit mère.
—Elle fait peut-être sa prière du soir en ce moment . . .
Mais dis-moi, Yniold, elle est souvent avec ton oncle Pelléas, n'est-ce pas?

YNIOLD: Oui, oui; toujours, petit-père; quand vous n'êtes pas là.

GOLAUD: Ah!
Tiens, quelqu'un passe avec une lanterne dans le jardin.—
Mais on m'a dit qu'ils ne s'aimaient pas . . .
Il paraît qu'ils se querellent souvent . . . non?
Est-ce vrai?

YNIOLD: Oui, c'est vrai.

GOLAUD: Oui?—
Ah! ah!—
Mais à propos de quoi se querellent-ils?

YNIOLD: A propos de la porte.

GOLAUD: Comment? à propos de la porte?—
Qu'est-ce que tu racontes là?—
Mais voyons, explique-toi; pourquoi se querellent-ils à propos de la porte?

YNIOLD: Parce qu'elle ne peut pas être ouverte.

GOLAUD: Qui ne veut pas qu'elle soit ouverte?—
Voyons, pourquoi se querellent-ils?

YNIOLD: Je ne sais pas, petit-père, à propos de la lumière.

GOLAUD: Je ne te parle pas de la lumière: je te parle de la porte.
Ne mets pas ainsi la main dans la bouche . . . voyons . . .

YNIOLD: Petit-père! petit-père! . . .
Je ne le ferai plus . . .
*(Il pleure.)*

GOLAUD: Voyons; pourquoi pleures-tu?
Qu'est-il arrivé?

YNIOLD: Oh! oh! petite-père, vous m'avez fait mal . . .

GOLAUD: Je t'ai fait mal?—
Où t'ai-je fait mal!
C'est sans le vouloir . . .

---

## SCENE IV.

*(In front of the Castle. Enter Golaud and little Yniold.)*

GOLAUD: Come, we will seat ourselves here, Yniold; come on my knees: we can see from here what goes on in the forest.
I don't see you at all for some time past.
You abandon me also.
You are always with little-mother.
Ah, here we are just exactly seated under the windows of little-mother.
She is, perhaps, saying her evening prayer at this moment . . .
But tell me.
Yniold, she is often with your uncle Pelléas, is she not?

YNIOLD: Yes, yes; always, little-father; when you are not there.

GOLAUD: Ah! hallo, someone passing with a lantern in the garden.
But I was told that they did not like each other . . .
It seems that they often quarrel . . .
No?
Is it true?

YNIOLD: Yes, it is true.

GOLAUD: Yes?
Ah, ha!
But what do they quarrel about?

YNIOLD: About the door.

GOLAUD: How, now? about the door?
What are you telling there?
But come, explain yourself.
Why do they quarrel about the door?

YNIOLD: Because it cannot be opened.

GOLAUD: Who doesn't want it to be opened?
Let us see, why do they quarrel?

YNIOLD: I do not know, little-father, because of the light.

GOLAUD: I am not talking of the light: I am talking to you of the door . . .
Do not put your hand that way in your mouth . . . come . . .

YNIOLD: Little father, little-father!
I will not do it again.
*(He cries.)*

GOLAUD: Come; why do you cry?
What has happened?

YNIOLD: Oh, oh, little-father, you hurt me . . .

GOLAUD: I hurt you?
Where did I hurt you?
It was without intending to . . .

---

YNIOLD: Ici, à mon petit bras . . .

GOLAUD: C'est sans le vouloir; voyons, ne pleure plus, je te donnerai quelque chose demain . . .

YNIOLD: Quoi, petit-père?

GOLAUD: Un carquois et des flèches; mais dis-moi ce que tu sais de la porte.

YNIOLD: De grandes flèches?

GOLAUD: Oui, de très grandes flèches.—
Mais pourquoi ne veulent-ils pas que la porte soit ouverte?—
Voyons, réponds-moi à la fin!—
non, non; n'ouvre pas la bouche pour pleurer.
Je ne suis pas fâche.
De quoi parlent-ils quand ils osnt ensemble?

YNIOLD: Pelléas et petite-mère?

GOLAUD: Oui; de quoi parlent-ils?

YNIOLD: De moi; toujours de moi.

GOLAUD: Et que disent-ils de toi?

YNIOLD: Ils disent que je serai très grand

GOLAUD: Ah! misère de ma vie! . . . je suis ici comme un aveugle qui cherche son trésor au fond de l'océan! . . .
Je suis ici comme un nouveau-né perdu dans la forêt et vous . . .
Mais voyons, Yniold, j'étais distrait; nous allons causer sérieusement.
Pelléas et petite-mère ne parlent-ils jamais de moi quand je ne suis pas là?

YNIOLD: Si, si, petit-père.

GOLAUD: Ah! . . .
Et que disent-ils de moi?

YNIOLD: Ils disent que je deviendrai aussi grand que vous.

GOLAUD: Tu es toujours près d'eux?

YNIOLD: Oui, oui; toujours, petit-père.

GOLAUD: Ils ne te disent jamais d'aller jouer ailleurs?

YNIOLD: Non, petit-père; ils ont peur quand je ne suis pas là.

GOLAUD: Ils ont peur? . . .
Comment vois-tu qu'ils ont peur?

YNIOLD: Ils pleurent toujours dans l'obscurité.

GOLAUD: Ah! ah! . . .

YNIOLD: Cela fait pleurer aussi . . .

GOLAUD: Oui, oui . . .

YNIOLD: Elle est pâle, petit-père.

GOLAUD: Ah! ah! . . . patience, mon Dieu, patience . . .

YNIOLD: Quoi, petit-père?

---

YNIOLD: Here, on my little arm.

GOLAUD: I did not mean it; come, do not cry any more, I will give you something tomorrow . . .

YNIOLD: What, little-father?

GOLAUD: A quiver and some arrows; but tell me what you know about the door.

YNIOLD: Great big arrows?

GOLAUD: Yes, very large arrows.
But why did they not wish that the door should be open?
Come, are you going to end by answering?—no, no, do not open your mouth to cry.
I am not angry.
What do they talk about when they are together?

YNIOLD: Pelléas and little-mother?

GOLAUD: Yes; what do they talk about?

YNIOLD: Of me; always of me.

GOLAUD: And what do they say of you?

YNIOLD: They say that I will be very big.

GOLAUD: Ah! misery of my life!
I am here like a blind man who seeks his treasure at the bottom of the ocean
I am here like one newly born, lost in the forest and you . . .
But, come, Yniold, I was absent minded; we will talk seriously.
Do Pelléas and little mother never speak of me when I am not there?

YNIOLD: Yes, yes, little-father.

GOLAUD: And
What do they say of me?

YNIOLD: They say that I will become as big as you.

GOLAUD: You are always near them?

YNIOLD: Yes, yes; always, little-father.

GOLAUD: They never tell you to go and play elsewhere?

YNIOLD: No, little-father; they are afraid when I am not there.

GOLAUD: They are afraid? . . .
By what do you see that they are afraid?

YNIOLD: They always weep in the darkness.

GOLAUD: Ah, ah!

YNIOLD: That makes one weep also . . .

GOLAUD: Yes, yes . . .

YNIOLD: She is pale, little-father.

GOLAUD: Ah, ah! . . . patience, my God, patience . . .

YNIOLD: What, little-father?

GOLAUD: Rien, rien, mon enfant.—
J'ai vu passer un loup dans la forêt.—
Ils s'embrassent quelquefois?—Non?

YNIOLD: Ils s'embrassent, petit-père?—
Non, non.—
Ah! si, petit-père, si; une fois . . . une fois qu'il pleuvait . . .

GOLAUD: Ils se sont embrassés?—Mais comment, comment se sont-ils embrassés?

YNIOLD: Comme ca, petit-père, comme ca! . . . .
(*Il lui donne un baiser sur la bouche; riant.*)
Ah! ah! votre barbe, petit-père!
Elle pique! elle pique!
Elle devient toute grise, petit-père, et vos cheveux aussi; tout gris, tout gris . . .
(*La fenêtre sous laquelle ils sont assis s'éclaire en ce moment, et sa clarté vient tomber sur eux.*)
Ah! ah! petite-mère a allumé la lampe.
Il fait clair, petit-père; il fait clair.

GOLAUD: Oui; il commence à faire clair . . .

YNIOLD: Allons-y aussi, petit-père.

GOLAUD: Où veux-tu aller?

YNIOLD: Où il fait clair, petit-père.

GOLAUD: Non, non, mon enfant: restons encore un peu dans l'ombre . . . on ne sait pas, on ne sait pas encore . . .
Je crois que Pelléas est fou . . .

YNIOLD: Non, petit-père, il n'est pas fou, mais il est très bon.

GOLAUD: Veux-tu voir petite-mère?

YNIOLD: Oui, oui; je veux la voir!

GOLAUD: Ne fais pas de bruit; je vais te hisser jusqu'a la fenêtre.
Elle est trop haute pour moi, bien que je sois si grand . . .
(*Ils soulève l'enfant.*)
Ne fais pas le moindre bruit; petite-mère aurait terriblement peur . . .
La vois-tu?
—Est-elle dans la chambre?

YNIOLD: Oui . . .
Oh! il fait clair!

GOLAUD: Elle est seule?

YNIOLD: Oui . . . non, non; mon oncle Pelléas y est aussi.

GOLAUD: Lui! . . .

YNIOLD: Ah! ah! petit-père! vous m'avez fait mal! . . .

---

GOLAUD: Nothing, nothing, my child.
I saw a wolf pass in the forest.
They embrace each other sometimes No?

YNIOLD: They embrace each other, little father?—
No, No.—
Ah, yes; once . . . once that it was raining . . .

GOLAUD: They embraced each other?
But how, how did they embrace each other?—

YNIOLD: This way, little-father, this way.
(*He gives him a kiss on the mouth; laughing.*)
Ah, ha, your beard, little father!
It prickles, it prickles.
It is becoming all grey, little-father, and your hair also; all grey, all grey . . .
(*The window, under which they sit, lights up at this moment and its reflection falls on them.*)
Ah, ah, little mother has lighted the lamp.
It is light, little-father; it is light.

GOLAUD: Yes; it begins to be light . . .

YNIOLD: Let us go there also, little-father . . .

GOLAUD: Where would you go?

YNIOLD: Where it is light, little-father.

GOLAUD: No, no, my child; let us remain a little in the shadow . . . one does not know, one does not yet know . . . I think that Pelléas is mad.

YNIOLD: No, little-father, he is not mad, but he is very good.

GOLAUD: Do you want to see little-mother?

YNIOLD: Yes, yes; I want to see her.

GOLAUD: Do not make a noise; I am about to hoist you up to the window.
It is too high for me, though I am tall . . .
(*He lifts the child.*)
Do not make the least noise; little-mother would be terribly frightened . . .
Do you see her?
Is she in the room?

YNIOLD: Yes . . . oh, it is light.

GOLAUD: She is alone?

YNIOLD: Yes . . . no, no, my uncle Pelléas is there too.

GOLAUD: He! . . .

YNIOLD: Ah, ah! little-father, you hurt me . . .

---

GOLAUD: Ce n'est rien; tais-toi; je ne le ferai plus; regarde, regarde, Yniold! . . .
J'ai trébuché; parle plus bas.
Que font-ils?—

YNIOLD: Ils ne font rien, petit-père.

GOLAUD: Est-ce qu'ils parlent?

YNIOLD: Non petit-père; ils ne parlent pas.

GOLAUD: Mais qu font-ils?

YNIOLD: Ils regardent la lumière.

GOLAUD: Tous les deux?

YNIOLD: Oui, petit-père.

GOLAUD: Ils ne disent rien?

YNIOLD: Non, petit-père; ils ne ferment pas les yeux.

GOLAUD: Ils ne s'approchent pas l'un de l'autre?

YNIOLD: Non, petit-père; ils ne bougent pas, ils ne ferment jamais les yeux.
J'ai terriblement peur . . .

GOLAUD: De quoi donc as-tu peur?
Regarde!
Regarde!

YNIOLD: Petit-père, laissez-moi descendre!

GOLAUD: Regarde!

YNIOLD: Oh!
je vais crier, petit-père!
Laissez-moi descendre! laissez-moi descendre!

GOLAUD: Viens! nous allons voir ce qui est arrivé.
(*Ils sortent.*)

# ACTE IV.

## SCENE I.

(*Un corridor dans le château.*)

PELLÉAS: Où vas-tu?
Il faut que je te parle ce soir.
Te verrai-je?

MÉLISANDE: Oui.

PELLÉAS: Je sors de la chambre de mon père.
Il va mieux.
Le médecin nous a dit qu'il était sauvé.
Il m'a reconnu.
Il m'a pris la main, et il m'a dit de cet air étrange qu'il a depuis qu'il est malade:
"Est-ce toi, Pelléas?
Tiens, je ne l'avais jamais remarqué, mais tu as le visage grave et amical de ceux qui ne vivront pas longtemps.
Il faut voyager; il faut voyager . . ."
C'est étrange; je vais lui obéir.
Ma mère l'écoutait et pleurait de joie.
Tu ne t'en es pas aperçue?

---

GOLAUD: It is nothing; be quiet; I will not do it again; watch, watch, Yniold!
I stumbled; speak lower.
What are they doing?

YNIOLD: They are doing nothing, little-father.

GOLAUD: Do they speak?

YNIOLD: No, little, father; they do not speak.

GOLAUD: But what are they doing?

YNIOLD: They look at the light.

GOLAUD: Both of them?

YNIOLD: Yes, little-father.

GOLAUD: They say nothing?

YNIOLD: No, little-father; they do not close their eyes.

GOLAUD: They do not come near one another?

YNIOLD: No, little-father; they do not stir, they never close their eyes . . .
I am terribly afraid . . .

GOLAUD: Of what are you afraid? Look, look!

YNIOLD: Little-father, let me down.

GOLAUD: Look!

YNIOLD: Oh!
I am going to cry out, little-father. Let me down, let me down!

GOLAUD: Come! we will go and see what has happened.
(*They go out.*)

# ACT IV.

## SCENE I

(*A passage way in the castle.*)

PELLÉAS: Where go you?
I must speak to you this evening. Shall I see you?

MELISANDE: Yes.

PELLÉAS: I am just leaving my father's room.
He is better.
The physician has told us that he is safe.
He knew me.
He took my hand and said to me with that strange expression he has assumed since he is ill:
"Is it you, Pelléas?
Ah, I had never remarked it, but you have the grave and friendly face of those who will not live long.
You must travel; you must travel . . ."
It is strange; I am about to obey him.
My mother listened to him and wept with joy.
You have not perceived it?

## Act IV, Scene I

Toute la maison semble déjà revivre, on entend respirer, on entend marcher . . .
Ecoute, j'entends parler derrière cette porte.
Vite, vite, réponds vite, où te verrai-je?

MÉLISANDE: Où veux-tu?

PELLÉAS: Dans le parc: près de la fontaine des aveugles?
Veux-tu?
Viendras-tu?

MÉLISANDE: Oui.

PELLÉAS: Ce sera le dernier soir.
Je vais voyager comme mon père l'a dit.
Tu ne me verras plus . . .

MÉLISANDE: Ne dis pas cela, Pelléas . . .
Je te verrai toujours; je te regarderai toujours . . .

PELLÉAS: Tu auras beau regarder . . . je serai si loin que tu ne pourras plus me voir.

MÉLISANDE: Qu'est-il arrivé, Pelléas?
Je ne comprends plus ce que tu dis . . .

PELLÉAS: Va-t-en, va-t-en, séparons-nous.
J'entends parler derrière cette porte.
(Ils sortent séparément.)
(Puis Arkel entre accompagné de Mélisande.)

ARKEL: Maintenant que le père de Pelléas est sauvé, et que la maladie, la vieille servante de la mort, a quitté le château, un peu de joie et une peu de soleil vont enfin rentrer dans la maison . . .
Il était temps!—
Car depuis ta venue, on n'a vécu ici qu'en chuchotant autour d'une chambre fermée . . .
Et vraiment, j'avais pitié de toi, Mélisande . . .
Je t'observais, tu étais là, insouciante peut-être, mais avec l'air étrange et égaré de quelqu'un qui attendrait toujours un grand malheur, au soleil, dans un beau jardin . . .
Je ne puis pas expliquer . . .
Mais j'étais triste de te voir ainsi; car tu es trop jeune et trop belle pour vivre déjà, jour et nuit, sous l'haleine de la mort . . .
Mais à présent tout cela va changer.
A mon age, —et c'est peut-être là le fruit le plus sûr de ma vie, —à mon âge, j'ai acquis je ne sais quelle foi à la fidélité des événements, et j'ai toujours vu que tout être jeune et beau, créait autour de lui des événements jeunes, beaux et heureux . . .
Et c'est toi, maintenant, qui vas ouvrir la porte à l'ère nouvelle que j'entre-vois . . .

The whole house seems to revive already, one hears people breathe, one hears them walk
Listen, I hear talking behind this door.
Quick, quick, answer quickly, where will I see you?

MELISANDE: Where would you?

PELLEAS: In the park; near the fountain of the blind?
Will you, will you come?

MELISANDE: Yes.

PELLEAS: It will be the last evening.
I am about to travel as my father said.
You will see me no more . . .

MELISANDE: Do not say that, Pelléas . . .
I will see you always; I will look on you always . . .

PELLEAS: You will look in vain . . .
I shall be so far that you will be unable to see me more.

MELISANDE: What has happened, Pelléas?
I no longer understand what you say . . .

PELLEAS: Go away, go away.
Let us separate.
I hear talking behind this door.
(They go out separately.)
(then Arkel enters accompanied by Melisande.)

ARKEL: Now that the father of Pelléas is saved, and that sickness, the old maidservant of death, has left the Castle, a little joy and a little sun are at last to re-enter the house . . .
It was time!
For since your coming, we have lived here only in whispering around a closed room . . .
And really I pitied you, Melisande . . .
I observed you, you were there, careless, perhaps, but with the strange and wild air of someone who awaited always a great misfortune, by sunlight, in a beautiful garden . . .
I cannot explain . . .
But I was sad to see you thus: for you are too young and too handsome to live thus, day and night, under the breath of death . . .
But at present all will be changed.
At my age.,—and there, perhaps, is the surest fruitage of my life,—at my age, I have acquired, I know not what faith in the truth of events, and I have always seen that every being, young and handsome, created about itself events that were young, handsome and happy . . .
And it is you, now, who will open the door to the new era that I fore-

Viens ici; pourquoi restes-tu là sans répondre et sans lever les yeux?—
Je ne t'ai embrassée qu'une seule fois jusqu'ici, le jour de ta venue; et cependant, les vieillards ont besoin de toucher quelquefois de leurs lèvres, le front d'une femme ou la joue d'un enfant, pour croire encore à la fraîcheur de la vie et éloigner un moment les menaces de la mort.
As-tu peur de mes vieilles lèvres?
Comme j'avais pitié de toi ces mois-ci!

MÉLISANDE: Grand-père, je n'étais pas malheureuse . . .

ARKEL: Laisse-moi te regarder ainsi, de tout près, un moment . . . on a tant besoin de beauté aux côtés de la mort . . .
(Entre Golaud.)

GOLAUD: Pelléas part ce soir.

ARKEL: Tu as du sang sur le front.—
Qu'as-tu fait?

GOLAUD: Rien, rien . . . j'ai passé au travers d'une haie d'épines.

MÉLISANDE: Baissez un peu la tête, seigneur . . .
Je vais essuyer votre front . . .

GOLAUD: (la repoussant). Je ne veux pas que tu me touches, entend-tu?
Va-t-en, va-t-en!—
Je ne te parle pas.—
Où est mon épée? . . .
Je venais chercher mon épée . . .

MÉLISANDE: Ici; sur le prie-Dieu.

GOLAUD: Apporte-là.—
(A Arkel.)
On vient encore de trouver un paysan mort de faim, le long de la mer.
On dirait qu'ils tiennent tous à mourir sous nos yeux.—
(A Mélisande.)
Eh bien, mon épée?—
Pourquoi tremblez-vous ainsi?—
Je ne vais pas vous tuer.
Je voulais simplement examiner la lame.
Je n'emploie pas l'épée à ces usages.
Pourquoi m'examinez-vous comme un pauvre?—
Je ne viens pas vous demander l'aumône.
Vous espérez voir quelque chose dans mes yeux, sans que je voie quelque chose dans les vôtres?—
Croyez-vous que je sache quelque chose?—
(A Arkel.)
Voyez-vous ces grands yeux?—
On dirait qu'ils sont fiers d'être riches . . .

ARKEL: Je n'y vois qu'une grande innocence . . .

see . . .
Come here: why do you remain there without answering and without lifting your eyes?
I have kissed you thus far only once, the day you came; and yet, old men want to touch sometimes with their lips, the forehead of a woman or the cheek of a child, to still believe in the freshness of life and to put farther away the threat of death.
Are you afraid of my old lips?
How I pitied you these past months . . .

MELISANDE: Grandfather. I was not unhappy . . .

ARKEL: Let me look at you, quite near, a moment . . . one has so much need of beauty by the side of death . . .
(Enter Golaud.)

GOLAUD: Pelléas goes away tonight.

ARKEL: You have blood on your forehead.
What have you done?

GOLAUD: Nothing, nothing . . .
I passed through a hedge of thorns.

MELISANDE: Bend your head a little, lord . . .
I will wipe your forehead . . .

GOLAUD: (pushing her off). I do not want you to touch me, do you hear?
Go away, go away!
I do not address you.
Where is my sword?
I came to get my sword . . .

MELISANDE: Here; on the praying stall.

GOLAUD: Bring it.
(to Arkel.)
They have just found the body of a peasant, starved to death, on the seashore.
One would think they all wanted to die under our eyes.
(to Melisande.)
Well, my sword?
Why do you tremble thus?
I am not going to kill you.
I simply wanted to examine the blade.
I do not use a sword for these purposes.
Why do you examine me like a pauper?
I do not come to beg of you.
You hope to see something in my eyes without my seeing anything in yours?
Do you think that I know anything?
(to Arkel.)
Do you see these big eyes?
One would imagine they were proud to be rich . . .

ARKEL: I only see a great innocence . . .

GOLAUD: Une grande inno-
cence! . . .
Ils sont plus grands que
l'innocence! . . .
Ils sont plus purs que les yeux d'un
agneau . . .
Ils donneraient à Dieu des lecons
d'innocence!
Une grande innocence!
Ecoutez-j'en suis si près que je sens
la fraîcheur de leurs cils quand ils
clignent; et cependant, je suis
moins loin des grands secrets de
l'autre monde que du plus petit se-
cret de ces yeux! . . .
Une grande innocence! . . .
Plus que de l'innocence!
On dirait que les anges due ciel y
célèbrent sans cesse un
baptême!
Je le conanis ces yeux!
Je les ai vus à l'oeuvre!
Fermez-les!
Fermez-les! ou je vais les fermer
pour longtemps! . . . —
Ne mettez pas ainsi la main à la
gorge; je dis une chose très sim-
ple . . .
Je n'ai pas d'arrière-pensée . . .
Si j'avais une arrière-pensée, pour-
quoi ne la dirais-je pas?
Ah! ah!—ne tâchez pas de fuir!—
Ici!—
Donnez-moi cette main!—
Ah! vos mains sont trop
chaudes . . .
Allez-vous-en!
Votre chair me dégoûte! . . .
Il ne s'agit plus de fuir à présent!—
(Il la saisit par les cheveux.)—
Vous allez me suivre à genoux!—
A genoux!—
A genoux devant moi!—
Ah! ah! vos longs cheveux servent
enfin à quelque chose!
A droite et puis à droite—
Absalon!
Absalon!—
En avant! en arrière!
Jusqu'à terre!
jusqu'à terre! . . .
Vous voyez, vous voyez; je ris déjà
comme un vieillard . . .

ARKEL: (accourant). Go-
laud!

GOLAUD: (affectant un calme
soudain). Vous ferez comme il
vous plaira, voyez-vous.—
Je n'attache aucune importance à
cela.—
Je suis trop vieux; et puis, je ne suis
pas un espion.
J'attendrai le hasard; et
alors . . .
Oh! alors! . . . simplement
parce que c'est l'usage; simplement parce que c'est
l'usage . . .
(Il sort.)

ARKEL: Qu'a-t-il donc?—
Il est ivre?

MÉLISANDE: (en larmes). Non,
non; mais il ne m'aime plus . . .
Je ne suis pas heureuse! . . .

---

GOLAUD: A great innocence!
They are bigger than innocence!
They are purer than the eyes of a
lamb
They would give God lessens in in-
nocence.
A great innocence!
Listen: I am so near that I feel the
freshness of their lashes when they
blink; and yet, I am less far from the
great secrets of the other world
than from the little secret of these
eyes! . . .
A great innocence! . . .
More than innocence!
One would think that the angels of
heaven were there ceaselssly celeb-
rating a baptism!
I know them, these eyes!
I have seen them at work.
Close them, close them! or I shall
close them for a long time . . .
Do not put your hand in that way to
your throat; I say a very simple
thing . . .
I have no hidden thoughts . . .
If I had a hidden thought, why
should I not speak it?
Ah, ah!—do not attempt to fly!
Here!
Give me this hand!
Ah, your hands are too hot . . .
Go away!
Your flesh disgusts me!
It is not, at present, a question of es-
cape . . .
(He seizes her by the hair.)
You must follow me on your knees!
On your knees!
On your knees before me!
Ah, ah, your long hair at last serves
some purpose! . . .
To the right and now to the left!
To the left and now to the right!
Absalom!
Absalom!
Front! now back!
Down to the ground! down to the
ground . . .
You see, you see, I laugh like an old
man . . .

ARKEL: (running forward.) Golaud!

GOLAUD: (affecting a sudden
calm.) You will do as you like, do
you see.
I do not attach any importance to
that.
I am too old; and then, I am not a
spy.
I shall await chance; and
then . . . oh, then; simply because it is the custom; simply because it is the custom . . .
(He goes out.)

ARKEL: What ails him?
He is drunk.

MELISANDE: No, no; but he loves
me no more . . .
I am not happy! . . .

---

ARKEL: Si j'étais Dieu, j'aurais
pitié du coeur des hommes . . .

## SCENE II.

(Une terrasse, dans la brume.)
(On apercoit le petit Yniold qui
cherche à soulever un quartier de
roc.)

YNIOLD: Oh!
Cette pierre est lourde . . . elle
est plus lourde que moi.—
Elle est plus lourde que tout le
monde.—
Elle est plus lourde que tout.
Je vois ma balle d'or entre le rocher
et cette méchante pierre, et je ne
puis pas y atteindre . . .
Mon petit bras n'est pas assez
long—et cette pierre ne veut pas
être soulevée . . .
On dirait qu'elle a des racines dans
la terre . . .
(On entend au loin les bêlements
d'un troupeau.)
Oh! oh!
J'entends pleurer les moutons.—
Tiens!
Il n'y a plus de soleil!
—Ils arrivent les petits moutons;
ils arrivent . . .
Il y en a! . . .
Il y en a! . . .
Ils ont eu peur du noir . . .
Ils se serrent. Ils se serrent!
Ils pleurent . . . et ils vont
vite!
Il y en a qui voudraient prendre à
droite . . .
Ils voudraient tous aller à droite.
Ils ne peuvent pas! . . .
Le berger leur jette de la
terre! . . .
Ah! ah! . . .
Ils vont passer par ici . . .
Je vais les voir de près.—
Comme il y en a! . . .
Maintenant, ils se taisent tous.
Berger?
Pourquoi ne parlent-ils plus?

LE BERGER: (qu'on ne voit pas).
Parce que se n'est pas le chemin de
l'étable!—

YNIOLD: Où vont-ils?
Berger?
Berger?
Où vont-ils? . . .
Il m'entend plus.
Ils sont déjà trop loin . . .
Ils ne font plus de bruit.—
Ce n'est pas le chemin de
l'étable . . .
Où vont-ils dormir cette
nuit? . . .
Oh! oh! il fait trop noir . . .
Je vais dire quelque chose à
quelqu'un!
(Il sort.)

## SCENE III.

(Une fontaine dans le parc.)
(Entre Pelléas.)

---

ARKEL: Were I God, I would have
pity for the hearts of men . . .

## SCENE II.

(A terrace, in the gloom. Yniold is
seen trying to lift a rock).

YNIOLD: Oh, this stone is
heavy . . .
It is heavier than I am.
It is heavier than all the world.
It is heavier than everything.
I see my golden ball between the
rock and this naughty stone and I
cannot reach it . . .
My little arm is not long enough—
and this stone will not be lifted
One would think it had roots in the
earth . . .
(The bleating of sheep is heard in
the distance.)
Oh, oh!
I hear the sheep cry.
Hallo, there is no more sun!
They come, the little sheep; they
come . . . what a lot . . . what
a lot!
They are afraid of the dark . . .
They press together . . . they
press together!
They cry . . . and they go quick-
ly!
There are some would go to the
right . . . they all want to go to
the right.
They cannot!
The shepherd throws earth at them!
Ah! ah! . . .
They will pass this way . . .
I will see them near by.
What a lot there are!
Now, they are all quiet.
Shepherd!
Why do they speak no more?

THE SHEPHERD: (who is not
seen). Because it is not the way to
the stable!—

YNIOLD: Where go they?
Shepherd?
Shepherd?
Where are they going?
He hears me no longer.
They are already too far . . . they
make no more noise
It is not the way to the stable . . .
Where will they sleep tonight?
Oh, oh! it is too dark . . .
I will go and say something to some-
body!
(He goes out.)

## SCENE III.

(A Fountain in the Park. Enter
Pelléas).

# Act IV, Scene III

**PELLÉAS:** C'est le dernier soir . . . le dernier soir . . .
Il faut que tout finisse.
J'ai joué comme un enfant autour d'une chose que je ne soupçonnais pas.
J'ai joué en rêve autours des pièges de la destinée . . .
Qui est-ce qui m'a réveillé tout à coup?
Je vais fuir en criant de joie et de douleur comme un aveugle qui fuirait l'incendie de sa maison.
Je vais lui dire que je vais fuir . . .
Il est tard; elle ne vient pas . . .
Je ferais mieux de m'en aller sans la revoir . . .
Il faut que je la regarde bien cette foisci . . .
Il y a des choses que je ne me rappelle plus . . . on dirait, par moment, qu'il y a plus de cent ans que je ne l'ai vue . . .
Et je n'ai pas encore regardé son regard . . .
Il ne me reste rien si je m'en vais ainsi.
Et tous ces souvenirs . . . c'est comme si j'emportais un peu d'eau dans un sac de mousseline . . .
Il faut que je la voie une dernière fois, jusqu'au fond de son coeur.
Il faut que je lui dise tout ce que je n'ai pas dit.
*(Entre Mélisande.)*

**PELLÉAS:** It is the last evening . . . the last evening . . .
It is needful that everything end . . .
I have played like a child around a thing that I did not suspect.
I have played in a dream around the traps of destiny . . .
Who has awakened me all of a sudden?
I shall fly crying with joy and sorrow like a blind man who runs from his house on fire.
I will tell her that I mean to fly . . .
It is late; she does not come . . .
I would do better by going away without seeing her . . .
I must look at her well this time . . .
There are things I no longer remember . . . one would think, at times that a hundred years had gone since I had seen her . . .
And I have not yet looked at her look . . .
There remains to me nothing if I go away thus.
And all these memories . . . it is as if I carried away a little water in a muslin bag . . .
I must look at her one last time, to the bottom of her heart . . .
I must tell her all that I have not told her . . .
*(Enter Melisande.)*

**MÉLISANDE:** Pelléas?

**MELISANDE:** Pelléas?

**PELLÉAS:** Mélisande!— Est-ce toi, Mélisande?

**PELLÉAS:** Melisande! Is it you, Melisande?

**MÉLISANDE:** Oui.

**MELISANDE:** Yes.

**PELLÉAS:** Viens ici: ne reste pas au bord du clair de lune.— Viens ici.
Nous avons tant de choses à nous dire.
Viens ici dans l'ombre du tilleul.

**PELLÉAS:** Come here: do not remain on the edge of the moonlight. Come here.
We have so many things to say to one another.
Come here in the shadow of the elm.

**MÉLISANDE:** Laisse-moi dans la clarté . . .

**MELISANDE:** Let me remain in the light . . .

**PELLÉAS:** On pourrait nous voir des fenêtres de la tour.
Viens ici; ici, nous n'avons rien à craindre.—
Prends garde; on pourrait nous voir . . .

**PELLÉAS:** They might see us from the windows of the tower.
Come here; here, we have nothing to fear.
Take care; they might see us . . .

**MÉLISANDE:** Je veux qu'on me voie . . .

**MELISANDE:** I want them to see me . . .

**PELLÉAS:** Qu'as-tu donc?— Tu as pu sortir sans qu'on s'en soit apercu?

**PELLÉAS:** What is the matter with you?
You were able to come out without anyone seeing you?

**MÉLISANDE:** Oui, votre frère dormait . . .

**MELISANDE:** Yes; your brother was sleeping.

**PELLÉAS:** Il est tard.—
Dans une heure on fermera les portes.
Il faut prendre garde.
Pourquoi es-tu venue si tard?

**PELLÉAS:** It is late.
In one hour they will close the gates.
We must take care.
Why have you come so late?

**MÉLISANDE:** Votre frère avait un mauvais rêve.
Et puis ma robe s'est accrochée aux clous de la porte.
Voyez, elle est déchirée.
J'ai perdu tout ce temps et j'ai couru . . .

**MELISANDE:** Your brother had a bad dream.
And then my grown got caught on the nails of the gate.
See, it is torn.
I lost all this time and I ran . . .

**PELLÉAS:** Ma pauvre Mélisande!
J'aurais presque peur de te toucher . . .
Tu es encore hors d'haleine comme un oiseau pourchassé . . .
C'est pour moi, pour moi que tu fais tout cela? . . .
J'entends battre ton coeur comme si c'était le mien.
Viens ici . . . plus près de moi.

**PELLÉAS:** My poor Melisande!
I would be almost afraid to touch you . . .
You are still out of breath like a hunted bird . . .
It is for me, for me that you do all this?
I hear your heart beat as if it were mine . . .
Come here . . . nearer, nearer to me.

**MÉLISANDE:** Pourquoi riez-vous?

**MELISANDE:** Why do you laugh?

**PELLÉAS:** Je ne ris pas;—ou bien je ris de joie, sans le savoir . . .
Il y aurait plutôt de quoi pleurer . . .

**PELLÉAS:** I do not laugh;—or else I laugh for joy, without knowing it . . .
There is rather cause for weeping . . .

**MÉLISANDE:** Nous sommes venus ici il y a bien longtemps . . .
Je me rappelle.

**MELISANDE:** We came here a long time ago . . .
I recall it.

**PELLÉAS:** Oui . . .
Il y a de longs mois.—
Alors, je ne savais pas . . .
Sais-tu pourquoi je t'ai demandé de venir ce soir?

**PELLÉAS:** Yes . . . Long months since.
Then, I did not know . . .
Do you know why I asked you to come tonight?

**MÉLISANDE:** Non.

**MELISANDE:** No.

**PELLÉAS:** C'est peut-être la dernière fois que je te vois . . .
Il faut que je m'en aille pour toujours . . .

**PELLÉAS:** It is perhaps the last time that I see you . . .
It is necessary that I go away forever . . .

**MÉLISANDE:** Pourquoi dis-tu toujours que tu t'en vas?

**MELISANDE:** Why do you say that you are going away? . . .

**PELLÉAS:** Je dois te dire ce que tu sais déjà?—
Tu ne sais pas ce que je vais te dire?

**PELLÉAS:** I am bound to say what you already know.
You do not know what I am about to say?

**MÉLISANDE:** Mais non, mais non; je ne sais rien . . .

**MELISANDE:** No, no; I know nothing . . .

**PELLÉAS:** Tu ne sais pas pourquoi il faut que je m'éloigne.
*(Il l'embrasse brusquement.)*
Tu ne sais pas que c'est parce que je t'aime . . .

**PELLÉAS:** You do not know why I must go far away.
*(He embraces her brusquely.)*
You do not know it is because I love you . . .

**MÉLISANDE:** *(à voix basse).* Je t'aime aussi.

**MELISANDE:** *(with lowered voice).* I love you, too.

**PELLÉAS:** Oh!
Qu'as-tu dit, Mélisande!
Je ne l'ai presque pas entendu!
On a brisé la glace avec des fers rougis!
Tu dis cela d'une voix qui vient du bout du monde!
Je ne t'ai presque pas entendue . . .
Tu m'aimes?—
Tu m'aimes aussi? . . .
Depuis quand m'aimes-tu?

**PELLÉAS:** Oh! what have you said, Melisande?
I almost failed to hear it . . .
They have broken the ice with red hot irons! . . .
You say that with a voice that comes from the end of the world . . .
I almost failed to hear you . . .
You love me?
You love me, too? . . .
Since when do you love me?

**MÉLISANDE:** Depuis toujours . . .
Depuis que je t'ai vu . . . .

**MELISANDE:** Since always . . .
Since I have seen you . . . .

PELLÉAS: Oh! comme tu dis cela! . . .
On dirait que ta voix a passé sur la mer au printemps! . . . je ne l'ai jamais entendue jusqui'ici . . . on dirait qu'il a plu sur mon coeur!
Tu dis cela si franchement . . .
Comme un ange qu'on tnterroge! . . .
Je ne puis pas le croire, Mélisande!
Pourquoi m'aimerais tu?—
Mais pourquoi m'aimes-tu!—
Est-ce vrai ce que tu dis?—
Tu ne me trompes pas?—
Tu ne mens pas un peu, pour me faire sourire? . . .

PELLÉAS: Oh, how you say that! . . .
One would say that your voice had passed over the sea in Springtime! I have not heard it up to now . . . one would think it had rained on my heart!
You say it so frankly . . . like an angel who is questioned.
I cannot believe it, Melisande!
Why should you love me?
But why do you love me?
Is what you say true?
You do not deceive me?
You do not lie a little, so as to make me smile? . . .

MÉLISANDE: Non; je ne mens jamais; je ne mens qu'à ton frère . . .

MELISANDE: No; I never lie; I only lie to your brother . . .

PELLÉAS: Oh! comme tu dis cela! . . .
Ta voix! ta voix . . .
Elle est plus fraîche et plus franche que l'eau! . . .
On dirait de l'eau pure sur mes mains
Donne-moi, donne-moi tes mains . . .
Oh! tes mains sont petites! . . .
Je ne savais pas que tu étais si belle! . . .
Je n'avais jamais rien vu d'aussi beau, avant toi . . .
J'étais inquiet, je cherchais partout dans la maison . . . je cherchais partout dans la campagne . . .
Et je ne trouvais pas la beauté . . .
Et maintenant je t'ai trouvée! . . .
Je ne crois pas qu'il y ait sur la terre une femme plus belle! . . .
Où es-tu?—
Je ne t'entends plus respirer . . .

PELLÉAS: Oh how you say that! . . .
Your voice, your voice!
It is fresher and franker than water.
One thinks of pure water on your lips.
One would imagine pure water on my hands.
Give me, give me, your hands
Oh, you hands are little! . . .
I did not know you were so beautiful!
I had, before you, never seen anything so beautiful . . .
I was anxious, I sought everywhere in the house
I sought everywhere in the country . . . and I did not find beauty . . .
And now I have found you . . . I have found you
I do not believe that on earth there is a woman more beautiful
Where are you?
I do not hear you breathe any more . . .

MÉLISANDE: C'est que je te regarde . . .

MELISANDE: It is that I look at you . . .

PELLÉAS: Pourquoi me regardes-tu si gravement!—
Nous sommes déjà dans la lumière.
Nous ne pouvons pas voir combien nous sommes heureux.
Viens, viens; il nous reste si peu de temps . . .

PELLÉAS: Why do you look at me so gravely?
We are already in the shadow.
It is too dark under this tree.
Come into the light.
We cannot see how happy we are.
Come, come; there remains so little time for us . . .

MÉLISANDE: Non, non; restons ici . . .
Je suis plus près de toi dans l'obscurité . . .

MELISANDE: No, no, let us stay here . . .
I am nearer to you in the darkness.

PELLÉAS: Où sont tes yeux?—
Tu ne vas pas me fuir?—
Tu ne songes pas à moi en ce moment.

PELLÉAS: Where are your eyes?
You are not going to run away from me?
You are not thinking of me at this moment.

MÉLISANDE: Mais si, mais si, je ne songe qu'à toi . . .

MELISANDE: Yes, I am, I only think of you . . .

PELLÉAS: Tu regardais ailleurs . . .

PELLÉAS: You were looking elsewhere . . .

MÉLISANDE: Je te voyais ailleurs . . .

MELISANDE: I saw you elsewhere . . .

PELLÉAS: Tu es distraite . . .
Qu'as-tu donc?—
Tu ne me semble pas heureuse . . .

PELLÉAS: You are absent minded . . .
What is the matter?
You do not seem happy to me . . .

MÉLISANDE: Si, si; je suis heureuse, mais je suis triste . . .

MELISANDE: Yes, I am; I am happy but I am sad . . .

PELLÉAS: Quel est ce bruit?—on ferme les portes! . . .

PELLÉAS: What is this noise?
They are closing the gates! . . .

MÉLISANDE: Oui, on a fermé les portes . . .

MELISANDE: Yes, they have closed the gates . . .

PELLÉAS: Nous ne pouvons plus entrer!—
Entends-tu les verrous!—
Ecoute! écoute! . . . les grandes chaînes!
Il est trop tard, il est trop tard!

PELLÉAS: We can no longer get in.
Do you hear the bolts?
Listen, listen! the great chains!
It is too late, it is too late! . . .

MÉLISANDE: Tant mieux! tant mieux!

MELISANDE: All the better, all the better!

PELLÉAS: Tu? . . .
Voilà, voilà! . . .
Ce n'est plus nous qui le voulons! . . .
Tout est perdu, tout est sauvé! tout est sauvé ce soir!—
Viens viens
Mon coeur bat comme un fou jusqu'au fond de ma gorge . . .
(Il l'enlace.)
Ecoute! mon coeur est sur le point de m'etrangler . . .
Viens! viens!
. . . Ah! qu'il fait beau dans les ténèbres! . . .

PELLÉAS: You? . . .
There, there . . .
It is no longer our will . . .
All is lost, all is gained!
All is gained this night!
Come, come . . .
My heart beats wildly even to the bottom of my throat . . .
(He enfolds her.)
Listen! my heart is on the point of strangling me.
Come, come!
Ah, how beautiful it is in the dark . . .

MÉLISANDE: Il y a quelqu'un derrière nous!

MELISANDE: There is some one behind us . . .

PELLÉAS: Je ne vois personne . . .

PELLÉAS: I see nobody . . .

MÉLISANDE: J'ai entendu du bruit . . .

MELISANDE: I heard a noise . . .

PELLÉAS: Je n'entends que ton coeur dans l'obscurité . . .

PELLÉAS: I only hear your heart in the darkness . . .

MÉLISANDE: J'ai entendu craquer les feuilles mortes . . .

MELISANDE: I heard the crackling of dead leaves . . .

PELLÉAS: C'est le vent qui s'est tû tout à coup.
Il est tombé pendant que nous nous embrassions . . .

PELLÉAS: It is the wind that suddenly became silent.
It has fallen while we were kissing.

MÉLISANDE: Comme nos ombres sont grandes ce soir!

MELISANDE: How long our shadows are tonight . . .

PELLÉAS: Elles s'enlacent jusqu'au fond du jardin.
Oh! qu'elles s'embrassent loin de nous!
Regarde!
Regarde!

PELLÉAS: They enfold each other to the end of the garden.
Oh, they embrace each other far from us!
Look, look!

MÉLISANDE: (d'une voix étouffée). A-a-h!—
Il est derrière un arbre!

MELISANDE: (with muffled voice). Aah!
He is behind a tree!

PELLÉAS: Qui?

PELLÉAS: Who?

MÉLISANDE: Golaud!

MELISANDE: Golaud!

PELLÉAS: Golaud?—où donc?—je ne vois rien

PELLÉAS: Golaud?
Where?
I see nothing . . .

MÉLISANDE: Là . . . au bout de nos ombres

MELISANDE: There . . . at the end of our shadows

**PELLÉAS:** Oui, oui; je l'ai vu . . .
Ne nous retournons pas brusquement . . .

**MÉLISANDE:** Il a son épée . . .

**PELLÉAS:** Je n'ai pas la mienne . . .

**MÉLISANDE:** Il a vu que nous nous embrassions . . .

**PELLÉAS:** Il ne sait pas que nous l'avons vu
Ne bouge pas; ne tourne pas la tête
Il se précipiterait
Il nous observe . . .
Il est encore immobile . . .
Va-t'en, va-t'en tout de suite par ici
Je l'attendrai . . .
Je l'arrêterai . . .

**MÉLISANDE:** Non, non, non! . . .

**PELLÉAS:** Va-t'en! va-t'en!
Il a tout vu!
Il nous tuera!

**MÉLISANDE:** Tant mieux! tant mieux! tant mieux! . . .

**PELLÉAS:** Il vient! il vient! . . .
Ta bouche!
Ta bouche! . . .

**MÉLISANDE:**
Oui! . . . Oui! . . . Oui! . . .
(*Ils s'embrassent éperdument.*)

**PELLÉAS:** Oh! oh!
Toutes les étoiles tombent! . . .

**MÉLISANDE:** Sur moi aussi! sur moi aussi! . . .

**PELLÉAS:** Toutes! toutes! toutes! . . .
(*Golaud se précipite sur eux l'épée à la main, et frappe Pelléas, qui tombe au bord de la fontaine. Mélisante fuit épouvantée.*)

**MÉLISANDE:** (*fuyant*). Oh! oh!
Je n'ai pas de courage! . . .
Je n'ai pas de courage! . . .
(*Golaud la poursuit à travers le bois, en silence.*)

**PELLÉAS:** Yes, yes; I saw him . . .
Do not let us turn around suddenly . . .

**MELISANDE:** He has his sword.

**PELLÉAS:** I do not have mine . . .

**MELISANDE:** He could see that we were embracing.

**PELLÉAS:** He does not know that we have seen him . . .
Do not move; do not turn your head . . .
He would precipitate himself . . .
He watches us . . .
He is still immovable
Go away, go off at once this way . . .
I will wait . . .
I will stop him . . .

**MELISANDE:** No, no, no! . . .

**PELLÉAS:** Go away, go away.
He has seen all!
He will kill us! . . .

**MELISANDE:** All the better! all the better! all the better!

**PELLÉAS:** He is coming, he is coming!
Your mouth . . . your mouth! . . .

**MELISANDE:** Yes . . .
Yes . . .
Yes!
(*They kiss one another wildly.*)

**PELLÉAS:** Oh, oh! all the stars are falling! . . .

**MELISANDE:** On me, too, on me too! . . .

**PELLÉAS:** All, all, all! . . .
(*Golaud, sword in hand, throws himself upon them and strikes Pelléas, who falls on the edge of the fountain. Melisande flees, terror-stricken.*)

**MELISANDE:** (*fleeing*). Oh, oh!
I have not the courage! . . .
I have not the courage! . . .
(*Golaud pursues her through the wood, in silence.*)

# ■ ACTE V.

## SCENE I.

(*Un appartement dans le château.*)
(*On découvre Arkel, Golaud et le médecin dans un coin de la chambre. Mélisande est étendue sur son lit.*)

**LE MÉDECIN:** Ce n'est pas de cette petite blessure qu'elle peut mourir; un oiseau n'en serait pas mort . . . ce n'est donc pas vous qui l'avez tuée, mon bon seigneur; ne vous désolez pas ainsi . . . Et puis, il n'est pas dit que nous ne la sauverons pas . . .

**ARKEL:** Non, non; il me semble que nous nous taisons trop, malgré nous, dans sa chambre . . . Ce n'est pas un bon signe . . . Regardez comme elle dort . . . lentement, lentement . . . on dirait que son âme a froid toujours . . .

**GOLAUD:** J'ai tué sans raison! Est-ce que ce n'est pas à faire pleurer les pierres! . . . Ils s'étaient embrassés comme des petits enfants . . . Ils étaient frère et soeur . . . Et moi, moi tout de suite! . . . Je l'ai fait malgré moi, voyez-vous . . . Je l'ai fait malgré moi . . .

**LE MÉDECIN:** Attention; je crois qu'elle s'éveille . . .

**MÉLISANDE:** Ouvrez la fenêtre . . . ouvrez la fenêtre . . .

**ARKEL:** Veux-tu que j'ouvre celle-ci, Mélisande?

**MÉLISANDE:** Non, non; la grande fenêtre . . . c'est pour voir . . .

**ARKEL:** Est-ce que l'air de la mer n'est pas trop froid ce soir?

**LE MÉDECIN:** Faites, faites . . .

**MÉLISANDE:** Merci . . . Est-ce le soleil qui se couche?

**ARKEL:** Oui; c'est le soleil qui se couche sur la mer; il est tard.— Comment te trouves-tu, Mélisande?

**MÉLISANDE:** Bien, bien.— Pourquoi demandez-vous cela? Je n'ai jamais été mieux portante.— Il me semble cependant que je sais quelque chose . . .

**ARKEL:** Que dis-tu?— Je ne te comprends pas . . .

**MÉLISANDE:** Je ne comprends pas non plus tout ce que je dis, voyez-vous . . . Je ne sais pas ce que je dis . . . Je ne sais pas ce que je sais . . . je ne dis plus ce que je veux . . .

**ARKEL:** Mais si, mais si . . . Je suis tout heureux de t'entendre parler ainsi; tu as eu un peu de délire ces jours-ci, et l'on ne te comprenait plus . . . Mais maintenant, tout cela est bien loin . . .

**MÉLISANDE:** Je ne sais pas . . . — Etes-vous tout seul dans la chambre, grand-père?

**ARKEL:** Non; il y a encore le médecin qui t'a guérie . . .

# ■ ACT V.

## SCENE I.

(*An apartment in the Castle. Arkel, Golaud and the physician discovered in a corner of the room. Melisande is extended on her bed.*)

**THE PHYSICIAN:** It is not from this little wound that she can die; a bird would not die from it . . . thus it is not you who have killed her, my good lord; do not take on so . . . And it is not said that we will not save her . . .

**ARKEL:** No, no; it seems to me that we are too silent, in spite of ourselves, in her room . . . It is not a good sign . . . Look how she sleeps . . . slowly, slowly . . . one would think her soul was cold forever . . .

**GOLAUD:** I killed without reason. Is it not enough to make the stones weep? . . . They were embracing each other like little children . . . They were brother and sister . . . And I, I at once! . . . I did it in spite of myself, you see . . . I did it in spite of myself . . . .

**THE PHYSICIAN:** Attention; I think she awakes . . .

**MELISANDE:** Open the window . . . open the window . . .

**ARKEL:** Do you wish me to open this one, Melisande?

**MELISANDE:** No, no; the great window . . . it is that I may see . . .

**ARKEL:** Is not the sea air too cold tonight?

**THE PHYSICIAN:** Do it, do it . . .

**MELISANDE:** Thank you. Is it the sun that is sinking?

**ARKEL:** Yes; it is the sun that is sinking in the sea; it is late. How do you find yourself, Melisande?

**MELISANDE:** Well, well. Why do you ask that? I was never in better health. It seems to me, however, that I know something . . .

**ARKEL:** What do you say? I do not understand

**MELISANDE:** I do not understand all that I say either, you see . . . I do not know what I say . . . I do not know what I know . . . I do not say any more what I want to . . .

**ARKEL:** Yes, you do . . . I am quite happy to hear you speak in this way; you have had a little delirium these past days, and we no longer understood you . . . But now, all that is long past.

**MELISANDE:** I do not know . . . Are you all alone in the room, grandfather?

**ARKEL:** No; there is also the physician who cured you . . .

MÉLISANDE: Ah . . .

ARKEL: Et puis il y a encore quelqu'un . . .

MÉLISANDE: Qui est-ce?

ARKEL: C'est . . . il ne faut pas t'effrayer
Il ne te veut pas le moindre mal, sois-en sûre . . .
Si tu as peur, il s'en ira . . .
Il est très malheureux . . .

MÉLISANDE: Qui est-ce!

ARKEL: C'est . . . c'est ton mari . . . c'est Golaud . . .

MÉLISANDE: Golaud est ici? Pourquoi ne vient-il pas près de moi?

GOLAUD: (se trainant vers le lit). Mélisande . . . Mélisande . . .

MÉLISANDE: Est-ce vous, Golaud Je ne vous reconnaissais presque plus
C'est que j'ai le soleil du soir dans les yeux
Pourquoi regardez-vous les murs?
Vous avez maigri et vieilli . . .
Y a-t-il longtemps que nous ne nous sommes vus?

GOLAUD: (à Arkel et au médecin.) Voulez-vous vous éloigner un instant, mes pauvres amis . . .
Je laisserai la porte grande ouverte . . .
Un instant seulement . . .
Je voudrais lui dire quelque chose; sans cela je ne pourrais pas mourir . . .
Voulez-vous?—
Vous pouvez revenir tout de suite . . .
Ne me refusez pas cela
Je suis un malheureux . . .
(Sortent Arkel et le médecin.)—
Mélisande, as-tu pitié de moi, comme j'ai pitié de toi? . . .
Mélisande? . . .
Me pardonnes-tu, Mélisande? . . .

MÉLISANDE: Oui, oui, je te pardonne
Que faut-il pardonner?

GOLAUD: Je t'ai fait tant de mal, Mélisande
Je ne puis pas te dire le mal que je t'ai fait . . .
Mais je le vois, je le vois si clairement aujourd'hui . . . depuis le premier jour . . .
Et tout est de ma faute, tout ce qui est arrivé, tout ce qui va arriver . . .
Si je pouvais le dire, tu verrais comme je le vois! . . .
Je vois tout, je vois tout!
Mais je t'aimais tant!
Je t'aimais tant!
Mais maintenant, quelqu'un va mourir
C'est moi qui vais mourir . . .

MELISANDE: Ah . . .

ARKEL: And then there is someone else . . .

MELISANDE: Who is it?

ARKEL: It is . . . you must not get frightened . . .
He does not wish you the least harm, be sure of that . . .
If you are afraid he will go away . . . he is very unhappy . . .

MELISANDE: Who is it?

ARKEL: It is . . . it is your husband . . . it is Golaud

MELISANDE: Golaud is here? Why does he not come close to me?

GOLAUD: (dragging himself toward the bed.) Melisande . . . Melisande.

MELISANDE: Is it you, Golaud? I hardly recognized you at all . . .
It is because I have the evening sun in my eyes . . .
Why do you look at the walls?
You have grown thin and older . . .
Is it long since we have seen one another?

GOLAUD: (to Arkel and the physician). Will you go away for a moment, my poor friends . . .
I will leave the door wide open . . .
A moment only . . .
I would like to tell her something; without it I shall not be able to die . . .
Will you?
You can come back at once . . .
Do not refuse me this . . .
I am an unfortunate.
(Arkel and the physician go out.)
Melisande, do you have pity on me as I have pity on you? . . .
Melisande? . . . do you forgive me, Melisande? . . .

MELISANDE: Yes, yes, I forgive you . . . what shall I forgive?

GOLAUD: I have done you so much harm, Melisande . . .
I cannot tell you the harm I have done you . . .
But I see it, I see it so clearly today . . . since the first day . . .
And all is of my fault, all that has happened, all that will happen . . .
If I could tell it, you would see it as I see it . . . I see all, I see everything . . .
But I loved you so much . . .
I loved you so much . . . It is I who will die
And I would like to know
I want to ask you . . .

Et je voudrais savoir . . .
Je voudrais te demander . . .
Tu ne m'en voudras pas? . . .
Il faut dire la vérité à quelqu'un qui va mourir . . .
Il faut qu'il sache la vérité, sans cela il ne pourrait pas dormir . . .
Me jures-tu de dire la vérité?

MÉLISANDE: Oui.

GOLAUD: As-tu aimé Pelléas?

MÉLISANDE: Mais oui; je l'ai aimé. Où est-il?

GOLAUD: Tu ne me comprends pas?—
Tu ne veux pas me comprendre?—
Il me semble . . .
Il me semble . . .
Eh bien, voici:
Je te demande si tu l'as aimé d'un amour défendu? . . .
As-tu . . . avez-vous été coupables?
Dis, dis, oui, oui, oui?

MÉLISANDE: Non, non; nous n'avons pas été coupables.—
Pourquoi demandez-vous cela?

GOLAUD: Mélisande! . . . dis-moi la vérité pour l'amour de Dieu!

MÉLISANDE: Pourquoi n'ai-je pas dit la vérité?

GOLAUD: Ne mens plus ainsi, au moment de mourir!

MÉLISANDE: Qui est-ce qui va mourir?—Est-ce moi?

GOLAUD: Toi, toi! et moi, moi aussi, après toi!
Et il nous faut la vérité . . .
Il nous faut enfin la vérité, entends-tu! . . .
Dis-moi tout!
Dis-moi tout!
Je te pardonne tout! . . .

MÉLISANDE: Pourquoi vais-je mourir . . .
Je ne le savais pas

GOLAUD: Tu le sais maintenant! . . .
Il est temps!
Il est temps! . . .
Vite! vite! . . .
La vérité! la vérité! . . .

MÉLISANDE: La vérité . . . la vérité . . .

GOLAUD: Où es-tu?—
Mélisande!—
Où es-tu?—
Ce n'est pas naturel!
Mélisande!
Où es-tu?—
(Apercevant Arkel et le médecin à la porte de la chambre.)—
Oui, oui; vous pouvez rentrer . . .
Je ne sais rien; c'est inutile . . .
Elle est déjà trop loin de nous . . .
Je ne saurai jamais! . . .
Je vais mourir ici comme un aveugle! . . .

You will not be angry with me?
The truth must be told to one about to die . . .
He must know the truth with out that he could not sleep . . .
Do you swear to tell me the truth?

MELISANDE: Yes.

GOLAUD: Did you love Pelléas?

MELISANDE: Why, yes; I loved him.
Where is he?

GOLAUD: You do not understand me?
You will not understand me.
It seems to me, it seems to me . . .
Well, then, here: I ask you if you loved him with a forbidden love? . . .
Have you . . . have you both been guilty?
Say it, say it, yes, yes, yes?

MELISANDE: No, no; we have not been guilty.
Why do you ask that?

GOLAUD: Melisande! . . . tell me the truth for the love of God!

MELISANDE: Why, have I not told the truth?

GOLAUD: Do not lie like this any more, at the moment of dying!

MELISANDE: Who is going to die? Is it me?

GOLAUD: You, you! and me, too, after you
And we must have the truth . . .
We must at last have the truth, do you hear?
Tell me all, tell me all.
I forgive you everything . . .

MELISANDE: Why am I about to die.
I did not know it

GOLAUD: You know it now!
It is time, it is time . . .
Quick! quick! . . .
The truth, the truth!

MELISANDE: The truth . . . the truth . . .

GOLAUD: Where are you?
Melisande! where are you?
It is not natural!
Melisande!
(Seeing Arkel and the physician at the door of the room.)
Yes, yes, you can come back . . .
I know nothing; it is useless . . .
She is already far from us . . .
I shall never know! . . .
I shall die here like a blind man! . . .

## Act V, Scene I

ARKEL: Qu'avez-vous fait? Vous allez la tuer . . .

GOLAUD: Je l'ai déjà tuée . . .

ARKEL: Mélisande . . .

MÉLISANDE: Est-ce vous, grand-père?

ARKEL: Oui, ma fille . . . Que veux-tu que je fasse?

MÉLISANDE: Est-il vrai que l'hiver commence?

ARKEL: Pourquoi demandes-tu cela?

MÉLISANDE: Parce qu'il fait froid et qu'il n'y a plus de feuilles . . .

ARKEL: Tu as froid?— Veux-tu qu'on ferme les fenêtres?

MÉLISANDE: Non, non . . . jusqu'à ce que le soleil soit au fond de la mer.— Il descend lentement, alors c'est l'hiver qui commence?

ARKEL: Oui.— Tu n'aimes pas l'hiver?

MÉLISANDE: Oh! non. J'ai peur du froid.— Ah! J'ai peur des grands froids

ARKEL: Te sens-tu mieux?

MÉLISANDE: Oui, oui; je n'ai plus toutes ces inquiétudes . . .

ARKEL: Veux-tu voir ton enfant?

MÉLISANDE: Quel enfant?

ARKEL: Ton enfant, ta petite fille

MÉLISANDE: Où est-elle?

ARKEL: Ici . . .

MÉLISANDE: C'est étrange . . . je ne puis pas lever les bras pour la prendre . . .

ARKEL: C'est que tu es encore très faible. Je la tiendrai moi-même; regarde . . .

MÉLISANDE: Elle ne rit pas . . . Elle est petite . . . Elle va pleurer aussi . . . J'ai pitié d'elle . . . (*La chambre est envahie, peu à peu, par les servantes du château qui se rangent en silence le long des murs et attendant.*)

GOLAUD: (*se levant brusquement*). Qu'y a-t-il?— Qu'est-ce que toutes ces femmes viennent faire ici?

LE MÉDECIN: Ce sont les servantes . . .

ARKEL: Qui est-ce qui les a appelées?

LE MÉDECIN: Ce n'est pas moi . . .

---

ARKEL: What have you done? You will kill her . . .

GOLAUD: I have killed her already . . .

ARKEL: Melisande . . .

MELISANDE: Is it you, grandfather?

ARKEL: Yes, my daughter . . . What do you wish me to do?

MELISANDE: Is it true that winter begins?

ARKEL: Why do you ask that?

MELISANDE: Because it is cold and there are no more leaves . . .

ARKEL: You are cold? Do you wish the windows closed?

MELISANDE: No, no . . . until the sun is at the bottom of the sea. It goes down slowly, then it is the winter that begins?

ARKEL: Yes. You do not like the winter?

MELISANDE: Oh, no. I am afraid of the cold. Ah, I am afraid of the great colds

ARKEL: Do you feel better?

MELISANDE: Yes, yes; I no longer have all those anxieties . . .

ARKEL: Do you wish to see your child?

MELISANDE: What child?

ARKEL: Your child, your little girl

MELISANDE: Where is she?

ARKEL: Here . . .

MELISANDE: It is strange . . . I cannot lift my arms to take her . . .

ARKEL: It is because you are still very weak . . . I will hold her myself; look . . .

MELISANDE: She does not laugh . . . She is little . . . She will also weep . . . I pity her . . . (*The room is invaded, little by little, by maid-servants of the Castle, who range themselves in silence along the walls and wait.*)

GOLAUD: (*rising suddenly.*) What is it? What are all these women doing here?

THE PHYSICIAN: It is the maid servants.

ARKEL: Who called them?

THE PHYSICIAN: It was not me . . .

---

GOLAUD: Pourquoi venez-vous ici?— Personne ne vous a demandées . . . Que venez-vous faire ici?—mais qu'est-ce que donc! Répondez! . . . (*Les servantes ne répondent pas.*)

ARKEL: Ne parle pas trop fort . . . Elle va dormir; elle a fermé les yeux . . .

GOLAUD: Ce n'est pas? . . .

LE MÉDECIN: Non, non; voyez, elle respire . . .

ARKEL: Ses yeux sont pleins de larmes.— Maintenant c'est son âme qui pleure . . . Pourquoi étend-elle ainsi les bras? Que veut-elle?

LE MÉDECIN: C'est vers l'enfant sans doute. C'est la lutte de la mère contre la mort . . .

GOLAUD: En ce moment?— En ce moment? Il faut le dire, dites! dites!

LE MÉDECIN: Peut-être . . .

GOLAUD: Tout de suite? . . . Oh! Oh! Il faut que je lui dise . . . — Mélisande! Mélisande! Laissez-moi seul! laissez-moi seul avec elle!

ARKEL: Non, non; n'approchez pas . . . Ne la troublez pas . . . Ne lui parlez plus . . . Vous ne savez pas ce que c'est qu l'âme . . .

GOLAUD: Ce n'est pas ma faute, ce n'est pas ma faute!

ARKEL: Attention . . . Attention . . . Il faut parler à voix basse.— Il ne faut plus l'inquiéter . . . L'âme humaine est très silencieuse . . . L'âme humaine aime à s'en aller seule . . . Elle souffre si timidement . . . Mais la tristesse, Golaud . . . mais la tristesse de tout ce que l'on voit! . . . Oh! oh! oh! (*En ce moment, toutes les servantes tombent subitement à genoux au fond de la chambre.*)

ARKEL: (*se tournant.*) Qu'y a-t-il?

LE MÉDECIN: (*s'approchant du lit tâtant le corps*). Elles ont raison . . . (*Un long silence.*)

ARKEL: Je n'ai rien vu.— Etes-vous sûr? . . .

---

GOLAUD: Why do you come here? Nobody asked you . . . What do you come to do here? But what is it? Answer! (*The servants do not answer.*)

ARKEL: Do no speak so loud . . . She is about to sleep; she has closed her eyes . . .

GOLAUD: It is not? . . .

THE PHYSICIAN: No, no; look, she breathes . . .

ARKEL: Her eyes are full of tears. Now it is her soul that weeps . . . Why does she stretch her arms this way? What does she want?

THE PHYSICIAN: It is toward the child, no doubt. It is the struggle of the mother against death . . .

GOLAUD: At this moment? At this moment? You must say it, speak, speak!

THE PHYSICIAN: Perhaps . . .

GOLAUD: At once? . . . Oh, oh! I must tell her . . . Melisande! Melisande! Leave me alone, leave me alone with her! . . .

ARKEL: No, no; do not approach . . . Do not trouble her. Do not speak to her any more . . . You do not know what the soul is . . .

GOLAUD: It is not my fault, it is not my fault!

ARKEL: Attention . . . attention . . . We must speak low. Do not annoy her any more . . . The human soul is very silent . . . The human soul likes to go away alone . . . It suffers so timidly . . . But the sadness, Golaud . . . but the sadness of all one sees! Oh, oh, oh! . . . (*At this moment all the servants fall suddenly on their knees at the end of the room*).

ARKEL: (*turning*). What is the matter?

THE PHYSICIAN: (*approaching the bed and feeling the body*). They are right . . . (*A long silence.*)

ARKEL: I have seen nothing Are you sure? . . .

LE MÉDECIN: Oui, oui.

ARKEL: Je n'ai rien entendu . . .
Si vite, si vite . . .
Tout à coup . . .
Elle s'en va sans rien dire . . .

GOLAUD: (*sanglotant*). Oh! oh! oh! . . .

ARKEL: Ne restez pas ici, Golaud . . .
Il lui faut le silence, maintenant . . .
Venez, venez . . .
C'est terrible, mais ce n'est pas votre faute . . .
C'était un petit être si tranquille, si timide et si silencieux . . .
C'était un pauvre petit être mystérieux, comme tout le monde . . .
Elle est là, comme si elle était la grande soeur de son enfant. —
Venez, il ne faut pas que l'enfant reste ici dans cette chambre . . .
Il faut qu'il vive, maintenant, à sa place . . .
C'est au tour de la pauvre petite . . .
(*Ils sortent en silence.*)

*FIN.*

THE PHYSICIAN: Yes, yes.

ARKEL: I heard nothing . . . so quick, so quick . . .
All at once . . .
She goes away saying nothing . . .

GOLAUD: (*sobbing*). Oh, oh, oh! . . .

ARKEL: Do not remain here, Golaud . . .
Now she needs silence . . .
Come, come . . .
It is terrible; but it is not your fault . . .
It was a little being so quiet, so timid, and so silent . . .
It was a poor little being, mysterious, like everybody . . .
She is there, as if she were the big sister of her child . . .
Come; it will not do for the child to stay here in this room . . .
It must live, now, in her place . . .
It is the turn of the poor little one . . .
(*They go out in silence.*)

*THE END.*

# Lakmé (1883)

MUSIC BY LÉO DELIBES ■ LIBRETTO BY EDMOND GONDINET & PHILLIPE GILLE

This three-act opéra comique, set to a libretto by Edmond Goudinet and Phillippe Gille (based on Goudinet's Poem "Le Mariage de Loti"), premiered at the Opéra-Comique in Paris on April 14, 1883. The story is about Lakmé, daughter of Nilakantha, a fanatical Brahmin (Hindu) Priest. He is forbidden to practice his religion by the British, rulers of India. Lakmé and other members of the Hindu religion pray to their gods as Nilakantha goes to another gathering of his followers. He leaves Lakmé alone with her companions, including Mallika, in the beautiful garden surrounding the temple. Lakmé and Mallika sing a beautiful barcarole together as they bathe in the stream, after which Lakmé takes off her jewelry and leaves it on a rock. Then they get into a boat and sail away. Now two British army officers are introduced, along with a couple of young girls and their governess. None of them has any understanding of the land in which they find themselves. They break through the fence surrounding the temple and exclaim at the beauty in front of their eyes. They are told about the priest and the joy of his life, his beautiful daughter, by Frédéric. The young girls want a sketch of the jewels, which Gérald promises to do. He speculates about the owner of the jewels, sees Lakmé and Mallika sailing back, and hides. Lakmé sends Mallika away, sees Gérald, and cries for help. When Mallika and Hadji enter, she sends them away. She is alone with Gérald and tells him that she could have had him killed. He is totally infatuated with her, and they sing together until she hears the entrance of her father. Nilakantha is enraged that his temple has been profaned and cries out for revenge. A festival is being held in a public square, where the governess is pick-pocketed until rescued by Frédéric. Nilakantha arrives, accompanied by Lakmé, and Gérald comes with his finacée, Ellen. Gérald is told by Frédéric that their regiment leaves before dawn. Nilakantha commands that Lakmé must sing in order to attract the man who has profaned the temple as he is sure that this man was drawn by her beauty. Nobody appears in response to her singing, and he tells his daughter to continue until she sees Gérald, at which she cries out and faints. Nilakantha thus knows his enemy and plans to destroy him during the procession of the goddess. Lakmé is left alone with Hadji, who promises to help her. Gérald comes to her, and they sing of their love. She admits her feelings for him and plans a new life for them. The procession enters, and the English young girls watch with their escort, Frédéric. He comments on his friend's infatuation but is not worried as they are leaving that night. As the procession continues, Gérald is stabbed, according to Nilakantha's plan. Lakmé finds that he has only a minor wound and, assisted by Hadji, moves him to a secret hiding place in the forest. Gérald awakens in this place, and she tells him that a group of lovers have come to drink the waters of the sacred spring. These waters give the gift of eternal love to those who drink them. She goes out, and Frédéric enters, having followed drops of blood which left a trail. Frédéric reminds Gérald of his duty, but Gérald is in love with Lakmé, forgetting about Ellen, his fiancée. But can Gérald truly forget his soldier's honor, asks Frédéric, and he leaves knowing that he has gotten through to his comrade. Gérald knows this as well when he hears the sounds of soldiers marching in the distance. Lakmé sees the change in him immediately, and as he listens to the sounds of the march, she tears a poisonous leaf off of the datura tree and eats it. She and Gérald drink water together and swear to love each other for all time. Then she tells him that he will not need to break his oath as she is dying. She tells her father before she dies that she and Gérald have drunk the sacred water together. Gérald cries out in grief as Nilakantha thinks about his daughter's journey to eternal life.

---

## ■ ACTE I

(Un jardin très ombragé où croissent et s'entremêlent toutes des fleurs de l'Inde. Au fond, une maison peu élevée, à demi chachée par es arbres. L'image du Lotus sur la porte d'entrée et plus loin un statue de Ganeça, idole à tête d'éléphant, dieu de la sagesse, donnent à cette mystérieuse habitation l'aspect d'un sanctuaire. Au fond, le commencement d'un petit cours d'eau qui se perd dans la verdure.—Le jardin est entouré d'une frêle clôture en bambous.—C'est le lever du jour.)

## ■ ACT I

A well-shaded garden, where flourish and intermingle the flowers of India. In the back-ground, near a little river, stands a building of modest proportions, half concealed by the trees, a figure of Lotus over the door; and near by, a statute of Ganesá, the God of Wisdom, an idol with the head of an elephant, give this mysterious abode the appearance of a sanctuary. The garden is enclosed by a light fence of bamboo. Time, daybreak.

(Hadji, Mallika, Nilakantha, puis Hindous, hommes et femmes.)
(Au lever du rideau, Hadji et Mallika vont ouvrir la porte du jardin à des Hindous, hommes et femmes, qui entrent avec recueillement.)

CHOEUR: A l'heure accoutumée.
Quand la plaine embaumée
Par l'aurore enflammée,
Fête le jour naissant,
Unissons nos prières,
Pour calmer les colères
De Brahma menaçant.

NILAKANTHA: (Sortant de sa demeure.) Soyez trois fois bénis, vous qui rendez hommage
Au prêtre abandonné qu'on raille et

(Hadji, Mall_ik_á, Nilakantha; then Hindu men and women. Hadji and Mallíká come to open the garden gate to the Hindus, who enter reflectively.)

PRAYER AND CHORUS: Here at the usual moment.
When the plain, perfume-freighted,
By the dawn's flame lighted,
Greets the new-born day,
Let our prayers rise united,
That the anger of Brahma
May from us pass away.

NILAKANTHA: (Coming from his dwelling). Thrice blessed may you be,
Who faithful homage render

qu'on outrage.
De nos vainqueurs odieux
Nous lasserons les colères;
Ils ont pu chasser nos dieux
De leurs temples séculaires!
Mais, sur leurs têtes, Brahma
A suspendu sa vengeance,
Et, quant elle éclatera,
Ce sera la délivrance,
Dans ma retraite, aujourd'hui
La puissance de Dieu brille,
Je le vois, je monte à lui
Quand j'entends prier ma fille.

**LAKMÉ:** (*A ce moment, on entend la voix de Lakmé, dans la demeure du brahmane. Tous les Hindous se prosternent.*) Blanche Douga,
Pâle Siva!
Puissant Ganeça!
O vous, que créa Brahma!
Apaisez-vous,
Protégez-nous!
(*A la fin du chant sacré, Lakmé a paru sur le seuil de la demeure du brahmane et mêle sa prière à celles des Hindous.*)

**NILAKANTHA:** (*Aux Hindous.*)
Allez en paix, redites, en partant
La prière au matin, allez, Dieu vous entend!
(*Toute le monde sort, à l'exception du brahmane, de Lakmé et de ses deux serviteurs.*)

**NILAKANTHA:** Lakmé, c'est toi qui nous protèges,
Et si je puis braver les haines sacrilèges
De l'ennemi triomphant
C'est que Dieu prend pitié de ta candeur d'enfant.

**LAKMÉ:** Lorsque Brahma, dans sa clémence,
En broyant une fleur, fit la terre et le ciel,
Il y laissa le miel.
Et ce fut l'espérance.

**NILAKANTHA:** Il faut que je te quitte à l'instant.

**LAKMÉ:** Quoi déjà?

**NILAKANTHA:** Sois sans crainte!
Dans la pagode sainte,
Qui reste encor debout à la ville ou m'attend,
La fête de demain m'appelle.
(*Aux serviteurs.*)
Restez près de Lakmé!

**HADJI:** Nous veillerons sur elle!

**MALL:** Nous veillerons tous deux!

**NILAKANTHA:** Je serai de retour
Avant la fin du jour!

**NILAKANTHA:** Que le ciel me protège,
Me guide par la main,
Chasse le sacrilège
Au loin de mon chemin!

---

To heaven's high priest in me,
Reviled, scoffed at, and outraged!
Of our base victors, the sway
We'll weary out, slowly;
They have driven our gods away
From the ancient temples holy.
But Brahma over their heads
His vengeance has suspended;
When that explodes and spreads,
Our bondage will be ended!
In my dwelling here, today,
I saw God's power displaying.
Up to him I soared away,
While I heard my daughter praying.
(*In the wing.*)

**LAKMÉ:** O Dourga fair, O Shiva great!
Powerful Ganesá, who Brahma did create.
(*Hindus kneeling.*)
(*Lakmé enters and joins in the prayer.*)
Calm yourselves!
Protect us!

**NILAKANTHA:** (*To Hindus.*) Go, now, in peace;
But as you leave, repeat
Your devout morning prayer.
God hears you
(*All now depart except Nilakantha, Lakmé, and the two servitors.*)

**NILAKANTHA:** (*Tenderly.*)
Lakmé! It is you who shall protect us!
And if I dare to brave the sacreligious hatred
Of the triumphant enemy;
It is that God takes pity on
Your childlike purity.

**LAKMÉ:** When Brahma great, in pity tender,
Bruising flowers on his way,
Made earth and sky,
He let their honey lie,
And from that hope did render!

**NILA:** I now must leave you for a while.

**LAKMÉ:** What? so soon?

**NILA:** Be fearless,
In that pagoda peerless
That's still allowed to stand,
Some are waiting my command.
The festival tomorrow calls me.
(*To the servants.*)
Stay here with Lakmé.

**HADJI:** Together we'll watch over her.

**MALL:** We will stay beside her.

**NILA:** I shall back find my way
Before the close of day.
(*Ensemble.*)

**NILA:** Kind heaven will guard and keep me.
And lead me by the hand,
And drive all foes away
That in my path may stand.

---

**LAKMÉ, HADJI, MALLIKA:** Que le ciel te protège,
Te guide par la main,
Chasse tout sacrilège
Au loin de ton chemin!
(*Nilakantha s'éloigne accompagné jusqu'à la porte par Lakmé et ses deux serviteurs. Hadji rentre dans la maison.*)

**LAKMÉ:** (*Après s'être débarrassée de quelques bijoux qu'elle a placer sur une table en pierre.*) Viens, Mallika, les lianes en fleurs
Jettent déjà leur ombre
Sur le ruisseau sacre qui coule, calme et sombre,
Eveillé par le chant des oiseàux tapageur

**MALL:** Oh, maîtresse, c'est l'heure où je te vois sourire,
L'heure bénie où je puis lire,
Dans le coeur toujours fermé
De Lahkmé!
(*Pendant les dernières measures du chant, Mallika détache une petite barque qui était amarrée dans les roseaux; Lakmé y monte, suivie de Mallika qui a pris l'aviron; à barque s'éloigne et leurs voix s'éteignent dans le lointain.*)
(*Gérald, Frédéric, Ellen, Rose, Mistress Bentson.*)
(*On entend des éclats de rire en dehors de la clôture du jardin.*)

**ROSE:** Que voyez-vous?

**FRÉDÉRIC:** Je vois un jardin

**ELLEN:** Et vous, Gérald?

**GÉRALD:** Je vois de très beaux arbres.

**ELLEN:** Il n'y a personne?

**GÉRALD:** Je ne sais pas.

**ROSE:** Regardez bien.

**FRÉDÉRIC:** Ce n'est pas commode, à travers une pareille clôture.

**ELLEN:** Essayez d'écarter les bambous!

**MRS. B:** Mesdemoiselles, mesdemoiselles, soyez prudentes.

**GÉRALD:** Tiens, je vois la statue de Ganeça, le dieu de la sagesse.

**FRÉDÉRIC:** Je vois une feuille de lotus dessinée sur la porte. C'est la demeure d'un brahmane.

**ROSE ET ELLEN:** D'un brahmane!

**FRÉDÉRIC:** Allons-nous-en!

**ROSE ET ELLEN:** Pourquoi?

**FRÉDÉRIC:** Parce qu'il ne faut pas plaisanter avec ces gens-là.

**ELLEN:** (*Écartant les bambous.*)
Oh! moi, je veux absolument voir le jardin d'un brahmane.

**MRS. B:** Miss Ellen, soyez prudente!

**ELLEN:** Oh! il est trop tard! (*Les bambous ont cédé, elle est entrée dans le jardin.*)

---

**LAKMÉ, MALL., HADJI:** May heaven guard and keep you.
And lead me (your) by the hand,
And drive all foes away
That in my (your) path may stand.
(*Nilakantha goes out followed to the door by the others. Hadji re-enters the house.*)

**LAKMÉ:** (*Taking off some jewels and laying them on stone table*)
Come, Malliká, the flowering vines
Are now their shadows throwing
Along the sacred stream,
That calmly here is flowing;
Enlivened by the songs of birds amid the pines.

**MALL:** O mistress, dear! it is now–
When I behold you smiling,
In this blessed hour, no cares beguiling,
That your oft-closed heart I may read. Lakmé! and more music
(*During the latter measures Mallika has unfastened a little boat which was anchored among the reeds in the stream. Lakmé steps into it, followed by Mallika, who sits at the helm. The boat moves on and their voices are lost in the distance.*)
(*Enter Gerald, Frederic, Ellen, Rose, Mrs. Benson.*)
(*Laughter heard outside the enclosure.*)

**ROSE:** What do you see?

**FREDERIC:** I see a garden.

**ELLEN:** And you, Gerald?

**GERALD:** I see lovely trees.

**ELLEN:** There are no people?

**GERALD:** I don't know.

**ROSE:** Look well.

**FREDERIC:** It's difficult, across this fence.

**ELLEN:** Try to move the bamboo.

**MRS. B:** Girls, girls, be careful.

**GERALD:** Wait! I see the statue of Ganesa, goddess of wisdom.

**FREDERIC:** There's a lotus leaf on the door. A Brahmin must live there.

**ROSE AND ELLEN:** A Brahmin!

**FREDERIC:** Let's go.

**ROSE AND ELLEN:** Why?

**FREDERIC:** You can't fool with these people.

**ELLEN:** (*Pushing aside the bamboo.*) Oh! I must see a Brahmin's garden.

**MRS. B:** Miss Ellen, be careful.

**ELLEN:** It's too late.
(*She pushes through the bamboo into the garden*)

## Act I

ROSE: La brèche est faite, on peut passer.

MRS. B: (*Éperdue.*) Miss Rose, vous aussi!

GÉRALD: Nous ne pouvons plus reculer, véné rable mistress Bentson.

MRS. B: (*Entrant en faisant la grimace.*) Mais je ne sais pas chez qui nous sommes.

FRÉDÉRIC: Moi, je le sais très bien. Je ne connais pas le propriétaire de ce petit temple, mais j'ai beaucoup entendu parler de lui.

GÉRALD: Très positivement, nous n'avons pas été presentés.

FRÉDÉRIC: Nous nous livrons là à une plaisanterie extrêmement dangereuse.

ROSE: (*Vivement.*) N'effrayez pas, mistress Bentson.

ELLEN: Oh! non, ne l'effrayez pas!

MRS. B: Permettez, mesdemoiselles, je suis votre gouvernante, la prudence est un devoir pour moi.

ROSE: La prudence, oui: mais la peur?

MRS. B: La peur aussi. Quand M. le gouverneur a diagné me confier sa fille et sa nièce, il m'a recommandé d'avoir peur. Je me suis engagée avoir peur. J'ai peur!

ELLEN: (*Gaiment, à Rose.*) Vois comme c'est joli.

ROSE: Quel adorable fouillis de feuilles et de fleurs!

FRÉDÉRIC: Prenez garde aux serpents, sous les fleurs, miss Rose!

ELLEN: Comme elle est coquette, cette rivière, toute bordée de verdure.

ROSE: Elle a l'air de s'allonger dans une courbe gracieuse pour arriver jusqu'ici.

ELLEN: Vois donc ces belles fleurs.

FRÉDÉRIC: N'y touchez pas, miss Ellen! ce sont des daturas, des daturas *stramonium*, très inoffensifs en Angleterre, mais, sous en beau ciel indien, il suffirait d'en mettre une feuille sous vos jolies dents.

MRS. B: Pour être empoisonnée?

GÉRALD: Pour être empoisonnée.

FRÉDÉRIC: Parfaitement, mistress Bentson.

MRS. B: C'est un pays abominable.

FRÉDÉRIC: Si vous me permettiez de vous parler raison.

ROSE: Nous ne voulons pas!

ELLEN: Non, non, nous ne voulons pas!

FRÉDÉRIC: Voyons, Gérald, toi qui as des droits ou du moins un semblant de droits, puisque tu auras le bonheur d'épouser miss Ellen dans quelques semaines.

ROSE: The opening is made, we can go through.

MRS. B: You too, Rose!

GERALD: We can't go back, ma'am.

MRS. B: (*Following after, making a face.*) But in whose place are we?

FREDERIC: I know. I don't know the owner of this temple but I've heard about him.

GERALD: Right! We haven't been introduced.

FREDERIC: Let's not fool around. It's dangerous.

ROSE: Don't worry, Mrs. Benson.

ELLEN: Of course, don't worry.

MRS. B: Please, girls, I am your governess and caution is my duty.

ROSE: Caution, yes; fear, no.

MRS. B: Fear, too. When the governor entrusted his daughter and his niece to me he told me to have fear. I was engaged to have fear. I have fear.

ELLEN: (*Gaily, to Rose.*) Isn't it lovely.

ROSE: Flowers and lovely buds–how adorable!

FREDERIC: Look out for snakes! Under the flowers!

ELLEN: And the river! How charming with its grassy banks.

ROSE: It seems to have gone to great lengths just to come here for us.

ELLEN: Look at these flowers.

FREDERIC: Don't touch them, Ellen! They're daturas stramonium–innocuous in England but here in India, if just one leaf–

MRS. B: They're poisonous.

GERALD: Poisonous.

FREDERIC: Right.

MRS. B: This is a terrible country.

FREDERIC: Now, if you'll listen to reason–

ROSE: We won't.

ELLEN: No, we won't.

FREDERIC: Look, Gerald, you have some rights, or seem to have since you're going to marry Ellen in a couple of weeks . . .

GÉRALD: Je n'userai jamais de mes droits pour contrarier ma femme.

ELLEN: (*Lui tendant la main.*) A la bonne heure, voilà une bonne parole!

FRÉDÉRIC: Oh! ces amoureux! (*A Gérald.*) L'aventure, d'ailleurs, ne te déplaît pas. (*A miss Ellen.*) Vous ne le connaissez pas bien, miss Ellen; il aime le danger, il y met de la poésie! c'est un rêveur de l'impossible, un enthousiaste de l'inconnu; il ai perd avec amour dans les nuages bleu.

ELLEN: (*Vivement.*) Je ne le lui reproche pas.

FRÉDÉRIC: (*Gaiement.*) Au contraire, n'est -ce pas? C'est moi qui suis prosaïque. Je vous jure pourtant que si j'étais seul.

ROSE: Quoi? Nous ne nous exposons pas beaucoup, puisque nous ne rencontrons personne. On dirait cette demeure inhabitée.

FRÉDÉRIC: Je vous répète qu'elle est parfaitement habitée par un brahmane fanatique qui se nomme Nilakantha. Il desservait une pagode que la conquête a ruinée, ce qu'il nous pardonne difficilement.

MRS. B: Mais j'en vois encore partout des pagodes!

FRÉDÉRIC: Dans les villes, oui; nous aurons même demain une des plus grandes fêtes indoues. Tous les brahmanes des environs vont se réunir à la grande pagode, mais dans les campagnes, le culte disparaît peu à peu. Nilakantha s'est retiré sur ce coin de terre qu'il a consacré à Brahma, de sa propre autorité, et il vit des modestes offrandes de quelques Hindous qui lui sont restés fidèles. Il a une fille.

ELLEN: Une fille?

MRS. B: C'est gens-là ont des filles?

FRÉDÉRIC: Elle se nomme Lakmé.

ELLEN: Oh! le joli nom: Lakmé!

ROSE: Je voudrais bien la voir.

FRÉDÉRIC: Il ne manquerait plus que cela. Mais vous ne savez donc pas, Européenne que vous êtes, que cette petite personne née dans une pagode, vouée à quelque Dieu ou à quelque déesse du ciel indien, se croit elle-même d'essence divine. Elle méprise tout ce qui se passe en dehors de cette enceinte et elle ne se montre pas.

ELLEN: Et vous croyez qu'elle est belle?

FRÉDÉRIC: Ravissante, dit-on.

ELLEN: Quand une femme est si jolie
Elle a bien tort de se cacher.

GERALD: I will never use my rights against my wife.

ELLEN: (*Giving him her hand.*) Well said, darling.

FREDERIC: Oh! these lovers! (*To Gerald*) The prospect does not displease, then. (*To Ellen*) You don't know him well. He loves danger and puts poetry into it. He's a dreamer of the impossible, an enthusiast of the unknown. He's lost with love in the blue shadows.

ELLEN: (*With spirit.*) I don't blame him.

FREDERIC: (*Gaily.*) On the contrary, eh? Well, I'm the prosaic one. But let me tell you, if only I could . . . .

ROSE: What? We're not taking a chance. We won't meet anyone. My guess is that no-one lives here.

FREDERIC: I tell you, this house certainly is inhabited by a fanatic Brahmin named Nilakantha. He built a pagoda here which was ruined in the conquest and now he hates all of us.

MRS. B: I see plenty of pagodas here.

FREDERIC: In the cities, yes. In fact, tomorrow's one of their big holidays. And all the Brahmins will gather in the main pagoda. But in the country the cult is gradually disappearing. Nilakantha has retired into this obscure place which he has dedicated to Brahma, living on the modest contributions of his few remaining faithful Hindus. He has a daughter.

ELLEN: A daughter.

MRS. B: Do these people have daughters?

FREDERIC: Her name is Lakmé

ELLEN: What a beautiful name: Lakmé!

ROSE: I'd like to see her.

FREDERIC: It's quite impossible. You don't understand, being European, that this little person born in a pagoda, vowed to some god or goddess in the Indian heaven, believes herself divine. Everything outside is profane and she never shows herself.

ELLEN: Do you think she's beautiful?

FREDERIC: They say she's ravishing.

ELLEN: When a woman is youthful and jolly,
She is wrong to hide herself;

FRÉDÉRIC: Dans ce pays tout est folie
Et j'admets tout, moi, sans brancher.

FREDERIC: But in this strange land all is folly.
Yet, we must abide by its rulings.

GÉRALD: Une idole qu'on divinise!

GERALD: Like an idol deified ever,

ROSE: Qu'l'on enferme avec ferveur!

ROSE: Shut up from the light by herself;

GÉRALD: Et qui jamais ne s'humanise!

GERALD: Stirred up with humanity never,

MRS. B.: Je la crois laide à faire peur!

MRS. B.: She'd be a perfect fright for me.

ELLEN: Une femme est toujours sensible
Au juste hommage qu'on lui rend.

ELLEN: Every woman listens with pleasure
To the praises that men bring to her;

FRÉDÉRIC: En Europe, c'est bien possible,
Mais ici, c'est tout différent!

FREDERIC: In Europe it is so in a measure,
But here it is a different thing!

GÉRALD, ROSE, ELLEN, MRS. B.:
Beaux faiseurs de systèmes,
Amoureux du changement,
Laissez là vos poèmes
Et raisonnons froidement;
Les femmes sont partout les mêmes
Fort heureusement.

GERALD, ROSE, ELLEN, MRS. B.:
Ah! adepts in plans aesthetic,
Loving changes and brilliant show;
Lay aside all your dreams poetic,
Let us reason with calmness now.

FRÉDÉRIC: Je hais tous les systèmes,
J'observe tout simplement
Sans faire de poèmes,
Les femmes changent vraiment
Et ne sont point partout les mêmes,
Fort heureusement!

FREDERIC: I hate all systems aesthetic,
And say and think what all know;
Without a fancy poetic,
I see only what the facts show.

ELLEN: Si nous cherchions un peu sa trace
Dans cet enclos mystérieux?

ELLEN: Should we seek them for gracious footprints,
In these calm, mysterious abodes?

FRÉDÉRIC: On! non—ce serait d'une audace
A faire bondir tous leurs dieux.

FREDERIC: Oh! no, it would be something audacious,
And a bustle it would make among their gods.

ROSE: (Railleuse.) A-t-elle une grâce divine?

ROSE: (Jestingly.) Then has she divine grace within her?

FRÉDÉRIC: (Avec bonhomie.) Mon Dieu! moi, je me l'imagine.

FREDERIC: My god! I would imagine so.

GÉRALD: (Raillant.) Fraudrait-il vivre à ses genoux?

GERALD: (Jestingly.) Must we live, then, on bended knee?

MRS. B.: (Ironique.) Dites donc qu'elle est mieux que nous!

MRS. B.: (Ironically.) Say then she's better than we!

FRÉDÉRIC: Je ne dis pas cete sottise.
Non. Mais, sous ce beau ciel de feu,
Les femmes que leur soleil grise,
Des nôtres diffèrent un peu.
Leur vertu bizarre
Manque d'apparat;
L'amour s'en empare
Sans loi ni contrat.
Ce n'est plus l'amour aux façons coquettes
Ce n'est plus ce tendre et doux sentiment
Un bonheur d'allures discrètes
Qui finit très moralement.
Non, leur coeur s'enivre
Du plaisir d'aimer,
Et pour elles, vivre
Ce n'est que charmer!

FREDERIC: I'll not speak in such foolish fashion,
But beneath this hot sky aflame,
The women here, burning with passion
As our own, are not quite the same.
Their peculiar virtue needs some outward show,
Though love engrossed, they neither love nor contract know.
It is not love, in our fine, coquettish manner,
Not a state of warm, gentle sentiment,
That often ends in moral sweet content.
No, their hearts are full while love is warm;
Life, for them, is knowing how to charm.
Living, is to charm.

ELLEN: Ce sont des femmes idéales
Qui charment instantanément
Et nous leur paraîtrons banales,
Nous, qui voulons plaire autrement.
Nous sommes conquises
Avec moins d'éclat;
De peur des surprises,
La raison combat.
Mais elles n'ont pas, vos enchanteresses,
Les effrois charmants des premiers aveux
Ni les troubles, ni les ivresses
D'un bonheur que l'on rêve à deux
Ces beautés célestes
Savent tout charmer,
Mais nous, plus modestes.
Nous savons aimer.

ELLEN: Such women we should call ideal,
Who charm all instantaneously;
And we seem commonplace and real
Who may be pleasing otherwise.
We're subdued, with less of brilliant noise and light;
Against surprises sudden we let reason fight.
But they've not, you know, your fine enchantresses,
Felt the sweet dismay when love is first declared.
Nor the pleasures, or the distresses,
Or the bliss, when one's dreams are shared.
Those celestial beauties know how to move hearts.
We know how to love with more modest feeling.

FRÉDÉRIC: Ne croyez pas que je compare.

FREDERIC: Do not think that I compare

ELLEN, ROSE ET MRS. B.: C'est votre esprit qui vous égare.

ELLEN, ROSE AND MRS. B.: It is but his wit that leads him straying.

GÉRALD: (Riant.) Il est naïf, en vérité!

GERALD: He deals with facts, we plainly see.

FRÉDÉRIC: Je dis ce qu'on m'a raconté.

FREDERIC: I say it as reported to me.

ROSE: (Apercevant les bijoux sur table de pierre.) Tiens! des bijoux de femme!

ROSE: (Perceiving jewels.) See! lovely jewels!

ELLEN: De la fille du brahmane!

ELLEN: The Brahmin's daughter's.

ROSE: Qu'ils sont gracieux de forme!

ROSE: They're grand.

FRÉDÉRIC: (Vivement.) Mesdemoiselles! n'y touchez pas.

FREDERIC: Girls! Don't touch them.
(Quickly.)

ELLEN: Rassurez-vous, je n'y toucherai pas puisqu'ils sont sacrés. Mais Gérald pourrait en prendre le dessin!

ELLEN: Don't worry. Since they're sacred, I won't touch them. But Gerald can copy the design.

FRÉDÉRIC: Vous voulez qu'il s'installe avec ses crayons?

FREDERIC: What! Start drawing right here?

GÉRALD: Pourquoi pas?

GERALD: Why not?

FRÉDÉRIC: Comment! pourquoi pas? Parce qu'en entrant ici, nous n'avons pas seulement commis une violation de domicile comdamnable en tous pays, mais un véritable sacrilège, la demeure d'un brahmane étant sacrée comme la pagode elle-même. Or, un sacrilége commis par un Européen n'est jamais reste impuni. Le coupable tombe un jour ou l'autre frappé par une main invisible.

FREDERIC: Why not? Because, in coming here, we have not only violated privacy, but have committed a sacrilege, the Brahmin's home being as sacred as his pagoda. A sacrilege committed by a European never remains unpunished. Sooner or later, an unseen hand strikes the fatal blow.

MRS. B.: Ah! mon Dieu, pourquoi ne nous avez-vous pas dit ça tout de suite?

MRS. B.: Why didn't you say so in the first place?

GÉRALD: Les officiers de Sa Majesté la reine d'Angleterre se moquent des brahmanes.

GERALD: The officers of Her Majesty the Queen just laugh at that nonsense.

FRÉDÉRIC: Il ne s'agit pas de courage avec des ennemis qui ne se montrent jamais, qui poursuivent leur vengeance dans l'ombre sans

FREDERIC: It's not a question of courage with enemies who never show themselves but pursue their vengeance, unhurried, waiting for

se hâter, attendant l'instant propice, sûrs que pas un des leurs ne les dénoncera. Rappelez-vous que nous sommes en pays conquis.

**MRS. B:** Oui! oui! en pays barbare. Quand je pense que nous serions si bien à Londres, à Hyde-Park, humant ce joli brouillard qui nous fait le teint frais. Maintenant, mesdemoiselles, j'userai de mon autorité.

**GÉRALD:** Je propose une transaction. Vous allez retourner à la ville, respectable mistress Bentson.

**MRS. B:** Merci.

**GÉRALD:** Avec ces demoiselles et Frédéric. Moi, je resterai pour copier ces bijoux qui plaisent à miss Ellen.

**ELLEN:** (*À Gérald.*) Si pourtant vous deviez courir un danger.

**GÉRALD:** (*Riant.*) Pas le moindre. Aussitôt que je vois arriver quelqu'un, je me sauve. Je n'y mettrai pas d'amour-propre.

**ELLEN:** Je porterai ces bijoux-là, le jour de notre mariage.

**GÉRALD:** C'est alors que je les trouverai jolis.

**MRS. B:** Eh bien, mesdemoiselles?

**ROSE:** (*À Ellen.*) Je regrette de m'en aller.

**ELLEN:** Je le regrette bien davantage.

**FRÉDÉRIC:** (*À Gérald.*) Rappelle-toi que tu as tort.

**MRS. B:** Monsieur Frédéric.

**FRÉDÉRIC:** (*En sortant.*) C'est un héros, lui! Tu es un héros! Et me je suis ridicule, parfaitement ridicule. Voilà, généralement en ce monde la vie des hommes sages.

**MRS. B:** Monsieur Frédéric.
(*Ils sortent.*)
(*Seul, se préparant à dessiner.*)

**GÉRALD:** Prendre le dessin d'un bijou,
Est-ce donc aussi grave? Ah!
Frédéric est fou!
(*Il se dirige vers les bijoux, puis s'arrête.*)
Mais d'où vient maintenant cette craint insensée;
Quel sentiment surnaturel
A troublé ma pensée
Devant ce calme solennel!
(*S'animant.*)
Fille de mon caprice
L'inconnue est devant mes yeux.
Sa voix à mon oreille glisse
Des mots mystérieux!
Fantaisie aux divine mensonges. Tu ne viens m'égarer encore. Va retourne au pays du songes. Ô fantaisie aux ailes d'or. O fantaisie aux ailes d'or. Va! va! ya, retourne au pays des songes. O fantaisie aux ailes d'or. Au bras polide la païenne Cet annelet dut s'en façer! Elle tiendrait ton te en la mienne, 'La main

the proper time and certain of secrecy. Remember you're in a conquered country.

**MRS. B:** Yes. A barbarous country. When I think how happy we were in London, in Hyde Park, breathing that beautiful invigorating fog! Well, girls, I'm going to use my authority.

**GERALD:** I have a suggestion to make. You go back to town, Mrs. Benson.

**MRS. B:** Thanks.

**GERALD:** With Frederic and the girls. I'll stay here to copy these jewels that Ellen likes.

**ELLEN:** (*To Gerald.*) If there's any danger.

**GERALD:** (*Laughing.*) Not the least. If anyone comes, I'll go. I won't be ashamed.

**ELLEN:** I'll wear these jewels on our wedding day.

**GERALD:** That's why I like them.

**MRS. B:** Well, girls.

**ROSE:** (*To Ellen.*) I hate to go.

**ELLEN:** I, too.

**FREDERIC:** (*To Gerald.*) I think you're making a mistake.

**MRS. B:** Mr. Frederic . . . .

**FREDERIC:** (*Leaving.*) A hero! He's a hero! And I am ridiculous. That's the way life is. Wisdom looks foolish.

**MRS. B:** Mr. Frederic . . .
(*They go out.*)
(*Gerald alone, preparing to sketch.*)

**GERALD:** Taking the design of a jewel, – is that so serious an action? Ah! Frederic is mad!
(*He moves toward the jewels, then stops.*)
But then, from where comes, this foolish forewarning of danger; what supernatural fancy has disturbed my reflections, amid these calm and solemn shades?
(*Becoming animated.*)
Daughter of my caprices, the unknown stands before my sight; her voice plain to my hearing, utters this one mysterious word, No! no! Idle fancy, cradled by delusion, You mislead me now, as of old. Go to dreamland, turn back in confusion, O phantom dove, with wings of Gold, O dove fantastic, with wings of gold! Go! go! to the dreamland, O sweet illusion! Fair dove fantastic, with wings of gold. Of some fair maid folding round her arm, This bracelet rich must oft ent-

qui seule y peut passer! Ce cercle d'or. Je le suppose. A suivi les pas voyageurs D'un petit pied qui ne se pose Que sur la mousse où sur les fleurs. Et ce collier encor parfumé d'elle, De sa personne encor tout enbaume A pu sentir battre son coeur fidele, Tout tressaillant au nom du bien aimé, Tout tressaillant au nom du bien aimé. non! non! Fuyez Fuyez, chimères Rêves ephèmres Qui troubles ma raison suives. Fantaisie aux divins mensonges, Tu reveins m'égarer encor. Va, retourne aux pays des songes. O fantaisie aux ailes d'or. O fantaisie aux ailes d'or. Va! va! va! retourne aux pays des songes. Ô fantaisie aux ailes d'or. Ô fantaisie Ô fantaisie aux ailes d'or!
(*Reconçant à dessiner.*)
Eh bien! non! Je ne veux plus toucher à ces bijoux. Ce serait, pour moi, comme une profanation. Lakmé, elle s'appelle Lakmé.
(*Il va pour s'en aller quand il entend la voix de Lakmé a la barque.*)
C'est elle, les mains pleines de fleurs. C'est elle!
(*Il se cache dans un massif d'arbustes.*)
*Gérald, caché, puis Lakmé et Mallika.*

wine. Ah! what delight would be the holding, The hand that passes there, in mine! This ring of gold .. my dream supposes, Often has followed, wandering for hours, With the small foot, that but reposes On moss banks or beds of flowers. This necklace too, with her own perfume scented . . . Embalmed as yet with sweets from her lips that came . . . Has felt the true heart, . . . beating glad, contented, Trembling with joy at the one well-love name, Trembling at sound of one . . . beloved name. No! No! Away fly, found illusions, Swiftly passing visions That my reason disturb . . . . . . . Idle fancy cradled by delusion, You mislead me now again Back to dream-land, go, in swift confusion! O fantastic dove, with wings of gold, O fantastic dove, with wings of gold! Go! Go! . . to the dream-land, O fair illusion, O fair illusion, with wings of gold. O fair illusion, with wings of gold!
(*Renounces his intention of sketching.*)
Well no! I'll not touch those jewels again.
It would be for me a sort of profanation.
Lakmé, she calls herself Lakmé!
(*He is about to leave when he hears the voice of Lakmé from the boat.*)
It is she! with her hands filled with flowers.
It is she!
(*He hides himself in a thicket of shrubbery.*)
Gerald, (*concealed*); then Lakmé, Mallika.

**MALLIKA, LAKMÉ:** (*Devant la statue de Ganeça.*) O toi qui nous protèges,
Garde-nous des pièges
De nos persécuteurs!
(*Elles posent des fleurs aux pieds de l'idole.*)

**LAKMÉ:** (*À Mallika.*) Et maintenant, dans cette eau transparente Qui, sur le sable frais, murmure insouciante, D'un soleil accablant vient braver les ardeurs.

**MALL:** Oui, profitons de l'heure propice
Où les arbres touffus
Répandent sur la rive une ombre protectrice.
(*Elle disparaît vivement derrière les arbres.*)
(*Lakmé, Gérald, caché.*)

**LAKMÉ:** (*Défait le manteau qui l'enveloppe, puis au moment de suivre Mallika, elle s'arrête rêveuse.*) Mais je sens en mon coeur des murmures confus,
Les fleurs me paraissent plus belles

**LAKMÉ and MALLIKA:** (*Standing before the statue Ganesá.*) O you who watches over us,
From our foes before us
Keep us unharmed we pray.
(*They place the flowers at the feet of the idol.*)

**LAKMÉ:** (*To Mallika.*) And briefly now,
In the stream cool and flowing,
Which over the golden sand murmurs
Heedless going,
Of an overpowering sun,
Come and brave the hot rays!

**MALL:** The moment, now, will find advantageous,
Where the the dense forest trees spread over the mossy bank,
A shelter cool, umbrageous!
(*She quickly disappears among the trees.*)
(*Lakmé, Gerald.*)
(*Concealed.*)

**LAKMÉ:** (*Having laid aside her mantle is about to follow her, but stops thoughtfully.*) But I feel in my heart sudden movements confused!
The flowers are seeming more fair

Le ciel est plus resplendissant,
Les bois ont des chansons nouvelles
L'air qui passe est plus caressant;
Je ne sais quel parfum m'enivre,
Tout palpite et commence à vivre.
Pourquoi dans les grands bois aimé-
je à m'égarer
Pour y pleurer?
Pourquoi suis-je attristée au chant
d'une colombe,
Par une fleur fanée, une feuille qui
tombe,
Et cependant ces pleurs ont des
charmes pour moi,
Je me sens heureuse! Pourquoi?
Pourquoi chercher un sens au mur-
mure des eaux
Dans les roseaux?
Pourquoi ces voluptés à sentir dans
l'espace
Comme un souffle divin qui
m'embaume et qui passe?
Parfois aussi ma bouche a souri
malgré moi,
Je me sens heureuse! Pourquoi?
(*Après avoir vu Gérald et pous-
sant un grand cri.*)
Ah! Mallika!
(*Entrent Lakmé, Hadji, Mallika.*)

MALL: Lakmé! Quel danger te menace?
(*Hadji paraît.*)

LAKMÉ: (*Maîtrisant son émotion.*)
Aucun! Je me trompais! Tout
m'effraie aujourd'hui!
Mon père ne vient pas, et pourtant
l'heure passe.
Allex tous deux vers lui!
(*Mallika et Hadji sortent en la regardant avec étonnement.*)
(*Lakmé, Gérald.*)
(*Lakmé, dès que les deux serviteurs sont sortis, va droit à Gérald
qui a fait un pas vers elle et qui la
regarde avec ravissement.*)

LAKMÉ: (*Courroucée.*) D'où
viens-tu? Que veux-tu? Pour punir
ton audace
On t'aurait tué devant moi.
Mais je rougis de mon effroi,
Et je ne veux pas qu'on sache,
Que le pied d'un barbare a souillé
d'une tache
La demeure sacrée où mon père se
cache,
Oublie et pour jamais ce qui frappe
les yeux.
Va-t-en! je suis fille des Dieux!

GÉRALD: Oublier que je t'ai vue
Te redressant tout émue
Sous un geste triomphant?
De colère frémissante,

to me,
The sky is more splendid in hue;
The wood is teeming with new
bird-songs,
Sweeter kisses the wind never
blew.
What's the perfume here that ex-
cites me,
And to new life now invites me!
But why?
Ah! why in these grand woods
Do I love to roam and creep,
Is it to weep?
Why is my heart so saddened
At voices of ring-doves calling,
At sight of flowers fading,
Or of brown leaflets falling?
And yet these tears have charms for
me,
Even though I sign.
And I feel that I still am happy,
But why?
Why seek a sense to find
In the stream's murmuring flow
Among the reeds below?
From where came all these sweet
delights,
While through space comes the
feeling,
Like a breath half divine,
Leaving balm, then on-stealing?
My lips, at times, with smiles with
sadness defy,
And I feel I am happy,
But why?

LAKMÉ: (*Perceiving Gerald, and
with loud cry.*) Ah, Malliká!

MALLIKÁ: (*Running back to
her.*) Lakmé! are you threatened
with danger?
(*Hadji runs in.*)

LAKMÉ: (*Conquering her emotion.*) Ah, no.
I was deceived. Trifles frighten me
to-day; my father does not come,
though the time is past already! Go,
both, in search of him. Away!
(*Malliká and Hadji depart, looking at her with astonishment.*)
(*Lakmé, Gerald.*)
(*So soon as the servants are gone,
Lakmé walks straight up to Gerald, who has taken a step towards
her, and gazes upon her with ravishment.*)

LAKMÉ: (*Angrily.*) From where
did you come? What do you want?
Your rash boldness to punish,
They should have killed you here
on sight!
I blush, ashamed of my fright!
To no one here shall it be said that a
barbarian has with the presence of a
task sealed the domain where my father hides. Be gone and forget forever what your eyes have seen. Depart! I'm the child of the gods!

GERALD: (*Warmly.*) Forget that I
saw you standing
There, erect, with eyes expanding,
In a posture of command?

Inflexible, menaçante
Avec ce regard d'enfant?

LAKMÉ: Jamais le plus téméraire,
Jamais un Hindou, mon frère,
N'oserait parler ainsi.
Et le Dieu qui me protège
Punira ton sacrilège
Va-t'en! va-t'en! sors d'ici!

GÉRALD: Oublier que je t'ai vue,
Et cette grâce ingénue,
Et ce charme pénétrant?
Ah! tu veux que je t'oublie
Lorsque je sens que ma vie
A tes lèvres se suspend?

LAKMÉ: (*Un peu radoucie.*) Tu ne
savais pas, sans doute,
Quel danger tu courais. Maintenant, suis ta route,
Va! c'est la mort dont rien ne saurait
a garder,
Va!

GÉRALD: (*Sans bouger.*) Laisse-
moi te regarder.

LAKMÉ: (*À part.*) C'est pour moi
dont il sait la haine,
Et c'est pour me voir un instant
Qu'il brave la mort, qu'il l'attend?
Quelle force vers moi l'entraîne?
Rien ne l'épouvante?
(*À Gérald.*)
D'où te vient
Cette audace surhumaine?
Quel est le Dieu qui te soutient?

GÉRALD: Ah c'est le Dieu de la jeunesse C'est la Dieu du printemps,
C'est le Dieu qui nous caresse De
ses baisers ardents, par qui
s'ouvrent les calices Des roses chaque jour; C'est le Dieu de tes caprices C'est l'amour!.

LAKMÉ: Il m'a semblé qu'une
flamme Avait passe sur mon âme,
L'empissant tout d'èmoi! Quels
sont ces mots nouveaux pour moi?
Ah! C'est le Dieu de la jeunesse
C'est le Dieu du printemps C'est
the Dieu qui nous caresse De ses
baisers ardent Par qui s'ouivrent les
calices Des roses chaque jour C'est
le Dieu de mes caprices! C'est
l'amour, C'est l'amour!

GÉRALD: Ah! reste, reste encor,
pensive et rougis sante, Laisse passer sur la douce pâleur, le charme
enchanteur De ta pudour naisante!

LAKMÉ, GÉRALD: Ah! C'est le
Dieu de la jeunesse. C'est le Dieu
du printemps C'est le Dieu qui
nous caresse De ses baisers ardents
Par qui s'ouvrent les calices Des
roses chaque jour. C'est le Dieu de
tes caprices, C'est l'amour C'est le

Trembling, with your anger lower-
ing;
Stern, unyielding, overpowering,
With that childlike gaze, so grand!

LAKMÉ: So boldly; never has an-
other,
If Hindu, or even my brother,
Dared address such speech to me,
And the gods still watching over
me;
Will chastise your sin before me,
Now, depart, away, quickly flee!

GERALD: Forget that I saw you
standing
There, with simple grace com-
manding,
And that penetrating charm?
Go, forget, are you decreeing,
When I feel my very being
Hangs upon your lips so warm?

LAKMÉ: (*Aside and softened.*)
Doubtless you had no suspicion
Of the danger you incur;
Now depart, with quick decision,
Or meet death, which no power can
deter.

GERALD: (*Without moving.*) Let
me stay and gaze.

LAKMÉ: (*Aside.*) It is for me,
though he knows I hate him;
To behold me, here he stays,
Braving death by his delays!
Strong the force is that draws him
towards me:
Nothing frightens him!
(*To Gerald.*)
From where comes to you that su-
perhuman courage?
What god is that who lends you aid?

GERALD: Ah it is the god of youth
and beauty; It is the young God of
Spring, Who repays love for duty
Brings ardent kisses; Opens for us
the delicious cups of roses in the
grove; It is the god of capricious
whims, Ah! It is love.

LAKMÉ: Saints inherit its breath
from the realms, Has seemed to pass
over my spirit, Filling me with ecstacy! What words are those, So new
to me? Ah! It is the god of youth and
beauty; It is the young god of
Spring, Who repays us love for
duty, And brings warm kisses.
Opens for us the cups delicious Of
roses in the grove; It is the god of capricious whims, Ah! It is love. Ah It
is love.

GERALD: Ah! stay you! remain
here. Thus pensive fair and blushing Let pass I pray . . over that pale
cheek again . . That sweetest Of
charms of mildest rosy flushing.

LAKME, GERALD: Ah! .. It is the
god of youth and beauty, It is the
sweet god of spring, Who repays
with love our duty, And brings
kisses warm; opens for us the delicious cups of roses in the grove; It is
the god of capricious whims, Ah! It

Dieu de la jeunesse! C'est l'amour!

is love roses in the grove; It is the god of capricious whims, Ah! It is love It is the god of youth and beauty! Ah! . . . It is love.

**LAKMÉ:** (*Poussant un grand cri.*)
Grands dieux! Mon père! Fuis!
(*Suppliant.*)
Par pitié pour moi!

**LAKMÉ:** (*With a loud cry.*) Great heaven! Behold, my father! Fly,
(*Beseechingly.*)
for my sake fly!

**GÉRALD:** (En sortant.) Non, je ne t'oublierai plus, ô douce vision!
(*Lakmé, Nilakantha, Hadji puis des Hindous.*)
(Gérald est sorti quand le Brahmane, guidé par Hadji paraît à la porte.)

**GERALD:** (*Departing.*) No, I'll never forget you; O fair vision!
(*Goes quickly out.*)
Lakmé, Nilakantha, Hadji; then Hindus (*Gerald is gone, when the Brahmin, guided by Hadji, appears at the door.*)

**HADJI:** (*Montrant la clôture brisée.*) Viens, là, là!

**HADJI:** (*Showing the broken enclosure.*) Come here!

**NILA:** Dans ma demeure?
Un profane est entré chez moi!

**NILAKANTHA:** (*Indignantly.*)
Here, in my dwelling, the profane one has defiled my home!

**LAKMÉ:** Je meurs d'effroi!

**LAKMÉ:** I die of fright!

**NILA:** Vengeance! Il faut qu'il meure!
(*Des Hindous qui sont entrés sur les pas du Brahmane répetent son cri de vengeance pendant que Lakmé reste terrifiée.*)

**NILAKANTHA:** The foe must die! Ah! Vengeance!
(*The Hindu entering, join the cry. Lakmé remains terrified.*)

# ◼ ACTE II

(*Une place publique.—Nombreuses boutiques chinoises, indiennes, des bazars, des étalages d'étoffes.—A droit, la tente d'une maison de repos ou confiserie, avec divans bas et chaises en bambou devant les petites tables à incrustation de nacre.—Au fond une grade pagode.*)

# ◼ ACT II

(*A public square. Numerous Indian and Chinese shops, bazaars, displays of rugs, stuffs, etc. An awning of a café or confectionery shop, divans, and two low bamboo chairs; little tables, encrusted with pearl. In the background, a grand pagoda. Time, near noon; the market hour.*
(*Chorus and market scene.*)

Promeneurs, Marchands, Matelots, un Domben, un Chinois, un Cipaye.
(*Au lever du rideau les marchands de fruits, de bijoux, en appellent les promeneurs venus pour la fête.*)

Promenaders, merchants, sailors, a soothsayer, a Chinaman, a sepoy. At the rising of the curtain, dealers in stuffs, jewels, and fruits call out to the promenaders who are come to the festival.

**CHOEUR:** Allons, avant que midi sonne
Venez, on ne vend plus, on donne,
Jamais nous ne trompons personne.
Venez, le marché va finir.

**CHORUS:** Come in before the noon bell rings;
We sell no more, but freely give you;
We give away, and don't deceive you.
So come, the market soon will close,
And we shall all repose.

**MARCHANDS HINDOUS:** (*1er Groupe.*) Admirez cette babouche
Et ce mouchoir merveilleux!

**HINDUS:** (*1st group.*) Look and see these slippers easy,
There gay kerchiefs, wondrous dyes.

**CHINOIS:** (*2e Groupe.*) Gâteaux exquis à la bouche
Et ravissants pour les yeux!

**CHINESE:** (*2nd group.*) Here are cakes, quite sure to please you,
And as tempting to the eyes.

**MARCHANDS DE FRUITS:** (*3e Groupe.*) Voyez ces fraîches bananes
Et ces feuilles de bétel,
Belles nattes de lianes,
Goûtez ces rayons de miel!

**FRUITERERS:** (*3rd group.*) See these golden, ripe bananas,
Leaves of betel, fresh and strong;
Braided mats of green lianas,
Taste, they will prolong you lives.

**MATELOTS:** (*4e Groupe.*) Servirez-vous les profanes,
Fils de Brahma, roi du ciel!
(*mistress Bentson puis Frédéric et Rose.*)

**SAILORS:** (*4th group. Rapping on a table.*) Come help us quick, you believers,
Sons of Brahma, come along.
(*Mrs. Benson; then Rose and Frederic.*)

**MRS. B:** (*Égarée dans la foule.*)
Ces égoïstes,
Peu formalistes,
Causent de leurs amours
Et me perdent

**MRS. B:** (*Lost in the crowd.*) These selfish lovers,
These careless rovers,
Talk love from morn till night,
And of me they quite lose sight.

**UN DOMBEN:** Madame, la bonne aventure?

**SOOTHSAYER:** (*To Mrs. Benson.*) My lady, I'll tell you your fortune.

**MRS. B:** Laissez-moi, je vous en conjure!

**MRS. B:** Let me pass, or I'll compel you.

**UN MARCHAND:** Voyez ces bijoux dorés.

**MERCHANT:** Look here! gold jewels are these.

**MRS. B:** Messieurs, vous m'exaspérez!

**MRS. B:** Sirs, you exasperate me!

**UN CIPAYE:** (*S'approchant.*) Laissez madame, on la désole!
(*Il lui vole sa montre.*)

**SEPOY:** (*Steals her watch.*) In peace leave madam; you treat her poorly.

**MRS. B:** Ah! merci. Mais il me vole!

**MRS. B:** Thank you, sir. But he robbed me!

**LE DOMBEN:** Je vais lire dans votre main
Quel bonheur vous attend demain!

**SOOTHSAYER:** In your hand pray let me read
What good luck you'll reach; take heed.

**MRS. B:** Mais, monsieur, laissez-moi tranquille!

**MRS. B:** But, sir, leave me tranquil only.

**LE MARCHAND:** Cet élixir rend la santé
Et donne aux femmes la beauté!

**MERCHANT:** This new elixir health restores,
And makes women beauteous by scores.

**MRS. B:** Merci, monsieur, c'est inutile!

**MRS. B:** Thank you sir; no use, I tell you.

**LE DOMBEN:** Encore un mot!

**SOOTHSAYER:** Spare me one word.

**LE MARCHAND:** A moi plutôt!

**MERCHANT:** To me speak fair.

**MRS. B:** (*Furibonde.*) Assez! je suis la gouvernante
De la fille du gouverneur!

**MRS. B:** (*Enraged.*) I'm governess—take notice—of the governor's young daughter here!

**FRÉDÉRIC:** (*Accourant.*) C'est mistress Bentson en fureur!

**FREDERIC:** (*Running in.*) Mrs. Benson! Mad, it is clear.

**ROSE:** Qu'avez vous?

**ROSE:** (*Running in.*) Mistress Benson, dear. What is here?

**MRS. B:** On me violente!

**MRS. B:** They insult me grossly.

**LE CHOEUR:** (*Reprend comme ai rien ne s'était passé.*) Allons, avant que midi sonne
Venez, on ne vend plus, on donne,
Jamais nous ne trompons personne,
Venez, le marché va finir!

**CHORUS:** (*As if nothing had happened.*) Come in before the noon bell rings;
We sell no more, but freely give you;
We give away and don't deceive you.
So come, the market soon will close,
And we shall all repose.

**FRÉDÉRIC ET ROSE:** Fault-il s'effrayer de la sorte
De quelques honnêtes marchands
Trop pressants?

**FREDERIC and ROSE:** Though afraid, must you speak crossly
What these honest men may hear?

**MRS. B:** Voilà qu'ils font les innocents,
Mai c'est ma montre qu'on emporte!
(*On entend la cloche du marché.*)
Ciel quel est ce nouveau tapage?

**MRS. B:** Observe how guileless they appear;
My watch, alas, they've stolen from me.
What's this new rumpus they are making?

FRÉDÉRIC: C'est le signal du départ,
Le marché déménage!
(*Les marchands se retirene peu à peu.*)
(*La musique continue en sourdine.*)

MRS. B: Ils sont assourdissants! Je demande calme, un peu de calme!

FRÉDÉRIC: Il faudra y renoncer pour aujourd'hui mistress Bentson. Moi, j'adore ce tapage!

MRS. B: Cependant, le marché est fini.

FRÉDÉRIC: Mais la fête commence.

MRS. B: Et que vont-ils faire encore?

FRÉDÉRIC: Ils vont danser sur toutes les places chanter à tous les coins de rue. La foule se plait à aller de l'une a l'autre tantôt ici, tantôt là, c'est très amusant.

MRS. B: Mais nous avons perdu miss Ellen.

FRÉDÉRIC: Elle est sous la garde de son fiancé.

ROSE: Oh! elle ne court aucun danger. Voici les danseuses.

MRS. B: Quelles danseuses?

FRÉDÉRIC: N'aviez-vous jamais entendu parler des bayadères de l'Inde?

MRS. B: Que font-elles ordinairement?

FRÉDÉRIC: Elles vivent dans les pagodes pour la plus grande joie des prêtres de Brahma.

MRS. B: Ce sont des vestales?

FRÉDÉRIC: Si vous voulez. Ce sont des vestales qui n'ont rien à garder.
(*Ballet.*)
(*Composé de différentes parties appelées Terana, Kaklah, Persian, etc. A la fin du ballet, la foule se retire suivant a bayadères. Pendant qu'elles sortent on voit passer Nilakantha et sa fille. Il est revêtu du costume de Sanniassy ou pétinent hindou.*)
(*Rose, Frédéric, Mistress Bentson, puis Gérald, et Ellen*)

ROSE: (*À Frédéric.*) Voyez donc ce vieillard et cette jeune fille ils ne ressemblent pas aux autres!

FRÉDÉRIC: C'est un moine mendiant ou Saniassy, qui vient à la fête dans l'espoir d'y trouver quelques menus profits.
Et la jeune fille?
Doit chanter des complaintes, des mystères ou des scenes dramatiques dont les Hindous raffolent.

MRS. B: Ah! voici miss Ellen. Ne nous séparons plus, je vous en conjure.
(*Miss Ellen est entrée au bras de Gérald.*)

FREDERIC: It is the signal for upbreaking;
It is the warning now to close.
(*The peddlers leave gradually. The music continues.*)

MRS. B: They are deafening! I ask for quiet –

FREDERIC: You must renounce that for to-day, Mrs. B.
Ah! I adore this rumpus!

MRS. B: Meanwhile the market is over.

FREDERIC: But the festival commences!

MRS. B: And what will they do now?

FREDERIC: They will dance on all the squares, and sing at the street corners. The crowds delight in going from one to another; now here, now there. It is quite amusing.

MRS. B: But we have lost Miss Ellen.

FREDERIC: She is in the care of her lover.

ROSE: Oh! She is not in any danger. Here are the dancers!

MRS. B: What dancers?

FREDERIC: Have you never heard tell of the Bayaderes of India?

MRS. B: What do they do, ordinarily?

FREDERIC: They live in the pagodas for the pleasure of the priests of Brahma.

MRS. B: Are they vestals?

FREDERIC: If you like. They are vestals with nothing to guard.
(*Ballet of the Bayaderes.*)
(*At the close of which Nilakantha and daughter are seen. He in the costume of a Hindu penitent or beggar. The Bayaderes retire, followed by the crowd. Nilakantha goes back with Lakmé.*)
(*Rose, Frederic, Mrs. Benson, and later on, Gerald and Ellen.*)

ROSE: Yonder see that old man
Leaning upon his daughter.

FREDERIC: It is a Sanniassay.
He wanders about
And scorns not the humblest of offerings,
While his daughter sings sacred ballads,
Which the Hindus will hearken to the live-long day.

MRS. B: Ah! Miss Ellen! at last!

FRÉDÉRIC: Ah! miss Ellen, comme on voit bien que vous êtes fière de donner le bras à un héros!

ELLEN: Ne plaisantez pas. J'ai été très inquiète et je me reprochais d'avoir laiseé Gérald dans le jardin de ce brahmane.

ROSE: Mais il n'a pas rapporté les dessins qu'on lui demandait.

FRÉDÉRIC: Bah! vraiment?

ELLEN: Il a eu raison.

GÉRALD: Le fille du brahmane était là cueillant des fleurs.

FRÉDÉRIC: Tu l'as vue!

GÉRALD: Je l'ai aperçue.

FRÉDÉRIC: Ah! ah!

ELLEN: J'aurais eu de vrais remords si ma curiosité avait causé le moindre chagrin à cette jeune fille. Voilà que maintenant elle va m'interesser, la petite déesse.

FRÉDÉRIC: (*A part.*) Elle ne s'aperçoit pas qu'il est tout à fait rêveur, l'ami Gérald. Il y a des grâces d'état.

GÉRALD: Vraiment?

FRÉDÉRIC: Le régiment part cette nuit, pour combattre des rebelles.

GÉRALD: Il faut absolument le cacher à ces dames.

FRÉDÉRIC: C'est cela.
(*A mistress Bentson.*)
Je vous conseille maintenant, mistress Bentson, de rentrer avec ces demoiselles au palais du gouverneur. Il n'y aura plus à voir que la cérémonie de la pagode et le passage de la déesse Dourga. Nous irons vous prendre.

ELLEN: Vous rentrez avec nous, Gérald?

GÉRALD: Mais certainement.

ELLEN: Vous ne m'avez pas dit si elle était vraiment belle, la fille du brahmane.

GÉRALD: Elle est étrange.
(*Il sort avec Ellen.*)

MRS. B: Je ne suis pas fâchée de rentrer, moi, et cependant on n'a plus rien à plus rien à me voler.
(*Elle sort.*)

ROSE: (*Au moment de les suivre, à Frédéric, en s'arrêtant.*) Est-ce que vous n'avez pas une revue aujourd'hui?

FRÉDÉRIC: Un simple appel.

ROSE: En tenue de guerre.

FRÉDÉRIC: Mais, non, pas en tenue de guerre.
Pourquoi en tenue de guerre?

ROSE: Vous ne nous dites pas que votre régiment part cette nuit? Oh! je sais qu'on le cache.

FRÉDÉRIC: Où avez-vous pris ces nouvelles?

FREDERIC: And how contented
She rests upon his arm!

ELLEN: Yes, in truth, I am happy!
See my heart,
Full of sunshine and love,
Is all gladness!

ROSE: He hasn't brought you the designs you wanted.

FREDERIC: Really?

ELLEN: He was right.

GERALD: The Brahmin's daughter was there, picking flowers.

FREDERIC: You saw her?

GERALD: Yes.

FREDERIC: Oh!

ELLEN: I hope my curiosity hasn't caused her any trouble. That goddess interests me.

FREDERIC: (*Apart.*) She doesn't see that he's just a dreamer. What a wonderful way to be.
(*To Gerald, undertone.*)
You know we must report at 3?

GERALD: Yes?

FREDERIC: The regiment leaves tonight to fight the rebels.

GERALD: We mustn't let the women know.

FREDERIC: Right.
(*To Mrs. Benson.*)
I advise you now, to go back with the girls to the governor's palace. There's only the pagoda ceremony and the passage of Dourga to see and we'll take you to that.

ELLEN: Ar you coming with us, Gerald?

GERALD: Certainly.

ELLEN: You didn't tell me whether this Brahmin's daughter was beautiful.

GERALD: She's sort of strange.
(*He goes out with Ellen.*)

MRS. B: I might as well go. I've nothing left that they can steal.
(*She goes out.*)

ROSE: (*Follows, then stops and to Frederic.*) No review today?

FREDERIC: Ordinary parade.

ROSE: With arms?

FREDERIC: No. Not with arms, why?

ROSE: Didn't you say your regiment was leaving tonight? Oh! I know you're trying to keep it quiet.

FREDERIC: Where did you hear this?

ROSE: Chez mon oncle le gouverneur, par hazard.
On ne se défie pas de moi.

FRÉDÉRIC: C'est-à-dire que nous devons faire a l'aube une promenade militaire.

ROSE: Dans une province révoltée. Je n'ai pas voulu en parler à Ellen parce quelle tremblerait à l'idée de voir partir sa fiancé. Ellen n'a pas mon courage et puis, moi, je n'air pas de fiancé.

FRÉDÉRIC: (À part.) Elle est ravissante!

ROSE: (Apercevant Nilakantha et Lakmé.) Voici encore ce vieillard et cette jeune fille.
Ils m'effraient.

FRÉDÉRIC: Prenez mon bras.

ROSE: Oh! volontiers! C'est parce que j'ai peur.

FRÉDÉRIC: Elle est adorable!
(Ils sortent.)
Lakmé, Nilakantha, puis La Foule.

NILA: C'est un pauvre qui mendie, Une diseuse de chansons.
Cette foule étourdie
S'éloigne quand nous passons!
Sous ce vêtement misérables!
Voit-on le justicier qui poursuit un coupable!
Ces Anglais sentent-ils tout leur sang de figer
En lisant sur mon visage?
Que je vais me venger?

LAKMÉ: Brahma nous défend-il d'oublier un outrage!

NILA: L'outrage d'un étranger!

NILAKANTHA: Lakmé, ton doux regard se voile, Ton sourire s'est attristé Comme on voit pâler une étoile, Une ombre assombrit ta beauté C'est que Dieu de nous se retire, C'est qu'il attend la mort du criminel Mais je veux retrouver ton sourire. Oui je veux retrouver ton sourire, Et dans tes yeux, et dans tes yeux! Je vous revoir le ciel! Le coeur rempli d'ardentes fièvres, J'ai voulu l'écouter dormir! Un rêve passait sur le lévres Et je voyons ton front rougir. C'est que Dieu de nous se retire, C'est qu'il attend la mort du criminel. Mais je veux retrouver ton sourire, Oui, je veux retrouver ton sourire Et dans les yeux Et dans les jeux, je veux revoir lé ciel!

ROSE: At my uncle's palace, by chance.

FREDERIC: Oh! It's just a dawn parade.

ROSE: In a revolting province. I wouldn't want Ellen to know because she trembles at the very idea of her lover leaving. As for me, I have no lover.

FREDERIC: (Apart.) She's ravishing.

ROSE: (Seeing Nilakantha and Lakmé.) Here's that old man and his daughter. He scares me.

FREDERIC: Take my arm.

ROSE: I will—because I am afraid.

FREDERIC: She's adorable.
(Lakmé, Nilakantha, then the crowd.)

NILAKANTHA: (Coming forward with Lakmé.) I, a beggar, alms imploring
And she, a ballad-singing maid.
(Frederic and Rose pass by, indifferent.)
All but self, the crowds ignoring.
They run when we reach for aid,
Beneath these faded robes defective
Who would think here to discover
A skillful, sharp detective?
Do these vile English foes
Feel their blood ceasing to flow
When they read upon my visage,
That I for vengeance go?

LAKMÉ: (Timidly.) Does Brahma ever forbid we should overlook an outrage?

NILA: The outrage of a wicked foe!
(Recitative.)

NILAKANTHA: (with much tenderness.) Lakmé, some grief your look is veiling; Your sweet smile, once gay, now is sad As we see a star that is paling A cloud shades your brow, once so glad It is that God hides from us His presence, It is that he waits the death of our base foe In your smile, let me see life's sweet essence, Yes, once more I would see life's sweet essence, And in your eyes, And in your eyes, would once more see the skies! Your beating heart with fever burning, While you slept, I listened to hear! A dream over your lips passed with yearning, A blush I saw your brow did wear. It is that God hides from us his presence, It is that He waits the death of our base foe In your smiles let me find life's sweet essence, Yes, I would, I would find life's sweet essence, And in your eyes, And in your eyes, would once more see the skies.

LAKMÉ: Ah! c'est de ta douleur que je me sens émue,
Ma gaîté reviendra, vois, elle est revenue.

NILA: Si ce maudit s'est introduit chez moi,
S'il a bravé la mort pour arriver à toi.
Pardonne-moi ce blasphème,
C'est qu'il t'aime!
Toi, ma Lakmé, toi, la fille des dieux!
Il va triomphant par la ville,
Nous allons retenir cette foule mobile,
Et s'il te voit, Lakmé, je lirai dans ses yeux.
Affermis bien ta voix—sois souriante,
Chante, Lakmé, chante,
La vengeance est là.
(Peu à peu la foule s'est approchée, attirée par la voix de Lakmé.)

NILA: (À la foule.) Pas les dieux inspirée,
Cette enfant vous dira
La légende sacrée
De la fille du paria.

LAKMÉ: Légende. Où va la jeune Hindoue,
Fille des parias,
Quand la lune se joue
Dans les grands mimosas?
Elle court sur la mousse.
Et ne se souvient pas
Que partout on repousse
L'enfant des parias!
Le long des lauriers roses,
Elle passe sans bruit.
Rêvant de douces choses
Et riant à la nuit!

Là bas dans la forêt plus sombre, Quel est-ce voyageur perdu? Autour de lui des yeux brillent dans l'ombre, Il march encore au hasard é perdu! Les fouves rugissent de joie, Ils vont se jeter sur leur proie La Jeune fille accourt et brave leurs furreurs. Elle a dans sa main la baquette, Où tinte la clochette, où tinte la clochette Des charmeurs. Ah! ah! ah! ah! L'étranger la regarde, Elle reste éblouie. Il est plus beau que les Rajahs! Il rougira, s'il sait qu'il doit la vie. A la fille des parias Mais lui, l'endormant dans un reve. Jasque dans le ciel il l'enlève. En lui disant; ta place est là! C'était Vishnou, fils de Brama! Depuis ce jour au fond des bois, Le voyageur entend parfais, Le bruit léger de la baguette Où tinte la clochette, Où tinte la clochette Ces chameurs. Ah! ah! ah! ah!

LAKMÉ: Ah! It is from your own grief I feel my heart yearning.
My gay thoughts will return! See!
Even now they are returning.

NILA: If that vile man has found access to me,
If he, too, has braved death, at your dear side to be,—
Forgive the anger that moves me,—
Ah! It is that he loves you!
You, my Lakmé, child of the gods,
He goes triumphant through the city;
We must draw the crowds by some motive of pity.
If he sees you Lakmé, in his eyes I shall read,
Now strengthen well your voice,
Look gay and smiling.
Sing now, Lakmé, vengeance awaits you here!
(Scene and legend of the Pariah's Daughter.)

NILA: Through the gods' inspiration,
This young girl will here relate
A legendic narration
Of the pariah's fair daughter's fate.

CHORUS: Let us hear this legend. Listen now!

LAKMÉ: Where goes the maiden straying,
This child of the pariah band?
When the bright moonlight is playing
Amid the forests grand,
Tripping light over the mosses,
Never remembers she
That a deadly hate ever crosses
The pariah's progeny.
Tripping light over the mosses,
Wanders the maiden free;
Through the pink oleanders,
With her sweet thoughts she wanders,
She moves on with steps light,
And laughs out at the night!

Down there, where shades more deep and glooming, What traveller's that, alone, astray?.... Around him flame bright eyes, dark depths illuming, But on he journeys, as by chance, on the way! The wolves in their wild joy are howling. As if for their prey they were prowling; The young girl runs forward, and their fury dares. A ring in her grasp she holds tightly, Whence tinkles a bell, sharply, lightly, A bell that tinkles lightly, That charmers wear. Ah! ah! ah! ah! While the stranger regards her Stands the dazed, flushed and glowing More handsome than the Rajahs, he! Yet with a blush, he'll learn his life he's owing To the Pariah's fair progeny, But he, in a dream her enfolding, Till to heaven she soars in his holding, To her he says, "Your mead is won." It was Vishnu, great Brahma's son! And since the day in that dark wood, The traveler hears, where Vishnu stood,

The sound of a little bell ringing.
The legend back to him bringing, a
small bell ringing like those the
charmers wear. Ah! ah! ah! ah!

NILA: (À part.) La rage me dévore,
Il n'est pas venu,
Je l'aurais reconnu.
(A sa fille.)
Chante, chante encore!

NILA: (Aside.) My fury doth overwhelms me! He has not yet come. I
should know him at once!
(To Lakmé.)
Sing out; repeat it!

LAKMÉ: (Hésitante.) Mon père!

LAKMÉ: My father!

LE CHOEUR: Ah! chante encore.
(Quelques officiers paraissent au
fond. Gérald et Frédéric sont parmi eux.)

CHORUS: Ah! Sing it again.
(Officers appear at the back, Gerald and Frederic among them.)

LAKMÉ: (D'une voix trem-
blante.) Où va le juene Hindoue,
Fille des parias,
Quand la lune se joue
Dans les grands mimosas?
(Elle aperçoit Gérald qui ne l'as
pas encore vue. — Très émue.)
Où va la jeune Hindoue,
Fille des parias.

LAKMÉ: Where goes the Hindu
straying,
Child of the pariah band?
Where the moonlight is playing
Through the mimosas grand,—
(She perceives Gerald, who has
not yet seen her.)
(Greatly moved.)
Where goes the Hindu straying,
Child of the pariah band?

NILA: Encor!

NILA: Sing on! once more, sing on!

LAKMÉ: (Chante le refrain de la
clochette et pousse un cri en voyant Gérald qui s'approche.) Ah!

LAKMÉ: (More and more disturbed.) Ah!
(Utters a cry at sight of Gerald approaching.)

GÉRALD: (S'élançant pour la
soutenir.) Lakmé.

GERALD: (Springing forward to
support her.) Lakmé!

NILA: (S'emparant de sa fille.)
C'est lui.

NILAKANTHA: (Catching at
Lakmé.) It is he!

LE CHOEUR: Qui la trouble ainsi?

CHORUS: What disturbs her thus?

LAKMÉ: (Cherchant à maitriser
son émotion.) C'est un mal que
j'ignore,
Ce n'est rien, c'est fini, je veux
chanter encore.
(D'une voix faible.)
Ah!

LAKMÉ: (Trying to conquer her
emotion.) It is a sudden pain –
nothing more.
It was unexpected;
Now it is gone. I'll try to be collect-
ed.
(With a faltering voice.)
Ah!—

GÉRALD: (À Frédéric.) La fille du
brahmane!

GERALD: (To Frederic.) Behold!
the Brahmin's daughter!

FRÉDÉRIC: Ici!

FREDERIC: What, here?

NILA: (À sa fille.) Ah! Brahma
t'inspirait! L'étranger s'est trahi!

NILAKANTHA: (To Lakmé.) You
are inspired by Brahma, and the
stranger is betrayed!

GÉRALD: (Avec exaltation.) C'est
Lakmé, c'est elle!

GERALD: (With emotion.) It is
herself; It is Lakmé!

FRÉDÉRIC: Sois prudent!

FREDERIC: Ah! prudent be.

GÉRALD: Laisse-moi la voir!

GERALD: Leave me free! Her once
more let me see.

FRÉDÉRIC: On nous appelle!

FREDERIC: On us they are calling.

GÉRALD: Attends!

GERALD: But stay.

FRÉDÉRIC: Par cette enfant es-tu
donc retenu!

FREDERIC: And that young girl;
does she then detain you?

GÉRALD: Non, non!
(Ils s'éloignent.)

GERALD: No, no.
(They go out.)

NILA: Je le connais! Dieu nous est
revenu!
(Les soldats anglais défilent au
fond du théâtre, fifres et tambours en tête. La foule les accompagne et s'éloigne lentement. Nilakantha et les Hindous se

NILA: I know him now! God is with
us again.
(The English soldiers file out the
back, headed by fifers and drummers. The crowd gathers slowly.
The Brahmin and conspirators
group on the front of the stage.)

groupent sur le devant de la
scène.)
(Nilakantha, Lakmé, Hadji, Hindous.)

(Nilakantha, Lakmé, Hadji, and
Hindus.)

NILA: Au milieu des chants
d'allégresse,
Ce soir, quand la foule suivra
Le cortège de la déesse!
Mon regard le designera!
Des siens séparant le coupable,
Sans bruit, pas à pas, vous irez,
Et dans un cercle infranchissable
Lentement vous l'enfermerez.

NILA: (Mysteriously to the conspi-
rators.) Amid the songs of joy and
pleasure,
When the crowd turns to go;
Where the priests march in stately
measure,
By a glance I'll point out the foe;
We'll then from his friends separate
him,
And noiselessly onward we'll go.
Till in a circle we instate him,
And will close on him sure and
slow.

LE CHOEUR: Des siens, séparant le
coupable,
Sans bruit, pas à pas, nous irons
Et dans un cercle infranchissable,
Lentement nous l'enfermerons!

CHORUS: We'll then from his
friends separate him,
And noiselessly onward we'll go.
Sure and slow,
And ready for the blow.

NILA: Alors, éloignez-vous sans
crainte,
Je serai là, j'air préparé
Mon bras pour cette tâche sainte,
Et c'est moi qi le frapperai!

NILA: Depart then without trepidation.
I shall be there, with arm trained
and strong;
It is mine, by heaven's consecration,
Ah! It is I who'll avenge the
wrong,–
To me the task belongs,

LAKMÉ: O mon père, je te suivrai!

LAKMÉ: O my father, with you I'll
go.

NILA: Non! non! mon coeur qui n'a
jamais faibli
Se troublerait. Non, reste avec Hadji!
(Les Hindous et Nilakantha sortent lentement. Lakmé reste seul
avec Hadji.)
(Lakmé, Hadji.)

NILA: No, daughter no!
My heart, that weakness never hath
known,
Would fail if you were at my side.
With faithful Hadji here abide.
(Nilakantha and the conspirators
depart slowly. Lakmé remains
with Hadji.)
(Lakmé, Hadji.)

HADJI: Le maître ne pense qu'à sa
vengeance, il n'a pas vu couler tes
larmes, ô maîtresse, mais Hadji était
là. Hadji sait lire sur les visages, et il
t'appartient, et la vie d'Hadji ne
compte pas; quand tu étais petite,
j'allais défier les tigres dans les
forêts sauvages pour cueillir la
fleur que tu aimais; j'allais au fond
de la mer chercher pour toi une
perle plus belle que toutes les
perles. Aujourd'hui, tu es femme,
ta pensée a d'autres caprices, ton
coeur a d'autres désirs. Si tu as un
ennemi à punir, parle, si tu as un
ami à sauver.
(Lakmé lui saisit vivement la
main.) Ordonne.
(A ce moment Gérald revient
rêveur. Lakmé fait signe à Hadji
de s'éloigner, puis court vers
Gérald.)

HADJI: The master thinks only of
his vengeance.
He has not seen your tears flow, O
mistress; but Hadji was nigh. Hadji
reads what the face tells, he knows
what traces grief leaves there; he
belongs to you and his life is of no
account. When you were a child I
defied the tigers in the jungle to
cull the flowers for which you
smiled. In the depths of the sea I
sought to find a pearl for you more
fair than others knew. A woman you
are to-day; your thoughts have other caprices, your heart other desires. If you have an enemy to punish, tell me! If you have a friend to
save, give me your order!
(Lakmé grasps his hand firmly.)
(At this moment Gerald returns
thoughtfully. Lakmé makes a sign
to Hadji to go farther away. Then
she runs toward Gerald.)

GÉRALD: Lakmé! Lakmé! c'est toi!
C'est toi qui viens à moi.
Dans la vague d'un rêve
Je t'ai vue en passant,
Le voile se soulève
Et l'idole descend.
Je subis ta puissance

GERALD: Lakmé! It is you I see?
You come to me!
(With warmth.)
In the fancies of dreaming,
I saw you as I neared;
The veil uplifted, seeming,
The the idol appeared.

Par ton charme enchaîné
Et je vais sans défense
Vers le ciel entraîne!

To your power I submitted,
By your charms drawn away;
And, defenceless, I quitted
Earth, for heaven's brighter day.

**LAKMÉ:** Mon ciel n'est pas le tien.
Le Dieu qui me protège
N'est pas celui que tu connais,
A lui si je te ramenais
Alors sans sacrilège,
Je pourrais te parler,
Tu ne courrais aucun danger.

**LAKMÉ:** (*Sadly.*) My heaven is not
your own,
The God you worship blindly
Is not the one whom I have known.
If I to mine could bring you heart,
Our Hindu brothers, kindly,
Would always take your part
(*Hesitating a little.*)
Against dangerous foes, or guileful
art.

**GÉRALD:** Viennent tous les dangers du monde!
Dans l'ivresse profonde
Où mon raison se perd
Verrais-je sous mes pas un abîme
entr'ouvrent
Quand de tes longs cheveux, document te m'effleures?

**GERALD:** Come! all the dangers of
creation!
In this wild adoration,
When reason's lost in bliss.
Should I see at my feet a yawning
abyss
While your long tresses
Sweep me, with tender caresses?

**LAKMÉ:** Je ne veux pas que tu
meures!

**LAKMÉ:** (*Resolutely.*) Your death
I'll never consent to.

**GÉRALD:** Ah! c'est l'amour endormi
Qui de son aile t'effleure,
Et ton coeur s'est raffermi,
Tu ne veux pas que je meure!

**GERALD:** (*Passionately*) Ah! this
is love, yet asleep,
Who with his wing has caressed
you;
Your heart though too strong to
weep,
My death assured, has depressed
you.

**LAKMÉ:** Hélas! c'est un ennemi
Dont le souffle ardent m'eáleure,
Tout mon être en a frémi,
Mais je ne veux pas qu'il meure!
Dans le fôret, près de nous,
Ce cache, tout petite,
Une cabane en bambous
Qu'un grand arbre vert abrite.
Comme un nid d'oiseaux peureux,
Dans les lianes posée
Et sous les fleurs écrasée
Elle attend des gens heureux.
Elle échappe à tous les yeux,
Dehors, rien ne la révèle,
Le grand bois silencieux
Qui l'enferme est jaloux d'elle.
C'est là que tu me suivras
Toujours à l'aube naissante
Je reviendrai souriante
Et c'est là que tu vivras.

**LAKMÉ:** Ah! yes, an enemy hold
It is, whose hot breath has caressed
me,
All my heart has shuddered with
cold,
While the thought of death oppressed me.
In the forest, quite near by,
A little cabin is hiding,
Built of bamboo, light and dry, –
Beneath a tall tree, shade providing,–
Like a nest for timid birds,
Amid flowering vines, there abiding,
And with welcomes plain as words,
It awaits
Two happy mates.
It escapes all curious eyes–
Outside no secret revealing,
While the wood all silent lies
And surrounds it with jealous feeling.
There it is, – you will follow me;
Each day when the dawn is breaking,
Smiling, there I'll come at waking,–
And it is there you will dwell.

**GÉRALD:** O douce enchanteresse,
Parle, parle, toujours!

**GERALD:** Sweetest of enchantresses.
Say more of that resort!

**LAKMÉ:** Ah! viens, viens, le temps
presse
Et les instants sont courts.

**LAKMÉ:** Ah! come; time now
presses,
And fleeting hours are short.

**GÉRALD:** Tu veux que je me
cache,
Tu ne peux pas savoir
Qu'ici l'honneur m'attache,
L'honneur et le devoir.

**GERALD:** You wish that I should
hide me,
But cannot understand
That honor must decide me
When duty makes demand,

**LAKMÉ:** Lakmé t'implore et te supplie!

**LAKMÉ:** Lakmé implores with supplication.

**GÉRALD:** Demande-moi plutôt ma
vie!

**GERALD:** Ask of me rather life than
station.

**LAKMÉ:** Ai-je donc perdu mon
pouvoir!

**LAKMÉ:** Have I lost my power to
command?

**GÉRALD:** Ah! Lakmé, Lakmé, tu
pleures.

**GERALD:** Ah! your eyes are filling!

**LAKMÉ:** Je ne veux pas que tu
meures!

**LAKMÉ:** That you must die I'm yet
unwilling. (*With great energy.*)

**GÉRALD:** Ah! c'est l'amour endormi, etc.

**GERALD:** Ah! this is love, yet
asleep, etc.

**LAKMÉ:** C'est fini, les nôtres sont
là.
Voici la déesse Dourga
(*Gérald, Frédéric, Ellen, Rose,
mistress Bentson, puis Nilakantha, Les Brahmanes, Les Danseuses Sacrées, Les Hindous, puis
Lakmé.*)
(*Des prêtres arrivent et se dirigent
vers la pagode.*)

**LAKMÉ:** Ah! It is too late–our people now are here!
Behold when the goddess is near.
(*Gerald, Frederic, Ellen, Rose,
Mrs. Benson; then Nilakantha,
Brahmins, Bayaderes, Hindus;
then Lakmé. Priests arrive and
move towards the pagoda.*)

**CHANT DES BRAHMANES:** O
Dourga, toi qui renais
Dans les flots du Gange,
A nos yeux, viens, apparais,
Toi par qui tout change!
Déesse d'or, entends nos voix,
Que ton bras nous protège!
Tu nous souris et tu nous vois
Saluant ton cortège.
De ta douce image
Nous venons fêter le passage,
Déesse d'or, entends nos voix!
*Les prêtres entrent dans la pagode. Ellen et Rose rentrent accompagnées de mistress Bentson,
puis Frédéric arrive avec Gérald.*)

**CHORUS:**
Dourga fair, you who was born
From the waves of Ganges,
To our eyes appear, and dawn,
Ruler of Time's changes.
Goddess of gold, hear us, we pray.
Give us here thy protection;
Over us still smile;
Look down meanwhile
On us with pure affection.
(*The Brahmins and Bayaderes enter the pagoda; Ellen and Rose reenter with Mistress Benson; then
Frederic arrives with Gerald.*)

**ELLEN:** Voyez cette ville en fête,
Et ces cris et ces hourrahs!

**ELLEN:** The town is gleaming with
splendor.
Hear the cries, the shouts of greetings glad.

**MRS. B:** Ils ont tous perdu la tête
Pour leur déesse aux dix bras!

**MRS. B:** They are crazed, or so are
seeming;
Their ten-armed goddess drives
them mad.

**FRÉDÉRIC:** (*Entrant avec
Gérald.*) C'est pour admirer la
déesse
Que tu nous as quittés ainsi?

**FREDERIC:** (*To Gerald.*) Was it to
admire this fair goddess
That you left us in the throng?

**GÉRALD:** (*Préoccupé.*) Oui, leur
fête m'intéresse!

**GERALD:** (*Preoccupied.*) Yes,
their festival amused me.

**FRÉDÉRIC:** (*Souriant.*) La fille du
brahmane a passé par ici!

**FREDERIC:** (*Smiling.*) The Brahmin's daughter
Has just now passed along.

**GÉRALD:** (*Éclatant.*) C'est un
rêve, une folie
Qui passe et qu'on oublie,
Mais dans mon coeur révolté
Je sens avec épouvante,
Que Lakmé scule est vivante
Je n'y vois que sa beauté!

**GERALD:** (*Breaking out.*) It is a
dream, a whim enthralling,
Which, flown, is past recalling,
But in my heart, dazed, confounded,
I feel, doubting and astounded,
That alone is Lakmé living.
No one else seems fair to me.

**FRÉDÉRIC:** (*Gaîment.*) Je te ferais
une belle morale
Si nous ne partions pas demain,
Mais la guerre a du bon, cette fille
idéale
Ne sera plus sur ton chemin!
(*Il s'éloigne.*)

**FREDERIC:** (*Gaily.*) Then I should
like a moral to borrow,
If we should not depart tomorrow,
But the war has some good;
That ideal maiden,
You'll no more meet, It is understood.
(*Goes out.*)

**ELLEN, ROSE ET MRS. B:** Comment fuir ce tapage! Ils ont juré, je le gage, De nous étourdir du soir au matin! (*Les brahames sortent de la pagode, escortant la déesse Dourga dont la statue est portée à bras dans une sorte de palanquin. La nuit est venue. Des porteurs de torches accompagnent le cortège. Les danses sacrées reprennent.*)

**CHORUS:** O Dourga, toi qui renais, etc. (*Les Hindous et Nilakantha guettent Gérald.—Nikalantha le désigne du doigt, la place se vide peu à peu.*)

**GÉRALD:** C'est un rêve, une folie Qui passe et qu'on oublie, Mais dans mon coeur révolté Je sens avec épouvante Que Lakmé seule est vivante Je n'y vois que sa beauté. (*Il aperçoit Lakmé qui se montre à droite. Il va vers elle, Nilakantha le suit et, au moment où Gérald est près de Lakmé, il le frappe et se sauve vivement en le voyant tomber. Lakmé se précipite vers Gérald, se penche sur lui, l'examine et sa figure s'éclaire lorsqu'elle reconnaît que la blessure n'ont pas dangereuse.*)

**LAKMÉ:** Ils croient leur vengeance assouvie, Tu m'appartiens pour toujours. Je ne vivias que de ta vie, Dieu protège nos amours! (*Elle appelle Hadji qui accourt.*)

## ■ ACTE III

(*Le théâtre représente un partie de forêt de l'Inde que le soleil éclaire de ses plus chauds rayons. Sous un arbre gigantesque une cabane à peine fermée et perdue dans les roses, les daturas à double calice blanc, les tulipias jaunes.*)

(*Au lever du rideau, Gérald est étendu sur un lit de feuillage. Lakmé, à demi penchée, inquiète, épie son sommeil en murmurant une chanson.*)

**LAKMÉ:** Sous le ciel tout étoilé, Le ramier blanc au loin s'en est allé Ah! reviens, ma vois l'appelle, Mon deux ami reviens ferme ton aile Sous le ciel tout étoilé, Le remier blanc au loin s'en est allé! Il dors! Puisse encor un moment Me naive chanson le bercer doucement Puisse-t-il près de moi reposer un moment. Sus le ciel leut étoilé, Le ramier blanc hélas s'en est allé. Sa compagne qui l'appelle, N'entrendra plus jamais battre son aille. Sous le ciel tous étoilé Le ram-

**ELLEN, ROSE and MRS. B:** How leave this noise tremendous? They've sworn, I'll make a bet stupendous, Our poor ears to smite From morning till night. (*The procession comes from the pagoda, escorting the ten-armed statue of the goddess Dourga, which is borne in a sort of palanquin. Night has come. Torch-bearers accompany the procession. The Bayaderes join in.*)

**CHORUS:** O Dourga bright, etc. (*While the procession marches on, Nilakantha points out Gerald to the conspirators.*)

**GERALD:** It is a dream, a whim enthralling, etc. (*Nilakantha and the Hindus watch Gerald; the square empties gradually.*) (*He perceives Lakmé, who enters at the right, and goes towards him. Nilakantha follows Gerald, and, at the moment when he is near Lakmé, he strikes him, and escapes quickly, after seeing him fall. Lakmé rushes towards Gerald, leans over and examines him. Her face lightens when she sees that the wound is not mortal.*)

**LAKMÉ:** They think that their vengeance is sated! Forevermore, love, you are mine. My life with yours is hence related. Over our loves may heaven's star shine. (*Calls Hadji, and runs out.*)

## ■ ACT III

(*The stage represents a forest in India, that the sun illumines with its fiercest rays. Under a gigantic tree a cabin is nearly concealed and crowned with brilliant flowers.*)

(*Gerald is extended upon a bed of foliage. Lakmé anxiously watches his slumbers while murmuring a song.*)

**LAKMÉ:** Beneath the starry canopy, The dovelet white has wandered far from me Ah! return from far dominions; My voice recalls you, Come and fold your pinions. Beneath the starry canopy, The dove-let white has wandered far away! He sleeps! Haply one moment more May my low, gentle song soothe his dream as before. At my side, it may be, Rest will new life restore. Beneath the starry canopy, the dove-let white has wandered from from me His fond mate in these dominions, Will

mer blanc hélas s'en est allé . . . Ah! reviens! .. Ah!

**GÉRALD:** (*S'éveillant sans voir Lakmé.*) Quel vague souvenir aloudit ma pensée? Et sur ma poitrine oppressée Quel rêve s'est appesanti? Sous un charme accablant je rest anéanti. Je me souviens, la ville était en fête, J'allais dans mon extase, à demi réveillé, Quand l'éclair d'un poignard à mes yeux a brillé, Et la nuit s'est faite!

**LAKMÉ:** (*Se penchant vers lui et continuant.*) Alors Hadji, dans l'ombre se glissant, T'a transporté sous ce toit de verdure, J'ai ramené la vie à ton front pâlissant; Les filles de ma caste apprennent en naissant Comment le suc des fleurs guérit une blessure.

**GÉRALD:** Je me souviens, sans voix, inanimée, Je te voyais sur mes lévres penchée, Mon âme à tes regards tout entière attachée, Revivait sous ton souffle ô ma douce Lakmé! Ah! viens, dans cette paix profonde L'aile de l'amour a passé, Et pour nous séparer du monde, Sur nous le ciel s'est abaissé. Ces fleurs courant capricieuses Ont des senteurs voluptueuses Qui jettent au coeur amolli L'ivresse et l'oubli. Ah! viens, dans cette paix profonde, Sur nous le ciel s'est abaissé. Pour nous faire oublier le monde L'aile de l'amour a passé!

**LAKMÉ:** Là, je pourrai t'entendre, Nous vivrons tous les deux, Et je pourrai t'apprendre L'histoire de nos dieux! Nous chanterons ensemble Ces dieux trois fois bénis Devant lesquels tout tremble, Qui nous ont réunis. Et ton âme enflammée De bonheur s'emplira, Sur la terre charmée Que protège Brahma! (*On entend des chants dans le lointain*).

**GÉRALD:** Ecoute! On passe sur la route Qui longe la forêt.

no more hear the beating of his pinions. Beneath the starry canopy, The pure white dove has wandered from from me. Ah! . . . return! .. Ah!

**GERALD:** (*Opens his eyes without observing Lakmé.*) What memories, strangely vague, On my thoughts are now weighing? All my weakened senses overlaying; What dream is this that does me oppress? As beneath some charm I lie without redress. I now recall; the town in guise was festive, Along the street I strolled with fancies suggestive, When the gleam of a poniard flashed quick on my sight; Then around me all was night!

**LAKMÉ:** (*Leaning over him.*) It was here that Hadji, through the shadows dark, Has borne you senseless to this verdant park; I soon brought the life to your pale brow again. The daughters of my caste, with early youth attain The power to heal all wounds, By juices of flowers applying.

**GERALD:** I too, recall,—still mute, inanimate,— I saw you bent over my lips; while thus lying, My soul upon your look was attracted and fastened; Beneath your breath life awoke and recovery hastened. O my charming Lakmé; ah, come! Through the forest depths secluded, Love's wing above us has passed; Earth-cares have not been intruded, And heaven on us falls at last. These flowering vines, with blooms capricious, Bear over our pathway scents delicious; Which soft hearts, with raptures beset, While all else we forget.

**LAKMÉ:** Here I may always reach you, And together we'll live; And while fondly I teach you, The gods' history will give. Here, with voices united, We will sing the gods blest, Before whom all bend, affrighted, But who give to us rest; And your spirit outflaming Shall with rapture be full, Over the charmed world proclaiming, Here that Brahma rules! (*Songs are heard in the distance.*)

**GERALD:** Oh, listen! Some persons are passing Along the forest road. No curious eyes will see us, Or find out our abode.

CHOEUR: (*Dans la coulisse.*)
Descendons la pente
Doucement,
La source qui chante
Nous attend!
Près de son murmure,
Deux à deux,
Puisons l'onde pure
Sous les cieux.

GÉRALD: Quel est ce chant plein de tendresse,
Qui passe comme une caresse?

LAKMÉ: Ce sont des couples amoureux
Qui, par les doux chemins ombreux,
Vont à la source vénérée
Pour puiser l'eau sacrée
Chère aux amants heureux.
Quand ils ont effleuré de leurs lèvres brûlantes
La même coupe, ils sont réunis pour toujours.
Et les déesses bienfaisantes
Veillent sur leurs amors.
(*Reprise du choeur.*)

LAKMÉ: Nous ne pourrions sans crainte
Suivre ces amoureux
Tous les deux,
Mais à la source sainte
J'irai seule, sans toi,
Attends-moi!
(*Elle s'éloigne lentement.*)

GÉRALD: (*En la suivant des yeux.*) O douce tentatrice,
Ton charme m'a dompté,
Je vis de ton caprice
Et de ta volonté!
(*Frédéric, entrant.*)

FRÉDÉRIC: Vivant!

GÉRALD: Ah!

FRÉDÉRIC: J'ai marché sous les hautes fougères
Qu'on venait de froisser.—J'ai vu sur les bruyéres
Et sur la mousse au reflet blanc,
Des gouttes de sang!
Je t'ai cru mort.—Que fais-tu là?

GÉRALD: Je rêve!

FRÉDÉRIC: Quand les nôtres vont partir?

GÉRALD: Laisse-moi me souvenir!

FRÉDÉRIC: Quand le pays tout entier se soulève?

GÉRALD: Hier on m'a frappé.
Lakmé m'a sauvé.

FRÉDÉRIC: La fille du Brahmane?

CHORUS: (*In the wings.*) Down along the mountain
Let's repair,
While the tuneful fountain
Waits us there,
From its rippling waters,
Two by two,
Drink we, sons and daughters,
Beneath skies blue.

GERALD: What's that song of tender feeling
That seems like kisses over us stealing?

LAKMÉ: Of lovers it is and amorous maids,
Who, wandering through the sylvan shades,
Go to the fountain pure, there springing,
And holy water come bringing,
To happy maids and lovers dear.
(*Sedately.*)
When this cool draught is drained
By their lips' burning fever,
From the same cup obtained,
They wedded are, and evermore
The goddesses, unthoughtful never,
Their love-life they watch over.

CHORUS: Down along the mountain, etc.

LAKMÉ: But we shall scarce be able
Those maids to follow through,
Two by two.
To this spring venerable
I'll go alone for you!
Wait for me!
(*Going out.*)

GERALD: O temptress, charming still!
Wait for me!
(*Gerald follows her with his eyes.*)
I live through your caprice,
And by your sovereign will!
(*Enter Frederic.*)

FREDERIC: He lives.

GERALD: Ah—

FREDERIC: I forced my way through the bushes–a painful task!
I found in the meadow and on the lawn traces of blood which led me here. I thought you dead; what do you here?

GERALD: I was dreaming.

FREDERIC: While the regiment was marching on?

GERALD: Let me collect my thoughts.

FREDERIC: The land rises in revolt against us.

GERALD: A dagger thrust nearly killed me; Lakmé saved and nursed me.

FREDERIC: The daughter of the Brahmin?

GÉRALD: Elle m'a fait revivre
Dans un monde où je reste éperdu,
sans force, ivre
De son charme et de son amour.

FRÉDÉRIC: Ah! je connais ces ivresses d'un jour.
Alors, il faut la fuir,
La fuir à l'instant même.
Garde-toi d'un remords,—si tu crois qu'elle t'aime
Ces enfants-là ne savent pas souffrir.

GÉRALD: Je l'envelloperai si bien de ma tendresse.

FRÉDÉRIC: Et miss Ellen?

GÉRALD: Je subis le pouvoir
D'une enchanteresse.

FRÉDÉRIC: Est notre passion—à nous tous, la meilleure,
Notre honneur de soldat?
C'est demain qu'on se bat.

GÉRALD: (*Avec résolution.*) J'y serai!
C'est Lakmé! C'est Lakmé qui m'apporte l'eau sainte!

FRÉDÉRIC: Oh! maintenant, tu peux la voir, je suis sans crainte.
(*En sortant.*)
En je t'attends.—Il est sauvé!

LAKMÉ: (*Revient triomphante, elle apporte l'eau consacrée.*) Ils allaient deux à deux
Et les mains enlacées,
Les jeunes amoureux.—
Moi, je marchais prés d'eux.—
Seule avec mes pensées.—
J'allais, le coeur tout en émoi,
Comme eux de tendresse altérée,
Et maintenant, écoute-moi.
(*Avec un accent religieux.*)
Quand à la même coupe on a bu l'eau sacrée,
On reste pour toujours unis.
(*Elle le regarde attentivement, puis comme frappée de stupeur elle pose la coupe en s'écriant.*)
Ce n'est plus toi! Quand tu parlais, ton âme
Sur tes lèvres se posait;
Ton regard n'a plus la flamme
Qui m'embrasait.
Sur ton visage
Un nuage
A passé
Et l'a glacé.

GÉRALD: N'es-tu plus l'enfant charmante
Pour qui j'ai tout oublié?
Es-tu moins belle te moins aimante?

LAKMÉ: (*Gravement.*) Veux-tu qu'à mon destin ton destin soit lié?

GÉRALD: Je veux ce que tu veux, je veux ce que t'inspire
Ton caprice, je veux, je veux et voir sourire!

GERALD: She restored me to life before the vital spark had fled. I was unconscious, helpless. Love only could work such wonders.

FREDERIC: These are but idle fancies! Tarry no more, and do not court remorse; if you think she loves you, spare her new grief.

GERALD: I will with tender care reward her kindness.

FREDERIC: And your betrothed?

GERALD: I am in the power of an enchantress!

FREDERIC: And your duties as a soldier? These you'll not forget. I know you too well.

GERALD: Count on me. But Lakmé comes, bringing the sacred water.

FREDERIC: Now you may see her, I have no fear! You will resist. I count on you. Now he is saved.
(*Exit Frederic.*)

LAKMÉ: (*Returns triumphant, bringing the cup of holy water.*)
So they walked two by two
With their arms interlacing,
These lovers young and true;
I walked quite near them, too,
With my thoughts figures tracing,
I walked; my heart did swiftly beat,
Like theirs,–all athirst,–hope embracing,
And now the tale hear me repeat:
(*Religiously.*)
When from one cup between them
They've drunk, each other facing,
United they will ever remain!
(*She looks at him attentively, and, struck with stupor, lays down the cup.*)
It is you no more!
Your soul, when you spoke sweetly,
On your lips was plainly posed
Fire has left your glance completely,
Which lately me enclosed.
Upon your face
Clouds I trace,
Which, though past,
Have frozen it fast.

GERALD: Aren't you still the charming maiden
For whom all else I have forgot?
Are you less fair, your heart with love less laden?

LAKMÉ: (*Seriously.*) Wish you that our two fates
Should be joined hence, evermore?

GERALD: I wish what you desire,—
Our wishes reconciling.
Your whims I still admire,
And wish to see you smiling.

LAKMÉ: (*De même.*) Quel que soit le Dieu clément Dont tu bénis la puissance, Quelle que soit ta croyance, Tu sais ce que vaut un serment. A cette coupe où l'amour te convie, Jure de m'aimer pour la vie! (*On entend au loin des chants militaire.*)

GÉRALD: Ciel! ce sont nos soldats!

LAKMÉ: Bois, et tu m'appartiendras! (*Avec force en posant la coupe.*) Tu n'oses pas. (*Elle regarde attntivement Gérald dont les yeux restent fixés du côté où l'on entend le chant des soldats.*) C'est là-bas que va sa pensée. Son coeur a tressailli, Et sa patrie à ses yeux s'est dressée. (*Avec déchirement après avoir essayé d'attirer son regard.*) Tout est fini! (*Pendant que Gérald, la tête penchée, suit de l'oreille les tambours qui s'éloignent, Lakmé, désespérée, arrache une feuille de datura et la mâche sans que Gérald s'en aperĉoive.*)

GÉRALD: Lakmé, qu'avez vous fait?

LAKMÉ: (*Allant à lui, avec tendresse et souriante.*) Tu m'as donné plus doux rêve Qu'on puisse avoir sous notre ciel, Reste encore pour qu'il s'achève Ici, loin du monde réel. Tu m'as dit des mots de tendresse Que les Hindous ne savent pas, Et tu m'as appris l'ivresse Des aveux murmurés tout bas.

GÉRALD: Ce que je lis sur ton visage, Ma Lakmé, me glace d'effroi. De tout mon âme se dégage Et je ne serai plus qu'à toi.

LAKMÉ: (*Avec passion.*) Ah! maintentant, je veux te croire, Voici la coupe où je vais boire. (*Elle y trempe ses lèvres et la lui tend.*)

GÉRALD: Pronds! (*La prenant avec exaltation.*) A toi, Lakmé, pour toujours!

LAKMÉ: C'est la fête de nos amours. (*Il boit.*)

GÉRALD: Qu'autour de moi tout sombre, Je ne veux pas une ombre, Je ne veux pas une ombre Sur ton frout enchanté Je reste sous le

LAKMÉ: (*Seriously.*) Whichsoever the god may be Whose power you worship blindly, Whatever your faith be, harsh or kindly, You know an oath's worth to me, Then drink from this cup holy, Where true love never fails. Drink! and swear to love me forever! (*Military music in the distance.*)

GERALD: Heavens! they are our soldiers!

LAKMÉ: Drink! and mine to be, thus vow! Drink! Ah! you dare not now! (*Throws down the cup violently.*) (*Gazes fixedly upon Gerald, who looks away at the side whence comes the chorus.*) It is here his thoughts are returning; His heart is falling now. For friends and native land he's yearning. (*With anguish, after trying vainly to attract his attention.*) Ah! all is ended now! (*While Gerald listens with bowed head, Lakmé desperately culls a flower of the datura, and eats it, smilingly, without notice from Gerald.*)

GERALD: Lakmé, what's that you do?

LAKMÉ: (*Goes to him, smiling tenderly.*) You've given me love, the sweetest dreaming That one may know beneath our sky; Longer stay, till exquisite seeming Is here made reality. To me you've whispered tender phrases, More sweet than Hindus ever know; You've taught me what delights and graces Dwell in vows murmured soft and low.

GERALD: That which I read upon your features Chills my heart, fear smitten, like a stone; My soul floats free from duller creatures, And from here I am yours alone.

LAKMÉ: (*With passion.*) Ah! it is now I'd fain believe you; Behold the cup that here I give you! (*She wets her lips from it, then holds it out to him.*) Drink!

GERALD: (*Taking it exaltedly.*) I am yours, Lakmé, forevermore!

LAKMÉ: It is to our love feast we outpour! (*Gerald drinks.*)

GERALD: (*With exaltation.*) Though doubt may shade our morrow, I'd have not cloud of sorrow, I'd have no cloud of sorrow On

cherme, Que jamais une larme Que jamais une larme, Ne me voile la beauté

LAKMÉ: C'est la fête de nos amours, C'est la fête de nos amours.

GÉRALD: Qu'autour de moi tout sombre Je ne veux pas une ombre Je ne veux pas une ombre Sur le frout enchanté Je reste sous le charme, Que jamais une larme Que jamais une larme Ne me voule ta beauté!

LAKMÉ: C'est ma première larme. Et je meurs sous le charme Par l'amour apporté!

GÉRALD: Toujours à toi, je te le jure!

LAKMÉ: C'est un serment que tu pourras té mir. Je ne crains pas, va! que tu sús parjure! Je vais mourir

GÉRALD: Mourir!

LAKMÉ: La mort ne sépare pas. C'est elle qui nour lie. Je te donne ma vie, Et je meurs dans tes bras.

GÉRALD: Lakmé!

LAKMÉ: Et je meurs dans tes bras!

GÉRALD: Non! ce n'est pas la mort. C'est la vie ardente Qui coule à plein bord Sur ta lèvre frémissante. Ah! Qu'autour de moi tout sombre, Je ne veux pas une ombre Je ne veux pas une ombre Je ne veux pas une ombre Sur ton front enchanté Je reste sous le charme Que jamais une larme Que jamais une larme, Ne me voile ta beauté Ne me voile to ta beauté!

LAKMÉ: A dieu! . . . . . . . . .Rêve que sombre Hélas, quelle ombre en mon coeur attristé! (*Les Memes, Nilakantha.*)

NILA: C'est lui! c'est! lui près de Lakmé!

GÉRALD: Frappez! Je suis désarmé!

LAKMÉ: (*Retenant son père d'un geste.*) Nous avons bu tous deux à la coupe d'ivoire. Il est sacré pour vous.

NILA: Lui!

LAKMÉ: S'il faut à nos dieux Une victime expiatoire, Qu'ils m'appellent vers eux!

GÉRALD: (*Effrayé.*) Quel éclair en ses yeux brille!

LAKMÉ: (*Avec extase.*) Ils m'ont parlé!

NILA: (*Éperdu, la saisissant.*) Lakmé, ma fille!

GÉRALD: (*Avec des sanglots.*) Elle meurt pour moi!

your enchanting brow, Beneath the charm I'm resting, That never a tear protesting, That never a tear protesting, Shall obscure you beauty's glow!

LAKMÉ: It is the festal of our young love, Of our love, It is the festal day.

GERALD: Though doubt may shade our morrow, I'd have no cloud of sorrow, I'd have no cloud of sorrow On your enchanting brow, Beneath the charm I'm resting, that never a tear protesting, That never a tear protesting, Shall obscure your beauty's glow!

LAKMÉ: It is my first tear of sorrow. A charm from death I borrow. Since it love bestows.

GERALD: (*plus anime*) I'm all your own, I truly swear it!

LAKMÉ: (*failing.*) Ah it is an oath that scarce your strength will try. I have no fear, Ah! Here I now declare it, I soon shall die!

GERALD: Shall die!

LAKMÉ: (*smiling*) But death does not lovers part, Our souls rejoined, foreseeing, I to you give my being, And I die on your heart.

GERALD: Lakme!

LAKMÉ: And I die . . . on your heart!

GERALD: No! it is no more death. Life it is strong and glowing, Passing a full breath From your pale lips overflowing. Ah! . . . . Though doubt may shade our morrow, I'd have no tear of sorrow, I'd have no tear of sorrow On your enchanting brow. Beneath the spell I'm resting, That never a tear protesting, That never tear protesting, Shall obscure your beauty's glow! Shall obscure you beauty's glow!

LAKMÉ: Farewell, . . . . . . . . .O dream of sorrow! Alas! what shadow on my heart lies now! (*Nilakantha, Hindus enter.*)

NILA: It is he! beside Lakmé. You must die!

GERALD: Strike now! All unarmed am I!

LAKMÉ: (*Withholding her father by a gesture.*) We have both taken a drink from the ivory flagon, which is sacred for you.

NILA: What, he?

LAKMÉ: (*With failing voice.*) If so it must be— A victim to the gods you offer, Let them claim one in me!

GERALD: (*Frightened.*) In her eyes what light is shining!

LAKMÉ: (*With ecstasy.*) Ah! they've spoken to me!

NILA: (*Lifting her.*) Lakmé, my daughter!

GERALD: (*Sobbing.*) She dies now for me.

# Act III

**LAKMÉ:** (*Mourant, le sourire su la lèvres.*) Tu m'as donné le plus doux rêve
Qu'on puisse avoir sous notre ciel.
Reste encore pour qu'il s'achève
Ici, loin du monde réel!

**GÉRALD:** Morte!

**LAKMÉ:** (*Failing.*) You have given me love, the sweetest dreaming
That one may know beneath our sky;
Let me stay, till exquisite seeming
Has become here reality!
Far from worldly.
(*She dies.*)

**GERALD:** Ah! heaven!

**NILA:** (*Avec extase.*) Elle a l'éternelle vie
Quittant cette terre asservie,
Elle porte là-haut nos voeux
Elle est dans la splendeur des cieux.

*FIN*

**NILA:** (*With exaltation.*) Her soul now has life eternal,
She leaves earth for regions supernal.
Upward bears she our vows on high,
Where angel glories fill the sky!

*END*

# L'Elisir d'Amore (1832)

## The Elixir of Love

MUSIC BY GAETANO DONIZETTI ■ LIBRETTO BY FELICE ROMANI

This two-act *opera comica*, set to a libretto by Felice Romani (based on Eugène Scribe's libretto *Le Philtre* written for Auber in 1831), premiered at the Teatro della Cannobiana in Milan on May 12, 1832. A group of harvesters and young women are resting under the trees on Adina's Basque country farm while she reads aloud the story of Tristan, whose love for Isolde is revived via a love potion. Nemorino is in love with Adina, but she completely ignores him, preferring Belcore, the sergeant of the garrison. Dulcamara, a fake doctor, gives Nemorino a potion that will heal all ills. Nemorino, remembering Tristan, is hopeful that it will help him. The doctor guarantees Adina will fall in love with Nemorino within twenty-four hours. Nemorino is so confident about the potion that his behavior changes radically. He ignores Adina, which angers her. She decides that she must marry Belcore at once, since the garrison is departing the following morning. Disconsolate, Nemorino begs Adina to wait for twenty-four hours (time enough for the potion to work), but she refuses. As preparations are being made for the wedding, Nemorino enlists, at Belcore's suggestion. He now has twenty crowns, enough to purchase another bottle of love potion. Nemorino is ignorant of the rumor that his uncle has died and left him a huge legacy. Surrounded by all of the village girls, he thinks the love potion is working. Adina is jealous and realizes at last that she is in love with Nemorino, with or without an inheritance. When she learns of all the things he has done to win her love, she buys back his enlistment papers. Nemorino sees a tear on her cheek and knows that she loves him. Doctor Dulcamara's potion becomes instantly popular, and the village celebrates the marriage of Adina and Nemorino.

## ■ ATTO I.

### SCENA I.

*(Ingreso d'una fattoria Campagna in fondo ove scorre un ruscello, sulla cui riva alcune lavandaje preparano il bucato. In mezzo un grand albero.)*
*(Gianetta, Mietitori e Mietitrici. Adina siede in disparte leggendo. Nemorino l' osserva da lontano.)*

**GIANNETTA e CORO:** Bel confoto al mietitore,
Quando il sol più ferve e bolle
Sotto un faggio appiè di un colle,
Ripposarsi e respirar!
Del meriggio il vivo ardore
Tempran l'ombre e il rio corrente;
Ma d'amor in vampa ardente
Ombra o rio no può temprar,
Fortunato il mietitore
Che da lui si può guardar.

**NEMORINO:** Quanto è bella, quanto è cara!
Più la vedo, e più mi piace . . .
Ma in quel cor non son capace
Lieve affetto ad inspirar.
Essa legge, studia, impara . . .
Non vi ha cosa ad essa igno-
ta . . .
Io son sempre un idiota,
Io non sò che sospirar.
Chi la mente mi rischiara?
Chi m'insegna a farmi amar?
*(Ridendo.)*

**ADINA:** Benedette queste carte!
E bizzara l'avventura.

**GIANNETTA:** Di che ridi? fanne parte
Di tua lepida lettura.

**ADINA:** E la storia di Tristano,
E una cronaca d'amor.

**CORO:** Leggi, leggi.

**NEMORINO:** (A lei pian piano
Vò accostarmi, entrar fra lor.)

**ADINA:** Della crudele Isotta
Il bel Tristano ardea,
Nè fil de speme avea
Di possederla un di.
Quando si trasse al piede
Di saggio incantator,
Che in un vasel gli diede
Certo elisir d'amore,
Per cui la bella Isotta
Da lui più non fuggi.

**TUTTI:** Elisir di sì perfetta,
Di sì rara qualità,
Ne sapessi la ricetta,
Conoscessi chi ti fa!

## ■ ACT I.

### SCENE I.

*(Homestead of a farm—an open Country at the back—River in landscape—a large tree, under which are seated Gianetta and Reapers—Adina is seated R., reading—Nemorino standing pensively observing her at the wing, L.—Curtain rises to Symphony of Introduzione and Chorus.)*

**CHORUS:** Beneath this leafy shade reclining,
Sweet repose with pleasure blending,
While the noontide sun is shining,
Here we pass an hour away;
Screened from heat by fragrant bowers,
Cooling streams, and beauteous flowers,
But when love exerts his power,
Nothing's impervious to his ray.
No; when love exerts his sway,
Neither tower nor bower's impervious to his ray.
*(Nemorino advances L., observing Adina).*

**NEMORINO:** Ah! how lovely! ah! how dear to me!
While I gaze, I adore more deeply;
Ah! what rapture that soft bosom
With a mutual flame to move.
But while reading, studying, improving,
She has learning and every attainment,
While I can do nothing but love,
etc.
*(Chorus repeated.)*

**ADINA:** Ah! ah! ah! It is a most amusing story! what a singular adventure!

**GIANETTA:** You are laughing! tell me why! Let us share the mirth that moves you.

**ADINA:** It is the story of Tristano. It is a legend, too, of love.

**GIANETTA and CHORUS:** Read it! read it!

**NEMORINO:** (I will listen to what she says, but so that she cannot perceive me.)

**ADINA:** Beauteous, but cruel Isotta,
With love inspired Tristano:
But though the knight adored her,
No prayers could move this fair one.
So at the feet low bent he,
Of a most sage enchanter,
Who in a vial gave him
A certain love elixir,
Through which the beauteous Isotta
In turn felt all the pangs of love.

**CHORUS:** Ah! elixir most divine,
I'd give the world if you were mine.
Ah! elixir most divine! etc.

**ADINA:** Appena ei bebbe un sorso
Del magico vasello,
Che tosto il cor rubello
D'Isotta intenerì.
Cambiata in un istante
Quella beltà crudele
Fu di Tristano amante,
Visse a Tristan fidele;
E quel primiero sorso
Per sempre ei benedì.
Elisir di sì perfetta,
Di sì rara qualità,
Ne sapessi la ricetta,
Conoscessi chi ti fa!

### SCENA II.

*(Suona il tamburo, tutti si alzano. Giunge Belcore guidando un drappello di soldati che rimangono schierati nel fondo. Si appressa ad Adina, la saluta e le presenta un mazzetto.)*

**BELCORE:** Come Paride vezzoso
Porse il pomo alla più bella,
Mia diletta villanella,
Io ti porgo questa fior.
Ma di lui più glorioso,
Più di lui felice io sono,
Poichè in premio del mio dono
Ne riporto il tuo bel cor.

**ADINA:** *(alle donne.)* È modesto il signorino!

**GIANNETTA e CORO:** Sì, davvero.

**NEMORINO:** Oh mio dispetto!

**BELCORE:** Veggo chiaro in quel visino
Ch'io fo breccia nel tuo petto.
Non è cosa sorprendente;
Son galente, son sargente;
Non v'ha bella che resista
Alla vista d'un cimiero;
Cede a Marte, iddio guerriero,
Fin la madre dell'amor.

**ADINA:** È modesto!

**CORO:** Sì, Davvero.

**NEMORINO:** Essa ride . . . oh! mio dolor!

**BELCORE:** Or se m'ami, com'io t'amo,
Che più tardi a render l'armi?
Idol mio, capitoliamo:
In qual dì vuoi tu sposarmi?

**ADINA:** Signorino, io non ho fretta;
Un tantin pensar ci vò.

**NEMORINO:** (Me infelice! s'elle accetta,
Disperato io morirò.)

**TUTTI e BELCORE:** Più tempo invan non perdere:
Volano i giorni e l'ore;
In guerra ed in amore
E fallò l' indugiar.
Al vincitore arrenditi
Da me non puoi scappar.

---

**ADINA:** Now, when Tristano tasted the magic draught of power, she, from that very hour, proved gentle as a lamb—quite changed even in the instant was the cruel lady, and when wedded to the knight; she proved most true and faithful, and ever blessed the magic draught which taught her how to love. O wonderful elixir! I wish I had the recipe of it, that I might know how to prepare it!

### SCENE II.

*(Martial Music, at the close of which, enter Belcore, R. U. E.—He presents flowers to Adina.)*

**BELCORE:** As the gay and gallant Paris
Gave the apple to the most lovely,
So to you, most fair Adina,
I present these flowers rare.
Yet while happy, even as he, love,
Fate grants me more glory, love,
If, in pledge for this, my token,
I bear away your heart.

**ADINA:** *(to the girls).* Isn't he modest?

**CHORUS:** So he is.

**NEMORINO:** Oh! my despair!

**BELCORE:** I read in your bright eyes,
That I have conquered your heart.
This is not at all surprising—
I am a gallant, a sergeant.
There is no girl who can resist
the sight of a soldier;
Was not the mother of love
Conquered by Mars, the god of battle?

**ADINA:** The modest man!

**CHORUS:** So he is.

**NEMORINO:** She laughs! Oh! torture!

**BELCORE:** If you love me as I love you,
Why not ground our arms instanter?
Make your conqueror your slave.

**ADINA:** Gentle Sergeant, I humbly crave
a few days' leisure to reflect.

**NEMORINO:** Ah! most unhappy! should she accept him,
Naught is left me but the grave.

**BELCORE:** Ah! waste not time so uselessly,
He's ever on the wing, dear,
In love, as in war, be sure
Victory brings speed
To the conqueror then yield,
Take shelter beneath a soldier's wing.

---

**ADINA:** Vedete di quest' uomini,
Vedete un pò la boria!
Già cantano vittoria
Inanzi di pugnar.
Non è, non è sì facile
Adina a conquistar.

**NEMORINO:** (Un po' del suo coraggio
Amor mi desse almeno!
Direi siccome io peno,
Pietà potrei trovar.
Ma sono troppo timido
Ma non poss' io parlar.

**GIANNETTA e CORO:** (Davver, saria di ridere
Se Adina ci cascasse.)
Se tutti vendicasse.
Cotesto militar!
Sì, sì; ma è volpe vecchia:
E a lei non si può far.)

**BELCORE:** Intanto, o mia ragazza,
Occuperò, la piazza.—Alcuni instanti
Concedi a miei guerrieri
Al coperto posar.

**ADINA:** Ben volontieri
Mi chiamo fortunata
Di potervi offerir una bottiglia,

**BELCORE:** Obbligato (Io son già della famiglia.)

**ADINA:** Voi ripigliar potete
Gl' interrotti lavori. Il sol declina.

**TUTTI:** Andiamo.
*(Partono Bel., Gia. e il coro.)*

### SCENA III.

*Nemorino e Adina.*

**NEMORINO:** Una parola, o Adina.

**ADINA:** L' usata seccatura!
I soliti sospir! Faresti meglio,
A recarti in città presso tuo zio,
Che si dice malato gravemente.

**NEMORINO:** Il suo mal non è niente—appreso al mio.
Partirmi non poss' io—
Mille volte il tentai—

**ADINA:** Ma s' egli more
E lascia erede un' altro?—

**NEMORINO:** E che m' importa—

**ADINA:** Morria di fame, e senza apoggio alcuno—

**NEMORINO:** O di fame o d' amor—per me è tutti.

**ADINA:** Odimi. Tu sei buono,
Modesto sei, nè nel parlar di quel Sargente
Ti credi certo d'inspirarmi affetto;
Così ti parlo schietto,
E ti dico che in vano amor tu speri,
Che in me tosto non muoja appena è desta.

---

**ADINA:** These men, these men,
how vain they are,
How forward, how presuming!
Before one blow struck for victory,
They sing a note of triumph
But Adina's not so easily caught
In a wedding ring, etc.

**NEMORINO:** If love would give me courage,
I'd tell of all my torture,
And then this fluttering bosom
Perchance would sing of victory.
But this poor heart's timidity
My bark to wreck will bring.

**CHORUS:** It truly would be laughable
If Adina should be caught now
By this gallant son of Mars,
Who conquers all he sees!
It would be very laughable.
But she, she's far too cunning
He never will victory sing.

**BELCORE:** Meanwhile, my dear girl, allow that my comrades may rest a little here, under these shady trees.

**ADINA:** With the greatest pleasure; and I shall be most happy in offering a bottle of wine to them.

**BELCORE:** Much obliged. I see I am already one of the family.

**ADINA:** *(to peasants).* The sun is setting, you may leave off working now.

**CHORUS:** Let us go.
*(Exeunt.)*

### SCENE III.

*Nemorino and Adina.*

**NEMORINO:** One word, Adina—

**ADINA:** Nemorino, it would be much better for you to go to town and see your uncle, who, it is reported, is seriously ill, than to waste your time in the indulgence of a fruitless passion.

**NEMORINO:** His illness is nothing compared with mine. I tried many times to leave this place, but it's impossible.

**ADINA:** But if he dies, and you lose the inheritance

**NEMORINO:** What do I care?

**ADINA:** You will die with hunger.

**NEMORINO:** Whether I die with hunger or with love, it's all the same.

**ADINA:** Listen to me. You are good and modest. I do not believe you so vain as that sergeant; and for that reason I speak to you plainly, and tell you that it is in vain to hope for love from me, because I can not love.

NEMORINO: Oh! Adina—e perchè mai?

ADINA: Bella richiesta!
Chiedi all' aura lusingiera
Perchè vola senza posa
Or sul giglio, or sulla rosa,
Or sul prato, or sul ruscel;
Ti dirà che è in lei natura
L'esser mobile e infedel.

NEMORINO: Dunque io deggio?—

NEMORINO: All' amor mio
Rinunziar, figgir da me.

NEMORINO: Cara Adina!—non poss' io.

ADINA: Tu nol puoi? perche?

NEMORINO: Perche?
Chiedi al rio perchè gemente
Dalla balza, ov' ebbe vita,
Corre al mar sen va a morir:
Ti dirà che lo strascina
Un poter che non sà dir.

ADINA: Dunque vuoi!—

NEMORINO: Morir com' esso
Ma morir sequendo te.

ADINA: Ama altrove: è a te concesso.

NEMORINO: Ah! possible non è.

ADINA: (illegible word) guarir da tal pazzia,
Chè è pazzia l' armor costante
Dêi seguir l' usanza mia.
Ogni dì cambiar d'amante.
Come chiodo scaccia chiodo,
Così amor discaccia amor.
In tal guisa io rido e godo,
in tal guisa ho sciolto il cor.

NEMORINO: Ah! te sola io vedo, io sento
Giorno e notte, in ogni oggetto;
E obbliarti invano io tento,
Il tuo viso ho sculto in petto—
Col cambiarsi qual tu fai,
Può cambiarsi in altro amor.
Ma non può giammai,
Il primiero uscir dal cor.
(*Partono.*)

## SCENA IV.

(*Piazza nel villagio. Osteria della Pernice da un lato.*)
(*Paesani che vanno e vengono. Odesi un suono di tromba: escono dalle case Donne con curiosità.*)

NEMORINO: And why not, O Adina?

ADINA: A wise question.
Go demand of yon light zephyr,
Why it roams from flower to flower,
Wand'ring on through sunshine and shower
Over mountain high or shady grange,
I will reply—it is my nature
That incites me thus to change.

NEMORINO: What remains then?

ADINA: This fruitless passion Renounce, and fly from me.

NEMORINO: Ah! I can not, dear Adina.

ADINA: You can not? and why? and why?

NEMORINO: You ask why?
Go demand of that fair river
Why parts it from its source and fountain,
Coursing on through dale, down mountain,
'Till lost in the far distant sea.
It will reply, some unknown power
Still drives me on, fate wills, so it must be.

ADINA: Then you will not.

NEMORINO: Like that fair river,
I'll be lost while following you.

ADINA: Seek some other, with her forget me.

NEMORINO: Ah! no, no, that never can be.

ADINA: Would you cure this idle madness—
For it is madness to think of constant love—
Then like me, with mirth and gladness,
You'll prove some new attachment each hour
As the night displaces day,
And in turn gives place to morn
So each fading elder passion
Should be the dawn of its younger.

NEMORINO: Ah! night and day, in every object
I do see and hear only you, love;
On this heart that form is graven,
And I would not, if I could, be free.
Other love perchance might waver,
Thus repelled with mirth and scorn;
But my true soul can never be driven
From the fond faith where it is born.
(*Exeunt, Adina, L. S. E., Nemorino, R. U. M.*)

## SCENE IV.

(*Enter Gianetta, Floretta, and Chorus, L. U. E., backing in on the Stage.*)

DON: Che vuol dire cotesta sonata?

UOM: La gran nuova, venite a vedere.

DON: Cos' è stato?

UOM: In carrozza dorata
E arrivato un signor forestiere.
Se vedeste che nobil sembiante!
Che vestito, che treno brilliante.

TUTTI: Certo, certo egli è un gran personaggio,
Un Barone, un Marchese in viaggio—
Forse un Duca—fors' anche di più.
Osservate—si avanza—si accosta;
Giù i berretti, i capelli giù, giù.

## SCENA V.

(*Il Dottore Dulcamara sopra una carrozza in piedi. Diero ad esso un servitore che suona la tromba. Tutti i Paesani lo circondano.*)

DULCAMARA: Udite, udite, o rustici;
Attenti, non fiatate.
Io già suppongo e imagino
Che al par di me sappiate
Ch' io sono quel gran Medico
Dotore enciclopedico,
Chiamato Dulcamara,
La cui virtù preclara,
E i portenti infiniti
Son noti in tutto il mondo—e in altri siti
Benefattor degli uomini,
Riparator de' mali
In pochi giorni io sgombero,
Io spazzo gli ospedali,
E la salute a vendere
Per tutto il Mondo io vò.
Compratela, compratela,
Per poco io ve la do.
È questo l' odontalgico
Mirabile liquore
Dei topi e delle cimici
Possente distruttore,
I cui certificati
Autentici, bollati,
Toccar vedere e leggere
A ciaschedun farò.
Per questo mio specifico
Simpatico, prolifico
Un uom settuagenario
E valeturinario,
Nonno di dieci bamboli
Ancora diventò.
*Per questo tocca e sana.*
In breve settimana
Più d' una affiitta vedova
Ei piangere cessò.
O voi matrone rigide,
Ringiovanir bramate?
Le vostre rughe incomode
Con esse cancellate.

CHORUS OF PEASANTS: What can Those strange sounds mean, echoing near us—
Great news it is! Come, now, and look!
What is it? what is it?
Oh! what wonder, all wonders excelling!
In a carriage of gold,
A traveller approaches our dwelling.
Whoever he looks on, he straightway confounds him!
He's a Baron, or Marquis, I think, boys,
Off hats, and he'll treat us to drink, boys!
He's a Baron, or Marquis, I'm sure, girls!
Here's a chance if you look but demure, girls!
See, he approaches,
How splendid his coach is,
All in flowers of gold and of green,
Such an equipage never was seen.

## SCENE V.

(*Enter Dulcamara and Attendant, L. U. E.*)

DULCAMARA: Give ear now, rustic ones,
Attention now, and silence all!
I think—yes, and imagine now,
That all who stand before me now,
Have heard of my wondrous fame,
And understand my glorious name—
The Italian Dulcamara,
A doctor from Ferrara!
And my wonderful renown
Is known through all the world—
And—and—and elsewhere, too!
Of all men, I am
The greatest, wondrous benefactor:
A doctor sans pareille.
I sell the "Magic Pain Extractor;"
I make the people happy all
In every place I go.
Come buy, come buy!
Cheap, you every one shall have it!
The famous odontalgicum is this—
Truly, an admirable mixture!
Which every sort of toothache cures,
And ne'er was known to fail.
Its infallible efficacy is corroborated,
As each of you himself may testify,
By certificates undoubted.
By this invaluable specific,
Sympathetic and prolific,
And old man, of eighty years,
Quickly changed was to youth
Of strong and active frame.
By this magic "Pain Extractor,"
Many an afflicted widow
Quickly of her tears was freed,
And, oh! all you stately matrons,
Do you wish to be young again?
If so, take this wondrous balsam,
And let your wrinkles disappear.

Volette voi donzelle
Ben liscia aver la pelle!
Voi giovani galanti
Per sempre avere amanti?
Per poco io ve lo do.
Ei move i paralitici,
Spedisce gli apopletici;
Gli asmatici, gli asfitici,
Gl' isterici, i diobetici;
Guarisce, timpanitidi,
E scrofole e rachitidi,
E fino il mal di fegato
Che in moda diventò.
Comprate il mio specifico,
Per poco io ve lo do,
L' ha portato per la posta
Da lontano mille miglia.
Mi direte: quanto costa?
Quanto vale la bottiglia?
Centro scudi—trenta—venti—
No—nessun osi sgomenti.
Per provarvi il mio contento
Di si amico accoglimento,
Io vi voglio, o buona gente,
Uno scudo regalar.

You maidens, too, who, I know,
All like to have a snowy skin;
And young gallants, who wish to win
Kind favor in their mistress' eye—
Come buy this great specific
Which I'll sell to you all cheaply.
This cures the apoplectical,
That asthmatical, the paralytical,
The dropsical, the diuretical,
Consumption, deafness, too,
The rickets and the scrofula—
All evils are at once upset
By this new and fashionable mode.
Come buy, come buy my grand specific,
For a mere trifle you shall buy it.
For you this mixture I have brought
More than ten thousand miles.
You will wonder what the price is—
One hundred dollars—thirty—twenty—
No! I think you'll scarce believe me,
But, to prove to you my friendship,
I am happy—yes, contented,
That all these good folks around me,
Now shall have it for one dollar.

CORO: Uno scudo! veramente?
Più brav' uom non si può dar.

CHORUS: One dollar, only! Truly
The most liberal offer we ever knew.

DULCAMARA: Ecco qua: così stupendo,
Si balsamico elisir,
Tutta Eurpoa sa ch' io vendo
Niente men di nove lire:
Ma siccome è pur palese,
Ch' io son nato nel paese,
Per tre lire a voi richiedo;
Cosi chiaro è come il Sole,
Che a ciascuno che lo vuole
Uno scudo bello e netto
In saccoccia io faccio entrar.
Ah! di patria il caldo affetto.
Gran miracoli può far.

DULCAMARA: Now, observe these
pills tremendous,
Their cures have been stupendous!
And you scarcely need be told,
At four dollars they are sold.
But you know, my friends most dear,
I was born among you here,
And you shall buy of me
This four-dollar box for three!
And for certain, it is most plain, sirs,
That each will gain a dollar, sirs!
But, to serve my native country,
I shall sacrifice my profits.

GIANNETTA: E verissimo: porgete,
Oh! il brav'uom, Dottor, che siete;
Noi ci abbiam del vostro arrivo
Lungamente a ricordar.

CHORUS: This is right, he tells us truly,
Let's accept his liberal offer.
Oh! most wise and wondrous doctor,
Your arrival at this place
Will be very long remembered.

## SCENA VI.

## SCENE VI.

*Nemorino e detti.*

*(Nemorino and Dulcamara.)*

NEMORINO: (Ardir. ha forse il cielo
Mandato espressamente per mio bene
Quest' uom miracoloso nel villaggio.)
Della scienza voglio far saggio,)
Dottore—perdonate—
E ver che possediate
Segreti portentosi?

NEMORINO: Courage! Heaven itself has sent this miraculous doctor into our village to save me. I will try his science.
Doctor! I beg your pardon—is it true that you are in possession of important secrets?

DULCAMARA: Sorprendenti.
La mia saccoccia è di Pandora il vaso.

DULCAMARA: Most surprising ones. My box is like that of Pandora!

NEMORINO: Avreste voi—per caso—
La bevanda amorosa
Della regina Isotta?

NEMORINO: Have you perhaps by chance, the amorous drink of the Queen Isotta!

DULCAMARA: Ah!—che?—che cosa?

DULCAMARA: Ah! the—what is it?

NEMORINO: Voglio dire—lo stupendo
Elisir che desta amore—

NEMORINO: I mean to say, the miraculous elixir that can awaken love.

DULCAMARA: Ah! sì, sì, capisco, intendo,
Io me son distillatore.

DULCAMARA: Oh! yes, yes; I understand you now. I prepare it.

NEMORINO: E fia vero?

NEMORINO: Is it possible!

DULCAMARA: Se ne fa,
Gran consumo in quest' età.

DULCAMARA: Oh! it is in great use nowadays.

NEMORINO: Oh! fortuna! e ne vendete?

NEMORINO: Oh! happiness! And do you sell it?

DULCAMARA: Ogni giorno, a tutto il mondo.

DULCAMARA: Daily, sir, to the whole world.

NEMORINO: E qual prezzo ne volete?

NEMORINO: And what will you have for it?

DULCAMARA: Poco—assai—cioè—secondo—

DULCAMARA: Little; it is according to—

NEMORINO: Un zecchin—null' altro ho qua—

NEMORINO: One eagle is all that I possess.

DULCAMARA: E la somma che ci va.

DULCAMARA: That's exactly the price for it.

NEMORINO: Ah! prendetelo. Dottore.

NEMORINO: Oh! there, take it, doctor.

DULCAMARA: Ecco il magico liquore.

DULCAMARA: Here is the magic liquid.

NEMORINO: Obbligato, ah! sì obbligato!
Son felice, son rinato.
Elisir di tal bontà,
Benedetto chi ti fa!

NEMORINO: Much obliged. How happy I am with this powerful elixir! Blessed be he who invented it!

DULCAMARA: Bei paesi che ho girato
Più d' un gonzo ho ritrovato
Ma un eguale in verità
Non ve n' e', non se dà.

DULCAMARA: (In the countries that I roamed through, I have found many a simpleton, but none to match this one.)

NEMORINO: Ehi! Dottore—un momentino—
In qual modo usar si puote?

NEMORINO: Eh! doctor, one moment. How am I to take this?

DULCAMARA: Con riguardo, pian pianino
La bottiglia un po' si scote—
Poi si stura—ma si bada—
Che il vapor non se ne vada.
Quindi al labbro la avvicini
E lo bevi a centellini,
E l' effecto sroprendente
Non è tardi à conseguir.

DULCAMARA: Shake the bottle a little, with great care, then open it—but beware that none of the vapor escapes; then put it to your mouth and drink it up, and the desired stupendous effect will be produced.

NEMORINO: Sul momento?

NEMORINO: Immediately?

DULCAMARA: A dire il vero,
Necessario è un giorno intero.
(Tanto tempo sufficiente
Per cavarmela e fuggir.)

DULCAMARA: To tell the truth, a whole day will be required. (After that time I shall be off.)

NEMORINO: E il sapore?

NEMORINO: How does it taste?

DULCAMARA: Egli è eccellente—
(È bordò, non elisir)

DULCAMARA: Oh! excellent. (It does taste rather more like wine than elixir.)

NEMORINO: Obbligato, ah! sì, obbligato!
Son felice, son rinato.
Elisir di tal bontà.
Benedetto chi ti fa!

NEMORINO: Thank you kindly, etc.

DULCAMARA: (Nei paesi che ho girato / Più d' un gonzo ho ritrovato; / Ma un eguale in verità / Non ve n' è, non se ne dà.) / Giovinotto! ehi! ehi!

NEMORINO: Signore!

DULCAMARA: Sopra più—silenzio—sai? / Oggidì spacciar l'amore / È un affar geloso assai. / Impacciar se ne potria / Un tantin l' Autorità.

NEMORINO: Ve ne do la fede mia: / Nè anche un' anima il saprà.

DULCAMARA: Va, mortale avventurato; / Un tesoro io t' ho donato: / Tutt' il sesso femminino / Te doman sospirerà. / (Ma doman di buon mattino / Ben lontan sarò di quà.)

NEMORINO: Ah! dottor, vi do parola / Ch' io berrò per una sola: / Nè per altro, e sia pur bella, / Nè una stilla avanzerà. / (Veramente amica stella / Ha costui condotto qua.) / (Dul. entra nell' ost.)

DULCAMARA: In all my travels I've seen many / Fools of every sort and size; / But of all the fools the biggest, / Now he stands before my eyes. Ah! / Yes, he surpasses, etc. / Eh! young man? eh! eh!

NEMORINO: Well, doctor!

DULCAMARA: Not a word, but keep silence; / Silence, silence, sir, I pray. / (Aside.) / Selling love in this queer fashion / May bring me no little trouble / So, not a word—not a look! / Discovered should it be this sale, / They may put me in jail. / Mind—not a word! be silent!

NEMORINO: Silent as a grave I'll be; / They'll get no word or look from me.

DULCAMARA: Go, and spend the day in pleasure; / I have given you a treasure; / All the women will adore you / When tomorrow shall arrive.

NEMORINO: Ah! Adina, each earthly blessing / Centered is in you alone, love. / Your loved image each thought possessing, / Makes this heart all your own. / Friendly powers, take thanks for guiding / This good doctor to my home.

DULCAMARA: (aside). But before tomorrow morning, / Dulcamara will be gone! / Go, and spend, etc. / Not a word, etc. / Not a word about the charming, / Fear the magistrates alarming, / But before, etc.

NEMORINO: Silent as the grave I'll be, etc.

(Exit Dulcamara, L. S. E., leaving Nemorino with the bottle in his hand.)

## SCENA VII.

NEMORINO: Caro elisir! sei mio! / Sì, tutto mio. Com' esser de possente la tua virtù, se, non bevuto ancora, / Di tanta gioia già mi colma il petto! / Ma perchè mai l' effetto non ne poss' io vedere prima che un giorno inter non sia trascorso? / Bevasi: oh! buono: oh! caro! un altro sorso. Oh! qual di vena in vena dolce calor mi scorre! / Ah! forse anch' essa—forse la fiamma istessa incomincia a sentir. / Certo la sente . . . me l' annunzia la gioia e l' appetito che in me si risveglia tutto in un tratto. / (Siede sulla panca dell' osteria: si cava di saccoccia pane e frutti e

## SCENE VII.

NEMORINO: Elixir of love! You're mine now, rarest of treasures! / How great must be your power, how strong your force! / Before I even taste you, my heart is floating and my pulse beats faster! / But what can be the reason that your magic virtue / Will not exert its spell until tomorrow? / (He shakes the bottle and drinks.) / Delicious! I love it! Let's have another! / (He drinks again.) / I feel a cozy burbling warming up my stomach. / Perhaps Adina feels it as well as I do and is longing for me. Yes, I am cer-

mangia cantando.) La rà, la rà.

## SCENA VIII.

ADINA: (Chi è mai quel matto? / Traveggo, o è Nemorino? / Così allegro! e perchè?)

NEMORINO: La la la . . . / (Diamine! è dessa— / (Se alza per correre a lei, ma si arresta.) Ma no—non, ci appressiam. De' miei sospiri / Non si stanchi per or. Tant' è . . . domani / Adorar mi dovrà quel cor spietato.)

ADINA: (Non mi guarda neppur! / Com' è cambiato!)

NEMORINO: La rà la rà; la rà! / Larà, larà, larà.

ADINO: (Non so se è finta o vera / La sua giocondità.)

NEMORINO: (Finora amor non sente.) / Lalleralla la la la.

ADINA: (Vuol far l' indifferente.) / (ride) / Ah! Ah!

NEMORINO: Esulti pu la barbara / Per poco alle mie pene! / Domani avranno termine, / Domani m'amerà.

ADINA: Spezzar vorria lo stolido, / Gettar le sue catene; / Ma gravi più del solito / Pesar le sentirà.

NEMORINO: Lallara, la, la, la.

ADINA: Bravissimo! / (Avvicinandosi a lui.) / La lezion ti giova.

NEMORINO: È ver: la metto in opera / Così, per una prova.

ADINA: Dunque il soffrir primiero?

NEMORINO: Dimenticarlo io spero.

ADINA: Dunque l' antico foco?

NEMORINO: Si estinguerà fra poco. / Ancora un giorno solo. / E il core guarirà.

tain, I feel it in my blood. She's my Isolda and I'm her happy love, I'm her Tristan! / (He sings.) / Lalalalalala! / (He sits down on a bench, takes fruit and bread from his pocket, and eats, while singing.)

## SCENE VIII.

ADINA: Now who's that idiot, I wonder? / Not Nemorino? And so happy? Why is that?

NEMORINO: (seeing Adina) Lalala . . . Hang it all! Adina! (He rises, as if to run toward her, then stops.) / But no, I'll take my time. / I will not burden her with my sighing just now. / Because . . . tomorrow, when the potion takes hold, she will adore me.

ADINA: (aside) He doesn't even look! / He dares ignore me!

NEMORINO: Lalalalalalalalalalala.

ADINA: Can he be really happy, / Or is it just put on?

NEMORINO: Lalalalalala . . .

ADINA: I think he wants to fool me.

NEMORINO: She's still as cold as ever. / She's laughing at my love for her, / That heartless, cruel Adina! / Tomorrow she will laugh no more, / She'll fall in love with me.

ADINA: The fool! He tries to tear in vain / The bond that holds him captive. / The more he strives to break his chain, / The stronger it will be.

NEMORINO: Lalalalala la la la . . .

ADINA: (approaching him) Not bad, my lad! / You learned your lesson quickly. / You're doing what I told you.

NEMORINO: I try to make the best of it / As long as I can't hold you.

ADINA: So you no longer love me?

NEMORINO: I'm hoping to forget you.

ADINA: Then you can live without me?

NEMORINO: I hope it won't upset you. / And by tomorrow morning / My heart will be all well.

ADINA: Davver? Me ne consolo . . .
Ma pure . . . si vedrà.

NEMORINO: (Esulti pur la barbara
Per poco alle mie pene!
Domani m'amerà.)

ADINA: (Spezzar vorria lo stolido,
Getar le sue catene;
Ma gravi più del solito
Pesar le sentirà.)

## SCENA IX.

(Belcore di dentro, indi in scena,
e detti.)

BELCORE: Tran tran, tran tran, tran
tran.
In guerra ed in amore
L' assedio annoja e stanca.

ADINA: (A tempo vien Belcore.)

BELCORE: Io vado all' arma bianca
In guerra ed in amor.

ADINA: Ebben, gentil Sargente,
La piazza vi è piaciuta?

BELCORE: Difesa à bravamente,
E invano ell' è battuta.

ADINA: E non vi dice il core
Che presto cederà?

BELCORE: Ah! lo volesse amore!

ADINA: Vedrete che vorrà.

BELCORE: Quando? saria possibile!

NEMORINO: (A mio dispetto io
tremo.)

BELCORE: Favella, o mio bell' Angelo.
Quando ci sposeremo?

ADINA: Prestissimo.

NEMORINO: Che sento?

BELCORE: Ma quando?

ADINA: Fra sei dì.
(Guardando Nem.)

NEMORINO: Oh! gioja! son contento.

BELCORE: Ah! ha! va ben così.
(Che cosa trova a ridere
Cotesto scimunito?
Or or lo piglio a scoppole
Se non va via di qua.)

ADINA: (E può sì lieto ed ilare
Sentir che mi marito!
Non posso più nascondere
La rabbia che mi fa.)

---

ADINA: Indeed? So much the better . . .
However . . . time will tell.

NEMORINO: She's laughing at my
love for her,
That heartless, cruel Adina!
Tomorrow she will laugh no more,
She'll fall in love with me.

ADINA: The fool! He tries to tear in
vain
The bond that holds him captive.
The more he strives to break his
chain,
The stronger it will be.

## SCENE IX.

(Enter Belcore, L. U. E.)
(Adina, Nemorino and Belcore.)

BELCORE: Tran, tran, tran, tran!
In love, boys, as in war,
A siege is wondrously trying.

ADINA: He comes most opportunely.

BELCORE: While both keen blades
require, boys,
Without a speck or flaw.

ADINA: How now most valorous
sergeant,
When will the siege be ended?

BELCORE: Alas! in vain I lay before
A place so well defended!

ADINA: Does not your heart inform
you,
That soon the place will fall!

BELCORE: Ah! if I dare imagine—

ADINA: Courage, you'll batter
down the wall!

BELCORE: Dearest! Oh! is it possible?—

NEMORINO: In spite of myself, I
tremble!

BELCORE: Then love, pray name
our wedding-day—
No longer dissemble.

ADINA: Tomorrow!

NEMORINO: Good heavens!

BELCORE: My angel!

ADINA: In three days.

NEMORINO: Ah!—what rapture
fills my bosom!
In three days—ha, ha, ha!—you'll
see

BELCORE: I wonder what he's
laughing at,
The stupid ignoramus!
I certainly shall punch his head,
Unless he march away.

ADINA: I can no longer hide my
rage!
That he, but now my vassal,
When hearing that I soon shall wed,
Is yet so blithe and gay.

---

NEMORINO: Gradasso! ei già
s'immagini
Toccar il ciel col dito:
Ma tesa è già la trappola,
Doman se ne avvedrà)

## SCENA X.

(Suona il tamburo: esce Giannetta con le contadine, indi accorrono i soldati di Belcore.)

GIANNETTA: Signor sargente, signor sargente
Di voi richiede la vostra gente.

BELCORE: Son qua: ch' è stato?
perchè tal fretta?

SOL: Son due minuti che una staffetta
Non so qual ordine per voi reco.

BELCORE: Il Capitano . . . ah!
ah! va bene.
(Leggendo.)
Su, camerata: partir conviene.

CORI: Partire . . . ! e quando?

BELCORE: Doman mattina.

CORI: O Ciel, sì presto!

NEMORINO: (Afflitta è Adina.)

BELCORE: Espresso è l' ordine—
che dir non so.

CORI: Maledettisima combinazione!
Cambiar sì spesso di guarnigione!
Dover le amanti abbandonar.

BELCORE: Espresso è l' ordine—
non so che far
Carino, udisti? domani, addio!
(Ad Adi.)
Almen ricordati dell' amor mio.

NEMORINO: (Sì, sì, domani ne
udrai la nuova.)

ADINA: Di mia costanza ti darò
prova:
La mia promessa rammenteró.

NEMORINO: (Sì, sì, domani te lo
dirò.)

BELCORE: Se a mantenerla tu sei
dispota,
Chè non anticip? che mai ti costa?
Fin da quest' oggi non puoi sposarmi?

NEMORINO: (Fin da quest' oggi!)

ADINA: (osservando Nem.). (Si
turba, parmi.)
Ebben; quest' oggi . . .

NEMORINO: Quest' oggi! o Adina,
Quest' oggi, dici? . . .

ADINA: E perchè no?

NEMORINO: Aspetta almeno fin
domattina.

BELCORE: E tu che c' entri? vediamo un po'.

---

NEMORINO: He thinks himself a
conqueror,
This man of war, so famous;
Tomorrow he will hide his head,
Through they exult today, ha, ha!

## SCENE X.

(Enter Gianetta, Floretta, and
Chorus, L. U. E.)

GIANETTA: O Mr. Sergeant, Mr.
Sergeant,
Your soldiers seek you through the
village

BELCORE: I am here, now: what's
the matter?

CHORUS OF SOLDIERS: An hour
ago, sir,
Was left below, sir,
This dispatch, sir, directed to you.

BELCORE: It is from the Captain.
Ah! ah! it is well! it will be something new.
Comrades, prepare: We change our
quarters.

CHORUS: You change! and when?

BELCORE: Faith, tomorrow at ten.

CHORUS: O heavens! so soon!

NEMORINO: Adina is pensive.

BELCORE: Ah, dear Adina, I must
go!

CHORUS: It is thus the garrison is
always changing
And thus the soldier is forever ranging
We might have guessed it is nothing
new.

BELCORE: Ah, dearest Adina, however unwilling,
Tomorrow, love, tomorrow,
I must say adieu.

NEMORINO: (aside). Yes, yes, tomorrow
You'll hear something new.

ADINA: I shall be faithful, you
have my pledge, sir;
I shall be faithful, faithful to you

NEMORINO: Yes, yes. Tomorrow,
dearest,
You'll hear something new!

BELCORE: If to be constant you are
disposed, love,
Why not anticipate our nuptials?
If in a week, love—why not today?

NEMORINO: Ah! not today

ADINA: He seems disturbed.
yes, today! why not, sir?

NEMORINO: Not today, O Adina,
Say not today!

ADINA: And pray, sir, why?

NEMORINO: Ah! wait till tomorrow!

BELCORE: Today or tomorrow,
Pray, sir, what have you to say?

NEMORINO: Adina, credemi, te ne scongiuro . . .
Non puoi sposarlo . . . te ne assicuro . . .
Aspetta ancora . . . un giorno appena
Un breve giorno . . . io so perchè.
Domani, o cara, ne avresti pena,
Te ne dorresti al par di me.

BELCORE: Il ciel ringrazi, o babbuino,
Che matto, o presso tu sei dal vino!
Ti avrei strozzato, ridotto in brani,
Se in questo istante tu fossi in te.
Ma finch' io tengo a fren le mani.
Va via, buffone, ti ascondi a me.

ADINA: Lo compatite, egli è un ragazzo:
Un mal' accorto, un mezzo pazzo:
Si è fitto in capo ch' io debba amarlo,
Perch'ei delira d' amor per me.
(Vo' vendicarmi, vo' tormentarlo,
Vo' che pentito mi cada al piè.)

GIANNETTA e CORI: Vedete un poco quel semplicione
Ha pur la strana presunzione:
Ei pensa farla ad un sargente.
A un uom di mondo che par non è.
Oh! sì per Bacco, è veramente
La bella Adina boccon per te!

ADINA: Andiamo, Belcore. Si avverta il notaro.

NEMORINO: Dottore! Dottore! . . . —Soccorso! riparo!

GIANNETTA e CORI: È matto davvero.

ADINA: (Me l' hai da pagar.)
A lieto convito—Amici, v' invito.

BELCORE: Giannetta, ragazze.—
Vi aspetto a ballar.

GIANNETTA e CORI: Un ballo, un banchetto!
Chi puó ricusar?

TUTTI: Fra lieti concenti,
Gioconda brigata,
Vogliamo contenti,
Passar la giornata;
Presento alla festa,
Amore sarà,
Ei perde la testa
Da rider mi fa.
Ah, ah, ah, ah,
Da rider mi fa,
Ei perde la testa,
Da rider mi fa.

NEMORINO: Wait till tomorrow, Adina, not today.
Adina, trust me, I beg you,
You cannot wed him.
I tell you truly, wait, I beg you,
Until tomorrow.
But one short day, love, but one short day.
The future, dearest, you'll spend in sorrow,
If to my suit, love, you now say no.

BELCORE: Thank heaven, you most consummate donkey,
You noodle, that nothing but contempt moves me;
If you had brains, I'd scatter 'em to the winds.
But when did an ass do anything but bray!
As I'm a soldier, I'll crack your crown, sir,
If you dare to stay here, you scoundrel,
I'll crack your crown, sir, if you stay.

ADINA: Oh! pray excuse him, he's young and foolish.
A stupid peasant half-mad with passion,
Whom I discarded this very morning,
So take no notice of him, I pray.
Revenge is pleasant:
I'll now torment him
Until he, repenting,
Shall mercy pray.

GIANETTA and CHORUS: Was ever seen such strange presumption!
This foolish fellow would fain outwit him.
Fight with a soldier!—why, we'd pit him
Against great Mars, in such a fray.

ADINA: Sergeant Belcore, send for the Notary.

NEMORINO: O Doctor, assist me!

CHORUS: He's mad, sirs! how sad, sirs.

ADINA: I pay in his own coin.
(To Peasantry.)
I know it will delight you
and therefore invite you—

BELCORE: To a ball and banquet,
On this happy day!

CHORUS: A ball and banquet!
It is their wedding day.

ENSEMBLE: These moments entrancing,
Such happiness bringing,
Enjoy them with dancing,
With feasting, with singing;
From love's cup of pleasure
We'll gladden the hours,
And fill up its measure
With joy and with flowers.

NEMORINO: Mi sprezza il sargente, mi burla l' ingrata,
Zimbello alla gente—mi fa la spietata,
L'oppresso mio core—più speme non ha.
Dottore! dottore!
Soccorso! pietà!
(Adina dà la mano a Belcore:
Nemorino si smania gli astanti lo dileggiano.)

*CALA IL SIPARIO*

# ■ ATTO II.

## *SCENA I.*

*Interno della fattoria d' Adina. (Adina, Belcore, Dulcamara, Giannetta seduti a tavola Gli abitanti del villaggio in piedi bevendo e cantando.)*

CORO: Cantiamo, faccian brindisi
A sposi così amabili.
Per lor sian lunghi e stabili
I giorni del piacer.

BELCORE: Per me l' amore e il vino
Due numi ognor saranno.
Compensan d' ogni effanno
La donna ed il bicchier.

ADINA: (Se fosse Nemorino!
Me la vorrei goder.)

CORO: Cantiamo, facciam brindisi, etc.

DULCAMARA: Poichè cancar vi alletta,
Uditemi, signori.
Ho qua una canzonetta
Di fresco data fuor
Vivace, graziosa
Che gusto vi può dar;
Purchè la bella sposa
Mi voglia secondar.

TUTTI: Sì, sì, l' avremo cara;
Dev' esser cosa rara,
Se il grande Dulcamara
E giunta a contentar.

DULCAMARA: (*Cava di saccoccia alcuni librettini, e ne da una ad Adi.*) La Nina Gondoliera
E il Senator Tredenetti
Barcaruola a due voci—Attenti

NEMORINO: The Sergeant is sneering,
Adina derides me,
The villagers leering—
Whatever betides me
I care not for all.
Now all is dark as night.
O Doctor, the nostrum
has ruined me!
(*At the close of this chorus, Nemorino is pushed about by all the characters.—Adina, in a coquettish manner, keeps near Belcore, who in return pays her attention.—Nemorino runs out, R. U. E. in a fit of distraction, amid the jeers and laughter of the chorus when the curtain falls.*)

*END OF ACT ONE.*

# ■ ACT II.

## *SCENE I.*

*(The interior of a village farmhouse with preparations for a feast. A table running across the back of the stage—another much smaller at which Dulcamara and Belcore sit.—Gianetta, Floretta, and Chorus seated at the other.*

CHORUS: A song, boys, a song! And a jovial one!
A toast, boys, and a noble one!
To them may pleasure, without measure,
Long and constant!

BELCORE: Thanks for your kindly greeting,
May pleasure, without measure,
Long and constant be.
This our merry meeting,
As pleasant be to every one
As it is now to me.
A health to all around, boys,
And a bumper let it be, etc.

ADINA: Would that Nemorino were here this sight to see.

CHORUS: A song, boys, a song! a song! a song, etc.

DULCAMARA: My friends, I have the last new barcarolle from Venice, in my pocket; it is for two voices, and, if the fair Adina will sing it with me, I shall be happy to let you hear it.

ALL: Yes, yes—we shall be delighted. It must be very clever to have pleased the learned Dulcamara.

## Act II, Scene I

TUTTI: Attenti.

DULCAMARA: Io son ricco, e tu sei bella,
Io ducatì e vezzi hai tu:
Perchè a me sarai ribella,
Nina mia, che vuoi di più?

ADINA: Quale onore!—Un senatore
Me d'amore—supplicar!
Ma, modesta gondoliera,
Un par mio vò sposar.

DULCAMARA: Idol mio, non più rigor;
Fa felici un Senator.

ADINA: Eccellenza, troppo onor,
Io non merto un Senator.

DULCAMARA: Adorata Barcaruola,
Prendi l' oro e lascia amor;
Lieve è questo, e lieve vola;
Pesa quello e resta ognor.

ADINA: Quale onore!—Un Senatore
Me d' amore—supplicar!
Ma Zanetto—e giovinetto;
Ei mi piace, e il vo' sposar.

DULCAMARA: Idol mio non più rigor;
Fa felice un Senator.

ADINA: Eccellenza! troppo onor.
Io non merto un Senator.

TUTTI: Bravo, bravo, Dulcamara!
La canzone è cosa rara,
Sceglier meglio non può certo
Il più esperto cantator.

DULCAMARA: Il Dottore Dulcamara
In ogni arte è professor.
(Viene un notaro.)

BELCORE: Silenzio!—E qua il Notaro.
Che vien a compier l'atto
Di mia felicità.

TUTTI: Sia il ben venuto!

DULCAMARA: T' abbraccio, e ti saluto
O medico d' Amor, spezial d' imene.

ADINA: (Giunto è il Notaro, e Nemorino non viene!)

BELCORE: Andiam, mia bella Venere . . .
Ma in quelle luci tenere
Qual veggo nuvolletto?

ADINA: Non è niente.
(S' egli non è presente.
Compita non mi par la mia vendetta.)

DULCAMARA: (Dulcamara presents Adina with one roll of music, and keeps the other himself.) You must—now, then, attention, silence! the subject is Nina, a pretty fish-woman, and old Tredenti, the Collector of Taxes.

DULCAMARA: I have riches, you have beauty,
I have gold, and you have charms,
Then fly, delightful Nina, to your fond adorer's arms.

ADINA: What an honor!—
My husband aspires to be, a collector!
But my heart goes with my hand, sir,
And your's is far too old for me.

DULCAMARA: Lovely girl, behold your slave,
At your feet I crave an answer.

ADINA: Ah! you're far too old and grave
Sir, to be a young girl's slave.

DULCAMARA: Most adored and beauteous creature,
Riches cleanse us from all stains;
Love is light, while gold is heavy,
This takes wing while that remains.

ADINA: What an honor!—a director
My husband aspires to be a director
But my heart goes with my hand, sir,
And I am far younger than you.

DULCAMARA: Dearest idol, relax your rigor,
And make your senator happy.

ADINA: Excellent sir, your proffered love
Is too much honor for me.

CHORUS: Bravo! bravo! Dulcamara,
It is a most amusing song, sir;
Taste and style belong to you, sir,
In no moderate degree.

DULCAMARA: Yes, I flatter myself, sirs,
That taste and style pertains to me.
(Enter Notary.)

BELCORE: Silence, I say. Here comes the Notary to accomplish my felicity.

ALL: And right welcome he is.

DULCAMARA: (to Notary). Great carpenter and joiner of Love and Hymen, I embrace and salute you.

ADINA: (The Notary has come, and Nemorino is not here.)

BELCORE: Adina, my love, you look sorrowful; brush away the little clouds that obscure the lustre of those eyes. What has happened to vex you?

ADINA: Nothing! (Aside.) If Nemorino is not present, my triumph will be but half complete.

BELCORE: Andiamo a segnar l' atto: il tempo affretta.

TUTTI: Cantiamo ancora un brindisi
A sposi così amabili
Per lor sian lunghi e stabili
I giorni del piacer.
(Partono tutti. Dul. ritorna indietro, e si rimette a tavola.)

## SCENA II.

Dulcamara, indi Nemorino.

DULCAMARA: La feste nuziali
Son piacevoli assai; ma quel che in esse
Mi dà maggior diletto.

NEMORINO: Ho veduto il Notaro.
(Sopra pensiero.)
Sì, l' ho veduto . . . Non v' ha più speranza;
Nemorino, per te; spezzato ho il core.

DULCAMARA: (Dettando fra i denti.) Idol mio non più rigor;
Fa felice un Senator.

NEMORINO: Voi, qui, Dottore!

DULCAMARA: Sì, m' han voluto a pranzo
Questi amabili sposi, e mi diverto
Con questi avanzi.

NEMORINO: Ed io son disperato!
Fuori di me son io. Dottore, ho d'uopo
D'essere amato . . . prima di domani . . .
Adesso . . . su du piè.

DULCAMARA (S'alza): (Cospetto è matto!)
Recipe l'elisir, e il colpe è fatto.

NEMORINO: E veramente amato
Sarò da lei . . .

DULCAMARA: Da tutte: io te 'l prometto.
Se anticipar l' effetto
Dell' elisir tu vuoi, bevine tosto
Un' altra dose. (Io parto fra mezzora.)

NEMORINO: Caro dottor, una bottiglia ancora.

DULCAMARA: Ben volontier. Mi piace
Giovare a' bisognosi.—Hai tu danaro?

NEMORINO: Ah! non ne ho più.

BELCORE: Come now, then, to sign the contract which makes you mine forever.

CHORUS: Let us sing and fill our glasses—bumpers, in honor of this amiable couple. May their days of mirth last for ever.
(Exeunt all but Dulcamara, who remains at the table eating and drinking.)

## SCENE II.

DULCAMARA: Witnessing a contract is all very well, if one has nothing better to do; but, as it is quite uncertain when the next dinner gratis may fall in, I'll even make the most of the one that's before me.

NEMORINO: All is lost! I saw the Notary—my poor uncle, too, who has ever been so kind to me, lies now, they say, upon his death-bed at Ravienna, and yet, madman as I am, I can not tear myself away.

DULCAMARA: (sings.) "Lovely girl, I crave an answer,
At your feet behold your slave!

NEMORINO: O Doctor! you here!

DULCAMARA: Yes, the amiable contracting parties are signing and sealing in the next room; they are feasting on love, but as that is rather short commons for lookers on, I stick to the lobster salad and champagne.

NEMORINO: I am desperate—I am mad, doctor. Where's the use of being loved tomorrow by one who is to be wedded today? I want to be loved now, instantly.

DULCAMARA: (Rising.) (By Heavens, he's mad!)
Take another dose of the elixir, and the thing's completely accomplished.

NEMORINO: I must be loved! before tomorrow! Instantly!

DULCAMARA: Undoubtedly: that I promise you. If you would anticipate the effect of the magic elixir, you have only to take another dose. (I go in half an hour).

NEMORINO: (impatiently). Give it me, give it me, Doctor!

DULCAMARA: With pleasure, my dear friend. (Producing it.) Nothing ever causes me so much happiness as being able to assist the unfortunate; the price is twenty crowns.

NEMORINO: I haven't one farthing in the world.

DULCAMARA: La cosa cambia aspetto. A me verrai
Subito che ne avrai.—Vieni a trovarmi
Quî presso alla Pernice.
Ci hai tempo un quarto d' ora.

## SCENA III.

*Nemorino indi Belcore.*

NEMORINO: (*Si getta sopra una panca.*) Oh! me infelice!

BELCORE: La donna è un animale
Stravagante davvero. Adina m' ama,
Di sposarmi è contenta, e differire
Pur vuol fino a sta sera!

NEMORINO: Ecco il rivale!
(Mi spezzerei la testa di mia mano?)

BELCORE: (Ebbene—che cos' ha questo baggiano?
Ehi, ehi, quel giovinotto!
Cos' hai che ti disperi?)

NEMORINO: Io mi dispero . . . Perchè non ho denaro . . . e non so come.
Non so dove trovarne.

BELCORE: Eh! scimunito!
Se danaro non hai.
Fatti soldato . . . e venti scudi avrai.

NEMORINO: Venti scudi!

BELCORE: E ben sonanti,

NEMORINO: Quando? adesso?

BELCORE: Sul momento.

NEMORINO: (Che far deggio?)

BELCORE: E coi contanti,
Gloria e onore al reggimento.

NEMORINO: Ah non è l' ambizione,
Che seduce questo cor.

BELCORE: Se è l' amore, in guarnigione
Non ti può mancar l' amor.

NEMORINO: Ai perigli della guerra
Io so ben che esposto sono;
Che doman la patria terra,
Zio, congiunti, ahimè, abbandono.
Ma so per che fuor di questa,
Altra strada a me non resta
Per poter del cor d' Adina
Un sol giorno trion far.
Ah! cri un giorno ottiene Adin
Fin la vita può lasciar.)

BELCORE: Del tamburo al suon vivace,
Fra le file e le bandiere
Aggirarsi amor si piace

---

## SCENE III.

(*Nemorino, and afterwards, Belcore.*)

NEMORINO: (*casting himself on a seat*) Oh, most unfortunate am I!

BELCORE: What an incomprehensible being is woman! Adina loves me, that is evident enough—wishes to be married to me—and yet insists on deferring the nuptials till tonight.

NEMORINO: Oh, there is my rival! How I should like to punch his head with this fist of mine!

BELCORE: That fellow here! what is the matter with the dolt, I wonder? Hark, friend, you seem disturbed.

NEMORINO: I am mad—desperate—heartbroken—Because I have no money, and don't know where to get any!

BELCORE: Enlist for a soldier, and you'll get twenty crowns!

NEMORINO: Twenty crowns!

BELCORE: Full weight, I vow, sir.

NEMORINO: Given directly! How determine!

BELCORE: Here, and now, sir!

NEMORINO: What shall I do?

BELCORE: And, besides the money, you will get glory and promotion in the regiment.

NEMORINO: It is not gold nor stern ambition that moves
My heart to this step.

BELCORE: Ah! if it is Cupid that enthralls you,
The soldier need never fall in love.

NEMORINO: I know full well that the path of war
Ever teems with fearful dangers—That, tomorrow, for strangers I abandon
My home, country, friends, relations,
But no other path is left me
To secure Adina's heart.
And, oh! what rapture unexampled,
To say I triumph before I part!
Once I have gained
Adina, I may die content.

BELCORE: At the drum's enlivening roll,
While flaunting banners grace the line,

---

Con le vispe vivandiere:
Sempre lieto, sempre gajo
Ha di bella un centinajo;
Dì costanza non s' annoja
Non si perde a sospirar.
Credi a me: la vera gioja
Accompagna il militar.

NEMORINO: Ebben, vada. Li prepara.

BELCORE: Ma la carta che tu vedi
Pria di tutto dei segnar
Qua una croce.
(*Nemorino segna e prende la borsa.*)

NEMORINO: (Dulcamara
Volo tosto a ricercar.)

BELCORE: Qua la mano, giovinotto,
Dell' acquisto mi consolo.
In complesso, sopra e sotto
Tu mi sembri un buon figlinolo,
Sarai presto caporale,
Se me prendi ad esemplar.
(Ho ingaggiato il mio rivale:
Anche questa è da contar.)

NEMORINO: Ah! non sai chi m' ha ridotto
A tal passo, a tal partito;
Tu non sai qual cor sta sotto
A quest' umile vestito;
Quel che a me tal somma vale
Non potresti immaginar.
(Ah! non v' ha tesoro eguale,
Se riesce a farmi amar.)
(*Partono.*)

## SCENA IV.

(*Campagna come nell' atto primo. Giannetta e paesane.*)

CORI: Saria possibile.

GIANNETTA: Possibilissimo.

CORI: Non è probabile.

GIANNETTA: Probabilissimo.

CORI: Ma come mai?—ma d' onde il sai?
Chi te lo disse? chi è? do' è?

GIANNETTA: No fate strepito: parlate piano:
Non anco spargere si può l' arcano.
E noto solo al merciajuolo;
Che in Confidenza l' ha detto a me.

CORI: Il merciajuolo l' ha detto a te!
Sarà verissimo . . . oh! bella affè!

GIANNETTA: Sappiate dunque che l' altro dî
Di Nemorino lo zio morì;
Che al giovinotto lasciato egli ha.

---

Love is pleased to wander round:
Amid the girls who sell provisions,
Always joyful, always gay,
You will find a hundred beauties.
Nor, by constancy if ennuied,
Need you waste much time in wooing.
Trust to me, there's no delight
To match a soldier's day and night.

NEMORINO: It is well—to enlist, then, I agree

BELCORE: But this paper must be signed,
First by you, and then by me. (*Both sign paper.*)
So, that's enough.

NEMORINO: Dulcamara, man of fame
I fly to claim
Your promised aid!

BELCORE: Now your hand—our bargain's ended;
I'm delighted to have gained you!
Your appearance will be splendid,
When the sergeant will have trained you;
And you'll soon become a corporal.
If you will but take example of me.
Yes, I have enlisted my rival
Now the field lies fair and free:
Thus success still waits on boldness,
And my triumph is decreed.

NEMORINO: To honor and glory, a name found in story,
All danger deriding, on, onward we march!
He knows not the motive my freedom I barter;
Nor ever can imagine its value to me.
The sun brightly gleaming, our arms gaily streaming,
The name of Adina shall be my bright star
(*They leave.*)

## SCENE IV.

(*Enter Gianetta, Floretta and Peasantry, L. U. E.*)

CHORUS: Is it possible?

GIANETTA: Yes, it is.

CHORUS: It can't be possible.

GIANETTA: Yes, it is.

CHORUS: But tell us how, who has told you, how do you know it; quick, tell us here.

GIANETTA: Hush! don't make a noise. This secret must not be known yet; because I have it from the peddler, who told me in the strictest confidence.

CHORUS: If he has told you of it, there can't be any doubt. O happy news!

GIANETTA: Know, then, that Nemorino's uncle died the other day, and left him a considerable inheritance. But silence! nobody must

Cospicua, immensa eredità.
Ma zitte . . . piano . . . per carità.
Non deve dirsi.

**CORI:** Non si dirà.
Or Nemorino è millionario . . .
E l' Epulone del circondai-
ro . . .
Un uom di vaglia, un buon parti-
to . . .
Felice quella cui fia marito!
Ma zite . . . piano . . . per
carità.
Non deve dirsi, non si dirà.
(*Veggono Nem. che si avvicina, si
ritirano in disparte.*)

know it yet.

**CHORUS:** Nobody shall know it.
Now, Nemorino is a millionaire; he
is the richest man in all the neighborhood—he is a worthy man—a
good match—happy the girl who
gets him. But be silent, nobody
must know it yet.
(*They see Nemorino coming, and
retire to one side, looking at him
anxiously.*)

## SCENA V.

*Nemorino e detti.*

**NEMORINO:** Dell' elisir mirabile
Bevuto ho in abbondanza,
E mi promette il Medico
Cortese ogni beltà.
In me maggior del solito.
Rinata è la speranza,
L' effeto di quel farmaco
Già, Già, sentir si fa.

**CORI:** (E ognor negletto ed ùmile:
La cosa ancor non sa.)

**NEMORINO:** (*per uscire*). ANdiam.

**GIANNETTA e CORI:** (*inchinan-dolo*) Serva umillissima.

**NEMORINO:** Giannetta!

**CORI:** (*L'una dopo l' altra*). A voi m' inchino.

**NEMORINO:** (Cos' han coteste giovani? (*Fra sè maravigliato.*)

**GIANNETTA e CORI:** Caro quel Nemorino!
Davvero ch' egli è amabile;
Ha l' aria da Signor.

**NEMORINO:** (Capisco, è questa l' opera
Del magico licor.)

## SCENA VI.

*Adina e Dulcamara.*

**ADINA:** Come sen va contento!

**DULCAMARA:** La lode è mia.

**ADINA:** Vostra o Dottor?

**DULCAMARA:** Sì, tutta.
La gioja è al mio comando,
Io distillo il piacer, l' amor lambic-co,
Come l' acqua di rose; e ciò che adesso
Vi fa maravigliar nel giovinotto,
Tutto portento egli è del mio decot-to.

**ADINA:** Pazzie!

## SCENE V.

**NEMORINO:** I have already drank so much,
Of this miraculous elixir,
That doubtless every beauty will court me,
As the great Doctor promised
I have now more hopes than ever;
And already I begin to feel the power,
The wonderful effects of this elixir.

**CHORUS:** At other times he is both humble and ignorant,
Now he is quite beside himself!

**NEMORINO:** Let us go. (*Going.*)

**GIANETTA and CHORUS:** Your humble servant, sir (*Bowing.*)

**NEMORINO:** Gianetta!

**CHORUS:** (*one after another*). I salute you.

**NEMORINO:** What is the matter with these young people?

**GIANETTA and CHORUS:** How dear is that Nemorino!
How exceedingly amiable he is!
He has quite the appearance of a Duke!

**NEMORINO:** I begin to comprehend—Their courtesy
Is the effect of the magic liquor.

## SCENE VI.

*Dulcamara and Adina.*

**ADINA:** How contentedly he goes with them.

**DULCAMARA:** It's all my doing!

**ADINA:** Yours, Doctor?

**DULCAMARA:** Yes, mine! I mix up happiness at twenty crowns a bottle, and distill love like rose-water. That which excites wonder in young men is a prodigy of my concoction.

**ADINA:** Psha!

---

**DULCAMARA:** Pazzie, voi dite?
Incredula! pazzie! Sapete voi
Dell' Alchimia il poter, il gran valore
Dell' Elisir d' amore
Della regina Isotta.

**ADINA:** Isotta!

**DULCAMARA:** Isotta.
Io n' ho ogni mistura e d' ogni cotta.

**ADINA:** (Che ascolto?) E a Nemori-no
Voi deste l' Elisir?

**DULCAMARA:** Ei me lo chiese
Per ottener l' affetto
Di non so qual crudele . . .

**ADINA:** Ei dunque amava?

**DULCAMARA:** Languiva, sospirava
Sena' ombra di speranza; e, per avere
Una goccia del farmaco incantato.
Vendè la libertà, si fe soldato.

**DUETTO:**

**ADINA:** (Quanto amore! ed io, spietata
Tormentai sì nobil cor!)

**DULCAMARA:** (Essa pure è innamorato;
ha bisogno del liquor.)

**ADINA:** Dunque . . . adesso—è Nemorino
In amor sì fortunato! . . .

**DULCAMARA:** Tutto il sesso femminino
E pel giovine impazzato.

**ADINA:** E qual donna è a lui gradita?
Qual fra tante è preferita?

**DULCAMARA:** Egli è il gallo delle Checca
Tutte segue; tutte becca.

**ADINA:** (Ed io sola, sconsigliata,
Possedea quel nobil cor!)

**DULCAMARA:** (Essa pure è innamorata;
Ha bisogno del liquor.)
Bella Adina! qua un momento
Più d' appresso . . . su la testa,
Tu sei cotta . . . io l' argomento
A quell' aria afflitta e mesta.
Se tu voi? . . .

**ADINA:** S' io vo'? che cosa?

**DULCAMARA:** Psha! do you say? I like that. Do you know the secrets of Alchemy? do you know the power of the love elixir of Queen Isotta? I have it in bottles of all sizes. Here, now, is one only ten crowns. (*Aside.*) A black drink—but never mind!

**ADINA:** Isota!

**DULCAMARA:** Isotta.
I have mixtures to suit all purposes.

**ADINA:** What do I hear? and you sold that elixir to Nemorino?

**DULCAMARA:** I did. He applied for it to try its effects upon some person who had refused him.

**ADINA:** Then he was in love?

**DULCAMARA:** He was—he languished, sighed—without a ray of hope—and now look at the effect; yonder he is (*Pointing, R. U. E.*) Sixteen women round him—look at that, there's an elixir for you! Sold his liberty, and became a soldier—sixteen women—very cheap, too, I think.

**DUET:**

**ADINA:** What affection! and I—how cruel
To torment that noble heart!
Ah! cruel! ah! cruel!

**DULCAMARA:** (She's in love and wants the elixir,
Faith, I won't depart so soon!)

**ADINA:** Then it's certain that Nemorino
has at length requited his love.

**DULCAMARA:** He's invited to every feast
All the women are delighted,
Every masculine is blighted.
Every feminine excited.

**ADINA:** And which fair damsel has
He made choice of; pray, on
Whom does his preference fall?

**DULCAMARA:** I think that, like a butterfly,
He flies from flower to flower.

**ADINA:** Some dark fiend, it was sure, tempted me—
To reject that noble heart.

**DULCAMARA:** She's in love and wants the elixir.
Hist, Adina, hear me a moment!
No, come nearer—
What! do you fear me?
You are caught now,
I see it plainly,
And
it is owing mainly
To my plans.
Now, if you will—

**ADINA:** Will what—what mean you?

**DULCAMARA:** Su la testa, schizzinosa!
Se tu vuoi, ci ho la ricetta,
Che il tuo mal guarir potrà.

**ADINA:** Ah! Dottor, sarà perfetta,
Ma per me virtù non ha.

**DULCAMARA:** Vuoi vederti mille amanti
Spasimar, languire al piede?

**ADINA:** Non saprei che far di tanti;
Il mio core un sol mi chiede.

**DULCAMARA:** Render vuoi gelose, pazze
Donne, vedove, ragazze?

**ADINA:** Non mi alletta, no mi piace,
Di turbar altrui la pace.

**DULCAMARA:** Conquistar vorresti un ricco?

**ADINA:** Di richezze io non mi picco.

**DULCAMARA:** Un Contino? un Marchesino?

**ADINA:** Io non vo' che Nemorino.

**DULCAMARA:** Prendi su la mia ricetta,
Che l' effetto ti farà

**ADINA:** Ah! Dottor, sarà perfetta,
Ma per me virtù non ha.

**DULCAMARA:** Sconsigliata! e avresti ardire
Di negare il suo valore?

**ADINA:** Io rispetto l'Elisire,
Ma per me n' ha un maggiore:
Nemorino, lasciata ogni altra
Tutto mio, sol mio sarà.

**DULCAMARA:** Ahi! Dottore! è troppo scaltra
Più di te costei ne sa.

**ADINA:** Una tenera occhiatina,
Un sorriso, una carezza,
Vincer può chi più si ostina,
Ammollir chi più si sprezza.
Ne ho veduti tanti e tanti
Presi, cotti, spasimanti,
Che nemmeno Nemorino
Non potrà da me fuggir.
La ricetta è il mio vicino
In quest' occhi è l'elisir.

**DULCAMARA:** Sì, lo vedo, o bricconcella,
Ne sai più dell' arte mia;
Questa bocca così bella
E d' amor la spezieria:
Hia lambicco ed hai fornello
Caldo più di un Mongibello,
Per filtrar l' amore che vuoi
Per bruciare e incenerir.
Ah! vorrei cambiar coi tuoi
I mie vasi d' Elisir.
*(Partono.)*

**DULCAMARA:** Oh! my dear, you're caught,
I see it very plainly,
But if art of man can save you,
It is the Doctor whom you see.
I've a wonderful receipt, dear,
For your identical disease.

**ADINA:** Ah! though your drugs are all powerful
They've no virtue for me.

**DULCAMARA:** Would you have a thousand lovers
Pining at your feet in anguish?

**ADINA:** What should I do with so many?
It is for one alone I languish!

**DULCAMARA:** Would you wish to render jealous
Every widow, wife and maiden?

**ADINA:** No, indeed, I'd add no burden
To the heart overladen with love.

**DULCAMARA:** Would you marry one with treasure?

**ADINA:** Ah! I find no pleasure in gold.

**DULCAMARA:** Would you like a nobleman to court you?

**ADINA:** I'd have none but Nemorino.

**DULCAMARA:** My receipt will surely cure you.

**ADINA:** No—no virtue, I assure you.

**DULCAMARA:** have you the presumption, maiden
To deny its great virtues?

**ADINA:** With respect to your elixir,
I have one more potent, sir,
Through whose great virtues Nemorino,
Leaving all to me will fly.

**DULCAMARA:** *(aside)*. Oh! she's far too wise and cunning
These girls know even more than I.

**ADINA:** With a tender look I'll charm him—
With a modest smile invite him—
With a tear or sigh alarm him—
With a fond caress excite him.
Never yet was a man so mulish,
That I could not make him yield,
Nemorino's fate's decided
When Adina takes the field.
My receipt is in my eyes,
There the true elixir lies.

**DULCAMARA:** Ah, you baggage! It is most certain
That your art far surpasses mine;
Your bright eyes are burning-glasses,
Within whose tremendous focus,
Just as though it were hocus-pocus—
Even the astutest heart must yield
You—you hussy, can distill
Just whatever love you will.
*(Exeunt.)*

---

*SCENA VII.*

*(Entra Nemorino.)*

**NEMORINO:** Una furtiva lacrima
Negli occhi suoi spuntò . . .
Quelle festose giovani
Invidiar sembrò.
Che più cercar io vo?
M' ama, lo vedo.
Un solo istante i palpiti
Del suo bel cor sentir! . . .
Co' suoi sospir, confondere
Per poco i miei sospir! . . .
Cielo, si può morir;
Di più non chiedo.
Eccola . . . Oh! qual le accresce
Beltà l' amor nascente!
A far l' indifferente
Si seguiti così, finchè non viene
Elle a spiegarsi.

*SCENA VIII.*

*Adina e Nemorino.*

**ADINA:** Nemorino!—ebbene?

**NEMORINO:** Non so più dove io sia; giovani e vecchie,
Belle e brutte me voglion per marito.

**ADINA:** E tu?

**NEMORINO:** A verun partito
Appigliarmi non posso: attendo oncora . . .
La mia felicità . . . (che è pur vicina.)

**ADINA:** Odimi.

**NEMORINO:** *(allegro.)* (Ah! ah! ci siamo.) Io v' odo Adina.

**ADINA:** Dimmi; perchè partire,
Perchè farti soldato hai risoluto?

**NEMORINO:**
Perchè! . . . perchè ho voluto
Tentar se con tal mezzo il mio destino
Io potea migliorar.

**ADINA:** La tua persona
La tua vita ci è cara . . Io ricomprai
If fatale contratto da Belcore.

**NEMORINO:** Voi stessa….(E Naturale: opera è d' amore.)

**ADINA:** Amico prendi or il contratto.
*(Nemorino lacera il contratto.)*
A tanta gioia è poco un core
Se pietoso d' un obb o
Copri o caro i torti miei
Fortunato appien son io
Fortunato appien tu sei
Amor brami? e il cor nel petto
Arderà per te d' affetto.

*SCENE VII.*

*(Enter Nemorino.)*

**NEMORINO:** In her dark eye embathed there stood
Trembling, the furtive tear;
While each gay smile that others wear,
Seemed parent to a fear.
What can this heart wish more?
She loves me! what joy in store.
Ah! but to feel for a moment
The throbbing of that heart!
While glance to glance, sigh echoes sigh
As though we never could part.
Death were a price too poor—I'd give
Eternity to share such bliss!
But here she comes. Oh, how her beauty grows with her growing love! I will, however, continue to affect indifference till she explains herself.

*SCENE VIII.*

*Adina and Nemorino.*

**ADINA:** Well, Nemorino!

**NEMORINO:** I scarcely know whether I stand on my head or my heels! the old, the young, the ugly, the pretty, all want to marry me.

**ADINA:** And you—

**NEMORINO:** I really don't know what to do. I feel it quite impossible to decide. *(Aside.)* My happiness and triumph are both near.

**ADINA:** Listen to me.

**NEMORINO:** *(joyfully).* Ah, she's coming to it. *(Aside.)* I'm all attention.

**ADINA:** Tell me, why do you leave us, why are you resolved to be a soldier?

**NEMORINO:** Because I'm tired of being idle, and would try in any way to better my condition.

**ADINA:** Nemorino, your life is dear to me—I have paid your smart money, and rebought the fatal contract from Sergeant Belcore.

**NEMORINO:** You! you love me, then? *(Aside.)* It is natural—the Elixir has done the business.

**ADINA:** Dearest, take this contract. *(Nemorino signs the contract.)* So much joy is more than my heart can contain,
If you can dismiss from your mind,
The wrongs that I have done you,
Then I shall be most happy.
And you, I know, will be the same.
Do you desire my love? my heart shall burn truly
With fondest love for you.

**NEMORINO:** La memoria del passato
Come un sogno svanirà
Il mio cor rigenerato
Al piacer rinascerà.

**NEMORINO:** The memorial of the past
Like a dream shall fade away;
And my heart, renewed with life,
Shall be born again to pleasure.

**ADINA:** Come mai nel nuovo incanto
Infelice a te d' accanto
La memoria dei tormenti.
In contenti fa cangiar
Ah! con te per sempre unita.
Sarà un estasi la vita
Nè più in cor saprà quest' alma
Che di gioia palpitar.

**ADINA:** Happy in the dear enchantment,
Which I feel while at your side,
The anguish which I've felt before
Is changed to supreme delight.
Ah, love, to you united ever,
Life will be one ecstasy;
And nothing but joy will ever possess
The heart that beats alone for you.

**CORO:** I moment dell' affanno
Più per te non spunteranno.
Per te alfin sfavilla un iride;
Hai cessato di penar.

**CHORUS:** Moments of sorrow and of grief
Shall no more have an existence;
For you, at last, a rainbow's beaming,
And your sufferings now shall cease.

## SCENA ULTIMA.

## SCENE IX.

*(Belcore con soldati e detti; indi Dulcamara con tutti i villaggianti.)*

*Belcore, with Soldiers, Dulcamara, and all the Villagers.*

**BELCORE:**
Alto! . . . fronte . . . che vedo? al mio rivale!

**BELCORE:** Attention! to the right, face!
What's this? my rival! present arms!

**ADINA:** Ella è così, Belcore,
E convien darsi pace ad ogni patto.
Egli è mio sposo; quel che è fatto.

**ADINA:** Exactly so, Belcore. You may as well submit placidly to your destiny. He is my husband: What is done—

**BELCORE:** E fatto.
Tientelo pur, briccona.
Peggio per te. Pieno di donne è il mondo;
E mille ne otterrà Belcore.

**BELCORE:** Cannot be undone. So much the worse for you, Madame Flirt: there are plenty of women in the world, and thousands will be glad to marry Belcore.

**DULCAMARA:** Ve le darà questo eliser d' amore.

**DULCAMARA:** I will let you have my elixir of love.

**NEMORINO:** Caro dottor, felice Io son per voi.

**NEMORINO:** Dear Doctor, through you I am happy.

**TUTTI:** Per lui!!!

**CHORUS:** Through him!

**DULCAMARA:** Per me. Sappiate.
Che Nemorino è divenuto a un tratto
Il più ricco castaldo del villaggio . . .
Poichè morto è lo zio—

**DULCAMARA:** Through me. Know that Nemorino has become the richest man in the village—his uncle is dead!

**ADINA e NEMORINO:** Morto lo zio!

**ADINA:** His . . .

**NEMORINO:** My . . .

**BOTH:** . . . uncle dead.

**GIANNETTA e CORI:** Io lo sapeva . . .

**GIANETTA AND CHORUS:** We knew it.

**DULCAMARA:** Lo sapeva anch' io.
Ma quèl che non sapete,
Nè potreste saper, egli è che questo
Sovrumano elisir può in un momento

**DULCAMARA:** And I knew it, too; but there is something that you do not yet know, and that is this, that my powerful elixir is the only thing

Non solo rimediare al mal d' amore
Ma arrichir gli spiantati.

that will procure you the affection of the girl you love in a moment. And besides this, it possesses the wonderful property of making the poor rich.

**CORI:** Oh! gran liquore.

**CHORUS:** Oh! the wonderful elixir.

**DULCAMARA:** Ei corregge ogni diffetto;
Ogni vizio di natura,
La più brutta creatura:
Caminar ei fa le rozze,
Schiaccia gobbe, appiana bozze,
Ogni incomodo tumore
Copre sì, che piu non è.

**DULCAMARA:** It corrects every imperfection, every natural defect of the person. It gives beauty to the most ugly creature; makes the most awkward and clumsy run as swift as the wind; and the largest tumors quickly disappear under its magic influence.

**CORI:** Qua, dottore, a me dottore . . .
Un vasetto . . . due . . . tre.

**CHORUS:** Doctor, let me have a bottle of it—give me one—two—three.

**DULCAMARA:** Egli è offa seducente
Pei guardiani scrupolosi;
E un sonnifero eccellente
Per le vecchie e pei gelosi;
Dà coraggio alle figliuole
Che han paura a dormir sole,
Svegliarino è per l' amore
Più potente del caffè

**DULCAMARA:** It exercises a most seductive effect over scrupulous guardians, producing profound sleep in old and jealous people. It inspires courage to such girls as are afraid to sleep alone; and to lovers gives a watchfulness more potent than coffee.

**CORI:** Qua, dottore . . . a me dottore . . .
Un vasetto . . . due . . . tre.
*(Tutte circondano a Dulcamara.)*

**CHORUS:** O Doctor! let me have a bottle—give me one—two—three. *(All surround Dulcamara.)*

**DULCAMARA:** Predilette dalle stelle,
Io vi lascio un gran tesoro;
Tutto è in lui; salute e belle,
Allegria, fortuna ed oro:
Rinverdite, rinfiorite,
Impinguate ed arricchite;
Dell' amico Dulcamara
Ei vi faccia ricordar.

**DULCAMARA:** Favored as you are by the stars, I give you the possession of this great treasure. By its means you will possess everything—good health, fortune, and gold. Prosperity will attend you, and you will think of your friend Dulcamara forever and ever.

**CORI:** Viva il grande Dulcamara
Dei dottori la fenice.

**CHORUS:** Viva the great Dulcamara,
The very Phoenix of all doctors.

**NEMORINO:** Io gli debbo la mia cara.

**NEMORINO:** I am indebted to him for my dearest love.

**ADINA:** Per lui solo io son felice!
Del suo farmaco l' effetto
Non potrò giammai scordar.

**ADINA:** He has made me happy. The effects of this elixir Can never be forgotten.

**BELCORE:** Ciarlatano maladetto,
Che tu possa ribaltar!
*(Il servo di Dulcamara suona la tromba—La carrozza si move—Tutti scuotono i loro cappelli e lo salutano.)*

**BELCORE:** Away, you cursed charlatan,
Who have thus frustrated my hopes. *(Dulcamara's Servant blows the trumpet—the chariot moves on—All take off their hats, wave them, and salute him.)*

**CORI:** Viva il grande Dulcamara,
La fenice dei dottori!
Con salute e con tesori
Possa presto a noi tornar.

**CHORUS:** Viva the great Dulcamara,
The very Phoenix of all doctors,
May he pay another visit quickly,
Will his health and treasures.

*FINE.*

*THE END.*

# Lucrezia Borgia (1833)

MUSIC BY GAETANO DONIZETTI ■ LIBRETTO BY FELICE ROMANI

This two-act opera *seria* with a prologue, set to a libretto by Felice Romani (based upon Victor Hugo's tragedy), premiered at the Teatro alla Scala in Milan on December 26, 1833. The story takes place during the early sixteenth century. At a feast in a Venetian palace, Maffio Orsini tells the gathering about an old man who prophesied the death of one of his friends at the hand of Lucrezia Borgia. Among those present is Gennaro, who saved Orsini's life during the battle of Rimini. Gennaro does not know his mother's identity; all he has is a letter from her in which she beseeches him never to look for her. While he is asleep on a sofa, a woman wearing a mask leans over to kiss him. His friends tell him that she is the infamous Lucrezia Borgia. Gennaro and his friends arrive in Ferrara. Lucrezia's husband, Alfonso, is jealous of the attention she pays to Gennaro. Gennaro's friends make fun of this and tease him that he has fallen prey to her attentions. He denies this, and on the Borgia crest he scratches out the first letter, "B," so that only "orgia" remains. Alfonso orders his arrest, and Lucrezia demands that the perpetrator be put to death at once for the offense. When she discovers that Gennaro is the offender, she changes her mind. She gives him an antidote to a poisoned drink which he has been given and arranges for him to escape through a secret door. At the last moment, Gennaro decides to go with his friends to a party at the Negroni palace. When the ladies have withdrawn to another room, a servant enters with drinks for the young men. The lights go out and death-like music is played. Lucrezia Borgia comes in with an armed guard and all exits are locked. She tells them that the wine they are drinking is poisoned because she is seeking revenge for their taunts. She recognizes Gennaro, too late. He refuses to drink the antidote as there is only enough to save himself and he dies as she sings that she is his mother.

## ■ PROLOGO.

### SCENA I.

*Terrazzo nel Palagio Gremani in Venezia. — Festa di notte. — Alcune Maschere attraversano di tratto in tratto il Teatro. — Dai due lati del Terrazzo si vede il Palagio spendidamente illuminato. In fondo, il Canale della Giudecca, sul quale si veggono passare ad intervalli nelle tenebre alcune Gondole. In lontano, Venezia il chiaror della luna.*

*Entrano in iscena lietamente, Gubetta, Gazella, Orsini, Petrucci, Vitellozzo e Liverotto. Quindi Gennaro che, com' Uomo affaticato, si riposa sovra un sedile appartato dagli altri.*

**GAZ:** Bella Venezia!

**PET:** Amabile;
D' ogni piacer soggiorno!

**ORS:** Men di sue notti è limpido
D' ogni altro cielo il giorno.

**TUTTI:** E l' orator Grimani,
Noi seguirem domani;
Tali avrem mai delizie,
Tai feste in riva al Po?

**GUB:** Le avrem; D' Alfonso è splendide,
Lieta la corte assai.
*(Inoltrandosi.)*
Lucrezia Borgia—

## ■ PROLOGUE.

### SCENE I.

*Terrace in the Grimani Palace, Venice. — Festival by night. — Several Masks traverse the stage from time to time. — From the two sides of the Terrace is seen the Palace, illuminated. At the back, the Canal of the Giudecca, on which Gondolas are dimly seen passing at intervals. In the distance, Venice by moonlight.*

*Enter gaily, Gubetta, Gazella, Orsini, Petrucci, Vitellozzo, Liverotto; afterwards, Gennaro, apparently weary: he rests himself on a seat apart from the rest.*

**GAZ:** Hail, lovely Venice!

**PET:** Fair Queen of earth!
Birthplace and home of pleasure!

**ORS:** Sunlight in less favored climates were shamed
By your sweet night's poetic azure.

**ALL:** We follow brave Grimani,
A charge preferred to any;
Think on the glories waiting our progress
Down fertile Po.

**GUB:** Well said, Alfonso's splendid court
Far will surpass all splendor.
*(Advancing.)*
Lucretia Borgia—

**ORS:** *(Interrompendolo.)* Acquetati!
Non la nomar giammai.

**VIT:** Nome esecrato è questo.

**LIV:** La Borgia! io la detesto!

**TUTTI:** Chi le sue colpe intendere,
E non odiar la può?

**ORS:** Io più di tutti; Uditemi.
*(Tutti si accosta.)*
Un vecchio, un indovino—

**GEN:** *(Interrompendolo.)* Novellator perpetuo,
Esser vuoi dunque, Orsini?
Lascia la Borgia in pace:
Udir di lei mi spiace.

**TUTTI:** Taci, non l' interrompere—
Breve il suo dir sarà.

**GEN:** Io dormirò, destatemi
Quando cessato avrà.
*(Si adagia, e a poco a poco si oddormenta.)*

**ORS:** Nella fatal di Rimini
E memorabil guerra,
Ferito e quasi esanimo,
Io mi giaceva a terra;
Gennaro a me soccorse,
Il suo destrier mi porse
E in solitario bosco
Mi trasse e mi salvò.

**TUTTI:** La sua virtù conosco;
La sua pietade io so.

**ORS:** *(Interrupting him.)* Forbear to name
Sin's very worst offender!

**VIT:** Italy's cankering fester.

**LIV:** The Borgia, gods! I detest her!

**ALL:** Her lightest crime where breathed alike
The deepest hate you sow.

**ORS:** Chiefest in my breast, I pray you listen.
*(They all gather about him.)*
An old man, a sage magician—

**GEN:** *(Interrupting him.)* To spin that same perpetual yarn
Seems your delight, Orsini.
Leave Borgia in peace:
Why have my patience tested?

**ALL:** Pray not to interrupt the tale;
Fortunately, it is brief enough.

**GEN:** So for a nap; awake me then
When he has finished off.
*(Wrapping his mantle round him, turns on his side and falls asleep.)*

**ORS:** There, where the field of Rimini
Swam with the blood of legions,
My prostrate and nearly breathless form
Spoke out how true my allegiance is.
Gennaro, till then a stranger,
Bore me from the danger,
And in a convent lonely
Assuaged the galling wound.

**ALL:** In him not virtue only,
But charity is found.

ORS: Là nella notte tacita,
Lena pigliando e speme.
Giurammo insiem di vivere,
E di morire insieme,
'E insiem morreto,' allora
Voce gridò sonora,
E un veglio in veste nera,
Gigante a noi s' offrì.

TUTTI: Cielo! Qual mago egli era,
Per profetar cosi!

ORS: 'Fuggite i Borgia, oh, giovani,
Ei prosequi più forte:
'Odio alla rea Lucrezia!
Dove è Lucrezia è morte!'
Sparve ciò detto; e il vento,
In suono di lamento,
Quel nome ch' io detesto,
Tre volte replicò.

TUTTI: Rio vaticinio è questo;
Ma fè puoi dargli?—no.

ORS: Fede a fallaci oroscopi
L' anima mia non presta;
Pur mio malgrado un palpito,
Tal sovvenir mi desta.
Spesso, dovunque io movo,
Quel vecchio orrendo io trovo,
Quella minaccia, orribile
Parmi la notte udir.
Te, mio Gennaro, invidio,
Che puoi così dormir.

TUTTI: Lenti. La danza invitaci;
Bando a sìtristre immagini!
Passiam la notte in gioja!
Assai quell' empia femina
Ne diè tormento e noja.
Finchè il Leon temuto
Ne porge a silo e ajuto,
L' arte e il furor de Borgia
Non ci portran colpir.
(Partono tutti, traendo seco Orsini.)

ORS: There, in the solemn hush of night,
Friendship bade gather fresh hopes
Vowing to pass life side by side,
We swore to end it together,
'Fate shall fulfil your forestalling,'
Thundered an appalling voice.
Shrouded in black, a
Gigantic phantom met our eyes.

ALL: Heavens! What was the import
Foretold by anything so wise?

ORS: Avoid the Borgia, gallant youths,
(These were his words ensuing)
'Wherever dwells Lucrezia
Destruction and ruin dwells also.'
This said, he vanished, and zephyr
Did waft presently and ever
The name that palsied our hearing
Three times echoed sad and slow.

ALL: Weighing its every bearing
Can we believe this? No.

ORS: Never to fallacious horoscope
Gave I the faintest credence;
But willing or not, a presentiment
This time asserts precedence,
That fatal spell enchants me,
That awful specter haunts me;
Still his ill-omened terrific threat
Night after night do I hear.
Ah! happy is Gennaro,
Quite free from boding fear.

ALL: Listen! Music invites us.
Banish doleful imaginings,
And drown night deep in all pleasure.
Long too, Lucrezia, that woman fiend,
Has given us trouble's full measure;
Our winged lion's assistance
Was ever Venice's existence.
Were there ten thousand more Borgias,
While he reigns who could fear?
(All go out, taking Orsini with them.)

## SCENA II.

Passo una Gondola—n' esce una Dama mascherata: è Lucrezia Borgia. S' inoltra guardinga; vede Gennaro addormentato, e si appressa a lui contemplandolo con piacere e rispetto.—Gubetta ritorna.

LUC: Tranquillo ei posa! Oh, sian così tranquillo
Sue notti sempre! e mai provar non debba
Qual delle notti mie, quanto è il tormento!
Sei tu?
(Si accorge di Gubetta.)

GUB: Son io. Pavento
Che alcun vi scopra: ai giorni vostri, è vero,
Scrudo è Venezia; ma vietar non puote
Che conosciuta non v' insulti alcuno.

## SCENE II.

A Gondola passes—a masked Lady issues from it: it is Lucretia Borgia. She advances cautiously; she sees Gennaro asleep and approaching him, remains gazing upon him with pleasure and interest.—Gubetta returns.

LUC: How calm a slumber! Ever be his reposings
Light as gentlest music, his visions undisturbed
By such appalling shapes as haunt me forever!
Is it you? (Perceiving Gubetta.)

GUB: Yea, madam, much dreading
Some here should know; for though assassination
Spare your days in Venice, her mighty power
Cannot shield you from the keener stab of insult.

LUC: E insultata sarei! M' abborre ognuno!
Pur per sì trista sorte
Nata io non era. Oh! potess' io far tanto
Che il passato non fosse, e in un cor solo
Destare un senso di pietà che invano
In mia grandezza all' universo io chiedo!
Quel giovin vedi?

GUB: Il vedo,
E da più di lo seguo.
Indarno io tento
Scoprir l' arcano che per lui vi tragge
Da Ferrara a Venezia in tanta ambascia.

LUC: Tu scoprirlo!—Non puoi—
Seco mi lascia.
(Gubetta si ritira.)

## SCENA III.

Lucrezia, e Gennaro addormentato. Mentre Lucrezia si avvicina a Gennaro non si accorge di due Uomini mascherati che passano dal fondo, e si fermano in disparte.

LUC: (Con affetto guardandolo.)
Com' è bello quale incanto in quel volto onestoe altero No: giammal leggiadro tanto non sel pinse il mio pensiero. L'alma mia di gioja e piena orchè afin lo puo mirar mi risparmia oh! ciel la pena ch'ei mi debba un di sprezzar ah! risparmi a oh! ciel la pena risparmi o della pena ci. ei mi debba un di sprezzar ah risparmi a oh ciel la pena ch'ei mi debba un di sprezzar.
Se il destessi? No, no, non oso.
(Piango.)
Nè scoprir il mio sembiante;
Pure il ciglio lagrimoso,
Terger debbo—un solo istante.
(Si toglie la maschera, e si asciuga le lagrime.)

DUCA: (Aparte.) Vedi? è dessa!
RUST: (Aparte.) E dessa, è vero.

DUCA: (Aparte.) Chi è il garzone?

RUST: (Aparte.) Un venturiero.
DUCA: (Aparte.) Non ha patria?
RUST: (Aparte.) Nè parenti;
Ma è guerrier fra i più valenti.

DUCA: (Aparte.) Di condurlo adopro ogn' arte
A Ferrara in mìo poter.

RUST: (Aparte.) Con Grimani all' alba ei parte—
Ei previene il tuo pensier.

LUC: Mentre geme il cor sommesso,
Mentre io piango a te d' appresso.
Dormi, e sogna, o dolce oggetto,

LUC: E insultata sarei! M' abborre ognuno! [English column]

LUC: Let them slay with their insults! all earth abhor us!
Why were we ever nurtured to a fate so hideous? Why were the feelings all torn out
And erased from our bosom, alone that render
A woman's breast the throne of virtue and of mercy,
For them we'd barter our Universe of Grandeur.
You see that young man?

GUB: I see him!
Long have my steps pursued him with fruitless effort
To filch the secret at whose back my lynx-eye
From Ferrara to Venice, tracked and spied him.

LUC: Learn our secret!—That you cannot. Leave me with him. (Exit Gubetta.)

## SCENE III.

Lucretia, and Gennaro asleep. While Lucretia draws near Gennaro, she does not perceive two Men in masks, who come from the back, and stand apart.

LUC: Holy beauty, child of nature,
Firstborn of the one great parent,
Graces gem your every feature. To your only self inherent, Your charms are given to these traits,
Gently blessing, while they win . . . Emblems of that purest Heaven, Heart of man untouched by sin, Emblems of that purest heaven, that purest heaven, heart of man untouched by sin. Emblems of that purest Heaven, Heart of man untouched by sin.
Should I awake him? dare I venture?
(Weeping)
This disguise albeit still keeping,
Its removal counts not censure,
But to dry up this bitter weeping.
(She removes the mask from her face and applies her kerchief to wipe her eyes.)

DUKE: (Aside.) Look: it is she—
RUST: (Aside.) You hit on the truth, sir!

DUKE: (Aside.) Who's the stranger?

RUST: (Aside.) A soldier youth, sir.
DUKE: (Aside.) With no country?
RUST: (Aside.) Nor relations.
Brave men find them in all nations!

DUKE: (Aside.) Then neglect no art, and lure him
Toward Ferrara in my leash.

RUST: (Aside.) Service duty must ensure him
To fulfil your very wish.

LUC: Would that ever I thus could linger,
Granting fond, though poor protection,

Sol di gioja e di diletto;
Ed un angiol tutelare
Non ti desti che al piacer!
Triste notti, e veglie amare
Debbo io sola sostener
Li volì il primo a cogliere,
Bacio d' unsanto amore
Quell' innocente core,
Riposè sul mio cor
Un dolce sogno un estasi
Un lusinghiero incanto.
La vita lui d' accanto,
Delizia fia d'amor.
(*Si alza: i due mascherati si ritirano.—Lucrezia ritorna indietro, e bacia la mano di Gennaro: egli si desta, e l' afferra per le braccia.*)

LUC: Ciel!
(*Per isciogliern da lui.*)

GEN: Che vegg' io?

LUC: Lasciatemi.

GEN: No, no, gentil signora;
No, per mia fede.
(*Trattenendola.*)
Ch' io vi contempli ancora!
Leggiadra e amabil siete;
Nè paventar dovete
Che ingrato ed insensibile
Per voi si trovi un cor.

LUC: Gennaro! E sia possibile
Che a me tu porti amor?

GEN: Qual dubbio è il vostro?

LUC: Ah! dimmelo!

GEN: Sì, quanto lice io v' amo.

LUC: (*Aparte.*) Oh, gioja!

GEN: Eppure uditemi:
Esser verace io bramo.
Avvi un più caro oggetto,
Cui nutro immenso affetto.

LUC: E ti è di me più caro!
Che mai?

GEN: Mia madre ell' e.

LUC: Tua madre!—O, mio Gennaro!
Tu l' ami?

GEN: Ah! più di me!

LUC: Ed ella?

GEN: Ah! compiangetemi,
Io non la vidi mai.

LUC: Come?

GEN: E funesta istoria,
Che sempre altrui celai;
Ma son da ignoto istinto
A dirla a voi sospinto:
Alma cortese e bella,
Nel vostro volto appar.

LUC: (*Aparte.*) Tenero cor! Favella:
Tutto mi puoi narrar.

While young Slumber's dainty finger
Gives that perfect more perfection!
With my dream joys never blending
Touched their darkness once with light;
Soon this too-bright vision ending
Shrouds me back in dawnless night.
To cull but a kiss the daintiest,
Laden with holy affection,
Yielding him more protection.
Reposing on my heart
One world of bliss, one ecstasy
Pervades me in his presence.
A mother's love!
The magic imparts love's essence.
(*She rises; the two Masks retire.—Lucretia goes back again, and kisses the hand of Gennaro: he awakes, and detains her by the arm.*)

LUC: Heavens! (*Endeavoring to break from him.*)

GEN: Who do I perceive?

LUC: Oh! leave me, sir!

GEN: No, no, my gentle lady;
No, on my honor.
(*Holding her.*)
I long to learn every feature, I am never blind
To beauty
So do not think to find me
Ungrateful or insensible
Where so much grace would charm.

LUC: Gennaro, can this be possible,
Your breast warms for me?

GEN: And why doubt it?

LUC: Speak candidly.

GEN: Then, by my knighthood, I love you!

LUC: (*Aside.*) Too joyous!

GEN: I love, but my sincerity
Faithfully will I prove to you;
There is a prior selection
To whom I owe more affection.

LUC: Even more than that you swore me?
To whom then?

GEN: To my mother!

LUC: Your mother?—O! dearest Gennaro,
You love her?

GEN: Far more than self.

LUC: And she?

GEN: Alas! that mother's face
Never have I beheld.

LUC: And why so?

GEN: It is a mournful story,
From every ear withheld;
Some strange resistless feeling
Now prompts the quick revealing:
Angel of light and beauty!
Hear what I yearn to relate.

LUC: (*Aside.*) Keep still, my heart!
(*Aloud.*) Proceed:
All then you may narrate!

GEN: Di pescatore ignobile esser figliuol credei e seco oscuri in Napoli vissi i prim' anni miei quandoun guerrier o incognito venne d'inganno a trarmi mi die cavallo ed armi e un foglio a me lascio Era mia madre ahi misera mia madre che scriveadirio possen te vittima per se per me temea di non parlar ne chiedere Il nome suo qual' era calda mi fe preghiera ed obbedita io l'ho calda mi fè preghiera ed obbedita io l'ho.

LUC: E il foglio suo?

GEN: Miratelo!
Mai dal mio cor non parte.

LUC: Oh! quante amare lagrime,
Forse in vergario ha sparte!

GEN: Ed io, signora, oh! quanto
Su quelle cifre ho pianto!
Ma che? voi pur piangete!

LUC: Ah sì! Per lei—per te!

GEN: Alma gentil! voi siete,
Ancor più cara a me.

LUC: Ama tua ma ire e tenero sempre perte i serba pregache l'ira plachi si della sua sorte acerba pregache un giorno stringerti ella ti possa al cor . . . pregache un giorno stringerti ella ti possa al cor pregache un giorno stringerti possa ah! stringerti possa al cor.

GEN: L'amo—sì l'amo! e sembrami
Vederla in ogni oggetto—
Una soave immagine
Me n' ho formata in petto!
Seco, dormente o vigile
Seco io favello ognor.

## SCENA IV.

*Si avvicinano da varie parti Orsini, Vitellozo, Petrucci, Gazella, Dame e Cavalieri in maschera.*

LUC: Gente appressa—io ti lascio.

GEN: (*Trattenendola.*) Ah! fermate!

ORS: Che mai veggo!
(*Riconosce Lucrezia, l' addita ai compagni, e seco loro favella.*)

LUC: Mi è forza lasciarti.

GEN: Deh! chi siete almen dirmi degnate.
(*Sempre trattenendola.*)

LUC: Tal che t' ama, e sua vita è t' amarti.

ORS: (*Inoltrandosi.*) Io dirollo.

GEN: Deemed of a fisher's lowly race, Where the wide beach, and wild wood Echoing smiles from Naples' sun Witnessed my humble childhood; One day there sought me an unknown knight, Breaking the spell that charmed me, Who having horsed and well armed me, A writing then bade me scan—Penned by a mother, ah misery The scroll was bearing each word, Told how a wretch seduced a breast For me, its child sore fearing, Hushed in my heart, I guard her will, Though look nor deed betray it, Honor and faith obey it, O as a son's only care! Honor and faith obey it, O as a son's only care.

LUC: But then her letter?

GEN: Here, look on it,
Safe near my heart long hidden.

LUC: How many bitter, bitter tears
Moistened these pages when written!

GEN: Mine, lady, without measure
Have bathed the priceless treasure!
You weep, so purely tender!

LUC: Ah yes! for her sake and yours.

GEN: Angel too kind, you render
No heart as blessed as mine.

LUC: O, with the fervent soul of youth, Always adore your mother, Pray that good heaven avert her fate, and change it for another. Pray for the day her longing kiss Welcomes you on her breast, Pray for the day her longing kiss welcomes you on her breast, Pray for the day her kiss shall welcome, yes . . . . welcome you unto her breast.

GEN: Fancy, induced by purest love,
Pictures her every feature;
Magical, bright imaginings
Depict her gentlest nature.
Until I can share that longing kiss,
Never will my step have rest.

## SCENE IV.

*Orsini, Vitellozzo, Petrucci, Gazella, Ladies and Cavaliers, in masks, approach from different parts of the stage.*

LUC: People approach us—I must leave you!

GEN: (*Detaining her.*) Please, wait!

ORS: Who do I see?
(*He recognizes Lucretia, points her out to this companions, and speaks with them.*)

LUC: It behooves me to leave.

GEN: Then do not be sorrowful of your name.
(*Still detaining her.*)

LUC: One who loves you, whose only duty is to love me.

ORS: (*Advancing.*) I will tell you.

## Scene I

**LUC:** Gran Dio!
(*Si copre colla maschera e vuola allontanarsi.*)

**ORS:** (*Appendendosi.*) Non partite!
Forza è udirne.
(*Riconducendola.*)

**LUC:** Gennaro!

**GEN:** Che ardite!
S' avvi alcun d' insultarla capace,
Di Gennaro più amico non è.

**ORS:** Chi siam noi sol chiarirla ne piace.
E poi fugga da te.

**LUC:** (*Aparte.*) Oh, cimento!

**GEN:** Favellate!

**ORS:** Maffio Osini, signora son' lo cui svenaste il dormente fratello.

**VIT:** Io Vitelli cui feste lo zio trucidar nel rapito castello.

**LIV:** Io Ne pote d' Appiano tradito che fu spento in infame convito.

**GEN:** Ciel che as colto.

**LUC:** Oh malvagia mia sorte:

**GEN:** Oh cielo oh cielo che as colto!

**GAZ:** Io, con guinto d' oppresso consorte,—

**LUC:** Ciel! . . . . ove fuggo che fare che dir!

**ORS:** Maffio Orsini signora son'—

**LUC:** Ah! . . . . ove fuggo che fare che dir.

**LUC:** (*Aparte*) Oh! malvagia mia sorte!

**CORO:** Qual rea donna!

**ORS:** Or che a lei l' esser nostro è palese,
Odi il suo.

**GEN, CORO:** Dite, dite!

**LUC:** Ah, pietade!

**A 5:** Ella è donna che infame si rese,
Che l' orrore sarà d' ogni etade!
Ella e donna venefica, impura,
Vilipese oltraggiò la natura
Com è odiata è temuta del paro;
Chè potente il destino la fa.

**GEN:** Oh, chi è mai? Ah! lo dite!

**LUC:** Non udirli, o Gennaro!
(*Supplichevole a' suoi piedi.*)

**A 5:** E la Borgia! Ravvisala!
(*Strapp. la maschera.*)

**TUTTI:** (*Con un grido d' orrore.*) Ah!
(*Lucrezia sviene.*)

---

**LUC:** Great heavens!
(*Covers her face with her mask, and attempts to go out.*)

**ORS:** (*Stopping her.*) You shall not go!
You must hear me!
(*Bringing her back.*)

**LUC:** Gennaro!

**GEN:** How dare you?
Whomever presumes to offend her
Boasts Gennaro no more for his friend.

**ORS:** Our intent here we merely would tender,
Then she may wend her ways!

**LUC:** (*Aside.*) Dark misfortune!

**GEN:** State your purpose!

**ORS:** Madam, I am Orsini, whose brother you did poison the while he was sleeping,

**VIT:** One Vitelli, the twin of my mother you have stabbed, and his birthright are keeping.

**LIV:** Know Appiano's young nephew! you drew him To the infamous banquet that slew him!

**GEN:** God, what do I hear?

**LUC:** Bitter curse on their onslaught!

**GEN:** Oh heaven! oh heaven! what do I hear?

**GAZ:** I am kin to the Spaniard, that consorts,—

**LUC:** Heaven . . . . strength would fail me, both power and breath!

**ORS:** Madam, I am Orsini,—

**LUC:** Or Heaven . . . . strength would fail me, both power and breath.

**LUC:** Deep curse on their onslaught!

**CHO:** Monstrous woman!

**ORS:** Since our names now are too well apparent,
Learn her own, then.

**GEN, CHO:** Say it!

**LUC:** Ah, have pity!

**ALL:** For her infamous crimes duly warrant
The approbrium and horror of ages.
She is a wanton! a faithless betrayer,
An incestuous night-loving slayer!
Nature, owning abortion so hideous,
Stands appalled at the awful offence.

**GEN:** But who is she? Ah! declare it!

**LUC:** Do not hear them, Gennaro!
(*At his feet, imploring him.*)

**ALL:** It is the Borgia! Yes, look on her!
(*Tearing off her mask.*)

**ALL:** (*With a cry of horror.*) Ah!
(*Lucretia faints.*)

---

*CALA IL SIPARIO.*

## ◼ ATTO I.

### *SCENA I.*

*Una Piazza di Ferrara.—Da un lato un Palazzo con un Verone, sotto al quale uno Stemma di Marmo ove e scritto con caratteri visibili di rame dorato, Borgia. Dal' altro una piccola Casa, le cui finestre sono illuminate di dentro.—Notte.*

*Il Duca Alfonso e Rustighello, coperti da lunge manto.*

**DUCA:** Nel Veneto corteggio
Lo ravvisasti?

**RUS:** E me gli posi al fianco,
E lo seguii come se l' ombra io fossi
Del corpo suo.—Quello è il suo tetto.
(*Addita la Casa di Gennaro ancora illuminata.*)

**DUCA:** Quello?
Appo il ducale ostello
Lucrezia il volle!

**RUS:** E in esso ancora, il vuole
Se non m' inganna di quel vil Gubetta
L' ire e il redir, e lo spïar furtivo.

**DUCA:** Entrarvi ei puote, non ne uscir mai vivo.
Odi?
(*Odonsi voci e suoni dalla Casa di Gennaro.*)

**RUS:** Gli amici in festa
Tutta notte accoglieva in quelle porte
Il giovin folle. Separarsi all' alba
Essi han costume.

**DUCA:** E l' ultim' alba è questa
Che al temerario splende,—
L' ultimo addio che dagli amici ei prende.

**DUCA:** Vieni la mia vendetta è meditata e pronta Ei l'assicu ra e affretta Col cieco suo fidar.
Ah! . . . . vie ni! la mia vendetta è meditata e pronta Ei l'assicura e affretta Col cieco suo col cieco suo fidar. Col cieco suo, col cieco suo . . . . fidar.

**RUS:** Ma se l' altier Grimani,
La si recasse ad onta?

**DUCA:** Mai per cotesti insani
Me non vorria sfidar.

---

*THE CURTAIN FALLS.*

## ◼ ACT I.

### *SCENE I.*

*A Public Place in Ferrara.—On one side, a palace with a gallery, under which is an escutcheon of marble, on which is written, in visible characters of metal, gilded, Borgia. On the other side, a small house, the windows of which are illuminated from within.—Night.*

*Duke Alphonso and Rustighello, covered with long mantles.*

**DUKE:** Have you observed him
With Lord Grimani's escort?

**RUS:** You could have made his shadow
Forget its substance easier than divorce me
From scent of his track.—Yonder, sire, he dwells.
(*Points to Gennaro's house, still lighted up.*)

**DUKE:** There?
Near to our Ducal Palace
Lucretia bade him!

**RUS:** Men thus would read the purpose,
If I mistake not, of that vile Gubetta,
Since he so often visits him in secret.

**DUKE:** And he shall enter, leaving only for burial.
Hear you?
(*Voices and sounds are heard from Gennaro's House.*)

**RUS:** Himself and comrades.
Night after night, sir, in too numerous wine cups
Temper their youthful folly. When the dawn is breaking
They break up also.

**DUKE:** And this shall prove the last one
That breaks over his rash head;
That final parting, which he takes with his friends!

**DUKE:** Hurry then to glut a vengeance Fraught with the fell rage of demons: Malice prepares her engines, Walk blindly toward your doom! Ah! . . . . Hasten! to glut a vengeance Fraught with the fell rage of demons: Malice prepares her engines, Walk blindly, walk blindly toward your doom, Walk blindly, blindly, walk blindly toward . . . . your doom.

**RUS:** But should the proud Grimani dream
Some purposed wrong here?

**DUKE:** Too slight the cause if any
Never would he so presume.

DUCA: Qua lunque sia, l'evento che può recar fortuna, ne mi co non pavento l'altero ambascia-tor. Non sempre piu sa ai popoli lù la fatal l'aguna non sempre, non sempre lù la fatal L'aguna nò e ad oltraggiato principe a prir si puote ancora ad oltraggiato principe aprir si puote ancor ad oltraggiato principe aprir-si puo . . . . te si puote ancor.
(*Le voci si fan più vicine: si spengono i lumi, ecc.*)
(*Si ritirano.*)

DUKE: My fame lies at stake in it, A heart that never winces, Would brave Venetia's senate Not fear . . . one poor puny lord? Unbounded power, unswerving will, ever appertains to Princes, unbounded, unswerving power appertains to princes, yes and woe to the daring worm who dares oppose their word then, and woe to the reckless worm who dares oppose their word, and woe to the reckless worm, the worm who dares . . . . oppose their word.
(*The voices sound nearer; the lights are extinguished.*)
(*Duke and Rus. retire.*)

## SCENA II.

*Gennaro, Orsini, Liverotto, Petrucci, Gazella, Vitellozzo. Escono tutti lieti dalla Casa di Gennaro. Egli solo è pensoso. Gubetta si fa vedere in disparte.*

TUTTI: Addio, Gennaro.

GEN: Addio!
Nobili amici.
(*Con serietà.*)

ORS: Ma che! degg' io sì mesto
Mirarti ognor?

GEN: Mesto? no gia! (*Aparte.*) Potessi,
Se non vederti, almen giovarti, o madre!

ORS: Mille beltà leggiadre
Laran stasera al genïal festino,
Cui la gentil me invita
Principessa Negroni. Ove qualcuno
Obblïato avess' ella, a me lo dica;
Di riparar l' errore è pensier mio.

TUTTI: Tutto fummo invitati.

GUB: (*Inoltrandosi.*) E il sono anch' io!

TUTTI: Oh, il Signor Beverano!
(*Tutti gli vanno incontro, tranne Gennaro e Orsini.*)

GEN: (*Aparte ad Orsini.*) Da per tutto è costui! Già da gran tempo
Ei mi è sospetto.

ORS: (*Aparte.*) Oh, non temer: uom lìeto
E, qual siam tutti, uno sventato è desso.

VIT: Or via; così dimesso
Io non ti vo', Gennaro.

LIV: Ammalïato
T' avria forse la Borgia?

## SCENE II.

*Gennaro, Orsini, Liverotto, Petrucci, Gazella, Vitellozzo. They all enter gaily from Gennaro's house, the latter alone pensive. Gubetta is perceived apart from the others.*

ALL: Farewell, Gennaro!

GEN: Farewell!
My noble friends. (*In a serious tone.*)

ORS: And why does your spirit bear
The tint of grief?

GEN: I am not sad. (*Aside.*) To see you,
Alas, forbidden, if only I could help you mother!

ORS: Beauties of fairest deeming
Tonight assemble, and give a festal banquet,
Unto which we're bidden
By the princess Negroni. Be there forgotten
Any qualified Signor, she has appointed
Straight to repair such error my happy office.

CHO: All of us are invited.

GUB: (*Advancing.*) And I, Sirs, among you.

ALL: O! It is the Count Beverano!
(*All saluting him, except Gennaro and Orsini*)

GEN: (*Aside to Orsini.*) This man dogs our footsteps. Long have I held Suspicion toward him.

ORS: (*Aside.*) Cast it aside: consider him
As all do, that is, a boon companion.

VIT: It grieves me to thus observe you
So very sad, Gennaro.

LIV: He is happily
In love, Sir, and with the Borgia.

GEN: E ognor di lei
V' udrò parlarmi? Giuro al Ciel, signori,
Scherzi non voglio. Uomo non v' ha che abborra
Al par di me costei—

PET: Tacete! è quello
Il suo palagio.

GEN: E il sia. Stamparle in fronte
Vorrei l' infamia, che a stampar son pronto
Su quelle mura dove scritto è Borgia.
(*Ascende un gradino innanzi alto Stemma, e col suo pugnale ne cancella la prima lettera: in quel mentre escono dal fondo due Uomini vestiti di nero.*)

TUTTI: Che fai?

GEN: Leggete adesso!

TUTTI: Oh, diàmin', Orgia!

GUB: Una facezia è questa,
Che può costar domani
Ben cara a molti.

GEN: Ove del reo si chieda,
Me stesso a palesar pronto son io.

ORS: Qualcun ci osserva—separiamci.

TUTTI: Addio!
(*Gennaro rientra in sua Casa; gli altri si disperdono.*)

## SCENA III.

*Astolfo e Rustighello, ambidue passeggiando: indi Scherani.*

RUS: Quì che fai?

AST: Che tu te 'n vada,
Questo aspetto;—e tu che fai?

RUS: Che tu sgombri la contrada,
Fermo attendo.

AST: Con chi l' hai?

RUS: Con quel giovane straniero
Che ha quì stanza;—e tu con chi?

AST: Con quel giovin forestiero,
Che pur esso alberga quì.

RUS: Dove il guidi?

AST: Alla Duchessa.
E tu dove?

RUS: Al Duca appresso.

AST: Oh, la via non è l' istessa!

RUS: Nè conduce al fine istesso.

AST: Una a festa—

RUS: L' altra a morte!
Delle due qual s' aprirà?

GEN: Signors, I bid you
Forbear that mention, else must the dawnlight
Reflect itself in our sword blades. No man on earth
Abhors the she-fiend more than I do.

PET: Be silent,
For there stands her palace!

GEN: Then if so, would I could thus
Write disgrace upon it as with ready dagger
I blot that scutcheon where is written Borgia.
(*He ascends a flight of stairs leading to the escutcheon, and with his dagger strikes out the first letter of the name "Borgia": while he is doing it, two men, habited in black, come from the back of the stage.*)

ALL: Your purpose?

GEN: Now read the inscription!

ALL: By Jove, Sirs! Orgia!

GUB: That letter off the name there
Will one day prove your shoulders
Minus the head, friend.

GEN: Should they demand the offender,
I gladly render my presence at the call!

ORS: Some one observes us—let us part here.

ALL: Adieu then!
(*Gennaro retires to his dwelling; the others disperse.*)

## SCENE III.

*Astolfo and Rustighello walking about, afterwards Bravos.*

RUS: What is your purpose?

AST: To see you vanish,
And the coast clear. Why do you tarry here?

RUS: Loiterers such as you to banish
Is now my duty.

AST: Whom your quarry?

RUST: Yonder young Venitian stranger
Who resides there.—Your business here?

AST: Just to save a youth from danger,
One who lodges somewhere near.

RUS: Where would you guide him?

AST: Unto the duchess.
Where would you, friend?

RUS: The duke's my preference.

AST: Between our roads the contrast such is—

RUST: That their ends have mighty difference.

AST: One means pleasure—

RUST: The other death!
What result our game then takes—

## Act I, Scene III

A 2: Del più destro—e del più forte
Dal voler dipenderà.
(*Rustighello fa un segno dal cantone della strada.—Entra un drappello di Scherani, i quali circondano Astolfo.*)

RUS, CORO: Non far motto! parti, sgombra.
Il più forte appien lo scorgi.
Guai per te se appena un' ombra
Di sospetto a lui tu porgi!
Solo Alfonso ancor quì:
Somma legge è il suo voler.

AST: Ma il furor della Duch essa.

RUS: Taci, e d' essa—non temer.

CORO: Al suo nome, alla sua fama
Fê l' audace estrema offesa:
Vendicarsi il Duca brama—
Impedirlo è stolta impresa.
Se da saggio oprar tu vuoi,
Dei piegar, partir, tacer.

AST: Parto, sì. Che avvenga poi
Vostro sia, non mio pensier.
(*Astolfo si ritira.—Rustighello e gli Scherani atterran le porte della Casa di Gennaro.*)

### SCENA IV.

Sala nel Palazzo Ducale.—Gran porta al fondo; a diritta un uscio chiuso da invetriata a sinistra un altr' uscio segreto. Tavolino nel mezzo coperto di velluto.

*Alfonso, poi Rustighello; indi un Usciere.*

ALF: Tutto eseguisti?

RUS: Tutto! Il prigioniero
Quì presso attende.

ALF: Or bada. A quell in fondo
Segreta sala, della statua a' piedi
Dell' avol mio, riposti armadj schiude
Quest' aurea chiave: ivi d' argento
un vaso
E un d' or vedrai. Nella propinqua stanza
Ambi li reca; nè desio ti tenti
Dell' aureo vaso—vin de' Borgia è desso.
Attendi—all' uscio appresso
Tienti di spada armato. Ov' io ti chiami
I vasi apporta; ov' altro cenno intendi,
Col ferro accorri.

---

BOTH: Most depends how best I smother
Points that my opponent makes.
(*Rustighello turns deftly aside and makes a signal: a troop of Sbirri enters and surrounds Astolfo.*)

RUST, CHO: Not a word, a thought, a motion:
Learn the force of overwhelming numbers.
Woe to you had your devotion
Broke his unsuspecting slumbers!
Our dread monarch has here created
His mere wishes supremest law.

AST: But the anger of the Duchess?

RUST: Silence; her mandate must bow in awe.

CHORUS: On her name and reputation
He has thrown the greatest slighting:
Not a man, though king in station
Dare neglect the duke's inditing.
If your wisdom equals your valor,
Take its presence from here at once.

AST: I depart! The coming sequel
Falls to your, not my, expense.
(*Astolfo retires.—Rustighello and the Sbirri steal into Gennaro's dwelling.*)

### SCENE IV.

Saloon in the Ducal Palace.—At the back, grand central entrance, to the right a small door, to the left another small door, partly hidden from observation. Behind this door, a recess is seen, in which a descending spiral staircase commences.

*Duke, Rustighello, afterwards an Usher.*

DUKE: All has been followed?

RUST: All, Sire. For here the prisoner
Awaits your pleasure.

DUKE: Then mark me: Those stairs conducts
To "Numa's chamber," beneath the panel painted
By Ludovico, a secret niche is hidden;
This key unlocks it; seek for a vase of silver
And one of gold there: In the adjoining lobby
Have them both ready; and beware—taste not
Of the golden: It is the wine of the Borgia!
One moment.—Take a stand behind us
Armed with you ready weapon. So when I call you
Bring in the vases; but should I touch this signal
Come sword in hand then.

---

USCIERE: La Duchessa!
(*Annunzia dalla porta di fondo.*)

ALF: Affretta.
(*Rustighello parte, e poco dopo si vede passeggiando dall' invetriata.*)

### SCENA V.

*Lucrezia ed Alfonso; indi Gennaro, fra le guardie.*

ALF: Così turbata?

LUC: A voi mi trae vendetta!
Colpa inaudita, infame,
A denunziarvi io vengo. Avvi in Ferrara
Chi della vostra sposa a pien meriggio
Oltraggio il nome, e mutilarlo ardisce.

ALF: Mi è noto.

LUC: E no 'l punisce!
E il soffre Alfonso in vita?

ALF: A noi dinanzi
Tosto ei fia tratto.

LUC: Qual ei sia, pretendo
Che morte egli abbia, e al mio cospetto; e sacra
Ducal parola al vostro amor ne chiedo.

ALF: E sacra io dôlla.—Il prigionier.
(*All' Usciere si presenta immantinente Gennaro disarmato fra le Guardie.*)

LUC: (*Aparte.*) Chi vedo!

ALF: (*Con un sorriso.*) Noto vi è desso?

LUC: (*Aparte.*) Oh, Ciel! Gennaro!
Ahi quale
Fatalità!

GEN: L' Altezza vostra, o Duca,
Toglier mi fece dal mio tetto a forza
Da gente armata. Chieder posso, io spero,
D' ond' io mertai questo rigore estremo?

ALF: Capitano, appressate.

LUC: (*Aparte.*) Io gelo! io tremo!

ALF: Un temerario osava
Testè, di giorno, dal ducal palagio
Con man profana cancellar l' augusto
Nome di Borgia.—Il reo si cerca.

LUC: Il reo—
Non è costui!

ALF: D' onde il sapete?

LUC: Egli era
Stammane altrove. Alcun de' suoi compagni
Commiso il fallo.

GEN: Non è ver.

---

USHER: Sire, the Duchess.
(*Announcing from the central door.*)

ALF: Admit her.
(*Rustighello enters the staircase.*)

### SCENE V.

*Lucrezia and Duke Alfonso; afterwards Gennaro and Soldiers.*

ALF: In trouble, Madam?

LUC: I look to you for vengeance!
Since there is lately committed
Crime of the blackest nature! One in Ferrara
Holds your spouse so lightly: in actual daylight
He insults her, and mutilates her scutcheon.

DUKE: I know it.

LUC: If you have known it
Why then have you not punished?

DUKE: He here is captive,
And waits our pleasure.

LUC: Let me urge then,
Whatever his guilty reason, be who he may be,
I ask of you, Don Alfonso, that he does not quit this room alive.

DUKE: I give my promise. Admit the man.
(*To the Usher.—Gennaro appears immediately, disarmed, among guards.*)

LUC: (*Aside.*) Who shall I see?

DUKE: (*Smiling.*) Know you the prisoner?

LUC: (*Aside.*) Oh heavens! Gennaro! Oh fatal,
Fatal day!

GEN: Your gracious Highness, my Lord Duke,
Has been pleased to drag me from my home
By armed men. Let me ask then, I pray you,
What great transgression calls for such rigorous treatment?

DUKE: Captain, pray approach us!

LUC: (*Aside.*) I shudder! I tremble!

DUKE: Some idle varlet has boldly,
By day, in public, on our ducal palace,
In profanation travestied the mighty name
Of Borgia! We seek the culprit!

LUC: No culprit
Have we here!

DUKE: How do you know that?

LUC: He passed
The morning elsewhere! Some one of his companions
Has wrought this insult.

GEN: No, in truth.

**ALF:** L' udite?
Siate sincero, e dite
Se il reo voi siete.

**LUC:** Uso a mentir non sono;
Chè della vita istessa
Più caro ho l' onor mio.
Duca Alfonso, il confesso—il reo
son io.

**LUC:** (*Aparte.*) Misera me!

**ALF:** (*Piano a Lucretia.*) Vi diedi
La mia ducal parola.

**LUC:** Alcuni istanti
Favellarvi in segreto, Alfonso, io
bramo.
Deh! secondami, o Ciel! (*Aparte.*)
(*Ad un cenno d' Alfonso, Genna-
ro e ricondotto via.*)

## SCENA VI.

*Lucrezia; Alfonso.*

**ALF:** Soli noi siamo.
Che chiedete?

**LUC:** Vi chiedo, o signore,
Di quel giovane illesa la vita.

**ALF:** Come?—E dianzi cotanto rigore!
L' ira vostra è si tosto sparita.

**LUC:** Fu capriccio! A che giova ch'
ei mora?
Giovin tanto! Perdòno gli do!

**ALF:** La mia fede io vi diedi, o signora;
Nè a mia fede giammai fallirò.

**LUC:** Don Alfonso, favoro ben lieve
Voi negate a sovrana, a consorte!

**ALF:** Chi v' offese irne impune non
deve—
Voi chiedeste; io giurai la sua
morte.

**LUC:** Perdoniam—siam clementi
del paro:
La clemenza è regale virtù.

**ALF:** No, non posso.

**LUC:** E sì avverso a Gennaro
Chi vi fa, caro Alfonso?

**ALF:** Chi?—tu!

**LUC:** Io, che dite?

**ALF:** Tu l' ami!

**LUC:** Che ascolto?

**ALF:** Sì, tu l' ami! In Venezia il seguisti.

**LUC:** (*Aparte.*) Giusto Cielo!

**ALF:** Anche adesso nel volto
Ti leggea l' empio ardor che nu-
dristi.

**LUC:** Don Alfonso!

**ALF:** T' acqueta.

**LUC:** Io vi giuro.

**DUKE:** You hear him?
Pray, Sir, be candid, say truly
Are you the culprit?

**GEN:** To tell but the truth's a max-
im
Which, though our life it perils
Can never risk our honor.
Duke Alfonso, I confess it, I only am
guilty.

**LUC:** (*Aside.*) Unhappy me!

**DUKE:** (*In an undertone.*) Remember
I gave my Ducal promise.

**LUC:** Let us a moment
Give this matter together more
close discussion.
(*Aside.*) Be my helper, oh heaven!
(*At a sign of the Duke, Gennaro is
taken away.*)

## SCENE VI.

*Lucretia; the Duke.*

**DUKE:** We are in private;
What do you wish to say?

**LUC:** I ask you, best beloved,
To spare that gentle youth his existence.

**DUKE:** How now? So lately his
death did you covet!
Has your anger taken wings such a
distance?

**LUC:** It was a mere whim! I am
ready to pardon.
What would his death now avail to
us!

**DUKE:** But we gave you our promise, fair lady.
When we promise we never do fail.

**LUC:** Don Alfonso; how trifling a favor
Do you deny to Lucretia, your consort!

**DUKE:** He has crimes even deeper
and graver.
You did ask me, and I vowed you
his life.

**LUC:** Is not mercy the brightest jewel
That should gleam from a great
prince's brow?

**DUKE:** No, I cannot.

**LUC:** What has made you so cruel
Toward Gennaro, my dear Alfonso?

**DUKE:** What?—You!

**LUC:** I have your meaning?

**DUKE:** You love him!

**LUC:** What say you?

**DUKE:** Yes, you love him! Straight
to Venice you pursued him.

**LUC:** (*Aside.*) Ha! gracious heaven!

**DUKE:** Guilty looks that betray you
Speak the passion that bade delude
him.

**LUC:** Don Alfonso!

**DUKE:** Pray calm yourself!

**LUC:** I implore you!

**ALF:** Non macchiarti di nuovo spergiuro.

**LUC:** Don Alfonso!

**ALF:** E omai tempo ch' io prenda
De' miei torti vendetta tremenda;
E tremenda da questo momento,
Sul tuo complice infame cadrà!

**LUC:** (*Inginocchiandosi.*) Grazia,
Alfonso!

**ALF:** L' indegno vo' spento!

**LUC:** Per pietà!

**ALF:** Più non odo pietà!

**LUC:** Oh! a te bada, a te stesso pon
mente don Alfonso mio quarto marito omai troppom' hai vista piangente omai troppo il mio coree
feerito al dolo re sottentra la rabbia
ti potria far la Borgia pentir bada
bada Alfonso, bada ti potria farla
Borgia pentir bada bada Alfonso
bada ti potria farla Borgia pentir.

**ALF:** Mi sei nota; nè porre in obblio
Chi sei tu, se il volessi, potrei
Ma tu pensa che il Duca son io—
Che in Ferrara, e in mia mano tu sei.
Io ti lascio la scelta s' egli abbia
Di veleno o di spada a perir.
Scegli.

**LUC:** (*Fuori di sè.*) Oh, Dio! Dio
possente!

**ALF:** Trafitto
Tosto ci sia.
(*Per uscire.*)

**LUC:** Deh! t' arresta!

**ALF:** Ch' ei cada.

**LUC:** Non commetter sì nero delitto!

**ALF:** Scegli! scegli!

**LUC:** Ah, non muoja di spada!

**ALF:** Sii prudente! D' appresso io ti
sono:
Nulla speme te è data nutrir.

**LUC:** L' infelice al suo fato abbandono!
Uom crudele! io mi sento morir!
(*Cade sopra una sedia.—Alfonso
accenna alle Guardie.*)

## SCENA VII.

*Gennaro ritorna fra i Custodi;
indi Rustighello.*

**ALF:** Della Duchessa ai preghi
Che il vostro fallo obblìa,
E forza pur ch' io pieghi;
E libertà vi dia.

**LUC:** (*Aparte.*) Oh, come ei finge!

**DUKE:** From additional falsehood
forbear now.

**LUC:** Don Alfonso!

**DUKE:** Now it is my time for action,
Mine to gain for my wrongs satisfac-
tion,
That tremendous revenge now I
cherish shall fall
On your hated accomplice!

**LUC:** (*Clinging to him.*) Mercy, Alfonso!

**DUKE:** No, the traitor must perish!

**LUC:** Oh, have mercy!

**DUKE:** I am deaf to your call!

**LUC:** Oh, though the fourth of my
husbands, you lord it, Don Alfonso,
too sternly, I assure you! They who
have wronged me have ever de-
plored it! They who slight me cannot shun my fury. I scorn all your
malice with derision, Know you
have to deal with the Borgia, wary,
wary Alfonso, wary, Know that you
have to deal with the Borgia, Wary,
wary Alfonso. Wary, know that you
have to deal with the Borgia.

**DUKE:** Well I know you! your
deeds have no covering,
You yourself duly tell to the world:
Yet think you once that I here am
sovereign
In Ferrara you dwell in my power.
I but leave you to fix the decision,
That he die by either poison or
steel.
Choose then!

**LUC:** (*Wildly.*) Oh, heaven! oh,
mighty heaven!

**DUKE:** It were shorter
By the sword—
(*As if going out.*)

**LUC:** Stay one moment!

**DUKE:** The word, then!

**LUC:** Oh, refrain from this horrible
murder.

**DUKE:** Choose the manner—

**LUC:** Let it not be the sword, then!

**DUKE:** Now be cautious, and do
not deceive yourself:
I reveal not one glimmer of hope.

**LUC:** Wretched boy! I must leave
you to your fate!
Cruel monster! how vain all appeal!
(*She sinks on a seat.—The Duke
makes a sign to the guards.*)

## SCENE VII.

*Gennaro returns amid his ward-
ers; afterwards Rustighello.*

**DUKE:** Her grace's intercession,
Anger at insult ceasing,
Commands our quick concession,
And grants you your releasing.

**LUC:** (*Aside.*) O, how he feigns!

ALF: E poi
Tanto è valore in voi,
Che d' Adria il mar privarno,
E Italia insiem, non vo'.

LUC: (*Aparte.*) Perfido!

GEN: Quai so darno,
Grazie, signor, ve'n do!
Pur—poichè dirlo è dato
Senza temer viltade—
In uom che l' ha mertato
Il beneficio cade.
Di vostra Altezza il padre
Cinto da avverse squadre
Perir, se scudo e aïta
Non gli era un venturier.

ALF: E quel voi siete?

LUC: (*Sorgendo.*) E vita
Voi gli serbaste?

GEN: E ver.

LUC: (*Aparte.*) Duca—

ALF: (*Aparte.*) L' indegna spera!

LUC: (*Aparte.*) S' ei si mutasse!

ALF: (*Aparte.*) E vano!
Seguir la mia bandiera
Vorreste, o capitano?

GEN: Al Veneto Governo
Nodo mi stringe eterno—
Mio fede io gli giurai;
E sacro è un giuro.

ALF: (*Volgendosi con intenzione
a Lucrezia.*) Il so!
Quest' oro almeno—
(*Presentendogli una borsa.*)

GEN: Assai
Da' miei signori io n' ho.

ALF: Almen, siccome antico
Stile è fra noi degli avi,
Libare a nappo amico
Spero che a voi non gravi.

GEN: Sommo per me favore
Questo sarà, signore.

ALF: Gentil la mia consorte
Coppiera a noi sarà.

LUC: (*Aparte.*) Stato peggior di
morte!

ALF: Meco, o Duchessa.—Olà.

*Esse Rustigbello.*

ALF: (*Prendendola per mano,
aparte.*) Guai se ti sfugge un
moto—
Se ti tradisce un detto!
Uscir dal mio conspetto
Vivo costui non dè.
Versa! Il licor ti è noto!
Strano è il ribrezzo in te.

DUKE: In sequel
Few lands show equal valor;
Shall ours appear deficient
Towards one so brave as you?

LUC: (*Aside.*) Perfidy!

GEN: All sufficient
Thanks, I, my lord, allow.
Sire; if you will please hear it,
And I may speak unhampered,
For one of some slight merit
Blame should be tempered with
grace.
Once, when around your father
Adverse the foe did gather,
His death was sure, till assistance
Was rendered by one poor youth.

DUKE: You then are he, Sir?

LUC: (*Rising.*) Existence
You restored him?

GEN: In truth.

LUC: (*Aside.*) Hear!

DUKE: (*Aside.*) False hope fans
her!

LUC: (*Aside.*) Can this not change
him?

DUKE: (*Aside.*) How vainly!
(*Aloud.*) Will you serve beneath
our banner,
Sir Captain? I ask it plainly.

GEN: Venice's lovely regions
Own my entire allegiance;
I've sworn and vowed my faith to
them;
And sacred shall my oath be.

DUKE: (*Turning significantly to
Luc.*) Just so!
This gold at least may—
(*Offering a purse.*)

GEN: The State, your grace,
Ample does allow.

DUKE: Since then our every offer
Meets with a similar rejection,
I proffer a parting cup,
To that, show no objection!

GEN: Such were a regal favor
Touched with the finest flavor.

DUKE: At your hands, gentle wife,
here
The generous wine shall flow.

LUC: (*Aside.*) Air with worst death
is rife here.

DUKE: Hear me, O Duchess!—
What ho!

(*Enter Rustigbello with a salver,
on which are two flagons, one of
silver, the other of gold, and two
cups; be places them on the table
and withdraws.*)

DUKE: (*Keeping Luc, by the band,
aside.*) Guard from all emotion,
Lull thought to subtlest essence;
This man, here, in our presence
Ceases to live this day.
As often as you pour that potion
Other than fear has swayed!

LUC: (*Aparte.*) Oh, se sapessi a
quale
Opra m' astringi atroce,
Per quanto sii feroce,
Ne avvresti orror con me!
Va—non v' ha mostro eguale—
Colpa maggior no v' è!

GEN: (*Aparte.*) Meco benigni tanto
Mai non credea costoro.
Trovar perdono in loro
Sogno pur sembra a me.
Madre, esser dee soltanto
Del tuo pregar mercè.

ALF: Or via mesciamo.
(*Si versa dal Vaso d' Argento.*)

GEN: Attonito
A tanta onor son io.

ALF: A voi, Duchessa.

LUC: (*Aparte.*) Il barbaro!

ALF: (*Aparte.*) Il vaso d' or.

LUC: (*Aparte.*) Gran Dio!
(*Versa dal Vaso d' Oro.*)

ALF: Vi assista il Ciel, Gennaro!

GEN: Fausto a voi sia del paro!
(*Bevono.*)

ALF: (*Aparte.*) Trema per te, spergiura!
Vittima prima egli è.

LUC: (*Aparte.*) Vanne! Non ha natura
Mostro peggior di te!

GEN: (*Aparte.*) Madre! è la mia
ventura
Del tuo pregar mercè!

ALF: Or, Duchessa, a vostr' agio potete
Trattenerlo, oppur dargli commiato.
(*Si allontana con Rustigbello.*)

LUC: (*Aparte, pensando.*) Oh,
qual raggio!

GEN: (*Inchinandosi.*) Signora, accogliete
I saluti di un cor non ingrato.

LUC: Infelice il veleno bevesti non
farmotto trafitto cadresti Prendi e
parti una goecia una soladi quel far-
macovita ti dà. Io na scondi,
t'affretta t'invola t'accompagni del
ciel la pietà t'accompagni del ciel
la pietà t'accompagni del ciel la
pietà Del ciel o del ciel la pietà del
cielo  . . . . del ciel la pietà.

GEN: Che mai sento? E tutt' altro
che morte
Aspettarmi io doveva in tua corte!
Un rio genio mi pose la benda,
M' inspiro sì fatal securtà.
Forse—ah! forse una morte più or-
renda,

LUC: (*Aside.*) O, could you know
the sequel
From such your atrocious deed
Even would your ferocious hate
Bid me stay in horror,
Monster without an equal,
And can you do nothing but slay?

GEN: (*Aside.*) Grace or benignant
favor
Scarce had I hoped as my guerdon,
But here to find a pardon
Must seem a dream always;
Mother, you are my saviour,
For your son's well-being, pray!

DUKE: Now, Madam! to help him!
(*Helps himself out of the silver
flagon.*)

GEN: Excuse the blush
Such regal kindness causes.

DUKE: We wait you, Duchess.

LUC: (*Aside.*) Barbarian!

DUKE: The vase of gold!

LUC: (*Aside.*) Great heaven!
(*Pours out for Gennaro from the
golden flagon.*)

DUKE: Young man, may long life
attend you!

GEN: Fortune the same befriend
you! (*They drink.*)

DUKE: (*Aside.*) Tremble, vile creature,
He falls, though first, not last.

LUC: (*Aside.*) Can there be in nature
Monster of crime so vast?

GEN: (*Aside.*) Life wears another
feature,
This hour of peril past!

DUKE: (*Aside to Lucrezia.*) Up,
fond Duchess, for your paramour
needs
All your love, his few moments remaining.
(*Retires with Rustigbello.*)

LUC: (*Aside, reflecting.*) What
thus inspires me!

GEN: (*Bowing.*) Your goodness so
overpowers me,
Such impression can scarcely be
forgotten.

LUC: Hapless victim of the poison
he gave you, This one antidote only
can save you, Take it! drink it! but a
drop from the vial, Precious life is
yours! Then again, Drink! and fly
from here! I brook no denial, Over
you, angels
forevermore reign . . . . Over
you, angels forevermore reign,
Over you, angels forevermore
reign, forever and evermore reign,
forever and evermore reign.

GEN: Deep designing could I else
have expected?
They that near you are selected for
death,
False the genius who now bending
over me
Whispers hope where all hope is in

La tua destra, o malvagia, mi dà?

**LUC:** Oh, in me fida!

**GEN:** In te, cruda!

**LUC:** Sì; parti!
Morto, in te vuole il Duca un rivale.

**GEN:** Oh, cimento!

**LUC:** Ei ritorna a svenarti!
Bevi, e fuggi!

**GEN:** Oh, dubbiezza fatale!

**LUC:** Bevi, e fuggi, io te 'n prego, o Gennaro!
Per tua madre—per quanto hai più caro!

**GEN:** Ti punisca, s' è in te tradimento,
Chi più speri che t' abbia pietà.
(*Beve.*)

**LUC:** Tu sei salve! Oh, supremo contento!
Quinci involati—affrettati—va!
(*Lucrezia lo fa fuggire per la porta segreta. Si presenta dal fondo Rustighello col Duca.—Ella dà un grido, e cade sovra una sedia.*)

*FINE DELL' ATTO PRIMO.*

# ATTO II.

## SCENA I.

*Piccolo Cortile che mette alla Casa di Gennaro. Una finestra della Case è illuminata.—E notte.*

*Un drappello di Scherani entra spiando.*

**RUST E CORO:** Rischiarata è la finestra:
In Ferrara egli è tuttora.
La fortuna al Duca è destra—
Del rival vendetta avrà.
Inoltriam! propizia è l' ora,
Buio è il cielo, alcun non v' ha.
(*Avvicinano alla Casa di Gennaro; odono rumore, e si arrestano.*)
Ma, silenzio, Un mormorio—
Un bisbiglio s' è levato:
E di gente calpestio
Più distinto udir si far.
Là in disparte—là in aggusto
Chi è si esplori, e dove va
(*Si ritirano.*)

**GEN:** Com' è soave quest' ora di silenzio
Al mio dolente cor! Quì non ascolto
Umana voce—e sembra
In dolce calma riposar natura.
Ah! non han posa le tempeste or-

vain.
A still more horrible ending,
Three times accursed one, your hand contains!

**LUC:** Do but trust me!

**GEN:** Trust you, vile fiend!

**LUC:** I pray you!
Your death, as a rival's, the Duke wills.

**GEN:** Fearful trial!

**LUC:** Comes he back, he will slay you!
Drink and fly from here!

**GEN:** Oh, this doubting is madness!

**LUC:** Dear Gennaro, I beg, I implore you
By that mother who lives to adore you!

**GEN:** May the gods with their utter resentment
Curse you ever if this be pretence!
(*Drinks.*)

**LUC:** You are saved! O supreme contentment;
Like the lightning, fly this moment from here!
(*Lucrezia makes him escape by a secret door. The Duke and Rustighello appear at the back of the stage. She gives a shriek and sinks on a seat.*)

*END OF ACT I.*

# ACT II.

## SCENE I.

*A small court adjoining the house of Gennaro. One window is lighted. Night.*

*Rustighello enters with a band of Bravos, all disguised.*

**RUST, CHO:** Yonder light is the guiding beacon
In Ferrara our man remaining,
Proves the Duke's only chance does not weaken;
He will be revenged at last.
Let us on the advantage now gaining,
Slumber and darkness over all seem cast.
(*Advancing towards the house of Gennaro, they hear voices and stop.*)
Yet, be silent! a sound encroaches
Like a breeze in leafy summer;
Softly, gently it approaches,
Clear, distinct, increasing fast.
Let us in ambush, noting the comer,
Well explore him till he has passed.
(*Retire.*)

**GEN:** Oh, how delightful this pleasing hour of silence
Comes over this lonely heart! No voice of discord
Can assail me here. In tranquil slumber

rende
Che mi premono il petto! Ove n' andaste
Giorni felici come un sogno scorsi,
Quando il mio cor non conoscea rimorsi!
Io pur sentii le placide
Gioie d' un puro amore,—
Conobbi io pure il fervido
Desio di gloria e onore;
E mi ridea nell' anima
De pace il bel seren!
Perderne la memoria,
Mi fosse dato almen!
Or da rimorsi lacero,
Calma non ho, ne speme.
Un affannoso palpito
Il cuor mi scuote e freme!
Mille funeste immagini,
Mi colmano d' orror!
Almen bastasse a uccidermi
L' immenso mio dolor!

## SCENA II.

*Entra Orsini e batta alla porta.*

**GEN:** Lei tu?

**ORS:** Son io.
Venir non vuoi, Gennaro, dalla Negroni?
Ogni piacer m' èscemo
Le nol dividi tu.

**GEN:** Grave cagione a te mi toglie
Per Venezia io parto fra pochi istanti.

**ORS:** E me qui lasci?
E uniti fem alla morte
Non giùrammo entrambi
Essere in ogni evento?

**GEN:** E ver.

**ORS:** Mitieni cosi tua fede
Com' io la tengo.

**GEN:** E tu vien meco.

**ORS:** All' alba attendi, e vengo.
Al geniale invito
Mancar non posso.

**GEN:** Oh! questa tua Negroni
M' d di sènistro auspicio.

**ORS:** E a me piultosto il tuo parter cosi,
Notturno è solo—così pensoso è mesto.
Restae, restae Gennaro!

**GEN:** Odi—e se il chiedi
Io resto!—Mi vacciata è la mia vita,
Alla morte io son presso.

**ORS:** Chè l' insidia? à me lo addita?
Che è costui?

**GEN:** Parla sommesso.

Wrapped, nature seems reposing.
Ah! quiet comes not to the fearful tempest
Still raging in this bosom. Where have you gone
Bright days of rapture, like a vision faded,
When my young heart had not one thought remorseful.
Oh, I have felt the rapture,
The joy of love's pure devotion,
Have known the burning eagerness
For fame and glorious promotion,
Yet peace within my bosom
Ever smiling so mild and fair!
Never will depart the memory
Till death relieves from care!
Now my soul's torn with agony,
Calmness and hope have departed,
Tremblings have seized and shaken me,
Borne me to earth faint-hearted.
Thousands of dark imaginings
My senses overpower—
Enough at least to wither me
The sorrows of this hour!

## SCENE II.

*Enter Orsini and raps at the door of Gennaro's dwelling.*

**GEN:** Is it you?

**ORS:** None else, friend.
Will you come with me and grace Negroni's supper?
There I can take no pleasure
If you do not share it.

**GEN:** Causes compel me now to refuse you,
Since I depart for Venice one hour from this time.

**ORS:** And will you leave me?
In life and death is our friendship
Sworn to share together
Equally cloud or sunshine?

**GEN:** It is true.

**ORS:** And think you I so could treat you
With like unkindness?

**GEN:** Come with me then.

**ORS:** Wait but the dawnlight, I'm with you.
Courtesy will not suffer
To slight Negroni.

**GEN:** This, her aforesaid banquet,
Rouses my worst suspicions.

**ORS:** Then rather, my friend, going away alone,
Unarmed, by night, too—through brigand-haunted regions,
Stay now, stay, dear Gennaro.

**GEN:** Well then, since you urge it
So be it!—Over my life there hangs a menace,
Death impends with fatal power.

**ORS:** Who asserts so? From where comes the menace?
Show me the man.

**GEN:** Speak lower.

## Act II, Scene II

**CORO DI SBIRRI:** Ci par tempo.

**RUST:** No s' aspetti
L' importunato partira.

**ORS:** Ah!

**GEN:** Taci! incanto!

**ORS:** Nè d' inganni tu sospetti
Quale in te credulita!
Non sai tu di donna l' arti:
Onde a lei ti mostri grato Ella ha finto, ella ha finto di salvarti; Di veleni, di veleni che ragioni dove fondi dove fondi il tuo ti mor? Gentil donna è la Negroni uom è il Duca uomo è il Ducad' alto cor!

**GEN:** Tu conosci apien tu sai se codardo io fui giammai se un ist ante in faccia a morte mai fu scemo il mio valor pure a desso in questa corte m' e di guai presago il cor m' e di guai presago il cor m' e di guai presago il cor presago il cor presago il cor, il cor.

**ORS:** Gentil dama è la Negroni uomo e il Duca d' alto cor uomo è il Ducad' alto cor uomo e il Duca d' alto cor d' alto cor d' alto cor.

**ORS:** Va se tu vuoi
Teutar m' ecaro
Afferrar la mia ventura.

**GEN:** Addio dungue—

**ORS:** Addio Gennaro.

**GEN:** Veglia a te!

**ORS:** Ti rassicura.

**GEN:** Ah, non posso abbandonarti.

**ORS:** Ah, non io lasciarti ouò.

**GEN:** Al feslin vuò seguitarti—

**ORS:** Teco all' alba partirò.

**A DUE:** Sì a qual vuolsi, si tuo destino,
Esse è mio, lo giuro ancora,
Tuo sempre, o viva amora.
Qual due fiori a un solo stello
Qual due fronde a un ramasol,
Noi vedremo sereno il cielo,
O saremo curvati al suol.
(*Li retirano.*)

**RUST AL SBIRRI:** Nol seguite!

**CORO:** A noi s' invola.

**RUS:** Stolti!
Ei corse alla Negroni.

**CORO:** Basta allora;
Al laccio eì corrè
Non v' ha dubbio al vert 'apponi,
E tenace è certo l' amo
Che gettato al cieco è la.

---

**CHORUS OF SBIRRI:** Now's the moment.

**RUST:** No, have patience
Till that meddling fool departs.

**ORS:** Ah!

**GEN:** Silence! you madcap!

**ORS:** These, your fears, are sad vexations;
Oh, how credulous your heart!
Look how the woman served you:
Thinking love must pay such kindness, She pretends, she pretends to have preserved you: As to poison, as to poison that lay only in your fear, your foolish fear and nothing more! O, a dove is the fair Negroni, As for the Duke, the Duke I know true to the core!

**GEN:** None but you are so empowered To declare me never a coward! But the snare of an assassin calls for energy yet more stern, Common valor even surpassing That pure courage men adore, That pure courage men adore, That pure courage men adore, we men adore, we men adore, adore.

**ORS:** O a dove is fair Negroni, and the Duke true to the core, and the Duke true to the core, and the Duke true to the core, true to the core, true to the core

**ORS:** I take the broad path,
You choose the narrow,
I must work out my adventure.

**GEN:** Adieu then, comrade.

**ORS:** Adieu, Gennaro.

**GEN:** Farewell!

**ORS:** Luck bless your venture.

**GEN:** Thus abandon you? ah never!
(*Rushing back.*)

**ORS:** Do you think I could leave you so?

**GEN:** Since tonight we do not sever—

**ORS:** I will go with you at dawn.

**BOTH:** O fortune, whatever it may be,
Shall be mine, again I swear it,
Life or death, together we share it.
Twin-born flowers, growing in union,
Twin-born leaflets upon a branch.
We show one smile, if summer be glowing,
Beneath the tempest we equally blanch.
(*Exit.*)

**RUST TO THE SBIRRI:** Do not follow!

**CHORUS:** But they escape us!

**RUS:** Madmen!
They seek Negroni's palace.

**CHORUS:** That is sufficient.
They rush into danger;
Then how useless such puny malice,
One with passion newly burning

---

Ir si lasci ritorniamo
Di ferir mestier non fa.

## SCENA III.

*Sala del Palazzo Negroni illuminata e addobbata per festivo banchetto.*

*Sono sedute ad una tavola riccamente imbandita la Principessa Negroni con molte Dame splendidamente vestite. Orsini, Liverotto, Vitellozzo, Gazella, Petrucci, ciascuno con una Dama al fianco. Da un lato della tavola è Gubetta; dall' altro è Gennaro.*

**LIV:** Viva il Madera!

**TUTTI:** Evviva!

**VIT:** Il Ren che scalda e avviva!

**GAZ:** De' vivi il Cipro è re!

**PET:** I vini—per mìa fè—Tutti so i buoni.

**ORS:** Io stimo quel che brilla,
Siccome la scintilla,
Che desta il Dio d' Amor
Nell' occhio seduttor,
Della Negroni!

**TUTTI:** Ben detto! A lei si tocchi!
Si beva ai suoi begli occhi!
Amore la formò!
Ciprigna in lei versò
Tutti i suoi doni!
(*Toccano e bevono.*)

**GUB:** (*Aparte.*) Ebbri son già: conviene
Tentar che restin soli.
(*S' alzn.*)

**GEN:** (*Aparte.*) Nojato io sono.
(*Si allontana.*)

**ORS:** Ebbene?
Gennaro, a noi t' involi?
Odi il novello brindisi
Da me composto un giorno.

**GUB:** (*Ridendo.*) Ah! ah!

**ORS:** Chi ride?

**GUB:** Ridono
Quanti ci sono intorno.

**ORS:** Come?

**GUB:** Oh l' esimio lirico!

**ORS:** M' insulteresti tu?

**GUB:** S' egli è insultarti il ridere,
Far no 'l potrei di più.

**ORS:** (*Alzandosi.*) Marrano di Castiglia!

**GUB:** Scheran Trasteverino!
(*Orsini afferra un coltello.*)

**DAME:** Cielo! costor si battono!

**TUTTI:** Che fai? T' acqueta, Orsini.
(*Trattenen.*)

---

Drags his friend where pitfalls lurk.
Let's be turning for other game,
Neater hands will do that work.
(*Exit.*)

## SCENE III.

*Saloon in the Negroni Palace; brilliantly illuminated and decorated.*

*On a table, covered with luxuries and rare flowers, the Princess Negroni is seated, with her ladies of honor. Orsini, Liverotto, Vitellozzo, Gazella, Petrucci, each with a lady seated at his side. At one end of the table Gubetta, opposite to him Gennaro.*

**LIV:** Long live Madeira!

**ALL:** Evviva!

**VIT:** Yet give us your Rhine wine forever!

**GAZ:** Cyprus the grape for me!

**PET:** God Bachus bids agree
Foeman and crony.

**ORS:** I praise the cup whose flowing
With golden, glorious glow,
Wakes Cupid from his trance
In your seducing glance,
Fairest Negroni!

**ALL:** Let us drink and sing her praises;
We sing the thousand graces
Love formed with so much art,
That Venus could impart
Such beauty only!
(*All touch their glasses and drink.*)

**GUB:** (*Aside.*) Half in their cups of those fair dames
I must bereave them.

**GEN:** (*Aside.*) I am weary.
(*Rising, as if about to go.*)

**ORS:** Such women,
Gennaro, can you leave them?
Hear but my last effusion
Composed the other morning.

**GUB:** (*Laughing rudely.*) Ha, ha!

**ORS:** Who laughs there?

**GUB:** All present,
Such absurd efforts scorning.

**ORS:** How so?

**GUB:** Ha, ha! a new Anacreon!

**ORS:** Would you insult me?

**GUB:** If laughing be insulting you,
More could I not, Sir dolt!

**ORS:** (*Rising*). You beggarly Castilian!

**GUB:** You gross Italian bully!
(*Orsini seizes a knife.*)

**LADIES:** Heavens, these men will come to swords!

**ALL:** What would you do? Be calm, Orsini.
(*Drawing him back.*)

ORS: Io ti darò, balordo—

GUB: —Tale di me ricordo, / Che temperante e sobrio / Per sempre ti farà.

TUTTI: Finitela, cospetto! / All' ospite rispetto. / O tutta quanta accorrere / Farete la città. / (*Le Dame si ritirano.*)

## SCENA IV.

*Gubetta, Orsini, Liverotto, Vitellozzo, Gazella, Petrucci, e Gennaro.*

LIV: Pace, pace, per ora!

VIT: Avrete il tempo / Di battervi doman da cavalieri; / Non col pugnal come assassin' di strada.

TUTTI: E ver.

GEN: Ma della spada / Che femmo noi?

ORS: L' abbiam deposta fuori.

TUTTI: Non ci si pensi più.

GUB: Beviam, signori.

GAZ: Ma intanto sbigottite / Ci han lasciate le dame.

GUB: Torneranno; / Ed umilmente chiederemo scusa. / (*Un coppiere vestito di nero porta in giro una bottiglia.*)

COPPIERE: Vino di Siracusa.

TUTTI: Ottimo vino, affè. / (*Tutti bevono: Gubetta versa il biechiere dietro le spalle.*)

GEN: (*Aparte.*) Maffio, vedesti? o Spagnuol non beve.

ORS: (*Aparte.*) Che importa? E naturale: ebbro esser deve.

GUB: Or, se gli piace, amior, / Può schiccherare Orsin versi a sua posta, / Poichè poeta lo farà tal vino.

ORS: Sì, a tu dispetto.

TUTTI: Una ballata, Orsini!

ORSINI: Il segreto peesser felice sò / per prova e l'insegno agli a mici sia / se reno sia nubilo ilcielo ogni tempo sia cal do sia gelo scherzo e bevo / e de ri do gl'insani che si dandel futuro pensier scherzo e bevo e derido gl'insani che si dandel futuro pensier Non curiamo l'incerto domani se quest' oggi n'è data goder. / (*Odesi un lugubre suono e voci lontane che cantano flobilmente:—*) / La gioja de' profani

E un fumo passeggier!

GEN: Quai voci?

ORS: Alcun si prende / Gioco di noi.

TUTTI: Che mi sarà?

ORS: Scommetto / Che delie dame una malizia è questa.

TUTTI: Un' altra strofa, Orsin!

ORS: La strofa è presta. / Profittiamo degli anni fiorenti,— / Il piacer li fa correr più lenti. / Se vecchiezza con livida faccia, / Stammi a tergo, e mia vita minaccia, / Scherzo e bevo, e derido gl' insani / Che si dan del futuro pensier!

TUTTI: Non curiamo l'imparto l' domani, / Se quest' oggie dato goder!

VOCI: Quitium sapicutiae / Est timor Domini. (*A poco a poco si spengono i lumi.*)

ORS: Gennaro!

GEN: Maffio! Vedi? / Si spengono le faci!

ORS: A farsi grave / Incomincia lo scherzo.

TUTTI: Usciam! Son chiuse! / Tutte le porte! Ove siam mai venuti?

## SCENA V.

*Si apre la porta dal fonde, e si presenta Lucrezia Borgia con gente armata.*

LUC: Presso Lucrezia Borgia!

TUTTI: (*Con un grido.*) Ah, siam perduti!

LUC: Sì, son la Borgia! Un ballo, un tristo ballo / Voi mi deste in Venesia: io rendo a voi / Una cena in Ferrara.

TUTTI: Oh, noi traditi!

LUC: Voi salvi ed impuniti / Credeste invano. Dell' ingiuria mia / Piena vendetta ho già: cinque son pronti

---

ORS: This small account I'll settle—

GUB: —With such a taste of metal, / As cannot fail to sober you / Forever and a day.

ALL: These ill-timed, ugly measures, / Have scarred our fairest treasures; / The total town will be aroused, / Inquiring of the fray. / (*The Ladies retire.*)

## SCENE IV.

*Gubetta, Orsini, Liverotto, Vitellozzo, Gazella, Petrucci, e Gennaro.*

LIV: Peace, peace, I implore!

VIT: The time is ample / To battle tomorrow at the sword's point, / Not here with knives, like your cutthroat butchers!

ALL: Well said.

GEN: Apropos of our swords: / Where have we left them?

ORS: Outside in that chamber.

ALL: Here let this matter end.

GUB: Now drink, my masters!

GAZ: Our harsh ill-mannered rudeness / Has dispersed all our ladies.

GUB: Each will come back / And smile on who woos her for humblest. / (*A cupbearer, clad in black, carries round a flask of wine.*)

CUPBEARER: Wine of Syracuse.

ALL: Best of the best—by Jove. / (*All drink, except Gubetta, who empties his goblet over shoulder.*)

GEN: (*Aside.*) Maffio, did you see that? That Spaniard, he drank not.

ORS: (*Aside.*) What does it matter? It is passing likely; why, he is reeling!

GUB: Now, if it please him, my comrades, / Bid the great bard Orsini verse us a strophe; / Gods, what a poet such wine as this should make him.

ORS: Yes, without your help, friend!

ALL: Tune us a stanza, Orsini!

ORSINI: O the secret of bliss in perfection, Is to never raise any objection Whether winter hang tears on the bushes Or the summer kiss deck them in blushes, Drink and pity the fool who on sorrow Ever wastes the pale shade of a thought; Drink and pity the fool who on sorrow Ever wastes the pale shade of a thought, Never hope for one jot from the morrow, Save a new day of joy by it brought. / (*They are interrupted by the dis-*

tant sound of a funeral bell, and voices chanting in a dismal tone, part of the Catholic funeral service.

CHORUS: (*Within.*) Et plusquam non videbunt / Si habent oculos.

CHORUS: (*Within, in response.*) Et nares habent omnes / Sed non odorabunt.

GEN: What means that?

ORS: While we pipe chansons / Echo sings vespers.

ALL: But yet, what is it?

ORS: Some dead monk; / With doleful chanting now to his grave they post him.

ALL: Let's drink to him, Orsini!

ORS: In this verse, I'll toast him. / On the springtime of life fully flowing, / On the ripe sun of youth gaily glowing, / Death may gloat with his bleary eye so yellow; / Here's a health for the jolly old fellow! / With a fig for the fool who on sorrow / Ever wastes the pale shade of a thought!

ALL: Life or death then must wait till tomorrow, / and not spoil this delight we have sought.

CHORUS OF PENITENTS: (*Entering and ranging themselves on each side of the banquet chamber.*) Quitium sapicutiae / Est timor Domini. / (*One by one the lights go out.*)

ORS: Gennaro!

GEN: Maffio! look round! / The lamps are expiring.

ORS: This wears an aspect / Surpassing even strangeness.

ALL: Let's fly! Our swords! / All exit is prevented! Have we a demon among us?

## SCENE V.

*The central door opens and Lucrezia appears, attended by armed men.*

LUC: No! but Lucrezia Borgia!

ALL: (*With a cry of horror.*) Ah! we are lost then!

LUC: See, it is the Borgia! how lately a sorry ball / All here did give me in Venice: / I now in turn bid you sup in Ferrara.

ALL: Hope! be banished!

LUC: You thought to pass unpunished; / Yet thought so vainly. Great as was your insult

Strati funèbri per coprirvi estinti,
Poichè il veleno a voi temprato è presto.

GEN: (*Avanz.*) Non bastan cinque: avvi mestier del sesto!

LUC: Gennaro! Oh, Ciel!

GEN: Perire
Io saprò cogli amici.

LUC: Ite: chiudete
Tutte le sbarre, e per rumor che ascolti,
Nessuno in questa sala entrar s' attenti.

TUTTI: Gennaro!
(*Strascinati.*)

GEN: Amici!

LUC: Uscite!

TUTTI: Oh, noi dolenti!
(*Escono fra gli armati, e la gran porta si chiude.*)

## SCENA VI.

*Lucrezia e Gennaro.*

LUC: Tu pur quì, nè sei fuggito?
Qual ti tenne avverso fato?

GEN: Tutto, tutto ho presentito!

LUC: Sei di nuovo avvelenato!

GEN: Ne ho il rimedio.
(*Cava l' ampolla del contraveleno.*)

LUC: Ah, me 'l rammento!
Grazie, grazie, al Ciel ne dò!

GEN: Cogli amici io sarò spento,
O con lor lo partirò.

LUC: Ah, per te fia poco ancora,
Ah non basta per gli amici.
(*Osservando l' ampolla.*)

GEN: Ei non basta? Allor! signora,
Morrem tutti.

LUC: Che mai dici?

GEN: Voi primiera di mia mano
Preparatevi a perir.

LUC: Io—Gennaro! Ascolta, insano!

GEN: Fermo io son!
(*Prende un coltello dalla tavola.*)

LUC: (*Sbigottita, aparte.*) Che far—che dir?

GEN: Preparatevi!
(*Ritornando.*)

LUC: Spietato! Ne ferir, svenar potresti?

My vengeance is as great: five narrow coffins
Now are in waiting to receive your bodies;
For one and all have taken poison!

GEN: (*Advancing.*) Five will suffice not—still you need a sixth one!

LUC: Gennaro! Oh, heavens!

GEN: Yes, Madam;
Here, to die with my comrades.

LUC: Hasten, and fast close
Every barrier; no matter, should you hear anything:
Let none else enter within this present chamber.

ALL: Gennaro!
(*Being led away.*)

GEN: Farewell then!

LUC: Remove them!

ALL: Heaven be our refuge.
(*Exit, among the armed men, and the great door closes.*)

## SCENE VI.

*Lucrezia, Gennaro.*

LUC: You are here, as if it were seeming
Fate must shadow your young horizon.

GEN: I foresaw this envisioned dreaming.

LUC: You have again taken the poison.

GEN: Here's the cure, still!
(*Shows the vial.*)

LUC: Ah! I remember!
I will thank for this with my latest breath!

GEN: Till my comrades all have drank
I will risk their chance of death.

LUC: Scarce that drop of life's restorer
Saves yourself, much less a friend.

GEN: Have no more? If so, Signora,
All must perish.

LUC: How will this end, then?

GEN: First, your course of more than badness
Ends beneath my vengeful steel.

LUC: I? I? Gennaro.—Withhold, oh, insensate—

GEN: Nothing can shake me.
(*Takes a knife from the table.*)

LUC: (*Terrified, aside.*) Must I reveal?

GEN: Quick, prepare yourself!
(*Seizing her.*)

LUC: Unkind one!
By your hand, too, shall I perish?

GEN: Lo posso io, son disperato!
Tutto, tutto mi togliesti.
Non più indugi.
(*Risoluto.*)

LUC: Ah! ferma, ferma!

GEN: Preparati!

LUC: (*Con un grido.*) Ah, un Borgia sei!
Son tuoi padri i padri miei.
Ti risparmia un fallo orrendo—
Il tuo sangue non versar.

GEN: Sono on Borgia! Oh Ciel! ce intendo?

LUC: Ah! ancora domandar.
M'odi ah m'odi io non t'imploro per voler serbarmi in vita ille volte al giorno io moro mille volte mille volte in cor ferita Perte prego ah teco al meno ah! non volere in crudelir bevi bevi il rio veleno ah, t'affretta deh t'affretta a prevenir Il tempo vola deh cedi cedi deh! t'affretta il velenoa prevenir deh cedi cedi il tempo vola ah deh t'affretta il veleno A prevenir. Bevi, cedi! cedi! Ah! t'affretta, il veleno A prevenir. Si, Gennaro! Bevi! cedi! ah! Deh t'affretta, il veleno A prevenir.

ORS: Gennaro!

GEN: Maffio muore!

LUC: Per tua madre!

GEN: Va!—tu sola
Sei cagion del suo dolore.

LUC: No, Gennaro!

GEN: L' opprimesti.

LUC: No 'l pensar.

GEN: Di lei che festi?

LUC: Vive! vive! E a te favella
Col mio duol, col mio terror.

GEN: Ciel! tu forse—

LUC: Ah sì, son quella!

GEN: Tu! Gran Dio! mi manca il cor!
(*Si abbandona sopra una sedia.*)
Madre, seognor lontano
Vissi al materno seno
Che a te pietò so.
Iddio—m' unisca in morte almeno,
Madre, l' estremo anelito
Ch' io spiri sul tuo cor.

LUC: Figlio mio! figlio mio! Aita! aita!
Ah, E spento! è spento!

GEN: See, how despair and grief can blind one.
Where are the comrades I did cherish?
No more talk!
(*Resolutely.*)

LUC: Ah! wait, wait!

GEN: Prepare to die!
(*Lifting the knife.*)

LUC: (*With a shriek.*) You're a Borgia;
You may call my fathers your own.
From an awful crime I stay you!
Do not spill your race's blood!

GEN: I a Borgia! Oh God, how say you!

LUC: Ask no more, for your own good.
Spurn, yes spurn me, I do implore you not to spurn my life's blighted blossom! Night and day too, in mourning over you a Thousand deaths, a thousand deaths do rack this bosom! Your existence a worthier jewel, Ah! must surmount this dark event, Drink, ah! drink then! that poison cruel, Hurry, hurry to prevent, yes to prevent. Ah, death will win. O yield, I pray, Hurry, hurry, To thus prevent cruel poison, O yield, I pray, Before death shall win ah, Hurry, hurry, To prevent the cruel poison. Drink it, yield! yield! Hurry, ah hurry, the cruel poison To prevent. Yes, Gennaro! Drink it! yield! ah! Hurry, to prevent the cruel poison.

ORS: (*Expiring within.*) Gennaro!

GEN: Maffio dies!

LUC: Save yourself, for your mother!

GEN: Hence! For in you lies
All her cause of sorrow.

LUC: No, no, Gennaro.

GEN: Did you molest her?

LUC: Never think it.

GEN: What fate opposed her?

LUC: Living she tells you yes, you, none other,
All her woe, her love, her faith.

GEN: Heaven, you perhaps?

LUC: I am that mother!

GEN: You! such tiding is worse than death.
(*Covering his face with his hands.*)
Mother, is this your welcome?
This your maternal blessing?
And must my daydream, my idol
Thus perish in this the possessing?
Mother, I've prayed, upon your breast
To pour out life's last breath.
(*Dies.*)

LUC: Child of sorrow! Help! succor! assistance!
Ah—it is ended!
(*Throwing herself upon the prostrate Gennaro.*)

## SCENA ULTIMA.

*Si spalancano le porte del fondo, e n' esce Alfonso con Rustighello e Guardie.*

**ALF:** Dove è desso?

**LUC:** Mira: è là.
(*Correndo ad Alfonso e additandogli Gennaro estinto.*)
Era desso il figlio mio!
La mia speme, il mio conforto:
Ei potea placarmi Iddio—
me parea far puro ancor!
Ogni luce in lui mi è spenta—

## LAST SCENE.

*The central door opens and admits Duke Alfonso and Rustighello, followed by guards.*

**DUKE:** Where then is he?

**LUC:** Look: at your feet.
(*Feebly raising her head and pointing to the body.*)
To my heart this hope was given:
His affection my soul redeeming,
Still might win me back to heaven,
With me share its holy shore.
Crushed in darkness, destroyed, ex-

Il mio cor non esso è morto!
Sul mio capo il Cielo avventa
Il suo strale punitor!
(*Cade sul Figlio.*)


**TUTTI:** Rio mistero! orribil caso!

**ALF:** Si soccorra!

**TUTTI:** Oh, Ciel! se 'n muor!

## LA FINE.

tinguished,
Fate has broken the magic dreaming;
Over this head too surely vanquished
See her wrathful vial pour now!
(*Sinks lifeless on Gennaro's body.*)

**CHORUS:** Wretched offspring, more wretched mother—

**DUKE:** Vain is help!

**CHORUS:** Vain is help; all is over.

## THE END.

# Lucia di Lammermoor (1835)

MUSIC BY GAETANO DONIZETTI ■ LIBRETTO BY SALVATORE CAMMARANO

This three-act opera, set to a libretto by Salvatore Cammarano (based upon Sir Walter Scott's novel, *The Bride of Lammermoor*) was first performed at the Teatro San Carlo in Naples on September 26, 1835. In Scotland at the end of the sixteenth century Lord Enrico Ashton finds himself in need of strong political allies. His home, Ravenswood castle, is not even rightfully his. Enrico's sister, Lucia, has been promised to Arturo Bucklaw but refuses to marry him. Normanno, captain of Lord Ashton's guard, is on to Lucia; she is in love with someone else. He discovers that Lucia's paramour is Sir Edgardo of Ravenswood. Lucia waits for Edgardo that night in the park, accompanied by Alisa, who pleads with her to end a relationship that can only come to grief because of the enmity between the Ravenswoods and the Ashtons. Edgardo wants to make peace with the Ashton family by asking for Lucia's hand in marriage. Although Lucia tries discourage him, they exchange rings as a pledge of their intentions. But, Enrico intervenes. He shows Lucia a forged letter from Edgardo to another woman, which convinces Lucia that she must marry Arturo after all. Edgardo interrupts the wedding after the marriage contract has been signed, accusing Lucia of unfaithfulness. Cursing the Ashtons, he draws his sword and attacks Enrico and Arturo. Raimondo, the chaplain, stops the fight. Enrico arrives at Wolf's Crag, the Ravenswood family's present home. He challenges Edgardo to a duel. The festivities continue, as the bride and groom retire for the night. Raimondo arrives suddenly with the news the Lucia has gone mad and, in her insanity, slain Arturo. In complete delirium, she acts out a wedding with the oblivious Edgardo. At the burial grounds, Edgardo hears the deathbell's toll and is told of Lucia's insanity and death. In the final dramatic moment of the opera, he dies, throwing himself on his own sword.

## ■ ATTO I

### SCENA 1

*Vestibula. NORMANDO e Coro.*

**NORMANDO E CORO:** Percorrete le spiagge vicine—Percorriamo le spiagge vicine—Della torre le vaste rovine. Cada il vel di si turpe mistero; Lo domanda, lo impone l'onor! Fia che splenda il terribile vero, Come lampo fra nubi d'orror!

### SCENA II

*ENRICO, RAIMONDO.*

**NORMANDO:** Tu sei turbato?

**ENRICO:** E n'ho ben d'onde. Il sai, del mio destin Si ottenebrò la stella; intanto Edgardo, Quel mortale nemico Di mia prosapia, dalle sue rovine Erge la fronte baldanzosa, e ride. Sola una mano raffermar mi puote Nel vacillante mio poter: Lucia Osa responger quella mano! Ah! suora Non m'è colei!

**RAIMONDO:** Dolente Vergin, che geme sull' urna recente Di cara madre, al talamo potria Volger io sguardo? Ah! rispettiam

## ■ ACT I

### SCENE I

*A Vestibule. NORMAN and Chorus.*

**NORMAN AND CHORUS:** Search well through the neighboring valley, through the ruins of the gloomy tower. This dark mystery that lowers around us it concerns our honor to clear. As the lightning up rends the storm cloud; so asunder this veil we will tear. (*Exeunt Chorus.*)

### SCENE II

*Enter HENRY and RAYMOND*

**NORMAN:** You seem troubled?

**HENRY:** And with reason; you know that the star of my destiny Darkly declines, This hated Edgar Bearing enmity deep and deadly to my race, laughing from his rock-bound tower To scorn my vows of vengeance, braves me! One hand alone can prop my falling fortune! There is just one thing that can save me now. Yet Lucy To Arthur still refuses her hand! Ah! sister She is no longer.

**RAYMOND:** A sorrowing Maiden, who mourns over the tomb of a parent, A dear loved mother, say how can you suppose She'll

quel core Che, traffitto dal duol, schivo è d'amore.

**NORMANDO:** Schivo d' amor! Lucia D' amore avvampa!

**ENRICO:** Che favelli?

**RAIMONDO:** (Oh, detto!)

**NORMANDO:** M'ascolta. Ella sen gia colà Del parco nel solingo vial Dove la madre giace sepolta— Impetuoso toro Ecco su lor s'avventa— Quando per l'aria sibilar si sente Un colpo, e al suol repente Cade la belva—

**ENRICO:** E chi vibrò quel colpo?

**NORMANDO:** Tal—che il suo nome ricopri d'un vela

**ENRICO:** Lucia, forse—

**NORMANDO:** L'amò!

**ENRICO:** Dunque il rivide?

**NORMANDO:** Ogni alba!

**ENRICO:** E dove?

**NORMANDO:** In quel viale.

**ENRICO:** Io fremo! Nè tu scopristi il seduttor:

**NORMANDO:** Sospetto Io n'ho soltanto—

**ENRICO:** Ah, parla!

think of marriage? Ah, respect that heart Which, enslaved by grief, dreams not of love.

**NORMAN:** Dreams not of love? You're fearfully mistaken.

**HENRY:** What are you saying?

**RAYMOND:** (*I tremble.*)

**NORMAN:** But listen. Lucy some few weeks ago. Was walking home alone in the park. As she was passing near her mother's tomb. A furious bull pursued her; Death at that time seemed certain, When through the still air came the short, sharp ring Of a rifle; the ball sped truly; The bull fell lifeless.

**HENRY:** And who was he that saved her?

**NORMAN:** One who in mystery still enshrouds himself.

**HENRY:** And you think Lucy—

**NORMAN:** She loves him!

**HENRY:** Then they have met since?

**NORMAN:** Each morning.

**HENRY:** Say where?

**NORMAN:** By that fountain.

**HENRY:** I tremble; Do you know the vile seducer's name?

**NORMAN:** Shrewdly I have suspicions—

**HENRY:** Proceed! speak!

**NORMANDO:** E tuo nemico!

**RAIMONDO:** (Oh, Ciel!)

**NORMANDO:** Tu lo detesti!

**ENRICO:** Esser potrebbe—Edgardo?

**NORMANDO:** Ah, lo dicesti!

**ENRICO:** Cruda, funesta smania tu m'hai svegliato in petto! è troppo, è troppo orribile, questo fatal sospetto! Mi fa gelare e fremere! solleva in fronte il crin, ah! mi fa gelare e fremere solleva in fronte, solleva in fronte il crin! Colma di tanto ob brobrio chi suora a me nascea! Ah! pria che d'amor si perfido a me svelarti rea se ti colpisse un fulmine, se ti colpisse un fulmine, fora menrio dolor ah, fora menrio fora menrio dolor fora menrio fora menrio dolor.

**NORMANDO:** Pietoso al tuo decoro,
Io fu con te crudel!

**RAIMONDO:** La tua clemenza imploro!
Tu lo smentisci, o Ciel!

## SCENA III

*Coro di Cacciatori, e detti.*

**CORO:** (*entrandi*). Il tuo dubbio è omai certezza.

**NORMANDO:** Odi tu?

**ENRICO:** Narrate!

**RAIMONDO:** (Oh, giorno!)

**CORO:** Como venti da stanchezza
Dupo lungo errare intorno,
Noi posammo della torre
Nel vesti bole cadente.
Ecco tosto lo trascorre
In silenzio un uom palente
Come appresoo ei n'è venuto,
Ravvisiam lo scono sciuto,
Ei su rapido destriero
S'involoò dal nostro guardo.
Qual s'appella un falconiero
Ne apprendeva qual s'appella.

**ENRICO:** E quale?

**CORO:** Edgardo!

**ENRICO:** Egli? Oh rabbia che m'accendi!
Contenerti un cor non può!

**RAIMONDO:** Ah no, non credere? no, no—
Deh sospendi—Ma—

**ENRICO:** No, no!

**RAIMONDO:** M'odi!

**ENRICO:** Udir non vuò.

---

**NORMAN:** That it is an enemy!

**RAYMOND:** (Oh, heaven!)

**NORMAN:** One you detest!

**HENRY:** Say who you mean. Is it Edgar?

**NORMAN:** Ah! You have named him!

**HENRY:** Each nerve with fury trembles at these dark thoughts you've awakened too frightful! too horrible! Say that you're mistaken! My blood congealed with rage freeze, And stagnant stands each vein, ah! My very blood congealed with rage freezes and stagnant, and stagnant stands each vein! Brother's counsel slighted, A sister's honor blighted! Ah! your black and matchless perfidy full soon shall be requited, On his head fall heaven's thunderbolt, On his head fall heaven's thunderbolt, Who our lineage, who our lineage would stain, Ah, who our lineage, who lineage, our lineage would stain.

**NORMAN:** It was cure for your wounded honor
That made me give you pain!

**RAYMOND:** Heaven, calm his angry feeling,
This fury now restrain!

## SCENE III

*Chorus of Hunters, and the above*

**CHORUS:** Your suspicions are now confirmed.

**NORMAN:** Do you hear?

**HENRY:** Proceed!

**RAYMOND:** Oh, dark hour!

**CHORUS:** Long we wandered over the mountain,
Searched each cleft around the fountain,
Dale and hill, and vale and bower,
Until we reached the ruined tower.
There we saw a man who silently strode
From out the portal; mounting
Straight his steed, he rapidly rode
Down the valley, at a bound
The torrent clearing.
Then like lightning disappearing.
From a falconer passing near us
We the intruder's name demanded.

**HENRY:** Who was it?

**CHORUS:** It was Edgar.

**HENRY:** Edgar? Ah, vengeance!
What deadly fury fires me.
Thus he dares to brave me!

**RAYMOND:** Ah, not believe it yet—
Suspend your anger—Lucy—

**HENRY:** No, no!

**RAYMOND:** Hear me!

**HENRY:** I'll hear no more!

---

**ENRICO AND CHORUS:** La pietade in suo favore miti sensi invan mi detta Se mi parli di vendetta solo in tenderti potrò! Sciagurati! il mio furore già su voi tremendo rugge, l'empia fiamma che vi strugge io colsangue spegnerò, io col sangue, io col sangue l'empia fiamma che vi strugge spegnerò, spegnerò, col sangue spegnerò, l'empia fiamma chei vi strugge, l'empia fiamma che vi strugge io col sangue spegnerò, si, spegnerò, si, si, col sangue spegnerò, si, spegnerò, si, spegnerò, spegnerò, spegnerò, col sangue spegnerò.

**NORMANDO E CORO:** Quell' indegno al nuovo albore L'iro tua fuggir non può. (Ahi! qual nube di terrore Questa casa circondò!) (*Partone.*)

## SCENA IV

*Parco. LUCIA ed ALISA.*

**LUCIA:** Ancor non giunse!

**ALISA:** Incauta a che mi traggi? Avventurarti or che il fratel qui venne E folle ardir!

**LUCIA:** Ben parli. Edgardo sappia Qual ne circonda orribile periglio!

**ALISA:** Perchè d' intorno il ciglio Volgi alterrita?

**LUCIA:** Quella fonte, ah! Mai senza temar non veggo. Ah tulo sai; un Ravenswood ardende Di geloso furor, l'amata donna Colà trafisse; e l' infelice cadde Nell' onda ed ivi rimanca sepolta. M'apparve l'ombra sua.

**ALISA:** Che dici?

**LUCIA:** Ascolta.

**LUCIA:** Regnava nel silenzio alta la notte bruna, colpia la fonte un pallido raggio di te tra Luna, quando un sommesso gemito fra l'aureudir si fè, ed ecco, ecco su quel margine l'ombra mostrarsi, l'ombra mostrarsi a me, ah! qual di chi parla muoversi il labbro suo vedea, e con la manoesanime chiamarmia separea; stette un momento immobile, poi ratta dile gnò e l'onda pria si limpida di sangue rosseggiò, si, pria si, limpida di sangue rosseggio, si, pria si, limpida, ah, di rosseggio. Ah, il pressagio orenda E questa cancellar, Dovrei dal petto Il fatale amato oggetto ma nol pos-

---

**HENRY AND CHORUS:** From my bosom all fear I banish, From my breast now mercy shall banish, For the wrongs this man has wrought me, Nothing but his blood can repay! Every pulse for revenge wildly bounding. Every nerve is strung to madness, And despair, with deadly fury, now to vengeance points the way, vengeance points the way. Nothing but blood my hate can allay, And despair with deadly fury unto vengeance points the way, Yes, points the way, Despair to vengeance points the way, Yes, despair points the way.

**NORMAN AND CHORUS:** He, your foe, can never escape you, Let that thought allay your rage. (Over your house dark clouds do lower On this inauspicious day.) (*Exeunt.*)

## SCENE IV

*A park. Enter LUCY AND ALICE.*

**LUCY:** Still, still he does not come!

**ALICE:** You dare much in venturing here;
Think, should your brother suspect, or discover, anything
Your doom would be dark.

**LUCY:** It is too true! Ah, Edgar does not know
What fearful perils, what dangers circle round me!

**ALICE:** Why did you turn toward the fountain
That glance of terror!

**LUCY:** Yonder fountain! ah! Alice, Whenever I behold it
Dark fears oppress me! A Ravenswood here
By jealousy inspired with mad fury.
His dear loved lady most foully murdered,
And she unhappy in those dark waters
Was cast, and there did find a sepulchre.
Her shade has once appeared to me.

**ALICE:** What are your saying?

**LUCY:** Dear Alice, ah, listen.

**LUCY:** Silence over all was reigning, Dark was the night and lowering, And over the fountain her pallid ray Yonder pale moon was pouring, Faintly a sharp but stifled sigh Fell on my startled ear, And straightway upon that same fountain's brink, The spectre did appear, spectre did appear, ah! Fast fixed it kept its bloodless lip, No further sound emitting, But slow on high its phantom hand, Threatening it did uprear, Stood for a moment immovable, Then vanished from my view, While that pure and limpid stream, had changed its hue to blood, While that pure limpid stream ah, had changed its hue.

so,
Egli è una luce e conforto al mio penar.

LUCIA: Quando rapita in estasi del più cocente ardore col favellar del core mi guira eterna fe gli affanni miei dimentico gioja di viene il pianto, parmi, che a lui d'accanto si schiuda il ciel per me si schiuda il ciel per me si schiuda il ciel per me a lui d'accanto si schiuda il ciel perme ah! si schiuda il ciel, il ciel per me, si, si, a lui d'accanto parche si schiuda il ciel per me.

ALISA: Egli s'avanza! La vicina soglia
Io cauta veglierò.

Oh, what horrid presage
Is this? I ought to banish
the fatal, Loved object, from my heart, but I cannot, No, I cannot; it is my life,
And comfort to my suffering.

LUCY: Then swift as thought up cleared the sky, Out shone the stars with brilliance, Soft sighted the breeze, and from on high The moon poured forth her light, All nature seemed in smiles to sleep, Unto my wandering sight, And heaven, in ten-fold splendor Enrobed then the waning night, Heaven robed then the waning night, ah! in tenfold splendor robed the night, Ah, yes, in splendor robed the night, Heaven in splendor robed the night.

ALICE: At length he comes! Concealed behind the foliage
I'll keep a careful watch.
(*Exit Alice.*)

## SCENA V

### EDGARDO E LUCIA.

EDGARDO: Lucia perdona
Se ad ora inusitata
Io vederti chiedea—
Ragion possente a ciò mi trasse.
Pria che in Ciel biancheggi
L'alba novella, delle patrie sponde
Luncicarò.

LUCIA: Che dici?

EDGARDO: Pe' Franchi lidi amici
Sciolgo le vele—ivi trattar m'è dato
Le sorti della Scozia.

LUCIA: E me nel pianto
Abbandoni cosi?

EDGARDO: Pria di lasciarti
Ashton mi vegga—stenderè placato
A lui la destra, e la tua destra, pegno
Fra noi di pace, chiederò.

LUCIA: Che ascolto?
Ah, no! Rimanga nel silenzio avvolte
Per or l'arcano affetto.

EDGARDO: Intendo. Di mia stirpe
Il reo persecutore
Ancor pago non è. Mi tolse il padre.
Il mio retaggio avito—nè basta?
Che brama ancor?
Quel cor feroce e rio?
La mia perdita intera? il sangue mio
Ei m'odia!

LUCIA: Ah, no!

EDGARDO: M'abborre!

LUCIA: Calma! Oh, Ciel, quell' ira estrema!

EDGARDO: Fiamma ardente in sen mi corre!
M'odi.

## SCENE V

### EDGAR AND LUCY

EDGAR: My Lucy, your pardon
That past the hour appointed
I've delayed our meeting.
Most powerful reasons detained me!
On the coming morn, love.
Before the break of dawn, I must depart my home and country.

LUCY: What are you saying?

EDGAR: To France I bend my steps, love!
Business of moment calls me early from you
Scotland needs my service!

LUCY: And unto misery
You abandon me!

EDGAR: Yet before I leave you
I'll seek your brother; to him in truth and friendship
This hand I'll tender, and as a pledge of peace
Between our houses I'll ask of him yours!

LUCY: What am I hearing?
Ah, no, I pray. In secrecy and silence
Still let our love be concealed!

EDGAR: I comprehend you. Your fell brother, My dark, relentless foe, Still yearns for blood, and will not forego vengeance. He killed my father,
He has taken away my heritage!
What more? That heart Ferocious, what would it? My entire utter ruin?
He'd take my life! Yes, he hates me!

LUCY: Ah, no!

EDGAR: Abhors me!

LUCY: Calm, oh, calm this fearful passion!

EDGAR: Deadly fury inflames my heart!
Hear me!

LUCIA: Edgardo!

EDGARDO: M'odi, e trema!
Sulla tomba che rinserra
Il tradito genitore,
Al tuo sangue eterna guerra
Io giurai nel mio furore!
Ma ti vidi, in cor mi nacque
Altro affetto, e l'ira tacque.
Pur quel voto non è infranto—
Io potrei compilrlo ancor!

LUCIA: Deh, ti placa! deh, ti frena!
Può tradirne un solo accento!
Non ti basti la mia pena!
Vuoi ch'io mora di spavento?
Ceda, ceda ogn' altro affetto,
Solo amor t'infiammi il petto!
Ah, il più nobile, il più santo
De tuoi voti è un puro amor!

EDGARDO: Qui, di sposa eterna fede
Qui mi giura, al Cielo innante!
Dio ci ascolta, Dio ci vede!
Tempio ed ara è un core amante.
Al tuo fato unisco il mio:
Son tuo sposo!

LUCIA: E tua son io!
A' miei voti amore invoco!
A' miei voti invoco il Ciel!
Ah soltanto il nostro foco
Spegnerà di morte il gel.

EDGARDO: Separarci omai conviene.

LUCIA: Oh, parola a me funesta!
Il mio cor con te ne viene!

EDGARDO: Il mio cor con te qui resta!

LUCIA: Ah, talor del tuo pensiero
Venga un goflio messaggia
E la vita fuggitiva
Di speranza nudrirò!

EDGARDO: Io di te memoria viva
Sempre, o cara, serberò!

LUCIA: Verrano là sull' aure i miei sospiri ardenti, udrai nel mar che mormora l'eco de' miei lamenti, pensando ch'io di gemiti mi pasco e di dolor, spargi un amara lagrima su' questo pegno allor, ah! su questo pegno allor, ah, sù questo pegno allor, ah! su quel pegno allor! si, su quel pegno allor, Edgardo. Il tuo scritto sempre viva la memoria in meterrà! Ah! verranno a te sull'aure i tuoi sospiri ardenti udro nel marche mormora l'eco de tuoi lamenti pensando che di gemiti mi pascoe di dolor. Spargi su questo pegno allor, ah! Su questo pegno allor. Ah! su questo pegno allor. Ah! questo pegno allor.

LUCY: My Edgar!

EDGAR: Hear me, and tremble!
By this lone tomb, over the cold grave Where my father's bones lie molding, I swore to wage eternal warfare with your kin, to the death.
Ah! when I saw you my heart relented Of my dark vow I half repented;
But my oath remains unbroken,
Still I've power to redeem my gage.

LUCY: Ah! pray calm yourself; ah, restrain yourself; Think what misery will soon enthrall me; I can scarce from fear sustain me;
Would you have me die with terror?
Yield yield to the dictates of affection. It is a nobler, purer passion,
Let that thought your wrath assuage.

EDGAR: Here, then! here in the eye of heaven Swear, your true faith is given to me, Him above, who sees and hears us,
Witness these mutual vows of love!
Your fate forever united with mine!
You are mine love!

LUCY: Yes, I am yours, love.
You who see us, You who hear us,
Witness these our vows of love!
Power eternal, oh, grant your blessing,
Look down kindly from above.

EDGAR: Now at length we must part, love!

LUCY: That word falls heavy on my heart, love,
this heart will bear with you.

EDGAR: Mine will stay forever with you!

LUCY: Ah! you will not fail to write me?
Each dear letter you send me,
Each fond word you indite me,
will cheer many a lonely hour.

EDGAR: A cherished memory of you,
Dearest, shall ever be treasured.

LUCY: My sighs shall be borne on the balmy breeze That wafts here, love; Each murmuring wave shall echo how I do mourn your absence, love! Ah! think of me when far away, with nothing to cheer my heart, I shall bedew each thought of you with many a bitter tear! Ah! with many a bitter tear! Ah! many a bitter. Ah! with many a bitter tear, Edgar. Ah! You will not fail to write me, many a lonely hour will cheer; Ah! my sighs shall be borne on the balmy breeze that wafts here, love; Each murmuring wave shall echo make how I your absence do mourn, love! Ah! think of me when far away, with nothing my heart to cheer; Ah! dear love! with many a bitter tear, ah! with many a bitter tear, ah, ah, many a bitter tear!

EDGARDO: Verrano a te sull' aure i miei sospiri ardenti; udrai nel mar che mormora l'eco de miei lamenti pensando ch'io di gemiti mi pasco e di dolor, spargi un amara lagrima su questo pegno allor, ah! su questo pegno allor! Ah! su questo pegno allor; ah, su quel pegno allor. Ah! sì! sì, sì, Lucia, sì, sì! ah! verrano a te sull' aure i miei sospiri ardenti, udrai nel marche mormora l'eco de miei lamenti! spargi un amara lagrima su questo pegno allor, ah! su questo pegno allor, ah! su questo pegno allor, ah! questo pegno allor.

*END OF THE FIRST ACT.*

# ■ ATTO II

## SCENA I

*Sala. ENRICO e NORMANDO.*

NORMANDO: Lucia fra poco a te verrà.

ENRICO: Tremante L'aspetto. A festeggiar le nozze illustri Già nel castello i nobili congiunti Di mia famiglia accolsi; in breve Arturo Qui volge; e s'ella pertinace osasse D'opporsi—

NORMANDO: Non temer; la lunga assenza Del tuo nemico—i fogli Da noi rapiti e la bugiarda nuova Ch'egli s'accese di altra fiamma— in core di Lucia spegneranno il cieco amore.

ENRICO: Ella s'avanza! Il simulato foglio Porgimi; ed esci sulla via che tragge Alla città regina Di Scozia; e qui fra plausi e liete grida Conduci Arturo. (*Parte Normando.*)

## SCENA II

*ENRICO e LUCIA*

ENRICO: Appressati, Lucia. Sperai più lieta in questo di vederti, In questo di, che d'imeneo le faci Si accendono per te. Mi guardi e taci?

LUCIA: Il pallor funesto orrendo che ricopre il volto mio ti rimprovero tacendo il mio strazio il mio dolore perdonare ti possa un

---

EDGAR: The balmy breeze that bears your sigh, will waft one back from me, love; The murmuring waves reechoing still I'm ever constant to you love, Ah! think of me when far away with nothing to cheer my heart, I shall, bedew each thought of you with many a bitter tear! Ah! with many a bitter tear, Ah! with many a bitter tear! Ah! many a bitter tear. Fear not! Have no fear, you shall hear! Ah! my sighs shall be borne on the balmy breeze that wafts here love; Each murmuring wave shall echo make how I your absence do mourn, love! I shall bedew each thought of you with many a bitter tear.

*END OF THE FIRST ACT.*

# ■ ACT II

## SCENE I

*An Apartment. HENRY and NORMAN.*

NORMAN: Your sister will shortly now be here.

HENRY: I tremble To meet her. The nuptial guests are fast assembling! Within the castle my noble friends and kinsmen Wait now to greet the bridegroom: for Arthur only We wait! Should she still pertinaciously persist In opposing—

NORMAN: Have no fear! She mourns his long absence, the letters We've intercepted, and the false news you'll tell her, Will quench all hope that may linger. Believing Edgar faithless, love will vanish, from her bosom.

HENRY: See, she approaches! You have that forged letter, Give it to me—Now hurry to the northern entrance, There keep watch, and wait The approach of Arthur, and with all speed, on his arrival Conduct him here! (*Exit Norman.*)

## SCENE II

*HENRY AND LUCY.*

HENRY: Draw nearer, my Lucy, On this fair morn accept a brother's greeting! May this glad day, sacred to love and Hymen, Prove auspicious to you. Do you hear me? You're silent!

LUCY: See these cheeks so pale and haggard, See these features so worn with sadness! Do they not betray too plainly all, my anguish, All my de-

---

Dio l'inumano tuo rigor, perdonarti possa un Dio, ah, l'i numano tuo rigor, l'inumano tuo rigor, il tuo rigor, il tuo rigor e il mio dolor.

ENRICO: A ragion mi fe' spietato, Quel che t'arse indegno affetto;— Ma si taccia del passato— Tuo fratello io sono ancor; Spenta è l'ira nel mio petto— Spegni tu l'insano amor. Nobil sposo—

LUCIA: Cessa! ah, cessa! Ad altr' uom giurai la fè.

ENRICO: Nol potevi.

LUCIA: Enrico!

ENRICO: Basti! Questo foglio appien ti dice, Qual crudel, qual empio amasti Leggi!

LUCIA: Il core mi balzò!

ENRICO: Tu vacilli!

LUCIA: Me infelice! (*Legge.*) Ahi la folgore piombò!

LUCIA: Soffriva nel pianto, languia nel dolore, la speme la vita riposi in un cor l'istante di morte e giunto per me quel core infedele ad altra ad altra si die!

ENRICO: Un folle t'acsese un perfido core tradisti il tuo sangue per vil sedetore ma degna del cielo ne avesti mercede quel core in fedele ad altra si die un folle t'acsese un perfido amore tradisti il tuo sangue per vil seduttore, ma degna del cielo ne avesti merce quel core infedele quel core infedele ad altra si diè, ad altra si diè, si, si, si diè, ad altra, ad altra ad altra si diè.

LUCIA: Ohime! l'istante tremendo e giunto per me si quel core infedele ad altra si die do, quel sore infedele ad altra si diè, quel core infedele quel core infedele ad altra si diè! ad altra si diè ad altra, ad altra, ad altra si diè de (*Gridi al di fuori.*)

LUCIA: Che fia?

ENRICO: Suonar di giubilio Odi la riva?

LUCIA: Ebbene?

ENRICO: Giunge il tuo sposo!

LUCIA: Un brivido Mi corse per le vene! Tremo!

---

spair, too? May you, not vainly, ask pardon from Heaven, for this your inhuman constraint, Pardon may you ask from Heaven for your inhuman, cruel constraint, This harsh, inhuman, cruel constraint, cruel constraint!

HENRY: Cease this wild recrimination, To both of us degrading, Of the past be silent! I, your brother will make no further complaint! My anger has flown! Banish your dejection, Buried be all that could taint your honor A noble husband—

LUCY: Cease to urge me! I have sworn to another true faith.

HENRY: To another!

LUCY: My brother!

HENRY: It is well! By this letter you may see How he keeps his faith with you. Read it! (*Hands her a letter.*)

LUCY: How beats my fluttering heart!

HENRY: You falter—

LUCY: Ah! great Heaven! (*Reads.*) Break, poor heart!

LUCY: My sufferings and sorrows I've borne without repining, I hoped with tomorrow some comfort might dawn! All's lost now, forsaken, deserted, forlorn, My last hope departed, my true love, my love turned to scorn.

HENRY: Your name you disgraced, your blood you debased, your love he disdains. Yourself he defames, The judgment of Heaven at length overtakes you, Your race's dark foeman treats you with scorn. Yes, yes, with scorn, he treats you, he treats you, he treats you with scorn!

LUCY: Ah me, my sufferings and sorrows I bore unrepining, I hoped that tomorrow some comfort might dawn All's lost now! forsaken, deserted, forlorn! My last hope departed, My love treated with scorn, Ah, my love turned to scorn! Deserted, forlorn, deserted, forsaken, deserted, forlorn. (*Noise heard without.*)

LUCY: What am I hearing?

HENRY: Those sounds of gladness Tell the arrival—

LUCY: Of whom?

HENRY: Your destined husband.

LUCY: Through every vein My blood seems to be congealing. I tremble!

ENRICO: A te appresta il talamo.

HENRY: The marriage rites await you now!

LUCIA: La tomba a me s'appresta!

LUCY: I would rather the dark grave be my refuge!

ENRICO: Ora fatale è questa!
Spento è Guglielmo ascendere
Vedremo il tron Maria.
Prostrata è nella polvere
La parte ch'io seguia;
Dal precipizio solo
Arturo può salvarmi sol egli.

HENRY: Oh, fatal hour of dark despair!
Hear me. The late rebellion
I was one who secretly abetted;
To Arthur, for my present safety
I'm alone indebted!
He from a foul, a traitor's doom,
Alone has power to save me.

LUCIA: Ed Io—

LUCY: And I then?

ENRICO: Salvarmi
Devi—

HENRY: You must
Wed him.

LUCIA: Enrico!

LUCY: My brother!

ENRICO: Vieni allo sposo.

HENRY: Come to the altar.

ENRICO: Ad altri giurai.

LUCY: I love another.

ENRICO: Devi salvarmi?

HENRY: Still do you falter?

LUCIA: Ma—

LUCY: But—

ENRICO: Il devi!

HENRY: To the altar!

LUCIA: Oh, Ciel!

LUCY: Oh, heaven!

ENRICO: Se tradirmi tu potrai,
La mia sorte è già compita
Tu m' involi onore e vita:
Tu la scure appresti a me!
Ne' tuoi sogni mi vedrai
Ombra irata e minacciosa.
Quella scure sanguinosa
Starà sempre innanzi a te.

HENRY: I'm your guardian, dare you to brave me?
I'm your brother—will you save me?
From your hands my sister,
Must I meet a traitor's doom?
See the axe, by one thread hanging;
Hark; the deep-toned deathbell clanging.
Has affection lost all power?
Will you consign me to the tomb?

LUCIA: Tu, che vedi il pianto mio,—
Tu, che leggi in questo core,—
Se respinto il mie dolore,
Come in terra. in Ciel non è!
Tu mi togli, eterno Iddio!
Questa vita disperata!
Io son tanta sventurata,
Che la morte è un ben per me!
(Partone.)

LUCY: I'm your sister, do you love me!
I am dying, will that move you!
From your hands my brother,
Must I meet now this dreadful doom!
Hopeless misery all surrounding,
Even while the marriage bell is sounding;
Fear and hate will be my dower;
Better had I wed the tomb.
(Exeunt.)

## SCENA III

*LUCIA & RAIMONDO.*

LUCIA: Ebben?

RAIMONDO: Di tua speranza
L'ultimo raggio tramontò.
Credei al tuo sospetto
Che il fratel chiudesse
Tutte le strade, onde sul Franco suolo,
All uom che amar giurasti
Non guingesser tue nuove;
Io stesso un foglio date vergato,
Per secura mano; recarglifeci
In vano! Tace mai sempre—
Quel silenzio assai d'infideltà ti parlà!

LUCIA: E me consigli?

RAIMONDO: Di piegarti al destino.

LUCIA: E il giuramento?

## SCENE III

*Corridor. LUCY and RAYMOND.*

LUCY: Your news?

RAYMOND: Hope has departed,
Even the last faint ray has fled!
Believing as you suspect,
That perchance your brother,
His ends to answer, your notes had intercepted,
And bared all correspondence
Between you and young Edgar,
I took your letter! I sent it to France
By secure conveyance. He did receive it
Five weeks since! Still is he silent!
It is too certain that he has proved unfaithful to you.

LUCY: What do you counsel?

RAYMOND: To submit to your destiny.

LUCY: The oath I pledged him?

RAIMONDO: Tu pur veneggi!
I nuziati voti
Che il ministro di Dio non bene,
Nè il ciel nè il mondo riconosce.

RAYMOND: You talk wildly—
The holy nuptial vow
Through the priest can alone be sworn, at the altar,
Nor heaven nor man holds anything else binding.

LUCIA: Ah! cede persuasa la mente,
Ma sordo alla ragion resisto il core.

LUCY: Ah, cease, pray; though my mind you're convinced,
Still deaf to reason's voice my heart resists!

RAIMONDO: Vincerlo è forza.

RAYMOND: Be firm and conquer!

LUCIA: Oh sventurato amore!

LUCY: What utter misery awaits me!

RAIMONDO: Ah, cedi, o più sciagure
Ti sovra stanti infe'ice,
Per te venere mie cure
Per l'estinta genitrice,
Il periglio d' un fratello
Deh ti muova e cangi il cor!
O la madre nell' avello
Fremerà per te d'orror.

RAYMOND: Ah, resign yourself to your destiny calmly.
Horrors greater far will else befall you;
Incline yourself to the voice of affection
From her grave your mother calls you.
Save your brother from this peril.
It is a parent that implores.
See the angry shade uprise before you.
Mark the blood-stained scaffold drenched with gore.

LUCIA: Taci—

LUCY: Cease—

RAIMONDO: Cedi—

RAYMOND: Save him!

LUCIA: Ah, vincerti.
Non son tano suatuarata.

LUCY: You have conquered.
I will act as you require.

RAIMONDO: Oh! qual giosa; in me tu dest!
Oh qual nube hai dissipata!
Al ben de' tuoi vittima
Offri, Lucia, te stessa,
E tanto sagrifizio
Scritto nel ceil sarà,
Se la pietà degli uomini
A te non fia concessa,
V' è un Dio, che tergere
Il pianto tuo saprà.

RAYMOND: O what rapture! Confide in me
Every cloud now disappears
This your heroic sacrifice,
Laid on the shrine of duty,
Shall be by holy angels
Recorded in heaven above.
Though man may not regard it,
Though earth may not reward it,
Your Maker who rules your destiny
marks this deed of love.

LUCIA: Guidami tu, tu reggime
Son fuori, di me stessa!

LUCY: Guide me, support me,
You have conquered, I confide in you!

## SCENA IV

*ENRICO, ARTURO, NORMANDO;
Cavalieri & Dame congiunti di
Ashton; Paggi, Armigeri; Abitanti
di Lammermoor, e Domestici.*

CHORUS: Per te d'immenso giubilo tuto s'avviva intorno, per te veggiam rinascera della speranza il giorno, qui l'amistà ti guida, qui ti conduce amore tutto ravviva intorno qui ti conduce amor, qual astro in notte infida qual riso nell dolor,—qual astro in notte infida qual riso nel dolor.

ARTURO: Per poco fra le tenebre
Sparsi la vostra stella,
Io la farò risorgere
Più fulgida e più bella,
La man mi porgi Enrico,
Ti stringi a questo cor,

## SCENE IV

*HENRY, ARTHUR, NORMAN;
Knights and Ladies related to Ashton; Pages, Squires; Inhabitants
of Lammermoor, and Domestics.*

CHORUS: Hope brightly beams before you now, Ah, day of joy and gladness. Heaven sheds its sunlight over you now, No more of grief or sadness. Dark though the clouds did gather round, Fierce the storm did lower, Each dreaded portent banishing, Love reasserts his power. Your star, but so late declining, Rises with tenfold glory, It is shining radiantly forth, In this thrice happy hour.

ARTHUR: My friend, I joy to meet you;
As brother here I greet you!
Ever may this, our union
In friendship's bonds combining,
In friendship's bonds entwining,

A te ne vengo amico, fratello, e defensor
Dov' è Lucia?

**ENRICO:** Qui guingere or la vedrem.
Se in lei soverchia è la mestizia,
Ma ravigliarti non dei
Dal duolo oppressa e vinta
Piange la madre estinta.

**ARTURO:** M'è noto. Orsolvo un dubbio
Famo suonò, ch' Edgardo
Sovr' essa temerario
Alzare osò lo sguardo.

**ENRICO:** E vero, quel folle ardia, ma—

**CORO:** S' avvanza a te Lucia!
(Entra Lucia.)

**ENRICO:** Piange la madre estinta.
Eco il tuo sposo. (Incauta!
Perdermi vuoi!)

**LUCIA:** Gran Dio!

**ARTURO:** Ti piaccia i voti accogliere
Del tenero amor mio!

**ENRICO:** Omai si compia il rito—
T'appressa!

**ARTURO:** Oh dolce invito!

**LUCIA:** (lo vado al sacrifizio!)

**RAIMONDO:** (Reggi, buon Dio, l'afflitta!)

**ENRICO:** Non esitar!

**LUCIA:** (Me misera!
La mia condanna ho scritta!)

**ENRICO:** (Respiro!)

**LUCIA:** (Io gelo ed ardo!
Io manco!)

**TUTTI:** Qual fragor!
Chi giunge?

## SCENA V

*EDGARDO, LUCIA, servi e detti.*

**EDGARDO:** Edgardo!

**LUCIA:** Edgardo!
Oh, fulmine!

**GLI ALTRI:** Oh, terror!

**EDGARDO:** Chi mi frena in tal momento, chi troncò dell'ire il corso? Il suo duolo il suo spavento son la prova, son la prova d'un rimorso! Ma qual rosa ina ridita, ella sta fra morte e vita! Io son vinto son commosso! T'amo ingrata, t'amo ingrata, t'amo ancor!

**ENRICO:** Chi mi frena il mio furore, e la manche al brando corso? Della misera in favore nel mio petto un grido corse! E mio sangue! L'ho

Prove prosperous to you;
This hand I give shall henceforth be your defender.
But where is Lucy?

**HENRY:** Shortly now will she be here.
If she in tears perchance appears;
I pray you pardon her demeanor;
Her mother's death she mourns,
By grief her heart is torn.

**ARTHUR:** It is well, One thing tell me.
Fame says that young Edgar
Some months since, with mad presumption's boldness,
Of you did ask her hand—

**HENRY:** It is true he had that boldness, but—

**CHORUS:** See, Lucy comes!
(*Enter Lucy.*)

**HENRY:** Still for our mother weeping?
There stands your husband—In grate!
(Would he be my ruin?)

**LUCY:** Great Heaven!

**ARTHUR:** Your lover kneels before you,
Lowly at your feet.

**HENRY:** Do you hear, girl? Approach,
And sign your dower. We wait thee.

**ARTHUR:** Oh, blissful hour!

**LUCY:** (I go to the sacrifice!)

**RAYMOND:** (Heaven shield her in this trying hour.)

**HENRY:** (You know my power.)—
Sign it!

**LUCY:** Ah, misery! (*She signs.*)
It is done! I have signed it.

**HENRY:** (I breathe again!)

**LUCY:** (My blood seems turned to ice.
All is over!)

**CHORUS:** What does this mean?
Who comes?

## SCENE V

*EDGAR and the above.*

**EDGAR:** It is Edgar!

**LUCY:** Edgar!
Oh, hide me, earth!

**CHORUS:** Fearful hour!

**EDGAR:** Instant vengeance, what restrains What stays my sword in scabbard? Is it affection that still remains And each angry thought, each angry thought enchains. Of your own blood you're betrayer! Now, between life and death she stands Ah! despair, my heart does wither, Yet, ungrateful one, I love you, yes, I love you still!

**HENRY:** Instant vengeance, what restrains What stays my sword in scabbard? Is it affection still remains And each angry, dark thought

tradita, ella sta fra morte e vita! Ah!
Che spegnere non posso i rimorsi
del mio core, del mio cor!

**LUCIA:** (Io sperai che e me la vita
Tronca avesse il mio spavento;
Ma la morte non m'aita—
Vivo ancor per mio tormento!
Da' miei lumi cadde il velo—
Mi tradi la terra e il Cielo!
Vorrei pianger, ma non posso;
Ah! mi manca il pianto ancor!)

**RAIMONDO:** (Qual terrible momento!
Più formar non so parole;
Densa nube di spavento
Par che copra i rai del sole.
Come rosa inaridita
Ella sta fra morte e vita!
Chi per lei non è commosso
Ha di tigre in petto il cor.)

**ENRICO, ARTURO, NORMANDO E CAVALIERI:** T' allontana! sciagurato,
O il tuo sangue fia versato.

**EDGARDO:** Morizò; ma insiem col mio
Altro sangue scorrerà.

**RAIMONDO:** Rispettate in me di Dio
La tremenda maestà!
In suo nome io vel comando,
Deponete l'ira e il brando.
Pace, pace;—egli abborrisce
L'omicida, e scritto sta—
Chi di ferro altrui ferisce,
Pur di ferro perirà.

**ENRICO:** Ravenswood in queste porte
Chi ti guida?

**EDGARDO:** La mia sorte!
Il mio dritto; si, Lucia
La sua fede a me giurò!

**RAIMONDO:** Questo amor per sempre obblia
Alla è d'altri.

**EDGARDO:** D'altri! ah, no!

**RAIMONDO:** Mira!

**EDGARDO:** Tremi, ti confindi!
Son tue ciffre? A me rispondi!
Son tue ciffre?

**LUCIA:** Si!

**EDGARDO:** Riprendi
Il tuo pegno, infido cor!
Il mio dammi.

**LUCIA:** Almen—

enchains. Of my own blood I'm betrayer! Now, between life and death she stands Ah! despair her heart does wither, And remorse, it fills my heart, it fills my heart.

**LUCY:** (I had hoped that death had found me,
And in his drear fetters bound me,
But he does not come to relive me!
Ah! of life will none bereave me?
Still in dark despair I languish,
For nothing to hope but ceaseless anguish;
Even tears mine eyes abandon,
My cup of woe to fill.)

**RAYMOND:** (Time, you have wrought your worst, terrible moment,
sense no longer has mastery over words;
Dense and impervious clouds of fear are seen,
As threatening even the brilliance of the sun,
Ah! like a rose that withers on the stem,
She now is hovering between death and life!
He who feels for he, no pity
Has the heart of a tiger.

**HENRY, ARTHUR, NORMAN, AND CHORUS:** You traitor, be gone!
Before our rage overwhelms us!

**EDGAR:** Dare advance one single step,
And other blood with mine shall flow!

**RAYMOND:** Stay, rash, impious men,
forego your sinful purposes
I stand here, a servant of heaven
In your Maker's name, I command.
Sheathe your weapons! Know that the murderer
He abhors! What does His work say?
"He that wields the sword in anger
By the sword shall be laid low,"

**HENRY:** Vile intruder, say what you see within these walls.

**EDGAR:** I came here
for my bride. Your sister
has sworn her faith to me.

**RAYMOND:** You must relinquish all hope of her.
She's another's!

**EDGAR:** Another's? no!

**RAYMOND:** Read!
(*to Lucy*).

**EDGAR:** You tremble? Are you confounded?
Did you write this? I wait for your answer!
Did you write this?

**LUCY:** Yes.

**EDGAR:** You behold
This token? Perfidious heart!
I return it.

**LUCY:** Ah, no—

EDGARDO: Lo rendi!
Hai tradito il Cielo e amor!
Maledetto sia l'istante
Che di te mi resi amante!
Stirpe iniqua, abbominata—
Io dovea da te fuggir!
Ah, di Dio la mano irata
Ti desperda!

TUTTI: Insano ardir!
Esci, fuggi il furor che m'accende,
Solo un punto i suoi colpi sospende,
Ma fra poco più atroce più fiero,
Sul tuo capo abborrito cadrà!

EDGARDO: Trucidatemi! e pronubo al rito
Sia lo scempio d'un core tradito!
Del mio sangue bagnata la soglia,
Dolce vista per l'empia sarà:
Calpestando l'e sangue mia spoglia
All'altare più lieta ne andrà.

LUCIA: Dio, lo salva! in si fiero momento
D'una misera ascolta l'accento.
E la prece d'immenso dolore
Che più in terra speranza non ha:
E l'estrema domanda del core,
Che sul labbro spirando mi sta!

RAIMONDO, ALISIA E DAME: Infelice, t'invola—t'affretta:
I tuoi giorni, il suo stato rispetta.
Vivi! e forse il tuo duolo fia spento
Tutto è lieve all'eterna pietà.
Quante volte ad un solo tormento
Mille gioje succeder non fa!

*FINE DELL'ATTO II.*

# ■ ATTO III

## SCENA I

*Sala terreno nella terre di Volfureng.*

EDGARDO: Orrida è questa notte
Come il destino mio! Si, tuona, o cielo—
Imperversate, o turbini—sconvolto
Sia l'ardin di natura, e pera il mondo—
Io non m'inganno! scalpitar d'appresse

EDGAR: Receive it—
You fallen traitress to heaven, to Love,
Accursed forever be the day on which I saw you.
Blotted from time be that dark hour when first I met you!
For your shameless, base desertion,
You shall ask pardon vainly from above.
May desolation grant your heart despair and anguish!

HENRY AND CHORUS: dare no further.
Be gone, before our anger overwhelms us.
Be gone, if you regard your life.
But a moment the blow is suspended;
Tempt us no longer, we bid you, beware!

EDGAR: Strike, the frail strings of life now dividing,
At her nuptials my pale corpse presiding.
Drain my heart's blood at they wedding banquet.
Strike! why do you pause? I'm ready; prepare.

LUCY: Heaven, in mercy, oh save him, protect him,
And through this fearful danger direct him!
By the woe thou hast now heaped upon me,
I do implore for him your kindly care.
Since you have doomed me to a life of misery,
Ah, refuse not my last, my dying prayer.

RAYMOND, ALICE AND LADIES:
Unhappy man, fly from here—let prudence haste you,
Your life, the claims of station, rank, respect.
Live! it may be your grief may find an end;
All woes must end by never-ending pity,
How often is it to a single torture
A thousand joys have in their turn succeeded!

*END OF ACT II.*

# ■ ACT III

## SCENE I

*A Room in the Tower of Wolf's Crag.*

EDGAR: Darkly the night is lowering,
Even as is my destiny! Yes! roll on, you thunders!
Flash, fierce forked lightning; convulsion,
Shake the vast womb of nature, the world overwhelming!
Ah! Is it deception? On the hard

Odo un destrier—s'arresta—
Chi mai della tempesta
Fra le minaccie e l'ire,
Chi puote a me venire?

## SCENA II

*Entra Enrico.*

ENRICO: Io.

EDGARDO: Quale ardire!—Ashton!

ENRICO: Si.

EDGARDO: Fra queste mura
Osi offrirti al mio cospetto?

ENRICO: Io vi sto per tua sciagura.
Non venisti nel mio tetto!

EDGARDO: Qui del padre ancor s'aggira
L'ombra inulta—e par che frema!
Morte ogn' aura a te qui spira!
Il terren per te qui trema!—
Nel varcar la soglia orrenda
Ben dovesti palpitar,
Come un uom che vivo scenda
La sua tomba ad albergar!

ENRICO: Fu condutta al sacra rito,
Quindi al talomo Lucia.

EDGARDO: (Ei più squarcia il cor ferito!
Oh tormento!—oh gelosia!)

ENRICO: Ascolta. Di letizia il mio soggiorno,
E di plausi rimbombava;
Ma più forte al cor d'intorno
La vendetta a me parlava!
Qui mi trassi—in mezzo ai venti
Le sua voce udia tuttor,
E il furor degli elementi
Rispondeva al mio furor.

EDGARDO: Da me che brami?

ENRICO: Ascoltami:
Onde punir l'offessa,
De' miei la spada vindice
Pende su te sospesa—
Onde punir l'offessa—
Ch'altri to spenga? Ah! mai—
Chi dee svenarti il sai!

EDGARDO: So che al paterno cenere
Giurai strapparti il core.

ENRICO: Tu!

EDGARDO: Quando?

ENRICO: Al primo sorgere del mattutino albore.

EDGARDO: Ove?

ENRICO: Fra I' urne gelide
De Ravenswood.

EDGARDO: Verrò.

earth beating
I hear a horse's hoof! It stops—
Who is it that through the tempest
With fierce and threatening gesture
Comes at this hour to meet me!

## SCENE II

*Enter Henry.*

HENRY: It is I.

EDGAR: Ha! what boldness! Ashton!

HENRY: Yes

EDGAR: Within these drear walls
You dare present yourself at this hour.

HENRY: Does my presence not content you?
I do but return your visit!

EDGAR: See my father's shade uprising,
For his wrongs revenge demanding!
Death is in the air you breath;
Even the earth shakes, trembles, where you're standing,
When you did cross the threshold
Did your heart not quake with fear,
As a living man descending
To your tomb with no help near?

HENRY: Even now the bridal chamber
Opens for the blooming bride!

EDGAR: Ah, infuriating this thought!
Oh, what torments! what torture!

HENRY: But listen though the sounds of mirth and gladness.
Echoed far and wide around me,
Stronger far than ties of pleasure
Are the bonds in which hate for you has bound me,
Friends, relations, guests forsaking,
Flew I straight to meet you here,
While the mad and furious tempest
Shouted vengeance in my ear.

EDGAR: What has brought you here?

HENRY: You now shall hear.
Think of the wrongs you have done me,
And dare not to falter or shun me;
Words were too poor to express them—
This arm alone can redress them!
I give you defiance to death—
Nothing else can wipe away the stain.

EDGAR: By my dead father's ashes,
Your heart's blood I will drain!

HENRY: You!

EDGAR: When shall we meet?

HENRY: At earliest dawning of the next approaching day.

EDGAR: Where?

HENRY: By the icy tombs
Of Ravenswood.

EDGAR: Agreed.

ENRICO: Ivi a restar preparati.

EDGARDO: Ivi t'ucciderò.

EDGARDO AND ENRICO: O sole più ratto a sorger t'appresta ti cinga di sangue ghirlanda funesta con quella rischiara, l'orribile gara d'un odio mortale d'un cieco furore, O sole più ratto risorgi è rischiara d'un odio mortale il cieco, il cieco furor.

## SCENA III

*Sala.*

CORO: D'immenzo giubilo
S'innalzi un grido
Corra di Scozia
Per ogni lido,
E avverta i perfidi
Nostri nemici,
Che più terribili,
Che più felici
Ne rende l'aura
D'alto favor;
Ch' a noi sorridono
Le stelle ancor.

## SCENA IV

*RAIMONDO, NORMANDO, e detti.*

RAIMONDO: Cessi, ah cessi quel contento!

CORO: Sei cosparso di pallore! Ciel, che rechi?

RAIMONDO: Un fiero evento!

CORO: Tu ne agghiacci di terrore!

RAIMONDO: Dalle stanze ove Lucia
Trassi già col suo consorte,
Un lamento, un grido uscia,
Come d'uom vicino a morte,
Corsi ratto in quelle mura:
Ahi! terribile sciagura!
Steso Arturo al suol giaceva
Muto, freddo, insanguinato;
E Lucia l'acciar stringeva—
Che fu già dei trucidato.
Ella in me le luci affisse:
"Il mio sposo ov' è?" mi disse;
E nel volto suo pallente
Un sorriso balenò.
Infelice! della mente
La virtude a lei mancò!

TUTTI: Oh! qual funesto avvenimento!
Tutti ne ingombra cupo spavento!
Notte, ricopri la ria sventura

HENRY: There you shall join your ancestors.

EDGAR: There too you shall fall.

EDGAR AND HENRY: Oh, haste, crimson morning, Bright sun of the morrow, Let red clouds give warning, Around you of sorrow. Like snails how you linger, slow moments delaying, That long the avenger from vengeance are staying, Oh haste, crimson morning, Bright sun of the morrow, Let the red clouds give the warning Of sorrow around.

## SCENE III

*Hall in Henry's Castle. Peasants and Domestics of the Castle.*

CHORUS: Ah, happy, happy day,
Swell high the choral lay
Through all Scotland,
To all her shores
Tell the wretches,
Our enemies,
That more terrible,
As more happy,
The presence renders us
Of our great joy.
Ah! even the stars themselves
Smile happily down on us.

## SCENE IV

*Raymond, Norman, and the above.*

RAYMOND: Cease, ah, cease these sounds of gladness!

CHORUS: You seem aghast with fear!
What has chanced?

RAYMOND: Horrible event!

CHORUS: You freeze our souls with terror.

RAYMOND: To their chamber the bride and bridegroom
Scarce a moment had departed,
When a shriek came, a cry of anguish!
As a man in death throes did languish.
Straight I forced the door; trembling entered;
terrible moment! sight of horror!
There poor Arthur, lay, upon the floor,
Pale and deathlike, besmeared with blood,
While Lucy, brandishing a sword,
Like some fell demon, stood threatening!
Then on me her eyes fast fixing,
"Where's the bridegroom?" she cried,
And a smile across her pallid face
With ghastly splendor shone.
Ah, unhappy maid! your reason
From you had forever flown!

CHORUS: Ah, dreadful moment, dire deed of horror;
Omen portentous, dark fears confound us.

Col tenebroso tuo denso vel!
Ah, quella destra di sangue impura
L'ira non chiami su noi del Ciel!

RAIMONDO: Eccolà!

## SCENA V

*LUCIA, ALISA, e detti.*

LUCIA: Il dolce suono
Mi colpi di sua voce. Ah! quella voce
M' è qui nel cor discesa!
Edgardo, io ti son resa—
Fuggita lo son da' tuoi nemici. Un gelo
Mi serpeggia nel sen—trema ogni fibbra
Vacilla il piè, presso la fonte meco
T'assidi alquanto. Ahimè! sorge il tremendo
Fantasma e ne separa!
Un serto io voglio. Un armonia celeste
Di, non ascolti? Ah! l'inno
Suona di nozze. Il rito
Per noi s'appressa! oh! me felice!
Oh! gioia che si sente e non si dice!
Ardon gl'incensi—splendono
Le sacre faci intorno!—
Ecco il ministro! Porgini
La destra—oh! lièto giorno!
Alfin son, tua, alfin sei mio,
A me ti dona un Dio
Ogni piacer più grato
Si ogni piacere mi fia conte diviso.
Del ciel demente un riso
La vitá a noi sarà.

RAIMONDO: S' avanza Enrico!

## SCENA VI

*ENRICO, e detti.*

ENRICO: Ditemi
Vera è l'atroce scena?

RAIMONDO: Vera, pur troppo!

ENRICO: Ah! perfida!
Ne avrai condegna pena—

ALISA, RAIMONDO E CORO: T'arresta oh, Ciel!

RAIMONDO: Non vedi
Lo stato suo?

LUCIA: Che chiedi?

ENRICO: O qual pallor!

LUCIA: Me misera!

Night, your dark mantle throw close around us;
Cover this deed with your densest veil.
Ah, let not the hand that this did compass
your wrath entail upon her kindred.

RAYMOND: Ah! she comes!

## SCENE V

*Lucy, Alice, and the above.*

LUCY: How sweetly, gently
Steals your voice on my ear. Ah, those dear accents
Once more, once more I hear.
My Edgar, at length I'm safe with you,
To you I've flown from all your enemies.
—What coldness
Shoots like ice through my veins!
Each fiber trembles;
My foot fails! Here, at the fountain.
Once more I'm at your side, love.
Oh, Heaven, do you see?
That dark, fearful phantom? Ah! it would part us!—
Hark, through the dark air heavenly harmony swells!
Say! do you hear it? Ah, it is the hymn
Of our nuptials! They wait us
At the altar; oh, I am happy
The joy that fills my bosom words cannot tell you.
They light the incense! See now
The sacred tapers brightly are burning;
The priest approaches. Place your hand
In mine now! oh, blissful moment,
At length you're mine, love, and I am yours;
What boundless rapture for me is now preparing!
Each pleasure doubly sharing.
Yes! doubly enjoying, if it is shared with you,
Thanks, bounteous Heaven!
You have given new life to me!

RAYMOND: Here comes her brother!

## SCENE VI

*Henry and the above.*

HENRY: Answer me.
Can this dark deed be real?

RAYMOND: But too surely.

HENRY: Abandoned one,
Your punishment condign shall be!

ALL: Stop yourself, oh, heaven!

RAYMOND: See you not
Her fearful state?

LUCY: What did you say?

HENRY: What death-like paleness!

LUCY: Ah, what misery!

# Act III, Scene VI

**RAIMONDO:** Ha la ragion smarrita!

**RAYMOND:** Her reason has for ever fled from her!

**ENRICO:** Gran Dio!—

**HENRY:** Great Heaven!—

**RAIMONDO:** Tremare, o barbaro! Tu dei per la sua vita.

**RAYMOND:** Tremble, heartless man, You should for her life.

**LUCIA:** Non mi guardar si fiero; Segnai quel foglio è vero; Nell' ira sua terribile Calpesta, oh Dio! l'anello— Mi maledice! Ah! vittima Fui d'un crudel fratello! Ma ognor t'amai—lo giuro. Chi mi nomasti—Arturo? Ah, non fuggir! perdone!

**LUCY:** Frown not so harshly on me, Although it is true, that I signed it; Ah, look not, love, so fearfully, Break not the ring I gave you; And do not curse me; I was the victim Of a cruel brother. I love only you, my Edgar! Whom did you name? was it Arthur? Ah! Do not leave me; have mercy, pray!

**LUCIA:** Spargi d'amaro pianto il mio terrestre velo mentre lassù nel cielo io preghero, preghero per te al giunge tuo soltanto fia bello il ciel per me, per me, al, si! ah, si! per me! fia bello il ciel, il ciel per me, ah, si! ah, si! per me, per me, si, per me, per me, per me.

**LUCY:** Shed one tear of sorrow Over my untimely grave, love: While there, above, in heaven I pray for you! yes, I'll pray for you! Even heaven, if you, love, are absent, will bring no joy to me! no joy, ah! no, even heaven will bring no joy to me! ah, no! even heaven, heaven will bring no joy to me.

**ENRICO:** (Giorni d'amaro pianto Serva il rimorso a me.) Si tragga altrove! Alisa, pietoso amico, Deh! voi la misera vegliate Io più me stesso in me non trovo!

**HENRY:** (Bitter remorse and misery Ever my lot will be.) With care remove her! Alice, kinsmen and friends, I pray you treat her with gentlest kindness; Remorse is from now on my earthly portion!

**RAIMONDO:** Delator! gioisci dell' opra tuo!

**RAYMOND:** Man of blood, in this your work now exult.

**NORMADO:** Che parli?

**NORMAN:** What do you mean?

**RAIMONDO:** Si, dell' incendio che divampa e strugge Questa casa infelice, Hai tu destata la primiera favilla.

**RAYMOND:** You brought the brand that this dire flame engendered. It was your fell hand that fired it! Each spark that kindled, you did fan to a blaze.

**NORMANDO:** Io non credei—

**NORMAN:** But I believed not—

**RAIMONDO:** Tu del versato sangue, impio! tu sei La rai cagion!—Quel sangue Al ciel t'accusa, e già la man suprema Segna la tua sentenza—or vanne, e trema. (Parte.)

**RAYMOND:** You are author of this crime. Traitor! Even now His blood cries for vengeance! At heaven's bar It accuses you and there the hand supreme signs your awful sentence! Depart from here and tremble. (*Exeunt.*)

## SCENA VII

*Parte esterna del Castello. Notte.*

**EDGARDO:** Tombe degli avi miei, l'ultimo avanzo D'una stirpe infelice, Deh! raccogliete voi! Cessò dell' ira il breve foco— Sul nemico acciaro Abbandonar mi vo'. Per me la vita E orrendo peso—l'universo intero E un deserto per me senza Lucia! Di faci tutta via Splende il castello! Ah! scarsa Fu la notte al tripudio! Ingrata donna!

## SCENE VII

*Exterior part of the Castle. Night.*

**EDGAR:** Tombs of my far-famed ancestors, open wide your portal, And the last fated scion Of your doomed race receive! My hate has vanished! Past is resentment. On his vengeful blade now How gladly would I fall. This life of misery. I cannot bear it! The vast universe Is but one desert, unless with her I share it! The sounds of mirth and feasting

Mentr' io mi struggo in disperato pianto, Tu ridi,—esulti accanto Al felice consorte! Tu delle gioje in seno, Io-della morte!

Echo around me. Ah, swiftly Flies the night mid their revelry. Ungrateful woman, While here I struggle, desperate in my anguish. With mockery you deride me! You most false, you most shameless! Your heart bounds with rapture, While death surrounds me.

**EDGARDO:** Fra poco a me ricovero darà negletto a vello, una pietosa lagrima non scenderà su quello, ah! fin degli estinti, ahi misero! manca il conforto a me. Tu pur, tu pur dimentica quel marmo dispreggiato: mai non passarvi o barbara, del tuo consorte a lato, ah! rispetta almen le ceneri di chi moria per te, rispetta almen leceneri di chi moria per te! Mai non passarvi, tu lo dimentica, rispetta al meno chi muore per te, mai non passarvi, tu lo dimentica rispetta almeno chi muore, chi muore per te, o barbara, io moro per te.

**EDGAR:** The wild flowers soon will shed their bloom Around my sad and lonely tomb, No kindly tear shall bless the spot Where blighted love's forgotten Ah! my weary wounded soul to heaven. Shall wing its rapid flight Oh! Lucy, should you with your spouse Roam near the tomb you've made, here, in silence pass, a word of love Would rouse my sleeping shade Oh! respect at least, you faithless girl, The dust of him who died for you. In silence pass then, a word of happy love Would rouse, would waken my sleeping shade. In silence pass then, Respect, respect at least, You faithless girl The dust of him, of him who died for you, who died for you.

## SCENA VIII

*Abitanti di Lammermoor dal Castello e detto.*

**CORO:** Oh meschina! oh, caso orrendo! Più sperar non giova omai. Questo di che sta sorgendo, Tramontar tu non vedrai!

**EDGARDO:** Guisto Cielo! ah, rispondete! Di, chi mai, di chi piangete?

**CORO:** Di Lucia!

**EDGARDO:** Lucia diceste?

**CORO:** Si; la misera sen muore. Fur le nozze a lei funeste di ragion la trasse amore s'avvicina all'ore estreme e te chiede per te geme. Questo di, questo sol chestà sorgendo tramontar, tramontar piu non vedra! di ragion le trasse amore, e te chiede per te geme.

**EDGARDO:** Ah Lucia! Lucia!

**CORO:** Rimbomba Già la squilla in suon di morte!

**EDGARDO:** Ahi! quel suono al cor mi piomba! E decisa la mia sorte: Rivederla ancor vogl' io; Rivederla, e poscia—

**CORO:** Oh Dio! Qual trasporto sconsigliato! Ah, desisti! ah, riedi in te!

## SCENE VIII

*Inhabitants of Lammermoor coming from the Castle, and Edgar.*

**CHORUS:** Poor forlorn one! oh, fate most fearful, Hope of life at length has vanished. Where on this dark night of sorrow Morning dawns she'll be no more.

**EDGAR:** Gracious heaven! say, what do you mean? What does this wailing cry mean?

**CHORUS:** It is for Lucy.

**EDGAR:** Did you say for Lucy?

**CHORUS:** She, alas, is surely dying. This unhappy, fatal marriage has quite deprived her of reason, All forlorn and brokenhearted, Life has near departed from her; Death his victim, his victim surely claims. Before the morning, the morning sun shall rise. Even while madness sense enthralls, Still on you for aid she calls.

**EDGAR:** Ah! Lucy, Lucy!

**CHORUS:** That sad And solemn bell her end does tell.

**EDGAR:** It rings both hers and my knell! Yes, my fate is now decided! In death we will not be divided. Soon I'll join you dearest Lucy!

**CHORUS:** Oh, heaven! Where are you going? O calm yourself, nothing can now the past recall.

## SCENA ULTIMA

*RAIMONDO, e detti.*

**RAIMONDO:** Ove corri, sventurato?
Ella in terra più non è.

**EDGARDO:** Lucia!

**RAIMONDO:** Sventurata.

**EDGARDO:** In terra più non è.
Ella dungue—

**RAIMONDO:** E in cielo.

**EDGARDO:** Tu che a Dio spiegasti l'ali, o bell' alma innamorata, ti rivolgi a me placata, teco ascendo teco ascendo il tuo fedel. Ah! se l'ira dei mortali fece a noi si cruda guerra, se divisi fummo in terra, ne congiunga il nume in ciel, o bell' alma innamorata, bell alma innamorata, ne congiunga il nume in ciel, o bell' alma innamorata bell' alma innamorata ne congiunga il nume in ciel.
Io ti seguo!

---

## SCENE THE LAST

*Raymond and the above.*

**RAYMOND:** Stay, rash man, what do you seek further?
She's forever lost to you.

**EDGAR:** My Lucy.

**RAYMOND:** All is over.

**EDGAR:** Forever lost to me!
She has departed—

**RAYMOND:** To heaven!

**EDGAR:** Though from earth you've flown before me, My adored, my only treasure, though from these fond arms they tore you, soon, soon, I'll follow you, I'll follow you above, Though the world frowned on our union, Though in this life they did part us, Yet on high in fond communion, shall our hearts be tuned to love. Though from these fond arms they tore you, from these fond arms they tore you soon I'll follow you above. Though from these fond arms they tore you,

---

**CORO:** Ah, che fai?

**EDGARDO:** Morir voglio.

**CORO:** Ritorna in te.
(*S' immerge il pugnale nel cuere.*)

**RAIMONDO E CORO:** Che facesti?

**EDGARDO:** A te vengo a bell' alma—
Ti rivolgi al tuo federl;
Ah, se l'ira demorteli
Fe cruda guerra—
Ne congiunga il nume in ciel.

**RAIMONDO:** Sciagurato, pensa al ciel!

**CORO:** Quale orror!
Ahi tremendo! ahi crudo fato!
Dio, perdona un tanto error!
(*Alzando le mani al cielo Edgardo spira.*)

*THE END.*

---

though from these arms they tore you, soon I'll follow, soon I'll follow you above.
Soon I'll join you.

**CHORUS:** Ah, what would you?

**EDGAR:** Die with her!

**CHORUS:** Forbear! or heaven forever is lost to you!
(*Edgar plunges his poignard in his breast.*)

**RAYMOND:** What has he done?

**EDGAR:** Die avenged then, O adored one:
Soon I'll follow you above—
Though in this world they did part us—
From these fond arms they did tear you,
Yet—we part not—above!

**RAYMOND:** Rash and impious, think of heaven!

**CHORUS:** Horror fills every breast, Horror dire. Ah, may kind heaven Grant him pardon from above.
(*Raising his hands to heaven, Edgar expires.*)

*THE END.*

# La Favorita (1840)

## The Favorite

MUSIC BY GAETANO DONIZETTI ■ LIBRETTO BY ALPHONSE ROYER, GUSTAVE VAËZ, AND AUGUSTIN EUGÈNE SCRIBE

This four-act grand opera, set to a libretto by Alphonse Royer, Gustave Vaëz and Augustin Eugène Scribe (based on Baculard d'Arnaud's play *Le Comte de Comminges*), was first performed at the Paris Opéra on December 2, 1840. The story takes place in Castille during the year 1340. Fernand, novice at the Monastery of St. James of Compostela, is disturbed by his love for a woman whom he has met. He confesses his feelings to Father Balthazar, his abbot, and chooses to give up life in the monastery. Blindfolded, he arrives on the island of St. León and is discovered by Inez. When Inez removes his blindfold, Fernand asks her if she knows the identity of the woman with whom he is in love, but she says nothing. This woman is Leonore of Gusman, mistress of King Alphonse of Castille, for whom the King has left the Queen. Fernand begs his mysterious lover to tell him who she is and to marry him, but she says this is impossible. She asks that they not meet again and gives him a letter which will greatly assist him in his new career in the army. Inez hurries in and announces that the King has arrived to pay a surprise visit. Fernand, still not realizing who his love is, decides that he must distinguish himself in the army so that he may win her over. The infidels are beaten in battle, and Fernand performs brilliantly—he saves the King's life and is to be honored for his bravery in a celebration at the Palace of the Alcazar. Leonore seeks her freedom from the King but is refused. During the festivities, the King intercepts a note from Fernand to Leonore. At this moment the Pope's messenger, Father Balthazar, bears a message to the King which criticizes his treatment of his wife. The Pope excommunicates the King. Fernand, unaware of the turn of events, comes to the King in triumph. The King asks Fernand how he would like to be rewarded for having saved his life and Fernand asks for Leonore's hand in marriage. She enters and is astonished to find that the King grants Fernand's request. Leonore, not wishing to deceive her future husband, asks Inez to tell Fernand the truth about her relationship with the King. Preparations are made for the wedding and the King confers many honors upon Fernand. Leonore believes that her beloved, who in fact still doesn't know the truth, accepts everything. When many of the courtiers refuse to shake Fernand's hand in congratulations for his marriage, Fernand becomes increasingly angry. Father Balthazar tells him why and Fernand believes that he has been deceived by Leonore and the King. He breaks his sword, tears off the decorations he has received and leaves with the abbot. Back at the monastery, Fernand is praying when an exhausted pilgrim arrives. It is Leonore, who has come to beg his pardon. He grants her forgiveness and she dies in his arms.

---

## ■ ATTO I

### SCENA I

(*Il teatro rappresenta l'estremità di una delle Galleri Interali che circondano il Convento di San Giacomo di Compostella. Dal lato diritto, fra le colonne della galleria, senopronsi gli alberi e le tombe del Chiostro. A sinistra si trova l'entrato della Cappella che rinserra le ceneri di San Giacomo. Il fondo del quadro è formato d'un muro di cinta, ove s'apre un cancello, I religiosi traversano la galleria per portarsi entro la Capella. Fernando, vestilo da Novizio, e Baldassre, il Superiore, compaiono gli ultimi.*)

**CORO DI RELIGIOSI:** O santo ricetto!
Securi al tuo tetto,
La nostra preghiera
Leviamo al Signor.
L'aiuto divino
Qui cerca, qui spera
Fedel pellegrino,

## ■ ACT I

### SCENE I

(*The stage represents the extremity of one of the galleries surrounding the Convent of St. James, of Compostella. On the right side, beyond the colonnade, are seen trees, and the tombs of the Cloister, on the left the entrance to the Chapel, which contains the relics of St. James. The background is formed by the outer wall, with a gate in the center. The Monks traverse the gallery on their way to the Chapel. Fernando, habited as a Novice, and Balthazzar, the Superior, follow.*)

**CHORUS OF MONKS, &c:** Sacred monastery!
May our prayer
From your sanctuary
Ascend to heaven!
In this holy house
With zeal inspired,
A faithful pilgrim

Con viva fervor. (*I Monaci entrano vella Cappella; Baldassare va per seguirli, ma scorgendo Fernando, che rimane immobile assorto ne' suoi pensieri, gli avvicina.*)

**BALDASSARE:** Né con essi pregar vuoi tu?

**FERNANDO:** Nol posso.

**BALDASSARE:** Compres' io dunque del tuo cor le pene?
Dio più non basta a te?

**FERNANDO:** Dicesti il vero! In quest' ora solenne
Che un voto eterno me all' altar congiunge
Mal mio grado uno sguardo ai ben terrestri
Getto d'amore e di dolor.

**BALDASSARE:** Prosegui.

**FERNANDO:** All' ara che del santo
Jacopo serra le reliquie estrem,
Agli angeli porgea prego fervente,
Una vergine, un angel di Dio
Presso all' ara pregava con me;
Una speme, un terrore, un disio
Scese all' alma e di gioia l' empie,
Ah! mio padre! com' essa era bella,

Proffers his vows. (*The Monks enter the Chapel. Balthazzar is about to follow, but perceiving Fernando wrapped in deep thought, he approaches him.*)

**BALTHAZZAR:** Do you not go to pray with them?

**FERNANDO:** I cannot.

**BALTHAZZAR:** Have I, then discovered the anguish of your heart? Does God no longer suffice?

**FERNANDO:** You have spoken truth. About to relinquish all my holy vows, despite myself, the world's bright joys excite my grief, regrets and love.

**BALTHAZZAR:** Proceed.

**FERNANDO:** At the holy altar of St. James, as my orisons I did offer to the radiant angels, one suddenly appeared to me: a virgin, an angel of God, by my side was praying at sight of whom I felt mixed joy and fear. Her beauty, holy father, has robbed my heart of peace; and

M' ha involato la pace del cor;
Volgo al nume la mente, ma quella
Allo sguardo presente m' é ognor!
L' onda santa le porsi, e mía mano
Di quell' angel la mano scontrò,
Questo chiostro, per impeto insa-
no,
Pari a tefra prigion mi sembrò.
A' suoi giuri quest' alma ribella
Un conforto ricerca al Signor.
E gemente l' imploro, ma quella
Allo sguardo presente m' è ognor!

**BALDASSARE:** E fia vero—son
desto o vaneggio?
Tu il sostegno, l' amor della fe,
Che me spento sull' inclito seggio
Dei sederti e succedere a me!

**FERNANDO:** Padre! Io l' amo!

**BALDASSARE:** Non sai tu che all'
augusta tiara
Dei regnanti lo sceltro piegò?
Che mia mano conglunge o separa?
Che l' Iberia a mia voce tremo

**FERNANDO:** Padre! Io l' amo!

**BALDASSARE:** Ma rispondi, chi è
dessa la bella
Che si facil trionfa di te?
La sua patria, i congiunti? favella;
Il suo nome, il suo rango qual' è?

**FERNANDO:** Io l' ignoro, ma l'
amo! (*Con passione.*)

**BALDASSARE:** Vanne dunque
frenetico, insano,
Lungi reca il profano tuo pie;
Ah! del nume la vindice mano
Non ricada tremenda su te!

**FERNANDO:** Cara luce, soave con-
forto,
Deh tu veglia propizia su me,
Tu mi salva, tu guidami al porto.

**BALDASSARE:** (*arresta con la
máno Fernando, già pronto a par-
tire, e gli dice con emozione*). La
perfidia, il tradimento,
Te, mio figlio, assalirà:
Fia tua vita un rio tormento,
Il dolor per te vivrà.
Forse, in grembo al flutto infido,
Un sospiro udrassi un dì;
Fia del naufrago che il lido
Va cercando che fuggi!

**FERNANDO:** (*Cadendo in ginocchio*). Io parto, O padre mio, mi benedici.

**BALDASSARE:** Vanne dunque,
frenetico, insano, ecc. (*Fernando
esce pel cancello in fondo, e da
lungi tende le braccia a Baldassare, che rivolge la faccia asciugandosi una lagrima, ed entra nella Cappella.*)

though to God I bend my knee, my
heart, of hope bereft, beats high alone for her. In offering holy water
to her, her angel hand encountered
mine; since when, these cloisters
seem a prison drear, which I would
flee. Faithless to my vows, my soul
rebels, though Heaven's aid I crave;
and while to God I bend my knee,
her image haunts my mind.

**BALTHAZZAR:** You! my son—my
only hope! The strength and honor
of our faith! Who, when the toils of
life have passed, will fill the place I
hold!

**FERNANDO:** Father! I love her.

**BALTHAZZAR:** Do you know that
to the august tiara even kingly
heads must bow? that I can join or
disunite? that Spain fear my voice?

**FERNANDO:** Father! I love her.

**BALTHAZZAR:** Say, who then is
she that has made this conquest?
her hand—her birth—her name—
her rank?

**FERNANDO:** (*passionately*). I
know not, but I love her.

**BALTHAZZAR:** Begone, insensate
youth! bear from here your profane
thoughts! may the avenging hand of
God not fall too heavy upon you!

**FERNANDO:** Light of my soul—
my heart's best joy, I live alone for
you. Propitiously watch over me,
and guide my erring steps.

**BALTHAZZAR:** (*takes Fernando
by the hand as he is about leaving,
and addresses him with much
emotion*). Treachery and perfidy,
my son, will mark your life's career.
Avoid the shoals where danger
lurks to embitter all your days.
Storm-tossed, perhaps you'll seek
again the happy port you leave.

**FERNANDO:** (*falling on his
knees*). I go, my father, bless me.

**BALTHAZZAR:** Begone! insensate
youth, etc., etc.
(*Fernando exit through the gate,
extending his arms imploringly to
Balthazzar, who turns away his
head, wiping away a tear, and enters the Chapel*).

## SCENA II

(*Il teatro rappresenta un luogo
delizioso sulla riva dell' isola di
Leon. Varie Giovinette sono rac-
colte sulla sponda del mare, ed
empiono canestri di fiori; alcune
schiave sospendono ai rami delle
ricche stoffe per rendere l' ombra
più spessa.*)

**INEZ, E LE GIOVANI SPAG-
NUOLE:**

**INEZ:** (*insieme al Coro*). Bei raggi
lucenti,
Bell' aure beate,
Il suolo smaltate
Di candidi fior,
Un genio divino
Ci veglia, ci guida,
Propizio ne affida,
D'un genio il favor,
Il lieto destino
Risponda il concento.
Ad esso l' accento Fia sacro del cor.

**INEZ:** Di gioie ridenti
Fragranza qui spira,
Ognor qui s' aggira,
La pace, l' amor.
Silenzio! è puro il mar,
L' aer sereno;
Il battello qui s' avanza
Lo dirige la speranza (*Tutte si ac-
costano alla riva e riguardano
lungi, poi ripigliano.*)
Dolce zeffiro, il seconda,
Lieve spira in sulla vela,
Finchè il tragga a questa sponda
L' amoroso suo distin:
Ed al giunger suo disvela,
Questo suolo a far più grato,
Il sospiro profumato
Degli arranci e gelsomin.

## SCENA III

*LE MEDESIME. FERNANDO*

(*che comparisce sur una barchetta circondato da alcune donzelle,
e avendo sugl' occhi un velo che
gli vien tolto*).

**FERNANDO:** (*a quella che lo aiu-
ta a scendere dalla barca.*) Mes-
saggera gentil, tacita ninfa,
Che ognor su queste sponde
Il mio venir proteggi e il mio ritor-
no,
A che non odo di tua voce il suono?
(*Le Donzelle volgono altrove la
faccia, e fan segno che non
possono rispondere.*)
Ma taciturna sempre!
(*Avvicinandosi ad Inez.*)
Ah! ti scongiuro!
La tua donna e la mia persiste an-
cora
Il suo rango a celarmi, il nome? Ah
parla!
Chi è dessa?

**INEZ:** (*sorridendo*). Vano è il dimandar.

## SCENE II

A beautiful view on the shores of
the island of St. Leon. Young girls
are grouped at the river side, filling baskets with flowers. Slaves
are busy in suspending from trees
rich bangings, to intercept the
sun's heat.

**INEZ AND SPANISH MAIDENS:**

**INEZ AND CHORUS:** The sun's
gold rays,
Mild zephyrs' breath,
This happy spot with perfumed
flowers bedeck;
Where nothing breathes but pleasure, peace and love.

**INEZ:** With laughing joy, with fra-
grant breath,
This spot is redolent.
Here peace and love dwell.
Silence! the sea is still, the air is
calm;
See, the barque advances, steered
by hope.
(*They all run to the river side, and
look out*).
Sweet zephyr, lightly swell the silk-
en sails
And calmly speed it on
To where true love dwells
The ripping waves with odors load,
As onwards speeds the barque;
With orange and with jessamine
Make grateful all the air.

## SCENE III

*THE SAME. FERNANDO*

(*appears in a boat, surrounded
by girls, a veil over his eyes, which
they remove.*)

**FERNANDO:** (*to the girl who assists him to descend from the
boat*). Gentle messenger, silent
nymph, who here each day protects
my arrival and departure, why hear
I not the sound of your voice? (*The
girls turn away, making signs
that they cannot answer*). What!
silent ever? (*Approaching Inez*). I
conjure you say, why your mistress,
and mine, still refuses to tell her
name and rank? Oh, speak! What are
they?

**INEZ:** (*smiling*). She alone must
tell.

FERNANDO: Tremendo dunque è l' arcan?

INEZ: Più assai che tu nol credi; Ella ver noi s' avanza, a lei lo chiedi.

## SCENA IV

*FERNANDO, LEONORA.*

LEONORA: Ah! mio bene, un dio t' invia. Vieni, ah! vien, ch' io viva in te: Tu sei gioia all' alma mia, Terra e ciel tu sei per me.

FERNANDO: Da' sacri altar lontano, Per te solcata ho l' onda.

LEONORA: Ma vegliai, e non invano, Quindi un pensier su te: E ver l' amica sponda Ei ti conduce a me.

FERNANDO: Felice io son!

LEONORA: Più misero Forse di te non v' è.

FERNANDO: Per pietade, a me disvela Qual periglio qui si cela: Del tuo cor è mio l' impero, Vo la morte ad incontrar.

LEONORA: Ah! che il fato è a me severo!

FERNANDO: Chi sei tu?

LEONORA: Nol dimandar.

FERNANDO: Tacerò–ma pria rispondi Se possente è in te l' amor. Tuo destin col mio confondi, Sposo tuo mi stringi al cor.

LEONORA: Il vorrei, ma nol poss' io.

FERNANDO: Che mai sento!–oh mio terror Un istante, oh crudo fato! Sventurato–appien mi fe'!

LEONORA: Ah! d' un Dio vendicator Il furor–piombò su me A te pensando ognor lo spirto amante, *(Mostrandogli poi una pergamena.)* Di queste cifre ti volea far dono, Ma dubbio il cor–

FERNANDO: Ebben?

LEONORA: Non hai tu detto Più fiate a me, Fernando, Che il solo onor t' alberga in petto?

FERNANDO: Il dissi.

LEONORA: Or certo l' avvenire io qui ti rendo, Ma giura–

FERNANDO: E che?

LEONORA: Fuggirmi.

FERNANDO: O ciel! che intendo? Fia vero? lasciarti! E tu il chiedi a me? Mia vita è l' amarti,

FERNANDO: The secret, then, is terrible?

INEZ: More so than you think. *(Inez and the girls exeunt.)*

## SCENE IV

*FERNANDO, LEONORA.*

LEONORA: Ah! my beloved Heaven has sent you! come, oh, come, I live for you alone—You brightest joy to my soul, to me you are both earth and heaven.

FERNANDO: For you alone have I abjured my vows—abandoned the Holy altar.

LEONORA: I have since watched over you—have thought of you, and you alone; and to this calm and friendly shore have guided secretly your steps.

FERNANDO: How blessed am I!

LEONORA: Perhaps not so; you may be wretched still.

FERNANDO: In pity's sake, at once confess what dangers we incur; if thus to me you yield your heart not death itself I fear.

LEONORA: Oh, cruel fate! sad destiny!

FERNANDO: Who are you?

LEONORA: Ask me not.

FERNANDO: I obey—one word only: if my ardent love meets a response then link your fate with mine; and, as my wife, rejoice my heart.

LEONORA: My heart consents, yet cannot.

FERNANDO: What do I hear? Be still, my heart, a moment yet—oh, cruel fate!

LEONORA: Ah! the wrath of an avenging God now falls upon me. *(Shows Fernando a parchment).* In you have centered all my thoughts, as this will prove—procured for you; but I have feared . . .

FERNANDO: Have feared?

LEOMORA: Have you not said, in confidence to me, Fernando, that honor was the goal of all your views?

FERNANDO: I have said so.

LEONORA: This, then, secures you a bright future, but it enjoins . . .

FERNANDO: Oh, speak!

LEONORA: That you shun me.

FERNANDO: Heavens! heard I aright? Impossible! shun you! you are all to me: my life—my love—my only hope! Cold shall be my

Spirare per te. Pria freddo il cor mio. Per morte sarà, Ma dirti l' addio Ah! mai non potrà Compiangermi ognora Il mondo dovrà, Non quei che t' adora Tacciar di viltà.

LEONORA: Deh, vanne! deh, parti, Deh fuggi da me: M' è gioia l' amarti, Delitto è per te. Ah! freddo il cor mio Per morte sarà, Ma dirti l' addio Dolente dovrà! Compiangerti ognora Il mondo potrà, Ma indarno s' implora Per me la pietà.

## SCENA V

*I MEDESIMI.*
*(Inez accorre tutta tremante.)*

INEZ: Ah! signora. Il Re!

LEONORA: Che sento! Giusti numi!

FERNANDO: *(sorpreso).* Il Re!

LEONORA: O spavento! *(Ad Inez.)* Io ti seguo. *(Rimettendo poi le carte a Fernando.)* Prendi e va.

LEONORA: Fuggi

FERNANDO: Ah! no.

LEONORA: Gran Dio, pietà!

FERNANDO: Fia vero? lasciarti! parti, ecc.

LEONORA: Deh! vanne, deh! parti, ecc. *(Leonora dà a Fernando un ultimo addio, poi esce precipitosamente.)*

## SCENA VI

*FERNANDO, INEZ*

FERNANDO: *(che ha trattenuto Inez disposta a seguire Leonora).* E l' uom che la desia, è il Re?

INEZ: Sì, è Alfonso: ma taci.

FERNANDO: È sciolto il vel, sua cuna, il rango L' avvicinano al soglio—ed io—chi sono? Sventurato ed oscuro e senza gloria!

INEZ: Prudenza! *(Gli fa segno di tacere, e fugge via.)*

heart—life's blood be stayed—but say farewell. Oh! never, never. Accursed on earth, where wend my steps? without you, love, I cease to live.

LEONORA: Depart! forget! you must not stay. My joy, my love, my heart's delight! Though cold in death my heart should be, we both must part, must bid farewell. With sighs and tears my heart bewails your absence. Kind. Heaven! pity him and me.

## SCENE V

*THE SAME.*
*(Inez enters with much trepidations.)*

INEZ: Ah! Signora. The King!

LEONORA: What is it? Oh, Heaven!

FERNANDO: *(surprised).* The King!

LEONORA: *(to Inez).* I follow you. *(Giving the parchment to Fernando).* Take this. Fly!

FERNANDO: Ah! no.

LEONORA: Great God, mercy!

FERNANDO: Impossible! Shun you etc., etc.

LEONORA: Depart! Forget, etc., etc. *(She bids Fernando a last farewell, and exit suddenly).*

## SCENE VI

*FERNANDO, INEZ.*

FERNANDO: *(who has withheld Inez about to follow Leonora).* He of whom you spoke is King?

INEZ: It is—Alphonso!

FERNANDO: I know all. Her rank—her birth, connects her with the throne, and I—what am I? An inglorious and obscure adventurer.

INEZ: Prudence! *(She makes signs to him to be silent, and exit.)*

## SCENA VII

**FERNANDO:** (*solo*). Io non meritava
Il suo amore, il suo cor!
(*Guarda le carte rimessegli da Leonora e manda un grido di gioia.*)
Gran Dio! Che degno
(*rango.*)
Io ne divenga or vuol! Sì—questo
Questo titol, e questo onor sublime!—
Io Capitan! - O donna, in un istante
Capitano e guerrier ti fai l'amante!
Sì, che un tuo solo accento
La voce egli è d'un Dio,
L'amor che in petto io sento
Accende il mio valor.
Ho dolce in cor la speme,
Se il tuo campion son io,
Che noi vivremo insieme
Beati nell'amor.
Addio terren diletto
Cui noto è il mio destin,
Tornare a te prometto
Cinto d'allori il crin.
Sì, che un tuo solo accento, ecc.

*FINE DELL'ATTO PRIMO.*

## ■ ATTO II

### SCENA I

(*Il Teatro rappresenta una Galleria aperta, attraverso la quale si scuoprono i Giardini e il Palazzo d'Alcazar.*)

*IL RE, DON GASPARE.*

**IL RE:** Giardini d'Alcazar, de' Mauri Regi
Delizie ascose! oh, quanto
Alla vostr'ombra riandar m'è grato
I sogni dell'amore
Onde s'inebria il cor!

**DON GASPARE:** Del vinto il tetto
S'aspetta al vincitor: per voi la Fede
Trionfa ed Ismael fugge paventa.

**IL RE:** Sì, di Marocco i Regi
E di Granata insiem, vider la luna
A Tarifa crollar.

**DON GASPARE:** Fu tua la gloria.

**IL RE:** Ah! non è ver : fu di Fernando, il prode
Nuovo guerrier, che un giorno sol fe' noto;
Che radunò l'armata,
Salvando il suo signor; ogg'io l'attendo
In Siviglia, e innanzi a tutti
Il suo valore d'onorar desio.

**DON GASPARE:** Del Pastor sommo or giunse
Un alto messagger.

## SCENE VII

**FERNANDO:** (*alone*). I do not merit either her heart or her love! (*Looks at the parchment Leonora gave him, and utters a cry of joy.*) Oh heavens! Her aspiration is, that I may prove worthy of it! Yes! this title, this rank, is indeed an unexpected honor. A captain!—it is joy indeed!—captain, warrior and lover! The accents of her tuneful voice breathe a god-like sound; and urged by deep-felt love, my courage shall astound. Hope still lingers in my heart that fate will yet relent, and, blessed in mutual love, we may end our days in joy. Farewell, beloved spot, for you my fate decides. To you I will return, my brows with laurel crowned.

*END OF ACT I.*

## ■ ACT II

### SCENE I

(*An open Gallery, through which are seen the Gardens and the Palace of Alcazar.*)

*THE KING, DON GASPAR.*

**THE KING:** Gardens of Alcazar—delight of Moorish kings, how much I prize your ancient sycamores, under whose shade I revel in dreams of love.

**DON GASPAR:** The palace of the conquered is now the conqueror's! The Faith, through you, has triumphed; and Ishmael wanders vanquished and forlorn.

**THE KING:** Yes; both the Kings of Morocco and Grenada, near Tarifa, have seen the crescent fall.

**DON GASPAR:** This glory, sire, is yours.

**THE KINGS** Not so. Fernando's arm the triumph claims!—the worthy warrior, till now unknown, who by his prowess my kingdom saved. This day, in Seville, I await his coming; and at my court let all due honor be shown unto him!

**DON GASPAR:** Some important message comes from the Holy Father.

---

**IL RE:** (*da sè, con impazienza*).
Ognor più grave
Omai divien suo scettro!
(*A un cenno del Re, Don Gaspare rispettosamente s'inchina, e parte.*)

## SCENA II

**IL RE:** (*solo, guardando dietro Don Gaspare che si allontana*).
Ma de' malvagi invan sul capo mio
Sventure impreca il rio livore; e a Roma
Congiunto io lo discerno!
Per te, mia vita, affronterei l'averno.
Vien, Leonora, a' piedi tuoi
Serto e soglio il cor ti dona;
Ah! se amare il Re tu puoi,
Mai del don si pentirà,
Che per soglio e per corona
Gli riman la tua beltà!
De' nemici tuoi lo sdegno
Disfidar saprò per te,
Se ti cessi e l' alma e il regno,
Io per gli altri ancor son Re.
De' miei dì compagna io voglio
Farti o bella innanzi al ciel,
Al mio fianco unita in soglio,
Al mio fianco nell' avel.
(*Andando verso Don Gaspare che appare in fondo, il Re gli dice.*)
Per la festa previeni
Tutta la corte.
(*Don Gaspare parte.*)

## SCENA III

*IL RE, LEONORA ED INEZ*
(*ch'entrano parlando a mezza voce*).

**LEONORA:** Ebben, così si narra?

**INEZ:** E il prode vincitor.

**LEONORA:** Egli, Fernando?
A lui la gloria, oh ciel! a me l'infamia!

**IL RE:** (*fa cenno ad Inez di ritirarsi, poi s'avvicina a Leonora*). Ah!
Leonora, il guardo sì mesto a che piegar?

**LEONORA:** Lieta mi credi
Se a te d'accanto io sono? Il cor non vedi?
Quando le soglie paterne varcai,
Debil fanciulla delusa nel cor,
Giunta qui teco divider sperai
Talamo offerto di sposa all'amor.

**IL RE:** Taci. (*Con tenerezza.*)

**LEONORA:** Sì, Alfonzo, traviata, avvilita,
M'hai tolto il padre, l' onore, la fe!
Fra l' ombre ascosa la bella e del Re,
Tacita e sola, dal mondo schernita,

---

**THE KING:** (*to himself, impatiently*). The sacred power exceeds its bounds!
(*At a sign from the King Don Gasper bows respectfully and exit*).

## SCENE II

(*The king alone, observing the departure of Don Gaspar*).

**THE KING:** Accursed courtiers! who, torn by envy, have formed a treacherous league with Rome. Against my love in secret they conspire; – for Leonora, alone, will I confront them. For her I'll quit my throne and kingdom! My heart is hers! My crown—nay; heaven—is nothing to me without her love! My foes I scorn for her bright eyes; nor see I aught on earth but she! To her my freedom I resign; and in her chains thy king and lover hold! With her my joy will know no end—this earth her charms a heaven will make! For her alone I wish to live. (*Re-enter Don Gaspar; the King advances towards him*). Let all the court prepare for the festival.
(*Don Gaspar exit*).

## SCENE III

*THE KING, LEONORA AND INEZ.* (*Leonora enters with Inez, conversing in a subdued tone*).

**LEONORA:** Is what I hear the truth?

**INEZ:** It is; he has achieved a glorious victory.

**LEONORA:** My Fernando! The glory his—the shame all mine.
(*The King signs Inez to retire and approaches Leonora*).

**THE KING:** Why sad, my Leonora? Some rankling care disturbs your calm.

**LEONORA:** You think it strange that I am joyless! The heart sees not! When I left my father's roof, fond hopes played round my youthful heart. I thought my fate had been happy; a husband's smiles I deemed were mine.

**THE KING:** (*tenderly*). No more.

**LEONORA:** Yes. Alphonso has betrayed, deceived me, my father, honor, love, and faith! These silent shades—these glittering domes, hide not contempt for the mistress of the king.

**IL RE:** In questo suolo, a lusingar tua cura
Regna il piacer, la via sparsa è di fior:
Se interno a te più bella appar natura,
Ahi! donde avvien che tanto è il tuo dolor?

**LEONORA:** In questo suol s'ammanta la sventura
Di gemme, d'oro e di leggiadri fior:
Ma vede il cielo la mortal mia cura,
Se ride il labbro, disperato è il cor.

**IL RE:** Ma di tue doglie la cagion primiera?

**LEONORA:** Ah! taci, indarno tu la chiedi a me.
Soffri che lungi da tua corte io pera?

**IL RE:** A ogni uom vo' noto l' amor mio per te.
Alfin vedrai se questo cor t'adora.

**LEONORA:** E vil Leonora, troppo grande è il Re.

**IL RE:** Ah! l' alto ardor che nutro in petto
In lei divien sterile affetto!
Non v'ha destin del suo miglior,
Pur grave, oh Dio! le pesa in cor!

**LEONORA:** Ah! l' alto ardor che nutro in petto
In lei divien soave affetto:
Ma splende invan, come fulgor,
Di tomba, oh Dio! nel muto orror!

**IL RE:** Poni tregua al dolor; siedi regina
Della festa che amore a te destina.

## SCENA IV

*IL RE, LEONORA, SIGNORI E DAME DELLA CORTE; PAGGI GUARDIE.*
*(I Signori e le Dame s' avanzano, ed inchinano al Re. Questo conduce Leonora per mano ai posti ove seggono per presiedere alla festa. I Signori si schierano ai lati. Al punto in cui la festa è per incominciare, Don Gaspare entra agitatissimo.)*

**DON GASPARE:** Ah, sire!

**IL RE:** Che mai fu!

**DON GASPARE:** *(a mezza voce).*
Tua fede intera
Al suddito fedele ognor negasti:
Ebben, lei che colmasti
Di fortuna e di gloria, il suo sovrano
In segreto tradia.

**IL RE:** Tu menti.

**DON GASPARE:** Un schiavo Ques-
to foglio recato avea per essa.
Ad Inez confidente. A quest'
Inez—*(Rimette una lettera nelle mani del Re)*
Il labbro mio non mente.

---

**THE KING:** Here pleasure reigns, and you alone its queen. Your steps are strewn with flowers—around, bright smiles appear to greet you; yet still dark grief corrodes your heart.

**LEONORA:** The palace walls resound with sighs, which gold and jewels fail to quell. And heaven knows my hapless state—a smiling face, but broken heart.

**THE KING:** From where comes the cause for so much grief?

**LEONORA:** Oh, do not ask that. These splendid scenes, in pity's sake oh, let me quit!

**THE KING:** My heart in love to no man yields. Its truth—its faith, I'll prove.

**LEONORA:** I dare not look so high.

**THE KING:** The ardor I in silence cherished meets no return—all fruitless seems—joyless—she whom my heart adores with anquish deep is torn.

**LEONORA:** The ardor I in silence cherished consumes my soul in hopeless joys, and ghastly burns, like a funeral lamp, within the deadly tomb.

**THE KING:** Oh do not speak this way. Be now the queen my love prepares for you.

## SCENE IV

*THE KING, LEONORA: LORDS AND LADIES OF THE COURT, PAGES AND GUARDS.*
*(The Lords and Ladies advance and salute the King. The King conducts Leonora to her seat by his side; the rest range themselves on both sides of the stage. As the fête is about to commence, Don Gaspar enters in agitation).*

**DON GASPAR:** Ah! sire!

**THE KING:** What means this?

**DON GASPAR:** You spurned the counsel a faithful subject dared to offer. She on whom you have conferred honor and glory has secretly betrayed her king.

**THE KING:** You lie!

**DON GASPER:** She gave this note to Inez, a slave, her confidante and friend. That Inez—*(Giving the letter to the King)* You'll find I have not lied.

---

**IL RE:** *(allontanando col gesto i cortigient).*
No, possibil non è!
*(Poi a Leonora ponendole sott' occhi la lettera.)*
Chi scriverti osa e parlarti d'amor?

**LEONORA:** *(avendo riconosciuto il carattere).* Un uomo che adoro.

**IL RE:** Oh! tradimento!—il nome?

**LEONORA:** Ah! pria la morte,
Che appagar tuo desire.

**IL RE:** Forse i tormenti l 'otterano.

**LEONORA:** Ah! sire!

## SCENA V

*I MEDESIMI, BALDASSARE*
*(seguito da un Monaco che porta una pergamena col sigillo papale.—All' arrivo di Baldassare si manifesta una grande agitazione fra gli assistenti).*

**IL RE:** Qual tumulto? Chi ardisce Inoltrar?

**BALDASSARE:** Io son quello, io son che l' ira
Or t'annunzio del ciel!

**IL RE:** Veglio! che parli?

**BALDASSARE:** Re di Castiglia, a te del Pastor sommo
Reco il voler di Dio.
Ove al dover t'opponi,
Il labbro mio pronunzia
L'anatema fatal che glì empi atterra.

**IL RE:** Ben so qual alto dessi
Rispetto al capo della Fe, ma obblio
Tu mai non prender che il tuo Re son io.

**BALDASSARE:** Si, per la scaltra e abbietta,
Che del tuo amor s' ammanta, a vil ripudio.
Dannar vuoi la regina

**IL RE:** E sacro è il mio voler! la fronte
Ornar della corona
D' altra donna mi piacque, e qual si fosse
Questa regal mia cura,
Giudice all'opra, il Re son io.

**BALDASSARE:** Sventura!
Ah! paventa il furor
D'un Dio vendicator;
Su' rei terribil scende
Se pace egli è al tapin.
Tu le procelle orrende
Affronti sconsigliato,
Ma già l'estremo fato
Minaccia il tuo destin.

---

**THE KING:** *(beckoning to courtiers to retire).* It cannot be! *(To Leonora, showing her the letter).* Who thus has dared to write to you, and speak of love?

**LEONORA:** *(aside, recognizing the handwriting).* One I love.

**THE KING:** Oh, treachery!—his name?

**LEONORA:** No, I'd rather die than ever divulge it.

**THE KING:** Torture may break your silence.

**LEONORA:** Ah! Sire!

## SCENE V

*THE SAME, BALTHAZZAR*
*(accompannied by a monk, with a parchment, to which is attached the papal seal. At the appearance of Balthazzar consternation prevails).*

**THE KING:** What means this tumult?

**BALTHAZZAR:** I am he who comes to proclaim to you the wrath of Heaven!

**THE KING:** What would you, Monk?

**INEZ:** King of Castile, I come to you with decrees from the papal throne, which if resisted, will carry with them the avenging anathema which seals your doom.

**THE KING:** I know my duty, and respect the Church; but you forget that I'm your king.

**BALTHAZZAR:** Enslaved by love, unholy and unchaste, you neglect your lawful queen repudiate.

**THE KING:** I will it so.

**ALL:** O Heaven!

**THE KING:** My will is sacred, and on her brow I'll place my crown. Alone I reign, nor master know. My words are law—my wish supreme! And I alone will judge myself.

**BALTHAZZAR:** Rash man! Avert Heaven's wrath, dare not its fury; it punishes sinners and pardons the righteous, brave not its rage; which even now impends. With timely repentence, you yet may be saved.

LEONORA: Io gelo di terror,
E sovra il mesto cor
L'ira terribil scende
Del crudo mio destin.
Fra le procelle orrende
E vedo estremo fato
Sorger dappresso alfin.

IL RE: Agli atti ed al furor,
Che gli arde in mezzo al cor,
Fiero il rimorso scende
Entro il mio petto alfin.
Ma le procelle orrende
Non mi vedran cangiato:
Tu trema sconsigliato
Sul nero tuo destin.

DON GASPARE E IL CORO: Io gelo di terror,
E sovra il mesto cor
L'ira terribil scende
Del barbaro destin.

BALDASSARE: Voi tutti che m'udite,
L'adultera fuggite;
Questa malnata femmina
Ha maledetta il ciel!

IL RE: Ah! Leonora!

TUTTI: Oh Dio!

LEONORA: Ch'io mora!

BALDASSARE: Ah! fuggite!

CORO: Ho agli occhi un vel.

IL RE: (con furore). E con qual dritto?

BALDASSARE: In nome Del gran gerarca, maledetti entrambi Sian, se doman gli stolti Non fian per sempre separati e sciolti.

IL RE: Ah! che diss'egli? Quel labbro infiammato
Di rovesciare il mio soglio ha tentato!
In petto m'arde tremendo disdegno
Pur la vendetta non scende del Re.
Ah! pria ch'io ceda, perisca il mio regno,
Lo scettro, il brando s'infranga con me.

LEONORA: Ah! che diss'egli? quel labbro infiammato
Me dalla terra, dal cielo ha scacciato:
Muta quest'alma non nutre un disegno,
Me la vendetta reclama del Re!
Amor, vergogna m'invade e disdegno;
Morte deh! scendi propizia su me.

DON GASPARE E CORO: Ah! che diss'egli, quel labbro infiammato
Face di guerra qui in mezzo ha gittato!
In petto gli arde tremendo disdegno,
Pur la vendetta non scende del Re!
Sia quest'infame bandita dal regno,
Sia maledetto chi asilo le diè!

BALDASSARE: (prendendo dalle mani del Monaco la pergamena spiegando agli occhi degli assistenti, tutti cadono genuflessi). Lo

---

LEONORA: I tremble with fear. My heart's pulse is stilled. This fearful anger by me is brought down. O my cruel fate! I sink with terror. Why was I born for such affliction?

THE KING: This act of frenzy afflicts my heart, and remorse at length will enter it. The dire dismay which seizes all, makes me tremble at the stern decree.

DON GASPAR AND CHORUS: We tremble with fear. Our hearts' pulse is stilled—how cruel is fate—we sink with horror.

BALTHAZZAR: All present hear. Shun the adultress Avoid her! Accursed of God is she!

THE KING: My Leonora!

ALL: Great God!

LEONORA: I die!

BALTHAZZAR: Her presence shun!

CHORUS: Let us go.

THE KING: By what right?

BALTHAZZAR: In the name of Heaven and the Holy Father, I pronounce anathema on all, if by to-morrow's dawn she still is here!

THE KING: His words inflame. His baneful hate with scorn I dare defy nor shall my vengeance sleep while here I reign a King No; rather than yield I'll throw my sceptre and crown to the winds.

LEONORA: His words inflame. His holy lips bar heaven from me! My secret soul has no design to keep a monarch's heart. The love he feels, I disdain. Oh! open, earth to me!

DON GASPAR, INEZ AND CHORUS: His words inflame! His holy lips shut heaven from us if we dare brave the decree our Holy Father issues. Let her be driven from here, or malediction dread!

BALTHAZZAR: (takes the parchment from the Monk, opens it, and shows it). Behold our Holy Father's bull! (All fall on their

---

stemma è questo del Pastor supremo.
Dio di vendetta decreto ha scagliato,
Di Gezzabelle rinnovisi il fato;
Quest'impia donna, a infame disegno,
Indarno spera vendetta dal Re.
Tutti fuggite, e del cielo lo sdegno.
Tutti invocate sovr'essa con me.

GLI ALTRI: Ah! che diss'egli? ecc., ecc.
(Leonora fugge nell'estrema confusione, nascondendo tra le mani la fronte.—Quadro.)

FINE DELL'ATTO SECONDO.

## ■ ATTO III

### SCENA I

*Una Sala nel Palazzo d'Alcazar.*

FERNANDO: (solo). A lei son presso alfin: partiva ignoto
E riedo vincitor! Mentre in sua corte
M'appella il Re, d'amor più che d'orgoglio
Mi freme in petto il cor! Colei, che tanto
Adoro, qui soggiorna;
E a conoscerla alfin l'alma ritorna.
(Vedendo avvicinarsi il Re si ritira modestamente.) Il Re!

### SCENA II

(Fernando in disparte; il Re che entra pensieroso senza vederlo; Don Gaspare, che segue il Re.)

DON GASPARE: Qual sarà di quell' empio il fato?

IL RE: (senza ascoltarlo parla tra sè).
D'un Monaco alle fole
Ceder dunque dev'io?

DON GASPARE: Ma il Re giustizia
A sè ricusa?

IL RE: Leonora inoltre: Inez complice sua, prigion rattieni.
(Don Gaspare s'inchina ed esce. Il Re scorgendo Fernando.)
Sei tu, mio nome tutelar, ti deve
La sua salvezza il Re.

FERNANDO: L'ambita gloria
Mi fe' contento appien.

IL RE: De'tuoi sudori,
Io stesso il vo' la ricompensa or chiedi.
All' accento del Re, t'affida e credi.

---

knees.) And mark! The clemency of heaven is withdrawn, as this decree will show, unless, indeed, the Jezebel be driven hence. The impious wretch abandon—fly; her base designs are now well known; yes, shun her—flee—nor o'er your heads draw down the Almighty's wrath.

CHORUS: His words inflame, etc., etc.
(Leonora exit, overpowered with emotion, concealing her face in her hands. Tableau.)

END OF ACT II.

## ■ ACT III

### SCENE I

*A saloon in the Palace of Alcazar.*

FERNANDO: , (alone). Near her once more. Unknown to fame I left, but now returned renowed. Summoned to court by royal command, my heart beats more with love than pride. The idol of my soul dwells here, I know, and soon shall see— know whom I love. (He perceives the king and retires modestly to back of stage.) It is the king!

### SCENE II

*The king enters in deep thought, not perceiving Fernando, followed by Don Gaspar.*

DON GASPAR: His fate have you decided?

THE KING: (not listening to Don Gaspar, and aside). To the menaces of a monk I then have yielded.

DON GASPAR: But will the king do justice to himself?

THE KING: Bring Lenora here— detain her accomplice Inez as prisioner.
(Don Gaspar bows and exit.)

THE KING (perceiving Fernando). Ah it is you, my guardian genius, to you the king owed his safety.

FERNANDO: The glory I have acquired is ample recompense, And I am well repaid with honor.

THE KING: Your valor claim some recompense. Ask, and by my kingly faith I promise all you ask.

FERNANDO: Sire, soldato misero,
Per nobil dama amor m' accende il petto,
E i mei trionfi io deggio,
La mia gloria al suo amor, questa ti chieggio.

IL RE:
Sia tua, la noma.
Ah, si, costei s' appella.
(*Vedendo venir Leonora.*)
Vedila. la più bella!

IL RE: (*stupefatto*). Leonora!

LEONORA: (*O ciel! l' amante!
Rea comparrgli innante!*)

IL RE: (*freddamente a Leonora*).
Ei del suo cor la brama,
Ch' ei ti' ama—or mi svelo!

LEONORA: (*da sè*). Quel sguardo m' agghiaccia!

IL RE: (*c.s.*). Potria piombar su te,
Poi che il tacer t' alletta,
La collera del Re.
Coll' alta sua vendetta!
(*S' arresta e poi ripiglia più fredaamente.*) Fernando, a te la mano desia di sposo offrir.
Il sovrano a lui ti dona.

LEONORA E FERNANDO: O cielo.

LEONORA: Oh che di' tu?

IL RE: Doman tu dei partir.
(*Volgendosi a Leonora con un po' di malcontento e tristezza.*)
A tanto amor, Leonora, il tuo risponda;
Quand' ei felice non vivrà che in te,
Dolce la speme del suo cor seconda,
Ch' ei mai non debba maledir tua fe.

LEONORA E FERNANDO: Se inganno o sogno è questo, a me s' asconda
Per sempre il ver che rischiarar mi de'.

IL RE: Entro un' ora il sacro rito fia compito

FERNANDO: O mio signor! A' tuoi piè col sangue mio
Or vogl' io donarti il cor.

LEONORA: Ed il giuro!

IL RE: Ei fia serbato: (*Piano a Leonora.*)
Se ingannato io fu' da te,
Vendicarsi appien sa il Re.
(*Il Re esce conducendo seco Fernando.*)

---

FERNANDO: Sire, a noble lady claims my love, though but a humble soldier; to her I owe my fame and glory, and her hand I ask from you.

THE KING: It is yours, Her name?

FERNANDO: The fairest of your court. (*Perceiving Leonora who enters.*) Behold her charms!

THE KING: (*stupified*). Leonora! O Heaven! my love!

LEONORA: Oh Heaven—my lover! Thus guilty to appear before him.

THE KING: (*coldly to Leonora*). I have learned just now of the love he bears

LEONORA: (*aside*). His looks freeze me with terror.

THE KING: Your silence, in another king, had drawn dark vengeance down. (*He stops suddenly, and resumes, with coldness.*) Fernando asks your hand in marriage.

FERNANDO: What do you say?

THE KING: And I, your king, bestow it.

LEONORA AND FERNANDO: Just heaven!

THE KING: Tomorrow you depart. (*Addressing Leonora with bitterness and sadness.*) Responsive beats your heart to his; his sole joy to live in you—second, then, his love with mutual warmth.

LEONORA AND FERNANDO: It is some delusion, sure–a joyous dream!
A vision rife with happiness.

THE KING: Within an hour the church's rites shall bind you in firm union.

FERNANDO: O noble sire! at your feet I fall, and vow eternal love and gratitude.

LEONORA: I vow the same!

KING: (*aside to Leonora*). And you will prove faithful? If I have been deceived in you, the king knows how to be avenged. (*Exuent the King and Fernando.*)

---

## SCENA III

(*Leonora, sola, cade sopra un divano*).

LEONORA: (*sola, cade sopra un divano*).
Fia dunque vero? O ceil! desso! Fernando!
Lo sposo di Leonora!
Tutto mel dice, e dubbia l' alma è ancora
All' inattesa gioia! O Dio! sposarlo!
Oh mia vergogna estrema! In dote al prode
Recare il disonor? no, mai! dovesse
Esecrarmi, fuggir: saprà in brev' ora
Chi sia la donna che cotanto adora!
O mio Fernando, della terra il trono
A possederti, avria donato il cor,
Ma puro l' amor mio come il perdono,
Dannato ahi lassa! e a disperato orror!
Il ver fia noto, e in tuo dispregio estremo
La pena aurommi che maggior si de'?
Se il giusto tuo disdegno allor fia scemo.
Piombi, gran Dio, la folgor tua su me.
Su, crudeli, e chi v' arresta!
Scritto è in cielo il mio dolor!
Su, venite, ell' è una festa,
Sparsa l' ara sia di fior!
Già la tomba a me s' appresta
E coperta in negro vel.
Sia la trista fidanzata
Che, rigetta, disperata.
Non avrà perdono in ciel!

## SCENA IV

LEONORA, INEZ.

LEONORA: Inez?

INEZ: Fia ver? Fernando a te consorte?

LEONORA: A me? che parli! la crudel fortuna
Tanta gioia al mio cor, no, non serbava.
Va di Fernando in traccia, e a lui disvela
Ch' io fu' del Re l' amante. Ah! s' egli m' abbandona,
Nè un lamento darò, ma, se a Dio pari
Generosa perdona,
Postrata ognor servirlo,
Amarlo, benedirlo
Fia poco ancor; per lui son presta a morte.
Così gli parla; almen ch' ei sappia il vero,
E per me primo il sappia.
(*Leonora parte.*)

INEZ: Il zelo mio risponda: Io corro
Ad obbedirti. (*S'incammina.*)

---

## SCENE III

(*Leonora, alone, seating herself on a couch.*)

LEONORA: Is this then true? O Heaven? Can it be, Leonora, wife of Fernando! yet all attests that it is so, although my heart still doubts such bliss is real. His wife–no, no–so dark a deed shall never be mine. Dishonor is my portion? Never! Though he spurn me from him, I will avow the truth–declare what I am. Fernando! the earth's best gifts were nothing compared to the possession of your heart; but though my love be pure as prayer, to drear despair it is doomed. I'll tell you attests that it is so, although my heart still all, even should contempt follow my avowal. If Heaven's justice be thus appeased. I'll die content, with joy quit life. Come on, then, hard of heart, my chastisement is written on high. Come on! to you it is festive sport! With flowers bedeck the altar, but let a tomb prepared be; cover with a somber veil the mourning bride, who accursed–repulsed, has lost all hope of heaven!

## SCENE IV

LEONORA AND INEZ.

LEONORA: Inez!

INEZ: O lady, they say you are the affianced bride of Fernando.

LEONORA: Fernando's bride? Oh! no! For so much joy by heaven I am not reserved. Go, seek him quick–the fact disclose that I am mistress to the king. If then he hates, no sigh shall escape my bursting heart. But if perchance his love still lives, to him I'll kneel, and worship, as unto Heaven. I'd die, For him! Go, tell him all. He soon will learn the dreadful truth, and best it is he know it first from me. (*Exit.*)

INEZ: Your orders quick shall be obeyed; with zeal I go to do them. (*She is going.*)

## SCENA V

*INEZ; DON GASPARE*
*(che entra per la dritta con la Pri*
*ma Cameriera).*

**DON GASPARE:** *(ad Inez).* Arresta. D' Alfonso ordin sovrano
T' impon che tosto a me prigion ti
rendi. *(Poi accennando la Camer*
*iera.)*
Dessa tu dei seguir.

**INEZ:** *(turbata).* Dio ci defendi!
*(Don Gaspare conduce Inez verso*
*la Prima Cameriera, che la mena*
*seco.)*

## SCENA VI

*DON GASPARE, TUTTA LA*
*CORTE, poi IL RE E FERNANDO.*

**CORO:** Già nell' augusta cella
Di cui la volta splende,
Voce soave appella
Gli sposi al sacro altar.
Regni in què petti eterno
L'amor che sì li accende
Ed il favor superno
Di gioie spanda un mar.

**FERNANDO:** *(entrando col Re).*
Ah! che da tanta gioia
Inebriato è il cor! Sogno avverato,
Insperato favor! Poss'io del pari
Ir dei più grandi al fianco.

**IL RE:** A ognun fia noto
Quant' io t' onori: O tu che mi salvasti,
Conte, e Marchese di Montreal t'
eleggo.
*(Fernando fa un gesto di sorpre*
*sa.)*
Quest' ordin t' abbi ancora.
*(Staccandosi una collana che gli*
*scendeva sul petto, e mettendola*
*al collo di Fernando, che pone un*
*ginocchio a terra.)*

**DON GASPARE:** *(a voce bassa ai*
*Signori che lo circondano.)* Ebben
che parvi?

**I SIGNORI:** Re son generosi!

**DON GASPARE:** Il prezzo è questo:
Dell' onta e dell' infamia.

**I SIGNORI:** È dunque vero l' imen?

**DON GASPARE:** Il Re gli unisce.
Insiem si concinaro, e il patto indegno
Del pontefice dee frenar lo sdegno.

**I SIGNORI:** Ma vien Leonora!

**DON GASPARE:** Oh! la novella illustre!

## SCENA VII

*I MEDESIMI (Leonora entra palli*
*da, vestita di bianco, e circondata*
*da alcune Dame. Vedendola il Re*
*esce con dolore.)*

## SCENE V

*INEZ; DON GASPAR (who enters*
*with the first Lady in waiting).*

**DON GASPAR:** *(stopping Inez).*
Stay! by order of the king I arrest
you; *(pointing to the lady in wait*
*ing)* you will accompany her from
here.

**INEZ:** *(with emotion).* May heaven
protect me!
*(Don Gaspar leads Inez to the*
*lady, who takes her away with*
*her.)*

## SCENE VI

*DON GASPAR, ALL THE COURT*
*IERS, THE KING AND FERNANDO.*

**CHORUS:** Already in the chapel,
under its splendid dome, the holy
voice calls bride and bridegroom.
May joy ever reign over faithful
love, and happy day be theirs for
age.

**FERNANDO:** *(who has entered*
*with the King).* My heart overflows
with joy! My dream proves true and
I am blessed! I now may consort
with Spain's best blood.

**THE KING:** That my esteem be
known to, you, my savior—the victor of the Moors–Count Zamora,
Marquis of Montreal, I you create.
*(Fernando expresses surprise.)*
This order, too, I now confer.
*(Fernando kneels, and the King*
*invests him with the order.)*

**DON GASPAR:** *(to the Lords who*
*are about him).* My lords, what
think you?

**A LORD:** The king is generous.

**DON GASPAR:** Thus honor is paid
with shame and infamy.

**A LORD:** And is this marriage true?

**DON GASPAR:** The king unites
them. It is all arranged. This shameful pact is made to stay the thunder
of the Church.

**A LORD:** Leonora comes.

**DON GASPAR:** The new-made
Marchioness.

## SCENE VII

*THE SAME.*
*(Leonora enters, pale, attired in*
*white, accompanied by some la*
*dies. As she enters, the King exit*
*mournfully.)*

**LEONORA:** *(da sè).* Io mi sorreggo
appena!— *(Accorgendosi che Fer*
*nando la guarda con amore.)*
Oh ciel! gli sguardi
Senza rancor mi volge! il mio messaggio
Inez recava, ei mi perdona: oh
sorte!

**FERNANDO:** *(avvicinandosela).*
L' ara è presta, o gentil—

**LEONORA:** Gran Dio!

**FERNANDO:** Tu tremi?

**LEONORA:** Ah! sì, di gioia!

**DON GASPARE:** *(ai Signori).* Oh
infame!

**FERNANDO:** Meco vieni,
E d' uno sposo al fianco ti sostieni.
*(Fernando esce conducendo Leo*
*nora per mano. Le Dame e una*
*parte dei Signori li seguono.)*

## SCENA VIII

*DON GASPARE E UNA PARTE DEI*
*SIGNORI.*

**DON GASPARE:** Oh viltade! obbrobrio insano!

**CORO:** Questo è troppo in mia fe!

**DON GASPARE:** Di consorte offrir
la mano—

**CORO:** Alla bella del Re!

**DON GASPARE:** Mortal di sangue
abbietto!—

**CORO:** Senza fama ed onor!

**DON GASPARE:** Marchese il Re l'
ha detto—

**CORO:** E sarà Prence ancor.

**DON GASPARE:** D' Alcantara l'
onore a lui fu dato—
E dei tesori—

**CORO:** Un rango ed un portar.

**TUTTI:** Di sue virtudi e del suo cor
bennato
Pagar fu dritto il vago avventurier.
*(Ritronano i Signori usciti dal*
*corteggio; gli altri vanno ad in*
*contrarli, e pare domandono rag*
*guagli della cerimonia. Il. matri*
*monito è fatto. Tutti manifestano*
*la loro indignazione.)*
Si tenti almen, se il nostro spregio
ei sfida,
Che al vile orgoglio mai la sorte arrida:
Che alcun di noi non cerchi il suo
favor,
Ch' egli abbia sol compagno il disonor!

## SCENA IX

*FERNANDO E I MEDESIMI.*

**LEONORA:** I scarce can stand! To
what, just heaven, am I still reserved! He knows now all. From
Inez he has learnt it. My courage
fails.
*(She perceives Fernando, who*
*contemplates her with joyful emo*
*tion.)*

**FERNANDO:** *(advancing).* How
rich in charms!

**LEONORA:** Oh! heaven!

**FERNANDO:** You dissemble.

**LEONORA:** With joy and love.

**DON GASPAR:** *(to the Lords).* The
shameless wretch!

**FERNANDO:** Come love, a husband greets you now.
*(Exit Fernando, leading Leonora*
*by the hand, followed by the La*
*dies, and part of the Lords.)*

## SCENE VIII

*DON GASPAR AND THE LORDS.*

**DON GASPAR:** What deceit, unheard-of shame!

**CHORUS:** It is beyond belief!

**DON GASPAR:** A mistress thus to
wed.

**CHORUS:** The mistress of the king!

**DON GASPAR:** By birth, of common blood!

**CHORUS:** With nor name nor honor!

**DON GASPAR:** A marquis is he
now.

**CHORUS:** And will be a prince ere
long.

**DON GASPAR:** The order, too of
Alcantara, with gifts of price.

**CHORUS:** With rank and power.
With his virtues and his goodness
he has recompensed an adventurer.
*(The lords who left return, and*
*are questioned relative to the*
*marriage ceremony, which has*
*been performed. All manifest*
*their indignation.)* Since thus he
braves our deep contempt, his
pride shall have a fall. Let all refuse
his proffered hand; and alone with
his dishonor leave him.

## SCENE IX

*THE SAME. FERNANDO.*

FERNANDO: (*nella massima gioia*). Per me, del ciel propizio Si dispiega il favor—ah! la mia gioia Dividete voi pur; meco esultate Di si lieto destin: ella è pur mia Questa donna adorata: avvi ad un core Ben più grande mel dite—

DON GASPARE E I SIGNORI: (*freddamente*). Avvi—l' onore!

FERNANDO: L' onor! sua nobil fiamma A me fu sacra ognora, e dalla culla Io la toglieva in dote, e tutti i beni, Che posseder m' è data, D' essa son fumo ai pari.

DON GASPARE E CORO: Un ve n' ha ch' è per te pensier più caro.

FERNANDO: Che diceste? Dell' ingiuria Vo' ragion—no, m' ingannai— Deh, parlate, io ve ne supplico, Qua le destre, amici—

TUTTI: (*ritirando le mani*). Ah! mai. E questo nome augusto In avvenir, Marchese, Più non s' udrà per noi.

FERNANDO: (*prorompendo*). Gli atti perversi Fian lavati col sangue.

TUTTI: Ebben si versi.

FERNANDO: Andiam. (*Tutti s' incamminano.*)

## SCENA X

I MEDESIMI, BALDASSARE.

BALDASSARE: Dove correte? Di quel cieco furo gl' impeti stolti Sospendete, o Cristiani.

FERNANDO: (*accorrendo a lui*). O Baldassare!

BALDASSARE: Figlio! (*Serrandolo tra le sue braccia.*)

DON GASPARE: (*ironico*). Lo sposo di Leonora!

BALDASSARE: (*sciogliendosi dalle braccia di Fernando e rispingendolo*). O Dio!

FERNANDO: Ma che mai fu?

BALDASSARE: Deh taci! Tu sei disonorato!

FERNANDO: O! come! oh! quando Il mio nome macchiai?

TUTTI: La destra or dando alla bella del Re!

FERNANDO: (*annientado*). Alla bella del Re! (*Poi con gran forza.*) Che!—Lenora!—l'inferno arde sul capo mio!

BALDASSARE: Tu l' lignoravi?

FERNANDO: (*con furore crescente*). Alla bella del Re!

BALDASSARE: Figlio!

---

FERNANDO: (*with much joy*). Heaven smiles upon me! my lords, partake my joy; be witness of my happiness. She is mine—she whom I loved. No greater boon in heaven's gift.

DON GASPAR AND LORDS: (*coolly*). Yes, honor.

FERNANDO: Honor to me was ever sacred. I drank it at my mother's breast; not all the gifts on earth or heaven are half so dear to me.

DON GASPAR AND LORDS: There's one appears of higher price.

FERNANDO: What say you? This insult shall not pass! I am deceived—it cannot be; your hands, my friends.

ALL: (*withdrawing their hands*). That sacred name in future, my lord, do not apply to us.

FERNANDO: Blood alone can wipe out this outrage.

ALL: It shall be so.

FERNANDO: Then follow! (*They are about to follow.*)

## SCENE X

THE SAME, BALTHAZZAR.

BALTHAZZAR: Where do you go all? With passion blind, you hasten on to acts unworthy Christians.

FERNANDO: (*running to him*). Balthazzar here!

BALTHAZZAR: (*embracing him*). My son!

DON GASPAR: (*ironically*). Leonora's husband!

BALTHAZZAR: (*disengages himself from Fernando, and rudely repulses him*). My God!

FERNANDO: What is my crime?

BALTHAZZAR: You are dishonored.

FERNANDO: Dishonored?—how and when? My name is unsullied.

ALL: By wedding the king's mistress.

FERNANDO: (*confounded*). The king's mistress! (*Passionately.*) What! Leonora!—hell's flames do sear my brain.

BALTHAZZAR: Did you not know?

FERNANDO: (*with increased rage*). The king's mistress!

BALTHAZZAR: My son!

---

FERNANDO: Il lor sangue! È a me devuto.

BALDASSARE: (*guardando fuori di scena*). Arrestati; alcun giunge.

FERNANDO: Io qui li attendo.

BALDASSARE: Fuggi.

FERNANDO: Ah no—vendetta Adesso io vo!

BALDASSARE: Fernando, figlio mio!

FERNANDO: Padre, mi lascia, ora in me parla Iddio.

CORO: Qual furore in quell' aspetto! Il Re!

## SCENA XI

I MEDESIMI, IL RE (*che tiene Leonora per mano*).

FERNANDO: (*andando gli incontro*). Sire, io ti deggio— Mia fortuna, mia vita. Di Conte il nome, ogni splendor novello, Dovizie, dignitá—beni supremi— Che l' uom desia, ma—tu volesti— O Dio! Darli al prezzo crudel dell' onor mio?

IL RE: Oh ciel! di quell' alma Il puro candor, Perduto ha la calma Si cangia in furor. L' oltraggio che scende Sul capo d' un Re, Immobil mi rende, Tremante mi fe'.

LEONORA: Se il ver di quell' alma Turbava il candor. Perchè nella calma Serrommi al suo cor? Ah! l' ire che intende Rivolger sul re, Crudeli tremende Ricadon su me.

FERNANDO: Un giuro dell' alma M' ha spento il candor, A rendermi in calma, Ritorna l'onor. Le pene che intende Rivolger su me, Ricadan tremende Sul capo del Re.

BALDASSARE: Oh ciel! di quell' alma Il puro candor. Perduto ha la calma, Si cangia in furor. L' oltraggio che scende Sul capo del Re, Immobil lo rende Tremante lo fe'!

DON GASPARE E TULTI GLI ALTRI: L' oltraggio che scende Sul capo d' un Re, Immobil mi rende, Tremante mi fe'.

IL RE: Or su, Fernando, ascoltami.

FERNANDO: Il tutto a me svelato.

---

FERNANDO: Their blood shall pay the outrage.

BALTHAZZAR: (*looking off*). Be calm—some one advances.

FERNANDO: Now, sweet revenge.

BALTHAZZAR: Fly.

FERNANDO: Oh! no, revenge and instantly.

BALTHAZZAR: Fernando, my son.

FERNANDO: Leave me, my father. 'Tis well they come!

CHORUS: What anger in his looks! The King.

## SCENE XI

THE SAME, THE KING (*leading on Leonora*).

FERNANDO: (*advancing to the King*). Sire, I owe you all – my fortune and my life—my noble titles, and my renown – wealth and dignity—supremest gifts that man can desire. But I have purchased them at the cruel cost of honor.

THE KING: The candor of his soul breaks forth in rage and indignation. This outrage, I own, sheds its shame upon me, and I feel all his pangs and despair.

LEONORA: If the candor of his soul is disturbed, why do not his pangs afflict my heart? The anger that now is reserved for the king should fall with force upon me.

FERNANDO: The vow that disturbs my soul's candor would be naught were my honor unsullied; the outrage intended to fall on me shall fall on the head of the king.

BALTHAZZAR: The candor of his soul breaks forth in rage and indignation. It would be nothing were his honor unsullied. The outrage intended to fall upon him shall fall on the head of the king.

DON GASPAR AND CHORUS: The outrage, etc., etc.

THE KING: A word, Fernando.

FERNANDO: I know all.

LEONORA: (*Ei non sapea mio fato!*)

FERNANDO: Manto d'infamia a tessermi,
Me sol sceglieva il Re.

IL RE (*sdegnato*). Marchese!—

FERNANDO: Io tal non sono.
Ogni pregiato dono
Saprà calcar mio pie.
Signori, a onor tornatemi;
Bersaglio della sorte,
In vado incontro a morte,
E il solo nome ognor
Avrò del genitor.

LEONORA: (*nel maggior smarrimento*). Inez, rispondi, ov' è? (*Piano a Don Gaspare.*)

DON GASPARE: (*piano a Leonora*). Inez, racchiusa in carcere—

LEONORA: (*annientata*). Or tutto è noto a me.

FERNANDO: (*distaccandosi dal collo l'ordine ricevuto dal Re*).
Quest' ordin venerato,
Prezzo d' infamia, io rendo.
(*squainando la spada.*)
Il brando profanato,
De' tuoi nemici al ciglio
Tanto finor tremendo,
Lo spezzo e sal perchè?
Sol perchè tu sei Re.

IL RE: Troppo, ah! troppo, in questo giorno.
Cadde in me d' oltraggio e scorno:
Trema, ingrato, i miei dolori
Tu raddoppi e il mio furor!
La vendetta che tu implori,
Nel rimorso è del mio cor.

LEONORA: Grazia, o Sire, in questo giorno!
Su noi cadde infausto scorno.
(*A Fernando.*)
Nobil alma, i tuoi furori
Sono strali pel mio cor.
La vendetta che tu implori,
Ben l' avrai ma m' odi ancor.
Maledetta è l' ora e il giorno
Che in me cadde un tanto scorno;
Che compenso a' miei sudori
Mi gittasti infamia ed or:
Serba, serba i tuoi tesori,
Lascia solo a me l' onor.

BALDASSARE: Re, sul capo in questo giorno
Ti ricadde e danno e scornio;
Del tuo manto agli splendori
Pur commisto è il disonor!
Vieni, o figlio, a' tuoi dolori
Calma implora dal Signor!

DON GASPARE E CORO: Su noi cadde in questo giorno
Il trimorso e insiem lo scorno!
Lo spregiammo, e di a' alti onori
Degno è assai quel nobil cor.
Vanne, o prode, e a' tuoi dolori
Calma implora dal Signor!
(*Movimento generale. Fernando esce seguito da Baldassare, i Sig-*

LEONORA: (*aside*). He did not know my cruel fate.

FERNANDO: By you I was chosen as a cloak for all your infamy.

THE KING: (*with anger*). Marquis!

FERNANDO: I disown that title, and all your gifts alike despise. My lords, recall your contempt. The sport of fate I go, and with me carry the unstained honor of my ancestors.

LEONORA: (*aside to Don Gaspar, wildly*). Answer me, where is Inez?

DON GASPAR: (*aside to Leonora*). She is a prisoner.

LEONORA: (*overshadowed*). I see all now!

FERNANDO: (*taking off the order he received from the king*). This order, the price of shame, I return. (*He draws his sword.*) This degraded blade, once the terror of Spain's worst foes, I break. My reason?—because you art king. Accursed be the day and hour when so much shame fell on me which you did deem with gold to recompense. Keep wealth and power; to me be left my only treasure, honor.

THE KING: You say too much, that I enshared thee to scorn and shame. Tremble, ingrate lest my ire should overlook your pangs of heart – lest my vengeance should displace the remorse I feel for your wrongs.

LEONORA: Mercy, O King! on us has fallen scorn and shame. (*To Fernando*) Oh! noble soul! your just despair lies heavy at my heart. The vengeance which you seek to wreak, oh! wreak on me alone.

BALTHAZZAR: King! on you, this day, be all the shame and scorn! The splendor of your robes will not conceal your dishonor. Come my son, your grief assuage in prayer to God most high.

DON GASPAR AND CHORUS: This day on us falls shame and scorn, together with remorse! We despised him but his noble heart is worthy of the highest honor. Go, then, oh! valiant one, and implore the Lord to calm thy griefs.
(*General movement. Fernando and Balthazzar exeunt. The Lords*

nori rispettosamente aprono le loro file per lasciarlo passare e s'inchinano innanci a lui.*)

*FIN DELL' ATTO TERZO.*

# ■ ATTO IV

(*Il teatro rappresenta il Chiostro del Convento di S. Giacomo. A dritto si trova il portico della Chiesa, in faccia una gran Croce sopra uno zocculo di marmo. Qua e la delle tombe e delle croci di legno. Il di nascente rischiora solamente la parte scoperta del Chiostro; i primi piani sono ancora attenebrati per l' ombre gettate dai muri della Chicsa.*)

## SCENA I

*RELIGIOSI, BALDASSARE.*

(*Alcuni Religiosi sono prostrati a pie della Croce: altri da lungi scavasse le loro tombe, e ad intervalli ripetono:*)

CORO: Scaviano l'asilo ove il dolore ha tregua.
(*Un religioso introduce de' Pellegrini, che si dirigono verso la Chiesa, c s' arrestano innanzi al portico ove comparisce Baldassare.*)

BALDASSARE E CORO: Splendon più belle—in ciel le stelle
De' penitenti il puro cor:
Lungi del mondo dalle procelle,
Al nume ascenda con vivo ardor.
(*I Religiosi si allontanano attraverso le arcute del chiostro: i Pellegrini entrano nella Cappella. Un solo Religioso è rimasto in piedi, immobile, col volto nascosto tra le mani: Fernando.*)

## SCENA II

*FERNANDO E BALDASSARE.*

BALDASSARE: O fratel mio, fra poco
Un giuramento eterno
Alla terra t'invola e ti congiunge
Eternamente al cielo.

FERNANDO: Allor che la bufera
Del mondo io scelsi, il porto
Abondonando, ben dicesti, "O figlio,
Tu riederai!" mi vedi!
Torno a cercar la pace
E l' obblio che qui dà la morte.

BALDASSARE: È vero. Su, coraggio, Fernando,
Se Dio t' appella, a lui pensar sol dei.
Giurato appena il santo voto, è pos-

respectfully making a passage for them, and saluting them as they pass.*)

*END OF THE THIRD ACT.*

# ■ ACT IV

(*The Cloisters of the Convent of St. James. On the right, the portico of the Church, opposite which is seen a large Cross on a stone base. The rising sun illumines that part of the cloister which is seen. The other portions are obscured by the shadows thrown by the Church walls.*)

## SCENE I

*MONKS, BALTHAZZAR.*

(*Some monks are seen kneeling before the Cross, others are seen in the distance digging their graves, who repeat at intervals:*)

THE CHORUS: We dig the haven where we shall rest in peace. (*A monk introduces some pilgrims, who proceed to the church and stop before the portico where Balthazzar appears.*)

BALTHAZZAR AND CHORUS: What sight so great as the stars of heaven! The pious chants of guileless hearts reach the gracious throne of mercy in welcome accents.
(*The monks exeunt through the arches of the Cloisters. The pilgrims enter the chapel; one monk remains, his face concealed in his hands, and motionless—it is Fernando.*)

## SCENE II

*FERNANDO, BALTHAZZAR.*

BALTHAZZAR: The time is near, my brother, when an eternal vow will sever you from earth, to join you unto heaven.

FERNANDO: When I left the haven of peace to brave the angry storms of the world, you then said, "O son! you soon again will seek its calm." I now return, and in its hallowed walls await that peace and oblivion which death alone can bring.

BALTHAZZAR: It is so! But courage, Fernando. When heaven calls upon you to it alone your thoughts devote. Your holy vow is now recorded, and henceforth between

ta
Fra te e i pensier del mondo
Una tomba, che porta obblio profondo.

**FERNANDO:** Mi lasci?

**BALDASSARE:** Inoltra al tempio
Un novizio mi attende: in questa notte
Ei qui giungeva, misero ed infermo
Il mio soccorso chiede.

**FERNANDO:** Giovine ancora?

**BALDASSARE:** Nell' età più verde,
Abbattuto, tremante, egli omai vide
L' ultimo giorno!

**FERNANDO:** Ah! sì, la doglia uccide!
(*Baldassare prende Fernando per le mani come per rinvigorirne il coraggio, poi parte.*)

## SCENA III

**FERNANDO:** (*solo*). Favorita del Re! Qual nero abisso,
Qual mai trama infernale, la gloria mia
Avvolse in un istante,
E ogni speme troncò del core amante.
Spirto gentil—ne' sogni miei
Brillasti un dì—ma ti perdei.
Fuggì dal cor—mentita speme,
Larve d'amor—fuggite insieme.
A te d'accanto—posi in obblio
Miei voti e Dio—virtù ed onor?
Nume clemente—torna a quest' alma
La dolce calma - sperdi l' amor!

## SCENA IV

*FERNANDO, BALDASSARE, RELIGIOSI.*

**BALDASSARE:** Ebben, sei presto?

**FERNANDO:** O padr, all' ara santa
Ti seguo già.

**BALDASSARE:** Deh vieni, e voglia Iddio
Rivelarsi al tuo core!
(*Baldassare e Fernando entrano nella cappella. I Religiosi li seguono in silenzio. Leonora comparisce sotto l' abito d' un Novizio, si pone innanzi al portico della Chiesa, cercando distinguere le sembianze del Religiosi, che passano col capo abbassato sotto i cappucci*)

## SCENA V

*LEONORA, sola.*

**LEONORA:** Fernando, ah! dov' egli è? di questo chiostro
Egli abita le mura! in tale ammanto
T' offendo, O Dio, ma fa che insino a lui
Mi fia dato inoltrar; dal rio dolore
Oh! Come affranta io sono!

---

the world and you no more remembrance must exist.

**FERNANDO:** Why leave me?

**BALTHZAAZR:** Near to the temple a novice, who this night arrived—young, but of infirm health, and suffering, claims my earliest care.

**FERNANDO:** Is he still young?

**BALTHAZZAR:** In the bloom of life, health-broken and forlon; his days, I fear, are numbered.

**FERNANDO:** Ah! yes, for grief may kill. (*Balthazzar takes the hand of Fernando as if to rouse him, and exit.*)

## SCENE III

*FERNANDO alone.*

**FERNANDO:** The king's mistress! The dreadful snare! Into what a dark abyss has all my glory sunk forever; and from this heart all hope is quite shut out. Gentle spirit, life of my dream, forever lost, though newly found—specious vision—deceitful love, no more my heart acknowledges you. For love of you my love for God grew weak, and virtue, honor nearly lost. In mercy's name restore my soul its former peace, and banish all memory of my love.

## SCENE IV

*FERNANDO, BALTHAZZAR AND MONKS.*

**BALTHAZZAR:** Are you ready?

**FERNANDO:** I will follow you to the sacred altar.

**BALTHAZZAR:** Stay not; and may Heaven reveal itself unto you. (*Balthazzar and Fernando enter the Chapel, the monks following, in silence. Leonora appears, in the habit of a novice, and places herself before the church, endeavoring to distinguish the features of the monks who pass with their cowls over their heads.*)

## SCENE V

*Leonora alone.*

**LEONORA:** Fernando! ah! where is he? Within these cloisters now he dwells. In this disguise, grant, O God, whom I have so offended that I may meet him. With grief overwhelmed, I scarcely can stand. My death draws near. Life's breath I

---

Pressa a morir, della mia vita il dono
Prendi, gran Dio, ma di Fernando al piede
Deh! m' ottieni il perdono.

**CORO DI RELIGIOSI:** (*nella Chiesa*). Che te, l' Eterno di sue grazie imprima
Voto d' un' alma in santa prece assorta!

**LEONORA:** Che ascolto? un voto che dall' ara sorge!
E vola al cielo.

**CORO:** (*c. s.*). Udite vo del monte sulla cima
Voce dell' angiol che salute apporta?

**LEONORA:** Oh! qual sarà quest' alma
Che si toglie alla terra?

**FERNANDO:** (*c. s.*). Io mi consacro al culto tuo, Signor!
Vieni, e d' un raggio illumina il mio cor.

**LEONORA:** È desso, è desso!
Perduto al mondo ! egli ritorna a Dio!
Fuggiam da queste soglie—ohimè!—noi posso!
La morte il cor m'agghiaccia!
(*Cade spossata al piede della Croce.*)

## SCENA VI

*LEONORA, FERNANDO.*

**FERNANDO:** (*esce agitato dalla Chiesa*). I voti miei
Fur pronunziati! e, mal mio grado, io sento
Terror segreto in l'agitato spirto,
Io fuggii dall'altare.

**LEONORA:** (*tentando levarsi*) O Dio! qual pena!
Qual freddo! ohimè!

**FERNANDO:** (*guardando intorno*) Che ascolto?
Un infelice al suol!
(*Avvicinandosi*).
Deh! ti rincora.

**LEONORA:** O Dio!

**FERNANDO:** (*riculando con orrore*). È dessa!

**LEONORA:** (*supplichevole*). Non maledir, Leonora!

**FERNANDO:** Ah! va, t'invola, e questa terra
Più non profana il rio tuo piè!
Fa che io tranquillo scenda sotterra,
Non maledetto al par di te,
Nelle sue sale il Re t'appella,
D'oro e d'infamia ti coprirà;
Al fianco suo sarai più bella,
Tuo nome infame ognor sarà.

**LEONORA:** In fra i ghiacci, le rupi, i sterpi, i sassi,
Ognor pregando, al chiostro tuo mi trassi.

---

freely yield to you my God; but grant me yet a little while, to crave Fernando's pardon.

**CHORUS OF MONKS IN THE CHURCH:** May Heaven's grace and holy joy succeed the vows you make.

**LEONORA:** What do I hear? Some blessed soul vowing eternal service to its Creator!

**THE CHORUS:** Hear you from the mountain top an angel's voice announcing salvation?

**LEONORA:** Oh! whose soul is it that is thus separated from the world?

**FERNANDO** (*in the church*). To your service I consecrate myself, O Lord! Oh! let your grace possess my soul.

**LEONORA:** It is he! it is he! to earth now lost! to heaven he now belongs. Oh! let me quit this spot!—Alas I cannot! My death-struck limbs refuse their office.
(*She falls overpowered at the foot of the Cross.*)

## SCENE VI

*LEONORA, FERNANDO.*
(*Fernando enters from the church in an agitated manner.*)

**FERNANDO:** I have pronounced my vows! yet despite all, some secret terror pervades my soul. I have left the altar.

**LEONORA:** (*endeavoring to rise*). What pains! O God! my limbs are frozen!

**FERNANDO:** (*looking around him*). What did I hear? A suffering wretch on the cold earth. Let me assist. (*Approaches.*)

**LEONORA:** It is he!

**FERNANDO:** Just Heaven! (*Recoiling from her.*)

**LEONORA:** Ah! do not curse me!

**FERNANDO:** Hence, begone! nor thus profane this holy spot. In peace I seek to end my days. My malediction comes from you. The king your presence in his palace waits, to deck your brows with gold and shame! His love will soften all your cares, though infamous thy name will ever be.

**LEONORA:** I came to these cloisters praying; and kneeling oft, my bleeding wounds are torn and chafed and bleeding sore.

**FERNANDO:** O tu che m ingannasti,
Che pretendi da me?

**Leonora:** D'ambo sul capo
Un solo error ricade,
Sperai che il nero arcano a te svelato
Inez avesse e il tuo perdon sperai,
Credimi, non si mente
Sull'orlo della tomba.
Infino, a te, Fernando,
Non giunse il messo, e fu celato il vero,
O ciel! Fernando, il tuo perdono io spero.
Clemente al par di Dio, ch'oggi accoglia tua fe,
Mira lo strazio mio. Abbi pietà di me
D'onta fatal segnata,
Null'altra speme ho in sen,
Che di morir beata
Del tuo perdono almen.
Al nero affanno, al mio tormento
Alfin pietà ti parli al cor.

**FERNANDO:** A quell'affanno, a quell'accento
Sento ahimè! stemprarsi il cor!
O giusto Dio, su me discondi,
Rendi all'alma il suo vigor.

**LEONORA:** Io tanto duolo, se non t'arrendi,
Io morrò più trista ancor.

**FERNANDO:** Addio, fuggir mi lascia.

**LEONORA:** Disarma il tuo furor.
Ah! di mia cruda ambascia
Pietà del mio dolor.
Al mio duolo, al mio spavento
Di conforto un solo accento!
Per tuo padre ei fia concesso,
Per la morte a cui son presso
Fa men crudo il mio dolore,
Per l'amor de'lieti di.

**FERNANDO:** O Leonora! il mio furore!
Come foglia inaridì!

**LEONORA:** Tua mercede alfin mi dona,
O mi spingi nell'avel.
(*Gettandosi a' piedi di lui.*)

**FERNANDO:** Io t'amo. Iddio perdona—

**LEONORA:** E tu dunque?

**FERNANDO:** Io t'amo.

**LEONORA:** O ciel!

**FERNANDO:** Vieni, ah! vieni, io m'abbandono
Alla gioia che m'inebria;
Del mio cor t'è reso il trono,
Teco allato io vo'morir.
Come lampo sorge all'anima
Una voce ed un pensiero.
Fuggi, ascondi al mondo intero.
la tua vita, il tuo gioir.

**LEONORA:** E fia vero? io m'abbandono
Alla gioia che m'inebria!
Del suo cor m'è reso il trono,
Pago appieno è il mio desir,
(*A Fernando.*)

**FERNANDO:** Deceived by you, what seek you now from me?

**LEONORA:** The pains of a single error fall on us both. I thought that Inez had revealed the dark secret; and hoped for pardon. My grave now gapes; and therefore I speak nothing but truth I deemed the revelation had been made, Fernando. Refuse not, then, forgiveness. That heaven to which you now are vowed, its mercy extend to me. My tear-dimmed eyes your pity crave. Victim of a fatal shame, the earth to me has lost its charms; nor can I die in peace, unless you say your pardon I have gained. Deep is my anguish at my dark crimes; compassion, then, bestow.

**FERNANDO:** Her accents of despair afflict my heart. O God! watch over me lest my faltering soul succumb.

**LEONORA:** Turn not away compassion's ear, or sad my death will be.

**FERNANDO:** Farewell! I must not stay.

**LEONORA:** Dispel your wrath and let my grief by pity now be soothed. One word from you will bring comfort—my heart-wrung prayers, oh heed! I ask it in your father's name I feel my veins are dry. Relieve the anguish of my soul in memory of past love.

**FERNANDO:** Just Heaven! my heart now throbs with all the love I bore her once.

**LEONORA:** Forgive! your mercy I implore, or I die at your feet.
(*Throws herself at his feet*).

**FERNANDO:** Ah! Leonora, Heaven forgives.

**LEONORA:** But you?

**FERNANDO:** I love you still.

**LEONORA:** Oh! joy!

**FERNANDO:** Come, ah! come! I yield to the intoxicating bliss. My heart's throne you resume with you I will live and die.

**LEONORA:** Fly then, and hide from the whole world thy past life, our fading joys. Can this be true? I yield to the intoxicating bliss. His heart's throne is once more mine, all my wishes are fulfilled. (*To Fernan-*

Ma risponder non sa l'anima
A tua voce, al tuo pensiero?
Deh, nascondi al mondo intero
La mia vita, il mio morir.

**FERNANDO:** Fuggiam, fuggiamo insieme.

**LEONORA:** Ah! taci, è vana speme.
(*Si sente il coro de' Religiosi nella Chiesa.*)

**CORO:** Che te l'Eterno di sue grazie imprima
Voto d'un'alma in santa prece assorta!

**LEONORA:** (*spaventata*). Quel concento odi ut?

**FERNANDO:** Fuggiamo.

**LEONORA:** È il cielo Che ti parla.

**FERNANDO:** Fuggiamo; in te riposto
Mio fato è sol, deh! vieni!

**LEONORA:** Pensa a'tuoi voti.

**FERNANDO:** Or più forte è l'amor; per possederti Io tutto affronterò, la terra e il cielo.

**LEONORA:** (*sentendo mancarsi sempre più*). Ah! del nume il favor, dal nero abisso
Ecco ti salva—addio!—poter supremo
Ti risparma un delitto, ah! di mia sorte
Io non mi lagno—Iddio, Fernando, il vuole.
Dell'onta—alfin ti lavo—
Colla morte—

**FERNANDO:** Fuggiam.

**LEONORA:** È vano—è vano!

**FERNANDO:** Leonora.

**LEONORA:** Il fier tormento—La mia vita è compiuta—

**FERNANDO:** O ciel! Leonora!

**LEONORA:** Io muoio perdonata—Fernando!—e son—beata— oltre la tomba—
Riuniti sarem—addio! (*Muore.*)

**Fernando:** Leonora! (*Piegandosi sul cadavere.*)
Al soccorso! al soccorso! È la mia voce
Che ti richiama; i lumi ancor dischiudi,
Son io, son io tuo sposo! ah! tutto è indarno!
Al soccorso! al soccorso!

## SCENA VII

(*Leonora distesa in terra, Fernando, Baldassare, che esce dalla Chiesa, seguito da' Religiosi.*)

**FERNANDO:** Oh! padre! è dessa!
Mira, Leonora!

**BALDASSARE:** Oh! chi veggio!

do). But my soul cannot respond to your words or to your thoughts. Oh! may both my life and death be concealed from the whole world. Like the lightning's vivid flash, a thought, a word illumes my soul.

**FERNANDO:** Then let us fly together.

**LEONORA:** Ah! forbear; vain is the hope.
(*The Chorus of monks is heard in the church*).

**THE CHORUS:** May Heaven's grace and holy joy succeed the vows you make.

**LEONORA:** Do you hear those words?

**FERNANDO:** Let's leave. On you alone my hopes are fixed.

**LEONORA:** Think of your vows.

**FERNANDO:** My love is still more dear—for you I brave both heaven and earth.

**LEONORA:** (*faintly*). Heaven's grace will save him still from despair and perdition. Farewell! Oh! power supreme! I save you from a crime. I pine not now at fate—Fernando.—It is God's will! From shame I now absolve you—by my death –.

**FERNANDO:** We'll fly.

**LEONORA:** In vain—in vain, you say it!

**FERNANDO:** Leonora!

**LEONORA:** My heart's anguish—I feel I die!—

**FERNANDO:** O God! My Leonora!

**LEONORA:** You've pardoned—Fernando—I am—blessed.—Beyond the tomb—we'll meet—farewell. (*She dies*).

**FERNANDO:** Help! oh! help! It is my voice recalls you. Oh! smile once more! 'Tis I—your husband! I call in vain! Oh! help! help!

## SCENE VII

(*Leonora, dead. Fernando, Balthazzar, who enters from the church, followed by the monks*).

**FERNANDO:** O father! it is she! See it is Leonora!

**BALTHAZZAR:** What do I see?

## Act IV, Scene VII

**FERNANDO:** Leonora!

**BALDASSARE:** Silenzio!
(*Si avvicina a Leonora, ed abbassa il cappuccio sui di lei cappelli sparsi, Poi volgendosi ai Religiosi.*)
Più non è! Spento è il novizio. Le vostre preci a lui, fratelli! (*Tutti si prostrano.*)

**FERNANDO:** Leonora!

**BALTHAZZAR:** Silence. (*He approaches the body of Leonora and covers her dishevelled hair with the hood of her dress*). Life is extinct; the novice is dead. My brethren, let us pray!
(*They all kneel*).

**FERNANDO:** O Dio! Avrò diman la stessa prece anch'io!

*CALA LA TELA.*

**FERNANDO:** O Heaven! tomorrow you will put up those same prayers for me.

*CURTAIN FALLS.*

# La Figlia Del Reggimento (1840)

## The Daughter of the Regiment

MUSIC BY GAETANO DONIZETTI ■ LIBRETTO BY JULES HENRI VERNOY DE SAINT-GEORGES & JEAN FRANÇOIS BAYARD

---

This two-act opera, set to a libretto by Jules Henri Vernoy de Saint-Georges and Jean Francois Bayard, premiered at the Opéra-Comique in Paris on February 11, 1840. *La Fille du Regiment* was Donizetti's first opera to be performed in French. The story takes place in Switzerland. Battle rages in a Swiss valley. The Marquise de Birkenfeld stops at a village and encounters Sulpice, sergeant of the Savoyard soldiers and Marie, the "daughter of the regiment," who grew up among the soldiers. Tonio, who is in love with Marie, is found following the troops and is arrested as a spy. Marie intervenes on his behalf, explaining that Tonio saved her life. Although she is in love with him, her regiment will only allow her to marry a grenadier. Tonio enlists. Sulpice, upon learning that the Marquise requires an escort to accompany her to Birkenfeld, remembers that a Captain Roberto Birkenfeld entrusted his daughter Marie to his regiment before his death. The Marquise is certain that Marie is her niece and takes her to her castle. Although she is happy to have found her family at long last, Marie misses Tonio and the regiment. Marie receives Sulpice at the castle; he finds her to be almost unrecognizable. Tonio, now an officer, arrives with the regiment at the castle. Tonio and Marie reaffirm their love, but the Marquise has arranged for Marie to marry the Duke of Krakentorp. The Marquise turns out to be Marie's mother and Marie feels that she must obey her wish. However, when faced with their mutual unhappiness, the Marquise has a change of heart and allows Marie and Tonio to marry.

---

## ■ Atto I

### SCENA I

*(Alla destra una casipola; alla sinistra le prime case d'un villaggio; da lontano delle montagne. La Marchesa di Birkenfeld è assisa sopra un banco rustico alla sinistra. Ortensio sta a lato di lei. Paesani Tirolesi son aggruppati sopra una collinetta di dietro come di guardia, intanto le loro mogli e figlie si sono prostrate avanti in ginocchio, verso il lato sinistro, innanzi all'Immagine di pietra della Vergine.)*

**CORO:** *(sulla colonna).* Armiamci in silenzio,
Ci assista l'ardir.—
Che l'oste avversaria,
Già sembra venir,
Andiam—andiam.

**CORO DI DONNE:** *(in ginocchio).*
Cielo elemente,
Cielo possente
Prostrate a te,
Chiediam consiglio
In tal periglio
Danne mercè.

**ORETENSIO:** Ma si calma—via Marchesa,
Si remetta faccia cor!

**LA MARCHESA:** Da nemicei, oh Dio! sorpresa
Qui—ad un tratto-è un vero orror.

**CORO:** *(un Paesan sulla Montagna).* Son da nemici i monti abbandonati;
Coraggio, amici mici, siam salvati!

**CORO:** Eh! niente paura
Viva il piacer,
La loro ventura
Non dessi temer.
La pace bramata
Rallegra ogni cor.
La terra salvata
Rinasce all'amor.
È salvo l'onor, eh! niente paura.
Mi viva il piacer.—La, la, la, la!

**LA MARCHESA:** Deh! mi reggete per pietà—Ragazzi—
Deh! non m'abbandonate.

**ORTENSIO:** E chi poteva immaginarsi mai,
Che il giorno appunto, in cui vostra Eccellenza, di Lauffen rispettabile
Marchesa, al nativo Castel volgea le Spalle, volesser le milizie di Savoja,
(Abbandonando a un tratto le frontiere)
Le marcie ripigliar?

**LA MARCHESA:** Ma che far deggio? andar inmanzi—
Oppur tornare addietro?

**ORTENSIO:** Ma—Eccellenza—

## ■ ACT I

### SCENE I

*(On the right is a cottage; on the left the first houses of a village; in the background are mountains. The Marchioness of Birkenfeld is seated on a rustic bench on the left, Ortensius standing by her side. Tyrolese Peasants are grouped on a rising ground behind, as if on the look-out, while their wives and daughters kneel in front, towards the left hand, before a stone Image of the Virgin.)*

**CHORUS OF MEN:** Up! the foe's advancing;
To arms, friends, to arms!
For home we battle!
Who, then, will shrink from war's alarms?

**CHORUS OF WOMEN:** Santa Maria,
Gentle and holy,
Lo, lo! to you
We bend in prayer;
Maiden and mother,
Behold our despair.

**ORTENSIUS:** Take heart, I pray, my noble lady:
Our friends approach, and soon they will be here.

**THE MARCHIONESS:** Yes, but I doubt the enemy is closer;
Those sounds!—they seem so very near.

**CHORUS:** *(Peasants entering from behind).* Friends, rejoice; see the French retreating:
All the danger is past.

**CHORUS:** Rejoice, brave companions, for the peril's over;
Their star, it has set, and it rises no more.
Peace, life's greatest blessing,
Returns again;
An our songs of triumph
Sound on hill and plain.—
The heavens be praised!
Our country is saved, and no more shall we fear.
But live happily in our villages here.

**THE MARCHIONESS:** Alas! support me, for pity, my friends!
Alas! do not abandon me.

**ORTENSIUS:** And who would ever have imagined
That precisely on the day on which your
Ladyship, the honored Marchioness of Laufen,
Returned to your native place, the castle.—
The armies of Savoy should have chosen
(Quitting, at once, the frontiers)
To resume their march?

**THE MARCHIONESS:** But what shall we do now? go on,
Or turn back?

**ORTENSIUS:** But—your ladyship—

LA MARCHESA: Indagate—vedete—esaminate—prendete
Lingua in somma; e la vettura, ditemi
Ortensio—sarà poi sicura?

ORTENSIO: In quanto a questo—

LA MARCHESA: Che fra costoro ad aspettarvi resto.
(*Entra Sulpizio, poi Maria.*)

SULPIZIO: Corpo di mille diavoli? che gambe hanno cotesti Svizzeri:
Temono della guerra ed invece abbiam la pace
Sul palmo della mano. In ogni vico sortito è il manifesto—
E tutti quelli che sdegnar di Savoja
Seguitar la bandiera,
Possono rimanersi e buona sera!
Ma chi arriva? Scommetto i camerati
No davvero—è Maria—la figlia nostra—
La perla e l'ornamento
dell'undecimo invitto reggimento.
Eccola quà.—Veh! un po' s'ella è gentile!
Più felice esser puote il reggimento,
Che tal figlia possiede?

MARIA: Il reggimento mio! ne vo propria superba!
E desso che ha vegliato con affetto paterno
Agli anni miei primieri!

SULPIZIO: Non è vero?

MARIA: Ma poi—senza adularmi—di fargli enore lo credo.

SULPIZIO: Senza dubbio! gentil come un amore—

MARIA: D'un militare io chiudo in petto il core.

Apparvi alla luce,
Sul campo gaerrier:
E il suon del tamburo,
Mio solo piacer.
S'affretta alla gloria
Intrepido il cor;
Savoja e vittoria!
E il grido d'onor.

SULPIZIO: Io l'ho educata, Non c'è che dire
Con quel sentire, Con quel vigor;
Una Duchessa Non può vantare
Più nobil fare,
Più amabil cor:—
No!

SULPIZIO: Oh! che bel giorno fu quel che il cielo,
Ancor fanciulla t'offerse a me
Quando il tuo pianto, turbò il silenzio
Del campo intero che accorse a te.

MARIA: Ognun qual padre dolce amoroso
Sul proprio dorso recommi allor.

SULPIZIO: E m'era il sacco di munizione, che bel di!

---

THE MARCHIONESS: Consider—see—examine—take counsel!
And the carriage, tell me, Ortensio.
Will it, then, be safe?

ORTENSIUS: As to that—

THE MARCHIONESS: Go—be quick—
I will wait for you among those people.
(*Enter Sulpizio, then Maria.*)

SULPIZIO: A thousand devils! what legs those Swiss have!
They fear war, and therefore have thrust Peace upon us. Everywhere
The manifesto has gone forth—and all those who disdained
To follow the standard of Savoy may stay behind!
And farewell to them! But who comes here?
I guess some comrades—
No, indeed, it is Maria, our daughter,
The pearl and ornament of the unconquered Twentieth.
There she is. Ah, how beautiful!
Oh, how happy is the regiment
That possesses such a daughter!

MARIA: My regiment! I am proud of it indeed!
And it has watched with paternal affection
Over my youthful years.

SULPIZIO: Is it not true?

MARIA: But now—without flattery—I think I do them honor.

SULPIZIO: Without question. You are graceful as a Cupid.

MARIA: A soldier's heart pants in my bosom.

The camp was my birth-place,
Amongst men brave and free;
And the drum is the music that
Sounds sweetest to me,
I march with the foremost
When dangers invite;
The fiercer the battle,
The more my delight.

SULPIZIO:
It is all my doing,
I own it freely;
And how genteelly
She marches on;
No duchess ever
Was half so clever
With pike, or sabre,
Or even with a gun.

SULPIZIO: How we then rejoiced to find you,
On the battle-field–deserted!
Each eye looked upon you in pity,
Each would claim you, then, for his own.

MARIA: You took me up, and bore me off,
With all the love that mothers feel.

SULPIZIO:
Glorious day!

---

MARIA: D'ogni altra culla ben più miglior!

SULPIZIO: E dolce sonno gustavi allor,
Mentre il tamburo facca rumor.

MARIA: E dolce sonno gustava allor,
Mentre il tamburo facea rumor.
Or poi che sono più grandicella
Ciascun la mano porta al bonnet.

SULPIZIO: E la consegna, ragazza bella,
E quest'omaggio dovuto a te.

MARIA: Con voi divido sul campo ognor
E strage, ieste e buon umor.

SULPIZIO: Ed ai feriti facendo cor
La destra stringi del vincitor.

MARIA: Quindi alla sera, alla cantina
Chi v'incoraggia? chi v'affascina?

SULPIZIO: In noi chi desta letizia e ardir?
Sei tu, sei tu—non c'è che dir.

MARIA: È quindi in merto del mio talento,
A voti unanimi il reggimento
Sua vivandiera mi nominò.

SULPIZIO: Sua vivandiera a voti unanimi.

MARIA: Ah! si.
Il reggimento mi nominò—

SULPIZIO: Il reggimento ti nominò.

MARIA: Son persuasissima che alla battaglia
Io pur cogli altri
Saprei pugnar.

SULPIZIO: Saprai pugnar.

MARIA: Si—e schioppi, e sciabole, bombe e mitraglia,
Con voi pugnando saprei sfidar.

SULPIZIO: Oh! saprei sfidar

MARIA: Se un figlio al padre dee somigliar.
Al mio somiglio.

SULPIZIO: Si—quest'è parlar.

MARIA: La gloria voglio.

SULPIZIO: Benone affè.

MARIA: Io vo' marciar.

SULPIZIO: Quest'è parlar!

MARIA: En avant—

SULPIZIO: En avant.

MARIA: Suol l'undecimo gridar—

SULPIZIO: Suol l'undecimo gridar.

MARIA: En avant—en avant—

---

MARIA: Yes, and then, instead of a cradle,
I was rocked in a cap of steel.

SULPIZIO: In which you seemed to be at home,
Sleeping to the rolling drum.

MARIA: In which I seemed to be at home.
Sleeping to the rolling drum.
But now, my friends, I've grown older
Sapperment!–they all salute me so.

SULPIZIO: Of course, of course; you fathers all
Salute à militaire, you know.

MARIA: On days of feast, in battle's tumult,
Still I'm first upon the field.

SULPIZIO: And give fresh courage to the wounded,
Making their shield of your breast.

MARIA: And then, who is it over the goblet
That sings at evening gay and wild?

SULPIZIO: Or plays a thousand tricks upon us?
It is still the regiment's gallant child.

MARIA: And better yet, to try my talent,
My fathers made me sutler to the corps–
There's an honor!–never conferred before.

SULPIZIO: We chose you by general consent.

MARIA: Oh yes;
All consented–sutler was I named by all.

SULPIZIO: All consented–sutler were you named by all.

MARIA: And in the day of glorious battle,
When cannons rattle,
I'm still the first.

SULPIZIO: She's still the first.

MARIA: Yes! I fear not swords nor the bullet,
And know to fight like one of you.

SULPIZIO: Ha! she fights like one of us!

MARIA: My kind father's fame, I hold, is sacred;
I've made it more.

SULPIZIO: Ha! she has made it more.

MARIA: And in the field–

SULPIZIO: And in the field–

MARIA: I'm still the first.

SULPIZIO: She's still the first.

MARIA: March away–

SULPIZIO: March away–

MARIA: Where the guns and sabres play–

SULPIZIO: Where the guns and sabres play–

MARIA: March away–march away–

SULPIZIO: En avant—en avant.

MARIA: Apparvi alla luce,
Sul campo guerrier.
E il suon del tamburo mio solo piacer
Rataplan, rataplan rataplan, rataplan.
En avant—rataplan, rataplan, March!
Mi chiama l'onor—present!
Present! March!
Sargente del reggimento,
En avant, rataplan, rataplan.
Rataplan, rataplan rataplan, rataplan.

SULPIZIO: Apparve alla luce,
Sul campo guerrier.
Il suon del tamburo suo solo piacer.
Rataplan, rataplan rataplan, rataplan.
E il suo grido d'onor.
Savoja, vittoria è suo grido d'onor.
Vivandiera del reggimento,
Rataplan, rataplan, rataplan.
Present!
Rataplan, rataplan rataplan, rataplan.

SULPIZIO: No, no Maria; non va ben: da noi
Tu fosti adottata, protetta ed allevata,
Colle nostre mensili economie;
E ci devi riguardo e confidenza.

MARIA: Ma, Sulpizio, mio caro, abbi pazienza.

SULPIZIO: Abbila tu pur ora, e stammi attenta;
Sai che non fu possibile scoprir la
Tua famiglia, il tuo paese, in onta
Ad una lettera trovata su di te:
Riposta quindi nel fondo del mio sacco
A posto fisso, e che—

MARIA: Ma se so tutto?

SULPIZIO: E perchè dunque soletta e pensierosa,
Sorti dalla cantina fuggendo i camerata,
Eh?

MARIA: Perchè?

SULPIZIO: M'han detto che nell'ultimo nostro accampamento
T'han sorpresa in colloquio con un—ma non
Sarà vero.

MARIA: Anzi è la verità—parlo sincero—
Con un giovine Svizzero, gentil, garbato.
E che mi tolse un giorno da sicuro

SULPIZIO: March away—march away—

MARIA: The camp was my birthplace,
Amongst men brave and free.
And the drum is the music that sounds sweetest to me.
Rataplan, rataplan, rataplan, rataplan.
Then advance– rataplan, rataplan! March!
For fame and for honor–
Fame and renown!
Present! March!
The Regiment is my glory!
Then advance, rataplan, rataplan.
Rataplan, rataplan, rataplan, rataplan.

SULPIZIO: The camp was her birthplace,
Amongst men brave and free.
The sound of the drum must be sweet music.
Rataplan, rataplan, rataplan, rataplan.
Rataplan, it is the roll of the drum,
It leads us to honor, fame, and renown.
Present!
Vivandiere beloved by our regiment.
Rataplan, rataplan, rataplan, rataplan.

SULPIZIO:
No, no, Maria; it is not well:
You were adopted, protected, and brought up by us
By our little savings on the passing month:
And you owe us regard and confidence.

MARIA: But, my dear Sulpizio, be patient.

SULPIZIO: Have patience yourself, this time, and attend to me,
You know that it was not possible to discover
Your family, your country, although
A letter was found upon you;
It now lies at the bottom of my knapsack,
Safely kept; and that–

MARIA: But suppose I know all this?

SULPIZIO: And why, then, lonely and pensive,
Do you leave the canteen, and quit our society.
Eh?

MARIA: Why?

SULPIZIO: They have told me that, when we were last encamped,
They surprised you in conversation with–but, no,
It cannot be true.

MARIA: It is true–I make no concealment–
With a young Swiss, handsome, agreeable, and who
Rescued me once from certain dan-

periglio:
Ma pure tutto adesso è finito; egli è là
—Noi siam qua.

SULPIZIO: (udendo rumore).
Che cosa è stato?
Cose'è questo rumore indiavolato?
(Entra Caporale e Coro.)

CORO E CAPORALE: Avanti; andiamo—tutto si sa.
Fra noi ti spinse curiosità.

MARIA: (da parte). Che vedo! Oh ciel, è lui!

SULPIZIO: Sia tratto altrove.

MARIA: (ai soldati). Fermate!
(Sottovoce a Sulpizio.)
E lui!

SULPIZIO: Davvero! lo straniero che t'ama?

TONIO: (fissando Maria). Ah! pel mio core qual tràsporto!

MARIA: (piano a Tonio). E che mai vi guida a noi?

TONIO: Posso cercarvi, o cara—altri che voi?

CORO: È un briccone, un villanzone,
Che qui venne a specular;
Ma gagliardi Savojardi
Ci sapremo vendicar.

MARIA: (precipitandosi in mezzo ai soldati). Un istante amici miei
Deh! cedete al mio desir.
Che! la morte a colui che mi salvò
La vita?

CORO: Che dice?

SULPIZIO: Ha il ver parlato.

CORO E CAPORALE: Questa parola ha il suo destin cangiato.

MARIA: D'un precipizio in fondo, io stave per cader
Ei m'a salvata esponendo i suoi giorni,
Volete ancor ch'egli perisca?

SULPIZIO: No, davver!
S'ella è cosi, mio bravo camerata,
Sii nostro amico.

TONIO: (tendendogli la mano). E il voglio
Che cosi potrò allora avvicinarmi
A lei che l'alma adora.

SULPIZIO: Or via festeggiar il salvator di questa amabil
Figlia, beviam! Trinchiam al suo liberator!

CORO: Trinchiam al suo liberator!

SULPIZIO: In giro il rum.
(A Maria.)
E festa di famiglia.

ger; but, indeed
All that is over–he is there–we are here.

SULPIZIO: (hearing a noise).
What noise is that?
What is that diabolical noise?
(Enter Corporal Spontoon and Chorus.)

CHORUS AND CORPORAL: Forward, go on–all is known!
Among us we punish curiosity.

MARIA: (aside).
What do I see? O heaven, it is he!

SULPIZIO: Let him be dragged here.

MARIA: (to the soldiers). Stay!
(Aside to Sulpizio.)
It is he!

SULPIZIO: Indeed! the stranger that loves you?

TONIO: (looking at Maria). Ah, what transport reigns in my heart!

MARIA: (aside to Tonio). And whatever led you to us!

TONIO: Can I seek, dearest, any other than you?

CHORUS: He's a rogue, a peasant,
Who came hither to spy;
But the gallant Savoyards
Well know how to avenge themselves.

MARIA: (throwing herself into the midst of the soldiers). One instant, my friends,–
Ah, yield to my wish.
What! death for him who saved my life?

CHORUS: What says she?

SULPIZIO: She has spoken the truth.

CHORUS AND CORPORAL: That word has changed his destiny.

MARIA: I was near falling from the top of a precipice to the bottom;
He saved me by venturing his own life.
Is it yet your will that he should perish?

SULPIZIO: No indeed!
If it be as you say, let the brave fellow
Become our friend.

TONIO: And I will,
(extending his hand to them).
That so
I shall then be able to approach her whom my soul adores.

SULPIZIO: And now, the savior to welcome
Of this our amiable daughter, let us drink!
Let us drink the health of her deliverer!

CHORUS: Let us drink to her deliverer!

SULPIZIO: Pass 'round the wine.
(To Maria.)
It is a family festival.

## Act I, Scene I

**CORO:** È festa di famiglia.

**CHORUS:** It is a family festival.

**SULPIZIO:** Sì, trinchiamo alla Svizzera, alla natal tua terra.

**SULPIZIO:** Drink to Switzerland, your native land.

**TONIO:** Oh no! giammai! rompo piuttosto il mio bicchier!

**TONIO:** Oh, no! never! Sooner would I break my glass.

**CORO E CAPORALE:** È pazzo?

**CHORUS AND CORPORAL:** Is he mad?

**TONIO:** Viva Italia! e i nuovi amici miei!

**TONIO:** Long live Italy! and my new friends!

**SULPIZIO, CORO E CAPORALE:** Viva, dunque, Italia, e tu con lei!

**SULPIZIO, CHORUS AND CORPORAL:** Long live Italy, then, and you too!

**SULPIZIO:** Perchè la festa sia completa, intuona, Figliuola mia, la nostra ronda usata.

**SULPIZIO:** That the festival may be complete, sing, My daughter, our usual round.

**CORO:** Del reggimento è la canzon più grata.

**CHORUS:** Ah! sing to us the song of the Regiment.

**MARIA:** Ciascun lo dice, Ciascun lo sa! È il reggimento Ch'egual non ha. Il sol cui credito Con amistà, Facciam le bettole Della città. Il reggimento Che ovunque andò; Mariti e amanti Disanimò, Della beltà, oh! ben supremo! Egli è là, egli è là davver; Vedi là, egli è là, sì, sì; Egli è là, dubbio non v'ha; Ecco l'undecimo ch'equal non ha.

**MARIA:** All men confess it, Go where we will. Our gallant Twentieth Is welcome still. Landlords, when surliest, To us are kind, And when we're merriest They then are blind. Husbands and lovers, They dread our sight; But oh! the fair, We are their delight! They are here, they are here, With sword and spear they are here! They are here, with sword and spear! See, our brave Twentieth–none are like them!

**CORO:** Egli è il davver! vedi là, sì, Ecco l'undecimo ch'egual non ha.

**CHORUS:** Hear the drum! They come, they come! Here in your land they pitch their tent, The gallant Twentieth Regiment.

**TONIO:** Viva l'undecimo!

**TONIO:** Long live the regiment! The Twentieth regiment!

**SULPIZIO:** Silenzio, silenzio!

**SULPIZIO:** Be still–be silent!

**MARIA:** Tante battaglie Ei guadagnò, Che il nostro principe Già decretò. Ch'ogni soldato, Se in salvo andrà, Generalissimo Diventerà. Perch'egli è Questo il reggimento, A cui sia facile Ogni cimento, Che un sesso teme, Che l'altro adora, Egli è là, ecc. (*Odisi un lontano suono di tamburo.*)

**MARIA:** (*resumed*). Highest and lowest, Heroes are we; Any amongst us May be Marshal. Foremost in victory, Last in retreat, Death we can suffer, But not defeat. First in the battle, First in the dance, The brave hussar, With sword and lance. They are here, etc. (*The sound of a distant drum is heard.*)

**SULPIZIO:** (*ai soldati*). È l'ora dell'appello; Andiamo e non si scherzi con il regolamento.

**SULPIZIO:** (*to the soldiers*). It is the hour of roll-call, Let us go, and not trifle with the regulations.

**MARIA E TONIO:** Ah, se ne vanno.

**MARIA AND TONIO:** Ah, they are going!

**SULPIZIO:** (*a Tonio*). E tu, ragazzo—via di qua.

**SULPIZIO:** (*to Tonio*). And, young man–away from here.

**MARIA:** Egli è nostro prigioniero, e di lui noi rispondiamo.

**MARIA:** He is my prisoner, and I will answer for him.

**SULPIZIO:** (*piano a Maria*). Ma non io, signorina! (*A Tonio che viene consegnato a due soldati, i quali lo conducono via per la montagna.*) Andiamo, andiamo.

**SULPIZIO:** (*to Maria*). But I will not, my little lady– (*To Tonio, who is placed under guard of two soldiers, and led away towards the mountains.*) Away! away with you.

**SULPIZIO, CORO E CAPORALE:** Talvolta è un poco duro Piegarsi ed obbedir, Ma suona già il tamburo, Plan e devesi servir. In tempi così strani Niun bada più al dolor, Pugnando all'indomani, Forse si vince o muor, Ma suona già il tamburo E devesi servir. (*Exeunt Sulpizio, Caporale e Coro.*)

**CHORUS, SULPIZIO AND CORPORAL:** This course is rather severe To carry him away; But already the drum beats, And we must obey. In times so strange as these, No one thinks much of grief, Before tomorrow, while fighting, Perchance we conquer or die. But already the drum sounds, And we must obey. (*Exeunt Sulpizio, Corporal and chorus.*)

**MARIA:** L'hanno condotto seco; ed io che avrei cotanto Volentier con lui parlato! Povero giovinetto! Per vedermi esporsi in questa guisa!

**MARIA:** They have led him away with them; And yet I wished so much To have spoken to him.–Poor young man! To have exposed himself to such danger for the sake of seeing me!

**TONIO:** (*correndo dalla montagna*). Signorina!

**TONIO:** (*running down from the mountain*). Fair lady!

**MARIA:** Ma come!—siete voi?

**MARIA:** How!–Is it you?

**TONIO:** Essi han creduto ch'io li seguissi; Eh sì? Non son venuto per chiacchierar con esse Che non sono gentili. Affatto, quel vecchio poi—quel vecchio?

**TONIO:** They thought I should follow them; But I did not come to gossip with them, Who are in fact scarcely civil. Yet, that old man–who is he?

**MARIA:** Egli è mio padre.

**MARIA:** He is my father also.

**TONIO:** Il vecchio?—allor mi son sbagliato. E l'altro?—quel piccolino!

**TONIO:** That old man?–then I am mistaken. And the other?–that little fellow!

**MARIA:** Egli è mio padre anch'esso.

**MARIA:** He is my father also.

**TONIO:** Anch'esso?—Gli altri adunque?

**TONIO:** He also! And the others?

**MARIA:** E gli altri pure.

**MARIA:** And the others as well.

**TONIO:** Che diamine! Ne avete un reggimento?

**TONIO:** The deuce! Have you a regiment of fathers?

**MARIA:** E appunto:—il reggimento è il mio padre Adottivo; e lor deggio il mio stato— L'educazione—tutto insomma—tutto. E dipendo da lor unicamente; ma Dite finalmente che volete da me, Qual mai segreto vi condusse fra noi?

**MARIA:** I have:–I was adopted by the whole regiment And to them I owe my present position– My education;–in fact, all–everything; And I depend entirely on them. But tell me, now, what do you wish from me– What secret motive has brought you among us?

**TONIO:** Egli è ch'io bramo tutto aprirvi Il mio cor—egli è che v'amo.

**TONIO:** It is that I wish to open all My heart–it is that I love you!

**MARIA:** Che? vio m'amate?

**MARIA:** What?–you love me!

**TONIO:** Non ci credete? udite poi decidete.

**TONIO:** Do you not believe me?–Hear me, and then decide.

**MARIA:** Vediam, udiam; ascoltiam e giudichiam.

**MARIA:** Let us hear and see–let us listen and judge.

**TONIO:** Da quell'istante che sul mio seno,
Io vi raccolsi venuta meno;
L'immagin vostra dolce e vezzosa,
Non mi dà posa la notte e il di.

**MARIA:** Ma carin quest'è memoria,
È memoria e nulla più.

**TONIO:** No, non e tutto—c'è di peggio,
Si, mia cara,—c'è di più.

**MARIA:** Vediam, udiam; ascoltiam e giudichiam.

**TONIO:** Il bel soggiorno de tempi andati,
Tutti gli amici cotanto amati,
Per voi, Maria!—Sin d'or lo sento;
Senza tormento potrei lasciar.

**MARIA:** Ma una tale indifferenza,
È impossibil perdonar.

**TONIO:** E finalmente da voi lontano,
Tanto la vita fu in odio a me;
Che sfidar volli furente insano;
La morte stessa—ma al vostro piè!

**MARIA:** Ah! ch'io lo so! lo capisco! anch'io!
Ma i giorni dennosi, amico mio,
Per quei che s'amano assicurar.

**MARIA:** A voti cosi ardente!
Il misero mio cor!
Consiglio più non sente,
Non sente che l'amor!

**TONIO:** A voti cosi ardente!
Il tenero suo cor!
Si mostrerà clemente
Al prego dell'amor!

**TONIO:** Cara voi ben vedete ma—v'ama.

**MARIA:** Si? decidete.

**TONIO:** Vediam, udiam, ascoltiam e giudichiam.

**MARIA:** Civetta un tempo felice e lieta,
Di niun amante sentia pietà;
Ma l'alma adesso turbata, inquieta
Sa che v'è un'altra felicità.

**TONIO:** Va ben! va ben!

**MARIA:** E fra i nemici che debbo odiar;
Per un di questi degg'io tremar.

**TONIO:** Di bene in meglio.

**MARIA:** E in un giorno d'orror che i sensi invigorino,
All'olezzar d'un fior cospersi io lo sentii;
Del vostro pianto quel caro fior tesor
Pieno d'incanto mai da quel giorno.

**TONIO:** From the instant when I clasped you to my bosom, reviving from affright,
Your fair and lovely image
Has left me no repose by night or day.

**MARIA:** (coquettishly). But my dear little friend, this is a recollection;—
And nothing more.

**TONIO:** No, indeed, it is more than a mere recollection;
It is true love.

**MARIA:** Let us see and hear, and—

**TONIO:** The beautiful abode of past days,
And all the friends so much beloved,
For you, Maria, I feel,
Without regret, I could leave them all.

**MARIA:** But such indifference as that
It is impossible to forgive.

**TONIO:** I could not live without you, dearest;
It were pain worse than death itself;
Hence, defying all, I've ventured here.
Let them now do their worst—I have seen you.

**MARIA:** Ah! I know it, I understand!
He who loves, my friend,
Respects his life!

**MARIA:** No longer can I doubt it!
His heart is given to me!
And mine, too, beats responding,
Oh, yes, it beats for you!

**TONIO:** No longer can I doubt it!
Her heart is given to me!
And mine, too, beats responding,
Oh, yes, it beats for you!

**TONIO:** You see it now, I love—
Perhaps, though, I love alone.

**MARIA:** Decide for yourself, sir.

**TONIO:** Well, then, tell your tale:
I will listen and decide it.

**MARIA:** Long time coquettish, so free and joyous,
I'd no notion of love's pains;
But too well now I read the secret,—
It is a lesson taught by love alone.

**TONIO:** Go on—go on.

**MARIA:** I loved only battle,
The noise and tumult of the camp,
But ah! I freely will confess it,
All my feelings now are changed.

**TONIO:** Oh, better still.

**MARIA:** Since the day when I met you,
Upon the steep abyss's edge depending
I plucked this flower, in its wild bed blooming
And wore it here as it had been your gift,
Till at length it withered on my heart.

**TONIO E MARIA:** Abbandonò il mio cor,
A voti così ardente, ecc., ecc.
Quest'alma è rapita nell'estasi d'amor.
Io perderò la vita ma fido al tuo bel cor.
(*Partono.*)
(*Entra Sulpizio, la Marchesa e poi Ortensio.*)

**SULPIZIO:** Lo dico con il cuore sulle labbra.
(*Alla Marchesa che legge.*)
Dovermi separar da quella cara
Amabile fanciulla è tal cordoglio
Che non lo so spiegar. Ma non c'è
Verso; se il Capital Roberto fu sposo
A lei segreto; a lei strettamente
Celate alla nobilissima casata dei Marchesi di Lauffen.

**LA MARCHESA:** Onde astretta venni a tener occulto
Quest'imeneo cotanto desperato!

**SULPIZIO:** Poi lo scritto trovato vicino alla fanciulla.
È a lei diretto, parla chiaro abbastanza,
E aperto mostra che la figliuola è sua;
Che il capitano mortalmente ferito
Raccomandava a le materne cure
Quell'angiol di bontà.

**LA MARCHESA:** Ma vi scongiuro, a nessuno palese
Si faccia questo arcano; e siate certo
Che un compenso condegno a tante cure—

**SULPIZIO:** Eh! se lo tenga pure;
che col perder
Maria, a tutto si perde!
Vado dunque a pigliarla.

**LA MARCHESA:** Io là v'aspetto.

**SULPIZIO:** Preferirci, le mille volte e mille
Morire dalla fame in alcuna città
Stretta d'assedio, che perderla cosi.
Non c'è rimedio.
(*Parte.*)

**LA MARCHESA:** Ortensio! presto, Ortensio! Andate
Subito a ordinar i cavalli! è necessario
Allontanarla testa da questi militari
Ad ogni costo.
(*Entrano Caprolae e Soldati.*)

**CORO:** Rataplan, rataplan, rataplan, rataplan!
Militar non v'ha
Cui non batta il cor.
Del tamburo al bel fragor.
Rataplan, rataplan, rataplan!
Pien di zel—pien d'ardor—
Di fervor—a questo fragor
Risponde con amor.
Viva la pugna! gli affanni suoi
E la vittoria, e il guerreggiar!

**MARIA AND TONIO:** No longer can I doubt it,
His [her] heart is given to me;
And mine, too, beats responding;–
Oh yes, it beats for you!
(*Exeunt.*)
(*Enter Sulpizio, the Marchioness, and afterwards Ortensio.*)

**SULPIZIO:** I speak it with my heart upon my lips. (*To the Marchioness, who is reading a letter.*)
To be obliged to part from that dear
Amiable girl, is such a grief,
That I cannot express it.
But it cannot be helped.
If Captain Roberto was married
To her in secret, from her carefully
Conceal the noble wardenship of the Marquis of Lauffen.

**THE MARCHIONESS:** Wherefore I have kept concealed
This unpropitious marriage!

**SULPIZIO:** Then, the writing found near the little girl,
And directed to you, speaks clearly enough;
And distinctly shows that the daughter
Is yours,—that the captain, when mortally wounded,
Commended to your maternal care
This angel of goodness.

**THE MARCHIONESS:** But, I conjure you, to none reveal
This secret; and be certain
That recompense adequate to such care–

**SULPIZIO:** Eh! Nothing will recompense me for losing
Maria! Yet I must bring her here.

**THE MARCHIONESS:** I will expect her.

**SULPIZIO:** (*aside*). I should prefer, a thousand times,
To die of hunger in any city
Closely besieged, to losing her this way.
Yet it cannot be helped.
(*Exit.*)

**THE MARCHIONESS:** Ortensio! Hurry Ortensio! Oh,
Go quickly, and order the horses;
For it is expedient at once to remove her
From these most fearful soldiers
At any cost.
(*Enter Corporal and soldiers.*)

**CHORUS:** Rataplan, rataplan, rataplan, rataplan.
There is not a soldier whose heart does not beat.
At the lively rattle of the drum.
Rataplan, rataplan, rataplan, rataplan.
Full of zeal–full of ardor–of fervor
To that sound he responds with delight.
Hail to the battle, its shouts and its din

# Act I, Scene I

Viva la morte! che ognun di noi
Nella battaglia vola a cercar.

IL CAPORALE: Ma chi diavolo viene? Oh! quel giovinotto
Che fra noi questa mane & è capitato.
Bravo! davvero, egli si fe' soldato.
(*Entra Tonio, con la coccarda francese al berretto.*)

TONIO: Miei cari amici, che lieto giorno!
Le vostre insegne io seguirò;
Sol per amore a voi ritorno.
E un grande eroe diventerò.
Ah, sì! colei ond'io sospiro
Ebbe pietade del mio martiro;
E questa speme desiata, ognor
Altera i sensi ed il mio cor.

CORO: Il camerata è innamorato.

TONIO: Ed in voi solo confida il cor.

CORO: Che?—Nostra figlia l'ha incatenato?

TONIO: Deh? m'ascoltate, deh!
Deh! m'ascoltate suo genitor
Le nozze stringere con lei non posso,
Se il vostro mancami saldo favor.

IL CAPORALE E CORO: La nostra figlia, s'è stabilito,
Un inimico non prenderà, no!
Le si conviene miglior partito,
Tal'è d'un padre la volontà.

TONIO: Vi ricusate?

IL CAPORALE E CORO: Con fondamento:
Mentr'ella da già promessa
Al nostro reggimento.

TONIO: Non lo poteva affatto,
Se appunto mi son fatto,
Per essa militar.

IL CAPORALE: Peggio per te!

TONIO: Signori miei—voi, suo buon padre,
Deh! m'ascoltate!

CORO: Peggio per te!

TONIO: La vostra figlia m'ama.

CORO: Possibil mai?—La nostra figlia!

TONIO: Sì, m'ama! lo giuro al ciel.

Hail to the victors, their laurels who win
Hail too to death, when we've fought the good fight!
The brave will never compass their safety by flight!

THE CORPORAL: Eh! but who comes? Oh, it is the youngster
Who was taken this morning; bravo! surely
He has enlisted–he has become a soldier.
(*Enter Tonio, with the French cockade in his cap.*)

TONIO: My brave companions, this day so joyful!
I've come to follow your much-prized flag.
For love alone do I return to you;–
And a great hero will I become.
Ah yes! even she for whom I'm sighing
Has pity on my deep felt passion,
And this fond hope and joy long wished for,
Affects my thoughts, enchants my heart!

CHORUS: Our comrade has fallen deeply in love.

TONIO: He confides his hopes to you alone!

CHORUS: What! has our daughter enthralled you?

TONIO: Ah! pray now hear me; hear!
You who are her father, hear me, I pray.
I cannot hope to gain her in marriage,
If the consent of all of you be denied.

THE CORPORAL AND CHORUS:
Our dearest daughter, it is resolved,
Shall not be wedded to a foe. No!
A match much better shall be accomplished,
Of that her father will take care.

TONIO: Do you refuse her?

THE CORPORAL AND CHORUS:
With good sound reason;–
She is pledged, not to marry
Without consent of the regiment.

TONIO: Of which I have the honor to be one.
I have become, for her sake,
One of your regiment.

THE CORPORAL: The worse for you!

TONIO: Gentlemen, hear me: you her good father–
Ah, pray now, hear me!

CHORUS: We do not want you.

TONIO: Your beauteous daughter loves me.

CHORUS: Can it be true?–our own dear daughter!

TONIO: She loves me; bear witness, Heaven!

CORO: Che dire! che fare? Poichè egli è piaciuto
D'un padre avveduto al nodo assentir.
Ma senza mistero, non sembra pur vero,
Che questo bamboccio, ce l'abbia ghermir.

TONIO: Ebben?

IL CAPORALE: Se dici il ver, suo padre adesso
Il suo consentimento ci fa promesso.

CORO: Sì;—il suo consentimento, ci fa promesso.

TONIO: Qual destino! qual favore!
La sua mano, ed il suo core!
Ah! finito è il mio penar—
Son marito e militar.
Suo padre me l'ha data!—è sposa mia!
(*Entra Sulpizio e Maria.*)

SULPIZIO: Esser non può d'alcun di che sua zia.
Se la porta con sè—

IL CAPORALE E CORO: Che! Nostra figlia portarla via? Sei pazzo.

TONIO: Lungi da me condurla! e sarà ver mio
Bene egli è un sogno crudel.

MARIA: Convien partir! o miei compagni d'arme;
E d'ora in poi lontan da voi fuggir,—
Ma per pietà celatemi quel pianto,—
Ha il vostro duol per il cor
Di Maria supremo incanto.
Convien partir, convien partir;
Ah! per pietà, celate il vostro pianto,
Addio, addio; convien partir!

SULPIZIO, TONIO ED IL CAPORALE: Io perdo, o cara, la sola speme
Ogni mio bene perdendo te.
A tant'affanno non regge il core
Simil dolore non v'è per me.

MARIA: Convien partir—o voi che nel mio core;
Destaste i primi palpiti d'amore!
Ed il piacer, con me partiste e il pianto.
M'offron dell'or—in cambio di quel ben puro soltanto.
Convien partir, ecc.

TONIO: Amici, ah! in ver ciò mai non sia;
Partir non de'—non de'—Maria.
Ah! no!

IL CAPORALE: A tanto affanno regge il core;
Simil dolore, non è per me.

CHORUS: What do we say in answer? It is the duty
Of a prudent father to give his consent.
It seems, though unlikely, beyond even belief
This youth should have won her, and call her his own.

TONIO: But speak!

THE CORPORAL: If he speaks truth, her fond loving fathers,
In promise most faithful, will give their consent.

CHORUS: Yes; in promise most faithful, we'll give our consent.

TONIO: O, happy fate! oh, joyous hour!
Her hand and heart I now have gained!
Ah! my anguish is all ended–
Now a husband and a soldier.
Her fathers now have given her–she's wholly mine!
(*Enter Sulpizio and Maria.*)

SULPIZIO: She can belong to none but to her aunt.
Should she take her away–

CHORUS AND CORPORAL: What, our own daughter! take her away! What madness!

TONIO: Take her away from Tonio? And shall, indeed,
My happiness pass away like a dream?

MARIA: Farewell! a long farewell! my dear companions,
In pity, do not strive to hide your sorrow,–
Those tears will be my comfort on the morrow.
Farewell, my friends; farewell, my friends, farewell,
In pity, do not strive to hide you sorrow,–
Farewell, farewell; I now must leave!

SULPIZIO, TONIO AND CORPORAL: Break not my heart!
Must we, then, part?
Glory and arms
Have now no charms.

MARIA: I must now go–but I can never forget you;
No, live where I may, my heart is yours!
I shall ever, in pomp and pleasure, still regret you;
No friends can be so dear as those I leave behind me.
Farewell, farewell, farewell, etc.

TONIO: My friends, in truth, this never must be;–
You should not ever depart from here, Maria
Ah! no!

THE CORPORAL: To lose you thus my heart is filled with pain;
Such grief as this will never be mine again.

SULPIZIO: Io perdo, o cara! la sola speme:
Ogni mio bene perdendo te.

CORO: Partir, no, non de'!

TONIO: Ah! se vi mi lasciate io vengo via.

SULPIZIO: Ma ingaggiato non sei, bellezza mia.

MARIA: Tonio!

TONIO: Mia bene amata!

MARIA: Questo colpo mancava al mio tormento.

TONIO: Maria!

MARIA: Perderlo adesso? Ah! che morir mi sento.

SULPIZIO: Ma ingaggiata tu sei.

MARIA E TONIO: Questo colpo mancava al mio cor.
Ahimè!

IL CAPORALE, SULPIZIO E CORO: Oh! duol, oh! sorpresa, lasciarla partir
Al diavolo Marchesa, che ce la vuol rapir.
In ogni cimento, che s'abbia a sfidar
Del nostro reggimento è l'angelo tutelar.

MARIA E TONIO: Ah! non più speranze—non più piacere,
D'un giorno solo potrò goder.
Ah! ch'ogni bene disprezza il cor,
Se a tante pene lo danna amor!

LA MARCHESA: Andiam, nipote.

MARIA: Miei cari amici, addio! per sempre!
La man, o Pietro—la tua, Matteo;
La tua, vecchio Tommaso.

LA MARCHESA: Ah, qual orror!

MARIA: Che ancor bambina in braccio mi portavi:—
Abbracciami, Sulpizio!
Ah! di costoro io son l'amor!

LA MARCHESA: Oh, l'orror!

TONIO: Oh, l'orror!

CORO: Nostra figlia nostro amor.

TONIO: Il mio core è a te serbato;
E fedele a te sarò.
Ah, s'il mio core è di Maria
E fido a lei lo serberò.

LA MARCHESA: Andiam, partiam.

ORTENSIO: Andiam, Marchesa; su via pertiam.

IL CAPORALE, SULPIZIO E CORO: Al diavol la Marchesa,
E con lei chi la porta.

---

SULPIZIO: I lose, beloved one, now my only hope;—
And every joy is gone in losing you!

CHORUS: To leave us!–No, it must not be!

TONIO: Yes, yes: if you do leave us, I must follow.

SULPIZIO: But are you not enlisted, my tender youngster?

MARIA: Tonio!

TONIO: My own beloved!

MARIA: This alone was wanted to complete my anguish.

TONIO: Maria!

MARIA: And I must leave him? Ah, I feel it worse than death.

SULPIZIO: But you are enlisted.

MARIA AND TONIO: This dread blow will surely crush my fond heart.
Alas!

THE CORPORAL, SULPIZIO AND CHORUS: O grief, O surprise! to let her depart
With the cruel Marchioness.
In every trial that we have endured
She has been the tutelary angel of our regiment.

MARIA AND TONIO: Ah! no longer hope–no longer pleasure,
May I enjoy for a single day.
Ah! let my heart despise every delight,
If love condemns it to such pains as this!

THE MARCHIONESS: My niece, now let us depart.

MARIA: My dear friends, farewell! farewell for ever!
Your hand, dear Pietro–yours, too, Matteo;
And yours, old Tommaso.

THE MARCHIONESS: Ah, I am shocked!

MARIA: When yet a little child, in his arms he bore me–
Embrace me, dear Sulpizio!
Ah! by them I am beloved!

THE MARCHIONESS: I am shocked!

TONIO: So am I!

CHORUS: Our daughter dear is our best treasure!

TONIO: My heart now beats for you alone;
And constant will I ever be.
Ah, yes; my heart is now Maria's
And faithfully will I devote it to her.

THE MARCHIONESS: Let us away.

ORTENSIUS: Even so, my lady–we'll journey there.

THE CORPORAL, SULPIZIO AND CHORUS: The deuce take the Marchioness,
And him along with her

---

FINE DELL'ATTO PRIMO.

# ATTO II

## SCENA I

*(Il teatro rappresenta un salone, che per mezzo di porte in fondo mette ad una galleria. Porte e finestre laterali. Un clavicembalo, tavolini, ecc.)*

*(Ortensio e Sulpizio, che avrà un braccio al collo, ma di tempo in tempo gestisce per provare che la ferita va meglio.)*

ORTENSIO: Ecco le carte che il notaro invia.
Il duca e la sua madre
'Per le sei saran qui.' Feste! allegria!
*(Via.)*

SULPIZIO: Povera figlia! Io più non ho coraggio
Di vederla soffrir. Già da quattr'ore
Le van storpiando i piedi, perchè impari
Il minuetto—e quella, abituata
A saltare con noi liberamente,
Pianage — e ripete: Non ne faccio niente!
Vestita da gran dama—
*(Entra Maria.)*

MARIA: Oh, mio Sulpizio!
Io non ne posso più—vonno ammazzarmi—
Ma tel dissi, e il ripeto schiettamente,
Hanno un bel dir: 'Non ne faremo niente.'
Io Tonio voglio—e non baroni o duchi.
Tonio per me si fe' soldato, ed io—

SULPIZIO: La zia!—

MARIA: Che importa?

SULPIZIO: Zitti.
Miseriocordia! che toelette.
*(Esce la Marchesa, in toupet.)*

LA MARCHESA: La romanza in quistione è ritrovata.
E cosa prelibata—
Venere scende—

SULPIZIO: (E monta il mal umore.)

LA MARCHESA: Che dite?

SULPIZIO: Io? Nulla affatto—

LA MARCHESA: Venere scende fra la notte opaca,
Per vedere colui, che amor le inspira—
*(Musica.)*

MARIA: (Sulpizio, senti?)

SULPIZIO: (Oh, bello!)

---

END OF ACT I.

# ACT II

## SCENE I

*(The Stage represents a Saloon opening by folding doors at the back on to a gallery. A clavecin, small tables, etc.)*

*(Ortensius and Sulpizio discovered, who has an arm in a sling, but makes signs from time to time, to show that the wound is better.)*

ORTENSIUS: Here are the cards sent by the notary.
The Duke and his mother
Will be here at six o'clock.'
What pleasure!
*(Exit.)*

SULPIZIO: Poor girl! I have no longer courage
To see her suffer. For four hours has she been
Twisting her feet in every direction, learning
The minuet; and she who has been used
To do just as she pleases with us,
Now weeps, and repeats: 'I can do nothing
Dressed as a grand lady.'
*(Enter Maria.)*

MARIA: Oh, Sulpizio,
I can do no more of it, if they kill me for it.
But I have already said, and I now repeat it.
We have a good saying: *'Against my will I will do nothing.'*
I will have Tonio, and not barons and dukes.
Tonio for my sake became a soldier, and I–

SULPIZIO: Your aunt!–

MARIA: I care not for her!

SULPIZIO: Gently.
Mercy on us! what a toilette.
*(Enter the Marchioness, in toupée.)*

THE MARCHIONESS:
The romance in question is found,–
It is an exquisite gem.
Venus descends–

SULPIZIO: (And bad humor ascends.)

THE MARCHIONESS: What do you say?

SULPIZIO: I? Nothing, truly.

MARCHIONESS: Venus descends in the midst of night,
To see him who has inspired her with love.
*(Music.)*

MARIA: (Sulpizio, do you hear?)

SULPIZIO: (Oh, splendid!)

## Act II, Scene I

LA MARCHESA: Ebben, Maria, stupida resti. Andiamo;
Voi zitto; tu sta attenta—incominciamo.
(*Si pone al clavicembalo, e suona con caricatura.*)

MARIA: Sorgeva il di del bosco il seno,
E Vener bella scendea dal ciel,
Scendeva in questo soggiorno ameno.
Sulle orme amiche del suo fedel.

SULPIZIO: Il nostro canto era più bel.
Rataplan, rataplan, rataplan, rataplan,
E il reggimento ch'egual non ha.

MARIA: Rataplan, rataplan, rataplan, rataplan,
E il reggimento ch'egual non ha.

LA MARCHESA: E—ma che sento mai?

MARIA: Perdon—perdono!
Confusa un po' mi sono.
Ero distratta: perdon! perdon!
È quest'amante a cui Ciprigna,
Donava il premio del valor,
Il più gentile della città
La cui beltà—

SULPIZIO: Oh, ben supremo della beltà.

MARIA E SULPIZIO: Eccolo qua.
Ecco l'undecimo ch'egual non ha!

LA MARCHESA: Oh, quale infamia—che dite la?

MARIA: (*a Sulpizio*).
(Ohimè, che noja!)

LA MARCHESA: Andiamo avanti.

MARIA: Sia pur cosi.
(*Alla Marchesa, con dispetto, poi piano a Sulpizio.*)
Ma non c'è case—non c'entra qui.
Vener scorgendo tanto vezzosa,
L'eco del monte, della valle
Di Filomela l'ansia gelosa
Ripeteranno col suon d'amor.

LA MARCHESA: Via, sospiriamo siccome lei.

SULPIZIO: Io preferisco a que' sospiri
D'un buon tamburo il bel fragor.

MARIA: Ah! non ho più pazienza,—
Troppo è ridicol cosa;
Io non ne posso più.

LA MARCHESA: Ohimè che sento!
ah, qual risposta!

MARIA: *En avant! En avant!*
Rataplan—plan—plan!

---

THE MARCHIONESS: Well, Maria, you stand there like a stupid.
Come, pay attention—we will begin.
(*She places herself at the piano, which she plays in an exaggerated style.*)

MARIA: The light of early day was breaking,
When from the skies above
Fair Venus to her grot descended.
To seek the object of her love.

SULPIZIO: Our songs in camp were much more gay.
Rataplan, rataplan, rataplan, rataplan.
Roll on, roll on, and march away.

MARIA: Rataplan, rataplan, rataplan, rataplan.
Roll on, roll on, and march away.

THE MARCHIONESS: Eh! what in the name of fate do I hear?

MARIA: Forgive me, forgive me;
I'm a little confused.
My thoughts were wandering; forgive me!
It is this lover, to whom Ciprynia
Gave the premium of valor,
The most charming in all the city,
Whose beauty—

SULPIZIO: Our regiment for beauty pre-eminent.

MARIA AND SULPIZIO: This is it.
The Eleventh remains without a rival.

THE MARCHIONESS: O, what infamy—what are you saying?

MARIA: (*to Sulpizio*).
(Oh, what an annoyance.)

THE MARCHIONESS: Let us continue.

MARIA: Be it so.
(*To the Marchioness, with spitefulness, afterwards whispering to Sulpizio.*)
But it is not so—it does not come in here.
Venus discovered so many charms,
That the echoes of the hills and valleys
Repeated with sounds of love
The jealous pangs of Philomel.

THE MARCHIONESS: Here you must sigh as she did.

SULPIZIO: I prefer to such sighs
The sound of a good drum.

MARIA: Ah! I have no more patience,—
It is truly ridiculous;
I will bear no more of it.

THE MARCHIONESS: What do I hear
Ah! what an answer!

MARIA: *En avant! En avant!*
Rataplan–plan–plan!

---

LA MARCHESA: Quale orror: possibil mai?
Che si possa avviluppar
Ad un canto si' gentile
La canzon d'un militar!
(*La Marchesa allontana, sdegnata. Maria entra nelle proprie stanzè, e, mentre Sulpizio sta per andarsene dal fondo s'incontra con Ortensio.*)

ORTENSIO: Giusto voi, granatiere.

SULPIZIO: Cos'è accaduto?

ORTENSIO: C'è abbasso un militar—ma di que' grossi!
Ha uno spallino d'or.

SULPIZIO: Uno spallino?
(Forse lui!—cospetton—ci vorria questa!
Che gazzabuglio allora e che tempesta.)
(*Parte.*)

ORTENSIO: Un giorno o l'altro—ed esser dee pur bello!
Dee cangiarsi in quartier tutto il castello.
(*Via.*)
(*Entra Maria.*)

MARIA: Per si' fatal contratto tutto è ietizia intorno,
La mia sventura io compirò in tal giorno—
Ma cosa sento io mai?
Ciel!—ah, m'illudessi?
Questa marcia guerriera—
Ah, so pur dessi!
Oh, trasporto! oh, dolce ebbrezza!
Son gli amici del mio cor.
Bei piacer di giovinezza
Ritornate almen con lor;
Evviva l'Italia!
E i prodi guerrier;
Son dessi mia gioia,
Mio solo pensier.
Ad essi soltanto
Aspira il mio cor;
Con essi ritrovo
La gloria, l'amor.

CORO: È lei, nostra figlia.
Qual piacer, qual destin!
L'antica tua famiglia
Ti vede alfin.
(*Entra Sulpizio, poi Tonio e Ortensio.*)

SULPIZIO: O camerati! amici!

CORO: Oh! veh, Sulpizio!

SULPIZIO: Si, Sulpizio in persona,
Che vi stringe e v'abbraccia tutti quanti.
Tommaso—Ambrogio—Pietro—
Nessun manca all'appello!

MARIA: (*cercando collo sguardo*). Oh, si, nessuno!

TONIO: E neppur Tonio.

MARIA: (*correndo ad esso*). Ah, Tonio mio! ma, guardo,—
(*A Sulpizio.*)
Ha uno spallino.

---

THE MARCHIONESS: For shame!
Is it possible?
Thus dare to disfigure
With a noisy military tune
A song so charming as this!
(*Exit the Marchioness, enraged.– Maria enter her own room; Sulpizio is also about to leave.– Ortensius enters.*)

ORTENSIUS: You are just the person I wanted to see, grenadier.

SULPIZIO: What has happened?

ORTENSIUS: There is a soldier below–but one of the great ones;
He has a wounded shoulder.

SULPIZIO: A wounded shoulder?
(Perhaps it is he. Zounds! that this should happen!
What an uproar there will be!)
(*Exit.*)

ORTENSIUS: Every day there is something happening,
And the whole castle is turned topsy-turvy.
(*Exit.*)
(*Enter Maria, alone.*)

MARIA: All around rejoice at the fatal contract,
While I in one day see my misery complete,
But what do I hear?
Heavens!–is it an illusion?
This martial music!
Ah! it is they!
Oh! what happiness, what delight!
It is my heart's best friends.
Sweet pleasure of youth,
With them you return.
Long live my country,
And all its brave warriors;
They are my delight–
They are my sole thought;
For them–them alone,
Does my heart now long;
With them I should find
Love and glory once more.

CHORUS: It is she, our daughter.
What happiness! what joy!
Your loving family
Sees you at length again. (*Enter Sulpizio, followed by Tonio and afterward Ortensio.*)

SULPIZIO: Oh, comrades, friends!

CHORUS: Oh Sulpizio!

SULPIZIO: Yes, Sulpizio himself,
And he embraces every one of you.
Thomas–Ambrose–Peter–
None are missing at my call.

MARIA: (*looking around*). Oh yes, all are here.

TONIO: Ay, even Tonio.

MARIA: (*running to him*). Ah, my own Tonio! But look (*To Sulpizio.*)
He has a wounded shoulder.

**TONIO:** Per Bacco!
Quand'un sì è messo in testa
Di morire sul campo dell'onore,
Non c'è a dir—o cale in alto, o
more.

**SULPIZIO:** Ma voi, miei buoni amici, un bicchierino
Forse ne bevereste?

**CORO:** Figurarsi!

**MARIA:** E se torna la zia?

**SULPIZIO:** Staran celati
In fondo al parco. Ortensio!

**ORTENSIO:** Misericordia!

**MARIA:** Senza tante smanie,
A costor fate dare una bottiglia.

**ORTENSIO:** Ce ne vuole una botte?

**SULPIZIO:** Meno ciarle,
Sien gli ordini eseguiti, e se resiste—

**ORTENSIO:** Io poi—

**SULPIZIO:** Già intesi ciamo.

**CORO:** Andiam.

**ORTENSIO:** No, che non vengo.

**CORO:** Andiamo—andiamo.
(*I soldati partono via da Ortensio.*)

**SULPIZIO, MARIA E TONIO:**
Stretti insiem tutti tre,
Qual favor! qual piacer!
Tanto ben, tal mercè
Non può il cor sostener.

**SULPIZIO:** Dolce memoria!

**TONIO:** Bel tempo andato!

**MARIA:** Da noi lontano—

**SULPIZIO:** S'è trasportato.

**TONIO:** Ma tornera.

**SULPIZIO:** Lo spero invano.
Il tempo andato tornò per me,
A lui vicino, vicino a te.

**SULPIZIO, MARIA E TONIO:**
Stretti insiem tutti tre.
Qual favor! qual piacer
Tanto ben, tal mercè
Non può il cor sostener.

**TONIO:** Tu parlerai per me—

**MARIA:** Per lui tu dèi parlar.

**TONIO:** Premiar la nostra fe'.

**MARIA:** Nè devi pi tardar.

**SULPIZIO:** Ma udite, udite almen.

**TONIO:** La tua promessa è urgente.

**MARIA:** Ei m'ama immensamente.

**TONIO:** Il core è la sua fe'.

**SULPIZIO:** Ma al diavolo voi e me.

---

**TONIO:** By Bacchus!
When a man has taken it into his head
To die on the field of honor,
No one can tell where the blow may fall.

**SULPIZIO:** But you, my dear friends,
Perhaps you would like a cup of wine.

**CHORUS:** Willingly.

**MARIA:** And if my aunt should return?

**SULPIZIO:** They shall be concealed
In the park. Ortensius!

**ORTENSIUS:** Good Heavens!

**MARIA:** Without more ado,
Go and get a cask of wine.

**ORTENSIUS:** Do you want a whole cask?

**SULPIZIO:** Without any prating.
Let the order be obeyed; and if you resist—

**ORTENSIUS:** I then—

**SULPIZIO:** We understand each other.

**CHORUS:** Let us go.

**ORTENSIUS:** No, do not come.

**CHORUS:** Let us go, let us go.
(*The soldiers depart from Ortensius.*)

**SULPIZIO, MARIA AND TONIO:**
All three united together again—
What a favor! what a pleasure!
The heart can scarcely sustain
Such unlooked-for happiness!

**SULPIZIO:** Sweet remembrances!

**TONIO:** Oh, days gone by!

**MARIA:** Far from us.

**SULPIZIO:** They are gone.

**TONIO:** But they will return.

**SULPIZIO:** I hope it, in vain;
But past times come again for him and me,
When near, oh, near to you.

**SULPIZIO, MARIA AND TONIO:**
All three united together again—
What a favor! what a pleasure!
The heart can scarcely sustain
Such unlooked-for happiness!

**TONIO:** You will speak for me—

**MARIA:** You must speak for him.

**TONIO:** And plead plighted faith.

**MARIA:** You must not delay.

**SULPIZIO:** But listen, listen at least.

**TONIO:** Your promise is urgent.

**MARIA:** He loves me immensely.

**TONIO:** With heart and soul.

**SULPIZIO:** The plague take you and me.

---

**SULPIZIO, MARIA E TONIO:**
Stretti insiem tutti tre.
Qual favor! qual piacer!
Tanto ben, tal mercè,
Non può cor sostener.
(*Entra la Marchesa.*)

**LA MARCHESA:** Che vedo! un ufiziale?—E voi, Sulpizio,
Qui rinchiuso con lor, che fate?

**MARIA:** Oh zia!
Questi è quel Tonio che salvommi un giorno
De certa morte—quest'è l'amor mio.
(*Timida.*)

**LA MARCHESA:** Che—amor!—che dite voi?

**TONIO:** Signora—

**LA MARCHESA:** Zitto!
Al Duca Krakentorp sposa è Maria.

**SULPIZIO:** Cioè (perdoni) sbaglia un po' la zia!
E promessa soltanto suo malgrado;
Ed or che Tonio capitano è fatto,
E che la vuol, va a monte ogni contratto.

**LA MARCHESA:** Come, Sulpizio?—voi—in tal guisa, voi—
Che sapete—

**TONIO:** Ma, signora—

**LA MARCHESA:** Escite!
(*A Tonio.*)
Nè qui osate mai più di porre il piede!

**TONIO:** (*offeso*). Qual baldanza è la vostra!
Vado e torno, Maria;
Sarai mia sposa al nuovo giorno.
(*A Maria, che piange, e parte.*)

**SULPIZIO:** Bravo!

**LA MARCHESA:** Che dite?

**SULPIZIO:** Addio le ho detto.

**LA MARCHESA:** (*a Maria*). Ritiratevi tosto; invan piangete.

**MARIA:** Parto—ma, Tonio—

**LA MARCHESA:** E quando ubbidirete?
(*A tutti e duve, che andavan via. Maria dà uno squardo a Sulpizio, e parte.*)
Fermatevi, Sulpizio—

**LA MARCHESA:** Un gran segreto confidar dovrei—
Alla vostra onestà. Lo leggete.

**SULPIZIO:** (*legge*) Educata nella mia gioventù troppo severamente, e toltami ogni via di conoscere la società—al primo comparir nel mondo vidi un giovane ufficiale—mi piacque—Io amai—partiva—e

---

**SULPIZIO, MARIA AND TONIO:**
All three united together again—
What a favor! what a pleasure!
The heart can scarcely sustain
Such unlooked-for happiness!
(*Enter the Marchioness.*)

**THE MARCHIONESS:** What do I see? and officer!—and you, Sulpizio,
You here with them—what are you about?

**MARIA:** Oh, aunt!
This is Tonio, who long ago saved me!
From certain death—this is my lover. (*Timidly.*)

**THE MARCHIONESS:** What—love! What do you say?

**TONIO:** Lady—

**THE MARCHIONESS:** Be silent!
Maria is betrothed to the Duke of Krakenthorp.

**SULPIZIO:** This is—(your pardon)—a little mistake of her good aunt's;
She is promised only in defiance of herself;
And, now that Tonio is made a captain,
And that he will marry her, the contract is ended.

**THE MARCHIONESS:** What, Sulpizio?–you–in this manner–you
Who well know—

**TONIO:** But, signora—

**THE MARCHIONESS:** Go!
(*To Tonio.*)
And never dare to put your foot here again.

**TONIO:** (*offended*). What presumption is yours!
I go, but will return, Maria;
You shall be my wife by break of day.
(*To Maria, who weeps.*)

**SULPIZIO:** Bravo!

**THE MARCHIONESS:** What say you?

**SULPIZIO:** I merely said 'Good bye.'

**THE MARCHIONESS:** (*to Maria*). Withdraw immediately; you weep in vain.

**MARIA:** I go–but, Tonio–

**THE MARCHIONESS:** And when will you obey?
(*To both, who are going. Maria gives a look at Sulpizio, and goes.*)
Remain, Sulpizio–

**THE MARCHIONESS:** I am about to confide a great secret
To your discretion. Read this.

**SULPIZIO:** (*reads*). Brought up in my youth too strictly, and deprived of the opportunities of mixing in society, at my first appearance in the world I saw a young officer—he pleased me—and a daughter was the

# Act II, Scene I

da un matrimonio clandestino n'ebbi una figlia. Ora, una mano celeste a me la guida; ma, per mio rossore, pubblicar non posso in faccia agli uomini, per legami di famiglia, per inimicizie nazionali, che fui sposa—e quella che ad ogni istante abbraccio—quella Maria che voi mi rendeste, quella è figlia mia.'
(*La Marchesa quasi piangendo si getta a' suoi piedi*)

**SULPIZIO:** Ah, signora!— Disponete di me come vi piace—

**LA MARCHESA:** Al Duca Krakentorp la persuadete A passar in isposa—e sopra tutto Non svelate il mistero—

**SULPIZIO:** Vado—volo.'
(*Entrano la Duchessa ed il Notaro.*)

**LA DUCHESSA:** Mio figlio il Duca Occupato alla corte, non può venir, Ma ov'è vostra nipote?

**LA MARCHESA:** Tuttora alla toilette; Ma verrà tosto.
(*Entrano Maria e Sulpizio.*)

**LA MARCHESA:** Maria!

**MARIA:** Cara madre!
(*Piangendo.*)

**LA MARCHESA:** Oh, figlia—zitto!

**SULPIZIO:** Giudizio—
(*Ad entrambe sotto voce.*)

**LA MARCHESA:** Un compimento avrà la festa!

**MARIA:** (*alla Marchesa*). Deggio segnar?

**LA MARCHESA:** Ah! la mia brama è questa.
(*Odesi un improvviso rumore.*)
(*Entrano Tonio e soldati.*)

**TUTTI:** Giusto Ciel! quali grida! qual chiasso!

**TONIO:** Mi seguite, compagni.

**CORO:** Ti rincora, amata figlia; Per giovarti siamo qua, Da ogni mal la tua famiglia, Te difendere saprà. Tergi il pianto, affrena il duolo. In noi fede aver puoi solo. Se ogni speme in te svanì, Per te sola ognum è qui.

**TONIO:** La misera forzata Si vuol da noi salvata: Lei sola è il nostro bene, Nè trarla ad un imene, Ch'ella non può compir.

**SULPIZIO:** Bravo, Tonio!

**LA MARCHESA:** Cosa fate?

**SULPIZIO:** Vivandiera al reggimento L'ha veduta e l'adorò.

---

offspring of a clandestine marriage. Now a heavenly hand has brought her to me; but shame prevents me revealing in the face of the world that I forgot family ties and national enmities–that I became a wife–that she whom I embrace every moment–that Maria whom you restored to me, is my daughter.
(*The Marchioness throws herself, weeping, at his feet.*)

**SULPIZIO:** Oh, lady! Dispose of me as you please.

**THE MARCHIONESS:** Persuade her to become the wife Of the Duke of Krakenthorp; and, above all, Do not reveal the secret.

**SULPIZIO:** I go–I fly.
(*Enter the Duchess and a Notary.*)

**THE DUCHESS:** My son the Duke Is at the court so occupied, That he cannot come.

**THE MARCHIONESS:** All things are here prepared, And we have been waiting for him.
(*Enter Maria and Sulpizio.*)

**THE MARCHIONESS:** Maria.

**MARIA:** Dear mother.
(*Weeping*)

**THE MARCHIONESS:** Oh, daughter, hush!

**SULPIZIO:** Justice.
(*Whispering to both.*)

**THE MARCHIONESS:** The feast will be complete.

**MARIA:** (*the Marchioness*). Must I sign?

**THE MARCHIONESS:** Yes! such is my wish.
(*An extraordinary noise is heard.*)
(*Enter Tonio and soldiers.*)

**ALL:** Just Heaven! What cries! What a bustle!

**TONIO:** Follow me, companions.

**CHORUS:** We have come to free our child Gallant, loving fathers we; Oh, we soldiers know our duty. Never fear them, never fear. Spite of velvet, silk, and feather, We'll the castle leave together. Welcome to the field and tent, Daughter of the regiment.

**TONIO:** From certain misery We shall save her: In her alone is our happiness, And she shall not be forced Into a detested union.

**SULPIZIO:** Bravo, Tonio.

**THE MARCHIONESS:** What are you doing?

**SULPIZIO:** When sutler of our regiment, He saw her and adored her.

---

**LA MARCHESA:** Oh, rossore! oh, avvilimento!

**SULPIZIO:** (La Marchesa in cor gelò.)

**MARIA:** Quando il destino in mezzo a stragi era, Nel lor seno fanciulla mi gettò, Essi han raccolto la miseria mia, E i primi passi miei ciascun guidò. Potrebbe mai dimenticarli il cor S'esisto per loro amor.

**CORO:** Infatti ella è gentile, Ne può tener sia vile! Se il vero ella confessa Se aperto mostra il cor. A vil non può tenersi, S'ella confessa il vero; S'è il labbro suo sincero, Se mostra schietto il cor.

**LA MARCHESA:** (Or tutto è noto; non mi rimane che segnar.)

**TONIO:** Che dirà mai?

**MARIA:** Ne morirò.

**LA MARCHESA:** T'arresta! Per me si' gran dolor—per me soltanto?

**ALTRI:** Cielo! che intende dir!

**LA MARCHESA:** Vieni, deh, vieni! Sacrificar non voglio un cor si' bello. In me taccia l'orgoglio, E quel ch'ella sceglieva, amante onesto. Alfin ottenga.

**ALTRI:** E qual'è desso?

**LA MARCHESA:** (*ponendo Tonio nelle braccia di Maria.*) È questo.

**SULPIZIO:** Bene!

**MARIA:** Tonio!

**TONIO:** Maria!

**SULPIZIO:** Brava, Signora Zia! Se non avessi il mustaccio Le darei proprio un militar abbraccio.

**CORO DI DONNE:** Oh, che scandalo, che orrore! Questo Imen fa inorridir. Andiam, partiam.

**TUTTI:** Salvezza alla Francia! Ai suoi lieti di Vivan le gioje Che amor nudrì.

**MARIA:** (*a Tonio*). Dolce tesoro, Han fin le pene; Ah! mai sostiene La gioia il cor. Quanto lo t'adoro Dir non saprei, Per me tu sei Un ciel d'amor.

*FINE.*

---

**THE MARCHIONESS:** Oh, shame! oh, disgrace!

**SULPIZIO:** (The Marchioness is melting.)

**MARIA:** When I was left, abandoned by all, Where in the death-sleep thousands lie. With these brave men I found protection, And shall I now my friends deny?

**CHORUS:** Her heart is really noble Although by soldiers nursed! Such thought should surely give her A place among the first. No one can think it wrong, That she the truth confesses: The bashfulness of her tongue Betokens the candor of her heart

**THE MARCHIONESS:** (Now everything is known, There is nothing left to me but to sign.)

**TONIO:** What will she say?

**MARIA:** It will be the death of me.

**THE MARCHIONESS:** Stop! Shall I cause such wretchedness–I alone?

**THE OTHERS:** Heavens, what do you mean?

**THE MARCHIONESS:** Come, oh come! I will not sacrifice such a noble heart Pride is silenced within me; And the one she has chosen– You, honest lover, shall obtain her.

**THE OTHERS:** And which is he?

**THE MARCHIONESS:** (*bringing Tonio to Maria*). This one.

**SULPIZIO:** Good!

**MARIA:** Tonio!

**TONIO:** Maria!

**SULPIZIO:** Bravo, Signora Aunt! Were it not for my moustache, I would give you a military salute.

**CHORUS OF LADIES:** What a scandal, what a horror! This marriage shocks us. Let us go and leave them.

**ALL:** Hurrah for France! For all their living days May the joys of love Attend upon them.

**MARIA:** (*to Tonio*). Dearest treasure, My griefs are ended; Ah, scarcely can this head Its joy sustain. How much I love you I cannot tell you. For me you are A heaven of love.

*THE END.*

# Madame Sans-Gêne (1915)

## The Lady Without Fear

MUSIC BY UMBERTO GIORDANO ■ LIBRETTO BY RENATO SIMONI

*Madame Sans-Gêne* premiered at the Metropolitan Opera House in New York on January 25, 1915. The three-act opera is set to a libretto by Renato Simoni based upon the comedy by Victorien Sardou and Emile Moreau. The opera opens in Paris on August 10, 1792, the day that the storming of the Tuileries takes place. Catherine Huebscher, a beautiful young Alsatian woman, is known as Madame Sans-Gêne for her carefree nature. She has a laundry, the customers of which include Fouché, am ambitious revolutionary whom Madame Sans-Gêne dislikes intensely. She prefers to take care of Napoléon Bonaparte, an officer who resides close to the laundry. Catherine is about to shut the door to the laundry when Count Neipperg, a wounded Austrian officer, enters and seeks shelter from his pursuers. A band of soldiers then arrives, led by Catherine's sweetheart, Sergeant Lefebvre. He finds the wounded officer but tells his soldiers that there is no one there. During the night Lefebvre and Catherine arrange Neipperg's escape. It is now September, 1811. Napoléon is at the pinnacle of his career. Madame Sans-Gêne is married to Lefebvre, who distinguished himself in the battle of Danzig and has been made Marshal and Duke of Danzig in return for his services. Catherine's behavior remains carefree as always, and the scandals surrounding her at court cause the Emperor to order Lefebvre to divorce her. Catherine and Lefebvre are deeply upset and are also concerned about Neipperg, whom the Emperor suspects of having an affair with his wife, Marie Louise. Catherine at a reception, makes a faux pas—the Emperor's sisters tease her, and she loses her temper at them. The Emperor's major-domo announces that Napoléon wishes to speak to her at once. Napoléon orders Catherine to get a divorce and to leave the court; she reminds him of the times when he was just a young officer and she served him. He is deeply moved by the recollection, but at that moment Neipperg is captured as he is about to enter Marie Louise's apartment. The Emperor orders his immediate execution. Catherine intervenes, proving Neipperg's innocence and saving his life. The Emperor is very impressed by her, and she leaves on his arm to begin the hunt.

## ■ ATTO PRIMO

*La lavanderia di Madame Sans-Gêne a Parigi il 10 Agosto 1792*

*Una bottega di lavandaia in via S. Anna. Grandi finestre a vetrate e porta principale anch'essa a vetrata, mostrano la strada. A destra, in primo piano, una porta d'ingresso dà sul cortile. A sinistra, ancora in primo piano, un'altra porta mette alla stanza da letto di CATERINA.*
*Su corde tese molta biancheria posta ad asciugare: sottane a righe tricoli, camicette insieme a pizzi aristocratici. Una vesta tinnoza, è posata sopra un treppiede. Vicino alla porta del cortile c'è una credenza. Sul fondo, un camino a cappa con fornello per riscaldare i ferri da stirare. Tavole ed assi posate su caralletti per stirare. Sgabelli di legno. Una grande poltrona presso la tavola.*

*All'aprirsi del velario, TONIOTTA, GUILIA e LA ROSSA stirano disattente e svogliate, sempre pronte a correre all'uscio a ogni strepito. Nella strada, una folla mobile, agitata e curiosa, di borghesi, di*

## ■ ACT I

*Madame Sans-Gêne's Laundry Paris, August 10, 1792*

*(Interior of a laundry in the rue Ste. Anne. Large windows and a door, with glass panes, show the street beyond. At the right front a door opens into a courtyard. At the left front another door leads to CATERINA'S bedroom. On cords stretched across the room a lot of laundry is hung up to dry: petticoats with three-colored lines, chemises with fine embroidery. A tub is placed on a three-legged stool. Near the door to the courtyard is a cupboard. At the back is a hooded stove with a little oven for heating the irons. Tables and boards on wooden horses for ironing. Wooden stools. A big armchair near the table.*

*(When the curtain rises, TONIOTTA, GIULLA and LA ROSSA are ironing with a distracted and unwilling air, always ready to run to the door at any sound. In the street a moving crowd, agitated*

*bottegai, guarda verso le Tuileries (a destra). C'è un via vai continuo. S'odono voci, commenti, esclamazioni. Da lontano, scoppi di fucilate e il rombo cupo del cannone.*

**TONIOTTA:** Sono in via della Scala! Li sentite?
Urli e strepiti orrendi il vento porta!

**GIULIA:** Che paura, mio Dio!

**LA ROSSA:** Se vengon qui!

**GIULIA:** *(cadendo ginocchioni)*
Vergine santa!

**TONIOTA:** No! Qui non verrano. L'han con le Tuileries
È il re che voglion mettere alla porta.
*(Romba, lontana, una cannonata)*

**LA ROSSA:** *(turandosi le orecchie)* Ci spezzeranno i vetri!
*(Movimento vivissimo nella via. Una guardia nazionale, ferita alla gamba, è portata a braccia entro la bottega del farmacista dirimpetto. Tutti si affollano davanti alla bottega, volgendo le spalle al pubblico)*

*and curious, of common people and shopkeepers, looks towards the Tuileries — right. — There is continuous coming and going. One hears voices, comments, exclamations. From afar comes the crack of rifles and the deep booming of the cannon.)*

**TONIOTTA:** They're in the rue d'Échelle! Do you hear?
The wind
Brings down their dreadful cries and groans this way!

**GIULLA:** O heaven! how terrible!

**LA ROSSA:** They're coming here!

**GIULLA:** *(falling on her knees)*
Mother in heaven!

**TONIOTTA:** No, no, they will not come.
The Tuileries and the king
Whom they would hurry out will keep them.
*(Far off a cannon booms.)*

**LA ROSSA:** *(stopping her ears)*
They'll break the windows!
*(A lively movement in the street. A national guard, wounded in the leg, is carried by the arm into the pharmacy opposite. All crowd around the shop, turning their backs to the audience.)*

# Act I

TONIOTTA: (*andando alla finestra*) Ecco un ferito!

GIULIA: Una guardia!

TONIOTTA: infelice!

GIULIA: Io tremo tutta!
(*Tuona ancora il cannone. Nella via la folla si agita; una parte di essa volge verso sinistra*)

LA ROSSA: Il cannon romba e tuona!

TONIOTTA: E la padrona che non torna ancora!

LA ROSSA: Dio l'assista, la povera padrona!

TONIOTTA: S'è intestata ad uscire ad ogni costo!

GIULIA: Ah! Ti ricorderò, dieci d'agosto!

LA ROSSA: (*guardando nella strada*) Zitte! Avremo notizie! . . . Ecco il cliente della casa vicina!

GIULIA: Ah, sì, il Natese . . .

LA ROSSA: . . . odiatore furente dell' Austriaca e del Re!

TUTTE: (*verso la strada, chiamando con la voce e con i cenni*) Olà, signor Fouché!
Signor Fouché! Signor Fouché!
(*FOUCHÉ entra rapido, guardandosi indietro, come chi sospetti d'essere spiato. Porta una valigia, e impugna un ombrello rosso*)

GUILIA: Signor Fouché! Che notizie recate?

FOUCHÉ: I patrioti hanno le beffe e il danno
e trionfa il tirano.
Su! La mia biancheria datemi presto,
ch'io la metta nel sacco insieme al resto.
(*TONIOTTA e GIULIA tolgono alcuni capi di biancheria non ancora lavata da un canestro. Egli ne fa dei rotoli, che caccia e stipa nella vaglia, sempre continuando a parlare*)

LA ROSSA: Ahimè! Scappate!

FOUCHÉ: La parola è dura, parto con un zinzino di premura.

GIULIA: Dunque le Tuileries non sono prese?

FOUCHE: Osso duro! Osso duro!
Prima il colpo pareva sicuro!
Ora invece il disastro è completo!
(*TONIOTTA dà a FOUCHE un fazzoletto di colore con un grosso strappo nel mezzo. FOUCHE lo esamina*)
Non è mio! E trionfa Capeto.

TONIOTA: Ma sì, è vostro! Tenetelo! E vostro!

---

TONIOTTA: (*going to the window*) See there! a wounded man!

GIULIA: A guard!

TONIOTTA: Poor thing!

GIULIA: Oh, how I'm trembling!
(*The cannon is heard again. In the street the crowd becomes agitated; part turn towards the left.*)

LA ROSSA: The cannon booms far off!

TONIOTTA: Our mistress does not come.

LA ROSSA: May no harsh rebuff Be keeping her!

TONIOTTA: If she would only stay Safe out of danger.

GIULIA: Ah!
I never can forget this dreadful day — the tenth of August!

LA ROSSA: (*looking into the street*) Be still! look there! here comes the man Next door.

GIULIA: Natese!

LA ROSSA: He who puts his ban Of hatred upon Austria and the king.

ALL: (*towards the street, calling and gesticulating*) Ha! monsieur Fouché! monsieur Fouché!
(*Fouché enters rapidly, looking about him, as if suspicious of being spied upon. He carries a valise and holds tightly a red umbrella.*)

GIULIA: Monsieur Fouché, what message do you bring?

FOUCHÉ: The patriots will lose by trick and wrong, —
The tyrant triumphs. Let me take my laundry along with my other things. Be quick!
(*Toniotta and Giulia take some piles of laundry, not yet washed, from a basket. He rolls them up and stuffs them into his valise, always talking.*)

LA ROSSA: Begone!

FOUCHÉ: That word is hard. With slight concern
I go, though.

GIULIA: Tell me now, when can we learn
The Tuileries is taken?

FOUCHÉ: It is hard to tell,
Alas! At first all seemed to be going well,
But now diaster seems complete.
(*Toniotta gives Fouché a colored handkerchief, torn badly in the middle. FOUCHÉ examines it.*)
No, no!
It is not mine.

TONIOTTA: It's yours — take it, and go!

---

FOUCHÉ: (*mette il fazzoletto nella valigia*)
La padrona?

GIULIA: É ancor fuori.

FOUCHÉ: Imprudente!
Star tappati oggi in casa conviene.
(*Si avvia verso la porta d'uscita*)

GIULIA: Le si è detto; mai, chi la tiene?

LA ROSSA: Vien chiamata Sans-Gêne della gente . . .

GIULIA: Ma quest'oggi Sans-Gêne si procura
anche il nome di Senza Paura!

FOUCHÉ: Tarda!

GIULIA: (*impensierita*) È vero! Dovbrebbe tornare!

FOUCHÉ: Purchè torni.

TUTTE: Ci fate tremare.
(*Due cannonate. Esclamazioni. Movimento nella via. Tamburi che battono la carica. FOUCHÉ che sta per uscire, si arresta*)

VOCI DI FUORI: Ecco Sans-Gêne! è qui Sans-Gêne!
(*CATERINA, seguita da un gruppo di gente, entra frettolosa e affannata, con un canestro di biancheria sotto il braccio. Tutte le giovani lavandaie le si affollano intorno festosamente*)

TUTTE: (*portando una sedia nel mezzo della scena, e offrendola a CATERINA.*) Ah, padrona! Finalmente!

FOUCHÉ: Si teneva, si tremava!

CATERINA: Son qui tutta.

GIULIA: Cara!

FOUCHÉ: Brava!

CATERINA: Ah! Non ne posso più!

FOUCHÉ: Dunque, là in fondo?

CATERINA: Un inferno, un finimondo.

FOUCHÉ: Bolle sempre?

CATERINA: Bolle!

FOUCHÉ: Bene!
Raccontate quel che avviene.

CATERINA: Non ho visto proprio nulla.

FOUCHÉ: (*deluso*) Nulla?

GIULIA: Nulla?

CATERINA: (*siede e parla affannata*) Nulla!
Mentre andavo via leggera
tra le grida, gli urli, i canti,
batto il naso in una schiera
di giganti
con la barba nera nera!
Un di quelli balza avanti
e comincia a domandare:
"Dove vai?,, "Dove mi pare!,,
Dice: "Chiuso t'è il passaggio
se non paghi il tuo pedaggio.,,

---

FOUCHÉ: (*putting handkerchief into his valise*) Your mistress?

GIULIA: She's still out.

FOUCHÉ: It is wiser to stay at home These days.

GIULIA: Yes — but she will roam.

LA ROSSA: They call her Without Care — the people here.

GIULIA: But these days that means also Without Fear.

FOUCHÉ: It's late.

GIULIA: (*thoughtfully*) It's true! I wish she would come back.

FOUCHÉ: Provided that she comes.

ALL: You make us tremble,
(*Two cannon-shots. Exclamations. Movements in the street. Drums beat the attack. FOUCHÉ, who is on the point of going out, stops.*)

VOICES OUTSIDE: Here is Sans-Gêne! here is Sans-Gêne!
(*CATERINA, followed by a group of people, enters hastily and in alarm, with a basket of linen under her arm. All the young women in crowd around her joyfully.*)

ALL: (*carrying a seat to the middle of the stage and offering it to CATERINA*) Our mistress! back at last!

FOUCHÉ: How did you save Yourself?

CATERINA: I'm quite all right.

GIULIA: So dear!

FOUCHÉ: So brave!

CATERINA: I am so faint!

FOUCHÉ: But what goes on? do tell.

CATERINA: Nothing but ruin — truly a perfect hell.

FOUCHÉ: It is more than bubbles?

CATERINA: Bubbles?

FOUCHÉ: Do say
What dreadful things have come to you today.

CATERINA: I have seen nothing.

FOUCHÉ: (*deceived*) Nothing?

GIULIA: Nothing?

CATERINA: (*sitting down and talking excitedly*) No!
While I tried to go with an easy gait
Where everyone was mad with groan and song
And desperate cries, I found myself among
A troop of giants, all with beards of black!
One of them seized on me and turned me back,
Asking, "Where are you going?" I

E m'afferra per la vita.
Mi solleva su su su
e mi schiaccia
un gran bacio sulla faccia
con quell'ispida baracca! (*si alza*)
— Bestia! — grido invipertia;
ride il mostro, epoi mi slancia
tra la barba folta folta
del vicin, che alla sua volta
mi scaciucchia sulla guancia!
(*facendo passare il paniere da un braccio all'altro, due volte*)
E così di bocca in bocca
passeggiare, ahime, mi tocca
tra le barbe di carbone
lungo tutto il battaglione!
Mi rassegno al mio destino,
lascio fare a quegli audaci
che m'azzecan centro baci,
profumati all'aglio e al vino!
Finchè libera mi stacco,
batto il tacco
svolto in fretta per la via
e son giunta a casa mia.
(*Tutti ridono*)

VOCI DI FUORI: Viva la Nazione!
(*Tutti si voltano e corrono alla porta*)

FOUCHÉ: (*Si fa largo e chiede, gridando, alla folla di fuori*) Dite, voi cosa c'è?

VOCI DI FUORI: Il popolo vince
ed hanno la peggio
l'Austriaca ed il re.
Si son già rifugiati al maneggio!

FOUCHÉ: E gli Svizzeri?

VOCI DI FUORI: Cessano il tiro, non han più munizioni.

FOUCHÉ: (*rientra e viene verso la ribalta fregandosi le mani*) Respiro!
(*Le voci, ripetendo, Viva la Nazione! si allontananoo. Restano in iscena FOUCHÉ, CATERINA e le ragazze*)

CATERINA: (*alle ragazze*) Il popolo laggiù, fa il bucato
e noi facciamo il nostro. Su, figliuole,
via dalla porta! Distendete al sole
questi panni lavati nel cortil.
(*TONIOTTA e GIULIA portano via la tinozza dalla porta di destra*)
(*alla ROSSA*)
E tu, Rousotte, fila via!
All'ufficiale di via dei Mulini
porta questa biancheria.
Non ne ha troppa. E non gli dare
il conto. No ha da pagare.
È all'asciutto. (*LA ROSSA, via*)

said, "Where I please."
"The road is closed." he said, "until the fees
We ask of you are paid." Then without grace
He picked me up and planted on my face
A kiss with his rough beard. (*She rises.*) "You beast!" I cried,
Maddened; the monster laughed, and at his side
Passed me on to the next man, who in turn
Made his foul kisses burn on my white cheek.
(*She passes the basket twice from one arm to the other.*)
Just so from mouth to mouth I had to pass,
And so be kissed by those black beards *en masse.*
I gave myself up then to destiny,
And let those hundred soldiers fling at me
Their kisses, sweet with garlic and with wine.
And then at last, when liberty was mine,
I did not seem to have much wish to roam
The streets, and so, my friends, I am at home.
(*All laugh.*)

VOICES OUTSIDE: Long live the Nation!
(*All turn and rush to the door.*)

FOUCHÉ: (*expanding himself, and calling to the crowd in the street*) Say, what is this burst?

VOICES: The people conquer, and have done their worst
To the Austrian and the king, who have taken flight
To the ministry!

FOUCHÉ: Where are the Swiss?

VOICES: Their fight
Is off — they have no powder.

FOUCHÉ: (*reentering, rubbing his hands*) I breathe again!
(*The voices calling out "Long live the Nation!" go farther away. There remain on the stage FOUCHÉ, CATERINA, and the GIRLS.*)

CATERINA: (*to the girls*) The people there begin to wash their hands
Of trouble. Let us do *our* wash. While
The sun stands so high, put out this pile of stuff
Upon the lines.
(*TONIOTTA and GIULIA take out the tub by the door at the right.*)
(*To LA ROSSA.*)
And you, Roussotte, be off,
And take this laundry to the officer
Who lives in the rue des Moulins.
Do not stir
His mind to payment, for he's not to pay.
Be off!
(*Exit LA ROSSA*)

CATERINA: (*chiamando un ragazzo ch'è in istrada*) Ehi, Maturino,
corri al posta di via Colbert,
a vedere se c'è
il sergente Lefebvre; e se c'è,
digli che venga da me.

(*Il ragazzo corre via. La scena si vuota. Restasolo FOUCHÉ non visto da CATERINA. Costei chiude i vetri delle finestre, lasciando aperte le imposte*)

(*Durante tutta la seguente scena con FOUCHÉ, CATERINA si dà gran da fare. Prende dal fornello il catino d'acqua e amido e lo depone sulla tavola; stende su questa i panni per stirare, immerge cuffie e cravatte nell'amido, poi le strizza, le fa sgocciolare, le distende sopra un salvietta piegata in due; poi, arrolgendole in essa, ne fa un pacchetto che spreme tra le mani; poi s'accinge a stirare. Prende un ferro, lo accosta alla guancia, per sentire se è caldo, lo rimette sul fornello, ne prende un altro, lo netta, stira; con un ferro da arricciare increspa le trine di una cuffia, ecc. ecc.*)

FOUCHÉ: Mia bella Caterina!

CATERINA: (*voltandosi sorpresa*) Voi siete ancora qui?

FOUCHÉ: Quel Lefebvre vi è assai caro, mi pare!?

CATERINA: È forse proibito d'amare?
È bello, è forte ed è cortese . . .
E poi è del mio paese,
Alsaziono come me.

FOUCHÉ: (*s'accomoda sulla poltrona*) Amore d'infanzia?

CATERINA: Ma che!
Lo conobbi non sono due mesi
al Wauxhall, a una festa da ballo.
. . . Un ceffo da scimmía m'apposta,
mi sbircia, mi segue, s'accosta.
Pareva Berlicche! Sghignazza;
— T'invito, mia bella ragazza,
la fricassée a far con me.
— Gnornò, dico io.
— Perchè? dice lui.
— Perchè, dico io,
ballar non mi garba, signor!
— Smorfiosa, mi grida Berlicche,
sei forse la dama di picche?
Ma giunto alle picche, una pacca
quell'orrido muso gli spacca.
La pacca era appunto . . .

FOUCHÉ: . . . Lefebvre!

(*Calling to a boy in the street*)
Ho! Maturino, without delay
Run to rue Colbert to the soldiers' post,
And see if sergeant Lefebvre is in the host
Of men that drift about there; if he's there,
Tell him that you have come from me.

(*The boy runs off. The stage is empty, except FOUCHÉ, unseen by CATERINA. She closes the windows, but leaves open the shutters.*)

(*During all of the following scene with FOUCHÉ, CATERINA gives herself a lot to do. She takes from the oven the basin of water and starch, and puts it on the table; she spreads out clothes to iron, dips collars and cuffs in the starch, squeezes them out, spreads them on a napkin, folded twice; then, wrapping them up in it, makes a packet, which she squeezes in her hands; then gets ready to iron. She takes an iron, tries it on her cheek to see if it is hot, puts it back in the oven, takes another out, scours it and sets to work; with another iron she curls the edge of a cuff, etc., etc.*)

FOUCHÉ: My fair
And lovely Caterina!

CATERINA: (*turning around in surprise*) You still here?

FOUCHÉ: Is this Lefebvre then to you so dear?

CATERINA: And is one not allowed to love? Command
And courtesy are his, and from my land
He comes—he is Alsatian like me.

FOUCHÉ (*making himself comfortable in the armchair*) A sentiment of childhood, then?

CATERINA: Not he.
We met a Vauxhall not two months ago,
Dancing.—A wretch, who thought himself a beau,
But had a monkey-face, made horrid eyes
At me, and followed me, through his disguise
Accosting me and laughing: "Pretty girl,"
He said, "come join with me the dancing whirl."
"Not I," I said. "Why not?" said he.
"Because
I like not dancing." And by now I was
Enraged, for now I knew this man to be
Berlicche. "Are you the queen of spades?" he cried.
But at that moment in a flash a blow
fell upon his ugly face.—

FOUCHÉ: Lefebvre!

CATERINA: — Mercè, dico io,
— Macchè, dice lui!
Con slancio m'afferra,
con slancio lo stringo,
si pestano i piè, si sgambetta,
si salta, si piroetta!
Così ci siam cotti d'amore
ballando la fricassée!

FOUCHÉ: Dunque presto le nozze?

CATERINA: Presto sì,
se quel geloso non guasta tutto
coi suoi sospetti senza costrutto.
(colta da un pensiero, espressivo
con un gesto della mano)
Anzi, filate!

FOUCHÉ: No!

CATERINA: Che aspettate?

FOUCHÉ: Che siano prese le Tuileries.

CATERINA: Ecco un uom formidabile a strillare
viva la libertà, morte al tiranno.
Ma quando invece i patrioti vanno
in battaglia, la zucca a cimentare,
voi ve ne state qui a scaldar la sedia
con le man sulla pancia. (ridendo)
Oh, che commedia!

FOUCHÉ: (calmo) Le parte compie ognun che gli è prescritta,
e le rivoluzion c'è che le fa . . .

CATERINA: . . . e c'è che ne profitta.
(con ironia)
Dicon che siete state in seminario.

FOUCHÉ: Fui prete.

CATERINA: Ed ora?

FOUCHÉ: Rivoluzionario!

CATERINA: (con ironia) Ciò vi dà
da mangiare?

FOUCHÉ: Non ancora!
Ma in seguito si spera.

CATERINA: (con sempre più viva
ironia) Alla buon'ora!
È per voi che si picchiano laggiù.
È per farvi ministro.

FOUCHÉ: (mezzo serio, mezzo
comico) Su per giù.

CATERINA: Ministro? Non della
Guerra.
Piuttosto di Polizia.
Avete un musetto tagliente . . .

FOUCHÉ: Per annusare la gente!

CATERINA: Vi piace curiosare . . .

FOUCHÉ: Frugare . . .

CATERINA: Spiare
con quegli occhi vivi e scaltri . . .

FOUCHÉ: Con questi occhi vivi e
scaltri . . .

CATERINA: . . . nei segreti degli
altri.

CATERINA: "Thank you," I said,
"But why?" said he!
He flung
His arms with force about me, and I
clung
Close to him, as at once we madly
let
Our feet turn, slide, jump, prance,
and pirouette.

FOUCHÉ: The marriage is at once?

CATERINA: At once, indeed,
Unless someone needs
To spoil it all with false suspicions.
(Struck by a thought, which she
expresses with a gesture.)
Come, now, be off!

FOUCHÉ: Not I!

CATERINA: Why do you wait?

FOUCHÉ: For the Tuileries to fall.

CATERINA: And you a perfectly
able man to call
Long live liberty! Death to the tyrant! When
your patriotic men
Go forth into the fight and face
things, you are safe from harm,
And keep the old armchair there
nice and warm.
Oh, what a comedy!

FOUCHÉ: (calmly) The party does
What is prescribed to it, so now it is
The revolution which—

CATERINA: Which profits.
(With irony.)
I have been told that your career
first was
In a seminary.

FOUCHÉ: Yes, I was a priest.

CATERINA: And now?

FOUCHÉ: A revolutionary.

CATERINA: (with irony) And
does that give you what you need
for food?

FOUCHÉ: Not yet! but I have hopes
of livelihood.

CATERINA: (with increasing irony) And is it to make you minister
they drown
Each other with their blows?

FOUCHÉ: (half serious, half joking) Life's up and down.

CATERINA: Minister? not of War,
but of Police.
You have a face of keenness.

FOUCHÉ: More to please
The people!

CATERINA: You have curiosity.

FOUCHÉ: I like to search.

CATERINA: No, more—you like to
spy,
With your sharp eyes—

FOUCHÉ: With my sharp eyes—

CATERINA: And get
Secrets from others.

FOUCHÉ: E sia,
vada per la polizia.

CATERINA: Ei ci crede e lo confessa!
(con uno scoppio di risa)
Ministro voi sarete quand'io sarò
duchessa!
(con un inchino burlesco a
FOUCHÉ)
Quando sarà chiamato al Ministero,
mi pagherà il suo conto, non è vero?
Sono tre mesi, sa, Vostra Eccellenza,
che la stiro e la inamido a credenza!

FOUCHÉ: (con malizia bonaria)
Non sono il solo! Un altro c'è
che nel pagare somiglia a me!
C'è l'ufficial d'artiglieria,
La Roussotte gli portò
la biancheria, ma il conto no . . .

CATERINA: Voi siete un fannul-
lon, quello è un soldato.

FOUCHÉ: Disperato!
Ha perso il grado,
briga, intriga
per riaverlo e non l'avrà!

CATERINA: Proveretto!

FOUCHÉ: Per mangiare,
l'orologio egli ha impegnato
iermattina da Fouvelet.

CATERINA: Non c'è vecchia por-
tinaia
ficcanaso come voi.

FOUCHÉ: Se aspettate che vi paghi
quel signor Timoleon . . .

CATERINA: (correggendo) Napoleon!

FOUCHÉ: (insistendo) Timoleon!

CATERINA: (irritata) Napoleone
Buonaparte!

FOUCHÉ: È un côrso selvatico,
verdognolo e secco,
dall'occhio enigmatico,
dal naso che è un becco!
Lasciate che vada,
farà poca strada,
credetelo a me!

CATERINA: Crepi l'astrologo!
(Le campane suonano a stormo.
Crescono lo strepito, lo scalpiccio
e le voci. Rombo di cannone. GIU-
LIA e TONIOTTA entrano dalla
porta di destra e corrono al fondo.
CATERINA corre anch'essa verso
il fondo. FOUCHÉ la segue. Guardano fuori.)

FOUCHÉ: Nuvole di fumo!

CATERINA: Brucian le Tuileries!

FOUCHÉ: Ah! so be it! let
Them come and question me.

CATERINA: You would confess!
(with a burst of laughter)
When I am duchess, you'll be minister!
(with a burlesque courtesy to
FOUCHÉ)
When you are at the Ministry in
state,
You'll pay your bill, perhaps a little
late?
In three months' time, my lord, it
will be due
For ironing and starching shirts for
you!

FOUCHÉ: (with good-natured
malice) But I am not alone. Do not
forget
There is another that is in your debt!
There is an officer of the artillery,
To whom Roussotte just now took
laundry—he
Was not to pay—

CATERINA: But you are of no use,
He is a soldier.

FOUCHE: Of bad character!
He's lost his rank, and strives with
low intrigues
To win it back, but that will never
be.

CATERINA: Poor fellow!

FOUCHÉ: And for cash to buy some
bread
He pawned his watch at Fouvelet's
yesterday.

CATERINA: There is no crabbed
portress with a nose
As sharp as yours for gossip.

FOUCHÉ: Do you think
You will be paid by this Timoleon?

CATERINA: (correcting him) Napoleon!

FOUCHÉ: (insisting) Timoleon!

CATERINA: (irritated) Napoleon
Bonaparte!

FOUCHÉ: That man
Is only a savage Corsican,
Of no experience and dry,
With an unfathomable eye,
And with a nose that's like a beak;
It's best to let him go and seek
What luck he can—he will not stir
Much trouble!

CATERINA: Hear the astrologer!
(The tocsin-bell is heard. Uproar,
tramping and voices grow louder.
The cannon booms. GIULIA and
TONIOTTA enter by the door at
the right and run to the back, CA-
TERINA joins them, FOUCHÉ fol-
lows her, and all look out.)

FOUCHÉ: Look! clouds of smoke!

CATERINA: The Tuileries is burning!

**FOUCHÉ:** Respiro! Evviva!
(*Grida e canti lontani di vittoria: Vittoria! Vittoria! Viva la Nazione! Entra VINAIGRE seguito e circondato dalla folla, nella quale è anche LA ROSSA*)

**CATERINA:** Ecco Vinaigre, il tamburo!

**VINAIGRE:** (*entrando, scalmanato, col tamburo alla cintola*) Vittoria! Vittoria!

**FOUCHÉ:** Dunque il palazzo . . . ?

**VINAIGRE:** È preso.

**FOUCHÉ:** Ed io trionfo!
(*Esce frettoloso abbandonando la sua valigia. VINAIGRE balza sul tavolo e grida alla folla che si addensa in fondo alla bottega e in istrada*)

**VINAIGRE:** Popolo di Parigi! L'austriaca e suo marito han dovuto sloggiare dalla reggia! Il palazzo è del popolo, ed il popolo governa!

**LA FOLLA:** Evviva il popolo!

**VINAIGRE:** La Francia va scalza alla vittoria, con le mani tinte di sangue . . .

**LA FOLLA:** Evviva il sangue e la Francia novella!

**VINAIGRE:** Cittadini! Chi vuol venir con me a visitare l'antro del tiranno?

**TUTTI:** (*con un urlo*) Tutti!

**VINAIGRE:** In marcia. Rataplan!
(*Si allontana battendo la carica, accompagnato dalla folla che grida: Viva la Nazione! TUTTI, meno CATERINA, lo seguono. GIULIA, TONIOTTA e LA ROSSA chiudono le imposte delle finestre, ed escono. CATERINA serra la porta d'entrata e ne chiude le imposte; la scena si oscura. Preso il mantello, ella si appresta ad uscire per la porta di destra. Si odono due colpi di fucile assai vicini. La porta di destra si apre. Entre NEIPPERG, che la richiude rapidamente come un uomo inseguito*)

**CATERINA:** (*sorpressa*) Ohè, dico . . .

**NEIPPERG:** (*origliando alla porta*) Per pietà! . . . Sono ferito . . .

**CATERINA:** Ferito?

**NEIPPERG:** (*quasi svendendo*) Hanno perduto le mie tracce . . . Sono il conte di Neipperg, austriaco . . .

**FOUCHÉ:** I breathe again! Hooray!
(*Cries and songs of victory in the distance: Victory! Victory! Long live the Nation! Enter VINAIGRE, followed and surrounded by the crowd, in which is also LA ROSSA.*)

**CATERINA:** Here is Vinaigre, The drummer!

**VINAIGRE:** (*coming in, excited, with his drum at his belt.*) Victory! Victory!

**FOUCHÉ:** And the palace?

**VINAIGRE:** Is taken.

**FOUCHÉ:** And I triumph!
(*He goes out hastily, abandoning his valise. VINAIGRE jumps onto the table, and cries out to the crowd that is becoming thick in the back of the shop and in the street.*)

**VINAIGRE:** People of Paris! The Austrian and her husband have been thrust Out of the palace; and the palace now Is ours, the people's, and the people rule!

**THE CROWD:** Hooray for the people!

**VINAIGRE:** France goes barefoot up To victory, with hands made red with blood—

**THE CROWD:** Hooray for the blood we shed and France, new France!

**VINAIGRE:** Good friends! Who wants to come with me and visit The den of the tyrant?

**THE CROWD:** (*with a yell*) All!

**VINAIGRE:** In line! Rataplan!
(*He goes away, beating his drum, and accompanied by the crowd, that cries out: Long live the Nation! All, except CATERINA, follow him. GIULIA, TONIOTTA and LA ROSSA close the shutters of the windows, and go out. CATERINA locks the entrance door and closes the shutters there. The stage is dark. Taking her cloak, she starts to go out by the door at the right. Two rifle-shots are heard quite near. The door at the right opens. Enter NEIPPERG, who closes it after him rapidly, like a man followed.*)

**CATERINA:** (*suprised*) What's this?

**NEIPPERG:** (*listening at the door*) Have pity!—I am wounded—

**CATERINA:** Wounded?

**NEIPPERG:** (*almost fainting*) I have lost my way—I am the Count of Neipperg, An Austrian—

**CATERINA:** (*a distanza, con accento di disprezzo*) Un realista . . . ?

**NEIPPERG:** Ho fatto il mio dovere cercando di salvare la Regina.

**CATERINA:** (*con sdegno*) L'austriaca!
(*Vedendo NEIPPERG pallido, quasi svenuto per la ferita, presa da pietà*)
Ma un ferito, è sacro! Non temete!

**NEIPPERG:** Ah! grazie!
(*CATERINA corre a cercare delle bende in un canestro di biancheria. Passi di fuori, e voci, che si fermano alla porta*)

**NEIPPERG:** (*atterrito*) Son scoperto!
(*Strepito di fucili che picchiano sul selciato*)

**LEFEBVRE:** (*di fuori, spingendo la porta per aprirla*) Caterina!

**CATERINA:** (*sottovoce, sbigottita*) Lefebvre!
(*Indicando a NEIPPERG la porta della sua stanza*)
Nella mia stanza, presto!

**LEFEBVRE:** (*di fuori*) Caterina! Sei qui?

**VOCI DI SOLDATI:** Madame Sans-Gêne!

**CATERINA:** (*forte*) Vengo!
(*a NEIPPERG, porgendogli le bende*)
Fasciatevi da solo. Verrò poi . . . Ma se vi sentono, siete morto!
(*NEIPPERG entra nella stanza di CATERINA, che chiude l'uscio e mette in tasca la chiave*)

**LEFEBVRE:** Che fai dunque, lumaca?
(*CATERINA corre ad aprire la porta. La scena si rischiara. LEFEBVRE entra con sei soldati. Uno di essi chiude l'uscio a vetri, lasciando aperte le imposte*)
Non lo vuoi abbracciare il tuo soldato?

**CATERINA:** (*con slancio*) Nespole, se lo voglio!

**LEFEBVRE:** Son tornato vincitore, intatto e intero.

**CATERINA:** (*maliziosa*) Eh, lo spero!

**LEFEBVRE:** (*presentando CATERINA ai suoi compagni*) La signorina Caterina Hubscher, alsazianetta giuliva e viva, piccante, petulante, spumeggiante, lesta di mano e schietta di parola,

**CATERINA:** (*at a distance, with an accent of scorn*) A royalist?

**NEIPPERG:** I have done My duty trying to save the Queen.

**CATERINA:** (*with contempt*) The Austrian!
(*Seeing NEIPPERG so pale, almost fainting from the wound, she begins to be sorry for him.*)
Your wound—a wound is sacred—do not fear!

**NEIPPERG:** Ah, thank you!
(*CATERINA runs to find some bandages in a basket of laundry. Steps outside and voices, which stop at the door.*)

**NEIPPERG:** (*alarmed*) I am discovered!
(*Sound of guns striking on the pavement.*)

**LEFEBVRE:** (*pushing at the door*) Caterina!

**CATERINA:** (*in a low voice, dismayed*) Lefebvre!
(*Indicating to NEIPPERG the door of her room*)
Quick, in my room!

**LEFEBVRE:** (*outside*) Caterina, are you there?

**VOICES OF SOLDIERS:** Madame Sans-Gêne!

**CATERINA:** (*full voice*) I'm coming!
(*to NEIPPERG, taking him the bandages.*)
Take these bands. You'll have to bind yourself, and then I'll see— But if they hear you it is certain death.
(*NEIPPERG goes into CATERINA'S room; she closes door and puts key in her pocket.*)

**LEFEBVRE:** What are you doing, snail?
(*CATERINA runs to open the door. The stage becomes light again. LEFEBVRE comes in with six soldiers. One of them closes the door but leaves the shutters open.*)
Have you no wish To kiss your soldier?

**CATERINA:** (*with abandon*) Kiss me, for I wish it.

**LEFEBVRE:** I have come back victorious, and sound In every limb.

**CATERINA:** (*maliciously*) For that fact I'll be bound.

**LEFEBVRE:** (*presenting CATERINA to his companions*) This is Mademoiselle Caterina Hubscher, Joyous and gay Alsacian, petulant, Piquant and brimming over with life, just light Enough of touch, sincere in happy

onde in tutto il quartier chiamata vien
Madame Sans-Gêne!

**TUTTI:** Madame Sans-Gêne!

**LEFEBVRE:** (*andando a deporre il fucile in un angolo*) Alle giubbe scarlatte diam la caccia,
ed ai vili sicari del tiranno!
Uno propio qui presso ci sfuggi.
Ma ha del piombo nell'ala e senza fallo
l'acchiapperemo! Intanto un gotto. Abbiamo
la gola asciutta ed arsa.
(*accennando a una bottiglia di vino che sta sul canterano*)
Ecco del vino!

**CATERINA:** Oh, ne ho di più meglio!
(*Va alla credenza, ne toglie due bottiglie, un cavatappi e alcune scodelle, che posa sulla tavola*)

**LEFEBVRE:** E venga il meglio!
(*sturando la bottiglia che gli appresta CATERINA*)
Ah, perdio, fu un travaglio rude. Dai tetti e dai balconi
che gragnuola di piombo!
Pan! Pan! ad agni colpo
era un grido, era sangue, era un caduto!
Or gli Svizzeri
inseguiti a fucilate
son dispersi, son distrutti!
Il Palazzo ora è nostro!
Adesso la folla vi penetra;
son piene le sale, le stanze
di grida, di canti e di danze!
Che gioia! La gente si abbraccia
lacera e straccia
fa man bassa,
rompe, spacca, fracassa,
scaraventa nella via
specchi, bottiglie, mobili,
pentole e sguatteri!
Oh! che allegria!
(*Risata generale. Ma LEFEBVRE si rabbuia ed esclama, mordendosi le mani*)
Penso a quel cane
che abbiam ferito
ed è fuggito!
Se lo riagguanto,
perdio, lo schianto!

**CATERINA:** Or che hai vinto, perdona e pensa a me.

**LEFEBVRE:** Tra un odio ed un amor sono diviso!
(*Rinboccandosi una manica*)
Guarda, su questo braccio,

words,
Whence comes it that in all this quarter men
Call her Madame Sans-Gêne!

**THE SOLDIERS:** Madame Sans-Gêne!

**LEFEBVRE:** (*going to put his gun in a corner*) To the red-jackets gives she merry chace,
And to the dirty cutthroats of the tyrant.
A moment ago one got away from us;
He had some lead in his wing, though— without doubt
We'll get him yet. And now a drink! Our throats
Are dry and burning.
(*indicating a bottle of wine on the chest of drawers.*)
There's some wine!

**CATERINA:** Oh, no!
I have some that is better.
(*She goes to the cupboard, takes out two bottles, a corkscrew, and some bowls, which she puts on the table.*)

**LEFEBVRE:** Here we are!
(*uncorking the bottle that CATERINA gives him.*)
By heaven! it's been a day of filthy work.
From roofs and balconies the shot hailed down,
Bang! bang! at every shot a cry, then blood,
And then a body lying there. The Swiss,
Driven back with rifles, are dispersed, destroyed;
The palace now is ours. The crowd already
Is thick inside, and furiously they prance
From room to room in their excited dance.
These people, bloody and in torn clothes, have gone
Madly about, and laid rough hands upon
Everything in sight, until you cannot pass
For all the tumult and the scattered mass
Of broken mirrors, bottles, furniture,
Of pots and pans — O, it is joy for sure!
(*General laughter. But LEFEBVRE'S face suddenly darkens and he exclaims*)
But I keep thinking of the dog we shot
And lost. If we should get him, he would not
Have much of life to boast of — ah! the beast!

**CATERINA:** Now you are here, do you think of me, at least?

**LEFEBVRE:** O, I am torn amid the double alarm
Of hate and love.
(*Turning back his sleeve.*)

un artista provetto
sotto al frigio beretto
questo motto m'ha inciso:
"Morte ai tiranni!,,

**TUTTI:** (*brindando con le scodelle colme di vino*) Morte ai tiranni!

**LEFEBVRE:** (*accennando all'altro braccio*) Ma su quest'altro invece,
bada, c'è un cuor trafitto,
e sotto il cuor sta scritto:
"Sans-Gêne mia per la vita!,,

**CATERINA:** (*pavoneggiandosi, ma insieme intenerita*) Sans-Gêne tua per la vita!

**LEFEBVRE:** Per la vita, in due . . .

**CATERINA:** . . . nella nostra piccola casa infiorata . . .

**LEFEBVRE:** Una casa con l'orto e il focolare
pieno di vampe e pieno di faville, come al nostro paese!

**CATERINA:** U una cucina grande . . .

**LEFEBVRE:** E Sans-Gêne che corre . . .

**CATERINA:** . . . e attizza il fuoco.

**LEFEBVRE:** . . . il mio fucile appeso presso all'uscio.

**CATERINA:** Tu fummi la tua pipa, il fumo danza
e Sans-Gêne canta!

**LEFEBVRE:** Canta ed io benedico il dì che l'ho incontrata
con la sua gota fresca e porporina . . .

**CATERINA:** (*accennando ai soldati*) Bada che i camerati ti sentono . . .

**LEFEBVRE:** (*volgendosi ai soldati*) Compagni,
sono il vostro sergente! attenti a me!
Obbedienza e disciplina!
Mentre io parlo a Caterina,
un, due e tre . . .
turatevi le orecchie! . . .
(*I soldati ridono*)
e poi mi piace
che sentan tutti,
l'esercito, la Francia, il mondo intero!
Oggi la vita è tutta una canzone!
Del vecchio tempo nulla più rimane;
mentre l'odio ha la voce del cannone,
l'amore squilla come le campane!
Nella luce del sol, giovine e bionda,
in cospetto degli uomini e di Dio
il mio braccio t'attira e ti circonda,
figlia del mio paese, amore mio . . .

**I SOLDATI:** (*a CATERINA e LEFEBVRE*)
Basta smorfie, ragazzi;
all'Assemblea!

But look upon this arm —
Once an old artist with his instrument
Inscribed there "Death to the tyrants!"

**THE SOLDIERS:** (*toasting with their bowls overflowing with wine.*) "Death to the tyrants!"

**LEFEBVRE:** (*pointing to the other arm*) But on this other is instead the dent
Of a heart, and under it, "Sans-Gêne mine for life."

**CATERINA:** (*walking about proudly, but at the same time affected*) Sans-Gêne yours for life!

**LEFEBVRE:** For life together —

**CATERINA:** — in our little house Covered with flowers.

**LEFEBVRE:** And its hearth aglow With flames and sparks, as in our own dear land!

**CATERINA:** A great big kitchen —

**LEFEBVRE:** And Sans-Gêne to run —

**CATERINA:** And rake the fire.

**LEFEBVRE:** My gun hung on the wall.

**CATERINA:** You smoke your pipe; the smoke floats idly up,
And Sans-Gêne sings.

**LEFEBVRE:** And while she sings I bless
The day I met her with her cheek so pink.

**CATERINA:** (*pointing to the soldiers*) That's all your comrades ought to hear.

**LEFEBVRE:** (*turning to the soldiers*) My friends,
Since what I have to say to Caterina appears
My own affair, obey — stop up your ears!
(*The soldiers laugh*)
And now I'd rather there should be unfurled
Before the army, France and all the world
My life, that is a song for evermore.
The past is gone; hate is the cannon's roar,
And love sounds sweeter than the evening bell.
And so in sight of men and God above
I draw you to me, happy in the spell
Of our dear fatherland and our own love.

**THE SOLDIERS:** (*to Caterina and Lefebvre*) Be done with affection, children, come,
Be off!

LEFEBVRE: (*guardandosi la mani*) Sacco in pacco, che mani!

CATERINA: Sono nere di polvere, ed è un nero che onora.

LEFEBVRE: Un po' d'acqua! (*Si dirige verso un catino che sta sopra una tavola e fa per lavarsi le mani*)

CATERINA: Che fai? Vuoi lavarti nell'amido?

LEFEBVRE: (*dirigiendosi verso la stanza di CATERINA*) Vado nella tua camera. (*si avvia dritto*)

CATERINA: (*con una certa inquietudine*) Ma no, veni qui alla fontana; ecco il sapone. (*Prende un pezzo di sapone di Marsiglia e apre la porta di destra che dà sulla corte*)

LEFEBVRE: (*che intanto ha cercato di aprire la porta di CATERINA*) Perchè hai chiusa la porta?

CATERINA: Perchè sto per uscire.

LEFEBVRE: Perchè hai tolto la chiave?

CATERINA: (*perdendo la pazienza*) Perchè mi pare e piace.

LEFEBVRE: (*minaccioso*) E se volessi entrare?

CATERINA: C'entrerai, ma da marito.

LEFEBVRE: (*cieco di gelosia*) C'è qualcuno lì dentro!

CATERINA: (*con Qudacia*) E se fosse? Son libera!

LEFEBVRE: Voglio la chiave! Là c'è un amante! . . . Lo sgozzo! (*Si slancia brutalmente su di lei. Ella, istintivamente, mette una mano alla tasca del gembiule. Egli vede l'atto e con violenza le strappa la chiave. I SOLDATI accorrono per difendere CATERINA. LEFEBVRE si divincola ed entra nella stanza. Silenzio*).

CATERINA: (*atterita*) Nessuna voce! Nessun remore! (*coprendosi le orecchie con le mani*) L'ucciderà! (*chiamando*) Lefebvre! (*LEFEBVRE riappare sulla soglia, pallido, turbato*)

I SOLDATI: Lefebvre, che c'è?

LEFEBVRE: (*con finta gaiezza, facendo un grande sforzo per dissimulare il violento dubbio che lo affanna*) C'è che mi ha peso in trappola!

LEFEBVRE: (*looking at his hands*) My gracious, what a sight, these hands of mine!

CATERINA: They're black with powder — it is the dirt of honour.

LEFEBVRE: A little water! (*He starts for a basin that is on a table, and is about to wash his hands.*)

CATERINA: What are you doing there! You're washing them in starch.

LEFEBVRE: (*going towards Caterina's room*) Then in your room — (*going straight ahead*)

CATERINA: (*with a certain uneasiness*) No, no — come here to the fountain; here's some soap. (*She places a piece of Marseilles soap and opens the door at the right which leads to the courtyard.*)

LEFEBVRE: (*who in the meantime has tried to open the door of CATERINA's room*) Why is the door locked?

CATERINA: I was going out.

LEFEBVRE: Why did you take the key?

CATERINA: (*losing patience*) It was my fancy.

LEFEBVRE: (*threateningly*) And if I wish to enter?

CATERINA: You should enter, But as my husband.

LEFEBVRE: (*blind with jealousy*) There is someone in there!

CATERINA: (*with daring*) And if there is? I'm free!

LEFEBVRE: I'll have the key! You've got a lover there — I'll cut his throat! (*He falls brutally upon her. She instinctively puts her hand on the pocket of her apron. He sees the action, and with violence wrenches the key from her. The soldiers rush forward to defend CATERINA. LEFEBVRE gets away, and goes into the room. Silence.*)

CATERINA: (*terrified*) No word! no sound! (*covering her ears with her hands*) He'll kill the man! (*calling*) Lefebvre! (*Lefebvre reappears at the threshold, pale and disturbed.*)

THE SOLDIERS: Lefebvre, what is it?

LEFEBVRE: (*with a feint of gaiety, making a great effort to hide the doubt that alarms him*) It is that I've been trapped! It is — (*with a false laugh*) that

C'è . . . (*Con un riso falso*) . . . che non c'è nessuno! (*Richiudendo la porta per impedir ai soldati di entrare*)

I SOLDATI: (*comicamente, invitandolo a far pace con CATERINA*) Riappiccia!

LEFEBVRE: (*con finta buffoneria*) Riappiccio! (*Fa un cenno ai soldati di allontanarsi. I sei uomini vanno verso il fondo senza far rumore, e mentre segue l'azione riprendono i fucili volgendo il dorso alla scena. LEFEBVRE intanto s'avvicina lentamente a CATERINA. Questa, con la faccia al pubblico, non lo guardo. LEFEBVRE la osserva attento*) Perchè non dirmi che là c'era un morto?

CATERINA: (*sorpresa*) È morto?

LEFEBVRE: Morto! Ha una palla nel fianco. Convien farlo portare alla sua casa.

CATERINA: Dove? Di lui soltanto so che ha nome Conte di Neipperg. Me l'ha detto. È tutto.

LEFEBVRE: Non lo conosci?

CATERINA: Entrò mentre chiudevo, e si reggeva appena. Voi giungeste feroci, se l'aveste trovato dilaniato l'avreste. (*Si volge e vede che egli la osserva attentamente*) Perchè dunque mi guardi?

LEFEVBRE: (*freddo, inquisitore*) E se fosse il tuo amante?

CATERINA: (*alzando la voce*) Il mio amante un austriaco?

LEFEBVRE: Parle piano, se t'odono . . .

CATERINA: (*facendo spallucce*) Ora è morto . . .

LEFEBVRE: (*sottovoce*) Ora è vivo!

CATERINA: (*volgendosi a lui contenta*) Ma che hai detto?

LEFEBVRE: Mentivo. Fu una prova perchè dubitavo di te. Or non dubito più . . . (*CATERINA presa da una subita commozione, fa per abbracciarlo*)

LEFEBVRE: (*continua sottovoce*) Via non farti capire: abbi cura di lui; questa notte verrò, lo faremo fuggiere.

there is no one there!

THE SOLDIERS: (*comically, inviting him to make peace with CATERINA*) Make up!

LEFEBVRE: (*with a feint of buffoonery*) Yes, I'll make up! (*He signals to the soldiers to go farther away. The six men go towards the back without a sound, and during the following action take up ther guns, keeping their backs turned. LEFEVBRE in the meantime goes slowly nearer to CATERINA. She, with her face to the audience, does not see him. He watches her attentively.*) And why did you not say There was a dead man in there?

CATERINA: (*surprised*) Is he dead?

LEFEBVRE: Dead! He has got a bullet in his side. We had better take him to his house.

CATERINA: But where? From him alone I know that he's the Count Of Neipperg. That he told me, and no more.

LEFEVBRE: You do not know him?

CATERINA: I was closing up, And suddenly he entered, almost fainting. Then you arrived outside, excitedly Trying to come in here — if you had found Him then, you would have torn the man in pieces. (*turns and sees him watching her attentively.*) Why do you watch me so?

LEFEVBRE: (*cole and inquisitive*) And if he was Your lover?

CATERINA: (*raising her voice*) Could an Austrian be my lover?

LEFEVBRE: Speak softly — if they hear you —

CATERINA: (*shrugging her shoulders*) Now he is dead —

LEFEVBRE: (*softly*) He is alive!

CATERINA: (*turning to him, relieved*) But you just said —

LEFEVBRE: I lied. It was a test of you — I had some doubt, But now I doubt no more. (*CATERINA, with sudden emotion, starts to embrace him.*) Don't let it out.

LEFEVBRE: (*continuing in a low voice*) Just take good care of him — tonight you'll see; In some way we'll arrange for him to flee.

(*CATERINA con le lagrime nelle voce*): Oh, mio Lefebvre, sei buono!

LEFEBVRE: Non mi serbi rancore?

CATERINA: Ti adoro e ti perdono!

LEFEBVRE: Sans-Gêne, qui sul mio cuore!
(*l'abbraccia*)

I SOLDATI: (*si voltano e vedono*) La pace è fatta, evviva!

LEFEBVRE: E le nozze imminenti!

I SOLDATI: (*aprendo la porta di fondo e le due finestre laterali*) Attenti! Attenti!
I nazionali della sezione vanno al maneggio! Olà! Si va?

LEFEBVRE: Si va.
(*CATERINA si getta nelle braccia di LEFEBVRE. Egli la baccia, poi si stacca da lei e va verso il fondo. Nella strada giungono da destra guardie nazionali e artiglieri col fucile in ispalla, preceduti da due tamburi, di cui una è VINAIGRE, l'altro MATURINO. Passano sul fondo cantando la Marsigliese. I sei soldati e LEFEBVRE, il quale manda ancora un bacio a CATERINA, si uniscono alla schiera che passa, seguiti dalla folla che acclama*)

*VERARIO.*

## ■ ATTO SECONDO

*Al castello di Compiègne. Settembre 1811*

(*Un grande e sontuoso salone del più puro stile impero. Sul fondo tre arcate, dalle quali entrano gli invitati. A destra, una grande porta, che conduce agli appartamenti interni*)

(*GELSOMINO attizza il fuoco nel caminetto. LEROY è in perdi presso la tavola, sulla quale sono tre scatole. Entra DESPRÉAUX*)

DESPRÉAUX: La Duchesa di Danzica?

GELSONINO: (*solenne*) Vien subito! E avvisata
Che il sarto
(*indicando LEROY*)
qui l'attende.
La . . . Duchessa di Danzica! (*sbotta a ridere*)

DESPRÉAUX: (*con grande sussiego*) Scusi, perchè mi ride in faccia?
. . .

CATERINA: (*with tears in her voice*) You are so kind!

LEFEVBRE: You blame me now no more?

CATERINA: I would do nothing but pardon and adore.

LEFEBVRE: Sans-Gêne, come to my heart.
(*He embraces her.*)

THE SOLDIERS: (*turning and looking*) Their peace is made, Hooray!

LEFEBVRE: Our wedding shall not be delayed.

THE SOLDIERS: (*opening the door at the back and the side windows*) Listen! listen! the winning people sway
Towards the administration! Shall we go?

LEFEVBRE: Away!
(*CATERINA throws herself in LEFEBVRE'S arms. He kisses her, then leaves her, and goes to the back. In the street there arrive from the right the national guard and artillery with guns on their backs, preceded by two drummers, one of whom is VINAIGRE, the other MATURINO. They pass across the back, singing the Marseillaise. The six soldiers and LEFEBVRE, who throws another kiss to CATERINA, join the battalion that is passing, followed by the acclaiming crowd.*)

*CURTAIN*

## ■ ACT II

*The château of Compiègne. September, 1811.*

(*A large and sumptuous drawing-room in the purest Empire style. At the back three arches, through which the guests enter. At the right a large door, leading to the inner apartments.*)

(*GELSOMINO is stirring the fire in the fireplace. LEROY stands by a table on which are three boxes. Enter DESPRÉAUX.*)

DESPRÉAUX: The Duchess of Danzig?

GELSOMINO: (*solemnly*) She will come at once.
She has been told the tailor awaits her here.
(*He indicates LEROY.*)
The — Duchess of Danzig!
(*He bursts out laughing.*)

DESPRÉAUX: (*with gravity*) I pray you, pardon me —
Why laugh you in my face?

GELSOMINO: Rido . . . ma non di Vostra Signoria!
Rido di certe nobiltà che sanno d'amido e ranno
e di lavanderia!
(*accostandosi, a DESPRÉAUX con un inchino*)
Signor Despréaux, io la conobbi quando
ell'era direttore del balletto all'Opéra
(*con pomposo orgoglio*)
ed io ero valletto
del Duca di Penthièvre.
(*con un sospiro*)
Bei tempi! tempi fini
e pieni di fragranza,
tempi d'ogni eleganza!

DESPRÉAUX: Che delicati inchini! Che grazie! che portento
di gesti e portamento!

LEROY: Le dame più squisite
io le vestivo, ed era
come una primavera!

LEROY, GELSOMINO, DESPREAUX: Oh tempi soavi svaniti così!

GELSOMINO: Adesso gran titoli ducati, contee . . .

LEROY: Ma modi da sguatteri e facce plebee!

DESPRÉAUX: È lustra la buccia, ma sotto . . . gentuccia.
(*a tre*)
Gentuccia, gentuccia, gentuccia!

LEROY: (*a GELSOMINO*) Il vostro padrone, sergente non era?

DESPRÉAUX: E lei vivandiera?

GELSOMINO: Or Duchi di Danzica! Capite! Capite!

LEROY: (*con comico orrore*) Danzica! Oh Dio! Che nome d'acquavite!

DESPÉAUX: Ah! per un uom di nascita e di gusto
che disgusto!

CATERINA: (*entre seguita dalla cameriera*) Bon dì, signor Despréaux! (*DESPRÉAUX e LEROY s'inchinano tre volte profondamente*)

DESPRÉAUX e LEROY: Madama la Duchessa!
(*GELSOMINO via*)

CATERINA: (*rivolgendosi a DESPRÉAUX*) Venir per me a quest'ora è grande cortesia!
Voi avete sposato la Guimard, se non sbaglio . . .

DESPRÉAUX: Madama la Duchessa si ricorda di lei?

GELSOMINO: I laugh, but not,
My kind Monsieur, at you. I laugh because
Of some nobility whose fancy was
Once on a time for laundry tubs and starch.
(*approaching DESPRÉAUX with a bow.*)
Monsieur Despréaux, I knew you in the march
Of strange events — it was when you trained the ballet
At the opera, (*with great pride*) and I was the valet
Of the Duke of Penthièvre. (*with a sigh*)
Times gone by!
O lovely times, when happy luxury
Did gracefully and gloriously enhance
Our daily life with every elegance!

DESPRÉAUX: What delicacy of gesture! what a grace!

LEROY: I used to dress with satin and with lace
Most charming ladies — it was the spring of life!

LEROY, GELSOMINO, DESPREAUX: Oh, lovely times, vanished so soon in strife!

GELSOMINO: Now they have wondrous titles — duke and count —

LEROY: With loutish ways, to what do they amount?

DESPRÉAUX: Their skin glows warm, but underneath it — what?
(*all three*)
Ay! underneath it, what?

LEROY: (*to GELSOMINO*) Your master was a sergeant, was he not?

DESPRÉAUX: And she a canteen-keeper?

GELSOMINO: Duchess now Of Danzig!

LEROY: (*with comic horror*) Danzig! Heavens! a name, I vow,
That sounds as if it ought to be a drink!

DESPRÉAUX: What a name to link to a man of breeding!

CATERINA: (*enters, followed by her maid.*) Good day, monsieur Despréaux!
(*DESPRÉAUX and LEROY bow three times very low.*)

DESPRÉAUX AND LEROY: Madame the Duchess!
(*Gelsomino goes out.*)

CATERINA: (*turning to DESPRÉAUX*) It is most kind of you to come tonight!
You married la Giumard — am I not right?

DESPRÉAUX: Madame the Duchess still remembers her?

CATERINA: Per bacco! Aveva certa biancheria!
(*rivolgendosi a LEROY*)
Caro signor Leroy, l'amazzone è già pronta?

LEROY: Pronta! Ed è un capo d'opera inaudito! Una cosa deliziosa, armoniosa...

CATERINA: (*interrompendolo e indicandogli una sedia*) Va bene ... Ma si metta a cuccia un momento, mentr' io dico due parolette al signor venditor di piroette.
(*DESPRÉAUX fa una smorfia*)
(*a DESPRÉAUX*)
Sono fuori dei gangheri!
Devo mettermi in ghingheri
per ricevere un mucchio di regine,
principesse, duchesse ed altri generi...
Se fosse gente del mio stampo, oh, allora
quattro frittelle, quattro capriole,
una padella di castagne arroste
e ci sarebbe da crepar dal ridere!
Ma son tutte damazze schizzinose
che ti parlano sempre a bocca storta
dimenando come anitre... la coda.
Ci vogliono, per loro, dei saluti
di prima qualità!
Ho detto: Despréaux mi insegnerà,
perchè lui... queste smorfie sono proprio
la sua specialità...

DESPRÉAUX: (*inchinandosi*)
Gran fortuna per me!
(*tra se, mortificato ed offeso*)
Smorfie!

CATERINA: (*a LEROY*) Voi là!
Svelto, proviamo.
(*La cameriera corre a prendere uno sgabello, che mette sotto ai piedi di CATERINA. LEROY s'inginocchia dinanzi a CATERINA e le calzi i coturni. Le sue abili mani avvolgono e stringolo il nastro attorno alle gambe della marescialla*)
Ehi, dico, sei giunto al polpaccio!
Fai conto di andare più in su?

LEROY: (*alzandosi*) Madama è servita...
(*CATERINA si alza per provare l'amazzone. Mentre LEROY e la cameriera l'aiutano a indossarla, si volge a DESPRÉAUX*)

CATERINA: Caro signor Despréaux,
vorrei qualche cosa di spiccio e insieme... di sopraffino...

---

CATERINA: My goodness, yes! I did her laundry, sir.
(*turning to LEROY*)
My good monsieur Leroy, is my court train Not ready?

LEROY: Ready? ah! you'll not refrain From greatest praise — it is a masterpiece Of style and delicacy —

CATERINA: (*interrupting him and indicating a seat*) I pray you cease Just for a moment. Sit down, while I get A word with the vendor of the pirouette.
(*DESPRÉAUX makes a face.*)
(*to DESPRÉAUX.*)
I'm out of graces — how to get me style In which I can receive this pile of queens, Princesses, duchesses and other folk? If they were folk of my own class, why, then A plate of pancakes, some capriole, A dish of roasted chestnuts would be quite Enough to make them have a splended time. But all are ladies of disdainful manner, Who always talk with pinched and twisted mouths, Wriggling, as ducks do with their tails. For them I need some graces of the finest class! They said Despréaux would show me what to do, Because his specialty is grimaces.

DESPRÉAUX: (*bowing*) What fortune!
(*to himself, mortified and offended*)
Grimaces!

CATERINA: (*to LEROY*) Ho, there! lets's try it — Be quick!
(*The maid goes and gets a stool, which she puts under CATERINA'S feet. LEROY kneels down before CATERINA and puts on her buskins. His hands put the lacing around her legs and tie it up.*)
Hey, there! you're almost to my knees! Pray, how much farther do you think of going?

LEROY: (*rising*) Madame is served.
(*CATERINA rises to try the court train. While LEROY and the maid are helping her to fasten it on her back, she turns to DESPRÉAUX.*)

CATERINA: My dear monsieur Despréaux,
I wish for something rich and bountiful, Together with the finest.

---

DESPRÉAUX: (*ispirato*) Il semplice e il fino? L'inchino!
Madama mi presti attenzione,
mi ascolti con religione!
L'inchino è l'essenza
del passo di danza,
è il ballo in potenza...
è il ritmo in sostanza...

LEROY: (*drappeggiando le pieghe della veste con gesti gravi e con sussiego*) È molto migliore di quella che ho avuto l'onore di far per l'Imperatrice. Ahimè, non ho avuto il permesso di fare'la prova io stesso! L'Imperatore non vuole...

DESPRÉAUX: Un... due... tre ...
leggermente...
soavemente...
non sia troppo commossa.
Un... due... tre... oplà,
vede?... c'è...

LEROY: È una cosa prodigiosa!
Che destrezza!
Che bellezza!

DESPRÉAUX: Madama la Duchessa può gareggiar con le più esperte dame!

CATERINA: (*si sveste*) Davvero? non son poi troppo salame?

DESPRÉAUX: (*inchinandosi*) Madama la Duchessa, servitore!

LEROY: (*inchinandosi*) Servitore, Madame la Duchessa!
(*Si avviano verso l'uscita. La cameriera esce a destra portando con se le scatole*)
(*Entra LEFEBVRE, mentre i due ministri d'ogni eleganza, escono rinculando e inchinandosi*)

CATERINA: Oh! Lefebvre!
(*CATERINA lo guardo e lo vede accigliato*)
Hai due spanne di muso.

LEFFEBVRE: Colpa tua.

CATERINA: (*con sorpresa*) Dico, ti gira?

LEFEBVRE: Sai, l'Imperatore

CATERINA: Di me? Perchè?

LEFEBVRE: Per i tuoi modi che gli dan fastidio.

CATERINA: Che modi?

LEFEBVRE: Questi, corpo d'una sciabola!
Torno, e ti trovo qui in camicia in mezzo
a servi e fornitori, a tu per tu...
Poi questa gente chiacchiera...

CATERINA: Lo so,
e me n'infischio.

---

DESPRÉAUX: (*inspired*) Simple and fine! The bow! Pray watch me well while I do mine, And listen with religious reverence! The bow and courtesy are the innate sense Of all the art of graceful step and time. —

LEROY: (*draping the folds of the garment with grave gestures and all seriousness*) This garment made for you is more sublime Than that I had the honor to create For the Empress. Ah! I had the tragic fate Of never trying it on! The Emperor Wished not —

DESPRÉAUX: One — two — three
Lightly and gracefully —
Do not be disturbed —
Hopla — you see?

LEROY: It is extraordinary Now — what grace! What great dexterity!

DESPRÉAUX: Madame the Duchess Will soon complete with the most expert ladies.

CATERINA: (*taking the robe off*) Really and truly? I am not too bad?

DESPRÉAUX: (*bowing*) Madame the Duchess, your servant!

LEROY: (*bowing*) Your servant, Madame the Duchess!
(*They go towards the door. The maid goes out at the right, taking the boxes. Enter LEFEBVRE, while the two retainers go out with every elegance, bowing and scraping.*)

CATERINA: Oh! Lefebvre!
(*She looks at him, and sees that he looks dejected.*)
You've got a dreadful look.

LEFEBVRE: It is your fault.

CATERINA: (*with surprise*) Tell me, what bothers you?

LEFEBVRE: The Emperor has spoken to me of you.

CATERINA: Of me? Why so?

LEFEBVRE: You grieve him with your ways.

CATERINA: What ways?

LEFEBVRE: These, body of a dagger! these! Here I come back, and find you so—half dressed, Gossiping here with furnishers and servants—

CATERINA: I know it, but I do not mind.

# Act II

LEFEBVRE: (con ira) Io no.
Sei o non sei duchessa, santo diavolo!?
Mondo assassino! agisci da duchessa,
e non de serva, corpo d'una pipa!

CATERINA: (ridendo) Farò come fai tu.

LEFEBVRE: Sono un soldato
e parlo da soldato, e da soldato bestemmio . . .

CATERINA: Insomma, che t'ha detto?

LEFEBVRE: Ha detto:
"Dove diavolo ha preso il suo linguaggio
vostra moglie? È uno scandalo! Si ride
alle sue spalle ed alle vostre. Ma c'è un rimedio per tutto!
C'è il divorzio!,,

CATERINA: (con un violento sussulto) Eh?! Il divorzio?

CATERINA: E invece, caro, siamo sempre qui,
io con la coda, e tu pieno di fiocchi!
Se quand'eri bambino,
venendo al villaggio vicino,
tu m'avessi incontrata . . .

LEFEBVRE: Se t'avessero detto:
quel ragazzo cencioso
sarà il duca tuo sposo . . . ?

CATERINA: Sarei crepata dal ridere! (ride)

LEFEBVRE: Sarei crepato dal ridere!
(ride: poi improvvisamente si tura la bocca, assumendo un aria seria)
Acciderba . . . che modo di parlare . . .
Non si dice: crepare . . .

CATERINA: Ah! per non dir spropositi,
sai quel che faccio? Taccio!
e t'abbraccio . . .
(Gli siede sulle ginocchia e lo bacia. Entra GELSOMINO: vedendoli in quella posizione fa un gesto di disdegno, poi tossisce)

CATERINA: (balzando in piedi) Accidenti!

GELSOMINO: (annunziando) Il signor Conte di Neipperg!

NEIPPERG: (entra rannuvolato. CATERINA e LEFEBVRE gli vanno incontro festosi) Vengo, a dirvi addio . . .

CATERINA: Partite?

NEIPPERG: (con un gesto di sconforto) Per l'esilio!

---

LEFEBVRE: (with rage) I do.
Are you or are you not a duchess? hell!
By this foul world, you ought to act as one,
Not as a slave, by the body of my pipe!

CATERINA: (laughing) I'll do as you do.

LEFEBVRE: But I am a soldier—
I have the right to talk and swear like one.

CATERINA: But seriously, what did he say?

LEFEBVRE: He said:
"Where in the devil did your wife pick up
The language that she uses? It is a scandal!
They laugh behind her back and in her face.
There is a remedy for all!—it is divorce!"

CATERINA: (with a violent start) Divorce!

CATERINA: And here instead, my love, we ever stay,
I with my court train, you filled up with schemes.
If we had met as children long ago,
And in our rags and tatters whispered low:
"This ragged girl will be my wife someday" —

LEFEBVRE: "This boy my duke and husband far away" —

CATERINA: We should have split our sides with laughter gay. (She laughs.)

LEFEBVRE: We should have split our sides with laughter gay.
(He laughs, then suddenly stops up his mouth, assuming a serious air.)
My heavens! what a way for us to talk!
One does not say 'to split one's sides with laughter'.

CATERINA: Well then, not to say foolish things like this,
What shall I do instead? Be still! and — kiss.
(She sits upon his knees and he kisses her. Enter GELSOMINO; seeing them in this position, he makes a gesture of disgust, then coughs.)

CATERINA: (junping to her feet) My heavens!

GELSOMINO: (announcing) Monsieur the Count of Neipperg.

(NEIPPERG enters, looking sad. CATERINA and LEFEBVRE go towards him joyfully.) I've come to say good-bye.

CATERINA: What! leaving?

NEIPPERG: (in a discouraged tone) It's exile.

---

CATERINA e LEFEBVRE: (a due con sorpreso) Per l'esilio?

NEIPPERG: (con sdegno e dolore) L'imperatore mi scaccia. Ha scoperto
un mio amor nella Reggia! Mi colpisce!
È un pretesto! Egli appaga un odio antico . . .

LAFEBVRE: (con tristezza, ma con dignità) E il padrone . . .

NEIPPERG: E obbedisco . . .

LEFEBVRE: Tristi gli addii quando la giovinezza
declinando s'annebbia di tristezza . . .
Scoloran lentamente i dì felici
e il cuore cerca solo i vecchi amici . . .

NEIPPERG: E l'amico che va, senza ritorno,
pensa la casa che gli fu ospitale
e sospira . . .

CATERINA: (con affettuosa malizia) E sospira la sua donna che lasacia qui . . .

NEIPPERG: (alza gli occhi, la fissa con dolore)

CATERINA: Perchè. perchè non dire
che soffrite per lei, povero amico . . . ?

NEIPPERG: (con profondo sconforto) Lasciar colei che si ama
e andarsene lontano
e sentir che ci chiama
invano, invano . . .

CATERINA: Oggi l'imperatore
Dichiara la guerra all'amore!

LEFEBVRE: Tutti tre
abbiamo una pena nel cuore,
abbiamo una pena d'amore
tutti tre!

NEIPPERG: (prorompendo) Ah, non posso tacere il mio martirio çon voi! È una febbre! E un delirio!
E voglio rivederla! E fingerò
di partir, ma stanotte tornerò.

LEFEBVRE: Voi siete pazzo.

NEIPPERG: (fuori di se) La rivedrò!
M'ha fatto dire di non partire
senza vederla . . . e obbedirò.

CATERINA: Non so chi sia costei!
Tremo per voi . . .
Non dovete tornar!

NEIPPERG: La rivedrò!
(a LEFEBVRE)
Se vi togliesserò questa
vostra donna diletta . . .

LEFEBVRE: Si provino, per Dio!

NEIPPERG: E volete ch'io fugga?

---

CATERINA AND LEFEVBRE: (surprised) Exile?

NEIPPERG: (with disdain and grief) The Emperor commands.
He has discovered that I have a love
In the palace! His keen eye has fallen on me.
It is a pretext — he repays old hatred.

LEFEBVRE: (with sadness and dignity) He is the master —

NEIPPERG: I obey.

LEFEBVRE: Sad are the partings when the flush of youth
Has sunk into the gloom of deeper truth;
When happiness with daylight slowly ends,
The heart turns back to find the old-time friends.

NEIPPERG: And now the friend who goes without return
Thinks of the house that was to him his home,
And sighs —

CATERINA: (deeply moved) And sighs the lady whom he leaves.

(NEIPPERG raises his eyes, and fixes them upon her with sorrow.)

CATERINA: Ah! why not say you suffer for her, friend?

NEIPPERG: (with deep sorrow) To leave her whom one loves and go afar,
To feel she calls in vain, in vain—

CATERINA: A war
Against love has been declared by the Emperor.

LEFEBVRE: We all have pain at heart, the pain of love.

NEIPPERG: (bursting out) I cannot hide my agony from you!
It is a fever! It is delirium!
Again I must behold her! I will feign
To go, but in the night come back again.

LEFEBVRE: You are unwise.

NEIPPERG: (beside himself) I must see her again!
She made me promise that I would not go
Without—and I obey.

CATERINA: I do not know who this person is. O, I tremble for you—
Do not come back!

NEIPPERG: I must see her again!
(to LEFEBVRE)
If they had taken your dear wife from you!—

LEFEBVRE: Heaven forbid!

NEIPPERG: Yet you would have me flee?

GELSOMINO: (*entra ed annunzia*) Sua Eccellenza il Ministro di Polizia!

CATERINA: Silenzio, è qui Fouché!

FOUCHÉ: (*entra*)

NEIPPERG: Amici, addio! (*CATERINA gli presenta le guance, egli le bacia, stringe la mano a LEFEBVRE ed esce in fretta commosso*)

FOUCHÉ: (*salutando NEIPPERG con un inchino ironico*) Buon viaggio, signor Conte. (*tre se*) E subito ritorno! . . . (*a CATERINA*) Marescialla, v'sannunzio le Loro Serenissime Altezze Imperiali. Badate, c' è per aria una congiura: vogliono provocarvi a parlare, far nascere uno scandolo! Sopportate prudente! Resistete all' attacco e cambiate discorso quando piglio tabacco. (*LEFEVBRE ha un gesto d'ira*)

CATERINA: (*sbuffando, minacciosa*) La corda troppo tesa alla fine si strappa. Vedremo! (*avviandosi verso l'uscio*) Perdonate! Vo' a metter la gualdrappa. (*Esce in fretta. Cominciano a giungere gli invitati*)

LEFEBVRE: Vengon gli ospiti già. (*inquieto*) La marescialla con è pronta . . . (*Dal fondo entra stuolo variopinto di dame e di cavalieri: ufficiali, accademici, diplomatici. Uniformi fastose. Azione. LEFEBVRE saluta, va sul fondo, si perde tra la folla, riappare*) (*Un gruppo di dame, sottovoce*)

LE DAME: Una notizia! Una notizia! —ch' è una primizia!— ch' è una primizia!

TUTTE: Neipperg partì! . . . Perchè? —Mah! . . . Chissà! Si buccina, si chiacchiera, si mormora Sotto voce—sotto vento—ma nessun conosce il vero. Ah! come provoca, irrita e stuzzica questo mistero! (*rivolgendosi a FOUCHÉ*) Ma qui, Fouché di tal partenza svelerà il perchè.

FOUCHÉ: E chi può mai saper, dame vezzose, il perchè delle cose? (*tra se*) Però, io lo so!

LE DAME: (*circondano FOUCHÉ*) O taciturno, che tutto sapete, dite il segreto; saremo discrete! Non appena in un orecchio

---

GELSOMINO: (*enters and announces*) His Excellency the Minister of Police!

CATERINA: Silence, here is Fouché!

(*Enter FOUCHÉ.*)

NEIPPERG: My friends, farewell! (*CATERINA presents her cheeks, which he kisses, grasps LEFEBVRE by the hand, and goes out in a hurry, much moved.*)

FOUCHÉ (*saluting NEIPPERG with an ironic bow*) A happy journey to you, monsieur Count! (*to himself.*) And soon return!— (*to CATERINA.*) My lady, I announce, Their Most Serene and Royal Highnesses. Look out—there is conspiracy in the air: They want to make you speak, and start a scandal! So bear up prudently! Be proud enough, And change the subject when I take my snuff. (*LEFEBVRE makes and angry gesture.*)

CATERINA: (*raging and menacing*) The cord that's pulled too tight will sometime snap. We'll see! (*going towards the door.*) Your pardon! I must robe myself. (*She goes out in a hurry. The guests begin to arrive.*)

LEFEBVRE: The guests are coming, and my wife Is not yet here to receive them. (*troubled*) (*From the back enters a motley band of ladies and cavaliers, officials, academicians, diplomats. Festive uniforms. Action. LEFEBVRE salutes, goes to the back, is lost in the crowd, reappears.*)

A GROUP OF LADIES: (*in a low voice*) A notice has been given!— there is some reason.

ALL: Neipperg is gone! But why? and where?— Who knows? One hears strange murmurings and whisperings Of something, but no person knows the truth. How irritating is this mystery! (*turning to FOUCHÉ.*) Surely, Fouché, you can unveil the reason Of this departure.

FOUCHÉ: Who, fair ladies, knows The reason for anything? (*to himself*) And yet—I know!

THE LADIES: (*surrounding FOUCHÉ*) O silent creature, who knows everything, Tell us the secret, please; beyond

---

il segreto profumato lieve sarà entrato, fuor dall'altro sortirà. Lo giuriamo.

FOUCHÉ: Lo giurate? Bene! Allora immaginate che sia entrato e uscito già. (*LE DAME protestano furiose, ma in quell' istante un confuso movimento che si propaga dal fondo, un brusìo improvviso, e il solenne silenzio che subito dopo si distende, preannunziano l'arrivo delle imperiali sorelle*)

GELSOMINO: (*dal fondo annunzia solennemente*) Sua Maestà la Regina di Napoli . . . Sua Altezza Imperial la Principessa di Lucca e di Piombino! (*Quadro. Tutti i presenti si levano in piedi e si allineano splendidi di ori, di galloni, di gioielli. Entrano CAROLINA ed ELISA, con dame di compagnia e cavalieri d'onore. LEFEBVRE si precipita incontro ad esse*)

CAROLINA: (*guardandosi intorno altera*) La Duchessa di Danzica non vedo!

LEFEBVRE: (*confuso*) Vostra Maestà . . . perdoni! È sofferente . . . Sarà qui tosto. (*tra se*) Io sudo e gelo insieme. (*Le due regina aggrottano le ciglia. Intorno è un pesante silenzio pieno di imbarazzo. Si precipita in iscena inciampando nella porta, frettoloso, affannata, turbata*)

CAROLINA: (*acida*) Vi fate ben desiderar, Duchessa!

CATERINA: Io prego Sua Maestà, Sua Altezza Imperiale e tutta la compagnia di scusare il ritardo. (*strizzando l'occhio*) Ma per mettersi in . . . pompa Ci vuole sempre un secolo. (*Risatina dietro i ventagli delle dame. FOUCHÉ tabacca rumorosamente. CATERINA rossa e impacciata, vede che tutte le dame si fanno vento, e, per darsi un contegno, si sventola anch'essa vivacemente. Poi, con subita risoluzione, come chi ha una trovata*) (*a LEFEBVRE*) Maresciallo suvvia, offri dunque da bere . . . (*chiamando il servo con voce acuta*) Pivert!

UNA DAMA: (*alle altre, piano*) Ah! Siamo all'osteria!

LE DAME: (*mormorando, con risa soffocate e sventolandosi*) — È incredibile!—È inespribimile! È incomparabile!—È inimitabile! (*Un valletto entra portando un*

---

our ring We will not breathe it! It will go in one ear And out the other—we then will not know. We swear it.

FOUCHÉ: Swear it? Well, then, without a doubt You can imagine it's gone in and out. (*The ladies protest furiously, but at this moment a confused movement starting at the back, an unforeseen excitement, and the solemn silence that suddenly spreads, announce the arrival of the imperial sisters.*)

GELSOMINO: (*announcing from the back solemnly*) Her Majesty the Queen of Naples— Her Imperial Highness the Princess of Lucca and Piombino! (*Tableau. All present arrange themselves, splendid in gold, lace, and jewels. Enter CAROLINA and ELSIA, with ladies-in-waiting, and cavaliers of honor. LEFEBVRE rushes towards them.*)

CAROLINA: (*looking around*) I do not see the Duchess of Danzig here!

LEFEBVRE: (*confused*) Pardon, your Majesty, she is not well. She will be here at once. (*to himself*) I burn and freeze. (*The two queens frown. An embarrassing silence. CATERINA rushes in, stumbling on the threshold, in a hurry and frightened.*)

CAROLINA: (*sourly*) You make yourself much wished for, Duchess!

CATERINA: I beg your Majesty, your Royal Highness, And all my guests to pardon my delay. (*winking*) To get me dressed for parties takes an age. (*Giggles behind ladies' fans. FOUCHÉ takes snuff, grumbling. CATERINA, red and confused, sees that the ladies are fanning themselves, and to give herself better deportment she begins to fan herself rapidly. Then, with a sudden resolution, as if finding something, to LEFEBVRE.*) My duke, be quick—offer them something to drink— (*calling the servant with a sharp voice.*) Pivert!

A LADY: (*to the others, softly*) Well, are we at a hostelry?

THE LADIES: (*murmuring, suffocating their laughter, and fanning themselves*) It is beyond belief, beyond all words, It is inimitable, beyond compare!

*vassoio di dolci che pone sulla tavola. Un altro valetto offre del punch agli uomini. CATERINA prende un bicchiere di punch dal vassoio e tocca, col suo, il bicchiere di un ufficiale)*

CATERINA: *(brindando)* Alla tua!
*(Ma nel momento in cui CATERINA allunga il braccio, FOUCHÉ tossisce e prende rumorosamente tabacco. Troppo tardi. CATERINA vede il gesto, e, intimidita, depone il bicchiere senza aver osato di bere. Poi va alla tavola, prende il vassoio di dolci e ne offre a CAROLINA)*
Vostra Maestà, gradisce due frittelle?

CAROLINA: *(con aria canzonatoria)* No, le frittelle non mi tentan punto!
*(Sorrisi, risatine in giro)*

CATERINA: *(a ELISA)* Vostra Altezza?

ELISA: *(ridendo con malizia)* No, no!

CATERINA: *(alle dame, con cortesia nelle quale bolle un principio di collera)* Signore belle?

LE DAME: *(tutte insieme, con aperta aria di derisione)* No, non ci fanno gola le frittelle.

LEFEBVRE: *(all' orecchio di CATERINA, con ira repressa)* Non insister, ti dico, non insistere!
*(FOUCHÉ tabacca ripetutamente, rumorosamente. CATERINA si volta per allontarsi, ma si trova con i piedi avviluppati nella coda. Tenta di liberarsi, e peggiora la sua posizione)*

CATERINA: *(gridando)* Accidenti alla coda!
*(Risata unanime. CATERINA sconcertata)*
Mille scuse, Maestà!
Un momento . . . e mi srotolo . . .

CAROLINA: *(con ironia sorridente)* È delizioso questo linguaggio
che usano solo le pescivendole
e le ragazze facili e grazii
del Palais Royal . . .
*(LEFEBVRE ha un gesto d'ira)*

CATERINA: *(fremendo, con le nari dilatate)* Sento odore di polvere.

CAROLINA: In quel quartiere, appunto,
mi fu detto, eravate . . .

CATERINA: *(tagliandole la parola, con orgoglio)* . . .lavandaia, Maestà!
*(Risata unanime, clamorosa, CATERINA, volge uno sguardo severo su chi ride)*

---

*(A valet enters, carrying a tray of sweets, which he puts on the table. Another valet offers some punch to the men. CATERINA takes a glass of punch from the tray and touches, with hers, the glass of an officer.)*

CATERINA: *(lifting her glass)* Your health!
*(But at the moment in which CATERINA puts her arm forward, FOUCHÉ coughs and takes snuff, grumbling. Too late. CATERINA sees the gesture, and, frightened, puts down the glass, without having dared to drink. Then she goes to the table, takes the tray of sweets and offers them to CAROLINA.)*
Your Majesty will take two fritters?

CAROLINA: *(with a scoffing air)* The—what do you call them—fritters do not tempt me.
*(Smiles and laughter among the people.)*

CATERINA: *(to ELISA)* Your Highness?

ELISA: *(smiling with malice)* No, indeed!

CATERINA: *(to the ladies with a courtesy in which is felt an undercurrent of wrath)* Fair ladies, you?

THE LADIES: *(all together, with an open air of derision)* No, no, we have no taste for things like that.

LEFEBVRE: *(in CATERINA'S ear, with repressed anger)* Do not insist, I tell you, do not insist!
*(FOUCHÉ takes snuff repeatedly. CATERINA starts to move away, but finds her feet tangled in her train. She tries to free herself, but makes her position worse.)*

CATERINA: *(screaming)* The devil take this train!
*(General laughter. CATERINA disconcerted.)*
Your Majesty,
A moment while I get myself unwound—

CAROLINA: *(with smiling irony)* This language is most charming, that one hears
From idle beggars and from fishmongers
About the Palais Royal.
*(LEFEBVRE makes a gesture of anger.)*

CATERINA: *(raging, with her nostrils dilated)* I smell powder.

CAROLINA: Pray, in what quarter was I told you were—

CATERINA: *(cutting off the word, with pride)* A laundress, Majesty!
*(General clamorous laughter. CATERINA turns a severe look on those who are laughing.)*
Yes, I have got the slang that the

---

Ed ho il gergo del popolo
e del popolo ho il gesto,
perchè popolo sono!
Siamo in tanti del resto!
Tutti usciti dal nulla! Non fu Brune
stampatore?
Ney bottaio? Bessières barbiere?
Lannes tintore?
Fu garzon d'osteria Murat, vostro marito,
sì che molti di quelli che lo chiaman Maestà,
gli avran detta: "ragazzo, porta un piatto pulito!,,

CAROLINA: *(con ira e con alterigia)* Ed avete l'audacia?

CATERINA: *(con impeto)* Oh! la gloria è sublime
se, partendo dal basso, si raggiungon le cime!
Della Rivoluzione tutti figli se è,
ed in questo palazzo ch'Ella sola ci diè,
chi rinnega la madre, è un perverso e un vigliacco!

FOUCHÉ: *(che tabacca invano, serra rumorosamente la tabacchiera esclamando)* Patatrac!

CATERINA: E voi, caro Fouché, risparmiate il tabacco!

CAROLINA: *(con acerbo disprezzo)* Con chi parlo stasera?
E con la marescialla o con la vivandiera?

CATERINA: *(con fierezza)* Con tutte e due, Maestà!

CAROLINA: *(esasperata)* Completò la caserna la bottega . . .

ELISA: *(furiosa, ironica)* . . .e la cantina . . . dove
si trinca e si bestemmia . . .

CAROLINA: . . . ed il bivacco dove si dorme, tra i soldati, sulla paglia!

CATERINA: *(interrompendo, con forza)* Se ce n' è!
Ma più spesso la terra era il giaciglio,
per i nostri riposi!
Sì, dormii tra i soldati, più di voi rispettosi
per la donna che sono, per nome che porto!
Ho trottato dal Reno al Danubio,
di battaglia in battaglia,
con la santa canaglia,
sotto neve, pioggia, mitraglia,
tra la fame e gli stenti,
raccogliendo i feriti,
consolando i morenti,
chiudendo gli occhi ai morti!
E versando una goccia
di liquore ai soldati
che vi davano un regno,
faticavo per voi,
per la vostra corona!
A voi facile fu
poi chinarvi, tuffare
dentro il sangue le dita
e raccoglierla su!

---

people use,
I've got their gestures, for I'm one of them!
We're all the same, all come right up from nothing.
Was not Ney a shoemaker, and Brune
A printer? Bersières a barbar? Lannes
A dyer? Murat, your husband, waiter in a tavern?
I bet you many that now call him Majesty
Have called to him: "Waiter, a clean plate!"

CAROLINA: *(with wrath and arrogance)* You have the audacity?

CATERINA: *(impetuously)* Sublime is glory
For those who leave the mire and reach the sky!
Sons of the Revolution are we all,
And in this palace that you give to us,
He who denies his mother is a villian!

FOUCHÉ: *(who takes snuff in vain, shuts noisily his snuff-box, exclaiming)* Patatrac!

CATERINA: And you, dear Fouché, save your snuff!

CAROLINA: *(with bitter disapproval)* I speak with whom this evening? with the duchess,
Or with the canteen-woman?

CATERINA: *(with pride)* Your Majesty,
With both!

CAROLINA: *(exasperated)* The scene of the barracks is complete—

ELISA: *(furious, ironical)* And the canteen, where they get drunk and swear.

CAROLINA: And the bivouac, where among the soliders
They sleep upon the straw.

CATERINA: *(interrupting with force)* And if it is!
More often was the earth the welcome couch
To our repose. I slept among the men,
Respected more than you for what I am.
I have travelled from the Danube to the Rhine,
From battle into battle, following on
After the blessed rabble, under the snow,
Rain, falling shot, hunger and misery,
Picking up wounded from the field, speaking
Some consolation to them as they died,
Closing their eyes a moment later. I poured
Water into their burning mouths—those men
Who've given to you your kingdom, toiled for you

(Le regine si alzano al colmo della sdegno)

CAROLINA: Rimpiangerete ben presto
Queste vostre parole.
CATERINA: Non più dell'altre, Maestà!
CAROLINA: Lo vedremo! Signore! Seguitemi!
(Le due sorelle dell'Imperatore escono seguite delle dame. Quadro)

BRIGODE: (entra dal fondo. Con fredda autorità) L'Imperatore invita la Duchessa
di Danzica a recarsi sull'istante da lui...
CATERINA: Vi seguo.
(BRIGODE fa un inchino profondo ed esce)

CATERINA: (volgendosi agli ufficiali) Camerati, vado
a combattere ancora una battiglia!
(tra scherzosa e commossa)
Presentate le armi!
(Tutti la salutano militarmente. CATERINA sulla porta, volgendosi con un sorriso pieno di bontà)
Buona notte!
(LEFEBVRE le va vicino, allarga le braccia)
Febvre! mio Febvre! Non ci commoviamo!
Vincerò, perchè t'amo!

QUADRO—VELARIO

# ■ ATTO TERZO

Il gabinetto dell'Imperatore.

A destra, davanti al caminetto, dove arde un fuoco basso, il tavolo da lavoro dell'Imperatore, ingombro di carte e di giornali. A sinistra, un canapè, poltrone ed X. A destra, in primo piano, la porta che conduce agli appartamenti dell'Imperatore. Sul fondo, sempre a destra, una larga porta a doppia battente si apre sopra un grande corridoio illuminato da lampade che non si vedono; di là dal corridoio, in coincidenza con la porta, l'uscio della camera dell'Imperatrice. Ancora sul fondo, verso sinistra, si apre con due grandi porte un vestibolo che dà sopra il parco imperiale. Sulla tavola, una lampada dal pesante abat-jour, due calamai, uno

And for your crown! For you it was so easy
To lean and put your fingers in their wounds,
And find that crown there and to lift it up!
(The queens rise, in haughtiest disdain.)

CAROLINA: You will regret these foolish words at once.
CATERINA: No more than others, Majesty!
CAROLINA: We'll see!
Ladies, you are to follow me!
(The two sisters of the Emperor go out, followed by the ladies. Tableau. Enter BRIGODE at the back.)

BRIGODE: (with cold authority) The Emperor invites the Duchess of Danzig
To come to him at once.

CATERINA: I follow you.
(BRIGODE makes a profound bow and goes out.)
(Turning to the officials)
Comrades, I go to fight another battle!
(Between fun and emotion.)
Present arms!
(All salute her in military fashion. CATERINA at the door turns with a smile full of kindness.)
Good night!
(LEFEBVRE goes up to her, extending his arms.)
Febvre! my Febvre! We will not be afraid!
Through love of you my conquest will be made!

TABLEAU—CURTAIN

# ■ ACT III

The cabinet of the Emperor.

At the right, before the fireplace, where a low fire burns, the Emperor's worktable, piled up with papers and journals. At the left a sofa, armchair, etc. At the right, front, the door leading to the apartments of the Empress. At the back, still at the right, a large double door opens upon a wide corridor, lighted by lamps that one does not see; beyond the corridor, in range with the door, the entrance of the Empress's room. Again at the back, towards the left, a vestibule with wide doors opens into the imperial park. On the table, a lamp with a heavy lampshade, two inkstands, one large and the other small, a bunch of violets, the Emperor's pocket-

grande ed uno piccolo, un mazzetto di violette, la cartella dell'Imperatore, una tazza ed una zuccheriera. La spada è sul caminetto. A sinistra, in primo piano, altra porta.

L'Imperatore, al suo tavolo, scorre qualche giornale. Roustan è in piedi, sul fondo, a destra. A sinistra, in fondo, stanno silenziosamente raccolti alcuni alti ufficiali e un capitano degli usseri. Tutta la scena è in una mezza luce. Solo il viso dell'Imperatore è vivamente illuminato dalla lampada che sta sul tavolo davanti a lui. Breve silenzio; poi Napoleone leva gli occhi dai giornali e si rivolge as capitano degli usseri.

NAPOLEONE: Ora il vostro rapporto, capitano.
(Il capitano va rapidamente al tavolo, saluta e presenta il rapporto. Entra FOUCHÉ. NAPOLEONE gli fa cenno. FOUCHÉ si avvicina al tavolo)
(sottovoce)
Dunque, Neipperg?
FOUCHÉ: Partì.
NAPOLEONE: Bene.
(Tabacca lentamente)
FOUCHÉ: (si allontana calmo, con la solita espressione di furberia sorniona e dice tra se:) E forse è ancor qui!...
(CONSTANT entra da destra con una caffettiera d'argento. Versa il caffè a NAPOLEONE e si pianta vicino alla porta di destra. Entra BRIGODE)
NAPOLEONE: (rivolgendosi a BRIGODE) La Duchessa di Danzica?
BRIGODE: Ora viene.
(Si apre la porta della stanza dell' Imperatrice. Si vedono in una luce rosa di veilleuse le dame d'onore inchinarsi per salutare la Sovrana che non si scorge. Poi le dame entrano in iscena; passano davanti a NAPOLEONE, inchinandosi; CAROLINA ed ELISA entrano prime. Le altre le seguono)
NAPOLEONE: (levandosi) La buona notte anch'io
or dò all' Imperatrice. Aspettate, Signore!
BRIGODE: (annunziando alla soglia, verso la stanza dell' Imperatrice) L'Imperatore!
(Napoleone entra nella stanza dell' Imperatrice. —LE DAME, in vari gruppi si accomodano sul canapè e sulle sedie. CAROLINA ed ELISA sono in primo piano)
ELISA: (bisbigliando) Ha la voce dei giorni cattivi.
CAROLINA: L'occhio torvo ed il gesto nervoso.

book, a cup and a sugar bowl. The sword is on the mantelpiece. At the left front another door.

The Emperor, at his table, is running through some journals. ROUSTAN stands at the back right. At the left back stand together in silence some high officers and a captain of the Hussars. The whole stage is in a dim light. Only the face of the EMPEROR is brilliantly illuminated by the light which stands on the table in front of him. A short silence; NAPOLEON raises his eyes from the journals and turns to the captain of the Hussars.

NAPOLEON: Now your report, captain.
(The captain goes rapidly to the table, salutes and presents the report. Enter FOUCHÉ. NAPOLEON signals to him. FOUCHÉ comes up to the table.)
(in a low voice.)
Well now, Neipperg?
FOUCHÉ: He's gone.
NAPOLEON: Good.
(takes snuff slowly.)
FOUCHÉ: (going away calmly, and saying to himself with an expression of knavery) But perhaps is back again!
(CONSTANT enters with a silver coffee tray. He pours out the coffee for NAPOLEON, goes and stands near the door at the right. Enter BRIGODE.)
NAPOLEON: (turning to BRIGODE) The Duchess of Danzig?
BRIGODE: She will come at once.
(The door of the Empress's room opens. One sees in a rosy shaded light the ladies of honor bending to salute the Sovereign, who is not visible. Then the ladies enter on the stage; they pass before NAPOLEON, bowing; CAROLINA and ELISA enter first, the others follow them.)
NAPOLEON: (rising) I also will go in to say good night
To the Empress. Ladies, await me.
BRIGODE: (announcing on the threshold, towards the Empress's room) The Emperor!
(NAPOLEON goes into the Empress's room. The ladies arrange themselves in various groups on the sofa and chairs. CAROLINA and ELISA remain in front.)
ELISA: (whispering) He has the voice of his bad days.
CAROLINA: His eye
Is wild and he is nervous with his hands.

**ELISA, CAROLINA e LE DAME:** È sdegnato, è furente, è geloso!
(*A FOUCHÉ, in tono di scherzo*)
Oh, Fouché, dite un po' . . . dite un po' . . .

**FOUCHÉ:** (*con esagerata galanteria, sorridendo*) Comandate, e obbedirvi saprò.

**ELISA, CAROLINA e LE DAME:** Si sussurra che egli apra indiscreto
Fin le lettere della sua sposa.

**FOUCHÉ:** (*con aria maliziosa*) Non so nulla!

**ELISA, CAROLINA e LE DAME:** Parlare non osa!

**FOUCHÉ:** So serbare, Signore, un segreto.

**ELISA, CAROLINA e LE DAME:** Oh, Fouché, dite un po' . . . dite un po' . . .

**FOUCHÉ:** Non affermo e non dico di no!

**BRIGODE:** (*annunziando*) L'Imperatore!
(*NAPOLEONE rientra. La stanza dell'Imperatrice si chiude*)

**NAPOLEONE:** (*alle Dame*) Alle quattro la caccia
comincia, Signore,
andate a riposare
e non manchi nessuna.

**BRIGODE:** (*annunziando*) La Duchessa di Danzica.
(*MADAME SANS-GÊNE entra lentamente con la pelliccia sullespalle, mentre le Dame escono. Sulla soglia, ELISA e CAROLINA hanno un tenue riso di scherno, e fulminano con occhiate superbe CATERINA, che si è fermata presso la porta. Quando tutti sono usciti, NAPOLEONE fa cenno bruscamente a MADAME SANS-GÊNE di sedere sul canapè. Poi si aggira un po' imbronciato per la stanza. Infine le si pianta davanti e le parla con ira continuata e con piglio imperioso*)

**NAPOLEONE:** Signora, voi coprite di redicolo
me, la mia Corte, il vincitor di Danzica . . .
Io non voglio! Lefebvre v'ha già parlato?

**CATERINA:** Sì, m'ha detto:
l'Imperator m'ha proposto
di separarmi da te.

**NAPOLEONE:** E che avete risposto?

**CATERINA:** (*con molta semplicità*) Io gli ho riso sul muso!
Ecco tutto, Maestà!

**NAPOLEONE:** (*con uno scatto d'ira*) E la mia volontà?

---

**ELISA, CAROLINA AND THE LADIES:** He is indignant, furious, and jealous!
(*To FOUCHÉ, in a playful tone.*)
Ah, good Fouché, tell us a little something.

**FOUCHÉ:** (*with exaggerated galantry, smiling*) Command, and I will know just how to obey.

**ELISA, CAROLINA AND THE LADIES:** It is whispered theat he opens even the letters of his wife without discretion!

**FOUCHÉ:** (*with a malicious air*) I know not.

**ELISA, CAROLINA AND THE LADIES:** You dare not speak.

**FOUCHÉ:** But I can keep a secret.

**ELISA, CAROLINA, AND THE LADIES:** Oh, good Fouché, tell us a little about it.

**FOUCHÉ:** I make no affirmation nor denial.

**BRIGODE:** (*announcing*) The Emperor!
(*NAPOLEON reenters. The Empress's room is closed.*)

**NAPOLEON:** (*to the Ladies*) At four o'clock, Ladies,
The hunt begins. Go now, and get repose,
And let no one be absent.

**BRIGODE:** (*announcing*) The Duchess of Danzig.
(*Madame SANS-GÊNE enters slowly with her pellisse on her shoulders, while the Ladies go out. On the threshold, ELISA and CAROLINA give a light laugh of scorn, and with superb eyes glare at CATERINA, who has stopped near the door. When all have gone out, NAPOLEON makes an abrupt sign to Madame SANS-GÊNE to sit on the sofa. Then he moves about the room in a irritated way. At last he plants himself in front of her and speaks to her with repressed wrath and with an imperious look.*)

**NAPOLEON:** Madame, you cover with your ridicule
Myself, my court, the conqueror of Danzig—
I like it not! Lefebvre has spoken of this?

**CATERINA:** He said to me: the Emperor has proposed
To separate me from you.

**NAPOLEON:** And you answered?

**CATERINA:** (*with great simplicity*) I simply laughed in his face—and that was all,
Your Majesty!

**NAPOLEON:** (*showing his anger*) But how about my will?

---

**CATERINA:** (*con calma, quasi con bonarietà, ma con fermezza*) Spazzare i troni, al mondo mutar faccia,
ah, questo sì, Vostra Maestà lo può!
Ma strappare Lefebvre dalle mie braccia
e dalle sue strapparmi . . . ah! questo no!

**NAPOLEONE:** (*facendo spalluccie*) Sentiremo Lefebvre . . .

**CATERINA:** Cambiar non mi vorrà con una principessa tutta boria,
che sempre in lui vedrà
il figlio d'un mugnaio . . .

**NAPOLEONE:** (*interrompendola con forza*) Il figlio della gloria!

**CATERINA:** (*sempre con semplicità*) Sì, ma un villan rifatto . . . come Vostra Maestà!

**NAPOLEONE:** (*una vampata di collera gli illividisce il volto; poi egli si domina e dice bruscamente*): E con questo linguaggio che stasera
uno scandalo avete provocato!

**CATERINA:** Uno scandalo! È vero! Le sorelle
di Vostra Maestà schernir così l'esercito . . .

**NAPOLEONE:** (*con stupore*) L'esercito?

**CATERINA:** Sì, nella mia persona, visto che servii sotto la bandiera.

**NAPOLEONE:** Voi?

**CATERINA:** La fiaschetta al fianco.

**NAPOLEONE:** Vivandiera?

**CATERINA:** (*con impeto crescente*) Con Febvre. Armata dei Vosgi,
Armata della Mosella,
Armata di Sambra e Mosa
ed Armata del Reno!
Trentasei mesi di battaglia, dodici combattimenti e una ferita al braccio!

**NAPOLEONE:** (*che s'è andato entusiasmando durante l'enumerazione*) Una ferita? Bene! Conservate
i galloni che avete guadagnato!
Duchessa, se la gloria
vi battezzò in un giorno di vittoria,
l'Imperator conferma!
(*sorridendo*)
Ma la Corte
non è fatta per voi . . .

**CATERINA:** (*allegra*) C'è troppa folla.

**NAPOLEONE:** (*con gaiezza bonaria*) C'è troppe cerimonie.

**CATERINA:** E troppa colla.

---

**CATERINA:** (*with calm, almost with good nature, but with firmness*) To empty thrones and change about the world,
Your Majesty can do this with scarcecly a blow!
But to imagine my Lefebvre hurled
Out of my arms and me from his—ah, no!

**NAPOLEON:** (*with a shrug*) We'll hear Lefebvre on this—

**CATERINA:** He would not exchange
Me for the proudest princess in the world,
For I will never see in him the son
Of the miller.

**NAPOLEON:** (*interrupting her with force*) No, the son of glory!

**CATERINA:** (*always with simplicity*) Yes,
But a remade peasant, like your Majesty.
(*A sudden fit of anger makes his face pale, but he controls himself, and says abruptly*)

**NAPOLEON:** And with such language did you start a scandal tonight!

**CATERINA:** A scandal! ah! your Majesty's
Two sisters thus to scorn the army!

**NAPOLEON:** (*stupified*) The army?

**CATERINA:** Yes, in my person—I served beneath its flag.

**NAPOLEON:** You?

**CATERINA:** My flask at my side.

**NAPOLEON:** A canteen-women?

**CATERINA:** (*with growing impetuosity*) With Febvre—in the army of the Vosges,
The army of the Moselle, the Sambre and Meuse,
The army of the Rhine! had thirty-six
Months of it, twelve battles, and a wound
In the arm.

**NAPOLEON:** (*who has been walking about enthusiastically during the enumeration*) A wound?
Splendid! Pray preserve
The ribbons you have won! If glory,
Duchess,
Baptized you in a day of victory,
The Emperor confirms it!
(*Smiling*) But the court
Is not made to your taste.

**CATERINA:** (*lightly*) It is too foolish.

**NAPOLEON:** (*with gay good nature*) It is too ceremonious.

**CATERINA:** And stiff necked.

NAPOLEONE: (*ridendo*) Dunque non ci venite. Io vi dispenso! (*con allegria*) Una festa al sobborgo è assai più gaia . . .

NAPOLEON: (*laughing*) You need not come. I will dispense with that. (*with joy*) A frolic in the suburbs is more fun—

CATERINA: (*con vivacità*) Mi ricordo quand'ero lavandaia . . .

CATERINA: (*with vivacity*) I remember when I was a washerwoman—

NAPOLEONE: (*furente, tagliantole la parola*) Lavandaia? Anche questo? Lavandaia? Tutti imestieri avete fatto?

NAPOLEON: (*furious, cutting off the word*) A washerwoman? That too? A washerwomen? Have you done every kind of trade?

CATERINA: Due; Ed ho dovuto chiudere bottega per colpa dei cattivi pagatori! Alla Corte c'è un tale che mi deve sessanta franchi e non se ne ricorda.

CATERINA: Just two; I had to close my shop because of those Who did not pay their bills! Here in the court There is a man who owes me sixty francs— He never remembers it.

NAPOLEONE: (*alzando le spalle*) Sia lode al cielo! (*Siede allo scrittoio e tenta di scrivere: la penna non va. La getta nervosamente; ne prende un'altra*)

NAPOLEON: (*shrugging his shoulders*) Praise be to Heaven! (*He sits down at his desk and tries to write; the pen does not go; he throws it away nervously, and takes another.*)

CATERINA: Gli ho portato il conto, così, per rinfrescargli la memoria. (*Estrae dal corsetto una logora lettera a cui è appuntato con uno spillo un conto. Apre la lettera, si avvicina alla lampada e legge a fatica*) "Con la mia magra paga di soldato "devo . . .,, È scritta da cane! . . . "devo . . . aiutar mia madre, "che ha lasciato la Corsica . . .,,

CATERINA: I've got the bill here to refresh my mind. (*She takes from her corsage a worn-out letter to which is pinned a bill. She opens the letter, goes the lamp and reads it with difficulty.*) "Out of my soldier's pay, which is but little, I must"—this devilish writing!— "I must aid My mother, who has come from Corsica."

NAPOLEONE: (*colpito*) La Corsica? Che dite? (*Si alza vivamente, le corre vicino, le strappa di mano la lettera, guarda la firma, legge sorpreso, sorridendo subito dopo*) "Buonaparte.

NAPOLEON: (*astounded*) From Corsica? What say you? (*He rises quickly, comes near her, snatches the letter from her hand, looks at the signature, reads with surprise, smiling immediately after.*) "Bonaparte."

CATERINA: Ecco, Sire, un cattivo pagatore. (*Siede sulla poltrona con comica aria di trionfo*)

CATERINA: This man pays badly, sir. (*She sits down in the armchair with a comic air of triumph.*)

NAPOLEONE: Lasciate che vi guardi! Ah, Vi ravviso! Siete voi . . . siete voi . . . (*Cerca nella memoria il nomignolo vivace della Duchessa*)

NAPOLEON: Let me look at you! I seem to recognize— but cannot quite— You are—you are— (*He searches his memory for the nickname of the Duchess.*)

CATERINA: (*suggerendoglielo*) . . . Madame Sans-Gêne.

CATERINA: (*suggesting it to him*) Madame Sans-Gêne.

NAPOLEONE: (*ridendo*) Madame Sans-Gêne, La mia allegra vicina!

NAPOLEON: (*laughing*) Ah, yes— My little neighbor!

CATERINA: In persona, Maestà!

CATERINA: In person, Majesty!

NAPOLEONE: Quella buona figliuola!

NAPOLEON: That charming girl!

CATERINA: In persona, Maestà!

CATERINA: In person, Majesty!

NAPOLEONE: (*reste assorto, guardando la lettera*) Questo logoro foglio scolorito, quanti ricordi suscita! Mi vedo

NAPOLEON: (*standing absorbed, as he looks at the letter*) This old, dicolored paper brings me back What memories! I see myself alone,

solo, pensoso, senza più speranza in una nuda stanza al quarto piano . . .

Thoughtful and hopeless, in an empty room Up four long flights of stairs, unknown, aloof.

CATERINA: . . . al quinto . . .

CATERINA: Up five—

NAPOLEONE: . . . al quarto . . .

NAPOLEON: Up four—

CATERINA: . . . al quinto! fin sotto i tetti v'eravate spinto!

CATERINA: Up five—it was on the roof.

NAPOLEONE: (*sorridendo*) È vero, è vero, mi ricordo, sì! (*raccogliendo nella sintesi di un gesto largo tutto il fasto della Reggia*) E fa piacere ricordarlo qui! (*scuotendosi, uscendo dai ricordi e ripredendo il tono vivace*) Madame Sans-Gêne, o discutiamo il conto. (*esaminandolo in tono di burla*) È salato!

NAPOLEON: (*smiling*) Yes, I remember—it is all quite clear. (*Stretching out his arms, as if to indicate by the gesture all the pomp of his kingdom*) It does me good to think of all that here! (*Shaking himself, he comes out of his dream and takes up his usual quick tone.*) Madame Sans-Gêne, we will dicuss the account. (*Examining it in a joking way.*) It is too much!

CATERINA: Ma no!

CATERINA: It's not.

NAPOLEONE: Ma sì! Via, via, quaranta frachi di soli rammendi!

NAPOLEON: It is! See here! You charged me forty frances for mending holes!

CATERINA: Ah, Sire, se sapeste che lavoro! La vostra biancheria era come un traforo!

CATERINA: Oh, sir, if you but knew how I had worked! Your laundry was as full of holes as lace.

NAPOLEONE: Non facciam paragoni! In breve, Bonaparte vi deve?

NAPOLEON: Comparisons are odious! In short Bonaparte owes you?

CATERINA: (*allungando la mano*) Tre Napoleoni!

CATERINA: (*putting out her hand*) Three Napoleons!

NAPOLEONE: (*si furga in tasca*) Ahimè, cara vicina, non li ho!

NAPOLEON: (*hunting in his pocketbook*) Alas! dear neighbor, I have not got it.

CATERINA: Pazienza, aspetterò . . . Vi fo credito ancora per qualche ora!

CATERINA: With patience I will wait—I'll credit you Still a few hours.

NAPOLEONE: (*sedendo vicino a lei, esaminandola tutta, rapidamente*) Madame Sans-Gêne, voi siete una donnina tutta malizia . . . (*Le tira scherzosamente l'orecchio*) con l'orecchia fina (*guardandole il viso*) e fino il viso, e vivido lo sguardo . . .

NAPOLEON: (*sitting down by her, examining her, rapidly*) Madame Sans-Gêne, you are A crafty lady— (*He pinches her ear playfully.*) With your pretty ear (*Looking at her face.*) And pretty face, and glance so fine and keen.

CATERINA: (*con allegro rimprovero e quasi confidenzialmente*) Vostra Maestà lo nota un po' in ritardo.

CATERINA: (*with slight reproach and half confidentially*) Your Majesty remarks it rather late.

NAPOLEONE: Che vuol dir?

NAPOLEON: What do you mean?

CATERINA: (*sorridendo*) Che in quel tempo io pensavo: "Accidenti, se questo tenentin mi domanda qualche cosa io gli dono anche il resto!,, Un giorno soprattutto! Ero venuta da voi tutta ridente e fresca e lucida, la sciarpa al vento e un ghirbizzo in testa! E salgo, oh, quante scale! E picchio! oh Dio, che palpiti!

CATERINA: (*smiling*) That in those times I thought: "By heaven! if this lieutenant only sought Something of me, why, he would have much more!" One day especially! Icame to you Happy and laughing, full of strange delight, Fancies within me, my scarf behind in flight! I mounted up such endless lengths

Ed entro . . . e mi tremavano i ginocchi!
Depongo il cesto della biancheria . . .
Vostra Maestà non leva neanche gli occhi
da una carta geografica. Io mi dico:
"Vediam se lascia la sui geografia
per occuparsi un poco della mia!,,
E m'aggiro, e vi sfioro, e fo tic tac
coi tacchetti inquieti sul piancito
e la stanza gelata vi riscaldo
di gioventù, di strepito e d'invito.
Ma voi, sempre più freddo e cieco e muto,
non vedeste l'amor ch'era venuto,
non vedeste l'amor che se n'è andato!
E così fu
che a casa riportai la mia tirtù,
intatta sì, ma furibonda . . .

NAPOLEONE: (prendendole la mano) Stolto ben fui quel giorno a non vedere
questa piccola man che m'era offerta,
caro pegno d'amore . . .

CATERINA: (in tono di burla)
Ecco un conquistatore.

NAPOLEONE: E la ferita?

CATERINA: (indicando il braccio) È qui.

NAPOLEONE: (facendo l'atto di baciarle il braccio) Voi permettete?

CATERINA: Il saluto ai feriti, sempre.

NAPOLEONE: (bacia la cicatrice e poicon le lebbra più in su, sempre più in su) No, Sire, no!
Non cercate più in su,
ferite non ce n è più!

NAPOLEONE: (insinuante) Via,
poichè pàgo i conti del tenente . . .

CATERINA: (alzandosi con un gesto dignitoso e inchinandosi)
L'Imperator non mi dovrà più niente!

NAPOLEONE: (serio) È giusto!
Ora vi faccio accompagnare.
(chiamando forte)
Roustan! (Entra Roustan)
Un ufficiale di servizio!

ROUSTAN: (attraversa la scena per obbedire all'Imperatore, che intanto si è avvicinato a CATERINA e l'ha aiutata a indossare la pelliccia. Ma il mammalucco ha appena varcata la porta di fondo, che si arresta e ascolta attentamente)
(NAPOLEONE fa un gesto de interrogazione)

of stair.
And knocked, and entered, and when I stood there
Before you I was trembling, and I laid
The box of laundry down. You never made
The slightest sign, you never raised your head
From the map that you were studying. I said:
"I'll see if for a moment I can trap
His fixed attention from this wretched map!
I moved about, I dropped some flowers, I kept
A dreadful noise up, as I madly stepped,
Filling the room with youth and charms to wind
About you. You, always more cold and blind,
Saw not the love that came and went away,
and so in virtue I was doomed to stay.

NAPOLEON: (taking her hand)
Stupid was I then not to see the hand
You offered me, the symbol sweet of love.—

CATERINA: (in a joking tone)
This is the conqueror.

NAPOLEON: And the wound?

CATERINA: (indicating her arm)
It is here.

NAPOLEON: (making the action of kissing her arm) You will permit?

CATERINA: Salute to the wounded always.

(NAPOLEON kisses the scar, and then moves his lips further and further upward.)
No, kiss no higher, there is no wound there!

NAPOLEON: (insinuatingly)
There, that is how I pay the lieutenant's bebts.

CATERINA: (rising with dignified gesture and bowing) The Emperor owes me nothing more!

NAPOLEON: (seriously) It is just.
Now I will have you accompanied.
(calling loudly.)
Roustan!
(Enter ROUSTAN.)
An officer of service.

(ROUSTAN crosses the stage to obey the Emperor, who at the same time approaches CATERINA and helps her put on her pellisse. But the officer has scarcely left the door at the back, when he stops and listens attentively.)
(NAPOLEON makes a gesture of interrogation)

ROUSTAN: (sottovoce) Hanno aperto la porta segreta . . .

NAPOLEONE: A quest'ora?

ROUSTAN: Odo un passo . . .

NAPOLEONE: (facendogli segno di prendere la lampada che illumina la stanza) Va e vedi!
(Poi, colto da un subito pensiero)
No.
(additando a ROUSTAN la porta della sua camera)
Là, e chiudi la porta . . . Se chiamo, corri.
(ROUSTAN esce con la lampada. La scena è tutta buia)

NAPOLEONE: (a CATERINA, duramente, a bassa voce) E silenzio!
(Nella stanza oscura entra furtiva la signora DE BOULOW; si guarda intorno, esamina il gabinetto che le sembra deserto, si inoltra nella direzione della stanza dell'Imperatore poi nell'antecamera. Rassicurata, torna sui suoi passi, riapre l'uscio dal quale è passata e fa cenno a NEIPPERG di avanzarsi. Quando NEIPPERG è entrato, essa lo prende per mano e lo conduce verso la porta dell'Imperatore. A questo punto l'Imperatore si avanza rapido, pone bruscamente una mano sulla spalla di NEIPPERG e chiama, gridando:)

NAPOLEONE: Roustan
(ROUSTAN entra subito con la lampada, che posa sulla tavola. La scena si illumina)

LA SIGNORA DE BOULOW: (atterrita) L'Imperatore!

NAPOLEONE: (con uno scoppio sordo di furore) Neipperg!

CATERINA: (tra se) Ah, disgraziato, era lui!

NAPOLEONE: (con voce suffocata, tutto fremente di collera) Voi!?
A quest'ora? Qui? Voi?
(a ROUSTAN, indicando la Signora de BOULOW)
Via questa donna! Via!
(ROUSTAN fa uscire la SIGNORA DE BOULOW, poi fitorna verso il fondo della scena e rimane immobile e attento)

NEIPPERG: Son venuto a prender commiato
dall'Imperatrice, com'è mio diritto.

NAPOLEONE: (con un grido suffocato, al colmo dello sdegno) Ed il mio,
trovandovi di notte, a quella porta,
è di trattarvi come un malfattore colto sul fatto e sopprimervi qui.

NEIPPERG: (con calma) Voi ne avete il potere . . .

ROUSTAN: (in a low voice) The secret door
Is open.

NAPOLEON: At this hour?

ROUSTAN: I hear a step.

NAPOLEON: (making a sign to him to take the lamp which lights the room) Go then and see!
(Struck by a new idea.)
No.
(indicating to ROUSTAN the door of his room.)
There, shut the door—
If I should call, hurry.
(ROUSTAN goes out with the lamp. The stage is entirely dark.)

(To CATERINA in a low, hard voice.)
Silence now!
Enter stealthily MADAME DE BOULOW; she looks carefully about, examining the cabinet which seems deserted; she advances in the direction of the Emperor's room, then towards the antechamber. Reassured, she retraces her steps, and opens again the door where she entered, and makes a sign to NEIPPERG to come in. When NEIPPERG has come in, she takes him by the hand and leads him towards the Empress's door. At this point the Emperor steps forward rapidly, puts roughly a hand on NEIPPERG'S shoulder, and calls out:)

NAPOLEON: Roustan!
(ROUSTAN enters at once with the lamp, which he puts on the table. The stage is light again.)

MADAME DE BOULOW: (terrified) The Emperor!

NAPOLEON: (with an explosion of fury) Neipperg!

CATERINA: (to herself) Disgrace! it's he!

NAPOLEON: (in a smothered voice, trembling with rage) You! at this hour! You? Here?
(To ROUSTAN, indicating MADAME DE BOULOW)
Away with her! away!
(ROUSTAN takes out MADAME DE BOULOW, then returns to the back of the stage, where he remains, motionless and attentive.)

NEIPPERG: I have come, your Majesty, to take my leave
Of the Empress, which I had the right to do.

NAPOLEON: (with a smothered cry, at the height of fury) And my right, finding your before this door
By night, is to treat you as a malefactor
Caught in the act and to suppress you here.

NEIPPERG: (calmly) You have the power—

NAPOLEONE: (con forza) E ne uso! Roustan, qui la tua gente!
(ROUSTAN corre alla porta, fa un segno e subito due mammalucchi appariscono sulla soglia)

NAPOLEONE: (a ROUSTAN) Portate via costui!

CATERINA: (interponendosi, fuor di se) Se fanno un passo, grido. (Gli uomini, che stavano per avvicinarsi a NEIPPERG, a questa minaccia s'arrestano incerti)

NAPOLEONE: E osate?!

CATERINA: Grido! Grido: "Qui si sgozza un uomo!,,

NAPOLEONE: (a ROUSTAN) E fatela tacere!

CATERINA: (disperata, piangente) E un assassinio! (Inginocchiandosi e aggrappandosi a NAPOLEONE, che la respinge) Ah, grazia, Sire, per la vostra gloria, grazia, grazia, vi supplico!

NAPOLEONE: (a ROUSTAN) Obbedite . . . (ROUSTAN e i due mammalucchi si avanzano verso NEIPPERG, che getta sul canapè il suo mantello e li ferma col gesto)

NEIPPERG: (a NAPOLEONE) Ma trattatemi almeno da soldato! Fattemi facilar vigliaccamente come il duca d'Enghien!

NAPOLEONE: (fuori di se) No! troppo onore per un bandito, degno solamente ch'io gli strappi le insegne e lo schiaffeggi con esse. (Gli strappa i cordoni delle insegne e fa il gesto di percuoterlo. — NEIPPERG fa un salto indietro e sfodera la spada)

NEIPPERG: Fate dunque! (I mammalucchi si gettano su di luie lo atterrano)

CATERINA: (gridando) Aiuto! Aiuto! (Accorrono tre ufficiali, ad uno dei quali ROUSTAN consegna la spada di NEIPPERG. L'ufficiale la depone sullo scrittoio)

NEIPPERG: (dibattendosi ancora) Un vero Côrso avrebbe tratto il suo coltello . . . (ai mammalucchi) Manigoldi! . . .

NAPOLEONE: (mostranandogli i cordoni delle insegne) Strangolare con queste io vi dovrei! Ma non lo faccio per rispetto del

---

NAPOLEON: (with force) Which I will use! Roustan, Bring in your people! (ROUSTAN hurries to the door, makes a sign and at once two men appear on the threshold.) (To ROUSTAN.) Take this man away!

CATERINA: (putting herself between them, beside herself) One step, and I will scream. (The men, who were about to approach NEIPPERG, at this menace stop uncertain.)

NAPOLEON: And you would dare?

CATERINA: I will cry out: "A man here cuts his throat!"

NAPOLEON: (to ROUSTAN) Make her be silent!

CATERINA: (desperate, weeping) He is an assassin! (Kneeling down and grasping NAPOLEON, who repulses her.) Ah, pity, pity, for your glory, pity!

NAPOLEON: (to ROUSTAN) Obey! (ROUSTAN and the men advance towards NEIPPERG, who throws his mantle on the sofa and stops them with a gesture.)

NEIPPERG: (to NAPOLEON) And you would treat me less than a soldier! You'd shoot me as a coward, like the Duke Of Enghien!

NAPOLEON: (beside himself) No! for that is too much honor! But as a bandit, whose desert is but That I should snatch his medals from his breast, And strike his face with them. (He snatches the strings of his medals and makes the gesture of striking him. NEIPPERG jumps back and unsheathes his sword.)

NEIPPERG: Then do it!

CATERINA: (crying out) Help! (Three officers rush in, to one of whom ROUSTAN consigns NEIPPERG'S sword. The officer puts it on the writing desk.)

NEIPPERG: (still striking) A true Corsican would have drawn his knife— (To the men.) Executioners!

NAPOLEON: (showing him the strings of his medals) I should strangle you With these! But I will not do so Out of respect to your Emperor!

---

vostro Imperatore! . . . (Getta lontano i cordoni con disprezzo e risàle a destra della tavola. — Ai tre ufficiali, con autorità) Quest' uomo su di me levò la spada! Fouché e Lefebvre sian chiamati qui e tutto sia finito avanti il giorno! (CATERINA, disperata, cade su una sedia)

QUADRO — VELARIO

## ■ ATTO QUARTO

Il gabinetto dell' Imperatore come nell' atto precedente.

(Le candele stanno per spegnersi, il fuoco muore. Accasciata sulla sedia, col mento tra le mani CATERINA pensa, dolorosamente assorta. Entra dalla sinistra LEFEBVRE, frettoloso e inquieto, in uniforme di servizio.)

CATERINA: (gli va incontro e gli prende la mano) Febvre, Febvre, mio Febvre! Neipperg fu colto là su quella porta (indicando la porta dell' Imperatrice) e alzò la spada sull' Imperatore!

LEFEBVRE: Ah, disgraziato, egli è perduto!

CATERINA: No, non dirlo, no, salvalo tu!

LEFEBVRE: (disperato) È perduto! è perduto! Ed io dovrò dir la parola che lo ucciderà!

CATERINA: (stringendosi a lui e parlando con la voce piena di lagrime) Febvre, la vita che gli concedesti un gioirno, or gli rotogli . . .

LEFEBVRE: (commosso) Ah, non guardarmi e taci! Se tu mi preghi, che risponderò? Il destino è segnato, io sono l'arma del destino, e spietato obbedirò! Ma quando torno, fa che non le vedo le tue lagrime, o cara! Ch'io non trovi il tuo pallido viso sulla soglia . . . . . . E fuggirò dove la casa è più

NAPOLEONE: Ah, la vostra paura, più sincera di voi, confessa e lo condanna! (con grande forza) Muoia, dunque!

CATERINA: (con un grido) No, Sire!

NAPOLEONE: (con un gesto imperioso) Entrate!

---

(He throws the strings away, and goes to the right of the table. To the three officers, with authority.) This man has dared to raise his sword against me! Let Fouché and Lefebvre be summoned here And everything be ended ere the dawn. (CATERINA, desperate, falls on a chair.)

TABLEAU—CURTAIN

## ■ ACT IV

The Emperor's cabinet, as in the preceding act.

(The candles are burning out, the fire is dying. Sitting weak on a chair, with her chin in her hands, CATERINA is tragically absorbed in her thoughts. Enter from the left LEFEBVRE hastily and restlessly, in service uniform.)

CATERINA: (going towards him and taking his hand) Febvre, Febvre, My Febvre! Neipperg was caught here at the door. (indicating the door of the Empress's room.) And raised his sword against the Emperor.

LEFEBVRE: He is disgraced—and lost!

CATERINA: No, say it not— No, you must save him!

LEFEBVRE: He is lost, he is lost! And I must give the word to seal his doom!

CATERINA: (clinging to him and speaking with a voice full of emotion) Febvre, the life we spared so long ago Comes wheeling back at us—

LEFEBVRE: Do not look at me— Be still! If you pleas thus, what shall I say? His destiny is signed, I am the arm Of destiny, and under careful watch I must obey! But when the deed is done, Let me not see your tears, let me not see Your pallid face in the doorway. I shall flee Away to where the house is solitary.

NAPOLEON: Your fear, sincerer than yourself, Confesses and condemns you! (With great force.) Will you go?

CATERINA: (with a cry) No, Sire!

NAPOLEON: (with an imperative gesture) Enter!

**CATERINA:** (*esitante, agitata tra propositi diversi, con la voce piena di pianto*) Che tortura!
(*Ancora ripugnante, si dirige lentamente verso la porta che mette all'appartamento dell'Imperatrice. NAPOLEONE la fissa con i suoi occhi pieni d'irresistibile comando. Smarita come un automa, ella si avanza, apre la porta. ROUSTAN, ch'è tuttora fermo nel vestibolo, le lascia il passo e rienta nel gabinetto imperiale. CATERINA, giunta all'uscio dell'Imperatrice, alza la mano per bussare, ma la mano le ricade ed ella si volge ancora in atto d'implorare verso l'Imperatore*)

**NAPOLEONE:** (*implacabile le comanda col gesto, di entrare. Abbassa la fiamma della lampada. La stanza si fa oscura; CATERINA bussa e apre la porta*)

**LA VOCE DELL' IMPERATRICE:** Ah, siete voi, signora de Boulow?

**CATERINA:** (*tremante, con un filo de voce*) Maestà, Neipperg è qui!

**LA VOCE DELL' IMPERATRICE:** Bene . . . Dategli questo . . .
(*s'intravede il braccio nudo dell' Imperatrice, che consegna a CATERINA una grande busta sigillata*) E addio! . . .
CATERINA chiude la porta, non ha la forza di avanzarsi verso l'Imperatore. Egli corre a lei, con una mano l'afferra per un polso, e la trascina mezzo svenuta verso la scrivania, con l'altra mano le strappa la lettera, alza convulsamente la fiamma, mentre CATERINA piomba spossata e disperta sopra una poltrona)

**NAPOLEONE:** (*leggendo l'indirizzo della lettera*) "A Sua Maestà l'Imperatore d'Austria . . .,, (*sorpreso*)
Suo padre?
(*Esita un momento, poi scrolla le spalle e rompe i suggelli, leggendo*)
"Signore e Caro Padre, poiché il ministro di
polizia apre le mie lettere, ricorro al conte di
Neipperg per inviarvi in segreto la presente . . .
Le sue assiduità . . . turbano me e l'Imperatore . . .
trattenetelo a Vienna . . .,,

**CATERINA:** (*con un'esplosione di gioia*) È innocente, è innocente!

**NAPOLEONE:** (*con l'espressione di chi è sollevato da un gran peso, e con calma voluta*) Il mio cuore non ne ha mai dubitato!

**CATERINA:** (*tra se*) Che razza disfacciata!

---

**CATERINA:** (*hesitating, agitated between different intentions, with a voice full of tears*) This is torture, torture!
(*Still hesitant, she goes towards the door which leads to the Empress's apartment with slow steps. NAPOLEON fixes her with eyes full of irresistible command. Bewildered, like an automaton she advances and opens the door. ROUSTAN, still standing firmly in the vestibule, makes way for her and reenters the imperial cabinet. CATERINA, arriving at the Empress's door, raises her hand to knock, but the hand falls powerless at her side and she turns toward the Emperor again in the act of supplication.*)

*NAPOLEON implacably commands her with a gesture to enter. He turns down the lamp. The room is dark; CATERINA knocks, and opens the door.*)

**THE VOICE OF THE EMPRESS:** Ah, it is you, Madame de Bulow?

**CATERINA:** (*trembling, very softly*) Majesty, Neipperg is here!

**THE VOICES OF THE EMPRESS:** It is well—Give this to him.— (*One catches the glimpse of a bare arm of the Empress, which consigns to CATERINA a large sealed packet.*) And my farewell!
(*CATERINA closes the door, has not the strength to advance towards the Emperor. He hurries to her, with one hand seizes her by the wrist and drags her half fainting to the writing desk, with the other he snatches the letter from her, and excitedly puts up the light, while she falls, weak and desperate, in an armchair.*)

**NAPOLEON:** (*reading the address of the letter*) "His Majesty the Emperor of Austria."
(*surprised*)
Her father!
(*He hesitates a moment, then shrugs his shoulders and breaks the seal, reading*)
"Honored and dear father, since the minister of police opens my letters, I am taking recourse to the Count of Neipperg, to send this by him in secret. His assiduity troubles me and the Emperor. Entertain him in Vienna."

**CATERINA:** (*with a burst of joy*) He's innocent, he's innocent!

**NAPOLEON:** (*with the expression of one from whom a great weight has fallen and with desired calm*)
My heart
Never doubted it!

**CATERINA:** (*to herself*) What bold impudence!

---

**NAPOLEONE:** (*consegnando a ROUSTAN la lettera*) Risigilla e riporta.
(*ROUSTAN esce.— Entrano LEFEBVRE, FOUCHÉ*)

**FOUCHÉ:** (*presentando a NAPOLEONE un foglio*) Sire, ecco la sentenza!

**CATERINA:** (*con un gesto vivacemente popolaresco*) Che sentenza d'Egitto!
(*Accorre a LEFEBVRE e gli parla frettolosamente sottovoce*)

**NAPOLEONE:** (*prende sul suo scrittoio la spada di NEIPPERG e la consegna a FOUCHÉ*) Consegnatela a Neipperg!
Fo'grazia! Parta subito!
(*FOUCHÉ esce.— NAPOLEONE, volgendosi con piglio burbero a LEFEBVRE*)
Quanto al vostro divorzio . . .
Il mio colere è questo:

(*accostandosi a CATERINA, tirandole l'oerecchio e cambiando tono di voce*)
Che tu la tenga sul tuo cor serrata, che tu ringrazi il Ciel che te l'ha data!
(*Volta le spalle ed entra nella sua stanza.— Si sentono fuori gli squilli dei corni da caccia. I servi aprono le porte di fondo. Penetra la luce a grandi fiotti nella stanaz.*)

**CATERINA:** (*a LEFEBVRE con gaia vivacità*) O vecchio mio, più mai
sfuggirmi non potrai!
Il tuo destino è al mio destin legato:
Dio mi ti ha dato
e chi ti tocca, guai!

**LEFEBVRE:** Il dì che splende già, sorridendo ci guarda, e ci ridà
e l'amore e l'amico!
Io benedico
la mia rinata felicità!

**CORO DI CACCIATORI:** (*di fuori*) Entro i sentieri, foschi dei boschi,
bisbiglia fresco il dì!
Alalì, alalì!
Nell' ombra già s'inselva la belva che dal covile uscì! Alaì, alaì!
Ma la ferina traccia la caccia tra l'erba discoprì! Alalì, alalì
(*L'atrio che dà sul parco si va popolando di cavalieri e di amazzoni. Il giardino imperiale appare luminoso, pieno di cavalleggeri, di cacciatori, di canattieri. E uno splendore di uniformi, un brusio, un parlare, un agitarsi, uno squillar di corni da caccia.*)
(*CAROLINA ed ELISA entrano nel gabinetto, in costume di amazzone, seguite dalla loro scorta d'onore*)

---

**NAPOLEON:** (*giving the letter to ROUSTAN*) Seal this again and take it.
(*ROUSTAN goes out. Enter LEFEBVRE and FOUCHÉ.*)

**FOUCHÉ:** (*presenting a paper to NAPOLEON*) Sire, the sentence!

**CATERINA:** (*with a quick common gesture*) Sentence of Egypt!
(*She hurries to LEFEBVRE and speaks to him rapidly in a low voice.*)

**NAPOLEON:** (*taking from his desk NEIPPERG'S sword and giving it to FOUCHÉ*) Consign this to Neipperg!
I thank you! Go at once!
(*FOUCHÉ goes out. NAPOLEON turns with a savage look to LEFEBVRE.*)
As to your divorce—
My wish is this:

(*Turning to CATERINA, taking her by the ear and changing the tone of his voice.*)
Hold her forever, true—
Give thanks to heaven for giving her to you!
(*He turns his back and goes into his room. From outside comes the sound of hunting-borns. Light in great waves comes into the room.*)

**CATERINA:** (*to LEFEBVRE, with gay vivacity*) My dear old friend, you'll not escape me now!
Your fate is bound to mine with more than a vow.
God gave me you—who touches you, beware!

**LEFEBVRE:** The smiling day, that looks upon us there,
Laughs with our love and friendship, and I bless
This glowing dawn, my newborn happiness!

**CHORUS OF HUNTSMEN:** (*outside*) Within the shaded paths beyond the lea
Whispers the freshness of the day! Alali!
Already through the brush there creeps along
The furious boar to meet us—hear our song!
The wild beast leads us on to his own woe
Among the open grasses there— halloa!
(*Through the opening to the park one sees crowds of cavaliers and amazons. The imperial garden seems luminous, full of riders, huntsmen, and dog-keepers. There is the color of uniforms, general noise and movement, the sound of hunting-borns. CAROLINA and ELISA enter the cabinet, in riding-costume, followed by their escort of bonor.*)

NAPOLEONE: (*ritornando dalla sua stanza in redingote grigia, cappello e stivaloni*)
(*a tutta la Corte*)
Signori, andiamo!
(*Volgendosi a CATERINA*)
Datemi la mano. Fino alla vostra soglia
vi condurrò, per farvi giusto onore!

CATERINA: (*a NAPOLEONE*) Ah, come potrò dirvi quanta sia
la gioia che mi palpita nel sen?

NAPOLEONE: (*sottolineando le parole e in modo che tutti possano intendere, soprattutto ELISA e CAROLINA*) La Duchessa di Danzica mi sia fida,
Come mi fu Madame Sans-Gêne!
(NAPOLEONE si inchina, prende la

NAPOLEON: (*returning from his room in a gray coat, hat and big boots, to the court*) My friends let us be off!
(*turning to CATERINA*) Give me your hand.
I will lead you back to your own threshold.
To do you worthy honour!

CATERINA: (*to NAPOLEON*) How can I describe
The joy that throbs within me?

NAPOLEON: (*emphasizing the words and in a way that all may hear, especially ELISA and CAROLINA*) May
The Duchess of Danzig be as true again
To me as was Madame Sans-Gêne!

mano di CATERINA e gliela bacia rispettosamente. CATERINA, al colmo della gioia, volge lo sguardo, con una mezza smorfia, a ELISA e CAROLINA. NAPOLEONE, tenendo sempre per mano CATERINA, si avvia verso il fondo, seguito da LEFEBVRE e da tutta la Corte. Quando è sulla soglia, ROUSTAN grida )

ROUSTAN: L'Imperatore!

UNA VOCE PIÙ LONTANA: (*annunciando*) L'Imperatore!

TUTTE LE VOCI: (*di fuori, in un grido formidabile*) Viva l'Imperatore!

*FINE*

(NAPOLEON bows, takes CATERINA'S hand and kisses it respectfully. CATERINA, at the height of joy, throws a glance, half of disdain, upon ELISA and CAROLINA. NAPOLEON, always holding CATERINA'S hand, goes towards the back, followed by LEFEBVRE and the whole court. When he is at the door, ROUSTAN cries out.)

ROUSTAN: The Emperor!

A VOICE FAR AWAY: (*announcing*) The Emperor!

ALL THE VOICES: (*outside, with a great cry*) Long live the Emperor!

*THE END*

# *André Chénier* (1896)

MUSIC BY UMBERTO GIORDANO ▪ LIBRETTO BY LUIGI ILLICA

This four-act dramma di ambiente storico, set to a libretto by Luigi Illica, premiered at the La Scala on March 28, 1896. The year is 1789. A ball is to be held at the Château de Coigny. Carlo Gérard, a servant, detests all of his noble masters except for Maddalena de Coigny, daughter of the house, whom he secretly loves. The guests to arrive; among them, the novelist Fléville, André Chénier, a poet, and the Abate. The Abate brings unfortunate tidings from Paris, but the guests are distracted by Fléville's reading of a pastoral. Chénier reads a poem that denounces the injustices of the church and the aristocracy against the common people. Cérard, leading a band of peasants, interrupts the ball; the Contessa gets rid of them, fires Gérard and orders the dancing to carry on. In Paris, the age of the Terror rages. Chénier is constantly under surveillance, watched by a spy for the revolutionary Government, to which Gérard has given his allegiance. Chénier tells Roucher, his friend, about an unknown woman who has written to him to ask for his protection. Roucher suggests that he flee Paris at once, but he insists on finding out the woman's identity. Gérard gives the spy a description of Maddalena with instructions to find her. She is Chénier's unknown letter writer; on seeing the two together, the spy reports back to Gérard. Not recognizing Chénier, Gérard challenges him to a duel. Chénier wounds Gérard, who finally recognizes Chénier, and warns him that he is in grave danger. The police arrive, Gérard says that he does not know his attacker. At the Revolutionary Tribunal, Gérard hears of Chénier's arrest; that he himself must write out the bill of indictment. He signs the documents, and Maddalena comes to plead for Chénier's life. She offers herself to her former servant if he will help Chénier, and Gérard agrees to her proposal. With the support of Gérard, Chénier defends himself eloquently in front of the Tribunal, but the poet is still sentenced to death. In the courtyard of St.-Lazare prison, Chénier reads his last poem to Roucher. Maddalena enters with Gérard, who makes one last plea for their lives. Maddelena bribes the jailer so that she may take another female prisoner's place. Thus she and Chénier, together until the end, can face their imminent death with the strength of their love for one another.

---

## ▪ QUADRO I

*(Sala da ballo al Castello di Coigny. All' alzarsi della tela, sotto i comandi di un gallonato Maestro di Casa, corrono Lacché, Servi, Valletti carichi di mobili e vasi, completando l'assetto dalla serra. Carlo Gerard, in livrea, entra sostenendo con altri servi un pesante sofà.)*

**IL MAESTRO DI CASA:** Questo azzurro sofà
la collochiam
*(Gérard e i lacchè eseguiscono, poi il Maestro di Casa accenna verso le sale interne e vi entra seguito da tutti i lacché. eccettuato Gérard che, inginocchiato avanti all'azzurro sofà ne liscia le frangie, sprimacciando i cuscini).*

**GÉRARD:** *(al sofà)*, Compiacente
a' colloqui
del cicisbeo
che a dame maturate
porgeva qui la mano!
Qui il Tacco Rosso al Neo
sospirando dicea:
"Oritia o Clori o Nice incipriate,
Vecchiette e imbellettate,
io vi bramo
ed, anzi sol per questo, forse, io
v'amo!"
Tal dei tempi il costume!
*(Dal giardino si avanza il padre di Gérard. — Questi guardando*

## ▪ ACT I

*(The Ball-room at the Château de Coigny. As the curtain rises enter the Major-domo, followed by Servants carrying furniture with which to ornament the rooms. Gerard, in livery, helps other servants to carry in a heavy sofa.)*

**MAJOR-DOMO:** Set the blue sofa down
There, in its place!
*(The Major-domo moves on to rooms beyond, leaving Gerard behind, who smoothes the cushions of the couch and dusts the faded silk.)*

**GERARD:** *(to the Sofa)*. You have patiently listened,
As gallant beaux to dames whose charms had ripened,
Their passion here protested!
Here, Corin came to woo,
As he said with a sigh:
"Orynthia! O Chloris! Oh, nymphs with paint bedizened
"To deck your features wizened
"I implore you,
"Have pity upon him who must adore you!"
It is the mode of the moment!
*(Gerard's father enters, carrying*

*commosso allontanarsi il padre).*
Son sessantanni, o vecchio, che tu servi!
A' tuoi protervi
arroganti signori
hai prodigato fedeltà, sudori,
la forza dei tuoi nervi,
l'anima tua, la mente
e—quasi non bastasse la tua vita
a renderne infinita
eternamente
l'orrenda sofferenza—
hai data l'esistenza
dei figli tuoi
Hai figliato dei servi!
*(si asciuga sdegnosamente le lagrime. e torna a guardare fieramente intorno a sè la gran serra.)*
T'odio, casa dorata!
L'imagin sei d'un secolo
incipriato e vano!
Fasti, splendori, orgogli di Re Sole!
Regno di Cortigiane tu, o Reggenza,
e dei Lebel
onnipotenza
tu, Luigi Lussuria!
O vaghi dami in seta ed in merletti,
volgono al fin le gaje vostre giornate
e le serate
a inchini e a minuetti!
Fissa è la vostra sorte!
Razza leggiadra e rea,
figlio di servi e servo,
qui—giudice in livrèa—
ti grido:—È giunta l'ora della

*a flower-stand, and as the old man departs by the garden-way, Gerard gazes at him wistfully.)*
Full sixty years, oh! my father,
You have served them,
Devoting ever to your arrogant masters
Strength of your manhood, loyally unbounded;
For them your limbs have toiled
They had your brain, your spirit,
And yet, as though your life were not sufficient,
A life of drudgery and toil unending,
Its load of shame and sorrow
Have been (by you) transmitted
to your sons! You are a father to slaves!
*(Surveying the sumptuous apartment.)*
Gilded house, I abhor you!
Of that vain world the image,
As fair, and false and painted!
Pretty ladies, in rich brocade and laces,
Swift advancing,
Dance minuets and gay gavottes
With your modish airs and graces!
Dance! yet your doom awaits you,
Frivolous, infamous gang!
Lackey, and son of a lackey,
Though a menial, yet your judge, I warn you:
The hour of doom is near!
*(The Countess, Madeleine, and Bersi appear at back. The Count-*

Morte!—
(*La contessa, Maddalena e Bersi appajono al di là dell'arco d'ingresso alla serra.—La contessa si sofferma a dare alcuni ordini al Maestro di Casa. Maddalena si avanza lentamente con la Bersi.*)

*ess stops to speak to the Major-domo. Madeleine with Bersi slowly enters.*)

**MADDALENA:** Il giorno intorno gia s'insera lentamente!
In queste misteriose ombre forme fantastiche assumono le cose!
Or l'anime s'acquetano umanamente!
(*Già si anima tutto il castello.—I valletti corono animatamente in su ed in giù apparecchiando le torcie nell'attesa delle slitte.*)

**MADELEINE:** The daylight fades;
And dusk around is gently falling:
Now, in the dim mysterious twilight,
Things take another shape,
Ethereal, fantastic:
Now to weary spirits Nature yields her solace!

**CONTESSA:** (*nervosa, imparte ordini, ora all'uno, ora all'altro.*) Presto avvertite i cori;
ed a tempo opportuno pastorelle e pastori!
E che non manchi alcuno!
Su, presto, i suonatori in cantoria!
(*Il Maestro di Casa annuncia ad alta voce.*)

**COUNTESS:** (*to her servants*).
Hasten to call the singers
And, at the proper time,
The shepherds and the shepherdesses;
See that none are missing;
Hurry! send the musicians up to the stand!

**MAESTRO DI CASA:** Madama de Bissy e il cavaliere di Villacerf!

**MAJOR-DOMO:** Madame de Bissy and Chev. Villacerf!

**CONTESSA:** (*al cavaliere di Villacerf.*) Oh! quanto commifò!
Come elegante e voi gentil Galante!

**COUNTESS:** Oh, How stylish
And fashionable you are!
A gallant cavalier indeed!
(*to Villacerf*).

**MAESTRO DI CASA:** La marchesa d'Entragnes e il barone Berwik!

**MAJOR-DOMO:** The Marquise d'Entragnes and Baron Berwick!

**CONTESSA:** (*al barone*) Vera galanteria!

**COUNTESS:** Vastly gallant, I vow!
(*to the Baron*).

**MAESTRO DI CASA:** La duchessa di Villemain e il marchese d'Harcout!

**MAJOR-DOMO:** The Duchess of Villemain and the Marquis of Harcourt!

**CONTESSA:** (*al marchese*) A ben più d'una brama
la vostra dama accender saprà l'esca!

**COUNTESS:** Oh! take care, my lord Marquis!
Your lady's eyes will surely work fresh havoc! (*to the Marquis*).

**MAESTRO DI CASA:** La principessa di Saint-Médard e il conte d'Aubetaire!

**MAJOR-DOMO:** The Princess of St. Médard and the Count of Aubetaire!

**CONTESSA:** (*alla principessa*). Mi ricordate
i dì della Reggenza
La Parabère, ecco, mi rassembrate!

**COUNTESS:** You remind me
Of the days under the Regency
And of the beautiful Parabére! (*to the Princess*).

**MAESTRO DI CASA:** Donna Anna da Torcy e don Enrico de Nangis!

**MAJOR-DOMO:** Donna Anna da Torcy and Don Henry de Nangis!

**CONTESSA:** (*a don Enrico de Nangis*). Quanta munificenza!

**COUNTESS:** What a kingly guest!
(*to Nangis*).

**MAESTRO DI CASA:** La contessa Etiolle d'Etoile e il reverendo Fragmont!

**MAJOR-DOMO:** The countess d'Etoile and Rev. Fragnont!

**CONTESSA:** (*alla vecchia dama, colla quale senza inchinarsi si abbracciano, vecchia dama che ha a cavaliere un grosso ecclesiastico*). Appariscente e fresca sempre!—Contessa, sempre, sempre la stessa!

**COUNTESS:** Why, you're as fair and young as ever!
Yes, Countess, just as youthful as ever! (*to the old dame*).

**MAESTRO DI CASA:** La marchesa di Lorge e il conte Fleuri!

**MAJOR-DOMO:** The Marquise of Sorge and Count Fleury!

**CONTESSA:** (*alla bella marchesina, accarezzandole la guancia*).
Come siete vezzosa!
Siete un amore!

**COUNTESS:** Oh! How sweet and charming;
How lovely you are! (*to the Marquise*).

**MAESTRO DI CASA:** La baronessa Boisguilbert e l'abate Crècy!

**MAJOR-DOMO:** The Baroness Boisguilbert and the Abbé Crecy!

**CONTESSA:** (*all'abate Crècy*). Con voi me ne congratulo Quale amica! Perfetta!
(*alla baronessa*). Sublime! Quanta grazia!
(*ad altra dama*). Dotta maestra! Invero è maestria! Mirabile toeletta!
(*Cavalieri e dame si affannano intorno alla Contessa interrogandola:*)
Chi avremo? Dite!
Mesmer?
Dugazon?
L'arlecchino Bordier?
Vestri?
Jeannot?

**COUNTESS:** I congratulate you;
Your friend is perfectly sweet!
(*to the Abbé*). Sublime! How graceful!
(*to the Baroness*). Very clever indeed!
You're wonderfully dressed!
(*to another lady*).
(*The hostess is being surrounded by inquisitive guests eagerly questioning her:*)
Do tell us who is coming!
Will he be Mesmer?
Or Dugazon?
That harlequin Bordier?
Is he Vestri?
or Jeannot?

**CONTESSA:** (*misteriosa abbassando la voce*). L'Abate!

**COUNTESS:** (*mysteriously, in a whisper*). The Abbé!

**TUTTI:** (*con gridi di gioja*). L'Abatino?
(*Entrano Fléville, l'Abate e Chénier.*)

**ALL:** (*joyously*). The little Abbé!

**MAGGIORDOMO:** Il cavaliere Anton Pietro Fléville.

**MAJOR-DOMO:** Chevalier Antoine Pierre Fléville.
(*Enter Fléville, the Abbé, and Chénier.*)

**FLÉVILLE:** Commosso lusingato a tanti complimenti
e a questo, più che omaggio amabil persiflaggio!
Ch'io vi presenti Flandro Fiorinelli, è cavaliere, italiano e musico!
e Andrea Chénier
un che fa versi e che promette molto.
(*Maddalena entra*).

**FLÉVILLE:** Delighted, I assure you,
At this auspicious meeting;
And flattered, vastly flattered,
By such a cordial greeting!
Let me present Fernando Fiorinelli,
A distinguished Italian musician—
André Chénier—writer of verses,
Who so they say, has talent!
(*Enter Madeleine*).

**IL MAGGIORDOMO:**
(*annuncia*). Sua Reverenza l'Abate
(*Le dame a questo annuncio si commuovono, rompono l'ordine fino allora tenuto e rumorosamente, con piccoli gemiti di gioja, attorniano il nuovo personaggio, soffocandolo quasi sotto le cortesie*).

**MAJOR-DOMO:** His reverence the Abbé!
(*The Ladies leaving their places in confusion rush toward the new comer and eagerly surround him. The Abbe is fairly smothered with courtesies.*)

**LE DAME:** L'Abate! É l'Abate!

**I CAVALIERI:** È l'Abate!

**I MARITI:** Finalmente!

**THE LADIES:** The Abbé at last! It is the Abbé.

**THE GENTLEMEN:** At last!

**LE DAME:** Venite da Parigi?

**MADELEINE:** So you've just come back from Paris!

**TUTTI:** Da Parigi?

**LE DAME:** Sì?

**I CAVALIERI:** Dite?

**I MARITI:** Che novelle della Corte?

**LE DAME:** Noi siam curiose!

**I CAVALIERI:** Presto!

**CHORUS:** From Paris?

**THE LADIES:** Is it true?

**THE GENTLEMEN:** Anything new?

**COUNTESS:** What news at Court, I pray you?

**MADELEINE:** We are dying to hear,

**THE LADIES:** Yes, do tell us, please!

**TUTTI:** Dite! dite!

**L'ABATINO:** Debole è il Re

**CHORUS:** Let us hear, quickly!

**ABBÉ:** The King, alas, is weak!

# Act I

MARITI: Ha ceduto?

L'ABATINO: Fu male consigliato!

CONTESSA: Necker?

L'ABATINO: Non ne parliamo! (*Degusta la marmellata sospirando in atto di suprema affizione.*)

TUTTI: Quel Necker!

DAME: Noi moriamo dalla curiosita!

L'ABATINO: (*questa volta attacca risolutamente la marmellata penetrandovi con tutto il cucchiajo.*) Abbiamo un Terzo stato!

TUTTI: Oh! Ah! Ah! Oh! Ma no! Ma no!

L'ABATINO: E ho veduto offender

TUTTI: Chi?

L'ABATINO: La statua di Enrico IV!

TUTTI: Orroe!

DONNE: Dove andremo a finire?

L'ABATINO: Cosi giudico anch'io!

CONTESSA: Non temono più Dio!

L'ABATINO: Assai, madame belle, sono dolente de le mie novelle

FLÉVILLE: Passiam la sera allegramente!—Della primavera a i zefiri gentili codeste nubi svaniranno! Il sole noi rivedremo e rose a gigli e viole e udrem ne l'aria satura de'fiori l'eco ridir l'egloghe de' pastori—

TUTTI: (*a vicenda*). O soave bisbiglio! È il vento! È zefiro! È mormorìo di fonte! È fruscìo d'ali Bacio è di nubi! Molce il cuor! Vallea veggiamo aprica! Io, un prato! Un ruscelletto ascolto mormorar! Parlan le fronde! Sospira un salce! Querula la canna di Dafne geme. Ecco il suo gregge! Rezzo divin!

FLÉVILLE: È questo il mio romanzo!

THE GENTLEMAN: Is he yielding?

ABBÉ: He has been ill-advised!

COUNTESS: Ah, Necker!

ABBÉ: (*Sadly helping himself to a marmelade.*) Let us not speak of him!

CHORUS: That Necker! We are dying to know; yes, we are!

ABBÉ: (*Vigorously attacking the marmelade with his spoon.*) We've now the "Third Estate"!

CHORUS: Oh! Oh! This seems absurd!

ABBÉ: And they've insulted even—

CHORUS: Whom?

ABBÉ: The statue of Henri Quatre!

CHORUS: Oh, horror!

THE LADIES: Gracious! where will it end?

ABBÉ: That's what I'd like to know!

COUNTESS: No fear have they of God!

ABBÉ: Enough, my beauteous ladies: I am sorry that I only bring bad news .

FLÉVILLE: What does that matter, my friends? We'll all be merry; And before returns the spring-tide, With light, and scent of flowers, Dispersed shall be the storm that lowers! There, on a bank of violets and fragrant roses, The breeze shall bear to us, on pinion light, Echoes of song, chants of the merry shepherd! It is the sigh of the breezes!

ABBÉ: It is the zephyrs!

CHORUS: It is the wind!

FLÉVILLE: It is the murmur of the fountain!

CHORUS: It is the sound of wings!

ABBÉ: I thought I heard the rippling stream!

FLÉVILLE: Behold, my dream comes true!

PASTORELLI: Pastorelli, addio! Ne andiamo verso, ahi! lidi ignoti e strani! Ahi! sarem lungi dimani! Questi lochi abbandoniamo! Non avrà, fino al ritorno, gioje il cuore! Non piacer fino a quel giorno, non amore!

PASTORELLI: O pastori, ahi! che dolori agli acerbi vostri detti! Treman dentro ai nostri petti languidetti i nostri cori! Ed ahi! ahi! fino al ritorno che crucïori! Non piacer fino a quel giorno, non amori!

L'ABATINO: "Il Volpe e l'Uva, favola. "Un volpe rodomonte—sospinto dalla fame "sovra alta vite tremula, vermilia "rama carca di grappoli "adocchia e cura "ammalïato. "Ma oh! come "tropp' alto pende il pampino! "E il volpe esclama! Oh, cosa vana "l'uva immatura!— "E, sospirando, s'allontana! "Del volpe chi sa il nome? "Terzo stato!"

CONTESSA: (*si avvicina a Chénier.*) Signor Chénier

CHÉNIER: Madama la Contessa?

CONTESSA: La vostra Musa tace?

CHÉNIER: È una ritrosa che di tacer desìa.

CONTESSA: La vostra Musa è la Malinconia! (*à Fléville*). Davver poco cortese!

FLÉVILLE: È un po' bizzarro!

ABATINO: Musa ognor pronta è donna a molti vieta!

CONTESSA: Musa ognor pronta! È ver Ecco il poeta! (*Prende il braccio dell'Abatino e con lui si avvicina a Fiorinelli, inducendolo gentilmente al clavicembalo*).

MADDALENA: (*alle compagne*) Io lo farò poetare! Scommettiamo? (*si avvicina a Chénier*).

MADDALENA: Al mio dire perdono ed al mio ardire! Ma viva bramosia. mi spinge Poi son donna e son curiosa riosa! Bramo di udire un'egloga da voi o una poesia per monaca o per sposa.

CHORUS: Oh, gentle nymphs, adieu! We're flying to lands afar. Oh, hear us, a-sighing! Heigho! Heigho! To distant lands we roam Before tomorrow; To part with you, alas! Brings bitter sorrow. Ah, well-a-day! Adieu! we must away!

CHORUS: Alas! The bitter pain In our trembling heart Now that we must part Heigho! Heigho! Until you come back How it will ache And our mind will rove For want of pleasure And of love!

ABBÉ: A hungry fox was spying With an envious eye The sweet ripe grape Hanging from a high vine But seeing that it was So hard to reach it She went away musing: It is sour after all! Now that fox has a name and it is?—"Third Estate."

COUNTESS: (*approaching Chénier*). Monsieur Chénier!

CHÉNIER: Madame, your most obedient!

COUNTESS: Your Muse, in truth, is silent!

CHÉNIER: Aye, for 'tis wayward, And rather would be dumb!

COUNTESS: Your Muse is Melancholy so it seems: (*to Fléville*). Indeed, 'twas scarcely courteous!

FLÉVILLE: He's so eccentric!

ABBÉ: Rare is the dower of ready song, we know it!

COUNTESS: Well said! Behold our poet! (*Takes the Abbé's arm and approaches Fiorinelli, whom she leads to the harpsichord*).

MADELEINE: (*to her companions.*) I'll make him rhyme, I warrant! Shall we wager? (*approaches Chénier*).

MADELEINE: I would pray you to pardon My seeming boldness; A woman, as you know, Is nothing if not curious. Will you not favor us with something of your own? Some harmless poem—that might amuse a school-girl?

**LE AMICHE:** Benissimo!
Per monaca o per sposa!

**CHÉNIER:** Desio che muove da due labbra rosa
è comando gentile a gentil cuore.
Ma—ohimè—la fantasia
non si piega a comando o a prece umìle
è capricciosa assai la poesia
a guisa dell'amore!
(*Maddalena e le ragazze ridono.*)

**CONTESSA:** Perchè ridete voi?
Che c'è?
Che c'è?
Che avviene?
Dite!

**LE AMICHE:** Udite! Udite che il racconto è bello!
Il poetino è caduto in un tranello.

**MADDALENA:** A tua preghiera, mamma, disdegnoso opponeva un rifiuto
Allor bizzarro
pensier mi venne

**LE AMICHE:** È vero
La vendetta!

**MADDALENA:** Io dissi: Scommettiano?

**CONTESSA E TUTTI:** Di che cosa?

**MADDALENA:** Che nel risponder alle preci nostre
volgarmente parlato avria d'amore.

**CONTESSA:** Ebben?

**TUTTI:** Ebben?

**CHÉNIER:** (*in atto di preghiera*).
No, signorina!

**MADDALENA:** Ebbene
(*imita Chénier*).
Levò la fronte al cielo!—
Chiamò la Musa!—E la implorata musa
per sua bocca ridisse la parola
che a me voi,
(*si rivolge ad un vecchio ridicolo*).
voi,
(*a un abate*).
e voi,
(*a un marchese grasso*).
e voi, più volte
(*a un giovinotto strano per la sua bruttezza*).
a me dite ogni sera senza Musa.
(*tutti ridono*).

**CHÉNIER:** Colpito qui m'avete
ov'io geloso
celo il più puro palpitar dell'anima.
Or vedrete, fanciulla, qual poema
è la parola "Amore" per voi scherno!
Un dì all'azzurro spazio
guardai profondo,
e ai prati colmi di viole,
pioveva l'oro il sole
e folgorava d'oro
il mondo;
parea la Terra un immane tesoro,

**CHORUS:** That might amuse a school-girl!

**CHÉNIER:** Your request, mademoiselle,
Is a command for me.
Yet, alas! sweet Fancy's coy,
Nor will heed, though commanded,
Or even entreated.
Most capricious is the Muse,
As fanciful as Love!
(*Madeleine and her friends burst out laughing*).

**COUNTESS:** What causes all this mirth?

**CHORUS:** What is it?
Oh, listen, for it is vastly diverting!
He is trapped in a way most disconcerting.

**MADELEINE:** When your entreaty, mother,
He curtly refused,
I thought I'd try—it was in sport—

**CHORUS:** Just for mischief!

**MADELEINE:** I said: Girls, let us wager—

**COUNTESS:** Wager what, pray?

**MADELEINE:** That I would make him speak of love!

**COUNTESS:** Yes—well?

**MADELEINE:** (*mockingly*). He summoned the Muse,
And she, the capricious nymph,
Through his lips has discoursed
Of the theme of which to me—
(*addressing a ridiculous dotard*).
You!
(*to an Abbé*). And you!
(*to a fat Marquis*). Ah, yes, and you, too—
(*to a singularly ugly youth*),
And you, often speak,
Unaided by the Muses!
(*General mirth*)

**CHÉNIER:** Your scorn has touched me here,
Where jealously
All the secrets of the soul inviolate are guarded:
You shall know, now, fair maiden,
What a poem lies in that little word "love,"
By you derided!
I gazed over the blue expanse of heaven unclouded;
Over fields with violets enamelled;
The world around, above me,

e a lei servia di scrigno il firmamento.
Dal cuore de la Terra a la mia fronte
veniva una carezza viva, un bacio.
Gridai, vinto d'amore: T'amo,
t'amo
tu che mi baci, tu divinamente
bella, o patria!
E volli pien d'amore
pregar!
Varcai d'una chiesa la soglia;
là un prete ne le nicchie
de' santi e de la Vergine
accumulava doni e al sordo orecchic
un tremulo vegliardo invano
chiedeva pane e invan stendea la mano!
(*Sensazione*).
Entrai nell'abituro;
un uom vi calunniava bestemmiando
il suolo che l'erario a pena sazia
e contra a Dio scagliava e contro a li uomini
le lacrime de' figli.
In cotanta miseria
e di cose e di genti—qui la patrizia prole
a che pensa e che fa?
Sol l'occhio vostro esprime umanamente
qui un guardo di pietà
ond'io ho guardato a voi sì come a ur angelo.
E dissi: Se bugiardo fu il miraggio
che mi venne dal sole,
eccola la bellezza della vita
nel glauco raggio
soave di pietà che vibra in voi!
Ma, poi,
a le vostre parole,
un novello dolore
m'ha còlto in pieno petto
O giovinetta bella, d'un poeta
non disprezzate il detto:
Udite!—Amate pria
e prima di schernir sappiate Amore!
(*Indignazione generale*).

**MADDALENA:** (*a Chénier*). Perdonatemi!

**CONTESSA:** Creatura strana assai!
Va perdonata!
È capricciosa e un po' romantichetta.
Ma udite! È il gajo suon de la gavotta.
Su, cavalieri!—Ognun scelga la dama!
(*Mentre i servi fanno posto e i cavalieri e le dame si preparano, lontanissimo, si sentono venire avvicinandosi confuse cantilene*).

In glimmering golden glory was shrouded;
The spacious earth seemed as one mighty gem
Enclosed within her casket, the boundless heaven!
Softly from earth, to me as a greeting,
There floated upon the wanton breezes a caress!
Then, in a transport I cried:
Ah! I love you, my country,
Divine in all your beauty, oh land, mine own!
By Love inspired, I sought to pray;
Swift through a church-door then I passed:
A priest collected offerings for the Virgin,
By all the faithful given; yet never heeded
Nor heard its piteous pleading
Of one poor aged beggar,
With hands held out in vain!
(*Sensation*).
And then I entered a workman's hut,
Where one in desperation loudly cursed his country;
He cursed his rich employers;
To God above in fury,
And unto men he hurled them,
His children's bitter tears!
Ah! ye pampered patricians,
How do you right all this wrong?
It was in your eyes alone,
Oh, lovely maiden, that gentle pity seemed to dwell,
And so I turned to you, as to an angel fair, and said
'Love is shining from out those beauteous eyes!"
But when, as in scorn you address me,
It was then that my heart by grief anew was shaken!
Believe me, beauteous maiden—
Do not despise—the word of a poet!
Oh, Listen! you know nothing of love!
Hear me—Love is divine;
Spare it your scorn!
The flame that lights the universe, Is Love!
(*General indignation.*)

**MADELEINE:** (*to Chénier*). I pray you, pardon me!

**COUNTESS:** (*to be Guests*) She's such a flighty girl!
(*to Madeleine*).
There, I forgive you!
She's so capricious!
Inclined to be romantic:
But listen! The merry sound of the gavotte!
Now, cavaliers, pray choose your partners!
(*As the dance is about to begin, a dismal sound of chanting is heard without. Gerard appears at the head of a group of ragged beggars.*)

# Act I

**LE VOCI:** (*si avviciano.—Sono lugubremente dolorose, gemiti che risuonano cupi e minacciosi*).
La notte e il giorno
portiamo intorno
il dolore;—
Siam genti grame
che di fame
or si muore;—
A mammelle avvizzite
chieggon le vite
de'bimbi moribondi!
Affamati, languenti
cadiam morenti
sovra suoli infecondi!
(*All'arco d'ingresso della serra appare Gérard alla testa di una folla di gente stracciata*).

**CHORUS OF PAUPERS:** Each day, each morrow,
Brings woe and sorrow;
For bread we're crying;
Our children are dying.
We're starving! Will no one hear us calling?
Oh, save us from famine appalling!

**GÉRARD:** (*imitando il maggior-domo*). È Sua Grandezza la Miseria!
(*mentre quegli straccioni, lamentosamente stendendo le mani, susurrano:*)
Anime umane,
deh, le nostre preghiere
non ci tornino vane!
Genti cristiane,
sollievo a queste fiere
torture aspre, inumane!

**GERARD:** (*mimicking the pompous Major-domo*). His Serene Highness, Prince Poverty!

**CONTESSA:** (*livida dall'ira*). Chi ha introdotto costoro?

**COUNTESS:** (*angrily*). Who admitted those beggars?

**GÉRARD:** Io, Gérard!

**GERARD:** I did, Gerard!

**CONTESSA:** (*ai suoi valletti, lacchè*). Questa ciurmaglia via!
(*a Gérard*).
E tu pel primo!

**COUNTESS:** Out! drive the rabble out!
And go you first!

**GÉRARD:** Sì, me ne vo—Contessa!
questa livrea—m'è di tortura;
è vile per me il pane
che qui mi sfama!
La voce di chi soffre a sè mi chiama!
Vien, padre mio, con me!
(*al padre che intercede*).
Perchè ti curvi ai piè
di chi non ode voce di pietà?
(*poi, strappandosi la livrea di dosso, grida:*)
Dalle mie carni via questa viltà

**GERARD:** Yes, I'll be gone, my lady!
I'll be rid of this hateful livery
That I loathe and detest!
Your bread, your food, it chokes me,
While round me all my fellow-men are starving!
(*to his father, who intercedes*).
Come, father, come with me!
Why do you bend the knee to them,
Since pity dwells not in their hearts!
(*stripping off his livery*).
Off with this vile livery!
Off accursed badge!
(*The footmen eject the beggars and Gerard is hustled out*).

**CONTESSA:** (*imbizzita*). Via! Via! Via!
(*Il Maestro di Casa, i servi, i lacchè gli staffieri, respingono la folla.—La Contessa si lascia cadere sul sofà ansante dalla bile*).
Ah! quel Gérard! L'ha rovinato il leggere!
Credetemi Fu l'Enciclopedia!
Ed io che tutti i giorni facevo l'elemosina
e a non fare arrossire di sé la povertà
perfin m'ho fatto un abito costume di pietà!
(*al Maestro di Casa che torna*).
Son tutti.andati?

**COUNTESS:** (*as she sinks prostrate upon a couch*).
Oh! that Gerard!
Reading has ruined him!
To me, of all people!
I who daily give to the poor!
Through regard for their feelings,
When I supply their needs,
I wear a modest gown, designed
For charitable deeds!
(*to the Major-domo*).
They have all gone, then?

**MAESTRO DI CASA:** Sì.

**MAJOR-DOMO:** Yes, my lady!

**CONTESSA:** (*agli invitati*) Scusate! L'interrotta,
mie dame, ripigliamo, gentil, nobil gavotta
Invitate le dame!
Ritorni l'allegria!

**COUNTESS:** (*to her guests*). Excuse me, ladies fair!
Our gavotte, by your leave, let us finish.
Now mirth once more shall reign!

*CALA LA TELA.*

*CURTAIN.*

# ■ QUADRO II

(*Parigi in un giorno del Giugno 1794, col Caffè Hottot e la Loggia dei Fogliantisti. A dritta un altare dedicato a Marat con su un busto diquesti. Dietro la, "Cours-la-Reine" e il ponte Perronet sulla Senna. Chénier seduto solo ad una tavola. Mathieu "Populus"indica ad Orazio Coclite il busto di Marat che egli ha tolto dall'altare e ripulisce, a sferzate energiche di fazzoletto, dalla polvere*).

# ■ ACT II

(*The Scene shows us Paris on a day in June, 1794, with the Café Hottot and the Terrasse des Feuillants. To the right an altar dedicated to Marat, on which stands his bust. At the back, the 'Cours la Reine' and the Peronnet Bridge across the Seine. At one of the tables Chénier is seated alone. Mathieu and Horace are arranging the altar, and Mathieu is dusting Marat's bust with a handkerchief. Bersi and the Spy are seen at one of the tables.*)

**MATHIEU:** Per l'ex inferno!
ecco ancor della polvere
sul capo di Marat!
(*strizza l'occhio all'amico e accenna alla Bersi seduta con la Spia.*)
Che ci covasse scherno?
Ah, troppo spesso
da un poco sgualdrineggiano
quelle donnine là!
E male! male! male!
Benedetto, o Rasojo nazionale!
Tu sol, tu solo non risenti il sesso!
(*Entrano degli strilloni. Mathieu compra un giornale, ma si accorge che é vecchio.*)
M'ha appioppato un giornale
di cinque mesi fa!

**MATHIEU:** By all that's infernal!
There's still such a heap of dust on the had of Marat!
(*Newsboys enter and Mathieu buys a paper. Soon he discovers that it is an old one.*)
Why, he's sold me a paper that's fully five months old!

**BERSI:** (*all'Incredibile.*) È ver che Robespierre allevi spie?

**L'INCREDIBILE:** Vuoi dire, cittadina "Osservatori dello spirito pubblico"

**BERSI:** Come tu vuoi.

**L'INCREDIBILE:** Non so, nè lo posso sapere! Hai tu a temere?

**BERSI:** Temer? Perchè? Perchè temer dovrò?
Non sono, come te, una vera figlia autentica della Rivoluzione?
Amo viver così! Vivere in fretta di questa febbre gaja d'un godere rapido, acuto e quasi inconsciente!
Qui il giuoco ed il piacere là la morte!
Qui il suon de le monete e il biribisso!
Laggiù il cannone e il rullo de'tamburi!
Qui inebria il vino laggiù inebria il sangue
Qui riso e amore;
là si pensa e s'odia!
Qui la Meravigliosa e l'Incredibile che brindan col Bordeaux, collo Sciampagna;

**BERSI:** (*to the Spy*). Is it true that Robespierre has chartered spies?

**SPY:** Not 'spies' my worthy citizen; 'Observers of the temper of the public!'

**BERSI:** As you will!

**SPY:** I know not;
Indeed, why do you ask me?
Are you afraid, then?

**BERSI:** Afraid? Not I!
What cause have I to fear?
Am I not, like yourself, a true and loyal child
Of the glorious Revolution?
No life but this for me!
Swift as a whirlwind, borne ever onward
Down the tide of pleasure;
Never a pause to think;
Not a moment of leisure;
Here, gambling, song, and laughter;
And yonder, death!
Here, chink of golden louis and rattle of dice-box;
There, boom of cannon, rolling of the drum!
Here, wine intoxicates;
Down there, they're drunk with

(*Verso l'ex Cours-la-Reine di dove sbocca il "piccolo paniere" carico di condannati condotti alla ghigliottina.*)
le mercatine là e le pescivendole
e la carretta di Sanson che passa!
(*esce.*)

L'INCREDIBILE: No, non m'inganno! Era proprio con lei la bella bionda! Ho scovato la traccia!
(*estrae di tasca un piccolo taccuino e vi scrive su rapidamente:*)
La cittadina Bersi, far sospetto di corruzione non spontanea; guardò Chénier di sottecchi. Osservarla!
Andrea Chénier per qualche ora in attesa con febbril ansia evidente. Osservarlo!
(*esce.*)
(*Roucher entra dal Cours-la-Reine.*)

CHÉNIER: (*vedendolo*). Roucher!

ROUCHER: Chénier! Tutto il giorno ti cerco! La tua salvezza tengo!

CHÉNIER: Un passaporto?

ROUCHER: Qui tutto intorno è periglio per te! La tua preziosa vita salva—parti!

CHÉNIER: Il mio nome mentir! Fuggire! No!

ROUCHER: Te ne prego, Chénier!

CHÉNIER: Credi al destino? Io credo! Credo a una possanze arcana che benigna o maligna i nostri passi or guida or svia pei diversi sentieri de l'esistenza umana!—Una possanza che dice a un uomo:—Tu sarai poeta! A un altro:—A te una spada, sii soldato! Or bene, il mio destin forse qui vuolmi! Se quel che bramo mi si avvera, resto!

ROUCHER: Se non si avvera?

CHÉNIER: Allora partirò! Seguo il destino umano dell'amore. Io non ho amato ancor! Pure sovente—nella vita ho sentita sul mio cammin vicina passar la donna che il destin fa mia; passare tutta bella—ideal, divina come la poesia; passar con lei sul mio cammin l'amor! Si più volte ha parlato la sua voce al mio cuore; udita io l'ho sovente

---

blood!
Here, smiles and friendship; there, undying hate!
While here we quaff our brimming bumper of champagne, Out in the market, there, Folk sell their fish and fruit—Meanwhile the headsman's cart goes past!
(*The death-cart passes, followed by an excited crowd.*)
(*Exit.*)

SPY: (*aside*). I'm not mistaken! It was with her I saw the blonde-haired beauty! Now I've discovered the clue!
(*writing in his book.*)
'Citoyenne Bersi rouses suspicion Of conduct one may call seditious. She gave Chénier such a sly glance Watch her closely! André Chénier has waited here several hours, No doubt for some important message. Watch him closely!'
(*Exit*).
(*Roucher enters from the Cours la Reine.*)

CHÉNIER: (*seeing Roucher*). Roucher!

ROUCHER: Chénier! All day long have I looked for you! Here I have it! your safeguard!

CHÉNIER: Ah! It's a passport!

ROUCHER: On every side there is danger for you; Ah! Save your life; It is precious; flee!

CHÉNIER: What? Escape like a coward? Not I!

ROUCHER: Nay, hear me, Chénier!

CHÉNIER: No! No! Do you believe in Fate, as I do? I have faith in a secret power That guides the steps of mortals, For good, or else for ill, Along the devious pathways of existence. It is this that says to one man: 'Be a poet!' And to another: 'Wield the soldier's sword!' Maybe Fate bids me to stay here! If what I long for comes to pass, I'll stay.

ROUCHER: If not, what then?

CHÉNIER: Why, then, my friend, I'll go! The destiny that guides me is none other than Love. I never yet have loved! Though the bright presence long-desired Of beauteous lady hath my life inspired; Of one alone That fate shall make mine own! Ideal divine; star of my stormy sea; With her, then life were Paradise for me!

---

con la sua voce ardente dirmi: "Credi all'amore; tu sei Chénier, amato!"
(*e preso sottobraccio Roucher la allontana dal caffè Hottot, narrandogli confidenzialmente.*)
Da tempo mi pervengon strane lettere or soavi ed or gravi—or rampogne, or consigli! Scrive una donna misteriosa ognora! In quelle sue parole vibra un'anima! Chi sia, indagato ho invano!

ROUCHER: Ancor?

CHÉNIER: Finora! Ma or guarda!

ROUCHER: (*legge*). Qui un ritrovo?

CHÉNIER: Ah! la vedrò!

ROUCHER: La misteriosa alfin solleva il velo!

CHÉNIER: Non ridere!

ROUCHER: Vediam! Calligrafia invero femminil! Carta elegante! Ma, ohimè! profumo "alla Rivoluzione!!" Questo gentil biglietto, a profumo di rosa, provocatore, non m'inganno, io giuro, esce da un salottino troppo noto all'amore: Chénier, te l'assicuro, il tuo destino ti ha dato il cuor d'una Meravigliosa Riprendi il passaporto e via la lettera.

CHÉNIER: Non credo!

ROUCHER: Tu non credi?

CHÉNIER: No, non credo!

ROUCHER: Le femminil marea parigina in gaje onde irrequiete o qui rovescia! Io le conosco tutte! Passeranno, ed io ti mostrerò la misteriosa!

CHÉNIER: (*colpito*). Una Meravigliosa la bella creatura del mio pensier sognata?! Non donna, ma

ROUCHER: una cosa.

CHÉNIER: Una caricatura?! Una moda?!

ROUCHER: Una faccia imbellettata!

CHÉNIER: La sconosciuta mia?

ROUCHER: La tua divina soave poesia

---

Often in my dreams, Like some strange haunting melody Her voice from out the midnight Calls me in tones enchanting, And murmurs: 'Love is divine!' 'Chénier, at last it's you!' For long while past, I've received strange letters; Sometimes charming, Or alarming, To reprove me or to warn me! It is a woman writes In such strange fashion; Her words upon the page They glow with passion; Vainly I sought to find her.

ROUCHER: Vainly, did you say?

CHÉNIER: Until now, But see here!

ROUCHER: A rendezvous?

CHÉNIER: At last I shall meet her!

ROUCHER: The mysterious woman unveils?

CHÉNIER: Why do you laugh?

ROUCHER: Let me see!
(*looking at letter*).
Yes, it's indeed a thorough woman's hand! Choicest of paper! But oh! the perfume reeks of Revolution! This little dainty letter, With its perfume designed to fetter the senses, Chénier, I swear it, believe me It comes from a salon noted For the cult of the tender passion. The Fate you trust rewards you with the heart Of some fine dame of fashion! Come! Take your passport; fling aside the letter!

CHÉNIER: I doubt you!

ROUCHER: Do you?'

CHÉNIER: Rather!

ROUCHER: The modish dames of Paris By way of diversion, frequent this café; I know them all by sight; and as they pass To you will I point out your most mysterious fair!

CHÉNIER: (*in amazement*). Some fine lady of fashion, She, the beautiful being divine Of whom I dreamed? Not a woman, but—

ROUCHER: A mere thing.

CHÉNIER: Just a caricature or a fashion plate?

ROUCHER: A painted face.

CHÉNIER: That of my unknown Dame?

ROUCHER: The beauteous lady that your life inspired Wears a Bastille Foulard.

| | |
|---|---|
| CHÉNIER: in fisciù a la Bastiglia! / ed il nero alle ciglia?! | CHÉNIER: And has darkened lashes? |
| ROUCHER: e con rimesse chiome! | ROUCHER: And hair all crimpled. |
| CHÉNIER: Oh, cosa senza nome! / Accetto il passaporto! | CHÉNIER: Oh! the nameless thing! / Here! Give me the passport! |
| ROUCHER: É provvido consiglio! / Vedi? al ponte Peronnet / s'agglomera la folla. | ROUCHER: Aye, take my good advice! / See how yonder, by the bridge, / A surging mob assembles. |
| CHÉNIER: La eterna cortigiana! / Vi si schiera / per incurvar la fronte / al nuovo iddio! | CHÉNIER: The eternal courtesan / Bending low, in abject adoration / To their new idol. |
| MATHIEU: Evviva Robespierre! | MATHIEU: Long live Robespierre! |
| CHÉNIER: (accennando a Robespierre). Egli cammina solo. | CHÉNIER: (pointing to Robespierre). He goes alone. |
| ROUCHER: E quanto spazio ad arte / fra il nume e / i sacerdoti! Ecco Tallien! | ROUCHER: And what gulf between / idol and adorers! / Here comes Gallien |
| CHÉNIER: L'enigma! | CHÉNIER: The sphynx. |
| ROUCHER: Ultimo, vedi? | ROUCHER: And Robespierre's brother / Comes last. |
| CHÉNIER: (ironico). Robespierre / il piccolo! | CHÉNIER: (ironical). A little Robespierre. / (Enter Gerard.) |
| LA FOLLA: Ecco laggiù Gérard! / Gérard! Viva Gérard! / (Entra Gérard.) (entra Robespierre). / Evviva Robespiere! / Barère! / Collot d'Herbois! / Quello è Couthon! / Saint-Just! / David. / Tallien! / Fréron! / Barras! / Fouché! / Le Bas / Sieyès! / Thuriot! / Carnot! / e Robespierre! | THE MOB: There goes Gerard! / Long live Gerard! / (Enter Robespierre.) / Long live Robespierre! / Barère! / Collot d'Herbois! / Here is Couthon! / Saint-Just! / David! / Tallien! / Fréron! / Barrar! / Fouché! / Les Bas, / Sieyès! / Thuriot! / Carnot! / Robespierre! |
| L'INCREDIBILE: (a Gérard). La / donna che mi hai chiesto di cercare / è bianca e bionda? | SPY: The lady whom you told me to seek, pray, tell me, / Is she pale and fair? |
| GÉRARD: Azzurro occhio di cielo / sotta una fronte candida: / bionda la chioma con riflessi d'oro / una dolcezza in viso / ed un sorriso / di donna non umano; / nel suo vestir modesto; / pudico velo / sovra il tesoro / d'un puro sen virgineo / ed una bianca cuffia sulla testa. / —Dammi codesta creatura vaga! / ti dissi—Cerca! Indaga! / Dinanzi mi è passata qual baleno / un di, ma poscia / io l'ho perduta! / Io piu non vivo; peno! / Mi salva tu da questa grande angoscia / e tutto avrai! | GERARD: Her eyes are blue as the heavens; / Her beauteous brow whiter than snow / And all her hair more bright than burnished gold; / The sweetest of all faces; / Her smile has graces / Entrancing to behold; / Most neat her dress and simple; / She wears a wimple, / White, yet not whiter than her bosom sweet; / It shrouds her head, and meets at her waist, / Find me this lovely maid that I adore; / I pray you search, explore! / Before my gaze she flashed / Like a flame in the night; / But now that I have lost her, / Life is void of delight! / If you can save me from this torture, / Then all is yours! |
| L'INCREDIBILE: Stasera la vedrai! | SPY: This evening you shall see her! |
| ROUCHER: (a Chénier). Eccole! / Strani tempi! Là vanno i pensatori. / Qui lo stormo chiassoso, di que' / vivi bagliori. / Tu presso a me ti poni! Di qui facile cosa / sarà scoprir chi sia la tua misterïosa! | ROUCHER: Here they come! / Strange times, indeed! / First march the careworn thinkers, / Then the seekers of pleasure! / And now, as they pass by us, / We'll mark your dame mysterious. |
| CHÉNIER: Partiamo! | CHÉNIER: Let us depart. |
| ROUCHER: Guarda! Guarda! | ROUCHER: Now just look there! |
| CHÉNIER: No! non voglio: partiamo! | CHÉNIER: No. Let's go. |
| BERSI: (a Roucher). Non mi saluti? / (Rapidamente gli susurra.) / Qui trattien Chénier. / Son spiata! qui fra poco tornerò! | BERSI: (to Roucher). Won't you salute me? / (In a rapid whisper.) / Beware! Keep Chénier here! / I'm being watched! |
| L'INCREDIBILE: Procace Bersi, / qui sono ancor per te! Meco giù scendi? | SPY: My good friend, Bersi, / I'm at your service, now; / Shall we go in, then? |
| BERSI: (sorridendogli indifferente). Per poco? | BERSI: If you like. |
| L'INCREDIBILE: Non ti chiedo che una Trenitz. | SPY: I should like some light refreshment. |
| BERSI: E perchè no? | |
| L'INCREDIBILE: Scendiam? | |
| BERSI: Scendiam! / (Scendono nei sotterranei del Caffè.) | BERSI: So should I! Let's go! / (They enter the café.) |
| LE MERAVIGLIOSE: (vedendo Barras discendere nei sotterranei del Caffè Hottot.) / Ah, riderem davver. / E là Barras! / La sua rivoluzion nome ha "piacer" / Ci aspetta là / fra il giuoco ed il bicchier. / Siam Riso, siamo Baci, siamo Amore / anche in di di Terror. / Uno oggidi baciato diman muor / Vedove e spose ognor. / Repubblicani, eroi o aristocratici / che importa a noi, / purché sia Amor? / Amante innamorato / cosi lo vuole il cuor / soltanto e ognor! / Siam Riso, siamo Baci, siam l'Amore / Vedove e spose ognor! / (Scendono nei sotterranei del Caffè.) | CHORUS: Ah! We will make merry / With that Barras / Whose revolution is 'pleasure.' / He's down here / Gambling and drinking. / Even in these days of terror / We like to laugh, to kiss and to love. / The man you kiss today will be dead by tomorrow, / And we are in turn widows and brides. / Republicans, heroes or aristocrats, / What do we care / As long as they love us? / A fervent lover, / That's what our hearts crave for. / We like to laugh, to kiss and to love, / And to be in turn widows and brides. / (They enter the café.) |
| CHÉNIER: Un meravigliosa! | CHÉNIER: A lady of fashion! |
| ROUCHER: Ho indovinato? / Son male esche d'abbocco! | ROUCHER: I guessed as much! |
| CHÉNIER: Tuttavia / Che mi vuol dir? | CHÉNIER: What could she tell me? |
| ROUCHER: É sera! Ora propizia! / E all'alba di domani Via! Il cammino! | ROUCHER: It's night-fall! Most propitious hour; / Before the morrow dawns, escape! Begone! |

CHÉNIER: O mio bel sogno, addio!
(*Si vede ritornare la Bersi.*)

BERSI: Andrea Chénier!
Fra poco, a te, una donna minacciata
da gran periglio qui verrà.
Là attendi!

CHÉNIER: Dimmi il suo nome!

BERSI: Il suo nome Speranza!
(*Bersi fugge via*).

ROUCHER: La ignota tua scrittrice!
No è un tranello!

CHÉNIER: Io là verrò!

ROUCHER: É un agguato.

CHÉNIER: M'armerò!

ROUCHER: Ah! veglierò su lui! (*Escono*).
(*E già sera.*)
(*Mathieu riappare. Viene a dar lume alla lanternina dell' altare a Marat.*)

L'INCREDIBILE: (*esce guardingo dal Caffé e va a porsi allo sbocco della via laterale al caffè, nascondendovisi dietro l'angolo.*)
Ed il mio piano è fatto!Ora attendiamo!
(*Una forma di donna si avanza cautamente*).

MADDALENA: Viene l'altare
(*si guarda intorno; è impaurita di quel silenzio*).
Nessuno! Ho paura!

L'INCREDIBILE: Ecco già il maschio!
(*entra Chénier*).

MADDALENA: Ah, è lui!
Andrea Chénier!

CHÉNIER: Son io!
(*Maddalena tenta parlare, la commozione sua è grande e non può profferire parola.*)
(*sorpreso di quel silenzio.*) Deggio seguirti?
(*Maddalena risponde con un gesto: No!*)
Sei mandata?
Dimmi da chi? Di' chi mi brama!

MADDALENA: Io, sono!

CHÉNIER: (*sorpreso ed ingannato all'abbigliamento da officiosa di lei*). Tu? Ebben, che sei?—Di'!

MADDALENA: Ancor ricordi?Ascolta!
(*e Maddalena, per richiamarglisi allamente, gli ricorda le parole che Chénier le ha rivolto la sera del loro incontro al castello di Coigny.*)

CHÉNIER: Ah! lovely dream, farewell!
(*Bersi hurries out of the café and approaches Chénier.*)

BERSI: André Chénier!
Before long a lady
Threatened by grievous peril
Will comes to you; await her here!

CHÉNIER: Tell me her name!

BERSI: Her name is "Speranza."
(*Exit.*)

CHÉNIER: Now we shall meet.

ROUCHER: Your unknown correspondent.
No it's a trap, an ambush!

CHÉNIER: I'll get my sword!

ROUCHER: Ah! I'll protect him, now!
(*Exeunt.*)
(*It is now growing dark. The patrol passes, and Mathieu enters with a lantern, which he places on the altar. The Spy enters, on the watch for Madeleine.*)

SPY: So! All my plans are laid!
Here I'll await them!
(*Hides.*)

MADELEINE: (*enters cautiously*).
Here is the altar!
As yet there's no one. How I tremble! (*Enter Chénier.*)

MADELEINE: It's him!
André Chénier!

CHÉNIER: It is I! Say, shall I follow? Who sent you here? Who needs my help?

MADELEINE: I do.

CHÉNIER: And who are you?

MADELEINE: Do you remember?

CHÉNIER: Yes–I remember!

MADELEINE: (*repeating his words addressed to her once at Coigny*). 'You know nothing of Love!
'Hear me–Love is divine;
'Spare it your scorn!'

CHÉNIER: Sì: mi ricordo! Udita io ti ho di già!
Ah nuova la tua voce non mi parla.
Ch'io ti vegga!

MADDALENA: Guardatemi!

CHÉNIER: Ah, Maddalena di Coigny!

L'INCREDIBILE: Ah è lei! La bionda! Or tosto da Gérard!
(*e cautamente si allontana*).

CHÉNIER: Voi? Voi!

MADDALENA: (*atterrsas*). Guardate là!

CHÉNIER: Dove?

MADDALENA: Là! Un'ombra!

CHÉNIER: (*va all'angolo dove prima era l'incredibile, ma non vede alcuno*). Nessun! Pur questo loco è periglioso
E qui sola

MADDALENA: Fu Bersi che l'ha scelto.
Or essa è là, giù, al giuoco e se un periglio
ne minacciasse Sono un'officiosa
che le viene a recar la sua mantiglia!

CHÉNIER: La mia scrittrice? Voi la mia celata
amica ognor fuggente?!

MADDALENA: Eravate possente,
io invece minacciata;—
pur nella mia tristezza
pensai sovente d'impetrar da voi
pace e salvezza,
ma non l'osai!
E ognora il mio destino
sul mio cammino
vi sospingea!
Ognora io vi seguivo, e strano assai,
ognor pensavo a voi
come a un fratello!—
E allora vi scriveva
quanto il cuore o il cervello
dettavami alla mente.
Sì, il cuore mi diceva che difeso
avreste quella che v'ha un giorno offeso.
Al mondo Bersi sola mi vuol bene
(è lei che m'ha nascosta). Ma da une mese
v'ha chi mi spia e m'insegue. E Bersi pure!
Mutammo nascondiglio, e più veemente
era la caccia!Ove fuggir?Fu allora
che pure voi non più potente seppi,
e son venuta.—Udite! Sono sola!
Son sola e minacciata! Io più non reggo!
Son sola al mondo! Sola ed ho paura
lo spero in voi! Proteggermi volete?

CHÉNIER: Where have I heard that strange, sweet voice?
Let me see you!

MADELEINE: Behold my face!

CHÉNIER: Ah! Madeleine de Coigny! You!

SPY: (*aside*). It is she! the blonde!
Now I'll inform Gerard!
(*Exit.*)

CHÉNIER: You? You!

MADELEINE: (*terror-struck*). See yonder there! A phantom!

CHÉNIER: There's no one!
And yet this place is one of peril!

MADELEINE: It was Bersi chose it;
But if danger now should threaten
I'll play the serving-maid
Who's brought a mantle for her mistress.

CHÉNIER: You, my fair scribe?
Was it you the friend so long unknown,
And lost so long?

MADELEINE: In the day of your power
By peril grave was I threatened;
Yet often in my sadness
I fondly hoped to gain, through you,
Safety and gladness.
I dared not, then; but not it is Fate's decree
That thrown together we should be.
Hope had I no other;
My trust I gave to you–
Gave, as to a brother.
Then, letters I wrote you often,
By heart or brain dictated,
In days and hours ill-fated.
I knew your loyal heart
Would have nobly requited
Her who long since your genius slighted.
In all the world no friend have I but Bersi;
(It was she who helped to hide me!)
But now for a month by spies am I hunted;
How to escape?
Then came the news that you had fallen from power;
To you I come!
Ah! Hear me! I'm alone, beset by danger;
All helpers fail me,
Dark fears assail me,
Oh! say, will you protect me?
In you I trust!

## ■ QUADRO III

*(L'aula del Tribunale rivoluzionario, Accanto a un' urna colossale su'l banco della presidenza Mathieu arringa la folla e sollecita contribuzioni).*

**MATHIEU:** Dumouriez traditore (muoja presto!)
è passato ai nemici (il furfantaccio!);—
Coburgo, Brunswick (Pitt crepi di peste!)
e il vecchio lupanare dell'Europa tutta, contro ci stanno! Oro e soldati!
Onde quest'urna ed io che parlo a voi
rappresentiam l'imagin della patria!
*(Un gran silenzio accoglie il discorso di Mathieu, però nessuno va ad ofrire).*
Nessun si muove? Che la ghigliottina
ripassi a ognun la testa e la coscienza!
*(Alcuni, pochi, vanno e gittano nella grande urna oggetti e denari. Mathieu riprende).*
E la patria in periglio! A Nostra Donna
il vessil nero sventola! Io pure
or, come già Barère, io levo il grido di Louverture: Liberta' e patate!
*(vedendo sopraggiungere Gérard)*
Ma, to' laggiù à Gérard! Convalescente
appena accorre ove il dover lo chiama.
Ei vi trarrà di tasca gli ex luigi
con paroline ch'io non so
M'infischio
io de'bei motti Ed anche me ne vanto!

**TUTTI:** Cittadino Gérard, salute! Evviva!

**MATHIEU:** La tua ferita?

**GÉRARD:** Grazie, cittadini!
La forte fibra mia m'ha conservato alla mia patria ancora!

**MATHIEU:** *(indicandogli l'urna)*. Ecco il tuo posto!
*(poscia sempre colla sua voce monotona accennando al drappo si rivolge al pubblico ripetendo).*
È la patria in pe
*(ma, accortosi che la pipa gli si è spenta, conclude indicando Gérard).*
Cedo la parola.

**GÉRARD:** *(con vero accento di dolore)*. Lacrime e sangue dà la Francia! Udite!
Laudun ha inalberato
yessillo bianco!
È in fiamme la Vandea!
E la Bretagna ognora ne minaccia!
E Austriaci, e Prussiani, e Inglesi, e tutti
nel petto della Francia

## ■ ACT III

*(The Court of the Revolutionary Tribunal. On the President's table a colossal urn, near which stands Mathieu, haranguing the crowd, and inviting contributions.)*

**MATHIEU:** Dumouriez the traitor, the villain,
Has gone over to the enemy! (lying scoundrel!)
Coburg and Brunswick,
(Pitt, the devil take him!)
That ancient lupanar called Europe,
All are in arms against us!
Money and soldiers! That's what we need.
This urn and I we're pleading now today
For funds to help our country!
*(Profound silence; yet no one contributes.)*
Will none come forward?
Then may the guillotine make short work of you all!
*(Some advance and throw contributions into the urn.)*
Our country's in danger!
Barére, he's told you so,
And to my cry now listen all: penny?'
*(As Gerard approaches.)*
But here's our worthy Gerard!
Maybe he'll draw the money from your pockets
With words that I could never find.
A plague on pretty speeches!
They're not my style at all!

**CHORUS:** To our worthy Gerard welcome and greeting!

**MATHIEU:** Your wound is better?

**GERARD:** Thank you, fellow-citizens: my constitution's sound;
This has saved me yet to serve my country.

**MATHIEU:** *(to Gerard)*. Your place is there.
*(Drawling out once more:)* And the country's in—
*(Finding that his pipe is out and stopping short.)*
*(to Gerard.)*
Speak to them yourself!

**GERARD:** Citizens!
France now sheds her tears of blood!
Loudun the white flag has hoisted;
La Vendée is in flames; Brittany threatens us;
While Austria, Prussia, England–all Europe
With vast and mighty armies
Now strives to crush our Father-

gli artigli armati affondano!
Occorre e l'oro, il sangue!
L'inutil oro e gemma ai vostri vezzi, donne francesi, date!
Donate i vostri figli alla gran madre, o voi, madri francesi!

**LE DONNE:** *(commosse, gittano dentro tutto quanto hanno in dosso di denaro o d'ornamento)*.
Prendi! È un ricordo!
A te! un anello!
È un braccialetto!
Otto dì di lavoro!
Una fibbia d'argento!
Quanto posseggo!
Son due bottoni d'oro!
*(S'avanza una vecchia cieca con un giovinetto guindicenne).*

**LA VECCHIA:** Fatemi largo, fatemi!
Son la vecchia Madelon; mio figlio è morto;
avea nome Roger; morì alla presa della Bastiglia; il primo figlio suo ebbe a Valmy galloni e sepoltura.
Ancora pochi giorni, e io pur morrò.
È il figlio di Roger! L'ultimo figlio, l'ultima goccia del mio vecchio sangue
Prendetelo!
Non dite che è un fanciullo!
È forte! Può combattere e morire!

**GÉRARD:** Noi l'accettiamo! Dinne il nome suo?

**LA VECCHIA:** Roger Alberto.

**GÉRARD:** A sera partirà!
*(allora la vecchia abbraccia forte il fanciullo che la bacia).*

**LA VECCHIA:** Prendetemelo via!
Chi mi dà il braccio?
*(Brancola intorno per un appoggio e vien condotta fuori).*

**CORO:** *(ballando al suona della Carmagnola)*
Amici, orsù! Beviam! Danziam ognor
Colmo bicchier—Allieta il cor!
Cantare e ber!
Viva la libertà!
Danziam la Carmagnola
al tuon, al suon—del cannon!
*(L'Incredibile si avvicina a Gérard).*

**L'INCREDIBILE:** L'uccello è nella rete!

**GÉRARD:** Lei?!

**L'INCREDIBILE:** No; il maschio. È al Lussemburgo!

**GÉRARD:** Quando?

**L'INCREDIBILE:** Stamattina.

**GÉRARD:** E come?

**L'INCREDIBILE:** Il caso!

land!
She needs your gold, your blood!
The useless gold on all your trinkets,
Women of France, now give!
And give your stalwart sons to the Great Mother,
Mothers of France!
*(The women fling coin and trinkets into the urn.)*

**THE WOMEN:** Take them! They're my earrings!
And this! Here's my bracelet!
My brooch! And here's my last week's wages!
Here's an old silver buckle!
And here are two gold buttons!
Here's all I possess!
Here's my little cross!
*(And old blind woman advances with a lad of fifteen.)*

**OLD WOMAN:** Make way, there!
I am old Madelon!
My son is dead; his name was Roger;
He was killed at the siege of the Bastille.
His eldest boy, who fought at Valmy,
Promotion won, yet perished.
It is but a little while and I shall die!
Here I've brought you Roger's son,
The youngest, the last;
He's all I live for; he is all I love!
Take him! Don't say he's but a child!
He's strong, though, and for France can fight and die!

**GERARD:** Yes we'll accept him. What is his name?

**OLD WOMAN:** Albert Roger!

**GERARD:** He'll be sent away to-night.

**OLD WOMAN:** *(as she tearfully bids the lad good-bye.)* Darling, good-bye!
Take my darling boy!
Who will give me an arm?
*(Groping for support, she is led out.)*

**CHORUS:** *(as they dance to the tune of the Carmagnole)*. Come dance and drink, good friends, to-day;
With song and wine drive care away!
The flagon fill that cheers the heart,
And bids all sorrow swift depart.
Drink, then, to Freedom's cause!
Dow with the despot's laws!
We'll dance the Carmagnole,
Though loud the cannon roar!

**SPY:** *(approaching Gerard)*. The bird is in the snare!

**GERARD:** She?

**SPY:** No, the man!
He's at the Luxembourg.

**GERARD:** Since when?

**SPY:** Since this morning.

**GERARD:** Why, how's that?

**SPY:** A mere chance!

GÉRARD: Dove?

GERARD: Where was he?

L'INCREDIBILE: Là a Passy, presso a un amico.

SPY: At Passy, at his friend's.

GÉRARD: E lei?

GERARD: And she?

L'INCREDIBILE: Nessuna traccia! Ma tal richiamo è il maschio per la femmina che volontariamente (penso e credo!) essa a noi ne verrà.

SPY: As yet, no trace of her; But for the 'she' the 'he' has such attraction, That, if I'm not mistaken, She'll come back of her own accord.

GÉRARD: No; non verrà! (*Lontano un gridìo acuto e confuso da ogni parte.*)

GERARD: Nay, she'll not come! (*Cries heard without.*)

L'INCREDIBILE: Ascolta!

GÉRARD: Grida son Monelli aizzati.

L'INCREDIBILE: No; i soliti strilloni! (*Passa—e lo si vede dall'arco di ingresso della sezione—venendo dalla via di destra—une strillone che urla a tutta gola:*) L'arresto importantissimo d'Andrea Chénier, nemico della patria!

SPY: Do you hear the street-lads selling papers? (*Boys passes shouting out, 'Arrest of André Chénier!'*) That cry is bound to reach her ears!

L'INCREDIBILE: Queste grida arriveranno a lei!

GÉRARD: Va, tentatore! E poscia? Ebben?

GERARD: What of that?

L'INCREDIBILE: Donnina innamorata che d'aspettar s'annoja, se è già passata l'ora e il perchè non sa di quel ritardo del suo amico al nido, sfido! (e ch'io muoja!) se la bella presaga all'ansia vinta non ti discende ratta per la via così, com'è, discinta! Esce correndo E indaga! E vola! E scruta! E spia! To'! passa uno strillone? E vocia un nome? Oh, come tutta impàllida! Ma non vacilla o china! Possanza dell'amor! In quel dolor cessa la donna ed eccola eroina! Tutto oserà! Laonde, per mia scienza tu la vedrai! Pazienza! Sì, a te verrà! Sì; questo è il mio pensiero un po' incredibil, ma altrettanto vero!

SPY: When a love-sick dame, complaining, Awaits her laggard lover, And trysting-time is over, What resource has she remaining? Alarmed and most dejected To find herself neglected, If love won't bind him, She'll go herself and try to find him! Swift through the streets she's flying, And watching, waiting, prying— Ha! There's a newsboy bawling; What's that he's calling? What name? Oh, Heaven, his name! Endowed with stoic courage, By Love's tremendous power, In grief's dark hour, Weak woman gains a fortitude heroic! For Love she would risk all! Mark what I say; it's true. Patience! She'll come to you Before the fall of night. It sounds unlikely; but I'm right!

MADDELENA: (*entrando*). Carlo Gérard?

MADELEINE: (*entering.*) Can I see Charles Gerard?

MATHIEU: Sì; c'è!—Entra!—Sta là!

MATHIEU: Here, this way, please!

MADDELENA: (*con voce tremante*). Se ancor vi sovvenite di me, non so! Son Maddalena di Coigny. Ah, non m'allontanate! Deh, mi udite!

MADELEINE: Maybe you remember me no longer? Who knows! I'm Madeleine de Coigny! Ah! Do not drive me away! Since, if you will not hear me, I am lost!

GÉRARD: Io t'aspettava! Io ti voleva qui! Io son che come veltri ho a te lanciato ordre di spie! Entro a tutte le vie la mia pupilla è penetrata e ad ogni istante! Io, per averti qui, preso ho il tuo amante!

GERARD: I was waiting for you; It's I that brought you here; It's I that have beset your path With swarms of crafty spies! Watching in street and by-way, Mine eye at every moment Was always fixed upon you; Thus, to secure you, I have seized your lover!

MADDELENA: A voi!—Qui sto! Signore, vendicatevi!

MADELEINE: Well, here I am! Take your revenge!

GÉRARD: Non odio!

GERARD: No, not revenge!

MADDELENA: Vendicatevi! Son l'ultima del nome mio!

MADELEINE: Take your revenge. I am the last survivor of my house.

GÉRARD: Non odio!

GERARD: No, not revenge!

MADDELENA: Perchè, dunque, m'avete qui voluta?

MADELEINE: Then wherefore would you have me here?

GÉRARD: Perchè ciò è scritto nella vita mia! Perchè ciò è scritto nella vita tua! Perchè ciò volle il mio voler possente! Era fatale, e, vedi, s'è avverato! Io l'ho voluto allora che tu piccina giù pel gran prato con me correvi lieta in quell'aroma d'erbi infiorate e di selvaggie rose! e poi lo volli il dì che mi fu detto: "Ecco la tua livrea!"—e, come fu lasera, entre tu studïavi il minuetto, Io, gallonato e muto, aprivo o rinchiudevo una portiera Ah, poscia un'altra sera io l'ho voluto! Fu quella sera allor che dentrol all'anima mi venne il gran disio di farti mia. Per te sognavo il genio! Ma, ironia! sovra altra fronte già splendea: Chénier! Ed il destin che trama le commedie de le diverse vite, quasi a prologo quella sera ci unìa! Vidi il tuo amore! Innamorato e odiando son fuggito! e poscia no non m'ha Chénier ferito ma il grido tuo d'orrore, il tuo: Gérard! Pure anche allora, e sempre, t'ho voluta! La poesia in te così gentile, di me fa invece un pazzo grande e vile! Ebben? Che importa? Sia! E, fosse un'ora sola, io voglio quell' ebrezza de' tuoi occhî profondi! Io pur, io pur, io pur voglio affondare le mani mie nel mare de' tuoi capelli biondi! Or dimmi che farai contro il mio amore?

GERARD: Why would I have you here? Because I desire you! Because it is written in the book of Fate; Because my will would have it so, my will supreme It is Fate's decree; and lo! It has come to pass! I longed for you while you were yet a little maid, With me you wandered Down the daisied meadows Through fragrant lane in blossom, Adorned with wilding roses! For you I longed that day they told me: 'Here! don thy livery' And when at evening, As there you practiced the measure of a minuet, I, rigid, mute, in livery, Threw back or closed the curtains at the doorway. And now, once more do I desire you! It is the charm, the poetry of your presence That enrages me, goads me on to madness! What matter? Be it so! Though were but one short hour, I'll feast me on the beauty of those enthralling eyes! I, too, I hunger for your soft caresses— Would plunge my hand within the ocean Of those bright golden tresses! Say, who shall save you now from my great love?

MADDELENA: Là giù! nella via corro! Il nome mio vi grido! Ed è la morte che mi salva! (*Gérard va a frapporsi tra Maddalena e le due uscite*)

MADELEINE: I'll rush through all the streets, Denounce myself to the mob!— From death, say, who shall save me, then?

GÉRARD: No, tu non lo farai!—No! tuo malgrado
tu mia sarai!

GERARD: (*barring her passage.*)
That you shall never do!
Ah! though you hate me, you are mine!

MADDELENA: (*gittando un grido di terrore fugge; ma, presa da improvvisa idea, movendo risoluta verso Gérard gli dice:*) Se de la vita sua
tu fai prezzo il mio corpo ebbene, prendimi!

MADELEINE: (*Shrieks and endeavors to escape; then, suddenly, with great calmness, she approaches him.*) If you will save his life
At the price of my honor—
I am yours! Take me!

GÉRARD: (*da sé*). Come sa amare!

GERARD: (*aside*) Ah! how she loves him!

MADDELENA: La mamma morta
m'hanno a la porta
là de la stanza mia;—
moriva e mi salvava!
poscia—a notte alta—io con la
Bersi errava,—
quando, ad un tratto, un livido bagliore
guizza e rischiara innanzi a' passi miei
la cupa via!—
Guardo! Bruciava il loco di mia culla!
Così fui sola! E intorno il nulla!
Fame e miseria!
Il bisogno e il periglio!
Caddi malata!
E Bersi, buona e pura
(ed a narrarlo mancan le parole)
ha del suo corpo fatto
un mercato, un contratto
per me!—Porto sventura
a chi bene mi vuole!
Fu in quel dolore
che a me venne l'amore!
Voce gentile piena d'armonia
che mi susurra: "Spera!"
e dice: "Vivi ancora! Io son la vita!
Ne' miei occhî è il tuo cielo!
Tu non sei sola! Le lagrime tue io
le raccolgo! Io sto sul tuo cammino
e ti sorreggo il fianco
affaticato e stanco!
Sorridi e spera ancora! Son l'amore!
Intorno è sangue e fango? Io son divino!
Io sono il paradiso! Io son l'oblio!
Io sono il dio
che sovra il mondo scende da
l'empireo,
muta gli umani in angioli,
fa della terra il ciel!
Io son l'amore!
L'angiol tremante allor le labbra smorte
della mia bocca bacia E or vi bacia
la morte!
Corpo di moribonda è il corpo mio!
Prendilo dunque! Io son già morta cosa!

MADELEINE: Before death had taken
My darling mother
Leaving me forsaken,
In dying, she strove to save me!
In darkest midnight I fled with Bersi;
Then suddenly a lurid glare
Lit up the path that lay before.
The cruel flames devoured my home.
And I was homeless, with nothing before me
But hunger, misery, and peril dire!
Then I fell sick, and Bersi nursed me,
Spent all her savings on me, noble soul!
To such as love me, see, I bring misfortune!
It was in such sorrow
That first I heard the voice of Love!
In accents sweet, it murmured:
'The Star of Love shall guide you,
'Even though grief betides me,
'Love, the immortal fire from heaven.
'Boon to mourners given,
'Am I Love's self; oh hear me calling:
'I'll guard you, guide you, save you from falling!
'Hope on, hope ever!
'Love fails you never!
'Though dark the road, and foes assail you,
'I will not fail you;
'I am Love whose magic power,
'My name is Love!
'Like golden sunlight falling from the skies,
'All this world can change to Paradise!
'Love's very self am I!'
And then the angel kissed me:
In me that hour the light of life did die!
Take me, then, take me; but a corpse am I!
(*Papers are handed to Gerard.*)

GÉRARD: (*guardando dei fogli che gli vengono consegnati*). Perduto!
Ah, la mia vita per salvarlo!

GERARD: (*reading*). He's lost. I'd give my life to save him!

MADDELENA: Voi lo potete!
Appena stamattina
egli arrestato fu.

MADELEINE: Ah! you can save him!
This morning only was he arrested!

GÉRARD: Ma per Chénier
un uomo che l'odiava ha preparato
per oggi il suo giudiziola sua morte!
(*A un tratto dalla strada viene un mormorio, un bisbiglio di folla.*)
La folla già! La maledetta folla
curiosa ed avida di sangue e lacrime
(*Rumore dei fucili e delle baionette*)
Sono i gendarmi!
E là sta già Chénier!

GERARD: But one who hates him
Has hurried on his case for trial;
And he must die!
(*Sounds of the noisy crowd heard without.*)
The cruel mob comes back,
Athirst for blood and tears and carnage!
(*Clatter of soldiers' arms.*)
Do you hear their sabres clanking?
They're the gendarmes; they've got him, in there!

MADDELENA: (*disperatamente*)
Salvatelo! Salvatelo! Salvatelo!

MADELEINE: (*despairingly*). Ah! save him!

GÉRARD: Ah, la Rivoluzione i figli suoi
divora! Non perdona! Fin di sangue per tutti
(*scrivendo un biglietto al Vice Presidente Dumas.*)
Io l'ho perduto? Lo difenderò!
Il tuo perdono è la mia forza! Io spero!
(*il pubblico, si rovescia tumultuante, rumoroso, eccitato, nell' aula.*)

GERARD: The Revolution does
devour the sons that serve her!
(*Writing a note for presentation to the President of the Court.*)
Your sweet forgiveness shall make me bold!
Courage! It is not too late;
I'll save him, if I can!
(*The mob now noisily enters the Court.*)

CORO DI VECCHIE: Mamma Cadet!
Presso alla sbarra, qui!
Di qui si vede e si ode
a perfezione.
Qui si gode
la vista d'ogni cosa.
Voi state bene?
Sì.
E voi?
—Così così
Dal mercato venite?
Vengo dalla barriera!
Notizie ce ne avete?
No! E voi nulla sapete?
Hanno cresciuto il pane!
Eh lo so è un tiro
Dite!
È un tiro di quel cane
d'inglese detto Pitt!

CHORUS: Well, how are you?
I'm just so-so!
Have you come back from market?
No, from the barrier.
You've heard the news? No!
Not heard the news?
They've raised the price of bread!
Yes, yes! I know!
They say it is all that scoundrel,
That English villain, Pitt!

UN'ALTRA: Venite?

ONE OF THEM: Are you coming?

L'AMICA: Sì!

A FRIEND: Here I am!

MATHIEU: Un po' di discrezione, cittidina!

MATHIEU: Now, then, what a noise you're making!

CORO DI VECCHIE: Più in là!
Venite qua, cittadina!
Dite, oggidì
grande infornata, pare!
Sì.
Molti ex!
(*Entrano giudici e giurati*).

CHORUS OF OLD WOMEN: Mother Cadet! sit by the barrier, here!
Here's the best place for seeing and hearing!
Come over here, good Mother Babet!
Here one sees things to perfections.
There'll be lots of prisoners!
There's Legray! And a poet! Come this way!
Move up, do! No, I shall not!
(*Enter the Judges and Jury.*)

MATHIEU: E c'e un poeta!
l'asso ai giurati, o popolo!

MATHIEU: Make way for the jury!

GÉRARD: (*A Maddalena*). Eccoli, i giudici.

GERARD: (*to Madeleine.*) Those are the judges.

LE MERCATINE: (*si levano ritte sulle panche esaminando i giudici*). Chi presiede é Dumas!

CHORUS: Here they come, the judges!
That's the President Dumas!
There's Vilate, the painter!

ALTRI: (*nominando i giudici.*) Vilate

MERCATINE: pittore! L'altro è lo stampatore tribuno Nicolas!

UNA VOCE: Ecco laggiù Fouquier!

TUTTI: L'accusatore pubblico!

MADDELENA: (*a Gérard*). E gli accusati?

GÉRARD: (*indicando la porta*). Di làpresso ai giurati!

MADDELENA: (*vedendo schiudersi la porta, soffocando un grido*). Ecco

GÉRARD: Tacete!

MADDELENA: Mi manca l'anima! (*Entrano i prigionieri*) Egli non guarda! Non mi crede qui! Ma pensa a me! Io sono in quel pensiero!

MATHIEU: Silenzio!

DUMAS: (*leggendo i nomi*). Gravier de Vergennes.

FOUQUIER TINVILLE: (*legendo una nota*). Un ex referendario! (*fa un rapido gesto e ripone la nota*)

PUBBLICO: È un traditore! (*succede un silenzio profondo*)

DUMAS: (*legge un altro nome*) Laval Montmorency

FOUQUIER-TINVILLE: (*c. s.*). Convento di Montmartre!

CALZETTAJE, MERCATINE, PESCIVENDOLE: (*urlano*). Aristocratica!

IL PUBBLICO: (*le grida ironico*) A che parlar? Sei vecchia! Taci.

DUMAS: Ti tolgo la parola! Abbiamo fretta! (*La monaca lascia. Cadere uno sguardo di sprezzo—poi siede dignitosa.—Il pubblico la applaude deridendola*)

DUMAS: (*c. s.*) Legray! (*Si leva una donna giovane che vuol parlare ma è zittita dal pubblico e si lascia cadere sulla panca piangendo.*)

DUMAS: Andrea Chénier!

GÉRARD: (*a Maddalena*). Coraggio!

MADDELENA: (*guardando Chénier*). O amore! o amore!

---

The other one's a printer, Tribune Nicolas! See! there he goes! That's Fouquier, The great Attorney-General!

MADELEINE: (*to Gerard*). Where are the accused?

GERARD: (*pointing to door*). In there, next to the jury!

MADELEINE: (*as the door opens*). Heavens! My courage fails me! (*The prisoners enter; Chénier walks last.*) He does not heed us! Perchance he thinks of me!

MATHIEU: Silence!

DUMAS: (*reading out the names.*) Gravier de Vergennes—

FOUQUIER-TINVILLE: (*consulting his notes.*) An ex-Chancery officer! (*Motions the accused to be seated.*)

CHORUS: Then he's a traitor!

DUMAS: (*reading*). Laval Montmorency—

FOUQUIER-TINVILLE: From the convent of Mont-Martre!

CHORUS: A cursed aristocrat! Best hold your tongue you hag! Silence! Die! Ha! ha! ha!

FOUQUIER-TINVILLE: I can't let you speak; we are in a hurry.

DUMAS: (*reading*). Legray—(*A woman rises, and would speak, but is silenced by the mob. She sinks back, sobbing piteously.*)

DUMAS: (*reading*). André Chénier—

GERARD: (*to Madeleine.*) Courage!

MADELEINE: (*gazing at Chénier*). Beloved one!

---

PUBBLICO: Ecco, è il poeta! Fouquier Tinville attentamente legge! Lunga è l'accusa dunque! È un accusato pericoloso? Sì!

MATHIEU: Scrittore e basta!

FOUQUIER TINVILLE: Andrea Chénier, poeta giornalista. Costui violento scrisse contro agli uomini de la Rivoluzione. Fu soldato con Dumouriez e

PUBBLICO: Un traditor!

CHÉNIER: (*a Fouquier Tinville*). Tu menti!

GÉRARD: (*fra sè, terribile, con disperazione a Maddalena*). Ah, Maddalena, io sono che ciò feci!

DUMAS: (*a Chénier*). Siediti e taci!

GÉRARD: (*fortissimo*). Parli!

ALCUNI: Parli!

TUTTI: (*interessandosi*) Parli!

DUMAS: (*violento*). No, nego la parola!

TUTTI: Parli! parli!

CHÉNIER: Sì, fui soldato
e glorios affrontata
ho la morte che vil qui mi vien data.
Fui letterato,
ho fatto di mia penna arma feroce
contro gli ipocriti!
Colla mia voce
ho cantato la patria!
Pura la vita mia
passa nella mia mente
come una bianca vela;
essa inciela
le antenne, ali allargate
ad un eterno volo,
al sole che le indora,
e affonda
la spumante prora
ne l'azzurro dell'onda
Va la mia nave spinta dalla sorte
a la scogliera bianca de la morte?
Son giunto? E sia!
Ma ancor io salgo a poppa e una bandiear
trionfal disciolgo ai venti!
De' mille e mille miei combattimenti
è la bandiera e su vi è scritto: "Patria!"
(*verso Fouquier Tinville*)
A lei non sale
il tuo fango, o Fouquier!
Essa ognora s'insola
immacolata.
Essa è immortale!
Non sono un traditore.
Uccidi? E sia! Ma lasciami l'onore.

FOUQUIER TINVILLE: (*subito*) Udiamo i testimoni!

GÉRARD: (*con voce possente*) Il passo datemi! Carlo Gérard.

---

CHORUS: There's the poet! Fouquier-Tinville reads the charge with interest; No doubt that he's a dangerous fellow.

MATHIEU: A writer—that's all!

FOUQUIER-TINVILLE: He has written against the Revolution; Was a soldier with Dumouriez—

CHORUS: He's a traitor!

CHÉNIER: (*to Fouquier*). You lie!

GERARD: (*to Madeleine.*) It was I who thus denounced him!

DUMAS: (*to Chénier.*) Silence!

GERARD: Let him speak!

CHORUS: Speak, then! Prove you're not guilty!

DUMAS: I will not allow it!

CHORUS: Let him speak!

CHÉNIER: Yes, as a soldier
Once I faced a glorious death,
Not such a vile one as you offer!
I was a writer; and I made my pen a scourge
Wherewith to lash all lying hypocrites!
And, as a poet, ever sang my country's praise.
Life was for me a ship
Set in a boundless ocean
With snowy sail outspread
To catch the morning glory;
It rode upon the crested waves,
Forth to remote horizons.
Now is my bark the sport of Fate,
And driven upon the rocks,
The ghostly rocks of Death,
Will it founder? Maybe!
But lo! from the mast
Floats a bright banner triumphant in the breeze;
Thereon is written My Country!'
(*to Fouquier-Tinville.*)
Your filth shall never soil that banner!
In truth am I no traitor!
Kill me, it is well! But leave my honor bright!

FOUQUIER-TINVILLE: Now we'll hear the witnesses!

GERARD: (*forcing a passage through the crowd.*) Let me pass! I'm Gerard!

ANDRÉ CHÉNIER  295

# Act III

DUMAS: Sta bene; puoi parlare.

GÉRARD: L'atto d'accusa è orribile menzogna.

FOUQUIER TINVILLE: (sorpreso). Se tu l'hai scritto?!

GÉRARD: E ho denunciato il falso Or lo confesso. (un gran movimento)

FOUQUIER TINVILLE: Io non ti credo!

GÉRARD: Giuro!

DUMAS: Dinne il perchè.

GÉRARD: L'odiavo!

DUMAS: Non ti credo!

FOUQUIER TINVILLE: (levandosi ritto e picchiando febbrilmente sul foglio scritto da Gérard). Mie faccio queste accuse e le rinnovo!

DUMAS: Ti do il consiglio de tacerti!

GÉRARD: No! Il tuo consiglio è una viltà!

FOUQUIER TINVILLE: Tu offendi la patria e la guistizia!

IL PUBBLICO: Basta! Taci! Imponigil silenzio tu, o Dumas!

MERCATINE: In istato d'accusa dichiaratelo!

SANCULOTTI: Sì; fuori della legge!

TUTTI: Alla lanterna Esso è un sospetto! Fu comprato! Taci!

GÉRARD: La patria! La guistizia osi tu dire! La tua Giustizia ha nome Tirannia! L'amore della patria? Qui?! No, è un' orgia d'odî e vendette! Il sangue della patria qui còla! E siam noi stessi che feriamo il petto della Francia! Basti il sangue! Andrea Chénier della Rivoluzione è figlio!—E il figlio più glorioso suo!

MERCATINE e CALZETTAJE: Con gli accusati tosto giudicatelo! Alla lanterna! Morte! Alla lanterna! (lontano rullare i tamburi)

---

FOUQUIER-TINVILLE: Fine! Speak!

GERARD: The indictment is a monstrous lie!

FOUQUIER-TINVILLE: (astonished). It was you who wrote it!

GERARD: But the charge is a false one, I confess it! (Sensation).

FOUQUIER-TINVILLE: I don't believe it.

GERARD: I swear it is true.

FOUQUIER-TINVILLE: Why did you do that, then?

GERARD: I hated him.

DUMAS: I don't believe it.

FOUQUIER-TINVILLE: (Pounding the papers containing the indictment.) I, too, have made these charges, Now I repeat them!

DUMAS: I advise you to keep silent.

GERARD: Then such an act is vile!

FOUQUIER-TINVILLE: It is an insult to country, to justice! Enough!

THE AUDIENCE: Let Dumas silence him!

FISHWIVES: Indict him!

SANCULOTS: Outlaw him!

ALL: Ha! most suspicious! They've bribed him! Silence!

GERARD: Here, all your justice is but cruel tyranny! An vile orgy of hate and vengeance! Can such as you be counted patriots? Bloodthirsty villains, who stab the heart of France! Chénier's a son of the glorious Revolution; Crown him with laurel, never let him die! (A sound of drums heard without.) Do you hear it, citizens? There speaks the real Fatherland, Whose gallant sons all perish for her now! Not here, where they are murdering her poets! (Rushes to Chénier and embraces him.)

---

GÉRARD: Laggiù, è la patria! Odila, o popolo! È la sua voce! Eccola! E là la patria; ove si muore colla spada in pugno! Non qui dove le uccidi i suoi poeti! (Gérard corre a Chénier e lo abbraccia).

CHÉNIER: O generoso! O grande! Vedi? lo piango!

GÉRARD: Guarda laggiù! Quel bianco viso È lei!

CHÉNIER: Lei? Maddalena! Ancor l'ho riveduta! Or muojo lieto!

GÉRARD: Io spero ancora! (i giurati rientrano.)

DUMAS: (dà una rapida occhiata al verdetto). Morte!

FOUQUIER TINVILLE: Via i condannati!

MADDELENA: (mentre Chénier esce) Andrea! Rivederlo!

CALA LA TELA

## QUADRO IV

(Il cortile delle prigioni di San Lazzaro a mezzanotte. Andrea Chénier scrive a tavolino. Roucher gli è vicino.)

SCHMIDT: (a Roucher). Cittadino, men duol, ma è tardi assai.

ROUCHER: (dandogli del denaro). Pazienta ancora un attimo!

CHÉNIER: (cessa di scrivere). Non più

ROUCHER: Ah, leggi!

CHÉNIER: Pochi versi

ROUCHER: Leggi! Leggi!

CHÉNIER: Come un bel dì di maggio che con bacio di vento—e carezza di raggio si spegne in firmamento, col bacio io d'una rima, carezza di poesia—salgo l'estrema cima de l'esistenza mia. La sfera che cammina per ogni umano sorte—ecco già mi avvicina all'ora della morte, e forse pria che l'ultima mia strofe sia finita,— m'annunciera il carnefiice la fine della vita. (con grande entusiasmo.) Sia!—Strofe, ultima Dea, dà ancor al tuo poeta—la sfolgorante idea, la fiamma consueta; io, a te, mentre tu vivida

---

CHÉNIER: Oh, noble heart and generous! See my tears! (Exeunt Jurors).

GERARD: Look, over there, that pallid face! It is she!

CHÉNIER: She? Madeleine? I've seen her once again! Now I die happy! (The jury come back into court.)

GERARD: I yet have hope!

DUMAS: (glancing at the verdict handed to him by the foreman). Death!

FOUQUIER-TINVILLE: Lead them away.

MADELEINE: (as Chénier is lead away). André! André! Farewell!

CURTAIN:

## ACT IV

(The Courtyard of the Prison of St. Lazare at midnight. André Chénier seated at a table, writing. Roucher is beside him.)

SCHMIDT: (to Roucher). I'm sorry, but the hour is late!

ROUCHER: (giving him money). No, wait a moment longer!

CHÉNIER: (as he stops writing). It is done! Verses?

CHÉNIER: Just a few lines.

ROUCHER: Read them!

CHÉNIER: 'Like summer day that closes 'While the breezes are sighing 'All for love of the roses, 'In dreamy twilight dying; 'So now my life is ending, 'As yet one last tender kiss 'The Muse now accords me 'Before I to Death surrender. 'The joys of life are over; 'Fond Hope now forsakes me; 'Love is lost to the lover; 'Lo! cruel Death must take me. 'As in these lines the Heavenly Muse 'Is calling farewell to me, 'The headsman grim shall summon me 'To meet my doom appalling! (with great enthusiasm.) 'Hail! Poetry, glorious goddess! 'Unto your votary, oh! grant, I pray you,

a me sgorghi dal cuore,—darò per
rima il bacio
ultimo di chi muore.
(*Roucher e Chénier si abbracciano e ●●● si separano.*)
(*Si picchia al portone della prigione. Entrano Gérard, e Maddalena.*)

SCHMIDT: (*gli s'inchina defer-
ente.*) Tu qui, Gérard?

GÉRARD: Viene a costei concesso
un ultimo colloquio

SCHMIDT: (*interrompendolo*). Il
condannato?
Il nome?

MADDELENA: Andrea Chénier!

SCHMIDT: Sta ben!
Attendi!

MADDELENA: (*a Gérard, risoluta*) Il vostro giuramento vi sovven-
go!
(*rivolgendosi a Schmidt*).
Odi! Fra i condannati di dimani
è una giovane donna.

SCHMIDT: La legray!

MADDELENA: Or ene viver deve!

SCHMIDT: Cancellare
or come da la lista il nome suo?

MADDELENA: Che importa il
nome se in sua vece
un' altra per lei risponderà?

SCHMIDT: Sta ben! Ma, e l'altra?

MADDELENA: Eccola!

SCHMIDT: Come?! Lei?
Tu, cittadina?

MADDELENA: (*a Schmidt porgendogli pochi giojelli e una piccola borsa contenente alcuni luigi*). A voi! Giojelli son! Questo è
denaro.

SCHMIDT: Evento strano in tempo
di assegnati!
Io non vorrei
Capite? Io non so nulla!
(*A Maddalena*)
Al nome di Legray salite in fretta!
(*esce*)

GÉRARD: O Maddalena, tu fai della
morte
la più invidiata sorte!

MADDELENA: Benedico il destino!
Benedico la morte!

GÉRARD: Salvarli! Ancor da Robespierre! Ancora!
(*esce*)
(*Schmidt ritorno con Chénier*).

CHÉNIER: Vicino a te s'aqueta
l'irrequïeta anima mia;
tu sei la mèta
d'ogni desio e bisogno

'The living flame of fancy, the fir
sublime, immortal!
'Behold this song I bring to you,
'Blended with my sighing,
'Let one last strain of melody
'Greet you from poet, dying!'
(*Roucher and Chénier embrace
and then part.*)
(*Knocking heard without. Enter
Gerard and Madeleine*).

SCHMIDT: (*lowing respectfully.*)
You here, Gerard?

GERARD: This lady is permitted to
have a final interview with—

SCHMIDT: (*interrupting*). Which
prisoner? Tell me his name.

MADELEINE: André Chénier!

SCHMIDT: Fine! Wait!

MADELEINE: (*to Gerard*). The
oath that you have sworn to me remember!
(*to Schmidt.*)
Listen! Among those who are to die
tomorrow, there is a young woman!

SCHMIDT: Yes, Legray!

MADELEINE: Well, mark you, she
must live!

SCHMIDT: But how can I now
strike her name off of the death-
roll?

MADELEINE: The name is nothing,
if, when she's called, another
should reply!

SCHMIDT: And who is that other?

MADELEINE: 'Tis I!

SCHMIDT: You? You would replace her?

MADELEINE: (*giving jewels and
gold.*) See here! I'll give you these!
Money and jewels!

SCHMIDT: It is an evil wind that
blows no good to some one!
(*to Gerard*).
I hardly like to risk it!
Well there! I know nothing!
(*Madeleine.*)
But—when I call for Legray, at once
come forward!
(*Exit.*)

GERARD: Oh! Madeleine your love
victorious
Make shameful death most glorious!

MADELEINE: Blessed Fate that requites us!
Blessed Death that unites us!

GERARD: (*aside*). How to save
them? I'll go once more to Robespierre!
(*Exit.*)
(*Schmidt returns with Chénier.*)

CHÉNIER: From you, beloved, my
restless soul
New joy and peace borrows;
You are the goal of my desire,

e d'ogni sogno
e d'ogni poesia!
Entro al tuo sguardo
l'iridescenza scerno
de li spazî infinit, lo son già eterno
Ti guardo;
e in questo fiotto verde
di tua larga pupilla erro coll'anima!
Questa è la luce arcana
delle plaghe serene!
Mi avvolge! Si allontana
lungi e si perde
ogni ricordo di cose terrene!
Tu sei la poesia
che alfin si dona tutta al suo poeta!
Tu sei la mèta
dell'esistenza mia!
Il nostro è amore d'anime!

MADDELENA: Il nostro è amore
d'anime!

CHÉNIER: Che tu viva se muojo,
di', che vale?
È l'anima immortale;
ovunque tu sarai, sì, io là sarò!

MADDELENA: Per non lasciarti
son qui; non è un addio!
Vengo a morire,
vengo a morire anch'io
con te!
Finì il soffrire
La morte nell'amarti
Chi la parola estrema
dalle labbra raccoglie
è Lui l'Amor! Come gemine foglie
da l'albero di vita
cadiamo e il vento
ne avvolge insieme dentro alla
infinita
luce del firmamento!
In quell'ora suprema
de l'ultimo cammino
ogni dolor finisce
col tuo bacio; il divino!
Ah, se anche è del carnefice
la man che insiem ci unisce,
quella sua mano è pia
se la tua boca—tocca
la morta bocca mia.
Salvo una madre! Maddalena
all'alba
ha nome per la morte Idia Legray!
Vedi? La luce incerta del crepuscolo
giù pe'squallidi androni già lumeg-
gia.
Abbracciami, mio amante! Amante,
baciami!

CHÉNIER: Orgoglio di bellezza!
Trïonfo tu de l'anima!
O mia fortuna il premio
di questa tua carezza!
Il tuo amore, sublime amante, è
mare,
è ciel, luce di sole e d'astri È il mondo!

CHÉNIER: La nostra morte è il trionfo d'amore!

MADDELENA: La nostra morte è il
trionfo d'amore!

CHÉNIER: Viva la morte!

MADDELENA: Viva la morte!

CHÉNIER: È la morte!

The solace of my sorrow;
In your blue eyes gazing,
All Heaven appears before me,
Starry spaces, bright and boundless;
The yard the gates, the shining por-
tal
Of a fair realm immortal,
Where I with you would dwell!

MADELEINE: Our love is of the
soul, divine

CHÉNIER: You are the life of me

MADELEINE: With you I'll stay to
the last
Nor say farewell!
With you I come to die!
All suffering ended! By death to you
united!
Let the last word upon my lips be
this:
"I love you!"
When comes the Morning,
Madeleine goes to death as Idia Le-
gray!

CHÉNIER: Pride of beauty.
Triumph of the soul!
You, my happy thought,
The prize of my good luck!
Your love, my queen, is for me
A sea, a heaven, a sun,
The very light of day, Tis all!

CHÉNIER: Our death is love's triumph!

MADELEINE: Our death is the
crown of love!

CHÉNIER: I welcome Death!

MADELEINE: Welcome, welcome!

CHÉNIER: It is coming!

MADDELENA: È la morte!

CHÉNIER: Ella viene col sole!

MADDELENA: Ella vien col mattino!

CHÉNIER: Benedico la sorte!

MADDELENA: Benedico il destino!

CHÉNIER: Vien come l'Aurora

MADDELENA: Col sole che la indora!

CHÉNIER: Ne viene a noi dal ciel velata entro ad un velo

MADDELENA: fatto di rose e viole!

CHÉNIER: Viene la misteriosa!

MADDELENA: La eterna innammorata!

CHÉNIER: Viene la Eterna Cosa

MADDELENA: La amante immacolata!

CHÉNIER: La fronte essa mi sfiora come raggio d'aurora!

MADDELENA: Ci bacia è ci accarezza
lene sî come brezza!

MADELEINE: Death is coming!

CHÉNIER: It is coming with the sun beams!

MADELEINE: Death comes in the wake of morn

CHÉNIER: Happy is my lot!

MADELEINE: Blessed is destiny!

CHÉNIER: Death comes on the wing of dawn!

MADELEINE: With the morning golden light!

CHÉNIER: From heaven to us it comes!
Shrouded in a wondrous veil

MADELEINE: Of violets and roses fair.

CHÉNIER: There is comes, the mysterious

MADELEINE: The ever restful Death!

CHÉNIER: There comes the everlasting end.

MADELEINE: The beloved maiden pure!

CHÉNIER: She, smites with her lips my forehead
Like the morning rays of dawn!

MADELEINE: Her loving fond embraces
New joy and peace afford.

CHÉNIER: Come una brezza lene la morte, eccola, viene!

CHÉNIER e MADDALENA: (*abbracciati l'uno all'altro*). Nell'ora che si muore
eterni diveniamo!
Eternamente amiamo!
Morte è infinito, è amore!

SCHMIDT, GENDARMI, SECONDIN: (*ripetono forte il nome appellato dai l'Usciere*). Andrea Chénier!

CHÉNIER: Son io!

SCHMIDT, GENDARMI, SECONDIN: Idia Legray!

MADDELENA: (*si fa arditamente innanzi*). Son io!

CHÉNIER: Inni alla morte!

MADDELENA: Viva la morte! (*si avviano al patibolo*).

*CALA LA TELA.*

CHÉNIER: New joys and peace affords us
Kind Death, Here it comes!
(*Chénier and Madeleine embracing.*)
The passing of our lives
Is the dawn of our eternal love!
Love be our everlasting bond!
And Death immortal love!

SCHMIDT, GENDARMES AND GUARD: (*calling the prisoners.*)
André Chénier.

CHÉNIER: It is I!

SCHMIDT, GENDARMES AND GUARD: Idia Legray!

MADELEINE: (*boldly coming forward.*) It is I!

CHÉNIER: Let us to death, united
Raise our song!

MADELEINE: O, blissful Death!
(*They go out to the scaffold*).

*CURTAIN.*

# Orfeo ed Euridice (1762)

MUSIC BY CRISTOPH WILLIBALD GLUCK ■ LIBRETTO BY RAINIERI DE CALZABIGI

This three-act azione teatrale, set to a libretto by Ranieri Calzabigi, was first performed at the Burgtheater in Vienna on October 5, 1762. A revised version, described as tragédie-opéra or drame héroïque, was performed at the Paris Opera on August 2, 1774. The story in Gluck's opera is somewhat different than that of Monteverdi. It opens in a grotto where, beside the tomb of Euridice, shepherds and nymphs mourn for her. Orfeo, desperate for his beloved, leaves behind his friends and prepares to go to Hades to rescue her. Amor, Jove's messenger, comes with the news that Orfeo has been given permission to go. If his singing can melt the heart of the demons, he can have Euridice back; however, if he turns around to look at her while leading her out of Hades, he will lose her forever. Orfeo goes off on his journey. Beyond the river Cocytus, the Furies and Shades dance gruesomely, trying their best to block Orfeo's path. However, Orfeo's singing is so beautiful that the demons fade away. Orfeo reaches the Elysian Fields, admiring their beauty, and the Blessed Spirits perform a dance especially for him. His only desire is to get to Euridice as quickly as possible—soon she is brought to him and, without looking at her, he takes her hand and leads her back to earth. As they continue on their journey, Euridice continually asks Orfeo questions—how was he able to get to Hades, why doesn't he look at her, doesn't he love her—and Orfeo, unable to help himself, turns around. At that moment, Euridice dies. Orfeo, in his grief, cries out that he would rather die than live without her. Once more Amor comes, and the gods give Euridice back to Orfeo. The opera ends at the temple dedicated to Amor, where the happy couple, heroes, heroines, nymphs and shepherds celebrate Euridice's return to life and the victory of love.

## ■ ATTO PRIMO

### SCENA I

*Il teatro rappresenta un ameno boschetto, ma solitario ove si vede la tomba di Euridice circondata d'allori e di cipressi. La scena è occupata da pastori e ninfe del seguito d'Orfeo e di Euridice. Altri portano ghirlande di mirto, altri vasi onde gli antichi servinansi nelle cerimonie fine-bri, alcuni poi sono intesi a sparger profumi e coprir di fiori la tomba, sulla quale sta appoggiata la statua d'Imene con la torcia rovesciata.*

*Orfeo, Pastori e Ninfe del seguito d'Euridice; coro del seguito d'Orfeo, e ballo delle Ninfe.*
*Orfeo seduto contra un albero ove ha appeso il caschetto e la lira interamente abbandonato al dolore, e non facendo altro che continuamente ripetere il nome di Euridice.*

**CORO:** S' in questo bosco oscuro e queto,
Euridice, il tuo spierto
Ode ancor?
Deh tu oscolta a' nostri preghi
Vedi il pianto, vedi il duol.
Abbi picta dell' infelice Orfeo
Ei sospira per te.
Compiange il suo destino.
L' amorosa tortorella
Cempre fida all' amor suo
Cosi sospira o muore di dolor.

## ■ ACT I

### SCENE I

*An attractive, secluded grove surrounding the tomb of Euridice. A group of shepherds and shepherdesses are performing funeral rites, strewing flowers on the tomb, carrying vases, garlands, etc.*

*Orpheus, slightly downstage from the others, is seen leaning against a tree. Occasionally he joins in the lament of the others by sighing the name of Euridice.*

**CHORUS:** Throughout this grove all joy has ended,
Wings of darkness have descended,
Our Euridice has died.
Hear our pleading,
Witness our sufferings,
See our anguish, see our sorrow,
See the tears our burning eyes have cried.
Orpheus, abandoned, lonely and forsaken,
See him weep at our side
In grief for his departed bride,

Like the tender dove is dying.
Weak and weary from bitter crying,
His ravished heart
Dies in pain and despair.

**ORFEO:** Il vostro sospirar
Aumenta il mio dolor : All' ombra fida
D' Euridice rendete
Onor, e ne coprite
L' avel di fior.

**CORO:** S'in questo bosco oscuro e queto, etc.

**ORFEO:** Lasciatemi, conviene
Che qui rimanga io sol,
Non vo compagni avere
Nel mio supremo duol.
(*Il sequito d'Orfeo si ritira, e si disperde nel bosco.*)

### SCENA II

**ORFEO:** (*solo*). Euridice! spirto caro,
Vieni a me. Del tuo fedel,
Deh tu ascolta il pianto amaro.
Egli invoca per te il ciel.
Nel dolore suo crudel,
Ma l'eco sol, aimè! risponde al prego.
Te cerco, o mia fedel,
Quando il dì torna in ciel,
Quando s' asconde.
O vano mio dolor,
L' idolo del mio cor,
Non mi risponde!
Euridice, del tuo nome,
E'l' aer pien : le valli, i boschi
Il colle, il pian,
Sulla pianta che muore,
Sulla scorza crescente

**ORPHEUS:** Your sorrow and your grief
Increase my desolation.
In final, devout invocation
Appeal to her gods in your gloom
By strewing flowers on her tomb!

**CHORUS:** Throughout this grove etc.

**ORPHEUS:** I bid you leave. Alone
My sorrow-stricken breast
Shall once more sigh her name
Where she will rest in death.
(*The Chorus leaves.*)

### SCENE II

**ORPHEUS:** (*Alone*)
Dearest shadow, my beloved,
My Euridice, why no reply, no hope?
Hear your husband, forlorn, in dismay
Crying out to the darkness forever,
Pleading in fear and horror.
The winds, alas, drown out
My cry of sorrow!
Now you, my love, have gone,
Vainly, I ask the dawn
Where I should go to be near you.
My heart shall call for you
Long after night must fall,
Hoping to hear you.
Ah, beloved, my beloved!
All that I see sings your name.
The brook sings its praise to the

Il nome tuo scolpi
La mano mia dolente.
Euridice morì,
Ed io respiro ancor.
O ciel, la rendi a me,
O chiudi anco i miei dì.
Ah! vinto dal mio duol,
Il più remoto suol,
Io vo cercando.
Pietoso il nome mio
Nel suo cammino il rio,
Va mormorando.
Divinità del cupo imper, ministri
Di terror; del soggiorno
Dell' ombre voi che nella trista valle
Fate che sia compito
Il voler di Plutone,
Voi che mai gioventù
Disarmò, ne beltade,
Da voi tolta mi fu,
La mia felicitade.
Oh memoria fatal! Aimè! le grazie
Del suo bel volto,
Dal più crudel destino
Non la poter salvar.
Implacabili Dei!
Ve la voglio involar.
Io saprò penetrar
Fino nel cupo abisso.
Ammolir tal rigor
La lira mia saprà,
Il vostro sdegno io sento
Che affrontare potrà.

trees,
And the leaves to the stones.
Cut in branches, the name of Euridice
Will sing of happiness and beauty.
Euridice has died,
I prefer death myself.
Gods, give her back to me
Or let me die with her!
Filled with woe and despair,
Rending the air with sighs.
My heart is sinking.
The brook alone shall know
How freely my tears can flow,
It is drinking tears.
You, gods of Acheron's domain,
You grim and fearsome lords
O the kingdom of darkness,
You, whom down among the shadows
Pluto's despotic power
So cruelly commands,
Heartless you are, and blind
To her youth and her beauty.
You have stolen from me
What made my world enchanted,
What has gladdened my life.
Alas, the blossom you have broken,
And in her tender heart
Have plunged your ruthless knife.
Fiendish ghosts of the night,
I ask of you my wife.
Without fear I descend
To your infernal regions
Where the pleas of my grief
Will at last cool your ire.
In your breast this eternal hatred?
Shall subside before my passion's fire!

## SCENA III

**AMORE:** (*entra*). Darà soccorso Amore
Al più tenero amante,
Non disperar, di te
Giove senti pietà,
Nel buio eterno
Tu scender puoi,
Va a trovar Euridice
Della morte nel sen.
Se col dolce suon di tua lira,
Se col tuo cantar divin,
De' numi dell' averno
Placar tu puoi l' ira,
A te ritornerà.
Dal tenebroso impero
A te ritornerà.

**ORFEO:** Ciel la rivedrò!

**AMORE:** Sì, ma per tanto aver
Esser pronto convien a compier l' ordine.
Che da me devi udir.

**ORFEO:** Chi mai potrà . . . a me 'l vietar
A tutto io son disposto.

**AMORE:** Odi dunque del ciel qual è il volere.
Su quest' amante . . . tanto adorata
T' è vietato lasciar,
Uno sguardo cader,
O per sempre da te

## SCENE III

**THE GOD OF LOVE:** (*enters*)
Your plea is not in vain.
Your appeal has been heeded.
The God of Love, I come here
To grant you your request.
For to your wish the gods have acceded:
You shall find your beloved
Where she rests in death.
Let your tender lyre's sweet endeavor
Fill the air with its harmony.
Its song the savage fiends
Shall becalm in their lair.
She will be yours once more,
Yours to behold forever.

**ORPHEUS:** Gods, I could see her again!

**LOVE:** Yes. Yet, before you go
You must know the will of the gods.
Mark their word and make your decision!

**ORPHEUS:** Nothing can alter my intent,
For her my heart shall never waver!

**LOVE:** Then learn from me the gods' decree:
You, when ascending from Hades,
Shall refrain from beholding
Your wife while you flee.
If you weaken but once
You will lose her forever.

Resterà separata.
Di Giove or sai la volontà qual è
Degno ti mostra della sua mercè.
L' adore raffrena,
Restringi il desio,
E tosto ogni pena
O duolo più rio
Sparito sarà.
Tu sai che un amante,
Discreto e costante
Nel cor d' un amata,
Ha sempre trovata
La dolce pietà.
(*esce Amore.*)

## SCENA IV

**ORFEO:** (*solo*). Chi vidi! chi parlò.
Euridice vivrài? Clemente cielo
Un dio propizio
La rende a me.
Ma che? io non potrò
Ritornando alla vita,
La serrar sul mio sen
O dolce amica!
O qual favor!
O qual ordin crudel!
Prevedo il suo timor
Il sospetto, il dolor.
A che il pensier soltanto
D' una prova si cruda
Mi fa di ghiaccio il cor,
Si lo potrò, lo giuro
Amore, m' assisterà,
Nell' immenso mio duolo
Temer di sua pietà,
Sarebbe a te far torto,
Fia così. Giove il vuol
A te sommesso io son.
(*Orfeo prende la lira e si mette il caschetto.*)
La speme in sen ritorna.
Fine avran le mie pene
Al mio supremo bene
La vita io vo ridar.
L' averno invan fra noi
Con tutti i mostri suoi
Non vincerà l' amor.
Al mio supremo bene
Vo dar la vita ancor.

*FINE DELL' ATTO PRIMO*

This is the gods' command
And you must obey it
To be worthy of their trust.
In silence to suffer,
Your loved one so near,
Is part of this offer.
But
Your torment and fear soon will be ended.
To love in distress
Shows faith and devotion.
Her tender caress
Will soothe your emotion,
You soon will confess.
(*The God of Love disappears.*)

## SCENE IV

**ORPHEUS:** (*alone*). How wondrous! Did I dream?
Euridice will return, be mine forever?
A god of light, a god of mercy
Will bring her back?
But I must turn away
From the one I love so dearly
Until we are back on earth
O, my beloved, harsh is the price
That restores you to me!
I can see all her doubts,
The despair which she feels
While this frightful ordeal,
So severe and inhuman
Turns my blood to ice.
I shall proceed without fear to endure it.
The God of Love will harden my heart,
Let his faith be defended!
If Love should fail me now,
My own life shall be ended!
Mighty gods, I proceed,
Obeying your command!
Oh Love, I call you to guide me,
To firmly stand beside me.
Your wondrous armor hide me
In danger and in fear!
Now death shall hold her no longer.
My heart will prove stronger,
And Love will guide her here,
Yes, Love will walk beside me
And gently guide her here.

*END OF THE FIRST ACT*

# ■ ATTO SECONDO

## SCENA I

*Il teatro rappresenta la porte dell' inferno, donde vedesi uscire denso fumo misto a fiamme.*
*Stuolo di demoni e di furie, Orfeo.*
*Ballo delle furie.*
*Orfeo fa sentire il suono della lira. Gli spettri, e le furie ne interrompono co' loro balli gli accordi, e cercano di fare a lui spavento.*

**CORO DEI DEMONI:** Chi mai dell' Erebo
Fra le caligini,
Sull' orme d' Ercole
Di morte impavido,

# ■ ACT II

## SCENE I

*A frightening, rocky landscape near the gates of the Underworld, veiled in a dark mist occasionally pierced by flames. The dance of the Furies and Monsters is interrupted by sounds of the lyre of the approaching Orpheus. When he comes into view they all join in the ensuing chorus.*

**CHORUS:** Who can the mortal be,
Wanton and bold,
Who has found the gate to this world of hate,
Daring a frightening fate,

Conduce il piò?
D' orror lo ingombrino
Le fiere Eumenidi
E lo spaventino,
Gli urli di Cerbero,
Se un dio non è.

**ORFEO:** (*avvicinandosi ai demoni, sempre suonando la lira*). Deh calmate tanto ardor!
Furie, larve, ombre sdegnate
Deh sentite alfin pietate,
Del mio barbaro dolor.

**CORO:** No, no, no.

**ORFEO:** Deh calmate, etc.

**CORO:** Misero giovane,
Che vuoi? che mediti?
Altro non abita
Che lutto e gemito,
In queste orribili
Soglie del duol.

**ORFEO:** Ah l' ardor che mi divora
Cento volte è ben più rio,
Ah l' inferno duol non ha
Pari a quel che in sen mi sta.

**CORO:** O quale incognito
Affetto flebile
Viene a sospendere
L' imperturbabile
Nostro furor.

**ORFEO:** Se il mio affanno, ah! voi sapeste
Se vedeste il mio dolore.
Dello strazio del mio core
Forse avreste allor pietà.
(*I demoni inteneriti al canto di Orfeo.*)

**CORO:** Le porte stridano
Su neri cardini.
E il passo lascino
Sicuro e libero
Al vincitor.
Tutto al dolcissimo
Suo canto piegasi,
E vincitor.
(*Durante questo coro le porte dell' inferno si schiudono Orfeo si apre il passo in mezzo agli spetri incantati al suono della lira, ed entra negli abessi.*)

*FINE DELL' ATTO SECONDO*

## ■ ATTO TERZO

### SCENA I

*Il teatro rappresenta i campi Elisi. Vi zi vedono degli archi fioriti, dei boschetti, delle fontane e de tapeti d' erbetta verde sopra i quali riposano le ombre dei giusti, divise in differenti gruppi.*

*Ballo delle ombre felice.*

---

Terror shall strike his heart,
Tearing his mind apart,
When howling hellhound's roar,
Foam-dripping fangs ajar,
Bar him from the door.

**ORPHEUS:** (*Playing the lyre*) Ah, have pity, have pity on me!
Furies! Monsters! Shadows so fearful,
Oh hear my song so tearful,
And your heart may heed my plea.

**CHORUS:** No! No! No! No!

**ORPHEUS:** Ah, have pity etc.

**CHORUS:** Having defied your fear
Tell us who brought you here!
Here there is no room for life -
Nothing but night and gloom,
Nothing but the cries of
The damned in their doom.

**ORPHEUS:** All the torments Hell has to offer
My heart must suffer hundredfold.
The world has never known such grief
As that from which I seek relief.

**CHORUS:** The song he sings, strangely,
Brings out of the night
Balm to our wild fury
Turning our beguiled hearts
Peaceful and mild.

**ORPHEUS:** Here before you
I implore you
So your wrath may soon abate.
Tears shall tell you and compel you
To allow me through the gate.
(*The Monsters and Furies are softened by the beauty of Orpheus' plea.*)

**CHORUS:** Beauty unknown to us,
Warm and melodious,
Melting our wrath away,
Holding our hearts in sway
Open his way!
So through the portals wide
In may the mortal stride.
He by the singer's art
Conquered the monsters' heart,
Winning his bride.
(*During the last chorus, the gates of the Underworld are thrown open. Orpheus makes his way through the monsters and descends into Hades.*)

*END OF THE SECOND ACT*

## ■ ACT III

### SCENE I

*The Elysian Fields, domain of the Blessed Spirits. An enchanting landscape with bushes, flowers, brooklets etc. Various groups of Spirits are seen on stage.*

*Ballet*

---

*Un ombra felice e coperta di lungo velo sequita da molte altre ombre. Aria alternativamente col Coro del seguito di Euridice.*

**L' OMBRA FELICE:** Questo prato sempre ameno
Del riposo è il dolce asil
Questo è il bel lido sereno
Ove sempre ha regno April.
Nulla qui la mente oscura
Qui si gode l' aura pura,
Dolce incanto infiamma il sen
E la misera tristezza,
Cessa in questo asilo amen.
Quest' è 'l suol ridente e tranquillo
Dove la pace in trono sta.

**CORO:** Quest' è il ridente asil
Della felicità.
(*Le ombre si allontano.*)

### SCENA II

**ORFEO:** (*entra*). Di qual splendor, qui brilla il sol?
Più puro è 'l ciel
Più chiaro il dì.
Dolce aura lusinghiera
Sento aleggiar nel bosco,
Degli augelli il gorgheggiar,
De' ruscelli il mormorar
E il dolce fiato dell' aura.
Si gode in questo asil,
Di vera pace il ben
Ma la calma che qui respiro
Il mio dolor blandir non val,
O mio ben d'amor soave oggetto,
Tu sola puoi calmar
Lo strazio del mio petto
Te mirar, la tua voce udir,
Star vicin sempre a te.
Ah il tuo sospiro,
E il solo ben, che ognor desire.

**CORO NELLA QUINTE:** Giunge Euridice.
Al soggiorno del riposo,
Vieni, o dolce amante e sposo
Vieni e scorda il tuo dolor.
Euridice amor ti rende
Euridice gia riprende
Di beltade il bel tesor.

### SCENA III

*Le ombre ed Orfeo.*

**ORFEO:** O larve che m' udite,
Ah tollerate in pace
I caldi miei sospir.
Se voi portaste in seno
L' ardor che mi divora
Gia stretto sul mio cor
Avrei l' amato ben,
Offrite al mio pregar
La beltà che qui cerco,
Che qui vengo a implorar.

**CORO DELLE OMBRE:** E il destin risponde a te.

---

**ONE BLESSED SPIRIT:** Lovely fields so gentle and peaceful
Where with joy is filled the air,
Friendly domain of Blessed Spirits,
Free of care.
Though the world beyond be grey and tearful,
Here our bond is gay and cheerful.
In timeless bliss the days go by
While all sadness turns to gladness
And to laughter every sigh.

**CHORUS:** Friendly domain of Blessed Spirits,
Free of care!
(*The chorus disperses.*)

### SCENE II

**ORPHEUS:** Out of the sky, wondrous and bright,
Down came a light to charm my eye.
Oh delight Abounds.
My feathered companions are singing
In their old, mysterious tongue.
The brooklet's lively song
Joins in the wind's gentle sighing
As everything around
Speaks of eternal peace.
Yet, this enchantment,
This quiet rapture
Cannot end my despair and grief.
For you, only you,
My beloved, my wife,
Euridice, can give me back my life!
Once again to listen to her voice,
Rejoice in her smile,
Once more to see her . . .
Grant me, you gods, this only favor!

**CHORUS:** Come, the Blessed Fields invite you,
Husband tender, love shall delight you,
Come, and banish sorrow and pain!
Soon your loving wife will greet you,
Yes, Euridice will meet you,
Never to depart again.

### SCENE III

*Orpheus and the Blessed Spirits*

**ORPHEUS:** But now, shadows that surround me,
Do not longer withhold my loved one
From my arms!
Ah, could you feel with me
The torments that confound me,
If you had known just once
A faithful lover's fire,
I should behold her face
Without all this delay.

**CHORUS:** So be it. Your wish shall be fulfilled!

## SCENA IV

Le ombre, Orfeo, Euridice velata
in tontananza.

Danza delle Ombre.

Durante il coro le ombre consegnano Euridice nelle mani di Orfeo, che la riceve senza guardarla, e manifestando il più vivo trasporto d' amore e di gioia.

**CORO DELLE OMBRE, AD EURIDICE:**
Torna, o bella at tuo consorte,
Che non vuol che più diviso,
Sia da te pietoso il ciel.
Non lagnarti di tua sorte
Che può dirsi un altro Eliso
Uno sposo io fedel.
(Le ombre felici seguono Orfeo ed Euridice.)

## FINE DELL' ATTO TERZO

# ■ ATTO QUARTO

## SCENA I

Il teatro rappresenta una caverna oscura, per sentieri interrotti e che conducono fuori dell' inferno.

Orfeo i Euridice.

Orfeo tenendo Euridice per la mano, ma senza alzarle gli occhi in volto comparisce in distanza, e s' innoltra con aria inquieta.

**ORFEO:** Ah! vieni Euridice,
Son io, del più constante amore il mio
Unico e dolce oggetto.

**EURIDICE:** Sei tu? se tu davver?
Ciel non è quest' un delir?

**ORFEO:** Si tu vidi il tuo amore,
Son io che vivo ancor.
E dal regno de' morti
Or ti vengo a salvar.
Del mio fedele ardor
Il pianto Giove udì,
Di nuovo tu vivrai.

**EURIDICE:** Che! vivrò! E per ti!
Sommi dei, qual bontà!

**ORFEO:** Euridice, partiam,
Ci affrettiam a godere
Di tal favor celeste.
Usciam da questo
Asil funesto,
Un' ombra più non sei
E la face d'amor ancor più viva
Arderà nel mio sen.

**EURIDICE:** Che ascolto? E sarà ver?
Oh sorte a noi felice!
E che noi risserrar
Potrem d' amore i nodi!

## SCENE IV

The Blessed Spirits, Orpheus, and Euridice, covered by a veil.

Ballet of the Blessed Spirits.

(During the ensuing chorus Euridice is brought to Orpheus who takes her hand without looking at her, but betraying great emotion.)

**CHORUS:** (To Euridice).
Near the one whose love so tender
Made the gods of death surrender
Shall you find a blissful life.
Be reborn, united with him
Whose undaunted heart is plighted
To his faithful, loving wife.
(The Blessed Spirits follow Orpheus and Euridice.)

## END OF THE THIRD ACT

# ■ ACT IV

## SCENE I

A dark subterranean vault indicating a labyrinth of passageways.

Orpheus and Euridice

(Orpheus appears, leading Euridice by the hand without looking at her. He is nervous and impatient.)

**ORPHEUS:** Oh come, Euridice, oh come!
Once more you return to blissful life,
And to my love.

**EURIDICE:** Is it you? Can it be?
Gods, I cannot believe it!

**ORPHEUS:** Yes, you see your husband.
My distress and my pain
Gave me courage to tear you
From Orcus again.
My pleas and bitter tears
Have wakened in the gods
Compassion and mercy.

**EURIDICE:** I, alive and with you?
Ah, great gods, what delight!

**ORPHEUS:** But, Euridice, come with me!
Let us tarry no more,
Blessed by our fortune's favor!
Away at last from all this horror,
From death and desolation!
Back to earth we ascend
Where all our sorrow shall end.

**EURIDICE:** But, tell me, how can this be?
Such ecstasy, such rapture!
And so, once again, you and I
Shall be united in happiness.

**ORFEO:** Si, presto andiam
Più non tardar.

**EURIDICE:** Ma la tua mano, o ciel,
io più non sento
Che! non son quella più,
Che tanto amasti un di!
Dal sen per Euridice
L' amore tuo fuggi?
O non trovi più in me
La beltà del mio volto.

**ORFEO:** (a parte). O cielo qual divieto!
Euridice andiam,
Di qui presto andiamo, preme il tempo,
Palesare vorrei
L' eccesso del mio amore
Legge fatal!
O barbaro destin!

**EURIDICE:** Ti chiedo un guardo sol.
Crudel son questi forse i lieti dì,
Che il tuo cuor mi prepara?
E questa ì la mercè
Di tanto amore?
O gelosa fortuna! Orfeo! aimè!
Tu rifiuti in tal dì
Gl' innocenti sospir,
Di quella che tant' ami?

**ORFEO:** Co' tuoi timor, or più non mi affannar.

**EURIDICE:** Tu mi dai vita sol
Per ricondurmi al duol.
Ciel, deh riprendi il don, io lo detesto
Sposo crudele, ah! lasciami.

**ORFEO:** Vieni, ah! vieni al tuo consorte

**EURIDICE:** No, crudel
M' è più caro ancor morir
Che di vivere con te.

**ORFEO:** Vedi il duol.

**EURIDICE:** Lasciami in pace.

**ORFEO:** No, mia vita, ombra seguace
Sarò sempre intorno a te.

**EURIDICE:** Parla, a chè sei si tiranno?

**ORFEO:** Potrò pria morir d' affanno
Ma giammai dirò perchè.

**EURIDICE E ORFEO:** Siate a me propizi, o Dei,
Ah vedete i pianti miei
Il dolor che in seno io porto
Più soffribile non è.
(Orfeo sta immerso nella più grande agitazione s' appoggia contra la rupe.)

**EURIDICE:** (a parte). Ma perchè a serbare
Tal silenzio persiste?
Quale arcan vuole a me celar?
Della pace all' asil,
Ei ritrar mi dovrà
Per me insultar can tantra indifer-

**ORPHEUS:** Yes.
Let us flee without delay!

**EURIDICE:** Yet, now your hand no longer touches mine.
Why, averting your eyes,
Do you flee my glance?
Your heart, has it forgotten
How to beat tender and warm?
Have I faded in death,
Lost my beauty and charm?

**ORPHEUS:** (Aside). Oh gods, how can I bear it?
(Aloud) Let us leave here at once,
Forsake this domain! We must hurry.
(Aside) How I wish I could show her
My delirious passion!
(Aside) It cannot be. O terrible decree!

**EURIDICE:** One look into my eyes!
Ah, you traitor!
Now I see in your heart
All the grief that awaits me.
Is this what love
May claim as sweet reward?
Oh deceitful mischance!
My husband's heart can no longer afford
To bestow on his wife
A single loving glance!

**ORPHEUS:** Oh do not yield, dear one,
To fear and doubt!

**EURIDICE.** Why return me to life
If now you cast me out?
Gods, your compassion is vain and unwanted.
Lonely and betrayed, leave me here!

**ORPHEUS:** Come! See how your sorrows aggrieve me!

**EURIDICE:** No, I stay. Death again relieve me
Of bitter deception and pain!

**ORPHEUS:** See my torment!

**EURIDICE:** Leave me behind you!

**ORPHEUS:** Ah, you wrong me.
How could I find you?
United, we never part again.

**EURIDICE:** Tell me your secret, I beseech you!

**ORPHEUS:** My secret I cannot teach you.
I still must remain silent.

**ORPHEUS AND EURIDICE.**
Mighty gods, I now implore you,
Oh see me weeping here before You!
My distress is past enduring.
Oh, what despair
Has my tortured heart to bear!
(Orpheus, overcome with grief, leans against a rock.)

**EURIDICE:** (aside). Yet, why should he persist
In this ominous silence?
What is the secret sealing his lips?
Could it be that he tore me
From heavenly bliss
To kill me anew by disdain and

enza.
O barbara sorte,
Mi togli da more
Per farmi la preda,
D' un nuovo dolor.
D' una tranquilla pace
Io gustava il riposo,
Gli affanni il pianto or sottentrati
sono
A quei felici dì.

**ORFEO:** Quel vano suo sospetto
Accresce il mio dolor,
Che dire mai? che fare?
Son quasi disperato,
Come poss' io calmar
Sa tema del suo cor.

**EURIDICE:** Io vacillo, io tremo
Io mi perdo, io gemo.

**ORFEO:** Quanto son da compian-
gere
Non mi so contenere.

**EURIDICE:** Oh barbara sort, etc.

**ORFEO:** Oh qual prova credele.

**EURIDICE:** Tu m' abbandoni,
Orfeo
Non hai pietà
La desolata sposa,
Soccorso invoca invan,
O Dei, sentite i miei martir.
Di vita devo uscir
Senza attenere un guardo solo.

**ORFEO:** Mi sento il coraggio man-
car,
Eperdo la ragion.
Da tanto amor portato,
Io scordo la difesa
Euridice e me stesso.
(*Fa un movimento per voltarsi in-
dietro, e a un tratto si trattiene.*)

**EURIDICE:** Caro sposo, appena
Io posso respirar.
(*Cade contro una rocca.*)

**ORFEO:** Non disperare
Or ti vo dire, o ciel che faccio
Giusti dei, quando avrà fine il mio
martire.

**EURIDICE:** Questo aimè sia l' estremo addio.
Non ti scordar d'Euridice.

**ORFEO:** Dove son? più resistere
non posso
Giusto ciel! chi soffrì si grave affa-
no?
O mia cara Euridice!

**EURIDICE:** Orfeo! Oimè! io moro.

coldness?
Oh fiendish delusion,
Treacherous illusion,
You give me back a life
Filled with torment and woe.
Why, gods above, oh why
Do you torture me so?
In recent enchantment,
Surrounded by beauty,
Now bitter, rejected,
Bereaved and dejected
My heart sighs in pain.

**ORPHEUS:** Her suspicion and
doubt
Sink daggers in my heart.
Her sorrow and sadness
Turn my despair to madness.
Where to find relief
For her distress and grief?

**EURIDICE:** I am failing, I tremble.

**ORPHEUS:** May the gods make me
stronger!
I can bear it no longer.

**EURIDICE:** Oh fiendish delusion
etc.

**ORPHEUS:** Gods, your command is
inhuman.

**EURIDICE:** Ah, do not flee, be-
loved husband!
Do not desert, in this hour of gloom
And sorrow, the one who needs
you,
Your wife.
O gods, lend your help to my plea!
Ere I shall end my life,
Grant me, my love, a final glance!

**ORPHEUS:** My heart can no longer
resist.
Slowly my mind turns mad,
As in a hellish trance.
My wife, myself, my prom-
ise . . .
I must cast you to your chance!
(*He starts turning towards her
but takes hold of himself immedi-
ately.*)

**EURIDICE:** On my heart I feel
The icy hand of death.
(*She sinks down against a rock.*)

**ORPHEUS:** You shall not
die . . .
For I shall tell you . . . I
have . . .
Great heavens!
Gods above, when will you relent
In your fury?

**EURIDICE:** So shall end
Euridice's great love . . .
Remember
her . . . farewell . . .

**ORPHEUS:** Where am I?
The command of the gods I defy.
No, my wife shall not die,
For the gods cannot will it!
(*Turns to her suddenly*)
Euridice beloved . . .

**EURIDICE:** (*tries to rise, but sinks
back again and dies*)
My Orpheus . . . farewell . . . forever . . .

**ORFEO:** Sventurato che fui!
In qual orrido abisso,
Mi gettò tal funesto amore
Cara sposa! Euridice!
Ella muor Dì fatal!
Più il miò ben non vedrò.
Io son, io che spensi i tuoi bei dì
Legge iniqua, destin crudel!
Dolor non avri eguale,
In ora sì funesta
Il mio delir, la morte
E sol quel che mi resta.
Che farò senz' Euridice
Dove andrò senza il mio ben,
Euridice, o Dio, rispondi,
Io son pure il tuo fedel.
Euridice, ah! non m' avvanza
Più soccorso, ne speranza.
Ne' dal mondo ne' dal ciel.
Mortal silenzio
Nulla m' avvanza,
Oqual martir!
Si spezza il cor.
Ah per sempre io t' ho perduta!
Ogni speme or disparì.
Del dolor l'ora è venuta.
Ogni ben da me fuggi,
Ah, possa il mio martir
Finir con la mia vita!
Sorviver non potrei
Ad un affanno egual.
Son presso ancor d'averno alla città
Raggiunto presto avrò,
La mia diletta sposa.
Sì, vengo a te, mio bene, mio sol
ben,
M'aspetto, più non mì sarai repita.
Sì la morte al tuo sen
Riconducami ancor.
(*Orfeo tira la spada per uccidersi,
ma l'Amore che gli appare ad un
tratto gli arresta il braccio.*)

**ORPHEUS:** What, great gods, have I
done!
What a frightful disaster
Brought on by my tortured love!
See me weeping here before you,
My beloved, I implore you!
She can hear me no more.
I have lost her again.
And I, yes, I, have sealed
Her final doom!
All is over, the end has come.
I can no longer bear it.
Gods, as a final favor let me remain
With her. In death we be united!
Now my love has gone forever.
All my days have turned to night.
From my heart, gone forever
Every ray of hope and light,
None can know my bitter plight.
My beloved, can you hear me?
Oh tell me, are you near me!
Hear my voice so sad and sighing
In tears and terror,
In fears and sorrow crying.
Can you hear me, are you near me?
No sound has found me.
Silence around me!
Sorrow has crowned me.
All has ended in pain and fright.
My overwhelming grief
Shall find its grim conclusion.
I never can survive
A fate too harsh to bear.
So once again I shall descend to Ha-
des
And soon shall be with her,
Euridice, my wife.
Yes, I shall follow you, my love,
To the grave, and stay with you for-
ever.
No one shall ever take you from me
After death does unite
What cannot live apart!
(*During the last words, Orpheus
has pulled a dagger and is now
about to stab himself when the
God of Love suddenly appears and
stops him.*)

## SCENA II

*Orfeo, Euridice, e L' Amore.*

**AMORE:** T'arresta Orfeo.

**ORFEO:** O Ciel!
Chi sei tu che ardisci or trattenare
Del miò core il trasporto?

**AMORE:** Deh! calma il tuo furor, o
uom demente,
T' arresta, e riconosci,
Amor che veglio sopra il tuo destino.

**ORFEO:** E che vuoi tu da me?

**AMORE:** Modello in te trovai
Di costanza e di fè
Or vo por fin a' tuoi guai.
(*Amore tocca Euridice e le dà ani-
ma.*)
Euridice respira!
Del più amoroso cor
Vieni a premiar l'ardor.

## SCENE II

*The God of Love, Orpheus, Eurid-
ice.*

**LOVE:** Desist, mortal!

**ORPHEUS:** Great gods, who can
mock my
Despair, can intrude on my grief,
On my sacred resolve?

**LOVE:** Master your despair and
your raving!
See here! I am the God of Love
Who rules the destiny you challenge.

**ORPHEUS:** What brings you here to
me?

**LOVE:** You have withstood the test
Of devotion and love,
And your suffering and pain shall
be ended.
Euridice, awaken!
He who loves you so truly,
Shall have his just reward!

## Act IV, Scene II

**ORFEO:** (*con trasporto*). Oh, Euridice!

**EURIDICE:** Orfeo!

**ORFEO:** Oh giusto ciel qual è
La mia riconoscenza!

**AMORE:** Più non negar
La mia potenza.
Dal doloroso imper,
Vi vengo a liberar.
Dato or v' è di goder
De' favor dell' amor.

## SCENA III

*Entra il seguito d' Orfeo e d' Euridice.*

**CORO:** Di Pafo il Signor e di Gnido
Infiamma sol il mondo inter,
Nel vuoto ciel giunger sa
L' augel veloce

---

**ORPHEUS:** My Euridice!

**EURIDICE:** My Orpheus!

**ORPHEUS:** Almighty gods,
Our gratitude shall be unbounded.

**LOVE:** Your fears and doubts
you find unfounded.
But now without delay
To brighter spheres above,
To enjoy, as you may,
The delights of your love!

## SCENE III

*Enter friends and companions of Orpheus and Euridice.*

**All:** Let love triumphant
Be your guide in all endeavors,
Rule forever beauty's domain!
His chains will unite us,

---

Le figliuole di Dori accende
Fin nel sen del vasto mar,
Più lieta fa giovinezza
Ei giunge in un la grazia e la beltà
E lui che adorna la saggezza
E di fior sparge il suo sentier,
E desso ancor che ne consola
Quando noi perdiam i suoi favor
E quando pur da noi s' invola
Ne lascia sempre l' amistà
Per temperare il duol.

*FINE*

---

Charm, and delight us.
Slaves, we are happy in his blessed reign.
Pained, in anguish, in doubt and sorrow,
Many a heart knows rain and storm.
Yet, the sun will shine tomorrow,
Loving and healing, so tender and warm.
Jealous and wild, my heart may suffer,
Tender thoughts may flee my breast;
Yet true love will have to offer
Healing balm and sweetest rest.
Let love triumphant etc.

*END*

# Armide (1777)

MUSIC BY CRISTOPH WILLIBALD GLUCK ■ LIBRETTO BY PHILLIPE QUINAULT

This heroic opera in five acts, set to a libretto by Philippe Quinault (adapted from Tasso's *Gerusalemme Liberata*), was first performed at the Paris Opéra on September 23, 1777. Glory and Wisdom praise Renaud's virtue, stating that he has the knowledge to follow honor's path. Armide seduces all other knights of the crusades except for Renaud, who does not fall for her. Her uncle Hidraot, King of Damascus, along with nymphs, shepherds and shepherdesses (who are in fact evil spirits), assist her in kidnapping Renaud. She takes him to an enchanted island where Hidraot, using his magical skills, causes Renaud to fall in love with her. Armide however, is torn between love and hate when she realizes that Renaud loves her not for her beauty but due only to the magic. Love wins out, and Armide persuades Renaud to stay with her. He lives a life of total pleasure there, forgetting entirely about the crusades. Two of his fellow crusaders come to look for him, and though initially stopped by Armide's magic, they eventually find him. They prove to him that he has been the victim of magical seduction. Renaud is ashamed of himself for his folly and chooses to resume his duties. Armide begs him to stay, but he has made his choice. She calls upon the gods of the Underworld to sink the enchanted island to the bottom of the sea.

---

## ■ ACTE PREMIER

*La scène représente une salle du palais d'Armide; au fond une place publique de la ville de Damas, ornée d'un arc de triomphe.*

### SCÈNE I

*Armide, Phénice, Sidonie.*

**PHÉNICE:** Dans un jour de triomphe, au milieu des plaisirs,
Qui peut vous inspirer une sombre tristesse?
La gloire, la grandeur, la beauté, la jeunesse,
Tous les biens comblent vos désirs.

**SIDONIE:** Vous allumez une fatale flamme
Que vous ne ressentez jamais;
L'Amour n'ose troubler la paix
Qui régne dans votre âme.

**PHÉNICE et SIDONIE:** Quel sort a plus d'appas
Et qui peut être heureux si vous ne l'êtes pas?

**PHÉNICE:** Si la guerre aujourd'hui fait craindre ses ravages,
C'est aux bords du Jourdain qu'ils doivent s'arrêter
Nos tranquilles rivages
N'ont rien à redouter.

**SIDONIE:** Les Enfers, s'il le faut prendront pour nous les armes.
Et vous savez leur imposer la loi.

**PHÉNICE:** Vos yeux n'ont eu besoin que de leurs propres charmes,
Pour affaiblir le camp de Godefroy.

**SIDONIE:** Ses plus vaillants guerriers contre vous sans défense.
Sonte tombés en votre puissance!

## ■ ACT I

*The scene represents a ball in the palace of Armide; at rear is shown a public square in the city of Damascus, in which is a triumphant arch.*

### SCENE I

*Armide, Phenice, Sidonie*

**PHENICE:** On the day of triumph, in the midst of pleasures,
Who can inspire you with dreary sadness.
Glory, grandeur, beauty, youth,
All benefits crown your wishes.

**SIDONIE:** You light a fatal flame
You do not feel;
Love dares not dim the peace
Which reigns in your heart

**PHENICE and SIDONIE:** What lot has more allurements?
And who can be happy if you are not?

**PHENICE:** If war brings its ravages today
Our peaceful land
Has nothing to fear.

**SIDONIE:** Hades, if need be, would take up arms for us
Your law rules there.

**PHENICE:** Your eyes only needed their charm,
To vanquish the camp of Godfrey.

**SIDONIE:** Before you his most valiant warriors are helpless,
They cede to your power!

**ARMIDE:** Je ne triomphe pas du plus vaillant de tous.
Renaud, pour qui ma haine a tant de violence.
L'indomptable Renaud échappe à mon courroux.
Tout le camp ennemi pour moi devient sensible.
Et lui seul, toujours invincible,
Fit gloire de me voir d'un oeil indifferent.
Il est l'âge aimable où sans effort on aime.
Non, je ne puis manquer, sansun depit extrême,
La conquête d'un coeur si superbe et si grand.

**SIDONIE:** Qu'importe qu'un captif manque à votre victoire?
On en voit dans vos fers assez d'autres témoins.
Et pour un esclave de moins,
Un triomphe si beau perdra de sa gloire.

**PHÉNICE:** Pourquoi voulez-vous songer
A ce qui peut vous déplaire?
Il est plus sûr de se venger
Par l'oubli que par la colère.

**ARMIDE:** Les Enfers ont prédit cent fois
Que contre ce guerrier nos armes seront vaines.
Et qu'il vaincra nos plus grands rois: de chaines,
Et d'arrêter le cours de ses exploits!
Que je le hais! Que son mépris m'outrage!
Qu'il sera fier d'éviter l'esclavage
Où je tiens tant d'autres héros!
Incessamment son importune image
Malgré moi trouble mon repos.
Un songe affreux m'inspire une fureur nouvelle
Contre ce funeste ennemi.

**ARMIDE:** I triumph not over the bravest of all.
Renaud—my most hated enemy he—
The unconquered Renaud escapes my fury.
The enemy's camp yields to me.
He alone, invincible always,
Takes glory in scorning me proudly.
Of a lovable age he is, when love comes readily . . .
No I cannot abandon that conquest beloved,
That heart so superb and so great.

**SIDONIE:** What matters one captive less to your victory? You lead so many others in chains
For but a single slave,
Little of your great glory is lost.

**PHENICE:** Why would you think
Of what displeases?
Surer vengeance lies
Not in anger, but—forgetting

**ARMIDE:** Hades has predicted a hundred times
That our arms are useless against this warrior.
He shall conquer our greatest kings.
How pleasing then to lead in chains
This warrior and end his prowess.
How I hate him! How his scorn rouses me!
How proud he is, escaping the bondage like this that
Other heroes must endure for me.
Constantly his ever present image
Haunts my sleep, despite me.
An awful dream inspires a new fury in me.

J'ai cru le voir, J'en ai frémi,
J'ai cru qu'il me frappait d'une at-
teinte mortello,
Je suis tombée aux pieds de ce cruel
vainqueur.
Rien ne fléchissait sa rigueur,
Et par un charme inconcevable,
Je me sentais contrainte à le trouver
aimable,
Dans le fatal moment qu'il me
perçait le coeur.

**SIDONIE:** Vous troublez-vous
d'une image légère
Que le sommeil produit?
Le beau jour qui vous luit
Doit dissiper cette vaine chimère,
Ainsi qu'il a détruit
Les ombres de la nuit.

## SCÈNE II

Hidraot et Sa Suite, Armide,
Phénice, Sidonie.

**HIDRAOT:** Armide, que le sang qui
m'unit avec vous
Me rend sensible aux soins que l'on
prend pour vous plaire!
Que votre triomphe m'est doux!
Que j'aime à voir briller le beau
jour qui l'éclaire,
Je n'aurais plus de voeux à faire,
Si vous choisissiez un époux.
Je vois de près la mort qui me
menace,
Et bientôt l'âge me glace
Va m'accabler sous son pesant far-
deau:
C'est le dernier bien où j'aspire
Que devoir votre hymen promettre
à cet Empire
Des rois formés d'un sang si beau,
Sans me plaindre du sort je cesserai
de vivre,
Si ce doux espoir peut me suivre
Dans l'affreuse nuit du tombeau.

**ARMIDE:** La chaine de l'hymen
m'étonnne,
Je crains les plus aimables noeuds.
Ah! qu'un coeur devient malheu-
reux.
Quand la liberté l'abandonne!

**HIDRAOT:** Pour vous, quand il
vous plait, tout l'Enfer est armé:
Vous êtes plus savante en mon art,
que moi-même:
De grands rois à vos pieds mettent
leur diadème,
Qui vous voit un moment, est pour
jamais charmé.
Pouvez-vous mieux goûter votre
bonheur extrême
Qu'avec un époux qui vous aime,
Et qui soit digne d'être aimé?
Pour vous, quannd il vous plaît,
etc.

**ARMIDE:** Contre mes ennemis, à
mon gré je déchaîne
Le noir Empire des Enfers,
L'Amour met des Rois dans mes
fers,
Je suis de mille amants maitresse

Against this deadly enemy.
I thought I saw him, and I trembled,
I thought he struck me a mortal
blow.
I fell before him, vanquished.
His rage, it was implacable;
Yet with inconceivable charm,
I found him admirable,
That fatal moment when he pierced
my heart.

**SIDONIE:** You but torment yourself— It is but the fleeting image of
a dream.
Before the light of day, that
chimera,
Like the shades of night,
Must vanish.

## SCENE II

Hidraot and her attendants, Armide, Phenice, Sidonie

**HIDRAOT:** May the blood, Armide,
which unites me to you,
Render me grateful for your care.
How sweet to me is your triumph!
I love the day which lights it with
beauty.
No further wish would I have
If you would choose a spouse.
My death draws near, menacing,
And soon I'll bow beneath the
weight of years
My last, and only longing is this—
To see the promise of a race of kings
Sprung from your union. Unregret-
ting I would die.
If I could only take such a hope as
this
Into the dark, deep tomb with me.

**ARMIDE:** Hymen's chain frightens
me,
I dread its loving ties.
Ah! How wretched is that heart,
From which all liberty has fled!

**HIDRAOT:** For you, if you but will,
all Hades arms itself:
In my art, far wiser you than I:
At your feet the mighty kings lay
down their crowns;
Who sees you for just an instant, is
forever charmed by you.
Can your happiness still be greater,
sweeter,
With a spouse you love—
One worthy of your trust?
For you, if you but will, etc.

**ARMIDE:** Against my enemies I unchain at will
The dreary Kingdom of the
doomed,
Kings are brought by Love, as my
slaves.

souveraine,
Mais je fais mon plus grand
bonheur,
D'être maîtresse de mon coeur.

**HIDRAOT:** Bornez-vous vos désirs
à la gloire cruelle
Des maux que fait votre beauté?
Ne ferez-vous jamais votre felicité
Du bonheur d'un amant fidèle?

**ARMIDE:** Si je dois m'engager un
jour,
Au moins vous devez croire
Qu'il faudra que ce soit la Gloire
Qui livre mon coeur à l'Amour.
Pour devenir mon maître,
Ce n'est point assez d'être roi:
Ce sera la valeur qui me fera con-
naître
Celui qui mérite ma foi:
Le vainqueur de Renaud, si
quelqu'un le peut être
Sera digne de moi.

## SCÈNE III

Troupe de peuples du royaume de
Damas.

Hidraot, Armide, Phénice, Sidonie.

Les peuples du royaume de
Damas, témoignennt par des
danses et par des chants, la joie
qu'ils ont de l'avantage que la
beauté de cette princesse (Armide) a remporté sur les chevaliers du camp de Godefroy.

**HIDRAOT:** Armide est encor plus
aimable
Qu'elle n'est redoutable:
Que son triomphe est glorieux!
Ses charmes les plus forts sont ceux
de ses beaux yeux.
Elle n'a pas besoin d'emprunter
l'art terrible
Qui sait, quand il lui plaît, faire
armer les Enfers,
Sa beauté trouve tout possible:
Nos plus fiers ennemis gémissennt
dans ses fers.

**HIDRAOT ET LE CHOEUR:** Ar-
mide est encor plus aimable
Qu'elle n'est redoutable:
Que son triomphe est glorieux!
Ses charmes les plus forts sont ceux
de ses beaux yeux.

**PHÉNICE ET LE CHOEUR:** Suivons
Armide, et chantons sa victoire,
Tout l'Univers retentit de sa gloire.

**PHÉNICE:** Nos ennemis, affaiblis et
troublés,
N'étendront plus le progrès de
leurs armes,
Ah! quel bonheur! Nos désirs sont
comblés,
Sans nous coûter ni de sang, ni de
larmes.

**LE CHOEUR:** Suivons Armide, etc.

I am Sovereign of a thousand lovers
But my greatest happiness is
to be Mistress of my heart.

**HIDRAOT:** Can you restrict your
wishes to that cruel glory
Of the ills your beauty causes?
Will you never find your happiness
In the joy of a faithful lover?

**ARMIDE:** If I must be entangled
one day
Believe, at least, that Glory only
My heart shall yield to Love.
My master must be more than king.
Valor alone shall win my faith:
Who conquers Renaud—if he can
be conquered
Will earn my love.

## SCENE III

Populace of the kingdom of Damascus.

Hidraot, Armide, Phenice, Sidonie

The people of the kingdom of Damascus, by dancing and singing,
evince the joy they feel at the advantage which the beauty of this
princess (Armide) has had over
the knights of Godfrey's camp.

**HIDRAOT:** More lovable is Ar-
mide,—
More lovable than redoubtable:
How glorious is her triumph!
Her strongest charms lie in her
eyes.
She has no need of using that terri-
ble art of hers,
Which, if she did, would arm all Ha-
des.
Her beauty is superme!
In her chains our proudest enemies
groan, enthralled.

**HIDAROT and CHORUS:** More
lovable is Armide,—
More lovable than redoubtable:
How glorious is her triumph!
Her strongest charms lie in her
eyes.

**PHENICE and CHORUS:** Let us follow Armide and her victory chant.
Her glory resounds through heaven
and earth.

**PHENICE:** Our enemies, afraid and
weakened,
No longer shall boast their prowess,
Ah! What joy! Our wishes are
crowned.
And we have shed no blood or tears.

**CHORUS:** Let us follow Armide,
etc.

PHÉNICE: L'ardent Amour qui la suit en tous lieux,
S'attache aux coeurs qu'elle veut qu'il enflamme,
Il est content de régner dans ses yeux,
Et n'ose encor passer jusqu'à son âme.

PHENICE: Ardent love, pursuing her
Stays with the hearts she wishes enflamed;
He is content to reign in her eyes,
Not daring to enter her soul.

LE CHOEUR: Suivons Armide, etc.

CHORUS: Let us follow Armide, etc.

SIDONIE ET LE CHOEUR: Que la douceur d'un triomphe est extrème,
Quand on n'en doit tout l'honneur qu'à soi-même!

SIDONIE and CHORUS: How extreme is the sweetness of triumph,
When all the honor is due to one's self!

SIDONIE: Nous n'avons point fait armer nos soldats,
Sans leur secours, Armide est triomphante,
Tout son pouvoir est dans ses doux appas,
Rien n'est si fort que sa beauté charmante.

SIDONIE: We have not armed our soldiers,
Unaided, Armide has triumphed;
In her sweet allurements lies all her power,
Nothing is so strong as her beauty.

LE CHOEUR: Que la douceur, etc.

CHORUS: How extreme is the sweetness, etc.

SIDONIE: La belle Armide a su vaincre aisément
De fiers guerriers, plus craints que le tonnerre,
Et ses regards ont en moins d'un moment
Donné des lois aux vainqueurs de la terre.

SIDONIE: Beautiful Armide has easily won,
She has conquered the warriors, more feared than the thunder.
In less than a moment her eyes have conquered;
Laws they have given to the victors of earth.

PHÉNICE ET LE CHOEUR: Que la douceur d'un triomphe est extrème,
Quand on n'en doit tout l'honneur qu'à soi-même!

PHENICE and CHORUS: How extreme is the sweetness of triumph,
When to one's self all the honor is due.

*(Le triomphe d'Armide est interrompu par l'arrivée d'Aronte, qui avait été chargé de la conduite des chevaliers captifs, et qui revient blessé, tenait à la main un tronçon d'épée).*

*Armide's triumph is interrupted by the arrival of Aronte, who had been charged with the care of the captive knights, and who returns wounded, carrying in his hand the half of a sword.*

## SCÈNE IV

*Aronte, Hidraot, Armide, Phénice, Sidonie.*

*Troupes de peuples de Damas.*

ARONTE: O ciel! O disgrâce cruelle!
Je conduisais vos captifs avec soin,
J'ai tout tenté pour vous marquer mon zèle,
Mon sang qui coule en est témoin.

ARMIDE: Mais, où sont mes captifs?

ARONTE: Un guerrier redoutable Les a délivrés tous.

ARMIDE ET HIDRAOT: Un seul guerrier! Que dites-vous? Ciel!

ARONTE: De nos ennemis c'est le plus redoubtable.
Nos plus vaillants soldats sont tombés sous ses coups,
Rien ne peut résister à sa valeur extrème . . .

## SCENE IV

*Aronte, Hidraot, Armide, Phenice and Sidonie.*

*Populace of Damascus.*

ARONTE: O Heaven! O cruel disgrace!
I led your captives with care;
I showed my zeal to you—
My blood bears witness.

ARMIDE: But where are my captives?

ARONTE: A redoubtable warrior Recued them all.

ARMIDE and HIDRAOT: A single warrior! What did you say?

ARONTE: Of all our enemies he is the most redoubtable.
Before him, our most valiant warriors succumb;
Nothing can resist him in his valor supreme.

ARMIDE: O ciel! C'est Renaud.

ARONTE: C'est lui-même. (*Il tombe mort sur la scène, son corps est emporté par deux guerriers.*)

ARMIDE ET HIDRAOT: Poursuivons jusqu'au trépas
L'ennemi qui nous offense:
Qu'il n'échappe pas
A notre vengeance.

*FIN DE L'ACTE I.*

ARMIDE: Oh, Heavens! It is Renaud!

ARONTE: He himself. (*He falls dead upon the stage; his body is borne away by two soldiers*).

ARMIDE and HIDRAOT: Vengeance pursue him,
This enemy who assails us;
He shall not escape
Our wrath.

*END OF ACT 1.*

## ACTE DEUXIÈME

*Le théâtre représente un désert.*

### SCÈNE I

*Artémidore, Renaud.*

ARTÉMIDORE: Invincible héros, c'est par votre courage
Que j'échappe aux rigueurs d'un funeste esclavage:
Après ce généreux secours,
Puis-je me dispenser de vous suivre toujours?

RENAUD: Allez, allez remplir ma place
Aux lieux d'où mon malheur me chasse.
Le fier Gernand m'a contraint à punir
Sa criminelle audace:
D'une indigne prison Godefroy me menace,
Et de son camp m'oblige à bannir.
Je m'en éloigne avec contrainte,
Heureux, si j'avais pu consacrer mes exploits
A délivrer la cité sainte
Qui gémit sous de dures lois.
Suivez les guerriers qu'un beau zèle
Presse de signaler leur valeur et leur foi:
Cherchez une gloire immortelle,
Je veux dans mon exil n'envelopper que moi.

ARTÉMIDORE: San vous, que peut-on entreprendre?
Celui qui vous bannit ne pourra se défendre
De souhaiter votre retour.
S'il faut que je vous quitte, au moins ne puis-je apprendre
En quels lieux vous allez choisir votre séjour?

RENAUD: Le repos me fait violence,
La seule gloire a pour moi des appas,
Je prétends adresser mes pas
Où la Justice et l'Innocence
Auront besoin du sécours de mon bras.

## ACT II

*The stage represents a desert.*

### SCENE I

*Artemidore, Renaud.*

ARTEMIDORE: Invincible hero, by your courage
I have escaped the rigors of a cruel slavery.
After this noble rescue,
Can I refuse to follow you ever?

RENAUD: Come, take my place,
Here from where misfortune drives me.
Proud Gernand compels me to punish
His rash audacity:
Godfrey menaces me with vile imprisonment,
And I am banished from his camp.
Reluctantly I keep away,
Happy, if I could devote my deeds
To the rescue of the holy city
Which groans beneath oppressive laws.
You follow those warriors whose noble zeal
Fires their valor and their faith:
Seek immortal fame,
I would, alone, conceal myself in exile.

ARTEMIDORE: Without you, what can be done?
One who banishes you, only wish
For your return
If I must leave you, then at least inform me
In what place you seek asylum.

RENAUD: Rest is distasteful to me,
Only glory draws me.
I shall turn my steps
Where Innocence and Justice
Need my arms' assistance.

## Act II, Scene I

**ARTÉMIDORE:** Fuyez les lieux où règne Armide,
Si vous cherchez á vivre heureux,
Pour le coeur le plus intrépide,
Elle a des charmes dangereux.
C'est une ennemie implacable,
Evitez ses ressentiments,
Puisse le ciel à mes voeux favorable
Vous garantir de ses enchantements.

**RENAUD:** Par une heureuse indifférence
Mon coeur s'est dérobé sans peine à sa puissance,
Je la vis seulement d'un regard curieux.
Est-il plus malaisé d'éviter sa vengeance
Que d'échapper au pouvoir de ses yeux?
J'aime la liberté, rien ne m'a pu contraindre
A m'engager jusqu'à ce jour.
Quand on peut mépriser le charme de l'amour,
Quels enchantements peut-on craindre?

### SCÈNE II

— Une Bois enchantée.

Hidraot, Armide.

**HIDRAOT:** Arrêtons-nous ici, c'est dans ce lieu fatal
Que la fureur qui nous anime
Ordonne à l'Empire infernal
De conduire notre victime.

**ARMIDE:** Que l'Enfer aujourd'hui tarde à suivre nos lois!

**HIDRAOT:** Pour achever le charme il faut unir nos voix.

**HIDRAOT ET ARMIDE:** Esprits de haine et de rage,
Démons, obéissez-nous.
Livrez à notre courroux
L'ennemi qui nous outrage.
Esprits de haine et de rage,
Démons, obéissez-nous.

**ARMIDE:** Démons affreux, cachez-vous
Sous une agréable image.
Enchantez ce fier courage
Par les charmes les plus doux.

**HIDRAOT ET ARMIDE:** Esprits de haine et de rage,
Démons, obéissez-nous.
(*Armide aperçoit Renaud qui s'approche des bords de la rivière*).

**ARMIDE:** Dans le piège fatal notre ennemi s'engage.

**HIDRAOT:** Nos soldats sont cachés dans le prochain bocage,
Il faut que sur Renaud ils viennent fondre tous.

**ARMIDE:** Cette victime est mon partage,
Laissez-moi l'immoler, laissez-moi l'avantage
De voir ce coeur superbe expirer de mes coups.

**ARTEMIDORE:** Fly to the place where reigns Armide,
If happy you would love;
For the most intrepid heart
She possesses dangerous attractions.
She is an implaceable enemy,
Beware her vengeance!
May heaven grant my wishes
And guard you from her charms.

**RENAUD:** A happy indifference.
My heart guards me easily from her power
I view her only with curiosity.
Is it harder to avoid her vengeance
Than to escape the power of her eyes?
Liberty I love, I am free,
My heart untouched, and if one
scorns the charms of love
What fear is there
That other allurements may beguile?

### SCENE II

— Enchanted Woods.

Hidraot, Armide.

**HIDRAOT:** Let us halt here, the fatal place is this,
Where fury, urging us,
Bids the infernal kingdom
Our victim lead.

**ARMIDE:** May Hades now our laws obey but slowly!

**HIDRAOT:** To complete the charm our voices raise in unison.

**HIDRAOT and ARMIDE:** Spirits of hate and rage,
Demons, obey us.
Deliver to our wrath
The outraging enemy.
Spirits of hate and rage,
Demons, obey us.

**ARMIDE:** Frightful demons, hide yourselves
Beneath a pleasing image.
This haughty courage now enchant
With sweetest charms.

**HIDRAOT and ARMIDE:** Spirits of hate and rage,
Demons, obey us.
(*Armide catches sight of Renaud, who is approaching along the bank of the river*).

**ARMIDE:** Our enemy comes to the fatal net.

**HIDRAOT:** Our soldiers are hidden in the wood, near by,
Ready to pounce on Renaud.

**ARMIDE:** This victim is mine; leave him to me,
Mine the advantage to destroy
That proud heart.
(*Hidraot and Armide retire. Renaud stops to admire the river; he*

(*Hidraot et Armide se retirent*).
(*Renaud s'arrête pour considérer les bords du fleuve et quitte une partie de ses armes pour prendre le frais*).

### SCÈNE III

**RENAUD:** (*seul*). Plus j'observe ces lieux et plus je les admire.
Ce fleuve coule lentement
Et s'éloigne à regret d'un séjour si charmant.
Les plus aimables fleurs, et le plus doux Zéphire
Parfument l'air qu'on y respire.
Non, je ne puis quitter des rivages si beaux.
Un son harmonieux se mêle au bruit des eaux.
Les oiseaux enchantés se taisent pour l'entendre,
Des charmes du sommeil j'ai peine à me défendre,
Ce gazon, cet ombrage frais,
Tout m'invite au repos sous ce feuillage épais.
(*Renaud s'endort sur en gazon, au bord de la rivière*).

### SCÈNE IV

Renaud (endormi), une Naïade (qui sort du fleúve), Troupe de Nymphes, Troupe de Bergers, Troupe de Bergères.

**UNE NAÏADE:** Au temps heureux où l'on sait plaire,
Qu'il est doux d'aimer tendrement!
Pourquoi dans les périls, avec pressement
Chercher d'un vain honneur et l'imaginaire?
Pour une trompeuse chimère,
Faut-il quitter un bien charmant?
Au temps heureux où l'on sait plaire,
Qu'il est doux d'aimer tendrement!
(*Les Démons sous la figure des Nymphes, des Bergers et des Bergères, enchantent Renaud, et l'enchaînent durant son sommeil avec des guirlandes de fleurs.*)

**UNE BERGÈRE:** On s'étonnerait moins que la saison nouvelle
Revînt sans amener les fleurs et les Zéphirs,
Que de voir de nos ans la saison la plus belle
Sans l'Amour et sans les plaisirs.
Laissons au tendre Amour la jeunesse en partage;
La Sagesse a son temps, il ne vient que trop tôt:
Ce n'est pas être sage
D'être plus sage qu'il ne faut.

### SCÈNE V

Armide, Renaud, endormi.

relieves himself of part of his armor, to enjoy the breeze*).

### SCENE III

**RENAUD:** (*alone*). The more I see this spot, the more am I charmed.
This river, gently flowing,
Quits regretfully these pleasant banks.
Flowers rare, and softest zephyrs
Perfume the air.
I cannot leave these pleasing brinks.
Sweet sounds are mingling with the rippling waters.
Feathered songsters pause to listen,
Sleep's dear charms assail me,
This grass, this cooling shade,
Invite me to repose beneath these sheltering leaves.
(*Renaud falls asleep upon the grass beside the river*).

### SCENE IV

Renaud (asleep), A Naiad (who comes out of the river), Troop of Nymphs, Troop of Shepherds and Shepherdesses.

**A NAIAD:** In the happy springtime,
How sweet it is to love!
Why then seek with haste the dangers
Of a vain and fleeting honor?
For deceiving chimeras
Shall one leave a charming present?
In the happy springtime,
How sweet it is to love!
(*The Demons disguised as Nymphs, and the Shepherds and Shepherdesses enchant Renaud, and bind him while asleep, with garlands of flowers*).

**A SHEPHERDESS:** One would be less astonished
If springtime came bereft of flowers and zephyrs,
Than to see our sweetest season
Bereft of Love and pleasures.
Let us leave to tender Love the care of youth;
Wisdom has its innings, but slow it comes;
It is not wisdom.
Needless to be wise.

### SCENE V

Armide, Renaud (asleep).

ARMIDE: (*tenant un dard à sa main*). Enfin, il est en ma puissance,
Ce fatal ennemi, ce superbe vainqueur.
Le charme du sommeil le livre à ma vengeance.
Je vais percer son invincible coeur.
Par lui, tous mes captifs sont sortis d'esclavage,
Qu'il éprouve toute ma rage . . .
(*Armide va pour frapper Renaud et ne peut exécuter le dessein qu'elle a de lui ôter la vie.*)
Quel trouble me saisit, qui me fait hésiter!
Qu'est-ce qu'en sa faveur la pitiè me veut dire?
Frappons . . . Ciel! qui peut m'arrêter?
Achevons . . . je frémis! Vengeons-nous . . . je soupire!
Est-ce ainsi que je dois me venger aujourd'hui!
Ma colère s'éteint quand j'approche de lui.
Plus je le vois, plus ma fureur est vain.
Mon bras tremblant se refuse à ma haine.
Ah! Quelle cruauté de lui ravir le jour!
A ce jeune héros tout cède sur la terre.
Qui croirait qu'il fût né seulement pour la guerre?
Il semble être fait pour l'Amour.
Ne puis-je me venger à moins qu'il ne périsse?
Hé! ne suffit-il pas que l'Amour punisse?
Puisqu'il n'a pu trouver mes yeux assez charmants,
Qu'il m'aime au moins par mes enchantements
Que s'il se peut, je le haïsse.
Venez, secondez mes désirs,
Démons, transformez-vous en d'aimables Zéphirs.
Je cède à ce vainqueur, la pitié me surmonte,
Cachez ma faiblesse et ma honte
Dans les plus reculés Déserts:
Volez, conduisez-nous au bout de l'Univers.
(*Les Démons transformés en Zéphirs, enlèvent Renaud et Armide*).

FIN DE L'ACTE II.

ARMIDE: (*holding an arrow in her hand*) He is in my power at last,
This fatal enemy, this mighty victor.
For my vengeance the charms of sleep ensnare him.
His invincible heart I now shall pierce,
Through him my captives all are free,
Now let him feel my rage.
(*Armide is about to strike Renaud, but stops in the act of taking his life.*)
What trouble now assails me, and halts my hand!
In his favor, what would pity whisper?
Let me strike . . . what would prevent me?
Be done . . . I tremble! Take vengeance . . . I falter!
Is it thus I must myself avenge today?
My anger fails beside him.
The more I see him, the vainer my fury grows.
My trembling arm responds not to my hate.
What cruelty to take from him the light!
All earthly things before him bow — this youthful hero.
And was he born for war alone?
He seems intended for Love.
My vengeance only comes by death!
Is not love's punishment enough?
Since he has found no charm within my eyes,
Then let him love at least my ravishment,
Whatever be, I hate him.
Come, second my desires.
Demons, the pleasing forms of Zephyrs take.
I bow before this victor, pity rules me now;
Hide my weakness and my shame
In farthest deserts:
Fly, conduct us to the ends of Earth.
(*The Demons transformed as Zephyrs, bear away Renaud and Armide*).

END OF ACT II.

Faut-il que malgré moi tu règnes dans mon cœur?
Le désir de ta mort fut ma plus chère envie,
Comment as-tu changé ma colère en langueur?
En vain, de mille amans je me voyais suivie,
Aucun n'a fléchi ma rigueur.
Se peut-il que Renaud tienne Armide asservie?
Ah! si la liberté me doit être ravie,
Est-ce à toi d'être mon vainqueur?
Trop funeste ennemi du bonheur de ma vie,
Faut-il que malgré moi tu règnes dans mon cœur?

## SCÈNE II

*Armide, Phénice, Sidonie.*

PHÉNICE: Que ne peut point votre art? La force en est extrême
Quel prodige, quel changement!
Renaud, qui fut si fier, vous aime,
On n'a jamais aimé si tendrement.

SIDONIE: Montrez-vous à ses yeux, soyez témoin vous-même
Du merveilleux effet de votre enchantement.

ARMIDE: L'enfer n'a pas encor rempli mon espérance,
Il faut qu'un nouveau charme assure ma vengeance.

SIDONIE: Sur des bords séparés du séjour des humains,
Qui peut arracher de vos mains
Un ennemi qui vous adore?
Vous enchantez Renaud, que craignez vous encore?

ARMIDE: Hélas! c'est mon coeur que je crains
J'ai recours aux Enfers pour allumer sa flamme,
C'est l'effort de mon art qui peut tout sur son âme,
Ma faible beauté n'y peut rien.
Par son propre mérite il suspend ma vengeance,
Sans secours, sans effort, même sans qu'il y pense,
Il enchaine mon coeur d'un trop charmant lien.
Hélas! que mon amour est différent du sien!
Quelle vengeance ai-je à prétendre
Si je le veux aimer toujours?
Quoi, céder sans rien entreprendre?
Non, il faut appeler la Haine à mon secours.
L'horreur de ces lieux solitaires
Par mon art va se redoubler.
Détournez vos regards de mes affreux mystères,
Et surtout, empêchez Renaud de me troubler.

Despite me, must you rule my heart?
Your death was once my dearest wish,
How have you changed my anger?
In vain a thousand lovers sought me,
None could touch my heart.
Must only Renaud hold Armide enslaved?
Ah! If liberty is lost to me,
Must you be my conqueror?
Too hated enemy of my life's sweet happiness,
Despite me, must you rule my heart?

## SCENE II

*Armide, Phenice, Sidonie.*

PHENICE: What can your art not accomplish?
Its power is irresistible. Ah! enchantment!
Renaud, once so proud, now loves you,
And never was love so tender.

SIDONIE: Reveal yourself to him, be witness
Of the marvellous enchantment you possess.

ARMIDE: Hades has not yet fulfilled my hope,
Another charm must bring my vengeance.

SIDONIE: On the secluded banks where mortals linger,
Who can release your enemy from you?
Renaud you have enchanted,
What do you fear now?

ARMIDE: Alas! I fear my heart.
I've called on Hades to light its flame,
This effort of my art can all accomplish
On his soul. — My feeble beauty is of little worth.
His own merit checks my vengeance.
Unaided, and with trifling effort,
He enchains my heart with far too charming ties.
Alas! how different is my love to his!
Towards what vengeance dare I now aspire,
If I would love him still?
What! shall I yield in helplessness!
No, to my aid I'll summon Hate.
The honor of these lonely places
Shall be increased by my art.
Turn your vision from my fearsome mysteries.
And keep Renaud from troubling me.

## ■ ACTE TROISIÈME

*Le théâtre représente un paysage sauvage.*

### SCÈNE I

ARMIDE: (*seule*). Ah! si la liberté me doit être ravie,
Est-ce à toi d'être mon vainqueur?
Trop funeste ennemi du bonheur de ma vie,

## ■ ACT III

*The stage represents a rough and wild landscape.*

### SCENE I

ARMIDE: (*alone*). Ah! If liberty is lost to me,
Must you be my conqueror?
Too hated enemy of my life's sweet happiness,

## SCÈNE III

**ARMIDE:** (*seule*). Venez, venez, Haine implacable,
Sortez du gouffre épouvantable
Où vous faites régner une éternelle horreur.
Sauvez-moi de l'Amour, rien n'est si redoutable,
Contre un ennemi trop aimable
Rendez-moi mon courroux, rallumez ma fureur.
Venez, venez, Haine implicable,
(*La scène se change en l'enfer.*)
Sortez du gouffre épouvantable
Où vous faites régner une éternelle horreur.
(*La Haine sort des Enfers accompagnée des Furies, de la Cruauté, de la Vengeance, de la Rage et des Passions qui dépendent de la Haine.*)

## SCÈNE IV

Armide, La Haine, Suite de la Haine.

**LA HAINE:** Je réponds à tes voeux, ta voix s'est fait entendre
Jusque dans le fond des Enfers.
Pour toi, contre l'Amour je vais tout entreprendre,
Et quand on veut bien s'en défendre,
On peut se garantir de ses indignes fers.

**LA HAINE ET SA SUITE:** Plus on connaît l'Amour, et plus on le déteste,
Détruisons son pouvoir funeste,
Rompons ses noeuds, déchirons son bandeau,
Brûlons ses traits, éteignons son flambeau.
(*Le choeur répète ces quatre derniers vers. La Suite de la Haine s'empresse à briser et à brûler les armes dont l'Amour se sert.*)

**LA HAINE ET SA SUITE:** Amour, sors pour jamais, sors d'un coeur qui te chasse,
Que la Haine règne en ta place,
Tu fais trop souffrir sous ta loi,
Non, tout l'Enfer n'a rien de si cruel que toi.
(*La Suite de la Haine témoigne qu'elle se prépare avec plaisir à triompher de l'Amour.*)

**LA HAINE:** (*approchant d'Armide*). Sors, sors du sein d'Armide, Amour, brise ta chaine.

**ARMIDE:** Arrête, arrête, affreuse Haine!
Laisse-moi, sous les lois d'un si charmant vainqueur,
Laisse-moi, je renonce à ton secours horrible,
Non, non, n'achève pas, non, il n'est pas possible
De m'ôter mon amour sans m'arracher le coeur.

## SCENE III

**ARMIDE:** (*alone*). Come, implacable Hate,
Quit your noisome depths,
Where terror of you reigns eternally,
Save me from Love, nothing so daring,
Against a foe too yielding,
Restore my anger, rekindle my fury.
Come, implacable Hate,
(*Scene changes to Inferno.*)
Quit your noisome depths,
Where terror of you reigns eternally.
(*Hate emerges from Hades, accompanied by the Furies, by Cruelty, Vengeance, Rage and the Passions who are dependents of Hate.*)

## SCENE IV

Armide, Hate, Attendants of Hate.

**HATE:** I obey your summons; your voice has reached
deepest Hades.
Against Love, for you, I'll undertake all things,
And when one meets him stubbornly,
There's no need to fear his chains.

**HATE and her ATTENDANTS:** The more one knows Love, the more one hates him,
Let us now destroy his wretched power,
Let us break his bonds, undo his chains.
Let us extinguish his torch.
(*The chorus repeats the four lines. The Attendants of Hate hurry to break and burn the arms used by Love.*)

**HATE and her ATTENDANTS:** Love, now and forever, quit the heart that chases you,
Let Hate reign in your place;
Your law oppresses.
Nothing so cruel exists in Hades.
(*The Attendants of Hate evince, by signs, that she is preparing with pleasure to triumph over Love.*)

**HATE** (*approaching Armide*). Here now from the bosom of Armide, Love, break your chain.

**ARMIDE:** Stop, frightful Hate!
Leave me beneath this charming victor's laws,
Leave me, renounce your aid,
No, no, it is not possible
To take my love without my heart.

**LA HAINE:** N'implores-tu mon assistance
Que pour mépriser ma puissance?
Suis l'Amour, puisque tu le veux
Infortunée Armide,
Suis l'Amour qui te guide
Dans un abime affreux.
Sur ces bords écartés, c'est un vain que tu caches
Le Héros dont ton coeur s'est trop laissé toucher:
La gloire à qui tu l'arraches,
Doit bientôt te l'arracher,
Malgré tes soins, au mépris de tes larmes,
Tu le verras échapper à tes charmes.
Tu me rappelleras, peut-être, dès ce jour
Et ton attente sera vaine.
Je vais te quitter sans retour,
Je ne puis te punir d'une plus rude peine
Que de t'abandonner pour jamais à l'Amour.
(*La Haine et sa Suite s'abîment.*)

## SCÈNE V

La scène se change en un paysage sauvage.

**ARMIDE:** O ciel, quelle horrible menace!
Je fremis . . . tout mon sang se glace!
Amour, pouissant Amour, viens calmer
Mon effroi, et prends jutré d'un coeur
Qui s'abandonne à toi.

*FIN DE L'ACTE III.*

## ACTE QUATRIÈME

### SCÈNE I

— Un Paysage Sauvage.

Ubalde et Le Chevalier Danois.

Ubalde porte un bouclier de diamant, et tient un sceptre d'or, qui lui ont été donnés par un magicien pour dissiper les enchantements d'Armide et pour délivrer Renaud.

Le Chevalier Danois porte une épée qu'il doit présenter à Renaud.

Une vapeur s'élève et se répand dans le Désert qui a paru au troisième acte. Des antres et des abîmes s'ouvrent, et il en sort des bêtes farouches et des monstres épouvantables.

**UBALE ET LE CHEVALIER DANOIS:** (*ensemble*). Nous ne trouvons partout que des gouffres ouverts.
Armide a dans ces lieux transporté

**HATE:** Did you implore my assistance
Only to mock my power?
Then follow Love, since you would follow.
Unfortunate Armide,
Follow the Love that leads you
Into an awful abyss,
Upon those lonely banks, in vain you hide
The Hero, by whom your heart is touched too deeply:
Glory, from whom you took him,
Soon shall take him from you,
Despite your care, your tears,
He shall escape your charms.
You may call me again that day,
But vain shall be your summons.
I quit you never to return,
For so rude a treatment
I abandon you to Love.
(*Hate and her Attendants sink out of sight*).

## SCENE V

Scene changes to a rough and wild landscape.

**ARMIDE:** O Heavens, what a terrible threat!
I shudder — my blood is frozen!
Love, all powerful Love, approach and calm
My fear. Pity a heart abandoned to them.

*END OF ACT III.*

## ACT IV

### SCENE I

— Wild, rugged landscape.

Ubalde and the Danish Knight.

Ubalde wears a shield studded with diamonds, and carries a golden sceptre both given to him by a magician to exorcise the enchantments of Armide, and to deliver Renaud.

The Danish Knight carries a sword, which he is to present to Renaud.

A vapor is rising and spreading over the desert shown in the third act. Caves and chasms open, from which come forth wild beasts and frightful monsters.

**UBALDE and the DANISH KNIGHT:** (*together*). On every hand we see these yawning gulfs.
Hades has Armide here transported.
Ah! what horrible sights!

les Enfers.
Ah! que d'objets horribles!
Que de monstres terribles?
(*Le Chevalier Danois attaque les monstres, Ubalde le retient, et lui montre le sceptre d'or qu'il porte et qui lui a été donné pour dissiper les Enchantements*).

UBALDE: Celui qui nous envoie a prévu ce danger
Et nous a montré l'art de nous en dégager.
Ne craignons point Armide ni ses charmes,
Par ce secours plus puissant que nos armes,
Nous en serons aisément garantis.
Laissez-nous un libre passage,
Monstres, allez cacher votre inutile rage
Dans l'abime profond d'où vous êtes sortis.
(*Les monstres s'abîment, la vapeur se dissipe, le Dèsert disparaît, et se change en une campagne agréable, bordèe d'arbres chargés de fruits, et arrosée de ruisseaux*).

LE CHEVALIER DANOIS: Allons chercher Renaud, le ciel nous favorise
Dans notre pénible entreprise
Ce qui peut flatter nos desirs,
Doit à son tour tenter de nous surprendre
C'est le connais du charme des plaisirs
Que nous voudrons à nous defendre

UBALDE ET LE CHEVALIER DANO: (*ensemble*). Redoublons nos soins, gardons nous
Des périls agréables,
Les enchantements les plus doux
Sont les plus redoutables.

UBALDE: On voit d'ici le séjour enchanté
D'Armide et du Héros qu'elle aime!
Dans ce palais Renaud est arreté.
Par un charme fatal dont la force est extrème
C'est là que ce vainqueur si fier, si redouté,
Oubliant tout jusqu'à lui-même,
Est réduit a languir avec indignité
Dans une molle oisiveté.

LE CHAVALIER DANOIS: En vain, tout l'enfer s'interéresse
Dans l'amour qui séduit un coeur si glorieux:
Si sur ce bouclier Renaud tourne les yeux,
Il rougira de sa faiblesse,
Et nous l'engagerons à partir de ces lieux.

## SCÈNE II

— Un Bois enchantée.

---

What terrible monsters!
(*The Danish Knight attacks the monsters, Ubalde lays hold of him and shows him the golden sceptre which he carries, and which was given to him to exorcise enchantments*.)

UBALDE: He who sent us here foresaw this danger,
And the means provided to escape it.
Fear neither Armide nor yet her charms.
By this aid, more potent than our arms.
We shall easily escape.
A free path open to us, monsters,
Your useless rage conceal
There in the depths from which you came.
(*The monsters sink out of sight, the vapor is dissipated, the desert disappears, and the scene becomes an agreeable country, bordered by fruit trees, and watered by brooks*).

THE DANISH KNIGHT: Come, let us seek Renaud, the heavens favor us
In our weighty enterprise.
What ever can flatter our wishes
Must seek to surprise us first.
Henceforth it is the charms of pleasures
We must beware.

UBALDE and the DANISH KNIGHT: (*together*). We must be more watchful,
Beware agreeable perils!
The best enchantments and the sweetest
Are those to fear the most.

UBALDE: From here see the enchanted dwelling,
Where lives Armide with him she loves!
In that palace Renaud lingers,
By a fatal charm, of force extreme;
It is there the proud and gallant victor stays.
Forgetting all, forgetting himself,
Reduced to shameful languor,
In weakest laziness.

THE DANISH KNIGHT: In vain all Hades interests itself
In this love that seduces a heart so glorious,
If Rennaud turns his eyes on this shield,
For his weakness he must blush,
And we shall lead him from here.

## SCENE II

— Enchanted Wood.

---

*Un Démon, sous la figure de Lucinde, Fille Danoise, aimée du Chevalier Danois. Troupe de Demons transformés en habitants champêtres de l'île qu'Armide a choisie pour y retenir Renaud enchanté.*

*Ubalde, Le Chevalier Danois.*

LUCINDE: Voici la charmante retraite
De la félicité parfaite,
Voici l'heureux séjour
Des Jeux et de l'Amour
(*Le choeur répète ce quatrain. Les habitants champêtres dansent*).

UBALDE: (*parlant au Chevalier Danois*). Allons, qui vous retient encore?
Allons, c'est trop nous arrêter.

LE CHEVALIER DANOIS: Je vois la beauté que j'adore,
C'est elle, je n'en puis douter.

LUCINDE ET LE CHOEUR: Jamais dans ces beaux lieux notre attente n'est vaine
Le bien que nous cherchons se vient offrir à nous,
Et pour l'avoir trouvé peine,
Nous ne l'en trouvons pas moins doux.

LE CHOEUR: Voici la charmante retraite
De la félicié parfaite,
Voici l'heureux séjour
Des Jeux et de l'Amour.

## SCÈNE III

LUCINDE (*parlant au Chevalier Danois*). Enfin, je vois l'amant pour qui mon coeur soupire:
Je retrouve le bien que j'ai tant souhaité

LE CHEVALIER DANOIS: Puis-je voir ici la beauté
Qui m'a soumis à empire?

UBALDE: Non, ce n'est qu'un charme trompeur
Dont il faut garder votre coeur.

LE CHEVALIER DANOIS: Si loin des bords glacés où vous prîtes naissance,
Qui peut vous offrir à mes yeux?

LUCINDE: Par une magique puissance
Armide m'a conduite en ces aimables lieux!
Et je vivais dans la douce espérance
D'y voir bientôt ce que j'aime le mieux.
Goûtons les doux plaisirs que pour nos coeurs fidèles,
Dans cet heureux séjour l'Amour a préparés.
Le devoir par des lois cruelles,
Ne nous a que trop séparés.

UBALDE: Fuyez, faites-vous violence.

---

*A Demon, disguised as Lucinde, a Danish Girl, beloved by the Danish Knight. A Troop of Demons, disguised as peasants of the islet where Armide has chosen to retain Renaud enchanted.*

*Ubalde, The Danish Knight.*

LUCINDE: Behold the sweet retreat
Of perfect bliss;
Behold the happy home
Of Play and Love.
(*The Chorus repeats this quatrain, the peasants dance*).

UBALDE: (*speaking to the Danish Knight*). Come, what keeps you here?
Come, we have lingered long.

THE DANISH KNIGHT: I see the beauty I adore,
It is she, I am not mistaken.

LUCINDE and the CHORUS: Never do we linger vainly in these pleasant places.
The good we seek comes ever to us.
And having found it easily,
Does not rob its sweetness from it.

CHORUS: Behold the sweet retreat
Of perfect bliss,
Behold the happy home
Of Play and Love.

## SCENE III

LUCINDE (*speaking to the Danish Knight*). At last I see the lover, for whom I sigh:
I find the good I so much wished.

THE DANISH KNIGHT: Here can I see that beauty
Which rules my heart supreme?

UBALDE: No, it is only a deceiving charm,
Protect your heart against it.

THE DANISH KNIGHT: So distant from the frozen shores that gave you birth,
What brings you here to my sight?

LUCINDE: By magic power
Armide has led me to this pleasant spot,
And I lived in sweetest hope
Of seeing, here, the one I love the best.
Let us taste the pleasure Love provides
For faithful hearts here meeting.
Duty's cruel laws
Have kept us both apart.

UBALDE: Fly, rouse yourself.

LE CHEVALIER DANOIS: L'amour ne me le permet pas, Contre de si charmants appas, Mon coeur est sans défense.

UBALDE: Est-ce là cette fermeté Dont vous vous êtes tant vanté?

LE CHEVALIER DANOIS ET LU-CINDE: (ensemble). Jouissons d'un bonheur extrême. Hé! quel autre bien peut valoir Le plaisir de voir ce qu'on aime? Hé! quel autre bien peut valoir Le plaisir de vous voir?

UBALDE: Malgrè la puissance infernale, Malgrè vous-même, il faut vous dètromper. Ce sceptre d'or peut dissiper Une erreur si fatale. (Ubalde touche Lucinde avec le sceptre d'or qu'il tient et Lucinde disparaît aussitôt).

## SCÈNE IV

Le Chevalier Danois, Ubalde.

LE CHEVALIER DANOIS: Je tourne en vain mes yeux de toutes parts, Je ne vois plus cette beauté si chère. Elle échappe à mes regards Comme une vapeur légère.

UBALDE: Ce que l'Amour a de charmant N'est qu'une illusion qui ne laisse après elle Qu'une honte éternelle. Ce que l'Amour a de charmant N'est qu'un funeste enchantement. D'une nouvelle erreur songeons à nous défendre. Evitons de trompeurs attraits. Ne nous détournons plus du chemin qu'il faut prendre Pour arriver à ce palais.

UBALDE et LE CHEVALIER DANOIS: Fuyons les douceurs dangereuses Des illusions amoureuses: On s'égare quand on les fuit, Heureux qui n'en est pas séduit!

FIN DE L'ACTE IV.

## ■ ACTE CINQUIÈME

Le théâtre représente un autre endroit du Jardin.

## SCÈNE I

Renaud, Armide.

RENAUD (sans armes, et paré de guirlandes de fleurs.) Armide, vous m'allez quitter!

---

THE DANISH KNIGHT: Love permits me not, Against such sweet allurements My heart is helpless.

UBALDE: Is this then that firmness You so vaunt about?

THE DANISH KNIGHT and LU-CINDE: (together). Let us enjoy this happiness. What other good is worth The pleasure of seeing one you love? Ah! what other good is worth The pleasure of seeing you?

UBALDE: Despite infernal influence, Despite yourself, you must be saved. This golden sceptre has the power To banish fatal errors. (Ubalde touches Lucinde with the golden sceptre which be carries, and Lucinde at once disappears).

## SCENE IV

The Danish Knight, Ubalde.

THE DANISH KNIGHT: Everywhere I turn my eyes in vain Seeking that beauty, dear. She escapes my vision Like thinnest vapor.

UBALDE: The charming things of Love Are only illusions, leaving naught But shame behind them. The charming things of Love Let us now beware of new errors, And of false attractions. Never must we leave the path before us To reach that palace.

UBALDE and the DANISH KNIGHT: Let us beware of dangerous attractions Such as Love's illusions: Happy is he who escapes Their blandishments.

END OF ACT IV.

## ■ ACT V

The stage represents another part of the Garden.

## SCENE I

Renaud, Armide.

RENAUD: (without his arms, and bedecked with garlands of flowers). Armide, can you leave me?

---

ARMIDE: J'ai besoin des Enfers, je vais les consulter, Mon art veut de la solitude. L'amour que j'ai pour vous cause l'inquiétude Dont mon coeur se sent agiter.

RENAUD: Armide, vous m'allez quitter!

ARMIDE: Voyez en quels lieux je vous laisse.

RENAUD: Puis-je rien que voir que vos appas?

ARMIDE: Les plaisirs vous suivront sans cesse.

RENAUD: En est-il où vous n'êtes pas?

ARMIDE: Un noir pressentiment me trouble et me tourmente, Il m'annonce un malheur que je veux prévenir, Et plus notre bonheur m'enchante, Plus je crains de le voir finir.

RENAUD: D'une vaine terreur pouvez-vous être atteinte, Vous qui faites trembler le ténébreux séjour?

ARMIDE: Vous m'apprenez à connaître l'Amour, L'Amour m'apprend à connaître la crainte. Vous brûliez pour la Gloire avant que de m'aimer, Vous la cherchiez partout d'une ardeur sans égale. La Gloire est une rivale Qui doit toujours m'alarmer.

RENAUD: Que j'étais insensé de croire Qu'un vain laurier donné par la victoire, De tous les biens fût le plus précieux! Tout l'éclat dont brille la Gloire Vaut-il un regard de vos yeux? Est-il un bien si charmant et si rare Que celui dont l'Amour veut combler mon espoir?

ARMIDE: La sévère Raison et le Devoir barbare Sur les Héros n'ont que trop de pouvoir.

RENAUD: J'en suis plus amoureux plus la Raison m'éclaire. Vous aimer, belle Armide, est mon premier devoir, Je fais ma gloire de vous plaire Et tout mon bonheur de vous voir.

ARMIDE: Que sous d'aimables lois mon âme est asservie!

RENAUD: Qu'il m'est doux de vous voir partager ma langueur!

ARMIDE: Qu'il m'est doux d'enchaîner un si fameux vainqueur!

RENAUD: Que mes fers sont dignes d'envie!

---

ARMIDE: I have need of Hades, I must consult with him, My heart needs solitude. The love I bear you causes unrest I feel it in my heart.

RENAUD: Armide, would you leave me?

ARMIDE: See in what place I leave you.

RENAUD: Can I see nothing but your allurements?

ARMIDE: Pleasures will follow you always.

RENAUD: Do they exist where you are absent?

ARMIDE: A dark presentiment haunts me, Announcing ills I would escape. The more our happiness enchants me, The more I dread its end.

RENAUD: Are you not afflicted by a vain terror, You who make all Hades tremble?

ARMIDE: You have taught me to know Love, Love teaches me to know Fear. Before you loved me, you burned for Glory, You sought her everywhere with matchless ardor: Glory is a rival whom I must always dread.

RENAUD: How foolish I was to believe That a vain laurel, given by victory, Was the most precious of gifts! All Glory's brilliant acclaims, Do they equal a glance from your eyes? Is there a boon, so charming, so rare, As that which fires my hope through Love?

ARMIDE: Stern Reason and inflexible Duty, These govern all heroes.

RENAUD: I am too much in love for Reason to teach me. To love you, my beautiful Armide, is my principal duty, It is my glory to please you, And all my happiness to see you, Armide.

ARMIDE: Under such gentle rule, how weak is my soul!

RENAUD: How sweet to see you share my leisure.

ARMIDE: How sweet to be enchanted by so famous a victor!

RENAUD: How enviable are my chain.

**RENAUD et ARMIDE:** (*ensembel*). Aimons-nous, tout nous y convie.
Ah! si vous aviez la rigueur
De m'ôter votre, coeur,
Vous m'ôteriez le vie.

**ARMIDE:** Témoins de notre amour extrême,
Vous, qui suivez mes lois dans ce séjour heureux,
Jusques à mon retour, par d'agréables jeux,
Occupez le Héros que j'aime.
(*Les Plaisirs, et une troupe d'Amants fortunés et d'Amantes heureuses, viennent divertir Renaud par des chants et par des danses*).

**RENAUD and ARMIDE:** (*together*). Let us love each other.
Ah! If your's was the power
To reclaim your heart,
You would take my life.

**ARMIDE:** Witnesses of our love extreme,
You, who here obey my laws,
Awaiting my return, with pleasant games,
Amuse the hero whom I love.
(*Pleasures, and a Troop of Happy Lovers come to entertain Renaud with songs and dances*).

## SCÈNE II

*Renaud, les Plaisirs, Troupe d'Amants Fortunês et d'Amantes Heureuses.*

**UN AMANT FORTUNÉ et LES CHOEURS:** Les plaisirs ont choisi pour asile
Ce séjour agréable et tranquille.
Que ces lieux sont charmants,
Pour les heureux amants!
(*Gavotte*).
C'est l'Amour qui retient dans ses chaînes
Mille oiseaux qu'en nos bois nuit et jour on entend
Si l'Amour ne causait que des peines,
Les oiseaux amoureux ne chanteraient pas tant.
(*Menuet, puis Sicilienne*).
Jeunes coeurs, tout vous est favorable.
Profitez d'un bonheur peu durable.
Dans l'hiver de nos ans, l'amour ne règne plus,
Les beaux jours que l'on perd sont pour jamais perdus.
Les plaisirs ont choisi pour asile
Ce séjour agréable et tranquille.
Que ces lieux sont charmants
Pour les heureux amants!

**RENAUD:** Allez, éloignez-vous de moi,
Doux Plaisirs, attendez qu'Armide vous ramène.
Sans la beauté qui me tient sous sa loi,
Rien ne me plaît, tout augmente ma peine.
Allez, éloignez-vous de moi,
Doux plaisirs, attendez qu'Armide vous ramène.
(*Les Plaisirs, les Amants fortunés et les Amantes heureuses se retirent*).

## SCÈNE III

*Renaud, Ubalde, Le Chevalier Danois.*

## SCENE II

*Renaud, Pleasures, Troop of Happy Lovers.*

**A HAPPY LOVER and CHORUS:** For its asylum, Pleasure has chosen
This tranquil, agreeable abode.
How charming is this place
For happy lovers.
(*Gavotte*).
It is Love which enchains
A thousand birds that sing, both night and day.
If love caused only trouble,
The feathered lover would sing much less.
(*Minuet, then a Sicilian dance*).
Youthful hearts, all favored,
Seize a fleeting happiness.
Love does not rule
The winter of our years.
Fine days, when lost are lost forever.
For its asylum, Pleasure hs chosen
This tranquil, agreeable abode.
How charming is this place
For happy Lovers!

**RENAUD:** Leave me, sweet Pleasures,
Await Armide's return.
Without that beauty nothing pleases me.
Leave me, sweet Pleasures,
Await Armide's return.
(*Pleasures and the Troop of Happy Lovers retire.*)

## SCENE III

*Renaud, Ubalde, The Danish Knight.*

**UBALDE:** Il est seul; profitons d'un temps si précieux.
(*Ubalde présente le bouclier de diamant aux yeux de Renaud*).

**RENAUD:** Que vois-je! Quel éclat me vient frapper les yeux?

**UBALDE:** Le ciel veut vous faire connaître
L'erreur dont vos sens sont séduits.

**RENAUD:** Ciel! quelie honte de paraître
Dans l'indigne état où je suis!

**UBALDE:** Notre général vous rappelle,
La Victoire vous garde une palme immortelle.
Tout doit presser votre retour.
De cent divers climats chacun court à la guerre,
Renaud seul, au bout de la Terre,
Caché dans un charmant séjour,
Veut-il suivre un honteux Amour?

**RENAUD:** Vains ornements d'une indigne mollesse,
Ne m'offrez plus vos frivoles attraits:
Restes honteux de ma faiblesse,
Allez, quittez-moi pour jamais.
(*Renaud arrache les guirlandes de fleurs et les autres ornements inutiles dont il est paré. Il reçoit le bouclier de diamants que lui donne Ubalde, et une épée que lui présente le Chevalier Danois*).

**LE CHEVALIER DANOIS:** Dérobez-vous aux pleurs d'Armide.
C'est l'unique danger dont votre âme intrépide
A besoin de se garantir.
Dans ces lieux enchantés la volupté préside,
Vous n'en sauriez trop tôt sortir.

**RANAUD:** Allons, hâtons-nous de partir.

## SCÈNE IV

*Armide, Renaud, Ubalde, Le Chevalier Danois.*

**ARMIDE:** (*suivant Renaud*). Renaud! Ciel! O mortelle peine!
Vous partez! Renaud! Vous partez!
Démons, suivez ses pas, volez, et l'arrêtez.
Hélas! tout me trahit, et ma puissance est vaine!
Renaud! Ciel! O mortelle peine!
Mes cris ne sont pas écoutés!
Vous partez! Renaud! vous partez!
(*Renaud s'arrête pour écouter Armide, qui continue à lui parler.*)
Si je ne vous plus, croyez-vous que je vive?
Ai-je pu mériter un si cruel tourment?
Au moins, comme ennemi, si ce n'est comme amant,
Emmenez Armide captive.
J'irai dans les combats, j'irai m'offrir aux coups

**UBALDE:** He's alone, let us seize the propitious moment. (*Ubalde holds the diamond shield before Renaud's eyes*).

**RENAUD:** What do I see! What dazzling light is this?

**UBALDE:** Heaven wills that you should know
The error cast over your senses.

**RENAUD:** Heavens! How ashamed am I to be
Seen thus attired!

**UBALDE:** Our general calls you,
Victory reserves immortal palms for you.
All must hasten your return.
From divers climates each one hastes to war,
Renaud alone, so far away,
A midst pleasant scenes conceared,
Would follow shameful Love?

**RENAUD:** Vain ornaments of a shameful leisure,
Your frivolous attractions cease from offering.
Hence, forever leave me.
(*Renaud tears off the garlands of flowers and other useless ornaments with which he is decked, he receives the diamond shield which Ubalde gives him and the sword presented by the Danish Knight*).

**THE DANISH KNIGHT:** Leave behind your Armide and her tears—
The only danger your intrepid soul fears.
Pleasure resides in such places as these.
The sooner you leave them the better.

**RENAUD:** Come, let us hasten.

## SCENE IV

*Armide, Renaud, Ubalde, The Danish Knight.*

**ARMIDE:** (*following Renaud*).
Renaud! O mortal pain!
You go! Renaud! You go!
Demons, follow in his footsteps, quick, detain him.
Alas! I am betrayed by all, my power is vain!
Renaud! O mortal pain!
My cries remain unheard!
You go! Renaud! you go!
(*Renaud stops to listen to Armide, who continues speaking to him.*)
If no more I see you, can I live?
How have I earned such cruel treatment?
If not my lover, as my enemy
Take Armide with you, a captive.
I will go to war, I'll stand between you
And the blows for you intended.
Renaud, if I can only follow you,

Qui seront destinés pour vous.
Renaud, pourvu que je vous suive,
Le sort le plus affreux me paraîtra
trop doux.

**RENAUD:** Armide, il est temps que
j'évite
Le péril trop chamant que je trouve
à vous voir.
La Gloire veut que je vous quitte,
Elle ordonne à l'Amour de céder au
Devoir.
Si vous souffrez, vous pouvez
croire
Que je m'éloigne à regret de vos
yeux,
Vous régnerez toujours dans ma
mémoire,
Vous serez après la Gloire
Ce que j'aimerai le mieux.

**ARMIDE:** Non, jamais de l'Amour
tu n'as senti le charme.
Tu te plais à causer de funestes
malheurs,
Tu m'entends soupirer, tu vois
couler mes pleurs,
Sans me rendre un soupir, san ver-
ser une larme.
Par les noeuds les plus doux je te
conjure en vain,
Tu suis un fier Devoir, tu veux qu'il
nous sépare.
Non, non, ton coeur n'a rien
d'humain,
Le coeur d'un tigre est moins bar-
bare.
Je mourrai si tu pars, et tu n'en peux
douter,
Ingrat, sans toi je ne puis vivre.
Mais après mon trépas ne crois pas
éviter
Mon ombre obstinée à te suivre.
Tu la verras s'armer contre ton co-
eur sans foi.
Tu la trouveras inflexible!
Comme tu l'as été pour moi;
Et sa fureur, s'il est possible
Egalera l'amour dont j'ai brûlé pour
toi . . .
Ah! la lumière m'est ravie!
Barbare, es-tu content?
Tu jouis, en partant.
Du plaisir de m'ôter la vie.
(*Armide tombe et s'évanouit.*)

The worst fate will seem to me but
sweet.

**RENAUD:** Armide, it's time I leave
behind
The far too charming peril of your
presence.
Glory bids me leave you,
She commands that Love should
yield to Duty.
If you suffer, then believe, Armide,
That I go with regret,
You always shall reign in my memo-
ry.
Next to Glory
I shall love you best.

**ARMIDE:** No, never have you felt
the charm of Love.
It pleases you to cause affliction,
My sighs you hear, my tears are
seen,
But you, hard hearted, sigh not, nor
weep in return.
By the tenderest ties I plead in vain,
You follow a vaunted Duty, you
obey gladly.
No, No, your heart has nothing hu-
man,
Less savage is the tiger's heart.
If you go I shall die, and well you
know
Ingrate, that without you I must
die.
But believe this, my shade shall
ever pursue you.
You shall see it armed against your
faithless heart.
You shall find it inflexible!
As you have been to me,
And its fury—be that possible—
Shall equal the love I bear you
Ah! the light has left me!
Rogue, are you content?
It pleases you in going,
To take from me my life.
(*Armide falls, fainting.*)

**RENAUD:** Trop malheureuse Armide, hélas!
Que ton destin est déplorable!

## SCÈNE V ET DERNIÈRE

**ARMIDE:** (*seule*). Le perfide Re-
naud me fuit,
Tout perfide qu'il est, mon lâche
coeur le suit.
Il me laisse mourante, il veut que je
périsse.
A regret je revois la clarté qui me
luit,
L'horreur de l'éternelle nuit
Cède à l'horreur de mon supplice.
Le perfide Renaud me fuit,
Tout perfide qu'il est, mon lâche
coeur le suit.
Quand le barbare éait en ma puis-
sance,
Que n'ai-je cru la Haine et la Ven-
geance!
Que n'ai-je suivi leurs transports!
Il m'échappe, il s'éloigne, il va
quitter ces bords,
Il brave l'Enfer et ma rage,
Il est déjà près du rivage,
Je fais pour m'y trainer d'inutiles ef-
forts
Traître, attends . . . je le tiens, je
tiens son coeur perfide.
Ah! je l'immole à ma fureur . . .
Que dis-je! où suis-je, hélas! Infor-
tunée Armide!
Où t'emporte une aveugle erreur?
L'espoir de la vengeance est le seul
qui me reste.
Fuyez, Plaisirs, fuyez, perdez tous
vos attraits.
Démons, détruisez ce palais.
Partons, et s'il le faut, que mon
amour funeste
Demeure enseveli dans ces lieux
pour jamais.
(*Les Démons détruisent le Palais
enchanté, et Armide part sur un
Char Volant*).

*FIN.*

**RENAUD:** Too unhappy Armide
alas!
How grievous is your lot!

## SCENE V AND LAST

**ARMIDE:** (*alone*). Perfidious Re-
naud had left me;
Perifidious though he be, my
wretched heart must follow him.
He leaves me dying, he wishes my
death;
With regret I see again the light of
day;
The horror of eternal night
Yields to the horror of my pain.
Perfidious Renaud has left me;
Perfidious though he may be, my
wretched heart must follow him.
When he was in my power,
Why thought I not of Hate and Ven-
geance!
Why followed not their transport!
He has escaped me, he has left these
shores;
He braves Hades and my wrath,
Already is he near the brink,
Useless are my efforts to restrain
him.
Traitor await . . . I hold him, I
hold his perfidious heart.
Ah! I immolate him to my
fury . . .
What say I! where am I, alas! Unfor-
tunate Armide!
Where does my blinding error lead?
Hope of vengeance is the only hope
remaining.
Hence, Pleasures, hence, all your
attractions hide.
Demons destroy this palace.
Let us leave it, henceforth let my
wretched love
Remain entombed here for ever.
(*The Demons destroy the en-
chanted Palace, and Armide
leaves in a flying Car*).

*THE END.*

# Roméo et Juliette (1867)

## Romeo and Juliet

MUSIC BY CHARLES GOUNOD ■ LIBRETTO BY JULES BARBIER & MICHEL CARRÉ ■ BASED ON THE PLAY BY WILLIAM SHAKESPEARE

---

This five-act opera, set to a libretto by Jules Barbier and Michel Carré and based on Shakespeare's tragedy, premiered at the Théâtre-Lyrique in Paris on April 27, 1867. Roméo, a Montague and thus an enemy of the Capulets, sneaks in to a Capulet ball wearing a mask. When he lays eyes on Juliette, a Capulet, he falls in love with her at once and she with him. Tybalt, Juliette's cousin, vows to seek vengeance. Roméo comes in secret to see Juliette, who waits for him on her balcony. Some Capulet servants catch him and try to kill him, but he escapes and returns later. The young lovers want to get married in spite of their families' enmity. Frére Laurent, Juliette's confessor, helps the young couple. Soon after the ceremony, a huge brawl erupts. Roméo tries to stop the fight between the Capulets and the Montagues, to no avail, refusing to take up Tybalt's challenge because of his love for Juliette. But when Mercutio is slain, he kills Typbalt in revenge. The Duke of Verona banishes him. Roméo spends the night with his bride before departing. Juliette's father tells her in Frére Laurent's presence that Tybalt's last request was for her to marry Count Paris. Frére Laurent comforts her and advises her to take a sleeping potion that will make everyone, except for Roméo, think she is dead. Roméo is the only one who will know differently. Juliette collapses at the wedding her family has arranged for her. Roméo, who fails to receive Frére Laurent's message explaining Juliette's "death," sneaks into the Capulet tomb to see his beloved one last time. He poisons himself; Juliette awakens. He dies, and as he does, she stabs herself with his dagger. They are united in death.

---

### Prologue.

**LE CHOEUR:** Vérone vit jadis deux familles rivales,
Les Montaigus, les Capulets,
De leurs guerres sans fin, à toutes deux la tales,
Ensanglanter le seuil de ses palais.
Comme un rayon vermeil brille en un ciel d'orage,
Juliette parut, et Roméo l'aima!
Et tous deux, oubliant le nom qui les outrage,
Un même amour les enflamma.
Sort funeste! aveugles colères!
Ces malheureux amants payèrent de leurs jours
La fin des haines séculaires
Qui virent naître leurs amours!

### Prologue.

**CHORUS:** There were once in Verona
Two rival families,
The Montagues and the Capulets.
By their endless wars,
To both fatal,
they stained their palaces with blood.
As a glittering ray in a cloudy sky
Juliette came and Romeo loved her;
Forgetting their family dissensions
The same love united them.
Sorrowful fate! Blind ill-fortune!
The unhappy lovers paid with their lives
For the hatred of centuries which had nurtured their love.

### ■ ACTE PREMIER.

### ■ ACT I.

#### SCÈNE I

#### SCENE I.

*Une galérie splendidement illuminée, chez les Capulets.*

*A ball magnificently decorated in Capulet's house.*

*Seigneurs et Dames, en dominos et masques.*

*Lords and Ladies in masks and dominoes.*

**CHOEUR:** L'heure s'envole,
Joyeuse et folle;
Au passage il faut la saisir!
Cueillons les roses
Pour nous écloses
Dans la joie et dans le plaisir!

**CHORUS:** Swift hours of pleasure
Pass to gay measure
Danced in the maze of glimmering feet;
While at the closes
Red wreck of roses
From our chaplets fall crushed but sweet!

**LES HOMMES:** Choeur fantasque
Des amours,
Sous le masque
De velours,
Ton empire
Nous attire
D'un sourire,
D'un regard!
Et, complice,
Le coeur glisse
Au caprice
Du hasard!

**LORDS:** Happy masks that kiss a fair maid,
Do but tell the grace they shade,
Half concealing,
Half revealing,
Love, in every charm arrayed!
Gleams of heaven—but sparely given—
Yet for these a heart is paid!

**LES FEMMES:** Nuit d'ivresse!
Folle nuit!
L'on nous presse,
L'on nous suit!
Le moins tendre
Va se rendre,
Et se prendre
Dans nos rêts.
De la belle
Qui l'appelle
Tout révèle
Les attraits.

**LADIES:** Night of fancy—lustrous night,
All your stars to love invite;
Sweet laugh calling,
Light foot falling,
And low cadence,
Sung by maidens,
Smooths a rough man to a woman's will!

**TOUS:** L'heure s'envole, etc.

**CHORUS:** Swift hours of pleasure, etc.

#### SCÈNE II

#### SCENE II.

*Les Mêmes, Tybalt, Pâris.*

*Paris, Tybalt, and the above.*

*(Tybalt et Pâris entrent en scène, leur masque à la main.)*

*(Enter Paris and Tybalt with their masks in their hands)*

**TYBALT:** Eh bien! cher Pâris, que vous semble
De la fête des Capulets?

**TYBALT:** Well, Paris, my friend, what do you think of the feast of the Capulets?

**PÂRIS:** Richesse et beauté tout ensemble
Sont les hôtes de ce palais.

**PARIS:** What earth holds of excelling beauty
Has assembled as a guest in these halls.

**TYBALT:** Vous n'en voyez pas la merveille; le trésor unique et sans prix Qu'on destine à l'heureux Pâris.

**PÂRIS:** Si mon coeur encore sommeille, Le moment est proche où l'amour Viendra l'éveiller à son tour.

**TYBALT:** (*souriant*). Il s'éveillera, je l'espère. Regardez! . . . la voici, conduite par son père.

## SCÈNE III

*Les Mêmes, Capulet, Juliette.*

(*Capulet entre en scène conduisant Juliette par la maison son aspect tout le monde se démasque.*)

**CAPULET:** Soyez les bienvenus, amis, dans ma maison! A cette fête de famille La joie est de saison! . . . Pareil jour vit naître ma fille; Mon coeur bat de plaisir encore en y songeant! . . . Mais excusez ma tendresse indiscrète! (*Présentant Juliette.*) Voici ma Juliette! . . . Accueillez-la d'un regard indulgent.

**LES HOMMES:** (*à demi-voix*). Ah! qu'elle est belle! On dirait une fleur nouvelle Qui s'épanouit au matin!

**LES FEMMES:** (*de même*). Ah! qu'lle est belle! Elle semble porter en elle Toutes les faveurs du destin! . . .

**TOUS:** (*à demi-voix*). Ah! qu'elle est belle! (*On entend le prélude d'un air de danse*).

**JULIET:** Ecoutez! écoutez! C'est le son des instruments joyeux; Qui nous appelle et nous convie! Ah! Tout un monde enchanté semble naître à mes yeux! Tout me fête et m'enivre, Tout me fête et m'enivre! Et mon âme ravie S'élance dans la vie, Comme un oiseau s'envole aux cieux!

**CAPULET:** Allons! jeunes gens! Allons! belles dames! Aux plus diligents. Ces yeux pleins des flammes. Ces yeux, ces yeux pleins de flammes! Nargue! Nargue! des censeurs qui grondent, qui grondent, qui grondent sans cesse! Fêtez la jeunesse! Fêtez la jeunesse! Fêtez la

**TYBALT:** Still you are thinking of just one, it seems, The marvel and pride of us all—Fariest Juliet—your promised bride!

**PARIS:** Ay! my heart ever dreams of her, And will dream, till, radiant and bright, She rises star-like on the dark of night!

**TYBALT:** Then you will awake—happy Paris! Lo! she comes—her father leads The timid maiden!

## SCENE III.

*Capulet, Juliet, and the above.*

(*Enter Capulet with Juliet, all the guests unmask.*)

**CAPULET:** I bid you welcome, gentlemen, To my house! And you, fair ladies; Tonight we hold an old accustomed feast. This, my child, I now commend unto you, A slip that has not seen the change Of many years. Of all earth's hopes She alone now is left me—my Juliet! Sweetest daughter! I pray you pardon me—A father's weak heart!

**LORDS:** (*in a low voice*) Ah! she is charming, No such beauty in all Verona, And our summer has no such flower!

**LADIES:** (*same as a bove*) Ah! she is charming, All the radiance of heaven indwelling, All the grace of earth for her dower!

**ALL:** Ah, she is charming, etc. (*Prelude of the dance heard.*)

**JULIET:** Listen all! listen all! It is the sound of joyous instruments; that calls us and bids us assemble, Ah! . . . The whole enchanted world, seems to be born in front of my eyes! All now fires me, all inspires me, All enflames and inspires me. Light to life now is flowing, Strange hopes are in me glowing. Bird-like the starry vault I'd dare For now my home seems lying there.

**CAPULET:** Come! gallant youths! Come! beautiful ladies! Come, champion, so bold. Your eyes filled with flames! Your eyes, your eyes filled with flames! Banish; banish each thought of care, That scolds us, us without ceasing. Celebrate youth! Celebrate youth! Celebrate

jeunesse: Et place aux danseurs! Qui reste à sa place Et ne danse pas De quelque disgrâce Fait l'aveu tout bas. O regret extrême! Quand j'étais moins vieux, Je guidais moi-même Vos ébats joyeux. Les douces paroles Ne me coûtaient rien. Que d'aveux frivoles Dont je me souviens! O folles années Qu'emporte le temps! O fleurs du printemps A jamais fanées! . . .

**LE CHOEUR:** Nargue des censeurs Qui grondent sans cesse! Fêtons la jeunesse! Et place aux danseurs! (*Tout le monde s'éloigne et circule dans les galéries sines, Juliette sort au bras de Pâris. Capulet et Tybalt suivant en causant. Roméo et Mercutio paraissent ave leurs amis.*)

## SCÈNE IV

*Roméo, Mercutio, Benvolio, et quelques de leurs amis.*)

**MERCUTIO:** La place est libre, mes amis! Pour un instant qu'il soit permis D'ôter son masque!

**ROMÉO:** Non! . . . non! vous l'avez promis; Soyons prudents! nul ne doit nous naître. Quittons cette maison sans affronter maître.

**MERCUTIO:** Bah! si les Capulets sont gens à se fâcher C'est lâcheté de nous cacher, (*Frappant sur son épée.*) Car nous avons tous là de quoi leur tenir tête!

**ROMÉO:** Mieux eût valu, ne pas nous mêler à la fête!

**MERCUTIO:** Pourquoi?

**ROMÉO:** J'ai fait un rêve!

**MERCUTIO:** O présage alarmant! La reine Mab t'a visité?

**ROMÉO:** Comment?

**MERCUTIO:** Mab, la reine des mensonges, Préside aux songes. Plus légère, plus légère que le vent Décevant, A travers l'espace, A travers la nuit, Elle passe, Elle fuit, Elle passe, Elle fuit. Son char, que l'atôme rapide Entraîne dans l'éther limpide, Fut fait d'une noisette vide

youth! Give pleasure its share. Ha! my mistresses—will you foot it now? If you do not—then your toes have corns, I'll vow! By're lady! my day For a measure is gone, Though gallant more gay Never vizor put on! To ladies' ear oft A love-tale I'd tell, And whispering soft, I'd please her right well! Gone! lady and lover—My beard now is hoar, I'll mask me no more My gay time is over! Come, gallant youths! Come! Give pleasure its share; Give pleasure its share.

**CHORUS:** Banish each thought of care that scolds without ceasing! Celebrate youth! And make way for the dancers! (*All the guests go off by the various entrances, Juliet leaning on Paris' arm. Capulet and Tybalt follow them. Enter Romeo, Mercutio, and Benvolio, with half a dozen friends.*)

## SCENE IV.

*Romeo, Mercutio, Benvolio, and friends.*

**MERCUTIO:** Al last we are alone, my friends! O beetle brows that blush for me, I now May be rid of you.

**ROMEO:** No, you have promised Be prudent still—that no one may suspect us! The Capulet's our foe—beware his anger!

**MERCUTIO:** Bah! If they think we come to scorn and jeer Their feast—why then we're not the cowards to hide! And should they question us, our swords shall give The answer!

**ROMEO:** Pray you, wait—My soul is sad with foreboding—

**MERCUTIO:** Why?

**ROMEO:** I had a dream!

**MERCUTIO:** Ah! but dreams often lie! So then Queen Mab has been with you?

**ROMEO:** Pardon?

**MERCUTIO:** Mab, the fairy queen of falsehood, presides over visions, Lighter than, lighter than the soft summer wind, Across time and space, Across the night, Journeying onward like a flash, Journeying onward like a flash. For atoms draw her, Up to poor sleeping mortals' noses,

Par Ver-de-Terre, le charron;
Les harnais, subtile dentelle,
Ont été découpés dans l'aile
De quelque verte sauterelle
Par son cocher, le moucheron;
Un os de grillon sert de manche
A son fouet, dont la mèche blanche
Est prise au rayon qui s'épanche
De Phoebé rassemblant sa cour;
Chaque nuit, dans cet équipage,
Mab visite sur son passage
L'epoux, qui rêve de veuvage,
Et l'amant, qui rêve d'amour!
A son approche, la coquette
Rêve d'atours et de toilette;
Le courtisan fait la courbette;
Le poète rim ses vers;
A l'avare, en son gîte sombre,
Elle offre des trésors sans nombre;
Et la liberté rit dans l'ombre
Au prisonnier chargé de fers!
Le soldat rêve d'embuscades,
De batailles et d'estocades;
Elle lui verse les rasades
Dont ses lauriers sont arrosés;
—Et toi qu'un soupir effarouche,
Quand tu reposes sur ta couche,
O vierge, elle effleure ta bouche,
Et te fait rêver de baisers!
Mab, la reine des mensonges, etc.

ROMÉO: Eh bien! . . . que
l'avertissement
Me vienne de Mab ou d'un autre,
Sous ce toit qui n'est pas le nôtre,
Je me sens attristé d'un noir pressentiment.

MERCUTIO: Ta tristesse, je le devine, Est de ne pas trouver ici ta Rosaline;
Cent autres dans ce bal te feront oublier
Ton fol amour d'écolier!
Viens! . . .

ROMÉO: (regardent au dehors).
Ah! voyez!

MERCUTIO: Qu'est-ce donc?

ROMÉO: Cette beauté céleste
Qui semble un rayon dans la nuit!

MERCUTIO: Le porte-respect qui
la suit
Est d'une beauté plus modeste!

ROMÉO: O trésor digne des cieux!
Quelle clarté soudaine a dessillé
mes yeux!
Je ne connaissais pas la beauté
véritable!

In a chariot then she reposes,
Made of a hazel-nut;
And the wagon-spokes, of the spinner's legs, slender and long;
The coachman, a small gray-coated gnat,
Who wields a cricket-bone whip,
filmed for a thong!
The traces are made of a small spider's web,
Collars of the moonshine's watery beam,
So she comes in royal state,
While we sleep and dream!
While he sleeps—the husband
dreaming of widowhood,
The lover dreaming of love,
And a better living to boot!
Then the miser in dreams beholds
Vain wealth that wicked Mab upholds,
And to a captive pining all alone,
Liberty smiles through bar and stone!
Over the neck of the soldier driving,
He dreams of swift foreign battle,
Of Spanish blade and cannon's rattle,
Then wakes—and swears a prayer or two!
To you Mab will come, gentle maiden,
Sleeping arrayed in your tender grace,
And, sly kisses bestowing on you,
Make you dream of love's kisses too!
Mab! Queen Mab, etc.

ROMEO: No more—Might the advice
Come from Mab or others,
In this home which is not ours.
My mind misgives me of some sad consequence.

MERCUTIO: Little marvel
Your sad demeanor. The pretty Rosaline
Is not among the dancers. But faces fair
There are here that, once you see them
Will make you think your swan is but a crow!
Come!

ROMEO: (looking off). Ah! Look!

MERCUTIO: What is it now?

ROMEO: Beauty that shows the torches
To burn more bright in the darkness!

MERCUTIO: The beldame that follows behind
Is not, by my word, so lovely!

ROMEO: Like a rich gem on an Ethiop's ear,
Her beauty hangs upon the cheek of night!
Oh, never till this hour

Ai-je aimé jusqu'ici? . . .

MERCUTIO: (en riant, à Benvolio
et aux autres jeunes gens).
Bon! Bon! voilà Rosaline au diable!
Et nous avions prévu ceci!
On la congédie
Sans plus de souci;
Et la comédie
Se termine ainsi!

TOUS: (moins Roméo, à demi-
voix, et en riant). On la congédie
Sans plus de souci, etc.
(Mercutio entraîne Roméo, au
moment où paraît Juliette suivie
de Gertrude.)

## SCÈNE V

Juliette, Gertrude.

JULIETTE: Voyons, nourrice, on
m'attend! parle vite!

GERTRUDE: Respirez un mo-
ment! . . . est-ce moi qu'on
évite,
Ou le comte Pâris que l'on
cherche?

JULIETTE: Pâris?

GERTRUDE: Vous aurez là, dit-on,
la perle des maris!

JULIETTE: (riant) Ah! ah! je songe
bien vraiment au mariage!

GERTRUDE: Par ma vertu! j'étais
marié à votre âge!

JULIETTE: Non, non; je ne veux
pas t'écouter plus longtemps;
Laisse mon âme à son prin-
temps!
Je veux vivre Dans le rêve qui
m'enivre ce jour encore! douce
flamme, Je te garde dans mon âme
Comme un trésor!
Cette ivresse
De jeunesse
Ne dure, hélas! qu'un jour!
Puis vient l'heure
Où l'on pleure
Le coeur cède à l'amour,
Et le bonheur fuit sans retour!
Loin de l'hiver morose
Laisse-moi sommeiller,
Et respirer la rose
Avant de l'effeuiller!
Je veux vivre, etc.
(Grégorio parait au fond et se ren-
contre avec Roméo.)

## SCÈNE VI

Les Mêmes, Grégorio, Roméo.

Have I met with true beauty! Did my
heart
Love them before? No—never till
now!

MERCUTIO: (In laughter, to Ben-
rolio and the other young gentle-
men).
Good!
Gone is Rosaline's dominion,
Dead the old desire lies!
The fair he groaned for, and would
gladly die,
With the tender Juliet matched, is
now not fair!

ALL: (except Roméo, half-voiced,
with laughter). Gone is Rosaline's
dominion, etc.
(Mercutio, Romeo, etc., exeunt
just as Juliet, followed by Gertrude, appears.)

## SCENE V.

Juliet, Gertrude.

JULIET: What is it you want to tell
me? Good nurse, speak!
Speak, I pray you!

GERTRUDE: Take breath! Is it me
you escape,
Or Paris you endeavor to meet?

JULIET: Paris!

GERTRUDE: A proper man, I think;
you've made a happy choice.

JULIET: (laughing). Ah, Ah! Good
nurse, my maiden heart
Thinks not of marriage.

GERTRUDE: Go to! go to!
At your age, I was married.

JULIET: No more! Leave me now, I
beg, to the fair dream
Of youth!
I want to live In the dream that ex-
hilarates me again today!
Sweet flames I am guarding in my
soul Like a treasure!
As in a fair dream enveloped,
Born of pure fantasy,
Spirits from fairy lands of old,
Come to me now!
Ah! forever would this gladness
Shine on me as brightly as now,
Would that never age and sadness
Threw their shade over my brow!
But short as day,
Youth passes away!
Then before the summer's failing,
Pluck the rose that blooms to die,
Love with its breath inhaling,
Love that steals in its odorous sigh!
In the calmness of a vision, etc.
(Gregorio enters at back and
meets Romeo.)

## SCENE VI.

(Romeo, Gregorio, and the
above)

**ROMÉO:** (*à Grégorio, en lui montrant Juliette*). Le nom de cette belle enfant?

**GRÉGORIO:** Vous l'ignorez? C'est Gertrude!

**GERTRUDE:** (*se retournant*). Plaît-il?

**GRÉGORIO:** (*à Gertrude*). Très-gracieuse dame,
Pour les soins du souper je crois qu'on vous réclame.

**GERTRUDE:** C'est bien! me voici!

**JULIETTE:** Va!
(*Gertrude sort avec Grégorio. Roméo arrête Juliette au moment où elle va sortir.*)

## SCENE VII

*Roméo, Juliette.*

**ROMÉO:** De grâce, demeurez!
(*Il se démasque et prend la main de Juliette.*) Ange adorable, Ma main coupable Profane, en l'osant toucher, La main divine Dont j'imagine Que une n'a droit d'approcher! Voila, je pense, La pénitence Qu'il convient de m'imposer, C'est qu'j'efface L'indigne trace De ma main par un baiser.

**JULIETTE:** Calmez vos craintes!
A ces étreintes
Du pélerin prosterné
Les saintes même,
Pourvu qu'il aime,
Ont d'avance pardonné;
Mais à sa bouche
La main qu'il touche
Doit prudemment refuser
Cette caresse
Enchanteresse
Qu'il implore en un baiser!

**ROMÉO:** Les saintes ont pourtant une bouche vermeille.

**JULIETTE:** Pour prier seulement.

**ROMÉO:** N'entendent-elles pas la voix qui leur conseille
Un arrêt plus clément?

**JULIETTE:** Aux prières d'amour leur coeur rest insensible
Même en les exauçant.

**ROMÉO:** Exaucez donc mes voeux, et gardez impassible
Votre front rougissant!
(*Il baise la main de Juliette.*)

**JULIETTE:** (*souriant*). Ah! je n'ai pu m'en défendre!
J'ai pris le péché pour moi!

**ROMÉO:** Pour apaiser votre émoi.
Vous plait-il de me le rendre?

**JULIETTE ET ROMÉO:** Non! je l'ai pris! . . . Laissez-le moi!
Vous l'avez pris! . . . rendez-le moi!

---

**ROMEO:** The name of that beautiful child?

**GREGORIO:** Easily told; that is Gertrude.

**GERTRUDE:** Who calls?

**GREGORIO:** (*to Gertrude*). Lady! they're seeking you; and the varlets Are alone without you to excite them.

**GERTRUDE:** Goodness! it's true!

**JULIET:** Go!
(*Juliet is following when Romeo restrains her.*)

## SCENE VII.

(*Romeo and Juliet*).

**ROMEO:** I pray you, do not go yet! Fair angel, my guilty hand profanes, To touch, The divine hand that I imagine; That no one is worthy of approaching! So then, I think, the punishment that should be imposed—A kiss, that effaces Unworthy traces This hand has left behind.

**JULIET:** Your hand, good pilgrim, this fine but wrongs,
For you blame it too much,
To pure devotion surely belongs,
Saintly palm that you may touch.
There are hands, sacred to pilgrim's greeting,
But, ah me! not such as this,
Palm to palm, not red lips meeting,
Is a holy palmer's kiss!

**ROMEO:** To palmer and to saint, have not lips too been given?

**JULIET:** Yes, but only for prayer!

**ROMEO:** Then grant my prayer, dear saint, or faith may else be driven
Into deepest despair!

**JULIET:** Know, the saints are never moved,
And if they grant a prayer, it is for the prayer's sake!

**ROMEO:** Then do not move, sweetest saint,
While the effect of my prayer,
I shall take from your lips!
(*He kisses her hand.*)

**JULIET:** (*smiling*). Ah! now my lips, from yours, burning,
Have the sin that they have taken.

**ROMEO:** O give that sin back again,
To my lips their fault returning.

**JULIET and ROMEO:** No, not again! no, not again!
O give the sin to me again!

---

## SCÈNE VIII

*Les Mêmes, Tybalt.*

**ROMÉO:** Quelqu'un! (*Il remet son masque.*)

**JULIETTE:** C'est mon cousin Tybalt.

**ROMÉO:** Eh! quoi! vous êtes? . . .

**JULIETTE:** La fille du seigneur Capulet.

**ROMÉO:** (*à part*). Dieu! . . .

**TYBALT:** (*s'avançant*). Pardon, Cousine! . . . nos amis déserteront nos fêtes,
Si vous fuyez ainsi leurs regards.
Venez donc!
(*Bas.*)
Quel est ce beau galant qui s'est masqué si vite
En me voyant venir?

**JULIETTE:** Je ne sais.

**TYBALT:** (*avec défiance*). On dirait qu'il m'évite!

**ROMÉO:** Dieu vous garde, seigneur. (*Il sort.*)

## SCÈNE IX

*Tybalt, Juliette, puis Capulet.*

**TYBALT:** Ah! je le reconnais à sa voix! . . . à ma haine!
C'est lui! C'est Roméo!

**JULIETTE:** (*à part*). Roméo!

**TYBALT:** Sur l'honneur,
Je punirai le traître, et sa mort est certaine!
(*Il sort.*)

**JULIETTE:** (*seule*). C'était Roméo!
Ah! je l'ai vu trop tôt sans le connaître!
La haine est le berceau de cet amour fatal!
C'en est fait, si je ne puis être
A lui, que le cercueil soit mon lit nuptial!
(*Elle s'éloigne lentement; les invités reparaissent.—Tybalt entre d'un côté avec Pâris, Roméo, Mercutio, Benvolio, et leurs amis masqués entrent de l'autre.*)

## SCÈNE X

*Tybalt, Pâris, Roméo, Mercutio, Benvolio, Invités, puis Capulet.*

**TYBALT:** (*apercevant Roméo*). Le voici!

**PÂRIS:** (*abordant Tybalt*). Qu'est-ce donc?

---

## SCENE VIII.

(*Tybalt, and the above.*)

**ROMEO:** Who comes?
(*Romeo remasks.*)

**JULIET:** Tybalt, my dear cousin!

**ROMEO:** Then say, who are you?

**JULIET:** Daughter
Of Capulet, sir, am I!

**ROMEO:** Ah!

**TYBALT:** (*coming down*). Pardon, sweet Juliet, though our sport
Be not yet at the best, still our guests will go,
And you are not there! Come away—come away!
(*Aside to Juliet.*)
And tell me true, sweet coz; Do you know
That strange pilgrim, who so quickly masked?

**JULIET:** No—not I!

**TYBALT:** (*with suspicion*) It would seem that he shuns me!

**ROMEO:** (*to Tybalt*). Sir, I bid you good night!
(*Exit.*)

## SCENE IX.

(*Tybalt, Juliet, afterwards Capulet.*)

**TYBALT:** Ah! I recognize his voice! It is he that I hate!
It's him! It's Romeo!
Even so—it is he, I'll swear!

**JULIET:** (*aside*). Romeo!

**TYBALT:** On my family's honor,
I'll punish the traitor, and his death is certain.
(*Exit.*)

**JULIET:** (*alone*).
It was Romeo, he said!
Ah! it was the only son of our great foe—
The cold grave then is to be my wedding-bed!
—Only love springing from my only hate!
Seen all too early—and known all too late!
(*She slowly withdraws; the guests reappear*).

## SCENE X.

(*Tybalt, Paris, Romeo, Mercutio, Benvolio, guests, afterwards Capulet.*)

**TYBALT:** (*Seeing Romeo*). There he stands!

**PARIS:** (*Approaching Tybalt*). What is it now?

**TYBALT:** (*lui montrant Roméo*). Roméo!
(*Tybalt va pour s'élancer vers le groupe dès qui rentre en scène; il lui montre Roméo; Capulet, d'un geste impérieux lui impose silence.*)

**ROMÉO:** (*à part*). Mon nom même Est un crime à ses yeux! O douleur! . . . Capulet est son père! et je l'aime!

**MERCUTIO:** (*bas à ses amis*). Voyez de quel air furieux Tybalt nous regarde! Un orage Est dans l'air!

**TYBALT:** Je tremble de rage!

**CAPULET:** (*à ses invités*). Quoi! partez-vous déjà! demeurez un instant! Un souper joyeux vous attend!

**TYBALT, PÂRIS ET QUELQUES JEUNES GENS:** Patience! patience! De cette mortelle offense Roméo, j'en fais serment, Subira le châtiment!

**MERCUTIO, BENVOLIO ET LEURS AMIS:** On nous observe! silence! Il faut user de prudence! N'attendons pas follement, Un funeste évènement!

**CAPULET:** (*à ses invités*). Que la fête recommence! Que l'on boive et que l'on danse! Nous autres, j'en fais serment, Nous dansions plus vaillamment!

**LE CHOEUR:** Que la fête recommence! Que l'on boive et que l'on danse! Le plaisir n'a qu'un moment, Terminons la nuit gaîment! (*Mercutio entraine Roméo; ils sont suivis de Benvolio et de leurs amis.*)

**TYBALT:** (*à demi-voix*). Il nous échappe! Qui veut me suivre! . . . —Je le frappe De mon gant au visage! (*Il se dispose à suivre Roméo avec Pâris et quelques jeunes gens.*)

**CAPULET:** (*qui s'est rapproché de Tybalt, à demi-voix*). Et moi, je ne veux pas D'esclandre, tu m'entends?. . . Laisse en paix ce jeune homme! Il me plaît d'ignorer de quel nom il se nomme! Je te défends de faire un pas! (*à ses invités.*) Allons! jeunes gens! Allons! belles dames! Aux plus diligents, Ces yeux pleins de flammes!

**TYBALT:** (*pointing off to Romeo*). Romeo's there! (*Tybalt is about to face the group of the Montagues when he is met by Capulet entering, who makes him silent at a sign.*)

**ROMEO:** (*aside*). To be Romeo is a crime in her eyes! fatal name! Capulet is her father; and I love her!

**MERCUTIO:** (*to his friends*). Beware— For see how with anger the fiery Tybalt is chafing: There's a storm brewing fast!

**TYBALT:** I burn for vengeance!

**CAPULET:** What! quit the floor so soon? No, then, gentlemen, Do not prepare to leave, for a trifling banquet awaits.

**TYBALT, PARIS, and FRIENDS:** Vengeance comes! Vengeance comes! And for this shameful intrusion, blood Alone shall make amends; death to Romeo I swear!

**BENVOLIO, MERCUTIO and FRIENDS:** See how they watch us! No, stir not—and use your wit more than valor; We heard the foe in their camp; let us not Wake their ire!

**CAPULET:** Rouse again the sound of pleasure, Crush the wine-cup, tread the measure, Time has been (I swear to you) When I danced and drank for two!

**CHORUS:** Rouse again the sound of pleasure, Crush the wine-cup, tread the measure, Youth will not endure, Nothing beyond the present's sure! (*Mercutio drags Romeo away, followed by Benvolio and friends. Exeunt.*)

**TYBALT:** Romeo will escape me! let who will, follow. I shall stroke his pretty face with my gauntlet. (*Makes as if to pursue Romeo.*)

**CAPULET:** (*aside to Tybalt*) Not so! I will not brook disorder! Do you hear? You shall not follow Romeo! What a plague it is to me what this youngster is called? From this place you shall not stir! (*To the guests.*) A hall, sirs, a hall! Lead forth now each maiden, Earth treading stars all, With bright beauty laden! Like to April on the heel

Nargue des rêveurs Qui grondent sans cesse, Fêtez la jeunesse, Et place aux danseurs!

**LE CHOEUR:** Nargue des rêveurs Qui grondent sans cesse, Fêtons la jeunesse, Et place aux danseurs! (*La toile tombe.*)

# ■ ACTE DEUXIÈME.

## *SCÈNE I*

*Un jardin. A gauche le pavillon habité par Juliette. La premier étage, une fenêtre avec un balcon. Au fond un balustrade dominant d'autres jardins.*

*Stéfano, Roméo.*

(*Stéfano, appuyé contre la balustrade du fond, tient une échelle de corde et aide Roméo à escalader la balustrade; puis il se retire en emportant l'échelle.*)

**ROMÉO:** (*seule*). O nuit sous tes ailes obscures Abrite moi!

**LA VOIX DE MERCUTIO:** (*au dehors*). Roméo! Roméo!

**ROMÉO:** C'est la voix de Mercutio! Celui-la se rit des blessures Qui n'en reçut jamais!

**MERCUTIO, BENVOLIO ET LEURS AMIS:** (*au dehors*). Mystérieux et sombre, Roméo ne nous entend pas! L'amour se plaît dans l'ombre; Puisse l'amour guider ses pas! (*Les voix s'éloignent.*)

**ROMÉO:** L'amour! . . . Oui, son ardeur a troublé tout mon être! (*La fenêtre de Juliette s'éclaire.*) Mais quelle soudaine clarté Resplendit à cette fenêtre! C'est la que dans la nuit rayonne sa beauté!

**ROMÉO:** Ah! lève toi soleil! fais pâlir les étoiles, qui, dans l'azur sans voiles, Brillent aux firmament. Ah! lève toi! ah! lève toi! parais! parais! astre pur et charmant! Elle rêve! elle dènoue Une boucle de cheveux qui vient caresser sa joue! Amour! Amour! porte lui mes voeux! Elle parle! Qu'elle est belle! Ah! je n'ai rien entendu! Mais ses yeux parlent pour elle, Et mon coeur a repondu! Ah! lève-toi, soleil! etc.

Of lame Winter pressing, Its coldness caressing, So love young hearts feel!

**CHORUS:** Like to April on the heel Of lame Winter pressing, Its coldness caressing, So love young hearts feel! (*The curtain falls.*)

# ■ ACT II.

## *SCENE I.*

*A garden. Juliet's apartments. Practicable window and balcony. At back a parapet overhanging the gardens.*

(*Stephano and Romeo.*)

(*Stephano, the page, discovered against the parapet, helping up Romeo by means of a rope ladder. Exit the page, bearing away the ladder.*)

**ROMEO:** O night! spread your pinions above me, And hide me now!

**MERCUTIO:** (*off*). Romeo! Romeo!

**ROMEO:** 'Tis Mercutio that mocking calls! Ever so He jests at scars that never felt a wound!

**MERCUTIO, BENVOLIO and CHORUS:** (*off*). Love sick, sad and pining, Here Romeo was seen to wend; May night, fond lovers shrining, Now to the pair a covert lend! (*The voices fade off.*)

**ROMEO:** Ah! it is love that has stirred all my being. (*A light is seen at the window.*) Soft! what is that light that so sudden and strange, Breaks from yonder window? O heart, It is the east and Juliet is the sun!

**ROMEO:** Rise, fairest sun in heaven! Pale the stars with your brightness, That over the vault at evening Shines with a feeble light.—Oh! rise again!—Oh! rise again;—and banish Night's dark shades, bid them vanish. She wakes, Ah! ever untwining From their bonds her tresses shining! If my prayer's, love, shall reach your hearing, Love; Love! All my fond vows bearing, Now she speaks. Ah! how lovely! What she said I have not heard, But her sparkling eyes speak for her and my heart responds Ah! fairest sun, arise. Etc. (*The window opens, Juliet comes onto the balcony. Romeo conceals himself.*)

## SCÈNE II

Roméo, Juliette.
(La fenêtre s'ouvre. Juliette paraît à son balcon. Roméo se cache dans l'ombre.)

JULIETTE: Hélas! . . . moi, le haïr! . . . haine aveugle et barbare!
O Roméo! pourquoi ce nom est-il le tien!
Abjure-le, ce nom fatal qui nous sépare,
Ou j'abjure le mien! . . .

ROMÉO: (s'avançant). Est-il vrai? . . . l'as-tu dit? . . . Ah! dissipe le doute
D'un coeur trop heureux!

JULIETTE: Qui m'écoute,
Et surprend mes secrets sous le voile des nuits.

ROMÉO: Je n'ose, en me nommant, te dire qui je suis!

JULIETTE: N'es-tu pas Roméo!

ROMÉO: Non! je ne veux plus l'être,
Si ce nom détesté me sépare de toi!
Pour t'aimer, laisse-moi renaître
Dans un autre que moi!

JULIETTE: Ah! Tu sais que la nuit te cache mon visage!
Tu le sais! . . . Si tes yeux en voyaient la rougeur.
Elle te rendrait témoignage
De la pureté de mon coeur? . . .
Adieu les vains
détours! . . . M'aimes-tu? Je devine
Ce que tu répondras. Ne fais pas de serments!
Phoebé, de ses rayons inconstants, j'imagine.
Eclaire le parjure et se rit des amants! . . .
Cher Roméo, dis-moi loyalement: je t'aime!
Et je te crois! . . . Et mon honneur
Se fie au tien, ô mon seigneur,
Comme tu peux te fier à moi-même! . . .
N'accuse pas mon coeur, dont tu sais le secret,
D'être léger, pour n'avoir pu se taire;
Mais accuse la nuit dont le voile indiscret
A trahi le mistère!

ROMÉO: Devant Dieu qui m'entend, je t'engage ma foi!

JULIETTE: Ecoute! . . . on vient!
. . . Silence! . . . éloigne-toi! . . .
(Roméo s'éloigne et disparait sous les arbres.—Juliette sa retire du balcon.)

## SCENE II.

(Romeo and Juliet.)

JULIET: Ah, me!—And still I love him!
Romeo, why are you Romeo?
Refuse then your name, for it is no part,
My love, of you! What rose we call
By any other name would smell as sweetly;
You are no foe, it is your name!

ROMEO: Can it be
That you are mine? Romeo
I never more will be!

JULIET: Who are you, say,
That, be-screened by the night,
So stumbles on my dream?

ROMEO: I do not know how
To tell you who I am by name.

JULIET: You are Romeo, I know!

ROMEO: No,
Never shall I be known again, dear saint,
By a name that is a foe to you!
Yet, oh, speak!—speak to my soul, bright angel,
To the night you are glorious, as a messenger from heaven!

JULIET: Ah! you know the mask of night
Is on my face,—or my brow would be red
With a maidenly blush for the words
I've spoken to you; wherefore yet deny
What I've said! then, compliment, farewell!
Do you love me?
If so, answer me, yes,
Swear not by the moon—
the inconstant moon
That changes monthly in circled orb;
But by your gracious self, and the oath I'll believe!
If you love me—pronounce it faithfully.
'I love you!'—and I am yours!
O impute not to light love
My passion so true, which the night has discovered!

ROMEO: Ah! my heart is true—and it is all, love, for you!

JULIET: But hearken!—a noise, ah, Romeo
Fly, if they come.
(Exit from balcony.)
(Romeo hides among the trees.)

## SCÈNE III

Grégorio, quelques valets, puis Gertrude.

(Grégorio et les valets entrent en scène avec des lanternes sourdes à la main.)

GRÉGORIO Et Les VALETS: Personne! personne!
Le page aura fui!
Au diable on le donne!
Le diable est pour lui!

GRÉGORIO: Le fourbe, le traître
Attendait son maître!
Le destin jaloux
L'arrache à nos coups;
Et demain peut-être
Il rira de nous!

GRÉGORIO Et Les VALETS: Personne! personne, etc.

GERTRUDE: (entrant en scène). De qui parlez-vous donc?

GRÉGORIO: D'un page
Des Montaigus—Maître et valet,
En passant notre seuil, ont osé faire outrage
Au seigneur Capulet.

GERTRUDE: Vous moquez-vous?

GRÉGORIO: Non, sur ma tête!
Un des Montaigus s'est permis
De venir avec ses amis
A notre fête!

GERTRUDE Et Les VALETS: Un Montaigu!

LES VALETS: (à Gertrude) Est-ce pour vos beaux yeux que le traître est venu?

GERTRUDE: Qu'il vienne encore, et sur ma vie!
Je vous le ferai marcher droit,
Si droit, qu'il n'aura pas envie
De recommencer!

GRÉGORIO: On vous croit!

LES VALETS: (riant). Pour cela, nourrice, on vous croit.

GRÉGORIO Et Les VALETS:
Bonne nuit, charmante nourrice!
Joignez la grace à vos vertus!
Que le ciel vous bénisse,
Et confonde les Montaigus!
(Grégorio et les valets s'éloignent.)

## SCÈNE IV

Gertrude, puis Juliette.

GERTRUDE: Béni soit le bâton qui tôt ou tard me venge
De ces coquins!

JULIETTE: (paraissant sur le seuil du pavillon). C'est toi, Gertrude?

GERTRUDE: Oui, mon bel ange!
Mais comment à cette heure
Ne reposez-vous pas?

JULIETTE: Je t'attendais! . . .

GERTRUDE: Rentrons!

## SCENE III.

(Gregorio, Servants, then Gertrude.)

(Gregorio enters with retainers, all have lanterns in their hands.)

GREGORIO and RETAINERS:
There's no one—there's no one,
The page has fled,
Satan his patron
Has protected him.

GREGORIO: The sorry, scurvy knave
Was waiting for his master!
Jealous fortune
Saved him from our blows;
He will tell tomorrow
How the slip he gave!

CHORUS: There's no one—there's no one! Etc.

GERTRUDE: (entering). Whom are you speaking of!

GREGORIO: Of a page of the Montagues!
Page and master have dared
To outrage Capulet,
In passing this door!

GERTRUDE: You are mad!

GREGORIO: No! By heavens!
With his friends, a Montague
Has come to this festival!

GERTRUDE and SERVANTS: One of the Montagues!

THE SERVANTS: (to Gertrude). Has love for you, Gertrude,
Brought him here?

GERTRUDE: Let him come again, and on my life
I will so well receive him
That he no more will fancy to return!

GREGORIO: This we believe.

SERVANTS: (laughing). This we believe!

GREGORIO and SERVANTS:
Good night, charming nurse!
May heaven bless your virtues,
And confound the Montagues!
(Gregorio and Servants exeunt.)

## SCENE IV.

(Gertrude, then Juliet.)

GERTRUDE: Blessed be the one
Who would avenge me
Of those rascals! . . .

JULIET: (appears at the door of the pavillon). Is it you, Gertrude?

GERTRUDE: Yes, my angel!
But how is it you aren't sleeping
At this time of night?

JULIET: I was waiting for you!

GERTRUDE: Come in!

JULIETTE: Ne gronde pas!
(*Elle jette un regard autour d'elle et rentre dans le pavillon, suivie de Gertrude. Roméo reparait.*)

## SCÈNE V

*Roméo, puis Juliette.*

ROMÉO: O nuit divine! je t'implore!
Laisse mon coeur à ce rêve enchanté!
Je crains de m'éveiller et n'ose croire encore
A sa réalité!

JULIETTE: (*reparaissant sur le seuil du pavillon, à demi-voix*). Roméo!

ROMÉO: (*se retournant*). Douce amie!

JULIETTE: (*l'arrêtant du geste et toujours sur le seuil*). Un seul mot! puis adieu!
Quelqu'un ira demain te trouver! . . . Sur ton âme,
Si tu me veux pour femme
Fais-moi dire quelque jour, à quelle heure, en quel lieu
Notre union sera bénie!
Alors, ô mon seigneur, sois mon unique loi!
Je te livre ma vie entière, et je renie
Tout ce qui n'est pas toi!
Mais, si ta tendresse
Ne veut de moi que de folles amours . . .
Ah! je t'en conjure alors
Par cette heure d'ivresse,
Ne me revois plus, et me laisse
A la douleur qui remplira mes jours!

ROMÉO: (*à genoux devant Juliette*). Ah! je te l'ai dit! . . . je t'adore!
Dissipe ma nuit! sois l'aurore
Où va mon coeur, où vont mes yeux!
Dispose en reine de ma vie!
Verse à mon âme inassouvie
Toute la lumière des cieux!

JULIETTE: On m'appelle!

ROMÉO: (*se relevant et saisissant la main de Juliette*) Ah! Déjà!

JULIETTE: Pars! Je tremble
Qu'on ne nous voie ensemble!
Je viens!

ROMÉO: Écoute-moi!

JULIETTE: Plus bas!

ROMÉO: (*attirant Juliette à lui l'amenant en scène*). Non! non! l'on ne t'appelle pas.

JULIETTE: Plus bas! Parle plus bas!

ROMÉO: Ah! ne fuis pas encore! Ah! ne fuis pas encore! Laisse, laisse ma main s'oublier dans ta main!

---

JULIET: Pray do not scold!
(*She looks around and, followed by Gertrude, steps inside, Romeo reappears.*)

## SCENE V.

(*Romeo, then Juliet.*)

ROMEO: Oh blessed night! I am fearful,
Being in night, this is all but a dream,
That, waking, I may find too flattering sweet,
To bide the dawn.
(*Enter Juliet from house.*)

JULIET: (*in a low voice*). Romeo!

ROMEO: (*turning around*). Speak, my dearest!

JULIET: (*stopping him*). But a word,
Then farewell!
If the faith you pledge be true,
If you want me as your wife,
The tomorrow, my love, send a message to me,
Telling me where and when the rite of marriage will be performed
Then all I have, my lord,
I'll lay low at your feet; through the whole world
I'll follow your steps, though my kinsmen,
Dearest, should say no!
If you are feigning true love,
And your vows all are vain,
I do beseech you then
Cease your wooing and leave me—
Leave me to my grief that will always fill my days!

ROMEO: (*kneeling before Juliet*).
Do not doubt my affection,
For so thrive my soul, I do love you!
And my life is in your love;
Like a queen dispose of my life!
Fill my unsatiated soul
With all the bliss of the heavens!

JULIET: She is calling!

ROMEO: (*seizing Juliet's hand*). Ah, not yet!

JULIET: Go! I tremble!
Someone might see us together!
I come!

ROMEO: A moment more!

JULIET: Speak low.

ROMEO: (*drawing Juliet to him*). No! no! they don't call you!

JULIET: Beware! I pray you, beware!

ROMEO: Ah! do not flee yet! Ah! do not flee yet! Let me, let me once more kiss your dear hand.

---

JULIETTE: Ah! l'on peut nous surprendre! Ah! l'on peut nous surprendre! Laisse, laisse ma main s'échapper de ta main. Adieu!

ROMÉO: Adieu!

JULIETTE: Adieu!

LES DEUX: Adieu! De cet adieu si douce est la tristesse Que je voudrais te dire adieu jusqu'a demain!

JULIETTE: Maintenant, je t'en supplie, Pars!

ROMÉO: Ah! cruelle! . . .
(*Roméo s'en va involontairement, elle lui fait signe à revenir.*)

JULIETTE: Pourquoi?
Te rappelais-je, ô folie?
A peine es-tu près de moi
Que soudain mon coeur l'oublie!
Je te voudrais parti, pas trop loin cependant
Comme un oiseau captif que la main d'un enfant
Tient enchaîné d'un fil de soie,
A peine vole-t-il, dans l'espace emporté,
Que l'enfant le remène avec des cris de joie,
Tant son amour jaloux lui plaint la liberté!

ROMÉO: Ah! ne fuis pas encore!

JULIETTE: Hélas! il le faut! Adieu!

ENSEMBLE: Adieu! De cet adieu si douce est la tristesse,
Que je voudrais te dire adieu jusqu'à demain!

JULIETTE: Adieu, mille fois! . . .
(*elle s'échappe des bras de Roméo et rentre dans le pavillon*).

ROMÉO: (*seule*). Va! . . . repose en paix! sommeille!
Qu'un sourire d'enfant sur ta bouche vermeille.
Vienne doucement se poser! . . .
Et, murmurant encore: Je t'aime! à ton oreille,
Que la brise des nuits te porte ce baiser! (*Il s'éloigne.—La toile tombe.*)

---

JULIET: Silence, a step is near us, someone, I fear will hear us, Let me, let me at least take my hand from your keeping. Good night!

ROMEO: Good night!

JULIET: Good night!

BOTH: Good night! Dearest, this sweet good night is such sorrow, That I should say, good night, good night—till it be dawn.

JULIET: Now indeed, I do entreat you—go!

ROMEO: Ah! cruel one! . . .
(*Is going, when she beckons him involuntarily to return.*)

JULIET: For what do I recall thee?
Ah, I know not! and when you're near me,
All the less do I remember. Yes!
I would have you gone, but no further from me,
Than hops the captive bird from lady's idle hand,
With silken gyves its flight restraining,
And as she plucks it back with a gentle command,
So, if you were my bird within my bower remaining,
I too would hold you captive, bound with silken hand!

ROMEO: Ah, might I stay forever?

JULIET: Alas, we must part! Farewell!

BOTH: Farewell, parting from you is, oh, so sweet a sorrow, That I could say 'good night' till dawn!

JULIET: Good night, O my love!
(*withdraws from Romeo's arms and exit to the house.*)

ROMEO: (*alone.*) Peaceful be your repose! . . . Sleep!
Let a youthful smile of thy rosy lips Whisper again! I love you! . . .
Let the night breeze bring this kiss to you.
(*Exit. Curtain falls.*)

---

## ■ ACTE TROISIÈME.

## SCÈNE I

*La cellule du Frère Laurent.*

*Frère Laurent, Roméo.*

ROMÉO: Mon père, Dieu vous garde! . . .

---

## ■ ACT III.

## SCENE I.

*The cell of Frair Lawrence.*

(*Friar Lawrence and Romeo.*)

ROMEO: Holy Father, may God have you in His mercy.

# Act III, Scene I

**FRÈRE LAURENT:** Eh! quoi! le jour à peine
Se lève, et le sommeil te fuit!
Quel espoir vers moi te conduit?
Quel amoureux souci t'amène?

**ROMÉO:** Vous l'avez deviné, mon père! c'est l'amour.

**FRÈRE LAURENT:** Eh! quoi! l'indigne Rosaline? . . .

**ROMÉO:** Quel nom prononcez-vous? Je ne le connais pas!
L'oeil des élus s'ouvrant à la clarté divine
Se s'ouvient-il encore des ombres d'ici-bas?
Aime-t-on Rosaline, ayant vu Juliette?

**FRÈRE LAURENT:** Quoi! . . . Juliette Capulet?
(*Juliette parait suivie de Gertrude.*)

## SCÈNE II

*Les Mêmes, Juliette, Gertrude.*

**ROMÉO:** La voici!

**JULIETTE:** (*s'élançant dans les bras de Roméo*). Roméo! . . .

**ROMÉO:** Mon âme t'appelait!
Je te vois! . . . ma bouche est muette! . . .

**JULIETTE:** (*à Frère Laurent*). Mon père, voici mon époux;
Vous connaissez ce coeur que je lui donne,
A son amour je m'abandonne.
Devant le ciel unissons-nous!

**FRÈRE LAURENT:** Oui! dussé-je affronter une aveugle colère
Je vous prêterai mon secours.
Puisse de vos maisons la haine séculaire,
S'éteindre en vos jeunes amours!

**ROMÉO:** (*à Gertrude*). Toi veille au dehors! . . .
(*Gertrude sort.*)

## SCÈNE III

*Roméo, Juliette, Frère Laurent.*

**FRÈRE LAURENT:** Témoin de vos promesses,
Gardien de vos tendresses.
Que le Seigneur soit avec vous!
A genoux!

**ROMÉO ET JULIETTE:** A genoux!
(*Ils s'agenouillent.*)

**FRÈRE LAURENT:** Dieu, qui fit l'homme à ton image,
Et de sa chair et de son sang
Créas la femme, et, l'unissant
A l'homme par le mariage,
Consacras du haut de Sion
Leur inséparable union! . . .

---

**LAWRENCE:** Romeo! Why do you come so early?
What brings you to me?
Are you uproused by some secret care,
Or is it love alone that brings you?

**ROMEO:** You have guessed right, holy father,
It is love.

**LAWRENCE:** How! Rosaline?

**ROMEO:** I do not know the name you pronounce,
Shall then the eye
That opens on the light of morning, weep,
With fond regret, the darkness that has fled!
Rosaline is no match, I say,
For my fairest Juliet.

**LAWRENCE:** What is it then, Juliet Capulet?
(*Juliet enters, followed by Gertrude.*)

## SCENE II.

(*The above, Juliet and Gertrude.*)

**ROMEO:** Lo! She comes!

**JULIET:** (*throwing herself into Romeo's arms*). Romeo!

**ROMEO:** My heart was calling you!
You are here now! I can speak no more!

**JULIET:** (*to Lawrence*). My father!
It is marriage we seek;
To none but Romeo shall I ever be wedded,
So we come to seek your office,
That holy church makes us one!

**LAWRENCE:** Strange! that children of two rival houses
Should marry; but in this your help
I shall prove;
Who knows this match may bind the foes
Together, and turn all their rancor to love!

**ROMEO:** (*to Gertrude*). Nurse, wait outside.
(*Exit Gertrude.*)

## SCENE III.

(*Romeo, Juliet, Friar Lawrence.*)

**LAWRENCE:** Guardian of your love,
And of your promises,
May the Lord be with you!
Let us pray.

**ROMEO and JULIET:** Let us pray.
(*They kneel.*)

**LAWRENCE:** God, who made man to his image,
Also created the woman,
And uniting them both
By the scared links of marriage,
On the heights of Sion,
Consecrated their inseparable

---

Regard d'un oeil favorable
Ta créature misérable
Qui se prosterne devant toi! . . .

**ROMÉO ET JULIETTE:** Seigneur, nous promettons d'orbéir à tu loi.

**FRÈRE LAURENT:** Entends ma prière fervente!
Fais que le joug de ta servante
Soit un joug d'amour et de paix!
Que la vertu soit sa richesse,
Que pour soutenir sa faiblesse
Elle arme son coeur du devoin.

**ROMÉO ET JULIETTE:** Seigneur!
Sois mon appui,
Sois mon espoir!

**FRÈRE LAURENT:** Que leur vieillesse heureuse
voie leurs enfants marchant dans ta loi,
Et les enfants de leurs enfants!

**ROMÉO ET JULIETTE:** Seigneur! du noir péché c'est toi qui nous défends!

**FRÈRE LAURENT:** Que ce couple chaste et fidèle,
Uni dans la vie éternelle,
Parvienne au royaume des cieux! . . .

**ROMÉO ET JULIETTE:** Seigneur, sur notre amour daigne abaisser les yeux!

**FRÈRE LAURENT:** Roméo, tu choisis Juliette pour femme?

**ROMÉO:** Oui, mon père!

**FRÈRE LAURENT:** (*à Juliette*). Tu prends Roméo pour époux?

**JULIETTE:** Oui, mon père.
(*Roméo et Juliette échange leurs anneaux.*)

**FRÈRE LAURENT:** (*mettant la main de Juliette dans celle de Roméo*). Devant Dieu qui lit dans votre âme,
Je vous unis! . . . Relevez-vous!
(*Roméo et Juliette se relèvant.*)

## SCÈNE IV

*Les Mêmes, Gertrude.*

(*Roméo et Juliette dans les bras l'un de l'autre.*)

**ENSEMBLE:** O pur bonheur! ô joie immense!
Le ciel reçoit nos serments amoureux!
Dieu de bonté, Dieu de clémence,
Sois béni par deux coeurs heureux!
(*Roméo et Juliette se séparent.—
Juliette sort avec Gertrude.—
Roméo sort avec Frère Laurent.*)

## SCÈNE V

*Une rue. A gauche la maison des Capulets.*

---

union.
O Lord, in your mercy,
Cast a favorable eye on them!
Who bows before your throne!

**ROMEO and JULIET:** O Lord, meekly we promise your laws to obey.

**LAWRENCE:** Support them in each good endeavor,
Grant that this union may be ever
One of peaceful joy and of love.
Bless them with virture's heavenly riches,
Make them pure and holy, O Lord,
In hearts like spirits above.

**ROMEO and JULIET:** O Lord, be our leader,
be our love.

**LAWRENCE:** Then, as old age advances,
May they behold their children walk uprightly,
As in your fear, from day to day.

**ROMEO and JULIET:** O Lord, preserve, we pray, our souls from error's way.

**LAWRENCE:** And when life and love both are over,
And death breaks the dream of the lover,
O grant that they yet meet above!

**ROMEO and JULIET:** O father of all! deign now to bless our love!

**LAWRENCE:** Romeo, say, for your wife you take now this woman!

**ROMEO:** Yes, my father!

**LAWRENCE:** (*to Juliet*). For your husband you take this man?

**JULIET:** Yes, my father!
(*They exchange rings.*)

**LAWRENCE:** (*joining their bands together*). In his name who marriage ordains,
I join your hands—be man and wife!
(*Romeo and Juliet rise.*)

## SCENE IV.

(*The above, Gertrude.*)

(*Romeo and Juliet embrace each other.*)

**ALL:** Holy father, O heavenly bliss,
Heaven has received our oaths!
To hearts now one, no more to sever!
Bless your name, O Lord.
(*Romeo and Juliet exeunt separately, Juliet with Gertrude, Romeo with Lawrence.*)

## SCENE V.

*A street in Verona. Capulet's house at left.*

*Stephano, seul*

**STEPHANO:** Depuis hier je cherche en vain mon maître! Est-il encor chez vous, ô Capulets? Voyons un peu si vos dignes valets A ma voix ce matin oseront reparaître!

*(Il fait mine de pincer de la guitare sur son épée.)*

Que fais-tu, blanche tourterelle, Dans ce nid de vautours? Quelque jour, déplayant ton aîle, Tu suivras les amours! Aux vautours il faut la bataille Pour frapper d'estoc et de taille, Leurs becs sont aiguisés! Laisse-là ces oiseaux de proie, Tourterelle qui fais ta joie Des amoureux baisers! . . . Gardez bien la belle! Qui vivra verra! Votre tourterelle Vous échappera! Un ramier, loin du vert bocage Par l'amour attiré, A l'entour de ce nid sauvage A, je crois, soupiré. Les vautours sont à la curée: Leurs chansons, que fuit Cythérée, Résonnent à grand bruit! Cependant qu'en leur douce ivresse Nos amants content leur tendresse Aux astres de la nuit! . . . Gardez bien la belle! Qui vivra verra! Votre tourterelle Vous échappera!

---

## SCÈNE VI

*Stephano, Grégorio, Valets.*

**STEPHANO:** Ah! ah! voici nos gens! . . .

**GRÉGORIO:** Qui diable à notre porte S'en vient roucouler de la sorte?

**STEPHANO:** *(à part, en riant).* La chanson leur déplaît!

**GRÉGORIO:** *(aux autres valets).* Mais parblue! n'est-ce point Celui que nous chassions heir la dague au poing?

**LES VALETS:** C'est lui-même!

**GRÉGORIO:** L'audace est forte!

**STEPHANO:** Gardez bien la belle!

**GRÉGORIO:** Est-ce pour nous narguer, mon jeune camarade, Que vous nous régalez de votre sérénade!

**STEPHANO:** J'aime la musique!

---

*(Enter Stephano)*

**STEPHANO:** Since yesterday, I've sought my master in vain. O Capulet, perchance he yet honors your house. I'll sing a tune, so the servants will rouse.

*(He seems to play guitar on his shoulder.)*

What do you do, white turtledove, In this nest of vultures? One day fly with outspread pinions, You follow the lovers! You battle with the vultures, Young, alone, with claws they will wound thee, Talons strong, and cruel beak. Unlike yours, soft and true and slender, Unlike yours, laid to lips more tender, In kisses warm and long! See you guard her safely, They that live will know; Or your dove may flutter From her cage and go! Now it happened that a ring-dove flying From his wood-land so green, To that eyrie came one evening sighing For her young love, I ween! Over a banquet of prey they'd mangled, In the vale the vultures loud wrangled, Harsh rose their cry afar; But the doves, for the past atoning, Heeded not, while their love-vows moaning; And rose the first bright star! See you guard her safely, They that live will know; Or your dove may flutter From her cage and go!

---

## SCENE VI.

*(Stephano, Gregorio and retainers)*

**STEPHANO:** At last the warriors come!

**GREGORIO:** In truth I'm in a passion! Disturbed in this fashion!

**STEPHANO:** *(aside, laughing).* They object to my song!

**GREGORIO:** What! By god It is the page, that, sword in hand, last night We hunted to the door!

**CHORUS:** It is the rascal!

**GREGORIO:** Audacious varlet!

**STEPHANO:** See you guard her safely!

**GREGORIO:** Do you seek a quarrel, O most alarming minstrel? And is it to provoke You serenade with songs so charming?

**STEPHANO:** I'm fond of music!

---

**GRÉGORIO:** C'est clair; On t'aura sur le dos, en pareille équipée, Cassé ta guitare, mon cher!

**STEPHANO:** Pour guitare j'ai mon épée, Et j'en sais jouer plus d'un air.

**GRÉGORIO:** Ah! pardieu! pour cette musique On peut te donner la réplique!

**STEPHANO:** *(dégainant).* Viens donc en prendre une leçon!

**GRÉGORIO:** *(dégainant).* En garde!

**LES VALETS:** *(riant).* Ecoutons leur chanson!

*(Pendant que Grégorio et Stephano se battent.)*

Quelle rage! Vertudieu! Bon courage, Et franc jeu! Voyez comme Cet enfant Contre un homme Se défend! Fine lame, Sur mon âme! Il se bat En soldat!

*(Mercutio et Benvolio entrent en scène.)*

---

## SCÈNE VII

*Les Mêmes, Mercutio, Benvolio, puis Tybalt, Pâris, Roméo et Partisans des deux maisons.*

**MERCUTIO:** Attaquer un enfant!

*(Il tire l'épée et se jette entre les combattants.)*

Morbleu! c'est une honte Digne des Capulets! Tels maîtres, tels valets!

*(Tybalt entre en scène suivi de Pâris et de quelques amis.)*

**TYBALT:** Vous avez la parole prompte, Monsieur!

**MERCUTIO:** Moins prompte que le bras!

**TYBALT:** C'est ce qu'il faudrait voir!

**MERCUTIO:** C'est ce que tu verras!

*(Au moment où ils se mettent en garde, Roméo entre en scène et se précipite entre eux.)*

**ROMÉO:** Arrêtez!

**MERCUTIO:** Roméo!

**TYBALT:** Roméo! Son démon me l'amène!

*(A Mercutio.)*

Permettez que sur vous je lui donne le pas!

*(A Roméo.)*

---

**GREGORIO:** Of course—of course! Yet I've known for such pranks the gay serenader Has had his guitar broke in two!

**STEPHANO:** Ah! Very likely—but then, good fellow, My guitar's a sword, hard to break!

**GREGORIO:** Save my soul! if that is your music, Perhaps we may give you the answer!

**STEPHANO:** *(drawing).* Let's try then, if we are in tune!

**GREGORIO:** *(drawing).* Have at you!

*(They fight.)*

**CHORUS:** *(laughing.)* We will hear how they play! How they parry —how they thrust, Quick as lightning; soon shall one bite the dust! Strong the boy is in defense; Faith! the issue's in suspense! Was a soldier ever bolder, Than this slip of a boy?

*(Enter Mercutio and Benvolio.)*

---

## SCENE VII.

*(The above, Mercutio, Benvolio, then Tybalt, Paris, Romeo and retainers of the two houses.)*

**MERCUTIO:** So you draw on a child! Go to! It's an achievement worthy of Capulet's fame: Like master—so, like man!

*(Enter Tybalt, Paris and friends.)*

**TYBALT:** *(drawing, to Mercutio).* Sir, your word Seems over-ready to me!

**MERCUTIO:** We'll join it With a blow!

**TYBALT:** You'll find me apt enough.

**MERCUTIO:** That I can prove at once!

*(They engage. Romeo enters hastily and throws himself between them.)*

**ROMEO:** Stop!

**MERCUTIO:** Romeo!

**TYBALT:** Romeo here! It is fate that has led him!

*(To Mercutio, with ironical politeness.)*

For a time peace be with you; here comes

---

Allons! Vil Montaigu! . . . flamberge
au vent! . . . dégaîne! . . .
Toi qui nous insultas jusqu'en no-
tre maison,
C'est toi qui porteras la peine
De cette indigne trahison!
Toi dont la bouche maudite
A Juliette interdite
Osa, je crois, parler tout bas,
Ecoute le seul mot que m'inspire
ma haine!
Tu n'es qu'un lâche! . . .
(*Roméo porte vivement la main à
son épée, la tire à moitié du four-
reau, puis l'y remet.*)

**ROMÉO:** Allons! tu ne me connais
pas,
Tybalt! . . . et ton insulte est
vaine!
J'ai dans le coeur des raisons de
t'aimer
Qui malgré moi me viennent
désarmer.
Je ne suis pas un lâche! . . . Adieu!
(*Il fait un pas pour s'éloigner.*)

**TYBALT:** Tu crois peut-être
Obtenir le pardon de tes offenses,
traître?

**ROMÉO:** Je ne t'ai jamais offensé
Le temps des haines est passé!

**MERCUTIO:** Tu souffrirais ce nom
de lâche?
O Roméo, t'ai-je entendu?
Eh bien, donc, si ton bras doit faillir
à sa tâche,
C'est à moi désormais que
l'honneur en est du!

**ROMÉO:** Mercutio, je t'en conjure!

**MERCUTIO:** Non! . . . Je vengerai ton injure! . . .
Misérable Tybalt, en garde, et
défends-toi!

**TYBALT:** Je suis à toi!

**ROMÉO:** Ecoute-moi!

**MERCUTIO:** Non! laisse-moi!

**STEPHANO, BENVOLIO et les
MONTAIGUS:** Bein! sur ma foi!

**PÂRIS et les CAPULETS:** En lui j'ai
foi!
Montaigus! . . . race immonde!
Frémissez de terreur!
Et que l'enfer seconde
Sa haine et sa fureur!

**STEPHANO, BENVOLIO et les
MONTAIGUS:** Capulets! race im-
monde!
Frémissez de terreur!
Et qu'l'enfer seconde
Sa haine et sa fureur!

The man I must fight!
(*to Romeo.*)
Now draw!
Draw for your life! Your are a spy
And traitor,—draw and you'll be a
man!
Do you think I forgot the night you
came
Without a bidding? Now for that in-
sult
You shall pay! . . .
Yes! and the more by this token,
That to my Juliet you have spoken.
Unhappy man, you'll rue the day!
No better term than this my hatred
affords me—
You are a villain!
(*Romeo half draws his sword,
then sheathes is calmly.*)

**ROMEO:** But no—I am no villain,
Tybalt.
I have reason to love you—which
excuses
All the rage of your words. Be satis-
fied,
Do no seek quarrel with me! I see
You do not know me—farewell!
(*Retires a step.*)

**TYBALT:** You cannot, boy, excuse
All the wrong that you have done
me!
Traitor!

**ROMEO:** Never have I wronged
you, I do protest!
Your name to me is dear as my own.

**MERCUTIO:** Calm and dishonora-
ble yielding!
How is this? Heard I right? So be it!
I'll reply with an à la stoccata.
(*Draws.*)
So, sir, pluck out your sword—for
now I am your man!

**ROMEO:** (*restraining him*). Put
up your rapier, Good Mercutio—

**MERCUTIO:** No! Come now, sir,
Show your passion; draw, you rat-
catcher, draw.

**TYBALT:** I am for you!

**ROMEO:** Listen to me!

**MERCUTIO:** No! let us be!

**STEPHANO, BENVOLIO and the
MONTAGUES:** It is well! On honor!

**PARIS and the CAPULETS:** I trust
in him!
Montagues—Montagues—offen-
sive race,
Tremble in alarm;
May demon, lending dark aid,
Now nerve his avenging arm!

**BENVOLIO, STEPHANO and MO-
NTAGUE'S RETAINERS:** Capu-
lets— Capulets—offensive race,
Tremble in alarm;
May demon, dark aid lending,
Now nerve his avenging arm!

**ROMÉO:** Haine en malheurs
féconde,
Dois-tu par ta fureur
Toujours donner au monde
Un spectacle d'horreur?
(*Tybalt et Mercutio se battent.*)

**MERCUTIO:** Ah blessé!

**ROMÉO:** Blessé? . . .

**MERCUTIO:** Que le diable
Soit de vos deux maisons! . . . Pour-
quoi
Te jeter entre nous?

**ROMÉO:** O sort impitoyable!
(*À ses amis.*)
Secourez-le!

**MERCUTIO:** (*chancelant*). Sout-
enez-moi!
(*On emmène Mercutio.*)

**ROMÉO:** Ah! maintenant, remonte
au ciel, prudence infâme!
Et toi, fureur à l'oeil de flamme,
Sois de mon coeur l'unique loi!
(*Tirant son épée.*)
Tybalt, il n'est ici d'autre lâche que
toi!
(*poussant une botte à Tybalt*).
À toi!
(*Tybalt est touché et chancelle;
Capulet entre en scène court à lui
et le soutient dans ses bras. — On
cesse de se battre.*)

## SCÈNE VIII

*Les Mêmes, Capulet, Bourgeois,
puis le Duc et sa Suite.*

**CAPULET:** Grand
Dieu! . . . Tybalt! . . .
(*Capulet, aidé des siens, étend Ty-
balt à terre lui soutient la tête.*)

**BENVOLIO:** (*à Roméo*). Sa blessure est mortelle!
Fuis sans perdre un instant!

**ROMÉO:** (*à part*). Ah! qu'ai-je
fait? . . . Moi, fuir! maudit par
elle!

**BENVOLIO:** C'est la mort qui
t'attend!

**ROMÉO:** (*avec désespoir*).
Qu'elle vienne donc! Je l'appelle!

**TYBALT:** (*d'une voix mourante*).
Un dernier mot! et sur votre
âme . . . exauces-moi!

**CAPULET:** Tu seras obéi! . . . Je
t'en donne ma foi!
(*Une foule de bourgeois a envahi
la scène.*)

**LE BOURGEOIS:** Qu'est-ce
donc? . . . C'est Tybalt! il meurt!

**CAPULET:** (*à Tybalt*). Reviens à
toi!
(*On entend des fanfares.*)

**LE CHOEUR:** O jour de deuil! ô
jour de larmes!
Un aveugle courroux,
Ensanglante nos armes!
Et le malheur plane sur nous.

**ROMEO:** Rancor and hate never
ending,
From age to age grow stronger;
Rending our homes
In sorrow and in woe!
(*They fight.*)

**MERCUTIO:** I am wounded!

**ROMEO:** Wounded?

**MERCUTIO:** Plague of your
houses, both! . . . but why
Did you come between us?

**ROMEO:** Alas!
Hurt for my honor!
(*To his friends.*) A surgeon, quick!

**MERCUTIO:** (*staggering*). Now
help me, there!
(*Exit, leaning on his friends.*)

**ROMEO:** Ah! he is slain!—Away to
heaven,
O shameful caution!
And you, O fire-eyed fury,
Shall be alone my conduct now.
(*Drawing sword and advancing.*)
Tybalt!
There is no coward here but you.
Fall on!
(*Wounds him mortally. Tybalt
totters, and falls. Enter Capulet,
who rushes to him, and supports
him in his arms. The fight ceases.*)

## SCENE VIII.

(*The above, Capulet, citizens, afterwards the Duke.*)

**CAPULET:** Ah heaven! Tybalt!
(*Capulet, assisted by his friends,
supporting Tybalt's head.*)

**BENVOLIO:** (*to Romeo*). He is
mortally wounded.
Away!
Quick, away!

**ROMEO:** (*aside*). O, evil fate—
dead!—
And he was her kinsman!

**BENVOLIO:** If you stay, death
awaits you!

**ROMEO:** Let it then be so.
(*With despair.*)
I am ready!

**TYBALT:** (*dying, to Capulet*). Yet
a word more—
This my last prayer—

**CAPULET:** On my soul I do swear
that your will
Shall be done!
(*Enter Citizens.*)

**CITIZENS:** How now? Tybalt is
slain!

**CAPULET:** (*to Tybalt*). Revive
again!
(*Procession march heard off.*)

**CHORUS:** O day of woe! O day of
weeping!
Blind revenge of our blades
In their blood now been steeping
And baleful stars hang over our

Le Duc! Le Duc!
(*Le Duc entre en scène suivi de son cortège de gentilshommes et de pages portant des torches.*)

CAPULET: (*se relevant*). Justice!

LES CAPULETS: Justice!

CAPULET: (*montrant le corps de Tybalt*). C'est Tybalt . . . mon neveu . . . tué par Roméo!

ROMÉO: Il avait le premier, frappé Mercutio!
J'ai vengé mon ami, que mon sort s'accomplisse!

LES MONTAIGUS: Justice!

TOUS: Justice!

LE DUC: Eh quoi! toujours du sang!—De vos coeurs inhumains Rien ne pourra calmer les fureurs criminelles!
Rien ne fera tomber les armes de vos mains,
Et je serai moi-même atteint par vos querelles!
(*à Roméo*).
Selon nos lois, ton crime a mérité la mort!
Mais tu n'es pas l'agresseur! . . . Je t'exile!

ROMÉO: Ciel!

LE DUC: Et vous, dont la haine en prétextes fertiles Entretient la discorde et l'effroi dans la ville.
Prêtez tous devant moi le serment solennel.
D'obéissance aux lois et du prince et du ciel!

ROMÉO et les AUTRES: Ah! jour de deuil et d'horreur et d'alarmes,
Mon coeur se brise éperdu de douleur!
Injuste arrêt qui trop tard nous désarmes,
Tu mets le comble à ce jour de malheur!
Je vois périr dans le sang et les larmes
Tous les espoirs et tous les voeux de mon coeur!

LE DUC: Tu quitteras la ville dès ce soir.

ROMÉO: O désespoir! l'exil!
Non! je mourrai—
Mais je veux la revoir!

CHOEUR: La paix? non! jamais!
(*La toile tombe.*)

# ■ ACTE QUATRIÈME

## SCÈNE I

La chambre de Juliette. Il fait nuit. La scène est éclairée par un flambeau.

*Roméo, Juliette.*

---

heads.
The Duke! The Duke!
(*Enter the Duke with suite and torch-bearers.*)

CAPULET: (*to Duke*). Avenge me!

RETAINERS: Avenge us!

CAPULET: (*pointing to Tybalt's corpse*). Tybalt's slain — my near friend; on Romeo
Is his blood.

ROMEO: From Mercutio first He struck out lusty life. Then I swore
His revenge; I am ready for my fate!

MONTAGUES: Avenge us!

ALL: Avenge us!

DUKE: How now? In ths sad fray Has your anger found vent? In your inhuman hearts,
Nothing can calm your criminal furies!
Nothing seems strong enough to keep your hands
From your hilts. Who knows, I May be next victim of your faction!
(*To Romeo.*)
For this offense, Romeo, you Deserve death; but as you did speak him fair,
Then you are banished!

ROMEO: Banished!

DUKE: And you, who in hate ever prone to occasion,
Do inflame in our town woeful strife and aggression,
Swear all on your lives, or at home or abroad,
You will obey the laws of the Duke and your God!

ROMEO and the OTHERS: Ah! direful day, day of woe and of mourning,
Breaking, my heart fails in pain and despair!
Though we disarm, how untimely the warning!
For we may never the ravage repair!
Every desire, every hope grimly scorning,
Only in weeping and blood may we share.

DUKE: Do avoid the city until the night.

ROMEO: Oh, I am banished! Despair!
No! Though I die, I will see her again.

CHORUS: Disarm? No! Revenge!
(*The curtain falls.*)

# ■ ACT IV.

## SCENE I.

The chamber of Juliet. It is night. The room is lit by a torch.

(*Romeo and Juliet*)

---

(*Juliette est assise; Roméo est à ses pieds.*)

JULIETTE: Va! je t'ai pardonné! Tybalt voulait ta mort;
S'il n'avait succombé, tu succombais toi-même
Loin de moi la douleur! loin de moi le remords!
Il te haïssait! . . . et je t'aime!

ROMÉO: Ah! redis-le, ce mot si doux!

JULIETTE: Je t'aime, ô Roméo! je t'aime, ô mon epoux!

JULIETTE ET ROMÉO: Nuit d'huménee! O douce nuit d'amour! La destinée M'enchaîne à toi sans retour. O volupté de vivre! O charmes tout puissants! Ton doux regard m'enivre, Ta voix ravit mes sens! Sous tes baisers de flamme voix ravit mes sens! Sous tes baisers de Sous tes baisers de flamme Le ciel, le ciel rayonne flamme Sous tes baiser de flamme Le ciel rayonne.
Je t'ai donne mon âme!
A toi! . . . toujours à toi! . . .
(*Les premières lueurs du jour éclairent les vitraux de la fenêtre.—On extend chanter l'alouette.*)

JULIETTE: Roméo, qu'as tu donc?

ROMÉO: (*se levant*). Ecoute, ô Juliette!
L'alouette déjà nous annonce le jour!

JULIETTE: (*le retenant*). Non! ce n'est pas le jour,
Ce n'est pas l'alouette Dont te chant a frappé ton oreille inquiète!
C'est le doux rossignol, confident de l'amour!

ROMÉO: C'est l'alouette, hélas! messagère du jour.
(*Ils s'approchent de la fenêtre.*)
Vois ces rayons jaloux dont l'horizon se dore!
Les flambeaux de la nuit pâlissent! . . . et l'aurore Dans les vapeurs de l'orient Se lève en souriant!

JULIETTE: Non! . . . ce n'est pas le jour!—Cette lueur funeste N'est qu'un doux reflet de l'astre des nuits!
Reste! Reste!

ROMÉO: (*serrant Juliette dans ses bras*). Ah! Vienne donc la mort! . . . je reste!

JULIETTE: Ah! tu dis vrai! . . . C'est le jour! . . . fuis!
Il faut quitter ta Juliette!

---

(*Juliet discovered on a couch, Romeo at her feet.*)

JULIET: Yes, I pardon you—
That Tybalt you have killed; for if Tybalt
Had lived, perchance you would have fallen.
Comfort me! It was your life he sought,
And I love you!

ROMEO: O speak again That word so fair!

JULIET: Ah, Romeo,
I love you—my husband—dear to me!

JULIET and ROMEO: Oh! blessed night hymenial, Oh sweet night of love! Destiny enchains me forever. Oh voluptuous life! Oh all powerful charms! Your sweet regard enraptures me, Your voice ravages Your sweet regard enraptures me, my senses Under your flaming kisses your voice ravages my senses, Under your flaming, Under your flaming kisses the sky, the sky, beams kisses, Under your flaming kisses, the sky beams.
I give you my soul It is your, yours forever.
(*Day breaks; the lark is heard.*)

JULIET: Romeo, what are you doing?

ROMEO: (*rising*). Ah, listen, Juliet!
Dearest Juliet, The lark that you hear,
Is the herald of morn.

JULIET: (*restraining him*). No! It is not yet near day,
No lark pierced your ear, love.
It is the nightingale's note,
That she nightly sings there!

ROMEO: No, it is the lark, alas!
Early herald of morn; look, love,
(*They come to the window.*)
What envious streaks, clouds in the east
Are lacing! now night's candles Are burning pale; on the mountains,
On tip-toe stands jocund day.

JULIET: No, love, it is not day—
Rather some wandering meteor.
Remain!
Remain!
(*Romeo embraces Juliet passionately.*)

ROMEO: Let me be put to death—
I'm staying.

JULIET: Ah! you were right, it is day!
Go! go away—wait no longer!

ROMÉO: Non! Non! ce n'est pas le jour, ce n'est pas l'alouette!
C'est le doux rossignol, confident de l'amour!

JULIETTE: C'est l'alouette, hélas! messagère du jour!
Pars, ma vie!

ROMÉO: Un baiser, et je pars! . . .

JULIETTE: (*s'abandonnant à l'étreinte de Roméo*). Loi cruelle!

ROMÉO: Ah! reste! reste encore dans mes bras enlacés!
Un jour il sera doux à notre amour fidèle
De se ressouvenir de ses tourments passés!

JULIETTE: Il faut partir, hélas!
Il faut quitter ces bras
Où je te presse,
Et t'arracher à cette ardente ivresse!

ROMÉO: Il faut partir, hélas!
Alors qu'entre ses bras
Elle me presse!
Et c'en est fait de cette ardente ivresse!

JULIETTE: Ah! que le sort
Qui de toi me sépare
Plus que la mort
Est cruel et barbare!

ROMÉO: Adieu, mon âme!
Adieu, ma vie! . . .
(*Roméo franchit le balcon et disparaît.*)

JULIETTE: Adieu! toujours à toi!
Anges du ciel, à vous je le confie! . . .

## SCÈNE II

*Juliette, Gertrude, puis Capulet et Frère Laurent.*

GERTRUDE: (*paraissant*). Juliette! . . . Ah! le ciel soit loué! . . . votre époux
Est parti! Voici votre père!

JULIETTE: Dieu! saurait-il? . . .

GERTRUDE: Rien, j'espère! . . . Frère Laurent le suit.

JULIETTE: Seigneur! protège-nous!
(*Entre Capulet suivi de Frère Laurent.*)

CAPULET: Quoi! ma fille, la nuit est à peine achevée,
Et tes yeux sont ouverts, et te voilà levée!
Hélas! notre souci, je le vois, est pareil,
Que l'hymne nuptial succède au bruit des armes!
Fidèle au dernier vœu que Tybalt à formé!

---

ROMEO: No, no! It is not yet near day,
It was no lark pierced thine ear, love;
It was the nightingale's note
On the pomegranate tree!

JULIET: No!
It is the lark; alas! early herald of morn,
Love, now leave me!

ROMEO: One more kiss,
And I go!

JULIET: (*leaving Romero's embrace*). Cruel fate!

ROMEO: Yet doubt not
That we'll meet, my Juliet, again!
And all these woes shall serve, love,
For sweet discourses in our time to come!

JULIET: But now indeed farewell!
For dawn does end the spell
With young love glowing,
And you my soul's delight
Are going afar!

ROMEO: But now indeed farewell!
For dawn does end the spell
With young love glowing,
From you my soul's delight
I'm going afar!

JULIET: O fortune, grant
Though we part now in sorrow,
Our love may blossom
More brightly tomorrow!

ROMEO: Farewell! my soul, my love!
(*Romeo goes off the balcony. Juliet watches his descent.*)

JULIET: Farewell, oh, dear one! Angels above,
To you, to you. I now confide my love!

## SCENE II.

*(Juliet, Gertrude, afterwards Capulet and Friar Lawrence.)*

GERTRUDE: (*entering*). Where is Juliet?
(*Sees her.*)
Ah! a mercy, my child,
That your husband is gone! your father is coming!

JULIET: Heaven! will he know?

GERTRUDE: Nay, that he will not;
The friar comes with him—

JULIET: In heaven
I put my trust!
(*Enter Capulet and Friar Lawrence.*)

CAPULET: How now, daughter?
the daylight yet is young
In heaven—and behold! you are awake,
As if you had not slumberred.
Alack!
On you too, weighs my care, I can see,
And a deep regret for the youth we have lost!

---

Reçois de lui l'époux que sa bouche à nommé
Souris au milieu des tes larmes!

JULIETTE: Cet époux, quel est-il?

CAPULET: Le plus noble entre tous.
Le comte Pâris!

JULIETTE: (*à part*). Dieu!

FRÈRE LAURENT: (*bas à Juliette*). Silence!

GERTRUDE: (*de même*). Calmez-vous!

CAPULET: L'autel est préparé;
Pâris a ma parole,
Soyez unis tous deux sans attendre à demain!
Que l'ombre de Tybalt, présente à cet hymen,
S'apaise enfin et se console!
La volonté des morts,
Comme celle de Dieu lui-même,
Est une loi sainte, une loi suprême;
Nous devons respecter la volonté des morts.

JULIETTE: (*à part*). Ne crains rien, Roméo, mon cœur est sans remords!

GERTRUDE: (*à part*). Dans leur tombe laissons dormir en paix les morts!

FRÈRE LAURENT: Elle tremble! et mon cœur partage ses remords!

CAPULET: Frère Laurent saura te dicter ton devoir.
Nos amis vont venir; je vais les recevoir.
(*Il sort, suivi de Gertrude.*)

## SCÈNE III

*Frère Laurent, Juliette.*

JULIETTE: (*avec désespoir*). Tout est perdu, mon père! tout m'accable!
J'ai pour vous obéir,
Caché mon désespoir et mon amour coupable!
C'est à vous de me secourir,
A vous de m'arracher à mon sort misérable!
Parlez, mon père! . . . ou bien je suis prête à mourir!
(*Elle lui montre un poignard.*)

FRÈRE LAURENT: Ainsi la mort ne trouble point votre âme?

JULIETTE: Non, non, plutôt la mort que ce mensonge infâme!

FRÈRE LAURENT: (*lui présentant un flacon*). Buvez donc ce breuvage, et des membres au cœur,
Va soudain se répandre une froide langueur

---

Let the nuptial hymns
Succeed to shocks of arm!
And faithful to Tybalt's last thought!
Receive the husband he has named!
And smile amid your tears!

JULIET: Who is he I'm to wed?

CAPULET: The noblest of us all!
Paris, brave and true!

JULIET: (*in terror*). Ah!

LAWRENCE: (*aside to Juliet*). Be silent!

GERTRUDE: (*aside to Juliet*). On your guard!

CAPULET: The altar is ready! Paris has my word!
Be married this very day!
That the soul of Tybalt,
Present to the marriage,
May rest in peace!
The will of the dead
As that of God itself,
Is a supreme and holy law
Which we must respect.

JULIET: (*aside*). Still my heart is yours, my love, for always.

GERTRUDE: (*aside*). Let the dead in cold obstruction rest forever!

LAWRENCE: How she trembles! still her heart will obey love.

CAPULET: You, holy father, can instruct her in duty, I know;
Our friends are coming, I go to receive them!
(*Exit, followed by Gertrude.*)

## SCENE III.

*(Friar Lawrence and Juliet.)*

JULIET: (*in despair*). My father!
I am past cure, past hope, past help;
Love, and my secret troth I've kept hid in my breast,
For you did so advise me. In my need
Now to you I turn; from out your long
Experience, O give present counsel.
O give me, my father, a hope—if not,
Then I'm ready to die!
(*She takes a dagger from her breast.*)

LAWRENCE: My child! then death has for you no terrors?

JULIET: No!—none—far worse than death
Living a wife, shame-stained!
(*Lawrence takes out a vial.*)

LAWRENCE: Drink then, drink of this potion,
When you are alone! quickly a drowsy humor.
Shall run though your veins: and

De la mort mensongère image;
Dans vos veines bientôt le sang
s'arrêtera;
Bientôt une pâleur livide effacera
Les roses de votre visage.
Vos yeux seront fermés ainsi que
dans la mort!
En vain éclateront alors les cris
d'alarmes
"Elle n'est plus!" diront vos com-
pagnes en larmes;
Et les anges du ciel répondront:
"Elle dort!"
Dans la nuit du tombeau vous dor-
mirez comme eux.
C'est là qu'après un jour votre
corps et votre âme,
Comme d'un foyer mort se ranime
la flamme.
Sortiront de ce lourd sommeil.
Par l'ombre protégés, votre époux
et moi-même
Nous épîrons votre réveil,
Et vous fuirez au bras de celui qui
vous aime!
Hésitez-vous?

**JULIETTE:** (*prenant le flacon*).
Non! non! à votre main
J'abandonne ma vie!

**FRÈRE LAURENT:** A demain!

**JULIETTE:** A demain!
(*Frère Laurent sort.*)

## SCÈNE IV

*Juliette, seule.*

**JULIETTE:** Dieu! quel frisson court
dans mes veines?
Si ce breuvage était sans pou-
voir! . . . craintes vaines!
Je n'appartiendrai pas au comte
malgré moi! Non!
(*Cachant le poignard dans son
sein.*)
Non! ce poignard sera le gardien de
ma foi!—Viens!
Amour, ranime mon courage,
Et de mon coeur chasse l'effroi!
Hésiter, c'est te faire outrage!
Trembler est un manque de foi!
Verse toi-même ce breu-
vage! . . .
O Roméo, je bois à toi!
(*Après avoir versé le contenu du
flacon dans une coupe, elle
s'arrête.*)
Mais, si demain pourtant, en ces ca-
veaux funèbres,
Je m'éveillais avant son retour! . . .
Dieu puissant!
Cette pensée horrible a glacé tout
mon sang!
Que deviendrai-je en ces ténèbres,
Dans ce séjour de mort et de
gémîssements
Que les siècles passés ont rempli
d'ossements?
Où Tybalt, tout saignant encore de

shall seize on
Each vital spirit: Then its progress
Shall keep no pulse, but shall cease
to beat!
All soon the roses on your lips, and
on
Your cheek shall wither and fade
into ashes;
Your eyelids too will close—as life
is shut
By death.
Loud will they raise the sound of
lamentation
'Juliet is dead!' 'Juliet is dead!' for
so
Shall they deem you reposing. But
The angels above will reply 'she but
sleeps!'
for two-and-forty hours, you shall
lie in death's seeming.
And then, to life awakening as from
a pleasant dreaming,
From the ancient vault you shall
haste away;
Your husband shall be there, in the
night, to watch over thee,
Nigh to you ever, on your waking
we will stay,
so shall this drink once more to life
and love restore you;
Are you afraid?

**JULIET:** (*taking the vial*). No! no!
in your hand
I give up my life!

**LAWRENCE:** Till tomorrow!

**JULIET:** Till tomorrow!
(*Lawrence exit.*)

## SCENE IV.

(*Juliet alone*)

**JULIET:** O Lord! what icy thrill per-
vades my veins!
Should this potion be without ef-
fect!
Vain fears! never against my will
Shall I be the Count's bride.
(*Hiding the dagger in her bosom.*)
No! this dagger shall be the keeper
of my faith! Come!
O Love! give strength and courage
To my heart. To hesitate is an out-
rage!
To tremble is a want of faith.
O! pour yourself this bever-
age! . . .
O Roméo, I drink to you!
(*Having poured the contents of
the vial in a cup, she stops.*)
Ah! But if in those funeral cells!
I should awake before his re-
turn! . . .
Almighty God! this awful thought
Has struck me with horror,
What shall I become in that
darkness!
In that abode of death and groans,
That the past centuries have filled
with corpses!
Where Tybalt, yet bloody from his
wounds
In the dark night, by my side shall
rest,

sa blessure
Près de moi, dans la nuit obscure,
Dormira? . . . Dieu! ma main
rencontrera sa main!
(*Avec égarement.*)
Quelle est cette ombre à la mort
échapée?
C'est Tybalt! . . . Il
m'appelle! . . . Il veut de mon
chemin
Ecarter mon époux, et sa fatale
épée . . .
Non! . . . fantômes, disparais-
sez!
Dissipe-toi, funeste rêve!
Que l'aube du bonheur se lève
Sur l'ombre des tourments pas-
sés! . . .
(*Saisissant la coupe.*)
Viens! Viens!
Amour, ranime mon courage,
Et de mon coeur chasse l'effroi;
Hésiter, c'est te faire outrage;
Trembler, est un manque de foi;
Verse toi-même ce breuvage,
O Roméo, je bois à toi!
(*Elle boit.—Gertrude parait au
fond suivie de jeunes filles. Juli-
ette va à leur rencontre et sort
avec elles.*)

## SCÈNE V

*Une galérie du palais.—Au fond,
les portes de la chapelle.*

*Capulet, Pâris, Frère Laurent,
Grégorio, Juliette, Gertrude,
jeunes filles, amies et serviteurs
des Capulets. Cortège nuptial.*

(*Un prélude d'orgue se fait entendre; les portes de la chapelle
s'ouvrent; un cortège de cleres et
d'enfants de choeur entre en
scène.*)

**CAPULET:** (*offrant la main à Juliette*). Ma fille, cède aux voeux du
fiancé qui t'aime;
Le ciel va vous unir par des voeux
éternels;
Le bonheur vous attend au pied des
saints autels;
De cet hymen béni voici l'instant
suprême!
(*Pâris s'avance et se dispose à
passer son anneau au doigt de Juliette.*)

**JULIETTE:** (*Retirant sa main et à
demi-voix, comme dans un rêve*).
La haine est le berceau de cet amour
fatal! . . .
Que le cercueil soit mon lit nuptial! . . .
(*Elle porte la main à sa tête et en
détache sa couronne de fiancée;
ses cheveux se déroulent et tombent sur ses épaules.*)

**CAPULET:** Juliette! . . . reviens
à toi! . . .

**JULIETTE:** Dieu . . . je chan-
celle! . . .
(*On l'entoure et on la soutient.*)
Quelle nuit m'environne? . . . et

Oh! should my hand meet his!
(*With madness.*)
What ghost is that, from death es-
caped?
It is Tybalt; he calls me! . . . he
wants
From my way to drive my husband
And his fatal sword! . . .
No!—Away, you ghosts—
And you! fatal dreams! away!
Let the dawn of happiness rise
Over the shadows of past torment.
(*Seizing the cup.*)
O Love! give strength and courage
To my heart! To hesitate is an out-
rage!
To tremble is a want of faith,
O pour yourself this beverage!
O! Romeo! I drink to you! . . .
(*She drinks,—enter Gertrude fol-
lowed by girls. Juliet goes to meet
them, and departs with them.*)

## SCENE V.

*A ball of the Palace—At back the
door of the chapel.*

*Capulet, Paris, Friar Lawrence,
Gregorio, Juliet, Gertrude, girls,
friends, and retainers of the Ca-
palets Wedding train.*

(*The organ is heard, the doors of
the Chapel open, a procession of
clergy and chorus children enter.*)

**CAPULET:** (*taking Juliet's hand*).
Daughter, yield to the will of the
betrothed who loves you.
God is going to unite you with eternal bonds;
Happiness waiting for you at the
foot of the holy altars,
From that blessed Hymn here is the
supreme moment.
(*Paris comes forward to place the
ring on the finger of Juliet.*)

**JULIET:** (*withdrawing her hand,
and as in a dream*). Hatred is the
source of this fatal love!
Let a coffin be my wedding couch.
(*She detaches her bridal wreath;
her hair falls on her shoulders.*)

**CAPULET:** O Juliet! come back to
your senses!

**JULIET:** O Lord!—I totter! . . .
(*They surround her.*)
Whose is that voice that calls me?
Can it be death!

quelle voix m'appelle?
Est-ce la mort? . . . j'ai
peur! . . . mon
père! . . . adieu!
(*Elle tombe inanimée dans les bras de ceux qui l'entourent.*)

**CAPULET:** Juliette! . . . ma
fille! . . . Ah! . . . morte! . . .
juste Dieu!

**TOUS:** Juste Dieu!
(*La toile tombe.*)

# ■ ACTE CINQUIÈME.

## SCÈNE I

*Une crypte souterraine; ça et là des tombeaux.*

*Frère Laurent, Frère Jean, Juliette.*

(*Au lever du rideau, Frère Laurent est debout prie du tombeau sur lequel est étendue Juliette endormie; une lampe funéraire, placée sur le tombeau, éclaire le théâtre; Frère Jean entre en scène.*)

**FRÈRE LAURENT:** Eh bien? ma lettre à Roméo?

**FRÈRE JEAN:** Son page,
Attaqué par les Capulets,
Vient d'être ramené blessé dans le palais
De son maître, et n'a pu s'acquitter du message.
(*Remettant une lettre à Frère Laurent.*)
Voici la lettre!

**FRÈRE LAURENT:** O funeste hasard!
Qu'un autre messager parte cette nuit même!
Venez! chaque instant de retard
Nous jette en un péril extrême.
(*Il sort, suivi de Frère Jean. — On entend une porte de fer se refermer sur eux. — Profond silence.*)

## SCÈNE II

*Juliette, puis Roméo.*

(*Au bout d'un moment, on entend le bruit d'un levier ébranlant la porte. — la porte cède avec bruit. — Roméo parait.*)

**ROMÉO:** (*un levier à la main.*)
C'est là! . . .
(*Il jette son levier.*)
Salut, tombeau sombre et silencieux!
Un tombeau! . . . non!—ô demeure plus belle
Que le séjour même des cieux,
Palais splendide et radieux,
Salut!
(*Apercevant Juliette et s'élançant vers le tombeau.*)
Ah! la voila! . . . C'est elle! . . .
Viens, funèbre clarté; viens l'offrir
à mes yeux!
(*Prenant la lampe funéraire.*)
O ma femme! ô ma bien-aimée!
La mort, en aspirant ton haleine embaumée,
N'a pas altéré ta beauté!
Non! cette beauté que j'adore
Sur ton front calme et pur semble régner encore
Et sourire à l'éternité.
(*Il repose la lampe sur le tombeau.*)
Pourquoi me la rends-tu si belle, ô mort livide!
Est-ce pour me jeter plus vite dans ses bras?
Va! c'est seul bonheur dont mon coeur soit avide,
Et ta proie aujourd'hui ne t'échappera pas.
(*Regardant autour de lui.*)
Ah! je te comtemple sans crainte,
Tombe, où je vais enfin près d'elle reposer! . . .
(*Se penchant vers Juliette.*)
O mes bras, donnez-lui votre dernière étreinte!
Mes lèvres donnez-lui votre dernier baiser!
(*Il embrasse Juliette, puis, tirant de son sein un petit flacon en métal et se tournant vers Juliette.*)
A toi! . . . ma Juliette!
(*Il vide le flacon d'un trait et le jette.*)

**JULIETTE:** (*s'éveillant peu à peu*).
Où suis-je? . . .

**ROMÉO:** (*tournant les yeux vers Juliette*). Dieu! . . . je rêve!
Sa bouche a murmuré! . . .
(*Saisissant la main de Juliette.*)
Mes doigts, en trémissant,
Ont senti dans les siens la chaleur de son sang!
(*Juliette regarde Roméo d'un air égaré.*)
Elle me regarde . . . et se lève!

**JULIETTE:** (*soupirant*).
Roméo! . . . . . Roméo! . . .

**ROMÉO:** (*avec éclat.*) Seigneur Dieu tout-puissant!
(*Juliette pose un pied sur les degrés du tombeau.*)
Elle vit! elle vit! Juliette est vivante!

**JULIETTE:** (*reprenant peu à peu ses sens*). Dieu! quelle est cette voix dont la douceur m'enchante? . . .

**ROMÉO:** C'est moi! C'est ton époux
Qui, tremblant de bonheur, embrasse tes genoux,
Qui ramène à ton coeur la lumière enivrante,
De l'amour et des cieux!

**JULIETTE:** (*se jetant dans les bras de Roméo*). Ah! c'est toi! . . .

**ROMÉO:** Viens, fuyons tous deux! . . .

**JULIETTE:** O bonheur!

---

O Heaven—my father!—farwell!
(*She falls insensible in his arms.*)

**CAPULET:** My Juliet!
My daughter!—lifeless!—dead!
Just God!

**ALL:** She is dead!
(*Curtain falls.*)

# ■ ACT V.

## SCENE I.

(*The Vault of the Capulets*)

*Friar Lawrence, Friar John, Juliet.*

(*As the curtain rises, Friar Lawrence is seen near the tomb on which Juliet is asleep—the stage is lighted by a lamp, burning over the tomb.*)
(*Enter Friar John.*)

**LAWRENCE:** Well! my letter to Romeo!

**FRIAR JOHN:** His page,
Attacked by the Capulets,
Has just now been taken wounded
In his master's palace,
And could not deliver the message.
(*Delivering the letter to Friar Lawrence.*)
Here is the letter!

**LAWRENCE:** O fatal doom!
Let another messenger leave this very night!
Come—each minute we lose
Brings us to great dangers.
(*Exeunt, an iron door is heard to shut behind them—great silence.*)

## SCENE II.

*Juliet, then Romeo.*

(*The noise of a crowbar is heard. The door yields. Enter Romeo with the iron bar in his hand.*)

**ROMEO:** (*Throws aside his bar.*)
Here!
All hail, O tomb, home of the silent dead!
Not a tomb! No! for here Juliet is lying,
Making the grim vault full of light.
All hail! O shrine radiant and bright.
(*Perceives and rushes towards her.*)
Ah, she is there—my Juliet!
(*Takes the lamp to see her more distinctly.*)
Burn,
O torch in the gloom! to me show her again!
Wife beloved—Ah! you are not conquered;
For death, though it has drawn from your breath
All the honey, to change you, yet lacked
The power. No, still beauty's ensign is crimson
In your lips, love—and death's pale flag
Is not advanced there.
(*Replaces the lamp on the tomb.*)
Oh, is it
Unsubstantial death of you is amorous,
And that the lean abhorred monster keeps
You here? for fear of that I'll stay with you,
My beloved, nor again depart from this palace
Of dim night,
Yes, my weary yoke
Offshaking, oh, here I will set up
My everlasting rest. Eyes, O look your last;
Arms, take your last embrace; and kiss her lips,
That are the doors of breath!
(*He embraces Juliet, then takes a vial of poison from a pouch.*)
My love,
Thus I pledge you!

**JULIET:** (*half awakening*). Where am I?

**ROMEO:** (*startled*). It was but fancy! Am I dreaming?
Yet surely she did speak!
(*Seizes her hand.*)
My hands,
Trembling the while, feel in hers
That the life-blood is still running warm!
(*She opens her eyes, raises her head slightly, and looks at him.*)
Now her eyes open! She arises!

**JULIET:** (*moving*). Romeo! Romeo!

**ROMEO:** O merciful Heaven!
(*Juliet sits up, and puts her feet on the ground.*)
She's alive! she's alive!

**JULIET:** (*coming to her senses*).
Ah! I thought that I heard
Tones that I loved, soft falling!

**ROMEO:** It is I! Romeo—your own—
Who your slumbers have stirred,
Led by my heart alone,
You, my bride, to love
And the fair world recalling!
(*Juliet falls into his arms.*)

**JULIET:** O mine own!

**ROMEO:** Come, let's fly hence!

**JULIET:** Happy dawn!

**ROMÉO ET JULIETTE:** Viens, fuyons au bout du monde!
Viens! soyons heureux,
Fuyons tous deux! Viens!
Dieu de bonté! Dieu de clémence!
Sois béni par deux coeurs heureux!

**ROMÉO:** (*chancellant*). Ah! les parents ont tous des entrailles de pierre!

**JULIETTE:** Roméo, que dis-tu?

**ROMÉO:** Les larmes, la prière,
Rien, rien ne peut les attendrir!
A la porte des cieux, Juliette . . . —Et mourir! . . .

**JULIETTE:** Mourir!—Ah! la fièvre t'égare,
De toi quel délire s'empare? . . .
Mon bien-aimé! Rappelle ta raison!

**ROMÉO:** Ah! je te croyais morte . . . et j'ai bu ce poison!

**JULIETTE:** Ce poison! . . . Juste Dieu! . . .

**ROMÉO:** (*serrant Juliette dans ses bras*). Console-toi, pauvre âme,
Le rêve était trop beau!
L'amour, céleste flamme,
Survit, même au tombeau!
Il soulève la pierre,
Et, des anges béni,
Comme un flot de lumière
Se perd dans l'infini! . . .

**JULIETTE:** (*égarée*). O douleur! . . . ô torture! . . .

**ROMEO and JULIET:** Come, the world is all before us!
Come! by joy our own, for woe departs!
Father of love, graciously bending,
You are blessed by two grateful hearts.

**ROMEO:** (*tottering*). Ah! hearts of stone—ay, harder than stone,
Have our fathers!

**JULIET:** (*frightened*). But your words are so wild!

**ROMEO:** Nor sorrow, nor entreaty, softened them
To their children's prayer! on the threshold
Of joy we are standing—yet we die!

**JULIET:** We die! Romeo, surely you wander!
What strange terrors seize on your fancy?
My love—my lord, recall yourself.

**ROMEO:** Alas! I believed you dead, love, and—
I drank of this drink!
(*Shows the vial.*)

**JULIET:** Of that drink?
It is death!
(*They embrace.*)

**ROMEO:** Do not yield to sorrow,
Our dream was all too bright,
Now dawns a fairer day, that
Shall never set in night!
From a dull slumber waking,
In a fair dawn I rise,
Chains my soul now is breaking,
To heaven dove-like it flies!

**JULIET:** O my heart—break; break in sorrow!

**ROMÉO:** (*d'une voix plus faible*).
Ecoute, ô Juliette! . . .
L'alouette déjà nous annonce le jour!
Non . . . ce n'est pas le jour . . .
Ce n'est pas l'alouette,
C'est le doux rossignol, confident de l'amour! . . .
(*Il glisse des bras de Juliette et tombe sur les degrés du tombeau.*)

**JULIETTE:** (*ramassant le flacon*). Cruel époux!—De ce poison funeste
Tu ne m'as pas laissé ma part! . . .
(*Elle rejette le flacon, et portant la main à son coeur de rencontre le poignard qu'elle avait caché sous ses vitesse et l'en tire d'un geste rapide.*)
Ah, fortuné poignard!
Ton secours me reste!
(*Elle se frappe.*)

**ROMÉO:** (*se relevant à demi*). Dieu! . . . qu'as-tu fait?

**JULIETTE:** (*dans les bras de Roméo*). Va! ce moment est doux!
(*Elle laisse tomber le poignard.*)
O joie infinie et suprême
De mourir avec toi . . .
Viens! . . . un baiser!
Je t'aime! . . .

**ENSEMBLE:** (*se relevant tous deux à demi dans un dernier effort*)
Seigneur, Seigneur, pardonnez-nous!
(*Ils meurent.*)

*FIN.*

**ROMEO:** (*wandering*). Yet hark!
Juliet my dearest—it is the lark,
Early herald proclaiming the day!
No, no!
It is not yet near day! It is no lark
You heard, love, but the lone nightingale
On the pomegranate tree!
(*He slips from her arms, and falls on the steps of the bier.*)

**JULIET:** (*taking the vial*). Ah! cruel spouse,
Drink all! no friendly drop you left me,
To help me, so I die with you!
(*She flings the vial away, then remembers the dagger, draws it from her breast.*)
Ah!
Here's my dagger still! I'd forgotten you,—
Friend: now, happy dagger, behold your sheath!
(*She stabs herself.*)

**ROMEO:** (*Romeo half raises himself.*) Hold! hold your hand!

**JULIET:** (*in his arms*). Ah, happy moment,
Stay! My soul with rapture is swelling,
Thus to die, love, with you,
(*She lets fall the dagger.*)
Yet one embrace!
I love you! (*They half rise in each other's arms.*)

**BOTH:** O, Heaven, grant us your grace!
(*They die.*)

*END.*

# Faust (1859)

MUSIC BY CHARLES GOUNOD ■ LIBRETTO BY JULES BARBIER & MICHEL CARRÉ

Faust, with libretto by Jules Barbier and Michel Carré based on Goethe's infamous novel premiered at the Théâtre-Lyrique in Paris on March 19, 1859. Faust, now an old man, looks back on life bereft of love. He is about to poison himself when the sound of girls singing in the street distracts him. He uses magic to conjure up Méphistophélès, who offers Faust a return to youth and happiness in exchange for his soul. Faust hesitates, but the devil tempts him with a vision of the beautiful young woman Marguérite. Faust signs the pact in his own blood, and he is changed into a handsome young knight. He sets off with the devil in search of earthly pleasures. Valentin, Marguérite's brother, is about to go off to war and he entrusts the care of his sister to Siebel, a young student (a mezzo-soprano) who is in love with her. The devil interrupts a toast being given by another student, Wagner, whose death he predicts. He also pronounces that any flower Siebel picks will fade and that Valentin will be killed by someone he knows. Faust asks Marguérite if he can walk her home while Siebel is detained by the devil. She refuses. Siebel picks flowers for his beloved, but they fade. He sprinkles them with holy water and places them on the porch. The devil and Faust set a jewelry box full of gifts alongside Siebel's humble offering. When Marguérite returns, she bedecks herself with the jewels and shows them to Marthe, her neighbor. Faust tells Marguérite of his love for her, which she returns. Now pregnant by Faust, Marguérite is eternally damned. Valentin returns from war. He challenges Faust to a duel, but is killed by a sword guided by the devil. On Walpurgis Night on the Brocken and Harz Mountains, the devil shows Faust a bacchanal. But Faust wants to be taken to Marguérite, now totally insane, imprisoned and awaiting execution for her son's murder. Faust tries to convince her to run away with him, but she reels from the sight of the devil and dies as she calls for mercy on her soul. An angel choir accompanies her to heaven as Faust prays for her.

---

## ■ ACTE I

### SCÈNE I

Le Cabinet de Faust.

(Faust, seul. Sa lampe est près de s'eteindre. Il est assis devant une table chargée de parchemins. Un livre est ouvert devant lui.

FAUST: Rien! . . . —En vain j'interroge, en ardente veille,
La nature et le Créateur;
Pas une voix ne glisse à mon oreille
Un mot consolateur!
J'ai langui triste et solitaire,
Sans pouvoir briser le lien
Qui m'attache encore à la terre! . . .
Je ne vois rien!—Je ne sais rien!
(Il ferme le livre et se lève. Le jour commence à naître)
Le ciel pâlit!—Devant l'aube nouveau
La sombre nuit
S'évanouit! . . .
(Avec désepoir.)
Encore un jour!—encore un jour en luit! . . .
O mort, quand viendras-tu m'a sous ton aile?
(Saisissani une fiole sur la table.)
Eh bien! puisque ia mort me fuit
Pourquoi n'irais-je pas vers elle?
Salut! ô mon dernier matin!
J'arrive sans terreur au terme du voyage
Et je suis, avec ce breavage,

## ■ ACT I

### SCENE I

Faust's Study.

(Night. Faust discovered, alone. He is seated at a table covered with books and parchments; an open book lies before him. His lamp is flickering in the socket.)

FAUST: No! In vain my soul has aspired, with ardent longing,
All to know,—all in earth and heaven.
No light illumines the visions, ever thronging
My brain, no peace is given,
And I linger, thus sad and weary,
Without power to sunder the chain
Binding my soul to life always dreary.
No do I see! No do I know!
(He closes the book and rises. Day begins to dawn.)
Again it is light!
Flying on its westward course
The somber night vanishes.
(Despairingly)
Again the light of a new day!
O death! when will your dusky wings
Hover above me and give me—rest?
(Seizing a flask on the table.)
Well, then! Since death thus evades me,
Why should I not go in search of him?

Le seul maître de mon destin!
(Il verse le contenu de la fiole dans une coupe de cristal ment où il va porter la coupe à ses lèvres, des voix de jeunes filles en font entendre au dehors.)

CHOEUR DE JEUNES FILLES: Paresseuse fille
Qui sommeille encor!
Déjà le jour brille
Sous son manteau d'or.
Déjà l'oiseau chante
ses folles chansons;
L'aube caressante
Sourit aux moissons;
Le ruisseau murmure,
La fleur s'ouvre au jour,
Toute la nature
S'éveille à l'amour!

FAUST: Vains échos de la joie humaine.
Passez, passex votre chemin!
O coupe des aïeux, qui tant fois fus pleine,
Pourquoi trembles-tu dans ma main? . . .
(Il porte de nouveau la coupe à ses lèvres.)

CHOEUR DES LABOUREURS: (dehors). Aux champs l'aurore nous rappelle;
Le temps est beau, la terre est belle;
Béni soit Dieu!
A peine voit-on l'hirondelle,

Hail, my final day, all hail!
No fears assail my heart,
On earth my days I number;
For this draught immortal slumber
Will secure me, and dispel care!
(Pours liquid from the flask into a crystal goblet. Just as he is about to raise it to his lips, the following chorus is heard, without.)

CHO. OF MAIDENS: Why your eyes so lustrous
Hide you from sight?
Bright Sol now is scattering
Beams of golden light;
The nightingale is warbling
Its carol of love;
Rosy tints of morning
Now gleam from above;
Flowers unfold their beauty
To the scented gale;
Nature all awakens—
Tells its tale of love

FAUST: Hence, empty sounds of human joys
Flee far from me.
O goblet, which my ancestors
Have filled so many times,
Why tremble in my grasp?
(Again raising the goblet to his lips.)

CHO. OF LABORERS: (without)
The morn summons us into the fields,
The swallow hastes away!
Why tarry, then?
To labor let's away! Let's on to

Qui vole et plonge d'un coup d'aile
Dans le profondeur du ciel bleu!

**JEUNES FILLES ET LABS:** Béni soit Dieu!

**FAUST:** (*reposant la coupe*) Dieu!
(*Il se laisse retomber dans son fauteuil.*)
Mais ce Dieu, que peut-il pour moi!
(*se levant.*)
Me rendra-t-il l'amour, l'espérance et la foi?
(*Avec rage.*)
Maudites soyez-vous, ô voluptés humaines!
Maudites soient les chaînes
Qui me font ramper ici-bas!
Maudit soit tout ce qui nous leurre,
Vain espoir qui passe avec l'heure,
Rêves d'amour ou de combats!
Maudit soit le bonheur, maudites la science,
La prière et la foi!
Maudite sois-tu, patience!
A moi, Satan! à moi!

## SCÈNE II

*Faust, Mephistopheles.*

**MEP:** (*apparaissant*). Me voici! . . . D'où vient ta surprise!
Ne suis-je pas mis à ta guise?
L'épée au côté, la plume au chapeau
L'escarcelle pleine, un riche manteau
Sur l'épaule;—en somme
Un vrai gentilhomme!
Eh bien! que me veux-tu, docteur!
Parle, voyons! . . . —Te fais-je peur?

**FAUST:** Non.

**MEP:** Doutes-tu ma puissance? . . .

**FAUST:** Peut-tre!

**MEP:** Mets-la donc à l'épreuve! . . .

**FAUST:** Va-t'en!

**MEP:** Fi!—c'est là ta reconnaissance!
Apprends de moi qu'avec Satan
L'on en doit user d'autre sorte,
Et qu'il n'était pas besoin
De l'appeler de si loin
Pour le mettre ensuite à la porte!

**FAUST:** Et que peux-tu pour moi?

**MEP:** Tout.—Mais dis-moi d'abord
Ce que tu veux;—est-ce de l'or?

**FAUST:** Que ferais-je de la richesse?

---

work,
The sky is bright, the earth is fair,
Our tribute, then, let's pay to heaven.

**CHO. OF MAIDENS AND LABORERS:** Praises to God!

**FAUST:** God! God!
(*He sinks into a chair.*)
But this God, what will he do for me?
(*Rising.*)
Will he return youth, love, and faith to me?
Cursed be all of man's vile race!
Cursed be the chain's which bind him in his place!
Cursed be visions false, deceiving!
Cursed the folly of believing!
Cursed be dreams of love or hate!
Cursed be souls with joy elate.
Cursed be science, prayer, and faith!
Cursed my fate in life and death! Infernal king, arise!

## SCENE II

*Faust and Mephistopheles.*

**MEP:** (*suddenly appearing*) Here am I! So, I surprise you?
SATAN, Sir, at your service!
A sword at my side; on my hat a gay feather;—
A cloak over my shoulder; and altogether,
Why, gotten up quite in the fashion!
(*Briskly*)
But come, Doctor Faust, what is your will?
Behold! Speak! Are you afraid of me?

**FAUST:** No.

**MEP:** Do you doubt my power?

**FAUST:** Perhaps.

**MEP:** Prove it, then.

**FAUST:** Begone!

**MEP:** Fie! Fie! Is this your politeness!
But learn, my friend, that with Satan
One should conduct in a different way.
I've entered your door with infinite trouble.
Would you kick me out the very same day?

**FAUST:** Then what will you do for me?

**MEP:** Anything in the world! All things. But
Say first what you would have. Abundance of gold?

**FAUST:** And what can I do with riches?

---

**MEP:** Bien! je vois où le bât te blesse!
Tu veux la gloire?

**FAUST:** Plus encor!

**MEP:** La puissance!

**FAUST:** Non! je veux un trésor
Qui les contient tous! . . . je veus jeunesse!
A moi les plaisirs,
Les jeunes maîtresses!
A moi leurs caresses!
A moi leurs désirs?
A moi l'énergie
Des instincts puissants,
Et la folle orgie
Du coeur et des sens!
Ardente jeunesse,
A moi tes désirs!
A moi ton ivresse!
A moi tes plaisirs! . . .

**MEP:** Fort bien! je puis contenter ton caprice.

**FAUST:** Et que te donnerai-je en retour?

**MEP:** Presque rien:
Ici, je suis à ton service,
Mais là-bas tu seras au mien.

**FAUST:** Là-bas? . . .

**MEP:** Là-bas.
(*Lui présentant un parchemin.*)
Allons, signe.—Eh quoi! ta main tremble!
Que faut-il pour te décider?
La jeunesse t'appelle; ôse la regarder! . . .
(*Il fait un gest. Au fond du théâtre s'ouvre et laisse voir Marguerite assise devant son rouet et filant.*)

**FAUST:** O merveille! . . .

**MEP:** Eh bien! que t'ensemble?
(*Prenant le parchemin.*)

**FAUST:** Donne! . . .
(*Il signe.*)

**MEP:** Allons donc!
(*Prenant la coupe restée sur la table.*)
Et maintenant,
Maître, c'est moi qui te convie
A vider cette coupe où fume en bouillonnant
Non plus la mort, non plus le poison;—mais la vie!

**FAUST:** (*prenant la coupe et se tournant vera Marguerite.*) A toi, fantôme adorable et charmant! . . .
(*Il vide la coupe et se trouve métamorphosé en jeune et élégant seigneur. La vision disparait.*)

**MEP:** Viens!

**FAUST:** Je la reverrai?

**MEP:** Sans doute.

**FAUST:** Quand?

**MEP:** Aujourd'hui.

**FAUST:** C'est bien!

**MEP:** En route!

---

**MEP:** Good. I see where the shoe pinches.
You will have glory.

**FAUST:** Still wrong.

**MEP:** Power, then.

**FAUST:** No. I would have a treasure
Which contains all. I wish for youth.
Oh! I would have pleasure,
And love, and caresses,
For youth is the season
When joy most impresses.
One round of enjoyment,
One scene of delight,
Should be my employment
From day-dawn till night.
Oh, I would have pleasure,
And love, and caresses;
If you restore me youth,
I'll renew my joys!

**MEP:** It is well—I can give you all you desire.

**FAUST:** Ah! but what must I give in return?

**MEP:** It is but little:
In this world I will be your slave,
But down below you must be mine.

**FAUST:** Below!

**MEP:** Below. (*Unfolding a scroll.*)
Come, write. What! does your hand tremble?
Where does dire trepidation come from?
It is youth that now awaits you—Behold!
(*At a sign from Mephistopheles, the scene opens and discloses Marguerite, spinning.*)

**FAUST:** Oh, wonder!

**MEP:** Well, how do you like it?
(*Taking parchment.*)

**FAUST:** Give me the scroll!
(*Signs.*)

**MEP:** Come on then! And now, master,
(*Taking cup from the table.*)
I invite you to empty a cup,
In which there is neither poison nor death,
But young and vigorous life.

**FAUST:** (*Taking cup and turning toward Marguerite.*) O beautiful, adorable vision! I drink to you!
(*He drinks the contents of the cup, and is transformed into a young and handsome man. The vision disappears.*)

**MEP:** Come, then.

**FAUST:** Say, shall I again behold her?

**MEP:** Most surely!

**FAUST:** When?

**MEP:** This very day!

**FAUST:** It is well.

**MEP:** Then let's away.

## Act I, Scene II

FAUST: A moi les plaisirs,
Le jeunes maîtresses!
A moi leurs caresses!
A moi leurs désirs!

MEP: A toi la jeunesse,
A toi ses désirs,
A toi son ivresse,
A toi ses plaisirs!
(*Ils sortent.—La telle tombe.*)

FAUST: 'Tis pleasure I covet,
'Tis beauty I crave;
I sigh for its kisses,
I demand its love!
With ardor unwonted
I long now to burn;
I sigh for the rapture
Of heart and of sense.
(*Exeunt. The curtain falls.*)

# ◼ ACTE II

## SCÈNE I

*La Kermesse.*

*Une des portes de la ville. A gauche un caborte à l'enseigne de Bacchus.*)

*Wagner, Etudiants, Bourgeois, Soldats, Jeunes Filles. Matrones.*

ETUDS: Vin ou bière,
Bière ou vin,
Que mon verre
Soit plein!
Sans vergogne,
Coup sur coup,
Un ivrogne
Boit tout!

WAG: Jeune adepte
De tonneau
N'en excepte
Que l'eau!
Que ta gloire,
Tes amours,
Soient de boire
Toujours!
(*Ils trinquent et boivent.*)

SOLDATS: Filles ou forteresses,
C'est tout un, morbleu!
Vieux burgs, jeunes maîtresses
Sont pour nous un jeu!
Celui qui sait s'y prendre
Sans trop de façon,
Les oblige à se rendre
En payant rançon!

BOURGEOIS: Aux jours de dimanche et de fête,
J'aime à parler guerre et combats;
Tandis que les peuples là-bas
Se cassent la tête.
Je vais m'asseoir sur les coteaux
Qui sont voisins de la rivière,
Et je vois passer les bateaux
En vidant mon verre!

# ◼ ACT II

## SCENE I

*The Kermesse.*

*One of the city gates. To the left, an Inn, bearing the sign of the god Bacchus.*

*Wagner, Students, Burghers, Soldiers, Maidens, and Matrons.*

STUDS: Wine or beer, now, which you will!
So the glass quick you fill!
And replenish at our need:
At our bouts we drink with speed!

WAG: Now, young tipplers at the cask,
Don't refuse what I ask—
Drink to glory! drink to love!
Drain the sparkling glass!

STUDS: We young tipplers at the cask
Won't refuse what you ask—
Here's to glory! here's to love!
Drain the sparkling glass!
(*They drink.*)

SOLDIERS: Castles, hearts, or fortresses, are all one to us.
Strong towers, maids with fair tresses,
Are won by the brave;
He, who has the art to take them,
Shows not little skill;
He, who knows the way to keep them, Has more wisdom still.

CITIZENS: On holy-days and feast-days,
I love to talk of war and battles.
While the toiling crowds around
Worry their brains with affairs,
I stroll calmly to this retreat
On the banks of the gliding river,
And behold the boats which pass
While I leisurely empty my glass.

(*Bourgeois et Soldats remontent vers le fond du théâtre.*)
(*Un groupe de jeunes filles entre en scène.*)

LES JEUNES FILLES: (*regardant de côté*). Voyez ces hardis compères
Qui viennent làbas;
Ne soyons pas trop sévères,
Retardons le pas.
(*Elles gagnent la droite du théâtre. Un second choeur d'etudiants entre à leur suit.*)

DEUXIÈME CHO. D'ETUDS: Voyez ces mines gaillardes
Et ces airs vainqueurs!
Amis, soyons sur nos gardes,
Tenons bien nos coeurs!

CHO. DE MATS: (*observant les étudiants et les jeunes filles*). Voyez après ces donzelles
Courir ces messieurs!
Nous sommes aussi bien qu'elles,
Sinon beaucoup mieux!
(*Ensemble.*)

MATS: (*aux jeunes filles*). Vous voulez leur plaire
Nous le voyons bien

ETUDS: Vin ou bière,
Bière ou vin,
Que mon verre
Soit plein!

SOLS: Pas be beauté fière!
Nous savons leur plaire
En un tour de main!

BOURG: Vidons un verre
De ce bon vin!

JEUNES FIILES: De votre colère
Nous ne craignons rien!

JEUNES ETUDS: Voyez leur colère,
Voyez leur maintien!
(*Les étudiants et les soldats séparent les femmes en riant. Tous les groupes s'éloignent et disparaissent.*)

## SCÈNE II

*Wagner, Siebel, Etudiants, Valentin.*

VAL: (*paraissant au fond; il tient une petite médaille à la main*). O sainte médaille,
Qui me viens de ma soeur,
Au jour de la bataille,
Pour écarter la mort, reste là sur mon coeur!

WAG: Ah! voici Valentin qui nous cherche sans doute!

VAL: Un dernier coup, messieurs, et mettre nous en route!

WAG: Qu'as-tu donc? . . . quels regrets attrist er nos adieux?

(*Citizens and soldiers go to back of stage.*)
(*A group of young girls enters.*)

GIRLS: Merry fellows come this way,
Yes, they now advance;
Let us, then, our steps delay,
Just to take one glance.
(*They go to right of stage. A second chorus of students enters after them.*)

STUDS: Sprightly maidens now advance,
Watch their conquering airs;
Friends be guarded, lest a glance
Take you unawares.

MATRONS: (*watching the students and young girls*). Behold the silly damsels,
And the foolish young men;
We were once as young as they are,
And as pretty again.
(*All join in the following chorus, each singing as follows.*)

MATS: (*to the Maidens*). You strive hard to please,
Your object is plain.

STUDS: Beer or wine, wine or beer,
I care nothing, with heart of cheer.

SOLDIERS: On, then, let's on;
Brave soldiers are we,
To conquest we'll on.

CITIZENS: Come, neighbor! In this fine weather
Let us empty a bottle together!

MAIDENS: They wish to please us, but it is in vain!
If you are angry, you'll gain little.

YOUNG STUDENTS: They are bright little maidens, it is plain;
We'll contrive to gain their favor.
(*The soldiers and students, laughing, separate the women. All the others depart.*)

## SCENE II

*Wagner, Siebel, Valentine, Students, and afterwards Mephistopheles.*

VAL: (*Advancing from the back of the stage and holding in his hand a small silver medal*). O sacred medallion, Gift of my sister dear To ward off danger and fear,
As I charge with my brave battalion,
Rest upon my heart.

WAG: Here comes Valentine, in search of us, doubtless.

VAL: Let us drain the parting cup, comrades,
It is time we were on the road.

WAG: What say you?
Why this sorrowful farewell?

VAL: Comme vous, pour long-temps, je vais quitter ces lieux; J'y laisse Marguerite, et, pour veiller sur elle, Ma mère n'est plus là!

SIE: Plus d'un ami fidèle Saura te remplacer a ses côtés!

VAL: (*lui serrant la main*). Merci!

SIE: Sur moi tu peux compter!

ETUDS: Compte sur nous aussi.

VAL: Avant de quitter ces lieux, Sol natal de mes aïeux, A toi, Seigneur et Roi des Cieux, Ma soeur je confie. Daigne de tout danger Toujours la protéger, Cette soeur si chérie. Délivré d'une triste pensée, J'irais chercher la gloire au sein des ennemis, Le premier, le plus brave au fort de la mêlée, J'irai combattre pour mon pays. Et si vers lui Dieu me rappelle, Je viellerai sur toi fidèle, O Marguerite!

WAG: Allons, amis! point de vaines alarmes A ce bon vin ne mêlons pas de larmes Buvons, trinquons, et qu'un joyeux refrain Nous mette en train!

ETUDS: Buvons, trinquons, et qu'un joyeux refrain Nous mette en train!

WAG: (*Montant sur un escabeau*) Un rat plus poltron que brave, Et plus laid que beau, Logeait au fond d'une cave, Sous un vieux tonneau; Un chat . . .

## SCÈNE III

*Les mêmes. Mephistopheles.*

MEP: (*paraissant tout à coup au milieu des étudiants et interrompant Wagner*). Pardon!

WAG: Hein?

MEP: Parmi vous, de grâce Permettez-moi de prendre place! Que votre ami d'abord achève sa chanson! Moi, je vous en promets plusieurs de ma façon!

WAG: (*descendant de son escabeau*). Une seule suffit, pourvu qu'elle soit bonne!

MEP: Je ferai de mon mieux pour n'ennuyer personne! I. Le veau d'or est toujours debout; On encense Sa puissance D'un bout du monde à l'autre bout! Pour fêter l'infâme idole,

VAL: Like you, I soon must quit these scenes, Leaving behind me Marguerite. Alas! my mother no longer lives, To care for and protect her.

SIE: You have more than one friend Who faithfully will supply your place.

VAL: My thanks!

SIE: On me you may rely.

STUDS: In us you surely may confide.

VAL: Even bravest heart may swell In the moment of farewell. Loving smile of kind sister, Quiet home I leave behind. I'll think of you often Whenever the wine-cup passes round, When my watch I keep alone. But when danger to glory shall call me, I still will be first in the fray, As blithe as a knight in his bridal array. Careless what fate shall befall me When glory shall call me.

WAG: Come on, friends! No tears nor vain alarms; We quaff good wine, to the success of our arms! Drink, boys, drink! In a joyous refrain Bid farewell, till we meet again.

CHO: We'll drink! Fill high! Once more in song our voices Let us raise.

WAG: (*mounting on a table*). A rat, more coward than brave, And with an exceedingly ugly head, Lodged in a sort of hole or cave, Under an ancient hogshead. A cat—

## SCENE III

*Mephistopheles and the preceding.*

MEP: (*appearing suddenly among the students and interrupting Wagner*). Good sir!

WAG: What!

MEP: If it please you I should wish To mingle with you a short time. If your good friend will kindly end his song, I'll tell a few things well worth hearing.

WAG: One will suffice, but let that one be good.

MEP: My utmost I will do Your worships not to bore. I. Calf of Gold! Always in the world To your mightiness they proffer, Incense at your fane they offer From end to end of all the world. And in honor of the idol

Peuples et rois confondus, Au bruit sombre des écus Dansent une ronde folle Autour de son piédestal? . . . Et Satan conduit le bal! II. Le veau d'or est vainqueur des dieux; Dans son gloire Dérisoire Le monstre abjecte insulte aux cieux! Il contemple, ô rage étrange! A ses pieds le genre humain Se ruant, le fer en main, Dans le sang et dans la fange Où brille l'ardent métal! . . . Et Satan conduit le bal!

TOUS: Et Satan conduit le bal!

CHO: Merci de ta chanson!

VAL: (*à part*). Singulier personnage!

WAG: (*Tendant un verre à Mephistopheles*). Nous ferez vous l'honneur de trinquer avec nous?

MEP: Volontiers! . . . (*Saisissant la main de Wagner et l'examinant.*) Ah! voici qui m'attriste pour vous! Vous voyez cette ligne?

WAG: Eh bien?

MEP: Fâcheux présage! Vous vous ferez tuer en montant à l'assaut!

SIE: Vous êtes donc sorcier?

MEP: Tout juste autant qu'il faut Pour lire dans ta main que le ciel a condamne A ne plus toucher une fleur Sans qu'elle se fane!

SIE: Moi!

MEP: Plus de bouquets à Marguerite!

VAL: Ma soeur! . . . Qui vous a dit son nom?

MEP: Prenez garde, mon brave! Vous vous ferez tuer par quelqu'un que je sais! (*Prenant le verre des mains de Wagner.*) A votre santé! . . . (*Jetant le contenu du verre, après y avoir trempé Peuh! que ton vin est mauvais! Permettez-moi de vous en offrir de mon cave!* (*Frappant sur le tonneau, surmonté d'un Bacchus qui est le seigne au cabaret.*) Holà! seigneur Bacchus! à boire! (*Le vin jaillit du tonneau. Aux étudiants*) Approchez-vous! Chacun sera servi selon ses goûts. A la santé que tout à l'heure Vous portiez, mes amis, à Marguerite!

Kings and peoples everywhere To the sound of jingling coins Dance with zeal in festive circle, Round about the pedestal. Satan, he conducts the ball. II. Calf of Gold, strongest god below! To his temple overflowing Crowds before his vile shape bowing, The monster dares insult the skies. With contempt he views around him All the vaunted human race, As they strive in abject toil, As they circle with souls debased Round about the pedestal. Satan, he conducts the ball.

ALL: Satan, he conducts the ball.

CHO: A strange story this of his.

VAL: (*aside.*) And stranger still is he who sings it.

WAG: (*offering a cup to Mephistopheles*). Will you honor us by partaking of wine?

MEP: With pleasure. Ah! (*Taking Wagner by the hand, and scrutinizing his palm.*) Behold what saddens me to view. See you this line?

WAG: Well!

MEP: A sudden death it presages,— You will be killed in mounting to the assault!

SIE: You are then a sorcerer!

MEP: Even so. And your own hand shows plainly To what fate condemns. What flower you would gather Shall wither in the grasp.

SIE: I?

MEP: No more bouquets for Marguerite.

VAL: My sister! How knew you her name?

MEP: Take care, my brave fellow! Some one I know is destined to kill you. (*Taking the cup.*) Your health, gentlemen! Pah! What miserable wine! Allow me to offer you some from my cellar? (*Jumps on the table, and strikes on a little cask, surmounted by the effigy of the god Bacchus, which serves as a sign to the Inn.*) What ho! god of wine, now give us drink! (*Wine gushes forth from cask, and Mephistopheles fills his goblet.*) Approach, my friends! Each one shall be served to his liking. To your health, now and hereafter! To Marguerite!

VAL: (*lui arrachant le verre des mains*). Assez! . . .
Si je ne te fais taire à l'instant, que je meure!
(*Le vin s'enflamme dans la vasque placée audessous du tonneau.*)

VAL: Enough! If I do not silence him,
And that instantly, I will die.
(*The wine bursts into flame.*)

WAG. ET LES ETUDS: Holà! . . .
(*Ils tirent leurs épées*).

WAG: Hola!

CHO: Hola!
(*They draw their swords.*)

MEP: Pourquoi trembler, vous qui me menacez?
(*Il tire un cercle autour de lui avec son épée—Valentin s'avance pour l'attaquer.—Son épée se brise.*)

MEP: Ah, ha! Why do you tremble so, you who menace me?
(*He draws a circle around him with his sword. Valentine attacks; the sword is broken.*)

VAL: Mon fer, ô surprise!
Dans les airs se brise! . . .

VAL: My sword, O amazement!
Is broken asunder.

VAL., WAG., SIE. ET LES ETUDS: (*forçant Mephistopheles à reculer et lui présentant la garde de leurs épées*). De l'enfer qui vient émousser
Nos armes!
Nous ne pouvons pas repousser
Les charmes!
Mais puisque tu brises le fer,
Regarde! . . .
C'est une croix qui, de l'enfer,
Nous garde!
(*Ils sortent.*)

ALL: (*Forcing Mephistopheles to retire by holding toward him the cross-shaped handles of their swords.*) Gainst the powers of evil our arms assailing,
Strongest earthly might is unavailing.
But you can not charm us,
Look here!
While we wear this blest sign
You cannot harm us.
(*Exeunt.*)

## SCÈNE IV

Mephistopheles, puis Faust.

MEP: (*remettant son épée au fourreau*). Nous nous retrouverons, mes amis!—Serviteur!

FAUST: (*entrant en scène*). Qu'as-tu donc?

MEP: Rien!—A nous deux, cher docteur!
Qu'attendez-vous de moi? par où commencerai-je?

FAUST: Où se cache la belle enfant
Que ton art m'a fait voir?—Est-ce un vain sortilège?

MEP: Non pas! mais contre nous sa vertu la protège;
Et le ciel même la défend

FAUST: Qu'importe? je le veux! viens! condui mois vers elle!
Ou je me sépare de toi!

MEP: Il suffit! . . . je tiens trop à mon nouveau emploi
Pour vous laisser douter un instant de mon zèle!
Attendons! . . . Ici même, à ce signal joyeux,
La belle et chaste enfant va paraitre à vos yeux!

## SCENE IV

Mephistopheles, then Faust.

MEP: (*replacing his sword*). We'll meet anon, good sirs,—adieu!

FAUST: (*enters*). Why, what has happened?

MEP: Oh, nothing! let us change the subject!
Say, Doctor, what would you of me? With what shall we begin?

FAUST: Where bides the beauteous maid your art
Did show to me?
Or was it mere witchcraft?

MEP: No, but her virtue protects her from you.
And heaven itself would keep her pure.

FAUST: It matters not!
Come, lead me to her,
Or I straightway abandon you.

MEP: Then I'll comply! It would be a pity should you think
So meanly of the magic power
which I possess.
Have patience! and to this joyous tune.
Right sure am I, the maiden will appear.

## SCÈNE V

Les étudiants et les jeunes filles, bras dessus, bras dessous, et precédés par des joueurs de violon, envahissent la scène. Ils sont suivant par les bourgeois qui ont paru au commencement de l'acte.

Les Mêmes, Etudiants, Jeunes Filles, Bourgeois, plus Siebel et Marguerite.

CHO: (*marquant la mesure en marchant*). Ainsi que la brise légère
Soulève en épais tourbillons
La poussière
Des sillons,
Que la valse nous entraîne!
Faites retentir la plaine
De l'éclat de nos chansons!
(*Les Musiciens montent sur les bancs; la valse commence.*)

MEP: (*à Faust*). Vois ces filles
Gentilles!
Ne veux-tu pas
Aus plus belles
D'entre elles
Offrir ton bras?

FAUST: Non! fais trêve
A ce ton moqueur!
Et laisse mon coeur
A son rêve! . . .

SIE: (*rentrant en scène*). C'est par ici que doit passer Marguerite!

QUELQUES JEUNES FILLES: (*s'approchant de Siebel*). Faut-il qu'une fille à danser Vous invite?

SIE: Non! . . . non! je ne veux pas valser!..

CHO: Ainsi que la brise légère
Soulève en épais tourbillons
La poussière
Des sillons,
Que la valse nous entraîne!
Faites retentir la plaine
De l'éclat de nos chansons! . . .
(*Marguerite parait.*)

FAUST: Ah! . . . la voici . . . c'est elle! . . .

MEP: Eh bien, aborde-la!

SIE: (*apercevant Marguerite et faisant un pas vers elle*). Marguerite!

MEP: (*se retournant et se trouvant face à face avec Siebel*). Plaît-il! . . .

SIE: (*à part*). Maudit homme! encor là! . . .

MEP: (*d'un ton milleux*). Eh quoi! mon ami! vous voilà! . . .
(*en riant*).
Ah, vraiment, mon ami!
(*Siebel recule devant Mephistopheles, qui lui fait faire ainsi un tour du théâtre en passant derrière le groupe des danseurs.*)

## SCENE V

Students, with Maidens on their arms, preceded by Musicians, take possession of the stage. Burghers in the rear, as at the commencement of the act.

Students, Maidens, Burghers, etc., afterwards Siebel and Marguerite.

CHO: (*marking waltz time with their feet*). As the wind that sportively plays,
At first will light dust only raise,
Yet, at last, becomes a gale,
So our dancing and our singing,
Soft at first, then loudly ringing,
Will resound over hill and dale.
(*The Musicians mount upon the table, and dancing begins.*)

MEP: (*to Faust*). See those lovely young maidens.
Will you not ask them
To accept you?

FAUST: No! desist from your idle sport,
And leave my heart free to reflection.

SIE: (*entering*). Marguerite can arrive this way alone.

SOME OF THE MAIDENS: (*approaching Siebel*). Pray seek a partner to join in the dance!

SIE: No: it has no charm for me.

CHO: As the wind that sportively plays,
At first will only raise light dust,
Yet, at last, becomes a gale,
So our dancing and our singing,
Soft at first, then loudly ringing,
Will resound over hill and dale.
(*Marguerite enters.*)

FAUST: It is she! behold her!

MEP: It is well! now, then, approach!

SIE: (*perceiving Marguerite and approaching her*). Marguerite!

MEP: (*turning round and finding himself face to face with Siebel*). What say you?

SIE: (*aside*). Malediction! here again!

MEP: (*coaxingly*). What, here again, dear boy?
(*laughing*).
Ha, ha! a right good jest!
(*Siebel retreats before Mephistopheles, who then compels him to make a circuit of the stage, passing behind the dancers.*)

FAUST: (*abordant Marguerite qui traverse la scène*). Ne permettrez-vous pas, ma belle demoiselle, Qu'on vous offre le bras pour faire le chemin?

MAR: Non, monsieur! je ne suis demoiselle, ni belle, Et je n'ai pas besoin qu'on me donne la main? (*Elle passe devant Faust et s'éloigne.*)

FAUST: (*la suivant des yeux*). Pas le ciel! que de grâce . . . et quelle modestie! O belle enfant, je t'aime! . . .

SIE: (*redescendant en scene sans avoir vu ce qui vient de se passer*). Elle est partie! (*Il va pour s'élancer sur la trace de Marguerite; mais, se trouvant de nouveau face à face avec Méphistophèles, il lui tourne le dos e s'éloigne par le fond du théâtre.*)

MEP: (*à Faust*). Eh bien?

FAUST: On me repousse! . . .

MEP: (*en riant*). Allons! à tes amours Je vois qu'il-faut prêter secours! . . . (*Il s'éloigne avec Faust du même côté que Marguerite.*)

QUELQUES JEUNES FILLES: (*s'adressant à trois ou quatre d'entre elles qui ont observé la rencontre de Faust et de Marguerite*). Qu'est-ce donc! . . .

DEUXIÈME GROUPE DE JEUNES FILLES: Marguerite, Qui de ce beau seigneur refuse la conduite! . . .

ETUDS: (*se rapprochant*). Valsons encor!

JEUNES FILLES: Valsons toujours!

## ■ ACTE III

### SCÈNE I

*Le Jardin de Marguerite.*

*Au fond, un mur percé d'une petite porte. A gauche, un bosquet. A droite, un pavillon dont la fenêtre fait face au public. Arbres massifs.*

SIE: (*seul*). (*Il est arrêté près d'un massif de roses et de lilas.*) I. Faites-lui mes aveux, Portez mes voeux, Fleurs écloses près d'elle, Dites-lui qu'elle est belle . . .

FAUST: (*approaching Marguerite, who crosses the stage*). Will you not permit me, my fairest demoiselle, To offer you my arm, and clear for you the way?

MAR: No, sir. I am no demoiselle, neither am I fair; And I have no need to accept your offered arm. (*Passes Faust and retires.*)

FAUST: (*gazing after her*). What beauty! What grace! What modesty! O lovely child, I love you! I love you!

SIE: (*coming forward, without having seen what has occurred*). She has gone! (*He is about to hurry after Marguerite, when he suddenly finds himself face to face with Mephistopheles—he hastily turns away and leaves the stage.*)

MEP: Well, Doctor!

FAUST: Well. She has repulsed me.

MEP: (*laughing*). Ay, truly, I see, in love, You know not how to make the first move. (*He retires with Faust, in the direction taken by Marguerite.*)

SOME OF THE MAIDENS: (*who have noticed the meeting between Faust and Marguerite*). What is it?

OTHERS: Marguerite. She has refused the escort Of yonder elegant gentleman.

STUDS: (*approaching*). Waltz again!

MAIDENS: Waltz alway!

## ■ ACT III

### SCENE I

*Marguerite's Garden.*

*At the back a wall, with a little door. To the left a bower. On the right a pavilion, with a window facing the audience. Trees, shrubs, etc.*

*Siebel, alone. He enters through the little door at the back, and stops on the threshold of the pavilion, near a group of roses and lilies.*

SIE: I. Gently whisper to her of love, dear flower; Tell her that I adore her, And for me, oh, implore her, For my heart feels love's power alone for her.

Que mon coeur nuit et jour Languit d'amour! Révélez à son âme Le secret de ma flamme! Qu'il s'exhale avec vous Parfums plus doux! . . . (*Il cueille une fleur.*) Fanée! . . . hélas! (*Il jette la fleur avec dépit.*) Ce sorcier que Dieu damne M'a porté malheur! (*Il cueille une autre fleur qui s'effeuille encore.*) Je ne puis sans qu'elle se fane Toucher une fleur! . . . Si je trempais mes doigts dans l'eau bénite? . . . (*Il s'approche du pavillon et trempe ses doigts dans un bénitier accroché au mur.*) C'est là que chaque soir vient prier Marguerite! Voyons maintenant! voyons vite! (*Il cueille deux ou trois fleurs.*) Elles se fanent? . . . Non! . . . Satan, je ris du toi . . . II. C'est en vous que j'ai foi; Parlez pour moi! Qu'elle puisse connaître L'ardeur qu'elle a fait naître, Et dont mon coeur troublé N'a point parlé! Si l'amour l'effarouche. Que la fleur sur sa bouche Sache au moins déposer Un doux baiser! . . . (*Il cueille des fleurs pour former un bouquet et disparait dans les massifs du jardin.*)

### SCÈNE II

*Méphistophèles, Faust, puis Siebel.*

FAUST: (*entrant doucement en scène*). C'est ici?

MEP: Suivez-moi!

FAUST: Que regardes-tu là?

MEP: Siebel, votre rival.

FAUST: Siebel!

MEP: Chut! . . . le voilà! (*Il se cache avec Faust dans un bosquet.*)

SIE: (*rentrant en scène, avec un bouquet à la main*). Mon bouquet n'est-il pas charmant?

MEP: (*à part*). Charmant!

SIE: Victoire! Je lui raconterai demain toute l'histoire Et, si l'on veut savoir le secret de mon coeur, Un baiser lui dira le reste!

MEP: (*à part*). Séducteur! (*Siebel attache le bouquet à la porte du pavillon et sort.*)

Say in sighing I languish, That for her, in my anguish, My aching heart beats alone, dearest flower. (*Plucks flowers.*) Alas! they are withered! (*Throws them away.*) Can the accursed wizard's words be true? (*Picks another flower, which, on touching his hand, immediately withers.*) 'You shall never touch flower again But it shall wither!' I'll bathe my hand in holy water! (*Approaches the pavilion, and dips his fingers in a little font suspended to the wall.*) When day declines, Marguerite hither Comes here to pray, so we'll try again. (*Plucks more flowers.*) Are they withered? No! Satan, you are conquered! II. I've faith in these flowers alone, For they will plead for me; They will reveal to her My hapless state. She is the sole cause of my woe And yet she knows it not. But in these flowers I've faith, For they will plead for me. (*Plucks flowers in order to make a bouquet, and disappears amongst the shrubs.*)

### SCENE II

*Mephistopheles, Faust, and Siebel.*

FAUST: (*cautiously entering through the garden door*). We are here!

MEP: Follow me.

FAUST: Who do you see?

MEP: Siebel, your rival.

FAUST: Siebel?

MEP: Hush! He comes. (*They enter the bower.*)

SIE: (*entering with a bouquet in his hand*). My bouquet is charming indeed?

MEP: (*aside*). It is indeed!

SIE: Victory! Tomorrow I'll reveal all to her. I will disclose to her the secret That lies concealed in my heart: A kiss will tell the rest.

MEP: (*aside, mockingly*). Seducer! (*Exit Siebel, after fastening bouquet to the door of the pavilion.*)

## SCÈNE III

*Faust, Mephistopheles.*

**MEP:** Attendez-moi là, cher docteur!
Pour tenir compagnie aux fleurs de votre élève,
Je vais vous chercher un trésor
Plus merveilleux, plus riche encor
Que tous ceux qu'elle voit en rêve!

**FAUST:** Laisse-moi!

**MEP:** J'obéis! . . . daignez m'attendre ici?
(*Il sort.*)

## SCÈNE IV

*Faust.*

**FAUST:** (*seul*). Quel trouble inconnu me pénètre!
Je sens l'amour s'emparer de mon être
O Marguerite! tes pieds me voici!
Salut! demeure chaste et pure, où se devine
La présence d'une âme innocente et devine! . . .
Que de richesse en cette pauvreté!
En ce réduit, que de félicité! . . .
O nature, c'est là que tu la fis si belle!
C'est là que cette enfant a grandi ton aile,
A dormi sous tes yeux?
Là que, de ton haleine enveloppant une âme,
Tu fis avec amour épanouir la femme
En cet ange des cieux!
Salut! demeure chaste et pure, où se devine!
La présence d'une âme innocente et divine!
Que de richesse en cette pauvreté!
En ce réduit, que de félicité! . . .
Salut! demeure chaste et pure, où se devine
La présence d'une âme innocente et divine! . . .

## SCÈNE V

*Faust, Mephistopheles.*

**MEP:** (*Mephistopheles reparait, une cassette sous le bras.*) Alerte! la voilà! . . . Si le bouquet l'emporte
Sur l'écrin, je consens à perdre mon pouvoir!
(*Il ouvre l'écrin.*)

**FAUST:** Fuyons! . . . je veux ne jamais la revoir!

**MEP:** Quel scrupule vous prend! . . .
(*Plaçant l'écrin sur le seuil du pavillon.*)
Sur le seuil de la porte,
Voici l'écrin placé! . . . venez! . . . j'ai bon es-

---

## SCENE III

*Faust and Mephistopheles.*

**MEP:** Now attend, my dear doctor!
To keep company with the flowers of our friend,
I go to bring you a treasure,
Which outshines them beyond measure,
And of beauty past believing.

**FAUST:** Leave me!

**MEP:** I obey. Deign to await me here.
(*Disappears.*)

## SCENE IV

*Faust.*

**FAUST:** (*alone*). What new emotion penetrates my soul!
Love, a pure and holy love, pervades my being.
O Marguerite, behold me at your feet!
All hail, dwelling pure and lowly,
Home of an angel fair and holy,
All mortal beauty excelling!
What wealth is here, a wealth outbidding gold,
Of peace, and love, and innocence untold!
Bounteous Nature! it was here by day your love was taught her,
You here with kindly care overshadowed your daughter
Through hours of night!
Here waving tree and flower
Made her an Eden bower
Of beauty and delight,
For one whose very birth
Brought down heaven to our earth.
All hail, dwelling pure and lowly,
Home of an angel fair and holy.

## SCENE V

*Faust, Mephistopheles.*

**MEP:** (*carrying a casket under his arm*). What ho! see here!
If flowers are more potent than bright jewels,
Then I consent to lose my power.
(*Opens the casket and displays the jewels.*)

**FAUST:** Let us fly; I never will see her again.

**MEP:** What scruple now assails you?
(*Lays the casket on the threshold of the pavilion.*)
See on yonder step,
The jewels snugly lie;
We've reason now to hope.

---

poir!
(*Il entraine Faust et disparait avec lui dans le jardin. Marguerite entre par la porte du fond et descend en silence jusque sur le devant de la scène.*)

## SCÈNE VI

*Marguerite.*

**MAR:** (*seule*). Je voudrais bien savoir quel était ce jeune homme,
Si c'est un grand seigneur, et comment il se nomme?
(*Elle s'assied dans le bosquet, devant son rouet, et prend son fuseau autour duquel elle prépare de la laine.*)
I.
'Il était un roi de Thulé,
Qui, jusqu'à la tombe fidèle,
Eut, en souvenir de sa belle,
Une coupe en or ciselé! . . . '
(*S'interrompant.*)
Il avait bonne grâce, à ce qu'il m'a en semble.
(*Reprenant sa chanson.*)
'Nul trésor n'avait plus de charmes!
Dans les grands jours il s'en servait,
Et chaque fois qu'il y buvait,
Ses yeux se remplissaient de larmes! . . . '

II.
(*Elle se lève et fait quelques pas.*)
'Quand il sentit venir la mort,
Etendu sur sa froide couche,
Pour la porter jusqu'à sa bouche
Sa main fit un suprême effort! . . . '
(*S'interrompant.*)
Je ne savais que dire, et j'ai rougé d'abord.
(*Reprenant sa chanson.*)
'Et puis, en l'honneur de sa dame,
Il but un dernière fois;
La coupe trembla dans ses doigts.
Et doucement il rendit l'âme!'
Les grands seigneurs ont seuis des airs résolus,
Avec cette douceur.
(*Elle se dirige vers le pavillon.*)
Allons! n'y pensons plus!
Cher Valentin, si Dieu m'écoute,
Je te reverrai! . . . me voilà
Toute seule! . . .
(*Au moment d'entrer dans le pavillon, elle aperçoit la bouquet suspendu à la porte.*)
Un bouquet! (*Elle prend le bouquet.*)
C'est de Siebel, sans doute!
Pauvre garçon! (*Apercevant la cassette.*)
Que vois-je là?
D'où ce riche coffret peut-il venir de n'ose
Y toucher, et pourtant . . . —
Voici la ciel je crois! . . .
Si je l'ouvrais! . . . ma main tremble! Pourquoi!
Je ne fais, en l'ouvrant, rien de mal je suppose! . . .

---

(*Draws Faust after him, and disappears in the garden. Marguerite enters through the doorway at the back, and advances silently to the front.*)

## SCENE VI

*Marguerite.*

**MAR:** (*alone*). Fain would I know the name
Of the fair youth I met?
Fain would I also know birth And station?
(*Seats herself at her wheel in the arbor, and arranges the flax upon the spindle.*)
I.
'Once there was a king in Thulé,
Who was until death always faithful,
And in memory of his loved one
Caused a cup of gold to be made.'
(*Breaking off.*)
His manner was so gentle! It was true politeness. (*Resuming the song.*)
Never treasure prized he so dearly,
Nothing else would use on festive days,
And always when he drank from it,
His eyes with tears would be overflowing.'

II.
(*She rises, and takes a few paces.*)
'When he knew that death was near,
As he lay on his cold couch smiling,
Once more he raised with greatest effort
The golden vase to his lips.'
(*Breaking off.*)
I knew not what to say, my face blushes red!
(*Resuming the song.*)
'And when he, to honor his lady,
Drank from the cup the last, last time,
Soon falling from his trembling grasp,
Then gently passed his soul away.'
Nobles alone can bear them with so bold a mien,
So tender, too, withal!
(*She goes toward the pavilion.*)
I'll think of him no more! Good Valentine!
If heaven heeds my prayer, we shall meet again.
Meanwhile I am alone!
(*Suddenly perceiving the bouquet attached to the door of the pavilion.*)
Flowers!
(*Unfastens the bouquet.*)
They are Siebel's, surely!
Poor faithful boy!
(*Perceiving the casket.*)
But what is this?
From whom did this splendid casket come?
I dare not touch it—
Yet see, here is the key!—I'll take one look!

(Elle ouvre la cassette et raisse tombre le bouquet.)
O Dieu! que de bijoux! . . . est-ce un rêve charmant
Qui m'éblouit, ou si je veille!
Mes yeux n'ont jamais vu de richesse pareille!
(Elle place la cassette tout ouverte sur une chaise et s'agenouille pour se parer.)
Si j'osais seulement
Me parer un moment
De ces pendants d'oreille!
(Elle tire des boucles d'oreilles de la cassette.)
Voici tout justement,
Au fond de la cassette,
Un miroir! . . . comment
N'être pas coquette?
(Elle se pare des boucles d'oreilles, se lève et se regarde dans le miroir.)
Ah! je ris de me voir
Si belle en ce miroir! . . .
Est-ce toi, Marguerite?
Réponds-moi, réponds vite!—
Non! non!—ce n'est plus toi!
Ce n'est plus ton visage!
C'est la fille d'un roi,
Qu'on salue au passage!
Ah! s'il était ici!
S'il me voyait ainsi! . . .
Comme une demoiselle
Il me trouverait belle! . . .
Achevons la métamorphose!
Il me tarde encor d'essayer
Le bracelet et le collier.
(Elle se pare du collier d'abord, puis du bracelet.—Se levant.)
Dieu! c'est comme une main qui sui mon bras se pose!
Ah! je ris de me voir
Si belle en ce miroir!
Est-ce toi, Marguerite?
Réponds-moi, réponds vit:—
Non! non!—ce n'est plus toi!
Ce n'est plus ton visage!
C'est la fille d'un roi,
Qu'on salue au passage! . . .
Ah! s'il était ici! . . .
S'il me voyait ainsi! . . .
Comme une demoiselle
Il me trouverait belle! . . .
Ah! s'il était ici! . . .

## SCÈNE VII

*Marguerite, Marthe.*

MART: (*entrant par le fond*). Que vois-je, Seigneur
Dieu! . . . comme vous voilà belle,
Mon ange! . . . —D'où vous vient ce riche écrin?

MAR: (*avec confusion*). On l'aura par mégarde apporté!

---

How I tremble—yet why?—can it be
Much harm just to look in a casket!
(*Opens the casket and lets the bouquet fall.*)
Oh, heaven! what jewels!
Can I be dreaming?
Or am I really awake?
Never have I seen such costly things before!
(*Puts down the casket on a rustic seat, and kneels down in order to adorn herself with the jewels.*)
I should just like to see
How they'd look upon me
Those brightly sparkling ear-drops!
(*Takes out the ear-rings.*)
Ah! at the bottom of the casket is a glass:
I there can see myself!—
But am I not becoming vain?
(*Puts on the ear-rings, rises, and looks at herself in the glass.*)
Ah! I laugh, as I pass, to look into a glass;
Is it truly Marguerite, then?
Is it you?
Tell me true!
No, no, no, it is not you!
No, no, that bright face there reflected
Must belong to a queen!
It reflects some fair queen, whom I greet as I pass her.
Ah! could he see me now,
Here, decked like this, I vow,
He surely would mistake me,
And take me for a noble lady!
I'll try on the rest.
The necklace and the bracelets
I fain would try!
(*She adorns herself with the bracelets and necklace, then rises.*)
Heavens! It is like a hand
Thank rests on my arm!
Ah! I laugh, as I pass, to look into a glass;
Is it truly Marguerite, then?
Is it you?
Tell me true!
No, no, no, it is not you!
No, no, that bright face there reflected
Must belong to a queen!
It reflects some fair queen, whom I greet as I pass her.
Oh! could he see me now,
Here, decked like this, I vow,
He surely would mistake me,
And take me for a noble lady!

## SCENE VII

*Marguerite and Martha.*

MART: Just heaven! what is it I see?
How fair you now do seem!
Why, what has happened?
Who gave to you these jewels?

MAR: (*confused*). Alas! by some mistake
They have been brought here.

---

MART: Que non pas
Ces bijoux sont á vous, ma chère demoiselle!
Oui! c'est là le cadeau d'un seigneur amoureux!
(*Soupirant.*)
Mon cher époux jadis était moins généreux!
(*Mephistopheles et Faust entrent en scène.*)

## SCÈNE VIII

*Les Mêmes, Mephistopheles, Faust.*

MEP: Dame Marthe Schwerlein, s'il vous plait

MART: Qui m'appelle?

MEP: Pardon d'oser ainsi nous présenter chez vous!
(*Bas à Faust.*)
Vous voyez qu'elle a fait bel accueil son bijoux?
(*Haut.*)
Dame Marthe Schwerlein?

MART: Me voici!

MEP: La nouvelle
Que j'apporte n'est pas pour vous en gaité:—
Votre mari, madame, est mort et vous salue!

MART: Ah! . . . grand Dieu! . . .

MAR: Qu'est ce donc?

MEP: Rien!
(*Marguerite baisse les yeux sous le regard de Mephistopheles se hâte d'ôter le collier, le bracelet et les pendants d'oreilles et de les remettre dans la cassette.*)

MART: O calamité! . . . O nouvelle imprévue! . . .
(*Ensemble.*)

MAR: (*à part*). Malgré moi mon coeur tremble et tressaille à sa vue!

FAUST: (*à part*). La fièvre de mes sens se dissipe à sa vue!

MEP: (*à Marthe*). Votre mari, madame, est mort et vous salue!

MART: Ne m'apportez-vous rien de lui!

MEP: Rien! . . . et, pour le punir, il faut dès aujourd'hui Chercher quelqu'un qui le remplace!

FAUST: (*à Marguerite*). Pourquoi donc quitter ces bijoux?

MAR: Ces bijoux ne sont pas à moi! . . . Laissez de grâce!

MEP: (*à Marthe*). Que ne serait heureux d'échanger avec vous La bague d'hyménée?

MART: (*à part*). Ah, bah!
(*Haut.*)
Plait-il?

---

MART: Why so?
No, beauteous maiden,
These jewels are for you;
The gift are they of some enamored lord.
My husband, I must say,
Was of a less generous turn!
(*Mephistopheles and Faust enter.*)

## SCENE VIII

*Mephistopheles, Faust, and the before-named.*

MEP: (*making a profound bow*).
Tell me, I pray, are you Martha Schwerlein?

MART: Sir, I am!

MEP: Pray pardon me,
If thus I venture to present myself.
(*Aside, to Faust.*)
You see your presents
Are right graciously received.
(*To Martha.*)
Are you, then, Martha Schwerlein?

MART: Sir, I am.

MEP: The news I bring
Is of an unpleasant kind:
Your much-loved spouse is dead,
And sends you greeting.

MART: Great heaven!

MAR: Why, what has happened?

MEP: Nothing!
(*Marguerite hastily takes off the jewels, and is about to replace them in the casket.*)

MART: Oh woe! oh, unexpected news!

MAR: (*aside.*) How beats my heart Now he is near!

FAUST: (*aside*). The fever of my love Is lulled when at her side!

MEP: (*to Martha*). Your much-loved spouse is dead, And sends you greeting!

MART: (*to Mephistopheles*). Sent he nothing else to me?

MEP: (*to Martha*). No. We'll punish him for it; Upon this very day We'll find him a successor.

FAUST: (*to Marguerite*). Wherefore lay aside these jewels?

MAR: (*to Faust*). Jewels are not made for me; I'll leave them where they are.

MEP: (*to Martha*).
Who would not gladly Present the wedding-ring to you!

MART: (*aside*). Indeed! (*to Mephistopheles*). You think so?

MEP: (soupirant). Hélas! cruelle destinée! . . .

FAUST: (à Marguerite). Prenez mon bras un moment!

MAR: (se défendant). Laissez! . . . Je vous en conjure!

MEP: (de l'autre côté du théâtre, à Marthe). Votre bras! . . .

MART: (à part). Il est charmant!

MEP: (à part). La voisine est un peu mûre!
(Marguerite abandonne son bras à Faust et s'éloigne avec Mephistopheles et Marthe restent seuls en scène.)

MART: Ainsi vous voyagez toujours?

MEP: Dure nécessité, madame!
Sans ami, sans parents! . . . sans femme.

MART: Cela sied encore aux beaux jours!
Mais plus tard, combien il est triste
De vieillir seul, en égoïste!

MEP: J'ai frémi souvent, j'en conviens,
Devant cette horrible pensée!

MART: Avant que l'heure en soit passée!
Digne seigneur, songez-y bien!

MEP: J'y songerai!

MART: Songez-y bien!
(Ils sortent. Entre Faust et Marguerite.)

FAUST: Eh quoi! toujours seule? . . .

MAR: Mon frère
Est soldat; j'ai perdu ma mère;
Puis ce fut un autre malheur,
Je perdis ma petite soeur!
Pauvre ange! . . . Elle m'était bien chere
C'était mon unique souci;
Que de soins, hélas! . . . que de peines!
C'est quand nos âmes en sont pleines
Que la mort nous les prend ainsi! . . .
Sitôt qu'elle s'éveillait, vite
Il fallait que je fusse là! . . .
Elle n'aimait que Marguerite!
Pour la voir, la pauvre petite,
Je reprendrais bien tout cela! . . .

FAUST: Si le ciel, avec un sourire,
L'avait faite semblable à toi,
C'était un ange! . . . Oui, je le crois

MAR: Vous moquez-vous? . . .

FAUST: Non! je t'admire!

---

MEP: (sighing). Ah me! ah, cruel fate!

FAUST: (to Marguerite). Pray lean upon my arm:

MAR: (retiring). Leave me, I humbly pray!

MEP: (offering his arm to Martha). Take mine!

MART: (aside). In truth, a comely knight!
(Taking his arm.)

MEP: (aside). The dame is somewhat tough!
(Marguerite yields her arm to Faust, and withdraws with him. Mephistopheles and Martha remain together.)

MART: And so you are always traveling!

MEP: It is a hard necessity, madame!
Alone and loveless, Ah!

MART: In youth it matters not so much,
But in late years it is sad indeed!
Right melancholy it is in solitude
Our olden age to pass!

MEP: The very thought makes me shudder.
But still, alas! what can I do?

MART: If I were you, I'd not delay,
But think on it seriously at once.

MEP: I'll think on it!

MART: At once and seriously!
(They withdraw. Faust and Marguerite re-enter.)

FAUST: Are you always alone?

MAR: My brother is at the wars,
My mother dear is dead!
By misadventure, too,
I have lost my dear sister.
Dear sister!
My greatest happiness was she.
Sad sorrows these;
When our souls are filled with love,
Death tears the loved one from us!
At morn, no sooner did she wake,
Than I was always at her side!
The darling of my life was she!
To see her once again.
I'd gladly suffer all.

FAUST: If heaven, in joyous mood,
Did make her like you,
An angel must she indeed have been!

MAR: You mock me!

FAUST: No, I do love you!

---

MAR: (souriant). Je ne vous crois pas
Et de moi tout bas
Vous riez sans doute! . . .
J'at tort de rester
Pour vous écouter! . . .
Et pourtant j'écoute! . . .

FAUST: Laisse-moi ton bras! . . .
Dieu ne m'a t il pas
Conduit sur ta route? . . .
Pourquoi redouter,
Hélas! d'écouter! . . .
Mon coeur parle; écoute! . . .
(Mephistopheles et Marthe reparaissent).

MART: Vous n'entendez pas,
Ou de moi tout bas
Vous riez sans doute!
Avant d'écouter,
Pourquoi vous hâter
De vous mettre en route?

MEP: Ne m'accusez pas,
Si je dois, hélas!
Me remettre en route.
Faut-il attester
Qu'on voudrait rester
Quand on vous écoute?
(La nuit commenoc à tomber.)

MAR: (à Faust). Retirez-vous! . . . voici la nuit.

FAUST: (passant son bras autour de la taille de Marguerite.) Chère âme!

MAR: Laissez-moi!
(Elle se dégage et s'enfuit.)

FAUST: (la poursuivant). Quoi! méchante! . . . on me fuit!

MEP: (à part, tandis que Marthe, dépitée, lui tourne le dos)
L'entretien devient trop tendre!
Esquivons nous!
(Il se cache derrière un arbre.)

MART: (À part). Comment m'y prendre?
(Se retournant.) Eh bien! il est parti! . . . Seigneur! . . .
(Elle s'éloigne.)

MEP: Oui! Cours aprés moi! . . .
Ouf! cette vieille impitoyable
De force ou de gré, je crois,
Allait épouser le diable!

FAUST: (dans la coulisse). Marguerite!

MART: (dans la coulisse). Cher seigneur!

MEP: Serviteur!

## SCÈNE IX

*Mephistopheles.*

MEP: (seul). Il était temps! sous le feuillage sombre
Voici nos amoureux qui reviennent! . . .
C'est bien!
Gardons nous de trouble un si doleur entretien!
O nuit, étends sur eux ton ombre!

---

MAR: (sighing). Flatterer! You mock me!
I don't believe you! You seek to deceive.
No longer will I stay, to hear your words

FAUST: (to Marguerite).
No, I do love you! Stay, oh stay!
Heaven has crowned my path with an angel.
Why do you fear to listen?
It is my heart that speaks.
(Re-enter Mephistopheles and Martha.)

MART: (to Mephistopheles). Of what now are you thinking?
You heed me not—perchance you mock me.
Now listen to what I say.—
You really must not leave us!

MEP: (to Martha). Ah, chide me not, if my wanderings I resume.
Suspect me not; to roam I am compelled!
Need I attest how gladly I remain.
I hear but you alone.
(Night comes on.)

MAR: (to Faust). It grows dark,—you must away.

FAUST: (embracing her). My loved one!

MAR: Ah! no more!
(Escapes.)

FAUST: Ah, cruel one, would you fly?
(Pursuing her.)

MEP: (aside, whilst Martha angrily turns her back to him). The matter's getting serious,
I must away.
(Conceals himself behind a tree.)

MART: (aside). What's to be done? he's gone!
What ho, good sir!
(Retires.)

MEP: Yes, look for me—that's right.
I really do believe
The aged beldame would
Actually have married Satan!

FAUST: (without). Marguerite!

MART: (without). Good sir!

MEP: Your servant!

## SCENE IX

*Mephistopheles.*

MEP: It was high time!
By night, protected,
In earnest talk of love,
They will return! It is well!
I'll not disturb
Their amorous confabulation!
Night, conceal them in your darkest shade.

Amour, ferme leur âme aus re-
mords importuns!
Et voux, fleurs aux subtils parfums,
Epanouissez-vous sous cette main
maudite!
Achevez de troubler le coeur de
Marguerite! . . .
(Il s'éloigne et disparait dans
l'ombre.)

Love, from their fond hearts
Shut out all troublesome remorse.
And you, O flowers of fragrance
subtle,
This accursed hand
Causes all to open!
Bewilder the heart of Marguerite!
(Disappears amid the darkness.)

## SCÈNE X

*Faust, Marguerite.*

**MAR:** Il se fait tard! adieu!

**FAUST:** (*la retenant*). Quoi! je
t'implore en vain!
Attends! laisse ma main s'oublier
dans la tienne!
(*S'agenouillant devant Marguer-
ite.*)
Laisse-moi, laisse-moi contempler
ton visage
Sous la pâle clarté
Dont l'astre de la nuit, comme dans
un nuage,
Caresse ta beauté! . . .

**MAR:** O silence! ô bonheur! ineffa-
ble mystère!
Enivrante langueur!
J'écoute!..Et je comprends cette
voix solitaire
Qui chante dans mon coeur!
(*Dégageant sa main de celle de
Faust.*)
Laissez un peu, de grâce! . . .
(*Elle ese penche et cueille une
marguerite.*)

**FAUST:** Qu'est se donc?

**MAR:** Un simple jeu!
Laissez un peu!
(*Elle effeuille la marguerite.*)

**FAUST:** Que dit ta bouche à voix
basse! . . .

**MAR:** Il m'aime!—Il ne m'aime
pas!—
Il m'aime!—pas!—Il m'aime!—
pas!
Il m'aime!

**FAUST:** Oui! . . . crois en cette
fleur éclose sous tes pas! . . .
Qu'elle soit pour ton coeur l'oracle
du ciel même! . . .
Il t'aime! . . . comprends-tu ce
mot sublime et doux? . . .
Aimer! porter en nous
Une ardeur toujours nou-
velle! . . .
Nous enivrer sans fin d'une joie
éternelle!

**FAUST ET MAR:** Eternelle! . . .

**FAUST:** O nuit d'amour . . . ciel
radieux!..
O douces flammes!
Le bonheur silencieux
Verse les cieux
Dans nos deux âmes! . . .

## SCENE X

*Faust and Marguerite.*

**MAR:** It grows late, farewell!

**FAUST:** I but implore in vain.
Let me take your hand, and clasp it,
And behold your face once again,
Illumed by that pale light,
That shines from yonder moon.
Shedding
Its faint but golden ray over your
beauteous features.

**MAR:** Oh, what stillness reigns
around,
Oh, ineffable mystery!
Sweetest, happiest feeling,
I listen; a secret voice
Now seems to fill my heart.
Still its tone again resounds in my
bosom
Leave me awhile, I pray.
(*Stoops and picks a daisy.*)

**FAUST:** What are you doing?

**MAR:** This flower I consult.
(*She plucks the petals of the daisy.*)

**FAUST:** (*aside*). What utters she in
tones subdued?

**MAR:** He loves me!—no, he loves
me not!
He loves me!—no!—He loves me!

**FAUST:** Yes, believe this flower,
The flower of loves.
To your heart let it tell
The truth it would teach,—
He loves you! don't you know
How happy it is to love?
To cherish in the heart a flame that
never dies!
To drink forever from the fount of
love!

**FAUST AND MAR:** We'll love for
ever!

**FAUST:** Oh, night of love! oh, radi-
ant night!
The bright stars shine above;
Oh, joy, this is divine!
I love, I do adore you!

**MAR:** Je veux t'aimer et te chérir!
Parle encore!
Je t'appartiens! . . . je
t'adore!
Pour toi je veux mourir! . . .

**FAUST:** Marguerite! . . .

**MAR:** (*se dégageant des bras de
Faust*). Ah! . . . partez! . . .

**FAUST:** Cruelle!
Me séparer do toi! . . .

**MAR:** Je chancelle! . . .

**FAUST:** Ah! cruelle! . . .

**MAR:** (*suppliante*). Laissez-
moi! . . .

**FAUST:** Tu veux que je te quitte
Hélas! . . . vois ma douleur.
Tu me brises le coeur,
O Marguerite! . . .

**MAR:** Partez! oui, partez vite!
Je tremble! . . . hélas! . . . J'ai
peur!
Ne brisez pas la coeur
De Marguerite!

**FAUST:** Par pitié! . . .

**MAR:** Si je vous suis chère,
Par votre amour, par ces aveux
Que je devais taire,
Cédez à ma prière! . . .
Cédez à mes voeux!
(*Elle tombe aux pieds de Faust.*)

**FAUST:** (*après un silence, la rele-
vant doucement*). Divine pur-
eté! . . .
Chaste innocence,
Dont la puissance
Triomphe de ma volonté! . . .
J'obéis! . . . Mais demain!

**MAR:** Oui, demain! . . . dès
l'aurore!
Demain toujours! . . .

**FAUST:** Un mot encore! . . .
Répète-moi ce doux aveu! . . .
Tu m'aimes! . . .

**MAR:** Adieu! . . .
(*Elle entre dans le pavillon.*)

**FAUST:** Félicité du ciel . . . Ah . . .
fuyons . . .

## SCÈNE XI

*Faust, Mephistopheles.*

**MEP:** Tête folle! . . .

**FAUST:** Tu nous écoutais.

**MEP:** Par bonheur.
Vous auriez grand besoin, docteur,
Qu'on vous renvoyât à l'école.

**FAUST:** Laisse-moi.

**MEP:** Daignez seulement
Ecouter un moment
Ce qu'elle va conter aux étoiles,
cher maitre.
Tenez; elle ouvre sa fenêtre.

**MAR:** I want to love and cherish
you
Speak, speak again!
Yours, I'll be yours
For you I'll gladly die.

**FAUST:** Oh, Marguerite!

**MAR:** (*suddenly tearing herself
from Faust's arms*). Ah, leave me!

**FAUST:** Cruel one!

**MAR:** Fly away! alas! I tremble!

**FAUST:** Cruel one!

**MAR:** Pray leave me!

**FAUST:** Would you have me leave
you?
Ah! Don't you see my grief?
Ah, Marguerite, you break my
heart!

**MAR:** Go hence! I waver! mercy,
pray!
Fly hence! alas! I tremble!
Break not, I pray, your Marguerite's
heart!

**FAUST:** In pity—

**MAR:** If I'm dear to you,
I conjure you by your love,
By this fond heart,
That too readily has revealed its se-
cret
Yield to my prayer,—
In mercy get
(*Kneels at the feet of Faust.*)

**FAUST:** (*after remaining a few
moments silent, gently raising
her*). O fairest child,
Angel so holy,
You shall control me,
Shalt curb my will.
I obey; but at morn—

**MAR:** Yes, at morn,
Very early,

**FAUST:** One word at parting.
Repeat thou lovest me.

**MAR:** Adieu!
(*Hastens towards the pavilion.*)

**FAUST:** Adieu! Were it already
morn!

## SCENE XI

*Faust, Mephistopheles.*

**MEP:** Fool!

**FAUST:** You overheard us?

**MEP:** Happily. You have great
need, learned Doctor,
To be sent again to school.

**FAUST:** Leave me!

**MEP:** Deign first to listen for a moment,
To the speech she rehearses to the
stars.
Dear master, delay. She opens her

**Act III, Scene XI**

*(Marguerite ouvre la fenêtre du pavillon et s'y appule un moment en silence, la tête entre les mains.)*

## SCÈNE XII

*Les mêmes. Marguerite.*

**MAR:** Il m'aime; . . . quel trouble en mon coeur,
L'oiseau chante! . . . le vent murmure! . . .
Toutes les voix de la nature
Semblent me répéter en choeur:
Il t'aime! . . . —Ah! qu'il est doux de vivre! . . .
Le ciel me sourit; . . . l'air m'enivre! . . .
Est-ce de plaisir et d'amour
Que la feuille tremble et palpite? . . .
Demain? . . . —Ah! presse ton retour,
Cher bien-aimé! . . . viens! . . .

**FAUST:** *(s'élançant vers la fenêtre et saisissant la main de Marguerite).* Marguerite! . . .

**MAR:** Ah! . . .

**MEP:** Ho! ho!
*(Marguerite rest un moment interdite et laisse tomber sa tête sur l'épaule de Faust; Mephistopheles ouvre la porte du jardin at sort en ricanant. La toile tombe.)*

■ **ACTE IV**

### SCÈNE I

*La Chambre de Marguerite.*

*Marguerite, Siebel.*

**SIE:** *(s'approchant doucement de Marguerite).* Marguerite!

**MAR:** Siebel! . . .

**SIE:** Encor des pleurs.

**MAR:** *(se levant).* Hélas!
Vous seul ne me maudissez pas.

**SIE:** Je ne suis qu'un enfant, mais j'ai le coeur d'un homme
Et je vous vengerai de son lâche abandon!
Je le tuerai!

**MAR:** Qui donc?

**SIE:** Faut-il que je le nomme?
L'ingrat qui vous trahit! . . .

**MAR:** Non! . . . taisez-vous! . . .

**SIE:** Pardon!
Vous l'aimez encore?

**MAR:** Oui! . . . toujours!
Mais ce n'est pas à vous de plaindre mon ennui
J'ai tort, Siebel, de vous parler de lui.

window.
*(Marguerite opens the window of the pavilion, and remains with her head resting on her hand.)*

## SCENE XII

*The preceding. Marguerite.*

**MAR:** He loves me! What trouble in my heart.
The night-bird's song,
The evening breeze,
All nature's sounds together say,
'He loves you!'
Ah! sweet, sweet indeed
Now is this life to me!
Another world it seems;
The very ecstacy of love this is!
With tomorrow's dawn,
O dear one, hurry
Hurry to return! Yes, come!

**FAUST:** *(rushing to the window, and grasping her hand).* Marguerite!

**MAR:** Ah!

**MEP:** *(mockingly).* Ho! ho!
*(Marguerite overcome, allows her head to fall on Faust's shoulder. Mephistopheles opens the door of the garden, and departs, laughing derisively. The curtain falls.)*

■ **ACT IV**

### SCENE I

*Marguerite's Room.*

*Siebel and Marguerite.*

**SIE:** *(quietly approaching).* Marguerite!

**MAR:** Siebel!

**SIE:** What, weeping still!

**MAR:** Alas! You alone are kind to me.

**SIE:** I am a mere youth
And yet I have a manly heart,
And I will sure avenge you.
The seducer's life shall forfeit pay.

**MAR:** Whose life?

**SIE:** Need I name him? The wretch
Who thus has deserted you!

**MAR:** In mercy, speak not thus!

**SIE:** Do you love him still, then?

**MAR:** Ay, I love him still!
But not to you, good Siebel, should I repeat this tale.
I.

**SIE:**
I.
Si la bonheur à sourire t'invite,
Joyeux alors, je sens un doux émoi;
Si la douleur t'accable, Marguerite,
O Marguerite, je pleure alors,
Je pleure comme toi!
II.
Comme deux fleurs sur une même tige
Notre destin suivant le même cours,
De tes chagrins en fière je m'afflige,
O Marguerite, comme une soeur,
Je t'aimerai toujours!

**MAR:** Soyez béni, Siebel! votre amitié m'est douce!
Ceus dont la main cruelle me repousse
N'ont pas fermé pour moi la porte de saint lieu;
J'y vais pour mon enfant . . . et pour le prier Dieu!
*(Elle sort; Siebel la suit à pas lents.)*

## SCÈNE II

*L'Eglisc.*

*Marguerite, puis Mephistopheles.*
*(Quelques femmes traversent la scène et entrent dans l'eglise. Marguerite entre après elles et s'agenouille.)*

**MAR:** Seigneur, daignez permettre à votre humble servante
De s'agenouiller devant vous!

**FAUST:** Non! . . . tu ne prieras pas! . . . Frappez-la d'épouvante!
Esprits du mal, accourez tous!

**VOIX DE DÉMONS INVISIBLES:** Marguerite!

**MAR:** Qui m'appelle?

**VOIX:** Marguerite!

**MAR:** Je chancelle!
Je meurs!—Dieu bon! Dieu clément!
Est-cd déjà l'heure du châtiment?
*(Mephistopheles parait derrière un pilier et se penche à l'oreille de Marguerite.)*

**MEP:** Souviens-toi du passé, quand sous l'aile des anges,
Abritant ton bonheur,
Tu venais dans son temple, enchantant ses louanges, Adorer le Seigneur!
Lorsque tu bégayais une chaste prière
D'une timide boix,
Et portais dans ton coeur les baisers de ta mère,
Et Dieu tout à la fois!
Ecoute ces clameurs! c'est l'enfer

**SIE:** When all was young, and pleasant May was blooming.
I, poor friend, took part with you in play;
Now that the dark cloud of autumn is glooming,
Now is for me, too, mournful the day.
Hope and delight have passed away from life.
II.
We were not born to trifle with true love,
Nor born to part because the wind blows cold.
What though the storm the summer garden rifle,
Oh, Marguerite! oh, Marguerite!
Still on the bough is left a leaf of gold.

**MAR:** Bless you, my friend, your sympathy is sweet.
The cruel ones who wrong me thus Cannot close
The gates of the holy temple against me.
I'll go there to pray
For him and for our child.
*(Exit. Siebel follows slowly after.)*

## SCENE II

*Interior of a Church.*

*Marguerite, then Mephistopheles.*
*(Women enter the church and cross the stage. Marguerite enters after them, and kneels.)*

**MAR:** O heaven!
Permit your lowly handmaiden
To prostrate herself before your altar.

**MEP:** No, you shall not pray!
Spirits of evil, hasten at my call,
And drive this woman from here!

**CHO. OF DEMONS:** Marguerite!

**MAR:** Who calls me?

**CHO:** Marguerite!

**MAR:** I tremble!—oh, heaven!
My last hour is surely near!
*(The tomb opens and discloses Mephistopheles, who bends over Marguerite's ear.)*

**MEP:** Remember the glorious days
When an angel's wings
Protected your young heart.
You came to church to worship,
Nor had you then sinned against heaven.
Your prayers then issued
From an unstained heart
And on the wings of faith
Did rise to the Creator.
Do you hear their call?
It is hell that summons you!
Hell claims you for its own!

qui t'appelle! . . .
C'est l'enfer qui te suite!
C'est l'éternel remords et
l'angoisse éternelle
Dans l'éternelle nuit!

MAR: Dieu! quelle est cette voix
qui me parle dans l'ombre?
Dieu tout puissant!
Quel voile sombre
Sur moi descend! . . .

CHANT RELIGIEUX: (accompagné par les orgues). Quand du
Seigneur le jour luira,
Sa croix au ciel resplendira,
Et l'univers s'écroulera . . .

MAR: Hélas! . . . ce chant pieux
est plus terrible encore! . . .

MEP: Non!
Dieu pour toi n'a plus de pardon!
Le ciel pour toi n'a plus d'aurore!

CHO. RELIGIEUX: Que dirai-je
alors au Seigneur?
Où trouverai-je un protecteur,
Quand l'innocent n'est pas sans
peur!

MAR: Ah! ce chant m'ètouffe et
m'oppresse!
Je suis dans un cercle de fer!

MEP: Adieu les nuits d'amour et les
jours pleins d'ivresse!
A toi malheur! A toi l'enfer!

MAR. ET LE CHO. RELIGIEUX:
Seigneur, accueillex la prière
Des coeurs malheureux!
Qu'un rayon de votre lumière
Descende sur eux!

MEP: Marguerite!
Sois maudite! A toi l'enfer!

MAR: Ah!
(Il disparait.)

## SCÈNE III

La Rue.

Valentin, Soldats, puis Siebel.

CHO: Déposons les armes;
Dans nos foyers enfin nous voici revenus
Nos mères en larmes,
Nos mères et nos soeurs ne nous attendront plus.

## SCÈNE IV

Valentin, Siebel.

VAL: (apercevant Siebel). Eh! parbleu! c'est Siebel!

SIE: Cher Valentin . . .

VAL: Viens vite!
Viens dans mes bras.
(Il l'embrasse.)
Et Marguerite!

SIE: (avec embarras). Elle est à
l'église, je crois.

---

Eternal pain, and woe, and tribulation,
Will be your portion!

MAR: Heaven! what voice is this
That in the shade speaks to me?
What mysterious tones are these!

RELIGIOUS CHO: When the last
day shall have come,
The cross in heaven shall shine
forth.
This world shall crumble to dust.

MAR: Ah me! more fearful still becomes their song.

MEP: Heaven has no pardon left for
you!
For you even heaven has no more
light!

RELIGIOUS CHO: What shall we
say to high heaven?
Who shall find protection
When innocence meets such persecution?

MAR: A heavy weight overpowers
my breast,
I can no longer breathe!

MEP: Nights of love, farewell!
Days of joy, adieu!
You are lost, lost for always!

MAR. AND CHO: Heaven! hear the
prayer
Of a sad, broken heart!
Send a bright ray
From the starry sphere
Her anguish to allay

MEP: Marguerite, you are lost, lost.

MAR: Ah!
(He disappears.)

## SCENE III

The Street.

Valentine, Soldiers, then Siebel.

CHO: Our swords we will suspend
Over the paternal hearth;
At length we have returned.
Sorrowing mothers no longer
Will bewail their absent sons.

## SCENE IV

Valentine and Siebel.

VAL: (perceiving Siebel, who enters). Ah, Siebel, is it you?

SIE: Dear Valentine!

VAL: Come, then, to my arms!
(Embracing him.)
And Marguerite?

SIE: (confused). Perhaps she's yonder at the church.

---

VAL: Oui, priant Dieu pour
moi . . .
Chère soeur, tremblante et craintive,
Comme elle va prêter une oreille
attentive
Au récit de nos combats!

CHO: Gloire immortelle
De nos aïeux,
Sois-nous fidèle
Mourons comme eux!
Et sous ton aile,
Soldats vainquerurs,
Dirige nos pas, enflamme nos coeurs!
Vers nos foyers hâiens le pas!
On nous attend; la paix est faite!
Plus de soupirs! no tardons pas!
Notre pays nous tend les bras!
L'amour nous rit! l'amour nous tête!
Et plus d'un coeur frémit tout bas
Au souvenir de nos combats!
L'amour nous rit! l'amour nous fête!
El plus d'un coeur frémit tout bas
Au souvenir de nos combats!
Gloire immortelle.

VAL: Allons, Siebel! entrons dans la
maison!
Le verre en main, tu me feras raison:

SIE: (vivement). Non! n'entre pas!

VAL: Pourquoi?.. —tu détournes la
tête?
Ton regard fuit le mien?.. —Siebel,
ex plique-toi!

SIE: Eh bien!—non, je ne puis!

VAL: Que veux-tu dire?
(Il se dirige vers la maison.)

SIE: (l'arretant). Arrête!
Sois clément, Valentin!

VAL: (furieux). Laisse-moi! laissi-moi!
(Il entre dans la maison.)

SIE: Pardonne-lui!
(Seul.)
Mon Dieu! je vous implore!
Mon Dieu, protégez-là.
(Il s'éloigne; Mephistopheles et
Faust entrent en scène; Mephistopheles tient une guitare à la
main.)

## SCÈNE V

Faust, Mephistopheles.

(Faust se dirige vers la maison de
Marguerite et s'arrête.)

MEP: Qu'attendez-vous encore?
Entrons dans la maison.

---

VAL: She doubtless prays for my return.
Dear girl, how pleased
She'll be to hear me tell
My warlike deeds!

CHO: Glory to those who in battle
fall,
Their bright deeds we can with
pride recall.
May we, then, acquire honor and
fame,
Our hearts will inspire their glorious deeds!
For that dear native land where we
first drew breath,
Her sons, at her command proudly
brave even death.
At their sacred demand who depend on us,
We will draw our swords, their
rights to defend.
We now will turn our steps homeward,
Joy and peace await us there!
On, on at once, nor loiter here;
On, then, to embrace our loved
ones,—
Affection calls, fond love summons
us,
Yes, many a heart will beat
When they shall hear our tale.

VAL: Come, Siebel, we'll to my
dwelling
And over a flask of wine hold conversation.
(Approaching Marguerite's
house.)

SIE: Nay, enter not!

VAL: Why not, I pray?—You turn
away;
Your silent glance seeks the
ground—
Speak, Siebel—what has happened?

SIE: (with an effort.) No! I cannot
tell you!

VAL: What do you mean
(Rushing toward house.)

SIE: (withholding him.) Hold,
good Valentine, take heart!

VAL: What do you mean!
(Enters the house.)

SIE: Forgive her!
Shield her, gracious Heaven!
(Approaches the church. Faust
and Mephistopheles enter at the
back; Mephistopheles carries a
guitar.)

## SCENE V

Faust and Mephistopheles.

(Faust goes towards Marguerite's
house, but hesitates.)

MEP: Why do you linger?
Let us enter the house.

FAUST: Tais-toi, maudit! . . . j'ai peur
De rapporter ici la honte et le malheur

MEP: A quoi bon la revoir, après l'avoir quitte
Notre présence ailleurs serait bien mieux fêtée!
La sabbat nous attend!

FAUST: Marguerite!

MEP: Je vois
Que mes avis sont vains et que l'amour l'emporte!
Mais, pour vous faire ouvrir la porte,
Vous avez grand besoin du secours de ma voix!
(*Faust, pensif, se tient à l'écart. Mephistopheles s'accompagne sur sa guitare.*)
I.
'Vous qui faites l'endormie,
N'entendez-vous pas,
O Catherine, ma mie, Ma voix et mes pas . . . ?'
Ainsi ton galant t'appelle, Et ton coeur l'en croit!
N'ouvre ta porte, ma belle,
Que la bague au doigt!
II.
'Catherine que j'adore,
Pourquoi refuser
A l'amant qui vous implore Un si doux baiser? . . . '
Ainsi ton galant supplie, Et ton coeur l'en croit!
Ne donne un baiser, ma mie, Que la bague au doigt!
(*Valentine sort de las maison.*)

---

FAUST: Peace! I grieve to think that I
Brought shame and sorrow here.

MEP: Why see her again, then, after leaving her?
Some other sight might be more pleasing.
To the sabbath let us on.

FAUST: (*sighing*). Oh, Marguerite!

MEP: My advice, I know,
Avails little
Against your stubborn will.
Doctor, you need my voice!
(*Throwing back his mantle, and accompanying himself on the guitar.*)
I.
Maiden, now reposing in peace,
Awake from sleep
Hear my voice with love imploring,
Will you take pity?
But beware how you confide
Even in your friend,
Ha! ha! ha!
If he does not have a
Wedding ring for you!
II.
Yes, sweet maiden, I implore you,—
Oh, refuse not this,—
Smile on him who adores you,
Bless him with your kiss.
But beware how you confide,
Even in your friend,
Ha!, Ha! ha!
If he does not have a
Wedding ring for you!
(*Valentine rushes from the house.*)

## SCÈNE VI

*Les mêmes. Valentin.*

VAL: Que voulez-vous, messieurs?

MEP: Pardon! mon camarade,
Mais ce n'est pas pour vous qu'était la sérénade!

VAL: Ma soeur l'écouterait mieux que moi, je le sais!
(*Il degaine et brise la guitare de Mephistopheles d'un coup d'épée.*)

FAUST: Sa soeur!

MEP: (*à Valentin*). Quelle mouche vous pique?
Vous n'aimez donc pas le musique?

VAL: Assez d'outrage! . . . assez! . . . .
A qui de vous dois-je demander compte
De mon malheur et de ma honte? . . .
Qui de vous deux doit tomber sous mes coups? . . .
(*Faust tire son épée.*)
C'est lui! . . .

MEP: Vous le voulez? . . . —Allons, docteur à vous! . . .

---

## SCENE VI

*Valentine and the before-named.*

VAL: Good sir, what do you want here?

MEP: My worthy fellow, it was not to you
That we addressed our serenade!

VAL: My sister, perhaps, would more gladly hear it!
(*Valentine draws his sword, and breaks Mephistopheles' guitar.*)

FAUST: His sister!

MEP: (*to Valentine*). Why this anger?
Do you not like my singing?

VAL: Cease your insults!
From which must I demand of you
Satisfaction for this foul outrage?
Which of you must I now slay?
(*Faust draws his sword.*)
It is he!

MEP: Your mind's made up, then!
On, then, doctor, at him, pray!

---

VAL: Redouble, ô Dieu puissant,
Ma force et mon courage!
Permets que dans son sang
Je lave mon outrage!

FAUST: (*à part*). Terrible et frémissant,
Il glace mon courage!
Dois-je verser le sang
Du frère que j'outrage? . . .

MEP: De son air menaçant,
De son aveugle rage,
Je ris! . . . mon bras puissant
Va détourner l'orage!..

VAL: (*tirant de son sein la médaille que lui a donnée Marguerite*). Et toi qui préservas mes jours,
Toi qui me viens de Marguerite,
Je ne veux plus de ton secours,
Médaille maudite!..
(*Il jette la médaille loin de lui.*)

MEP: (*à part*). Tu t'en repentiras!

VAL: En garde! . . . et défends-toi! . . .

MEP: (*à Faust*). Serrez-vous contre moi! . . .
Et poussez seulement, cher docteeur moi, je pare.

VAL: Ah!
(*Valentin tombe.*)

MEP: Voici notre héros étendu sur le sable!
Au large maintenant! au large! . . .
(*Il entraine Faust. Arrivent Marthe et des bourgeois portent des torches.*)

## SCÈNE VII

*Valentin, Marthe, Bourgeois, puis Siebel et Marguerite*

MART. ET LES BOURG: Par ici! . . .
Par ici, mes amis! on se bat dans la rue! . . . —
L'un d'eux est tombé là! . . . —
Regarde le voici! . . .
Il n'est pas encore mort! . . . on dire qu'il remue! . . . —
Vite, approchez! . . . il faut le secourir!

VAL: (*se soulevant avec effort*). Merci!
De vos plaintes, faites-moi grace!
J'ai vu, morbleu! la mort en face.
Trop souvent pour en avoir peur!
(*Marguerite parait au fond soutenue par Siebel.*)

MAR: Valentin! . . . Valentin! . . .
(*Elle écarte la soule e' tombe à genoux près de Valentin.*)

VAL: Marguerite! ma soeur! . . .
(*Il la repousse.*)
Que me veutx-tu? . . . va-t'en

---

VAL: Oh, heaven, aid afford,
Increase my strength and courage,
That in his blood my sword
May wipe out this fell outrage!

FAUST: What fear is this unnerves my arm?
Why falters now my courage?
Dare I to take his life,
Who but resents an outrage?

MEP: His wrath and his courage
I laugh alike to scorn!
To horse, then, for his last journey
The youth right soon will take!

VAL: (*Taking in his hand the medallion suspended round his neck*). Oh gift of Marguerite,
Which till now has ever saved me,
I'll no more of you—I cast you away!
Accursed gift, I throw you from me!
(*Throws it angrily away.*)

MEP: (*aside*). You'll regret it!

VAL: (*to Faust*). Come on, defend yourself!

MEP: (*to Faust, in a whisper*). Stand near to me, and attack him only;
I'll take care to parry!
(*They fight.*)

VAL: (*falling*). Ah!

MEP: Behold our hero, Lifeless on the ground!
Come, we must go—quick, fly!
(*Exit, dragging Faust after him.*)

## SCENE VII

*Enter Citizens, with lighted torches; afterwards Siebel and Marguerite.*)

CHO: Here, come this way—
They're fighting here hard by!
See, one has fallen;
The unhappy man lies prostrate there.
Ah! he moves—yes, still he breathes;
Quick, then, draw near
To raise and succor him!

VAL: It is useless, cease these vain laments.
I have gazed too often
On death, to heed it
When my own time has come!
(*Marguerite appears at the back, supported by Siebel.*)

MAR: (*advancing, and falling on her knees at Valentine's side*).

VAL: Valentine! ah, Valentine!
(*thrusting her from him*).
Marguerite!
What are you doing here?—away!

MAR: O Dieu! . . .

VAL: Je meurs par elle! . . .
J'ai sottement
Cherché querelle
A son amant!

LA FOULE: (*à demi voix, montrant Marguerite*). Il meurt, frappé par son amant!

MAR: Douleur cruelle!
O châtiment! . . .

SIE: (*À Valentin*). Grâce pour elle! . . .
Soyez clément!

VAL: (*soutenu par ceux qui l'entourent*). Ecoute-moi bien, Marguerite! . . .
Ce qui doit arriver arrive à l'heure dite!
La mort nous frappe quand il faut,
Et chacun obéit aux volontés d'en haut!..
—toi! . . . te voilà dans la mauvaise voie!
Tes blances mains ne travailleront plus!
Tu renîas, pour vivre dans la joie,
Tous les devoirs et toutes les vertus!
Va! la honte t'accable
Le remords suit tes pas!
Mais enfin l'heure sonne!
Meurs! et si Dieu te pardonne,
Soit maudite ici-bas.

LA FOULE: O terreur, ô blasphème
A ton heure suprême, infortuné,
Songe, hélas, a toi-même,
Pardonne, si tu veux tre un jour pardonné!

VAL: Marguerite! Soit maudite!
La mort t'attend sur ton grabat!
Moi je meurs de ta main
Et je tombe en soldat!
(*Il meurt.*)

LA FOULE: Que le Seigneur ait son âme
Et pardonne au pêcheur.
(*La toile tombe.*)

# ■ ACTE V

## SCÈNE I

*La prison.*

*Marguerite, endormie, Faust, Mephistopheles.*

FAUST: Va t'en!

MEP: Le jour va luire.—On dresse l'échafaud!
Décide sans retard Marguerite à te suivre.
Le geôlier dort.—Voici les clefs.—
Il faut
Que ta main d'homme la délivre.

FAUST: Laisse-moi!

---

MAR: O heaven!

VAL: I die for her! Poor fool!
I thought to chastise her seducer!

CHO: (*in a low voice, pointing to Marguerite*). He dies, slain by her seducer!

MAR: Fresh grief is this! ah, bitter punishment.

SIE: Have pity on her, pray!

VAL: (*supported by those around him*). Marguerite, give ear awhile;
That which was decreed
Has duly come to pass.
Death comes at its good pleasure:
All mortals must obey its behest.
But for you intervenes an evil life!
Those white hands will never work more;
The labors and sorrows that others employ,
Will be forgotten in hours of joy.
You dare to live, ingrate?
You dare to still exist?
Go! Shame overwhelm you! Remorse follow you!
At length your hour will sound.
Die! And if God pardons you hereafter,
So may this life be a continual curse!

CHO: Terrible wish! Unchristian thought!
In your last sad hour, unfortunate!
Think of your own soul's welfare.
Forgive, if you would be forgiven

VAL: Marguerite; I curse you!
Death awaits me.
I die by your hand; but I die a soldier.
(*Dies.*)

CHO: God receive your spirit!
God pardon your sins!
(*Curtain.*)

# ■ ACT V

## SCENE I

*A Prison.*

*Marguerite asleep; Faust and Mephistopheles.*

FAUST: Go!

MEP: The morn appears, black night is on the wing.
Quickly prevail upon Marguerite to follow you.
The jailer soundly sleeps—here is the key,
Your own hand now can open the door.

FAUST: Good! Leave me!

---

MEP: Hâtez-vous.—Moi, je veille au dehors.
(*Il sort.*)

FAUST: Mon coeur est pénétré d'épouvante!—O torture
O source de regrets et d'éternels remords!
C'est elle!—La voici, la douce créature
Jetée au fond d'une prison
Comme une vile crminelle!
Le desespoir égara sa raison
Son pauvre enfant, ô Dieu! tué par elle!
Marguerite!

MAR: (*s'eveillant*). Ah! c'est lui!—c'est lui! le bien-aimé!
(*Elle se lève.*)
A son appel mon coeur s'est ranimé.

FAUST: Marguerite!

MAR: Au mileiu de vos éclats de rire,
Démons qui m'entourez, j'ai reconu sa voix!

FAUST: Marguerite!

MAR: Sa main, sa douce main m'attire!
Je suis libre! Il est là! je l'entends la vois.
Oui, c'est toi, je t'aime,
Les fers, la mort même
Ne me font plus peur!
Tu m'as retrouvé,
Me voilà sauvé!
C'est toi, je suis sur ton coeur!

FAUST: Oui, c'est moi, je t'aime,
Malgré l'effort même
Du démon moquer,
Je t'ai retrouvé,
Te voilà sauvé,
C'est moi, viens sur mon coeur!

MAR: (*se dégageant doucement de ses bras*). Attends! . . . voici la rue
Où tu m'as vue
Pour la première fois! . . .
Où votre main osa presque effleurer mes doigts!
'—Ne permettez-vous pas, ma belle demoiselle,
Qu'on vous offre le bras pour faire le chemin?'
'—Non, monsieur, je ne suis demoiselle ni belle,
Et je n'ai pas besoin qu'on me donne la main!'

FAUST: Oui, mon coeur se souvient!—Mais fuyons! l'heure passe!

MAR: Et voici le jardin charmant,
Perfumé de myrte et de rose,
Où chaque soir discrètement
Tu pénétrais à la nuit close.

FAUST: Viens, Marguerite, fuyons!

MAR: Non, reste encore.

FAUST: O ciel, elle ne m'entends pas!

---

MEP: Be sure you do not linger!
I will keep watch without.
(*Exit.*)

FAUST: My heart is wrung with grief!
O, torture! oh, source of agony
And remorse eternal! Behold her there
The good, the beauteous girl,
Cast like a criminal
Into this vile dungeon;
Grief must her reason have disturbed,
For, with her own hand, alas!
She slew her child!
Oh, Marguerite!

MAR: (*waking*). His voice did sure Resound unto my heart.
(*Rises.*)

FAUST: Marguerite!

MAR: At that glad sound it wildly throbs again
Amid the mocking laugh of demons.

FAUST: Marguerite!

MAR: Now am I free. He is here. It is his voice.
Yes, you are the one I love.
Fetters, death, have no terrors for me;
You have found me. You have returned.
Now am I saved! Now I rest on your heart!

FAUST: Yes, I am here, and I love you,
In spite of the efforts of yon mocking demon.
(*Faust attempts to draw her with him. She gently disengages herself from his arms.*)

MAR: Stay! this is the spot
Where one day you did meet me.
Your hand sought to clasp mine.
'Will you not permit me, my fairest demoiselle,
To offer you my arm, and clear for you the way?'
'No, sir. I am no demoiselle, neither am I fair;
And I have no need to accept your offered arm.'

FAUST: What is it she says? Ah me! Ah me!

MAR: And the garden I love is here,
Odorous of myrtle and roses,
Where every eve you came in
With careful step, as night was falling.

FAUST: Come, Marguerite, let us fly!

MAR: No! stay a moment!

FAUST: O heaven, she does not understand!

## SCÈNE II

*Les mêmes. Mephistopheles.*

**MEP:** Alerte! alerte! ou vous êtes perdus!
Si vous tardez encor, je ne m'en mêle plus!

**MAR:** Le démon! le démon!—Le vois-tu? . . . là..dans l'ombre
Fixant sur nous son oeil de feu!
Que nous veut-il?—Chasse-le du saint lieu!

**MEP:** L'aube depuis longtemps a percé la nuit sombre,
La jour est levé
De leur pied sonore
J'entends nos chevaus frapper le pavé
(*Cherchant à entrainer Faust.*)
Viens! sauvons-la. Peut-être il en temps encore!

**MAR:** Mon Dieu, protégez-moi!—Mon Dieu je vous implore!
(*tombant à genoux.*)
Anges purs! anges radieux!
Portez mon âme au sein des cieux!
Dieu juste, à toi je m'abandonne!
Dieu bon, je suis à toi!—pardonne!

**FAUST:** Viens, suis-moi! je le veux!

## SCENE II

*Mephistopheles and the preceding.*

**MEP:** Away at once, while yet there's time!
If longer you delay longer,
Not even my power can save you

**MAR:** Do you see yon demon crouching in the shade?
His deadly glance is fixed on us;
Quick! drive him from these sacred walls.

**MEP:** Away! we'll leave this spot,
The dawn has appeared;
Do you not hear the fiery chargers,
As with they paw the ground sonorous hoof?
(*Endeavoring to drag Faust with him.*)
Hurry, then,—perchance there yet
Is time to save her!

**MAR:** O Heaven, I crave your help!
I do implore your aid alone!
(*Kneeling.*)
Holy angels, blessed in heaven,
My spirit longs to rest with you!
Great Heaven, grant pardon, I implore you,
For soon shall I appear before you!

**FAUST:** Marguerite! Follow me, I implore!

**MAR:** Anges purs, anges radieux!
Portez mon âme au sein des cieux!
Dieu juste, à toi je m'abandonne!
Dieu bon, je suis à toi!—pardonne!
Anges purs, anges radieux!
Portez mon âme au sein des cieux!
(*Bruit au dehors.*)

**FAUST:** Marguerite!

**MAR:** Pourquoi ce regard menaçant?

**FAUST:** Marguerite!

**MAR:** Pourquoi ces mains rouges de sang!
(*Le repoussant.*)
Va! . . . tu me fais horreur!
(*Elle tombe sans mouvement.*)

**MEP:** Jugée!

**CHO. DES ANGES:** Sauvée! Christ est ressuscité!
Christ vient de renaître!
Paix et félicite
Aux disciples du Maître!
Christ vient de renaître.
Christ est ressuscité!.
(*Les murs de la prison se sont ouverts. L'âme de Marguerite s'élève dans les cieux. Faust la suit des yeux avec désespoir à genoux et prie. Mephistopheles est à demi renversé par l'épée lumineuse de l'archange.*)

*FIN.*

**MAR:** Holy angels, in heaven blessed,
My spirit longs to rest with you!
Great Heaven, grant pardon, I implore you.
For soon shall I appear before you.

**FAUST:** O Marguerite!

**MAR:** Why that glance fraught with anger?

**FAUST:** Marguerite!

**MAR:** What blood is that which stains your hand!
Away! your sight causes me horror!
(*Falls.*)

**MEP:** Condemned!

**CHO:** Saved!
Christ has arisen!
Christ has arisen!
Christ is born again!
Peace and felicity
To all disciples of the Master!
Christ has arisen!
(*The prison walls open. The soul of Marguerite rises towards heaven. Faust gazes despairingly after her, then falls on his knees and prays. Mephistopheles turns away, barred by the shining sword of an archangel.*)

*END OF THE OPERA.*

# Giulio Cesare (1724)

## Julius Caesar

MUSIC BY GEORGE FREDERIK HANDEL ■ LIBRETTO BY NICOLÒ FRANCESCO HAYM

This three-act opera, set to a libretto by Nicolò Haym, was first performed in London at the King's Theatre on February 20, 1724. The opera begins with Pompeo, who has been beaten in the battle of Pharsalus, seeking refuge with Tolomeo, the king of Egypt. His wife and son, Cornelia and Sesto, beg for peace from Giulio Cesare, the Roman conqueror. Achillas, captain of the Egyptian king, brings the head of Pompeo to Cesare, who orders that his enemy be honored as a hero for having died so savagely. Cesare extends his kindness to Cornelia and Sesto; meanwhile, Achillas falls in love with Cornelia. Sesto vows to seek vengeance for his father's death. Cleopatra, Tolomeo's sister, seeks Cesare's help in order to secure her succession to the Egyptian throne. Tolomeo arranges with Achillas that Cesare will be assassinated in exchange for Cornelia marrying Achillas. Sesto challenges Tolomeo and is arrested; Cornelia is made prisoner in Tolomeo's harem. Cesare is told of the plot to kill him—he saves himself by leaping off Cleopatra's terrace into the sea. Achillas reports Cesare's death to Tolomeo, but Tolomeo has now fallen in love with Cornelia and thus will not permit Achillas to marry her as promised. The Egyptians and Romans are in battle; the Romans flee as they believe Cesare to be dead. Cesare, who has saved himself from drowning, overhears a conversation between Sesto and Achillas in which Achillas, dying, confesses his culpability in Pompeo's death. He gives Sesto a gold seal which will give him the ability to gather a hundred men to kill Tolomeo. Cesare himself takes the seal, leads the revolt and emerges victoriously. Sesto kills Tolomeo, and Cleopatra is crowned Queen of Egypt. The people and the army are exultant, and Cesare and Cleopatra vow eternal love.

## ■ ACT I

### SCENA I

*Una pianura vicino Allessandria*

*(Cesare, Curio entrano can qualche Egiziano del popolo)*

**EGYPTIANS:** Viva, viva il nostro Alcide!
Goda, goda il Nilo in questo di!
Ogni, spiaggia per lui ride,
ogni affanno giá sparí.

**CESARE:** Presti omai l'Egizia terra
le sue palme al vincitor!
*(mentre gli Egiziani escono)*
Curio, Cesare venne e vide e vinse;
giá sconfitto Pompeo
invan ricorre per rinforzar
de' suoi guerrier lo stuolo d'Egitto
al re.

**CURIO:** Tu qui, Signor, giungesti a tempo appunto,
a prevenir le trame.
*(mentre Cornelia e Sesto entrano)*
Ma chi ver noi sen viene?

**CEASARE:** Questa é Cornelia.

**CURIO:** O sorte—
del nemico Pompeo l'alta consorte?

**CESARE:** *(a Cornelia)* Da Cesare che chiedi,
gran germe de' Scipioni, alta Cornelia?

**CORNELIA:** Da' pace all'armi!

## ■ ACT I

### SCENE I

*A plain near Alexandria*

*(Caesar, Curio and some of the Egyptian populace enter.)*

**EGYPTIANS:** Long live our Alcides!
May the Nile rejoice today!
Every land smiles for him,
every anguishy disappears.

**CAESAR:** Let Egypt's land, at last,
offer her palms to the victor!
*(as the Egyptians leave)*
Curio, Caesar came, saw and conquered;
Pompey, already routed,
seeks help in vain from Egypt's king
to reinforce his army.

**CURIO:** You, my lord, came here just in time
to thwart the plots.
*(as Cornelia and Sextus enter)*
But who is this who comes toward us?

**CAESAR:** This is Cornelia.

**CURIO:** O destiny—
the great consort of Pompey, our foe?

**CAESAR:** *(to Cornelia)* What do you seek from Caesar,
O great Cornelia, descendant of the Scipios?

**CORNELIA:** Give us peace!

**SESTO:** Dona l'asta la tempio,
ozio al fianco, ozio alla destra!

**CESARE:** Virtú de' grandi é il perdonar le offese,
venga Pompeo, Cesare abbracci,
e resti l'ardor di Marte estinto,
sia vincitor del vincitore il vinto.

**ACHILLE:** *(entrado, accompagnato da quattro soldati Egiziani portando un elaborato cofano dorato)* Sua reggia Tolomeo t'offre in albergo,
eccelso eroe, per tuo riposo.
Accio'l'Italia ad adorarti impari,
in pegno d'amistrade e di sua fede
questa del gran Pompeo superba testa
di base al regal trono offre al tuo piede.
*(lui apre il cofano, rivelando la testa di Pompey)*

**CESARE:** Giulio, che mira?

**SESTO:** O Dio! Che veggio?

**CORNELIA:** Ahi, lassa? Consorte!
Mio tesoro!

**CURIO:** Grand' ardir!

**CORNELIA:** To Jomeo, barbar o traditor!
lo manco, io moro—
*(Essa sviene.)*

**SEXTUS:** Give your spears to the temple,
rest your men's bodies and their weapons.

**CAESAR:** Great men's virtue lies in their forgiving offense.
Let Pompey come, let him embrace Caesar,
let the wrath of Mars be quenched,
let the conqueror be conquered by the conquered.

**ACHILLAS:** *(entering, accompanied by four Egyptian soldiers bearing an elaborate golden casket)* Ptolemy offers you his palace
as a place for your to rest, great hero.
So that all Italy may learn to love you,
as a pledge of friendship and his good faith,
this proud head of the great Pompey
he offers as a base on which to build your throne.
*(He opens the casket, revealing the head of Pompey.)*

**CAESAR:** Julius, what do you look upon?

**SEXTUS:** O God, what do I see?

**CORNELIA:** Alas! My husband! My beloved!

**CURIO:** How daring!

**CORNELIA:** Ptolemy, barbarous traitor!
I am fainting, I am dying—
*(She faints.)*

## Act I, Scene I

ACHILLE: (*a se stesso*) Questa é Cornelia?
Oh, che beltá! Che volto!

SESTO: Padre! Pompeo! Mia genitrice! O Dio!

ACHILLE: Cesare, frena l'ire.

CESARE: Vanne! Verró alla reggia, pria ch' oggi il sole a tramontar si veggia.
(*Achille ed i soldati escono*)
Empio, diró, tu sei, togliti a gli occhi miei, sei tutto crudeltá.
(*Lui esce*)

CURIO: (*guardando a Cornelia*) Giá torna in sé.

SESTO: Madre!

CURIO: Cornelia!

CORNELIA: O stelle! Ed ancor vivo?
(*Lei cerca di portar via la spada di Sesto*)

CURIO: (*trattenendo Cornelia*) Ferma! In van tenti tinger di sangue in quelle nevi il ferro.
Curio, che ancor t'adora, e sposa ti desia, se pur t'aggrada, vendicarti sapra con la sua spada.

CORNELIA: Sposa a te?

CURIO: Si.

CORNELIA: Ammutisci!

SESTO: Madre!

CORNELIA: Viscere mie!

SESTO: Or che farem?

CORNELIA: (*mentre Curio se ne va*) Priva son d'ogni conforto, e pur speme di morire per me misera non v'é.
Il mio cor. da pene assorto, é giá stanco di soffrire, e morir si niega a me.
(*Essa eshe*)

SESTO: Vani sono lamenti; é tempo, o Sesto, cmai di vendicar il padre; si svegli alla vendetta l'anima neghittosa, che offesa da un tiranno in van riposa.
Svegliatevi nel core furie d'un'alma offesa, a far d'un traditor aspra vendetta!
L'ombra del genitore accorre a mia difesa, e dice: A te il rigor, figlio, si aspetta.

### SCENA 2

La stanza di Cleopatra nel Palazzo di Tolomeo

(*Cleopatra entra con una processione di giovani Egiziani*)

ACHILLAS: (*to himself*) Is this Cornelia?
Oh, what beauty! What a face!

SEXTUS: Father! Pompey, Mother! O God!

ACHILLAS: Caesar, restrain your wrath.

CASEAR: Go! I shall come to the palace, today, before the sun has set.
(*Achillas and the soldiers leave.*) I shall say, "You are a villain, leave my sight— you are wholly cruel."
(*He leaves.*)

CURIO: (*looking at Cornelia*) She is reviving now.

SEXTUS: Mother!

CURIO: Cornelia!

CORNELIA: O stars! And still alive?
(*She tries to wrest Sextus' sword away from him.*)

CURIO: (*restraining Cornelia*) Cease! To stain the knife with your blood be piercing this snowy breast would be in vain.
Curio, who loves you still and wants you as his wife, if you accept, will avenge you with his sword.

CORNELIA: Your wife?

CURIO: Yes.

CORNELIA: Be silent!

SEXTUS: Mother!

CORNELIA: My flesh and blood!

SEXTUS: Now what shall we do?

CORNELIA: (*as Curio leaves*) I am deprived of all consolation, yet for me, wretched one, there is no hope of death.
My heart, consumed with sorrow, is already weary of suffering yet death denies itself to me.
(*she leaves*)

SEXTUS: It is useless to lament; now is the time, O Sextus, to avenge your father; awaken to revenge your slothful soul which now, offended by a tyrant, cannot rest.
Awaken in my heart the wrath of an offended soul, so I may wreak upon a traitor my bitter vengenance!
The ghost of my father hastens to my defense, saying, "From you, my son, ferocity is expected."

### SCENE II

Cleopatra's Room in Ptolemy's Palace

(*Cleopatra enters with a retinue of young Egyptians*)

CLEOPATRA: Regni Cleopatra; ed al mio seggio intorno, popola adorator Arabo e Siro, su questo crin la sacra benda adori.

NIRENUS: (*entrando*) Regina, infausti eventi!

CLEOPATRA: Che fia? Che tardi?

NIRENUS: Troncar fé Tolomeo il capo de gran Pompeo.
(*l giovani Egiziani se ne vanno*)

CLEOPATRA: Stelle! Tu qui resta; alle Cesaree tende son risolta portarmi.
(*Tolomeo appare*)

NIRENUS: Che dirá Tolomeo?

CLEOPATRA: Non parventar; in vano aspira al trono; egli é il germane, ma la regina io sono.

TOLOMEO: Tu di regnar pretendi, donna superba e altera?

CLEOPATRA: Io ció é mio contendo.

TOLOMEO: Vanne, e torna omai, folle, a qual di donna é l'uso di scettro invece a trattar l'ago e il fuso!

CLEOPATRA: Non disperar; chi sa? Se al regno non l'avrai, avrai sorte in amor.
Mirando una beltá in essa troverai a consolar un cor.
(*Essa e Nirenus escono; Achille entra*)

ACHILLE: Sire, Signor!

TOLOMEO: Achille! Come fu il capo tronco da Cesare gradito?

ACHILLE: Sdegnó l'opra.

TOLOMEO: Tant' osa un vil Romano?

ACHILLE: Io ti prometto darti estinto il superbo al regio piede, se di Pompeo la moglie in premio a me il tuo voler concede.

TOLOMEO: É costei tanto vaga?

ACHILLE: Lega col crine, e col bel volto impiaga.

TOLOMEO: Amico, il tuo consiglio é la mia stella; vanne, pensa, e poi torna.
(*mentre Achille esce*) Muora, Cesare, muora, e il capo altero sia del mio pié sostegno.
L'empio, sleale, indegno, vorria rapirmi il regno, e disturbar cosí la pace mia.

CLEOPATRA: Long may Cleopatra reign.
And, around my throne, O adoring Arab and Syrian people, worship the holy band that binds these tresses.

NIRENUS: (*entering*) O queen, ill-omened happenings!

CLEOPATRA: What can it be? Why do you hesitate?

NIRENUS: Ptolemy has decapitated the great Pompey.
(*The young Egyptians leave.*)

CLEOPATRA: O stars! You stay here;
I am resolved to go to Caesar's tents.
(*Ptolemy appears.*)

NIRENUS: What will Ptolemy say?

CLEOPATRA: Fear not; in vain he aspires to the throne; he is the half brother, but I am the queen.

PTOLEMY: You dare to claim the throne, proud, haughty woman?

CLEOPATRA: I claim only what is mine.

PTOLEMY: Go now, mad woman, return to women's usual things— the needle and the distaff— not the scepter!

CLEOPATRA: Do not despair. Who knows?
Though you shall not have the kingdom, you shall have good fortune in love.
Looking upon your beauty, there you shall find a heart to comfort.
(*She and Nirenus go out; Achillas enters*)

ACHILLAS: Sire, my lord!

PTOLEMY: Achillas! How did Caesar like the severed head?

ACHILLAS: He loathed the deed

PTOLEMY: Does a vile Roman dare so much?

ACHILLAS: I promise to bring this proud man, dead, to your royal feet, if you will give me Pompey's wife as a reward.

PTOLEMY: Is she so beautiful?

ACHILLAS: Her tresses ensnare men, her glance wounds them.

PTOLEMY: Friend, your counsel is my star; go now, think about it, then return.
(*as Achillas goes out*) Let Casear die, and let his haughty head serve as my footrest.
The impious one, the unworthy traitor, would take my kingdom from me

Ma perda pur la vita,
prima che in me tradita,
dall'avido suo cor la fede sia!

## SCENA 3

*Il Campo di Cesare*

*(In fondo, il cofano di Pompea, con la sua spada sopra)*

CESARE: (*entrando*) Alma del gran Pompeo,
fur ombra i tuoi trofei,
ombra la tua grandezza,
e un'ombra sei.
Cosí termina al fine
il fasto umano.
Ieri chi vivo occupó
un mondo in guerra
oggi risolto in polve
un'urna serra.
Tal di ciascuno—ahi, lasso!—
il principio é di terra,
e il fine é un sasso.
Misera vita!
Oh, quanto é fral tuo stato!
Ti forma un soffio,
e ti distrugge un fiato.

CURIO: (*entrando, seguito da Cleopatra*) Qui nobile donzella chiede chinarsi al Cesare di Roma.

CESARE: Sen vengo pur.

CLEOPATRA: Tra stuol di damigelle
io servo a Cleopatra.
Lidia m'appello,
e sotto il ciel d'Egitto
di nobil sangue nata;
ma Tolomeo mi toglie,
barbaro usurpator,
la mia fortuna.

CESARE: (*a se stesso*) Quanta bellezza!

CLEOPATRA: (*Inginocchiandosi di fronte a Cesare*) Avanti al tuo cospetto,
avanti a Roma,
mesta, afflitta e piangente
chieggio giustizia.

CESARE: (*a se stesso*) O Dio, come innamora!
(*lui aiuta Cleopatra ad alzarsi*)

CLEOPATRA: Piangeró sorte mia,
si crudele e tanto ria,
finché vita in petto avró.
Ma poi morta d'ogn'intorno
il tiranno e notte e giorno
fatta spettro agiteró.

CESARE: (*mentre Curio se ne va*) Sfortunata donzella, in breve d'ora
deggio portarmi in corte,
oggi cola
stabiliró tua sorte.
(*Lui se ne va*)

NIRENUS: (*entrando*) Ferma, Cleopatra, osserva
qual femina dolente con grave passo
e lacrimoso ciglio quivi si porta.
(*Lui e Cleopatra si nascondono mentre Cornelia entra*)

## SCENE III

*Caesar's camp*

*(Pompey's coffin with his sword upon it is at the rear.)*

CAESAR: (*entering*) Soul of great Pompey,
your trophies were but a shadow,
your greatness was but a shadow,
you yourself but a shadow.
Thus ends finally
the pomp of man.
The man who yesterday occupied
a world at war
is today reduced to dust,
held in an urn.
Thus everyone—alas!—
has his beginning in dust,
and his end is a stone.
Wretched life!
Oh, how frail you are!
A breath forms you,
a breath destroys you.

CURIO: (*entering, followed by Cleopatra*) Here a noble maiden asks to bow before Rome's Caesar.

CAESAR: Let her approach.

CLEOPATRA: Together with a band of maidens
I serve Cleopatra.
My name is Lydia;
I was born under Egypt's sky
of noble blood.
But Ptolemy, a barbarous usurper,
is taking from me
my fortune.

CAESAR: (*to himself*) What beauty!

CLEOPATRA: (*kneeling before Caesar*) Before your gaze,
Before Rome,
saddened, distraught and weeping,
I ask for justice.

CAESAR: (*to himself*) O God, how she awakens love!
(*He helps Cleopatra to her feet.*)

CLEOPATRA: I shall weep for my fate,
so cruel and so evil,
so long as I have life in my breast.
But then in death, from every side,
my ghost shall prod the tyrant
night and day.

CAESAR: (*as Curio leaves*) Unfortunate maiden,
soon I must go to the court.
There, I shall see
that you are treated justly.
(*He leaves.*)

NIRENUS: (*entering*) Stop Cleopatra,
see how sorrowful a woman comes here,
with heavy step and tearful eye.
(*He and Cleopatra conceal themselves as Cornelia enters.*)

CORNELIA: (*Fissando al cofano di Pompeo*) Nel tuo seno, amico sasso,
sta sepolto il mio tesoro.
(*Sesto entra*)
Ahimé! Vile e negletta
sempre starai Cornelia?
Ah no! Tra questi arnesi
un ferro sceglierò;
con mano ardita contro di Tolomeo
dentro la reggia—
(*Lei prende la spada di Pompeo*)

SESTO: Madre, ferma! Che fai?

CORNELIA: Lascia quest'ormi;
voglio contro il tiranno,
uccisor del mio sposo,
tentar la mia vendetta.

SESTO: (*prendendo la spada da Cornelia*) Questa vendetta a Sesto sol si aspetta.

CORNELIA: Oh, dolci accenti! Oh, care labra!

SESTO: Ma, o Dio, chi al re fellone ci scorterá?
(*Cleopatra e Nirenous emergono dal loro nascondiglio*)

CLEOPATRA: Io stessa.

NIRENUS: (*a Cleopatra, con un soffio*) Non ti scoprir!

CORNELIA: E chi ti sprona, amabile donzella,
oggi in nostro soccorso offrir te stessa?

CLEOPATRA: La fellonia d'un re tiranno, il giusto.
Sotto nome di Lidia io servo a Cleopatra;
se in virtú del tuo braccio
ascende al trano, sari felice.

CORNELIA: Chi a noi sará scorta?

CLEOPATRA: (*Indicando Nirenus*) Questi, che alla regina é fido servo,
saprá canto condurvi all'alta impresa.

SESTO: Figlio non é, chi vendicar non cura
del genitor la morte.
Armeró questa destra,
e al suol trafitto cadrà punito
il gran tiran d'Egitto.
(*Cleopatra, Nirenous e Cornelia escono*)
Cara speme, questo core tu cominci a lusingar.

## SCENA 4

*Il palazzo di Tolomeo*

*(Cesare entra con Curie e seguaci Romani; Tolomeo entra con Achille e seguaci Egiziani.)*

SEGUACI: Oh, quanto bella gloria é quella del vincitor.

TOLOMEO: Cesare, alla tua destra stende fasci di scettri generosa la sorte.

CORNELIA: (*gazing at Pompey's coffin*) Within your breast, O friendly stone,
is buried my treasure.
(*Sextus enters.*)
Woe to me! Shall Cornelia be forever wretched and alone?
Ah, no! Among these weapons
I shall choose a blade;
with daring hand, against Ptolemy
here in the palace—
(*She takes Pompey's sword.*)

SEXTUS: Mother, stop! What are you doing?

CORNELIA: Leave me this weapon;
I would try my revenge
against the tyrant,
slayer of my husband.

SEXTUS: (*taking the sword from Cornelia*) This revenge must come from Sextus alone.

CORNELIA: Oh, sweet words! Oh, dear lips!

SEXTUS: But, O God, who will lead us to the villainous king?
(*Cleopatra and Nirenus emerge from their hiding place.*)

CLEOPATRA: I myself.

NIRENUS: (*to Cleopatra, softly*) Do not reveal yourself!

CORNELIA: Dear maiden, who spurs you on
to offer yourself for our help today?

CLEOPATRA: Justice and the villainy of a tyrant king.
Under the name of Lydia, I serve Cleopatra;
if, through the strength of your arm
she ascends the throne, you will be happy.

CORNELIA: Who will be our escort?

CLEOPATRA: (*indicating Nirenus*) This man, a trusted servant of the queen,
will lead you on your great exploit.

SEXTUS: Unworthy is the son who does not accept
to avenge his father's death.
I shall take up arms,
and he shall fall in punishment to earth,
this great tyrant of Egypt.
(*Cleopatra, Nirenus and Cornelia leave.*)
Dear hope, you begin to give joy to this heart.

## SCENE IV

*Ptolemy's palace*

*(Casear enters with Curio and Roman followers; Ptolemy enters with Achillas and Egyptian followers.)*

FOLLOWERS: Oh, what a splendid glory is that of the victor.

PTOLEMY: Caesar, generous fate proffers sheaves of scepters to your right hand.

and thus disturb my peace.
But he shall lose his life
before my faith shall be betrayed
by his ambitious heart!

**CESARE:** Tolomeo, a tante grazie io non so dir,
se maggior lume apporti,
il sole in cielo o Tolomeo qui in terra,
Ma sappi, ch'ogni mal opra
ogni gran lume oscura.

**CAESAR:** Ptolemy, I cannot say whether
the gracious receive more light
from the sun in the sky or from Ptolemy on earth.
But know this: every evil deed darkens every bright light.

**ACHILLE:** (*a Tolomeo, con un soffio*) Sino al real aspetto egli to'offende,

**ACHILLAS:** He offends even your royal presence?

**TOLOMEO:** (*a se stesso*) Temerario Latin!

**PTOLEMY:** (*to himself*) Rash Roman!

**CESARE:** (*a se stesso*) So che m'intende.

**CAESAR:** (*to himself*) I know he understands me.

**TOLOMEO:** (*a Cesare*) Alle stanze reali
questi che miri t'apriran le porte,
e a te guida saranno.
(*a se stesso*)
Empio, tu pur venisti in braccio a morte.

**PTOLEMY:** (*to Caesar*) These men whom you see
will open the royal rooms to you,
and they will be your guide.
(*to himself*)
Rascal, you have walked into the arms of death.

**CESARE:** (*a se stessio*) Scorgo in quel volto un simulato inganno.
(*I seguaci se ne vanno*) Va tacito e nascosto,
quand' avido é di preda,
l' astuto cacciator.
E chi é a mal far disposto,
non brama che si veda
l'inganno del suo cor.
(*lui e Curio se ne vanno, Cornelia e Sesto entrano*)

**CAESAR:** (*to himself*) I see the deceit hidden in his face
(*The followers leave.*)
Silently, unseen,
Intent on his prey,
the clever huntsman goes.
And the man disposed to evil
wants for no one to see
the deceit within his heart.
(*He and Curio leave; Cornelia and Sextus enter.*)

**ACHILLE:** Sire, con Sesto il figlio questa é Cornelia.

**ACHILLAS:** Sire, this is Cornelia, with Sextus, her son.

**TOLOMEO:** (*a se stesso*) Oh, che sembianze, che amore!

**PTOLEMY:** (*to himself*) Oh, what beauty, what love!

**CORNELIA:** Ingrato, a quel Pompeo,
tu recidesti il capo in faccia Roma?

**CORNELIA:** Ungrateful one, you severed
the head of Pompey before the Romans?

**SESTO:** Empio, ti sfido a singolar certame.

**SEXTUS:** Wretch, I challenge you to single combat.

**TOLOMEO:** O lá Da vigil stuol
sian custoditi questi Romani arditi.

**PTOLEMY:** Enough! A vigilant band
will take care of these brave Romans.

**ACHILLE:** Alto Signor, condona il lor cieco furor!

**ACHILLAS:** Great lord, forgive their blind fury!

**TOLOMEO:** Per or mi basta.
(*a Achille, con un soffio*) Io per te serbo
questa dell'alma tua bella tiranna.

**PTOLEMY:** For now, it's enough for me.
(*to Achillas, softly*) For you I shall save
this lovely mistress of your soul.

**ACHILLE:** Felice me!

**ACHILLAS:** How happy I am!

**TOLOMEO:** (*a se stesso*) Quanto costui s'inganna.
(*lui va furoi*)

**PTOLEMY:** (*to himself*) How this man deceives himself.
(*he goes out*)

**ACHILLE:** Cornelia, se all'amor mio
giri sereno il ciglio,
ci talami concedi,
sará la madre in libertá col figlio.

**ACHILLAS:** Cornelia, if you will look upon
my love with favor,
if you will permit our marriage,
the mother shall have freedom,
with her son.

**CORNELIA:** Barbaro, a te consorte?
Ah, no! Pria della morte.

**CORNELIA:** Barbarian—your wife?
Ah, no! Rather death.

**ACHILLE:** Tu ferma il piede,
e pensa di non trovar piedtade
acció che chiedi,
se pietade al mio amor pria non concedi.

**ACHILLAS:** Then stay
and expect no mercy
for what you ask
if you do not show mercy for my love.

Tu sei il cor di questo core,
sei il mio ben, non t'adirar!
(*lui se ne va*)

You are heart of this heart,
my love, do not be angry!
(*He leaves.*)

**SESTO:** Madre!

**SEXTUS:** Mother!

**CORNELIA:** Mia vita!

**CORNELIA:** My life!

**SESTO:** (*mentre i soldati lo catturano*) Addio.

**SEXTUS:** (*as soliders take him captive*) Farewell.

**CORNELIA:** (*afferandosi al braccio di suo figlio*) Dove, dove, inumani,
l'anima mia guidate?
Empi, lasciate,
che al mio core, al mio bene
io porgo almen gli ultimi baci.
ahi, pene.
Son nato a lagrimar
e il dolce mio conforto,
ah, sempre piangeró.

**CORNELIA:** (*clinging to her son's arm*) Where, inhuman wretches,
are you taking my soul?
Wretches, grant me
at least a last kiss
to my son, my heart, my love.
Ah, my suffering
I was born to weep,
and for my sweet comforter
I shall ever weep.

**SESTO:** Son nato a sospirar,
e il dolce mio conforto,
ah, sempre piangeró;
son nato a sospirar, ecc.

**SEXTUS:** I was born to sigh,
and for my sweet comforter
I shall ever weep.
Ah, I shall ever weep;
I was born to sigh, etc.

**CORNELIA:** Ah, sempre piangeró;
son nato a lagrimar, ecc.

**CORNELIA:** Ah, I shall ever weep;
I was born to weep, etc.

# ■ ACT II

## SCENA I

"Monte Parnasso"

(*Cleopatra, la sua attendente e Nirenus*)

**CLEOPATRA:** E seguisti, o Niren, quanto t'imposi?

**NIRENUS:** Adempito é il comando. Ma, che far pensi?

**CLEOPATRA:** Amore giá suggerí all'idea
stravagante pensier;
ho giá risolto sotto finte apparenze
far prigionier d'amor ch'il cor m'ha tolto.

**NIRENUS:** Io che far deggio

**CLEOPATRA:** Attendi Cesare in quel parte;
e lui dirai
che, per dargli contezza
di quanto dal suo re gli si contende,
pria che tramonti il sol Lidia l'attende.
(*essa se ne va*)

**NIRENUS:** Da Cleopatra apprendo
chi é seguace d'amor l'astuzie e frodi.

**CESARE:** (*entrando*) Dov'é, Niren, dov'é l'anima mia?

**NIRENUS:** In questo loco in breve verrá Lidia, Signor.
(*si sente una bellissima sinfonia*)

**CESARE:** Taci!

**NIRENUS:** Che fia?

**CESARE:** Cieli, e qual della sfere
scende armonico suon, chi mi rapisce?

# ■ ACT II

## SCENE I

The "Mount Parnassus"

(*Cleopatra, her attendants and Nirenus*)

**CLEOPATRA:** Nireno, have you done as I commanded?

**NIRENUS:** Your command has been carried out.
But, what is your plan?

**CLEOPATRA:** Love has put a wild thought in my mind.
I have decided, in disguise,
to imprison in love
the man who has stolen my heart.

**NIRENUS:** What must I do?

**CLEOPATRA:** Wait for Caesar here,
and tell him
that at sundown Lydia
will come to him with news
of how she fared with the king.
(*She leaves.*)

**NIRENUS:** From Cleopatra he shall learn
that cleverness and fraud are love's henchmen.

**CAESAR:** (*entering*) Where is she, Nirenus, where is my love?

**NIRENUS:** In a little while
Lydia will come, my lord.
(*A beautiful symphony is heard.*)

**CAESAR:** Silence!

**NIRENUS:** What can it be?

**CAESAR:** Heavens, from which of the spheres
comes this music which enchants me?

**NIRENUS:** Avrá di selce il cor chi non languisce.
(*lui se ne va*)

**NIRENUS:** Only a man whose heart is stone
would not be moved.
(*He leaves.*)

**CESARE:** (*mentre Cleopatra diventa visibile*) Giulio, che miri?
E quando con abisso di luce scesero i Numi in terra?

**CAESAR:** (*as Cleopatra becomes visible*) Julius, what are you gazing on?
When did these gods come to earth in all their radiant glory?

**CLEOPATRA:** V'adoro, pupille, saette di'amore,
le vostre faville son grate nel sen.
Pietose vi brama il mesto mio core,
ch'ogn'ora vi chiama l'amato suo ben.

**CLEOPATRA:** I adore you, O eyes, love's darts,
your sparks are pleasing to my heart.
My sad heart, which never ceases calling you beloved.
begs for your mercy.

**CESARE:** Non ha in cielo il Tonante melodia,
che pareggi un sí bel canto.

**CAESAR:** The Thunderer in heaven lacks a melody
to rival so lovely a song.

**CLEOPATRA:** V'adoro, pupille, ecc.

**CLEOPATRA:** I adore you, O eyes, etc.

**CESARE:** (*mentre Cleopatra va da lui*) Vola, vola, mio cor, al dolce incanto!

**CAESAR:** (*as Cleopatra comes to him*) Fly, my heart to the sweet enchantment!

**CLEOPATRA:** Caro!

**CLEOPATRA:** Dear!

**CESARE:** Bella!

**CAESAR:** Beautiful!

**CLEOPATRA:** Piú amabile beltá mai non si troverá
del tuo bel volto . . .

**CLEOPATRA:** No more lovable beauty
will ever be seen
than your handsome face . . .

**CESARE:** Piú amabile beltá mai non si troverá
del tuo bel volto.
Piú amabile beltá, ecc.

**CAESAR:** No more lovable beauty will even be seen
than your lovely face.
No more lovable beauty, etc.

**CLEOPATRA:** . . . del tuo bel volto.
Piú amabile beltá, ecc.

**CLEOPATRA:** . . . than your handsome face.
No more lovable beauty, etc.

## SCENA 2

*Il giardino serraglio nel Palazzo di Tolomeo)*

**CORNELIA:** (*entrando*) Deh, piangete, o mesti lumi,
giá per voi non v'é piú speme.

## SCENE II

*The seraglio garden in Ptolemy's palace*

**CORNELIA:** (*entering*) Ah, weep, my saddened eyes,
for you there is no hope.

**ACHILLE:** (*entrando*) Bella, non lagrimare!
Cangerá il tuo destin le crude tempre.

**ACHILLAS:** (*entering*) Beautiful one, do not weep!
Your destiny will change its cruel temper.

**CORNELIA:** Chi nacque a sospirar, piange per sempre.

**CORNELIA:** The one born for sighing, forever weeps.

**ACHILLE:** Se a me non sei crudele, ogn' or sará fedele
a te questo mio cor.
Ma se spietata sempre,
ver me non cangi tempre,
aspetta sol rigor!
(*lui se ne va*)

**ACHILLAS:** If you are not cruel to me,
then this heart of mine shall be ever faithful to you.
But if you are forever pitiless,
unchanging in your temper,
then expect only severity from me!
(*He leaves.*)

**TOLOMEO:** (*entrando*) Bella, placa lo sdegno.

**PTOLEMY:** (*entering*) Beautiful one, quiet your disdain.

**CORNELIA:** Lasciami, iniquo re!

**CORNELIA:** Leave me, evil king!

**TOLOMEO:** Tanto rigore?
Ma se un re ti bramasse—

**PTOLEMY:** Such harshness?
But if a king desired you—

**CORNELIA:** Freni l'anima insana lo stimolo del senso;
pensa che con romana.

**CORNELIA:** Your mad soul must restrain
the prodding of your senses.
Remember, I am a Roman.

**TOLOMEO:** Tanto ritrosa a un re?
Perfida donna!
Si spietata, il tuo rigore
sveglia l'odio in questo sen.

**PTOLEMY:** So reluctant toward a king
Treacherous woman!
So pitiless, your harshness

awakens hatred in my breast.
(*He leaves, Sextus enters and finds Cornelia with a dagger about to take her life.*)

(*lui se ne va. Sesto entra e trova Cornelia con una daga in mano, cercando di togliersi la vita*)

**SESTO:** Madre! Ferma! Che fai!

**SEXTUS:** Mother! Stop! What are you doing?

**CORNELIA:** Figlio, Sesto, mio core,
come qui ne venisti?

**CORNELIA:** My son, Sextus, my beloved,
how have you come here?

**SESTO:** Chi alla vendetta aspira, vita non cura, o madre!

**SEXTUS:** The man intent on vengeance
cares not about his life, O mother!

**NIRENUS:** (*entrando*) Cornelia, infauste nove.
Il re m'impone,
che tra le sue dilette io ti conduca.

**NIRENUS:** (*entering*) Cornelia—unhapping tidings.
The king commands me
to take you to his harem.

**CORNELIA:** O Dio!

**CORNELIA:** O God!

**SESTO:** Numi, che sento?

**SEXTUS:** O gods, what do I hear?

**NIRENUS:** Non vi turbate, no;
unqua sospetto a Tolomeo non fui;
ambi verrete lá dove il re tiranno
é in preda alle lascive.
Colá Sesto nascoso
in suo potere avrá l'alta vendetta.

**NIRENUS:** Do not be troubled.
Ptolemy has no suspicion of me;
both of you must come there,
where the tyrant king
lies prey to his lascivious women.
There Sextus, in hiding,
will find his great revenge within his power.

**CORNELIA:** Assista il cielo una si giusta impresa!
Cessa omai di sospirare!
Non é sempre irato il cielo contro i miseri;
suol fare, benché tardo le vendette.
(*essa se ne va*)

**CORNELIA:** May heaven favor so righteous an endeavor!
Cease now your sighing!
Not always is heaven wroth against the wretched;
it grants revenge however late.
(*She leaves.*)

**SESTO:** Figlio non é, chi vendicar non cura
del genitor lo scempio.
Sú dunque alla vendetta
ti prepara 'alma forte
e prima di morir altrui da' morte!
(*Nirenua se ne va*)
L'angue offeso mai riposa
se il veleno pria non spande
dentro il sangue all'offensor.
Cosí alma mia non osa
di mostrarsi altera e grande,
se non svelle l'empio cor.

**SEXTUS:** He is no son who would not strive
to avenge the slaughter of a parent.
Up, then, and may your stout heart
prepare you for revenge;
before you die, bring death to another!
(*Nirenus leaves.*)
The angry serpent never rests
until he has spread his poison
in his tormentor's blood.
So my soul dares not show itself
so haughty and so grand,
until it has torn out the evil heart.

## SCENA III

*Il "Monte Parnasso"*

*(Cesare e Cleopatra)*

**CESARE:** Bella Lidia,
ben potresti sperar dalla tua sorte
d'essermi forse un dí sposa e consorte.

## SCENE III

*The "Mount Parnassus"*

*(Caesar and Cleopatra)*

**CAESAR:** Beautiful Lydia,
well might you hope one day
for Fate to make you my wife, my consort.

**CLEOPATRA:** Sposa? T'adoreró fino alla morte.

**CLEOPATRA:** Wife? I shall love you until I die.

**CURIO:** (*entrando*) Cesare, sei tradito.

**CURIO:** (*entering*) Caesar, you are betrayed.

**CESARE:** Io tradito?

**CAESAR:** I, betrayed?

**CLEOPATRA:** Che sento?

**CLEOPATRA:** What do I hear?

**VOCI:** (*dietro i scenarii*) Mora, mora, Cesare more!

**VOICES:** (*offstage*) He shall die, Caesar shall die!

**CESARE:** Cosí dunque in Egitto regna la fellonia?
Bella, rimanti;
sono infausti per noi cotesti lidi.

**CAESAR:** So then perfidy reigns in Egypt?
My beauty, remain here.
these shores are an evil omen for us.

**CLEOPATRA:** Fermati, non partir.

**CELOPATRA:** Stop—do not leave.

**CESARE:** Lascia, Lidia!

**CAESAR:** Let me go, Lydia!

## Act II, Scene III

**CLEOPATRA:** Son Cleopatra,
e non piú Lidia in cambio.

**CESARE:** Sei Cleopatra? Lidia é
Cleopatra?
Che udisti, cor mio?

**CLEOPATRA:** Fuggi, Cesare, fuggi!
Dalle reggi volano
i congiurati.

**CESARE:** Vengano pure, ho core.

**CLEOPATRA:** Oh, salvati, oh, mio
bel sol!
Cesare, fuggi!

**VOCI:** (*dietro i scenarii*) Mora,
mora, mora.

**CESARE:** Al lampo dell'armi
quest'alma guerriera vendetta fará.
(*lui e Curio se ne vanno*)

**VOCI:** (*dietro i scenarii*) Mora,
mora, Cesare mora!

**CLEOPATRA:** Che sento? O Dio!
Morrá Cleopatra ancora.
Anima vile, che parli mai?
Deh, taci!
Avró, per vendicarmi
in bellicosa parte,
di Bellona in sembianza
un cor di Marte.
Intanto, o Numi,
voi che il ciel reggete.
difendete il mio bene!
Ch'egli é del seno mio
conforto e speme.
Se pietá di me non senti,
guisto ciel, io moriró.
Tu da' pace a miei tormenti,
o quest'alma spireró.

### ■ ACT III

#### SCENA I

*Sulle sponde del Mediterraneo*

(*Al suono della Sinfonia comincia la battaglia tra i soldati di Tolomeo e quelli di Cleopatra. Le Forze de Tolomeo vince. A Sinfonia finita, Tolomeo e Cleopatra entrano seguiti dai soldati.*)

**TOLOMEO:** Vinta cadesti al balenar,
di questo mio fulmine reale.

**CLEOPATRA:** Tolomeo non mi
vinse.

**TOLOMEO:** Olá! Sí baldanzosa del
vincitor
al riverito aspetto?
(*ai soldati*)
S'incateni costei.

**CLEOPATRA:** Empio crude! Ti puniranno i dei.
(*Tolomeo si ritira; Cleopatra e le guardie seguono*)

---

**CLEOPATRA:** I am Cleopatra,
no more the changeling Lydia.

**CAESAR:** You are Cleopatra? Lydia
is Cleopatra?
What do I hear?

**CLEOPATRA:** Flee, Caesar, flee!
The conspirators are hastening
from their palaces.

**CAESAR:** Let them come: I am
brave.

**CLEOPATRA:** Oh, save yourself,
oh, my sun!
Caesar, flee!

**VOICES:** (*offstage*) He shall die.

**CAESAR:** Amidst the flash of arms
the warrior's heart shall take its revenge!
(*He and Curio leave.*)

**VOICES:** (*offstage*) He shall die,
Caesar shall die!

**CLEOPATRA:** What do I hear? O
God!
Let Cleopatra also die.
Cowardly soul, what are you saving?
Ah, be silent!
I shall have,
for my revenge in battle,
the features of Bellona,
with the heart of Mars.
Meanwhile, O gods,
you who reign in heaven,
defend my lover!
For he is both
my hope and my comfort.
If you do not feel mercy for me,
just heaven, I shall die.
Give you peace to my torment,
or this soul will die.

### ■ ACT III

#### SCENE I

*At the edge of the Mediterranean Sea*

*To the strains of a warlike Sinfonia the battle between Ptolemy's soliders and those of Cleopatra takes place. Ptolemy's forces win. At the end of the Sinfonia, Ptolemy and Cleopatra enter, followed by soldiers.*)

**PTOLEMY:** You have fallen, conquered by
the flash of the royal sword.

**CLEOPATRA:** Ptolemy has not
conquered me.

**PTOLEMY:** Enough! Still so
haughty
before the revered face of the conqueror?
(*to the soliders*) Put this woman in
chains.

**CLEOPATRA:** Cruel villain! The
gods will punish you.
(*Ptolemy goes off; Cleopatra and
guards follow.*)

---

**CESARE:** (*entrando*) Dall' ondoso
periglio
salvo mi porto al lido il mio propizio fato.
Qui la celeste parca non tronca ancor
lo stame alla mia vita!
Ma dove andró?
E chi mi porge aita?
Ove son le mie schiere?
Ove son le legioni,
che a tante mie vittorie il varco
apriro?
Solo in queste erme arene
al monarca del mondo errar conviene?
Aure, deh, per pietá
spirate al petto mio,
per dar conforto, o Dio,
al mio dolor.
Dite, dov'é,
che fa l'idolo del mio sen,
l'amato e dolce ben di questo cor?
Ma d'ogni intorno i' veggio
sparse d'arme e d'estinti
L'infortunate arene,
segno d'infausto annunzio al fin
sará.
(*lui si ritira mentre Sesto e Nirenus entrano. Achille entra
pure*)

**SESTO:** Cerco in van Tolomeo
per vendicarmi.

**ACHILLE:** (*cadendo*) Hai vinto, o
fato!

**NIRENUS:** É questi Achilla,
in mezzo al sen piagato.

**ACHILLE:** Tu sai che quell 'Achilla
consiglió
del gran Pompeo la moret—

**SESTO:** (*a se stesso*) Ah, scelerato!

**ACHILLE:** Sol per aver Cornelia in
moglie,
contro Cesare ordí l'alta
congiura—

**CESARE:** (*a se stesso*) Fellone!

**ACHILLE:** Questo sigil tu prendi;
nel piú vicino speco
cento armati querrieri
a questo segno ad ubbidir son pronti;
cosi tu puoi e in breve d'ora
torre all'empio Cornelia,
e insieme far
che vendicato io mora.
(*dando il sigillo a Sesto lui
muore*)

**CESARE:** (*rivelando se stesso*) Lascia questo sigillo!

**SESTO:** Che veggio! Cesare vivo.

**CESARE:** Teco Niren mi segua;
o che torró alla sorte Cornelia
e Cleopatra, o avró la morte.
Quel torrente, che cade dal monte,
tutto atterra ch' incontra lo stá.

---

**CAESAR:** (*entering*) From the perilous waves,
my propitious Fate has brought me
safe to shore.
The heavenly Fate does not yet sever
the thread of my life!
But where shall I go?
And who will help me?
Where are my troops?
Where are the legions,
which opened the pass to so many
of my victories?
Among these ancient sands
must the conqueror of the world
wander?
Gentle breezes, ah, for mercy's sake
blow upon my breast,
to give comfort, O God,
to my grief.
Tell me, where is she
who is the idol of my breast,
the beloved, sweet love of this
heart?
But on every side I see,
covered with weapons and our
dead,
the unlucky sands,
which in the end will be an unlucky
sign.
(*He withdraws as Sextus and Nirenus enter. Achillas also enters.*)

**SEXTUS:** I am seeking Ptolemy,
to take my revenge, but in vain.

**ACHILLAS:** (*falling*) You have
conquered, O fate!

**NIRENUS:** This is Achillas,
wounded in the chest.

**ACHILLAS:** You know that this
Achillas
counseled the killing of Pompey—

**SEXTUS:** (*to himself*) Ah, wretched man!

**ACHILLAS:** Only to take Cornelia
as his wife
did he plan the conspiracy against
Caesar—

**CAESAR:** (*to himself*) Villain!

**ACHILLAS:** Take this seal;
is a cave nearby
a hundred armed men wait
to obey this sign;
thus you can quickly
save Cornelia from the villain,
and at the same time
see to it that I die avenged.
(*Giving the seal to Sextus, he
dies.*)

**CAESAR:** (*revealing himself*)
Give me that seal!

**SEXTUS:** What is this I see! Caesar—alive.

**CAESAR:** Follow me with Nirenus;
either I shall save Cornelia
and Cleopatra, or I shall die.
The torrent that floods down from
the mountain
levels everything that stands in its
way.

## SCENA 2

*Il Campo di Tolomeo*

*(Cleopatra e le sue attendenti. Soldati stanno alla Guardia.)*

**CLEOPATRA:** Voi, che mie fide ancelle
un tempo foste, or lagrimate invan,
piú mie non siete.
Il barbaro germano,
che mi privó del regno,
a me vi toglie,
e a me torrá la vita.
*(fuori si sente un battito d'armi.)*
Ma qual strepito d'armi?
Ah, sí! Piú mie non siete,
spirar l'alma Cleopatra or or vedrete.
*(Cesare e i sui soldati entrano. Lui fa motto alle guardie di uscire, e Cleopatra e' lasciata libera)*
Cesare, o un' ombra sei?

**CESARE:** Cara! Ti stringo al seno;
ha cangiato vicende il nostro fato.
Per conquister, non che l'Egitto,
un mondo, basta l'ardir
di questo petto solo.
*(lui va fuori, seguito dai suoi soldati)*

**CLEOPATRA:** Da tempeste il legno infranto,
se pai salvo giunge in porto,
non sá piú che desiar.
Cosí il cor tra pene e pianto,
or che trova il suo conforto,
torna l'anima a bear.

## SCENA III

*Il Serraglio di Tolomeo*

**TOLOMEO:** Cornelia, é tempo omai,
che tu doni pietade
a un Re che langue.

**CORNELIA:** Speri in vano mercede.
Come obliar poss'io
l'estinto mio consorte?

**TOLOMEO:** Altro ten'offre il regnator d'Egitto;

**SESTO:** *(entrando con la spada in pugno)*
A me, tiranno!
*(lui ferisce Tolomeo)*

## SCENE II

*Ptolemy's camp*

*(Cleopatra and her attendants. Soldiers stand guard.)*

**CLEOPATRA:** You, who were my faithful handmaidens,
now weep in vain—
you are no longer mine.
The barbarous brother,
who took my kingdom from me
takes you too,
and from me he will take my life.
*(There is a clash of arms outside.)*
But that clash of arms?
Ah, yes! You are no longer mine,
and now you shall see Cleopatra die.
*(Caesar and his soldiers enter. He motions the guards out, and Cleopatra is released.)*
Caesar—or his ghost?

**CAESAR:** Beloved! I hold you in my arms;
our destiny has changed its course.
To conquer not only Egypt but the world,
the daring of this heart
alone suffices.
*(He goes out, followed by his soldiers.)*

**CELOPATRA:** When, broken by the storms,
the ship comes safe to port,
the sailor has no other desire.
So the heart, torn with suffering and tears,
when at last it is comforted,
brings ecstasy anew to the soul.

## SCENE III

*Ptolemy's seraglio*

**PTOLEMY:** Cornelia, the time has come
for you to take pity
on a king who languishes for you.

**CORNELIA:** You hope in vain for mercy.
How can I forget
my husband who is dead?

**PTOLEMY:** The one who reigns in Egypt offers you more;
beloved, close to me—

**SEXTUS:** *(entering, with sword in hand)* You are mine, tyrant!
*(He stabs Ptolemy.)*

**TOLOMEO:** Io son tradito, o Numi!
*(lui muore)*

**CORNELIA:** Or sí, ti riconosco,
figlio del gran Pompeo,
e al sen ti stringo.

**SESTO:** Giace il tiranno estinto;
or, padre, sí,
tu benché vinto hai vinto.
*(lui bacia la mano di Cornelia e si inginocchia difronte a lei)*

**CORNELIA:** Non ha piú che temere
quest'alma vendicata;
or si sará beata—
comincio a respirar!

## SCENA 4

*Alessandria*

*(Durante la Sinfonia, Cesare e Cleopatra entrano con il seguito di Egiziani. Dopo entra Nirenus, poi Cornelia e Sesto.)*

**CESARE:** *(a Sesto, che si inginocchia)* La vendetta del padre
é ben dovuta al figlio;
sorgi, Sesto,
ed amico al sen t'accolgo.

**SESTO:** Ogni affetto di fede in te rivolgo.

**CORNELIA:** Dell'estinto tiranno
ecco i segni reali;
a te li porgo.

**CESARE:** *(a sua volta dando a Cleopatra i segni reali)* Bellissima Cleopatra, regina del Egitto,
darai norma alle genti,
e legge al trono.

**IL POPOLO:** Ritorni omai nel nostro core
la bella gioia ed il piacer;
sgombrato é il sen d'ogni dolore,
ciascun ritorni ora goder.

**CLEOPATRA E CESARE:** Un bel contento il sen giá si prepara,
se tu sarai costante orgn' or per me;
cosí sortí dal cor la doglia amara,
e sol vi resta amor, costanza e fé.

**IL POPOLO:** Ritorni omai nel nostro core, ecc.

*FINE*

**PTOLEMY:** I am betrayed, O gods!
*(He dies.)*

**CORNELIA:** Now indeed I see in you
great Pompey's son,
and I clasp you to my breast.

**SEXTUS:** The tyrant lies dead;
now, indeed, father,
you although vanquished, have conquered.
*(He kisses Cornelia's hand and kneels before her.)*

**CORNELIA:** This soul, now avenged,
no longer fears;
henceforth it will be blessed—
I breathe again!

## SCENE IV

*Alexandria*

*(During the Sinfonia, Caesar and Cleopatra enter with a following of Egyptians. Then Nirenus enters, and then Cornelia and Sextus.)*

**CAESAR:** *(to Sextus, who kneels)* The father's revenge
comes indeed from the son;
arise, Sextus,
I embrace you as my friend.

**SEXTUS:** My loyalty I will give to you.

**CORNELIA:** Here are the royal symbols
of the dead tyrant;
I give them to you.

**CAESAR:** *(in turn giving the symbols to Cleopatra)* Loveliest Cleopatra, Egypt's queen
you shall be the model for the people
and bring your law to the throne.

**POPULACE:** Let there return to our hearts
fairest joy and pleasure;
with our hearts free from all sorrow,
let each one again rejoice.

**CLEOPATRA and CAESAR:** A great joy will fill my breast,
if you will always be faithful;
thus bitter grief will leave my heart;
there will remain only love, constancy and faith.

**POPULACE:** Let there return to our hearts, etc.

*THE END*

# Alcina (1735)

## Music by George Frederick Handel

This three-act opera, set to a libretto by an unknown author (adapted from the opera *L'isola di Alcina*, based upon an episode in Ariosto's *Orlando furioso*), was first performed in London in 1735. This opera includes the use of ballet and full chorus (as opposed to an ensemble of soloists). Bradamante, dressed as a soldier, and her guardian Melisso are searching for Ruggiero, Bradamante's fiance. They are shipwrecked on an island ruled by Alcina, a sorceress. Morgana, Alcina's sister, meets them and falls in love with Bradamante in her disguise. Alcina is in her palace with Ruggiero. She welcomes the strangers and sings of her love for him. Bradamante, posing as her brother Ricciardo, and Melisso beseech him to remember Bradamante, but Ruggiero now loves Alcina. Oronte, Alcina's general, is in love with Morgana. He tells Ruggiero that Alcina is attracted to "Ricciardo" and that Ruggiero will soon become a beast or a tree as is the fate of Alcina's other former lovers. Bradamante tries to convince Ruggiero of her true identity; however, he doesn't believe her. Morgana and Melisso urge her to leave the island, but she refuses to do so. Melisso, dressed as Ruggiero's old tutor, comes to him and places a magic ring on his finger that breaks Alcina's spell. Ruggiero remembers his love for Bradamante but still doesn't believe "Ricciardo" is in fact she. Alcina is about to cast a spell on Ricciardo but is stopped by Morgana. Ruggiero assures Alcina that he still loves her (which isn't true), and Oronte tells Alcina that her lover intends to leave her. Bradamante and Ruggiero are at last re-united, but Morgana sees them together and rushes off to inform Alcina, who is enraged. Morgana, realizing that she has been in love with a woman, bemoans her fate to Orontes, who is still in love with her. Alcina swears revenge upon Ruggiero and later learns that the lovers are intent on conquering the island and breaking Alcina's spells. Alcina tries to convince them of her desire for friendship, which they don't believe; Ruggiero breaks the urn containing Alcina's magical powers. Alcina and Morgana vanish, and Alcina's former lovers return to life. The opera ends with their choruses of joy and a ballet.

## ■ ATTO I

### SCENA I

*Luogo de deserto chiuo da alti, e scoscesi Monti, a' piedi de' quali è cavata un picciolo Antro.*

*Bradamante in Abito virile guerriero, Melisso pure in Abito guerriero: e' poi Morgana.*

**BRA:** Oh! Dei! quivi non scorgo alcun sentiero!

**MEL:** Taci. Da quello speco Donna, mi sembra, ad incontrar ne viene.

**MOR:** Qual felice ventura Animosi Guerrieri, a noi vi reca?

**MEL:** Il Mar turbata, il Vento Qui ne sospinse.

**BRA:** E a chi è 'l felice suolo?

**MOR:** Della possente Alcina il Regno è questo.

**MEL:** Oh! noi felici!

**BRA:** Intesi Il suo poter, la sua beltà. Ma dinne, Lice a noi d' inchinar l' alta Reina?

## ■ ACT I

### SCENE I

*A desert Place terminated by high craggy Mountains, at the Foot of which opens a little Cave.*

*Bradamante in warlike Man's Habit, Melisso also in warlike Habit; and afterwards Morgana.*

**BRA:** No Path or human Footstep can I trace!

**MEL:** Be silent. From the Cave a Lady comes; By her kind Look she seems to welcome us.

**MOR:** Say, unknown Warriours, what happy Chance Has brought you hither?

**MEL:** The trouble Seas, and rude opposing Winds, Have forc'd us on these Shores.

**BRA:** But on what Coast are we arriv'd?

**MOR:** Here fam'd Alcina holds her sumptuous Court.

**MEL:** Then we may bless the Chance that drove us hither.

**BRA:** Both of her Beauty and her Pow'r I've heard. Is it permitted, gentle Fair, That we may kneel before the Potent Queen?

**MOR:** Per te nobil Guerriero, un dolce amore.
(*Guardando teneramente Bradamante.*)
Mi si desta nell' Alma. In questo loco
Attendete la sì: verrà fra poco.
O s' apre al riso
O parla, o tace,
Ha un non sò chè
Il tuo bel Viso,
Che troppe piace
Caro al mio cor.
Al primo sguardo,
Che in Voi fissai
Provar me se,
Vezzosi rai,
Quanto è col dardo
Possente Amor.
O s', ec.
(*Parte.*)

### SCENA II

*(S' ode sirepito di Tuoni, e Folgori, aprindosi improvvisamente da piu lati rovinando il Monte; e dileguandosi appàre la deliciosa Reggia di Alcina, d' ond' ella in atto di adornarsi siede presso a Ruggiero, che le sostiene al Volto uno specchio. Il Giovinetto Oberto si tiene da uncanto, Paggi, e Damigelle, che le apprestano vari abbigliamenti. Altri giovani Cavalieri, e Dame coronati di Fiori formano il Coro.)*

**MOR:** Your Look, brave Youth, I feel has pass'd
Already to my Heart, and fixes there.
Wait you the Princess here, she soon will come.
Your Smile, your Words,
Even your Silence
Shoot thro' my Soul
A sweet unwonted Pleasure.
Soon as I fix'd on you
My ravish'd Sight,
I prov'd within
The utmost Power of Love.
Your Smile, etc.
(*Exit.*)

### SCENE II

*A Noise of Thunder and Lightning; the Mountain suddenly opens, and breaks to pieces, and vanishing, leaves to View the beautiful Palace of Alcina, where she, adorning herself, sits by Rogero, who holds a Mirrour. Oberto at her Side, Pages and Damsels, who bring in different Habits; other young Knights and Ladies, with Chaplets of Flowers on their Heads, form the Chorus.*

CORO: Questo e il Cielo de' contenti,
Questo è il centro del goder.
Qui è l' eliso de Viventi,
Qui, gli eroi, forma il piacer.
*Bradamante, e Melisso; si arrestano alquanto ad ammirare la magnificenza del luoco, e delle feste.*

*Bradamante, Melisso, Alcina, Ruggiero, ed Oberto.*

BRAD: (Ecco l' infido.)

MEL: (Taci.) Alta Reina
*(Avvanzando verso Alcina.)*
Con Ricciardo Guerriero,
Melisso à piedi tuoi umil s' inchina.

ALC: Fu vostra forte, amici,
Al mio Regno approdar.

MEL: Diam lodi al Cielo.
Ti preghiam, che pietosa,
Sin che 'l mar sia placato
Ne permetti restar

ALC: Tanto m' è grato.
E' tu, odi Ruggiero, anima mia
Mostra lor la mia Reggia, e Caccie, e Fonti.
Veggan dove scorprimmo, all' ombra amica
D' un scambievole Amor, fiamma pudica.
Dì, cor mio, quanto t' amai.
Mostra il Bosco, il Fonte, il Rio
Dove tacqui, e sospirai
Pria di chiederti mercè.
Dove fisso ne miei rai,
Sospirando al sospir mio,
Mi dicesti con un sguardo
Peno, ed ardo al par di tè.
Dì, ec.
*(Parte.)*

CHORUS: Here's the Seat of endless Pleasure,
Centre of unbounded Joy,
Bless'd Elisium! Nothing here
Can our happy Peace destroy.
*Bradamante and Melisso stay some time admiring the Magnificence of the Place and Pomp.*

*Bradamante, Melisso, Alcina, Rogero, and Oberto.*

BAD: (Behold the base Ingrate!)

MEL: (Be still.) Great Queen, Melisso and the brave Richard
Bow now before you.

ALC: Worthy unknown.
It was kind Fate that drove you on our Coast.

MEL: We thank the Fate that guided us so well,
And beg your kind Compassion, that we may
Here take our Shelter, 'till the troubled Sea
Is more appeas'd.

ALC: I bid you Welcome, Strangers.
And you, my Dear Rogero, entertain them;
Shew them our Palace, Gardens, bubbling Fountains;
Shew them some pleasing Chase; shew them the Shade,
The ever grateful Shade where first we breath'd
The modest Fervour of our mutual Loves.
Tell, O tell, how much I lov'd thee;
Shew the Fount, the Rill, the Grove,
Where first by Sighs alone I ask'd
Your gentle Pity of my Love.
When your Eyes on mine intent,
And returning Sigh for Sigh,
First in pleasing Sounds you said
With equal Flames, I burn, I die.
Tell, etc.
*(Exit.)*

## SCENA III

*Melisso, Bradamante, Ruggiero ed Oberto.*

OBER: Generosì Guerrier; deh! per pietade
Udiste mai del Palladino Astolfo?

MEL: D' Astolfo?

BRA: Del Cugin?

MEL: Perche?

OBER: E mio Padre.
Dal naufragio scampati
Il Genitor ed io
Quivì approdamno; e la clemente Alcina
Generosa ne accolse, anzi d' onori
Colmò il mio Genitor.

MEL: Che arrivò poì?

## SCENE III

*Melisso, Bradamante, Rogero and Oberto.*

OBERT: Brave Warriors, for Pity let me know,
Have you heard of the Paladin Astolfo?

MEL: Astolfo?

BRAD: My Cousin?

MEL: Why seek you him?

OBERT: He is my Father.
We, by good Chance, escap'd the raging Sea,
And to this happy Place kind Fate directed us;
Where fair Alcina, generous and mild,
Receiv'd us hospitably; and still more,
With Honours deck'd my Father.

MEL: What then could happen?

BRA: (Sarà con gli altri in Fera.) (*a Melisso.*)

OBER: Più non lo trovo, è l' alma mia dispera. (*piange*)
Chì m' insegna il caro Padre?
Chi mi rende il Genitor?
Per far lieto questo cor.
Mi abbandona la speranza;
Langue in me bella constanza;
Agitato è me l' amor.
Chi, ec.
*(Parte.)*

## SCENA IV

*Bradamante, Melisso, e Ruggiero.*

BRA: Mi ravviso, Ruggier, dimmi?

RUG: Il tuo Volto
Di Ricciardo rassembra.

BRAD: Io pur son quello.
Germano alla tua cara Bradamante.

RUG: Mia? Nò: t' inganni. Io son s' Alcina amante.

MEL: Signor: tu senza il Brando, e senza scudo?

RUG: Servo ad Amor, che và senz' Arme, e nudo.

MEL: Della tua prima Fama Nulla curi?

BRAD: E la fede,
Che Alla Germana mia di sposo desti?

RUG: E Alcina mia non vien? Siete molesti?
Guardando all' intorno. (*a Bra. e Mel.*)
Di te mi rido
Semplice stolto. (*a Bradamante.*)
Sieguo Cupido,
Amo un bel Volto (*a Melisso.*)
Nè sò mancare di fedeltà.
Il caro bene
Che minnamora
A me non viene?
Non torna ancora?
Dov' è? Che fà?
Di te, ec.
*(Parte.)*

## SCENA V

*Oronte, Melisso e Bradamante.*

OR: Quà dunque ne veniste,
D' una Donna incostante
A involarmi l' Amor? Grand' è l' offesa.
Decida il Brando fol la ria contesa.
*(Sfodera la spada.)*

BRAD: A savage Beast he, with the rest, will range
The horrid Wilds. (*Aside to Mel.*)

OBERT: Alas! in vain I've sought him; he is lost,
And with him all the Comfort of my Soul. (*Weeps.*)
Ah! who will tell me where to find
My dearest Father? Who again
Can give him to my longing Sight?
And ease my troubled Mind.
Of Grief alone I am possest
My Courage fails, Hope flies,
And leaves no Gleam of Joy within my Breast.
Ah! etc.
*(Exit.)*

## SCENE IV

*Bradamante, Melisso and Rogero.*

BRAD: Think you, Rogero, that you ever saw me?

ROG: Your Face bears much resemblance of Richard.

BRAD: I am the same,
The Brother of your dearest Bradamante.

ROG: You are deceiv'd; Alcina has my Love.

MEL: What mean you, Sir, thus without Shield and Sword?

ROG: Love now I serve, and need nor Shield nor Sword.

MEL: Have you thrown off all Care For glorious Deeds, and for your former Fame?

BRAD: Have you forgot the Faith You plighted to my Sister.

ROG: Why comes not my Alcina?
(*Looking round him.*)
Away, you trouble me.
Thy idle Talk
I laugh to Scorn. (*To Bradamante.*)
Cupid I serve; (*To Melisso.*)
To Beauty bow,
And miss not of my Faith.
Why does the Fair
Whom I adore
With Absence wound me so?
Oh Cruel, stay!
Why comes she not? Why this Delay?
Thy, etc.
*(Exit.)*

## SCENE V

*Orontes, Melisso and Bradamante.*

OR: Here are you come to tempt a fickle Fair,
And rob me of her Love? Great the Offence,
Not to be born. The Sword shall do me right. (*Draws.*)

## Act I, Scene V

**BRAD:** Qual ingiuria? Qual' onta? Ricevesti da Noi

**OR:** La spada il dica.

**BRAD:** We know not of the Charge: What Injury have you receiv'd from us!

**OR:** Let this pronounce your Crime.

## SCENA VI

*Morgana, e Detti.*

**MOR:** Io sono tura disesa. Io tua nemica. (*a Bradam.*) (*ad Oronte.*)

**BRA:** E Gelosia: (*ad Oron.*) Forza d' Amore (*a Morg.*) Che il fen t'affanna (*ad Or.*) Che senti al core, (*a Mor.*) Ma questa è ancora la pena mia. (*a Morg.*) Ma pur tiranna la provo in me. Per un bel volto, che ne vien tolto Tu mesto gemi. (*ad Oronte.*) Noi ci sdegnamo (*a Morgana.*) E tutti amiamo, senza mercè. E Gelosia, ec. (*Parte con Mel.*)

## SCENE VI

*To them Morgana.*

**MOR:** I will maintain your Cause (*to Brad.*) and your's oppose (*to Or.*)

**BRAD:** 'Tis Jealousy torments your Breast. (*To Or.*) 'Tis Love that warms your Heart. (*To Mor.*) Your Tyrant gives me equal Pain. (*To Or.*) Yours too I prove within. (*To Mor.*) For a lost Beauty you complain. (*To Or.*) You love and meet Disdain (*To Mor.*) Alike our Fate is hard, Doom'd to Love, without Reward. 'Tis, etc. (*Exit with Mor.*)

## SCENA VII

*Camera, che guarda agli Appartamenti di Alcina. Ruggiero, che torna dal cercare; e poi Oronte.*

**RUG:** La cerco in vano, e la crudel non torna.

**OR:** (Nuovo inganno si trovi; Un geloso Amator all' altro giovi.) Senti, Ruggiero, senti; E' credi ai sguardi, alla mentita frode D' Alcina tua?

**RUG:** Cosi favella Oronte?

**OR:** Cosi. Tu sol non fai, Che Chiudon queste selve Mille Amanti infelici Conversi in Onda, in fredde Ruppi, e Belve?

**RUG:** Io fo ben dì quai laccj. Per me la strinse Amore

**OR:** Il laccio è sciolto

**RUG:** Me sol' ama, e desia.

**OR:** Va, che sei stolto, Ricciardo è l' Idol suo.

**RUG:** Già di lui s'invaghi?

**OR:** Lui solo adora; E' per lui cangeratti in Belva ancora. Semplicetto; a Donna credi?

## SCENE VII

*A Galley leading to the Apartments of Alcina, Rogero, returning from seeking her, and afterwards Orontes.*

**ROG:** I've sought the Cruel, but in vain; She does not yet return.

**OR:** New Arts arise to mitigate my Grief; A jealous Lover joys in another's Pains. (*Aside.*) Hear me, Rogero; Do you so easily believe the Arts, The false designing Looks of your Alcina?

**ROG:** What says Orontes?

**OR:** E'en thus he says: Do you not know that in these fatal Woods. Thousands of hapless Lovers lie inanimate, Some chang'd to Streams, Some to wild Beasts, to Trees and Rocks?

**ROG:** Well, well I know that Love has bound her to me With Chains not be loos'd.

**OR:** Already they are loos'd.

**ROG:** No; me alone she loves, I am her only Wish.

**OR:** Too fond Credulity, Alone Richard has her very Thought.

**ROG:** Hah! what say'st thou, does he possess her Thought?

**OR:** Him fondly she beholds, and for his Sake Will change you to some brutal Form.

---

Se la vedi, che ti mira, Che sospira: pensa, e di; Ingannar potrebbe ancor. Quell sospiri lusinghieri, Quelli sguardi a voglier tardi, Menzogneri san cosi, Senza amar, mostrare Amor. Semplicetto, ec. (*Parte.*)

Can you a Woman thus believe? Shou'd you see her gently sigh And gently gaze, e'en then think and say, That still she may deceive. Their flatt'ring Sighs, and practis'd Smiles Not following the Heart, Make Shew of Love they do not feel. Can, etc. (*Exit.*)

## SCENA VIII

*Ruggiero ed Alcina.*

**RUG:** Ah! infedel, infedel! Questo è l' Amore?

**ALC:** Mio tesoro, mio ben, anima mia, Chiami Alcina infede?

**RUG:** Si, che lo sei, crudele. Và; Ricciardo t'attende, Egli a' tuoi prieghi Qui volse il piè: quivi per te dimoreà.

**ALC:** Tu geloso m' offendi, e piaci ancora.

## SCENE VIII

*Rogero and Alcina.*

**ROG:** Ah, faithless Fair! is this your boasted Love?

**ALC:** Thou Treasure of my Heart, my only Joy. Call you Alcina faithless?

**ROG:** Yes, and most justly, cruel as thou art: Away to thy Richard, he expects thee; Hither he comes according to your Wish; Here waits he for you.

**ALC:** Your Jealousy offends, and yet you please me.

## SCENA IX

*Bradamante e Detti.*

**BRAD:** Reina: il tuo soggiorno Quanto di raro ha il Mondo, ha in fe raccolto; Ma il portento maggior' è il tuo bel volto.

**AL:** Bello è sol per Ruggiero.

**BRAD:** Egli lo merta.

**RUG:** Eh! torna al Patrio Nido, Torna Ricciardo a tratar l' arme

**BRAD:** (Infido!)

**ALC:** Lascia prima, che sia l' Onda placata.

**BRAD:** E pietade.

**ALC:** E dovere.

**RUG:** E Amore, ingrata. (*ad Alcina sdegnato.*)

**ALC:** Alla costanza mia, cosi favella Il tuo core crudele? E pur ti son fedel', e pur son quella. Sì: son quella Non piu bella, Non piu cara agli occhj tuoi; Ma fe amar tu non mi vuoi, Infedel, deh! non mi odiar. Chiedi al guardo, alla favella Se non quella, ohjd ingrato Al tuo core mentitore, Che mi vuole rinfacciar. Sì, ec. (*Parte.*)

## SCENE IX

*To them Bradamante.*

**BRAD:** The World's best choicest Treasures seem collected In this your splendid Palace; yet, fair Queen, Your Beauty far exceeds those Ornaments, And is its chiefest Treasure.

**ALC:** Rogero owns that Praise.

**BRAD:** True, he deserves it.

**ROG:** Ah! haste away to serve your Country's Need; Return, Richard, to repel the Foes.

**BRAD:** (Ungrateful Man!)

**ALC:** First, let the stormy Sea be more appeas'd.

**BRAD:** This is most kind Compassion.

**ALC:** It is a Due to all.

**ROG:** No, no, Ingrate! 'tis Love.

**ALC:** Have you the Heart thus cruelly to wound My firmest Truth? And yet I am the same, the faithful She. I am the same, though now no more Dear or pleasing to your Eyes: But, cruel, if you cannot love, For Pity don't despise. Question my Words and ev'ry Look, If they denote a Change: As your false Heart, 'tis that alone, That will upbraid my Love. I am, etc. (*Exit.*)

## SCENA X

*Bradamante e Ruggiero.*

**BRAD:** Se nemico mi sossì,
Potresti peggio far?

**RUG:** Rival mi sei.
T'odio Ricciardo.

**BRAD:** Odii il German diletto
Della tua Bradmante?

**RUG:** E perciò t'odio ancor.

**BRAD:** Perfido amante;
Tu così mi dispreggi?

**RUG:** Forse d'Amor vaneggi?

**BRAD:** Indegno Amante!

**RUG:** Che favelli? ed a chi?

**BRAD:** Mirami altero.
Bradamante cosi parla a Ruggiero.

## SCENA XI

*Malisso, e Detti.*

**RUG:** Bradamante favella?
Bradamante in tali Arme?
Reina sei tradita

**MEL:** Eh! non è quella.

**BRAD:** Sì: và della tua Maga a' es-
pormi all' ira.

**MEL:** Ruggier non l' ascoltar.

**RUG:** Sò, che delira.
La bocca vaga: quell' occhio nero
Lo sò, t' impiaga; ma è fida ancora.
Chi t' innamora
Per to non è
Và, che sei stolto. Cangia pensiero.
Piace quel Volto; ma datti pace
Non è per tè.
La bocca, ec
(*Parte.*)

## SCENA XII

*Melisso e Bradamante.*

**MEL:** A quai strani perigli
N' espone il tuo parlare.

**BRAD:** Nell' altrui mal, facile è il
dar configli.
(*Melisso parte.*)

## SCENA XIII

*Morgana e Bradamante.*

**MOR:** Fuggi cor mio, ti affretta.
Al geloso Ruggiero
Concesse al fin l' innamorata Maga
In Belva di cangiarti

## SCENE X

*Bradamante and Rogero.*

**BRAD:** Were I your Enemy,
What worse cou'd you have done?

**ROG:** Thou art my Rival, and I hate
thee for't

**BRAD:** And do you hate
The Brother of your once-lov'd Bradamante?

**ROG:** Therefore I hate thee too.

**BRAD:** Perfidious Lover,
Am I so much your Scorn?

**ROG:** Does your Love make you
rave?

**BRAD:** Oh! most unworthy of my
Love!

**ROG:** What mean your Words? to
whom, if what I know not?

**BRAD:** Then look, proud Man,
Thus to Rogero, Bradamante
speaks.

## SCENE XI

*To them Melisso.*

**ROG:** Thus Bradamante speaks?
Bradamante! and thus arm'd!
My Queen, you are betray'd.

**MEL:** Ah no! it is not she.

**BRAD:** I am: now haste to your Inchantress,
And rouse her Rage against me.

**MEL:** Rogero, listen not.

**ROG:** I see it is but Madness.
Each Look, I know, has pierc'd thy
Heart;
But all your Hopes are vain:
What you would gain,
Is not for Thee.
Go, fond Believer; cease that
Thought.
This Face does please;
But be at Peace,
'Tis not for Thee.
Each, etc.
(*Exit.*)

## SCENE XII

*Melisso and Bradamante.*

**MEL:** To what known Dangers do
we stand expos'd
By your incautious Words?

**BRAD:** 'Tis easy to advise in others
Ills.
(*Exit Mel.*)

## SCENE XIII

*Morgana and Bradamante.*

**MOR:** Fly, fly, my Dearest, haste far
hence;
Jealous Rogero has at length prevail'd

**BRAD:** Và, la ritrova, e dilli,
Che Alcina non desio,
Che amarla non saprei:
Ch' ardo per altro Volto.

**MOR:** Il corro, e 'l mio

**BRA:** Dia l' inganno ristoro al miro
gran duolo.
(*Le dà la mano, e poi parteno.*)

## SCENA XIV

*Alcina.*

**ALC:** Tiranna Gelosìa.
Dell' amato Ruggier tormenta il
core,
E pur solo per lui mì strugge
Amore,
Tornami a vagheggiar,
Te solo vuole amar
Quest' Anima fedel
Caro mio bene.
Già ti donai 'l mio cor:
Fido sarà el mio amor.
Mai ti sarò crudel,
Cara mia spene.
Tornami, ec.

*Fine dell' Atto Primo.*

## ■ ATTO II

### SCENA I

*Ricca, e maestosa Sala del Palaz-
zo incantato di Alcina.*

*Ruggiero, e poi Melisso nella for-
ma di Atlante, che lo aveva educa-
to.*

**RUG:** Col celarvi, a chi v' ama, un
momento
Care luci, crudeli Voi sietè.
(*Col, ec.*)

**MEL:** Taci: taci codardo
Rimira il mio sembiante,
Ed arrossisci in rivedere Atlante.

**RUG:** Oh! de primi anni miei
Fedel educator

**MEL:** Menti.

**RUG:** T'abbraccio, (*vuole abbracciarlo, una esso risospinge.*)

On the Inchantress to employ her
Power,
And change you to some Brute or
senseless Form.

**BRAD:** Go, find him, courteous
Fair One, and inform him
That I nor seek, nor yet desire Alci-
na;
That I not want her Love, nay can-
not love her;
For to another all my Wishes tend.
I find some Comfort in deceiving
her.
(*Aside.*)

**MOR:** My Soul is full of you alone,
My dearest Youth,
You only can I love.
Since now I've given you my Heart,
I never more will change;
But ever will be kind and true,
My Dear, alone to you.

## SCENE XIV

*Alcina.*
*She alludes to Rogero's Jealousy.*

**MOR:** My Soul is full of you alone,
My dearest Youth,
You only can I love.
Since now I've given you my Heart,
I never more will change;
But ever will be kind and true,
My Dear, alone to you.

*The End of the First Act.*

## ■ ACT II

### SCENE I

*A rich and splendid Hall of the In-
chanted Palace of Alcina.*

*Rogero, and afterwards Melisso in
the Form of Atlante who had
brought him up.*

**ROG:** Oh cruel! for a Moment to de-
prive
Your Lover of the Sight of your dear
Eyes.
Oh cruel, etc.

**MEL:** No more, soft wanton Coward, lost to Glory;
But look on me, awaken your Remembrance,
And blush to see Atlante thus again.

**ROG:** My more than Friend!
Thou tender Guardian of my Infant
Years.

**MEL:** Thy Deeds belye thy Words.

**ROG:** Oh! let me clasp thee to my
Breast.

## Act II, Scene I

MEL: Vanne lunge; io ti scaccio.
Molle, insame Ruggiero,
Così tu corrispondi
A tanti miei per te sosserti assanni?

RUG: Amor! Dovere!

MEL: E poi?

RUG: Cortesia di gentil

MEL: Segui.

RUG: Pietato

MEL: Ti arresti, e ti confondi?
D' Amor vile Guerriero:
E questo della Gloria il bel sentiero?

RUG: Un Fato.

MEL: Questa, in Dito ora ti poni.
(*Li dà un' Anello.*)
Verace Gemma, e fe piu a me non credi,
Mira Ruggiero, e la tua infamia vedi.
(*Non così tosto Melisso porge a Ruggiero l' Anello stato già di Angelica, che la Sala tutta si cangia in luoco orrido, e deserto. Melisso in tanto riprende la sua prima forma.*)

RUG: Qual portento mi richiama
La mia Mente a richiarar?
Atlante, dove fei?

MEL: Io quel sembiante
Presi per liberarti.

RUG: Ah! Bradamante!

MEL: A te appunto mi manda

RUG: Or và ad Alcina,
Dille pur, che Ruggiero piu non l' ama;
Che 'l mio core ha tradito, e a mia Fama.

MEL: Il tuo sdegno sia cara a Bradamante.

RUG: Dì a quella, che l' adoro
Che bramo E che far deggio?

MEL: Ora rivesti
Tutte pria l' Arme usate;
Ma taci con Alcina,
E fingi il primo amor', il primo Volto.
Mostra desìo di Caccia,
Così fuga, e salute a te procaccia
Pensa a chi geme d' Amor piagata,
E sempre teme abbandonata,
Crudel, da tè.
Pensa, ec.
(*Parte.*)

---

MEL: Away far hence; I bid you from this Chace,
Idle luxurious Rogero.
Are these the Fruits of all my former Pains,
To foster thy weak Infancy?

ROG: Love! Duty!

MEL: What else?

ROG: Kind Courtesy

MEL: Go on.

ROG: The Gentle Pity

MEL: You are confus'd, and know not what to answer,
Love's wanton Champion:
Is this the great, the shining Path to Glory?

ROG: My Destiny

MEL: Put on your Finger This,
A true inestimable Gem;
And if you care not to believe my Words,
Be a Self-witness of your Infamy.
*Melisso puts the Ring (formerly Angelica's) on Rogero's Finger, and the Hall immediately changes to a horrid desart Place. Then Melisso resumes his former Shape.*

ROG: What mighty Cause has rous'd my drowsy Soul,
Shewn my lost Life, and bid me be my self.
Atlante, where art thou?

MEL: I took that Form to draw you from the State
Of idle Luxury in which you sunk.

ROG: Ah Bradamante!

MEL: From her I come on Purpose to

ROG: Go to Alcina, tell the Sorceress,
Rogero has at length thrown off her Love;
Tell her she has betray'd my Heart and Fame.

MEL: How dear this brave Resolve, this just Disdain
Will be to faithful Bradamante!

ROG: And tell that best unparagon'd in Truth,
Her only do I love Oh! what can I?

MEL: Again assume your wonted Dress and Arms;
But let it be all hidden from Alcina,
To her shew no Abatement of your Love,
But dress your Face in all its former Smiles
Desire to hunt, and thus in Safety we
May aid your Flight.
Think of the Fair, who left by thee,
Sadly complains;
Whose Tears and Pains
Are for your Cruelty.

## SCENA II

*Bradamante, e Ruggiero.*

BRAD: Qual' odio ingiusto contro me?

RUG: Perdona;
Vinse la mia Ragion, forza d' incanto.
Fin' ora vaneggiai: ecco, a me torno;
Rompo l' indegno laccio,
E se Rival mi sei,
Il tuo crudel Destin piango, e t' abbraccio.

BRAD: Ed è ver, mi rammembri?

RUG: Sì. Ah! sosse teco ancora
L' adorata mia sposa, tua fore la.

BRAD: Ruggier non mi conosci! e pur son quella.

RUG: Numi! è ver! Bradamante!
Ma Bradamente? e come? Un nuovo Incanto
Sì, che d' Alcina è questo.
Non l' avria nò tacciuto
Chi m' osserse il bel dono.
Và insidiosa Maga,
Della mia Donna amata
Tu mentir vuoi la forma, e la favella.

BRAD: Crudel, tu mi discacci, e pur son quella.
Vorrei Vendicarmi
Del perfido cor.
Amor dammi l' Armi
M' appresta il furo.
Vorrei, ec.
(*Parte.*)

---

## SCENE II

*Bradamante and Rogero.*

BRAD: What unjust Cause for your Disdain to me?

ROG: Oh! pardon me:
At length my Reason has subdu'd the Force
Of foul Inchantment; till now I was bewilder'd
In a dark Maze, but now have found my Path.
I'll break th' unworthy Chain so long I've borne,
And if you are my Rival, I'm your Friend,
And weep your cruel Fate.

BRAD: Is it then true? Do you remember me?

ROG: Full well.
Ah! was my dearest Fair, your Sister with you.

BRAD: Do you not know me still? e'en I am she.

ROG: Ye Powers! Is't possible? this Bradamante!
Ah how? it cannot be! Surely this is
Some new invented Spell of base Alcina.
But she shall not sully my Reason more,
And rob me of the Gift so late obtain'd.
Away, designing Sorceress, away,
Falsely thou tak'st my much-lov'd Fair One's Form,
And dost abuse her Speech.

BRAD: You, cruel, drive me from you, yet I am She.
Cou'd I revenge me of thy faithless Heart,
Love give me Arms,
And Fury drive me on.
Cou'd, etc.
(*Exit.*)

## SCENA III

RUGGEIERO: Chi scopre al mio pensiero,
Se tradito pur son, o s' odo il vero?
Mi lusinga il dolce assetto
Con l' aspetto del mio bene.
Pur chi sà? Temer convience,
Che m' inganni amando ancor.
Ma se quella fosse mai
Che adorai, e l' abbandono;
Infedele, ingrato io sono.
Son crudele e traditor.
Mi, ec.
(*Parte.*)

---

## SCENE III

ROGERO: (*alone.*) Who can resolve the Doubtings of my Mind?
Am I betray'd, or is it Truth I hear?
Love, every ready with fond Views,
Tells me the best, it is my Fair;
Yet I know not, and whilst there's room
To doubt, 'tis best to fear;
Then sweet is the Deceit to come.
But shou'd it be her I adore,
And I thus leave her still,
I shall deserve the worst Reproach,
As Traytor, base Ingrate.
Love, etc.
(*Exit.*)

## SCENA IV

*Luogo, che conduce ai Giardini Reali con Statua di Circe nel mezzo, che cangia gli Uomini in Fiere. Alcina, i poi Morgana.*

---

## SCENE IV

*A Place leading to the Royal Gardens, with the Statue of Circe (who changes Men to Beasts) in the Middle. Alcina, and then Morgana.*

ALC: S' acquieti il rio sospetto, / Che tormenta il mio ben. Vesta Ricciardo / Ferina í poglia. O voi / Temute Larve, al noto imper scendete. / A te Figlia del sole / Porgo i miei prieghi usati.

MOR: Ancor per poco / Sospendi il suon di Magiche parole.

ALC: Importuna: mi arresti?

### SCENA V

*Ruggiero, e detti.*

MOR: E la tua pace, (*a Ruggiero.*) / Con tanta crudeltà comprar si dee?

ALC: Caro ti vò appagar.

RUG: Ciò basta, Alcina, / Piu non chiede il mio Amor.

### SCENA VI

*Alcina, e Ruggiero.*

ALC: Non scorgo nel tuo Viso / Il contento di pria. Dì: che ti offende?

RUG: Una noiosa Virtùte or mi riprende.

ALC: Pensa a goder

RUG: Concedimi, o Reina / Almen, che nel mio Usbergo / Faccia guerra alle Fiere, / Per ravvivar lo spirto mio languente.

ALC: Al tuo voler s' unì sempre mia mente. / Vanne, ma sia per poco: / Ma pensa al mio martiro. / Temo. Partir ti lascio, e ne sospiro.

RUG: Mil bel tesoro, / Fedel son' io, / (Ma non a te) / Al ben, che odoro / All' Idol mio / Prometto Fè. / Il caro amante / Non siegue il Piede, / E fido resta, / (Ma non con te) / Con chi li chiede / Costante, e mesta / Pace, e mercè. / Mio, ec. / (*Parte.*)

### SCENA VII

*Alcina ed Oberto.*

---

ALC: Calm the black Jealousy that has possess'd / And wracks my Charmer's Breast; / Invest Richardo with a brutal Shape; / And you, dread Spectres, haste to the Command, / But chief to Thee, great Daughter of the Sun, / I give my wonted Prayers.

MOR: Oh! for a while break off those Magick Sounds,

ALC: Why this your Importunity?

### SCENE V

*To them Rogero.*

MOR: Gentle Rogero, / Wou'd you buy Peace with with so much Cruelty?

ALC: I go to end your Pains.

ROG: Enough, Alcina, my Love demands no more.

### SCENE VI

*Alcina and Rogero.*

ALC: Your Brow seems wanting of its fair Serene; / I miss its former Peace: Say what disturbs you?

ROG: With tedious Leisure, tir'd my Soul, / Burns now for active Sports.

ALC: Think but of Joys

ROG: Suffer me, Queen, in Arms to range the Woods, / And through the pathless Wilds the Chase pursue, / And there by glorious Toils, my drooping Spirits raise

ALC: Your Inclination ever has my Will: / Go, but, my Love, be quick in your Return; / Think of the Pains I suffer in your Absence. / I'm full of Fear, / I let you go, yet oh! I sigh to leave Thee.

ROG: Joy and Treasure of my Heart, / My Love is true / (But not to you) / To her whom I alone desire; / To the Object of my Vows / I promise deathless Truth. / I go and leave my Heart behind / (But not with you) / That's firm and true / To her who sweetly complains, / And asks my Pity of her Pains. / Joy, etc. / (*Exit.*)

### SCENE VII

*Alcina and Oberto.*

---

OBER: Reina; io cerco in vano / L' amato Genitore!

ALC: Spera, Oberto, e sta lieto

OBER: Oh Dei! non posso

ALC: Il riso, il brio, la gioia, / Qui t' invita a goder.

OBER: Tutto mi annoja.

ALC: Dispon de' miei Tesori.

OBER: Io non li curo.

ALC: Al mio matterno amore / Cosi mal corrispondi?

OBER: Sempre grato / Ti sarò, se m' insegni il Genitore.

ALC: (Mi sà pietade; or si lunsinghi) ascolta; / Vedrai in breve tuo Padre, Io tel prometto.

OBER: Comincia a respirar l' anima in petto. / Trà speme e timore / Mi palpita il core, / Nè sò ben ancora / S' è gioia ò dolor. / Trà, ec. / (*Parte.*)

### SCENA VIII

*Oronte, e Alcina.*

OR: Reina, sei tradita / Con segreto Configlio / Degli Ospiti malvagj / A fuggir s' apparecchia il tuo Ruggiero.

ALC: Numi! che intendo, Oronte! e questo è vero?

OR: Pur troppo: ed

ALC: Ora intendo / Perchè l' Arme vesti; crudel, spergiuro! / Di lui, di lor, sarne vendetta io giuro. / Ah! mio cor! schernito sei / Stelle! Dei! Nume d' Amore! / Traditore! t' amo tanto; / Puoi lasciarmi sola in pianto, / Oh Dei! perchè? / Ma che sà gemendo Alcina? / Son Reina, e tempo ancora? / Resti, o Mora. Peni sempre, / O torni a me. Ah! mio, / Ah! mio, ec. (*Parte.*)

---

OBER: O Queen, all Search is vain, / I cannot find / My dearest Father.

ALC: Hope still, and be of Comfort.

OBER: Ah me! I never can.

ALC: Dispel that sad Despair. / Here Mirth and Joys alone invite to Pleasure.

OBERT: They are to me but troublesome and tasteless.

ALC: My Treasures all use as you will.

OBER: I care not for them.

ALC: Is this Return for all my tender Cares / And Mother's Love?

OBER: If you will shew me where to find my Father, / My Gratitude shall never know an End.

ALC: Those Words move Pity in me. (*Aside.*) / Then here I promise, you e'er long shall be / Blest with your Father's Sight.

OBER: Again my Soul admits some small Content. / Now Hopes succeed my former Fears, / Now hasty throbs my trembling Heart; / But whether greater Joy or Woe / Creates this Change I cannot know. / Now, etc. / (*Exit.*)

### SCENE VIII

*Orontes and Alcina.*

OR: My Queen, you are betray'd, / The secret Councils of the faithless Guests, / Have wrought on your Rogero, and prepar'd / His speedy Flight.

ALC: Ah me! what do I hear? / Orontes, is it true?

OR: Oh were it not! It is too true.

ALC: Now I perceive his Earnestness to bear / His warlike Arms with him; false perjur'd Man! / On Them, on Him, I vow a full Revenge. / Ye gentle Gods of Love, / Am I thus left despis'd! / Dear Traytor, thee I love alone, / Can you then leave me here, / To make a fruitless Moan / In what have I deserv'd your Hate? / But why these dull Complaints? / I've Time and Pow'r. / Traytor, return or die; / Return, or feel the Misery / I can inflict on Thee. / Ye, etc. / (*Exit.*)

# Act II, Scene IX

## SCENA IX

*Oronte, e Morgana.*

**OR:** Or, che dici Morgana?
Il tuo novello amante
Con perfidia, ed inganno
Ti abbandona. Lo sai?

**MOR:** Nol credo Oronte.
La gelosia ti sprona:
Ma piu gli affetti miei per te non
sono.
Libera son, nè chieggo a te perdo-
no.
(*Parte.*)

## SCENA X

**ORONTE:** All' offesa, il disprezzo
Giunge l' ingrata? Sù: corraggio;
Oronte
Scaccia costei dall' Alma; e se mai
torna
Pentita a riamarti.
Deludi l' arti sue con l' istess' arti.
E un solle, è un vile affetto,
Non è la sua beltà,
Che trionfar la fa
Superba dei mio cor.
E un, ec.
(*Parte.*)

## SCENA XI

*Bradamante ed Oberto.*

**OBER:** Ed è ver? Che mi narri?

**BRA:** Amato Oberto,
Del mio Cugino Astelfo
Tuo caro Genitor presto il sembi-
ante
Vedrai; e l' empia Maga,
Che in Lion lo cangiò, error confuso
Guarda cauto il secreto.

**OBER:** Non temer

**BRA:** Tienti pronto; or' và, stà lieto.
(*Oberto Parte.*)

## SCENA XII

*Ruggiero, Bradamante, e Morga-
na, che ascolta in disparte.*

**RUG:** Eccomi a' piedi tuoi
Generosa Donzella (*vuole ingi-
nocchicarse.*)
Doppio error mi sà reo

---

## SCENE IX

*Orontes and Morgana.*

**OR:** What say you, now, Morgana?
Your new, your gentle Lover proves
unkind,
And, by perfidious Arts, abandons
you.
You know th' unpleasing Truth?

**MOR:** Nor do I know it, nor believe.
Thy Jealousy drives Thee to odious
Fancies:
But be at Rest, you share not my Re-
gards;
I'm free, and care not for thy Love
or Hate.
(*Exit.*)

## SCENE X

**ORONTES:** What, does she height-
en her Offence with Scorn?
No more, Orontes, stoop thus vilely
low,
But drive the proud Inconstant
from your Heart:
E'en shou'd she e'er, repenting of
her Folly,
Return to Love, give back her
Scorns,
And use the Arts she taught.
'Tis ill-plac'd Love, and foolish
Airs,
More than her Beauty's Power,
That make her triumph o'er
My long subjected Heart.
'Tis, etc.
(*Exit.*)

## SCENE XI

*Bradamante and Oberto.*

**OBER:** Is it then true? What joyful
Sounds I hear!

**BRA:** Yes, my Oberto,
You soon shall see the Likeness of
Astolfo,
Your dearest Father, and my more
than Friend;
And the Inchantress too, whose im-
pious Spells
Transform'd him to a Lion, soon
confus'd,
Wandring disconsolate.
Be cautious of the Secret.

**OBER:** Fear not.

**BRA:** And be you ready. Now go
contented.
(*Exit Oberto.*)

## SCENE XII

*Rogero, Bradamante and Morga-
na, who listens apart.*

**ROG:** See, prostrate at your Feet,
kind injur'd Fair,
One conscious of his Crimes,
Black with a double Error

---

**BRAD:** Sorgi Ruggiero.
Serbiamo a miglior uso
Tu le discolpe, io le querele. Andia-
mo.
Temo sempre dovunque il guardo
volga
Vedere Alcina ria, che mi ti tolga.

**RUG:** Bradamante cor mio

**BRAD:** Ruggiero ameto, (*Si abbracciano.*)
Fuggiam l' infame loco.
(*Morgana si presenta loro insu-
riato.*

**MOR:** Mentitrice che vuoi? (*a Bra-
damante.*)
Che pensi ingrato? (*a Ruggiero.*)
Alcina vi dara giusta mercede,
Ospite ingannatrice: Uom senza
Fede. (*a Bradam.*) (*a Ruggiero.*)
(*Parte sdegnata.*)

**RUG:** Verdi Prati, e selve amene
Perderete la beltà.
Vaghi Fior, correnti Rivi
La vaghezza, la Bellezza
Presto in voi si cangerà.
Verdi Prati, e Selve amene
Perderete la beltà.
E cangiato il vago oggetto
All' orror del primo aspetto
Tutto in voi ritornerà.
Verdi Prati, e Selve amene
Perderete la beltà.
Verdi, ec.
(*Parte.*)

## SCENA XIII

*Stanza sotterranea delle Magie,
con varie Figure e Strumenti, che
appartengono a quesi' uso.*

**ALCINA:** Ah! Ruggiero crudel, tu
non mi amasti!
Ah! che fingesti amore, e m' ingan-
nasti!
E pur ti adora ancor fido il mio core.
Ah! Ruggiero crudel, sei traditor!
Del pallido Acheronte.
Spiriti abitatori, e della notte
Ministre di vendetta
Cieche Figlie crudeli, a me venite.
Secondate i miei voti,
Perche Ruggiero amato
Non fugga da me ingrato.
*Guarda d' intorno, e sospesa.*
Ma; ahime! Misera! e quale
Insolita tardanza! Eh! Non mi udite?
(*sdegnata.*)
Vi cerco, e vi ascondete?
Vi comando, e tacete?
Evvi inganno? Evvi frode? (*Infuria-
ta.*)
La mia Verga fatal non ha poslanza?
Vinta, delusa Alcina, e che ti avan-
za.
Ombre pallide, lo sò, mi udite.
D' intorno errate, e vi celate.

---

**BRAD:** Arise, Rogero, and let us re-
serve
For more and better Leisure,
You your Repentance, and I my Re-
proaches.
Let us away, for ever while I'm here
I fear to see Alcina, who depriv'd
me
Of Thee, my All.

**ROG:** My dearest Bradamante!
(*They embrace.*)

**BRAD:** My dear Rogero! let's fly this
hateful Place.

**MOR:** What will you, Faithless! (*to
Brad.*)
What will you, Ingrate! (*to Rog.*)
Alcina shall give you both due Re-
ward,
Deceitful Stranger! (*to Brad.*)
Most perfidious Man! (*to Rog.*)
(*Exit angrily.*)

**ROG:** Verdant Meadows, pleasant
Shade,
All your Beauties soon shall fade.
Fragrant Flow'rs, crystal Rills,
Soon your Sweets will all decay,
And your Pride will soon away.
Verdant Meadows, pleasant Shade,
All your Beauties soon will fade.
Each gay Prospect now we see
Rising in its full Delight,
In its first Horror soon shall be
A rude unpleasing Sight.
Verdant Meadows, pleasing Shade,
All your Beauties soon shall fade.
Verdant, etc.
(*Exit.*)

## SCENE XIII

*A Subterraneous Apartment of the
Inchantresses, with various
Figures and Instruments for their
Use.*

**ALCINA:** Cruel Rogero! have I not
your Love!
Did you but feign it? Am I then de-
ceiv'd!
Ah! still my Heart reserves its Love
for Thee,
Cruel Rogero! Art thou then a Tray-
tor!
Ye Spirits that on Acheron's dark
Shores
For ever dwell, ye Ministers of
Night,
Offspring of blind Revenge, haste,
haste to me,
Second my Will, employ your Pow-
er to stay
My dear Rogero's intended Flight:
But, hah! whence this unwonted
Disobedience?
Alas! why this Delay? Do you not
hear me?
I seek you, and do you avoid my
Sight?
I now command; do you refuse to
obey?
Do you betray me too? Are these

Sorde da me. Perchè? Perche?
Fugge il mio bene; voi lo fermate
Deh! per pietatè,
Se in questa Verga, ch' ora disprezzo,
E voglio frangere, forza non v' è.
Ombre, ec.
(*Parte con impeto gittando via la Verga Magica, ed allora mamsestandonsi diversi Spiriti, e Fantasmi.*)

*Fine del Atto Secondo.*

# ■ ATTO III

## SCENA I

*Atrio del Palaggio.*

*Oronte, e Morgana.*

**OR:** Voglio amare, e disamar
Così mi piace. Voglio, ec.

**MOR:** Vendicarti tu vuoi.
Di un' innocente inganno, e pur t' adoro,
Oronte, Anima mia.

**OR:** Và, tuo non sono.

**MOR:** Se t' offesi mio ben, chiego perdono.
Credete al mio dolore
Luci tiranne, e care.
Per voi languo d' amore,
Bramo da voi pietà.
Credete, ec.
(*Parte.*)

**OR:** M' inganna, me n' avveggo,
E pur' ancor l' adoro
Se ben mi su crudel', è 'l mio tesoro.
Un momento di contento
Dolce rende a' un fido amante
Tutto il pianto, che verso.
Suol Amore, dal dolore
Tirar Balfamo alle pene,
E sanar, chi pria piagò.
Un ec.
(*Parte.*)

## SCENA II

*Ruggiero, ed Alcina per parte opposta.*

**RUG:** (Molestissimi incontro!)

**ALC:** Ahimè! Ruggiero.
E ver, che mi abbandoni?

your Arts?
My fatal Rod then has no Power to charm!
Left, left Alcina! nought is left for Thee!
You hear, I know, false airy Forms,
And wander here to me conceal'd;
But why is your Observance now with-held?
My Lover proves to me unkind
And flies; his Flight, for Pity, stay.
If in this Rod no Pow'r I find
When now most wanted, let it hence away.
You hear, etc.
*Goes out in a Rage, throwing away her Magick Wand, when divers Spectres appear.*

*The End of the Second ACT.*

# ■ ACT III

## SCENE I

*A Court of the Palace.*

*Orontes and Morgana.*

**OR:** I'll love or hate
But as I please

**MOR:** Will you pursue so much so deep Revenge
For Arts of harmless Kind; for still, Orontes,
You are the only Object of my Wish.

**OR:** Then is your Wish mis-plac'd;
mine tends elsewhere.

**MOR:** If I've been guilty of the least Offence,
Forgive me now.
Believe, dear Tyrant, that I grieve
Full much for my so small Offence.
For you I sigh, of you I ask
Kind Pity of my Pains.
Believe, etc.
(*Exit.*)

**OR:** I was abus'd, but I must love her still;
Tho' she was cruel, yet I cannot change.
A Moment of Content o'er pays
A faithful Lover's Pains,
Waking Nights and restless Days.
Love ever heals the Wounds he gives;
E'en from the Torments we endure
He draws a pleasing Cure.
A Moment, etc.
(*Exit.*)

## SCENE II

*Rogero and Alcina differently.*

**ROG:** (Unlucky Meeting!)

**ALC:** Alas! Rogero, must I find it true,
That you abandon me despis'd?

**RUG:** M' invita la Virtute,
Che langue nell' Amore.

**ALC:** E non pensi, mio caro, al mio dolore?

**RUG:** Il passato, suo inganno
Rimira con orrore un' Alma grande.

**ALC:** Ah! che sei mentitore:
Fuggi da me per darti a' un' altra amante:

**RUG:** Quella è mia sposa.

**ALC:** Oh! Dei!
E scordar tu mi puoi, mia cara speme?

**RUG:** Dover', Amor, Virtu pugnano assieme.

**ALC:** Per questi sospir miei

**RUG:** Li spargi al vento.

**ALC:** Ti sui sempre fedel.

**RUG:** Scorda il passato.

**ALC:** Ti adoro ancor.

**RUG:** Non è piu tempo.

**ALC:** Ingrato!

**RUG:** Mi richiama la Gloria.

**ALC:** E un van pretesto.

**RUG:** Mi stimola l' Onore.

**ALC:** Và: m' oltraggiasti assai. Và traditore
Ma quando tornerai
Di laccj avvinto il piè,
Attendi pur da me
Rigore, e crudeltà,
E pur, perche t' amai,
Ho ancor di te pietà.
Ancor placar mi puoi
Mio ben, cor mio; non vuoi?
Mi lascia infido, e và.
Ma, ec.
(*Parte.*)

## SCENA III

*Melisso, Ruggiero, e Bradamante.*

**MEL:** Tutta d' armate Squadre
L' Isola è cinta, e d' incantati Mostri.

**RUG:** Mi sarò via col braccio.

**BRAD:** Io con la spada.

**MEL:** Non basta umana forza.
Prendi il Gorgoneo scudo,
Prendi il Destriero alato, e a me lo presta.

**RUG:** Partur da te mio ben l' Alma funesta.
Stà nell' Ircana pietrosa Tana
Tigre sdegnosa, e incerta pende,
Se parte, o attende il Cacciator.
Dal teso Strale guardar si vuole,
Ma poi la Prole lascia in periglio.
Freme, e l' assale desio di sangue,
Pietà del Figlio; poi vince amor.

**ROG:** Virtue excites me to those glorious Deeds,
Which idle Love has so long robb'd me of.

**ALC:** Oh! have you lost all Sense of what I bear.

**ROG:** A noble Soul looks e'en with Horror back
On his past Errors.

**ALC:** Oh! then am I betray'd:
You fly my Love, to hasten to another's.

**ROG:** She is my Spouse.

**ALC:** Oh killing Sound!
And can you then forget me?

**ROG:** Duty, Love, Virtue wage a cruel War.

**ALC:** For Pity of my Sighs

**ROG:** I must not hear, but give them to the Wind

**ALC:** I ne'er was missing in my Faith.

**ROG:** I must forget the past.

**ALC:** And still I love Thee.

**ROG:** Then now no more.

**ALC:** Barb'rous Ingrate!

**ROG:** 'Tis Glory calls, I must obey.

**ALC:** That's but a vain Pretext.

**ROG:** Great Honour drives me on.

**ALC:** Go, Traytor, Go.
Enough you've wrong'd me, to excite my Hate.
When you shall return again,
Not thus, but bound in Chains;
Then you may expect from me
Severest Rigour, justest Cruelty.
But as I once have lov'd,
Still Pity will have Place,
Still you have Pow'r to please
And calm my Rage. Do you refuse?
Go worthless Traytor, go. When, etc.
(*Exit.*)

## SCENE III

*Melisso, Rogero and Bradamante.*

**MEL:** With armed Troops and with inchanted Monsters
The Isle is all surrounded.

**ROG:** My Arm will force my Way.

**BRAD:** The Sword shall mine.

**MEL:** All human Power, I fear, will not avail.
Take you the Gorgon Shield,
Get you the winged Horse, and haste to me.

**ROG:** O, my Delight, my Soul is griev'd to part
But for a Moment from Thee.
The Hyrcanian Tygress, when pursu'd,
Flies to her rocky Den, and knows not
If to depart or wait the Hunter's Coming;

# Act III, Scene III

Stà, ec.
(*Parte.*)

Is willing to avoid the threat'ned Shaft.
But cannot leave her Young in Danger:
In Rage she foams, her Safety bids her thence,
But Nature for her Young strongly assails,
And Love at last prevails
The, etc.
(*Exit.*)

## SCENA IV

*Melisso, e Bradamante.*

**MEL:** Vanne tu seco ancora;
Dov fà seno il mare,
Ed è la Nave ascosa, ambo vi attendo.

**BRAD:** Non partirò, se pria,
Sciolto ogni infame incanto
A chi privo ne stà Vita non rendo.
(*Melisso Parte.*)
All' Alma sedel
Amore placato,
Il Fato, ed il Ciel
Promette pietà.
In mezzo ai martiri
La gioia ravviso,
E dopo i sospiri
Il riso verrà
(*Al. ec. Parte.*)

## SCENE IV

*Melisso and Bradamante.*

**MEL:** Go you too with him,
Where the Sea forms a Bay;
A secret Bark is ready, there I expect you.

**BRAD:** No, I shall not depart
Till I have quite destroy'd this Magick's Force,
And given back to Life those who so long
Have lain inanimate.
(*Melisso Exit.*)
A faithful Soul will ever find,
Tho' late, its due Reward;
The Heavens promise Peace to all
Who much and truly love.
Amidst my Pains I see a Dawn
Of smiling Joy come swiftly on,
And after all the Torments past
I shall be blest at last.
(*Exit.*)

## SCENA V

*Oronte, ed Alcina.*

**OR:** Niuna forza lo arresta.
Vinse Ruggiero.

**ALC:** Ahime! perfide Stelle!
Ma i miei Guerrier?

**OR:** Giaccion distesi? al suolo.

**ALC:** E i Mostri miei

**OR:** Son vinti.

**ALC:** E quell' ingrato
Dunque fuggi?

**OR:** Nò. L' Isola minaccia.
Rende Amore a costei giusta mercede
Di tanti, ch' oltraggiò miseri amanti.
Val questa pena sua tutti i lor pianti.
(*Parte.*)

**ALC:** Mi restano le lagrime.
Direi dell' Alma i voti;
Ma i Dei resi ho implacabili,
E non mi ascolta il Ciel.
*Alc. Mi, ec.*

## SCENE V

*Orontes and Alcina.*

**OR:** No Force can stay Rogero's conqu'ring Arm,
He bears down all before him.

**ALC:** Oh inauspicious Stars!
Where are my Warriours?

**OR:** All lie subdu'd.

**ALC:** And the devouring Monsters?

**OR:** They are tam'd.

**ALC:** Is the Ingrate then fled?

**OR:** No, no, the Ruin of the Isle he threatens;
Love justly gives her this Reward
For the Severity she us'd
Against so many hapless sighing Lovers.
And now the Pains she feels exceed
Those that she made them undergo.
(*Exit.*)

**ALC:** Still Fears I have,
A needy Soul's best Arguments.
But cruel Heav'n hears me not,
Th' offended Gods are now no more
Inclined to pity me.

## SCENA VI

*Prospetto della Reggia meravigliosa di Alcina, attorniata di Alberi, di Statue, di Obbelischi, e di Trofei, con Seragli di Fiere, chè vanno girando: ed Urna rilevata nel mezzo, che racchiude la forza di tutto l' Incanto.*

**CORO:** Sin per le vie del sole
Una gloriosa Prole
Il volo sà innalzar.

*Oberto, e poi Alcina con Dardo alla mano.*

**OBER:** Già è vicino il momento
Di cangiar il mio duol tutto in contento; (*Alcina ascolta a parte.*)
E Parmi già con amoroso core
Di stringer in al mio seno il Genitore. (*Alcina gli si presenta.*)

**ALC:** Come lo sai? (*Oberto si consonde nel responderle.*)

**OBER:** Perche il Destino i pianti
Il dover.

**ALC:** Ti confondi?

**OBER:** Alta Regina; (*Oberto si dà corragio.*)
Io ben lo sò; melo promise Alcina.

**ALC:** (Ah! che ancora costui pensa a' miei danni;
Ingrato! or proverai gli estremi affanni.)
(*Alcina si volge verso il Seraglio delle fiere, e mormorando qualche parola, si avvanza un Lione mansueto verso Oberto, quando Alcina dà il suo Dardo al medesimo dicendogli.*)

**ALC:** Prendi, Oberto, il mio Dardo, e ti difendi
Da quella Fiera. (*Il Lione si corica vicino ad Oberto, e gli và lambendo i piedi.*)

**OBER:** Eh! mi fi mostra amica.

**ALC:** Non ti fidar; la uccidi.

**OBER:** Ah! non hò core.

**ALC:** Ubbidisci il commande. (*risoluta.*)

**OBER:** (Ah! ch' io ben ricconosco il Genitore.)

**ALC:** Rendimi 'l Dardo; Io ferirolla appieno.) (*Sdegnata.*)

**OBER:** Crudel; lo immergerò pria nel tuo seno.
(*Oberto ritirandosi volge il Dardo contro Alcina, mentre*)
*Lione ritorna nel Seraglio.*
Barbara; Io ben lo sò,
E' quello il Genitor,
Che l' empio tuo furor

## SCENE VI

*A Prospect of the splendid Palace of Alcina surrounded with Trees, Statues, Obelisks and Trophies, and Dens of wild Beasts; an Urn rais'd in the Middle which incloses the whole Power of the Inchantment.*

**CHORUS:** A glorious Offspring on a daring Wing
Can raise its noble Flight
To an immeasurable Height.

*Oberto, and then Alcina, with a Dart in her Hand.*

**OBER:** The happy Moment now comes smiling on,
Whence all my Griefs shall change to sweet Content. (*Alcina listens apart.*)
When I again shall in a dear Embrace
With matchless Joy take to this Breast my Father.

**ALC:** How know you that?

**OBER:** My pitying Fate, my Plaints Duty

**ALC:** Your doubting Tongue knows not its Answer.

**OBER:** Great Queen, I know it well;
For so Alcina promis'd.

**ALC:** He also joins to aggravate my Woes:
But thou, Ingrate, shall prove extreamest Grief. (*Aside.*)
(*Alcina turns towards the Den of wild Beasts, and muttering some Words, a Lion comes meekly towards Oberto and Alcina gives him a Dart.*)

**ALC:** Oberto, take my Dart,
And guard you from this hungry Lion's Rage.
(*The Lyon lies down near Oberto, licking his Feet.*)

**OBER:** I see no savage Fierceness;
He rather seems my Friend.

**ALC:** Oh trust him not, kill the devouring Beast.

**OBER:** Nature points out my Sire in any Shape. (*Aside.*)

**ALC:** Give me the Dart, I'll strike the unerring Blow.

**OBER:** Inhuman, first I'll drench it in your Heart.
(*Oberto retiring, turns the Dart on Alcina, mean while the Lyon returns to the Den.*)
More savage than the brutal Kind;
This is, I know, my dearest Sire
In this senseless Form confin'd

Cangiato hà in fera.
Barbara, ec.
(*Parte, portando via il Dardo di Alcina.*)

By thy black Spells and impious Power. Etc.
(*Exit, carrying away the Dart.*)

## SCENA VII

*Bradamante, Ruggiero, e Alcina.*

BRAD: Le lusinge, gl' inganni,
Non udir piu, mio caro sposo amato.

ALC: Che inganni? Anzi ho pietà.
Piango il suo Fato.

RUG: Non la ascoltar.

BRAD: Detesto
Le sue offerte, e gli Auguri.

ALC: Per questa cara Destra (*a Ruggiero.*)

RUG: Ormai mi lascia.

ALC: Bradamante, à tuoi piedi. (*a Bradamante.*)

BRAD: A me t' invola,

ALC: A morir tu ten vai. (*a Ruggiero.*)

RUG: Cura è del Cielo.

ALC: Tu, Vedova dolente. (*a Bradamante.*)
Lo piangerai.

RUG: Non l' ascoltar, che mente.

ALC: Non è Amor, nè Gelosia
è Pietà. (*a Ruggiero.*)

BRAD: Che ascose Frodi!

ALC: E' desio, che lieta godi. (*a Bradamante.*)

RUG: Che fallaci indifi accenti!

ALC: Non t' offendo. (*a Bradamante.*)

RUG: Indegna taci.

ALC: Non t' inganno.

BRAD: Iniqua, menti.

ALC: Cruda Donna: rio Tiranno

RUG: Non vogl' io da Voi

BRAD: Non sperar da Noi

RUG, BRAD: mercè.

BRAD: Caro sposo!

RUG: Animà mia!

ALC: Solo affanni, e solo pene

BRAD, RUG: Solo gioie, e solo bene:

ALC: Premio fian di nostra Fè.

BRAD, RUG: Premio fian di vostra Fè.
(*Partono Alcina per una parte e Bradamante per un' altra.*)

## SCENE VII

*Bradamante, Rogero, and then Alcina.*

BRAD: Her Smiles, her Blandishments, and other Arts,
Oh hear them not, my Dear.

ALC: How much are you deceiv'd?
'Tis Pity moves me thus, I weep his Fate.

ROG: Heed not her Words.

BRAD: I scorn your Offers and your Auguries.

ALC: By this Dear Hand (*To Rog.*)

ROG: Away, and leave me.

ALC: Bradamante at your Feet (*To Brad.*)

BRAD: Speak not to me.

ALC: To certain Death you go. (*To Rog.*)

BRAD: That is as Heaven will.

ALC: And you become a Widow,
Will mourn his hapless Fate.

BRAD: Neither believe nor hear her.

ALC: Nor is this Love, nor Jealousy,
But kindest Pity all. (*To Rog.*)

BRAD: What hidden Arts are these!

ALC: 'Tis my Desire that you have Peace. (*To Brad.*)

ROG: Betraying Sounds!

ALC: In this I wrong not you. (*To Brad.*)

ROG: No more.

ALC: Nor is it to betray you. (*To Rog.*)

BRAD: That is alone your Will.

ALC: Oh cruel Fair! ungrateful Tyrant!

RUG: I ask not from you

BRAD: Hope not from us

RUG, BRAD: Pity.

BRAD: Joy of my Life!

ROG: My Heart's Delight!

ALC: May endless Fears and Pains alone

BRAD, ROG: May endless Peace and Joy alone

ALC: Be your Faith's Reward.

BRAD, ROG: Be our Faith's Reward.
(*Exeunt Alcina and Bradamante differently.*)

## SCENA VIII

*Ruggiero con Oronte a cui rende la Spada.*

RUG: Prendi, e vivi.
Vuol la tua libertà, non il tuo sangue,

OR: Signor, m' è grato il dono,

RUG: Or l' Urna infame
Si spezzi.

OR: Eroico oprar.

RUG: Và, se paventi;
Io basto solo.
(*Ruggiero si avanza per rompere l' Urna coll' Anello incantato: ed Alcina fretolosa lo tratiene.*)

## SCENA IX

*Alcina e Detti, e poi Bradamante.*

ALC: Ah mio Ruggiero, che tenti?

RUG: Voglio la libertade
Degl' infelici, che quì chiudi.

ALC: Ed io Lo sarò

BRAD: Non fidarti.
Lascia, che faccia il colpo, il braccio mio.
(*Và per spezzar l' Urna.*)

*Morgana, e detti,*
(*Quando Bradamante và per spezzar
l' Urna, Morgana le si oppone.*)

## SCENA X

*Melisso, Oberto e detti.*

ALC: Misera, Ah! nò!

MOR: Per quella
Vita, che ti serbai, lascia

## SCENA ULTIMA

*Melisso, Oberta, e detti.*

MEL: A che tardi?
Struggi l' infame Nido: (*a Ruggiero.*)
Rendi altrui la salute.

RUG: Sì.

OR: Sì.

BRAD, OBER, MEL: Spezza, Ruggiero.

ALC, MOR: O noi perdute! (*Si ritirano.*)
(*Ruggiero spezza l' Urna, e subitamente precipita, e si dilegua tutto ciò appariva all' intorno, sorgendo su quelle ruine il Mare, che si vede da una vasta, e sotterranea caverna, dove molti sassi si cangi-*

## SCENE VIII

*Rogero and Orontes, to whom he gives his Sword.*

ROG: Take it and live: I do not seek your Life,
But give you Liberty.

OR: Thanks for the grateful Gift.

ROG: Now to destroy this most destructive Urn.

OR: Good noble Work.

ROG: Go if you fear, alone I can perform
The needful Deed.
(*Rogero goes to break the Urn with the inchanted Ring, and Alcina hastily holds him.*)

## SCENE IX

*To them Alcina, and then Bradamante.*

ALC: What wou'd you, my Rogero?

ROG: The Liberty of these
Unhappy here confin'd.

ALC: I will desolve the Charm

BRAD: I shall not trust the glorious Task to you.
Let my Hand give the Blow.
(*Goes to break the Urn, when Morgana enters and hinders her.*)

## SCENE X

ALC: Ah! No

MOR: For Pity of the Life which I've kept for you,
Suffer I may

## SCENE THE LAST

*To them Melisso and Oberto.*

MEL: Why this Delay?
Dissolve the hateful Spell,
Restore to every one their former State.

ROG: I go.

OR: On.

BRAD, OBER, MEL: Haste, Rogero.

ALC, MOR: Oh we are lost!
(*Retire.*)
(*Rogero throws down the Urn and breaks it, when the Scene wholly disappears, changing to the Sea, which is seen thro' a vast subterraneous Cavern, where many Stones are chang'd into Men;*

ano in Uomini, trà quali è Astolfo, che abbraccia Oberto: Che formano il Coro.)

**CORO:** Doppo tanta amare pene,
Già proviam consorto all' alma;
Ogni mal si cangia in bene,
Ed al fin trionfa amor.
Fortunato è questo giorno,
Che ne reca bella calma,

among them is Astolfo, who embraces Oberto: They form the Chorus.)

**CHORUS:** After the bitter Torments past,
Our Souls find Peace and smiling Joys at last;
Now each Misfortune's chang'd to Bliss,

Dell' inganno e infidie a scorno
Gia festeggia il nostro cor.

*Fine dell' Opera.*

And all exult with Love and Happiness.
How blest this Day,
That brings such Ease;
And now forgetting what we bear,
Our Hearts know nought but present Peace.

*The End.*

# Serse (1738)

## MUSIC BY GEORGE FREDERICK HANDEL ■ LIBRETTO ADAPTED FROM NICCOLÒ MINATO

This three-act opera, set to a libretto partly adapted from Niccolò Minato, premiered at the Haymarket Theatre in London on April 15, 1738. Serse, King of Persia, falls in love with Romilda after hearing her sing. However, he is betrothed to Amastre. Romilda is in love with Arsamene, the king's brother, and thus rejects Serse's repeated proposals. The king wants her at any cost and decides to send Arsamene into exile. Amastre, who discovers this, sees death as her only way out (but she doesn't die). Atalanta, Romilda's sister, appears—she, too, is in love with Arsamene. Atalanta encourages Romilda's marriage to Serse so that she herself may marry Arsamene. She intercepts a letter to Romilda, sent from Arsamene through the servant Elviro, and convinces the king that the letter is meant for her. She then begs the king to arrange a wedding immediately. Serse uses the letter to convince Romilda that Arsamene has betrayed her. The plot is revealed, and Romilda and Arsamene vow their loyalty to each other. Serse is still determined to marry Romilda, who states that she will do so if he gets Ariodate's consent (Ariodate is her father). Serse indeed asks Ariodate but does so in such a fashion that Ariodate believes he is giving permission for Arsamene and Romilda to marry—this is the outcome. Serse, once he realizes his mistake, resigns himself to the situation and at last returns the love of Amastre, who has waited for him all this time. Atalanta has to find another lover to replace Arsamene.

Note: This libretto was taken from an original facsimile and has not been edited, in order to preserve historical context.

## ■ ATTO I

### SCENA I

*Belvedere accanto di un Giardino in mezzo di cui vi è un Platano.*

**Serse:** (*Sotto il Platano*). Frondi tenere e belle
Del mio Platano amato,
Per voi risplenda il Fato.
Tuoni, Lampi, e Procelle
Non vi oltraggino mai la cara pace,
Nè giunga a profanarvi Austro rapace.
Ombra mai su
Di Vegetabile,
Cara ed amabile,
Soave più.
(*Sta ammirando il Platano.*)

### SCENA II

*Arsamene, Elviro addormentato, e Romilda nel Belvedere.*

**ARS:** Siam giunti Elviro.
**EL:** Intendo.
**ARS:** Dove alberga.
**EL:** Seguite.
**ARS:** L' Idol mio.
**ELV:** Dite pure.
**ARS:** Oh se fortuna—
**ELV:** Sì così è—
(*in atto di partire.*)

## ■ ACT I

### SCENE I

*A summer house on one side of a garden, in the middle of which is a plane tree, and Xerxes under it.*

**XER:** May fate, ye tender and ye beauteous leaves,
Of my beloved plane to you prove kind;
May thy dear peace be undisturb'd by storms,
By thunder's rage, or by the light'nings blast;
Nor may'st thou be, by ruffl'ing winds, prophaned.
No, never vegetable made
A dearer and a lovelier shade;
And never from the sun's fierce heat,
Was more agreable retreat.
(*Stands and admires the tree.*)

### SCENE II

*Arsamenes, Elviro, who looks drowzy, and Romilda in the summer house.*

**ARS:** We are, Elviro, come.
**ELV:** Enough, I know.
**ARS:** Where's lodged.
**ELV:** Proceed.
**ARS:** The idol of my soul.
**ELV:** Forward.
**ARS:** Oh if fortune e'er—
**ELV:** Ay, that's true.
(*going.*)

---

**ARS:** Tu dove vai?
**ELV:** Men vado
Ad appoggiarmi, che di sonno io cado.
**ARS:** Vien quì pronto, ti dico
(*Si ode breve sinfonìa.*)
Sento un soave concento.

**ELV:** Andiam vicini.
**ARS:** Andiam.
**ELV:** Son di Romilda
Questi Villaggi?
**ARS:** Sì. Lasciami udire.
**ELV:** Così dalla Città poco discosti?
(*sieguela sinfonia.*)
**ARS:** Non parlar più.
**ELV:** Me n' anderò a dormire.

**ARS:** Non ti partir.
**ROM:** (*Nel Belvedere.*) O voi—
**ARS:** Questa è Romilda.
**ROM:** —O voi che penate.

**ELV:** Romilda è ver?
**ARS:** Sì, taci.
**ELV:** E chi favella?
**ROM:** O voi, che penate
Per cruda beltà,
Un Serse.

### SCENA III

*Serse e detti.*

---

**ARS:** Where dost thou go?
**ELV:** I go
To take a nap, for I'm half dead with sleep.
**ARS:** Quickly, I say, come hither strait to me;
Strains of sweet musick strike upon my ear.
(*a short symphony heard.*)

**ELV:** Let us draw near.
**ARS:** We'll go.
**ELV:** Romilda then
Owns all these villages.
**ARS:** Yes, let me hear.
**ELV:** So near the town!

**ARS:** Be hushed, and talk no more.
**ELV:** I'll go, and of my pillow ask advice.
(*Romilda in the summer house.*)
**ARS:** No, do not go—
**ROM:** O, ye.
**ARS:** This sure Romilda is.
**ROM:** Ye, who for cruel beauties sigh.
**ELV:** Romilda sure enough.
**ARS:** Peace then.
**ELV:** Who speaks?
**ROM:** The loving Xerxes.

### SCENE III

*To them Xerxes.*

**SER:** Quì si canta il mio Nome.

**ROM:** Un Serse mirate,
Che d' un ruvido tronco acceso sta;
E pur non corrisponde
Altro al suo amor, che 'l mormoriò
di fronde.

**SER:** Arsamene.

**ARS:** Mio Sire.

**SER:** Udiste?

**ARS:** Udii.

**SER:** Conoscete chi sia?

**ARS:** Io, no Signore.

**SER:** Io sì.

**ARS:** (Aimè che gelosià m' accora.)

**SER:** Che dite?

**ARS:** Ch' amerei sentirla ancora.

**ROS:** Va godendo vezzoso e bello
Quel ruscello la libertà.

**SER:** Quel canto a un bell' amor l'
anima sforza.
Per mia Dama la scelgo.

**ARS:** (Oh Dei che sento!)
Signor, ella è Romilda; è Principes-
sa:
Ma parmi non convenga—

**SER:** Eh mi diceste
Non conoscerla. Or come?

**ARS:** Sol la conosco al Nome.

**SER:** E al canto ancora.
Se Dama non convien, Sarà mia Spo-
sa.
L' approvate?

**ARS:** Signor a un Re non lice
Ergere al Trono chi non è Regina.

**SER:** Per Dama non convien, Sposa
non lice.
Nulla vi piace: è rigido il consiglio.
Mi sia compagna al Soglio.
Le direte che l'amo, io così voglio.

**ARS:** Io?

**SER:** Sì voi.

**ARS:** Non ò il modo di parlarle.

**SER:** Cercatelo.

**ARS:** Ma Sire e se non posso—

**SER:** Perchè?

**ARS:** Ma la modestia—e al fine.

**SER:** Intesi.
Io gliel dirò, che a parlar meglio ap-
presi.
Io le dirò che l' amo,

**XER:** My name, I hear is mentioned
in this song.

**ROM:** The loveing Xerxes see,
Who on a plane, has fix'd his eye
Enamour'd with a tree.
Yet no return to love it gives,
But the soft murmurs of its leaves.

**XER:** Arsamenes.

**ARS:** Sir.

**XER:** Did'st hear?

**ARS:** I did.

**XER:** And who is it, dost know?

**ARS:** I? no my lord.

**XER:** But well I know.

**ARS:** (How jealous do I grow!)

**XER:** Say'st thou?

**ARS:** That fain, this voice, I'd hear
again.

**ROM:** That wanton lovely rivulet
Its winding liberty enjoys.

**XER:** To love's soft passion, does
this voice impel
My glowing heart, the fair one there
shall reign.

**ARS:** (Ye gods, what's this I hear)
Romilda 'tis;
She is a princess, true, but then,
methinks
She does not suit.

**XER:** Thou said'st thou knew'st her
not,
Now how?

**ARS:** I know her by her name alone.

**XER:** Yes, also by her voice it does
not suit
She shou'd my fav'rite be. She shall
my spouse;
Do'st this approve?

**ARS:** It is not lawful, sir,
That you, a king, shou'd, to the
throne advance,
One who is not a sov'reign princess
born.

**XER:** That she my fav'rite be, it does
not suit;
And 'tis not lawful that my spouse
she be;
Thus nothing's to thy mind. Thy
counsel's harsh;
But she, however, shall adorn my
throne.
Tell her, I love her. Such is my command.

**ARS:** I!

**XER:** Yes, you.

**ARS:** The opportunity to do't?

**XER:** Seek it.

**ARS:** Suppose I cannot speak your
love?

**XER:** Why?

**ARS:** Bashfulness prevents—and,
when all's done—

**XER:** I understand thee well; I'll
count my love
Who have much better learn'd
t'explain my mind.

Nè mi sgomenterò
E perchè mia la bramo,
So quel che far dovrò.
(*Parte.*)

**ARS:** Tu le dirai che l' ami
Ma non ti ascolterà
Quella beltà che brami
Solo di me sarà.

## SCENA IV

*Romilda, Atalanta, Arsamene, ed
Elviro.*

**ROM:** Arsamene.

**ARS:** Romilda, oh Dei! pavento
Che 'l tuo più volte a me giurando
amore,
Tu non sparga d' oblio.

**ROM:** Perchè parli così.

**ARS:** Lo so ben io.
Il Re.

**ROM:** Chi? Serse!
E che da me richiede?

**ARS:** Tenterà la tue fede.

**ATA:** (Se può vincerle il cor, oh me
felice!)
Vien acceso ogni cor dal tuo bel
guardo.
(*a R.*)

**ROM:** Io non temo.

**ARS:** Io pavento.

**ATA:** (Ed io tutt' ardo.)
Dimmi Arsamene, e credi
Che la Germana mia tradir ti possa?

**ARS:** Crollan le Quercie annose a
una gran scossa.

**ROM:** Ma Romilda resiste.

**ATA:** (Ah fosse infida!)

**ROM:** Mia sarà l' alma mia da te dis-
ciolta.

**ARS:** Che diletto!

**ATA:** (Che doglia!) ascolta ascolta.
Sì sì ben sì sì
Io per te vivo sol,
Io per te moro.
Amo che mi ferì,
E pure al mio gran duol
Non ò ristoro.
Romilda notte e dì
Va esclamando così,
Io per te moro.

**ELV:** Presto, Signor, vien Serse.

**ARS:** Io quì mi celo.

## SCENE V

(*Serse, Romilda, Arsamene ed Elviro nascosi.*)

My love I'll to the fair one speak;
Nor will my heart the task decline;
I know what method I've to take,
As I do ardent wish her mine.
(*Exit.*)

**ARS:** To her thou'lt 'count thy
am'rous fire,
To which she will no ear incline;
That beauty, which thou dost de-
sire,
She is, and shall be, only mine.

## SCENE IV

*Romilda, Atalanta, Arsamenes
and Elviro.*

**ROM:** Arsamenes!

**ARS:** Romilda! O ye Gods!
That love, I fear, which oft thou'st
sworn to me;
Thou'lt in oblivion cast.

**ROM:** Why talk'st thou so?

**ARS:** Too well I know it. The king.

**ROM:** Who, Xerxes?
And what of me can Xerxes wish?

**ARS:** He'll tempt
Thy faith.

**ATA:** (He her heart may move,
bless'd am I!
There's not a heart but what thy
eyes enflame.
(*To Romilda.*)

**ROM:** I nothing fear.

**ARS:** I fear.

**ATA:** (I'm all on fire.).
Say, Arsamenes, canst thou e'er believe
My sister can thy love sincere deceive?

**ARS:** By vi'lent shocks the sturdy
oak's o'erthrown.

**ROM:** But Romilda not.

**ATA:** (Ah were't thou but false!)

**ROM:** My heart from thee shall never be estranged.

**ARS:** What flow of joy?

**ATA:** (What tide of grief!) but hear
My treasure, does Romilda cry,
Thou hast no cause to grieve;
It is for thee alone I live;
It is for thee alone I die.
Him, him I love, who gave my
wound,
And yet, to my too piercing grief,
No remedy can e'er be found,
To give my panting heart relief.
This night and day's Romilda's cry,
It is for thee, it is for thee I die.

**ELV:** Quick, quick, my lord, for
Xerxes comes.

**ARS:** I here will hide.

## SCENE V

SER: Come qui Principessa al Ciel sereno?
Forse agl' inviti d' Arsamene usciste?

ROM: Egli non mi chiamò.

SER: Parlovvi almeno.

ROM: Ma Sire—

SER: Basta, udite,
Romilda. Il Fato al Trono
Oggi vi scorge; amor v' ingemma il serto.

ROM: Non aspiro tant' alto. Io non ò merto.

SER: Ne so ben la cagione.
(escono Arsam. ed Elv.)
Arsamene m' offende, ma—

ARS: Io? Sire
Tolga il Ciel, che vi offenda.

ROM: Ei non sapea—

SER: Tacete. E voi veloce
Lunge da questa Corte, qual Torrente
Volgere il piede.

ARS: Andrò benchè innocente.

SER: Pure se promettete
Lasciar Romilda—

ELV: Eh dite, io lo farò.
(ad A.)

SER: Posso usarvi pietate.

ARS: Oh questo no.
Meglio in voi col mio partire
Gelosìa si estinguerà.
Io men vado al mio morire
Voi restate in libertà.
(Parte con Elv.)

## SCENA VI

Serse e Romilda immobile e pensofa.

SER: Bellissima Romilda, eh non celate
L' adorato sembiante.
Uditemi Romilda, io sono amante.
E pur tacete ancora?
Dite un sì, dite un no, dite ch' io mora.
Di tacere e di schernirmi
Ah crudel, chi t' insegnò?
O lasciate d' esser belle
Care luci amate stelle,
O ceslate di ferirmi
Che mai più vi seguirò.
(Parte.)

ROM: Aspide sono a detti tuoi d' amore,
Nè vuò macchiar d' insedeltà il mio cuore,
Nè men coll' ombre d' infedeltà

XER: How, princess? here, expos'd
to th' evening damps?
At Arsamenes' invitation 'tis,
Perhaps, you ventured forth?

ROM: He asked me not.

XER: He spoke to you, at least.

ROM: But, sir.

XER: No more.
But listen thou, Romilda. Fate does guide,
Thee to the throne, where love the diadem
Does, by enriching, still more brilliant make.

ROM: So high aspire I not; nor merit have.

XER: I know full well the cause. I suffer thus
(Ar. and Elv. appear.)
By Arsamenes; but howe'er.

ARS: By me—
Heav'n forbid I shou'd offend thee e'er.

ROM: He knew not—

XER: No more.
And thou, swift as a torrent's rapid course,
Hence; far, far distant from this court withdraw.

ARS: I'll go, tho' innocent.

XER: But yet, if thou,
Romilda, promisest to quit—

ELV: Ah! say
You'll turn her off.

XER: I may compassion show.

ARS: Ah no; with this I never can comply.
My going hence may prove, to you,
Th' extinction of your jealousy;
I now to death depart, adieu;
Remain thou here in liberty.
(Exit.)

## SCENE VI

Xerxes and Romilda, pensive and motionless.

XER: Romilda, lovely fair, ah do not hide
Thy charms adored; in me, Romilda, hear
Thy ardent lover. Art thou silent yet?
Say yes, say no; or say, that I must die.
Who taught thee, cruel, thus to be
Scornful and silent still with me?
Ah do thou cease to be so fair;
Let those dear piercing eyes forbear,
And wound my tortured breast no more;
I'll then my present suit give o'er.
(Exit.)

ROM: To all professions of thy love, I'm deaf,
And never will, with falsehood, stain my heart.
My heart I never will betray,

Voglio tradire l' anima mia.
E se il mio bene suo mai si sa
Incolpi amore, non gelosìa.
(Parte.)

## SCENA VII

Cortile.

Amastre in abito da Uoma seguita da uno Scudiere.

Se cangio Spoglia,
Non cangio core,
Ma nell' amore
Son pur l' istessa.
(Si ritira in disparte.)

## SCENA VIII

Ariodate seguito da Soldati con Prigionieri ed insegne prese a Nemici, ed Amastre.

ARIO: Pugnammo Amici, e stette
Per noi bella Vittoria.

AMA: Dunqu' è vinto il Re Moro?
Oh noi felici!

ARIO: Ed accresce di Serse ognor la Gloria.

CORO DI SOLDAT: Già la tromba,
Che chiamò le schiere all' armi,
Or si scioglie in dolci carmi,
E vittorte a noi rimbomba.

## SCENA IX

Serse, Ariodate, ed Amastre in disparte.

AMA: (Ecco Serse: Oh che volto!
Oh che splendore!)

SER: Ariodate, vi abbraccio. Il vostro ferro
Sempre porta vittoria.

ARIO: Del vostro Nome sol questa è la Gloria.

SER: In premio de' Disagj, ch' ora diamo
Alla vostra Città, che di nostr' armi
Fatta è Piazza, a sostener l' Impresa
Dì Atene; or vi prometto,
Romilda vostra Figlia
Avrà Sposo Reale
Della Stirpe di Serse a Serse eguale.

ARIO: Così arditi Fantasmi
Nel pensier non ammetto.

SER: Ite, così prometto.

Nor e'en to falsehood's shade give way:
If he who is belov'd by me,
Of his own harm the author be,
Let him blame love, not jealousy.
(Exit.)

## SCENE VII

A court yard.

Amastre, in a man's habit, followed by a page.

Altho' my sex my dress belies,
My heart will never wear disguise;
That still the same shall ever prove,
And never will be false to love.
(Withdraws to one side.)

## SCENE VIII

Ariodates, followed by soldiers, with prisoners, and colours, taken from the enemy. Amastre apart.

ARI: We've fought, my friends, and glorious vict'ry gained.

AM: (Is then the moor o'ercome? O happy we!)

ARI: And Xerxes daily does fresh laurels reap.

CHORUS OF SOLDIERS: The trumpet which, to arms did sound,
Shall sweetly breath to flowing verse;
Which shall our victories rehearse,
And the soft note, the shriller blast shall drown.

## SCENE XI

Xerxes, Ariodates, and Amastre, apart.

AMA: See, Xerxes comes; how glorious is his mien?
And with what splendor does the king appear!

XER: O, Ariodates, welcome to these arms,
Conquest does still attend upon thy sword.

ARI: The glory to your name alone is due.

XER: To recompence the trouble, we now give
To this your town, which, of th' Athenian war,
The place of arms, and grand support has been.
Romilda shall a royal spouse embrace,
Equal to Xerxes, and of Xerxes' line.
To this I do engage our royal word.

ARI: Thoughts so aspiring, can I ne'er admit.

XER: Keep on your march; our promise is engaged.

ARIO: Soggetti al mio volere
Gli Astri non chieggio no.
Ma quel che fan le sfere
Sempre lodar saprò
(*Parte col medesimo seguito. Replica Coro—Già la trombai*)

ARI: I do not ask, I can't expect,
The stars shou'd do as I direct;
Tho' to whatever they think fit,
I do, with thankfulness submit.
(*He goes off with his followers, the chorus repeating. The trumpet, &c.*)

## SCENA X

*Serse ed Amastre col suo Scudiere in disparte.*)

SER: Queste Vittorie io credo,
Predicono trionfi anco al mio amore.

AMA: (Parla di me: ai vento sì mio core.)

SER: Impaziente io vivo,
Di abbracciar quell' amato mio tesoro.

AMA: (E di gioja non moro?)

SER: Ma pur, che dirà Amastre,
E l' offeso suo Padre
Del mio Imeneo, del mio novello amore?

AMA: (E così mi Schernisce il traditore?)

SER: Benchè di Regio sangue
Non sia l' Idolo mio,
Una Vassalla illustrar poss' io
Colle mie nozze. Al fin; crede decenti
I voler d' un gran Rege il Mondo.

AMA: Menti.

SER: Chi parla olà? Chi siete?

AMA: Forastieri Signor.

SER: Ma a chi mentita
Tu desti?

AMA: Al mio compagno,
Che volea sostener, che il vasto Eufrate—
E che 'l Ponte che fate—
Sarebbe esposto ai venti;
Io per discorso allor, dissi tu menti.

SER: Sciocchi mi rassembrate. Ite lontani.
(*Am. Parte*)
Non dee render ragione il mio decoro.
Sempre mi torna in mente il ben che adoro.
Più che penso alla fiamma del Core
Più l' ardore crescendo sen va.
E 'l mio petto è ricetto ben poco
Di quel foco che pena mi dà.
(*Parte.*)

## SCENE X

*Xerxes and Amastre, with her page, apart.*

XER: These victories, I hope, fore-runners are
Of my triumphing, also, in my love.

AMA: (Of me he speaks. My heart the conquest's thine.)

XER: How slowly do the lazy moments creep,
Which lead me to embrace my life's sole joy?

AMA: (Beneath this tide of pleasure, live I still!)

XER: What will Amastre; what her father say;
With this new passion, these new nuptials wrong'd?

AMA: (And dost thou, traitor, scorn Amastre thus?)

XER: Altho' the fair, who triumphs in my heart,
Draws not her birth from a long race of kings;
Yet, o'er my vassal, will my nuptials spread
The rays of dazzling royalty. But more,
Whate'er great monarchs do, the world approves.

AMA: Thou ly'st.

XER: How now! who's that who speaks? who art?

AMA: A stranger.

XER: But to whom the lie did'st give?

AMA: To my companion, who wou'd needs maintain,
That great Euphrates—That the bridge thou build'st,
Wou'd be expos'd to winds. To this discourse
I then return'd the lie.

XER: Thou seem'st of judgment little found. Be gone.
(*Exit. Amastre.*)
It don't become our state, to reasons give.
The beauty which I love, will still return,
And take up all my thoughts.
More on the flame I turn my mind,
Which does my heart devour;
It gathers greater strength, I find,
Increasing ev'ry hour,
Receptacle' too small's my breast,
For th' fire which robs me of my rest.
(*Exit.*)

## SCENA XI

*Arsamene ed Elviro.*

ARS: Eccoti il foglio Elviro
A Romilda lo porta.

ELV: Siete pur risoluto?

ARS: Sì, vanne.

ELV: Io vi saluto.
Che parlar le volete,
Altro non le scrivete?

ARS: No.

ELV: Ma son, voi sapete,
Con voi bandito: e se son conosciuto?
Siete pur risoluto?

ARS: Vanne, non tardar più.

ELV: Come glie l' ò da dar?

ARS: Pensaci tu.

ELV: Che stravagante Scena!
(*pensa un poco, e poi risoluto dice.*)
Signore, Signore lasciate sare a me;
Io l' ò pensata bene,
Corro, volo, parto, vo.
E più presto tornerò
Che se avessi l' ale al piè.
(*Parte.*)

ARS: Non so se sia la speme
Che mi sostenga in vita,
O l' aspro mio dolor.
Sio che quest' Alma geme,
Da che mi su rapita
La gioja del mio cor.
(*Parte.*)

## SCENA XII

AMASTRE: Tradir di regia Sposa
La fe promessa? e chiamerallo il mondo
Un decente Voler? No che dei Regi
Son giustizia e Clemenza i più gran pregj.
Saprà delle mie offese
Ben vendicarsi il cor.
Colui, che l' ira accese
Proverà il mio furor.

## SCENA XIII

*Atalanta, e Romilda.*

ATA: Al fin Sarete Sposa al vostro Serse.

## SCENE XI

ARS: Do thou this letter to Romilda give.

ELV: Is't possible? Art sure thou art resolved?

ARS: I am; be gone.

ELV: Well! Gods be with ye, then.
You nothing else have scarwl'd but that you wish
With tittle tattle to disturb her brain?

ARS: That I wou'd speak with her, is all I wrote.

ELV: But I, you know, thanks to your caterwawling,
As well as you, am on the common turn'd.
And are you still as obstinate?

ARS: I am.
No longer loiter.

ELV: Good, But how, I pray,
Must I this billet to her hands convey?

ARS: Look you to that.

ELV: 'Tis whimsical enough.
(*He thinks awhile, and then, as having fallen on an expedient, he says,*)
My lord,, my lord, let me alone,
Already thought expedient brings;
I run, I fly, I go, am gone,
As if my heels were arm'd with wings.
(*Exit.*)

ARS: Whether 'tis cruel grief, or hope,
Which gives to life a greater scope,
Is what I cannot say.
But this poor heart does nought but sigh,
Since that its only darling joy,
Is from it forc'd away.
(*Exit.*)

## SCENE XII

AMASTRE: The faith that's to a royal princess giv'n,
Shall then be broke, and this the world approve?
Can royalty so mean an action grace?
No; for those kings with greatest lustre shine,
Whom clemency and justice make divine.
My heart will find, for injured love,
Means of revenge a thousand ways;
And he the effects of rage shall prove,
Who did my strong resentment raise.

## SCENE XIII

*Atalanta and Romilda.*

ATA: At length thou wilt thy Xerxes' consort be.

ROM: Che? mio, Serse non è.

ATA: Meno Arsamene.

ROM: Egli sì, perchè l'amo.

ATA: Egli no, perchè parte esule errante.
Perdete un Re per un perduto amante.

ROM: Perduto amante? e come?

ATA: A il core acceso
D'altre fiamme.

ROM: Di chi?

ATA: Ben lo saprete.

ROM: Dunque odiarò Arsamene; e al Re gli affetti
Tutti darò: che dite?

ATA: Allor prudente
Certo vi chiamerò; ed Arsamene
In Sposo io chiederò

ROM: E che dunque l'amate?

ATA: No, ma poi l'amerò.

ROM: E sì tosto potrete
Render di amore i vostri voti accesi?

ARS: Mi sforzerò.

ROM: Ah che pur troppo intesi.
Se l'Idol mio
Rapir mi vuoi,
Cangia desio, ch'è vanita.
Quei dolci lacci
Snodar non puoi,
Che mi legaro la libertà.
(*Parte.*)

## SCENA XIV

ATALANTA: Per rapir quel tesoro,
Che te colma di gioja, e me d'affanni
Se amor non basta, adoprerò gl'inganni.
Un cenno leggiadretto,
Un riso vezzosetto,
Un moto di pupille
Può fare innamorar.
Lusinghe pianti e frodi
Son' anco certi modi,
Che destano faville
E tutti io li so far.

*Fine dell'Atto Primo.*

# ◼ ATTO II

## SCENA I

*Piazza della Città.*

---

ROM: How? Mine he is not.

ATA: Arsamenes less.

ROM: Yes, he is mine, for my whole heart is his.

ATA: He? no, he is a wand'ring exile gone.
You'll lose a monarch, for a lover lost.

ROM: A lover lost? and how?

ATA: His heart avows
Another flame.

ROM: For whom?

ATA: That wilt thou know.

ROM: Then Arsamenes will I truly hate,
And, to the king, my whole affection turn.
What say'st to this resolve?—

ATA: Then truly prudent shall I say thou art,
And I, for spouse, will Arsamenes ask.

ROM: Thou lov'st him then?

ATA: No; but hereafter may.

ROM: And canst thou, then, so readily enflame
With love thy wish?

ATA: I some constraint may use.

ROM: Ah now I understand thee but too well.
If of my treasure thou'dst bereave me,
Let not those idle thoughts deceive thee;
Change thy desires, for they are vain;
Do thou thy purposes forsake;
Not all thy arts, those bands shall break,
Which do my liberty enchain.
(*Exit.*)

## SCENE XIV

ATALANTA: That I may on that treasure seize, the which
Fills thee with joy, and me with grief o'erwhelms.
If love does not suffice, I'll fraud employ.
A graceful and consenting nod,
Allureing smiles, and rowling eyes,
Assisted by the wanton god,
May, with soft love, his heart surprize.
So tears deceit, and flatt'ring praise;
Are also known, as methods sure,
Within the breast a flame to raise,
And I, all these will put in ure.

*End of the First Act.*

# ◼ ACT II

## SCENE I

*A square of the city.*

---

*Amastre, e poi Elviro (che vende fiori, e parla la lingua franca.)*

AMA: Speranze mie fermate,
Non mi lasciate ancor.

ELV: (Ah chi voler fiora di bella Giardina
Giancinta Indiana, Tulipana Gelsomina.)
E chi direbbe mai ch'io sono Elviro?
Ma se del foglio poi sapesse il Re?

AMA: (Che parla egli del Re?)

ELV: Credo, Arsamene,
Pianti e sospiri al vento spargerà:
E che per moglie, al fine il Re l'avrà.

AMA: (Il Re? per moglie? chi? Cieli che sento!)

ELV: Serse però dovrebbe aver per Sposa
Dama di regio sangue, e non Vassalla:
Questa non gli sa onore.

AMA: (Dunque io sono schernita. Ah traditore!)
Amico.

ELV: Ah ci sui colto.
(*vuol fuggir.*)

AMA: Ferma, olà, dico a te: perchè scappar?

ELV: Da mia che cercar?
(Voler fiora comprar? ma—)

AMA: (No.) Si dice,
Che Serse farà Sposo in questo di:
Vorrei saper di chi?

ELV: Ma dire, tu chi star?
E perchè dimandar?

AMA: Viaggiante curioso, e chi ama il Re.

ELV: Poichè tì star bon Uom, mi dir a te;
Ma teser, non parlar.

AMA: Dì pur, non dubitar.

ELV: Ariodate, de Chista.
Città Signor, che stare al Re Vassallo,
Aver figlia Romilda; e Re voler
Chista sposar: ma chista sempre dir,
Se mi sposar, morir.

AMA: Ma Romilda ama i Re?

ELV: No: ma fratello
Ch'aver nome Arsamene.

AMA: E questo, forse
I dolor suoi le Scrive?

---

*Amastre, and after her Elviro, (who carries flowers, and speaks in a broken dialect.)*

AMA: Ah! stay your course, ye fleeting hopes,
And do not leave me yet.

ELV: (Who vant de vine vlower dat in garden be seen,
Te jacint, te tulip, te sweet jessamine.)
Who, now, wou'd say, that I Elviro am?
But should the king of this same billet know.

AMA: (What says he of the king?)

ELV: I greatly doubt,
Altho' my master burst his belt with sighs,
Xerxes will gain the prize; she'll be his wife.

AMA: (The king? a wife? who? heav'ns! what is't I hear?)

ELV: Yet, for a consort, Xerxes ought to chose
A dame of royal blood; a vassal's wrong.

AMA: (Am I, traitor, then despis'd!) friend, a word.

ELV: Ah! I am catched.
(*Getting off.*)

AMA: Stop, holoa; to thee I speak—why woud'st fly?

ELV: Vat vid me you vant? (you flower buy? but—)

AMA: (No flow'rs I want;) I've by rumour heard,
That Xerxes on this day take a wife,
And I wou'd know who is the happy fair.

ELV: Say vat you be, and vy, for vat you you ask?

AMA: A curious traveller, who love the king.

ELV: Since you be one good man, me tell to you;
But hold your tongue; you no be for to speak.

AMA: You may proceed; you nothing need to doubt.

ELV: Ariodates, who be dis town lord?
Be too one vassal to te king. 'Tis lord
One dautre ave, dat be Romilda name.
Dis she te king vou'd make one vife; but her
Say, marry me, me soon be sure will die.

AMA: But this Romilda; does she love the king?

ELV: No; but te king browder, Arsamenes.

AMA: And he, perhaps, now writes her all his grief.

ELV: Aimè! tì star devina.
(Chi voler fiora di bella Giardina.)

AMA: Dimmi.

ELV: Nu saper altro.
(Tulipana Gelsomina.)

AMA: Perchè m' uccida il duolo
Mancava solo esser tradita ancora.

ELV: Chi voler fiora? chi voler fiora?

AMA: Or che siete speranze tradite,
Sì fuggite, fuggite da me.
E in quest' anima oppressa dal duolo
Resti solo la bella mio fe.
(*Parte.*)

## SCENA II

*Elviro, poi Atalanta.*

ELV: Quel curioso è partito: oh! che indiscreto!
Matto non son per dirgli il mio segreto.
La Signora Atalanta a me sen viene.
Oh! bene: bene: bene!

ATA: A piangere ognora
Amor mi distina.

ELV: Ah! Chi vuol Fiora-di bella Giardina?
Voler Giancinta? voler Gelsominà?

AMA: Oà! vien quà. (Degli aspri miei dolori
Le acute spine adornerò co' Fiori.)

ELV: Ma mi chi star?

ATA: Non so.

ELV: Mi ben guardar.

ATA: Tu quivi? o sventurato! guarda bene-
Che porti?

ELV: Porto un foglio di Arsamene
All' amata Romilda.

ATA: A me lo porgi.

ELV: Glielo darete poi?

ATA: Sì.

ELV: Ma dov' è?

ATA: Sta nelle stanze sue scrivendo al Re.

ELV: Al Re? ma che gli scrive?

ATA: Che in lui spera, in lui vive.

ELV: E di Arsamene?

ATA: Punto non si sovvienne.

ELV: Ah tigre infedele!
Cerasta crudele!

ATA: Parti, il Re si avvicina.

ELV: Ah, to be sure, you one great conj'rer be.
(Who buy te vine vlower dat ever be seen.)

AMA: But tell me—

ELV: Me no more know.
(Te tulip ant te vine jasmine.)

AMA: Grief only wanted this assisting stroke
Of infidelity to end my life.

ELV: Who vant te vine vlower, te vine vlower vant.)

AMA: My hopes betray'd, fly, hence depart,
And quit this over-burthen'd heart:
In this, in which strong grief bears sway,
Let faith, untainted, only stay.
(*Exit.*)

## SCENE II

*At the distance Atalanta and Elviro.*

ELV: Th' impertinent is gone. O silly toad!
But I'm no fool, to blurt my secrets out.
This way the lady Atalanta comes.
Well, well.

ATA: Love to incessant tears
Has destined me.

ELV: Who vant de vine vlower dat ever be seen.
Who vant hyacint, who vant te jasmine?

ATA: Here, this way turn. (The pungent thorns of grief,
With gaudy, and with fragrant flow'rs, I'll deck.)

ELV: But vat me be?

ATA: I know not.

ELV: look me vell.

ATA: Thou here? o wretch unfortunate! take care—
What hast thou there?

ELV: From Arsamenes 'tis,
A note, which I must to Romilda give.

ATA: Give it to me.

ELV: Will you then give it her?

ATA: Yes.

ELV: Where is she tho'?

ATA: In her chamber, where She's writing to the king.

ELV: To th' king! pray what?

ATA: That all her hopes, nay, life, depend on him.

ELV: Of Arsamenes then?

ATA: She has no thought.

ELV: A! faithless tygress!
A! the viperous spawn!

ATA: Be gone; the king draws near: away.

ELV: Ah! chi vuol fiori di bella Giardina?
(*Elv. Parte in fretta.*)

## SCENA III

*Serse, ed Atalanta, che legge il foglio d' Arsamene.*

ATA: (Con questo foglio mi sarò contenta.)

SER: E tormento troppo fiero
L' adorar cruda beltà.
Di quel foglio, Atalanta
(*ad Atal. che legge.*)
Lice saper gli Arcani?
Saran forse amorosi?

ATA: E' ver, ma strani.

SER: Son più curioso.

ATA: Ma.

SER: Ma che?

ATA: Io temo—
Mi perdonate?

SER: Sì.

ATA: Dunque leggete.
(Deh seconda l' inganno o ignudo Arciero.)
(*Serse prende la lettera, e guarda la firma.*)

SER: Scrive Arsamene.

ATA: E' vero.

SER: (*legge.*) "Allorchè nell Ibero ascoso è il sole
Verrò notturno, ove talor mi suole
Il raggio balenar di vostre stelle.
Ivi a dispetto di maligna, sorte,
O sarò vostro o pur sarò di morte."
A chi serive Arsamene?

ATA: A me.

SER: A voi?

ATA: Vi sdegnate?

SER: Stupisco. Ma s' egli ama Romilda?—

ATA: No Signor: ella ben l' ama,
Ma lui finge d' amarla, affinchè quieta
Non sturbi il nostro amore.

SER: Strana Avventura! Godi sì mio core!

ATA: Dunque vi prego o Re, se l' approvate,
Che pubblico Imeneo lo faccia mio.

SER: Bella, farò che sia,
O vostro Sposo o preda all' ira mia.

ATA: Dià che amor per me
Piagato il cor non gli à.
Ma non gli date se
Ch' egli fingendo va.

ELV: Ah who vant te vlower, ov te vine garden.
(*Exit hastily.*)

## SCENE III

*Xerxes and Atalanta, who reads Arsamenes' letter.*

ATA: My heart will from this letter find some ease.

XER: The torment is too great to bear,
When we adore a cruel fair.
Say, Atalanta, is't allow'd to know
The secrets which that letter does contain?
Perhaps of love they treat?

ATA: 'Tis true, but strange.

XER: It makes me still more curious.

ATA: But—

XER: But what?

ATA: I apprehend—Do you my pardon seal?

XER: I do.

ATA: Then read (o love, aid thou this fraud)

XER: This Arsamenes writes.

ATA: It is from him.

XER: (*reads.*) "When in the streams of ebro Phoebus hides,
I'll visit, in the night, the place where oft
Thy brilliant eyes have blessed my aching sight.
Then, spight of adverse fate, I will be thine,
Or my warm blood, my destiny shall sign."
To whom writes Arsamenes this?

ATA: To me. Does it displease thee?

XER: I am quite amazed.
But 'tis Romilda's object of his love?

ATA: Far diff'rent is it. She loves him 'tis true:
But he a passion only feigns for her,
That, thus amus'd, she mayn't our love impede.

XER: A strange adventure! thou my heart exult!

ATA: If I your approbation meet, I pray
That publick nuptials may secure him mine.

XER: Fair one, I will that he thy spouse shall be,
Or of my anger feel severe effects.

ATA: That love, for me, ne'er touch'd his heart
He'll say; don't thou believe;
For this is but concerted art,
On purpose to deceive.

SER: Voi quel foglio lasciate a me per prova.

ATA: (Bella frode, se giova.)

SER: Itene pur.

ATA: Ma vi ricordo.

SER: E che?

ATA: Dirà che non mi amò
Che mai per me languì,
Ma non credete nò
Che fingerà così.
(*Parte.*)

## SCENA IV

*Serse e Romilda.*

SER: Ingannata Romilda! ecco leggete.
Dite poi se Arsamene amar dovete.

ROM: Leggo.

SER: Nè vi sdegnate?

ROM: A chi Scrive?

SER: Alla sua cara Atalanta.
Sapete già, s' io mento.

ROM: (Non mi uccider tormento!)

SER: Che farete?

ROM: Piangendo ognor vivrò.

SER: L' amarete?

ROM: L' amerò.

SER: E pur sempre vi tradì.

ROM: L' empia forte vuol così.

SER: Se ben fiero v' ingannò
L' amarete?

ROM: L' amerò.

SER: Se bramate d' amar chi vi sdegna,
Vuò sdegnarvi, ma come non so.
La vostr' ira crudel me l' insegna;
Tento farlo e quest' alma non può.
(*Parte.*)

## SCENA V

ROM: (*sola.*) L' amerò? non sia vero.
Amante traditor! sorella infida!
Godete di mie pene.
Barbara, menzognero!
L' amerò? non sia vero.
Ma voi, che delirate, mi ascoltate,
Forse saper bramate
La mia furia crudel ora chi sia?
E' gelosia,
Quella tiranna
Che tanto affanna
L' anima mia.
Del suo veleno
Mi aspersa il seno,
E mi condanna
A pena rìa.
(*Parte.*)

---

XER: Leave me that letter for my stronger proof.

ATA: Ingenious is the fraud, if it avails.

XER: Thou may'st withdraw.

ATA: But call to mind—

XER: And what?

ATA: He'll say, that me he never lov'd,
Nor for me languish'd e'er:
Let not thy faith, by this, be mov'd;
In this he's not sincere.

## SCENE IV

*Xerxes and Romilda.*

XER: Deceiv'd Romilda! read thou this, and then
Speak Arsamenes worthy of thy love.

ROM: I've read.

XER: And anger does not dye thy cheek?

ROM: He writes, to whom?

XER: To Atalanta's this.
Thou know'st if I speak truth.

ROM: (Kill me not, grief!)

XER: What wilt thou do?

ROM: I'll waste my life in tears.

XER: And wilt thou love him yet?

ROM: My love I can't forget.

XER: Yet you're betray'd, you know.

ROM: 'Tis fate will have it so.

XER: Altho' deceiv'd, thou'lt love him still.

ROM: I'll love him, tho' he use me ill.

XER: If thou with love do'st meet disdain,
I'd slight thee too, but know not how.
Your anger teaches me in vain;
My heart can't e'n the thought allow.

## SCENE V

ROMILDA: (*solo.*) Shall I then love him? let it not be said,
Deceitful lover! treach'rous sister! who
Now basely triumph in my misery.
Sister inhumane, and with fraud replete!
And shall I love him? be it never said.
But you, perhaps, who do my raving hear,
May ask what fury on my breast has seiz'd?
'Tis jealousy, that tyrant foul,
Which gives this torture to my soul,
Which sheds her venom in my breast,
And dooms me stranger to all rest.

---

## SCENA VI

*Amastre in atto di uccidersi, ed Elviro.*

AMA: Giacchè il duol non m' uccide,
M' uccida questo ferro.

ELV: Oibò, che fate?
Pensate: e poi se mi volete credere
Vivete sol per ben mangiare e bevere.

AMA: Via su, pria di morire
A quell' alma crudel corriamo a dire.
Anima infida
Tradita io sono.
Vien, tu m' uccida
Io ti perdoho.
(*Parte.*)

## SCENA VII

*Elviro, poi Arsamene.*

ELV: E pazzo affè.

ARS: Elviro—

ELV: Voi quì Signor? fuggiamo.

ARS: Che ti disse Romilda?

ELV: Ad Atalanta
Diedi il foglio, e mi disse,
Che la vostra Romilda amava il Re:
Che stava a lui serivendo.

ARS: Di nera infedeltade o mostro orrendo!
Ma, non bene intendesti? parla a me.

ELV: V' ò detto già, ch' ama e che scrive al Re.
Che volete di più?

ARS: Forse scherzò.

ELV: Oibò oibò; parlò troppo da vero.

ARS: O di Tigre crudel core più fiero!
Quella che tutta se
Per me languia d' amore,
No che più mia non è,
Perduto ò il core.
Che pensa il Ciel? che fa?
Non sa col suo rigore
Punir chi reo fen va
Di tanto errore.
(*Partono.*)

---

## SCENE VI

*Amastre going to kill herself. Elviro.*

AMA: Since grief don't end my days, this trusty sword—

ELV: Hold. What art about? think well, and then,
If my advice thou'lt take—live—were it but
For th' bottle, and a little jaw work sake.

AMA: But hold. Let us th' inhuman lover find,
And, e'er we die, in dying accents say,
Faithless man, by thee betrayed,
Life is now a burthen made;
'Tis death alone, that can relieve me;
Take thou my life, and I forgive thee.
(*Exit.*)

## SCENE VII

*Elviro, and to him Arsamenes.*

ELV: By the lord Harry, the poor creature's mad.

ARS: Elviro.

ELV: You here? Let us quick brush off.

ARS: What said Romilda to thee?

ELV: I, my lord,
To Atalanta did the letter give,
Who told me, your Romilda lov'd the king,
And even then, to him a billet-doux,
Well as she cou'd spell, was, sir, in-diteing.

ARS: Monster most black of infidelity!
Did'st understand her well? answer me strait.

ELV: I've once already told you, that she loves
The king, and to the king love-letters writes.
And what a plague can you require more?

ARS: Perhaps this Atalanta jesting spoke.

ELV: O laud, in jest! no, no, she spoke plain truth.

ARS: O heart more cruel than the tyger fierce!
The fair, who was all faith before,
And loving me did languish;
Is mine, alass! is mine no more.
My heart is lost in anguish.
What think the Gods? what is't they do?
Will they such crimes forbear?
Will they not perjury pursue,
With punishment severe?
(*Exeunt.*)

## SCENA VIII

*Ponte costrutto sopra il Mare, che si unisce a due rive.*
*Serse, Ariodate, e Coro di Marinari.*

**CORO:** La Virtute sol potea
Giunger l' Asia all' altra riva.
Viva Serse, viva viva.

**SER:** Ariodate.

**ARIO:** Signor.

**SER:** Del Mare ad onta
E fin del vento infido
Seppi giunger ancor Sesto ad Abido.
Tu vanne pronto ad ordinar le Schiere.

**ARIO:** Ubbidirò.

**SER:** Pria della terza Aurora
Di passar in Europa è il mio volere,

**ARIO:** Per essempio dei Regi
I tuoi gloriosi preggi
Con caratteri d' or la fama scriva;
(*Parte.*)

**CORO:** La Virtute sol potea, &c.

## SCENA IX

*Arsamene, e Serfe.*

**ARS:** Per dar fine alla mia pena
Chi mi svena per pietà?

**SER:** Arsamene, ove andate?

**ARS:** A ber l' onda di Lete,
Sol per scordarmi che fratel mì siete.

**SER:** Cessi lo sdegno.

**ARS:** E in voi la tirannia.

**SER:** Voglio sposarvi al bel, che v' innamora.

**ARS:** E mi schernite ancora?

**SER:** So di qual fiamma ardete.
Lessi le vostre note, invan tacete.
(lio!)

**ARS:** (Ah che Romilda, Oh Dei!
mostrò il mio fog.)
Ed or che lo confesso,
E che già lo sapete?

**SER:** Per Consorte l' avrete.

**ARS:** Ora lasciate
Ch' io vi baci la man.

**SER:** Tanto l' amate?

**ARS:** Più che l' Anima mia.

---

## SCENE VIII

*A bridge built over the sea, uniting the two shores.*
*Xerxes, Ariodates, and a chorus of mariners.*

**CHORUS:** Virtue alone, nought else beside,
Cou'd Asia join to Europe's side;
Live, Xerxes, live, great nature's pride.

**XER:** Ariodates.

**ARI:** Sir.

**XER:** In spight thou seest
Of mountain seas, and of the faithless wind,
I Sestos, thus, and Abydos have joined.
Go quickly, thou, the warlike squadrons range.

**ARI:** I shall obey.

**XER:** Before the third day's dawn,
I am resolv'd to pass to Europe's side.

**ARI:** Fame will, in golden characters, record
Thy glorious deeds, that monarchs, yet to come,
From them may bright examples take.
(*Exit.*)

**CHOR:** Virtue alone, &c.

## SCENE IX

*Arsamenes and Xerxes.*

**ARS:** Who is there will compassion shew,
And give me death to end my woe.

**XER:** Say, whether, Arsamenes, dost thou go.

**ARS:** From Lethe's muddy streams to take a draught,
That thou'rt my brother, I must thus forget.

**XER:** No longer am I wroth.

**ARS:** Thou tyranniz'st.

**XER:** I'll wed thee to the fair whom thou ador'st.

**ARS:** And do'st thou even make me too thy jest.

**XER:** I know the flame which preys upon they heart,
Thy note I've read, thy silence is in vain.

**ART:** (Romilda has, o gods! my letter shewn!)
And now that I my am'rous flame avow?
Now that thou know'st the whole, what does't avail?

**XER:** She shall thy consort be.

**ARS:** Ah now permit,
That I thy royal hand, may grateful kiss.

**XER:** So greatly do'st thou love her?

**ARS:** More than life.

---

**SER:** Che nol diceste pria?
Lieti saremo in un istesso dì.
Io Sposo di Romilda.

**ARS:** Ed io di chi?

**SER:** Di Atalanta.

**ARS:** E così voi m' ingannate?

**SER:** So, che Atalanta amate.

**ARS:** Amo Romilda.

**SER:** Eh non fingete più.

**ARS:** Dunque Romilda a me non concedete?

**SER:** Lo so, non la volete.

**ARS:** Sì la voglio, e la otterrò
E se il Ciel per me non Splende,
Gli empj Mostri, e l' ombre orrende
Di Cocito invocherò.
(*Parte.*)

## SCENA X

*Atalanta, e Serse.*

**ATA:** V' inchino eccelso Re.

**SER:** Negò Arsamene
D' essere vostro amante,
E per Romilda sol egli è costante.
Dunque da ver non v' ama; e voi lasciate
Di fuggir tante pene, e non lo amate.

**ATA:** Voi mi dite che non l' ami
Ma non dite, se potrò.
Troppo belle
Son le stelle
Che al suo volto il Ciel donò.
Troppo stretti quei legami
Onde amor m' incateno.
(*Parte.*)

**SER:** Saria lieve ogni doglia,
Se potesse un amante
Amar e disamar sempre a sua voglia.
Il core spera e teme,
Penando ognor così,
Se goderà in amore
Sapere ancor non può.
Lo chieggio alla mia speme
Ella mi dice, sì.
Ma poi freddo timore
Sento che dice no.
(*Parte.*)

## SCENA XI

**ELVIRO:** (*solo.*) Me infelice! ò smarrito il mio Padrone!
Ma mi confesso reo; son pazzo affè.
Egli à smarrito me.
Forse per questo Ponte ei sen andò

---

**XER:** Why did'st not sooner let me know this love?
One day, the happiness of both shall see,
I, with Romilda blessed.

**ARS:** And I, with whom?

**XER:** With Atalanta.

**ARS:** Do you mock me thus?

**XER:** I know, that thou dost Atalanta love.

**ARS:** Romilda, only does engross my heart.

**XER:** Ah, give dissembl'ing o'er.

**ARS:** Romilda then
Thou dost not yield me?

**XER:** Thou'lt that fair refuse.

**ARS:** Yes, he I'll have, I'll her obtain,
And if my pray'rs to heav'n prove vain;
The monsters of th' infernal shade,
I will invoke to lend their aid.
(*Exit.*)

## SCENE X

*Atalanta and Xerxes.*

**ATA:** To thee, great monarch do I lowly bend.

**XER:** That Arsamenes loves you, he denies,
And constant only to Romilda proves
Wherefore, in truth, his passion's not for thee,
Avoid thy fruitless pain, nor love him thou.

**ATA:** To love no more, thou do'st advise,
But do'st not say, if thou hast pow'r,
Too many darts are in his eyes,
Which charms incessant round him show'r;
That chain which love on me imposed,
Is for my strength too streightly closed.
(*Exit.*)

**XER:** How trifling wou'd be grief, if lovers cou'd
At pleasure love, or from their love desist.
Both love and fear the heart possess,
Alternate tyrants to our joy;
Nor can the ardent lover guess,
If he the fair one shall enjoy.
If of my hopes I ask the fair,
My hopes a flatt'ring answer give;
But then, if I consult my fear,
A flat denial I receive.
(*Exit.*)

## SCENE XI

**ELVIRO:** (*solos.*) Wretch that I am,
I have my master lost;
But 'tis my fault, I own. I'm quite turn'd fool.
He, by my troth, has turn'd my

No, ch' io nol veggo no
Ma qual adombra il Ciel nubilo os-
curo?
Sento che l' onde fremono,
Sento che l' aria sibila:
Son restato all' oscuro;
Voglio partir, e vò partir in fretta
Si spezza il Ponte, a te, fa cor Gam-
betta,
Perchè nemico al mio temperam-
ento
E l' acquoso elemento.
Del mio caro Bacco amabile
Nell' Imperio suo potabile
Amo Solo d' arbitar.
L'acqua rende Ipocondriaco;
Il buon vin sin al Zodiaco
La mia testa sa imalzar.
(*Parte.*)

head, perhaps
O'er this bridge he's gone. No; I see
him not.
But what a foggy cloud obscures the
sky?
The billows roar, and whistling
winds I hear,
'Tis now quite dark, I will brush off,
And that with speed, for if the
bridge shou'd break,
'Twere best to shew a nimble pair
of heels;
The wat'ry Elements I ne'er did
like.
In Bacchus' liquid realms, I own,
I wou'd my habitation chuse;
'Tis there that I wou'd fix alone,
His potables I'll ne'er refuse.
The spleen does from mere water
rise;
But glorious wine revives the foul.
I strike my head against the skies,
Whene'er I hug the flowing bowl.
(*Exit.*)

AMA: (Tornerò per tua pena, o
traditore.)
(*Si ritira in disparte.*)

AMA: (Yes, traitor, to thy grief)
(*She withdraws to one side.*)

## SCENA XII

*Luogo di ritiro contiguo alla Cit-
tà.*
*Serse da una parte, Amastre dall'
altra.*

SER: Gran pena è gelosìa!

AMA: Lo sa il mio cor piagato.

SER: Per altri son sprezzato.

AMA: Per altri anch' io tradita.

SER: E la mia fe schernita.

AMA: Schernita è l' Alma mia.

A 2: Gran pena è gelosìa.

SER: Aspra sorte!

AMA: Empie stelle!

SER: O Romilda crudel!

AMA: Serse rubelle!

SER: Chi parla?

AMA: Un Infelice.

SER: E chi fei tu?

AMA: Un che vi servì in Guerra, e
fu ferito.

SER: Vuoi tornar a servirmi?

AMA: Ci penserò.

SER: Perchè?

AMA: Perchè non vuò servir senza
mercè.

SER: Che? mi trovasti ingrato?

AMA: Son rimaso ingannato.

SER: (Ma sen viene il mio ben)
scostati. Appresso
Noi Parlarem. Tengo un affar che
importa,
Ritorna a me in brev' ore.

## SCENE XII

*A place of retirement contiguous
to the town.*
*On one side Xerxes, on the other,
Amastre.*

XER: How great a pain is jealousy.

AMA: My wounded heart the proof
has made.

XER: Another is prefer'd to me.

AMA: And for another I'm betrayed.

XER: My constant faith with scorn's
receiv'd.

AMA: My constant heart by scorn
deceiv'd.

BOTH: How great a pain is jealousy!

XER: O rigid fate!

AMA: O stars severe!

XER: Romilda cruel!

AMA: Xerxes disloyal!

XER: Who is't that speaks?

AMA: A wretch.

XER: And who art thou?

AMA: One serv'd thee in the wars,
and wounded was.

XER: To serve me woud'st thou
willingly return.

AMA: I will consider on't.

XER: And why?

AMA: Because I will not serve,
without I meet reward.

XER: How? did'st find me, then, ungrateful e'er?

AMA: I've been deceiv'd

XER: My treasure comes this way.
Withdraw; anon we will have far-
ther talk.
A business of great weight I have;
return
In a short space.

## SCENA XIII

*Serse, Romilda, ed Amastre in dis-
parte.*

SER: Romilda, e farà ver, che
sempre in vano
Pianger mi lasciarete?
Che dite? rispondete.

ROM: Val più contento core
Che quanto il Mondo aduna.
Più vale un ben d' amore
Che cento di fortuna.

SER: Vuò, ch' abbian fine i miei dolori immensi.

ROM: Lasciate, ch' io ci pensi.

SER: No, datemi la destra.

AMA: Olà fermate.
Che il Re v' inganna.

SER: Che ardimento è questo?
Olà, condotto sia
In oscura prigion.

AMA: Morirò pria.
(*Si mette in difesa colla Spada in
mano.*)

SER: Temerità importuna!
(*Serse parte sdegnato.*)
Strano disturbo!

ROM: (O buona mia fortuna!)
(*Le Guardie attaccano Amastre
che si defende.*)
Cessate olà. E voi prode Guerriero
Riponete quel brando.
Ite—Approverà Serse il mio co-
mando.
(*Le Guardie Partono.*)

AMA: La fortuna, la Vita, e l' esser
mio
In eterno obligate.

ROM: Ite, non vi fermate.
Che se venisse il Re—Ditemi solo,
Che v' indusse del Re a sturbar le
voglie?

AMA: Perchè vi vuol sforzar d' ef-
fergli Moglie;
E fiamme più gradite
V' ardono il sen.

ROM: Partite.
(*Am. Parte.*)
Chi cede al furore
Di stelle rubelle
Amante non è.
Trionfa in amore
Del Fato Spietato
L' invitta mia fe.

## SCENE XIII

*Xerxes, Romilda, and Amastre
apart.*

XER: And art thou, fair Romilda,
then resolv'd
To be regardless of thy lover's
sighs?
What say'st thou, charmer? deign
some answer give,

ROM: Search the world's stores,
and you'll not find
Treasures to weigh with peace of
mind.
And Fortune, with her immense
store,
Compar'd with love, is truly poor.

XER: Wilt thou, one day, that my
fierce torments cease?

ROM: Allow me, sir, some little
space for thought.

XER: No, bless me with thy hand.

AMA: Holloa, take heed;
The king deceives thee.

XER: What is this boldness? Who is
there that waits?
To a dark dungeon let him be convey'd.

AMA: I first will die.
(*Puts herself in a posture of defence.*)

XER: Strange interruption! rash impertinence!
(*Exit in anger.*)

ROM: (How fortunate am I.)
(*The guards attack Amastre, who
defends herself.*)
Halt there, forbear. Warrior, do
thou replace
Thy fearless sword. Withdraw.
What I command,
Great Xerxes will approve.
(*The guards go off.*)

AMA: My fortune, life, and all my
faculties,
For ever to thy service hast thou
bound.

ROM: Go, stay not, hero, for, if the
king shou'd come—
But tell me, only, why thou were't
induced
Thus to oppose the pleasure of the
king?

AMA: Because he'd make thee, by
constraint, his queen,
While a more pleasing flame thy
breast does warm.

ROM: Retire from hence.
(*Amastre goes off.*)
A lover's name he don't deserve,
Who to malignant stars does yield.
My faith, unconquer'd, ne'er shall
swerve;
But love triumphing over fate,
Howe'er severe and fierce its hate,
Shall bear the laurels from the field.

*Fine dell' Atto Secondo.*

## ATTO III

### SCENA I

*Galleria.*

*Arsamene, Romilda, ed Elviro che trattiene Arsamene e poi Atalanta.*

**ARS:** Sono vani i presti—

**ROM:** Scrivesti ad Atalanta. Elviro parlerà.

**ARS:** Sì Atalanta dirà—(Oh amate pene!)

**ROM:** Ecco, Atalanta viene.

**ATA:** (Ahi! scoperto è l' inganno, e che farò?)

**ELV:** Brutti imbrogli son questi. O la febre, e la voce—Deh Signora Dite per carità Quel che diceste a me.

**ATA:** Dissi, Romilda scrive, ed ama il Re.

**ARS:** Che volete di più?

**ROM:** Dunque ingannate?

**ATA:** Piano; non vi adirate. Dissi così, per far partire il Servo, Che voleva parlarvi.

**ROM:** Seguite pur, son pronta ad ascoltarvi.

**ATA:** Serse mi sopragiunse, e prese il foglio. Io per giovarvi, dissi, è scritto a me, Mi finsi Amante, ed ò ingannato il Re.

**ARS:** Or che dite Romilda?

**ROM:** Or che dite Arsamene?

**ARS:** Che vi adoro—

**ROM:** Che siete il caro Bene. Fate Atalanta pur quanto sapete, Arsamene il mio ben non mi torrete.

**ATA:** No, se tu mi sprezzi, Morir non vuò. Fo certi vezzi Col mio sembiante, Che un altro amante Trovara saprò. *(Parte.)*

### SCENA II

*Romilda, Arsamene, Elviro, e poi Serse.*

**ROM:** Ecco in segno di se la destra amica.

**ELV:** Ecco Serse, ecco Serse.

**ARS:** Oh che sciagura!

*End of the Second Act.*

## ACT III

### SCENE I

*A gallery.*

*Arsamenes, Romilda, and Elviro, who stops Arsamenes, and to them Atalanta.*

**ARS:** Vain is all pretence—

**ROM:** Thou to my sister wrot'st. Elviro, speak.

**ARS:** Thy sister too shall say—(o cruel pain!)

**ROM:** See Atalanta comes.

**ATA:** (Discover'd is my fraud, what must I do?)

**ELV:** What filthy broils, what squabbling work is here. I've catch'd an ague, and my voice—Madam, For pity sake, say, what you said to me.

**ATA:** My sister lov'd, and to the king did write.

**ARS:** Woud'st thou have more?

**ROM:** Art a deceiver then?

**ATA:** Softly, and do not to thy wrath give way, To fend the servant hence, I this devis'd, For he wou'd speak to thee.

**ROM:** Proceed, I pray, For I with eagerness thy tale attend.

**ATA:** Xerxes surpriz'd me, and the letter took; I said it was, to skreen you, wrote to me, And feigning that I lov'd, deceiv'd the king.

**ARS:** What says Romilda?

**ROM:** Arsamenes what?

**ARS:** That I adore thee.

**ROM:** That in thee I live. Go on now, sister, ev'ry art employ; Thou shall't not rob me of this only joy.

**ATA:** With patience I thy slights will bear, Nor will romantick die. I still have beauty, still an air, Another lover to ensnare, And still bear light'ning in my eye. *(Exit.)*

### SCENE II

*Romilda, Arsamenes, Elviro, and to them Xerxes.*

**ROM:** Behold, my hand in token of my faith.

**ELV:** See Xerxes, Xerxes comes.

**ARS:** What luckless fate!

**ELV:** Ed io vi aspetterò fuor delle mura. *(fugge.)*

**ROM:** Nascondetevi.

**ARS:** Oh sorte! *(Si nasconde.)*

**SER:** Che vi mosse, Romilda, a quel Guerrioro Donar la libertate?

**ROM:** Il suo valore.

**SER:** Tutto potete; è vostro il Regno e il Core. Già siete mia Reina.

**ROM:** Signor, volo tanto alto è gran ruina.

**SER:** Deh non negate puì.

**ROM:** Negherò sempre.

**SER:** Franger io ben saprò— Intendete Romilda?

**ROM:** (Ah che farò?)

**SER:** Non partirò, se pria—basta— che dite?

**ROM:** Che del mio Genitor vi vuol l' assenso.

**SER:** E poi che dubbio v' è?

**ROM:** Ubbidirò il mio Re.

**SER:** Vado a chiederlo; e intanto Mi stillo in gioia.

**ROM:** Ed io mi struggo in pianto.

**SER:** Per rendermi beato Parto vezzose stelle, E poi pupille belle A voi ritornerò. Farfalla al vostro lume Il core innamorato Ardendo le sue piume Fenice io scorgerò. *(Parte.)*

### SCENA III

*Arsamene e Romilda.*

**ARS:** Ubbidirò al mio Re. Oh che limpido amor! che bella se!

**ROM:** Ah ch' io mi moro. *(Sviene sostenuta dalle sue damigelle.)*

**ARS:** Romilda?

**ROM:** Vi fermate.

**ARS:** Romilda?

**ROM:** Andate andate, Serse il Re Sovvenirmi potrà, Quando m' ucciderà.

**ARS:** Tanto m' odiatè?

**ROM:** Tantò vi adoro, Addio, vi lascio, addio.

**ARS:** Vi fuggo.

**ELV:** I'll wait you, sir, without the city walls. *(runs off.)*

**ROM:** Hide thee.

**ARS:** O fate!— *(He hides.)*

**XER:** What could, Romilda, move thee to release That soldier?

**ROM:** 'Twas his bravery, Sir.

**XER:** Thou hast all pow'r; our heart and kingdom's thine.

**ROM:** So high a flight, an equal ruine threats.

**XER:** Refuse no more.

**ROM:** I ever shall refuse.

**XER:** I shall find ways to break— Heark thee, Romilda.

**ROM:** (Ah! what shall I do?)

**XER:** I will not part, before— enough—what say'st?

**ROM:** That first my father shou'd approve your will.

**XER:** And then, what doubts?

**ROM:** I shall my king obey.

**XER:** I go for his consent. In th' int'rim I Feel thro' my heart of sudden flow of joy.

**ROM:** While I in tears do waste away.

**XER:** The choicest blessing to receive, I now those lovely brilliants leave; And then shall joyfully return, To view those stars by which I burn. Thus, like the moth, around those eyes, Th' enamour'd heart does wanton play; But if 'tis scorch'd by too much day, It, phoenix like, again shall rise.

### SCENE III

*Arsamenes and Romilda.*

**ARS:** I shall my king obey. O love most pure? Oh glorious faith!

**ROM:** Ah me, I faint, I die. *(She falls into the arms of her women.)*

**ARS:** Romilda?

**ROM:** Stay.

**ARS:** Romilda?

**ROM:** Away, be gone, for Xerxes, The king, will give me ease in giving death.

**ARS:** Am I so much the object of thy hate?

**ROM:** Thou art so much the object of my love. Adieu, I leave thee; but farewel.

**ARS:** I flie thee.

ROM: E dove andate Idolo mio?

ARS: Dove vuol fiera sorte. E voi, dove?

ROM: Alla morte.

ARS: Eh dite, al Trono, Che promesso vi sù.

ROM: Vi lascio, addio, non mi vedrete più.
(*La damigelle la conducono via sostenendola.*)

ARS: Amor, tiranno amor
Per me non à pietà.
Farmi languir ognor,
E troppa crudeltà.
Un core, un petto sol
Tanto soffrir non sa,
O cangia tempre al duol,
O dammi libertà.

ROM: Whither wilt thou go, my life?

ARS: Where cruel fate shall guide. And whither thou?

ROM: To death.

ARS: Ah, rather to the promis'd throne.

ROM: Adieu; I quite thee ne'er to see thee more.
(*Her women lead her off, supporting her.*)

ARS: O love, thou too tyrannick pow'r,
No pity do'st thou shew to me:
To make me sigh away each hour,
Is too great cruelty in thee.
One heart, one breast, without relief,
Can't bear what thou inflict'st on me.
O change and moderate my grief,
Or give me back to liberty.

## SCENA IV

*Bosebetto.*

*Serse, ed Ariodate.*

SER: Come già v' accennammo
Sposo del nostro sangue, a piacer vostro,
Destiniamo a Romilda.

ARIO: Alto e' l' onore—e—

SER: L' approvate? assentite?

ARIO: Bramo sol d' ubbidirvi.

SER: Dunque udite.
Verrà tra poco nelle vostre stanze
Persona eguale a noi, del nostro sangue:
Fate che vostra figlia
Per suo Sposo l' accetti.

ARIO: Del vostro sangue? e così noto a me?
(*S. Parte.*)

SER: Quanto Serse.

ARIO: Arsamene, altri non è.
Del ciel d' amore
Sorte sì bella
Chi mai sperò.
Per mio Splendore
Qual fu la stella
Che lampeggiò.
(*Parte.*)

## SCENE IV

*A grove.*

*Xerxes and Ariodates.*

XER: As we already hinted you before,
If you approve, we to Romilda give
A consort of our royal blood.

ARI: Sublime's the honour—and—

XER: Do'st thou approve? do'st thou to this consent?

ARI: My only wish is, to obey they will.

XER: Hear then; to thy apartment there will come,
In a short space, a person whom thou'lt own
Equal to us, and of our royal stem.
Do thou engage thy daughter to receive
This consort.

ARI: Of thy high blood? and known to me as such?

XER: As well as Xerxes is.

ARI: This cannot be
(*Exit, Xerxes.*)
Other than Arsamenes.
Who, from the sphere of love,
Cou'd ever hope to prove
So happy in his fate!
What lucky star, to me,
Cou'd so propitious be,
To raise me to such state!

## SCENA V

*Romilda sdegnata che poi s' incontra in Serse.*

ROM: Il ferto rifiuto:
E dite a Serse in riportargli il dono,
Che fida Amante, ad altri Sposa io sono.
(*vuol Par.*)

## SCENE V

*Romilda in anger, who meets with Xerxes.*

ROM: His offer'd diadem I do reject,
And with his gift return'd, let Xerxes know;
Another's wife I am, and true to love.

SER: Fermatevi mia Sposa, e mia Reina.

ROM: Che dite? oimè! così non mi chiamate.

SER: Perchè?

ROM: Perchè oscurate
Il Decoro real.

SER: Come?

ROM: Ascoltate.
Arsamene mi amò—

SER: Principio infausto.

ROM: Fu modesto e fedel.

SER: Basta.

ROM: Servimmi
Tacito adoratore.

SER: Ah m' uccidete!

ROM: Ma ardito al fin.

SER: Che?

ROM: Non ardisco, o Sire,
Mi arrosiisco, Signor; non lo dirò.
Parto, lo scriverò.

SER: No no, seguite.

ROM: Non so se ardire, o se fortuna fu—

SER: Ah che non posso più.

ROM: Le sue labbra accostò—

SER: Dove?

ROM: Alle mie.
E— E— E—

SER: E vi baciò, non è? Ditelo.

ROM: Appunto.

SER: Per fuggir le mie nozze, ora mentite.
Ma siasi ver o no; delle sue colpe
Abbia il castigo. Olà, pronti volate;
Arsamene uccidete.
(*alle Guardie.*)
Vedova di quel bacio
Poi Sposa mia sarete.
(*Parte sdegnato.*)

ROM: Mio Re, mio Sposo, sì: Oh amare pene!
Fermate, e viva il caro mio Arsamene.

## SCENA VI

*Romilda, ed Amastre con lettera in mano.*

ROM: Prode Guerrier.—

AMA: Signora.

ROM: A me venite.
Se nel petto nudrite
Alma cortese e pia,
Le mie preghiere udite.

XER: Stay thee, my spouse, stay my beloved queen.

ROM: What's this I hear? Alas! don't term me such.

XER: And why?

ROM: Thou'lt bring a blemish on thy crown.

XER: And how?

ROM: Do thou attend. I once was lov'd
By Arsamenes.

XER: Luckless exordium.

ROM: Within the bounds of faithful modesty.

XER: Enough.

ROM: A silent adoration prov'd.

XER: You give me death.

ROM: His love: but grown, at length,
More bold.

XER: What?

ROM: I dare not, sir, my blushes
Do preclude my words. No, I cannot speak;
But I will hence and write it.

XER: No, go on.

ROM: I know not, if it boldness was, or fate—

XER: Ah! I can bear no more.

ROM: His lips he did approach.

XER: To what?

ROM: To mine, and, and—

XER: And kiss'd thee; is't not so? speak out.

ROM: 'Twas so.

XER: This, to avoid my nuptials, hast thou feign'd;
This instant feign'd; but be it so or not,
He shall chastisement for his boldness meet.
Who's there? quick, fly, and Arsamenes slay.
(*To the guards.*)
First shalt thou widdow of that kiss be made,
And then the spouse of Xerxes shalt thou be.
(*Exit in rage.*)

## SCENE VI

*Romilda and Amastre, with a letter in her hand.*

ROM: Brave warrior.

AMA: Lady.

ROM: Draw thou near to me.
If in thy breast thou gentle pity bear'st,
Hear my request.

**AMA:** Comandi, e non preghiere
A me porger dovete. Io mi sovven-
go,
Che toglieste il mio piede
Da' lacci di quell' empio ingrato
Re.

**ROM:** Ingratissimo appunto. Egli
comanda,
Ch' Arsamene s' uccida.
In voi il mio cor si fida;
Cercatelo, e per voi nota gli sia
Quella sentenza rìa.

**AMA:** Vado pronto a servirvi, ed io
vi priego
Di far recare al Re questo mio foglio.

**ROM:** Volo per ispedirlo. (Oh mio
cordoglio!)

**AMA:** Cagion son io
Del mio dolore,
E so perchè.
Ama il cor mio
Un traditore,
Con troppo amore
Con troppa fe.
(*Parte.*)

## SCENA VII

*Arsamene, e Romilda.*

**ARS:** Romilda infida, e di me pensa
ancora?

**ROM:** Romilda, che vi adora
Di voi pensa ad ognora.

**ARS:** Per spronarmi a partire,
Non per salvar chi v' ama,
Dite che Serse brama il mio morire.

**ROM:** Troppo oltraggi la mia fede.

**ARS:** Troppo inganni la mia fede.

**A 2:** Alma fiera, ingrato core.

**ROM:** E tiranna la Mercede.

**ARS:** Non è questa la Mercede.

**ROM:** Che riceve.

**ARS:** Che si deve.

**A 2:** Al mio petto innamorato.
(*Partono per diverse parti.*)

## SCENA VIII

*Gran Tempio, col simulacro del
Sole, ed Ara accesa
Coro di Ministri all' intorno del si-
mulacro.*

---

**AMA:** Commands, and not requests,
Become thee more with me; I bear
in mind,
From the ungrateful king thou
sett'st me free.

**ROM:** Ungrateful, truly, to the last
degree.
He has commanded Arsamenes'
death.
In thee my heart confides, ah, seek
him out,
And let him know this wicked sentence pass'd.

**AMA:** To serve thee, I with readiness do go,
And to the king this note I beg
thou'lt give.

**ROM:** I fly to give it. (O my piercing grief!)

**AMA:** The cause of my own grief
am I,
And well I know the reason why:
My heart a traitor does pursue,
With too fond love, and faith too
true.
(*Exit.*)

## SCENE VII

*Arsamenes and Romilda.*

**ARS:** Faithless Romilda, think'st
thou still of me?

**ROM:** Thou do'st Romilda's every
thought employ,
As thou'rt alone, the fond Romilda's joy.

**ARS:** To hasten my departure hence
with speed,
And not to have thy lover, do'st
thou say,
That angry Xerxes has my death decreed.

**ROM:** Too many wrongs my faith
does meet.

**ARS:** My faith does find too great
deceit.

**BOTH:** Thy cruel heart denies me
rest.

**ROM:** Tyranical is the reward.

**ARS:** This is not the just reward.

**ROM:** Which does receive.

**ARS:** Which thou do'st give.

**BOTH:** This faithful and enamour'd
breast.
(*Exit, on different parts of the
stage.*)

## SCENE VIII

*A large temple, with the image of
the sun. An altar lighted. A chorus
of priests round the statute.*

---

**CORO:** Ciò the Giove destinò
Impedir l' Uomo non sa.
(*Ariodate, Romilda, Arsamene
dal fondo della Scena.*)

**ARIO:** Ecco lo Sposo. Io ben ne fui
presago.
Quanto m' arride il Fato.

**ARS:** Alma fiera

**ARS:** Core ingrato

**ARS, ROM:** Troppo oltraggi la mia
fede.

**ARIO:** A colmarmi d' onore
Signor, so che veniste

**ROM:** Ah il Genitore!
(*vuol P.*)

**ARIO:** Romilda, non partite.

**ARS:** Ariodate, che dite?

**ARIO:** Che a voi dò la mia figlia
Per serva umile e Sposa,
Come m' impose il Re.

**ARS:** Serse l' impose?

**ARIO:** A me stesso.

**ROM:** Che Ascolto!

**ARIO:** E voi veniste
Per prenderla in consorte?

**ARS:** Altro non bramo.

**ROM:** (Oh me Beata! oh sorte!)

**ARIO:** Romilda, acconsentite?

**ROM:** Sì mio Padre, e Signore.

**ARIO:** Stringete omai le Destre

**ROM, ARS:** e in un il core.

**ARIO:** Ora corriamo a Serse
Per render grazie d' un si grande
onore.
(*Partono.*)

**CORO:** (*replica.*)
Chi infelice si trovò
Pien di gioja or lieto va.

## SCENA IX

*Serse, poi Ariodate.*

**SER:** Se ne viene Ariodate. è tempo
omai
Di scoprir, che son Io,
Che Romilda desiò.
Eccomi Ariodate.

**ARIO:** Invitto Sire
V' inchino.

**SER:** Or che vi sembra?
Lo Sposo egual vi dissi?

**ARIO:** E un alto onore.

**SER:** Romilda vaga
Ne sarà paga?

**ARIO:** Non brama più.

**SER:** Ma perchè mai non viene?
Dov' è?

---

**CHOR:** Whate'er all ruleing Jove
commands;
Vainly all human force withstands.
(*Ariodates, Romilda, Arsamenes,
at the farther end of the stage.*)

**ARI:** Behold the bridegroom. This I
well presaged.
How does fate smile on me this day.

**ARS:** Too cruel soul

**ROM:** Ungrateful heart

**ARS, ROM:** Too much my faith you
wrong.

**ARI:** With honours to o'erwhelm
me art thou come,
I know, my lord.

**ROM:** : Ha! is my father here!
(*Going.*)

**ARI:** Stay thee, Romilda; thou must
not go hence,

**ARS:** What was it, Ariodates, thou
did'st say?

**ARI:** That, in obedience to the
king's commands,
For humble handmaid, and obedient wife,
I give thee here my daughter.

**ARS:** Did Xerxes
This Command?

**ARI:** To my myself.

**ROM:** What hear I?

**ARI:** And come you not to take her
for your spouse?

**ARS:** Nothing I wish more.

**ROM:** (Happy me! O fate!)

**ARI:** Romilda, do'st consent?

**ROM:** My lord, I do.

**ARI:** Join then your hands.

**ROM, ARS:** And join in one our
hearts.

**ARI:** Now let us strait to Xerxes
haste away,
And thank him for the might honour done.
(*Exit.*)

**CHORUS:** (*replies.*) And he who
was depress'd with woe,
Does rising joy and comfort know.

## SCENE IX

*Xerxes, to him Ariodates.*

**XER:** See Ariodates comes, 'tis
time, at length,
To let him know, 'tis I, Romilda ask.
Thou seest, my Ariodates,

**ARI:** that I'm here;
Now what's thy thoughts?

**XER:** equal the spouse I said?

**ARI:** The honour is sublime.

**XER:** Romilda fair,
Is she content.

**ARI:** She nothing more does wish.

**XER:** But say, why comes she not?
where is she then?

ARIO: Con Arsamene.

SER: Che?

ARIO: Collo Sposo.

SER: Come?

ARIO: Collo Sposo Signor?

SER: Che Sposo? Aimè!

ARIO: Come imponeste.

SER: Che v' imposi? che?

ARIO: Eguale a voi, del vostro sangue; e venne
Nelle mie stanze—

SER: E sono Sposi?

ARIO: Sono.

SER: Empio, perfido, indegno.

ARIO: Mio Re?

SER: Tu m' ai tradito,
E per tuo Re tenti chiamarmi ardito,
(*Un paggio porta un Lettera a Serse, e gli parla basso.*)
Romilda a me l' invia? Perfida donna!
crede co' inchiostri rei
Incantar follemente i sdegni miei?
(*Dà la Lettera ad Ariodate, che legge.*)

ARIO: (Perchè non moro oh Ciel!)

SER: Leggi, che fai?

ARIO: "Ingratissimo amante.

SER: Come? ingrato mi chiama; e tanto ell' osa?

ARIO: "Venni per esser vostra

SER: E altrui si Sposa?

ARIO: Trovai che mi sprezzate.

SER: Ah note Scelerate!

ARIO: "Partò, ma il Ciel punitrà vostra colpe.

SER: Colpe di averti amato.

ARIO: "Io piangerò
"Sino all' ultimo fiato;
"Amastre.

SER: Che?

ARIO: Non di Romilda è il foglio.
(*Serse prende con isdegno la Lettera e guarda la firma.*)

SER: Amastre? vanne, e ti allontana indegno;
(*Ariodate si ritira in disparte.*)
Non mancava altro tedio in tanto sdegno.
Crude furie degli orridi abissi
Aspergetemi d' aspro veleno.
Crolli il Mondo, il sole s' eclissi
A quest' ira, che spira il mio seno.
(*Nel partire gli si fanno innanzi Arsamene, Romilda, Amastre, Atalanta, ed Elviro.*)

---

ARI: With Arsamenes.

XER: What?

ARI: She's with her spouse.

XER: How?

ARI: She's with her spouse, my lord?

XER: Her spouse? alas!

ARI: Whom thou enjoin'st

XER: What? whom did I enjoin?

ARI: Equal to you, and of your royal blood
In my apartments.

XER: Are they married then?

ARI: They are.

XER: Thou treach'rous, impious, worthless wretch.

ARI: What means my king?

XER: I am by thee betray'd,
And hast thou confidence to call me king?
(*A page brings a letter to Xerxes, and speaks softly to him.*)
Romilda send me this? woman most base!
Thinks she by writing to appease my wrath?
(*Gives the letter to Ariodates, who reads.*)

ARI: Why still, o heavens, do I life retain.

XER: Read, what do'st thou do?

ARI: "Lover ungrateful.

XER: How? dares she tax me with ingratitude?

ARI: "To be thine I came.

XER: And weds another?

ARI: "By thee, I found myself despis'd.

XER: Wicked!

ARI: "From hence I go, thy crimes will heav'n o'ertake.

XER: The crime of loving thee.

ARI: "I shall in tears
"Draw my last gasp of breath.
Amastre.
(*Xerxes takes the letter in a passion and examines the subscription.*)

XER: Amastre! hence, hence from my sight thou wretch.
(*Ariodates withdraws to one side of the stage.*)
What worse could happen to encrease my pain.
Ye cruel furies of the lake,
On me, o'er me, your venome shake.
Crush'd by the world, and let yond light,
T' assuage my wrath, be drown'd in

---

night.
(*In going off, he is met by Arsamenes, Romilda, Amastre, Atalanta, and Elviro.*)

## SCENA ULTIMA

*Tutti.*

SER: Perfidi, e ancora usate
Venirmi innanzi

ARIO: Che furor

ARS: Cessate.
Umili al vostro pie—

SER: Sol per schernirmi

ARS: Come, Signor?

SER: Tu m' ai Romilda tolta.

ARS: Fu pur vostro comando.

ARIO: E ver.

ROM: Confermo.

SER: E quando?
Temerarj pretesti!
(*tira la Spada.*)
Questo ferro a quell' empia in seno immergi.

ARS: Ch' io sveni la mia Sposa?
Svenerò pria il tuo core.

AMA: Datelo a me Signore.
(*a Serse.*)

SER: E chi sei tu che ognor sempre mi sturbi?

AMA: Uno, che cerca far giusta vendetta.
Volete chi si sveni
Un alma che tradì chi pur l' adora?

SER: Sì.

AMA: E si squarci quel core.

SER: Sì.

AMA: Mori dunque ingrato, e traditore.
(*gli rapisce a forza il ferro, presentandoglielo el petto.*)
Ecco Amastre tradita, e ognor fedele:
E tu spietato e rìo
La disprezzi così.

SER: Uccidetemi sì.

AMA: Morir degg' io.

SER: Fermate. Ora mi pento—

AMA: E torni a amarmi?

SER: Sì, ma di tua pietade indegno sono.

AMA: Amami pur, o cara, io ti perdono.
(*si abbracciano.*)

ELV: Sono tutto tremante.

ARS: Or sparve il duolo.

ARS: Io respiro, e stupisco.

ROM: Io mi consolo.

---

## SCENE LAST

*All.*

XER: Dare ye, ye wretches, meet me face to face.

ARI: How great's his rage!

ARS: No more. We prostrate come.

XER: T' insult.

ARS: How, my lord?

XER: Thou hast depriv'd me
Of Romilda.

ARS: It was by your command.

ARI: That's truth.

ROM: And I confirm it.

XER: When, I pray?
Most vain pretence, Here, do thou plunge this sword
(*draws.*)
Into that impious breast.

ARS: How, kill my wife?
No, sooner would I spilt thy cruel heart.

AMA: Give me, my lord, the sword—
(*to Xerxes.*)

XER: And who art thou, who'rt momently my plauge.

AMA: One who does seek a just revenge to take.
Wouldst that I should pierce th' ungrateful heart
Which has with treachery repaid true love?

XER: Most willingly.

AMA: The faithless heart transfix?

XER: 'Tis what I wish.

AMA: Then, thankless traitor, die.
(*She snatches the sword out of his hand, and claps it to his breast.*)
Behold Amastre, traitor, faithful still.

XER: Give me then death.

AMA: 'Tis I that ought to die.

XER: Hold, I now repent—

AMA: Do'st thou return again to love and me?

XER: I do; but still thy pity don't deserve.

AMA: Give me thy love, and I can all forgive—
(*They embrace*)

ELV: I've got, methinks, an ague fit.

ARI: Let ev'ry grief now vanish.

ARS: I do again respire, tho' still amaz'd,

ROM: And I now comfort know.

## Act III, Last Scene

**ATA:** Ed io cercherò altrove un altro amante.

**SER:** Amici, compatite i miei furori,
E godete felici: i vostri amori.

**ROM:** (*à Ars.*) Caro voi siete all' Alma
Dolce voi siete al cor.
Son dalla vostra palma
Fatta Trofeo d' amor.

**ATA:** And I else where another love will seek.

**XER:** Forgive, my friends, the vi'lence of my rage,
And be ye happy in each others love.

**ROM:** (*to Ars*) Thou to my heart art ever dear,
Such to my soul thoul't ever prove.
I am the palm, which thou shall't bear,
As trophy of a constant love,

**CORO:** Ritorna a noi la Calma
Riede la gioja al Cor.
Per riportar la palma
S' uniro amore e onor.

*IL FINE.*

**CHORUS:** Now, at length, returns the calm
Joy and peace, the heart's delight;
And, to bear away the palm,
Love and honour do unite.

*FINIS.*

# Semele (1744)

MUSIC BY GEORGE FREDERIK HANDEL ■ LIBRETTO BY WILLIAM CONGREVE

This three-act opera, set to a libretto by William Congreve, premiered at Covent Garden, London, on February 10, 1744. The story opens with religious ceremonies taking place at the Temple of Juno in Thebes. The daughter of King Cadmus, Semele, is engaged to Athamas, Prince of Boeotia. However, she is in love with Jupiter, who has come to her in disguise. Her father and Athamas urge her to cease delaying the wedding, and she prays to Jove to help her. Ino, Semele's sister, is in love with Athamas. Semele begs Ino to speak about her feelings; Cadmus tells her off, and the altar fire dies down, a sign of Jupiter's displeasure. The crowd is upset by this and rushes out of temple. In a scene between Ino and Athamas, he realizes her feelings for him. Cadmus enters and says that Semele has been taken by an eagle. Her disappearance is mourned until the priests tell Cadmus that Jupiter now favors his family—this cannot be explained. Semele appears from a cloud and reassures everyone that she is well. Juno, seeking revenge, is looking for Semele. Iris, Juno's attendant, tells her that Jupiter is protecting Semele with two dragons. Juno says that Somnus, god of sleep, will cause the two dragons to sleep so that she may exact her revenge. Semele is now asleep at her palace, surrounded by Zephirs and Loves. Jupiter appears and reassures her of his love. Semele brings up the matter of her mortality as opposed to Jupiter's immortality. Jupiter decides to bring Ino to her for company, and he takes them to Arcadia. Ino realizes that she is brought to this hallowed place at Jupiter's direct order. Somnus is asleep at his cave. Juno and Iris appear and ask his help to remove the protection Jupiter has placed around Semele. Somnus hesitates, but Juno mentions the name Pasithea and he agrees to help her in return for Pasithea. Juno orders that Jupiter be distracted by dreaming of Semele and that the dragons and Ino be put to sleep by Somnus' rod. Juno appears to Semele disguised as Ino and asks her if Jupiter has made her immortal yet; she suggests to Semele that she refuse Jupiter all favors until he grants her immortality and he appears to her in his godly state—Juno knows that Semele will be destroyed should he do so. Semele believes her and thanks her; Juno departs as Jupiter enters. Jupiter tells Semele that he has dreamt she refused him all favors, and she sticks to her decision to do just that. Jupiter promises to grant her whatever she should desire, and she asks him to appear to her in his immortal state. Jupiter is agitated by this request, but she insists that he comply. Jupiter mourns his promise as he realizes the consequences. He appears to her in his godly splendor and she dies. Back at Cadmus' court, Ino announces that her marriage to Athamas is prophesied. Apollo appears on a cloud and announces that a phoenix will rise out of Semele's ashes.

NOTE: THE MUSIC FOR THIS OPERA WAS WRITTEN FOR THE FOLLOWING ENGLISH LIBRETTO AND THEREFORE HASN'T BEEN EDITED IN ANY WAY.

## ■ PART I.

### SCENE I.

*The SCENE is the Temple of Juno: Near the Altar is a Golden Image of the Goddess. Priests are in their Solemnities, as after a Sacrifice newly offered; Flames arise from the Altar, and the Statute of Juno is seen to bow.*

*Cadmus, Athamas, Semele, Ino, and Chorus of Priests.*

**RECITATIVE:** (*accompanied.*)
BEHOLD! auspicious Flashes rise!
Juno accepts our Sacrifice;
The grateful Odour swift ascends,
And see, the golden Image bends.

**CHORUS:** Lucky Omens-bless our Rites,
And sure Success shall crown your Loves;
Peaceful Days and fruitful Nights
Attend the Pair that she approves.

**CADM:** Daughter, obey,
Hear and obey;
With kind Consenting
Ease a Parent's Care;
Invent no new Delay,

**ATHA:** O hear a faithful Lover's Pray'r;
On this auspicious Day,
Invent no new Delay.
Hear—

**CADM:** And obey—

**BOTH:** Invent no new Delay,
On this auspicious Day.

**RECITATIVE:** (*accompanied.*)

**SEMELE:** (*Apart.*) Ah me!
What Refuge now is left me?
How various, how tormenting
Are my Miseries!
O Jove! assist me:
Can Semele forgo thy Love,
And to a Mortal's Passion yield?
Thy Vengeance will o'ertake
Such Perfidy.
If I deny, my Father's Wrath I fear.
O Jove! in Pity teach me which to chose,
Incline me to comply, or help me to refuse.

**SONG:**
The Morning Lark to mine accords his Note,
And tunes to my Distress his warbling Throat;
Each setting and each rising Sun I mourn,
Wailing alike his Absence and Return.
The Morning Lark, &c.

**ATHA:** See, she blushing turns her Eyes;
See, with Sighs her Bosom panting:
If from Love those Sighs arise,
Nothing to my Bliss is wanting.

**SONG:**
Hymen, haste, thy Torch prepare,
Love already his has lighted;
One soft Sigh has cured Despair,
And more than my past Pains required.
Hymen, haste, &c.

**INO:** Alas! she yields,
And has undone me:
I can no longer hide my Passion;
It must have Vent—
Or inward Burning
Will consume me.
O Athamas!—
I cannot utter it.

**ATHA:** On me Fair Ino calls
With mournful Accent,
Her Colour fading,
And her Eyes o'erflowing.

**INO:** O Semele!

**SEMELE:** On me she calls,
Yet seems to shun me:
What would my sister?
Speak—

**INO:** Thou hast undone me.

**A FOUR-PART SONG:**

**CADM:** Why dost thou thus untimely grieve,
And all our solemn Rites prophane?
Can He, or She thy Woes relieve?
Or I? of whom dost thou complain?

**INO:** Of all; but all I fear in vain.

**ATHA:** Can I thy Woes relieve?

**SEMELE:** Can I asswage they Pain?

**CADM, ATHA, SEMELE:** Of whom dost thou complain?

**INO:** Of all, but all I fear in vain.
(*Thunder is heard, and the Fire is extinguished on the Altar.*)

**CHORUS OF PRIESTS:**
Avert these Omens, all ye Pow'rs!
Some God, averse, our holy Rites controlls;
O'erwhelmed with sudden Night the Day expires!
Ill-boding Thunder on the right hand rolls.
And Jove himself descends in Show'rs,
To quench our late propitious Fires.

**RECITATIVE:** (*accompanied*)
(*Flames are rekindled on the Altar.*)
Again auspicious Flashes rise,
Juno accepts our Sacrifice.
(*The Fire is again extinguished.*)
Again the sickly Flame decaying dies:
Juno assents, but angry Jove denies.

**ATHA:** Thy Aid, pronubial Juno,
Athamas implores.

**SEMELE:** (*Apart.*) Thee, Jove, and thee alone, thy Semele adores.
(*A loud Clap of Thunder, the Altar sinks.*)

**CHORUS OF PRIESTS:**
Cease, cease your Vows, 'tis impious to proceed;
Be gone, and fly this holy Place with Speed:
This dreadful Conflict is of dire Presage;
Be gone, and fly from Jove's impending Rage.
(*Exeunt*)

## SCENE II.

**ATHAMAS AND INO:**

**ATHA:** O Athamas, what Torture hast thou born!
And O, what hast thou yet to bear!
From Love, from Hope, from near Possession torn,
And plunged at once in deep Despair.

**SONG:**
**INO:** Turn, hopeless Lover, turn thy Eyes,
And see a Maid bemoan;
In flowing Tears and aching Sighs,
Thy Woes too like her own.
Turn, hopeless Lover, &c

**ATHA:** She weeps!
The gentle Maid, in tender Pity,
Weeps to behold my Misery!
So Semele wou'd melt
To see another mourn.

**SONG:**
Your tuneful Voice my Tale would tell,
In pity of my sad Despair;
And with sweet Melody compel
Attention from the flying Fair.
Your tuneful Voice, &c.

**INO:** Too well I see
Thou wilt not understand me.
Whence cou'd proceed such Tenderness?
Whence such Compassion?
Insensible! Ingrate! —
Ah no, I cannot blame thee:
For by Effects unknown before
Who cou'd the hidden Cause explore;
Or think that Love cou'd act so strange a Part,
To plead for Pity in a Rival's Heart?
**ATHA:** Ah me, what have I heard?
She does her Passion own.

**DUET:**
**INO:** You've undone me;
Look not on me;
Guilt upbraiding,
Shame invading,

**ATHA:** With my Life I wou'd atone
Pains you've born, to me unknown.
Cease to shun me.

**INO:** You've undone me;

**BOTH:** Love, Love alone,
Has both undone.

## SCENE III.

*To Them, Enter Cadmus, attended.*

**CADM:** Ah, wretched Prince, doomed to disastrous Love!
Ah me, of Parents most forlorn!
Prepare, O Athamas! to prove
The sharpest Pangs that e'er were born;
Prepare with me our common Loss to mourn.
**ATHA:** Can Fate, or Semele invent
Another, yet another Punishment?

**RECITATIVE:** (*accompanied.*)
**CADM:** Winged with our Fears, and pious Haste,
From Juno's Fane we fled;
Scarce we the brazen Gates had passed,
When Semele around her Head
With azure Flames was graced;
Whose lambent Glories in her Tresses played.
While this we saw with dread Surprize,
Swifter than Light'ning downward tending,
An Eagle stooped, of mighty Size,
One purple Wings descending;
Like Gold his Beak, like Stars shone forth his Eyes;
His silver plumy Breast with Snow contending:
Sudden he snatched the trembling Maid,
And soaring from our Sight conveyed;
Diffusing ever as he lessening flew
Celestial Odour, and ambrosial Dew.

**ATHA:** O Prodigy, to me of dire Portent!

**INO:** To me, I hope, of fortunate Event.

## SCENE IV.

*Enter to them Chorus of Priests and Augurs.*

**CADM:** See, see, Jove's Priests and holy Augurs come:
Speak, speak, of Semele and me declare the Doom.

**CHORUS OF PRIESTS AND AUGURS:**
Hail Cadmus, hail! Jove salutes the Theban King.
Cease your Mourning,
Joys returning,
Songs of Mirth and Triumph sing.

**SONG:**
Endless Pleasure, endless Love,
Semele enjoys above;
On her Bosom Jove reclining,
Useless now his Thunder lies;
To her Arms his Bolts resigning,
And his Lightning to her Eyes.

**CHORUS:**
Endless Pleasure, endless Love,
Semele enjoys above.

# ▪ PART II.

## SCENE I.

*The SCENE is a pleasant Country.*

*Juno and Iris.*

**JUNO:** Iris, impatient of thy Stay,
From Samos have I winged my Way,
To meet thy slow Return.

**IRIS:** With all his Speed, not yet the Sun
Thro' half his Race has run,
Since I to execute thy dread Command
Have thrice encompassed Sea and Land.

**JUNO:** Say, where is Semele's Abode?

**RECITATIVE:** (*accompanied.*)
**IRIS:** Look where Citheron proudly stands,
Bœotia parting from Cecropian Lands.
High on the Summit of that Hill,
Beyond the Reach of Mortal Eyes,
By Jove's Command, and Vulcan's Skill,
Behold a new erected Palace rise.

**SONG:**
There from Mortal Cares retiring,
She resides in sweet Retreat;
On her Pleasure, Jove requiring,
All the Loves and Graces wait.
There from, &c.

**RECITATIVE:** (*accompanied.*)

**JUNO:** No more—I'll hear no more.
Awake Saturnia from thy Lethargy;
Seize, destroy the cursed Semele.
Scale proud Citheron's Top:
Snatch her, tear her in thy Fury,
And down to the Flood of Acheron
Let her fall, let her fall, fall, fall,
Rolling down the Depths of Night,
Never more to behold Light.
If I th' imperial Scepter sway—I swear
By Hell—
Tremble thou Universe this Oath to hear,
Not one of cursed Agenor's Race to spare.

**IRIS:** Hear, mighty Queen, while I recount
What Obstacles you must surmount.

**RECITATIVE:** (*accompanied.*)
With Adamant the Gates are barred,
Whose Entrance two fierce Dragons guard;
At each Approach they lash their forky Stings,
And clap their brazen Wings:
And as their scaly Horrors rise,
They all at once disclose
A thousand fiery Eyes
Which never know Repose.

**SONG:**

**JUNO:** Hence, Iris, hence away,
Far from the Realms of Day;
O'er Scythian Hills to the Meotian Lake
A Speedy Flight we'll take:
There Somnus I'll compel
His downy Bed to leave, and silent Cell:
With Noise and Light I will his Peace molest,
Nor shall he sink again to pleasing Rest,
'Till to my vowed Revenge he grants Supplies,
And seals with Sleep the wakeful Dragons Eyes.
Hence, Iris, &c.
(Exeunt)

## SCENE II.

*An Apartment in the Palace of Semele, she is sleeping, Loves and Zephirs waiting. Semele awakes and rises.*

**SONG:**
O Sleep, why dost thou leave me?
Why thy Visionary Joys remove?
O Sleep again deceive me,
To my Arms restore my wand'ring Love.

## SCENE III.

*To them enter Jupiter.*

**SEMELE:** Let me not another Moment
Bear the Pangs of Absence;
Since you have formed my Soul for Loving,
No more afflict me
With Doubts and Fears, and cruel Jealousies.

**SONG:**

**JUPITER:** Lay your Doubts and Fears aside,
And for Joys alone provide;
Tho' this Human Shape I wear,
Think not I Man's Falshood bear.
Lay your Doubts, &c.
—I was not absent;
You are Mortal, and require
Time to rest and to repose.
I was not absent,
While Love was with thee
I was present:
Love and I are one.

**SONG:**

**SEMELE:** With fond Desiring,
With Bliss expiring,
Panting,
Fainting,
If this be Love, not you alone
But Love and I are one.
Causeless doubting,
Or despairing,
Rashly trusting,
Idly fearing,
If this be Love, not you alone
But Love and I are one.
With fond desiring, &c.

**CHORUS OF LOVES AND ZEPHIRS:**
How engaging, how endearing,
Is a Lover's Pain and Care!
And what Joy the Nymph's Appearing
After Absence or Despair!

**SEMELE:** —Ah me!

**JUPITER:** Why sighs my Semele?
What gentle Sorrow
Swells thy soft Bosom?
Why tremble those fair Eyes
With interrupted Light?
Where hov'ring for a Vent,
Amidst their humid Fires,
Some new-formed Wish appears.
Speak, and obtain.

**SEMELE:** At my own Happiness
I sigh and tremble;
For I am Mortal,
Still a Woman;
And ever when you leave me,
Tho' compassed round with Deities
Of Loves and Graces,
A Fear invades me,
And conscious of a Nature
Far inferior,
I seek for Solitude,
And shun Society.

**JUPITER:** (*Apart.*) Too well I read
her Meaning,
But must not understand her:
Aiming at Immortality
With dangerous Ambition.

**SONG:**
I must with speed amuse her;
Lest she too much explain,
It gives the Lover double Pain,
Who hears his Nymph complain,
And hearing, must refuse her.

**CHORUS OF LOVES AND ZEPHYRS:**
Now Love that everlasting Boy invites
To revel while you may in soft Delights.

**JUPITER:** By my Command,
Now at this Instant,
Two winged Zephyrs
From her downy Bed
Thy much-loved Ino bear,
And both together,
Waft her hither,
Thro' the balmy Air.

**SEMELE:** Shall I my sister see!
The dear Companion
Of my tender Years.

**JUPITER:** See, she appears,
But sees not me;
For I am visible
Alone to thee.
While I retire, rise and meet her,
And with Welcomes greet her.
Now all this Scene shall to Arcadia turn,
The Seat of happy Nymphs and Swains;
There, without Rage of Jealousy, they burn,
And taste the Sweets of Love without its Pains.

**SONG:**
Where'er you walk, cool Gales
shall fan the Glade;
Trees, where you sit, shall croud
into a shade:
Where'er you tread, the blushing
Flow'rs shall rise;
And all things flourish where you
turn your Eyes.
Where'er, &c.
(*Exit.*)

## SCENE IV.

*Semele, Ino, and Chorus of
Nymphs and Swains.*

**SEMELE:** Dear Sister, how was your
Passage hither?

**INO:** O'er many States and peopled
Towns we passed,
O'er Hills and Valleys, and o'er Desarts waste;
O'er barren Moors, and o'er unwholesome Fens,
And Woods, where Beasts inhabit
dreadful Dens.
Thro' all which pathless Way our
Speed was such,
We stopped not once the Face of
Earth to touch.
Mean time they told me, while thro'
Air we fled,
That Jove did thus ordain.

**ACCOMPANIED:**
But hark! the heav'nly Sphere turns round,
And Silence now is drowned
In Ecstacy of Sound.
How on a sudden the still Air is charmed,
As if all Harmony were just alarmed!
And ev'ry Soul with Transport filled,
Alternately is thawed and chilled.

**DUET:**
Prepare then, ye Immortal Choir,
Each sacred Minstrel tune his Lyre,
And all in Chorus join.

**CHORUS:** Bless the glad Earth with
heav'nly Lays,
And to that Pitch th' eternal Accents raise,
That all appear Divine.

## ■ PART III.

### *SCENE I.*

*SCENE, the Cave of Sleep, the God
of Sleep lying on his Bed. A soft
Symphony is heard afterwards.*

*Juno and Iris appear.*

**JUNO:** Somnus, awake,
Raise thy reclining Head.

**IRIS:** Thyself forsake,
And lift up thy heavy Lids of Lead.

**SONG:**

**SOMNUS:** (*waking.*) Leave me,
lothsome Light.
Receive me, silent Night.
Lethe, why does thy ling'ring Current cease?
O murmur, murmur me again to
Peace.
(*Sleeps again.*)

**IRIS:** Dull God, canst thou attend
the Water's fall,
And not hear Saturnia call?

**JUNO:** Peace Iris, Peace, I know
how to charm him,
Pasithea's Name alone can warm him.
Somnus, arise!
Disclose thy tender Eyes;
For Pasithea's Sight
Endure the Light.
Somnus, arise!

**SONG:**

**SOMNUS:** More sweet is that Name
Than a soft purling Stream;
With Pleasure Repose I'll forsake,
If you'll grant me but her to sooth
me awake.
More sweet, &c.

**JUNO:** My Will obey,
She shall be thine.
Thou, with thy softer Pow'rs,
first Jove shall captivate:
To Morpheus then give order,
Thy various Minister,
That with a Dream in Shape of Semele,
But far more beautiful,
And more alluring,
He may invade the sleeping Deity;
And more to agitate
His kindling Fire,
Still let the Phantom seem
To fly before him,
That he may wake impetuous,
Furious in Desire,
Unable to refuse whatever Boon
Her Coyness shall require.

**SOMN:** I tremble to comply.

**JUNO:** To me thy leaden Rod resign,
To charm the Centinels
On Mount Citheron,
Then cast a Sleep on mortal Ino:
That I may seem her Form to wear,
When I to Semele appear.

**DUET:**

**JUNO:** Obey my Will, they Rod resign,
And Pasithea shall be thine.

**SOMN:** All I must grant, for all is due
To Pasithea, Love, and You.
[*Exeunt.*]

### *SCENE II.*

*An Apartment. Semele alone.*

**SONG:**
My racking Thoughts by no kind
Slumbers freed,
But painful Nights do joyful Days
succeed.

### *SCENE III.*

*To her enter Juno as Ino, with a
Mirrour in her Hand.*

**JUNO:** (*apart.*) Thus shaped like
Ino,
With Ease I shall deceive her,
And in this Mirrour she shall see
Herself as much transformed as me.
(*To Semele.*) Do I some Goddess
see!
Or is it Semele?

**SEMELE:** Dear Sister, speak,
Whence this Astonishment?

**JUNO:** Your Charms improving
To Divine Perfection,
Shew you were late admitted
Amongst Celestial Beauties.
Has Jove consented?
And are you made Immortal?

**SEMELE:** Ah! no, I still am Mortal,
Nor am I sensible
Of any Change, or new Perfection.

**ARIOSO:**
(*Juno giving her the Glass.*)
Behold in this Mirrour
Whence comes my Surprize,
Such Lustre and Terror
Unite in your Eyes;
That mine cannot fix on a Radiance
so bright,
'Tis unsafe for the Sense, and too
slipp'ry for Sight.

**SEMELE:** O Ecstacy of Happiness
Celestial Graces
I discover in each Feature!

**SONG:**
Myself I shall adore,
If I persist in gazing;
No Object sure before
Was ever half so pleasing.

**JUNO:** Be wife, as you are beautiful,
Nor lose this Opportunity.
When Jove appears
All ardent with Desire,
Refuse his proferred Flame
'Till you obtain a Boon without a
Name.

**SEMELE:** Can that avail me?
But how shall I attain
To Immortality?

**RECITATIVE:** (*accompanied*)

**JUNO:** Conjure him by his Oath
Not to approach your Bed
In Likeness of a Mortal;
But like himself, the mighty Thunderer,
In Pomp of Majesty,
And heav'nly Attire;
As when he proud Saturnia charms,
And with ineffable Delights
Fills her encircling Arms,
And pays the Nuptial Rites,
You shall partake then of Immortality,
And thenceforth leave this Mortal
State
To reign above
Adored by Jove,
In spite of jealous Juno's Hate.

**SONG:**

**SEMELE:** Thus let my Thanks be
paid,
Thus let my Arms embrace thee;
And when I'm a Goddess made,
With Charms like mine I'll grace
thee.

**JUNO:** Rich Odours fill the fragrant
Air,
And Jove's Approach declare.
I must retire—

**SEMELE:** Adieu—your Counsel I'll
pursue.

**JUNO:** (*apart.*) And sure Destruction will ensue.
Vain wretched Fool—
Adieu.—
(*Exit.*)

## SCENE IV.

*Enter Jupiter to Semele.*

**SONG:**

**JUPITER:** Come to my Arms, my
lovely Fair,
Sooth my uneasy Care:
In my Dream late I wooed thee,
And in vain I pursued thee,
For you fled from my Pray'r,
And bid me despair.
—O Semele
Why art thou thus insensible?

**SONG:**
Semele. I ever am granting,
You always complain;
I always am wanting,
Yet never obtain.

**JUPITER:** Speak, speak your Desire,
Say what you require,
I'll grant it—

**SEMELE:** Swear by the Stygian Lake.

**RECITATIVE:** (*accompanied.*)

**JUPITER:** By that tremendous
Flood, I swear,
Ye Stygian Waters, hear;
And thou, Olympus, shake,
In Witness to the Oath I take.
(*Thunder is heard at a distance,
and underneath.*)

**SEMELE:** You'll grant what I require.

**JUPITER:** I'll grant what you require.

**SEMELE:** Then cast off this human
Shape which you wear,
And Jove since you are, like Jove too
appear.

**ACCOMPANIED:**

**JUPITER:** Ah, take heed what you
press,
For, beyond all Redress,
Should I grant your Request I shall
harm you.

**SONG:**

**SEMELE:** No no! I'll take no less
Than all in full Excess;
Your Oath it may alarm you,
Yet haste and prepare,
For I'll know what you are,
With all your Powers arm you.
No no! &c.
(*Exit.*)

## SCENE V.

*Jupiter pensive and dejected.*

**RECITATIVE:** (*accompanied.*)
Ah! whither is she gone! unhappy
Fair!
Why did she wish?—why did I rashly swear?
'Tis past, 'tis past recall,
She must a Victim fall.
Anon when I appear
The mighty Thunderer,
Armed with inevitable Fire,

She needs must instantly expire,
'Tis past, &c.
My softest Lightning yet I'll try,
And mildest melting Bolt apply;
In vain—for she was framed to
prove
None but the lambent Flames of
Love.
'Tis past, &c.

## SCENE VI.

*Juno alone.*
**SONG:**
Above measure
Is the Pleasure
Which my Revenge supplies.
Love's a Bubble
Gained with Trouble,
And in possessing dies.
With what Joy shall I mount to my
Heav'n again,
At once from my Rival and Jealousy
freed!
The Sweets of Revenge make it
worth while to reign,
And Heav'n will hereafter be
Heav'n indeed.
Above measure, &c.

## SCENE VII.

*The Scene discovers Semele under
a Canopy, leaning pensively: She
looks up, and sees Jupiter descending in a Cloud: Flashes of
Lightning issue from either side,
and Thunder is heard.*

**RECITATIVE:** (*accompanied.*)
Ah me! too late I now repent
My Pride and impious Vanity.
He comes! far off his Lightning
scorch me.
—I feel my Life consuming:
I burn, I burn, I faint, for Pity I implore—
O help, O help—I can no more—
(*She dies.*)
The Cloud bursts, and Semele with
the Palace instantly disappear.

## SCENE VIII.

*Cadmus, Athamas, Ino, and Chorus of Priests.*
**INO:** Of my ill-boding Dream
Behold the dire Event.
**ALL:** O Terror and Astonishment!

**CHORUS:**
Nature to each allots his proper
Sphere,
But that forsaken, we like Meteors
err:
Tossed thro' the Void, by some rude
shock we're broke,
And all out boasted Fire is lost in
smoke.

**INO:** How I was hence removed,
Or hither how returned, I know
not:
So long a Trance withheld me.
But Hermes in a Vision told me
(As I have now related)
The Fate of Semele;
And added, as from me he fled,
That Jove ordained I Athamas
should wed.

**CADM:** Be Jove in ev'ry thing
obeyed. (*Joins their Hands.*)

**ATHA:** Unworthy of your Charms
myself I yield;
Be Jove's Commands and your's fulfilled.

**SONG:**
Despair no more shall wound me,
Since you so kind do prove;
All Joy and Bliss surround me,
My Soul is tuned to Love.
Despair no more, &c.

**CADM:** See from above the bellying
Clouds descend,
And big with some new wonder this
way tend.

## SCENE THE LAST.

*A bright Cloud descends and rests
on Mount Citheron, which opening, discovers Apollo seated in it
as the God of Prophesy.*

**RECITATIVE:** (*accompanied.*)

**APOLLO:** Apollo comes to relieve
your Care,
And Future Happiness declare.
From Semele's Ashes a Phœnix shall
rise,
The Joy of this Earth, and Delight of
the Skies;
A God He shall prove
More mighty than Love,
And Sighing and Sorrow for ever
present.

**CHORUS:**
Happy, happy shall we be,
Free from Care, from Sorrow free;
Guiltless Pleasures we'll enjoy,
Virtuous Love will never cloy;
All that's Good and Just we'll
prove,
And Bacchus crown the Joys of
Love.

*FINIS.*

# Hänsel und Gretel (1893)

## Hansel and Gretel

MUSIC BY ENGLEBERT HUMPERDINCK ■ LIBRETTO BY ADELHEID WETTE

---

This three-act musical fairy story (*märchenspeil*), set to a libretto by Adelheid Wette, Humperdinck's sister, is based on a story by the Brothers' Grimm. It premiered at the Hoftheater in Weimar on December 23, 1893. In a poor hut, Hänsel and Gretel are supposed to be doing chores. Their mother, Gertrude, yells at them when she sees them sitting by the fire. In anger, she knocks over a jug of milk, their only food for dinner. She sends them into the woods to pick strawberries instead. Peter, their father, comes home from work drunk as always, but with an armload of food. He is upset when he hears that the children are in the woods because a wicked witch who eats children lives there. Gertrude and Peter rush off to look for Hänsel and Gretel.

The children have picked plenty of strawberries but are afraid to go home because they've eaten them all. The Sandman sprinkles sand in their eyes; they say their prayers and go to sleep, guarded by angels. The next morning, they see the witch's house, made of marzipan and sugar, in the distance. Enticed, they make their approach. The witch captures them and forces Gretel to set the table while she fattens Hänsel up for dinner. Gretel seizes the witch's magic wand and frees Hänsel from his cage. As they push the witch into the oven and close the door, the house collapses, and a group of children appear, singing their thank-yous to Hänsel and Gretel for saving them. Their parents arrive just in time to find the children preparing to eat the witch, who they have baked into a gigantic cake.

---

## ■ ERSTES BILD

*DAHEIM*

### ERSTE SCENE

*Dürftige Stube. Im Hintergrunde rechts eine niedrige Thür, in der Mitte ein kleines Fenster mit Aussicht in den Wald. Links ein Herd mit einem Rauchfang darüber. As den rechten Wand hängen Besen in verschiedenen Formen. Hänsel an der Thüre mit Besenbinden, Gretel, am Herde, stricken beschäftigt, sitzen einander gegenüber.*

**GRETEL:** Suse, liebe Suse, was raschelt im Stroh?
Die Gänse gehn barfuss und haben kein' Schuh.
Der Schuster hat's Leder, kein'n Leisten dazu.
Drum kann er den Gänslein auch machen kein' Schuh.

**HÄNSEL:** Eia popeia, das ist eine Not!
Wer schenkt mir einen Dreier zu Zucker und Brot?
Verkauf ich mein Bettlein und leg mich auf's Stroh, sticht mich keine Feder und beisst mich kein Floh!
Ach, käm doch die Mutter nun endlich nach Haus!

**GRETEL:** Auch ich halt's kaum noch vor Hunger aus

## ■ ACT I

*AT HOME*

### SCENE I

*(A small and poorly furnished room. In the background a door; a small window near it, looking on to the forest. On the left a fireplace with chimney above it. On the walls are hanging brooms of various sizes. Hansel is sitting by the door, making brooms, and Gretel opposite him by the fireplace, knitting a stocking.*

**GRETEL:** Susy, little Susy, pray what is the news?
The geese are running barefoot, because they've no shoes!
The cobbler has leather, and plenty to spare,
Why can't he make the poor goose a new pair?

**HÄNSEL:** Then they'll have to go barefoot!
Eia-popeia, pray what's to be done?
Who'll give me milk and sugar, for bread I have none?
I'll go back to bed and I'll lie there all day;
Where there's nought to eat, then there's nothing to pay!

**GRETEL:** Then we'll have to go hungry!

**HÄNSEL:** Seit Wochen nichts als trocken Brot;
ist das ein Elend! Potz schwere Not!

**GRETEL:** Still, Häsel, denk daran, was Vater sagt
wenn Mutter manchmal so verzagt:
Wenn die Not auf's höchste steigt, Gott der Herr die Hand euch reicht!''

**HÄNSEL:** Jawohl, das klingt ganz schön und glatt,
aber leider wird man davon nicht satt.
Ach, Gretel, wie lang' ist's doch schon her, das wir nichts Gutes geschmauset mehr!
Eierfladen und Butterwecken—kaum weiss ich noch, wie die thun schmecken.
Ach, Gretel, ich wollt' . . .

**GRETEL:** Still, nicht verdriesslich sein:
Gedulde dich fein, sieh freundlich drein!
Dies lange Gesicht,—hu, welcher Graus!
Siehst ja wie der leibhaftige Griesgram aus!
Griesgram, hinaus!
Fort aus dem Haus!
Ich will dich lehren,
Herz zu beschweren,
Sorgen zu mehren,
Freuden zu wehren:
Griesgram, Griesgram, greulicher

**HÄNSEL:** If mother would only come home again!
Yes, I am so hungry,
I don't know what to do!
For weeks I've eaten nothing but bread—
It's very hard, it is indeed!

**GRETEL:** Hush, Hänsel, don't forget what father said,
when mother, too, wished she were dead:
"When past bearing is our grief,
The Lord God, will send relief!"

**HÄNSEL:** Yes, yes, that sounds all very fine,
but of course off maxims we cannot dine!
O Gretel, it would be such a treat if we had something nice to eat!
Eggs and butter and suet paste,
I've almost forgotten how they taste.
O Gretel, I wish—

**GRETEL:** Hush, don't give way to grumps;
have patience awhile, no doleful dumps!
This woeful face, whew! what a sight!
Looks like a horrid old crosspatch fright!
Crosspatch, away!
Leave me, I pray!
Just let me reach you
how to make trouble,
soon mount to double!
Crosspatch, crosspatch,

Wicht,
griesiges, grämiges Galgengesicht,
packe dich, trolle dich, schäbiger
Wicht!

**HÄNSEL:** Griesgram, hinaus!
Halt's nicht mehr aus!
Immer mich plagen,
Hungertuch nagen,
muss ja verzagen,
mag's nicht ertragen!
Griesgram, Griesgram, greulicher
Wicht,
griesiges, grämiges Galgengesicht,
packe dich, trolle dich, schäbiger
Wicht!

**GRETEL:** So recht! Und willst du
nun nicht mehr klagen,
so will ich dir such ein Geheimnis
sagen.

**HÄNSEL:** Ein Geheimnis? Wird
wohl was Rechtes sein!

**GRETEL:** Ja, hör nur, Brüderchen!
Darfst dich schon freun,
Guck her in den Topf, Milch ist darin,
die schenkte uns heute die Nachba-
rin.
Mutter kocht uns, kommt sie nach
Haus,
gewiss einen leckeren Reisbrei daraus.

**HÄNSEL:** Reisbrei, Reisbrei, herr-
licher Brei!
Giebt's Reisbrei, da ist Hänsel da-
bei!
Wie dick ist der Rahm auf der
Milch! Lass schmecken!
Herrjemine, den möcht' ich ganz
verschlecken!
Wie, Hänsel, naschen? Schämst du
dich nicht?

**GRETEL:** Fort mit den Fingern, du
naschhafter Wicht!
(*Giebt ihm eins auf die Finger.*)
Und jetzt an die Arbeit zurück,
geschwind,
dass wir beizeiten fertig sind!
Kommt Muter heim, und wir thaten
nicht recht,
Dann, weisst du, geht es den Faul-
pelzen schlecht.

**HÄNSEL:** Arbeiten? Brr! Wo denkst
du hin?
Danach steht mir jetzt nicht der
Sinn.
Immer mich plagen, das fällt mir
nicht ein,
jetzt lass uns tanzen und fröhlich
sein!

**GRETEL:** (*Entzückt.*) Tanzen? Das
wär' auch mir eine Lust!
Dazu ein Liedchen aus froher Brust,
Wie's uns die Muhme gelehrt zu
singen:
Tanzliedchen soll jetzt lustig
erklingen!
(*Klatscht in die Hände.*)

what is the use,
growling and grumbling,
full of abuse?
Off with you, out with you,
shame on you, goose!

**HÄNSEL:** Crosspatch away!
Hard lines, I say.
When I am hungry,
surely I can say so,
cannot allay so,
can't chase away so!

**GRETEL:** If I am hungry,
I'll never say so,
will not give way so,
chase it away so!
that's right. Now, if you leave off
complaining,
I'll tell you a most delightful secret!

**HÄNSEL:** O delightful! it must be
something nice!

**GRETEL:** Well, listen, brother-
kin—won't you be glad!
Look here in the jug, here is fresh
milk,
It was given today by our neighbor,
and mother, when she comes back
home,
will certainly make us a rice-blancmange.

**HÄNSEL:** Rice-blancmange!
When blancmange is anywhere
near,
then Hänsel, Hänsel, Hänsel, is
there!
How thick is the cream on the milk;
let's taste it! O Gemini!
wouldn't I like to drink it!

**GRETEL:** What, Hänsel, tasting?
Aren't you ashamed?
Out with your fingers quick,
greedy boy!
(*Gives him a rap on the fingers.*)
Get back to your work again, be
quick,
that we may both have done in time!
If mother comes and we haven't
done right,
then badly it will fare with us tonight!

**HÄNSEL:** Work again? No, not for
me!
That's not my idea at all;
It doesn't suit me! It's such a bore!
Dancing is jollier far, I'm sure!

**GRETEL:** (*Delighted.*) Dancing,
dancing! O yes, that's better far;
and sing a song to keep us in time!
One that our grandmother used to
sing us;
sing then, and dance in time to the
singing!
(*Claps her hands*)

Brüderchen, komm, tanz' mit mir,
beide Händchen reich' ich Dir; einmal hin, einmal her,
rund herum, es ist nicht schwer!

**HÄNSEL:** Tanzen soll ich armer
Wicht,
Schwesterlein, und kann es nicht.
Darum zeig' mir, wie es Brauch,
dass ich tanzen lerne auch!

**GRETEL:** Mit den Füsschen tapp
tapp tapp,
mit den Händchen klapp klapp
klapp,
einmal hin, einmal her,
rund herum, es ist nicht schwer.

**HÄNSEL:** Mit den Füsschen tapp
tapp tapp
mit den Händchen klapp klapp
klapp,
einmal hin, einmal her,
rund herun, es ist nicht schwer.

**GRETEL:** Ei, das hast Du gut gemacht,
ei, das hätt' ich nicht gedacht!
Seht mir doch den Hänsel an,
wie der tanzen lernen kann!
Mit dem Köpfchen nick nick nick,
mit den Fingerchen tick tick tick,
einmal hin, einmal her,
rund herum, es ist nicht schwer!

**HÄNSEL:** Mit dem Köpfehen nick
nick nick,
mit dem Fingerchen tick tick tick,
einmal hin, einmal her,
rund herun, es ist nicht schwer!

**GRETEL:** Hänsel, komm und gieb
mal acht,
wie's die Gretel weiter macht!
Lass uns Arm in Arm verschränken,
unsre Schrittchen paarweis lenken!
Ich liebe Tanz und Fröhlichkeit
und bin nicht gern allein;
ich bin kein Freund von Traurigkeit,
und fröhlich will ich sein.
Tralala, tralala, tralala la la,
Dreh dich herum, mein lieber
Hans!

**GRETEL:** Komm her zu mir, komm
her zu mir,
zum Ringelreigentanz!

**HÄNSEL:** Geh weg von mir, geh
weg von mir,
ich bin der stolze Hans!
Mit kleinen Mädchen tanz ich
nicht,
das ist mir viel zu dumm!

**GRETEL:** Geh, dummer Hans, geh,
stolzer Hans,
ich krieg dich doch herum!
Tralala, tralala, tralala la la,

Brother, come and dance with me,
both my hands I offer thee;
right foot first,
left foot then,
round about and back again!

**HÄNSEL:** I would dance, but don't
know how,
when to jump, and when to bow;'
show me what I ought to do,
so that I may dance like you.

**GRETEL:** With your foot you tap,
tap, tap;
with you hands you clap, clap,
clap;
right foot first,
left foot then,
round about and back again!

**HÄNSEL:** With your hands you
clap, clap, clap;
with your foot you tap, tap, tap;
right foot first,
left foot then,
round about and back again!

**GRETEL:** That was very good indeed,
O, I'm sure you'll soon succeed!
Try again, and I can see
Hänsel soon will dance like me!
With your head you nick, nick,
nick;
with your fingers you click, click,
click;
right foot first,
left foot then,
round about and back again.

**HÄNSEL:** With your head you nick,
nick, nick;
with your fingers you click, click,
click;
right foot first,
left foot then,
round about and back again!

**GRETEL:** Brother, watch what next
I do,
you must do it with me too.
You to me your arm must proffer,
I shall not refuse your offer!
Come!
What I enjoy is dance and jollity,
love to have my fling;
in fact, I like frivolity.
and all that kind of thing.
Tralala, tralala, tralala!
Come and have a twirl, my dearest
Hänsel,
come and have a turn with me, I
pray;
come here to me, come here to me,
I'm sure you can't say no!

**HÄNSEL:** Go away from me, go
away from me,
I'm much too proud for you:
with little girls I do not dance,
and so, my dear, adieu!

**GRETEL:** Go, stupid Hans, conceit-
ed Hans,
you'll see I'll make you dance!
Tralala, tralala, tralala!

dreh dich herum, mein lieber Hans!

**HÄNSEL:** Ach, Schwesterlein, ach, Gretelein,
Du hast im Strumpf ein Loch!

**GRETEL:** Ach Brüderlein, ach Hänselein,
Du willst mich hänseln noch!
Mit bösen Buben tanz ich nicht,
das ist mir viel zu dumm!

**HÄNSEL:** Nicht böse sein, lieb Schwesterlein,
ich krieg Dich doch herum!
Tralala, tralala, tralala, la la,
Dreh dich doch herum, mein Gretelein!

**HÄNSEL:** Tanz lustig, heissa, lustig tanz! Lass dich's nicht gereu'n;
und ist der Strumpf auch nicht mehr ganz,
die Mutter strickt dir 'n neu'n! Dreh dich doch herum! Sei nicht so dumm! Tralala, tralala u. s. w.

**GRETEL:** Tanz lustig, heiss, lustig tanz! Lass dich's nicht gereu'n;
und ist der Schuh' auch nicht mehr ganz,
der Schuster flickt dir 'n neu'n! Dreh dich doch herum! Sei nicht so dumm! Tralala, tralala u. s. w.
*(Dann fassen sie sich bei den Haenden und drehen sich immer schneller im Kreise, bis sie schliesslich das Gleichgewicht verlieren und uebereinander auf den Boden hinpurzeln. In diesem Augenblicke geht die Thuere auf; die Mutter wird sichtbar, worauf die Kinder schnell vom Boden aufspringen.)*

## ZWEITE SCENE

**MUTTER:** Holla!

**HÄNSEL UND GRETEL:** Himmel, die Mutter!

**MUTTER:** Was ist das für eine Geschichte?

**GRETEL:** Der Hänsel . . .

**HÄNSEL:** Die Gretel . . .

**MUTTER:** *(In Zorn ausbrechend.)*
Wartet, ihr ungezogenen Wichte!
Nennt ihr das Arbeit? Johlen und singen?
Wie auf der Kirmes tanzen und springen?
Indes die Eltern vom frühen Morgen
bis spät in die Nacht sich mühen und sorgen?
Dass dich!
*(Giebt Hänseln einen Puff.)*
Lässt seh'n, was habt ihr beschickt?
Wie, Gretel, den Strumpf nicht fertig gestrickt?
Und du?—Du, Schlingel! In all den

Come and have a twirl, my dearest Hänsel,
come and have a turn with me, I pray!

**HÄNSEL:** O Gretel dear, O sister dear,
your stocking has a hole!

**GRETEL:** O Hänsel dear, O brother dear,
do you take me for a fool?
With naughty boys I do not dance,
and so, my dear, adieu!

**HÄNSEL:** Now don't be cross.
you silly goose,
you'll see I make you dance!

**GRETEL:** Tralala, tralala, tralala!
Come and have a twirl, my dearest Hänsel,
come and have a turn with me, I pray.
Sing lustily hurrah! hurrah!
While I dance with you;
and if the stockings are in holes,
why mother'll knit some new!

**HÄNSEL:** Tralala, tralala, tralala!
Sing lustily hurrah! hurrah!
while I dance with you;
and if the shoes are all in holes,
why mother'll buy some new!
tralala, tralala, tralala!
*(They dance round each other as before. They then seize each other's hands and go round in a circle, quicker and quicker, until at last they lose their balance and tumble over one another on the floor. Suddenly the door opens, the mother appears and the children jump up.)*

## SCENE II

**MOTHER:** Hallo!

**HÄNSEL AND GRETEL:** Heavens! Here's mother!

**MOTHER:** What is all this disturbance?

**GRETEL:** It was Hänsel, he wanted—

**HÄNSEL:** It was Gretel, she said I—

**MOTHER:** Silence, idle and ill-behaved children!
*(The mother comes in, unstraps the basket, and puts it down.)*
You call it working, yodelling and singing? As though it were fair time, hopping and springing!
And while your parents from early morning
Are slaving and toiling till late at night!
Take that!
*(Gives Hänsel a box on the ear.)*
Now come, let's see what you've done.
Why, Gretel, your stocking not

Stunden
nicht mal die wenigen Besen gebunden?
Ihr unnützigen Kinder! Den Stock will ich holen,
den Faulpelz werd' ich euch beiden versohlen!
*(In ihrem Eifer hinter den Kindern her stösst sie den Milchtopf vom Tisch, das erklirrend zu Boden fallt.)*
Jesses! Nun auch den Topf noch zerbrochen!
*(Weinend.)*
Was soll ich nun zum Abend kochen?
*(Besieht ihren mit Milch begossenen Rock; Hänsel kichert verstohlen.)*
Was, Bengel, du lachst mich noch aus?
*(Mit dem Stock hinter Hans her, der zur offenen Thür hinausrennt.)*
Wart, kommt nur der Vater nach Haus—
*(Reist einen kleinen Korb von der Wand und drängt ihn Gretel in die Hand.)*
Marsch, fort-in den Wald!
dort sucht mir Erdbeeren!—Nun, wird es bald?
*(Treibt auch Gretel zur Stube hinaus und droht mit dem Stocke den sich furchtsam umschauenden Kindern.)*
Und bringt ihr den Korb nicht voll bis zum Rand,
so hau ich euch, dass ihr fliegt an die Wand!
*(Setzt sich erschöpft an den Tisch.)*
Da liegt nun der gute topf in Scherben!
Ja, blinder Eifer bringt immer Verderben.—
Herrgott, wirf Geld herab! Nichts hab' ich zu leben,
kein Krümchen den Würmern zu essen zu geben;
kein Tröpfchen im Topfe, kein Krüstchen im Schrank,
schon lange nichts als Wasser zum Trank
*(Stützt den Kopf mit der Hand.)*
Müde bin ich—müde zum Sterben—
Herrgott, wirf Geld herab—
*(Legt den Kopf auf den Arm und schläft ein.)*

## DRITTE SCENE

*Man hört eine Stimime von weitem:)*

Ach, wir armen, armen Leute!
Alle Tage so wie heute: In dem Beutel ein grosses Loch und im Magen ein gröss'res noch—
Rallalala, rallalala,
Hunger ist der beste Koch!
*(Am Fenster wird der Kopf des Vaters sichtbar, der während des Folgenden in angeheitertem Zu-*

ready yet?
And you, you lazybones, have you nothing to show?
Pray how many brooms have you finished?
I'll fetch my stick, you useless children,
and make your idle fingers tingle!
*(In her anger at the children she gives the milk-jug a push, and it smashes.)*
Gracious! there's goes the jug all to pieces!
What now can I cook for supper?
*(She looks at her skirt, down which the milk is streaming. Hänsel covertly titters.)*
How saucy, how dare you laugh?
*(Going with a stick after Hänsel, who is running out of the open door.)*
Wait, wait till the father comes home!
*(She snatches a basket from the wall, and pushes it into Gretel's hands.)*
Off, off, to the woods!
There seek for strawberries! Quick, away!
And if you don't bring the basket back full,
I'll whip you so that you'll both run away!
*(The children run off into the forest. She sits down exhausted by the table.)*
Alas! there my poor jug lies all in pieces!
Yes, blind excitement only brings ruin.
O Heaven, send help to me!
I have nothing to give them—
*(Sobbing.)*
No bread, not a crumb, for my starving children!
No crust in the cupboard, no milk in the pot—
*(Resting her head on her hands.)*
Weary am I, weary of living!
Father, send help to me!
*(Lays her head down on her arm and drops to sleep.)*

## SCENE III

*(A voice is heard in the distance.)*

Tralala, tralala! little mother, here am I!
Tralala, tralala! bringing luck and jollity!
O, for you and me, poor mother, every day is like the other;
with a big hole in the purse, and one in the stomach, even worse.

*stande mit einem Kober auf dem Rücken in die Stube tritt.)*
Ja, ihr Reichen könnt euch laben!
Wir, die nichts zu essen haben,
nagen, ach, die ganze Woch'
sieben Tag an einem Knoch'!
Rallalala, rallalala,
Hunger ist der beste Koch!
Ach, wir sind ja gern zufrieden,
denn das Glück ist so verschieden,
aber, aber wahr ist's doch:
Armut ist ein schweres Joch!
Rallalala, rallalala,
Hunger ist der beste Koch!
*(Er setzt seinen Kober nieder und tritt an die Rampe.)*
Ja ja, der Hunger kocht schon gut,
sofern er kommandieren thut.
Allein was nutzt der Kommandör,
fehlt euch im Topf die Zubehör?
Rallalala, rallalala,
Kümmel ist mein Leiblikör!
Rallalala, rallalala,
Mutter, schau, was ich bescheer!
*(Giebt ihr einen derben Schmatz.)*

**MUTTER:** *(Sich die Augen reibend.)* Hoho!—
Wer spek—spektakelt
mir da im Haus
und rallalakelt
aus dem Schlaf mich heraus?

**VATER:** *(Lallend.)* Das tolle Tier,
im Magen hier,
das bellte so, das glaube mir!
Rallalala, rallalala,
Hunger ist ein tolles Tier.
Rallalala, rallalala,
beisst und kratzt, das glaube mir!

**MUTTER:** So, so!
Das tolle Tier,
es ist wohl schier
stark angezecht—das glaube mir!

**VATER:** Nun ja, 's war heut ein heitrer Tag!
Fondst du nicht such, lieb' Weib?

**MUTTER:** *(Ärgerlich.)* Ach geh!
Du weisst, nicht leiden mag
ich Wirtshaus-Zeitvertreib!

**VATER:** Auch gut! So sehen wir,
wenn's beliebt,
was es für heut zu schmausen giebt.

**MUTTER:** Höchst einfach ist das Speiseregister.
der Abendschmaus—zum Henker ist er!
Teller leer,
Keller leer,
und im Beutel ist gar nichts mehr.

---

Tralala, tralala!
Hunger is the poor man's curse!
Tralala, tralala!
Hunger is the poor man's curse!
*(The father appears at the window, and during the following he comes into the room in a very happy mood, with a basket on his back.)*
It isn't much that we require;
just a little food and fire!
But alas! it's true enough,
life on some of us is rough!
Hunger is a customer tough!
Yes, the rich enjoy their dinner,
while the poor grow daily thinner!
Strive to eat, as well he may,
somewhat less than yesterday!
Tralala, tralala.
hunger is the devil to pay!
tralala, tralala!
hunger is the devil to pay!
*(He puts down his basket.)*
Yes, hunger's all very well to feel,
if you can get a good square meal;
but when there's nothing, what can you do,
supposing the purse be empty too?
Tralala, tralala!
O for a drop of mountain dew!
Tralala, tralala!
Mother, look what I have brought!
*(Reels over to his sleeping wife and gives her a smacking kiss.)*

**MOTHER:** *(Rubbing her eyes.)* Oho!—
Who's sing-sing-singing
all around the house,
and tra-la-la-ing me
out of my sleep?

**FATHER:** *(Inarticulately.)* How now!—
The hungry beast
within my breast
called so for food
I could not rest!
Tralala, tralala!
Hunger is an urgent beast!
Tralala, Tralala!
pinches, gnaws, and gives no rest!

**MOTHER:** So, so!
And this wild beast,
you gave him a feast.
He's had his fill,
to say the least!

**FATHER:** Well, yes! It was a lovely day,
don't you think so, dear wife?

**MOTHER:** *(Angrily.)* Oh Please!
You have no troubles to bear,
it is I must keep the house!

**FATHER:** Well, well,—then let us see, my dear,
what we have got to eat today.

**MOTHER:** Most simple is the bill of fare,
our supper's gone, I know not where!
Larder bare, cellar bare,
nothing, and plenty of it to spare!

---

**VATER:** Rallalala, rallalala,
lustig, Mutter, bin auch noch da!
Rallalala, rallalala,
bringe Glück und Gloria!
*(Nimmit den Kober und kramt aus.)*
Schau, Mutter!
Wie gefällt Dir dies Futter?

**MUTTER:** Mann, was seh' ich?
Speck und Butter!
Mehl und Würst! . . . vierzehn Eier—
—Mann! Sie sind jetztunder teuer!—
Bohnen, Zwiebeln und—herrjeh!
Gar ein viertel Pfund Kaffee!

**VATER:** Rallalala, hopsassa!
Heute woll'n wir lustig sein!
Ja, hör nur, Mütterchen, wie's geschah!
*(Er setzt sich nieder, die Mutter kramt inzwischen die Sachen ein, zuendet Feuer im Herd an, schlaegt Eier in eine Pfanne u.s.w.)*
Drüben hinterm Herrenwald
prächt'ge Feste giebt's da bald,
Kirmes, Hochzeit, Jubiläum,
Böllerknall und gross Tedeum.
Mein Geschäft kommt nun zur Blüte;
dessen froh sei Dein Gemüte!
Sieh! wer feines Fest will felern,
der muss kehren, schrubben und scheuern.
Bot drum meine Waren aus,
zog damit von Haus zu Haus:
"Kauft Besen! Gute Feger!
Feine Bürsten! Spinnejäger!"
Sieh, da verkauft' ich massenweise
meine Waren zum höchsten Preise!—
Schnell nun her mit Topf und Pfanne,
her mit Kessel, Schüssel, Kanne!

**MUTTER:** Vivat hoch die Besenbinder!

**VATER:** Doch halt—wo bleiben die Kinder?
Hänsel! Gretel!—Wo steckt der Hans?

**MUTTER:** Wo er steckt? Ja, wüsste man's!
Nur das weiss ich klar wie Tag,
dass der Topf in Scherben lag!

**VATER:** *(Zornig.)* Was? der neue Topf entzwei?

**MUTTER:** Und am Boden quoll der Brei!

**VATER:** *(Mit der Faust auf den Tisch schlagend.)* Donnerkeil! So haben die Rangen
Unfug wieder angefangen?

**MUTTER:** Unfug viel und Arbeit keine
hatten sie getrieben alleine.
Hörte schon draussen sie juchzen

---

**FATHER:** Tralalala, tralalala!
Cheer up, mother, for here I am,
bringing luck and jollity!
*(He takes his basket and begins to display the contents.)*
Look, mother, doesn't all this food please you?

**MOTHER:** Man, what do I see?
Ham and butter,
flour and sausage—
eggs, a dozen . . .
(Husband, and they cost a fortune!)
Turnips, onions, and—for me!
Nearly half a pound of tea!

**FATHER:** Tralala, tralala,
hip hurrah!
Won't we have a festive time!
Tralala, hip hurrah!
Won't we have a happy time!
Now listen how it all came to pass!
*(Sits down. Meanwhile the mother packs away the things, lights a fire, breaks eggs into a saucepan, etc.)*
Yonder to the town I went,
there was to be a great event,
weddings, fairs, and preparation
for all kinds of jubilation!
Now's my chance to do some selling,
and for that you may be thankful!
He who wants a feast to keep,
he must scrub and brush and sweep.
So I brought my best goods out,
tramped with them from house to house:
"Buy! good! brooms!
Buy my brushes! sweep your carpets,
sweep your cobwebs!"
And so I drove a roaring trade,
and sold my brushes at the highest prices!
Now make haste with cup and platter,
bring the glasses, bring the kettle—
here's a health to the broom-maker!

**MOTHER:** Here's a health to the broom-maker!

**FATHER:** But stay, why, where are the children?
Hänsel, Gretel, what's gone with Hans?

**MOTHER:** Gone with Hans? O, who's to know?
But at least I do know this,
that the jug is smashed to bits.

**FATHER:** What! the jug is smashed to bits?

**MOTHER:** And the cream all run away.

**FATHER:** *(Striking his fist on the table in a rage.)* Hang it all! So those little scapegraces have been again in mischief!

**MOTHER:** Been in mischief? I should think so!
Nothing have they done but their mad pranking;

und johlen,
hopsen und springen wie wilde Fohlen,
wusste nicht, wie mir stand der Kopf.
Und vor Zorn

VATER: —zerbrach der Topf. Hahahaha!
(*Beside lachen aus vollem Halse.*)
Na, Zornmütterchen, nimm mir's nicht, krumm,
solche Zorntöpfe find' ich recht dumm!.
Doch sag, wo mögen die Kinderchen sein?

MUTTER: (*Schnippisch.*) Meinethalben am Ilsenstein!

VATER: (*Erschrocken.*) Am Ilsenstein?—Ei, juckt Dich das Fell?
(*Nimmt einen Besen von der Wand.*)

MUTTER: Den Besen lass nur an seiner Stell.

VATER: (*Lässt den Besen fallen und ringt die Hände.*) Wenn sie sich verirrten im Walde dort,
in der Nacht, ohne Stern und Mond!
Kennst Du nicht den schauerlich düstern Ort?
Weisst nicht, dass die Böse dort wohnt?

MUTTER: Die Böse? Wen meinst Du?

VATER: (*Mit geheimnisvollem Nachdruck.*) Die Knusperhexe!—

MUTTER: (*Fährt zusammen.*) Die Knusperhexe!—
Mein! Sag doch, was soll denn der Besen!

VATER: Der Besen! Der Besen!
Was macht man damit? Was macht man damit?
Es reiten drauf, es reiten drauf die Hexen!
Eine Hex' steinalt,
haust tief im Wald,
vom Teufel selber hat sie Gewalt!
Um Mitternacht,
wann niemand wacht,
dann reitet sie aus zur Hexenjagd,
Zum Schornstein hinaus
auf dem Besen, o Graus!
Braus!
Über Berg und Kluft,
Über Thal und Gruft
durch Nebelduft
im Sturm durch die Luft:
Ja so reiten, ja so reiten,
juchheissa, die Hexen!

MUTTER: Entsetzlich!

VATER: Ja, bei Tag, o Graus:
zum Hexenschmaus
ins Knisper-Knasper-Knusperhaus
die Kinderlein,
Armsünderlein,
mit Zauberkuchen lockt sie herein.
Doch übelgesinnt
ergreift sie geschwind
das arme Kuchen knuspernde Kind.

as I came home I could hear them hopping and cutting the wildest capers,
till I was so cross that I gave a push—
and the jug of milk was spilt!

FATHER: And the jug of milk was spilt!
Ha ha ha ha!
(*Both laughing.*)
Such anger, mother, don't take it ill,
seems stupid to me, I must say!
But where, where think you the children can be?

MOTHER: (*Snappishly and curtly.*) For all I know, at the Ilsenstein!

FATHER: (*Horror-struck.*) The Ilsenstein! Come, come, have a care!
(*Fetches a broom from the wall.*)

MOTHER: The broom, just put it away again!

FATHER: (*Lets the broom fall and wrings his hands.*) My children astray in the gloomy wood,
all alone without moon or stars!
Do you not know the awful magic place,
the place where the evil one dwells?

MOTHER: The evil one! What do you mean?

FATHER: (*With mysterious emphasis.*) The gobbling ogress!
(*The mother draws back, the father takes up the broom again.*)

MOTHER: The gobbling ogress!
But—tell me, what help is the broom!

FATHER: The broom the broom, why what is it for?
They ride on it, they ride on it, the witches!
An old witch dwells within that wood and she's in league with the powers of hell!
At midnight hour, when nobody knows,
away to the witches' dance she goes.
Up the chimney they fly,
on a broomstick they hie—
over hill and dale,
o'er ravine and vale,
through the midnight air
they gallop full tear—
on a broomstick, on a broomstick,
hop hop, hop hop, the witches!

MOTHER: O horror!
But the gobbling witch?

FATHER: And by day, they say, she stalks around,
with a crinching, crunching, munching sound,
and children plump and tender to eat
she lures with magic gingerbread sweet.
On evil bent,

In den Ofen, hitzhell,
schiebt's die Hexe blitzschnell;
dann kommen zur Stell,
gebräunt das Fell,
aus dem Ofen, aus dem Ofen
die Lebkuchenkinder!

MUTTER: Und die Lebkuchenkinder?

VATER: Die werden gefressen!

MUTTER: Von der Hexe?

VATER: Von der Hexe.

MUTTER: (*Händeringend.*) O Graus!
Hilf, Himmel! die Kinder! Ich halt's nicht mehr aus!
(*Rennt aus dem Hause.*)

VATER: (*Nimmt die Kümmelflasche vom Tisch.*)
He, Alte, so wart' doch! Nimm mich mit!
Wir wollen ja beide zum Hexenritt!
(*Eilt ihr nach: Der Vorhang fällt schnell.*)

## ■ ZWEITES BILD

*IM WALDE*

### ERSTE SCENE

(*Im Hintergrunde der Ilsenstein, von dichtem Tannengehölz umgeben. Rechts eine mächtige Tanne; darunter sitzt Gretel auf einer moosbedeckten Wurzel und windet einen Kranz von Hagebutten; neben ihr liegt ein Blumenstrauss. Links, abseits im Gebüsch, Hänsel, nach Erdbeeren suchend. Abendrot.*)

GRETEL: Ein Männlein steht im Walde ganz still und stumm;
es hat von lauter Purpur ein Mäntlein um.
Sagt, wer mag das Männlein sein,
das da steht im Wald allein
mit dem purpurroten Mäntelein?
Das Männlein steht im Walde auf einem Bein
und hat auf seinem Kopfe schwarz Käpplein klein.
Sagt, wer mag das Männlein sein,
das da steht im Wald allein
mit dem kleinen schwarzen Käppelein?

HÄNSEL: (*Kommt hervor und schwenkt jubelnd sein Körbchen.*) Juchhe!
Mein Erbelkörbchen ist voll bis oben;
wie wird die Mutter den Hänsel loben!

with fell intent,
she lures the children, poor little things,
in the oven red-hot
she pops all the lot;
she shuts the lid down
until they're done brown,
in the oven, in the oven,
the gingerbread children!

MOTHER: And the gingerbread children?

FATHER: Are served up for dinner!

MOTHER: For the ogress?

FATHER: For the ogress!

MOTHER: O horror!
Heav'n help us! the children!
O what shall we do?
(*Runs out of the house*)

FATHER: Mother, mother, wait for me!
(*Takes the whiskey bottle from the table and runs after her.*)
We'll both go together to seek the witch!
(*The curtain falls quickly.*)

## ■ ACT II

*IN THE FOREST*

### SCENE I

(*The curtain rises. The middle of the forest. In the background is the Ilsenstein, thickly surrounded by fir-trees. On the right is a large fir-tree, under which Gretel is sitting on a mossy tree-trunk and making a garland of wild roses. By her side lies a nosegay of flowers. Amongst the bushes on the left is Hänsel, looking for strawberries. Sunset.*)

GRETEL: There stands a little man in the wood alone,
he wears a little mantle of velvet brown.
Say, who can the mankin be,
standing there beneath the tree,
with the little mantle of velvet brown?
His hair is all of gold, and his cheeks are red,
he wears a little black cap upon his head
Say, who can the mankin be,
standing there so silently,
with the little black cap upon his head?

HÄNSEL: (*Comes out, swinging his basket joyfully.*) Hurrah! my strawberry basket is nearly full!
O won't Mother be pleased with Hänsel!

GRETEL: Mein Kränzel ist auch schon fertig, sieh!
So schön wie heute ward's noch nie!
(*Will den Kranz Hänsel auf den Kopf setzen.*)

HÄNSEL: (*Barsch abwehrend.*) Buben tragen doch so was nicht, 's passt nur für ein Mädchengesicht.
(*Setzt ihr den Kranz auf.*)
Hei, Gretel, feins Mädel!
Ei, der Daus,
siehst ja wie die Waldkönigin aus!

GRETEL: Seh ich wie die Waldkönigin aus,
so reich' mir auch den Blumenstrauss!

HÄNSEL: Waldkönigin mit Scepter und Kron',
da nimm auch die Erbeln, doch nasch' nicht davon!
(*Reicht ihr das Körbchen voll Erdbeeren und hockt, gleichsam huldigend, vor ihr nieder. In diesem Augenblick hört er den Ruf eines Kuckucks.*)

HÄNSEL: Kuckuck! Eierschluck!

GRETEL: (*Schalkhaft.*) Kuckuck! Erbelschluck!
(*Nimmt eine Beere aus dem Körbchen und hält sie Hänsel hin, der sie schlürt, als ob er ein Ei austränke.*)

HÄNSEL: (*Springt auf.*) Hoho! Das kann ich auch! Gieb nur acht!
(*Nimmt einige Beeren und lässt sie Gretel in den Mund rollen.*)
Wir machen's, wie der Kuckuck schluckt,
wenn er in fremde Nester guckt,
(*Es beginnt zu dämmern.*)

HÄNSEL: (*Greift wieder zu.*) Kuckuck! Eierschluck!

GRETEL: (*Ebenso.*) Kuckuck! Erbelschluck!

HÄNSEL: Setzest Deine Kinder aus! Kuckuck!
Trinkst die fremden Eier aus! Gluckgluck!
(*Lässt sich eine ganze Handvoll Erdbeeren in den Mund rollen.*)

GRETEL: Sammelst Beeren schön zuhauf! Kuckuck!
Schluckst sie, Schlauer, selber auf! Schluckschluck!
(*Sie werden übermütiger und raufen sich schliesslich um die Beeren. Hänsel trägt den Sieg davon und setzt den Korb vollends an den Mund, bis er gänzlich leer geworden. Indessen hat die Dunkelheit immer mehr zugenommen.*)

GRETEL: (*Hänsel den Korb entreissend.*) Hänsel, was hast Du gethan! O Himmel!
Alle Erbeln gegessen, Du Lümmel!
Wart' nur, das giebt ein Strafge-

GRETEL: My garland is ready also! Look! I never made one so nice before!
(*Tries to put the wreath on Hänsel's head.*)

HÄNSEL: (*Drawing back roughly.*) You won't catch a boy wearing that!
It is only fit for a girl!
(*Puts the wreath on her.*)
Ha, Gretel, "Fine feathers!"
O the deuce!
You shall be the queen of the wood!

GRETEL: If I am to be queen of the wood,
then I must have the nosegay too!

HÄNSEL: Queen of the wood, with sceptre and crown,
I give you the strawberries, but don't eat them all!
(*He gives the basket full of strawberries into her other hand, at the same time kneeling before her in homage. At this moment the cuckoo is heard.*)
Cuckoo, cuckoo, how d'you do?

GRETEL: Cuckoo, cuckoo, where are you?
(*Takes a strawberry from the basket and pokes it into Hänsel's mouth; he sucks it up as though he were drinking an egg.*)

HÄNSEL: (*Jumping up*). Oho, I can do that just like you!
(*Takes some strawberries and lets them fall into Gretel's mouth.*)
Let us do like the cuckoo too.
who takes more than his lawful due!
(*It begins to grow dark.*)

HÄNSEL: (*Helping himself again*). Cuckoo, cuckoo, how are you?

GRETEL: Cuckoo, where are you?

HÄNSEL: In your neighbour's nest you go.
Cuckoo, why do you do so?
(*Pours a handful of strawberries into his mouth.*)

GRETEL: And you are very greedy too!
Tell me, cuckoo, why are you?
(*They get rude and begin to quarrel for the strawberries. Hänsel gains the victory, and puts the whole basket to his mouth until it is empty. During this time, it has grown dark.*)

GRETEL: (*Horrified, clasping her hands together.*) Hänsel, what have you done?
O Heaven! all the strawberries eaten.

richt,
denn die Mutter, die spasst heute nicht!

HÄNSEL: (*Ruhig.*) Ei was, stell Dich doch nicht, so an,
Du, Gretel, hast es ja selber gethan!

GRETEL: Komm nur, wollen rasch neue suchen!

HÄNSEL: Im Dunkeln wohl gar, unter Hocken und Buchen?
Man sieht ja nicht Blatt, nicht Beere mehr!
Es wird schon dunkel rings umher!

GRETEL: Ach, Hänsel, Hänsel! Was fangen wir an?
Was haben wir thörichten Kinder gethan?
Wir durften hier gar nicht so lange säumen!

HÄNSEL: Horch, wie rauscht es in den Bäumen!—
Weisst Du, was der Wald jetzt spricht?
"Kindlein!" sagt er, "fürchtet ihr euch nicht?"
(*Späht unruhig umher.*)
Gretel! Ich weiss den Weg nicht mehr!

GRETEL: (*Bestürzt.*) O Gott! Was sagst Du? den Weg nicht mehr?

HÄNSEL: (*Sich mutig stellend.*) Was bist Du doch für ein furchtsam Wicht!
Ich bin ein Bub', ich fürchte mich nicht!

GRETEL: Ach, Hänsel! Gewiss geschieht uns ein Leid!

HÄNSEL: Ach, Gretel, geh, sei doch gescheit!

GRETEL: Was schimmert denn dort in der Dunkelheit?

HÄNSEL: Das sind die Birken im weissen Kleid.

GRETEL: Und dort, was grinset daher vom Sumpf?

HÄNSEL: (*Stotternd.*) D— d—das ist ein glimmender Weiden stumpf!

GRETEL: Was für ein wunderlich Gesicht
Macht er soeben—siehst Du's nicht?

HÄNSEL: (*Sehr laut.*) Ich mach' dir ne Nase, hörst du's, Wicht?

GRETEL: (*Ängstlich.*) Da, sieh', das Lichtchen—es kommt immer näh'r!

HÄNSEL: Irrlichtchen hüpfet wohl hin und her!
Gretel, Du musst beherzter sein—wart, ich will einmal tüchtig schrein!

You glutton! Listen, you'll have a punishment
from the mother—this is more than a joke!

HÄNSEL: (*Quickly.*) Now come, don't make such a fuss;
You, Gretel, you did the same thing yourself!

GRETEL: Come, we'll hurry and seek fresh ones!

HÄNSEL: What, here in the dark, under hedges and bushes?
Why, we can see nothing of fruit or leaves!
It's getting dark already here!

GRETEL: O Hänsel! O Hänsel! O what shall we do?
What bad disobedient children we've been!
We ought to have thought and gone home sooner!
(*Cuckoo behind the scenes rather nearer than before.*)

HÄNSEL: Hark, what a noise in the bushes!
Know you what the forest says?
"Children, children," it says,
"Are you not afraid?"
(*Hänsel spies all around uneasily, at last he turns in despair to Gretel.*)
Gretel, I cannot find the way!

GRETEL: (*Dismayed.*) O God! What did you say?
You do not know the way?

HÄNSEL: (*Pretending to be very brave*). Why, how ridiculous you are!
I am a boy, and not know fear!

GRETEL: O Hänsel, some dreadful thing may come!

HÄNSEL: O Gretel, come, don't be afraid!

GRETEL: What's glimmering there in the darkness?

HÄNSEL: That's only the birches in silver dress.

GRETEL: But there, what's grinning so there at me?

HÄNSEL: (*Stammering.*) Th—that's only the stump of a willow-tree.

GRETEL: (*Hastily.*) But what a dreadful form it takes,
and what a horrid face it makes!

HÄNSEL: (*Very loud.*) Come, I'll make faces, you fellow!
D'you hear?

GRETEL: (*Terrified.*) There, see! a lantern,
It's coming this way!

HÄNSEL: Will-o'-the-wisp is hopping about—
Gretel, come, don't lose heart like this!
Wait, I'll give a good loud call!

(*Ruft durch die hohlen Hände.*)
Wer da?

ECHO: Er da!
(*Die Kinder schmiegen sich erschreckt aneinander.*)

GRETEL: Ist jemand da?

ECHO: Ja!
(*Die Kinder schaudern zusammen.*)

GRETEL: Hast du's gehört? 's rief leise: Ja!
Hänsel, sicher ist jemand nah'!
(*Weinend:*)
Ich fürcht' mich, ich fürcht' mich!—O wär ich zu Haus!
Wie sieht der Wald so gespenstig aus!

HÄNSEL: Gretelchen, drücke Dich fest an mich!
Ich halte Dich, ich schütze Dich!
(*Ein dichter Nebel steigt auf und verhüllt den Hintergrund gänzlich.*)

GRETEL: Da, kommen weisse Nebelfrauen,
sieh', wie sie winken und drohend schauen.
Sie schweben heran!
Sie fassen uns an!
(*Schreiend:*)
Vater! Mutter!
(*Eilt entsetzt unter die Tanne und verbirgt sich, auf die Kniee stürzend, hinter Hänsel. In diesem Augenblicke zerreisst links de Nebel; ein kleines graues Männchen, mit einer Säckchen auf dem Rücken, wird sichtbar.*)

HÄNSEL: Sieh' dort das Männchen, Schwesterlein!
Was mag das für ein Männchen sein?

## ZWEITE SCENE

SANDMÄNNCHEN: (*Nähert sich mit freundlichen Gebärden den Kindern die sich allmählich beruhigen, und wirft ihnen beim Singen Sand in die Augen.*) Der kleine Sandmann bin ich—s-t!
und gar nichts Arges sinn ich-s-t!
Euch Kleinen lieb ich innig—s-t!
bin euch gesinnt gar minnig—s-t!
Aus diesem Sack zwei Körnlein euch Müden in die Äugelein;
die fallen dann von selber zu,
damit ihr schlaft in sanfter Ruh.
Und seid ihr fein geschlafen ein,
dann wachen auf die Sterne,
und nieder steigen Engelein
aus hoher Himmelsferne
und bringen hold Träume.
Drum träume, Kindchen, träume!
(*Verschwindet. Völlige Dunkelheit.*)

HÄNSEL: (*Schlaftrunken.*) Sandmann war da!

---

(*Goes back some steps to the back of the stage and calls through his hands.*)
Who's there?

ECHO: You there!
There!
(*The children cower together.*)

GRETEL: Is some one there?

ECHO: Where?
Here!

GRETEL: Did you hear? a voice said, "Here!"
Hänsel, surely some one's near.
(*Crying.*)
I'm frightened, I'm frightened,
I wish I were home!
I see the wood all filled with goblin forms!

HÄNSEL: Gretelkin, stick to me close and tight,
I'll shelter you, I'll shelter you!
(*A thick mist rises and completely hides the background.*)

GRETEL: I see some shadowy women coming!
See, how they nod and beckon, beckon!
They're coming, they're coming,
they'll take us away!
(*Crying out, rushes horror-struck under the tree and falls on her knees, hiding herself behind Hänsel.*)
Father! mother! Ah!
(*At this moment the mist lifts on the left; a little grey man is seen with a little sack on his back.*)

HÄNSEL: See there, the mankin, sister dear!
I wonder who the mankin is?

## SCENE II

SANDMAN: (*The little man approaches the children with friendly gestures, and the children gradually calm down. He is strewing sand in the children's eyes.*) I shut the children's peepers, sh!
and guard the little sleepers, sh!
for dearly do I love them, sh!
and gladly watch above them, sh!
And with my little bag of sand,
By every child's bedside I stand;
then little tired eyelids close,
and little limbs have sweet repose.
And if they're good and quickly go to sleep,
then from the starry sphere above
the angels come with peace and love,
and send the children happy dreams,
while watch they keep!
(*Disappears. Darkness.*)

HÄNSEL: (*Half asleep.*) Sandman was there!

---

GRETEL: (*Ebenso.*) Lass uns den Abendsegen beten!
(*Sie kauern nieder und falten die Hände.*)

BEIDE: Abends, will ich schlafen gehn,
vierzehn Engel um mich stehn,
zwei zu meinen Häupten,
zwei zu meinen Füssen,
zwei zu meiner Rechten,
zwei zu meiner Linken,
zweie, die mich decken,
zweie, die mich wecken,
zweie, die mich weisen
ze Himmelsparadeisen.
(*Sie sinken aufs Moos zurück und schlummern Arm in Arm verschlungen alsbald ein.*)

## DRITTE SCENE

*Vierzehn Engel, die kleinsten voran, die grössten zuletzt, schreiten paarweise, während das Licht an Helligkeit zunimmt, in Zwischenräumen die Wolkentreppe hinab und stellen sich, der Reihenfolge des Abendsegens entsprechend, um die schlafenden Kinder auf, das erste Paar zu Häupten, das zweite zu Füssen, das dritte rechts, das vierte links; dann verteilen sich das fünfte und sechste Paar zwischen die übrigen Paare, sodass der Kreis der Engel vollständig geschlossen wird. Zuletzt tritt das siebente Paar in den Kreis und nimmt als "Schutzengel" zu beiden Seiten der Kinder Platz waehrend sie sich zu einem malerischen Schlussbilde ordnen, schliesst sich langsam der Vorhang.*)

## ■ DRITTES BILD

### DAS KNUSPERHÄUSCHEN

### ERSTE SCENE

*Scene wie vorhin. Der Hintergrund noch von Nebel verhüllt, der sich während des Folgenden langsam verzieht. Die Engel sind verschwunden. Früher Morgen. Taumännchen tritt auf und schüttelt aus einer Glockenblume Tautropfen auf die schlafenden Kinder.*)

TAUMÄNNCHEN: Der kleine Tau-Mann heiss' ich—kling!
Mit Mutter Sonne reis' ich—klang!
Von Ost bis Westen weiss ich—kling!

---

GRETEL: (*Ditto*) Let us first say our evening prayer.
(*They cower down and fold their hands.*)

BOTH: When at night I go to sleep,
fourteen angels watch do keep:
two my head are guarding,
two my feet are guiding,
two are on my right hand,
two are on my left hand,
two who warmly cover,
two who over me hover,
two to whom it's given
to guide my steps to Heaven.
(*They sink down on to the moss, and go to sleep with their arms twined round each other. Complete darkness.*)

## SCENE III

(*Here a bright light suddenly breaks through the mist which forthwith rolls itself together into the form of a staircase, vanishing in perspective, in the middle of the stage. Fourteen angels, in light floating garments, pass down the staircase, two and two, at intervals, while it is getting gradually lighter. The angels place themselves, according to the order mentioned in the evening hymn, around the sleeping children; the first couple at their heads, the second at their feet, the third on the right, the fourth on the left, the fifth and sixth couples distribute themselves amongst the other couples, so that the circle of the angels is completed. Lastly the seventh couple comes into the circle and takes its place as "guardian angels" on each side of the children. The remaining angels now join hands and dance a stately step around the group. The whole stage is filled with an intense light. Whilst the angels group themselves in a picturesque tableau, the curtain slowly falls.*)

## ■ ACT III

### THE WITCH'S HOUSE

### SCENE I

(*The curtain rises. Scene the same as the end of Act II. The background is still hidden in mist, which gradually rises during the following. The angels have vanished. Morning is breaking. The Dew Fairy steps forward and shakes dewdrops from a bluebell over the sleeping children.*)

DEW FAIRY: I'm up with early dawning,
and know who loves the morning,
who'll rise fresh as a daisy,
who'll sink in slumber lazy!

# Act III, Scene I

Wer faul ist und wer fleissig—
klang!
Ich komm mit lichtem Sonnenschein
und strahl in eure Äugelein,
und weck mit kühlem Taue,
was schläft auf Flur und Aue.
Dann springet auf, wer fleissig
zur frühen Morgenstunde,
denn sie hat Gold im Munde.
Drum, Schläfer, auf, erwachet,
der lichte Tag schon lachet!
(Ab.)
(Öffnet die Augen, richtet sich
halb auf und blickt verwundert
um sich, während Hänsel sich auf
die andere Seite legt, um weiter zu
schlafen.)

**GRETEL:** Wo bin ich? Wach ich? Ist
es ein Traum?
Hier lieg' ich unterm Tannenbaum.
Hoch in den Zweigen lispelt es
leise,
Vöglein singen so süsse Weise.
Wohl früh schon waren sie aufge-
wacht
und haben ihr Morgenlied dargebracht.
Guten Morgen, liebe Vöglein, guten Morgen!
(Sie erblickt Hänsel.)
Sieh da, der faule Siebenschläfer!
Wart nur, Dich weck' ich! Tirelireli,
's ist nicht mehr früh!
die Lerche hat's gesungen
und hoch sich aufgeschwungen.
Tirelireli,

**HÄNSEL:** (Aufspringend.) Kikeri-
iki!
's ist noch frü!
Ja, hab's wohl vernommen,
der Morgen ist gekommen,
Kikeriki!
Mir ist so wohl, ich weiss nicht wie;
so gut wie heute schlief ich nie.

**GRETEL:** Doch höre nur! Hier unter dem Baum,
da hatt' ich einen wunderschönen
Traum.

**HÄNSEL:** Richtig! Auch mir
träumte so was!

**GRETEL:** Mir träumt' ich hört' ein
Rauschen und Klingen,
wie Chöro der Engel ein himmlisches Singen;
lichte Wölkchen im rosigen Schein
wallten und wogten ins Dunkel
herein.
Siehe, hell ward's mit einem Male,
lichtdurchflossen vom Himmels-
strahle;
eine goldene Leiter sah ich sich
neigen,
Englein zu mir herniedersteigen,
Engel mit goldenen Flügelein—

**HÄNSEL:** Vierzehn müssen's
gewesen sein!

**GRETEL:** (Erstaunt.) Hast Du
denn alles das auch gesehn?

ding! dong! ding! dong!
And with the golden light of day
I chase the fading night away,
fresh dew around me shaking,
and hill and dale awaking.
Then up, with all your powers
enjoy the morning hours,
the scent of trees and flowers—
then up, sleepers, awaken!
The rosy dawn is smiling,
then up, sleepers, awake, awake!
(Hurries off singing. The children
begin to stir. Gretel rubs her eyes,
looks around her, and raises herself a little, while Hänsel turns
over on the other side to go to sleep
again.)

**GRETEL:** Where am I? Waking? Or
do I dream?
How come I lie in the wood?
High in the branches I hear a gentle
twittering,
birds are beginning to sing so
sweetly;
from early dawn they are all awake,
and warble their morning hymn of
praise.
Dear little singers, little singers,
good morning!
(Turns to Hänsel.)
See there, the sleepy lazybones?
Wait, now, I'll wake him!
Tirelireli, it's getting late!
Tirelireli, it's getting late!
The lark his flight is winging,
on high his morning singing,
Tirelireli! tirelireli!

**HÄNSEL:** (Suddenly jumps up
with a start.) Kikeriki! it's early
yet!
Kikeriki! it's early yet!
Yes, the day is dawning;
awake, for it is morning!
Kikeriki! kikeriki!
I feel so well, I don't know why!
I never slept so well, no, not I!

**GRETEL:** But listen, Hans; here beneath the tree
a wondrous dream was sent to me!

**HÄNSEL:** Really! I, too, had a
dream!

**GRETEL:** I fancied I heard a murmuring and rushing,
as though the angels in Heaven
were singing;
rosy clouds above me were floating—
hovering and floating in the distance away,
Sudden-all around a light was
streaming,
rays of glory from Heaven beaming,
and a golden ladder saw I descending,
angels gliding, down it
such lovely angels with shining
golden wings.

**HÄNSEL:** Fourteen angels there
must have been!

**GRETEL:** (Astonished.) And did
you also behold all this?

**HÄNSEL:** Freilich! 's war halt wun-
derschön—
Und dort hinaus sah ich sie gehn!
(Er wendet sich nach dem Hintergrunde. In diesem Augenblick
zerreisst der letzte Nebelschleier.
An Stelle des Tannengehölzes
erscheint glitzernd im Strahl der
aufgehenden Sonne das "Knusperhäuschen" am Ilsenstein.
Links davon in einiger über ein
grosser Käfig, beide mit dem
Knusperhäuschen durch einen
Zaun von Kuchenmännern verbunden.)

## ZWEITE SCENE

**GRETEL:** (Hält Hänsel betroffen
zurück.) Bleib stehn! Bleib stehn!

**HÄNSEL:** Himmel, welch Wunder
ist hier geschehn!
Nein, so was hab ich mein Tag
nicht' gesehn!

**GRETEL:** (Gewinnt allmählich
die Fassung wieder.)
Wie duftet's von dorten,
O schau nur die Pracht!

**BEIDE:** Von Kuchen und Torten
Ein Häuslein gemacht!
Mit Fladen, mit Torten
ist's hoch überdacht!
Die Fenster wahrhaftig
wie Zucker so blank,
Rosinen gar saftig
den Giebel entlang!
Und—traun!
Rings zu schaun
gar ein Lebkuchen-Zaun!
O herrliches Schlösschen,
Wie bist du schmuck und fein
Ach wär' doch zu Hause
die Wald-Prinzessin fein
Sie lüde zum Schmause
bei Kuchen und Wein
zum herrlichen Schmause
sie lüde zur Klause
uns beide wohl ein!

**HÄNSEL:** (Nach einer Pause.)
Alles bleibt still. Nichts regt sich da
drinnen.
Komm lass uns hineingehn!

**GRETEL:** (Erschrocken ihn
zurückhaltend.) Bist du bei Sinnen?
Junge, wie magst du so dreist nur
sein?
Wer weiss, wer da drin wohl im
Häuschen fein?

**HÄNSEL:** O sieh nur, wie das
Häuschen uns lacht!
(Begeistert.)
Die Englein haben's uns herge-
bracht!

**GRETEL:** (Sinnend.) Die Englein?—Ei, so wird es wohl sein!

**HÄNSEL:** Ja, Gretel, sie laden
freundlich uns ein!
Komm, wir knuspern ein wenig
vom Häuschen!

**HÄNSEL:** Truly, it was wondrous
fair!
And upward I saw them float.
(He turns towards the background; at this moment the last
remains of the mist clear away. In
place of the fir trees is seen the
"Witch's house at the Ilsenstein,"
shining in the rays of the rising
sun. A little distance off, to the
left, is an oven; opposite this, on
the right, a large cage, both joined
to the Witch's house by a fence of
gingerbread figures.)

## SCENE II

**GRETEL:** (Holds Hänsel back in
astonishment.) Stand still, be still!

**HÄNSEL:** (Surprised.) O Heaven,
what wondrous place is this,
as never in all my life have I seen!

**GRETEL:** (Gradually regains her
self-possession.) What delicious
odor!
O say, do I dream?

**BOTH:** A cottage all made
of chocolate cream.
The roof is all covered
with Turkish delight
the windows with lustre
of sugar are white;
and on all the gables
the raisins invite,
and think! all around
is a gingerbread hedge!
O magic castle,
how nice you'd be to eat!
Where hides the princess
who enjoys so great a treat?
Ah, could she but visit
our little cottage bare,
she'd ask us to dinner,
her dainties to share!

**HÄNSEL:** (After a while.) No
sound do I hear; no, nothing is stirring!
Come, let's go inside!

**GRETEL:** (Pulling him back horrified.) Are you senseless?
Hänsel, however can you be so
bold?
Who knows who may live there,
in that lovely house?

**HÄNSEL:** O look, do look how the
house seems to smile!
(Enthusiastically.)
Ah, the angels did our footsteps beguile!

**GRETEL:** (Reflectively.) The angels? Yes, it must be so!

**HÄNSEL:** Yes, Gretel, the angels
are beckoning us in!
Come, let's nibble a bit of the cottage.

**BEIDE:** Ja, knuspern wir, wie zwei Nagemäuschen!
(*Sie büpfen Hand in Hand nach dem Hintergrunde, bleiben wiederum stehen und schleichen dann vorsichtig auf den Fuss-spitzen bis an das Häuschen heran. Nach einigem Zögern bricht Hänsel an der rechten Kante ein Stäckchen Kuchen heraus.*)

## DRITTE SCENE

**TIMME AUS DEM HÄUSCHEN:** Knusper, knusper Knäuschen, wer knuspert mir am Häuschen?

**HÄNSEL:** (*Lässt erschrocken das Stück su Boden fallen.*)

**GRETEL:** (*Zaghaft.*) Der Wind!

**HÄNSEL:** Der Wind!

**BEIDE:** Das himmlische Kind.

**GRETEL:** (*Hebt das Stück wieder auf und versucht es.*) Hm!

**HÄNSEL:** (*Gretel begehrlich anschauend.*) Wie schmeckt das?

**GRETEL:** (*Ihn beissen lassend.*) Da hast du auch was!

**HÄNSEL:** (*Legt entzückt die Hand auf die Brust.*) Hei!

**GRETEL:** (*Ebenso.*) Hei!

**BEIDE:** O köstlicher Kuchen, Wie schmeckst du nach mehr! Mir ist ja, als wenn ich im Himmel schon wär!

**HÄNSEL:** Hei, wie das schmeckt! 's ist gar zu leckeri

**GRETEL:** Vielleicht gar wohnt hier ein Zucker-bäcker!

**HÄNSEL:** He, Zuckerbäcker, nimm dich in acht, Ein Loch wird dir jetzt vom Mäuselein gemacht! (*Bricht ein grosses Stück aus der Wand heraus.*)

**STIMME AUS DEM HÄUSCHEN:** Knusper, knusper Knäuschen, wer knuspert mir am Häuschen?

**HÄNSEL UND GRETEL:** Der Wind, der Wind, das himmlische Kind! (*Der obere Teil der Hausthüre öffnet sich leise, und der Kopf der Knusperhexe wird sichtbar. Die Kinder bemerken sie nicht und schmausen lustig weiter.*)

**GRETEL:** Wart, du näschiges Mäuschen, gleich kommt die Katz' aus dem Häuschen!

**HÄNSEL:** Knuspre nur zu und lass mich in Ruh!

**GRETEL:** (*Entreisst ihm ein Stück Kuchen.*) Nicht so geschwind, Herr Wind, Herr Wind!

---

**BOTH:** Come, let's nibble it. like two mice persevering! (*They bop along, band in hand, towards the back of the stage; then stand still, and then steal along cautiously on tiptoe to the house. After some hesitation Hänsel breaks off a bit of cake from the right-hand corner.*)

## SCENE III

**A VOICE FROM THE HOUSE:** Nibble, nibble, mousekin, who's nibbling at my housekin? who's nibbling at my housekin?

**HÄNSEL:** (*Hänsel starts, and in his fright lets the piece of cake fall.*)

**GRETEL:** (*Somewhat timidly.*) The wind—

**HÄNSEL:** The Wind!

**BOTH:** The heavenly wind!

**GRETEL:** (*Picks up the piece of cake and tastes it.*) H'm!

**HÄNSEL:** (*Looking longingly at Gretel.*) Do you like it?

**GRETEL:** (*Lets Hänsel bite it.*) Just taste and try it!

**HÄNSEL:** (*Lays his hand on his breast in rapture.*) Hi!

**GRETEL:** (*Ditto*) Hi!

**BOTH:** Hi, hi! O cake most delicious, some more I must take! It's really like Heaven to eat such plum-cake!

**HÄNSEL:** O how good, sweet, how tasty!

**GRETEL:** How tasty, how sweet! It's perhaps the house of a sweet maker!

**HÄNSEL:** Hi, sweet maker! Have a care! A little mouse your sweets would share! (*He breaks a big piece of cake off the wall.*)

**A VOICE FROM THE HOUSE:** Nibble, nibble, mousekin, who's nibbling at my housekin?

**HÄNSEL AND GRETEL:** The wind, the wind, the heavenly wind! (*The upper part of the house-door opens gently and the Witch's head is seen at it. The children at first do not see her, and go on feasting merrily.*)

**GRETEL:** Wait, you gobbling mousekin, here comes the cat from the housekin!

**HÄNSEL:** Eat what you please, and leave me in peace!

**GRETEL:** (*Snatches the piece from his hand.*) Don't be unkind, Sir wind, sir wind!

---

**HÄNSEL:** (*Nimmt es ihr wieder ab.*) Himmlisches Kind, ich nehm, was ich find!

**HEXE:** (*Kichernd.*) Hihi, hihi, hih-ihi!

**HÄNSEL:** (*Entsetzt.*) Lass los!— Wer bist du?

**HEXE:** Engelchen! Und du, mein Zuckerbengelchen! Ihr kommt mich besuchen?—Das ist nett! Liebe Kinder!—So rund und fett!

**HÄNSEL:** Wer bist du, Garstige?— Lass mich los!

**HEXE:** Na, Herzchen, zier dich nicht erst gross! Wisst denn, dass euch vor mir nicht graul: Ich bin Rosina Leckermaul, höchst menschenfreundlich stets gesinnt, unschuldig wie ein kleines Kind. Drum hab ich die kleinen Kinder so lieb. So lieb—ach zum Aufessen lieb!

**HÄNSEL:** (*Barsch abwehrend.*) Geh!—bleib mir doch aus dem Gesicht! Hörst du? Ich mag dich nicht!

**HEXE:** Hihihi! Was seid ihr für leckere Teufelsbrätchen. besonders du, mein herzig Mädchen! (*Lockend.*) Kommt, kleine Mäuslein, kommt in mein Häuslein! Sollt es gut bei mir haben, Will drinnen köstlich euch laben. Schokolade, Torten, Marzipan, Kuchen, gefüllt mit süsser Sahn', Johannisbrot und Jungfernleder und Reisbrei—auf dem Ofen stecht er— Rosinen, Mandeln und Feigen, 's ist alles im Häuschen eur eigen!

**HÄNSEL:** Ich geh nicht mit dir, garstige Frau!— Du bist gar zu freundlich.

**HEXE:** Schau, schau, wie schlau, Ihr Kinder, ich mein's doch so gut mit euch, seid ja bei mir wie im Himmelreich! Kommt, kleine Mäuslein! kommt in mein Häuslein! Sollt es gut bei mir haben, will drinnen köstlich euch laben!

**GRETEL:** Was willst du meinem Bruder thun?

**HEXE:** I nun, ich will ihn fuettern und nudeln mit allerhand vortrefflichen Sachen will ich ihn zart und wohlschmeck-

---

**HÄNSEL:** (*Takes it back from her.*) Heavenly wind, I take what I find!

**BOTH:** (*Laughing.*) Ha, ha, ha!

**THE WITCH:** Hi, hi! hi, hi!

**HÄNSEL:** (*Horror-struck.*) Let go! Who are you? Let me go!

**THE WITCH:** Angels both! (And goosey-ganders!) You've come to visit me, that is sweet! You charming children, so nice to eat!

**HÄNSEL:** Who are you, ugly one?

**THE WITCH:** Now, darling, don't give yourself airs! Dear heart, what makes you say such things? I am Rosina Dainty-mouth, and dearly love my fellow-men. I'm artless as a new born child! That's why the children to me are so dear, so dear, so dear, ah, so charming to eat!

**HÄNSEL:** (*Turning roughly away.*) Go, get you gone from my sight! I hate, I loathe you quite!

**THE WITCH:** Hi hi! hi hi! These dainty morsels I'm really gloating on, and you, my little maiden, I'm doting on! Come, little mouse, come into my house! Come with me, my precious, I'll give you sweetmeats delicious! Of chocolate, tarts, and marzipan you shall both eat all you can, and wedding-cake and strawberry ices, blancmange, and everything else that nice is, and raisins and almonds, and peaches and citrons are waiting— you'll both find it quite captivating!

**HÄNSEL:** I won't come with you, hideous fright! You are quite too friendly!

**THE WITCH:** See, see, see how sly! Dear children, you really may trust me in this, and living with me will be perfect bliss! Come, little mouse, come into my house! Come with me, my precious, I'll give you sweetmeats delicious!

**GRETEL:** But say, what will you with my brother do?

**THE WITCH:** Well, well! I'll feed and fatten him up well, with every sort of dainty delicious, to make him tender and tasty. And if he's brave and patient too,

end machen
und ist er dann recht zahm und brav,
geduldig und fügsam wie ein Schaf,
dann—höre, Hänsel, ich sag dir's ins Ohr:
dir steht eine grosse Freude bevor!

**HÄNSEL:** So sag's doch laut und nicht ins Ohr!
Welche Freude steht mir bevor?

**HEXE:** Ja liebe Kinder, Hoeren und Sehen
wird euch bei diesem Vergnügen vergehn!

**HÄNSEL:** Ei, meine Augen und Ohren sind gut,
haben wohl acht, was Schaden mir thut.
Gretel, trau nicht dem gleissenden Wort
(*Leise.*)
Schwesterchen, komm, wir laufen fort!
(*Er hat sich inzwischen von der Schlinge befreit und will mit Gretel fortlaufen, sie werden aber von der Hexe zurück gehalten, die gebieterisch einen Stab gegen die Beiden erhebt.*)

**HEXE:** Halt!
(*Die Bühne verfinstert sich.*)
Hocus pocus, Hexenschuss!
Rühr dich, und dich deisst der Fluss!
Nicht mehr vorwärts, nicht zurück,
bann dich mit dem bösen Blick;
Kopf steh starr dir im Genick!
Hocus pocus, nun kommt Jocus!
Kinder, schaut den Zauberknopf!
Äuglein, stehet still im Kopf!—
Nun zum Stall hinein, du Tropf!
Hocus pocus, bonus jocus,
Malus locus, hocus pocus!
(*Leitet Hänsel zum Stalle und schliesst hinter ihm die Gitterthüre.*)
(*Vernügt zu Gretel.*) Nun, Gretelchen, sei vernünftig und nett!
Der Hänsel wird nun balde fett.
Wir wollen ihn, so ist's am besten,
mit Mandeln und Rosinen mästen.
Ich geh ins Haus und hol sie schnell—
Du rühre dich nicht von der Stell!
(*Hinkt ins Haus.*)

**GRETEL:** (*Starr und unbeweglich.*) Hu—Wie mir vor der Hexe graut!

and docile and obedient like a lamb,
then, Hänsel, I'll whisper it you,
I have a great treat in store for you!

**HÄNSEL:** Then speak out loud and whisper not.
What is the great treat in store for me?

**THE WITCH:** Yes, my dear children, hearing and sight
in this great pleasure will disappear quite!

**HÄNSEL:** Eh? both my hearing and seeing are good!
You'd better take care you do me no harm!
(*Resolutely.*)
Gretel, trust not her flattering words,
come, sister, come, let's run away!
(*He has in the meantime got out of the rope and runs with Gretel to the foreground. Here they are stopped by the Witch, who imperiously raises against them both a stick which hangs at her girdle, with repeated gestures of spellbinding.*)

**THE WITCH:** Hold.
(*The stage becomes gradually darker.*)
Hocus, pocus, witches' charm!
Move not, as you fear my arm!
Back or forward do not try,
fixed you are by the evil eye!
Head on shoulders fixed awry!
Hocus, pocus, now comes jocus,
children, watch the magic head,
eyes are staring, dull as lead!
Now, you atom, off to bed!
(*Fresh gestures; then she leads Hänsel, who is gazing fixedly at the illuminated head, into the stable, and shuts the lattice door upon him.*)
Hocus pocus, bonus jocus,
malus locus, hocus pocus,
bonus jocus, malus locus!
(*The stage gradually becomes lighter, whilst the light of the magic head diminishes.*)
Now Gretel, be obedient and wise,
while Hänsel's growing fat and nice.
We'll fatten him up, you'll see my reason,
and with sweet almonds and raisins season.
I'll go indoors, the things to prepare,
and you remain here where you are!
(*She grins as she holds up her finger warningly, and goes into the house.*)

**GRETEL:** (*Stiff and motionless.*)
O, what a horrid witch she is!

**HÄNSEL:** Gretel! Pst! sprich nicht so laut!
Sei hübsch gescheit und gieb fein acht
auf jedes, was die Hexe macht.
Zum Schein thu alles, was sie will—
da kommt sie schon zurück—Pst! Still!
(*Dem Hänsel aus einem Korbe Mandeln und Rosinen his streuend.*)

**HEXE:** Nun, Jüngelchen,
ergötze dein Züngelchen!
Friss, Vogel, oder stirb—
Kuchen-Heil dir erwirb!
(*Wendet sich zu Gretel und entzaubert sie mit einen Wachbolderbuach.*)
Hocus pocus, Holderbusch!
Schwinde, Gliederstarre, husch!
Nun wieder kregel, süsses Kleinchen,
rühr mir geschwind die runden Beinchen!
Geh, Zuckerpüppchen, flink und frisch
und decke drinnen hübsch den Tisch!
Schüsselchen, Tellerchen, Messerchen, Gäbelchen,
Serviettchen für mein Schnäbelchen;
und mach nur alles recht hurtig und fein,
sonst sperr ich auch dich in den Stall hinein!
(*Sie droht kichernd; Gretel eilt ins Haus.*)

**HEXE:** (*Zu dem sich schlafend stellenden Hänsel.*) Der Lümmel schläft ja nun—sieh mal an,
wie doch die Jugend schlafen kann!
Na, schlaf nur brav, du gutes Schaf,
bald schläfst du deinen ewigen Schlaf.
Doch erst muss mir die Gretel dran;
mit dir, mein Liebchen, fang ich an,
bist so niedlich, zart und rund,
wie gemacht für Hexen-Mund!
(*Sie öffnet die Backofenthür und riecht hinein.*)
Der Teig ist gar, wir können voran machen
Hei, wie im Ofen die Scheite krachen!
Ja, Gretelchen,
wirst bald ein Brätelchen!
Schau, schau,
wie ich schlau bin, so schlau!
Sollst gleich im Backofen hucken
und nach dem Lebkuchen gucken.
Und bist du dann drin—schwaps,
geht die Thür—klaps!
Dann ist fein Gretelchen
mein Brätelchen!
Das Brätelchen soll sich verwandeln
in Kuchen mit Zucker und Mandeln!
Im Zauberofen mein
wirst du ein Lebkuchen fein!
Hurr, hopp, hopp, hopp!
Galopp, Galopp!
mein Besengaul,

**HÄNSEL:** Gretel, sh! don't speak so loud!
Be very sharp, watch well and see
whatever she may do to me!
Pretend to do all she commands—
O, there she's coming back, sh! hush!
(*The Witch comes out, satisfies herself that Gretel is stil standing motionless, and then spreads before Hänsel almonds and raisins from a basket.*)

**THE WITCH:** Now, little man,
come, I pray you, enjoy yourself!
(*Sticking a raisin into Hänsel's mouth.*)
Eat, minion, eat or die!
Here are cakes, O so nice!
(*Turns to Gretel and disenchants her with a juniper-branch.*)
Hocus pocus, elder-bush!
Rigid body lossen, hush!
(*Gretel moves again.*)
Now up and move again, bright and blithesome,
limbs are become again supple and lithesome.
Go, my poppet, go my pet,
you the table now shall set,
little knife, little fork, little dish, little plate,
little napkin for my little mate!
Now get everything ready and nice,
or else I shall lock you up too in a trice!
(*She threatens and titters. Gretel hurries off.*)

(*The Witch, to Hänsel, who pretends to be asleep.*)
The fool is slumbering, it does seem queer how youth can sleep and have no fear!
Well, sleep away, you simple sheep,
soon you will sleep your last long sleep!
But first with Gretel I'll begin—
off you, dear maiden, I will dine;
you are so tender, plump, and good,
just the thing for witches' food!
(*She opens the oven door and sniffs in it, her face lighted up by the deep red glare of the fire.*)
The dough has risen, so we'll go on preparing.
Hark, how the sticks in the fire are crackling!
(*She pushes a couple more faggots under, the fire flames up and then dies down again. The Witch, rubbing her hands with glee.*)
Yes, Gretel mine,
how well off you I'll dine!
See, see, O how sly!
When in the oven she's peeping,
quickly behind her I'm creeping!
One little push, bang
goes the door, clang!
Then soon will Gretel be
just done to a T!
and when from the oven I take her
sh'll look like a cake from the bak-

hurr, hopp, nit faul!
Sowie ich's mag
am lichten Tag
spring kreuz und quer
um Häuschen her!
Bei dunkler Nacht,
wann niemand wacht,
zum Hexenschmaus
am Schornstein raus!
Aus fünf und sechs,
so sagt die Hex,
mach sieb und acht,
so ist's vollbracht;
und neun ist eins,
und zehn ist keins,
und viel ist nichts,
die Hexe spricht's.
So reitet sie
bis morgens früh—
Prr! Besen! hüh!
Auf, auf, mein Jüngelchen!
Zeig mir dein Züngelchen!
(*Hänsel streckt die Zunge heraus.*)
(*Schnalzend.*)
Schlicker, schlecker,
lecker, lecker!
Kleines leckres Schlingerchen,
Zeige mir dein Fingerchen!
(*Hänsel streckt ein Stöckchen heraus.*)
Jemine, je!
Wie ein Stöckchen, o weh!
Bübchen, deine Fingerchen
sind elende Dingerchen!
(*Ruft.*)
Mädel! Gretel!
(*Gretel zeigt sich an der Thür.*)
Bring Rosinen und Mandeln her;
Hänsel meint, es schmeckt nach
"mehr!"
(*Gretel springt in's Haus und kehrt alsbald mit einen Körbchen voll, Rosinen und Mandeln zurueck. Sie stellt sich, waebrend die Hexe den Haensel fuettert, hinter sie und macht mit dem Wachboolder die Entzauberungagebaerde.*)

GRETEL: (*Leise.*) Hocus pocus,
Holderbusch!
Schwinde, Gliederstarre—husch!

HEXE: (*Sich rasch umwendend.*)
Was sagtest du, mein Gänselchen!

er,
by magic fire red
changed into gingerbread!
See, see how sly!
Hi hi! hi hi!
(*In her wild delight she seizes a broomstick and begins to ride upon it.*)
So, hop, hop, hop,
gallop, lop, lop!
my broomstick nag,
come do not lag!
(*She rides excitedly round on the broomstick.*)
At dawn of day
I ride away,
am here and there
and everywhere!
(*She rides again; Gretel meanwhile is watching at the window.*)
At midnight hour, when none can know,
to join the witches' dance I go!
And three and four
are witches' lore,
and five and six
are witches' tricks,
and nine is one,
and ten is none,
and seven is nil,
or what she will!
And thus they ride till dawn of day!
(*Hopping madly along, she rides to the back of the stage and vanishes for a time behind the cottage. Here the Witch becomes visible again; she comes to the foreground, where she suddenly pulls up and dismounts.*)
Prr, broomstick, hi!
(*She hobbles back to the stable and tickles Hänsel with a birch twig till he awakes.*)
Up, awake, my mankin young;
come show to me your tongue!
(*Hänsel puts his tongue out. The Witch smacks her lips.*)
Dainty morsel! dainty morsel!
Little toothsome mankin come,
now let me see your thumb!
(*Hänsel pokes out a small bone*)
Gemini! Oho!
O how scraggy, how lean!
Urchin, you're a scraggy one,
as bad as a skeleton!
(*Calls.*)
Maiden, Gretel!
(*Gretel appears at the door.*)
Bring some raisins and almonds sweet,
Hänsel wants some more to eat.
(*Gretel runs into the house and returns immediately with a basket full of almonds and raisins. Whilst the Witch is feeding Hänsel, Gretel gets behind her and makes the gestures of disenchantment with the juniper-branch.*)

GRETEL: (*Softly.*) Hocus pocus,
elder-bush,
Rigid body loosen, hush!

THE WITCH: (*Turning suddenly round.*) What were you saying, little goose?

GRETEL: Meint' nur: wohl bekomm's, mein Hänselchen!

HEXE: Hihihi! Mein gutes Tröpfchen!
da—steck dir, was ins Kröpfchen!
Friss, Vogel, und stirb—
Kuchen-Heil dir erwirb!
(*Sie öffnet die Backofenthür; Hänsel giebt Gretel lebbate Zeichen.*)

HÄNSEL: (*Leise die Stallthür öffnend.*) Schwesterlein,
hüt dich fein!

HEXE: (*Gretel gierig betrachtend.*) Wie wässert mir das Mündchen
nach diesem süssen Kindchen!
Komm, Gretelchen!
Zuckermädelchen!
Sollst in den Backofen hucken
und nach den Lebkuchen gucken,
sorgfältig schaun—ja,
ob sie schon braun da,
oder ob's zu früh—
's ist kleine Müh!

HÄNSEL: (*Aus dem Stall schleichend.*) Schwesterlein,
hüt dich fein!

GRETEL: (*Sich ungeschickt stellend.*) Ei, wie fang ich's an,
dass ich komme dran?

HEXE: Musst dich nur eben
ein bisschen heben,
Kopf vorgebeugt—
's ist kinderleicht!

HÄNSEL: Schwesterlein,
hüt dich fein!

GRETEL: (*Schüchtern.*) Bin gar so dumm,
nimm mir's nicht krumm;
drum zeige mir ieben,
wie soll ich mich heben?

HEXE: (*Macht eine ungeduldige Bewegung.*) Kopf vorgebeugt!
's ist kinderleicht!
(*Sie schickt sich murrend an, in den Backofen zu kriechen indem sie sich mit halbem Leibe vorbeugt, geben ihr Hänsel und Gretel einen derben Stoss, so dass sie vollends hinaus fliegt, und schlagen dann rasch die Tuere zu.*)

HÄNSEL UND GRETEL: Und bist du dann drin—schwaps!
Geht die Thür—klaps!
Du bist dann statt Gretelchen ein Brätelchen!
(*Hänsel und Gretel fallen sich jubelnd in die Arme, fassen sich bei der Hand und tanzen.*)
Juchhei! Nun ist die Hexe tot, mausetot!

GRETEL: (*Confusedly.*) Only—much good may it do to Hans!

THE WITCH: Eh?

GRETEL: (*Louder.*) Much good may it do to Hans!

THE WITCH: He he he, my little miss,
I'll stop your mouth with this!
(*Sticks a raisin into Gretel's mouth.*)
Eat, minion, eat or die!
Here are cakes, O so nice!
(*She opens the oven door; the heat has apparently diminished. Meanwhile Hänsel makes violent signs to Gretel.*)

HÄNSEL: (*Softly opening the stable door.*) Sister dear,
O beware!

THE WITCH: (*looking greedily at Gretel.*) She makes my mouth water,
this pretty little daughter!
Come, Gretel mine,
sugar-maiden mine!
(*Gretel comes towards her.*)
Peep in the oven,
be steady,
see if the gingerbread's ready!
Carefully look, pet,
whether it's cooked yet,
but if it wants more,
shut quick the door!
(*Gretel hesitates.*)

HÄNSEL: (*Slipping out of the stable.*) Sister dear,
Now take care!

GRETEL: (*Making herself out very awkward.*) I don't understand what I have to do!

THE WITCH: Just stand on tip-toe,
head bending forward;
try it, I pray,
it's merely play!

HÄNSEL: (*Pulling Gretel, back by her frock.*) Sister dear,
now take care!

GRETEL: (*Shyly.*) I'm such a goose, don't understand!
You'll have to show me how to stand on tip-toe!

THE WITCH: (*Makes a movement of impatience.*) Do as I say,
it's merely play!
(*She begins creeping up to the oven, muttering all the time, and just as she is bending over it, Hänsel and Gretel give her a good push, which sends her toppling over into it, upon which they quickly shut the door.*)

HÄNSEL AND GRETEL: (*Mocking her.*) Then "One little push, bang goes the door, clang!"
You, not Gretel, then will be just done to a T!
(*Hänsel and Gretel fall into one another's arms.*)
Hurrah! now sing the witch is dead, really dead!
No more to dread!

Nun ist geschwunden Angst und Not!
Junchhei! Nun ist die Hexe still, mäuschenstill,
Und Kuchen giebt's die Hüll und Füll!
Juchhei! Nun ist zu End der Graus, Hexengraus!
Und böser Zauberspuk ist aus!
Drum lasst uns fröhlich sein,
tanzen im Feuerschein,
halten im Knusperhaus
herrlichsten Freudenschmaus!
Juchhei, juchhei!

**GRETEL:** Da sieh nur die artigen Kinderlein,
wo mögen die hergekommen sein?
(*Sie umfassen sich und walzen mit einander, erst im Vordergrund, dann allmaehlich in der Richtung auf das Knusperhaeuschen zu. Als sie beim Knusperhaeuschen angekommet sind, reisst sich Hänsel von Gretel los, eilt in's Haeuschen, indem er die Tuere hinter sich zuschlaeget, und wirft Gretel durch die obere Luke Aepfel, Birnen, Apfelsinen, vergoldete Nuesse und allerhand Zuckerwerk in die aufgehaltene Schuerza, Mittlerweile faengt der Hexenofen gewaltig an zu knistern; die Flamme Schlaegt hoch empor. Dann gibt's einen starken Krach, und der Ofen stuerzt donnernd zusamnien.*)

Hurrah! now sing the witch is still, deathly still!
We can eat our fill!
Now all the spell is over, really over!
We fear no more!
(*They seize each other's hands.*)
Yes, let us happy be,
dancing so merrily;
now the old witch is gone,
we'll have no end of fun!
Hey! hurrah, hurrah!
Hip hurrah! Hip hurrah!
Hurrah!

**GRETEL:** (*Spoken.*) There, see those little children dear,
I wonder how they all came here!
(*They take each other around the waist and waltz together, first in the front of the stage, and then gradually in the direction of the Witch's house. When they get there Hänsel breaks loose from Gretel and rushes into the house, shutting the door after him. Then from the upper window he throws down apples, pears, oranges, gilded nuts, and all kinds of sweetmeats into Gretels outstretched apron. Meanwhile the oven begins crackling loudly, and the flames burn high. Then there is a loud crash, and the oven falls thundering into bits. Hänsel and Gretel, who in their terror let their sweetmeats all fall down, hurry towards the oven startled, and stand there motionless. Their astonishment increases when they become aware of a troop of children around them, whose disguise of cakes has fallen from them.*)

## VIERTE SCENE

**DIE KUCHENKINDER:** (*Ganz leise.*) Erlöst—befreit
für alle Zeit!

**GRETEL:** Geschlossen sind ihre Äugelein;
sie schlafen und singen doch so fein!

**KUCHENKINDER:** (*Leise.*) O rühre mich an,
dass ich erwachen kann!

**HÄNSEL:** (*Verlegen.*) Rühr du sie doch an—ich traue mir's nicht.

**GRETEL:** Ja, streicheln will ich dies hübsches Gesicht!
(*Sie streichelt das nächste Kind; dieses öffnet die Augen und lächelt.*)

## SCENE IV.

**THE GINGERBREAD CHILDREN:** (*Motionless and with closed eyes, as the cake figures were before.*)
We're saved, we're freed
for evermore!

**GRETEL:** Your eyes are shut—pray who are you?
You're sleeping, and yet you're singing too!

**THE GINGERBREAD CHILDREN:** (*Always very softly.*) O touch us, we pray,
that we may all awake!

**HÄNSEL:** (*To Gretel embarrassed.*) O touch them for me,
I dare not try!

**GRETEL:** Yes, let me stroke this innocent face!
(*She caresses the nearest child, who opens its eyes and smiles.*)

**ANDERE KUCHENKINDER:** O rühre auch mich—auch mich rühr' an,
dass ich die Äuglein öffnen kann.
(*Gretel geht streichelnd zu den übrigen Kindern, die lächelnd die Augen öffnen, ohne sich zu rühren; endlich ergreift Hänsel den Wachholder.*)

**HÄNSEL:** Hocus pocus, Holderbusch!
Schwinde, Gliederstarre—husch!

**DIE KUCHENKINDER:** Habt Dank, habt Dank euer Leben euer Leben lang!
Juchhei!
Die Hexerei
ist nun vorbei;
nun singen und springen wir froh und freil
Kommt, Kinderlein,
zum Ringelreihn,
reicht allzumal die Händchen fein!
Drum singt und springt,
drum tanzt und singt,
dass laut der Jubelruf durchdringt den Wald,
und rings erschallt
von Lust der Wald.

**HÄNSEL UND GRETEL:** Die Englein haben's im Traum gesagt in stiller Nacht,
was nun so herrlich uns der Tag hat waht gemacht.
Ihr Englein, die uns so treu bewacht bei Tag und Nacht,
habt Lob und Dank für all die Pracht, die uns hier lacht.

**DIE KUCHENKINDER:** Habt Dank, habt Dank
euer Leben lang!

## LETZTE SCENE

**VATER:** Rallalala, rallalala,
wären doch unsre Kinder da!
Rallalala, rallalala.—
(*Er erblickt Hänsel und Gretel.*)
Juch—! Ei, da sind sie ja!

**HÄNSEL UND GRETEL:** (*Den Eltern entgegen eilend.*) Vater! Mutter!

**MUTTER:** Kinderchen!

**VATER:** Da sind ja die armen Sünderchen!
(*Frohe Umarmung; unterdes haben zwei Knaben die Hexe ais grossen Lebkuchen aus den Trümmern des Zauberofen gezo-*

**OTHER GINGERBREAD CHILDREN:** O touch me too, O touch me too,
that I also may awake!
(*Gretel goes and caresses all the rest of the children, who open their eyes and smile, without moving; meanwhile Hänsel seizes the juniper-branch.*)

**HÄNSEL:** Hocus pocus, elderbush!
Rigid body loosen, hush!

**SOME OF THE CHILDREN:** (*Jump up and hurry towards Hänsel and Gretel from all sides.*) We thank, we thank you both!

**THE CHILDREN:** The spell is broken and we are free,
We'll sing and we'll dance and we'll shout for glee!
Come, children all, and form a ring,
join hands together while we sing,
Then sing and spring,
then dance and sing,
for cakes and all good things we bring.
Then sing and spring,
then dance and sing,
that through the wood
our song of praise my sound,
and echo repeat it all around!
We thank, we thank, we thank!

**HÄNSEL AND GRETEL:** The angels whispered in dreams to us in silent night
what this happy, happy day has brought tonight.

**THE GINGERBREAD CHILDREN:** We'll thank you both all our life!

## LAST SCENE

**FATHER:** Tralala, tralala!
Were our children only here!
Tralala, tralala!
(*The Father appears in the background with the Mother, and stops when he sees the children.*)
Ha! Why, they're really there!

**HÄNSEL:** (*Running towards them.*) Father! mother!

**GRETEL:** (*The same.*) Father! mother!

**MOTHER:** Children dear!

**FATHER:** O welcome, poor children innocent!
(*Joyfully embracing. Meanwhile two of the boys have dragged the Witch, in the form of a big gingerbread cake, out of the ruins of*

gen.)

VATER: Kinder, schaut das Wunder an,
wie solch Hexlein hexen kann,
wie sie hart,
knusperhart
selber nun zum Kuchen ward!

*the magic oven. At the sight of her they all burst into a shout of joy. The boys place the Witch in the middle of the stage.)*

FATHER: Children, see the wonder wrought,
how the Witch herself was caught
unaware in the snare
laid for you with cunning rare!
Such is Heaven's chastisement;

Merkt des Himmels Strafgericht:
böse Werke dauern nicht!
Wenn die Not aufs höchste steigt,
Gott der Herr die Hand uns reicht!

ALLE: Wenn die Not aufs höchste steigt,
Gott der Herr die Hand uns reicht!

*THE END*

evil works will have an end.
"When past bearing is our grief,
Then God, the Lord, will send us relief!"

ALL: "When past bearing is our grief,
Then God, the Lord, will send relief!"

*THE END*

# I Pagliacci (1892)

### MUSIC & LIBRETTO BY RUGGIERO LEONCAVALLO

This two-act opera with a prologue, set to a libretto by the composer, premiered at the Teatro dal Verme in Milan on May 21, 1892. The libretto incorporates characters that are part of the *Commedia del Arte* tradition, which was popular in Italy during the last half of the nineteenth century and which laid the foundations for the mime tradition in France. Tonio, a member of a company of actors, announces that a performance is about to begin and tells the audience what the opera is about. The company arrives in a Calabrian village to the cheers of the crowd. Tonio offers a hand to Nedda, wife of the company leader, to help her down from the wagon. Canio, her husband, won't allow anyone near her and pushes Tonio away. The actors go inside the inn. Nedda, left alone, sings of freedom. Tonio comes to her and confesses his love. When she rejects him, he persists, and she hits him across his face with a whip. Tonio, utterly humiliated, overhears Silvio, her lover, asking her to run away with him; Nedda hesitates, but says she will meet him after the performance. Canio appears but Silvio escapes without Canio recognizing him, and Nedda refuses to say who he is. It is almost performance time, and Canio must hide his wrath behind a clown's face. Silvio is in the audience. After a serenade, Beppe, dressed as Harlequin rendezvous with Nedda, who is dressed as Columbine; Canio, playing Pagliacci, Columbine's husband, enters, and Harlequin flees. Canio thus finds himself acting out his own real-life drama. He hurls himself at Nedda, ordering her to tell him who her lover is, and when she refuses; he stabs her. Silvio rushes to her, and Canio kills him as well. He then addresses the audience, saying, "the comedy is ended."

---

## ■ ATTO PRIMO.

### PROLOGO.

*Tonio, in costume da Taddeo come nella commedia, passando a traverso al telone.*

**TONIO:** Si può? . . . (*poi salutando*) Signore! Signori! . . . Scusatemi se solo mi presento.—
Io sono il Prologo. Poichè in scena ancor le antiche maschere mette l' autore, in parte ei vuol riprendere le vecchie usanze, e a voi di nuovo inviami. Ma non per dirvi come pria: "Le lagrime che noi versiam son false: Degli spasimi e dei nostri martir non allarmatevi!" No: L'autore ha cercato invece pingervi uno squarcio di vita. Egli ha per massima sol che l' artista è un uomo e che per gli uomini scrivere ei deve.—Ed al vero ispiravasi. Un nido di memorie in fondo a l' anima cantava un giorno, ed ei con vere lacrime sorisse, e i singhiozzi il tempo gli battevano! Dunque, vedrete amar si come s' amano gli esseri umani; vedrete de l' odio i tristi frutti. Del dolor gli spasimi, urli di rabbia, udrete, e risa ciniche! E voi, pruttosto che le nostre povere gabbane d' istrioni, le nostr' anime considerate, poichè noi siam uomini di carne e d' ossa, e che di quest' orfano mondo all pari di voi spiriamo l' aere! Il concetto vi dissi.—Or ascoltate com' egli è svolto. (*Gridando verso la scena.*) Andiamo. Incominci-

## ■ ACT I.

### PROLOGUE.

*Tonio, dressed as Taddeo of the Comedy, comes in front of the curtain.*

**TONIO:** A word—allow me! (*bowing*) sweet ladies and gentlemen, I pray you, hear, why alone I appear, I am the Prologue! Our author loves the custom of a prologue to his story, And as he would revive for you the ancient glory, He sends me before you to speak the prologue! But not to prate, as once of old, That the tears of the actor are false, unreal, That his sighs and cries, and the pain that is told, —He has no heart to feel! No! No! Our author to-night a chapter will borrow From life with its laughter and sorrow. Is not the actor a man with a heart like your? So 'tis for men that our author has written, And the story he tells you is—true! A song of tender memories deep in his listening heart One day was ringing; with trembling heart, he wrote it, And marked the time with sighs and tears. . . . Come then, Here on the stage you shall behold us, in human fashion,

ate!
(*Rientra e la tela si teva.*)

And see the sad fruits of love and passion! Hearts that weep and languish, cries of rage and anguish, And bitter laughter. . . . Ah, think then—sweet people, When you look on us, clad in our motley and tinsel, Ours are human hearts, beating with passion, We all are men like you, for gladness or sorrow. 'Tis the same broad Heaven above us, The same wide lonely world before us! Will you hear then the story, how it unfolds itself, surely and certain? Come then! ring up the curtain! (*Exit. The curtain rises.*)

### SCENA I.

*La scena rappresenta un bivio di strada in compagna, al l'entrats di un villaggio. La destra occupata obliquamente da un teatro di fiera. All' alzarsi della tela si sen ono squilli di tromba stonata alternantisi con dei colpi di cassa, ed insieme risa e, grida allegre, fischi di monelli e vociare che vanno appressandosi.—Attirati dal suono e dal frastuono i contadini di ambo i sessi, in abito da fes a, accorrono a frolte dal viale, mentre Tonio il gobbo, va a guardare verso il strada a sinistra, poi, annojato dalla folla che arriva, si*

### SCENE I.

*SCENE: The entrance of a village, —where two roads meet. On right, a travelling theatre. As the curtain rises, sounds of a trumpet out of tune and a drum are heard. Laughing, shouting, whistling voices approaching. Enter Villagers in holiday attire. Tonio looks up road on left. Then, worried by the crowd which stares at him, lies down in front of the theatre. Time 3 o'clock. – Bright sunlight.*

*sdraia, ainanzi al teatro. Son tre ore dopo mezzogiorno; il sole di agosto splende cocente.*
*Coro di Contadini, Nedda, Canio, Tonio, e Peppe.*

**CORO DI UOMINI E DONNE:** (*arrivando a poco a poco*). Son quà!
Ritornano . . .
Pagliaccio è là.
Tutti lo seguono grandi e ragazzi e ognuno applaude ai motti, ai lazzi.
Ed egli serio saluta e passa e torna a battere su la gran cassa
In aria gittano i lor cappelli, fra strida e sibili, tutti i monelli.

**MEN AND WOMEN:** (*entering one by one*) This way they come
With pipe and drum,
This way they come,
This way they come,
Here's a pretty Columbine
And Punchinello,
A merry fellow.
With laugh and jest
They come, they come
Look how sedately
He smiles and passes,
Beating his drum
With a nod to the lasses.

**RAGASSI:** (*di dentro*). Ehi, sferza l'asino, bravo Arlecchino!

**BOYS:** (*behind*) Hi there! Harlequin!
Whip up your donkey!

**CANIO:** (*di dentro*). Itene al diavolo!

**CANIO:** (*behind*) Go to the devil!

**PEPPE:** (*di dentro*). To, birichino!
(*Un gruppo di monelli entra, correndo, in scena dalla sinistra.*)
Indietro, arrivano . . .
Ecco il carretto . . .
Che diavolerio
Dio benedetto!
(*Arriva una pittoresca carretta dipinta a varfi colori e tirata da un asino che Peppe, in abito da Arlechino, guida a mano camminando, mentre collo scudiscio allontana i ragazzi. Sulla carretta sul davanti e sdrajata Nedda in un costume tra la zingara e l'acrobata. Dietro ad essaiè piazzata la gran cassa. Sul di dietro della carretta è Canio in piedi, in costume di Pagliaccio, tenendo nella destra una trombe e nella sinistra la mazza della gran cassa.— I contadini e le contadine attorniano festosamente la carretta.*)

**BEPPE:** (*behind*). Take that, you monkey!
(*Crowd of boys run on from left.*)
Keep back! They're coming now,
The wagon's coming!
Oh what an awful row!
Oh what a drumming!
(*Enter Beppe, dressed as a harlequin leading donkey, which draws a gaily painted cart, in which Nedda is lying. Behind her, the drum, and Canio, dressed as Punchinello in back of cart, trumpet in his right hand, drumsticks in left. The villagers surround the cart.*)

**TUTTI:** Evviva! il principe se' dei pagliacci
Tu i guai discacci
co 'l lieto umor.
Evviva!

**VILLAGERS:** Hail, Punchinello!
Long live the merry king,
Who keeps us mellow!
He is the blithest fellow!
Long life to him we sing!
Hail, Punchinello!

**CANIO:** Grazie . . .

**CANIO:** Thank you!

**CORO:** Bravo!

**VILLAGERS:** Bravo!

**CANIO:** Vorrei . . .

**CANIO:** Allow me.

**CORO:** E lo spettacolo?

**VILLAGERS:** Now then begin the play!

**CANIO:** (*picchiando forte e ripetutamente sulla cassa per dominar le voci*). Signori miei!

**CANIO:** (*beating drum*) Gentlemen all. (*Drowning the voices of the crowd.*)

**TUTTI:** (*scostandosi e turandosi le orecchie*). Uh! ci assorda! . . . finiscila.

**VILLAGERS:** (*stopping their ears*). You deafen us. Do stop, I say!

**CANIO:** (*affettando cortesia e togliendosi il berretto con un gesto comico*). Mi accordan di parlar?

**CANIO:** (*politely*) A word, a word, I pray! (*Taking off his cap and bowing.*)

**LA FOLLA:** (*ridendo*). Oh! con lui si dee cedere.
tacere ed ascoltar.

**VILLAGERS:** Hush! Hush! be quiet, pray,
Begin and say your say!

**CANIO:** Un grande spettacolo a ventitrè ore
prepara il vostr' umile
e buon servitore.
(*Riverense.*)
Vedrete le smanie
del bravo Pagliaccio;
e come ei si vendica
e tende un bel laccio.
Vedrete di Tonio
tremar la carcassa,
e quale matassa
d'intrighi ordirà.
Venite, onorateci
Signori e Signore.
A ventitrè ore!
A ventitrè ore!

**CANIO:** This evening at seven o'clock I invite you
To see our performance, I know it will delight you.
We'll show you the troubles of poor Punchinello
And the vengeance he wreaked on a treacherous fellow;
And Tony the clown with his big corporation,
And strange combination of love and of hate.
O come then, and honor us,
You'll all be delighted,
At seven you're invited,
At seven you're invited!

**LA FOLLA:** Verremo, e tu serbaci il tuo buon umore.
A ventitrè ore!
A ventitrè ore!
(*Tonio ai avanza per ajutar Nedda a discendere dal carretto Canio, che è già saltato giù, gl'dà un ceffone dicendo.*)

**VILLAGERS:** With pleasure, with pleasure!
We are all delighted.
At seven we're invited!
At seven we're invited!
(*Tonio advances to help Nedda down from the cart, but Canio, who has already alighted, boxes his ears.*)

**CANIO:** Via da lì. (*Pol prende fra le bracci Nedda e la depone a terra.*)

**CANIO:** Get away! (*Takes Nedda by the arms and lifts her down.*)

**LE DONNE:** (*ridendo, a Tonio*). Prendi questo, bel galante!

**WOMEN:** (*laughing at Tonio*). How do you like it, pretty lover!

**I RAGAZZI:** (*fischiando*). Con salute!
(*Tonio mostra il pugno al monelli cne scappano, poi si allonta bron olando e scommoare sotto la tenda a destra del teatre.*)

**BOYS:** (*whistling*). How do you like it?
(*Tonio shakes his fists at the boys, who run away, and goes off, grumbling, right of theatre.*)

**TONIO:** (*a parte*). La pagherai! . . . brigante. (*Intanto Peppe conduce l'asino col carretto dietro al teatro.*)

**TONIO:** (*aside.*) Oh, he shall pay me, you'll discover!
(*Beppe leads off donkey and cart behind theatre.*)

**UN CONTADINO:** (*a Canio*). Di', con noi vuo' tu bevere un buon bicchiere sulla crocevia?

**VILLAGER:** (*to Canio*). Say! will you drink with me a measure?
They sell good liquor at the tavern yonder.

**CANIO:** Con piacere.

**CANIO:** With pleasure!

**PEPPE:** Aspettatemi . . . Anch' io ci sto! (*Poi entra dall' altro lato del teatro per cambian costume.*)

**BEPPE:** I say! Wait, you two!
I'll come with you!
(*Enters theatre to change his dress.*)

**CANIO:** (*gridando verso il fondo*). Di Tonio, vieni via?

**CANIO:** (*calling towards theatre*). Hi! Tonio, are you coming?

**TONIO:** (*di dentro*). Io netto il somarello. Precedetemi.

**TONIO:** (*behind*). I've got to clean the donkey.
I'll soon be after you.

**UN CONTADINO:** (*ridendo*). Bada, Pagliaccio, ei solo vuol restare per far la corte a Nedda.

**VILLAGER:** (*laughing to Canio*). Take care, my master. He waits till you're departed, to go a-courting Nedda!

**CANIO:** (*ghignando, ma con cipiglio*). Eh! Eh! vi pare?
(*tra il serio e l'ironico*). Un tal gioco, credetemi, è meglio non giocarlo.
con me, miei cari; e a Tonio . . . e un poco a tutti or parlo.
Il teatro e la vita non son la stessa cosa;
e se lassù Pagliaccio sorprende la sua sposa
col bel galante in camera, fa un

**CANIO:** (*smiling and frowning*). You think so?
(*half in earnest, half ironically*) Such a game, believe me, friends, is hardly worth the playing.
Let Tonio ponder what I am saying.
For the Stage and Life are different, you'll discover;
For if up there
(*pointing to the theatre*)
I caught her—my lady, with a lover,

comico sermone,
poi si calma od arrendesi ai colpi di
bastone! . . .
Ed il pubblico applaude, ridendo
allegramente.
Ma se Nedda sul serio sorprendes-
si . . . altramente
finirebbe la storia, com'è ver che vi
parlo . . .
Un tal gioco, credetemi, è meglio
non giocarlo.

NEDDA: (a parte). Confusa io
son! . . .

ALCUNI CONTADINI: Sul serio
pigli dunque la cosa!

CANIO: (un po' commosso). Io?
. . . Vi pare! . . . Scusatemi . . .
Adoro la mia sposa!
(Canio va a baciar Nedda in
fronte. Un suono di cornamusa si
fa sentire all'interno; tutti si precipitano verso la sinistra, guardando fre le quinte.)

I MONELLI: (gridando). I zampognari! . . . I zampog-
nari! . . .

GLI UOMINI: Verso la chiesa vanno
i compari
(Le campane suonano a vespero
da lontano.)

I VECCHI: Essi accompagnano la
comitiva che a coppie al vespero
sen va giuliva.

LE DONNE: Andiam.—La campana
ci appella al signore.

CANIO: Ma poi.. ricoratevi, A ventitrè ore.
(I zampognari arrivano dalla sinistra in abito da festa con nastri
da colori vivaci e fiori ai cappelli
acuminati. Li seguono una frotta
di contadini e contadine anch'
essi parati a festa. Il coro, che è
sulla scena, scambia con questi
saluti e sorrisi, poi tutti si dispon-
gone a coppie ed a gruppi, si uniscono alla comitiva e si allontanano, cantando, pel viale del fondo,
dietro al teatro)

CORO GENERALE: Din, don,—
suona vespero,
ragazze e garzon,
a coppie affrettiamoci,
al tempio—din, don!
Il sol diggia i culmini,
Din, don, vuol baciar;
Le mamme ci adocchiano,
attenti, compar.
Din, don.—Tutto irradiasi
di luce, d'amor;
Ma i vecchi sorvegliano,
gli arditi amador.
Din, don—suona vespero,
ragazze e garzon.
Le squille ci appellano
al tempio—din, don!
(Durante il coro, Canio entra dietro al teatro e va a lasciar la sua

---

I'd preach a little sermon, and get
into a passion,
Then calmly I would seat me there,
And let her lover beat me there,
while the people would applaud
me in the usual silly fashion!
But if Nedda—in earnest should
deceive me,
The ending would be different, believe me.
Mark the words that I am saying,
such a game, believe me, friends, is
hardly worth the playing!

NEDDA: (aside). What can he
mean?

VILLAGERS: But surely you cannot
suspect her?

CANIO: (slightly moved). No, no,
of course not. That could not be.
I love her and respect her!
(Kisses Nedda on her forehead.)
(Bagpipes heard from within. The
villagers run to the left and look
off.)

BOYS: Hark! hark the bagpipes!
The pipers are coming!

MEN: See where the people
churchward are going!

OLD PEOPLE: Hark to the bagpipes so merrily blowing!
Gaily the couples to vespers are going!

WOMEN: Come away!
The gray twilight falls,
The Angelus calls!

CANIO: Yes, but remember, pray,
At seven you're invited!
(Enter bagpipe Players from left,
in holiday attire. A troop of villagers follows. Villagers on stage
greet them. All disperse in couples, and at close of chorus go off
singing, down road behind theatre.)

CHORUS: Ding, dong! the shadows
fall,
Then come, one and all!
To the church come away
Ding, dong! we roam along,
In love's dream so fair.
But mothers have watchful eyes,
Beware! oh beware!
Soon in the twilight
Love will be told;
But the old folks are watching,
Be not too bold!
Ding, dong! all above,
All around, is bright with love.
Ding, dong! the shadows fall,
Come one and all!
(During the above, Canio goes
into theatre, and after taking off
his Punchinello's dress, returns,

---

giubba da Pagliaccio, poi ritorna,
e dopo aver fatto, sorridendo, un
cenno d'addio a Nedda, parte con
Peppe a cinque o sei contadini per
la sinistra.—Nedda resta sola.)

## SCENA II.

*Nedda sola, poi Tonio*

NEDDA: (pensierosa). Qual fiamma avea nel guardo!
Gii occhi abbassai per tema ch'ei ei
leggesse
Il mio pensier segreto.
Oh! s'ei mi sorprendesse . . .
brutale come egli è . . . Ma basti,
orvia.
Son questi sogni paurosi e fole!
O che bel sole
di mezz' agosto! Io son piena di
vita, e tutta illanguidita
per arcano desio, non so che bramo!
(Guardando in cielo.) Oh! che
volo d' augelli, e quante strida!
Che chiedon? dove van? chissà ..La
mamma
mia, che la buona ventura ann o
nciava,
comprendeva il lor canto e a me
bambina così cantava:
Hui! stridono lassù, liberamente
lanciati a vol come frecce, gli augel.
Disfidano le nubi e 'l sol cocente,
e vanno, e vanno per le vie del ciel.
Lasciateli vagar per l' atmosfera
questi assetati d' azzurro e splendor:
seguono anch' essi un sogno, una
chimera,
e vanno, e vanno fra le nubi d'or.
Che incalzi il vento e latri la
tempesta,
con l' ali aperte san tutto sfidar;
la pioggia, i lampi, nulla mai li
arresta,
e vanno, e vanno, sugli abissi e i
mar.
Vanno laggiù verso un paese strano,
che sognan forse e che cercano invan.
Ma i boëmi del ciel seguon l'arcano
poter che li sospinge . . . e vanno.. e van!
(Tonio durante la canzone sarà
uscito di dietro al teatro e sarà ito
ad appoggiarsi all' albero, ascoltando beato.—Nedda, finito il
canto fa per rientrare e lo scorge.)

NEDDA: (bruscamente contrariata). Sei là? credea che te ne fossi
andato.

---

nods good-bye to Nedda with a
smile, and goes off with Beppe and
five or six villagers, left. Nedda remains.)

## SCENE II.

*Nedda, alone, then Tonio.*

NEDDA: (musing). How fierce he
looked and watched me!
I hung my head, fearing lest he
should discover
My secret thoughts of my lover.
Heavens! if he should suspect me,
With all his brutal ways! No matter!
I fear not,
These are but empty dreams and
idle fancies.
Shine, oh glorious sun, upon me!
Every pulse is throbbing, glowing,
Like the tide, my passion flowing,
Oh my heart, my restless heart,
where are you going?
(Looking to the sky.)
Ah, beautiful song-birds! I hear
your pinions.
What do you seek? Where are you
going? Who knows?
My mother knew the meaning of
your sweet voices,
And the song she sang me in happy
childhood
Comes back forever! High! high
aloft they fly,
Through Heaven's blue ether
launched in their flight,
Like arrows of light, in the sky,
The storm clouds and the tempest
and the sunlight defying,
For ever flying,—through the
boundless sky!
Afar, ever they journey! on, upward
for ever!
On! wearying never, their fetterless
wings unfold.
They have their visions, their tender, beautiful visions,
They soar forever through clouds of
gold.
What though the wind howls, and
night is dark above them,
Spreading their pinions by planet
and star,
No night dismays them, no storm
delays them,
They soar forever over sea and scar.
Far! oh so far they fly on wings un-
tiring,
Seeking sweet regions they may
never know,
For what can bar their dreams and
their desiring?
It is fate that leads them;—still on
they go!
(during the song, Tonio comes
from behind theatre, leans
against tree listening. As Nedda
moves to go off, she sees him.)

NEDDA: (crossly). What! You? I
thought that you had gone to market!

TONIO: (*ridiscendendo, con dolcezza*). E colpa del tuo canto. Affascinato io mi beava!

NEDDA: (*ridendo con scherno*). Oh! quanta poesia! . . .

TONIO: Non rider, Nedda . . .

NEDDA: Va, va all' osteria.

TONIO: So ben che difforme, contorto son io;
che desto soltanto lo scherno o l' orror.
Eppure ha 'l pensiero un sogno, un desio, e un palpito il cor!
Allor che sdegnosa mi passi d' accanto
non sai tu che pianto mi spreme il dolor,
perchè, mio maìgrado, subito ho l' incanto m' ha vinto l' amor!
(*Appressandosi.*) Oh! lasciami, lasciami or dirti . . .

NEDDA: (*interrompendolo e beffeggiandolo*). che m'ami?
Hai tempo a ridirmelo stasera, se il brami,
facendo le smorfie colà, sulla scena.
Intanto risparmiati per ora la pena.

TONIO: (*delirante con impeto*).
No, è qui che voglio dirtelo,
e tu m' ascolterai.
che t' amo ti desidero,
e che tu mia sarai!

NEDDA: (*seria ed insolente*). Eh!
dite, mastro Tonio!
La schiena oggi vi prude, o una tirata d' orecchi è necessaria
al vostro ardor?

TONIO: Ti beffi? sciagurata!
Per la croce di Dio, bada che puoi
pagarla cara! . . .

NEDDA: Tu minacci? . . . Vuoi
che vada a chiamar Canio?

TONIO: (*movendo verso di lei*).
Non prima chio ti baci

NEDDA: (*retrocedendo*). Bada!

TONIO: (*s'avanza ancora aprendo le braccia per ghermir la*). Oh,
tosto sarai mia! . . .

NEDDA: (*sale retrocendo verso il teatrino, vede la frusta lasciata de Peppe, l' afferra e dà un colpo faccia a Tonio, dicendo*). Miserabile! . . .

TONIO: (*coming forward*). The fault lies in your singing.
(*Caressingly.*)
The song bewitched me,
And I could not leave you.

NEDDA: (*laughing scornfully*).
Ha! ha! How very poetic.

TONIO: Do not laugh, Nedda.

NEDDA: Go to the tavern!

TONIO: I know that you hate me and laugh in derision,
For what is the Clown? he plays but a part.
Yet he has his dream, and his hope and his vision,
The Clown has a heart.
And ah when you pass me, uncaring, unseeing,
You know not my sorrow, so cruel and sweet.
I give you my spirit, my life, and my being,
I die at your feet.
(*Approaching her.*)
Ah, hear me then, hear me then,
Let me tell you—

NEDDA: (*interrupting and scoffing at him*). —You love me.
It's time enough to tell me this evening,
Tonight when you're playing the fool,
With sighs and grimaces,
Why not postpone the confession till then?

TONIO: (*passionately*). No, it is now I will tell you,
And you shall hear me now.
I love you, worship and long for you,
To make you mine for ever.

NEDDA: (*with studied insolence*)
Tell me, silly varlet,
Do your shoulders itch for a drubbing?
Or do your ears want a rubbing?
How shall I teach you to cool your love?

TONIO: You mock me? Too long I've borne it.
By the cross of the Saviour, I'll make you pay,
I've sworn it!

NEDDA: You threaten?
Must I then call Canio to you?

TONIO: (*moving towards her*).
But not before I kiss you!

NEDDA: (*drawing back*). Hands off!

TONIO: (*advancing and putting out his arms to embrace her*). No!
No! you shall be mine.
(*Nedda goes up stage backwards, sees whip left by Beppe, takes it up and strikes Tonio in the face.*)

NEDDA: Unhand me, wretch!

TONIO: (*dà un urlo e retrocede*).
Ah! Per la vergin pia di mezz' agosto
Nedda, lo giuro . . . me la pagherai! . . .
(*Esce minacciando dalla sinistra.*)

NEDDA: (*immobile guardandolo allontanarsi*). Aspide! va.—Ti sei svelato ormai
Tonio lo scemo!—Hai l' animo
Siccome il corpo tuo difforme . . . lurido!..

## SCENA III.

*Silvio, Nedda, e poi Tonio.*

SILVIO: (*sporgendo la metà dei corpo arrampicandosi dal muretto a destra, e chiama a bassa voce*). Nedde!

NEDDA: (*affrettandosi verso di lui*). Silvio! a quest' ora . . . che imprudenza.

SILVIO: (*saltando allegramente e venendo verso di lei*). Ah bah! sapea che non rischiavo nulla.
Canio e Peppe da lunge a la taverna no scorto con gli amici! . . . Ma prudente per la macchia a me nota qui ne venni.

NEDDA: E ancora un poco in Tonio t' imbattevi.

SILVIO: (*ridendo*). Oh! Tonio il gobbo!

NEDDA: Il gobbo è da temersi.
M' ama . . . Ora qui mel!
disse . . . e nel bestiale delirio suo, baci chiedendo, ardiva correr su me . . .

SILVIO: Per Dio!

NEDDA: Ma con la frusta
del cane immondo la foga calmai.

SILVIO: E fra quest' ansie in eterno vivrai?
Decidi il mio destin,
Nedda, Nedda rimani!
Tu il sai; la festa ha fin e parte ognun dimani.
E quando tu di qui sarai partita che addiverrà di me . . . de la mia vita? . . .

NEDDA: (*commossa.*) Silvio!

SILVIO: Nedda, rispondimi.
Se è ver che Canio non amasti mai,
se è vero che t' è in odio
il ramingare e il mestier che tu fai,
se l'immenso amor tuo fola non è
questa notte partiam! . . . fuggi con me.

TONIO: (*screaming and drawing back*). By the Holy Virgin of the Assumption, Nedda,
I swear it, I'll be revenged upon you.
(*Exit left, with threatening gestures.*)

NEDDA: Viper, begone! You have revealed your nature.
Tonio—the Fool! You have a heart as foul
And ugly as your body, ay! fouler still!

## SCENE III.

*Silvio, Nedda; then Tonio*
*Silvio leans half over wall, right, and calls in a low voice.*

SILVIO: Nedda!

NEDDA: (*hurrying towards him*) Silvio! at this hour. What madness!

SILVIO: (*jumping over and coming towards her*). Bah! Bah! No danger, dear, I'm thinking.
Canio I left at yonder tavern drinking.
By the pathway that we love,
through the bushes, I came here.

NEDDA: A moment sooner and Tonio would have caught you.

SILVIO: (*laughing*). Ha! ha! The fool!

NEDDA: The fool is to be feared.
He loves me,
Just now he told me.
With burning words and brutal fire,
He tried to kiss me in his mad desire.

SILVIO: By Heaven!

NEDDA: No, don't be anxious! For such a passion,
A whip's the fashion.
(*Pointing to Beppe's whip.*)

SILVIO: Why will you live, then, for ever like this, Nedda?
My fate is in your hands.
Nedda, pity my sorrow.
Tonight the fair is over,
You will be gone tomorrow.
Ah, what of me, when you have departed?
How shall I live apart from you
And broken-hearted?

NEDDA: (*deeply moved*). Silvio!

SILVIO: Nedda, hear, I implore you!
If for your husband no passion inspires you,
If all this roving life sickens and tires you,
If this great love of yours is not empty delight,
Fly with me, fly with me, dearest, tonight!

NEDDA: Non mi tentar!... Vuoi tu—perder la vita mia?
Taci Silvio, non più . . . —E deliro . . . è follìa
Io mi confido a te—a te cui diedi il cor
Non abusar di me—de 'l mio febbrile amor! . . .
Non mi tentar!..E poi . . . —Chissè! meglio è partir
Sta il destin contro noi.—E vano il nostro dir.
Eppure da 'l mio cor—strapparti non poss' io,
Vivrò sol de l' amor—ch' hai destato al cor mio.
(*Tonio appare dal fondo a sinistra.*)

SILVIO: No, più non m' ami!

TONIO: (*scorgendoli, a parte*). T' ho colta, sgualdrina!
(*Fugge dal sentiero minacolando.*)

NEDDA: Si, t' amo! t' amo!

SILVIO: E parti domattina?
(*Amorasamente, cercando ammaliaria.*)
E allor perchè, di', tu m' hai stregato
se vuoi lasciarmi senza pietà?
Quel bacio tuo perchè me l' hai dato
fra spasimi ardenti di voluttà?
Se tu scordasti l' ore fugaci
io non lo posso, e voglio ancor
que' spasmi ardenti, que' caldi baci
che tanta febbre m' han messo in cor!

NEDDA: (*vinta e smarrita*). Nulla scordai—m'ha sconvolta e turbata
questo amor che ne 'l guardo ti sfavilla.
Viver voglio a te avvinta, affascinata
una vita d' amor calma e tranquilla.
A te mi dono; su me solo impera.
Ed io ti prendo e m' abbandono intera.

SILVIO: (*stringendoia fra le braccia*). Verrai? . . .

NEDDA: Si—baciami! . . .

SILVIO: Tutto scordiamo . . .

NEDDA: Negli occhi guardami!

SILVIO: Si, ti guardo e ti bacio, t'amo . . . t'amo!

## SCENA IV.

*I precedenti, Canio e poi Peppe.*

*Mentre Silvio e Nedda s' avviano parlando verso il muriccluo arrivano, camminando furtivamente dalla scorciatoia, Canio e Tonio*

---

NEDDA: Ah, tempt me not! Has not life enough of sadness?
Silvio, tempt me no more. It is folly, it is madness!
Have I not given you my heart? You have my love for all time.
Then say good-bye and part. You will not then betray.
Ah, tempt me not, for pity's sake, my heart will break!
Who knows, dear heart, it is best to part!
Tears are vain, all is vain; we must not meet again.
And yet remembering all our love, since first I met you.
I shall dream of you, live for you, never forget you.
(*Tonio appears at back, left.*)

SILVIO: No! you do not love me!

TONIO: (*aside, watching*). I've caught you, you strumpet!
(*Runs down pathway, with threatening gestures.*)

NEDDA: I love you, love you!

SILVIO: And yet you leave me tomorrow.
(*Lovingly, trying to move her.*)
Why have you taught me Love's magic story, If you will leave me, hopeless, alone?
Why press to mine your lips in their glory, Why fold your heart unto mine?
If you forget all our caresses, I still remember that dream divine,
I want your heart, your passionate kisses, I want your spirit to melt in mine!

NEDDA: (*overcome and yielding*). Can I forget, as I see you before me,
The spell of love your heart has woven over me?
By the words you have spoken, the ties that have bound me,
All I want is your love, folded around me.
Ah, do not leave me! why must we sever?
You have my heart, and I am yours forever!

SILVIO: (*clasping her in his arms*). Will you come?

NEDDA: Yes! Kiss me, love!

SILVIO: Forget the past, think not of tomorrow!

NEDDA: Look in my eyes, and kiss away my sorrow.

SILVIO: In your dear eyes, I kiss away my sorrow.

## SCENE IV.

*The same. Canio, and then Beppe.*

*As Nedda and Silvio go off towards the wall, talking, Canio and Tonio come stealthily by the short path.*

---

TONIO: (*ritenendo Canio*). Cammina adagio e li sorprenderai.
(*Canio s' avanza cautamente sempre ritenuto da Tonio noe potendo vedere, dal punto ove si trova, Silvio che scavalca il muricciuolo.*)

SILVIO: (*che ha già la metà del corpo dall' altro lato ritenendosi al muro*). Ad alta notte laggiù mi terrò.
Cauta discendi e mi ritroverai.
(*Silvio scompare e Canio si appressa all' angolo del teatro.*)

NEDDA: (*a Silvio che sarà scomparso di sotto*). A stanotte—e per sempre tua sarò!

CANIO: (*che dal punto ove si trova ode queste parole, dà un urlo*). Oh! . . .

NEDDA: (*si volge spaventata e grida verso il muro*). Fuggi!
(*D' un balzo Canio arriva anch' esso al muro; Nedda gli si para dinante ma dopo breve lotta egli la spinge da un canto, scavalca il muro e scompare.—Tonio resta a sinistra guardando Nedda che come inchiodata presso il muro cerca sentire se si ode rumore di lotta mormorando.*)

NEDDA: Aitalo . . . Signor! . . .

TONIO: (*ridendo cinicamente*). Ah! . . . ah!

LA VOCE DI CANIO: (*di dentro*). Vile! t' ascondi!

NEDDA: (*al riso di Tonio si è voltata e dice con disprezzo fissandolo*). Bravo! Bravo il mio Tonio!

TONIO: Fo quel che posso!

NEDDA: E quello che pensavo!

TONIO: Ma di far assai meglio non dispero.

NEDDA: Mi fai schifo e ribrezzo.

TONIO: Oh, non sai come lieto ne son!
(*Canio intanto scavalca di nuovo il muro e ritorna in iscena pallido, asciugando il sudore con un fazzoletto di colore oscuro.*)

CANIO: (*con rabbia concentrata*). Derisione e scherno!
Nulla! Ei ben lo conosce quel sentiero
Fa lo stesso; poichè del drudo il nome
or mi dirai.

NEDDA: (*volgendosi turbata*). Chi?

CANIO: (*furente*). Tu, pel padre eterno! . . .
(*Cavando dalla cinta lo stiletto.*)
E se in questo momento qui scannata non t' ho già, gli è perchè pria di lordarla nel tuo fetido sangue, o

---

TONIO: (*holding Canio back*). Tread lightly, lightly, and you will catch them so!
(*Canio advances cautiously, still held back by Tonio; they cannot see Silvio getting over the wall.*)

SILVIO: (*half over the wall*). At midnight, dearest, I wait you below!
Come to me, love, when the star-beams shine.
(*Silvio disappears, and Canio approaches the corner of the theatre.*)

NEDDA: Tonight, love, and forever I am yours!

CANIO: (*who overhears*). Ha!

NEDDA: (*turns round, frightened, and calls toward the wall*). Fly, love!
(*Canio with one bound reaches the wall; Nedda places herself in front of him. After a short struggle he pushes her into a corner, gets over the wall and disappears. Tonio remains on left, watching Nedda, who, as if pinned to the wall, tries to hear whether they are fighting.*)

NEDDA: Ah, Heaven, preserve him now!

TONIO: (*laughing ironically*). Ha! ha!

CANIO: (*outside*). Coward! where are you?

NEDDA: (*turning at Tonio's laugh, looking with disgust at him*). Well done, well done, then, Tonio.

TONIO: Yes—yes, I did it.

NEDDA: Just like you, you coward!

TONIO: But next time, I expect to do better!

NEDDA: You make me hate and loathe you.

TONIO: Love me, or hate me! It is nothing to me.
(*Canio re-enters, over the wall, pale, and wiping the perspiration from his forehead.*)

CANIO: So again, she's fooled me. Baffled again!
He knows the path too well.
But no matter. This moment you shall tell me
Your lover's name.

NEDDA: (*turning in confusion*). Who?

CANIO: (*furiously*). You, by Heaven eternal!
And if here now this moment, I have not cut your throat,
(*drawing dagger from his belt*)
It's because before I kill you, and

svergognata, codesta lama, io vo' il suo nome.—Parla.

NEDDA: Vano è l' insulto.—È muto il labbro mio.

CANIO: (urlando). Il nome, il nome, non tardare o donna!

NEDDA: No, nol dirò giammai...

CANIO: (slanciandosi furente col pugnale alzato). Per la madonna!...
(Peppe, che sarà entrato dalla sinistra, sulla risposta di Nedda corre a Canio e gli strappa il pugnale che gitta via tra gli alberi.)

PEPPE: Padron! che fate!... Per l' amor di Dio... La gente esce di chiesa e a lo spettacolo qui muovo... andiamo Canio, via, cal matevi!

CANIO: (dibattendosi). Lasciami Peppe—Il nome, il nome.

PEPPE: Tonio vieni a tenerlo. Andiamo arriva il pubblico.
(Tonio prende Canio per la mano méntre Peppe si volge a Nedda.)
Vi spiegherete.—E voi di lì tiratevi. Andatevi a vestir—Sapete, Canio, è violento, ma buono...
(Spinge Nedda sotto la tenda e scompare con essa.)

CANIO: (stringendo il capo frat le mani). Infamia! infamia!

TONIO: (piano a Canio, spingendolo sul davanti della scena). Calmatevi padrone.—E meglio fingere; il ganzo tornerà.—Di me fidatevi.
(Canio ha un gesto disperato, ma Tonio spingendolo col gomito, prosegue piano.)
Io la sorveglio—Ora facciam la recita. Chissà ch' egli non venga a lo spettacolo e si tradisca! Or via.—Bisogna fingere per riuscir...

PEPPE: (uscendo dalle scene). Andiamo, via, vestitevi padrone.—E tu batti la cassa, Tonio.
(Tonio va di dietro al e teatro Peppe anch esso ritorna al' interno, mentre Canio accasciato si avvia lentamente verso la cortina.)

CANIO: Recitar!... mentre preso dal delirio non so più quel che dico e quel che faccio! Eppur... è d' uopo...sforzati! Bah, se' tu forse un uom? Tu se' Pa-

your blood stains my dagger, You shameless woman, you will tell me Who is your lover. Tell me!

NEDDA: Vain are your insults. My lips are sealed forever.

CANIO: (shouting). His name, I tell you. This moment, you shall tell me.

NEDDA: No! No! Never will I tell you.

CANIO: (rushing on her furiously with dagger raised). By Heaven, I'll kill you.
(Beppe, entering left, hearing Nedda's answer, snatches dagger from Canio and throws it away among the trees.)

BEPPE: Ah, stay, good master, for the love of God! The people! see! they're coming. Look, where they come from church, to see the play. Come away. Be calm, I pray.

CANIO: (struggling). Leave me, I tell you. His name, then, his name!

BEPPE: Tonio, come here and hold him. The people come this way. Don't let them see you.
(Tonio takes Canio by the hand, while Beppe turns to Nedda.)
And Nedda, you go, I say. Go and dress yourself. You know well, Canio Is hasty but tender.
(Pushes Nedda under the curtain and exits with her.)

CANIO: (holding his head in both hands). It is shameful, shameful!

TONIO: (in a low voice to Canio, pushing him towards front of stage). Ah! calm yourself, my master. It is best to make believe! The gallant will return. I am convinced of it. Trust me to watch her. Now it is time the play began.
(Canio makes a fierce gesture, but Tonio, pushing him by the elbow, comes forward slowly.)
Who knows? Haply the lover will be here tonight, And will betray it. Come, then, we must dissemble, If we would win.

BEPPE: (entering, to Canio). Come, come, go dress yourself, I pray you.
(To Tonio.)
And you play up your drum there, Tonio!
(Tonio goes behind, Beppe re-enters theatre. Canio, worn out with emotion, walks slowly towards the curtain.)

CANIO: To act, with my heart saddened with sorrow. I know not what I'm saying or what I'm doing. Yet I must face it. Courage, my heart!

gliacci! Vesti la giubba e la faccia infarina. La gente paga e rider vuole quà. E se Arlecchin t' invola Colombina, ridi, Pagliaccio... e ognuno applaudirà! Tramuta in lazzi lo spasmo ed il pianto; in una smorfia il singhiozzo e 'l dolor... Ridi Pagliaccio, sul tuo amore infranto! Ridi del duol che t' avvelena il cor!
(Entra commosso sotto la tenda, mentre la tela cade lentamente.)

(Fine del' atto primo.)

# ATTO SECONDO.

La stessa scena dell' atto primo.

## SCENA PRIMA.

Tonio compare dall'altro lato del teatro colla gran cassa e ra a piazzarsi sull' angolo sinistro del proscenio del teatrino. Intanto la gente arriva da tutte le parti per lo spettacolo e Beppe viene a metters nel banchi per le donne.
Donne, Uomini, Tonio, Nedda, Silvio, Peppe, Canio a Coro.

DONNE: (arrivando). Presto, affrettiamoci svelto, compare, chè lo spettacolo dee cominciare. Cerchiam di metterci ben sul davanti.

TONIO: (picchiando la cassa). Si dà principio; avanti! avanti!

UOMINI: Veh, come corrono le bricconcelle! Accomodatevi comari belle O Dio, Che correre per giunger tosto!
(Silvio arriva dal fondo e va a pigliar posto sul devanti a sinistra salutando gli amici.)

TONIO: Si dà principio pigliate posto!

LE DONNE: (cervando sedersi, spingendosi).—Ma non pigiatevi, fa caldo tanto! —Su; Peppe ajutaci. V' è posto accanto!
(Nedda esce vestita da Colombina col piatto per incassare i posti.—Peppe cerca di mettere a posto le donne.—Tonio rientra ad teatro portando via la gran cassa.)

You are not a man; you're but a jester! On with the motley, the paint and the powder, The people pay you and want their laugh, you know. If Harlequin your Columbine has stolen, Laugh, Punchinello! The world will cry 'Bravo!' Go hide with laughter your tears and your sorrow, sing and be merry, playing your part, Laugh, Punchinello, for the love that is ended, Laugh for the sorrow that is eating your heart.
(Passes under the curtain of the stage theatre, while the curtain slowly falls.)

(End of the first act.)

# ACT II.

Scene as in Act I.

## SCENE I.

Tonio appears with big drum and takes up his position at the left angle of the theatre. People come from different directions for the performance. Beppe places benches for the women.

WOMEN: (arriving). Quickly, sweet gossips come, The show's beginning, Hark, how they beat the drum, Oh, what a dinning! Come, quickly, come, I say, Let's get good places.

TONIO: (beating drum). Walk up and see the play, All take your places.

MEN: Look how they rush and run, Ribbons and laces, Come here and see the fun, My pretty faces! Oh, what a crush and rush, Just for first places!
(Silvio comes from back, and takes his place in front, left, nodding to his friends.)

TONIO: Walk up, walk up, I say, All take your places!

WOMEN: (sitting down, pushing each other). Why are you pushing, you? I'm nearly baking; Help, Beppe, help us, do! Our places taking.
(Nedda enters dressed as Columbine, holding plate to receive money. Beppe tries to settle the women. Tonio re-enters theatre, carrying away the drum.)

## Act II, Scene I

**UNA PARTE DEL CORO:** (*a Peppe*). Suvvia, spicciatevi incominciate.
Perchè tardate?
Siam tutti là.

**PEPPE:** Che furia, diavolo!
Prima pagate.
Nedda, incassate

**TUTTI:** (*volendo pagare nelio stesso tempo*). Di qua—di qua!

**UN'ALTRA PARTE DEL CORO:**
Veh, si accapigliano! . . .
chiamano ajuto! . . .
Ma via, sedetevi
senza gridar.

**SILVIO:** (*piano a Nedda, pagando il posto*). Nedda!

**NEDDA:** Sii cauto!
Non t' ha veduto.

**SILVIO:** Verrò ad attenderti.
Non obliar! . . .
(*Nedda dopo aver lasciato Silvio riceve ancora il prezzo della sedie da altri, e poi rientra anch' essa nel teatro con Peppe.*)

**CORO GENERALE:** Questa commedia incominciate.
Perchè tardate?
Perchè indugiar?
Facciamo strepito.
facciam rumore,
ventitrè ore
suonaron già.
Allo spettacolo
ognuno anela! . . .
(*Si ode una lunga e forte scampanellata.*)
S' alza la tela!
Silenzio.—Olà.
(*Le donne sono parte sedute sui banchi, situati obliquamente, volgendo la faccia alla scena del teatrino; parte in piedi formano gruppe cogli uomini sui rialzo di terra ov' è il grosso albero. Altri uomini piedi lungo le prime quinte a sinistra. Silvio è innanzi ad easi.*)

**SOME OF THE CROWD:** (*to Beppe*). Now, then, begin the play,
Have done your prating!
Why keep us waiting?
We all are here!

**BEPPE:** Keep back, keep back, I say!
First you must pay, please,
This way, this way, please!

**ALL:** (*trying to pay at once*). This way!
This way!

**OTHERS:** See how they fight their way
To get between us!
You, there! sit down, I say,
Take care, take care!

**SILVIO:** (*in a low voice to Nedda as he pays for his seat*). Nedda!

**NEDDA:** Be careful,
He has not seen us!

**SILVIO:** Tonight, remember, love!
I shall be there!
(*Nedda, leaving Silvio, takes money for more seats, and then re-enters theatre with Beppe.*)

**FULL CHORUS:** Now, then, begin the play,
Have done your prating!
Why keep us waiting?
Begin, I say!
Time to begin!—
Let's make a din!
It's seven o'clock, that's certain!
Ring up the curtain!
Time to begin! We all are in.
(*Bell rung loudly.*)
Ring up the curtain.
Silence, you there!
Begin! Begin!
(*Some of the women sit on benches placed obliquely towards the stage of theatre, others stand with the men on rising ground under tree. Others at wing, left. Silvio among them.*)

---

## SCENA II.

*Commedia.*

Nedda (Colombina), Peppe (Arlecchino), Canio (Pagliacci), Tonio (Taddeo), e Silvio.

*La tela del teatrino si alza.—La scena, mal dipinta, rappresenta una stanzetta con due porte laterali ed una finestra praticabile in fondo. Un tavolo e due sedie rozze di paglia son sulla destra del teatrine—Nedda in costume da Colombina passeggia ansiosa.*

**COLOMBINA:** Pagliaccio, mio marito,
a tar la notte sol ritornerà.
E quello scimunito

---

## SCENE II.

*The Play.*

Nedda (Columbine), Beppe (Harlequin), Canio (Punchinello), Tonio (Taddeo), and Silvio.

*Curtain of the theatre rises. Scene: a small room with two side doors, practicable window at back. Nedda as Columbine is walking about anxiously.*

**COLUMBINE:** My husband Punchinello does not
Come till morning; empty lies the street!

---

di Taddeo perchè ancora non è quà!
(*Si ode un pizzicar di chitarra all' interno; Colombina corre alla finestra e dà segni d' amorosa impazienza.*)

**LA VOCE DI ARLECCHINO:**
(*Peppe, di dentro*). O Colombina, il tenero
fido Arlecchin
È a te vicin!
Per te chiamando,
e sospirando—aspetta il poverin!
La tua faccetta mostrami,
ch' io vo' baciar
senza tardar
la tua boccuccia.
Amor mi cruccia—e mi sta a tormentar!
O Colombina schiudimi
il finestrin,
che a te vicin
ver te chiamando
e sospirando—è il povero Arlecchin!

**COLOMBINA:** (*ritornando ansiosa sul davanti*). Di far il segno covenuto appressa
l' istante, ed Arlecchino aspetta! . . .
(*Siede ansiosa volgendo le spalle alla porta si destra. Questa si apre e Tonio entra sotto le spoglie del servo Taddeo, con un paniere infilato al braccio sinis tro. Egli si arresta a contemplare Nedda cant aria esageratamente iragica, dicendo.*)

**TADDEO:** È dessa! (*Poi levando bruscamente al cielo le mani ed il paniere.*)
Dei, com'è bel a!
(*il pubblico sul teatro ride.*)
Se a la rubella
io disvelassi
l' amor mio che commuove sino i sassi!
Lungi è lo sposo.
Perchè non oso?
Soli noi stamo
e senza alcun sospetto! Orsù Proviamo
(*Sospiro lungo, esagerato.*)
Oh! . . .
(*Il pubblico ride.*)

**COLOMBINA:** (*volgendosi*). Sei tu, bestia?

**TADDEO:** (*immobile*). Quell' io sono, si!

**COLOMBINA:** E Pagliaccio è partito?

**TADDEO:** (*come sopra*). Egli parti!

**COLOMBINA:** Che fai così impalato?
Il pollo hai tu comprato?

**TADDEO:** Eccolo, vergin divina!
(*Precipitandosi in ginocchio, offrendo colle due mani il paniere. Colombina che si appressa.*)
Ed anzi eccoci entrambi ai piedi

---

Taddeo's at the market—lazy fellow!
All is safe and sweet!
(*A guitar is heard off. Columbine runs to window, with signs of love and impatience.*)

**HARLEQUIN:** (*behind the scene*).
O Columbine, unbar to me
Your lattice high.
I watch and sigh,
Longing to hear you
And be near you, as the hours go by.
Ah, show your little face to me.
So dear you are
You have my heart.
Ah, do not vex me,
Tease and perplex me! how can I live
Without your loving heart?
O Columbine, then listen to me,
Unbar, the door.
Come down, my star!
Come down, and love me,
See, where alone I sigh!
For if you love me not,
Then let me die!

**COLUMBINE:** (*returning anxiously to front*). Ah, yes! it is now love's hour entrancing!
The moment's advancing!
And Harlequin is waiting there!
(*Seats herself, with troubled looks, with her back to door on right, through which Tonio, dressed as Taddeo, enters with basket on left arm. He stops, and gazes at Nedda with exaggerated expression of love.*)

**TADDEO:** Behold her! (*Suddenly raising his hands and the basket to ceiling.*) Ah! how surpassing fair!
(*The audience laugh.*)
Ah! just to tell her, rebellious maiden,
Just to tell her the love with which I'm laden!
All safe and clear, now!
No husband near, now!
Why should I fear, now!
There's no one to suspect me.
Come, Love! Direct me!
(*Loud and exaggerated sigh. The audience laugh.*)

**COLUMBINE:** (*turning*). Well, fool? Is it you?

**TADDEO:** (*without moving*). Yes, it is I.

**COLUMBINE:** Have you seen Punchinello?

**TADDEO:** (*as before*). He went just now.

**COLUMBINE:** Come, then, what were you sent for?
Where is the fowl you went for?

**TADDEO:** (*throwing himself on his knees before Columbine and offering basket as he approaches*).
Low at your feet it is lying,
See us both.

---

400    I PAGLIACCI

tuoi.
Poichè l' ora è suonata, o Colombina,
di svelarti il mio cor. Di', udirmi vuoi?
Dal dì . . .
(*Colombina va alla finestra la schiude e fa un segno; pol va versa Taddeo.*)

COLOMBINA: (*strappandogli il paniere*). Quanto spendesti dal trattore?

TADDEO: Una e cinquanta. Da quel dì il mio core . . .

COLOMBINA: (*presso alla tavola*). Non seccarmi Taddeo!
(*Arlecchino scavalca la finestra, depone a terra una bottiglia che h (sotto il braccio, e poi va verso Taddeo mentre questi finge non verderlo.*))

TADDEO: (*a Colombina, con intenzione*). So che sei pura
E casta al par di neve! E ben che dura
Ti mostri, ad obliarti non riesco!

ARLECCHINO: (*lo piglia per l' orecchio dandogli un calcio e lo obbliga a levarzo*). Va a pigliar fresco!
(*Il pubblico ride.*)

TADDEO: (*retrocedendo comicamente verso la porta a destra*). Numi! s' aman! m' arrendo ai detti tuoi.
(*Ad Arlecchino.*)
Vi benedico!. . .là . . . veglio su voi!
(*Taddeo esce. Il pubblico ride ed applaude.*)

COLOMBINA: Arlecchin!

ARLECCHINO: (*con affetto esagerato*). Colombina! Alfin s'arrenda Ai nostri prieghi amor!

COLOMBINA: Facciam merenda!
(*Colombina prende dal tiretto due posate e due coltelli Arlecchino va a prender labottiglia, poi entrambi sieaono a tavola uno in faccia all'altro.*)

COLOMBINA: Guarda, mio ben, che splendida cenetta preparai!

ARLECCHINO: Guarda, amor mio, che nettare divino t' apportai!
(*A due.*)
L' amor ama gli effluvi del vin, de la cucina!

ARLECCHINO: Mia ghiotta Colombina!

COLOMBINA: Amabile beon!

(*Pointing to fowl in basket.*)
Ah! I implore you,
Luckless couple here before you,
O Columbine—be mine, be mine!
Hear, O maiden tender!
From the day—
(*Columbine opens window and makes signal.*)

COLUMBINE: (*turning to Taddeo*). How much, I say?
(*Snatching basket.*)

TADDEO: Just one and three-pence!—Hear me say
How I love and adore you!

COLUMBINE: (*near to table*). Get away, get away!
(*Harlequin enters by window, places bottle which he is carrying under his arm on floor, and goes towards Taddeo, who pretends not to see him.*)

TADDEO: (*to Columbine pointedly*). Pure! Yes, I know you are,
Pure as the snowflake falling.
Why will you close your heart,
Unto my calling?
Must I leave you and forsake you?

HARLEQUIN: (*taking him by the ear and kicking him up*). Yes, or I'll make you!
(*The audience laugh.*)

TADDEO: (*retiring comically to door, right; to Harlequin*). Heavens! You love her!
Then I must hand her over!
(*Raising his hands.*)
Bless you, my children!
(*Retiring to door.*)
Yonder I will watch over you!
(*The audience laugh and applaud.*)

COLUMBINE: Dear Harlequin!

HARLEQUIN: (*in exaggerated style*). Sweet Columbine! Ah, how we've prayed, dear,
And Love has heard our prayer.

COLUMBINE: (*pointing to the table on which she has placed the fowl, knives, and forks, etc.*) The supper's laid, dear!
See here, see here, my dearest dear,
The supper that I've bought you!

HARLEQUIN: (*pointing to the wine which he places on the table*). See here, my love, my dainty dove,
The splendid wine I've brought you!

BOTH: (*sitting down opposite each other*). For love is very fond of wine,
And partial to the kitchen.

HARLEQUIN: My greedy little Columbine!

COLUMBINE: My most bewitching friend!

ARLECCHINO: (*prendendo un' ampolletta che ha nella tunica*). Prendi questo narcotico, dallo a Pagliaccio pria che s' addormenti, e poi fuggiamo insiem.

COLOMBINA: Si, porgi.

TADDEO: (*spalanca la porta a destra a traversa la scena tremando esageratamente*). Attenti! . . .
Pagliaccio è là tutto stravolto. . .ed armi cerca! Ei sa tutto. Io corro a barricarmi!
(*Entra precipitoso a sinistra e chiude la porta. Il pubblico ride.*)

COLOMBINA: (*ad Arlecchino*). Via!

ARLECCHINO: (*scavalcando la finestra*). Versa il filtro ne la tazza sua.
(*Scompare.*)
(*Canio in costume da Pagliaccio, compare sulla porta a destra.*)

COLOMBINA: (*alla finestra*). A stanotte.—E per sempre io sarò tual!

CANIO: (*porta la mano al cuore e mormora a parte*). Nome di Dio! . . . quelle stesse parole! . . .
coraggio!
(*Forte.*)
Un uomo era con te.

NEDDA: Che fole! Ser briaco?

CANIO: (*fissando la*). Briaco! si . . . da un' ora!

NEDDA: (*riprendendo la commedia*). Tornasti presto.

CANIO: (*con intezione*). Ma in tempo!
T' accora dolce sposina.
(*Reprende la commedia.*)
Ah! sola ti credea
(*mostrando la tavola*)
e due posti son là.

NEDDA: Con me sedea Taddeo che là si chiuse per paura.
(*Verso la porta a sinistra.*)
Orsù, parla! . . .

TONIO: (*di dentro fingendo tremare ma con intenzione*). Credetela. Essa è pura! . . .
E abborre dal mentir quel labbro pio!
(*Il pubblico ride forte.*)

CANIO: (*rabbioso al pubblico*). Per la morte!
(*Poi a Nedda sordamente.*)
Smettiamo. Ho Dritto anch' io d' agir come ogni altr' uomo. Il nome suo.

NEDDA: (*fredda e sorridente*). Di chi?

HARLEQUIN: (*taking a vial from his breast*). Take then this little philter fine,
Give it to your husband,
Pour it in his wine,
And then let's fly, my dear!

COLUMBINE: Yes—give it to me!

TADDEO: (*entering by door, on right, crosses stage, trembling in exaggerated style*). Beware! Your husband is here!
For weapons seeking, with anger stamping,
All's discovered! I'd better be leaving now.
(*Exit hurriedly through door, left. The audience laugh.*)

COLUMBINE: (*to Harlequin*). Fly, then.

HARLEQUIN: (*getting through window*). Pour the philter in his wine, love!
(*Disappears.*)
(*Canio, dressed as Punchinello, appears at door, right.*)

COLUMBINE: Tonight and for ever, I am yours love!

CANIO: (*with his hand to his heart, aside*). God! am I dreaming? What she said this morning! Courage!
(*Advancing for his part.*)
Someone was with you here!

NEDDA: What nonsense! You've been drinking.

CANIO: (*looking at her*). Been drinking! . . . I think so!

NEDDA: (*resuming the play*). You're back too early.

CANIO: (*pointedly*). Too early! You fear!
I'm sorry, my sweetest, my dearest?
(*Resuming the play.*)
Ah, no you were not lonely.
(*Pointing to the table.*)
Who has been with you here?

NEDDA: The Fool Taddeo—only! In fact, he's in the cupboard hiding!
(*Pointing to door, left.*)
Come out! . . . explain!

TONIO: (*from within*). Believe me, sir, your wife is true. She'd never grieve you!
(*Pretending to be afraid, pointedly.*)
Those pious lips of hers would never deceive you.
(*The audience laugh.*)

CANIO: (*furious; to the audience*).
To the death.
(*To Nedda, quietly.*)
Do not trifle, false woman,
Do you forget that I am also human?
Tell me his name!

NEDDA: (*coldly, with a forced smile*). Whose name?

## Act II, Scene II

CANIO: Vo' il nome de l' amante tuo, del drudo infame a cui ti desti in braccio
O turpe donna!

NEDDA: (*sempre recitando la commedia*). Pagliaccio! Pagliaccio!

CANIO: No, Pagliaccio non son; se il viso è pallido
è di vergogna, e smania di vendetta!
L' uom riprende i suoi dritti, e il cor che sanguina
vuol sangue a lavar l'onta, o maledetta!
No, Pagliaccio non son! . . . Son quei che stolido
ti raccolse orfanella in su la via
quasi morta di fame, e un nome offriati
ed un amor ch' era febbre e follìa!
. . .
(*Cade come affranto sulla seggiola.*)

GRUPPI DI DONNE A PARTE: Comare, mi fa piangere!
—Par vera questa scena!

UN GRUPPO DI UOMINI: Zitte laggiù.—Che diamine!

SILVIO: (*a parte*). Io mi ritengo appena!

CANIO: (*riprendendosi ed animandosi a poco a poco*). Sperai, tanto il delirio accecato m' aveva, se non amor, pietà . . . mercè!
Ed ogni sacrifizio
al cor, lieto, imponeva,
e fidente credeva,
più che in Dio stesso, in te!
Ma il vizio alberga sol ne l' alma tua negletta;
tu viscere non hai . . . sol legge è 'l senso a te . . .
Va, non merti il mio duol, o meretrice abbietta,
vo' ne lo sprezzo mio schiacciarti sotto i piè! . . .

LA FOLLA: (*estusiasta*). Bravo! . . .

NEDDA: (*fredda, ma seria*). Ebben se mi giudichi
Di te indegna, mi scaccia in questo istante.

CANIO: (*sogghignando*). Ah! ah! di meglio chiedere
Non dèi che correr testo al caro amante.
Sei furba!—No, per Dio, tu resterai
E 'l nome del tuo ganzo mi dirai.

NEDDA: (*cercando riprendere la commedia sorridendo forzatemente*). Suvvia, così terribile davver non ti credeo!
Qui nulla v' ha di tragico.
(*Verso la porta a sinistra.*)
Vieni a dirgli, o Taddeo,
che l' uom seduto or dianzi a me vicino
era . . . il pauroso ed innocuo

CANIO: Tell me, then, by God who made me, Within whose shameless arms have you betrayed me?

NEDDA: (*continuing the play*). Punchinello! Punchinello!

CANIO: No! Punchinello no more! I am a man again,
With aching heart and anguish deep and human,
Calling for blood to wash away the stain,
Your foul dishonor, you shameless woman!
No! Punchinello no more! Fool that I sheltered you!
And made you mine by every tender token!
Of the love that I gave you, what is there left to me?
What have I now, but a heart that is broken?
(*Falls on chair, overcome.*)

WOMEN:
(*aside to each other*). Sweet gossip, ah, it makes me weep,
So true it all is seeming.

MEN: Silence, down there. Keep quiet.

SILVIO: (*aside*). Ah, can it be I'm dreaming?

CANIO: (*recovering himself, and becoming gradually more excited*). I hoped in my passion so blindly confiding,
If not for love, for pity sweet.
I loved you more than God in heaven abiding,
All my life and my being I laid at your faithless feet!
I dreamt you were true! I wish I never had met you!
I thought of you, pure and stainless as the morn.
You have broken my heart, I live but to forget you,
You had my love, but now you have my hate and scorn!

AUDIENCE: (*with enthusiasm*). Bravo!

NEDDA: (*coldly, and in earnest*). Well, then, if you deem me so unworthy,
Come, let me go and leave you.

CANIO: (*laughing*). No doubt! no doubt! and set you free,
And let your lover's arms receive you!
No! you shall remain, I swear it.
I want your lover's name—Come, then—declare it!

NEDDA: (*trying to resume the play, with forced smile*). I never knew, my dear, that you
Were such a tragic fellow!
(*going left, towards the door.*)
You here will see no tragedy,
My dearest Punchinello!
The man who's been to dine with me,
And caused you all this bother,

Arlecchino!
(*Risa tosta represse dall' attitudine di Canio.*)

CANIO: (*terribile*). Ah! tu mi sfidi
E ancor non l' hai capita
Ch' io non ti cedo? Il nome, o la tua vita! (*Assieme.*)

NEDDA: (*prorompendo*). No, per mia madre! Indegna esser poss' io, quello che vuoi, ma vil non son, per Dio!
Di quel tuo sdegno è l' amor mio più forte . . .
Non parlerò. No . . . A costo de la morte! . . .

VOCI TRA LA FOLLA: Fanno davvero? Sembrami seria la cosa e scura!
(*Peppe vuol uscire dalla porta a sinistra, ma Tonio lo ritiene.*)

PEPPE: Bisogna uscire, Tonio.

TONIO: Taci sciocco! . . .

PEPPE: Ho paura! . . .

SILVIO: (*a parte*). Oh la strana commedia!
Io non resisto più! . . .

CANIO: (*urlando dà di piglio a un coltello sul tavolo*). Il nome! Il nome!

NEDDA: (*sfidandolo*). No!

SILVIO: (*snudando il pugnale*). Santo diavolo . . .
Fa davvero . . .
(*Le donne che indietreggiano spaventate, rovesciano i banchi ed impediscono agli uomini di avanzare, ciò che obbliga Silvio a lottare per arrivare all scena. Intanto Canio al parossismo della collera, ha afferrata Nedda in un attimo e la colpisce per di dietro mentre essa cerca di correre verso il pubblico.*)

CANIO: (*a Nedda*) Di morte negli spasimi Lo dirai.

LA FOLLA E PEPPE: (*che cerca svincolarsi da Tonio*). Ferma!

CANIO: A te!

NEDDA: (*cadendo agonizzando*). Soccorso . . . Silvio!

SILVIO: (*che e quasi arrivato alla scena*). Nedda!
(*Alla voce di Silvio, Canio si volge come una belva, balza presse di tui è in un attimo lo ferisce, dicendo.*)

CANIO: Ah! sei tu? Ben venga!
(*Silvio cade come fulminato.*)

GLI UOMINI DEL CORO: Arresta aïta!

LE DONNE: (*urlandino*). Gesummaria! . . .
(*Mentre parecchi si precipitano verso Canio per disarmarlo ed arrestarlo, egli, immobile, istupidito lascia cadere il coltello dicendo.*)

CANIO: La commedia è finita! . . .
(*La tela cade.*)

FINE.

Was only Harlequin, you see,
Poor Harlequin, no other!
(*Stops laughing, seeing Canio's attitude.*)

CANIO: (*in fury*). Ah! do you mock me? My rage you still defy.
Say who's your lover—this moment—or you die!

NEDDA: (*bursting out*). No! By my mother's soul, unworthy though you call me,
I will not tell you, whatever fate befalls me!

VOICES in the CROWD: Are they in earnest?
What are they doing?
(*Beppe tries to pass through door on left; Tonio detains him.*)

BEPPE: Let us be going, Tonio!

TONIO: Silence, fool!

BEPPE: I am afraid!

SILVIO: (*aside*). Oh, the play is a strange one,
I can bear it no more!

CANIO: (*yelling, takes knife from table*). His name! His name!

NEDDA: (*defiantly*). No!

SILVIO: (*drawing his dagger*). What in the devil's name!
. . . He's in earnest!
(*The women draw back frightened, overturning the benches, preventing the men from getting to the front. Silvio struggles to get clear. Meantime Canio has seized Nedda, and stabbed her from behind, as she tries to escape to the audience.*)

CANIO: Take that, and that!
In your last dying agony you'll tell!

VOICES IN AUDIENCE: Stop him!

NEDDA: Ah! Help me, Silvio!
(*Dies.*)

SILVIO: (*nearly reaching her*). Nedda!
(*At the voice of Silvio, Canio turns savagely, leaps at him, and stabs him.*)

CANIO: So! It is you, then? It is well! (*Silvio falls dead.*)

MEN: Help! help! arrest him!

WOMEN: (*screaming*). Father of pity!
(*Several of the audience throw themselves on Canio to disarm and arrest him; he stands stupefied and drops the knife.*)

CANIO: The comedy is ended.

Curtain.

# Zazà (1900)

## Music and Libretto By Ruggiero Leoncavallo

This four-act opera, set to a libretto by the composer (based upon a play by Charles Simon and Pierre Berton), premiered at the Teatro Lirico in Milan on November 10, 1900. The setting is France at the end of the 19th century. Zazà is a café singer at the Alcazar Theatre in Saint-Étienne, presented by the impresario Courtois. She has a major success there with her partner, Cascart—she is also Cascart's mistress. After the performance a journalist, Bussy, introduces her to his friend Milio Dufresne from Paris. She falls in love with him, but he treats her with disdain as he thinks that performers are flighty and that relations with them spell trouble. She arranges to see him alone several evenings later, and he is unable to resist her charms. Three months later, Dufresne and Zazà are living together. He now tells her that he must go to America for an indefinite period of time. Her former lover, Cascart, informs her that he has seen him with another woman in Paris. He suggests that she accept the way things are and return to her career. She is enraged and jealous and immediately goes to Paris. Dufresne is back at his home in Paris, where he has a wife and daughter. Conscious of his responsibility to them, he knows that he must leave the country in order to break off his affair once and for all. Zazà comes to his house disguised as a friend of his wife's. She sees a letter left open on a table and realizes the truth of the situation, compounded by the entrance of Dufresne's daughter. She doesn't have the heart to destroy Dufresne's family and leaves in deep despair. She returns to Saint-Étienne and is offered a contract by Courtois, but she refuses to return to work until she meets Dufresne one last time. Their meeting is stormy: Zazà tells him that she knows the truth, and as he grows more and more angry she pretends that she has told his wife about their affair. His anger grows uncontrollable, and he declares his total love and devotion to his wife and his disgust at his relationship with her. Zazà admits that she lied about telling his wife and sends him away.

## ■ Atto Primo.

*Il Palcoscenico Dell 'Alcazar di St. Étienne, visto lateralmente. — Una buona metà della scena a sinistra rappresenta il camerino di Zazà.—A destra della scena, sul davanti, un tavolo con varie sedie per gli assidui del concerto che hanno libero accesso sulla scena.—Nell'angolo, sempre sul davanti a destra, la porta che dà nella sala di spettacolo.—Indi tutto 'il lato destro della scena presso le quinte è occupato in senso longitudinale dal fondale che per mezzo di una porta dà sulla scena del Caffè-Concerto.—In faccia a questa porta, pure in senso longitudinale, è il fondino che maschera al pubblico che si suppone essere nella sala del caffè-concerto, l'interno del palcoscenico.—Il fondo della scena che rappresenta l'altro muro laterale del palcoscenico, è ingombro di quinte, scene arrotolate, oggetti di ginnastica, ecc.—Nel camerino di Zazà, nel quale si entra per una porta situata nel mezzo della scena, quasi in faccia al tavolo, sono due o tre sedie, una toletta, un paravento; e sui muri, sospesi gli abiti di Zazà.— All'alzarsi della tela la porta che dà sulla scena è aperta, e si vede Floriana che saluta mientre si sentono all'interno applausi e grida di bis. Floriana esce di nuovo, e siccome la porta resta aperta la si sente cantare la strofa della sua canzone accompagnata dal vociare della folla.— Intanto Michelin, Courtois ed un altro signore insiemea Claretta, in costume corto da concerto, vengono a sedersi al tavolo sul davanti a destra, e comandano le bibite ad Augusto.—In fondo si scorgono il pompiere di servizio che gira sorvegliando, due macchinisti e varî artisti del concerto.—Movimento continuo sulla scena.—Qua e là grossi avvisi con: È vietato fumare, ma tutti fumano sigari e sigarette, compreso il pompiere di servizio.*

FLORIANA: (*cantando all'interno*) So che son capricciosa e sventatella,
che, come l'api, adoro svolazzar;
non son nata per far la monachella
e vivo sol per ridere e scherzar.
So pur che ad ogni giogo son rubella,
che in amore mi piace di cangiar,
che mi diverto ad ogni gherminella,
eppur, s'io vo', la testa fo' girar!
Che s'io vi fo' l'occhietto,
mio signor,
se lancio un sorriseto
seduttor! . . .
tremante, io ci scommetto,
a' piedi miei v'udrò
giurarmi eterno affetto
mentr' io riderò!

## ■ Act I.

*Side view of stage of the "Alcazar" at St. Étienne; left half of stage shows Zazà's dressing-room. At r. front, a table with some chairs for the habitués of the Concert Hall, who have free access to stage. In the corner r. front of stage, a door leads to auditorium of Hall. Thence all the right side of the stage near the wings is occupied longitudinally by the back drop through which a door opens on the stage of the Concert Hall. In front of this door, also longitudinally placed, is a screen which hides rear of stage from the audience supposed to be in the Concert Hall. The back drop is supposed to represent the other side wall of the stage, and is littered with rolled-up scenery, wings, flies, tumbling apparatus, trapeze, etc. Entrance to Zazà's dressing-room in center partition, almost in line with table r.; there are two or three chairs, a dressing table, a screen; along the walls hang Zazà's costumes. When the curtain rises, the door l. which leads to stage of Concert Hall is open, and Floriana is seen bowing in response to applause and encore calls offstage. As the door remains open, Floriana is visible as she repeats her song, which the audience cheers. Meanwhile Michelin, Courtois and another gentleman with Claretta, in short stage costume, take seats around the table at r. front, and give orders for drinks to Augusto. At back of stage a fireman is on duty, two machinists and many vaudeville artists standing about. Lively coming and going on stage. Signs with "No Smoking" prominent about stage, but all smoke cigars and cigarettes, the fireman on duty included.*

FLORIANA: (*singing offstage*)
I know well that I am gay and capricious;
Like the bees I flutter on from flower to flower!
I was not born for weeping and for sighing,
I live but for the pleasure of the hour.
Free as a bird, no tie can ever hold me,
My heart I give now here, now there awhile:
My life is just a round of love and laughter,
None can resist the magic of my smile:
If I give you just one smile,
Yes, just one,
All your reason, gentle sirs,
Will be gone.

# Act I

<table>
<tr><td>

MICHELIN: (*mentre Floriana canta*) Augusto!

AUGUSTO: (*accorrendo al tavolo*) Pronti!

MICHELIN: Birra.
(*poi a Claretta*)
E voi, su, che prendete?

CLARETTA: Un kümmel, grazie.

COURTOIS: Io prendo una gran tazza; ho sete.

DUCLOU: (*gridando mentre appare a destra*)
Attenti i clowns!
(*Due clowns portando bizzarri strumenti musicali giungono dal fondo a sinistra e dopo aver scambiato saluti amichevoli con le persone sedute al tavolo vanno a guardarsi ad uno specchio che sarà situato sul muro di divisione nel mezzo, accanto alla porta del camerino di Zazà, e si tengono pronti ad entrare in iscena.—Floriana finisce' la strofa; grandi applausi, essa saluta nuovamente e si avanza verso il tavolo mentre Duclou suona il campanello elettrico per annunciare l'entrata dei clowns.*)

MICHELIN, COURTOIS, CLARETTA ed IL SIGNORE: (*a Floriana*)
Ma brava! ma brava! che successo!

FLORIANA: Stasera sono in voce.

COURTOIS: (*galantemente*)
Sempre!

FLORIANA: (*squadrandolo con fare insolente*) Ma guarda!
Adesso divien galante!
È vero che Zazà l' ha piantato!

COURTOIS: Come?!

FLORIANA: Come si pianta!
(*ironica*) Il mio turno è arrivato?
(*salutando con affettazione*)
Troppa grazia!

DUCLOU: (*ai due clowns*) In iscena!
(*I clowns entrano in iscena suonando stonato e sono salutati da applausi.—Duclou che si terrà presso alla porta che dà sulla scena, la socchiude di tanto in tanto come per guardare nella sala; e si sentono dei frammenti musicali eseguiti da istrumenti strani.*)

MICHELIN: (*a Floriana che si sarà seduta ed avrà ordinato da bere*) Di', stasera si prova finito lo spettacolo la gran "rivista" nuova di Bussy?

FLORIANA: (*di cattivo umore*)
Ma . . . purtroppo!

</td><td>

Here at my feet you'll be sighing,
Vowing you'll love me forever!
While for my favor you're vying,
Laughing, I'll trip away!

MICHELIN: (*while Floriana sings*) Augusto!

AUGUSTO: (*hurries to table*)
Here, sir!

MICHELIN: Beer —
(*then to Claretta*)
And you, what can I get you?

CLARETTA: A cocktail, thank you.

COURTOIS: I'm dry—buy me a big one, I'll let you!

DUCLOU: (*shouting as he appears from right*) You clowns! you're next!
(*Two clowns with bizarre instruments come from upstage l. and greet those seated at table. They take a final look at themselves in mirror hung against center partition, near Zazà's dressing-room door and then make ready to go on. Floriana finishes her encore to hearty applause. She returns bowing and comes towards table while Duclou rings electric bell announcing the clown number.*)

MICHELIN, COURTOIS, CLARETTA AND THE OTHER GENTLEMAN: (*to Floriana*) Bravo, splendid—an ovation!

FLORIANA: My voice is in condition.

COURTOIS: (*gallantly*) Always!

FLORIANA: (*looks at him insolently*) You fill me with elation.
I think you flatter!—
So Zazà gave you the mitten?

COURTOIS: How?!

FLORIANA: As is her habit:
(*ironically*)
Is it my turn now to be smitten?
(*bows low with affectation*)
This is an honor!

DUCLOU: (*to the two clowns*)
You go on now!
(*Clowns run off to concert stage banging instruments discordantly. Wild applause offstage. Duclou remains near door, opening on stage, which he leaves ajar from time to time, as though looking offstage into hall; whenever door is opened, the weird clown music becomes audible.*)

MICHELIN: (*to Floriana who sits down and orders drink*) Tell me—is it true
That after the show you try the new "Review" by Bussy?

FLORIANA: (*crossly*) More's the pity!

</td><td>

MICHELIN: (*sorridendo*) Ciò non ti garba?

FLORIANA: (*scattando*) Affatto!
Questo sarà un bel fiasco!
Già, quasi tutto l'atto è per Zazà! . . .
la Diva! . . .

MICHELIN: (*ridendo*) Sempre la stessa storia! Contro Zazà!!

FLORIANA: (*levandosi di scatto*)
Perdono!
Che sciocca!
La sua gloria, come Bussy, tu canti sempre nel *Gazzettino*, ed io me lo scordavo! . . .
So a mente il fervorino!
(*Simona arriva. Saluta e siede al tavolo. Tutti ridono. Natalia arriva dal fondo a sinistra, va ad aprire il camerino di Zazà ed entra.*)

COURTOIS: (*interrompe Floriana vedendo Natalia*) È qui che arriva.
All'erta!

FLORIANA: (*stizzosa*) All'inferno la stella con l'astronomo!

COURTOIS: (*sorpreso*) Che astronomo? farnetichi!

FLORIANA: Cascart, l'amante suo che l'ha scoperta!
(*Floriana siede volgendo le spalle al fondo del teatro donde giunge Zazà, che tutti si volgono a salutare.*)

ZAZÀ: (*allegramente appressandosi al tavolo*) Salute, ragazzi.

MICHELIN, COURTOIS, CLARETTA e SIMONA: Zazà, buona sera.

ZAZÀ: (*a Claretta e Simona*) Addio, mie piccine.
(*Scambia un'occhiata di odio con Floriana e poi chiede a Courtois e Michelin*)
È giunto Bussy?

MICHELIN: No, ancora il collega non vidi stasera.

ZAZÀ: (*con interesse*) E il suo fido amico Dufresne?

MICHELIN: Non è qui.

ZAZÀ: (*delusa*) Ah! . . . vado a vestirmi.
(*fa un passo verso il camerino*)

DUCLOU: (*che sarà venuto avanti al giunger di Zazà*) Però, senza fretta;
C' è tempo, sai.

ZAZÀ: (*dando la mano a Duclou*) Grazie.
(*entra nel camerino*)

DUCLOU: A te, su, Claretta.
(*In questo punto i clowns rientrano salutando mentre si sentono applausi prolungati all'interno.—Poi Duclou suona il campanello come prima, si*)

</td><td>

MICHELIN: (*smiling*) You do not like it?

FLORIANA: (*spitefully*)
Frightful!!
This show is doomed to failure—
I'm not spiteful,
But it's all star—all Zazà—

MICHELIN: (*laughing*) Always the same old story:
Down with Zazà!

FLORIANA: (*rises abruptly*) Excuse me—this is foolish!
With her glory,
Like Bussy, you fill columns—rank and rotten—
I know your stuff by heart—but I'd forgotten!
(*Simona enters; she greets the others and sits down. All are laughing except Floriana. Natalia enters from back of stage l., opens door of Zazà's dressing-room and goes in.*)

COURTOIS: (*seeing Natalia, interrupts Floriana*) I think she is coming—be careful!

FLORIANA: (*viciously*) Confound the astronomer and star!

COURTOIS: (*surprised*) Astronomer?—
You must be dreaming!

FLORIANA: Cascart, her lover, who has made her!
(*Floriana sits down with her back turned to rear of stage, whence Zazà approaches; all others greet her effusively.*)

ZAZÀ: (*gayly approaching the table*) Hello, everybody!

MICHELIN, COURTOIS, CLARETTA AND SIMONA: Hello, Zazà, how are you?

ZAZÀ: (*to Claretta and Simona*) Well, girls, how are things going?
(*Exchanges a glance of hatred with Floriana; then addresses Courtois and Michelin*)
Have you seen Bussy?

MICHELIN: No, my colleague seems to be still absent.

ZAZÀ: (*eagerly*) And how about his faithful friend Dufresne?

MICHELIN: He's not here.

ZAZÀ: (*disappointed*) Oh!—I must dress for business!
(*turns to go to her dressing-room*)

DUCLOU: (*who had come forward before Zazà's entrance*) Don't get in a flurry—
There is time a-plenty.

ZAZÀ: (*shakes hands with Duclou*) Thank you.
(*Goes into dressing-room*)

DUCLOU: Next, Claretta—hurry!
(*The Clowns here reënter, while hearty applause is heard offstage. Then Duclou rings bell as before—prelude to Claretta's song is heard, she goes off through door*)

</td></tr>
</table>

sente il preludio della canzone di Claretta, questa entra in iscena, e Duclou chiude la porta. — Zazà, entrata nel suo camerino, comincia a svestirsi, si trucca ed avrà finito di mettere l'abito corto da concerto solo quando Bussy giungerà. — Mentre Claretta entra in iscena, dalla porta a destra che dà nella sala entra Malardot, il proprietario del Concerto, con la pipa in bocca, ed intanto appare dal fondo Lartigon in abito nero e cravatta bianca. — Quando Claretta sarà uscita, due cantanti in costume arrivano dal fondo, vanno al tavolo, siedono e bevono con Simona, Courtois e l'altro Signore.)

**MICHELIN:** (andando incontro a Malardot) Ecco il padron.

**MALARDOT:** (levando il berretto per salutare Michelin, Courtois e l'altro Signore) Signori!

**MICHELIN:** (allegramente) Va bene. . . !
Quanta gente! È contento?

**MALARDOT:** Non troppo.
Si beve poco o niente!
(scorgendo Lartigon) Ah! udite!

**LARTIGON:** (salutando con affettazione) Direttore!

**MALARDOT:** Spero che ci direte un monologo allegro, e non in versi.
Avete un repertorio . . .

**LARTIGON:** (interrompendolo con severità) Classico!
La morte d'Ermione:
Amleto fra le tombe:
La funebre orazione di Bossuet! . . .

**MALARDOT:** (scoppiando) Saranno classici, ma, per Dio, non sono punto allegri!

**LARTIGON:** (con ironia) Nè Bossuet, nè io teniamo a farvi ridere.

**MALARDOT:** E torto entrambi avete.

**LARTIGON:** Ma l'arte . . .

**MALARDOT:** (interrompendolo) L'arte . . .
(vede un cameriere che traversa la scena con un vassojo di tazze di birra) Caspita! rovinarmi volete? La birra senza spuma si serve? Nel versare, una tazza su cinque bisogna-guadagnare con tanto di solino! Andate! . . .
(poi a Lartigon)
Mio signore, l'arte è ciò che i clienti mette di buon umore.

to concert stage; Duclou closes door. Zazà, having entered her dressing-room, begins to undress, then makes up and does not finish with change to short stage costume until Bussy arrives. When Claretta goes to concert stage, Malardot, the proprietor of the Concert Hall, enters from auditorium, through the door extreme r. He has a pipe in his mouth. Meanwhile Lartigon, in a dress suit and white tie, comes from upstage. As soon as Claretta goes off, two singers in costume enter from upstage and sit down at table to drink with Simona, Courtois and the other gentleman.)

**MICHELIN:** (meeting Malardot) See who is coming!

**MALARDOT:** (raises cap to Michelin, Courtois and the other man) Good evening!

**MICHELIN:** (brightly) How's business?
Fine, I'm thinking—
Sold-out houses?

**MALARDOT:** It's crowded—but they're slow at drinking.
(catches sight of Lartigon) Say—listen!

**LARTIGON:** (bows formally) At your service.

**MALARDOT:** I hope you are reciting
Some funny monologue—not one in verses—exciting!
Or full of spice—

**LARTIGON:** (interrupts with dignity) Hamlet's soliloquy, that grand creation,
Hermione's death and Bossuet's funeral oration,
Are all classics—

**MALARDOT:** (explosively) They may be classics, I admit,
But they're not funny—

**LARTIGON:** (with irony) Neither Bossuet nor I are bent on mirth and laughter—

**MALARDOT:** Then you won't make a hit!

**LARTIGON:** For Art's sake—

**MALARDOT:** (interrupting) Art—
(sees waiter crossing stage with tray full of beer glasses)
See here! is it my ruin you are after,
To serve beer without foam?
From each five glasses
With collars you make six; that always passes!
Now run along!
(then to Lartigon)
Remember, you there, sonny,
Art is what pleases patrons and what brings in real money.

**MICHELIN:** (ridendo a Malardot) Bravo!!
(va verso il fondo con Malardot)
(Lartigon crolla le spalle con disprezzo e va a sedersi al tavolo. — Augusto giunge dalla porta che dà nella sala portando un gran mazzo di fiori, delle carte da visita, due bottiglie di sciampagna, e va a bussare al camerino di Zazà. — Natalia socchiude un po' l'uscio, ed Augusto fa passare i fiori e lo sciampagna; poi si allontana e scompare dal fondo. — Courtois addita a Floriana ciò che Augusto porta a Zazà, questa si leva di scatto furibonda e va via pel fondo, in collera. — In questo punto Claretta finisce, la porta si schiude e la si vede salutare mentre si applaude, poi essa ridiscende sul davanti della scena. — Dal fondo ritornano Malardot e Michelin mentre Lartigon si alza per prepararsi ad entrare in iscena.)

**DUCLOU:** (a Lartigon, mentre suona il campanello) Che dite?

**LARTIGON:** (con importanza) Il monologo di Ruy-Blas!
(Entra in iscena, si sentono le prime parole del monologo; poi la porta si chiude.)

**MALARDOT:** (sul davanti, in collera) Ehi, Duclou!
(Duclou accorre)
appena termina, una buona fischiata, e poi gli lacero la scrittura!

**DUCLOU:** Sta ben.
(Corre all'uscio che dà nella sala di spettacolo, esce e ritorna dopo un istante. — Cascart viene dal fondo in costume di città.)

**MALARDOT:** Vedrem che cèra farà!!
(scorge Cascart e lo saluta)
Signor Cascart!

**CASCART:** (rispondendo al saluto di entrambi) La buona sera!
(entra da Zazà senza battere all'uscio)
Buona sera, mia Zazà.

**ZAZÀ:** (lietamente, continuando a vestirsi) Ah, sei tu, Cascart! mio core!
(Natalia esce dal camerino e scompare dal fondo.)
Amor mio!
Donde venite?
Raccontate, mio signore
Dove foste ad ingannarmi?

**CASCART:** (ridendo) Come va, cattiva cèra?

**ZAZÀ:** Bene.
Siedi là, mi narra: che notizie questa sera?

**CASCART:** (sedendo a cavalcioni sulla sedia) C'è l'agente che mi scrive da Marsiglia: offre la piazza . . .

**MICHELIN:** (laughing, to Malardot) That's right!
(He goes upstage with Malardot)
(Lartigon shrugs shoulders contemptuously and sits at table. Augusto comes from door r. front, carrying large bouquet, some visiting cards and two bottles of champagne. He knocks at Zazà's door; Natalia receives flowers and champagne. Augusto then withdraws upstage. Courtois calls Floriana's attention to the offerings brought for Zazà and she rises in a temper; exit at back of stage. Claretta here ends her number, the door is opened and she is seen bowing while audience applauds. Then she comes downstage. Malardot and Michelin return from upstage, while Lartigon gets ready to go on for his number.)

**DUCLOU:** (to Lartigon, while he rings bell) What's yours now?

**LARTIGON:** (very important) The soliloquy Of Ruy-Blas!
(He goes on; the first words of monologue are heard—then the door closes.)

**MALARDOT:** (comes forward angrily) See here, Duclou!
(Duclou hurries over to him)
When he has finished, I want a storm of hisses and then I can cancel his engagement!

**DUCLOU:** All right.
(He hurries to door leading into Hall and exit, returning shortly after. Cascart comes from back of stage in street clothes.)

**MALARDOT:** I'll teach him what to do for Art!
(notices Cascart—greets him) Hello, Cascart!

**CASCART:** (greeting all present) Good evening to you!
(enters Zazà's room without knocking) Good evening, dearest Zazà.

**ZAZÀ:** (joyfully, but continuing her dressing) Oh—it's you, Cascart, my dear one!
(Natalia retires from dressing-room and disappears upstage.)
Sweetheart mine, where did you come from?
Sir, you might at least come near one.
And confess where you've been flirting!

**CASCART:** (laughs) How are you? How are things going?

**ZAZÀ:** Fine!
Sit here and tell me all the news that is worth knowing.

**CASCART:** (sits astride chair) The agent at Marseilles has offered double: I won't be losing.

# Act I

ZAZÀ: Per noi due?
Non vuoi piantarmi già?

CASCART: (*crollando le spalle*)
Sarebbe cosa pazza!
Offre il doppio!

ZAZÀ: E dire, amico, ch'è per te
che sono artista!
(*Courtois e l'altro Signore con le
due cantanti si allontanano pel
fondo e scompajono.*)
Ti rammenti?
Alle taverne per cantar che vita
trista!
Io col piatto andava intorno . . .
Che dolori abbiam sofferti
Con mia madre!

CASCART: Certamente ch'eran
magri i vostri incerti!
Se per caso trenta soldi raccoglievi
nel tuo piatto, ne beveva almen
quaranta la tua madre d'un sol
tratto!
Vecchia spugna insaziata!

ZAZÀ: Basta . . . ! sai che mi dà
pena!

CASCART: Va il gran male e che
prosegue . . . oggi, vedi, una
dozzena!

ZAZÀ: (*con dolcezza*) Via, non mi
torturare!
È madre mia, e ha sorriso sì poco ai
suoi prim'anni:
ha pianto molte lacrime per via,
povera donna, ed ebbe molti
affanni!
(*seria*)
Lo sai tu che vuol dire un uom che
fugge e che ti lascia con un bimbo,
sola?
Ogni seme di bene in te si strugge, e
diventa l'amore una parola!
Che farà, dove andrà, dimmi, una
madre con un figliuol tremante fra
le braccia!
Annoja tutti un bimbo . . . anche
suo padre . . . e la povera donna ognun discaccia!!
Io la mamma rivedo in abbandono:
rammento i suoi dolori, e le
perdono!!

CASCART: (*levandosi un po'
commosso, bonariamente*) Sei
buona . . . troppo buona!
(*la bacia*)
Ora a vestirmi vado.

ZAZÀ: (*allegramente*) Ti spiccia,
e vieni a prevenirmi.
(*Cascart esce dal camerino e
scompare dal fondo a destra mentre un cantante vestito da soldato
si prepara ad entrare in iscena gi-
ungendo dalla sinistra. — Pure
dal fondo ritornano Malardot e
Michelin nel tempo stesso che Du-*

ZAZÀ: For both of us?
You would not leave me now?

CASCART: (*shrugs shoulders*) I'd
be a fool refusing a splendid contract!

ZAZÀ: My art, dear, it was you
alone who taught me!
(*Courtois and the other man with
the two singers withdraw upstage
and exit.*)
You remember?
From such a wretched life you have
brought me to stardom!
I passed the plate in taverns—I suffered sore privations—
Then, with my mother—

CASCART: Yes, they were rather
meagre, those donations,
I believe that thirty cents was most
that you collected daily.
But your mother drank her forty
cents' worth of strong spirits gaily.
She could soak it up like sponges!

ZAZÀ: Hush—you know I hate to
hear it!

CASCART: She drinks whiskey by
the gallon, though she knows she
shouldn't go near it!

ZAZÀ: (*gently*) Don't you see how
much you hurt me?
She's my mother—
Her youth was sad, all tears and
grief and sighing,
Drink was her solace and she knew
no other;
And that one comfort would you be
denying?
(*gravely*)
Think what it means, when by a
man forsaken,
You have a child—the world is
black before you,
Your faith in man and even heaven
is shaken,
A cruel mockery the love he bore
you!
Where can she turn, poor mother,
who will aid her?
She is condemned—the child an
accusation,
No help, not even from the God
who made her.
What wonder if she craves some
consolation?
I know well how mother to drink
was driven,
I know how much she suffered—
and have forgiven.

CASCART: (*rises; he is touched,
and speaks very gently*) You're a
good girl—much too good, dear,
(*kisses her*)
I'll go—if you will let me, to dress.

ZAZÀ: (*brightly*) Yes, hurry—
then come and get me.
(*Cascart leaves dressing-room
and exit at back of stage r., while a
singer in soldier's uniform prepares to go on, coming from
upstage l. Malardot and Michelin
also return from back of stage at
this moment and Duclou runs to*

clou corre ad aprire la porta che
dà sulla scena e si sentono le ultime parole del monologo di Ruy-
Blas.*)

DUCLOU: (*a Malardot*) Attento,
direttore!
(*Appena la voce di Lartigon finisce ed egli appare sulla porta, si
sente una salva di fischi.*)

LARTIGON: (*mostrando il pugno
al pubblico e venendo sul davanti*) Oh, i vili! oh, gli asini!
Fischiano Vittor Hugo!

MALARDOT: No, no, fischiano
Voi, mio signore.
Ed alla porta io mettovi.

LARTIGON: (*nel partire, con disprezzo*) Va! mercante d'assenzio
verde!
(*esce.*)

MALARDOT: (*correndogli dietro*) Stupido!
Sei tu che al verde resti! . . .
(*esce seguito da Michelin che
ride*)

DUCLOU: (*all'artista vestito da
soldato suonando il campanello*)
A voi, cominciano.
(*L'artista entra in iscena, Duclou
chiude la porta e poi scompare dal
fondo a destra mentre Natalia ritorna dalla sinistra ed entra nel
camerino.*)

ZAZÀ: (*a Natalia, che rientra*)
Dimmi: Bussy . . . o Dufresne
visto non hai lì fuori?

NATALIA: No, mia signora.

ZAZÀ: (*preoccupata*) È strano! . . .
Chi mandò questi fiori?

NATALIA: (*leggendo le carte da
visita*) Courtois . . .
Camus . . .
Qui ognuno per voi d'amor si
strugge.

ZAZÀ: (*pensierosa*) Sì, ma il solo
che bramo è quello che mi fugge!
(*Anaide appare dal fondo a sinistra mentre Augusto entra dalla
porta che dà nella sala; essi si incontrano a mezza scena. — Augusto avrà un vassojo con un bicchiere ripieno.*)

ANAIDE: (*graziosa*) Augusto,
buona sera!

AUGUSTO: Buona sera, Signora
Anaide!
Avete buona cèra.

ANAIDE: (*subito, in tono desolato*) No, sto mal! . . . ne lo stoma-
co ho un gran fuoco! (*indicando il
bicchiere*) Che porti?

AUGUSTO: Un grog.

open stage door just as the last
words of Ruy Blas' monologue are
heard.*)

DUCLOU: (*to Malardot*) Now, sir,
you'll see what happens!
(*As Lartigon finishes his monologue and reappears in door, a
storm of hisses and catcalls is
heard.*)

LARTIGON: (*shakes his fist at audience, then advances*) O, you villains, O you jackasses,
To hiss at Victor Hugo!

MALARDOT: No—not Hugo,—
You they are hissing—and you are
fired this very moment!

LARTIGON: (*contemptuously*)
Bah—go drown in your vile green
liquor!
(*Exit*)

MALARDOT: (*after him*) You
idiot!
You're greener than my absinthe is!
(*Exit followed by Michelin, laughing*)

DUCLOU: (*to singer in uniform,
as he rings bell*) Your turn beginning!
(*The singer goes on; Duclou closes
door and passes out at back r.
while Natalia enters from l. and
goes into dressing-room.*)

ZAZÀ: (*to Natalia, as she enters*)
Tell me:
Bussy and Dufresne—did they
bring me these roses?

NATALIA: No, dearest lady—

ZAZÀ: (*thoughtfully*) Peculiar!
Who sent the pretty posies?

NATALIA: (*reads cards*) Courtois
. . . Camus . . .
I've noticed they all are mad about
you.

ZAZÀ: (*pensively*) Not all—
there's one quite sane—so I'm inclined to doubt you!
(*Anaide comes on from back of
stage l. as Augusto enters by door
leading to hall. They meet in center stage. He is carrying a tray
with a glass of liquor.*)

ANAIDE: (*sweetly*) Good evening,
dear Augusto!

AUGUSTO: Well, how are you?
You're looking fine tonight.
Can I do something for you?

ANAIDE: (*suddenly in whining
tone*) No—I'm ill!
My stomach pains me
It's turning—
(*points to glass he carries*)
What is that?—

AUGUSTO: Some gin—

ANAIDE: Dà qui. (*lo beve*) Ciò calma un poco.
Mettilo in conto di mia figlia.

AUGUSTO: Bene. Ah! vostra figlia che successo!
Tiene tutta da voi!
Che ai vostri tempi! . . .

ANAIDE: Augusto! Quand'io cantavo!!

AUGUSTO: Che grazia! che gusto!

ANAIDE: Il repertorio classico!

AUGUSTO: Il Pompiere! . . .

ANAIDE: Le oche!!
Oh, miei trionfi. . . !
Or vo' a vedere Zazà.
Mi porta un punch nel camerino.

AUGUSTO: Sta ben.

ANAIDE: (*appressandosi all'uscio del camerino*)
Ahi! brucio . . .
è proprio all'intestino.
(*apre l'uscio e grida facendo la graziosa*)
Addio tesoro!

ZAZÀ: (*sorpresa*) Toh! sei tu, Mammà.

ANAIDE: Sì, la mammina de la sua Zazà.

ZAZÀ: Datele un bacio tosto alla Zazà.—
Ma via non portate il rossetto.

ANAIDE: (*bacia Zazà, saluta Natalia e siede*) Signora Natalia!

NATALIA: Signora!

ANAIDE: (*a Zazà*) Alfin ti trovo sola, e si può parlare senza Cascart che sindaca! . . .

ZAZÀ: Mamma, non cominciare!

ANAIDE: (*riscaldandosi*) Già, non si può toccarlo; sempre i consigli suoi segui!

ZAZÀ: Nella miseria ci avean costretti i tuoi!

ANAIDE: (*tragicamente*) Va pure, ingrata, insultami! su me le accuse aduna.

AUGUSTO: (*entrando col vassojo*) Ecco il punch.
(*esce subito e ritorna nella sala*)

ANAIDE: (*in tono gentile*) Mille grazie.
(*prende il bicchiere e prosegue tragicamente*)
Ciò non porta fortuna!

ZAZÀ: Mamma, bevi e sta zitta.

---

ANAIDE: All right.
(*drinks it*)
That soothes the burning.
And you can charge it to my daughter.

AUGUSTO: Yes, ma'am!
Your daughter is a star and nothing less, ma'am.
She's you all over in your days of glory!

ANAIDE: I delighted all by my singing!

AUGUSTO: What grace and charm united!

ANAIDE: A classic repertoire was mine!

AUGUSTO: Fireman's ending!

ANAIDE: The Goose and Gander!
What a triumph!
—I must be attending Zazà.—
Please bring me a drink; my hand is shaking.

AUGUSTO: Yes, ma'am!
(*Exit*)

ANAIDE: (*going to dressing-room door*) Mercy!
Frightful—this burning here inside, and aching!
(*She opens door and cries out effusively*)
My darling treasure!

ZAZÀ: (*surprised*) Is it you, Mother?

ANAIDE: Yes, your own dear little mother, my Zazà.

ZAZÀ: Come, give me a kiss, dear—you see I am busy—
Don't get my rouge all smeared and mussy!

ANAIDE: (*kisses Zazà—nods to Natalia and sits down*) How are you, Natalia?

NATALIA: Quite well, ma'am.

ANAIDE: (*to Zazà*) At last we are alone, dear, no one here to bother,
And no Cascart between us—

ZAZÀ: Please drop the subject, Mother.

ANAIDE: (*annoyed*) There—he, of course is perfect; his advice you follow blindly.
Always—

ZAZÀ: That your own people would not help, you oftentimes remind me.

ANAIDE: (*tragically*) Ungrateful daughter, to insult me!
All blame on me you're laying!

AUGUSTO: (*enters with tray and glass*) Here is your punch.
(*exit quickly, returning to Hall*)

ANAIDE: (*sweetly*) Thank you so much.
(*takes glass and continues tragically*)
The outlook is dismaying!

ZAZÀ: Mother—drink it and be quiet.

---

ANAIDE: (*fingendo scoppiare in pianto*) Ahi! sono sventurata!

ZAZÀ: Ci siamo! eccoci al pianto! la solita scenata!
(*levandosi a calmarla*) Baciami, bevi e dimmi perchè sei qui.

ANAIDE: (*dopo averla baciata e bevuto sorride imbarazzata*) Zazà, Per vederti!

ZAZÀ: E per chiedermi?

ANAIDE: L'affitto . . .

ZAZÀ: Lo so già. Farò pagare; e dopo?

ANAIDE: Un vecchio conto . . . un nulla . . .
Tre luigi. . . !

ZAZÀ: (*balzando*)
Sei matta. . . !

ANAIDE: Zazà, cara fanciulla . . .

ZAZÀ: Darò un luigi, e smettila.

ANAIDE: Oh! due!

ZAZÀ: Mamma, prevedo . . .

ANAIDE: Due, ti farò le carte!

ZAZÀ: (*sorridendo*) Le carte! . . . ah furba! io cedo.

DUCLOU: (*di fuori forte*) Avanti i ballerini!

ZAZÀ: (*ad Anaide*) Il mio turno è vicino. Vieni domani.

ANAIDE: (*baciandola*) Amore!
(*esce, e dice allontanandosi:*)
Oh, Dio, questo intestino. . . !
(*Due donne e due uomini in costume di ballerini spagnuoli arrivano vivamente dal fondo e vanno a guardarsi allo specchio mentre l'artista vestito da soldato rientra, e di dentro si applaude. Poi Duclou suona il campanello, l'orchestra preludia all'interno un movimento di danza spagnuola ed i ballerini entrano in iscena fra grandi applausi. Nel tempo istesso Bussy giunge vivamente dal fondo, picchia alla porta di Zazà ed entra. Zazà sarà completamente vestita.*)

ZAZÀ: (*abbracciando Bussy, allegra*) Alfin! sei tu, poeta del cuor mio!

BUSSY: (*sorpreso allegramente*) Che accoglienza!
Davver fiero son io!
Saresti incapricciata di Bussy?

ZAZÀ: Che pretesa!

BUSSY: Ti par?

ZAZÀ: (*ansiosa*) Sei solo?

---

ANAIDE: (*pretending to weep*) O dear, I shall die of sorrow!

ZAZÀ: There, there dear!
I know these scenes of weeping.
You'll do the same tomorrow.
(*rises to soothe her*)
Now kiss me, drink this and tell me what you want.

ANAIDE: (*after having kissed her and gulped down the liquor, smiles somewhat embarrassed*) Zazà, just to see you.

ZAZÀ: And then you wanted?

ANAIDE: The rent, dear—

ZAZÀ: Dearest Mamma, that will be settled.
And further?

ANAIDE: A trifling matter long due now,—Three Louis—

ZAZÀ: (*jumps up*) Good gracious!

ANAIDE: Zazà, I appeal to you, now—

ZAZÀ: I will give one Louis—that is settled.

ANAIDE: O, two, dear!

ZAZÀ: Mother, you dun me!

ANAIDE: TWO, dear, I will tell your fortune—

ZAZÀ: (*smiling*) Card fortune?—
How clever!—
You've won me!

DUCLOU: (*outside—calls*) All ready—the dancing number.

ZAZÀ: (*to Anaide*) My turn is near—and I am busy; come back tomorrow.

ANAIDE: (*kisses her*) My darling!
(*As she goes out, holding her stomach*)
O heavens!
Pain has made me dizzy!
(*Exit*)
(*Two men and two women dancers in Spanish costume come on quickly from back of stage and go to take a final survey in the mirror; while the singer in soldier's uniform returns, applause off-stage. Duclou rings bell—Spanish dance music offstage and the dancers go on, received with loud applause. Simultaneously Bussy enters quickly from back of stage, knocks at Zazà's door and enters. Zazà has now finished dressing.*)

ZAZÀ: (*embracing Bussy effusively*) At last, my poet, eagerly awaited!

BUSSY: (*surprised and delighted*) What a reception!
I am quite elated!
You like me just a little, is that so?

ZAZÀ: Why, what conceit!

BUSSY: Indeed?

ZAZÀ: (*anxiously*) No one with you?

**BUSSY:** Sì.

**ZAZÀ:** (*delusa*) Ah!

**BUSSY:** Ti portavo il *duo* per la "Rivista".

**ZAZÀ:** (*annojata*) Ah!

**BUSSY:** Vuoi vederlo?

**ZAZÀ:** (*c. s.*) Grazie, fa lo stesso. E facile?

**BUSSY:** Lo impari a prima vista; il l'ho letto a Dufresne adesso adesso.

**ZAZÀ:** (*balzando di gioja*) È qua?

**BUSSY:** Da Floriana . . .

**ZAZÀ:** (*scoppiando*) Oh! addirittura si vede che di lei non può far senza!
Certo al tuo Milio piace la pittura se al vecchio quadro dà la preferenza.

**BUSSY:** (*ridendo*) Tu meglio ameresti vederlo da te!

**ZAZÀ:** (*dissimulando*) Io . . . no . . . non ci tengo . . . non l'amo!

**BUSSY:** Ma che! Ei non ti vagheggia, e, naturalmente, chi poco ti cura tu brami.

**ZAZÀ:** (*ridendo*) Insolente! Al tuo bel Dufresne sol ch'io dica: voglio! lo vedi ai miei piedi. . . !

**BUSSY:** Zazà . . . troppo orgoglio!

**ZAZÀ:** Tu dunque mi sfidi?

**BUSSY:** Scommetto. Ci stai? Ciò ch'egli rifuta a me tu darai.

**ZAZÀ:** (*ridendo*) Stai fresco!

**BUSSY:** Tu temi?

**ZAZÀ:** Temer? Poveretto. . . !

**BUSSY:** Se Milio non cede. . . ?

**ZAZÀ:** (*ridendo*) Mi vinci; l'hai detto!
(*Intanto dal fondo arriva Cascart in costume da concerto con Michelin, mentre dalla porta che dà nella sala rientrano Courtois e l'altro signore, la scena si va popolando e durante la prima parte del dialogo tornano dal fondo Claretta e Simona che siedono al tavolo. Cascart va alla porta di Zazà e l'apre.*)

**CASCART:** Ebben, Zazà?

**ZAZÀ:** Ho finito; ci siamo?

---

**BUSSY:** No.

**ZAZÀ:** (*disappointed*) Oh!

**BUSSY:** I brought the song for the "Review," dear lady.

**ZAZÀ:** (*annoyed*) Oh!

**BUSSY:** Shall we rehearse it?

**ZAZÀ:** (*as above*) Thank you—later, maybe.
Is it easy?

**BUSSY:** I'm sure it's to your liking. I showed it to Dufresne; he thought it striking.

**ZAZÀ:** (*starts up joyfully*) He's here?

**BUSSY:** With Floriana.

**ZAZÀ:** This fad for her seems funny.
I think your friend is fond of antique treasure.
Doubtless for old masters he would squander money, if such old painted faces give him pleasure.

**BUSSY:** (*laughing*) Of course you'd rather have him admiring you!

**ZAZÀ:** (*pretending indifference*) I—no—I don't want him!— No, not I!

**BUSSY:** You do! We all are devoted—he by far the coldest, so he attracts you more than others—

**ZAZÀ:** (*laughing*) You are boldest! As for your friend Dufresne—if I'd only let him, he'd be here at my feet—

**BUSSY:** Don't be too sure you'd get him!

**ZAZÀ:** You dare me to do it?

**BUSSY:** We'll wager! You agree? Whatever he refuses—you'll grant it to me!

**ZAZÀ:** (*laughing*) You'll wait long!

**BUSSY:** Afraid, dear?

**ZAZÀ:** Afraid? That's not in me!

**BUSSY:** If Milio's unyielding?

**ZAZÀ:** (*laughs*) You've said it— you win me!
(*Cascart, in dress clothes, meanwhile enters with Michelin from back of stage; Courtois and the other gentleman come through door from Hall; the stage fills and during first part of following conversation Claretta and Simona return from back of stage and sit at table. Cascart goes to Zazà's door and opens it.*)

**CASCART:** Ready, Zazà?

**ZAZÀ:** I am ready! Is it our turn?

---

**CASCART:** Non ancora. (*salutando Bussy*) Addio.

**ZAZÀ:** Beviamo allora un bicchier di sciampagna.

**BUSSY:** Ciò mi va.

**ZAZÀ:** (*a Michelin e Courtois che son presso all'uscio rimasto aperto*) Signori, avete udito? Entrate, dunque, andiamo!

**MICHELIN:** (*entrando con Courtois*) Se non v'importuniamo. . . !

**COURTOIS:** Mille grazie.

**CASCART:** (*scorgendo l'altro signore mentre si adopera ad aprire la bottiglia di sciampagna.*) Signore! e lei che fa?

**ZAZÀ:** (*facendosi all'uscio*) Via, ci faccia l'onore. . . ! entri anche lei, . . . le pare. . . ! (*Il signore entra salutando, quando appajono dal fondo Milio Dufresne con Floriana.*)

**CASCART:** (*a Bussy*) Guarda! . . . veggo spuntare l'amico tuo, Bussy.

**BUSSY:** (*avanzandosi all'uscio*) Dufresne?

**CASCART:** Sì. è là con Floriana . . .

**ZAZÀ:** (*ritenendosi appena*) Ah! . . .

**CASCART:** (*a Bussy*) Se ti fa piacere, invita anch'esso a bere.

**BUSSY:** (*chiamando*) Ehi, Dufresne!

**DUFRESNE:** Che c'è?

**BUSSY:** Venite qui.

**DUFRESNE:** Or vengo. (*a Floriana*) Mi scusate! (*Va anche egli nel camerino di Zazà, saluta e prende la coppa che gli offre Bussy.*)

**ZAZÀ:** (*dopo aver salutato Dufresne*) I calici colmiamo.

**CASCART:** È fatto . . .

**BUSSY:** Noi beviamo a Zazà!

**TUTTI GLI UOMINI:** Ai trionfi di Zazà!! (*bevono*)

**FLORIANA:** (*presso al tavolo, a Bussy che si accosta alla porta del camerino*) Un uomo sol restavaci da questo lato, e l'hai condotto via! Sei proprio gentilissimo!

**BUSSY:** (*ridendo*) E tu perchè con lui non vieni qua?

---

**CASCART:** No—too early. (*greets Bussy*) How are you?

**ZAZÀ:** Come have a drink with me, then, champagne will make us brighter.

**BUSSY:** I'm with you!

**ZAZÀ:** (*to Michelin and Courtois, who are near the open door*) Well, boys, did you hear me? Come in—don't be exclusive.

**MICHELIN:** (*enters with Courtois*) If we are not intrusive?

**COURTOIS:** Thank you, thank you!

**CASCART:** (*noticing the other man, while he is opening a bottle of champagne*) Come on, sir, why don't you join us?

**ZAZÀ:** (*coming to door*) Come— come and do us the honor! Come right in—you're very welcome! (*The gentleman enters bowing; Milio Dufresne with Floriana comes forward from back of stage.*)

**CASCART:** (*to Bussy*) Look here! See who is with us! Your friend is coming, Bussy.

**BUSSY:** (*goes toward door*) Dufresne?

**CASCART:** Yes. And with him Floriana.

**ZAZÀ:** (*scarcely controlling herself*) Ah!

**CASCART:** (*to Bussy*) Ask Dufresne—if you care to, to join us—if he dare to!

**BUSSY:** (*calls*) Hey there—Dufresne!

**DUFRESNE:** What now?

**BUSSY:** Will you come here?

**DUFRESNE:** I'm coming. (*to Floriana*) Please excuse me! (*He joins the others in Zazà's dressing-room, greets all and takes the glass which Bussy offers him.*)

**ZAZÀ:** (*after having greeted Dufresne*) Now have the glasses clinking!

**CASCART:** We've done so!

**BUSSY:** We are drinking to Zazà!

**ALL THE MEN:** All success to our Zazà! (*They drink*)

**FLORIANA:** (*beside table, to Bussy, who stands in door of dressing-room*) One single man was left us here, And you have coaxed him in there too. That was a kindly thing to do!

**BUSSY:** (*laughing*) And why did you not follow him inside?

FLORIANA: (*forte, con astio*) Io
là?!
No, tante grazie!
Ci resti sol.
Se cerca compagnia, da quella
parte non ne mancherà!!

ZAZÀ: (*che ba sentito, grida dal
camerino*) Da te certo altrettanta
non ne trova!

FLORIANA: Se non ti basta prendi
anche il pompier!

ZAZÀ: Vederlo teco non è cosa
nuova: s'egli ti vuole te lo lascio
inter!
(*In questo punto i ballerini ban
finito e rientrano applauditi, ma
restano in iscena vedendo Zazà
che esce furibonda dal camerino
seguita dagli uomini. Gli altri artisti arrivano in iscena attirati
dal tumulto; le donne tengono per
Floriana e gli uomini per Zazà.*)

FLORIANA: (*urlando*) Ah, bald-
racca!

ZAZÀ: Vil mezzana!

CASCART e BUSSY: (*cercando ri-
tenere Zazà*) Via cessate!

PARTE DELLE DONNE: (*tenendo
per Floriana*) Essa ha ragione.
(*Zazà afferra pel ciuffo Floriana,
ma gli uomini le separono.*)

LE DONNE: (*Iª parte*) Dalli, dalli,
Floriana!

ALTRA PARTE: (*a Zazà*) Su, Zazà,
dalle un ceffone!

ZAZÀ: Linguacciuta!

FLORIANA: Svergognata!

UOMINI: La tempesta è scatenata!
Dividiamole—smettetela!
Teniamole—finitela!
(*Malardot arriva dal fondo con
Duclou.*)

MALARDOT: (*urlando*) Basta,
basta, che mai fu?
Zitto, sentono di giù!

DUCLOU: Via Zazà, ch'or tocca a
voi.

ZAZÀ: (*a Cascart mentre si riac-
concia innanzi allo specchio.*)
No, paura non mi fa.

CASCART: Sì, lo so, ma spetta a noi:
su, preparati Zazà.

ZAZÀ: Se pel ciuffo la ripig-
lio . . .

FLORIANA: (*dal fondo mentre la
portono via*) Che. . . ?!

---

FLORIANA: (*loud and vindictive-
ly*) In there?!—
No thank you, no, not I!
I hate a crowd.
In there you're one of many.
It's like a streetcar—everyone piles
in.

ZAZÀ: (*who beard her—calls
from dressing-room*) With you he
would be sure to have no rivals.

FLORIANA: If you want more, the
fireman might be willing!

ZAZÀ: I've noticed he was all that
you could capture,
Poor thing, and so I'll leave that
ONE to you.
(*Dancers, baving finished, return
while applause is heard; they remain on stage when Zazà, furious, comes from her dressing-
room, followed by the men. Other
performers, hearing the noise,
come on stage; the women side
with Floriana and the men with
Zazà.*)

FLORIANA: (*shrieks*)
Ah! you hussy!

ZAZÀ: Hateful cat, you!

CASCART AND BUSSY: (*trying to
restrain Zazà*) Stop this scrapping!

SOME OF THE WOMEN: (*siding
with Floriana*) She knows what
she's saying.
(*Zazà seizes Floriana by the hair,
but the men separate them.*)

WOMEN: (*first balf*) Give it to her,
Floriana!

WOMEN: (*second balf*) Slap her,
quick, without delaying!

ZAZÀ: Dirty liar!

FLORIANA: Shameless devil!

MEN: Now the fight is growing evil,
Keep them still and make them stop
it,
Hold them back and make them
drop it!
(*Malardot comes from back of
stage with Duclou.*)

MALARDOT: (*yelling*) Stop that
noise—shut up, you all!
They can hear you in the Hall!

DUCLOU: Come, Zazà, your turn is
next.

ZAZÀ: (*to Cascart, while she
takes final look in mirror*) No—
of her I have no fear!

CASCART: No—of course—but
don't be vexed!
Are you ready now, my dear?

ZAZÀ: If I ever catch her nap-
ping—

FLORIANA: (*who is being led
away, turns again*) What?!!!

---

MALARDOT: (*a Floriana e Zazà*)
Cessate lo scompiglio!
(*poi a Duclou*)
Date il segno.
(*agli artisti che si allontanano*)
Zitti, olà!

DUCLOU: (*suonando*) Fate posto.

CASCART: (*prendendo Zazà per
la mano per entrare in iscena*) A
noi, Zazà.
(*Appena Cascart e Zazà si presen-
tano sulla porta per entrare in
iscena si sente una salva di applausi dalla sala. Gli artisti saranno tutti ritirati nelle quinte.*)

MALARDOT: (*dando un sospiro*)
Oh! le donne!!

MICHELIN: (*a Bussy e Dufresne*)
Venite?

BUSSY: No, restiamo.

MICHELIN: (*a Courtois ed
all'altro Signore*) La nostra diva a
festeggiar andiamo!
(*Escono Michelin, Courtois,
l'altro Signore con Malardot per
la porta che dà nella sala. Restano
in iscena Bussy e Dufresne passeggiando sul davanti della scena
mentre Duclou ba chiusa la porta
che dà sulla scena e resta dietro
l'uscio.*)

BUSSY: Dufresne, contarvene voglio una bella! . . .

DUFRESNE: Che?

BUSSY: Ma pria ditemi: la nostra
stella, la irresistibile nostra Zazà,
come vi va?

DUFRESNE: Come? benissimo. . .!
la trovo un frutto saporosissi-
mo . . . davver farei pazzie per
lei!

BUSSY: (*sorpreso*) Ne imparo
delle belle!
e la fuggite?

DUFRESNE: Come tutte quelle che
al primo incontro turbano il mio
cuore.
Io non voglio un amore violento,
nel mio stato . . .

BUSSY: (*sorpreso quasi interrogando*) Oh. . . !?

DUFRESNE: (*correggendosi*) Non
mi va lo scherzare col fuoco; ci si
abbrucia! . . .

BUSSY: E Zazà?

DUFRESNE: Pericolosa!

BUSSY: E perchè mai?

DUFRESNE: Sentirlo è facil
cosa . . . eppure io non so
dirlo! . . .
È un riso gentile

---

MALARDOT: (*to Floriana and
Zazà*) Girls, stop this foolish scrapping!
(*to Duclou*)
Give them the signal!
(*to artists who are leaving stage*)
Quiet back there!

DUCLOU: (*rings bell*) Take your
places!

CASCART: (*Cascart takes Zazà's
band to go on concert stage*)
Now then, Zazà!
(*Cascart and Zazà barely appear
when a storm of applause is heard
offstage from Hall. The other artists have all retired.*)

MALARDOT: (*gives a sigh*) O,
these women!

MICHELIN: (*to Bussy and Dufresne*) Coming along?

BUSSY: No, we're remaining.

MICHELIN: (*to Courtois and the
other gentleman*) Let's hear how
much applause our star is gaining!
(*Michelin, Courtois and the other
gentleman leave with Malardot
through door leading to Hall; Bussy and Dufresne stay on, walking
to and fro. Duclou has closed
door to concert stage and remains
standing behind it.*)

BUSSY: Dufresne, I must tell you
Something very funny!

DUFRESNE: Well?

BUSSY: However, first pray tell
How do you like her,
The radiant and sunny,
Quite irresistible,
Bright shining star?

DUFRESNE: Like her?
Why certainly!
She's like a lovely peach,
Growing—not out of reach.
We want a bite,
Though it's not right.

BUSSY: (*surprised*) Then I wonder, friend and brother,
You avoid her?

DUFRESNE: Just like any other
Who at our first meeting
Sets my heart to beating.
People of our social station
Should avoid a wild, mad pas-
sion—

BUSSY: (*dumbfounded—ques-
tioningly*) Oh?!

DUFRESNE: (*explaining*) I'm
afraid
If I play with fire, I'll suffer—I'll
burn my fingers!

BUSSY: And Zazà?

DUFRESNE: She is a danger.

BUSSY: But tell me why?

DUFRESNE: I feel it like strong
conviction—and yet I cannot reveal it!
Like a zephyr of May

# Act I

Qual' alba d'aprile che inebria e
conquide le fibre del cuor!
È un brivido arcano se porge la
mano, e baldi si destano i sogni
d'amor!
Soavi misteri han gli occhî severi e
par che dischiudan del cielo il
confin;
E l'anima oblìa per dolce malìa al
suon di sua voce, la vita, il destin!
Pur belle cotanto ci passano accanto, ma è *lei* che il destino ci impone
adorar!
Chi folle d'amore la strinse sul
cuore a *lei* sempre vinto dovrà
ritornar!
È l'ebbro vicino al nappo di vino.
Se fugge lontano resister potrà.
Se il nappo egli tocca, se il porta
alla bocca,
sin l'ultima goccia del nappo berrà!

**BUSSY:** Allor tutto va bene! gua-
dagno la scommessa.

**DUFRESNE:** Quale?

**BUSSY:** Zazà ha un debole per voi,
e lo confessa!

**DUFRESNE:** (*balzando*) Davver?

**BUSSY:** Le ho raccontato ch'essa
v'è indifferente
e ha scommesso
di vincervi. . . !

**DUFRESNE:** (*turbato*) Che v'è saltato in mente!
E poi perchè ripetermi. . . ! pensate un poco . . . tale
ragazza innamorata. . . !

**BUSSY:** (*ridendo*) Si monta il col-
legiale!
Sarà come vorrete, in fondo! . . .

**DUFRESNE:** Oh, mio Bussy!
Sarà com'essa vuole; . . . non fu
sempre così!
(*A questo punto si sente una salva
di applausi all'interno: dalla porta laterale arrivano Malardot,
Michelin, Courtois e l'altro Signore. Zazà e Cascart salutano fra
grida insistenti di bis: Malardot li
spinge a salutare mentre tutti si
appressano alla porta, anche Bussy e Dufresne.*)

**MALARDOT:** Son tutti in delirio!
Andiam, salutate!
(*Le voci di dentro domandano
con insistenza: Il bacio, il bacio!*)
*Il bacio* reclamano!

**MICHELIN, DUFRESNE, COUR-
TOIS, BUSSY:** Sì, *il bacio!*

Her laughter can sway,
Can make you forget what the
world would call wise;
By a sweet, gentle bond,
To her touch you respond,
And wonderful visions before you
arise.
Love's light you behold
In the eyes that were cold,
You see a promise of rapture un-
bounded!
So potent their spell,
That heaven and hell,
Life, honor and truth will be
forgotten!
You pass all unseeing,
Till you meet with the being,
The one whom by Fate you are
doomed to adore,
Who sets your heart beating,
Sweet madness each meeting,
To her you are bound like a slave
evermore!
Where wine means temptation
And intoxication,
The drunkard must flee, or he strug-
gles in vain.
If his lips wine have tasted,
Resistance is wasted,
He empties the flagon again and
again!

**BUSSY:** Then I shall win the wager!
I might have guessed it!

**DUFRESNE:** Wager?

**BUSSY:** Zazà is badly smitten with
you and has confessed it.

**DUFRESNE:** (*starts*) Truly?

**BUSSY:** I had said you were like
marble, cold and quite unbending.
And she has wagered she could win
you!

**DUFRESNE:** (*perturbed*) And
what, pray, will be the ending?
And why betray it and tell me?
Impossible to conceive it—
This woman by love affected!

**BUSSY:** (*laughing*) You schoolboy—do you believe it?
It will end exactly as you elect it.

**DUFRESNE:** O no, Bussy!
It will end as she may decide it.
It has always been thus.
(*Wild applause offstage; Malardot, Michelin, Courtois and the
other man come through the side
door. Zazà and Cascart are seen
bowing, while shouts of "encore"
are heard. Malardot urges them to
respond, while all come nearer to
stage door, including Bussy and
Dufresne.*)

**MALARDOT:** The crowd is wild
with pleasure—
Go on to please them!
(*Calls outside for "The Kiss! The
Kiss!"*)
They want "The Kiss" repeated!

**MICHELIN, DUFRESNE, COUR-
TOIS, BUSSY:** Yes, repeat it!

**DUCLOU:** Attaccate!
(*Suona il campanello e lascia la
porta aperta, di maniera che si
senton distintamente le due voci
di Zazà e Cascart all'interno.*)

**LUI:** Non so capir perchè,
se m'ami tu,
non vuoi venir qui sola a me vicin!

**LEI:** No, mio signor, venir non posso giù;
è buja troppo l'ombra del giardin!

**LUI:** Dunque paura io faccio a te?!

**LEI:** Ma alfin che vuoi tu, giù,
da me?

**LUI:** Io che mai voglio. . . ? un sol
bacin!

**LEI:** Uh! . . . che mai dite, sig-
norin! . . .
(*Insieme*)

**LEI:** Un bacin!
Giù in giardin! . . .
è peccar:
nol vo' far!

**LUI:** Perchè no?
Io lo vo'!
Cedi orsù,
vieni giù!

**LEI:** Ma se mamma ci arriva repente
chi la sente!
che terror!

**LUI:** No, fa cor!

**LEI:** Vieni invece un po' su dalle
scale,
e se giunge nasconderti io so!

**LUI:** Cara! io salgo; c'è niente di
male;
più d'un bacio allor darti potrò!
(*Appena Zazà e Cascart hanno
finito, nuovi applausi; essi poi si
avanzano giulivi tra gli amici.*)

**BUSSY, MICHELIN, COURTOIS,
DUFRESNE:** Ma bravi! che delizia!

**CASCART:** (*trionfante*) Eh. . . ?
quando noi
vogliamo. . . !

**BUSSY:** Siete straordinarî!

**MALARDOT:** Su, tempo non perdiamo; la "Rivista" or si prova. Ognun sia pronto!

**CASCART:** (*andando via*) È detto!
(*esce dal fondo*)

**BUSSY:** Duclou, mi raccomando!

**ZAZÀ:** (*sull'uscio del camerino*)
Ehi, Bussy! quel duetto Vorrai farmi
ripetere . . .

**BUSSY:** Non posso . . . ho un
gran da fare!
(*con intenzione*)
Ma l'amico Dufresne può fartelo
passare!

**DUCLOU:** Pay attention!
(*He rings bell and leaves door
open so the voices of Cascart and
Zazà can be distinctly heard from
offstage.*)

**HE:** If you love me, how can you be
so cold?
Why do you leave me all alone
down here?

**SHE:** No, no, dear boy, 't is dangerous, I'm told,
The garden is too dark at night, I
fear!

**HE:** Are you afraid?
Am I so awful to you?

**SHE:** What do you want me for—
tell me, now do?

**HE:** What do I want of you?
One kiss, my dear!

**SHE:** Go—you're a naughty boy, I
fear!
(*together*)

**SHE:** One small kiss
Might not be amiss,
Still, at night
It's not right.

**HE:** Don't say no!
Before I go,
Come, give in,
It's no sin!

**SHE:** It is dangerous, my mother has
told me!
She would scold me
If she knew!

**HE:** Come now, do!

**SHE:** I'll not come down, but you
come up to me, dear!
If mother comes, safe hidden you'll
be.

**HE:** Sweetheart, I'm coming!
Love can be no sin, dear!
(*When Zazà and Cascart end
their song, renewed applause offstage. They join their friends joyfully.*)

**BUSSY, MICHELIN, COURTOIS,
DUFRESNE:** Just splendid, quite
delightful!

**CASCART:** (*triumphantly*)
Well—we impressed them rather!

**BUSSY:** You are just splendid!

**MALARDOT:** Come, gather for rehearsal!
The new "Review" we're trying—
be quick, get ready!

**CASCART:** (*goes upstage*) I'm going.
(*Exit at back of stage*)

**BUSSY:** Duclou, I'd like to see you!

**ZAZÀ:** (*in the door of her room*) I
say, Bussy, how about it?
Shall we go over that one number?

**BUSSY:** I cannot—I shall have to
be here.
Perhaps (*with meaning*) my friend
Dufresne can substitute for me
here.

ZAZÀ: (*lieta*) Davvero? non v'incomoda?

DUFRESNE: (*un po' imbarazzato*) Vi pare . . . !

BUSSY: (*ridendo*) Andiamo, su!

ZAZÀ: (*a Dufresne*) Oh, come siete buono!
(*entra vivamente nel camerino e dice piano a Natalia:*)
Fila, e non tornar più!
(*Natalia esce e si allontana dal fondo.*)

BUSSY: (*andando verso il fondo con Malardot*) Duclou, tutto sia pronto!

DUCLOU: Fidate pure in me!
(*Malardot e Bussy escono dal fondo a sinistra*)
(*gridando e uscendo dalla porta che dà sulla scena*)
Fuori di scena. . . ! All'opra. . . !

MICHELIN: (*a Courtois*) Noi scendiamo al Caffè.
(*Escono dalla porta che dà nella sala in modo che la scena resta vuota e scura. Il camerino di Zazà è rischiarato come prima, Dufresne è presso all'uscio.*)

ZAZÀ: Signore, entrate; è un gentile pensiero il vostro . . .
(*Dufresne entra; Zazà chiude l'uscio.*)

DUFRESNE: È un debole ajuto!

ZAZÀ: Modesto troppo!

DUFRESNE: È la prima campagna!

ZAZÀ: Davvero? Le attrici agli amanti domandan questo. . . ; ne conoscete?

DUFRESNE: Qualcuna . . .
(*Dufresne siede*)

ZAZÀ: Ero certa! Dite, e Floriana?

DUFRESNE: La trovo piacente . . .

ZAZÀ: Ma non è il vostro ideal?!

DUFRESNE: Veramente non ho idĕali!

ZAZÀ: Davver? Che scoperta! Amate il vario . . .

DUFRESNE: Ecco . . . il vario . . .

ZAZÀ: Capisco! . . . Ma, in fede mia, non sposatevi!

DUFRESNE: (*ridendo come colto da un'idea comica*) Io? mai. . . !!!

ZAZÀ: Io son diversa da voi—Non ardisco dirvelo, e pur d'un sogno mi beai!
(*chinandosi sino alla faccia di Dufresne*)

ZAZÀ: (*pleased*) O, will you? It will not bore you?

DUFRESNE: (*a little embarrassed*) Indeed, no—

BUSSY: (*laughing*) Then go ahead!

ZAZÀ: (*to Dufresne*) You are so kind to help me!
(*She hurries into dressing-room and says softly to Natalia*)
Leave us and don't return here!
(*Natalia exit back of stage.*)

BUSSY: (*going upstage with Malardot*) Duclou, are you all ready?

DUCLOU: You can depend on me.
(*Malardot and Bussy exeunt back of stage l.; Duclou through door which opens on stage, shouting*)
Clear the stage—all ready!

MICHELIN: (*to Courtois*) Let us go to the Café.
(*Exit through door which opens into hall; half of stage is empty and darkened. Zazà's room is lighted as before. Dufresne is near the door.*)

ZAZÀ: Come in! Perhaps I shall impose unduly upon you—
(*Dufresne enters—Zazà closes door.*)

DUFRESNE: I fear small help I'll render.

ZAZÀ: To please me, try it!

DUFRESNE: My first venture at coaching.

ZAZÀ: Truly? The actresses all have their lovers coach them—it's easy. Do you know any?

DUFRESNE: A number.
(*He sits down.*)

ZAZÀ: I could guess it. Tell me, this Floriana?

DUFRESNE: I think her entertaining.

ZAZÀ: But she is not your own ideal?

DUFRESNE: I confess it, I have no ideal!

ZAZÀ: Really? Ah, I see then you like variety?

DUFRESNE: Just so —variety.

ZAZÀ: Exactly! But, take my advice and do not marry!

DUFRESNE: (*laughs as though struck by a comical idea*) I?— Never!

ZAZÀ: I am not like you at all—I feel timid to tell it. A dream is haunting me ever!
(*Bends close to Dufresne*)
There is one man who means all the

C'è un uomo al mondo ch'è tutto per me . . . e ha nome . . . il nome è un mistero. . . !

DUFRESNE: (*freddo*) Perchè?

ZAZÀ: Perchè non so; pur questo mi turba e mi confonde . . . ma a voi poco ne importa . . .

DUFRESNE: (*con fredda cortesia*) No, dite!

ZAZÀ: Si nasconde forse l'indifferenza? Voi non la nascondete; e allora a che parlare?

DUFRESNE: E il duetto?

ZAZÀ: (*contrariata dandogli i fogli*) Tenete! . . .
(*sospirando*)
Ripetiamo . . . ma prima vo' cambiar veste; avvezzo ai nostri camerini voi siete già da un pezzo!
(*fingendo chiamare*)
Natalia! . . . Non avete scrupoli . . . Natalia!

DUFRESNE: (*alzandosi*) La chiamo?

ZAZÀ: No; vorreste, signore, in cortesia darmi un poco d'ajuto, slacciarmi il corsaletto?

DUFRESNE: Ben lieto . . .

ZAZÀ: Cominciate di sopra, dal laccetto.

DUFRESNE: (*sempre freddo*) Scusate; non ho pratica, son così poco destro . . .

ZAZÀ: (*piegandosi indietro voluttuosamente*) Che! fate così bene. . . ! siete un vero maestro! . . .

DUFRESNE: Grazie!

ZAZÀ: (*sfiorando il volto di Dufresne colla nuca*) Con che piacere voi slaccereste il busto d'una donnina bella . . .

DUFRESNE: (*tirando indietro la testa*) Già! . . .

ZAZÀ: Ma di vostro gusto . . .

DUFRESNE: Ahi! mi son punto!

ZAZÀ: Al diavolo! ho la maledizione! Vi duole?

DUFRESNE: Oh, no.
(*Zazà passa un accappatojo.*)

ZAZÀ: Son lieta!! Ed ora alla lezione.
(*Siede in faccia a Dufresne che si dispone a leggere presso il tavolo.*)
Oh! strano. . . !
(*si alza e si accosta a Dufresne*)

DUFRESNE: A che guardate, signorina?

world to me— And this one man—his name is a mystery!—

DUFRESNE: (*coldly*) And why?

ZAZÀ: I cannot tell; the mere thought can fill me with sweet confusion. But that can never interest you.

DUFRESNE: (*coldly courteous*) No—tell me!

ZAZÀ: No illusion have I that you are curious—it causes you no worry; Then why discuss the subject?

DUFRESNE: Shall we rehearse now?

ZAZÀ: (*handing song to him*) There's no hurry.
(*sighs*)
We'll rehearse it—but first I want to change my costume slightly. You know our dressing-rooms and that we take conventions lightly.
(*pretends to call Natalia*)
Natalia!—I'm sure you will excuse me—Natalia!

DUFRESNE: (*jumps up*) Shall I call her?

ZAZÀ: No—instead I'll ask you to assist me. Kindly unfasten my bodice for me—if you don't mind it!

DUFRESNE: With pleasure!

ZAZÀ: Begin at the top hook, if you can find it.

DUFRESNE: (*still frigid*) Have patience!— I have had no experience as a maid to ladies.

ZAZÀ: (*bending backward enticingly*) Why, I can scarce believe this is your "first appearance!"

DUFRESNE: Thank you!

ZAZÀ: (*grazing his face with her hair*) You would unlace a bodice to perfection for some nice little woman—

DUFRESNE: (*drawing back*) True!

ZAZÀ: Of your own selection—

DUFRESNE: There—a pin pricked me!

ZAZÀ: O darn those pins—they make you feel like cursing! Does it hurt you?

DUFRESNE: Oh no—
(*Zazà puts on a negligée.*)

ZAZÀ: All right then—now let us begin rehearsing.
(*She sits down facing Dufresne, who is beside table—ready to read.*)
How funny!
(*She goes close to Dufresne.*)

DUFRESNE: Now what is holding your attention?

# Act I

ZAZÀ: Guardo i vostri capelli: han lampi d'oro!

DUFRESNE: (*ridendo*) Ma con lega d'argento; è lega fina ma disprezzata . . .

ZAZÀ: (*carezzandogli i capelli*) No; sono un tesoro! Oh, guarda! un segno voi portate presso la nuca: oh, grazioso! Ce l'ho anch'io . . . ma più piccino e quasi al luogo istesso . . . (*piegandosi*) No, più presso l'orecchio. Eccovi il mio . . . (*Un servo di scena traversa il fondo suonando la campana.*)

DUFRESNE: (*freddo*) La campana . . .

ZAZÀ: (*sdegnata*) Oh, la sento la campana, per Bacco!

DUFRESNE: E il duetto? . . .

ZAZÀ: So tutto: (*fra sè*) mi pagherai lo smacco! (*Arrivano dal fondo Duclou, Malardot, Bussy, Cascart e Claretta*) (*Dufresne esce lentamente dal camerino.*)

CASCART: (*aprendo la porta del camerino*) Su, Zazà!

BUSSY: (*vedendola in accappatojo*) Che! in quello stato?

ZAZÀ: (*nervosa*) Per servirti. È un gran peccato?

BUSSY: Ma c'era ben tempo . . .

ZAZÀ: Da sola dovevo vestirmi?

CASCART: Non c'era la sarta?

ZAZÀ: È partita . . .

MALARDOT: Parola d'onore la multo stasera!

BUSSY: (*piano a Malardot*) Ha i nervi, lascia . . .

MALARDOT: Dà il segno, Duclou!

DUCLOU: Al posto, batto i tre colpi!

BUSSY: (*a Malardot*) Andiam giù . . . (*Malardot e Bussy escono dalla porta che dà nella sala. Gli artisti che prendono parte alla Rivista si perdono tra le quinte. Zazà, in collera, leggendo il duetto, siede presso ad una quinta sul davanti a destra. Dufresne passeggia guardandola.*)

DUCLOU: (*batte i tre colpi*) A te, Cascart . . . (*Cascart entra in iscena.*) (*appressandosi a Zazà*) Zazà, dopo tu sei di scena . . . sta

ZAZÀ: Your hair is golden where the reflections strike it!

DUFRESNE: (*laughing*) But mingled with silver—and I would call it a common alloy—

ZAZÀ: (*playing with his hair*) No—precious is more like it! O—lovely! You have a mole—till now I did not know it— Right by the ear, where I have mine; come nearer— It's in the selfsame spot—just wait, I'll show it! (*bending close to him*) There—on my neck. Bend down, you'll see it clearer. (*A stagehand crosses at back, ringing bell.*)

DUFRESNE: (*coldly*) The call sounding.

ZAZÀ: (*angry*) Oh, I can hear that bell, don't worry!

DUFRESNE: And the song number?

ZAZÀ: I know it! (*aside*) For this I'll make him sorry! (*Duclou, Malardot, Bussy, Cascart and Claretta come downstage from back. Dufresne slowly leaves dressing-room.*)

CASCART: (*opens door to dressing-room*) Come, Zazà!

BUSSY: (*noticing the negligée*) What—in this condition?

ZAZÀ: (*nervously*) No, not dressed. Pray pardon the omission!

BUSSY: You had time enough, though.

ZAZÀ: Left lonely, how could I change dresses?

CASCART: Was the maid not with you?

ZAZÀ: She had left me!

MALARDOT: She is paid to wait on you, and on you only!

BUSSY: (*softly to Malardot*) Let her go—she is nervous.

MALARDOT: Give the signal, Duclou!

DUCLOU: All ready—three knocks I'll give you.

BUSSY: (*to Malardot*) We'll go too. (*Malardot and Bussy out through door into Hall; the singers who take part in the "Review" disappear in the wings.*) (*Zazà, angry, sits down near one of the wings, r. front, reading the duet. Dufresne passes her, watching her.*)

DUCLOU: (*gives three loud knocks*) On stage, Cascart! (*Cascart goes on concert stage.*) (*coming over to Zazà*) Zazà, he goes on just before you.

pronta, te ne prego: potrò guardarti appena; debbo dall'altra parte fare il rumor del cocchio.

ZAZÀ: (*secca*) Lo so.

DUCLOU: Mettiti calma, te ne prego in ginocchio. Quando Cascart ti dice: *"Chi dunque mi conduce?"* entra; non mi sbagliare!

ZAZÀ: (*come sopra*) Lo so. (*Duclou gira dietro al fondaletto e scompare al di là del fondo a destra.*)

DUFRESNE: (*arrestandosi presso Zazà*) Non vi seduce ripetere il duetto insieme un pò?

ZAZÀ: (*sgarbata*) No, grazie; ne fo' senza!

DUFRESNE: Aspetterò! . . . (*Dufresne si china e la prende alla cintura col braccio mentre la bacia con forza sul collo: Zazà si volge raggiante e lo avvinghia con le braccia.*)

ZAZÀ: Perchè, cattivo, non me l'avevi prima tu detto?

DUFRESNE: È forse tardi per riparare?

ZAZÀ: No, mio diletto!

CASCART: (*di dentro*) *"Chi dunque mi conduce?"*

ZAZÀ: (*estasiata*) Oh! come bene m'hai tu baciata qui, sul collo!

DUCLOU: (*riapparendo dietro al fondaletto: con angoscia*) Ebbene? Zazà! . . . Psst. . . !

ZAZÀ: (*sempre nelle braccia di Dufresne*) Dunque ti divertiva la mia tortura? Allor tu m'ami?!

DUCLOU: Zazà. . . !

MALARDOT: (*di dentro*) L'entrata non è sicura!

BUSSY: (*di dentro*) Zazà è di scena!

CASCART: (*in collera appare sull'uscio della scena*) Per Dio! non entri?

ZAZÀ: (*stordita*) Che?

CASCART: Come, che? Non entri in tempo! mi pianti in asso!

ZAZÀ: (*in collera*) Basta, perchè tu m'hai seccata!

CASCART: (*stupito*) Ah!

ZAZÀ: (*proseguendo*) Vo'mancare alle mie entrate quando mi piace! Ti proibisco queste scenate!

CASCART: (*a Duclou*) Che diavolo ha in corpo? (*Duclou crolla le spalle, Cascart rientra.*)

Be ready—I can't call you—don't fail me, I implore you! I have to make the noise for carriage wheels approaching.

ZAZÀ: (*dryly*) I know!

DUCLOU: Don't get excited, don't forget your coaching! As soon as Cascart says: *"Who then would dare resist you?"* Run on—don't keep them waiting!

ZAZÀ: (*as before*) All right! (*Duclou goes behind the back drop and disappears r.*)

DUFRESNE: (*stops beside Zazà*) Can I assist you? Shall we rehearse the number after all?

ZAZÀ: (*curtly*) No thank you—I don't need you!

DUFRESNE: I'm at your call! (*He bends over her and, putting his arms around her, kisses her passionately on the shoulder.—Zazà, radiant, clasps him in her arms.*)

ZAZÀ: But why, you rascal, why did you keep me waiting forever?

DUFRESNE: I'll make amends, or is it too late now?

ZAZÀ: No, dearest, never!

CASCART: (*from offstage*) "Who then would dare resist you?"

ZAZÀ: (*in ecstasy*) Oh, you were kissing me on my neck—just where I like it!

DUCLOU: (*reappears behind drop—in agonized tone*) She's missing! Zazà—Psst!

ZAZÀ: (*still in Dufresne's arms*) For fun you just made me suffer—just confess it! And now you love me?!

DUCLOU: Zazà!

MALARDOT: (*from offstage*) If you're too late, you will mess it!

BUSSY: (*offstage*) Zazà—this is your scene!

CASCART: (*angry, appears in door to stage*) Confound it! Where are you?

ZAZÀ: (*amazed*) What?

CASCART: Nothing "what"! You missed your entrance; your cue I shouted!

ZAZÀ: (*furious*) Enough of that— You have annoyed me!

CASCART: (*nonplussed*) Ah!!!

ZAZÀ: (*as above*) If I choose, I can miss my cue! And this I'll tell you—I'll not stand for being bossed by you!

CASCART: (*to Duclou*) What devil is she possessed of? (*Duclou shrugs his shoulders; Cascart goes on stage again.*)

ZAZÀ: Ora vengo:
(*a Milio con dolcezza*)
Scusate . . .

CASCART: (*di dentro*) "Chi dunque mi conduce?"

ZAZÀ: (*sempre a Milio*) Udrete il mio pezzo?
(*Dufresne fa un segno di affermazione e le bacia la mano.*)

CASCART: (*più forte c. s.*) "Chi dunque mi conduce?"

ZAZÀ: (*entra in iscena facendo dei gorgheggi*) Io. . . !

*La tela cala rapidamente.*
*Fine Del Primo Atto.*

# ■ Atto Secondo.

*Il Salotto in Casa Di Zazà. — Scena parapettata: a sinistra camino con sopra una specchiera, un orologio, un servizio per cognac, fotografie, ecc.; sulla campana dell'orologio sarà posto un cappello di Zazà. Subito dopo il camino una porta che conduce all'interno dell'appartamento; poi sul muro in isbieco una porta che dà in un gabinetto di sbarazzo; dalla porta aperta si scorge un portamantello con delle vesti, e per terra delle scatole di cappelli. Sul muro di fondo, nel mezzo una finestra che dà sulla via; a sinistra della finestra un tavolo da toletta; a destra un pianoforte verticale. Indi sulla destra, in fondo in isbieco, la porta che dà nell'anticamera; poscia un paravento; presso al paravento una chaise-longue e verso la sinistra un tavolo. Qua e là sedie. Mobili modesti. È pieno giorno. Milio è mezzo sdrajato sulla chaise-longue, Zazà è presso a lui, in piedi, con un ginocchio appoggiato sul divano.*

ZAZÀ: (*con tristezza*) È deciso: tu parti per questo gran viaggio?

MILIO: (*con affetto*) Dovrei: ma di lasciarti ancor non ho coraggio.

ZAZÀ: Quanto starai lontano?

MILIO: . . . Tre, quattro mesi . . .

ZAZÀ: Ahimè che quattro lunghi mesi saranno senza te! . . . Prendimi teco!

MILIO: Mia Zazà, mio bene, ragiona dunque; che follìe son queste? Sai?
L'America è lungi e sono modeste le mie sostanze; lavorar conviene. Perciò solo io men vado. Ed è già tardi!

---

ZAZÀ: (*Now I'm coming:*)
(*to Milio, sweetly*)
Excuse me—

CASCART: (*offstage*) "Who then would dare resist you?"

ZAZÀ: (*still to Dufresne*) Will you stand by and listen?
(*Dufresne nods and kisses her hands.*)

CASCART: (*louder, offstage*)
"Who then would dare resist you?"

ZAZÀ: (*runs off on concert stage, trilling*) I!

*Quick Curtain.*
*End of Act I.*

# ■ Act II.

*(Living-room in Zazà's apartment. Box scene; at left a mantel with mirror; a clock, a liqueur set, photographs on the mantel. On top of the clock is Zazà's hat. Close to fireplace a door leading into apartment; in sidewall a door opening into dressing-room; through open door a portmanteau is visible, with some clothes; on the floor are boxes with hats. In center of rear wall a window looking on street; at left of window a dressing-table; at right an upright piano; to right of piano, in rear, a door leading to anteroom; then a screen; near the screen, a lounge; toward left of stage a table; chairs here and there; modest furnishing. It is broad daylight. Milio Dufresne is half reclining on the lounge. Zazà beside him, standing, with one knee on lounge.*)

ZAZÀ: (*sadly*) Is it settled: Upon this journey you are starting?

MILIO: (*tenderly*) I must—although my courage fails at thought of parting.

ZAZÀ: How long will you be absent?

MILIO: Four months or over.

ZAZÀ: Poor Me!
Four endless months without you, as many years will be!
Do take me with you!

MILIO: My Zazà—my dearest, be good; you know it's folly what you say, and the United States are very far away.
I am not wealthy—there my work is waiting;
And I must go alone, tho' it's exasperating!

---

ZAZÀ: (*sedendo ed abbracciandolo stretto*) Amor mio, che farà non più vicina a te, la tua Zazà, la tua piccina, essa che vive solo dei tuoi sguardi?
Quando vai a Parigi e la sera ritorni, ch'io non ti veggo, o Milio, mi sembran mille giorni . . .
Hai detto: quattro mesi . . . due piccole parole, ma quanto strazio, amore, in queste voci sole!
Quattro mesi a domandarmi: Tornerà? m'amerà ancora?
Tornerai, dimmi, ad amarmi? come un tempo? come allora che mi desti il primo bacio? come adesso?
Dimmi o mio bene, mi farai soffrire? . . .
No, tu m'ami! . . . e t'amo anch'io!
(*si getta al collo di Milio profondamente commossa.*)

MILIO: (*commosso*) Zazà, Zazà, non ti attristare sai che mi strazia questo abbandono!
Sai, da tre mesi dovevo andare e a te vicino ancora io sono.
Perchè, s'io parto, l'ore del pianto sul mio deserto cuor scenderanno, e queste labbra baciate tanto più le tue labbra non bacieranno! . . .

ZAZÀ: (*quasi sperando*) Tu pur sei triste! . . .
Vedi? avrai coraggio di partire?

MILIO: (*levandosi serio*) L'avrò! questo viaggio è necessario . . .

ZAZÀ: (*con dolce rimprovero*) Ancora?

MILIO: (*guardandola*) Ebbene, no . . . se sarai buona . . .

ZAZÀ: (*ansiosamente*) Che?

MILIO: Ritarderò!

ZAZÀ: (*con impeto di gioja gettandosi nelle sue braccia*) Ah! lo sapevo!
T'amo! sei buono.

MILIO: T'amo, ma troppo debole io sono!
Or tempo e baci per guadagnare tosto a Parigi lasciami andare.

ZAZÀ: (*lieta*) Oh, certo!
(*chiamando*) Natalia! . . .
(*Natalia entra dalla destra*)
Dà l'abito e il cappello
(*Natalia eseguisce.*) al signore.

---

ZAZÀ: (*sitting down and holding him close*) My dearest love!
I live for you only!
Your own Zazà, your girl will be lonely!
The world is dark without your smile, your glances—
When you go on to Paris and are late in returning,
On the days you are absent, Milio, I nearly die of yearning!
You said four months of absence; those two brief words mean grieving and tears, and sorrow, dearest, that is beyond believing!
Four months of endless question: Will he come?
Does he love no more?
Dearest—say you'll come back and love me just the same as you did before!
As you did with the first sweet kisses!
Just as now—O tell me true!
Tell me, will you make me suffer?
No, you love me and I adore you!
(*She throws herself passionately into his arms.*)

MILIO: (*deeply moved*) Zazà, Zazà, you must not be downhearted!
You know it rends my soul to leave you lonely.
You know three months ago I should have started,
And still I'm beside you—I think of you only!
For if I leave, the bitter hours of yearning will torture me with memory of blisses.
Alone—my lips, still with your kisses burning, can not meet yours in hungry, endless kisses!

ZAZÀ: (*hopefully*) You too are sorry!
There now—you cannot stand it to be parted—

MILIO: (*rises, seriously*) I must— the Fates demand it.
This awful journey—

ZAZÀ: (*with gentle reproach*) Still cruel?

MILIO: (*looking at her fondly*) O well then, no, if you'll be good, dear—

ZAZÀ: (*anxiously*) How?

MILIO: I will not go.

ZAZÀ: (*in a transport of joy, throwing herself into his arms*) Ah, how I love you—Dearest! I adore you!

MILIO: I love you too, and yield too much before you!
Now let me go to Paris; there I'm earning the time for kisses that shall still my yearning.

ZAZÀ: (*joyfully*) Oh—surely!
(*calls*)
Natalia!
(*Natalia enters from r.*) Bring Mr. Dufresne's hat and coat here.

# Act II

(*a Milio*)
Il bastone? . . . i guanti? . . .
Tornerai? . . .

**MILIO:** Posdomani . . .

**ZAZÀ:** Due giorni? sono lunghi! . . . Ora vai!

**MILIO:** (*con finto rimprovero*) Con che fretta mi scacci!

**ZAZÀ:** Ritornerai più presto.

**MILIO:** Passo per le valigie dall'albergo . . .

**ZAZÀ:** Io mi vesto vengo alla stazione a vederti . . . mi vuoi?

**MILIO:** Sì

**ZAZÀ:** (*prendendolo fra le braccia*) Ma prima baciami forte . . . laggiù non puoi! Che tu pensa! Baciami! . . . Addio! . . .

**MILIO:** Fanciulla mia, amo e ti penso: Addio! . . . (*Esce strappandosi da Zazà*)

**ZAZÀ:** Fa presto, Natalia! stivaletti, il velo, il mantello . . .

**NATALIA:** (*correndo allo spogliatojo*) Ecco quà . . . Signor Milio parte?

**ZAZÀ:** No, va a Parigi. (*con un grido*) Àh! la che ancor lo veda alla finestra! (*va alla finestra e la spalanca per seguire Milio coll'occhio*) che mi batte il cuore, o Natalia! Ora traversa già la via maestra . . . nobiltà nel passo e che malìa . . . apisce che è un uomo, al portamento, io, franco, leale, . . . un uomo raro! bene alta la testa! Ecco, un momento olge; vedi, s'è voltato . . . Caro! (*mandandogli dei baci*) manca di voltarsi . . . mi ha sentito . . . Li'io lo guardo! È all'angolo . . . È sparito! (*sospira*)

**NATALIA:** Ecco gli stivaletti, signora . . .

**ZAZÀ:** Ed il cappello? fa presto . . .

**NATALIA:** È là; lo vede? sul caminetto

He is leaving.
(*to Milio*)
Your walking-stick—your gloves? When will you be here?

**MILIO:** Day after next.

**ZAZÀ:** Two days! They will be endless; now go, dear!

**MILIO:** (*pretending to be reproachful*) You're in great haste to lose me!

**ZAZÀ:** I'll have you back here sooner.

**MILIO:** I'll stop at the hotel for my valises.

**ZAZÀ:** I'll get ready and see you on your train down at the station.—Shall I?

**MILIO:** Yes, come!

**ZAZÀ:** (*clasping him in her arms*) First kiss me good and hard—later we'll have no time. You'll not forget me? One more kiss now! —Good-by!

**MILIO:** My own girl! I think of you and love you: Now, good-by! (*He breaks away from Zazà.*) (*Exit*)

**ZAZÀ:** Make haste—it is not early! Natalia—bring my boots, my veil, my wraps—where are they?

**NATALIA:** (*running to dressing-room*) Here they are. Is Mister Milio leaving?

**ZAZÀ:** No—he goes to Paris— (*cries out*) Àh!— From the window I can see him as he is going— (*runs to window and opens it, looking after Milio*) O, how my heart is beating—while I am waiting! Now—there he crosses the street, the distance is growing. See, how noble his bearing—how fascinating! One can see he is grand—his manner is royal! Yet he's kind and gentle and frank and loyal— How high he carries his head: See, he is turning and smiling; he has seen me—Dearest! (*throws kisses*) He never fails to turn—O, how endearing! He knows I'm watching—he turns the corner—disappearing— (*sighs*)

**NATALIA:** Here are your walking boots, Miss Zazà.

**ZAZÀ:** I want my hat on! Please hurry!

**NATALIA:** It's there—before you upon the mantel.

**ZAZÀ:** Quello? Vuoi che Milio mi creda un istrice od un riccio?! . . . (*Va da sè, trascinandosi con una sola scarpa ad un piede a prendere il cappello che le conviene nello spogliatojo.*)

**NATALIA:** (*segendola*) Signora! mia signora! . . . che fa? . . .

**ZAZÀ:** Così mi spiccio.

**NATALIA:** Ma signora! . . . (*suono di campanello*)

**ZAZÀ:** (*spaventata*) Si suona!? Non ci sono: partita, ammalata . . . defunta . . . tutto!! . . . (*Natalia esce.*) Sarei spedita! Una visita! . . . (*cercando i guanti*) i guanti dove sono? Oh, disdetta! Fa nulla . . .

**NATALIA:** (*annunziando*) È la signora Anaide.

**ANAIDE:** (*a Zazà, entrando, cerimoniosa*) Benedetta . . .

**ZAZÀ:** (*lieta, ma rapidamente*) Mamma, se avete fame, mangiate! Avete sete? Bevete! Avete sonno? un letto troverete: avete da parlarmi? Ritornerò . . . (*esce correndo*)

**ANAIDE:** (*interdetta*) Zazà! . . . (*a Natalia*) Adesso dove corre quella saetta?

**NATALIA:** Va a salutar l'amico alla stazione . . .

**ANAIDE:** (*lieta*) Parte?

**NATALIA:** Sì.

**ANAIDE:** Oh! non ritornasse mai, da nessuna parte!

**NATALIA:** Torna domani l'altro . . .

**ANAIDE:** (*seccata, sedendo presso il tavolo*) Maleducato! (*Suonano*)

**NATALIA:** Vado ad aprir . . .

**ANAIDE:** Che noja! . . . (*Visto il cognac sul camino va a versarsene un bicchierino che beve rapidamente.*) (*Entrano Cascart e Natalia*)

**CASCART:** (*a Natalia*) Non c'è? perchè vorrei

**NATALIA:** Fra poco . . . la signora (*accenna Anaide*) l'aspetta ancora lei . . .

**CASCART:** (*con spiacevole sorpresa, salutando*) Signora . . .

**ZAZÀ:** That one? He'll take me for a porcupine with stickers—I won't wear it! (*She hops off with one shoe on to select another hat from dressing-room.*)

**NATALIA:** (*following*) Miss ZaZà—wait one moment—just one!

**ZAZÀ:** He cannot bear it!

**NATALIA:** (*trying to put on her shoe*) Please, Miss Zazà— (*The bell rings.*)

**ZAZÀ:** (*frightened*) Who's ringing? I've gone walking—departed— I've a headache—say I'm dead—anything— (*Exit Natalia*) I'll not get started If it's a caller.— (*hunting for her gloves*) Where can my gloves be hiding? How unlucky! No matter—

**NATALIA:** (*announces*) It's only Madam Anaide—

**ANAIDE:** (*enters, to Zazà, ceremoniously*) May God bless you!

**ZAZÀ:** (*joyously, very quickly*) Mamma, if you are hungry, there's plenty—for that dry feeling, Take this here.— If you are sleepy, the lounge may look appealing! And if you want to see me,—I will return— (*runs off*)

**ANAIDE:** (*upset*) Zazà! . . . (*to Natalia*) Where is she running now, the crazy creature?

**NATALIA:** Off to meet her friend down at the railroad station.

**ANAIDE:** (*pleased*) Leaving?

**NATALIA:** Yes.

**ANAIDE:** Well—if he returned no more, I should not be grieving!

**NATALIA:** Day after next he comes.

**ANAIDE:** (*annoyed, sits down beside table*) I hate that rascal! (*bell rings*)

**NATALIA:** I'll see who is there.

**ANAIDE:** Annoying! (*She sees cognac on the mantel—fills a glass and gulps it down.*) (*Cascart and Natalia enter.*)

**CASCART:** (*to Natalia*) Not here? Now, if I knew?

**NATALIA:** She's coming—here, the lady is waiting for her too. (*indicates Anaide*)

**CASCART:** (*unpleasantly surprised, bows*) Beg pardon—

ANAIDE: (con affettata amabilità) Riverenza!!

CASCART: (a Natalia) Aspetterò . . .
Pazienza!
(Natalia esce dalla destra.)
(Cascart siede sul divano. Anaide siede presso al caminetto facendo il possibile perchè Cascart attacchi la conversazione. Momento di silenzio. Poi, visto il fermo proposito di Cascart nel suo silenzio, non potendone più, Anaide si alza decisa e va a sedere sul divano accanto a Cascart.)

ANAIDE: Che ne dite, Cascart? suvvia, parlate!

CASCART: E voi, che cosa dunque ne pensate?
Or siete lieta!

ANAIDE: Io, lieta!
Dio buono!!! . . .

CASCART: Non m'odiavate?

ANAIDE: (con dignità) Domando perdono!
Voi di Zazà m'avevate rubato il cuore! . . .

CASCART: (ridendo) Il cuore?! . . .

ANAIDE: (levandosi) Perciò, nel mio stato di madre, v'odio, e vi copro di fango! . . .
Uomo, vi stimo, v'ammiro e compiango!
Con voi non fece pazzie . . .

CASCART: Voi trovate Ch'ora ne faccia?

ANAIDE: Pazzie da legnate. . . !
(sedendo nuovamente)
E dove corre?
Che cosa pesca?

CASCART: (levandosi serio) Chi può supporre?
Vattelapesca!!
Sapete; è sdrucciolevole la strada della vita: quando una donna ruzzola . . . buona notte, è finita. . . !

ANAIDE: (sospirando) Purtroppo!
(levandosi)
Ma conoscere almen la verità Saper di quel suo Milio le generalità!

CASCART: (con mistero) Io ne so qualche cosa . . .

ANAIDE: (balzando) Davvero? oh Dio, parlate! salvatemi la figlia!

CASCART: Dirò . . . non dubitate . . .
(Zazà entra lieta e si arresta ridendo francamente come colta da un'idea comica vedendo Cascart e Anaide accanto.)

ANAIDE: (pretending joy at seeing him) I'm delighted!

CASCART: (to Natalia) I'll wait for her—don't worry.
(Exit Natalia)
(Cascart sits on sofa. Anaide sits near fireplace trying every possible means to induce Cascart to begin a conversation. A pause; then seeing that Cascart is determined not to speak first, she can stand it no longer, rises resolutely and goes to sit beside him on the sofa.)

ANAIDE: What's your opinion, Cascart?
Speak freely, frankly!

CASCART: And you?
I guess it pleases you to see me— now you are happy!

ANAIDE: I happy?
God forbid it!

CASCART: You did not hate me?

ANAIDE: (very dignified) Excuse me—YOU did it.
You stole my daughter's heart from me, and no other—

CASCART: (laughs) Heart, you call it?

ANAIDE: (rising) And therefore as her mother, I detest you—fling mud at you, berate you, but as a man I esteem you—I pity and not hate you.
With you she tried no nonsense.

CASCART: You suspect then that this is different?

ANAIDE: She is simply crazy!
(sits down again)
Where is she going?
Where is she straying?

CASCART: (rising gravely) There is no knowing,
There is no saying!
The road of life is steep and slimy
Unto the heights ascending,
And when a woman stumbles blindly,
She'll fall before long—then comes the ending.

ANAIDE: (sighing) I know it!
(rises)
If I only knew the facts about this man!
About her precious Milio;
I'll find out all I can!

CASCART: (mysteriously) There's something I could tell you—

ANAIDE: (jumping up) What! really?
Tell me about it!
O save my daughter, tell me!

CASCART: I'll tell you—you need not doubt it!
(Zazà enters joyfully and stops, laughing openly, as though struck by a comical idea, on seeing Cascart and Anaide together.)

ZAZÀ: (ad Anaide e Cascart) Ah, ah, ah!
Che quadretto!
È molto, è poco che m'aspettate insieme? . . .
Ed i vicini non han gridato al fuoco . . . ai ladri . . . agli assassini. . . ?
Non credo alla mia vista . . .

ANAIDE: (offesa) L'hai sempre avuta trista!
Ma tua madre e Cascart sono persone piene d'educazione, e fra noi sedie o tazze non sono mai volate!

ZAZÀ: (sorridendo) Eh!!

ANAIDE: (seria) Basta—
Ei vuol parlarti—
Io vo di là.
(a Cascart)
Scusate!
(saluta ed esce dalla sinistra)

ZAZÀ: Cascart, mio camerata, mi piace il rivederti . . .
Siedi . . .

CASCART: Son qui a proporti affari . . .

ZAZÀ: (sedendo distratta) Ah!

CASCART: (sedendo a sua volta presso al tavolo) M'hanno offerti Dei buoni patti.

ZAZÀ: (sempre con aria sbadata) Ah?!!

CASCART: (serio) È tempo di mettere giudizio o tutte le scritture ci vanno a precipizio!

ZAZÀ: Offrono?

CASCART: Da Marsiglia . . .

ZAZÀ: (balzando) Non vado in capo al mondo!
Perchè non al Tonkino, allora?

CASCART: (perdendo la calma) Cioè Dove lui vuole!

ZAZÀ: (severamente) Questo riguardo solo me!
(siede volgendo le spalle a Cascart)

CASCART: (dopo un momento, cercando riprendere la calma) Buona Zazà del mio buon tempo, ascolta: è il vecchio amico che ti parla al cuore: non è il geloso che domanda amore ma l'uom che a la miseria un dì t'ha tolta!
Per te sola io son qui: per te m'increbbe di veder l'arte da te tradita!
Hai avuto un capriccio! . . . e chi non l'ebbe? ma il capriccio è di un dì . . . lunga è la vita!! . . .

ZAZÀ: (come assorta) Peggio se questa dolce— illusion non dura!

ZAZÀ: (to Cascart and Anaide)
Ha ha ha ha! what a picture!
You can't be waiting for me together long?
Or there's no telling but that I'd find the neighbors all excited, police or fire or murder yelling!
I thought my eyes deceived me!

ANAIDE: (offended) You never were sharp-sighted!
Your mother, child, and Cascart both have good breeding, always etiquette heeding.
I did not throw the dishes and he would not abuse me!

ZAZÀ: (smiling) Eh!!?

ANAIDE: (gravely) Enough—he wants to see you!
I'll go in there!
(to Cascart)
Excuse me.
(Bows and goes into room at left)

ZAZÀ: Cascart, my friend and partner, sit down, I'm glad to see you!
How are you?

CASCART: I came to you on business.

ZAZÀ: (sits down abstractedly) Ah!

CASCART: (takes chair near table) They have made us a splendid offer!

ZAZÀ: (as before) Ah?

CASCART: (gravely) To future business we must now be looking, or for the good engagements we'll fail to get a booking.

ZAZÀ: What offers?

CASCART: Marseilles wants us!

ZAZÀ: (jumps up) I'll not go to the backwoods!
I might as well go off to China!

CASCART: (losing his temper) I see his wishes guide you—

ZAZÀ: (curtly) That's something which concerns but me!
(Sits with her back to Cascart)

CASCART: (after a pause, trying to regain composure) My dearest Zazà, for old times' sake hear me!
It is your good old pal to you appealing,
And not the lover out of jealous feeling—
The man who saved you from want and degradation.
For your sake I am here, for you I'm grieving,
To see your art betrayed for something hollow.
You have a passing fancy!—it is deceiving
Our fancies last but for a day, and years will follow!

ZAZÀ: (as though far away) Pity me, if from dreaming I should awaken later!

CASCART: (*incalzando*)
T'inganni! se durasse sarebbe una sventura!

ZAZÀ: (*estasiata*) Fosse tal gaudio eterno com'ei me l'ha giurato.

CASCART: Ricco non è: Che aspetti? che t'abbia abbandonato?

ZAZÀ: Niuna promessa: amore solo Zazà gli chiese!

CASCART: E s'anco ti sposasse? saresti . . . una borghese!
No: resta libera: resta la limpida gola squillante del rosignuolo: serbati all'ilare tuo ritornello irresistibile e civettuolo . . . !
Serbati al plauso, alla vertigine, dea della folla china al tuo piè.
E questo il vivere, è questo il bello!
Illusa! destati, ritorna in te!!

ZAZÀ: (*animandosi*) Bello è soltanto il vivere sempre con l'uomo amato!

CASCART: (*impaziente*) Tutte le cose passano . . .

ZAZÀ: (*rivoltandosi*) Io non ho ancor mutato!

CASCART: (*incalzando sempre*) Ma puoi cangiare! . . .

ZAZÀ: Amare un altro? . . .

CASCART: E perchè no?

ZAZÀ: Tu scherzi!

CASCART: (*prorompendo*) Un dì m'amasti!

ZAZÀ: (*gridando*) Io?! non t'ho amato, no!

CASCART: (*stupito*) Neghi?

ZAZÀ: (*sorridendo quasi con compassione*) M'illusi, amore non conoscevo: tutto che mi cresceva intorno era cattivo e brutto.
Ti conobbi, eri buono; ti piacqui e mi piacesti. fui tua . . . com'ero d'altri; nè tu te ne dolesti . . .
(*nervosa*)
E dici che t'amavo? e amor questo è per te?!
Cascart, lasciami ridere, . . . ridi tu pur con me!

CASCART: (*irritato*) Pazza! tu sogni!

ZAZÀ: La sciami sognar! son paga, e basta!

CASCART: (*earnestly*) Believe me—if this lasted, your sorrows would be greater!

ZAZÀ: (*ecstatically*) He swore our joy would be endless!—
Your bitterness deceives you!

CASCART: He is not rich:
—What prospect other than that he leaves you?

ZAZÀ: No binding promise:
His love was all I asked him!

CASCART: And even should he wed you? What are you?
Only a housewife!
No—stay free, unfettered: cling to your calling!
Your golden voice was not meant for seclusion!
Cling to your gay little songs, light and airy,
Bringing you plaudits and flowers in profusion!
Do not renounce the applause and the laurel,
To crowds a goddess—their idol remain!
Keep to the pathway all strewn with roses:
You dreamer, awake! Be yourself again!

ZAZÀ: (*with animation*) Life is sweet only when united with the beloved forever!

CASCART: (*impatiently*) That is soon past and forgotten.

ZAZÀ: (*turning on him*) But I will not change—no, never!

CASCART: (*still more urgently*) You might forget it.

ZAZÀ: And love another?

CASCART: And why not, pray?

ZAZÀ: You're joking!

CASCART: (*impulsively*) Once you loved me!

ZAZÀ: (*with an outcry*) I?—I never loved you, no!

CASCART: (*dazed*) Never?

ZAZÀ: (*smiling almost pityingly*) So young was I, yet often heard the power of love derided; my inner self was crude—my youthful soul was all unguided.
I met you and you were kindly; we liked each other truly,
And I was yours—like many who scrupled not unduly.
(*nervously*)
And you say that I loved you?
Love means no more to you?
Cascart—we'll laugh together—that is the best we can do!

CASCART: (*irritated*) Stop—you are dreaming!

ZAZÀ: Then let me dream on, and do not try to awaken!

CASCART: No! l'ora del risveglio saria per te nefasta:
Un' altra può rapirtelo, Zazà!

ZAZÀ: (*con impeto di passione*)
Io sfido Iddio a togliermelo!
È mio, e non lo cedo! è mio. . . !

CASCART: Cieca e stolta! e se avesse un'amante?

ZAZÀ: (*come folle lo afferra disperatamente per le mani*)
Menti!! . . .

CASCART: (*concitato*) No, dissi il vero, e costante Fido amico ti son nel dolore!
Ha un' amante a Parigi . . .

ZAZÀ: (*tremante di emozione, portando le mani al cuore, quasi senza voce*) Ah! . . . mio core. . . !
Come sai?
Chi t'ha detto?

CASCART: (*commosso e turbato*)
Sei bianca . . .
Sei tremante . . . la voce ti manca . . .

ZAZÀ: (*insistendo*) Chi t'ha detto? la prova! la prova. . . !

CASCART: Tio dirò: ma sii calma, disperarsi che giova?
A Parigi una sera ero alle "Varietà".
Milio vid'io con una donna . . .

ZAZÀ: Una donna . . .

CASCART: Ma elegante, distinta . . .
Pareva una moglietta . . .
Li rividi all'uscita: poi montarono in fretta in carrozza . . . e ridevano. . . !

ZAZÀ: Ridevano! e non sai altro?

CASCART: Non basta?

ZAZÀ: (*al colmo dell'orgasmo*)
Infatti, chi potrebbe esser mai fuor che un'amante?
(*scoppiando*)
e questo sapevi? e me lo dici ora soltanto!
Adesso che sono là, felici, a Parigi ad amarsi!

CASCART: Non m'ascoltavi!

ZAZÀ: Ed io son qui a rodermi! . . .
(*urlando*)
Bene non finirà, per Dio!
(*Anaide appare sull'uscio a sinistra e si avanza.*)

ANAIDE: Dite figliuoli . . . che mai succede?

CASCART: No—for the hour has come—your faith must now be shaken.
Another woman might claim him, Zazà.

ZAZÀ: (*passionately*) Not Power Divine can rob me of him!
He's mine—I will not yield him!—
He's mine!

CASCART: You are blind and foolish!
What if he loves another?

ZAZÀ: (*seizes his hands wildly*)
Falsehood!!

CASCART: (*excitedly*) No—I'm not lying!
Like a brother I grieve at what I am revealing.
He has another love in Paris!

ZAZÀ: (*trembling with emotion, puts her hands over her heart and says in a toneless voice*) Ah—I am reeling!
How do you know?—
Who told you?

CASCART: (*moved and troubled*)
You feel ailing—
You are trembling—your voice is failing—

ZAZÀ: (*insisting*) Who has told you?
And prove it—yes, prove it!

CASCART: I'll tell you—but be quiet, you must not get excited.
One fine evening while in Paris I went to a Variété—
And saw Milio there with a woman—

ZAZÀ: With a woman?

CASCART: Looking distinguished—a wifely look about her.
I met them at the exit—he did not leave without her.
I saw them take a cab—both laughing—

ZAZÀ: Laughing!
And is that all
You know?

CASCART: You want more?

ZAZÀ: (*in high excitement*) No question—what else could this woman be except a sweetheart—?
(*turning on him wildly*)
And you said nothing?
You kept it from me until this minute?
Meanwhile those two are there in town, united, to love and laugh together!

CASCART: You would not listen!

ZAZÀ: And now I sit here fuming!
(*fiercely—very loud*)
This thing will not end well—I vow!
(*Anaide appears in door l. and comes forward.*)

ANAIDE: Why so excited? Tell me, my children—

ZAZÀ: (*disperatamente*) Egli ha un'amante . . .

ANAIDE: (*stupefatta*) Cascart?!

ZAZÀ: (*in collera*) Si vede che voi vivete dentro la luna! Milio ha un'amante!

ANAIDE: (*scattando*) Oh! che fortuna.
(*correggendosi tosto*) Cioè che scandalo! . . .

ZAZÀ: Che infamia, intendi? . . .

CASCART: Non sei sua moglie, poi . . .

ZAZÀ: (*furente*) Lo difendi? Ah!
Cascart . . . quanto soffro . . . quanto male mi fa!
(*Scoppia in pianto e cade fra le braccia di Cascart.*)

CASCART: (*commosso*) Hai ragione; ti calma, è una malvagità . . .

ZAZÀ: (*sempre piangendo*) Oh! sì.

CASCART: Convien punirlo! . . .

ZAZÀ: Sì, sì!

CASCART: Piantarlo!

ZAZÀ: (*decisa sciogliendosi dall'abbraccio*) Ah no!! . . .

CASCART: Che farai?

ANAIDE: Figlia mia, la dignità . . .

ZAZÀ: Non l'ho!
Me ne infischio!!
Lasciarlo? . . . ora vi mostrerò.
(*chiama mentre corre alla toletta*)
Natalia!

ANAIDE: Che vuoi fare?

CASCART: Ma insomma . . .

ZAZÀ: Natalia!
(*Natalia entra dalla destra.*)
Il cappello, il mantello . . . fa presto . . . vado via!
(*Natalia esce dallo spogliatojo e torna con gli effetti di Zazà.*)

ANAIDE: Ma pensa . . .

CASCART: Rifletti!

ZAZÀ: Io parto.

ANAIDE: Che tenti?

ZAZÀ: Lo seguo a Parigi!

CASCART: Ma calmati, senti. . . !

ZAZÀ: Saper voglio il vero!

ANAIDE: E sola tu vai?

ZAZÀ: (*desperately*) I hear he has a sweetheart!

ANAIDE: (*bewildered*) Cascart?

ZAZÀ: (*impatiently*)
Good gracious!
One might believe that you are benighted!
Milio has a sweetheart—

ANAIDE: (*jumps up*)
I'm delighted—
(*Catching herself*)
I mean—what a scandal!

ZAZÀ: It's an outrage, I tell you!

CASCART: You are not his wife—so—

ZAZÀ: (*furious*) You defend him? Ah, Cascart—how I suffer—it is breaking my heart!
(*Breaks into tears and falls sobbing into Cascart's arms.*)

CASCART: (*moved*) There, don't worry, be quiet—it is a shame! a disgrace!

ZAZÀ: (*still weeping*) Oh yes!

CASCART: He must be punished!

ZAZÀ: Yes, yes!

CASCART: You will leave him!

ZAZÀ: (*frees herself resolutely from his arms*) Oh no!

CASCART: Well, what then?

ANAIDE: Dearest child, show dignity!

ZAZÀ: Not I!
I have no dignity.—
But leave him?
I'd rather die!
(*Calls as she runs to dressing-room*)
Natalia!

ANAIDE: Where are you going?

CASCART: Be careful!

ZAZÀ: Natalia!
(*Natalia comes from right.*)
Bring me my hat—my coat—get ready; and hurry—I am leaving!
(*Exit Natalia to dressing-room and returns with Zazà's hat and wrap*)

ANAIDE: Consider—

CASCART: Take counsel!

ZAZÀ: I'm going!

ANAIDE: And where to?

ZAZÀ: I'll follow him to Paris!

CASCART: Be calm before you dare to!

ZAZÀ: I want to know the truth now!

ANAIDE: You go all alone?

ZAZÀ: (*a Natalia che le ba portato il cappello e il mantello*) Su, su, Natalia, tu meco verrai; ma spicciati presto!
(*Natalia esce.*)

CASCART: Zazà, via, m'ascolta, t'invito a riflettere un'ultima volta.

ZAZÀ: (*a Natalia che ritorna in cappello e scialle*) Sei pronta? partiamo!

CASCART: Zazà! . . .

ANAIDE: Figlia mia! . . .

ZAZÀ: Bisogna ch'ei scelga—
O me o l'altra . . .
Via!
(*Prende per la mano Natalia e la trascina rapidamente.—Anaide levando le braccia va verso l'uscio donde Zazà è partita.— Cascart siede con un gesto desolato.*)

Cala la tela.
Fine Del Secondo Atto.

## ■ Atto Terzo.

*Il Salotto Di Milio Dufresne A Parigi, Riva Di Mazzarino: mobili elegantissimi; pianoforte a coda nel mezzo colla tastiera verso il fondo della scena; poltroncine, causeuses, divanetti all'ingiro; a destra finestra che dà verso la Senna; innanzi alla finestra elegante scrivania sulla quale, tra le altre carte, sarà una lettera colla busta lacerata; in fondo, nel mezzo, porta che dà nell'anticamera; altra porta a sinistra che dà negli appartamenti.*

*Milio solo, in costume da viaggio, è seduto al tavolo presso la finestra a destra; sta ordinando alcune sue carte sparse alla rinfusa sullo scrittojo; dopo rimane un momento come malinconico ed assorto, la testa fra le mani.*

MILIO: Oh mio piccolo tavolo ingombrato sì come è ingombro di sgomenti il cuore!
Domani a Saint-Étienne sarò tornato . . . l'ultima volta . . . a salutar l'amore! . . .
Come dirle ch'io parto? oh come fare a lasciarla? a mentire? il labbro mio come le giurerà di ritornare mentre che il cuore le dirà l'addio?
Mai più, Zazà, raggiar vedrò da gli occhi tuoi la fiamma de l'amor! . . . e mormorar mai più t'udrò calde parole, stretta sul mio cor . . .
Oh baci, oh nostre tenere ebbrezze, notti incantate, lunghe carezze, sereni dì! . . .
Il nostro amore è naufragato, e ci ha travolti l'onda del fato!
Tutto finì! . . .
(*Signora Dufresne entra dalla*

ZAZÀ: (*to Natalia, who bands her bat and coat*) Come, come, Natalia—I'll take you with me, but hurry—time is pressing!
(*Exit Natalia*)

CASCART: Zazà, I pray you, listen! I ask you to consider this thing that you would do!

ZAZÀ: (*to Natalia who returns with hat and shawl*) All ready? then follow!

CASCART: Zazà!

ANAIDE: Dearest daughter!

ZAZÀ: Now he must choose between us—I or the other!— Come!
(*She takes Natalia's hand and draws her off quickly. Anaide raises her arms imploringly and goes after her to door. Cascart sits down dejectedly.*)

Curtain.
End of Act II.

## ■ Act III.

*Drawing-room in Milio Dufresne's home at Paris. Very elegantly furnished, grand piano in center of stage, with keyboard away from audience; armchairs, sofas, lounge chairs; at right a window overlooking the Seine; in front of window an elegant desk on which, with other papers, is a letter with the envelope torn open; in center back a door opening on reception hall; another door at left leads to the other dwelling-rooms.*

*Milio, alone, in travelling costume, is seated at the desk, near the window at right; he is arranging some papers scattered over the desk. He sits silently a moment in sad thoughts, with his head resting in his hands.*

MILIO: Oh, my poor desk, encumbered with this confusion. Just like my heart, that is beating beneath a load of care!
Tomorrow I am returning to St. Étienne; to see my dearest in a last fond meeting!
How can I tell her gently—O, how betray her?
How can I lie and swear to leave her never?
And while my lips may vow I'm soon returning, my heart knows well it is farewell forever.
No more, Zazà, shall I behold within your eyes the fire of love aglow! Nor hear your whispered words grow more ardent when I fold your trembling form in my arms.
O rapture!
O joy of our kisses unending!
Clinging caresses, when night was descending—

ZAZÀ    417

# Act III

*porta a sinistra, seguita da Marco, il cameriere.)*

**SIGNORA DUFRESNE:** Ecco son pronta, Milio, . . .
*(al cameriere)*
La valigia è al suo posto?

**MARCO:** È giù nella carrozza.

**MILIO:** *(si è alzato, ha preso il cappello, il soprabito, alcune carte)* Bene, scendiamo tosto . . .

**SIGNORA DUFRESNE:** *(a Marco)* Vegliate a tutto . . .
*(fa per avviarsi, poi si trattiene ancora)* oh, Marco, . . . mi scordavo . . .
Aspetto una signora Dunoyer . . .
Se giunge, trattenetela: le dite che tornerò . . . che sono alla stazione . . .

**MARCO:** Sta bene.

**SIGNORA DUFRESNE:** *(fa qualche passo poi si rivolge)* Ricordate . . .
*(sillabando)*
Dunoyer . . .
*(Esce con Milio.)*
*(Marco li accompagna e compare in anticamera con essi; poi ricompare.)*

**MARCO:** Dunoyer? . . .
Chi è? . . .
Ora veniamo a noi!
*(Va al tavolo a destra, apre il tiretto, prende la scatola dei sigari del padrone, ne sceglie uno e lo accende.)*
La fumatina solita . . .
*(aspirando il fumo, da buon conoscitore)*
Peuh! non c'è male, poi! . . .
*(prende un giornale dal tavolo)*
Ora un po' di notizie politiche: fa bene! . . .
*(Si sente il canto delle lavandaje, come venendo di sotto alla finestra, accompagnato dai colpi di battitojo, mentre Marco va al canapè a sinistra e si allunga per leggere comodamente.)*

**LE LAVANDAJE:** *(giù dalla Senna)* Perchè soletta sei laggiù? Margot?
Sparve il riso dal tuo viso.
Il tuo ben fuggì nè più torna qui!
E canti il labbro non ha piu!
Ma rinnovare amor si può Margot!
Prendi il mazzuol, ritorna ancor
Come l'onda fugge amor.
Ridi con noi—Margot!
*(risate e colpi di mazzuolo.)*

---

Days of delight!
Our love has been wrecked in life's mighty ocean, and swept in the deep is our tender emotion—
Joy takes to flight!
*(Mme. Dufresne enters from door l., followed by Marco, the butler.)*

**MME. DUFRESNE:** Now I am ready, Milio—*(to butler)*
The baggage has all departed?

**MARCO:** It's down in the cab, ma'am!

**MILIO:** *(Has risen, taken his hat and coat and some papers.)* All right—it's time that we started.

**MME. DUFRESNE:** *(to Marco)* Be watchful and careful!
*(She is about to go, but stops and turns back.)*
O Marco, that reminds me.
I am expecting a Mme. Dunoyer;
Please ask her if she will wait, and tell her I will return—I've merely gone to the station.

**MARCO:** Very good, ma'am.

**MME. DUFRESNE:** *(goes a few steps, then turns back)* Now remember—*(distinctly)* Dunoyer!
*(Exit with Milio)*
*(Marco goes out with them to reception hall and then reappears.)*

**MARCO:** Dunoyer?
Who's that?
Well, of this chance I am glad!
*(He goes to desk at r., opens drawer, takes out box of cigars, chooses one and lights it.)*
The usual daily smoke—
*(blowing off smoke with air of connoisseur)*
Puh!—
After all, not bad!
*(taking newspaper from desk)*
Now for a little political discourse—it broadens!
*(While Marco goes to the sofa at l. and lies down to read in comfort, the song of washerwomen on the bank of the Seine floats through the window—to the beating of the wooden paddles used in washing the clothes.)*

**THE LAUNDRESSES:** *(from the riverbank)* Why are you walking all alone, Margot?
Your smile has faded,
Your face looks jaded,
Your own sweetheart dear
Has left you, we fear,
And songs from your lips we no longer hear!
A new love soon in your heart will grow, Margot!
Come, take your washing, love comes and goes,
Just like the water it surges and

---

**MARCO:** Ecco la nenia solita che dalla Senna viene: Oh, queste lavandaje! . . .
*(si sprofonda nella lettura del giornale)*
*(Scampanellata, Marco butta via sigaro e giornale ed esce dal fondo.—Entrano Zazà e Natalia con Marco dopo un istante.)*

**MARCO:** *(introducendole, a Zazà)* Lei dunque è la signore Dunoyer?

**ZAZÀ:** *(coglie l'occasione)* Sì, sì, Dunoyer . . .

**MARCO:** Sia buona di trattenersi qui un istante: madama è andata alla stazione; accompagna il signore che parte per Lione.

**ZAZÀ:** Grazie: l'aspetterò . . .
*(Marco saluta ed esce dal fondo chiudendo la porta.)*

**NATALIA:** Che turbamento! . . .

**ZAZÀ:** Tremi? Perchè?

**NATALIA:** Se dalla casa ci scacciano. . . ?

**ZAZÀ:** Che temi?
Non sono io forse teco?

**NATALIA:** Voi? che potreste fare? in casa sua?

**ZAZÀ:** La loro casa la puoi chiamare!
Il domestico ha detto: il signore . . . madama . . . qui fiorisce l'idillio! qui si sorride ed ama!!

**NATALIA:** Ebben, fuggiam, signora: ormai tutto v'è noto!

**ZAZÀ:** Perchè fuggir? sei folle: tutto m'è invece ignoto! . . .

**NATALIA:** *(dopo una pausa, guardando il salotto)* Han scelto un incantevole, elegante soggiorno . . .

**ZAZÀ:** Più del mio! . . .
Troppo bello! . . .

**NATALIA:** Perchè?

**ZAZÀ:** Guardati intorno:
Non odi la tacita stanza da un' onda di baci pervasa?
non senti l'acuta fragranza d'amore, che corre la casa?
E un' orma invisibile, un segno di giunco sul lido del mare . . . chè dove la donna ha suo regno un nulla può tutto svelare! . . .
Lo vedi quel cantuccio? i cuscini! . . . il divano? là s'abbraccian

---

flows;
Smile with us—laugh, Margot!
*(Laughter and beating of paddles)*

**MARCO:** It is the daily song that floats to us from up the river!
Oh, these young washerwomen!—
*(He buries himself in his newspaper. Bell rings energetically; Marco throws away cigar and paper, and exit to reception room. Presently, Marco reenters, with Zazà and Natalia.)*

**MARCO:** *(holding door for them to enter, to Zazà)* Pardon me—you are Mme. Dunoyer.

**ZAZÀ:** *(grasping opportunity)* Yes, yes!
Dunoyer!

**MARCO:** Be good enough to enter here, and wait.
Madame went to the station to the Lyons train,
To see the Master off—he's leaving town again.

**ZAZÀ:** Thank you—then I will wait.
*(Marco bows and exit at back, closing door.)*

**NATALIA:** I am so worried.

**ZAZÀ:** Worried?
And why?

**NATALIA:** Suppose they drive us from the house!

**ZAZÀ:** You're flurried!
Why fear when I am with you?

**NATALIA:** You?
What could you do for me?
In his own home?

**ZAZÀ:** In their own home might be as well to call it:
The Master and the Madam—I heard the butler saying.
And here they live their idyl, with love like children playing!

**NATALIA:** Now you know all!
Come with me, and endeavor to get home!

**ZAZÀ:** Why run away?
How foolish!
I now know less than ever!

**NATALIA:** *(after a pause, looking about her)* They have selected lovely quarters—I know it must wound you.—

**ZAZÀ:** Finer than mine—far too lovely!

**NATALIA:** But why?

**ZAZÀ:** Just look around you!
I fancy a flood of caresses
From every corner is sweeping,
I scent the sweet fragrance of roses
Where love lies sleeping in seclusion.
A sound, that is swaying like a reed,
A mark in the sand by the sea—
Small trifles are betraying the truth,
Wherever a woman may be!
See there, the corner sofa—the

la sera, si stringono la mano e si parlan d'amore! . . .
Oh, li vedo, son là, e non posso dividerli! . . .
—Folle divengo già!

NATALIA: Posson udir, calmetevi . . . signora! . . .

ZAZÀ: (mal contenendosi) Chi sarà questa donna? . . .
Se il servo interrogassi . . .
(gli occhi suoi cadono sulla lettera ch'è sul tavolo; sordamente.) Ah!

NATALIA: Che è?

ZAZÀ: Guarda: una lettera . . . sopra quel tavolino . . .

NATALIA: (si avvicina al tavolo e si china a leggere la soprascritta) "A madama Dufresne, riva di Mazzarino" (spaurita)

È ammogliato! . . . signora, signora . . . andiamo via!

ZAZÀ: (fissando la lettera, convulsa, angosciata, con voce spenta) Ammogliato?!
No, è l'uso, vivendo in compagnia di dare il proprio nome . . .
(poi afferrando convulsamente la lettera)
Tra poco lo saprò!

NATALIA: (spaurita, supplichevole) Non l'oserete!?

ZAZÀ: (risoluta) È aperta . . . e poi?
Venni per ciò!
(legge rapidamente)
"Quando, amica, a Parigi verrà vostro marito" . . . (lascia cadere la lettera, accorata dalla subìta rivelazione)
Dunque è vero? . . .
Ammogliato!
Non aveva mentito quel povero Cascart . . .
Ammogliato?!

NATALIA: Signora, buona signora, andiamo
Perchè soffrire ancora?
tutto è scoperto . . .

ZAZÀ: (come pazza) Andare?
No: qui restar conviene: egli è certo già stanco di queste sue catene!
Me sola ama! io l'aspetto ferma; egli giungerà, lascerà la sua sposa . . . e meco partirà!

NATALIA: (bruscamente scuotendola) Ah! vengono
(La porta a sinistra si apre; una bambina entra senza vedere le due donne e va verso l'etagère vicino al piano per cercare della

cushions soft and warm,
There they embrace at evening—
he holds her in his arm;
And all their love confessions—I see them—I can hear—
And can not separate them:—My brain will turn, I fear!

NATALIA: Try to be calmer, I beg,—I implore you!

ZAZÀ: (hardly able to contain herself) Who is she, the other woman?
Maybe I might ask the butler—
(Her eyes are attracted by letter on desk—softly) Ah!

NATALIA: What now?

ZAZÀ: See here: there is a letter lying upon the table!

NATALIA: (goes to table and bends over to read address) It is plainly addressed to Mme. Dufresne, Paris!
(frightened) He is married!
Oh, Madam, dearest lady!
What shall we do?

ZAZÀ: (looks at letter—then in an agonized, breaking voice) Married?!
No—no—it is the custom to take the man's name too
When people live together—
(seizes letter convulsively)
The contents soon will show—

NATALIA: (frightened, imploringly) You would not dare to?

ZAZÀ: (resolutely) It is open—why not?
I want to know!
(reading quickly)
"My dearest friend:—When in Paris I hope to meet your husband"—
(drops letter—overcome by the revelation)
Then it is true—he is married—it was not a falsehood poor Cascart told me!
He is married!

NATALIA: Dearest lady, dearest Madam—do come away!
Why should you suffer longer?
All is discovered—

ZAZÀ: (as though crazed) Leave here?
No, we surely must remain, for I know well he's weary and hates the galling chain.
He loves only me!
I believe him—he will not betray!
He'll leave his wife—I know it—and go away with me!

NATALIA: (taking her by the arm and shaking her) Oh—they're coming!
(Door opens and a little girl enters without seeing the two women; she goes to music rack near the

musica.)
(a bassa voce, rapidamente)
Signora . . . guardate: una bambina.

ZAZÀ: (nello spavento) Dove? chi è? . . .

NATALIA: Signora, . . . certo è la sua piccina, è sua figlia! . . .

ZAZÀ: Sua figlia! . . .
(La bambina si accorge delle straniere e resta interdetta.)

NATALIA: Le abbiam fatto paura . . .

ZAZÀ: Parlale tu . . . non oso . . .

NATALIA: (osservando Totò) Che dolce creatura!
(parlando alla bambina)
Signorina, vi abbiamo spaurita?

TOTÒ: (sempre semplicemente)
No, signora, venivo al pianoforte . . .

NATALIA: Vi disturbiamo . . .

TOTÒ: No . . . la mamma è uscita: l'aspettate?

NATALIA: Da un pezzo . . .
Ora più corte saran l'ore con voi.

TOTÒ: (confusa) Signora, come siete gentile . . .
(Fa cenno a Zazà ed a Natalia di sedere e siede anch'essa nel mezzo.)

ZAZÀ: (facendosi forza) Angioletto, il tuo nome?

TOTÒ: Antonietta Dufresne è il nome mio . . . ma mi dicon Totò . . .

ZAZÀ: (con soavità)
Totò . . . Perchè?

TOTÒ: Voi mi date del tu? Perchè?

ZAZÀ: Perchè . . . tu rassomigli . . . voi rassomigliate ad uno . . . che amo tanto . . .

TOTÒ: Uno che amate?
Io somiglio a papà . . . lo conoscete?

ZAZÀ: (con slancio) No! . . .

TOTÒ: Mi vuol tanto bene, . . . è tanto buono . . . io da sei mesi nol vedea, sapete . . .

ZAZÀ: Sei mesi! . . .

TOTÒ: Or lo rivedo e lieta sono . . .
Presso la nonna in Algeria siam stati . . . babbo, al ritorno, al circo ci ha portati . . .
Ma insieme a noi tra breve partirà.

piano to look for some music.)
(Natalia softly, speaking quickly)
See, Madam! look—the little girl!

ZAZÀ: (startled) Who? and where?

NATALIA: O madam, it surely must be his daughter, his little girl!

ZAZÀ: His daughter!
(The child sees the strangers and stops shyly.)

NATALIA: She is afraid of strangers.

ZAZÀ: You speak to her—I dare not!

NATALIA: (looking at Totò) O, what a little darling!
(to the child)
Were you frightened, little lady, when you saw us?

TOTÒ: (ingenuously) No, madam, I had come to play the piano.

NATALIA: Do we disturb you?

TOTÒ: No—my mamma is not here yet!
You've been waiting?

NATALIA: Quite awhile now —time will pass quickly since you are with us here.

TOTÒ: (shyly) How very lovely of you to say that!
(She motions Zazà and Natalia to seats and sits down between them.)

ZAZÀ: (forcing herself to composure) What's your name, dear, will you tell me?

TOTÒ: Antonietta Dufresne I was baptized, but they call me Totò.

ZAZÀ: (sweetly) Totò?—and why?

TOTÒ: Now your voice is more friendly—why?

ZAZÀ: Perhaps you may resemble—indeed you have great likeness
To someone—whom—I love dearly—

TOTÒ: Whom you love dearly?
I look just like my papa—do you know him?

ZAZÀ: (with sudden resolution) No!

TOTÒ: He loves me very much—my darling papa!
You see, for six whole months I had not seen him.

ZAZÀ: For six months?

TOTÒ: But now he's back and I am very happy!
We were with Grandma in Algiers to visit;
Then Papa came, and took us to the circus,
And soon we'll go away—all three together!

**ZAZÀ:** (*ansiosa*) E dove andate? . . .

**TOTÒ:** In America.

**ZAZÀ:** (*commossa*) Ah . . .

**TOTÒ:** Voi non avete, dunque, una Totò?

**ZAZÀ:** No, il cielo, Totò, non me l'ha data!
S'io l'avessi, Totò,
l'adorerei . . . come adorata dal tuo babbo sei . . .

**TOTÒ:** Certo che mamma e babbo amano assai la piccola Totò! . . .
V'ama, signora, la vostra?

**ZAZÀ:** (*con profonda tristezza*) Mamma?! io non l'ho avuta mai!
Mamma usciva di casa in sull'aurora . . . ed ero sola . . . fin che ritornava . . .
Ma la sera . . . al ritorno . . .

**TOTÒ:** (*interessandosi*) Vi baciava?

**ZAZÀ:** (*dolorosamente*) No: non volea destarmi . . .
Avea ragione, c'era sì poco da vedere al mondo!
Lo sai, piccina mia? ci son persone che devi amare d'un amor profondo!
sono cattive . . . e il mondo le disprezza . . . pure han tanto sofferto . . . in fanciullezza . . .

**TOTÒ:** (*con interesse crescente*) I bimbi senza pane e senza tetto?

**ZAZÀ:** (*amaramente*) Vi sono bimbi ai quali manca molto più! . . .

**TOTÒ:** (*alzandosi ed andando verso di lei*) Sono i bimbi che non han l'affetto del babbo? . . .

**ZAZÀ:** I bimbi senza padre . . . hai colto!
(*con le lagrime agli occhi abbracciando Totò*)
Questa per un fanciullo è la maggior sventura!
Ma tu . . . vivi tranquilla . . . soave creatura; il padre tuo . . . nessuno . . . ti strapperà!

**TOTÒ:** (*guardandola*) Signora . . . piangete? . . .

**ZAZÀ:** No, non piango . . .
Un ricordo m'accora . . .
(*levandosi come per nascondere la sua angoscia*)
A studiar tu venivi . . .
Ti prego . . . suona un poco . . .

**TOTÒ:** Non oso: di me certo voi vi farete gioco! . . .

---

**ZAZÀ:** (*anxiously*) Where are you going?

**TOTÒ:** To America.

**ZAZÀ:** (*agitated*) Ah!

**TOTÒ:** You haven't got a little Totò, have you?

**ZAZÀ:** No, dear, for heaven did not send me any.
If I might have a Totò, I would love her,
Just as your father loves his own dear little girl.

**TOTÒ:** My mamma and my papa both love
Their own little Totò dearly.
Do yours love you, Dear lady?

**ZAZÀ:** (*very sadly*) Mamma?
I scarcely ever saw her.
My mamma left the house at early morning
And I was lonely—all day long, till evening,
When she came home again—and then—

**TOTÒ:** (*eagerly*) And then she kissed you?

**ZAZÀ:** (*sadly*) No—for she feared to wake me—she had reason,
For there was little joy in life to wake to.
You know, my little dear, there are some people
Whom you must love more tenderly than others,
For they are wicked and the world condemns them,
But they have suffered deeply when they were little—

**TOTÒ:** (*with rising interest*) The children with no homes, nor bread and butter?

**ZAZÀ:** (*bitterly*) And there are children who lack more than bread, dear.
Much more!

**TOTÒ:** (*gets off chair and goes to Zazà*) Are they the children who have no dear daddies
To love them?

**ZAZÀ:** The children without fathers—poor babies—
(*She clasps Totò in her arms with tears in her eyes*)
For little girls that is a great misfortune,
But you need never fear it, you sweet darling,
Your father, dear, no one will take away—

**TOTÒ:** (*regarding her*) Dear lady, you are crying—

**ZAZÀ:** No, not crying—I remember something.
(*rises to hide her anguish*)
You came in here to practice—will you not play something?

**TOTÒ:** I dare not—you might laugh at me if I play badly!

---

**ZAZÀ:** (*protestando*) Totò, che dici! . . .

**TOTÒ:** Allora, suono un' "Ave Maria"; è bella e piace tanto alla mammina mia.
(*Totò parlando si è accostata al pianoforte, lo apre, sceglie un foglio di musica, e siede.*)

**ZAZÀ:** (*mal frenando il pianto*) Sì, Totò, va!
(*Cade sul divano a sinistra piangendo a dirotto mentre Totò comincia a suonare l' "Ave Maria" di Cherubini.*)

**NATALIA:** (*piano, sorreggendo Zazà*) Coraggio!

**ZAZÀ:** È finita! . . .
Ammogliato . . . e un angiolo ha per figlia!
ho sognato . . . ho sognato . . .
(*Totò tutta assorta nel pezzo non s'accorge di Zazà che accasciata dal dolore piange dirottamente.*)
Dir che ci sono al mondo crëature nate fra gli agi e contro il mal protette, che a l'uom prescelto se ne vanno pure spose felici e madri benedette!
E non son paghe!
E ignorano i dolori di noi cresciute al freddo ed alla fame che stanche alfine di cotanti orrori cerchiamo scampo ne la vita infame!
Noi siam le maledette!! il nostro cuore alla speranza invano si aprirà?!
Il mondo ci rifiuta anche l'amore!
Quanto dolor! . . . di me che addiverrà?!

**TOTÒ:** (*levandosi dal pianoforte*) Ho finito! . . . baciatemi . . .

(*la bacia ardentemente*) Non piangete!
(*in ascolto, udendo rumore nell'anticamera*)
È Mammà.
(*va verso l'uscio del fondo*)

**NATALIA:** Dio! che succede adesso?!

**ZAZÀ:** (*levandosi e rassicurandola*) Nulla . . .
(*La porta si apre. La signora Dufresne appare e resta un po' interdetta vedendo delle straniere, poi si avanza mentre Zazà a parte*)
Oh, come è bella!
(*salutando*)
Voi, signora, aspettavate una signora Dunoyer . . .
E il nome mio.
Noi di porta ci siamo sbagli-

---

**ZAZÀ:** (*protesting*) Oh no—I would not!

**TOTÒ:** Then I will play "Ave Maria" for you—
It's very nice and pleases my mamma when I play it.
(*While speaking, Totò goes to the piano and takes a piece of music which she puts on rack, then sits down.*)

**ZAZÀ:** (*scarcely able to restrain her tears*) Yes, Totò, do!
(*She sinks on sofa l. weeping, while Totò begins to play Cherubini's "Ave Maria".*)

**NATALIA:** (*softly soothing Zazà*) Have courage!

**ZAZÀ:** It is ended—he is married
And has a little angel daughter—I was dreaming, I was dreaming!
(*Totò, all engrossed in her piece, does not notice Zazà, who, overcome by sorrow, is weeping heartbrokenly.*)
And there are beings in this world, I know,
Who born to wealth, and shielded more than others,
Are led before the altar pure as snow,
Becoming happy wives and blessed mothers!
What do they know of us, whose childhood dreary
Was nothing but cold and want and rank starvation,
And who, at last of hopeless struggle weary,
Gave up the fight and yielded to temptation!
We are the outcast kind, our hearts are crying
For one small ray of hope to bring relief,
But love to us the whole world is denying,
It is too much—how can I bear this grief?

**TOTÒ:** (*rising from piano*) Now it is finished.
Will you kiss me?

(*Zazà kisses her passionately*)
Please stop crying.
(*offstage a noise in reception hall*)
That's Mamma!
(*goes toward door at back of stage*)

**NATALIA:** Lord help us—what will happen!

**ZAZÀ:** (*rising and reassuring her*) Nothing!
(*Door opens, Mme. Dufresne appears and stands a little embarrassed at finding strangers—then advances*) (*Zazà says, aside*)
Great heaven!
How lovely!
(*bowing*)
I understand that you expected a Mme. Dunoyer—which is my name.

ate . . .
Volli spiegar l'equivoco e restai.
Intanto con la bimba conversai . . .
E un angiolo! . . .
Felice voi
Men vo . . .
(*andando verso l'uscio seguita da Natalia*) Scusate!

TOTÒ: (*presso alla sua mamma*)
Addio, signora . . .

ZAZÀ: (*rivolgendosi con intensa emozione*) Addio, Totò! . . .
(*Zazà e Natalia escono. Totò corre ad abbracciare la madre che sembra interrogarla confusa.*)

*Il sipario cala lentamente.*
*Fine Dell'Atto Terzo.*

■ **Atto Quarto.**

*Il salotto di Zazà come nel secondo atto.*
(*Anaide seduta presso al tavolo.—Malardot inquieto in piedi vicino a lei.*)

MALARDOT: Così, nessuna nuova?

ANAIDE: Forse verrà più tardi; non so . . . qualche disgrazia forse? Dio ce ne guardi!

MALARDOT: Non si dovea lasciarla allontanare nemmen di quattro passi!
Con quei nervi, vi pare. . .?!
Ora mi avete messo in un impiccio serio! mi mangio il meglio degli incassi per ogni suo capriccio!!
Ieri sera, ad esempio: hanno imparato che Zazà non cantava . . . e m'han piantato!

ANAIDE: (*balzando in piedi*)
Qualcuno! s'apre l'uscio . . .
E lei. . .!
(*Anaide scompare, correndo incontro e poscia rientra in iscena con Zazà, che camminando quasi automaticamente, traversa la stanza senza vedere Malardot.—Zazà si getta sulla sedia presso al tavolo come oppressa; Malardot passa a destra impacciato.—Dalla destra in fondo entrano Cascart e Natalia che rapidamente sembra mettere Cascart al corrente dell'avvenuto a Parigi.*)

ANAIDE: (*accompagnando Zazà*) Figliuola mia . . .
Mia Zazà!

ZAZÀ: (*sedendo*) Buondì, Mamma . . .

We came to the wrong house, but soon detected
Our own mistake, remaining to explain.
Your little girl was here to entertain;
She is an angel.
You are fortunate—Adieu!
(*goes to door followed by Natalia*) Excuse us!

TOTÒ: (*beside her mother*) Good-by, dear lady!

ZAZÀ: (*turning to her, with deep emotion*) Good-by, Totò!
(*Exit Zazà and Natalia—Totò runs to embrace her mother, who bends to question her wonderingly.*)

*Slow Curtain.*
*End of Act III.*

■ **Act IV.**

*Zazà's living-room, as in Act II.*
(*Anaide seated near table. Malardot standing near her—restlessly shifting his feet.*)

MALARDOT: So you know nothing further?

ANAIDE: Perhaps she will come later!
Who knows—perhaps some awful scandal?
I await her in fear!

MALARDOT: You never should have let her go four paces out of your sight unguarded.
And she high-strung—hot-headed!
This escapade my box receipts retarded more than you think; my business goes to pieces.
The people want their favorites, last night the house was empty when they discovered that Zazà was not singing.
I pay for her caprices!

ANAIDE: (*jumps to her feet*) The door is being opened:
It is she!
(*Exit Anaide, running to meet Zazà and reentering with her. Zazà walks as though dazed, crosses stage without noticing Malardot, then drops on chair near table, exhausted. Malardot passes to right, embarrassed. From r. back Cascart and Natalia enter. She is hurriedly explaining to him what happened in Paris.*)

ANAIDE: (*close beside Zazà*) My beloved daughter, my Zazà!

ZAZÀ: (*sitting down*) Good morning, Mamma!

ANAIDE: (*riprende una sedia e siede come per cominciare un lungo discorso*) Che orribile agonia!
Ma tu ci darai subito notizie . . . stavo in pena . . .

ZAZÀ: Oh no, Mamma, non posso . . .
Mi reggo in piede appena: tutta notte ho vegliato . . .
Racconterò . . . ma dopo!

ANAIDE: (*insistendo*)
Vorrei . . .

ZAZÀ: La sciami in pace.
(*volgendosi scorge Malardot—irritata e sorpresa*)
Voi qui! per quale scopo?

MALARDOT: (*imbarazzato*)
Io . . . venivo a sentire . . .

ZAZÀ: (*amaramente*) Oh! già lo sò!! . . . se canto!!
Voi pagate!
Che importa a voi se ho il cuore infranto!
Sì, canterò. . .!
(*levandosi, ad Anaide*)
Ma portalo, Mamma, lontan di qua!

MALARDOT: (*scusandosi*) Io non pensavo . . .

ZAZÀ: (*a Malardot*) Andate . . .
(*a Anaide*)
Mamma . . . va via!
va . . . va . . .
(*Anaide esce con Malardot.—Zazà ricade spossata sul canapè.*)

NATALIA: (*a Cascart, dolcemente*) Signore! è adesso—la vostra volta . . . ditele qualche—mite parola . . . se voi non siete—chi la consola?

CASCART: (*un po' risentito, bonariamente, avanzando*) Che debbo dirle—se non m'ascolta?

ZAZÀ: (*supplichevole*) Ah, tu non puoi, Cascart, dire così—i tuoi consigli io seguirò . . .
Sei tu ch'io stimo!
Oh, mio Cascart, non reggo più . . . perdo la testa!
Che far debbo? . . .
Di'!?
(*Natalia esce dalla sinistra.*)

CASCART: (*commosso*) Zazà, piccola zingara, schiava d'un folle amore, tu non sei giunta al termine ancor del tuo dolore!
Quanto convien di lacrime che sul tuo volto scenda pria che il tuo solo ed umile pellegrinar riprenda!
Tu lo credesti libero . . . or la speranza è spenta . . .
Ora sei tu la libera, e il tuo dover rammenta!
Ahi! del sognato idillio sparve l'incanto a un tratto!
una manina d'angelo indietreggiar t'ha fatto!

ANAIDE: (*drawing up a chair and sitting down, as though for a long talk*) What an awful time of waiting!
But now you must tell me all—I have such an anxious feeling!

ZAZÀ: Oh no, Mamma, I couldn't—my head is simply reeling—
All night I could not sleep—I'll tell you all—but later!

ANAIDE: (*insisting*) I would—

ZAZÀ: Let me alone, I beg you!
(*Turns and sees Malardot; annoyed and surprised*)
You here?
What are you bringing?

MALARDOT: (*embarrassed*) I—came to inquire—

ZAZÀ: (*bitterly*) Oh, it's about my singing!
You pay me!
So what's the odds if I'm heartbroken?
Yes—I will sing!
(*rises;—to Anaide*)
Take him away, Mamma—but far from here.

MALARDOT: (*apologetically*) I was not thinking—

ZAZÀ: (*to Malardot*) Please leave me!
(*to Anaide*)
Mamma, please hurry—go—go!
(*Anaide exit with Malardot; Zazà drops on sofa again, exhausted.*)

NATALIA: (*to Cascart, softly*)
Now, sir, it is your turn for consolation.
Say something kindly—show consideration.
Of your good counsel she is sore in need.

CASCART: (*a little hurt but kindly—going toward Zazà*) What can I tell her, if she will not heed?

ZAZÀ: (*pleadingly*) Ah, Cascart, do not talk like that to me!
I know your counsel good and wise will be.
Cascart, I have no faithful friend but you,
I can not stand this—tell me what to do!
(*Exit Natalia, left.*)

CASCART: (*with emotion*) Zazà, you wild little Gipsy,
The folly of love you are tasting.
The cup is not drained, and not ended
The tears that for him you are wasting!
Many will flow from your lovely eyes
Before you awaken from this dream,
Before you go onward alone again,
Faith in humanity shaken!
You had believed he was fancy-free,

ZAZÀ: (*come mormorando*) Ah, quella figlia . . .

CASCART: Piangi la pace tua svanita . . .
Ma rammenta che un altro dovere hai nella vita:
Quell'uomo ha una famiglia . . . Rendilo!

ZAZÀ: Abbandonarlo?

CASCART: È tuo dovere: rendilo!
Che? . . .
Non vorresti farlo?

ZAZÀ: Ciò non dissi . . .

CASCART: Che pensi?

ZAZÀ: Nulla . . . che lo farò . . . dovessi anche morire . . . oggi . . . gli parlerò . . .

CASCART: No! non vorrai riceverlo? ti rovini! . . .

ZAZÀ: Ha promesso di tornare oggi!

CASCART: Pazza tu, che glie l'hai concesso!
Pazza le mille volte! . . .
Se lo vedi . . . sei persa!
Scrivigli . . . se gli scrivi la cosa è assai diversa. . .
Egli sen va . . . tu all'arte ritorni come pria . . .

ZAZÀ: Non sarebbe cortese . . .

CASCART: (*brutale*) Parli di cortesia?!
Qui si tratta di moglie, di figlia, di dovere!

NATALIA: (*entrando in fretta*)
Oh signora, signora . . .
Venitelo a vedere . . . il signor Milio è all'angolo della via . . .

ZAZÀ: (*corre alla finestra*) Milio!!

NATALIA: E là; Ei conversa ridendo con il signor Courtois.

ZAZÀ: (*con gioia delirante*) Mio Cascart, ti ringrazio dei tuoi consigli . . . di . . . li seguirò . . . ma parti, ch'ei non ti trovi qui . . . va . . . va . . .

CASCART: Men vo: Ma presto su te discenderà l'ora del pentimento! . . .
Ahi povera Zazà! . . .
(*esce*)

ZAZÀ: Natalia, guarda! si vede che ho pianto?

For vanished hopes you are crying!
You have no fetters to hold you,
Duty before you is lying!
Alas, the dream that you cherished so
Proved a deception hollow;
It was the hand of an angel that
Pointed to the path you must follow!

ZAZÀ: (*murmurs*) Ah—little Totò!

CASCART: Weep for the hopes and dreams you loved so dearly,
But remember your duty is outlined very clearly.
Your lover has a family—release him!

ZAZÀ: How can I stand it?

CASCART: It is your duty: release him!
What?
Does not right demand it?

ZAZÀ: I cannot tell!

CASCART: You're thinking?

ZAZÀ: Nothing—I'll tell him, though,
And if it kills me, Cascart, today I'll know my fate!

CASCART: No—you must not receive him—that is fatal.

ZAZÀ: He will be here,
Today, as he has promised.

CASCART: To see him is a great mistake, I fear.
You must refuse to see him, for if you do, you'll falter.
But write him—written reasons the case are bound to alter.
He'll go his way—you to your art once more restoring.

ZAZÀ: It would not be polite, though—

CASCART: (*harshly*) You're talking politeness?
The question here is wife and child!—
Your duty is to free him!

NATALIA: (*enter excitedly*) O Madam—dearest madam!
Come quick if you would see him!
It's Mister Milio—standing on the corner!

ZAZÀ: (*runs to window*) Milio!

NATALIA: He's there!
Talking and laughing with Mr. Courtois.

ZAZÀ: (*wild with joy*) Dear Cascart—I am grateful for your advice and—I—
Will follow it—but leave now—he's coming—so good-by!
Go—go!

CASCART: I'll go!—
But soon your hour of sorrow and penitence will reach you!
—Alas—poor little Zazà!
(*Exit*)

ZAZÀ: Natalia—look if you can discover traces of tears?

NATALIA: Anzi non fosti mai bella così!

ZAZÀ: La colazione preparagli intanto . . .
(*osservando intorno*)
Dio! quale orrendo disordine, qui!
Ei che a Parigi ha quel ricco salotto. . . !
(*volgendosi*)
Sulla poltrona m'hai lasciato il busto?!
Vedi; quel pajo di scarpe là sotto!
(*accenna il tavolo*)

NATALIA: (*prendendo il busto e le scarpe*) Siam giunte or ora, poi! mi sembra giusto!

ZAZÀ: Taci. . . ! la polvere . . . sul pianoforte!
l'accappatojo sul paravento . . .
(*si serve dell'accappatojo per pulire il piano. — Scampanellata: Zazà si rivolge.*) E quel cappello . . .
(*indicando quello sulla campana dell'orologio*)
(*Natalia sempre tenendo le scarpe e il busto corre a cercare il cappello; quando si volta, Zazà le getta l'accappatojo; allora Natalia va a gettar tutto nello spogliatojo, ne chiude la porta e corre a destra ad aprire a Milio.*)

ZAZÀ: (*dando un ultimo sguardo*) Per buona sorte tutto è a suo posto.
Dio! che momento!
(*Milio appare sulla porta.*)

ZAZÀ: Eccoti, amore e vita!
Deh, ch'io ti guardi e baci: oh, t'amo: ancor ti stringono le braccia mie tenaci!

MILIO: (*abbracciandola*) Che hai? perchè m'abbracci sì forte, stamattina?

ZAZÀ: Oh, il cattivo! io son sempre uguale a te vicina!

MILIO: No: conosco i tuoi baci; so del tuo amore immenso!
(*Natalia prepara la tavolo.*)
T'amo troppo, e il mistero indovinare io penso!

ZAZÀ: (*in un abbraccio lungo*)
M'ami troppo?
Mai quanto basta! . . .
Ti par tedioso l'amor mio? . . .
E che ho fatto un sogno tormentoso!
Tu non m'amavi più . . . non ti vedevo più . . .
Dei dolci tempi andati, dei baci innumerati, del nostro amor che fu, altro non rimanea che una parola . . . anzi due voci e una minaccia sola: Mai più!
E ridestandomi—ancor ti vedo!
m'ami, ai tuoi baci—ancora io

NATALIA: You never looked more lovely, young and fair!

ZAZÀ: Prepare some lunch meanwhile—he may be hungry.
(*notices disorder around her*)
Lord—what a wild disorder everywhere!
And he has such a fine house—what a contrast!
(*turning around*)
Now who has left my corset on the chair?
Those shoes were lying there for two days past!
(*She scans table.*)

NATALIA: (*taking shoes and corset*) We've only just arrived—we have excuses.

ZAZÀ: Silence!
The piano—there the dust is thickest!
The bathrobe on the screen will clean it quickest!
(*She takes the robe to wipe the piano; bell rings*)
(*starts and turns*) And that old hat there—
(*points to the bat on the clock*)
(*Natalia still with shoes and corset runs to get the bat; when she turns back, Zazà throws her the bathrobe; Natalia then throws everything into the dressing-room, pell-mell, closes door and runs r. to open the door for Milio.*)

ZAZÀ: (*giving a last glance around*) Now all is right, I guess.
All is in order!
Heavens—such a mess!
(*Milio appears in door.*)

ZAZÀ: My love!
My life!
What rapture to kiss you, to behold you!
O dearest, once more my longing arms can fold you to my bosom!

MILIO: (*embracing her*) Why are you so impassioned this morning, so excited?

ZAZÀ: O you bad boy!
When you come here, I'm always so delighted!

MILIO: No—I know too well your kisses and your great love—all mine!
(*Natalia sets table*)
And I love you far too much!
Your thoughts I would divine.

ZAZÀ: (*in a long embrace*) Too much you say—I want still more, dear!
These warm caresses
May have a cause—I had a horrid dream, and that depresses:
Your love for me was dead,
You left me all alone—
Joy gone beyond returning,
Our kisses fond and burning,
Our love—one long regret.
One haunting phrase remains, no pledge, no token,
By two strange voices like a menace

credo!
Come felice,—Milio, mi
fai . . . lasciami pian-
gere . . .

MILIO: (*asciugandole gli occhi*)
Zazà, che hai?

ZAZÀ: Nulla: i miei nervi! solita
storia!
Non ti dar penna . . . facciam
baldoria!
Vogliamo ridere . . . far vita lieta . . . Hai appetito?

MILIO: Come un poeta!

ZAZÀ: (*gridando a Natalia*) Presto! servi!
E tu siediti, come sedesti, qui,
all'indomani della "Rivista" di Bussy . . .
(*Natalia serve. Zazà fingendo calma ed allegria.*)
Come la prima volta! . . .
Che notizie mi porti da Parigi?

MILIO: (*allegro*) Le solite: le nas-
cite, le morti, le corse . . . oh!
mi scordavo; i cani ammaestrati al
circo!

ZAZÀ: (*interrogando ansiosa*) E
ci sei stato?

MILIO: Cioè: ci *siamo* stati!

ZAZÀ: (*contenendosi*) *Ci siete* stati! . . .

MILIO: Avevo due miei amici
meco . . .

ZAZÀ: (*fissandolo seria*) Due
amici?

MILIO: Che hai? . . .
Mi fissi e mi fai l'eco!

ZAZÀ: Nulla; pensavo che sono
felici
Di venire a teatro con te; quei tuoi
amici!
Zazà, tu non la prendi, Zazà! . . .

MILIO: Tu hai ragione . . .
Vuoi? stasera . . .

ZAZÀ: (*vivamente*) Ah, davvero?

MILIO: Ho visto il cartellone che
annuncia una commedia . . .
Quindici giorni fa ero . . .

ZAZÀ: (*interrompendo*) Con un
amico . . .

MILIO: Ero . . .

ZAZÀ: (*come sopra*) Alle "Varietà".

MILIO: (*fissandola*) Che hai?

spoken:
No more!
And now to your return once more I
waken.
In your love and your kisses my
faith is not shaken!
I am so happy since you are here—
The tears are coming—

MILIO: (*drying her eyes*) What is
it, dear?

ZAZÀ: Nothing—I'm only
nervous—the same old story;
Let us be festive—and do not wor-
ry!
Laugh with me—life is sweet!
Clouds have all vanished!
Dear, are you hungry?

MILIO: Yes—I am famished!

ZAZÀ: (*calls to Natalia*) Serve the
luncheon!
And you sit here, as on the day
we two
Sat here, just after Bussy's new
"Review"!
(*Natalia serves; Zazà pretends to
be calm and merry.*)
Like that first, blessed morning!
Now tell the news you brought me.
From the City—

MILIO: (*merrily*) The same old
thing—some births, some
deaths—the races,
O yes—some new trained dogs put
through their paces
At the circus—

ZAZÀ: (*questioning anxiously*)
You went to see them?

MILIO: I went—or rather *we*!

ZAZÀ: (*controlling herself*) You
went with others?

MILIO: I took two friends of mine,
so we were three.

ZAZÀ: (*looks at him gravely*) You
took two friends?

MILIO: What now?
You stare and echo what I'm
saying?

ZAZÀ: Nothing—my thoughts had
gone a-straying.
You do not take your Zazà out at all
To theatres with you—like your
two friends.

MILIO: We might be going this evening, if you like?

ZAZÀ: (*eagerly*) Ah, really?

MILIO: I saw a poster showing
announcement of a funny play,
about two weeks ago.
I went—

ZAZÀ: (*interrupting*) You took a
friend?

MILIO: I went—

ZAZÀ: (*as above*) To the *Variétés*!

MILIO: (*looking at her surprised*)
What ails you?

ZAZÀ: Sono nervosa . . .
Cascart ieri è venuto a propormi
Marsiglia . . . ed io non ho volu-
to . . .

MILIO: Perchè?

ZAZÀ: Non hai affari laggiù da
quelle parti . . .

MILIO: Ed io delle scritture non
voglio più privarti. Il mio viaggio . . .

ZAZÀ: (*scattando, si alza e passeggia nervosa*) Alfine!! . . .
Eccolo il gran discorso!! . . .
Morivi se di nuovo non lo mettevi
in corso!!
Il tuo viaggio!!! invero che ci mancava questo! . . .

MILIO: Via, ti calma, bambina . . . sai che ritorno presto, fra
tre o quattro mesi . . .

ZAZÀ: O cinque, o sci . . .
Che fa?
Misura forse il tempo la gelosia?!

MILIO: (*con rimprovero*)
Zazà . . . tu sai che parto solo!

ZAZÀ: (*si volge impetuosa*) Solo?
Tu menti!
Vai . . . bugiardo!
*Con tua moglie* parti!! . . .

MILIO: (*levandosi sorpreso*) Mia
moglie! . . .
Sai?! . . .
(*Ricade seduto. Un silenzio.*)

ZAZÀ: Ebbene, sì, so tutto!
Che hai moglie . . . che mi
fuggi!
(*un silenzio*)
Senti; io non vo' dolermi di ciò: tu
non sapevi il futuro . . .
Mi dolgo di ciò che in me distruggi!
So che nel mio destino entrar tu non
dovevi!
Perchè m'hai tanto amata! . . .
Perchè! . . .

MILIO: Zazà!

ZAZÀ: Ah! no! tu non avevi il diritto di fare tutto ciò!
La mia vita era quella che tu
sai . . . io sorridevo . . . non
pensavo al male . . . tu
m'apparisti allora . . . e t'adorai,
dolce amor mio fatale!
E sognai di passar lieta al tuofianco,
una vita d'amor rigenerata! e mi vedevo già col crine bianco sposa e
madre adorata!
Come tornar qual fui, dopo tal sogno?! del mio passato io stessa mi
vergogno!!
No, tu dovevi dir la verità . . .
Che non t'avrei ama-
to . . . allor! . . .

ZAZÀ: I am nervous—
Cascart urges making
A contract with Marseilles—and I
should hate to do it.

MILIO: But why?

ZAZÀ: You would be taking no
business trips into those parts.

MILIO: I'd not prevent your book-
ings any longer, if I knew it!
There is my journey—

ZAZÀ: (*jumps up—nervously
pacing room*) Now for it! Here we
have the awful subject!
You had to bring it up again—you
couldn't do without it!
This journey that you plan—I simply cannot bear to talk about it!

MILIO: Come, calm yourself, my
girlie, you know I'll only stay three
months or maybe four—

ZAZÀ: Or five or six—one day of
absence to a jealous heart is torture!

MILIO: (*reproachfully*) Zazà,
alone you know I'm going—

ZAZÀ: (*turns impetuously*)
Alone?
You're lying!—
Go, deceiver!
You're going with your own wife.

MILIO: (*jumps up surprised*)
My wife?
You know?
(*Falls back in chair—a pause.*)

ZAZÀ: Yes—it is so—I know it!
You have a family—you will leave
me!
(*A silence*)
Listen: You could not see the fu-
ture; the past I'm not regretting,
But what you have destroyed in me,
and that you could deceive me!
It was wrong to enter into my life—
to keep me from forgetting;
Why did you ever love me? Ah why?

MILIO: Zazà!

ZAZÀ: Ah no, you had no right to
do this thing and make me suffer so!
You knew my past—and what I was
you know,
I gaily smiled, no thought of evil
bearing,
And then you came and I adored but
you,
And love was sweet beyond comparing!
I dreamt, transfigured by my love
unbounded,
By your side I would walk through
life, protected!
I saw myself with silvery hair,
surrounded
As wife and mother, loved, adored,
respected!
How can I live the old life after
dreaming,
All of my past seeming to me a
horror?

MILIO: Zazà!!
(*Zazà cade tra le braccia di Milio, piangendo*)

ZAZÀ: No! tu lo sai ch'io mento; che t'avrei sempre amato!
eri il mio solo ed unico amor predestinato!
Ma mi dovevi, o Milio, il pianto risparmiare d'una felicità . . . che non potevi dare!
(*Cade sul canapè piangendo a dirotto. Milio è presso a lei.*)

MILIO: Zazà, tu mi rimproveri d'averti troppo amata?
Forse io potea riflettere?
Tu mi domandi ciò!
La tua carezza prima forse m'hai tu negata?
Forse potevo amarti diversamente? No!
Dimmi: ho avuta la forza io di lasciarti? di fuggire lontano? . . .
Io sono qui, presso le labbra tue, chino a baciarti, a desiarti, come il primo dì!
No! mia colpa non è.
Eravam nati l'uno per l'altra: era fatalità!
bisognava non essersi incontrati per non volersi bene, o mia Zazà!
(*A poco a poco egli si è seduto su di una sedia dietro il divano, e a questo punto Zazà, piegandosi indietro, si trova fra le sue braccia, piangendo.*)

ZAZÀ: (*in lacrime, perdutamente*) Sì! sì!

MILIO: (*susurrando, tenendola tra le braccia*) Tu sei buona; m'hai tanto adorato . . .

ZAZÀ: E sempre t'adoro. . . !

MILIO: Tuo sempre son stato! lo sai. . . !

ZAZÀ: So che parti . . . mi lasci . . .

MILIO: Ma torno! . . .

ZAZÀ: Amor che finisce non ha più ritorno!

MILIO: Che pensi?

ZAZÀ: (*risoluta*) Non torni! . . .
L'ha detto . . . Totò! . . .

MILIO: (*levandosi bruscamente*) Totò!! . . .
Tu hai veduta mia figlia!!

ZAZÀ: Sì . . .

You should have told the truth and spared me—Ah!
I would not then have loved you—oh no!

MILIO: Zazà!
(*Zazà falls weeping into Milio's arms.*)

ZAZÀ: No—you must not believe me. I would have loved you knowing
You were not free, bestowing my only true love on you;
But Milio, all the tears that flow so bitterly
For joy you cannot give, you might have spared me.
(*Sinks on sofa sobbing; Milio is beside her*)

MILIO: Zazà, can you reproach me for loving you too madly?
I could not think or reason—I will admit it gladly!
That first caress decided—and you did not deny it.
Could any man resist you or leave you coldly?—No!
Tell me, had I the courage to go away and miss you,
To flee from danger wisely? I still am here,
Close to the lips I love—waiting to kiss you,
Warm with desire whenever you are near!
No—it is not my fault—we two were fated
To love each other—it is destiny!
That Power by whom all beings were created,
My Zazà, willed that you should meet with me!
(*He has meanwhile approached a chair behind the divan and is about to sit down, when Zazà turns, weeping, and finds herself in his arms.*)

ZAZÀ: (*sobbing*) Yes, yes!

MILIO: (*soothingly, holding her close*) Dear, you are good—you loved me well, I know it—

ZAZÀ: And still I love you!

MILIO: I am yours as ever, believe me!

ZAZÀ: You are going—to leave me—

MILIO: Not long, dear,

ZAZÀ: Since love is ended, you depart forever!

MILIO: Who told you?

ZAZÀ: (*firmly*) Forever—she told me—Totò!

MILIO: (*jumps up brusquely*) Totò!
You mean to say you saw my daughter?

ZAZÀ: Yes!

MILIO: No . . .
Smentisci! . . .
Ma dove?
(*silenzio*)
Ma dove?

ZAZÀ: Da te!

MILIO: Sei stata a Parigi?! sei stata da me?!

ZAZÀ: Sì . . .

MILIO: Hai visto mia moglie?

ZAZÀ: L'ho vista!

MILIO: Hai parlato?

ZAZÀ: Sì! . . .

MILIO: Questo delitto hai compiuto?
Hai osato. . . !

ZAZÀ: (*levandosi diritta, terribile*) Io! . . . perchè no?

MILIO: (*con furore crescente*) Che hai detto? che hai fatto, malaccorta!

ZAZÀ: Nulla!
Ma s'io son quella che adori, . . . che t'importa?

MILIO: Che le hai detto? hai potuto la pace sua turbare?

ZAZÀ: Ah, come l'ami!
Vedi l'ami! non puoi negare!!

MILIO: (*cercando scuse*) È mia moglie . . . e tu sei . . .

ZAZÀ: (*fra l'ira e i singhiozzi*) Lo so! . . . sono un piaga putrida, che tu celi giù nel tuo cuor profondo!
Lo so; sono una stolta che col suo pianto paga il marchio dell'infamia che la segnò nel mondo!
"Mia moglie!" quando hai detto "mia moglie" hai detto tutto!
Va, che mi bolle il sangue!
Non vale il mio più brutto costume di cantante, quella tua donna! . . .
Va!

MILIO: (*folle*) Tuoi. . . !

ZAZÀ: Oso!! Le ho detta tutta la verità!

MILIO: Le hai parlato?
Ah, l'infame!
Tu non le hai detto . . .

ZAZÀ: Ho detto tutto: sì, tutto!
I nostri baci, l'ardente affetto, le notti innamorate; sai? le follie! . . .
Che sei mio, tutto mio! . . .

MILIO: (*l'afferra come per batteria, poi la getta a terra, urlando*) Sgualdrina!

ZAZÀ: (*a terra*) Ah, come l'ami, lei!!!
(*silenzio*)

MILIO: No!
Deny it!
But where?
(*pause*)
But where?

ZAZÀ: At home!

MILIO: You went into the City?—You went to my house?

ZAZÀ: Yes!

MILIO: And did you see my wife?

ZAZÀ: I saw her!

MILIO: Did you meet her?

ZAZÀ: Yes!

MILIO: You dared to do this thing, you dared to greet her?

ZAZÀ: (*rises up straight and terribly tense*) I—and why not?

MILIO: (*with growing fury*) What did you say—what did you do, blundering creature!

ZAZÀ: Nothing!
But if you are "still mine as ever," what do you care?

MILIO: What did you tell her?
To destroy her peace of mind—ah!—did you dare?

ZAZÀ: Oh, how you love her!
I know it—you cannot deny it!

MILIO: (*seeking excuses*) She is my wife—while you, of course—

ZAZÀ: (*sobbing with anger*) I know!
I'm something foul to hide away in secret—deep where no one will find it!
I know—poor fool, I'm paying with tears the price of living!
The brand of shame is scarlet with which the world has marked me.
"My wife"—the way you said it—"my wife"—that told the story!
Go—for my blood is boiling!
Your woman is no better
Than we who wear the spangles and gauzy raiment—GO!

MILIO: (*furious*) How dare you?

ZAZÀ: I dare!
And what is more—the truth I let her know!

MILIO: You spoke together?
Ah—outrageous!
And what did you tell her?

ZAZÀ: I told her all that has happened!
About our kisses, our glowing passion,
The nights of mad delight—do you remember?
That you
Are mine—all mine!

MILIO: (*Seizes her as though to strike her, then flings her from him to the floor, shouting.*) You harlot!

ZAZÀ: (*crushed*) Ah! how you worship her!
(*silence*)

MILIO: (*tremante di rabbia, con voce soffocata, mentre prende il soprabito ed il cappello*) Ed ora io mi domando come, vicino a te, potei scordar la dolce mia buona creatura; come insozzare il nome mio, ch'ella porta, e me in quell'immondo amplesso della tua carne impura!
(*Zazà poco a poco si alza e si ritrae verso il caminetto a sinistra*)
Oh! tu m'hai ben guarito dalla fatal follia!
ora chi sei conosco; so il fondo del tuo cor!
e al rientrar domani nella dimora mia, d'averti conosciuta mi resterà il rossor!
(*Va a passo concitato sino alla porta a destra.*)

ZAZÀ: (*in uno sforzo ultimo*) Basta! non più!
Pitorna pur nella tua dimora: vi troverai la pace . . .

MILIO: (*che stava per uscire, ritornando indietro vivamente*) Che?

ZAZÀ: Nulla io dissi . . .

MILIO: Allora, Zazà, perchè mentire?

ZAZÀ: Nulla han saputo . . . .
Io sola or so quanto volevo. . . . !
(*senza voce*)

MILIO: Zazà, una parola!

ZAZÀ: Tua moglie . . . . tu l'ami . . . mi basta!

MILIO: (*appressandosi*) Zazà!

---

MILIO: (*trembling with rage—in a choked voice, goes to get his hat and coat*) How could I ever forget her—how could I leave her for you?
That pure, sweet, lovely being, and with you be enraptured?
And how defile and dishonor the name she bears with me,
Lowered in your embrace, by your vile arts captured!
(*Zazà has slowly risen and withdrawn to fireplace l.*)
Oh, rest assured you have cured me of this unspeakable madness!
Now I have learned to know you, now I have looked into your heart!
When I return to my fireside, dark and bereft of all gladness,
Shame that I ever have touched you will be my inglorious part.
(*He goes to door r. in great agitation.*)

ZAZÀ: (*after a last struggle*) That is enough!
Your fireside is undisturbed and waiting—
You will find peace and gladness—

MILIO: (*who was about to go out, turns back*) How?

ZAZÀ: I told her nothing.

MILIO: Then wherefore Zazà, did you deceive me?

ZAZÀ: She suspects nothing—I only learned what I wanted to know.
(*Her voice breaks.*)

MILIO: Zazà, can you forgive me?

ZAZÀ: Your wife—you love her—that ends it!

MILIO: (*going closer to her*) Zazà!

---

ZAZÀ: Va via! vorrei dirti che t'odio e ti sprezzo!
Non posso: ma parti: mi metti ribrezzo .
Va . . . taci . . .
(*lo respinge*)

MILIO: (*dopo un istante di lotta, disperatamente*) Ah!?!
(*Fugge*)
(*Un silenzio*)

ZAZÀ: Che ho fatto?
(*corre alla porta*)
Egli parte! egli va?
Non torna indietro . . .
(*esce correndo nell'anticamera e là si sente gridare*)
Milio! Milio!
(*nessuna risposta*)
(*rientra*)
Ed io l'ho scacciato!
(*un'idea*)
Ah! posso richiamarlo!
(*corre alla finestra*)
Dio!
(*chiama*)
Milio!!
(*un lampo di speranza*)
S'è voltato! . . .
(*disillusa*)
No . . .
(*chiamando più forte*)
Milio! torna!
Milio . . .
(*Lo segue coll'occhio come nell'Atto II*)
E all'angolo . . .
E sparito!
(*disperata*)
Sparito! . . .
E non ritorna . . . mai più!
Tutto è finito!
(*Cade seduta sui gradini della finestra piangendo.*)

*Fine.*

---

ZAZÀ: Go, leave! I'd like to tell you "I hate you"—I'm glad to free you—
I cannot!
But go now—I do not want to see you.
Say—nothing—
(*She pushes him from her.*)

MILIO: (*after a moment's struggle—desperately*) Ah!
(*runs off*)
(*Pause*)

ZAZÀ: What have I done?
(*runs to door*)
He is leaving!
He has gone
And never will I see him!
(*runs to anteroom and calls offstage*)
Milio! Milio!
(*No reply*)
(*reentering*)
Why did I not restrain him?
(*struck with an idea*)
Perhaps I still can reach him!
(*runs to the window*)
Heavens!
(*calls*)
Milio!!
(*with a ray of hope*)
He is turning—
(*disappointed*)
No!
(*calls louder*)
Milio!
Come back, Milio!
(*follows him with her eyes as in Act II*)
He's at the corner—disappearing!
(*despairing*)
He's gone—no more I'll see him—no more—
Now all is ended!
(*She drops to the window seat, weeping.*)

*End.*

# Cavalleria Rusticana (1890)

## Rustic Chivalry

MUSIC BY PIETRO MASCAGNI ■ LIBRETTO BY GIUDO MENASCI & GIOVANNI TARGIONI-TOZZETTI ■ BASED ON A PLAY BY GIOVANNI VERGA

*Cavalleria Rusticana* premiered at the Teatro Costanzi in Rome on May 17, 1890. This one-act opera, set to a libretto by Giovanni Targioni-Tozzetti and Giudo Menasci (based on a short story by Giovanni Verga), launched the vogue of operatic verismo. The story, based on an actual event, takes place in Sicily. Upon returning to his village after serving in the military, Turiddu finds his girlfriend, Lola, married to the carter, Alfio. Turiddu turns his affections to the beautiful Santuzza. The villagers celebrate Easter at the piazza in front of the church. Santuzza pays a visit to Turiddu's mother, Lucia, to inquire about her son. While they are talking, the crack of a whip announces Alfio's arrival. Santuzza begs Turiddu for his love and faithfulness, but when he hears Lola's voice, he spurns Santuzza for his first love. Santuzza goes to Alfio and reveals his wife's infidelity. Alfio swears to kill both Lola and Turiddu in revenge. After a beautiful *intermezzo sinfonico*, Turiddu invites the peasants to drink wine with him. Alfio enters, and Turiddu offers him a cup, but he refuses; only a duel will settle this matter. The two men embrace in the Sicilian manner, and Turiddu bites off Alfio's right ear, symbolizing the challenge. Turridu asks his mother to bless him and to look after Santuzza. They fight the duel outside the village. Santuzza rushes in only to find her beloved dead and collapses to the ground, crying out, "They have murdered Turiddu."

**TURIDDU:** O Lola, bianca come fior di spino, .. quando t'affaci te s'affaccia il sole; .. Chi t'ha bacciato il labbro
porporino .. Grazia più bella a Dio chiedernon vole .. C'è scitto sangue sopra la tua porta; .. Ma di restarci a me non me n'inporta; .. se per te mojo e vado in paradiso, Non c'entro se .. non vedo il tuo bel viso, Se per te mojo e vado in paradiso Non e'entro se .. non vedo il tuo bel viso.
Ah! . . . Ah! . . . Ah! . . . Ah!

**TURIDDU:** (*Behind the scenes.*) O Lola, fair as flowers smiling in beauty, Love from your soul lit eyes is glowing softly; .. He who would kiss your lips, red and beguiling .. blissful and favored were he, Knowing such heaven! .. Though your threshold blood, crimson, is staining, .. Caring for nothing, I seek you; scorning to hide me; .. What though I forfeit life, your presence gaining? What were the joy of heaven, were you denied me! What though I forfeit life, your presence gaining, What were the joy of heaven were you denied me.
Ah! . . . Ah! . . . Ah! . . . Ah!

## SCENA I

*La scena rappresenta una piazza in un paese della Sicilia. Nel fondo, a destra, Chiesa con porta practicabile. A sinistral'o steria e la casa di Mamma Lucia. E il giorno Pasqua.*
*(Campane interne dalla Chiesa. Si alza la tela. Lascena sul principio è vuota. Albeggia. Paesani, contadini, contadini e ragazzi traversano la scena. Si apre la chiesa e la folla vi entra. Il movimento del popolo continua fino al Coro punto in cui rimane la scena vuota.)*

**CORO:** (*Donne di dentro,*) Ah! (*Uomini di dentro.*) Ah!
(*Donne di dentro.*)
Gil aranci olezzano sui verdi

## SCENE I

*A public place or square in a Sicilian village. At right, in background, a church. At left, the inn and dwelling of Mamma Lucia. Time, Easter morning.*
*(Peasants, countrymen, countrywomen, and children, cross the stage.)*
*(The church doors open and the throng enters.)*
*(The movement continues until the following:)*

**CHORUS OF WOMEN:** (*Behind scenes.*) Ah! Ah!
**CHORUS OF MEN:** (*Behind scenes.*) Ah! Ah!
**CHORUS OF WOMEN:** (*Behind*

margini,
Cantan le allodole tra i mirti in fior;
Tempo è si mormori da ognuno il tene ro canto che i palpiti—
Raddoppia al cor
(*Le donne entrano in iscena.*)
(*Uomini di dentro.*)

**CORO:** In mezzo al campo tra le spiche d'oro
Giunge il rumore delle vostre spole,
Noi stanchi riposando dal lavoio A voi pensiamo, o belle occhidisole.
O belle occhidisole, a voi corriamo,
Come vola l'augelo—al suo richinmo.
(*Gli uomini entrano in issena.*)

**DONNE:** Cessin le rustiche opre: (tor;)
La Virgine serena allietasi del Salvator;
Tempo è si mormori da ognuno il tenero canto che i palpiti—
Raddoppia al cor.
**UOMINI:** (*Allontanandosi.*) In mezzo al campo, etc.

**DONNE:** (*Allontanadosi.*) Gil aranci olezzano, etc.

*scenes.*) Sweet is the air with the blossoms of oranges;
Sings now the lark from the myrtles in flower;
Murmurs of tender song tell of a joyful world,
And of thankful hearts. Ah! gladsome hour!
(*The women enter.*)

**CHORUS OF MEN:** (*Behind scenes.*) Your spinning wheels now busily are humming, Over fields of golden corn the sound is coming;
We linger where the leafy shade is restful;
Of you we think, and every heart is zestful.
Oh lovely women! Allured by you and enraptured,
Like the bird held by the lure, now we are captured.
(*The men enter.*)

**WOMEN:** Work in the field now is ended;—
The Holy Mother mild
Fondles the Child in ecstasy.

**ALL:** (*Withdrawing from stage.*)
Murmurs of tender song tell of a joyful world,
And of thankful hearts.
Ah! gladsome hour!
(*Enter, Santuzza, approaching Lucia's dwelling.*)

## SCENA II

*Sortita di Alfio.*

**SANTUZZA:** (*Entra e si dirige alla casa di Lucia.*) Dite, Mamma Lucia—

**LUCIA:** (*Sortendo.*) Sei tu? che vuoi?

**SANTUZZA:** Turiddu ov'è?

**LUCIA:** Fin qui vieni a cercare il figlio mio?

**SANTUZZA:** Voglio saper soltanto, Perdonatemi voi, dove trovarlo.

**LUCIA:** Non lo so, non lo so, non voglio brighe!

**SANTUZZA:** Mamma Lucia, vi supplico piangendo, Fate come il Signore a Maddalena, Ditemi per pietà, dov' è Turiddu.

**LUCIA:** E andato per il vino a Francofonte.

**SANTUZZA:** No! l'hanvisto in paese ad alta notte.

**LUCIA:** Che dici? che dici! se non è tornato casa! Entra!

**SANTUZZA:** Non posso entrare in case vostra. Sono scomunicata!

**LUCIA:** E che ne sai del mio figliuolo?

**SANTUZZA:** Quale spina ho in core!
(*Dall' interno schiocchi di frusta e tintinnio di sonagli*
(*Entrano in iscena i coristi indi Alfio.*)

**ALFIO:** Il cavallo scalpita, i sonagli squillano, schiocchi la frusta, Ehi là! . . . Soffiil vento gelido cada l'acquao nevichi, a me che cosa fa! . . . Il cavallo scalpita, i sonagli squillano, schiocchia la frusta, schiocchi la frusta, Ehi là! .. schiocchi la frusta, schiocchi la frusta, Ehi là! Ehi là!

**TENORS:** O che bel mestiere fare il carrettiere andar di qua e di là! . . . Oh che bel mestiere fare il carrettiere andardi quà e di là! andardi qua e di là! andardi qua e di là! andardi quà e di là! andar di quà e di là!

**ALFIO:** (*Andante rit.*) M'a spetta a casa Lola che m'a ma e mi consola, ch'e tutta fedeltà . . . M'a spetta a casa Lola! che m'ama e mi consola, ch'è tutta fideltà . . . Il cavallo scalpiti, i sonagli squillino, è Pasqua, ed io son quà, . . . è Pasqua ea' io son quà . . . son quà! . . .

## SCENE II

(*Santuzza, Lucia, Alfio, and chorus.*)

**SANTUZZA:** Tell me, mother Lucia—

**LUCIA:** (*Coming from house.*) It is you? What will thou?

**SANT:** Where is Turiddu?

**LUCIA:** You ask for him? For him, my son Turiddu!

**SANT:** I ask you only for him. Pardon, but answer! Where is Turiddu?

**LUCIA:** Ask me not! I know not; I want no trouble.

**SANT:** Mamma Lucia, with weeping I pray you!
Even as spake the Saviour to the Magdalen,
Say, in pity say, where is Turiddu!

**LUCIA:** He's gone to bring some wine from Francofonte.

**SANT:** No! Last night someone in the village saw him.

**LUCIA:** What say you? Who told it? No, he has not yet returned. Enter!

**SANT:** I may not step across your threshold,
I cannot pass it, I, most unhappy outcast!
Excommunicated!

**LUCIA:** What of my son? What have you to tell me?

**SANT:** Ah! the torture, the heart-pain.
(*Cracking of whips and jingling of bells behind scenes.*)
(*Chorus enters, followed soon by Alfio.*)

**ALFIO:** Gaily moves the tramping horse, Joyful sound the ringing bells; Snap, now, the lash goes, A-hi! . . . The wind may blow cold today, Rain or snow do what it may, I do not care, not I! . . . Gaily moves the tramping horse, Joyful sound the ringing bells; Snap, now, the lash goes, Snap, now, the lash goes! A-hi! .. Snap, now, the lash goes. Snap, now, the lash goes, A-hi! A-hi!

**TENORS:** Who has a calling merrier than the life of a carrier? Where is a jollier man? . . . Who has a calling merrier than the life of a carrier? Where is a jollier man? Where is a jollier man? Where is a jollier man, a jollier man than he?

**ALFIO:** My loving Lola calls me! Her gentle grace enthralls me, Ah! .. faithfully she calls . . . My loving Lola calls me, Her gentle grace enthralls me, Ah! fondly I reply . . . . . Gaily moves the tramping horse, Joyful sound the ringing bells; It's Easter and I come home . . . It's Easter and I come

(*Women of the chorus enter the scene.*)

**CORO:** O che bel mestiere fare il carrettiere andar di quà e di là, andar di quà e di là! andar di quà e di là, andar di quà e di là, di quà e di là.

**ALFIO:** Ehi là! Ehi là! schiocchi la frusta, Ehi là! schiocchi la frusta, schiocchi la frusta, schiocchi la frusta, Son quà! Oh che bel mestiere fare il carrettiere, oh che bel mestiere, andar de quà, andar di là, andar di quà, andar di là! Pasqua ed io son quà, . . . andar di quà e di là, andar di quà e di là, E Pasqua ed io son quà, . . . sou qua!
(*Il Coro esce, alcuni entrano in chiesa, altri prendone direzioni diverse.*)

## SCENA III

**LUCIA:** Beato voi, compar Alfio, Che siete sempre allegro così!

**ALFIO:** (*Spigliato.*) Mamma Lucia, N'avete ancora di quel vecchio vino?

**LUCIA:** Non so; Turiddu è andato a provvederne.

**ALFIO:** Se è sempre qui! L'ho visto stamattina vicino a casa mia

**LUCIA:** (*Sorpresa.*) Come?

**SANTUZZA:** (*A Lucia rapidamente.*) Tacete.

**ALFIO:** Io me ne vado, ite voi altre in chiesa
(*Esce.*)

**CORO:** (*Interno.*) Regina Coeli, laetare—
Alleluja!
Quia, quem meruisti potare—
Alleluja!
Resusrexit sicut dixit—
Alleluja!

**CORO:** (*Esterno.*)
(*Uomini e donne entrano e si schierano innanzi alla Chiesa in atteggiamento devoto*.)
Inneggiamo, il Signor non è morto!
Ei fulgente ha dischiuso l'avel,
Inneggiamo al Signore risorto
Oggi asceso alla gloria del ciel!
Inneggiamo, il Signor non è morto!
Ei fulgente ha dischiuso l'avel,
Inneggiamo al Signore risorto
Oggi asceso alla gloria del ciel!
(*Tutti entrano in chiesa tranne Santuzza e Lucia.*)

home! . . . come home! . . . It's Easter and I come home . . . come home . . .
(*Women of the chorus enter the scene.*)

**CHORUS:** Who has a calling merrier, Than the life of a carrier, Where is a jollier man? Where is a jollier man? Where is a jollier man? Where is a jollier man, a jollier man?

**ALFIO:** A-hi! A-hi! Snap, now, the lash goes, A-hi! Snap, now, the lash goes, Snap, now, the lash goes Snap, now, the lash goes, I come! I'm the merry carrier! I'm the merry carrier, Who has a calling merrier than the life, the life of a carrier, than the life, this life of mine, A happier man than I? . . . Where is a jollier man, where is a jollier man? It's Easter, I, come home I come home!
(*Chorus withdraws into the church; others separate in various directions.*)

## SCENE III

*Scene And Prayer.*

**LUCIA:** Your are blessed, friendly Alfio!
So favored, ever to be gay!

**ALFIO:** Mamma Lucia, have you that rare old wine,
The same as ever?

**LUCIA:** Not now; Turiddu has gone to buy plenty.

**ALFIO:** No; he is here! I saw him here this morning;
He lingered near my cottage.

**LUCIA:** (*Surprised.*) What now!

**SANTUZZA:** (*Rapidly, to Lucia.*) Be silent!

**ALFIO:** I will not linger, You will to church devotedly?
(*Exit.*)

**CHORUS:** (*In church.*) Queen of the Heavens, sorrow flies!
**PEOPLE:** (*External chorus.*) Hallelujah!
**CHORUS:** (*In church.*) Your holy Son lives, nor dies!
**PEOPLE:** Hallelujah!
**CHORUS:** (*within.*) From the dead He now has risen,
Truly has He risen.
**PEOPLE:** Hallelujah.

**CHORUS:** (*External. Grouping in devotional attitudes.*) We will sing of the Lord now victorious! All the terrors of death were in vain! Let us sing of the Christ ever glorious;
He is risen, in glory to reign!
(*All enter the church, except Santuzza and Lucia.*)

## Scene IV

### SCENA IV

**LUCIA:** Perchè m'hai fatto segno di tacere?

**SANTUZZA:** Voi lo sapete, o mamma, prima d'andar soldato Turiddu aveva a Lola eterna fe giurato.
Tornò, la seppe sposa; e con un nuovo amore
Volle spegner la fiamma che gli bruciava il core
M'amò, l'amai, l'amai, ah!
Quell' invida d'ogni delizia mia,
Del suo sposo dimentica, arse di gelosia.
Me l'ha rapito. Priva dell' onor mio,
Dell' onor mio rimango:
Lola e Turiddu s'amano, io piango!

**LUCIA:** Miseri noi, che cosa vieni a dirmi
In questo santo giorno?

**SANTUZZA:** Io son dannata.
Andate, o mamma, ad implorare Iddio,
E pregate per me. Verrà Turiddu,
Vo' supplicarlo un' altra volta ancora!

**LUCIA:** Ajutatela voi, Santa Maria!
(*Lucia entra in chiesa.*)

### SCENA V

**TURIDDU:** (*Entrando.*) Tu qui Santuzza?

**SANTUZZA:** Qui t'aspettavo

**TURIDDU:** È Pasqua in chiesa non vai!

**SANTUZZA:** Non vo. Debbo parlarti.

**TURIDDU:** Mamma cercavo.

**SANTUZZA:** Debbo parlarti.

**TURIDDU:** Qui no! qui no!

**SANTUZZA:** (*Parlato.*) Dove sei stato?

**TURIDDU:** (*Parlato.*) Che vuoi tu dire? A Francofonte.

**SANTUZZA:** No, non è ver.

**TURIDDU:** Santuzza credimi.

**SANTUZZA:** No, non mentire
Ti vidi volgere giù dal sentir,
E stamattina all' alba t'hanno
Scorto presso l'uscio di Lola.

**TURIDDU:** Ah! mi hai spiato!

**SANTUZZA:** No! te lo giuro, a noi l'ha raccontato
Campar Alfio il marito poco fa.

### SCENE IV

**LUCIA:** (*To Santuzza.*) And why with signals would you gain my silence?

**SANTUZZA:** Now shall you know, kind mother:
Before he went forth as a soldier,
Turiddu pledged his love to Lola,
All his faithfulness renewing
But; ah! homeward returning,
Married he found his Lola!
And, her falsity shaming—
All the old love subduing—
Loved me!
And I loved him!
With jealousy, hatefully, and with madness,
Scorning wifely duty, envious of my gladness,
Lola, in malice shameful, regains Turiddu!
Disgraceful fate overtakes me,
My own Turiddu forsakes me!
He and Lola in joy remain,
Having each other's love again!
Ah me! alone I weep, I weep!

**LUCIA:** Grief is upon us!
Such dire and woeful tidings to hear this holy morning.

**SANTUZZA:** I am accursed! I am accursed!
Good mother, go pray for me to the Saviour!
You'll beseech Him for me!
I'll seek Turiddu, and pray to him
That he again may love me!

**LUCIA:** Holy Mary be with you—the blessed Mary!
(*Lucia enters the church*)

### SCENE V

**TURIDDU:** (*Entering.*) Are you here, Santuzza?

**SANTUZZA:** Here I await you.

**TURIDDU:** Attending not the service of Easter?

**SANTUZZA:** Not now! I would speak with you.

**TURIDDU:** I seek my mother.

**SANTUZZA:** I would speak with you!

**TURIDDU:** Not here, not here!

**SANTUZZA:** From where have you come?

**TURIDDU:** Why do you ask me?—From Francofonte.

**SANTUZZA:** Ah, that is false!

**TURIDDU:** Santuzza, believe me!

**SANTUZZA:** No! You are lying!
Over yon path I saw you approach:
And you were seen today returning homeward
From the dwelling of Lola!

**TURIDDU:** Ah! you were spying!

**SANTUZZA:** No, I do swear it!
Her husband, Alfio, saw you
Here within the town, and told it me!

**TURIDDU:** Cosi ricambi l'amor che ti porto?
Vuoi che m'uccida?

**SANTUZZA:** Oh! questo non lo dire.

**TURIDDU:** Lasciami dunque, lasciami invari tenti sopire
Il giusto sdegno colla tua pietà.

**SANTUZZA:** Tu l'ami dunque?
**TURIDDU:** No!
**SANTUZZA:** Assai più bella è Lola!
**TURIDDU:** Taci, non l'amo.
**SANTUZZA:** L'ami, l'ami, Oh! maledetto!

**TURIDDU:** Santuzza!

**SANTUZZA:** Quella cattiva femmina ti tolse a me!

**TURIDDU:** Bada, Santuzza, schiavo non sone
Di questa vanatua gelosia.

**SANTUZZA:** (*Con angoscia.*) Battimi, insultami, t'amo e perdono
Ma è troppo forte l'angoscia mia.
(*Troncando nel sentire avvicinarsi Lola.*)

### SCENA VI

**LOLA:** (*Dentra alla scena.*) Fior di giaggiolo
Gli angeli belli stano
A mille in cielo
Ma belli come lui
Ce n'è uno solo.
(*Entra in iscena e s'interrompe.*)
Oh! Turiddu, e passato Alfio?

**TURIDDU:** Son giunto ora in piazza non so.

**LOLA:** Forse è rimasto dal maniscalco ma non può tardare!
E voi sentite le funzioni in piazza?

**TURIDDU:** (*Confuso affret.*) Santuzza mi narrava—

**SANTUZZA:** Gli dicevo che oggi è Pasqua
E il Signor vede ogni cosa.

**LOLA:** Non venite alla messa?

**SANTUZZA:** (*Subito.*) Io no, ci deve andar chi sa
(*Con intensione.*)
Di non aver peccato!

**LOLA:** (*Con forza.*) Io ringrazio il Signore, e bacio in terra!

**SANTUZZA:** (*Esprimendosi.*) Oh! fate bene, fate bene,
(*Con amarezza.*)
Lola!

**TURIDDU:** So you reward the love I gave you,
Now he will slay me!

**SANTUZZA:** Ah! Tell me not of murder!

**TURIDDU:** Leave me, I tell you! leave me!
The rage burning within me—
My righteous wrath, you can not assuage!

**SANTUZZA:** Then, you do love her!
Lola is more fair than I am—
False friend! Oh, curses on her!

**TURIDDU:** Santuzza!

**SANTUZZA:** She—vilest woman, steals the love that should be mine!

**TURIDDU:** I am no slave to your envy
Scornfully showing, jealously showing

**SANTUZZA:** Beat me, insult me!
Yet do I love you,
Even though anguish my heart is rending,
Even though in sorrow my life is ending.

### SCENE VI

**LOLA:** (*Behind scenes.*) Bright flower, so radiant!
Angelic thousands stand arrayed in heaven,
Yet none so fair as you have yet been given!
(*Enters. Pauses suddenly.*)
Oh! Turiddu, have you seen Alfio?

**TURIDDU:** I came but this moment: I have not.

**LOLA:** Then perhaps he awaits at the forge.
Here I must not linger.
And you?
Is it here in public that you are praying?

**TURIDDU:** (*Confusedly.*) Santuzza here was telling—

**SANTUZZA:** I was saying this is Easter!
(*Meaningly.*)
And the Lord beholds all things!

**LOLA:** (*To Santuzza.*) You will not go to the service?

**SANTUZZA:** No, no! None shall attend but those
Who know they are not guilty!

**LOLA:** (*Vehemently.*) In the grace of the Saviour
I bow before you!

**SANTUZZA:** (*Bitterly.*) O, well you speak!—
Lola!

TURIDDU: (A Lola.)
(Impacciato.)
Andiamo, andiamo, Oni non abbia-na che fare.

LOLA: (A Turiddu.) Oh!
(Con ironia.)
Rimanete.

SANTUZZA: (A Turiddu con fermezza.) Si, resta, resta,
Ho da parlarti ancora.

LOLA: (Sempre ironica.) E v'assista il Signore,
(Con caricatura.)
Io me ne vado.
(Entra in chiesa.)

## SCENA VII

TURIDDU: (Con ironia.) Ah! lo vedi, che hai tu detto.

SANTUZZA: (Fredda.) L'hai voluto e ben ti sta!

TURIDDU: (S'avventa.) Ah! per Dio!

SANTUZZA: Squarciami il petto.

TURIDDU: (S'avvia.) No!

SANTUZZA: (Trattenendolo.) Turiddu ascolta!

TURIDDU: Va!

SANTUZZA: (Andante appassionato.) No, no, Turiddu, rimani, rimani ancora abbandonarmi dunque tu vuoi? no, no, Turiddu! rimani ancora dunque tu vuoi abbandonarmi? No, no, Turiddu, rimani, rimani ancora, no, Turiddu, Turiddu rimani ancora.

TURIDDU: Perchè seguirmi, perchè spiarmi sullimitare fin della chiesa? Perchè seguirmi perchè spiarmi?

SANTUZZA: (con dolore.) La! tua Santuzza piangè e t'implora . . . come cacciarla cosi tu puoi, la tua Santuzza? no, Turiddu! rimani ancora! Oh! Turiddu! no, Turiddu! rimani ancor no, Turiddu! Ah! .. no, Turiddu, rimani, rimani ancora, ancor. No! no! no! la tua Santuzza piangè e t'implora come cacciarla come cacciarla tu puoi?

TURIDDU: Va ti ripèto, va non te diarmi pentirsi è vano dopo l'offesa. Non te diarmi va! va! va! va Ti ripeto non te diarmi, pentirsi è vano, dopo l'offesa pentirsi è vano, dopo l'offesa. va! va! va! (reprimendosi.) va, ti ripeto, va, pentirsi e vano dopo l'offesa. Va! va! Ti ripeto Va! Ah! va! ti ripeto, va non te diarmi. va! Pentirsi e vano dopo

TURIDDU: (Embarrassed.)
(To Lola.)
Away then! Come, Lola;
Here there is nothing to hold us.

LOLA: (Ironically.) Oh, stay with her!

SANTUZZA: (To Turiddu.) Yes stay!
(Firmly.)
I have something yet to tell you:

LOLA: (Mockingly.) May the Saviour assist you!
(Going.)
So, I will leave you.
(Enters the church.)

## SCENE VII

TURIDDU: (To Sant.) Ah! how foolish! nothing availing!

SANTUZZA: (Coldly.) I have spoken; it is well—it is the truth.

TURIDDU: (Threateningly.) Ah! by heaven!

SANTUZZA: My heart is ripped open!

TURIDDU: (Approaching her.) No!

SANTUZZA: (Warding him away.) Turiddu, ah! hear me!

TURIDDU: Go!
(Turns from her.)

SANTUZZA: No, no, Turiddu, remain with me yet, and forever! Love me again! How can you forsake me! (with dolorous vehemence.) Into your arms .. loving again, Say you will take . . . me! No, no, Turiddu! Remain with me yet and for ever! No Turiddu, Turiddu remain with me ever!

TURIDDU: Why do you follow me? Why do you watch me? Why do you spy even at the church-door? Why do you follow, Why watch me ever?

SANTUZZA: Lo! here your Santuzza now do implore . . . you; . . . Ah! can you leave me weeping before you! Love your Santuzza! No, Turiddu! Stay, I implore you! (entreatingly.) Oh! Turiddu! No, Turiddu, remain, remain! No! Turiddu! Ah!.. No, Turiddu, remain, remain, I implore you, again! No, no, no! See your Santuzza now does implore you, Ah! can you leave me, thus weeping before you!

TURIDDU: Go! I repeat it! Go! you make me weary! All repentance for such offending is in vain! You shall leave me! Go! Go! Go! Go! I repeat it; Go, I tell you, repenting is in vain, repenting is in vain, for all your offending, all your offending! Go! go! go! Go! I repeat it! Go! repentence for such offending is in vain. Go! Go! I repeat it, Go! Ah! Go!

l'offesa, pentirsi è vano dopo l'offensa.

SANTUZZA: (Minacciosa.) Bada!

TURIDDU: (Con moltissima forza.) Dell' ira tua non mi curo!
(La getta a terra e fugge in chiesa.)

SANTUZZA: (Nel colmo dell' ira.) A te la mala Pasqua, spergiuro!
(Cade affranta ed angosciata.)

## SCENA VIII

(Sorte Alfio e s'incontra con Santuzza.)

SANTUZZA: (Ad Alfio rianimandosi.) Oh! Il Signore vi manda, compar Alfio.

ALFIO: (Tranquillo.) A che punto è la messa?

SANTUZZA: È tardi ormai, ma per voi
(Con intenzione.)
Lola è andata con Turiddu!

ALFIO: (Sorpreso.) Che avete detto?

SANTUZZA: Che mentre correte All' acqua e al vento a guadagnarvi il pane,
Lola v'adorna il tetto in malo modo!

ALFIO: Ah! nel nome di Dio, Santa che dite?

SANTUZZA: Il ver. Turiddu mi tolse, mi tolse l'onore,
E vostra moglie lui rapiva a me!

ALFIO: (Minaccioso.) Se voi mentite, vo' schiantarvi il coro.

SANTUZZA: Uso a mentire il labbro mio, il labbro mio non è!
Per la vergogna mia, pel mio dolore
La trista verità—vi dissi, ahimè!

ALFIO: (Dopo un poco di pausa.) Comare Santa, allor grato vi sono.

SANTUZZA: Infame io son che vi partai così.

ALFIO: Infami loro, ad essi non perdono
Vendetta avrò pria che tra monti il di!
Io sangue vo glio, all'ira m'abbandono,
In odio tutto l'amor mio finì!
(Escono.)

## SCENA IX

(Tutti escono di chiesa. Lucia attraversa la scena de entra in casa. A gruppi soto voce fra loro.)

I repeat it, Go! I repeat it! Go! Go! repentence for your offending is in vain! Once more I tell you, go! And forever!

SANTUZZA: (Threateningly.) False! false!

TURIDDU: (With increased rage.) Thus I reward you in my anger.
(Throws her down, and hastens into the church.)

SANTUZZA: (In the height of fury.) Accursed! accursed at Easter, you false one.
(Falls, despairingly.)

## SCENE VIII

(Enter, Alfio.)

SANTUZZA: (Calming herself.) Oh! did the Saviour send you, neighbor Alfio?

ALFIO: At what point is the service?

SANTUZZA: It is now at closing. But I tell you Lola has gone with Turiddu!

ALFIO: (Surprised.) What are you saying?

SANTUZZA: While you labor to earn an honest living, Lola is giving her love unfaithfully.

ALFIO: Ah! in the name of heaven, Santuzza, What are you saying?

SANTUZZA: The truth! Turiddu forsakes me—and he has betrayed me! It was your wife who enticed him away from me!

ALFIO: (Threateningly.) And if you are lying I'll have your heart's blood!

SANTUZZA: Lies, as yet, my lips have never uttered. Prone to be truthful am I.

ALFIO: (After a pause.) Santuzza, I am thankful that you have spoken.

SANTUZZA: But ah! what shame! And I have told it to you!

ALFIO: (Suddenly, in fury.) It is they who are shameful! I'll have revenge upon them! This day and hour my wrath Shall fall upon them!

## SCENE IX

(The people enter from the church. Lucia crosses and enters the inn.)

# Scene IX

CORO: (*Uomini.*) A casa, a casa, amici, ove ci aspettano Le nostre donne, andiam, Or che letizia reasserena gli animi.

CHORUS OF MEN: (*sotto voce.*) Now homeward, now homeward neighbors, Good cheer is awaiting there; And wives our joy will share, Now Easter day shall be for all a time of rest, Without sorrow or care.

CORO: (*Donne.*) A casa, a casa, amiche, ecc. (*Lola e Turiddu escono dalla chiesa.*)

CHORUS OF WOMEN: Now homeward, now homeward neighbors, etc. (*Lola and Turiddu come from the church.*)

TURIDDU: Comare Lola, ve ne andante via Senza nemmeno salutare?

TURIDDU: My pretty Lola! Have you not a greeting, When honest people we are meeting?

LOLA: Vado a casa; Non ho visto compar Alfio!

LOLA: I must leave you. I must go and welcome Alfio!

TURIDDU: Non ci pensate, verrà in piazza. (*Rivolgendosi al Coro che s'avvia.*) Intanto, amici, qua, Beviamone un bicchiere. (*Tutti si avvicinano alla tavola dell' osteria e prendono in mano i bicchieri.*)

TURIDDU: Here he will seek you. Do not hasten! (*To the people.*) Meanwhile, good friends, come here. (*All come forward.*) We'll try the merry wine! (*All take cups from the bar of the inn.*)

TURIDDU: Viva il vino spumeggiante, nel bicchiere scintillante Come il riso dell' Amante; mite infonde il giu .. bilo, viva il vino spumeggiante, nel bicchiere scintillante come il riso dell' amante, mite infonde il giu .. bilo! Viva il vino ch'è sincero che ciallieta ogni pensiero, e che af foga l'umor nero nell' ebbrezza tenera . . . Viva il vino ch'è sincero che ci allieta ogni pensiero, e che af foga l'umor nero nell' ebbrezza tenera.

TURIDDU: Hail! the ruby wine now flowing, Brightly in the cup now showing, Merry spell upon you throwing, Like a smile from happy love Hail! the ruby wine now flowing, Brightly in the cup now showing, Merry spell around you throwing, Like the smile of happy love! Hail! ah, wine so richly gleaming! In your crimson joy is beaming! All your comfort lend us, With your cheer attend us—Hope and love! . . . Hail! ah, wine so richly gleaming! In your crimson joy is beaming! All your comfort lend us, With your cheer attend us—Hope and love!

CORO: Viva, beviam! Rinnovisi la giostra!

CHORUS: Welcome!

TURIDDU: (*A Lola.*) Ai vostri amori! (*Beve.*)

TURIDDU: (*To Lola.*) To those who love you! (*Drinks.*)

LOLA: (*A Turiddu.*) Alla fortuna vostra! (*Beve.*)

LOLA: (*To Turiddu.*) May fortune give you favor! (*Drinks.*)

TURIDDU: Beviam!

TURIDDU: We will!

CHORUS: Drink it!

LOLA, TURIDDU E CORO: Beviam, beviam! rinnovisi la giostra! (*Entra Alfio.*)

CHORUS: Welcome! and drink! (*All drink.*) Come, let us drink another!

ALL: Come, drink; yes, let us drink another! Hail! the ruby wine now flowing, etc.

ALFIO: A voi tutti salute.

ALFIO: To all of you, greeting!

CORO: Compar Alfio, salute.

CHORUS: Neighbor Alfio, greeting!

TURIDDU: Benvenuto! con noi dovete bere, (*Empie un bicchiere.*) Ecco pieno e il bicchiere. (*Troncando.*)

TURIDDU: (*To Alfio.*) Hearty welcome! Now join with us in revel. (*Fills a glass for him.*) Look you! drink you this measure!

ALFIO: Grazie, ma il vostro vino io non l'accetto, Diverrebbe veleno entro il mio petto!

ALFIO: Thank you! but I must refuse the offer! A cup of deadly poison perhaps you proffer!

TURIDDU: (*Parlato.*) A piacer vostro. (*Getto il vino.*)

TURIDDU: Then suit your pleasure! (*Throws away the wine.*)

LOLA: Ahimè che mai sarà? (*Alcune donne nel Coro si consigliano fra loro poi si su vicinano a Lola dicendole sotto voce.*)

LOLA: Ah me! what now befalls! (*Some of the women consult together, and then approach Lola*)

CORO: Comare Lola, andiamo via di qua. (*Tutte le donne escono conducendo Lola.*)

CHORUS: Neighbor Lola, come, haste away from here! (*Exit, all the women, with Lola.*)

TURIDDU: Avete altro a dirmi?

TURIDDU: (*To Alfio.*) Perhaps you have something to tell me!

ALFIO: Io nulla.

ALFIO: I? nothing!

TURIDDU: Allota sono agli ordini vostri—

TURIDDU: Then hear me! You will find me at your service!

ALFIO: Or ora?

ALFIO: This moment?

TURIDDU: Or ora! (*Si abbracciano. Turiddu morde l'orecchio destro o Alfio.*)

TURIDDU: This moment! (*They embrace, Turiddu bites Alfio's ear, viciously.*)

ALFIO: Compar Turiddu, a vete morso, a buono (*Con intenzione.*) Cintenderemo bene a quel che pare!

ALFIO: Neighbor Turiddu, you give a ready challenge! And I accept it! you understand me!

TURIDDU: Compar Alfio. Lo so che il torto è mio; E ve lo giuro nel nome di Dio Che al par d'un cane mi fare! sgozzar— Ma s'io non vivo, (*Dolorosamente.*) Resta abbandonata povera Santa! Lei che mi s'è data! (*Con impeto.*) Vi saprò in core il ferro mio piantar!

TURIDDU: Neighbor Alfio! I own you should have vengeance, And I admit, in the name that is holy, That I should be dealt with as a dog! But, should you kill me—if I perish By your arm—yes, if I perish,— Unhappy Santa, she whom I have cherished— Lone, unhappy Santa, my dagger Will embed within her heart!

ALFIO: (*Freddamente.*) Compare fate come più vi piace, Io v'aspetto qui fuori dietro l'orto. (*Esce.*)

ALFIO: Good neighbor, act upon it as may suit you! You will find me yonder in the orchard. (*Exit.*)

TURIDDU: (*Chiamando.*) Mamma— (*Entra Lucia.*) Mamma—quel vino è generoso, E certo oggi troppi bicchier Ne ho traccannati— Vado fuori all' aperto— Ma prima voglio che mi benedite— Come quel giorno che partii soldato: E poi mamma, Sentite, s'io non tornassi— Voi dovrete fare da madre a Santa, Ch'io le avea giurato di condurla all' altare.

TURIDDU: (*Calling.*) My mother! (*Enter Lucia.*) Mother! the wine-cup too freely passes! Exciting, crazing! I have drunk too many cups! —I must leave you, good mother! But first let me ask for a kindly blessing, As on that day when I became a soldier. And, mother, hear me—and heed it: If I return not, You must be a kindly mother to my Santa! Santa, whom I promised I would lead to the altar! —If I return—

LUCIA: Perchè parli cosi, figliolo mio?

LUCIA: Why say you this to me? What is it? tell me!

TURIDDU: (*Con disinvoltura.*) Oh! nulla, è il vino che m'ha suggerito! M'ha suggerito il vino— Perme pregate Iddio,

TURIDDU: Ha—nothing! It is wine—that I have drunk so freely. —For me oh! pray to heaven, That I may be forgiven!

Un bacio mamma! un altro bacio
Addio!
(*Fugge disperatamente.*)

LUCIA: Turiddu! che vuoi dire!
(*Va in fondo alla scena a disperatamente chiama.*)
Turiddu! Turiddu! ah!
(*Entra Santuzza.*)
Santuzza.

SANTUZZA: Oh! madre mia!
(*Le getta le braccia al colla. La scena si popolo. L'agitazione si scorge sul volto di tutti. Che scambievolmente s'interrogano con terrore. Si ode un mormorio confuse da lontano. Una donna sola,*

One kiss, one kiss, my mother!
And yet—and yet another!
Farewell!
(*Rushes off, desperately.*)

LUCIA: Turiddu! Ah!
(*Retires to back of stage, crying.*)
(*Enter, Santuzza.*)
Santuzza!

SANTUZZA: Ah! good mother!
(*Throws her arms around Lucia's neck.*)
(*People crowd upon the stage.*)
(*Excitement and agitation.*)
(*Enter a woman in the distance crying, "Neighbor Turiddu is

*assai lontano, gridando.*)
Hanno ammazzato compare Turiddu!
(*Si sentono delle voci confuse piu vicine. Alcune donne entrano atterite correndo, ed una di esse grida disperatamente.*)
Hanno ammazzato compare Turiddu!
(*Tutti si precipitano sulla scena.*)

SANTUZZA, LUCIA E CORO:
(*Gridando.*) Ah!
(*Santuzza cade priva di sensi, Lucia sviene ed è sorrettidalle donne del Coro. Tutti restano atterriti.*)

*CALA RAPIDAMENTE LA TELA.*

murdered.''*)
(*Several women hastily enter, terrified. One of them shrieks—*)
''Neighbor Turiddu is murdered.''
(*All rush upon the stage.*)

ALL: Ah!
(*Santuzza falls; swooning. Lucia faints, and is supported by some of the women.*)

THE CURTAIN FALLS RAPIDLY.

# L'Amico Fritz (1891)

## Friend Fritz

MUSIC BY PIETRO MASCAGNI ■ LIBRETTO BY P. SUARDON

L'Amico Fritz, a three-act lyric comedy, is set to a libretto by P. Suardon (whose real name was Nicola Daspuro) based on L'Ami Fritz by Emile Erckmann and Alexandre Chatrian. The opera premiered at the Teatro Costanzi in Rome on October 31, 1891. Fritz, a middle-aged, well-to-do Alsatian landowner, doesn't understand why people like to marry. He wagers one of his vineyards with David, the Rabbi, that he will never give up the life of a bachelor that he enjoys with his friends, Federico and Hanezo. At Fritz' birthday party, he sees Suzel, the daughter of one of his tenants, and asks her to sit next to him. David tells her that she will soon be the most beautiful bride in Alsace. Fritz, on vacation in the country, helps Suzel pick cherries in an orchard. David realizes that Suzel is in love with Fritz, and he tells Fritz that she is about to marry a country boy. Fritz is very upset to hear this as he is in love with her, and he leaves without saying good-bye in order to get over his unwelcome feelings. She is upset and mystified by his actions. Fritz cannot forget Suzel; David enters and announces the arrival of Suzel's father, who asks for Fritz' consent to her marriage as mentioned earlier. Fritz is jealous and opposes the match. When he finds out from Suzel that she does not want this marriage, he at last tells her that he loves her. David wins the bet and gives the vineyard to Suzel.

---

## ■ ATTO I

### SCENA I

*Sala da pranzo in case de Fritz Kobus.*

*Fritz e David.*

**FRITZ:** Ma questa è una pazzia! vuoi maritare
Tutti e per colmo di sventura io debbo
Sborsar la dote! . . .

**DAVID:** Son ragazzi e si amano . . .

**FRITZ:** Ci pensin loro . . . ho in odio il matrimonio,
Non so che sia l'amore . . . e chi sospira
E piange e si dispera per le donne,
Rider mi fa. Ma chi del mio danaro
Resta garante?

**DAVID:** Io firmerò per loro . . .

**FRITZ:** (*sorridendo*). Bravo! di te posso fidarmi. Scrivi!

**DAVID:** Grazie! grazie!

**FRITZ:** (*dettando*). "M'impegno io sottoscritto . . ."

### SCENA II

*Hanezò, Caterina, Federico e i precedenti.*

**HANEZÒ:** Evviva Fritz!

## ■ ACT I

### SCENE I

*Scene: Fritz Kobus' dining parlor.*

*Fritz and David.*

**FRITZ:** But this is merely nonsense,
You'd have them all be wedded.
And to crown all this misery,
It is I who must furnish the dowry.

**DAVID:** They love—and loving—they—

**FRITZ:** At least they think so.
The very thought of marriage disgusts me.
I look upon this love as naught by folly.
This sighing for the bright eyes of some young woman
Seems so absurd—
Who'll guarantee that I won't lose my money?

**DAVID:** I! Will you take my word for it?

**FRITZ:** Bravo! Of course that's quite sufficient.
Write then—

**DAVID:** Thanks! thanks!—

**FRITZ:** "I, the undersigned—"

### SCENE II

*Hanezo, Caterina, Federico and the preceding.*

**HANEZO:** Hurrah! for Fritz.

**FEDERICO:** Evviva!

**HANEZÒ:** (*a Fritz*) Per la tua festa i nostri voti accogli.

**DAVID:** Deh! tacete. Bisogna che io gli scriva . . .

**FRITZ:** Debbo sbrigare uno dei tanti imbrogli
Del rabbino . . .

**FEDERICO:** Ha qualcun da maritare?

**HANEZÒ:** Sempre! . . .

**DAVID:** Scrivo: "M'impegno io sottoscritto,
Di rendere al signor Fritz Kobus mille
Trecento lire al sei per cento, quando . . ."

**FRITZ:** (*interrompendo*). Il detto signor Fritz compiuti avrà
Due secoli d'età!

**HANEZÒ E FEDERICO:** (*ridendo*). Ah! ah!

**DAVID:** Che dici?

**HANEZÒ:** Bella davver!

**DAVID:** (*con dolore*). È inutile; tu vuoi
Farti giuoco di me.

**FRITZ:** Su via, scherzavo.
Ecco il danaro.

**DAVID:** O mio diletto Fritz,
Come potrò ricompensarti?

**FRITZ:** Voglimi
Sempre bene!

**CATERINA:** (*entrando colla zuppiera*). Signori. È pronto.

**FRITZ:** Andiamo
A tavola! Ed ancor Beppe non venne?

**FEDERICO:** Hurrah! boys.

**HANEZO:** (*to Fritz*). Now, on your birthday, we offer you our greeting.

**DAVID:** Hold your tongue lad! Just let me put my name here.

**FRITZ:** I must take care of some of the troubles that beset the old Rabbi.

**FEDERICO:** Any one else here to marry?

**HANEZO:** Certainly!

**DAVID:** Now, then—
"I, the undersigned, do covenant with Master Fritz Kobus
To pay thirteen hundred ducats, at six per cent., when—"

**FRITZ:** The aforesaid Fritz shall have attained—two hundred years of age!

**FEDERICO AND HANEZO:** Ha! ha!

**DAVID:** What's that, now?

**HANEZO:** Faith that is good!

**DAVID:** It is nonsense! You are playing a trick on me.

**FRITZ:** Your pardon; I was joking. Here, take the money.

**DAVID:** Oh! my good fellow, Fritz, How can I ever thank you enough?

**FRITZ:** Think of me always kindly. (*Enter Caterina.*)

**CATERINA:** The dinner is served!

**FRITZ:** Come, then!—to table!

FEDERICO: (*a David che si dispone ad uscire*) E tu che fai?

DAVID: Verrò per far un brindisi! (*Si mettono a tavola, meno David.—Caterina esce.*)

FRITZ: (*servendo la zuppa agli amici*). Lascialo! In palpiti saran gli sposi . . .
Se tarda, possono d'ansia morir.

FEDERICO: Vada! s'affretti!

HANEZÒ: Corra!

DAVID: Noiosi! . . .
D'amor dovrete voi pur languir! (*esce dalla terrazza.*)

FRITZ: (*chiamando David a traverso la finestra*). Ohè, David! David! oggi, perchè
Anche una sposa non hai per me?

DAVID: (*sulla terrazza*). O Fritz, rammentalo! tu pur sarai
Marito un giorno!

FRITZ: Ma tu non sai
La mia divisa? Amico a tutti e sempre . . .
Marito . . . no!

DAVID: Vedremo! (*si allontana.*)

FRITZ: Oh! che bel matto!

HANEZÒ: (*alzando il bicchiere*). Viver tu possa sempre giocondo!

FEDERICO: (*come sopra*). Salute ai celibi di tutto il mondo!

CATERINA: (*rientrando, a Fritz*). Signore, è giunta Suzel, la figliuola
Del fattor . . . vi vorrebbe salutare . . .
Ha dei fiori per voi . . .

FRITZ: Fatela entrare. (*Caterina fa entrare Suzel e poi esce.*)

## SCENA III

*Suzel e i precedenti, poi David.*

SUZEL: Son pochi fiori, povere viole,
Son l'alito d'aprile
Dal profumo gentile;
Ed è per voi che la ho rapite al sole
. . .
Se avessero parole,
Le udreste mormorar:
"Noi siamo figlie timide e pudiche
Di primavera,
Siamo le vostre amiche;

---

HANEZO: But where can Beppe be lingering?

FEDERICO: (*to David, who is going*). Where are you going?

DAVID: I'll soon be back to drain a glass. (*Exit; the rest seat themselves at the table.*)

FRITZ: (*helping the soup*). Let him go!
The lovers' hearts are beating with joy.
Hearts are ticklish things to play with,
Timid and coy.

FEDERICO: Off, then! Don't tarry!

HANEZO: Hurry!—

DAVID: You rascal!
Or may your heart be made of love the toy
(*Exit by terrace.*)

FRITZ: (*seeing David through the window*). Hey! David! David! have you, I say,
Such a thing as a wife for me? Tell me, I pray!

DAVID: (*through the window*). Oh! Fritz, I tell you true,
There will be a little wife for you.

FRITZ: The lady's name I pray you tell me.
You know I always was your friend,
But—marriage!—No!

DAVID: We shall see! (*Exit.*)

FRITZ: (*reflecting*). Sharp as a needle!

HANEZO: (*raising his goblet*). Here's to good fellows, wherever they be!

FEDERICO: (*same business*). Here's to all bachelors, merry and free! (*Enter Caterina.*)

CATERINA: (*to Fritz*). Good master, the steward's daughter, Suzel, waits outside.
She comes to bid you welcome, and brings some flowers.

FRITZ: Good! She is welcome! (*Enter Suzel, with a bunch of violets in her hand. She advances with downcast looks.*)

## SCENE III

*Suzel and the preceding, then David.*

SUZEL: Sweet, purple violets, emblems of spring's beauty,
Perfumed by April's showers,
Upspringing in sweet bowers,
For you, with humble duty,
I bring my ravished booty.
For though they are but mute, he
That loves will hear their sighs:
"Daughters of Spain, we hide our faces,
Striving to shun Phœbus' burning

---

Morremo questa sera,
Ma morremo felici
Di dire a voi, che amate gl'infelici:
Il ciel vi possa dar
Tutto quel bene che si può sperar."
Ed il mio cor aggiunge una parola
Modesta, ma sincera:
Eterna primavera
La vostra vita sia, ch'altri consola
. . .
Deh, vogliate gradir
Quanto vi posso offrir!
(*Suzel, con gli occhi bassi, offre il mazzolino a Fritz.*)

FRITZ: (*sorridendo*). Tu sei molto gentil; dei fiori tuoi
L'olezzo mite giunge caro a me.
Grato ti sono . . . Orsù, vieni fra noi,
Al fianco mio . . .
(*Suzel esita.*) Ti vergogni? E di che?

SUZEL: (*timidamente*). Oh . . . no . . .

FRITZ: Bambina! (*Suzel siede.*)

HANEZÒ: (*sottovoce*). Com'è carina!

FEDERICO: (*c. s.*). Quanto candor!

HANEZÒ: (*c. s.*). Dei campi è un fior!

FRITZ: E babbo come va, povero vecchio?

SUZEL: Babbo sta bene; egli, però, vi aspetta.

FRITZ: Certo, verrò Di' . . . come vanno i campi?

SUZEL: Tutto si allieta: il cielo è uno splendore,
L'aria è dolce, sottile, e il prato è in fiore.

FRITZ: Bevi, Suzel.—Verrò fra pochi di.—
Bevi! Non star così!

DAVID: (*entrando*). Vi saluto!

FEDERICO: Sei qui, vecchio rabbino!

HANEZÒ: Giungi in buon punto . . .

FRITZ: Ecco un bicchier di vino! (*David siede e beve.*)

FEDERICO: Un brindisi chi fa?

DAVID: (*a Suzel*). Tu pur, bimba sei qua?
(Come la bricconcella
S'è fatta grande e bella!)
(*Dalla terrazza, arriva un dolce suono di violino.*)

HANEZÒ: Chi mai sarà?

FRITZ: Lo zingaro!

DAVID: Ah! questi è Beppe!

---

embraces.
Each flower fades in blooming,
In death the air perfuming.
We comfort those who sorrow,
From hope our sweets we borrow.
May joy crown this fair morrow."
Then these gifts I offer,
Love's own flowers I proffer.
Enjoy love before he flies.
Take, then, these flowers,
Types of sweet, happy hours.
(*She offers the violets to Fritz.*)

FRITZ: (*smiling as he smells them*). How good and kind you are,
Your flowers shed fragrance on my inmost heart.
Thanks, lovely maid.—Nay, do not now depart,
Come, sit beside me. (*She wavers.*)
What affrights you? Is it I?

SUZEL: Oh! no.

FRITZ: Come nearer.

HANEZO: (*in a whisper*). He might say "dearer."

FEDERICO: (*aside*). How sweet and fair.

HANEZO: (*aside*). A lily rare.

FRITZ: Tell me, my child, how is it with your father?

SUZEL: Well, honored sir, and longing much to see you.

FRITZ: Soon shall I come. Are all the meadows blooming?

SUZEL: The fields are gemmed with roses, redly blowing,
The air is full of fragrance, the skies with sunshine, glowing,
All Nature rejoices with all her myriad voices.

FRITZ: Some wine, Suzel! Be sure I'll not delay.
Drink, then—you'll not say nay? (*Enter David.*)

DAVID: Sir, I greet you!

FEDERICO: What! back again so soon?

HANEZO: Glad to meet you!

FRITZ: Drink, your person is a boon. (*David sits and drinks.*)

FRITZ: Who knows a lively song?

DAVID: (*noticing Suzel*). I've not seen you for long.
How these young ones do spring up,
And what sad thoughts they bring up! (*A violin is heard outside.*)

HANEZO: What's that?

FRITZ: The gypsy lad.

FEDERICO: Udite il violino!

FRITZ: (*guardando Suzel*).
Perchè piangi, perchè?

SUZEL: (*timidamente*). Mi commove la musica . . .
Scusatemi.

FRITZ: (*sottovoce*). Di che? . . .
Se commove anche me?

HANEZÒ: (*ascoltando la musica*). Oh, quanto è bella!

FEDERICO: Silenzio! . . . taci.

FRITZ: Che dolci note!

DAVID: Paiono baci!
(*La musica cessa.*)
(*Tutti si alzano. Fritz corre verso la terrazza e s'incontra con Beppe.*)

### SCENA IV

*Beppe e i precedenti.*

BEPPE: Salute, amico Fritz!

FRITZ: (*abbracciandolo*). Ah!
n'ero certo
Che saresti venuto . . .

BEPPE: Amico, avrei sofferto
Di non farti per oggi il mio saluto
. . .

FRITZ: Beppe, siediti qua . . .
So quel che mi vuoi dir . . .
Non voglio udir . . .

DAVID: Allor, canta per noi!
(*Beppe imposta il violino all'uso zingaresco, e, dati alcuni accordi, canta.*)

BEPPE: Laceri, miseri tanti bambini
Languiano qua:
Senza la mamma quei poverini
Facean pietà.
Era uno strazio! Quando amoroso,
Per essi stringersi, un cor sentì,
Fu il nostro amico quel generoso
Che li nutrì.

FRITZ: (*con dispetto*). La vuoi finir?

DAVID, HANEZÒ E FEDERICO:
Oh, canta, seguita, lascialo dir!

BEPPE: Preso dal turbine d'una bufera
Persi il cammino;
Ansante, gelido, sfinito, a sera,
Caddi supino.
Scendea la morte! Quando, pietoso,
Un braccio valido mi sollevò:
Fu il nostro amico quel generoso
Che mi salvò!

---

HANEZO: Ah! Beppe? surely. Eh!
can't he play divinely?

FRITZ: (*looking at Suzel*). You are
crying. And why?

SUZEL: (*timidly*). The music is so
sad—forgive me, sir.

FRITZ: (*aside*). And I? Those notes
stir my feelings.

HANEZO: (*listening to the music*). Oh! how delightful. Silver—
hark!
What lovely strains!

DAVID: Like song of lark.

### SCENE IV

*Beppe and the preceding.*

BEPPE: Ah! Fritz. How do you do?

FRITZ: Welcome, dear friend! I am
glad to see you.

BEPPE: Dear fellow, on this day,
above all others, you might expect
me.

FRITZ: Beppe, I know you well!
Come, join our party.

DAVID: Come, sing a song!
(*Beppe plays his fiddle like a gypsy and sings.*)

BEPPE: Sad and forlorn,
Starving, tattered and torn,
We crouched in despair—
For our dear mother we mourn.
Full of care,
Oh! it was piteous.
But help came quickly.
A brave defender came to aid
Our dearest friend—a hero, strictly,
Brought me back hope, all fear allayed.

FRITZ: Be silent, pray!

HANEZO: Sing on!

DAVID: Make an end!

CHORUS: Go on! Go on!

BEPPE: In the fierce blasts of the
wild tempest raging
Forth I was hurled,
Chilled to the bone, strange misfortune presaging.
Out of the world,
Death was approaching,
When a defender
Came to the rescue,
And all the shadows that now were
encroaching
Far away whirled.

---

DAVID, HANEZÒ E FEDERICO:
Viva lo zingaro! Evviva! Bravo!

FRITZ: (*celiando*). D'esser sì
grande io non pensavo!

CATERINA: (*rientrando ed appressandosi a Suzel*).
Suzel, fermo alla porta è il barocci-
no . . .

SUZEL: (*alzandosi rapidamente*).
Sì, chè è tardi!

FRITZ: Ci vuoi lasciar di già?

SUZEL: Il babbo attende . . .

FRITZ: Va, cara piccina . . .
Presto verrò. Salutalo per me.

SUZEL: Grazie, vi servirò.

FRITZ: Ringrazio te
Dei vaghissimi fior . . .
(*Suzel fa un inchino ed esce.*)

HANEZÒ: Come s'inchina!

BEPPE: Ha nello sguardo amor . . .

FEDERICO: Quanto è gentil!

DAVID: E a me susurra il core:
Bisogna farne subito
La più vaga sposina
Di tutta Alsazia!

FRITZ: Ma Suzel è bambina.

DAVID: Presto, vel giuro, la mariterò.

FRITZ: Che pazzo!

HANEZÒ: Oh, tu vaneggi . . .

DAVID: Io so quel che mi fo!

FRITZ: Va alla malora
Tu, le tue femmine,
E chi le adora!

HANEZÒ E FEDERICO: Rabbin,
questa è per te!

DAVID: (*levandosi, irritatissimo*). Per voi, ghiottoni inutili,
La vita è nel goder:
Passar i giorni a tavola,
Ecco il più gran piacer
Ma chi nel petto ha un'anima,
Chi crede in Dio, che disse:
"Getta nel fuoco l'albero
Che senza frutti visse,"
Chi preferisce al vivere
Randagio e senza amor,
Una famiglia, un placido
Nido che allieti il cor,
Vi deve disprezzar,
Deve chiamarvi piante da bruciar!

BEPPE: Il suo sermone è splendido!

FEDERICO: Ma predica al deserto
. . .

FRITZ: Oh! grida, strilla, arrabbiati!

DAVID: (*a Fritz*). Eppure . . . io ne
son certo
Noi presto accompagnar
Ti dovremo all' altar.

---

DAVID: Long live the Zingara!

CHORUS: Bravo! Bravo!

FRITZ: I never thought you were so
clever.

CATERINA: Suzel, the farmer's
cart is near by.

SUZEL: Ah! yes, it is late.

FRITZ: And must you go?

SUZEL: Yes, my father calls me.

FRITZ: Go, pretty maid, then
I will follow. Remember me to
papa.

SUZEL: Thank you; I'll not forget.

FRITZ: Many thanks for the pretty
flowers.

HANEZO: What a sweet bow!

BEPPE: "Love in her eyes sits playing."

FEDERICO: "And wanting in her
breath."

DAVID: My heart whispers to me
that our little lass
Will be soon the fairest bride in all
Alsace.

FRITZ: But Suzel is a child.

DAVID: I'll take my oath she soon
will find a mate.

FRITZ: Don't be an ass!

HANEZO: What cursed nonsense!

DAVID: Then my job will come in.

FRITZ: Oh! to the devil
You and your women, all are
naught but evil.

FEDERICO AND HANEZO: (*to
David*). You want her for yourself!

DAVID: You lazy, loafing loiterers
on naught but pleasure think,
You spend your days in idleness,
your nights in brawl and drink.
But who puts his trust in God, and
never with evil clashes,
Knows that the barren, withered
tree is good for naught but ashes.
But who lives a virtuous life,
And lets the girls alone,
Will still be free from care or strife
Nor dread misfortune's frown.
So I might such as you despise,
And deem you very fit
To follow the "lust of your eyes"
Unto the yawning pit.

BEPPE: That's a splendid sermon.

FEDERICO: He preaches to the
stones.

FRITZ: Oh! bellow. Hollo! Tear
your clothes!

DAVID: For all that, I am certain we
shall soon go with her to the altar.

**FRITZ:** All' altare?

**DAVID:** Ne debiti?
Lo affermo e ci scommetto!

**BEPPE:** Oh, che bel matto!

**HANEZÒ:** Stolido!

**FRITZ:** La tua scommessa accetto:
Giuoco la vigna mia di Clairefontaine!

**DAVID:** Ad ufo beverò! Vada!

**FRITZ:** Sta ben!

**HANEZÒ:** Son gli orfanelli . . .

**BEPPE:** (*a Fritz*). Portanò
A te, benefattor,
Il saluto del cor!
(*Beppe, Federico e Hanezò corrono ala terrazza.*)

**HANEZÒ:** Oh, quanta gente!

**BEPPE:** Vengona qua!

**FEDERICO:** Oh, come marciano!

**BEPPE:** Guardali là!

**HANEZÒ:** (*a Beppe*). Son tuoi discepoli?

**BEPPE:** Amico, sì!

**HANEZÒ:** La folla applaude!

**FEDERICO:** Sono già qui!

**BEPPE:** (*che batte il tempo con le mani*). Oh vieni, Fritz, vieni a veder!

**FEDERICO:** È uno spettacolo che fa piacer!

**FRITZ:** (*battendo sulla spalla di David*). I figli miei saranno quelli ognor!
(*poi, agli altri*)
Andiamo, tutti, i bimbi a salutar!
(*Raggiunge gli amici sulla terrazza.*)

**DAVID:** Eppure, o stolti, vi vedrò cascar!

**CORO:** (*di fuori*). Salute a Fritz!
Viva il benefattor!
(*Tutti agitano i cappelli, salutando la folla.*)

[*Fine Del Primo Atto.*]

# ▪ ATTO II

## *SCENA I*

*Cortile nella fattoria di Mèsanges.*

*Suzel, Coro interno.*

**SUZEL:** Oh! le belle ciliege! Stamattina,
Appena il signor Fritz sarà disceso,
Vo' che la assaggi . . . sono già mature.

**CORO:** (*da lontano*). Chi l'amor
suo non seppe conservar
Perde il tempo a sperar:
L'amore che lontano se ne va

---

**FRITZ:** To the altar?

**DAVID:** Aye, to the altar. Will you wager on it?

**BEPPE:** Oh! what a madman!

**HANEZO:** Yes, what an ass!

**FRITZ:** I'll take your bet. My vineyard at Clairfontaine I stake.

**DAVID:** Done! Here's my hand.
Your bet I take.
(*Trumpets sound afar off.*)

**HANEZO:** Here come the children!

**BEPPE:** The orphans come to greet
Their lord with voices sweet.
(*Beppe, Federico and Hanezo go to the window.*)

**HAENZO:** Oh! what a lot!

**BEPPE:** They are coming hither!

**FEDERICO:** Don't they march bravely!

**BEPPE:** Only look at them!

**HANEZO:** (*to Beppe*). Are they your pupils, then?

**BEPPE:** You've hit the mark!

**HANEZO:** Hear the applause!

**FEDERICO:** Yes, here they come!

**BEPPE:** (*beating time*). Oh! come here, Fritz,
Just come and see!

**FEDERICO:** Oh! ain't it jolly! It just suits me.

**FRITZ:** (*slapping David's shoulder*). I'll adopt the whole lot.
(*To the others.*)
Come, salute my children, dear!
(*Goes to window.*)

**DAVID:** You are an idiot!

**CHORUS:** Hurrah! for Fritz. Hurrah! Hurrah!

[*Curtain.*]

# ▪ ACT II

## *SCENE I*

*Scene: Courtyard of the farm.*

*Suzel and chorus behind the scenes.*

**SUZEL:** Oh! what lovely cherries!
I'll pluck some for Master Fritz. He will enjoy them,
They're so nice and ripe.

**CHORUS:** (*outside*) Ah! (*Chorus approaches, but is not seen.*)
(*Close at hand.*)
Who knows not how true love to

---

Mai più non tornerà.

**SUZEL:** I contadini sono andati all'opre,
Era tempo: oggi devono tagliare
L'orzo maturo nella prateria.

## *SCENA II*

*Suzel, poi Fritz.*

**SUZEL:** Il padrone tra poco sarà desto,
Voglio per lui comporre un mazzolino.
(*Cogliendo fiori.*)
—Bel cavalier, che vai per la foresta . . .
—Che volete da me, cara figliuola?
—Bel cavaliere dalla faccia mesta . . .
—Cogliete fiori, allegra boscaiuola!
—Bel cavaliere, ti darò una rosa . . .
—Grazie, piccina, rose non ne vo'!
. . .
—Bel cavalier, sarà per la tua sposa . . .
—Piccina, grazie! la sposa non l'ho!
(*Fritz si mostra in cima alla scala, ascoltando.*)

**FRITZ:** Suzel, buon dì. D'un gaio rosignuolo
La voce mi svegliò.

**SUZEL:** Che dite mai?

**FRITZ:** Mi piace come canti . . .

**SUZEL:** Oh, signor Fritz . . .
Canto così come mi vien dal core.

**FRITZ:** (*scende la scala*). Quei fiori son per me?

**SUZEL:** Per voi li ho côlti
Ed oltre i fiori ho pronta una sorpresa . . .

**FRITZ:** Una primizia certo . . .

**SUZEL:** Le ciliege.

**FRITZ:** Ah! le ciliege! e son di già mature?

**SUZEL:** Han della porpora vivo il colore,
Son dolci e tenere . . .

**FRITZ:** (*da sè guardandola dolcemente*). Di Maggio è simile a un vago fiore
Fragrante e roseo . . .

**SUZEL:** Son pronta a coglierne un mazzettino,
Debbo gettarvele?

**FRITZ:** Gettale subito,
bell'augellino,
Le saprò prendere . . .
(*Suzel esce dalla porta dell'orto,*

---

keep
Will waste his time in wooing.
The love that nods and falls asleep
Will work its own undoing.

**SUZEL:** Ah! the peasants are going to their labor.
The crops are ready for the sickle.

**CHORUS:** (*afar off*). The love that nods and falls asleep
Will work its own undoing.

## *SCENE II*

*Suzel, then Fritz.*

**SUZEL:** The master will soon be awaking. I must cull him a bunch of flowers. (*Sings.*)
"Brave knight, who through the wood
Now goes so gaily riding!"
"What would you with me, prettiest of maidens?"
Brave sir knight, I see
That something sore does grieve you."
"Go cull your flowers, dear girl,
For surely I must leave you."
"Brave cavalier, take then these rosebuds, blushing."
"Thanks, pretty maid, the flowers I should be crushing."
"Fair cavalier, your bride they'll suit right well."
"Sweetest of girls, no bride have I. Farewell!" (*Enter Fritz.*)

**FRITZ:** Good day Suzel, I thought I heard a nightingale.

**SUZEL:** And found it was a raven.

**FRITZ:** You sing like any lark.

**SUZEL:** Good Master Fritz, I sing as my heart prompts me.

**FRITZ:** (*pointing to flowers*). Are those for me?

**SUZEL:** For you I've culled them, and a sweet surprise awaits you.

**FRITZ:** The first sheaf of the harvest?

**SUZEL:** No, these sweet cherries.

**FRITZ:** Cherries! And are they ripe so early?

**SUZEL:** See how their purple cheeks are softly blushing.
See, from their rosy lips sweetness is gushing.

**FRITZ:** (*gazing at her*). Fragrance of spring all around your breathing.

**SUZEL:** (*passing through the gate and picking cherries*). Catch them in bunches. See, them I am wreathing.

**FRITZ:** Them throw here quickly,
you darling, you beauty,
I'm here to catch them—a most pleasant duty.

*appare in cima alla scala, dall'altra parte del muro, coglie le ciliege e le getta a Fritz.)*
Son fresche e morbide, di brina ancora
Son tutte roride . . .
Ma . . . è da quell'albero, che, sull'aurora,
Pispiglia il passero?

**SUZEL:** Sì, da quell'albero . . .

**FRITZ:** Ciò ch'egli dice
Sai tu comprendere?

**SUZEL:** Io lo so intendere . . . ch'egli è felice
Nel canto mormora:
Sui rami floridi ha i suoi piccini . . .
Lieti lo aspettano;
Agili scherzano dei bianco-spini,
Tra i fiori candidi.

**FRITZ:** Come ne interpreti bene il linguaggio!

**SUZEL:** Sembra che parlino . . .
Sembra salutino coi canti il raggio
Del dì che nasce! . . .

**FRITZ:** (*solo, al proscenio*). Tutto tace . . .
Eppur tutto al cor mi parla . . .
Questa pace
Fuor di qui, dove trovarla?
Tu sei bella,
O stagion primaverile!
Rinnovella
Fiori e amori il dolce aprile!

**SUZEL:** (*rientrando dalla porta dell'orto, col grembialino pieno di ciliege*). Qual incanto
Nel risveglio d'ogni fiore!
Riso e pianto,
Tutto è palpito d'amore!
Tutto il prato
D'un tappeto s'è smaltato . . .
Al Signore
S'alza l'inno di ogni core!

Fresh as the dew they are, new fallen daily.
Is this the tree where the birds sang so gaily?

**SUZEL:** This is the tree.

**FRITZ:** Of what were they singing? Teach me the song that the birds' throats were singing.

**SUZEL:** I know the singing well. Birds gaily caroling high on the tree Sing of the pleasures of life, gay and free.
No care have they, nor thought of the morrow,
Leaving to human souls trouble and sorrow.

**FRITZ:** Oh! let me know what their carol is telling.

**SUZEL:** Oh! I can hear them within their snug dwelling.

**FRITZ:** What do they say? Come, tell me, I pray.

**SUZEL:** They sing of the glory of sun-risen day.
(*Exeunt.*)

**FRITZ:** (*alone*). All is silent. Yet to my heart a message,
Comes from the silence, bringing Love's sweet presage.
Oh! lovely spring, season of hope and joy,
Fair April's promise all my thoughts employ.
(*Enter Suzel.*)

**SUZEL:** (*at the gate with her apron full of cherries*). What bliss and sadness from these flowers arise,
All Nature seems to yield to Love's surprise.
The meadows praise the God with sweet incense of flowers,
The birds chant hymns excelling songs of ours.

## SCENA III

*David, Beppe, Hanezò, Federico e. i. precedenti.*

(*Si ode il rumore di un baroccino che arriva.*)

**FRITZ:** Oh! chi è che giunge? Ragazza, guarda!
Odo i sonagli . . .

**SUZEL:** (*guardando a sinistra*). È un baroccino . . .
I vostri amici! Beppe, il Rabbino . . .

**FRITZ:** (*che è corso a vedere*). E Federico! Visto il bel cielo,
Vengono qui.

**SUZEL:** Scesi son già.

## SCENE III

*David, Beppe, Hanezo, Federico and the preceding.*

(*Bells are heard, a whip cracks, and wheels rumble.*)

**FRITZ:** Ah! who comes here?
Oh! Suzel, listen!
I hear bells clanging.

**SUZEL:** (*looking off*). A carriage comes,
And all your friends,
Beppe, the Rabbi—

**FRITZ:** (*looking*). And Federico!
The day is fine,
And now they come.

**FRITZ:** Incontro andiamo!
(*Escono. Dopo popo rientrano, accompagnati da David, Beppe, Hanezò e Federico.*)

**SUZEL:** Bene arrivati!

**FRITZ:** Il sol vi attrasse? . . .

**BEPPE:** Tu ci hai scordata:
Ti ripeschiamo!

**DAVID:** (*guardando Fritz meravigliato*) Sei fresco e bello.

**FRITZ:** Sì, sto benone . . . Merito a lei . . .
(*Addita Suzel.*)

**DAVID:** Brava, davver!
(*Suzel entra nella fattoria.*)

**FRITZ:** Nelle mie terre
Facciamo un giro?

**BEPPE, HANEZÒ E FEDERICO:** Sì! sì!

**FRITZ:** (*a David*). Non sei
Tu pur dei nostri?

**DAVID:** Io no; darei
Disturbo e noia; mi sento stanco . . .

**BEPPE, HANEZÒ E FEDERICO:** Andiamo noi!

**DAVID:** Vi attenderò . . .

**FRITZ:** Salute a David . . . Andiam, andiamo! . . .

**DAVID:** Sin che torniate riposerò!
(*Tutti escono, meno David.*)
(*David siede.*)
Vediamo un po'! L'amico
In volto è colorito e d'umor gaio

Non ci fa saper nulla
E, sorridendo, elogia la fanciulla . . .

Ch'egli sia già rimasto al paretaio?
Quando Suzel vedrò, tutto conoscerò.

## SCENA IV

*David e Suzel.*

**SUZEL:** (*con una brocca dirigendosi al pozzo*). Ah! siete ancora qui?

**DAVID:** Sì, mi riposo.

**SUZEL:** Io l'acqua attingerò.

**DAVID:** Dammene un sorso.

**SUZEL:** Vo a prendere un bicchier . . .

**DAVID:** Oh! non importa . . .
La broca basterà . . .

**SUZEL:** Come volete . . .

**DAVID:** (*da sè*) La ragazza è carina . . .

**SUZEL:** (*gli proge da bere*). A voi! prendete!

**SUZEL:** Yes, they are here!
Let's haste to greet them!

**SUZEL:** (*to David, helping him off with his coat and seating him*). You are welcome!

**FRITZ:** You bring the sunshine with you!

**BEPPE:** We thought we were forgotten and came to put you in mind.

**DAVID:** I hope you're well?

**FRITZ:** Yes, well and happy. (*Pointing to Suzel.*) Thanks to her.

**DAVID:** God bless her for it.

**SUZEL:** (*going into the house*). Will you not come and look around you?

**CHORUS:** Of course we will.

**FRITZ:** (*to David*). Will not you come, too?

**DAVID:** I? No! I don't wish to offend you, but I am tired.

**CHORUS:** Come, then, let's go!

**DAVID:** I'll see you later.

**FRITZ:** Good-bye, then. Come on! Come on!

**DAVID:** I'll take a snooze while you are gone.
(*Takes snuff.*)
Our good friend is very jolly. His face is radiant.
Ah! ha! I smell a rat. He was eloquent in praise of that young girl.
When I see Suzel alone I'll find out what's in the wind.

## SCENE IV

*David and Suzel.*

**SUZEL:** Ah! you are here still?

**DAVID:** Yes, at my ease.

**SUZEL:** Shall I bring you some water?

**DAVID:** Yes, just a drop.

**SUZEL:** I'll bring a goblet.

**DAVID:** Don't trouble, give me the pitcher.

**SUZEL:** As you please.

**DAVID:** (*aside*). She's as pretty as a peach.

**SUZEL:** Here is the water.

DAVID: (*dopo aver bevuto*). È purissima e fresca...

SUZEL: (*c. s.*). Eccone ancora!

DAVID: Per ora no... fammi riprender fiato...
Ragazza, tu non sai ciò che pensavo?

SUZEL: In verità... signor...

DAVID: Presso la fonte,
Porgendomi da ber, tu mi sembravi
Rebecca e mi credetti Eleazaro.

SUZEL: Vi ridete di me?

DAVID: Non rido, no.

SUZEL: Ma che volete dir?

DAVID: Non sai la Bibbia?

SUZEL: Sì; la leggo ogni sera al padre mio.

DAVID: Ridimmi un po' la storia de Rebecca!

SUZEL: (*impacciata*). Signor mio, non potrò...

DAVID: Che! ti vergogni?

SUZEL: Ho soggezione...

DAVID: Via! fatti coraggio!

SUZEL: (*dopo un po' d'esitazione*). "Faceasi vecchio
Abramo, ed il Signore
Lo aveva benedetto. Ei disse un giorno
Al suo più vecchio servo: "Parti, va
Nella natal mia terra ed una sposa
Scegli ad Isacco mio""

DAVID: "Che tra le figlie
Di Canahan, donna per lui non v'ha."

SUZEL: "Ed in Mesopotamia il vecchio servo
Fedele, se ne andò; ma, giunto ai possi
Nei pressi di Nachor..."

DAVID: Proprio così

SUZEL: "Signore—ei disse—fa che la donzella
A cui prima dirò: Progimi l'anfora
E che dirammi "Bevi" sia la sposa
D'Isacco."

DAVID: Brava!

SUZEL: E tempo non passò
Che comparve Rebecca...

DAVID: Amata figlia,
Di Bathuel, figlio a Nachor, bellissima!

SUZEL: E il vecchio servo disse:
"Oh! fa ch'io beva
Un sorso di quell'acqua, per favore!"
Ed essa a lui: "Ne bevi, o mio signore,"
E l'anfora piegò verso quel vecchio.

DAVID: (*after drinking*). Ah! that is refreshing.

SUZEL: Is that enough?

DAVID: Quite enough, thank you! Let me take breath.
Do you know what I was thinking?

SUZEL: (*hesitating*). Truly, good sir, I—

DAVID: I was thinking how like Rebecca you are,
And I like Eleazar.

SUZEL: (*quickly*). Ah! now you are laughing at me.

DAVID: Not I, indeed!

SUZEL: Then what do you mean?

DAVID: You read your Bible?

SUZEL: Yes, I read a chapter every day to my dear father.

DAVID: Then tell me the story of Rebecca at the well.

SUZEL: (*agitated*). Oh! no, indeed I cannot!

DAVID: What! Are you shy?

SUZEL: The tale is too suggestive.

DAVID: Take courage, lass!

SUZEL: (*bashfully at first, but gaining courage as she goes on, the first part almost speaking*).
"Now Abraham was stricken in years
"And God had blessed him above all men.
"And he said to his trusty and beloved servant Eleazar:
"'Go, seek the land where I was born and choose there
"'A wife for my son Isaac'"—

DAVID: "'For, verily, among the daughters of Canaan
"'I find none worthy.'"—

SUZEL: "And the old servant came to Mesopotamia,
"And when he had come to the well near the house of Nahor"—

DAVID: You tell it well, my daughter—

SUZEL: "'Oh! Lord,' cried he, 'grant that the maiden
"'I first shall ask: 'Give me to drink,' and who
"'Shall fill her pitcher for me, may be wife to Isaac!'"—

DAVID: Very good!—

SUZEL: "And so it befell, for Rebecca came from the house,"—

DAVID: "Rebecca, the daughter of Bethuel—Nahor's son—
"And she was fair to look upon."—

SUZEL: "Then spoke Eleazar: 'Give me to drink, I beseech thee,'
"And the damsel answered: 'Drink freely,' and to
"The aged stranger she offered the pitcher."

DAVID: E sposa fu Rebecca... Ed ora, o Suzel,
Se a te dicessi, che porgesti l'acqua:
"Sono un messo del cielo; il mio Signore,
Che ha dovizia di case e campi e armenti,
Non attende che te," che mi diresti?

SUZEL: Che dir potrei?... Non so... Giammai pensiero...

DAVID: (*fissandola negli occhi*). Giammai, davver?... E se come Eleazaro,
Ti dicessi: "Chi viene a noi dai campi?
Risponderesti tu come Rebecca
Nascondendoti il viso?

FRITZ: (*da fuori*) O Beppe, qua!

SUZEL: (*nascondendosi il viso*). Ahimè! Mio Dio!
(*Fugge nella fattoria.*)

DAVID: (*con un sorriso di soddisfazione*). La sposa sua sarà!

## SCENA V

*David e Fritz.*

FRITZ: Come va?

DAVID: Meglio assai... son riposato...
Ma... la campagna a te non viene a noia?

FRITZ: No; qui Suzel con garbo m'intrattiene...

DAVID: Suzel... di fatti, ha qui con me parlato...
Mi piace... troverà presto marito.

FRITZ: Marito a lei! Ti pare?... è una bambina!...

DAVID: Ho il giovinotto che ci vuol per lei...

FRITZ: (*scaldandosi*). Essa rifiuterà...

DAVID: Non ci pensare!

FRITZ: Dell'antica manìa non sei guarito?

DAVID: E mai ne guarirò. Parlo a suo padre
E le nozze, vedrai, si faran presto.

FRITZ: (*scattando*). Oh! no, non si faran perchè non voglio...
Ah! finalmente... tu mi vieni a noia.
Lasciami in pace!

DAVID: A un vecchio amico parli
In questo modo?... Ma non mi spaventi
Colle tue grida: non mi fai paura!
(*Fa l'atto d'andarsene.*)

FRITZ: David! David!

DAVID: (*ritornando*). Che c'è?

FRITZ: Vattene al diavolo!
(*David esce.*)

DAVID: And Isaac won Rebecca.
And now, Suzel, must I teach you,
you who have given me your pitcher, that I am a herald from on high?
Know that the owner of this house, these flocks and herds, would wed you, my daughter,
What will you answer?

SUZEL: I do not know. I never thought.

DAVID: (*looking fixedly at her*). Never? Come, trust me. Now if I should ask:
"What manner of man is he that comes" would you answer, like Rebecca: "Hide your face from your handmaid?"

FRITZ: (*outside*). Beppe, come here!

SUZEL: (*hiding her face in her apron*). Oh! heaven! (*Runs into the house.*)

DAVID: (*smiling*). She shall be his wife.

## SCENE V

*David and Fritz.*

FRITZ: How do you do?

DAVID: Much better since I've rested.
But, tell me, do you not find the country irksome?

FRITZ: No, Suzel's prattle amuses me.

DAVID: Suzel? Good! I've just been chatting with her.
She is charming, and I must find her a good husband.

FRITZ: A husband! For her? She's only a child!

DAVID: I know a young fellow who will suit her.

FRITZ: (*angry*). She'll not consent!

DAVID: Don't be so sure of that.

FRITZ: Always matchmaking! Why don't you drop it?

DAVID: It suits me. I've only to tell her father, and she'll be wedded in short order.

FRITZ: Not it! I will forbid the banns!
What am I saying? I do declare, I've lost my temper!
Leave me in peace!

DAVID: Why so rough with an old friend? But, never mind,
You can't frighten me.

FRITZ: David! David!

DAVID: Well? What?

FRITZ: Confound your impudence!
(*Exit David.*)

## SCENA VI

**FRITZ:** (*solo*). Uno strano turbamento
Improvviso ora m'assale . . .
Da qual nuovo sentimento
Agitato io sento il cor?
È l'amor da me deriso,
Che si vendica ad un tratto . . .
Dovran ridere sul viso
Alla vittima d'amor?
No . . . son salvo . . . il rabbin m'aperse gli occhi . . .
Vo' fuggir . . . Suzel qui non mi trattiene . . .

## SCENA VII

*Fritz, Hanezò, Federico poi Beppe.*

**FEDERICO:** Fritz, noi partiamo . . . addio!

**FRITZ:** Con voi ritorno anch'io . . .

**HANEZÒ:** Come, vieni in città?

**FRITZ:** Sì . . . voglio tornar via.

**FEDERICO:** Così presto, perchè . . .

**FRITZ:** Mi son seccato già.

**HANEZÒ:** Ma il Rabbino dov'è?

**FRITZ:** Resta alla fattoria.

**FEDERICO:** Ma qui si perde tempo.

**FRITZ:** (*da sè*). Oh! povera mia Suzel!

**BEPPE:** Il baroccino si move già.

**FEDERICO:** Che più s'aspetta?

**FRITZ:** Lesti! in città!

## SCENA VIII

*David e Suzel.*
(*Si sente il rumore del baroccino che si allontana.*)

**DAVID:** Sono i sonagli del baroccino . . .
E Fritz ov'è? On sta a vedere
Che ha preso il volo! . . .

**SUZEL:** Signor Rabbino

**DAVID:** (*additando il baroccino*). Non vedi . . . là?

**SUZEL:** (*con un grido*). È lui!

**DAVID:** (*de sè*) Il disertor!

**SUZEL:** (*desolata*). Ahimè. partì!

**DAVID:** Piangi? . . . perchè? . . .

**SUZEL:** (*confusa*). Non so . . .

**DAVID:** Via, fatti cor?
(*Da sè.*)
Son lagrime d'amor.

---

## SCENE VI

**FRITZ:** (*alone*). What a strangely troubled feeling
Fills my heart with doubt and fear,
While my brain with hope is reeling
And I'm happy while she's near.
Can it be that Love has slain me
With his arrow, sharp and strong?
That his net has taken me prisoner,
I who mocked at him so long?
No, I'm safe! The Rabbi has opened my eyes!
I will fly! Suzel shall not make a fool of me!

## SCENE VII

*Fritz, then Beppe, Hanezo and Federico.*

**FEDERICO:** Fritz, we must depart. Farewell!

**FRITZ:** I shall go with you!

**HANEZO:** What! back to town?

**FRITZ:** Aye, I will go with you!

**FEDERICO:** And why so soon?

**FRITZ:** I hate the country!

**HANEZO:** And where is David?

**FRITZ:** In the house, resting.

**FEDERICO:** But time is flying. Come!

**FRITZ:** Oh! Suzel, my little darling!

**BEPPE:** The cart is all ready!

**FEDERICO:** We can stay no longer!

**FRITZ:** Let us go back!

## SCENE VIII

*David and Suzel.*

**DAVID:** Bells ringing! Carriage starting! Where is Fritz?
Ho! Fritz, why have you left us?

**SUZEL:** Oh! Rabbi, he's gone?

**DAVID:** (*pointing to carriage*). Don't you see him?

**SUZEL:** (*with a scream*). It is he!

**DAVID:** (*aside*). The rascal! The deserter!

**SUZEL:** (*disconsolately*). Alas! he's gone. Alas!

**DAVID:** Why do you weep?

**SUZEL:** I don't know.

**DAVID:** Then don't do it!

**SUZEL:** Alas! he's gone away! He's gone away!

**DAVID:** (*aside*). Those tears are tears of love.

---

**CORO INTERNO DI DONNE:** L'amore, che lontano se ne va,
Mai più non tornerà!

**SUZEL:** (*disperata*). Mai più . . . non tornerà!

*[Fine Del Secondo Atto.]*

# ■ ATTO III

## SCENA I

*La stessa scena del primo atto.*

**FRITZ:** (*solo*). Tutto ho tentato . . . tutto! e sempre invano . . .
L'ho lasciata laggiù, senza un addio:
Ma l'imagine sua, pur da lontano,
M'appare mesta e mi richiama a se.

**VOCI INTERNE:** Intrecciate ghirlande, o giovinette!
Giovani, un fior mettetevi all'occhiello!
La bionda molinara è andata sposa
Stamane col suo bello!

**FRITZ:** E da per tutto amor! Sempre il destino
Mi perseguita . . . Ahimè! si sposa a Franges,
A Mesnil si battezza . . . e fin due vecchi,
Bianchi ed allegri, fan le nozze d'oro! . . .
Oh! questa pace come turba il core!
Come tutto mi canta: "Amore! Amore!"

## SCENA II

*Fritz e Beppe.*

**BEPPE:** Buon giorno, Fritz! Ti volli salutare . .
Perchè triste così?

**FRITZ:** Nulla . . .

**BEPPE:** Una volta,
Venivi incontro con un bel sorriso . . .
Che cos'hai?

**FRITZ:** La tristezza mi tortura!
Pace trovar non so . . .

**BEPPE:** Povero amico!
Oh! lo conosco il male che tu soffri . . .
E l'ho provato anch'io, nè son guarito! . . .
E scrissi una canzon per consolar-

---

**CHORUS:** (*outside*). The love that loves and runs away
Won't live to love another day.

**SUZEL:** He'll never return to me! Alas!
(*Bursts into tears.*)

*[Curtain.]*

# ■ ACT III

## SCENE I

*Scene: Same as in Act First, but without the table equipage.*

**FRITZ:** (*discovered*). I have tried everything, but in vain! I fled from her presence without a farewell, but her face still pursues me and seems to call me back!

**CHORUS:** (*outside*). It is the miller's daughter
Going to be wed
To the man who sought her.

**GIRLS:** Come, take this flower, red,
And wear it in your bosoms.

**FULL CHORUS:** In honor of the fair
These white and rosy blossoms,
Of tint and fragrance rare.

**FRITZ:** Ah! Love, you follow me everywhere! It is my fate! Alas!
At Franges will be the wedding,
At Mesnil babes will come,
And bye and bye two white haired old folk
Will hold their golden wedding.

**CHORUS:** It is the miller's daughter, etc.

**FRITZ:** Oh! how this peace disturbs my heart!
The whole world seems to echo: "Love! Love! Love!"

## SCENE II

*Fritz and Beppe.*

**BEPPE:** Good morning, Fritz! I'm very glad to see you.
But why so sad?

**FRITZ:** No matter!

**BEPPE:** You used to meet me with a smile of welcome.
What is the matter?

**FRITZ:** I'm broken hearted. I shall never more find peace.

**BEPPE:** Poor old boy! I, too, have felt love's smart.
But as there is no cure for it, I ease it with a song. Perhaps it may do you good. I'll sing it.
Oh! pale one, who so long ago

---

mi.
Non la conosci tu? vuoi che la canti?
O pallida, che un giorno mi guardasti,
In sogno tornami!
Una dolcezza tal mi procurasti,
Che ancor ne ho l'estasi!
Oh! che chiedevi tu, con gli occhi tuoi?
Ebbrezze o lagrime?
Pallida, torna a me, dimmi che vuoi,
Dimmi i tuoi palpiti!
Nulla ti so negar, pallida mia,
T'ho dato l'anima . . .
E, se un tuo bacio dà la morte . . . sia!
Oh! vieni, baciami!

FRITZ: Anche tu, Beppe, giungi a torturarmi
Con le mendaci ebbrezze del pensiero?
Lasciami in pace . . . lasciami!

BEPPE: Men vo!
Povero amico!
(Beppe esce.)

## SCENA III

FRITZ: (solo). Ed anche Beppe amò . . .
Anche al suo cor s'apprese
Questa febbre fatale della vita!
Anch'ei s'accese
Del male che delizia e fa soffrir!
(Sospira.)
O amore, o bella luce del core,
Fiammella eterna che il mondo ha in sè,
Mesta carezza lieto dolore,
La vita è in te!
Blanda è la luce che a notte scende,
Sfolgora il sole possente ognor,
Pure il tuo raggio su tutti splende,
Luce del cor!
Oh! splendi, eterna limpida face,
Spanditi, o palpito generator!
Oh! Cielo canta l'inno di pace:
La vita è amor!

## SCENA IV

*Fritz e David.*

DAVID: (da sè). L'amico Fritz fantastica d'amore!
(Avanzandosi.)
Ebbene, come va?

FRITZ: Lasciami stare!

DAVID: Lo so, lo so che non ti senti bene . . .
Dice la Bibbia: "Al solitario guai!"
(Con mistero.)
Ho combinato tutto . . .

FRITZ: Io non intendo . . .

DAVID: Per le nozze di Suzel . . .

FRITZ: Che mi dici?

DAVID: Impallidisci?

Gave kisses kind,
Come back, though but in dreams, to me,
You'll find welcome.
Your eyes are stars of destiny
None can resist,
Come back, my love, come back to me,
Come and be kissed.
I can refuse you nothing,
My maiden mild,
I'm yours and you are mine, dear
Flower undefiled.

FRITZ: And even you, Beppe, would tease me with these mists of the imagination! I pray you leave me!

BEPPE: I'm off! Poor old boy!
(Exit.)

## SCENE III

FRITZ: (alone). So Beppe, too, has loved! He, too, has felt the archer's dart and knows the unrest that gives no rest!
Oh! Love, sunlight of the heart, everlasting flame, pleasing pain, exquisite torture, all the world is yours!
Fair as the moon in the evening's still splendor,
Glorious as sun in the beauty of day,
But Love, royal Love, to your I render homage,
More than sun, moon or stars gleams your bright, shining ray.
Oh! shine, then, eternal, fair child of Dame Venus,
Sing on your sweet carols of music and joy,
No darkness nor sorrow can ever come between us,
For Love still is Life, Love our life shall employ.

## SCENE IV

*Fritz and David.*

DAVID: (aside). Friend Fritz, sunk in a dream of love!
(Aloud.)
Good morning, Fritz! How goes it?

FRITZ: Let me be!

DAVID: I see you are not happy. What says the Scriptures? "It is not good for man to be alone."
(Mysteriously.)
Everything is working for the best.

FRITZ: What do you mean?

DAVID: For Suzel's wedding.

FRITZ: (hastily). What do you say?

DAVID: Why are you so pale?

FRITZ: Non mi sento bene!
Ma . . . di'la verità . . . Suzel è sposa?

DAVID: Con un bel giovinotto allegro e ricco . . .
Suo padre oggi verrà pel tuo consenso.

FRITZ: Ma . . . Suzel non sa nulla?

DAVID: Approva tutto.

FRTIZ: Io nego il mio consenso . . .

DAVID: Oh! non lo dire!

FRITZ: Per farti rabbia m'opporrò . . .

DAVID: Fa pure!
(Fritz esce.)

## SCENA V

*David, poi Suzel.*

DAVID: (sorridendo). Povero Fritz, l'amore in te si desta . . .
E una vera tempesta
S'agita nel tuo core!
(Entra Suzel—David voltandosi.)
Caterina . . . Ah sei tu, Suzel!

SUZEL: Signore,
Venni a portare i frutti al mio padrone.

DAVID: Perchè mesta così? . . . piccina mia,
Ti voglio sempre veder lieta, sai?
Che? ti spuntan le lagrime? Fa' cuore!
Quando ritornerò, sorriderai!
(Exce.)

## SCENA VI

SUZEL: (sola.) Non mi resta che il pianto ed il dolore . . .
Io non sogno che ai piedi suoi cader,
Dirgli che tutto il core
Vive del suo pensier!
Vorrei dirgli: ma tu dei miei tormenti
Non comprendi l'orribile martir?
Ah! nel tuo cor non senti
Che mi farai morir!

## SCENA VII

*Suzel e Fritz.*

FRITZ: Suzel!

SUZEL: Signor!

FRITZ: (da sè.) Come s'è fatta pallida!
(A Suzel.)
Che mi vuoi dire?

SUZEL: Io? . . . nulla . . .

FRITZ: E che mi venne
Allora a raccontare David? . . . Ch'eri
Già fidanzata ad un bel giovinotto?

FRITZ: I am not well. But, tell me, is Suzel going to be married?

DAVID: Yes; a rich, good looking fellow, of a pleasant temper. Her father will come today for your approval of the match.

FRITZ: Then Suzel consents?

DAVID: She does, with joy.

FRITZ: But I don't! Nor will I!

DAVID: Oh! pray, don't say that!

FRITZ: Just for spite I'll not consent!

DAVID: I fancy not. (Exit Fritz.)

## SCENE V

*David, then Suzel.*

DAVID: (smiling). Poor Fritz, he is in a bad state! Love's fever has caught him.
(Calls.)
Caterina!
(Enter Suzel.)
Ah! you, Suzel?

SUZEL: I have brought the fruit for the master.

DAVID: Why do you look so sad, poor little child, you who should always be gay? What! tears? Cheer up, you will be laughing bye and bye. (Exit.)

## SCENE VI

SUZEL: (alone). Now nothing is left but bitter tears of sorrow,
Never more shall I see his godlike features.
Hope from his presence never more may I borrow,
My life is very weary, my dream of love is over.
On his dear smile I'd live and love forever,
But without him my heart is bleak and drear.
Since from his presence I must sadly sever,
Sure I shall die of grief too deep for tear.

## SCENE VII

*Suzel and Fritz.*

FRITZ: Suzel!

SUZEL: Master!

FRITZ: (aside). How pale she is! What do you want?

SUZEL: I? Nothing!

FRITZ: What did David mean by telling me that you were going to be married to a young and handsome fellow?

SUZEL: Ahimè!

FRITZ: (*con amarezza*). Credevo inver che tu venissi
A portarmi l'invito per le nozze.

SUZEL: Ah! non lo dite!

FRITZ: Perchè piangi? Forse
Non l'ami? . . . E perchè mai lo sposi?

SUZEL: Così vuol.

FRITZ: Ma non l'ami?

SUZEL: Io no . . .

FRITZ: Rifiuta
La nozze!

SUZEL: Io non ho core . . .
Ma, voi che lo potete,
Salvatemi, signore!
(*Supplichevole.*)
Ah! ditela per me quella parola,
Ditela al padre mio:
E se dovrò nel mondo restar sola,
M'assisterà il buon Dio!
Pel babbo, questa è certo una gran pena,
Io lo farò soffrir . . .
Ma, pria d'avere al cor quella catena,
Preferisco morir!

FRITZ: Suzel, tu n'ami un altro!

SUZEL: Un altro? Ah no!

FRITZ: Confessa! dimmi il nome suo qual è?

SUZEL: Ahimè!

FRITZ: Saper lo voglio! Ed io farò
Ch'egli ti sposi.

SUZEL: No!

FRITZ: Sì, dillo a me!

SUZEL: Giammai, giammai, signor, prima morir!

FRITZ: Te ne scongiuro!

SUZEL: Ah, no!—voglio partir!

FRITZ: Ma . . . s'io t'aprissi le mie braccia?

SUZEL: Oh Dio!

FRITZ: Se ti dicessi: io t'amo!

SUZEL: È sogno il mio?!

FRITZ: Io t'amo, t'amo, o dolce mio tesor,
Soave immagine d'amor!
Di te soltanto
Vivea, mio bene,
E sol di te vivrò!

SUZEL: Alas!

FRITZ: I thought you were bringing me an invitation to the wedding.

SUZEL: Ah! do not say that!

FRITZ: Do you not love him, then? If you do not, why marry him?

SUZEL: I must obey my father.

FRITZ: Your father! You do not love him, then?

SUZEL: No!

FRITZ: Then break the engagement!

SUZEL: I dare not. But you, who can do everything,
Save me! Save me! Ah!
Say to my father that I would not marry.
That I would rather live out my days alone.
To my life's end I would carry deep regret
Bound to a husband whom I would disown.
Tell him, I pray, that I am loath to grieve him,
But thus to wed would break my very heart.
And though I never will trouble or deceive him,
I cannot wed with one in whom I have no part.

FRITZ: Suzel, do you love some other?

SUZEL: Another? No!

FRITZ: Come, tell me his name.

SUZEL: Alas!

FRITZ: He shall be your husband. I will see to that.

SUZEL: No!

FRITZ: Yes, I will know!

SUZEL: No! Never! I rather would die!

FRITZ: I entreat you!

SUZEL: Ah! no! I must go.

FRITZ: But if I hold you in my arms—

SUZEL: Oh! heaven!—

FRITZ: And say that I love you?

SUZEL: Ah! it is my dream.

FRITZ: I love you! I love you! treasury of my soul, sweet jewel of my heart! Tell me you love me, and we will live for each other.

SUZEL: Oh! parla, parla, imparadisa il cor!
Non oso gli occhi volger su di te!
O vivo raggio d'amor,
Oh splendi, splendi per me!
Il duolo, il pianto
E le mie pene,
Tutto ora scorderò!

FRITZ: O Suzel mia, giammai, giammai si amò di più!

SUZEL: Io t'amo, t'amo tanto! La vita mia sei tu!

## SCENA ULTIMA

*I Precedenti, David, Beppe, Federico, Hanezò e Caterina.*

DAVID: (*comparendo, seguito dagli altri, sul limitare della terrazza*). Amici! ho vinto, ho vinto!

FRITZ: O buon Rabbino,
Vinse l'amor! La vigna è tua!

DAVID: La vigna
È di Suzel!

FRITZ: Che dici?

DAVID: E non si strinse
Patto fra noi che ne sarei padrone?
E sia data alla tua sposa la vigna
Di Clairefontaine!

BEPPE E CATERINA: Bravo, Rabbino! bravo!

FEDERICO: (*a Fritz*). Tu sposi, Fritz?

HANEZÒ: E noi che mai faremo?

DAVID: Per voi ci penseremo . . .
Se avete in petto il core,
Lontana no sarà l'alba d'amore!

FRITZ: O amore, o bella—luce del core,
Fiammella eterna—che il mondo ha in sè,
Mesta carezza—lieto dolore, La vita è in te!

TUTTI: O amore, o bella—luce del core,
Fiammella eterna—che il mondo ha in sè,
Mesta carezza—lieto dolore, La vita è in te!

[*Fine.*]

SUZEL: Oh! speak, your words bring heaven to my heart! I scarce dare raise my eyes to look on you. Bright sun of love, oh! shine upon me still! All grief is past, my soul is full of joy.

FRITZ: Oh! Suzel, sure none ever loved before?

SUZEL: I love you, love you dearly, as none ever loved before!

FRITZ: My heart speaks, loud and clearly, each day I'll love you more!

## LAST SCENE

*The preceding, David, Beppe, Federico, Hanezo and Caterina.*

DAVID: (*on the threshold*). I've won, my friends, I've won!

FRITZ: No, good Rabbi, it was Love! The vineyard is yours!

DAVID: I give it to Suzel!

FRITZ: What do you say?

DAVID: According to our bargain the vineyard is mine, and I give it to Suzel—the vineyard of Clairefontaine.

BEPPE AND CATERINA: Bravo, Rabbi! Bravo!

FEDERICO: So, Fritz, you'll wed?

HANEZO: And, pray, what shall we do?

DAVID: We'll find you wives. If in your hearts love's fire is glowing, His favor Cupid will be soon bestowing.

FRITZ: Oh! Love! fair as moon in the evening's still splendor, Glorious as sun in the beauty of day, Love, royal Love, to you I render homage, More than sun, moon or stars gleams your bright, shining ray.

CHORUS: Oh! shine, then, eternal, fair child of Dame Venus, Sing on your sweet carols of music and joy, No darkness nor sorrow can ever come between us, For Love still is life, Love our life shall employ.

[*Curtain.*]

# Iris (1898)

## MUSIC BY PIETRO MASCAGNI ■ LIBRETTO BY LUIGI ILLICA

This three-act melodrama, set to a libretto by Luigi Illica, was first performed at the Teatro Costanzi in Rome on November 22, 1898. In a Japanese village, Osaka, a wealthy young rogue, is in love with Iris, a simple laundry girl. He asks the owner of a teahouse, Kyoto, to kidnap her. They plan a public marionette show at which this scheme will take place. The marionettes perform the story of the love of Dhia and Jor; Osaka himself performs the part of Jor, the son of the Sun God. Iris, attracted by his singing, joins the crowd watching the show; she is grabbed and dragged away. Kyoto sends Iris' old father, who is blind, money along with a note that says she has gone of her own free will to Yoshiwara, an area of bad reputation. The old man searches for his daughter so that he may curse her. Iris regains consciousness in Osaka's apartment. She recognizes his voice as that of Jor, and she rejects his attempts to woo her. He tires of her, and Kyoto dresses her up and shows her off to the crowd. Her father finds her thus and curses her, throwing mud as he does so. She throws herself into a sewer in her sadness. Her body is found at the bottom of the sewer by ragpickers who attempt to remove her clothes and jewelry, but they realize that she is still alive and run away in fright. The dawn comes as Iris is dying, comforting her in her grief. Flowers open in full bloom around her body as she dies, and she rises into the sky surrounded by color and light.

---

## ■ ATTO PRIMO

*La Notte. I Primi Albori. I Fiori.
L'Aurora. I Primi Raggi.*

*La luce e l'idioma de'gli eterni!
Udetelo!*

IL SOLE: Son Io! Son Io la Vita.—
Son la Belta Infinita!
la Luce ed il Calor!
Amate, O Cose dico:
Sono il Dio novo e antico! amate!—
Son l'Amor!
Per me gli augelli han canti i flor
profumi e incanti!
Dei Mondi Io la Cagione!
Dei Cieli Io la Ragione!
Uguale Io scendo ai Re, si come a te,
Mousme!
Pieta la esenza mia
Eterna Poesia—Amor!

IRIS: (*Sul limitare della casa*). Ho
fatto un triste sogno pauroso
Un sogno tutto pieno
di draghi, mostri, volante chimera,
e di striscianti colubri.
S'era malata la amica bambola
ond' io—tutta piangente—
l'avea posta in giardino a riposare
entro un cespo di rose.
Intorno a lei tacea tutto il giardino:
non piu canti di gigli,
canzoni di gardenie porporine
ne voli di libellule;
Avevo detto ai flor— "Tacete, O
fiori!
Malata e mia bambola!"
Quand'ecco in ciel vol di bianche
cicogne
fuggire spaventate!
Guardo!—Pieno e il giardin di
mostri terribile
che la mia bimba insidiano!
Accorro a sua difesa! Prego! La gri-
mo!
"Lasciatemi, l'amica!
Ma una fenice spiega in ruote e giri
fantastici la coda
che come serpe avvinghia la piccina
allarga l'ali—e fugge!
Ma, Sol, tu vieni, ed il sogno e bugia,
Guarita e la mia bambola!
(*Corre entro la casa, vi prende
una bambola, poi rapidamenta
tornando sui limitare della casa
alza verso il sole la sua bambola,
e con grazia, le agita le manine, a
guisa di saluto*).
Vieni e saluta il Sole!

IL CIECO: (*dall' interno*). Con che
parli?

IRIS: O padre mio, col Sole!
(*depone la bambola su un vaso di
fiori ed entra nella casa*).
(*Gia di tempo si sono veduti
spiare il luogo-nascosti dietro il
gruppo di bambou*).
(*cautamento si sono avanzati
lungo la siepe, finche Osaka ba
sconto Iris nel momento in cui
essa entra nella casa—Osaka la
indica a Kyoto*).

OSAKA: E lei! e lei!

KYOTO: E la figlia del Cieco.

OSAKA: La voglio!

KYOTO: Tu l'avrai!

OSAKA: Non farle male!

KYOTO: Non sciupo la mia merce!

OSAKA: Che se! Bada!

KYOTO: Son noto al Yoshiwara!
Non temere!

OSAKA: Sta ben!

## ■ ACT ONE

*The Night. Daybreak. Flowers.
The Dawn. Sunrise.*

*Light is the language of the im-
mortals, Hear it!*

CHORUS — THE SUN: I am! I am
the Life. I am the Infinite Beauty!
The Light; and the Heat!
Love O things — I say —
I am the god, new and old!
Love! I am Love!
By me the birds have their songs!
The flowers their perfume and in-
cense!
I am the Cause of the world!
I am the Reason of the Heavens!
On equal terms I go to the King
And to you, Wash-girl!
Compassion is my nature;
Eternal Poesy — Love!

IRIS: (*At the door of her cottage*) I
have had a sad and fearful dream
A dream all filled.
With dragons, flying chimeras,
And hissing serpents.
My dear doll-baby was sick
So I, all weeping,
Had put it in the garden to sleep
Under a rose-bush.
Everything around her was silent,
in the whole garden.
No more sang the lilies
The songs of the purple flowers,
Wish not to disturb her
I said to each flower, "Silence,
flower,
My doll-baby is sick."
When lo! in heaven white storks
were flying.
They flew away, frightened.
I watch! The garden is full of
horrible monsters
That threaten my doll-baby!
I run to her defense. I pray. I weep.
"Leave me! my friend."
But a phoenix spread its tail like a
wheel
And made fantastical motions
As a serpent came near my baby.
Then it spread its wings, and flew!
But, Sun! you came back, and the
dream was a lie!
Guard my doll-baby!
(*She goes into the house, picks up
a doll-baby, returns quickly to the
door, lifts the doll high, gracefully
moving its hands saluting*)
Come! Salute the Sun!

CIECO: (*Within*) With whom are
you speaking?

IRIS: O, my father, with the Sun!
(*She places her doll by a vase of
flowers and goes into the house*)
(*At the same time, Osaka and
Kyoto are seen watching the place
from behind a group of bamboo*)
(*Cautiously they creep along the
hedge until Osaka has seen Iris.
He points her out to Kyoto*)

OSAKA: It is she! It is she!

KYOTO: She's the blind man's
daughter.

OSAKA: I want her.

KYOTO: You'd have her?

OSAKA: Do her no harm!

KYOTO: Don't covet my property!

OSAKA: Look out! Beware!

KYOTO: I'm known at the Yoshiwara! Don't be frightened.

OSAKA: Very well!

# Act I

KYOTO: Soltanto. Ho d'uopo di tua voce all trammi ch'io medito— Sottile e pieghevol come salce e la tua voce.

OSAKA: E ver! ho voce acuta: imita il sono, il bisbiglia d'augelli e il chiacchierare d'irrequiete fanciulle. La mia voce vibra nell'aria, desta gli echi ai monti, e vola alta nel ciel come cigne o falco.

KYOTO: Essa ni occorre!

OSAKA: E la fanciulla?

KYOTO: Supponi ch'esso gia sia cosa tua. Andiamo a prepararci un viso!

OSAKA: Andiamo!

KYOTO: Prudenza vuol cosi! ignoti, e cauti!

OSAKA: Cauti! Ignoti!

KYOTO: Si.

OSAKA: Gia mi diverto e godo gia.

OSAKA E KYOTO: La vita e cosi bella. (s'avviano verso il fondo della scena). (passano il ponte e scompaino). (sul limitare della casa appare il cieco, che la figlia Iris guida amorosamente. scendono nel giardino).

CIECO: Voglio posare ove a piu caldo il sole!

IRIS: (fa sedere il padre su di un piccolo sgabello).

CIECO: Si, Oh, il buon raggio! M'avviva! Or dammi il mio rosario. Vio pregare!

IRIS: (porgendo al padre il rosario). Ecco il rosario!

CIECO: E tu pai pregato?

IRIS: Si! inaffiero i mei fiori, intanto. (Iris si aggiro pel piccolo giardino, inaffiando i fiori; ammiradore aciuno-coglie un crisantemo a se lo pone fra i capelli).

CIECO: Io prego. (Il cieco prega silenziosamente, immobile, movendo solo la d'ita per fare scorrere la grana del rosario).

(Dal villaggio si avanza un gruppo di mousme portano a braccio, o sul capo, della cestedi giunchi— Sono giovani lav—daji che vengono a lavore del ruscello bianchi lini, e varlotinte mussoline).

CORO DE MOUSME: Al rio! al rio! E il plenilunio! A rio! (si dispongono in vari e pittoresqui gruppi pe cominciare il lavoro). L'acqua e limpida e tiepida!

KYOTO: Only I wish I had your voice For the trick I'm planning — Your voice is subtle and flexible as the willow.

OSAKA: It is true. I have a sharp voice. It imitates sound; the whirr of Birds; the chatter of noisy children. My voice vibrates in the air, Echoes from the mountains, and Flies up like a stork or a falcon!

KYOTO: She's runnning here!

OSAKA: Is it the girl?

KYOTO: Suppose the girl is yours, Let's go and prepare a show.

OSAKA: We'll go.

KYOTO: Such affairs demand prudence, caution, disguise!

OSAKA: Caution! disguise!

KYOTO: Yes.

OSAKA: It will be a good diversion for me.

OSAKA and KYOTO: "For life is thus made lovely!" (They go toward the back of the scene) (They cross the bridge and disappear) (At the door of the cottage Cieco appears guided lovingly by his daughter, Iris. They go into the garden)

CIECO: I wish to sit where the sun is warm.

IRIS: (Placing her father on a small bench) Here, father!

CIECO: Yes! Oh! good warmth! It revives me! Now give me my rosary. I wish to pray.

IRIS: (Handing the rosary) Here is the rosary.

CIECO: And have you prayed?

IRIS: Yes, I will go and water my flowers the while. (Iris moves about her little garden, watering the flowers, admiring them. She picks a chrysanthemum, and puts it in her hair)

CIECO: I pray. (The blind man prays silently, immobile, only moving his finger to slip the beads of the rosary)

(From the village come a group of Mousme, working girls; they carry in their arms or on their heads rush baskets filled with muslins of various colors)

CHORUS OF MOUSME: To the river! The river! The moon is full! To the river! (They dispose themselves in picturesque groups to commence their work)

Sciuga il bucato il sole e la lavanda in fiore! E il plenilunio! Fra loti ed iridi, felci e ninfe e nenufare gelsominee scorre la rapida carezza il pie delle Mousme. Viene il suo bacio dalla sorgente, Bacio di rio, bacio di Dio Contorci e attorta Acqua correnti da lungi porta cento profumi l'odor del muschio, cotto dall'onde fra zolle e dumi di cento sponde!

IRIS: In pure stille—gaie scintilla scende la vita! L'acqua s'effonde per vie profonde Bevi la vita alga cerulea. Tu, Margharita, leva il candore, della chioma. O celestrino! fiore di mey. neve odorante, tu, gelsomino e tu, olezzanto, fiore di amoma! La varia chioma leva, o coriando. fiore di monte!

CHORUS: Fra zolle e dumi di cento sponde.

CIECO: (recitando). Tu mi, hai tolta la vista. Ma io verdo la Tua Grandezza: La tua Grandezza la sento. essa parla all'anima mia! la belleza della Vita creato da te mi penetra col sole, nella mia Vecchia persona! Tu sei Grande e Buono! La Vita e pur tuttavia sempre un cammino faticoso, Ma e aggradevole se io penso che conduce a Nirvana! Io cammino anelando alla meta! Tu mi hai tolta la vista Ma mi hai dato degli occhi d'Iris; Mi hai dato un Genio. Buono e gentile non son solo! Io dico la tua Grandezza!

IRIS: Ristoria! Irrora! Thea dorosa, fiore divino, gardenia, rosa, vita bevete! Bevete, fiori, mente, verbene e olezzi e balsami pel mio giardino fiore espandete!

CORO: Ha raggi il sole; ha timi il prato, il lino candido, bioncheggia ed ole. (Suoni lontani di striduli samisen, di gongs, e di tamburelli—

The water is clear and warm! Drying our wash in the sunshine And working away among the flowers. Now is it full moon! Mid ferns and irises, water-lilies Nymphs and jassamines They follow rapidly. Wavelets whirl, Caressing the feet Of the Mousme. Come now and kiss us, rising still higher Kiss of the river; yet kiss of fire! Now twisting; now turning Swift running water Carrying perfume. The odor of musk, borne by the wave- From sweet briars and thorns Of a hundred strands!

IRIS: Dropping so purely — gaily, demurely, So Life is falling! To the deep journey — soaring upward with lightness! Drink! and be living, Your fragrance giving! Thou, Margarita, Hold to your title named for your whiteness! Sky-colored fennel! — Sweet-scented snow-flower! Thou, yellow jessamine! And you, with aroma, flower of amoma, Named as you may be — Up! coriander! Over mountains to wander!

CHORUS: From the clay and the thorns Of a hundred strands.

CIECO: (reciting). You have robbed me of my sight But I see all your grandeur — I know your greatness! It speaks to my soul! The beauty of life from you Penetrates my old body with the sunshine! You are great and good! Life is, by every road, A toilsome journey. But I love it, since it leads me to Nirvana! I walk impatiently toward the goal! You have robbed me of vision But have given me the eyes of Iris. You have given me an angel, Gentle and good. I am not alone, I say to your grandeur!

IRIS: Refresh! Bedew! Odorous Thea, divine flowers Garden of roses, Life now drink ye. Drink, pretty flowers, mint and verbena! That grow in my garden, To increase, now, I think ye!

CHORUS: The sun has rays; and thyme has the meadow, Linens are whitering, drawn from the shadow. (Far away are beard the sounds of

*Iris e le mousme guardono con sorpresa verso la strada che conduce al ponte).*

**IRIS:** Gui per la via ne viene un gaio suono.

**CORO:** *(ascoltando ansiose).* Son samisi, tamburi e risonati cymbali e gongs!

**CIECO:** *(ad Iris).* Lontano?

**IRIS:** S'avvicina.

**CIECO:** Iris! chi son? li vedi? Guarda!

**IRIS:** Guardo! *(si avvicina alla slepe guardando verso il fondo).*

**CORO:** Son commendianti! Sono guechas! Vengono

**IRIS:** O padre!

**CIECO:** Di!

**IRIS:** E il Teatro dei Pupi!

**CIECO:** Stammi presso, fanciulla!

**IRIS:** Obbediro.

**CIECO:** Sono vagabondi! *(Iris torna presso il padre e lo rassicura).*

**CORO:** Ritordiamo il ritorno? *(Osaka e Kyoto entrambi camuffati da istrioni girovaghi sbucano del fondo con un codazzo, di sounatori guecha e samovrai; al suono di samisen gongs, tamburelli; le mousme corrono incontro curiose, a battono festamente le mani nei vedere che si tratti d'una rappresentazione di Pupi— Osaka e Kyoto scendono li ponte, sequlti della loro compagnia: Le mousme, curiose, fanne cerchio—mentre ad un cenno di Kyoto alcuni degli istrioni pianto il Teatro del Pupi).*

**CORO:** Rimaniamo! Col bucato piu tardi torneremo! Ecco il guechas! Tutte a veli E numerosa assai la campagnia! Veh! quattro guechas: sono due attori! Son quattro suonatori! Eccoli! Vengono!

**IRIS:** *(attratta dalla curiosita, si pone ad osservare dietra la slepe).* Dietro allo biancho spine me mettro.

**KYOTO:** *(rivolto alle mousme, pur tenedo d'occhio Iris, che se se avvincinata all a siepe del suo giardino, guardando ansiosamente).* Io son Danjuro il padre dei Fantocci che nelle mie commedie faccio sposi alle gentili bambole. *(rivolto*

*the samisen, of gongs and tambourines. Iris and the Mousme look with surprise toward the street which leads to the bridge)*

**IRIS:** Up from the street comes very gay music!

**CHORUS:** *(Listening anxiously)* There are samisens, tambourines, High resounding cymbals, and gongs!

**CIECO:** Away, far?

**IRIS:** They are coming near.

**CIECO:** Iris, who are they? Do you see them? Watch you!

**IRIS:** I'll watch. *(She goes to the hedge and looks beyond)*

**CHORUS:** They are comedians; And some Geishas. They're coming.

**IRIS:** O father!

**CIECO:** Speak!

**IRIS:** It's a puppet-show.

**CIECO:** Keep near me, my child.

**IRIS:** I'm standing here.

**CIECO:** They are vagabonds. *(She returns to her father, and reassures him)*

**CHORUS:** Shall we delay our going home? *(Osaka and Kyoto, both disguised as wandering players, enter. They are followed by a crowd of musicians, geishas and vagabonds, at the sound of the music) Yes; we'll stay here! (The Mousme run about, moved by curiosity, and clap their hands joyfully at the prospect of seeing the puppet-show) (Osaka and Kyoto cross the bridge followed by the whole company) (The Mousme look at them curiously. Meanwhile at a sign from Kyoto some of the others set up the theatre for the puppets)*

**CHORUS:** We'll stretch out our washing, delaying return. Look at the Geishas! all clothed in gauzes, See what a company! See! Four Geishas! Two actors! Four musicians! Look at them! They're coming!

**IRIS:** *(Drawn by curiousity she posts herself so as to see behind the hedge)* I will place myself behind the white-thorn.

**KYOTO:** *(Kyoto turns to the Mousme while holding the eyes of Iris, who comes near the edge of the garden peering anxiously beyond)* I am Danjuro, the father of the puppets, which, in my comedy, become husbands to the gentle doll-babies.

*al suonatori).* Ola, musica! mousme! tenete pupe da marito?

**CORO:** Si che ne abbiamo, e sono buone e belle.

**IRIS:** Come la mia, no; non ve n'ha. Sto certa!

**CORO:** E un Teatro di lusso!

**CIECO:** — *(chiamando).* Iris!

**IRIS:** *(al padre).* Sto qua.

**KYOTO:** Ora daremo representazione! Udrite i Pupi miei dirtante cose tutte maravigliose e dotta assai Parlai udrite Jor, figlio del Sole e Dhia la bella figlia sventurata! Ma piu non voglio dir — Udrite, e basta Ehi — Musica! Preparo la scena! *(Osaka! attento!)*

**OSAKA:** *(Non die temer).*

**KYOTO:** *(La parte?)*

**OSAKA:** *(Io la ricordo e non ne fallo un ette!)*

**LE MOUSME:** Poniamici tutte intorno. *(Duranti gli ultimi preparativi le Mousme seggono, ginnochioni, facendo cerchio intorno al teatrino).*

**KYOTO:** *(E la piccina?)*

**OSAKA:** *(Guarda con occhi larghi come foglie di loto e di nelumbo! sta alla siepe!)*

**KYOTO:** *(Vedrai, ne la trarremo!)* *(Ora l'adesco! E la curiosita infallibil amo).*

**LE MOUSME:** Facciam silenzio! Gia danno principio. *(Osaka e Kyoto si collocano dietro il paravennto a destro del Teatrino, da dove possono spiare i vovimenti d' Iris, pure sequendo le loro respettive parti).* *(Kyoto fa cenno d' introdurri in Scena Dhia).*

**DHIA** *(una guecha).* Misera! *(un gran sospiro).* Ogno qui sola! Unque mai mi consola! . . . Morte rapi mia madre ridotta e mia famiglia a un collerico padre che non ama la figlia! . . . *(un gemito).* Ho vesti brutte a lacere . . . *(altro gemito).* scarne braccia e sottili *(terzo gemito).* gote pallide e grame son malata ed ho fama e sono le mie lacrime mie gemmi e mie monili! . . . *(un singhiozzo).*

*(To the Musicians)* Ho, there! Music! Mousme, have you had the puppets of marriage?

**CHORUS:** Yes, we have had them; and they ar just lovely!

**IRIS:** As for me, no; I have not. That's certain.

**CHORUS:** As a show, it is charming!

**CIECO:** Iris!

**IRIS:** I'm here.

**KYOTO:** Now we give the representation. You shall hear my puppets tell many things. All marvellous and very learned; You shall hear Jor, Son of the Sun, And Dhia, the beautiful unfortunate daughter. But more, I won't say. You'll hear plenty. Ho, there! Music! Prepare the scene! *(Osaka, attention!)*

**OSAKA:** *(Never fear!)*

**KYOTO:** *(Your part.)*

**OKASA:** *(I remember it. I'll not miss a point.)*

**THE MOUSME:** Let's place ourselves around. *(The Mousme seat themselves around the theatre knee-fashion, forming a circle, while the preparations go on)*

**KYOTO:** *(And the young maiden.)*

**OSAKA:** *(She's looking With large eyes, like a lotus flower. She's at the hedge.)*

**KYOTO:** *(You'll see how we'll draw her!)* *(Now she's attention!)* *(Curiosity's certain to lead to love!)*

**THE MOUSME:** Let us keep silence! They give the beginning! *(Osaka and Kyoto arrange themselves behind a large screen at the right of the puppet theatre, where they are able to spy out the movements of Iris, while following out their respective parts) (Kyoto makes a sign to bring on Dhia).*

**DHIA:** *(A Geisha)* Miserable *(A long breath)* Always here alone! No one even consoles me! Death took my mother— my family is broken up I've a bad, ill-tempered father, Who does not love his daughter! *(A sigh)* I am all wounds and bruises. *(Another sigh)* My arms are scrawny and thin *(Third sigh)* My cheeks are sad and pale. I am sick and hungry. I have only my tears, My sighs and my weepings. *(A great sob)*

# Act I

chi ascolta i mie dolori? . . .
(lamento).
non ho amiche ne fiori! . . .

OSAKA: (sotto voce). (Brava!)

KYOTO: (a clever actress)

LE MOUSME: (fanno i loro commenti). come forza le lacrime la povera fanciulla!
Davvero fa pieta!

OSAKA: (Ve come stanno attente!)

LE MOUSME: (chiamando Iris).
Iris, vientene qua; di la tu vedi nulla!

IRIS: (alle Mousme). Vedo. Qui resto: grazie!
(Kyoto imitanda la voce rauco de un vecchio catarroso fa le plu strane grida del mondo, picchiondo forte sul legno del Teatro, a dare l'idea dell' avvicinarse del vecchio, irraconda ed inumono genitore).

DHIA: Ah, mia padre!
(Apparizze sul teatrino il pupo Padre).

CORO: Ecco il padre!

DHIA: (tremolo voce). Lo sento. Tremo dallo spavento

LE MOUSME: Che ceffo! Me lo sogno stanotte!

IL PADRE: (Kyoto, con voce terribile).
Ah! sciagurata putta! Sono stanco di mantenermi questo sciocca, vana,
inutile, neghittosa, scioperata!

DHIA: Ah, padre mio!

IL PADRE: Preparati! Io ti vendo al gran mercato di Simonosaky!

DHIA: (grande strida). No, padre, no non vendermi!

IL PADRE: Preparati!

OSAKA: (La piccina si muove! Forza al dialogo!)

DHIA: (cade ai piedi del pupo padre). Per la luce del sole, e delle stelle
tienmi ancora con te!
Che vuoi ch'io faccia?
(gurgli inghiozzi).

OSAKA: (Ha gli occhi rossi, rossi!)

CIECO: (chiamando). Iris!

IRIS: Sto qua!

IL PADRE: (Kyoto, forzando terribilmente la voce). Al gran mercato di Simonosaky
Tu troverai padrone!
Io sono stanco
d'averti con me!
Tu mangi troppo
e non rendi mi nulla!
Ond io te vendo!

---

Alas! who hears my grieving?
(Lamentations)
I've neither friends nor flowers!
(A sigh, a sob and a lament)

OSAKA: (sotto voce). (Brava!)

KYOTO: (A clever actress!)

THE MOUSME: (Commenting among themselves) The poor young woman is moved to tears! It is most pitiful!

OSAKA: (See how attentive they are!)

THE MOUSME: (Calling Iris) Iris! why don't you come here? You can see nothing from there.

IRIS: (to the Mousme). I can see. I'll stay here,—thank you.
(Kyoto, imitating the nasal voice of a rough old croaker, with catarrh, knocks loudly on the wooden frame of the puppet theatre to announce the arrival of the irate and wicked old father)

DHIA: Ah! my father! (The puppet father appears)

THE CHORUS: See the father!

DHIA: I know him!
(Voice trembling)
I tremble from fear.

THE MOUSME: What a face! I'll dream of it to-night!

THE PUPPET FATHER: (Kyoto, in a terrible voice) Ah! wicked wench! I am tired of keeping. Such a stupid, vain, useless, lazy, idle—

DHIA: O, my father!

THE FATHER: Get ready, I will sell you
To the great whiskey merchant.

DHIA: (Great shriek) No! father! Do not sell me!

THE FATHER: Get ready!

OSAKA: (Our, little girl is moved. Force of the dialogue!)

DHIA: (Falls at the feet of her father) By the light of the sun and of the stars
I'll work again for you. What would You have me do?
(Gurgling sighs)

OSAKA: (Her eyes are blood red!)

CIECO: (calling). Iris!

IRIS: I'm here!

THE FATHER: (Forcing terribly his voice) In the great whiskey merchant
You may find a father!
I am tired
Of having you near me!
You eat much,
And earn me nothing,
Therefore I sell you.

---

(impressionate di tanta crudelta, Le Mousme sono furenti contro il pupo Padre).

LE MOUSME: Vecchio lercio! Furfonte! Muso da vecchia arpia!

DHIA: (con grida strazianto e disperato). Uccidimi, piuttosto!

IL PADRE: Basta! Ho detto.
(se ne va).

CORO: E sordo alle sue tante lacrime disperate!
Pigliamolo a sassate?
Orco!
Vampiro!
Via!
(urlando, e minniciando coi pugni il padre tiranno).

OSAKA: (Si scalda il nostro pubblico).
(E in furora)

DHIA: Morire! . . . Si . . . Finire!

OSAKA: Quasi, quasi, t'uccidono davvero il pupo padre.

IRIS: Ah! la istoria pietosa!
Mi pai che centro al core
Mano me prema e tocchi
che me vende affanosa.

DHIA: (con esaltazione) Deh prendimi con te, genio il Bene! Portami teco dov non si soffre!

KYOTO: (ad Osaka). Or torcati! Dolcissimo!

OSAKA: Dolcissimo.

JOR: (figlio del Sole). (Osaka invisible.) Apri la tua finestra — or son io
che venga al tuo chiamar, povera Dhia
Apri la tua finestra al raggio mio
Apri il tuo cor a mia calda malia
Jor ha ascolta, O Dhia, la tua preghiera
Apri l'anima tua, fanciulla al Sole
Apri l'anima tua alle mi parole!
Apri il tuo cuore a me, fanciulla, e spera!
Tu vuoi morir? Morire io ti faro,
ma ti faro morir dal sol baciata,
Poscia paese eterno ti traro
Ove, O fanciulla tu sarai amata!

KYOTO: (a Osaka). (videndo i impressione che la voce di Jor ha fatto sull' anima di Iris). E questa poesia gran ciurmatrice
Due motti, due bisticci, ch'uno dice.
E una fanciulla inconscia come questa
Vi si sdilinque e vi perde la testa. (e ride).
(Poco a poco una finestra del Teatrino si illumina, poi si apre e si scorge il pupo de Jor figlio del Sole:

---

(Impressed by the great cruelty of the Father, as shown by the rough voice of Kyoto, the wash girls are furious against the wicked man)

THE MOUSME: You old scoundrel! You thief! The face of an old harpy.

DHIA: (With a cry of distress and desolation) O kill me rather!

THE FATHER: Shut up! I've spoken! (He goes out)

CHORUS: He has no feeling for her tears of desperation. Let's catch him and kill him! Old Death-head. Vampire! Away!
(Howling, and threatening to fight the wicked Father with their fists)

OSAKA: (Our public is warm over it.)
(It's in a fury.)

DHIA: To die——yes——end it!

OSAKA: (Thus, indeed, they'd kill the puppet father.)

IRIS: Ah! this play is affecting! It goes straight to my heart! My hands I press with heavy grief, My thoughts are torn apart.

DHIA: (With exaltation) Then take me to you, angel of Good! Take me where there is no weeping!

KYOTO: (To Osaka) Now comes your part. Sweetly!

OSAKA: Most sweetly.

JOR: (Osaka invisible) Open your lattice window to Jor! He that comes at their call, poor Dhia,
Open your window to my gentle power,
Open your heart to my love for you! Jor has heard, O Dhia, your prayer Open your soul, dear child, to the sun!
Open your soul to my words so fair! Open your heart, though all hope be gone!
You wish to die? To die I will make you;
But you shall die of the kiss of the Sun,
Then to eternal worlds I'll take you To be loved, where all weeping is done!

KYOTO: (Seeing the impression Jor's voice has made on the mind of Iris) This fine-sentiment's always deceiving With innocent girls who are sweetly believing;
For a quibble and distich, so it is said,
A girl such as this one will lay down her head!
(Little by little a window of the theatre is illuminated, then it opens and there is seen the puppet

*Dhia s'inginocchia innanzi a lui — Iris, quasi affascinata da tale spettacola, obbandona la slepe del suo giardino e si accosta al Teatro).*

**IRIS:** Dei sogni il triste verde
disvanisce e si perde!
Quali i vani bagliori
d'errantim, misteriose
lucciole luminose
se ne vanno i dolori!

**KYOTO:** (*alla danzatrici*). Or,
Guechas, quando termina il duetto
dansate e fate! senza dar sospetto.

**DHIA:** Io muorio! Prendimi! Tua
m'abbondono!
Portami al mondo eterno della
luce!
Salgo a Nirvana! E Jor che me conduce!
Jor, son tua! A te tutta mi dono!

**IRIS:** (*a Dhia*). No, tu non muori,
Dhia!
Tu ascendi alle alte nuvole
di rose e di viole
Con Jor tu ascendi, o bambola
al paese del sole, e del Poesia.

**JOR:** (*Osaka*). Or muori dunque!
(*Dhia cade stecchita, mentre Jor
invoca sulla morta pupa le danze
celesti*).
Danzatrice alato!
Intorno a lei che a me ne vien dan-
zate!
(*a Dhia*).
Ti copriro di zaffiri e topazi!
Vieni agli amori degli eterni spazi!
(*con gran stupore del pubblico,
Jor avvinghia Dhia, e cosi abbra-
ciati si vedono i due pupi innal-
zarsi lentamente per salire al —
Nirvana, mentre cala il siparito del
Teatrino; in pari tempo le tre
Guechas mascherate si collocono
innanzi pronte alla danza*).

**LA BELLEZZA, LA MORTE, IL
VAMPIRO:** (*Durante le danze,
Kyoto gira intorno, e cosi riesce
scaltramente a distrare
l'attenzione, mentre le tre Guecho
danzatrici circondano Iris, la
quale rimane ad un tratto isolato
dal gruppo delle mousme al posto
piu avanti*).
(*con vorticosi giri e con voli del
loro veli le tre danzatrici riescono
a nascondere Iris, la quale ingen-
umente ammira*).
(*I samourais rapidi
s'impossenano della fanciulla:
una mano sulla bocca le strozza
un grido*).
(*Le tre Guechas continuano la
danza avvicinandosi di nuovo al
gruppo delle mousme: col larghi
giri de i loro veli impediscono alle
spettatrici di vedere i Samourais
che trasportano Iris, completamente inanimata verso la citta*).

*Jor, son of the Sun. Dhia kneels be-
fore him. Iris, who is fascinated
by this spectacle, leaves the garden hedge and comes near the theatre*)

**IRIS:** The earth is but sad dreaming.
It's pleasures only seeming
Short flashes, gone before the mor-
row.
We are wandering in mystery
On vanities still pondering
Until all ends in its sorrow.

**KYOTO:** (*to the dancers*). Now
Geishas, at the end, this your mis-
sion;
Dance widly, to keep off suspicion!

**DHIA:** I'm dying! O take me! Here
do not leave me
With you to the world of Light eternal.
O Jor, we will dance to Nirvana
supernal.
I am yours, Jor, I give myself to you.

**IRIS:** (*to Dhia*). No! You'll die nev-
er, Dhia.
Among high clouds forever
Of violets and roses,
Where evil never opposes,
From Jor none shall sever
From Love and Poesy.

**JOR:** (*Osaka*). And die therefore!
(*Dhia falls like a stick, meanwhile
Jor invokes over the dead puppet
the dances celestial*)
Now dancers, prance!
Around her, but not me, dance!
(*to Dhia*)
Thou shall be covered with topaz
and sapphire,
Come to eternal love's desire!
(*To the amazement of the public,
Jor is tied to Dhia, and thus bound
together the two puppets are seen
slowly to dance away to Nirvana;
meanwhile the puppet curtain de-
scends; at the same time the three
Geishas put on their masks ready
for their dances*)

**BEAUTY, DEATH, THE VAM-
PIRE:** (*During the dances Kyoto
goes around and thus cunningly
succeeds in distracting the attention; meanwhile the three dancing Geishas surround Iris, who remains at a spot isolated from the
Mousme farther to the front*)
(*With whirling motions and the
folds of their veils the three dancers contrive to hide Iris, who is absorbed in her unsuspecting wonder*)
(*The Samourais quickly seize the
young girl; with a hand on her
mouth they smother a cry*)
(*The three Geishas continue their
dance again approaching the
group of Mousme; with wide
swings of their garments they prevent the spectators from seeing
the Samourais, who carry Iris,
quite inanimate, toward the city*)

**KYOTO:** Grazie, Mousme! A rived-
erci! Musica!
(*Le Mousme si alzano in piedi per
andarsena*).

**CORO:** Andiamo? E tardi! Andiamo!

**KYOTO:** (*ad Osaka*). Or lascio
questo scritto e del denaro al
Cieco . . . e il colpo e fatto).

**OSAKA:** Il colpo e fatto!
(*Partono tutto ripassando il
ponte; Kyoto corre entro il giardino d'Iris rapidamente depone sulla soglia della casetta un foglio
scritto, poi raggiunge correndo la
comitiva che si allontana*).

**CIECO:** Questo drammo e menzogna . . . tutto, tutto
Malvagio intento e talento malvagio.
(*credendo Iris sempre presente*).
Iris, tu che ne dice? Non rispondi?
Comprendo; sei commossa!
(*credendo sempre di pariare ad
Iris*).
No; non credervi!
Tu sei si buona che ogni pianto
breccia fa nel tuo cuore! Andiamo.
(*stendono, il tremulo braccio*).
Dammi il bracchio! Perche non credo
ai genito di Dhia? Ebben . . . vi
credo!
(*stendo ancora il bracchio*).
Vieni! Dammi il bracchio. Una carezza. al vecchio Cieco..Iris!
(*sorpreso*).
Ancora non rispondi!
Iris! . . . Iris . . . Iris . . . Mia figlia! . . .
Vita! . . . Non ei sei piu!
(*alcuni mercialuoli ambulanti
che passano per andare allo citta,
undendo le grida strazianti del
Cieco entravo nel giardino a lo ri-
alzono compassionevoli*).

**CORO:** Cieco, a che grida despera-
mente!

**CIECO:** Iris! Mia figlia! In casa! La!
Cercatela!
(*ajunl mercialuoli entrano nella
casa ed appariscono pol alla finestra spalancata*).

**I MERCIAIUOLO:** (*alla finestra*)
E vuota la tua casa! Iris non c'e!

**TUTTI:** Iris!
(*ascoltono*).
Iris!
(*ascoltano ancora*).
Neppur l'eco risponde!

**CIECO:** La mia Vita! . . . Pupilla
da' mei occhi!
(*tonnano dalla casa, uno del merciaiuoli. nell' uscire, vede e il fogi-

**KYOTO:** Thanks, Mousme! Now we
are going. Music!
(*The Mousme arise to their feet
and disperse*)

**CHORUS:** Shall we go? It is late
now! Let us go.

**KYOTO:** (*To Osaka*) Now I'll
leave this letter and the money to
the blind man and the deed is done.

**OSAKA:** (The deed is done.)
(*All separate, crossing the bridge;
Kyoto runs into the garden of Iris,
quickly places on the threshold of
the cottage a note with money for
the blind man. He then runs to
join his companions, who are far
away*)

**CIECO:** This play is false—utter-
ly—totally.
It was of evil intent and badly given.
(*Believing Iris still present*)
Iris, do you not say so? Don't you an-
swer? I see it! She is overcome!
(*Smiling pleasantly, believing
still that he is speaking to Iris*)
No; I'll not believe it!
You are so good that every sorrow
Breaks through to your heart.
(*Stretching out his trembling
arms*)
Let us go, give me your arm.
Why not believe in the sighs of
Dhia?
(*Smiling again*)
Very well. I believe! Come!
Give me your arm! One caress
For poor old Cieco! Iris!
Again do you not answer?
(*Surprised*)
Iris! Iris! My daughter!
My Life! Are you not here!
Iris! My Iris! Iris!
(*He gets up, staggering; he
searches around him; stumbles;
falls. Some of the peddlers passing
toward the city, bearing the cries,
mock the blind man, but coming
into the garden are moved with
pity*)

**CHORUS:** Ah, that wailing! It is of
desperation.

**CIECO:** Iris! My daughter! In the
house!
There! Please look for her!
(*Some of the peddlers go into the
house; and appear at the wide
open window*)

**PEDDLERS:** (*At the windows*) The
house is empty. Iris is not here!

**CIECO:** Call her loudly, for pity's
sake!

**ALL:** Iris! Iris!
(*They listen*)
Iris! Iris!
(*Again they listen*)

**CHORUS:** There is not the least answer.

**CIECO:** She's my life! The sight of
my old eye balls!
My only daughter! And she so good!
(*Coming away from the house

## Act I

lo e il denaro lasciato da Kyoto sulla soglia).

UN MERCIAIUOLO: Tu la piange! Non piangerla!

CIECO: Che dici? Ohime, che dici?

IL MERCIAIUOLO: Qui sulla soglia t'ha lasciato un foglio e del denaro!
(*mostrando foglio e denaro ai compagni*).

CORO: E al Yoshiwara!
(*il cieco tocca e ritocca, unsendo in grid; soffocati, il foglio e il denaro*).
(*l'ive, il dolore, rendo il Cieco come pazzo, ed allontanando con violenza alcuni fra i Merciaiuoli che gil stanno vicinl verebe correre da solo verso la citta: ma incespica e cade—I Merciaiuoli si affrettono a rialzan il Cleco, il quale prorompe in dirotto pianto*).

CIECO: (*piangendo, se rivolge ai Merciaiuoli che sono invasi di un gran sento di pieta*).
La Casa! Il mio giardino. Quel che tengo
a chidi voi mi guida al Yoshiwara?
(*Con voce terribile*).
Or voglia la-la schieffeggiarla!
Vogli sputarle in volto voglio e Maladirla! Iris! Mia Vita!
(*le lagrime gle troncano le parole*).
(*quasl rergognoso di quell'affetto che gli trabocca dall'anima, esclama minaccioso*).
E posica . . . e poscia . . . e poscia..
(*pietosamente i Merciaiuoli lo sorrengono e lo accompagnano, barcollante, inebetito quesi fantasma verso la citta*).

*Fine dell'Atto Primo*

one of the peddlers at the doorway sees and picks up the letter, and the money left on the threshold by Kyoto)

PEDDLER: You are crying! Don't cry any more.

CIECO: What do you speak of? Alas, what say you?

PEDDLER: Here on the threshold was left a letter, and this money. (*Showing the note and money to his companions*)

ALL: She's at the Yoshiwara!
(*The blind man touches and retouches the letter and money, sending out great suffocating cries. His anger and grief take away his senses, and at length for his violence, some of the peddlers wish to run away to the city but he stumbles and falls. The peddlers hesitate to raise the blind man up, who again breaks out into weeping; turning to the peddlers who are filled with a feeling of pity*)

CIECO: My cottage! To my garden! All I love! Ah! who among you Will guide me to the Yoshiwara? I must go there! To whip her! I will spit in her face and curse her! Iris! My life!
(*Weeping breaks off his words*)
(*As if looking at those who had caused the downfall of her soul, he exclaims, threatening*)
And then!—and then,—and then—
(*Pitying, the peddlers surround him and accompany him, stumbling, toward the city*)

*End of Act I*

## ■ ATTO SECONDO

Dov'è ora l'umile casetta tua così modesta e semplice colle sue stuoie colorate e i battenti di quercia, o piccola Iris;—la bianca siepe di biancos-pine fiorite?;-il sentiero coverto dal fiore delle scabbiose che conduce al rio?;—

Dov'è la pace dei campi intorno e il silenzio ristoratore come il riposo della tua vallea entro all'ampia circolare distesa di monti e, in alto, la solenne maestà del Fousiyama?;—dove l'aria purissima?;—dove la luce libera?—

## ■ ACT II

Where now, O little Iris, is your tiny simple cottage with its colored blinds and wooden doors? Where the white hedge of flowering hawthorn? Where the flowered path that leads to the river?

Where is the peace of the fields all around it, and the silence, healing as slumber, of your valley nestling in the vast amphitheatre of the mountains? Where the solemn majesty of Fushi Yama? Where the limpid air? Where the light and freedom?

Tu ora gianci nel cuore affannoso della città gaudente ove più accelerato batte il palpito delle esistenze nelle diverse febbri che agitano le genti—quella della gloria, quella del piacere, quella del denaro.—La più appariscente delle sue case è ora la tua abitazione—tu vi riposi sul rialzo di lacca ed oro di un fion ricchissimo, abbandonata la fragile persona alla stanchezza che ti hi affranto.

Tu sei nella casa di Kyoto.

Qui, nella dolcissima ora del drago, non verrà il Sole a dissipare i piccoli sogni paurosi della tua infantile fantasia!;—qui, nella misteriosa ora del cignale, non la luna scenderà a posarsi con te!—

Qui, ricche stuoie a tessiture fantasiose, impediscono alla luce di penetrarvi.

No, il Sole non penetra in questa casa!—Qui tutto è riflesso di metallo che scoppia a vivi e rapidi sfavillii dalle profumiere cesellate dove brucia esalando l'olio di camelia odorosa, dai vasi smaltati, dalle grandi chimere e mostri di smalto e cobalto che adornano la stanza.

Là in un angolo un bouddah ridè, i piccoli occhi sfuggenti.

Non la luce, non l'armonia del Sole! Solo, su dalla tumultuante via, per le stuoie che la dimenticanza dei kamouro ha lasciato semiaperte, entra l'affannoso moto della vita cittadina, le strida dei merciaioli, le minacce dei samouraïs, le ansanti cadenze dei djin, i diversi idiomi dei dragomanni, la bestemmia e la risata.

Presso al tuo letto, come spettri, stanno ancora le guèchas. La guècha della commedia accoscia sussurra a bocca chiusa un 'Anakomitasani" accompagnandosi al suono del sàmisen.

Kyoto le coglie appunto in quell'abbandono di oziosa trascuratezza— e le investe.

Accosciata presso il letto ove giace Iris susurranda "Ana Komitasansa" accompagnandosi al suono di samisen e tamtam delle altre guechas.

UNA GUECHA (*a bocca chiusa*).

Now you are lying in the fiercely beating heart of the City of Joy, where the pulse of existence beats faster with the fevers that distract mankind—that of Glory, that of Pleasure, that of Gain. The most gaudy of its houses is now your dwelling; you are now reposing on a couch rich with gold, your fragile body abandoned to the weariness which overcomes you.

You are in the house of Kyoto.

Here, in the sweetest hour of the mid-day sleep, the sun will not come to dissipate the tiny timid dreams of your childish fancy. Here in the mysterious hour of the curfew the moon will not rise to rest with you.

Here, rich hangings fantastically woven forbid the light to enter.

No, the sun does not penetrate within this house. Here, all is sheen of metal glancing back in swift rays from the chiselled censers in which burns, exhaling sweet perfume, the fragrant oil of camelia; from the enamelled vases; from the huge dragons and monsters of enamel and dark blue which adorn the chamber.

There in the corner smiles a Buddha, his eyes half hidden.

Not the light, not the harmony of the sun. Only from the bustle of the street below, through the shutters which the negligence of the attendants has left half open enters the frenzied roar of the life of the City; the cries of the peddler, the threats of the police, the panting cadence of the ricksha men, the varied idioms of the dragomans, blasphemy and loud laughter.

Near your couch, like spectres, still stand the Geishas, still disguised in their horrible masks. The Geisha of the comedy sitting beside you is humming with closed lips an "Anakomitasani" to the accompaniment of the sâmisen and the tam-tams of the other Geishas.

Kyoto comes upon them in this attitude of careless indolence and scolds them.

(*Gathered near the bed where Iris is lying, humming "Anakomitisana," accompanied by the sound of samisens and tam-tams, are three Geishas*)

A GEISHA: (*Hums with closed mouth*)

**KYOTO:** La che ci fate
ancora mascherate?
O che siete bonzi? e . . . stz!
Tacete! silenzio; non voglio appena
desta
abbia ricordi tristi, ognor dolori!
Tutta una festa, un giorno d'ori,
di bronzi e fiori!
(*sorpreso nel vedere aperta una
delle imposte*).
Toh! fuori spalancata e ancora
l'impannata?
(*vorebbe gridare, ma si ritiene*).
Silenzio, dico! Rispondermi volete?
Oh, le sfaccite! Udite! Da la strada
Salgon le voci chiocce de le genti,
Vandari ed il venire, de djin correnti!
O che avete gli orecchi falla in gia-
da?
Con tal baccano o chi puo mai dormire?
Echete! Mogie! Vostre voce acute.
son vespe, son cicale, son zanzare!
Mute!
vi voglio, mute, e se possibili, senza
respirare!
(*va a chiudere l'imposta, guardando nella strada vede un elle-
gante norimon entrare nella
casa*).
Toh! Vien gente! E Osaka in palan-
chino!
Giu tutti col migliore nostro inchino!
(*entra con inusata vivacita in-
drizzandosi a Kyoto*).

**OSAKA:** Ch'io vegga, ov'e la
Mousme
da li occhi simila a camelie!

**KYOTO** (*calmandole*). La voce
tua moduta in suon piu grave
Come punta d'agrave
Va ne le orecchio a chi posa
Ripsoa!
(*l'astuto taikomati mostra all'
annoiato signori Iris addormentata*).
(*allontanando brutalmente le
Guechas, che scompaiono rapide*).
Donne, vampiri della casa, via!

**OSAKA:** Sollevani il velario!

**KYOTO:** Parla Piano!
(*sollevando il velario*).
Toh! guardala! E perfetta!
Non ti Pare?

**OSAKA:** Spande l'oro dal loto, la
piccina!

**KYOTO:** Sogguardo a quella bocca
porporina.

**OSAKA:** E cilieggia da cogliene e
mangiare!

**KYOTO:** Vedi che braccio! e vedi
un po'che mano!

**KYOTO:** Shall we have again the
masquerade
Or do you wish the priests?
(*Preventing them from answer-
ing*)
Quiet! Be silent!
I want nothing to disturb her!
She remembers only grief and sor-
rows.
It's a feast day; a day of money;
Of bells and flowers.
(*Surprised to see a window open*)
Toh! without, that panel is wide
open!
(*They would answer; but he stops
them*)
Silence! I tell you.
You want to answer back! You bra-
zens!
Now listen! From the street comes
The chattering voices of the people
As they go here and there,
And of the djins running.
Or are your ears filled with cotton?
With that bacchanal going on
Who would be able to sleep?
Now quiet, stupids! Your voices
Are as sharp as the sound of wasps,
Tree-frogs or mosquitos! Mute
I want you! Mute! And, if possible,
Don't breathe!
(*He goes to close the window, and
looking into the street he sees an
elegant nobleman enter the
house*)
Toh! they're coming! And Osaka
In a palanquin! We must bow
down.
(*Quickly all bow as they touch
their foreheads*)

**OSAKA:** (*Entering with unusual
vivacity and going toward Kyoto*)
Now that I am here, where is the
Mousme,
With the eyes like camelias?

**KYOTO:** Modulate your voice to
something lower.
Like the point of a thorn it goes into
The ears of the sleeper.—She's
sleeping.
(*He calls brutally to the Geishas*)
Ladies! Vampires of the house!
Away!
(*Osaka and Kyoto come near the
bed of Iris*)

**OSAKA:** Let us lift the veil.

**KYOTO:** Speak softly.
(*Lifting the veil*).
Here! Look at her! She's perfect!
Don't you think so?

**OSAKA:** She sends out the fragrance of the lotus! The beauty!

**KYOTO:** Look at that beautiful purple mouth!

**OSAKA:** Lips like cherries, ready to
be eaten!

**KYOTO:** See what arms! And look
at that little hand!

**OSAKA:** (*con grande entusiasmo*). Crea in quegli occhi il lampo
d'un desio.
Vibri in quegliocchi il senso,
l'uman dio,
Una scintilla, un fuoco uno favilla,
che di piace ne incenda la pupilla,
e dimmi, come lei ne sai tu alcuna?

**KYOTO:** Nessuna, in fede mia nessuna!

**OSAKA:** In questa noia matta
Ogni di soddisfatta e insoddisfatta
costei nel cuor m'ha cacciata
una spina di brama che m'offana!
Non e mousme leziosa di citta
ordigno fatto per la voluttà!
Qui c'e l'anima!
(*torno presso il letto a guardare e
lasoia il velario sulla fanciulla
addormentata, poi trae con se
lontano in disparte Kyoto onde il
loro chiacchierio non risvegli
Iris*).
Lunga lotta m'annoia
a ritrosie io mal m'addato
s'ella resistesse?

**KYOTO:** Abbi denaro
E il paradiso e ovunque! Comprendi tu?

**OSAKA:** Parla un linguaggio chiaro!

**KYOTO:** Son fior le frasi,
le parole foglie,
ma il frutto e l'or,
che satolla le voglie,
Comprendi tu?

**OSAKA:** Abborro dai proverbi!

**KYOTO:** Regali! . . . Doni . . . ap-
pariscenti!
Ricchi! Vistosi! Mi comprendi?
Larga mano! aperti borsellino!
Mi comprendi?
Vesti! Fiori! Giovelli!
Mi comprendi?

**OSAKA:** Oh, fauce ingorda!
Oh, fauce sazia mai!

**KYOTO:** Dapprima gia ci vuol che
moino
per rasciugar gli occhietta da le lacrime,
Poi, una nuora poi doventa suocera!

**OSAKA:** E aggiunge, in oltre, il piu
fantazioso
e armonico linguaggio figura-
ta . . .

**KYOTO:** Desta e la piccina! Vieni
via.
Va a preparti un romanzesco viso!
Porta gemme, regali, mi comprendi?
(*escono cautamente*).

**IRIS:** (*si sveglia e guarda intorno
a se sorpresa*). Ognora sogni, sogni
e sogni . . .
(*con dolcezza*).
Oh, il bel velario . . . oh, il lieve
drappo

**OSAKA:** (*With great enthusiasm*)
I believe that such eyes are the
lamps of desire!
In these eyes there is sensibility!
The true human feeling!
A spark, a twinkling of fire,
Of pleasure in these burning pu-
pils!
And, tell me, have you ever
Seen any one like her?

**KYOTO:** I, never! On my faith, no
one!

**OSAKA:** In love's annoying
madness
Every day satisfaction is unsatisfied.
This one has taken my heart.
She has put a thorn in my breast
That tortures me! She is no
Wanton Mousme from the city!
Made to go the rounds of pleasure!
Here is a soul!
(*He comes near the bed to look at
her, and then goes away a little
distance with Kyoto, where their
talk will not disturb Iris*)
For waywardness I'm not fit
Who could resist her?

**KYOTO:** They have money in Para-
dise
As everywhere else!
Do you understand me?

**OSAKA:** You speak in a moonshiny
language!

**KYOTO:** The phrase is the flower
The words are its leaves!
But its fruit is the gold
I would harvest in sheaves!
Understand me?

**OSAKA:** I hate the proverb!

**KYOTO:** Presents, showy gifts!
Riches, are comely!
Understand me?
A liberal hand! An open purse!
Understand me?
Garments, flowers, jewels!
Understand me?

**OSAKA:** Jaws of a glutton, never to
be satisfied!

**KYOTO:** First we try coaxing; then
work on her fears
To rescue her eyes from the folly of
tears!
A sister-in-law requires a mother-
in-law!

**OSAKA:** You add to the others a
still more fantastic and figurative
language.

**KYOTO:** Stz! You disturb the girl!
Come, this way!
Go and get up a romantic face.
Bring gems, presents!
Understand me?
(*They go out cautiously*)

**IRIS:** (*She awakes and looks
around surprised*). Always vi-
sions! Visions and visions!
(*Sweetly*)
Ah! this beautiful drapery!
And this light dress all covered with

tutto sparsa a. or la a
vesta e un velo e ha trasparenze
a'onda e di nube! Or io cosi ho
vergogna! non piu le mie pianelle
in lacca nera, ho sandali
dorati, e il pie vi posa cosi
morbidamente . . . che ne me
pare
di comminar sopra un prato
dipiume!
(*Ed ecco svolgersi nella mente tra-
sonata dell'ingenua fanciulla le
scene del teatrino, la danza delle
Guechas e . . . la rapimento*).
Ecco! or ricordo! si! il teatro!
Dhia! La danza delle geuchas!
Il nero manto m'avvolve del
Vampiro!
Ove son io? Morta son? dunque?
Si; sono una morta!
E questa casa bella e il Paradiso!?
(*guardando intorno piu attentamente mormora fra l'angoscia e
la gioia*).
(*si ode un dolcissimo suono di
samisen interno; Iris ascolta*).
(*un samisen attira i suoi sguardi*).
chi e morto tutto so, diceva il bonzo!
Mi voglio accompagnai l'Uta di Na-
niva!
Sorge dal mar la luna e luna piena:
una giunca laggiu, me mena
Io vo coll' onda che mi porta.
La voce canta, ma il suon non accompagna!
(*getta indispettita l'istromento,
mentre riprende il suono interno
del samisen*).
Dicon di gran bugie nel mondo ai
vivi!
Chi da vivo non sa, non sa da morto!
(*si aggira curiosa e meravigliata,
ammirando i ricchi paraventi ed i
preziosi dipinti*).
(*verde pennelli e colori su di una
tavola*).
(*essa vi si accosta ed attratt a dal
mestero del colori siedo presso la
tavola tentando dipingere*).
(*Iris getta indispetti a il foglio di
carta*).
(*ed ora vorrebbe dipingere un
cielo azzurro*). (*sfiduciata lascia
cadere i pennelli*).
Io pingo . . . pingo, ma il mio
pennilo
invano stendo, intengo!
Va la mia mano invano!
Io peso a un fiore.
E n'essce invece un'angue tutto terrore!
Tutto un rosso di sangue!
Se voglio un cielo azzurro in mio
pensiero
e un fosco velo un velo tinto in
nero!
La fantasia con se m'invola porta
di casa mia a la picciola porta:
la—la pupilo d'un Cieco finalmente ha una scintula una favilla
d'una luce rovente che fulge e brilla
ma e il lucer d'una lacrima

irises!
Now my clothing is a veil;
And has the transparency of water
and the clouds!
I am ashamed of such things!
No more slippers lacquered black,
But I have lovely sandals!
And my feet on these soft cushions,
They will nevermore walk for me
over the meadow!
(*She revolves in her mind, dream-
ily, the innocent girl scene in the
puppet theatre; the dances of the
Geishas, and then her capture*)
Let's see! Now I remember! Yes!
The theatre! Dhia! The dances of the
Geishas!
The black mantle that covered the
Vampire!
Where am I? Am I dead? Truly?
Yes! I am dead! And this beautiful
house
Is Paradise!
(*She looks about her attentively
murmuring both from anguish
and from joy*)
(*She hears the sweet sound of a
samisen near. She listens*)
"Whoever is dead, knows all," so
said the priest.
(*She takes the samisen*)
I will accompany "The Fall of Nine-
vah."
"Rises the moon over the ocean,
And now it is for me!"
(*She tries to accompany herself
but makes only meaningless
sounds*)
"A bulrush below I would carry
With the wave upon the sea."
(*Breaks off*)
My voice sings but the sound does
not accompany it.
(*Throws away the samisen*)
They tell a great lie in the living
world.
What the living know not
The dead know not!
(*She looks around, with curiosi-
ty, wondering and admiring the
rich folding screen, and the beau-
tiful pictures. She sees brushes
and colors on a table. She seats
herself near the table and tries to
paint. She would paint a flower,
but instead makes a snake. She
lets fall the brush*)
I paint — paint — but my brush
I employ in vain! My hand
Moves without purpose!
I think of a flower, and a snake
All terrible, with a red, bloody
mouth
Comes instead. If I would make
The azure sky; there comes a dark
veil;
A spot of black! My fancy takes me
To the door of my cottage;
My pretty little doorway;
There the eye of a blind man
At last has a spark, a ray
Of red light, which sparkles and
dazzles,
But it shines through tears slowly
falling.

che lentamente stilla!
(*accasciata, nasconde il viso le
mani*).
In paradiso (*ha detto*) non si
piange!
Ed io de lacrime ho i miei occhi
pieni!
(*una cortina si solleva lentamente e Kyoto introduce Osaka*).
(*i due uomini soffermano sul limitare della porta e guardano la
fanciulla seduta al tavalino del
colori*).

OSAKA: A un cenno mio manda le
vesti e i doni

KYOTO: Si, mandero!

OSAKA: or . . . quanto a te—
inutil qui . . . va, via!

KYOTO: A meraviglia, Vo!
(*il talkomati scompare dietro la
cortina, insciando soli il giov-
anne signore voluttuoso e
l'ingenua Mousme*).
(*alle parole di Osaka Iris si volge
sorpressa,*)

OSAKA: Oh, come al tuo sottile
corpo s'aggira e
s'informa di tela flessuosa notturna
Vesta! senza posa lo sguarda ti
rimira da capo a pie
e l'anima s'appago nella sorpresa
vaga, nel portento gentile di tua
belta, che in festa alta trionfa in te!
(*Osaka si avvincia sempre piu ad
Iris Questa si ritrae ancor piu,
sordesa e impaurita*).

IRIS: Conosca questa voce! O gia
l'udivi
In ogni sera parola si rivela
E la voce d'Jor! E Jor! E Jor!

OSAKA: Perche il piede vitragge se
a te vicin
mi porta il mio desio. Dentro
a'tuoi lascia lo sguardo mio desirio-
so
penetravar! Io ne tuoi occhi vego
tut
ti i cieli! Gli olezzi io bevo in te di
tutti maggi!
(*Osaka accarezza la testa di Iris;
questa chiude timorosa gli occhi.
Al tocco del giovine gli spilloni cadono e disciolgono liberi i lunghi
capille che fluiscono giu per le
spalie di Iris recoprendola come
de un manto*).

OSAKA: (*tuffando con volutto le
mani nel cappeli di Iris*).
Ah i tuoi capelli son si lunghi e tanti
da incatenarti intorno.. tutto gli
uomini!
Tu m'incatena e per la via,
Mousme,
d'ogni tua brama, deh, tu mi mena!

(*She hides her face with her
hands*)
In Paradise they say there's no
weeping,
And I of tears have my eyes full.
(*A curtain is slowly raised and
Kyoto brings in Osaka*)
(*The two men pause a little at the
entrance, and watch Iris seated at
the table with the colors*)

OSAKA: (*Speaking sotto voce to
Kyoto*) At a sign from me hand me
the garments and the gifts.

KYOTO: Yes; I'll hand them.

OSAKA: Now — as to you —
you're useless here.
Go away.

KYOTO: That's wonderful! Go!
(*Kyoto, the taikomati, disappears
behind the curtain leaving alone
the young man and the innocent
Mousme*)
(*At the words of Osaka Iris turns
herself, surprised*)

OSAKA: Oh how cunningly your
body
Is surrounded and shut in by that
Flexible night-robe! Without rest-
ing
I stare at it, admiring you from head
to foot.
The soul is pleased of the surprised
lover
In the wonderful gentility of your
beauty!
Which in the high feast will bring
Triumph to you!
(*Osaka comes nearer and nearer
to Iris, who draws back again
through surprise and fear*)

IRIS: (I know that voice! I have
heard it!
In every word is he revealed.
It is the voice of Jor! It is Jor!
It is Jor!)

OSAKA: Why do you draw back
your foot
At the very beginning of my longing?
Within the veil let me look
Where my strong love would enter!
In your eyes I see all the heavens!
In your fragrance I drink in all May!
(*Osaka caresses the head of Iris,
who timorously closes her eyes. At
the young man's touch her comb
falls, and frees the long hair,
which falls on her shoulders, and
covers her as with a mantle*)

OSAKA: (*Toying with his hands
in her hair*) Ah! your hair, so abun-
dant and beautiful!
It weaves chains around you,
For all men! You have enchained
Me by your manner, Mousme,
By every motion do you draw me!

IRIS: (*incredula, quasi sorridendo e riannodandosi i capelli*). Da niuno ho udito dirmi tanta cosa. Iris tanta belleza? Niun lo crede! M'ha detto un sol finor che son grazosa,
il babbo mio, ch'e Cieco e non me vede.

OSAKA: Il tuo corpo s'iniglia d'un candore piu
bianca del Fousiaama! Bocca sana vermiglio.
Fresca fontana ove zampillan tutte le dolcezza e tutte le carezze!
Ove il mio sangue vivo si ristora!
(*Iris sorride nell' udiere le arole entusiastiche di Osaka*).
Tu ridi? Ridi? Ridi! Ridi ancor!

IRIS: Ho fatto male a rider, ma non so
se muovermi o star fermia a sue parole
se fargli reverenza! Gli diro "Signor,"
No. Re? E poco.. Figliuol del Sole!

OSAKA: Arrossia mie parole? Non arrossir!
Lascia arrossire il Sole! egli ogni di ha tramonti tu? sali,
sali altissima a le superbe aurore ai superbi orrizzonti del mio amore!

IRIS: Figlio del Sol! (*da in una stridente risata Iris si ritral ancora, impaurita*).

OSAKA: Ah! tu fanciulla ancor me credi
Jor della commedia? Or recito la Vita.
T'ho in vesta d'istrion per farti mia rapita!
Apri gli occhi, Mousme! vede ed impara la Vita!
Il vero nome mio vuoi tu sapere? Ebben, Mousme, io mi chiamo "Il Piacere!"

IRIS: (*ricordando con accento di terrore*). Un di (ero piccino) al tempio vidi un bonzo
a un paravento tutto fatto a simboli, sciorinare il velame d'un Mistero—
Era una plaga d'un gran mare morto color del bronzo; e vera un Cielo rosso livido
e una gran spiaggia, una grau spiaggia
morta di grigio e nero—una fanciulla
giaceva adagiata, scorne le membra,
sparsi i capelli, e nella bocca
un riso che era uno spasimo—
su dal mar morta unagran
piovra intanto il capo ergeva.
e la fanciulla col grande
occhio falcato fuor guatava—
questa domata a quel terror di
sguardo tutto affisava.
su dal mai morto, e viscidi tentacole
moveva il mostro, e per le gambe, pei reni e per le spalle, poi perle

IRIS: (*Incredulous, smiling, and rearranging her hair*) From no one did I ever hear such things! Iris so beautiful! No one will believe it. Only one has ever spoken so graciously. He was my father. He was blind, and never saw me!

OSAKA: Your body is of lilies. whiter than Fujiama. Your mouth is vermilion; a fresh fountain overflowing with caressing sweetness, where my mounting blood would fain restore itself! You smile! You smile! Smile! Smile again!

IRIS: I did wrong to smile! But I know not whether to stay or run from your words. I make my reverence! Shall I say "Signor?" No! King? It is too small. Son of the Sun!

OSAKA: You are blushing at my words! Don't blush! Let the sun blush! Has he not drawn you every day higher and higher, up to the highest? You are the glorious dawn — the great horizon of my love!

IRIS: Son of the Sun! (*After a shrill laugh, Iris again draws back, frightened*)

OSAKA: Ah! you child! Again do you believe me Jor of the comedy? Now I play Life! I have stage clothes exactly fitted for my bride. Open your eyes, Mousme! See
And get ready for Life.
My true name would you like to know?
Very well, Mousme, I am called Pleasure!

IRIS: (*Recoiling with accents of terror*) One day (I was a child) at the temple
I saw a priest, with a large screen All made over with symbols,
To show the veil of Mystery.
There was the shore of a great dead sea
Of the color of bronze. And there was a heaven
Red as blood, an ugly livid red, And a great seashore of dead Gray and black. There a child Was lying, lean in limbs, with scattering hair,
And on its mouth a laugh, which was a spasm.
On this dead sea a great monster its head
Was raising. And the child
With large eye peeping,
Was captivated, by a look it was transfixed.
By this sea of the dead, with its viscid tentacles,
The monster moved; and by the legs,

chiome e il fronte e gli occhi e il petto esile ansante, e per le bracchia,
le stringe e alloecia! La stringe e allacia in viso! Essa sorride ognor! essa sorride e muor . . . con un estremo
spasima che par un riso, essa sorrida e muor! e muor!
E il bonzo a voce forte:
"Quella piovra e Piacere!"
"Quella piovra e Morte!"
(*Iris lascia cadere ai piedi del givovane, piangendo, e rimanendo accocciata dalla paura e dal dolore*).
Deh . . . ch'o torni a mio padre!

OSAKA: (*con cinismo*). Son le folle dei bonzi spavaldi e i ipocriti che all' alito d'un bacio si sbugiardono!
(*a an cenno di Osaka le Koumaro portano e stendono ai piedi di Iris stoffe, gioielli, ventagli, fiori*).
(*sallevando Iris e stringendola a se poco a poco*).

OSAKA: Or dammi il braccio tuo braccio de neve e avorio!
intorno al callo
cosi m'annoda!
sciogli i capelli
la testa bruna sovra il mio petto tu m'abbandona!
Cogli occhi, gli occhi miei tu, ed io, labbra le labbra
vi, scendo e tocco
la dolce bocca.
(*Osaka abbondona la sua bocca su quella di Iris quasi svenuta mormorando e supplicando*).
E questo il baccio
(*Iris staccadosi da Osaka rimane atterrita poi prorompe i pianto*).

OSAKA: (*guardandola, sorpreso*). Piangi?

IRIS: Penso a mia padre!

OSAKA: Gli daro vesti e denaro.

IRIS: Io penso alla mia casa!

OSAKA: Palazzi avrai!

IRIS: Io penso al mio giardino!

OSAKA: Ne avrai d'immense e a serre in fiore!

IRIS: ma non sono i mie flori

OSAKA: (*E una puppetola!*) Nulla desio
ti desca di codesto splendore. Vesti, ori? E bacio e un esca cui non morde il tuo cuore?
chiedi, fanciulla, Brama! . . . Ta pur abbi un desio!

IRIS: Voglio il giardino mio!
Io voglio il mio giardino,
Colla sua siepe intorno, la mia casetta bianca
col mormorate rio, col suo villagio

By the loins, and by the shoulders And then by the hair, the forehead and the eyes.
And the chest, lean, panting,
And by the arms, with strings Bound it. Bound, with strings over its face,
It smiled on, ever! It smiled and died,
In a terrible convulsion that seemed a laugh
It smiled and died.
And the priest, in a loud voice, said: "This monster is Pleasure!
This monster is Death!"
(*Iris lets herself fall at the feet of Osaka, weeping, and lies powerless through grief and fear*)
Oh! that I could return to my father!

OSAKA: (*With cynicism*) There are the lies of the impudent priest And hypocrite, which the delights of one kiss will overcome!
(*At a sign from Osaka, the female servants bring and place at the feet of Iris gifts, silks, jewels, fans and flowers*)
(*They lift Iris up and she gathers strength little by little*)

OSAKA: Now give me your arm;
Your arm of snow and ivory —
Around my neck as a love bond Scatter your hair. Your head on my bosom,
Give yourself to me; your eyes to mine!
And I, lips to lips, will come down And touch your sweet mouth!
(*Osaka puts his mouth on that of Iris, as subdued, she supplicates and murmurs*)
This is a kiss!
(*Iris disengages herself from Osaka, and terrified, breaks out into weeping*)

OSAKA: (*Looking at her, surprised*) Crying?

IRIS: I think of my father!

OSAKA: I'll give you clothes and money!

IRIS: I think of my cottage!

OSAKA: Palaces you shall have!

IRIS: I think of my garden!

OSAKA: Immense fields that you can plant
All in flowers!

IRIS: But they are not my flowers!

OSAKA: (*annoyed and angry*)
She's but a little puppet!
Have you no love for all this splendor?
Garments? Gold? Is a kiss a monster That will bite your heart?
You seek Bramma, child! Have you not one desire?

IRIS: I want my garden! I want my garden with its hedge around it!
My white cottage, with the murmuring brooklet,
With the village to buy in!

a manca
con la vallata a prati, col sol che
oppena e giorno
appar sugli elevati fianchi del Fousiyama
e mi chiama, mi chiama!

**OSAKA:** (*seccato vivolgendosi a Kyoto*). Da un' ora essa m'attedia!
E pupa da commedia! pupa di leg-
no; or io me sdegno!
Un mio consiglio accetta!

**KYOTO:** (*con finta sollomis-
sione*). Ognora Kyoto impara!

**OSAKA:** (*imitando Iris*). "Torni
alla sua casetta!"

**KYOTO:** E questo il tuo consiglio?
La espongo al Yoshiwara!

**OSAKA:** Fa pur. Ah, me! che noia
Vo! sbadglio.

**KYOTO:** (*con astuzia parlando fra se*). Colle piccine, gran maestra
natura;
O moina, o paura!
Osaka e giovin, ve de ratto
E ratto e i vuole il suo desio tradotto
in fatto.
Esperienza e pazienza!
Ah me! Vedlam!
(*con occhio conoscitore osserva e studia attentomenta Iris*).
E in una vesta ancor piu trasparente
codesta
Come se indosso avesse a vesta il
nulla
Vedrite quol trionfo di fanciulla!
(*sceglie una veste e fa cenno a le donne di vistirne Iris*).
alla toeletta . . . Ol'a—
(*le donne accorrono; Iris impaurita vuol fuggire*).

**KYOTO:** Con me retrosa?
(*Imperioso*).
Qui s'obbedisce! Bada!
Per le putte cattive c'e la morte!
(*apre la parete a destra e mostra ad Iris un precipizio oscuro e fon-
do; Iris indietreggia impaurita*).
Chiamo il Vampiro, e fatta e latua
sorte!

**IRIS:** (*implorando*). No—non me
fate male!
(*rabbonito*).

**KYOTO:** Non lo voglio!
(*Insinuante-prende il pupo che nella commedia rappresentava Jor e lo porge ad Iris*).
E se obbedisci, guardo! tuo!

**IRIS:** E Jor

---

With the valley, and the meadow!
With the sun rising in the morning!
Shining over the broad sides of Fuji-
ama
And calling me! calling me!

**OSAKA:** (*Dryly, and turning to Kyoto*) For an hour she has wearied
me!
She's a comedy puppet. A puppet
of wood.
She makes me tired.
Now take my counsel!

**KYOTO:** (*With a pretense of submission*) Kyoto must always be
learning.

**OSAKA:** (*imitating Iris*) "Take
her to her home!"

**KYOTO:** And that is your counsel!
I'll expose her in the Yoshiwara.

**OSAKA:** So do! Ah me. I'm tired. I
go.
I yawn.
(*He goes out yawning*)

**KYOTO:** (*With cunning, talking to himself*) With children, Nature
is the grand master.
Either by coaxing or by fear.
Osaka is young; after rapine.
Forcing in his pleasure, his ecstasy.
Experience and patience! Ah me!
We shall see!
(*With the eye of a connoisseur he looks at Iris, and studies her at-
tentively*)
Perfect—and in a garment again
More transparent than this one;
As appearing to have clothes of
nothing;
We shall see the triumph of the
child.
(*He selects a garment and makes a sign to the women to put it on Iris*)
To the toilet. Ho there!
(*The women come, running. Iris, frightened, would run away*)

**KYOTO:** (*Irritated*) Stubborn,
with me! Here you must obey!
Careful! For a bad wench it is death!
(*Opening the wall at the right, he shows Iris a precipice, dark and deep. Iris draws away, frightened*)

**KYOTO:** I'm called the Vampire!
And I am your husband!

**IRIS:** (*Imploringly*) No. Don't treat
me badly.

**KYOTO:** I don't want to. But you
must obey!
Remember!
(*He takes the puppet which repre-
sents Jor in the comedy, and hands it to Iris*) It is yours!

**IRIS:** Jor!

---

**KYOTO:** (*dietro le stuoje, spiando nella via*). Annoto! La gente dotta
e ghiotta
d'ogni cosa vaga e rara
s'accalca e indagi
Arrossa di lumiere il Yoshiwara!
Oh, febre de Il Piacere!
(*intanto le esperte donne com-
minciano ad abbigliare Iris dietro un paravento*).
La parete sottile scorre e si schiude
a uno sciame gentile di donne ignude
Qualch altro Osaka certo passeva
e in questa onesta rete
di giovinezza incappera.
(*mentre abbigliano, Iris tutta intenta al pupo, si risovviene la dol-
cissima cantilena del dramma, e mentre repete, infantilemente lo fa agire*).

**KYOTO:** Vediam . . . cosi stai
bene!
(*strappa ruvidamente il pupo ad Iris, e io gitta in alto; ana guecha lo offerra a volo*). Ha sonno il piccol Jor; poniamolo a dormire! sovra
la bocca un vaga punta in or!
(*prende an pennello, e designa un neo d'oro sulla labbra d'Iris*).
Cosi! Vediam ove posarti . . .
In alto! Ti voglio qui!
(*collora Iris sulla veranda*). (*con enfasi*).
superba erette le divin tua forma!
Ed or vediam se la gente abbocca!
Attente, streghe, attente, attente!
(*colpo di mani-gridato*).
Via le cortime!
(*le guechas fanno scorrere rapidamente le mobili pareti*).
(*si scorge la strada del Yoshiwara tutta affollata*).
(*L'improvisa apparizione di Iris, attrae subito l'attenzione della folla, che prorompe in entusiasmo*).

**CORO-LA FOLLA:** Oh, maraviglia
del maraviglie!
La vaga figlia—E rosa thea
Fior verbena! Fior da vaniglia!
Fra le piu vaghe figlie
O vaga mervaviglia!
Giorno di rose e di viole notte sere-
na:
Parla bella Mousme!
Udiamo l'armonia di tue parole!
L'anima ti desia!

**KYOTO:** (*esultandosi fregandosi le mani*). Son uomo di talento, si o
no?
Ve' che furore!
Strana e la genti in fregula d'amore.
Io ci guadagnero a staia i rios!

**OSAKA:** Datemi il passo!

**KYOTO:** E Osaka.

**OSAKA:** Indietro.

---

**KYOTO:** (*Behind the screen, peer-
ing into the street*) Just look at it!
The people, ready and hungry for
any rare attraction, are searching.
They are red with the light of the
Yoshiwara! Ah! this fever of Plea-
sure!
(*The women experts commence to dress Iris behind the screen*)
The thin little wall will safely hide
Our thinly clad women from peo-
ple outside.
Some other Osaka is sure to pass by;
And in this honest net the youth
will be caught!
(*While being dressed, Iris, always intent on the puppet, sings the cantilena of Jor, and fondles the puppet*)

**KYOTO:** We shall see. Just now it's
all right.
(*He snatches rudely the puppet, and throws it away*)
Enough of little Jor; let him go to
sleep!
Now, above the mouth, there wants
a little bit of color.
(*Takes a brush and paints a mole above the lips of Iris*)
So! Let me see where to put you!
Here? Up on high!
(*Placing Iris on the veranda*)
(*With enthusiasm*)
Supurbly erect is your beautiful
form!
And now we'll see the public cap-
tured!
Attention, witches! Attention! At-
tention!
(*Clapping his hands*)
Away with the curtain!
(*The Geishas quickly take away the light, moveable wall*)
(*The street of the Yoshiwara is seen to be crowded*)
(*The improvised apparition of Iris quickly attracts the attention of the throng, which breaks out in enthusiasm*)

**CHORUS:** O wonder of wonders!
Lovely maiden! A tea rose!
Verbena, flower, vanilla!
Of all pretty maidens
The most wonderful!
Speak! lovely Mousme!
We hear harmony in your words,
Our souls love you!
Purest gem! O diadem!

**KYOTO:** (*Elated and rubbing his hands*) Am I a man of talent—yes,
or no?
See, what a furore! The people
struggle
In the fire of passion! I'll make
more than a bushel of rios!

**OSAKA:** Here, let me pass!

**KYOTO:** It is Osaka!

**OSAKA:** Get back there!

KYOTO: Eccolo ancor! E pazzo! Io godo!

KYOTO: He here again! He's a fool. I'm glad of it.

OSAKA: Indietro! Indietro. (*aggrappandosi sale sulla veranda*). Iris, son io; io sono Osaka, Jor tutto saro per te quel che vorrai! Osaka puo donar gemme ed oro; quanto puo m'darti Jor di luce orai! qui or io m'inchino innazi a te, qui giu! qui giu nel fango a tuoi piedi, curvo a tuoi pie, fanciulla. Osaka vedi qui giu! qui giu nel fango! qui a tuoi pie. Qui la pazzia prostemo del mio orgoglio che cieco e vil mia fatta a tue bellezza! Iris ancor! ancor! ti voglio. Dammi l'immenso ciel di tue carezza! (*si slancio verso, Iris, ma Kyoto se framette Osaka e la fanciulla*).

OSAKA: Get back there. (*Clinging to the veranda*) Iris! It is I! I am Osaka; Jor! You shall have whatever you want! I am able to give you gems and gold! Pray to Jor for whatever you will! And here now I bend before you! Down here! Here down in the mud and at your feet! Bent down at your feet, dear child, see Osaka! Here, the folly of my pride Has brought all this on your beauty! Iris, once more! Once more! Once more I love you, Give me the heaven of your caresses! (*He urges himself towards Iris, but Kyoto puts himself between Osaka and the child*)

KYOTO: Osaka! io qui son servo a tutti pubblico.

KYOTO: Osaka! here I serve the whole public.

OSAKA: (*impetuosa e minnacciando Kyoto*). Io primo fui che tol tesoro vidi! Kyoto La voglio ancor! I son penti-tol . . . Ebben chi gareggar potra con me? Do tutto quel che chiedi, ladra, arpia! Iris divina, deh sia mia, Iris! (*appare nella fola il cieco accompagnato da due merciaiuoli*).

OSAKA: (*Impetuous and threatening Kyoto*) I was the first to find the treasure. Kyoto! I want her again—I'm sorry. For how much will you sell her to me? I will give you all you ask; you thief! You harpy! (*To Iris*) Iris, divine! Come! be mine! Iris! (*The blind man appears in the crowd, accompanied by two peddlers*)

CIECO: Iris! . . . Essa e qui dunque? (*rimasta nno allora intonititta, alla voce del padre sobbolza per le gran gioia*).

CIECO: Iris! (*Iris, who had been silent, at the voice of her father, sobs with joy*) Here do I find her?

IRIS: Si! son io! Padre! Son Iris! (*protendendo le braccia verso il padre mentre la fola sorpresa circonda curiosmente il cieco*).

IRIS: Yes! I'm here! (*Extending her arms towards her father while the crowd, in curiosity, surrounds the blind man*) Father! I am Iris! Ah! You are here!

CORO: Suo padre! E un cieco!

CHORUS: Her father! He's a blind man!

IRIS: Ah, qui vieni!

IRIS: Here!

CIECO: (*implorando i circostanti; la folla presa subitamente da un senso di pieta fa largo intorno al Cieco*). Conducetemi sotto a la finestra!

CIECO: (*Imploring those around; the crowd quickly affected with a feeling of pity gives plenty of room for the blind man*) Lead me up to the window!

CORO: Fate largo! Il passo!

CHORUS: Make room! Make room!

CIECO: ovi sta la fanciulla svergognata.

CIECO: Where stands the disgraced hussy.

KYOTO: (*sorpreso dall apparizione del cieco urla per giustificarsi*). Egli venduto m'ha la figlia sua!

KYOTO: (*Surprised at the apparition of the blind man and shrieking out to justify himself*) "He sold his daughter to me!"

CIECO: Iris! rispondi! Ove sei tu?

CIECO: (*Imperiously*) Iris! answer me! Where are you?

IRIS: Qui padre! (*guidata dallo voce della figlia, si avvicina, e raccoglienda manate di fango lo scaglia contro la veranda; gran movimento disorpresa nella folla*).

IRIS: Here, father! (*Guided by the voice of his daughter he goes near, and gathering his hands full of mud, he throws it toward the veranda. A great movement in the surprised throng*)

CIECO: To! sul tuo viso! To sovra il fronte! To! nella bocca! To! ne tuoi occhi fango!

CIECO: There! in your face! There, on your forehead! There! in your mouth! There, in your eyes! Mud!

CORO: Ah! (*le maledizione del padre rende Iris pazza di dolore, e respingendo tutti da se con improvviso slancio se precipita dalla finestra nelli abissa prima mostratole la Kyoto, prorompendo in grido terribile*). (*Osaka, che non arriva in tempo per salvare Iris rimane terrorizzato alla finestra, davanti al abisso*).

CIECO: (*The curses of her father make Iris crazy, and pushing all from her, with an impetuous rush, she throws herself from the window into the abyss which Kyoto had shown her, making a terrible outcry*) (*Osaka, who arrived too late to save Iris, stands terrified at the window before the abyss. Kyoto tears his hair*)

IRIS, OSAKA, KYOTO E CORO: Ah!

IRIS, OSAKA, KYOTO and CHORUS: Ah!

*Fine dell'Atto Secondo*

*END OF ACT II*

# ■ ATTO TERZO

# ■ ACT III

*O bel Genio nipponico, bello e antico Genio delle poesie, leggende, paurosi drammi, grottesche commedie e ute dolcissime agli amori che animano i silenzii delle sere,—bello e antico Genio dei fiori e dei pittori, non dunque gaiezza di colori vivaci, non bianchi chiarori di cune o distese di prati verdi correnti ai declivii di azzurri monti rispecchiati da laghi candidi, non trionfi di cieli e stormi di migranti uccelli, o mari d'argento ed agili saettii di awabis, intorno alla agonia di Iris?*

*A Waste Space outside the City Boundary.* Oh! beautiful genius of Nippon, beautiful ancient Genius of Poesy, Legend, awe-inspiring Drama, grotesque Comedies, and sweet Melodies which waken the silences of night to Love; beautiful ancient Genius of flowers, of painters, have you, then, no sheen of bright colors, no silvery glow of moonlight, no horizons of green fields sloping down the blue mountain side mirrored in gleaming lakes, no triumphs of the sky, no flights of wandering birds, no sea of silver wherewith to surround the deathbed of Iris?

*Sul dilicato corpo, capolavoro distrutto, giù nell'abisso incombono solo le tre sinistre notti, la notte senza stelle del cielo,—la notte senza riflessi delle acque morte,—la notte senza lacrime della insensibilita dellà della natura.*

Over her dainty frame, now lying at the foot of the precipice with all its beauty marred, brood only the three dark Nights—the starless Night of Heaven, the Night of the waters on which no sun shines, the Night of unresponsive Nature that sheds no tears.

*Così qui muore la vergine, il picciol corpo abbandonato all'abbraccio della bombèria velenosa e della scirpa pungente.*

Thus, then, Iris died her shattered body, once so fair, abandoned to the deadly embrace of the venomous swamp, rent by cruel thorns.

*Di lassù non un riflesso di una delle mille gaie lumiere della città!*

From above not one gleam from the thousand gay lights of the city.

*Nell'aria greve e letale pur tuttavia vagano incerte ombre strane.*

Yet in through the fetid death-bearing mists wander strange vague shadows.

# Act III

*Bella e antica fantasia nipponica, sono essi forse gli Oni del tuo mondo superstizioso che scendono radendo gli squallidi fianchi della squallida montagna, i tuoi grotteschi, bonarii o perversi folletti dalle facce sinistramente buffone? È Bénkei a cavallo della sua gran campana di bronzo? È Kintoki abbracciato ad un orso che ride? È Momotaro gobbe e sbilenco? O sono forse gli Incubi in forma di granchi o nani dall'orribile rictus quelle strane ombre?*

*In Verità rassembrano fantastiche creazioni, così la penombra caliginosa li trasfigura! No; non sono gli enti permalosi e ora bonaccioni delle tue fole infantili, bello e antico Genio nipponico; sono dei cenciaioli, quaggiù sospinti dalla lotta per la esistenza!*

*Colle loro lanternuzze, bizzarre umano lucciole della Vita cittadina, errano, l'uncino acuto a mano, guardando, desiderando, sognando i più pazzi tesori del mondo, giù in questo fango di cose morte.*

*(Poche voce di donne in lontananza).*

*(I cenciaiuoli alcune figure strane errane con piccolo lanterne e con uncini, rovistando).*

**IL CENCIAIUOLO:** (*canticchia un Elogia allo Luna*). Adora brunna e tarda
la luna e tutta gaia
se in due la si reguarda
soli, e luna scialba
Se notte not te appaia
amico invoco l'Alba!

**ALCUNI CENCIAIUOLI:** (*frugando inutilmente*). La fogna e avara e muta
(*sarresta-gli occhi fissi nell'ancino trattenutto da un presso l'acqua morta*).

**UNO:** Tacete! Il mio s'intrica!
(*il cenciaiuolo ritira con paziente cautela l'uncino, e trae a se un inviluppo d'ortiche. Gli altri ridono*).

**I CENCIAIUOLI:** (*Ridono*). Ah, ah! E il cespo d'un' ortica!

**UNO:** Ola! Non muover passo!
(*respinge brutalmente il colega che gli stavacino*).
(*il suo uncino ha fatto resa in un blocco di fango e resiste contro un oggetto, pesante, come fosse davvero uno serigno colmo di rios d'oro*).

*O beauteous and ancient mystic lore of Nippon, are they perhaps the Oni of your world of fancy who descend skirting the squalid sides of the squalid hillocks; are they your goblins, grotesque, good-humored, or malicious, with faces sinister yet mocking? Is it Ben Kei, astride on his great bell of bronze? Is it Kintoki who embraces the grinning bear? Is it Momotaro, maimed and halt? Are they dwarfs or strange monsters of the sea, these shadows that smile so horribly?*

*Of a truth they resemble the creatures of fancy, so strangely does the misty halflight transform them. No, they are not the beings, now playful, now helpful, of your tales of childhood. O fair and ancient Genius of Nippon, they are rag-pickers, driven hither by the struggle for existence.*

*With their little lamps, strange human will-o'-the-wisps of the city's life, they wander with their sharp hooks in their hands, searching, desiring, dreaming of the maddest treasures of the world here amid the slime and by the margin of the dead sea.*

*(Voices of women far away)*

*(Rag-pickers, some of them in strange guises, with small lanterns and grappling hooks, roving around)*

**RAG-PICKER:** (*Sings a Eulogy to the Moon*) The hour of night is tedious;
The moon is ever gay,
If either one regards you,
Whitewashed, the Moon, they say.
If Night now does not please you
Then call, my friend, for the day.

**CHORUS OF RAG-PICKERS:** (*Probing uselessly*) The sewer is mean and stingy;
Gives nothing to us, here, dingy!
(*He stops, his eyes fixed on the hook drawn out by one of those near the motionless water*)

**ONE:** Hush, now! This is my find!
(*He patiently draws at the hook, which brings up a bag of thorny bushes. The others laugh*)

**CHORUS OF RAGPICKERS:** It's a bag of thorns!

**ANOTHER:** Ho there! It won't budge an inch!
(*He rudely pushes away those nearby*)
(*His hook, stuck in the mud, was held by a heavy stone which seemed as if it might be a chest full of gold*)

**I CENCIAIUOLI:** Un tesoro! Del oro!
Grand oro! gran tesoro!
(*con enorme sforzo i fortunato cenciaiuci lo estrae dal fango un sasso—e qui altri ridono*).
Ah, ah, ah! E il tesoro d'un sasso!
(*il cenciaiuolo bestemmia*).

**UNO:** (*riprende il suo Elogie alla Luna*). Adora bruna e tarda
la Luna e tutta gaia
se in due la si riguarda
soli e una Luna scialba
se Notte—
(*un rapido bagliore luccica sotto il monte tagliata a picco; un grido di sorpresa strozza al cantelina cenciaiuolo l'Elogio all Luna*).

**UN CENCIAIUOLO:** Il bagliore!
(*il bagliore e gia svanita, e innalzino abbassono le lanterne per richiamare nel oggetto misterioso il bagliore intravveduto*).

**I CENCIAIUOLI:** Svanito
via . . . spento..
D'avida fantasia
e il tormento.
(*ecco di nuova e piu distinto il bagliore prima; e la veste d'Iris*).

**CORO:** Ancor! E raggio d'or !
Traluce!
E veste!
E luce!
Ha dentro ancor il corpo che la porta!

**UNO:** che importa? E l'una morta!
(*I cenciaiuoli, che sono accorsi avidamente s'arrestano avanti il corpo d'Iris, e non osono stenderne le mani*).
(*si slanciarno sul corpo d'Iris*).
(*la veste e strappata con gran violenza, uno respingendo l'altro a pugne, a ceffate, si contendono gli orpelli di Kyoto*).
(*un moto di vita sfugge dai piccolo corpo di Iris*).
(*i cenciaiuoli, atterrite, supestiziosi, pauroso, fuggono*).

**IL CENCIAIUOLO:** (*la voce del cenciaiuolo dentro alle scene, lontanissimo*). Amico, invoca l'Alba!

**IRIS:** (*rinvenendo un poco, come trasognata mormora, quasi rampogua contro il mondo, il destino o la divinita*).
Perche? . . . Perche?
(*e rimane immobile: nell'aere freddo e muto le sembra di udire strane e beffarde voci, che rassembrano quelle del tre personaggi della sua breve existenza*)
(*il giovane della volutta, il Taikomati Kyoto, e il Padre cieco*).

**THE RAG-PICKERS:** Of Gold! A treasure!
Great gold! Large measure!
(*With great force he pulls up the hook*) It is a treasure of a stone!
(*The disappointed rag-picker swears*)

**A RAG-PICKER:** (*Taking up his song*) The hour of night is tedious,
The moon is ever gay,
If either now regards you,
Is whitewashed the moon, they say,
If night——
(*A quick flash of light from a mountain peak; a cry of surprise interrupts the rag-picker's song*)

**A RAG-PICKER:** A flash!
(*The light vanishes, and in vain they seek a mysterious object which the light had revealed*) It's gone
It has vanished.

**ONE RAG-PICKER:** From greedy fancy is this torment!
(*Again they see the flash, more distinctly than before. It is the dress of Iris*)

**CHORUS:** Again! A flash of gold.
Transparent,
Splendid,
A garment! Has in it also
The body it has carried!

**A RAG-PICKER:** What does it matter? It's a dead one.
(*The rag-pickers, running greedily, stop before the body of Iris, but do not dare to touch it with their hands*)
(*They rush again toward the body of Iris. They violently tear off the dress. They push and strike each other contending for the ornaments put on Iris by Kyoto*)
(*A motion, indicating life, comes from the body of Iris*)
(*The rag-pickers, superstitious, frightened, terrified, run away*)

**A RAG-PICKER:** (*A voice heard from away behind the scenes*) My friend, then call for the day!

**IRIS:** (*Reviving a little, as dreaming, she murmurs, as if reproaching the world, destiny, or divinity, sotto voce*)
Why? Why?
(*She remains immobile, in the air, cold and silent; she seems to hear strange and mocking voices which resemble those of the three persons associated with her short life—the young man, the taikomati Kyoto, and the blind father*)
(*The voice of Osaka*)

**L'EGOSIMA DI OSAKA:** (*La voce di Osaka*). Ognun pel suo cammino
va spinto dal destino
di sua fatal natura!
Il tuo gentile vezzo
calma a desio divino,
e un umana tortura.
Tu muori come il fior
che pel suo olezzo muor!
Nel mio egoismo tetro
or porto altrove
il mio riso canto di spetro cosi la Vita!
Addio!

**THE EGOISM OF OSAKA:** Every step in your journey
Was thrust on you from destiny
By your fatal nature!
In your gentle sporting,
Cool to desire divine
There was human torture.
You die as a flower—
Shedding fragrance in death!
In my gloomy egoism
Now I carry elsewhere
My spectral laughter and song.
Such is life.
Farewell!

**L'EGOISMA DEL KYOTO:** Rubai,
fai bastonato
onde mutai mestiere;
ho la livrea indossata
del piu gran re; Il Piacere!
Or siamo qui cosi,
io per la mia vilta
carnefice, tu, vittima
per questa tua belta
Perche? Io non lo so.
Cosi la Vita
Vo!

**THE EGOISM OF KYOTO:** I robbed; was bastinadoed,
Wherefore I changed my occupation,
I have worn a livery
Of a great king—Pleasure.
Now we are here—in this plight.
I, by my cowardly hangman;
You, the victim
Of your own beauty.
Why? I do not know.
Such is life.

**L'EGOISIMO DEL CIECO:** Ahime!
che allumera
nell'inverno il mio foco
e all'ombro fresco loco
la state m'addura?
Tale e il pensiero che in fondo
dispreme il pianto mio
e fa il mio duol profondo!
Cosi la Vita!
Addio!
(*Le voce misteriose, cosi come hanno favellato alla fantasia dalla morente fanciulla, si estinguono bizarramente*).

**THE EGOISM OF CIECO:** Alas!
Who will rekindle
My fire in winter;
Or in the shade place me a summer?
This is the thought, in the deep
Extremity of my weeping,
Which makes my grief profound!
Such is life!
Farewell!
(*The mysterious voices having thus fabled to the fancy of the dying child, end strangely*)

**IRIS:** (*credendo sempre di sognare*). ancora il triste sogno pauroso!
Visioni! affani! angoscie!
Personne ignote!
ignote cose e lochi . . .
e strane risa . . .
e lacrime!
(*La voce di Osaka—Lontanissima*).
Tu vuoi morir? Morir io ti faro
Ma ti faro morir dal sol baciata,
ed al paese eterno te traro.
Ove, O fanciulla tu sarai amata!

**IRIS:** (*Believing always that she dreams*) Again the evil dream so fearful!
Visions! Agitations! Anxieties!
Unknown persons! Unknown places and things!
Strange laughter, and tears. (*The voice of Osaka, far away*)
You wish to die? To die I will make you;
But you shall die of the kiss of the Sun,
Then to eternal worlds I'll take you
To be loved where all weeping is done!

**IRIS:** Apri l'orecchio a mie dolce parole
Apri l'anima tua alla fede, e spera!
Jor ha oscoltata O Dhia, la tua preghiera

**IRIS:** Jor has heard, O Dhia, your prayer,
Open your soul, dear child, to the Sun!
Open your soul to my words so fair!
Open your heart, though all hope be gone!

**OSAKA:** Tu muori come il fior
che pel suo olezzo muor!
(*il pensiero della sua misera vita le si affaccia dolorosamente*).

**OSAKA:** You die as a flower
That sheds its fragrance in death.
(*The thought of her sad life affects her sorrowfully*)

**IRIS:** Il picciol mondo del mia cassetta perche dispar? Perche?
Giardin, rondini, fior.
echi a miei canti

**IRIS:** Why destroy the little world of my cottage?—Why?
Gardens; swallows; flowers; my songs

tutto dilegua e tace.
Perche codesti strazii
e queste tenebre?
E perchi piango e muoio
e m'abbondona ogni persona
e cosa, e vita, e luce, e tutto.
Il picciol mondo della mia cosetta
e silenzio e paura. Perche? perche?
(*sempre l'angoscia la stessa domanda*).
(*nel cielo cominciano i primi bagliore*)
(*la luce si fa piu viva quasi volesse riani mare la morento Iris che guarda, fissa nelle immense profonditta dell'azzuro cielo. I primi raggi del sole scendono a carezzare Iris; essa creda sentire in se rinnovellarsi la vita; e con entusiasmo alzandosi a protendendo le braccia in alto*).
Un grand occhio me guarda!
E il sole! tu sol non m'abbandoni!
A me tu vieni;
io reposi al tuo raggio!
Riposo nella luce!
Aure di canti! mari splendore!
Plaghe, cieli di fiore.

all dissolved in silence!
Why these tearings-away? And this darkness?
And why do I weep and die?
Every person, every thing leaves me!
And Life, and Light, and All.
The little world of my cottage
Is silent and afraid. Why? Why?
(*Always asked with anxiety*)
(*In the sky there come the first flashes. The light gives her more life, as if to reanimate the dying Iris, who looks with fixed gaze on the immense profundity of heaven's azure. The first rays of the sun descend, to caress Iris. She believes them intended to reanimate and restore her life, and with exaltation extends her arms on high, saluting the sun, which now illuminates everything*)
The great eye I see!
It is the Sun!
You alone do not abandon me!
To me you come!
I rest on ray.
I sleep in your light
Aura of singing!
Ocean of splendor!
Lands and heavens of flowers!

**CORO-IL SOLE:** Ancor! son Io! la Vita!
son la Belta infinita
la Luce ed il Calor!
Amate o cose! dico:
sono il Dio novo e antico
son l'Amor!

**CHORUS—THE SUN:** Once more!
I am the Life!
I am the Infinite Beauty!
The Light and the Heat!
Love! O things!
I am the god new and old! I am Love!

**FIORI:** (*tutta una fantasia di fiori, che sbocciano sotto la potenza del raggi solari, si stendo poco a poco intorno al corpo d'Iris non piu gli squalidi dirupi, la melmosa fogna, ma una immensita di fiori ad un mare di luce*).
(*gli steli del fiori si annodano intorno al corpo d'Iris, come braccia umane, e la sollevano su per l'azzuro e l'infinito, verso il sole*).

**THE FLOWERS:** (*A fancy of flowers, which flow out under the power of the sun's rays. They extend themselves little by little*)
(*The flowers knot themselves around the body of Iris, as human arms, and lift her up toward the Azure, the Infinite and to the Sun!*)

**CORO:** Dei Mondi Io la Cagione!
Dei Cieli Io la Ragione!
Uguale Io scendo ai Re
si come a te, Mousme!
L'anima tua e mia!
D'un fior all'agonia!
Venite, o fior!
Venite tutti!
O fior!

**CHORUS—THE SUN:** I am the Cause of the world!
I am the Reason of the heavens.
Alike I descend to the King
And to you, O Mousme!
Your soul is mine!
From a Blossom to Death!
Come, O Flower! Come, O Flower!
Come all,
O Flowers!

*Tutto un sussuro di fiori intorno alla morente! .. — Piove il sole sul picciolo corpo aureole irradiate! .. Nella suprema agonia Iris finalmente non ha più angoscia, affanni, paure, dolori. — Il suo sogno è di luce—è di fiori! —E raggi e fiori parlano il linguaggion eterno della pietà, dell'amore!—*

*The air is filled with the rustling of flowers around the dying girl. The Sun irradiates her with a crown of gold. In her last death struggle Iris feels neither pain, frenzy, fear, nor grief. Her dream is all of light and flowers and the Sun and flowers speak to her the eternal language of the Pity of Love.*

## Act III

Muore la Vergine colla visione splendente della immortalità; essa vede intorno a sè una fantasia di fiori—tutti i fiori della terra—che allungano a lei gli steli, steli che si snodano e si stendono intorno al corpo suo come braccia umane.

Ed è in questa trionfante visione che gli occhi della mousmè si chiudono, onde sul suo pallido viso è ancora la calma della tenera giovinezza innocente che la lotta della

She dies with the splendid vision of immortality before her eyes; she sees all around her a glorious fantasy of flowers—all the flowers of the Earth—which spread out their arms towards her, which wrap her body in their embrace like the arms of the beloved.

In this triumphant vision the eyes of the Mousmé close in death and on her wan face is still the calm of tender innocent youth which the squalid battle of the life of this

vita terrena lasciò immacolata. Sotto a quegli abbracci e baci di fiori il piccolo corpo della morta dispare. L'anima della mousmè è fiore, luce, armonia!

O Morte, Signora Misteriosa, quanto sei grande nella tua pietà, Tu che tanti mari e cieli eterni poni fra gli umani e i loro dolori!

FINE.

earth has left unstained. Beneath the embraces and kisses of the flowers her body is lost to sight. The soul of the Mousmé has fled to the World of Flowers, Light, Harmony.

O Death, Lady of Mystery, how great you are in your infinite pity. You, who place such vast oceans, such boundless heavens between Humanity and its grief.

FINIS.

# Hérodiade (1881)

## Herodias

MUSIC BY JULES MASSENET ■ LIBRETTO BY PAUL MILLIET, "HENRI GREMONT" (GEORGES HARTMANN), & ANGELO ZANARDINI

This four-act opera with seven tableux is set to a libretto by Paul Milliet, "Henri Gremont" (Georges Hartmann) and Angelo Zanardini based upon *Hérodias* by Gustave Flaubert. It was first performed at the Théâtre de la Monnaie in Brussels on December 19, 1881. Salomé, left behind when her mother Hérodiade married Hérode, is a follower of the prophet Jean. She is in love with Jean; however, Hérode, her stepfather, is deeply and openly attracted to her. Hérodiade decides to use her husband's fixation on her daughter to destroy Jean, who attacks her behavior publicly. Hérode realizes that Jean and his followers are the only real Jewish opposition to Roman rule. Jean refuses to cooperate with Hérode, and he is thrown into prison when Hérode finds out about Salomé's love for the prophet. Salomé joins him there, prepared to die with him, and he finally accepts her love since it is purified by her sacrifice. The guards take her away to a banquet at the palace where Salomé throws herself at the feet of her mother and stepfather. Hérodiade recognizes her daughter at last, but their joint pleas for Jean's life are in vain. He has already been beheaded, and Salomé takes her own life in her mother's presence.

---

## ■ ACTE PREMIER

*Une grande cour extérieure du palais d'Hérode.—A gauche, un portique qui sert d'entrée au palais; à droite, bocages d'oléandres, de sycomores et de cèdres; en face, une balustrade avec colonnade à jours qui domine la vallée; dans le loitain la mer Morete entourée des collines de la Judée.*

### SCÈNE PREMIERE

*Chefs, Marchands, Jeunes Esclaves, puis Phaneul, puis Salomé.*

*C'est l'aurore, presque la nuit encore; des chefs sont endormis à terre pres de la baricde qui domine la vallee où repose la caravane en attendant le jour.—Peu après le lever du rideau, le jour paraît, les chefs s'éveillent, se lèvent et appellent les marchands.*

**LES CHEFS:** Alerte! levez-vous! le palais est ouvert!
Debout! vous tous qui venez du désert!
(*Des marchands de différents pays, des esclaves portant de lourds fardeaux gravissent lentement la côte.*)

**MARCHANDS ET ESCLAVES:** Voici que le jour se lève,
Nous avons touché le but!
Notre voyage s'achève,
O Jérusalem! salut!
Au bord des claires fontaines

## ■ ACT I

*A large outer court in Herod's palace.—To the left, a portico serving as an entrance to the palace; to the right, thickets of oleander, sycamore and cedar.—In front, a balustrade with colonnade dominating the valley.—In the distance, the Dead Sea, surrounded by the hills of Judea.*

### SCENE I

*Chiefs, Merchants, Young Slaves; then Phanuel, afterward Salome.*

*It is dawn of day, but as yet almost as dark as night.—When the curtain rises, the Chiefs are asleep on the ground, near the barrier which separates the palace from the depression where the caravans are resting while waiting for daylight.—Day dawns; the Chiefs awake, arise, and call to the Merchants.*

**CHIEFS:** Awake! Arise! The palace is open.
All who come from the desert Awake! Arise!
(*Merchants of different lands and Slaves, carrying heavy burdens, come slowly up the slope.*)

**MERCHANTS AND SLAVES:** The day is breaking!
We have reached our goal.
Our journey is ended.
O Jerusalem, all hail!
Beside the clear fountains

Nous pourrons nous rafraichir,
Quand de plus chaudes haleines
Sur les sables vont courir.

**LES CHEFS:** Que dès l'abord on remarque,
Dans ce que vous apportez,
Les dons offerts au tétrarque
Par ses nombreuses cités!
Séparez l'or et les baumes,
Les ivoires et l'argent,
Rangez l'encens, les arômes
Et la nacre au ton changeant.
(*Les esclaves ouvrent les ballots, et étalent les parfums, les étoffes, etc.*)

**LES ESCLAVES:** Voici l'ambre de Judée!
Voici les parfums d'Ophir!
Les pistaches d'Idumée!
Voici les agrès de Tyr!

**MARCHANDS:** (*premier groupe.*)
Nous arrivons des plus lointaines villes
Sans fatiguer nos chevaux de Saron!

**MARCHANDS:** (*deuxième groupe*): Mais nos chevaux ne sont pas moins agiles,
Nous avons pris cette pourpre a Sidon!

**PREMIER GROUPE:** (*avec mépris.*) Oh! le Pharisien!

**DEUXÌEME GROUPE:** (*de même.*) Ah! le Samaritain!

**PREMIER GROUPE:** Nos chevaux ont des ailes . . .

**DEUXÌEME GROUPE:** (*raillant.*) Comme les sauterelles Des rives du Jourdain!

We may refresh ourselves
While the hot winds
Blow across the desert.
Our journey is ended,
O Jerusalem, all hail!

**CHIEFS:** First of all set aside
Of what you have brought
The gifts offered to the Tetrarch
By his numerous cities!
Set apart the gold from the balm,
The ivory from the silver!
Set in place the incense and the perfumes!
(*The Slaves open the bales and spread out the presents, perfumes and fabrics.*)

**THE SLAVES:** Here is amber from Judaea!
Here are the perfumes of Ophir!
Here are the species from Idumaea!
Set apart the silver from the gold,
Separate the gold from the silver!

**MERCHANTS:** (*first Group.*) We have come from the farthest cities,
Without wearying our horses of Sharon!

**MERCHANTS:** (*second Group.*) Our horses are no less fleet!
These purples have we brought from Sidon—

**FIRST GROUP** (*contemptuously*): Fie on the Pharisees!

**SECOND GROUP** (*same*): Fie! Samaritans are these!

**FIRST GROUP:** All our horses are arrows.

**SECOND GROUP** (*mockingly*): And swifter than the sparrows Of Jordan's banks they fly!

TOUS: (*prêts à en venir aux mains.*) Quoi! cette indigne race
Ose nous outrager!
D'une pareille audace
Nous saurons nous venger!

PREMIER GROUPE: Va, va, Samaritain! nous acceptons la lutte!

DEUXIÈME GROUPE: Croient-ils vraiment nous egaler?
(*Phanuel paraît*)

TOUS: (*apercevant Phanuel.*) Le Chaldéen!

PHANUEL: (*au milieu des groupes qui se séparent*) Encore une dispute!
Eh quoi! toujours se quereller!
Le monde est inquiet, la patrie est en larmes!
Et les voilà! contre eux-mêmes tournant leurs armes!
Les insensés! les débiles humains!
Ils en viennent aux mains
Et restent sourds à la voix immortelle
Qui leur répète: "Amour! Pardon! Vie éternelle!"

TOUS: L'avenir est trompeur!
Faut-il ouvrir son coeur
A l'espérance vaine?

PHANUEL: Non! Contre les Romains
La révolte est prochaine!
J'arrive de pays lointains
Où les actes suivront de très près les paroles;
Bientôt tout changera, les lois et les symboles!

TOUS: Jusqu'à ce jour ce qu'on nous a promis
N'allège pas le joug des ennemis!

PHANUEL: Soit! N'espérez donc rien! Poursuivez votre route
Ou descendez à la cité;
Pour moi, j'attends, calme et sans doute,
Des jours meilleurs pour notre humanité.
(*Les marchands et les esclaves s'éloignent, se dirigeant vers la ville, les chefs, suivis d'esclaves portant les présents destinés au roi, entrent dans le palais par le portique.–Salomé est sortie par la gauche du palais, elle est inquiète, indécise, et semble chercher une issue pour s'enfuir, quand elle aperçoit subitement Phanuel.*)

PHANUEL: (*avec surprise.*) Salomé! . . . Quelle destinée T'amène dans ces lieux?
(*A part.*)
Ignore-t-elle encore de quel sang elle est née?
(*A Salomé.*)
De Siloé pourquoi quitter les bords heureux?

SALOMÉ: (*avec tristesse.*) Sans cesse, je cherche ma mère! . . .
Une voix me criait: "Espère, Cours à Sion! . . . –Je ne l'ai pas

---

ALL: (*on the point of active hostilities*). What! Does this ignoble race Dare to insult us? For such audacity We shall have our revenge!

FIRST GROUP: We are ready to fight, Samaritans!

SECOND GROUP: Do they really suppose they are equal to us? (*Phanuel appears.*)

ALL (*perceiving Phanuel*): The Chaldean!

PHANUEL (*stepping between the disputants, who separate*). Another quarrel! Why must they always wrangle? The world is full of unrest; Their country is in tears. And behold them! They turn their arms against themselves! Insensate Madmen! Depraved creatures! They will come to blows! They are deaf to the eternal voice Which calls to them and says: Love, pardon, life everlasting!

ALL: The future is full of uncertainty Dare I trust my heart to doubtful hopes!

PHANUEL: Revolt against Rome is at hand. I returned of late from distant lands, Where deeds follow swiftly upon words. Soon all laws and the symbols of laws will change.

ALL: All that has been promised us as yet Has not lightened the yoke of our oppressors!

PHANUEL: True! Better have no hopes. Take your own course! As for me, steadfast and calm, I wait for better days for all mankind. (*The Merchants and the Slaves go down to the city; the Chiefs, followed by Slaves carrying the presents destined for the King, enter the palace by the portico.*) (*Salome comes out of the palace on the left, anxious, undecided. She seems to be seeking an avenue of escape when she sees Phanuel and approaches him.*)

PHANUEL (*in surprise*): Ah, Salome, what fate has brought you to the palace? (*Aside.*) Can it be that she does not yet know from what blood she is sprung? (*To Salome.*) Why have you left the happy banks of Silo?

SALOME: Still without ceasing, O Phanuel. I search for my mother. I heard a voice cry: "Hope on! Go to Jerusalem!" Alas, I have not found

---

trouvée, hélas!
Et je reste seule ici-bas.
Celui dont la parole efface toute peine,
Le prophetè est ici! . . . C'est vers lui aue je vais! . . .
Il est doux, il est bon; sa parole est sereine,
Il parle, tout se tait . . . Plus léger sur la plaine
L'air attentif passe sans bruit.
Partout mon souvenir le suit,
Ah! quand reviendra-t-il? Quand pourrai-je l'entendre?
Je souffrais, j'étais seule, et mon coeur s'est calmé
En écoutant sa voix mélodieuse et tendre!
Puis-je vivre sans toi, prophète bien-aimé?
C'est là, dans ce désert où la foule étonnée
Avait suivi ses pas,
Qu'il m'accueillit un jour, enfant abandonnée
Et qu'il m'ouvrit ses bras!
Ah! quand reviendra-t-il? Quand pourrai-je l'entendre?
Je souffrais, j'étais seule, et mon coeur s'est calmé
En écoutant sa voix mélodieuse et tendre!
Puis-je vivre sans toi, prophète bien-aimé!

VOIX: (*dans le lontain.*) Jérusalem! Jérusalem! Salut.

PHANUEL: Tu le veux! pars, enfant, la foi t'éclaire Elle te guidera Et dans de palais veillera Un ami fidèle et sincère.

VOIX: (*s'éloignant encore.*) Jérusalem! Jérusalem! Salut! (*Salomé s'éloigne par la droite. –Phanuel accompagne Salomé du regard et remonte au palais. –A ce moment sortent par la droite des jardins les Esclaves du Roi qui, sous la conduite de leurs gardiens, traversent la scène et se dirigent vers le Palais; c'est la Promenade Des Danseuses Du Palais.*)

## SCÈNE II

*Hérode entre précipitamment en scène par la porte qui a précédemment livré passage à Salomé; il parcourt d'un regard inquiet les groupes des Danseuses qui s'éloignent et voit que Salomé n'est parmi elles.*

HÉRODE: (*fiévreusement.*) Elle fui le palais, elle a quitté ces lieux, Et l'angoisse soudain a pénétré mon âme! . . . Déesse ou femme Au charme séducteur,

---

her; and I am still alone in this world. But he whose words can dispel all griefs, the Prophet, is here. I shall go to him. He is kind, he is good. His words are calm. He speaks and all keep silence. The wind blows more softly over the meadows, and listens to him. He speaks-. . .! Ah, when will he return; we shall I hear him? I was sick, I was alone, but my heart grew peaceful when I heard his voice, so melodious, and so tender. O Prophet, much beloved, how can I live without you! It was there in the desert, with the people who had followed him in awe, that one day he took me to him; me, an abandoned child! And to me he opened his arms. He is kind, he is good, and his words are sublime.

VOICES (*in the distance*): Jerusalem! Jerusalem! Hail!

PHANUEL: As you will! Go my child, Thy faith shall enlighten you Thy faith shall guide you And in this palace a friend, Sincere and faithful, Will watch over you Farewell, Salome!

VOICES (*still more distant*) Jerusalem! Jerusalem! Hail! (*Salome goes off toward the right. Phanuel follows Salome with his eyes and goes up toward the palace.—The Slaves of the King appear at the right of the garden, under the escort of their guardians, and go toward the palace.—This is the Promenade of the Dancers of the Palace.*)

## SCENE II

*Herod enters suddenly by the door at which Salome has just gone out; he anxiously passes in review the various groups of dancers as they go out, and perceives that Salome is not among them.*

HEROD (*feverishly*): She has fled from the palace. She has left this place. And a sudden anguish strikes into my soul. Goddess or woman whose seductive charm,

Forme à peine entrevue et qui déjà m'est chère,
Reviens, reviens, rêve enchanteur!
Salomé, Salomé! c'est ma voix qui t'implore!
Une ivresse ineffable illumine mes cieux!
Mon rayon de soleil c'est l'éclat de tes yeux!
C'est toi, toi que j'attends! Ah! reviens, je t'adore!
(*Hérodiade paraît, pâle, égarée.*)

## SCÈNE III

*Hérode, Hérodiade, puis Jean.*

**HÉRODIADE:** Hérode, venge-moi d'une suprême offense!
C'est de toi, de toi seul que j'attends ma vengeance!
J'allais ce matin au désert,
Quand un homme a peine couvert,
Le front menaçant, la voix brève,
Se dresse au milieu du chemin!
Comme un vent d'orage se lève,
Sa voix, invoquant le destin,
Me poursuit, me trouble et m'outrage
"Tremble, me dit-il, Jézabel!
"Que de fléaux sont ton ouvrage!
"Il faut en rendre compte au ciel!
"Va, la colère du prophète
"A fait appel aux nations,
"Bientôt tu courberas la tête
"Devant leurs malédictions!"

**HÉRODE:** Qui est cet homme?

**HÉRODIADE:** C'est Jean! C'est l'apôtre infâme
Qui prêche le baptême et la nouvelle foi!

**HÉRODE:** (*brusquement.*) Que puis-je? Que veux-tu de moi?

**HÉRODIADE:** C'est sa tête que je réclame!
Ne me refuse pas, toi, mon seul bien.
Pour qui j'ai tout quitté, mon pays et ma fille.
N'es-tu pas mon soutien?
Et ma seule famille?
Rappelle-toi le Tibre avec ses bords ombreux!
Nous vivions sans compter les heures fugitives;
Nos timides baiser étaient nos seuls aveux;
Nous n'avions pour témoins que ses vagues plaintives;
Le soir, sous les grands pins, nos serments répétés
Eveillaient des échos inconnus à la terre
Et l'astre de la nuit dans ses molles clartés
Enveloppait nos coeurs d'amour et de mystère!

---

Though scarcely seen by me,
Has yet become most dear,
Come back once more!
Come back enchanting dream!
Salome! Come back! I call you! I implore!
Salome! What ineffable intoxication
Brightens the world for me!
The light of your eyes is the radiance of my sun.
I await you! I adore you!
Salome! Return once more!
(*Herodias appears, pale and distraught.*)

## SCENE III

*Herod, Herodias; then John.*

**HERODIAS:** Avenge me of insult; one most deep! By you alone, can I be avenged. I was walking this morning out upon the desert, when a man, well near naked, with threatening brow, and of rough voice, sprang up before me in my path, as springs up a whirlwind. Calling upon the Fates he followed me; frightened and insulted me! "Tremble," he cried, "tremble, Jezabel! For you have been a flail, and must give account to heaven. Go! The wrath of the Prophet has called aloud to the nations of the earth, and soon you will bow your head before their maledictions."

**HEROD:** Who is this man?

**HERODIAS:** It is John! He is the impious apostle, who preaches baptism, and the new faith.

**HEROD:** What can I do? What would you have me do?

**HERODIAS:** It is his head that I demand!
Herod! Herod! Do not refuse me this!
Herod, remember. Do not refuse me this!
I have none but you. I left all for you.
My country and my child.
Are you not my sole support and family?
Do not refuse me this. Remember.
Remember the Tiber, with its shady banks,
Where we lived, nor ever counted the happy hours;
Our furtive kisses were our only vows,
Our only witnesses the phantom waves.
At night beneath the great pines
Our vows awoke unearthly
And the moon, with radiance tender,
Wrapped us in mystery and love

---

**HÉRODE:** Non! je ne puis . . . je dois céder à la raison.
Aimé des Juifs, consolant leur misère.
Cet homme est fort . . . partout on le révère!

**HÉRODIADE:** (*méprisante.*) Ah! la peur te conseille?

**HÉRODE:** Et toi, c'est le démon.

**HÉRODIADE:** (*de même.*) Quel nouveau favori t'inspire?

**HÉRODE:** (*résolu.*) Je prétends demeurer seul maître dans l'empire!

**HÉRODIADE:** (*avec rage.*) Tu ne m'aimes plus? Soit! seule j'accomplirai
Ce que j'ai résolu . . . Jean, je te frapperai!

**JEAN:** (*il est entré sur les dernières paroles d'Hérodiade.*) Frappe donc!

**HÉRODE ET HÉRODIADE:** (*avec un cri d'epouvante.*) Jean!

**JEAN:** Il n'est plus d'ombre pour tes crimes,
Je réveillerai tes victimes!
Jézabel! . . . Tes sanglots te briseront le coeur!
Nul ne prendra pitié de ta douleur!

**HÉRODIADE:** (*à Hérode.*) Sa malédiction me glace de terreur.
Ne prendras-tu pitié da ma douleur?

**HÉRODE:** Sa malédiction me frappe de terreur.
Il me brave, il l'outrage, et moi, le roi, j'ai peur! . . .
(*Hérode et Hérodiade entrent précipitamment dans le Palais, fuyant la malédiction de Jean.*)

## SCÈNE IV

*Jean, Salomé.*

**JEAN:** (*les regardant s'éloigner.*) Allez! ne parlez pas d'offense,
Vous que le Seigneur tient déjà dans sa balance!
(*Salomé est apparue; elle reconnaît Jean et s'élance vers lui.*)

**SALOMÉ:** (*embrassant les genoux de Jean.*) Ah! Jean! je te revois!

**JEAN:** (*avec bonté.*) Enfant, que me veux-tu?

**SALOMÉ:** Ce que je veux, oh Jean! te dire que te t'aime
Et que je t'appartiens! . . . que je vis par toi-même
Et qu'au son de ta voix mon être est suspendu!

**JEAN:** C'est toi, Salomé? . . .
Pauvre enfant . . . qu'ai-je entendu?

---

**HEROD:** No! I cannot. I must do what is wise.
I am liked by the Jews,
And I alleviate their sufferings.
This man is powerful; he is revered by all.

**HERODIAS:** Ah, you counsel of your fears.

**HEROD:** And you are a devil!

**HERODIAS:** What new favorite rules over you?

**HEROD:** It is my purpose to be sole ruler in this empire!

**HERODIAS:** You have ceased to love me! It is vile!
Alone then I shall accomplish what I have resolved!
John! I shall strike you down!
(*John enters in time to hear the last words of Herodias.*)

**JOHN:** Strike me then!

**HEROD and HERODIAS** (*with a cry of terror*). John!

**JOHN:** No more your crimes shall in the shadows lurk,
I will awake your victims!
Jezabel! . . . Your sobs your heart shall break
And none upon your tears shall pity take!

**HERODIAS:** His curses and his threats have filled my heart with fears!
Ah! Will you not take pity on my tears!

**HEROD:** With terror I hear his maledictions.
He braves, insults me, and I, I go in fear!
(*Herod drags Herodias, shaking with fear, away.—They go quickly into the palace, as if fleeing in terror before John's attitude of malediction.*)

## SCENE IV

*John and Salome.*

**JOHN** (*watching them go*): Oh, calm your rage: and talk not, forsooth, of insult, you whom the Lord already holds in the balance!
(*Salome appears; she runs to John and falls at his feet.*)

**SALOME:** John! I have found you!

**JOHN** (*kindly*): My child! What do you want of me?

**SALOME:** What do I want, O John?
What I want is to tell you that I love you, and that I belong to you; that in you alone I live; that by the sound of your voice my whole being is held in suspense!

**JOHN:** It is you, Salome? Poor child, what did I hear?

**SALOMÉ:** Loin de toi je souffrais et me voilà guérie!
Dans ton regard est ma patrie;
Mon visage est baigné de larmes, et mon coeur
Tessaille de bonheur!

**JEAN:** Que me veut ta splendeur dans l'ombre de ma vie?
Que ferait ta jeunesse à peine épanouie
Dans les pierres de mon chemin?
Pour toi, c'est la saison où les voeux moins timides
Appellent des baisers sur les lèvres avides;
Pour moi, tout autre est le destin!
Je ne veux pas t'entendre.
Va, laisse-moi!
Ame naïve et tendre,
Eloigne-toi!

**SALOMÉ:** Non, l'amour n'est pas un blasphème
Et c'est ton amour que je veux!
Qu'à tes genoux, ô toi que j'aime,
S'épande l'or de mes cheveux!

**JEAN:** (*inspiré.*) Aime-moi donc alors, mais comme on aime en songe
Dans la mystique ardeur où l'idéal te plonge,
Transfigure l'amour, esclave de nos sens!
Dannis tous les transports d'un sentiment profane,
Elève, jusqu'au ciel, ton âme! qu'elle plane
Au milieu des parfums de nuageux encens!
Enfant, regarde cette aurore
De vie et d'immortalité!
La foi nouvelle est près d'éclore
Dans cette sublime clarté!
N'entends-tu pas les saints cantiques
Que prennent leur essor
Et les voeux des âmes mystiques
Ouvrant leurs ailes d'or?

**SALOMÉ:** (*avec ravissement.*)
Parle, j'écoute . . . je t'adore!
Et l'éclat de tes yeux
Plus resplendisssants que l'aurore
Illumine les cieux.
(*Jean se délivre des bras de Salomé que tombe à genoux, extasiée; il s'éloigne en lui montrant le ciel.*)

*FIN DE L'ACTE PREMIER.*

## ■ ACTE DEUXIÈME

*Premier Tableau*

*La Chambre d'Hérode.*

*Les hautes murailles sont couvertes de tentures rouges à bandes noires. Des poutrelles de cèdre, avec des dorures dans les noeuds du bois, encadrent les parois auxquelles sont suspendues des armes de toute espece. —La cham-*

**SALOME:** I am yours! I love you! Away from you, I was sick; ah, so sick! And now I am whole. In your look is my country; my cheeks are bathed in tears, yet my heart trembles with hapiness.

**JOHN:** What place has your beauty in this gloom of my life? How would your youth fare, that has scarcely come to bloom, upon my stony pathway? For you it is the season when tenderer avowals, call for kisses upon thirsty lips. For you it is the time to love. Another fate awaits me. No, I will not hear you. Leave me. Go your way. Sweet, tender, innocent soul. Leave me; leave me. Go!

**SALOME:** Love is no blasphemy! It is your love I desire. I love you! And you alone do I love. I would spread the glory of my hair upon your knees; for you alone do I love! O John!

**JOHN** (*inspired*): Love me then, but as one loves in dreams, where in contemplation of the ideal one is wrapped in a mystic flame which passes away that love which destroys the body. Banish these transports of unholy desire! Raise up your soul, till it shall soar, most perfumed clouds of incense! My child, behold the dawn, and life everlasting. Harken! Can you not hear the holy canticles that even now arise, and the prayers of mystic spirits that spread their golden wings? My child, behold the dawn. The new faith is breaking; and life everlasting.

**SALOME:** Ah, I hear you speak, and I adore you!
The light of your eyes more splendid than the sun, illumines the sky!
(*John releases himself from Salome's arms.—She falls at his feet in ecstasy.—He goes off pointing toward the sky.*)

*END OF FIRST ACT.*

## ■ ACT II

*First Tableau*

*Herod's Chamber.*

*The high walls are covered with red hangings banded with black. Beams of cedar-wood, their projections gilded, frame panels from which hang weapons of every kind. The room is in the shape of a regular pentagon; small doors at*

*bre forme un pentagone régulier; petites portes au premier plan, au fond, à droite.—L'ameublement se compose d'escabeaux d'ébène, de coussins de pourpre, de tapis épais, de peaux de lynx et d'un lit d'ivoire placé au second plan à la gauche de spectateur. Ce lit très bas est fait de courroies blanches et recouvert de riches étoffes; candélabres de bronze soutenus par des sphynx; cassolettes d'argent remplies de nard et de cinnamone; gigantesques morceaux d'ambre; vasques de porphyre, cornes d'antilopes garnies de bagues et de bracelets.—Au lever du rideau, Hérode est nonchalamment étendu sur le lit; des esclaves nubiennes, grecques et babyloniennes sont couchées au fond de la chambre et autour du lit du roi, dans des poses lascives et pittoresques, une d'entre elles est appuyée contre le pied du lit.*

*SCÈNE V*

*Hérode. Une Babylonienne, Esclaves.*

**LES ESCLAVES:** Roi, tu peux t'assoupir sur ta couche d'ivoire,
Tu peux rêver d'amour, tu peux rêver de gloire!
Les ardeurs du midi font taire les échos,
Rien ne troublera ton repos.
Le matin s'est enfui de perles tout humide,
L'oiseau cherche un abri sous le feuillage aride,
C'est l'heure où le soleil monte dans le ciel bleu
Et couvre le désert des ses vagues de feu.

**HÉRODE:** Non! le sommeil me fuit et ses chaudes haleines
Font circuler un sang plus brûlant dans mes veines! . . .
Dans les clartés de l'aube au dans l'ombre du soir
C'est elle que j'attends . . . elle que je veux voir! . . .
Que votre danse, au moins, me la rappelle encore.
(*Les Esclaves dansent.*)

**DANSE BABYLONIENNE:** (*Sur un geste d'Hérode les danseuses arrêtent.*)

**UNE JEUNE BABYLONIENNE:** (*désignant à Hérode la coupe que lui tient une esclave.*) Que ce philtre amoureux dissipe ton ennui! . . . . .
Maître, bois dans cette amphore
Le vin rosé d'Engaddi
C'est un rayon de l'aurore
Enchâssé dans l'or poli
Et dans l'ivresse du breuvage
Dont notre pays est fier
Tu retrouveras limage
De l'être qui t'est si cher!

*the front, at the back, and to the right. The furniture consists of ebony stools, purple cushions, heavy rugs, lynx skins, and an ivory couch placed in the center to the left of the spectator. The low couch is made of white leather and covered with rich stuffs; candelabra of bronze supported by sphynx; silver vessels filled with nard and cinnamon; gigantic pieces of amber; porphyry bowls; antelope-horns garnished with rings and bracelets. As the curtain rises Herod appears, negligently reclining on the couch; Nubian, Greek and Babylonian slavegirls, lie around the back of the chamber, and about the king's couch, in lascivious and picturesque poses. One of them leans against the foot of the couch.*

*SCENE V*

*Herod; A Babylonian Slave-girl; other slaves.*

**SLAVES:** Take your rest, O king, upon your ivory couch,
You may dream of love and of glory.
The heart of the day has silenced the echoes,
You may dream of love nothing shall disturb your rest!
It is the hour when the sun ascends the azure sky,
And bathes the desert in his waves of fire.
You may dream of love!

**HEROD:** No! Sleep has deserted my couch, but his hot breath sends my blood burning through my veins! In the light of the morning, or in the shadows of eve, I wait for her! It is she whom I desire to see.
Let your dances recall her to me once more!
(*The Slaves dance.*)

**BABYLONIAN DANCE:** (*At a sign from Herod the dance ends.*)

**YOUNG BABYLONIAN WOMAN** (*calling Herod's attention to the cup a Slave holds out to him*). Let this amorous drink dispel these cares of yours!
This love portion will dispel your cares.
Drink, master, from this amphora, Of the roseate wine of Engadi;
It is rays of the sun
Chaliced in burnished gold!
And in the intoxication of this drink,

**HÉRODE:** (*se soulevant, à lui-même, troublé et radieux.*) Ce breuvage pourrait me donner un tel rêve!
Je pourrais la revoir . . . contempler sa beauté!
Divine volupté
A mes regards promise! Espérance trop brève!
Qui viens bercer mon coeur et troubler ma raison . . .
Ah! ne t'enfuis pas . . . douce illusion! . . .
Vision fugitive et toujours poursuivie,
Ange mystérieux qui prends toute ma vie,
C'est toi que je veux voir,
O mon amour, ô mon espoir!
Te presser dans mes bras! te dire ma tendresse,
Sentir battre ton coeur
D'une amoureuse ardeur!
Puis, mourir enlacés . . . dans une suprême ivresse! . . .
Ah! pour connaître ces transports
Et pour te voir partager cette flamme,
Je donnerais mon âme
Sans regrets, sans remords!
Si l'esclave mentait cependant . . . ce breuvage . . .
Si c'était un poison mortel! . . .
Lâche terreur! . . . Voir son image!
Puis-je hésiter encor quand on m'offre le ciel! . . .
Donne la coupe, esclave!
(*Il boit et pousse un cri.*)
Ah! déjà . . . je chancelle,
Mes yeux sont obscurcis
. . . mais je la vois . . . c'est elle.
Que de cris sur ma levre . . . et je ne puis parler
Je sens là . . . dans mon coeur qui s'agite et soupire
Comme un aveu brûlant qui ne peut s'exhaler
Ah! prends pitié de mon martyre!
Viens! plus près . . . Je le veux!
Que ma lèvre effleure
L'or de tes cheveux!
Qu'à tes pieds je meure!
Car dans mon vertige
Je ne veux que toi . . .
Viens . . . plus près . . . te dis-je!
Encor! . . . Sois à moi!
(*Il tombe accablé sur le lit.–Phanuel paraît.*)

## SCÈNE VI

*Hérode, Phanuel.*

---

Of which our land is so proud,
You shall see once more,
The features of the one
Who is most dear to you.

**HEROD:** (*anxious, yet pleased; aside.*) This drink might well bring me a dream!
I might see her! Behold her beauty!
A divine pleasure is promised to my sight!
An all too fleeting hope,
That comes to ease my heart,
And to disturb my mind;
Fly not, O sweet illusion!
You fleeting vision that I must pursue,
Mysterious angel that steals my life
Ah, it is you whom I would see!
O my love, O my hope!
It is a fleeting vision.
That steals away my life.
Ah, to hold you in my arms!
To feel your heart beat with loving flame,
And to die, in your arms, in mutual intoxication!
Ah, for such fire of joy,
Would I surrender my soul.
For your love, oh my hope,
It is a fleeting vision,
That steals my life away!
Yes, it is you, my love!
you, my only hope!
What if the slave is lying after all?
This draught may be some deadly poison!
Cowardly fear! To see her form!
How can I any longer hesitate
When it is heaven that is offered me?
Slave, give me the cup!
(*He drinks. Casting away the goblet with a cry.*)
Ah!
Already do I tremble, and my eyes
Grow dim! And yet I see her! It is she.
What words rush to my lips, and I cannot speak! I feel here, in my heart,
That beats and sighs, a flood of burning vows
I cannot utter. Oh, take pity,
Take pity on my pain. Come nearer, come!
Come nearer still, and let my lips caress
Your golden hair! For at your feet I'd die.
Ah, in my madness it is you alone
Whom I desire! Come nearer! It is my will!
Be mine! Come nearer! Come! And at your feet
Let me expire. Come nearer! Nearer! Ah!
(*He falls on his couch, overcome, and sleeps.–Phanuel enters.*)

## SCENE VI

*Herod, Phanuel.*

---

**PHANUEL:** Voilà l'homme qui fait trembler tout un empire!
Qu'importe si l'aurore à des voiles de sang!
Qu'importe le ciel menaçant!
Cet homme . . . c'est le roi . . . flétri par le délire!
Une femme l'occupe . . .

**HÉRODE:** (*revenant à lui et cherchant à se rappeler le rêve qui l'oppresse.*) Ah! Là! . . . n'ai-je pas vu
Sa vivante image? . . .
Tout à disparu! . . .
Impuissante rage.
(*il se lève, chancelant.*)
A moi! . . .
(*Apercevant le Chaldéen.*)
Phanuel! . . . Est-ce toi? . . . Réponds!

**PHANUEL:** Hérode tristement je reviens dans Sion;
La misère s'accroit selon la prophètie
Et le peuple inquiet réclame le Messie!

**HÉRODE:** Explique-moi d'abord le mal que je ressens
Et guéris un amour qui consume mes sens!
Nuit et jour, je l'appelle et je vois son image;
Un instant, j'ai cru la posséder . . . vain mirage!
Ce n'était qu'un fantôme, une ombre une vapeur! . . .
Parle! . . . Est-ce le délire? . . . Est-ce un songe trompeur? . . .

**PHANEUL:** (*avec fermeté.*) Roi, tu dis vrai, c'est le délire!
Une femme t'occupe, alors que tout respire
Autour de toi la révolte et le sang!
Roi, le ciel deviet menaçant,
Parcourant en ton nom les cités et la plaine,
Partout j'ai demande l'appui de nos voisins,
Nos plus sûrs alliés sont soumis aux Romains!

**HÉRODE:** Je le sais! mais ici la révolte est prochaine,
Et le peuple est pour moi!

**PHANUEL:** Le peuple est inconstant.

**HÉRODE:** Ce n'est pas un consul c'est un roi qui réclame!

**PHANUEL:** Il tremble devant toi, mais c'est Jean qu'il acclame.

**HÉRODE:** Ce Jean me servira peut-être dans l'instant
Où les Romains chassés je vaincrai les prophètes!
(*Avec energie.*)
Tu verras à mes pieds tomber toutes les têtes
De ces fous dangereux que la gloire a tentés! . . .

**PHANUEL:** Des fous? Eux? Des croyants!

---

**PHANUEL:** There lies the man who makes an empire tremble!
A woman fills his thoughts. And the king,
Lies there! Blasted by his delirium.

**HEROD:** (*waking, and trying to remember the dream by which he is still oppressed.*)
Ah! did I not see her living image?
There! All has disappeared
(*He rises, trembling.*)
Help!
(*Seeing the Chaldean.*)
Phanuel, is it you?

**PHANUEL:** Sadly, oh, Herod, I return to Zion.
Evils increase apace, as foretold by the prophet. The people are ill at ease, and demand the Messiah!

**HEROD:** First tell me what are those troubles that I feel! Ah, cure this love that is consuming me. Cure this love that is killing me. Night and day I call her, and I see her face. For a moment I believed her mine. It was an empty vision. Alas, it was but a shade, a phantom and a mist! Oh, cure this love of mine! Speak! Tell me, is it delirium? Or a deceptive dream? Speak! Speak!

**PHANUEL:** You have said the word, O king—delirium it is! A woman fills your mind, while all about you foreshadows slaughter and blood. Heaven has begun to threaten, O king. As in your name I passed through the cities of the plain, from all our neighbors I asked assistance. Our foremost friends are subject to Rome!

**HEROD:** That I know. But here, the revolution is at hand, for the people are with me.

**PHANUEL:** The people are fickle.

**HEROD:** It is not a Consul, it is a King who demands.

**PHANUEL:** They tremble before you, but it is John whom they receive with acclamation.

**HEROD:** This John will serve my turn. And when the Romans are once driven out, I shall conquer the prophets! (*With energy.*) You shall see fall at my feet the heads of each one of these dangerous madmen, whom the hope of glory has led astray.

**PHANUEL:** Madmen? They? They are believers!

HÉRODE: (*s'animant.*) Ce sont des révoltés!

PHANUEL: Que tu glorifieras, ô roi! par le martyré!

HÉRODE: On ne les plaindra pas où je les veux proscrire!

PHANUEL: On entendra leurs cris.

HÉRODE: Je les étoufferai!

PHANUEL: Leurs temples resteront.

HÉRODE: Je les renverserai!

LE PEUPLE: (*au loin, acclamant Hérode.*) Gloire au tétrarque! à l'alliance
Qui nous promet la libérté
Et renverse un joug détesté!

HÉRODE: Entends-tu, Phanuel? . . . Ai-je encor la puissance? . . .
Ce sont les messagers
De nos voisins, tributaires de Rome!
Mon oeuvre se consomme,
Je puis braver tous les dangers!
(*Ils sortent.–Changement à vue.*)

*Deuxieme Tableau*

*La Place Publique.*
*Le Xyste, place publique de Jérusalem.–A droite, l'entrée principale du Palais d'Hérode, avec un vaste escalier, des tapis de laine en couvrent les marches.–A gauche, une fontaine, une suite de terrasses aboutissant à la porte dorée.–Dans le lointain, la vue de la ville, l'aspect, du temple de Salomon sur le mont Moriab.–La multitude aux vêtements bigarrés s'y presse, sous l'ombrage. des sycomores et des sophoras.–Prêtres juifs. – Pharisiens, scribes, marins, marchands et soldats de toutes les tribus, envoyés arabes, chefs du désert, tous sont debout attendant l'arrivée d'Hérode. Des femmes et des enfants à la fontaine.–Marchands de colombes.– Une grande animation règne sur la place.–Dernières heures du jour.*

## SCÈNE VII

Hérode, Hérodiade, Phanuel, des Messagers, La Multitude, puis Vitellius, Les Romains, puis Jean. Salomé et Les Femmes Chananéennes, etc., etc.

LA MULTITUDE: Roi, que ta superbe vaillance
Nous sauve d'un joug détesté!
Gloire au tétrarque! à l'alliance
Qui nous promet la liberté!
(*Hérode et Phanuel descendent les degrés du Palais avec les envoyés du désert.*)

HÉRODE: Le moment est venu de te faire connaître,
O peuple, le projet que caresse ton maître,

HEROD: They are insurgents!

PHANUEL: Whom you would glorify by making martyrs of them!

HEROD: They shall be prosecuted!

PHANUEL: Their cries will be heard!

HEROD: I will stifle them!

PHANUEL: Their temples will remain.

HEROD: I shall demolish them!

VOICES OF THE PEOPLE: (*distant.*) Hail to the Tetrarch!
Hail to the alliance
That promises us our freedom!

HEROD: Do you hear, Phanuel? I still hold the power!
These are the messengers.
Of our neighbors, who are subject to Rome! These are the deputies!
My work nears fulfilment. I can face all dangers.
(*They go out!·The scene changes.*)

*Second Tableau*

*The Grand Square in Jerusalem (the Xyst.) On the right, the principal entrance to Herod's palace with a great flight of steps covered with woolen carpets. To the left a fountain and a series of terraces leading to the Golden Door. The city can be seen in the distance, with Solomon's temple on Mount Moriah. A crowd in variegated raiment, surges beneath the shadow of the sycamore and sophoras-trees; Jewish Priests, Saduccees, Pharisees, sailors, merchants, soldiers of all the tribes, Arabian envoys, desert chieftains, all await the arrival of Herod. There are women and children by the fountain. Vendors of doves. Great animation reigns in the Square. The day is drawing to a close.*

## SCENE VII

Herod, Herodias, Phanuel: Envoys, the Crowd, then Vitellius, the Romans, then John, Salome and Women of Canaan.

CHORUS: O king, may your sublime courage,
Save us from the yoke we detest!
All hail! Hail to the Alliance
That promises to us our freedom!
(*Herod comes down the steps of the palace, followed by the Envoys.*)

HEROD: (*to the people.*) The time has come, O my people, when you should be informed of the project which your master has at heart. For

Depuis assez longtemps, nous nous courbons flétris
Par le joug! . . . Le Romain n'a que notre mépris,
Mais, installé chez nous, avec un front superbe
Il donne à ses troupeaux le meilleur de notre herbe!
Peuple, pour le chasser, seconds mon effort:
Voici mes alliés! Es-tu prêt?

TOUS: Oui, la mort!
Ou notre indépendance!

HÉRODE: Et vous mourrez en braves?

TOUS: Oui! nous ne voulons plus d'entraves!

HÉRODE: Si leurs cohortes, là, surgissaient tout à coup?

TOUS: Nous n'aurions qu'un seul cri: debout!

HÉRODE, PHANUEL, LES MESSAGERS, LES CHOEURS: Aux Romains orgueilleux de nous avoir soumis
Faisons une guerre sacrée!
Jetons-nous bravement dans les rangs ennemis,
Frappons une race abhorrée!

HÉRODE: C'est bien! Vous, messagers, dites quels sont vos gages?

LES MESSAGERS: (*s'avançant.*) Tu nous garderas comme otages!

PHANUEL: Que nos apportez-vous?

PREMIER GROUPE: Quinze mille chevaux

DEUXIEME GROUPE: Des hommes!

TROISIEME GROUPE: Nous, cent chariots!

LES CHOEURS: Faisons une guerre sacrée
Aux Romains orgueilleux de nous avoir soumis.
Frappons cette race abhorrée.
Jetsons-nous bravement dans les rangs ennemis.
(*Fanfares romaines au loin.–Hérodiade, paraissant subitement au haut de l'escalier, fait un gest pour imposer silence à la foule qui, frappée de stupeur, écoute les fanfares encore très lontaines.*)

HÉRODIADE: Vous qui tenez conseil sur les places publiques,
Cessez vos appels héroiques
Et prêtez l'oreille! . . . Là-bas
Vous entendrez monter les pas
Du consul et de son escorte!
(*Elle descend. Le jour baisse peu à peu.*)

LES CHOEURS: O Dieux!

HÉRODE ET PHANUEL: Vitellius?

HÉRODIADE: Il est à votre porte!

HÉRODE: Que faire?

a long time we have bowed down, crushed by the yoke of Rome. The Romans we despise, yet they have established themselves among us, and have given to their flocks the best of our harvests. Help me, therefore, O my people, to cast them out! Here are my allies! Are you ready?

MESSENGERS AND CHORUS: Aye! Death or independence!

HEROD: And you will die like brave men?

MESSENGERS AND CHORUS: Aye, we swear it! Away with truces!

HEROD: What if their cohorts, here, were suddenly to rise?

MESSENGERS AND CHORUS: "Death or independence!" would be our only battle cry!

HEROD, PHANUEL AND THE REST: ALL. On Rome that was proud to bring us to our knees,
We'll now wage a holy war.
Let us rush bravely on against our proud enemies.
Let us conquer the race we abhor.

HEROD: It is well. And you the deputies,
What pledges do you bring?

THE MESSENGERS: You shall hold us as hostages.

PHANUEL: What do you bring us?

FIRST GROUP: Fifteen thousand horses!

SECOND GROUP: And men! And arms!

THIRD GROUP: One hundred chariots!

CHORUS: We will wage a sacred war
Against the Romans!
Let us fling ourselves bravely upon the ranks of our enemies!
We will strike down this race that we abhor.
(*Fanfare of Roman trumpets, in the distance. Herodias suddenly appears at the top of the steps. With a motion of her hand she silences the crowd, which listens in amazement to the Roman trumpets, still far off.*)

HERODIAS: You who hold your concerts in public place, cease for a moment your heroic clamor. Hark! Hark! You will hear the approaching foot—
(*She comes down. The daylight slowly fades.*)
steps of the Consul, and his guard!

CHORUS: O, God!

HEROD, PHANUEL: Vitellius!

HERODIAS: Is at your doors!

HEROD: What's to be done?

**LES CHOEURS:** Nous sommes perdus!

**HÉRODIADE:** Peut-être . . . .
(*A Hérode.*)
Toi, ne tremble plus:
Ton existence m'est plus chére que la mienne,
Je saurai les tromper.
(*Les fanfares se rapprochent.*)

**TOUS:** Ah! le Romain!

**HÉRODIADE:** Qu'il vienne!
(*Des femmes envahissent la place, tout le monde s'agite confusément. –la nuit est venue.*)

**LE CHOEUR:** Voici les Romains
Avec leurs cohortes,
C'est en souverains
Qu'ils ouvrent nos portes!
L'airain retentit
Et, sur leur passage,
Sinistre présage,
Tout céde et s'enfuit!
(*Une nouvelle fanfare annonce l'arrivée des Romains, le cortège du proconsul est précédé de porteurs de torches éclairant les enseignes et les aigles dorées qui surmontent les drapeaux de pourpre; vélites et licteurs, légionnaires.–Hérode confus et troublé va à la rencontre de Vitellius.*)

**VITELLIUS:** Quel trouble à mon approche
Fait détourner les yeux?
S'il me faut réprimer un complot odieux,
Qu'ils tremblent! car le châtiment est proche
Pour ce peuple orgueilleux!

**HÉRODE:** Quel trouble à son approche
Me fait baisser les yeux?
Sachons cacher encore ma haine et mes voeux,
Qu'il tremble, car notre vengeance est proche
Contre un joug odieux!

**HÉRODIADE:** Quel trouble! A leur approche
Il a baissé les yeux!
L'ingrat qui m'oubliait se courbe devant eux.
Il tremble! Mais le jour de ma vengeance est proche
Le sort comble mes voeux!

**PHANUEL:** Quel trouble à leur approche
Leur fait baisser les yeux?
Est-ce le châtiment qui commence pour eux?
Ils tremblent! O Jean, ton heure est proche! . . .
Dieu va combler tes voeux!

**PEOPLE:** We are lost!

**HERODIAS:** It may be so.
(*to Herod aside*) Tremble no more.
Your life is dearer to me than my own. Herod, I love you! I shall outwit them.
(*The fanfares are heard more distinctly.*)

**CHORUS:** The Roman! The Roman! The Roman!

**HERODIAS:** Let him come!
(*Women rush into the square and run about distractedly. General commotion. Night has fallen gradually.*)

**PEOPLE:** Here are the Romans
Their cohorts march on,
Seeming like victors
To seize on our town!
And at their passage,
Ominous presage,
How the brass rings,
Let us fly from the sound!
(*Another fanfare announces the arrival of the Romans. The Proconsul's train is preceded by torchbearers lighting the standards, and the golden eagles surmounting the purple banners; velites, lictors, legionaires.*)

**VITELLIUS:** Why do they lower their eyes at my approach? If it be some vile plot to be suppressed, let them beware! The punishment of this rebellious people is at hand!

**HEROD:** At his approach, what compels me thus to avert my eyes?
We must cover our plot!
I must conceal, as yet, both my hate and my vow! Beware, then!
I must hide for a while my hate and my plot!
For the punishment comes against a power we like not!

**HERODIAS:** Unworthily he bows to them, and I'm forgot!
He trembles, and fate grants what I sought!
What causes you to avert your eyes?
He trembles! yet is my triumph nearing!
And the gods will grant what I long have sought!

**PHANUEL:** When they approach them,
What causes them to avert their eyes?
In this vengeance, at last, that has come on them now?
They tremble! John, your hour is nearing!
By God you are not forgotten!

**LE PEUPLE JUIF:** Quel trouble à leur approche
Nous fait baisser les yeux?
Sachons dissimuler notre haine et nos voeux,
Qu'ils tremblent! car notre vengeance est proche
Contre un maître odieux!

**LES ROMAINS:** Quel trouble à notre approche
Fait détourner les yeux?
S'il nous faut réprimer un complot odieux,
Qu'ils tremblent! car le châtiment est proche
Pour ce peuple orgueilleux!

**VITELLIUS:** Je représente ici César et la justice:
Peuple, dis-moi quels sont tes voeux?

**LES PRETRES JUIFS:** (*revenant de leur surprise et entourant Vitellius.*) Rome nous est propice!
Qu'elle nous rende alors le temple d'Israël
Et fasse respecter le grand prêtre à l'autel!

**VITELLIUS:** Tiberè exaucera ce voeu trop légitime!
Célébrez le pouvoir d'un vainqueur magnanime!

**LA FOULE:** Salut au proconsul, aux Romains, aux soldats
Dont la gloire grandit encore à chaque pas!
(*Tandis que la foule se presse autour du proconsul et qu'Hérodiade invite Vitellius à monter au palais, tandis que les Romains retirent les lances plantées sur le sol et passent leurs boucliers à leurs bras, Jean paraît près de la Porte dorée suivi de Salomé, et de femmes chananéennes.–Jean, Salomé, et les Chananéennes semblent enveloppés dans la blanche clarté des étoiles, ils chantent: Hosannah! Gloire à celui qui nous vient du Seigneur.–Vitellius s'arrête, surpris des témoignages de respect que l'on donne à Jean.–Hérode reconnait Salomé et la désigne à Phanuel.–Enfin Hérodiade considère toute la scène avec jalousi et fureur.*)

**HÉRODE:** (*a Phanuel.*) Vois! C'est elle! mon coeur l'avait bien reconnue!

**HÉRODIADE:** (*à part.*) Il connaît cette enfant! Il pâlit a sa vue! D'où vient-elle?

**VITELLIUS:** Quel est ce mortel triomphant?

**SALOMÉ:** (*s'avançant.*) Le prophète du Dieu vivant!

**VITELLIUS:** Un fou?

**CHORUS OF THE JEWS':** When they approach us,
What causes us to avert our eyes?
Wherefore should we tremble?
Beware, then! We must conceal both our hate and our plot!
Against an odious master!

**ROMAN SOLDIERS:** When we approach them,
What causes them to avert their eyes? Beware then! Vengeance is now upon them!
Swift retribution waits
For haughty peoples who rise!

**VITELLIUS:** (*to the people.*) I represent here, Caesar, and justice!
What does this people demand?

**The JEWISH PRIESTS** (*having recovered from their surprise, surround Vitellius.*) Is Rome propitious to us?
Then let her give us back the Temple of Israel,
And cause to be respected, the High Priest at the altar!

**VITELLITUS:** Tiberius will grant your reasonable petition.
Hail then the power of so generous a conqueror!

**MESSENGERS AND PEOPLE:** All hail the Proconsul! All hail Tiberius!
Caesar all hail! All hail the soldiers!
(*The crowd presses about the Proconsul, and Herodias invites Vitellius to enter the palace, while the Romans take up the lances planted on the ground and place their shields on their arms.–John and Salome appear followed by the Canaanite women.–The moonlight surrounds them like an aureole. They sing "Hosanna! Hosanna! Hosanna! Bless him that comes in the name of the Lord!" Vitellius stops, surprised at the honor and respect shown to John. Herod recognizes Salome and points her out to Phanuel. Herodias contemplates the scene with jealous fury.*)

**HEROD:** See! It is she, Salome! I felt it in my heart!

**HERODIAS:** He knows this young girl! He grows pale at sight of her.

**VITELLIUS:** Who is this triumphant mortal?

**SALOME:** He is the prophet of the living God!

**VITELLIUS:** He's mad!

**HÉRODIADE:** (*bas et vivement à Vitellius.*) Qui rêve la puissance! Regarde!
(*A part.*)
Ah! je tiens ma vengeance!
(*Sur l'ordre du proconsul, des licteurs se mêlent au cortège de Jean et entourent le précurseur.*)

**JEAN:** (*très calme.*) Toute justice vient du ciel!
Homme, ta puissance fragile
Se brise aux pieds de l'Éternel
Comme un vase d'argile!
*Les Femmes chananéennes et Salomé reprennent leur chant: Hosannah! Hosannah!—La foule crie de nouveau: Salut au proconsul.—Hérodiade et Vitellius entrent dans le Palais.—Phanuel entraîne Hérode qui ne peut détacher ses regards de Salomé.—Tableau.—Rideau.*

*FIN DE L'ACTE DEUXIÈME.*

■ **ACTE TROISIÈME**

*Premier Tableau*

*La demeure de Phanuel.—Au fond une large ouverture qui laisse voir la nuit étoilée, et d'où l'on domine Jérusalem.*

**PHANUEL puis Hérodiade.**

*SCÈNE VIII*

**PHANUEL:** Dors, ô cité perverse! . . . Ignore le destin
Qui frappera tes fils au milieu de leurs fêtes!
Dors, et n'écoute pas la plainte des prophètes,
Moi, j'interrogerai le ciel jusqu'au matin!
Astres étincelants que l'infini promène
Enfermant l'avenir dans vos cercles de feu;
Astres qui dévoilez la destinée humaine,
Parlez! Quel est ce Jean? Est-ce un homme? Est-ce un Dieu?
Sa voix tonne comme la foudre;
Il dit: Vous trouverez, cherchez!
Les sceptres vont tomber en poudre!
Peuples! ceignez vos reins! . . .
Et les humbles, sur son passage,
Paraissent attendre un signal;
Et les rois cachent leur visage
Dans les plis du manteau royal!
Astres étincelants que l'infini promène
Enfermant l'avenir dans vos cercles de feu;
Astres qui dévoilez la destinée humaine,
Parlez, Quel est ce Jean? Est-ce un homme? Est-ce un Dieu?

---

**HERODIAS:** (*to Vitellius, in a low voice angrily.*) Who has dreams of power. See! (*aside.*)
My revenge is at hand!

**JOHN:** (*to Vitellius and to People.*) Justice cometh from the Lord! Man, your power is a frail thing, And will break at the feet of the Eternal As a vessel of clay!
*The Canaanites and Salome take up their chant again: "Hosannah! Hosannah!" The crowd again cries, "All Hail, Proconsul!" Herodias and Vitellius go into the palace, while Phanuel leads away Herod, who cannot take his eyes off Salome.*

*END OF SECOND ACT.*

■ **ACT III**

*First Tableau*

*Phanuel's house.-At the back, a large opening overlooking Jerusalem, and showing the starlit sky.*

*SCENE VIII*

**PHANUEL:** Sleep, O foolish city! Heed not the fate that will overwhelm your children in the midst of their festivities! Sleep, and listen not to the cries of your prophets! I shall question the stars until the morning.
O burning stars that heaven spreads out, and who compass the future with your orbits of fire,-O stars who can unveil the destiny of mankind, shining stars,-speak! Who is this John? Is he a man, tell me,-or a god? His voice resounds like thunder; he cries "Seek and you shall find! Sceptres will crumble into dust! Gird up your loins, people and walk!" And the lowly, as he passes, seem to await some sign. And kings hide their faces in their royal robes. Who is this John? Is he a man or a god? Shining stars, speak! Speak!
(*He remains wrapt in contemplation of the starry night. Herodias enters suddenly, disturbed and agitated.*)

---

(*Il reste absorbé dans la contemplation de la nuit étoilée, Hérodiade entre tout à coup, inquiète, agitée.*)

**HÉRODIADE:** Ah! Phanuel!

**PHANUEL:** (*surpris.*) Vers ma demeure
Quel souci t'amène à cette heure?

**HÉRODIADE:** Puis-je m'inquiéter de l'heure où du danger?
La reine vient ici pour se venger!

**PHANUEL:** Te venger?

**HÉRODIADE:** Le ciel et notre âme
Ont un lien secret! Phaneul, montremoi
L'astre auquel est lié le sort de cette femme
Qui m'a volé l'amour du roi!

**PHANUEL:** (*hésitant.*) Tu le veux?

**HÉRODIADE:** Je l'ordonne!

**PHANUEL:** Ecoute:
J'ai souvent contemplé to astre, et je l'ai vu
Par un autre toujours obscurci dans sa route! . . .
Ce soir encore . . .
(*Il remonte.*)

**HÉRODIADE:** Ah! que dis-tu?

**PHANUEL:** (*considérant le ciel.*)
Vos deux étoile sont comme une âme jumelle
Avec la même vie et la même clarté!
Le destin vous sépare . . . , et l'amour vous appelle . . .

**HÉRODIADE:** (*avec angoisse.*)
Regarde encore! Et dis la vérité, Phanuel, je veux tout connaître!

**PHANUEL:** (*sombre.*) L'horizon devient menaçant;
Je vois l'étoile disparaître,
Tu restes seule! . . . Ah!
Que de sang!
Que de sang couvre ton étoile!

**HÉRODIADE:** (*fremissante.*) Du sang . . . Je suis vengée! . . .

**PHANUEL:** (*sans l'écouter.*)
Hélas! un dernier voile
Se déchire . . . tu fus mère . . . et tu ne l'es plus!

**HÉRODIADE:** (*d'abord stupefaite, puis s'attendrissant.*)
Oui . . . mère! . . . Je le fus!

**PHANUEL:** (*se rapprochant d'elle.*) Ah! songe au passé, reine!
Reine, qu'il t'en souvienne!

**HÉRODIADE:** Si Dieu l'avait voulu!
Si j'avais pu garder auprès de moi cet ange,
J'aurais tout oublié, vengeance, amour deçu!

**PHANUEL:** (*a part.*) Son coeur se trouble (charme étrange!)
Au souvenir de son enfant perdu . . .

**HÉRODIADE:** Oui, Phanuel, mon âme à besoin de tendresse!
Je voudrais mon enfant; j'ai soif de ses caresses . . .

---

**HERODIAS:** Ah, Phanuel!

**PHANUEL:** What cares bring the Queen to my house at this hour?

**HERODIAS:** Shall I trouble myself as to the hour, or the danger? The Queen comes here for vengeance.

**PHANUEL:** For vengeance?

**HERODIAS:** The heavens and my soul are bound together by a secret bond! Phanuel, point out to me the star that is united to the fate of the woman who has stolen from me the love of the King!

**PHANUEL:** You wish it?

**HERODIAS:** I command it!

**PHANUEL:** Listen! I have often beheld your star. And ever, on its way, I have seen it obscured by another even tonight . . . !

**HERODIAS:** Ah! What do you say?

**PHANUEL:** Your star and hers are like twins, that have one life, one light! Fate separates you, but love draws you together.

**HERODIAS:** Look again! And tell me the truth. Phanuel! Phanuel! I would know all!

**PHANUEL:** The horizon becomes threatening! I see the star disappear . . .
Yours alone remains . . . Ah, and blood, blood quenches your star!

**HERODIAS:** Blood! I am revenged!

**PHANUEL:** And now, one last veil is rent asunder. You are mother no more.

**HERODIAS:** Mother! Sacred word.

**PHANUEL:** Think of the past, O Queen.

**HERODIAS:** Had it been God's will . . . !If I could have kept my angel with me. I should have forgotten it all! Vengeance, and love betrayed.

**PHANUEL:** Her heart is troubled.

**HERODIAS:** My soul is in need of love-I want my child. I thirst for her caresses!

PHANUEL: (*se rapprochant encore.*) Espère donc!

HÉRODIADE: La voir? . . . la presser sur mon cœur?

PHANUEL: Oui, tu le peux!

HÉRODIADE: O ciel! pour moi plus de douleur! Et c'en est fait de ma misère!

PHANUEL: Ah! tu le vois, le ciel te permet d'être mère! (*Subitement et rémontant la scène. il l'entraine ver l'ouverture du fond et lui montre Salomé qui se dirige vers le temple.*) Ta fille . . . tiens! regarde! Là-bas . . . entrant Dans le temple . . .

HÉRODIADE: (*reculant et poussant un cri de rage.*) Elle! ma rivale! Non! non! ma fille est morte, et je n'ai plus d'enfant!

PHANUEL: (*terrible et chassant Hérodiade.*) Reine impitoyable et fatale! Et tu disais que tu l'aimais! Va! tu n'es qu'une femme . . . une mère, jamais!

(*Hérodiade fuit épouvantée sous la malédiction de Phanuel.*) (*Changement à vue.*)

*Deuxième Tableau*

*Partie immense du temple de Solomon précédant le Sanctuaire.—Murailles de bois de cédre, dont la dorure est éblouissante; colonnes de marbre et de porphyre, corniches en formes de lis avec feuillage d'or.—Des chaînes de bronze, des tapisseries rattachent les colonnes les unes aux autres.—A droite, grille fermée conduisant au souterrain du temple. Au fond, portes d'argent sur lesquelles pendent des voiles de lin.—Des voiles à fleur de pourpre cachent l'entrée du Sanctuaire.—Au lever du rideau, la scène est déserte.*

## SCÈNE IX

VOIX AU DEHORS: Hérode, à toi ces palmes, A toi, reine, ces fleurs! A tous deux, richesse et bonheurs Que vos jours soient nombreux et calmes! (*Salomé, entre faible, se soutenant à peine.*) L'aube renaît à peine . . . on s'éveille au palais On acclame Hérode et la reine! Ah! qu'ils soient maudits à jamais Ceux qui poursuivent de leur haine Jean mon bien-aimé! Ils l'ont pris . . . enchainé! Quel supplice s'apprête! Ou peut-être . . . déja . . . quel

PHANUEL: Hope on!

HERODIAS: To see her! To hold her to my heart!

PHANUEL: You may see her!

HERODIAS: Can it be I shall see her? O Heaven! For me then there would be no more pain!

PHANUEL: Oh, you see, Heavens permit you To be a mother again! (*leading her to the opening at the back and showing her Salome who is going toward the temple.*) Your child! There! Look! She is about to enter the Temple! Down there! Entering the temple!

HERODIAS: My daughter? She? My rival! No, no! My daughter is dead! I have no child.

PHANUEL: Queen, pitiless as fate-go! You are but a woman; a mother, never!

HERODIAS: Ah!

*Second Tableau*

*A large portion of the Temple before the Sanctuary.-Walls of cedar, richly gilded; columns of marble and periphery with lily-shaped cornices with golden foliage. Bronze chains and tapestries interconnect the columns. To the right, a barred gate leading to the Temple vaults. At the back, silver doors, over which fall linen vails; these veils, embroidered with purple and hyacinth flowers, hide the entrance to the Sanctuary.-When the curtain rises, the stage is empty.*

## SCENE IX

VOICES OF WOMEN (*heard off*): O Herod! for you the palms, For you, Queen, the flowers! To them both, long life, happy hours! To him, the palms! To her, the flowers! (*Salome enters, half-fainting, scarcely able to stand.*) Dawn is scarcely appearing, Yet I hear them before Herod's palace servilely cheering! Ah! Be they accursed evermore, Those who to death, perhaps, are bearing John, whom I adore! In their chains he was bound! Is he waiting their torture?

tombeau s'est fermé? Je souffre! . . . Et là toujours ces chants de fête!

VOIX AU DEHORS: A toi, reine, ces fleurs, Hérode, à toi ces palmes! A vous deux, richesse et bonheurs! Que vos jours soient nombreux et calmes!

SALOMÉ: La force m'abandonne . . . hélas! toute la nuit J'ai veillé . . . (*Elle regarde craintivement autour d'elle.*) C'est ici pourant qu'ils l'ont conduitô (*Avec désespoir.*) Dieu! tu n'entends donc pas leur injuste sentence! Charme des jours passés où j'entendais sa voix, Où je sentais mon cœur renaître a l'espérance, As-tu donc disparu pour le dernière fois? Vais-je rester encor seul avec ma souffrance? Les cieux s'ouvraient plus brillants et plus clairs, La tendresse et la foi palpitaient dans les airs, A peine ai-je entrevu cette heure fortunée Que tu viens me frapper, cruelle destinée! Qui prendra pitié de mes pleurs? Qui m'ouvrira la porte de sa tombe! Ah! permettez qu'avec lui je succombe, Bourreaux! . . . s'il doit mourir . . . je meurs! (*Elle tombe épuisée au moment où Hérode entre et se dirige vers la grille de souterraiu à droite.*)

## SCÈNE X

*Hérode, Salomé.*

HÉRODE: (*il s'arrête sombre et préoccupé*) C'en est fait! . . . La Judée appartient à Tibère! A quio m'a-t-il servi de flatter les Romains Pour devenir le roi de ce pays prospère? Je suis chef de tribu chez les Galiléens! Tu l'emportes, César! . . . Mais ma vengeance est prête. Tremble! Je sauverai Jean, ce hardi prophète Qui n'attend rien de ta faveur, Et les Juifs briserout ton joug envahisseur! (*Il aperçoit Salomé toujours accroupie dans l'ombre.*) On m'écoutait! . . . qui donc était la? Femme! femme! Que fais-tu là?

Salomé: (*comme dans un rêve douloureux.*) Qui parle?

Or, it may be, even now, he lies dead in the ground! I suffer-these festal songs, how they resound!

VOICES (*without*): Riches and hapiness be yours! May your days be long, and peaceful! For you the flowers; for you the palms.

SALOME: I suffer! And ever about me these festal songs. My strength fails me! Alas, I kept watch all night. It was here, indeed, they bought him. Some dark conspiracy threatens the prophet! This Herod, cowering before the Romans; and these Pharisees, fearing lest they rose their power, have thrown him into the dungeons beneath. O God, you will not heed their unjust condemnation! God have pity, have mercy! How sweet were the days that are gone, When I listened to his voice; When I felt my hopes revive in my heart. Have you then vanished forever? Shall I be left alone with my grief? Heaven opened then more bright and clear, Mercy and faith breathed in the air. But scarce had I beheld this happiness, When you, O cruel Fate, did strike me down. God, O God, have pity on my tears! Have pity on me. Have pity Murderers! Murderers! If he must die, Let me die with him! (*She falls exhausted at the bars of the prison.*)

## SCENE X

*Herod, Salome.*

HEROD: (*stops, preoccupied and gloomy*). It is done! Judaea belongs to Tiberius. What use to me was it to flatter the Romans only to become king of this pretty province? I am chief of a tribe-the tribe of Galileeans! You have conquered, O Caesar! But my vengeance is at hand, Beware! Beware! I shall save this John, this bold prophet, who asks no favors of you! And the Jews will break your conqueror's yoke. (*He sees Salome.*) I have been overheard! Woman! Answer. What do you want here?

SALOME: (*as though in a painful dream.*) Who speaks?

HÉRODE: (*avec violence.*) Sur ton âme,
Réponds!
(*La reconnaissant.*)
Ah! Salomé! . . . C'est elle que je vois . . . Rêves réalisés!

SALOMÉ: (*interdite.*) Que voulez-vous de moi?

HÉRODE: Demande au prisonnier qui revoit la lumière,
À la fleur qui s'entr'ouvre aux premiers feux du jour,
Au coeur désespéré qui renaît à l'amour,
Demande-leur, enfant, ce qu'ils veulent sur terre?
Ils oublient tout, la nuit, le froid et la misère,
Ils ne désirent rien car ils ont le soleil,
Ils ont la joie, ils ont un horizon vermeil! . . .
Et pour moi c'est ainsi: j'ai tout ce que j'espère! . . .
Laisse-moi contempler ta beauté douce et fière!
Une ivresse ineffable illumine mes cieux;
Mon rayon de soleil, c'est l'éclat de tex yeux
Toi seule es le trésor que je cherche sur terre!
(*Salomé s'est relevée, elle fait un effort pour chasser le souvenir qui la possède, et, comprenant tout enfin, elle repousse Hérode avec horreur.*)

SALOMÉ: Ah! que m'oses-tu dire?

HÉRODE: Oui, je n'aime que toi;
Oui, c'est toi que veux; oui, ton corps et ton âme
Vont m'appartenir, car je suis le roi!

SALOMÉ: (*fremissante.*) Le roi! . . . C'est lui, l'infâme!

HÉRODE: (*cherchant à l'entraîner.*) Viens! viens! sois à moi!

SALOMÉ: Non!

HÉRODE: Faveur suprême
Du ciel en ce jour!
Esclave, je t'aime
Et veux ton amour!

SALOMÉ: (*lui résistant.*) Non!

HÉRODE: Vois quelle aurore
S'ouvre devant toi!

SALOMÉ:
Lui! . . . C'est lui que m'aime!

HÉRODE: C'est moi qui t'implore
Et je suis le roi!

SALOMÉ: O douleur suprême!

HÉRODE: Tu m'appartiendras!

SALOMÉ: Non! jamais!

HEROD (*violently*): Upon your soul, reply!
(*recognizing her*)
Ah, Salome, Salome, it is she! My dream is realized!

SALOME: What do you wish of me?

HEROD: Salome! Ask of the prisoner who regains the light of day; ask of the hopeless heart that feels its love revive, ask these, my child, why they wish to live on the earth. They forget all, night, cold, and suffering. There is nothing they wish, for they have the sun; joy they have and the future is roseate for them. So it is with me: I have everything for which I hoped. Salome, let me behold your beauty, sweet and proud! Salome, what ineffable intoxication fills my sky! The rays of my sun are the light of your eyes. You alone are the treasure which I seek on this earth. Salome! Let me love you, Salome!
(*Salome rises and making an effort to drive away the memories that hold her, then as she realizes Herod's meaning, repulses him with horror.*)

SALOME: How dare you speak to me this way!

HEROD: I love you! Yes, you alone I love! And you are my desire! Ah, your body and your soul must be mine; for I am the King!

SALOME: The King! It is he! Monster!

HEROD (*seeking to persuade her.*) Come! Be mine! Salome, I love you!

SALOME: Never!

HEROD: It is the highest gift the world affords today. Slave, I love you and I will have your love!

SALOME: No!

HEROD: See what a future opens before you. Come, Salome, I implore!

SALOME: He loves me! He!

HEROD: See what a future opens before you. I am the King, and I implore!

SALOME: O—to suffer so! Have pity!

HEROD: I love you, and you shall belong to me.

SALOME: Never!

HEROD: I'll make you smart!

SALOME (*braving him*): What care I for death . . .

HÉRODE: Crains ma fureur!

SALOMÉ: (*le bravant.*) Je te méprise, toi, ton amour, ta puissance . . .
J'aime! . . . Un autre, entends-tu? possède tout mon coeur.

HÉRODE (*avec violence.*) Un autre! . . . dis-tu vrai?

SALOMÉ: Cet autre qui t'offense
Est plus fort que César, plus grand que les héros!

HÉRODE: (*terrible.*) Qu'il soit César où bien esclave,
Je connaîtrai cet homme qui me brave
Et je vous livrerai tous les deux aux bourreaux!

DES VOIX: (*dans les profondeurs du sanctuaire.*) Schmah Isroël! Adonaï Eloheinou!

HÉRODE: (*revenant à Salomé et suppliant.*) Ecoute, enfant! Le peuple anvahit ces portiques,
Et des Juifs j'entends les cantiques.
Ne me repousse pas . . . Pitié! viens au palais!

SALOMÉ: (*se dégageant.*) Tu me fais horreur! je te hais!

HÉRODE: (*avec fureur.*) Depuis trop longtemps, Hérode supplie!
Va! je châtierai tes amours!

SALOMÉ: Que m'importe la mort! que m'importe la vie,
Si le ciel protège ses jours!
(*Hérode sort précipitamment en faisant un dernier geste de menace à Salomé qui, palpitante, se laisse tomber auprès du grand voile de lin, devant le sanctuaire.–La foule envahit le temple.*)

HEROD: Beware of my anger!

SALOME: I despise you; your love and your power! I, too, love! Another has my heart!

HEROD: Is this the truth?

SALOME: I, too, love! And that other who offends you, is mightier than Caesar, and greater than any hero!

HEROD: Is this the truth? I shall discover this man, who defies me, and I will send you both to eternity!

VOICES (*from the Temple*): Schmah Isroël! Adonaï Eloheinou!

HEROD: (*taking Salome by the arm, beseechingly.*) You hear them? The arches with voices are ringing!
It is the Jews, singing their ancient anthem.
Repel me not! Be kind, come home with me!

SALOME (*breaking away.*) Ah, disgusting brute!

HEROD (*fiercely.*) Good! it will be your fault! I will chastise your contemptible love!

SALOME: What care I for death! What care
I for living! If heaven but guard him!
(*Herod goes out hurriedly, with a final threatening gesture toward Salome (who, trembling, sinks down beside the great veil which conceals the Holy of Holies.–The crowd invades the temple.*)

## SCÈNE XI

*Les Princes Des Prêtres, Une Voix dans la sanctuaire, La Foule.*

*Par les portiques de droite et de gauche la foule pénètre dans le temple, lentement, avec calme et en donnant les marques du plus profond respect.–Puis des serviteurs du temple ouvrent les grilles d'argent qui défendent l'accès du sanctuaire et le grand voile se sépare laissant apercevoir le sanctuaire dont la large colonnade et les vastes profondeurs sont brillamment éclairées; seul, le tabernacle reste encore voilé.–Une procession sainte sort lentement par la droite du sanctuaire, ce sont: Les Serviteurs du Temple, des Prêtres, les Femmes de Jérusalem portant des offrandes, les Princes des Prêtres, les*

## SCENE XI

*The Priestly Nobles. A Voice (within the Sanctuary). The Crowd.*

*(The people go into the temple slowly and quietly, by the doors at the right and left, exhibiting the greatest reverence. The servitors of the temple open the silver gratings that prevent access to the Sanctuary and the great veil slowly separates. The great colonnade and extensive depth of the Sanctuary appear in a brilliant illumination; the Tabernacle alone remains veiled. A sacred procession moves slowly out from the right of the Sanctuary, comprising: Temple Servitors, Priests; Women of Jerusalem bearing offerings; the Priestly Nobles; Levites carrying golden censers in which incense is burning; Young Israelites; the*

*Lévites tenant les cassolettes d'or où brule l'encens, De Jeunes Israélites, les Filles Sacrées et enfin le Grand Prètre; toute la foule se prosterne.*

**VOIX:** (*dans le sanctuaire.*): Schemah Israel! Adonaï Eloheinou!

**LA FOULE:** (*prosternée.*) Schemah Israel! Adonaï Eloheinou!

**LE GRAND PRETRE:** Accurez tous, revenez dans le temple!! Le Seigneur trois fois saint permet qu'on le contemple O peuples d'Israël, Prosternez-vous! Adorez l'Eternel!

**LA FOULE:** Gloire au Dieu des armées! Hosannah! Gloire à Dieu! Revenez, tribus alarmées, Prier dans le saint lieu! Hosannah! Gloire à Dieu! (*Le lin qui cachait encore le tabernacle se soulève, et le Saint des Saints, éclairé de mille lumières, apparaît aux yeux de la foule frémissant de joie.*)

**DANSE SACRÉE:** (*Les filles de Manahim.*)

## SCÈNE XII

*Les Mêmes, Hérode, Hérodias, Phanuel, Vitellius, Les Romains, puis Jean, puis Salomé.*

**VITELLIUS:** Peuple juif! rends justice à la grandeur de Rome, Sa gloire et ses bienfaits emplissent l'univers!

**HÉRODE:** (*à part.*) Oui, célébrez César qui vous donne des fers! (*Les princes des prêtres s'avancent vers Vitellius.*)

**LES PRETRES:** Achève donc ton oeuvre en condamnant un homme Qui preche la discorde et méconnait ta loi: Il pervertit le peuple des Juifs et se dit roi . . . Rends la paix au royaume en frappant cent impie! . . .

**VITELLIUS:** (*a Hérode.*) Jean est Galiléen, Hérode, c'est à toi De le juger.

**HÉRODE:** (*avec un mouvement de joie bientôt réprimé.*) Moi! . . .

**VITELLIUS:** N'es-tu as son roi?

**LES PRINCES DES PRETRES:** On t'amène ce faux Messie, Pour l'Etat et pour nous mesure le danger!

**HÉRODE:** (*a Vitellius.*) Je consens à l'interroger. (*A part.*) Qu'il serve mes projets, je lui donne la vie! (*Entrée de Jean, amené par les serviteurs et les gardes du temple.*)

---

*Daughter of Manahim; and, last, the High Priest. The people fall prostrate).*

**A VOICE** (*within the Sanctuary*): Schemah Israel! Adonaï Eloheinou!

**THE CROWD:** Schemah Israel! Adonaï Eloheinou!

**THE HIGH PRIEST:** Come one, come all, to the Temple. For this day you may see the Lord, who is thrice holy! People of Israel! Now bow down, and adore the Eternal!

**THE CROWD:** Glory to the Lord of Hosts! Hosannah! Sing His praise Come, tribes affrighted, in this holy place Your prayers to Him upraise! Hosannah! Sing His Praise! (*The sacred veil of the Temple rises little by little and the Holy of Holies appears, lit by a thousand lights. The people rise, joyful and excited*).

**SACRED DANCE:** (*The Daughters of Monahim*).

## SCENE XII

*Herodias, Herod, Vitellius, and Phanuel enter, followed by the Romans; then John, afterward Salome.*

**VITELLIUS** (*to The People*): People of Judea, render justice to the greatness of Rome, whose great deeds and glories fill the world.

**HEROD:** Aye! Shout for Caesar, who keeps you in chains. (*The Priests advance toward Vitellius.*)

**PRIESTS:** Finish your work, by the condemnation of a man who preaches discord, and disregards the law! He stirs up the people, and calls himself King of the Jews. Restore peace of the realm, by punishing this offender.

**VITELLIUS** (*to Herod*): John is a Galilean, it is for you to pass judgment.

**HEROD** (*with a movement of ill-conceled joy*). For me?

**VITELLIUS:** Are not you his King?

**PRIESTS** (*to Herod*): They are bringing you this false Messiah! Judge well of the danger to the State, and to us.

**HEROD:** I consent to question him. (*Aside.*) If he will serve my purpose, I will give him his life. (*John appears, led in by the guards of the Temple.*)

---

**LES FEMMES:** Comme il est beau dans sa misère! Il est rempli de majesté, Son regard n'a rien de sévère, Il rêve d'immortalité! . . .

**VITELLIUS:** (*à Hérode.*) Je plains cet homme en sa misère, Je crois à sa sincérité. Hérode, ne sois pas sévère, Le voilà plein d'humilité! . . .

**LES PRETRES:** Roi, cet homme feint la misère, Pour éveiller la charité; Craignant que te ne sois sévère, Le voilà plein d'humilité! . . .

**HÉRODIADE:** (*à Hérode.*) Vois cet homme qui feint la misère, Il abandonne sa fierté; Craignant que tu ne sois sévère, Le fourbe est plein d'humilité!

**PHANUEL:** Comme il est grand dans sa misère! Il est rempli de majesté, Son regard n'a rien de sévère, Il rêve d'immortalité!

**HÉRODE:** Voilà donc ce mortel qui soulève le monde! . . .

**JEAN:** Seigneur! donne à mon coeur les clartés de la foi, Que ma parole soit plus ardente et féconde; Soutiens ton défenseur! Je vais parler pour toi! . . . (*Hérode, Vitellius, Phanuel: ont pris place sur les sièges placés devant les grandins.*)

**HÉRODE:** (*avec une faveur marquée.*) Homme, ton nom?

**JEAN:** Je suis Jean, fils de Zacharie.

**HÉRODE:** Est-il donc vrai que par ta prophétie Le peuple est agité?

**JEAN:** J'ai dit: Paix aux mortels de bonne volonte!

**HÉRODE:** Quelle armes as-tu pour fonder ton symbole?

**JEAN:** Je n'ai qu'une arme: La parole!

**HÉRODE:** Quel est ton but enfin?

**JEAN:** Mon but: La liberté! (*Rumeurs diverses.*)

**LA FOULE:** La liberté! la liberté!

**LES PRETRES:** César! A mort! à la torture! . . .

**HÉRODIADE:** Roi, souffriras-tu cette injure? A mort! . . . A la torture!

**VITELLIUS ET PHANUEL:** Quoi! la mort! la torture!

**HÉRODE:** (*profite de ce moment de confusion pour se rapprocher de Jean.*) On ne peut condammer cet homme en vérité:

---

**THE WOMEN OF JERUSALEM:** Ah, what distress, and yet what beauty! See! see him stand there in his misfortune! Ah, behold! Ah, he is full of majesty.

**VITELLIUS** (*to Herod*): He does not lack humility. See, he seems in humble mood to me! It is he! And, Herode, there is no need to be severe . . .

**THE PRIESTS:** King, this man but acts his misery. That it may arouse our charity He thinks you will not be severe Therefore behold him all humility!

**HERODIAS** (*to Herod*): See, the rogue is all humility! See, he's lost his old audacity! It is he! Here he is! Behold him all humility! He's before us at last!

**PHANUEL:** Is he not grand in his misfortune? He is imbued with majesty, He dreams of immortality! He stands there clothed in majesty!

**HEROD:** Here is the man who would uplift the world!

**JOHN:** Pour, O Lord, into my heart the light of your faith, that my words may be fervent and fruitful. Sustain, O Lord, your advocate, for I speak for you! (*Herod, Vitellius, and Herodias take their places on the seats before the steps. The crowd is held back by the guards. Phanuel remains apart.*)

**HEROD** (*to John*): Man, what is your name?

**JOHN:** I am John, son of Zacharias.

**HEROD:** Is it true that the people are stirred up by your prophecies?

**JOHN:** I have preached, "Peace on earth, good will towards men!"

**HEROD:** What weapons have you with which to establish your pretension?

**JOHN:** I have no arms but my words.

**HEROD:** What end have you in view?

**JOHN:** My end is liberty! (*Clamor.*)

**ALL:** Liberty! Liberty! Liberty!

**PRIESTS:** Caesar! It is death! It is torture!

**HERODIAS:** Will you, O King, suffer this outrage? It is death! It is torture!

**HEROD** (*taking advantage of the confusion, he rises and imposes silence on the crowd.*) This man cannot be condemned. He is mad.

## Act III, Scene XII

C'est un fou!

BAS, (*à Jean.*) Grace à moi, la foule est incertaine;
Serviras-tu mes projets et ma haine?

JEAN: (*a Hérode.*) Dieu n'abaisse pas son regard
Sur les complots des rois!

LES PRÊTRES: Il insulte César! A mort! à la torture!
Roi, souffriras-tu cette injure? . . .
(*Avec exaltation croissante.*)
Il à méconnu notre loi!
Des Juifs cet homme se dit roi!
Crucifiez ce faux Messie!
A mort! à mort! Mort à l'impie!

HÉRODIADE: Crucifiez ce faux Messie!
A mort! mort! . . . Mort à l'impie!

LA FOULE: (*entraînée par la voix des prêtres.*) A mort! qu'on l'attache à la croix!
Et s'il doit vivre
Nos verrons si Dieu le délivre!

HÉRODE, PHANUEL, VITELLIUS: Non! il doit vivre! Mon/ton pouvoir le délivre! . . .
(*Au milieu du tumulte produit par cette scène, Salomé sort des rangs de la foule et se précipite cu-devant de Jean que les gardes du temple vont saisir.*)

SALOMÉ: J'ai vécu de sa vie et mourrai de sa mort,
Laissez-moi partager son sort!

HÉRODE: (*à part, à la vue de Salomé.*) Malédiction! C'était lui! cet homme!
(*Salomé tombe aux pieds de Jean.-La foule interdite se retourne vers elle.*)

SALOMÉ: C'est Dieu que l'on te nomme,
Car il n'est pas un homme
Qui garde ta sérénité! . . .
Toi, dont la vie entière
Ne fut qu'une prière
A l'amour, à la charité!
Je veux quitter la vie,
Divin maître, ravie
Dans l'extase de ta clarté,
Loin des vaines pensées,
Nos âmes enlacées
Montent dans l'immortalité.

LA FOULE: (*attirée.*) Que dit-elle? etrange mystère
Elle veut partager son sort?
Victime volontaire,
Elle affronte la mort!

---

(*Going near to John and saying to him:*) Thanks to me the people is divided. A word. Will you further my projects and my revenge?

JOHN: God does not stoop to look upon the petty plots of kings.

PRIESTS: It is insult to Caesar! To death with him! To the torture! Will you, O King, suffer this outrage? He had disregarded our laws! To death with him. Nail him to the cross; and if he is to live, let his God deliver him! Death to the imposter.

HERODIALS: Death to the impostor! Crucify this false Messiah!

THE CROWD (*incited by the priests*) Death to the traitor! Crucify him!
If he's to live,
Then his God must deliver!

HEROD, PHANUEL, VITELLIUS: No! He should live! My power shall deliver him. / No! He should live! Your power shall deliver him.
(*Great movement in the crowd. At a signal from the Priests, the guards of the Temple advance to seize John. In the midst of the tumult, Salome comes suddenly out of the crowd and runs to John.*)

SALOME: I have lived in his life; and in his death I shall die! Let me share his fate.
(*Salome falls at John's feet; the crowd contemplates them in silence.*)

HEROD: (*aside, seeing Salome*): Fool that I am! It is he that she loves, and I would have saved him.

SALOME (*to John*): It is a god they call you! For no man could maintain your serenity! You, whose whole life was an appeal for love, for charity! It is a god they call you. I would leave this life, Divine Master, and follow you, exalted in the ecstacy of your brightness! I would follow you! Far from vain thoughts our souls together joined, will soar upward to immortality. It is a god that they call you! God!

PEOPLE and OTHERS: Ah! What does she say? How strange a mystery!
A voluntary victim!
She faces death!

HEROD: It is he that she loves!
And I would have saved him!

---

PHANUEL ET VITELLIUS: Que dit-elle? O sombre mystère!
Ile veut partager son sort?
Victime volontaire,
Elle s'offre à la mort!

HÉRODIADE: Que dit-elle? etrange mystère!
Elle veut partager son sort?
Mon coeur jaloux espère!
Pour elle, c'est la mort!

HÉRODE: C'est lui! c'est cet homme.
Qu'elle aime! Et j'allais le sauver! . . .
(*Revenant à lui et s'adressant avec véhémence aux prêtres, aux Romains et à la foule.*)
Prêtres, vous disiez vrai! contre César et Rome
C'est bien le peuple juif qu'il voulait soulever!
Il menaçait les grands d'un châtiment sévère,
Il prêchait la révolte aux humbles de la terre,
Et lui! . . . le saint prophète! est l'amant odieux
De Salomé, la courtisane!
Frappez-les! Frappez-Les! car ma voix les condamne!

Tous: A mort! Hérode les condamne!

HÉRODE: (*s'avançant, et bas à Salomé.*) Je te l'avais bien dit! vous périrez tous deux.

HÉRODIADE: (*à part.*) Quelle étrange pitié saisit mon âme!

PHANUEL: (*à Hérodiade.*) O reine!
Ton coeur est rassuré! Ta jalousie est vaine!

JEAN: (*inspiré.*) Vox yeux sont grands ouverts et ne voient pas le jour!
Frappez donc, frappez les apôtres
Dont le dernier soupir est un long cri d'amour!
Oui, frappez-moi! vous en lapiderez bien d'autres!
Toi, Rome, dans l'horreur des nuits
Tu veux étouffer ma prière
Mais je vois tes palais et tes temples détruits,
Il n'en restera plus bientôt pierre sur pierre!

HÉRODE ET HÉRODIADE: Qu'ils périssent tous deux
Si la foi les inspire!
Pas de pitié pour eux . . .
Sous mes yeux qu'elle expire!

LES PRETRES ET LA FOULE:
Qu'ils périssent tous deux
Si la foi les anime!
Pas de pitié pour eux,
Non! La mort pour leur crime!

---

VITELLIUS AND PHANUEL: What does she say?
O dark mystery!
A voluntary victim!
She offers to die!

HERODIAS: What does she say?
She wishes to share his fate!
My jealous heart has hopes!
Death for her.

HEROD: (*regaining his self-possession and speaking very forcibly to the Priest, the Romans and the Crowd*). Priests! you have said what is true! He has endeavored to rouse the people against Rome and Caesar. He has threatened the mighty with dire punishments. He has preached revolt to the lowly of the earth, and he, the holy Prophet, is the vile lover of Salome the Courtesan! Slay them! Slay them. It is I who condemn them!

ALL: To death! To death! Herod has condemned them!

HEROD (*to Salome*): I told you that you both should perish.

HERODIAS (*aside*): What strange feeling of pity takes possession of my soul?

PHANUEL (*to Herodias*): O Queen, your jealousy is in vain; for your heart has lost its fears.

JOHN (*with inspiration*): Slay me, then. Kill the apostles, whose last breath is a great cry of love! Your eyes are open wide, but ye see not the light of day! Aye slay me! Many others will you also stone! And you, O Rome, you would strangle my prayers in horror and darkness! But I see your palaces and your temples overturned, and soon there shall not be left one stone upon another! Slay one! Kill the apostles-slay!

HEROD AND HERODIAS: Let them both perish! The faith that upholds them is a fresh crime. Yea, I wish them both to perish now! O Rome, they have insulted your gods! This is their crime! Let them both perish! This is their fresh crime! Let them both perish! Aye, both!

PRIESTS AND CROWD: Destroy them! Have them both put to death It is faith's expression!
Pity not their obsession!
Have them both put to death!

**LES FEMMES:** Il meprise la mort,
Innocente victime!
Un Dieu puissant et fort
Le soutient et l'anime!

**VITELLIUS et LES ROMAINS:** Ils méprisent la mort,
Quelle foi les anime?
Ils bénissent leur sort
En dépit de leur crime.

**JEAN:** Que m'importe la mort?
C'est la foi qui m'inspire!
O Dieu puissant et fort,
Je bénis mon martyre!

**SALOMÉ:** Que m'importe la mort
C'est la foi qui m'anime,
En partageant ton sort,
O prophète sublime!

**PHANUEL:** Ils mésprisent la mort
Et la foi les inspire!
Quel Dieu puissant et fort
Apaise leur martyre?
(*Les gardes et les serviteurs du temple eniourent Jean et Salomé.*)

*FIN DE L'ACTE TROISÌEME.*

■ **ACTE QUATRÌEME**

*Premier Tableau*

*Un Souterrain du Temple.*

*Sorte de crypte creusée jusqu'au tuf sous le temple de Jérusalem; les piliers trapus qui forment les assises du temple, sont très rapprochés les uns des autres.–A gauche, sur une stèle, une lampe funéraire brûle dans une coquille de bronze faisant un demi-circle de clarté douteuse au milieu de laquelle se trouve Jean.–A droite, la vasque de la fontaine où se désaltéraient les prisonniers.*

*SCÈNE XIII*

*Jean, puis Salomé puis le Grand Prètre.*

**JEAN:** (*est assis dans une attitude de résignation contemplative.*)
Ne pouvant réprimer les élans de la foi,
Leur impuissante rage à frappé ton prophète.
Seigneur, ta volonté soit faite,
Je me repose en toi!
Adieu donc, vains objets qui nous
Charment sur terre.
Salut! premiers rayons de l'immortalité!
L'infini m'appelle et m'éclaire;
Je meurs pour la justice et pour la liberté!
Je ne regrette rien de ma prison d'argile,
Fuyant l'humanité,
Je vais, calme et tranquille,
M'envelopper d'éternité!
Je ne regrette rien, et pourtant, ô

**WOMEN:** He despises death!
He holds to his faith!
How strong in God his faith!
He despises even death!

**VITELLIUS AND ROMANS:** They despise death, which faith provokes that?
They praise their fate
Braving their crime!

**JOHN:** Blest be the martyr's pyre,
It is faith that inspires
O God, more strong than death,
Bless your martyr's pyre.

**SALOME:** Ah, what is death to me,
If faith be in possession!
I'll share your fate with you.
Though death mark my transgression!

**PHANUEL:** This faith that's in possession,
Leads to the martyr's pyre!
May God this fresh oppression
Reprove in his just ire!
(*The guards of the Temple seize John and Salome.*)

*END OF THIRD ACT.*

■ **ACT IV**

*First Tableau*

*(A Dungeon in the Temple.)*

*(A sort of circular vault, arched to the top under the Temple at Jerusalem. Thick-set pillars forming the foundation of the edifice are set closely together. At the left on a stool burns a funeral lamp in a bronze stand, shedding a semi-circle of faint light, in the middle of which John sits. To the right, a fountain-basin for the refreshment of prisoners.)*

*SCENE XIII*

*John, then Salome, then the High Priest.*

**JOHN** (*in an attitude of contemplative resignation*). Since they could not repress the power of Thy Truth, their impotent rage has struck at Thy prophet, O Lord! Thy will be done. I trust in Thee! Farewell, then, vain things of earthly charm. Hail! Hail! first rays of immortality. The infinite calls me, and lights my way. I die for justice and for liberty! I do not regret this prison of clay, for when I leave this humanity I shall be clothed in eternity! I do not regret anything, yet, such is my weakness, I dream of that child. I dream of that child, whose radiant features are present to my eyes. Her memory weighs upon me. Ever do I dream of her! I am your son, O Lord. Why do you permit love to come to me and dis-

faiblesse!
Je songe à cette enfant dont les traits radieux
Sont toujors presents à mes yeux,
Souvenir qui m'oppresse! . . .
O Seigneur, si je suis ton fils, dis-moi pourquoi
Tu souffres que l'amour vienne ébranler ma foi?
Et si je sors meurtri, vaincu de cette lutte,
Qui l'a permis! . . . à qui la faute de la chute?
(*Avec angoisse, comme si un doute subit s'emparait de lui.*)
Ah! Seigneur, suis-je bien le héraut du vrai Dieu
Et l'elu des apôtres?
Ou nes suis-je qu'un homme en tout semblable aux autres?
(*Il retombe accablé. La clarté bleuâtre du temple fait tout à coup une traînée lumineuse dans le souterrain, et, enveloppée dans cette lumière, Salomé paraît.*)

**JEAN:** (*avec un cri.*) Salomé!

**SALOMÉ:** (*de même.*) Jean!

**JEAN:** C'est toi! toi, dans ce sombre lieu!
Mais qu'as-tu donc, Salomé
. . . tu frissonnes . . .

**SALOMÉ:** Oui, Jean c'est de bonheur!

**JEAN:** Ah! c'est donc vrai,
Seigneur, que tu pardonnes?
Que je puis respirer cette enivrante fleur,
La presser sur ma bouche et murmurer: Je t'aime.
Ces mots ne sont pas un blasphème:
Tu m'as donné la voix pour te nommer,
Seigneur, et l'âme pour aimer!

**SALOMÉ:** Mon coeur se brise . . . et j'ai peur de l'entendre . . .
Jusqu'à moi tu veux bien descendre?

**LES PRÊTRES:** (*dans le temple.*)
Mort au prophète.

**JEAN:** (*égaré.*) Pars! enfant, pars! il le faut.

**SALOMÉ:** (*presque bas.*) C'est le supplice qui s'apprête!

**JEAN:** S'élever jusqu'au ciel et retomber si tôt!

**LES PRETRES:** Mort au prophète!

**JEAN:** (*avec déchirement.*) Hôlas, le rêve était trop beau!
Va, fuis l'horreur de ce tombeau!

**SALOMÉ:** Te quitter, moi? quand le ciel nous appelle!
Ami, la mort n'est pas cruelle
Qui nous prend tous les deux et va nous réunir!
Si Dieu l'avait permis, l'âme heureuse et ravie,
A tes côtés, j'aurais passé ma vie;

turb my faith? If I should be wounded or worsted in this struggle, whose fault would be my fall? I am your son, O Lord.
(*He falls, overcome.*)
(*The azure light of the Temple suddenly casts a luminous glow into the dungeon and enveloped in this radiance, Salome appears.*)

**JOHN** (*with a cry*): Salome!

**SALOME** (*with a cry*): John!

**JOHN:** Is it you? You in this dismal place? But . . . what is it, Salome? You tremble!

**SALOME:** Yes, John with happiness.

**JOHN:** Ah, then it is true, O Lord, that you forgive me! That I may breathe of this intoxicating flower, To press it to my lips, and murmur, "I love you!"
Such words are not blasphemy.
You have given a voice to pray to you, O Lord
And a soul for love!

**SALOME:** My heart is bursting . . .
I am afraid to listen!
And would you then stoop to me?

**THE PRIESTS** (*in the Temple*):
Death to the Prophet! Death to the Prophet!

**JOHN** (*disturbed*): Go, Salome! Go! You must!

**SALOME:** They are preparing for you the torture!

**JOHN:** Ah, to be lifted up to heaven, to fall again so soon.

**THE PRIESTS:** Death to the Prophet!

**JOHN** (*in anguish*): Alas! It was too fair a dream!
Go, flee from the horrors of this tomb!

**SALOME:** Leave you? I? When heaven is calling us? O John! I leave you? No! Never! My friend, there is no cruelty in a death that takes us both, only to reunite us! Had God permitted it, with a happy and joyous heart I could have spent my life with you. God has not willed it so.

# Act IV, Scene XIII

Dieu ne l'a pas voulu; je saurai donc mourir
Près de toi, dans tes bras, ô sublime martyr!

**JEAN ET SALOMÉ:** (*elacés dans une étreinte suprème.*) Il est beau de mourir en s'aimant ma chère âme!
Quand nos jours s'éteindront comme une triste flamme,
Notre amour, dans le ciel rayonnant de clarté,
Trouvera le mystère et l'immortalité!
(*Le grand prêtre paraît accompagné des gardiens de temple et des esclaves éthiopiens du Tétrarque.*)

**LE GRAND PRETRE:** (*à Jean.*)
Hérodiade veut qu'on te mène au supplice!
Jean! ton heure est venue . . . (*à Salomé.*)
Enfant, rends grâce au roi
Pour toi, pour ta jeunesse, il brave la justice
Et t'appelle au palais!

**SALOMÉ:** (*résistant aux esclaves éthiopiens qui s'emparent d'elle.*)
Non! jamais! . . . Laissez-moi!

**LE GRAND PRETRE:** (*bas à Jean.*)
Maintenant dis un mot: Hérode te délivre!
Il veut régner sur ce pays,
Viens le proclamer roi, viens armer tes amis,
Consens à le servir enfin . . . si tu veux vivre!

**JEAN:** (*se livrant lui-même aux gardes du temple.*) Je suis le serviteur du Dieu puissant et fort
Et non du lâche Hérode! Allons, j'attends la mort.
(*Il suit les gardes, pendant que les esclaves éthiopiens entraînent Salomé sur l'ordre du grand prêtre.*)

*Deuxième Tableau*

*La Salle Du Festin.*

Salle immense du palais du Proconsul. –Aux colonnes de marbre sont suspendus des trophées militaires, des boucliers d'or, des éperons de trirèmes et des lampadaires d'argent. –Les corniches des colonnes sont ornées de feurs et de guirlandes. – Un velarium aux couleurs éclatantes abrite cette salle à ciel ouvert. –A gauche au premier plan, la statue colossale, en or, de Rome.–Au fond, de vastes marches conduisent à une terrasse qui domine Jérusalem. –Au lointain l'aspect ensoleillé de la ville.

---

So I shall gladly die, with you, in your arms. Oh, martyrdom sublime!

**JOHN AND SALOME:** (*Clasped in a supreme embrace.*)
When our life shall be quenched, as if it were a sacred fire,
Still our love up in heaven will be more radiant.
And will solve the Unknown in immortality.
(*The Chief Priest appears with the Ethiopian slaves of the Petrarch.*)

**HIGH PRIEST:** John, your hour has come! Herodias commands that you be put to death.
(*to Salome.*)
My child, give thanks to the King! As for you, by reason of your youth, he waives the law, and calls you to the palace.
(*The Slaves seize Salome, who resists desperately, holding out her arms to John.*)

**SALOME:** John! No! Let me go! Never!

**THE HIGH PRIEST** (*low to John*):
And now say but a word and Herod frees you!
For in this land he thinks to reign. Proclaim him king, arm all your friends;
Serve him, in short—and life you gain!

**JOHN:** (*placing himself voluntarily in the hands of the Guards of the Temple.*) I am the servitor of God alone, not of the coward Herod!
Enough! Enough! I am ready for death!
(*He follows the guards, while the black slaves drag away Salome at the command of the High Priest.*)

*Second Tableau*

*The Festival.*

(*A great ball in the palace of the Proconsul. Marble columns hung with military trophies; shields of gold, prows of triremes, and lamp-brackets of silver. The cornices of the columns are ornamented with garlands and flowers. A blue velarium (awning) is stretched above the hall, which is open to the sky. To the left, in front, a colossal golden statue of Rome. Jerusalem, lying sunlit in the distance, is seen through the porticos in the back, which open on broad steps leading to a terrace overlooking it.*)

---

## SCÈNE XIV

*Les Romains, puis Hérode, Hérodiade, Vitellius et leur cour.*

**LES ROMAINS:** Romains! nous sommes Romains!
A ce nom seul le monde entier frémit de crainte
Devant Jérusalem, devant la cité sainte
Arrêtons-nous en souverains!
Nos aigles d'un coup d'aile étendent notre gloire.
A travers la plaine et les mers;
Et nous parcourons l'univers
En marquant tous nos pas avec une victoire! . . .
Quel charme tout-puissant Possèdes-tu, Patrie?
Pour toi, mere chérie,
Nous versons notre sang!
Rome, de nous sois fiere!
Et toi, Tibère,
Regarde tes enfants,
Leur front à l'auréole
Des Césars triomphants!
Nous monterons au Capitole!
Romains! nous sommes Romains!
A ce nom seul le monde entier fremit de crainte!
Devant Jérusalem, devant la cité sainte
Arrêtons-nous en souverains!
(*Entree d'Hérode, d'Hérodiade et de Vitellius; on acclame le proconsul: Gloire à César!*)

**BALLET:**
1. Les Egyptiennes.
2. Les Babyloniennes.
3. Les Gauloises.
4. Les Phéniciennes.

## SCÈNE XV

*Les Mêmes, Salomé, Phanuel, Le Peuple.*

(*Salomé, les cheveux épars et s'arrachant des mains des esclaves êthiopiens, se precipite sur la scène.*)

**SALOMÉ:** (*suppliante.*) Pourquoi me retirer cette faveur suprême,
Le bonheur de mourir avec celui que j'aime?

**HÉRODE:** Elle me doit la vie, et c'est lui seul qu'elle aime?

**HÉRODIADE:** Quel trouble m'envahit! Puis-je oublier qu'il l'aime!

**PHANUEL:** Espère-t-elle encore sauver celui qu'elle aime!

**VITELLIUS:** Pourra-t-il faire grâce au prophète qu'elle aime!

**LE CHOEUR:** Elle espère sauver le prophète qu'elle aime!

**SALOMÉ:** (*s'adressant à Hérode, puis à la reine.*) Qu'il vive! sois clément et doux!
Salomé te prie à genoux!

---

## SCENE XIV

*The Romans, then Herod, Herodias, Vitellius and the Court.*

**THE ROMANS:** Romans, Romans, Romans are we!
At this name alone the world trembles with fear.
Before Jerusalem, before the Holy City,
Let us halt, as conquerors!
With the strokes of their wings our eagles spread our glory
Over land and sea!
And we overrun the universe!
And mark our steps with victories!
Romans, Romans are we, etc.
For you, our mother country dear,
We pour out our blood!
Rome shall be proud of us,
And you, Father Tiber, look upon your sons!
Our brows wear the glory of triumphant Caesars!
We shall ascend to the capitol!
Romans, Romans are we!
At this name alone the world trembles with fear.
Before Jerusalem, before the Holy City,
Let us halt, as conquerors!
(*Enter Vitellius, Herod and Herodias, followed by the court. The proconsul is acclaimed with shouts of, "Hail to Caesar!"*)

**BALLET:**
I. Egyptian Women.
II. Babylonian Women.
III. Women of Gaul.
IV. Phenecian Women.

## SCENE XV

*The Same, Salome, Phanuel, the People.*

(*Salome, her hair in disorder, tearing herself from the hands of the Ethiopian slaves, rushes on the stage.*)

**SALOME:** (*supplicating*) Why refuse me this last favor,
The joy of dying with him I love?

**HEROD:** She owes her life to me; but she loves him alone!

**HERODIAS:** What troubles me? Can I forget that he loves her?

**PHANUEL:** Can she hope to save the one she loves?

**VITELLIUS:** Could he show mercy to the prophet whom she loves?

**CHORUS:** She hopes to save the Prophet!

**SALOME** (*to Herod*): Let him live! Let him live! Be kind and merciful! Salome implores you! (*To Herodias:*) No, it is you, I implore! O

Non! c'est toi qu'elle implore! . . . ô reine, vois mes larmes!
Une femme comprend de pareilles alarmes!
Pitié! si tu fus mère!

HÉRODIADE: (*frissonnant à ce mot.*) Ah! que dis-tu . . . tais-toi! Quel souvenir! . . . c'est vrai, dieux puissants, je suis mère!

SALOMÉ: (*avec des sanglots.*) Si je vous fais pitié, connaissez ma misère; Laissez-vous émouvoir, ô reine! écoutez-moi! Lorsque m'abandonnait une mère inhumaine . . . C'est lui qui m'accueillit . . . et consola ma peine . . .

HÉRODIADE: Ses pleurs ont calmé ma fureur! De l'enfant oublié c'est le spectre vengeur! Qui comme cette enfant ma fille eût été belle! Sa voix me rappelle sa voix, Le remords me crie: oui, c'est elle. Il me semble que je la vois!

SALOMÉ (*douloureusement.*) Pour un hymen infâme, Ma mère, je l'ai su . . . Ma mère à brise l'âme Du pauvre enfant perdu! . . .

HÉRODIADE: Elle maudit sa mère! Je lui tendais les bras, Mais non, je veux me taire, Je ne parlerai pas!

SALOMÉ: Connaissez ma misère, Laissez-vous émouvoir! Reine, vous fûtes mère, Voyez mon désespoir!

Queen, behold my tears! A woman will understand my agony! Have pity! If you ever were a mother, have pity!

HERODIAS (*trembling at the word*): Ah! What do you say? Be still! What memories . . . ! It is true! Oh, ye gods! I was once a mother!

SALOME (*with deep feeling*): Save him for me! save him! If I have touched your heart, Then try to feel my pain, do not smother your pity When I was cast aside by a mother ignoble, It was he who took me in, it was he who consoled my trouble.

HERODIAS: By tears I am of rage bereft! It is a shade of revenge of the child that I left Ay, as fair as this child might now have been that other! Her voice, too, recalls me her voice! My remorse proclaims me her mother! Ay, as fair as this child might have been that other!

SALOME (*with deep grief*): To make an infamous alliance my mother, oh, I knew of it, my mother crushed the soul of her poor lost child.

HERODIAS: But no, I must beware. Alas! that she should curse her mother! To her my arms I'd strain. Yet silent I remain! That she should curse her mother!

SALOME: Ah, try to feel my pain, And look on my despair! Be kind! My tears are falling! O look on my despair.

HÉRODE: Au bonheur que j'espère En vain je tends les bras, A toi ma vie entière Enfant! ne t'en va pas!

VITELLIUS, PHANUEL: Grâce pour sa misère, Voyez son dèsespoir! Reine, vous fûtes mere, Laissez-vous émouvoir!

SALOMÉ: Reine! . . . laissez-le vivre! Parlez! qu'on le délivre . . . (*Au moment où Hérodiade, hèsitante, émue, va céder aux supplications de Salomé, le bourreau paraît au fond, sur le haut de la terrasse, tenant à la main le glaive teint de sang.*)

SALOMÉ: (*avec un cri terrible.*) Ah!

LE CHOEUR: (*attéré.*) Le prophète est mort!

SALOMÉ: (*fait un effort désespéré tire un poignard de sa ceinture et se précipite sure Hérodiade.*) Il est mort de ta main . . . Tu mourras donc aussi! . . . Tu m'implores en vain!

HÉRODIADE: (*recule épouvantée.*) Pitié! je suis ta mère!

SALOMÉ: Ah! reine détestée, S'il est vrai que tes flancs odieux m'aient portée, Tiens! reprends ton sang et ma vie. (*Elle se frappe.*)

HÉRODE: Ah! morte! Horreur!

HÉRODIADE: Ma fille! morte!

LE CHOEUR: O jour de rage et de terreur!

*FIN.*

HEROD: I stretch my arms to you! My child, fly not again! With you I'd share my life! Fly not again, I love you child, I give my life to you!-Come! ah, come!

VITELLIUS AND PHANUEL: Ah, let your heart be moved, And try to feel her pain And her despair! Ah, look, look on her pain! Ah, save his life for her!

SALOME: Queen! spare his life! Speak! and deliver him . . . (*Herodias, hesitating and moved, is about to yield to Salome's supplications, when the Executioner appears at the back on the terrace, holding in this hand a sword dripping with blood.*)

SALOME (*with a terrible cry*): Ah!

ALL: The Prophet is dead!

SALOME: (*with a frantic effort drawing a dager from her girdle and flinging herself upon Herodias*). He is slain by your hand! And you shall die as well!

HERODIAS: Mercy! I am your mother!

SALOME: Ah, hated Queen, if it be true that it was your odious womb that bore me . . . Here! take back your blood and my life. (*She stabs herself and dies.*)

HEROD: Salome, dead!

HERODIAS: My daughter!

CHORUS: O day of horror!

*END.*

# *Werther* (1892)

MUSIC BY JULES MASSENET ■ LIBRETTO BY EDOUARD BLAU, PAUL MILLIET & GEORGES HARTMANN ■ BASED ON GOETHE'S *LEIDEN DES JUNGEN WERTHERS*

This four-act *drame lyrique*, set to a libretto by Edouard Blau, Paul Milliet and Georges Hartmann is based on Goethe's *Lieden des jungen Werthers*, and premiered at the Hofoper in Vienna on February 16, 1892. In Wetzlar, near Frankfurt, during the year 1780, the burgomaster, whose wife has died, is teaching his children a Christmas carol when Johann and Schmidt enter with an invitation to dinner. However, his eldest daughter, Charlotte, is going to a ball and he must stay home with the other children. Werther, Charlotte's escort, arrives; Albert, Charlotte's fiance, returns unexpectedly, disappointed not to find her at home, but Sophie, the next eldest daughter, tells him that her sister has not forgotten about him. Werther confesses his love to Charlotte. But, the burgomaster calls out, announcing Albert's return, and she tells Werther that she gave her word to her dying mother that she would marry Albert. Werther goes off, deeply disappointed. In the town square, at the celebrations for the golden wedding anniversary of the village Pastor, Johann and Schmidt make a toast to Albert and Charlotte; they have been married for the past three months. Werther watches from a distance, unconsolable. Albert tells Werther how happy he is and suggests that Sophie might be of interest to him. Werther goes to see Charlotte, who pleads with him to stay away until Christmas. Werther considers killing himself. Sophie asks him to dance; he turns her down, saying he is going to go away and never come back. She bursts into tears. On Christmas Eve, Charlotte rereads Werther's letters. She misses him terribly and cannot hide this fact from Sophie. At Charlotte's window, Werther recites some Ossian, which he translated especially for her. Moved to tears, she lets him kiss her and then runs away from him, vowing never to set eyes on him again. Albert suspects Werther's visit. A servant delivers a note from Werther, asking to borrow Albert's pistols. Albert tells Charlotte to give them to the servant, and she is afraid that Werther might shoot himself. She finds him in his room, mortally wounded, and she tells him that she has loved him ever since they met. As he dies in her arms, the faint sound of children singing a Christmas carol can be heard.

## ■ ACTE PREMIER

### SCÈNE I

**LE BAILLI:** (*grondant*) Assez! Assez! . . . Va-t-on m'écouter cette fois?
Recommençons! . . . surtout pas trop de voix!

**LES ENFANTS:** (*chantant très fort et sans nuances.*) Noël! Jésus vient de naître,
Voici notre divin maître . . .

**LE BAILLI:** (*se fâchant*) Non! ça n'est pas cela!
Osez-vous chanter de la sorte
Quand votre soeur Charlotte est là!
Elle doit vous entendre au travers de la porte!
(*Les enfants ont paru tout émus au nom de Charlotte. Ils reprennent le Noël avec gravité.*)

**LES ENFANTS:** Noël!
Jésus vient de naître,
Voici notre divin maître,
Rois et bergers d'Israël!
Des anges gardiens fidèles,
Dans le firmament,
Ont ouvert leurs grandes ailes
Et s'en vont partout chantant:
Noël!

## ■ ACT I

### SCENE I

**BAILLIE.** Enough! Enough! Will you listen to me this time? Begin again. Above all not too loud.

**CHILDREN SING:** Christmas! Jesus came this day,
To lead us in the heavenly way!

**BAILLIE:** No, it's not that! How dare you sing that way when your sister Charlotte is there? She'll hear you through the door.

**CHILDREN SING:** Christmas!
Jesus came this day,
To lead us in the heavenly way.
Israel's king and shepherds all
Heard the startled Magis call—
Stir the firmament!
All the world its offering brings
When the Christmas carol rings.
Christmas!

**LE BAILLI:** C'est bien!
Jésus vient de naître!
Voici notre divin maître . . .
(*Johann et Schmidt, qui s'étaient arrêtés pour écouter les enfants, sont entrés dans la cour.*)

### SCÈNE II

*Les Mêmes, Johann et Schmidt.*

**JOHANN:** Bravo pour les enfants!

**SCHMIDT:** Bravo pour le couplet!

**LES ENFANTS:** (*accourant joyeusement.*) Ah! monsieur Schmidt! monsieur Johann!

**JOHANN:** (*au bailli.*) Eh! mais j'y pense!
Vous chantez Noël en juillet,
Bailli, c'est s'y prendre à l'avance!

**LE BAILLI:** Cela te fait rire, Johann; mais quoi!
Tout le monde n'est pas artiste comme toi;
Et ce ne sont point bagatelles
Que d'apprendre le chant à ces jeunes cervelles!
(*Entrée de Sophie.*)

### SCÈNE III

*Les Mêmes, Sophie.*

**SCHMIDT:** Bonjour, Sophie! . . . Eh! eh! Charlotte n'est pas loin!

**BAILLIE:** That's good.
Christmas! Jesus came this day.
To lead us in the heavenly way.

### SCENE II

(*Enter Johann and Schmidt.*)

**JOHANN:** Bravo for the children!

**SCHMIDT:** Bravo for the rhyme!

**CHILDREN:** Ah! Herr Schmidt! Herr Johann!

**JOHANN:** Eh?–but I think when you sing of Christmas in July, you rush the season.

**BAILLE:** That makes you laugh, Johann; but why? All the world is not as artistic as I am, and it's a mere bagatelle when I teach children.

### SCENE III

(*Enter Sophie*)

**SCHMIDT:** Good day, Sophia! Eh? but Charlotte isn't far off.

SOPHIE: (*lui faisant une révérence.*)
En effet, monsieur Schmidt, puisque nous prenous Charlotte et moi, de la famille.

JOHANN: (*au bailli*) Ah! Ce superbe temps
Viens-tu?

LE BAILLI: Dans un instant.

SOPHIE: (*à Johann.*) Ma sœur s'habille
Pour le bal . . .

LE BAILLI: (*se retournant, à Schmidt*) Oui, le bal d'amis et de parents
Que l'on donne à Wetzlar . . . On vient prendre Charlotte.

SCHMIDT: C'est donc cela! . . . Keeffel a mis sa redingote,
Steiner a retenu le cheval du brasseur,
Hoffmann a sa calèche et Goulden sa berline . . .
Enfin, monsieur Werther m'a paru moins rêveur!

LE BAILLI: (*à ses deux amis.*) Fort bien, ce jeune homme!

JOHANN: Oui, mais pas fort en cuisine!

LE BAILLI: (*insistant*) Il est instruit, très distingué.

SCHMIDT: (*vivement*) Un peu mélancolique . . .

JOHANN: Ah! certes! jamais gai!

LE BAILLI: (*poursuivant son idée.*) Le Prince lui promet, dit-on, une ambassade!
Il l'estime et lui veut du bien . . .

JOHANN: (*avec mépris.*) Un diplomate! Ah! bah! ça ne vaut rien
A table.

SCHMIDT: (*de même*) Ça ne sait pas boire une rasade!

JOHANN: (*au bailli, en lui tendant les mains*) A tout-à-l'heure, au Raisin d'Or.

SCHMIDT: (*de même*) Oui, tu nous dois une revanche.

LE BAILLI: (*se récriant*) Encore!

JOHANN: Dame! . . . et puis c'est le jour des écrevisses . . .
Grosses comme le bras . . . Gretchen nous l'a promis.

LE BAILLI: Oh! les gourmands! les deux complices!
(*Cédant un peu.*)
Vous n'attendez donc pas Charlotte, mes amis?

SCHMIDT: (*à Johann*) Nous la verrons ce soir, nous voulons faire
Un petit tour sur le rempart.

LE BAILLI: (*souriant, à Johann*) Pour t'ouvrir l'appétit? . . .

SOPHIE: We are looking for the family, Herr Schmidt, Charlotte and I.

JOHANN: Ah, this is lovely weather. Will you come now?

BAILLIE: In a moment.

SOPHIE: My sister is dressing for the ball.

BAILLIE: Yes; the family ball which they are giving at Wetzlar. They are coming for Charlotte.

SCHMIDT: That's it. Keeffel has put on his frock coat. Steiner has hired the brewer's horse. Hoffman has his carriage, Goulden, his. In fact, Herr Werther seems less dreamy.

BAILLE: The young man is well enough.

JOHANN: Yes, but he is not much of a cook.

BAILLIE: He is well educated—well mannered.

SCHMIDT: A little melancholy.

JOHANN: He is certainly never very lively.

BAILLIE: They say that the Prince promised him an embassy. He esteems him, and wishes him well.

JOHANN: A diplomat. Bah That's no good at the dinner-table.

SCHMIDT: He does not know how to drink a bumper.

JOHANN: See you later, Baillie, at the Golden Grapes.

SCHMIDT: Yes, you owe us our revenge, you know.

BAILLIE: What, still?

JOHANN: Why not? Besides, this is crayfish day—big as your arm, Gretchen promised us.

BAILLIE: Oh, the gluttons! They are of a kind. Won't you wait for Charlotte, then, my friends?

SCHMIDT: We shall see her this evening. Johann and I are going to take a turn on the ramparts.

BAILLIE: (*to Johann*). To give you an appetite?

JOHANN: (*à Schmidt*) Toujours il exagère
Allons, viens; il est tard!

SCHMIDT: (*revenant, au bailli*) A propos, quand Albert revient-il?

LE BAILLI: Je l'ignore.
Il ne m'en parle pas encore,
Mais il m'écrit que ses affaires vont au mieux.

SCHMIDT: Parfait! Albert est un garçon brave et fidèle;
C'est un mari modèle
Pour ta Charlotte; et nous, les vieux,
Nous danserons à perdre haleine
A la noce prochaine.

JOHANN: (*gaiement*) Eh! bon soir! les enfants!

SCHMIDT: (*au bailli, plus bas*) A tantôt!

LE BAILLI: (*et les enfants*) Au revoir!
(*Les deux hommes s'en vont bras dessus bras dessous en chantant un refrain bacchique: Vivat Bacchus semper vivat!*)

## SCÈNE IV

Le Bailli, Sophie, Les Enfants, puis Werther.

LE BAILLI: (*aux enfants*) Rentrez! nous redirons notre Noël ce soir,
Avant goûter, note par note!
Sophie, il faut aller voir ce que fait Charlotte.
(*Sophie sort*)
(*Werther, accompagné d'un jeune paysan, s'avance dans la cour et regarde curieusement la maison.*)

WERTHER: (*au paysan*) Alors, c'est bien ici
La maison du bailli? . . .
(*Congédiant son guide.*)
Merci.

WERTHER: (*seul, pénètre plus avant dans la cour et s'arrête devant la fontaine.*) Je ne sais si je veille ou si je rêve encore:
Tout ce qui m'environne a l'air d'un paradis!
Le bois soupire ainsi qu'une harpe sonore:
Un monde se révèle à mes yeux éblouis.
O nature, plein de grâce,
Reine du temps et de l'espace,
Daigne accueillit celui qui passe
Et te salue, humble mortel!
Mystérieuz silence! ô calme solennel!
Tout m'attire et me plaît! ce mur, et ce coin sombre,
Cette source limpide et la fraîcheur de l'ombre;
Il n'est pas une haie, il n'est pas un buisson
Où n'éclose une fleur, où ne passe un frisson.

JOHANN: (*to Schmidt*). How that man exaggerates. Come along; it's late.

SCHMIDT: When does Albert come back?

BAILLIE: I don't know. He says nothing about it in his letters. But he writes me that his business is going on well.

SCHMIDT: Glad to hear it. Albert is a good fellow. There's a model husband for your Charlotte, and we old fellows will dance ourselves breathless at the wedding.

JOHANN: Well, good-night, children.

SCHMIDT: See you later.

BAILLIE AND CHILDREN: Until we meet again.
(*Exeunt Schmidt and Johann.*)

## SCENE IV

BAILLIE: (*to the children*) Come, children, we'll sing over our Christmas carol this evening before supper, note by note. Sophie, go and see what Charlotte is doing. (*Exit.*)

WERTHER: (*appears with a peasant*). Well, here we are at the Baillie's house.
(*Dismisses guide.*)

GUIDE: Thanks.

WERTHER: I know not if I sleep or wake!
I seem to move in Paradise,
The winds make soft music.
A new world meets my eyes.
Oh, nature full of grace—
Queen who reigns on high
Bend your beauteous face—
On me—a passer-by.
Mysterious silence! brooding peace.
That lurks within this shadowy dell;
Beneath these trees one finds release,
From worldly sorrows' sodden spell!
There's not a bush but hides a flower;
The whole scene breathes of spring—the hour.
Oh, Nature
Eternal mother, ever young,
Defend me. Sun, that shines so red,

## Act I, Scene IV

Mère éternellement jeune, nature, adorable et pure
Enivre-moi de tes parfums! et toi, soleil,
Viens m'inonder de ton rayon vermeil!
(*Voix des enfants, dans l'intérieur de la maison, répétaut le Noël.*)
Oh! chers enfants! . . . Autant notre vie est amère
Autant leurs jours sont pleins de foi,
Leurs âmes pleines de lumière!
Ah! comme ils sont meilleurs que moi!

Fling down your blessings over my head.
(*Children sing.*)
Children, with childhood's golden love,
With faithful voices fresh and glad
Would I could pray the God above,
To give me back the faith I had.

### SCÈNE V

*Les Mêmes, puis Charlotte.*

**LES ENFANTS:** Charlotte! Charlotte!

**CHARLOTTE:** (*au bailli*) Eh bien! père,
Etes-vous content d'eux?

**LE BAILLI:** Content, content! ce n'est pas merveilleux.

**LES ENFANTS:** (*entourant Charlotte*) Si! père est très content!

**LE BAILLI:** (*embrassant sa fille et admirant sa toillette*) Comme te voilà belle,
Mignonne!

**LES ENFANTS:** Oh! mais c'est vrai!

**LE BAILLI:** (*prenant les mains de Charlotte*) Venez, mademoiselle!
Qu'on vous regarde . . . nos amis seront jaloux.

**CHARLOTTE:** (*souriante*) Nos amis ne sont pas exacts au rendez-vous.
Voilà ce dont je suis bien sûre;
Et j'en vais profiter
Pour donner le goûter
Aux enfants.

**LE BAILLI:** Hâte-toi, car j'entends la voiture!

**LES ENFANTS:** Merci, grande sœur! . . .

**LE BAILLI:** (*apercevant Werther et allant au-devant de lui*) Ah! monsieur Werther!
Vous venez visiter mon petit ermitage . . .
Mieux . . . mon petit royaume, et j'eu suis vraiment fier.
(*Lui présentant Charlotte*)
Ma fille, qui prend soin de ce ménage
Et de tous ces enfants gâtés
Depuis le jour où leur mère nous a quittés.

**CHARLOTTE:** Pardonnez-moi, monsieur, de m'être fait attendre,
Mais je suis, en effet, une maman très tendre,
Et mes enfants exigent que ma main
Leur coupe chaque jour leur pain.

### SCENE V

(*Enter Charlotte.*)

**CHILDREN:** Charlotte! Charlotte!

**CHARLOTTE:** Well, father, are you pleased with the children?

**BAILLIE:** Yes, yes; it's not wonderful.

**CHILDREN:** Yes, father is satisfied.

**BAILLIE:** How lovely you are, pet.

**CHILDREN:** Oh yes, indeed.

**BAILLIE:** Come when they see you, our friends will be jealous.

**CHARLOTTE:** Our friends are not punctual, evidently, and I shall take advantage of their absence to give the children their supper.

**BAILLIE:** Make haste I hear the carriage.

**CHILDREN:** Thank you, sister.

**BAILLIE:** (*sees Werther*). Ah, Herr Werther! You have to see my little hermitage, or rather my little kingdom. I am very proud of it. My daughter and housekeeper has had charge of these spoiled little ones since the mother left us.

**CHARLOTTE:** Pardon me, sir, if I have made you wait, but I am a tender mother, and my children insist that their daily bread and butter must be cut by me.

### SCÈNE VI

*Werther, Charlotte, Le Bailli, Sophie, Les Invités.*

**LE BAILLI:** Arrivez donc, Brühmann! Charlotte est prête; On vous attend! . . .
(*Brühmann et Kathchen marchent côte à côte.*)

**BRÜLHMANN:** (*avec un soupir d'extase*) Klopstock! . . .

**KATCHEN:** (*avec ravissement*) Divin Klopstock! . . .

**LE BAILLI:** (*à Brûlhmann*) Bavard!
Vous direz le reste à la fête . . .
Un aussi long discours vous mettrait en retard.

**CHARLOTTE:** (*à l'enfant*) Embrasse ton cousin! . . .

**WERTHER:** (*se redressant, étonné*) Cousin? suis-je bien digne De ce nom? . . .

**CHARLOTTE:** (*enjouée*) En effet, c'est un honneur insigne,
Mais nous en avons taut qu'il serait bien fâcheux
Que vous fussiez le plus mauvais d'entre eux.
(*A Sophie, avec autorité, mais sans sévérité, en lui montrant les enfants.*)
Tu me remplaceras, Sophie;
Tu le sais, je te les confie . . .
(*Aux enfants.*)
Vous serez tous sages comme avec moi.

**SOPHIE:** Oui, mais ils aimeraient bien mieux que ce fût toi.

**WERTHER:** (*avec extase, tandis que Charlotte embrasse les enfants*) O spectacle idéal d'amour et d'innocence,
Où mon cœur et mes yeux sont ravis à la fois!
Quel rêve de passer une entière existence
Calmé par ses regards et bercé par sa voix!

**LE BAILLI:** (*saluant Werther*) Monsieur Werther . . .
(*A Charlotte.*)
Adieu, ma chérie . . .

**CHARLOTTE:** Adieu, père! . . .
(*Charlotte et Werther s'éloignent, suivis d'un groupe d'invités; Brûlhmann et Kathchen s'en vont les derniers sans avoir dit une parole.*)

**LE BAILLI:** (*les regardent en souriant.*) Ne souhaitons rien à ceux-là!
L'extase magnétique!
Klopstock! divin Klopstock! cela Me paraît sans réplique!
(*Sophie a fait rentrer les enfants dans la maison.*)

### SCÈNE VII

*Le Bailli, puis Sophie.*

### SCENE VI

**BAILLIE:** Come along, Brülhmann, Charlotte is ready. You are waited for.
(*Brülhmann and Kathchen enter.*)

**BRÜLHMANN:** (*with a bit of ecstasy in his voice*) Klopstock!

**KATCHEN:** Divine Klopstock!

**BAILLIE:** Charlotte! You can tell us the rest at the festival. Such a long discourse will delay us now.

**CHARLOTTE:** Kiss your cousin.

**WERTHER:** Cousin?—am I indeed worthy of that name?

**CHARLOTTE:** Really, it's a great honor! We have so many cousins that it would be a pity if you were the worst in the lot. Take my place, Sophie. I trust the children to you. Children, you must be as good as though you were with me.

**SOPHIE:** Yes, but they'd rather have you with them.

**WERTHER:** Visions so holy, sent from the skies
My heart is enraptured, my senses beguiled.
A man might live on for the light of your eyes,
And count the world better and bright when you smiled.

**BAILLIE:** Adieu, Herr Werther. (*To Charlotte*) Adieu, my dear one.

**CHARLOTTE:** Adieu, father.
(*Exeunt omnes, except the Baillies.*)

**BAILLIE:** We needn't waste our wishes on those two, They're in a magnetic ecstasy. Klopstock! Divine Klopstock! Even you could add nothing to their bliss.
(*Enter Sophie.*)

### SCENE VII

SOPHIE: Et qui donc a promis d'aller au Raisin d'Or?

LE BAILLI: (*d'un ton embarrassé.*) Qui? moi, te laisser seule . . .

SOPHIE: Eh bien! . . .

LE BAILLI: Non!

SOPHIE: (*gravemeut.*) Je l'exige! Schmidt et Johann doivent t'attendre encore.

LE BAILLI: (*se laissant convaincre, et prenant le chapeau et la canne des mains de Sophie.*) Rien qu'un moment alors . . . (*Il s'éloigne, puis se retournant, à Sophie.*) Au fait, promesse oblige!

SOPHIE: And your promise to go to the Golden Grapes?

BAILLIE: What! Leave you alone?

SOPHIE: That's all right.

BAILLIE: No

SOPHIE: I insist on it Schmidt and Johann will wait for you.

BAILLIE: Well! Only for a moment. If it was not for my promise— (*Exit.*) (*Albert enters.*)

## SCÈNE VIII

*Albert, Sophie.*

ALBERT: Sophie!

SOPHIE: Albert! toi de retour?

ALBERT: Oui, moi, petite sœur, bonjour! (*Il l'embrasse.*)

SOPHIE: Que Charlotte sera contente De te revoir!

ALBERT: Elle est ici?

SOPHIE: Non, pas ce soir, Elle qui jamais ne s'absente! Aussi pourquoi n'as-tu prévenu?

ALBERT: J'ai voulu la surprendre . . . Parle-moi d'elle, au moins; il me tarde d'apprendre Si de moi l'on s'est souvenu? Car c'est bien long, six mois d'absence!

SOPHIE: Chez nous, aux absents chacun pense, Et n'es-tu pas, d'ailleurs, son fiancé?

ALBERT: (*joyeux.*) O chère enfant! . . . Et que s'est-il passé?

SOPHIE: Rien! . . . On s'est occupé de votre mariage . . . On y dansera, dis?

ALBERT: Beaucoup . . . et davantage! Oui, je veux que pour tous, il y ait du bonheur; Ah! j'en ai tant au fond du cœur! Va! rentre.. j'ai peur qu'on t'appelle Et qu'on apprenne mon retour: N'en dis rien, je serai prè d'elle Dès le lever du jour.

SOPHIE: (*restant*) A demain monsieur mon beau-frère. (*Elle ferme la porte vitrèe.*)

## SCENE VIII

ALBERT: Sophie!

SOPHIE: Albert—you are back?

ALBERT: Yes, my little sister. How are you?

SOPHIE: Charlotte will be delighted to see you again.

ALBERT: She is here?

SOPHIE: No, not this evening, she who is never away– why didn't you let us know you were coming?

ALBERT: I wanted to surprise you. Tell me of her, at least. I can hardly believe that she has thought of me. How long I have been away! Six months!

SOPHIE: Our thoughts go ever to the absent, and are you not, besides, her betrothed?

ALBERT: Oh, dear child! Now, what news is there?

SOPHIE: None. Every one talks of your marriage. Will there be dancing?

ALBERT: Plenty. And more. Yes, I wish every one to have a good time! Ah I have so much hidden in my heart. There, go in. I am afraid that you are called and that they suspect I am here. Say nothing. I shall be with her early tomorrow.

SOPHIE: Tomorrow, my dear brother-in-law. (*Exit.*)

## SCÈNE IX

ALBERT: (*seul*) Elle m'aime . . . elle pense à moi!.. quelle prière De reconnaissance et d'amour

## SCENE IX

ALBERT: She loves me! She thinks of me: What a prayer of thankfulness and love rises to my lips Ah! When one returns after an absence,

Monte de mon cœur à ma bouche! Ah! comme à l'heure du retour Un rien nous émeut et nous touche. Et comme tout possède un charme! Je voudrais qu'en rentrant Charlotte retrouvât les pensers que je laisse: Tout mon espoir et toute ma tendresse! (*Il s'éloigne.*)

## SCÈNE X.

*Charlotte et Werther paraissent à la porte du jardin.*

CHARLOTTE: Il faut nous séparer. Voici notre maison: C'est l'heure du sommeil.

WERTHER: Ah! pourvu que je voie Ces yeux toujours; ces yeux, mon horizon, Ces doux yeux, mon espoir et mon unique joie, Que m'importe à moi le sommeil! Les étoiles et le soleil Peuvent bien dans le ciel tour à tour reparaître, J'ignore s'il est jour, s'il est nuit, et mon être Demeure indifférent à ce qui n'est pas toi!

CHARLOTTE: (*souriant.*) Mais vous ne savez rien de moi.

WERTHER: Mon âme a rencontré votre âme. Je vous ai vue assez Pour savoir quelle femme Vous êtes!

CHARLOTTE: Vous me connaissez?

WERTHER: (*grave et tendre*). Vous êtes la meilleure ainsi que la plus belle Des créatures . . .

CHARLOTTE: (*confuse*) Non!..

WERTHER: Faut-il que j'en appelle A ceux que vous nommez vos enfants?

CHARLOTTE: (*pensive et se rapprochant de Werther.*) Hélas! oui . . . Mes enfants . . . vous avez dit vrai!.. C'est que l'image De ma mère est présente à tout le monde ici. Et pour moi, je crois voir sourire son visage Quand je prends soin de ses enfants . . . de mes enfants. Ah! je souhaiterais que dans cette demeure Elle revînt et vît, an moins quelques instants, Si je tiens les serments faits à la dernière heure. Chère, chère maman, que ne peux-tu nous voir?

WERTHER: O Charlotte, ange devoir, La bénédiction du ciel sur toi repose!

how everything interests, touches one and possesses a penetrating charm. I wish that when we meet, Charlotte could know all the thoughts that I have had of her, all my hopes and all my tenderness. (*Exit.*)

## SCENE X

(*Enter Charlotte and Werther.*)

CHARLOTTE: Our ways divide; here is our house. It is time for sleep.

WERTHER: Asleep–and can it be your eyes With lids downcast in slumber deep. Can so conceal their dear blue skies? I cannot think of them–asleep. The golden sun may cease to shine, The stars to sparkle over the sea I only know those eyes of yours Are sun and stars and sky to me.

CHARLOTTE: But you know nothing of me.

WERTHER: 'Tis fate I have seen you; It is enough to make me know you

CHARLOTTE: You know–

WERTHER: That you are the best and the most beautiful of women.

CHARLOTTE: No!

WERTHER: Shall I call the little ones you call yours to testify?

CHARLOTTE: My children? You say truly. They recall the image of my mother. I seem to see her smiling above me when I am caring for them–for my children. Ah I wish that she could come back to this old dwelling, if only for an instant to see that I have kept my oath made in her last hour. Dear, dear mother, if you could only see us.

WERTHER: Oh, Charlotte, angel of devotion. The blessings of Heaven be upon you.

## Act I, Scene X

**CHARLOTTE:** Si vous l'aviez connue!..Ah! la cruelle chose
De voir ainsi partir ce qu'on a de plus cher!
Quels tendres souvenirs et quel regret amer!
Pourquoi tout est-il périssable?
Les enfants ont senti cela très vivement;
Ils demandent souvent, d'un ton inconsolable,
Pourquoi les hommes noirs ont emporté maman.

**WERTHER:** Douce extase! ô bonheur! Je donnerais ma vie
Pour garder à jamais ces yeux, ce front charmant,
Cette bouche adorable, étonnée et ravie,
Sans que nul à son tour les contemple un moment! . . . Le céleste sourire!.. Je vous aime et je vous admire!

**CHARLOTTE:** Nous sommes fous! . . . rentrons!

**WERTHER:** (d'une voix altérée et la retenant.) Mais nous nous reverrons? . . . (Voix du bailli appelant: Charlotte!)

### SCENE XI

Werther, Charlotte, Le Bailli:

**LE BAILLI:** (accourant, monte rapidement les marches de la terrasse et disparaît dans la maison.) Charlotte! . . . Albert est de retour! . . .

**WERTHER:** (dans le plus grand trouble.) Ah! votre père . . . Ce retour et ce nom! . . .

**CHARLOTTE:** (à demi voix.) Oui; celui que ma mère M'a fait jurer d'accepter pour époux. Dieu n'est témoin qu'un instant, près de vous, J'oubliai le serment que ce nom me rappelle.

**WERTHER:** A ce serment restez fidèle! . . . Moi, j'en mourrai, Charlotte! . . . (Charlotte, qui a gravi les marches du perron. se retourne une dernière fois avant de disparaître à son tour dans la maison.)

**WERTHER:** (seul, désespéré.) Un autre son époux!

### ◼ ACTE DEUXIÈME

#### SCENE I

A Wetzlar.

Johann et Schmidt ensemble et le verre en main.

---

**CHARLOTTE:** If you had seen her fluttering breath
Die out at last! Her gentle brow
Grow cold and white and stern in death–
You'd weep–you'd weep as I do now.
Ah Why must all things fade?
My little sisters cannot see
Why death is such a mystery.

**WERTHER:** Oh ecstasy Oh, dream divine–
If I were yours and you were mine?
How pure, how fair you are.
Your little tender mouth, your eyes–
They speak to me of Paradise,
Of love–the guiding star.

**CHARLOTTE:** We are mad! Let us part!

**WERTHER:** But we must meet again?
(Baillie's voice is heard: Charlotte!)

### SCENE XI

**BAILLIE:** Charlotte! Albert has come back.

**WERTHER:** Ah, your father. The return of whom–

**CHARLOTTE:** He whom my mother made me promise to accept for my husband. God witnessed, but for a moment, that I forgot my sacred oath in your presence. The name of Albert now recalls it.

**WERTHER:** If you keep that oath, Charlotte, I shall die.
(Charlotte exit.)

**WERTHER:** (alone). Another–to be her husband.
(Curtain.)

### ◼ ACT II

#### SCENE I

(At Wetzlar.)

---

**JOHANN:** L'admirable journée!
De ce joyeux soleil, j'ai l'âme illuminée!
Qu'il est doux de vivre, quand l'air
Est si léger, le ciel si bleu, le vin si clair!

**SCHMIDT:** Allez! chantez l'office et que l'orgue résonne!
De bénir le Seigneur, il est bien des façons.
Moi je le gloritie en exaltant ses dons.

**JOHANN:** Oui, gloire à Celui qui nous donne
De si bon vin et fait l'existence si bonne!
Du monde! encore du monde! on vient de tous côtés!
Le pasteur verra bien fêté
Ses cinquante ans de mariage!

**SCHMIDT:** C'est bon pour un pasteur cinquante ans de ménage.
Dieu le soutient! Mais moi, je n'aurais pu jamais
En supporter autant . . .
(Charlotte et Albert paraissent.)

**JOHANN:** Et cependant j'en sais
Qui ne s'effraieraient guère
De semblable félicité.
(Les désignant.)
Tieus! ceux-là, par exemple!..

**SCHMIDT:** Eh bien! à leur santé
Allous vider encore un verre!
(Ils rentrent tous les deux dans la Wirthschaft.)

### SCENE II

Albert, Charlotte.

**ALBERT:** (avec tendresse.) Trois mois! voici trois mois que nous sommes unis!
Ils ont passé bien vite et pourtant il me semble
Que nous avons vécu toujours ensemble!

**CHARLOTTE:** (doucement.) Albert!

**ALBERT:** Si vous saviez comme je vous bénis!
Mais moi, de cette jeune fille,
Que naguère entourait
Tant de calme bonheur au foyer de famille,
Ai-je fait une femme heureuse et sans regret?

**CHARLOTTE:** Quand une femme a près d'elle à toute heure
Et l'esprit le plus droit et l'âme la meilleure
Que pourrait-elle regretter?

**ALBERT:** Ah! la douce parole et comme à l'écouter
Je me sens tout heureux et j'ai l'âme ravie!
(Ils sortent.)

---

**JOHANN:** What a charming day! I love this sunshine. Ah Life is a pleasant thing when the air is so balmy, the sky so blue, and the wine so pure.

**SCHMIDT:** Go on! Sing the office while the organ sounds! It is a good thing to praise the Lord. I glory in extolling his gifts.

**JOHANN:** Yes, let us praise Him who has given us good wine and a pleasant life. Ah! people come from every side to gaily celebrate the pastor's golden wedding.

**SCHMIDT:** It's a good thing for a pastor to be fifty years married: the Lord favors it. As for me, I couldn't stand it so long.
(Charlotte and Albert appear.)

**JOHANN:** And yet married life is not always war under the semblance of felicity. As for instance (pointing to Charlotte and Albert), those two.

**SCHMIDT:** Good Let us drink to their health. We'll empty another glass.
(Exit.)

### SCENE II

**ALBERT:** Three months! Three months since our union. They have passed quickly, and yet it seems to me that we have always been together.

**CHARLOTTE:** Albert!

**ALBERT:** If you only knew how I bless you! But the young girl, but lately surrounded with all happiness in her own family, have I made her contented without regret?

**CHARLOTTE:** When a woman has always with her the sense of doing right, of loving what is good, what should she regret?

**ALBERT:** Ah when I hear you talk like that it makes me very happy and delights my soul.
(Exit.)

## SCENE III

**WERTHER:** Un autre est son epôux! Ô Dieu, Dieu de bonté, Si tu m'avais permis de marcher dans la vie Avec cet ange à mon côté, Mon existence entière N'aurait jamais été Qu'une ardente prière . . . Et maintenant, parfois, j'ai peur de blasphémer! (*Douloureusement.*) C'est moi qu'elle pouvait aimer! J'aurais pressé sur ma poitrine La plus belle, la plus divine Créature que Dieu lui-même ait su former! C'est moi qu'elle pouvait aimer! Lorsque s'ouvrait le ciel qui s'illumine Soudain. je l'ai vu se fermer! C'est moi qu'elle pouv ait aimer! Tout mon corps en frissonne, et tout mon être en pleure!

## SCENE IV

*Werther, Johann, Schmidt, Brülhmann.* (*Johann et Schmidt reparaissent sur le seuil de la Wirthschaft.*)

**SCHMIDT:** (*à Brülhmann.*) Si . . . Kathchen reviendra, je vous dis! . . . A quelle heure. Et quel jour aura lieu ce retour Qu'importe, elle reviendra . . .

**JOHANN:** Tu l'entends! Des fiancailles de sept ans Ca ne peut pas s'oublier de la sorte!

**SCHMIDT:** Dépêchons! j'entends le signal . . . Si nous manquons l'office, an moins, ouvrons le bal! (*Ils sortent, en trébuchant.*)

## SCENE V

*Werther, Albert.*

**ALBERT:** Au bonheur qui remplit mon âme, Ami, parfois il vient se mêler un remord.

**WERTHER:** (*étonné.*) Un remord?

**ALBERT:** (*avec franchise.*) Je vous sais un cœur loyal et fort; Mais celle qui devint mas femme Vous apparût un jour Qu'elle était libre encore, et peut-être près d'elle Avez-vous fait un rêve envolé sans retour! A la voir si douce et si belle, Je connais trop le prix du bien qui m'est donné Pour ne comprendre pas que sa perte est cruelle . . . Comprende ce tourment, c'est l'avoir pardonné . . .

## SCENE III

**WERTHER:** Wedded to another Oh, God of mercy if you had permitted me to pass my life with such an angel by my side, my whole existence would have been one prayer. And now there are times when I fear I blaspheme. She could have loved me. I might have pressed to my bosom the loveliest, the most divine creature that God ever made. She could have loved me! I have had one lightning glimpse of Paradise! She could have loved me! At the thought I tremble and weep. (*Enter Schmidt and Johann.*)

## SCENE IV

**SCHMIDT:** Yes, Kathchen will come back, I warrant. But when she'll come back–matters not.

**JOHANN:** A seven years' engagement can't be forgotten in that fashion.

**SCHMIDT:** Hurry I hear the signal. If we miss the ceremony, don't let's miss the dance. (*Exit.*)

## SCENE V

(*Enter Albert and Werther.*)

**ALBERT:** My friend, remorse sometimes mingles with the happiness that fills my soul.

**WERTHER:** Remorse?

**ALBERT:** I know that your heart is strong and loyal. But she who is now my wife will cross your path some day as if she were still free and, perhaps, when near her, seeing her so sweet and so beautiful, dreams may come. I know so well the value of what I have gained that I can comprehend the misery of its loss. To understand is to forgive.

**WERTHER:** Vous l'avez dit: mon âme est loyale et sincère, Si j'avais du passé trop amer souvenir, Retirant cette main de la main qui la serre, Je fuirais loin de vous pour ne plus revenir. Mais, comme après l'orage une onde est apaisée. Mon cœur ne souffre plus de son rêve oublié, Et celui qui sait lire au fond de ma pensée N'y doit trouver jamais que la seule amitié! Et ce sera ma part de bonheur sur la terre! (*Sophie accourt, des fleurs dans les mains.*)

## SCENE V

*Les Mêmes, Sophie.*

**SOPHIE:** (*à Albert, gaîment.*) Frère, Voyez le beau bouquet! J'ai mis, pour le pasteur, le jardin au pillage. Et puis on va danser . . . Pour le premier menuet, C'est sur vous que je compte . . . Oh! le sombre visage! Mais aujourd'hui, monsieur Werther, Tout le monde est joyeux, le bonheur est dans l'air Du gai soleil, plein de flamme, Dans l'azur resplendissant, La pure clarté descend De nos fronts jusqu'à notre âme, Et l'oiseau que monte aux cieux, Dans la brise qui soupire, Est revenu pour nous dire Que Dieu permet d'être heureux.

**WERTHER:** (*à part.*) Heureux! pourrai-je l'être encore?

**ALBERT:** (*à Sophie.*) Va porter ton bouquet, chère petite sœur, Je te rejoins . . . (*Sophie s'éloigne de quelques pas.*) (*A Werther.*) Werther, nous parlons de bonheur! On le cherche bien loin, on l'appelle, on l'implore, Et voici que peut-être il passe en nos chemins, Un sourire à lèvre et des fleurs dans les mains.

**SOPHIE:** (*sur le seuil du presbytère, à Albert.*) Frère, revenez vite. Pour le premier menuet, je vous invite, Vous entendez, monsieur Werther! Tout le monde est heureux, le bonheur est dans l'air! (*Albert a rejoint Sophie et disparaît avec elle.*)

**WERTHER:** My friend, if I have dreamed too late, I ask forgiveness. Here's my hand. I will not follow after fate I go to some for alien land. And if these haunting fancies flee Or fade away and leave no trace I shall return ennobled, free To meet you, greet you, face to face (*Enter Sophie.*)

## SCENE V

**SOPHIE:** Oh, brother, see this pretty nosegay. I have quite robbed the garden for the pastor. And they're going to dance. I count on you for the first minuet. Why, what a gloomy countenance But today, Herr Werther, all the world is gay. Happiness is in the very air. The bright sun, high above, The clear and balmy air Breathe everywhere of love; The whole wide world is fair. The gentle whispering breeze, The bird upon the wing, The silent sexéd trees Feel love's eternal spring.

**WERTHER:** Happy? Can I ever again be happy?

**ALBERT:** (*to Sophie*). Go present your nosegay, dear little sister. I will rejoin you. (*Sophie retires.*) Werther, we steep of happiness; we seek it afar; we call it; we implore it; and perhaps it stands in our way with a smile on its lips and flowers in its hands.

**SOPHIE:** Make haste, brother, I shall keep the first minuet for you. You hear, Herr Werther. All the world is gay. Happiness is in the very air. (*Exeunt.*)

## SCENE VI

**WERTHER:** (*seul d'abord, puis Charlotte.*) Ai-je dit vrai? L'amour que j'ai pour le
N'est-il pas le plus pur comme le plus sacré?
En ce coeur, malgré lui rebelle,
Un coupable désir est-il jamais entré?
Oui! je mentais! . . . ô Dieu! souffrir sans cesse,
Ou bien toujours mentir!
C'est trop de honte et de faiblesse!
Je dois, je veux partir!
(*Charlotte a paru sur le seuil du temple et se dirige vers le presbytère. Werther l'aperçoit, très ému.*)
Partir! Non! je ne veux que me rapprocher d'elle!

**CHARLOTTE:** (*sans remarquer Werther.*) Comme on trouve en priant une force nouvelle!

**WERTHER:** (*de loin.*) Charlotte! . . .

**CHARLOTTE:** (*se détournant, simplement.*) Vous venez aussi chez le pasteur?

**WERTHER:** (*se rapprochant, tristement.*) À quoi bon? pour vous voir danser avec un autre!
Ah! qu'il est loin ce jour plein d'intime douceur
Où mon regard a rencontré le vôtre
Pour la première fois; . . . où nous sommes tous deux
Demeurés si longtemps . . . tout près . . . sans nous rien dire . . .
Cependant que tombait des cieux
Un suprême rayon qui semblait un sourire
Sur notre émoi silencieux!

**CHARLOTTE:** (*froidement.*) Albert m'aime et je suis sa femme! . . .

**WERTHER:** (*avec emportement*) Albert vous aime! . . . Qui ne vous aimerait? . . .

**CHARLOTTE:** (*plus doucement.*) Werther! . . . N'est-il donc pas D'autre femme ici-bas Digne de votre amour et libre d'elle-même?
Je ne m'appartiens plus; pourquoi donc m'aimez-vous?

**WERTHER:** Eh! demandez aux fous D'où vient que leur raison s'égare!

**CHARLOTTE:** (*resolument.*) Eh bien! puisqu'à jamais le destin nous sépare
Eloignez-vous, partez! partez! . . .

**WERTHER:** Quel mot Ai-je entendu?

**CHARLOTTE:** (*gravement.*) Celui qu'il faut De moi que l'on entende!

**WERTHER:** (*violemment.*) Eh! qui donc le commande?

## SCENE VI

**WERTHER:** Have I spoken truly? Is not the love I feel for her pure and sacred? No wish has ever entered this rebellious breast? Yes! I have lied. Oh Heaven! To suffer eternally–or to lie eternally. It is too shameful and weak. I must–will go away.
(*Sees Charlotte.*)
Go away? No! I only wish to be near her!

**CHARLOTTE:** (*aside*). What new strength comes to us from prayer!

**WERTHER:** Charlotte!

**CHARLOTTE:** Are you also going to the pastor's?

**WERTHER:** Why should I? To see you dance with another? Ah! There was once a golden day,
How long ago–how far away
How precious is its memory–
This day that never more can be.
We sat enthralled and neither spoke,
And love alone the silence broke.
The sunshine fell on you and me.

**CHARLOTTE:** Albert loves me and I am his wife.

**WERTHER:** Albert loves you! Ah who would not love you?

**CHARLOTTE:** Is there no other woman who is free and worthy of your love? I am not my own mistress. Why do you love me?

**WERTHER:** Ask a madman why his reason wanders!

**CHARLOTTE:** Then, since fate divides us, leave me! Go!

**WERTHER:** What do I hear?

**CHARLOTTE:** The only word that I should speak and you listen to.

**WERTHER:** What do you ask of me?

**CHARLOTTE:** Le devoir!
(*Plus doucement.*)
L'absence rend parfois la douleur moins amère.

**WERTHER:** Ah! me donner l'oubli n'est pas en son pouvoir!

**CHARLOTTE:** (*plus douce encore*) Pourquoi l'oubli?..Pensez à Charlotte, au contraire
Pensez à son repos; soyez fort, soyez bon.

**WERTHER:** (*apaisé peu à peu.*) Oui! . . . j'ai pour seul désir que vous soyez heureuse
Mais ne plus vous revoir, c'est impossible, non.

**CHARLOTTE:** Ami, je ne suis pas à ce point rigoureuse
Et ne saurais vouloir un exil èternel.
Vous reviendrez . . . bientôt . . . tenez . . . à la Noël!

**WERTHER:** (*suppliant.*) Charlotte!

**CHARLOTTE:** (*s'éloignant.*) A la Noël!
(*Elle disparait.*)

## SCENE VII

(*Werther veut la rappeler, mais il revient sur ses pas, découragé, abattu.*)

**WERTHER:** Oui, ce qu'elle m'ordonne
Pour son repos, je le ferai;
Et si la force m'abandonne,
Ah! c'est moi, pour toujours, qui me reposerai!
(*Songeant fiévreusement.*)
Pourquoi trembler devant la mort . . . devant la nôtre?
On lève le rideau; puis on passe de l'autre
Côté! Voilà ce qu'on nomme mourir.
Offensons-nous le ciel en cessant de souffrir?
Lorsque l'enfant revient d'un voyage avant l'heure,
Bien loin de lui garder quelque ressentiment,
Au seul bruit de ses pas tressaille la demeure,
Et le pére, joyeux, l'embrasse longuement.
O Dieu qui m'a créé, serais-tu moins clément!
Non! tu ne saurais pas, dérobé sous tes voiles,
Rejeter dans la nuit tou fils infortuné!
Devinant ton sourire au travers des étoiles,
Il reviendra vers toi d'avance pardonné!
Père! Père!
Que je ne connais pas, en qui pourtant j'ai foi,
En qui j'espère.

**CHARLOTTE:** Your duty! Absence will assuage your grief.

**WERTHER:** It cannot make me forget.

**CHARLOTTE:** Why should you forget? Think of Charlotte as of a friend. Be strong! Be noble!

**WERTHER:** Your happiness is my sole wish. But to see you no more–I cannot bear it.

**CHARLOTTE:** And I do not exact eternal absence. Come back— at Christmas.

**WERTHER:** Charlotte!

**CHARLOTTE:** At Christmas!

## SCENE VII

**WERTHER:** We know that all who lived have died
It is in the circle of the soul.
It is but to cross the silent tide.
It is but to reach ambition's goal.
As when a little child has strayed
And stands reluctant at the door,
How glad the Father's heart is made,
To have him back once more.
Oh, God who created me, receive me so
To him who dwells and reigns on high,
And smiles through mist and starry space,
From out the night I send my cry–
That before I ask–he'll grant me grace.
Father! Father! I do not know you, but
I trust, in whom I hope–call me.
I will obey her, for her own peace; and if any strength fail me, my peace shall be eternal.

Appelle-moi!
(*Werther va s'éloigner, lorsque paraît Sophie sur le seuil du pres-bytère.*)

## SCENE VIII

*Werther, Sophie, puis Charlotte, Albert et tout le cortège.*

SOPHIE à WERTHER: Mais venez donc! le cortège s'approche, Et soit dit sans reproche. C'est vous seul qu'ou attend!

WERTHER: (*brusquement.*) Pardonnez-moi; je pars!

SOPHIE: Vous partez!

WERTHER: A l'instant!

SOPHIE: Mais sans doute . . . Vous reviendrez . . . demain . . . bientôt . . .

WERTHER: (*violemment.*) Jamais! Adieu!
(*Il s'enfuit.*)

SOPHIE: (*très émue, l'appelant et courant après lui jusqu'à la route.*) Monsieur Werther! . . . Au tournant de la route Il disparaît . . . plus rien!
(*Fondant en larmes.*)
Mon Dieu!
Tout à l'heure
J'étais si joyeuse!
(*Le cortège de la Cinquantaine paraît. On vient de différents côtés.*)

CHARLOTTE: (*apercevant Sophie et accourant près d'elle.*) Ah! qu'est ce donc: elle pleure!

SOPHIE: Ah! soeur! monsieur Werther est parti! . . .

CHARLOTTE: Lui!

SOPHIE: Et pour toujours! . . . A l'instant méme Il vient de me le dire. et puis il s'est enfui Comme un fou!

CHARLOTTE: (*à part.*) Pour toujours!

ALBERT: (*sombre et regardant Charlotte.*) Il l'aime!

## ■ ACTE TROISIÈME

### SCENE I

(*La maison d'Albert.*)

CHARLOTTE: (*seule.*) Werther! Werther . . . Qui m'aurait dit la place aujourd'hui. Depuis qu'il est parti, magré moi, tout me lasse Et mon âme est pleine de lui! Ces lettres . . . ah! je les relis sans cesse . . . Avec quel charme, mais aussi quelle tristesse. Je les devrais détruire . . . je ne puis!
(*Lisant.*)
'Je vous écris

## SCENE VIII

(*Enter Sophie.*)

SOPHIE: Why don't you come? The wedding party draws near and you are the only absent one.

WERTHER: Forgive me. I am going away.

SOPHIE: Going away?

WERTHER: This moment.

SOPHIE: But you will come back soon? To-morrow?

WERTHER: Never! Farewell!
(*Exit.*)

SOPHIE: Herr Werther. Ah he vanishes around the bend of the road. Oh dear—and I was so happy.
(*Procession appears.*)
(*Enter Charlotte.*)
What's this?—weeping.

SOPHIE: Oh, sister! Herr Werther is gone.

CHARLOTTE: He?

SOPHIE: And forever. This moment he bade me farewell and fled madly from my sight.

CHARLOTTE: (*aside.*) Forever!

ALBERT: He loves her.
(*Curtain.*)

## ■ ACT III

### SCENE I

(*The Home of Albert.*)

CHARLOTTE: (*alone.*) Werther! Werther! Who could have told me that he should hold such a place in my heart today. Since he has left me, my mind is full of him. These letters—Ah I read them over and over again with delight—and with sadness. I should destroy them—but I cannot
(*Reads*)
I write today

De ma petite chambre;
Un ciel gris
Et lourd de décembre
Pèse sur moi, comme un lin-ceul . . .
Et je suis seul, seul, toujours seul!'
Non, Werther, dans leur souvenir
Votre image reste vivante,
Et quand vous reviendrez . . . Mais doit-il revenir!
Ah! ce dernier billet me glace et m'épouvante!
Personne près de lui! . . . Pas un seul témoinage
De tendresse . . . ou pitié! Comment
M'est venu ce triste courage
D'ordonner cet exil et cet isolement!
(*Elle a pris une autre lettre et l'ouvre.*)
'Des cris joyeux d'enfants montent sous ma fenêtre,
Et je pense à ce temps si doux
Où tous vos chers petits jouaient autour de nous.
Ils m'oublieront peut-être!'
'Tu m'as dit: A Noël! et j'ai crié: Jamais!
On va bientôt connaître
Qui de nous deux disait vrai! . . . Mais . . .
Si je ne dois reparaître
Au jour fixé, devant toi,
Ne m'accuse pas, pleure-moi!
Qui, de ces yeux si pleins de charmes,
Ces lignes, tu les reliras,
Tu les mouilleras de tes larmes,
O! Charlotte, tu frémiras!'
(*Sophie entre.*)

## SCENE II

*Charlotte, Sophie.*

SOPHIE: (*gaiement.*) Bonjour, grande soeur! je viens aux nouvelles,
Sans attendre que tu m'appelles . . .
On ne te voit plus. Albert est absent Et le père est très mécontent.

CHARLOTTE: (*encore préoccupée.*) Enfant! . . .

SOPHIE: (*prenant Charlotte par la taille.*) Mais souffres-tu?

CHARLOTTE: Pourquoi cette pensée?

SOPHIE: Cette main est glacée Et tes yeux sont rougis, je le vois bien.

CHARLOTTE: (*avee embarras.*) Non, ce n'est rien!
Je me sens quelquefois un peu triste . . . . isolée.
Mais si d'un vague émoi mon âme était troublée.
Je ne m'en souviens plus maintenant . . . et tu vois.
Je souris . . .

In my lonely room.
The sky is gray;
December's gloom
Has found my hopes, my fancies flown.
I am always alone, dear, always alone.
All alone! No one to witness his pity or tenderness. How could I have had courage to condemn him to exile, to this loneliness.
(*Reads another letter.*)
Below my window the children cry.
They bring back many a game
I've had with your children in days gone by—
And now—they're forgetting my name.
No, Werther; in their remembrance your image still lives. And when you come back—but should you come back——Ah This last note chills and terrifies me!
That blessed day—the day you set
For my return to you again,—
Can never dawn! Could I forget
The past with all its grief and pain?
I could not, dear one, though I tried.
And then—the memories of the place
Wherein I saw you as a bride
In all your beauty, youth and grace
If your dear form no more I see,
Accuse me not—but pity me!

## SCENE II

(*Enter Sophie*)

SOPHIE: Good morning, my big sister! I have news for you. I don't wait to be sent for, you see. You never come out now-a-days, and Albert is away too. Our father is displeased.

CHARLOTTE: Child!

SOPHIE: Are you ill?

CHARLOTTE: Why do you think so?

SOPHIE: Your hand is as cold as ice, and your eyes bloodshot.

CHARLOTTE: It is nothing! Sometimes I feel a little sad—lonely. But if my soul were troubled by some vague emotion—I have forgotten it—you see, I smile.

SOPHIE: (*câline.*) Ce qu'il faut, c'est rire, rire encore. Comme autrefois.

CHARLOTTE: (*à part.*) Comme autrefois!

SOPHIE: (*gaiemet*) Ah! le rire est béni, joyeux, léger, sonore! Il a des ailes; c'est un oiseau de l'aurore! C'est la clarté du coeur qui s'échappe en rayons! Écoute! je suis d'âge à savoir les raisons De bien des choses! Qui! tous les fronts ici sont devenus moroses Depuis que Werther s'est enfui! Mais pourquoi laisser sans nouvelles Ceux qui lui sont restés fidèles?

CHARLOTTE: (*se dégageant des bras de Sophie, se lève, à part.*) Tout, jusqu'à cet enfant, tout me parle de lui!

SOPHIE: (*revenant à Charlotte.*) Des larmes! Oh! pardonnne, je t'en prie! Oui, j'ai tort de parler De tout cela . . .

CHARLOTTE: (*ne se contraignant plus.*) Va! laisse couler les larmes Elles font du bien, ma chérie! Les larmes qu'on ne pleure pas Dans notre âme retombent toutes, Et de leurs patientes gouttes Martèlent le coeur triste et las. Sa résistance enfin s'épuise; Le coeur se creuse et s'affaiblit; Il est trop grand, rien ne l'emplit; Et trop fragile, tout le brise!

SOPHIE: (*effrayée.*) Tiens, Charlotte, crois-moi, ne reste pas ici . . . Viens chez nous; nous saurons te faire Oublier ton souci; Le père A fait apprendre à ses enfants De magnifiques compliments Pour la Noël . . .

CHARLOTTE: (*à part, très troublée.*) Noël! oh! cette lettre: (*Répétant d'un ton sombre.*) 'Si tu ne me vois reparaître, Au jour fixé, devant toi. Ne m'accuse pas; pleure-moi!'

SOPHIE: (*revenant vers Charlotte.*) Alors, c'est convenu! tu viendras . . .

CHARLOTTE: Oui . . . peut-être . . .

SOPHIE: Non! non! certainement!

CHARLOTTE: (*essayant de sourire.*) Certainement . . .

SOPHIE: Bien vrai!

---

SOPHIE: But you must laugh, as you used to.

CHARLOTTE: (*aside.*) As I used to.

SOPHIE: Laughter is blessed by God, the God who reigns on high. It is the smile of the happy heart! It has wings to soar and fly, It is the light of the joyous soul that escapes in beams of cheer, In rays of sound and mirth. There is no laughter here. Since Werther went away. A spell seems over all. And those who love you best? Can they not win your true - Your old self back once more. Ah, Charlotte, have not we, Who share with you your grief,–who love you so, and see You fade and weep and mourn,–some power to comfort you?

CHARLOTTE: Everything! Even this child reminds me of him.

SOPHIE: Tears! Ah, forgive me, I pray. It was wrong to speak of this.

CHARLOTTE: Go! Let them flow. It does me good to weep, darling. What bitter tears we shed in grief, That comes at memory's haunting call But sadder far beyond belief Are tears that never, never fall! The tears that spring from out the heart Are never dry–the source is deep. Ah She who plays the saddest part Is she who–cannot–will not–weep.

SOPHIE: Come with us, Charlotte. Do not stay here. Come with us. We will find a way to make you forget your troubles. Father has made the children learn magnificent Christmas greetings.

CHARLOTTE: Christmas Oh, that letter. (*Reads.*) If I shall not see you anymore, Accuse me not–but pity for me!

SOPHIE: Then it's all settled? You'll come.

CHARLOTTE: Perhaps!

SOPHIE: No, no. Certainly.

CHARLOTTE: Certainly, then.

SOPHIE: You're sure?

---

CHARLOTTE: J'irai, je te le promets, mignonne . . .

SOPHIE: Tu viendras!

CHARLOTTE: Oui! j'irai! . . . Que je t'embrasse encore! (*Sophie s'éloigne.*)

## SCENE III

*Charlotte, puis Werther*

CHARLOTTE: La force m'abandonne! Seigneur Dieu, Seigneur! J'ai fait et veux faire Toujours mon devoir! En toi seul j'espère. Car bien rude est l'épreuve et bien faible mon coeur! Seigneur Dieu, Seigneur! Tu lis dans mon âme; hélas! tout la blesse! Si mes pleurs t'offensaient, j'en demande pardon; Viens à mon secours – ô Dieu fort! Dieu bon! Prends pitié de moi! soutiens ma faiblesse! (*Werther paraît.*) Ciel! Werther!

WERTHER: Oui, c'est moi . . . je reviens . . . et pourtant . . . Loin de vous . . . je n'ai pas laissé une heure, Un instant, Sans dire que je meure Plutôt que la revoir . . . Puis, lorsque vînt le jour Que vous aviez fixé pour le retour . . . Je suis parti . . . sur le seuil de la porte Je résistais encore . . . je voulais fuir . . . Qu'importe D'ailleurs tout cela . . . me voici!

CHARLOTTE: Pourquoi cette parole amère? Pourquoi ne plus revenir, quand ici Chacun vous attendait . . . mon pére . . . Les enfants . . .

WERTHER: (*s'approchant*). Et vous? vous aussi?

CHARLOTTE: Voyez la maison est restée Telle que vous l'avez quittée A la revoir ainsi Ne vous semble-t-il pas qu'elle s'est souvenue?

WERTHER: Oui, Je vois . . . Ici, rien n'a changé . . . que les coeurs Toute chose est encore á la place connue. Voici le clavecin qui chantait mes bonheurs Ou qui tressaillait de ma peine Alors que votre voix accompagnait la mienne Ces livres sur qui tant de fois Nous avons incliné nos têtes rap-

---

CHARLOTTE: I promise you, darling, that I will come.

SOPHIE: You will come?

CHARLOTTE: Yes. Kiss me once more. (*Exit Sophie.*)

## SCENE III

CHARLOTTE: My strength fails me. Oh, God! To whom I kneel, You know all I feel. I never swerved from you. Do but comfort me– Hear my appeal If tears offend you, Lord of light, Send down your grace into the night Within my soul! In deep despair I beg–command you–heed my prayer! (*Werther appears.*) Heavens! Werther!

WERTHER: Yes. It is I! I have come back. Notwithstanding that when away from you, I have not passed an hour, an instant without telling myself that I would rather die than see you again. Well, when the day came that you had fixed for my return, I left—even at the gate I hesitated again—I wished to fly—what do all these struggles amount to—I am here.

CHARLOTTE: Why do you speak so, my friend? Why should you not come back? Everyone awaits you— my father—the children—

WERTHER: And you—you also?

CHARLOTTE: Yes! The house is just as it was when you left. Doesn't it seem to give you a welcome?

WERTHER: Yes, I see? Nothing is changed here—except hearts. Everything is in the familiar place. There is the harpsichord that pleased my merry hours or responded to my sad moods,—then your voice accompanied mine. These books—how many times have we bent our heads together over them. (*Looks at pistols.*) And these weapons—one day my

prochées.
(*Allant au secrétaire sur lequel est placée la boîte aux pistolets.*)
Et ces armes . . . un jour ma main les a touchées.
Déjà, j'étais impatient
Du long repos anquel j'aspire! . . .

CHARLOTTE: Et voici ces vers d'Ossian
Que vous aviez commencé de traduire.

WERTHER: (*prenant le manuscrit.*)
Traduire . . . Ah bien souvent mo n rêve s'envola
Sur l'aile de ces vers, et c'est toi, cher poête,
Qui, bien plutôt, étais mon interpréte!
Toute mon âme est lá
"Pourquoi me réveiller, ô souffle du printemps?
Sur mon front je sens tes caresses.
Et pourtant bien proche est le temps
Des orages ct des tristesses
Demain, dans le vallon, viendra le voyageur,
Se souvenant de ma gloire premiére.
Et ses yeux vainement chercheront ma splendeur:
Ils ne trouverout plus que deuil et que misère!"

CHARLOTTE: (*trés troublée.*)
N'achevez pas!
Hélas!
Ce désespoir . . . ce deuil . . . on dirait . . . il me semble! . . .

WERTHER: Ah ciel ai-je compris . . . Dans cette voix qui tremble
Dans ces yeux remplis
De larmes, n'est-ce pas un aveu que je lis! . . .
A quoi bon essayer de nous tromper encore.

CHARLOTTE: Je vous implore!

WERTHER: Va nous mentions tous deux en nous disant vainqueurs
De l'immortel amour qui tressaille en nos coeurs.
Ah ce premier baiser, mon rêve et mon envie,
Bonheur tant espéré qu'aujourd'hui j'entrevois,
Il brûle sur ma lèvre encore inassouvie
Ce baiser demandé pour la premiére fois!

CHARLOTTE: (*défaillante.*)
Werther?

WERTHER: Ah ma raison s'égare.
Tu m'aimes . . .

CHARLOTTE: (*le repoussant.*)
Non . . . tout ce qui nous sépare
Ne peut être oublié!

WERTHER: (*se jetant à ses pieds.*)
Tu m'aimes! . . . tu m'aimes! . . .

CHARLOTTE: Pitié!

---

hands sought them. Already I had become impatient for the long, breathless sleep.

CHARLOTTE: And here are the poems of Ossian that you commenced to translate.

WERTHER: Translate! Ah! how often my dreams have soared on the wings of these poems, and it is you, dear poet, who often interpreted my feelings! All my soul is there Oh wake me not, breath of spring, breath of spring.
Let me dream on, as one who knows Bleak winter with its chill and snows,
And dreads awakening.
The stranger found me fair to see—
And now—in scorn, he passes me,
To see so sad a thing!

CHARLOTTE: No more! Alas! This despair—this mourning—it appeals to me.

WERTHER: Ah! Heaven! Do I understand correctly? In your trembling voice—in your eyes filled with tears—is it not an avowal that I see? And we were deluding ourselves with our good endeavors.

CHARLOTTE: I implore you!

WERTHER: There All the lies between us are over. Immortal love has driven them from our hearts.
The first long lingering kiss Burns in my eager soul— yet I know it's bliss— Love is beyond control!

CHARLOTTE: Werther?

WERTHER: Ah My reason deserts me You love me

CHARLOTTE: No. We must separate. We must forget.

WERTHER: You love me, you love me.

CHARLOTTE: Pity me!

---

WERTHER: Je t'aime! . . .
Il n'est plus de remords, il n'est plus de tourment.

CHARLOTTE: (*éperdue.*) Seigneur clément,
Défendez-moi contre moi-même.

WERTHER: Hors de nous rien n'existe et tout le reste est vain
Mais l'amour, seul est vrai, car c'est le mot divin.
Défendez-moi, Seigneur

WERTHER: Viens!

CHARLOTTE: (*dans les bras de Werther.*)
Ah! pitié!

WERTHER: Je t'aime!

CHARLOTTE: (*se redressant, affolée.*) Ah! moi! moi! dans ses bras!

WERTHER: (*suppliant.*) Pardon!

CHARLOTTE: (*résolument.*) Vous ne me verrez plus . . .

WERTHER: Grâce, Charlotte! . . .

CHARLOTTE: Non!
C'est vous, vous que je fuis l'âme désesperée.
Adieu, pour la derniére fois!

WERTHER: (*se précipitant sur ses pas.*) Mais non! c'est impossible . . . écoute-moi . . . ma voix
Te rappelle . . . reviens . . . Tu me seras sacrée! Rien! . . . pas un mot . . . elle se tait.
Soite adieu doue! Charlotte a dicté mon arrêt! Prends le deuil, ô nature!
Ton fils, ton bien-aimé, ton amant va mourir!
Emportant avec lui l'éternelle torture!
Ma tombe peut s'ouvrir!
(*Il s'enfuit.*)

## SCÈNE IV

*Albert, puis Charlotte.*

ALBERT: (*entrant, préoccupé, sombre.*) Werther est de retour . . . on l'a vu revenir . . .
Personne ici . . . la porte ouverte sur la rue . . .
Charlotte! . . .

CHARLOTTE: (*poussant un cri à la vue de son mari.*) Ah!

ALBERT: Qu'avez-vous?

CHARLOTTE: (*de plus en plus troublée.*) Rien! . . .

ALBERT: Pourtant vous voilà Troublée, émue . . .

CHARLOTTE: Oui! . . . la surprise . . .

ALBERT: (*presque violent.*) Et qui done était là?

CHARLOTTE: Qui? lá . . .

---

WERTHER: I love you—No more remorse, no more torment.

CHARLOTTE: Merciful Savior, defend me against myself.

WERTHER: Except ourselves, nothing exists. Everything is void. Love alone is real, for it is the word of God.

CHARLOTTE: Defend me, Lord.

WERTHER: Come with me!

CHARLOTTE: Pity!

WERTHER: I love you.

CHARLOTTE: Ah I—I—In his arms!

WERTHER: Pardon me.

CHARLOTTE: You shall see me no more.

WERTHER: Have mercy, Charlotte.

CHARLOTTE: No. It is from you that my desperate soul is flying. Good by—for the last time.

WERTHER: No. It is impossible! Listen to me; let my voice recall you. Come back! You shall be sacred to me. Nothing—not one word—I will keep silent. So be it. Farewell, then! Charlotte has condemned me.
Nature, make room within your breast
For one who bore the stings of grief,
Now bears them with him of the tomb—
His only—last relief.
(*Exit.*)

## SCENE IV

(*Enter Albert.*)

ALBERT: Werther has returned. He has been seen—Nobody here—The street door open—Charlotte!

CHARLOTTE: Ah!

ALBERT: What is the matter?

CHARLOTTE: Nothing.

ALBERT: Then why are you so agitated?

CHARLOTTE: The surprise—

ALBERT: And who has been here?

CHARLOTTE: Who—here?

## Act III, Scene IV

ALBERT: Répondez!
(*Un domestique est entré apportant une lettre.*) Un message!
De Werther . . .

CHARLOTTE: Dieu!

ALBERT: (*lisant, sans perdre Charlotte de vue.*) "Je pars pour un lointain voyage . . . Voulez-vous me prêter vos pistolets?"

CHARLOTTE: (*à part, se sentant défaillir.*) Il part!

ALBERT: (*continuant.*) "Dieu vous garde tous deux."

CHARLOTTE: (*à part, avec terreur.*) Ah l'horrible présage!

ALBERT: (*à Charlotte, froidement.*) Donnez-les-lui! . . .

CHARLOTTE: (*reculant épouvantée.*) Qui? moi?

ALBERT: Sans doute . . .

CHARLOTTE: (*comme fascinée par le regard de son mari, se dirige vers le secrétaire où est déposée la boîte au pistolets.*) Quel regard! Dieu! tu ne voudras pas que j'arrive trop tard!
(*Elle sort désesperée.*)

---

ALBERT: Answer me. (*Enter Servant.*) A note–From Werther.

CHARLOTTE: My God!

ALBERT: (*reads*). "I am going on a long journey. Will you lend me your pistols?"

CHARLOTTE: He goes—

ALBERT: (*reading*). "God keep you both."

CHARLOTTE: Ah! Horrible presentiment.

ALBERT: Give them to him.

CHARLOTTE: Who?–I?—

ALBERT: Why not?— (*The servant takes the pistols.*)

CHARLOTTE: (*aside*). How he looks at me! God! You would not let me reach Werther–too late.
(*Exits.*)
(*Curtain.*)

---

## ■ ACTE QUATRIEME

### SCÈNE I

*La nuit de Noël.*
*La morte de Werther.*

*Werther puis Charlotte.*

CHARLOTTE: (*entrant brusquement et appelant, avec angoisse.*) Werther! . . . Rien!
(*Tout à coup, elle aperçoit le corps de Werther et se jette sur lui, puis pousse un cri et recule, épouvantée.*)
Dieu! du sang!
Non! non! c'est impossible!
Il ne peut ètre mort!—Werther!
Werther! reviens à toi!
Réponds! réponds!— Ah! c'est horrible!

WERTHER: (*ouvrant les yeux, reconnaissant Charlotte.*) Qui parle? . . . Charlotte, ah! c'est toi, pardonne-moi!

CHARLOTTE: Te pardonner, quand c'est moi qui te frappe,
Quand le sang qui s'échappe
De ta blessure, c'est moi qui l'ai versé! . . .

WERTHER: (*qui s'est soulevé un peu.*) Non!
Tu n'as rien fait que de juste et de bon!
Mon âme reconaissante
Te bénit pour cette mort
Qui te garde innocente
Et m'épargne un remord!

---

## ■ ACT IV

### SCENE I

(*Christmas night scene changes from exterior to Werther's study.*)

CHARLOTTE: (*calling*). Werther—No answer!
(*Throws herself on the body of Werther.*)
My God! Blood! No, no! It is impossible. He cannot be dead! Werther! Werther! Come to your senses! Answer me! Answer me! Ah, this is horrible.

WERTHER: Who speaks?—It is you. Pardon me.

CHARLOTTE: Pardon you?–when it is I who have killed you. I who have spilled the blood which flows from your wounds?

WERTHER: No! You have done only what is just and right! From my soul I feel the blessing of my death–which saves your innocence and my remorse.

---

CHARLOTTE: (*affolée et se tournant vers la porte.*) Mais il faut du secours!

WERTHER: (*se soulevant sur un genou.*) Non! n'appelle personne . . .
Tout secours serait vain!
Donne
Seulement ta main . . .
Vois! . . . je n'ai pas besoin d'autre aide que la tienne!
Et puis, il ne faut pas qu'on vienne
Encore ici
Nous séparer . . . On est si bien ainsi!
A cette heure suprême:
Je suis heureux; je meurs en te disant
Que je t'adore! . . .

CHARLOTTE: (*avec élan.*) Et moi, Werther, et moi je t'aime!

WERTHER: Dieu puissant!

CHARLOTTE: Qui, du jour même
Où tu parus devant mes yeux,
J'ai senti qu'une chaine
Impossible à briser nous liait tous les deux
A l'oubli du devoir j'aí préféré ta peine
Et pour ne pas me perdre, hélas je t'ai perdu
Mais si la mort approche, avant qu'elle te prenne..
Ah ton baiser, du moins, je te l'aurait rendu
Que ton âme en mon âme eperdúment se fonde
Qu'elle oublie, à jamais, en ce baiser, le monde
Les maux, les douleura, tout . . .

WERTHER ET CHARLOTTE ENSEMBLE: Oublious tout!
(*Voix des enfants dans la maison du bailli.*)

VOIX DES ENFANTS:
Noël!

CHARLOTTE: (*douleureusement.*) Ces cris joyeux, ce rire en ce moment cruel!

VOIX DES ENFANTS: (*au dehors.*) Jésus vient de naître
Voici notre divin maître
Rois et bergers d'Israël.
Noël! . . .

WERTHER: (*se soulevant un peu, avec une sorte d'hallucination.*) Ah les enfants . . . les anges . . . oui, Noël,
C'est le chant de la délivrance,
C'est l'hymne de pardon
Redit par l'innocence!

CHARLOTTE: (*se rapprochant, effrayée de ce délire qui commence.*) Werther!

WERTHER: (*de plus en plus halluciné.*) Pourquoi ces larmes? . . . Crois-tu donc Qu'en ce instant ma vie est achevée?
Elle commence, vois-tu

---

CHARLOTTE: We must have help.

WERTHER: No! Call no one. All assistance will be vain. I only need your hand. See—I have need of no other aid but yours. And besides, it is better that no one comes to separate us again. In this supreme hour I am happy. I die telling you that I adore you.

CHARLOTTE: And I, Werther, and I, I love you.

WERTHER: Father almighty!

CHARLOTTE: But death cannot unlink the chain
Of lové like ours. It was to be
No you shall smile on me again.
Werther Your spirit lives in me.
And when we meet in Heaven above.
And lose ourselves in boundless bliss,
In memory of our earthly love
We'll consecrate this last sad kiss,
Now death has set a captive free
And soul to soul at last are we—
Waiting God's great eternity!

WERTHER AND CHARLOTTE: Let us forget everything.
(*Voices of children heard.*) Christmas!

CHARLOTTE: These joyous cries, this laughter in this cruel moment.

(CHILDREN'S VOICES): Christmas! Jesus came this day
To lead us in the heavenly way.
Israel's king and shepherds all
Heard the startled Magis' call—
Christmas!

WERTHER (*his mind wanders*).—Ah! The children—the angels—Yes, Christmas! This is the song of deliverance, of pardon repeated by the innocent.

CHARLOTTE: Werther!

WERTHER: Why these tears? Do you not know that at this instant I have achieved all? Life begins! See I go to my Father and yours. He will comfort me until you come.

bien . . .
Voici que je m'en vais vers mon père . . . et le tien!
Il me consolera jusqu'à ton arrive!

**VOIX DE SOPHIE:** Dieu permet d'être heureux!
Le bonheur est dans l'air tout le monde est joyeux!

**VOIX DES ENFANTS:** Noël! Noël!

**WERTHER:** Dieu permet d'être heureux! . . .

**CHARLOTTE:** (*le regardant avec angoisse.*) Ses yeux se ferment . . . sa main se glace . . . Il va mourir . . . mourir . . . ah pitié. Grâce!
Je ne veux pas . . . je ne veux pas . . .
Werther, réponds . . . tu peux encore m'entendre
La mort entre mes bras
N'osera pas te prendre
Tu vivras . . . Tu vivras . . . vois je ne crains plus rien . . .

**WERTHER:** (*d'une voix éteinte.*) Ah . . . Charlotte . . je meurs . . . oui . . . mais écoute bien.

**(VOICE OF SOPHIE):** The bright sun high above; the clear and balmy air,
Breathe everywhere of love; the whole wide world is fair!

**(CHILDREN'S VOICES.):** Christmas! Christmas!

**WERTHER:** The whole wide world is fair—

**CHARLOTTE:** His eyes are closing—his hand is cold—he is dying. dying. Ah Pity—grace! It cannot be! This cannot be! Werther! Answer me! Can you not hear me? Death dare not take you from my arms! You shall live! You shall live I fear nothing.

**WERTHER:** Ah, Charlotte—I am dying, yes—Listen—
Within the vale below
Two stern old lindens grow;

Là-bas, au fond du cimetière,
Il est deux grand tilleuls . . . C'est là
Que je voudrais reposer . . . Si cela
M' était refusé, si la terre
Chrétienne est interdite au corps d'un malheureux,
Près du chemin ou dans le vallon solitaire
Allez placer ma tombe . . . en détournant les yeux
Le prêtre passera . . . Mais à la dérobée
Quelque femme viendra visiter le banni
Et d'une pure larme en son ombre tombée
Le mort, le pauvre mort, se sentira béni!

**CHARLOTTE:** Ah!
**VOIX DES ENFANTS:** Jésus vient de naître
Voici notre divin maître . . . Noël!

**CHARLOTTE:** (*appelant désespérément.*) Werther! . . . Tout en fini! . . .

*Fin.*

Beneath their sacred shade
Bid my new grave be made.
Yet if God's priests, more stern than He,
Refuse a sinner soil so blest,
Till day shall break and shadows flee,
Beside some woodland path. I'll rest.
And though the church may scorn the dead,
Some fair sweet soul one tear may shed—
Then shall my tomb be hallowéd.

**CHARLOTTE:** Ah!
**(VOICES OF CHILDREN:)** Christmas! Jesus came this day
To lead us in the heavenly way. Christmas!

**CHARLOTTE:** Werther—All is ended!

*Curtain.*

# Thaïs (1894)

**Music by Jules Massenet ■ Libretto by Louis Gallet ■ Based on the novel by Anatole France**

First performed at the Paris Opéra on March 16, 1894, this three-act *comédie-lyrique*, is set to a libretto by Louis Gallet (based on Anatole France's novel). At the refuge of the Cenobites along the banks of the Nile, Athanaël bemoans the corruption of Alexandria's inhabitants which he blames on Thaïs, a beautiful courtesan. He sees her in a dream and decides to save her from her sins. Thaïs is expected as Nicia's guest that evening; Nicias invites Athanaël to join them. Thaïs tries to seduce him, but he angrily rejects her. Athanaël comes to see Thaïs. She is terrified of becoming an old woman, and he tries to convince her to give up the dissolute life she is leading. He almost succeeds in persuading her, but she changes her mind. Athanaël falls asleep on the stairs leading to her house. Now deeply moved by what he has said, she asks him how she may be saved. He urges her to go the convent. He offers to take her if she will agree to burn everything from to her previous life. She sets fire to her home and leaves, dressed in a simple woolen tunic. Athanaël entrusts Thaïs to the nuns at the convent and departs. Back at the Cenobite retreat, he is unable to forget her. Palémon, an elderly Cenobite, chides him, reminding him that he must resist temptation. Athanaël prays and falls asleep, and dreams that Thaïs is dying, surrounded by nuns. He goes to see her one last time, arriving at her bedside just before she dies. She thanks him for all he has done. He tells her of his love for her, but she doesn't understand what he is saying. She dies thinking of heavenly forgiveness.

## ■ ACTE PREMIER

### PREMIER TABLEAU

(*La Thébaïde.—Les cabanes des Cénobites aux bords du Nil. Ce n'est pas encore la fin du jour; douze Cénobites et le vieux Palémon sont assis autour d'une longue table. au milieu, Palémon préside le frugal et paisible repas. Une place est vide, celle d'Athanael*).

**UN CENOBITE:** Voici le pain.

**UN AUTRE:** Et le sel.

**UN AUTRE:** Et l'hysope.—

**UN AUTRE:** Voici le miel.

**UN AUTRE:** Et voici l'eau.—

**PALEMON:** (*se levant, avec onction*). Chaque matin le ciel répand sa grâce—sur mon jardin, ainsi qu'une rosée.—Bénissons Dieu dans les biens qu'il nous donne—et prions-le qu'il nous garde en sa paix!—

**LES CENOBITES:** (*presque murmuré*). Que les noirs démons de l'abîme—s'écartent de notre chemin!—
(*Paisiblement les Cénobites continuent leur repas*).

**UN CENOBITES:** (*rompant le silence*). Sur Athanael, notre frère,—étends, Seigneur, la force de ton bras!—

**PLUSIERS CENOBITES:** (*avec regret*). Athanaël! . . .

**D'AUTRES CENOBITES:** (*de même*). Bien longue est son absence!—

## ■ ACT I

### SCENE I

(*The Thebald. Huts of the Cenobites on the bank of the Nile. It is the declining day. Twelve Cenobites and old Palemon are seated at a long table. In their midst Palemon presides at the frugal and peaceful repast. One seat is empty, that of Athanael*).

**A CENOBITE:** Here is bread.

**ANOTHER:** And salt.

**ANOTHER:** And hyssop.

**ANOTHER:** Here is honey.

**ANOTHER:** And here is water.

**PALEMON:** (*rising with unction*). Each morning Heaven spreads its mercies—on my garden as a dew.—Let us thank God for the things that He gives us—and let us pray that He keep us in peace!—

**THE CENOBITES:** (*almost in a murmur*) That the black demons of the abyss—leave our path clear!—
(*Quietly, the Cenobites continue their repast*.)

**A CENOBITE:** (*breaking the silence*.) Upon Athanael, our brother—extend, oh Lord, the strength of your arm!—

**SEVERAL CENOBITES:** (*with regret*). Athanaël! . . .

**OTHERS:** (*same tone*). His absence is very long! . . . —

**D'AUTRES:** (*avec intérêt*). Quand donc reviendra-t-il? . . . —

**PALEMON:** (*mystérieusement*). L'heure de son retour est proche . . . —Un songe, cette nuit, me l'a montré vraiment—hâtant vers nous sa marche!—

**LES CENOBITES:** (*avec foi*). Athanaël est un élu de Dieu! . . . —
(*Pieusement.*) Il se révèle dans les songes! . . . —
(*Athanael paraît; il s'avance lentement comme épuisé de fatigue et de chagrin*).

**LES CENOBITES:** (*avec respect*). Le voici! Le voici!

**ATHANAEL:** (*au milieu d'eux, douloureusement*). La paix soit avec vous!—

**PALEMON ET LES CENOBITES:** Frère, salut! (*Tous s'empressent autour de lui.*) La fatigue t'accable!—la poussière couvre ton front . . . —repose-toi! . . . reprends ta place! . . . —mange, bois!—

**ATHANAEL:** (*il s'est assis avec accablement et repousse doucement les mets qu'on lui présente*). Non! mon coeur est plein d'amertume . . . —Je reviens dans le deuil et dans l'affliction! . . . —La ville est livrée au péché! . . . —une femme, Thaïs, la remplit de scandale—et par elle l'enfer y gouverne les hommes!—

**LES CENOBITES:** (*avec une curiosité calme et simple*). Quelle est cette Thaïs?

**OTHERS:** (*interested*). But when will he return?—

**PALEMON:** (*mysteriously*). The hour of his return is near . . . —A dream, this night, showed him truly to me—hastening his march toward us!—

**THE CENOBITES:** (*with faith*). Athanael is an elect of God! . . . (*Piously*) He reveals Himself in dreams! . . . —
(*Athanael appears; he advances slowly, as if exhausted with fatigue and sorrow*.)

**THE CENOBITES:** (*with respect*). He is here! he is here!

**ATHANAEL:** (*in their midst, painfully*). Peace be with you!—

**PALEMON AND THE CENOBITES:** Brother, salutation (*all gather about him*). Fatigue crushes you—dust stains thy forehead . . . — Rest . . . take your place once more!—eat, drink!—

**ATHANAEL:** (*he sits down, overcome with fatigue, gently declining the food they offer him*). No! my heart is full of bitterness . . . —I return in mourning and affliction . . . —The city is given over to sin! . . . —A woman, Thais, fills it with scandal—and, through her, hell there governs men!—

**THE CENOBITES:** (*with calm and simple curiosity*). Who is this Thais?

ATHANAEL: (*sortant un peu de sa torpeur*). Une prêtresse infâme—du culte de Vénus . . . (*Humblement, et comme se souvenant d'un passé lointain.*) Hélas! enfant encore—avant qu'à mon coeur la grâce ait parlé,—je l'ai connue! . . . (*Plus sombre, plus agité.*) Un jour, je l'avoue à ma honte,—devant son seuil maudit, je me suis arrêté . . . —mais Dieu m'a préservé de cette courtisane—et j'ai trouvé le calme en ce désert,—maudissant le péché que j'aurais pu commettre! . . . Ah! mon âme est troublée—La honte de Thaïs et le mal qu'elle fait—me causent une pein amère;—et je voudrais gagner cette âme à Dieu!—

PALEMON: (*simplement, sagement*). Ne nous mêlons jamais, mon fils, aux gens du siècle;—craignons les pièges de l'Esprit;—voilà ce que nous dit la sagesse éternelle.—(*La nuit vient peu à peu.*) La nuit vient; prions et dormons!—

LES CENOBITES: (*avec une crainte mystérieuse, les mains jointes, se séparent, tout en priant*). Que les noirs démons de l'abime—s'écartent de notre chemin!—Seigneur, bénis le pain et l'eau.—Bénis les fruits de nos jardins.—Donne-nous le sommeil sans rêves—et l'inaltérable repos!—
(*Athanael s'est étendu devant sa cabane, la tête appuyée sur un petit chevalet de bois, les mains jointes*).

ATHANAEL: (*seul, dans l'omber*). O Seigneur, je remets mon âme entre tes mains.—(*Il s'endort.*)
(*Nuit presque noire. Après un instant de calme, au milieu des ténèbres, une blancheur se fait; dans un brouillard apparaît l'intérieur de théâtre à Alexandrie; foule immense sur les gradins. En avant se trouve la scène sur laquelle Thaïs, à demi vêtue, mais le visage voilé, mime les amours d'Aphrodite.—Dans le théâtre d'Alexandrie, immenses acclamations d'enthousiasme très prolongées.—Effet extrêment lointain.—On peut distinguer, le nom de Thaïs hurlé par la foule.—Les acclamations augmentent jusqu'à la fin de la vision, la mimique s'accentuant de plus en plus.—La vision disparaît subitement; le jour revient.—Aurore*).

ATHANAEL: (*qui s'est éveillé peu à peu, se lève; avec épouvante et colère*). Honte! horreur! ténèbres éternelles!—Seigneur, assiste-moi!—(*Il s'est jeté à terre et il y reste proterné.*) Toi qui mis la pitié

ATHANAEL: (*recovering from his torpor*). An infamous priestess—of the worship of Venus (*humbly as if remembering the long gone past*). Alas, when still a child—before that to my heart grace had yet spoken,—I had known her!(*sombre and excited*). One day, I say it to my shame, I had stopped before her accursed doorstep . . . —but God had preserved me from this courtezan—and I found calm in this desert,—cursing the sin that I might have committed . . . —Ah my soul is troubled . . . —the shame of Thaïs and the harm that she has done—cause me bitter pain—and I would win this soul to God!—

PALEMON: (*simply, sagely*). Let us never meddle, my son, with the people of the time . . . let us fear the traps of—the Spirit;—this is what eternal wisdom tells us (*night begins to fall*). Night comes; let us pray and sleep.

THE CENOBITES: (*with a mysterious fear, hands clasped, separate while they pray*). May the black demons of the abyss—move from our way. Lord bless the bread and the water. Bless the fruits of our gardens—give us the sleep without dreams—and the unalterable rest—
(*Athanael has stretched himself before his hut, his head on a wooden pallet, his hands clasped.*)

ATHANAEL: (*alone in the shadow*). Oh, Lord, I place my soul in your hands—(*he sleeps*). (*Night is almost black. After a moment of calm in the midst of the darkness light is seen; in a mist appears the interior of the theatre at Alexandria. Immense crowd, in rows. In foreground the state on which Thaïs, half clothed, but, the face veiled, mimics the lovers of Aphrodite. In the theatre of Alexandria great, very prolonged, acclamations of enthusiasm. The effect is of great distance. The name of Thaïs, howled by the mob, can be distinguished. The acclamations increase to the end of the vision, the mimicry being more and more accentuated. The vision disappears; suddenly day begins. Dawn*).

ATHANAEL: (*who gradually awakes, rises. With fear and anger*). Shame! horror! eternal darkness!—Oh Lord, assist me—(*He throws himself prone and remains thus*). You who put pity in

dans nos âmes,—Dieu bon, louange à toi!—J'ai compris l'enseignement de l'ombre,—je me lève et je pars!—(*Il s'est relevé avec enthousiasme.*) Car je veux délivrer cette femme—des liens de la chair!—Dans l'azur, je vois penchés vers elle—les anges désolés!—N'est-elle pas, Seigneur, le souffle de ta bouche!—Ah! plus elle est coupable et plus je dois la plaindre!—Mais, je la sauverai, Seigneur! Donne-la-moi—et je te la rendrai pour la vie éternelle!—(*Il appelle ses frères qui reparaissent et se pressent autour de lui.*) Frères, levez-vous tous! venez!—ma mission m'est revélée!—Dans la ville maudite il faut que je retourne —Dieu défend que Thaïs s'enfonce davantage—dans le gouffre du mal!—et c'est moi qu'il choisit pour la lui ramener!—(*Athanael s'incline devant Palémon.*)

PALEMON: (*à Athanael avec une douce expression*). Ne nous mêlons jamais, mon fils, aux gens du siècle.—Voilà la sagesse éternelle! . . . —
(*Les Cénobites qui ont entouré Athanael l'accompagnent jusqu'à la route, puis, s'agenouillant par groupes, ils répondent à Athanael dout la voix se perd dans les solitudes du desert*).

LA VOIX D'ATHANAEL: (*déjà éloignée*). Esprit de lumière et de grâce,—arme mon coeur pour le combat.—

LES CENOBITES: (*à genoux*). Arme son coeur pour le combat.—

LA VOIX D'ATHANAEL: (*encore plus éloignée*). Et fais-moi fort comme l'archange—contre les charmes du démon.

LES CENOBITES: (*comme un murmure*). Et fais-le fort comme l'archange—contre les charmes du démon!—
(*Le rideau s'abaisse lentement*).

## DEUXIEME TABLEAU

(*La terrasse de la maison de Nicias à Alexandrie.—Cette terrasse domine la ville et la mer; elle est ombragée de grands arbes; à droite, vaste tenture derrière laquelle se trouve la salle préparée pour le banquet*).

(*Lentement, Athanael paraît et s'arrête au fond; à sa vue, un serviteur se léve sous le portique, et marche à sa rencontre*).

LE SERVITEUR: Va, mendiant, chercher ailleurs ta vie!—Mon maître ne recoit pas les chiens comme toi!—

our souls.—Good God, praise!—I have understood the teaching of the darkness—I rise and go. (*He has risen with enthusiasm*). For I will deliver this woman—from the thraldom of the flesh. In cerulean heights I see leaning toward her—the angels sorrow stricken—Is she not, Lord, the breath of your mouth—Ah the more guilty she the more I compassionate her!—But I will save her, Lord! Give her to me—and I shall give her back to you for life eternal!—(*He calls his brothers who reappear and press about him*). Brothers, rise all of you! come—My mission is revealed to me—I must return to the accursed city . . . —God forbids that Thaïs should sink deeper—in the pit of wickedness! and I am the one He chooses to bring her back! (*Athanael bows before Palemon.*)

PALEMON: (*to Athanael, with a gentle expression*). Let us never meddle, my son, with the people of this time—That is the eternal wisdom.—
(*The Cenobites who have surrounded Athanael, accompany him to the road, then kneeling by groups, they respond to him as his voice is lost in the solitude of the desert.*)

THE VOICE OF ATHANAEL: (*far away*). Spirit of light and grace—strengthen my arm for the combat—

THE CENOBITES: (*on their knees*). Arm his spirit for the combat.

THE VOICE OF ATHANAEL: (*still further*). And make me stronger than the archangel—against the charms of the demon.

THE CENOBITES: (*like a murmur*). And make him stronger than the archangel—against the charms of the demon!—
(*The curtain falls slowly*).

## SCENE II

(*The terrace of the house of Nicias at Alexandria. The terrace dominates the town and sea. Shaded with great trees. At right, vast drapery, behind which is the banqueting room.*)

(*Slowly Athanael appears and stops at rear. Seeing him, a servant rises under the portico and comes to meet him.*)

THE SERVANT: Go, beggar, get your living elsewhere—My master does not receive dogs like you!—

ATHANAEL: (*doucement*). Mon fils, fais, s'il te plaît, ce que je te commande.—Je suis l'ami de ton maître, et je veux—lui parler à l'instant.

LE SERVITEUR: Hors d'ici, mendiant!—(*Il lève sur Athanael son bâton.*)

ATHANAEL: (*fermement et avec calme*). Frappe, si tu le veux, mais avertis ton maître.—Va. (*Se serviteur recule, s'incline et disparaît*).

ATHANAEL: (*seul, après avoir un instant contemplé la ville*). Voilà donc la terrible cité!—Alexandrie, où je suis né dans le péché,—l'air brillant où j'ai respiré—l'affreux parfum de la luxure!—Voilà la mer voluptueuse—où j'écoutais chanter la sirène aux yeux d'or!—Oui, voilà mon berceau selon la chair,—Alexandrie!—Mon berceau, ma patrie! . . . —De ton amour j'ai détourné mon coeur! . . . —pour ta richesse je te hais!—pour ta science et ta beauté—Je te hais! je te hais!—Et maintenant je te maudis—comme un temple hanté par les esprits impurs!—Anges du ciel, souffles de Dieu,—venez! parfumez du battement de vos ailes—l'air corrompu qui va m'environner!—
(*On entend des voix et des rires.—Presque aussitôt, Nicias paraît à s'avance, les bras appuyés sur les épaules de Crobyle et de Myrtale, deux belles esclaves rieuses. A la vue D'Athanael, il s'arrête, les quitte et s'approche les bras ouverts*).

NICIAS: (*avec vivacité*). Athanaël, c'est toi! mon condisciple,—mon ami, mon frère! oh! va! je te reconanis,—bien qu'à la vérité—tu sois bien plus semblable à la bête qu'à l'homme!—Embrasse-moi donc; sois le bienvenu.—Tu quittes le désert?—tu nous reviens?

ATHANAEL: O Nicias!—je ne reviens que pour un jour, que pour une heure!—

NICIAS: Dis-moi tes voeux!—

ATHANAEL: Nicias, tu connais cette comédienne,—Thaïs, la courtisane?—

NICIAS: (*riant*). Certes, je la connais! pour mieux dire, elle est mienne—encore pour un jour!—J'ai vendu pour elle mes vignes—et ma dernière terre et mon dernier moulin,—et composé trois livres d'élégies;—et cela ne compte pour rien!—Je voudrais la fixer que je pedrais ma peine.—son amour est léger et fuyant comme un rêve! Athanaël, qu'attends-tu d'elle?—

ATHANAEL: Je veux la remener à Dieu!

ATHANAEL: (*gently*). My son, do, if you please what I command you.—I am the friend of your master and I must—speak to him at once.

THE SERVANT: Out of here, beggar. (*He is about to strike Athanael with his stick.*)

ATHANAEL: (*firm and calmly*). Strike if you will but tell your master.—Go. (*The servant steps back, bows and disappears.*)

ATHANAEL: (*after having contemplated the city.*) There is the terrible city!—Alexandria, where I was born in sin;—the brilliant air where I breathed—the perfume of luxury—There is the voluptuous sea—where I listened to the siren of the golden eyes!—Yes, there is my cradle according to the flesh,—Alexandria! My cradle, my country!—I turn my love away from you!—for your riches I hate you—for your science and your beauty—I hate you! I hate you!—and now that I curse you—as a temple haunted by impure spirits!—Angels of heaven breath of God,—come perfume with the whirring of your wings—the corrupt air that is about to surround me.
(*Voices and laughter are heard.—Soon after Nicias appears and advances, leaning on the shoulders of Crobyle and Myrtale, two beautiful, smiling slaves. At the sight of Athanael, he stops, quits them and approaches with open arms.*)

NICIAS: (*with vivacity*). Athanael, it's you! my co-disciple—my friend, my brother oh, I know you—though in sober truth—you're much more like a beast than a man—Embrace me, you're welcome—you would quit the desert? You will come back to us?

ATHANAEL: Oh Nicias!—I return just for a day, just for an hour.

NICIAS: Tell me your wishes!

ATHANAEL: Nicias, you know this comedienne,—Thais, the courtezan?—

NICIAS: (*laughing*). Of course, I know her! to say more, she is mine—for yet a day!—I have sold, for her, my vines—and my last estate and my last mill,—and composed three books of elegies;—and that counts for nothing! I would retain her that I'd lose my pains:—her love is light and fitful as a dream! Athanael, what would you do with her?

ATHANAEL: I would lead her back to God.

NICIAS: (*éclatant de rire*). Mon pauvre ami!—crains d'offenser Vénus dont elle est la prêtresse.—

ATHANAEL: (*avec plus de force*). Je veux la ramener à Dieu! Va, Nicias,—j'arracheria Thaïs à ces amours immondes—et je la donnerai pour épouse à Jésus.—Pour entrer dans un monastère—Thaïs va me suivre aujourd'hui!—

NICIAS: (*à l'oreille d'Athanael et en riant*). Crains d'offenser Vénus, la puissante déesse!—Elle se vengera!

ATHANAEL: Dieu me protégera.—(*Après un temps.*) Où puis-je voir cette femme?

NICIAS: Ici même!—Pour la dernière fois—elle y doit souper avec moi—en très joyeuse compagnie!—Elle joue aujourd'hui;—en sortant du théâtre, elle viendra.—

ATHANAEL: Prête-moi donc, ami, quelque robe d'Asie—afin que dignement je puisse figurer-à ce festin que tu vas lui donner.—

NICIAS: Crobyle et Myrtale, mes chères,—hâtez-vous de parer mon bn Athanaël.—
(*Tandis que Nicias et Athanael se sont assis et s'entretiennent amicalement, Myrtale a frappé dans ses mains; le serviteur a paru auquel elle donne un ordre. Il sort et revient aussitôt avec des esclaves portant un coffret dont Crobyle et Myrtale tirent les objets qui doivent servir à la toilette D'Athanael, ainsi qu'un miroir de métal.*
(*Puis, elles commencent à lui verser sur la tête des parfums, à lui accomoder les chevuex et la barbe. Nicias souriant, les regarde faire*).

NICIAS: Je vais donc te revoir brillant comme autrefois!—

ATHANAEL: Oui, j'emprunte à l'Enfer des armes contre lui.—

NICIAS: Philosphe orgueilleux, lâme humaine est fragile.—

ATHANAEL: Je ne crains pas l'orguel quand le Ciel me conduit.—

CROBYLE: (*à Myrtale, à part*). Il est jeune!

MYRTALE: (*à Crobyle, même jeu*). Il est beau!

CROBYLE: Sa barbe est un peu rude!

MYRTALE: —Ses yeux sont pleins de feu!

CROBYLE: Ce bandeau lui sied bien!—

MYRTALE ET CROBYLE: Cher Satrape, voici tes bracelets!

MYRTALE: Tes bagues!—

CROBYLE: Donne tes bras!

NICIAS: (*bursting out laughing*). My poor friend—fear to offend Venus of whom she is the priestess.—

ATHANAEL: (*with more force*). I would bring her back to God! there, Nicias—I shall tear Thais from these filthy amours—and shall give her for spouse to Jesus—To enter a monastery—Thais will follow me today!—

NICIAS: (*at the ear of Athanael, laughing*). Fear offense to Venus the powerful goddess!—She will avenge herself.

ATHANAEL: God will protect me (*after a lapse*). Where can I see this woman?

NICIAS: Here!—For the last time—she is to sup with me—in very joyous company.—She plays today—on leaving the theatre, she will come.—

ATHANAEL: Lend me then, friend, some robe of Asia—that I may assume decent appearance—at this festivity that you will give her.—

NICIAS: Crobyle and Myrtale, my dears,—hasten to embellish my good Athanael.—
(*While Nicias and Athanael have seated themselves and amicably entertain one another, Myrtale has clapped her hands. Servant appears to whom she gives an order. He exits and returns with slaves carrying a coffer, from which Crobyle and Myrtale draw out things that will serve for the toilet of Athanael, as well as a mirror of metal. Then they begin to pour perfumes over his head and to arrange his hair and beard. Nicias, smiling, looks on*).

NICIAS: I am then to see you again brilliant as of yore!—

ATHANAEL: Yes, I borrow from Hell arms against itself.—

NICIAS: Proud philosopher, the human soul is fragile.—

ATHANAEL: I fear not pride when Heaven leads me.—

CROBYLE: (*to Myrtale, aside*). He is young!

MYRTALE: (*to Crobyle, aside*). He is handsome!

CROBYLE: His beard is a trifle rude!

MYRTALE: —His eyes are full of fire.

CROBYLE: This band becomes him well—

MYRTALE AND CROBYLE: Dear Satrap, here are your bracelets.

MYRTALE: Your rings.—

CROBYLE: Lend your arms.

MYRTALE: Tes doigts!

MYRTALE ET CROBYLE: (à part). Il est jeune, il est beau!—Ses yeux sont pleins de feu!—

MYRTALE: (continuant la toilette). La robe, maintenant!

CROBYLE: (avec câlinerie). Quitte ce noir cilice!—

ATHANAEL: (se levant comme pour leur échapper). Ah! femmes, pour cela, jamais!—

CROBYLE ET MYRTALE: (d'abord effarouchées par le brusque refus reviennent auprès de lui). Soit! (Lui passant une robe brodée par-dessus sa tunique.) Cache tes rigueurs sous cette robe souple!—

NICIAS À ATHANAEL: Ne t'offense pas de leur raillerie,—ne baisse pas devant elles les yeux!—admire-les plutôt!

ATHANAEL: (à lui-même). Viens, esprit de lumière!—arme mon cœur pour le combat!—contre ies charmes du démon!—

CROBYLE ET MYRTALE: (à part). Il est beau comme un jeune dieu!—Si Phoebé le rencontrait,—sa divinité farouche—s'humaniserait!—(Continuant la toilette).

MYRTALE: (à Athanael). Laisse-nous te chausser de ces sandales d'or!—

CROBYLE: Laisse-nous te verser ce parfum sur les joues.—

CROBYLE ET MYRTALE: (à part). Il est beau comme un jeune dieu!—(Grandes acclamations lointaines et prolongées). (Au bruit des acclamations, Nicias est remonté vers la terrasse, et il a regardé du côté de la ville).

NICIAS: (revenant vers Athanael, en souriant). Garde-toi bien! Voici ta terrible ennemie!—(Des groupes d'histrions et de comédiennes mêlés à des philosophes amis de Nicias paraissent sur la terrasse, précédant la venue de Thaïs).

HISTRIONS, COMEDIENNES, PHILOSOPHES: (entourant Thaïs et s'inclinant devant elle). Thaïs! soeur des Karites!—Rose d'Alexandrie!—Belle silencieuse!—Thaïs! tant désiree!—Thaïs!—Thaïs! Thaïs!—

NICIAS: (accueillant ses hôtes et leur désignant la salle du banquet dont les esclaves soulèvant les tentures.) Thaïs! Chère Thaïs!—Hermodore! Aristobule!—Callicrate! Dorion!—mes hôtes! mes amis! les dieux soient avec vous!—(Tous se rendent dans la salle. Thaïs a été retenue doucement par Nicias au moment où elle se

MYRTALE: Your fingers.

MYRTALE AND CROBYLE: (aside). He is young and handsome!—His eyes are full of fire!—

MYRTALE: (continuing the toilet) Now, the robe.

CROBYLE: (playfully). Give up this black cowl!—

ATHANAEL: (rising so as to escape them). As for that, women, never!—

CROBYLE AND MYRTALE: (at first frightened by the savage refusal, come toward him again). Very well (passing an embroidered robe over his tunic). Hide your rigors under this yielding stuff.—

NICIAS: (to Athanael). Take no offense at their raillery. Do not lower your eyes before them—rather admire them.

ATHANAEL: (to himself). Come, spirit of light—strengthen my arm for the combat against the charms of the demon.—

CROBYLE AND MYRTALE: (aside). He is handsome as a young god—If Phoebe should encounter him—her fierce divinity—would be humanized. (Continuing the toilet).

MYRTALE: (to Athanael). Let us invest you with these sandals of gold—

CROBYLE: Let us pour this perfume on your cheeks. —

CROBYLE AND MYRTALE: (aside). He is handsome as a young god.—(Great acclamations far off and prolonged. At the sound, Nicias mounts the terrace and looks in direction of the town).

NICIAS: (returning to Athanael, smiling). Guard yourself well! Here is your terrible enemy!—(Groups of histrions and comediennes, intermingled with philosophers, friends of Nicias, precede the coming of Thaïs).

HISTRIONS, COMEDIENNES PHILOS: (surrounding Thaïs and bowing before her). Thaïs! sister of the Karites—Rose of Alexandria—Oh silent Beauty—Thaïs all desired!—Thaïs! Thaïs! Thaïs!

NICIAS: (receiving his guests and designating the banquet hall, of which slaves lift the draperies). Thaïs, dear Thaïs,—Hermodore! Aristobule—Callicrate—Dorian!—My guests, my friends; the gods be with you!—(All go to banquet room. Thaïs has been gently detained by Nicias at the moment when she was

disposait à suivre ses amis. Nicias tombe assis; Thaïs est près de lui; celle-ci reste debout).

THAÏS: C'est Thaïs, l'idole fragile—qui vient pour la dernière fois—s'asseoir à ta table fleurie . . . —Demain, je ne serai pour toi plus rien qu'un nom! . . . —

NICIAS: Nous nous somes aimés une longue semaine . . . —C'est beaucoup de constance, et je ne me plains pas . . . —et tu vas t'en ailer, libre, loin de mes bras . . . —

THAÏS: Pour ce soir, sois joyeux.—Laissons s'épanouir les heurs bienheureuses,—et ne demandons rien plus rien à cette nuit—qu'un peu de folle ivresse et de divin oubli.—Demain . . . je ne serai pour toi plus rien qu'un nom . . . —(Quelques philosophes, parmi lesquels se trouve Athanael, sortent de la salle tout en discutant gravement.—Athanael s'est détaché du groupe: il demeure immobile dans une attitude sévère, en regardant Thaïs).

THAÏS: (à Nicias). Quel est cet étranger dont le regard farouche—s'attache ainsi sur moi?—Je ne l'ai jamais vu paraître en nos festins . . . —d'où vient-il? quel est-il?—

NICIAS: (asez bas et négligemment). Un philosophe à l'âme rude!—un solitaire du désert!—Il est ici pour toi; prends garde!—

THAÏS: Qu'apporte-ti-il? L'amour?

NICIAS: Nulle faiblesse humaine—ne saurait amollir son cœur.—Il veut te convertir à sa sainte doctrine.—

THAÏS: Qu'enseigne-t-il?

ATHANAEL: (s'avancant). Le mépris de la chair,—l'amour de la douleur,—l'austère pénitence!—

THAÏS: (après l'avoir regardé longuement). Va; passe ton chemin! je ne crois qu'à l'amour—et nulle autre puissance—ne pourrait rien sur moi!—

ATHANAEL: (va vers elle et dit avec éclat). Ah! ne blasphème pas! (Les philosophes cessent leur entretien et descendent. Tous les invités, ont quitté la salle du banquet, et, se joignent, à Thaïs et à Nicias).

THAÏS: (à Athanael, avec une sorte de câlinerie ironique). Qui te fait si sévère—et pour-quoi démens-tu la flamme de tes yeux?—Quelle triste folie—te fait manquer à ton destin?—Homme fait pour aimer, quelle erreur est la tienne!—Homme fait pour savoir, qui t'aveugle à ce point!—Tu n'as pas effleuré la coupe de la vie!—Tu

about to follow his friends. Nicias falls on a seat. Thaïs, near him, remains standing).

THAÏS: It's Thaïs, the fragile idol—who comes for the last time—to sit at your enflowered table . . . —Tomorrow, I shall be nothing for you but a name!—

NICIAS: We have loved each other one whole, long week—It is great constancy and I do not complain . . . —you are about to go, free, far from my arms . . . —

THAÏS: For tonight, be joyful.—Let the happy hours fade away—and let us ask nothing, nothing more from this night—than a little mad bliss and divine forgetfulness.—Tomorrow—I shall be no more to you than a name.—(A few philosophers, among them Athanael, leave the banquet room gravely arguing. Athanael detaches himself from the group. He stands still, severely looking at Thaïs).

THAÏS: (to Nicias). What is this stranger, the fierce eyes of whom—look on me thus—I have not seen him at our feasts—Whence comes he? Who is he?

NICIAS: (low and negligently). A philosopher of rude soul—a solitary of the desert.—He comes here for you; take care!—

THAÏS: What does he bring? Love?

NICIAS: No human weakness—could soften his heart.—He would convert you to his sacred doctrine.

THAÏS: What teaches he?

ATHANAEL: (advancing). Contempt of the flesh—love of pain—austere penance.—

THAÏS: (gazing at him long). Go, pass on your way. I believe but in love—and no other power—can swerve me from it!—

ATHANAEL: (going toward her, exclaiming). Ah! blaspheme not. (The philosophers cease their talk and come down. All the guests have left the banquet room and joined Thaïs and Nicias).

THAÏS: (to Athanael, with ironic playfulness). Who makes you so severe—and why forswear the flame of your eyes? What sorrowful folly—makes you fail in your destiny—Man made for love, what error is yours—Man made for knowledge, who blinds you to this extent?—You have not tasted of the cup of life—you have not spelled

n'as épelé l'amoureuse sagesse!—Assieds-toi près de nous, couronne-toi de roses,—rien n'est vrai que d'aimer, tends les bras à l'amour!—

**NICIAS ET LA FOULE:** Assieds-toi près de nous, couronne-toi de roses,—rien n'est vrai que d'aimer, tends les bras à l'amour!—

**ATHANAEL:** (*ardemment*). Non! je hais vos fausse ivresses!—Non! ici, je me tais, mais j'irai, pécheresse,—j'irai dans ton palais te porter le salut—et je vaincrai l'Enfer en triomphant de toi!—

**THAÏS, NICIAS, LA FOULE:** Couronne-toi de roses!—rien n'est vrai que d'aimer, tends les bras à l'amour!—

**ATHANAEL:** (*se dispose à s'éloigner; il dit avec autorité*). J'irai dans ton palais te porter le salut!—

**NICIAS, LA FOULE:** Ose venir, toi qui braves Vénus!—

**THAÏS:** (*se disposant à reproduire la scène des amours d'Aphrodite à Athanael, avec provocation*). Ose venir, toi qui braves Vénus!! . . . —
(*Des esclaves s'apprêtent à détacher les vêtements de Thaïs.—Athanael a fui avec un geste d'horreur*).

## ■ ACTE DEUXIEME

### PREMIER TABLEAU

(*Chez Thaïs.—Une figure de Vénus est au premier plan.—Il y a, devant la stèle, un brûle-parfums. Le sol est couvert de tapis de Byzance, d'oreillers brodés et de peaux de lions lybiques. Grands vases d'onyx d'où s'élancent des perséas en fleurs*).

(*Thaïs paraît, accompagnée de quelques histrions et d'un petit groupe de comédiennes.—Bientôt elle les éloigne tous d'un geste*).

**THAÏS:** (*seule, avec lassitude et amertume*). Ah! je suis fatiguée à mourir! . . . Tous ces hommes—ne sont qu'indifférence et que brutalité.—Les femmes sont méchantes; et les heures pesantes!—J'ai l'âme vide . . . Où trouver le repos? . . . —Et comment fixer le bonheur!—(*Rêveuse, elle prend un miroir*.) O mon miroir fidèle,—rassure-moi; dis-moi que je suis toujours belle,—que je serai belle éternellement;—que rien ne flétrira les roses de mes lèvres,—que rien ne ternira l'or pur de mes cheveux;—dis-moi que je suis belle et que je serai belle—éternellement! éternellement!—

amorous wisdom?—Sit by us, we'll crown you with roses—nothing is true but loving, spread out your arms to love!—

**NICIAS AND THE CROWD:** Sit near us, we'll crown you with roses—nothing is true but loving, extend your arms to love.

**ATHANAEL:** (*ardently*). No. I loathe your false intoxication—No, here I am silent, fair sinner, but I shall go—I shall go to thy palace and carry salvation—and I shall vanquish Hell in triumphing over thee!—

**THAÏS, NICIAS, THE CROWD:** We'll crown you with roses—nothing is true but loving—spread out your arms to love.

**ATHANAEL:** (*about to go; be says with authority*). I shall go in your palace and bring you salvation.

**NICIAS AND THE CROWD:** Dare it, you who braves Venus!—

**THAÏS:** (*disposing herself to reproduce scene of loves of Aphrodite, to Athanael with provocation*.) Dare to come, you who braves Venus! . . .
(*Slaves prepare to detach the robe of Thaïs. Athanael escapes with a gesture of horror*).

## ■ ACT II

### SCENE I

(*At the house of Thaïs. A figure of Venus is in the foreground. Before it a censer. The floor is covered with rugs of Byzantium, embroidered pillows and lion skins. Onyx vases full of flowers*).

(*Thaïs appears, accompanied by some actors and a group of comediennes. Soon she dismisses them with a gesture*).

**THAÏS:** (*alone, with lassitude, bitterly*). Ah, I am tired to death . . . All these men—are but indifference and but brutality.—The women are wicked—and the hours heavy!—My soul is empty . . . where find peace?—And how assure happiness (*dreamily, she takes a mirror*). Oh, my faithful mirror—reassure me; tell me that I am always beautiful—that I shall be beautiful eternally;—that nothing shall tarnish the roses of my lips,—that nothing shall dull the pure gold of my hair;—tell me that I am beautiful and that I shall be beautiful—eternally, eternally!—(*Listening as if a voice spoke*

(*prêtant l'oreille, comme si une voix lui parlait dans l'ombre*.) Ah! tais-toi, voix impitoyable,—voix qui me dis: Thaïs, tu vieilliras!—Un jour, ainsi, Thaïs ne serait plus Thaïs! . . . —Non! non! je n'y puis croire;—et s'il n'est point pour garder la beauté—de secrets souverains, de pratiques magiques,—toi, Vénus, réponds-moi de son éternité!—(*S'adressant à l'image de Vénus, avec dévotion*.) Vénus, invisible et présente! . . . —Vénus, enchantement de l'ombre!—réponds-moi! . . . —Dis-moi que je suis belle et que je serai belle—éternellement!—que rien ne flétrira les roses de mes lèvres,—que rien ne ternira l'or pur de mes cheveux;—dis-moi que je suis belle et que je serai belle—éternellement!—éternellement!—éternellement!—
(*Elle apercoit Athanael qui est entré silencieusement et s'est arrêté sur le seuil*).

**THAÏS:** (*avec charme*). Etranger, te voilà comme tu l'avais dit . . . !—

**ATHANAEL:** (*murmurant une prière*). Seigneur, fais que son radieux visage—soit comme voilé devant moi!—fais que la force de ses charmes—ne triomphe pas de ma volonté!—

**THAÏS:** (*avec un sourire*). Allons parle, à présent!—

**ATHANAEL:** On dit qu'aucune femme ne t'égale!—Et c'est pourquoi j'ai voulu te connaître,—et c'est pourquoi, te voyant, j'ai compris—combien il me serait glorieux de te vaincre!—

**THAÏS:** Tes hommages sont hauts; ton orgueil les dépasse—Présomptueux, prends garde de m'aimer!—

**ATHANAEL:** (*avec chaleur*). Ah! je t'aime, Thaïs, et j'aime à te le dire,—mais je t'aime, non comme tu l'entends!—moi, je t'aime en esprit, je t'aime en vérité,—je te promets mieux qu'une ivresse fleurie—et songes d'une brève nuit;—cette félicité qu'aujourd'hui je t'apporte—ne finira jamais! . . .

**THAÏS:** Montre-moi donc ce merveilleux amour!—Un amour vrai n'a qu'un language: les baisers.—

**ATHANAEL:** Thaïs, ne raille pas! L'amour que je te prêche—c'est l'amour inconnu!

**THAÏS:** (*légèrement*). Ami, tu viens bien tard;—je connais les ivresses.—

**ATHANAEL:** L'amour que tu connais n'enfante que la honte.—Celui que je t'apporte est le seul glorieux!—

in the shadows). Oh, be quiet, unpitying voice—voice that to me says: 'Thaïs, you will grow old!'—Some day then, Thaïs would no longer be Thaïs!— No! No! I cannot believe it;—and if there are not, to safeguard beauty,—sovereign secrets and magic practices,—Venus, answer me for its eternity—(*addressing the image of Venus, with devotion*). Venus invisible and ever present! Venus enchantment of the gloom—answer me!—Tell me that I am beautiful and that I shall be beautiful—eternally—that nothing shall tarnish the roses of my lips,—that nothing shall dull the pure gold of my hair;—tell me that I am beautiful and that I shall be beautiful—eternally—eternally—eternally!—
(*She perceives Athanael, who has entered silently and who remains at the door*).

**THAÏS:** (*with charm*). Stranger, you're here as you said you'd be.

**ATHANAEL:** (*murmuring a prayer*). Lord, have it that her radiant visage—be as veiled before me—make it that the strength of her charms—do not triumph over my will!—

**THAÏS:** (*smiling*). Come speak at once.—

**ATHANAEL:** It is said that no woman equals you!—It is for this I wished to know you—and why, seeing you, I understood—how glorious it would be to vanquish you—

**THAÏS:** Your homage is great; Your pride greater.—Presumptuous, beware in case you might love me.—

**ATHANAEL:** (*hotly*). Ah, I love you, Thais, and I like to tell you so—but I love you not as you understand!—for me, I love you in spirit, I love you in truth—I promise you better than flowery bliss—and dreams of a brief night—this felicity that I bring you today—will never end!—

**THAÏS:** Show me then this marvelous love!—A true love has but one language; Kisses.—

**ATHANAEL:** Thaïs, rail not! The love that I preach to you is the unknown love—

**THAÏS:** Friend, you come very late. I know every bliss.—

**ATHANAEL:** The love that you know begets only shame—That which I bring you is the only glorious love!—

**THAÏS:** Je te trouve hardi d'offenser ton hôtesse.—

**THAÏS:** I find you bold to offend your hostess.

**ATHANAEL:** T'offenser! . . . je ne songe—qu'à te conquérir à la vérité!—(*Avec un enthousiasme croissant.*) Ah! qui m'inspirera des discours embrasés—pour qu'à mon souffle, ô courtisane—ton coeur fonde comme une cire!— Qui pourra te livrer à moi—et qui changera ma parole—en un Jourdain dont les flots répandus— Prépareront ton âme à la vie éternelle.—

**ATHANAEL:** Offend you! I would not dream—but to make you yield to truth (*With increasing enthusiasm.*) Ah! who will inspire me with words of fire—so that at my breath, oh courtezan—your heart melts like wax!—Who is able to deliver you to me—and who will change my words—to a Jordan the widening waves of which shall prepare your soul for the life everlasting.—

**THAÏS:** (*le regarde avec un vague sentiment de crainte*). A la vie éternelle! . . .

**THAÏS:** (*looking at him with a vague sentiment of fear*). For the life everlasting!—

**ATHANAEL:** A la vie éternelle! . . .

**ATHANAEL:** For the life everlasting!

**THAÏS:** (*prenant une résolution, mais d'abord tout en tremblant*). Eh bien, fais-moi connaître—tout cet amour mystérieux,—je t'obéis . . . je suis à toi! . . . (*Thaïs, avec une spatule d'or, puise dans une coupe quelques grains d'encens qu'elle jette dans le brûle-parfums.*)

**THAÏS:** Well, then, let me know— all this mysterious love,—I obey you . . . I am yours! . . . (*Thaïs, with a spatula of gold, takes from a cup a few grains of incense which she throws in the censer*).

**ATHANAEL:** (*à part, avec fièvre*). vn tumulte effrayant s'élève en ma pensée! . . .—Seigneur, fais que son radieux visage—soit comme voilé devant moi! . . .— (*Une fumée légère enveloppe Thaïs en même temps que la Déesse, et elle murmure une sorte d'incantation mystérieuse*).

**ATHANAEL:** (*aside, feverishly*). A frightful tumult arises in my mind . . .—Lord, have it so that her radiant visage—be as veiled before me!— (*A light mist envelopes Thaïs as well as the goddess and she murmurs a sort of mysterious incantation*).

**THAÏS:** Vénus, invisible et présente!—Vénus, enchantement de l'ombre!—

**THAÏS:** Venus, invisible and here present—Venus, enchantment of the darkness.

**ATHANAEL:** (*à part, priant avec ardeur*). Fais que la force de ses charmes—ne triomphe pas de ma volonté.—

**ATHANAEL:** (*aside, praying with ardor*). Make it so that the force of her charms—shall not triumph over my will.

**THAÏS:** Vénus, éclat du ciel et blancheur de la neige!—Splendeur, Volupté, Douceur! . . .

**THAÏS:** Venus, descend and reign!—Venus, flash from heaven and white as snow—Splendor, Voluptuousness, Gentleness!

**ATHANAEL:** (*Déchire, arrache sa robe d'emprunt sous laquelle il a gardé son cilice*). Je suis Athanaël, moine d'Antinoé!—Je viens du saint désert et je maudis la chair— et me voici devant toi, femme— comme devant un tombeau;—et je te dis: Thaïs, lève-toi, lève-toi!—

**ATHANAEL:** (*tearing away his borrowed robe, under which he has kept his cowl*). I am Athanaël, monk of Antinous! I come from the sacred desert and I curse the flesh—and I curse the death that possesses you—and I am here before you, woman—as before a tomb; and I say to you: Thaïs, arise, arise!

**THAÏS:** (*pâle d'épouvante, pleurant et gémissant, se jette aux pieds d'Athanaël*). Ne me fais pas de mal. Parle, que me veux-tu?—Je sais que les saints du désert détestent celles qui s'asservissent aux hommes!—pourtant ne me méprise pas;—je n'ai pas plus choisi mon sort que ma nature;—et ce n'est pas ma faute enfin si je suis belle! . . .—Ne me fais pas mourir! Ah! je crains tant la mort!—

**THAÏS:** (*pale with fear, weeping, groaning, throws herself at the feet of Athanael*). Do not harm me. Speak! what would you?—I know that the saints of the desert—detest those who lend themselves to men!—Yet, do not despise me; I no more chose my lot than my nature;—and it is, after all, not my fault if I am beautiful!—Do not make me die—Ah! I so fear death.—

**ATHANAEL:** (*avec enthousiasme*). Non, tu vivras de la vie éternelle;—sois à jamais la bien-aimée—et l'épouse du Christ dont tu fus l'ennemie.—

**ATHANAEL:** (*with enthusiasm*) No, you shall live of the life everlasting—be forever the well beloved—and the spouse of the Christ of whom you were the enemy.—

**THAÏS:** (*avec ardeur et joie*). Je sens une fraîcheur en mon âme ravie—Je frissonne et demeure charmée! . . .—Quel pouvoir est le sien?

**THAÏS:** (*with ardor and joy*). I feel a freshness in my ravished soul!—I shiver and remain as one charmed!—What would you do?

**LA VOIX DE NICIAS:** (*au loin et se rapproche graduellement*). O Thaïs, idole fragile,—je veux une dernière fois—l'amour de ta lèvre fleurie! . . .—

**THE VOICE OF NICIAS:** (*in the distance, gradually approaching*). Oh, Thaïs, fragile idol—I want for one last time—the love of your fragrant lip!—

**THAÏS:** (*écoutant avec un sentiment de répulsion*). Ah! Nicias! . . . encor! . . . (*Avec agitation.*) Mon âme n'est plus mienne.—M'aimer! . . . (*Avec dédain.*) Il n'a jamais aimé personne . . .—il n'aime que l'amour! . . .

**THAÏS:** (*listening, with a sentiment of repulsion*). Ah, Nicias! again—(*agitated*) My soul is no more mine.—Love me! (*with disdain*). He has never loved anyone.—He loves only love! . . .

**ATHANAEL:** Tu l'entends?

**ATHANAEL:** Do you hear?

**THAÏS:** (*avec énergie*). Eh bien, va!—Dis-lui que je déteste—tous les riches, tous les heureux! . . .—qu'il m'oublie, entends-tu! Dis-lui que je le hais! . . .—

**THAÏS:** (*with energy*). Well then, go—Tell him that I detest—all rich men, all happy ones!—That he must forget me! Tell him that I hate him!—

**ATHANAEL:** (*avec autorité*). A ton seuil, jusqu'au jour, j'attendrai ta venue! . . .—

**ATHANAEL:** (*with authority*). On your doorstep until dawn, I shall await your coming!—

**THAÏS:** (*avec un dernier mouvement de révolte*). Non! . . . je reste Thaïs, Thaïs la courtisane.—Je ne crois plus à rien et je ne veux plus rien.—Ni lui, ni toi, ni ton Dieu! (*Elle est prise d'un rire nerveux, qui s'achève en des sanglots, et se jette le visage dans ses coussins, tandis que lui s'éloigne*). (*Les rideaux se ferment lentement*).

**THAÏS:** (*with a last movement of revolt*). No! I remain Thaïs, Thaïs the courtezan—I believe in nothing more and I want nothing more.—Not him, not you, not your God! (*She laughs nervously, which ends in sobs and throws herself face down on the pillows, while he departs. The curtains come together slowly*).

*MEDITATION RELIGIEUSE.—SYMPHONIE.*

*RELIGIOUS MEDITATION.—SYMPHONY.*

## DEUXIEME TABLEAU

## SCENE II

(*Avant le jour.—Sur une place, devant la maison de Thaïs.—Sous le portique, une petite statuette d'Eros; devant l'image, une lampe allumée.—Au bas des degrés du portique dort Athanaël.—Au fond, à droite, une maison dans laquelle sont réunis Nicias et ses amis; les baies sont éclairées*).

(*Before daylight.—A square facing the house of Thaïs. Under the portico a small statuette of Eros; facing it a small lighted lamp. On the last of the steps of portico, Athanael sleeps. At rear, on right, a house in which are Nicias and his friends. The windows are lighted*).

(*Après un temps, la porte de la maison de Thaïs s'ouvre. Thaïs paraît; elle prend la lampe, qu'elle élève audessus de sa tête pour voir sur la place. Elle apercoit Athanael, repose la lampre et revient vers lui*).

(*After a time the door of Thaïs opens. She appears; she takes the lamp, which she extends over her head to view the square. She perceives Athanael, puts down the lamp and comes to him*).

**THAÏS:** (*se penchant vers Athanael mystérieusement.*) Père, Dieu m'a parlé par ta voix! me voici!—

**THAÏS:** (*leaning over Athanael, mysteriously*). Father, God has spoken by your voice! I am here.

# Act II, Scene II

ATHANAEL: (*se levant, à Thaïs, mystérieusement*). Thaïs, Dieu t'attendait!

THAÏS: (*avec humilité*). Ta parole est restée—en mon coeur comme un baume divin.—J'ai prié, j'ai pleuré . . .—il s'est fait en mon âme une grande lumière.—Ayant vu le néant de tout volupté,—vers toi je viens, ainsi que tu l'as commandé.—

ATHANAEL: Va, courage, ô ma soeur!—l'aube du repose se leve! . . .

THAÏS: (*humblement*).—Que faut-il faire? . . .

ATHANAEL:—Non loin d'ici vers l'occident,—il est un monastère où des femmes élues—vivent pareilles à des anges—dans un parfait recueillement:—pauvres, pour que Jésus les aime,—modestes, pour qu'il les regarde,—et chastes pour qu'il les épouse!—C'est là que je te conduirai.—A leur pieuse mère, Albine,—je te consacrerai!—

THAÏS: Albine, fille des Césars!

ATHANAEL: (*simplement*). Et la servante—la plus pure du Christ!—(*Avec mystère.*) Là, je t'enfermerai dans l'étroile cellule—jusqu'au jour où Jésus te viendra délivrer!—(*Avec un enthousiasme grandissant.*) Va! n'en doute pas! Il viendra lui-même—et quel tressaillement dans la chair de ton âme—quand tu sentiras sur tes yeux—se poser ses doigts de lumière—afin d'en essuyer les pleurs!

THAÏS: (*avec joie*). Ah mène-moi, mon uère, à la maison d'Albine!

ATHANAEL:—Oui. Mais, d'abord, anéantis—ce qui fut l'impure Thaïs:—ton palais, tes richesses,—tout ce qui proclame ta honte!—Brûle tout! anéantis tout!—

THAÏS: (*résignée*). Père, qu'il en soit ainsi.—(*Elle se dirige vers la maison, puis s'arrête devant la petite image d'Eros.*) Je ne veux rien garder de mon passé,—rien que cela . . . (*Prenant l'image qu'elle présente à Athanael.*) Cette image d'ivoire,—cet enfant, d'un travail antique et merveilleux,—c'est Eros! c'est l'amour! Considère, ô mon père,—que nous ne le pouvons traiter cruellement.—L'amour est une vertu rare,—j'ai péché, non par lui, mais plutôt contre lui.—Ah! je ne pleure pas de l'avoir eu pour maître,—mais d'avoir méconnu sa volonté!—Il défend qu'une femme—se donne à qui ne vient point en son nom:—et c'est pour cette loi qu'il convient qu'on l'honore.—Prends-le, pour le placer dans quelque monastère,—et ceux qui le verront se tourneront vers Dieu.—car l'amour nous élève aux célestes pensées—(*Après un temps.*) Quand Nicias m'aimait, il m'offrit cette image.—

ATHANAEL: (*avec une explosion de colère*). Nicias! ah! maudis la source empoisonnée—d'où te vient ce présent! qu'il soit anéanti.—(*Il a saisi la statuette qu'il jette violemment sur le pavé où elle se brise.*) Et tout le reste à la flamme, à l'abime!—Viens, Thaïs—que tout ce qui fut toi retourne à la poussière,—à l'éternel oublie!—

THAÏS: Que tout retourne à la poussière—à l'éternel oubli!—Viens!

ATHANAEL: Viens! (*Quand Thaïs et Athanael sont sortis, paraissent Nicias et tous les personnages du second tableau.—Ils descendent joyeusement.—Nicias les mène, très animé*).

NICIAS ET LE CHOEUR:—Suivez-moi tous, amis!—La nuit n'est pas finie!—Le jeu m'a rendre trente fois le prix—dont je payai la beauté de Thaïs!—Donc, réjouissons nous, encore, encore, encore!—Evohé!—Appelez les danseuses d'Asie—les psylles et les baladins!—Faisions durer jusqu'à l'aurore-les danses, les jeux et les cris!—Evohé! Frappons aux portes des tavernes.—Allumons des flambeaux.—Faisons honte au soleil!—Qu'on serve des vins à la neige!—Qu'on jette là d'épais tapis!—A mes côtes, Crobyle, et toi, Myrtale!—Evohé!—Rien n'est vrai que la vie!—Rien n'est sage que la folie!—Evohé! (*On a dans un grand mouvement, exécuté les indications de Nicias.—Il tombe paresseusement parmi les coussins.—Autor de lui, Crobule, Myrtale, les femme, les histrions*) DIVERTISSEMENT. (*Après plusieurs danses, paraît la Charmeuse*).

NICIAS: (*à l'apparition de la Charmeuse*). Voilà l'Incomparable! Prends la lyre, Crobyle, et, toi, prends la cithare,—Myrtale! Et toutes deux chantez—le cantique de la Beauté. (*Alors Crobyle et Myrtale chantent en s'accompagnant de leurs instruments; tandis que la Charmeuse développe ses poses lentes et ses pas légers*).

---

ATHANAEL: (*rising, to Thaïs, mysteriously*). Thaïs, God awaited you!

THAÏS: (*humbly*). Your word has remained—in my heart as a balm divine.—I prayed, I wept . . .—There took place in my soul a great light.—Having seen the nothingness of all passion,—I come toward you as you command.—

ATHANAEL: Courage, oh my sister! the dawn of rest begins . . .

THAÏS: (*humbly*).—What am I to do?

ATHANAEL: Not far from here, toward the West,—there is a monastery, where the elect among women—live similar to the angels—in a perfect introspection:—poor, that Jesus may love them,—modest, that he may look upon them,—chaste that he may espouse them!—it is there I shall conduct you.—To their pious mother Albine,—I shall consecrate you!—

THAÏS: Albine, daughter of the Caesars!

ATHANAEL: And the servant—the purest, of Christ!—(*Mysteriously.*) There, I shall shut you up in the narrow cell—until the day that Jesus shall come to deliver you!—(*With increasing enthusiasm.*) Ah, do not, do not doubt it, he will himself come—and what trembling in the flesh of your soul—when you feel on your eyes—the touch of his fingers of light—so as to wipe away the tears!—

THAÏS: (*joyfully*). Oh, take me, my father, to the abode of Albine.

ATHANAEL: Yes, but first destroy—all that was the impure Thaïs:—your palace, your wealth,—all that proclaims your shame! Burn all, destroy all!—

THAÏS: (*resigned*). Father, so be it,—(*she goes toward house but stops before the image of Eros*). I will keep nothing of my past,—nothing but this. (*Taking the image which she presents to Athanael*). This ivory image,—this child of a fashion antique and marvelous, it is Eros, it is Love. Consider, oh my father,—that we cannot treat it cruelly.—Love is a rare virtue,—I have sinned, not by him, but rather against him.—Ah, I do not weep to have had him for master,—but to have misconceived his will!—He forbids that a woman—should give herself to whoever comes not in his name;—and it is for this that he claims to be honored.—Take it, and place it in some monastery,—those who see it will turn themselves toward God,—for love, raises us to heavenly thoughts—(*Pauses*). When Nicias loved me he gave me this image.—

ATHANAEL: (*explosion of anger*). Nicias! then curse the poisoned source—that brought this present! Destruction to it!—(*He seizes the statuette, throws it violently on the pavement where it is smashed.*) And all the rest to the flames, to the abyss!—Come, Thaïs—that all which was you returns to dust,—to eternal forgetfulness!—

THAÏS: That all returns to dust—to eternal forgetfulness!—Come.

ATHANAEL: Come. (*When Thaïs and Athanael have gone, Nicias and all the personages of the second scene appear. They descend joyously. Nicias leads them, very animated*).

NICIAS AND THE CHORUS: Follow me, all my friends! The night is not over!—The game has given thirty times the price—that I paid for the beauty of Thaïs!—Then, let us rejoice, again, again, again!—Evoh'e!—Call in dancers of Asia—the pyslles and the baladins,—Let it last until dawn—dances, games and shouts!—Evoh'e! Let us knock on the doors of the taverns.—Light the torches.—Let us shame the sun!—That wine with snow be served.—That thick rugs be laid here!—To my side Crobyle and Myrtale!—Evoh'e!—Nothing is true but life!—Nothing is wise but folly!—Evoh'e! (*The orders of Nicias have been carried out. He falls lazily among the pillows. Around him are Crobyle, Myrtale, the women and the actors*). (*Diversion*). (*After several dances, appears the Charmer*).

NICIAS: (*at her apparition*). There is the Incomparable! Take the lyre, Crobyle and thou, the cythera, Myrtale, and both of you sing—the canticle of Beauty. (*Crobyle and Myrtale sing to the accompaniment of their instruments. Meanwhile the Charmer develops her slow poses and her light steps*).

**CROBYLE ET MYRTALE:**

I
Celle qui vient est plus belle
Que la reine de Saba
Qui dansait sur des miroirs!

II
Et de l'ombre de ses voiles
Partent les traits de sa voix
Comme des flèches de feu!

III
Elle a le teint d'ambre pâle,
Les lèvres couleur de sang,
Et ses yeux sont pleins de nuit!

IV
Elle vient, aérienne,
Flexible comme un roseau,
Légère comme un oiseau!

V
Ses regards jettent des chaînes,
Qui font les hommes captifs,
Ses beaux regards alanguis!

VI
Elle entraîne, elle caresse,
Elle a le charme mortel,
A qui nul n'a résisté!

VII
Comme une idol impassible
Elle va sans rien savoir
De son effrayant pouvoir!
(*A ce moment, Athanael sort vivement de la maison, une torche allumée à la main*).

**NICIAS:** (*avec ironie*). Eh! c'est lui! . . . c'est Athanaël!—

**AMIS:** Athanaël!—Salut, sage des sages!—Thaïs a donc désarmé ta raison?—(*En riant.*) Ah! ah! Voyez sa face glorieuse!—

**ATHANAEL:** (*jetant sa torche sur le sol*). Ah! taisez-vous! Thaïs est l'épouse de Dieu,—elle n'est plus à vous! La Thaïs infernale—est morte à tout jamais . . . et la Thaïs nouvelle,—la voici! (*Paraît Thaïs, les cheveux défaits, vêtue d'une tunique de laine. Ses esclaves la suivent attristées, regardant vers la maison d'où montent de légères fumées que vont bientôt suivre des lueurs d'incendie et des flammes.—La foule attirée par les cris et les rires envahit la place*).

**ATHANAEL:** (*à Thaïs*). —Viens, ma sœur, et fuyons à jamais cette ville;

**LA FOULE:** (*s'interposant*).—Ah! jamais! non! jamais!

**LA FOULE ET LES AMIS DE NICIAS:** L'emmener! que dit-il?—

**THAÏS:** Il dit vrai!

**NICIAS:** Thaïs! tu nous quitterais!—Est-ce possible? (*Nicias a pris le bras de Thaïs*).

**ATHANAEL:** (*la lui arrachant*). Impie!—crains de mourir si tu touches à celle-ci.—Elle est sacrée! elle est la part de Dieu!—(*Prenant Thaïs, près de lui*). Passage!

---

**CROBYLE AND MYRTALE:**

I.:
She who comes is finer
Than the Queen of Sheba
When dancing on the mirrors!

II.:
From the shade of her veils
Leap the darts of her voice
Like arrows of fire!

III.:
She has the tint of pale amber,
And lips of blood color,
And her eyes are full of night!

IV.:
She comes aeriel,
Flexible as a reed,
And light as a bird!

V.:
Her looks cast the chains,
That make captives of men,
Those fine looks so languid!

VI.:
She leads on, she caresses,
She has the mortal charm,
To which none has resisted!

VII.
Like an idol impassive
She will know nothing
Of her fearful power.
(*At this moment Athanael comes quickly from the house, a lighted torch in his hand*).

**NICIAS:** Ah, it is he . . . it is Athanael!—

**FRIENDS:** Athanael!—salutation, wise of the wise—Thaïs then has robbed you of reason?—(*laughing*) Ha, ha, see his face, how glorious!—

**ATHANAEL:** (*throwing his torch on ground*). Be silent. Thaïs is the spouse of God,—She is no longer yours! The infernal Thaïs—is dead forever . . . and the new Thaïs,—is here! (*Thaïs appears, hair in disorder and meanly clad, her slaves sadly follow her, looking at the house from which smoke arises, to be followed shortly by gleams of fire and flames. The crowd, attracted by the cries and the laughter, invade the scene*).

**ATHANAEL:** (*to Thaïs*). —Come, my sister, and let us fly this town forever;—

**THE CROWD:** (*interposing*).—No never, oh never!

**THE CROWD AND FRIENDS OF NICIAS:** Take her away! What does he say?

**THAÏS:** He speaks true.

**NICIAS:** Thaïs, you would leave us—Is it possible? (*Nicias holds Thaïs by the arm*).

**ATHANAEL:** (*tearing her away*). Impious!—fear death. Do not touch this one—She is sacred, she is the share of God—(*taking Thaïs to him.*) Make way!

---

**LA FOULE:** (*excitée*). Non! Que lui veut donc cet homme!—Qu'il retourne au désert!

**UN PETIT GROUPE DE GENS DU PEUPLE:** (*menaçant Athanael*). Va-t'en! Cynocéphale!—

**LA FOULE:** (*par groupes*). Nous reprendre Thaïs!—Eh! de qui vivrons-nous?—Mes robes! mes colliers! mes chevaux! mes bijoux!—qui nous paiera! Pour qui donc sont les lois!—Il nous vole Thaïs!

**LES FEMMES AFFOLEES:** (*désignant la maison incendiée*). La flamme! l'incendie!—le palais brûle!

**LA FOULE:** (*hurlante*). Qu'elle reste!—et lui qu'on l'assomme! aux corbeaux!—au gibet! à l'égout!—

**UN HOMME DU PEUPLE:** (*jetant une pierre à Athanael qu'il blesse au front*). Tiens, satyre, à toi!—

**ATHANAEL, THAÏS:** (*très calme, regardant la foule*). Ah! mourons, si c'est notre heure!—Achetons-en un instant—une éternelle allégresse—au prix de tout notre sang!—

**LA FOULE:** (*avec fureur*). A mort!

**NICIAS:** (*parvenant à s'interposer*). Arrêtez! de par tous les dieux!—voilà de quoi vous apaiser! (*Il jette de l'or à poignées.*)

**LA FOULE:** (*Tous se précipitent sur l'or qu'ils se disputent.*) De l'or!

**NICIAS:** (*à Athanael et à Thaïs*). Allez!—Adieu, Thaïs, en vain tu m'oublieras;—ton souvenir sera le parfum de mon âme!—(*Nicias jette de nouveau de l'or.*) (*Nouvelles clameurs de la foule.—Athanael et Thaïs s'enfuient. Le palais brûle*).

# ■ ACT TROISIEME

## PREMIER TABLEAU

('*Oasis.—Sous les palmeirs, un puits. Plus loin, pour les voyageurs, un abri dans la verdure. Plus loin encore, à la lisière du sable, incendié de soleil, les cellules blanches de la retrait d'Albine*).

(*Le soleil est très haut; sous les palmiers, une à une quelques femmes viennent en silence, descendent au puits, en romontent et s'éloignent. Après un instant, Thaïs et Athanael paraissent. Thaïs, accablée de fatigue se soutient à peine*).

---

**THE CROWD:** (*excited*). No! what does this man want of her?—Let him return to the desert.

**A LITTLE GROUP OF COMMON PEOPLE:** (*threatening Athanael*). Go away! Cynocephalus—

**THE CROWD:** (*by groups*). Take from us Thaïs!—And from whom shall we live?—My robes! my necklaces! my horses! my jewels!—Who will pay us? For whom then are the laws?—He is robbing us of Thaïs.

**CRAZY WOMEN:** (*pointing to house in flames*). Flames, fire!—The palace burns!

**THE MOB:** (*howling*). Let her stay.—As for him, brain him. To the crows! to the scaffold! to the gutter!—

**A MAN OF THE PEOPLE:** (*throwing a stone at Athanael that wounds him in forehead*). There, satyr, for you.—

**ATHANAEL AND THAÏS:** (*very calm, looking on crowd*). Let us die if it is our hour!—Let us purchase in an instant—an eternal triumph—at the price of all our blood!—

**THE CROWD:** (*with fury*). Death!

**NICIAS:** (*managing to interpose*). Stop! by all the gods!—Here is something to appease you. (*He throws handfuls of gold*).

**THE MOB:** (*Throwing themselves on the gold and fighting over it*). Gold!—

**NICIAS:** (*to Athanael and Thaïs*). Go!—Farewell, Thaïs, in vain will you forget me;—remembrance will be the perfume of my soul!—(*Nicias throws more gold*). (*Renewed clamor of the mob.—Athanael and Thaïs escape. The palace burns*).

# ■ ACT III

## SCENE I

(*The Oasis.—Under the palms, a well. Further, for travelers, a shelter amid the verdure. Further still, on the edge of the sand, the white cells of Albine's retreat*).

(*The sun is high; under the palms, one by one, some women come in silence, descend to the well and return again. After a while Thaïs and Athanael appear. Thaïs is overcome by fatigue and hardly endures*).

THAÏS: L'ardent soleil m'écrase,—comme un fardeau trop lourd!—Ah! je succombe au poids du jour!—Arrêtons nous!

ATHANAEL: Non! Marche encore!—Brise ton corps, anéantis ta chair!

THAÏS: (humblement). —Père, tu dis vrai. Ma torture,—je l'offre au divin rédempteur.

ATHANAEL: —Seul, le repentir nous épure.—Marche! Ce corps parfait, que tu livras—aux païens, aux infidèles,—(Avec un furie soudaine.) à Nicias! Dieu l'avait pourtant formé—pour qu'il devint sontabernacle!—Et maintenant que tu conanis la vérité.—tu ne peux plus unir tes lèvres,—tu ne peux plus joindre tes mains,—sans concevoir le dégoût de toi-même.

THAÏS: (humblement). —Père, tu dis vrai.

ATHANAEL: Marche! Expie!

THAÏS: —Sommes-nous loin encore de la maison de Dieu?

ATHANAEL: (avec rudesse). —Qu'importe? Marche!

THAÏS: (chancelante). Je ne puis!—Pardon, vénéré père! (Comme elle va défaillir, il la soutient dans ses bras, puis la fait asseoir à l'ombre. Il la contemple un instant. Tout à coup alors l'expression de son visage s'adoucit).

ATHANAEL: —Ah! des gouttes de sang coulent de ses pieds blancs.—La pitié s'émeut en mon âme!—Pauvre enfant, pauvre femme!—O sainte Thaïs! O ma soeur! . . . —J'ai trop prolongé cette dure épreuve.—Pardonne-moi! (Il se prosterne. Il pleure. Il baise les pieds saignants de Thaïs. Avec adoration). —O sainte, très sainte Thaïs!

THAÏS: —Ta parole a la douceur d'une aurore!—Marchons maintenant!

ATHANAEL: (la retenant avec douceur) Pas encore.—De l'eau fraîche, des fruits—te rendront quelque force.—Attends que je descende vers le puits,—que j'aille vers la halte hospitalière.—Vois, là-bas, ces cellules blanches:—c'est le couvent d'Albine, où nous allons.—Le but est proche. Espère, prie! (Il s'éloigne lentement; va vers l'abri sous le feuillage, rapporte des fruits dans une corbeille, puis descend ver le puits).

THAÏS: (seule). —O messager de Dieu, si bon dans ta rudesse,—sois béni, toi qui m'as ouvert le ciel.—Ma chair saigne, et mon âme est pleine d'allégresse.—Un air léger baigne mon front brûlant.—Plus fraîche que l'eau de la source,—

THAÏS: The ardent sun stifles me,—like a load that is too great!—Ah, I give way to the weight of the day.—Let us stop.

ATHANAEL: No, walk on!—Break your body, destroy your flesh!

THAÏS: (humbly). —Father, you speak truly. My torture,—I offer to the divine Redeemer.

ATHANAEL: —Only repentance purifies us—Walk! This perfect body that you gave—to pagans and infidels,—(with sudden fury.) To Nicias! Ah, yet God formed it—that it should become his tabernacle—and now that you know the truth,—you can no longer unite your lips—you can no longer join your hands,—without conceiving disgust at yourself.

THAÏS: (humbly). —Father, you speak truly.

ATHANAEL: Walk! Expiate!

THAÏS: —Are we far from the house of God?

ATHANAEL: (rudely). —What matters it? Walk!

THAÏS: (swaying). I cannot.—Pardon, venerated father. (As she is about to fall, he holds her in his arms, then seats her in the shade. He contemplates her a moment. All at once the expression of his face softens).

ATHANAEL: —Ah, drops of blood flow from her white feet—. Pity moves my soul.—Poor child, poor woman!—Oh saint Thaïs, oh my sister!—I have prolonged this hard trial too much.—Forgive me. (He prostrates himself. He weeps. He kisses the bleeding feet of Thaïs. With adoration). Oh saint, very saint Thaïs!

THAÏS: —Your words resemble the softness of the dawn.—Now let us go on.

ATHANAEL: (detaining her gently). Not yet.—Fresh water, fruits—will give you strength.—Wait until I go down to the well,—to the hospitable halting place.—Look, over there, those white cells:—it is the convent of Albine, where we go.—Our object is near. Hope, pray! (He passes on slowly, goes to the shelter under the trees, and brings back fruit in a basket, then descends to well).

THAÏS: (alone). —Oh messenger of God, so good in your rudeness,—Blessed be you that has opened Heaven to me.—My flesh bleeds and my heart is full of happiness.—Light breezes bathe my burning forehead.—Fresher than

plus douce qu'un rayon de miel,—ta pensée est en moi, suave et salutaire—et mon esprit, dégagé de la terre—plane déjà dans cette immensité.—Sois béni, très vénéré père! (Athanael revient).

ATHANAEL: —Baigne d'eau tes mains et tes lèvres.—Goûte à ces fruits, apaise cette fièvre—qui fait étinceler tes yeux!—Ta vie est maintenant mon trésor précieux,—elle m'appartient; Dieu me la confie. (Il répand l'eau sur les mains de Thaïs, approche la coupe de ses lèvres. Elle boit, puis, élevant vers lui la coupe).

THAÏS: Bois à ton tour!

ATHANAEL: Non? à te voir revivre,—je goûte une douceur meilleure et je m'enivre—rien que de ton mal apaisé!—douceur ineffable!

THAÏS: O divine bonté! (Il lui présente les fruits. Tandis qu'elle mange, il va de nouveau remplir la coupe d'eau et la lui rapport. Scène muette, durant laquelle s'élève à distance une lente psalmodie, qui va se rapprochant graduellement, jusqu'à l'entrée en scène d'Albine et des filles blanches).

VOIX: (à distance). Pater noster, qui es in coelis . . . Panem nostrum quotidianum da nobis.

THAÏS: —Qui vient!

ATHANAEL: Ah! Providence divine!—Voici la vénérable Albine—et ses soeurs rapportant le pain noir du couvent.—Elles viennent vers nous et marchent en priant.

LES VOIX: (très proches). —Et ne nos inducas in tentationem,—sed libera nos a malo. (Albine et ses compagnes paraissent).

ATHANAEL: Amen! (A la vue d'Athanael, Albine, s'est arrêtée, ainsi que les filles blanches, avec de grandes marques de respect. Thaïs qui s'est levée, est aux côtés d'Athanael).

ATHANAEL: (à Albine). —La paix du Seigneur soit avec toi, sainte Albine.—J'apporte à ta ruche divien—une abeille que j'ai, par la grâce d'en haut,—trouvée un jour perdue en un chemin sans fleurs.—Dans le creux de ma main je l'ai prise, très frêle.—De mon souffle je l'ai réchauffée et voici—que pour la consacrer à Dieu je te la donne. (Thaïs s'est agenouillée devant Albine).

ALBINE: —Ainsi soit-il!—Venez ma fille. (Elle prend Thaïs dans ses bras).

spring water—softer than a ray of honey—Your thought is in me, suave and salutary—and my spirit, disengaged from Earth—floats already in this immensity.—Blessed be you, father, most venerated.

ATHANAEL: (returns). —Bathe your hands and lips in water.—Taste these fruits, appease this fever—that sparkles in your eyes.—Your life is now my precious treasure,—it, to me, belongs; God confides it to me. (He pours water on her hands, puts the cup to her lips. She drinks and then presents cup to him).

THAÏS: —Drink in turn.

ATHANAEL: No, to see you revive,—I taste a softer pleasure and I rejoice—from nothing but your pain appeased.—Oh, ineffable sweetness!

THAÏS: Oh, divine goodness! (He presents the fruits to her. While she eats he goes once more to the well and brings water. In the distance is heard a slow psalmody, that gradually approaches, until the entrance on scene of Albine and the White Ladies).

VOICES: (in distance). Pater noster, qui es in coelis . . . Panem nostrum quotidianum da nobis.

THAÏS: Who comes?

ATHANAEL: Oh, divine Providence! Here is the venerable Albine and her sisters bringing the black bread from the convent—They come toward us and pray as they walk.

VOICES: (nearby). Et ne nos inducas in tentationem,—sed libera nos a malo. (Albine and her companions appear.)

ATHANAEL: Amen! (At sight of Athanael, Albine has stopped and also the White Ladies, with every mark of respect. Thaïs, who has risen stands beside Athanael).

ATHANAEL: (to Albine.) —The peace of the Lord be with you, Saint Albine.—I bring to your divine hive—a bee that I, by the favor of the grace on high—found one day, lost on a flowerless way.—I took her in the hollow of my hand very frail. I warmed her with my breath and here—to consecrate to God, I give her to you. (Thaïs kneels before Albine.)

ALBINE: —So be it.—Come, my daughter. (She takes Thaïs in her arms.)

ATHANAEL: —Je n'irai pas plus loin. Mon oeuvre est accomplie!—Adieu, chère Thaïs—reste recluse en 'l'étroite cellule.—Fais pénitence et prie, à chaque heure, pour moi!

THAÏS: (lui prenant les mains). —Je baise tes mains secourables—je pleure à te quitter—ô toi qui m'as rendue à Dieu!

ATHANAEL: —O parole touchante!—O larmes adorables!—Bienheureuse la pécheresse—gagné à l'éternel amour! (Avec exaltation.) —Que son visage est beau! Quel rayon d'allégresse—émane de ses yeux!

THAÏS: —Adieu, mon père, adieu! . . . —Pour toujours!

ATHANAEL: (comme frappé). Pour toujours?

THAÏS: Dans la cité céleste,—nous nous retrouverons.

ALBINE et LES FILLES BLANCHES: Amen! (Elles s'éloignent).

ATHANAEL: (seul) —Elle va lentement parmi les filles blanches. —Les palmiers inclinent leurs branches—comme pour rafraîchir son front—et les jours, les ans passeront—sans qu'elle m'apparaisse encore. (Un cri d'angoisse). Je ne la verrai plus! . . . je ne la verrai plus! . . . je ne la verrai plus! (Appuyé sur son bâton, il regarde encore vers le chemin qu'a pris Thaïs. La toile tombe).

## DEUXIEME TABLEAU

(La Thébaïde. —Les cabanes des Cénobites au bord du Nil. —Les Cénobites regardent le ciel avec une vague terreur. —Rafales lointaines du simoun).

LES CENOBITES: Que le ciel est pesant! quelle torpeur accable—les êtres et les choses!—On entend au loin le cri du chacal!—Le vent va déchaîner ses meutes rugissantes—avec le tonnerre et l'éclair!—

PALEMON: (aux Cénobites). Rentrons dan nos cabanes—et nos grains et nos fruits!—Redoutons une nuit d'orage—qui les disperserait!—

UN CENOBITE: Athanaël! . . . qui l'a vu? . . .

PALEMON: Depuis vingt jours qu'il nous est revenu,—mes frères, je crois bien qu'il n'a mangé ni bu!—Le triomphe qu'il a remporté sur l'enfer—semble l'avoir brisé de corps et d'âme!—
(Athanael sort de sa cabane).

ATHANAEL: I shall go no further. My work is accomplished! Farewell, dear Thaïs—remain secluded in the narrow cell.—Do penance and pray, each hour, for me.

THAÏS: (taking his hands). —I kiss your helping hands—I weep to leave you—Oh you that gave me to God.

ATHANAEL: —Oh touching words!—Oh adorable words!—Happy indeed is the sinner—saved for the eternal love (with excitation). How beautiful is her visage. What a ray of joy emanates from her eyes.

THAÏS: —Farewell, my father, farewell . . . —forever.

ATHANAEL: (shocked). Forever?

THAÏS: We shall find one another again in the celestial city.

ALBINE AND THE WHITE LADIES: Amen! (They move away).

ATHANAEL: (alone). —She moves slowly among the White Ladies. —The palms lower their branches as if to refresh her forehead—and the days and the years will pass—that she will never appear to me again (A cry of anguish.) I shall see her no more . . . I shall see her no more!
(Leaning on his stick he looks at the road Thaïs has taken. The curtain falls).

## SCENE II

(The Thebald. Huts of the Cenobites on the bank of the Nile. These look on the heavens with a vague terror. Distant sounds of the simoon).

THE CENOBITES: How heavy the air is. A torpor overwhelms us—human beings and all things.—We hear in the distance the cry of the jackal.—The wind will unchain its howling bands—with thunder and the lightning!—

PALEMON: (to the Cenobites). Let us put both our grains and our fruits in our huts.—We fear a night of storm would disperse them.—

A CENOBITE: Athanael . . . who has seen him? . . .

PALEMON: For the twenty days since he has returned,—my brothers, I think he has not eaten nor drunk.—The triumph he has had over hell—appears to have broken him body and soul.—
(Athanael comes from his hut.)

LES CENOBITES: (avec respect). C'est lui qui vient!
(Athanael passe au milieu d'eux comme s'il ne les voyait pas).

UN GROUPE: Sa pensée est absente . . . —

UN AUTRE GROUPE: Elle est auprès de Dieu!

LES CENOBITES: (en s'éloignant). Respectons son silence . . . —laissons-le seul! . . .

ATHANAEL: (à Palémon, avec humilité). Demeure auprès de moi;—il faut que je confesse—le trouble de mon âme à ton âme sereine. —Tu sais, ô Palémon, que j'ai reconquis l'âme—de celle qui fut l'impure Thaïs. —Une orgueilleuse joie a suivi ce triomphe—et je suis revenu vers ce désert de paix! . . . Eh bien, en moi, la paix est morte! . . . —En vain, j'ai flagellé ma chair,—en vain je l'ai meurtrie! un démon me possède!—La beauté de la femme hante mes visions!—Je ne vois que Thaïs, ou mieux, ce n'est pas elle,—c'est Hélène et Phryné, c'est Vénus Astarté,—toutes les splendeurs et toutes les voluptés—en une seule créature!—
(Il tombe comme écrasé de honte aux pieds de Palémon).

PALEMON: (doucement et simplement). Ne t'avais-je pas dit:—"Ne nous mêlons jamais, mon fils, aux gens du siècle"—craignons les pièges de l'esprit!"—Ah! pourquoi nous as-tu quittés? . . . Que Dieu t'assiste!—Adieu!—
(Athanael se lève. —Palémon l'embrasse et s'éloigne. —Athanael seul s'agenouille sur sa natte. —Après quoi, il s'allonge et s'endort. Après un temps, la forme de Thaïs apparaît, lumineuse, dans l'ombre).

THAÏS: (à Athanael, avec un grand charme). —Qui te fait si sévère,—et pourquoi démens-tu la flamme de tes yeux?—

ATHANAEL: (comme en rêvant). Thaïs! . . .

THAÏS: Quelle triste folie—te fait manquer à ton destin?—Homme fait pour aimer, quelle erreur est la tienne!—

ATHANAEL: (se levant). Ah! Satan! arrière! . . . ma chair brûle!

THAÏS: —Ose venir, toi qui braves Vénus!

ATHANAEL: (éperdu). —Je meurs!
Thaïs! . . . Viens! . . . —
(Rires stridents de Thaïs dont l'image disparaît subitement).
(Le ciel s'éclaircit. —Une vision nouvelle montre à Athanael le jardin du monastère d'Albine. —A

THE CENOBITES: (with respect). He is coming!
(Athanael passes amid them without seeing.)

A GROUP: His thoughts are far off . . . —

ANOTHER GROUP: They are near to God.

THE CENOBITES: (moving away). Let us respect his silence . . . —We will leave him alone.

ATHANAEL: (to Palemon, with humility). Remain by me;—I feel I must confess—the trouble of my soul to your serene soul. —You know oh Palemon, I regained the soul—of that was the impure Thaïs. —A proud joy had followed this triumph—and I came back to this desert of peace . . . —Well then, peace is dead in me . . . —In vain I flagellated my flesh,—in vain I bruised it; a demon possesses me. The beauty of the woman haunts my visions,—I only see Thaïs, or rather it is not she,—Helen and Phryne. Venus Astarte.—all the splendors and the enjoyments—in one single creature!—
(He falls stunned with shame at Palemon's feet).

PALEMON: (gently and simply). Did I not tell thee:—"Let us never meddle, my son, with the people of the time,—let us fear the traps of the Spirit." Ah, why did you leave us? . . . May God assist you. Adieu.—
(Athanael rises. —Palemon embraces him and goes . . . Athanael alone, kneels on his mat. After which, he stretches out and sleeps. After a time, the form of Thaïs appears, luminous in the gloom).

THAÏS: (to Athanael with great charm). —What makes you so severe,—and why do you deny the flame of your eyes?—

ATHANAEL: (dreaming). Thaïs! . . .

THAÏS: What sad folly—makes you false to your destiny?—Man made to love, what error is yours?—

ATHANAEL: (rising). Ah Satan! away, my flesh burns.

THAÏS: —Dare to come, you that braves Venus!

ATHANAEL: (beside himself). —I die, Thaïs! . . . Come! . . . —
(Strident laughter of Thaïs who disappears. The sky clears. A new vision shows to Athanael the garden of the monastery of Albine. In the shadow of a fig tree, Thaïs is stretched out motionless.—

*l'ombre d'un grand figuier, Thaïs est étendue immobile.—Autour d'elle sont agenouillées les Filles blanches du Monastère).*

**ATHANAEL:** (*apercevant la vision. Avec un cri d'épouvante et reculant*). Ah! . . .

**LES VOIX:** Une sainte est près de quitter la Terre.—Thaïs d'Alexandrie—va mourir! Thaïs va mourir!—

**ATHANAEL:** (*avec égarement*). Thaïs va mourir! Thaïs va mourir! . . . —(*Avec une passion furieuse*). Alors, pour quoi le ciel, les êtres, la lumière!—A quoi bon l'univers!—Thaïs va mourir! Ah! la voir encore! La revoir! la saisir! la garder! . . . je la veux! Oui, fou, fou que je suis de n'avoir pas compris—qu'elle seule était tout! . . . qu'une de ses caresses—valait plus que le ciel! Oh! je voudrais tuer tous ceux qui l'ont aimée!—Non, Thaïs, ne meurs pas! Non! je vais te reprendre!—Sois à moi! sois à moi!
(*Il s'élance et disparaît dans la nuit*).
(*Obscurité complète.—Nuages envahissants, éclairs sinistres.— Tonnerre La musique continue jusqu'au changement*).

## TROISIEME TABLEAU

(*Le jardin du monastère d'Albine.—A l'ombre d'un grand figuier, Thaïs est étendue, immobile, comme morte.—Ses compagnes et Albine sont autour d'elle*).

**LES FILLES BLANCHES DU MONASTERE:** (*à genoux*). Seigneur, ayez pieié de moi—selon votre mansuétude!—effacez mon iniquité—selon votre miséricorde!—

**ALBINE:** (*à part, contemplant Thaïs*). Dieu l'appelle, et, ce soir, la blancheur du linceul—aura voilé ce pur visage!—Durant trois mois, elle a veillé, prié, pleuré;—son corps est détruit par la pénitence,—mais ses péchés sont effacés!—

**LES FILLES BLANCHES:** Seigneur, ayez pitié de moi—selon votre mansuétude!—
(*Athanael, paraît à l'entrée du jardin. Ayant été aperçu par Albine, il contient son émotion et s'arrête humblement. Albine est allée au-devant de lui avec respect.—Les filles blanches forment un groupe qui tout d'abord dérobe à Athanael la vue de Thaïs*).

*Around her are kneeling the White Ladies of the Monastery*).

**ATHANAEL:** (*perceiving the vision, terror stricken*). Ah! . . .

**THE VOICES:** A saint is about to quit the Earth.—Thaïs of Alexandria is about to die.—

**ATHANAEL:** (*wildly*). Thaïs must die! Thaïs must die . . . (*With furious passion.*) Then, why Heaven, human beings, light?—Of what good is the universe?—Thaïs must die. Oh, to see her again. To see her, hold her, keep her! . . . I must have her. Yes, fool that I was, not to have understood—that she alone was all, that one of her caresses was worth more than Heaven! Oh I would kill all those who have loved her! No, Thaïs, do not die. No, I'll come to take you.—Be mine, be mine!
(*He rushes into the night. Complete obscurity. Thunder. Music continues*).

## SCENE III

(*The garden of the monastery. In the shade of a fig tree, Thaïs stretched, as if dead. Her companions and Albine surround her*).

**WHITE LADIES OF THE MONASTERY:** (*kneeling*). Lord have pity on me—according to your grace!—Wipe out my iniquity—according to your mercy.—

**ALBINE:** (*aside, looking at Thaïs*). God calls her and tonight the whiteness of the winding-sheet—will have hidden this pure face.—During three months, she has watched, prayed, wept; her body is destroyed by penance,—but her sins are effaced!—

**THE WHITE LADIES:** Lord, have pity on me—according to your grace!—
(*Athanael appears at entrance of garden. Being seen by Albine, he restrains his emotion and stops, humbly. Albine has gone toward him with respect. The White Ladies form a group which at first conceals from Athanael the sight of Thaïs*).

**ALBINE:** (*à Athanael, simplement*). Sois le bienvenu dans nos tabernacles,—ô père vénéré!—car sans doute tu veins pour bénir cette sainte—que tu nous as donnée . . .

**ATHANAEL:** (*avec un égarement qu'il essaie de contenir*). Oui . . . Thaïs! . . .

**ALBINE:** Ayant fait—ce que ton esprit pur lui commanda de faire,— voici qu'elle va voir l'éternelle lumière!— (*Athanael l'apercoit*).

**ATHANAEL:** Thaïs! . . . Thaïs! . . . (*Ecrasé de douleur, il est tombé prosterné. Albine et ses filles blanches s'élognent de un peu pas Athanael s'est trové sur les genoux et se trouve pres de Thaïs*).

**ATHANAEL:** (*basse et douleurment*). Thaïs! . . . —

**THAÏS:** (*ouvrant ses yeux et regardant Athanael*). C'est toi mon père . . . —Te souvient-il du lumineaux voyage—lorsque tu m'as conduite ici? . . . —

**ATHANAEL:** (*avec attendrissement*). J'ai le seul souvenir de ta beauté mortelle!

**THAÏS:** —Te souvient-il de ces heures de calme—dans la fraîcheur de l'oasis! . . .

**ATHANAEL:** (*avec ardeur*). Ah! je me souviens seulement—de cette soif inapaisée—dont tu seras l'apaisement . . .

**THAÏS:** Surtout te souvient-il de tes saintes paroles—en ce jour—où par toi j'ai connu le seul amour! . . . —

**ATHANAEL:** Quand j'ai parlé, t'ai menti . . . —

**THAÏS:** Et la voilà l'aurore!—et les voilà les roses de l'éternel matin!—

**ATHANAEL:** Non! le ciel . . . rien n'existe . . . — rien n'est vrai que la vie et que l'amour des êtres . . . —Je t'aime! . . .

**THAÏS:** Le ciel s'ouvre!—Voici les anges, les prophètes . . . et les saints! . . . —ils viennent avec un sourire—les mains toutes pleines de fleurs!–

**ATHANAEL:** Entends-moi donc, ma toute aimée! . . . —

**THAÏS:** (*debout, frissonnate*). Deux séraphins aux blanches ailes—planent dans l'azur!—et comme tu l'as dit, le doux consolateur—posant sur mes yeux ses doigts de lumière—en essuie à jamais les pleurs! . . .

**ATHANAEL:** (*de plus en plus exalté*). Viens! dis-moi: je vivrai! je vivrai!

**ALBINE:** (*to Athanael, simply*). You are welcome in our tabernacles,—oh venerated father—for, no doubt. You come to bless this saint—whom you gave us . . .

**ATHANAEL:** (*with a wildness he tries to contain*). Yes . . . Thaïs! . . .

**ALBINE:** Having done—what your pure spirit commanded her to do,—she is now about to see the eternal light.— (*Athanael sees Thaïs*)

**ATHANAEL:** Thaïs! . . . Thaïs! . . . (*Broken with grief he falls. Albine and the White Ladies move away a little. Athanael has dragged himself on his knees close to Thaïs*).

**ATHANAEL:** (*low and sorrowfully*). Thaïs! . . .

**THAÏS:** (*opening her eyes and seeing Athanael*). It's you, my father! . . . Do you remember the luminous voyage,—when you brought me here? . . . —

**ATHANAEL:** (*tenderly*). I have alone the memory of your mortal beauty!

**THAÏS:** —Do remember those hours of calm—in the freshness of the oasis?—

**ATHANAEL:** (*with ardor*). Ah, I remember only—this unappeased thirst of which you alone shall be the appeasement.

**THAÏS:** Above all, do you remember your saintly words—on that day—when through you I knew the only love? . . . —

**ATHANAEL:** When I spoke, I lied to you . . . —

**THAÏS:** And there is the dawn; and there are the roses of the eternal morning!—

**ATHANAEL:** No. Heaven— nothing exists . . . —nothing is true but life and the love of beings . . . —I love you!

**THAÏS:** Heaven opens itself.— Here are the angels, the prophets, and the saints! . . . —they come smiling—their hands all full of flowers!—

**ATHANAEL:** Listen to me, my all beloved!—

**THAÏS:** (*standing, trembling*). Two seraphim with wings of white—soar in the azure—and as you said, the gentle Consoler— placing on my eyes His fingers of light—wipes away the tears forever!—

**ATHANAEL:** (*more and more exalted*). Come, say to me: 'I shall live, I shall live'!—

**THAÏS:** Le son des harpes d'or m'enchante!—de suaves parfums me pénètrent! . . . Je sens—une exquise béatitude—endormir tous mes maux!—Ah! Le ciel! je vois Dieu! . . . —

**THAÏS:** The sound of the harps of gold, enchants me—soft perfumes penetrate my being . . . I feel— an exquisite beatitude—put all my ills to sleep— Ah! . . . Heaven! . . . I see

*(Ells meurt.)*
*(Athanael avec un cri terrible se jette à genoux devant elle)*

*FIN.*

God! . . . —
*(She dies).*
*(Athanael with a terrible cry falls prostrate beside her).*

# Cendrillon (1899)

## Cinderella

Music by Jules Massenet ■ Libretto by Henri Cain ■ Based on the Story by Charles Perrault

This four-act *conte de fées* with six tableaux, set to a libretto by Henri Cain (based upon Charles Perrault's fairy story *Cinderella*), premiered at the Opéra-Comique in Paris on May 24, 1899. The opera begins at the home of Madame de la Haltière. The Prince of the kingdom is giving a grand ball which will be attended by Noémie and Dorothée, Madame de la Haltière's daughters. Lucy, her stepdaughter (also known as Cendrillon), will not be attending. The family leaves for the ball and Cendrillon falls asleep. She has a dream in which she is magically able to go to the ball and is fêted by all as a great beauty. A fairy waves a magic wand and turns Cendrillon's rags into a beautiful gown. As Cendrillon rushes off to the ball, she is warned that she must be home by midnight. The Prince is alone as he has not yet met the girl of his dreams. He is totally uninterested in Cendrillon's stepsisters. A beautiful woman appears, and the Prince falls in love with her immediately. He begs her to tell him who she is, but she tells him that he must never learn her identity. He tries to keep her there, but at the stroke of midnight she runs away. In her flight she loses one of her glass slippers. Cendrillon returns to Madame's house and collapses, weeping. The stepsisters return and tell Cendrillon about the mysterious guest. Cendrillon thinks that the Prince must doubt her innocence and decides to run away to the farm where she and her father, Pandolfe, lived after her mother's death. Cendrillon, in the fairies' forest, asks the fairy to comfort her. The Prince finds her there and offers her his heart as a token of his love, and the fairies put them both to sleep. Cendrillon is now back in her own room, having been found unconscious in the forest. She is recovering from a long illness, and during her fever her father says she spoke of love and a shoe. The voice of a herald announces that the Prince will receive young maidens to try on the slipper lost by the mysterious guest. Cendrillon realizes that she did not dream about the ball after all. Once all of the maidens have tried on the slipper, the fairy leads Cendrillon, who carries the heart given to her by the Prince, to him. The crowd watches in excitement as the Prince embraces his true love.

---

## ■ ACTE PREMIER

### SCÈNE PREMIÈRE

*Chez Madame de la Haltière*

*(Vaste chambre. Grande cheminée avec son âtre.)*

*(Coups de sonnette répépés. Des Domestiques troublés, ahuris ne savent qui entendre. Quelques-uns courent, affolés.)*

DOMESTIQUES, SERVITEURS:
*(hommes et femmes).* On appelle, on sonne!
On carillonne!
Que de scènes! Que de cris!
Nous sommes ahuris!
On appelle, on sonne!
C'est par ici! non! c'est par là!
On ressonne, on recarillonne!
Voilà, voilà,
On y va!
Mieux vaudrait servir le diable en personne
Que cette femme-là! . . .
*(Les uns aux autres)*
O mon cher, ô ma chère!
C'est une mégère! *(A la vue de Pandolfe, qui paraît, tous s'arrêtent, troublés, interdits.)*
Monsieur!

## ■ ACT I

### SCENE I

*HOME OF MADAME DE LA HALTIÈRE.*

*A large room. Big fireplace.*

*Repeated ringing of a bell. Servants in a flurry. Know not whom to wait upon. Some rush about distracted.*

SERVANTS, MEN AND WOMEN:
They call, they ring!
And ring again!
What scenes! What shouts!
We are befuddled!
They call, they ring!
Not here! no! nor there!
They ring again, again.
There now, there now,
They are coming!
Better serve the devil himself
Than that woman! . . .
*(to one another)*
O my dear, my dear!
She is a vixen!
*(At sight of Pandolfe, who appears, they all stop troubled and bewildered).*
The master!

PANDOLFE: Continuez. Ce n'est que moi. Pourquoi
Vous taisez-voux? Pas besoin de prudence;
ne soyez pas ainsi troublés par ma présence
Et dites, que se passe-t-il?

LES DOMESTIQUES: Monsieur, chacun proclame
Que monsieur est gentil, très gentil, très gentil!
Mais c'est madame! Ah! madame! ah! madame!

PANDOLFE: Hein! Qu'est-ce à dire?
*(A part)*
Au fond, ils ont raison!
*(Nouveaux et très forts coups de sonnette.)*
Allez, allez . . . on vous réclame!

LES DOMESTIQUES: Monsieur est si gentil, si gentil . . .

PANDOLFE: Eh, c'est bon!
*(En sortant, les domestiques se retournent en disant: "Mais c'est madame! Ah! Madame!")*

### SCÈNE II

PANDOLFE: Du côté de la barbe est la tout-puissance . . .
Oui, je devrais le faire voir Et savoir
Obtenir de ma femme un peu

PANDOLFE: Go on. It is only I.
Why be silent? no need for prudence,
Do not be troubled by my presence.
Tell me, what is happening?

THE SERVANTS: Master, every one proclaims
That you are kind, very kind, very kind!
But the mistress! Ah the mistress! ah, the mistress!

PANDOLFE: Well! What do you mean?
*(Aside)*
Really, they are right!
*(The ringing of the bell begins again, stronger).*
Go, go . . . you are wanted!

THE SERVANTS: Master is so kind, so kind . . .

PANDOLFE: Ah, well!
*(As they go out the servants turn and say: "But the mistress, Ah, the mistress".)*

### SCENE II

PANDOLFE: Power lies with the bearded one
Yes, I must make her see it and know it.—

d'obéissance.
Hélas! vouloir n'est pas pouvoir!
Pourquoi, grands dieux, veuf et tranquille,
Vivant chez moi, loin de la ville,
Exempt de soucis et d'émois
Près de ma fillette adorable
Ai-je quitté ma ferme et nos grands bois!
Pourquoi? Pou m'en aller tenter le diable, En étant le mari
Re-mari, très marri
D'une comtesse fière et d'humeur redoutable
Qui m'apportait en dot, non! c'est épouvantable,
Deux belles filles, deux! mon sort est lamentable!
A les chérir, je suis condamné par la loi!
Ombre de Philémon, plaignez-moi! plaignez-moi!
Mon sort est vraiment effroyable!
Encore, si j'étais seul à gémir, mais non,
Pour toi, c'est l'abandon,
O ma fillette!
Ah! que je souffre en te voyant, Lucette, Sans affiquets, ni collerette,
Te cacher pour venir me donner un baiser,
Sans un regard pour m'accuser
Quand au logis, seulette
Je te laisse pendant le bal!
Que veux-tu! Je sens que c'est mal!
Mais si ma femme gronde et rage
Je tremble et je ne peux résister à l'orage!
(*Avec agitation et nervosité*)
Ah! par ma foi,
Ce sera pénible, peut-être,
Mais il faudra qu'un jour, chez moi,
(*Avec autorité*)
Je finisse par être maître!
(*Les domestiques entrent, précédant Madame de la Haltière et ses deux filles.*)

**PANDOLFE:** (*changeant de ton et s'enfuyant*). Ma femme! hélas! Partons! Vouloir n'est pas pouvoir!

Obtain from my wife a little obedience.
Alas! to wish is not to do!
Why on earth, in my peaceful life as widower,
Living far from the city,
Free from care and strife,
With my dear little daughter,
Did I leave my farm and the beautiful woods.
Why? To go and tempt the devil, as the husband,
The second husband
Of a proud and haughty Countess
Who brought me as her dowry
—No! it is abominable!—
Two step-daughters, two! oh my lot is pitiable!
The law compels me to support them!
Shade of Philemon, pity, pity me!
My lot is truly lamentable!
And if it was only I who suffered, but no,
For you it means desertion,
Oh, my daughter!
Ah, how I suffer, Lucette, seeing you without collar or trinket.
Hiding to give me a kiss,
Never a look of reproach,
When alone in the house
I leave you during the ball!
What can I do! I feel how cruel it is!
But if my wife gets in a rage
I tremble and succumb to the storm!
(*With agitation and nervousness*)
Ah! on my faith,
It would be dreadful, perhaps,
But some day I must really
(*With determination*)
Assert my power.
(*The servants enter, preceded by Madame de la Haltière and her two daughters.*)

**PANDOLFE:** (*changing his tone and making his escape*). My wife! Alas! We must go! To wish is not to do!

## SCÈNE III

*Madame de la Haltière et ses filles.*

**MADAME DE LA HALTIÈRE:** (*à ses filles, avec une importance comique*). Faites-vous très belles, ce soir; J'ai bon espoir.

**NOÉMIE ET DOROTHÉE:** Pourquoi, maman?

**MADAME DE LA HALTIÈRE:** Peut-on jamais savoir?
Faites-vous très belles, ce soir!
(*A part*)
Non, cela n'aurait rien qui me puisse surprendre
Car c'est plus d'une fois
Que l'on a vu des rois . . .

## SCENE III

*MADAME DE LA HALTIÈRE AND HER DAUGHTERS.*

**MADAME DE LA HALTIÈRE:** (*to her daughters, with comical importance*). Make yourselves very beautiful, tonight, I have great hopes.

**NOEMIA AND DOROTHY:** Why, mama?

**MADAME DE LA HALTIÈRE:** One can never know.
Make yourselves very beautiful tonight!
(*aside*)
No, it would not surprise me though . . .
Since more than once
We have seen kings . . .

**NOÉMIE ET DOROTHÉE:** Quoi donc, maman? Plus d'une fois Qu'est-ce donc qu'ils ont fait, les rois?

**MADAME DE LA HALTIÈRE:** A tout nous devons nous attendre.

**NOÉMIE ET DOROTHÉE:** Nous attendre à tout? Mais pourquoi?

**MADAME DE LA HALTIÈRE:** Parce qu'on va, ce soir, vous présenter au roi!

**NOÉMIE ET DOROTHÉE:** Ah! quel bonheur! nous allons voir le roi!

**MADAME DE LA HALTIÈRE:** Il vous remarquera, j'espère!

**NOÉMIE ET DOROTHÉE:** Alors, qu'est-ce qu'il faudra faire?

**MADAME DE LA HALTIÈRE:** Il faudra faire comme moi! Le bal est un champ de bataille

**NOÉMIE ET DOROTHÉE:** Comment, Maman, Le bal est un champ de bataille? . . .

**MADAME DE LA HALTIÈRE:** Tenez-vous bien, Ne perdez rien De votre taille, Pas de mouvements trop nerveux . . .

**NOÉMIE ET DOROTHÉE:** Non, maman!

**MADAME DE LA HALTIÈRE:** A-t-on bien frisé vos cheveux?

**NOÉMIE ET DOROTHÉE:** Oui, maman!

**MADAME DE LA HALTIÈRE:** (*à part avec volubilité, comme se parlant à elle-même*). Car je ne veux, ni ne puis me résoudre, A croire qu'il existe seulement Dans la roman Le coup de foudre!

**NOÉMIE ET DOROTHÉE:** Le coup de foudre!

**MADAME DE LA HALTIÈRE:** (*à ses filles*). Prenez un maintien gracieux En arrondissant votre bouche. Bien! N'ayez pas l'aire trop farouche!

**NOÉMIE ET DOROTHÉE:** Voilà, maman!

**MADAME DE LA HALTIÈRE:** Parfait! on ne peut mieux! Ne soyez pas banales! Ni trop originales!

**MADAME DE LA HALTIÈRE:** Faites-vous très belles ce soir! Quel succès nous allons avoir! Mais vous ne devez pas savoir Quel est mon espoir!

**NOÉMIE ET DOROTHÉE:** Nous serons très belles ce soir! Quel succès nous allons avoir! Et nous croyons déjà savoir Quel est votre espoir!

**NOEMIA AND DOROTHY:** What is it, mama? More than once What did they do, the kings?

**MADAME DE LA HALTIÈRE:** We must expect everything.

**NOEMIA AND DOROTHY:** Expect everything? But why?

**MADAME DE LA HALTIÈRE:** Because this evening you will be presented to the king!

**NOEMIA AND DOROTHY:** Ah! what luck! We shall see the king.

**MADAME DE LA HALTIÈRE:** I hope he will notice you!

**NOEMIA AND DOROTHY:** Then, what must we do?

**MADAME DE LA HALTIÈRE:** Do as I do!
The ball room is a battle field . . .

**NOEMIA AND DOROTHY:** How, Mama, The ball room is a battle field? . . .

**MADAME DE LA HALTIÈRE:** Carry yourselves well, Be careful of your figures, And don't get too nervous . . .

**NOEMIA AND DOROTHY:** No, mama!

**MADAME DE LA HALTIÈRE:** Have they curled your hair?

**NOEMIA AND DOROTHY:** Yes, mama!

**MADAME DE LA HALTIÈRE:** (*aside, volubly, as if speaking to herself*). For I do not wish, nor can I bring myself To believe that it is only In romance That the unexpected happens!

**NOEMIA AND DOROTHY:** The unexpected!

**MADAME DE LA HALTIÈRE:** (*to her daughters*). Assume a gracious manner, And smile pleasantly. Good! Don't appear too haughty!

**NOEMIA AND DOROTHY:** There, mama!

**MADAME DE LA HALTIÈRE:** Splendid! could not be better! Don't be commonplace! Nor too original!

**MADAME DE LA HALTIÈRE:** Make yourselves beautiful this evening! What success we shall have! But you do not know How much I hope!

**NOEMIA and DOROTHY:** We will be beautiful this evening! What success we shall have! And we already know How much you hope!

## SCÈNE IV

Les memes, Les Domestiques.

**LES DOMESTIQUES:** (*affairés*). Madame, ce sont les modistes.

**D'AUTRES:** Madame, ce sont les tailleurs.

**D'AUTRES:** Madame, ce sont les coiffeurs.

**MADAME DE LA HALTIÈRE:** (*avec ostentation*). Qu'on introduise ces artistes!
(*Pendant que les modistes, les coiffeurs et les tailleurs s'occupent de la toilette des trois femmes.*)
De sa robe, il faut que les plis
Soient plus légers, plus assouplis.
(*A ses filles*)
Qu'en dites-vous? . . . La ligne est pure . . .
Très bien cela. Cette coiffure
Est concordante à la figure!

**LES DOMESTIQUES:** (*au fond, pouffant de rire*). Cheveux garantis sur facture.

**NOÈMIE ET DOROTHÉE:** (*s'interrogeant mutuellement*). Sommes-nous bien ainsi? Oui, véritablement Sans compliment, C'est charmant! C'est charmant!

**MADAME DE LA HALTIÈRE:** Charmant!

**NOÈMIE ET DOROTHÉE:** (*flattant leur mère*). Un éblouissement!

**LES DOMESTIQUES:** (*au fond, même jeu*). Est-elle fagotée?

**MADAME DE LA HALTIÈRE:** (*flattant ses filles*). Un émerveillement!

**LES DOMESTIQUES:** (*au fond, même jeu*) Et Noémie! Et Dorothée?

**MADAME DE LA HALTIÈRE:** (*et ses deux filles*). On en parlera sûrement!

**LES DOMESTIQUES:** (*même jeu*). Oui, oui, sûrement!
(*Les fournisseurs sont reconduits par les domestiques*).

**PANDOLFE:** (*entrant en grande toilette*) Félicitez-moi donc de mon exactitude.

**NOÈMIE ET DOROTHÉE:** Oui . . . ce n'est pas votre habitude.

**MADAME DE LA HALTIÈRE:** Vous êtes toujours en retard Enfin . . . cette fois . . . par hasard . . .

**NOÈMIE ET DOROTHÉE:** (*se montrant avec prétention*). Ne sauriez-vous trouver un mot aimable à dire En voyant nos beautés? . . .

## SCENE IV

THE SAME. THE SERVANTS.

**THE SERVANTS:** (*busy*). Madame, the dressmakers.

**OTHERS:** Madame, the tailors.

**OTHERS:** Madame, the hairdressers.

**MADAME DE LA HALTIÈRE:** (*ostentatiously*). Let these artists enter!
(*The dressmakers, tailors and hairdressers become busy with the toilets of the three women*)
Your robe must have the plaits
Hang lighter, in graceful lines.
(*To her daughters*)
What think you? . . . Is the linen fine . . .
That is very nice. The headdress
Is becoming to the figure!

**THE SERVANTS:** (*at rear, stifling with mirth*). The hair is as per invoice.

**NOEMIA AND DOROTHY:** (*mutually examining each other*). Do we look well this way? Yes, without doubt, or compliment, It is charming! It is charming!

**MADAME DE LA HALTIÈRE:** Charming!

**NOEMIA AND DOROTHY:** (*flattering their mother*). A marvel!

**THE SERVANTS:** (*at rear, same manner*). Isn't she a fright?

**MADAME DE LA HALTIÈRE:** (*flattering her daughters*). Ravishing!

**THE SERVANTS:** (*at rear, same play*). And Noemia! And Dorothy!

**MADAME DE LA HALTIÈRE:** (*and her two daughters*). They will talk of it surely!

**THE SERVANTS:** (*same play*). Yes, yes, surely!
(*The workwomen are conducted away by the servants*).

**PANDOLFE:** (*entering in grand attire*). Congratulate me on my promptness.

**NOEMIA AND DOROTHY:** Yes . . . it is not your habit.

**MADAME DE LA HALTIÈRE:** You are always late, At last . . . for once . . . by chance . . .

**NOEMIA AND DOROTHY:** (*showing themselves off, pretentiously*). Can you not find a word of commendation When you see our beauty? . . .

**PANDOLFE:** (*préoccupé*). Excusez-moi . . . j'admire . . .
(*A part, pendant que les trois femmes se pavanent*)
Ne disons rien, restons tranquille en notre coin,
Ne voulant de près ou de loin
Ajouter même une parole,
Un doux espoir me soutenant,
Me caressant, me consolant . . .
(*Montrant sa femme, joyeusement*)
On va l'enfermer, elle est folle!

**MADAME DE LA HALTIÈRE:** (*brusquement*). Eh! bien! Qu'avez-vous donc? Vous restez comme un pieu Planté là!

**NOÉMIE:** Venez donc!

**DOROTHÉE:** Et partons!

**MADAME DE LA HALTIÈRE:** Venez vite!

**PANDOLFE:** Tout de suite! de suite!
(*A part, avec émotion*)
Ma Lucette . . . je pars sans t'avoir dit adieu! . . .
Je te laisse encore seule . . . ô ma pauvre petite!
Je pars sans même oser
Te donner un baiser!
Sans bercer ta tristesse
D'un seul mot de tendresse! . . .

**MADAME DE LA HALTIÈRE:** (*regardant ses filles*). Quand le prince aura vu leurs attraits enchanteurs,
La fortune est à nous . . . Le trône et ses grandeurs!

**MADAME DE LA HALTIÈRE, NOÈMIE ET DOROTHÉE:** De la race
De la prestance,
De l'audace,
De l'élégance,
De la finesse,
Ensorcelante,
Une souplesse
Un peu troublante,
Lèvre mutine
Et délicate,
Le mot qui flatte,
Grâce assassine,
Des yeux de chatte.
Elles ont tout, oui, vraiment tout!
Le prince est pris, s'il a du goût!
(*Sortie générale. Les domestiques emportent les candélabres et les flambeaux pour accompagner le départ.—Obscurité.*)

## SCÈNE V

**CENDRILLON:** (*paraissant*). Ah! que mes soeurs sont heureuses! Pour elles
C'est chaque jour nouveau plaisir!
Elles n'ont pas le temps de former un désir . . .
Et le bonheur aussi, je crois, les rend plus belles! . . .
Elles vont à la cour . . . à la cour . . . !oh! ce bal!
On y viendra de toutes les prov-

**PANDOLFE:** (*preoccupied*). Excuse me . . . I admire . . .
(*aside, while the three women strut along*).
Let's say nothing, but stay quiet in our corner,
Not wishing near or far
To add one word even,
A sweet hope sustaining me,
Caressing me, consoling me.
(*Pointing to his wife, merrily*)
They will lock her up, she is mad!

**MADAME DE LA HALTIÈRE:** (*brusquely*). Well! What is wrong with you? You stand there.

**NOEMIA:** Come along!

**DOROTHY:** Let us go!

**MADAME DE LA HALTIÈRE:** Hurry!

**PANDOLFE:** Immediately! Immediately!
(*Aside, with emotion*)
I go, my Lucette, without bidding you farewell!
I leave you alone again . . . O my little one!
I go without daring
Even to kiss you!
Without comforting you
With a single word of tenderness.

**MADAME DE LA HALTIÈRE:** (*looking at her daughters*). When the prince sees their enchanting attractions,
Fortune is ours . . . the throne and its splendors!

**MADAME DE LA HALTIÈRE, NOEMIA AND DOROTHY:** Of birth,
Deportment,
Audacity
And elegance,
Daintiness,
Bewitchment,
Carriage
Distracting,
Pouting lips
And delicate,
The word that flatters,
Grace assassinates,
Cats' eyes
They have all of these, yes all!
The prince is captured, if any taste he has!
(*All go out. The servants carry with them the candle sticks. Obscurity.*)

## SCENE V

**CINDERELLA:** (*appearing*). Ah! how happy my sisters are! For them
Each day brings some newer pleasure!
They have scarcely time to form a wish . . .
And fortune, too, I think, makes them beautiful!
They go to court! Oh, that ball! . . .
From everywhere they'll come to

inces;
Tous les seigneurs seront au moins
marquis ou princes
A l'entour du trône royal!
Et mes soeurs seront
là . . . tandis que moi . . . je
rêve . . .
Et j'ai tort, oui, j'ai tort. Ces rêves-là
font mal!
Ma besogne est là qu'il faut que
j'achève!
Reste au foyer, petit grillon,
Car ce n'est pas pour toi que brille
Ce superbe et joyeux rayon . . .
Ne vas-tu pas porter envie au papil-
lon?
A quoi penses-tu, pauvre fille?
Travaille, Cendrillon,
Résigne-toi, Cendrille!
C'est une joie aussi de faire son de-
voir!
Débarrassons la table et rangeons le
dressoir!
Je suis décidément paresseuse ce
soir.
J'ai beau vouloir . . . j'entends
toujours des bruits de fête
Dont les échos troublants bourdon-
nent dans ma tête . . .
Reste au foyer, petit grillon,
Car ce n'est pas pour toi que brille
Ce superbe et joyeux rayon . . .
Ne vas-tu pas porter envie au papil-
lon?
A quoi penses-tu, pauvre fille?
Résigne-toi, Cendrille,
Travaille, Cendrillon!
Voyons, j'ai bien fait tout ce que
j'avais à faire.
Je puis me reposer.
Comme la nuit est claire!
Les étoiles ont l'air de me sourire,
aux cieux!
C'est étrange! on dirait que le som-
meil m'accable!
Je ne suis plus à l'âge où le marc-
hand de sable
Venait si tôt, jadis, fermer mes
yeux!
Dormons; souvent on est heureux
Quand on dort . . . et qu'on fait
des songes merveilleux!
(En s'endormant, Cendrillon dit
encore:)
Reste au foyer petit grillon
Fésigne-toi! Résigne-toi!

## SCÈNE VI

Cendrillon endormie, La Fée, puis
Les Esprits et Les Follets.

**LA FÉE:** (apparaissant, à Cendrillon, endormie) Douce enfant, ta
plainte légère
Comme l'haleine d'une fleur,
Vient de monter jusqu'à mon coeur.
Ta marraine te voit et te
protège . . . espère! . . .

**VOIX LOINTAINS:** Espère!

**LA FÉE:** Sylphes, lutins, follets, accourez à ma voix,
De tous les horizons, à travers les
espaces . . .

it;
The lords, at least, will surely be
marquises and princes
Around the royal throne!
And my sisters will be
there . . . while I . . . I
dream.
And I do wrong, yes
wrong . . . These dreams are
bad!
My work is here, I must perform it!
Stay by the fireside, little cricket,
For it is not for you that shines
That superb and joyous ray . . .
Do not go and envy the butterfly?
Of what do you think, poor girl?
Work, Cinderella,
Resignation, Cinderella.
Pleasant it also is to do your duty!
Let us clear the table and wash the
dishes!
I feel decidedly lazy tonight.
I wish in vain . . . I still hear the
sounds of merriment
Whose disturbing echos burden my
head . . .
Stay by the fireside, little cricket,
For it is not for you that shines
That superb and joyous ray . . .
Do not go and envy the butterfly?
Of what do you think, poor girl?
Resignation, Cinderella,
Work, Cinderella!
See, I have done all I had to do.
I can go to bed.
How clear the night is!
The stars appear to smile on me,
from heaven!
Strange! one would think sleep
weighed on me!
No longer am I of the age when the
Sandman
Came so early, as he used to do, to
close my eyes.
Let us sleep; often is one happy
When asleep . . . and dreaming
marvelous dreams!
(As she goes to sleep, Cinderella
still says.)
Stay by the fireside, little cricket,
Resignation! Resignation!

## SCENE VI

CINDERELLA, asleep, THE FAIRY,
then SPIRITS AND GOBLINS.

**THE FAIRY:** (appearing, to Cinderella, asleep). Sweet child, your
gentle complaint
Like the breath of a flower,
Has reached my heart,
Your Godmother sees and protects
you . . . hope!

**DISTANT VOICES:** Hope!

**THE FAIRY:** Sylphs, goblins, spirits, come at my bidding
From out the air, through spaces
vast . . .

(Les esprits et les follets apparais-
sent)
Suivez exactement mes lois.
Apportez-moi tous vos talents,
toutes vos grâces!
Je veux que cette enfant charmante,
que voici,
Soit aujourd'hui hors de souci
Et que par vous, splendidement
parée,
Elle connaisse enfin le bonheur à
son tour . . .
Je veux qu'aux fêtes de la cour
Elle soit la plus belle et la plus ad-
mirée.

**LA FÉE:** O Cendrillon, ma fleur
d'innocence et d'amour,
Sur toi je veille!

**CENDRILLON:** (endormie). Vision ravissante! Étonnante merveille!

**LES ESPRITS:** Cendrillon, tu seras
la beauté sans pareille!

**LA FÉE:** (aux follets). Pour en faire
un tissu magiquement soyeux
Dont vous composerez sa robe,
Que votre main adroitement
dérobe
Aux astres radieux
La subtile splendeur de leurs rayons
joyeux,
A l'arc-en-ciel ses harmonies,
Au clair de lune empruntez ses
pâleurs,
Et que pour son bouquet soient par
vous réunies
En un philtre d'amour les plus
douces senteurs.
(A un groupe de follets).
Et vous, préparez l'attelage!
(A un follet)
Toi, tu seras cocher.

**UN ESPRIT:** Et moi?

**LA FÉE:** Tu seras page!
(A d'autres)
Et vous serez les postillons!

**LA FÉE ET LES ESPRITS:** (aux fol-
lets). Tous les petits oixeaux vous
prêteront leurs ailes,
Les coursiers seront les insectes
frêles,
Les phalènes, les papillons
Et les légères demoiselles. Habiles
artisans,
Fournissez-nous des pierreries
En butinant dans les prairies,
Coccinelles et vers luisants!
Que les moucherons et les scar-
abées
Égalent des rubis les purs scintille-
ments.
Aux larmes de la nuit, sur les rose
pâmées
Donnez l'éclat des diamants.
Vous cacherez des lucioles,
Pour éclairer tout son chemin,
Au fond des tremblantes corolles
Des tulipiers et du jasmin.

**LA FÉE:** (à Cendrillon, toujours
endormie). Tout est donc prêt.
Éveille-toi, petite!

(Spirits and goblins appear.)
Follow my commands exactly,
Bring me all your talents, all your
graces!
I wish this charming child
Free from all care today,
And that you dress her splendidly,
So happy she may be at last . . .
At court I wish her to appear
The prettiest and most admired.

**THE FAIRY:** O Cinderella, my
flower of purity and love,
I watch over you.

**CINDERELLA:** (asleep). Ravishing
vision! Astonishing marvel.

**THE SPIRITS:** Cinderella, you will
be beauty itself!

**THE FAIRY:** (to the goblins). To
make the finest silken fabric,
Needed for her gown,
Your hands must rob
The brightest stars
Of the subtle splendor of their bril-
liant rays.
And the harmonies of the rainbow
take.
And the paleness of the moonlight
too.
And for her bouquet you must gath-
er
In love's philtre the sweetest es-
sences.
(To a group of goblins)
And you, prepare the escort!
(To a goblin)
You shall be the coachman.

**A SPIRIT:** And I?

**THE FAIRY:** You shall be the page!
(To others)
And you will be the postillions!

**THE FAIRY AND THE SPIRITS:**
(to the goblins). All the birds will
lend their wings,
The horses will be feeble insects,
Moths and butterflies
And nimble dragon-flies. Clever
workers
Furnish us the jewels
Stealing from the meadows
Lady bugs and glossy worms!
Let the gnats and beetles
Match the purest rubies scintillat-
ing.
The tears of night, on drooping
roses
Give the brilliancy of diamonds.
You will catch the fireflies
To light your path,
Searching in the trembling corols,
Of the tulip trees and jasmines.

**THE FAIRY:** (to Cinderella, still
asleep). Everything is ready now,
Awake, little one!

**LES ESPRITS:** (*à Cendrillon*) C'et ta marraine qui t'invite,
O Cendrillon! ô fleur d'amour!
On t'attend au bal de la Cour!
Tes voeux sont exaucés. Eveille-toi, petite!

**CENDRILLON:** (*en rêvant*). Enfin . . . je connaîtrai le bonheur à mon tour!
(*Tristement*)
On ne va pas au bal, à la cour, en guenille . . .
(*Avec ravissement*)
Que vois-je? Suis-je folle?
(*Avec stupeur et joie, en se voyant superbement parée.*)
Est-ce de l'or qui brille?
A la place de mon haillon,
Cette robe splendide et ce manteau qui traîne!
Ah! je ne suis plus Cendrillon!
Ni Lucette! . . . je suis princesse . . . je suis reine . . .
(*A la fée avec effusion.*)
Merci, merci, bonne marraine!

**LA FÉE:** Écoute bien. Quand sonnera minuit,
Ici, je veux que tu sois revenue.
Donc, par quelque plaisir que tu sois retenue,
Du bal tu partiras sans bruit.

**LES ESPRITS:** Quand sonnera minuit . . .

**CENDRILLON:** Je serai revenue . . .

**LA FÉE ET LES ESPRITS:** Souviens-toi bien.

**CENDRILLON:** A l'heure convenue.
(*Cendrillon, sur le point de partir, s'arrête et avec un découragement soudain.*)
Mais hélas! c'en est fait déjà de mes bonheurs!

**LA FÉE:** Que dis-tu?

**CENDRILLON:** Ma mère et mes soeurs
Sont à ce bal . . . Je serai reconnue. Et . . .

**LA FÉE:** Calme tes vaines frayeurs.
Cette pantoufle mignonne Que je te donne,
Est un talisman précieux
Qui rendra ma Lucette inconnue à leurs yeux.
En route, maintenant, en route, le temps presse
(*Montrant le carrosse*)
Voici ton carrosse, princesse!

**CENDRILLON:** (*avec une joie naïve*) Qu'il est joli! . . . qu'il est petit!

**LA FÉE:** Tous les esprits
Lutins, follets, seront à tes ordres.

**CENDRILLON:** (*avec une gaieté débordante*). Je ris!
Ne fût-ce qu'une fois, qu'une heure dans ma vie,
Moi qui ne connaissais encore que les mépris,

**THE SPIRITS:** (*to Cinderella*). It is your godmother who invites you,
O Cinderella! Flower of love!
At the court ball they await you!
Your wishes are granted. Awake, little one!

**CINDERELLA:** (*dreaming*). At last . . . I shall know happiness too!
(*sadly*)
One cannot go to the ball, at court, in rags . . .
(*rapturously*)
What do I see? Am I mad?
(*With stupefaction and joy, seeing how she is dressed.*)
Is this gold that glitters?
Instead of my rags,
This splendid robe and this mantle with train!
Oh! I am no longer Cinderella!
Nor Lucette! . . . I am a princess . . . I am a queen . . .
(*To the Fairy effusively*)
Thanks, thanks, kind godmother!

**THE FAIRY:** Listen carefully, when midnight sounds,
Here I wish you to return.
However great the pleasure that detains you then,
From the ball retire quietly.

**THE SPIRITS:** When midnight sounds . . .

**CINDERELLA:** I will return . . .

**THE FAIRY AND THE SPIRITS:** Do not forget.

**CINDERELLA:** At the hour fixed.
(*Cinderella, on the point of going out, stops, suddenly discouraged.*)
But alas! My happiness already ends!

**THE FAIRY:** What do you mean?

**CINDERELLA:** My mother and sisters
Are at the ball . . . I will be recognized. And . . .

**THE FAIRY:** Calm your idle fears.
This tiny slipper that I give you,
Is a talisman most precious
That will make my Lucette to their eyes unknown.
Now go, be off, time presses.
(*Pointing to the carriage*).
Behold your coach, my Princess!

**CINDERELLA:** (*with naive joy*). How pretty it is! . . . how small it is!

**THE FAIRY:** All the spirits,
All the goblins will obey you.

**CINDERELLA:** (*with excessive gaiety*). I laugh!
If only for once in my life, for a single hour,
I who have known only scorn until now

Des plus belles j'aurai pu mériter l'envie!
Je ris! Je ris!

**LA FÉE ET LES ESPRITS:** Partez, madame la princesse,
Le coeur content, le front joyeux!
Mais, fidèle à votre promesse,
Minuit sonnant, soyez de retour en ces lieux!

**CENDRILLON:** Fidèle à ma promesse,
A minuit, je serai de retour en ces lieux!

**LA FÉE ET LES ESPRITS:** Partez! partez! madame la princesse!

*FIN DE L'ACTE PREMIÈR.*

■ **ACTE DEUXIÈME**

*SCÈNE PREMIÈRE*
___

*Chez Le Roi.*

(*La salle des fêtes et les jardins du palais. Le tout brillamment illuminé.*)

*Le Prince Charmant. Auprès de lui trois musiciens, [luth, viole d'amour et flûte de cristal] font entendre pendant toute la scène comme un concert mystérieux. Le Surintendant des Plaisirs, avec un groupe de Courtisans, saluant Le Prince, puis Les Docteurs et Les Ministres.*

**LE SURINTENDANT:** (*au prince*). Que les doux pensers sur vos lèvres Viennent éclore souriants.
Laissez la tristesse et ses fièvres,
Fuyez les chagrins décevants.
Noble prince,
Répondez!

**LES COURTISANS:** (*entre eux*). Non. Il ne nous répond rien.

**LE SURINTENDANT:** Messieurs, je crois qu'on nous évince.

**TOUS:** Aucun moyen
De prolonger cet entretien.
Pauvre Prince!
(*Ils se retirent et sont remplacés par un groupe de docteurs*).

**LE DOYEN DE LA FACULTÉ:** (*au Prince*). Par Hippocrate et docta lex
Volumus vos auscultare,
Chère Altesse, atque drogare
Suivant les règles du Codex.
Noble Prince
Écoutez!

**LES DOCTEURS:** (*entre eux*). Non. Il n'écoutera rien.

**LE DOYEN:** Messieurs, je crois qu'on nous évince.

**TOUS:** Aucun moyen
De prolonger cet entretien.
(*Les docteurs s'éloignant font place au groupe des ministres.*)

Will merit the envy of the most beautiful ones.
I laugh! I laugh!

**THE FAIRY AND THE SPIRITS:**
Go, Madame the Princess,
With happy heart and smiling face!
But remember to keep your promise,
At midnight you must return!

**CINDERELLA:** I'll remember my promise,
At midnight I will return!

**THE FAIRY AND THE SPIRITS:**
Go! Go! Madame the Princess!

*END OF ACT I.*

■ **ACT II**

*SCENE I*
___

*THE KING'S COURT.*

(*The Court room and gardens of the Palace, all brilliantly illumined.*)

*Prince Charming. Around him three musicians (lute, love violin and cristal flute) compose a mysterious Concert during the entire scene. The Guardian of Pleasures with a group of Courtiers, saluting the prince, then the Doctors and Ministers.*

**THE GUARDIAN:** (*to the Prince*). May sweet thoughts on your lips Break ever smilingly.
Leave sadness and its gloom,
Fly from deceptive sorrow.
Noble Prince,
Reply!

**THE COURTIERS:** (*to each other*). No! He answers nothing.

**THE GUARDIAN:** Gentlemen, I think we are dismissed.

**ALL:** No means
Of entertaining further.
Poor Prince!
(*They retire aside and are replaced by a group of doctors.*)

**THE DEAN OF FACULTY:** (*to the Prince*). By Hippocrates and docta lex
Volumus vos auscultare,
Dear Highness, atque drogare.
Following the rules of the Codex.
Noble Prince,
Listen.

**THE DOCTORS:** (*among themselves*). No, he will hear nothing.

**THE DEAN:** Gentlemen, I think we are dismissed.

**ALL:** No means
Of entertaining further.
(*The Doctors retire aside and make place for a group of ministers.*)

LE PREMIER MINISTRE: (*au Prince*). Nous sommons Votre Seigneurie
De venir s'amuser au bal
Et de chasser sa rêverie,
Aux termes d'un décret royal.
Noble Prince,
Consentez.

THE PRIME MINISTERS: (*to the Prince*). We summon Your Lordship
To the amusements of the ball,
To drive your pensive thoughts away,
By royal decree.
Noble Prince,
Consent.

LES MINISTRES: (*entre eux*). Non. Il ne consent à rien.

THE MINISTERS: (*among themselves*). No. He consents to nothing.

LE PREMIER MINISTRE: Messieurs, je crois qu'on nous évince.

THE PRIME MINISTER: Gentlemen, I think we are dismissed.

TOUS: Aucun moyen
De prolonger cet entretien.

ALL: No means
Of entertaining further.

LES TROIS GROUPES: (*légèrement, changeant de ton, avec indifférence, en s'éparpillant*). Pauvre Prince! Pauvre Prince! Pauvre Prince!

THE THREE GROUPS: (*lightly, changing their tone, with indifference and dispersing*). Poor Prince! Poor Prince! Poor Prince!

## SCÈNE II

LE PRINCE CHARMANT: (*seul*).
Allez, laissez-moi seul . . . seul avec mes ennuis . . .
Coeur sans amour, printemps sans roses!
Pour moi, tous les jours sont moroses
Et moroses toutes les nuits! . . .
Pourtant, de doux frissons glissent par tout mon être . . .
Si, me tendant les bras, je la voyais paraître,
Celle que veut mon âme! Enivré, radieux,
Je lui dirais dans mon ivresse:
"De nous l'amour fera des dieux,
Je suis à toi. Prends ma jeunesse!"
Mais je vis triste et seul, le coeur brisé d'ennuis . . .
Pour moi, tous les jours sont moroses
Et moroses toutes les nuits! . . .
Coeur sans amour! Printemps sans roses!
Ah! si je la trouvais, oubliant la grandeur,
Dédaigneux des richesses,
Du trône je prendrais en pitié la splendeur,
Pour ne plus rien goûter que nos chères tendresses!

## SCENE II

PRINCE CHARMING: (*alone*).
Go, leave me alone! . . . alone with my boredom . . .
Heart without love, spring without roses!
All days for me are sombre
And sad all my nights! . . .
Yet, sweet emotions flit through my being . . .
If, her arms extending, I should see her come,
Her whom my soul desires! Elated, jubilant,
I would tell her in my ardor
"Love shall make us as the gods,
I am yours; accept my youth!"
But alone and sad I live, my heart oppressed by boredom . . .
All days to me are sombre,
And sad all my nights,
Heart without love, spring without the rose.
Ah! If I found her, forgetting grandeur,
Scorning riches,
I'd take its splendor from the throne,
Henceforth to enjoy only our sweet caresses.

## SCÈNE III

LE PRINCE CHARMANT. *Entrée du Roi et de la COUR.*

LE ROI: Mon fils, il vous faut m'obéir.
Vous allez voir à cette fête
Les filles de noblesse! Or, vous devrez choisir
Celle qui vous fera le mieux tourner la tête,
Et l'épouser . . . Mon fils, tel est mon bon plaisir!

PREMIÈRE ENTRÉE: (*Les Filles de Noblesse.*)

## SCENE III

PRINCE CHARMING. THE KING *and* COURT *enter.*

THE KING: My son, you must obey me.
At this entertainment you will see
The daughters of the nobility! You must choose
The one that turns your head the most
And marry her . . . My son, such is my pleasure!

FIRST ENTRY:
(*Daughters of the Nobility.*)

DEUXIÈME ENTRÉE: (*Les Fiancés.*)

SECOND ENTRY:
(*The Lovers.*)

TROISIÈME ENTRÉE: (*Les Mandores.*)

THIRD ENTRY
(*The Mandores.*)

QUATRIÈME ENTRÉE: (*La Florentine.*)

FOURTH ENTRY:
(*The Florentine.*)

CINQUIÈME ENTRÉE: (*Le Rigodon du Roy.*)
(*Entrent Madame de la Haltière, ses deux filles, Pandolfe, le Surintendant, le Doyen et le premier Ministre. Aussitôt après les révérences.*)

FIFTH ENTRY:
(*The King's Rigadoon.*)
(*Enter Madame de la Haltière, her two daughters, Pandolfe, the Guardian, the Dean, the Prime Minister. Immediately after, homage is paid.*)

LE DOYEN, LE SURINTENDANT ET LE PREMIER MINISTRE: (*Aux trois femmes*) Ah! vous êtes on sa présence!
Par votre superbe prestance
Jouez de tous vos attraits,
C'est l'instant où jamais!

THE DEAN, THE GUARDIAN AND THE PRIME MINISTER: (*to the three women*). Ah! You are in his presence!
Through your superb deportment
Enhance all your charms,
It is now or never!

MADAME DE LA HALTIÈRE, SES DEUX FILLES ET PANDOLFE: (*Confidentiellement entre elles*). Ah! nous sommes en sa présence!
Par notre superbe prestance
Jouons de tous nos attraits,
C'est l'instant où jamais!
(*Pendant la danse à laquelle prennent part madame de la Haltière et ses deux filles.*)

MADAME DE LA HALTIÈRE, HER TWO DAUGHTERS AND PANDOLFE: (*Confidentially and among themselves*). Ah! in his presence we are!
Through our superb deportment
Enhance all our charms,
It is now or never!
(*During the dance in which Madame de la Haltière and her two daughters take part*).

PANDOLFE: (*à part dans le plus grand trouble*). Que je suis donc ému! Mon auguste maître,
Sa Majesté, va me parler
Elle m'a reconnu . . . peut-être . . .
Ah! je voudrais bein m'en aller!
(*Pendant la danse, quand les couples se rencontrent.*)

PANDOLFE: (*aside, in great trouble*). How moved I am! My august master,
His Majesty, will speak to me.
Perhaps already he recognizes me . . .
Ah! I would like to get away!
(*During the dance, when the couples come together*).

NOÈMIE ET DOROTHÉE: (*à leur mère, rapidement, en passant*). Maman, nous sommes angoissées . . .

NOEMIA AND DOROTHY: (*to their mother, rapidly, as they pass*). Mama, we are distressed . . .

MADAME DE LA HALTIÈRE: (*à ses filles, même jeu*). Ne soyez pas embarrassées . . .
Le prince vient . . . c'est le moment

MADAME DE LA HALTIÈRE: (*to her daughters, same play*) Don't be embarrassed . . .
The Prince is coming . . . it is the moment

DOROTHÉE: Je défaille . . . Ah! maman!

DOROTHY: I am fainting . . . Ah! mama!

MADAME DE LA HALTIÈRE: Vos robes vont être froissées!
(*Cendrillon paraît. Le Prince, qui semblait l'attendre, la contemple de loin, en extase. — Grand étonnement de toute l'assistance. Stupeur et dépit des dames de la Haltière. Chacun observe tour à tour Cendrillon qui s'avance lentement.*)

MADAME DE LA HALTIÈRE: Your gowns will be crushed!
(*Cinderella appears. The Prince, who seems to be awaiting her, looks at her from a distance, in ecstasy. Great astonishment of the assembly. Stupefaction and chagrin of the de la Haltière ladies. Each in turn observes Cinderella, who advances slowly.*)

LA FOULE: Voyez! L'adorable beauté!

THE CROWD: Look! The adorable beauty!

MADAME DE LA HALTIÈRE ET SES FILLES: (*avec dépit*). Le prince paraît transporté!

MADAME DE LA HALTIÈRE AND HER DAUGHTERS: (*spitefully*). The Prince appears transported!

## Act II, Scene III

**LA FOULE:** (*entre groupes*). Qui la connaît?
Personne!
Rien ne la trouble et ne l'étonne.
Elle est exquise en vérité!

**LA FOULE:** O la surprenante aventure!
O la charmante créature!
La voilà
Notre reine future!
Saluons-la!

**MADAME DE LA HALTIÈRE, ET SES FILLES:** (*avec dépit*). O la décevante aventure!
O la bizarre créature!
Est-ce là
Notre reine future!
Évitons-là!

**PANDOLFE, LE DOYEN, LE SURINTENDANT ET LE PREMIER MINISTRE:** O la surprenante aventure!
O la charmante créature!
C'est bien là
Notre reine future!
Saluons-là!

**LE ROI:** O la suprenante aventure!
O la charmante créature!
La voilà!
C'est la reine future!
Saluez-la!
(*Le Prince s'est rapproché de Cendrillon.*)
(*Le Roi, ravi, fait retirer tout le monde avec discrétion de l'autre côté, Madame de la Haltière éloigne ses filles avec un geste de pudeur offensée, puis retourne vivement chercher son mari qui était resté en contemplation devant la beauté de l'inconnue, et elle le fait partir d'un air d'autorité scandalisée.*)

### SCÈNE IV

*Le Prince, Cendrillon, La Fée.*

**LE PRINCE:** (*à Cendrillon*). Toi qui m'es apparue,
O beau rêve enchanteur, beauté du ciel venue
Ah! par pitié, dis-moi de quel nom te salue,
O Reine, la céleste cour
Qui, dans le paradis, t'invoque avec amour . . .
Par pitié, dis-le moi! Toi qui m'es apparue!

**CENDRILLON:** Pour vous, je serai l'Inconnue!

**LE PRINCE:** Beauté du ciel venue
Qui donc es-tu . . . ?

**CENDRILLON:**
L'Inconnue! . . .
Vous l'avez dit, je suis le rêve et dois passer
Sans qu'il en reste trace,
Comme s'efface

Un reflet du ciel que l'on voit glisser
Sud l'eau, que le vent ride et pousse.
Et qui bientôt ira se perdre dans la mousse . . .

**LE PRINCE:** Je te perdrais, moi, non . . . non . . . plutôt le trépas!
Qui que tu sois, partout, je veux suivre tes pas . . .

**CENDRILLON:** Non, je vais fuir, hélas!
Et vous ne me reverrez pas! . . .

**LE PRINCE:** Ah! cette parole cruelle,
Est-ce bien toi qui l'as dite? Comment
Ta lèvre si douce peut-elle
La prononcer? Ton oeil candide la dément . . .

**CENDRILLON:** (*tendrement*).
Vous êtes mon prince Charmant,
Et, si j'écoutais mon envie,
Je voudrais consacrer ma vie
A vous complaire seulement . . .
Vous êtes mon prince Charmant.
Vous êtes mon prince Charmant,
Et mon âme gémit, blessée
Jusqu'à mourir à la pensée
De vous attrister seulement . . .
Vous êtes mon prince Charmant.

**LE PRINCE:** Eh bien, laisse ta main dans la mienne pressée
Car, si de toi j'étais abandonné,
Lors, je serais ton prince infortuné!

**CENDRILLON:** (*à part, très émue*). Sa voix est comme une harmonie
Qui ravit mon oreille et tient mon coeur charmé . . .

**LE PRINCE:** Ah! reste et prends pitié de mon coeur alarmé! . . .
Éveille en mon esprit la douceur infinie
Et le charme innocent de l'avril embaumé!

**CENDRILLON:** Oui, du seul souvenir de cette heure bénie,
Mon esprit restera pour toujours embaumé! . . .

**LE PRINCE:** Je t'aime et t'aimerai toujours . . .

**CENDRILLON:** (*Elle écoute anxieuse le premier coup de minuit qui sonne au loin.*) Ah! je frissonne!

**LE PRINCE:** (*tendre et pressant*). Rien ne m'éloignera de toi . . . rien, ni personne!

**CENDRILLON:** (*se détachant peu à peu des étreintes du Prince*). L'heure! déjà! mon Dieu! déjà l'heure qui sonne! . . .

---

**THE CROWD:** (*in groups*). Who knows her?
No one!
Nothing troubles or surprises her . . .
She is in truth exquisite!

**THE CROWD:** O surprising adventure!
O charming creature!
See her!
Our future queen!
Salute her!

**MADAME DE LA HALTIÈRE AND HER DAUGHTERS:** (*spitefully*). O deceptive adventure!
O strange creature!
Is that
Our future queen!
Avoid her!

**PANDOLFE, THE DEAN, THE GUARDIAN AND THE PRIME MINISTER:** O surprising adventure!
O charming creature!
She surely is
Our future queen!
Salute her!

**THE KING:** O surprising adventure!
O charming creature!
See her!
The future queen!
Salute her!
(*The Prince has approached Cinderella. The King, delighted, commands all to retire discretely to the other side of the room. Madame de la Haltière moves away with her daughters in offensive dignity, then turns quickly in search of her husband who had remained in contemplation of the unknown beauty, and with an air of scandalized authority, compels him to leave.*)

### SCENE IV

*THE PRINCE, CINDERELLA, THE FAIRY.*

**THE PRINCE:** (*to Cinderella*). You who have appeared to me,
O enchanting dream, beauty from heaven descended,
Ah! in mercy, tell me, by what name are you saluted,
O Queen, in the celestial court
Which, in paradise, invokes you with its love . . .
In mercy, tell me! You who have appeared to me!

**CINDERELLA:** To you I will remain The Unknown!

**THE PRINCE:** Beauty from heaven descended
Who then are you? . . .

**CINDERELLA:** The Unknown! . . .
As you said, I am a dream and must fade
Leaving no trace behind,
As vanishes
A reflection of the sky when seen to glide
Over water, when roughened by the breeze,
Soon lost within the shadow of the mossy bank.

**PRINCE:** I shall lose you,
no . . . ah, no . . . sooner death!
Wherever you go I shall follow you . . .

**CINDERELLA:** No, I shall flee, alas!
And you shall not find me! . . .

**THE PRINCE:** Ah! that cruel word,
Is it you who speak it? How
Can lips so sweet pronounce it?
Your candid eye belies it . . .

**CINDERELLA:** (*tenderly*). You are my prince Charming,
And if I hearkened to my wish,
I would consecrate my life
To pleasing only you . . .
You are my Prince Charming,
My Prince Charming you are,
And my soul sighs, wounded
Even unto death, at thinking
I could cause you sadness even . . .
You are my Prince Charming.

**THE PRINCE:** Then, let your hand lie close in mine,
For, if I am abandoned by you,
Then, I shall be your luckless Prince! . . .

**CINDERELLA:** (*aside, much moved*). His voice is like sweet harmony
That my ear enravishes and holds my heart encharmed . . .

**THE PRINCE:** Ah! stay and have mercy for my afrighted heart! . . .
Wake in my spirit infinite sweetness
And the pure charm of perfumed April . . .

**CINDERELLA:** Yes, by the recollection of this happy hour,
My spirit ever shall remain perfumed! . . .

**THE PRINCE:** I love you and shall ever love you . . .

**CINDERELLA:** (*she listens anxiously to the first strokes of midnight which sound afar off*). Ah! I shudder!

**THE PRINCE:** (*tender and urging*). Nothing shall take me from you . . . nothing, nor any one!

**CINDERELLA:** (*releasing herself by degrees from the embrace of the Prince*). The hour! already! my God! already the hour sounds! . . .

**LE PRINCE:** L'heure? Qu'importe l'heure? Il la faut oublier!
Je suis à tes genoux pour te mieux supplier!
Je t'aime!
(*Cendrillon s'enfuit. La Fée, voilée, surgit rapidement. Elle arrête le Prince Charmant qui allait s'élancer à la poursuite de Cendrillon, puis disparaît immediatement.*)

**LE PRINCE:** (*avec saisissement et égarement*). Suis-je fou?
(*On danse comme si rien ne s'était passé, et tout s'aperçoit du bal comme à travers un brouillard.*)

**LE PRINCE:** (*à lui-même avec désespoir*). Qu'est-elle devenue?
(*Pendant les danses.*)
Inconnue! Inconnue! O céleste Inconnue!

*FIN DE L'ACTE DEUXIÈME.*

# ■ ACTE TROISIÈME

## ■ Premier Tableau

### *SCÈNE PREMIÈRE*

(*Comme au premier acte.*)
**CENDRILLON:** (*Cendrillon paraît. Furtivement, puis avec agitation.*) Enfin, je suis ici . . .
La maison est déserte . . .
A revenir, j'ai réussi
Sans être découverte.
Mais que de peine et de souci! . . .
Fuyant dans la nuit solitaire
Par les terrasses du palais,
En courant j'ai perdu ma pantoufle de verre! . . .
Marraine, voudrez-vous me pardonner jamais? . . .
Oui, car pour tenir ma promesse,
J'ai fait tout ce que je pouvais.
Vous avez dû voir ma détresse
Quand, tremblante, je me sauvais
Dans mes habits de pauvresse.
A l'heure dite je fuyais
Parmi les noires avenues,
Et je voyais
Se dresser de grandes statues . . .
Ah! quel effroi!
Blanches sous les rayons de lune! . . .
Leurs yeux sans regard se fixaient sur moi,
Elles me montraient du doigt
Se riant de mon infortune.
Dans les profondeurs du jardin
Je m'égarais . . . tout était sombre . . .
Je courais toujours, puis m'arrêtais soudain.
J'avais peur de mon ombre!
Interrogeant les horizons,
Craignant partout des trahisons

**THE PRINCE:** The hour? What matter the hour? Let us forget it!
I am here at your knees to beseech you more!
I love you!
(*Cinderella makes her escape. The Fairy, veiled, suddenly rises up. She stops Prince Charming who was about to hasten after Cinderella, then she immediately disappears*).

**THE PRINCE:** (*bewildered*). Am I mad?
(*The dance is resumed the same as if nothing had happened and everything is seen as through a mist.*)

**THE PRINCE:** (*to himself, in despair.*) What has become of her?
(*During the dance*)
Unknown! Unknown! O heavenly Unknown!

*END OF ACT II.*

# ■ ACT III

## ■ First Tableau

### *SCENE I*

(*As in the first act.*)
**CINDERELLA:** (*Cinderella appears. Furtively, then with agitation.*) Here I am at last . . .
The house is deserted . . .
I returned safely
Without being seen.
But what trouble and care! . . .
Fleeing in the lonely night
Across the palace terraces,
Running I lost my glass slipper! . . .
Godmother, will you ever pardon me? . . .
Yes, for I kept my promise,
I did all I could to keep it.
You must have seen my great distress
When, so troubled, I escaped
In my poor old garb.
At the very hour I fled
Through the dark avenues,
And I saw
Great white statues there . . .
Oh, how frightened I was!
Ghost-like in the moonlight! . . .
Their eyes unseeing fixed upon me,
They pointed at me,
Mocking my misfortune.
In the depths of the garden
I lost my way . . . it was so dark . . .
Still, I ran, then stopped, suddenly.
My shadow frightened me!
Searching the horizon,
Fearing treachery everywhere,
I crept along the houses,
Dreading to cross the square . . .

Je glisse le long des maisons,
N'osant pas traverser la place . . .
Un grand bruit éclate et me glace
De sinistres frissons . . .
C'était le carillon du beffroi dans l'espace! . . .
Réconfortant mon coeur
Il me disait dans son language:
Je veille, calme ta frayeur,
Reprends courage!
(*Avec un découragement subit, regardant autour d'elle.*)
Mais c'en est fait, hélas! du bal et des splendeurs! . . .
Et je n'entendrai plus les paroles si tendres
Qui me berçaient d'espoirs menteurs
(*Machinalement, elle se rapproche de la cheminée et montrant le foyer éteint.*)
Mon bonheur s'est éteint . . . il n'en reste que cendres! . . .
Résigne-toi, petit grillon
Car ce n'est pas pour toi que brille
Le superbe et joyeux rayon
Résigne-toi, Cendrille . . .
(*Comme sortant d'un rêve, subitement et avec frayeur.*)
Ah! j'entends revenir mes parents et mes soeurs! . . .
A tous il faut cacher mes pleurs . . .
(*Elle se sauve dans sa chambre.*)

### *SCÈNE II*

*Madame de la Haltière, Noémie, Dorothée, Pandolfe.*

(*L'entrée de Madame de la Haltière et de ses deux filles est tumultueuse. Une grosse discussion est déchaînée. Pandolfe essaie de se disculper, mais il est accablé par les trois femmes.*)

**MADAME DE LA HALTIÈRE:** (*furibonde, à Pandolfe.*) Vous êtes, je vous le déclare,
Un sot, un faquin, un ignare,
Un portefaix,
Un grand dadais,
Un pauvre sire,
J'ose le dire . . .
Dans le seul but de me contrarier
Vous avez le front de nier
Que cette fille,
Cette guenille,
Cette guenon,
Cette chiffon,
Que vous dirais-je encore?
Etait une pécore.
Rien en un mot, et moins que rien!

**NOÉMIE ET DOROTHÉE:** Ah! maman! que vous parlez bien!

**PANDOLFE:** Pourquoi tant vous mettre en colère?

**MADAME DE LA HALTIÈRE:** Espérez-vous que, pour vous plaire,
Je vais me taire?
Non, mais voyez un peu, quelle au-

A great noise scared me,
Freezing my blood . . .
It was the clock in the belfry far above me!
Comforting my heart,
It told me in its language:
I keep watch, fear nothing,
Regain your courage!
(*Suddenly discouraged, looking about her.*)
But it is all over, alas! the ball and its splendors! . . .
I will never hear again such tender words
Which filled me with deceptive hopes . . .
(*Mechanically, she approaches the chimney corner and points to the ashes.*)
My happiness is extinguished . . . only the ashes remain! . . .
Resignation, little cricket,
It is not for you it shines,
That superb and joyous ray . . .
Resignation, Cinderel . . .
(*As if awakening from a dream, suddenly and with fear.*)
Ah! I hear my parents and my sisters coming back! . . .
From all I must conceal my tears . . .
(*She escapes into her room.*)

### *SCENE II*

*MADAME DE LA HALTIÈRE, NOEMIA, DOROTHY, PANDOLFE.*

(*Madame de la Haltière and her daughters enter boisterously. A noisy discussion starts. Pandolfe tries to excuse himself, but he is overwhelmed by the three women.*)

**MADAME DE LA HALTIÈRE:** (*furiously to Pandolfe*). I do declare, you are
A fool, a puppy, a numskull,
A street-porter,
A dolt,
A sad fellow,
I mean it . . .
Simply to contradict me
You had the nerve to deny
That that girl,
That rag,
That fright,
That thing,
What more can I call her?
Was a fool.
In short a good-for-nothing!

**NOEMIA AND DOROTHY:** Ah! mama! How rightly you speak!

**PANDOLFE:** Why do you get so angry?

**MADAME DE LA HALTIÈRE:** Do you think, to please you,
I will shut my mouth?
No, but what a nerve she had,
That worthless adventuress! . . .

dace elle avait
Cette maudite aventurière! . . .
Aussi, notre prince a bien
fait . . .

**PANDOLFE:** (*s'apercevant que
Cendrillon chancelle et est prête à
défaillir.*) Mais ma fille pâit . . .
(*A Cendrillon.*)
Qu'as-tu, ma pauvre enfant?
(*Aux trois femmes.*)
Assez de vos caquets! . . .

**MADAME DE LA HALTIÈRE:**
Qu'un homme est énervant!

**PANDOLFE:** (*tout à Cendrillon*).
Mon Dieu! la force l'abandonne?
(*Aux trois femmes avec force.*)
Sortez!

**MADAME DE LA HALTIÈRE:** (*suffoquée, se retournant*). Hein!
Quoi?

**PANDOLFE:** (*plus accentué encore*). Je vous l'ordonne! . . .

**MADAME DE LA HALTIÈRE:** (*à
ses filles*) Ah! mes filles, venez; par
ma foi, c'en est trop!
(*A Pandolfe.*)
Je ne vous connais plus . . . vous
êtes un rustaud!

**TOUTES LES TROIS:** Un rustaud! . . . Un lourdaud!

**PANDOLFE:** (*violemment.*).
Vous, sortez au plus tôt . . .
(*Les trois femmes ont, en même
temps, trois attaques de nerfs. Fu-
ribond*).
Vous pouvez trépigner! . . . Je
vous jette à la porte!

**MADAME DE LA HALTIÈRE ET
SES DEUX FILLES:** Rétractez, insolent!

**PANDOLFE:** Le diable vous emporte!
(*Les trois femmes sortent comme
des furies.*)

## SCÈNE III

*Pandolfe, Cendrillon.*

**PANDOLFE:** (*à Cendrillon, pres-
que évanouie dans les bras de son
père*). Ma pauvre enfant chérie, ah!
tu souffres donc bien . . .
Va, repose ton coeur douloureux
sur le mien . . .
Et laisse-toi bercer dans mes bras,
ma petite! . . .
Je t'ai sacrifiée, en venant à la Cour.
Mais tu pardonneras, quant nous ri-
rons un jour,
De mon ambition maudite . . .
Viens, nous quitterons cette ville
Où j'ai vu s'envoler ta gaieté
d'autrefois
Et nous retournerons au fond de nos
grands bois,
Dans notre ferme si tranquille.
Là, nous serons heureux
Tous les deux
Bien heureux!

Our Prince did well . . .

**PANDOLFE:** (*seeing Cinderella
stagger and ready to faint.*) But
my daughter is pale.
(*to Cinderella*).
What ails you, my poor child?
(*To the three women*).
Enough of your prattle! . . .

**MADAME DE LA HALTIÈRE:** How
a man gets on your nerves!

**PANDOLFE:** (*to Cinderella*). My
God! her strength deserts her!
(*To the three women*).
Get out!

**MADAME DE LA HALTIÈRE:** (*suffocating, turning around*). Hey!
What!

**PANDOLFE:** (*more emphatically*). I command you to!

**MADAME DE LA HALTIÈRE:** (*to
her daughters*). Ah! my daughters,
come, faith, it is too much!
(*To Pandolfe*).
I don't recognize you . . . you
are unmannerly!

**ALL THREE:** Unmanner-
ly! . . . Unmannerly!

**PANDOLFE:** (*violently*). Get out
of here at once . . .
(*The three women have simultaneously an attack of nerves. Furiously*).
You can stamp your feet! . . . I
throw you out!

**MADAME DE LA HALTIÈRE AND
HER TWO DAUGHTERS:** Take it
back, insolent!

**PANDOLFE:** The devil take you.
(*The three women go out like furies*).

## SCENE III

*Pandolfe, Cinderella.*

**PANDOLFE:** (*To Cinderella, al-
most fainting in his arms*). My
poor dear child, ah! You suffer
so . . .
Come, repose your grieving heart
on mine . . .
And let me cradle you in my arms
my love!
I have sacrificed you going to the
Court.
But you will pardon me, when we
shall laugh one day,
At my cursed ambition . . .
Come, we shall leave this town
Where I have seen your gaiety take
wings
And will return to the shade of our
dear woods,
On our peaceful farm.
There, we shall be happy.
Both of us

Le matin, nous irons, comme deux
amoureux,
Cueillir les blancs muguets . . .

**CENDRILLON:** Et les liserons
bleus,
Dès que les cloches argentines
S'éveilleront

**PANDOLFE:** Sonnant matines!

**CENDRILLON:** Le soir, nous enten-
drons le chant si doux, si frais,
Du rossignol des nuits . . .

**PANDOLFE:** Au profond des
forêts.

**ENSEMBLE:** Oui nous quitterons
cette ville
Où nous vu s'envoler notre gaîté
d'autrefois.
Et nous retournerons au fond de nos
grands bois,
Dans notre ferme si tranquille.
Là, nous serons heureux
Tous les deux,
Bien heureux!

**CENDRILLON:** Maintenant, je suis
mieux et je me sens renaître
Tu peux me laisser seule.

**PANDOLFE:** Oui, si tu veux promettre
De ne plus être triste et de ne plus
pleurer:
Pour nous sauver d'ici je vais tout
préparere!
(*Il sort.*)

## SCÈNE IV

**CENDRILLON:** (*seule*). (*Avec
résolution*) Seule, je partirai, mon
père.
Le poids de mon chagrin serait trop
lourd pour toi.
Je ne veux pas te voir souffrir de ma
misère! . . .
(*Puis, sous le coup d'une idée
fixe.*)
Non . . . je ne peux plus
vivre . . . Il a douté de moi,
Lui! . . . mon doux maître et
mon seul roi! . . .
Lui que j'adore! . . . Il me renie
et me repousse! . . .
Pourtant, sa voix était bien douce,
Pourtant, ses yeux étaient bien
doux!
O mes rêves d'amour, hélas! envo-
lez-vous!
(*Enveloppant la chambre d'un
long regard.*)
Adieu, mes souvenirs de
joie . . . et de souffrance,
Qui, malgré tout, me parliez
d'espérance! . . .
Témoins et compagnons de mon si
court destin! . . .
Partez, mes tourterelles,
Pour qui chaque matin,
J'allais, par les venelles,
Cueillir le vert plantin . . .
Je ne vous verrai plus, fleurs d'aube
printanière . . .
(*Allant à la cheminée.*)

Very happy!
In the morning we shall go, like lov-
ers,
To gather white May-lilies . . .

**CINDERELLA:** And blue bind-
weed
As soon as the silvery bells
Shall awake

**PANDOLFE:** Calling to matins!

**CINDERELLA:** In the evening, we
shall hear the sweet and gentle
Nightingale sing in the
night . . .

**PANDOLFE:** In the depths of the
forest.

**TOGETHER:** Yes, we will leave this
town
Where we have seen our gaiety take
wings
And we will return to the shade of
our dear woods,
On our peaceful farm.
There, we shall be happy
Both of us,
Very happy!

**CINDERELLA:** Now, I am better
and my senses return,
You can leave me alone.

**PANDOLFE:** Yes, if you will promise—
To be sad no more, nor weep no
more,
I'll go get ready to escape from
here!
(*He goes out*).

## SCENE IV

**CINDERELLA:** (*alone*). (*with res-
olution*). Alone, I shall go, my fa-
ther.
The weight of my shame will bear
you down.
I wish not that you see my mis-
ery . . .
(*Then, struck with a fixed idea*)
No . . . I can live no longer. He
doubts me,
He! . . . my lover and my only
king!
Him whom I adore! . . . He de-
nies me and repulses! . . .
Yet, his voice is very sweet,
And his eyes are very soft,
O my dream of love, alas! dispelled!
(*Casting a long look around the
room*).
Adieu, pleasant memo-
ries . . . and sad,
Memories that spoke to me of hope!
Witnesses and companions of my
too brief fate!
Go, my turtle-doves,
For whom each morning,
I went through the lanes
To gather green herbs.
I shall never see you again, flowers
of springtime . . .
(*Going to the chimney*).
Nor you, my old familiar
nook . . .
(*Detaching the little branch hang-
ing in the chimney*).

Ni toi, ma place familière . . .
(*Détachant la petite branche pendue à la cheminée.*)
Que je t'embrasse encor, tout séché, tout jauni,
Relique d'un beau jour, humble rameau béni.
(*Avec un sentiment très profond.*)
Comme on aime ce que l'on quitte! . . .
Adieu, le grand fauteuil
Où, quand j'étais petite,
Avant de m'être vue, en ma robe de deuil,
Je courais me blottir, bien vite, Frileusement,
Sur les genoux de ma maman
Au sourire indulgent, plein de mélancolie . . .
De maman,
(*Avec des larmes.*)
De maman, si bonne et si jolie! . . .
Qui fredonnait en me berçant:
"C'est l'Angelus,
Dors, mon petit ange,
Dors, comme Jésus
Dormait dans la grange."
(*La nuit, qui venait de commencer un peu, s'assombrit plus rapidement; le tonnerre gronde, l'éclair brille.*)
(*Avec un subit désespoir.*)
Ah! puisque tout bonheur me fuit,
Montant par les roches sacrées,
Sans crainte, j'irai dans la nuit,
Malgré les revenants et le follet qui luit . . .
(*Avec décision.*)
J'irai mourir sous le chêne des Fées! . . .
(*Elle s'enfuit rapidement dans la nuit qui est devenue complète.*)

FIN DU PREMIER TABLEAU.

(*Le deuxième tableau apparaît en se dégageant peu à peu dans l'ombre.*)

## ■ Deuxième Tableau

### SCÈNE PREMIÈRE

*Chez la Fée.*

(*Un grand chêne, au milieu d'une lande pleine de genêts en fleurs.— Au fond la mer.—Nuit claire.— Lumière très bleutée.*)

VOIX LONTAINES DES ESPRITS; danse silencieuse des gouttes de rosée, accompagnée par la VOIX DE LA FÉE.

**LA VOIX DE LA FÉE:** Ames ou follets,
Fugitives chimères,
Lueurs éphémères,
Glissez sur les bruyères!
Flottez sur les genêts!

---

Let me kiss you again, all dried, all yellowed,
Relic of a happy day, poor little twig.
(*With very deep sentiment*).
How we love what we must leave!
Adieu, big armchair,
In which, when I was small,
Before I wore my sombre garb of grief,
I ran to hide my face,
Roguishly,
On my mother's knees.
Her smile of kindness, mingled with sadness . . .
My mother . . .
(*Tearfully*).
My good, pretty mother!
Humming as she cradled me: "It is the Angelus,
Sleep my little angel,
Sleep, as Jesus
Slept in the manger."
(*Night which has begun to fall, darkens rapidly; thunder rolls, there are flashes of lightning.*)
(*With sudden despair*).
Ah! since all happiness has fled,
Scaling the sacred rocks,
Without fear, I shall go into the night,
Despite the ghosts and goblins that prowl . . .
(*With decision*).
I shall go and die beneath the Fairies' Oak.
(*She runs out into the night which has completely closed in*).

END OF FIRST TABLEAU.

(*The second tableau appears gradually out of the shadows.*)

## ■ Second Tableau

### SCENE I

*AT THE FAIRY'S.*

*A large oak, in the centre of a moor covered with flowering broom.—At rear the sea.—A clear night.—The atmosphere is very blue.*

*Distant Voices of the Spirits; silent dance of dew drops, accompanied by the Voice of the Fairy.*

**VOICE OF THE FAIRY:** Ghosts or goblins,
Wandering chimeras,
Ephemeral glimmers,
Glide over the heath!
Skim over the broom!

---

**CHOEUR INVISIBLE DES ES-PRITS:** (*en écho*). Glissez sur les bruyères
Flottez sur les genêts.
(*La Fée paraît dans les branches du chêne.*)

**TROIS ESPRITS:** (*accourant*).
Mais là-bas, au fond de la lande obscure,
Par le chemin, on voit venir
Sur le doux tapis de verdure,
Une enfant qui semble gémir . . .

**TROIS ESPRITS:** (*accourant*). Regardez au fond de la lande obscure! . . .

**LA FÉE:** (*dans les branches du chêne*). Et, de l'autre côté, voyez-vous pas, mes soeurs,
Ce pauvre garçon tut en pleurs?

**LES SIX ESPRITS:** Narguant les dangers, la froidure,
Cé sont de jolis amoureux . . .
Comme ils sont malheureux!
D'ombre voilées
Invisibles pour eux,
Mes soeurs, écoutons bien leurs plaintes désolées.

**LA FÉE:** (*étendant le bras*). A fin qu'ils ne puissent se voir,
Sylvains, obéissez au magique pouvoir!
Entre le Prince et son aimée,
Fermez-vous, une muraille embaumée!
(*Les esprits s'éloignent doucement.—La Fée se dissimule dans les branches et devient invisible.—Un mur de feuillage et de fleurs magiques sépare le milieu de la scène.*)

### SCÈNE II

*Cendrillon et le Prince Charmant, entrent chacun de leur côté. Ils s'agenouillent sans se voir. Ils sont séparés par les fleurs et ils adressent leur prière à la Fée.*

**CENDRILLON:** A deux genoux,
Bonne marraine,
J'implore mon pardon de vous
Si je vous ai fait moindre peine.

**LE PRINCE:** Je viens à vous,
Puissante reine,
Et vous demande à deux genoux
De vouloir terminer ma peine.

**CENDRILLON:** (*à la Fée avec ardeur*). Bonne marraine,
A deux genoux
J'implore mon pardon de vous
Si je vous ai fait moindre peine.

**LE PRINCE:** (*à la Fée avec ardeur*). Puissante reine,
Je viens à vous
Et vous demande à deux genoux
De vouloir terminer ma peine.

---

**INVISIBLE CHORUS OF SPIRITS:** (*echoing*). Glide over the heath,
Skim over the broom.
(*The Fairy appears in the branches of the oak*).

**THREE SPIRITS:** (*hastening*). But yonder, across the darkened moor,
By the path there comes
A child that seem to moan
Down the soft green grass . . .

**THREE SPIRITS:** (*hastening*).
Look across the darkened moor! . . .

**THE FAIRY:** (*in the branches of the oak*). And from the other side, see, my sisters,
That poor boy in tears?

**SIX SPIRITS:** Defying the dangers, the cold,
They are pretty lovers . . .
How unhappy they are!
Veiled shadows
Invisible to them,
My sisters, heed their wailing.

**THE FAIRY:** (*extending her arms*). That they may not see each other,
Sylvans, obey the magic power!
Between the Prince and his beloved,
Raise a perfumed wall!
(*The spirits move away softly.— The Fairy conceals herself in the branches and becomes invisible.—A wall of foliage and magic flowers parts the scene in two*).

### SCENE II

*CINDERELLA AND PRINCE CHARMING. (They enter on either side. They kneel without seeing each other. They are separated by the flowers and address their prayer to the Fairy.*)

**CINDERELLA:** On both knees,
Kind Godmother,
I implore your pardon
If I have caused you pain.

**THE PRINCE:** I come to you,
Powerful queen,
And ask you on both knees
To end my pain.

**CINDERELLA:** (*to the Fairy, with ardor*). Kind Godmother,
On both knees
I implore your pardon
If I have caused you pain.

**THE PRINCE:** (*to the Fairy, with ardor*). Powerful queen,
I come to you,
And ask you on both knees
To end my pain.

**LE PRINCE:** (*à la Fée*). Vous qui pouvez tout voir
Et tout savoir
Vous n'ignorez pas ma souffrance
Vous n'ignorez pas comment
Pendant un trop court moment
Du plus divin bonheur j'ai conçu l'espérance!
Ah! ce bonheur, je l'ai vu de mes yeux!
Ce fut un éclair radieux
Dont mon âme fut traversée,
Dont mon regard fut ébloui.
Et un instant, hélas! tout s'est évanoui,
Et j'en garde un mortel regret dans ma pensée!

**CENDRILLON:** (*qui a écouté palpitante*). Une pauvre âme en grand émoi
Est là qui prie et désespère . . .
Puisqu'il n'est plus pour moi
Que tristesse et misère,
Que je souffre en rachat de ce coeur tant meurtri . . .
Marraine, frappez-moi. Mais que lui soit guéri!

**LE PRINCE:** (*ayant entendu cette prière*). Pauvre femme inconnue,
Doux ange de bonté
Dont un enchantement me dérobe la vue,
Je te bénis pour ta sublime charité!
Pauvre femme inconnue!

**LE PRINCE:** (*avec effusion*). Suis-je assez malheureux!
Mais celle que j'aime est si belle
Que tu dirais, voyant ses yeux:
Pas une étoile n'étincelle
Plus pure au firmament des cieux!
Asservissant la terre et l'onde,
Pour la revoir et la chérir,
Pour la reconquérir,
Je soumettrai le monde.

**CENDRILLON:** (*radieuse*). Vous êtes le Prince Charmant!

**LE PRINCE:** Toi qui as eu pitié de ma détresse extrême
Qui donc es-tu m'interrogeant?

**CENDRILLON:** Je suis Lucette qui vous aime . . .

**LE PRINCE:** (*avec ivresse*). Ineffable ravissement!

**CENDRILLON:** Vous êtes mon Prince Charmant!

**LE PRINCE:** (*en adoration, avec la plus profonde émotion*). Tu me l'as dit, ce nom que je voulais connaître,
Lucette, de ton doux secret, me voilà maître . . .
De tes lèvres, mon âme a recueilli l'aveu!

**CENDRILLON:** (*à part*) Sa chère voix d'extase me pénètre . . .
Mais l'entendre, hélas! c'est trop peu!

**LE PRINCE:** (*à la Fée avec ardeur*). Bonne fée, à mes yeux, laissez-la reparaître . . .
Laissez-moi la revoir . . . et recevez mon voeu;
A la branche du chêne enchanté, bonne fée,
Je suspendrai mon coeur, pur et sanglant trophée . . .
Laissez-moi la revoir! . . . Laissez-moi la revoir!

**LA FÉE:** (*apparaissant de nouveau dans les branches du chêne*). J'accepte ton serment. J'exauce ton espoire.

**LE PRINCE:** (*revoyant Cendrillon*). Lucette! ma Lucette! ah! je t'ai retrouvée!

**CENDRILLON:** (*dans les bras du Prince, tendrement et innocemment.*) Vous êtes mon Prince Charmant!

**LE PRINCE:** Viens! viens! mon âme est comme au ciel ravie!
Je jure que tout la vie
A vous aimer fidèlement!

**CENDRILLON:** A vos douces lois asservie,
Je consacre tout ma vie
A vous aimer fidèlement!
(*Un sommeil magique s'empare d'eux et ils s'endorment bercés par la voix des Esprits. Les Esprits et les Gouttes de Rosée apparaissent de tous côtés et s'avancent silencieusement.*)

**LES ESPRITS:** (*aux deux amants*). Dormez! rêvez!

**LA FÉE:** (*toujours dans les branchs du chêne*). Aimez-voux, l'heure est brève;
Vous croirez, tous les deux, n'avoir fait qu'un beau rêve! . . .

**LES ESPRITS:** Dormez! Rêvez!

*FIN DE L'ACTE TROISIÈME.*

# ■ ACTE QUATRIÈME

## ■ Premier Tableau

### SCÈNE PREMIÈRE

(*La Terrasse de Cendrillon. — Matinée de printemps.*)

*Pandolfe, affectueusement attentif et presque à voix basse pendant que Cendrillon sommeille.*

**PANDOLFE:** O pauvre enfant! depuis que l'on t'a ramenée
Des bords du ruisselet où nous t'avons trouvée
Gisant près des roseaux, glacée, inanimée . . .
Voilà des jours . . . des mois . . . quel souvenir affreux,
Quelle angoisse cruelle!

---

**THE PRINCE:** (*to the Fairy*). You who can see all things
And know all things,
You are not ignorant of my suffering,
Nor ignorant of how,
For a brief moment,
I conceived the hope of divine happiness . . .
Ah! that happiness, I saw it plainly!
It was a brilliant ray,
Which entered my very heart,
And by which my eyes were dazzled.
In an instant, alas! all vanished,
And in my mind I keep a deep regret!

**CINDERELLA:** (*who has listened with heaving bosom*). A poor soul in great distress
Here prays in desperation . . .
Since he is henceforth for me
Only sadness and misery,
Let me suffer instead of this poor wounded heart . . .
Godmother, strike me down. But let him be cured!

**THE PRINCE:** (*having heard this prayer*). Poor unknown girl,
Sweet Angel of goodness
Snatched from my sight by enchantment,
I bless you for your great charity!
Poor unknown girl!

**THE PRINCE:** (*with effusion*). I am so unhappy!
But she whom I love is so beautiful,
You would say, if you saw her eyes:
No star shines
Purer in heaven!
Through land and sea,
To see her again and cherish,
To conquer her again,
I will overcome the world.

**CINDERELLA:** (*radiant*). My Prince Charming you are!

**THE PRINCE:** You, who have taken pity on my distress,
Who is speaking!

**CINDERELLA:** I am Lucette who loves you . . .

**THE PRINCE:** (*with ecstasy*). Ineffable joy!

**CINDERELLA:** You are my Prince Charming!

**THE PRINCE:** (*in adoration, with strongest emotion*). You have told me the name I wished to know,
Lucette, I am now the master of your sweet secret . . .
From your lips my soul has won avowal . . .

**CINDERELLA:** (*aside*). His sweet voice fills me with ecstasy
But, alas! to hear him is not enough.

**THE PRINCE:** Her sweet voice fills me with ecstasy
But, alas! to hear her is not enough.
(*to the Fairy, with ardor*). Good Fairy, let her reappear to me . . .
Let me see her again . . . and receive my vow;
On the branch of the enchanted oak, Good fairy,
I will hang my heart, a pure and bleeding trophy . . .
Let me see her again! . . .
Let me see her again! . . .

**THE FAIRY:** (*again appearing in the branches of the oak*). I accept your vow, I grant your wish.

**THE PRINCE:** (*seeing Cinderella again*). Lucette! my Lucette! ah! I have found you again!

**CINDERELLA:** (*in the Prince's arms, tenderly and innocently*). You are my Prince Charming!

**THE PRINCE:** Come! Come! my soul is jubilant!
I swear that all my life
I shall love you faithfully!

**CINDERELLA:** To your sweet rule, I consecrate my life
I shall love you faithfully!
(*A magic sleep comes over them and they are lulled to rest by the voices of the Spirits. The Spirits and Dew Drops appear from all sides, advancing silently.*)

**THE SPIRITS:** (*to the two lovers*). Sleep! dream!

**THE FAIRY:** (*still in the branches of the oak*). Love each other, the hour is brief;
You both will believe it was only a beautiful dream! . . .

**THE SPIRITS:** Sleep! Dream!

*END OF ACT THREE.*

# ■ ACT IV

## ■ First Tableau

### SCENE I

(*Cinderella's Terrace. — A spring morning.*)

*Pandolfe, affectionately attentive and in a low voice while Cinderella sleeps.*

**PANDOLFE:** O poor child! since we found you
By the banks of the stream, frozen and unconscious,
Days and months have passed . . . how terrible
And how cruel our anguish!
In taking you death might have taken us both . . .

En te prenant, la mort nous aurait pris tous deux
Mais la mort n'osa pas en te voyant si belle.

**CENDRILLON:** (*s'éveillant, à son père*). Je n'étais rendormie . . . Et toi, tu restais là . . . Me soignant sans repos . . .

**PANDOLFE:** Ah! mon enfant chérie, Ne me plains pas. Je suis bien heureux; te voilà Vaillante, maintenant, et tout à fait guérie. (*Mouvement de Cendrillon*). Reste calme . . . il te faut encore ménager.

**CENDRILLON:** (*l'interrogeant doucement, mais gentiment et résolument*). Dis-moi la vérité!

**PANDOLFE:** (*embarrassé*). Pourquoi m'interroger?

**CENDRILLON:** (*sérieuse*). J'étais donc insensée.

**PANDOLFE:** (*fêné*). A quo vas-tu songer?

**CENDRILLON:** Alors, père, c'était comme si ma pensée M'avait tout à coup délaissée . . .

**PANDOLFE:** Tu riais, tu pleurais Sans motif et sans trêve. Tu vivais comme dans un rêve . . . Comme au hasard tu murmurais Des mots confus . . .

**CENDRILLON:** Quoi donc?

**PANDOLFE:** Pauvre enfant, tu souffrais! . . .

**CENDRILLON:** Et je parlais? . . .

**PANDOLFE:** Du bal de la cour . . . oui, vraiment! . . . Et surtout du Prince Charmant, Du Prince que tu n'as jamais vu seulement . . . De brillant avenir . . . et de promesses folles D'un grand chêne enchanté . . . d'un petit coeur sanglant D'une pantoufle en verre . . . et de riche parure . . . (*Volant la faire rire.*) Tu voyais des lutins qui traînaient ta voiture!

**CENDRILLON:** (*anxieuse*). Quoi! Rien de tout cela ne serait arrivé! . . .

**PANDOLFE:** Rien, ma chère fillette! . . .

**CENDRILLON:** Hélas! j'ai donc rêvé! . . .

**PANDOLFE:** Tu riais . . .

**CENDRILLON:** Je pleurais Sans motif . . .

**PANDOLFE:** Et sans trêve.

---

But death dared not touch one so beautiful.—

**CINDERELLA:** (*awaking, to her father*). I have been sleeping again . . . and you have stayed by me Watching while I slept.—

**PANDOLFE:** Ah! my dear child, Do not blame me. I am very happy; Now you are brave again and quite recovered. (*Cinderella makes a movement*) Rest calmly . . . we must still cradle you.

**CINDERELLA:** (*gently interrogating him, but resolute*). Tell me the truth!

**PANDOLFE:** (*embarrassed*). Why ask me?

**CINDERELLA:** (*seriously*). Was I then so foolish . . .

**PANDOLFE:** (*awkwardly*). Of what do you think?

**CINDERELLA:** Father, it seems as though my mind Had suddenly left me . . .

**PANDOLFE:** You did laugh and weep. Needlessly and without pause . . . You lived as in a dream . . . Fitfully you did murmur Confused words . . .

**CINDERELLA:** What?

**PANDOLFE:** Poor child, you did suffer! . . .

**CINDERELLA:** And I talked?

**PANDOLFE:** Of the court ball . . . yes, really! . . . And especially of Prince Charming, The Prince whom you have never seen Of a brilliant future . . . and of wild promises . . . Of a great enchanted oak . . . of a bleeding heart.— Of a glass slipper . . . and of rich attire . . . (*Trying to laugh*). You did see goblins drawing your coach! . . .

**CINDERELLA:** (*anxiously*). What! nothing like that happened to me! . . .

**PANDOLFE:** Nothing, my dear girl! . . .

**CINDERELLA:** Alas! I have only dreamed! . . .

**PANDOLFE:** You laughed . . .

**CINDERELLA:** I wept Needlessly . . .

**PANDOLFE:** And without pause.

---

**CENDRILLON:** Je vivais comme dans un rêve . . . Et je parlais?

**PANDOLFE:** De riche parure!

**CENDRILLON:** D'un petit coeur sanglant . . .

**PANDOLFE:** Et surtout du Prince Charmant!

**CENDRILLON:** Du Prince . . .

**PANDOLFE:** Que tu n'as jamais vu seulement.

**CENDRILLON:** Je croyais aux lutins . . .

**PANDOLFE:** (*en riant*) Qui traînaient ta voiture!

**CENDRILLON:** Rien de cela n'est arrivé! . . .

**PANDOLFE:** Oui! tout cela tu l'as rêvé!

**CENDRILLON:** (*attristée, mais convaincue par son père*). Mon papa! J'ai rêvé!

## SCÈNE II

*Les Memes, Voix de Jeunes Filles.*

**VOIX DE JEUNES FILLES:** (*au loin*). Ouvre ta porte et ta fenêtre. Ouvre-les, mais pas à demi . . . Ouvre, pour que l'avril ami Chez toi pénètre! . . . (*LEs voix sous le balcon de la terrasse*) Comment vas-tu ce matin, Lucette?

**CENDRILLON:** (*qui s'est approchée du balcon et finissant de se dégager de son obsession*). Merci, je vais bien et m'apprête Avec mon père à descendre au jardin . . . (*Heureuse et comme transfigurée*). Printemps revient en ses habits de fête! Allons cueillir la pâquerette Et les muguets au fond du bois. Les ramures sont en émois! Les frelongs butinent les roses Les prés semblent brodés de fleurs. Charmés les yeux! charmés les coeurs! Les marjolaines sont écloses!

**LES VOIX:** (*gaîment*). Bon espoir!

**CENDRILLON:** (*de même*). Au revoir!

**LES VOIX:** (*en s'éteignant peu à peu*) Ouvre ta porte et ta fenêtre, Ouvre-les, mais pas à demi Ouvre, pour que l'avril ami Chez toi pénètre! (*Bruit dans la pièce*)

---

**CINDERELLA:** I lived as in a dream . . . And I talked? . . .

**PANDOLFE:** Of rich apparel! . . .

**CINDERELLA:** Of a bleeding little heart . . .

**PANDOLFE:** And especially of Prince Charming! . . .

**CINDERELLA:** Of the Prince . . .

**PANDOLFE:** That you have never seen.

**CINDERELLA:** I thought of goblins . . .

**PANDOLFE:** (*laughing*). That drew your coach!

**CINDERELLA:** Nothing like that happened! . . .

**PANDOLFE:** Yes! You dreamed it all.

**CINDERELLA:** (*saddened, but convinced by her father*). My father! I have dreamed! . . .

## SCENE II

THE SAME, VOICES OF YOUNG GIRLS.

**VOICES OF YOUNG GIRLS:** (*at a distance*). Open your door and your window. Open them wide, very wide . . . Open, that friendly Spring May come in to you! . . . (*Voice under the balcony of the terrace*). How are you this morning, Lucette?

**CINDERELLA:** (*who has approached the balcony and completely throwing off her obsession*) Thanks, quite well and ready to walk in the garden With Father. (*Happy and as if transformed*). Spring has come in its festal dress! Let us go gather Easter daisies And May lilies in the woods. The branches are aflutter! The bees pilfer the roses, The meadows seem embroidered with flowers, Charmed are all eyes! Charmed all hearts! The sweet marjorams are opening!

**THE VOICES:** (*gaily*). Good luck!

**CINDERELLA:** (*gaily*). Good Bye!

**THE VOICES:** (*growing fainter gradually*). Open your door and your window, Open them wide, very wide . . . Open, that friendly Spring May come in to you . . . (*Noise in the adjoining room.*)

PANDOLFE: (*joyeusement*). Ah! c'est ma femme que j'entends tends . . .
Pour éviter cris et gourmades,
Viens retrouver tes camarades! . . .
Profitons du beau temps!
(*Il emmène doucement Cendrillon*)
Tous tes chagrins sont finis, je l'espère!

CENDRILLON: (*en sortant avec lui*). Comme vous êtes bon, mon père!

PANDOLFE: (*joyfully*). Ah! It is my wife who comes . . .
To escape from her scolding,
Come, let us join your companions! . . .
Enjoy the beautiful weather!
(*He gently leads away Cinderella*).
All your griefs are over, I hope!

CINDERELLA: (*going out with him*). How good you are, my father!

## SCÈNE III

Entrée tumultueuse de Madame de la Haltière, Noémie, Dorothée, puis les Domestiques.

MADAME DE LA HALTIÈRE: (*à tous, avec importance*). Avancez! Reculez! Apprenez qu'aujourd'hui L'ordre de notre Roi convoque près de lui
Les princesses sans nombre à appel venues
De régions qui sont ou ne sont pas connues.
Il en vient du Cambodge,
Il en vient du Japon, de l'Espagne et de Tyr,
Des bords de la Tamise et du Guadalquivir,
Il en vient du Cambodge,
Il en vient de Norvège . . .
Et tout à l'heure, ici, passera le cortège
(*Changeant de ton*).
Puis . . . comme le ciel clair succède à l'ouragan,
La source murmurante au fracas du torrent,
Vous verrez sur la fin s'avancer noblement,
Comme une vision idéale et céleste,
Trois femmes au maintien radieux et modeste.
(*Comme devant la plus suave des apparitions*).
Alors, vous entendrez un long frémissement,
Car le peuple dira; "Voyez ces inconnues,
Pour le Prince Charmant, du ciel bleu descendues" . . .
Sans penser que ce sont deux filles et moi,
Nous rendant au palais pour saluer le Roi.
(*Roulements de tambours et sonneries de trompettes dans la rue*.)

MADAME DE LA HALTIÈRE: C'est le héraut du Roi!
(*Tous se précipitent au balcon, Mêlée*).

## SCENE III

Noisy entry of Madame de la Haltière, Noemia, Dorothy and the Servants.

MADAME DE LA HALTIÈRE: (*to all, impatiently*). Go on! Move back! Don't you know that today The King summons to him
Every princess from wherever she may come,
Be it Japan or Spain or Tyre,
From the banks of the Thames or Guadalquivir,
From Cambodia—or from Norway . . .
Past here the procession will go.
(*Changing her tone*.)
Just as clear weather follows the storm,
The murmuring brook, the roar of the torrent,
You will see in the rear, advancing nobly,
Like heavenly visions, no less,
Three women radiantly and modestly robed.
(*as if in the presence of the sweetest of apparitions*.)
Then, you will hear a long murmur of voices,
For the people will say: "Behold these unknown ladies,
Sent for Prince Charming expressly from heaven . . . "
Not thinking they are my two daughters and I,
Going to the palace to greet the King.
(*A sound of drums and the sound of trumpets in the street*.)

MADAME DE LA HALTIÈRE: It is the King's herald!
(*All rush to the balcony, mingling together*.)

MADAME DE LA HALTIÈRE: (*bousculant ceux qui encombrent*.) Eh bien! s'il vous plaît, après moi!
(*Cendrillon vient d'entrer sans être aperçue des personnes présentes. Elle écoute anxieuse*.)

LA VOIX DU HÉRAULT: (*dans la rue*). Bonnes gens, vous êtes avertis qu'aujourd'hui même, le Prince va recevoir en personne dans la grande cour du Palais, les Princesses qui viennent essayer la pantoufle de verre perdue par la femme inconnue dont le départ a déchiré le coeur du fils du Roi et dont l'absence le fait mourir de langueur et de désespoir . . .

VOIX: (*dans la rue*). Hurra! le cortège s'avance!

CENDRILLON: (*frappée*). Mon rêve était donc vrai!
Maintenant, j'en ai l'assurance,
Si mon ami me revoyait, chère espérance,
A mon aspect il revivrait . . .
Je sais qu'il m'aime . . .
Il me l'a dit . . . il me l'a dit lui-même.
O marraine, venez à mon appel fervant!
Et faites-moi revoir mon doux prince Charmant!
(*Pendant que les acclamations rdoublent au dehors et au balcon, derrière Cendrillon apparaît la Fée*.)
(*La musique joue jusqu'au changement.—Marche des Princesses*.)

## ■ Deuxième Tableau

### SCÈNE PREMIÈRE

Chez le Roi.

(*La cour d'honneur.—Grand soleil.—Les Princesses sont là*.)

Les Mêmes, Le Prince Charmant, Les Princesses, Le Roi, La Fée, La Foule.

LA FOULE: Salut aux Princesses! Salut aux Altesses!

LE PRINCE CHARMANT: (*d'une voix faible*). Posez dans son écrin, sur un coussin de fleurs,
La pantoufle d'azur déteinte par mes pleurs.
(*Avec fièvre, se soutenant à peine*.)
Au'à mon regard avide enfin elle apparaisse . . .
La divin princesse
Qui croit pouvoir la réclamer . . .
Je ne puis vivre encor que si je puis

MADAME DE LA HALTIÈRE: (*shoving aside those who crowd her*.) Here! if you please, after me!
(*Cinderella has just entered unseen by those present. She listens anxiously*.)

THE HERALD'S VOICE: (*in the street*). Good people, you are informed that today the Prince will receive in person in the great Court of the Palace, the Princesses who are coming to try on the glass slipper lost by the unknown woman whose departure has distressed the King's son and from whose absence has caused him to languish and despair . . .

VOICES: (*in the street*). Hurrah! The procession is coming!

CINDERELLA: (*impressed*). Then my dream was real!
Now, I am sure of it,
If my friend behold me again, dear hope,
At the sight of me he will revive . . .
I know that he loves me . . .
He told me so . . . he told me himself.
O Godmother, come at my earnest appeal!
And make me see my sweet Prince Charming again!
(*While the acclamations redouble without and on the balcony, behind Cinderella the Fairy appears*.)
(*The music plays during the change of scenery "March of the Princesses."*)

## ■ Second Tableau

### SCENE I

THE KING'S COURT.

The Court of honor.—Bright sunlight.—The Princesses are assembled.

THE SAME PERSONS, PRINCE CHARMING, THE PRINCESSES, THE KING, THE FAIRY, THE CROWD.

THE CROWD: Long live the Princesses!
Long live the Highnesses!

PRINCE CHARMING: (*in a weak voice*). In its casket on a cushion of flowers,
Place the blue slipper, my tears besprinkled.
(*Feverishly sustaining himself with difficulty*).
To my hungry gaze may she at last appear,
My divine princess,
Who thinks to claim it . . .
I can live no longer if I may not love her!

l'aimer!
*(Les princesses s'avancent. Il les regarde anxieusement. Mais il les arrête, d'un geste triste et très doux, avant qu'elles n'arrivent jusqu'à la pantoufle de verre.)*

LE PRINCE CHARMANT: Chacune de vous est bien belle,
Mais je cherche, et ce n'est pas elle!
Il faudra donc que rien n'apaise ma douleur
Il faudra donc que sans baisers reste ma lèvre!
Point ne se calmera ma fièvre.
On ne m'a pas rendu mon coeur!
*(est prêt à s'évanouir.)*

LA FOULE: *(anxieuse)*. Sur sa tête pâlie
Quelle mélancolie!

LE ROI: *(avec émotion)*. Ses yeux vont se fermer. Parle-moi, mon enfant!

LA FOULE: *(avec recueillement)*.
Dans un appel fervent
Tout un peuple supplie.
Nous implorons les cieux!

## SCÈNE II

Les Memes.

*(Le chant de la Fée se fait entendre au loin.)*

LA FOULE: *(interdite et comme un murmure)*. Enchantement! merveille!

LA FOULE: Voyez la beauté sans pareille!

LA FÉE: *(au Prince, lui montrant Cendrillon)*. Prince Charmant, rouvrez les yeux!
*(Le Prince voit Cendrillon et la désigne du doigt en tremblant dans une joie d'extase.)*

LE PRINCE: Ah! c'est elle, c'est ma Lucette! . . .

CENDRILLON: *(simplement)*. Cendrillon, la pauvrette!
*(Elle va vers le prince qui l'attend joyeux et timeide; en lui rendant son coeur.)*

*(The princesses advance. He looks at them anxiously; but he stops them with a sad, yet gentle gesture, before they reach the glass slipper.)*

PRINCE CHARMING: Each of you is beautiful,
But still I seek for her!
Shall nothing then appease my grief,
Shall my lips no kisses ever know!
Shall my fever never end?
They have not returned my heart to me?
*(He almost faints)*.

THE CROWD: *(anxiously)*. On his pale countenance
What melancholy broods!

THE KING: *(with emotion)*. His eyes are closed. Speak to me, my son!

THE CROWD: *(drawing back)*. In a fervent appeal
All people beseech.
We implore the heavens!

## SCENE II

THE SAME.

*The Chant of the Fairy is heard at a distance)*.

THE CROWD: *(puzzled and like a murmur.)* Enchantment! Marvel!

THE CROWD: See the matchless beauty!

THE FAIRY: *(to the Prince, showing him Cinderella)*. Prince Charming, open your eyes!
*(The Prince sees Cinderella and points to her with a trembling finger, in an ecstasy of joy)*.

THE PRINCE: Ah! it is she, it is my Lucette! . . .

CINDERELLA: *(simply)*. Cinderella, the poor girl! . . .
*(She goes towards the prince who awaits her joyfully; returning him his heart.)*

Vous êtes mon Prince Charmant
Laissez-vous renaître à la vie . . .
C'était là toute mon envie . . .
Reprenez-le ce coeur sanglant . . .
Vous êtes mon Prince Charmant.

LE PRINCE: Ah! garde-le, chère maîtresse!
De tes yeux, la douce caresse
Fait renaître ce coeur flétri.

LA FÉE: Avril pour eux a refleuri!

LE PRINCE ET CENDRILLON: Avril pour nous a refleuri!

LA FOULE: *(joyeuse)*. Honneur à notre souveraine!
*(Pandolfe arrive avec Madame de la Haltière et ses filles, les trois dames sont accompagnées par le Doyen, le Surintendant et le premier Ministre. Pandolfe se précipite vers Cendrillon qui s'élance vers son père.)*

PANDOLFE: Grands dieux! . . . c'est . . .

MADAME DE LA HALTIÈRE: *(écartant vivement son mari et recevant dans ses bras Cendrillon qu'ell câline)*. Ma fille!

PANDOLFE, NOÉMIE ET DOROTHÉE, LE DOYEN, LE SURINTENDANT ET LE PREMIER MINISTRE: *(stupéfiés)*. Ah! quel aplomb est le sien!

MADAME DE LA HALTIÈRE: *(continuant et accentuant)*. Lucette que j'adore!

PANDOLFE: *(au public)*. Ici tout finit bien.
Voici nos amoureux maintenant hors de peine.

TOUS: *(au public, en saluant ou en faisant la belle révérence)*. La pièce est terminée. On a fait de son mieux
Pour vous faire envoler par les beaux pays bleus.

*FIN.*

You are my Prince Charming,
Return to life again . . .
All my desire is there . . .
Take back this bleeding heart . . .
You are my Prince Charming.

THE PRINCE: Ah! keep it, mistress dear!
Your eyes, your sweet caress
Will cure this wounded heart.

THE FAIRY: April has bloomed for them.

THE PRINCE AND CINDERELLA: April for us has bloomed!

THE CROWD: *(joyfully)*. All honor to our sovereigns!
*(Pandolfe arrives with Madame de la Haltière and her daughters; the three ladies are accompanied by the Dean, the Guardian and the Prime Minister. Pandolfe rushes toward Cinderella who hastens to meet her father.)*

PANDOLFE: Great Heavens! . . . it is . . .

MADAME DE LA HALTIÈRE: *(quickly thrusting her husband aside and receiving Cinderella into her arms, and fondling her.)*
My daughter!

PANDOLFE, NOEMIA, DOROTHY, THE DEAN, THE GUARDIAN AND THE PRIME MINISTER: *(stupefied)*. Oh! what assurance she has!

MADAME DE LA HALTIÈRE: *(continuing with emphasis)*. Lucette whom I adore!

PANDOLFE: *(to the public)* Here all ends well.
Behold our lovers now out of trouble.

ALL: *(to the public, bowing low)*. So ends the play. We have done our best
To take you all through Fairy Land.

*THE END.*

# Don Quichotte (1910)

## Don Quixote

Music by Jules Massenet ■ Libretto by Henri Cain

This five-act opera, set to a libretto by Henri Cain (based on Jacques Le Lorrain's play *Le Chevalier de a Longue Figure,* after Cervantes' romance), premiered at the Théâtre du Casino in Monte Carlo on February 19, 1910. In a square in front of Dulcinée's house, the people are singing praises to her beauty. Don Quichotte, a knight, and his companion, the comical Sancho, enter on horseback. As he serenades Dulcinée, Juan, her lover, becomes jealous, and Dulcinée prevents them from duelling. Amused by Don Quichotte, she agrees to give him her love if he can retrieve a necklace of hers that was stolen by a band of thieves. The famous fight with the windmill ensues on the way to the camp. Arriving there, Don Quichotte attacks the thieves as Sancho retreats. They capture the gallant knight, who expects to die at their hands, but they are moved by his courage, his politeness and his love for Dulcinée; the thieves give him her necklace and set him free. Dulcinée is ecstatic when Don Quichotte returns with the necklace. She embraces him, and he begs her to marry him. Touched by his love, she shatters his illusions, telling him of her many, well hidden faults. Don Quichotte is now in a forest, quickly approaching death. He tells Sancho that he is giving him the most beautiful island in the world as he promised during their travels together. Feverish, he sees his beloved before him one last time. His lance falls from his hand, and he dies, a tragic figure dressed in a rusty suit of armor.

## ■ ACTE PREMIER

*LE JOUR DE LA FERIA*
*(La scène représente une place publique en Espagne.)*
*(A droite, une hôtellerie.)*
*(A gauche, la demeure de la Belle Dulcinée.)*
*(Foule, grand mouvement, danses, beuveries.)*
*(On danse.)*
*(Acclamations de la foule.)*

JUAN, RODRIGUEZ, GARCIAS, PEDRO: ) *(sous le balcon de Dulcinée)* Belle, dont le charme est l'empire,
Faites l'aumône d'un sourire
Et d'un regard de vos grands yeux
A nos pauvres coeurs amoureux;
Dulcinée, enchantresse,
Pour un instant
Délaisse
Le nouvel amant
Que t'a choisi ta fantaisie,
Et parais
Devant tes sujets,
Ô Dulcinée!
ô souveraine!
Gentille Reine!
*(On danse.)*

LA FOULE: Vivat!
Anda!
pour notre Reine!

DULCINÉE: *(apparaissant au balcon et répondant à la foule amusée.)* Quand la femme a vingt ans, la majesté suprême
Ne doit pas avoir grands attraits!

## ■ ACT I

*SPAIN: A FESTIVAL*
*(A public square. On the right, an Inn. On the left, the house of the lovely Dulcinea.)*
*(A gay and animated Crowd, singing, dancing and making merry.)*

PEDRO, GARCIAS, RODRIGUEZ AND JUAN: *(beneath Dulcinea's balcony.)* Lady, Queen of earth in your splendor,
Smile upon us, of your mercy,
Deign that one glance of your sweet eyes
Will soothe and heal our love-stricken hearts;
Dulcinea, lovely sorceress,
Set aside
For awhile
This new lover of yours,
This victim and slave of your fancy!
And let your subjects
Gaze on you,
Oh, Dulcinea, Queen transcendent,
Beautiful Empress!
*(They dance.)*

CROWD: Vivat!
Anda!
beautiful Queen!

DULCINEA: *(appearing on the balcony, to the crowd, amused.)*
When her years are twenty, woman pines not for glory,
Nor for queenly joys of a throne!

L'on possède un beau diadème,
Mais après, mes amis, après? . . .
On vit dans une apothéose,
Nos jours sont de gloire entourés,
Mais il doit manquer quelque chose . . .
Ou quelqu'un . . . comme vous voudrez.

TOUS: Vivat pour Dulcinée,
Fantasque et fêtée!

DULCINÉE: *(rieuse.)*
D'hommages, l'on vous environne
Durant le jour; oui, mais, la nuit,
Parce qu'on porte une couronne,
Le temps divin d'amour s'enfuit.
Et pour calmer le coeur morose
Et les ennuis exaspérés,
Il doit bien manquer quelque chose . . .
Ou quelqu'un . . . comme vous voudrez.

TOUS: Vivat pour Dulcinée,
Fantasque et fêtée! . . .

DULCINÉE: *(joyeuse.)* Amis, à tous ici . . .
Merci!
*(Elle disparaît pendant les acclamations joyeuses de la foule qui se répand sur la place.)*

Though she wears a crown and a sceptre,
Yet there must come a day—
And then?
What then?
All is glitter and all is splendor,
She reigns throned in glory supreme,
But she frets for the lack of something—
Or some one—take your choice!

ALL: Long live Dulcinea,
Our fanciful Beauty!

DULCINEA: *(merrily)* When her years are a score
This Queen may be honored and flattered,
Morn till evening; yes, but in lonely night—
Because she is caged in this splendor,
Love's rare moments slip by.
And to soothe her poor heart so heavy,
And so weary in lassitude,
She will thankfully turn to something—
Or some one—you may take your choice!

ALL: Long live Dulcinea,
Our fanciful Beauty!

DULCINEA: *(gratefully.)* Dear friends, to you, to all,
My thanks!
*(She disappears, amid the acclamations of the crowd, which begins to open out.)*

**RODRIGUEZ:** (*légèrement.*) Dulcinée est certes jolie,
Mais on doit l'aimer seulement
Comme on cueille une fleur, un matin de printemps,
Autrement, c'est folie!

**JUAN:** (*avec un soupir attristé.*)
Je l'adore pourtant,
Cette perverse enchanteresse.

**RODRIGUEZ:** (*avec pitié.*) Si tu l'aimes d'amour fervent . . .
Mon pauvre ami, que de tristesse
Tu te réserves!

**JUAN:** (*attristé.*) Ah!
(*Très au loin, on entend des rires et un choeur éloigné:*)
"Vive le Chevalier
Don Quichotte de la Manche!"
Etc.
((*Voir plus loin les paroles.*))

**RODRIGUEZ:** (*rieur, ayant regardé au loin pour se rendre compte d'où venaient ces rumeurs joyeuses.*) Pour te désennuyer,
Regarde Don Quichotte et son gros écuyer.

**JUAN:** (*avec un rire méprisant, sans même se retourner.*) Ce fantoche grotesque,
Ce vieux fou pédantesque,
Qui déclare que Dulcinée
Est la "Dame de sa pensée,"
Tandis que celle-ci
Se rit de lui.

**RODRIGUEZ:** (*avec fermeté.*)
Tant pis! car il est brave et franc comme une lame.

**JUAN:** (*moqueur.*) Et beau!

**RODRIGUEZ:** (*sincère.*) De la beauté merveilleuse de l'âme.

**JUAN:** (*méprisant.*) Il n'est qu'extravagant,
Toqué, cocasse, inélégant.

**RODRIGUEZ:** Mais il secourt la veuve et les enfants sans mère.

**JUAN:** Apôtre halluciné!

**RODRIGUEZ:** Porté par la chimère,
Il parcourt plaines et vallons,
Escalade les pics, poursuit les chemins longs.

**JUAN:** (*ricanant.*) Ah! c'est un être exquis! . . .

**RODRIGUEZ:** (*sérieux.*) De très haute envergure
Que le bon Chevalier . . .

**JUAN:** (*moqueur, achevant la phrase.*) De la Longue Figure!
(*Arrivée de Don Quichotte et de Sancho. Don Quichotte est monté sur Rossinante, il a la lance au poing. Sancho est sur son grison. Entrée comique. Les enfants les entourent en faisant la roue, en*

**RODRIGUEZ:** (*lightly.*) Dulcinea is fair as a blossom,
But a man should love her no more
Than a flower that is plucked on a morning in spring;
To do more would be folly!

**JUAN:** (*with a doleful sigh.*) Yet I love and adore
This wayward and enchanting beauty.

**RODRIGUEZ:** (*pityingly.*) If your love is so desperate—
To what misery must you be fated,
Poor love-sick boy!

**JUAN:** (*dejected.*) Ah!
(*Laughter and shouting heard in the distance.*)
"Here's to Don Quixote," etc.

**RODRIGUEZ:** (*laughing, having ascertained the cause of the merriment.*) To cure your dumpish mood,
See yonder Don Quixote and his fat esquire.

**JUAN:** (*with a scornful laugh.*)
That fantastic old waxwork,
That pedantic old numskull,
Who proclaims the fair Dulcinea
As the "Lady of his thoughts!"
While she only mocks
And jeers at him.

**RODRIGUEZ:** (*with emphasis.*) It is ill!
For he is brave, and chivalrous and noble—

**JUAN:** (*with a laugh.*) And handsome!—

**RODRIGUEZ:** (*with sincerity.*)
Within his soul shines a transcendent beauty.

**JUAN:** (*sneering.*) Come, he's a shatter-pate,
A dolt, a loon, a clumsy fool.

**RODRIGUEZ:** He rescues lonely widow and defenceless orphan.

**JUAN:** A mad, blundering clown!

**RODRIGUEZ:** Inspired by some fine frenzy,
He roams and scours the vale and plain,
Scaling mountain and peak, careening far and wide.

**JUAN:** (*laughing.*) A truly precious fool!

**RODRIGUEZ:** Full of high aspiration
Is this large-hearted Knight—

**JUAN:** (*sarcastically finishing the sentence.*) Of the Rueful Countenance!
(*Entrance of Don Quixote, mounted on Rosinante, lance in rest. Sancho rides his ass, Dapple: Children precede them, turning cart-wheels, the crowd welcome*

*dansant une ronde. La foule s'amuse en les acclamant. Les bonnets sautent en l'air. Don Quichotte est revêtu de sa vieille armure, casqué de son armet. Clinquaille moyen âge.*)

**LA FOULE:** (*entourant Don Quichotte impassible et Sancho radieux.*) Vive le Chevalier
Don Quichotte de la Manche!
Vive son écuyer,
Le fidèle et bon Sanche!
Vivat pour Rossinante . . . et l'âne . . . et l'écuyer!
Allégresse!
Allégresse!

**DON QUICHOTTE:** (*sur son cheval, brandissant sa lance, ravi, à Sancho.*) C'est merveille de voir comme l'on me connaît!
(*Don Quichotte descend de cheval. Sancho de son âne. Les deux montures sont remises à un valet.*)

**SANCHO:** (*la bouche s'épatant d'un énorme rire.*) Même moi, gros benêt,
Je prends ma large part des vivats qu'on adresse.
(*Ils serrent joyeusement les mains tendues.*)
Des pauvres, en loques, viennent, tendant leurs chapeaux rapiécés.)

**DON QUICHOTTE:** (*à Sancho.*)
Sancho, vide ta poche, et réjouis ces gueux,
Car il faut qu'aujourd'hui nous soyons tous heureux!
(*Brandissant sa lance, les yeux au ciel.*)
Vivent les Séraphins, les Archanges, les Trônes!

**SANCHO:** (*piteux.*) Notre pauvre souper qui se fond en aumônes.
(*Il distribue l'argent à toute la canaille qui est accourue.*)

**DON QUICHOTTE:** Donne à profusion, mon fils, sois généreux
Et tâche, comme moi, d'être jeune . . . amoureux.
(*Avec enthousiasme—entouré par la foule—jeune, ardent.*)
Ah! c'est beau la jeunesse, et bon quoi qu'on en dise!
Cette gaîte m'emparadise!
Je voudrais que la joie embaumât les chemins,
La bonté, le coeur des humains,
Qu'un éternel soleil illuminât les plaines,
Que les bois éventés par de fraîches haleines
N'eussent que des parfums et des fruits savoureux,
Des ruisseaux chantant clair et que tout fût heureux!
(*Un défilé passe devant Don Quichotte. On rechante: "Vive Don Quichotte de la Manche." On lui jette des brassées de fleurs. Hur-*

*them boisterously, throwing hats and caps in the air, etc. Don Quixote wears his old-fashioned armour and morion. Don Quixote sits impassive and Sancho beams with delight as the crowd surround them.*)

**CROWD:** (*enthusiastically.*) Long live the worthy Knight,
Don Quixote de la Mancha!
Here's to the good and faithful Sancho!
And Rosinante too–the ass—the portly squire!
All acclaim them!

**DON QUIXOTE:** (*mounted, poising his lance, says delightedly to Sancho.*) It is a marvel to note how all the world knows me!
(*Don Quixote and Sancho dismount; a servant takes charge of the two animals.*)

**SANCHO:** (*with a broad grin and a fat laugh.*) Even I, portly fool,
I share in full and goodly measure this grand welcome.
(*They gleefully shake the hands stretched out to them; beggars, ragged, maimed, and halt, hold out their tattered hats for alms.*)

**DON QUIXOTE:** (*to Sancho.*) Sancho, turn out your wallet, and let these beggars feast,
For on this day I wish that every heart is glad!
(*Raising his lance and gazing upward.*)
Hail, angels and saints, Archangels, heavens!

**SANCHO:** (*woefully.*) No soup for us tonight, we must go empty.

**DON QUIXOTE:** (*while Sancho distributes money to the Riff-Raff.*) Give now, freely, freely!
And stint them not, my son!
Take example from me, cling to youth—live for love!
(*With enthusiasm, surrounded by a young and eager crowd.*)
Ah! Good and sweet is youth, though there are fools that flout it!
This laughter fills me with rejoicing!
Come, gladness, and make our pathways sweet with perfume,
Oh, kindness, cleanse the heart of man,
Come, endless sunshine, and illumine plain and meadow!
Oh, woods, lightly sway in the gentlest of zephyrs,
Streamlets, sing aloud; all the world, shout for joy!
(*Loud applause, Don Quixote is pelted with flowers; a regular pro-*

rabs frénétiques. La place se vide peu à peu. Le crépuscle commence.)

DON QUICHOTTE: (envoie un long baiser à la fenêtre de Dulcinée et montrant le balcon, il chante:) "O Dulcinée!
"Voici l'heure fortunée! . . . "

SANCHO: (l'interrompant.) Vous allez ameuter alcade, régidor,
(Riant.)
Peut-être réveiller le Cid Campéador! . . .
Maître, je serais fier de voir la noble dame,
Mais c'est plus fort que moi, mon gosier me réclame.
Cette rouge lueur qui me clignote au loin:
C'est l'auberge où j'aurai grand soin
De me soûler, non d'allégresse,
Mais de la vraie et bonne ivresse!

DON QUICHOTTE: (avec froideur.) Laisse-moi.

SANCHO: (goguenard.) Seigneur! Sous ce balcon, goûtez votre bonheur,
(Lui retirant son bonnet.)
Je suis votre assoiffé, mais humble serviteur.
(Sancho s'en va, tout en chantant un vieux refrain:)
"Ah! comme on vous héberge Dans cette auberge! . . . "
(La nuit très bleue, très claire, tombera tout doucement. Sous un rayon de lune, Don Quichotte est resté absorbé dans sa contemplation, devant le balcon de Dulcinée; il esquisse une ritournelle sur sa mandoline. Sancho, au son de la mandoline est revenu sur ses pas et, désignant de loin Don Quichotte, il dit avec grandiloquence:)
Cet homme a fait le voeu, prononcé le serment
D'être jusqu'à la fin, étonnant, stupéfiant . . .
(Puis il s'éloigne rapidement)

DON QUICHOTTE: (seul, très amoureusement.) Quand apparaissent les étoiles
Et quand la nuit du fond des cieux
Couvre la terre de ses voiles . . .
Je fais ma prière à tes yeux!
Dans la fleur . . .
(Il est interrompu par Don Juan.)

JUAN: (railleur, lui coupant la parole.) Qu'est cela, mon beau mandoliniste?

DON QUICHOTTE: (ingénument.) Une chanson d'amour.

JUAN: Est-elle gaie ou triste?

cession passes before him, with shouts of: "Long live Don Quixote!" The stage now gradually empties: Twilight begins to fall.)

DON QUIXOTE: (throws a long kiss to Dulcinea's window.) Oh, Dulcinea!
The hour of joy!

SANCHO: Would you provoke to wrath alcaid or regidor,
(With a laugh.)
Perchance awake the Cid, mighty Campeador?
Sir Knight, right proud were I to see this noble lady.
But stronger than my will, my stomach grows impatient—
Yonder cheery red glow winks at me from afar.
It is the hostel, there shall I regale
My pressing needs, not with romancing.
But good and downright heavy drinking!

DON QUIXOTE: (curtly.) Be gone!

SANCHO: (bantering.) My lord, Beneath that balcony enjoy your sweets.
(Taking off his cap)
Your thirsty liegeman, sir, but humble still withal.
(Sancho goes out, singing an old burden.)
Ah! Good food and good housing, Mirth and carousing!
(Night falls gently, blue and serene. Don Quixote, absorbed in contemplation before Dulcinea's balcony, breaks the silence with a ritournelle on his mandoline. Hearing the mandoline, Sancho comes back, and, pointing to Don Quixote, says pompously:)
That man has vowed and sworn To amaze and stupefy mankind—
(He goes out hurriedly.)

DON QUIXOTE: (alone, passionately.) When the stars in countless number,
When the night's veil beclouds the skies,
When the earth falls to rest and slumber—
Here I breathe my prayer to your eyes!
To your tender lips—
(He is interrupted by Juan.)

JUAN: (breaking in with a polite sneer.) What may that be, gallant mandoline-player?

DON QUIXOTE: (simply.) It is a song of love.

JUAN: A song of joy or sadness?

DON QUICHOTTE: (avec enthousiasme.) Elle peut être l'une et l'autre également,
Car c'est une chanson d'amant;
Pour ma Dame d'Amour: la Belle Dulcinée!

JUAN: (insolent.) Vieux fou, je vous défends . . .

DON QUICHOTTE: (bondissant sous l'insulte.) Avez-vous une épée?

JUAN: (dégaînant.) A me servir, monsieur, elle est trop ocupée Pour me quitter jamais.

DON QUICHOTTE: (dégaînant à son tour.) Que la chanson du fer Remplace le refrain qui montait pur et clair
Vers vous, étoiles innocentes! . . .
(Ils commencent à ferrailler. Soudain Don Quichotte se frappe le front, remet son épée au fourreau.)
Oh! pardon, cher monsieur, des rimes sont absentes
Au cantique d'amour que j'allais réciter;
Avant de vous tuer, je tiens à les chanter.
(Dulcinée, à son balcon, à moitié cachée, répète les paroles de l'inconnu qui chante, sans être vue ni de lui ni de Juan. Don Quichotte continue perdu dans son rêve.)
Et c'est dans la fleur de tes lèvres
Qui ne sauraient jamais mentir
Qu'Amour tout palpitant de fièvres
S'est fait un nid pour s'y blottir.
(Il termine sa ritournelle, puis il envoie un baiser vers la fenêtre de Dulcinée qui vient de quitter son balcon. Il rejette sa mandoline derrière son dos et tire son épée. Les deux adversaires se remettent en garde. Intervention de Dulcinée qui sépare les épées d'un coup d'éventail, et passe entre les combattants.)

DULCINÉE: (gaie à Don Quichotte en s'éventant.) Tiens! c'est vous qui lanciez des vers à ma fenêtre?

DON QUICHOTTE: (simple et ravi.) C'est moi!

DULCINÉE: (légèrement.) Les strophes sont d'un maître.
(Désignant la mandoline.)
Et vous jouez, mon cher, de ce noble instrument
Comme de votre épée, avec un air charmant.

JUAN: (jaloux.) Madame!

DULCINÉE: (à part, à Juan en lui souriant.) Riez donc, grand jaloux que vous êtes! . . .
(Revenant vers Don Quichotte ravi.)
J'aime paladins et poètes,
L'amour est avec eux d'une distinc-

DON QUIXOTE: (with enthusiasm.) It is a song sad and joyful too, or one, or both.
For is it not a lover's song
For my Lady of Love, the Princess Dulcinea?

JUAN: (insolently.) Old fool, I forbid—

DON QUIXOTE: (starting at the insult.) Do you carry a weapon?

JUAN: (drawing.) No sword of mine, good sir, has the time to be idle,
And here it serves my need.

DON QUIXOTE: (also drawing.) The music of our swords
Shall now supplant that song which arose pure and clear
To seek the stars lofty and stainless!
(They cross swords. Suddenly Don Quixote claps his hand to his forehead and sheathes his sword.)
Your pardon, good sir, a rhyme or two is wanting
To the love-serenade I had set out to sing.
I would finish my task before I settle with you.
(Dulcinea, half-hidden, on the balcony, repeats the words of the unknown singer, unobserved by Juan and Don Quixote; Don Quixote continues his rhapsody.)
And to your lips so tender
Sweet as a flower, too pure to lie,
Love faint and fluttering—seeking a nest, weary will hie—
Yield him to them, in eager surrender!
(As he finishes, Dulcinea comes down from the balcony. He tosses his mandoline behind his back, and draws. The combatants cross swords again. Dulcinea intervenes, knocks up the weapons with her fan, and separates the combatants.)

DULCINEA: (to Don Quixote, fanning herself.) Ah! it was you I heard singing just under my window!

DON QUIXOTE: (artlessly, in rapture.) It was I.

DULCINEA: (lightly.) You are truly a poet.
(Pointing to the mandoline.)
It would seem you wield this noble weapon, too.
No less than your good sword, with charming skill and grace.

JUAN: (jealous.) My lady!

DULCINEA: (aside to Juan, smiling at him.) Laugh with me, It is ill to be jealous!—
(Turning again to the delighted Don Quixote.)
None save the paladin and poet
Can write or sing of love

tion
Parfaite et qui contraste avec la passion
Dont un autre amant nous opprime.
(*Don Quichotte ferme les yeux; bas à Juan qui s'avancait jaloux, furieux.*)
Délicieusement
d'ailleurs . . . et c'est un crime
Que je te pardonne.
(*Elle lui envoie un baiser du bout de son éventail.*)

JUAN: (*fiévreusement.*)
Ah! . . .

DULCINÉE: (*l'arrêtant dans son élan d'amour.*) Mais allez me chercher
Ma mantille.

JUAN: (*furieux, montrant Don Quichotte toujours extasié.*)
Mais . . .

DULCINÉE: (*hautine, presque méchante.*) Quoi?
(*Puis souriante à Juan derrière son éventail, en haussant les épaules.*)
Laissez-moi m'amuser!
(*Juan sort, malheureux de la coquetterie de la belle.*)

DON QUICHOTTE: (*rouvrant les yeux, regardant avec stupeur partir Juan. Surpris, à Dulcinée.*)
Comment!
Vous m'empêchez
De couper la gorge à mon adversaire?

DULCINÉE: (*paraissant trembler.*) Que dites-vous?
Qu'alliez-vous faire?

DON QUICHOTTE: (*majestueux.*) Mais l'occire à l'instant.

DULCINÉE: (*gentiment.*) Vous êtes, monseigneur, plus que compromettant.
Pour un peu de musique, un brin de poésie,
Vous auriez donc la fantaisie
De répandre du sang!
Que non! . . .
Je veux modérer votre ardeur.
(*Le frôlant au passage.*)

DON QUICHOTTE: (*tremble de joie, mais cherche à paraître implacable.*) Le nom
De cet homme?

DULCINÉE: (*ayant l'air de supplier.*) Qu'importe!
Il est de mon cortège.
Pitié, mon chevalier!
Ma bonté le protège,
Il est de mes amis, attachés à mes pas.

DON QUICHOTTE: (*tranquille.*)
Vous n'avez aujourd'hui qu'ajourné son trépas!

---

With your true consummate perfection,
You have no jealous fancy and caprice
That fret me in one other lover—
(*Aside to the jealous Juan, while Don Quixote closes his eyes.*)
Charming and sweet in all but this—
Yet is is a fault I cannot pardon.
(*Throws him a kiss on the tip of her fan.*)

JUAN: (*passionately.*) Ah!—

DULCINEA: (*cutting short his outburst.*) Go within now and bring me
My mantilla.

JUAN: (*discontentedly pointing to Don Quixote still ecstatic.*)
But—

DULCINEA: (*haughty and mischievous.*) But?—
(*Then smiling at Juan behind her fan, with a shrug.*)
Do not grudge me my jest!
(*Juan goes out, ill-pleased with Dulcinea's coquettish humor. Don Quixote opening his eyes, is amazed to see Juan go; he says to Dulcinea, in surprise*)
DON QUIXOTE: How now?
Must I be thwarted
In cutting down my rival?

DULCINEA: (*feigning fright.*)
What do you mean?
What was your purpose?

DON QUIXOTE: (*grandly.*) Why, to strike him dead.

DULCINEA: (*prettily.*) Most brave and worthy knight is your mood too fiery!
For one short strain of music—
One simple little poem—
Would you indulge a mad fantastic whim
For the shedding of blood?—
No, no!
(*Following up her advantage.*)
I would I could make you relent.

DON QUIXOTE: (*trembling with joy, but trying to appear implacable.*) The name of this fellow!
His name!

DULCINEA: It matters not!
(*Pleading.*)
It is but a poor admirer—
Be kind, my gentle knight!
He is a friend devout, and one who serves me well—

DON QUIXOTE: (*quietly.*) He is spared for now, but before long he shall die!
(*Dulcinea makes a show of emotion, and puts a hand to his lips with a sweet smile.*)

---

DULCINÉE: (*paraissant troublée, lui mettant la main sur la bouche et lui faisant un doux sourire.*)
Vous me faites pleurer . . .
Puis-je vous croire encore? . . .

DON QUICHOTTE: (*balbutie, étranglé d'émotion.*)
Moi . . . mais . . . je vous adore!
(*Avec force, largement.*)
Pour vous choyer et vous servir,
Je vous offre un château sur le Guadalquivir.
Les jours y passeront duvetés de tendresse,
Parfumés d'idéal et fleuris de caresses!

DULCINÉE: (*avec élan.*)
Alors . . . vous devriez,
O mon héros superbe, à l'âme valeureuse,
Pour me voir très heureuse,
Tenter de ravoir le collier
Qu'hier, sur ma poudreuse,
Le bandit Ténébrun osa me dérober . . .

DON QUICHOTTE: (*fièrement.*)
Devrais-je succomber,
Demain, je partirai l'âme claire et joyeuse,
Heureux de vous donner cette preuve d'amour.
(*Dulcinée reprend les paroles de Don Quichotte.*)

DULCINÉE: (*follement coquette et prometteuse.*) Si vous êtes vainqueur! . . .
Vous verrez au retour! . . .
(*Don Quichotte pose la main sur son coeur et met un genou en terre devant Dulcinée dont il baise la main. On entend les amoureux de Dulcinée conduits par Juan qui rapporte la mantille de la Belle. A Don Quichotte.*)
Mais voici mes amis . . .
Don Quichotte est légèrement interloqué en voyant Dulcinée prendre le bras de Juan.)

DULCINÉE: (*à Don Quichotte, jouant la sévérité. Souvenez-vous . . . Messire!*

DON QUICHOTTE: (*avec un sentiment d'étonnement.*) Partir . . . avec celui? . . .

DULCINÉE: (*rieuse et faisant la grosse voix.*) Que vous vouliez occire!
(*Lui rappelant sa promesse.*)
Vous aviez pardonné . . .

DON QUICHOTTE: (*avec un geste de condescendance, laisse tomber un "oui" plein d'indulgence.*)
Oui.

DULCINÉE: (*follement prometteuse à Don Quichotte radieux.*)
Au retour . . . grand ami! . . .
(*Dulcinée va rejoindre ses amis*

---

DULCINEA: I weep for your words—
Can I believe and trust you?—

DON QUIXOTE: (*stammering, choking with emotion.*) Me?—
But—
I do adore you!
(*With great vigour and warmth.*)
For your behest I'd give my all,
I offer you my keep on broad Guadalquivir,
There let us while the hours, rapt in dalliance enchanting,
In a dream of delight, and a feast of caresses!—

DULCINEA: (*quickly.*) Well then—
Now prove your boast,
My transcendental hero—My lion-hearted champion,
Would you make me truly happy—
Go forth then and win back for me my necklace—
That yester eve the brigand chief Tenebrun
Did dare to steal from me.

DON QUIXOTE: (*proudly.*)
Though death be my reward,
Tomorrow I go forth—
Well pleased to show you thus one small token of love.
(*Dulcinea catches up his words.*)

DULCINEA: And if you return in triumph,
You shall see when we meet!
(*Don Quixote, with his hand on his heart, has knelt and is kissing Dulcinea's hand when the voices of the four admirers are heard, led by Juan with the mantilla. To Don Quixote.*)
My friends are coming near!
(*Don Quixote is somewhat disconcerted at seeing Dulcinea take Juan's arm.*)

DULCINEA: (*to Don Quixote, assuming severity.*) Do not forget—
Your honor!

DON QUIXOTE: (*in astonishment.*) Would you—leave me—for him?

DULCINEA: (*laughing, with mock solemnity.*) Whom you have doomed to slaughter!
(*Reminding Don Quixote of his promise.*))
You have pardoned his fault—

DON QUIXOTE: (*with a fine gesture of condescension, utters a magnanimous "Yes."*) Yes.

DULCINEA: (*to the radiant Don Quixote, making mischievous promises.*) Until we meet—noble friend!

rieurs après avoir envoyé un baiser à Don Quichotte tremblant de bonheur.)

JUAN: (avec la bande joyeuse, ayant Dulcinée au bras.) Son amour vous amuse?

DULCINÉE: (s'amusant.) Il est drôle!
Je suis sa désse! . . .

JUAN: (s'esclaffant.) Sa muse! . . .
(Éclats de rire.)

DON QUICHOTTE: (montant sa garde, seul, grave, immobile, fier, la lance au poing, dans le silence.)
Elle m'aime, c'est clair, et va me revenir
Bientôt avec des yeux mouillés de repentir.
Ah! son rire d'enfant, sa démarche onduleuse,
Son oeil tendre, câlin et sa voix enjôleuse!
Je ne bougerai pas, quoi qu'il puisse advenir;
Ma parole est sacrée, et je veux la tenir.
(Au loin, on entend la voix rieuse de Dulcinée. Tout est calme dans la ville.)

■ ACTE DEUXIÈME

Un lever d'aurore très rose dans la campagne. Les buées enveloppent encore le fond du théâtre. Les moulins sont invisibles dans le brouillard.)
(Don Quichotte entre sur Rossinante, sa lance à l'arçon; il joue de sa mandoline, et les yeux au ciel "cherche des rimes" pour des couplets, en l'honneur de Dulcinée.)
(Sancho suant, soufflant, conduit à la fois par bride Rossinante et le grison.)

DON QUICHOTTE: (cherchant, avec difficulté, ses rimes.) C'est vers ton amour
Que je soupire . . . nuit et jour,
Ma Dulcinée,
Ah! ah!
Ma Dulcinée
Ah! ah!
Dame de ma pensée!
Ah! ah!
De toi mon âme est oppressée,
(Il semble heureux d'avoir trouvé sa rime au mot: pensée.
Ma Dulcinée,
Ah! ah! ah!
Mais j'ai vu ton émoi,
Ah! ah!
Je sais que tu penses à moi,
Ah! ah!
Ma Dulcinée,
Ah! ah!
Je crois en toi!
Ah! ah!
(Les yeux au ciel.)
Ah! ah!

(Dulcinea rejoins her laughing friends after throwing a kiss to the enraptured Don Quixote.)

JUAN: (to Dulcinea, taking her arm.) Does his passion divert you?

DULCINEA: (enjoying the fun.)
He is crazy!—
And he calls me his goddess!

JUAN: (convulsed.) His muse!
(Peals of laughter.)

DON QUIXOTE: (dignified, motionless and proud, lance in hand, alone in the silence.) Ah, she loves me, she will return to me
Weeping and penitent, craving grace.
Ah, she laughed as a child, and she moved as a goddess,
Bewitching me, while her voice coaxed and cajoled me!
I will not yield, though it cost me my life,
My word is sacred, I will stand by my pledge.
(In the distance Dulcinea is heard laughing. All is silent in the town.)

■ ACT II

Crimson dawn in the country. A haze still obscures the horizon. The windmills are blotted out by the mists.)
(Don Quixote enters on Rosinante, lance in sling; he is playing his mandoline and, with upturned gaze, searches for rhymes to couplets composed to Dulcinea. Sancho, panting and perspiring, leads Rosinante and Dapple.)

DON QUIXOTE: (racking his brain for rhymes.) To love you always—
My heart is yearning night and day!
Dulcinea!
Ah! ah!
Queen of beauty!
I worship you in duty!
Ah! ah!
By you my spirit is oppressed—
(Delighted at finding a rhyme to "oppressed.")
Lady blessed!
Ah! ah! ah!
I did see your trembling—
Ah! ah!
I know that you think of me!
Ah! ah!
Sweet Dulcinea!
Ah! ah!
I trust in you!
Ah! ah!
(In rapture.)
Ah! ah!
(Don Quixote dismounts, still ab-

(Don Quichotte continue son improvisation tout en descendant de cheval. Sancho s'essuie le front et va conduire les bêtes dans un fourré.)

SANCHO: (revenant, mécontent, exaspéré, interrompant les "Ah! ah!" de Don Quichotte.) Croyez-moi, Chevalier, nous nous sommes trompés,
Les ennemis qu'hier vous avez dissipés
En chargeant à grands cris de: "Vive Dulcinée
Et mort aux mécréants!"
(Riant.)
C'était tout simplement la troupe combinée
De petits cochons noirs et de gros moutons blancs!

DON QUICHOTTE: (très calme, tout en tirant de sa poche de quoi écrire, commence à noter une chanson d'amour.) Tes paroles me font sourire . . .
(Don Quichotte est de suite dans le feu de sa composition.)

SANCHO: (lève les bras au ciel.)
Enfin, il est heureux . . . respectons son délire.
(Mais il pousse un cri, se tâtant l'échine.)
Pour peu qu'on marche encor, à la fin de l'été
(Regardant Don Quichotte absorbé dans son travail et battant la mesure.)
Je lui rendrai des points pour la gracilité;
Tout se volatilise en moi, si cela dure . . .
(Geignant et se contemplant avec douleur.)
J'ai déjà resserré trois crans à ma ceinture!

DON QUICHOTTE: (ravi, composant son air.) Tra la la la la la!
Tra la la la!
(Sancho, subitement fou en l'entendant chanter, se frappe la tête avec son pain, saute en l'air, crie, montre les poings au ciel. Don Quichotte surpris le regarde avec stupeur.)
Deviens-tu fou, Sancho!

SANCHO: (éclatant.) Oui!
Tout de même . . . être ici!
(Il rage.)
Parce que Doña Dulcinée
Usant de son pouvoir . . .
(A part, en croquant rageusement dans son pain.)
La coquine damnée!
(Haut.)
Vous a dit un beau soir:
(Imitant une voix de femme.)
Qu'il existait dans la Sierra voisine
Un bandit qui pille, assassine . . .
Mais . . . qui lui déroba tel bijou de valeur.
(Avec sa voix naturelle, en colère.)

sorbed in his poem. Sancho wipes his forehead and leads the animals to a thicket.)

SANCHO: (comes back, annoyed to exasperation; he interrupts Don Quixote's apostrophes.)
Please your grace, good sir Knight, but I think we were fooled.
The foes that yesterday you scattered and routed,
And charged with shouts and cries of: "Long live Dulcinea!"
And "Death to rogues and thieves!"
(Laughing.)
Were no foes indeed, but simple harmless cattle,
A drove of small black pigs mixed with big white sheep!

DON QUIXOTE: (is quite calm; bringing tablets from his pocket, he begins jotting down a love-song.) Your suspicions make me smile—
(Don Quixote settles down to the throes of composition.)

SANCHO: (throwing up his arms.) At last—he's happy now—all respect to his frenzy.
(Gives a cry, feeling his backbone.)
It wants but little more, and before summer is over
(Looking at Don Quixote, who is beating time, absorbed in his work.)
My portly shape will find itself more lean than his.
I shall evaporate in air—if this continues—
(Moaning and surveying his figure in distress.)
For I have tightened up three holes in my poor girdle!

DON QUIXOTE: (absorbed in composition,) La, la la la la!
Tra, la, la, la!
(Sancho, suddenly maddened by the singing, strikes his forehead with his bread, gives a wild leap into the air, and shakes his fists.)
DON QUIXOTE: (looks at him, surprised and amazed.) Are you possessed, good Sancho?

SANCHO: (exploding.) Yes!
I am mad to be here!
(Raging.)
Because the Doña Dulcinea
Has ill-used her power—
(Aside, munching savagely.)
Curse that impudent sauce-box!—
(Aloud.)
And told you, that night,
(Mimicking a woman's voice.)
That in the neighbouring Sierra
Lived a bandit chief, a thieving cutthroat—
That he had plundered her of a jewel of worth.
(In his natural voice, angrily.)
For this we sally forth, hard on the heels of the thief!

Voilà que nous courons sus au hardi voleur!
Cette dame se rit de nous deux, mon bon maître.

**DON QUICHOTTE:** (*avec sérénité.*) Pour en parler ainsi, c'est ne pas la connaître, C'est ignorer son coeur.

**SANCHO:** (*haussant les épaules en levant les bras au ciel.*) Au contraire, seigneur!

**DON QUICHOTTE:** (*calme, doux, souriant.*) Mon Sancho, tu m'amuses.

**SANCHO:** (*dans une explosion de colère et d'indignation.*) Les femmes, chevalier, c'est tout mensonge et ruses!

**DON QUICHOTTE:** (*bondissant, indigné.*) Quoi?

**SANCHO:** (*cette fois, têtu comme une mule en faisant signe qu'il ne démordra pas de son idée.*) Oui. (*Puis se frottant les mains et clignant de l'oeil.*)
Ce qui m'enchante en notre beau métier
C'est que j'ai pu laisser au logis ma moitié.
Ça me console, je le jure,
Quand je sens les nodosités
(*Se passant les mains sur les reins.*)
De mon asinesque monture
M'entrer dans les . . . rotondités
Dont m'a doté Dame Nature.
Comment peut-on penser du bien
(*Avec une indignation comique, s'adressant à Don Quichotte incrédule, qui sourit avec pitié.*)
De ces coquines, ces pendardes,
Ces menteuses, ces bavardes,
Dont la meilleure ne vaut rien?
Regardez cette dévote
(*Sancho jouant la scène.*)
Qui passe en baissant les yeux,
Et par les rues trotte, trotte,
Édifiant jeunes et vieux.
Tout à coup sous sa mantille
Pourquoi ce regard qui brille?
C'est qu'elle a vu s'entr'ouvrir
Une porte dérobée . . .
Par où va s'évanouir
La coquine embéguinée!
(*Se tordant de rire.*)
Et le mari se morfond,
Trouvant bien longue la messe,
Tout en se grattant le front
Qui le picotte sans cesse . . .
(*Sentencieusement.*)
La femme est un démon vicieux et malin
Créé pour le malheur du sexe masculin!
(*S'enrageant.*)
Qu'elles viennent d'Afrique,
D'Asie ou d'Amérique,
Qu'elles aient le nez fin,
Camus, aquilin,
Qu'elles soient brunes, rousses, blondes,
Plates, dodues, minces our rondes,
Nous sommes les souris de ces êtres

---

But my lady mocks us both, honored master.

**DON QUIXOTE:** (*unruffled.*) To rail upon her betrays your own folly—
You can not know her heart.

**SANCHO:** (*with a shrug and a wave of his arms.*) On the contrary, my lord!

**DON QUIXOTE:** (*with a quiet smile.*) No, good Sancho, you amuse me.

**SANCHO:** (*exploding with anger and indignation.*) A woman, honored Knight, is all deceit and lying!

**DON QUIXOTE:** (*starting indignantly.*) What?

**SANCHO:** (*now obstinate as a mule and sticking to his point.*) Yes!
(*Then with a wink, rubbing his hands.*)
It is my one joy in this mad pilgrimage
That I contrive to leave behind me—my wife!
It doth consoles me in discomfort,
When all those nodulated humps
(*Rubbing his back.*)
On Dapple's asinine old backbone
Stick into those rotundities
With which Dame Nature has endowed me.
What good can a man expect to find
(*With comic indignation, to the smiling and incredulous Don Quixote.*)
In saucy minxes, pert and brazen,
Deceitful hussies, shameless baggages,
The very best is not worth one straw!
See, here comes a woman saintly,
(*Acting as he speaks.*)
She goes by with downcast eyes,
Along the street moves tripping, tripping,
A model wife for all to see.
But behind her drawn mantilla—
Why this sudden glance that sparkles?
She has seen a secret gate
At a sign half open slyly—
Through the doorway disappears
This little jade infatuated!
(*Squirming with laughter.*)
Meantime her lord cools his heels,
He finds the Mass long and tedious,
Scratching his unhappy head
He frets and chafes unceasingly—
(*Sententiously.*)
A woman is a fiend and a plague and pestilence
Created for the ruin of us luckless men.
(*Flying into a passion.*)
Be she African, or Asian or American,
Be her nose long or short, a snub or a pug,

---

félins,
(*Avec énergie.*)
L'homme est une victime, et les mairs . . . des Saints!
(*Les brumes s'élèveront doucement; peu à peu les moulins apparaîtront.*)

**DON QUICHOTTE:** (*désignant le fond.*) Homme de peu, regarde! . . .

**SANCHO:** (*sursautant, regardant autour de lui.*) Pourquoi?

**DON QUICHOTTE:** (*désignant le premier moulin.*) Sancho! . . . En garde!
Vois là-bas se dresser dans le fond opalin
Ce terrible géant . . .

**SANCHO:** (*ahuri.*) Maître, c'est un moulin!
(*D'autres moulins apparaissent vaguement dans le fond.*)

**DON QUICHOTTE:** (*transporté d'une noble impatience.*) Rustre, c'est les géants qui dans leur arrogance
Tentent de m'arrêter.
Folle et leur insolence,
Je vais les châtier!

**SANCHO:** (*avec pitié.*) O fatale démence!
Le pauvre recommence!
(*Il court chercher Rossinante, qu'il ramène avec effarement.*)

**DON QUICHOTTE:** (*tirant son épée et lançant le défi au premier moulin.*) Géant, monstrueux cavalier,
Si votre coeur n'est pas cuirassé de vaillance,
Faites-nous place, ou bien à la dague, à la lance,
Je vous porte un défi, moi le Haut-Chevalier!
(*Les moulins se mettent à tourner. On entend leur tic-tac, Don Quichotte brandit son épée.*)
Vos grands gestes ne font qu'exalter mon courage!
Arrière! ou bien à l'instant
Je m'ouvre un large passage
Dans votre chair et votre sang!

**SANCHO:** (*navré.*) Mon Dieu! quelle folie!

**DON QUICHOTTE:** (*s'élance sur Rossinante, l'enfourche, saisit ensuite sa lance, puis d'une voix tonnante.*) Ecuyer, avec moi, dis que je les défie!

**DON QUICHOTTE:** (*et Sancho, qui, tremblant de peur sous les regards furibonds de son maître, crie aussi fort qu'il peut.*) Géant,

---

Or be she flaxen, dark or carroty,
Weedy, or fleshy, dumpy, bouncing,
The man is but a mouse to play with,
And the woman a cat.
(*Beside himself.*)
We men are helpless victims, and married men are Saints!
(*The haze begins to lift, the windmills gradually become visible.*)

**DON QUIXOTE:** (*pointing to the horizon.*) Craven of heart! Look yonder!

**SANCHO:** (*startled, looking around him.*) What is it?

**DON QUIXOTE:** (*pointing to the first windmill.*) Now, Sancho!
On guard!
Look—down there—a gaunt shape!
In the blue of the haze,
That huge monster's a giant—

**SANCHO:** (*amazed.*) Master, that is a windmill!
(*Other windmills appear, dimly outlined.*)

**DON QUIXOTE:** (*magnificently impatient.*) Blockhead, those forms are giants, that, haughty, proud and boastful,
Dare to hinder me,
Dare to affront my knighthood;
I mean to punish them!

**SANCHO:** (*pityingly.*) A curse on this madness!
Once more the craze has got him—
(*Runs to fetch Rosinante, bringing him back in bewilderment.*)

**DON QUIXOTE:** (*with drawn sword, hurling defiance at the first windmill.*) Avaunt, monster foe, grisly knight!
Unless your heart is armed with triple brass of courage,
Stand aside now,
If not, in the combat, at the spear-point,
Here I fling my gage, I, the Knight of Knights!
(*The windmills begin to revolve: the whirring of the sails becomes audible; Don Quixote waves his sword.*)
Your wild gestures serve to add fire to my courage,
Stand back! stand back! if not, in a trice,
Through your gross carcass steeped in blood
I'll carve and cleave me a pathway!

**SANCHO:** (*aghast.*) Good Lord! This madness!

**DON QUIXOTE:** (*leaps on to Rosinante's back, seizes his lance, then cries in a voice of thunder:*) Now repeat, after me, Say I bid them all defiance!

**DON QUIXOTE AND SANCHO:** (*who, cowed by his master, shouts at the top of his voice.*) Avaunt! etc.

monstrueux cavalier,
Si votre coeur n'est pas cuirassé de vaillance,
Faites-moi place, ou bien à la dague, à la lance,
Je vous porte un défi, moi le Haut-Chevalier!

SANCHO: Faites-lui place, ou bien à la dague, à la lance,
Il vous port un défi, lui le Haut-Chevalier!
(*Puis Don Quichotte bien couvert de son écu, la lance en arrêt, frappe furieusement les flancs de Rossinante et charge contre les moulins à vent aux cris répétés de: "Dulcinée! Dulcinée! pour toi, ma Dame de Beauté!" Tandis que le pauvre Sancho, à genoux, se lamente en criant: "Quel malheur! Au secours! Au secours! Mon bon maître! Hélas! Hélas! Jésus, Marie, venez le délivrer!" Le meunier, ahuri, paraît à la fenêtre du moulin. Le rideau se ferme très vite au moment où Don Quichotte fonce sur le moulin.*)
(*Le rideau se rouvrira et l'on apercevra Don Quichotte, accroché, par le fond de son haut de chausses, voltigeant par les airs, enlevé par une aile du moulin. On l'entendra toujours crier désespérément: "Dulcinée! Dulcinée pour toi, ma Dame de Beauté! . . . " Sancho poussera des cris en essayant de l'arrêter au vol. Soleil levant. Ciel incendié.*)

(*Don Quixote, crouching behind his shield, lance in rest, gives Rosinante a furious cut across his lean flanks, and charges the Windmills, with repeated cries of "Dulcinea! Dulcinea! This for thee, my Lady of Beauty!" Meanwhile Sancho, on his knees, groans and shouts: "Oh, oh! Help, help! My dear Master! Oh, oh! The Lord deliver him!" The bewildered miller appears at the windmill casement, and the curtain descends rapidly just as Don Quixote charges the sails.*)
(*When the curtain is raised again, Don Quixote is seen whirling round, entangled in the sails of the Windmill; he still cries desperately: "Dulcinea! Dulcinea! This for thee, my Lady of Beauty!" Sancho shrieks and attempts to catch him as he revolves. Sunrise in a flaming sky.*)

# ■ ACTE TROISIÈME

*DANS LA SIERRA*)
(*Le crépuscule rouge, magnifique. Fourrés à droite et à gauche. Profils vagues de montagnes.*)

DON QUICHOTTE: (*contemplé par Sancho, tenant par la bride Rossinante et le grison, est à quatre pattes; il regarde attentivement les traces du chemin. Il s'écrie radieux:*) C'est ici le chemin que prennent les bandits
Quand ils rentrent en leur taudis.
(*Se relevant.*)
Débâte le grison, desselle Rossinante,
(*Les caressant.*)
Peut-être fatigués par notre course ardente!
(*Don Quichotte embrasse le museau de son cheval.*)

# ■ ACT III

*SIERRA*
(*The gorgeous red of a setting sun. Clumps of trees right and left. Mountains faintly outlined in the distance.*)
(*Don Quixote is on all fours, with his eyes fixed on footprints. Sancho watches him, holding Rosinante and Dapple; Don Quixote exclaims with delight:*)

DON QUIXOTE: Here are tracks, it is the path by which the bandits come
In their passage to their retreat—
(*Rising.*)
Unharness your good Dapple, unsaddle Rosinante,
(*Patting them.*)
For rest well earned by lightning speed of fiery gallop!
(*Don Quixote rubs his cheek against Rosinante's muzzle.*)

SANCHO: (*très peu rassuré.*) Ce lieu dégage une épouvante
Qui hérisse mon poil et celui du grison.
(*Il tire les animaux au dehors, dans un pré.*)
Allez, mes chers agneaux, brouter l'épais gazon!

DON QUICHOTTE: (*tendant l'index.*) Ne vois-tu rien qui bouge au fond de la clairière?

SANCHO: (*poltron, prêt à fondre en larmes.*) Seigneur, je voudrais bien revenir en arrière!
Maître, j'ai peur de l'ombre et des bruits angoissants
Dont s'emplissent la brande et les bois frémissants.
Que va-t-il se passer?

DON QUICHOTTE: (*héroïque.*)
Quelque chose d'immense!
Sancho . . . notre gloire commence!
(*Solennel.*)
Les preux, les paladins et les héros passés
Vont être, en un clin d'oeil, oubliés, éclipsés.
Je bous d'impatience héroïque et de fièvre.

SANCHO: Et moi, je tremble comme un lièvre.
Mais si l'on s'asseyait un brin?
Je suis fourbu . . .
Non d'avoir trop mangé, trop bu! . . .

DON QUICHOTTE: (*stupéfait.*)
S'asseoir!
Un chevalier qui tente l'aventure
Doit toujours paraître en posture
De déjouer la ruse et de parer le coup.

SANCHO: (*s'allongeant sur l'herbe.*) Je vous laisse le soin de veiller sur mon cou:
Qu'on ne le tranche point, seigneur, à l'improviste.

DON QUICHOTTE: Sois tranquille.

SANCHO: (*s'allongeant davantage.*) Je dors, vous . . . restez sur la piste.
(*Le ciel devient plus sombre. Harassé de fatigue, Don Quichotte s'est endormi, debout, appuyé sur sa lance. Il rêve . . . et murmure:
Quand apparaissent les étoiles . . .
(Bruit de pas.*)

DON QUICHOTTE: (*se réveillant et envoyant un baiser au ciel. O mes rêves divins . . .
(Soudain il sursaute et regarde dans le fond.*) Cette fois ce sont eux!
(*Joyeux et fier.*)
Ils sont plus de deux cents, fils!

SANCHO: (*not at all reassured.*) This spot exudes a ghostly horror
Which makes Dapple's grey bristles and mine stand on end.
(*Taking the animals to a patch of turf.*)
Come on, my little dears, and browse upon the turf!

DON QUIXOTE: (*pointing a forefinger.*) Look yonder down the glen, do you see something moving?

SANCHO: (*frightened, almost in tears.*) My lord, I vow we would do well to be returning!
Master, the creeping shadows and ghostly sounds
Of the brushwood and bracken harrow my soul!
Tell me, what can it mean?

DON QUIXOTE: (*grandly.*) Something great and stupendous!
Sancho,—the dawn of our glory is breaking!
All knights, all paladins of bygone chivalry
Shall now be put to shame in a flash, and eclipsed.
Heroic frenzy rages in me like a fever!

SANCHO: And I am trembling like a rabbit.
But—shall we not sit down awhile?
My knees are shaky—not from surfeit of meat or drink!

DON QUIXOTE: (*scandalized.*)
Sit down?
The prudent knight consigned to deed of venture
Holds him upright and prepared
To guard against a snare and foil a crafty foe.

SANCHO: (*stretching his limbs on the grass.*) To you I leave the task to guard my head from harm:
Let no man cut if off, my Lord, without my permission!

DON QUIXOTE: Rest in peace.

SANCHO: (*stretching himself at full length.*) I sleep, you—remain on guard.
(*The sky begins to darken. Worn out with fatigue Don Quixote goes off to sleep standing, leaning on his spear. He dreams and murmurs:*)
When the stars gleam in countless number—
(*Footsteps heard.*)

DON QUIXOTE: (*waking and throwing a kiss to heaven.*) It was of heaven I did dream—
(*Suddenly, standing bolt upright, he scans the horizon.*)
At last, it is they!
(*Happy and proud.*)
There are more than two hundred!

SANCHO: (*piteux, arrivant tremblant près de Don Quichotte. Il se signe.*) Et nous sommes deux!

DON QUICHOTTE: Nous les vaincrons, s'il plaît à la cause servie.

SANCHO: (*fou de terreur.*) Maître, j'ai les bras courts et je tiens à la vie!

DON QUICHOTTE: (*riant.*) Va te cacher, mon fils, au plus noir des forêts.

SANCHO: (*en se sauvant.*) Ah! si j'avais moins peur, quel héros je ferais!
Il disparaît.)

DON QUICHOTTE: (*d'une voix tonitruante, aux brigands qui sont en face de lui.*) Halte-là! rendez-vous, gens de peu, valetaille, Ou je vous charge et je vous taille.
(*Bataille. Cris. Au milieu de la bagarre, la voix de Don Quichotte domine avec ces mots: "Dulcinée! . . . Dame de mes pensées!" En un clin d'oeil il est renversé et solidement maintenu.*)

LE CHEF: Voilà, certe, un gaillard d'une audace superbe!
Si nus avions été brins d'herbe, Il nous eût tous fauchés du coupant de son fer!
Mais d'où sort-il?
Du Purgatoire ou de l'Enfer?
(*Le chef s'immobilise à l'écart et ne quitte plus des yeux Don Quichotte, impassible.*)

UN BANDIT: A quelle sauce allonsnous mettre sa chair rance?

DEUXIÈME BANDIT: Remarque son indifférence.

PREMIER BANDIT: (*à Don Quichotte. Indique-nous ton choix. (Don Quichotte hausse les épaules sans répondre.*)

TROISIÈME BANDIT: (*le bousculant.*) Nous feras-tu l'honneur De répondre aux larrons que nous sommes, seigneur?
(*Silence hautain de Don Quichotte.*)

PREMIER BANDIT: (*le souffletant.*) Voilà pour ta morgue imbécile.
(*Hilarité générale.*)

QUATRIÈME BANDIT: (*même jeu.*) Voilà qui te rendra la langue plus facile.

LE CHEF: (*énervé.*) Il faut en finir!
Saignez-le, brûlez-le, pendez-le: qu'on m'évite
Le trouble où son regard me plonge . . .
Faites vite!
(*Quelques-uns allument un feu.*)

---

SANCHO: (*in a pitiable state of terror, runs to Don Quixote, and crosses himself.*) We are only two!

DON QUIXOTE: If it seem good to the cause that we serve, we shall conquer—

SANCHO: (*wild with terror.*) Master, I'm weak and frail, and I cling to my life!

DON QUIXOTE: Go hide in the depths of the forest!

SANCHO: (*making off.*) Ah! Were I less afraid, what a hero I should be!
He vanishes.

DON QUIXOTE: (*in a voice of thunder, to the brigands confronting him.*) Halt, I say! and surrender, craven curs, filthy vermin! Else I charge and hew you down!
(*A struggle—shouts—above the din Don Quixote is heard crying "Dulcinea! Lady-of-my-thoughts!" In a twinkling Don Quixote is thrown and bound.*)

CHIEF BANDIT: A fine brave fellow, I believe!
Had we been blades of grass, The swish of his sword would have mown us down!
But where does he come from? From Purgatory or from hell?
(*The Chief stands motionless apart, his eyes fixed on the impassive Don Quixote.*)

A BANDIT: What sauce for this tough old morsel?

SECOND BANDIT: See how proud he is.

FIRST BANDIT: (*to Don Quixote.*) Name your choice.
(*Don Quixote shrugs his shoulders without replying.*)

THIRD BANDIT: (*jostling him.*) Will you condescend to answer us poor thieves, my lord?
(*Don Quixote is scornfully silent.*)

FIRST BANDIT: (*cuffs him.*) That for your silly churlishness.
(*General laughter.*)

FOURTH BANDIT: (*does the same.*) This will loosen your tongue.

CHIEF: (*unnerved.*) Enough! Stab him!
Burn him, hang him!
Rid me of that strange look that troubles me—
Finish him!
(*Some bandits busy themselves lighting a fire. Others sing and dance around the calm and impassive Don Quixote, whom the Chief watches with bewilderment.*)

---

LES BANDITS: (*chantant et dansant autour de Don Quichotte impassible et calme que le chef contemple avec stupeur.*) Voir un corps long comme un jour sans pain Pendre à la branche d'un pin Est un spectacle cocasse!
(*Rires.*)
Ah!
Ah!
Ah!
Le repas fait avec sa carcasse Sera pour les corbeux un plus maigre régal Qu'un corps d'hidalgo colossal!
(*Rires.*)
Ah!
Ah!
Ah!

DON QUICHOTTE: (*les mains jointes, loin de tout, faisant sa prière.*) Seigneur, recois mon âme, elle n'est pas méchante, Et mon coeur est le coeur d'un fidèle chrétien.
Que ton oiel me soit doux et ta face indulgente!
Étant le chevalier du droit, je suis le tien.
(*Le chef est visiblement ému. Don Quichotte se relève. Les bandits se regardent confondus, interdits.*)

LE CHEF: (*d'une voix grave.*)
Vraiment je crois rêver, voyant ta face pâle,
Tes grands traits innocents d'où le divin s'exhale
Et tes yeux fulgurants de sublimes clartés!
Où vas-tu?
Que veux-tu?

DON QUICHOTTE: (*fièrement.*)
Qui je suis?
Écoutez!
Je suis un chevalier errant et qui redresse
Les torts; un vagabond inondé de tendresse
Pour les mères en deuil, les gueux, les opprimés,
Pour tous ceux qui du sort ne furent pas aimés.
Je suis fou de soleil ardent, d'air pur, d'espace,
J'adore les enfants qui rient lorsque je passe,
Et ne déteste point les bandits, quant ils ont
De la force au jarret et de l'orgueil au front.
(*D'un effort il brise ses liens puis dresse sa grande taille.*)
Et me voici debout, jouant un nouveau rôle,
Libre dans mon effort comme dans ma parole;
Et je vous dis ceci, moi "le Haut-Chevalier":
C'est qu'il faut à l'instant me rendre le collier
Pris au cou délicat d'une femme adorée.
Le joyau, lui, n'est rien, mais la cause est sacrée.

---

BANDITS: This lean lank body, long as a hungry day, Hung on the bough of a pine, Invites to jesting and laughter!
(*Laughing.*)
Ha! ha! ha! ha!
Meat is scarce on his old bony carcass,
Most disappointing meal for the carrion crows!
Not so plump or sweet as a fine fat hidalgo!
(*Laughing.*)
Ha! ha! ha!

DON QUIXOTE: (*apart, with hands bound, offers up a prayer.*)
O Lord, receive my spirit, not wholly vile or worthless,
For my heart is faithful to you; Deal kindly with me, judge me in mercy!
Since I do stand for truth and right, I stand for you!
(*The Chief is visibly affected. The other bandits exchange glances of amazement and bewilderment.*)

CHIEF: (*awed.*) I seem to dream of a truth, in looking upon your pallor,
Those fine inspiring features, suffused with sancity,
Those eyes that flash sublime and transparent!
Where are you going?
What is your mission?

DON QUIXOTE: (*proudly.*) The True Knight-Errant, sirs, am I, Who guards the good, and rights the wrong;
A wanderer whose heart overflows with tenderness
For the mother that mourns, the poor, weak and oppressed,
For all whom fate denies the precious boon of love.
I am fey with the flaming sun, the air, the heavens!
I love the little child that crows aloud to see me,
Nor do I bear ill-will to a bandit, be he fearless,
And stalwart of limb and brave and proud of mien.
(*With a supreme effort he breaks his bonds and draws himself up to his full height.*)
Here I stand erect, you see me, in new guise,
I stand free and unfettered in speech as in movement,
And this I here demand, I, the Knight of all Knights:
Now must you yield to me that necklace which you have,
Filched from the fair slender throat of a maid whom I worship.
Gems are dross, nothing to me, but the cause I serve is holy.

PREMIER BANDIT: Ah! je me sens trembler!
(*Le chef retire de sa ceinture le collier qu'il remet à Don Quichotte respectueusement.*)

FIRST BANDIT: Ah! My heart is strangely troubled!
(*The Chief draws the necklace from his girdle, bares his head and kneels; he surrenders the necklace to Don Quixote.*)

LE CHEF: (*se découvrant et mettant un genou en terra.*) Voici. Le joyau dérobé, monseigneur!

CHIEF: The stolen jewel, Sire!

DON QUICHOTTE: (*très simplement.*) Bien, merci.

DON QUIXOTE: (*quite simply.*) Good. I thank you.
(*The other bandits also kneel.*)

LE CHEF ET LES BANDITS: (*s'agenouillant à leur tour, avec recoellien ent.*) Et maintenant, sur nous, placez votre main pure, O noble Chevalier de la Longue Figure!

BANDITS: (*fervently.*) Before you go, we would pray, that you grant us your blessing, O great and noble Knight of the Rueful Countenance!

DON QUICHOTTE: (*d'une voix éclatante; éclairé par l'éclat du feu allunti par les bandits, sa tète auréolée d'un dernier rayon.*)
Sancho, rustre au coeur timoré, Viens voir le miracle opéré!
(*Sancho sort timidement de l'ombre. Se montant jusqu'à la fin dans une fièvre de sublime exaltation.*)
Les manants, les pillards, fils du vol et du crime,
Ceux que la peur redoute et que la force opprime,
Les sans-logis, les gueux aux rires menacants,
Ont deviné mon but, en ont saisi le sens!
Courbés sous l'âpre vent qui vient des cimes hautes,
Tremblants d'un grand frisson, regarde-les, mes hôtes,
Les élus de mon coeur, mes fils prédestinés,
Vois-les, comme ils sont beaux, dociles, fascinés!
(*Radieux, les mains étendues en avant comme pour bénir les bandits.*)

DON QUIXOTE: (*in a burst of enthusiasm; as he stands in the light throw by the Bandits' fire, a flaming aureole encircles his head.*)
Sancho, blockhead, craven of heart, Come see the Miracle performed!
(*Sancho crawls from his hiding-place in the shadows. In a rising frenzy of exaltation.*)
These poor wights, wretched thieves, born in crime, nursed in evil,
Whom nothing but fear can chasten, whom nothing but force coerces,
Vagrant strays, and rogues that mocked me with threats,
These have divined my aim, and fathomed my intent!
Struck down beneath the blast, laid low by wrath of heaven,
They shiver cowering, my erstwhile savage hosts,
Henceforth my chosen folk, my children fore-ordained,
Behold!
Devoted slaves, in homage to my thrall!
(*High-wrought and ecstatic, with hands outstretched in blessing.*)

# ■ ACT QUATRIÈME

*LA FÊTE DANS LE PATIO DE LA BELLE DULCINÉE*
Dulcinée, Rodriguez, Juan Pedro, Garcias, Foule Des Invités, Valets
(*Musique invisible. On danse au loin. Dulcinée est dans un angel du patio, entourée de galants; elle est pensive.*)

# ■ ACT IV

*FÊTE IN THE COURTYARD OF THE LOVELY DULCINEA'S HOUSE*
Dulcinea, Rodriguez, Juan, Pedro, Garcias, Guests, Servants.
(*Dance-music heard in the distance, groups appear from time to time, Dulcinea, pensive, sits in a corner, surrounded by admirers.*)

JUAN: (*chagrin, à Dulcinée.*) Alors je n'ai plus rien, traîtresse, à espérer?

JUAN: (*vexed, to Dulcinea.*) And so—deceiver—there is no hope for me?—

DULCINÉE: (*préoccupée, distraite.*) Plus rien . . . mais Pepita saura te consoler.

DULCINEA: (*preoccupied, absently.*) No, none— But fair Pepita may console you still.

RODRIGUEZ: (*s'empressant à son tour, galamment.*) De ma grande détresse Quand aurez-vous pitié?

RODRIGUEZ: (*gallantly seizing his opportunity.*) Have my torment and anguish No power to move your heart?—

GARCIAS: (*de même.*) Et resterez-vous la maîtresse . . .

GARCIAS: (*likewise.*) Will you deign to be the beloved—

PEDRO: (*terminant la phrase.*) De celui qui souffre à vos pieds?

PEDRO: (*finishing the phrase.*) Of one who sighs and pleads to you?—

DULCINÉE: (*nonchalamment.*) Pauvres amis, vous m'ennuyez!
(*A part.*)
J'ai bien assez de ma tristesse . . .
(*Ils s'éloignent dépités. Des danses lentes et silencieuses continment a lointain.*)

DULCINEA: (*with indifference.*) No, no, good friends—you weary me!—
(*Aside.*)
Enough for me is mine own sadness—
(*They withdraw in high dudgeon. Stately and noiseless, the distant dancing continues, to the accompaniment of invisible musicians.*)

DULCINÉE: (*dans un rêve.*) Lorsque le temps d'amour a fui Que reste-il de nos bonheurs? . . .
Que reste-ii donc des splendeurs Des soirs d'été, lorsque la nuit Dans ses voiles ensevelit L'or des courchants, l'éclat des fleurs? . . .
(*Les danses ont cessé dans le lointain; la musique s'est tue; toute la foule envahit le patio; Dulcinée s'est levée et est aussitôt entourée des amoureux qui s'empressent autour d'elle; mais voici que Rodriguez observe Juan se rapprochant de Dulcinée; même jeu de la part de Juan.*)

DULCINEA: (*musing.*) When our brief hour of love has fled, Gone are those joys that make life sweet—
Gone are those summer nights, When twilight grey, softly falling, Veils the nodding flowers closed in sleep—
(*The distant dancing has ceased, the music has stopped, the whole company swarms on to the stage. Dulcinea rises, and is quickly besieged by a host of admirers. Rodriguez and Juan observe each other trying to attract Dulcinea's attention.*)

RODRIGUEZ ET JUAN: (*à part.*) Par fortune!
serait-ce son tour?
Aurait-il plus de chance en lui parlant d'amour?

RODRIGUEZ AND JUAN: (*aside.*) Is he favored, her choice of today? Will his suit better prosper if he tells of his love?

DULCINÉE: (*à part, malicieusement.*) Vous n'aurez pas de chance en me parlant d'amour.
(*Puis changeant de ton et d'allure.*)
Non! j'ai pour le moment le désir d'autre chose,
Je rêve et je pleure sans cause;
Ah! je suis très à plaindre, et c'est pitié vraiment
De n'être pas ravie ayant de tels amants.

DULCINEA: (*aside, with sly glances.*) All your labor is vain if you whisper of love!
(*Changing her tone, with a new charm.*)
No! though I should be happy, yet something is wanting.
I brood and I weep without reason, As one to be pitied, and a sad plight is mine
Who can take no delight in this surfeit of lovers.

RODRIGUEZ: Que dit-elle?

RODRIGUEZ: What can she mean?

JUAN, PEDRO ET GARCIAS: Hein?

JUAN, PEDRO AND GARCIAS: Ha!

DULCINÉE: (*étrange.*) Autrement que par vous et . . . qu'à l'accoutumée,
Ou . . . soyez imprévus, superbes, éclatants,
Car c'est de l'inédit que mon rêve demande
Et d'inconnus frisson mordant ma chair gourmande!

DULCINEA: (*dully.*) Would that men could but love in far different wise,
In more novel a fashion—
Now woo me like men, with passion fierce as the sun!
For the glow of new ecstasy long have I hungered;
For the thrill that is new am I faint to dying!

TOUS: Vivat pour Dulcinée Indomptable! Indomptée!

ALL: Long live fair Dulcinea! Undefeated, triumphant!
(*Dulcinea, picking up a guitar, sings with passion.*)

DULCINÉE: (*saisissant une guitare (avec un accent de fièvre).*)
Alza! ne pensons qu'au plaisir d'aimer,
A la fièvre des heures brèves Où l'on sent le coeur se pâmer

DULCINEA: Alza!
Live for love and love's joys alone, Live for passion all too soon over, Let souls enraptured, two as one, Melt in the kiss of maid and lover! Ollé!

Sous les baisers cueillis aux lèvres!
Ollé! que les yeux plongent dans les yeux.
Désirs, courez la pretentaine;
Et jeunes gens, qu'il vous souvienne
Que l'amour sourit aux audacieux.
Anda! ne pensons qu'aux minutes brèves
Où les âmes vont se pàmer
Sur les baisers pris sur les lèvres
Dans l'ivresse de s'adorer!
(*Elle danse.*)

**TOUS:** Alza!
Ollé!
Anda!
(*Après les cris d'enthousiasme, des valets paraissent à la porte de la salle où aura lieu le souper dont on apercoit les tables somptueusement servies.*)

**LES INVITÉS:** (*en se rendant au souper.*) L'aube bientôt va pourprer l'horizon! . . .
En soupant, verre en main, nous salûrons l'aurore,
Tandis que les vieux vins emporteront encore
Ce qui nous reste de raison.
(*Les tentures se referment. Quelques instants après la sortie de tous. Sancho est introduit par deux !aquais.*)

**SANCHO:** (*faisant l'important, au premier valet aburi.*) Annonce le grand don Quichotte de la Manche,
Baron et Chevalier de la Longue Figure,
(*Au second valet.
Arrivant en Estramadure
Avec son écuyer le valeureux don Sanche.*)

**LE PREMIER VALET:** (*intimidé par les regards de Sancho.*) El señor . . . el señor Quichotte Estramadure . . .
(*Il cherche son souffle.*)

**SANCHO:** Idiot!

**LE DEUXIÈME VALET:** (*finissant l'annonce.*) Le Chevalier de la Longue Figure . . .

**SANCHO:** (*avec un geste condescendant.*) Mieux . . .
(*Don Quichotte entre, compassé, solennel, sa salade sous le bras: il fait dans le salon vide un salut effarant que Sancho s'efforce en vain de reproduire, puis le chevalier pousse un soupir en ne voyant personne.*)

**LE DEUXIÈME VALET:** (*éclatant de rire, bas à son camarade.*) Sont-ils drôles!
J'augure Que cet homme n'a rien mangé depuis deux ans!

**LE DEUXIÈME VALET:** Encor s'il nous faisait quelques riches présents!
(*Ils ricanent.*)

You that gaze and sigh in despair,
Feed the flame of passions that fire you,
You that are young, let this inspire you,
Love befriends him that fears not to dare!
Anda!
Live for love, for joys too soon over,
Let twin souls commingle as one,
Let love's glorious ecstasy won
Crown with its kisses maid and lover!
(*She dances.*)

**ALL:** Alza!
Ollé!
Anda!
(*When the enthusiasm has subsided, servants appear at the doors of the supper-room, through which can be seen groaning tables.*)

**ALL:** (*making a move to the supper-room.*) Soon will the dawn make the skies bright and clear!
Greet the new morrow with toasting and merriment!
Let good old wine work its will on our wits tonight,
Wine shall have all the wit left us!
(*The curtains are drawn: some seconds after the general exit, Sancho is introduced by two menservants.*)

**SANCHO:** (*overweighted with importance, to the first servant, who gazes open-mouthed.*) Announce the noble Don Quixote de la Mancha,
Baron, Duke, and Knight of the Rueful Countenance,
(*To the second servant.*)
Just come to Estramadura
Attended by his Squire, the valorous Don Sancho—

**FIRST SERVANT:** (*cowed by Sancho's gaze.*) The Señor—Quixote—Estramadura—
(*Gasping.*)

**SANCHO:** Idiot!

**SECOND SERVANT:** (*finishing.*) Noble Knight of the Rueful Countenance—

**SANCHO:** (*condescendingly.*) Better!
(*Don Quixote enters, stiff and formal, he sweeps the stage with an extravagant gesture of salutation which Sancho tries in vain to copy; he breathes a sigh of disappointment.*)

**FIRST SERVANT:** (*guffawing, aside to his fellow-servant.*) What a sight!
I warrant that man has eaten nothing for two years!

**SECOND SERVANT:** Think of the handsome presents he will give us!
(*They giggle.*)

**SANCHO:** (*s'apercevant de leur manège, court sur eux, furieux.*) Que le Grand Chevalier rève, chante ou soupire,
Moi seul, entendez-vous, ai le droit de sourire!
(*Ils disparaissent vivement.*)

**DON QUICHOTTE:** (*épanoui.*) J'entre enfin dans la joie et l'immortalité!

**SANCHO:** (*geignant.*) Quand donc dans l'abondance et dans l'oisiveté?
Quand pourrai-je palper le plus mince pécule . . .

**DON QUICHOTTE:** (*le réconfortant joyeusement.*) Mais biens vont t'échoir, j'en jure par Hercule.
(*Avec gravité.*)
Pour ton dévoûment, ta vertu, Je songe à t'enrichir.

**SANCHO:** (*ravi.*) Enfin!

**DON QUICHOTTE:** (*très sérieusement.*) Que dirais-tu D'une île . . . ou d'un château festonné de tourelles,
Ceint d'un parc, où le soir glissent des tourterelles?

**SANCHO:** (*la figure épatée par un large sourire.*) Ce rêve me sourit. Mais dans combien de temps?

**DON QUICHOTTE:** (*réfléchissant.*) Ce soir . . . demain peut-être . . .

**SANCHO:** (*paradant.*) O bienheureux moment
Où, vêtu d'or, de brocatelles,
Le jabot fleuri de dentelles,
Devant mes gens je paraîtrai,
Moi, leur Seigneur et Maître, en habit chamarré!

**DON QUICHOTTE:** (*avec assurance.*) Radieuse pour nous s'ouvre la destinée!

**SANCHO:** (*ravi, pousse un formidable:*) Oh!

**DON QUICHOTTE:** (*avec une tendre émotion.*) D'abord, ce soir, j'épouse Dulcinée
(*Regard étonné de Sancho à cette nouvelle.*)
Et l'emmène au pays charmant
Où tout est rêve, enchantment,
L'heure y coule exquise et se savoure toute.

**SANCHO:** (*intrigué.*) Où perche cet Eden?

**DON QUICHOTTE:** (*avec mystère.*) Moi seul en sais la route.
(*Des domestiques soulèvent la tapisserie. Avec une indicible émotion.*)
Mais, voici Dulcinée . . .
Ah! que je suis heureux!
Mon Sancho, tu vas voir cet accueil chaleureux!

**SANCHO:** (*furious at their behaviour, rushes at them:*) The great Knight dreams or sings or sighs,
It is mine, and mine alone, to smile!
(*They vanish.*)

**DON QUIXOTE:** (*excitedly.*) At last I taste of joy!
The sweets of immortality!

**SANCHO:** (*grumbling.*) But when may I expect a taste of plenteous ease?
And when shall I enjoy the handling of a stiver?

**DON QUIXOTE:** (*joyfully reassuring him.*) All of these shall be yours, I swear, by Hercules!
(*Gravely.*)
You have been loyal, faithful, true,
And you shall have riches.

**SANCHO:** (*in rapture.*) At last!

**DON QUIXOTE:** (*in all seriousness.*) What do you say to an island?
Or castle keep, with serrated battlements,
In a park, where doves at night sing songs of rapture?

**SANCHO:** (*a broad smile coming over his face.*) The picture pleases me.
But when shall these things be?

**DON QUIXOTE:** (*reflecting.*) To-night—perhaps—tomorrow.

**SANCHO:** (*strutting about.*) Oh! great will be the day.
When, tired in brocatel and satin,
Broidered lawn and frills, lace and jewels,
I appear before my household,
As overlord and master, in gorgeous panoply!

**DON QUIXOTE:** (*confidently.*) To us the fates have opened out a glorious vista!

**SANCHO:** (*fiercely exultant.*) Oh! Oh!

**DON QUIXOTE:** (*with tenderness and emotion.*) This night I wed the lovely Dulcinea,
(*Sancho is staggered at this announcement.*)
Then away to that fair domain—
Where souls enchanted—may find oblivion—
And the blissful ecstasy of amaranthine rapture.

**SANCHO:** (*curious.*) And where may this Eden be?

**DON QUIXOTE:** (*mysteriously.*) I alone know the secret.
(*The curtains of the supper-room are drawn aside.*)
DON QUIXOTE: (*deeply moved.*)
Ah!—
It is she—
Dulcinea!—
I am happy now!

(*Tous les invités arrivent les coupes en mains, rieurs, moqueurs. Soudain Dulcinée apercoit Don Quichotte. Vivement elle s'avance et l'examine. Grand brouhaba joyeux et moqueur de la part de toutes et de tous les invités de Dulcinée.*)

DULCINÉE: (*rieuse, étonnée, s'avancant.*) Tiens, c'est vous, chevalier . . .
Mais pas une blessure?
Quoi, sans un bras coupé, sans une égratignure?

DON QUICHOTTE: (*souriant et calme avec un large geste.*) Intact!
(*Il reste un instant le bras levé dans sa fière attitude.*)

DULCINÉE: (*souriante, malicieuse.*) Intact? . . .
(*Gaiment.*)
Vivat!

RODRIGUEZ, JUAN, GARCIAS, PEDRO: (*moqueurs, à Don Quichotte et Sancho.*) On ne s'explique pas
Qu'à deux vous ayez pu vous tirer de ce pas.
Donnez, de vos exploits, la preuve, malepeste!

SANCHO: (*désignant Don Quichotte.*) Ne la voyez-vous pas, chers seigneurs, à son geste?

TOUS: (*répètent avec insistance, à Don Quichotte.*) Comment avez-vous pu vous tirer de ce pas?..
La preuve! . . .

DULCINÉE: (*rieuse, mais incrédule aussi.*) Auriez-vous les trente perles fines?

DON QUICHOTTE: (*navré.*) O mes illusions, mes croyances divines! . . .
Elle a douté! . . .
(*Il exhume du fond de sa pauvre cape le collier qu'il tend d'un geste douloureux à Dulcinée.*)
Voici, madame, le collier.

DULCINÉE: (*stupéfaite, vivement.*) Mon collier!

TOUS: Ah!

DULCINÉE: (*folle de joie, sautant au cou de Don Quichotte après avoir mis son collier.*) Mon Chevalier,
Il faut que je t'embrasse!
Les plus illustres faits des héros de jadis
Sont ici dépassés, même ceux d'Amadis!

TOUS: (*regardant Don Quichotte.*) Voyez de quels transports s'illumine sa face!

DON QUICHOTTE: (*fou d'amour, s'avance vers Dulcinée.*) Marchez dans mon chemin
Et prêtez-moi l'appui léger de votre main:
A deux nous aimerons davantage le monde,

Now good squire, you shall see her delight at my coming!
(*Goblet in hand, the guests crowd on to the stage, laughing and joking. Dulcinea catches sight of Don Quixote, she comes forward quickly and scrutinises him. General animation and amusement.*)

DULCINEA: Ah, it is you, gallant Knight!—
But not one single wound?
Not one damaged limb, not one tiny scratch?—

DON QUIXOTE: (*smiling and self-possessed, with a fine gesture.*) Intact!

DULCINEA: (*with a roguish smile.*) Intact?
(*Gaily.*)
Holà!

RODRIGUEZ, PEDRO, etc.: (*together, mocking at Don Quixote and Sancho.*) A pretty tale, indeed, that two like you
Could come unharmed through such peril as that.
The burden rests on you to prove it, caballeros!

SANCHO: (*pointing to his master.*) Have you not proof enough, good masters, in his comportment?

ALL: (*insisting, to Don Quixote.*) Unharmed in peril such as that?
Come, prove it!

DULCINEA: (*also laughing incredulously, to Don Quixote.*) Then have you really brought me back my pearls?

DON QUIXOTE: (*crestfallen.*) Alas for my illusions, and my cherished hopes,
She doubts me!
(*He extracts the necklace from his seedy cloak and sorrowfully hands it to Dulcinea.*)
Here, my lady, is your necklace!

DULCINEA: (*eagerly, dumbfounded.*) My necklace?

ALL: Ah!

DULCINEA: (*wild with delight, puts on her necklace and flings herself on Don Quixote's neck.*) Beautiful Knight!
For this I must embrace you!
All the heroes of old and their marvellous deeds
Are extinguished by you, even great Amadis!

ALL: (*point to Don Quixote.*) What joy shines in his eyes—and illuminates his features!

DON QUIXOTE: (*madly in love, advances to Dulcinea.*) Life's journey is lonely,
Oh, guide and direct my path with a gentle hand,
Then shall you learn with me to make life worth living,

Le temps sera plus court, la moisson plus féconde . . .
Les maux dont geint l'humanité
Ont besoin de la femme et de sa charité!
Allons vers l'Idéal, montons à grands coups d'aile!
(*En lui offrant la main.*)
Soyez mon épouse fidèle!

DULCINÉE: (*éclatant de rire.*) Me marier, moi!
Que j'abandonne ma maison,
Ma ville!
eh!
mais . . . vous perdez la raison!
J'aime trop la folie et le rire,
Et l'amour, mon charmant empire,
Je vous estime fort!
Vous êtes un galant
Fantasque, glorieux, étrange infiniment . . .
Mais laissez-moi . . . très libre, en ma ville natale.
Me marier! ah! ah!

DON QUICHOTTE: (*courbant la tête.*) O réponse fatale!
Peu de mots ont suffi pour me désespérer.

DULCINÉE: (*d'un geste lent, éloignant la foule. Sancho lui-même s'efface. Seule, avec Don Quichotte.*) Oui, je souffre votre tristesse
Et j'ai vraiment chagrin à vous désemparer;
Mais je dois vous désabuser . . .
Et en n'acceptant pas ce que vous proposez,
Vrai . . . je vous prouve ainsi ma sincère tendresse.
Vous . . . j'aurais de la peine, ami, de vous tromper . . .

DON QUICHOTTE: (*très ému.*) Dulcinée! Dulcinée! . . .

DULCINÉE: (*émue, tristement, mais en souriant.*) Car c'est ma destinée
De donner de l'amour à ceux dont le désir
Est d'avoir ou mon âme ou ma bouche à saisir.
(*Avec un tendre élan.*)
Puisque vous souffrez et que je suis impure,
Indigne, vengez-vous, lancez sur moi l'injure . . .
Mais restez avec nous . . .
(*Don Quichotte tombe à genoux.*)
Oui, restez à genoux . . .
Là, devant Dulcinée! . . .
Ah! restez avec nous! . . .

DON QUICHOTTE: (*à deux genous, avec une infinie bonté.*) O toi, dont les bras nus sont plus frais que la mousse,
Laisse-moi te parler
De ma voix la plus douce
Avant de te quitter.
(*Avec une gravité triste.*)

The days shall fly swifter, Earth give more of its fullness—
The wounds that chafe the souls of men
Shall be healed by the love and charity of woman!
Away to the Perfect Life, triumphant soaring,
(*Offering her his hand.*)
Be mine adored, beloved wife!

DULCINEA: (*laughing.*) I! A lawful wife!
And would you bid me leave my home?
Surely—your senses are bewitched!—
My heart is given to folly, laughter, mirth
And love, they and I hold revel here.
I hold you well esteemed!
I know you for a brave fantastick,
Valiant, true, and passing strange indeed—
But leave me in freedom where I was born and nurtured.
A lawful wife! Ha! ha!

DON QUIXOTE: (*with bowed head.*) You have spoken my doom!—
Simple words, but enough, henceforth my heart is dead.

DULCINEA: (*quietly dismisses her guests, Sancho makes himself scarce also. Alone with Don Quixote.*) I, too, suffer, your anguish is mine,
And I am sorely pained to lose your gentle heart,
Yet must I undeceive you now,
That so denying you the answer you crave,
I may prove how sincere my affection is.
You,—dear friend, I should be unhappy deceiving you.

DON QUIXOTE: (*deeply moved.*) Dulcinea!

DULCINEA: (*with emotion, smiling bitterly.*) For the fates have ordained me
To surrender in love unto all whose desire
Is to feast on my soul or my lips as they will.
(*In an outburst of tenderness.*)
Ah! since through unworthy, tainted me, you suffer
Exact the forfeit of revenge from me!—
But remain here with us!—
(*Don Quixote falls on his knees.*)
Yes, on your knees
At Dulcinea's feet!—Ah, leave us not!—

DON QUIXOTE: (*on his knees, with infinite tenderness.*) O lady, whose gleaming arms thrill me, soft as swan-down,
I would say to you
Words most gentle and tender—
Before I bid farewell.
(*Grave and sad.*)

Comme réponse à ma prière,
Pour m'avoir dit des vérités,
Femme, je te bénis: Reste toujours sincère
Tu m'as brisé le coeur . . . et je suis à tes pieds.
(*Dulcinée se penche vers lui et l'embrasse au front avec ferveur en répétant les dernières paroles qu'elle lui a dites, puis, au bruit de la foule qui revient, elle quitte Don Quichotte et rejoint ses amis. Le chevalier se relève, soutenu par Sancho qui le premier, est entré et s'est élancé vers son pauvre maître.*)

**TOUS ET TOUTES:** (*revenant bruyamment, à Dulcinée.*) Enfin, te revoilà! Rends-nous ton clair sourire!
(*Le Chevalier, à bout de forces, s'assoit dans un coin. Pendant ce qui suit, Sancho reste près de Don Quichotte et essaie de le consoler; le chevalier cherche à sourire à Sancho.*)

**RODRIGUEZ:** (*en montrant Don Quichotte qui s'est relevé.*) Non, ce n'est pas pour en médire . . .

**JUAN:** (*moqueur, achevant la phrase.*) Mais tu prends trop souci de cet être falot.

**DULCINÉE:** (*rudement à Juan, déconcerté.*) Si vous aviez son coeur, alors vous seriez beau!

**JUAN:** (*à des amis.*) C'est un fou simplement qui pose à la victime.

**DULCINÉE:** (*interrompant Juan et très émue, envoyant avant de sortir un grand baiser au pauvre chevalier.*) Oui, peut-être est-il fou . . .
Mais c'est un fou sublime!
(*Elle sort.*)

**TOUS:** (*entre eux, après le départ de Dulcinée, éclatant de rire.*) Tout ça pour ce débris vermoulu du passée!
Pour ce corps de héron! Pour ce masque plissé!
(*Sancho, frémissant sous les insultes, a cherché à empêcher son maître d'entendre; mais le coup est trop rude; Don Quichotte est prêt à fondre en larmes; il se lève, va vers la porte. Sancho énergique l'arrête dans son mouvement.*)

**SANCHO:** (*d'un geste terrible et d'une voix tonnante, à la foule qui demeure interdite.*) Ca, vous commettez tous un acte épouvantable,
Belles dames, seigneurs, en outrageant ici
Le héros admirable
Et hardi que voici.
Riez, allez, riez du pauvre idéologue
Qui passe dans rêve et vous parle d'églogue,
D'amour et de bonté somme autre-

Since in denying my petition
You have not hid the truth from me—
Lady, here I bless you,
True to yourself God keep you!
You have broken my heart—still do I kneel to you!
(*Dulcinea bends down to Don Quixote and fervently kisses him on the forehead, repeating his words; then, bearing her guests returning, moves away and rejoins her friends. Don Quixote rises, assisted by Sancho, who is the first to enter and has hurried to his master's side.*)

**ALL:** (*rushing in and besieging Dulcinea.*) Once more we find you here!
Now for us smile your sweetest!
(*The Knight, at the end of his tether, sinks to a seat in the corner during the following. Sancho remains at his side, trying to console him. Don Quixote smiles feebly at Sancho in return.*)

**RODRIGUEZ:** (*indicating Don Quixote, who has arisen.*) No, though I scorn to speak unkindly—

**JUAN:** (*breaking in with a sneer.*) Come, do not waste your charms on this foolish old loon.

**DULCINEA:** (*sharply rebuking Juan, who winces.*) If you had his great heart, indeed, you would be a man!

**JUAN:** (*to his friends.*) Just a madman, nothing more, who poses as a martyr!

**DULCINEA:** (*with great emotion, cutting Juan short.*) Yes, a madman, maybe—but—with the soul of an angel!—
(*She goes out, throwing a kiss to the unhappy Knight.*)

**ALL:** (*bursting into laughter, after Dulcinea's exit.*) All this for that moth-eaten, worm-eaten relic!
That moulting old stork!
That death's head and bones!
(*Sancho, quailing under the shower of insults, tries to prevent his master from hearing; but the taunts are too brutal; Don Quixote, almost in tears, rises and makes a move towards the door. Sancho quickly detains him.*)

**SANCHO:** (*overawes the crowd with a menacing gesture and thunders a rebuke.*) Stop!
You propose a crime that is wicked and cruel,
Gentle ladies, my lords, in reviling with scorn
This brave man, true and honest,
Great in heart and in soul.
Laugh on, and mock this poor champion of chimeras
Whose thoughts are noble dreams, and whose speech is an idyll
Of tenderness and love inspired by

fois Jésus!
Moquez-vous sans pitié des ses bas décousus,
De son pourpoint usé, de ses chausses boueuses,
Vous, bas fripons, courtisans, gueuses,
Qui devriez tomber aux pieds
De l'être saint dont vous riez.
Viens, mon grand!
Viens! scrutons les profondeurs cachées;
Viens, viens! recommencons les belles chevauchées, Foncons sur tout lâcheté
Et donnons au malheur le pain de la bonté!
(*Il embrasse son vieil ami lui a tendu les bras.*)

## ■ ACTE CINQUIÈME

*DANS LE CHEMIN RAVINÉ DE LA VIEILLE FORÊT*
(*C'est la nuit, Une nuit étoilée, très claire; Jupiter brille dans tout son éclat.*
*Don Quichotte repose, debout, contre un grand chêne.*
*Sancho le veille comme un enfant, il attise un feu de sarments qui réchauffera son "grand." Il retirera silencieusement sa grosse veste pour en couvrir les pieds du pauvre chevalier; puis sa prière s'élèvera attendrie et fervente.*)

**SANCHO:** O mon maître, ô mon grand! dans des splendeurs de songe
Que ton âme s'élève aux cieux loin du mensonge
Et que ton coeur si doux plane dans les clartés,
Où tout ce qu'il rêva devient réalité!

**DON QUICHOTTE:** (*se réveillant, d'une voix douce.*) Écoute, mon ami, je me sens bien malade!
Délace mon pourpoint, enlève la salade
Qui recouvre le front basané qu'est le mien;
Mets ton bras sous mon cou, sois l'ultime soutien
De celui qui pansa l'humanité souffrante,
Et survécut à la Chevalerie errante.
(*Sancho murmure: "Mon maître" pendant que Don Quichotte continue à parler (avec un doux sourire) à son brave Sancho.*)
Sancho, mon bon Sancho, nous allons nous quitter . . . Ingrat, vas-tu me regretter? . . .
Déjà tes yeux revoient le village
Où tu fus enfant quant j'étais en âge . . .
Et te voici rêvant aux jolis prés,

source divine!
Spare him not as you mock his shabby attire,
His doublet soiled and worn, and his hose patched and threadbare.
You—vulgar boors—underbred—ribald—
Scarce fit to grovel on your knees
To the saint whom you revile!
Come, my Prince!
We will probe unfathomed depths!
Once more we will sally forth together,
To smite and scourge the profligate,
And heal the suffering, with love and tenderness!
(*He embraces his aged friend, who holds out his arms to him.*)

## ■ ACT V

*ROAD THROUGH THE GORGE OF AN ANCIENT FOREST*
(*It is night, starry and clear. Jupiter is at his brightest. Don Quixote is resting, leaning against the trunk of an oak. Sancho watches over him like a child; he makes a fire of sticks and faggots for his "Prince," covers the poor knight's feet with his cloak, then sings, simply, affectionately and fervently:*)

**SANCHO:** Oh, my Lord, oh, my Prince!
Bright visions crown your dreaming,
May your spirit find rest in heaven from earthly falsehood,
And may your gentle soul soar through celestial realms,
Where all its dreamland forms become reality!

**DON QUIXOTE:** (*waking, in a low voice.*) Good Sancho, faithful friend, I am faint, I am dying!
Let my head rest on your arm, be the last to uphold
Him who championed the right, fought for the poor that suffered,
Outlived true chivalry, and survived the Knights-Errant!
(*Sancho murmurs: "My master!" while Don Quixote continues with a smile.*)
Good Sancho, faithful friend, we are fated to part—
Do you care, will you mourn for my loss?
Even now your eyes once more see the village
Of early childhood—
And you dream again of the forest and glades,
The silent woods, the broidered vales,
The all-compelling charms of the

## Act V

Aux bois mystérieux, aux vallons diaprés,
Aux charmes obsesseurs de la terre natale!

SANCHO: (*désolé.*) Non! non!

DON QUICHOTTE: (*avec une infinie douceur.*) Mais, mon pauvret, c'est la chose fatale!
Tu n'es qu'un homme enfin, tu veux vivre . . . et je meurs!

SANCHO: Mon maître! . . .

DON QUICHOTTE: (*fièrement et simplement, en un suprême et sublime effort se redressant. Oui! je fus le chef des bons semeurs! J'ai lutté pour le bien, j'ai fait la bonne guerre!
(Il retombe . . . il étouffe . . . )*
Sancho, je t'ai promis naguère
Des coteaux,
Des châteaux,
Même une île
Fertile . . .

SANCHO: (*très doux.*) C'était un simple îlot que je voulais avoir! . . .

DON QUICHOTTE: (*souriant.*)
Prends cette île qu'il est toujours en mon pouvoir
De te donner! . . .
Un flot azuré bat ses grèves.

hamlet that gave you birth!

SANCHO: (*distraught*) No! no!

DON QUIXOTE: (*with infinite tenderness.*) Ah, my poor friend, fate will brook no denial!—
You are only a man, you would live,—I must die—

SANCHO: (*sobbing.*) Oh, master!

DON QUIXOTE: (*proudly and simply, straightening himself with a mighty effort.*) Yes!
I was the prince of kindly men!
I strove to right the wrong, I fought for truth and honor!
(*He reels and chokes.*)
Good Sancho, of late I promised you
Boundless lands,
Castles fair,
Then an island,
A pleasance—

SANCHO: (*gently.*) A simple little islet was my heart's desire!—

DON QUIXOTE: (*continuing with a smile.*) Take that island, the sole possession that is still
Mine own to give—wavelets blue and clear lave its margin—

Elle est belle, plaisante . . . et c'est l'île des Rêves! . . .
(*Sancho pleure.*)
Ne pleure pas, Sancho, mon bon, mon gros Sancho!

SANCHO: Laisses-vous délacer; comme dans un cachot Vous étouffez, mon grand, dans cet habit d'apôtre!

DON QUICHOTTE: (*l'arrête. Je meurs . . . Fais ta prière et dis la pâtenôtre . . .
(Don Quichotte baisse la tête et défaille. Un court instant. Sancho avec précaution le cale contre l'arbre. le bon Sancho pleure. Don Quichotte reprend, désignant Jupiter à qui il tend les bras.)*
L'Étoile! Dulcinée! . . . avec l'astre éclatant
Elle s'est confondue! . . . O Sancho, c'est bien elle,
La lumière, l'amour, la jeunesse immortelle,
Vers qui je vais, qui me fait signe, qui m'attend . . .
(*Ses bras retombent. Il meurt. On entend un cri, puis sangloter Sancho qui embrasse son vieux maître adoré.*)

*FIN.*

It is lovely, enchanting—
It is the Island of Dreams!
(*Sancho weeps.*)
No, Sancho, weep not so, my fine, my mighty Sancho!

SANCHO: Give leave to loose your mail, you are imprisoned like this,
Liked to be choked indeed, trussed in your champion's armor!

DON QUIXOTE: (*waves him away.*) I am dying—
Whisper a prayer and a last Pater-Noster—
(*His head droops, he collapses. Sancho carefully props him up against the tree. Don Quixote continues, stretching out his arms to Jupiter.*)
The Star!—
Dulcinea!—
With that bright shining star
Finds her soul sweet communion—
It is my Goddess!—
She is Light, she is Love, she is Beauty!—
I go to her—for she has called me—and awaits me!
(*His arms drop lifeless, he dies. With a cry and a sob Sancho embraces his aged master.*)

*THE END*

# Sapho (1897)

## Sappho

MUSIC BY JULES-ÉMILE FRÉDÉRIC MASSENET ■ LIBRETTO BY HENRI CAIN AND BERNÈDE ■ BASED ON THE NOVEL BY ALPHONSE DAUDET

This five-act pièce lyrique, set to a libretto by Henri Cain and Arthur Bernède (based upon Alphonse Daudet's novel) premiered at the Opéra-Comique in Paris on November 27, 1897. The story begins in the drawing-room of Caoudal's house. A masquerade ball is taking place there, and Caoudal and his friend, La Borderie enter with his guests. La Borderie says he is tired and tries to leave, only to be brought back by the female guests. Jean Gaussin, a young man from the country, is also a guest at the ball. Jean is about to depart when he hears Fanny, a model of Caoudal's, sing with the rest of the guests. Jean is homesick and yearns to leave just as he spots Fanny and falls in love with her at first sight. She manages to speak with him and finds out that he is not an artist, knows nothing of the artist's life and has just arrived from Provence. Afraid that he will find out about her past and anxious to be his friend, she talks him into leaving with her quietly. Caoudal sees Fanny leaving with Jean, calls some of his friends over, and they all laugh with pity for the innocent young man.

At Jean's lodgings in the Rue d'Amsterdam, he is at work with his father, Césaire. Césaire and Divonne, Jean's parents, came to Paris to find their son a job and take Jean's cousin, Irene, home with them. After his family returns to the country, Jean is not lonely for long. Fanny enters and finds him in a mood for company. She sees a statuette of Sappho by Caoudal for which she herself had been the model and almost reveals her identity to Jean. She stops herself in time and hums a melody which reminds Jean of his home. He declares his love for her and they pledge eternal devotion to each other. One year later, Jean and Fanny are husband and wife. He is more in love with her now and she is truly in love with him. She believes that she has left her old bohemian life behind forever. But things go awry when Caoudal and Jean meet, and Caoudal asks Jean if he is still living with "Sappho" (the name under which Fanny is know amongst the artists). Jean at first doesn't realize who this is, but soon he understands that the model of the statuette Caoudal gave him is in fact his beloved. He is disgusted by this, and he denies to Caoudal that Fanny is still with him. Caoudal tells him about Fanny's former life, including the fact that she has a child living with her father by a former lover. Jean is overcome with anger and expresses his hatred of Fanny. Fanny enters at this instant, and when she sees Caoudal and La Borderie with Jean and the look on Jean's face, she knows that she has been betrayed. Jean reviles her and she curses her old friends. She thinks that they have deliberately told Jean about her in order to take away the one happiness in her life.

Jean goes home to Provence. While his family tries to comfort him, Césaire enters and asks Divonne and Irene to go out for a while. When they do, he tells Jean that "Sappho" has come to see him. Césaire departs as Fanny enters. She can not stand being away from him. He is touched by her beauty and her pleas and is about to reconcile with her when his parents enter. Fanny begs her forgiveness from Divonne. As Jean goes away, she reaches out to him and leaves in tears. It is now winter, and Fanny is alone in the room where she and Jean lived together for that blissful year. She is sad, but she tears up Jean's letters and decides to devote herself to her child. Jean suddenly comes in as he could no longer stay away. He has come back to live with her, giving up everything else. When she calls him, "my love", he once again becomes jealous. He is reminded of Caoudal's story of another lover of Fanny's. He becomes tired, falls into a chair and goes to sleep. Fanny realizes that she and Jean can never live together again, writes him a farewell note, and leaves him as he sleeps.

---

## ■ ACTE I

*Un salon précédant l'atelier du sculpteur Caoudal—une nuit de bal costumé.*

### SCÈNE PREMIÈRE

*Au lointain, dans l'atelier, bruit continu de conversations très animées, mêlées d'exclamations bruyantes dominant parfois un orchestre de faux tziganes installé dans cet atelier. Dans le salon, va-et-vient d'invités. Bientôt paraissent Caoudal et La Borderie, costumés et entourés d'amis et de petites femmes travesties.*

**CAOUDAL:** Eh! jeunesse, regardez-nous,
Les vieux sont maintenant les plus gais, les plus fous.

**LA BORDERIE:** Je n'en puis plus!

**CAOUDAL:** Tu veux filer peut-être? . . .

**LA BORDERIE:** Je n'en puis plus, cher maître!

## ■ ACT I

*Large drawing-room, behind which is the studio of Caoudal, the sculptor.—A masked ball is in progress.*

### SCENE I

*From the studio, off, comes the continuous hum of animated conversation, mingled with sharp exclamations.—Some of the guests come into the room from the studio behind.—A make-believe Gypsy orchestra is playing noisily in the studio, off.*

**CAOUDAL:** Hey, my children!
Hear, everyone!
We may be old, but we have the fun!

**LA BORDERIE:** I'm quite worn out.

**CAOUDAL:** You would escape, no doubt!

**LA BORDERIE:** Dear master, I am quite worn out.

## Act I, Scene I

**CAOUDAL:** Allons donc!
Regarde autour de toi . . .
(*En charge.*)
Bayadère à l'oeil noir, colombine charmante,
Andalouse gentille, arlequine troublante
Se donnent rendez-vous chez moi . . .
Ohé! jeunesse! . . .

**TOUS:** (*sauf La Borderie*). Ohé! jeunesse! . . .
Faisons les fous,
Amusons-nous!
Des baisers cueillons la caresse!

**LA BORDERIE:** Faites les fous!
Bonsoir!
Amusez-vous!
Mais laissez moi m'esquiver!

**CAOUDAL:** Empêchez-le de se sauver!

**TOUS:** Non, tu ne peux pas t'esquiver
Avant que le jour ne paraisse!

**CAOUDAL:** Et ça s'appelle la jeunesse!

**LA BORDERIE:** Caoudal a vingt ans!

**CAOUDAL:** Non! soixante printemps!

### SCÈNE II

*Caoudal, Jean, La Borderie et quelques invités.*

**CAOUDAL:** (*à Jean*). Vous aussi, vous fuyez la danse?
Et pourtant, à votre âge, on est plein de vaillance . . .

**JEAN:** Je n'ai jamais dansé.
Et me sens tout embarrassé!

**CAOUDAL:** Ça vous change de la Provence?

**JEAN:** Ah! je ne puis dire combien!

**LA BORDERIE:** Té, mon petit, je le vois bien!

**CAOUDAL:** Allons! courage! confiance!

**LA BORDERIE:** Le premier pas est tout, et le reste n'est rien.

**CAOUDAL:** Connaissez-vous ces belles filles?

**JEAN:** Non, monsieur.

**CAOUDAL:** Comment les trouvez-vous?

**JEAN:** Mais, gentilles.

**CAOUDAL:** Faut-il vous présenter?

**JEAN:** Elles riraient de moi.
Les femmes me font peur!

**UN GROUPE:** Ah! ah! vraiment!

---

**CAOUDAL:** (*To La Borderie*).
Don't say that!
Wait a bit!
Look around you.
(*Indicating the girls, who are listening.*)
And tell me what you see: Bayadère dark of eye,
Columbine most enchanting, Andalusian divine.
Have all come here to sup with me:
Hurrah! for youth!

**ALL:** (*except La Borderie*). Hurrah! Hurrah! Do what we choose,
So it amuse!
And gather kisses while we may!
Hurrah! Hurray!

**LA BORDERIE:** Do what you choose; so it amuse!
Do what you choose,
But please let me get away!

**CAOUDAL:** We must not let him get away!

**ALL:** We must not let him get away!
No, not before the break of day!

**CAOUDAL:** And this is what they call their youth!

**LA BORDERIE:** Caoudal's twenty-one!

**CAOUDAL:** I'm sixty, my son!

### SCENE II

*Caoudal, Jean, La Borderie and some of the guests.*

**CAOUDAL:** (*to Jean*). What! you too would escape the dance?
My dear boy, at your age one has courage to prance.

**JEAN:** I don't know how to dance,
I'm ashamed to take my chance.

**CAOUDAL:** It is different from your Provence!

**JEAN:** How different, you do not know!

**LA BORDERIE:** Hey, young man! You here tonight?

**CAOUDAL:** Come, come! Be brave, and advance.

**LA BORDERIE:** One step, and it is done.
It will then go all right.

**CAOUDAL:** But have you met these pretty ladies?

**JEAN:** I have not.

**CAOUDAL:** What do you think of them?

**JEAN:** Why—most charming.

**CAOUDAL:** Let me present you— come!

**JEAN:** No!
They would laugh, I know.
Girls put me in a fright.

**SOME OF THE WOMEN:** Ha! Ha!
Should we?

---

**LA BORDERIE:** Pourquoi?
C'est être un peu naïf, ma foi!

**CAOUDAL:** (*à Jean*). Venez-vous?

**JEAN:** Non, je reste!
(*Tous se dirigent vers l'atelier, à l'exception de Jean.*)

### SCÈNE III

**JEAN:** (*seul*). Est-ce vraiment un songe,
Qui trouble mon esprit et déroute mon coeur?
Voilà donc ce qu'on nomme ici-bas le bonheur!
Mensonge!
(*Tout le monde est rentré dans l'atelier; au dehors, cris: "Silence! Taisez-vous! chante!"*)
(*Vieille Chanson dans la coulisse.*)

**LA VOIX DE FANNY:** (*puis les femmes et les hommes qui reconnaissent la vieille chanson de l'atelier.*)
La reine des modèles,
Le plus beau . . .
Qui pose sans ficelles,
C'est Sapho!
Zoé, Paulette, Angèle,
La grande Adèle
Et Rebecca,
Sont d'la p'tit' bièr' à côté d'ça!
Le plus beau,
C'est Sapho!
(*On reprend en choeur, puis un ban formidable est exécuté par toute la foule.*)

**JEAN:** Ce monde que je vois, ces chansons que j'écoute,
Tout dans ce bal me trouble et me déroute . . .
Qu'il est loin mon pays de clarté, de soleil!
Où mille fleurs odorantes,
Dans le couchant vermeil,
Exhalent par les airs leurs senteurs pénétrantes;
Où le Rhône bondit et roule impétueux
Ses flots couleur d'azur que jalousent les cieux.
Mon pays où le soir dans la verte oseraie,
L'on peut aller rêver sans que rien vous effraie,
Où l'on entend passer dans les grands arbres verts
Le vent, chantant plus fort durant les courts hivers . . .
Mon pays où tout dit l'amour et l'espérance,
Qu'il est loin de mes yeux! . . . Qu'elle est loin ma Provence!

---

**LA BORDERIE:** Why so?
A wee bit artless, that!

**CAOUDAL:** (*to Jean*). Will you come?

**JEAN:** I'll wait!
(*All go into the studio, with the exception of Jean.*)

### SCENE III

**JEAN:** (*alone; to himself*). What are these dreams that rise,
And trouble so my soul, and my heart put to flight?
Here I see what they tell me is earthly delight:
What lies!
(*All go into the studio; cries heard off: "Silence! Be still! Keep still! Sing!"*)
(*Old Song heard off*).

**VOICE OF FANNY:** (*also of the men and women who recognize the old studio song.*) The queen of pretty poses,
As you know,
Who all her charms discloses,
Is Sappho!
Louise, Pauline, Angèle,
And big Adèle, if you prefer,
Are all cheap goods alongside of her!
That is so,
O Sappho!
(*Noisy demonstration by the whole company.*)

**JEAN:** These people that I see, and the songs that I hear,
All, at this ball, disturbs—fills me with fear.
Ah, but I'm far from home, from the land of the sun!
There, where my flowers now are blowing,
And, since the day was done,
Upon a purer air their sweet scent have been strowing:
Ah, but I'm far from my home, my dear land of the sun!
Where the Rhone bounds along, and rolls its waters by,
In waves that are so blue that they laugh at the sky;
My dear land, where at eve along the willow way one
May wander with one's thoughts, and there's naught to dismay one.
Where, if one hears at times among the tall, green trees
A wind that louder sighs, it is the winter breeze.
Dearest land, where all voiced the hopes that lay before me,
Ah, you are far from my sight, land of promise that bore me.

## SCÈNE IV

*Fanny, Caoudal, La Borderie, Hommes, Femmes, Etc.*
*De bruyantes exclamations gaies et prolongées, mêlées de rires, éclatent dans l'atelier.—Aussitôt, tous entrent en tumulte à la suite de Fanny.—Caoudal, La Borderie et quelques hommes très empressés.*

DES HOMMES: Un baiser!

FANNY: Non!
Taisez-vous!

DES HOMMES: Un seul!

FANNY: Voyons!

DES HOMMES: Pour nous!

FANNY: (*cherchant à se dégager de tous les hommes qui l'entourent*). Allez, jolis farceurs, vrai, vous me faites rire! Adorateurs, poètes, courtisans, Amoureux, flatteurs, médisants, Cachant mal votre jeu sous un charmant sourire! Allez! jolis farceurs, vrai, vous me faites rire!
(*Mouvements dans les groupes, impressions de mécontentement, de déceptions et d'indifférence aussi. Tous vont et viennent, Jean regarde Fanny avec trouble. Sa physionomie semble s'éveiller à un nouveau sentiment qui l'émeut et le transfigure.*)

FANNY: (*à Caoudal, lui montrant Jean*). Quel est ce beau garçon?

CAOUDAL: (*distrait*). Je ne sais.

FANNY: Tiens, il faut
Que je lui parle!

CAOUDAL: Bien!
Allons . . . toujours Sapho!
(*Il s'éloigne en riant.*)

FANNY: (*qui s'est rapprochée, à Jean*). Comment vous nommez-vous?

JEAN: Jean Gaussin.

FANNY: De Provence?

JEAN: Ça s'entend?

FANNY: Pas beaucoup. Artiste, je le pense?

JEAN: Non, madame.

FANNY: Ah! tant mieux!
Mais pourquoi baissez-vous les yeux?
Je ne suis pas méchante . . .

JEAN: Vous vous moquez de moi.

## SCENE IV

*Fanny, Caoudal, La Borderie, men, women.*
(*Prolonged cries, gay and noisy, come from the studio.—Thereupon all enter in confusion, following Fanny: Caoudal, La Borderie, and the other men, eagerly.—They surround Fanny, with eager entreaties.*)

THE MEN: A kiss!

FANNY: No, no!
Have done!

THE MEN: For me!

FANNY: Ah, please!

THE MEN: Just one!

FANNY: (*trying to free herself from the men who surround her*).
Go on!
You're a nice lot!
Yes, I shall die laughing!
Ha, ha!
Adores you!
Hypocrites!
Hypocrites!
Ha, ha!
And poets, lovers too!
What cheats!
O you wits!
But you can't hide your game with your smiles or your chaffing!
Ha, ha!
Ha, ha!
Ha, ha!
(*The guests move about here and there, wearing expressions of displeasure, disappointment, or indifference.—Jean looks at Fanny, disturbed; his face seems to light up with some new feeling which moves and transfigures him.*)

FANNY: (*aside to Caoudal, pointing out Jean*). Who is that handsome boy?

CAOUDAL: (*absently*). I don't know.

FANNY: What?
I must make his acquaintance!

CAOUDAL: Good!
Go on!
You're Sappho still!
(*He goes away laughing.*)

FANNY: (*who has approached; to Jean*). Tell me, what is your name?

JEAN: Jean Gaussin.

FANNY: From Provence?

JEAN: Does it show?

FANNY: Not so much!
An artist, I suppose?

JEAN: No, madame.

FANNY: Ah! I'm glad!
But why do you lower your eyes?
I am not really bad.

JEAN: Are you laughing at me?

FANNY: Moi, me moquer de toi!
Pas artiste! mais ça m'enchante!

LA BORDERIE ET CAOUDAL: (*sortant de l'atelier*). Le couvert est mis!

FANNY: (*bas à Jean*). A bientôt!

CAOUDAL: Hé! les amis!
(*Entraînant un groupe de femmes et rentrant dans l'atelier.*)
A table! à table!

TOUS: (*en parodie*).
Plaisir de la table,
Bonheur véritable!

LA VOIX DE CAOUDAL: (*dans l'atelier*). Sapho!

TOUS: Sapho!

FANNY: (*baletante, barrant le passage à Jean qui veut rentrer dans l'atelier*). N'y va pas!
Viens avec moi plutôt!
Viens donc!

JEAN: Mais . . .

FANNY: Viens, te dis-je.

JEAN: Je sens que malgré moi je vais où vont ses pas!

FANNY: Viens donc, m'ami . . .

JEAN: J'ai le vertige!
(*Ils s'enfuient.*)
(*Cris dans l'atelier: Sapho! Sapho!*)
(*La grande tapisserie du fond est entièrement écartée. On aperçoit tous les invités assis à de petites tables . . . souper bruyant. Caoudal, comprenant la fuite de Fanny et de Jean, appelle autour de lui quelques amis; puis, ils échangent entre eux des gestes de commisération, tout en plaisantant. Au fond, les tziganes accentuent avec virtuosité une sorte de czardas.*)

*FIN DE L'ACTE PREMIER.*

## ■ ACTE DEUXIÈME

*Le logement de Jean Gaussin, a Paris, Rue D'Amsterdam.*

### SCÈNE PREMIÈRE

*Jean, Césaire.*

JEAN: (*chantonnant*). O Magali, ma tant amado
Mete la testo au fenstroun.

CÉSAIRE: Escouto un pau aquesto aubado
De tambourin et de vioulon.

JEAN: Vous vous donnez bien de la peine,
Père . . .

FANNY: I—making fun of you!
Not an artist!
Oh!
I'm so glad!

LA BORDERIE and CAOUDAL: (*coming out of the studio*). Supper's ready now!

FANNY: (*whispering to Jean*).
Bye-and-bye!

CAOUDAL: (*urging the guests to go into the studio*). To supper!
To supper!

ALL: (*in parody*). Pleasures of the table,
They only are stable!

THE VOICE OF CAOUDAL: (*from the studio*). Sappho!

ALL: Sappho!

FANNY: (*breathlessly, as she blocks Jean's way into the studio*). Do not go!
Do not go!
No!
Come with me.
Yes, come—with me!

JEAN: But—

FANNY: Come, I say!

JEAN: Ah! I know, in spite of me, that where she goes, I go!

FANNY: Come, come, my dear!

JEAN: Ah!
I am dizzy!
(*They go off.*)
(*From the studio come cries of "Sappho! Sappho!"—The great curtain at the back is drawn aside; all the guests are disclosed sitting at small tables: a gay supper.—Caoudal, who has noticed the departure of Fanny and Jean, calls some friends to him, and they jokingly exchange gestures of commiseration.—The gypsies at the back brilliantly execute a sort of czardas.*)

*END OF FIRST ACT.*

## ■ ACT II

*Lodgings of Jean Gaussin in the rue d'Amsterdam, Paris.*

### SCENE I

*Jean, Césaire.*

JEAN: (*singing at his work*). O Magali, beloved maidie,
Look out and let your face be seen.

CÉSAIRE: And listen while we serenade you
With violin and tambourine.

JEAN: Why, how much trouble you are taking, Father!

## Act II, Scene I

**CÉSAIRE:** Tais-toi!

**JEAN:** (*regardant avec amour un tableau accroché au mur*). Notre maison . . .
Avec ses bois de myrtes dans la plaine
Et ses vignes à l'horizon;
Maman Divonne est sur la porte.
En la voyant toujours, toujours devant mes yeux,
Je travaillerai mieux;
Sa présence me réconforte.

**CÉSAIRE:** A nous tu penseras souvent?

**JEAN:** Oui, Père.
Mais où donc est ma mère?

**CÉSAIRE:** Au couvent,
Pour y chercher Irène, l'orpheline,
Notre nièce.

**JEAN:** Ah! Je devine;
Vous l'emmenez?

**CÉSAIRE:** Nous l'adoptons.
Elle nous tiendra compagnie
Remplaçant le fils que nous regrettons.

**JEAN:** Pour toutes vos bontés,
Mère, soyez bénie!

### SCÈNE II

*Les Mêmes, Divonne, Irène.*

**DIVONNE:** C'est nous!
Jésus!
Quelle villasse que ce Paris!
Que de tours et de pas!
Que de voitures, de brouhahas
Et ce monde qui passe et passe!
Tous ces gens-là font les pressés . . .
Si ça leur plaît, grand bien leur fasse! Tous ces gens-là sont insensés . . .
Que je préfère être là-bas!
Ah! bou Dïou que je suis lasse!
Eh! qué!
Rien n'est encore en place!
Pauvre petit!

**CÉSAIRE:** C'est fini n'gronde pas!

**JEAN:** Bonjour, Maman!

**DIVONNE:** Bonjour, pitchoun!
Té! c'est Irène,
Ta cousine!

**IRÈNE:** Mon cousin, bonjour.

**DIVONNE:** (*à Jean*). Hein! qu'en dis-tu? fraîche comme le jour,
Belle comme une reine!
Vous vous êtes connus jadis sur mes genoux . . .
(*A Césaire.*)
Césaire, il faudra partir tout à l'heure
Allons, nous,
En attendant, visiter la demeure,
Voir s'il ne manque rien.
(*A Jean.*)
Pécaïre!
Embrasse-moi, vaurien!
(*Ils sortent.*)

---

**CÉSAIRE:** Keep still!

**JEAN:** (*looking affectionately at a picture which hangs on the wall*).
Home that I love,
With all its groves of myrtle in the lowlands,
And its vineyards that rise above.
Mother Divonne is at the door,
And when I see her there each day anew,
How well I'll do my work,
For my courage she will restore.

**CÉSAIRE:** And you will often think of us?

**JEAN:** Yes, Father.
And now, where is my mother?

**CÉSAIRE:** At the convent.
She's gone to fetch Irene, a niece of ours,
Who is an orphan.

**JEAN:** Ah! I suppose—
You'll take her home?

**CÉSAIRE:** We shall adopt her;
With her we shall not be so lonely,
She will take the place of the son we lose.

**JEAN:** For all your loving care,
Mother, take my blessing!

### SCENE II

*The same, Divonne, Irene.*

**DIVONNE:** At last!
Good Lord!
What a monstrous place
This Paris is!
How they go, how they come!
Ah!
Good Lord! and the crowds, how they race!
The time that I have had!
All these people must be mad!
Oh, how I wish I were at home!
Ah!
Lordy me!
But I am weary!
Eh, what! still all upset, my deary?
Oh, you poor boy!

**CÉSAIRE:** All is done!
Don't you scold!

**JEAN:** Good-morning, Mother!

**DIVONNE:** Good-morning, ducky!
Eh! here's Irene!
She's your cousin.

**IRENE:** Cousin Jean, good-day!

**DIVONNE:** (*to Jean*). Well, what do you say?
Sweet and fresh as the day,
And as fair as a queen!
You have sat, you and she,
Together on my knee!—
Césaire! we must all be off before long!
Let us go, while we have time,
For a look round the place
To see that nothing's wrong.
Come, Piggy-wig!
Give me a kiss, scapegrace!
(*Divonne and Césaire go out.*)

---

### SCÈNE III

*Jean, Irène.*

**JEAN:** Chers parents!
(*A Irène.*)
Vrai, je vous envie
D'aller avec eux passer votre vie,
De revoir mon pays de clarté, de soleil,
Les vergers rougissants dans le couchant vermeil . . .
(*A lui-même.*)
Mon pays où tout dit l'amour et l'espérance . . .
Qu'il est loin de mes yeux!
Qu'elle est loin ma Provence!

**IRÈNE:** C'était bien gentil autrefois
Quand nous allions tous les deux par les bois,
Avec Blanchet, notre âne si fidèle;
Ses clochettes sonnaient, il allait trottinant . . .
J'étais bien fière sur la selle!

**JEAN:** Et moi donc!
Vous tenant
Par la main, je me disais: "Qu'elle est belle!"

**IRÈNE:** Et vous rappelez-vous quand nous nous amusions,
Pour imiter l'image de la Bible . . .

**JEAN:** A la fuite en Égypte!

**IRÈNE:** Où nous étions,
Vous saint Joseph, et moi sainte Marie.

**JEAN:** Je m'en souviens, petite amie.

**IRÈNE:** Puis nous nous sauvions,
Pour fuir l'ordre d'Hérode, un monarque terrible,
Qui faisait massacrer par ses centurions
Les pauvres innocents . . .

**TOUS DEUX:** Ah! que nous tremblions!

**IRÈNE:** Vous souvient-il aussi lorsque nous revenions?
Que c'était beau, dans la prairie,
D'écouter l'appel du courlis
Ou le vent qui sifflait ses joyeux frizzelis!

**JEAN:** Je m'en souviens, petite amie.

**IRÈNE:** Et quand venait la nuit,
Tous les contes de la veillée
Revivaient á nos yeux.
Alors au moindre bruit
Je prenais votre bras, frissonnante, effrayée,
Et, sans oser parler, tous deux nous rentrions.

**IRÈNE ET JEAN:** Comme nous tremblions!

---

### SCENE III

*Jean, Irene.*

**JEAN:** Parents dear!
(*To Irene*)
Yes, I envy you
A life to be passed in peace with those two,
Where you'll see our dear home of the land of the sun,
(*To himself.*)
And hopes that lay before me.
Ah, you are far from my sight,
Land of promise that bore me!

**IRENE:** It was sweet when in our childhood
We would journey through the wood,
We would journey through the wood together!
And good Blanchette, our donkey so confiding,
And her bells used to ring,
As along she would swing:
Oh, how proud I felt when riding!—Ah!

**JEAN:** Yes, and I, with your hand held in mine,
I used to think: "She is lovely!"

**IRENE:** Do you remember, too the things we played?
We'd make believe we were the Bible story—

**JEAN:** Of the flight into Egypt—

**IRENE:** When we would be Saint Joseph you, and I the Virgin Mary.

**JEAN:** It all comes back, my little fairy!

**IRENE:** Then we would run away
From Herod, to escape that fearful monster gory,
Whose fierce centurions he had sent forth to slay
Poor little innocents!
**JEAN:** Ah, great was our dismay!

**BOTH:** Ah, great was our dismay!

**IRENE:** Do you remember, too.
As homeward we would stray,
How sweet it was upon the prairie,
To listen to the curlew's cry,
Or to the joyful breezes that went whisp'ring by?

**JEAN:** I do, indeed, my little fairy!

**IRENE:** And when the night closed round,
All the tales we were wont to hear
Would take shape in the dark, and then, at ev'ry sound,
I would cling to your arm, all a-tremble, full of fear;
And, too afraid to speak, we'd steal along our way!

**BOTH:** Ah! great was our dismay!

JEAN: Puis, sur le seuil, en arrivant,
Irène m'embrassait, gentiment,
doucement . . .

IRÈNE: Une soeur, sans pécher,
peut embrasser son frère,
Et vous l'étiez pour moi . . .

JEAN: Ai-je changé pour toi?

IRÈNE: Ah!

JEAN: Donc en t'embrassant, je ne
peux te déplaire, dis?

IRÈNE: Non, puisqu'une soeur
peut embrasser son frère.

JEAN: Comme autrefois . . .

IRÈNE: Comme autrefois dans la
prairie,
Par les sentiers et par les bois.

JEAN: Comme autrefois, petite
amie!
(*Jean embrasse Irène sur le front,
très chastement.*)

## SCÈNE IV

*Jean, Irène, Divonne, Césaire.*

DIVONNE: (*paraissant sur le
seuil de la porte en tenant une
lampe allumée. A Césaire*). Regarde-les, bon Dieu!

CÉSAIRE: L'on ne vous en veut pas!
Non! sangdiou! au contraire.

DIVONNE: Il faut nous dire adieu!

JEAN: Moi, je vous recon-
duis . . .

DIVONNE: Reste là, bien tranquille,
Devant ta table et ne va pas te
déranger.
C'est le travail qui dans la grande
ville
Te préservera du danger.

CÉSAIRE: O ma brave Divonne!

DIVONNE: Petit, voici ta
lampe . . .
Elle est vieille, mais bonne . . .
Jadis à sa clarté,
Dans la sérénité
Des soirs d'automne,
Je cousais tes habits
d'enfant . . .
L'âme en repos, le coeur content,
Lorsque tu dormais dans ta berce.
A sa lueur je t'ai surpris,
Derrière les rideaux de Perse,
Souriant comme un ange à ceux du
paradis.
Pour la dernière fois, aujourd'hui je
te donne
Ce doux nom de petit . . .

JEAN: Maman!

CÉSAIRE: Divonne!

DIVONNE: Adieu!
Travaille!
Espère et sois un homme
Sous l'oeil consolant du bon Dieu.

JEAN: And at the gateway, very oft,
Irene gave a kiss, very sweet, very
soft—

IRENE: It is not wrong for a sister so
to kiss her brother,
And that you were to me—

JEAN: And have I changed for you?

IRENE: Ah!

JEAN: So, if I kiss you, you will not
be offended?
What?

IRENE: No—because a sister may
kiss her brother—

JEAN: As long ago—

IRENE: As long ago together
Among the woods we used to do!

JEAN: As long ago—
(*Jean kisses Irene on the forehead.*)

## SCENE IV

*The same, Divonne, Césaire.*

DIVONNE: (*appearing at the door
carrying a lighted lamp; to
Césaire*). Just look at them, good
Lord!

CÉSAIRE: We are not finding fault!
No, my word! we approve!

DIVONNE: (*to Jean*). And now bid
us good-bye!

JEAN: No. I must see you off!

DIVONNE: No—you stay here, you
sit down
And be still before your table here,
And do not let us break the charm.
It is your work, here in this mon-
strous town,
That will keep you safe from harm.

CÉSAIRE: O, my splendid Divonne!

DIVONNE: My child, now here's
your lamp!
It is my old one, and by it
Many a winter's night,
I've sat beneath its light
When all was quiet,
Making you a baby vest,
Peace in my soul, my heart at rest.
In the shadows soft and uncertain
Asleep my cradled baby lies
Behind his flowery muslin curtain,
Smiling up like an angel to those in
Paradise!
So now, for the last time, my dear
son,
I will call you that sweet name,
"Little One."

JEAN: Mamma!

CÉSAIRE: Divonne!

DIVONNE: Good-bye!
Be faithful!
Have courage to be a man
And live in the light of God's love!

JEAN: Ah! vous deux, comme
Je vous aime!

DIVONNE: (*à Césaire*). Eh! vas-tu
pleurer aussi . . .

IRÈNE: (*à Jean*). Vous laisser seul
ici . . .
C'est triste!

JEAN: Il le faut!
A bientôt, j'espère.

CÉSAIRE ET DIVONNE: Oui, mon
enfant . . .
Allons, adieu!

JEAN: Adieu, chers par-
ents . . . bonne mère . . .
(*A Irène.*)
Petite soeur . . .

IRÈNE: Pauvre grand frère!

DIVONNE, CÉSAIRE ET IRÈNE:
Nous prierons pour toi le bon Dieu.
Nous prierons pour vous le bon
Dieu.

TOUS: A bientôt!
Adieu!
Adieu!

## SCÈNE V

*Jean seul, puis Fanny.*

JEAN: (*seul*). Ils s'en vont, c'est la
solitude!
Maintenant que je les ai vus
Et que j'ai respiré cet air de
quiétude,
De bonheurs à peine entrevus,
Je voudrais retourner vers la chère
demeure.
Ah! pourquoi faut-il se quitter,
Au moment où l'on a tant besoin de
s'aimer?
J'ai froid au coeur, je m'attriste et je
pleure!
Hélas! ils sont partis et déjà loin de
moi.
Me voilà seul à Paris dans la foule,
Qui gronde autour de moi comme
gronde la houle.
Tant de monde et personne à soi!
Ils reverront notre chère demeure!
J'ai froid au coeur, je m'attriste et je
pleure!
(*Il se dirige vers la table, et
s'asseyant, avec un soupir.*)
À l'ouvrage!
(*Il veut lire, mais s'interrompt
bientôt.*)
Pauvre Maman!
Que n'es-tu donc toujours auprès
de ton enfant
Pour lui dire si tendrement:
"C'est le travail qui dans la grande
ville
Te préservera."
Le travail serait facile
En t'écoutant!
Et mon bon père . . . et ma pe-
tite amie . . .
Elle est si douce, si jolie!
Son baiser de chaste pureté
A laissé son parfum tout embaumer

JEAN: Parents dear,
Whom I have loved so well!

DIVONNE: (*to Césaire, aside*).
Well, so you'll cry a little, too?

IRÈNE: (*to Jean*). It is sad to leave
you here, so lonely!

JEAN: You must, but not for long I
hope!

CÉSAIRE and DIVONNE: Yes, my
child!
Come!
Good-bye!

JEAN: Good-bye, parents dear!
Little sister; dearest mother!

IRÈNE: My poor big brother!

DIVONNE, CÉSAIRE and IRENE:
And we shall pray for you.

ALL: Farewell!
Farewell!

## SCENE V

*Jean alone, afterwards Fanny.*

JEAN: (*alone*). They are gone!
Ah, but this is lonely!
Now, indeed, since they all were
here,
And since I now have breathed,
though for a moment only,
Breathed that reposeful, sweet,
happy air.
I could wish to return to the home
of my childhood:
Why, ah why are we torn apart,
When most one feels the need of
love in one's heart?
In Paris here, all alone!
While unheeding the crowd goes
surging by
With the sound of a torrent:
Millions round me, yet alone am I!
They will see all for which I here
am sighing;
My heart is sick—I am sad, I am cry-
ing!
Alas! they now are gone, already far
from me!
(*Sits down to work, taking his
books, etc.*)
Now to work! (*with a sigh.*)
Ah, Mother dear!
Why are you not with me, your
child, and ever near
To repeat, so sweet and clear:
"It is your work here in this mon-
strous city
That will keep you safe."
—My work would all be easy
If you were here!
And my good father, my little cous-
in, too,
She is so sweet, so true.
And her kiss, so innocent and
chaste,

mon âme . . .
Je pourrais être heureux, si j'en faisais ma femme . . .

FANNY: (*entre sans frapper et s'approche doucement*). Bonjour, m'ami!

JEAN: Comment! c'est vous Fanny!

FANNY: Moi-même!
Tu croyais que c'était fini?
Non pas, quand j'aime
C'est pour longtemps.
Si depuis quelque temps
J'avais cessé de te rendre visite,
C'est que je savais
Que tu recevais
Tes parents . . . et cette petite . . .
Pas mal du tout . . . ta sœur? . . . mon compliment . . .

JEAN: Non, ma cousine.

FANNY: (*plus froidement*). Elle est gentille.
Il n'y a qu'un moment,
J'ai vu s'éloigner ta famille,
Je guettais son départ et me voici!

JEAN: Ma mère a voulu m'installer ici . . .
Dans mon petit chez moi, pour que mieux je travaille.

FANNY: Je comprends . . . il faut que je m'en aille.

JEAN: J'ai travaillé parfois lorsque vous étiez là . . .

FANNY: (*s'installant*). Alors, je reste et serai sage.
Voilà!
(*Examinant la pièce.*)
De jolis meubles . . . le grand paysage!
Du caractère et de la vérité!

JEAN: C'est notre maison de là-bas!

FANNY: Sous cet arbre
Comme on serait bien abrité
Pour s'aimer là!
(*Apercevant la Sapho de Caoudal.*)
Tiens, vous avez ce marbre?

JEAN: C'est la Sapho de Caoudal
Ne le connais-tu pas?

FANNY:
Mais . . . oui . . . c'est bien possible . . .
J'ai contre tout artiste un haine invincible . . .
Faut jamais m'en parler!
(*A part.*)
Ils m'ont fait tant de mal!

JEAN: Pourtant, l'art c'est bien beau pour égayer la vie,
Rendre le cœur meilleur, la route plus fleurie.

---

Has cast a perfumed spell over my soul for life:—
How happy might I be, should she become my wife!

FANNY: (*entering without knocking, and approaching him softly*). Good-morning, dear!

JEAN: What! Fanny! Not you?

FANNY: It is, though!
Did you fancy that all was over?
No no!
Once given, my love will last!
If now, for some time past,
I've not been here, but have kept myself shady,
It is because I knew your parents both were with you,
And that little lady—
Your sister, eh?
Not bad!
My compliments!

JEAN: No, she's my cousin.

FANNY: (*more coldly*). She's very sweet:—
But a moment ago I saw them go off down the street:
I was waiting for that, and now appear!

JEAN: My mother thought best to install me here,
So I might have a home, for the work I am doing.

FANNY: Oh, I see!
That means, I must be going—

JEAN: I've often done some work when you were with me here.

FANNY: Well then, I'll stay; I shall be good—so there!
(*Looking round the room.*)
What handsome pieces—what a splendid landscape!
That has some force!
What truth is there revealed!

JEAN: Yes, that is our house and the grove.

FANNY: In the grove one could be so nicely concealed,
While making love.
(*Seeing Caoudal's Sappho*).
Ah, you've one of these statues?

JEAN: Yes, that is Caoudal's Sappho.
You know it, do you not?

FANNY: Why—yes—I may have seen it—
I have for every artist an invincible hatred!
Never name one to me.
(*Aside.*)
They have injured me so!

JEAN: And yet, art is good, to make our life the lighter,
Art lifts the heart on high, and our path of life seems brighter.

---

FANNY: Ce que j'appelle beau,
c'est d'avoir tes vingt ans,
Et comme toi, m'ami, d'être fier, d'être brave,
Et de sentir son cœur si fort que nulle entrave
Ne s'en vienne arrêter ses sublimes élans.
Ce que j'appelle beau, c'est toute créature
S'élevant par l'amour au-dessus des rancœurs
Ou subissant la loi d'éternelle nature,
Deux êtres réunis par le sang de leurs cœurs.
(*Jean l'embrasse. Fanny montrant sa table et l'y conduisant.*)
Travaille!

JEAN: Viens!

FANNY: (*le forçant à s'asseoir à sa table*). Travaille!
(*A part et assombrie.*)
Est-ce un rêve . . .
Mensonger
Venant, comme l'oiseau léger,
Bercer mon cœur et le frôler?
N'est ce qu'un rêve mensonger,
Une caresse vaine et brève?
Pauvre Sapho! n'est-ce qu'un rêve?
(*Elle commence à fredonner:*)
O Magali, ma tant amado,
Mete la testo au fenestroun:
Ecouto un pau aquesto aubado
De tambourin et de viouloun.
Ei plen d'estello aperamount,
L'auro es toumbado;
Mai lis estello paliran
Quand te veran!

JEAN: (*qui a écouté, fasciné, court à Fanny*). Le vieil air du pays! ô ma Fanny que j'aime,
Je voudrais t'entendre toujours
Chanter ainsi la chanson des amours.
En t'écoutant, je ne suis plus moi-même . . .
Je t'aime!

FANNY: Il m'aime!
Et cependant, il faut se dire adieu!
Mieux vaut en finir tout de suite . . .
Pourrais-je m'en aller ensuite?

JEAN: Tu n'es pas libre?

FANNY: Dieu!
Libre de tout amour, puisqu'à toi je me donne!

JEAN: Tu m'appartiens, Fanny!

FANNY: (*grave*). Je ne sui à personne.

JEAN: (*inquiet*). A personne!

FANNY: A toi seul si tu veux de moi!
Ah! garde-moi toujours
là . . . toujours avec toi.

JEAN: Je suis pauvre.

---

FANNY: Ah, what I call the good, is to be twenty-one,
And like you, my friend, to be proud and noble,
To feel one's heart so strong, no fears nor any trouble
Can prevent or delay things superbly begun.
Yes, what I call the good, is any living creature
That can rise through its love high above petty arts,
And will submit alone to the law of its nature,
Ah, yes!
Two beings who are joined by the blood of their hearts!
(*Jean kisses Fanny, who then leads him to his table.*)
To work now!

JEAN: Come!

FANNY: (*forcing him to sit down at his table*). To work now!
(*Aside, as if saddened.*)
Do I dream an empty thing,
That like a bird would lightly wing
Its way into my heart, and sing?
Do I but dream an empty thing?
Alas!
A single kiss, to nothing streaming—
Poor Sappho—ah! am I dreaming?
(*She begins to hum.*)
O Magali, beloved maidie,
Look out and let your face be seen.
And listen while we serenade you
With violin and tambourine.
Full many a star in golden sheen
Shines on high, fair lady;
But all the stars will pale and flee
When they see you!

JEAN: (*listens fascinated and runs to Fanny*). It is the old country air!
It is you that I adore,
My Fanny, and would hear
For ever singing, as you do now,
That old love-song so dear!
When you I hear, I know myself no more!
I love you!
I love you!

FANNY: He love mes, but we two must say good-bye;
Best end this at once, and for ever—
If not, I could not leave you then, ah, never!

JEAN: Are you not free?

FANNY: I?
Free from all other love,
Since mine is yours alone.

JEAN: Then you belong to me!

FANNY: (*seriously*). I belong to no one.

JEAN: (*anxiously*). What, to no one?

FANNY: To you, then—that is, if you care!
Ah! keep me here with you, dear,
Oh, let me stay here, always here!

JEAN: I am poor—

FANNY: Qu'importe!

JEAN: Oh! non, c'est impossible!

FANNY: Pourquoi, dis, n'est-ce possible? . . .
Pendant que tu travaillerais,
Sans bruit, moi je m'occuperais
Du ménage,
Si bien que toi me regardant,
Fraîche et coquette en mon tablier blanc,
Tu m'en aimerais davantage.
Et le dimanche nous irions
Tous les deux, des chansons aux lèvres,
Près de l'étang de Villebon!
Nous perdre dans les bois de Meudon
Et de Sèvres,
Ah! comme nous ririons!
Puis, nous déjeûnerions
Sur l'herbe . . .
Et reprenant notre chemin . . .
Je te cueillerais une gerbe
De beaux lilas et de jasmin.

JEAN: Tu me cueillerais une gerbe
De beaux lilas et de pasmin.
Ah! laisse-moi t'aimer de toute ma tendresse,
Reste là dans mes bras, tes beaux yeux dans mes yeux.
Qui plus que nous peut être heureux!
Viens, ma Fanny, viens ma maîtresse!

FANNY: Ah! laisse-moi t'aimer de toute ma tendresse,
Je suis là, dans tes bras, tes chers yeux dans mes yeux.
Qui plus que nous peut être heureux!
De mes baisers, prends la caresse!

JEAN: Aimons-nous!

FANNY: Aimer est si doux.

ENSEMBLE: Voici la nuit, enfermons-nous!

*FIN DE L'ACTE DEUXIÈME.*

## ■ ACTE TROISIÈME

*Dans le Jardin d'un Restaurant a Ville D'Avray, un Dimanche.*

### SCÈNE PREMIÈRE

*Jean, Fanny (à la fenêtre d'un petit chalet du jardin.)*

FANNY: Le beau soleil pour les amours!
*(A Jean qui paraît à côté d'elle.)*
Sortons-nous?

JEAN: Sortons?
*(Il va pour l'embrasser.)*

FANNY: Prends bien garde, . . .
Un vieux ménage . . . on nous regarde.

---

FANNY: What matter!

JEAN: Oh no, that is impossible!

FANNY: But why? come, tell me why it should be?
Say why?
While you are hard at work, you see,
I quietly shall busy be
With housekeeping;
In fact, no doubt when I am seen
In my coquettish apron clean,
You will love me best when I'm sweeping!
Our Sunday holiday we'd take
At Villebon beside the lake;
Or we will both get lost in the woods
Of Meudon, or at Sèvres!
In joy the hours will pass:
We'll lunch upon the grass,
And gaily, as we return on our way
For you I'll gather a bouquet,
Of every flower that blows in May.

JEAN: For me you'll gather a bouquet,
Of every flower that blows in May.
Ah, let me, dear, love you with all my affection!
Ah, you must stay in my arms,
Let your eyes look in mine:
Who else could know such love divine?
Come, my sweet mistress, Fanny mine!

FANNY: Ah, let me, dear, love you with all my affection!
Ah, I am here in your arms,
Let your eyes look in mine:
Who else could know such love divine?
Ah, take my kisses, take my love!

JEAN: I love you!

FANNY: It is sweet to love!

BOTH: Forever more, as time shall prove!

*END OF SECOND ACT.*

## ■ ACT III

*In the garden of a restaurant at Ville d'Avray.*
*(On Sunday.)*

### SCENE I

*Jean, Fanny (by the window of a small chalet in the garden.)*

FANNY: *(to Jean who appears beside her).* Shall we go out?

JEAN: We will!
*(about to kiss her.)*

FANNY: Oh, take care!
So old a pair—
Some one might spy us!

---

JEAN: Un ménage d'un an!
Les jours
Ont passé vite!
Oh! Fanny, ma maîtresse!
Tu me prends tout entier.

FANNY: Non, pas encore assez!
Je te veux plus à moi, je veux que ma tendresse
N'ait plus le souci des instants passés.

JEAN: Voilà pourquoi cette campagne
Me plaît, car pendant la belle saison,
Dans notre petite maison,
Nous vivrons tous les deux bien seuls . . .

FANNY: Ta compagne
Chaque soir t'attendra . . .

TOUS DEUX: Lorsque son ami reviendra,
Dans les chemins où le soleil décline,
Nous irons en rêvant de baisers, de chansons,
Sous les bois dont la cime s'incline,
Au doux gazouillement des merles, des pinsons.

JEAN: *(lui prenant la main et voulant l'attirer à lui.)* Ah! Fanny!

FANNY: Voyons, soyons sages,
Donne-moi ton bras; te sentir ainsi,
Tout près de moi, comme ceci . . .
Je suis fière, m'ami.

TOUS DEUX: Viens, sur nos deux visages.
Plus radieux que ce beau jour.
Ceux qui passent liront notre fervent amour.
*(Tous deux s'éloignent.)*

### SCÈNE II

*(Au moment où Jean et Fanny disparaissent, entrent Caoudal, La Borderie, quelques Jeunes Gens et Jeunes Femmes.)*
*(Caoudal paraît au fond, il regarde l'enseigne du restaurant et fait signe, gaiement, aux amis que l'on ne voit pas encore. La Borderie le suit de près et agit de même.)*

CAOUDAL: Par ici! par ici!

LA BORDERIE: Nous serons à merveille.

CAOUDAL: *(montrant l'enseigne):* "A la friture sans pareille!"

---

JEAN: You've been mine for a year!
The days fly swiftly by us!
Oh my dear, my Fanny,
You hold me all in all!

FANNY: No, not enough as yet!
You must be still more mine;
My love will not brook
Any yearnings for the past,
Nor permit regret!

JEAN: And that is why I shall be glad to come here;
Here, my love, when summer has come,
We'll live in our own little home,
And can have it all to ourselves.

FANNY: Your companion every night will be here,
And then,

BOTH: When her love shall appear,
In a dream full of kisses and song we shall roam
Through the woods, we shall roam in a dream
Where tree-tops above us are swaying,
And hear the murmuring stream
Where the chaffinches come—we shall roam in a dream!

JEAN: *(taking her hand and trying to draw her to him).* Fanny dear!

FANNY: Come come!
Don't disgrace us!
Let me take your arm,
Let me feel you there quite close to me,
That is the way—so!
There, I feel proud today!

BOTH: Come!
Now upon our faces,
Brighter than those bright skies above,
Those who see us will read
Our ardent, fervent love!
*(They go off slowly.)*

### SCENE II

*(As Fanny and Jean disappear, enter Caoudal, La Borderie and some young people.)*
*(Caoudal has appeared at the back. He looks at the sign of the restaurant and beckons gaily to his friends, who are not yet in sight. La Borderie follows him closely, and does the same.)*

CAOUDAL: This way!
This way!

LA BORDERIE: This way!
This way!

CAOUDAL: *(pointing to the sign, and reading).* "The Sans Pareil Restaurant."—

LA BORDERIE: (*même jeu*). Ce restaurant
Est excellent.
(*Apparaît alors toute la petite troupe des amis et amies, tous très gais, très bruyants.*)

CAOUDAL, LA BORDERIE: Ohé! Patron.

TOUS: Ohé patron!

CAOUDAL: Qu'on se dépêche! Nous avons tous la gorge sèche . . .

TOUS: Non! non! pas le garçon! Le patron! le patron!

LE PATRON: Bonjour messieurs, bonjour mesdemoiselles. Ah! monsieur Caoudal! voulez-vous déjeuner Dans l'arbre ou bien sous les tonnelles?

CAOUDAL: Il s'agit de nous apporter . . . De ton vin fameux entre mille.

LES HOMMES: Nous nous y connaissons, Corbleu!

CAOUDAL: Donne du blanc.

LES HOMMES: Mais pas du bleu!

LE PATRON: Ah! monsieur, soyez tranquille, Vous serez bien servi!

CAOUDAL: Puis, ce soir pour dîner Nous reviendrons . . . Que vas-tu bien nous cuisiner?

LE PATRON: Mais, ce que vous voudrez . . .

CAOUDAL: Une énorme friture!

LE PATRON: Deux poulets marengo . . . Plus, un fort beau gigot.

CAOUDAL: Ce sera bon . . .

LE PATRON: Je vous le jure!

TOUS: (*en charge*). C'est entendu! C'est convenu!

CAOUDAL: Quant à toi, tavernier du diable! Si nous ne trouvons pas en nous mettant à table Des mets délicats, onctueux, Délicieux, Et copieux, C'est toi qu'avec furie Et frénésie, Nous embrochons, Découpons, Et mangeons A la sauce tartare. Donc, agis de ton mieux Si tu ne veux, Par nos estomacs creux, Être l'hôte du Styx ou de l'affreux Ténare!

LA BORDERIE: (*continuing to read the sign*). "This restaurant is quite the best."
(*Enter the entire little troop of friends of both sexes, all very jolly and noisy.*)

CAOUDAL and LA BORDERIE: What ho! The House!

THE FRIENDS: What ho! The House!

CAOUDAL: Come, get a gait on! You've got some thirsty throats to wait on!

ALL: No, no, no! No waiters, no! Send the Boss! Send the Boss!

KEEPER OF RESTAURANT: Good-morning, Sirs! Good-morning to you, ladies! Ah, Monsieur Caoudal! Which do you prefer—the tree-top, Or below, where it's shady?

CAOUDAL: First, there's this: Go bring us some wine, Your marvelous wine, in a hurry!

THE MEN: We are all connoisseurs! That's flat!

CAOUDAL: Let us have white—

THE MEN: Not if it's flat!

KEEPER OF RESTAURANT: Pray do not worry, I've the best wine there is!

CAOUDAL: And tonight we will all come back to dine. What have you in the way of fish?

KEEPER OF RESTAURANT: Ah—why, whatever you wish!

CAOUDAL: An enormous "friture!"

KEEPER OF RESTAURANT: Two nice chickens with ham. Then a fine leg of lamb.

CAOUDAL: That will be good.

KEEPER OF RESTAURANT: You may be sure!

ALL: It is agreed! and understood!

CAOUDAL: As for you, caterer to the devil, Unless we all shall find, When we sit down to table, Food that's to our mind, Positive, comparative, superlative, It is you whom we, With fierce and frantic fury, Tonight shall split And roast as meat On your own spit, And shall eat With a sauce tartare! So do your best, Unless you wish to fare Through stomachs void and bare, To play host on the Styx!— Now you know where you are, sir!

TOUS: C'est toi qu'avec furie Et frénésie, Nous embrochons, Découpons, Et mangeons!

LE PATRON: C'est promis!

LA BORDERIE: (*tragiquement*). Il y va de ta vie!

CAOUDAL: Ecoute encore: Il faut que notre table soit servie A sept heures . . . ou la mort!

TOUS: Ou la . . .

LE PATRON: (*pressé, il achève la phrase*). Mort! (*aux garçons.*) Qu'on apporte d'abord Des biscuits et du vin . . . qu'on se presse! Allez . . . courez! Dépêchez et servez! (*On apporte les verres et le vin.*)

CAOUDAL: Attention! croyez en ma vieillesse Qui regrette bien ses vingt ans, Amusez-vous quand il est temps: (*Levant son verre.*) A la santé de la jeunesse!

TOUS: A la santé de la jeunesse!!! (*Des musiciens ambulants traversent la route au fond du jardin, ce qui permet aux joyeux compagnons d'esquisser un pas de quadrille. Mais bientôt les musiciens sont chassés par les garçons du restaurant et s'éloignent.*)

## SCÈNE III

*Les Mêmes, Jean.*

CAOUDAL: (*apercevant Jean*). Tiens, vous voilà!

JEAN: (*saluant*). Messieurs!

CAOUDAL: La rencontre opportune! Ces cheveux, ce teint de soleil Si jeune et si vermeil, Pour eux je donnerais bien plus que ma fortune!

LA BORDERIE: Vous habitez par ici?

JEAN: Là, tout près! J'aime les bois et leurs ombrages frais, On vit mieux qu'à Paris, et tranquille on respire L'air embaumé dans un calme infini.

CAOUDAL: Toujours avec Sapho?

JEAN: (*très surpris, ne comprenant pas encore*). Sapho!

CAOUDAL: Mais oui, Fanny! Fanny Legrand, Sapho, le beau modèle.

LA BORDERIE and FRIENDS: It is you whom we, With fierce and frantic fury, Tonight shall split And roast as meat On your own spit, And shall eat, etc.

KEEPER OF RESTAURANT: No mistake!

LA BORDERIE: (*tragically*). Your life pays the forfeit!

CAOUDAL: Once more draw near: We wish to have our dinner Laid before us at seven—or you die!

ALL: Or you—

KEEPER OF RESTAURANT: (*hurriedly spoken*). Die! (*To the waiters.*) Go and fetch, first of all, Some biscuits and wine: Make haste! Don't crawl! (*They bring glasses and wine.*)

CAOUDAL: Give ear to me: I'm old, but I'm truthful, And wish I were twenty today; Have the time of your lives while you may: Let us drink, then, to all that's youthful! (*raising his glass.*)

LA BORDERIE and FRIENDS: Let us drink now to all that's youthful! Hurrah! Hurray! and away! (*Some strolling musicians pass the restaurant, and stop at the back of the garden.—They go off, playing.—Jean appears, and is seen by Caoudal.*)

## SCENE III

*The Same, Jean.*

CAOUDAL: (*to Jean*). Ah! is it you?

JEAN: (*greeting them*). Good-day!

CAOUDAL: What a fortunate meeting!— What a skin, what hair on his head! So young, so rosy-red! For those I would exchange All fame and fortune fleeting!

LA BORDERIE: And do you live out here?

JEAN: There, quite near. I love these woods, with shadows cool beneath; What is Paris to this, Where one breathes at one's leisure Pure, fragrant air in such infinite peace?

CAOUDAL: And you're with Sappho still?

JEAN: (*much surprised, failing to understand*). Sappho?

CAOUDAL: Fanny, of course— Fanny Legrand, The lovely model, Sappho!

JEAN: (à part). Quoi!
Sapho!
Ma Fanny!
La Sapho!
C'était elle!
(Après avoir hésité.)
Non, c'est fini!
Je ne la vois plus.

CAOUDAL: Elle est jolie . . . et pire!
On ne la quitte pas facilement . . .
Elle s'attache à vous . . . et l'on souffre pour elle.
L'amour de Sapho causa plus d'un tourment.

LA BORDERIE: La rupture toujours fut terrible et cruelle.

JEAN: (à part). Ah! mon Dieu!

UN GROUPE D'AMIS: C'est bien vrai.

CAOUDAL: Vraiment.
En ménage, elle a peu de chance!
Et tenez, ce graveur . . .

LA BORDERIE: Froment!

CAOUDAL: N'eut-il pas la démence
De faire un faux billet, et ce fut la prison . . .
Ah! je la vois encore
Envoyant un baiser à ce pauvre garçon,
Criant: je t'aime, je t'adore!
Courage! nous nous reverrons!
M'ami, m'ami je suis ta femme,
Et de toute mon âme!
Oui, nous nous aimerons!

JEAN: (à lui-même, brisé). M'ami!

CAOUDAL: Fini, maintenant!

LA BORDERIE: Je l'espère!

CAOUDAL: Elle doit être chez son père . . .
A la campagne, avec son enfant.

LA BORDERIE: Oui, le fils de ce pauvre Froment.

JEAN: Son enfant!

CAOUDAL: Qu'avez-vous?

JEAN: Je mentais!
Auprès de cette femme,
Depuis un an, j'avilissais mon âme,
Grisé par le mensonge et lui donnant mon coeur,
Croyez-moi, je vous en conjure,
J'ignorais tout, ma parole d'honneur!
Je vous avais menti, mais, vrai Dieu!
Je vous jure
Que tout est fini désormais;
Je la méprise autant qu'autrefois je l'aimais.
(Fanny à ce moment apparaît radieuse.)

---

JEAN: (aside). What!
Sappho!
Fanny, she?
She, Sappho?
Can it be so?
(after some hesitation.)
No, that is past—
She's not with me now.

CAOUDAL: Pretty, at least—good measure!
It's sometimes rather hard to get away!
When she becomes attached, one's case is distressing.
Ah, Sappho! your love caused much pain in its day!

LA BORDERIE: And the breach, when it came, always painful, depressing!

JEAN: (aside). Oh my God!

THE FRIENDS: Eh, Sappho!

CAOUDAL: In all her affairs unlucky, chaotic!—
Then there was—that engraver—

LA BORDERIE: De Kay!

CAOUDAL: Who was so idiotic,
He counterfeited notes—that was jail, fast enough;
Oh, I can see her now,
Standing kissing her hand to the poor, silly muff,
And she: "I love you, I adore you!
Have courage! we must bear the pain!
My love! my love!
I am your wife,
Your wife—you're my soul and my life!
My love! yes! we shall meet again!"

JEAN: (to himself; overcome). My love!

CAOUDAL: But now, it is done!

LA BORDERIE: (laughing). Well, rather!

CAOUDAL: I fancy she is with her father;
She goes to see her child, I dare say.

LA BORDERIE: Yes, the son of that poor De Kay.

JEAN: Her child!

CAOUDAL: What's the matter?

JEAN: (breathlessly). It was a lie—yes!
For a year,
By living with this creature,
I have defiled my soul,
And have been drunk with lies,
While giving her control
Of my heart:
—I did not know—
Yes, I swear that is so!
I lied at first, I own,
But before God now I swear,
All's over and done—evermore,
I shall despise her
As much as I loved her before!
(At this instant Fanny appears, radiant.)

---

## SCÈNE IV

Les Mêmes, Fanny.

CAOUDAL: (l'apercevant).
Grands dieux! Sapho!

JEAN: (se jetant sur elle). Sapho! quelle infamie!
Je t'ai tenue entre mes bras,
Et je t'appelais mon amie!
Non . . . non . . . je ne me doutais pas
Qu'une femme pouvait ainsi briser une âme!
Ah! j'ai honte! je souffre et je voudrais partir,
Rachetant mon erreur par un cruel martyr,
Et maudire à jamais le nom de cette femme.
Fanny, moi qui t'aimais, maintenant je sais tout,
Je connais d'aujourd'hui ton passé misérable
Que tu m'avais caché . . . tu te riais de moi;
En captivant mon coeur, tu surprenais ma foi;
Ma tendresse
Est changée en dégoût;
Redeviens la Sapho, redeviens leur maîtresse,
Tu m'entends, je sais tout!

FANNY: (à part). Ils ont parlé, les lâches!
(A Jean).
C'est fini, n'est-ce pas? . . . Tu te fâches,
C'est bon! retourne chez les tiens . . .
Il fallait que ça se termine,
C'est fait!
Va donc retrouver ta cousine . . .
Tu seras bien heureux là-bas,
A moi, tu ne penseras pas . . .
Tu vivras tranquille,
Entre ton papa, ta maman . . .
Allons . . . décampe,
file . . .
Je te donne congé . . . va-t'en!

JEAN: Eh bien! . . . je pars . . . brisé par la souffrance,
Je pars . . . pour ne plus te revoir,
Le coeur meurtri de honte et d'affreux désespoir!
Adieu bonheur, douce espérance! Adieu!
(Jean s'éloigne précipitamment.)

FANNY: (terrifiée, courant après lui). M'ami! m'ami! Ils t'ont menti!
(Revenant sur le groupe formé par Caoudal, La Borderie et leurs amis.)
Mais, maintenant qu'il est parti,
Messieurs les beaux parleurs, les malins, les bravaches . . .
Non, je ne vous crains pas, vous êtes tous des lâches!

---

## SCENE IV

The Same, Fanny.

CAOUDAL: (seeing her). Ye gods! Sappho!

JEAN: (starts to rush at her). Sappho!
(to Fanny, very violently). Oh shame on you!
To me, to me who loved you so,
And poured my affection on you,
Yet I did not, could not know,
Alas! that a woman
Could be so cruel, so inhuman!
Ah! the shame!—
I suffer,
And I must leave this place,
Till my fault I redeem
In pain and in disgrace,
While for ever I curse
The name of such a woman!
Ah, Fanny, I loved you well!
Oh, Fanny! and today I know all:
For today I have heard
Of your hideous past
That you concealed from me;
You held my heart so fast,
You stole my faith most dear.—
Fanny! go laugh and jeer
At me!
All my love
Has been changed to gall!
Go, be Sappho once more,
Go and be as before!
Understand, I know all!

FANNY: (aside). Ah, they've told him, the cowards.
(To Jean:)
Here it ends, does it not?
You are angry—all right!
Go back where you belong,
It was time there should be an end:
It's done! go back to your dear little friend:
For me you need not have a thought.
You'll be happy in that sweet spot,
(ironically and vulgarly.)
Where you will not worry
Papa and Mamma, no doubt.
Go on! be off there! hurry!
You have got your discharge—get out!

JEAN: All right!
I'll go!
I'll go!
And I shall not return!
Good-bye!
(He goes quickly away.)

FANNY: (terrified, calls despairingly). My love! my love! it is a lie!
And now he's gone—but here I am.
(Advancing, and growing more excited.)
And so you had to tell,
Oh you beasts and blowhards!
No, I am not afraid,
You are a pack of cowards!

**LA BORDERIE ET TOUS LES AMIS:** Tu nous insultes, toi?
(*Rires moqueurs.*)

**FANNY:** Et vous savez pourquoi.
Mon bonheur vous a fait envie;
Cet enfant dont l'amour avait
changé ma vie,
Par votre faute m'a quittée!
(*A tous.*)
Ici, l'on s'est vanté
Racontant tout, ma honte, ma
misère,
Étalant au grand jour autant de
lâcheté!
(*A La Borderie.*)
Et toi, vipère,
Toi qui m'a fais tant pleurer, tant
souffrir,
Ta haine est donc inassouvie,
Puisqu'en brisant mon coeur qui se
régénérait,
Tu me prends plus que cache la vie!
Je cachais mon amour, comme on
un trésor,
Vous me l'avez volé . . . mais je
veux vivre encore,
Pour vous maudire tous, pour me
venger, peut-être . . .
Et vous faire souffrir ce que souffre
mon être.

**TOUS:** (*avec un geste de révolte contre Fanny*). Sapho!

**FANNY:** (*les bravant*). Laissez-moi!
Désormais,
Mon âme est morte pour aim-
er . . .
Mais, je vous hais!
(*S'élançant sur La Borderie qui souriait méchamment.*)
Canaille!

*FIN DE L'ACTE TROISIÈME.*

■ **ACTE QUATRIÈME**

*En Avignon.*
(*Le domaine des Gaussin. — A droite, la maison. — Devant, un jardin de ferme, avec un puits à gauche. — Au fond, le Rhône et le panorama de Villeneuve.*)

*SCÈNE PREMIÈRE*

*Jean, Irène, Césaire, Divonne sont à table, silencieux et inquiets de la tristesse de Jean. Bientôt, sur un signe de Divonne, Césaire et Irène se lèvent et s'éloignent.*

**DIVONNE:** (*s'approchant alors de Jean*). Eh bien?

**JEAN:** Mère!

**DIVONNE:** Pitchoun! tu de
tournes, la tête!
Ecoute-moi, voyons, qui t' arrête?

**JEAN:** Je ne sais . . .

**ALL THE OTHERS:** So, you insult us, you!
(*They laugh sneeringly.*)

**FANNY:** And you—know why—
you do:—
You hated—to see me—so hap-
py.—
And this boy, whose pure love
Had changed my very nature,
Through what you've done, has
gone away—
And here you've all made gay
In telling him my story, my afflic-
tion,
Laying bare your vile souls
Here in the light of day!
And you, vile creature!
(*To La Borderie.*)
You who caused me so much pain,
so much grief,
Is not your hatred sated yet,
But you must break a heart
Beginning to forget,
And destroy more than my life, alas?
For my love I concealed
As a miser his gold,
And this you stole from me:
But I shall live, you'll see,
And I shall curse you all,
And make you suffer, too,
As I myself have suffered!

**ALL:** (*roused against Fanny*). Sap-pho!

**FANNY:** (*defying them*). Let me go!
From now on
My heart is dead to love!
But I can hate!—
You blackguards!

*END OF THIRD ACT.*

■ **ACT IV**

*AT AVIGNON.*
(*The homestead of the Gaus-sins. — To the right, the house. — In front a garden with a well on the left. — At the back the Rhone, and the country Villeneuve.*)

*SCENE I*

*Jean, Irene, Césaire, Divonne, are at table, silent and distressed at Jean's sadness. Presently at a sign from Divonne, Césaire and Irene get up and go off.*

**DIVONNE:** (*going to Jean*). And now?

**JEAN:** Mother!

**DIVONNE:** My dear!
You won't look at your mother!
Answer me, come now! what's the bother?

**JEAN:** I don't know.

**DIVONNE:** Vé, ne mens pas!
Raconte un peu . . . là-bas
Quelque chose, j'en suis bien
sûre . . .

**JEAN:** Rien, rien, je vous as-sure . . .

**DIVONNE:** Té, ce brusque
retour!
Tu te sauvais . . .

**JEAN:** Non, non!

**DIVONNE:** Quelque mauvaise
femme
Qui me prenait ton âme,
Quelque méchant amour!
Ne cache rien à ta maman Di-vonne . . .
Tu sais comme elle t'aime, et qu'au
fond elle est bonne.

**JEAN:** Eh bien, vous m'avez de-viné . . .
Mais c'est fini.

**DIVONNE:** Tu crois?

**JEAN:** C'était une folie
Qu'aujourd'hui je regrette et que
j'oublie.
Dites, Maman, m'avez-vous par-donné?

**DIVONNE:** Te pardonner, petit!
C'est déjà fait, je t'aime . . .
Et mon coeur, pour le tien, donner-ait tout son sang.

**JEAN:** Si vous lisiez au profond de
moi-même
Ah! vous verriez ce que le mien res-sent.

**DIVONNE:** Une maman
Devine tout, les chagrins, les
alarmes.

**JEAN:** Pour les partager.

**DIVONNE:** Oui, pour les chasser,
Et d'un fils, effacer les larmes
Par un baiser!
Allons . . . pas de faiblesse,
Et si par instants la tristesse
Te prend encore, dis-moi tout,
n'est-ce pas?

**JEAN:** Ouvrez-moi donc bien
grands vos bras . . .

**DIVONNE:** Viens, mon petit, que je
te presse
Comme autrefois,
Lorsque à ma voix
Tu t'endormais chaque soir dans ta
berce.

**JEAN:** Comme autrefois,
A votre voix,
Je ne sens plus le chagrin qui
m'oppresse.

**DIVONNE:** Pooh!
Do not lie!
Come, tell me now; up there,
I am sure, something strange befell
you!

**JEAN:** No, no! or I should tell you!

**DIVONNE:** Eh, then why not stay
there?
You ran away—

**JEAN:** No, no!

**DIVONNE:** Some wicked girl, I
know, dear,
Who would not let you go, dear;
Some wretched love-affair!
So tell me all, for I shall not reprove
you;
You know that I am just, and you
know that I love you!

**JEAN:** Well then, what you say is
the truth.
But, it is past.

**DIVONNE:** You think?

**JEAN:** I very much regret it,
For I see it was folly, and shall for-get it.
Can you forgive such a madness of
youth?

**DIVONNE:** Can I forgive, my dear!
Why, it is done: I love you,
And my heart would pour out all its
lifeblood for thine.

**JEAN:** Could you but read all my
thoughts, it would prove you
How very grateful is this heart of
mine.

**DIVONNE:** A mother quickly
guesses
A son's distress
And his fears.

**JEAN:** Suffers in his place!

**DIVONNE:** Yes, or would efface
And wipe away her loved one's
tears
In her embrace!
But come! we must be brave,
And if for a while you should have
Times of sadness still,
Tell me all, do you see?

**JEAN:** Then open wide your arms
to me!

**DIVONNE:** Come, little one, and
let me hold you,
As long ago I'd hold you so,
And sing to sleep, and in my arms
enfold you.
Be at rest, my darling child,
No more regrets, nor any anger,
And always now we'll stay together,
Always keep each other's love!
We shall, for ever, for ever!

**JEAN:** As long ago, as long ago,
Your voice has ended all my trou-ble!
It is done!
It is done!
No more regrets, nor any anger.
Together! together! keep each oth-er's love!
We shall, for ever, for ever!

DIVONNE: Ah! calme-toi, mon pauvre enfant!

JEAN: Maman!
C'est fini, je n'ai plus ni regrets, ni colère . . .
Ensemble, nous resterons!

DIVONNE: Oh! comme nous nous aimerons!

TOUS DEUX: Oui, comme nous nous aimerons!

DIVONNE: Courons prévenir ton père;
Ah! qu'il sera joyeux
De voir enfin renaître dans tes yeux
L'espoir des jours meilleurs et des moments heureux!
Mon chéri . . .

JEAN: Ma bonne mère!
(*Divonne sort.*)

## SCÈNE II

*Jean, Irène.*

IRÈNE: (*qui est rentrée, à Jean*).
Vous souffrez donc?
Pourquoi songer ainsi?
Dites-moi . . .

JEAN: Pas à vous!

IRÈNE: Mais je suis votre amie . . .
Souvenez-vous, saint Joseph et Marie . . .
Quel est votre souci?
Si j'avais un jour quelque peine,
Pour la conter, ja m'en irais
Vers mon ami; je lui dirais
Le chagrin dont mon âme est pleine.
Sans doute, il me prendrait la main,
Il me dirait une parole
Qui fait sourire, vous console,
Et rend plus doux le lendemain.
Ce serait un rayon d'aurore
Qui dissiperait mes tourments.
Mon coeur refleurirait encore
Sous le clair baiser du printemps.

## SCÈNE III

*Les Mêmes, Césaire.*

CÉSAIRE: (*accourant*). Jean!

JEAN: Mon père!

CÉSAIRE: (*à Irène*). Va-t'en vite
Retrouver Divonne!

IRÈNE: Mais qu'avez-vous?

CÉSAIRE: Rien! rien, obéis, ma petite!

DIVONNE: But come, let us tell your father;
Ah! with what glad surprise
Will he perceive returning to your eyes
The hope of better days, and happy times to come!
Dearest son!

JEAN: My darling mother!
(*Divonne goes off.*)

## SCENE II

*Jean, Irene.*

IRENE: (*who has entered, to Jean*). Are you not well?
Why so sadly inclined?
Tell me all!

JEAN: Not to you!

IRENE: Am I not still your friend?
Please recollect, we were "Joseph and Mary!"
Now what is on your mind?
If some day my heart should be aching,
I'm very sure
That I should go and seek my friend,
And tell him all
The distress that my heart was breaking,
And he no doubt my hand would hold,
He'd bid me speak, and he would hear me,
And give some counsel that would cheer me,
And day would seem less dark and cold.
On my path would he sunshine pour,
Far away the clouds would he fling;
Ah, until my heart should bloom once more
Beneath the glowing kiss of the spring!

## SCENE III

*The Same, Césaire.*
(*Césaire hurries in, in consternation.*)

CÉSAIRE: (*entering hastily*). Jean!

JEAN: Why, Father!

CÉSAIRE: (*to Irene*). Run away, Irene, and find Divonne!

IRENE: (*anxiously*). But—what is this?

CÉSAIRE: Go, go! run away, as I tell you!

IRÈNE: Vous semblez en courroux
Et . . .

CÉSAIRE: Va donc, et laisse-nous!
(*Irène sort.*)

## SCÈNE IV

*Césaire, Jean.*

CÉSAIRE: (*à Jean*). Mon pauvre enfant là! . . . chez nous, elle arrive!

JEAN: (*comprenant*). Elle est là?

CÉSAIRE: Te demandant.

JEAN: Sapho!

CÉSAIRE: Pour ignorer ton amour imprudent,
Je n'ai pas l'âme assez naïve.
Du courage, surtout!

JEAN: Oh! désormais,
Je serai courageux . . .
Je tremblais tout à l'heure . . .
Mais maintenant, qu'elle menace ou pleure,
Je ne faiblirai pas . . .
Père . . . je le promets!
(*Césaire s'éloigne.*)

## SCÈNE V

*Fanny, Jean.*
(*Fanny, qui s'avance lentement, regarde autour d'elle. Elle aperçoit Jean, va vers lui très vite, puis tout à coup s'arrête. Un silence.*)

FANNY: (*très douce*). Ne m'en veux pas d'être venue . . .
L'on ne se quitte pas sans les derniers adieux.
Loin de toi je souffrais d'une peine inconnue,
Maintenant, je te vois, je vais mieux.

JEAN: Je ne vous en veux pas.

FANNY: (*avec douleur*). Tu dis: vous!
Je suis lasse . . .
J'ai tant pleuré . . . je ne sais pas comment
Je suis vivante et parle encore en ce moment.
Toute autre en fut morte à ma place.
(*Anxieusement.*)
Je suis changée?
Oui, n'est-ce pas?

JEAN: Toujours vous habitez là-bas?

FANNY: Mais où veux-tu que j'aille?
J'ai là des souvenirs qui me font espérer . . .
Et parfois, cessant de pleurer
Ne pensant à rien, je travaille . . .
Quelquefois, le matin, je m'éveille en riant;

IRENE: Why, you seem to be cross!—And—

CÉSAIRE: Go, please go, and leave us here!
(*Irene goes away.*)

## SCENE IV

*Césaire, Jean.*

CÉSAIRE: (*to Jean*). Ah, my poor boy!
She has come, she is here!

JEAN: (*with comprehension*). She is here!

CÉSAIRE: And asks for you!

JEAN: Sappho!

CÉSAIRE: Ah, I am not such a simple old soul
As not to know your foolish passion.
Above all things, be brave!

JEAN: Oh! after this I shall be strong enough.
I've behaved like a coward,
But after this, though she should weep and threaten,
I never shall give way:
Father, I promise you!
(*Césaire goes out.*)

## SCENE V

*Fanny, Jean.*
(*Fanny comes in slowly and looks about her.—She sees Jean and runs towards him, as if to throw her arms about his neck.—She stops.—A pause.*)

FANNY: (*very sweetly*). Oh, blame me not that I have sought you!
You left without a word to me, never a one;
I have known unendurable sorrow without you:
Now I see you again, it is gone!

JEAN: I am not blaming you.

FANNY: You are cold!
So much grieving
Has worn me out, and I do not know how
I still should be alive, and speak as I do now.
No one in my place would be living—
(*Anxiously.*)
And I have changed?
Yes! have I not?

JEAN: You still are living where you were?

FANNY: Why, where should I be going?
For there are all the hopes, that as memories I keep,
And sometimes, when I cease to weep,
With nothing, mornings, on my mind,
I do sewing;

C'est quand le ciel est pur et le soleil brillant.
Alors, je prends ma robe blanche,
J'arrange mes cheveux comme tu les aimais,
A la fenêtre je me mets
Et jusqu'au soir je me penche,
Pour guetter ton retour, pour entendre tes pas . . .
C'est en vain que j'espère, et m'ami ne vient pas!

JEAN: L'hiver est toujours triste . . . il serait préférable
De rentrer à Paris.

FANNY: Qu'y ferai-je, sans toi?
Ces gens que je connais, ce monde misérable
Où j'ai vécu, tout est pour moi
Un sujet de douleur et de cruel émoi.
Pendant un an je fus ta femme
Et j'entends rester à toi pour toujours;
Tu vas revenir, les beaux jours
Viendront à nouveau parfumer mon âme.
Viens, m'ami, je serai si douce
Et si bonne pour toi que ton coeur s'ouvrira,
Et que la main qui me repousse
Tendrement me caressera.
Ah! viens, car tu m'aimes encore . . .
Vois ma douleur . . . seul, tu peux l'apaiser . . .
Cède à mon amour qui t'implore,
Ta bouche ne saurait oublier mon baiser.

JEAN: Non, je ne puis!

FANNY: Pourquoi?

JEAN: Si grande est ma faiblesse
Que si je te suivais, je ne m'en irais plus.

FANNY: Vois mon chagrin, vois ma tendresse
Mon attachement!

JEAN: Espoirs superflus!
Et ton passé?

FANNY: (avec désespoir). Mais ce n'est pas ma faute . . .
Et je l'ai tant maudit qu'il devrait être mort!

JEAN: Il existe toujours et nous ôte,
A moi, le droit de vivre avec toi sans remord,
A toi, celui d'aimer sans scrupule et sans honte . . .
D'ailleurs, je dois partir.

And at times I awake with delight:—
That's when the sky is clear, and when the sun is bright;
I put on something fresh and white,
And I put up my hair in your favorite way,
And at the window I stay,
Waiting till it shall be night,
When I shall hear your step and see you coming home.
But in vain have I waited, my lover does not come.

JEAN: The winter is always dreary;
It would surely be better to back into town.

FANNY: Ah, how could I, without you!
The people that I knew, the miserable gutter
In which I lived, all, all for me
Is a story of pain and cruel misery!
For one sweet year I was your wife,
And yours I mean to remain forever;
And you will come back,
The happy days will come again
To renew my life!
Come, my love!
I shall love so well,
And so sweet will I be, that your heart will expand:
The hand with which you now repel me
Will tenderly caress my hand.
Come! for I know that you love me;
See how I grieve—you could console me yet.
Yield then to my love, I implore you,
These lips of yours can never forget
All my kisses!
Come, my love! come!

JEAN: No, I can not!

FANNY: But why?

JEAN: I can not!
If today I should heed you,
My weakness is so great, I'd never leave again!

FANNY: See my distress—

JEAN: No!

FANNY: See how I need you,
See how I cling to you!

JEAN: No!
Such hopes are in vain!
What of your past?

FANNY: (in despair). But—it was not my doing!
And I so hate it now, you know it's dead, of course:
Be kind!

JEAN: But your past does exist,
even now, and destroys
My power to live with you and yet be free from remorse—
In you, the right to love free from shame and dishonor!
And now I ought to go—

FANNY: Je sais la vérité . . .
Ici, contre moi l'on te monte . . .
L'on veut te marier . . . et toi, sans volonté,
Faisant fi de mes pleurs, riant de ma détresse,
Tu brises froidement le coeur de ta maîtresse . . .
C'est mal!

JEAN: (violent). Tu dis . . .

FANNY: (humble). J'ai tort! . . . pardonne-moi . . .
Je crois, j'espère et je ne veux que toi . . .
Viens, m'ami, je serai si douce
Et si bonne pour toi que ton coeur s'ouvrira,
Et que la main qui me repousse
Tendrement me caressera.

JEAN: Tu sais bien que c'est impossible . . .
Que tout est fini désormais . . .

FANNY: Je t'aime!
Je t'aime! et jamais
Tu ne me fus plus cher; vois ma peine indicible,
Pitié! pitié!
Je tombe à tes genoux!

JEAN: (éperdument). Fanny!

## SCÈNE VI

Les Mêmes, Césaire, Divonne. (Césaire entre avec Divonne.)

CÉSAIRE: Mon fils, rentre chez nous!

JEAN: Ah! mon père!

FANNY: Je ne le quitte pas!
(Elle veut s'élancer sur Jean. Elle trouve Divonne en face d'elle.)

DIVONNE: Partez!

FANNY: Mais qui donc êtes-vous?

DIVONNE: Sa mère!

FANNY: (balbutiant). Ah! madame . . .
Pardonnez-moi . . . je ne savais . . .
(Fanny tend les bras à Jean que Césaire emmène. Fanny la voix coupée par les sanglots.)
Jean . . . là . . . je m'en vais . . .
(Elle s'éloigne en chancelant.)

DIVONNE: (détourne la tête, puis, très pâle, les yeux au ciel.)
La pauvre femme!

FIN DE L'ACTE QUATRIÈME.

FANNY: Oh, I can see it all!
These people have set you against me,
They've chosen you a wife, and you've no will at all;
You make light of my tears, you laugh at my distress,
And you can coolly break the heart of your mistress!
It's wrong!

JEAN: (angrily). What's that?

FANNY: (humbly). No, no!
Forgive me!
I hope—I trust you—and all I want is you!
Come, my love!
I shall love so well,
And so sweet will I be, that your heart will expand—
The hand with which you now repel me
Will tenderly caress my hand.

JEAN: No!
You know well—
It cannot be!
All's at an end, after this!

FANNY: I love you!
I love you!
And to me you never were more dear!
Mercy! ah, see how I suffer!
Forgive! forgive!
I beg upon my knees!

JEAN: (recklessly). Fanny!

## SCENE VI

The Same, Césaire, Divonne. (Césaire enters with Divonne.)

CÉSAIRE: My son!
Go into the house!

JEAN: Ah!
My father!

FANNY: (wishing to go to Jean, finds herself face to face with Divonne). I will not go away!

DIVONNE: You will!

FANNY: Who are you, if you please?

DIVONNE: His mother!

FANNY: (stammering). Ah! Madame, I beg your pardon—
I did not know—
(Stretching her arms to Jean; going off, her voice broken by sobs.)
Jean—there—I will go!

DIVONNE: (turning away her face and then raising her eyes to heaven).
Oh, poor woman!

END OF FOURTH ACT.

## ■ ACTE CINQUIÈME

*C'est l'hiver. Dans la chambre déserte de la petite maison à Ville-d'Avray.*
*(Au fond porte vitrée donnant sur la campagne couverte de neige.)*

### SCÈNE PREMIÈRE

**FANNY:** (*seule, pensive, triste, résignée*). Demain, je partirai puisqu'il le faut . . .
Allons, mon coeur, ne meurs pas à la tâche . . .
Je pleure . . .
Vraiment! comme je suis lâche!
Pauvre Sapho!
A jamais j'ai perdu ma vie,
Toute espérance m'est ravie,
Tout bonheur a fui désormais.
Je disparais,
Du monde je m'exile,
Je ne dois rien espérer maintenant.
Oublier sera difficile,
Je l'aimais tant!
(*Ouvrant le tiroir d'une commode.*)
Ses lettres:
"Ma Fanny, ma femme bien aimée,
"Le temps est pur et clair . . . la campagne embaumée
"Nous appelle . . . demain . . .
(*Les embrassant.*)
Je vais encore pleurer . . .
Ne les relisons pas, mieux vaut les déchirer . . .
Un tas d'objets à lui . . . Ces pauvres fleurs fanées,
C'est lui jadis qui me les a données.
Faut-il avoir aimé pour un jour tant souffrir!
Faut-il avoir vécu de si douces journées,
Pour renoncer à tout, s'en aller . . . et mourir,
Sans l'espoir consolant des fautes pardonnées!
Je comprends aujourd'hui, j'aurais perdu son âme . . .
C'était le condamner à l'amère douleur,
J'aurais fait son malheur:
Hélas! je blasphémais en me disant sa femme!
Là-bas, un tout petit être, frêle, innocent,
M'appelle d'une voix qui m'attire et me touche.
Ce petit, c'est mon fils . . . cet être, c'est mon sang.
Je veux le retrouver, entendre de sa bouche
Ce doux nom de maman! Tout mon bonheur futur
Est là, je le sens bien, et dans l'espoir suprême
De faire de mon fils le coeur honnête et pur
Que je n'ai pas été moi-même.

## ■ ACT V

*(Winter.—The dismantled room of the little house at Ville d'Avray.—At the back a glass door, showing the country covered with snow.)*

### SCENE I

**FANNY:** (*Alone: pensive, sad, resigned*). And now, seeing I must, at last I go.—
Break not, my heart, by your task overpowered.
I'm weeping—in truth, am I not a coward!
Ah, poor Sappho!
Now my life once for all is over,
My hopes can not again recover.
All my joy is gone: From now on
From all the world I'll hide me; I shall vanish,
For it is useless to hope—that I know.
Thoughts of him will be hard to banish,
I loved him so!
I loved him so!
(*Opening the drawer of a bureau.*)
His letters:—"My Fanny, my wife whom I adore,
The skies are bright and blue, and the country once more
Is calling! Tomorrow—" I'm going to cry again—
I'd better read no more, to keep them would be vain!
(*Tears up the letters.*)
And all these things of his, these sad and faded flowers,
He gave to me in those lost, happy hours!
Can one then only love but to mourn and to sigh?
Can one then only live a few moments in heaven,
But one must lose it all, go away, and die?
And without even the hope, one's sins have been forgiven!
Yet today I can see, I should have wrecked his life,
He would have been condemned to despair, or to worse,
For my love is a curse:
It was wicked of me, to call me his wife!
Yet there—is a helpless little one—and so good!
That wakens in my heart thoughts that draw me, yet grieve me:
For the child is my son, that being is my blood,
And I must go to him and teach him, ah! to give me
The sweet name of mamma! All happiness for me lies there,
It is my one hope—for me there is no other,
Except to give my son a heart sincere and pure,
Such as she never had—his mother!

### SCÈNE II

*Fanny, Jean.*

**JEAN:** (*entrant tout à coup*). Fanny!

**FANNY:** (*interdite*). C'est vous?

**JEAN:** C'est moi!
Je ne pouvais rester plus longtemps loin de toi!

**FANNY:** Vous êtes revenu, pourquoi?

**JEAN:** Ma maîtresse chérie,
C'est toi qui me dis: vous, maintenant . . .

**FANNY:** Je t'en prie,
Laisse-moi . . .
Je m'en vais, Jean, tu dois m'oublier.

**JEAN:** (*exaspéré*). Si tu pars, c'est pour te lier
Avec un autre amant.

**FANNY:** Non! non! je te le jure.

**JEAN:** Ainsi, pour toi je fus parjure,
J'ai tout brisé, là-bas, pour revenir,
Le coeur des miens, mon avenir,
J'ai quitté notre vigne et nos beaux lauriers roses,
Oui, j'ai quitté de douces choses . . .
J'ai vu pleurer ma mère, et j'ai senti sa main
Me retenir encore au détour du chemin.
Tout s'écroule pour moi, rêve, amour, espérance!
Ah! tu veux m'oublier, partir . . . en ce moment!
Va, ne prolonge pas plus longtemps ma souffrance,
Et cours rejoindre ton amant.

**FANNY:** (*avec élan*). Ah! tu m'aimes encore!
Non, ne t'en défends pas, car je lis dans tes yeux
L'amour des jours passés, des jours délicieux.
Je reste, je t'adore!
(*Ils restent un instant enlacés.*)

**FANNY:** Mais tu pâlis, m'ami . . .

**JEAN:** Qu'as-tu dit?
M'ami! . . . rien que se mot rappelle
Un souvenir affreux!

**FANNY:** (*éplorée*). Vas-tu recommencer
A me tenailler l'âme en parlant du passé?
Est-ce donc pour cela que tu venais vers celle
Qui croyait au pardon, en sentant ton baiser.

### SCENE II

*Fanny, Jean.*

**JEAN:** (*entering suddenly*). Fanny!

**FANNY:** (*surprised*). Not you!

**JEAN:** Yes, I!
I could not stay at home any longer without you!

**FANNY:** You mean you have come back; but why?

**JEAN:** Ah, my dearest, my dearest,
It is you who now are cold—cold to me.

**FANNY:** I must ask you, Jean, to leave me;
I must go, and you must forget.

**JEAN:** (*forcibly*). If you go, it must mean you've met
Of course, some other lover!

**FANNY:** No! no!
You must believe me!

**JEAN:** It is true!—and you could so deceive me?
I have destroyed my home, to come to you,
Their love for me, my future, too!
I've left our pleasant vines, with rosy laurels girted,
Yes, sweeter things have I deserted:
I've seen my mother weeping, her hand put out to stay;
I've felt upon my shoulder at the turn of the way;
All is crumbling away, the past and the future!
It is you that would forget, it is you that make the move.
Go!
Do not wait, I say, to prolong me my torture;
But go to meet your new love!

**FANNY:** (*with spirit*). Ah! you love me, still love me!
No, that you can't deny!
I read in your eyes
The light of love that in them lies!
I'll stay, then—I adore you, I adore you!
(*They remain in each other's arms.*)

**FANNY:** But you are pale, my love!

**JEAN:** What was that?
"My love!"
The words alone awaken
Those accurst memories!

**FANNY:** (*tearfully*). Oh, must you speak like this,
And crush my very soul by recalling the past?
And was it then for this
This course with one you've taken
Who believes you forgave,
When you gave her your kiss!

JEAN: Ah! . . . c'est vrai . . . je suis fou . . .
(*Il s'est dirigé vers le fauteuil sur lequel il s'est laissé tomber épuisé.*)

FANNY: Tu me fais peur, ta lèvre Tremble et tes yeux sont tout rouges de fièvre . . .

JEAN: Je suis brisé . . .

FANNY: Calme-toi maintenant.

JEAN: Je n'avais plus dormi . . .

FANNY: Repose doucement.

JEAN: Reste là . . .

FANNY: Si tu veux.

JEAN: O ma Fanny! je t'aime!

FANNY: Oublie et sois heureux.

JEAN: Oui . . . c'est l'oubli . . . suprême!


FANNY: Comme il dort!
(*Après s'être dégagée et un peu éloignée de lui doucement.*)
Vais-je rester ici?
Mais non, mieux vaut partir ainsi . . .
Gardant étroitement dans mon âme blessée
Son cher baiser d'amour, sa dernière pensée!

JEAN: Ah, it is true—I am mad—
(*He sinks wearily into a chair.*)


FANNY: You frighten me!
Your lips are trembling, and your eyes
Are red with fever.

JEAN: I am worn out—

FANNY: You must rest.
There, be still.

JEAN: I could not go to sleep—

FANNY: I know—but now you will.

JEAN: Do not go—

FANNY: I will not.

JEAN: O Fanny mine, I love you!

FANNY: Be happy, for all's forgot!

JEAN: Yes!
It is gone—for ever!
(*Fanny releases herself and goes to a little distance.*)

FANNY: How he sleeps!—
Shall I stay here, or no?
No, no!
Far better I should go.
While I can take away in my heart torn and riven
His last dear kiss of love—when he thought he'd forgiven!
But he would not forget, that I know well today;

Jamais il n'oubliera, je le sens maintenant,
Chaque baiser sera suivi d'un mot méchant.
C'est l'heure!
(*Elle se dirige vers la table.*)
Allons!
(*Elle écrit.*)
Adieu m'ami, je par à tout jamais . . .
Ne m'en veux pas, car je t'aimais . . .
Je t'aime toujours et je pleure.
J'accomplis mon devoir, et j'en suis toute fière.
S'il est vrai que là-haut il existe un bon Dieu,
Je pourrai maintenant lui faire une prière
Et lui parler de toi . . .
C'est tout! Adieu!
(*S'approchant de Jean endormi, la voix brisée.*)
Un baiser . . . le dernier, et de toute mon âme . . .

JEAN: (*rêvant endormi*). Ma femme!

FANNY: (*anxieuse*). Il se réveille?
Non, non, toujours endormi.
(*En s'éloignant.*)
Adieu! adieu! m'ami!
(*Elle sort lentement en le regardant toujours.*)

FIN.

With every kiss some cruel word his lips would say.
So come!
Time's flying!
(*Writing.*)
Good-bye, my love!
This is my last farewell;
Ah, blame me not, I love you well!
I love you still—I am crying:
I have done what is right, even gladly and proudly.
If it is true there's a God who dwells there on high,
I can pray to Him now without fear, and devoutly.
And I can pray for you:—
No more!
Good-bye!
Just a kiss—it is the last,
And I leave him—my life!


JEAN: (*dreaming*). My wife!


FANNY: Is he awaking?
No, he does not move!
Good-bye, good-bye, my love!
(*Going away.*)
(*She goes out slowly, still looking at him.*)

END.

# Gli Ugonotti (1836)

## The Huguenots

MUSIC BY GIACOMO MEYERBEER ■ LIBRETTO BY EUGÈNE SCRIBE

This five-act opera, set to a libretto by Eugène Scribe (after Emile Deschamps), premiered at the Paris Opéra on February 29, 1836. In August, 1572, the Catholic Count de Nevers invites the Huguenot Raoul de Nangis to a banquet in accordance with the king's wishes that hostilities between the two groups come to an end. Raoul makes a toast to a mystery woman whom he defended from an attack. The mystery woman enters, and Raoul, who is in love with her, assumes that she is the Count's mistress. She is actually Valentine de Saint-Bris, sent by the Queen to ask the Count to allow the betrothal of Valentine and Raoul. The Queen's page invites Raoul to a rendezvous with an anonymous lady. In the gardens of Chenonceaux, Marguérite de Valois suggests to the blindfolded Raoul that Valentine marry him. Valentine's father, de Saint-Bris, is a prominent Catholic leader, and the union would solidify the peace between the Catholics and the Huguenots. Valentine, now in love with Raoul, is happy to comply, but Raoul still believes her to be Count de Nevers' mistress and refuses to marry her. His decision insults the Catholics. In Paris, Valentine and the Count de Nevers are about to be married when Raoul challenges de Saint-Bris to a duel. Valentine hears of a plot to ambush Raoul at this duel and warns his servant, Marcel, who rounds up Raoul's followers; fighting between the Catholics and Huguenots breaks out. The Queen arrives and Raoul finally realizes the truth about Valentine. Raoul tries to talk to her, but has to hide when her father and de Nevers enter. De Saint-Bris wants to wipe out the Huguenots, but de Nevers refuses and is arrested. Raoul overhears the plan and leaves Valentine to warn his followers, who are celebrating the marriage of the King and Queen. At the Huguenot churchyard, Raoul finds Marcel mortally wounded; Raoul is determined to die with his servant. Valentine comes to Raoul, telling him of Nevers' death and that the Queen will pardon him if he renounces his faith. Raoul refuses, and Valentine chooses his faith over her own. They die together at the hands of her father's army.

---

## ■ ATTO I

### SCENA I

*Sala nel Castello di Nevers, corrispondente a deliziosi giardini.—A destra una porta, che conduce agli appartamenti.—A sinistra una finestra, che si suppone guardar in un Oratorio.*

*Il Conte di Nevers, Tavannes, De Cossé, De Retz, Meru, Raul, ed altri Signori, seduti a tavola.*

**CHOR.:** Piacer della mensa, piacer della mensa, Piacer veritiero, piacer vetiero, Che guai non dispensa, Che guai non dispensa; Che sempre è sincer, che sempre è sincer. Beviam senza tema, Beviam senza tema, Che Bacco è la stella, Che Bacco è stella, Bacco è La guida più bella, La guida più bella, la guida più bella, Di tutti i piacer, Di tutti i piacer.

**NEV:** Della Turrena versate il vino.

**TAV:** A tazza piena, versiam da ber.

## ■ ACT I

### SCENE I

*A Salon in the Castle of Count de Nevers, opening onto a beautiful Garden.—On the right hand, a door opening to an inner apartment.—On the left, a window, supposed to command a view into a chapel.*

*The Count de Nevers, Tavannes, De Cossé, De Retz, Meru, Raoul, and other Noblemen, seated at table.*

**CHOR.:** Fill, fill, fill, fill, fill to the joys of the table; Crown, crown, crown, crown, crown every cup in foam, sir, Kill, kill, kill, kill, kill time as fast as we're able; Drown, drown, drown, drown, drown him in bright wine. Rosy Bacchus over our revels presiding, To his care our evening's pleasure confiding, To his care all, all confiding; While thus gaily onward the moments are gliding, All our souls to wine, sirs, we'll resign.

**NEV:** Old care defying with joyous song,

**TAV:** Beneath his bright banner we march along:

**TUTTI:** E nell' ebbrezza facciam tacer E la sagezza e il dispiacer.

**NEV:** Versate ancor del vino, e senza fren versate; sú via Raul, beviam a nostri amori. Ma, nel mirar quell' aria di langnore, scommetto che di già amor vi accende il core.

**RAU:** Che dite—a me?

**NEV:** Gioventù lo richiede. Ma sotto il suo poter doman me stringe Imene; promesso l'ho, per me non v'è più amor. E da questo momento io non potrei bastare di tante mie beltà il duolo a temperare.

**TAV:** Ci narra, or sù, racconta, e poi ciascuno con fedele ragguaglio ne seguirà l'esempio.

**NEV:** Si, la prova facciamo, e all' ospite novello il comminciare. (*A Raul.*)

**TUTTI:** È ver!

**RAU:** Lo faccio volentier: ma senza compromettere quella che ferito ha il mio cor.

**NEV:** Puoi dir almen chi sia.

**RAU:** Altro non so.

**NEV:** Il nome suo?

**RAU:** L'ignoro.

**ALL:** We pour to him sparkling libations— Bacchus, bright Bacchus, we adore you.

**NEV:** Come, let us touch glasses, Sir Raoul, and drink to those we love. Now, by your looks and your soft languishing tone, I know that you are already in love.

**RAO:** Who—I?

**NEV:** But at your age you have a right to be so. For my own part, I marry tomorrow, and I must therefore forswear love, in doing which I feel that I shall cause desolation in the heart of many a fair one.

**TAV:** Now, sirs, new zest to our feast to give, suppose we all in turn recount the history of our love lives.

**NEV:** Agreed, with all my heart! It is for the last newcomer to begin. (*to Raoul.*)

**ALL:** Most true!

**RAO:** I believe I am he; and I have no objection, sirs, so that all pass in honor.

**NEV:** Tell us first, then—who is she?

**RAO:** I do not know.

**NEV:** Her name?

**RAO:** I am ignorant even of that.

**NEV:** Davver! Signori, udiam, il suo racconto; ci deve interessar.

**NEV:** Indeed! Gentlemen, silence, pray: the tale bids fair to be piquant.

**RAU:** Un dì presso al castello dell' antica Amboise errava mesto e solo, quand' ad un tratto apparve una ricca lettiga, sul volger del sentiere. Un numeroso stuolo di giovani studenti l'investir, le grida lor, l'ardir ben mi fer noti i lor vili pensieri. Io mi slanciai, ciascun fugge lontano, allor timido avvanzo, oh qual soave vision, oh qual beltade, a miei sguardi appari!

**RAO:** Not far from the old towers and time-worn ramparts of Amboise, I chanced to lose my way; when, at the turn of the road, I saw before me a richly-housed litter: a band of wild young students were discourteously crowding round it, and their shouts and insolent demeanor left me no doubt of their audacious projects. I rushed forward—at sight of me they fled: I advanced still nearer—ah! what an enchanting vision met my view!

**RAOUL:** Più bianca del più bianco relo, Più pura, più pura d'un giorno d'April, Un angel, ò vergindel cielo, La sua vista rapì il mio cor. Vergin divina, Quant' era belia! Malgrado me innanzi d'ella m'inchinai. Le dissi allor, Bell angel, dea, dea de gl'amor, Beltà dei ciel, Te voglio amar ognor, ognor, ognor, ognor, ognor, Te voglio amar, amar . . . oh! dea de gl'amor, Te vo glio amar, amar . . . amar!

**RAOUL:** Fairer far even than fairest lily, Than spring morn, more pure and more lovely and bright, An angel of heaven-born beauty Burst upon my ravished sight. Oh! she was charming past all expression! And as I bent my knee before her divine form, I faltered, I faltered, Fair angel, surely you come from heaven above, For evermore will I love none but you! Forever, forever, forever, will I love none but you! Forever will I love none but you, for ever, forever; No, none . . . but you.

**TUTTI:** È davver quel candore leggiadro, Se lo fan due begli occhi tremar.

**ALL:** I vow, his candor is really most charming— Bright eyes, how very bewitching!

**RAU:** Nell'ascoltarmi, un dolce riso Tradi gli affanni del suo bel sen; Legger potei sovra il suo viso Scritto il presagio d'ogni mio ben. Fiamma novella, ma fido amante, D'amor costante arde il mio cor. E dirò ognor, Bell'angiol, dea, etc.

**RAO:** Sweetly she smiled as I stood by her side, Sighing the love which even her tongue denied to speak; And in her eyes the love-light gleamed, And on her brow affection beamed, Bidding me hope to gain her love, Bidding me echo still the strain, Fairer than, etc.

**TUTTI:** È davver quel candore leggiadro, Se lo fan due bei lumi tremar.
*Entra Marcello.*

**ALL:** I vow, his candor is really most charming— Bright eyes, how bewitching!
(*Enter Marcel.*)

**DE COS:** (*Attentamente guardando a Marcello.*) Qua! mai strana figura quì veggio comparire?

**DE COS:** (*Looking earnestly at Marcel.*) But what strange-looking mortal here makes his appearance.

**RAU:** È un servo mio fedele, che mi vide fanciullo.

**RAO:** It is a faithful old follower, who from my childhood hath served me.

**MAR:** (*Avvicinandosi a Raul.*) Sir, Raul! con essi a mensa! Ah! Signore, disse il ciel, fuggi l'empio e il suo festin.

**MAR:** (*Perceiving Raoul.*) Sir Raoul! Eh! at table with them! Ah! dear master, we are told— "With the wicked feast you not nor have anything to do."

**MER:** (*Ridendo.*) C'Israele è desso un santo.

**MERU:** (*Laughing.*) It is a saint of Israel—

**MAR:** Si, nel campo Filisteo.

**MAR:** In the camp of the Philistines.

**NEV E CORO:** Che vuol dir?

**NEV AND CHO:** What said he?

**RAU:** Ah, perdono! religioso e guerriero gli avi miei l'educar, dalla sua prima età, e l'amore a spregiar, e il papa, e il suo poter. Marcel, non è cosi?

**RAO:** Pardon him! he knows no manners but those of a rough soldier, having been taught to hate the Pope and his power.

**MAR:** (*Con satisfazione.*) Pur troppo egli è cosi!

**MAR:** (*With earnestness.*) Truly, it is so!

**RAU:** Ma fedele, valente e in cor sensibile, gemma è gentil in ruvido metal. Orsù, vieni, ne servi. (*A Marcello.*) È non parlar—se pur ti tia possibile.

**RAO:** Still he loves me, and is sterling as an uncut diamond. (*To Marcel.*) Come, attend us, and be silent, if you can.

**MAR:** Obbedisco. (*Da se.*) Da lor come salvarlo?

**MAR:** I obey. (*Aside.*) How shall I guard his soul from their wiles?

**NEV:** (*Bevendo.*) Beviam, beviam a chi ne accende sene!

**NEV:** (*Drinking.*) Now, sirs we drink to our mistresses!

**RAU:** (*Bevendo.*) Si, al solo e dolce affetto del mio core!

**RAO:** (*Drinking.*) To her whom alone I adore!

**DE COS:** Beviam, beviamo al loro ardente amore.

**DE COS:** Yes, let us drink to their true love.

**MAR:** Deh vieni, divo amor, il salva tu dal mal, E di tua voce il suon mesci al canto infernal! O, tu che ognor in guardia stai Del giusto cha t'adora.

**MAR:** Had I great Calvin's voice, whoever might frown, I'd raise it high to drown their impious songs. Oh! you, who are our only guide And guard from every earthly ill—

**NEV:** Vieni, bevi!

**NEV:** Come, drink!

**RAU:** No, no!

**RAO:** No!

**MAR:** Umile o altero invano mai Alcun fedel t'implora!

**MAR:** Do not turn your face from us in each strait But protect us!

**MERU:** (*A Raul.*) Ma che dicendo va?

**MERU:** (*To Raoul.*) What's that?

**RAU:** (*Con voce soffocata.*) È la santa preghiera che noi diciamo ognor, ne' rischi e nel dolor.

**RAO:** (*In an impressive voice.*) That is the prayer that was written by Calvin which we offer when grief or danger threatens.

**MAR:** Per nostro mal, Contro di noi L'oste infernal Levossi ancor! Sommo Signor, Ne reggi e salva Dal suo furor.

**MAR:** The serpent tempter's net He spreads for his prey; He besets our path Our souls he would betray! Oh, do not forget your servants! But save us now, we pray!

**DE COS:** (*Attentamente guardando a Marcello.*) Ma, più lo vedo, e più ricordami un guerrier, che un di vicino alla Rochelle—?

**DE COS:** (*Attentively regarding Marcel*) If my eyes serve me, this is a soldier whom we encountered beneath the walls of Rochelle?

**MAR:** (*Con piacere.*) Mi rammentate voi?

**MAR:** (*Much pleased.*) You know me, then?

**DE COS:** Si, davver, per mia fe, questa ferita.

**DE COS:** Too well; and this scar—

**MAR:** (*Con orgoglio.*) Essa venia da me.

**MAR:** Was given to you by me.

**RAU:** Orsù, Marcel!

**RAO:** Peace, Marcel!

**DE COS:** (*Lietamente.*) E fu di buona guerra, e per darten la prova, mesciam beviamo insieme.

**DE COS:** (*Gaily.*) Ah, that was a good fight! Come, commemorate it in a glass!

**MAR:** Perdon, non posso ber.

**MAR:** Thank you: I cannot drink.

**DE COS:** (*Ridendo.*) No, con un infedel!

**DE COS:** (*Laughing.*) With a son of sin like me!

**RAU:** Grazia gli fate ancor.

**RAO:** No, excuse him, I pray you.

**NEV:** Ebben, se ber non vuol, che canti.

**NEV:** Well, if he won't drink, he must sing, sirs.

**RAU:** Ma, Signor—

**RAO:** But, gentlemen—

**DE COS:** Si, vogliam, che canti!

**DE COS:** Oh, yes, yes; he must sing!

**MAR:** Con piacere;—una vecchia canzone contro la fè di Roma, e la stirpe donnesca. Vo la sapete ben—la canzone guerresca; quella della Rochelle, quando al rumore,

**MAR:** Sirs, I will; an old Huguenot song against the snares of Rome and the dark wiles of woman. You, sirs, should know it well—it is our battle song; you heard it at Rochelle, it

el suon di tamburi e cimballi, accompagnato dal piff, paff del fuoco de' fucili, cantava.

**MARCEL:** Finita è pe' frati, Abbasso i lor covi, De' finti beati Pietà non si provi! Al ferro ed al fuoco Lor tempii poniam; Al fuoco i tempii poniam, Al ferro al fuoco i tempii poniam. Battiamo, par sterminiam, uccidiam, distruggiam! Battiamo, par steminiam, uccidiam, distruggiam—Piff, paff, piff, Abbattiam—Piff, paff, piff, uccidiam! Piff, paff, piff, paff, paff, piff, paff, piff, paff, Che piangan, che moran, Ma grazia giammai, Che piangan, che moran, Ma grazia giammai; Nò, nò, nò! giammai! Nò, nò, nò, giammai! Nò, nò, nò, giammai! Nò, nò, nò, nò, nò, nò, nò, nò, nò, giammai!

**CORO:** Ha! ha! bontà senza par! Mercè dell' avviso!

**MAR:** Mia man mai non trema A' pianti di donna: Sventura a chi piega Innanzi a una gonna. Tronchiam con l'acciar L'incanto infernal. Di donna l'amor Fuggiamo, abborriamo: Che piangan, che moran, Ma grazia giammai! *Entra un servo del Conte di Nevers, dal fondo del teatro, conducendo una Dama coperta d'un velo. Ella scompare nei giardini, ed il servo si accosta al Conte, e gli parla sotto voce.*

**NEV:** Ignota dama a me brama parlare! E cosa strana in vero come inseguito ia sono. Signori, perdonate, or m'è uopo partir, ma voi quívi restate del banchetto a gior che l'amor disturbò;—ma, che per quanto par, fra breve tornerà a blandir l'amistà. *(Nevers esce ed il Servo, accompagnato fino alla porta dagli espiti, che ritornano in scena ridendo.)*

**TAV:** L'avventura è stravagante.

**DE RETZ:** De' più belli è il suo destin. *(Alcuni Signori s'avvincinano alla finestra, e guardano nell'oratorio.)*

**RAU:** *(Guardando e maravigliato.)* O, Cielo!

**TUTTI:** Che mai fù?

**RAU:** *(A Marcello.)* Ah! la vergin così giovine e bella, che e il mio braccio salvò, ond' or parlato v'ho, e quella!

**TUTTI:** È quella?

---

was sung amid the din of drums and trumpets; with a full accompaniment—piff, paff, piff, paff—bullets from our ranks, it rang out:

**MARCEL:** Old Rome and her revelries, Her pride and her lust, boys, The monks and their devilries, We'll grind them to dust, boys! Deliver to fire and sword their temples of Hell, Till of the black demons none live to tell, none live to tell, none live to tell. Down, down with them! Slay them all, every soul! Slaughter them! Down, down with them! Slay them all, every soul! Slaughter them—Piff, paff, piff; Slay them all, Piff, paff, piff, every soul! Piff, paff, piff, paff, paff, piff, paff, piff, paff, All vainly for aid or for mercy they call; No pity for them! No, they die, no, they die; No, slay all! slay all! No, no, no, slay all! No, no, no, no, no, no, no, slay all!

**CHO:** Ha! ha! ha! what a dear lamb-like soul! Have mercy on us, pray?

**MAR:** Woe to all defilers fair! I never heed their shrieking—Woe to the Dalilahs fair, Who men's souls are seeking! Deliver to fire and sword Those children of hell, Till of the black demons None live to tell! All vainly for aid or for mercy they call! No pity for them! no, they die—slay all!

*(Enter a Servant of the Count de Nevers from the back of the stage, leading a Lady, veiled. The Lady passes into the garden, the Servant comes forward, and whispers to the Count.)*

**NEV:** A lady you say? Truly, the request I am in amongst them surpasses belief! Gentlemen, may I beg you will excuse me; but do not let me disturb you; continue, I pray, the feast we had begun, and which, though partially interrupted by love, shall be concluded in friendship. *(Exeunt De Nevers and Servant, followed to the doorway by the Guests, who afterwards return, laughing, to the front.)*

**TAV:** This is a singular adventure.

**DE RETZ:** He is certainly in great luck. *(Several of the party approach the window, and peep into the adjoining Chapel.)*

**RAO:** *(With astonishment, after looking.)* Oh, heaven!

**ALL:** What is it?

**RAO:** *(To Marcel.)* This lady, this young beauty, is the same I once saved, of whom I told you.

**ALL:** Are you sure?

---

**RAU:** Ah si, certo ne son. *(Si vede nel fondo traversar il giardino Nevers, con una Donna coperta d'un velo, cui rispettosamente saluta, e lascia.)* *Entra Nevers, in scena astratto e quasi senza accorgersi de' convitati, che gli aprono il passaggio, e subito dopo lui entra Urbano.*

**NEV:** Paggio gentil, che cerchi in questo albergo?

**URB:** Nobil Signori, salute.

**URBAIN:** Nobil donna, e tanto onesta, Che far lieto un repotria, Messaggiero quì m' invia, Cavalier, cavalier, per un di voi. Senza nomarlo, si renda onor A chi fù degno Di tanto amor, Di tanto amor! A me credete, Mai niun signor A tanto gloria fù eletto ancor, a . . . tanta gloria, a tanta gloria eletto ancor.

Non temete inganno ò frode, Cavalier, nel mio parlar. Ora addio; e il Ciel vi regga Nell' amare e nel pugnar.

**NEV:** Troppa virtù talora Per verità importuna; Ma, poichè infin non mi potrei sottrarre Dai colpi di fortuna, porgi quel foglio a me.

**URB:** Siete voi Sir Raulfo di Nangis?

**NEV:** Che di' tù?

**URB:** È a lui che questo foglio io reco.

**TUTTI:** O Ciel!

**MAR:** *(Con orgoglio.)* È pel mio sire—eccolo là.

**RAU:** È per me?

**URB:** Sì, per voi. *(Presentandogli il foglio.)*

**RAU:** *(Lo prende e legge.)* 'Prima che cada il di, Sir Raulfo di Nangis, Di corte un legno a prendervi verrà, Voi sommesso obbedite; e posto agli occhi un vel In silenzio partite—avrete tal coraggio.' Andiam, a spese mie, quì ridere si vuole, Potria caro costar ma ciò pur sia, m' arrendo—Or leggete voi stesso. *(Presenta la lettera a Nevers, che le legge, e poi la dà ad un altro, e così passa per le mani di tutti.)*

**NEV:** *(Maravigliato.)* Giusto Cielo!

**MER:** Qual sorpresa!

**DE COS:** Il suo stemma!

**TAV:** Le sue ciffre.

---

**RAO:** Tis she, I'm certain. *(De Nevers is seen to pass through the garden with a Lady veiled, whom he salutes respectfully, and takes leave.)* *(Enter Nevers—pensively advances up the stage, without taking notice of his Visitors—all the Guests make way for him—Urbain enters after him.)*

**NEV:** My gentl page, what brings you to my chateau?

**URB:** Nobel Signors, I salute you.

**URBAIN:** A most charming noble lady, whom kings might view with envy, has charged me with a message here, Cavaliers, cavaliers, to one of you. I do not name him; but honor be Unto the good knight, whoever he may be, whoever he may be! And until now, sirs, there never has been Mortal so favored by beauty's queen, Mortal so favored, so favored by beauty's queen.

Do not fear the least deception, Noble knights, in my discourse; Now farewell, may heaven kindly protect you in love or war.

**NEV:** The sky today rains females in a shower On me, I think; but so it must be! For to resist the sex I have no power;—Give me the note—give it to me.

**URB:** Are you, then, Sir Raoul de Nangis?

**NEV:** What say you?

**URB:** I've brought this note for him.

**ALL** Ah! great Heaven!

**MAR:** *(Proudly.)* For my master! he is here—that is he!

**RAO:** What! for me?

**URB:** Yes, for you. *(Handing him the letter.)*

**RAO:** *(Reading.)* 'Before the close of day, Sir Raoul de Nangis, A carriage from the court will be wating for you, Ascend in strictest silence; closely veil your eyes, Trust to other guidance—unless your courge fails Indeed! they seek to have a joke at my expense; But it may cost them dearly! Still, be it so—I do consent. *(Handing the letter to Nevers, who reads it, and in turn hands it to another, and so it passes through the hands of all.)*

**NEV:** *(Astonished.)* Ah! great Heaven!

**MER:** Surprising!

**DE C:** Her Seal!

**TAV:** Her arms!

## Act I, Scene I

**TUTTI:** E, fia vero? la sua mano!
Certo ormai è il suo destin.
(*Tutti si avvicinano a Raul, e gli serrano la mano.*)

**NEV:** Voi sapete ch' io sono vostr' amico sincero.

**MER. E DE COS:** Se scortarvi—servirvi è mestiero.

**DE RET, NEV. E TAV:** Sì, sapremo, adoprarci davvero.

**CORO:** Voi penserete a noi, nol scorderete poi.

**RAU:** Qual cambiamento è questo? Che posso, o miei signor?

**TUTTI:** Tutto.

**URB. I SETTE SIGNORI E NEV:** I piaceri, l' onor, l' opulenza
Compiran i desir, la speranza,
Dell' ardir, ed ognor la potenza,
Va per dritto a chi sa la colpir.

**NEV:** Ah! per voi, oh qual gloria novella!
La beltade in tal giorno v' appella.

**RAU:** (*Solo*) I piaceri, gli onor, l' opulenza!
Che vuol dir non intendo davver.

**MAR:** Che vuol dir questa gran differenza,
Per mia fè non intendo davver.

**CORO:** I piaceri, gli onor, l' opulenza,
Compiran la speranza, i desir.

**MAR:** Te Deum, laudamus!
E Sansone atterrava i Filistei.

**TUTTI:** (*A Raul.*) Ah! per te, o qual gloria novella!
La betade in tal giorno t' appella.
Portiamo alle stelle chi vince le belle.
O nostro compione, orsù parti, vola,
Ti spinge l' onore, l' amor ti consola;
Addio, parti, va!

### SCENA II

*Il teatro rapprescenta il Castello ed i Giardini Chenonceaux, con una gran scalinata alla destra.*

*Margarita circondata dalle Damigelle, arrà appena finito la sua toletta.*

**MARG:** O, vago suol della Turrena,
Erbette e fior, fresche sorgenti,
Chiaro ruscel che s' ode appena,
O, qual piacer di voi sognar!
O l' una, o l' altra fede vermiglio
faccia il suolo,
In lor varia e divota opposizione,
De' ministri del cielo sia la morale austera,
D' un Dio supremo, santo timor.

---

**ALL:** Can it be true? Her hand!
Then now is his fortune made.
(*All approach Raoul and shake him by the hand.*)

**NEV:** You know that I have ever been your friend.

**MER & DE COS:** I am at your service, whenever required.

**DE RET, NEV & TAV:** I shall be happy to serve you.

**CHO:** You will not forget the promise you made.

**RAO:** How? what change is this?
I do not understand—what can I do?

**ALL:** Everything!

**URB, KNIGHTS & NEV:** Here pleasure, and honor, and wealth,
High power and rank, will be yours;
And all that ambition could crave,
In your fortune and state will combine.

**NOVE:** Ah, what glory now awaits you
You are chosen by beauty this day!

**RAO:** (*Alone.*) What? pleasure, and honor and wealth!
I cannot believe what they say.

**MAR:** I see the difference in their conduct,
Though I do not know what they design.

**CHO:** Pleasure, honor, and wealth will be his.
Oh, how happy such joys to combine.

**MAR:** We praise you, oh Heaven!
Samson overcame the Philistines.

**ALL:** (*To Raoul.*) Quick, away! for this beautiful
that glory and love will be yours:
For he must be favored, for whom
Both beauty and fortune combine.
Then no longer stay here;—
Adieu, depart away!

### SCENE II

*The scene represents the Castle and Garden of Chenonceaux, with a broad flight of steps on the right hand.*

*Margaret is discovered, surrounded by her Maids, who have just finished her toilet.*

**MARY:** Oh, lovely land of fair Touraine!
Your vine-clad hills, your sparkling fountains,
Your green banks, and your murmuring zephrys,
All fill my soul with peace and love!
Yet, for a difference in belief,
This fair scene may be stained by war,

---

**MARG., URB. E UNA DAMA D' ONORE:** Fosche chimere! forme severe!
Non v' appressate al nostro cuor;
Sotto, al mio regno, non avvi impegno;
Che far onore al dio d' amor.

**CORO:** Triste follie, riserbe vane,
Ite lontane dal nostro cor.
Sotto, il tuo, impero, non v' è pensiero.
Che render gloria al dio d' amor.

**MARG:** Sotto il mio impero,
Non v' è pensiero
Che di dar vanto
Al dio d' amor.

**MARGARET:** A questa voce sola
Natura par più bella La terra l' aura,
il ciel . . . D' amor favalla. La terra, l' aura, il cielo, D' amor si dè e favella; La terra, il cielo, la terra il ceil, Favella, favella, d' amor.

**CORO:** La terra, l' aura, il cielo, favellano d' amor.

**URB:** (*Guardando a Margarita sospirando.*) Oh! quanto dessa è bella, oimè!

**MARG:** Chi giunge?

**URB:** Ve', la più bella fra le damigelle,
(*La dame si ritirano.*)
*Entra Valentina.*

**MARG:** Valentina!—T' innoltra, e non tremare!

**URB:** Già tutto è per lei sola,—
Di già la favorita.

**MARG:** Afflitta io la trovai,
E il dolor sempre sa
In noi svegliar pietà.

**URB:** A! Più rider non vo'.
(*Esce.*)

**MARG:** (*A Valentina.*) Mia figlia, andiam, coraggio.
Dimmi che risultò dal tuo ardito viaggio.

**VAL:** Il Conte di Nevers mi promise e guirò
Di rifiutar mia man.

**MARG:** Or d' accordo saremo:
Fra poco un altro Imene
Conchiuder si potrà.

**VAL:** Che sento, o cielo?

**MARG:** Io ti vedo arrossir!
Dunque tu l' ami inver?

**VAL:** In non lo debbo amar, ma il padre mio—

**MARG:** Non temer, io di lui gli parlerò.

**VAL:** Sì—ma Raul?

---

Oh, that men could observe the moral,
To love and fear the all-powerful Being!

**MARG, URB, & LADIES:** But hence with sorrow!
Care we will banish;
Quick, let it vanish,
Far, far away.

**CHO:** Youth is a treasure,
Which while enjoying,
To love and pleasure
Our court we'll pay!

**MARG:** In the land where I reign,
From the mount to the main,
All re-echo the strain
That's devoted to love!

**MARGARET:** For at that word of power, Each Bird, each beast, each flower, All nature springs, rejoicing, Through earth and air and sky. The rippling stream repeats it, In gentle murmurs greets it; The winds, the waters, with tuneful voice echoing, echoing, reply.

**CHO:** All echo the strain that's devoted to love!

**URB:** (*Looking towards Margaret and sighing.*) Oh! how beautiful is she!

**MARG:** See, who comes here!

**URB:** More fair than all the maids of honor.
(*The Maids of Honor retire.*)
(*Enter Valentina.*)

**MARG:** It is Valentina! Approach and fear not!

**URB:** All sympathize with and would console her
Who is the favorite of her sovereign.

**MARG:** Yes, I have marked her sorrows:
Grief is indeed all powerful
To wake the heart to pity.

**URB:** Ah! I shall laugh no longer.
(*Exit.*)

**MARG:** (*To Valentina.*) Approach, my child, take courage,
And tell me now of your most bold adventure.

**VAL:** The Count of Nevers has, on his honor,
Promised to refuse my hand.

**MARG:** All will then be easy:
Leave everything to me.
I will soon arrange another match for you.

**VAL:** Oh, Heaven! what do I hear?

**MARG:** What, you blush!
Oh! I see you love him.

**VAL:** Nay—I must not venture—but my father—

**MARG:** Have no fear, I will confer with him.

**VAL:** Yes—but Raoul?

MARG: Ebben l' aspetto quì.

VAL: Ah! mai non oserò—

MARG: Allor per te son io che lo vedrò.

*Reintrano le Damigelle d' Onore, seguite da Villanelle.*

UNA DAM: Andiam, regina, in queste amene sponde
Del sol control l'ardor rifugio a ritrovar,
Del vivido ruscel o fortunate l' onde
Che d'un lucente vel il dono a voi può far.

*(Alcune si pongono a sedere sul margine del fiume, altre cantano, ed altre ballano.)*

CORO DI VILLANELLE: Giovin beltà, sù questa riva,
Che ne difende dall' aura estiva
Possiam del dì sfidar l'ardor.
Mirate come son l' onde chiare;
Nel lor seno possiam trovare
Dolcezza all' alma, calma e ristor.

*Entra Urbano, comparisce fra un gruppo di Damigelle.*

MARG: Ancora quì! ma, quale audacia, Urbano?

URB: Ma non son io! è un cavalier.

*(Valentina e le Damigelle dan segni di agitazione.*

VAL: Un cavalier!

TUTTI: Un cavalier!

URB: Lasciate ogni timor, l' avventura ascoltate.

URBAIN: No, no, no, no, no, no!
Caso egual giammai scommetto,
No, non udiste ancor, Raccontar de un giovin paggio, No No, no, no, no, no, no! E le figlie del villaggio,
Giammai non lo . . . scorderan!
Circondato gran folla, Sorra gl' occha un relo, un velo nero. Ecco appar un cavalier! E simil ad ombra, a nube fuggente, Traversa lo spazio con piè leggier; Con gl' occhi ciascun, Seguendole va, E dicon dov'è? E poi dove andò, Che cosa cercò? E fan gran rumor! No, no, no, no, no. Caso egual giammai, scommelto, No, non udiste pria raccontar d' un giovin paggio.
Ah! . . . No, no, no, no, no, no, no! E le figlie del villaggio giammai, no lo scorderan.

Il gioco è bello davvero!
Ma sott' occhio sol ridiamo
Qualche arcan quì acoso sta;
Non dobbiam scoprir mistero
Che celar si studia amor,
L'amor scesso, e potente,
Fra le piante quì sovente
Corte tien.

CORO: Ah! il gioco è bello davvero!
Ma sott' occhio sol ridiamo,—
Un arcan quì si celò.
In tal di, che mai pensar?

MARG: Know he is coming here. '

VAL: Ah! never shall I dare—

MARG: Never! Then I must see him for you.

*(Re-enter the Maids of Honor, followed by Village Girls.)*

1ST LA: Come, rest beneath the verdant trees' broad shade,
And seek a shelter from the burning sun,
Where brooks meander through the grassy glade,
And crystal streams in cooling current run.

*(Some go towards the river, and seat themselves upon the bank, others sing, and others dance.)*

CHO. OF VILLAGE GIRLS: Youth and beauty may rest here,
Or sport beneath the shady vest
Of gently waving trees.
Sheltered from the burning sun,
Waves of purest crystal run,
And woo the freshening breeze.

*(Enter Urbain, from amidst a group of Damsels.)*

MARG: You here again! What assurance, Urbain!

URB: I come to announce the approach of a cavalier.

*(Valentina and the Ladies show signs of agitation.)*

VAL: A cavalier!

ALL: A cavalier!

URB: Calm your fears and listen to this adventure.

URBAIN: No, no, no, no, no, no! You have not heard, I will engage, So strange a tale as this told by a youthful page. No, no, no, no, no, no! And the maidens of the village Will not forget the vision: Crowds of persons flocked around him; Over his eyes a veil of black he'd bound him: Thus this cavalier appeared, Gliding like a shadow all around, With feet that do but lightly touch the ground: And young ones and old the vision behold, Saying, "what is it!" and then, "where is it? And whom does it seek?" It makes a great noise! No, no, no, no, no! you have not heard, I will engage, So strange a tale as this, told by a youthful page. Ah! . . . No, no, no, no, no! And the maidens of the village will not forget the vision.

Oh, what a joke!
But let us stem our laughter,
There must be some secret
That I cannot discover,
Which love would fain conceal.
Ah, Love!
That powerful king disports here
will hold his court,
And amid these groves.

CHO: Oh, what a joke!
But let us stem our laughter.
Some secret here must be concealed,

Uno scherzo egli è d'amor.
Ah, davver un gioco egli è
Dell' astuto dio d' amor,
Che l' amore spesso quì
La sua corte tiene—ah! sì.

URB: *(Ridendo.)* Nulla vede il cavaliere.

CORO: *(Ripetendo.)* Nulla vede il cavaliere.

URB: A tenton cerca il sentiere.
Ragazzi a stuolo seguendo il van,
Gioco ne fan.

CORO: Ragazzi a stuol seguendo il van,
Gioco ne fan.

URB: Ma le suore lor
Gli gettan de' fior.

CORO: *(Ridendo.)* Ah, ah!

URB: No, no! giammai scommetto, etc.
E un gran corteggio ridente e bello!

CORO: Qual corteggio quanto è bello!

URB: Agli occhi un vel; dal lieto piè
Di giovin figlie seguito egli è.

CORO: Lo scherzo è bel,—oh, qual piacer?

URB: E già vicino è del castel.
O, qual mai festa vi si farà?

CORO: Ei vien costì

URB: O, qual mai festa?
E vien—costì—
Egli è già quì!
*(Indicando verso la scala.)*
*Entra Raul, con gli occhi bendati—è condotto in scena della parte della scalinata.—Alcune Damigelle lo guar dando attentamente, e chi si ritira, e chi lo circonda.*

MARG: È Raul de Nangis, il misterioso eroe.
Tanta lealtà, o Signor, merta il suo premio.
Della vostra, promessa io vi disciolgo;—
Levar potete il velo.

RAU: O Ciel! dove som io?
Illusione non è? non è prestigio agli occhi miei?

RAU: Beltà divina, incantatrice,
Che egual mai vidi in uman vel,
Parla ten prego mortale o dea,
In terra sono, oppur nel ciel?
Ah! mi rispondi un detto sol.

MARG: *(Da se.)* Della sua dolce ardente brama.
Appen comprendo tutto il fervor.
Quant' è leggiadro! Regina, o dama

That may this day, perhaps, be revealed.
Sly Cupid is playing his part,
And in jest will exert all his art.
The merry god disports here
And delight to hold his court
Amidst these groves and bowers.

URB: *(Laughing.)* Nothing can this knight behold.

CHO: *(Repeating.)* Nothing can this knight behold.

URB: But groping tries to find his way.
Groups of boys, with shouting noise,
Follow, in sport.

CHO: Troops of boys, with shouting noise,
Follow, in sport!

URB: But their sisters, in showers,
Throw on him sweet flowers.

CHO: *(Laughing.)* Ha, ha!

URB: You have not heard, etc.
An astonishing pageant, quite charming to see.

CHO: An astonishing pageant, quite charming to see.

URB: A veil conceals his eyes from view,
Yet the young maids pursue his form.

CHO: Oh, what a joke—this is a treat!

URB: Nigh to the castle he comes, we may see,
Oh, what a treat now for us there will be!

CHO: Yes, he approaches.

URB: Oh, what a treat!
He comes—he is near—
Behold! he is here! *(Pointing towards the steps.)*
*(Enter Raoul, with his eyes bandaged—he is led from the steps to the front.—Some of the Ladies look at him attentively and retreat, while others surround him.)*

MARG: It is Sir Raoul de Nangis, our mysterious hero.
Such loyalty deserves to be rewarded.
I absolve you from your oath;—
You may remove the veil.

RAO: Oh, Heaven! where am I?
Do I see rightly? Is it an illusion or a dream?

RAO: Beauty bright! divine enchantress!
Who to my raptured sight are given,—
Are you mortal, or are you goddess?
Am I on earth, or am I in Heaven?
Speak! oh speak, lovely being!

MARG: *(Aside.)* Ah! now indeed I well can all divine
She, too, has obeyed the voice of love!

# Act I, Scene II

Far non potria scelta miglior.

RAU: D' un umil cavalier, aggradite i servigi.

MARG: Dell' ubbidienza sua M' è duopo ancora un pegno.

RAU: Lo giuro a vostri piè. Ogni vostro desir, obbedirò.

MARG: (*Da se.*) Ah, d' una tal conquista, Se ne bramassi il vanto! Si, nulla è facil tanto; Ma no, or sol sì dè! Poichè la sua bella Si fida al mio zelo, Piacergli per ella, E non gia per me.

RAU: A voi la vita e il core, A voi la spada io sacro, Per cielo e per l' amore La morte affronterò.

MARG: O, come, a quel suo ardore Mi batte il core in seno! Sperate, e lieti appieno Io rendervi saprò.

RAU: Ah! poichè questa bella Riposa sul mio zel, Punire saprò quella Che mi mancò da fe. *Entrano i Signori di Corte. — Cattolici si mettono da una parte, i Protestanti dell' altra. — La Regina presenta Raul a San Bris e Nevers, che gli fanno lieta accoglienza. — Un Gentiluomo della Corte presenta un foglio a Margarita.*

MARG: (*A San Bris e Nevers, dopo aver letto in foglio.*) Carlo, mio buon fratello, Che il vostro zel conosce, ambo a Parigi Questa sera vi vuol per un disegno Ch' io non conosco.

NEV. E SAN BRIS: Sommessi entrambi al suo desir noi ciamo.

MARG: Sì, ma siate prima al mio. Grazie all' Imen che quì stringer desio, Ogni rancor obliando, è mestiero a ciascuno, Come a piè dell' altare, d' un inviolabil pace Il giuro pronunciare; e voi pure, o Signori, Un voto sol congiunga. (*Raul, Nevers, San Bris, e i Signori si radunano presso Margarita e fanno il giuramento:—*) Per la fè, l' onore, che i nostri avi esaltarò, Noi giuriam per l' acciaro che a no il ciel confidò, Per quel Dio, che punisce chi mentitor si fà, Innanzi a voi giuriamo un eterna amistà.

---

He's really charming; not queen nor princess Could ever have made better choice.

RAO: A humble cavalier begs his services to offer.

MARG: But first of his obedience It is meet he give some token.

RAO: At your feet now hear me swear, In all things I'll be true to you!

MARG: (*Aside.*) Ah! if I were coquettish— Heaven! here's a situation! I declare I feel a palpitation;— But no, it would not do! On my faith relying, She is dying for him; And though it is rather trying, I will be true to her!

RAO: To you my heart I proffer, My honor and my sword. And even death would suffer For heaven and my adored.

MARG: How strongly my heart beats,— How much I like his zeal! Believe me, sir, I only wish To seal your happiness.

RAO: Ah! since this lady confides And places her faith in me, I shall forget the beauty Who proved to be faithless. (*Enter the Nobles of the Court.— The Catholics range themselves on one side, the Protestants on the other. The Queen presents Raoul to St. Bris and Nevers, who receive him with great courtesy.—A Gentleman of the Court presents a royal dispatch to Margaret.*)

MARG: (*To St. Bris and Nevers, after reading dispatch.*) Charles, my good brother, Well knowing your great zeal, Wills that you both forthwith go to Paris, On private matters not revealed to me.

NEV. & ST. BRIS: His will is our law,—we obey.

MARG: Yes, but first attend to mine. First swear that, by the marriage vow, Which each this day shall plight, No more shall enmity prevail,— No more each others' lives assail, In party feud or fight. (*Raoul, Nevers, St. Bris, and the Nobles, gather round the Queen, and take the oath:—*) We swear by our forefathers bold, The Queen, and all her powers, That kindly acts and generous thoughts Shall evermore be ours.

---

MAR: Per le fè, per l'onore, etc. Giammai non sia tra noi Nè amistà, nè pietà!

CHO: Noi giuriam, noi giuriamo, Per la fè, per l' onore, etc. Un eterna amistà.

RAU. NEV. E SAN BRIS: Providenza, dolce madre, Fa che scenda sulla terra La concordia che ci serra In fraterna pace ognor!

MAR: Providenza, dolce madre, Sul mio sire fa che scenda L' alma luce che lo renda Co' tuoi figli in pace ognor!

MARG: Voglia il Cielo ascoltar, E benedir i giuramenti vostri!

URB E DAMIGELLE: I giuramenti vostri Degni il Ciel benedir!

RAU. E NEV: Si, innanzi a voi giuriamo Al Cielo d' obbedir.

MAR: Guerra e morte, giammai Amità ne pietà.

TUTTI: Innanzi a voi giuriam Pel Cielo di morir! (*Esce San Bris.*)

MARG: Or deggio presentar a vostri sguardi La bella fidanzata. La promessa a tenere de voi lieve sorà. *Ricomparisce San Bris, conducendo Valentina verso Raul.*

RAU: (*Con voce quasi soffocata.*) Giusto Ciel! che mai veggio?

MARG: Onde il terrore?

RAU: È lei, è lei che iu un tal dì m' offrite?

MARG: Con l'Imeneo, e l'amor.

RAU: Tradimento, o perfidia! Io sposo suo?—giammai, giammai!

TUTTI: O, Cielo!

MARG., URB., VAL., E DAME: O, delir! qual oltraggio crudele! A spezzar chi lo sforza un tal nodo.

RAU: Mi tradir, o perfidio crudele! Io per sempre rifiuto un tal nodo.

NEV. E SAN BRIS: O, rossor, qual affronto crudele! Di vendetta or la voce sol odo.

MAR: All' onor per mostrarsi fedele, Si doveva spezzar questo nodo.

---

MAR: By my faith and hope I swear, etc., That kindly acts and generous thoughts, For them, can never be ours.

CHO: By faith and honor we now swear, etc., That for each other friendly acts Shall alone be ours.

RAO., NEV. & ST. BRIS: Great Providence! oh, gentle mother, Consecrate this holy rite, Once again our hearts unite, Make each respect his brother!

MAR: Great Providence! oh, gentle mother! To him I serve dispense the power, In this solemn trying hour, To guard the faith of each true brother!

MARG: May Heaven above your hearts direct, That so you may respect your oaths!

URB. & LADIES: The oath they've sworn, oh Heaven, bless, And ever in their hearts impress!

RAO. & NEV: Before you all we swear, this day to obey, The will of Heaven.

MAR: War and death, but friendship never,— With them strife soon their oath will sever.

ALL: We swear, before great heaven on high, That for our faith we'd freely die! (*Exit St. Bris.*)

MARG: And now you shall be presented to the lady, Your beauteous betrothed. To fulfill your promise you will not find difficult. (*Re-enter St. Bris, leading Valentina towards Raoul.*)

RAO: (*With a stifled voice.*) Great Heaven! what do I see?

MARG: Why this astonishment?

RAO: What! is this the bride you would offer to me?

MARG: Yes, to marry and to love.

RAO: What perfidy! what treachery! I her husband? never, never!

ALL: Oh, Heaven!

MARG., URB., VAL. & LADIES: What dire madness can possess him, To thus reject her hand?

RAO: Perfidiously am I betrayed,— Her hand with scorn reject!

NEV. & ST. BRIS: Oh, what disgrace! what outrage deep! I live but for revenge.

MAR: He by refusing thus her hand, Avenges the insult.

**CORO:** O, delir, qual oltraggio crudele,
Chi lo sforza a spezzar un tal nodo!

**VAL:** L' como io mai potei
Mertar cotanto oltraggio?
Vinta dal duol perdei
La speme ed il coraggio.

**RAU:** E soffrir io dovrei
Tant' ont e tanto oltraggio!

**NEV. E SAN BRIS:** Tremar, languir io sento
Il core a tanto oltraggio!

**MARG., URB., VAL. E DAME:** O deliro, o demenza!
Ite lontau da quì.

**RAU:** Non più Imen, tradimento, perfidia!
Ma l' oltraggio saprò col valore
Sì, più tardi saprò col valore
Lavar l' onta, far salvo l' onor.

**NEV. E SAN BRIS:** Mio furor sol col sangue fia calmo!
Sì, l' oltraggio saprò vendicar;—
Vien partiam, che purir l' offensore
A me tocca e far salvo l' onor.

**MAR:** Il mio core fa plauso al valore
Di Raul, che spezzò quest' Imene.
Ah! partiam, nel suo giusto furore,
Saprà bene far salvo l' onor.

**VAL:** Nel mio cor più non avvi speranza;
In un giorno il coraggio mancò;
Ho perduto la pace, l' amore,
E per me più non v' è che dolor.

**MARG:** D' un amor che ignorava il potere
Prese impero avvampò nel suo cor.

**CORO:** Ah, partiamo! Ei punir l' offensore
Saprà bene, e far salvo l' onor.

*FINE DELL ATTO PRIMO.*

# ■ ATTO II

## SCENA I

*Un prato sulle sponde della Senna.—A sinistra un osteria, presso la quale molti, giovani studenti, Cattolici sono seduti in compagnia delle loro belle.—A destra un altra osteria, ove sono varii Sol-*

**CHO:** What madness! oh, what insult dire,
To thus reject her hand!

**VAL:** Oh, how have I deserved this stain,
This outrage at his hands?
Grief now dispels all hope while he brands
My brow with shame.

**RAO:** Oh, how can I endure this shame?
This outrage deep efface?

**NEV. & ST. BRIS:** My heart with bursting rage is filled,
At this severe disgrace!

**MARG., URB., VAL. & LADIES:** Oh, what outrageous madness!
Away, and leave this place!

**RAO:** Though treason and malice my hopes may overturn,
No power shall make me confirm this marriage.
No more shall I hold myself bound by my vow,
And the fury is vain that you wreak on me now.

**NEV. & ST. BRIS:** I tremble with rage when I think of the shame;
But mine be the task to avenge her fair fame.
His blood shall flow for this outrage in torrents,
For honor insulted has called for the blow.

**MAR:** It is the pride of his heart has his courage inspired,
It is a proper disgust that his feelings have fired;
There is honor and faith in breaking his vow,
And your fury is vain that you wreak on him now.

**VAL:** Oh, what have I done to deserve this great scorn?
My poor heart is breaking, and shaken each nerve;
I have lost at one blow all my heart held most dear,
And nothing can avail in my misery here.

**MAR:** Ah! she knew not how great the power of love,
In the heart that she gave so freely.

**CHO:** Ah, away! to punish this offender, we trust,
He knows how, and his honor thus save.

*END OF THE FIRST ACT.*

# ■ ACT II

## SCENE I

*A meadow on the banks of the Seine.—On the left an inn, near which several Catholic students and young girls are seated.—On the right another inn, where various Huguenots are seen drinking*

*dati Ugonotti che bevono e giocano a dadi.—Più verso il fondo l' esterno d' una Capella.—La scena è ingombra di gente d' ogni classe che va e viene.*

**CORO DI PASSAGGERI:**
Quest' è giorno di festa,
Tregua diamo al lavor,
E in allegria modesta
Scordiam ogni dolor.

**CORO DI SOLDATI UGONOTTI:**
Rataplan, rataplan, rataplan!
*(Imitando con le mani il battere del tamburo.)*
Con la spada di battaglia
Che non teme la mitraglia
A' guerrieri della fè
Dissi andiam, venite a me.
Sono il vostro capitano,
A vi guido alla vittoria,
O del Cielo all' alma gloria;—
Presto andiam, venite a me.
A noi bravi Calvinisti,
Son le figlie de' papisti;
A noi gloria, a noi bottino,
A noi gioia, a noi buon vino.
Tutto al forte quì appartiene,
E il buon vin serbato in cella:
Per gli altari, e per le cene
Colmerà il nostro bicchier.
Rataplan, rataplan, rataplan! etc.
Sì, beviam, viva la guerra!
Sì, beviamo a Coligny.
*In questa momento una Processione di giovane Figlie Cattoliche, compare a destra, accompagnando il corteggio dello sposalizio di Nevers e Valentina, che, sequiti da lor parenti ed amici, si diriggono verso la capella a manca.*

**LITANIE:**
Ave Maria,
O Vergin pia,
Prega il Signor
Pel peccator!
Sempre sei stella
Nella procella,
E dall' error,
Ne salvi ognor!
Salve, o Maria,
O Vergin pia!
*Entra Marcello in scena col capello in testa.*

**MAR:** Il Signor di San Bris?

**COR:** Tu parlargli non puoi.

**MAR:** Perchè?

**CORO:** La fronte inclina!

**MAR:** Per qual ragion ciò fare?
Quivi non avvi altar.

**CORO:** Ah, l' empio!

**BOIS:** Egli ha ragion.

**CORO:** Rataplan, etc.

*and playing at dice.—In the background, the exterior of a Chapel.—The back of the stage is crowded with persons of every description, passing to and fro.*

**CHORUS OF CITIZENS:**
From our labors reposing,
With dance and with song,
In mirth and in revelry
The hours pass along.

**CHORUS OF HUGUENOT SOLDIERS.:**
Rataplan, rataplan, rataplan!
*(Imitating with hands the beating of the drum.)*
Upon the foe like lightning flying,
The Papal wolves to the death defying,
He cried, "Who would be free, follow me!
Your old faithful captain leads you,
To death or victory he precedes you—
to death or victory, follow me!"
Long live our captain—long live he!
Drink to our father, Coligny!
Warriors brave our armies swell,
Riches great our coffers tell,
While daughters of our foemen fell
Yield to our power.
To us belongs all strength in arms;
While store of wine our spirit charms,
And with its potent draughts inspired,
We pass the hour.
Rataplan, rataplan, rataplan!
Yes, war—drink to war!
A health to Coligny!
*(At this moment a Procession of young Catholic maidens enters on the right, accompanying the bridal cortège of Nevers and Valentina, who, followed by their relations and friends, advance towards the chapel on the left.)*

**LITANY:**
Ave Maria,
Oh, holy Virgin,
Look down upon us!
Raise your voice for us,
And pardon ask!
You can protect us,
You can direct us,
This is your task!
Ave Maria,
Oh, holy Virgin!
*(Enter Marcel, without removing his hat.)*

**MAR:** His lordship of St. Bris?

**CHO:** You cannot speak to him.

**MAR:** Why not?

**CHO:** Bend, sir, your knee!

**MAR:** Why should I do so?
I see no altars here.

**CHO:** Heretic!

**BOIS:** He is right.

**CHO:** Rataplan, etc.

# Act II, Scene I

CORO DI CATTOLICI: L' alme lor son già perdute:
O i profani ch' esser denno
Arsi in terra, e che salute
Non avranno estinti ancor.
(Danso.)
Entrano San Bris, Nevers, Maurevert, uscendo dalla Capella.

NEV: (A San Bris.) Per adempir ad un solenne voto,
Fin a stasera a piè del sacro altar
Rimanersi domanda Valentina in preghira;
Obbedirele voglio, e, degli amici insieme,
A riprender verro la sposa mia,
Per quindi accompagnarla al mio castello.
(Esce.)

SAN BRIS: Così s' estinguerà con queste illustra
Nodo l' oltraggio che Raul ne fece
Col suo rifuto; ma scordare nol posso;
S' ei s' offre a' colpi miei—

MAR: (Entrando con una lettera in mano, e con aria d' importanza.) Al Signor di Sant Bris,
Il mio Signore questa lettera invia, ed io che.

SAN BRIS: (Interrompendolo.) Porgi!
E di Raul alfine ei tornera.
(Prende la lettera e legge.)

MAR: Con la Regina, tutti tre pocanzi
Lasciammo la Turrena, e giungemmo a Parigi.

SAN BRIS: E grazie al Ciel ne rendo!
Sfidare ei' m' osa, e mandami il cartello!

MAR: O, Cielo! qual sorpresa!

SAN BRIS: Quest' oggi istesso al Prè an Clercs, di notte
Quando l' ombre faran sgombre le vie,
Ei promette di venir.

MAU: Un Dio vendicatore
Lo spinge al suo destin!

SAN BRIS: (A Marcello.) L' aspetteremo.
(A Maurevert.) La sfida de Nevers
Si tenga ascosa in un giorno d' Imen correr non de?
In certame fatal periglio alcuno.

MAU: E voi neppur, per castigare un empio
Altri mezzi vi son che approva il Cielo.

SAN BRIS: E quai son dessi?

MAU: Meco venite, e chiara
L' opra saprete ch' oggi il Ciel prepara.
(Rientrano nella Capella.)
Comincia a Fare oscuro.—S' ode la campana del Coprifuoco.—

CHO. OF CATHOLICS: Their souls are wholly lost,
Profane and impious men,
Who ought to suffer once on earth,
And after death again.
(A Dance.)
(Enter St. Bris, Nevers and Maurevert, from the Chapel.)

NEV: (To St. Bris.) To fulfill a cherished vow,
At the altar's foot, in solemn prayer,
Valentina desires to linger silent there;
It is well; and followed by my numerous friends,
I will return to seek the joys most dear,
And bid her welcome home with heart sincere.
(Exit.)

ST. BRIS: And thus by this alliance great and politic,
May I punish Sir Raoul's insolent refusal;
But not so soon shall I forget it,
And should he cross my path—

MAR: (Entering with a letter in his hand, and with an air of importance.) For the Count de St. Bris
My master sends this letter, and bids me say—

ST. BRIS: (Interrupting him.) Give it to me!
Sir Raoul has returned, then, at last.
(Takes and reads letter.)

MAR: With the Queen we three have lately quitted
Fair Touraine, and come to Paris.

ST. BRIS: And now I thank you Heaven!
He dares defy me, and sends a challenge!

MAR: Oh, Heaven! what do I hear?

ST. BRIS: At evening this day, near to the Pré-aux-Clercs,
When shades of night in peace shall wrap the spot,
He will come.

MAU: Here, then, he'll shortly be;
With Heaven's aid the wretch shall not escape!

ST. BRIS: (To Marcel.) We shall await him.
(To Maurevert.) Conceal this from De Nevers;
I would not on his bridal day
He should be mixed up in this fray.

MAU: Neither should you, for to punish such a crime
Heaven will surely divine some chastisement.

ST. BRIS: What do you say?

MAU: Heaven wills it; come, and you shall know
What means are in your reach to end your woe.
(Exeunt into the Chapel.)
(Night comes on.—The Curfew-

Vari borghesi traversano la scena.—Un Arciero seguito bella veglia notturna fa la guardia.

L' ARC: Rientrate, abitanti di Parigi,
E nell' albergo suo ognun sen vada.
Partir è uopo da questo loco,
Che questa è l' ora del coprifuoco.

CORO: Rientrate, etc.
(La folla si desperde.—Soldati entrano in un osteria, i borghesi, le donne, e gli Studenti nell' alta.)
Entrano San Bris e Maurevert, dalla Capella.

SAN BRIS: (Con mistero a Maurevert.) Or d' accordo noi siam, ben intendesti?

MAU: In men d' un ora
Tu poi contar su nostri amici ancora.
(Escono.)
Valentina comparisce alla porta della Capella.

VAL: O terror! mi spaventa l' eco de' miei piè.
Perd to ho la ragione!
E vaneggia il mio cor!
A ognun nascosta dietro a quell' altare,
Sentii tremando, aimè!
Quella trama crudele!
Sottrar lo deo dalle nemiche squadre.
Non per lui solo, o Ciel?
Ma per l' onor d'un padre.
Come mai prevenir potrò Raul?
Entra Marcello.

MAR: L' aspetterò, anch' io combatterò;
E s' egli muore, io pure morirò.

MAR: Nella notte io sol quì veglio—
Ah! mi par che alcun quì viene;
Ma prudenza mi trattiene—
Da lontano osserverò.

VAL: Ciel, pietà del mio dolore!
Quest' è il loco, e incalzan l' ore,
Come mai, con qual destrezza
Dal periglio il salverò?

MAR: Chi va là?

VAL: L, lieta sorte!
Di Marcel la voce essa è.

MAR: A quest' ora, in questo loco,
Chi mi chiama, chi va là?

VAL: Di quà vieni!

MAR: Chi va là?
La parola, o sei tu morto!

VAL: Raul.
(Avvanzando.)

MAR: Ah, questo basta! Una donna e velata!

VAL: Tremi tu?

bell is heard.—Various Citizens traverse the stage.—An Officer, followed by the Night Watch, comes on guard.)

OFF: Retire, citizens of Paris,
Shut yourselves within your houses,
Let all noise cease, depart in peace:
The curfew hour has come.

CHO: Retire, etc.
(The crowd disperses—Soldiers enter one inn, the Citizens, the Women, and the Students, the other.)
(Enter St. Bris and Maurevert, from the Chapel.)

ST. BRIS: (mysteriously to Maurevert.) It is agreed then—you well understand me?

MAU: In one hour from this time
Your friends will all be here assembled.
(Exeunt.)
(Enter Valentina, from the porch of the Chapel.)

VAL: Oh, Heaven! at my own footfall I tremble!
My brain is sore distraught!
Have I heard them aright?
Behind yon sainted shrine, concealed from view,
Each word fell on my ear:
A horrid plot to take away his life!
I seek to save him from their treachery,
Not for his sake alone, oh Heaven!
But to preserve a father's honor.
How can I warn Raoul of his peril?
(Enter Marcel.)

MAR: I'll wait for him here—I too, will fight;
If he falls, I will die with him!

MAR: Here by night I wander alone—
Ah! what sound?—footsteps come this way!
Prudence counsels to conceal me.
Yes, I'll watch, and still be near.

VAL: Oh, great Heaven! pity my anguish!
The dread moment fast approaches!
How, ah! how shall I inform him
Of all I know; and all I fear?

MAR: Who goes there?

VAL: Oh, how fortunate!
It is the voice of good Marcel.

MAR: At this hour, in this place,
Who calls on me?—who goes there?

VAL: Pray, come here!

MAR: Who goes there?
Give the word, quickly, or you die!

VAL: Raoul.
(Advancing.)

MAR: Ah, all is well! What! a woman, veiled?

VAL: Are you afraid?

**MAR:** Che? io timor! No, son Marcel
Son la spada d'Israel,
E 'l terror dell' infedel.

**VAL:** Or m' odi ben, Raul,
Or dovrà quì recarsi.

**MAR:** È ver.

**VAL:** Per un duello.

**MAR:** È ver: contro un profano,—
A vendicar verrà
L' onor e i dritti suoi.

**VAL:** Ch' ei non venga quì solo,
Ma forte scorta il segua.
(*Esce Marcello.*)
Ah! l' ingrato d' offesa mortale
Ha ferito un cor puro e fedele!
Ed ancor quell' immagin crudele
Cerco invan cancellar dal mio cor.
Voglio dunque salvar la sua vita
Come un giorno ei salvava il mio
onor;—
Se poi deggio scordarlo, morrò.
*Rientra Marcello.*

**MAR:** Io volea prevenirlo e salvar-
lo,
Ma scordai che di casa egli uscì;
Egli quì m' ordinò d' aspettarlo.
Ove adesso trovarlo potrò
Come adesso poterlo avvisar?
Giusto Ciel! se di quà m' allontan
Può quell' orda assalirlo ad un trat-
to,
Cercherà di difendersi invano
Domandando Marcello ei morrà.
Ah, restiam! ma quì sol che potrò?
Qual fedel servitore morire
Sul suo corpo, tu, o Ciel, mi
concedi;
Tu l' angoscia del core che vedi,
A miei voti pietà non negar.

**VAL:** Intesi siamo;—addio!

**MAR:** No, chi sei tu, pria dimmi.

**VAL:** Io son—

**MAR:** Ebben!

**VAL:** Io sono—
Una donna, o Marcello, che l'adora,
E che morrà ma per salvar suoi dì.

**MAR:** E fia vero?

**VAL:** Tu comprender non puoi ne
sapere,
Qual m' affanna indicibil tormento
Se la fede, l' amore, il dovere
A vicenda mi straziano il cuor.
Per salvare una vita si cara,
Padre, onore, tradisco ed oblio!
Ma il perdono che spero de Dio
Mi sostiene, m' infonde vigor.

**MARCEL:** Non pentirtio giovinetta,
Dell' affetto a lui mostrato; Deh non
pianger, ed accetta il tributo del
mio cor! La preghiera del vegliardo,
paria un ben dal ciel

**MAR:** Who? I afraid! No, I am Mar-
cel!
The old sword of Israel,
As the vile infidels know full well.

**VAL:** Now hearken, pray;
Raoul has here an assignation?

**MAR:** It is true.

**VAL:** For a duel.

**MAR:** True: with a man of sin,—
Which, by the aid of his good
sword,
Fear not, he'll bravely win.

**VAL:** Let him not venture here,
Unless his friends are near.
(*Exit Marcel.*)
Victim of unrequited love,
My heart for ever dead!
Yet, spite of all, this bosom throbs
For him I never must wed.
I'll watch over his life and honor,
As he did over mine;
And oh, to save him, life resign.
(*Re-enter Marcel.*)

**MAR:** How, oh, how can I warn
him?
He has left his abode,
And at this spot we are to meet,
This fated place I must not leave,
For where to find him I know
not,—
No guide have I to direct my steps.
The assassins may fall upon him—
Then his servant should be near to
him.
He shall never vainly call upon me;
No, no, I will wait for him here.
Oh, Heaven! at least this concede,
That I freely may share his peril;
To the anguish of one faithful heart,
Oh, listen, and grant his sad prayer.

**VAL:** You know enough:—farewell!

**MAR:** No, say first, who are you?

**VAL:** I am—

**MAR:** Proceed!

**VAL:** I am—
A woman, Marcel, who loves
him,—
Who would give my life away for
him.

**MAR:** Can this be true?

**VAL:** Ah! my bosom is tortured
with anguish,
To which no tongue can give ex-
pression;
In torments unceasing I languish,
In the conflict between duty and
love!
To preserve one whose life I must
cherish,
I betray both a parent and honor!
Every hope upon earth now per-
ishes—
All I ask for is pardon above!

**MARCEL:** Grieve not, grieve not,
noble child! Marcel is confessing
his wrongs, Here gives you now an
old man's blessing, Yes, his blessing and his love! Weep not, weep

bramato: Di pietà per te un sguardo; Si, otterrà dal tuo signor.

Dir intesi che la donna
Ha lo sguardo e il cor fallace,
Ma costei non è mendace
Quì venir sembra dal Ciel.
(*Esce Valentina, e prende rifugio
nella Capella.*)
Grave danno il minaccia,
Ed io ignoro qual sia.
Eh! voi mie vecchie gambe all' erta
state,
Per sottrarre il meschin dal suo
periglio
Ciela! è lui, e San Bris!
*Entrano San Bris, Raul e quattro
Testimonii.*

**SAN BRIS:** (*A Raul.*) Ah! nel me-
desmo tempo
Ambo esser quì. Va ben.

**RAU:** Che dubitaste forse dell' esa-
tezza mia.

**MAR:** (*Da se.*) Or come mai del tradimento infame
Sventar le trame?

**RAU:** (*A Marcello.*) Sei tu, mio
buon Marcello?

**MAR:** Sì, dal Ciel scese un angelo,
Che annunziò la tempesta.
Signor, quì ascoso nu tradimento v'
è.

**RAU:** Deliri tu, Marcel?
I patti del certame, ora fissar io las-
cio a voi.
Signori, m' affido al vostro onor.
(*Indirizzandosi a' quattro Testi-
monii.*)

**TUTTI:** (*Meno Marcello.*) De dritti
miei ho l' alma accesa—
Per vendicarmi dall' offesa
Il ferro sol gindicar de'.
Voglio ragione del vile oltraggio,
Temprato acciaro, e buon coraggio,
Per tutti il Cielo, ciascun per sè.

**MAR:** (*Da se.*) Oh, qual dolore il
ciel mi dona!
Piangi, Marcel, Dio n' abbandona!
Povero amico, tradito egli è!
Pietà Signore, per lui mercè!

**MAR. E SAN BRIS:** La tema in lor
già si palesa,
La spada in mano or già lor pesa,
Ma dell' assalto si vegga il fin.

**TUTTI GLI ALTRI:** Sì, noi sprezzia-
mo un tale oltraggio,
Felloni or su, presto in difesa,—
Già del pugnar desio la fin!
Andiam, Signori, la spada in man
A uostri piè cader dovran;
In guardia, in guardia, felloni in
guardia!
Si alfine esangui al suol cadran!
(*Mentre stanno per azzufarsi,
Marcello, osservando infondo
vede avvanzar qualcuno, e tosto*

not, I implore you, Heaven may yet
restore you to peace: It shall be my
humble prayer; For, whatever your
creed. It is from above!

I have ever been led to believe,
That all women were born to de-
ceive;
But on her face sweet truth is im-
pressed,
And with Heaven's own goodness
seems blessed.
(*Exit Valentina, taking refuge in
the Chapel.*)
Some great danger hovers over him,
Though what it is I cannot tell.
You must be watchful now, old sol-
dier,
To save his life you love so well.
Ah! he comes, and with him St. Bris!
(*Enter St. Bris, Raoul, and four
Seconds.*)

**ST. BRIS:** (*To Raoul.*) Ah! both are
here met
At the appointed hour. It is well.

**RAO:** Doubted you that I should
keep my word?

**MAR:** (*Aside.*) How can I frustrate
their treachery,
And impart to him their designs?

**RAO:** (*To Marcel.*) You here, my
good Marcel?

**MAR:** Yes, an angel appeared to
me,
Foretelling the coming danger.
Treason lurks beneath your feet.

**RAO:** You're surely mad, Marcel!
These gentlemen fix the rules of
our combat.
I have confidence in their honor.
(*Turning to the Seconds.*)

**ALL:** (*Except Marcel.*) In a good
cause relying,
In death the foe defying,
Content to stand or fall,
While this quarrel just defending,
On the sword alone depending,
Each for himself, and Heaven for
all.

**MAR:** (*Aside.*) Oh, what a sight for
these old eyes!
Weep, oh Marcel! God hears you
not!
For him, my master, heed my cries!
Look down in mercy from the skies!

**MAR. & ST. BRIS:** With fear their
faces now turn pale,
Their swords are trembling in their
hands.
Let us now the attack begin.

**ALL THE OTHERS:** We all despise
your base conduct,—
Come on, let each himself de-
fend,—
Let's hasten to the combat's end!
Proceed; let each with steel against
steel,
Fight on until his foeman fall;—
Soon our deep vengeance you shall
feel;
Come on, though death may grasp
us all!

## Act II, Scene I

*(si precipita fra i combattenti.)*

*(Just as they are on the point of fighting, Marcel sees some one approaching, and throws himself between the combatants.)*

MAR: Arrestatevi olà! alcun quì giunge.
*(Rau., i suoi Testimonii, e Marcello, vengosi circondati dai Seguaci di Maurevert.)*
Un tradimento è questo—il Ciel vi mira!
*(S' ode nell' interno dell' osteria il canto dei Soldati Ugonotti.)*

MAR: Hold, hold! some one approaches.
*(Raoul, his Seconds, and Marcel, are surrounded by the followers of Maurevert.)*
Ah, what treachery—Heaven sees you!
*(From the inn on the right is heard the song of the Huguenot Soldiers.)*

CORO INTERNO: Rataplan, viva la guerra, etc.

CHO: (*inside.*) Rataplan, upon the foe, etc.

MAR: (*Forte battendo alla porta dell' osteria.*) Coligny!—difensor della fede!
Tutto il nemico è sorto—
Reca il Ciel la vittoria alle nostr' armi.

MAR: (*Knocking loudly at the door of the inn.*)
Coligny!—defend your faith!
Hasten, the foe is rising—
May Heaven crown us with victory!

SAN BRIS: A me, studenti miei, quivi accorrete;
Quest' è un vil tradimento—ormai venite!
*Cattolici escono in folla dall' osteria a manca; da quella a destra escono gli Ugonotti. Ambo i partiti si guardano con aria minacciosa.*

ST. BRIS: Students, come out—haste to our aid;
Help, help! for we are betrayed!
*(The Catholics come out from the inn on the left, the Huguenots from that on the right. They look at each other in threatening attitudes.)*

TUTTI: Siam quì, felloni—indietro!

ALL: We are here—begone, varlets!

CAT: Facitor di preghiero,
Turba di fantucchiere!

CAT: You regiment of hypocrites,
Mutterers of Prayers!

UG: Riponete le spade,
Pinzocheri guerrier!

HUG: Put up your swords,
You cowards' heirs!

CAT: Onor di Calvinisti!

CAT: You honor to Calvin!

UG: Beì fregi di Papisti!

HUG: You jewels of Rome!

CAT: Si abbruci l' infedel!

CAT: The infidels let us destroy!

UG: A morte l' impostor!

HUG: By our hands the impostors shall die!

DONNE CAT: Cenare alla caserna,
A miscredenti insiem!

CAT. WOMEN: Supping in the barracks there
With unbelievers vile!

DONNE UG: Danzare alla taverna,
Agli studenti insiem!

HUG. WOMEN: While you in public-houses
Have been reveling the while!

CAT: Quetatevi, sfrontate!

CAT: Away, degraded ones!

UG: Tacete, svergognate!

HUG: Hypocrites, hold your tongues!

CAT: Gioielle d' Ugonotti!

CAT: Chaste dames of the Huguenots!

UG: Amiche de bigotti!

HUG: Pure mistresses of bigots!

TUTTI: Scaldata abbiam la testa;
Zitto, lontan di quà!
La morte a chi resiste;
Tacete, zitto là!
*In questo momento entrano alcune Guardie reale con torce, schiarando la via alla Regina, che entra in scena a cavallo. I disputanti si arrestano.*

ALL: Our brains are on fire,—
Hence, be silent, away!
Death to all who resist,
Or who dare disobey!
*(At this moment enter the Royal Guards, bearing torches, and preceding the Queen, who enters on horseback. The disputants desist.)*

MAR: Alto là! ognun rispetti la Regina.

MAR: Desist! the Queen approaches!

MARG: Come, in Parigi ancora,
Del fratel mio in presenza,
Gli eccessi de' partiti
Si denno paventar? Entrar non pos-

MARG: What, even here in Paris,
Beneath the eyes of my brother,
Still the excess of your party spirit
Have I to fear? My palace, even,

so
In seno a lari miei
Senza udire, ò trovar, discordie e guerra?

I cannot enter in tranquility;
But sounds of strife, instead, greet my ear.

SAN BRIS: E chi dessi accusar?
Colui che ne tradiva,
*(Mostrando Raul.)*
E ne sforzava a domandar giustizia.

ST. BRIS: And who is to be blamed?
With him was the fault;
*(Pointing to Raoul.)*
I'm forced to insist on justice.

RAU: (*Mostrando San Bris.*) La colpa è di lui so lo,
Che contro ogni ragione
Del più vile attentato
Quì colpevol s' è reso.

RAO: (*Pointing to St. Bris.*)
The fault must rest with him,
Who did begin the assault
Against treachery, and in defense,
I but pursue what they commence.

MARG: O ciel! chi creder deggio!
Chi d'un sospetto tal mi puo dar prova?

MARG: Oh Heaven! whom shall I believe?
Who can give me proof of this suspicion?

MAR: La prova io dar vi posso!
Essi han voluto assassinare il mio padron.

MAR: I've proof that none can ever gainsay,
They basely would slay my master.

SAN BRIS: Menzogna!

ST. BRIS: It is false!

MAR: Del tradimento infame,
Quivi una donna mi svelò l'arcano.
E tal donna è costei!
*(Indicando Valentina ch' esce dalla Capella.)*
*Entra Valentina.*

MAR: A lady appeared upon this spot
And disclosed to me their treachery,
That is the lady approaching!
*(Pointing to Valentina, who is seen leaving the Chapel.)*
*(Enter Valentina.)*

SAN BRIS: Mia figlia!

ST. BRIS: My daughter!

CORO: O Cielo!

CHO: Oh Heaven!

SAN BRIS: Quale audacia! è credibil? oh, perfidia!

ST. BRIS: What audacity! can I believe it? oh, perfidy!

RAU: Come esser può?

RAO: Can this be true?

MARG: Raul, tutto saprete!

MARG: The truth must be disclosed!

VAL: Signora, per pietà!

VAL: Oh, my Queen, have pity on me!

RAU: E quel reo tradimento
Di cui fui testimone
Al castel di Nevers?

RAO: But her breach of faith, her perfidy,
To which I myself was witness,
In the house of De Nevers?

MARG: Ella v' andava
Per ispezzar un odiato imene.

MARG: She went to supplicate
That her hated marriage might be broken off.

SAN BRIS: E da questo mattin
D' un altro ella è la sposa!

ST. BRIS: Before the morn shall dawn,
She will be the bride of another!

CORO: D' un altra? oh, sommo Ciel!
*(Odesi lontano suono.)*

CHO: Another? oh, great Heaven!
*(Distant music is heard.)*

SAN BRIS: Ma che! ascoltate del trionfante sposo
Il corteggio s' avvia.
Sì, lo sento esultar d' alta allegria.
Tal pompa è degna in ver
De' San Bris, de' Nevers.
*Vedesi approdare una scialuppa, riccamente addobbata ed illuminata. Essa è occupata da Musici, Paggi, Cavalieri, e Dame, che formano il corteggio delle nozze di Nevers che sbarca il primo.*

ST. BRIS: Hark! even now the bridegroom comes!
The escort approaches with speed;
Yes, I hear its exulting tones.
And well such splendor suits, indeed,
The Saint Bris and De Nevers.
*(A boat, richly decorated, is seen to approach, occupied by Musicians, Pages, Knights and ladies of Nevers' brilliant nuptial suite. Nevers steps first from the boat.)*

NEV: (*A Valentina.*) Nobil donzella,
Deh vieni, ove l' amore d' uno sposo ti chiama. Soddisfatti i tuoi voti, o rispondi a misi?
Venite a celebrar si lieto giorno.

NEV: (*To Valentina.*) Noble lady,
Come where joy and hope await you;
True to your vow, accept of mine!
And make my happiness encompass you.

*(A Signori.)*
Ove amistà v' aspette,
Al festin d' Imeneo.
Schiavo ognor ti sarò,
*(A Valentina.)*
Orgoglioso e altero
De' miei lacci d' amore.
*(Tutti fanno onore agli Sposi. Nevers prende Valentina per le mano, e la guida alla barca, seguiti da San Bris e tutto il corteggio.)*

**GRAND CHORUS:** Il destin che dal ciel lor s' appresta; Di piacer i lor dì colmerà; Il castel che risuon dalla festa, Di fortuna il soggiorno or sarà!

**CHO:** S' unirà delle danze all' incanto
Il fragor degli evviva e del canto;
Per lodare in lor metro la bella,
La gentil che piegava all' amor.

**SOL:** Non più pace all' acciaro,— oramaì
Noi dobbiam nostra sorte affidare;
E il meschin più non sappia trovare
Che di nostra vendetta il furor.
*(Il corteggio si scosta dalla riva, ansiosamente guardato dalla moltitudine—Raul sostenuto da Marcello mostrasi in preda al dolore—I soldati de' due partiti si ritirano da opposti lati et con aria minacciosa.)*

*FINE DELL' ATTO SECONDO.*

# ■ ATTO III

## SCENA I

*Sala nel Castello di Nevers, ornata di ritratti di famiglia.—Gran porta in fondo—A sinistra una porta che conduce agli appartamenti di Valentina.—A destra una porta segreta, e una finestra che guarda sulla strada.*

*Valentina uscendo da' suoi appartamenti, immersa in profondi pensieri.*

**VAL:** Eccomi sola ormai, sola sel mio dolore!
A pianti senza fine condannar mi voleste,
O padre mio, Raul ebbe il mio core,
E a un altro voi lo prometteste! E Tu,
Che supplica invan ne' miei martiri,
Tu che permesso l' hai quest' imeneo funesto—
Gran Dio! tu raddolcir degna almeno il miomal,
Disperdi un sovvenir al viver mio fatal!
In preda al duol, un sogno ancor mi bea
Che per lui sol in sen mi batte il cor.

---

*(To the Suite.)*
Before our friends who here await
To join our Hymeneal fête,
I'll pledge my life to you.
*(To Valentina.)*
I ever shall prize, all joys above,
The silken bonds of your sweet love!
*(All pay their homage to the bride. Nevers takes Valentina by the hand, and leads her to the boat, followed by St. Bris and the cortege.)*

**GRAND CHORUS:** May kind Heaven ever shed blessings over them: May content, peace, and joy, gird them round; May no care ever annoy: but, before them, In their path, oh may love still be found!

**CHO:** Loved and happy, now we hail you!
May no sorrows ever assail ye!
But joy be ever, ever yours,
Such as true love alone ensures.

**SOLDIERS:** No more peace, no more quiet,—
Nothing but revelry and riot;
Nothing but battle's fell disquiet,
Till our latest breath.
*(The boat leaves the shores, anxiously observed by the crowd. Raoul, supported by Marcel, seems a prey to grief. The Soldiers of both parties, from opposite sides, regard each other with threatening attitudes.)*

*END OF THE SECOND ACT.*

# ■ ACT III

## SCENE I

*A Room in the Castle of De Nevers, decorated with family portraits.—A large door at the further end.—On the left a door leading to Valentina's apartments.—On the right a door covered with tapestry, and a window overlooking the street.*

*Enter Valentina from her apartment, with an air of profound pensiveness.*

**VAL:** At length I am alone,—alone with my sorrows!
To eternal woe my father has condemned me;
Raoul alone can ever possess my heart,
While you have given my hand to another!
Oh, You whom I in vain have supplicated,—
You who has allowed this fatal marriage—
High Heaven! deign at least to aid me now,
And shed sweet oblivion over dark memory!
A prey to grief which I can never

---

Crudo pensier! Ah, non mi far più rea,
Fuggirlo vò, ed a lui penso ognor!
Da lunge ancor sua voce cara
L' amor del ciel fa in me tacer.
L' imagin sua, a piè dell' ara,
Fin sull' altar parmi veder!
*Entra Raul, dalla porta in fondo.*
*(Vendendo comparir Raul.)*
Giusto cielo? e sei tu? tu il cui temuto aspetto
Qual rimorso crudel m' insegue ognora!

**RAU:** Si, sì, son io che vengo, dell' ombre fra l'orrore,
A colpevole eguale sotto pena mortale,
Che dell' afflitto cor soccombe al gran dolor!

**VAL:** Ma che vuoi tu da me?

**RAU:** Nulla: vederti sol pria di morire.

**VAL:** *(Spaventata.)* Che sento? e ver pur fia?
E mio padre? e Nevers?

**RAU:** *(Freddamente.)* Sì, quì incontrarli posso.
E vero,—io lo sapea.

**VAL:** Di cor feroci entrambi,
T' uccideran. Ah! vanne!

**RAU:** Io quì li attendo.

**VAL:** Alcun quì viene; ah! vanne!

**RAU:** No, quì resto,—è per te non paventare.

**VAL:** *(Tutta tremante.)* Il padre, il mio consorte!
*(Vendendoli venire.)*
Per me, pel mio onor,
Deh! ne schiva il furora!
*(Raul si nasconde dietro le cortine.*
*Entrano San Bris, Nevers, Tavannes, con altri Signori, Cattolici, e detta.*

**SAN BRIS:** *(A' Signori.)* Un cenno della corte ora quì vi raduna,
È giunta l' ora alfine, in cui debbo ad ognuno
Un progretto svelare che già protegge il cielo,
Ch' è da gran tempo in cor della Regina!*
*Caterina de' Medici.

**VAL:** Io tremo!

**SAN BRIS:** *(A Valentina.)* Tu, mia figlia, or esci.

**VAL:** Ah, padre!

---

banish,
My love the only thought I ponder over;
And though I know to love him is a crime,
The more I would forget, I love the more!
Alas! powers who know my inmost thought,
Vain is the succor I implore;
For while in prayer I kneel at the altar,
The while I pray, I do but love him more!
*(Enter Raoul, from the door in the centre.)*
*(On discovering Raoul.)*
Gracious Heaven! is it he? or is it a vision
That ever haunts my every thought!

**RAO:** Yes, is it I, who come in the darkness of night,
Gliding like a criminal, borne down with sorrow,
Yet still living on, overwhelmed in despair!

**VAL:** But what would you with me?

**RAO:** Nothing: I hoped to see you before I die.

**VAL:** *(Alarmed.)* What do I hear?—impossible!
But my father? My husband?

**RAO:** *(Coldly.)* Yes, that I may meet them here
I know but too well.

**VAL:** They are still inflexible—
They will kill you. Ah, fly!

**RAO:** I will await them here.

**VAL:** Hear you not footsteps? Ah, fly!

**RAO:** No, I will remain; fear not for me.

**VAL:** *(Trembling.)* My father! My husband!
*(Seeing them coming.)*
For my sake, for my honor's sake,
Avoid them; oh, hasten and conceal yourself!
*(Raoul hides himself behind the tapestry.*
*(Enter St. Bris, Nevers, Tavannes, followed by Noblemen, Catholics, etc.)*

**ST. BRIS:** *(To the Nobles.)*
By order of the Queen, we assemble in this place;
The time has arrived when the plot must be known.
For the project which brings us salvation forever,
Is worthy the lady who sits on the throne!*
*Catherine de Medici.

**VAL:** I tremble!

**ST. BRIS:** *(To Valentina.)* Leave us, my daughter.

**VAL:** Ah, my father!

NEV: Perchè? Lo zel ch' ella ha di nostra fede
Lascia che senza rischio lei presente si possa
Del ciel, della regina le brame disvelar.

SAN BRIS: Di guai crescenti ognor e d' un empio conflitto
Volete insieme a me liberar questo suol?

I SIG: Sì, lo vogliam!

SAN BRIS: Del nostro eccelso Rè, del cielo e della patria,
Volete voi con me colpire i traditor?

I SIG: Sì, lo vogliam!

SAN BRIS: Ebben! del Nume che noi tutta ainta
Il minaccioso acciar su lor sta per piombar:
Degli Ugonotti l' empia setta e ria
Fra poco sparirà.

NEV: Chi li condanna?

SAN BRIS: Il ciel?

I SIG: Il ciel!

NEV: E chi li colpirà?

SAN BRIS: Voi!

I SIG: Noi?

NEV: Io?
(Con orrore.)

SAN BRIS: D' un sacro zel l' ardore
Vi elevi e scaldi l' alma,
A voi dan forza e palma
Il Ciel, l' onore, e il Rè.
V' accenda un pio furore
Contro quel popol rio;
V' infiammi l' ardir mio,
L' amor di vostra fè.

NEV: Tradir degg' io l' onore?
Sì vil no non son io,
Ne può incolparmi il Rè.

VAL: Chi frena il suo furore?
(Indicando San Bris.)
Tu mi sostieni, o Dio?
Abbi pietà di me!

TAV: Eguale al tuo furore,
Sarà lo giuro il mio,
In sostenar le fé,

CORO: Salviam la nostra fè,
Obbediamo al Rè.

SAN BRIS: (A' Signori che lo circondano.) Può il Rè su voi contar?

I SIG: (Meno Nevers.) Sì, lo giuriam!

SAN BRIS: Io duce a voi sarò.

I SIG: (Meno Nevers.) Noi vi seguiamo.

VAL. E SAN BRIS: Ma che? Nevers solo è rimasto muto?

VAL: (Da se.) Che pensa ei mai? O Ciel! io gelo e tremo.

---

NEV: Why? Her virtues and zeal for the faith
Give assurance that she is worthy our confidence
And to receive the orders of our Queen.

ST. BRIS: From growing troubles, and this impious war,
You will, like me, your country still deliver?

NOBLES: We will!

ST. BRIS: Of the King, of Heaven, and our country,
You will, like me, annihilate the enemies?

NOBLES: We will!

ST. BRIS: It is well! the sword on high is swung,
Threatening vengeance on their heads;
And every Huguenot shall fall,
While far and near our fury spreads.

NEV: Who condemns them?

ST. BRIS: Heaven!

NOBLES: Heaven!

NEV: Who shall strike the blow?

ST. BRIS: You!

NOBLES: We?

NEV: I?
(With horror.)

ST. BRIS: To your country, for her honor,
You must your help afford;
And you will be victorious,
For Heaven will guide your sword.
Justice, in its vengeance
Against that impious band,
Inspires our hearts and guides our arms
To slay them from the land.

NEV: Can I my honor stain?
Disgrace it would on me bring,
Though prompted by my King.

VAL: Who can his fury now restrain?
(Pointing to St. Bris.)
Oh Heaven, I call on you!
Have mercy—pity me!

TAV: Like you I boldly swear,
Whatever, may chance, despite
To fight for our true faith.

CHO: Our faith we will defend,
Our King's command attend.

ST. BRIS: (to the Noblemen who surround him.) May the King on you depend?

ALL: (Except Nevers.) We swear it.

ST. BRIS: And I will be your leader.

ALL: (Except Nevers.) And we your followers.

VAL. & ST. BRIS: What! is Nevers alone silent!

VAL: (Aside.) What does he think? Heaven! I tremble.

---

NEV: I traditor feriamo, ma non senza difesa:
Non è il pugnal del vile che noi brandir dobbiamo.

SAN BRIS: Quand' il Rè tel comanda?

NEV: Ei mel comanda invan;
Del mio nome macchiar, non vola fama antica,
Fra gli antenati miei, che quì mi fanno onore,
Prodi guerrier tu vedi, non un solo assassin.

SAN BRIS: E per te la sant' opra dunque fallita audrà?

NEV: No; ma dal disonore io salvo la mia spada.
Tieni; eccola! tra noi giudichi il cielo.
(Spezzando la spada, e gettandogliela a piedi.)

VAL: Ah d' ora in poi tutto confido in voi.
Andiam, più non tardare; vi voglio far palese.
In questo momento s' aprono le porte in fondo, e compariscono Eschiorini e Capi del San Bris armati.

SAN BRIS: (Indirizzandosi a loro, e indicando Nevers.) Sia fatto prigioniere,—a noi mostrossi avverso,—
Fin a doman vegliato sia da voi.

VAL: (Da se.) Possa il ciel disarmar gli sdegni suoi.

NEV: Ragion è meco e onore,
Non preme il cor timore,
Contrastar devo al Rè.

TAV: M' accende un pio furore,
Dover mi sprona e onore,
Obbedir devo al Rè.

SAN BRIS: V' accenda un pio furora,
Dover vi sprona e onore,
Obbedir dessi al Rè.

VAL: Ah! d' un mortal timore
Tutto ho compreso il core;
O Ciel, pietà di me!

CORO: M' accende un pio furora,
Dover mi sprona e onore,
Obbedir de si al Rè.
(Parte degli armati conducon via Nevers.)

SAN BRIS: E voi fedeli al Rè, e al ciel, che in sen vi vede,
Nobili cor, sostegni della fede,
Cittadini e guerrieri, udite i miei pensieri.
Per la città la schiera sparsa sia
Tetra e silente, occupi ogni via.
Indi al date segnal tutti a ferir corriamo!

---

NEV: Strike down our foes, but bravely, face to face;
The soldier's, not the assassin's, wreath we'd claim.

ST. BRIS: But should the King command?

NEV: He would command in vain;
For, though in honor's cause my blood may flow,
Amongst my ancestors, I'd have you know,
Were heroes brave, but no assassins vile.

ST. BRIS: Through you may our purpose be betrayed?

NEV: For murder was my good sword never made.
Take it; and Heaven my judge must be.
(Unsheathing his sword, and throwing it at his feet.)

VAL: From this day forth I will confide in thee!
You must know all—a secret I would tell—
(At this moment the doors in the background open, and Officers and Soldiers of the St. Bris faction enter.)

ST. BRIS: (Addressing them, and pointing to Nevers.) I cannot trust him,—see you guard him well,—
Give him no liberty till morning dawns.

VAL: (Aside.) May Heaven their angry feelings soothe.

NEV: Honor is on my side.
Although I have denied
Obedience to my King.

TAV: My heart's inflamed within me
By honor, faith, and duty,—
Let us obey the King.

ST. BRIS: Honor now combines with duty,
Inflames your hearts and guides your minds
In fealty to your King.

VAL: A mortal fear seizes my mind
With terror's chill my heart freezes—
Will Heaven bring no comfort?

CHO: Our hearts are on fire with fury,—
In faith and duty we desire
To serve our King with zeal.
(Soldiers surround Nevers and lead him off.)

ST. BRIS: And you who listen to the call of Heaven,
Devoted to the cause with fearless zeal,
Citizens and soldiers, attend to my command:
In every quarter where the rebels meet,
Cautious and silent fill each neighboring street;
And at the signal given, strike on every hand!

CORO: Sì, corriamo a ferir!

SAN BRIS: (*Indirizzandosi ad uno de' Signori.*) Tu, De Bresme, co' tuoi cingi l' albergo Di Coligny, fa che primiero ei mora!

CORO: Sì, mora pel primier!

SAN BRIS: (*Indirizzandosi a varii altri.*) Voi alla Torre di Nesle, Ove de traditori I condottieri infidi uniti sono, Preparando la festa a Margarita Ed al Re di Navarra.

CORO: Noi alla Torre di Nesle!

SAN BRIS: Ascoltate! Allorchè di San Germano La prima volta undrete, a rimbombar la squilla, Attenti e muti a quel segnal d' allarme Sia pronto il cor, pronta a ferir sia l' arme. A quel funebre suon tu ovunque corri E raddoppia il furor. M' affido al tuo coraggio. E quando alfin dell' Auxerrois voi udrete, Squillare il sacro bronzo, per la volta seconda, Del ciel vendicatore nunziator di rigore;— Ciascun l' acciaro altor dovrà brandire! Ciuscuno allor de' rei dovrà perire! Quel Dio, che qui v' ascolta o benedice, Fidi guerrieri, a voi sarà di scorta!

VAL: O Cielo! o Ciel, come salvarlo posso? Ei tutto sente ne fuggir gli è dato. A lui correr vorrei, ma pur non oso! Pietoso Ciel, in tal periglio estremo Salva Raul,—per me, per me non temo! *La porte in fondo sischiudono, e compariscono tre Monaci, con un paniere di ciarpe bianche.*

I MONACI: Sia gloria eterna e onore Al buon guerrier fedel Ch' oggi l' acciar brandisce Per obbedire al Ciel. (*Tutti snudano la spada,—I Monaci la benedicono.*)

SAN BRIS. E MONACI: Nobili acciari e santi, che d' un reo sangue impuro Or, or vi bagnerete, O voi per cui d' Eterno Strugge un culto infedel, O santi acciar, voi benedice il Ciel!

---

ALL: Yes, we'll strike on every hand!

ST. BRIS: (*Addressing some of the Officers.*) De Bresme, with your friends, fly to the Admiral's For Coligny must be the first to die!

ALL: Yes, he first shall die!

ST. BRIS: (*Addressing others of the Officers.*) You repair to the Tour de Nesle Where, mingling in the throng, You'll find our deadliest foe, At a fête which they prepare For Margaret and the King of Navarre.

ALL: We'll to the Tour de Nesle!

ST. BRIS: Now, mark me well! When first from St. Germain, The solemn peal pours forth over hill and plain Telling in accents loud of dire alarms, Summon in silent night your men to arms; Inspire their minds with zeal to act their part, And by your own example fire each heart; And when at length from Auxerrois The sacred bell a second time shall peal, Then, sword in hand, arise! let all the accursed fall! It is Heaven's holy cause: nerve every arm—slay all! Servants of Heaven! the path lays well before you, It is Heaven that calls! respond, then, we implore, And God will be your guide, whom we adore!

VAL: Oh Heaven, direct me how to save him! He hears their plot, and yet cannot escape. If I only knew how my troubled course to shape! Merciful Heaven, save him from danger near! O save Raoul—for him alone I fear! (*The door in front opens, and three Monks approach, carrying a basket of white scarfs.*)

MONKS: Honor and glory to the brave! Glory to them our cause who save— Who draw the sword in Heaven's just cause, And thus uphold its sacred laws. (*They all draw their swords,—the Monks bless them.*)

ST. BRIS AND THE MONKS: Swords of the faithful, consecrated arms, Soon in their faithless blood you steeped shall be; Now the Most High shall strike the impious race, Be blessed, Heaven pour its blessings on you!

---

SAN BRIS: (*Mostrando la ciarpa e la croce.*) A questa bianca benda, a questa doppia croce, Sian distinti gli eletti.

SAN BRIS ED I MONACI: Nè grazia, nè pietade! ferite senza tregna, Chi pugna ò si dilegua,—lo chiede il ciel, lo vuol.

CORO: Corriam, corriam; feriamo! Dal fuoco e dalla spada, Imune alcun non vada, il guerriero invano Domandi a voi pietà. Cada il fanciul, la madre Non si risparmi età;—Il ciel lo vuol, l' impone! Così de' nostri falli la grazia s' otterà.

SAN GRIS ED UN MONACO: Silenzio, amici! un detto Svegliar potria sospetto; Nessun rumor ci scopra Sia muto il labbro e il piè.

CORO: D' un sacro zel l' ardore Ci elevi e scaldi l' alma, A noi già dan la palma Il ciel, l' onore e il Rè.

SAN BRIS: V' accenda un pio furore Contro del popol rio, V' infiammi l' ardir mio Il ciel, l' onore e il Rè.

CORO: Niun avvisar lor possa, Nessun rumor ci scopra; Andiamo alla sant' opra Il ciel lo vuole, e il Rè. (*Escono in silenzio.*) *Raul soleva lentamente la cortina, si assicura che tutti sono partiti, e si slancia verso la porta in fondo, ma s' arresta sentendola chiudere al di fuori. Allora se dirigge verso la porta a manca, a ne vede uscir Valentina.*

VAL: O Ciel, dove vai tu? Raul, a me rispondi!

RAU: Vado a salvar gli amici, Un delitto inumano ad impedire. A pugnare, a ferire, Di si rei traditoria a sventare il furor!

VAL: Ma v' è fra lor mio padre, e v' è lo sposo, Ch' or reverir degg' io. Vuoi tu punir costoro?

RAU: Gl' infidi punirò!

VAL: Lor spinge all' opra il ciel!

---

ST. BRIS: (*Pointing to the scarf and the white cross.*) By this white cross, surmounted by the scarf, Heaven's messengers be ever known.

ST. BRIS AND THE MONKS: No pardon, no pity! strike all and spare none, Though they meet us with valor, or like cowards run.

CHO: Though humble and suppliant before us they fall, No pity, no mercy, slay all—yes, slay all! Be they bowed down with age, be it child or a mother, Let our curses descend on the one and the other! For this will Heaven pardon whatever may befall.

ST. BRIS AND ONE OF THE MONKS: Silence, lest we raise suspicion By some incautious act or word; Still each rumor, move in secret, Let not even your step be heard!

CHO: May honor, faith and duty, Our minds and hearts inflame, And we shall be victorious, Who fight in our king's name.

ST. BRIS: May honor, faith, and duty, Incite to strike the blow, Then you will be victorious, Against an impious foe.

CHO: Let every rumor cease, Lest we may warn the foe; Such is the will of Heaven— To this great deed we go! (*Exeunt all in silence.*) (*Raoul slowly raises the tapestry, and when he perceives that they are all gone rushes to the door in the center, but finds it fastened on the other side.—He then runs to the door on the left, and meets Valentina coming out of it.*)

VAL: Oh, Heaven, where are you going? Raoul, reply to me!

RAO: I would now fly to save my friends, And cheat these plotters of their deadly ends. I'd have them take revenge, and, sword in hand, Hew down these desecrators of the land!

VAL: But amongst these enemies are some most dear— A father whom I love, a husband I revere! And would you see them slain?

RAO: I would punish their treason!

VAL: It is Heaven's high mandate they obey!

RAU: (*Con ironia.*) Lor spinge all' opra il ciel!
Or ecco il nume che il tuo altar consacra,
Un dio, che tra fratelli cruda strage comanda.

VAL: Ah, non parlar così.
Egli è per sua pietà
Ch' or vuol serbare in te
Un alma pura e forte,
Deh! non uscir.

RAU: Mio dover!

VAL: Tu corri a certa morte.

RAU: Se quì resto io tradisco
L' onore e l' amistà, giammai, giammai.
Stringe il periglio, il tempo,
Ai! rapido s' invola, ah! lasciami partir!

VAL: Così inerme cadresti,
Per pietà non partir, Raul!

RAU: Aimè!

VAL.: Tu mio cospir, tu l' amor mio, Abbandonarti saria marir! Io ben saprò salvar tuoi dì! salvar tuoi dì, Ah, per pietà! ascolta almen, ascolta al ciel, tu l' amor mio, io ben saprò salvar.

RAU.: I mei fratei morir vegg'iso! Me lascia, oimè, da te partir; m' impon l' onor da te fuggir; Mi lascia oimè, mi lascia oimè! m'impon l' onor, — da te fuggir, Mi lascia oimè, partir m' impon l' onor!

(*Raul corre verso la porta, Valentina lo sequee lo trattiene.*)

VAL: No, Raul, questa soglia
Tu varcar non potrai!
Non mi stacco da te!

RAU: L' udirti è colpa.

VAL: E colpa è pur la mia?

RAU: Ciel!

VAL: Ma t' ascolto però! in quest' ora suprema,
Non veggo altri che te, già vicino a perir!
Resta, o Raul, se non mi spregi ancora,
Io t' imploro per me!
Sappi, — se muori, — oimè! io pur morrò.
Ah! resta, resta — io t' amo!

RAU: Tu m' ami? — O, qual brillò
Raggio d' amor celeste!
Qual suon si fece udir!
Il fato mio cambiò!
Fia ver! troppo è gioire!
Venga or la morte a me, —
Dolce sarà il morir!

VAL: O terror! che diss' io?

RAU: Ah, dillo ancor tu m' ami!
Nel fosco orro qual stella
In Ciel per me brillò!
Per sempre tuo se il brami,

RAO: (*Ironically.*) Heaven's high mandate!
Is this the creed of which you vainly boast?
Those are most virtuous who destroy the most!

VAL: Condemn them not,
But spare them pity's tear;
And, if you'd save your life,
Oh, stay you here!
Go not away!

RAO: I must not stay!

VAL: You run to certain death.

RAO: Longer to remain were treason,
When friendship, duty, honor call.
Now danger threats from deadly foe,
I cannot stay — ah, let me go!

VAL: Without your arms you'd surely fall!
For pity's sake, Raoul remain!

RAO: Alas!

VAL.: You are my only hope on earth now, And can you leave me here to die? I will save you — You shall not fly! I will save you! For pity's sake, for pity's sake, will you leave me, here to die . . . here to die!

RAU.: It is my brethren whom they'd murder! Detain me not, but let me fly; — honor calls; Even if I die, I must fly, I must fly! honor calls, I must fly: honor calls, I must fly!

(*Raoul runs towards the door, but is followed by Valentina, who stops him.*)

VAL: No, Raoul, this threshold
Your foot shall never pass!
In death I'll cling to you!

RAO: It is sin to listen or to hesitate.

VAL: And do I not sin also?

RAO: Heaven!

VAL: Yet still I remain here, and in this dreadful hour
Think of nothing but you, for you are all to me!
Stay, then, Raoul, if I'm still dear to you;
If you still love me, stay here!
If you should die, I cannot live.
Stay, I implore — oh, stay — I love you!

RAO: Oh, rapture entrancing!
Oh, transport divine!
Your words, how they change me!
What joy is now mine!
Sweet airs greet my senses!
Come, death, I'd meet your blow,
Here at the loved one's feet!

VAL: O, spare me! what have I said?

RAO: That you love me — repeat it again!
Now all clouds disappear,
While the rays of love shine!

Per sempre tuo sarà!
(*S'ode il suono di lontana squilla.*)

VAL: Eccò l' ora! che faccio? o mio terror!

RAU: Ah! parla ancor; prolunga
L' ineffabile sogno del mio core;
S' è un sogno il ben ch' io provo,
Fa che in eterno duri il dolce errore!

VAL: Che faccio? O, mio periglio!

RAU: Ah! parla ancor; prolunga
Di questo cor l' ebbrezza!
S' è un sogno tal dolcezza
Non resti a me avvenir!

VAL: È l' ora, or con la morte
Svanisce l' avvenir!

RAU: Notte lieta d' amor!

VAL: Notte funesta!

RAU: Vieni, fuggiam!

VAL: Ah, no!

RAU: Tu lo dicesti m' ami; —
Vieni, fuggiam!

VAL: T' arresta!

RAU: Odi quel suon funebre?
(*Odesi in distanza suonar la campana.*)

VAL: Ei m' agghiaccia di terror!

RAU: Dal sen di cupe tenebre qui giunge,
Un grido di furor! —
Dov' era io dunque?

VAL: Vicino a me, Raul.

RAU: Ah, sovvenir fatal!
Della strage dei miei
E l' orribil segnal!
Non più amor, non più amor!
O, rimorso! o, dolor!
Io li vedo perir!
Invano or tu mi parli, —
Io volo a salvarli,
O con essi a morir!

VAL: Che Raul, il mio dolor dunque non può toccarti il core? Dunque vuoi, vuoi, tradir, l' amor tuo, l' amor, la mia fè? E fuggire, fuggire da me, Per volare, per volare a morir! Ah, tu lo puoi, Ah, si! lo puoi Ma col veder . . . mi a tuoi piedi, a tuoì piedi spirar! E puoi nel tuo dolore? Obbliar tanto amore, aimè! aimè!

RAOUL: Non piu lai, non amore! O rimorso, o terrore!

RAU: Ah corriam, — quest' è l' ora.

VAL: No!

RAU: Il Ciel vuol or ch' io mora!

VAL: No!

RAU: Io saprò seguitarli!

VAL: No!

RAU: Io volo a salvarli!

VAL: No!

Oh, forever, at your bidding,
For ever I'll be yours.
(*The sound of a distant bell is heard.*)

VAL: This is the hour! — I shake with terror!

RAO: You have said you have loved me
Through darkness and night,
But a bright star has risen
And lent us its light!

VAL: Oh, how shall I save him? Oh, terror!

RAO: Oh, repeat the sweet words
That brought balm to my heart!
And should all be a dream,
Let it never depart!

VAL: What dreadful hour is this?
Now all must end in death!

RAO: Oh, night of love!

VAL: Oh, fatal night!

RAO: Let us fly, love!

VAL: Ah, no!

RAO: You have said that you love me —
Come, let us away!

VAL: Ah, stay!

RAO: Do you hear the fatal bell?
(*The bell is heard in the distance.*)

VAL: It chills me with terror!

RAO: Ah those cries too plainly tell
What follows that sad knell!
Where am I?

VAL: By my side, Raoul.

RAO: Ah, fatal remembrance!
They murder my friends —
It is the signal of death!
Oh, remorse fills my heart
As for aid from my brethren
Resounds the shrill cry!
It is I who betray them —
I cannot defend them,
But with them will die!

VAL.: Ah! Raoul, my despair has no power to touch your heart! And you will even here, now consent to part from me? From my arms, from my arms you may fly, With your friend, with your friend, now to die; Yes, you may — yes, you may; But, before . . . you do this, my course you'll pass over! Can you part from me? From these arms will you fly? Alas! alas!

RAOUL: Oh, despair fills my heart! Fell remorse overwhelms me!

RAO: I must away, — the hour is come!

VAL: No!

RAO: My blood must also be shed!

VAL: No!

RAO: I must fly to my friends!

VAL: No!

RAO: I'll speed to their rescue.

VAL: No!

RAU: Ah, mi trattieni invan'

RAO: It is in vain you would detain me!

VAL: Io non ti lascio—ah, no!
Crudel mi squarcia il seu,—
Sii tu il mio uccisor!

VAL: You shall not go—ah, no!
Cruel!—sooner than from you to part,
Oh, pierce this bosom to the heart!

RAU: Ciel reggi il mio coraggio!
(*Raul mostrando a Valentina dalla finestra ciò che succede nella strada.*)
Vedi di sangue piena e d' estinti è la Senna!

RAO: Heaven, grant me courage!
(*Raoul shows from the window, to Valentina, what happens in the street.*)
The river's waves with gory streams are red!

VAL: Ah, mia ragion s' invola! o, delitto esecrando!
Raul, t' uccideranno!
Pietà, pietade—io moro, ah!
(*Cade svenuta.*)

VAL: Ah, fearful deed!—my senses fail!
Raoul, they will kill you!
Oh, in pity stay! Alas! I die!
(*She swoons.*)]

RAU: (*Nel più grande affanno.*)
Ritorna in te! che fare?
O, terribil momento!
Potrei così obbliarla?
(*In disperazione.*)
Aimè! fuggiam, fuggiamo!
Tu veglia a giorni suoi, O Ciel, che imploro!
(*Parte per la finestra.*)

RAO: (*In the utmost affright.*)
What shall I do? how see you die!
Oh! terrible moment!
How can I leave her thus?
(*In despair.*)
But go I must at honor's call!
Heaven, spare her life, though I may fall!
(*Exit from the window.*)

*FINNE DELL' ATTO TERZO.*

*END OF THE THIRD ACT.*

# ■ ATTO IV

# ■ ACT IV

## SCENA I

## SCENE I

*Sala di Ballo nell' Hotel de Nesle, ove molte Dame e Cavalieri Protestanti si sono riuniti per festeggiare il matrimonio di Margarita con Enrico di Navarra. La danza viene di tratto in tratto interotta dal suono della Campana di San Germano, finchè tutti spaventati escono precipitosamente.*

*A Ballroom in the Tour de Nesle, where many Ladies and Gentlemen are assembled to celebrate the Marriage of Margaret with Henry, King of Navarre. — The dance is often interrupted by the sound of the great bell of St. Germaine, until all, in alarm, hurry out of the room.*

## SCENA II

## SCENE II

*Cimetero. Da un lato chiesa con porta praticabile. Da un altro lato cancello che mette a una piazza.*

*A Cemetery.—On one side a Church, with a practicable door; on the other a gate opening into a square.*

*Traversano la scena, Donne, Uomini, Fanciulli, che corrano a rifuggiarsi nella chiesa.*

*Men, Women, and Children cross the stage, and take refuge in the Church.*

RAU: (*Entrando da uno lato.*) Sei tu, mio buon Marcello?
Non credea rivederti.

RAO: (*Entering from one side.*) Is it you, my faithful Marcel?
I had no thought to see you again.

MAR: (*Entrando dall' altro.*) Ah! mio Signore, io vi rìtrovo ancora?

MAR: (*Entering from the other side.*) Ah! dear master, are you living still?

RAU: Ferito sei?

RAO: You are wounded?

MAR: L' ignoro.

MAR: I know it not.

RAU: Vendetta?

RAO: Vengeance!

MAR: Che mai dite?
De' codardi assassini resto ancora
Cingon d' eroi, per ogni lato;
Entro quel tempio o mai, rifugio estremo
Di donne e di fanciulli,
La folla in pianti accorre
Santamente a morir. Andiam;
l' unica sorte
Che a noi rimane è d' incontrar la morte!
*Entra Valentina scapigliata e tutt' anelante.*

MAR: What say you?
Bands of soldiers and assassins on every side
Surround our few remaining friends;
In that sacred edifice, their last and only refuge,
Women and children crowd around in tears;
And, praying, seek to die at peace with Heaven!
Let us join them: all hope is vain;
Nothing remains for us but to partake their doom!
(*Enter Valentina, with hair disheveled, and breathless.*)

VAL: Ove correte?

VAL: Where are you going?

RAU: Alla gloria!

RAO: To glory!

MAR: Al martirio?

MAR: To martyrdom!

VAL: No, no, tu non morrai;
Or che senza delitto, amarti posso.

VAL: No, no, you must not die;
I now may love you, and commit no crime.

RAU: E Nevers?

RAO: But De Nevers?

MAR: Generoso guerrier!—
Fu lui che mi salvò da morte!
E del suo zelo vittima, i ribaldi l' assassinar!

MAR: That generous warrior!—
He bravely fought to save my life;
But found, in doing so, a hero's grave!

RAU: Nevers morì?

RAO: Is Nevers dead?

VAL: Ah, vieni, partiamo.

VAL: Come; do not stay here.

RAU: No: presso a lui rimango per morir.

RAO: No; I must remain, and die with him.

VAL: E così dunque io ti vedrò perire?
Io senza te n' andrò raminga sulla terra,
In cui sofferto abbiam, in cui ci stringe amor?
E tu pensarlo puoi?
Ah! sì, dell' uom ben rado un fido amore
Pon radice nel core: ebben, conoscerai
Or l' amor d' una donna.
Or che tutto noi arride, tu vuoi da me fuggir.
Il crudele contrasto di quest' alma.
Di ragion mi privò!
Tu la mia fè disprezzi;—
Io mi arrendo alla tuo!

VAL: Now that my pride may be to live,
Now that I dare sweet hope to cherish,
Now that I give my heart to you,
Can you desert and see me perish?
Alas! but you have yet to learn,
In woman's heart, how love may burn.
How true affection there may glow
And only cease with life to flow!
Since life and love are smiling now on you,
In Heaven or earth we'll be no more parted!
Listen, Raoul, and judge this heart of mine;
You have abjured my faith, I'll welcome yours!

RAU: O, delir!

RAO: Oh, rapture!

MAR: Il Signor del fuoco suo l' accende e irraggia.

MAR: Heaven has enlightened her mind!

VAL: O Cielo, la mia fede sei tu!
L' uom mi maledrià, mio buon Marcel, mio padre,
Accogli i voti miei, consacra il nostro amor!

VAL: Yes, Heaven smiles upon my new-born faith.
Guide my steps, that I may act aright.
Marcel, my father, here give your blessing!

RAU: (*A Marcello.*) Niun ministro del ciel avvi con noi:
Questo nodo tu sol puoi benedir.

RAO: (*To Marcel.*) No minister can press his hand on us,
Consecrate our union and bless.

## Act IV, Scene II

**MAR:** Io, con trasporto accetto il sacro incarco,—
Il servo tuo fedel
Sia il ministro del ciel.

**CORE:** (*Di donne nella Chiesa.*)
Signor che ognor proteggi
Il giusto che t' adora,
Il tentator ne preme,
Deh salva chi t' implora!

**MAR:** L' innocenza e la fè
Alzan lor preci al Ciel;
E del Signor fan risuonar le lodi,
Nell' aspettar la morte,
In questo tristo asilo.
Rispondi il vostro cor
come innanzi al Signor,
Nell' unir vostre mani in tai fosche tenebre.
Io consacro il festin d' un tristo addio
Ed un nodo funebre.

**RAU. E VAL:** Noi sappiam che il Ciel sol
Le nostr' alme unirà.

**MAR:** E vigore avrai tu i tormenti a sfidar?
E la fè d' un sol dì
Non saprai più negar,
A fronte del martir?

**RAU. E VAL:** A noi diede il Ciel vigor
Quando in noi sveglio l' amor.

**CORE:** (*Di donne nella Chiesa.*)
Signor, tu che proteggi, etc.
(*Qui il cantico viene ad un tratto interrotto da rumor d' armi e alte grida.*)

**CORO DEGLI ASSASSINI NELL' INTERNO DELLA CHIESA:** Abbiurate, Ugonotti, il Ciel l' impone! Abbiurate, o morrete!

**VAL:** (*Guardando dalla finestra.*)
Ah, crudeli! son donne,—
Ah, pietade, malvagi!

**CORO D' ASSASSINI:** Non v' ha scampo,—il Ciel l' impone!

**CORO DI DONNE:** Signor ne reggi ancor!
(*S' Ode una scarica di archibugi nella chiesa.*)

**VAL. E MAR:** Cantano ancor?

**RAU:** Ora non cantan più!
(*Tutti i tre restano in un silenzio funebre, celandosi il volta nelle mani, poi Marcello, come sorpresi da improvvisa visione e guardando al Cielo.*)

**MAR:** With joy do I accept the sacred office;
Your old and faithful servant will at once fulfil
The holy rite.

**CHO:** (*Of Women in the Church.*)
Oh you, who protect
The just who you adore,
Oh, shield us from the foe,
Your servants now implore!

**MAR:** Now innocence and faith
To Heaven their prayers raise,
And, while awaiting death,
They render praise to God.
May He, amidst this scene,
Direct your hearts aright,
While thus, before high Heaven,
I do unite your hands,
By this blessed rite again you'll be
United in eternity.

**RAO. & VAL:** Ah yes, we know we soon shall be
United in eternity.

**MAR:** And will your courage you sustain
All torture to defy,
And in the faith you now have sworn
Persist, till both shall die!

**RAO. & VAL:** Yes, Heaven will its strength impart
When love devoted fills the heart.

**CHO:** (*Of Women in the Church.*)
Oh you, who protects, etc.
(*Here the Chorus is interrupted by a loud din of arms and cries.*)

**CHORUS OF ASSASSINS WHO HAVE ENTERED THE CHURCH:** Huguenots, abjure—your faith deny,
Or Heaven commands that you must die!

**VAL:** (*Looking through the window.*) Hold, murderers, hold,—
They are women and children!

**CHORUS OF ASSASSINS:** No! It is Heaven's command—they die!

**CHORUS OF WOMEN:** Oh Heaven, do you protect us!
(*Firing heard from within the Church.*)

**VAL. & MAR:** Still does their song resound?

**RAO:** They sing no more!
(*They all remain in profound silence, burying their faces in their hands; then Marcel, as if inspired, looks towards heaven.*)

**MAR:** Ah, vedete! il Ciel s' apre e sfavilla!
Gloria a Dio! l' eterea tromba squilla.
E degli angioli il cauto risuona
Che il stuol guida de' martiri al Ciel!

**RAU. E VAL:** Vedi come lo sguardo gli brilla!
E di folgori il capo incorona;
La sua voce nell' aura risuona,
Come un angiol disceso dal Ciel!

**TUTTI:** L' ammiro, l' ascolto?
M' addita il sentiere.
Che al cielo si ascende,
Supremo piacere!
O morte ti segno.
O terra un addio!
(*S' apre il cancello e varii assassini si precipitano in scena.*)

**CORO:** Abbiurate, Ugonotti, il Ciel l' impone;
Abbiurate, o morrete, il Ciel lo vuol!

**RAU. E VAL:** No, no: timor no ho,—
Nè mi resto desio,
Venite, ormai ferite!
Osanna—terra—addio!
(*Tutti partono a destra, mentre a sinistra s' odono scariche di fucile.*)

### SCENA ULTIMA

Strada in Parigi presso la Senna nel 1572.—E' notte stellata.

San Bris, Valentina, Raul, Marcello, Soldati Cattolici, Urbano, e infine La Regina.

**CORO DE' SOLDATI, D' OLTRA:**
Sian tutti messi a fil di spada,
Ormai lo stuolo degli empii cada;
Pietà non s' abbia, neppur d' un sol:
Del Ciel soldati, gl' empi Ugonotti
Feriam, struggiam;—è Dio che 'l vuol,
(*Durante questo Coro Raul appare a destra, mortalmente ferito, e sostenuto da Valentina e da Marcello.*)

**SAN BRIS:** (*Entra a sinistra, dirigendo una compagnia di Archibugieri.*) Chi vive?

**VAL:** (*Sostenendo Raul, e mettendogli una mano sulla bocca per impedirgli di rispondere.*) Per pietada, oimè! deh taci!

**RAU:** (*Facendo un ultimo sforzo grida.*) Ugonotti!

**MAR:** Ah, see! the effulgent Heavens open wide!
The clarion sounds Hosanna from on high!
And music from the angel choir resounds,
Now welcoming the martyrs to their side!

**RAO. & VAL:** Ah! see upon his face a heavenly ray!
His brow is crowned with the eternal light;
And, with his voice inspired, the vaults resound;
Hosanna! the archangel leads the way!

**ALL:** His harp's gentle sound
Tells where rest may be found;
Where the wretched may fly
To a home in the sky!
For the faith that is true,
Earth, we bid you adieu!
(*The gate flies open, and a crowd of Assassins rush upon the stage.*)

**CHO:** Huguenots, abjure—deny your faith,
Or Heaven commands that you must die!

**RAO. & VAL:** No! Heaven is our guide—
We fear nothing from you!
Advance, this bosom strike!
Hosanna!—earth, adieu!
(*All rush off on the right, at the same time firing is heard on the left.*)

### SCENE THE LAST

A Street on the Quays of Paris, in 1572—Starlight Night.

St. Bris, Valentina, Raoul, Marcel, Catholic Soldiers, Urban, and afterwards the Queen.

**CHO. OF SOLDIERS, FROM WITHOUT:** By the sword and by the fagot
Shall their race become extinct.
Let every true Catholic
Hunt down the heretic;—
Heaven on high has sent their doom.
(*During this Chorus Raoul appears on the right, mortally wounded, supported by Valentina and Marcel.*)

**ST. BRIS:** (*Entering on the left, at the head of a company of Musketeers.*) Who's there?

**VAL:** (*Supporting the drooping head of Raoul, and placing her hand on his mouth to prevent an answer.*) For mercy's sake, speak not!

**RAO:** (*Making a final struggle, cries out.*) Huguenots!

**MAR. E VAL:** E noi pur!

**SAN BRIS:** (*A' Soldati.*) Ferite, il re l'impone!
(*I Soldati fan fuoco su loro, e Valentina e Marcello cadono, mortalmente feriti.*)

**VAL:** Cielo! mio padre!

**SAN BRIS:** (*Precipitandosi su lei.*) Ah! che vegg' io mia figlia?

**VAL:** (*Sollevandosi con stento.*) Sì, sì,—son io che vo a pregar per voi!
Per voi, padre, nel Ciel!
(*Muore.*)

---

**MAR. & VAL:** And we also!

**ST. BRIS:** (*To the Soldiers.*) In the King's name, fire!
(*The Soldiers fire on them, and Valentina and Marcel fall mortally wounded.*)

**VAL:** Heaven! my father!

**ST. BRIS:** (*Rushing towards her.*) Ah! what do I see?—my daughter!

**VAL:** (*Raising herself with difficulty.*) Yes, yes, it is I—who go to pray for you,
For you, my father in Heaven!
(*Dies.*)

---

**URB:** (*Entro le scene.*) Vien la Regina!
(*In questo momento entra la Regina, portata in una lettiga. Ella ritorna dal ballo al Louvre.—Alla vista dell' estinta Valentina gitta un grido, e fa segno a' Soldati di arrestarsi.*)

**CORO:** Sian tutti messi a fil di spada;
Alfin lo stuol degli empi cada;
Feriam, struggiam,—è Dio che 'l vuol!
(*Cade il sipario.*)

*FINE.*

---

**URB:** (*From without.*) The Queen approaches!
(*At this moment the Queen enters, borne on a litter, returning from a ball at the Louvre.—At the sight of the lifeless Valentina she screams, and makes signs to the Soldiers to stop.*)

**CHO:** By the sword and by the fagot
At last their race becomes extinct;—
Heaven on high has sent their doom!
(*The curtain falls.*)

*THE END.*

# Le Prophète (1849)

## The Prophet

MUSIC BY GIACOMO MEYERBEER ■ LIBRETTO BY AUGUSTIN EUGÈNE SCRIBE

This four-act opera, set to a libretto by Eugène Scribe, premiered at the Paris Opéra on April 16, 1849. In Holland during the time of the Anabaptists, Berthe and Jean of Leyden are in love and ask Count Oberthal to give them permission to wed. But the Count himself falls in love with Berthe and refuses, ordering Berthe to his castle. Berthe obeys but does not go alone—Fides, Jean's mother, goes with her. The Anabaptists hear about the Count's abuse of his powerful position and invite Jean to join them. They foresee that he will be crowned. Berthe escapes from the Count's castle and attempts to rejoin Jean, but the Count forces her to return to him as he still has Fides in his clutches. At the Anabaptists' camp, Jean is now their prophet. They decide to launch an attack on the Count's castle. Oberthal's son is there, hiding in the crowd. He is discovered and is about to be killed when Jean saves him. Jean finds out that Berthe has escaped yet again; Fides has also successfully escaped, and the women curse the Anabaptists. Berthe swears to kill their prophet. Three of the Anabaptists betray their prophet, who is now under siege. Berthe commits suicide when she finds out the Jean and the prophet are the same man. Jean blows up the castle rather than surrender, killing himself and Fides (who has forgiven him) as well as the enemies seeking his capture.

---

## ■ ACTE I.

*(Le théâtre représente les campagnes de la Hollande, aux environs de Dordrecht. Au fond on aperçoit la Meuse: à droite un château-fort avec point-levis et tourelles: à gauche, fermes et moulins dépendant du château. Du même côté, sur le premier plan, des sacs de blé, des tables rustiques, des bancs, etc.)*

### SCÈNE I.

*Paysans, Paysannes, Ouvriers, Etc.*
*(Au lever du rideau le théâtre est vide. Un berger arrive, et avec son chalumeau, donne l'éveil. Un autre berger (censé dans les coulisses) lui répond de loin, alors les portes des cabanes s'ouvrent, les paysans sortent avec leurs outils, les meuniers avec des sacs de farine sur le dos, etc., etc.)*

**CHOEUR PASTORAL:** La brise est muette,
Le jour est serein!
D'échos en échos,
Sonne la clochette,
Sonne nos gais troupeaux!

**UNE PAYSANNE:** Trop souvent l'orage,
Attriste nos coeurs!

**CHOEUR:** Attriste nos coeurs.

**UNE PAYSANNE:** D'un jour, d'un jour sans nuages,
Goûtons tous les douceurs,
La brise est muette,
Le jour est serein!

## ■ ACT I.

*(A rural scene in Holland, in the vicinity of Dordrecht. At the back the Meuse may be seen. On the right a fortress with drawbridges and towers; on the left, farms and mills connected with the castle. On the same side, in the foreground, sacks of wheat, rustic tables, benches, etc.)*

### SCENE I.

*Peasants and Laborers.*
*(When the curtain rises the stage is empty. A shepherd enters and on his reed-pipe sounds the matinal. Another shepherd answers him from the distance; then the doors of the cottages open; the peasants come out with their tools, the millers with their sacks of meal on their backs, etc.)*

**PASTORAL CHORUS:** The wind is hushed,
The day is still!
Echo to echo answering,
Ring the bell,
Summon our gay flocks.

**A PEASANT GIRL:** Too often the storm
Saddens our hearts.

**CHORUS:** Saddens our hearts.

**A PEASANT GIRL:** Of this day, of this cloudless day,
Let us sup the pleasures,
The wind is hushed,
The day is still,

D'un jour heureux,
Goûtons le bonheur,
Le jour, oui, le jour est serein!
Oui, Le vent qui s'arrête
Arrête le moulin.
Qu'ici pour nous s'apprête,
Le repas du matin! oui,
Le vent qui s'arrête,
Arrête le moulin.
Qu'ici pour nous s'apprête,
Le repas du matin.

### SCÈNE II.

*Les mêmes, Fidès.*
*(Berthe voit arriver de loin Fidès. Elle court à sa rencontre, prend son bras, et la conduit doucement jusque sur le devant de la scène. Fidès est fatiguée de la route et marche pesamment. Quand elle est arrivée sur l'avant-scène, elle embrasse Berthe, la bénit et met à son doigt un anneau de fiancée, envoyé par Jean.)*

**BERTHE:** Fidès, ma bonne mère, enfin donc vous voilà!

**FIDÈS:** Tu m'attendais?

**BERTHE:** Depuis l'aurore!

**FIDÈS:** Et Jean, mon fils, attend plus ardemment encore
Sa fiancée!
"Allez, allez, bonne mère,
Allez-allez, amenez là,"
A-t-il dit, et je viens!

**BERTHE:** Ainsi moi, pauvre fille,
Orpheline et sans biens,
Il m'a daigné choisir?

Of one happy day
Let us take the treasures.
The day, yes, the day is still!
Yes, no longer blows the wind,
No longer moves the mill,
Which now prepares for us
The morning meal.

### SCENE II.

*The same, Fides.*
*(Bertha sees Fides in the distance. She runs to meet her, takes her arm, and leads her gently to the foreground. Fides is tired from the journey and walks heavily. When she reaches the forestage she embraces Bertha, blesses her and places on her finger an engagement ring sent by Jean.)*

**BERTHA:** Fides, my dear mother, at last you are here!

**FIDES:** You were waiting for me?

**BERTHA:** Since the dawn!

**FIDES:** And Jean, my son, even more ardently
Awaits his bride! "Go, dear mother, go,
Go, bring her to me!"
Said he, and here I am!

**BERTHA:** But me, a poor girl,
An orphan and dowerless,
Me, he has deigned to choose?

**FIDÈS:** (*babillant avec bonho-mie*). Des filles de Dordrecht
Berthe est le plus gentille,
Et le plus sage, et je veux vous unir,
(*S'animant toujours davantage.*)
Et je veux dès demain,
Que Berthe me succède,
Dans mon hotellerie
Et dans mon beau comptoir;
Le plus beau, vois-tu bien,
De toute la ville de Leyde!
Partons, partons, partons!
Hâtons-nous, hâtons-nous,
Car mon fils nous attend pour ce
soir, partons!

**BERTHE:** Non pas vraiment!
Vassale, je ne puis
Me marier, ni quitter ce pays,
Sans la volonté souveraine
Du comte d'Oberthal, seigneur de
ce domaine,
Dont vous voyez d'ici les créneaux
redoutés!

**FIDÈS:** Auprès de lui courons!
(*Fidès veut entraîner Berthe vers
le château à droite. Au moment
où les deux femmes viennent de
franchir les marches de l'escalier
qui conduit au château, les trois
Anabaptistes paraissent au baut
des marches, ils s'approchent
d'eux et les examinent avec curiosité. Fidès redescend avec
crainte les marches de l'escalier.*)

## SCÈNE III.

*Les mêmes, Zacharie, Jonas,
Mathisen.
Le Prêche Anabaptiste.
(Les trois Anabaptistes sur la col-
line, etendent les mains sur le peu-
ple comme pour le bénir.)*

**JONAS:** Ad nos, ad salutarem un-dam,
Iterum venite miseri!
Ad nos, ad nos, venite populi!

**LES PAYSANS:** Ecoutons le ciel
qui les inspire, qui les inspire!
(*Les trois Anabaptistes descendent l'escalier et s'approchent des
paysans.*)

**ZACHARIE:** (*montant sur une
borne pour baranguer le peuple*).
De ces champs fécondés longtemps
par vos sueurs,
Voulez-vous, voulez-vous être en-
fin les maîtres et seigneurs?
Le voulez-vous, le voulez-vous?
Ad nos salutarem undam,
Iterum venite miseri.

**LES TROIS ANABAPTISTES:** Ad
nos salutarem undam,
Iterum venite miseri.

**MATHISEN:** Esclaves et vassaux
trop longtemps à genoux,
Ce qui fut abaissé s'élève.
Levez-vous!

**FIDES:** (*gossiping good natured-ly*). Of all the girls in Dordrecht
The finest is Bertha,
And the wisest! I wish to unite you,
(*Getting more excited.*)
And that from tomorrow,
Bertha succeed me
At the counter, in my inn,
The best, Bertha, you well know,
In all the village of Leyden!
Come, come, let us go!
Let us hasten, let us hasten,
For my son expects us this evening,
Let us go!

**BERTHA:** No, indeed no!
I—a vassal—
Cannot marry, nor leave this coun-try,
Without the sovereign will
Of the Count of Oberthal, Lord of
this domain,
Whose dread battlements you now
behold.

**FIDES:** Let us hasten to him!
(*Fides wishes to drag Bertha to the
castle on the right. Just as the two
women mount the steps of the
stairway which leads to the castle,
three Anabaptists appear at the
top. They advance quietly, while
the peasants approach them and
examine them with curiosity.
Fides descends the steps in fear.*)

## SCENE III.

*The same, Zacharia, Jonas and
Mathisen.
The Anabaptists' Sermon.
(The three Anabaptists on the hill,
stretching their hands over the
people as if to bless them.)*

**JONAS:** Ad nos, ad salutarem un-dam,
Iterum venite miseri!
Ad nos, ad nos, venite populi!

**THE PEASANTS:** Let us listen to
Heaven who inspires them!
(*The three Anabaptists descend
the stairway and approach the
peasants.*)

**ZACHARIA:** (*mounting a stone to
barangue the people*). Of these fair
fields, fertile by your long labors,
Do you wish to be at last the masters
and lords?
Do you, do you?
Ad nos salutarem undam,
Iterum venite miseri.

**THE THREE ANABAPTISTS:** Ad
nos salutarem undam,
Iterum venite, miseri.

**MATHISEN:** Slaves and vassals
kneeling too long,
What was abased, arises.
Rise!

**LES TROIS ANABAPTISTES:** Levez-vous, Levez-vous, Levez-vous!
(*Les paysans commencent à
s'émouvoir, et se consultent entre
eux. Ils engagent un des leurs à
parler aux prêcheurs. Le paysan
ne veut pas d'abord, mais ses
compagnons le poussent en
avant.*)

**SIX CORYPHÉES:** (*timidement*).
Ainsi ces beaux châteaux?

**JONAS:** Ils vous appartiendront.

**SIX CORYPHÉES:** (*timidement*).
La dime et la couvée?

**JONAS:** Elles disparaîtront.

**SIX CORYPHÉES:** Et nous serfs et
vassaux?

**MATHISEN ET ZACHARIE:** Libres
en ce séjour.

**SIX CORYPHÉES:** Et nos anciens
seigneurs?

**MATHISEN ET ZACHARIE:** Esclaves à leur tour.

**LE PREMIER ET LE DEUXIÈME
PAYSANS:** (*avec les basses du
Choeur entr'eux se consultant*).
Oui!

**CHOEUR:** Ils ont raison, écoutez-
les!
Oui!
Ils disent vrai, Dieu parle ainsi!
Nous les suivrons, point de retard!
Allons!
Et nous aussi!
Point de merci!
Venez!
(*Aux paysans.*)
Vous êtes forts!
Vous êtes grands!
Vous êtes forts, puissants, grands!
Allez!
(*Les Anabaptistes parcourent les
différents groupes de Paysans
pour les exciter.*)

**LES TROIS ANABAPTISTES:** Ad
nos!
Ad nos!
Ad nos!
Ad nos!

**LES PAYSANS:** Ces vils, ces vils
tyrans!
Cruels ces appresseurs indignes,
seigneurs!
Ah!
Vengeons-nous sur nos tyrans!
Vengeons-nous sur nos tyrans!
Qu'ils meurent tous!
Qu'ils meurent tous!

**LES TROIS ANABAPTISTES:** Ad
nos!
Ad nos!
Ad nos!
Ad nos!

**THE THREE ANABAPTISTS:**
Arise, arise, arise!
(*The peasants begin to move
about and to consult each other.
They select one of their number to
speak to the preachers. The peasant does not wish to at first, but
his companions push him forward.*)

**SIX CORYPHÉES:** (*timidly*). Then
these beautiful castles?

**JONAS:** They will belong to you.

**THE SIX CORYPHÉES:** (*timidly*).
Tithes and feudal labor?

**JONAS:** They will disappear.

**THE SIX CORYPHÉES:** And we
serfs and vassals?

**MATHISEN AND ZACHARIA:**
Free in this abode.

**THE SIX CORYPHÉES:** And our
former lords?

**MATHISEN AND ZACHARIA:**
Slaves in their turn.

**FIRST AND SECOND PEASANTS:**
(*and some of the chorus consult-
ing each other*). Yes, they are right,
Let us listen to them!
God speaks thus!
We shall follow them!
No delay! Come!

**CHORUS:** We too!
No delay!
Come!
(*To the peasants*).
You are strong!
You are mighty!
You are strong, powerful, mighty!
Go!
(*The Anabaptists run among the
different groups of peasants to ex-
cite them.*)

**THE THREE ANABAPTISTS:** Ad
nos!
Ad nos!
Ad nos!
Ad nos!

**THE PEASANTS:** These unworthy
oppressors,
These vile tyrants!
Cruel lords!
Ah! let us have revenge on our tyr-
ants!
Let them die!
Let them die!

**THE THREE ANABAPTISTS:** Ad
nos!
Ad nos!
Ad nos!
Ad nos!

**LES PAYSANS:** Levons-nous!
Levons-nous!
Levons-nous!
Levons-nous!
Malheur á qui nous combattrait,
malheur!

**THE PEASANTS:** Let us rise, rise,
rise, rise!
He is doomed who opposes us,
Doomed!

**LES TROIS ANABAPTISTES:** *Ad nos salutarem undam, Iterum venite!*

**THE THREE ANABAPTISTS:** Ad nos salutarem undam, Iterum venite!

**LES PAYSANS:** Son supplice est tout prêt,
Dieu signe l'arrêt.
(*Les Paysans courent au fond du théâtre où sont déposé les fourches à fâner, les faux et les pioches: ils les brandissent, s'alignent et marchent en ordre militaire, en promenant les trois Anabaptistes en triomphe.*)

**THE PEASANTS:** His punishment is all prepared,
God signs the warrant!
(*The peasants run to the background where pitchforks, scythes and spades are piled; they brandish them, form into lines and march in military order, parading the three Anabaptists in front.*)

**MATHISEN ET ZACHARIE:** (*avec enthusiasme*). O roi des cieux,
c'est la victoire,
Dieu des combats, veille sur nous,
sur nous!
Les nations verront ta gloire,
Ta sainte loi luira pour tous, pour tous!
Suivez nous, amis, Dieu le veut,
Dieu le veut!
C'est le grand jour
Que la liberté, que la liberté soit notre amour,
Et du monde entier, Dieu le veut!
Son drapeau fera le tour!

**MATHISEN AND ZACHARIA:** (*enthusiastically*). O heavenly king, this foretells victory!
God of combats, guard over us!
The nations will observe your glory!
Your sacred law will shine for all!
Follow us, comrades, God wishes it,
It is the day of days!
Let liberty be our love,
And through the whole world, as God wishes,
His flag shall be unfurled!

**LES TROIS ANABAPTISTES:** Dieu le veut!
Dieu le veut!
Suivez-nous, chers compagnons!
Aux armes! aux armes!

**THE THREE ANABAPTISTS:** God wishes it!
Follow us, dear comrades!
To arms!
To arms!

**LES PAYSANS:** Ah! viens!
Ah! viens! viens! viens! viens!
(*Tous les paysans se sont armés de fourches, de pioches et de bâtons, et se sonts élancés sur les marches de l'escalier qui conduit au château.*)

**THE PEASANTS:** Ah! come,
Ah! come, come, come!
(*All the peasants arm themselves with the pitchforks, spades and cudgels, and rush up the steps of the stairway leading to the castle.*)

## SCÈNE IV.

## SCENE IV.

*Les Mêmes, Oberthal, Seigneurs, Gardes, Etc.*
(*Les portes due château s'ouvrent. Oberthal sort; il est entouré de seigneurs, ses amis avec lesquels il cause en riant. À sa vue les paysans s'arrêtent, ceux qui avaient déjà gravi les marches de l'escalier, les redescendent avec effroi, et cachent les bâtons dont ils étaient armés, Oberthal s'avance tranquillement au milieu des paysans qui le saluent.*)

*The same, Oberthal, Nobles and Guards.*
(*The doors of the castle open, Oberthal comes out; he is surrounded by nobles, his friends, with whom he chats and laughs. Upon his appearance the peasants stop, those who have already ascended the stairs, return in terror, and hide the cudgels with which they are armed. Oberthal advances calmly into the midst of the peasants, who greet him.*)

**BERTHE:** Le Comte d'Oberthal, le seigneur châtelain!

**BERTHA:** Count of Oberthal, Lord of this domain,—

**OBERTHAL:** De quels cris menaçants, ces visages si tristes,
Troublent-ils dans nos murs la gaité du festin?
(*Rappelant ses souvenirs.*)
Ah!
Ceux là ne sont-ils pas de ces Anabaptistes,

**OBERTHAL:** Whose menacing cries and somber faces,
Disturb the gaiety of our festival?
(*Recollecting.*)
Ah!
Are these not the Anabaptists,
These pernicious Puritans, those boring preachers,

Ces fougueux puritains, ces ennuyeux prêcheurs,
Semant partout, dit-on, leurs dogmes imposteurs?
Eh! mais vraiment, vraiment, je crois le reconnaître.
Oui, c'est maître Jonas, mon ancien sommelier;
Il me volait mon vin, dont il se disait maître!
(*Aux soldats.*)
Que le fourreau du sabre aide à le chatier
Soldats qu'on le chasse!
Eloignez sa figure infernale!
(*Les soldats emmènent les trois Anabaptistes.*)
(*Apercevant Berthe.*) Ah! celle-ci vaut mieux!
Que veux-tu, ma vassale?
Avance et parle sans frayeur!

Sowing everywhere their heretical creed!
But, truly, I think I recognize him,
Yes, it is Jonas, my former cellar-keeper;
He used to steal my wine, which he said was his!
(*To the soldiers.*)
Let the scabbard aid in punishing him!
Let the soldiers beat him!
Remove his infernal face!
(*The soldiers take the three Anabaptists away.*)
(*Noticing Bertha.*)
Ah! here is a more welcome sight!
What do you wish, my vassal?
Approach and speak without fear!

**BERTHE:** (*à part*). Ma mere, ma mere, helas!
J'ai bien peur!

**BERTHA:** (*aside*). Mother, mother, alas, I am afraid!

**FIDÈS:** (*rassurant Berthe*). Sois sans crainte.
Sois sans crainte;
Je suis là, je suis là, pour te donner du coeur!

**FIDES:** (*assuring Bertha*). Have no fear!
Have no fear!
I am here, to give you courage!

**BERTHE:** (*doux*). Un jour dans les flots de la Meuse,
J'allais périr, j'allais périr,
Jean me sauva!

**BERTHA:** (*softly*). One day in the waves of the Meuse
I was about to perish,
When Jean rescued me!

**FIDÈS:** (*faisant la révérence*).
Jean, Jean la sauva!

**FIDES:** (*bowing*). Jean, Jean saved her!

**BERTHE:** Orpheline et bien malheureuse,
Depuis ce jour,
Jean me protegea!

**BERTHA:** An orphan most unhappy,
Since that day
Jean protected me!

**FIDÈS:** (*faisant la révérence*). Jean la protegea!

**FIDES:** (*curtsying*). Jean protected her!

**BERTHE:** Je connais votre droit, je connais votre droit supreme!
Mais Jean m'aime de tout son coeur, de tout son coeur!
Ah! mon seigneur, mon doux seigneur!
Permettez-moi d'être sa femme!
Permettez-le!
Permettez-le, mon doux seigneur.

**BERTHA:** I knew your law, I knew your law supreme!
But Jean loved me with all his heart!
Ah! my lord, my sovereign, my gracious sovereign,
Allow me to become his wife, do, do!

**OBERTHAL:** (*regardant Berthe avec amour*). Eh quoi! tant de candeur,
D'attraits et d'innocence,
Seraient perdus pour nous
Et quitteraient ces lieux!
Non, non, non, non, je refuse!

**OBERTHAL:** (*looking at Bertha tenderly*). Ah! truly that such candor,
Such beauty and such innocence,
Should be lost for us
And should leave this place!
No, no, no, no!
I refuse!

**BERTHE:** (*se jetant dans les bras de Fidès*). Ah! quel malheur!

**BERTHA:** (*throwing herself into Fides' arms*). Oh! What an affliction!

**FIDÈS:** (*se jetant au milieu des paysans*). Ah! ah! quel malheur!

**FIDES:** (*rushing among the peasants*). Oh! What an affliction!

**BERTHE:** (*poussant un cri d'indignation*). O nouvelle infamie!
O mortelles alarmes!
Faut-il, hélas! se soumettre à ce sceptre d'airain?
Fuyons!
(*Fidès à gauche, au milieu des paysans leur fait honte de leur la-*

**BERTHA:** (*uttering a cry of indignation*). Oh! new misfortune!
Oh! mortal terror!
Alas! must we submit, submit to this scepter of iron?
Let us flee!
(*Fides on the left, in the midst of the peasants, shames them for their cowardice, begs them to de-*

cheté, les supplie de defendre Berthe, et de réclamer justice pour elle. Les paysans excités par ces reproches s'avancent d'un air résolu et menaçant vers Oberthal, qui sans les voir cause avec les autres seigneurs, à leur approche Oberthal se retourne, les vassaux s'arrêtent interdits et tremblants.)

**OBERTHAL:** Je l'ai dit, je le veux, moi seigneur châtelain
Cedez tous, cedez tous aux desirs du seigneur châtelain
Cedez tous, cedez tous, cedez tous, ou si non, soldats!
(Pendant ces derniers vers, des gardes de la suite d'Oberthal ont entouré Berthe et Fidès, qu'ils entraînent dans le château. Oberthal et ses amis les suivent, et les portes se referment derrière eux. Les paysans muets de surprise et de frayeur, se retirent en silence et tête baissée. A ce moment on entend dans le lointain le psaume des Anabaptistes.)

**LES ANABAPTISTES:** (dans les coulisses). Ad nos, ad salutarem undam,
Iterum venite, Miseri! Venite!
(Le peuple entendant le chant des Anabaptistes court au devant eux.)
(Les trois Anabaptistes reparaissent sur les marches de l'escalier du château, étandant leur mains sur le peuple (qui s'agenouille devant eux) et menaçant du geste et du regard le château d'Oberthal.)

*RIDEAU.*

# ■ ACTE II.

## SCÈNE I.

Jean, puis paysans et paysannes, puis Jonas, Mathisen, Zacharie.
(Le théâtre représente l'auberge de Jean et de sa mère dans les faubourgs de Leyde. Portes au fonds, et croisée donnant sur la campagne. On entend au dehors un air de valse. Jean tenant des broc qu'il pose sur une table sort de la chambre de la droite et va ouvrir les portes du fond; il aperçoit devant les portes et devant les croisées des paysans et des paysannes qui s'amusent à valser, et qui toujours en valsant entrent dans l'interieur de l'auberge, plusieurs se mettent à table et chantent le choeur suivant, tandis que les autres continuent leur danse.)

fend Bertha and to demand justice for her. The peasants, incited by these reproaches, advance resolutely and menacingly against Oberthal, who without noticing them chats with the other nobles. At their approach Oberthal turns; the vassals cease, confused and trembling.)

**OBERTHAL:** I have said it; I wish it, I, your sovereign.
Yield everything, yield everything to the desires of your lord!
Yield everything, everything, everything!
If not!—soldiers!
(During this last speech, the guards of Oberthal's train have surrounded Bertha and Fides, whom they are dragging to the castle. Oberthal and his friends follow them and the door closes behind them. The peasants, speechless from surprise and fright, retire in silence and with bowed heads. Just then the psalm of the Anabaptists is heard in the distance.)

**THE ANABAPTISTS:** (in the wings). Ad nos, ad salutarem undam,
Iterum venite, Miseri! Venite!
(The people hearing the song of the Anabaptists run to meet them.)
(The three Anabaptists reappear on the steps of the stairway of the castle, extending their hands over the people (who are kneeling before them) and threatening the castle by look and gesture.)

*CURTAIN.*

# ■ ACT II.

## SCENE I.

Jean, then some peasants, then Jonas, Mathisen and Zacharia.
(The inn of Jean and his mother in the suburbs of Leyden. Door at the back and a casement with a view of the fields. Outside a waltz tune is heard. Jean, carrying some flasks which he sets on a table, enters from a room on the right and opens the doors at the back. In front of the door and the casement he sees peasants who are enjoying a waltz, and who enter the inn, without stopping their dance. Several sit down at the tables and sing the following chorus, while other continue their dance.)

**VALSE VILLAGEOISE:** Valsons toujours,
Oui, la valse a mes amours;
Valsons, chantons, chers amis!
Valsons toujours.
Oui, la valse a mes amours;
Valsons, chantons, chers amis!
Vive, vive, vive Jean!

**JEAN:** (à part). Le jour baisse, et ma mère bientôt sera de retour
Avec ma fiancée, ma Berthe, mon amour,
Ma Berthe, mon amour, ma Berthe, mon amour.

**JONAS:** (regardant Jean). O ciel!

**ZACHARIE:** Qu'as-tu donc?

**JONAS:** (à voix basse). Regarde ce jeune homme!

**ZACHARIE:** (à voix basse). En effet!

**MATHISEN:** (à voix basse). Oui, ces traits et cet air.

**ZACHARIE:** La ressemblance est inouie.

**JONAS:** Et, devant moi, vivant, j'ai cru voir à son air,
David, le roi David, qu'on adore à Munster!

**MATHISEN:** Ce tableau qu'on admire en notre Westphalie,
Et qui fait tous les jours des miracles!

**JONAS:** Silence!

**CHOEUR:** Allons, verse, viens ici!

**UN SOLDAT:** Jean!

**JONAS:** (à un paysan). Ami, quel est cet homme?

**UN PAYSAN:** Jean, le maître du logis!
Son coeur est excellent
Et son bras est terrible!

**JONAS:** Tête ardente?

**UN PAYSAN:** Oui, vraiment.

**JONAS:** Il est brave?

**UN PAYSAN:** Et dévot!
Il sait par coeur toute la Bible!

**ZACHARIE:** (à part à ses compagnons). Chers amis, n'est-ce pas la l'apôtre qu'il nous faut?

**MATHISEN:** Celui qu'à nous aider appelle le Très Haut!

**JEAN:** La nuit couvre la terre
Et le repos est doux;
J'attends Berthe et ma mère,
Allez, allez, amis, retirez-vous!

**LES PAYSANS:** Partons, partons, il songe à sa belle!
Partons, le ciel est noir!
Partons!
(Dans les coulisses.)
Bonsoir!
Bonsoir!
Bonsoir!
(Les paysans sortent en valsant

**VILLAGER'S WALTZ:** Let us dance forever,
Yes, dancing is our delight;
Let us dance, let us sing; comrades!
Let us dance forever.
Yes, dancing is our delight;
Let us dance, let us sing, comrades!
Long live Jean, long live Jean!

**JEAN:** (aside). The day dies, and soon my mother will return
With my bride, Bertha, my love,
My Bertha, my love, my Bertha, my love!

**JONAS:** (looking at Jean). Heavens!

**ZACHARIA:** What's the matter now?

**JONAS:** (aside). Look at that youth!

**ZACHARIA:** (aside). Indeed!

**MATHISEN:** (aside). Yes, the very features and that air.

**ZACHARIA:** The resemblance is unheard of.

**JONAS:** Yes, before me I fancy I see alive,
David, the King David whom Munster adores!

**MATHISEN:** That picture worshipped in our Westphalia,
And which performs miracles every day!

**JONAS:** Silence!

**CHORUS:** Come, fill up, come here!

**A SOLDIER:** Jean!

**JONAS:** (to a peasant). Friend, who is that man?

**A PEASANT:** Jean, our most worthy host!
Of excellent good heart
And most powerful arm.

**JONAS:** An ardent spirit?

**A PEASANT:** Yes, truly.

**JONAS:** Is he brave?

**A PEASANT:** And devout.
He knows the whole Bible by heart.

**ZACHARIA:** (aside to his companions). Comrades dear, is he not the apostle whom we need?

**MATHISEN:** The very one whom the Lord has called to aid us!

**JEAN:** Night covers the earth
And sweet is repose;
I am waiting for Bertha and my mother,
Go, friends, go, depart!

**THE PEASANTS:** Let us depart, let us depart, he is dreaming of his beloved!
Let us go, the sky is dark!
Let us go!
(In the wings.)
Good night!
Good night!
(The peasants withdraw dancing.

après leur depart restent en scène les trois Anabaptistes et Jean, qui va s'asseoir rêveur près de la table à droite.)

After their departure the three Anabaptists and Jean, who sits in reverie at a table on the right, remain on the stage.)

## SCÈNE II.

## SCENE II.

*Jonas, Mathisen, Zacharie, Jean. (Les Anabaptistes se lévent et s'approchent de Jean.)*
Le songe.

*Jonas, Zacharia, Mathisen and Jean.*
*The dream.*

ZACHARIE: (*à Jean lui frappant sur l'épaule*). Ami, quel nuage obscurcit ta pensée?

ZACHARIA: (*to Jean, slapping him on the shoulder*). What cloud hangs over your thoughts?

JEAN: J'attends ma mère avec ma fiancée,
Leur retard m'inquiète; déjà l'autre nuit,
Un sinistre présage a troublé mon esprit!

JEAN: I am waiting for my mother and my bride,
Their delay disturbs me; the other night
A sinister vision troubled my soul!

ZACHARIE: Qu'est-ce donc?
Parle ami!

ZACHARIA: What was it?
Speak, friend!

JEAN: Qu'ici votre science
Eclaire par pitié ma faible intelligence,
Sur mille objets bizarres et confus,
Et que deux fois en dormant j'air revus!
Sous les vastes arceaux un temple magnifique,
J'etais debout, le peuple à mes pieds prosterné,
Et du bandeau royal, mon front était orné!
Et pendant qu'ils disaient dans un pieux cantique:
C'est l'élu le Messie!
C'est le fils de Dieu!
Je lisais sur le marbre écrit en traits de feu:
Malheur a toi!
Malheur a toi!
Ma main voulait tirer le glaive,
Mais un fleuve de sang, et m'entoure et s'élève,
Pour le fuir sur un trône, en vain j'etais monté;
Et le trône et moi-même, il à tout emporté,
Au milieu des eclairs, au milieu de la flame,
Pendant qu'aux pieds de Dieu, Satan trainait mon âme,
S'élèvait de la terre une clameur:
Qu'il soit maudit!
maudit!
maudit!
Mais vers le ciel et dans l'abîme immense,
Une voix s'éléva, qui répéta:
Clémence!
Clémence!
Clémence!
Ici je me réveillai . . .
Muet . . . anéanti d'épouvante et d'horreur.

JEAN: For pity's sake, with your wisdom,
Enlighten my weak intelligence,
A thousand confused mysteries
Twice have I dreamed!
Beneath the vast arches of a magnificent temple,
I was standing; the people prostrate at my feet,
With an imperial diadem my brow was crowned!
And while they chanted a sacred strain:
"The Messiah has come!
Behold the son of God!"
I read upon the marble walls inscribed in blazing characters:
"Woe to you!
Woe to you!"
My hand was about to draw my sword,
But a river of blood arose and surrounded me,
To escape it, I tried in vain to ascend a throne;
But the throne and I were entirely swept away,
Amid lightning, amid flame,
While to the feet of God, Satan was dragging my soul,
There arose from the earth a clamor:
"Perdition unto him!
Perdition!
Perdition!"
But to Heaven and into the vast abyss,
A voice arose repeating: "Mercy,
Mercy!
Mercy!
Mercy!"
Then I awakened . . .
Speechless, filled with fear and horror.

LES TROIS ANABAPTISTES: Sur ce songe prophetique,
Le ciel même à nous s'explique,
L'avenir s'offre à nos yeux!
Jean tu règneras!

THE THREE ANABAPTISTS: This dream prophetic Heaven itself
Has explained to us,
The future is revealed to our eyes,
Jean, you shall reign!

JEAN: Moi! mes amis, ah! vous n'y pensez pas!
Pour Berthe moi je soupire,
Je me veux pas d'autre empire;
Oui, son coeur est tout pour moi,
Son amour, son amour m'à fait Roi!
Pour moi le plus beau royaume, le plus beau royaume,
Ne vaut pas ce toit de chaume,
Humble empire, doux sejours,
De la paix et de l'amour!
Où Berthe sera toujours,
Mes seuls amours, toujours,
Toujours mes seuls amour.

JEAN: I! dear friends, do not think of it!
I am sighing for Bertha,
I want no other kingdom;
Yes, her heart is all mine,
Her love, her love has made me a king.
For me the most beautiful kingdom
Needs not even this roof of thatch,
Humble empire, sweet retreat,
Of peace and of love,
Where Bertha will be forever
My only love, forever,
Forever my only love, forever!

LES TROIS ANABAPTISTES: Ah, quelle folie extrême!
Dédaigner le rang suprême!
Et bientôt tu régneras!

THE THREE ANABAPTISTS: Oh, what absurd folly!
To refuse the highest rank!
For soon you shall reign!

JEAN: Loin de moi portez vos pas!
(*Les trois Anabaptistes sortent.*)

JEAN: Away from me!
Away!
(*The three Anabaptists go out.*)

## SCÈNE III.

## SCENE III.

*Jean seul.*

*Jean (alone).*

JEAN: Ils partent, grâce au ciel!
Leur funeste présence,
M'empêchait d'être heureux!
Oui, demain quant j'y pense,
Demain mon mariage, ô riant avenir!

JEAN: They are gone, thank Heaven!
Their solemn appearance
Banished my happiness!
Yes, when I think of tomorrow
Of my marriage, tomorrow, of smiling future!

## SCÈNE IV.

## SCENE IV.

*Jean, puis Berthe.*

*Jean, then Bertha.*

JEAN: Quel bruit retentit à cette heure?
N'entends je pas le galop des coursiers? les armes des soldats?
(*Berthe entre en courant, pâle, nupieds et échevelée elle court se jeter dans les bras de Jean.*)
Ah, Berthe, ma bien aimée!
Et d'où vient cet effroi?

JEAN: What does that noise at this hour mean?
Do I not hear the gallop of horsemen? the arms of soldiers?
(*Bertha, pale, barefooted, and dishevelled runs in and throws herself into Jean's arms.*)
Ah! Bertha, my beloved!
Why this terror?

BERTHE: (*bors d'haleine*). Des fureurs d'un tyran . . . sauve moi . . .
Comment fuir ces regards?
Juste ciel!
(*Jean lui montre sous l'escalier un enfoncement caché par un rideau.*)

BERTHA: (*out of breath*). From the fury of a tyrant . . . save me . . .
How can I escape his glances?
Merciful Heaven!
(*Jean shows her a recess hidden by a curtain under the stairway.*)

JEAN: Là! là!
(*Berthe près de l'escalier pendant que Jean regard avec crainte au dehors.*)

JEAN: There!
There!
(*Bertha, near the stairway, while Jean looks outside in fear.*)

BERTHE: (*avec une expression douleureuse*). Ah! d'effroi je tremble encore!
Au trépas, viens m'arracher!
Dieu puissant, toi que j'implore,
A leurs yeux viens me cacher, Mon Dieu!

BERTHA: (*with a sorrowful expression*). Ah! with fright I am still trembling!
From this fate, come rescue me!
God Almighty, I implore you,
Come hide me from their eyes,
Oh, my God!

## SCÈNE V.

## SCENE V.

*Les mêmes, Oberthal, des Gardes. (Berthe se cache dans l'enfoncement à droite.)*

*The same, Oberthal and Guards. (Bertha hides in the recess on the right.)*

**OBERTHAL:** Loin de ces rives, au château de Harlem
Je menais deux captives, deux captives,
Quand près de ta chaumière, et dans un bois épais,
Dont les sombres détours l'ont cachée à ma vue,
L'une d'elles a fui, qu'est elle devenue?
Réponds! réponds! Tu vas me la livrer,
Ou ta mère à l'instant, à tes yeux va périr
Si tu ne parles pas!

**JEAN:** (*poussant un cri, et étendant ses mains suppliantes*).
Ma mère!
Ah! grâce!

**OBERTHAL:** (*souriant*). Ah! le moyen est bon!
Vois!
Choisis!

**JEAN:** (*d'une voix entrecoupée par les sanglots*). Ah! cruels, prenez ma vie!
Tout mon sang, oui, le voilà!
Mais, ma mère, tant chérie,
Ah! de grâce épargnez la!
Ah! Cruels, grâce, grâce, grâce,
Prends pitié de mes alarmes,
Ah! suspends l'arrêt cruel!
Laisse un fils, un fils en larmes,
T'implorer comme le ciel,
T'implorer, hélas, comme le ciel!

**OBERTHAL:** Te voilà reduit aux larmes
M'implorant comme le ciel,
Prends conseil de tes alarmes,
Et préviens l'arrêt mortel, Eh, bien?

**JEAN:** (*avec fureur*). Qu'entre nous deux le ciel juge et decide,
Qu'il fasse sur toi seul tomber le parricide!
(*Oberthal remonte le théâtre, ouvre la porte et fait signe à ses soldats d'amener Fidès. Pendant ce temps Berthe, pâle et tremblante, entr'ouvre le rideau. Jean fait un pas vers elle, mais en ce moment on a traîné Fidès à la porte du fond. Elle tombe à genoux en étendant les bras vers son fils, des soldats lèvent la hache sur sa tête, Jean se retourne, l'aperçoit; il pousse un cri, s'élance vers Berthe et le fait passer devant lui, aù moment où Oberthal redescend le théâtre.*)

**JEAN:** (*avec fureur en jetant Berthe aux mains des soldats*).
Ah! Va-t'en, va-t'en!
Tu le vois,
Il le faut!
Va-t'en!
(*Les soldats entraînent Berthe; Jean tombe hors de lui sur une chaise, ne regardant pas sa mère et se cachant le visage dans ses mains.*)

**OBERTHAL:** Far from these shores, to my Harlem castle,
Two captives I was leading, two captives,
When near your hut, and in a thick wood
Whose dark paths hid her from my sight
One of them escaped. What has become of her?
Reply! Reply! You must deliver her to me,
Or your mother straight away will perish before your eyes,
If you do not speak.

**JEAN:** (*uttering a cry, and extending his hands in supplication*). My mother!
Ah! Mercy!

**OBERTHAL:** (*smiling*). Ah! it was a good means!
See!
Choose!

**JEAN:** (*sobbing*). Cruel man, take my life, yes, here,
But my mother, so dear,
For pity's sake spare her!
Ah! Cruel one, mercy, mercy, mercy!
Take pity on my fright,
Suspend this cruel arrest.
Let a son's tears
Implore you as Heaven,
Implore you, alas, as Heaven.

**OBERTHAL:** Ah! At last I see you weeping,
Imploring me as the Heaven,
Take counsel from your fright,
And prevent the mortal arrest,
Well, then?

**JEAN:** (*furiously*). Between us two let Heaven judge and decide,
That the guilt of parricide may fall on you alone.
(*Oberthal crosses the stage, opens the door and gives the signal to his soldiers to bring Fides in. Meanwhile Bertha, pale and trembling, draws the curtain back. Jean motions to her, but at that moment Fidès is dragged to the door at the back. She falls on her knees stretching her arms toward her son. The soldiers raise an axe over her head. Jean turns around and sees this; he utters a cry, rushes toward Bertha, lets her pass in front of him, just as Oberthal crosses the stage again.*)

**JEAN:** (*throwing Bertha furiously into the hands of the soldiers*). Ah!
Go! Go!
You see!
It is our fate!
Go!
(*The soldiers take Bertha away. Jean falls distractedly on a chair without noticing his mother and hiding his face in his hands.*)

## SCÈNE VI.

*Jean, Fidès.*

**FIDÈS:** (*d'une voix timide, et pleurant*). Ah! mon fils, sois beni,
Ta pauvre mère, toi plus chère,
Que ta Berthe, que ton amour!
Ah! mon fils!
Ah! mon fils!
Tu viens, hélas! de donner pour ta mère,
Plus que la vie, en donnant ton bonheur, ton bonheur!
Ah! mon fils!
Ah! mon fils!
Que vers le ciel s'élève ma prière,
Et sois beni dans le Seigneur, mon fils,
Sois beni, dans le Seigneur! sois beni!
(*Elle embrasse Jean avec transport.*)
Jean! ah! sois beni!
(*Jean par un geste indique à sa mère qu'il est calme, et l'invite à se retirer dans sa chambre pour se reposer. Fidès inquiète, hésite, puis obéit, en se retirant lentement.*)

## SCÈNE VII.

*Jean, puis Jonas, Mathisen et Zacharie.*

**JEAN:** (*cessant de se contraindre et éclatant*). O fureur!
Le ciel ne tonne pas sur ces têtes impies!

**LES TROIS ANABAPTISTES:** (*dans les coulisses, de très loin*).
Ad nos, ad salutarem undam!

**JEAN:** (*à voix basse*). Ah! c'est Dieu qui m'entends!
Dieu qui me les envoie!
(*D'une voix etouffée.*)
Venez! venez!
Entrez, nous sommes seuls!
Dans mes rêves tantôt lisant le rang suprême,
Ne m'avez-vous dit pas: suis nous, tu régneras?

**LES TROIS ANABAPTISTES:** Et nous t'offrons encor un diadême,
Sois roi!
Sois roi!

**JEAN:** Que faut-il faire alors? parlez, et je vous suis!

**ZACHARIE:** (*à demi voix*).
Gémissant sous le joug et sous la tyrannie,
Nos frères d'Allemagne attendent le Messie,
Qui doit briser leurs fers! prêts à se soulever
Au seul nom de Prophète
Que Dieu leur a promis et que j'ai su trouver!

**JEAN:** Que dites-vous?

## SCENE VI.

*Jean, Fides.*

**FIDES:** (*timidly and weeping*).
Ah! my son, God bless you!
Your poor mother, more dear to you,
Than your Bertha, your love.
Ah! my son!
Ah! my son!
Alas!
You have just given for your mother,
In giving your happiness, more than life.
Ah! my son! ah, my son!
To Heaven, to Heaven let my prayer rise,
And blessed be my son, blessed!
(*She embraces Jean in a transport.*)
Jean!
Ah! God bless you!
(*Jean shows his mother by a gesture that he is calm, and invites her to withdraw to her room to rest. Fides, anxious, hesitates, then obeys, withdrawing gently.*)

## SCENE VII.

*Jean, then Jonas, Mathisen and Zacharia.*

**JEAN:** (*bursting out*). Oh! Fury!
And Heaven does not burst upon these impious heads!

**THE THREE ANABAPTISTS:** (*in the wings; from afar*). Ad nos, ad salutarem undam!

**JEAN:** (*softly*). Ah! God hears me!
He sends them to me!
(*Choking.*)
Come, come!
Enter!
We are alone!
Interpreting my dreams the highest rank
Have you not said to me: Follow us and you shall reign?

**THE THREE ANABAPTISTS:** And we still offer you a crown,
Be king!
Be king!

**JEAN:** What must I do then! Speak! and I follow you.

**ZACHARIA:** (*whispering*). Groaning beneath the yoke of tyranny,
Our brothers in Germany await the Messiah,
Ready to raise himself
To the name of Prophet alone,
Who will shatter their fetters! Whom God has promised them and whom I know I have found!

**JEAN:** What do you say?

**JONAS:** Le ciel dont il est l'interprète,
Le ciel nous a lui-même,
À des signes certains,
Révélé cet élu marqué par les destins!

**LES TROIS ANABAPTISTES:** Jean, Dieu t'appelle!
Ah! viens, viens avec nous, mon frère!
(*À demi voix.*)
Oui, c'est Dieu qui t'appelle, qui t'éclaire,
A tes yeux a brillé sainte lumière,
En tes mains sa bannière,
Avec elle apparais dans nos rangs,
Et des grands cette foule si fière,
Va par toi se reduire en poussière,
Car le ciel t'a choisi sur la tèrre,
Qui, j'irai sous ta sainte bannière,
A ta voix les reduire en poussière,
Car ton bras m'a choisi sur la tèrre,
Pour frapper et punir les tyrans!
Ne sais-tu pas qu'en France, une chaste héroïne,
Qu'inspiraient comme toi de saintes visions,
Jeanne d'Arc, a sauvé son pays?

**JEAN:** Oui, partons!

**ZACHARIE:** Mais envoyé du ciel, songe bien desormais
Que tout lien terrestre est brisé pour jamais!
Que tu ne verras plus ton pays, ni ta mère!

**JEAN:** Partir sans voir ma mère?

**ZACHARIE:** Il le faut!
Dieu le veut!

**JEAN:** (*s'approche la chambre de Fidès*). Silence, elle dort . . .
Et pendant son sommeil murmure une prière!
(*Ecoutant et répétant à mesure les paroles de sa mère.*)
C'est pour moi qu'elle prie!
Dieu veillez sur mon enfant!
Et son enfant la fuit et la délaisse!
Non, non, non, partez sans moi,
Je reste!
Je reste à sa veillesse!
Ma mère est le seul bein qui me reste à présent!

**ZACHARIE:** (*s'approche mystérieusement de Jean d'une voix étouffée*). Et le vengeance?

**MATHISEN:** (*s'approchant de l'autre côté de Jean*). Et l'espérance . . .
De voir tomber nos oppresseurs?

**JONAS:** Et la couronne,
Que le Ciel donne,
A ses élus, à ses vengeurs!
O sainte extase,
Qui nous embrâse,
Viens le guider dans les combats!

**JONAS:** Heaven whose interpreter he is,
Heaven has revealed itself to us
By certain signs,
This chosen one designated by destiny!

**THE THREE ANABAPTISTS:** Jean, God calls you!
Ah! come, come with us, my brother!
(*Whispering.*)
Yes, it is God who calls you!
Ah! who calls you, who instructs you,
For your eyes sacred light shines,
In your hands His banner;
With it appear in our ranks,
And all the vast host so arrogant,
Will be reduced by you to dust,
For Heaven has chosen you
To punish the tyrants on earth.
Yes, I am going to bear your sacred banner,
At your command to reduce them to dust,
For your arm has chosen me
To punish the tyrants on earth.
Do you know that in France, a virgin,
Who, inspired as you were by sacred visions,
Joan of Arc, saved her country?

**JEAN:** Yes, let us go!

**ZACHARIA:** But since you have been sent by Heaven,
Consider all earthly ties forever broken!
You shall never more see your native land, nor your mother!

**JEAN:** Go away without seeing my mother?

**ZACHARIA:** Your fate is so decreed!
God desires it!

**JEAN:** (*going to Fides' room*). Silence!
She sleeps!
And sleeping murmurs a prayer!
(*Listening and repeating the words of his mother.*)
She prays for me!
"God guard my child!"
And her child is fleeing and forsaking her!
No, no, go without me!
I shall remain to watch over her old age!
My mother is the only treasure I have left!

**ZACHARIA:** (*approaching Jean mysteriously*). And your vengeance?

**MATHISEN:** (*from the other side*). And the hope of seeing our oppressors fall?

**JONAS:** And the crown,
Which heaven gives
To her elect, to her avengers!
Oh sacred ecstasy
Which enfolds us,
Come, guide him in the combats!

**JEAN:** Non, non, non!
Si je l'embrassais
Je ne partirais pas!
Allons!
Partons!
Partons!
(*Tous les quatre sortent.*)

*RIDEAU.*

## ■ ACTE III.

(*Le camp des Anabaptistes dans une forêt de Westphalie. En face du spectateur un étang glacé qui s'étend à l'horizon et qui se perd dans les brouillards et dans les nuages. À droite et à gauche une antique forêt dont les arbres bordent un côté de l'étang. Du l'autre côté de cet étang les tentes des Anabaptistes. Le jour est sur son déclin, on entend dans le lontain un bruit de combat qui augmente et se rapproche. Des soldats Anabaptistes se précipitent sur le théâtre par la droite. Des femmes et des enfants sortant du camp, accourent à leur rencontre, au moment où un autre groupe de soldats entre par la gauche traînant enchaînés plusieurs prisonniers, hommes et femmes, richement vêtus, hauts barons et dames châtelaines, un moine, des enfants, etc.*)

### SCÈNE I.

**MATHISEN:** (*prenant Zacharie à part*). Voici la fin du jour, nos fidèles soldats,
Depuis l'aurore ont tous combattu!

**ZACHARIE:** Pour la gloire!

**MATHISEN:** Aux estomac à jeun elle ne suffit pas!

**ZACHARIE:** Voici venir pour eux les fruits de la victoire!
Sur cet étang glacé de tous les environs,
De nombreux pourvoyeurs, le front haut, le pied leste,
Accourent vers le camp!

**MATHISEN:** (*se frappant joyeusement les mains*). C'est la manne céleste!
Qui vient reconforter nos pieux bataillons.

**ZACHARIE:** (*en riant*). C'est la manne celeste!

(*L'arrivée des patineurs.*)
(*Pendant ce choeur on voit dans le fond du théâtre défiler sur l'étang glacé des traineaux attelés de chevaux, de petites voitures à quatre roues, chargées de provisions. La fermière est assise sur la banquette de devant, et un homme, debout derrière elle, pousse le traineau en patinant. Des hommes, des femmes et des enfants, portant sur leur têtes des*

**JEAN:** No, no, no, no!
If I should kiss her
I would not go!
Come!
Let us go!
Let us go!
(*The four go out.*)

*CURTAIN.*

## ■ ACT III.

(*The Anabaptist camp in a Westphalian forest. A frozen lake extends to the horizon and disappears in the mist and clouds. To the right and left an ancient forest whose trees border one side of the lake. On the other side of this lake are the tents of the Anabaptists. It is near the close of day. In the distance a noise of fighting which increases and comes nearer is heard. The Anabaptist soldiers rush in on the right. Women and children coming out of the camp, run to meet them, just as another group of soldiers enters on the left dragging several prisoners in chains, men, women richly dressed, lords and ladies, a monk, some children, etc.*)

### SCENE I.

**MATHISEN:** (*taking Zacharia aside*). Behold the day's decline!
Our faithful soldiers have fought Since the dawn!

**ZACHARIA:** For glory!

**MATHISEN:** That does not appease the call of hunger.

**ZACHARIA:** Behold!
The fruits of victory are coming for them
Over this icy lake from every side,
Purveyors are coming, heads high and light of foot.

**MATHISEN:** (*clapping his hands in glee*). It is manna from Heaven!
Sent to comfort our pious battalions!

**ZACHARIA:** (*smiling*). It is manna from Heaven.

(*The arrival of the skaters.*)
(*During this chorus, in the background, passing over the frozen lake, are horses and wagons, small four-wheeled carriages, laden with provisions. A farmer's wife sits on the front seat, and men, women and children, carrying baskets or bowls of milk on their heads, skate in all directions over the lake, and stop near the camp.*)

paniers ou des pots du lait, sillonnent l'étang glacé dans tous les sens en patinant, et abordent auprès du camp.)

**CHOEUR:** Voici les fermières,
Lestes et légères,
Sur leurs têtes fières,
Portant leur fardeaux;
Leur pieds sur la glace,
Courant avec grâce,
Sans laisser de trâce
Glissent sur les flots.

**CHORUS:** The maidens are coming,
So swiftly and lightly,
With heads held high,
Carrying their burdens;
Over the ice, over the ice,
Sliding with grace,
Without leaving a trace,
They glide over the paths!

## SCÈNE II.

**ZACHARIE:** (allant à Mathisen). Tu reviens de Munster?

**MATHISEN:** J'ai sommé de se rendre
Son gouverneur, le vieil Oberthal!

**ZACHARIE:** Qu'a-t-il dit?

**MATHISEN:** Le château de son fils par nous réduit en cendres,
L'a rendu furieux;
Il ne veut rien entendre, l'impie!

**ZACHARIE:** Il a beau faire, il cèdera bientôt!

**MATHISEN:** Oui, mais en attendant, si Munster nous résiste,
C'en est fait dès demain du dogme.
Anabaptiste,
Car l'empereur accourt!

## SCENE II.

**ZACHARIA:** (going over to Mathisen). You return from Munster?

**MATHISEN:** To surrender have I ordered its governor,
The old count Oberthal.

**ZACHARIA:** What did he say?

**MATHISEN:** His breast was filled with rage, for we had
Reduced his son's castle to ashes;
He would have nothing to do with us.

**ZACHARIA:** That was beautifully done!
He will soon yield.

**MATHISEN:** Yes, but if Munster still holds out, after tomorrow
Nothing will be left of our Anabaptist creed.
The Emperor is making all haste to go there.

## SCÈNE III.

Zacharie, Jonas, et Oberthal amené par plusieurs soldats.

**ZACHARIE:** Qui marche là? Qui vive?

**JONAS:** Un voyageur errant,
Que je viens de surprendre
Aux environs du camp!

**OBERTHAL:** (avec embarras). Egaré dans la nuit et dans ce bois immense . . .

**JONAS:** Il venait, m'a-t-il dit, se joindre à nous.

**ZACHARIE:** (s'adressant à Oberthal puis à Jonas). Avance!
Tu dis donc qu'en nos rangs il venait s'engager?

**OBERTHAL:** (à part). Laissons-lui son erreur, seul moyen, je pense!
De pénétrer plus tard à Munster sans danger!

**JONAS:** Mais pourquoi dans l'ombre, demeurer ainsi?
Chassons la nuit sombre, qui nous couvre ici.
(Battant le briquet.)
La flamme scintille, scintille,
Et grâce à ce fer,
Du caillou pétille, pétille,
Et jaillit l'éclair!

## SCENE III.

Zacharia, Jonas and Oberthal led by several soldiers.

**ZACHARIA:** Who is approaching? Who goes there?

**JONAS:** This traveler loitering,
I have just found
Within our lines.

**OBERTHAL:** (hesitating). Lost in this vast forest at night . . .

**JONAS:** He was coming, he told me, to join our ranks.

**ZACHARIA:** (addressing Oberthal first, then Jonas). Come forward!
You say then that he was coming to ally himself with us?

**OBERTHAL:** (aside). I must let him have it so!
The only way, I fear,
Of later reaching Munster without peril.

**JONAS:** Buy why in the darkness do you remain this way?
(Striking light with flint and steel.)
The flame scintillates,
And thanks to this steel,
Gives sparks, sparks,
And bursts into light!

**JONAS, OBERTHAL ET ZACHARIE:** O douce rencontre,
Qui sans doute ici
L'un à l'autre nous montre,
Les traits d'un ami, d'un ami!
(Il bat de nouveau le briquet.)
La flamme scintille, etc.

**JONAS:** (reconnaissant Oberthal). O ciel! cet infame!

**OBERTHAL:** (reconnaissant Jonas). C'est lui!
Brigand!

**ZACHARIE:** Oberthal.

**OBERTHAL:** Mon sommelier, fils de satan!

**JONAS:** Mon ancien maître! ah! mon tyran!
Toi qui fis couler notre sang!

**ZACHARIE:** Le ciel nous éclaire, frère,
À notre bannière sainte,
Tu sera pendu, j'espère,
Pendu, mon cher frère,
O destin prospère,
A notre bannière,
Tu seras, j'espère,
Pendu par un frère, par un ami.

**OBERTHAL:** Vous qui tous deux l'enfer reclâme,
L'enfer reclâme tous deux!
Grand Dieu, ta juste colère,
Aneantira, j'espère,
Cette race sanguinaire!
Soyez tous maudits!
Ta juste colère
Chatiera, j'espère,
Ces bandits maudits!
(Les soldats qui étaient en sentinelles à la porte de la tente sont accourus au bruit et entourent Oberthal.)

**ZACHARIE:** (à Jonas lui montrant Oberthal). Qu'on le mene au supplice!
Ah! qu'un moine l'escorte!

**JONAS:** (s'arrêtant et reflechissant). Sans consulter le Prophète!

**ZACHARIE:** Il m'importe!
C'est lui . . . va-t'en!
(Jonas sort par la gauche avec Oberthal et les soldats.)

## SCÈNE IV.

Zacharie et Jean.
(Jean entre par la droite, l'air pensif et la tête baissée.)

**ZACHARIE:** (s'approchant de Jean). Quel air pensif et soucieux,
Quand le guerrier prophète, inspiré par les cieux,
Apparait dans sa gloire à l'Allemagne entière,
Comme l'ange vengeur que la France revère.

**JONAS, OBERTHAL AND ZACHARIA:** Oh, happy meeting,
Which doubtless will reveal
To one another
The features of a friend!
(Strikes the light again.) The flame scintillates!

**JONAS:** (recognizing Oberthal). O Heaven!
That wretch!

**OBERTHAL:** (recognizing Jonas). It is he!
The robber!

**ZACHARIA:** Oberthal.

**OBERTHAL:** My butler, the son of Satan!

**JONAS:** My former master!
My tyrant!
You who have shed so much of our blood!

**ZACHARIA:** Heaven clears for us, brother,
From our sacred banner,
You will hang, I hope,
Hang, dear brother!
O happy fate,
From our banner,
You will hang, I hope!
Hung by a brother, by a friend!

**OBERTHAL:** May perdition reclaim both of you!
Great God, your just wrath
Will destroy, I hope,
This bloodthirsty race
Cursed be all!
Your just wrath,
Will punish, I hope,
These accursed bandits!
(The sentinels at the door of the tent on hearing the noise run in and surround Oberthal.)

**ZACHARIA:** (to Jonas, pointing to Oberthal). Have him led to the gallows!
Let a monk escort him!

**JONAS:** (stopping to reflect). Without consulting the Prophet?

**ZACHARIA:** It is my affair!
It is he . . . Away!
(Jonas goes out left with Oberthal and the soldiers.)

## SCENE IV.

Zacharia and Jean.
(Jean enters on the right, with pensive air and bowed head.)

**ZACHARIA:** (going up to Jean). What a pensive and worried air,
When the warrior Prophet, inspired by Heaven,
Appears in his glory to all Germans
Like the avenging angel whom France reveres.

## Act III, Scene IV

**JEAN:** Jeanne d'Arc, sur ses pas, fit naître des héros,
Et je n'ai sur les miens trainé que des bourreaux!
Je n'irai pas plus loin!

**ZACHARIE:** Qu'oses tu dire?

**JEAN:** Que je veux voir ma mère, ma mère chérie!

**ZACHARIE:** Où plustôt son trépas,
Car si tu la revois,
Ne t'en souvient-il pas?
Dans l'interêt du ciel elle expire!

**JEAN:** (*se levant et jetant son épée*). Pour m'immoler d'abord reprenez donc ce fer,
Je vous le rend, adieu!
L'Allemagne enchaînée
Est libre par mon bras!
Ma tâche est terminée!
Je n'irai pas plus loin!
Non! non!

**ZACHARIE:** (*portant la main à son poignard*). Par l'enfer! par mort!

## SCÈNE V.

*Les mêmes, Oberthal.*
(*Oberthal, la tête baissée, conduit par Jonas et des soldats traverse le fond de théâtre, en dehors de la tente. Le moine qui a paru à la première scène est à côté d'Oberthal et l'exhorte. Deux soldats portent des torches.*)

**JEAN:** (*se retournant*). Ou va ce prisonnier?

**OBERTHAL:** Il est juste,
Mon crime a merité la mort!
Du haut de mes créneaux,
Berthe, pure et chaste victime,
Pour sauver son honneur,
S'élance dans les flots!

**JEAN:** Morte!
Morte!
Et comment?
Parle!

**OBERTHAL:** Hier un avis sûr m'apprend
Qu'on l'a vue à Munster.

**JEAN:** À Munster?

**OBERTHAL:** J'aillais implorer d'elle,
Et du ciel, mon pardon,
Et en tes mains me voilà!
J'ai tout dit. Frappe!

**JEAN:** (*aux soldats qui s'avance la hache levée*). Epargnez l'infidèle,
Berthe sur lui prononcera!
(*Les soldats emmènent Oberthal.*)

## SCÈNE VI.

*Jean seul.*

## Act III, Scene IV

**JEAN:** Joan of Arc, in her steps,
Made heroes spring up, and I
Have dragged in mine only butchers!
I will go no further!

**ZACHARIA:** What do you dare say?

**JEAN:** How I long to see my dear mother!

**ZACHARIA:** Or rather her doom,
For if you see her again,
Do you not recall?
She will die in Heaven's cause!

**JEAN:** (*rising and brandishing his sword*). To slay me first take back this blade,
I return it to you, farewell!
Germany, enslaved,
Is freed by my arm!
My task is over!
No further will I go!
No!
No!

**ZACHARIA:** (*putting his hand on his poniard*). Through Hell!
Through death!

## SCENE V.

*The same, Oberthal.*
(*Oberthal, with head bowed, led by Jonas and some soldiers, crosses the back of the stage outside of the tent. The monk seen in the first scene is at Oberthal's side and exhorts him. Soldiers bear torches.*)

**JEAN:** (*turning around*). Where is this prisoner going?

**OBERTHAL:** Heaven is just!
My crime deserves death!
From my highest towers,
Bertha, pure and chaste victim,
To preserve her honor,
Plunged into the waves.

**JEAN:** To death?
To death?
But how?
Speak!

**OBERTHAL:** Yesterday a trustworthy spy informed me
He had seen her at Munster.

**JEAN:** At Munster?

**OBERTHAL:** I was bound there to beg her pardon
And also Heaven, and behold I am in your hands!
I have told all.
Strike!

**JEAN:** (*to the soldiers who advance with raised axes*). Spare the infidel!
Bertha will pronounce his sentence!
(*The soldiers lead Oberthal away.*)

## SCENE VI.

*Jean (alone).*

---

**JEAN:** Remparts, que ma pitié
N'osait réduire en cendre,
Vous qui me cache Berthe,
Il faudra me la rendre!
Fidèles compagnons, vous me suivrez!

## SCÈNE VII.

*Jean, Mathisen.*

**MATHISEN:** (*accourant éffrayé*).
O terreur!
Toi seul peux desarmer ces cohortes rebelles;
Des portes de Munster, des guerriers sont sortis
Et les notres par eux mis en fuite!

**JEAN:** (*suivi de Mathisen. Il se précipite par la gauche hors de la tente*). Courons!
Courons!

## SCÈNE VIII.

*Jean, Mathisen, Jonas, Zacharie.*

**JEAN:** (*aux soldats d'un ton sévère*). Qui, vous a, sans mon ordre,
Entrainés aux combats?

**PREMIER ANABAPTISTE:** (*montrant Mathisen*). C'est lui!

**MATHISEN:** (*éffrayé montrant Zacharie*). C'est lui!

**DEUXIÈME ANABAPTISTE:** C'est lui!

**JEAN:** Perfides, que mon bras devrait punir!
Et vous insensés que vous êtes,
Depuis quand au trépas ai-je voué vos têtes,
Sans y marcher devant vous?
Du Dieu qui dans ses mains tenait les palmes prêtes,
Votre rebellion excita le courroux!
L'éternel dites-vous, à l'ennemi vous livre:
C'est que l'impiété règne encor dans vos coeurs!
Ils n'avaient pas la foi, ces tièdes serviteurs,
Que Dieu dans ses décrets juge indignes de vivre!
Craignez plutôt comme eux le celeste courroux,
Et pour le calmer, peuple impie,
Peuple à genoux! à genoux! à genoux!
Et sous son bras vengeur—coupables, courbez-vous!

**CHOEUR:** À ses accents d'un saint effroi,
J'ai tressailli
Car l'Eternel, car Dieu,
Est encor avec lui!
(*On entend du loin un bruit de clairons et de trompettes.*)

---

**JEAN:** Battlements, which my pity
Dared not reduce to ashes,
You that hid from me
My Bertha, ought to return her to me!
Faithful companions, you will follow me!

## SCENE VII.

*Jean, Mathisen.*

**MATHISEN:** (*running in fright*).
O terror!
You alone can disarm these rebel cohorts;
From the gates of Munster, warriors have come
And have put ours to flight!

**JEAN:** (*followed by Mathisen. He rushes out of the tent, on the left*). Run!
Run!

## SCENE VIII.

*Jean, Mathisen, Jonas, Zacharia.*

**JEAN:** (*to the soldiers severely*). Who, without command from me,
Who has dared lead you into battle?

**FIRST ANABAPTIST:** (*pointing to Mathisen*). It was he!

**MATHISEN:** (*frightened, pointing to Zacharia*). It was he!

**SECOND ANABAPTIST:** It was he!

**JEAN:** Faithless ones, whom my arm
Should punish!
And you senseless ones,
Since when to death
Have I dedicated you,
Without marching before you?
Of God who in His hands was holding in readiness
The palms, your rebellion will excite the wrath!
The Eternal One delivers you to the enemy, you say:
It is because impiety still reigns in your hearts!
They have no faith, these indifferent servants,
Whom God in His decrees judges unworthy to live!
Fear rather like them the celestial wrath,
And to appease it, impious people,
On your knees!
Fall on your knees!
And beneath His arm revenging
Guilty ones, bow!

**CHORUS:** At his words I tremble with fright,
For the Eternal One, for God is with him, still with him!
(*In the distance a sound of clarions and trumpets is heard.*)

**JEAN:** Écoutez!
Écoutez! quels sons se font entendre?
Les clairons de Munster, reveillent nos clairons!
Dieu m'inspire! ah! venez, et demain sur vos fronts
La victoire sainte va descendre!
Et la grâce du Seigneur va s'étendre.

**MATHISEN:** (*accourt suivi d'une foule de paysans armée*). Grand prophète, ton peuple se rélève, er tu regnes,
Oui, tous les paysans, en agitant leurs fers,
Courent se ranger sous tes saintes enseignes!

**PREMIER ANABAPTISTE:** Maître, un seul cri s'élève: l'assaut à Munster!

**JEAN:** (*sans écouter Mathisen et comme frappé d'une vision*). Que vois-je! le ciel est ouverte!
(*D'une voix mystérieuse.*)
Sur les harpes les voix des anges,
Chantent en cheour:
À Munster!
À Munster!

**TOUS:** À Munster!

**JEAN:** (*avec exaltation*). Roi du ciel et des anges,
je dirai tes louanges,
Comme David ton serviteur!

**CHOEUR:** En marche, en marche, en marche!

**JEAN:** Car Dieu nous suit de ses regards.

**CHOEUR:** Vous clairons, répétez notre chant triomphant,
Marchons!
À Munster! oui! oui!
En marche!
Dieu nous suit!
(*Dans ce moment le brouillard qui couvrait l'étang et la forêt se dissipe. Le soleil brille et laisse apercevoir dans le lointain, au-delà de l'étang glacé, la ville et les remparts de Munster, que Jean montre de la main. L'armée pousse des cris de joie, et incline devant lui les bannières. La toile tombe.*)

*RIDEAU.*

■ **ACTE IV.**

(*Le théâtre représente une place publique de la ville de Munster. À droite la porte de l'Hôtel de la ville; plusieurs marches y conduisent. Plusieurs rues aboutissent à la place publique. Au lever du rideau plusieurs bourgeois, portant des sacs d'argent où des vases précieux, montent les marches de l'Hôtel de ville; d'autre descen-*

**JEAN:** Listen!
Listen!
What sounds do we hear?
The trumpets of Munster, awakening our clarions!
O God, inspire me!
Ah!
Come, and tomorrow, on our heads
The blessed victory will descend!
And the grace of the Lord will fall on us!

**MATHISEN:** (*running in followed by a crowd of armed peasants*). Great Prophet, your people awaken and you reign,
Yes, all the peasants, unsheathing their swords,
Hasten to gather under your sacred ensigns!

**FIRST ANABAPTIST:** Master, one cry alone arises: Down with Munster!

**JEAN:** (*without hearing Mathisen and as if entranced*). What do I see?
Heaven opens up!
(*Mysteriously.*)
Above the harps the voices of angels,
Sing in chorus: On to Munster!
On to Munster!

**ALL:** On to Munster!

**JEAN:** (*exalted*). Ruler of Heaven and the Angels,
I will sound your praises,
As David thy servant!

**CHORUS:** March, march, march, march!

**JEAN:** For God follows us with His eyes.

**CHORUS:** You, clarions, repeat our song triumphant,
March!
To Munster!
Yes, yes!
March!
God follows us!
(*Just then the fog begins to disappear. The sun shines and in the distance above the frozen lake the battlements of Munster appear. Jean points to them. The army utters cries of joy and lowers its banners. The curtain falls.*)

*CURTAIN.*

■ **ACT IV.**

(*A square in Munster. On the right the gates of the Town Hall; several steps leading to it. Various streets meet at the square. When the curtain rises a number of citizens carrying sacks of gold or precious vases, ascend the steps of the Town Hall: others descend with empty hands. Many arrive by different streets and form groups*

*dent les mains vides. Plusieurs arrivent par les différentes rues, s'avancent au bord du théâtre et forment des groupes. Ils regardent autour d'eux avec inquiétude et se parlent à voix basse.*)

*SCÈNE I.*

**BOURGEOIS DE MUNSTER:** Courbons notre tête,
Craignons les mechants!
Voici la tempête,
Voici la tempête,
Et tous les noirs autans!
(*Voyant venir une patrouille de soldats anabaptistes ils crient à haute voix:*)
Vive le prophète,
Vivent ses soldats, ses soldats!
(*À voix basse entr'eux.*)
À bas ses soldats!
À bas le prophète!
À bas!

*SCÈNE II.*

*Les mêmes, Fidès.*

**LE TROISIÈME BOURGEOIS:** (*seul, voyant Fidès assise*). Assise sur cette pierre,
Femme, que fais-tu là?
(*Quelques bourgeois conduisent Fidès qui parait épuisée de fatigue, sur l'avant scène.*)

**FIDÈS:** (*d'une voix plaintive*). Donnez, donnez, pour une pauvre âme,
Ouvrez-lui le paradis, le paradis!
Donnez, donnez à la pauvre femme,
Qui prie, hélas! pour son fils!
Donnez! donnez! nobles seigneurs,
Donnez de grâce,
Au sein de votre richesse,
Pitié, seigneur opulent!
Donnez, pour dire une messe,
Hélas! à mon pauvre enfant!
(*Sanglottant.*)
Pitié!
Donnez!
Ah! ah! ah!
Hélas! Pitié!

**DEUXIÈME BOURGEOIS:** (*à demi voix*). C'est l'heure!
(*On entend le son d'un crecelle dans une des cours interieures du palais.*)

**CHOEUR:** On nous attend!

**DEUXIÈME BOURGEOIS:** Et si nous differons—

**PREMIER BOURGEOIS:** Il y va de nos jours!

**TROISIÈME BOURGEOIS:** (*il donne de l'argent à Fidès*). Tiens! Tiens!

**FIDÈS:** Merci!
(*Ils reprennent leurs sacs d'argent et rentrent tous dans l'interieur du palais.*)

*at the front of the stage. They look about them anxiously and whisper to each other.*)

*SCENE I.*

**CITIZENS OF MUNSTER:** Let us bend our heads,
Let us fear the wicked!
Look! here comes the storm
With all its dark blasts.
(*Seeing a troop of Anabaptist soldiers coming, they exclaim:*)
Long live the Prophet,
Long live his soldiers!
(*Aside to each other.*)
Down with his soldiers!
Down with the Prophet!
Down!

*SCENE II.*

*The same, Fides.*

**THIRD CITIZEN:** (*seeing Fides*). Seated upon that stone,
Woman, what do you want here?
(*Some of the citizens lead Fides, who seems overwhelmed with fatigue, to the front of the stage.*)

**FIDES:** (*plaintively*). Give, oh, give, to save a poor soul,
Open for her paradise, paradise!
Give, oh, give, to save a poor soul
Who prays, alas, for her son,
Give, oh, give, noble lords,
A portion of your wealth.
Pity! oh, opulent master!
Give for one mass
For my son, alas!
(*Sobbing.*)
Pity!
Give an alms!
Pity!

**SECOND CITIZEN:** (*in a low tone*). The hour has come!
(*The sound of a racket in one of the interior courts of the palace is heard.*)

**SOME:** They now await our coming!

**SECOND CITIZEN:** And if we delay!

**FIRST CITIZEN:** That will be the end of our days.

**THIRD CITIZEN:** (*giving Fides money*). Here! Here!

**FIDES:** Thanks!
(*They take up their sacks again and all return to go back into the palace.*)

LES TROIS BOURGEOIS: Et courons!

THE THREE CITIZENS: Let us hurry!

## SCÈNE III.

*Fidès, un jeune pélerin.*
*(Il sort de la rue à droite et*
*marche avec peine.)*

FIDÈS: Un pauvre pélerin
De fatigue, mon frère,
Vous semble accablé!

BERTHE: Dieu, quelle est cette
voix?

FIDÈS: Berthe, Berthe!
Ces traits!

BERTHE: Fidès, ma bonne mère!

FIDÈS: Sous ces habits, c'est toi que
je revois.
*(Elles se jettent dans les bras l'une*
*de l'autre, et semblent*
*s'interroger.)*

BERTHE: Pour garder à ton fils le
serment qui m'engage.
J'ai cherché vainement le trépas
dans les flots;
Un pêcheur m'a portée expirante
au rivage,
Où des soins généreux l'ont cachée
aux bourreaux!
Et plus tard j'ai couru.
J'ai revu ta chaumière!
Où sont-ils?
Où sont-ils? disparus pour jamais!
Loin d'ici, disaient-ils, et le fils et la
mère,
Pour Munster sont partis!
Suivons-les! ai-je dit,
Vers Munster, j'ai tourné mon es-
poir!
La naguère
Mon aïeul, vieux soldat, fut guar-
dien du palais,
Et j'accours!
Je te vois, mon amie et ma mère,
Guide moi vers ton fils! conduis-
moi dans ses bras!
O bonheur!
O transport!
O bonheur!
O transport!
Je te vois!
Ah! conduis-moi vers ton fils! viens!
J'accours, je te vois, conduis-moi
dans ses bras!
O mon bonheur!
Conduis-moi dans ses bras!
Hatons-nous!
Dans quels lieux est il donc?

FIDÈS: (*à part*). Pauvre fille!
Si joyeuse, comment faire,
Pour t'apprendre ta misère,
Pour te dire ici, moi, sa mère, moi,
sa mère,
De Jean, hélas le trépas!
*(Avec embarras et contenant à*
*peine ses larmes.)*
Mon fils!
Mon fils!
Il est mort!
Il est mort!

## SCENE III.

*Fides, a young pilgrim.*
*(He comes from the street on the*
*right and walks with difficulty.)*

FIDES: A poor pilgrim
You seem weighed down
With fatigue, brother!

BERTHA: Heavens!
Whose voice is that?

FIDES: Ah, Bertha, Bertha!
Those features!

BERTHA: Fides, my mother!

FIDES: In this attire, it is you whom
I see again.
*(They embrace each other, and*
*seem to ask each other questions.)*

BERTHA: To keep the vow which
bound me to your son,
I sought in vain death amid the
waves;
A fisherman bore me, dying to the
shore,
Where generous care hid me from
the tyrant.
Later while searching about, I saw
once more your cot!
"Where are they?
Where?"
"Gone forever,
Far from here," they said,
"Both the son and the mother
Have departed to Munster."
"Let us follow them," I said.
I turned my hope to Munster.
The swimmer,
My god-father, an old soldier, is
warden of the palace,
And I hastened here.
I now behold you, my beloved
mother.
Take me to your son!
Lead me to his arms!
O happiness!
O transport!
O happiness!
O transport!
I am seeing you!
Lead me to your son.
Come!
I hurried here; I am here!
Oh, lead me to his arms!
O happiness!
Lead me to his arms!
Hurry!
Where is he now?

FIDES: (*aside*). Poor girl, full of
joy,
How can I acquaint you of your mis-
ery?
How can I tell you here, I, his moth-
er,
Of Jean, alas, of his fate.
*(Embarrassed and restraining*
*her tears with difficulty.)*
My son!
My son!
He is dead!

BERTHE: Il est mort! il est mort!
Dernier espoir, lueur dernière!
Qui pour jamais, qui pour jamais,
ont disparu,
Que faire encor sur cette terre?
Mon bien-aimé, mon bien-aimé, je
t'ai perdu! je t'ai perdu!

FIDÈS: Hélas! non, plus d'espoir,
plus d'espoir, mon bonheur
Tout mon bonheur a disparu!
Que faire encor sur cette terre?
Mon pauvre enfant, je t'ai perdu!

FIDÈS ET BERTHE: Non plus
d'espoir en ma misère,
Tout mon bonheur n'est plus!

FIDÈS: Un matin j'ai trouvai dans
mon humble logis,
Des habits teints de sang, c'étaient
ceux de mon fils!
Une voix s'écriait:
Le ciel voulait sa tête;
Tu ne le verras plus,
C'est l'arrêt du prophète!

BERTHE: Qui? lui? ce tyran!
Qui remplit l'Allemagne de sang!

FIDÈS: Il a tué mon fils!

BERTHE: Punissons ses forfaits!

FIDÈS: Hélas! tu ne peut rien!

BERTHE: Peut-être!
Si je puis seulement entrer dans son
palais!

FIDÈS: Et que veux-tu?

BERTHE: Ce que je veux?
Frapper! frapper ce traitre!
Dieu me guidera!
Dieu m'inspirera!

FIDÈS: O vierge, o vierge immor-
telle,
À toi ma plainte fidèle,
Mon esperance,
Est dans ta présence,
Ah! mon fils, près de toi!
Mon fils, rappelle-moi!
*(Berthe se précipite vers une des*
*rues à gauche qui conduit au Pa-*
*lais. Fidès qui ne peut courir aussi*
*vite la suit de loin en tendant ses*
*bras vers elle.)*

## SCÈNE IV.

*(Le théâtre change et représente la*
*Cathédrale de Munster. Une par-*
*tie du cortège est censée déjà en-*
*trée; l'autre moitié continue à dé-*
*filer; au fond de l'Eglise des*
*trabans de la garde du prophète*
*forment la baie. Marche des*
*grands électeurs portant l'un la*
*couronne, l'autre le sceptre,*
*l'autre la main de justice, celui-ci*
*le sceau de l'État, et l'autres les*
*ornements impériaux. Jean pa-*
*rait après eux, la tête nue et ha-*
*billé en blanc. Il traverse la nef*
*principale et se rend dans le Cho-*
*eur au maître-autel qui est dans le*
*fond à droite et qu'on ne voit pas.*

BERTHA: He is dead!
He is dead!
My last gleam of hope,
Which has disappeared forever.
What shall I now do on this earth?
My beloved, my beloved, I have lost
you forever.

FIDES: Alas! No more hope!
My happiness!
All my happiness has gone!
What shall I now do on this earth?
My poor child, I have lost you.

FIDES AND BERTHA: No more
hope in my misery!
All my happiness is no more!

FIDES: One morning I found in my
humble cottage,
Garments stained with blood, those
of my son!
A voice cried out: Heaven desired
his head;
You shall never see him again;
It is the Prophet's will!

BERTHA: Whose? His? That tyran?
Who has spilled all Germany's
blood?

FIDES: And killed my son.

BERTHA: Let us punish his misdeeds.

FIDES: Alas, you can do nothing.

BERTHA: Perhaps!
If I could but enter his palace!

FIDES: What would you do?

BERTHA: What would I do?
Kill!
Kill this traitor!
God will guide me!
God will inspire me!

FIDES: To you my faithful lament,
My hope is in your presence.
Jean, my son near to you,
My son remember me!
*(Bertha rushes up one of the*
*streets leading to the Palace.*
*Fides, who cannot run as fast, fol-*
*lows her at a distance, extending*
*her arms toward her.)*

## SCENE IV.

*(The Cathedral of Munster. A part*
*of the procession has already en-*
*tered; the other is still filing in; at*
*the back of the church the hal-*
*berds of the Prophet's guard form*
*a railing. The electors enter bear-*
*ing the crown, the sceptre, the*
*band of justice, the state seal, and*
*other imperial insignia. Jean,*
*clothed in white and with uncov-*
*ered head, follows them. He*
*crosses the principal aisle and en-*
*ters the cloister on the right which*
*is not seen. The people in the front*
*rush after him. They are kept back*
*by the railing of the side chapel.*
*All go out. Fides who has just en-*

*Le peuple qui est sur le devant du Théâtre, veut se prècipiter sur ses pas. Il est repoussé par les trabans dans les chapelles latérales. Tous disparaissent, Fidès qui vient d'entrer est seule, à gauche, à genoux, sur le devant du théâtre, ne s'occupant pas de ce qui se passe autour d'elle, et plongée dans la rêverie et la prière. Tout à coup on entend un grand bruit d'orgues, de clairons et de trompettes, c'est la marche du couronnement.)*

*tered is alone on her knees, in the front of the theatre on the left, not paying any attention to what is going on about her, plunged in reverie and praying. Suddenly sounds of clarions and of trumpets, and the organ are heard. The crowning is taking place.)*

**LES TROIS ANABAPTISTES ET LE CHOEUR:** *(dans les coulisses).* Domine salvum fac regem nostrum, Et exaudi nos in die qua invocaverimus te!

**THE THREE ANABAPTISTS:** *(and the chorus in the wings).* Domine salvum fac regem nostrum, Et exaudi nos in die qua invocaverimus te!

**FIDÈS:** Que Dieu sauve le roi prophète, disent-ils?
*(Avec force.)*
Grand Dieu, exaucez ma prière!
Et qu'errant, miserable et proscrit,
Il soit chatié sur la terre,
Et que dans le ciel il soit maudit!

**FIDES:** God save the Prophet King, do they say?
*(Forcefully.)*
God in Heaven, answer my prayer!
May he alone, in misery and shunned,
Be scourged on the earth
And in Heaven be cursed!

**LES ANABAPTISTES:** Domine, salvum fac regem! Domine!

**THE ANABAPTISTS:** Domine salvum fac regem! Domine!

**FIDÈS:** *(avec exaltation).* Ah! ma fille, o Judith nouvelle,
Que Dieu protège ton dessein!
Va!
Qu'en ta main le glaive étincelle!
Et de leur roi frappe le sein!
Dieu lui-même, permet son trépas!
Va!
Va!
Le Seigneur conduira ton bras!

**FIDES:** *(exalted).* Oh, my daughter, a second Judith,
May God protect you in your task!
Go!
May the blade flash in your hand!
And strike the bosom of their king!
God himself permits his death!
The Lord will guide your arm!

**LES ANABAPTISTES:** Domine salvum, salvum fac regem, salvum fac!

**THE ANABAPTISTS:** Domine salvum fac regem, salvum fac!

**CHOEUR D'ENFANTS:** *(pendant ce choeur a lieu une marche religieuse. Les enfants de choeur l'encensoir à la main, ouvrent la marche; d'autres frappent sur des timbres, par lesquels ils invitent le peuple à s'agenouiller; puis viennent les jeunes filles jetant des fleurs sur la route où doit passer le Prophète; dans le fond du théâtre on voit passer les grands dignitaires, qui portent les objets du couronnement que l'on passe alternativement aux enfants de choeur qui les encensent).* Le voilà, le roi prophète!
Le voilà le fils de Dieu!
À genoux! courbez la tête,
À genoux! à genoux! à genoux,
Devant son sceptre de feu,
C'est le sceptre de feu.

**CHORUS OF CHILDREN:** *(during this chorus a religious march is played. The children of the chorus with censors in their hands, start the procession; others ring bells which call the people to kneel; then girls throw flowers in the Prophet's path. In the front of the stage pass grand dignitaries carrying the insignia of the coronation which they hand to the children who perfume them).* Behold the Prophet King!
Behold the son of God!
Let every head incline,
Let every knee be bent.
Before his sceptre of fire!

**JEAN:** Jean, tu règneras!
Ah!
C'est donc vrai! oui je suis
L'élu, je suis le fils de Dieu!
*(En ce moment Fidès qui est en prière sur le devant du théâtre à droite, vient de se relever. Elle seule et Jean sont debout dans l'Eglise. Elle regarde le nouveau roi et pousse un cri.)*

**JEAN:** Jean, you will reign!
Ah!
It is true! Yes, I am
The chosen one, the son of God.
*(At this moment Fides who was praying in the front on the right has arisen. Jean and she are the only ones standing in the church. She looks at the new King and utters a cry.)*

**FIDÈS:** Mon fils!
*(Jean à la voix de sa mère veut courir vers elle, mais Mathisen qui est près de lui l'arrête et lui dit à voix basse.)*

**MATHISEN:** Si tu parle, sa mort!

**FIDES:** My son!
*(Jean at the sound of his mother's voice is about to run to her, but Mathisen who is near him stops him and whispers to him.)*

**MATHISEN:** One word and your mother dies!

**CHOEUR:** Son fils?

**CHORUS:** Her son?

**JEAN:** *(avec effroi et modérant son émotion se retourne vers sa mère et dit froidement).* Quelle est cette femme?
*(Fidès bors d'elle-même se frappe les mains; elle veut parler mais le saisissement lui coupe la parole.)*

**JEAN:** *(frightened and restraining his emotion he turns to his mother and says coldly).* Who is this woman?
*(Fides beside herself strikes her hands; she wants to say something but a chill prevents her.)*

**FIDÈS:** *(d'une voix tremblante).* Qui je suis?
*(Avec indignation.)*
Moi, qui je suis?
*(Avec une douloureuse tendresse et en pleurant.)*
Moi! qui je suis!
Ce que je voudrait, hélas! la pauvre femme?
Elle voudrait pardonner à l'ingrat,
Elle voudrait même au prix de son âme,
Un seul instant, une seul instant te presser dans ses bras!
*(Avec force.)*
Hélas!
L'ingrat ne me reçonnaît pas!

**FIDES:** *(trembling).* Who am I?
*(Indignantly.)*
Who am I?
*(With pitiful tenderness and weeping.)*
What do I want, I, a poor soul?
I wish to pardon the ingrate,
I wish even at the risk of my life,
To press you for one moment in my arms!
*(Forcefully.)*
Alas!
The ungrateful one did not recognize me.

**LES ANABAPTISTES:** O Ciel!

**JEAN:** Blasphème affreux!

**THE ANABAPTISTS:** Heavens!

**JEAN:** Outrageous blasphemy!

**MATHISEN ET ZACHARIE:** C'est trop souffrir, divin Prophète!
Et son blasphème et son erreur!

**MATHISEN AND ZACHARIA:** It is too much to stand, Prophet!
Her blasphemy and her delusion.

**CHOEUR:** Qu'entends-je? o Ciel! et quel aveu!

**CHORUS:** What do we hear?
O Heaven!
What a fraud!

**MATHISEN ET ZACHARIE:** Éclate enfin notre fureur!

**MATHISEN AND ZACHARIA:** Our fury may burst!

**JONAS:** Livrez-la donc à nous, à nous, à nous.

**JONAS:** Give her to us, to us!

**CHOEUR:** Quoi le saint prophète
Serait-il donc un imposteur?
Malheur à lui!
Malheur à lui!
*(Entr'eux menaçant Jean.)*
L'élu du ciel, le saint prophète,
ne serait-il qu'un imposteur?
Juste ciel!
Malheur à lui!
*(Jonas et les Anabaptistes qui ont entouré Fidès lèvent leurs poignards sur sa tête.)*

**CHORUS:** Can the sacred Prophet
A base imposter, be?
Woe to him!
Woe!
*(To each other, threatening Jean.)*
The elect of Heaven, sacred Prophet,
Can it be that he is an imposter?
Merciful Heaven!
May our fury burst!
*(Jonas and the other Anabaptists who have surrounded Fides raise their swords over her head.)*

**JEAN:** *(avec effort).* Arretez!

**FIDÈS:** *(avec joie).* Il prend ma dèfense.

**JEAN:** *(with an effort).* Cease!

**FIDES:** *(joyfully).* He takes my part!

**JEAN:** Qu'on respecte ses jours!
Ne voyez vous donc pas,
Que cette femme est en dèmence?
*(Fidès s'éloigne avec indignation.)*
Un miracle seul lui rendre la raison!

**JEAN:** You must respect her age!
Do you not see,
This woman is demented?
*(Fides withdraws indignantly.)*
A miracle alone can cure her mind.

**LES TROIS ANABAPTISTES ET LE CHOEUR:** Tout est possible au roi prophète,
Tout est possible au fils de Dieu!

**THE THREE ANABAPTISTS AND THE CHORUS:** The Prophet King can all achieve!
The son of God can all achieve!

## Act IV, Scene IV

**JEAN:** Que Dieu m'inspire donc!
*(Il s'avance lentement vers Fidès. Avec solennité.)*
Que la sainte lumière
Descende sur ton front,
Pauvre insensée, et t'éclaire!
*(À Fidès.)*
Femme, à genoux!
*(Fidès fait un geste d'indignation.)*
*(Jean s'approche de Fidès, étend les mains sur sa tête et la fascine tellement de son regard qu'involontairement elle tombe à genoux.)*

**JEAN:** *(avec intention à Fidès).* Tu cherissais ce fils,
Dont je t'offre les traits?

**FIDÈS:** *(émué)* Si je l'aimais!

**JEAN:** Eh! bien! que maintenant
Vers moi ton oeil se lève!

**FIDÈS:** *(d'une voix tremblante).*
Mon Dieu!
Mon Dieu!

**JEAN:** *(au peuple).* Et vous qui m'écoutez, peuple, tirez le glaive!
*(Tous tirent leurs épées et leurs poignards.)*

**FIDÈS:** Ah! je frémis!

**JEAN:** Eh bien!
Eh bien!
Si je suis son enfant,
Si je vous ai trompés,
Punissez l'imposteur!
Frappez!
Voici mon sein!
Frappez!
Voici mon sein!
*(Sur un signe de Jean plusieurs Anabaptistes mettent la pointe de leurs poignards sur sa poitrine.)*
*(À Fidès.)*
Suis-je ton fils?
Suis-je ton fils?

**CHOEUR:** Parlez!
Parlez!

**FIDÈS:** *(d'une voix entrecoupée pouvant à peine parler).* Ah! Peuple! . . . je vous trompais . . .
C'est ne pas mon fils!
Non, non!
*(Avec effort.)*
Je n'ai plus de fils, hélas!

**CHOEUR:** Miracle! miracle du grand Prophète!
Miracle!
Miracle!
Miracle!

**FIDÈS:** *(à part).* O doûleur!
Il faut donc pour le sauver,
À jamais le quitter!
Mon Dieu! veillez sur lui!
*(Il encensent Jean qui part avec sa suite.)*

**LES TROIS ANABAPTISTES:** Domine salvum fac regem!
Salvum fac prophetam nostrum.

**CHOEUR:** Sublime spectacle!
Oui, sa voix rend la raison,
Oui, sa voix rend la raison, aux insensés!

---

**JEAN:** Inspire me, Heaven!
*(He advances slowly toward Fides. Solemnly.)*
May the sacred light
Descend on your forehead
And illumine you, poor senseless one!
On your knees, woman!
*(Fides show her indignation.)*
*(Jean approaches Fides, extends his hands over her head, and so fascinates her with his look that she involuntarily falls on her knees.)*

**JEAN:** *(pointedly to Fides).* You loved this son, whom I resemble?

**FIDES:** *(moved).* Did I love him?

**JEAN:** Well, then,
Turn your eyes to me now!

**FIDES:** *(trembling).* My God!
My God!

**JEAN:** *(to the people).* You who hear me, unsheath your swords!
*(All unsheathe their swords and their poniards.)*

**FIDES:** Ah! I tremble!

**JEAN:** Now, if I am her child,
If I have deceived you,
Punish the impostor!
Strike
Here on my bosom!
Strike!
*(At a sign from Jean several Anabaptists place their sword points on his chest.)*
*(To Fides.)*
Am I your son?
Am I?

**CHORUS:** Answer!

**FIDES:** *(sobbing and scarcely able to speak).* Ah! people . . . I have deceived you . . .
He is not my son!
No, no!
*(With an effort.)*
I have no son anymore, alas!

**CHORUS:** A miracle!
The Great Prophet's miracle.
A miracle!
A miracle!

**FIDES:** *(aside).* O grief!
To save you, I must
Forever leave you!
My God, watch over him!
*(Jean and his retinue depart perfumed with incense.)*

**THE THREE ANABAPTISTS:** Domine salvum fac regem!
Salvum fac prophetam nostrum.

**CHORUS:** Sublime spectacle!
Yes, his word restores reason,
Yes, his word restores reason to the insane.

---

Ah! quel miracle du prophète, fils du Dieu!
Miracle!
Miracle!
Miracle!

**FIDÈS:** Et Berthe, o ciel!
Qui veut l'assasiner!
Courons!
*(Elle veut se précipiter sur les pas de Jean. Les Anabaptistes lui présentent la pointe de leurs lances, et l'empêchent de passer. Elle voit Jean qui s'éloigne sans pouvoir le réjoindre.)*

*RIDEAU.*

## ■ ACTE V.

*(Le théâtre représente un caveau vouté dans le palais de Munster. À gauche un escalier de pièrre par lequel on descend dans le caveau. Au fond au milieu du mur une dalle saillante sur laquelle des caractères sont tracés. À droite une porte de fer donnant sur la campagne.)*

### SCÈNE I.

*Fidès seule.*
*(Apparraissent sur les marches de l'escalier à gauche plusieurs soldats; l'un tient un flambeau, les autres entrainent Fidès. Les soldats montrent à Fidès un banc de pièrre, lui font signe de s'asseoir, et remontent l'escalier par où ils partent.)*

**FIDÈS:** O prêtres de Baal,
Où m'avez vous conduite?
Quoi! les murs d'un cachot!
Ah! l'on retient mes pas,
Quand de mon fils Berthe veut le trépas!
Mon fils! il ne plus!
Il renia sa mère!
Que sur son front coupable éclate ta colère!
Frappe!
Frappe!
Toi qui
Punis tous les enfants ingrats!
Non, non, non, grâce pour lui!
O toi qui m'abandonnes,
Mon coeur, mon coeur, est désarmé,
Ta mère te pardonne,
*(Pleurant.)*
Adieu, adieu, adieu, adieu!
Mon pauvre enfant.
Mon bien-aimé! sois pardonnez!
Je t'ai donnez mon coeur,
Je t'ai donnez mes voeux,
Et maintenant pourque tu sois heureux,
Je te donne ma vie,
Et mon âme ravie,
T'attendra dans les Cieux!
Adieu!

---

Unheard of deed of the Prophet, the son of God!
A miracle!
A miracle!

**FIDES:** And Bertha, O Heaven!
Wishes to assassinate him! Haste!
*(She rushes after Jean. The Anabaptists present the points of their lances to prevent her from passing. She sees Jean going off without being able to join him.)*

*CURTAIN.*

## ■ ACT V.

*(A vaulted cavern in the Palace of Munster. On the left a stone stairway. At the back in the center of the wall a slab on which various characters are traced. On the right an iron door leading to the open country.)*

### SCENE I.

*Fides, alone.*
*(Several soldiers appear at the top of the stairway on the left; one holds a torch, the others lead Fides. The soldiers show Fides a stone bench, tell her to sit down and return by way of the stairway.)*

**FIDES:** O priests of Baal,
Where have you brought me?
What! the walls of a dungeon!
Oh!
Why were my steps hindered
When Bertha wished my son's death!
My son!
No longer mine!
He has renounced his mother.
May your wrath burst on his guilty Forehead!
Strike!
You who punish all ungrateful children!
No, no, no mercy for him!
Ah!
You who abandoned me,
My heart is appeased,
Your mother pardons you.
*(Weeping.)*
Farewell, farewell, farewell!
Farewell, my poor child!
My beloved, I pardon you!
I have given you my heart
I have given you my vows,
And now that you may be happy
I have given you my life!
And my soul at ease,
I will await you in Heaven!
Farewell!

## SCÈNE II.

*(L'officier descendant par l'escalier à gauche.)*

**UN OFFICIER:** Femme, prosterne-toi, prosterne toi
Devant ton divin maître!
Le Roi prophète à tes yeux va paraître!
*(Il sort.)*

**FIDÈS:** *(d'une voix suffoquée par l'émotion)*. Il va venir! je vais le voir!
Hélas!
Bien coupable peut-être!
Dieu!
Dieu!
*(Avec exaltation.)*
Comme un éclair précipité,
Dans son âme,
Frappé mon fils, ô vérité!
De ta flamme!
Frappé mon fils, o vérité!
De ta flamme!
Qu'il soit dompté!
Comme l'airain par le feu!
Céleste flamme,
Touche enfin son âme!
Sainte phalange,
Rends lui son ange,
Esprit divin, descends vainqueur,
De tes rayons, perce son coeur,
Et du crime, sous ses pas
L'abime ne s'ouvre pas!
Je ramène mon enfant,
Mon enfant au Dieu sauveur!

## SCÈNE III.

*Fidès, Jean, un Officier.*
*(Jean est habillé comme au quatrième acte, mais enveloppé d'un manteau et la couronne sur la tête, il fait un signe à l'officier qui s'éloigne.)*

**JEAN:** Ma mère!
Ma mère!
Ma mère!

**FIDÈS:** *(d'un ton sévère et solennel)*. Arrière
Prophète et fils de Dieu,
Tu n'es plus dans ce temple,
Où debout tu m'osais braver!
Et maintenant que Dieu seul nous contemple,
À genoux, à genoux!

**JEAN:** Ah! Pardons pour un fils égaré!

**FIDÈS:** Mon fils! je n'en ai plus!
Ce fils tant pleuré,
Etait pur, pur devant Dieu!
Mais toi! mais toi!

**JEAN:** De honte je rougis!

**FIDÈS:** Mais toi qu'on déteste,
Tyran, sous la colère céleste,
Tremblant, toi dont les mains
Sont teintes de sang,
Va-t'en, va-t'en!
Tu n'est

## SCENE II.

*(An officer descends the stairway on the left.)*

**AN OFFICER:** Woman, kneel, yes, kneel
Before your divine master
The Prophet King will appear before you!
*(Exit.)*

**FIDÈS:** *(in a voice choking with emotion)*. He is coming!
I shall see him!
Alas!
Guilty perhaps!
O God!
*(Exalted.)*
Like a bolt of lightning
Strike my son
In his soul, O Truth!
With your flame
Strike my son, O Truth!
May he be softened
As bronze by fire!
Celestial flame,
Warm at last his soul!
Sacred band
Restore his guardian angel!
Spirit divine, conquering come,
Pierce his heart with your beams!
And for his crime,
Let no dark abyss open beneath his steps!
I will restore my son to God,
My son to God, our Savior!

## SCENE III.

*Fides, Jean, an officer.*
*(Jean is dressed as in the fourth act, but wrapped in a mantle, and with the crown on his head. He motions to the officer to withdraw.)*

**JEAN:** My mother!
My mother!

**FIDES:** *(severely and solemnly)*.
Away!
Prophet and son of God!
You are no longer in that temple
Where you dared stand and brave me!
Now where God alone beholds us,
Kneel, kneel!

**JEAN:** Ah! Pardon an erring son!

**FIDES:** My son!
I have none anymore!
That son for whom I wept,
Was pure, pure in the eyes of God!
But you! But you!

**JEAN:** I blush with shame!

**FIDES:** But you whom they detest,
Tyrant, beneath the celestial wrath,
Trembling, you whose hands
Are stained with blood,
Away!
Away!

Plus rien pour moi, va-t'en!
Tu n'est plus rien pour moi!

**JEAN:** Ma mère, me maudit, me déteste,
Quand j'allais la presser dans mes bras!
Et son courroux est le courroux céleste!
Hélas!
*(Avec égarement.)*
Autour de moi cachez ces flots de sang!
Image horrible, éloigne-toi, va-t'en!
Ah! mon coeur, éloigne-toi,
Va-t'en, remords vengeur,
Éloigne-toi, va-t'en!

**FIDÈS:** Va-t'en, tyran, va-t'en,
Tu n'est plus rien pour moi!
Eh bien! si le remords
S'eveille dans ton âme,
Et si tu peux encor
Être digne de moi,
Renonce à ton pouvoir,
À ceux qui t'ont fait roi!

**JEAN:** *(d'une voix suffoquée, presque parlé)*. Deserter mes soldats.

**FIDÈS:** C'est Dieu qui te réclâme!

**JEAN:** Par eux je fus vainqueur!

**FIDÈS:** Par eux tu fus infâme!

**JEAN:** Ils diront que j'ai fui!

**FIDÈS:** Vers le ciel!
Vers l'honneur!
*(Elle conduit Jean sur le devant du théâtre lui montrant le ciel.)*
À la voix de ta mère,
Le ciel peut se rouvrir!
Dieu n'a plus de colère,
Devant le repentir,
Le ciel peut se rouvrir!
À la voix de ta mere,
Le ciel peut se rouvrir,
Ah! les jours d'innocence
A ma voix renaîtront.
Et le pardon céleste
Descendra sur ton front!

**JEAN:** En moi quels combats!

**FIDÈS:** Viens, mon fils!

**JEAN:** Quoi! se pourrait-il?

**FIDÈS:** Oui, mon fils!

**JEAN:** Mais mon crime?

**FIDÈS:** S'effacera!

**JEAN:** Le pardon?

**FIDÈS:** Descendra!

**JEAN:** Le ciel pourrait me pardonner!

**FIDÈS:** Viens à ta mère, viens!
*(Elle ouvre les bras à son fils qui s'y jette avec transport.)*

You are no longer
Anything to me!
Away!
You are nothing to me!

**JEAN:** My mother detests and curses me
When I was about to embrace her!
Both her wrath and the wrath of God!
*(Wildly.)*
Hide these rivers of blood from me!
Hateful image!
Away!
Away!
Ah! from my heart, remove yourself,
Vengeful remorse!
Away!
Remove yourself!
Away!

**FIDES:** Go, tyrant, go!
You are nothing to me!
Ah, if remorse really
Awakens in your soul,
And if you wish once more
To be worthy of me,
Renounce your power,
To those who made you King!

**JEAN:** *(scarcely able to speak)*.
Desert my soldiers?

**FIDES:** It is God who reclaims you!

**JEAN:** Through them I conquered!

**FIDES:** Through them you grew infamous!

**JEAN:** They will say that I have deserted them!

**FIDES:** For Heaven!
For honor!
*(She leads Jean to the front of the stage and points to the sky.)*
Your mother's prayer
Can open the Heavens!
God has no anger
Against the penitent!
The Heavens can open!
Your mother's prayer
Can open the Heavens,
Ah! Your days of innocence,
Will come back at my word,
And the forgiveness of Heaven
Will descend on your head.

**JEAN:** Ah! the strife within me!

**FIDES:** Come, my son!

**JEAN:** What!
Can it really be?

**FIDES:** Yes, my son!

**JEAN:** But my crime?

**FIDES:** Will be effaced.

**JEAN:** And the pardon?

**FIDES:** Will be granted.

**JEAN:** Heaven can pardon me?

**FIDES:** Come, my son, to your mother!
*(She opens her arms to her son who rushes into them in a transport.)*

JEAN: Ma mère!
Ma mère!

FIDÈS: Mons fils!
Mon fils!
Ah!
Il en est temps encor,
Sois à l'honneur fidèle,
Le Dieu t'appelle!
Et bientôt le pardon céleste
Descendra sur toi!

JEAN: Oui, je le veux,
Il en est temps encor,
Et trop longtemps rebèlle,
Changeons enfin mon sort!
Le Dieu du ciel m'appelle!
Et bientôt du Seigneur
Le pardon descendra,
Et bientôt le pardon céleste
Descendra sur moi!

JEAN: My mother!
My mother!

FIDES: My son!
My son!
There is still time!
Be true to honor!
God calls you!
And soon the pardon of the Lord
Will descend on your head.

JEAN: Yes, it is my desire, and
There is still time.
Too long rebellious,
Let me change my destiny!
God in Heaven calls me!
And soon the pardon of Heaven
Will be granted!
And soon the celestial pardon
Will descend on me!

## SCÈNE IV.

(Les mêmes, Berthe, babillée du blanc et vanant un flambeau à la main. Elle entre par la porte de droite.)

BERTHE: (s'avançant vers le mur du fond et touchant la dalle de pièrre qui s'ouvre). Voici le souterrain . . . et la dalle de pièrre!
Fidès!

FIDÈS: (courant vers Berthe).
Berthe!
Ici que viens-tu faire?

JEAN: O ciel!

BERTHE: Par mon aieul, gardien
Du palais de Munster,
Je savais les amas
De salpetre de fer,
(Montrant le flambeau qu'elle tient.)
Caches dans ce caveau.
Cette flamme propice
Peut en quelques instants
Embrâser l'édifice!
Ce Prophète et les siens,
Et moi-même, et moi-même avec eux!

FIDÈS: (à Jean). Que dit-elle?
grand Dieu! Mon fils!

BERTHE: (apercevant Jean). Ah!
qu'ai-je vu!
Toi, mon bien-aimé!
C'est toi qui m'es rendu!

## SCENE IV.

(The same, Bertha, dressed in white and bearing a torch in her hand. She enters by a door on the right.)

BERTHA: (advances along the wall at the back, touching a slab of stone which opens). Here is the cavern and the stone!
Fides!

FIDES: (running toward Bertha).
Bertha, what are you doing here?

JEAN: Heavens!

BERTHA: From my god-father, guardian
Of the palace of Munster,
I knew of the store of sulphur,
Hidden in this cavern.
(Holding out the torch.)
This propitious flame,
In a few moments can
Envelop this palace;
The Prophet and his friends, and
Myself, and myself with them.

FIDES: (to Jean). What is she saying?
Great God!
My son!

BERTHA: (seeing Jean). Whom do I see?
You, my beloved!
You are returned to me!

## SCÈNE V.

(Les mêmes, un officier, suivi de plusieurs soldats, descend precipitamment l'escalier à gauche.)

UN OFFICIER: (à Jean). On t'a trahi!
Par ruse en ce palais s'est glissé l'ennemi!

JEAN: L'ennemi!

## SCENE V.

(The same, and officer, followed by several soldiers, descends the stairway on the left in haste.)

AN OFFICER: (to Jean). You are betrayed!
By a ruse
The enemy has stolen into this palace!

JEAN: The enemy!

UN OFFICIER: (s'adressant toujours à Jean). Ils veulent t'immoler
au milieu de la fête
De ton couronnement . . .
Viens les punir, Prophète!

BERTHE: (avec un cri d'épouvanté. D'une voix suffoquée presque parlé). Prophète!
Prophète!
Non!
Non!

FIDÈS: Grâce!

JEAN: Grâce!
Grâce!

BERTHE: Va! Va!
Je t'aimais, toi que je maudis . . .
Je t'aimais encor
Peut-être et m'en punis!
(Berthe se frappe d'un poignard et tombe dans les bras de Fidès.)

JEAN: Ah!
Morte! morte!
(Jean fait signe aux soldats d'enmener sa mère et Berthe, puis il reprend la couronne qui était restée sur la table de pièrre et la remet sur son front.)
Veillez sur ma mère!
Moi je reste en ces lieux
Pour punir les coupables!

FIDÈS: Mon fils!
Mon fils!
Mon fils!
(Silence pendant lequel Jean regarde si Fidès est assez éloignée.)

JEAN: Et maintenant, vous qui m'avez perdu,
Tous vous serez punis!
(Il remonte vivement l'escalier à gauche après avoir regardé le caveau que Berthe a montré au commencement de la scène.)

AN OFFICER: (addressing Jean all the time). They wish to kill you in the midst of the feast
Of the coronation . . .
Come, punish them, Prophet!

BERTHA: (with a cry of terror. Scarcely able to speak). Prophet!
No, No!
Prophet!

FIDES: Mercy!

JEAN: Mercy!
Mercy!

BERTHA: Away!
Away!
But I love you, even when I cursed you!
I love you even yet, perhaps,
And punish myself!
(Bertha stabs herself with a poignard and falls into Fides' arms.)

JEAN: Dead!
Dead!
(Jean motions to the soldiers to take his mother away, and Bertha also. Then he takes his crown which had been lying on a stone table and puts it on his forehead.)
Take care of my mother!
I will remain in this palace
To punish the guilty!

FIDES: My son!
My son!
(Silence, while Jean watches to see that his mother is far enough away.)

JEAN: And now you who have betrayed me,
You shall all be punished!
(He quietly ascends the stairway on the left after looking into the cavern that Bertha had revealed at the beginning of the scene.)

## SCÈNE VI.

(Le théâtre représente la grande salle du palais de Munster. Une table placée sur une estrade s'élève au milieu du théâtre. On monte de chaque côté par des degrés. Autour de l'estrade circulent des pages, des valets portant des vins et des corbeilles chargées de fruits. Au fond à droite et à gauche de grandes grilles en fer conduisant en dehors du palais. Jean est assis seul, pâle et triste devant une table couverte de mets où étincellent des vases d'or. De jeunes filles le servent, d'autres dansent autour de la table, pendant que des anabaptistes celèbrent les louanges du Prophète. De tous côtés les flambeau étincellent, des lustres brillent au plafond.)

CHOEUR: Hourra!

## SCENE VI.

(The banquet hall of the palace of Munster. In the center a raised table. About the platform are pages, and footmen carrying wines, and baskets of fruit. At the back, on the right, high gates of iron leading out of the hall. Jean is seated alone, pale, sad, before a table covered with meats and sparkling with vases of gold. Young girls serve him; others dance about the table, while the Anabaptists sing the praises of the Prophet. On all sides torches gleam and candles shine on the ceiling.)

CHORUS: Hurrah!

JEAN: (*à part et à voix basse à deux de ses officiers*). . . .
Quand vous verrez entrer nos ennemis,
Que ces grilles d'airain
Se ferment sur ce gouffre,
D'où vont jaillir
Le salpetre et le souffre!
Puis, hâtez-vous de fuir,
Loin de ces lieux maudits,
Vous mes seuls, mes derniers amis!
(*Les officiers sortent.*)
(*Jean se retourne avec un air riant vers les convives invitant du geste les jeunes filles à lui présenter la coupe et le vin.*)
(*Dans des jeunes filles, lesquelles, sur un geste de Jonas, viennent offrir à genoux à Jean une coupe dorée que d'autres femmes se hâtent de remplir.*)

JEAN: (*avec force et une gaité sauvage*). Versez que tout respire,
L'ivresse et le délire.
Que tout cède à l'empire
De ce nectar brûlant!
O la céleste fête,
O triomphe si brillant!
Compagnons du prophète,
La recompense vous attend!
Venez!
Venez!
Venez!
Versez que tout respire,

JEAN: (*aside to two of the officers*). When you see the enemy enter,
Close the gates of iron
Over this whirlpool,
From which the flames of sulphur
Are going to pour.
Then with all haste fly,
Far from this cursed place,
You, my only, my last friends.
(*The officers go out.*)
(*Jean, smiling, turns around to the banquetters and invites the young girls to bring him refreshment.*)
(*A dance by the young girls who have just offered Jean a golden cup which others hasten to refill.*)

JEAN: (*forcefully and with savage gaiety*). Let us drink that all may breathe
Frenzy and delirium,
That all may yield to the sway
Of this burning nectar.
Oh heavenly fête,
O brilliant triumph!
Companions of the Prophet,
You will be rewarded!
(*The dances begin again.*)

L'ivresse et le délire!
Versez que tout cède
A ce nectar brûlant!
(*Les danses recommencent.*)

CHOEUR: Vive, vive, vive, le prophète!
(*Dans ce moment les portes s'ouvrent avec fracas, Oberthal à la tête des troupes imperiales s'élance dans la salle.*)

LES TROIS ANABAPTISTES: La mort, la mort, la mort au faux prophète!

JEAN: Versez que tout respire,
L'ivresse et le délire,
Que resonne la lyre et . . . .
(*On entend fermer en dehors les grilles du fond.*)
Que ces portes d'airain
Soient celles du tombeau!
Qu'on les ferme sur eux!

JONAS: Le tyran est à nous!

JEAN: À Dieu seul j'appartiens!

OBERTHAL: Il est en mon pouvoir!
(*Bruit souterrain, la fumée se fait jour par le plancher.*)

JEAN: Vous êtes tous au mien!
(*L'estrade élevée sur laquelle Jean et sa mère se tiennent, s'écroule au milieu des flammes qui penetrent de toute part. Tout s'embrâse, le palais s'écroule.*)

*RIDEAU.*

CHORUS: Long live, long live the Prophet!
(*At that moment the doors gates open with a crash; Oberthal at the head of the imperial troops rushes into the hall.*)

THE THREE ANABAPTISTS: Death to the Prophet!

JEAN: Let us drink that all may breathe
Frenzy and delirium,
Sound the lyre and . . .
(*Outside the gates at the back may be heard closing.*)
That these gates of bronze
May prove to be our tombs!

JONAS: The tyrant is in our power!

JEAN: I belong to God alone!

OBERTHAL: He is in my power!
(*A noise from below, and smoke appears through the floor.*)

JEAN: You are all mine!
(*The platform on which Jean and his mother were standing crumbles in the flames which penetrate the whole building. All embrace each other and the palace falls.*)

*CURTAIN.*

# L'Africana (1865)

## The African Maid

MUSIC BY GIACOMO MEYERBEER ■ LIBRETTO BY AUGUSTIN EUGÈNE SCRIBE

This five-act opera, set to a libretto by Eugène Scribe, was first performed at the Paris Opéra on April 28, 1865. The story opens in Lisbon at the King's Council Chamber. Ines is told by her father, Don Diego, that the King has decided that she will marry Don Pedro, President of the Royal Council. Vasco da Gama, with whom she is in love, is presumed to have drowned in a shipwreck during a voyage. The Council meets in order to decide whether to send assistance to the survivors. Vasco himself arrives and speaks of his adventures. He presents a petition which demonstrates the possibility of sailing around the Cape of Storms, beyond which lie unknown territories. He brings two prisoners from a strange race of that region and presents them to the Council—they are Selika and Nelusko. The Grand Inquisitor accuses him of heresy and imprisons him along with the slaves. Vasco, in prison, dreams about his voyages and Ines. Selika wakes him and protects him from Nelusko, who wants to kill him as he is in love with Selika. Selika shows Vasco a secret way to reach her country beyond the Cape. Vasco hugs her in appreciation just as Ines and Don Pedro enter with a pardon. Ines, who no longer believes that Vasco still lovers her, has obtained the pardon by promising to marry Don Pedro. Vasco learns that Don Pedro has been chosen to lead the next voyage. Ines, Selika and several other women are on board Don Pedro's flagship. He is consulting his charts as Nelusko, who is piloting and has already wrecked two ships, steers perilously close to a reef. Vasco, sailing aboard an unknown ship bearing the Portuguese flag, boards Don Pedro's ship to warn of the impending danger. Don Pedro does not heed his warning and orders his execution, but a storm arises. Members of Selika's tribe take over the ship, killing the Portuguese. Now on the island of Madagascar, where Selika is the queen, celebrations are taking place to honor her and Nelusko's return. She invokes the law of the ancestors which calls for death to any stranger who sets foot on the island. She pretends that Vasco is her husband in order to spare his life, and the High Priest calls for the gods to bless them. Vasco promises to stay with her forever, but as he does so he hears Ines mourning for him. Ines and Vasco are discovered together in Selika's garden, but he assuages her by promising that he will keep his promise and that Ines can never marry him as he is already married and she is Catholic. Selika, however, can feel the strength of their love, and frees them. She orders them to return to the ship. She then goes to a place where the manchineel tree grows, a tree whose smell is poison to all who breathe it. She hears the firing of the guns announcing the departure of the ship. She refuses to be saved by Nelusko, and they die together as a choir sings that everyone is equal when they die.

---

## ■ ATTO I

### SCENA I

*Sala di consiglio del Rè di Portogallo. Porte al fondo. Porte laterali. Al diritta, il seggiolone del Presidente, a diritta ed a sinistra le sedie dei Consiglieri.*

*(Inez e Anna entra)*

**INEZ:** Che intesiamica . . . al consiglio m'attendon E comparirvi debbo alla voce del padre?

**ANNA:** E question mi fu detto, d'un importante affare.

**INEZ:** Che mai si vuol? Io temo e spero al tempo stesso; Che si sa della flotta; e del mio caro Vasco?

**ANNA:** Voi l'aspettate ancor, dopo due anni?

**INEZ:** Si Vasco vincera. Lo sento là in fondo all' alma. La sua canzon d'addio. Nel core risuonar, Mi sento come allor Che sotto al mio verron, La notte che parti Cosi cantò. Del Tago sponde addio, Addio mio sol' amore, O patrio suol addio Addio mio solo amor! Per quella che m'e cara, I voti miei saran. Addio! Addio! Voi zeffiri leggieri. Portate i miei sospir Amor dell' infanzia Si caro al mio core, Bei sogni di speme, Con voi morro. Addio mio sol natal Addio mio sol' amor!

## ■ ACT I

### SCENE I

*The Council Chamber of the King of Portugal. Doors at back and at each side. To the right is seen the President's chair, on either side of which are the seats destined for the Councillors.*

*(Enter Ines and Anna.)*

**INES:** What do I hear? I am expected at the council chamber, Where, at my father's summons I must appear?

**ANNA:** He would speak with you, it would seem on matters of grave importance.

**INES:** What can he wish to tell me? I vainly struggle between fear and hope. What tidings have we of the fleet, and of my much loved Vasco?

**ANNA:** And do you still expect him, though twice twelve months have flown?

**INES:** Vasco will triumph yet. My inmost soul tells me so! His farewell song Even now resounds within my heart. As on the night, When beneath my balcony He thus, in tender accents, sang. Farewell, fair shores of Tagus. Farewell my only love, Farewell land of my dear fathers, My mistress sweet adieu! For her my prayers to heaven shall be forever dear to me! Farewell! You playful zephyrs Waft her my sighs, You visions of infancy, So dear to my heart. Bright day-dream of hope, With you will I die! Land of my fathers, farewell! Farewell, my only love!

## SCENA II

*(I suddetti, Don Diego, poi Don Pedro.)*

**INEZ:** O padre, a' tuoi cenni . . .

**DON DIEGO:** Inez, tu dei saper
Pria che il consiglio qui venga ad unirsi,
Quale sposo glorioso in sua bontà suprema,
Sceg{lier} degnò per te il monarca lui stesso..
E Don Pedro!

**INEZ:** Chi lui! giammai, giammai mio padre!

**DON DIEGO:** Il Rè lo vuol . . . lo voglio io
pur . . . l'ira mia temi.
*(Abbassando la voce.)*
A quest' illustre imen, immola un folle amor
Per quel garzon oscur!

**INEZ:** Ei sara grande un di!
Il suo nobile ardir . . .

**DON DIEGO:** ha condotto a perire!
*(Volgendosi a Don Pedro.)*
Vera forse e la nuova che correa questa man,
E che Bernardo Diaz perito mai sarebbe.

**DON PEDRO:** I piani suoi fallir . . . la tempesta in cammin,
Le sue navi scagliò contro rive deserte,
Si! il ciel lo colpi! ei fu breda del mar!

**INEZ:** E lui stesso perì?

**DON PEDRO:** E si teme . . . e s'ignora.

**INEZ:** *(tremante.)* E l' ufficiale . . . Vasco di Gama . . . vive egli ancora.

**DON DIEGO:** Vasco di Gama! e chi mai di tal gente ignota,
Si cal . . . chi mai . . . Vediam fra i morti . . .
Si, guardate . . . spento è pur!
*(Dando a Inez una carta.)*

**INEZ:** *(Guardando la carta.)* Egli e spento!
*(Inez e Anna escono.)*

**DON PEDRO:** La novella che qui ne giunge
Perchè turbar cotanto puotè i sensi suoi!
Crudel sospetto or m'entra nel cor.

**DON DIEGO:** Che importa, si teme il sovvenir d'un estinto rival!

## SCENE II

*(The above, Don Diego, and afterwards Don Pedro.)*

**INES:** Father, at your bidding I have come—

**DON DIEGO:** Ines, it is time that you learn,
Before the members of the council that have come here,
The noble spouse our monarch, in his sovereign goodness,
Has deigned to choose for you;
None other than Don Pedro!

**INES:** He! O father, this must never be!

**DON DIEGO:** The King has willed it, and I myself approve the royal choice,
*(lowering his voice.)*
If you would escape thy father's wrath,
You'll sacrifice your senseless love for an ignoble youth
To nuptials glorious as those that are now offered you!

**INES:** The youth you scorn will one day become great!
His dauntless courage—

**DON DIEGO:** Has lured him to his doom!
*turning to Don Pedro.*
Is it true, as was this morning noised abroad,
That Bernard Diaz has perished?

**DON PEDRO:** It is most true; his every plan has failed;
A fearful storm has thrown his ships upon rude barren coasts,
Yes! heaven has stricken him; the sea has claimed him as its prey!

**INES:** And he himself—has perished?

**DON PEDRO:** It is feared so! but his fate is shrouded in uncertainty.

**INES:** *(trembling.)* And the young officer—Vasco di Gama—
Does he live still?

**DON PEDRO:** *(scornfully.)* Vasco di Gama! Tush! who ever thinks him of anything so obscure?
Wait, we'll look among the list of perished—
Yes, see here, he too is dead.
*(hands document to Ines.)*

**INES:** *(glancing at the document.)* Alas! he is no more
*(exeunt Ines and Anna.)*

**DON PEDRO:** Why does this sudden news so disturb and agitate her senses?
What dread suspicion assails my heart?

**DON DIEGO:** It matters not, you surely cannot fear
The memory of a rival now no more.
*(Enter an Usher.)*

**UN USIERE:** I membri del consiglio
Entran in seduta!

## SCENA III

*Don Diego, Don Pedro, il Grande Inquisitore vescovi, Don Alvar e gli altri Consiglieri.*

**CORO:** Tu che la terra adora
Pace ne infonda in sen,
Colla tua santà face
Tu ci rischiara ognor,
Che la tua grazia immensa
Mite ci renda il cor
Ah signor del ciel,
Sii nostro appoggio in vita
Sii nostra guida ognor!

**DON PEDRO:** *(levandosi.)* Dal di ch'allo spagnuol, mortal nostro rival,
Colombo un nuovo mondo e suoi tesori apri,
Con qualche audace impresa o qualche gran scoperta,
Il grande Emmanuel, nostro Rè nostro signor
Vuol segnalar il regno . . .

**L'INQUISITORE:** *(conseverità.)* O cernar il suo danno!

**DON PEDRO:** Il Portoghese, gia ardito navigante.
D'una strada novella presentendo il fato,
Ove il turbin ruggiva fondò la speranza!

**L'INQUISITORE:** Qual fatale speranza!

**ARCH:** Qual fatale speranza.

**L'INQUISITORE:** Ben presto egli credè
Di passare gli scogli del Cape temuto
Voce corre che Diaz negli abissi furiosi,
Ha visto sugli scogli la sua squadra ingojata!

**CORO:** Ingojata!

**DON PEDRO:** Per conoscer sua sorte, e a lui reca soccorso,
Ci riunisce il Rè, Signori l' avviso a dar.

**L'INQUISITORE:** Invochiamo l' Eterno!

**CORO:** Colla tua santa face,
Tu ci rischiara ognor
Sii nostro appoggio in vità,
Sii nostra guido ognor!

**DON PEDRO:** Don Alvar, qual avviso è il vostro?

**USHER:** *(announcing.)* The members of the council
The sitting now commence!

## SCENE III

*Don Diego, Don Pedro, the Grand Inquisitor, several Bishops, Don Alvar, and other members of the Council.*

**CHORUS:** You whom the universe adores,
Infuse peace into our souls,
May your celestial beams
Forever light us on our way.
O may your boundless mercy
Teach clemency to our hearts,
O gracious Lord of Heaven,
Be our stay in life,
Our guide for evermore!

**DON PEDRO:** *(rising.)* Ever since Columbus did reveal to the haughty Spaniard.
A new world with all its untold treasures,
The great Emanuel, our sovereign lord and king
With some bold enterprise or great discovery,
Has also wished to signalize his reign—

**GRAND INQUISITOR:** *(angrily.)* Or bring about his ruin!

**DON PEDRO:** The hardy Portuguese, in bold navigation, had already long foreseen the existence of a new route,
And near the Cape of storms, where the dread tempest
Does ever loudest roar, his fondest hopes had
Centered of success.

**GRAND INQUISITOR:** Rash, fatal hopes were those!
He fondly thought right soon to pass the rocks
Of that dread Cape—but it is said that Diaz' ships,
Tossed by the furious waves—were dashed to pieces!

**CHORUS:** Were dashed to pieces!

**DON PEDRO:** To ascertain his fate, or lend him succour,
The king has summoned you this day
That each may express his separate opinion.

**GRAND INQUISITOR:** We'll first invoke the aid of heaven!

**CHORUS:** May your holy beams
Forever light us on our way—
Be our stay in life,
Our guide for evermore!

**DON PEDRO:** Say, Don Alvar, what plan would you recommend?

**DON ALVAR:** Per Diaz preghiam! Dio disponea dei suoi di!

**DON PEDRO:** Chi lo sa?

**DON ALVAR:** Un marinar quasi solo sfuggito Al naufragio fatal, dell' intero equipaggio Ed in premio dei di disputato alla morte, Non chiede che l' onor di potervi parlar.

**DON PEDRO:** S' appressi . . . il suo nome. (*Due uscieri escono.*)

**DON ALVAR:** Vasco di Gama.

**DON PIEDRO e DON DIEGO:** Desso o ciel!

## SCENA IV

E suddetti, e Vasco Di Gama. (*Vasco Di Gama saluta con rispetto i membri del consiglio. Don Pedro gli fa cenno di parlare.*)

**VASCO DI GAMA:** Io vidi . . . miei signori, sfondare negli abissi, Ed il capo ed i soldati . . . vidi quei valorosi, In cui nessun d'Europa giammai non penetrò Quante volte quei luoghi deserti e selvaggi, Quei torrenti furiosi e quelle nuove spiagge . . .

**DON ALVAR:** Da voi esul afflitto ah! maladette fur!

**VASCO DI GAMA:** (*con esaltazione.*) No! ma conquistati saran, si saran da noi, Credo in Dio chi m' ispira! Che questo scritto sia da voi consultato E che il Rè per favor mi confidi un vascello, Pronto allor varchero quello scoglio fatal, Del commercio e dei mar io vi prometto l'impero, A voi, a voi novelli climi a voi ricchi tesor, A voi prosperita!

**L'INQUISITORE:** E voi . . . qual parte avrete?

**VASCO DI GAMA:** Io! . . . l'immortalita! A costo pur del sangue mio, Io vi prometto di riuscir, E pel mio Rè . . . per la mia terra, Signori udir . . . degnate accettar!

**DON ALVAR:** Pray for the soul of Diaz—it has pleased heaven to end. His days.

**DON PEDRO:** What proof have we of this?

**DON ALVAR:** A mariner waits without— The sole survivor of that fatal wreck; As guerdon for the deadly strife which he has waged against the elements, He craves the honor of addressing you.

**DON PEDRO:** Bid him approach. (*exeunt ushers.*) His name, I pray you!

**DON ALVAR:** Vasco di Gama!

**DON PEDRO AND DON DIEGO:** (*aside.*) He! O heaven!

## SCENE IV

The above, and Vasco Di Gama. (*Vasco Di Gama bows respectfully to the members of the Council. Don Pedro motions to him to speak.*)

**VASCO DI GAMA:** Noble sirs! these eyes have seen our chief and his stout warriors Struggling in the ocean's yawning gulf! Where none, born in Europe, have ever set foot before, How often when wandering amid those pathless wastes, Those raging torrents, those wild thickets, How often

**DON ALVAR:** How often luckless exile, they were cursed by you—

**VASCO DI GAMA:** (*enthusiastically*). Not so! but often I swore they soon should own our sway— It is heaven, I feel, that inspires me; Consult this scroll, I pray you If our King will but entrust a ship to me, I'll undertake to pass the dreaded rocks. And promise increase of commerce, No, the empire of the seas—new climes, Rich treasures—boundless fortune!

**GRAND INQUISITOR:** And for your own share what will you claim?

**VASCO DI GAMA:** (*enthusiastically.*) Why—immortality! I swear to you I will succeed, Even should it cost me my own life: Hear me, great sirs, for our King's sake, For our own dear native land, vouch-safe to grant my prayer.

**L'INQUISITORE, DIE:** (*ecc.*) Per tanto ardir e tal follia Al la pieta m' assale già, E non si può con seria mente, Prestar orecchio al suo desir

**DON ALVAR:** (*i giovani consigliere, ecc.*) A tanto ardir . . . a tanto genio Mi sento in sen il cor tremar E per l' onore della patria Si deva udirlo Sicuro egli e di riuscir!

**VASCO DI GAMA:** Un motto ancor in pria che voi deliberate . . . E che il mio re mi confidi un vascello; Senza danno ei la può. Certo sono di me, Due schiavi di razza ignota fin ora, Dei neri sul mercato m' avean colpito gli occi, In Africo! Sono là!

**L'INQUISITORE:** E che pretendi tu?

**VASCO DI GAMA:** Di gente ignota ancor, ei provan l' esistenza, Sotto l' ardente sol, dell' Asia non son nati! Ne pur nel nuovo suol, allo Spagnuol sommesso! Li vedete!

**DON DIEGO:** Si! entrar si faccian. (*Ad un cenno di Don Pedro l' usciere fa entrare Selika e Nelusko.*) I suddetti, Selika e Nelusko.

## SCENE V

**DON PEDRO:** O schiavi v' appressate . . .

**DON DIEGO:** Qual è la patria vostra? (*Nelusko. crolla ferocemente la testa. Selika rifiuto con un gesto altiero.*)

**DON PEDRO:** Quì fra noi chi guidati v' ha!

**DON DIEGO:** Tu risponder non vuoi?

**NELUSKO:** No! no!

**DON PEDRO:** Donna . . . à tè a parlar.

**SELIKA:** Fatti fummo prigioni sopra l' immenso mar, Un di che da feroce tempesta sorpresi, Ben lungi errammo, ohime! dall' isola natal!

**GRAND INQUISITOR, DON DIEGO, ETC:** For so much courage joined to such madness I can feel nothing but pity, No one of serious mind, I think Can listen such rash designs!

**DON ALVAR:** *the younger counsellors, etc.* Such dauntless courage mated with such genius Causes my heart to throb within my breast, For our own country's honor We even must listen to his prayer, Right sure are we that he'll succeed.

**VASCO DI GAMA:** Another word I pray, before you commence your deliberations. I again even solicit that the King entrust to me a ship, This he may safely do. No doubt, my errand! In Africa, two slaves, of race till now unknown, While in the slave mart, met my eye! They wait without!

**GRAND INQUISITOR:** And where would all this tend?

**VASCO DI GAMA:** It tends to prove the existence of a race to us unknown, Who never beneath Africa's sun drew breath, Nor in the new world by the Spaniards conquered— Judge for yourselves, I pray you!

**DON DIEGO:** Let them be brought before us! (*At a sign from Don Pedro the usher leads in Selika and Nelusko.*)

## SCENE V

The above, Selika and Nelusko.

**DON PEDRO:** Slaves! draw near!

**DON DIEGO:** Of what country are you? (*Nelusko shakes his head with an air of fierce denial. Selika refuses with a haughty gesture.*)

**DON PEDRO:** Who brought you here! (*to Nel.*)

**DON DIEGO:** Will you not answer?

**NELUSKO:** No!

**DON PEDRO:** Woman, yours be it then to speak.

**SELIKA:** We were prisoners taken upon the open seas, One day—when surprised by a fearful storm, Our bark, alas! had drifted far from our dear native isle.

**VASCO DI GAMA:** Ah di grazia mirate le linee di quel volto, (*accenando Nelusko.*) Quei vestimenti e quel color Palesan un popolo ignoto.

**DON ALVAR:** Ever . . . è ver! (*tutti fanno segno di assenso.*)

**DON DIEGO:** La patria vostra dite!

**VASCO DI GAMA:** Ma parla dunque o Selika, Son io che te ne prego!

**SELIKA:** La voce sua mi prega Ah! resistere no posso!

**NELUSKO:** (*piano a Selika.*) Regina . . . die giuri tuoi mantien la fè! La schiava incatenata da un tiranno Per essere nei ferri è men sovrano? Di? Per gli dei che la patria adora, pel gran Brama tuo signor. Ah! il popol tuo, Regina, ah! il popol non tradire! Ah! per pietà deh taci!

**DON PEDRO:** La tua patria, odi tu? Donna, io quì commando, Bisogno al fin la tua patria far nota . . .

**SELIKA:** Nomarla a te non so! non la conobbi mai, Lo schiavo non e ha!

**NELUSKO:** (*con mal celata rabbia.*) Ma quando voi mercate Un bue per il lavor, purchè sia di misura, E fortemente sempre esso lavori, Del suo paese mai non vi curate giá! Che cosa importa allor da dove vien un uomo, Che sol sara una bestia di soma?

**DON PEDRO:** Qual indomito orgoglio!

**VASCO DI GAMA:** Vani i' sforzi saran. Non parleranno, no! e pur tutto dice, Che d' Affrica nativi non sono, ma d'un suo Dove mai l'ocean portò le nostre vele, Quei remote paesi io voglio discoprir, Deh! li mezzi mi date per veli conquistar.

**DON PEDRO:** Va ben! ora attendete . . . Il consiglio s'apre!

**L'INQUISITORE:** (*ed otto Vescove.*) Dio che la terra adora. Pace ci enfondi in sen!

**VASCO DI GAMA:** I pray you note the contour of those features. (*pointing to Nelika.*) That garb—that hue—all indicate A race till now unheard of.

**DON ALVAR:** It is true—most true! (*Counsellors, etc., interchange signs of assent.*)

**DON DIEGO:** Reveal to us your country!

**VASCO DI GAMA:** Selika, speak! It is I who now implore you!

**SELIKA:** Ah! It is *his* voice that now beseeches, I can resist no longer!

**NELUSKO:** (*aside to Selika*). O Queen, preserve your oath inviolate, Remember, though you now wear a tyrant's fetters, You're none the less a queen! By all the gods your countrymen adore, By the great Brahma's self,—I conjure you, Do not betray people!

**DON PEDRO:** Your country—do you hear? Know, woman, that it is I who here command, I now do *bid* you to reveal your country.

**SELIKA:** Alas! I cannot–I never knew my country, No country has the slave!

**NELUSKO:** (*with difficulty mastering his rage*.) When you have purchased an ox for the plough, If he be of fitting stature, and strong enough To bear the yoke, what do you care of his country? Why ask then where the man comes from, Who will merely be a beast of burthen?

**DON PEDRO:** Unconquerable pride!

**VASCO DI GAMA:** Your efforts are vain, They never will speak, and yet all tends to prove That they were not born in Africa, But in a clime to which the ocean Never has wafted our sails; Those climes, I say, however remote, I will discover If you'll but grant the means.

**DON PEDRO:** It is well; await the decision of the council, Which even now commences its deliberations

**GRAND INQUISITOR AND BISHOPS:** O you whom the universe adores, Infuse peace into our breasts!

**CORO:** Che la tua grazia immensa Mite ci renda il cor!

**DON PEDRO:** (*dopo di aver consultato da parte coi consiglieri, etc.*) Il consiglio sovran che per il rè comanda, In nome dei vantaggi in poter suo fidati Respinto ha l' inchiesta vostra E gl' insensati progetti vostri.

**VASCO DI GAMA:** (*con indegnazione.*) Insensati voi dite! Fu così non ha guari, Che dal suolo natal, come il son, fu Colombe respinto, Sì egli pur, quel Genovese illustre oggi alfin venerato, I sapienti d' allor insensato gridar.

**DON PEDRO:** Silenzio tèmerario!

**DON DIEGO, L'INQUISITORE E CORO:** Silenzio temerario!

**VASCO DI GAMA:** No! Io parlerò! Or a me di giudicarvi, e vi diffamerò! Ah! che l' onta della patria Da voi tradita Su voi ricada tutti un dì Voi tribunal cièco, invidioso, e geloso!

**DON PEDRO, DON DIEGO, L'INQUISITORE, e CORO:** La morte a lui per tanto ardir!

**DON ALVAR:** No! indulgenza e perdon!

**L'INQUISITORE:** Per simile insolenza, un' eterna prigion.

**VASCO DI GAMA:** Si, giusto è quel furor, miei carnefici siate, Ah! voi ch' abborrite la luce In ria prigion la racchiudete, Guai, se ad onta vostra, a rischiararvi giunge!

**CORO:** Ribelle . . . insolente, Tua sorte e in nostra man Gui dicarti saprem! Iniquo ribelle Da noi dipende il tuo destin! Il ciel sia vendicato, E in una la maestà Del dritto, dell' onor!

**VASCO DI GAMA:** Da iniquo . . . da ribelle, Io son trattato in van Da ora n' ho appellato Alla posterita, E per domar l'invidia La patria e l' avvenire E il vano suo furor! Sapranmi vendicare!

**CHORUS:** O may your boundless mercies Teach clemency to our hearts.

**DON PEDRO:** (*after having consulted aside with the council, etc.*) The sovereign council now acting for the king, In virtue of the high prerogative conceded it, Now refuses your request, And rejects your insensate projects!

**VASCO DI GAMA:** (*indignantly*). Insensate, you call them! Even the great Columbus Was spurned by his own native land. The immortal Genoese, whom now all men revere, Was even by the *wise* of those days, treated as a madman!

**DON PEDRO:** Rash youth, be silent.

**DON DIEGO, GRAND INQUISITOR, AND CHORUS:** Peace, we pray you.

**VASCO DI GAMA:** No, I'll be heard! Mine be it now to judge,—and to expose you, May the shame you now inflict upon your much wronged country, One day recoil upon yourselves. Blind, partial judges, that you are!

**DON PEDRO, DON DIEGO, GRAND INQUISITOR, AND CHORUS:** His life shall pay the forfeit of this overweening boldness!

**DON ALVAR:** No—rather extend pardon to his fault!

**GRAND INQUISITOR:** Such insolence as his, richly merits eternal imprisonment

**VASCO DI GAMA:** (*bitterly*) No, check not your wrath, become my executioners! Ah! You who abhor the light of truth, And would forever immure her in a gloomy cell, Woe, woe, to you, should she ever shine in spite of you!

**CHORUS:** Insolent rebel! Impious slave! Your fate is in our hands; Your sentence we'll at once pronounce, Your fate depends on us. This outrage against heaven shall be revenged, We vindicate the eternal majesty Of right and honor!

**VASCO DI GAMA:** (*indignantly*). Of rebellion, of impiety; You would vainly accuse me. From the injustice of the present hour I appeal to posterity; To mar rash envy And her malicious train, My country will suffice me, And the avenging future!

# Act I, Scene V

**DON ALVAR:** Da iniquo . . . da ribelle
Egli e tratto in van.
Per lui ne appello,
Alla posterità
E il vano suo furor
E per domar l' invidia
La patria e l' avvenire
Sapran lo vendicar!

**L'INQUISITORE:** Per mia voce . . . Dio lui stesso
Nel suo giusto rigor
Sull' empio capo tuo
Anatemà scagliò!

**CORO:** Al ribelle scagliam l' anatemà!

*FINE DELL' ATTO PRIMO.*

## ■ ATTO II

*Prigione dell' Inquisizione à Lisbona. Al fondo una panca, nel centro della scena una colonna massiccia, sul quale si vede una carta geografica.*

### SCENA I

*Vasco Di Gama addormentato sulla panca, Selika.*

**SELIKA:** In grembo a me del sol figliuol,
Glorioso in campo aperto,
In grembo a me vieni a cercar,
Il sonno ed il riposo
Tutto intorno a te
Pace spirà e amor'
La stella brilla
In puro cielo
Canta il Bengallin.
Ah si, della notte in sen!
Riposa in pace in questa selva oscura.
Vieni a goder, ah vien! ah vien!
(*Contemplando Vasco.*)
Tranquillo e già.
Ah gia succombo al duol
Io soffro, in se vaccilla il cor.
Dolor mortale, ah!
Presso di te pia go appena
La dolce terra mia natal
La reggia avita, il popol mio!
I numi che il cor tradè
Ah! io t' amo!
Mio ben supremo
Ah si! sei tu, sei tu!
(*S'inchina versa di lui ed è sul punto di baciarlo sul fronte, quando ella osserva Nelusko che entra dal diritta. Selika si rileva con prestezza, e si nasconde dietro della colonna.*)

---

**DON ALVAR:** Of rebellion, of impiety;
You would vainly accuse him,
In his name I appeal
Unto posterity!
To mar rash envy
And her malicious train,
His country will suffice him,
And the avenging future!

**GRAND INQUISITOR:** Heaven itself in righteous wrath.
Now speaks through my lips;
And on your impious head
launches Eternal Malediction!

**CHORUS:** Malediction—Eternal Malediction on his head!

*END OF THE FIRST ACT.*

## ■ ACT II

*The prison of the Inquisition at Lisbon. At the back of the stage is a bench. In the centre is a massive column, on which is seen a map.*

### SCENE I

*Vasco Di Gama asleep on bench, Selika.*

**SELIKA:** Lulled in my arms, bright sun's child,
Right valiant in the tented field,
Lulled in my arms, enjoy in peace
Sweet slumber and repose.
There's nothing around but breathes of tranquil peace and love;
The bright star shines
In the pure sky above,
The Bengalli trills its liquid note,
Yes, shrouded in the night's dark bosom
Sleep secure amid waving woods around,
Lulled in my arms, bright sun's child,
Enjoy sweet rest!
O, come! O, come!
(*Contemplating Vasco Di Gama.*)
He is tranquil now.
Alas! my grief overcomes me.
What suffering is mine!
My heart wildly throbs within my bosom
And yet, when near to you I scarce regret
My own sweet native land,
My ancestral palace, my devoted subjects,
Nor even the deities I've so forsworn!
Yes, I dearly love you,
My heart's own idol fond
Is you!
(*She bends over Vasco Di Gama and is about to press her lips to his forehead, when she perceives Nelusko, who has meanwhile entered from the right; she hastily rises and conceals herself behind the column.*)

---

### SCENA II

*Nelusko, Selika nascosta, Vasco dormente.*

**NELUSKO:** (*pensoso cogli occhi abbassati*) L' oltraggiato onor della sovrana lo vuol,
L' onor suo lo vuole, e l' odio mio!
(*Esitando.*)
O ciel che miro, egli dorme, malè stà!
Ferir ripugna a me uno rival che dorme,
Si compia, morir dè!

**SELIKA:** (*slanciandosi verso di Nelusko.*) Ciel, che far mai tenti,
Egli è al par di noi prigionier.

**NELUSKO:** Egli è christian, io gli detesto tutti!

**SELIKA:** Fu nostro salvator ed inerme egli giace.

**NELUSKO:** Sul mercato a lui fummo venduti a prezzo d' or!
Davver! fu gran bontà. Al comprator giammai,
La merce riconoscenza non deve!

**SELIKA:** Ei ti comprò e ver! ma generoso e buon,
Allor che lo pregava cogli occhi lagrimosi,
Di non mai separar, almen nel lor dolor,
Color che uniti fur dall' ira del destin
Per me vendettè allor, le gioje e l' arme sue,
A lui solo degg' io, in mezzo a tanto duol,
Di trovar presso a te, la mia patria adorata!
Senza lui da te divisa, sola in terra sarei.
Sarei più trista ancor!
E tu, nobil guerriero macchiando un ferro illustre,
Tu vuoi ferir quel cor si generoso!

**NELUSKO:** Io lo vo!..io lo devo, aborro quel christian!

**SELIKA:** E senza altra ragion . . .

**NELUSKO:** Oh, forse.

**SELIKA:** Ti spiega.

**NELUSKO:** Io nol posso.

**SELIKA:** Io tel comando. Io lo voglio!

**NELUSKO:** Figlia dei Rè a tè l' omaggio,
Che ti deve mia fedeltà.
Tu la sventura o schiavitude
Non tolgan nulla alla tua maestà!
Ma per lui per quel uom, quel christian,
Odio . . . rabbia . . . pensaci

---

### SCENE II

*Nelusko, Selika concealed, Vasco Di Gama sleeping.*

**NELUSKO:** (*advancing thoughtfully, his eyes bent on the ground*). The honor of my sovereign Queen wills it.
*Her* honor and my hate both demand it!
O Heaven! what is it I see! he sleeps!
(*Hesitating*). No, this may not be!
I scorn to strike a sleeping rival!
And yet it must be so—he dies!

**SELIKA:** (*rushing toward Nelusko*). Heavens! what would you do?
Is he not, like us, a prisoner?

**NELUSKO:** He is a Christian, and I loathe the hateful race!

**SELIKA:** It was he who saved us, and he now lies defenseless.

**NELUSKO:** Yes! in the slave-mart we were sold to him
For price of gold—his great kindness!
Mere merchandize like me can owe but slender thanks
Unto its purchaser!

**SELIKA:** He purchased you, it's true, but he was generous and kind,
For when I did beseech him with tearful eye,
Not to part those whose fate had been linked together,
He at once sold his jewels, no his arms,
That he might buy me too!
To him alone I owe, amidst all my woes,
That you're still by my side, and that I find in you
Some vestige of my much loved country!
But for his timely aid, torn from your side, I should have been
Friendless and alone, and even more wretched still
Than I am now! And you, brave warrior that you are,
Would stain your noble blade with the heart's blood
Of one so kind, so generous?

**NELUSKO:** It must—it shall be done.
I abhor yon Christian!

**SELIKA:** Have you no other reason?

**NELUSKO:** Perchance I have.

**SELIKA:** Explain, I pray you.

**NELUSKO:** I cannot.

**SELIKA:** I entreat, no, I insist that you tell me!

**NELUSKO:** Daughter of kings, the homage
Which your faithful subject swore to you,
Nor slavery, nor misfortune's frowns,
Can affect your queenly state,
But for him, hateful Christian,

ben.
Quando amor m' infiamma
Oppur quando l' odio,
Improvviso, ardente
Si sveglia, nel cor,
Nel mio sen s' accende
Fiamma disperato,
Che da noi s' aumenta
Al fuoco del sol!
Un fatale segreto io credei scoprir,
E se pur fosse vana mia tema,
Non l' ho giurato in van che costui
deve perir!

**SELIKA:** Nelusko!

**NELUSKO:** L'ira mia paventando
Ch' ei tremi quel pagan . . .

**SELIKA:** Per pietà!

**NELUSKO:** Ah per lui! più funesto
E il tuo pregar!
(*S' avvicina di Vasco Di Gama per colpirlo.*)

**SELIKA:** (*slanciandosi verso di Vasco Di Gama.*) Mio signor ti desta!
Sorgi signor!

**VASCO DI GAMA:** (*svegliandosi.*)
Che si vuol!
(*Nelusko nasconde il suo pugnal.*)

**SELIKA:** Il tuo pasto!
Che te recò il tuo schiavò!

**VASCO DI GAMA:** Va
ben . . . ci lascia!
(*Vedendo che Nelusko sta immobile.*)
M'odi tu?
(*Nelusko esce gettando un ultimo sguardo su Selika.*)

**VASCO DI GAMA:** (*guardando la carta geografica.*) Terribil, fatal promontorio
Che niun ancor potè passar,
Avrò la gloria di varcarti.
Il varco è qui,

**SELIKA:** (*avvicinadosi e guardando la carta.*) No!

**VASCO DI GAMA:** (*altonito.*)
Perchè.

**SELIKA:** Sarebbe perir!

**VASCO DI GAMA:** Che dite?

**SELIKA:** Sulla dritta.

**VASCO DI GAMA:** Sulla dritta?

**SELIKA:** V' è una terra!

**VASCO DI GAMA:** Qual terra?

**SELIKA:** Isola immensa . . .

**VASCO DI GAMA:** O ciel!

**SELIKA:** A Brama caro suol . . .

---

nothing else save deadly detestation can I feel!
You know me well, when love or hatred fierce and burning,
Takes possession of my soul, a raging desperate fire
Is kindled in my heart, which the sun's warmth
Irritates even unto madness!
A fatal secret methinks I have discovered.
And even should my dread presentment prove vain.
I have sworn, and may not vainly swear,
That he shall perish!

**SELIKA:** Nelusko!

**NELUSKO:** Yes, let yon accursed Christian
Beware my hate!

**SELIKA:** I entreat you.

**NELUSKO:** Entreat me not for *him.*
Each prayer you breathe
Just insures his doom.
(*Approaches Vasco to strike the blow.*)

**SELIKA:** (*rushing toward Vasco.*)
Good master, wake up!
Wake, I pray!

**VASCO DI GAMA:** (*waking*).
What would you?
(*Nelusko conceals his dagger.*)

**SELIKA:** Your slave has brought
Your morning meal.

**VASCO DI GAMA:** It is well; now leave me.
(*Perceiving that Nelusko remains motionless.*)
Do you hear?
(*Nelusko exit, glancing passionately at Selika.*)

**VASCO DI GAMA:** (*contemplating the map*). You fatal promontory
Whom none as yet has ever rounded.
The glory of first doubling you shall yet be mine!
The passage must lie here!

**SELIKA:** (*who has meanwhile approached him, looking at map*).
Not so!

**VASCO DI GAMA:** (*surprised*).
And why not?

**SELIKA:** To venture there would be to seek death!

**VASCO DI GAMA:** What did you say?

**SELIKA:** To the right

**VASCO DI GAMA:** (*eagerly*). To the right—proceed!

**SELIKA:** There lies a land—

**VASCO DI GAMA:** (*eagerly*).
What land, I pray you?

**SELIKA:** A vast island—

**VASCO DI GAMA:** O heaven!

**SELIKA:** A land dear to Brahma!

---

**VASCO DI GAMA:** Prosegui . . .

**SELIKA:** Ei fù la che la mia fragil barca,
Sorpreso in cheto mar da repentina tromba,
Battuta senzo fiu da procella fatal,
Strascinata fu al fin verso rive nemiche.

**VASCO DI GAMA:** Trionfo! io detto l' ho . . .
Trionfo il varco e là.
Non mi illudeva dunque . . . è là!
Ah per te or certo ne son!
Alfin ha il ciel di me pieta!

**VASCO DI GAMA:** (*Abbracciando Selika.*) Ah! quanto m' è caro,
Quest' angel custode
Pel qualo la luce,
Intera si fè.
Immenso favore,
O gioja inattesa,
Ah per sempre il mio core
Memoria ne avra!

**SELIKA:** (*Tutta commossa.*) Ciel io gli son cara,
O qual dolce raggio
L' alma mia rischiara
E m' inebria il sen,
I moti costanti
Di speme, d' amore,
Deh! frena pietosa
O madre d' amor!
(*Verso la fine del ensemble la porta del prigione si apre. Don Pedro e Inez entrano al momento quando Vasco Di Gama tiene Selika nelle sue braccia.*)

## SCENA III

I suddetti, Don Pedro, Inez, e Nelusko.

**DON PEDRO:** (*à Inez, accenando Vasco Di Gama e Selika.*) E la fortuna amica,
Avevan detto il ver!
Or ven offre la prova.

**VASCO DI GAMA:** (*accorgendosi di Inez.*) Guisto ciel . . . è fia ver!
Inez amato bene!

**SELIKA:** (*con un sgrido di dolore.*) Dessa . . . o ciel, che sarà!
(*Traversando il tèatro e avvicinandosi di Inez con un aria minacciosa.*)
Com' e bianca . . . e qual gel nelle vene mie si scorre.
(*Selika contempla Inez con un sentimento d' invidia.*)

**INEZ:** (*a Vasco Di Gama.*)
Udii..ohime . . . che nel orror
Di questo carcer cupo,
Gemevi tu . . . ma il tuo perdon
E compro al fin
E rèco a te la libertà!

**VASCO DI GAMA:** La libertà!

---

**VASCO DI GAMA:** Proceed, I pray you.

**SELIKA:** It was there that my frail bark
While sailing on the calm, unruffled sea,
Was suddenly overtaken by the typhoon,
And driven onward by the fatal storm,
Thrown on hostile shores!

**VASCO DI GAMA:** (*eagerly*). Ah! I triumph, it is even as I predicted!
The passage does lie there!
I was not mistaken! it is there!
Yes, thanks to you, I now am sure of it!
Heaven at length has granted my fondest wish!

**VASCO DI GAMA:** (*embracing Selika*). O guardian angel,
By whom the light of truth
So clearly is revealed,
The service you have rendered me,
Shall ever be treasured
In this most grateful heart!

**SELIKA:** (*in great agitation*). O heaven! am I then dear to him!
What bright ray of happiness
Illumes my soul—intoxicates my sense
Restrain fond goddess of love these ceaseless emotions
Of hope and affection,
In mercy.
(*Towards the end of the ensemble the prison door is opened, Don Pedro and Ines enter just as Vasco di Gama is clasping Selika in his arms.*)

## SCENE III

The above, Don Pedro, Ines, Nelusko.

**PEDRO:** (*to Ines, pointing to Vasco and Selika.*) The tale was true, it would seem,
Fortune most kindly offers you the proof!

**VASCO DI GAMA:** (*perceiving Ines*). Great heaven! do I see aright!
Ines! my beloved!

**SELIKA:** (*with a cry of anguish*).
She! Ines—here!
(*Crossing the stage and approaching Ines with a threatening air.*)
How fair she is—what icy thrill pervades my veins.
(*She contemplates Ines with evident envy.*)

**INES:** (*to Vasco.*) I heard, alas! that amid this dreary prison's gloom,
You were languishing—but I have obtained your pardon at last:
I bring you liberty!

**VASCO DI GAMA:** Liberty!

## Act II, Scene III

**INEZ:** Si! leggio quel foglio . . . pago sei tu.
(*Rimettendo gli una pergamena che porta il sigillo reale.*)
Deh! ed or dividerci dobbiamo.
Dividerci per sempre
Fuggir mi dee,
Addio! (*a Don Pedro*) Andiam, signora, andiam!
Sortiamo!

**VASCO DI GAMA:** (*ritenendolo.*)
No! i tuoi sospetti il mio core scopre,
*Accennando Selika.* Quella schiava . . .

**INEZ:** Da voi la nell' Affrica presa.

**VASCO DI GAMA:** Non è che la mia schiava . . .
Un sol cenno mi basta
Per calmar il vostro cor,
Inez io ve la dono!

**SELIKA:** (*con indegnazione.*) Ah crudel! ah crudel!

**VASCO DI GAMA:** Io ve la cedo . . . io ve la dono.

**NELUSKO:** Ed io?

**VASCO DI GAMA:** Si! la segui il mio cor . . .
Ah il mio sangue il mio cor
Tutto quel che possiedo per un suo sguardo!

**SELIKA:** (*da parte.*) Ah! il crudel.

**INEZ:** Ah! sventurato . . .

**DON PEDRO:** Noi accettiam . . .
Entrambi ve li pago . . .
(*Accennando Selika e Nelusko.*)
Ed or non più (*a Inez.*) partiam!

**VASCO DI GAMA:** (*sorpreso.*)
Che dite voi?

**DON PEDRO:** Del Rè la bontade paterno
A miei lumi confido, o se vuoi al mio zelo,
La gloria di tentar quel passaggio fatal
Che più d' un folle orgoglio in van tentò.

**VASCO DI GAMA:** Voi! a chi dato avea con intera fiducia,
Dei mie perigli i frutti, le mie veglie, i pensieri.

**DON PEDRO:** Di quei sogni la fiamma giustizia fè . . .

**VASCO DI GAMA:** Gloria che m'appartien e che strappate a me!

**NELUSKO:** (*piano a Don Pedro.*)
Tu l' otterrai per me, se teco, bordo io son,
Signor, ti servirò da guida e da pilota.

---

**INES:** Yes, read this document,— you are free.
(*Handing him a parchment scroll bearing the royal seal.*)
And now we must part,—
Yes, forever part!
Henceforth you must shun me.
Farewell!
(*To Don Pedro.*)
Come, sir, let us leave this place.

**VASCO DI GAMA:** (*detaining her.*) No! no! my heart has divined your suspicions. (*pointing to Selika.*)
Yon slave—

**INES:** Purchased by you in Africa!

**VASCO DI GAMA:** Is nothing else than my slave!
One sign, one word of mine, will prove this
To your doubting heart—Ines, I give her to you!

**SELIKA:** (*indignantly*). Ah! cruel one!

**VASCO DI GAMA:** She's yours, I say—I give her to you!

**NELUSKO:** And I?

**VASCO DI GAMA:** (*to Ines*). You even may follow her.
My life, my heart's best blood,
All would I give for one sole glance
From those loved eyes.

**SELIKA:** (*aside*). Ah! cruel one!

**INES:** (*aside*). Unhappy man!

**DON PEDRO:** (*to Vas.*) It is well! we accept your offer.
(*pointing to Selika and Nelusko.*)
I'll purchase both the slaves from you.
And now (*to Ines*) we will set out!

**VASCO DI GAMA:** (*surprised.*)
What did you say?

**DON PEDRO:** The King, of his sovereign goodness,
Has been pleased to trust to my skill,
Or rather to my zealous care,
The glory of attempting the dread passage;
A feat which more than one proud boaster has already tried,
But has never yet accomplished!

**VASCO DI GAMA:** (*astounded.*)
You! to whom I I had confidently entrusted
The results of all my perilous escapes, my wakeful nights,
My hours of thought—

**DON PEDRO:** Mere senseless dreams! which
Have long since been committed to the flames!

**VASCO DI GAMA:** Not so! The glory of this discovery belongs to me,
And you would wrest it from me!

**NELUSKO:** (*aside to D. Ped.*) That glory you'll obtain through me,
On board your ship if you'll take me,
As guide and pilot I will serve you.

---

**DON PEDRO:** (*osservandolo.*) Io vi contavo ben allor che ti comprai.
Il Rè, dei paesi scoperti da me,
Concessa m' ha il governo.

**VASCO DI GAMA:** Che sento!

**DON PEDRO:** Quest' oggi stesso
Sulpera la mia squadra; (*a Inez.*)
Andiam la vostra man . . .
Tempo è gia . . .

**VASCO DI GAMA:** Di quel dritto.

**DON PEDRO:** Di quel dritto che a piè degli altar
Ricevei di Dio stesso . . .

**VASCO DI GAMA:** Che mai dice?

**INEZ:** (*piano a Vasco Di Gama.*)
Per voi che dicean infidele
E per sottrarvi all' orror d' una prigion eternal
Mia man io l' ho sacrata . . .

**VASCO DI GAMA:** Ah!

**INEZ:** E da voi lungi io muojo.

**VASCO DI GAMA:** Anatemà sull' infame,
Maledetto è il mio destin!

**VASCO DI GAMA:** Stupefatto da sorpresa
Dal dolor ho il cor straziato
Come creder che l' onore,
Del suo giuro infranto essa ha.
E per tanto egli proclama
Egli dice che è sua moglie,
Anatema sull' infame,
Maledetto e il mio destin.

**DON PEDRO:** Stupefatto da sorpresa,
Dal dolor ha il cor straziato
A mie leggi essa è sommessa
Vincitor io son alfin.
Tremo in van . . . esa e mia moglie
Più rival il cor non teme
E sfidare posso altero,
La vendetta, il suo furor.

**NELUSKO:** Stupefatto da sorpresa.
Dal dolor ha il cor straziato,
Quel cristiano che detesto
E mi pasco dal suo duol!
E quest' altro . . . quest' infame
Che l' orgoglio già consuma,
Sì paventi del mio core,
La vendetta ed il furor!

**INEZ:** Stupefatto da sorpresa,
Dal dolor ha il cor straziato,
Ho tradito i giuri miei
Maledetto è il mio destin
Ma l' onor ed il decoro,

---

**DON PEDRO:** (*scrutinizing him, aside to Nelusko.*) It was my intention, when I purchased you.
(*aloud.*)
The King already has proclaimed me governor
Of the new lands I discovered.

**VASCO DI GAMA:** Do I hear right?

**DON PEDRO:** This very day will
My squadron set sail.
(*to Ines.*)
Madam, the hour draws near—your hand.

**VASCO DI GAMA:** And by what right, do you address this lady thus?

**DON PEDRO:** By the right, which at the altar's foot,
I have received from heaven itself!

**VASCO DI GAMA:** (*surprised.*)
What is it he says?

**INES:** (*aside to Vas.*) They told me you were faithless,
To save you from the wretchedness of an eternal prison,
To him I sacrificed my hand.—

**VASCO DI GAMA:** Great heaven!

**INES:** And I go far from you—to die!

**VASCO DI GAMA:** I'm overcome with mute surprise,
My heart is wrung with cruel grief;
Can I believe that she has forsworn her plighted faith
And yet he loudly proclaims,
That she's his wife, and calls her by that sacred name!
Accursed be such base treachery
And thrice accursed my wretched fate!

**DON PEDRO:** He is overcome by mute surprise,
His heart is wrung with cruel grief;
But she is mine,—my word is law,
I am the victor after all!
My fears were in vain, she is my bride
No rival need this heart ever fear,
With head erect, I laugh to scorn
His vengeful threats—his wild fury.

**NELUSKO:** He is overcome by mute surprise,
His heart is wrung with cruel grief;
The pangs of him whom I so hate,
Do fill my soul with wild delight,
And *he* too (*glancing at Don Pedro.*)
That haughty wretch,
Whom pride even now consumes,
Let him beware the vengeful hate
My heart feels for all his race!

**INES:** He is overcome by mute surprise,
His heart is wrung with cruel grief;
I have betrayed my plighted faith,
Accursed is my luckless faith.

Tutto grida che son moglie,
Anatema sul mio capo,
Maledetto è il mio destin!

**SELIKA:** Stupefatto da sorpresa
Dal dolor ha il cor straziato
E l' ingrato che mi spezza
Non si cura del mio duol,
Ma d' un altro ella è sposa!
E la rabbia che lo rode . . .
Ma sua rabbia fa rinascer
E la speme ed il piacer.

**INEZ:** (*à Vasco Di Gama.*) M' ascolta per pieta!

**SELIKA:** Seguirlo tenta!

**NELUSKO:** Egli cede!

**INEZ:** Ebben per me sei libero . . .
La gloria a se ti chiama
E sul mio solo cor fedele,
Deh vien al tuo ritorno . . .
Ah! nei sospir del mar che geme
Ascolta lar del mio core,
D' un cor che langue e muor
Addio! lassù ti rivedro,
Lassù ci rivedrem!
Godremo eterno amor!

**SELIKA:** L' esiglio e il disprezzo
O ciel qual colpo . . . qual martir.
Si m' abbandona il barbaro,
Lasciar mio solo ben,
Men crudo fià il morir!
Addio! Addio!

**VASCO DI GAMA:** Destin fatal . . . ci la perdè
Qual colpo . . . qual martir,
Ah, si! perduta ci l' ha,
Per me fia men crudo il morir!
Inez, addio! addio!

**NELUSKO:** Quel vil Chrisitan spietato
Convinto al fin sarà
Lode a te, o Brama!
Di sua fronto il pallor,
Già tradisce il suo duol
E salva alfin . . . addio!

**DON PEDRO:** Trionfo alfin di quel rival,
Ei vinto è già,
Si vendicato io sono appiena
Di sua fronte il pallor.
Già tradisce il suo duol
Trionfo alfin . . . addio!
(*Don Pedro parte con Inez. Vasco Di Gama cade mezzomorto sopra una sedia. Selika vuol slanciarse verso di lui, ma Nelusko ritiene e la stringe a seguire i passi Don Pe-*

But honor's voice alone proclaims,
That I am now another's bride;
I must subdue this guilty love,
What wretched destiny is mine!

**SELIKA:** I am overcome by mute surprise,
My heart is wrung with cruel grief;
While he who tortures me,
Heeds not the pain I feel.
But she's another's bride,
His heart is wrung with vengeful hate,
Alas! his torments are to me
A source of joy and gladness.

**INES:** (*to Vasco.*) Hear me, in mercy hear me!

**SELIKA:** (*aside.*) Even now he fain would follow her.

**NELUSKO:** (*aside.*) He yields!

**INES:** (*to Vasco.*) Yes, through my efforts you are free
The voice of glory now calls you here,
But when, O faithful one! you shall return
You will not pass by my grave unheeded.
Ah! let the murmurs of the surging sea,
Convey to you the yearnings of my heart,
A heart that's languishing and soon will cease to throb.
Farewell! in heaven above we'll meet again,
And never know separation more!

**SELIKA:** Exile and contempt!
O heaven! what fearful martyrdom is this.
The ruthless one abandons me
I am severed from him I love,
Ah! death itself were far less fearful.
Farewell! Farewell!

**VASCO DI GAMA:** O cruel fate, he has destroyed her happiness,
What fearful martyrdom is this.
Ah, yes! her peace of mind has flown forever.
Ah! death itself were far less terrible.
Ines, farewell! Farewell

**NELUSKO:** This thrice-accursed Christian will meet;
His punishment right soon;
Thanks be to you, O Brahma!
The ashy paleness of his brow reveals,
The bitterness of his grief.
But *she* is safe at last. Farewell!

**DON PEDRO:** Over my rival now I triumph,
Yes, my victory is complete;
Revenged am I and that right fully
The ashy paleness of his brow reveals.
The bitterness of his grief.
Yes, yes,—I triumph. Farewell!
(*Exeunt Don Pedro and Ines. Vasco falls half fainting on a seat. Selika is about to rush towards him, but Nelusko withholds her, and*

dro. Selika getta su Vasco Di Gama un ultimo sguardo di dolore d' amore.*)

*FINE DELL' ATTO SECONDO.*

# ■ ATTO III

La scena rappresenta il ponte a parte del interiore d' un gran vascello. colle entrate dei camerini principali.

## *SCENA I*

(*Si vede sul ponte diversi marinari ed ufficiali di marina. Inez è stesa sopra d' un lettuccio, circondata dalle sue donne.*)

**CORO DEI MARINARI:** Su, su marinar,
L'equipaggio è in piè,
La ridente aurora,
Sorge e gia colora,
I campi del mar!
Su, su marinari!
Si torni al lavor!
(*Si ode la campana che annunzia la preghiera della mattina . . . i marinari. gli ufiziali. Inez e le sue donne s' inginocchiano.*)

**PREGHIERA DEI MARINAR:** O gran' San Domènico,
Dell' infedel terrore
Ci proteggi e guida ognor!
Ogni di l'inno tuo vogliam dire,
Gran' San Domenico!

**SELIKA, INEZ, E LE SUE DONNE:** O celeste providenza,
O ricorso nostro sol
Signor, ci assisti ognora,
Ci proteggi e guida ognor!

**NELUSKO:** (*parendo sul primo ponte.*) Olà! marinar!
Muta il vento . . . pronti alle vele
Tutti correte . . . il vento muta
Volgete al nord . . . Vedete in fondo là
I segni precursor del terribil uragan,
Volgete al nord . . . oppur persi siam!
(*Scende dal primo ponte.*)

**ALVAR:** (*à Don Pedro, accennando Nelusko.*) Siete ben sicuro che non è un traditor?

**NELUSKO:** (*à Don Pedro con finta dolcezza.*) Io che v' ho guidati . . . io che interi vi svelai,
I projetti ed i piani di Vasco di Gama.

**DON PEDRO:** Ha detto il ver . . . io son ancor suo debitor.

compels her to follow Don Pedro. As Selika departs she bends on Vasco a last lingering look of love and anguish.*)

*END OF THE SECOND ACT.*

# ■ ACT III

The scene represents the 'between decks' of a large ship with entrances to the principal Cabins.

## *SCENE I*

(*Several sailors and naval officers are discovered. Ines is reclining on a couch, surrounded by her attendants.*)

**CHORUS OF SAILORS:** Up, up, mariners,
The crew is now astir,
The smiling morn looks forth,
And paints in gay colors
The vast expanse of ocean.
Up, up, mariners,
To work with right good will!
(*The bell is heard announcing the morning prayer. The sailors, officers, Ines, and her ladies kneel.*)

**PRAYER OF MARINERS:** O great Saint Dominic,
Terror of the infidel,
Protect and guide us evermore!
Daily we will repeat your hymn,
O great Saint Dominic!

**SELIKA, INES, AND ATTENDANTS:** O, Providence benign,
Our only hope in trouble,
Assist us when we call on you,
Guide and protect us evermore!

**NELUSKO:** (*appearing on main deck.*) What ho, mariners!
The wind has changed, quickly man the yards!
Keep well round to the north,
Do you not see, afar, the dread precursors of the fearful hurricane?
Keep to the north, I say, or we are lost!
(*He descends from main deck; during the above Don Pedro and Don Alvar have entered from their cabins.*)

**ALVAR:** (*to Don Pedro, pointing to Nelusko.*) Are you sure that fellow does not play us false?

**NELUSKO:** (*to Don Pedro with assumed meekness.*) I play you false!
I, who of my own accord, revealed to you
The whole of Vasco's plans and projects!

**DON PEDRO:** He speaks the truth—I'm much indebted to him.

# Act III, Scene I

DON ALVAR: (à Don Pedro.) E fede aver potete in quel perfido schiavo, Che il suo primier signor tradi, E tradir vi pur ei saprà, Gia, sua mercè, due navi perdute abbiam.

NELUSKO: Il gigante delle tempesta, Adamastor, Condannate le avea . . . ed il suo sdegno fatal, Cadrà sul capo vostro si di cammino non cambiate,

DON ALVAR: E non vuoi tu guidarci . . .

NELUSKO: Qual tema avete in cor?

DON PEDRO: Ebben . . . sia. Si diriga sul nord . . .

NELUSKO: (contando.) Tra, la, la, la, la.

UN MARINAR. Ehi Nelusko! che cosa canti la?

NELUSKO: (solennamente.) Io canto la canzone del Rè di questo mari, Del tremendo Adamastor che su voi la morte tien.

MARINARI: Ascoltiamo la leggenda del tremendo Adamastor.

NELUSKO: Adamastor . . . rè dell' onde profonde, Al suon del vento sull' acque s' avanza E se col piè urta il mar Guai a voi! Guai a voi, Se col piè urta il mar! Guardate . . . è le. Al chiaror cupo dei lampi, del fuoco, Ei gia s' inoltra . . . gia regna sul mar, Fino al ciel l' onde nere solleva Scampo non v' ha . . . non v' ha tomba por l' empio!

CORO: Ne scampo ne tomba per voi non v' ha.

NELUSKO: No per voi non v' ha! E vano il tremar! e vano il pregar! (Con un riso studente.) Ha! ha! ha! Corraggio . . . alle vele Fin che n' è tempo ancora, Su gli alberi sospesi, Prevenite l' Uragan fatal Ei gia minacciosa s' avanza, Ed apre ad inghiottirvi Gli abissi profondi del mar!

DON ALVAR: (to Don Pedro.) And can you trust the treacherous slave, Who betrayed his former master? He'll soon betray you to, I expect, Through him you know we have lost two ships already.

NELUSKO: Adamastor, the Giant of the Tempest, had pronounced their doom, His dread wrath will soon overtake even you And you change not soon your course, By steering quickly towards the north.

DON ALVAR: (to Nelusko.) Where would you guide us?

NELUSKO: What fear has taken possession of your heart?

DON PEDRO: Well, be it so! steer northward!

NELUSKO: (singing.) Tra, la, la, la, la.

A SAILOR: Why, Nelusko—what are you singing, man?

NELUSKO: (gloomily.) I sing the song of the king of the seas, It is the legend of the dread Adamastor, Whose mighty hand is even now suspended over your heads.

SAILORS: Let's hear the legend of the dread Adamastor!

NELUSKO: Adamastor, monarch of the pathless deep, Rides over the waves to the wild wind's sound. Beware, beware, for should he draw near, Woe, woe to the wretch who crosses his path! See, he is there! how swiftly he glides. Illumed by the lightning's lurid glare, High up to the skies, he piles the dark waters, All hope now is lost, for the doomed wretch no tomb, None, none, but a watery grave!

CHORUS: All hope is lost, for the doomed wretch no tomb, None, none, but a watery grave.

NELUSKO: For you, none but a watery grave. Neither trembling nor prayers will avail. (with a demoniac laugh.) Ha! ha! ha! Come, courage! up, up with the sails While yet there be time, Quick, man the masts, and prepare For the storm which darkly advances, And bids the vast depths of the sea Yawn wide to engulf you!

CORO: E già minaccioso s' avanza, Ed apre ad inghiottirci Gli abissi profondi del mar!

UN MARINARO: (dalla poppa.) Un vascello che porta la nostra bandierà, Spiccato ha verso noi una barca leggiera, Essa avanza . . . giunta è già,

NELUSKO: (da parte.) Ohimè! se fosse mai Qualche avviso importuno che per salvarli Vien in quest' ora fatal.

## SCENA II

I suddetti . . . Vasco Di Gama.

DON ALVAR: Ah che vedo! Vasco! su questo ignoti mar, In un con voi venir? Chi mai potè condurvi?

VASCO DI GAMA: E Dio che m inspiri le sue mire a compir Ei giudò i passi miei. e gonfiò le mie vele.

DON PEDRO: Per seguirci costi?

VASCO DI GAMA: Per precedervi dite!

DON PEDRO: E dunque allor per disfidarci!

VASCO DI GAMA: No! s' e v' è tempo ancor, signor ti vo salvar! (Don Pedro fa cenno a tutti di ritirarsi.)

## SCENA III

Vasco Di Gama, Don Pedro.

VASCO DI GAMA: Qual destin, o piu tosto qual cieco delirio Vi conduce allo scoglio fatal, Ove Don Bernard Diaz mio fido ammiraglio, Ha infranto il suo vascello. Non bastan le insidie del mar Tu vedrai contro tè, di mille e mille schifi, Ricoprarsi il mar, da cui guerrier selvaggi, Gli avanzi del vascel a saccheggiare verran.

## SCENA IV

I suddetti, Don Alvar, Nelusko, Marinari e Soldati, poi Inez, Selika e donne.

(I Marinari ed i Soldato accorrono, si precipitano se Vasco Di Gama, e lo desarmono.)

CHORUS: Yes, prepare for the storm which darkly advances, And bids the vast depths of the sea Yawn wide to engulf us!

A SAILOR: (from the poop of the vessel.) A ship sailing under our own colors, Has just put forth a boat, Which pulls rapidly towards us, It nears us quickly—it is already alongside!

NELUSKO: (aside, anxiously.) Should this be some ill-timed message, Sent forth to save them in this fatal hour!

## SCENE II

The above, and Vasco Di Gama.

DON ALVAR: What is it I see? Vasco! You, a fellow traveler On these remote sequestered seas? What can have brought you here?

VASCO DI GAMA: Inspired by heaven, I am here come A holy mission to fulfil; It is heaven my steps that guides, and swells my flowing sail!

DON PEDRO: Have you then followed us here!

VASCO DI GAMA: Not followed, but preceded!

DON PEDRO: (angrily.) Is then your objective to defy us?

VASCO DI GAMA: Not so—if there be yet time, I have come here To save you! (Don Pedro motions to the bystanders to withdraw.)

## SCENE III

Vasco Di Gama. Don Pedro.

VASCO DI GAMA: What fatality, or rather what blind delirium Brings you to the fatal promontory, Where Don Bernard Diaz, my trusty admiral Was lost with all his crew? It is not alone the ocean's treachery you have to fear, The sea will soon be covered with a thousand barks, Each with wild savage warriors filled, And bent on ravaging your hapless ship!

## SCENE IV

The above, Don Alvar, Nelusko, Soldiers and Sailors, and afterwards Ines, Selika, and Women.

(The Soldiers and Sailors who have hastened to obey Don Pedro's summons, rush hastily upon Vasco, whom they disarm.)

**DON PEDRO:** (*ai Soldati che ritengo Vasco Di Gama.*) Si leghi al grand albero tosto:
E che il fuoco dell' arme vostra
Giustizia ne faccia . . .

**SELIKA:** Giusto ciel! e desso!

**INEZ:** Vasco! e desso . . . o ciel!

**VASCO DI GAMA:** Vile!

**DON PEDRO:** (*ai Soldati accennarde Vasco Di Gama.*) Tosto a morte sia tratto!

**INEZ e SELIKA:** (*inginocciandosi.*) Ah! per pietade mio signor
Mitigate un tal rigor,
Signor pietà, signor pietà.

**DON PEDRO:** No! Ola! obbedite!
(*Il temporale, che fin adesso è stato sentito da lontano, s' avvicina.*)

**SELIKA:** Ah! se non m' ode il ciel
L' averno al men m' ajùti.
(*A. Don Pedro con rabbia.*)
Tosto Vasco fia salvo, oppur Inez io sveno,
Velo giuro per Brama che m' ascolto nel cielo.
Pronunziar spetta a voi la lor grazia
O lor morte!

**CORO:** O ciel da terror il suo cor e colpito,
Muto e titubante già freme quel cor!

**DON PEDRO:** Strascinato egli sia al fondo del vascel.

**DON ALVAR:** La sua nave l' aspetta . . .

**DON PEDRO:** S' allontani! è mio prigioniero costui.

**DON ALVAR:** Ma promesso l' hai ei vivra!

**DON PEDRO:** Si ma nulla io non promisi a Selika,
E mia giustizia ben punir sapra,
La schiava che sulla signora,
Il ferro alzar osò
Ch' essa sia sino al sangue al instante sferzata,
In presenza di tutti!

**INEZ, SELIKA, e NELUSKO:** (*con un fremito d' indegnazione.*) Ah!

**NELUSKO:** La maesta suprema in essa ingiuriata,
Chi l' osera tentar?
(*Il temporale diviene ad un tratto violentissim.*)

**DON ALVAR:** Alle velle, all sarte! . . .
Il turbin giunge.
(*Ad un tràtto il vascello è assalito da Indiani, che abbordano a traverso le cannoniere. I marinari,*

**DON PEDRO:** (*to the soldiers who have hold of Vasco.*) Bind him fast unto the mainmast,
And let your bullets dispatch him!

**SELIKA:** Heavens! it is he—it is Vasco.

**INES:** Vasco! it is he, O heaven!

**VASCO DI GAMA:** (*to Don Pedro.*) Coward!

**DON PEDRO:** (*to his soldiers, pointing to Vasco Di Gama.*) Quick, to death with him!

**INES AND SELIKA:** (*kneeling.*) In mercy's name, great sir, we beseech you
Restrain this fearful wrath.
Mercy mercy, we implore!

**DON PEDRO:** No mercy, will I show, what ho! obey there!
(*The storm which has for some time been gathering in the distance gradually approaches.*)

**SELIKA:** Ah! heaven heeds not my prayer,
Ye powers of ill assist me!
(*To Don Pedro, angrily approaching Ines.*)
Set Vasco free at once, or Ines straight I kill!
I swear it by Brahma, who now in heaven hears me!
Pronounce at once their sentence—their pardon or their death!

**CHORUS:** O heaven! He is overcome with fear!
Mute and irresolute—he tremblingly stands!

**DON PEDRO:** Drag him to the vessel's lowest recesses!

**DON ALVAR:** But, by your leave, his ship awaits him.

**DON PEDRO:** Let her proceed on her course, this man's my prisoner!

**DON ALVAR:** Did you not promise he should live!

**DON PEDRO:** I gave no promise to Selika,
And I'll soon find a right punishment
For the rebellious slave, who
Dared to raise the dagger's point over her mistress!
Let her be bound, and straight severely scourged,
In presence of the crew!

**INES, SELIKA, AND NELUSKO:** (*with a shudder of indignation.*) Ah!

**NELUSKO:** (*menacingly.*) This fearful outrage injured majesty,
Who here will dare inflict?
*The storm suddenly increases in violence.*

**DON ALVAR:** (*hastily.*) Reef the sails, man the yards, the hurricane is at hand!
(*The ship is suddenly invaded by Indians, who board it through the port holes. The crew endeavor to*

soldati, Ec. cercano di rispingerli, ma sono sopraffatti dai loro numerosi assalitori.*)

**TUTTI:** Oh ciel;

**CORO:** Oh cielo tu da forza ai figli tuoi,
Proteggi lor dallo stranier,
Infondi nel cor d' ognun la pace
E da tregua al fier dolor!

*FINE DELL' ATTO TERZO.*

## ■ ATTO IV

La Scena rappresenta (*à sinistra*) l' entrata d' un tempio Indiano . . . a diritta un palazzo. Al fondo altri monumenti sontuosi.

### *SCENA I*

(*Selika, Nelusko, il Gran Prete Di Brama, ed Indiani di varie. Marzia, Cortège, Ballo.*)

**NELUSKO:** Noi giuriamo per Brama
E per Vischiù, per Schiva,
Onnipotente Dei che l' Indostan adora,
Non giuriamo obbedienza,
Al rampol dei nostri Rè!

**CORO:** Noi giuriam obbedienza,
Al rampol dei nostri Rè!

**NELUSKO:** Selika pur . . . or da noi coronata,
Giura di mantener, delle legge il vigor,
Sopra il libro divin, la nel tempio!
Altre volte affidato da Brama!

**SELIKA:** (*estendendo la mano sopra il libro d' oro.*) Si . . . lo giuro! (*da parte.*) Il tuo destin, O Vasco,
(*Guardando il Gran Prete e Nelusko.*)
Qual' è?
Io tremo, non oso interrogar!
(*S' ode un colpo del tem-tam seguito da un grido stridente.*)

**GRAN PRETE:** (*a Selika.*) Giammai nessun stranier, rammenta il giuro tuo
Non lordera di sua presenza impura,
Il sacro suol del Indostano!

**NELUSKO:** Regina, il sacro ferro tutti gia gl' immolava!

**SELIKA:** Ciel! tutti!

drive them back, but are overpowered by the overwhelming numbers of their assailants.*)

**ALL:** (*in terror*). O heaven!

**CHORUS:** (*kneeling*). O heaven! grant strength your prostrate sons,
Protect them from the foeman's ire,
Restore peace unto our hearts,
Vouchsafe to end our grievous woes!

*END OF THE THIRD ACT.*

## ■ ACT IV

The scene represents, on the left hand, the entrance of an Indian temple; on the right, a palace; at back, other sumptuous monuments.

### *SCENE I*

(*Selika, Nelusko, the High Priest of Brahma, Indians of various Castes. March, Procession, Ballet.*)

**NELUSKO:** We swear by Brahma
By Vishnu, too, and Siva,
All powerful deities whom Hindostan reveres—
We swear, I say, obedience to the daughter
Of our ancient kings!

**CHORUS:** Obedience we here swear
Unto the daughter of our ancient kings!

**NELUSKO:** And you, Selika, whom we now do crown,
Swear to maintain inviolate our laws
Swear it on the book divine, in yonder temple formerly enshrined by Brahma!

**SELIKA:** (*advancing her hand towards the Golden Book.*) I swear it! (*aside.*) O Vasco! what dreadful fate
May have overtaken you?
(*Looking towards the High Priest and Nelusko.*)
Alas! I tremble—I dare not question them.
(*A stroke of the tam-tam is heard, followed by a piercing shriek.*)

**HIGH PRIEST:** (*to Selika.*) Remember your oath—no stranger, whoever he is,
Shall with defiling presence stain
The sacred soil of Hindostan!

**NELUSKO:** O Queen! the sacred weapon is even now.
Destroyed them all!

**SELIKA:** O heaven! all! Did you say All?

# Act IV, Scene I

**UN PRETE:** (*piano a Nelusko.*) Tranne un sol, che avean incatenato. Della nave al fondo . . . ei sol respira ancora.

**A PRIEST:** (*aside to Nelusko.*) All, but one Whom we found chained in the vessel's hold, He alone is left alive!

**NELUSKO:** (*a parte, con rabbia.*) E Vasco forse. (*piano al Prète.*) Va! Che sia spento egli pur— (*Il Prète esce.*)

**NELUSKO:** (*aside, angrily.*) Perchance it is Vasco! (*aside to Priest.*) Go! See that he too be dealt with speedily. *Exit Priest.*

**GRAN PRETE:** La corona t' aspetta, al piè degli altar, Andiam! (*Entra nel tempio insieme Selika ed i Prèti.*)

**HIGH PRIEST:** The crown awaits you at the altar's foot. On, then, to the temple! (*Enters temple, together with Selika, Priests, etc.*)

**NELUSKO:** (*agli Indiani.*) Noi seguiam la regina! (*S' ode un rumore.*) Ma qual rumor.

**NELUSKO:** (*to Indians.*) We follow our Queen. (*A noise is heard without.*) What do these sounds mean?

**UN PRETE:** Dei pagani le donne al supplizio son guidate. Verso il mancennillier, del nero e folto aspetto.

**A PRIEST:** The stranger women are even now conducted to the slaughter, Where the mancanilla tree frowns dark and gloomy!

**NELUSKO:** Nel sacro limitar guidate i passi lor, Là, sotto l' ombre chete, le lor stanche membra, Il sonno troveran e in un . . . la morte! (*Esce.*)

**NELUSKO:** (*to soldiers.*) Guide their steps to the sacred groves, Beneath the tranquil shade their weary limbs will seek repose, And find—the sleep of death! (*Exit.*)

**CORO DI SACRIFICATORI:** O sol che nel ciel cocente t' innalzi, Tu vittime chiedi cruenti, Che a fèrir s' appresti il ferro, E che l' eco ancor ripeti. La morte! la morte! O Schiva su noi discendi, La vittima e pronta discendi!

**CHORUS OF SACRIFICERS:** O sun that now rise with beams red and angry. You call for victims and blood. Prepare we the steel then! make ready the glaive, And let the loud echo resound with wild shriek. Death! death! O Siva! descend among us! The victims are ready—descend! descend!

## SCENA II

*Vasco (seguiti da Soldati.)*

## SCENE II

*Vasco, followed by Soldiers.*

**VASCO DI GAMA:** (*guardando il sito con admirazione.*) O ridente suol . . . vago e bel giardin, Salute a voi, O Paradiso in terra, Ciel azzur senza equal . . . che incantate mio cor, Tu m' appartieni o nuovo mondo, Dono feci di tè, all' amato mio suolo natal A noi queste apriche campagne! A noi quest' incanto divin; Ricchi tesori! O meraviglie! Ah salute a voi! O bel paese! Alfine mio sei tu . . . si nuovo sol. Si mio sei. O bel paese Alfine mio sei tu!

**VASCO:** (*contemplating the prospect with evident admiration.*) Hail! fruitful land of plenty, beauteous garden, hail! Indeed an earthly paradise you are! That sky of matchless azure, All—all enchants my soul! O New World, you are mine; you belong to *me*, And as a gift I will present you to my dear native land! These sunny plains are ours! Ours these matchless scenes! Hail! priceless treasures! wondrous marvels, hail! O beauteous country—you are mine at last! Yes—land till now unknown, you're mine! Mine! yes, mine!

## SCENA III

*VASCO DI GAMA: Bramini, e Soldati.*

## SCENE III

*Vasco, Brahmins, and Soldiers*

**CORO.:** Si la morte allo stranier! Pietà . . . pietà non v' ha!

**CHORUS:** Death—death to the stranger! We will show no mercy!

**VASCO DI GAMA:** Ebben! moriam da eroe, da Cristian, Oh Dio . . . tu m' accogli nel ciel, Ah! marciam!

**VASCO DI GAMA:** It is well—at least I'll meet my death As becomes a hero and a Christian! On then!

**CORO:** Sol che t' innalzi cocente nel ciel, Pronto sia il ferro e la mano a ferir! E ripeti l' eco morte il suon! (*Tutti hanno levato lor scure e sono sul punto di amazzare, Vasco Di Gama.*)

**CHORUS:** O sun that now rises with beams red and angry, You call for victims and blood, Prepare we the steel then, make ready the glaive, And let the loud echoes with wild shrieks resound, Death! death! (*The soliders have all raised their axes, and are on the point of despatching Vasco di Gama.*)

## SCENA IV

*I suddetti, Selika, seguita da Nelusko, Il Grande Prete, Ec., Ec.*

## SCENE IV

*The above—Selika followed by Nelusko, The High Priest, Ec., Ec.*

**SELIKA:** (*vedendo Vasco Di Gama.*) V' arrestate!

**SELIKA:** (*perceiving Vasco Di Gama.*) Hold!

**VASCO DI GAMA:** Selika! (*Alla voce di Selika i soldati stanno immobili, Selika corre a Vasco Di Gama.*)

**VASCO DI GAMA:** Selika! (*At Selika's voice the soldiers remain motionless. Selika rushes eagerly to Vasco Di Gama.*)

**NELUSKO:** (*piano à Selika.*) Volerlo sottrarre al supplizio!

**NELUSKO:** Would you then save him from his impending doom?

**GRAN PRETE:** E per uno stranier, le leggi qui violar, Che ai piè degli altar Il labbro tuo giurò.

**HIGH PRIEST:** And, for an unknown stranger, violate the laws. Which at the altar's foot even now you swore Forever to preserve?

**CORO:** Si! morte agli stranier E che la legge si compia!

**CHORUS:** Death—death to the stranger, Let our laws be fulfilled!

**GRAN PRETE:** La legge eseguita gia fu, Sino alla donne tutti immolati gia son.

**HIGH PRIEST:** The decree already has been put in force. Even the women have all met their fate!

**VASCO DI GAMA:** (*disperato.*) Inez, non sei più?

**VASCO DI GAMA:** (*despairingly.*) Ines, are you no more?

**SELIKA:** (*a parte con dolore.*) Ah crudele!

**SELIKA:** (*aside, in tones of anguish.*) Ah, cruel one!

**GRAN PRETE ED IL CORO:** La morte à quel stranier!

**HIGH PRIEST AND CHORUS:** Death to the stranger!

**SELIKA:** (*prendendo la mano di Vasco Di Gama.*) E se costui non fosse uno stranier!

**SELIKA:** (*taking Vasco's hand.*) And should he *not* prove a stranger!

**VASCO DI GAMA:** Che sento?

**VASCO DI GAMA:** What is it I hear?

**SELIKA:** Silenzio . . . io voglio ancor . . . la vita à te salvar . . . Indi m' obblia se vuoi. (*Volgendosi al popolo ed ai prèti.*) Se per prodigio strano Fratel nostro ei fosse?

**SELIKA:** Hush—not a word—I yet would save your life Anon you may forget me, and your will! (*Turning to the bystanders, priests, Ec.*) Should he, by a marvel strange, be Our brother!

**CORO:** O ciel!

**CHORUS:** O heaven!

**SELIKA:** E se il destin, Con sacri nodi unita a lui m' avesse, Che far dovreste allor!

**SELIKA:** (*continuing.*) Should fate have linked my fate with his with sacred ties indissoluble? What course would ye pursue then?

**NELUSKO:** (*piano.*) Ciel! quanto tentar osa!

**NELUSKO:** Heavens! and would she dare—

**SELIKA:** Si! quando schiavo gemea in lontane contrade, (*Accennando Vasco Di Gama.*) Quel prode mi salvò la vita e insiem l'onor!
(*à Nelusko.*)
E mia man, lo sai tu, fu sua ricompensa.

**NELUSKO:** Chi . . . io?

**SELIKA:** Tu sol smentirmi puoi . . .
Ma tu ben sai che s' egli muor . . . io pur morro! (*Dirigendosi verso i prèti ed il popolo.*) In tua presenza attestarlo può Nelusko ancor.

**GRAN PRETE:** Attestarlo dè innanzi agli dei,
E sopra il libro d' or.
(*Ad un cenno del Gran Prete un Bramino cerca il libro consecrato.*)

**NELUSKO:** (*esitando e guardando Selika.*) Averla tanto amata E in questo dì fatal,
Doverla dar io stesso,
In braccio al mio rival?

**CORO:** Vedete si turba . . . ei trema, vacilla.

**SELIKA:** Ah! tu sol giurando Puoi finir mia pena,
L' affianno mio tu vedi,
Il mio duolo . . . il mio pianto,
Pietà! favella!
(*piano.*)
Ei piange!

**NELUSKO:** (*ad un sguardo supplichevole di Selika.*) Ancor un sacrifizio
Il cor perisca
Insieme col' onor!

**CORO:** (*à Nelusko.*) Ti spiega . . . favella.

**NELUSKO:** Ah! vo calmar sua gioja Contenta alfin mi vegga morir! . . .
Morir ah! del suo piacer!

**CORO:** Potresti giurando Calmare sua pena,
Giura!

**NELUSKO:** (*con sforzo.*) Ebben! innanzi a voi io giuro,
Ch' essa l' ama, e ch' egli e sposo suo!

**CORO:** Sposo suo!
(*Tutti s' inchinano dinanzi a Vasco Di Gama.*)

**NELUSKO:** (*da parte.*) Al mio penar da fine
Ciel, coi strazii tuoi!
Ma che l' infame che l' ha rapita,
Sia meco fulminato ancor!
Averlo tanto amato
E l' idol mio veder rapito
A questo cor . . . o dolor!

**SELIKA:** (*continuing.*) Yes, when I languished, a slave in far off lands (*pointing to Vas.*) Yon hero did preserve my life and honor. (*to Nel.*)
And as you well know, my hand was his reward!

**NELUSKO:** (*astounded.*) I! Do you appeal then to me?

**SELIKA:** (*aside to Nelusko.*) You alone can contradict the tale;
But, mark me well, should *he* be doomed to death,
I, too, will die!
(*turning to priests, etc.*)
Before all, Nelusko will attest to the truth
Of what I've said

**HIGH PRIEST:** That must he then straightway before our gods,
And over the Golden Book!
(*At a sign from the High Priest a Brahmin fetches the consecrated book.*)

**NELUSKO:** (*hesitating and glancing anxiously at Selika.*) And have I then so fondly loved her,
And yet must on this fatal day,
By my own act, resign her to a rival's arms!

**CHORUS:** Observe him! he's troubled—he hesitates, trembles!

**SELIKA:** (*to Nelusko.*) Take the oath, for this way alone,
Can you assuage my woes,
You see my grief, my bitter tears,
Have mercy, mercy—speak, I pray!
(*aside, anxiously.*)
He weeps—he's moved!

**NELUSKO:** (*overcome by Selika's suppliant glance.*) One more struggle!
Nelusko's honor and his heart's fond dream,
Must now perish together!

**CHORUS:** (*to Nelusko.*) Speak then! explain.

**NELUSKO:** (*aside.*) I will be no barrier to her bliss;
She shall see me die contented
Yes, *die!* to make *her* happy!

**CHORUS:** Swear! swear!
By swearing, you may lessen her grief. Swear!

**NELUSKO:** (*with a violent effort.*) Then here in presence of all, I swear
That she does love him, and that he is her husband!

**CHORUS:** Her husband!
(*All incline themselves respectfully before Vasco di Gama.*)

**NELUSKO:** (*aside.*) O heaven! let thunderbolts end
My fearful sufferings,
But let the miscreant who has won her love,
Share your vengeance with me!
I have loved her—ah how fondly!
And yet must see my heart's sole

Al mio penar da fine
O ciel coi strazzii tuoi!
Son io che l' abbandono,
Si! in braccio al mio rival!
Su me . . . su lui . . . l' ira del ciel cadi!
(*Esce.*)

**GRAN PRETE:** Popol . . . Odi il mio parlar
Gli Dei dell' Indostan . . . di cui seguiam le leggi,
Vogliono che l' union sotto altro ciel giurata,
Sia, dell' ara innanzi, per sempre consacrata.
O Brama! O Vichnou! O Siva!
(*Tutti escono, eccetti Vasco Di Gama e Selika.*)

## SCENE V

**VASCO DI GAMA:** (*da parte.*) Dove son . . . e qual gioja m' in-onda di piacer?
Dei mali che soffrì . . . io perdo il sovvenir,
Mi par veder un mar di fuoco e di splendor,
E da cocente ardor il cor s' agita in sen.

**SELIKA:** Ebben? fuggi da me crudel . . . colla tua gloria,

**VASCO DI GAMA:** Me lasciar il dolor!

**SELIKA:** Non comprendesti mai,
Che si può amar, soffrir e morir di dolor!

**VASCO DI GAMA:** Che sento . . . e qual error fu il mio,
Qual velo?—ti nascose a me?

**SELIKA:** Qual velo . . . lo spreggo . . .

**VASCO DI GAMA:** Deh taci! non bestemmiar! giammai mortal imago
Al rapito sguardo mio, non s' offerse si bella,
E del tuo ciglio o ciel il divorante ardor
Come di fiamma un raggio passò nel mio seno!
Ah! lasciarti ora mai è impossibile al mio cor!
No! giammai!

**SELIKA:** Fatale errore, non m' hai tu forse già venduta alla rivale!

**VASCO DI GAMA:** Ah! vedi il mio rossor, Regina io son ai piedi tuoi!
O Selika pel sposo tuo perdon!

idol,
Thus cruelly torn from me.
Ah woe is me!
O heaven, let thunderbolts
End My fearful sufferings,
But let the miscreant who
has won her love,
Share your vengeance with me!
It is I—who now yields her
To a rival's arms.
Accursed fate,—on me—on *him*.
May heaven's indignation fall!
(*Exit.*)

**HIGH PRIEST:** O people, listen to my words.
The gods of Hindostan, whose righteous laws we obey
Have willed it that a tie contracted beneath other skies
Must over the altar of our sacred faith *again* be solemnized!
Brahma; Vichnu! Siva!
(*At the conclusion of chorus, all withdraw, except Vasco and Selika.*)

## SCENE V

**VASCO DI GAMA:** (*aside as though in in a dream.*) Where am I? What unknown joy is this that steeps my soul in wild delight?
I've lost the memory of past sufferings,
A brilliant sea of dazzling brightness rolls before mine eyes.
While my rapt heart throbs fast with glowing ecstacy!

**SELIKA:** O cruel one, heedless of anything save glory would you fly me?
And leave me then to mourn!

**VASCO DI GAMA:** Leave me, pain!

**SELIKA:** Do you not understand that one may love and suffer,
And of that suffering—die?

**VASCO DI GAMA:** What is it I hear? How mistaken was I
What veil did shroud you from me!

**SELIKA:** The dark veil of—scorn!

**VASCO DI GAMA:** Ah say it's not so! Ah do not blaspheme!
Never did mortal form
Appear so beauteous to my ravished sense!
The all devouring brightness of your eyes,
Even like a ray of flame penetrates my breast.
What leave you now? No, no, it is impossible!
My heart would never consent—
No! never.

**SELIKA:** O fatal error,—did you not sell me to your rival?

**VASCO DI GAMA:** You see my shame! O Queen, behold me at your feet!
Selika, pardon, for your *husband*, pardon!

SELIKA: Tu! sposo mio!

SELIKA e VASCO DI GAMA: O trasporto . . . o dolce ebbrezza, Che commove il cor amante, Diva fiamma che allegrezza, Nel mio cor infonde amor. Suprema gioia, piacer del ciel Ah! io mi sento in' ciel rapita, Ah! sul tuo cor amare è la vita, Oh trasporto o dolce ebbrezza Che commuove il cor amante! Diva fiamma che allegrezza Nel mio cor infonde amor!

VASCO DI GAMA: Selika mio ben . . . ah tu regni sul mio core!

SELIKA: Non proferir dolci accenti, Vaneggiare non farmi . . .

VASCO DI GAMA: Inanzi al tuo ed al mio Dio Sei mia sposa . . .

SELIKA: Tua sposa! Ma rifletti ben . . . foss' io sposa tuo Io geloso sarei tutto. Ah, si! Anche del sovvenir di quella che non è più . . . E che bandir dovrai . . . Di' ne avrai tu la forza.

VASCO DI GAMA: Presso a te, Tutto scordo o Selika!

SELIKA: Tu lo giuri . . . davanti a Dio!

VASCO DI GAMA: Io lo giuro . . . davanti a Dio!

ELIKA: A me . . . ognor a me!

VASCO DI GAMA: A te . . . ognor a te!

VASCO DI GAMA e SELIKA: O trasporto o dolce ebbrezza, Che commuove il cor amante Diva fiamma che allegrezza Nel mio cor infonde amor Il ciel ci dona sulla terra, L' amor che sola inebria i sensi, E sul mio cor quando ti stringo, Felice io son . . . si son rapito in ciel! Ah! sul tuo cor amare è la vita!

## SCENA VI

*I suddetti. I prèti ed il popolo.*

GRAN PRETE: (*alzando le mani sopra di Vasco Di Gama e Selika che s' inchinano dinanzi à lui.*) Divina Trinita! ai spergiuri tremen-

---

SELIKA: You, my husband?

SELIKA AND VASCO DI GAMA: What transport wild, what sweet delight, My fond heart now feels A Godlike flame that joy inspires, And teaches us to love! Bliss supreme—bright gift of heaven, To worlds above I seem to soar Pressed to your heart, ah, love is life indeed. What transport wild, what sweet delight, My fond heart now feels A Godlike flame that joy inspires, And teaches us to love.

VASCO DI GAMA: Beloved Selika, you are sole mistress of my heart.

SELIKA: Ah, utter not these accents fond, They drive me to the verge of madness!

VASCO DI GAMA: Before your god, before my own, I ask you. Will you be my wife—

SELIKA: Your wife! Think, if I, were your wife, I should be jealous of all—Ah, yes! Even of the memory of her who is no more, And whose very image I would have you strive To banish from your mind. Say, has it the strength to do this?

VASCO DI GAMA: When at your side, All, all, do I forget, save you, Selika!

SELIKA: Will you swear it—before heaven—will you swear it?

VASCO DI GAMA: I swear it—before heaven—I swear it!

SELIKA: (*fervently.*) Yours, then, forever yours!

VASCO DI GAMA: Yours, forever yours!

VASCO DI GAMA AND SELIKA: What transport wild, what sweet delight, My loving heart feels A godlike flame that joy inspires, And teaches us to love! Heaven has given to mortals on this earth, This bliss divine, that exalts the senses. Yes to my heart, when I press you, I am thrice blessed! I soar towards heaven. Ah! love like this is life indeed!

## SCENE VI

*The above, the priests, populace, etc.*

HIGH PRIEST: (*raising his hands over Vasco Di Gama and Selika who kneel before him.*) Mystic deities! of perjurors the dread

---

da, Di questi sposi accogli i voti, Uniti . . . siate felici ognor!

CORO: Uniti . . . siate felici ognor!

(*Le donne circondano Selika sulla sua testa esse pongono una corona di fiori, e la coprono d' un velo . . . altre donne formano coi loro veli intorno à Selika una siepe diafana.*)

CORO: Siepe leggiera L' estasi cela, Che gli circonda, In si bel dì! Dolce speranza Infiamma i cori, Della costanza, D' eterno amore.

(*Vasco Di Game contempla la regina con amore; ad un tratto un canto lontano gli giunge al orecchio.*)

INEZ E CORO DI DONNE: (*di dentro.*) Addio sponde del Tago, Io più non vi vedrò, Addio mio suol natale Addio! Addio!

VASCO DI GAMA: O qual prodigio, O qual magia! O Inez! L' ombra tua Là dal ciel . . . ancor m' invia Un estremo addio!

(*Non potendo resistere alla sua emozione, tenta di slanciarsi dal lato dove si ode il coro di donne, ma un gruppo di fanciulle lo circonda e lo strascina verso di Selika, chi in questo punto si dirige verso del suo palazzo, insotto alle volte di tocca, formate dar veli delle bayadères.*)

CORO: Siepe leggiera L' estasi cela, Che gli circonda, In si bel dì. Dolce speranza Infiamma i cori, Della costanza D' eterno amore!

*FINE DELL' ATTO QUARTO.*

## ■ ATTO V

*Giardini della Regina. Alberi tropici, fiori, frutti, Ec. A sinistra l' entrata del palazzo.*

## SCENA I

*Selika, Inez (circondata di Soldati).*

SELIKA: Ah, che intesi mai! Son io già tradita ed ingannata? Cosi tu serbasti la fè.

---

Receive now the vows of this fond pair United,—be happy ever more!

CHORUS: United,—be happy ever more!

(*Indian maidens surround Selika, they place a crown of flowers on her head, and cover her with a veil. The others surround Selika with their veils, thereby forming round her a transparent rampart of gauze.*)

CHORUS: Light fluttering veil, The ecstasies conceal, Of the fond pair, On this auspicious day! Sweet hopes of happiness Now fill their hearts, With vows of constancy And love eternal.

(*Vasco gazes on the Queen with looks of ardent affection, when of a sudden a mournful strain from afar meets his ear.*)

INES AND CHORUS OF WOMEN: (*off the stage.*) Oh shores of Tagus, farewell! I never shall see you again; My own sweet native land, farewell! Forever—farewell!

VASCO DI GAMA: What strange marvel is this? It is magic sure! O Inez—your dear shade sends me From heaven itself, A last sorrowing farewell! (*Vasco, unable to control his emotion, attempts to rush towards the side whence the strains proceed, but a group of maidens now surround him, and drag him towards Selika, who is at this moment bending her steps towards the palace, beneath the archway of gauze formed by the veils of the bayaderes.*)

CHORUS: Light fluttering veil, The ecstacies conceal, Of the fond pair, On this auspicious day! Sweet hopes of happiness Now fill their hearts With vows of constancy, And love eternal.

*END OF THE FOURTH ACT.*

## ■ ACT V

*The Queen's gardens. Tropical trees, flowers, fruits, etc. On the left side is the entrance to the palace.*

## SCENE I

*Selika, Ines. (surrounded by soldiers.)*

SELIKA: What do I hear? Deceived—betrayed already! Is it thus you keep faith?

INEZ: Deh tu m' ascolta.

SELIKA: No, un istante avvilito ho ripreso i miei dritti, / Or la Regina vedi, non la sposa, / L' oltraggiata Regina che giudice diventa, / E ti sapra punire.

INEZ: Ah, Selika, perdon!

SELIKA: Chi dunque tanto osa la voce d' innalzar, / Innanzi alle sovrana? Tu paventa lo sdegno, / Che gia raffreno appena! / In pria che mia vendetta, comandi il tuo supplizio, / T' appressa o schiava e rispondi a me! / Per quale tradimento e per qual' artifizio, / Quell' indegno era egli in questo luogo / Presso à te?

INEZ: Il caso sol venne ad offrirmi a sua vista.

SELIKA: E che uniti, diceva tremante e l' alma scossa?

INEZ: Ei diceva che l' Imen i vostri giorni unì, / Che vostra sol è la sua vita, / La sua fe . . . sua riconoscenza.

SELIKA: E per tanto ei t' ama ancor!

INEZ: No, No! Che il vostro cor gli perdoni, / Si fedel all' onor! Ohime! ei m' abbandona, / E da me fuggira.

SELIKA: Ma per tanto ognor ei t' amerà!

INEZ: Se per te, quest' e un delitto / Cada su me lo sdegno vostro, / Egli e giusto il riconosco, / Sol mio pregare e questo, / E l' imploro al vostro piè, / Quando più gioja non v' ha su questa terra / Di dolor senza fin quando i di pieni son, / Venga la morte . . . / Su me il tuo rigor ricada . . . ferisci! / (riguardando Selika che fin adesso è stata immobile.) / Piangi tu?

SELIKA: Ah giovinetta sventurata, / Come mai colpevol far la, / Del mio martir . . . del mio crudel dolor, / E questo sol il mio penar!

INEZ: E questo sol il mio penar, / Si queto sol è il mio delitto, / Si mi punite . . . mi ferisci . . . / Ah! che la morte é un ben per me!

INES: Ah, would you just listen—

SELIKA: No! for a brief space I did forget my queenly state, / But now resume my rights. The wife no more, / The Queen alone you see in me. / An outraged Queen, who now becomes your judge / And straight will punish you!

INES: Selika, I implore forgiveness!

SELIKA: (angrily). Who is it that dares to raise her voice, / While in her sovereign's presence. / Beware the wrath / Which I can scarcely control! / Before mine indignation just your death ordains, / Draw near, O slave, and answer me / By what base treachery—what subtle artifice, / Did Vasco just now gain access to you, / Here—on this very spot?

INES: It was chance alone that brought about our meeting!

SELIKA: (bitterly.) And what did he say to you, all trembling with emotion?

INES: He said you two were now united in wedlock's holy bonds. / And that his life, his faith, his gratitude, / Are henceforth yours alone

SELIKA: And yet he loves you still?

INES: No, no. Your heart may freely pardon him, / For being faithful honor's law. / Alas! he has forsaken me—-he'll spurn me evermore!

SELIKA: But still he'll love you, none the less.

INES: Ah! if you deem that love a crime, / Then let your indignation fall on me / Just is your anger—I avow it; / This only do I wish, and / I do implore you at your feet, / Grant my prayer. When in this world all joy has fled / And nothing but bitter grief remains, / Then welcome death. Let then, I say, your anger falls on me / Strike! (watching Selika, who until now has remained motionless.) / I think you weep!

SELIKA: Hapless maiden, / How could I ever accuse you / Of this my grief—my direful woe; / The fault, alas, is mine alone!

INES: I've told you now my torments cause, / You know my only crime; / Quick, punish me,—no, quickly strike, / No greater boon than death is there to me!

SELIKA: Provi dunque pensando all' amato tuo ben . . .

INEZ: E l' amor e lo sdegno nel cor indeciso.

SELIKA: E senti là come una ferrea man.

INEZ: Si . . . che tormenta e spezza.

SELIKA: Ah! giovinetta sventurata / Come mai colpevol farla, / Del mio martir . . . del mio crudel dolor, / E questo sol il mio penar. / Io stesso provo il suo martir, / Il suo dolor mi fa pietà.

INEZ: E questo sol il mio penar, / E questo sol il mio delitto, / Si mi punite . . . mi ferisci, / Ah! che la morte è un ben per me. / Ah si . . . io vo morir! / Del mio martir . . . alfin pietà! / Ebben non tardar! ambidue tu ne svena.

SELIKA: Lui svenar! la suora sua! / Io, sua amicà, che data avrei per lui / Il torno e la mia vita . . . / Ma se, per sua piacer, lo potessi seguir.

INEZ: Io lo respinger- ei . . . perche sposo egli t' è / La morte sol, fra noi e sceglier tai nodi può.

SELIKA: Desiarla ei vorra . . . eccesso di dolore! / Ohimè! Lungo dolore / Che di già comincia / Ed il cor vacilla / Ad abandonnar. / Dio che vedi il duolo / Per spezzar miei lacci / D' ispirarmi degni almen.

INEZ: Lungo dolore / Che di già comincia / Ed il cor vacilla / Ad abandonnar. / Dio che vedi il duolo, / Per spezzar miei lacci / D' ispirarmi degni al fino.

SELIKA: Ah già dell' odio gl' impeti furenti, / Non turban più il mio sen. / E già succede à mia febbre cocente, / Un repentin stupor.

INEZ: Si . . . un ripentino stupor.

SELIKA: Il riposo torna / E l' afflitto core, / Più dolce vendetta, / Libero fara.

SELIKA: What do you feel then when thinking of your love?

INES: Fierce hate and love within my doubting breast / Do struggle for the mastery.

SELIKA: (eagerly pressing her hand to her heart.) And do you feel here as it were an iron hand?

INES: Yes—that tortures and oppresses me!

SELIKA: Hapless maiden, / How could I ever accuse you / Of this my grief—my dreadful woe! / The fault, alas, is mine alone! / Her very torments I experience, / Her grief itself excites my pity!

INES: I've told you now my torment's cause, / You know my only crime. / Ah! punish me—no—quickly strike, / No greater boon than death could you concede. / Yes, yes, I'll gladly die, / You then will feel some pity for my woes! / Why do you tarry? Slay both me and him!

SELIKA: Slay him! I, his loving mate who would have sacrificed / Both life and throne for him / But tell me, were it granted you to follow him?

INES: Even then I'd spurn him— for he is your husband, / And, in our land, it is death alone can rend such ties asunder.

SELIKA: And even my death he will desire. / O bitter grief! Ah! woe is me! / O misery unceasing, / Your bitter pang I feel / And yet my heart hesitates / To set itself free. / O heaven, you see my grief, / Inspire me, I pray you, / Teach me how to end my woes.

INES: O unceasing misery, / I feel your bitter pangs, / And yet my heart hesitates. / To set itself free. / O heaven, you see my deep grief, / Inspire me I pray you, / Teach me how to end my woes.

SELIKA: The furious dictates of relentless hate. / No longer agitate my tortured breast: / A sudden stupor already has succeeded / The all-consuming fever which but now possesed me.

INES: Yes!—a sudden stupor!

SELIKA: Yes! my peace of mind returns, / A sweeter vengeance far / Will rid my tortured heart / Of its dread load.

## Act V, Scene I

INEZ: Il suo cor vacilla,
Fra l' odio ed il pieta,
Il dio de, miei padri,
Ha visto il mio duolo,
E ad ispirarla la vien!

### SCENA II

*I suddetti . . . Nelusko (seguito
da soldati.)*

SELIKA: Via . . . sia tratta colei!
*(i soldati escono con Inez.)*
*(a Nelusko.)*
E tu, da qui lontan
Conduci Vasco.

NELUSKO: Con essa?

SELIKA: *(scivendo sulle taro-
lette.)* Si . . . ambedue
Tu devi all' istante condurli
Su quel vascel.
Che ancor si vede la sul mar.

NELUSKO: O ciel!

SELIKA: E poi . . . m' ascolta
ben; quando à bordo ei sarà.
E partira . . . questi noti gli porgi,
Ma non prima . . . m' intendi tu!

NELUSKO: Ah! li credete in man di
chi fu ognor discreto,
O fausto dì chea ai tormenti miei da
fin,
Regina, ei rendi a te la possanza e la
gloria!

SELIKA: E quando tu verdrai dai
nostri lidi,
Uscir per sempre il lor vascello
Vien à trovarmi allor, alla punta del
capo,
E se quel promontorio che s' erge
sul mar!

NELUSKO: *(con terrore.)* Ah! non
ve n' appressate!
Là, se vene sovvien si stende la
grand ombra,
Del ner mancenillier, dell' albero
mortal.

SELIKA: Io lo so.

NELUSKO: Sciagura all' impru-
dente
Che respira quei fior. Dall' odor fa-
tal
Per poco egli si crede in ciel rapito,
Quel estasi così menzognera e fatal
Lo conduce pian pian dal delirio al
morir!

SELIKA: Io lo so . . . ma di quei
luoghi si scopre il mar,
Ed è quel che vogl' io!
*(Nelusko esce e Selika entra nel
Palazzo.)*
*(Cambiamento di scena, che rap-
presenta adesso un promontorio
dominando il mare. Un albero sta
nel centro della scena.)*

---

INES: Between hate and pity
Her heart wavers still;
God of my fathers, you have seen
my suffering,
Now inspire her with mercy!

### SCENE II

*The above. Nelusko. (followed by
soldiers.)*

SELIKA: *(to soldiers.)* At once remove that woman!
*(soldiers remove Ines.)*
*(to Nelusko.)* And you conduct
Vasco Far, far away!

NELUSKO: With her?

SELIKA: *(writing on her tablets.)*
Yes, conduct them both
To yonder ship, which still remains
in sight.

NELUSKO: O heaven!

SELIKA: And then—now mark me
well—when Vasco is on board,
And even about to sail—no sooner,—mind—
Give him these tablets—do you understand?

NELUSKO: *(taking tablets.)* You
may safely entrust them to the hand
of one.
Who never has proved indiscreet;
Thrice happy day that puts an end
to my torments,
And to you, O Queen, restores your
power and glory!

SELIKA: And when you see that
bark depart
For ever, from these shores, rejoin
me at the Cape's remotest point,
You'll find me on the promontory
which steeply rises over the sea!

NELUSKO: *(in terror.)* Beware!
approach not that dread spot.
Remember, it is there the fatal
trees,
The lowering mancanilla readily
unfolds his leaves

SELIKA: I know it well.

NELUSKO: Woe to the luckless
wretch who inhales
The fragrance of its blossoms; their
fatal perfume
At first seems to waft the soul to regions of celestial bliss,
But soon this false and fleeting ecstacy subsides.
And wild delirium gives place to—
death

SELIKA: I know all this; but this
dread spot overlooks the vast expanse of ocean.
And it is this spectacle I would enjoy.
*(exit Nelusko, Selika enters pal-
ace.)*
*(The scene changes to a view of
the promontory overlooking the
sea, a large tree occupying the
center of the stage.)*

---

### SCENA III

*Selika sola, s'inoltra lenta fin al
margine del mare ch' ella contempla in silenzio.*

SELIKA: Da qui io veda il mar immenso e senza fine,
Al par del mio dolor,
E il suo flutto in fluror che si rompe
e si muove,
Ohime! come il mio cor!
*(appressandosi del mancenilli-
er.)*
O tempio sontuoso, o volta di fogliame,
Che ondeggiate ognor i letali vostre
rami,
Io vengo a voi cercar dopo il tumulto
La calma ed il riposo e l' oblio del
dolor,
L' ombra vostra eterna è l' ombra
del sepolcro,
*(cogliendo i fiori che cadono dai
rami del mancenillier.)*
Già l' odio m'abbandona . . . nel
cor non ho livor
Ricevi il mio perdono . . . addio
mio caro ben,
Addio mio Vasco caro . . . io ti
perdono, Addio!
O ridente color . . . o firo ver-
miglio e
Vie sopra il sen della sposa novella,
Vieni . . . tu sei la mia corona
nuzial,
Si dice che il tuo odor fatale gioja
da,
Che un instante del ciel egil aprir sa
le porte,
E poi d'un lungo sonno fa per
sempre dormir,
Come l' amor esso v' inebbria,
E come luivi fa morir.
Ah! dicon ver; i sensi sopiti già vaci-
lan,
Il mio cor di piacer e di gioja bolzò.
Qual celeste suon . . . non è un
prodigio.
Quanto splendor . . . al mio
sguardo s'aprono le porte del ciel,
Brama sul mio passaggio risplen-
dente m' appar
E lui! è la sua imago! ah si! ei mi ri-
ceve in ciel!
Dal dolce canto un cigno sopra bi-
anca nube,
Trae leggiero un carro; le Uri sorri-
denti
Presso lui dansando e vezzegiando
volano,
Vien egli quel che adoro, ei m' ama
egli ancora.
No! non m' obliò!
Ah ch' io respiro appena, O qual
trasporto è il mio,
Desso egli é! si Vasco egli è!
Ei vien! colui ch' adore,
Su bianca nuo vien,
A miei piedi già s' arresta,
Poi risale ah! egli è la!
*(Selika sul punto di dormire è ca-
duto al piè del mancenillier. S'ode
un colpo di canone. A questo ro-*

---

### SCENE III

*Selika enters and slowly advances
to the edge of the sea, which she silently contemplates.*

SELIKA: Yes! here I look upon the
mighty sea—boundless—infinite
As is my woe!
Its waves break in angry fury and
then anon their course renew,
As my sorrowing heart!
*(advancing towards the mancan-
illa tree.)*
Oh leafy temple, vault of dark foliage,
That waves your deadly branches in
the wind ceaselessly,
After life's weary tumult I now
come
To seek repose, and find oblivion
from my woes,
Yes! your shade eternal is like the
darkness of the tomb!
*(gathering flowers which have
fallen from the branches of the
mancanilla tree.)*
All thought of hate now forsakes
me!
No envious wish now racks my
heart.
Loved one, farewell! my pardon I
now waft to you;
Farewell, my Vasco, I forgive you.
Ah! farewell!
*(contemplating flowers.)*
Glittering hues! Oh beauteous
crimson flowers
Rest on the bosom of the new-made
bride,—
Come,—you are my nuptial crown!
It is said your dread perfume in-
spires a joy,
Which for a moment yields un-
earthly joy,
And then causes an eternal sleep.
Even like love which first intoxi-
cates,
And then, like you kills!
Yes the tale was true, my sense is
lulled and seems to wander,
My heart wildly bounds with plea-
sure.
What heavenly sounds now meet
my ear,
It is enchantment sure! To my rav-
ished eyes
The gates of heaven are opened;
Brahma, in all his mystic splendor
appears,
It is he! it is he! to heaven he wel-
comes me,
A graceful swan lightly draws his
chariot
Over that white cloud; the smiling
Houris dance
Round him with luring wiles.
See, my Vasco comes, he loves me
still.
No! he has not forgotten me!
With joy's excess I scarce can
breathe, what fond transport is
mine!
It is he! it is Vasco's self,
My loved one comes,

*more Selika apre gli occhi, guarda verso il mare, e vedendo il vascello che s' allontana, proferisce un grido di dolore.*)

**SELIKA:** Ah! son svegliata ancor! Io sono in terra!

## SCENA ULTIMA

*Selika e Nelusko.*

**NELUSKO:** O trasporti di gioja! al fin partiti son! Già sparir le lor navi vedete . . .

**SELIKA:** Ah! mi rendete il ciel!

---

On you white cloud he comes,— He stops, and he kneels at my feet.— He rises now,—Ah! see, he's there! (*Selika, overcome by sleep, falls at the foot of the mancanilla tree. The report of a cannon is now heard, at the sound of which Selika opens her eyes, looks toward the sea, and perceiving the ship, now pursuing its homeward course, she utters a cry of grief.*)

**SELIKA:** Ah! it was a dream! I am awake once more! Ah yes, it is earth indeed I tread!

## SCENE IV

*Selika and Nelusko.*

**NELUSKO:** O boundless joy! at length they're gone, for ever gone! See, see! even now their vessel disappears.

**SELIKA:** Ah! the heavenly vision restore to me!

---

**NELUSKO:** (*avvendendosi di Selika, proferisce un grido e si getta ai suoi piedi.*) Ritorna in te, o mia giovin sovrana, Ma già sua mano è fredda e gelata, O terror! è la morte . . .

**SELIKA:** No! è il piacer! (*Essa muore cogli occhi volti al cielo. Nelusko s' inginocchia vicino a' Selika ch' egli solleva nelle sue braccia.*)

**NELUSKO:** Giusto ciel, O mio dolor! Vicino a te restar io vò Con te vogl' io morir!

**CORO:** Questo sol è il soggiorno d' eterno amor, Sol qui regna eterno amor! (*Nelusko cade, morendo ai piedi di Selika.*)

*FINE.*

---

**NELUSKO:** (*suddenly perceiving Selika, he utters a cry and throws himself at her feet.*) Ah! Your senses wander, be yourself once more, O youthful Queen! Alas! her hand is icy cold.— O horror, it is death!

**SELIKA:** No! it is bliss eternal! (*She dies with her eyes fervently turned toward heaven. Nelusko kneels by the side of Selika, whom he raises in his arms.*)

**NELUSKO:** Great heaven! she is dead! O bitter woe! Selika! I will remain at your side. With you—with you I'll die!

**CHORUS:** Of Love eternal, the abode is this! Here Love reigns eternal! (*Nelusko falls lifeless at Selika's feet.*)

*THE END.*

# L'Amore Dei Tre Re (1913)

## The Love of Three Kings

Music by Italo Montemezzi ■ Libretto by Sem Benelli

This three-act tragic opera, set to a libretto by Sem Benelli, was first performed at the Teatro alla Scala in Milan on April 10, 1913. The story begins at a remote castle in Italy in the tenth century, forty years after barbarians have invaded. An Italian princess, Fiora, is betrothed to an Italian prince, Avito, when she is forced to marry Manfredo, son of King Archibaldo, Italy's barbarian conqueror. Manfredo is out on a campaign and his father suspects Fiora of being unfaithful to his son. As the old King is blind, Flaminio, one of his guards, guides him through the castle. Fiora and Avito rendezvous on the night that Manfredo returns, but Avito escapes just before Archibaldo enters. Fiora is unable to convince the king of her innocence, but she uses Manfredo's arrival as a way to pretend that she was walking around in her desire to see him again. Manfredo is going out on yet another campaign and requests that Fiora wave to him from the castle battlements until he is out of view. Fiora is touched by his request, but even as she waves goodbye Avito comes to her. They sing of their love for one another and Archibaldo overhears them. Flaminio stops Avito from killing the king and urges him to escape. Flaminio then meets Manfredo, who sees that Fiora has ceased waving and decides to return home as he feels that something is wrong. Fiora and Archibaldo are left together, and she teases him, not revealing Avito's name, until Archibaldo strangles her to death. Manfredo hears about this but forgives Fiora; she is laid out in the castle crypt and is mourned by those who loved her. Avito enters and kisses her, and he dies from the poison which Archibaldo has spread on her lips in order to find out her lover's identity. Manfredo also kisses her lips and dies. Archibaldo finds Manfredo's body, which he at first assumes is that of Fiora's lover, and discovers his own dead son.

---

## ■ ATTO PRIMO

*Spaziosa sala del Castello. Due archi ben misurati aprone le belle curve alla vista di una terrazza a colonne, e della notte poco innanzi l'alba. Una lanterna, come un segnale, rossastramente splende rivolta verso la campagna. Nel buio della sala rilucono i mosaici del colonne e i capitelli medioevali, incroci bizzarri me armoniosi di stili, s'intrecciano e s'incontrano paurosamente.*

*(Un po' silenzio; quindi entra da sinistra Archibaldo vecchio e cieco barone; è condotto da Flaminio sua guida, che indossa il vestito delle guardie del castello.)*

*(Le vesti di ognuno, ampie e lunghe, hanno linee pure, ieratiche.)*

**ARCHIBALDO:** Grazie, Flaminio: guarda quella porta. E chusa bene?

**FLAMINIO:** Accostata; signore . . .

**ARCHIBALDO:** Chiudila bene, ma senza rumore . . .

## ■ ACT I

*Spacious hall in the castle. Through the fine curves of two well proportioned arches a view of a terrace with pillars, and of the night, just before dawn, is obtained. A lantern, employed as a signal, sheds its reddish light across the country. The mosaics on the ceiling above the arches, and above the doors on the right and left, shine out through the gloom of the hall. The pillars and their mediæval capitals, twisted in a curious but harmonious style, intersect and cross one another gloomily.*

*(A short silence; then there enters from the left Archibaldo, an old and blind baron; he is led by his guide, Flaminio, who wears the dress of the castle-guards.)*

*(The garments of both men are full and long, with pure, priestly lines.)*

**ARCHIBALDO:** Thanks, good Flaminio: look at that door. Is it quite shut?

**FLAMINIO:** Not quite, my Lord . . .

**ARCHIBALDO:** Then shut it quite, but make no noise . . .

**FLAMINIO:** *(attraversa la stanza, s'avvicina alla porta di faccia)*

**ARCHIBALDO:** *(pentito; con premura)* No; lasciala! Che credí tu? Che senta?

**FLEMINIO:** Chi, mio signore?

**ARCHIBALDO:** *(amaro)* Ma che sei? Stordito dal sonno? Chi ci dorme mai, di là?

**FLAMINIO:** Fiora! La sposa del figliuolo vostro!

**ARCHIBALDO:** Dorma; dorma: che giovinezza è sogno . . . Non altro! A me negato ora è sognare Chè il sonno mi tradisce e come un'ape molesta scherza con le mie palpebre, poi che lo sorte m'ha seccato gli occhi . . . *(Dolorosamente)* Flaminio, guarda il cielo; tu che puoi . . .

**FLAMINIO:** E notte ancora; ma l'alba è vicina . . .

**ARCHIBALDO:** Flaminio, guarda, indaga nella valle. Io sento che Manfredo tornerà

**FLAMINIO:** Non può darsi, se ancora egli combatte i castelli dei nostri oltre qué monti . . .

**ARCHIBALDO:** Che dici tu: dei nostri?

**FLAMINIO:** *(crosses the room and approaches the door opposite).*

**ARCHIBALDO:** *(changing his mind; hastily)* No; leave it so! What do you think? or hear?

**FLAMINIO:** Who, my lord?

**ARCHIBALDO:** *(bitterly)* But what are you? Are you dazed With slumber? Who is it that sleeps in there?

**FLAMINIO:** Fiora! your son's wife sleeps there!

**ARCHIBALDO:** Well, let her sleep: since youth is but a dream . . . Nothing else! Dreams are denied me since sleep betrays me and like a buzzing bee Plays with my eyelids; Since fate has sealed my eyes . . . *(mournfully)* Flaminio, look at the sky; you that can see . . .

**FLAMINIO:** It is dark still, but the dawn is near . . .

**ARCHIBALDO:** Flaminio, look beyond, and scan the valley. I feel that Manfred will return

**FLAMINIO:** That cannot be if he still fights the castles Of our men beyond these mountains.

**ARCHIBALDO:** What are you saying? Our men?

FLAMINIO: Si; dei miei che voi già soggiogaste . . . Io sono nato sulle cime del colle là d'Altura, dove nacque la nostra principessa Per aver pace vi donammo Fiora . . . Avito il giovane principe nostro l'avrebbe sposata . . .

ARCHIBALDO: (con insistenza) Guarda, Flaminio; guarda nella valle . . .

FLAMINIO: Nessuno, mio signore! Tutto è pace!

ARCHIBALDO: Sono stanco ed il sonno che mi fugge mi lascia ancora più sperso nel buio . . .

FLAMINIO: (distrattamente) Chi non dorme di notte o smania o prega . . .

ARCHIBALDO: O ricorda! . . . Il pensiero mio stanotte ripercorre solingo la pianura sconfinata del viver mio trascorso . . .

FLAMINIO: Ricordate la vostra giovinezza . . .

ARCHIBALDO: Italia! Italia . . . è tutto il mio ricordo! . . . (Maestoso) Son quarant'anni che discesi in questa bella serra di fiori; e sento ancora le mie narici dilatarsi al fiero ricordo . . . Era la nostra gioventù ardente, esercitata alla conquista . . . Ed in noi tutti era la volontà possente come una mazza di ferro. Tornavano da questra terra alcuni dei nostri e, nella lingua scalpitante metallica di nostra gente, ai cieli esaltavano questa preziosa gemma; ed il bel nome d'Italia a noi squillava forte come la lusinga d'una marcia di guerra . . . Finalmente il re nostro di noi scelse i migliori; e movemmo: masnada scintillante argentea verde e d'oro come serpe immane che si desta e si divincola dall'ombra e muove, risuonando, al sole. Tesi nell'acceso impeto i cavalli; e gli uomini, su loro, i menti aguzzi: tutti sentimmo ai primi aliti italici il caldo aroma della bella preda! E questa Dea, natante fra due mari, ci parve sola . . . . . . E qui con lei sedemmo e qui giacemmo e qui l'amammo e mai nessun di noi la lascerà, l'amante novella, tutta fresca, tutta verde, tutta d'oro; ed amandola si piange ch'ella ci sia la schiava e non la madre,

FLAMINIO: Yes; of my men Whom, long ago, you conquered . . . I was born Upon the hilltops, yonder, of Altura, Where our princess was born . . . For sake of peace we gave you Fiora . . . . . . Avito, our young prince Was to have wedded her . . .

ARCHIBALDO: (insistently) Look out, Flaminio, look into the valley.

FLAMINIO: No one, my lord! All is quiet!

ARCHIBALDO: I'm weary, and the sleep that shuns me Leaves me yet more distracted in the gloom . . .

FLAMINIO: (absently) He who does not sleep at night must either rave or pray . . .

ARCHIBALDO: . . . Or else remember! . . . My thoughts tonight Are wandering lonely over the boundless plain Of my past life . . .

FLAMINIO: Remember your young days . . .

ARCHIBALDO: Italy! Italy! is all I can remember! (majestically) It has been forty years since first I came into This lovely park of flowers; and still I draw My breath more quickly at the proud Remembrance Our youth was ardent And all intent on conquest . . . And deep in every breast there was A will of iron Some of our kinsmen came back from this land, And in the strident tongue that marks our race They praised its wonderous beauties to the skies; Until the name of Italy rang out As loud and luring as a war march . . . At last The king picked out the best among us; And forth we rode, our cohort glittering Silvery green and golden, like a snake That, being roused, uncoils its monster lengths And drags them from the shadow to the sun. Keen were the horses on the eager charge; And keen were the minds of them that rode them: With the first balmy breeze from Italy We all inhaled the stirring breath of conquest! And this fair goddess, swimming

chè, se ci fosse madre, allora si, c'insegnerebbe a dominare il mondo. (Pausa. A Flaminio) Taci? . . . con odio forse tu mi guardi! . . .

FLAMINIO: (guardando il vecchio cieco ipocritamente) Io vi son servo; e voi siete mio re! (volendo sviare il suo pensiero) Ma . . . il cielo imbianca e la lanterna cede al giorno la sua luce.

ARCHIBALDO: Adunque, spengila . . . inutile segnale! Egli non giunge!

FLAMINIO: (spegne la lanterna sulla terrazza e poi:) Andiamo, allora, mio signore. (Lontano il suono di un flauto campestre) (Turbato) Andiamo! . . . (Quasi lo trascina verso le sue stanze, à sinistra)

ARCHIBALDO: Torniamo, si; torniamo nella notte . . . (Esce guidato da Flaminio.) (Avito ravvolto in un mantello esce dalla porta di destra. Muove due o tre passi verso la terrazza. Indaga fuori; scruta il cielo; ascolta, esita un po'. Si riavvicina alla porta d'onde è uscito, ma sulla soglia gli apparsa la bianca figura di Fiora: i bei capelli corti inanellati, vivi intorno alla testa. Sul suo corpo snello una toga sottilissima bianca e avorio.)

AVITO: È ancora notte fonda. Troppo presto Geronte ha dato il segno.

FIORA: Ritorniamo . . .

AVITO: No: restiamo cosi sul limitare della notte d'amore a dirci addio.

FIORA: Si; restiamo cosi . . . (Avvincendosi a lui) Come chi appena si sveglia . . . e teme il giorno e aborre il sole.

AVITO: (tremante; accenna a sinistra) È chiusa quella porta?

FIORA: È chiusa; è chiusa. Tu tremi, Avito! E una infinita pace è nel mio petto . . .

between two seas, Appeared alone to us . . . And here we sat with her; And here we lay; and here we loved her; and never Will one of us forsake her, our fair new mistress So fresh, so green, so golden; And as we love her, so we weep That she should be the slave and not the mother, Since, if she were the mother, she in truth Would teach us how to dominate the world. (Pause. To Flaminio) You're silent? Perchance you look on me with hatred?

FLAMINIO: (looking at the blind man hypocritically) I am your servant; and you are my King! (wishing to turn his thoughts) But now . . . the sky grows light; our lantern pales Before the daylight . . .

ARCHIBALDO: Put out the lantern then . . . A useless signal! He comes not! . . .

FLAMINIO: (extinguishes the lantern on the terrace; then:) Then let us go, my lord . . . (In the distance the sound of a rustic flute.) (Uneasily) Let us go! (He almost drags him to his apartments on the left.)

ARCHIBALDO: Let us go back, then; back into the night . . . (Exit, led by Flaminio.) (Avito, wrapt in a mantle, comes out from the door on the R. He takes two or three steps towards the terrace. He looks about; examines the sky; listens; hesitates a little. Again he approaches the door whence he came; but on its threshold has appeared the white figure of Fiora: her lovely short hair hangs in disorder 'round her face. Her slender figure is draped in a very fine ivory-white garment.)

AVITO: The night is still profound. Geronte has given the signal too early.

FIORA: Let us go back . . .

AVITO: No: let us remain like this, upon the threshold of this night of love, bidding each other adieu.

FIORA: Yes; let us stay like this . . . (clinging to him) Like one who scarcely Has walked . . . and fears the day and loathes the sun.

AVITO: (shuddering; points to the left) Is that door closed?

FIORA: It is closed; it is closed. You're trembling, Avito! Infinite peace Is in my breast . . .

AVITO: Fiora sì; lo sento,
ed ho paura di quella tua
pace . . .

FIORA: Dammi le labbra e tanta ti
darò
di questa pace! . . . E poi la ri-
vorrò
implorandola dispertamente,
chè senza le tue labbra non ho
pace . . .

AVITO: Se poi mi renderai tanta
dolcezza
quanta è quella che dare ti vorrei,
struggimi tutto con il fuoco tuo,
perchè rinascerò.

FIORA: Sì, mio diletto!
Mio cuore ardente! la tua bocca è
un fiore
d'ongi momento . . . Sì;
perch'io lo colgo
ad ogni istante e sempre rifior-
isce . . .

AVITO: (perdutamente, come un
fanciullo ammalato) Sì . . . ri-
fiorisce . . . Senza te pa-
tisce . . .

FIORA: (con lo stesso smarrimento) E se lo bacio aulisce . . . E il-
languidisce
l'anima che stacurva su quel
fiore
Avito; molle sogno . . .

AVITO: (c. s.) Eterna febbre!

FIORA: Incanto lungo . . . senza fine!
(Si stringono perdutamente e si
smarriscono nel bacio)

AVITO: (come svegliandosi, si
scioglie da lei)
Ahimè! Guarda; la luce già comincia,
il cielo imbianca . . .

FIORA: Tu mi vuoi lasciare . . .

AVITO: (per fuggire) È tardi!
(Scorge la lanterna spenta . . .
Atterrito)
Fiora! Guarda! La lanterna
è stata spenta . . . Qualcuno è
venuto
qui, nella notte . . .

FIORA: Il vento è stato . . .

AVITO: No;
che la notte era cheta! . . . Non
rammenti?

FIORA: Ascolta! . . . Corri! . . .

AVITO: (fugge dalla terrazza verso destra. Fiora lo guarda, lo segue come a proteggerlo, poi corre
verso le sue stanze. Ma s'è aperta
la porta di sinistra ed è apparso
Archibaldo solo).

---

AVITO: Yes, Fiora, I can feel it,
And I am frightened at such
peace . . .

FIORA: Give me your lips and I will
give you
Of this peace! . . . And then I'll
want it back,
Beseeching, in despair,
That there's no peace for me without your lips . . .

AVITO: If you then gave me your
sweetness,
As much as I should wish to give to
you,
Consume me wholly with your fire
That I may come to life again.

FIORA: Yes, my belovèd!
My glowing heart! Your mouth is as
a flower
That never can die . . . Yes,
though I pluck it
Every instant, it always flowers afresh.

AVITO: (passionately — like a
sick child) Yes . . . it flowers afresh . . . and droops without
you . . .

FIORA: (in the same rapt manner) And if I kiss you, it revives . . . The soul that's bending
Over that flower, is languishing.
Avito; sweetest dream . . .

AVITO: (as above) Eternal ecstasy!

FIORA: Divine enchantment!
. . . without end!
(They embrace passionately and
are strained, lip to lip, in a long
kiss.)

AVITO: (as though awaking, frees
himself from her) Alas! See there,
the light begins to dawn,
The sky grows paler . . .

FIORA: You want to leave
me . . .

AVITO: (about to fly) It is late!
(He perceives the lantern is extin-
guished. Terrorstruck)
Fiora! look! The light has been
Extinguished . . . Someone has
been here
In the night . . .

FIORA: The wind has done
it . . .

AVITO: No:
The night has been quite calm,
have you forgotten?

FIORA: Listen! Fly!

AVITO: (escapes from the terrace
towards the right. Fiora watches
him, follows him as if to protect
him, then runs towards her
rooms. But the door on the left has
opened and Archibaldo has appeared by himself).

---

ARCHIBALDO: Fiora! Fiora! Fiora!
(Celando agli orecchi del vecchio
ogni suo movimento, Fiora cerca
sparire silenziosa)

ARCHIBALDO: (pertinace) Tue
sei costà . . . Ti sento rifiatare!
Affanni? Affanni?
O Fiora, di': con chi parlavi, tu?

FIORA: (con fermezza nuova)
Con me stessa parlavo! . . .

ARCHIBALDO: (lentamente
s'avvicina a lei) Non fuggire!
Resta! Voglio sapere!
(Ghermisce lei che s'è appoggiata
ad una colonna. L'attira a sè: con
la mano le indaga il volto, la sente
fra le sue grandi braccia di vecchio eroe. Con voce placata e con
maraviglia:)

Non può darsi!
Tu mentire così! Così tradire! . . .
(Più amoroso, con la gola quasi
stretta da una mascente bontà paterna, senile)
Tu sei come una bimba . . . Se
mentisci
È per nulla . . . Chi, adunque,
era con te?

FIORA: (con risolutezza continua; senza piegarsi; rigidamente;
ma con lieve tremito) Nessuno,
mio signore!

ARCHIBALDO: (indagando)
Perchè tremi,
se dici il vero? . . .

FIORA: (subitamente pungendo-
lo) Ed anche voi tremate
e non mentite . . .

ARCHIBALDO: (impetuoso)
Fiora!
(Lieve pausa)
E vero! Tremo . . .
Ma tremo . . . tremo per la tua
menzogna!

FIORO: (con ingenuità feroce) Io
son venuta, qua, sulla terrazza . . .
Non potevo dormire . . . col
pensiero . . .

ARCHIBALDO: (improvviso, urlando) Di chi? Di chi? . . .

FIORO: (con semplicità) Del mio
sposo Manfredo! . . .

ARCHIBALDO: Orrore! Orrore!
Oh, buio senza fine!
Tu sei di ferro; tu sei di catene
intorno alla mia testa!

FIORA: (riaccostandosi a lui con
inganno) Mio signore!

ARCHIBALDO: No! Ferma! Non avvicinarti più!
Ho per te come il terrore d'un bimbo . . .
E la persona tua, che dentro
l'ombra
sentivo sorvolare come un'ala

---

ARCHIBALDO: Fiora! Fiora! Fiora!
(concealing every movement
from the old man's ears, Fiora
tries to escape silently).

ARCHIBALDO: (persisting)
You're close at hand . . . I hear
you breathing!
You're breathless! and excited!
O Fiora say: with whom have you
been speaking?

FIORA: (with new firmness) I
have been speaking to myself!

ARCHIBALDO: (slowly ap-
proaching her)
Do not escape!
Stay! I wish to know!
(He seizes her as she leans against
a pillar. He draws her to him, he
touches her face with his hand, he
feels her within his fine old arms.
In pacified tones and with amazement:)

That you should lie so! should deceive so!
(More lovingly, almost choked
with a growing fatherly and pro-
tective kindness)
You're like a baby . . . if you
lie . . .
it is for nothing . . . Who, then
was with you?

FIORA: (with unfaltering resolu-
teness; without bending; rigidly
but with a slight tremor) No one,
my lord!

ARCHIBALDO: (feeling her) Why
do you tremble,
If what you say is true? . . .

FIORA: (suddenly touching him)
You also are atremble
And are not lying . . .

ARCHIBALDO: Fiora! (slight
pause)
It is true! I'm trembling . . .
But I am trembling . . . trembling for your lie!

FIORA: (with fierce ingenuity) I
came out here, on the terrace . . .
I could not sleep . . . for thinking . . .

ARCHIBALDO: (shouting, suddenly) Of whom? of whom?

FIORA: (simply) Of my husband,
Manfred . . .

ARCHIBALDO: O horror! horror!
Oh, unending night!
You're made of iron; You're made
of chains
Inside my head!

FIORA: (approaching him deceit-
fully) My lord!

ARCHIBALDO: No! stay where you
are! and come no nearer!
I have an almost childish terror of
you
And your person, which I heard
gliding
Through the shadows like a snowy

di candore, mi par soffio di gelo,
brivido accusatore; . . . si che ancora,
mentre sento che tu qui, qui tradivi,
io mi debbro abbracciar la tua menzogna,
e per non arrossire giudicandoti
debbo gridare: "No . . .
No . . . Non tradiva!

**FIORA:** Signore!

**ARCHIBALDO:** Va: non ti potrei toccarre
altro che per ucciderti!

**FLAMINIO:** (*di dentro*)
Signore!
(*Comparendo dalla terrazza*)
Monsignore! Un drappello se'è fermato
sul ponte e m'è sembrato che vi fosse
il barone Manfredo . . .
(*Giungono dal basso del castello squilli di trombe. La luce del giorno è molto cresciuta*) . . .
Udite! Udite! Lo salutano!

**ARCHIBALDO:** (*tremante*) È lui!
Flaminio, va! . . .
Corrigli incontro . . .
(*Col pianto nella voce*)
Io . . . sono cieco . . . Va!

**FLAMINIO:** (*esce correndo*)

**ARCHIBALDO:** (*a Fiora dopo una lunga pausa*) Tu non gli puo; correie incontro . . . No!

**FIORA:** (*tace*)

**ARCHIBALDO:** No! . . . Tu dormivi . . . Torna nel tuo letto . . .

**FIORA:** (*s'avvia lentamente verso le sue stanze. Un lieve sorriso crudele di vittoria è sul suo giovane viso bello . . . Sparisce*).

**ARCHIBALDO:** (*aspetta il figlio dolorosamente immobile . . .* )

**MANFREDO:** (*ài dentro*) Padre!
(*Apparisce dalla terrazza*)

**ARCHIBALDO:** Figliuolo mio! Giunge la luce con te!
(*Si abbaracciano*)

**MANFREDO:** Troppo era lungo e tedioso
l'assedio per la mia brama ardentissima . . .
E son fuggito: e resterò con te qualche giorno.

**ARCHIBALDO:** Potessi tu restare sempre!

**MANFREDO:** Oh, sì; presto finirà la guerra.
(*Lieve pausa*)
E Fiora; dorme? . . .

**ARCHIBALDO:** Dorme.

wing,
Seems like a frosty breath to me,
Coldly accusing . . . To that extent,
While I feel that you were here deceiving,
I must myself embrace your lie,
And, so as not to blush while judging you,
I have to cry; No, she did not deceive me!

**FIORA:** My lord! . . .

**ARCHIBALDO:** Go: for I could not touch you.
Unless it were to slay you!

**FLAMINIO:** (*from within*) My lord!
(*appearing on the terrace*)
My liege! a troop of soldiers has drawn up
Upon the bridge and I do think the Baron Manfred
is among them! (*Trumpet blasts sound from the foot of the castle. Daylight has grown much stronger*).
Listen! listen!
They are saluting!

**ARCHIBALDO:** (*trembling*) It is he! Flaminio, go!
Run forth to meet him . . .
(*with tears in his voice*)
I-am-blind-go!

**FLAMINIO:** (*runs out*).

**ARCHIBALDO:** (*to Fiora after a long pause*) You . . . can not run to meet him - No!

**FIORA:** (*is silent*).

**ARCHIBALDO:** No! You were sleeping . . . Go back to bed . . .

**FIORA:** (*goes off slowly towards her rooms. A faint cruel smile of victory is on her beautiful young face . . . She disappears.*)

**ARCHIBALDO:** (*awaits his son, sadly motionless*)

**MANFREDO:** (*from within*) Father!
(*He appears on the terrace*)

**ARCHIBALDO:** My dearest son!
You bring light
With you!
(*They embrace.*)

**MANFREDO:** Too long and wearisome
Was the siege for my impatient longing . . .
So I escaped; and shall remain with you
Some days.

**ARCHIBALDO:** If only you could stay here
Always!

**MANFREDO:** Oh yes! the war will soon be over.
(*slight pause*)
And Fiora? Is she asleep?

**ARCHIBALDO:** Asleep.

**MANFREDO:** Oh, padre mio,
questo ritorno m'e caro siccome
un premio lungamente atteso
Nelle guerre
combattute, nel sangue, nella strage,
nell'orgia di vittoria, io sono stato
ferma colonna di virtù, si come
tu m'hai insegnato, padre! . . . E Fiora, Fiora
amare mi sprà; chè tu educata
l'avrai come un'agnella di candore..

**ARCHIBALDO:** Godi la giogia tua! . . . Fiora ti aspetta . . .
Anzi, ella giunge; . . . sento i passi suoi . . .

**MANFREDO:** Io non sento: ella vola . . .
(*Si rivolge alla porta di destra. Apparisce Fiora*)
Fiora! Fiora!

**FIORA:** (*con freddezza crudele, ma simile a bontà*) Siete tornato, signor mio?! Stamani,
prima dell'alba mi sono destata
e son venuta qui sulla terrazza;
ed ho guardato tanto nella valle . . .
Ero certa che voi sareste giunto . . .
(*Ad Archibaldo*)
E vero, padre mio?

**ARCHIBALDO:** (*tace*)

**MANFREDO:** E vero, padre moi?

**ARCHIBALDO:** Si, si; l'ho . . . colta . . .
(*Riprendendosi*)
mentr'ella ti aspettava . . .

**MANFREDO:** Oh; Fiora! Fiora!
Piccolo fiore, vieni sul mio petto;
qui, qui tra le mie braccia, ch'io ti rechi,
come agnella sperduta e manuseta,
all'ovile dal mio cuore intessuto.
Oh; come tremi! . . .
(*Avviandosi*)
Cosi ti porterò nel tuo bel letto d'avorio . . .
(*Al padre*)
Padre mio, certo tu vedi,
ora, che il figlio ha trovato il suo bene!
Certo tu vedi, perchè troppa luce
esce dal cuore mio che si confonde
e si mischia e moltiplica con questa
luce odorosa che dal mio tesoro
si libera, dal mio tesoro aulente.
(*Entra nelle stanze di destra con Fiora abbracciata*)

**MANFREDO:** O dearest father,
This return is dear to me as a reward
That's long expected
Throughout the war,
The fights, the bloodshed and the slaughter,
The revelries of victory, untarnished
Have I kept my virtue, as you
Have taught me, father! And Fiora, Fiora,
Will learn to love me: since you have
Brought her up as spotless as a lamb..

**ARCHIBALDO:** Enjoy your happiness! Fiora awaits you
Hark, she is coming . . . I hear her footsteps . . .

**MANFREDO:** I do not hear: she flies . . .
(*He turns toward the door on the R. Fiora appears*)
Fiora! Fiora!

**FIORA:** (*with cruel coldness, but with a semblance of kindness*)
Have you returned, my lord? This morning
I awoke before the dawn
And came onto this terrace . . .
And looked so long for you down in the valley . . .
I was so certain you would come . . .
(*to Archibaldo*)
It is true–father . . . you . . . heard me.

**ARCHIBALDO:** (*remains silent*).

**MANFREDO:** Is it true, my father?

**ARCHIBALDO:** Yes, yes–I caught her..
(*correcting himself*)
While she was waiting for you.

**MANFREDO:** Oh, Fiora, Fiora!
Come to my breast, my little flower;
Here, here, within my arms, that I may bear you
Like to a lost and gentle lamb,
Unto the fold and shelter of my heart.
Oh, how you tremble! . . .
(*approaching her*)
Thus let me bear you to your soft White bed . . .
(*to his father*)
Now, Father mine, you needs must see
Your son has found his happiness!..
You needs must see, because too strong a light
Streams from my heart and flashes
And multiplies and mingles with this perfumed light,
Which flows forth from my treasure,
From this my fragrant treasure.
(*With his arm around her he goes into the room on the right.*)

## Act I

**ARCHIBALDO:** (*solo, Pausa*)
Signore mio, se tu m'hai tolto gli occhi,
fa ch'io non veda . . . che sia cieco . . . cieco!
(*Cala la tela.*)

**ARCHIBALDO:** (*Alone. Pause*) O Lord my God, since you have taken my eyes,
Let me not see . . . let me be blind . . . be blind!

## ■ ATTO SECONDO

*Terrazza sulle alte mura del castello; una terrazza tondeggiante. In cima al muro che la cinge, smerlato, più alto d'un uomo, si giunge con una scaletta a metà del fondo. Una panchina di pietra larga un metro, altra fino al ginocchio, gira torno torno, accosto al muro. Si giunge per due porte laterali. Pomeriggio: il cielo scoperto è corso da nubi cangianti, estive. Squilli di tromba chiamano a raccolta.*

*(Etrano da sinistra Manfredo e Fiora abbracciati. — Fiora è adorna semplicemente e mirabilmente.)*

**MANFREDO:** (*a Fiora*) Dimmi, Fiora, perchè ti veggo ancora così chiusa dinanzi al mio dolore? . . .
Io parto, Fiora, io parto ancora, . . . ancora, . . . e sono così scosso che mi pare per un viaggio eterno, di partire . . .

**FIORA:** Mio signore, v'ho detto che la vostra
partenza così prossima turbò la gioia ch'ebbi dal vostro ritorno . . .
E perciò son così, senza parole . . .
Io poco vi conosco, chè voi siete sempre lontano; e quando ritornate pur mi dite: fra poco partirò . . .

**MANFREDO:** No; Fiora, Fiora: tu mi parli come
ad un nemico che ti chiede pace. Intendi, Fiora? Intendi il mio dolore?
O dimmi tu: che cosa t'addolora?

**FIORA:** Nulla, signore, m'addolora; solo
che voi partiate; . . .

**MANFREDO:** Tornerò per te, per te, per te, per la tua cara vita che voglio tutta cingere d'amore . . .
(*Con altro modo*)
Oh, Fiora: dammi alcuna cosa tua che mi possa tenere presso al cuore, mentre sarò lontano.

**FIORA:** Che volete?

**MANFREDO:** Che scegli tu?

## ■ ACT II

*A circular terrace on the high castle-walls. On the top of the wall which surrounds it, battlemented higher than a man's stature, is a single staircase halfway from the back. A little stone bench, about a yard wide and knee-high, winds around the wall. Two side-doors give access to the terrace. It is afternoon: the sky is covered with changing fleeting clouds. Trumpet blasts sound a retreat.*

*(Enter from the left Manfredo, his arms around Fiora. Fiora is beautifully and simply attired.)*

**MANFREDO:** (*to Fioro*) Tell me, Fiora, why do I see you
Still so reserved before my sorrow?
I leave you, Fiora, once more — once more . . .
And I am moved like this because it seems to me
As if I left you for an eternal journey . . .

**FIORA:** My lord, have I not told you how your
Speedy parting has cast a gloom Upon the joy your coming brought me . . .
And therefore I am thus, bereft of words . . .
I do not know you well, since you are
Always distant; and yet when you return
You always say: soon I must leave you . . .

**MANFREDO:** No; Fiora, Fiora: You speak to me
As to an enemy that sues for peace. Do you hear me, Fiora? Do you grasp my grief?
O tell me: what is it that grieves you?

**FIORA:** Nothing, my lord, is grieving me; only
That you are going . . .

**MANfREDO:** For you, for you, for that dear life of yours
That I am longing to surround with love . . .
(*In different tones*)
Oh, Fiora mine, give me some little token
That I can keep close to my heart While I am far away.

**FIORA:** What do you want?

**MANFREDO:** What will you choose?

**FIORA:** (*con arcado dolore traboccetto*) Volete la mia vita! . . .

**MANFREDO:** (*con pietosa mansuetodise*) Fanciulla, tu non puoi mulla donarmi,
per placare il mio cuore che per ora.
t'è ignoto! Solamente lo posso chiederti
un dono che mi dia per poco pace; e te lo chieggo.

**FIORA:** Che?

**MANFREDO:** (*dopo una pausa dolorosamente*) Suonata è l'ora della partenza. I miei prodi compagni
m'aspettano sul ponte: impazienti sono i cavalli; un fremito di vita e di conquista tremola nell'aria rossa. Si parte. I miei compagni fidi sono lieti. Si Giù giù per l'ampia valle
si scende. Si divincolano i sogni d'ebbrezza dalle loro menti giovani.
In mezzo a loro io sono cupo e solo . . .
Dentro mi piange lacrime dogliose tutta l'umanità, perch'io mi dolgo dell'amor mio lasciato e vado solo, senza conforto . . . Ho perso ogni mio bene,
sono forse cacciato dalla gioia Perchè, se tanto amore è dentro me? . . .
E mi volto e riguardo sopra il colle questo castello che rosseggia al sole . . .
Giù si scende disperatamente . . .
E la valle si snoda e incontra il fiume
che piange e piange e mormora e rimproverta;
e il castello si perde, . . . trascolora
fra gli alberi . . . Soltanto questa torre
si vede, questa dove siamo . . .
Ora, ti prego,
anima mia, mia consolazione, resta qui un poco, monta qui sul muro,
e col tuo velo manda il tuo saluto allo sposo che parte e mi parra, ti giuro, anima mia, che tu m'asciughi
le lacrime sul mio cuore scoperto Questo ti chiedo, anima mia non più! (*pause*)

**FIORA:** (*finalmente commossa, con sincere pietá.*) E questo sarà fatto . . .

**MANFREDO:** Ora ti lascio . . . E volerò, perche qua si m'è caro partire, per vederti salutarmi . . .
Addio, Fiora . . .

**FIORA:** (*overflowing with secret grief*) You want my life?

**MANFREDO:** (*with compassionate gentleness*) My child, there's nothing you can give me,
That will appease my heart which is as yet
Unknown to you! There's only one gift I can ask
Of you, to give me peace awhile; And I do ask it.

**FIORA:** What?

**MANFREDO:** (*after a pause, sorrowfully*) The hour has struck Of my departure. My brave companions
Await me on the bridge: the horses Champ their bits; a thrill of life And conquest pulses through the air.
We're going. My trusty companions Are joyful.
Down through the open valley We descend. Their youthful minds Are drunk with dreams of prowess. I only in their midst am sad and alone . . .
Within me all humanity weeps tears
Of grief, because I'm racked with bitter grief
At my abandoned love, and go alone . . .
Uncomforted . . . For I have lost my joy,
And am bereft of all my happiness . . .
But why, if so much love is in me? And then I turn and look where on the hill
This castle crimsons in the evening sun . . .
Down, down we travel, swift and strenuous . . .
The valley twists and meets the river
Which weeps and weeps and murmures and reproves;
The castle's lost to sight . . . fading
Among the trees. Only this tower Where now we stand, can still be seen
Now, I entreat you,
My dearest love, my consolation, Stay here a little longer, climb on the wall
And wave a greeting with your scarf To your departing husband; and I swear
It will seem to me, that you are drying
The tears upon my heart . . .
I ask you this, my love, no more! (*Pause.*)

**FIORA:** (*moved at last with sincere pity*) And this shall be done . . .

**MANFREDO:** Now I must leave you
And I shall fly, for almost do I love our
Parting, to see you wave your greet-

(La bacia; si stacca subito dal bacio; fugge quasi voli, perchì lo punge.)

FIORA: (pur liberata da lui cerca come sciogliersi da quell'abbraccio che le da rimasto alla persona . . . Si avvicina poi al muro smerlato; monte i gradini della scaletta; si aporge . . . Ma ecco cautamente e como un sogno Avito, da destra. E vestito come Flaminio, come la guardia del castello).

AVITO: (si guarda attorno, scorge Fiora lassù . . . ) Oh! . . . Fiora! Fiora! (Ella si volta; prima non lo riconosce con quelle sue vesti.) Sono Avito! Avito!

FIORA: Ma che?! che?! Forse da quella notte . . .

AVITO: Fui qui, fui qui, sempre vicino a te con l'anima e la mente mia che perdesi Flaminio m'ha vestito ora cosi per potermi nascondere . . . e vederti . . .

FIORA: (con improvvisa disperazione). Non posso più vederti . . . Non ti debbo amar più . . . La tua voce, oh, non risuoni più nell'orecchie mie . . . Ti prego; va . . .

AVITO: Io non intendo, Fiora! Sei tu, Fiora, Fiora, che parli a me?

FIORA: Si; mille volte; sì, mille, mille: disperatamente.

AVITO: Sei mille volte mia? Che dici?

FIORA: No! Silenzio fosco è dentro la mia vita e terrore d'intorno . . . Vinta, vinta sono dalla pietà . . . dalla bontà . . . Ohimè: non senti il mio sposo che parte? . . .

AVITO: Perchè non dici, il mio sposo che giunge?

FIORA: Lasciami in pace. Lasciami al mio pianto.

AVITO: Lasciarti, Fiora! E dove andare, Fiora? Dove vo? Dove cerco la mia vita? . . .

FIORA: Nasconditi. Qualcuno deve giungere.

AVITO: (sempre come trasognato) Andrò; si: fuggirò . . . (S'avvia)

FIORA: Fuggi: ti prego!

ing . . . Farewell, my Fiora . . . (He kisses her; then wrenches himself from her, and rushes off, shaken by sobs.)

FIORA: (Freed from him, she tries to shake off the sensation of his embrace . . . Then she approaches the battlemented wall, ascends the steps of the staircase; stands forth there . . . But suddenly Avito appears on the R, cautiously and as in a dream. He is dressed like Flaminio, as a castle-guard).

AVITO: (looks about him and sees Fiora up there) Oh! Fiora! Fiora! (She turns; at first she does not recognize him in that garb) I am Avito! Avito!

FIORA: Why, how is this? Can it be, since that night . . .

AVITO: I have been here, here, close to you, Close with my soul and my tormented mind Flaminio dressed me thus that I might Hide . . . and watch you . . .

FIORA: (in sudden desperation) I cannot see you any more . . . I must not Love you . . . Your voice must never Sound on my ears again . . . I beseech you . . . go . . .

AVITO: I am bewildered, Fiora! Can it be you, You, Fiora, who are speaking to me?

FIORA: Yes—a thousand times: Yes, a thousand, thousand, desparately.

AVITO: Your're mine a thousand times? Is that it?

FIORA: No! A gloomy silence is within my life And terror all around me . . . I'm conquered, Conquered by kindness . . . by compassion . . . Alas: do you not hear my husband going?

AVITO: Wherefore not say: my husband coming?

FIORA: Leave me in peace. Leave me to my sorrow . . .

AVITO: Leave you, Fiora! and where should I go? Where can I go? Where seek my life?

FIORA: Conceal yourself. Someone is coming.

AVITO: (as if in a dream) Yes, I will go . . . I will escape . . . (He goes.)

FIORA: Escape! I beg you!

AVITO: (fugge da destra) (Fiora scende la scaletta. Entra dopo un istante l'Ancella da sinistra).

ANCELLA: (recando un cofanetto intarsiato) Il barone Manfredo questo dono vi manda, baronessa . . .

FIORA: (con infinita malinconia) Metti là! (Addita la panchina di pietra)

ANCELLA: (posa il cofanetto sulla panchina. Esce)

FIORA: (si approssima al cofano; lo apre lentamente; trae fuori lentissimamente un velo bianco lungo . . . Le braccia le cadono giù come morte; e con esse il velo . . . Resta un poco immobile, muta, senza pianto e senza vita. Poi si ricorda della promessa e s'accosta, recando il velo, al muro. Monta sulla scaletta; guarda giù; vede nella valle i cavalieri che si allontanano ed agita per la prima volta il velo . . . per la seconda ancora; e per la terza; e sempre il braccio le cade giù stanco . . . . Ma ritorna Avito).

AVITO: Addio, Fiora; ho voluto rividerti . . . Debbo partire; ma senza ritorno . . . Addio, Fiora; se non vuoi dareme un bacio che sarebbe principio della vita. fammi toccare quel tuo velo bianco che certo sa la tua molle fragranza . . . (Cerca prendere il velo di Fiore)

FIORA: (che ha ascoltate le sua parole) . . . Non toccarlo!

AVITO: Nulla di te più, dunque m'appartiene? . . .

FIORA: (guardandolo compassione volmente e e tutte dimentirando all'improvvisa . . . con altra voce!) Come sei bianco . . . Come sei disfatto . . . Sembri un giglio, amorosa creatura . . .

AVITO: Il veleno d'amore è assai più forte del sonno e della fame; ed ormai più forte della vita . . .

FIORA: Vita tua. è vita mia! Ma che pietà, che arcano gorgo di bene ora m'invade! . . . Avito, ahimè . . . Tu sei come una frasca troppo esposta ai venti; il male t'ha stremato. il male ch'io t'ho dato.

AVITO: (escapes on the R.) (Fiora comes down the staircase. A moment after the handmaid comes in from the L.)

HANDMAID: (handing her an inlaid casket) Baron Manfredo sends you this offering Madam . . .

FIORA: (with intense melancholy) Place it there! (The maid places the casket on the bench and goes off.)

FIORA: (approaches the casket; opens it slowly, and very slowly draws forth a long white scarf. Her arms hang down like dead; and the scarf with them . . . She remains motionless, without tears and life, for awhile. Then she remembers her promise and approaches the wall, with the veil. She ascends the staircase; looks down, sees the horsemen disappearing in the valley and waves the veil for the first time; then the second; then the third; and each time her hand drops wearily; . . . But Avito returns).

AVITO: Farewell, Fiora . . . I wished to see you once again . . . For I must go, but I shall not return . . . Farewell, Fiora . . . if you refuse me The kiss which is the source of life, Let me at least caress your snowy scarf Which has been nestling in your fragrance . . . (Tries to take her scarf.)

FIORA: (who has been listening to his words wearily, drawing back) No, do not touch it!

AVITO: Is nothing of you then, belonging to me still?

FIORA: (looking at him compassionately and forgetting all, suddenly, in different tones:) How white you are . . . and how distraught . . . Your're like a lily, amorous creature.

AVITO: Love's poison is by far more strong Than sleep and hunger, and now indeed More strong than life . . .

FIORA: Your life Is my life! But what compassion, what mysterious Wave of kindness has engulfed me! . . . Avito, Woe is me! . . . Your're like a branch that's too Exposed unto the winds; the evil has destroyed you, The evil I have done you.

# Act II

**AVITO:** (*avidamente*) E tutto il bene rendimi senza indugio con un bacio! Oh, Fiora, scendi, scendi . . .

**FIORA:** No: non debbo! (*Si ricorda dolorosamente del voto e agita il velo.*)

**AVITO:** (*si avvicina a lei*)

**FIORA:** Non salire quassù!

**AVITO:** Fiora; perchè?

**FIORA:** Non domandarmi . . . (Agita Il vela.)

**AVITO:** Allora fuggirò . . . Io sono cosi stanco che non posso quasi più transcinarmi . . .

**FIORA:** Avito! Resta . . . Non domandare . . . Avvicinati . . . Bacia la mia veste giù sulla balza d'oro . . . Io l'ho trapunta!

**AVITO:** (*corre subito. Stringe la sua veste: la bacia*). Ah! Sento le tue dita ancora sopra,- accarezzanti il bel ricamo! Io bacio le tue mani, cosi . . . Ma stranamente: aspri sono i miei baci, quasi che l'ago tu avessi qui lasciato infisso . . . (*Le sue labbra avidamente si dissetano.*)

**FIORA:** (*vuole ancora agitare il velo; ma non può: le braccia cadono: Il capo si piega*). Ah; tortura! indicibile contrasto!

**AVITO:** (*come un fanciullo*) Io non ascolto più! Dentro il rosaio ho immerso la mia testa . . . Nelle orecchie sento i fuchi ronzarmi i loro incanti di vecchi maghi, e il petto mi si piena di liquori olezzanti (*La stringe a' ginocchi.*) I tuoi ginocchi! A quale scoglio morbido di musco m'aggrappo, dopo tanto navigare, dopo tanto morire! . . .

**FIORA:** (*accasciata, attratta*) Avito, ahimè; tu pesi come piombo! . . . Tu mi trascini!

**AVITO:** Ah! La tua fresca voce ch'io sento costassu, come m'incanta! . . .

**FIORA:** Avito! Avito!

**AVITO:** Io stringo al petto mio un gran fascio di fiori soavissimi! Ma i lunghi steli solamente stringo! Non vorrò, dunque, immergere la testa nelle corolle?!

**FIORA:** Avito! ahimè, non sai!

---

**AVITO:** (*eagerly*) Then give me back The good without delaying, in a kiss! Come down, O Fiora, come . . .

**FIORA:** No I must not! (*She sadly remembers her vow, and waves the scarf.*)

**AVITO:** (*approaches her*).

**FIORA:** You must not come up here!

**AVITO:** Fiora, why not?

**FIORA:** No, do not ask me . . . (*waves the scarf*)

**AVITO:** Then I will fly from here . . . I am so weary that I can hardly Drag myself away . . .

**FIORA:** Avito! stay.. No — do not ask . . . Come closer . . . Kiss my garment . . . Down on the golden fringe . . . I embroidered it!

**AVITO:** (*runs hastily to her. Seizes her dress and kisses it*) Ah! still I feel your fingers on it, Lingering on the broidery. I kiss Your hands, like this . . . But strangely stinging Are my kisses, almost as though Your needle you has left inserted. (*His lips drink kisses greedily*)

**FIORA:** (*wants to wave her scarf again, but cannot; her arms drop; her head droops*) Oh agony! the dreadful contrast!

**AVITO:** (*like a child*) I will no longer listen! I've thrust My head into the rosebush . . . And in my ears The drones are humming their spells Of ancient magic, my breast is full Of fragrant balm (*Seizes her knees*) Your knees! I cling to them, as to a kindly Mossgrown reef, after so much journeying, So much dying!

**FIORA:** (*weakening, fascinated*) Avito, woe is me, you are like lead! You drag me down!

**AVITO:** Ah! Your fresh voice That's souding there above, how it enthralls me!

**FIORA:** Avito! Avito!

**AVITO:** Unto my breast I strain A bunch of sweetest flowers! But it is the long stems only that I grasp! May I not, dearest, plunge my head Into the petals?

**FIORA:** Avito! woe is me, you know not!

---

**AVITO:** Fossi tu pure, non un fascio bello di fiori; ma una ruvida forcata di spini, che bruciassero lassù, vorrei tuffar nel fuoco la mia vita per trovarvi la morte e la tua bocca!

**FIORA:** Avito, no!

**AVITO:** La bocca tua! La bocca tua, Fiora! Fiora! Disperatamente io chieggo la tua bocca!

**FIORA:** (*abbandonandosi, vinta*) Ahimè! Si peiga il voto mio, com'albero pietoso a chi muroe di sete . . .

**AVITO:** Ho sete! Ho sete! (*Accoglie lei che, scendendo i gradini, cade nelle sue braccia. Si baciane come fossero moribondi d'amore. Muovono quindi la panchina. Fiora si abbandona appoggiando la testa sul petto di Avito.*)

**FIORA:** (*dopo una pausa*) Come tremi, diletto! . . .

**AVITO:** L'amor tuo, che mi ricopre tutto, ora mi fa sentire il gelo della solitudine . . .

**FIORA:** (*carezzosa: tutto dimenticando*) Pensando a Fiora, non dormivi più . . .

**AVITO:** (*quasi imitanda la sus voce*) Pensando a Fiora, non vivevo più . . .

**FIORA:** Mio diletto! . . .

**AVITO:** . . . Guarda in sù . . . siamo in cielo . . . Si naviga nel cielo; si molleggia sull'etere . . .

**FIORA:** (*come in sogno*) Nel cielo . . .

**AVITO:** Oh, Fiora, dove siamo? Io mi smarrisco . . . Il viso tuo; che piu non lo rammento! . . . (*Le prende il volto con dolce furore e lo contempla follemente*) Oh; bello; oh, bello! Oh; piccola stelluccia! O firmamento, tu che me l'hai data, grazie! . . .

**FIORA:** (*con estasi*) . . . Incatenami, dunque In un occhio si può chiudere il cielo . . . Tu potrai con la tua bocca chiudere la mia vita . . . Prendi . . . Prendila . . .

**AVITO:** Eccoti, Fiora, un bacio bello, . . . l'ultimo, l'ultimo d'un'infinità di baci, liprimo, il primo d'un'eternità . . .

---

**AVITO:** Oh would to heaven you were, not a fair bunch Of flowers; but a rough clump of thorns, That I might burn upon it, And plunge my life into the fire To find death and your lips there! . . .

**FIORA:** Avito! No!

**AVITO:** Your lips! Your lips, my Fiora! Fiora! Fiora! Desparately I crave your lips!

**FIORA:** (*yielding to him, conquered*) Alas! my will Bows down to yours as does a kindly tree To one who dies of thirst . . .

**AVITO:** I'm thirsting — thirsting — (*He receives her, as she, coming down the steps, falls into his arms. They kiss each other as if dying of love. Then they move to the bench. Fiora drops onto it, leaning her head on Avito's breast*).

**FIORA:** (*after a pause*) How you are trembling, dearest!

**AVITO:** Your love Which wraps me round completely, now lets me Feel the cold of solitude . . .

**FIORA:** (*caressingly — oblivious of all*) Thinking of Fiora, he no longer slept . . .

**AVITO:** (*almost imitating her voice*) Thinking of Fiora, I no longer lived . . .

**FIORA:** My dearest . . .

**AVITO:** We are in heaven . . . We float in heaven . . . We drift upon the ether . . .

**FIORA:** (*as in a dream*) In heaven

**AVITO:** Fiora, where are we? I have lost my way . . . Show me your face; for I cannot recall it! . . . (*Takes her face in a gentle ecstasy and gazes at it madly*) Oh, fair, most fair! Oh, little star of mine! I thank you firmament, for this your gift To me!

**FIORA:** (*ecstatically*) Enchain me, then The whole of heaven Can be held within an eye . . . And you can hold my life With your dear lips . . . Take . . . take it . . .

**AVITO:** Here, Fiora, is a glorious kiss . . . the last, The last of an infinity of kisses, The first, the first of an eternity . . .

---

*(baciano e restano avvinti perdutamente aboliti nella loro nube amorosa . . . )*

ARCHIBALDO: *(di dentro)* Fiora! *(Subito fuori seguito da Flaminio).* Fiora!

*(Gli due amanti che non hanno sentito il primo grido del vecchio, si svegliono ora come da un sogno)*

AVITO: *(riacquistata la pienezza delle sue forze, si slancia contro il vecchio, avendo levato il pugnale).*

FLAMINIO: *(che segue Archibaldo lo fermo col gesto).*

FIORA: *(rispondendo al vecchio col gesto scongiuza Avito di faggire).* Son qua!

ARCHIBALDO: *(con anala e sospetta à Flamino)* Guarda, Flaminio, chi c'è? . . .

FLAMINO: . . . Non c'è nessuno! . . .

AVITO: *(esce).*

ARCHIBALDO: *(che ha sentito il suo passo, amaramente dice:)* Sta bene! . . . Fiora, dove sei?

FIORA: Son qua! . . . *(Ella resta più indietro a destra. Archibaldo ha la prova del vero: ha udito: ha visto.)*

ARCHIBALDO: *(violento).* Va via, Flaminio!

FLAMINIO: *(quasi balbettando).* Udite, Monsignore . . . Il Barone ritorna: ha rivoltato il cavallo *(Salta sulla panchina e guarda nella valle).*

ARCHIBALDO: *(fremente).* Ritorna certamente!

FIORA: *(ricordando il suo voto).* Ritorna?!

ARCHIBALDO: Su: Flaminio; vagli incontro

FLAMINIO: *(insistendo)* Signore! . . .

ARCHIBALDO: Va!

FLAMINIO: *(esce correndo).*

ARCHIBALDO: Fiora, dove sei tu?

FIORA: Signore! . . .

ARCHIBALDO: *(tremante d'ira e di giustizia).* La tua voce menzognera ancora mi ferisce?!

FIORA: Monsignore! . . .

ARCHIBALDO: Chi era qui con te? chi ci tradiva? . . .

FIORA: Nessuno!

ARCHIBALDO: Fiora!

*(They kiss, and remain locked in each other's arms, and lost to everything, in their love-trance.)*

ARCHIBALDO: *(from within)* Fiora! *(He comes out quickly, followed by Flaminio.)* Fiora! *(The two lovers, who did not hear the old man's first call, now start asunder, as if roused from a dream.)*

AVITO: *(who has hardly recovered his full consciousness, hurls himself on to the old man, with his drawn dagger.)*

FLAMINIO: *(who is following Archibaldo, stops him with a gesture)*

FIORA: *(replying to the old man, entreats Avito by a gesture to escape)* I am here!

ARCHIBALDO: *(anxiously and suspiciously, to Flaminio)* Look, Flaminio, Who is there?

FLAMINIO: No one is there! *(Avito goes out.)*

ARCHIBALDO: *(who has heard his footsteps, says bitterly)* It is well! . . . Fiora, where are you?

FIORA: I am here! . . . *(She remains a little behind on the right. Archibaldo has proof of the truth; he has heard; he has seen.)*

ARCHIBALDO: *(with violence)* Be gone, Flaminio!

FLAMINIO: *(almost stammering)* Listen, my Lord . . . The Baron is returning: he has turned back His horse . . . *(He jumps onto the bench and looks into the valley.)*

ARCHIBALDO: *(trembling)* In truth, he is returning! . . .

FIORA: *(remembering her vow)* Returning? . . . .

ARCHIBALDO: Quick! Flaminio, go to meet him

FLAMINIO: *(urgently)* My lord!

ARCHIBALDO: Go!

FLAMINIO: *(runs off).*

ARCHIBALDO: Fiora, where are you?

FIORA: Sire!

ARCHIBALDO: *(trembling with anger and loyalty)* Your lying voice Once more offends me?!

FIORA: My lord! . . .

ARCHIBALDO: Who has been here with you? Who Betrayed us?

FIORA: No one!

ARCHIBALDO: Fiora!

FIORA: *(accovacciandosi, come per isparire, sulla panchina, accosta al muro).* Nessuno! Nessuno!

ARCHIBALDO: . . . Ho udito il passo suo . . . *(La ghermisce).*

FIORA: *(improvvisamente ergendosi come la serpe).* Allora . . . Allora . . . Quello ch'è fuggito era l'amore mio; era il mio bene E voi, tremendo vecchio, che mi siete adosso come la vendetta, come la morte, . . . non mi fate più terrore, ora che penso a lui!

ARCHIBALDO: Dimmi il suo nome! Fa ch'io lo conosca . . .

FIORA: Ch'io parli con Manfredo, che ritorna . . . La sua bontà!

ARCHIBALDO: *(buttandola, con violenza, distesa sulla panchina)* No! No! Perdonerebbe, e gli ho insegnato io questa virtù senza gioia! *(Ha preso la sua gola)* Il suo nome! Il nome suo!

FIORA: *(è distesa sulla panca; il vecchio la ricopre con la sua vasta persona. Si sente la sua voce ferma).* Ei non ha nome, poi ch'è più di tutto . . .

ARCHIBALDO: Traditrice . . . La tua gola i oserra questo nome . . . La mano mia lo stringe . . . Dillo! . . . Bada: Manfredo s'avvicina e perdona . . . Non io, se tu non parli . . . Dillo; dillo!

FIORA: *(chiaramente)* Si chiama: dolce morte!

ARCHIBALDO: Ma se tu muori, io lo saprò ghermire l'amor tuo . . .

FIORA: *(ergendosi improvvisamente).* No! No! Allora, fammi vivere per difenderlo: non per accusarlo . . .

ARCHIBALDO: *(stringendo la sua gola).* Ah! gola audace! Gola menzognera! *(Il vecchio si stacca dal corpo di lei atterrito.)* *(Pausa orrenda)* Silenzio! Notte fonda! La ferocia del sangue mio soltanto alita intorno *(Con terrore e disperazione.)* Ecco! . . . Giunge Manfredo! . . . S'avvicina Enon sa . . . Teme, il figlio mio perduto Lo sento . . . giunge . . .

FIORA: *(cowering down on the seat close to the wall, and if to disappear)* No one! No one!

ARCHIBALDO: I heard his footsteps. *(He seizes hold of her.)*

FIORA: *(suddenly rearing like a serpent)* Well then . . . well then . . . He who has fled Was my true lover — my beloved . . . And you, you dread old man, who dog my Steps like vengeance, or like death, You can no longer fright me, Now that I think of him!

ARCHIBALDO: Tell me his name! Tell me, that I may know him . . .

FIORA: Nay, let me speak to Manfred, who's returning . . . He is so kind!

ARCHIBALDO: *(striking her violently, as she lies on the beach)* No! no! He would forgive you; And I myself have trained him to this joyless Virtue! *(He seizes her by the throat.)* His name! his name!

FIORA: *(lying full length on the seat; the old man covers her with his huge person. Her voice is heard, firm and steady)* He has no name, since he is more than all . . .

ARCHIBALDO: Traitress . . . Tis lurking in your throat This name . . . My hand is clutching it . . . Say it! . . . Listen: Manfred is nearing And will pardon . . . Not so I, if you don't speak Say it; say it!

FIORA: *(clearly)* His name is: welcome death!

ARCHIBALDO: But if you die, I shall know how to track him . . . Your love . . .

FIORA: *(suddenly raising herself)* No! No! Then let me live To defend him—not to accuse him.

ARCHIBALDO: *(throttling her)* Ah! wicked throat! ah lying throat! *(The old man recoils from her body in horror.)* *(A gruesome pause.)* Silence around me! Night is falling! The fury Of my blood alone is breathing . . . *(In terror and despair)* And here . . . Manfred is coming He nears . . . And does not know . . . He fears, my poor unhappy son, I feel it . . . he draws near . . . he runs to his de-

Corre alla sua gioia . . .
*(Ritorna presso il corpo di Fiora come a nasconderlo dietro la sua persona: così attende il figlio).*
*(S'avvicina il tramonto. Nel cielo nubi rossastre.)*

*(He goes back near to Fiora's body as if to hide it behind his person—thus he awaits his son.)*
*(The dawn approaches. Pale pink clouds in the sky.)*

**MANFREDO:** *(di dentro, a pena, con voce anelante).* Fiora! Mia Fiora! Sei caduta, sei? . . .
*(Eccolo.)*
Padre! È caduta forse giù dal muro. mentre col velo suo m'accarezzava da lontano? Chè più non l'ho veduta . . .

**MANFREDO:** *(from within, panting and calling with difficulty)* Fiora! my Fiora! Have you fallen?
*(He appears.)*
Father! Has she perchance fallen from the wall. While she was waving her long veil to me From far? when I no longer saw her . . .

**ARCHIBALDO:** *(disperatamente)* La tua spada, perch'io me la conficchi nel peto e cada sopra lei ch'è morta! . . .

**ARCHIBALDO:** *(desperately)* Your sword, that I may plunge it In my breast and fall on her that's died!

**MANFREDO:** Morta! Morta!

**MANFREDO:** Dead! Dead!

**ARCHIBALDO:** Deh! Non avvicinarti! Io l'ho uccisa!

**ARCHIBALDO:** Alas! Do not come nearer! I have slain her!

**MANFREDO:** Che dici tu? Che dici? Morta ella?! Non più esistere?! Non più?! C'è così grande orrore che pareggi quest'orrore della mancanza di lei per il mondo? . . .

**MANFREDO:** What are you saying? What?
. . . That she is dead? Exists No longer?! No longer?! Is there another horror In the world so great as this one, that she is gone?

**ARCHIBALDO:** Impura ell'era sì come la notte!

**ARCHIBALDO:** She was impure as she was fair!

**MANFREDO:** Impura?! Che di' tu? Come ragioni?

**MANFREDO:** Impure?! What are you saying? Are you raving?

**ARCHIBALDO:** Impura! Ti tradiva in casa tua, qui, qui, mentre la mano sua mendace agitava quel velo che le desti, la vampata d'amore le lambiva la veste e nella colpa più crudele la trancinava ancora: io l'ho sorpresa! . . .

**ARCHIBALDO:** Impure! Betraying you in your own house, Here, here, the while her treachirous hand Waved the long veil you gave her; The blaze of love enveloped her, And dragged her down into the cruellest guilt, I caught her in the act!

**MANFREDO:** *(a sè stesso, profondamente)* Di tanto amore era dunque capace quel suo cuore fanciullo: e non per me?

**MANFREDO:** *(to himself, in profound thought.)* Of such great love that child-heart Then was capable, and not for me?

**ARCHIBALDO:** Figlio, il tuo cuore è più freddo di lei! . . .

**ARCHIBALDO:** My son, the heart is colder still than she!

**MANFREDO:** *(con disperazione)* Ed ama tanto! Ed ama oltre la vita! Lascia ch'io pianga sopra il petto suo!

**MANFREDO:** *(brokenly)* And she could love so much!.. Even beyond her life!.. Then let me weep upon her breast! . . .

**ARCHIBALDO:** Tu puoi; tu puoi sposare la tua bocca a quella dell'ignoto predatore? . . .

**ARCHIBALDO:** You can't: you can't unite your lips To those of the unknown betrayer!

**MANFREDO:** *(disperatamente)* Ma dimmi, dunque! Dimmi tu: chi era?

**MANFREDO:** *(brokenhearted)* But tell me then! tell me, who was he?

**ARCHIBALDO:** *(dolorosamente)* Ahime ch'io sono cieco, e non l'ho scorio! Ma, illuminato dalla mia vendetta. io frugherò nell'ombra dove il male

**ARCHIBALDO:** *(dolorously)* Alack that I am blind and could not see him! But, lighted by my vengeance, Amoung the shadows will I grope;

s'annida e lo vedrò e ferocemente. lo ghermirò per la tua gioia! . . .

and where the traitor's Hiding will I see him, and fiercely will I seize him For your pleasure!

**MANFREDO:** *(ripreso dal pensiero di Fiora, implorando)* . . . Padre mio!

**MANFREDO:** *(thinking of Fiora again, entreatingly)* . . . My father!

**ARCHIBALDO:** No! Fermati. Vedresti alla sua gola la collana di morte delle mie dita paterne . . .

**ARCHIBALDO:** No! stay where you are! For you would see the collar of death, Around her neck, wrought by your father's fingers.

**MANFREDO:** *(indietreggia).*

**MANFREDO:** *(draws back)*

**ARCHIBALDO:** Additami la strada con il suono dei tuoi passi, che poi ti seguirò

**ARCHIBALDO:** Show me the way by the sound Of your footsteps and I will follow you

**MANFREDO:** *(esce lentamente da sinistra, muto nell'immenso dolore).*

**MANFREDO:** *(goes out slowly on the left, mute in his intense grief)*

**ARCHIBALDO:** *(si carica sul petto la morta e s'avvia seguendo il figlio).*
*(Cala la tela.)*

**ARCHIBALDO:** *(hoists the dead body across his chest and follows his son out).*
*(The curtain falls.)*

# ■ ATTO TERZO

# ■ ACT III

**CORO:** Morte in gelido stupore; vita in orrida paura giaceranno quel dì che il Creatore trarrà dal buio la sua creatura. Ogni affetto è cosa vana ogni luce ottenebrata L'amore nascerà come fontana dal seno della terra liberata il dì che il Creatore darà la luce alla sua creatura.
*(Finita la muta preghiera, le donne rialzano le teste addolorate.)*

**CHOIR:** In leaden stupor Death shall lie; And life shall shrink in fright, The day that the creator calls His creatures from the night. Desire is but an empty thing, All light must clouded be . . . Love like a fountain forth shall spring From out a world set free, The day that the Creator lifts His creatures to the light. *(After a silent prayer the women raise their sorrowful heads.)*

**UNA GIOVINETTA:** *(si leva di mezzo al grouppo delle donne:)* Venni piangendo in questa strana terra a rivederti, o nostra principessa! Ho trovato di pianto il mondo pieno . . . Mi vedi? Io torno per la terzavolta.

**A YOUNG GIRL:** *(rises from amongst the group of women)* I have come weeping to this foreign land To see you O our princess, once again! And I have found the whole world weeping . . . Do you see me? For the third time I'm returning.

**UOMINI:** *(dal fondo con voci soavi).* Fiora, Fiora, non dài tu la risposta? . . .

**MEN:** *(from the back, with stubbued voices)* Fiora, Fiora, will you not answer us?

**UN GIOVANETTO:** *(levandosi di mezzo al gruppo).* Ella par viva . . . Stanca, pare . . .

**A YOUTH:** *(rising from the center of the group)* She seems alive . . . she seems weary.

**DONNE:** Siamo tutte per la gran doglia persc e morte! . . .

**WOMEN:** We are distraught And almost dead with such great sorrow!

**IL GIOVANETTO:** Anche prima era un sogno ed era vival!

**THE YOUTH:** At first it was a dream and she was living! . . .

**UOMINI:** Lamento senza fine! . . . Chi ci rende il giglio, che venuto è ormai l'autunno . . . La primavera fu uccisa tra' fiori! . . .

**MEN:** Oh, endless lamentation! Who will restore to us The lily, who came among us in the autumn . . . And in the spring was slain among the flowers! . . .

**UNA VECCHIA:** (*che si sarà accostata a Fiora indagando*) (*Improvvisa e furibonda*). Alzate, tutti, gli occhi in volto a lei . . . Ella ha sul volto scritta la vendetta!

**AN OLD WOMAN:** (*who has groped her way to Fiora's side*) (*suddenly and frenziedly*) Raise, all of you your eyes to Fiora's face For on her face "revenge" is written clearly!

**LE DONNE:** (*si accostano a Fiora, si fermano a due passi dalla bara e scrutano la morta*). La vendetta? Si Si Parla con gli occhi . . . Ci vuol dire che il vecchio . . . Il vecchio forse . . . Il vecchio certo . . . Prima che tornasse Manfredo . . . Era già morta al suo ritornol Nefanda impressa! Orribile delitto! Reliquia violata! Cuore infranto! Vendicata sia! Si Fiore! Fiora . . . (*Si riode improvvisamente il coro sacro dentro la chiesa. Le donue si inginocchiano ancora.*)

**THE WOMEN:** (*approach Fiora, stand two steps from the bier and examine the dead woman*) Revenge? Yes! . . . Yes! Her eyes are sparkling . . . She wants to tell us that the old man . . . Perhaps the old man . . . Undoubtedly the old man . . . Before Manfred returned That she was dead ever he returned . . . Oh wicked deed! Abhorrent crime! Atrocious desperation! Oh broken heart! We will revenge her! Yes! Fiora! Fiora! . . . (*Suddenly the sacred choir is heard again from the church. The woman grow calmer and kneel down once more.*)

**UOMINI:** Silenzio. Siamo in chiesa . . .

**MEN:** Silence. We are in church . . .

**DONNE:** Oriamo . . . (*Suon di campane.*)

**WOMAN:** Let us pray . . . (*Tolling of bells.*)

**LA VECCHIA:** E l'oral

**THE OLD WOMAN:** It is the hour!

**UOMINI:** (*alzandosi*) Andiamo . . .

**MEN:** (*rising*) Let us go . . .

**DONNE:** Si fa notte . . .

**WOMEN:** The night is falling.

**TUTTI:** Fiora, addio! . . .

**ALL:** Fiora, farewell!

**LA VECCHIA:** (*che ha scorto Avito che s'avvicina lentamente dalla scala di sinistra: con sorpresa*) Cè il principe d'Altura . . .

**THE OLD WOMAN:** (*has caught sight of Avito, who is approaching slowly from the steps on the left: with surprise*) It is the Prince of Altura . . .

**DONNE:** Avito!

**WOMEN:** Avito!

**UOMINI:** Andiamo . . . Andiamo. Si fa notte . . . (*escono salendo la scala che mette in chiesa*).

**MEN:** Let us go . . . Let us go. Night is falling . . . (*They go off, mounting the steps leading to the church.*)

**AVITO:** (*rimane impietrato presso l'arco d'entrata e, come se nel mausoleo non fosse che una gran fiamma abbagliante, il suo capo è ripiegato, quasi nascosto. Resta immobile, fino a che tutti non sono usciti. Indi s'inoltra. Quando giunge presso la morta;*) Fiora, Fiora . . . E silenzio: siamo soli . . . E tu, parlami. Aspetto, Io non ti voglio guardare, prima che tu parli, amata, eletta, sempre viva, anima mia . . . (*Con improvviso pianto*). Ahimè, no, no! Tu sei morta! Tu sei spenta! . . . Inganno! Ed ora toccherò le tue mani che paìon morbide di vita; saranno fredde; baccerò la tua: bocca che sembra custodirmi il bacio

**AVITO:** (*remains rigid near the vaulted entrance, and, as if the Mausoleum held nothing but a huge dazzling flame, his head remains bowed, almost hidden. Thus he stands motionless till all have gone out. Then he comes forward. When he has come close to the body:*) Fiora, Fiora . . . Silence surrounds us: we are alone . . . Speak to me, then. I'm waiting. I will not Look at you, beloved, before you speak to me, My soul, my chosen, ever-living . . . (*with sudden tears*) Alas! No, no! you're dead! you are No more! — Delusion! And now I'll touch your hands Which seem to throb with life;

che tanto tanto sopra v'ho cercato: anch'ella sarà fredda, irrigidita . . . (*con altra voce:*) Povera vita mia! Quanto travaglio, per non avere mai tutto per me quel ch'era mio! Si, mia! Dunque, si cara sempre, anche spenta! Un ultimo sospiro dell'anima tua bella è certo in te . . . Fiora lo voglio! E sopra la tua bocca: ed è la bocca tua che più rammenta . . . (*Piangendo si getta follemente sulla bocca di lei. Dopo un breve istante si rialza.*) Qual effluvio! Oh, miracolo! Mi perdo dunque con te?! Si; si: perch'io mi sento torcere il cuore! Ahimè!, che più di tutto il dolore è possente. (*Si leva improvviso e fa qualche passo verso l'uscita vacillando, come colpito.*) Oh, giovinezza, sei attaccata forte alla tua roccia! (*Ode qualcuno avvicinarsi.*) Qualcuno giunge?! Ed io sarò scoperto! (*Ecco simile ad un'ombra Manfredo! Giunge da destra, si avvicina ad Avito che non può fuggire. Lentamente lo scorge.*) (*Si avvicina il tramonto.*)

They will be cold; and I will kiss your lips Which seem to guard the kiss I sought On them so often, ah so often: And those, too, will be cold and stark (*in different tones*) Oh my poor life! What agony, No more to have and hold as mine, All that was mine! Yes mine! For you are Ever dear, even dead! One last sigh Of your fair soul is surely still within you Fiora, I want it! It lingers over your mouth; And it is your mouth that recalls most clearly . . . (*Weeping, he throws himself beside her desperately and presses his lips on hers. After a brief instant he raises himself again.*) What curious exhalation! Oh miracle! Do I then Perish with you? Yes, yes: I feel my heart Is being wrund! Ah me! How far more powerful Than all is pain! (*He rises suddenly and takes a few tottering steps towards the exit, as if struck*) Oh youth, How strongly are you fettered to your rock! (*He hears some one approach.*) Some one approaches?! I shall be discovered! (*Manfred appears like a shadow. He advances from the R. and approaches Avito, who is unable to escape. Slowly he perceives him.*) (*Sunset approaches.*)

**MANFREDO:** Eccoti alfine, si: t'abbiamo colto! (*Riconoscendolo.*) Sei tu, Avito? Tu? Tu, ch'ella adorava?

**MANFREDO:** Yes, here you are at last then: we have caught you! (*recognizing him*) Is it you, Avito? You? You, whom she adored?

**AVITO:** Che vuoi tu? Ma non vedi ch'io non dosso quasi parlare? . . .

**AVITO:** What do you want? Can you not see that I can scarcely speak? . . .

**MANFREDO:** E bene! . . . E bene! E bene! Tu sei già morto! Sopra alla sua bocca. per poterti ghermire, fu disteo un veleno possente . . .

**MANFREDO:** It is well . . . it is well! it is well! You are already dead! Upon her lips, To track and snare you, there was spread A powerful poison . . .

**AVITO:** (*atterrito*) . . . No! NO! NO! Sulla sua bocca . . .

**AVITO:** (*terrorstruck*) No! No! No! Upon her lips . . .

**MANFREDO:** Tu l'hai baciata: tu l'hai profanata; e muori! . . .

**MANFREDO:** Yes, you have kissed her, have profaned her And you shall die!

**AVITO:** Questo facesti, tu Tu potesti in questo modo macchiare la sua bocca sacra?

**AVITO:** And you have done this? you could in this wise Sully her sacred lips?

**MANFREDO:** Io, no! Ma fu mio padre che volle sapere chi tu fossi! . . . Per me per la mia gioia! . . .

**MANFREDO:** No, not I! It was my father, who would know Who you were! For me . . . and for my pleasure!

**AVITO:** E giusto: godi della morte mia . . .

**AVITO:** It is just: rejoice then in my death . . .

**MANFREDO:** (*con disperazione*)
Ma dimmi quello, quello ch'io non so!
Dimmi: t'amava ella?

**AVITO** Come la vita
che le fu tolta . . . No . . . di più; . . . di più
Ma se vuoi vendicarti, non tardare
che presto io muoio; vendicati, uccidimi . . .
(*Vacilla, è per cadere.*)

**MANFREDO:** (*le sorregge e lo aiuta fino in terra. Poi levando le braccia al cielo:*) Dio mio! Dio mio! Perchè non posso odiare!
(*Si rivolge verso il cadavere di Fiora*)
Ma tu, ma tu non mi lasciare al mio squallore, alla mia fonda solitudine!
Fa ch'io torni con te, ch'io ti raggiunga! . . .
Fiora, sorreggi me, nell'ora estre-

**MANFREDO:** (*in desperation*) But tell me this, this that I do not know! Tell me: did she love you?

**AVITO:** She loved me as the life
That they took from her . . . No, more, far more . . .
But if you thirst for vengeance, do not delay.
For I am nearly dying; avenge yourself and kill me . . .
(*He totters and nearly falls.*)

**MANFREDO:** (*supports him and then lays him on the ground. Then, raising his arms to the sky:*)
My God! My God! Why can't I hate!
(*He turns to Fiora's corpse.*)
But you, you cannot leave me in my Misery, my utter loneliness!
Let me come back to you and join you once again!
Fiora, help me in my hour of need! . . .
Let me come back to you, come

ma! . . .
Ch'io torni a te; ch'io torni a te per sempre! (*Si getta su lei e la bacia anch'egli sulla bocca e quivi rimane sussultando per la morte che si spande nelle sue vene. Ma ecco Archibaldo a tastoni nella sua ombra perpetua.*)

**ARCHIBALDO:** Un gemito! T'ho colto predatore!
(*Si avvicina alla bara, cerca e sente il corpo di Manfredo. Subito lo abbranca*) Predatore! . . . Il tuo cuore vo' sentire nella morte!

**MANFREDO:** (*con voce morebonda*) No, padre! Tu t'inganni!

**ARCHIBALDO:** (*alzandosi improvviso con tutta la persoua*) Ah! Manfredo! Manfredo! Anche tu, dunque,
senza rimedio sei con me nell'ombra! . . .
(*Cala la tela.*)

back to you, for ever!
(*He throws himself on her and also kisses her on her lips and remains there, quivering, while death slowly creeps through his veins. Archibaldo now comes groping through his eternal darkness.*)

**ARCHIBALDO:** A groan! Now I have caught you, thief!
(*He approaches the bier, feels for and finds Manfredo's body. He catches hold of it quickly.*)
Thief! I want to feel your heart In death!

**MANFREDO:** (*with dying voice*)
No Father! You're mistaken!

**ARCHIBALDO:** (*suddenly rising to his full height*) Ah! Manfredo! Manfredo! You also, then,
Are with me past salvation in the shadows!
(*The curtain falls.*)

# L'Incoronazione di Poppea (1642)

MUSIC BY CLAUDIO MONTEVERDI ▪ LIBRETTO BY FRANCESCO BUSENELLO

This three-act opera, set to a libretto by Giovanni Francesco Busenello, was premiered in Venice at the Teatro SS. Giovanni e Paolo in 1642. It opens with a prologue—the goddesses of Fortune and Virtue are arguing over which one of them has greater power over man. However, the goddess of Love claims to have the greatest power as evidenced by the story of Nerone and Poppea. The actual story begins as Ottone returns from war, looking forward to a reunion with his mistress, Poppea. He sees two imperial guards outside her home and realizes that the Emperor Nerone has become her lover in Ottone's absence. Nerone almost promises Poppea the throne, and Poppea rejoices in her success. Her nurse, Arnalta, warns her of the jealousy of the Empress Ottavia. Ottavia seeks vengeance from the gods against Nerone which the Senator Seneca urges her not to do. Seneca also tries to persuade Nerone to see reason, but Nerone angrily states that he will marry Poppea. Poppea is overjoyed and convinces Nerone that Seneca is a threat; Nerone sentences him to death. Ottone seeks comfort in Drusilla, a court lady. Seneca is executed; Ottavia convinces Ottone to kill Poppea, which Ottone attempts to do with Drusilla's willing assistance. Poppea is protected by Venere, goddess of Love, from being murdered; Drusilla is arrested for the crime. Despite her pleas of her innocence, she is about to be executed when Ottone confesses his guilt. The Emperor banishes him, and Drusilla shares his exile. Ottavia is also banished for instigating the plot, and Nerone and Poppea celebrate the triumph of their love.

## ▪ ATTO I

*The Palace of Poppea*
*Two guards are asleep at the gate*

**OTTONE:** E pure io torno qui
Qual linea al centro
qual foco a sfera
e qual ruscello al mare . . .
E, se ben luce alcuna non appare, se ben io che sta il mio sol qui dentro . . .
E pur io torno qui qual linea al centro.
Caro tetto amoroso albergo di mia vita e del mio bene il passo l'cor ad inclinarti viene!
Apri un balcon, Poppea!
Con bel viso, in cui son le sorti mie, previeni, anima mia, precorri il die.
Sorgi e disgombra homai da questo ciel caligini e tenebre con il beato aprir di tue palpebre!
Sogni, portate a volo su l'ali vostre, in dolce fantasia questi sospir alla diletta mia!
Ma che veggio, infelice? Non già fantasmi o pur notturne larve . . .
Son questi i servi di Nerone.
Ahi!
Dunque a l'insensati versi io diffondo i lamenti necessito le pietre a deplorarmi, adoro questi marmi, amoreggio con lagrime un balcone e, in grembo di Poppea dorme Nerone!
Ah!
Perfida Poppea!
Son queste le promesse ed i guiramenti che accesero il cor mio?
Questa è la fede, o Dio!
Io son quell'Ottone che ti seguì che ti bramò che ti servì!
quell'Ottone che t'adorò che, per

## ▪ ACT I

*The Palace of Poppea*
*Two guards are asleep at the gate*

**OTTONE:** (*Poppea's husband*) I am drawn here Like a line to the center, Like fire to the sphere, Or the river to the sea.
And though there is No light, I know My sun is here.
Like the line, I am drawn to the center,
Beloved dwelling, Home of my life And my possessions, I come here With a trembling heart.
Open your window, Poppea!
And show your face, My fate is there Forerunner of light, My love, my life.
Come forth and dispel The darkness, Open your eyes, and Fill the sky with light.
O dreams, carry My tears and my sighs On your wings In sweet fantasy To my beloved.
What do I see?
Phantoms, or shadows Of the night? No!
They are Nero's servants.
O, so I lament In passionate verse That move the stones to pity And but address The balcony While Nero sleeps In happiness In Poppea's arms.
O, treacherous Poppea!
Where are the promises And the oath That fired my heart?
This is fidelity?
I am you Ottone who has followed you Loved and adored you.
Ottone who worshipped you, Who, to win your heart prayed in tears with pious sacrifice and vows.
You promised me That I would

peigarti ed intenerirti il core di lagrime imperò prieghi devoti gli spirti a te sacrificando in voti.
M'assiscurasti al fine ch'abbracciate haverei nel tuo bel seno le mie beatitudini amorose; io di credula speme il seme sparsi ma l'aria e'l ciel a danni miei rivolto tempestò di ruine il mio raccolto.

**PRIMO SOLDATO:** Chi parla?

**SECONDO SOLDATO:** Chi parla?

**PRIMO SOLDATO:** Chi va lì?

**SECONDO SOLDATO:** Camerata, che fai?
Perchè parli sognando?

**PRIMO SOLDATO:** Sorgono pur dell'alba i primi rai . . .
Non ho dormito in questa notte mai.

**SECONDO SOLDATO:** Su, risvegliati tosto, guardiamo il nostro posto.

**PRIMO SOLDATO:** Sia maledetto amor, Poppea e Roma, maledetto Nerone e la milizia, soddisfar io non posso la pigrizia un giorno un hora sola.

**SECONDO SOLDATO:** La nostra imperatrice stilla se stessa in pianti e Neron per Poppea la vilipende.
L'Armenia si ribella ed egli non ci pensa, la Pannonia da all'armi ed ei se ne ride.
Impariamo da gl'occhi a non trattar da sciocchi.

**PRIMO SOLDATO:** Ma già s'imbianca l'alba e viene il dì.

**SECONDO SOLDATO:** Tacciam!
Nerone è qui.
(*Nero comes out of the palace.*)

hold you In my arms In amorous bliss.
I sowed the seeds of hope but the heavens destroyed my harvest of happiness.

**1ST SOLDIER:** Who speaks?

**2ND SOLDIER:** Who speaks?

**1ST SOLDIER:** Who goes there?

**2ND SOLDIER:** Friend, what are you doing?
Why do you talk in your sleep?

**1ST SOLDIER:** I see the first rays of dawn . . .
I haven't slept all night.

**2ND SOLDIER:** Let us get up and keep watch.

**1ST SOLDIER:** Cursed be love Poppea and Rome.
Cursed Nero and the army.
Not one hour a day Can be given to sloth.

**2ND SOLDIER:** Our empress weeps, Nero insults her Forsakes her For Poppea.
Armenia is in revolt, Nero is unmoved.
Pannonia is in arms, And Nero laughs.
We must learn to see Without speaking.

**1ST SOLDIER:** It is getting light, Day is coming.

**2ND SOLDIER:** Silence!
Nero is coming.
(*Nero comes out of the palace.*)

**POPPEA:** Signor, deh, non partire. Sostien che queste braccia ti circondino il collo come le tue bellezze circondano il cor mio.

**NERONE:** Poppea, lascia ch'io parta.

**POPPEA:** Non partire signor! Appena spunta l'alba e tu, che sei l'incarnato mio sole, la mia palpabil luce e l'amoroso dì della mia vita vuoi si repente far da me partita?
Deh! Non dir di partir che di voce si amara al solo accento, ahi, spirar quest'alma io sento.

**NERONE:** La nobiltà de' nascimento tuoi non permette che Roma sappia che siamo uniti infin' ch'Ottavia . . .

**POPPEA:** Infin che . . .

**NERONE:** Infin che Ottavia non rimane esclusa col ripudio da me.

**POPPEA:** Vanne, ben mio.
*(She throws herself into Nero's arms)*

**NERONE:** In un sospir che vien dal profondo del cor includo un bacio, o cara, ed un a Dio.
Si rivedrem bien tosto idolo mio.

**POPPEA:** Signor, sempre me vedi anzi mai non mi vedi perchè s'è ver che nel tou cor io sia entra l'tuo sen celata non posso da tuoi lumi esser mirata . . .
Tornerai?
*(Nero draws away gently)*

**NERONE:** Se ben io vò pur teco io stò

**POPPEA:** Tornerai?

**NERONE:** Il cor dalle tue stelle mai non si disvelle.

**POPPEA:** Tornerai?

**NERONE:** Io non posso da te viver disgiunto se non si smembra l'unità dal punto.

**POPPEA:** Tornerai?

**NERONE:** Tornerò.

**POPPEA:** Quando?

**NERONE:** Ben tosto.

**POPPEA:** Ben tosto . . . me l'prometti?

**NERONE:** Te l'giuro.

**POPPEA:** E me l'osserverai?

**NERONE:** E se a te non verrò tu a me verrai.

**POPPEA:** A dio, Nerone

**NERONE:** A Dio, Poppea
*(exit Nero)*

**POPPEA:** Speranza, tu mi vai il cor accarezzando, speranza tu mi vai il genio lusingando e mi cirondi intanto di regio si ma imaginario manto.
No!
Non temo di noia alcuna; per me guerreggia Amor e la Fortuna!

**POPPEA:** Do not go My Lord. Let my arms Enfold you again As your beauty Envelopes my heart.

**NERO:** Let me go, Poppea.

**POPPEA:** Do not go!
It is hardly dawn, And you who are My sun, The blinding light of day, Of my love's life, Must you think Of departing so soon?
Do not speak of departure, My whole being changes As I hear This bitter word.

**NERO:** The nobility Of your birth Forbids that Rome Should know of our union Before Octavia . . .

**POPPEA:** Before . . .

**NERO:** Before Octavia Is banished And repudiated.

**POPPEA:** Then leave, my love.
*(She throws herself into Nero's arms)*

**NERO:** With a sigh From the depth of my heart I kiss you, my love And say farewell.
My idol, we shall meet Soon again.

**POPPEA:** My Lord, you see me always Though I am invisible For how can your eyes See me if I am hidden In your heart.
You will return?
*(Nero draws away gently)*

**NERO:** As I go, I promise you.

**POPPEA:** You will return?

**NERO:** My heart will never Forsake you.

**POPPEA:** You will return?

**NERO:** I cannot live Far from you Without your filling My whole being.

**POPPEA:** You will return?

**NERO:** I shall.

**POPPEA:** When?

**NERO:** Soon.

**POPPEA:** Soon, you promise?

**NERO:** I swear it.

**POPPEA:** Will you keep your word?

**NERO:** And if I do not come to you, You will come to me.

**POPPEA:** Farewell, Nero.

**NERO:** Farewell, Poppea.
*(exit Nero)*

**POPPEA:** Hope caresses My heart, Hope flatters My mind; I feel the royal mantle On my shoulders.
I fear no hindrance, Love and Fortune Are fighting for me.

**ARNALDA:** *(enters preoccupied)* Ahi, figlia, voglia il cielo, che questi abbracciamenti non siano un giorno i precipizi tuoi.

**POPPEA:** No!
Non temo di noia alcuna . . .

**ARNALDA:** L'imperatrice Ottavia ha penetrati di Neron gli amori onde temo e pavento ch'ogni giorno, ogni punto sia di tua vita il punto estremo.

**POPPEA:** Per me guerreggia Amor e la Fortuna!

**ARNALDA:** Mira, Poppea, dove il prato è più ameno e dilettoso stassi il serpente ascoso; dei casi le vicende son funeste la calma è profezìa de le tempeste

**POPPEA:** No!
Non temo di noia alcuna . . .
Per me guerriggia Amor e la Fortuna.

**ARNALDA:** Ben sei pazza se credi che ti possano far contenta e salva un garzon cieco ed una cieca calva.

**OTTAVIA:** Disprezzata regina! del monarca romano!
Afflitta moglie, che fò, ove son, che penso?
O delle donne miserabil sesso.
Se la natura e 'l cielo libere ci produce il matrimonio c'incatena serve.
Se concepiamo l'huomo al nostro empio tiranno formiam le membra, allattiamo il carnefice crudele che ci scanna e ci svena e siam costrette per indegna sorte a noi medesme fabbricar la morte.
Nerone empio, o Dio, marito bestemmiato, per sempre maledetto dai cordogli miei dove, hoimè, dove sei?
In braccio di Poppea tu dimori felice e godi e intanto il fraquente cader de' pianti miei pur va quasi formando un diluvio di specchi in cui tu miri dentro alle tue delizie i miei martiri!
Destin che stai lassù Giove, ascoltami tu.
Se, per punir Nerone, Fulmini tu non hai d'impotenza t'accuso d'ingiustizia t'incolpo.
Ahi!
Trapasso trop'oltre e me ne pento . . . sopprimo e seppellisco in taciturne angoscie il mio tormento.
*(she sinks onto a bench)*

**SENECA:** Ecco la sconsolata donna assunta all'imperio! per patir il servaggio!
O gloriosa del mondo imperatrice, sovra i titoli eccelsi de l'insigni avi tuoi cospicua e grande la vanità del pianto de gl'occhi imperiali è ufficio indegno.
Ringrazia la Fortuna che, con i colpi suoi t'accresce gli ornamenti.
La cote non percossa non può mandar faville.
Tu, dal destin colpita, produci a te medesma alti splendori di vigor, di

**ARNALTA:** *(enters preoccupied)* O, my daughter Pray to the heavens That this love May not be Ill-fated.

**POPPEA:** No!
I fear nothing.

**ARNALTA:** The Empress Octavia Has discovered Nero's love.
I fear that each day May be your last.

**POPPEA:** Love and Fortune Are with me.

**ARNALTA:** Reflect, Poppea, Where the grass is greenest There the serpent hides.
Fate is often solemn And calm predicts the storm.

**POPPEA:** I fear No hindrance Love and Fortune Are fighting for me.

**ARNALTA:** You are mad If you believe In a blind boy Or in a despoiled blind woman.

**OCTAVIA:** *(concealed by a cloak)* Despised queen!
Unhappy wife of Rome's sovereign.
Where then am I?
What shall I do?
O, the misery Of women!
Nature Makes us free But marriage Enslaves us.
Our own sons Become our Masters; We suckle our Own executioneers.
By giving birth, Such is our fate, We bring about Our own deaths.
Nero, Ungodly And cursed husband, Source of all my misery, Where are you?
In the arms of Poppea In happiness While I am Washed by the Tears of my Unhappiness.
In the midst of your joy, You can see, As in a mirror, My heart breaking.
O Destiny above, Jupiter harken: If you have no thunderbolts To punish Nero, I accuse you of weakness and injustice!
Woe!
I blaspheme.
I repent it.
I shall suppress My sufferings In silent anguish.
*(she sinks onto a bench)*

**SENECA:** There is the unhappy woman, Raised to authority To suffer slavery.
O glorious empress Of the world, You are great By ancestry.
The hopelessness Of your tears Is unworthy Of your regal eyes.
Give thanks to Fortune Who, through your sufferings Increases your virtue.
Steel which is not tempered Does not shine.
Stricken by Destiny Your strength And your dignity Surpass even Your

fortezza, glorie maggiori assai che la bellezza!
La vaghezza del volto e i lineamenti che, in apparenza illustre, risplendon coloriti e delicati da pochi ladri di ci son rubati, ma la virtù costante il fato e 'l caso giammai non vede accaso.

**OTTAVIA:** Tu mi vai promettendo balsamo dal veleno e gloria da tormenti.
Scusami!
Questi son, Seneca mio, vanità speziose, studiati artifizi, inutili rimedi agl' infelici!
Neron tenta il ripudio de la persona mia per isposar Poppea.
Si divertisca se divertir si può si indegno esempio . . .
Tu per me prega il popol e 'l senato ch'io mi riduco a porger voti al tempio.

**SENECA:** Le porpore regali e le grandezze d'acute spine e triboli conteste, sotto forma, di veste sono martirio a principi infelici: le corone eminenti servono solo a indiademar tormenti.
Delle regie grandezze si veggono le pompe e gli splendori ma stan sempre invisibili i dolori.
(*Octavia exits rapidly*)

**NERONE:** (*enters, followed by a group of courtiers and goes over to Seneca*) Son risoluto alfine o Seneca, o maestro, di rimover Ottavia dal posto di consorte e di sposar Poppea.

**SENECA:** Signor, nel fondo alla maggior dolcezza spesso giace nascosto il pentimento.
Consiglier scellerato è il sentimento ch'odia le leggi a la ragion disprezza.

**NERONE:** La legge è per chi serve e, se voglio, posso abolir l'antica e indur la nova.
E partito l'imperio: è il ciel di Giove ma del mondo terren lo scettro è mio.

**SENECA:** Sregolare voler Non è volere.
Ma dirò con tua pace, egli è furore.

**NERONE:** La ragione è misura rigorosa per chi ubbidisce e non per chi comanda.

**SENECA:** Anzi, l'irragionevole comando distrugge l'obbedienza.

**NERONE:** Lascia i discorsi. Io voglio a modo mio.

**SENECA:** Non irritar il popolo e 'l senato.

**NERONE:** Del senato e del popolo non curo.

**SENECA:** Cura almeno te stesso e la tua fama.

**NERONE:** Trarrò la lingua a chi vorrà biasmarmi.

**SENECA:** Più muti che farai Più parleranno.

beauty.
The grace of your body, Your perfect features, The passing of time Can destroy them, But no misfortune Can touch Your constant virtue.

**OCTAVIA:** You offer balm For poison And glory for torment.
Forgive me, Seneca, But this is specious And artificial, Useless remedies For the miserable.
Nero wishes to reject me To marry Poppea.
Were it amusing I would be amused By his disgraceful example.
Speak for me To the senate and the people While I take refuge In the temple.

**SENECA:** The royal purple And its trappings Is woven with thorns And torments.
Under the guise of dress It strikes torment To an unhappy prince.
Crowns serve only To bruise heads.
We see the pomp, The royal grandeur And the splendour, But the sufferings Remain concealed.
(*Octavia exits rapidly*)

**NERO:** (*enters, followed by a group of courtiers and goes over to Seneca*) I have decided, Seneca, To remove Octavia From her position as my wife And to install Poppea.

**SENECA:** My Lord, the greatest joy Often conceals Remorse.
Any feeling That hates law And despises reason Is wicked.

**NERO:** Laws are made for the user! If I wish, I can abolish an old one And proclaim a new law.
The empire is divided: The heavens belong to Jupiter But the sceptre of earthly Power is mine.

**SENECA:** An irrational wish Is no wish at all.
With your permission I call this folly.

**NERO:** Reason is compulsory For those who obey, Not for him who commands.

**SENECA:** Unreasonable orders Destroy obedience.

**NERO:** Enough speechmaking. I rule in my own way.

**SENECA:** Do not annoy The people and the senate.

**NERO:** I take no account of The people and the senate.

**SENECA:** At least, consider Yourself and your honor.

**NERO:** I shall cut out the tongue Of anyone who finds fault.

**SENECA:** The more the mutes, The more will talk.

**NERONE:** Ottavia è infrigidita e infeconda.

**SENECA:** Chi ragione non ha cerca pretesti.

**NERONE:** Tu mi sforzi allo sdegno . . .
Al tuo dispetto e del popolo in onta e del senato e d'Ottavia e del cielo e dell'abisso, siansi giuste od ingiuste le mie voglie hoggi Poppea sarà mia moglie.
(*exit Nero and courtiers*)

**SENECA:** Il partito peggior sempre sovrasta quando la forza alla ragion contrasta.

**NERO:** Octavia is frigid and sterile.

**SENECA:** When one is in the wrong One looks for excuses.

**NERO:** You incite me to anger! In spite of you, The people The senate and Octavia, Of heaven and hell, Be my wishes just Or unjust, Today I shall marry Poppea.
(*exit Nero and courtiers*)

**SENECA:** When force apposes reason, One may always expect Unworthy actions.

# ■ ATTO II

**POPPEA:** Come dolci, come soavi riuscirono a te, la notte andata, di questa bocca i baci!

**NERONE:** Più cari i piò mordaci.

**POPPEA:** Di questo seno i pomi?

**NERONE:** Mertan le mamme tue più dolci nomi.

**POPPEA:** Di queste braccia i dolci amplessi?

**NERONE:** Idolo mio, deh, in braccio ancor t'havessi.
Poppea, respiro appena, miro le labbra tue e, mirando recupero con gli occhi quello spirto infiammato che nel baciarti, o cara, in te diflussi.
Non è più in cielo il mio destino, ma sta dei labbri tuoi nel bel rubino.

**POPPEA:** Signor, le tue parole son si dolci ch'io nell'anima mia le ridicò à ma stessa e l'interno ridirle necessita al deliquio il cor amante.
Come parole le odo, come baci io li godo . . .
son de' tuoi cari detti i sensi si soavi e si vivaci che, non contenti di blandir l'undito mi passano al stampar sul cor i baci . . .
Ma troppo attraversa ed impedisce di si regie promesse il fin sovrano.
Seneca, il tuo maestro, quello stoico sagace, quel filosofo astuto che sempre tenta perturbar altrui . . .
Che il tuo scettro dipenda da lui . . .

# ■ ACT II

**POPPEA:** How fresh and sweet Were your kisses Last night.

**NERO:** Most sweet and passionate.

**POPPEA:** And my breasts?

**NERO:** They deserve The sweetest names.

**POPPEA:** The caresses of my arms?

**NERO:** Your lover Desires always, My idol . . .
I can hardly breathe, I look at your lips And as I look, My soul becomes fire As before, when Loving you. My Destiny is not In heaven. But in the rubies Of your lips.

**POPPEA:** Your words Are so sweet That I repeat them Within my soul. The words I hear, The kisses I accept.
My whole being Is caressed And you plant Your kisses only On my heart.
But there is nevertheless Something in the way Which hinders the fulfillment Of your promises. Seneca, your teacher, The wise Stoic, The astute philosopher Who always attempts To worry others . . .
Does your crown Depend on him?

**NERONE:** Che?
Quel decrepito pazzo ha tanto ardire?
Olà!
Vada un di voi a Seneca volando e imponga a lui che in questa sera ei mora.
Poppea, sta di buon coro, hoggi vedrai ciò che può far Amore.

**OTTONE:** Ad altri tocca in sorta ber il licor e a me guardar il vaso.
aperte son le porte a Neron ed Otton fuori è rimaso.

**NERO:** What?
On that old fool?
Is he so rash?
Here!
Let one of you go To Seneca And order him to kill Himself this night.
Poppea, be of good cheer.
Today you will see What love can achieve.

**OTTONE:** It is the fortune of others To drink the wine, I am merely the cupbearer.
The doors are open to Nero But I re-

Sied egli a mensa a sattolar sue brame: in amaro digiun mor'io di fame.

POPPEA: Chi nasce sfortunato di se stesso si dolga e non d'altrui; del tuo penoso stato l'aspra cagion Otton, non son nè fui.
Il destin getta i dadi e i punti attende; l'evento buono o reo da lui dipende.

OTTONE: La messe sospirata delle speranze mie de'miei desiri in altra mano è andata e non consente Amor ch'io più v'aspiri.
Neron, felice, i dolci pomi tocca e il solo pianto a me bagna la bocca.

POPPEA: A te le calve tempia ad altri il crine la Fortuna diede S'altri i desiri adempie hebbe di te più fortunato il piede.
La disventura tua non è mia colpa te solo dunque il tuo voler incolpa.

OTTONE: Sperai che quel macigno, bella Poppea, che ti circonda il core fosse d'amor benigno intenerito a prò del mio dolore.
Hor del tuo bianco sen la selce dura di mie morte speranze è sepoltura.

POPPEA: Deh, più non rinfacciarmi, porta il martellino in pace, cessa di più tentarmi.
Al cenno imperial Poppea soggiace.
Ammorza il fuoco homai, tempra gli sdegni, io lascio te per arrivar ai regni.

OTTONE: E così l'ambizion sopra ogni vitio tien la monarchia.

POPPEA: Così la mia ragione. Incolpa i tuoi capricci Di pazzia.

OTTONE: È questo del mio amore il guiderdone?

POPPEA: Non più, non più, son di Nerone!

OTTONE: Otton, torna in te stesso.
Il più imperfetto sesso non ha, per sua natura, altro d'human in se che la figura.
Costei pensa al comando e, sè ci arriva, la mia vita è perduta.
Ella temendo che risappia Nerone i miei passati amori ordirà insidie all'innocenza mia, indurrà colla forza un che m'accusi di lesa maestà, di fellonia . . .
La calumnia, da grandi favorita, idstrugge agl'innocenti honor e vita.
Vo' prevenir costei col ferro o col veleno.
Non min vuò più nutrir il serpe in seno.
A questo fine dunque arrivar dovea l'amor tuo, perfidissima Poppea!

DRUSILLA: Pur sempre con Poppea o con la lingua o col pensier discorri?

---

main outside.
He sits at the table Partakes of the feast, While I die from hunger In bitter fasting.

POPPEA: Those born unfortunate Can only lament that They are not otherwise; I am not responsible for your pitiful condition.
Fate throws the dice And waits for the score.
Events depend On that.

OTTONE: The harvest of my wishes, My hopes and my desires Has fallen into other hands, Amor did not consent.
Happy Nero gathers the fruit And I am left With tears.

POPPEA: Fortune has made you bald To others she gave hair.
Those who achieve Their desire Are more adept Than you.
Your misfortune Is not my fault.
I can do nothing Against your unhappiness.

OTTONE: I had hoped, beautiful Poppea, That the stone Which surrounds your heart Could be softened By a worthy love.
But the stone Of your heart Is the grave Of my dead hopes.

POPPEA: Trouble me no more And calm yourself,
I accept and I bow Before the supreme will.
You must now quench Your fire and your fury, I leave you To ascend a throne.

OTTONE: So ambition is The strongest vice In the kingdom.

POPPEA: It is my wish.
Accuse yourself Of stupidity.

OTTONE: Such is the reward Of my sincere love?

POPPEA: Enough, enough. I belong to Nero.

OTTONE: Ottone, be calm The weaker sex Is inhuman, but for Their appearance.
Poppea thinks of ruling And if she wins, My life is lost.
And if she deceives Nero to conceal Her past, If by force she obliges A base villain to accuse me Of high treason,
Slander, favored By the great Destroys the honor Of the innocent.
I must destroy That cunning serpent With the sword Or with poison.
To such and end Our love has come, Treacherous Poppea!

DRUSILLA: (the former mistress of Ottone) Are your thoughts And your words Still concerned with Poppea?

---

OTTONE: A te di quanto son, bellissima donzella, hor fo libero don.
Ad altri io mi ritolgo e solo tou sarò.
Drusilla mia, perdona, o Dio, al passato scortese mio costume.
Finchè io vivrò t'amerà sempre, o bella, quest'alma che ti fu cruda e rubella.
Già pentito dell'errore antico, mi ti consacro homai servo ed amico.

DRUSILLA: Già l'oblio seppelli gli andati amori?
E ver, Otton, che questo fido cor al suo s'uni?

OTTONE: È ver, Drusilla.

DRUSILLA: Temo che tu mi dica la bugìa.

OTTONE: No, no! Drusilla, no!

DRUSILLA: Otton, Otton, no so.

OTTONE: Teco non poù mentir la fede mia.

DRUSILLA: M'ami?

OTTONE: Ti bramo.

DRUSILLA: E come? In un momemto?

OTTONE: Amore è foco e subito s'accende.

DRUSILLA: Lieta men vado, Otton resta felice.
M'indirizzo a riveder l'imperatrice.
(exit Drusilla)

OTTONE: Le tempeste del cor tutto tranquilla.
D'altri Otton non sarà che di Drusilla.
Eppure, a mio dispetto, iniquo Amore, Drusilla ho in bocca e ho Poppea nel core.
(The house of Seneca)

SENECA: Solitudine amata eremo della mente, romitaggio a pensieri, delitia all'intelletto, che contempla l'imagini celesti sotto le forme ignobili e terrene a te l'anima mia lieta sen viene.
E lunge dalla corte ch'insolente e superbe fa della mia patienza anatomia qui tra le frondi e l'erbe m'assido in grembo della pace mia.

LIBERTO: Il comando tiranno esclude ogni ragione e tratta solo o violenza o morte.
Io devo riferirlo e nondimeno relatore innocente mi par esser partecipe del male che a riferire io vado.
Seneca, assai m'incresce di trovarti mentre pur ti ricerco.
Deh, non mi riguardar con occhio torvo se a te sarò d'infausto annunzio il corvo.

SENECA: Rido mentre mi rechi un si bel dono.

LIBERTO: Nerone a te mi manda . . .

SENECA: Non più.
Ho inteso e obbedisco hor, hora.
Vanne homai; e se parli a Nerone avanti sera, ch'io son morte e sepolte gli dirai.
Amici, è giunta l'hora di praticar in

---

OTTONE: I make a gift of Myself to you, O beauty.
I shall withdraw from others And be yours alone.
Drusilla, Forgive my Former negligence.
I shall love you As long as I live.
I repent my fickleness I am your servant And your friend.

DRUSILLA: The old passion Is therefore gone?
Can my faithful heart Be united with yours?

OTTONE: It is true.

DRUSILLA: I fear that you lie.

OTTONE: No, no Drusilla!

DRUSILLA: I don't know, Ottone.

OTTONE: My honor cannot lie.

DRUSILLA: Do you love me?

OTTONE: I desire you.

DRUSILLA: How so? In a moment?

OTTONE: Love is a fierce Fire.

DRUSILLA: I leave happy.
Ottone, stay happy.
I go to see the Empress.
(exit Drusilla)

OTTONE: The storm in my heart Is calling itself.
I shall belong to none But Drusilla.
But still, though I speak Of Drusilla, I have Poppea in my heart.
(The house of Seneca)

SENECA: Beloved solitude Sanctuary of mind And thought, Contemplation Which looks toward heaven, My soul longs for you.
Here I am in peace Far from the pride And pomp of the court, Seated among the flowers And the grass.

OFFICER: The tyrant's order Is quite without reason, It deals of violence And death.
I must communicate the order, Yet nevertheless Though an innocent messenger, I feel an accomplice Of evil.
Seneca, although I seek you, I am sorry To have found you.
Do not look at me So sad, Though I am the bearer Of ill news.

SENECA: I laugh while you Bring me such a great gift.

OFFICER: I am sent by Nero . . .

SENECA: Enough.
I understand And I obey.
Go, and should you see Nero Before the evening Say that I am dead And buried by his wishes.
My friends, the hour Has come to

fatti quella virtù que tanto celebrai.
Breve angoscia è la morte: un sospir peregrino esce dal core ove è stato molt'anni quasi in hospitio come forestiere e se ne vola all'Olimpo della felicità, soggiorno vero.

**FAMIGLIARI:** Non morir, Seneca.

**UNO:** Io per me morir non vò . . .

**TUTTI:** Questa vita è dolce troppo. Questo ciel troppo è sereno. Ogni amar, ogni veleno finalmente è lieve intoppo. Se mi corco al sonno lieve mi risveglio in sul mattino ma un avel di marmo fino mai non dà quel che riceve.

**SENECA:** Itene tutti a prepararmi il bagno chè se la vita corre come rivo fluente, in un tepido rivo questo sangue innocente io vò che vada a imporporarmi del morir la strada.

**NERONE:** Idolo mio, celebrarti io vorrei ma son minute fiaccole cadenti dirimpetto al tuo sole i detti miei. Son rubini amorosi i tuoi labbri preziosi, il mio core costante di saldo amante. Così le tue bellezze ed il mio core di care gemme ha fabbricato amore.

**OTTONE:** I miei subiti sdegni, la politica mia già poco d'hora m'indussero a pensare d'uccidere Poppea. O mente maledetta, come sei tu mortale ond'io non possa svenarti e castigarti. Sprezzami quanto sai, odiami quanto puoi voglio esser Clizia al sol degli occhi tuoi. Amerò senza speme al dispetto del fato fia mia delizia l'amarti disperato. Blandirò i miei tormenti nati del tuo bel volto, sarò dannato sì, ma in paradiso.

**OTTAVIA:** Tu che dagli avi miei avesti la grandezze se memoria conservi dei benefici avuti hor dammi aita.

**OTTONE:** Maestà che prega è destin che necessita, son pronto ad obbedirti, o regina, quando anche bisognasse sacrificare a te la mia ruina.

**OTTAVIA:** Voglio che la tua spada scriva gli obblighi miei col sangue di Poppea. Vuò che l'uccida.

**OTTONE:** Che uccida chi?

**OTTAVAIA:** Poppea!

**OTTONE:** Che uccida Poppea? O ciel, o Dei! In questo punto estremo ritoglietemi i giorni e i spirti miei.

practice The prophetic virtue That we respect. Death is merely A slight breath, Leaving the heart Where it stayed many years As a stranger Who found shelter To fly up to Olympus, The true abode Of happiness.

**ATTENDANTS:** Do not die, Seneca.

**ONE ATTENDANT:** I do not want to die . . .

**ALL TOGETHER:** Life is beautiful and sweet, The sky is clear, Every love and every poison In the end passes away. When I sleep in my bed, In the morning I awake; But the tomb in finest marble Brings an end to destiny.

**SENECA:** Go all, Prepare my bath. Life passes Like a river. May my innocent blood Redden the noble course Of death.

**NERO:** My idol, I wish to praise you, But my words Are as sparks Compared with your light. Your precious lips Are like rubies. Love has made Priceless jewels Of your heart And your beauty.

**OTTONE:** A short while ago My violent rage Had made me want To kill Poppea. O cursed mind Of mortals, How can I kill And punish you? Despise me as you will, Hate me as you can, I wish to be a fury In your eyes. I shall love without hope, Regardless of fate It will be my pleasure To love hopelessly. Finally I will calm The torments that you caused, I shall be damned But be in paradise.

**OCTAVIA:** (*taking him unawares*) If you recall My great ancestors, Help me now.

**OTTONE:** When a queen begs, Destiny commands. I am ready to obey, Even if it causes My ruin.

**OCTAVIA:** I want your sword To write my orders In Poppea's blood. I want you to kill her.

**OTTONE:** To kill . . . ?

**OCTAVIA:** Poppea!

**OTTONE:** That I kill Poppea? O, gods in heaven, Take my life This instant.

**OTTAVIA:** Se tu non m'ubbidisci, t'accuserò a Nerone ch'abbi voluto usarmi violenza inhoneste e farò che ti si stancheranno intorno il tormento e la morte in questo giorno.

**OTTONE:** Ad obbedirti, o imperatrice, io vado. O ciel, etc.

**DRUSILLA:** Felice cuor mio festeggiami in seno. Dopo i nembi e l'horror godrò il sereno. Hoggi spero che Ottone mi riconfermi il suo primiero amore.

**OTTONE:** Io non so dov'io vada; il palpitar del core il moto del piè non van del pari. L'aria che mentra in seno quando io respiro trova il mio cor si afflitto ch'ella si cangia in subitaneo pianto. E così mentre io peno l'aria per compassion mi piange in seno.

**DRUSILLA:** E dove, signor mio?

**OTTONE:** Te sola cerco.

**DRUSILLA:** Eccomi ai tuoi piaceri.

**OTTONE:** Io vò fidarti un secreto gravissimo. Prometti e silenzio e concorso.

**DRUSILLA:** Ciò che del sangue mio più che dell'oro può giovarti e servirti è già tuo più che mio. Palesami il secreto che del silenzio mio ti do l'anima in pegno e la mia fede.

**OTTONE:** Non esser più gelosa di Poppea.

**DRUSILLA:** Felice cor mio, festeggiami in seno.

**OTTONE:** Senti! Io devo hor, hora per terribile comando immergerli nel sen questo mio brando. Per coprir me stesso in misfatto si grande io vorrei le tue vesti.

**DRUSILLA:** E le vesti e le vene io ti darò.

**OTTONE:** Se occultarmi potrò viveremo più uniti sempre in dilettosi amori, se morir converrammi ne l'idiomo d'un pietoso pianto dammi essequie o Drusilla, se dovrò fuggitivo scampar l'ire mortal di chi comanda socorri a mie fortune.

**DRUSILLA:** Andiam pur ch'io mi spoglio e di mia man travestirti io voglio. Ma vò saper da te più addentro e a fondo di così horrenda impresa la cagione.

**OTTONE:** Andiam homai che con alto stupore il tutto udrai.

**POPPEA:** Hor che Seneca è morto Amor, ricorro a te. Guida mia speme in porto e fammi sposa al mio re.

**ARNALTA:** Pur sempre sulle nozze canzoneggiando vai.

**OCTAVIA:** If you do not obey me, I shall accuse you of violating me And you will die This very day.

**OTTONE:** Empress, I obey. Ye gods, Take my life, etc.

**DRUSILLA:** Be happy, My heart. After so much misery, I shall be happy. I hope that today Ottone will return To his first love.

**OTTONE:** My heart throbs, my feet do not obey. I know not where to hide. The very air I breathe, As it enters my body Is transformed Into tears.

**DRUSILLA:** How so?

**OTTONE:** I seek only you.

**DRUSILLA:** I am devoted to you.

**OTTONE:** I will tell you My secret. Promise silence And you help.

**DRUSILLA:** Whatever I can do To please and To serve you, Is all yours. Tell me your secret And I shall pledge My silence.

**OTTONE:** Be jealous of Poppea No more.

**DRUSILLA:** My heart is Joyful.

**OTTONE:** Listen! I have been ordered To plunge my sword Into her heart. To conceal myself I want your clothes.

**DRUSILLA:** I will give you the clothes And my blood as well.

**OTTONE:** If I could hide, We would live together Happily forever. And if I die, You will weep Over me. If I have to flee From the tyrant's wrath, Look after my Possessions.

**DRUSILLA:** I shall take off my gown And disguise you With my own hands. But I want to know The precise reason For your decision.

**OTTONE:** Let us go. You shall hear all. It will surprise you.

**POPPEA:** Now that Seneca is dead I pray you, Love, That I may marry The Emperor.

**ARNALTA:** You think always Still of marriage.

# Act II

**POPPEA:** Ad altro, Arnalta mia, non penso mai.

Perchè il sonno m'alletti a chiuder gli occhi alla quiete in grembo, qui nel giardin, Arnalta, fammi apprestar del riposare il modo ch'alla fresc'aria addormentarmi godo.

**ARNALDA:** Adagiati, Poppea, acquetati, anima mia, sarai ben custodita.

Oblivion soave, i dolci sentimenti in te, figlia, addormenti.

Posatevi, occhi ladri aperti, deh, che fate se, chiusi, ancor rubate?

Poppea, rimanti in pace, luci care e gradite, dormite, homai, dormite.

Amanti vagheggiate il miracol nuovo.

E luminoso il dì si come suole, e pur vedete addormentato il sole.

**LOVE:** Dorme l'incauta.

Ella non sa ch'hor verrà il punto micidiale.

Così l'umanità vive all'oscuro e quando ha chiusi gli occhi crede essersi dal mal posta in sicuro.

O sciocchi, o frali sensi mortali; mentre cadete in sonnacchioso oblio sul vostro sonno è vigilante Dio.

Siete rimasi gioco de casi oggetti al rischio e del periglio prede se Amor, genio del mondo, non provedde.

Dormi, Poppea, terrena dea.

Ti salverà dall'armi altrui rubelle Amor che move il sol a l'altre stelle.

Già s'avvicina la tua ruina ma non ti nuocerà strano accidente ch'Amor picciolo è, sì, ma omnipotente.

**OTTONE:** Eccomi trasformato non d'Ottone in Drusilla ma d'huomo in serpe il cui veleno è rabbia.

Non vide il mondo e non vedrà simile . . .

Ma che veggio, infelice?

Tu dormi, anima mia, chiudesti gli occhi per non aprirli più.

Care pupille al sonno in seno acciò che non vediate questi prodigi strani; la vostra morte uscir dalle mie mani.

Ma che tardo?

Costei m'aborre e sprezza e ancor io l'amo?

Ho promesso ad Ottavia e se mi pente accelero a miei dì funesto il fine.

Esca di corte chi vuol esser pio.

Colui chi ad'altra guarda che all'interesse suo merta d'esser cieco

Il fatto resta occulto la macchiata coscienza si lava con l'oblio.

Poppea, io t'uccido.

Amor, rispetto, a Dio.

**AMOR:** Forsennato!
Inimico del mio nume.
Tanto dunque si presume?
Fulminarti io dovrei, ma non merti di morire per la mano degli dei.

**POPPEA:** I think of nothing else. Bring my bed Into this garden. I must relax in sleep And I like To fall asleep In the open air.

**ARNALDA:** Lie down, Poppea, And rest.
You will be well Protected. Rest your enchanting eyes. Why are they still open If even closed they enchant?
Poppea, rest in peace. Dear child, rest quietly, Sleep now, sleep. Behold the miracle! The day is bright As it should be And yet the sun Is asleep.

**LOVE:** Regardless, she sleeps, Unaware that soon The fatal moment Is coming.
Thus is humanity In the dark, and by Closing their eyes They think themselves Safe.
O weak mortals! While you sink Into obliviion A god watches Over your sleep.
You are in the Clutches of chance, The prey of danger, If Love, the spirit Of the world, Does not protect you.
Sleep, Poppea Earthly Goddess. Love will save you From the treacherous attack, Love that moves the sun And the stars.
Your ruin approaches, But will not harm you.
Love is small But all powerful .

**OTTONE:** I am transformed, Not from Ottone into Drusilla But from a human being Into a serpent full of venom.
The world has never seen Such crime.
But what do I see?
You are asleep, beloved, Your eyes are closed, Closed forever.
You will never see The death-bringing Hand.
But why do I wait?
She despise me, And I still love her?
I have promised Octavia And If I stay, I seal my fate.
Anyone who wishes to remain Honest should leave the court.
Anyone who considers other Than his own interest Ought to be blind.
The crime remains secret, A stained conscience Is washed by time's passing.
Poppea, I kill you!
Farewell, love.

**AMOR:** Miserable creature!
Enemy of my realm.
I should kill you But you do not deserve To die by the hand Of a god.
You may go free From my sharp ar-

Libero va da questi strali acuti . . .
Non tolgo ai manigoldi i lor tributi.

**POPPEA:** Drusilla in questro modo con l'armi ignude in mano mentre nel giardin dorma soletta?

**ARNALTA:** Accorete, o servi, o damigelle!
Inseguite Drusilla.
Dallì, dallì!
Tanto mostro a ferir non sia chi falli.

**AMOR:** Ho difeso Poppea.
Vò farla imperatrice.

# ■ ATTO III

**DRUSILLA:** O felice Drusilla! O che sper'io?
Corre adesso per me l'hora fatale.
Perirà la mia rivale e Otton finalmente sarà mio.
Se le mie vesti havran servito a ben coprirlo, con vostra pace, o dei, adorar io vorrò gli arnesi miei.

**ARNALTA:** Ecco la scellerata che, pensando occultarsi, di vesti s'è mutata.

**LITTORE:** Fermati!
Morta sei!

**DRUSILLA:** Qual peccato mi conduce a morte?

**LITTORE:** Ancor t'infingi sanguinaria indegna?
A Poppea dormiente macchinasti la morte.

**DRUSILLA:** Ahi, caro amico, sorte, sorte, Ahi, mie vesti innocenti.
Di me dolermi deggio e non d'altrui.
Credula troppo e troppo incauta fui.

**ARNALTA:** Signor, ecco la rea che trafigger tentò la matrona Poppea.
Dormiva l'innocente nel suo proprio giardino, sopragiunse costei col ferro ignudo; se non si risvegliava la tua devota ancella sopra di lei scendava il colpo crudo.

**NERONE:** Onde tanto ardimento?
E chi t'indusse, rubella, al tradimento?

**DRUSILLA:** Innocente son io, Lo sa la mia coscienza e lo sa Dio.

**NERONE:** No!
Confessa homai s'attendesti per odio o se ti spinse autorità o l'oro al gran misfatto.
Flagelli, funi e fuochi cavino da costei il mandante e i correi.
Prima ch'aspri tormenti ti facciano sentir il mio disdegno o persuadi all'ostinato ingegno di confessar gli orditi tradimenti.

**DRUSILLA:** Signor, io fui la rea che uccider volli l'innocente Poppea.

rows . . .
You will be killed By unclean hands.

**POPPEA:** Drusilla, in such guise, Sword in hand, While I sleep alone In the garden?

**ARNALDA:** Run, servants, Ladies, run!
Follow Drusilla.
There, there!
Arrest the terrible monster Without fail.

**AMOR:** I have saved Poppea.
I shall make her empress.

# ■ ACT III

**DRUSILLA:** Fortunate Drusilla! How I hope.
Now is the fatal hour When my rival dies And Ottone will be mine.
If my garments Have helped him In his undertaking I shall worship them.

**ARNALDA:** Here is the villain.
She changed her clothes To flee and hide.

**OFFICER:** Stay! you shall die!

**DRUSILLA:** For what crime Am I to die?

**OFFICER:** Miserable girl, You dare pretend?
You tried to kill Poppea.

**DRUSILLA:** O dear friend!
I have been given away by my clothes.
I must blame nobody But myself.
I lack cunning.

**ARNALDA:** There is the criminal Who tried to kill The innocent Poppea.
She was sleeping In the garden, When this woman Suddenly entered.
If she had not a awoken She would have died By this sword.

**NERO:** Whence this courage?
Who has driven you To such treason?

**DRUSILLA:** I am innocent, As God and my Conscience know.

**NERO:** No! Confess If you thought of the crime Either by hate or for money Or were driven by some power.
Extract from her with Whips, ropes and fire The name of her accomplice.
Confess before You feel my rage By torture.
Do not be stubborn.

**DRUSILLA:** I am the criminal Who wished to kill Innocent Poppea.

**NERONE:** Conducete costei al carnefice homai.
Fate ch'ei ritrovi con una morte a tempo qualche lunga amarissima agonia, ch'in difficile forme inasprisca la morte a questa rea.

**DRUSILLA:** Adorato mio bene!
Amami anche sepolta e sul sepolcro mio mandino gli occhi tuoi una sol volta, do le fonti del core, lagrime die pietà se non d'amore.
Ch'io vada, fida amica e vera amante, fra i manigoldi irati a coprir col mio sangue i tuoi peccati.

**NERONE:** Che si tarda, o ministri?
Con una atroce fine provi costei mille morti hoggimai, mille ruine.

**OTTONE:** No, no!
Questra sentenza cada sopre di me che ne son degno.

**DRUSILLA:** Io fui la rea ch'uccider volli l'innocente Poppea.

**OTTONE:** Innocente è costei Io, con le vesti di Drusilla andai, per ordine d'Ottavia l'imperatrice, ad attentar la morte di Poppea.
Dammi, o signor, con la tua man la morte.

**DRUSILLA:** Io fui la rea.

**OTTONE:** Giove, Nemesi, Astrea fulminate il mio capo chè per guista vendetta il patibolo a me s'aspetta.

**DRUSILLA:** A me.

**OTTONE:** A me.

**DRUSILLA:** A me s'aspetta.

**OTTONE:** Dammi, o signor, con la tuo man la morte.

**NERONE:** Vivi!
Ma va ne' più remoti deserti di titoli spogliato e di fortuna e serva a te mendico e derelitto di flagella e spelonca il tuo delitto.
(*To Drusilla*) E tu che ardisti tanto, o nobile matrona, per ricoprir costui d'apportar salutifere bugie, vivi alla fama della mia clemenza, vivi alla gloria della tua fortezza, e sia del sesso tuo nel secol nostro la tua costanza un adorabil mostro.

**DRUSILLA:** In esilio con lui, deh, signor, consenti ch'io tragga i giorni ridenti.

**NERONE:** Vanne, come ti piace.

**DRUSILLA:** Ch'io viva o mora teco; altro non voglio.
Dono alla mia fortuna tutto ciò che mi diede pur che tu riconosca in cor di donna una costante fede.

**NERONE:** Delibero e rosolvo con editto solenne il ripudio d'Ottavia e, con perpetuo esilio de Roma io la proscrivo.
Mandisi Ottavia al più vincino lido, le si appresti in un momento qualche spalmato legno e sia

**NERO:** Take her to the scaffold.
Discover a refined way Of killing her, To make the criminal's Death more terrible.

**DRUSILLA:** O my beloved!
Love me still When I am dead.
May your tears Fall on my grave If only once, Tears of pity If not remorse.
As your true and faithful love I will cover your sins With my blood, at the hands Of the torturers.

**NERO:** What are you waiting for?
Take her to her death, To ruin and a thousand Deaths.

**OTTONE:** No
Thus fury fall on me Who deserves it.

**DRUSILLA:** I am guilty.
I wanted to kill Poppea.

**OTTONE:** She is innocent.
It is I, with these clothes, Who went to kill Poppea At the order of the Empress Octavia.
Sire, Kill me with your own hands.

**DRUSILLA:** I am guilty.

**OTTONE:** Jupiter, Nemesi, Astra, Strike me down.
Because for just vengeance The gallows await me.

**DRUSILLA:** No, I.

**OTTONE:** No, I.

**DRUSILLA:** They wait for me.

**OTTONE:** Kill me, my lord, With your own hands.

**NERO:** Then live!
But hence To distant deserts, Shorn of your titles.
A lonely beggar, that is Your punishment.
(*to Drusilla*)
And you, noble matron, Who dared so much To shield and free him, Live also, in memory Of my clemency And may your loyalty Be proof of the nobility Of the women Of this century

**DRUSILLA:** Allow me to live With him in exile, Allow me those happy days.

**NERO:** Go then, as you wish.

**DRUSILLA:** With you to live or die Is all I ask for.
I give back to Fortune All she has given me.
If only you admit The constancy of my heart.

**NERO:** I decree and resolve, With solemn edict That Octavia is repudiated And banished forever From Rome.
May she be taken To the nearest shore, A boat be prepared And set adrift At the mercy of the winds.

commessa al bersaglio dei venti.
Convengo giustamente risentirmi.
Volate ad ubbidirmi. (*The Palace of Nero*)

**POPPEA:** Signor, hoggi rinasco ad primi fiori di questa nova vita.
Voglio che sian sospiri che ti faccian sicuro che, rinata, per te languisco e moro e, vivendo e morendo ogn'hor t'adoro.

**NERONE:** Hoggi, come promisi, mia sposa tu sarai.

**POPPEA:** Si caro dì veder non speravo mai.
giunto è pur l'hora che del mio ben godrò.

**NERONE:** Non più s'interporrà noia o dimora.

**A DUE:** Cor nel petto non ho. me l'rubasti
Dal cor me lo rapi de'tuoi begli occhi un lucido sereno.
Per te, ben mio, non ho più core in seno.
Stringimi fra le braccia innamorate, Non interotte havrai l'hore beate.

**POPPEA:** Se ben in te perduta, in te mi troverò.

**NERONE:** E tornerò riperdermi, ben mio, che sempre in te perduto mi troverò.

**OTTAVIA:** A Dio, Roma!
A Dio, partia!
Innocente, da voi partir conviene, Vado a patir l'esilio, in pianti amari. navigo disperata i sordi mari.
L'aria che, d'hora in hora, riceverà i miei fiati, li porterà per nome del cor mio a veder, a baciar le pattie mura ed iio starò solinga alternando le mosse ai pianti, ai passi insegnando pietade ai freddi sassi.
Denigrate hoggimai, perverse genti allontanandomi dagli amati lidi.
Ahi!
Sacrilego duol, tu m'interdici il pianto quando lascio la partia.
Ne stillar una lagrime poss'io mentre dico a parenti a Roma A Dio!

**NERONE:** Ascendi, mia diletta alla suprema altezza, all'apice sublime!
Blandita dalle glorie ch'ambiscono servirti come ancelle, acclamata dal mondo e dalle stelle.
Siano del tuo trionfo tra i più cari trofei, adorata Poppea, gli affetti miei.

**POPPEA:** Il mio genio confuso al non usato lume quasi perde il costume, signor, di ringraziarti.
Su quest'eccelse cime ove mi collocasti per venerarti appieno io non ho cor che basti.
Doveva la natura al soprapiù degli eccessivi affetti un core a parte fabbricar ne' petti.

My sentiments are justified, Hasten to obey me.
(*The Palace of Nero*)

**POPPEA:** My lord, today I am reborn With the first flowers Of this new life.
I want my sighs To assure you that being Reborn for you, I languish and die and That living and dying I adore you.

**NERO:** As I promised, Today you will be my wife.

**POPPEA:** I did not expect To see so great a day.
Idol of my heart, The moment is come When I shall really live.

**NERO:** We must wait no longer.

**BOTH:** I have no more heart In my breast.
You have stolen it. The serenity of your Eyes has taken it From me.
Take me in your arms My love, The time of happiness Will never end.

**POPPEA:** I shall always be lost In love for you.

**NERO:** And I shall always, O my dear, be lost In love for you.

**OCTAVIA:** Farewell, Rome!
Farewell, my country!
Innocent I take my leave In bitter tears, To wander hopelessly On the boundless Sea.
The wind which every hour Will catch my sighs,
Will carry them back To the walls of my city.
And I shall be alone In sadness and wandering Even the stones Will take pity on me.
Wretched creatures, To drive me From my own Beloved land.
Sacrilegious grief Prevents my weeping.
I cannot shed a single tear In taking leave of my family And of Rome.
O Rome, farewell!

**NERO:** (*ascending the throne*) Ascend, my love, To the greatest height.
Protected by glory, Eager to serve you And acclaimed by the earth And the stars.
May my love be The dearest prize Of your triumph, Beloved poppea.

**POPPEA:** My mind, confused By the brilliance of the light Knows not how to thank you.
At the height To which you have raised me I am too abashed To express my devotion.
Nature should have Given us a special heart To answer so great a joy.

# Act III

**NERONE:** Per capirti negli occhi Il sol s'impiccioli per albergarti in seno l'alba dal ciel partì e, per farti sovrana a donne e dee,
Giove nel tuo bel volto stillò le stelle e consumò l'dee.

**POPPEA:** Dà licenza a mio spirto ch'esca dall'amoroso labirinto di tanta lodi e tante e che s'umilii a te come conviene, mio re, mio sposo, mio signor, mio beno.

**NERONE:** Ecco vengono i consoli e tribuni a riverirti, o cara.
Nel solo rimirarti, il popolo e 'l senato homai comincia a divenir beato.

**CONSOLI E TRIBUNI:** Te sovrana augusta, con il consenso universal di Roma indiademiam la chioma.
A te l'Asia e l'Africa s'atterrra,

A te l'Europa e il mar che cinge e serra quest'imperio felice hora consacra e dona questa del mondo imperial corona.

**POPPEA:** Pur ti miro!

**NERONE:** Pur ti godo!

**POPPEA:** Pur ti stringo!

**NERONE:** Pur t'annodo!

**POPPEA:** Più non peno!

**NERONE:** Più non moro!

**POPPEA:** O mia vita!

**NERONE:** O mio tesoro!

**POPPEA:** Io son tua!

**NERONE:** Tuo son io!

**A DUE:** O mia vita, mio tesoro!

*FINE*

---

**NERO:** The sun has left the sky To enter into your eyes, The dawn has left heaven To whiten your breasts. And to make you queen Of women and goddesses, Jupiter has awarded you The ideal of beauty.

**POPPEA:** Let me emerge From the labyrinth Of your praise, To prostrate myself At your feet, My king, my spouse.

**NERO:** Here come the consuls And the tribunes To praise you.
The people and the senate Consider themselves blessed Just by seeing you.

**CONSULS AND TRIBUNES:** August sovereign, With the universal Consent of Rome We crown you. Asia and Africa Bow before you.

Europe and the sea That surrounds This happy empire Award you The imperial crown.

**POPPEA:** I gaze at you.

**NERO:** I rejoice in you.

**POPPEA:** I hold you.

**NERO:** I bind myself to you.

**POPPEA:** No more suffering.

**NERO:** No more death.

**POPPEA:** My love.

**NERO:** My treasure.

**POPPEA:** I am yours.

**NERO:** And I yours.

**TOGETHER:** O life, o love.

*THE END*

# Le Nozze di Figaro (1786)

## The Marriage of Figaro

MUSIC BY WOLFGANG AMADEUS MOZART ■ LIBRETTO BY LORENZO DA PONTE

Le Nozze di Figaro, set to a libretto by Lorenzo Dan Ponte, is based on the second play in a trilogy by Pierre Augustin Caron de Beaumarchais. Mozart himself conducted the premiere of this masterpiece of opera buffo on May 1, 1786, at the Burgtheatre in Vienna. The opera, in four acts, opens on Figaro (formerly a barber — see Il Barbiere di Siviglia) and his bride-to-be Susanna, both servants of Count Almaviva and his wife Rosina, who are measuring the room the Count has given them. The Count flirts with Susanna; meanwhile, Dr. Bartolo, who bears a grudge against Figaro, discovers that Figaro has promised to marry the elderly Marcellina in repayment for a debt. Cherubino, an adolescent page (performed by a soprano or mezzo-soprano) is in love with the Countess, who laments the loss of her husband's love. Susanna and the Countess lament together, and Figaro lets them in on his plot to help the Countess win back the Count's affections—by letting the Count think that Cherubino is the Countess' lover! Figaro and Susanna are preparing to get married when, amongst other twists and turns in this marvelous plot, Marcellina and her lawyer enter and demand that Figaro marry her! Later it is discovered that Figaro, who has a particular birthmark, is Marcellina's and Bartolo's long-lost son. The never-ending intrigue continues throughout this beautiful opera, which concludes with the Countess forgiving the Count (and all of the couples back together with their rightful partners).

---

## ■ ATTO I

### SCENA I

*Oumera quasi smobiliata con un seggiolone nel mezzo.)*

*Figaro sta misurando con una canna il pavimento per lungo e per largo. Susanna si aggiusta davanti uno specchio un cappellino in testa.*

**FIG:** Cinque—dieci-venti—trenta—
Trantasei—quarantatre—

**SUS:** Ora si ch' io son contenta,
Sembra fatto inver per me.

**FIG:** Cinque—dieci—&c.
(*come sopra.*)

**SUS:** Guarda un po', mio caro Figaro,
Guarda adesso il mio cappello.

**FIG:** Sì, mio core, ora è più bello,
Sembra fatto inver per te.

**FIG & SUS:** Ah! il mattino alle nozze vicino,
Quanto è dole al mio, tuo tenero sposo
Questo bel cappellino vezzoso,
Che Suanna ella stessa si fe!

**SUS:** Cosa stai misurando,
Caro il mi mio Figaretto?

**FIG:** Io guardo se quel lettò,
Che ci destina il Conte,
Farà buona figura in questo loco,

**SUS:** In questa stanza!

## ■ ACT I

### SCENE I

*A half-furnished room, with a large arm-chair in the middle.*

*(Figaro measuring the length and breadth of the floor with a rod; Susanna is putting on a little hat before a glass.)*

**FIG:** Five—ten—twenty—thirty—
Thirty-six, and forty-three—

**SUS:** Now, indeed, I feel quite happy,
It seems truly made for me

**FIG:** Five—ten, etc.
(*as above.*)

**SUS:** Just look, my dearest Figaro,
Look at this new hat of mine.

**FIG:** Yes, my love, it is now finer:
It seems truly made for you.

**FIG & SUS:** Ah! how nice on the morn of the marriage,
Ah! how nice for (my/your) tender sweet love
This charming and pretty little hat,
Which was made by Susanna herself.

**SUS:** My dear little Figaro, what are you measuring?

**FIG:** I am looking whether the bed the Count intends for us will look well here.

**SUS:** In this room?

**FIG:** Certo! a noi la cede
Generoso il padrone.

**SUS:** Io per me te la dono.

**FIG:** Io non capisco
Perchè tanto ti spiace
La più comoda stanza del palazzo.

**SUS:** Perch' io son la Susanna, e tu sei pazzo.

**FIG:** Grazie!—non tanti elogi!
Guarda un poco
Se potria meglio stare in altro loco.
Se a caso Madama
La notte ti chiama:
Din—din—in due passi
Da quella quoi gir.
Vien poi l' occasione,
Che vuolmi il padrone:
Don—don—in tre alti
Io vado a servir.

**SUS:** Così se il mattino (*ironica.*)
Il caro Contino
Din—din—din—ti manda
Tre miglia lontan,
Don—don—allo porta
Il diavol lo porta,
Ed ecco in tre salti—

**FIG:** Susanna, pian pian!

**SUS:** Ascolta—

**FIG:** Fa presto.

**SUS:** Se udir brami il resto,
Discaccia i sospetti
Che torto mi fan.

**FIG:** Udir bramo il resto,
I dubbj, i sospetti
Gelare mi fan.

**SUS:** Or bene, ascolta, e taci.

**FIG:** Certainly! our master generously gives it up to us.

**SUS:** I don't care for it.

**FIG:** I do not understand why you dislike the most convenient room in the castle.

**SUS:** Because I am Susanna, and you are mad.

**FIG:** Thanks! not so many compliments! See then if it could be better somewhere else.
If Madame by chance
Calls you in the night—
Ding—ding—in two steps,
You may go that way.
Should master require me,
Dong—dong—in three jumps,
I wait upon him.

**SUS:** So, if in the morning
(*ironically*)
The dear charming Count,
Ding, ding, ding, sends you
Three miles far away,
Dong, dong, and the devil
Brings him at the door,
And then in three jumps—

**FIG:** Gently, gently, Susanna.

**SUS:** Hear me—

**FIG:** Hurry.

**SUS:** The rest you would hear,
Drive away your suspicions,
For they wrong me.

**FIG:** I wish to hear the rest;
The doubts and suspicions,
They chill my blood.

**SUS:** Well, then, listen, and be silent.

## Act I, Scene I

FIG: Parla, che c'è di nuovo?

SUS: Il signor Conte,
Stanco d' andar cacciando
Le straniere bellezze,
Vuole ancor nel castello
Ritentar la sua sorte;
Ne già di sua consorte, bada bene,
Appetito gli viene.

FIG: E di chi dunque?

SUS: Della tua Susannetta.

FIG: Di te?

SUS: Di me medesma. E tu credevi,
Che fosse la mia dote
Merto del tuo bel viso?

FIG: Me n' ero lusingato,
(suona un campanello.)
Chi suona!—la Contessa.

SUS: Addio, Figaro bello.

FIG: Coraggio, mio tesoro.

SUS: E tu cervello!
(parte.)

FIG: Bravo, signor padrone! Ora incomincio
A capire il mistero, e vede schietto
Tutto il vostro progetto—A Londra, è vero?
Voi ministro, io corriero; e la Susanna
Secreta ambasciatrice!—
Non sarà—non sarà, Figaro il dice.
Se vuol ballare, signor Contino,
Il chitarrino le suonerò.
Se vuol venire nella mia scuola,
La capriolo le insegnerò.
Saprò ma piano—meglio ogni arcano
Dissimulando scoprir potrò.
L' arte schermendo, l' arte adoprando,
Di quà pusando, di là scherzando,
Tuttu le macchine rovescero.
(parte.)

### SCENA II

Bartolo e Marcellina con un contratto in mano.

BAR: Ed aspettate i giorno
Fissato per le nozze
A parlarmi di questo?

MAR: Io non mi perdo,
Dottor mio, di coraggio.
Per romper dei sponsali
Più avanzati di questo
Bastò spesso un pretesto. Ed egli ha meco,
Oltre questo contratto,
Certi impegni—so io —basta—conviene
La Susanna atterrir, convien con arte
Impuntigliarla a rifiutare il Conte.
Egli, per vendicarsi,
Prenderà il mio partito,
E Figaro così fia mio marito.

BAR: Bene, io tutto farò: senza riserva
Tutto a me palesate. (Avrei pur gusto
Di dare in moglie la mia serva antica

---

FIG: Speak, what is the matter?

SUS: My lord Count, tired with seeking strange beauties, wishes again to try his chance in the castle; but mind well, he does not feel inclined toward his wife.

FIG: Towards whom, then?

SUS: Towards your dear Susanna.

FIG: Towards you?

SUS: Me! And you thought that my portion was for your sweet sake.

FIG: I flattered myself so.
(a bell rings.)
Who rings? the Countess.

SUS: Adieu, my pretty Figaro.

FIG: Cheer up, my lovely.

SUS: And you have sense!
(exit.)

FIG: Well done, my Lord! now I begin to understand the mystery, and see too plainly all your schemes. To London, it is true? You minister, I messenger; and Susanna secret ambassadress.
It shan't be; Figaro says so.
If my dear Count wishes to dance,
I shall play the guitar for you.
If you will come to learn about me,
I will teach you to caper about.
I shall know—softly; better shall learn
Dissimulating every secret.
Foiling art, by using art,
Now in right earnest, then in joking;
I shall surely spoil their plans.
(exit.)

### SCENE II

Bartolo and Marcellina with a written agreement in her hand.

BAR: And you waited until the day appointed for the wedding, to speak to me about this?

MAR: My dear doctor, I do not lose courage. Often a mere pretense has been enough to break off matches in a more forward state than this. And he has with me, besides this agreement, certain engagements. I know—well—we must terrify Susanna; we must cleverly pique her, that she may refuse the Count; then, in order to be revenged, he will take my part, and so Figaro will be my husband.

BAR: Well, I shall do all: let me know every thing without reserve. (I should be delighted if I could give my old servant in marriage to one who has made me lose my

---

A chi mi fece un dì rapir l' amica.)
(La vendetta—oh! la vendetta
E un piacer serbato ai saggi
L' obbliar l' onte, gli oltraggi
È bassezza, è ognor viltà.)
Coll' astuzia, coll' arguzia,
Col giudizio, col criterio
Si potrebbe—il fatto è serio!
Ma credete si farà.
Se tutto il codice dovessi volgere,
Se tutto l' indice dovessi leggere,
Con un equivoco, con un sinonimo
Qualche garbuglio si troverà.
Tutta Siviglia conosce Bartolo,
Il furbo Figaro vinto sara.

### SCENA III

Marcellina; indi Susannna, con una cuffia da notee, ed un nastro in mano, ed una vesta da camera sui braccio.

MAR: Tutto ancor non ho perso,
Mi resta la speranza;
Ma Susanna s' avanza—io vo' provarmi—
Fingiam di non vederla.
E quella buona perloa
La vorrebbe sposar.

SUS: (Di me favella.)

MAR: Ma da Figaro, alfine,
Non può meglio sperarsi: argent fait tout!

SUS: Che lingua! manco male
Che ognun sa quanto vale!

MAR: Brava! questo è giudizio!
Con quegli occi modesti,
Con quell' arla pietosa!
E poi—

SUS: Meglio è partir.

MAR: Che cara sposa!
(troniche a chi parte la prima)
Via resti servita, madama brillante.

SUS: Non sono sì ardita, madama piccante.

MAR: No, prima a lei tocca.

SUS: No, no, tocc' a lei

MAR & SUS: Io so i dover miel non fo incivilità.

MAR: La sposa novella,
Del Conte ia bella,
I meriti, il posto—
Per Bacco! precipito
Se ancor resto quà.

SUS: La donna d' onore,
Di Spagna l' amore,
Stimabile età!
Sibilla decrepita
Da rider mi fa!
(Marc. parte)

### SCENA IV

Susanna, poi Cherubino.

---

sweetheart.)
(Oh! revenge! Oh! yes; revenge
Is a pleasure for the wise;
To forget affronts and insults,
Is both cowardly and base:
With both pleasantry and cunning,
With good sense and judgment too.
One might do it. The affair is serious
But, believe me, I'll succeed.
If all the code I ought to turn,
If all the index I ought to read
With an equivoque or synonym;
I'll create some great confusion.
Well all Seviglia Don Bartolo knows;
The cunning Figaro shall be quite foiled.
(exit.)

### SCENE III

Marcellina; then Susanna, with a night-cap and a ribbon in her hand, and a dressing-gown on her arm.

MAR: I have not lost all, I still have hopes left; but Susanna is coming—I will try—let me pretend not to see her. To think my sweet creature wishes to marry her.

SUS: (She speaks of me.)

MAR: However, nothing better can be expected from Figaro—"Money does everything."

SUS: What a tongue! luckily every one knows what it is worth!

MAR: Well said! that is sensible! with those modest eyes, that pious look! And then—

SUS: I had better go.

MAR: What a charming bride!
(ironically, both watching who goes first.)
Pray walk ahead, my grand lady.

SUS: I am not so bold, my pert lady.

MAR: No, you, madam, must go first.

SUS: No, no, you, madam.

MAR & SUS: I know good breeding, and never commit an incivility!

MAR: The young new-made bride,
The Count's own fair choice,
The great worth and station,
By Jove I shall lose,
If I stay here any longer.

SUS: The woman of honor,
The love of all Spain!
O respectable age!
The stupid old sybil!
I must indeed laugh!
(exit Mar.)

### SCENE IV

Susanna, then Cherubino.

---

SUS: Va là vecchia pedante,
Dottoressa arrogante.
(*Vien Cherubino.*)

CHE: Susannetta sei tu?

SUS: Son io, coa volete?

CHE: Ah! cor mio, che accidente!

SUS: Cor vostro! cos' avvenne?

CHE: Il Conte ieri,
Perchè trovommi sol con Barberina
Il congedo mi diede:
E se la Contessina,
La mia bella comare,
Grazia non m'intercede, io vado via,
Io nen ti vedo più, Susanna mia.

SUS: Non vedete più me? Bravo! ma dunque
Non più per la Contessa
Segretamente il vostro cor sospira?
(*Cher. sospira.*)

CHE: Cos, hai lì? dimmi un poco.

SUS: Ah! il vago nastro, e la notturna cuffia
Di comare sì bella!

CHE: Deh dammelo, sorella—
(*vuol prenderle il nastro, Sus. si schermisce.*)
Dammelo per pietà.
(*la raggiunge, e glielo strappa di mano.*)

SUS: Presto quel nastro.

CHE: Eh via, via! sta cheta;
In ricompensa poi
Questa mia canzonetta io ti vo dare.
(*cava di tasca un foglio.*)

SUS: E che ne debbo fare?
(*glielo strappa di mano.*)

CHE: Leggila alla padrona,
Leggila tu medesma,
Leggila a Barberina, a Marcellina,
Leggila ad ogni donna del Palazzo.

SUS: Povero Cherubin, siete vio pazzo?

CHE: Non so più cosa son, cosa faccio,
Or di fuocco, ora son ghiaccio;
Ogni donna cangiar di colore,
Ogni donna mi fa palpitar.
Solo ai nomi di' amore, e diletto,
Mi si turba, mi s' altera il petto,
E a parlare mi forza d' amore
Un desio che non posso spiegar.
Parlo d' amor vegliando,
Parlo d' amor dormendo,
All' acqua, all ombra, ai monti,
Ai fiori, all' erbe, ai fonti,
All' eco, ail' aria, ai venti,
Che il suon de' miei lamenti
Portano via con se.
E se non ho chi m' oda,
Parlo d' amor con me.

---

SUS: Go along, pedantic old woman, proud prattler!
(*Enter Cherubino.*)

CHE: My pretty Susanna, is it you?

SUS: Yes, what do you want?

CHE: O my dear! what an accident!

SUS: Your dear? what has happened?

CHE: Because yesterday the Count found me alone with Barberina, he gave me warning; and if the dear Countess, my pretty godmother, does not obtain my pardon, I must go; I shall see you no more, my Susan.

SUS: You see me no more! well done. Then you no longer sigh secretly for the Countess?
(*Cher. sighs.*)

CHE: What have you got there? tell me now.

SUS: Ah! the beautiful ribbon and night-cap of such a pretty godmother.
(*mimicking him.*)

CHE: Pray, sister, give it me!
(*tries to take the ribbon from her. Sus. defends herself.*)
Give it to me for mercy's sake?
(*overtakes her, and snatches it out of her hand.*)

SUS: Quick, here, that ribbon.

CHE: Come, come, be quiet. In return I will give you my little song that you see here.
(*pulls a paper from his pocket.*)

SUS: Well, what am I to do with it?
(*snatches it from him.*)

CHE: Read it to my lady, read it yourself, read it to Barberina, to Marcellina, read it to all the women in the castle.

SUS: Poor Cherubino, are you mad?

CHE: Who I am, what I do, I know not,
I am now all on fire, then all ice;
Every woman I see makes me blush,
Every woman quite makes my heart throb,
The mere mention of love or delight
Both disturbs and unsettles my heart.
A desire that I can not explain
Of affection compels me to speak.
I speak of love awake,
I speak of love in sleep,
To water, shades, and hills,
To flowers, herbs, and fountains,
To echo, air, and winds,
Which bear along with them
The sounds of my laments.
And if no one hears me, I speak of love to myself.

## SCENA V

*Detti: poi Il Conte; indi Basilio.*

SUS: Taci, vien gente—il Conte! oh! me meschina!
(*Cher. si nasconde nietro il seggiolone; e viene Il Conte.*)

IL C: Susanna, tu mi sembri
Agitata e confusa.
(*siede sul seggiolone.*)

SUS: Signor—io chiedo scusa—
Ma se mai qui sorpresa—
Per carità partite

IL C: Un momento e ti lascio:
Odi.

SUS: Non odo nulla.

IL C: Due parole: tu sai,
Che ambasciatore a Londra
Il Re mi dischiarò; di condur meco
Figaro destinai—

SUS: Signor—se osassi—

IL C: Parla parla, mia cara; e con quel dritto,
Ch' oggi prendi su me, fin che tu vivi,
Chiedi, imponi, prescrivi—
(*Bas. di dentro.*)

BAS: È uscito poco fa.

IL C: Chi parla?

SUS: O Dei!
(*Il Con. si alza.*)

IL C: Esci, ed alcun non enri.

SUS: Ch' io vi lasci quì—solo?
(*turbata*)

BAS: Da madama sarà; vado a cercarlo.
(*di dentro.*)

IL C: Quì dietro mi porrò.

SUS: Non vi celate.

IL C: Taci, e cerca ch' ei parta.

SUS: Ohimè! che fate?

*Il Con. va a celarsi dietro il seggiolone; ma Sus. sì pone destramente avanti di lui; e fa cenni a Cher. il quale gira lestamente quasi carpone, e si getta rannicchiato nel seggiolone. Sus. lo copre colla vesta, che ha recata. Vien Bas. .*

BAS: Susanna, il ciel vi salvi; avreste a caso
Veduto il Conte?

SUS: E cosa
(*arrabbiata.*) Deve far meco il Conte? Animo, uscite.

BAS: Aspettate, sentite—
(*lo spinge fuori.*)
Figaro di lui cerca.

## SCENE V

*The same, then The Count; afterwards Basilio.*

SUS: Hush! some body comes—the Count! O wretched me!
(*Che. conceals himself behind the great chair, and the Count enters.*)

COUNT: Susanna, you seem agitated and confused.
(*sits down in the great chair.*)

SUS: Sir—I beg pardon—but if I should be surprised here? For mercy's sake, go!

COUNT: One moment and I quit you—hear me.

SUS: I will hear nothing.

COUNT: Two words—You know that the King has named me for ambassador at London; I intend to take Figaro with me.

SUS: Sir—if—

COUNT: Speak, speak, my dear; and with the right which you take over me, as long as you live. ask, order, direct.

BAS: (*from within.*) He has just gone out.

COUNT: Who speaks?

SUS: O gods!
(*Count. rises.*)

COUNT: Go, and let no one come in.

SUS: What! Leave you here—alone?
(*troubled.*)

BAS: Perhaps he is with my Lady, I will go and look for him.
(*from within.*)

COUNT: I will put myself here, behind.

SUS: Do not conceal yourself.

COUNT: Hush! and try to send him away.

SUS: Alas! what are you doing?

*Count goes to conceal himself behind the great chair, but Sus. places herself adroitly before him; makes signs to Cher. who goes cleverly round, almost on all fours, and squats down in the great chair. Sus. covers him with the gown she brought. Enter Bas.*

BAS: Susanna, heavens preserve you! have you any chance seen the Count?

SUS: And what (*vexed*) has the Count to do with me? Come, march.
(*pushes him out.*)

BAS: Stay, hear me—Figaro wants him.

**SUS:** O cielo! ei cerca
Chi, dopo voi, più l' odia.

**IL C:** (Vediam come mi servo.)

**BAS:** Io non ho mai
Nella moral sontito,
Che uno ch' ami la moglie odii il
marito.

**SUS:** Uomo maligno, un' impostura
è questa.

**BAS:** È un maligno con voi chi ha
gli occhi in testa.
E quella consonetta
(*confidente.*)
Ditemi in confidenza, io sono ami-
co,
Ad altrui nulla dico,
È per voi? per madama?

**SUS:** (Chi davol gliel' ha detto!)

**BAS:** Aproposito figlia
Cherubino si regoli;
Guarda madama a tavola sì spesso,
E con tale immodestia,
Che se il Conte s' accorage—e sul
tal punto
Sapete, egli è una bestia.

**SUS:** O scellerato! perchè andate
voi
Tai menzogne spargendo?

**BAS:** Io! ehe ingiustiza!
Io quel che compro vendo:
A quel che tutti dicono
Io non aggiungo un pelo. (*Il Con.
si leva turbato.*)

**IL C:** Come! che dicon tutti?

**BAS:** (O bello!)

**SUS:** (O cielo!)

**IL C:** Cosa sento? tosto andate
(*a Bas.*)
F scacciate il traditor.

**BAS:** (In qual punto son quì giunto!)
Perdonate, mio signor.

**SUS:** (Che ruina! me meschina!)
Sono oppressa dal dolor!
(*vaccilla fingenao.*)

**IL C, BAS:** Ah! già svien la poverina!
Come, oh Dio! le batte il cor!
(*la sostengone.*)

**BAS:** Pian pianin su questo seggio—
(*la vuol porre a sedere, Sus. lo
rispinge con forza.*)

**SUS:** Dove sono?—cosa veggio?
Che insolensa! andate fuor.

**IL C, BAS:** Siamo quì per aiutarvi,
È sicuro il vostro onor.

**BAS:** Ah! del paggio quel che ho
detto
Era solo un mio sospetto.

**SUS:** È un' insidia, una perfidia.
Non credete, è un impostor.

---

**SUS:** O heavens! he is looking for
one who hates him most, after you.

**COUNT:** (Let me see how she
serves me.)

**BAS:** I never heard in morality, that
one who loved the wife, hated the
husband.

**SUS:** Wicked man, this is a falsehood.

**BAS:** According to your opinion, a
man who is not stupid, is wicked.
And that little song (*with an air of
confidence*)—tell me as a friend,
trust to me, I shall tell it to nobody—is it for you? for Madame?

**SUS:** (Who the deuce told it him?)

**BAS:** Now I think on it, my dear
Cherubino must mind; he looks so
often at Madame when at table, and
with such impudence, that if the
Count perceives it—and upon
such a subject you know he is inexorable.

**SUS:** O the wicked man! and why do
you go about spreading such reports?

**BAS:** I! how you wrong me! I only
say what I heard
I do not add a syllable to what every
body says.
(*Count rises with a troubled
look.*)

**COUNT:** How! what does every
body say?

**BAS:** (This is a fine one.)

**SUS:** (O heavens!)

**COUNT:** What do I hear? Go quickly away, and dismiss the scoundrel!

**BAS:** (At what a moment am I arrived!)
Pray forgive me, my good sir.

**SUS:** (What disaster! woe is me!)
I am overwhelmed by grief.
(*staggers, dissembling.*)

**COUNT, BAS:** Ah! the poor creature is fainting!
Heavens, how her heart is beating.
(*they support her.*)

**BAS:** Slowly and gently on this
chair.
(*tries to place her on the chair,
Sus. pushes him vigorously
away.*)

**SUS:** Where am I? what do I see?
What impertinence! go away

**COUNT, BAS:** We are here to give
you help;
Your honor is in safety.

**BAS:** Now, what I said of the page
Was no more than my suspicion.

**SUS:** It is a falsehood, and a scandal;
Do not believe him, he is a cheat.

---

**IL C:** Parta parta il damerino.

**SUS, BAS:** Poverino! poverino!

**IL C:** Poverino! poverino!
(*ironico.*)
Ma da me sorpreso ancor. (*serio.*)

**SUS:** Come?

**BAS:** Che?

**IL C:** Da tua cugina
L' uscio ier trovai rinchiuso
Picchio; m' apre Barberina
Paurosa fuor dell' uso
Io dal muso insospettito
Guardo, cerco in ogni sito,
Ed alzando pian pianino
Il tappeto al tavolino,
Vedo il paggio—
(*alsa, in imitazione, la vesta che
copre il seggiolone, e scorpre Che-
rubino.*)
Ah! cosa veggio?

**SUS:** (rude stelle!)

**BAS:** (Ah! meglio ancora!)

**IL C:** Onestissima signora!
(*a Sus.*)
Or capisco come va!

**SUS:** (Accader non può di peggio!
Giusti Dei! che mai sarà!)

**BAS:** Così fan tutte le belle,
Non c' è alcuna muovità.
(*Cher, ch' è fin qui rimaso ranni-
chiate nel seggiolone si leva su
quasi a sedere.*)

## SCENA VI

*Detti.*

**IL C:** Basilio, in traccia tosto
Di Figaro volate; io vo' che veda—

**SUS:** Ed io che senta; andate.
(*con siourezza.*)

**IL C:** Restate: che baldanza! E quale
scusa
Se la colpa è evidente?

**SUS:** Non ha d' uopo di scusa un' innocente.

**IL C:** (O ciel!) dunque he sentito
(*a Sus.*)
Quello chi' io ti dicea?

**CHE:** Feci, per non sentir, quante
potea.

**IL C:** O perfidia!

**BAS:** Frenatevi, vien gente.

**IL C:** E voi restate quì piccol serpente?
(*prende per un braccio Cher. e lo
mette in piedi.*)

---

**COUNT:** Let the coxcomb soon depart.

**SUS, BAS:** Ah! poor fellow! Ah!
poor fellow!

**COUNT:** Ah! poor fellow! Ah! poor
fellow!
(*ironically.*)
But surprised by me, too.
(*seriously.*)

**SUS:** How?

**BAS:** What?

**COUNT:** I found the door shut at
your cousin's
I knock, Barberina opens,
And appears quite frightened;
Filled with suspicion at her looks,
I search and examine everywhere:
Then lifting the cloth from the ta-
ble,
I see the young man—
(*he lifts, as he describes, the gown
that covers the great chair, and
discovers Cherubino.*)
Ha! what do I see?

**SUS:** (Cruel stars!)

**BAS:** (Better still!)

**COUNT:** Most honest lady!
Now I see how it is!

**SUS:** (Nothing worse can happen!
Good gods, what will it be!)

**BAS:** All the fair do so;
This is nothing new.
(*Cher. who till now remained
squatted in the great chair, rises
and is almost seated.*)

## SCENE VI

*The same.*

**COUNT:** Fly, Basilio, immediately,
To fetch Figaro; I will have him
see—

**SUS:** And I, that he may hear; go.
(*with a confident air.*)

**COUNT:** Stay! What assurance! and
what excuse can you make, if the
guilt is evident?

**SUS:** Innocence wants no excuse.

**COUNT:** (O heavens! Then he has
heard all that I was saying to you?)
(*To Sus.*)

**CHE:** I did all that I could do not to
hear.

**COUNT:** O treachery!

**BAS:** Check your passion; some
body is coming.

**COUNT:** And you stay here, you little serpent?
(*takes Cher. by the arm, and
makes him stand up.*)

## SCENA VII

*Detti. Figaro, Barberina che porta in mano un cappallino ornato di piume, e nastri bianchi. Contadini, e Contadine.*

**CORÒ:** Giovanni lieti, firio spargete
Davinti al nobile nostro Signor;
Il suo gran core vi serba intatto
D' un più bel fiore l' almo candor.

**TUTTI:** Evviva?

**FIG:** E voi non applaudite?
(*a Cher, che sta affitto.*)

**SUS:** È affitto poveretta,
Perchè il padron lo scaccia dal castello

**FIG:** Ah! in un giorno sì bello!
(*al Con*)

**SUS:** In un giorno di nozze.

**FIG:** Quando ognuno vi ammira!

**CHE:** Perdono, mio signor!
(*s' inginocchia*)

**IL C:** Nol meritate.

**SUS:** Egli è ancora fanciullo.

**IL C:** Men di quel che tu credi.

**CHE:** È ver mancai; ma dal mio labbro alfine—

**IL C:** Bene ben, vi perdono;
Anzi farò di più—vacante è un posto
D' ufizial nel reggimento mio;
Io scelgo voi; partite tosto: addio.

**SUS, FIG:** Ah! fin domani sol—

**IL C:** No, parta tosto.

**CHE:** A ubbidirvi, signor, son già disposto.

**IL C:** Via per l' ultima volti
(*con ironia a Cher.*)
La Susanna abbracciate.
(*Inaspettato è il colpo.*)
(*parte con Sus.*)

**FIG:** Ehi, Capitano,
A me pure la mano. (Io vo' parlarti,
*basso a Cher.*)
Pria che tu parta;) addio,
Piccolo Cherubino;
Come cangia in un punto il tuo destino!
Non più andrai, farfallone amoroso,
Notte e giorno d' intorno girando,
Delle belle turbando il riposo,
Narcisetto, Adoncino d' amor.
Non più avrai, questi bei pennacchini,
Quel cappello leggero e galante,
Quella chioma, quell' aria brillante,
Quel vermiglio donnesco color.
Fra guerrieri, poffarbacco!
Gran mustacchi, stretto sacco,
Schioppo in spalla, spada al fianco,
Collo dritto, musco franco,
Un gran casco, un gran turbante,
Molto onor, poco contante;
Ed invece del fandango
Una morcia in mezzo al fiango.
Per montagne e per valloni,
Colle nevi, e i solleoni,
Al concerto di tromboni
Di bombarde, e di canoni,
Che le palle in tutti i tuoni
Alle orecchie fan fischiar.
Cherubino, allo vittoria,
Alla gloria militar.
(*partono tutti.*)

*FINE DELL' ATTO PRIMO*

# ■ ATTO II

## SCENA I

*Magnifica Camera con alcova da letto in fondo Allato all'alcova, alla sinistra degli attori porta practicabile di un gabinetto; dalla parte opposta finestra practicabile. A sinistra, alla quinta di mezzo, porta di entrata; dal lato opposto, all' ultima quinta, porta di un gabinetto. Varie sedia.*

*La Contessa; poi Susanna; indi Figaro.*

**LA C:** Porgi, amor, qualche ristoro
Al mia duolo, ai miei sospir:
O mi rendi il mio tesoro,
O mi lascia, almen morir!
(*siede*)
(*Vien Susanna.*)

**LA C:** Vieni, cara Susanna, Finiscimi la storia.

**SUS:** È già finata.

**LA C:** 'Dunque volea sedurti?
(*Fig. di dentro, poi esce.*)

**FIG:** Là ra, là, là

**SUS:** Eccolo: vieni, amico,
Madame è impaziente—

**FIG:** A voi non tocca.
Stare in pena per questo,
Alfin di che si tratta? Al Signor Conte
Piace la sposa mia.

**SUS:** Ed hai coraggio di trattar scherzando
Un negozio sì serio?

**FIG:** Non vi basta
Che scherzando io ci pensi! Ecco il progetto:
Per Basilio un biglietto
Io gli fo capitar, che l' avvertisca
Di certo appuntamento,
Che per l' ora dell' ballo
A un amante voi deste.

**LA C:** O ciel! che sento?
Ad un uom sì geloso?

**FIG:** Ancora meglio!
Empiendol di sospetti,
Rovesceremo tutti i suoi progetti.

## SCENE VII

*The same, then Figaro; Barberina brings a hat in her hand, ornamented with white feathers and ribbons. Countrymen and women.*

**CHORUS:** My merry youths, strew flowers about,
Before our noble and gentle lord;
His heart for you preserves the bloom,
The rarest flower of sincerity.

**ALL:** Huzza!

**FIG:** And you, don't you applaud?
(*to Che. who, looks sad.*)

**SUS:** Poor fellow! he is grieved because my lord turned him out of the castle.

**FIG:** What! on such a happy day?
(*to the Count.*)

**SUS:** On a wedding-day!

**FIG:** When every one admires you!

**CHE:** Pardon, my lord!
(*kneels.*)

**COUNT:** You do not deserve it.

**SUS:** He is yet a boy.

**COUNT:** Less than you think.

**CHE:** I erred, it is true; but at last, from my lips—

**COUNT:** Well, well, I forgive you; no, I will do more. an officer's commission is vacant in my regiment; I appoint you—set out immediately, adieu.

**SUS, FIG:** Oh! pray, only till tomorrow!

**COUNT:** No, let him set out without delay.

**CHE:** I am ready to obey you, my lord.

**COUNT:** Come, for the last time,
(*ironically to Che.*) embrace Susanna. (The blow is unexpected.)
(*exit with Sus.*)

**FIG:** Halloo, Captain; shake hands with me too. (I want to speak to you *softly to Che.*) before you go.) Adieu, my little Cherubino—how in a moment your destiny changes! You, amorous butterfly, shall no longer go
Fluttering about, day and night,
Troubling the repose of beauties—
Pretty Narcissus, little Adonis of love.
No longer will you have those pretty feathers,
That light and graceful hat,
That head of hair, that lively look,
Nor those rosy girlish cheeks.
Among warriors, by Jupiter!
Bushy whiskers and small jackets;
On your shoulder a heavy gun;
A stiff neck and bold face;
A big helmet, a large turban.
Much honor, little cash;
And, instead of the fandango,
A nice march all through the mud
Climbing mountains, crossing valleys;
Now through snow, then under heat;
To the sound of blunderbusses,
Of howitzers, and of cannon,
Which send hissing and whizzing shot
In variety about your ears.
Cherubino, haste to victory,
To the glory of the soldier.
(*exeunt all.*)

*END OF ACT I.*

# ■ ACT II

## SCENE I

*A magnificent Room, with an alcove for a bed at the bottom; close to the alcove, on the left of the Actors, a door which leads into a Closet: on the opposite side, a window that opens. On the middle side-scene, on the left, a door to come in at: opposite, at the last side-scene, the door of a Closet. Several chairs.*

*The Countess, then Susanna; afterwards Figaro.*

**COUN:** King Cupid, some consolation
To my grief and sorrows send
Ah! restore to me my love,
Or at least take away my life.
(*takes a seat.*)
(*Enter Susanna.*)

**COUN:** Come, dear Susanna, finish the story.

**SUS:** It is already finished.

**COUN:** "Then he wanted to seduce you?"
(*Fig. from within then enters.*)

**FIG:** Larà, larà.

**SUS:** Here he is; come, friend,
Madame is impatient.

**FIG:** You need not be uneasy for that:
At last, what is this about?
The Count likes my bride.

**SUS:** And have you the courage to treat
Such a serious affair as a joke?

**FIG:** Is it not enough
That I think on it joking?
Here is my scheme;
Basilio shall take a note to him from me,
To warn him of a certain appointment made by you
With some admirer for the ball.

**COUN:** Heavens! what do I hear?
To such a jealous man?

**FIG:** So much the better!
In filling him with suspicion,
We shall overthrow all his projects.

SUS: È ver, ma, in di lui vece
Si opporrà Marcellina.

SUS: It is true,
But Marcellina will oppose it.

FIG: Aspetta! Al Conte
Farai subito dir, che verso sera
Attendati in giardino;
Il picciol Chuerubino,
Per mio consiglio, non ancor parti-
to.
Da femmina vestito
Faremo che in sua vece ivi sen vada;
Questa è il unica strada
Onde monsù sorpreso de madama
Sia constretto a far poi quel che si
brama.

FIG: Stay! send word to the Count,
That towards evening
He may expect you in the garden:
Little Cherubino
Has delayed his departure by my ad-
vice,
We shall dress him in woman's
clothes,
And make him go instead;
This is the only way to get
Monsieur to be surprised by Ma-
dame,
And then compel him to do what
we want.

LA C: Che ti par?
(a Sus.)

COUN: What do you think of it?
(to Sus.)

SUS: Non c' è mal.

SUS: Not bad.

LA C: Nel nostro caso—

COUN: In our case—

SUS: Quand' egli è persuaso—E
dov' è il tempo?

SUS: If he is persuaded—
But where's the time?

FIG: Il Conte è andato a caccia, e
per qualche ora
Non sarà di ritorno. Io vado, e tosto
Cherubino vi mando. Lascio a voi
La cura di vestirlo.

FIG: The Count has gone a hunting,
And for some hours he will not be
back.
I shall go, and send
Cherubino to you soon.
I leave you to dress him.

LA C: E poi?

COUN: And then?

FIG: E poi—
Se vuol ballare,
Signor Contino,
Il chitarrino
(parte.)
Le suonerò.

FIG: And then—
If my dear lord
Wishes to dance,
I will
Play the guitar for you.
(exit.)

## SCENA II

La Contessa, e Susanna, poi Cherubino.

## SCENE II

The Countess and Susanna, then
Cherubino.

LA C: Quanto duolmi, Susanna,
Che questo giovinetto abbia del
Conte
Le stravaganze udite!—ah! tu non
sai
Ma per qual cosa mai
Da me stessa non venne?
Dov' è la canzonnetta?

COUN: How sorry I am, Susanna,
That this youth has heard
The foolish things the Count said!
Ah! you do not know—
But why then did he not come to
me?
Where is the little song?

SUS: Eccola appunto,
Facciam che la canti.
(Vien Cherubino.)
Zitto! vien gente—è desso. Avanti,
avanti,
Signor uffziale.

SUS: Here,
Let us make him sing it.
(Enter Cherubino.
Hush! some body is coming—
It is he. Come on, come on, Mr. Of-
ficer.

CHE: Ah! non chiamarmi
Con nome sì fatale; ei mi rammenta
Che abbandonar degg' io.

CHE: Ah! do not call me by so fatal a
name;
It puts me in mind that I must quit
A godmother that is so good—

SUS: E tanto bella.

SUS: And so beautiful!

CHE: Ah! sì certo!
(sospirande)

CHE: Ah! (sighing.) Yes, certainly!

SUS: Ah! si certo! (contraffacendo-
lo.) Ipocritone!
Via presto la canzone,
Che stamane a me deste,
A madama cantate.

SUS: Ah! (mimicking him.)Yes,
certainly!
Great hypocrite!
Come, be quick,
Sing the song to Madame
Which you gave me this morning.

LA C: Chi n' è l' autor?

COUN: Who wrote it?

SUS: Guardate, egli ha due braccia
Di rossor sulla faccia.

SUS: Look! the red is two feet deep
on his cheeks with blushing.

LA C: Prendi la mia chittarra, e l' accompagna.

COUN: Take my guitar, and accompany him.

CHE: Io sono sì tremante—
Ma se madama vuole—

CHE: I am trembling all over;
But if Madame chooses—

SUS: Io canterò per te, poche pa-
role.
Voi che sapete—che cos' è amor,
Donne vedete—s' io l' ho nel cor.
Quello ch' io provo—a voi dirò,
È per me nuovo—capir nol so.
Sento un affetto—pien di desir,
Ch' ora è diletto—ora è martir,
Gelo, e poi sento—l' alma avvam-
par,
E in un momento—torno a gelar.
Ricerco un bene—fuori di me,
Non so ch' il tiene—non so cos' è.
Sospiro, e gemo—senza voler.
Palpito e tremo—senza saper.
Mon trovo pace—notte nè di;
Eppur mi piace—languir così.

SUS: I shall sing for you, that's
enough.
You who know what is love,
Ladies, see if it is in my heart.
What I feel I shall now tell,
It is new to me, I can not under-
stand it.
I feel a passion, full of desire,
Which now delights and then tor-
ments.
Now I am frozen and then all flame
And in an instant am frozen again.
I seek for happiness which is not in
me,
I know not who possesses it;
I sigh, lament without desire;
My heart does beat, I know not why.
I find no peace by night nor day,
Yet I am pleased to languish thus.

LA C: Bravo! che bella cosa! io non
sapea
Che scrivesse sì bene.

COUN: Well done! What a pretty
thing!
I did not know he could write so
well.

SUS: Oh! in verità
Egli fa bege tutto quel che fa.
Presto, a noi, bel soldato:
Figaro v' informò—

SUS: Oh! indeed, he does well all
that he does.
Quick, come here my pretty soldier.
Figaro told you—

CHE: Tutto mi disse.

CHE: All.

SUS: Lasciatemi vedere—andrà
benissimo;
(osservando Cher.)
Siamo d' egual strature. Giù quel
manto.
(gli leva il manto.)

SUS: Let me see—it will go very
right.
(observing Che.)
We are of the same height.
Down with that cloak.
(takes his cloak off.)

LA C: Che fai?

COUN: What are you doing?

SUS: Niente paura.

SUS: Fear nothing.

LA C: E se qualcuno entrasse?—

COUN: And if some body were to
come in?—

SUS: Entri, che mal facciamo?
(va a chiuder la porta.)
La porta chiuderò; ma come poi
Acconciargli la testa?

SUS: Well, what harm?
(goes to shut the door.)
I shall shut the door;
But how shall his hair be dressed?

LA C: Una mia cuffia,
Presto—che carta è quella?

COUN: One of my caps;
Quick—what paper is that?

CHE: La patente,
(Sus. entra nel gabinetto; La
Cont. prende la cara, e la guar-
da.)

CHE: The commission.
(Sus. goes to the closet; the Coun.
takes the paper and looks at it.)

LA C: Che sollecita gente!

COUN: How active they have been!

CHE: L' ebbi or or da Basilio.

CHE: I just now had it from Basilio.

LA C: Dalla fratta obbliato hanno il
sigillo.
(torna Sus. con una cuffia; La
Cont. rende le la patente a Cher.)

COUN: In their haste they forgot
the seal.
(Sus. returns with a cap; the
Coun. gives back Che. his commission.)

SUS: Il sigillo di che?

SUS: The seal of what?

LA C: Della patente.

COUN: Of the commission.

SUS: Cospetto, che premura!
Ecco la cuffia.

SUS: Indeed! what haste!
Here is the cap.

LA C: Spicciati—va bene;
Oh! disgraziati noi se il Conte
viene.
(*Sus. siede vicino alla Cont.; Che.
se le inginocchia davanti, e Sus.
gli mette la cuffia.*)

SUS: Venite, inginocchiatevi,
Restate fermo lì:
Pian piano or via giratevi;
Brave! va ben così.
La faccia rivolgetemi—
Olà quelgi occhi a me.
Dritissimo guardatemi,
Madama qui non è
Sù alto quel colletto;
Quel ciglio un po' più basso,
Le mani sotto il petto,
Vendromo poscia il passo
Quanto sarete in piè.
Mirate il bricconcello,
(*alla Cont.*)
Vedete quanto è bello!
Che furba guardatura!
Che vezzo, che figura!
Se l' amano le femmine
Han certo il lor perchè.

LA C: Finiana io raggazzate! or
quelle maniche
Oltre il gomita gli alza,
Onde più agiatamente
L' abito gli si adatti.
(*Sus. eseguisce.*)

SUS: Ecco.

LA C: Più indietro.
Così—Che nastro è quello?
(*Che. lo ha legato al braccio.*)
Chi picchia alla mia porta?

COUN: Hurry—it is right;
Oh! woe be to us if the Count
comes!
(*Sus. sits by the Coun.; Cher.
kneels before her. Sus. puts the cap
on his head.*)

SUS: Come now, I pray, kneel
down,
And remain there, tranquil,
And now turn gently round;
That's well, it is right so.
Now turn your face to me;
Your eyes do fix on me.
Look straight upon my face;
Madame, he is not here.
Hold up your necks still higher,
Cast down those wicked eyes!
Your hands under your breast.
And when you stand up,
We shall see how you walk.
Look at the little rogue,
(*to the Coun.*)
See how pretty he is!
What cunning looks he has!
What charms! and what a figure
If women do love him,
They surely have good reason.

COUN: Let us leave off such ridicu-
lous language:
Tuck up those sleeves above the el-
bow,
That the dress may sit easier.
(*Sus. does as she is bid.*)

SUS: There!

COUN: Farther back.
So—what ribbon is that?
(*Che. has one tied round his
arm.*)
Who knocks at my door?
(*a knocking is heard at the principal door.*)

## SCENA III

*Il Conti di fuori, e detti poi Susan-
na, che torna portando una vesta
di mussolino.*

LA C: Perchè chiusa?

LA C: Il mio sposo—
O Dei! son morta!
(*si alzano agitati.*)
Voi quì senza mantello!
In questo stato—un ricevuto fog-
lio—
La sua gran gelosia!—

IL C: Cosa indugiate?

LA C: Son sola—sì, son sola.

IL C: E a chi parlate?

LA C: A voi—certo a voi stesso—
(*confusa.*)

CHE: Dopo quel ch' è successo—
Il suo furor—non trovo altro consiglio.
(*corre a celarsi nel gabinetto.*)

LA C: Ah! mi difena il Cielo in tal
periglio!
(*leva la chiave dal gabinetto, e
corre ad aprire al Conte che entra.*)

## SCENE III

*The Count without, and the same,
then Susanna who returns, bringing a muslin dress.*

COUNT: Why locked in?

COUN: My husband—
O God! I am dead!
(*they rise flurried.*)
You here without a cloak—
In this condition—
A letter received—
His great jealousy—

COUNT: Why do you delay?

COUN: I am alone—Yes, I am alone.

COUNT: Then, who are you speaking to?

COUN: To you—certainly to you.
(*confused.*)

CHE: After what has happened—
his rage—I find no other means.
(*runs to conceal himself in the
closet.*)

COUN: Ah! May Heaven defend me
in so great a danger!
(*takes the key from the closet, and
runs to open the door to the
Count, who comes in.*)

IL C: Che nuovità? Non fu mai vostra usanza
Di rinchiudervi in stanza.

LA C: È ver—ma io—
Io stava quì mettendo—

IL C: Via mettendo—

LA C: Certe robe—era meco la Susanna,
Che in sua camera è andata.

IL C: Ad ogni modo
Voi non siete tranquilla.
(*esaminandola, e mostrandole
una lettera.*) Guardate questo foglio.

LA C: (Numi! è il foglio,
Che Figaro gli scrisse.)
(*si fa rumore nel gabinetto dov' è
Cher.*)

IL C: Cos' è cotesto strepito?
Là dentro al gabinetto
Qualche cosa è caduto.

LA C: Io non intesi niente.
(*più confusa.*)

IL C: Convien che abbiate gran pensieri in mente.

LA C: Di che?

IL C: Là v' è qualcuno.

LA C: Chi volete che sia?

IL C: Lo chiedo a voi;
Io vengo in questo punto.

LA C: Ah! sì—Susanna—appunto—

IL C: Che passò, mi diceste alla sua
stanza—

LA C: Alla sua stanza, o là, non vidi
bene.

IL C: S' ò Susanna, onde viene,
Che siete sì turbata?

LA C: Per la mia cameriera?

IL C: Io non so nulla;
Ma turbata senz' altro.

LA C: Ah quella serva
Più che non turba me, turba vio
stesso.

IL C: È vero, è vero e lo vedrete
adesso.
(*va al gabinetto*)
Susanna, or via sortite,
Sortite, io così vo'.

LA C: Fermatevi—sentite—
Sortire ella non può.
(*Susanna, esce dalla sua camera
con una vesto ed ascolta indietro.*)

SUS: (Cos' è codesta lite—
Il paggio dove andò?)
(*entra nell' alcova*)

IL C: E chi vietarlo o osa?

LA C: Lo vieta l' onestà.
Un abito di sposa
Provando ella si sta.
*a 3.*

IL C: (Chiarissima è la cosa,
L' amante quì sarà!)

COUNT: What novelty is this?
You never used to lock yourself in
the room.

COUN: It is true—but I—
I was putting here—

COUNT: Well putting—

COUN: Some things—
Susanna was here with me,
And is now gone to her room.

COUNT: At all events, you are not
composed.
(*examining her, and showing her
a letter.*)
Look at this paper.

COUN: (Gods! It is the letter Figaro
wrote to him!)
(*a noise is heard in the closet
where Che. is.*)

COUNT: What noise is that?
Something fell down in that closet.

COUN: I heard nothing.
(*more confused.*)

COUNT: You must have some great
thoughts in your head.

COUN: About what?

COUNT: Some body is there.

COUN: Who will you have it to be?

COUNT: I ask you? I am only just
come.

COUN: O yes—Susanna—Precisely.

COUNT: Who, as you told me,
Is gone to her room.

COUN: To her room, or there,
I did not see well.

COUNT: If it is Susanna,
From where does your confusion
arise?

COUN: For my maid.

COUNT: I know nothing;
But undoubtedly you are confused.

COUN: Ah! that maid confuses
You much more than me.

COUNT: It is true, it is true, you
will see it now.
(*goes to the closet.*)
Susanna, now come out,
Come out; I will have it so.

COUN: Remain, hear what I say,
Susanna can come out.
(*Sus. comes out of her chamber
with a gown, keeps back and listens.*)

SUS: (What does this quarrel
mean—
Where has the page now gone?
(*goes into the alcove.*)

COUNT: Who dares prevent it now?

COUN: Modesty prevents it.
She is now trying on a wedding-
dress in her room.

COUNT: (It is a clear affair the lover must be here!)

LA C: (Bruttissima è la cosa,
Veggiamo come va!)

SUS: (Capisco qualche cosa,
Chi sa cosa sarà!)

IL C: Dunque parlate almeno,
(alla porta)
Sussanna se quì siete?

LA C: Questo non vo' nemmeno,
(alla porta)
Io v' ordino, tacete.

IL C: Consorte mio, giudizio!

LA C, SUS: Un scandalo, un disordine,
Schiviam per carità!

SUS: Quì certo nascerà.

IL C: Dunque, vio non aprite?

LA C: E perchè deggio
Le mie camere aprir?

IL C: Ebben, lasciate,
L' aprirem senza chiavi: Ehi? gente?

LA C: Come?
Porreste a repentaglie
D'una dama l' onor?

IL C: È vero, io sbaglio.
Voi la condiscendenza
Di venir meco avrete:
Madama, eccovi il braccio; andiamo.

LA C: Andiamo.
(alzando la voce.)

IL C: Susanna starà là finchè torniamo.
(Sus. esce in fretta dall' alcova, e va alla porta del gabinetto.)

SUS: Aprite, presto aprite,
Aprite, è la Susanna
Sortite via, sortite,
Andate via di quà.
(Che. esce fuori.)

CHE: Ahimè! che scena orribile!
Che gran fatalità!

SUS: Partite, non tardate.

CHE: Ahimè! che scena orribile!

SUS: Di quà—di là—di quà—

CHE: Che gran fatalità!

SUS, CHE: Le porte son serrate; O
ceil! che mai sarà?

CHE, SUS: M' uccide se mi trova. V'
uccide se vi trova.
(Che. guarda fuori della finestro)

CHE: Veggiamo un po' quì fuori,
Dà proprio nel giardino.
(accena di saltar giù Sus. lo tiene.)

SUS: Fermate Cherubino,
Fermate per pietà.

CHE: Un vaso o due di fiori
Più mal non avverrà.
(come sopra.)

SUS: Tropp; alto è per un salto
Fermate per pietà!

---

COUN: (It is an ugly affair;
Let us see how it will end!)

SUS: (I have made something out;
Who knows how this shall turn out!)

COUNT: At least then speak, Susanna,
(towards the closet door.)
If you are in the room.

COUN: No, I will not, neither;
(towards the closet door.)
I order you to be silent.

COUNT: My wife, be prudent!

COUN, SUS: For Heaven's sake, let us avoid an exposure and quarrel.

SUS: Here certainly will happen—

COUNT: Then you do not open?

COUN: And why must I open my rooms?

COUNT: Well, never mind;
We shall open without keys:
Who is there?—people?

COUN: How? would you expose the honor of a lady of rank to danger?

COUNT: It is true, I am wrong.
You will have the goodness to come with me.
Madame, here is my arm; let us go.

COUN: Let us go.
(raising her voice.)

COUNT: Susanna will stay there till we return.
(Sus. runs out of the alcove, and goes to the closet door.)

SUS: Open, be quick, open;
Open—'tis Susanna; come out,
Now then come out,
Get quick away from here.
(Che. comes out.)

CHE: Mercy on me! what a horrible scene.
What a sad fatality!

SUS: Go, do not delay.

CHE: Mercy on me! what a horrible scene

SUS: This way—that way—this way.

CHE: What a sad fatality!

SUS, CHE: The doors are locked; O heavens! How will it end?

SUS, CHE: He will kill (me/you), if he finds (me/you).
(Che. looks out of the window.)

CHE: Let me look a little here; it is just over the garden.
(prepares to jump down, Sus. stops him.)

SUS: Stop, Cherubino; stop, for mercy's sake.

CHE: A flower-pot or two, that is all the mischief.
(as above.)

SUS: It is too high for a leap!
Pray stop for mercy's sake.

---

CHE: Lasciami, pria dinuocerle,
Nel fuoco volerei.
Abbraccio te per lei;
(baccia Sus.)
Addio—così sì fa.
(salta nel giardino. Sus. spaurita, si getta un momento sopra una sedia; poi s' alza, e guarda dalla finestra.)

SUS: Oh! guarda il demonietto,
'come fugge!'
Entriam nel gabinnetto;
Venga poscia il Gradasso, io quì l' aspetto.
(entra nel gabinetto.)

La Conte, Il Conte, poi gli altri a loro tempo. Il Conte porta in mano una leva per aprir l' uscio del gabinetto, che posa sopra la tavola, mentre esamina intorno la stanza.)

IL C: Tutto è come il lasciai—volete dunque
Aprir voi stessa, o deggio—

LA C: Ahimè! fermate,
E ascoltatemi un poco:
Mi credete capace
Di mancare al dover?

IL C: Come vi piace,
Entro a quel gabinetto;
Chi sta chiuso vedrò.

LA C: Sì lo vedrete—
Ma uditemi tranquillo.
(turbata.)

IL C: Non è, danque, Susanna?
(alterato.)

LA C: È un fanciullo.

IL C: Un fanciul.

LA C: Sì Cherubino.

IL C: (E mi farà il destino
Ritrovar questo paggio in ogni loco?)
Come? Non è partito?—Scellerati!
Ecco i dubbi spiegati; ecco l' imbroglio,
Ecco il raggiro, onde m' avverte il foglio.
Esci ormai, garzon malnato;
(al gabinetto.)
Sciagurato, non tardar!

LA C: Ah! signore, quel furore,
Per lui fammi il cor tremar!

IL C: E d' opporvi ancora osate?

LA C: No, sentite!

IL C: Via parlate.

LA C: Giuro al ciel che ogni sospetto—(tremando.)
E lo stato, in che il trovate—
Sciolto il collo, nudo il petto—

IL C: Sciolto il collo, nudo il petto!

LA C: Per vestir feminee spoglie—

IL C: Ah! comprendo, indegna moglie,
Mi vo' tosto vendicar.
(prende infuriato la leva.)

---

CHE: Leave me, before hurting her,
I would fly into the fire.
I salute you for her;
(kisses Sus.)
Adieu! This is the way.
(leaps into the garden. Sus., frightened, throws herself for a moment on a chair; then rises, and looks through the window.)

SUS: O see, the little devil, "how he runs." I now shall go into the closet; then let the fury come, I am ready for him here.
(goes into the closet.)

The Countess, the Count, then the others in their turn. The Count brings an iron crow to break the closet-door open; he lays it on the table, then searches the room.

COUNT: Every thing is as when I went away; will you then open the door yourself, or must I—

COUN: Alas! stop and hear me a little: do you think me capable of failing in my duty?

COUNT: As you like. I will see who is shut up in that closet.

COUN: Yes, you shall—but hear me coolly.
(confused.)

COUNT: Then it is not Susanna?
(angrily.)

COUN: It is a boy.

COUNT: A boy!

COUN: Yes, Cherubino.

COUNT: (And will my unlucky stars make me find this page everywhere?) How? Is he not sent out?—Wretches!—Here are my suspicions verified; this is the scheme, this is the plot, that I am warned of by the letter. Come out, wicked boy, (towards the closet.) wretched fellow, do not delay!

COUN: Ah! sir! that rage makes me tremble for him!

COUNT: And do you still dare oppose?

COUN: No, hear me.

COUNT: Come, speak.

COUN: I swear by Heaven that any suspicion—(trembling) and the condition you will find him in—his neck and breast bare—

COUNT: His neck and breast bare!

COUN: To put on woman's clothes.

COUNT: Oh! I understand—worthless wife! I will be revenged immediately.
(takes the crow in a rage.)

LA C: Mi fa torto quel trasporto, / M' oltraggiate a dubitar.

IL C: Quà la chiave.

LA C: Egli è innocente— / Voi sapete—

IL C: Non so niente. / Va lontan dagli occhi miei, / Un' infida, un' empia sei, / E mi cereni d' infamar.

LA C: Vao sì—ma—

IL C: Non ascolto.

LA C: Non so rea—

IL C: Vel leggo in volto, / (gli dà la chiave.) / Mora mora, e più non sia / Rea cagion del mio penar.

LA C: (Ah! la ceca gelosia / Qualche eccesso gli fa far.) / (Il Conte apre la porta; La Contessa si getto afiannosa sopra una sedia, coprendosi gli occhi. Susanna esce dal gabinetto con aria grave, ed ironica.)

LA C, IL C: Susanna!

SUS: Signore / Perchè tal stupore? / Il brando prendete, / Il paggio uccidete, / Vedetelo quà.

LA C: (Che storia è mai questa! / Susanna era là!)

IL C: Che scuola! la testa, / Girando mi va!

SUS: Confusa han la testa, / Non san come va.

IL C: Sei sola?

SUS: Guardate, / Là ascoso sarà.

IL C: Guardiamo, guardiamo, / Quì ascoso sarà. / (entra nel gabinetto. La C. si alza)

LA C: Susanna, son morta, / Il fiato mi manca.

SUS: Più lieta, più franca, / In salvo è di già. / (Il. C ese confuso)

IL C: (Che sbaglio mai presi / Appena la credo!) / Se a torto vi offesi / Perdono vi chiedo, / (alla C.) / Ma far burla simile / È pio crudelta.

LA C, SUS: le vostre follie / Non mertan pietà.

IL C: Io v' amo.

LA C: Nol dite.

IL C: Vel giuro.

LA C: Mentite. / Son l' empia, l' intida, / Che ognora v' inganna.

IL C: Quell' ira, Susanna, / M' adjuta a calmar!

COUN: That passion wrongs me; you offend me by your doubts.

COUNT: Give here the key.

COUN: He is innocent. You know—

COUNT: I know nothing. Go far from my sight; You are a faithless and false woman, and seek my dishonor.

COUN: Yes, I go—but—

COUNT: I will not hear.

COUN: I am not guilty.

COUNT: I read it in your face; / (she gives him the key.) / Let him die, and be no longer / The sad cause of all my sufferings.

COUN: (Ah! his jealousy, too blind, / Will urge him to some catastrophe.) / (the Count opens the door; the Countess throws herself on a chair, overwhelmed with grief, covering her eyes. Susanna comes out of the closet with a grave and ironical air.)

COUN, COUNT: Susanna!

SUS: Sir—why such astonishment? / Take up your sword, and kill the boy; / See—he is here.

COUN: (What can this mean? / Susanna now there!)

COUNT: (How great is this school! / My head turns giddy!)

SUS: (Their heads are confused, / They know not how it ended.)

COUNT: Are you alone?

SUS: Look, he may be concealed there.

COUNT: Let us look, let us look; / He may be concealed here, / (goes into the closet; the Coun. rises.)

COUN: Susanna, I am dead! / My breath is quite gone!

SUS: More cheerful, more frank; / Take courage, he is safe. / (The Count comes out, composed.)

COUNT: (What a mistake I made! / I can hardly believe it!) / If I have wronged you. / I beg your pardon; / (to the Coun.) / But such foolish jokes indeed are too cruel.

COUN: Your follies deserve no pity at all.

COUNT: I love you.

COUN: Do not say so.

COUNT: I swear it.

COUN: It is false! I am the false, faithless woman, that always deceives you.

COUNT: Susanna, help me to appease this anger!

SUS: Così si condanna / Chi può sospettar.

LA C: Ah! dunque la fede / D' un' anima amante / Sì fiera mercede / Doveva sperar! / (Sus. e Il Con. pregano La Cont.)

SUS: Signora!

IL C: Rosina!

LA C: Consorte crudele! / Più quella non sono, / Ma il misero oggetto / Del vostro abbandona, / Che avete diletto / Di far disperar.

SUS: (Confuso, pentito. / (piano alla Cont.) / E troppo punito, / Abbiate pietà!

LA C: Soffrir sì gran torto / Quest' alma non sa!

IL C: Ma il paggio rinchiuso?

LA C: Fu sol per provarvi.

IL C: Ma i tremiti, i palpiti?

LA C: Fu soi per bularvi. / (Il Con. mostra la lettera.)

IL C: Ma un foglio sì barbaro!

LA C: Dí Figaro è il foglio. / E a voi, per Basilio—

IL C: Ah! perfidi! io voglio—

LA C: Perdono non merita / Chi agli altri nol dà.

IL C: Ebben se vi piace, / Commune è la pace, / Rosina inflessibile / Con me non sarà.

LA C: Oh! quanto Susanna, / Son dolce di core! / (dà la mano al Conte.) / Di donna al furore, / Ch più crederà!

SUS: Cogli uomin, Signora, / Girate, volgete, / Vedrete, che ognora / Si cade poi là.

IL C: Guardatemi!

LA C: Ingrato!

IL C: Ho torto; mi pento / Da questo momento.

COUN, COUNT, SUS: Quest' alma a conoscer la, mi, vi / Apprender potrà. / (Vien Figaro.)

FIG: Signore, di fuori / Son già i suonatori; / Le trombe sentite, / I piferi udite; / Tra canti, tra balli / De' vostri vassalli / Corriamo, voliamo / Le nozze a compir. / (partendo Il C. lo ferma.)

IL C: Pian piano, men fretta.

FIG: La turba m' aspetta.

SUS: Who is capable of suspicion, / Must be punished so.

COUN: Ah! then the faith / Of one who loves / Was to expect such cruel return.

SUS: Madam!

COUNT: Rosina!

COUN: Oh husband most cruel! / No more I am the same, / But am the unfortunate / Object of your contempt, / Which you delight / In driving to madness.

SUS: (Confused and repenting, (in a low voice to Coun.) / He is punished too much / Have pity upon him.)

COUN: My soul can not bear / So great an insult.

COUNT: But the page locked up?

COUN: It was only to try you.

COUNT: But the trembling, the agitation?

COUN: Only to laugh at you. / (the Count shows the letter.)

COUNT: But so cruel a letter?

COUN: It is by Figaro, and to you by Basilio.

COUNT: Wretches! I will—

COUN: He is undeserving of pardon that will not grant it to others.

COUNT: Well if you like, the peace shall be general; / Rosina will not be inexorable with me.

COUN: O Susanna! how tender-hearted I am! / (gives her hand to the Count.) / Who will believe any more the anger of a woman?

SUS: Madam, with the men, turn and twist the business as you please, you will see that always ends so.

COUNT: Look at me!

COUN: Ungrateful man!

COUNT: I am in the wrong! / I repent from this moment!

COUN, COUNT, SUS: This soul will now learn to know (her/me/you) quite well. / (Enter Figaro.)

FIG: The musicians, dear sir, have already arrived; / Hear how the trumpets; / Hark! list to the fifes! / Let us run, let us fly / To celebrate the wedding / In singing and dancing / With your vassals. / (as he goes the Count stops him.)

COUNT: Gently, gently; do not be in haste.

FIG: The people expect me.

# Act I, Scene IV

**IL C:** Un dubbio toglietemi In pria di partir.

**COUNT:** Before you go, rid me of a doubt.

**LA C, SUS, FIG:** (La cosa è scabrosa, Com' è da finir?)

**COUN, SUS, FIG:** (It is a knotty point; how is it to end?)

**IL C:** (Con arte le carte Convien quì scoprir.)
(*mostra la lettera a Fig.*) Conoscete, signor Figaro, Questo foglio chi vergo?

**COUNT:** (With skill I must play my cards.)
(*shows the letter to Fig.*) Do you know, Mr. Figaro, who wrote this letter?

**FIG:** Nol conosco.

**FIG:** I do not.

**SUS, IL C:** Nol conosci?

**SUS, COUNT:** You do not?

**FIG:** Nol conosco, no, no, no.

**FIG:** I do not know it, no, no, no.

**SUS:** E nol desti a Don Basilio?

**SUS:** And did you not give it to Don Basilio?

**LA C:** Per recarlo—tu c' intendi.

**COUN:** To deliver it—you understand us.

**FIG:** Non v' intendo; oibò! oibò!

**FIG:** I do not understand you, no, no! no, no!

**SUS:** E non sai del damerino, Che stasera nel giardino—

**SUS:** And do you not know of the young spark who was in the garden tonight

**IL C:** Già capisci—

**COUNT:** You make out now—

**FIG:** Io nulla so!

**FIG:** I know nothing!

**IL C:** Corichi invan difesa, e scusa, Il tuo ceffo già t' accuse, Vedo ben, che vuoi mentir.

**COUNT:** It is in vain for you to defend yourself and seek excuses; your face accuses you already; see you want to lie.

**FIG:** Mente il ceffo, io già non mento.

**FIG:** My face lies, not I.

**LA C, SUS:** Il talento anguizzi invano Palesato abbiam l' arcano, Non v' è nulla da ridir.

**COUN, SUS:** It is in vain for you to sharpen your wit; we have discovered the secret; there is no reply.

**IL C:** Che respondi?

**COUNT:** What do you answer?

**FIG:** Niente, niente.

**FIG:** Nothing, nothing.

**IL C:** Dunque accordi?

**COUNT:** Then you agree?

**FIG:** Non accordo.

**FIG:** I do not agree.

**LA C, SUS:** Eh! vi chetati, balordo, La burletta hai da finir.

**COUN, SUS:** Come, have done, mad fellow; you must finish the farce.

**FIG:** Per finirla lietamente All' usanza teatrale, Un' azoin matrimoniale Noi faremo ora seguir.

**FIG:** To finish it joyfully according to theatrical custom, we shall have a matrimonial entertainment follow now.

**LA C, SUS:** Deh! signor, nol contrastate, Consolate i miei desir!

**COUN, SUS:** Pray, sir, do not oppose it.
Make me happy—grant my wishes!

**IL C:** Marcellina, Marcellina, Quanto tardi a comparir!
(*viene Ant., mezzo ubriaco, portando un vas di viole co' steli schiacciati.*)

**COUNT:** Marcellina, Marcellina, Oh! how long you are a coming!
(*enter Ant., half drunk, bringing a pot of violets with the stalks broken.*)

**ANT:** Ah! signore, signor.

**ANT:** Ah! sir, sir!

**IL C:** Cos' è stato?

**COUNT:** What is the matter?

**ANT:** Che insolenza! chi il fece? chi fu?

**ANT:** What impudence! who did it? who was it?

**LA C, IL C, FIG, SUS:** Cosa dici? cos' hai? cos' è nato?

**COUN, COUNT, FIG, SUS:** What do you say? what is the matter with you? what has happened?

**ANT:** Ascoltate.

**ANT:** Hear me.

**LAC, IL C, FIG, SUS:** Via parla, dì su.

**COUN, COUNT, FIG, SUS:** Come, speak out.

**ANT:** Dal balcone che guarda in guardino,
(*al Con*)
Mille cose ogni dì gettar veggio, E poc' anzi, può darsi di peggio! Vidi un uom, signor mio, gettar giù.

**ANT:** From the balcony that looks into the garden,
(*to the Count.*)
I see a thousand things thrown down; and not long ago (can they do worse?) I saw a man, sir, thrown out.

**IL C, LA C, SUS:** Dal balcone?

**COUNT, COUN, SUS:** From the balcony?

**ANT:** Vedete i garofani.

**ANT:** See the pinks.

**IL C:** In giardino?

**COUNT:** In the garden?

**LA C, SUS:** (Su, Figaro all' erta.)

**COUN, SUS:** (Now, Figaro, look sharp.)

**IL C:** (Cosa sento?)

**COUNT:** What do I hear?

**LA C, SUS:** (Costui ci sconerta!)

**COUN, SUS:** (This fellow puts us out!)

**LA C, SUS, FIG:** (Quel briaco che venne a far quì!)

**COUN, SUS, FIG:** (What is that drunken man come to do here?)

**IL C:** Dunque un uomo?—ma dov' è egli gite?
(*ad Ant.*)

**COUNT:** Then a man—but where is he gone?
(*to Ant.*)

**ANT:** Ratto ratto il birbone è fuggito, E ad un tratto di vista m' usci.
(*Sus. piano a Fig.*)

**ANT:** The scoundrel ran away full speed, and I lost sight of him in a moment.
(*Sus. whispers to Fig.*)

**SUS:** (Sai che il paggio?—)

**SUS:** (You know that the page?)

**FIG:** (So tutto!) Ah!—ah!—
(*ridendo.*)

**FIG:** I know all; ha! ha!
(*laughing.*)

**IL C:** Taci là, taci là!

**COUNT:** Silence there, silence there!

**ANT:** Cosi rida?

**ANT:** Why do you laugh?

**FIG:** Ah! ah! ah! ah! ah! ah!

**FIG:** Ha! ha! ha! ha! ha! ha!

**IL C:** Taci lì.

**COUNT:** Silence there!

**FIG:** Tu sei cotto dal sorger del dì.
(*ad Ant.*)

**FIG:** You are half seas over by daybreak.
(*to Ant.*)

**IL C:** Or ripetimi: un uom dal balcone?—
(*ad Ant.*)

**COUNT:** Now tell me again—a man from the balcony?
(*to Ant.*)

**ANT:** Dal balcone.

**ANT:** From the balcony—

**IL C:** In giardino?

**COUNT:** In the garden?

**ANT:** In giardino.

**ANT:** In the garden.

**LA C, SUS, FIG:** Ma, signore, se in iui parla il vino!

**COUN, SUS, FIG:** But, sir, if it is the wine that speaks in him!

**IL C:** Segui pur: nè tu in volto il vedesti?

**COUNT:** Go on, then;—and did you not see his face?

**ANT:** No, nol vidi.

**ANT:** No I did not.

**LA C, SUS:** (Olà, Figaro all erta!)

**COUN, SUS:** (Mind, Figaro, look sharp!)

**FIG:** Via, piagnone, sta zitto una volta,
(*ad Ant.*)
Per tre soldi far tanto tumulto!
(*accennando i fiori.*)
Giacchè il fatto non può stare occulto, Son io stesso saltato di lì.

**FIG:** Come, crying booby, hold your tongue!
(*to Ant.*)
To make such a noise for three-pence!
(*pointing to the flowers.*)
Since it can no longer be concealed, it was I who jumped down from there.

**IL C, ANT:** Chi? voi stesso?

**COUNT, ANT:** Who? You yourself?

**LA C, SUS:** (Che testa! che ingegno!)

**COUN, SUS:** (What a head! How clever!)

**FIG:** Che stupore?

**FIG:** Why wonder?

**IL C:** (Ah! creder nol posso!)

**COUNT:** (Oh! I can not believe it!)

ANT: Come mai diventaste sì grosso?
Dopo il salto non eri così.

FIG: A chi salta succede così.

ANT: Chi il direbbe?

LA C, SUS: Ed insisti? che pazzo!
(*ad Ant.*)

IL C: Tu che dici?

ANT: A me parve il ragazzo—

IL C: Cherubin?

LA C, SUS: (Maledetto!)

FIG: Esso appunto
Per la posta a cavallo quì giunto
Da Saviglia, egli forsi sarà!

ANT: Questo no, questo no, che il cavallo
Io non vidi saltare di là.

IL C: Che pazienza! Finiam questo ballo.

LA C, SUS: (Come mai, giusto ciel, finirà;)

IL C: Dunque tu?—

FIG: Saltai giù.

IL C: Ma perchè?

FIG: Il timor—

IL C: Che timor?

FIG: Là rinchiuso;
Aspettando quel caro visetto—
Tippe—tappe—un susurro fuor d'uso—
Voi gridaste—lo scritto biglietto—
Saltai giù dal balcone confuso,
E stravolto m' ho un nervo del piè.
(*stropicciandosi il piede; Ant.
cava fuori delle carte.*)

ANT: Vostre dunque saran queste carte,
Che perdeste?

IL C: Olà porgile a me.
(*Ant. gliele dà.*)

FIG: (Sono in trappola!)

LA C, SUS: (Figaro all' erta!)

IL C: Dite un po' questo foglio cos' è?
(*mostrandoglielo da lontano.*)

FIG: Tosto il dico—ne ho tanti, aspettate.
(*cava di tasca molte carte, e le esamina.*)

ANT: Sarà forse il sommario de debiti.

FIG: No, la lista degli osti.

IL C: Parlate!
(*a Fig.*)
E tu lascialo.
(*ad Ant.*)

LA C, SUS: Lascialo, e parti.

ANT: Parto sì, ma se torno a trovarti—

---

ANT: What has made you become so big? You were not so after the jump.

FIG: It happens so to people who jump.

ANT: Who would suppose it?

COUN, SUS: And you insist?—how stupid!
(*to Ant.*)

ANT: I thought it was the boy—

COUNT: Cherubino!

COUN, SUS: (Curse him!)

FIG: He is just come from Seville, and is arrived here—perhaps it is he!

ANT: Not so, not so, for I did not see the horse jump down.

COUNT: What patience! Let us finish this dance.

COUN, SUS: (Good heavens! how will it end?)

COUNT: Then you?

FIG: I jumped down.

COUNT: Why then?

FIG: Fear.

COUNT: Of what.

FIG: Shut up there,
Waiting for that dear pretty face—
Knock, knock—an unusual noise I hear.
You cried out—The note that was written—
I leaped down from the balcony confused,
And have sprained my foot.
(*rubs his foot; Ant. pulls out some papers.*)

ANT: Then these papers are yours, which you dropped?

COUNT: Here! Give them to me.
(*Ant. gives them to him.*)

FIG: (I am caught!)

COUN, SUS: (Figaro, mind!)

COUNT: Tell me a little what is this paper?
(*showing it him at a distance.*)

FIG: I shall tell it immediately—I have so many—stay.
(*pulls many papers out of his pocket and examines them.*)

ANT: Perhaps it is the list of his debts.

FIG: No, it is that of the guests.

COUNT: Speak!
(*to Fig.*)
And you leave him.
(*to Ant.*)

COUN, SUS: Leave him and go.

ANT: I go, yes, but if I find you again—

---

FIG: Vanne, vanne, non temo di te.
(*Ant. parte: Il Conte mostra ancor il foglio; e La Contessa vede ch' Lè la patente.*)

IL C: Dunque?

LA C: (O ceil! la patente.)
(*piano a Sus.*)

SUS: (Giusti Dei! la patente!)
(*a Fig.*)

IL C: Coraggio.
(*a Fig.*)

FIG: Oh che testa! quell' è la patente
Che poc' anzi il fanciullo mi diò.

IL C: Perchè fare?

FIG: Vi manca—

IL C: Vi manca?

LA C: (Il suggello.)

SUS: (Il suggello, il suggello.)
(*piano a Fig.*)

FIG: E l' usanza di porvi il suggello.

IL C: (Questo birbo mi toglie il cervello!
Tutto, tutto è mistero per me!
(*guaicisce il foglio*)

LA C, SUS: (Se mi solve da questa tempesta, Più non havvi naufragio per me!)

FIG: (Sbuffa invano, la terra calpesta,
Poverino! ne sa men di me.)
(*vengono Bar., Mar., e Bas.*)

MAR, BAR, BAS: Voi, signor, che giuto siete, Ci dovete ora ascoltar.

IL C: (Son venuti a vendicarmi,
E mi sento consolar!)

LA C, SUS, FIG: Son venuti a sconcertarmi, Qual rimedio ritrovar!

FIG: Son tre stolidi, tre pazzi,
al Con.)
Cosa mai vengono a far?

IL C: Pian pianin, senza schiamazzi
Dica ognun quel che gli par.

MAR: Un impegno nuziale
(*al Con. parlando di Fig.*)
Ha costui con me contratto,
E pretendo che il contratto
Deva meco effettuar.

LA C, SUS: Come! come!

IL C: Olà! silenzio!
Io son quì per giudicar.

BAR: Io com' uomo al mondo cognite
Vengo quì per testimonio,
Del promesso matrimonio
Con prestanza di danar.

LA C, SUS, FIG: Son tre matti, son tre matti!

IL C: Ehi! silenzio, lo vedremo,
Il contratto leggeremo,
Tutto in ordin deve andar.

---

FIG: Go, go, I do not fear you.
(*exit Ant., the Count shows the paper, and the Countess sees it is the commission.*)

COUNT: Then.

COUN: (O heavens! the commission!)
(*whispering to Sus.*)

SUS: (Just heavens! the commission!)
(*to Fig.*)

COUNT: Cheer up.
(*to Fig.*)

FIG: O what a head! That is the commission which that boy gave me not long ago.

COUNT: To do what?

FIG: It wants—

COUNT: It wants?

COUN: (The seal.)

SUS: (The seal, the seal.)
(*softly to Fig.*)

FIG: It is usual to put the seal to it.

COUNT: This rogue turns my brain!
All, all is mystery for me!
(*he twists and rumples the paper about.*)

COUN, SUS: (If I save myself from this storm, I shall never be wrecked!)

FIG: (In vain the poor fellow raves and stamps, he knows less about it than I.)
(*Enter Bar., Mar., and Bas.*)

MAR., BAR., BAS: You, sir, who are just, must hear us now.

COUNT: They are come to revenge me, and I feel myself comforted!)

COUN, SUS, FIG: They are come to put me out; what remedy can I find!

FIG: They are three stupid ones, three madmen.
(*to the Count.*)
What can they be coming about?

COUNT: Softly and gently, without confusion, let every one say what he likes.

MAR: This man has signed articles of marriage with me:
(*to the Count, speaking of Fig.*)
And I demand the performance of it.

COUN, SUS: How! how!

COUNT: Mind there! be silent! I am here to judge.

BAS: I, as a man known to the world, come here as a witness of the promise of marriage, and money lent.

COUN, SUS, FIG: They are all three mad, they are all three mad.

COUNT: Mind! be silent! We shall see it, we shall read the articles, all must proceed regularly.

**LA C, SUS, FIG:** (Son confusa, o, son stordita!, o! Disperata, o, sbalordita!, o! Certo un diavol del inferno Quì gli ha fatti capitar!)

**IL C, MAR, BAR, BAS:** (Che bel colpo! che bel caso! È cresciuto a tutti il naso! Qualche Nume a noi propizio Quì ci ha fatti capitar!)

*FINE DELL' ATTO SECONDO*

**COUN, SUS, FIG:** I am confused, I am astonished! in despair and confounded! Certainly some devil from Tartarus sent them here.

**COUNT, MAR., BAR., BAS:** What a fine blow! what a fine case! They are all out of countenance! Some propitious deity has sent us here.

*END OF ACT II.*

# ■ ATTO III

## SCENA I

*Gran Sala, ornata per una Festa Nuziale.* Il Conte, che passeggia turbato, e riflessivo; poi La Contessa, e Susanna in fondo.

**IL C:** Che imbarazzo è mai questo! Un foglio anonimo— La cameriera in gabinetto chiusa— La padrona confusa—un uom che salta Dal balcone in giardino— Non so cosa pensare! (*vengono La Cont. e Sus.*)

**LA C:** Via fatti core, digli Che t' attenda in giardino.

**IL C:** Saprò se Cherubino Era giunto a Siviglia; e a tale oggetto Ho mandato Basilio.

**SUS:** O Dio! non oso!

**LA C:** Pensa che sta in tua mano il mio riposo. (*si ritira.*)

**IL C:** È Susanna! Chi sa ch' ella tradito Abbia il segreto mio— Oh! se à parlato, a Figaro Farò sposar la vecchia.

**SUS:** (Marcellina!) (*Sus. si avanza.*) Signor?

**IL C:** Cosa bramate?

**SUS:** Mi par che siate in collera?

**IL C:** Volete qualche cosa?

**SUS:** Signor, la vostra sposa Ha i soliti vapori, E vi chiede il vasetto degli odori.

**IL C:** Prendete.

**SUS:** Or vel riporto.

**IL C:** Ah no! potente

**IL C:** Riternelo per voi.

**SUS:** Per me, signore? Questi non son mali Da donne triviali.

**IL C:** Un' amante che perde il caro sposo, (*ironico.*) Sul punto d' ottenerlo—

# ■ ACT III

## SCENE I

*A large Room fitted up for a Wedding. The Count walks up and down with an air of trouble and reflection; then the Countess and Susanna at the farther end.*

**COUNT:** What perplexity is this! An anonymous letter—the maid locked up in the closet—the mistress in confusion—a man jumps from the balcony into the garden—I know not what to think! (*the Coun. and Sus. come forward.*)

**COUN:** Come, take courage, tell him to wait for you in the garden.

**COUNT:** I shall know if Cherubino had arrived at Seville for that purpose I sent Basilio.

**SUS:** O gods! I do not dare!

**COUN:** Remember that my peace of mind is in your hands. (*withdraws.*)

**COUNT:** It is Susanna! Who knows whether she has betrayed my secret?—Oh! if she has spoken, I will make the old woman marry Figaro.

**SUS:** (Marcellina!) (*SUS. comes forward.*) Sir?

**COUNT:** What do you want?

**SUS:** You seem angry?

**COUNT:** Do you want any thing?

**SUS:** Your lady has her usual vapors, and begs for the smelling-bottle.

**COUNT:** Take it.

**SUS:** I shall bring it back immediately.

**COUNT:** Oh! no, you may keep it for yourself.

**SUS:** For me, sir? those are not complaints for women of low estate.

**COUNT:** An affectionate girl, who loses her beloved promised husband, (*tronically,*) on the point of having him—

**SUS:** Pagando Marcellina colla dote Che voi mi prometteste—

**IL C:** Ch' io vi promisi! quando?

**SUS:** Credea d' averlo—inteso—

**IL C:** Sì—se—aveste voluto Intendermi voi stessa.

**SUS:** È mio—dovere— E quel di sua Eccellenza—è mie volero.

**IL C:** Crudel! perchè finora Farmi languir così?

**SUS:** Signor, la donna ognora Tempo à di dir di sì.

**IL C:** Dunque, in giardin verrai?

**SUS:** Se piace a voi, verrò.

**IL C:** È non mi mancherai?

**SUS:** No, non vi mancherò.

**IL C:** Mi sento dal contento Pieno di gioja il cor!

**SUS:** (Scusatemi se mento, Voi che intendete amor.)

**IL C:** Ma la Contessa attenderà il vasetto.

**SUS:** Eh, fu solo un pretesto, Parlato non avrei senza di questo.

**IL C:** Carissima!

**SUS:** Vien gente.

**IL C:** (È mia senz' altro!) (*parte*)

**SUS:** Forbitevi la bocca, signor scaltro. (*parte, ma Fig. l' incontra*)

**FIG:** Ehi, Susanna, ove vai?

**SUS:** Taci; senz' avvocato Hai già vinta la causa.

**FIG:** Cos' è nato? (*Sus. fugge; Fig. la seque; Il Con. che ha sentito dal fondo le ultime parole, torna.*)

**IL C:** Hai già vinta la cause!—Cosa sento? In qual laccio cadea!—Perfidi! io voglio In tal modo punirvi—Ma piacer mio La sentenza sarà—Ma se pagasse La vecchia pretendente? Pagarla? in qual maniera?—E poi v' è Antonio, Che all' incognito Figaro ricusa Di dare una nipote in matrimonio— Coltivando l' orgoglio Di questo mentecatto— Tutto giova a un raggiro: il colpo è fatto. Vedrò, mentr' io sospiro, Felice un servo mio! E un ben che invan desio, Ei posseder dovrà! Vedrò per man d' amore

**SUS:** Paying Marcellina with the portion that you promised me—

**COUNT:** That I promised you? when?

**SUS:** I thought I heard it—

**COUNT:** Yes—if—you would have listened to me yourself.

**SUS:** It is my—duty—and your lordship's pleasure—is mine.

**COUNT:** Cruel maid! why make you me to languish like this until now?

**SUS:** Sir, a woman always has time to say yes.

**COUNT:** Then you will come to the garden?

**SUS:** If it pleases you, I will come.

**COUNT:** And you will not disappoint me?

**SUS:** No, I will not disappoint you.

**COUNT:** I feel my heart delighted, and filled with joy.

**SUS:** (You who know what love is, pardon me if I deceive.)

**COUNT:** But the Countess is waiting for the box.

**SUS:** Oh! it was only a pretense; without this I could not have spoken.

**COUNT:** You are quite certain!

**SUS:** Some body is coming.

**COUNT:** (She is mine without a doubt!) (*exit.*)

**SUS:** You'll lose your trouble, Mr. Fox. (*exit, but is met by Fig.*)

**FIG:** Here, Susanna, where are you going?

**SUS:** Hush! without an attorney, you have already won your cause.

**FIG:** What has happened? (*Sus. runs; Fig. follows her; the Count, who heard the last words from a distance, comes back.*)

**COUNT:** You have already won your cause!—What do I hear? In what snare was I falling? You two are both false-hearted! I will punish you in such a manner—the sentence shall be according to my pleasure—But if he paid the old pretender, I pay her? how?—besides, there is Antonio, who refuses to give a niece in marriage to the unknown Figaro.—In feeding the pride of this booby—All is useful in a scheme; the blow is struck. Shall I behold my happy servant while I sigh? And is he to possess A treasure I wish for in vain? Shall I see joined by love To an unworthy object One who has raised a passion She does not feel for me? Oh no! I will not leave

Unita a un vile oggetto
Chi in me destò un affetto,
Che per me poi non ha!
Ah no! lasciarti in pace
Non vo' questo contento:
Tu non nascesti, audace,
Per dare a me tormento,
E forse ancor per ridere
Di mia infelicità!
Già la speranza sola
Della vendetta mia
Quest' anima consola,
E giubbilar mi fa!

You so much bliss in peace:
Bold man, you were not born
To give me this torment,
And afterwards, perhaps,
To laugh at my misfortune.
Already the mere hope
That I shall have revenge,
gives my soul content,
And fills my heart with joy.

## SCENA II

*Mentre Il Conte sta per partire, vede arrivar Don Curzio, che parla con Figaro, Marcellina, Bartolo; indi Susanna.*

**D. C:** È deci-sa la li-te;
O pagarla, o sposarla.

**IL C:** È giusta la sentenza;
O pagare, o sposar, bravo Don Curzio!

**FIG:** Son gentiluomo, e senza
L' assenso de' miei nobili parenti—

**IL C:** Dove sono? chi sono?

**D. C:** Il te-sti-imonio?

**FIG:** L' oro, le gemme, i ricamati panni,
Che ne' più teneri anni
Mi ritrovaro addosso i masnadieri,
Sono gl' indizj veri
Di mia nascita illustre, e soprattutto
Questo al mio braccio impresso
geroglifico.
*(va per alzar la manica)*

**MAR:** Una spatola impressa al braccio destro.
*(con premura)*

**FIG:** A voi chi il disse?

**MAR:** O Dio! È desso.

**FIG:** È ver son io.

**D. C:** Chi-i?

**IL C:** Chi?

**BAR:** Chi? Raffaello.
E i ladri ti rapir!

**FIG:** Presso un castello

**BAR:** Ecco tua madre.
*(di Mar.)*

**FIG:** Balia.

**BAR:** No, tua madre.

**IL C:** (Sus madre!)

**FIG:** (Cosa sento?)

**MAR:** Ecco tu padre.
*(mostrando Bar.)*

**MAR:** Riconosci in questo amplesso
Una madre, amato figlio.
*(si abbracciano.)*

**FIG:** Padre mio, fate lo stesso,
Non mi fate più arrossir.

**BAR:** Resistenza la conscienza
Far non lasciar al tuo desir.
*(come sopra.)*

## SCENE II

*While the Count is going he sees Don Curzio coming, who is speaking with Figaro, Marcellina, and Bartolo; then Susanna.*

**DON C:** The su-uit is deci-ded: or pay her, or marry her.

**COUNT:** The sentence is just; or pay or marry, "well done, Don Curzio."

**FIG:** I am a gentleman, and without the consent of my noble relatives—

**COUNT:** Where am I? who am I?

**DON C:** The proo-of?

**FIG:** The gold, jewels, embroidered clothes, which in my infancy the robbers found upon me, are the true indications of my noble birth, and particularly this hieroglyphic printed on my arm.
*(goes to turn up his sleeve.)*

**MAR:** A spatula printed on your right arm?
*(with eagerness.)*

**FIG:** Who told it you?

**MAR:** Oh god! It is he.

**FIG:** It is true I am myself.

**DON C:** Who-o?

**COUNT:** Who?

**BAR:** Who? Raffaello. And the thieves carried you away?

**FIG:** Near a castle.

**BAR:** Behold your mother.
*(pointing to Mar.)*

**FIG:** Nurse.

**BAR:** No, your mother.

**COUNT:** (His mother!)

**FIG:** (What do I hear?)

**MAR:** Behold your father.
*(showing Bar.)*

**MAR:** Beloved son, know your mother by this kiss.
*(they embrace.)*

**FIG:** My father, do the same; do not make me blush any longer,

**BAR:** Conscience does not let me oppose your wish.
*(as above.)*

**D. C:** È-ei su-uo pa-adre? è-ella su-ua ma-adre?
*(al Con. che lo spinge.)*

**IL C:** (Son smarrito, son stordito!)

**D. C:** L' ime-neeo non puo-ò seguir.

**MAR:** Figlio amato!

**FIG:** Cara madre!

**BAR:** Cara figlio!

**FIG:** Amato padre!

**IL C:** (Meglio è assai di quà partir!)
*(partendo, vien Sus. con una borsa in mano di denari, e lo trattiene.)*

**SUS:** Alto alto, signor Conte,
Mille doppie son quì pronte,
A pagar vengo per Figaro, Ed a porlo in libertà.

**IL C, D. C:** Non sappiam com' è la cosa, Osservate un poco là.
*(accennando Fig. abbracciato con Mar.)*

**SUS:** Già d' accordo con la sposa!
Giusti Dei! che infedeltà!
*(vuol partire; Fig. la trattiene.)*
Lascia, iniquo!

**FIG:** No, t' arresta
Senti, o cara—

**SUS:** Senti questa.
*(gli da uno schiaffo.)*
(Fremo! smanio di furore
Una vecchia me la fa!)

**IL C:** (Fremo! smanio dal furore
Il destino me la fa!)

**D. C:** Fre-eme-sma-nia da-al fu-uro-ore, Il destino, gliela fa!

**MAR, FIG, BAR:** È un effetto di buon cuore, Tutto amore è quel che fa.

**MAR:** Lo sdegno calmate
*(a Sus.)*
Mia cara figliuola,
Sua madre abbracciate,
Che or vostra sarà.

**SUS:** Sua madre?

**IL C., D.C.:** Sua madre?

**SUS:** Tua madre?

**FIG:** Mia madre,
E questo è mio padre,
*(di Bar.)*
Che a te lo dirà.

**SUS, MAR, FIG, BAR:** Al dolce contento—di questo momento Quest' anima appena—resistere or sa!

**IL C, D. C:** Al fiero tormento—di questo momento Quest' Quell' anima appena—resistere or sa
*(Il Cont. e D. C. partono.)*

**DON C:** He-e hi-is father? She-e hi-is mother.
*(to the Count. who pushes him.)*

**COUNT:** (I am surprised, I am astonished!)

**DON C:** The mar-ri-age can-no-ot take place.

**MAR:** Beloved son!

**FIG:** Dear mother!

**BAR:** Dear son!

**FIG:** Beloved father!

**COUNT:** (It is much better for me to go!)
*(as he goes, Sus. comes in with a purse of money in her hand, and stops him.)*

**SUS:** Stop, stop, Count; a thousand pistoles are ready here, and I am come to pay for Figaro, and restore him his liberty.

**COUNT, DON C:** We do not know how the business goes on; look there a bit.
*(pointing to Fig. who is embracing Mar.)*

**SUS:** Already agreed with the bride! Just gods! what infidelity!
*(going, Fig. stops her.)*
Leave me, villain!

**FIG:** No, stay; hear me, my love—
*(gives him a slap.)*

**SUS:** Hear this one.
(I fret, I rave with fury,
An old woman plays me a trick!)

**COUNT:** (I fret, I rave with fury,
Fate plays me a trick!)

**DON C:** (He fre-ets, he ra-aves with fu-ury,
Fate plays him a fine trick.)

**MAR, FIG, BAR:** It arises from goodness of heart;
Whatever he does in from love.

**MAR:** Your anger appease;
*(to Sus.)*
My daughter so dear,
His mother embrace,
Who now will be yours.

**SUS:** His mother?

**COUNT, DON C.:** His mother?

**SUS:** Your mother?

**FIG:** My mother, and this is my father
Who will tell it you.
*(pointing to Bar.)*

**SUS, MAR, FIG, BAR:** The unusual content of this happy moment My mind can hardly sustain with firmness.

**COUNT, DON C:** The cruel torment of this fatal moment (My/His) mind can hardly sustain with firmness.
*(exeunt the Count. and Don C.)*

## SCENA IV

*Susanna, Marcellina, Figaro, e Barberina.*

**MAR:** Prendi questo biglietto
Del denar che a me devi, ed è tua dote.
(*lo dà, e gli altri*)

**SUS:** Prendi ancor questa borsa.

**BAR:** E questa ancora.

**FIG:** Bravi! gettate pur, ch' io piglio ognora.

**SUS:** Voliamo ad informar di ogni avventura
(*a Fig.*)
Madama e nostro zio.
Chi al par di me contento?

**FIG:** Io.

**BAR:** Io.

**MAR:** Io.

**SUS, MAR, BAR, FIG:** E schiatti il signor Conte al gusto mio!
(*partono.*)

## SCENE IV

*Susanna, Marcellina, Figaro and Bartolo.*

**MAR:** Take this note for the money you owe me; it will be your portion.
(*gives it and the others.*)

**SUS:** Take this purse too.

**BAR:** And this one also.

**FIG:** Well done all! throw and welcome, I shall always take.

**SUS:** Let us fly (*to Fig.*) to inform Madame and our uncle of all that has happened. Who can be as happy as I?

**FIG:** I.

**BAR:** I.

**MAR:** I.

**SUS, MAR, BAR, FIG:** And may the Count go mad with rage at hearing of my happiness!
(*exeunt.*)

## SCENA V

*Bar. che tira per la mano Cherubino.*

**BAR:** Andiamo, andiam, bel paggio; in casa mia
Tutte ritroverai
Le più belle ragazze del Castello.

**CHE:** Ah! se il Conte mi trova,
Misero me! tu sai;
Che partito mi crede per Siviglia.

**BAR:** Odi: vogliamo adesso
Vestirti come noi;
Tutti insieme andsem poi
A presentar de' fiori a madamina;
Fidati, Cherubino a Barberina.
(*partono.*)

## SCENE V

*Barberina, pulling Cherubino by the band.*

**BAR:** Come, come, by pretty page: you will find at my house all the prettiest girls of the castle.

**CHE:** Oh! if the Count finds me, I am finished! You know he thinks I've gone to Seville.

**BAR:** Hear me; we want to dress you like one of us: we then shall all go to present some flowers to my lady. Cherubino, trust Barberina.
(*exeunt.*)

## SCENA VI

**LA CONTESSA:** (*sola*). E Susanna non viene! Sono onsiosa
Di saper come il Conte
Accolse la proposta; alquanto ardito
Il progetto mi par—Ad uno sposo
Sì vivace, e geloso
Ma che mal c' è? Cangiando i miei vestiti
Con quelli di Susanna, e i suoi co' miei—
Al favor della notte—O cielo! e a quale
Umil stato fatale io son ridotta
Da un consorte crudel, che dopo avermi
Con un misto inaudito
D' infedeltà, di gelosia, di sdegno—
Prima amata indi offesa, e alfin tradita.
Fammi or cercar da una mia serva aita!
Dove sono i bei momenti
Di dolcezza e di piacer?

## SCENE VI

**COUN:** (*alone*). And Susanna does not come! I am anxious to know how the Count received the proposal: the plan seems to me a bold one—to a husband so quick and jealous—but what harm is it? In changing my dress with Susanna, and she putting on mine—Favored by night—O Heavens! To what state of humiliation am I reduced by a cruel husband! who after having with an unheard-of mixture of infidelity, of jealousy, of anger—first beloved, then offended, and at last betrayed. I am now compelled to employ the assistance of a servant of mine!
Where have those charming moments fled
Of great sweetness and delight?
Where have those frequent oaths flown
Of that false deceitful mouth?
Why, if all is changed to sorrows
And to tears, for my poor heart,

Dove andaro i giuramenti
Di quel labbro menzogner?
Perchè mai, se in pianto e in peno
Per me tutto si cangiò
La memoria del mio bene
Dal mio sen non trespassò!
Ah! se almen la mia costanza
Nel languire amando ognor,
Mi portasse una speranza
Dan cangiar l' ingrato cor!
(*parte*)

The remembrance of my happiness
Is not flown away with them!
Ah! my constancy in loving,
And in suffering such pains,
Could at least afford me a hope
To change that ungrateful heart.
(*exit.*)

## SCENA VII

*Il Conte, ed Antonio col cappello da uffiziale di Cherubino in mano.*

**ANT:** Io vi dico, signor, che Cherubino
È ancora nel castello,
E vedete per prova il suo capello.

**IL C:** Ma come se a quest' ora
Esser giunto a Seviglia egli dovria?

**ANT:** Scusate, oggi Seviglia è in casa mia.
Là vestissi da donna, e là lasciati
Ha gli altri abiti suoi.

**IL C:** (Perfidi!)

**ANT:** Andiamo, e gli vedrete voi.
(*partono.*)

## SCENE VII

*The Count, and Antonio with Cherubino's regimental hat in his band.*

**ANT:** I tell you, sir, that Cherubino is still in the castle. and, as proof, here is his hat.

**COUNT:** How then, if by this time he ought to have arrived at Seville?

**ANT:** Pardon me, today Seville is in my house. He put on a female dress, and has left his own clothes in my house.

**COUNT:** (Deceivers!)

**ANT:** Let us go, and you may see them yourself.
(*exeunt.*)

## SCENA VIII

*La Contessa, e Susanna, che vengono insieme.*

**LA C:** Cosa mi narri? E che ne disse il Conte?

**SUS:** Gli si leggeva in fronte
Il dispetto e la rabbia.

**LA C:** Piano, chè meglio or lo porremo in gabbia.
Dov' è l' appuntamento
Che tu gli proponesti?

**SUS:** In giardino.

**LA C:** Fissiamogli ora un loco. Scrivi, scrivi—

**SUS:** Ch' io scriva? ma signora—

**LA C:** Eh, scrivi, dico; tutto
Io prendo su me stessa.
(*Sus. siede.*)

**LA C:** Canzonetta sull' aria—

**SUS:** —sull' aria.

**LA C:** Che soave zefiretto—

**SUS:** Zefiretto.

**LA C:** Questa sera spirera—

**SUS:** Questa, etc.

**LA C:** Sotto i pini del boschetto.

**SUS:** Sotto, etc.

**LA C, SUS:** Ei già, certo il reso capirà. (*Sus. piega il biglietto.*)

**SUS:** Piegato è il foglio; or come si sigilla?

## SCENE VIII

*Enter the Countess and Susanna together.*

**COUN:** What do you tell me? And what did the Count say about it?

**SUS:** One could read on his face vexation and rage.

**COUN:** Gently, we will catch him better now.
Where did you propose to meet him?

**SUS:** In the garden.

**COUN:** Let us now give him a place. Write—

**SUS:** I write? but, madam—

**COUN:** Come, write, I say; I take all upon myself.
(*Sus. takes a chair.*)

**COUN:** A song to the tune—

**SUS:** —To the tune.

**COUN:** Of sweet Zephyr—

**SUS:** Sweet Zephyr?

**COUN:** This night will marry—

**SUS:** —Will marry,

**COUN:** Under the pines in the grove—

**SUS:** —The grove.

**COUN, SUS:** (Of course/Certainly), he will understand the remainder.
(*Sus. folds up the note.*)

**SUS:** It is folded; now how is it to be sealed?

LA C: Ecco prendi una spilla,
Servirà di sigillo—attendi—scri-
vi—
Sul rovescio del foglio:
Rimandate il sigillo.
(*Sus. scrive.*)

SUS: È più bizzarro
Di quel della patente.

LA C: Presto nascondi, io sento venir gente.

## SCENA IX

*La Contessa e Susanna. Viene Cherubino in abitedi contadinella; e Barberina con varie altre contadine, che portano dei mazetti di fiori; poi Il Conte, ed Antonio in fondo; indi Figaro)*

**Cherubino e Barberina:** Ricevete, padroncina,
Queste rose e questi fior,
Che abbiam colti stammattina
Per mostrarvi il nostro amor
Siamo tante contadine,
E siam tutte poverine,
Ma quel poco che rechiamo
Ve diamo di buon cuor.

BAR: Queste sono. Madama,
Le ragazze del loco,
Che il poco ch' han vi vengono ad
offrire,
E vi chiedon perdon del loro ardire.

LA C: Venite quà, datemi i vostri
fiori.
(*prende il mazzetto di Cher. e lo bacia in fronte. Il Con. e Ant. entrano, ed Ant. esamina le ragazze.*)
Come arrossì! Susanna, non ti pare
Che somigli ad alcuno?

SUS: Al naturale!
(*Ant. scuopre Cher. gli leva la cuffia, gli pone il cappelo da uffiziale in testa, e dice al Con.*)

ANT: Eh! cospettaccio, quest' è l'
uffiziale.

LA C: (O stelle!)

SUS: (Malandrino!)

IL C: Ebben, madama?—
(*alla Cont.*) E perchè non partiste?
(*a Cher. che si cava il cappello.*)

CHE: Signor—

IL C: Saprò punire
La tua disubbidienza.
(*Vien Figaro.*)

FIG: Signor, se trattenete
Tutte queste ragazze,
Addio festa addio danza.

IL C: E che! vorresti
Ballar col piè stravolto?
(*ironica.*)

FIG: Eh, non mi duol più molto.
Andiam, belle faniculle.

LA C: (Come si caverà dall' imbarazzo?)
(*a Sus.*)

---

COUN: Here, take a pin, it will serve for a seal—
Mind—write on the back, send back the seal.
(*Sus. writes.*)

SUS: It is more odd than that of the commission—

COUN: Be quick, hide it; I hear some body coming.

## SCENE IX

*The Countess and Susanna. Enter Cherubino, dressed as a Country girl; and Barberina, with several Country Lasses, bringing nosegays; then the Count and Antonio at the farther end; afterwards Figaro.*

**CHERUBINO and BARBERINA:**
Receive, my dear mistress,
These roses and flowers,
Which we gathered this morning
To show you our love.
We are country girls,
And we are all poor;
But what little we offer,
We give with good heart.

BAR: Madam, these are the girls of this place, who come to offer you what little they have, and beg your pardon for their presumption.

COUN: Come here, give me your flowers.
(*takes Cher.'s nosegay, and kisses his forehead. Enter the COUNT and Ant.; he examines the girls.*) What blushes! Susanna, do not you think there is a great resemblance to some body?

SUS: To the life.
(*Ant. discovers Cher., pulls his cap off, claps his regimental hat on, and says to the Count,*)

ANT: Ha! by Jupiter, this is the officer.

COUN: (O heavens!)

SUS: (Wicked dog!)

COUNT: Well, madam?
(*to the Coun.*)
And why didn't you set out?
(*to Cher., who pulls off his hat.*)

CHE: Sir—

COUNT: I shall know how to punish your disobedience.
(*Enter Figaro.*)

FIG: Sir, if you stop all these girls, there is an end of the entertainments and the dance.

COUNT: Would you dance with a sprain in your foot?
(*ironically.*)

FIG: Oh! it does not give me much pain now. Come, my pretty girls.

COUN: (How will he get through the scrape?)
(*whispering to Sus.*)

---

SUS: Lasciate fare a lui.

IL C: Per buona sorte,
(*a Fig.*)
I vasi eran di creta.

SUS: Senza fallo!
Andiamo, dunque, andiamo.

ANT: Ed intanto a cavallo
Di galoppo a Siviglia andava il paggio.

FIG: Di galoppo o di passo, buon viaggio.
Venite belle giovani.
(*si sente la marcia in lontano.*)
Ecco la marcia, andiamo,
Ai vostri posti, o belle;
(Susanna, dammi il braccio!

SUS: Eccolo.

IL C: (Temerarj! io son di ghiaccio!)
(*partono tutti; eccetio Il Con. e La Cont.*)

IL C: Contessa!

LA C: Or non parliamo,
Ecco quì le due nozze,
Riceverle dobbiamo: alfin si tratta
D' una vostra protetta.
*ironica.*)
Sediam.

IL C: Sediamo; (e meditiam vendetta!)

## SCENA X

*Il Conte e La Contessa seduti sul sofà; Susanna a braccio con Figaro, e Marcellina con Bartolo; Basilio ed Antonio; Contadini e Contadine, Servi e Guardie.*

*Varie Contadinelle portano il cappellino verginale, ornato di piume bianche, il velo, i guanti, ed il mazzetto per Sus. e per Mar. Bart. e Fig. vengono insieme. Ant. conduce Sus. dinanzi al Conte, ed ella s'inginocchia. Mentre Il Conte le pone in testa il cappellino, ed il velo, e la da i guanti ed il mazzetto, si canti il Coro. Sus. dà al Conte, furtivamente un biglietto, ed egli se lo pone in seno con desirezza. Fig. viene a ricever Sus. dalle mani del Conte e si ritira dall' altra parte vicino a Mar. Segue intanto una lieta danza.*

CORO: Amanti costanti—seguaci d' onor,
Cantate, lodate—sì saggio signor.
A un dritto cedendo—che—oltraggia, che offende,
Ei caste vi rendo—ai vostri amator.

TUTTI: Cantiamo, lodiamo, sì saggio signor.
(*Il Con. nell' aprire il biglietto si punge, e getta via lo spillo.*)

IL C: È già solita usanza;
Le donne ficcan gli aghi in ogni loco
Ah! ah! capisco il giuoco!
(*cerca lo spillo.*)

---

SUS: (Let him alone.)

COUNT: Luckily the pots were of clay.

FIG: Without doubt! let us go then, let us go.

ANT: And in the mean time the page was galloping away to Seville.

FIG: Galloping or cantering a good journey. Come, my pretty damsels.
(*a March is heard at a distance.*)
Here is the march, let us go; take your places, my beauties. (Susanna, give me your arm.)

SUS: Here it is.

COUNT: (Impudent ones, I am frozen!)
(*exeunt all, except the Count and Coun.*)

COUNT: Countess!

COUN: Let us not speak now; here are the two weddings, we must receive them: mind, it is a protégé of yours that is in question.
(*ironically.*)

COUNT: Let us sit down and think of revenge!

## SCENE X

*The Count and Countess seated on a sofa. Enter Sus. and Fig. arm in arm, and Mar. with Bart., Basillo and Ant. Country people, Servants, and Guards.*

*Some country girls bring the little virginal hat adorned with white feathers, the veil, the gloves, the nosegays, for Sus. and Mar. Enter Bart. and Fig. together. Ant. leads Sus. before the Count, and she kneels. While the Count puts the little hat on her head, and the veil, and gives her the gloves and nosegay, the Chorus is sung. Sus. gives slyly the Count a note, and he puts it dexterously into his waistcoat. Fig. comes to receive Sus. from the hands of the Count, and withdraws on the other side, near Mar. Then follows a merry dance.*

Chorus: You constant lovers, who follow honor,
Do sing, do praise so good a lord;
Who gives up a right, insulting, degrading,
And return chastely to your lovers.

ALL: Let us sing, let us praise so good a lord,
(*the Count on opening the note pricks himself, and throws away the pin.*)

COUNT: (It is the usual custom, women thrust pins everywhere.)
Oh! oh! I understand the trick now!
(*looks for the pin.*)

## Act III, Scene X

FIG: (Un biglietto amoroso!
(*a Mar. e Sus.*)
Che gli diè nel passar qualche galante,
Ed era sigillato d' uno spillo
Ond' ei si punse il dito;
Il Narciso or lo cerca: oh, che stordito!)
(*Il Con. trova lo spillo, e lo prende. Finisce il ballo.*)

IL C: Andate amici, e sia per questa sera
Disposto l' apparato nuziale,
Colla più ricca pompa; io vo' che sia
Magnifica la festa; e canti, e fuochi,
E gran cena, e gran ballo; ognuno impari
Com' io tratto color che a me son cari.
(*partono tutti.*)

*FINE DELL' ATTO TERZO*

## ■ ATTO IV

Gran Viale del Giardino, che conduce al Castello.

Barberina, che tiene in mano un' arancia, una ciambella, ed un lanternino nell' altra, cercando qualche cosa per terra con ansietà. Indi Fig. e Mar. Notte.

BAR: L' ho perduta—me meschina!
Ah! chi sa dove sarà?
La mia povera cugina,
Il padron cosa dirà?
(*piango.*)
(*Vengono Fig. e Mar.*)

FIG: Barberina, cos' hai?

BAR: L' ho perduta cugino.

FIG: Cosa?

MAR: Cosa?

BAR: La spilla,
Che a me dette il padrone
Per recare a Susanna.

FIG: A Susanna la spilla?

BAR: A te già niente, preme?

FIG: Oh! niente, niente?

BAR: Addio, mio bel cugino;
Vo' da Susanna, e poi da Cherubino!
(*parte.*)

FIG: Madre?

MAR: Figlio?

FIG: Son morto!
Ah! quella spilla, o madre, è quella stessa
Che poc' anzi raccoiso.

MAR: È ver, ma questo,
Al più, ti porge un dritto
Solo di stare in guardia.

FIG: All' arte dunque, il loco del congresso
So dov' è stabilito.

---

FIG: (A love letter? (*to MAR. and SUS.*) which some lover's friend gave him in passing, and it was sealed with a pin, which pricked his finger. The Adonis is now looking for it: oh! what a foolish fellow!)
(*the Count finds the pin, and takes it; the dance ends.*)

COUNT: Go, my friends, and let the nuptial preparations be ready for to-night, with the richest pomp: I will have the entertainment be magnificent; singing, fire-works, a great supper, and a grand ball; let all learn how I treat those who are dear to me.
(*exeunt all.*)

END OF ACT III.

## ■ ACT IV

A great Alley in the Garden, leading to the Castle.

Barb. with an orange and a cake in one hand, and a little lantern in the other, looking uneasily for something on the ground. Then Fig. and Mar. Night.

BAR: I have lost it—how unlucky?
Oh! who know where it is? my poor cousin, my master, what will he say?
(*cries.*)
(*enter Fig. and Mar.*)

FIG: Barberina, what is the matter?

BAR: I have lost it, cousin.

FIG: What?

MAR: What?

BAR: The pin my master gave me to carry to Susanna.

FIG: A pin to Susanna.

BAR: It is of no consequence to you?

FIG: Oh! none, none!

BAR: Adieu, my pretty cousin; I shall go to Susanna, then to Cherubino.
(*exit.*)

FIG: Mother?

MAR: Son?

FIG: I am dead!
Oh! that pin, my mother, is the very same which not long ago he picked up.

MAR: It is true; but this gives you, at most, a right to be upon your guard.

FIG: I must look sharp then; I know where the meeting place is.

---

MAR: Dove vai, figlio mio?

FIG: A vendicar tutti i mariti, addio!
(*parte.*)

MAR: Presto avvertiam Susanna;
Io la credo innocente: quella faccia,
Quell' aria di modestia.
Ah! quando il cor non ci arma
Personale interesse,
Ogni donna è portala alla difesa
Del suo povero sesso,
Da questi uomini ingrati a torto oppresso.
Il capro e la capretta
Son sempre in amistà;
L' agnello, all' agnelletta
La guerra mai non fa.
Le più feroci belve
Per selve e per campagne
Lascian le lor campagne
In pace e libertà.
Sol noi povere femmine,
Che tanto amiam questi uomini,
Trattate siam dai perfidi
Ognor con crudeltà.
(*parte.*)

### SCENA XII

Giardino. In fondo un Viale di Pini. Dai lati due Padiglioni chiusi praticabili.

Barberina, Figaro, Bartolo, e Basilio, con alcuni sgherri.

BAR: Nel padiglione a manca, ei così disse:
È questo, è questo—e poi se non venisse?
Ebben che cosa importa?
Sempre avrò fatto ben—oh Dio! son morta.
(*vede venir gente, ed entra nel padiglioni a sinistra. Vengono da una parte Fig. e Bar. dall' altra Bas. e varj sgherri.*)

FIG: È Barberina—chi va là?

BAS: Son quelli, che invistaste a venir.

BAR: Che brutto ceffo!
Sembri un conspirator; (che diamin sono
Quegli infausti apparati?)

BAS: (Ora capisco come Accordati si son senza di me.)

FIG: Voi da questi contorni
(*agli sgherri.*)
Non vi scostate: intanto
Io vado a dar certi ordini,
E torno in pochi istanti;
A un fischio mio, correte tutti quanti.
(*si ritira con ossi.*)

BAS: Ha i diavoli nel corpo!

BAR: Ma cosa pensi?

---

MAR: Where are you going, son?

FIG: To revenge all the husbands; adieu!
(*exit.*)

MAR: Quick, I must let Susanna know; I believe she is innocent; her face, her modest air. Ah! when personal interest does not harden our hearts, every women is inclined to defend those of her poor sex, wronged and oppressed by men. The goat and his dear mate Are ever tender friends; The lamb never molests His gentler companion. The most ferocious beasts Grant their partners In peace and liberty to live, Through forests and through fields. It is only we poor women, Who love these men so much, That are so cruelly treated By these treacherous men.
(*exit.*)

### SCENE XII

A Garden. At the bottom, an Alley of Pines. On the sides, two Pavilions, with the doors shut.

Barberina, Figaro, Bartolo, and Basilio, with some Ruffians.

BAR: In the pavilion on the left as he said; it is this, it is this—and then, if he doesn't come—Well, what does that signify? I shall always have done right—O gods! I am dead!
(*sees people coming, goes into the Pavilion on the left. Enter from one side, Fig. and Bar.; from the other side, Bas. and some Ruffians.*)

FIG: It is Barberina—Who goes there?

BAS: The men you invited to come.

BAR: What an ugly face! you look like a conspirator. (What the deuce are those ill-looking appearances?)

BAS: (Now I understand how they have agreed without me.)

FIG: Do not go (*to the ruffians*) far from here; mean while I shall go to give certain orders, and shall be back in a few moments; when I whistle all of you, run!
(*withdraws with them.*)

BAS: He has the devil in his body!

BAR: But what are you thinking about?

**BAS:** Nulla;
Susanna piace al Conte, ella d'accordo
Gli diè un appuntamento,
Che a Figaro non piace.

**BAR:** E che? Dunque dovria soffrirlo in pace?

**BAS:** Nel mondo, amico mio,
L'accozzarlo co' grandi,
Fu pericolo ognora,
Da novanta per cento, e han vinto ancora.
In quegli anni, in cui val poco
La mal pratica ragion,
Ebbi anch' io lo stesso fuoco,
Fui quel pazzo che or non son.
Che col tempo, co' perigli
Donna Flemma capitò,
E i capricci, ed i puntigli
Dalla testa mi cavò.
Presso un piccolo abituro
Seco lei mi trase un giorno,
E togliendo giù dal muro
Del pacifico soggiorno
Una pelle di somaro,
Prendi, disse, o figlio caro,
Poi disparve, e mi lasciò.
Mentre ancor tacito, guardo quel dono,
Il ciel si annuvola, rimbomba il tuono,
Mista alla grandine, scroscia la piova;
Ecco le membra coprir mi giova
Col manto d'asino che mi donò.
Finisce il turbine, io fo due passi:
Che fiera orribile innanzi a me fassi;
Già già mi tocca l'ingorda bocca;
Già di difendermi speme non ho.
Ma il fiuto ignobile del mio vestito.
Tolse alle belva sì l'appetito,
Che disprezzandomi si rinselvò.
Così conoscere mi fe la sorte,
Ch' onte, pericoli, vergogna e morte
Col cuoja d'asino fuggir si può.
(*si ritirano.*)

## SCENA XIII

*Figaro solo.*

**FIG:** 'Tutto è disposto: l'ora
Dovrebbe esser vicina—io sento gente—
Edessa—non è alcun: buja è la notte,
Ed io comincio amai
A far lo scimunito!
Mestiere di marito!
Ingrata! nel momento
Della mia cerimonia
Ei godeva leggendo, e vederlo,
Io rideva di me senza saperlo!
O Susanna! Susanna!
Quanta pena mi costi!
Con quell' ingenua faccia—
Con quegi occhi innocenti—
Chi creduto l' avria—
Ah! che il fidarsi a donna è gran follia!

**BAS:** Nothing; the Count likes Susanna; she consenting, fixed a meeting which Figaro does not like.

**BAR:** What? Should he bear it patiently?

**BAS:** My friend, in this world it was always dangerous to oppose the great; if they give ninety points in a hundred, they still win any game. In those years when inexperienced Reason is of little avail. I too had the same great fire; I was that madman, I am no more. That time no less than dangers, Have brought me, madam, patience, Who drove out of my head My whims and all punctilios. One day she took me to A humble dwelling place, And took down from the wall Of the peaceful abode The skin of an old ass; Take this, she said, dear son, Then she left me and disappeared, while I still beheld the gift. I saw the clouds come on, I heard the thunder, And hail and rain flew around the land; I therefore found it good to cover myself With the mantle of the skin she gave me. The storm ceased. I went on a little; I saw a wild beast rushing near me; I saw his mouth voracious upon my limbs All hopes I had to defend myself had fled But the ignoble scent of my dress Cured the beast of its appetite, That, despising me, it went into the wood. Thus fate made me discover, That disgrace, danger, shame, and death, May be avoided with an ass's skin. (*they withdrew.*)

## SCENE XIII

*Figaro alone.*

**FIG:** "All is prepared: the hour ought to be near—I hear somebody—it's her—No, it is nobody: the night is dark, and I begin now to play the silly part of a husband! Ungrateful woman! At the moment of my ceremony, he was enjoying what he read, and on seeing him, I was laughing at my own expense without knowing it! O Susanna! Susanna! What anguish you cost me!—With that air of sincerity—with those innocent eyes—who could have believed it!—Ah! trusting to a woman is a great folly! "Open your eyes a little, imprudent and silly men; look at these women—see what they are. These called goddesses by the deceived

Aprite un po' quelgi occhj,
Uomini incauti, e sciocchi,
Guardate queste femmine,
Guardate cosa son.
Queste chiamate Dee
Dagl' ingannati sensi,
A cui tributa incensi
La debole ragion,
Son streghe, che incantano per farci penar;
Sirene che cantano per farci affogar;
Civette che allettano per trarci le piume,
Comete che brillano per toglierci il lume;
Son rose spinose, son volpi vezzose!
Son orse benigne, colombe maligne:
Maestre d'inganni, amiche d'affanni,
Che fingono, mentono,
Amore non sentono,
Non senton pietà.
Il resto nol dico.
Già ogouno la sa'
(*si ritiro.*)

## SCENA XIV

*La Contessa, Susanna, Marcellina, Figaro, che passeggia.*

**SUS:** Signora, ella mi disse,
Che Figaro verravvi.

**MAR:** Anzi venuto,
Abbassa un po' la voce.

**SUS:** Dunque un ci ascolta, e l'altro
Dee venir a cercarmi:
Incominciam.

**MAR:** Io voglio quì celarmi.
(*si ritira*)

**SUS:** Madama, voi tremate; avreste freddo?
(*alla Con.*)

**LA C:** Parmi umida, la notte: io mi ritiro;
(*si ritira: comparisce Fig.*)

**FIG:** Eccoci della, crisi al grand' istante!
(*passeggia e si ritira, poi subito ricomparisce ed ascolta.*)

**SUS:** Il birbo è in sentinella,
Divertiamci anche noi,
Diamogli la mercè dei dubbj suoi.
Giunse al fine il momento,
(*Fig. ascolta.*)
Che godrò senza affanno
In braccio all' idol mio: timide cure,
Uscite dal mio petto,
A turbar non venite il mio diletto.
Oh! come par che all' amoroso fuoco
L' amenità del loco,
La terra, il ciel risponda,
Come la notte i furti miei seconda!
Deh! vieni, non tardar, o gioja bella,
Vieni ove Amore per goder t' appella;
Finchè risplende in ciel notturna face,
Finchè l' aria è ancor bruna, e il

senses to whom altars are raised by weak reason. "They are witches that bewitch, to put us to torment; sirens who sing but to drown us; owls to ensnare us, to pick our feathers; comets which shine to dazzle and blind us; they are roses full of thorns, they are beautiful foxes; they are kind bears, wicked doves; skillful in fraud, creatures of sorrow, who dissemble, lie, feel neither love nor pity. "I say no more, for it is needless." (*withdraws.*)

## SCENE XIV

*The Countess, Susanna, Marcellina, Figaro, walking about.*

**SUS:** Madam, you told me that Figaro would come.

**MAR:** No, he is here; speak softly.

**SUS:** Then one hears us, and the other has come to seek me; let me begin.

**MAR:** I will conceal myself here. (*draws aside.*)

**SUS:** Madame, you tremble; are you cold?
(*to the Coun.*)

**COUN:** I think it is a damp night: I withdraw.
(*withdraws. Fig. appears.*)

**FIG:** We are now at the moment of the great crisis!
(*walks about, withdraws, then immediately reappears.*)

**SUS:** The rogue is upon the watch; I will amuse myself too, and reward him for his suspicions. At last the moment has come (*Fig. listens.*) that I shall be happy with my love; timid apprehensions, begone from my breast; come not to trouble my happiness. Oh! how it seems that the beauty of the place, the earth, the sky, answer to my amorous wishes! How night favors my secret love! Then come, do not delay, my dearest jewel. Ah! come where love invites you to be happy. Come, while the stars of night shine in the sky. While darkness reigns, the world is wrapped in silence. The brook here murmurs, here the

# Act IV, Scene XIV

mondo tace.
Quì mormora il ruscel, quì scherza l' aura,
Che col dolce susurro il cor ristaura;
Quì ridono i fioretti, e l' erba fresca
Ai piaceri d' amor quì tutto adesca.
Vieni, ben mio, fra queste piante ascose,
To vo' la fronte incoronar di rose.
(*si ritira.*)

## SCENA XVI

*Fig., Che. da uffiziale; poi tutti gli altri a loro tempo. La Con. esce subito cogli abiti di Sus.*

FIG: Perfida! e in questa forma
Meco mentià!—non so s' io vegli, o dorma!

CHE: Là, là, là, là, là, lerà.

LA C: Il picco! paggio.

CHE: Io sento gente, entriamo
Dove entrò Barberina—
Oh! vedo quì una donna.

LA C: Ahimè meschina!

CHE: M' inganno? a quel cappello,
Che nell' ombra vegg' io, parmi Susanna.

LA C: Ah! se il Conte ora vien!—
sorte tiranna!

CHE: (Pian pianin le andrò più presso;
(*si avvicina.*)
Tempo perso non sarà.)

LA C: Ah! se il Conte arriva adesso,
Qualche imbroglio accaderà.

CHE: Susannetta? (non risponde;
Or la burlo in verità.)
(*la prende per la mano.*)

LA C: Arditello!—sfacciatello,
Ite presto via di quà.

CHE: Smorfiosa, maliziosa,
Io già so perchè soi quà.
(*Vengono Il Con. e Fig.*)

LA C: Ah! se arriva quì il Conte,
siam perduti!

CHE: Dunque tu mi rifiuti
Una semplice occhiata, e al Conte poi—

LA C: Partite tosto, o chiamo gente!

CHE: Ingrata!

IL C: Questa mi par Susanna.

LA C: (Ecco quì il Conte.)

FIG: (Teniam le mani pronte.)

CHE: (Il Conte! O Dio! Son morto,
La tempesta prevedo, e vado in porto.)
(*entra dove è andato Bar.*)

zephyrs play,
And their sweet sounds give comfort to the heart.
Here the gay little flowers seem to smile around,
And the fresh grass invites us all to love.
Ah! come, my love, in these sequestered bowers;
And I encircle your head with roses.
(*withdraws.*)

## SCENE XVI

*Fig., Che. in an Officer's regimentals; then all the others in their turn. The Countess comes out immediately, in Susanna's dress.*

FIG: False woman! And in this manner did she impose upon me! I don't know whether I am awake or asleep!

CHE: La, la, la, la, la lera.

COUN: The little page.

CHE: I hear people about, I'll go where Barberina went! Oh! I see a woman here.

COUN: Alas! I am undone!

CHE: Do I mistake? By the hat I perceive in the dark, I think it is Susanna.

COUN: Ah! if the Count should come now! Cruel fate.

CHE: (I will go softly nearer to her.
It will not be lost time.)
(*approaches her.*)

COUN: Oh! If the Count should come now, something bad will happen.

CHE: Dear Susanna? (She gives no answer; I shall now catch her indeed.)
(*takes her by the hand.*)

COUN: Little bold fellow!—Little impudent fellow, begone quickly from here.

CHE: Madame affectation, madame deep-one, I know why you are here.
(*Enter the Count and Figaro.*)

COUN: If the Count should happen to come now, we are undone!

CHE: Then, you wicked creature, you deny me a single glance, and with the Count—

COUN: Begone, or I will cry out for help!

CHE: You ungrateful hussy!

COUN: 'Tis Susanna, I think.

COUN: (Here is the Count.)

FIG: (Let us be prepared for blows.)

CHE: (Oh! I see the Count, I am undone; the storm is at hand, let us take shelter here.)
(*enters where Barb. went.*)

IL C: Son quì, dammi la mano,
Amabile Susanna—ah! vieni—

FIG: (Indegni!)

LA C: O ciel! di là vien gente!

IL C: Chi va là?

FIG: Un galantuom.

IL C: Figaro parmi
Precedimi, verrò; voglio celarmi.
(*La Cont. entra nel padiglione a dritta, Il Con. va in fondo.*)

FIG: Tutta è tranquillo e placido;
Entrò la bella Venere,
Col vago Marte prendere
Nuovo Vulcan del secolo
In rete la potrò.
(*Vien Susanna.*)

SUS: Ehi? Figaro, tacete.

FIG: (Oh! questa è la Contessa.)
A tempo quì giungete,
Vedrete da voi stessa
Il Conte, e la mia sposa;
Di propria man la cosa
Toccare vi farò.

SUS: Parlate un po' più basso:
(*con voce alterata.*)
Di quà non movo il passo,
Ma vendicar mi vo'.

FIG: (Susanna!) Vendicarsi?

SUS: Sì.

FIG: Come potria farsi?

SUS: (L' iniquo io vo' sorprendere,
Poi so quel che farò.)

FIG: (La volpe vuol sorprendere,
E secondar la vo'.)
(*Sus. vuole schiaffeggiar, Fig. che si difende con grazia.*)

FIG: Pace, pace, mio dolce tesoro;
Conosciuto ho la voce che adoro,
E che impressa ognor serbo nel cor.

SUS: La mia voce?

FIG: La voce che adoro.

FIG & SUS: Pace, pace, mio dolce tesoro,
Pace pace, mio tenero amor.
(*Viene Il Con.*)

IL C: Non la trovo, girai tutto il bosco.

SUS, FIG: (Questi è il Conte, alla voce il conosco.)

IL C: Ehi? Susanna? Sei sorda? Sei muta?

SUS: (Bella! bella! non l' ha conosciuta!)

FIG: (Chi?)

SUS: Madama.

FIG: Che dici! Madama?

SUS, FIG: La commedia, idol mio, terminiamo, Consoliamo il bizzarro amator.
(*Fig. s' inginocchia avanti a Sus.*)
Sì Madama, voi siete il ben mio.
(*a Sus.*)

COUNT: Here I am, dear Susy, give me your hand. Come!

FIG: (O you wretched creature!)

COUN: (Heavens! some body is coming!)

COUNT: Who goes there?

FIG: Friends.

COUNT: 'Tis Figaro, I think; go before; I will conceal myself for a moment.
(*the Coun. goes into the Pavilion on the right, the Count goes towards the farther end.*)

FIG: All here is quiet and tranquil,
The fair Venus has gone
With her beloved Mars,
A Vulcan of this age;
I'll catch her in my net.
(*Enter Susanna.*)

SUS: Hear me? Figaro, be silent.

FIG: (Oh! this is the Countess.)
You come in the right time,
You will yourself behold
The Count and my bride:
I will you quite convince!
Of it with your own eyes.

SUS: Speak softer;
(*changing her voice a little*)
I shall not stir a step,
But will be revenged.

FIG: (Susanna!) Revenged?

SUS: Yes.

FIG: How can it be done?

SUS: (I will surprise the villain;
then I know what I shall do.)

FIG: (The fox wants to surprise,
and I will assist.)
(*Sus. goes to box Fig's ears, who defends himself gracefully.*)

FIG: Peace, peace, my sweet love;
I discovered the voice I adore,
And which is ever imprinted on my heart.

SUS: My voice?

FIG: The voice I adore.

FIG & SUS: Peace, peace, my sweet treasure;
Peace, peace, my tender love.
(*Enter the Count.*)

COUNT: I can not find her. I have gone all over the wood.

SUS, FIG: (This is the Count; I know him by his voice.)

COUNT: Here, Susanna, are you deaf? Are you dumb?

SUS: (A fine one, a fine one indeed! He did not know her!)

FIG: (Who?)

SUS: Madame.

FIG: What do you say? Madame?

SUS, FIG: My love, let us finish this farce, let us comfort the whimsical lover.
(*Fig. kneels before Sus.*)

IL C: (La mia sposa, e senz' arme son io!)

FIG: Un ristoro al mio cor concedete.

SUS: Io son quì, faccio quel che volete.

IL C: (Ah! ribaldi!)

SUS, FIG: Ah! corriamo, mio bene, E le pene compensi piacer.
(Sus. entra nel padiglione a sinistra, Il Cont. chiama gente.)

IL C: Gente? all' armi!

FIG: Ohimè il padrone! (finge pauro.)

IL C: Gente, ajuto!

FIG: Son perduto! (vengono in fretta Bart., Basil., Anton., contadini con torce.)

BAR, BAS, ANT: Cos' avvenne?

IL C: Il scellerato (dì Fig.) M' ha tradito, mi ha infamato, E con chi, state a veder, (entra nel padiglione a sinistra)

BAR, BAS, ANT: Son stordito, sbalordito! Non mi par che ciò si aver.

FIG: Son stordito sbalordito! (Oh che scena! che piacer!) (Il Con. tira Cher. per un braccio senza guardarlo.)

---

FIG: Yes, Madame, you are my love. (to Sus.)

COUNT: (My wife! and I unarmed!)

FIG: Grant comfort to my heart.

SUS: I am here, ready to please you.

COUNT: (Villains!)

SUS, FIG: Let us run, my love, that pleasure may compensate pain. (Sus. goes into the Pavilion on the left. The Count calls out for assistance.)

COUNT: People? To arms!

FIG: Alas! my master! (pretending fear.)

COUNT: People! help!

FIG: I am undone. (enter in haste Bart., Basil., Ant., and Countrymen, with torches.)

BAR., BAS., ANT: What is the matter?

COUNT: The villain (of Fig.) has betrayed me, has disgraced me? and with whom? go and see. (goes into the pavilion on the left.)

BAR. BAS. ANT. FIG: I am surprised, I am astonished! It does not seem to me true. I am surprised, I am astonished! (What a scene what a delight!) (the Count pulls Che. along by the arm without looking at him.)

---

IL C: Invan resisti; uscite, Madama, Il premio ora avrete di vostra onestà. (si avanzano Sus., Mar., Barb., sorpressa generale.)

IL C: Il paggio!

ANT: Mia figlia!

FIG: Mia Madre!

FIG, BAR, ANT: Madama!

IL C: Scoperta è la trama, la perfida è quà. (Sus. si copre il viso col ventaglio.)

SUS: Perdono! perdono!

IL C: No, no, non vo' darlo.

FIG, BAS, ANT, SUS: Perdono!

IL C: No, no! (La Contessa viene dal padiglione alla destra.)

LA C: Almeno per loro perdono otterrò.

FIG, BAS, ANT, SUS: O cielo! che veggio, delirio! vaneggio! E creder non so!

IL C: Contessa, perdono!

LA C: Più docile io sono, E dico di sì.

TUTTI: Ah! tutti contenti saremo così. Questo giorno di tormenti, Di capricci e di follia, In contenti, e in allegria Solo Amor può terminar. Sposi, amici! al ballo, al giuoco Alle mine date fuoco, Ed al suon di lieta marcia Corriam tutti a festeggiar.

*END OF OPERA*

---

COUNT: In vain you resist; come out, Madame; you shall now receive the reward of your honesty. (Sus., Mar., Bar. come forward; a general surprise ensues.)

COUNT: The page!

ANT: My daughter!

FIG: My mother!

FIG, BAS, ANT: Madame!

COUNT: The plot is discovered, the traitress is here. (Sus. hides her face with her fan.)

SUS: Pardon! Pardon!

COUNT: No, no, I will not grant it.

FIG, BAS, ANT, SUS: Pardon!

COUNT: No, no! (the Coun. comes out of the pavilion on the right.)

COUN: At least I shall obtain pardon for them.

FIG, BAS, ANT, SUS: O heavens! What do I see? am I right? am I in my senses? I can not believe it.

COUNT: Countess, pardon?

COUN: I am more condescending, and say yes.

ALL: Then we shall be most pleased and happy For this sad day of torments, Of strange whims, and of folly In contentment and in mirth, Love alone will terminate. Bride and bridegroom, friends, advance, Repair to the merry sports, Let us all be merry here To the sound of lively music.

*END OF OPERA*

# Don Giovanni (1787)

## Don Juan

MUSIC BY WOLFGANG AMADEUS MOZART ■ LIBRETTO BY LORENZO DA PONTE

This two-act *dramma giocoso*, set to a libretto by Lorenzo da Ponte, premiered at the National Theater in Prague on October 29, 1787. It is said that Mozart wrote the overture for this magnificent opera the night before its premiere in 3 hours' time! There is also a story that, at the first rehearsal, Mozart was not satisfied with Zerlina's cry of terror; leaving the orchestra pit, he hid behind the wings and, at her cue, he pinched her. When she shrieked, Mozart said, "that is the way I want it." The opera opens with Leporello, Don Giovanni's servant, declaiming the number of Don Giovanni's conquests—1,003 in Spain. Don Giovanni comes in, followed by Donna Anna and then her father, the Commandant. Don Giovanni murders the Commandant in a duel. Donna Anna, in her grief, swears vengeance. Next enters Donna Elvira, whom Don Giovanni has deserted just as he was eloping with her. The action now moves to a country spot where villagers are singing and dancing in celebration of the upcoming marriage of Zerlina and Masetto. Don Giovanni decides to seduce Zerlina; Leporello invites the merry-makers to the castle and detains Zerlina. Just as Don Giovanni is about to win her over, Donna Elvira denounces him. Donna Anna and Don Ottavio, Donna Anna's fiancé, also enter and it is during this scene that Donna Anna recognizes the voice of her father's murderer. After many dramatic developments, a man in stone appears at a banquet held at Don Giovanni's castle; it is the statue of the Commandant. The statue asks Don Giovanni, I have been your guest. Will you be mine? and, when Don Giovanni wrenches himself free from the statue's grip and refuses to repent, a fiery pit opens and engulfs Don Giovanni in its flames.

---

## ■ ATTO I

### SCENA I

*Piazza. Da un lato il Palazzo del Commendatore; dall'altro una Locanda.—S'appressa l'alba.*

*Leporello; indi Don Giovanni e Donna Anna.*

**LEPORELLO:** Notte e giorno faticar,
Per chi nulla sà gradir;
Piòva e vento sopportar,
Mangiar male e mal dormir.
Voglio far il gentiluomo,
E non voglio più servir;
Nò, nò, nò, non voglio più servir.
Oh che caro galantuomo:
Vuol star dentro colla bella,
Ed io far la sentinella!
Voglio far il gentiluomo,
E non voglio più servir,
Nò, nò, nò, non voglio più servir.
Ma mi par, che venga gente,
Non mi voglio far sentir, Ah!
*(Entra Don Giovanni, e Donna Anna.)*

**ANNA:** Non sperar, se non m'uccidi,
Ch'io ti lascio fuggir mai.

**GIOVANNI:** Donna folle, indarno gridi!
Chi son io tu non saprai.

**LEPORELLO:** (Che tumulto! oh, ciel, che gridi)
Il padron in nuovi guai!

**GIOVANNI:** (Taci, e trema al mio furore.)

**ANNA:** Scelerato!

**GIOVANNI:** Sconsigliata!

**ANNA:** Genti, servi! traditore!
Come furia disperata
Ti saprò perseguitar.

**GIOVANNI:** (Questa furia disperata
Mi vuol far precipitar.)

**LEPORELLO:** (Sta a veder ch'il malandrino
Mi farà precipitar.)
*(Esce Donna Anna).*

### SCENA II

*Don Giovanni, il Commendatore, Leporello.*

**COMMENDATORE:** Lasciala, indegno;
Battiti meco.

**GIOVANNI:** Va, non mi degno
Di pugnar teco.

**COMMENDATORE:** Così pretendi
Da me fuggir?

**LEPORELLO:** (Potessi almeno
Di quà partir.)

**COMMENDATORE:** Batti!

---

## ■ ACT I

### SCENE I

*A Square. On one side, the Palace of the Commandant; on the other, an Hotel with a Balcony. Time, Daybreak.*

*Leporello; afterwards Don Juan and Donna Anna.*

**LEPORELLO:** I'm tortured night and day,
And no thanks I ever get;
Now I'm chilled by piercing winds,
Now with rain I'm dripping wet.
I'm resolved to change my state,
And be a gentleman so great;
Yes, yes, yes, and be a gentleman so great.
I've a precious master truly;
While within he woos the ladies,
I must sentinel without be!
I'm resolved to change my state,
And be a gentleman so great.
Softly now, there's someone coming,
And I must not be seen here.
*(Enter Don Juan, followed by Donna Anna.)*

**ANNA:** Till your name I've learned, you viper,
From this spot you shall not go.

**JUAN:** Foolish girl, beware my fury! Who I am you shall never know.

**LEPORELLO:** (What a tumult! oh, dear, what screaming).
My master's in some new trouble!

**JUAN:** (Be silent, or my rage you'll rue.).

**ANNA:** Miscreant!

**JUAN:** Imprudent woman!

**ANNA:** Villain, tremble! Help! what, ho!
I'm desperate,
Any my persecutor fain would know.

**JUAN:** (Some fearful act she'll surely
Make me do.).

**LEPORELLO:** (Some fearful act! and
I must share it, too.).
*(Exit Donna Anna).*

### SCENE II

*Don Juan, the Commandant, and Leporello.*

**COMMANDANT:** Unhand her, villain;
Turn and defend yourself.

**JUAN:** Hence, fool! I deign not to fight with you.

**COMMANDANT:** Do you fear me? Do you from me fly?

**LEPORELLO:** (I wish I could—I think I'll try.).

**COMMANDANT:** Coward!

GIOVANNI: Misero! attendi,
Se vuoi morir.
(*Si battono—il Commendatore cade*)

COMMENDATORE: Ah soccorso!
son tradito.
L'assassino m'ha ferito,
E dal seno palpitante
Sento l'anima partir.

GIOVANNI: Ah! già cade il sciagurato,
Affannoso e agonizzante;
Già dal seno palpitante
Veggo l'anima partir.

LEPORELLO: (Qual misfatto! qual eccesso!
Entro il sen dallo spavento
Palpitar il cor mi sento—
Io non so che far, che dir!)

GIOVANNI: (*Sotto voce*). Leporello, ove sei?

LEPORELLO: Son quì mia disgrazia, e voi—

GIOVANNI: Son quì.

LEPORELLO: Chi è morto—voi, o il vecchio?

GIOVANNI: Che domanda da bestia! il vecchio!

LEPORELLO: Bravo! due imprese leggiadre: sforzi la figlia, ed ammazzar il padre!

GIOVANNI: L'ha voluto suo danno.

LEPORELLO: Ma Donn'Anna cos'ha voluto?

GIOVANNI: Taci! Non mi seccar, vien meco;
—se non vuoi qualche cosa ancor tu—
(*Minacciandolo*.)

LEPORELLO: Non vo' nulla, Signor! non parlo più.
(*Partono*).

## SCENA III

*Donna Anna, Don Ottavio, e Servi con fiaccole.*

ANNA: Ah, del padre in periglio! in soccorso voliam.

OTTAVIO: Tutto il mio sangue verserò, se bisogna.
Ma dov'è il scelerato!

ANNA: In questo loco (*Vedendo il corpo del suo Padre.*) Ma qual mai s'offre, oh Dei! spettacolo funesto agli occhi miei! Padre mio! mio caro padre!

OTTAVIO: Signore!

ANNA: Ah, l'assassino mel trucidò! Quel sangue, quella piaga—quel volto tinto e coperto del color di morte! Ei non respira più— fredde le membra! Padre mio! caro padre! padre amato! Io manco—io moro!

---

JUAN: Tremble! for you must
Most surely die.
(*They fight—the Commandant falls*).

COMMANDANT: Ah, great Heaven! Powers of Mercy!
'Neath the assassin's hand expiring,
Forth, from out my quivering bosom,
Fast the life-blood wells away.

JUAN: There the meddling fool lies prostrate:
Agony his frame is wringing;
Fast his soul its flight is winging,
As his life-blood wells away.

LEPORELLO: (Horror, horror! deed of darkness!
Terror, dire, my blood congealing,
Through my veins like ice it is stealing—
I know not what to do or to say.).

JUAN: (*in a low voice*). Leporello, where are you?

LEPORELLO: Here, master, to my disgrace; and you—

JUAN: Here.

LEPORELLO: Oh! which is dead— you or the old man?

JUAN: Fool! what a question!

LEPORELLO: Two pretty exploits, truly, for one night: seduce the daughter, and kill the father!

JUAN: He was bent on his ruin.

LEPORELLO: And was Donna Anna bent on her's?

JUAN: Silence! Question not, but follow me;
—breathe not a word, or—
(*Threatening him*.)

LEPORELLO: I won't, I won't, Sir! I'll never speak again.
(*Exeunt*).

## SCENE III

*Donna Anna, Don Octavio, and Servants with torches.*

ANNA: Ah, my father is in danger! let us fly to his succor.

OCTAVIO: To the last drop of my blood you may command me. But where is the villian?

ANNA: Here I left him. (*Seeing the body of her Father.*) But, just Heaven, what sight of horror presents itself! My father! my dear father!

OCTAVIO: My lord!

ANNA: Ah, he is slain! This blood, these wounds—his face covered with the pale hue of death! He no longer breathes—his limbs are cold. My father! my dear, my beloved father! I faint—I die!

---

OTTAVIO: Ah soccorrete, amici, il mio tesoro! Cercatemi, recatemi qualche odor, qualche spirito. Ah non tardate! Donn'Anna, sposa, amica! Il duolo estremo la meschinella uccide.

ANNA: Ahi!

OTTAVIO: Già riviene! Datele nuovi ajuti.

ANNA: Padre mio!

OTTAVIO: Celate, allontanate agli occhi suoi quell'oggetto d'orrore. Anima mia! consolati, fa core!

ANNA: Fuggi, crudele, fuggi!
Lascia che mora anch'io!
Ora ch'è morto, oh Dio!
Chi a me la vita diè!

OTTAVIO: Senti cor mio, deh senti!
Guardami un solo istante!
Ti parla il caro amante.
Che vive sol per te!

ANNA: Tu sei, perdon! mio bene!
L'affanno mio, le pene!
Ah, il padre mio dov'è?

OTTAVIO: Il padre lascia, o cara!
La rimembranza amara:
Hai sposo e padre in me!

ANNA: Ah, vendicar, s'il puoi,
Giura quel sangue ognor!

OTTAVIO: Lo giuro agli occhi tuoi.
Lo giuro al nostro amor!

A 2: Che giuramenti oh Dei!
Che barbaro momento!
Fra cento affanni e cento
Vammi ondeggiando il cor!
(*Partono*)

## SCENA IV

*Strada.—Don Giovanni e Leporello.*

GIOVANNI: Orsù spicciati presto—cosa vuoi?

LEPORELLO: L'affar di cui si tratta è importante.

GIOVANNI: Lo credo.

LEPORELLO: Importantissimo.

GIOVANNI: Meglio ancora. Finiscila.

LEPORELLO: Ma giurate di non andar in collera.

GIOVANNI: Lo giuro sul mio onore, purchè non parli del Commendatore.

LEPORELLO: Siamo soli?

GIOVANNI: Lo vedo.

LEPORELLO: Nessun ci sente?

GIOVANNI: Via!

LEPORELLO: Vi posso dire tutto liberamente.

GIOVANNI: Tutto si.

---

OCTAVIO: Hasten, my friends, to assist your unfortunate mistress! Fetch water, scents—try all means to restore her. Hasten, I entreat you! Donna Anna, beloved mistress! Her grief, I fear, is fatal.

ANNA: Ah, me!

OCTAVIO: She revives! Redouble your efforts.

ANNA: Oh, my father!

OCTAVIO: Quickly remove her from this scene of horror. Console yourself, love! oh, cease this sorrow!

ANNA: Leave me, forever leave me! Heaven of life bereave me! With him who being gave me, Oh, let me perish too!

OCTAVIO: Forbear this wild appealing!
Oh, calm your frantic feeling!
And hear your lover, kneeling,
Who lives alone for you!

ANNA: My love, alas! forgive me!
My maddening mind will leave me!
My father, you I call!

OCTAVIO: Console yourself,
soothe your mind, love
Ever in me you'l find, love,
A father, lover, all!

ANNA: Swear for my bleeding sire
You will prove a stern avenger.

OCTAVIO: I swear by your eyes' soft fire!
I swear by all our love!

A 2: Oh, moment full of anguish,
That such on oath makes needful!
Our hearts with grief still languish,—
Our cup's with sorrow full!
(*Exeunt*).

## SCENE IV

*A Street.—Don Juan and Leporello.*

JUAN: Come, then, out with this mystery—what is it?

LEPORELL: The affair I am about to speak of is of consequence.

JUAN: No doubt.

LEPORELLO: Of great consequence.

JUAN: Better and better. To the point, then.

LEPORELLO: Promise me not be in a passion.

JUAN: I give you my honor, provided it does not relate to the Commandant.

LEPORELLO: We are alone?

JUAN: For aught I see.

LEPORELLO: No one hears us?

JUAN: Away, fool!

LEPORELLO: But may I speak my whole mind freely?

JUAN: You may.

LEPORELLO: Dunque quand'è così, caro signor padro-ne, la vita che menate è da briccone—

GIOVANNI: Temerario! in tal guisa!

LEPORELLO: E il giuramento.

GIOVANNI: Zitto! Non si parli di giuramento, taci, o ch'io— (*Minacciandolo*).

LEPORELLO: Non parlo più! non fiato, pardon mio.

GIOVANNI: Così saremo amici. Or odi un poco sai tu perchè son qui?

LEPORELLO: Non ne so nulla. Ma essendo l'alba chiara, non sarebbe qualche nuova conquista: io lo devo saper per porla in lista.

GIOVANNI: Va là che sei 'l grand'uom! Sappi ch'io sono innamorato d'una bella dama, e son certo che m'ama. La vidi, le parlai: meco al Casino questa notte verrà; zitto mi pare sentir odor di femina.

LEPORELLO: (*aparte*). Cospetto! che odorato perfetto!

GIOVANNI: All'aria mi par bella.

LEPORELLO: (*aparte*). E che occhio, dico!

GIOVANNI: Ritiriamoci un poco, e scopriamo terren.

LEPORELLO: (Già prese foco.)

## SCENA V

*Donna Elvira; Don Giovanni, e Leporello, in disparte.*

ELVIRA: Ah! chi mi dice mai Quel barbaro dov'è?
Che per mio scorno amai, Che mi mancò di fè.
Ah se ritrovo l'empio, E a me non torna ancor,
Vò farne orrendo scempio, Gli vò cavar il cor.

GIOVANNI: (*a Leporello*). Udisti? Qualche bella del vago abbandonata. Poverina! poverina! cerchiam di consolar il suo tormento.

LEPORELLO: (*aparte*). Così ne consolò mille e ottocento.

GIOVANNI: Signorina! signorina!

ELVIRA: Chi è là!

GIOVANNI: Stelle! che vedo?

LEPORELLO: (*aparte*). Oh bella! Donna Elvira!

ELVIRA: Don Giovanni! Sei quì? Mostro, fellon, nido d'inganni!

---

LEPORELLO: Well, since you give me leave, dear master, I must say that the life you lead is horrible, and the sooner you amend it—

JUAN: What, rascal! do you dare to talk to me thus?

LEPORELLO: No, but your promise.

JUAN: No more, knave! Promise or no promise, be silent or— (*Threatening him*).

LEPORELLO: I am dumb! I say nothing, dear master.

JUAN: It is the way to keep us friends. Now, hark Leporello: do you know what brings me here?

LEPORELLO: I know nothing, but I guess it's some new love affair: you must tell me the lady's name, that I may put it in my list.

JUAN: Spoken like a clever fellow! Know, then, that I am enamored of a most beautiful woman, and I am sure she returns my love. I have seen her and conversed with her: she is to meet me to-night at the Casino; but hush! a female approaches.

LEPORELLO: (*aside*). Zooks! what an exquisite ear he has!

JUAN: At the first glance I see she is handsome.

LEPORELLO: (*aside*). With an eye like a hawk!

JUAN: Let us retire a little, and reconnoitre.

LEPORELLO: (He is on fire already.)

## SCENE V

*Donna Elvira; Don Juan and Leporello concealed.*

ELVIRA: Ah! how shall I discover Where this barbarian lives?
Though I may not call him mine, My heart still homage gives.
But should I find the traitor, And find he loves no more,
It will then be mine to torture, And wound his bosom's core.

JUAN: (*to Leporello*). Do you hear? This fair damsel is complaining of some faithless lover. Poor girl! I must seek to console her.

LEPORELLO: (*aside*). He has consoled, in this manner one thousand and eight hundred only!

JUAN: Madam, madam!

ELVIRA: Who is there?

JUAN: Heaven! what do I see?

LEPORELLO: (*aside*). Excellent! It is Donna Elvira!

ELVIRA: What do I see? Don Juan! Monster, robber, mountain of deceit!

---

LEPORELLO: (*aparte*). Che titoli cruscanti! Manco male che lo conosce bene.

GIOVANNI: Via, cara Donna Elvira, calmate quella collera! sentite— lasciatemi parlar!

ELVIRA: Cosa puoi dire dopo azion sì nera? In casa mia entra furtivamente, a forma d'arte, di giuramenti e di lusinghe arrivi a sedurre il cor mil! m'innamori, o crudele! Mi dichiari tua sposa, e poi,—mancando della terra e del Ciel al santo dritto,—con enorme delitto, dopo tre dì da Burgos allontani.
M'abbandoni, mi fuggi—e lasci in preda al rimorso ed al pianto per pena forse che t'amai cotanto!

LEPORELLO: (*aparte*). Pare un libro stampato!

GIOVANNI: Oh, in quanto a questo ebbi le mie ragioni. (*a Leporello*). E vero?

LEPORELLO: È vero (*Ironicamente*.) E che ragioni forti?

ELVIRA: E quali sono, se non la tua perfidia, la legerezza tua? Ma il giusto Cielo vuole, ch'io ti trovassi per far le sue, le mie vendette.

GIOVANNI: Via, cara Donna Elvira, siate più ragionevole! (*Aparte*.) Mi pone a cimento costei. (*Forte*.) Se non credete al labbro mio, credete a questo galantuomo.

LEPORELLO: Salvo il vero?

GIOVANNI: (*forte*). Via dille un poco.

LEPORELLO: (*piano*). E cosa devo dirle?

GIOVANNI: (*forte, pariendo*). Si, si, dille pur tutto.

ELVIRA: (*a Leporello*). Ebben, fa presto.

LEPORELLO: (*esitando*). Madama—veramente—in questo mondo conciò—sia cosa—quando—fosse che—il quadro non è tondo—

ELVIRA: Sciagurato! Così del mio dolor gioco ti prendi? Ah voi— (*Verso Don Giovanni che non crede partito*.) Stelle! l'iniquo fuggì! Misera me! dove? In qual parte.

LEPORELLO: Eh, lasciate che vada! Egli non merita ch'a lui voi più pensiate.

ELVIRA: Il scelerato m'ingannò, mi tradi!

LEPORELLO: Eh consolatevi! Non siete voi, non foste, e non sarete nè la prima, nè l'ultima. Guardate questo non piccolo libro: è tutto pieno dei nomi di sue belle. Ogni

---

LEPORELLO: (*aside*). What choice epithets! One may see that she is an old acquaintance.

JUAN: Come, dear Elvira, restrain this anger! Hear me—let me speak!

ELVIRA: What can you say in excuse for your black conduct? To enter secretly my house, and, by artifice, by oaths and flattery, to become master of my affections! To make me your wife, and then, defying Heaven and earth, as it were,—denying my sacred right,—and with unheard of treachery departing, in three days, from Burgos. To fly, to abandon me—to leave me a prey to remorse and anguish! A sad return for having loved so well!

LEPORELLO: (*aside*). This is as true as if it was printed!

JUAN: Yes, I confess it all; but know, Elvira, that I had my strong reasons for this; (*to Leporello*) had I not, Leporello?

LEPORELLO: Oh, yes, very strong reasons. (*Ironically*.) But what were they?

ELVIRA: What can they be but levity and want of faith? But heaven has permitted me to discover you, that I may avenge its wrongs, and my own.

JUAN: My dearest Elvira, be a little more rational, I entreat you! (*Aside*.) This woman embarrasses me. (*Aloud*.) If you will not believe me, you will at least believe this worthy gentleman.

LEPORELLO: That's me, exactly!

JUAN: (*aloud*). You will explain the whole to her.

LEPORELLO: (*aside to him*). And what can I explain?

JUAN: (*aloud, and going*). Yes, yes, you will explain all.

ELVIRA: (*to Leporello*). Well, make haste, then.

LEPORELLO: (*besitating*). Madam—assuredly—in the strange world in which we live—it may—be safely asserted—that a square is not a circle—and, therefore—

ELVIRA: Abominable villain! is my grief a fit subject for mockery? And you, Don Juan—(*Turns, and discovers that he has gone*.) Heaven! the reprobate has left me! Unhappy me! what shall I do? Which way did he go?

LEPORELLO: Ah, let him go! He does not deserve that you should bestow a thought upon him.

ELVIRA: He betrays, he abandons me!

LEPORELLO: Do not be unhappy! You are not the first lady he has deserted, neither will you be the last. See, here is a large book: it is filled entirely with the names of his mis-

villa, ogni borgo—ogni paese, è testimone di sue donnesche imprese.

Madamina!
Il catalogo è questo,
Delle belle, che anò il padron mio!
Un catalogo egli è ch'ho fatto io:
Osservate, leggete con me!
In Italia seicento e quaranta,
In Alemagna duecento trent'una;
Cento in Francia, in Turchia novant'una,
Ma, ma in Ispagna, son già mille e tre!
V'han fra queste contadine.
Cameriere cittadine,
V'han Contesse, Baronesse,
Marchesane, Principesse,
E v'han donne d'ogni grado,
D'ogni forma d'ogni età.
Nella bionda, egli ha l'usanza
Di lodar la gentilezza,—
Nella bruna la costanza,
Nella bianca la dolcezza.
Vuol d'inverno la grassotta
Vuol d'estate la magrotta;
E la grande, maestosa;
La piccina, ognor vezzosa.
Delle vecchie fa conquista
Per piacer di porle in lista:
Sua passion predominante
E la giovin principiante
Non si picca, se sia ricca—
Se sia brutta, se sia bella!
Purchè porti la gonnella,
Voi sapete quel che fa!
(*Parte*).

ELVIRA: In questa forma dunque mi tradì lo scelerato? è questo il premio che quel barbaro rende all'amor mio? Ah vendicar vogl'io l'ingannato mio cor! Pria ch'ei mi fugga, si ricorra—Si vada; io sento in petto sol vendetta parlar, rabbia, e dispetto!
(*Parte*).

## SCENA VI

*Il Contado, con una veduta del Palazzo di Don Giovanni.*

*Zerlina; Masetto; Contadini, e Contadine.*

ZERLINA: Giovinette, che fate all'amore,
Non lasciate, che passi l'età;
Se nel seno vi bulica il core,
Il rimedio vedetelo quà!
La la la, la la la!
Che piacer, che sarà.

CORO: Ah, che piacer che sarà,
La la la lera, la la la lera.

tresses. Every country, every city— No, every village, has witnessed his exploits in gallantry!

Pray behold, ma'am!
In this long list I've made, is
An account of my master's fair ladies!
Not Jove so renowned for his trade is:
Pray observe it, and read it with me!
First in Italy, ma'am, seven hundred,
Then in Germany, eight may be numbered;
Then in Turkey and France, one and ninety.
But, but, in Spain, ma'am,
One thousand and three!
Here are chambermaids by dozens.
City dames and country cousins;
Countesses and Baronesses,
Marchionesses and Princesses,
All descriptions, ages, classes,
Not a woman could go free.
First the fair ones he bewitches
By the softness of his speeches,—
Makes the brown ones in a fever,
Warmly vowing love for ever!
With the pale ones he will languish,
Melt and sigh in tender anguish;
The great and tall ones sometimes warm him,
High and low, ma'am, old and young, ma'am.
Own the music of this tongue, ma'am:
Though, if I must tell the truth, ma'am,
I know he'd give the choice to youth, ma'am,
But ugly, pretty, fat, or thin—
Something a petticoat within!
It matters not, for, short or tall,
It is very plain he loves them all!
(*Exit*).

ELVIRA: Am I thus become the victim of perfidy? and is this the return for all my affection? but my wrongs, shall not go unpunished! Before he escapes me, let the arm of justice— Love sleeps in my breast; I feel but rage and hatred.
I will be revenged!
(*Exit*).

## SCENE VI

*The country with a view of Don Juan's Palace.*

*Zerlina; Masetto. Male and Female Peasants.*

ZERLINA: Pretty lasses, love's summer, remember, Ever flies upon gossamer wing; Suffer not, then, life's chilly December To destroy Cupid's bow and his string!
La la la, la la la! But make haste and be happy like me.

CHORUS: Ah, But make haste and be happy, Like you, la la la lira.

MASETTO: Giovinetti leggieri di testa, Non andate girando quà e là Poco dura dei matti la festa, Ma per me cominciata non ha!
Lera, lera la!
Che piacer, che piacer, che sarà! Lera la, lera la!

CORO: Che piacer! La, la, lera!

ZERLINA E MASETTO: Vieni, vieni, carina godiamo, E cantiamo, e balliamo, e suoniamo! Che piacer, che piacer, che sarà!

CORO: Che piacer! La, la, lera!

## SCENA VII

*Don Giovanni; Leporello; e detti.*

GIOVANNI: Manco male è partita! Oh guarda, guarda, che bella gioventù! Che belle donne!

LEPORELLO: (Tra tante per mia fe, vi sarà qualche cosa anche per me.)

GIOVANNI: Cari amici, buon giorno! Seguitate a star allegramente;— seguitate a suonar, o buona gente. C'è qualche sposalizio!

ZERLINA: Si, signore; e la sposa son io.

GIOVANNI: Me ne consolo. Lo sposo?

MASETTO: Io per servirla.

GIOVANNI: Oh bravo! per servirmi! Questo è vero parlar da galantuomo.

LEPORELLO: Basta che sia marito.

ZERLINA: Oh, il mio Masetto è un uom d'ottimo core!

GIOVANNI: Oh anch'io, vedete: voglio che siamo amici. Il vostro nome?

ZERLINA: Zerlina.

GIOVANNI: E il tuo?

MASETTO: Masetto.

GIOVANNI: Oh, caro il mio Masetto! cara la mia Zerlina, v'esibisco la mia protezione. Leporello! cosa fai là, birbone?

LEPORELLO: (*Chi fa amore a qualcune delle Femine.*) Anch'io caro padrone, esibisco la mia protezione.

GIOVANNI: Presto va con costor, nel mio palazzo conducili sul fatto: ordina ch'abbiano cioccolatte, caffe, vini, presciutti—cerca divertir tutti. Mostra loro il giardin, la galleria, le camere; in effetto fa che resti contento il mio Masetto. Hai capito?

MASETTO: And, you lads who are constantly changing, For a time though It is pleasant to run From this beauty to that, ever ranging, Yet, at last, pray be constant to one! Lira, lira la! And be happy, be happy, like me! Lira la, lira la!

CHORUS: And be happy, be happy like you!

ZERLINA AND MASETTO: Oh, what rapture! the marriage-bells ringing, To be dancing and playing and singing! Who is so happy, so happy as we!

CHORUS: Lira la, lira la! Who is so happy, so happy as we!

## SCENE VII

*Don Juan; Leporello; the same.*

JUAN: Heaven be praised, she is gone! But look, look, what a lively group! What pretty girls!

LEPORELLO: (Faith! among so many, one or two may fall to my share.)

JUAN: Friends, good day! Pray go on with your sports, your singing and dancing. Is this a wedding?

ZERLINA: Yes, my lord; and I am the bride.

JUAN: I give you joy. Where is the bridegroom?

MASETTO: Here, my lord, at your service.

JUAN: Very good! at my service! Spoken like a youth of spirit.

LEPORELLO: It is enough to be the husband.

ZERLINA: Oh, my dear Masetto has such an excellent heart!

JUAN: And so have I, be assured; that is why we should be friends. And your name?

ZERLINA: Zerlina.

JUAN: And your's?

MASETTO: Masetto.

JUAN: Ah my dear Masetto! my dear Zerlina! accept my protection. Leporello! what are you doing there, knave?

LEPORELLO: (*Who is making love to some of the women.*) I too, master, am making an offer of my protection.

JUAN: Instantly conduct these happy people to my palace: give orders to supply them with coffee, chocolate, wine, sweetmeats—do your best to entertain them. Show them the gardens, the gallery, the hall; and above all, pay particular attention to my dear Masetto. Do you understand?

**LEPORELLO:** Ho capito. Andiam.

**MASETTO:** Signore!

**GIOVANNI:** Cosa c'è?

**MASETTO:** La Zerlina senza me non può star.

**LEPORELLO:** In vostro loco ci starà sua eccellenza—e saprà bene fare le vostre parti.

**GIOVANNI:** Oh la Zerlina è in man d'un cavalier. Va pur; fra poco ella meco verrà.

**ZERLINA:** Va; non temere: nelle mani son io d'un cavaliere.

**MASETTO:** E per questo—

**LEPORELLO:** E per questo non c'è da dubitar.

**MASETTO:** Ed io, sospetto!

**GIOVANNI:** Olà! Finiam le dispute; se subito senz'altro replicar, non te ne vai, Masetto, guarda ben, ti pentirai.

**MASETTO:** Ho capito, signor sì!
Chino il capo, e me ne vò
Giacchè piace a voi così Altre repliche non fò.
Cavalier voi siete già,
Dubitar non posso affè,
Me lo dice la bontà,
Che volete aver per me.
Bricconaccia! malandrina!
(*a Zerlina*). Fosti, ognor, la mia ruina!
(*a Lep.*) Vengo, vengo. (*a Zer.*).
Resta! resta!
È una cosa molto onesta;
Faccia il nostro cavaliere, Cavaliera ancora te.
(*Parte con Leporello, Masetto, e Paesani*).

## SCENA VIII

*Don Giovanni e Zerlina.*

**GIOVANNI:** Alfin siam liberati, Zerlinetta gentile da quel sioccone. Che ne dite, mio ben, so far pulito?

**ZERLINA:** Signore, è mio marito.

**GIOVANNI:** Chi! colui? Vi par ch'un'onest'uomo, un nobil cavalier, qual io mi vanto, possa soffrir che quel visetto d'oro, quel viso inzuccherato da un bifolcaccio vil sia strapazzato.

**ZERLINA:** Ma, signore, io gli diedi parola di sposarlo.

**GIOVANNI:** Tal parola non vale un zero, voi non siete fatta per esser paesana. Un'altra sorte vi procuran quegli occhi bricconcelli, quei labretti sì belli, quelle dituccia candide, e odorose, parmi toccar giuncata, e fiutar rose.

**ZERLINA:** Ah, non vorrei—

**GIOVANNI:** Che non vorreste?

---

**LEPORELLO:** I understand. Friends, let us go.

**MASETTO:** My lord!

**JUAN:** What say you?

**MASETTO:** My Zerlina cannot stay here without me.

**LEPORELLO:** His lordship will well supply your place—he knows how to play your part to perfection.

**JUAN:** Fear not, Zerlina is in the care of a nobleman. Go, then; she shall soon follow with me.

**ZERLINA:** Go; fear nothing: I am in the care of a nobleman.

**MASETTO:** And for that reason—

**LEPORELLO:** For that reason you have nothing to fear.

**MASETTO:** And I, indeed!

**JUAN:** Oh, reply no more! If without more words, you do not immediately depart, Masetto, you shall repent it.

**MASETTO:** Yes, my lord, I understand you! and, since you are pleased to command my absence, will go without farther reply. You say you are a nobleman; and I can not doubt your world, but something within tells me that your designs are not honorable. (*To Zerlina.*) Traitress! viper! you were born to be my ruin!
(*To Leporello.*) I come, I come. (*To Zerlina.*) Ay now! do stay! It is quite prudent in you to trust him; let my lord here make a lady of you.
(*Exeunt Leporello, Masetto, and Peasants*).

## SCENE VIII

*Don Juan and Zerlina.*

**JUAN:** At length, my sweet Zerlina, we are rid of this troublesome fellow. Say, then, my angel, have I not well contrived?

**ZERLINA:** My lord, he is my lover.

**JUAN:** What! he? Do you think that a nobleman, a man of rank, as I am, can suffer such bewitching beauty to be profaned by a base clown?

**ZERLINA:** But, my lord, I have promised to marry him.

**JUAN:** Such a promise is void in itself; you were not born to be the wife of a country booby. Those roguish eyes, those pouting lips, those pretty little fingers, so white and tapering, ensure you a better fortune.

**ZERLINA:** Ah, but I would not—

**JUAN:** Would not what?

---

**ZERLINA:** Alfine ingannata restar. Io so che rado colle donne voi altri cavalieri siete onseti e sinceri.

**GIOVANNI:** È un'impostura della gente plebea: la nobiltà ha dipinta negli occhi l'onestà. Orsù non perdiamo tempo in quest'istante io vi voglio sposar.

**ZERLINA:** Voi?

**GIOVANNI:** Certo io. Quel casinetto è mio: soli saremo: e là giojello mio, ci sposeremo.

**GIOVANNI:** La ci darem la mano,
La mi dirai di sì!
Vedi, non è lontano
Partiam, ben mio, da qui!

**ZERLINA:** Vorrei, e non vorrei;
Mi trema un poco il cor:
Felice, è ver sarei,
Ma può burlarmi ancor.

**GIOVANNI:** Vieni nio bel diletto!

**ZERLINA:** Mi fa pietà Masetto.

**GIOVANNI:** Io cangierò tua sorte.

**ZERLINA:** Presto, non son più forte.

**GIOVANNI:** Vieni! Vieni! La ci darem la mano,
La mi dirai di sì!

**ZERLINA:** Vorrei e non vorrei;
Mi trema un poco il cor.

**DUETTO:** Andiam, andiam mio bene,
A ristorar le pene
D'un innocente amor.

## SCENA IX

*Donna Elvira; e detti.*

**ELVIRA:** Fermati, scelerato! Il Ciel mi fece udir le tue perfidie; io sono a tempo di salvar questa misera innocente dal tuo barbaro artiglio.

**ZERLINA:** Meschina! cosa sento!

**GIOVANNI:** (*aparte*). Amor, consiglio! (*A Elvira.*). Idol mio, non vedete ch'io voglio divertirmi.

**ELVIRA:** Divertirti, è vero, divertirti? Io so, crudele, come tu diverti.

**ZERLINA:** Ma, signor cavaliere, è ver quel ch'ella dice?

**GIOVANNI:** (*a Zerlina.*) La povera infelice è di me innamorata, e per pietà deggio fingere amore, ch'io son per mia disgrazia uom di buon core.
(*Don Giovanni parte*).

---

**ZERLINA:** Not like to be imposed on. I have heard that noblemen are seldom frank and sincere with women.

**JUAN:** It is a vile slander of the vulgar: nobility and honor always go together. But do not let us lose time: this very moment I will marry you.

**ZERLINA:** You?

**JUAN:** Certainly. That house you see is mine: there we shall be alone; and there, my angel, we will be married.

**JUAN:** Then with your hand in mine, dear,
You'll whisper gently yes!
The castle's lord by yours dear,
Come, and lover bless!

**ZERLINA:** I would, and yet I would not;
My breast with terror heaves:
It would be the happiest lot,
Unless this lord deceives.

**JUAN:** Come, then, with me, my beauty!

**ZERLINA:** Masetto claims my duty.

**JUAN:** I wish to change your state, love.

**ZERLINA:** I yield myself to fate, love.

**JUAN:** Come, then! Then with your hand in mine, dear,
You'll whisper gently yes!

**ZERLINA:** I would, and yet I would not;
My breast with terror heaves.

**TOGETHER:** Then come, and share with me the pleasure Of innocence and love.

## SCENE IX

*Donna Elvira, the same.*

**ELVIRA:** Stay, wicked one, stay! Heaven has permitted me to overhear your perfidious design; and I may yet save this poor artless girl from your barbarian grasp.

**ZERLINA:** Oh, me! what is it I hear?

**JUAN:** (*aside*). Cupid befriend me! (*To Elvira.*) My love, do you not see that I am amusing myself?

**ELVIRA:** Amusing yourself! Yes, cruel man, I know too well how you amuse yourself.

**ZERLINA:** But, my lord, does this lady speak truly?

**JUAN:** (*to Zerlina*). This poor forlorn damsel almost adores me, and I cannot but seem, out of pity, to return her love, for I am so tender-hearted; that is my only misfortune.
(*Exit Don Juan*).

ELVIRA: In qual eccessi. oh, Numi! ini quali misfatti orribili, tremendi, è avvolto il sciaguarato! Ah, no! non puote tardar l'ira del Cielo. La giustizia tardar sentir già parmi la fatale saetta, che gli piomba sul capo,—aperto veggio il baratro mortal.
Misera Elvira!
Che contrasto d'affetti in sen ti nasce!
Perchè questi sospiri, e queste ambasce?

Mi tradì quell'alma ingrata,
Infelice oh Dio! mi fa!
Mi tradita abbandonata
Provo ancor per lui pietà
Quando sento il mio tormento,
Di vendetta il cor favella;
Ma se guardo il suo cimento,
Palpitando il cor mi va.
(*Partono*).

## SCENA X

*Don Giovanni, Don Ottavio, Donna Anna; indi Donna Elvira.*

GIOVANNI: Mi par ch'oggi il demonio si diverta d'opporsi ai miei piacevoli progressi, vanno mal tutti quanti.

OTTAVIO: Ah! ch'ora, idolo mio, son vani i pianti! Di vendetta si parli. Oh, Don Giovanni!

GIOVANNI: (*aparte*). Mancava questo intoppo!

ANNA: Amico! a tempo vi ritroviam! Avete core, avete anima generosa?

GIOVANNI: (*aparte*). Sta a vedere ch'il diavolo gli ha detto qualche cosa? (*Forte*). Che domanda! perchè?

ANNA: Bisogno abbiamo della vostra amicizia.

GIOVANNI: (*aparte*). Respiro. (*Forte*.) Comandate,—i congiunti, i parenti; questa man, questo ferro, i beni, il sangue spenderò per servirvi. Ma voi, bella Donn'Anna, perchè cosi piangete? Sì crudel chi fu, ch'osò la calma turbar del viver vostro?
(*Entra Elvira*).

ELVIRA: Ah ti ritrovo ancor, perfido mostro.

ELVIRA: (*a Anna*). Non ti fidar, o misera!
Di quel ribaldo cor!
Me già tradì queì barbaro—
Ti vuol tradir ancor.

ANNA E OTTAVIO: Cieli! che aspetto mobile!
Che dolce maestà!
Il suo dolor, le lagrime
M'empiono di pietà.

## SCENE X

ELVIRA: Oh, Heaven! into what excesses, into what horrible, unheard-of crimes is this wretched man plunged! The wrath of Heaven can no longer be averted. Already I see the fatal bolt launched at his devoted head,—already I see the abyss opened beneath him.
Hapless Elvira!
What contending feelings agitate my bosom!
Why these sighs? what checks my utterance?

Though by him I've been neglected,
Though my peace has fled, alas!
Though his falseness I've detected,
Prayers for him my lips still pass.
When I think on wrongs I'm bearing
Vengeance only steels my heart;
When I see him perils sharing,
I'd avert the poisoned dart.
(*Exeunt*).

## SCENE X

*Don Juan, Don Octavio, Donna Anna; afterwards Donna Elvira.*

JUAN: My evil genius seems to take pleasure to-day in crossing all my pleasant schemes—everything goes wrong.

OCTAVIO: Dearest Donna Anna, cease these unavailing tears! Let us think only of vengeance. Ah, Don Juan here!

JUAN: (*aside*). There wanted but this encounter!

ANNA: Ah, at length we have found you! Have you, my friend, a noble, a generous heart!

JUAN: (*aside*). I wonder whether my ill stars have put any suspicion into her head? (*Aloud.*) What a question, Madame! Why do you ask it?

ANNA: We have need of all your friendship and advice.

JUAN: (*aside*). I breathe again. (*Aloud.*) Pray command me,—command my relations, my friends; this arm, this sword, shall be devoted to your service. But fairest Donna, why these tears? What wretch has dared disturb your bosom's wonted calm?
(*Enter Elvira*).

ELVIRA: Ha! do I find you again, perfidious monster!

ELVIRA: (*to Anna*). Oh, do not listen to those witching tones!
They come not from the heart!
On me they fell but to betray—
He'll play on you that part.

ANNA AND OCTAVIO: Oh, Heaven! what beauty's in that form!
What softness and what grace!
Her patient grief, her looks forlorn,
In my fond heart find place.

GIOVANNI: La povera ragazza
È pazza, amici miei:
Lasciatemi con lei!
Forse si calmerà.

ELVIRA: Ah non credete al perfido!

GIOVANNI: È pazza; non badate.

ELVIRA: Restate, oh Dei! restate.

ANNA E OTTAVIO: A chi si crederà?

ANNA, OTTAVIO E GIOVANNI:
(Certo moto d'ignoto tormento
Dentro l'alma girare mi sento,
Che mi dice per quella infelice
Cento cose che intender non sa.)

ELVIRA: (Sdegno, rabbia, dispetto, spavento
Dentro l'alma girare mi sento,
Che mi dice di quel traditore
Cento cose che intender non sa.)

OTTAVIO: Io di quà non vado via,
Se non so com'è l'affar.

ANNA: Non ha l'aria di pazzia
Il suo tratto, il suo parlar.

GIOVANNI: (Se men vada, si potria
Qualche cosa sospettar.)

ELVIRA: Da quel ceffo si dovria
La ner'alma giudicar.

OTTAVIO: (*a Giovanni*). Dunque quella?

GIOVANNI: È pazzarella.

ANNA: (*a Elvira*). Dunque quegli?

ELVIRA: È un traditore.

GIOVANNI: Infelice!

ELVIRA: Mentitore!

ANNA E OTTAVIO: Incomincio a dubitar.

GIOVANNI: Zitto, zitto, che la gente
Si raduna a noi d'intorno:
Siate un poco più prudente—
Vi farete criticar.

ELVIRA: Non sperarlo, o scelerato!
Ho perduta la prudenza—
Le tue colpe ed il mio stato
Voglio a tutti palesar.

ANNA E OTTAVIO: Quegli accenti sì sommessi!
Quel cangiarsi di colore
Sono indizj troppo espressi
Che mi fan determinar.
(*Elvira parte*)

GIOVANNI: Povera sventurata! i passi suoi
Voglio seguir, non voglio
Che faccia un precipizio.
Perdonate,
Bellissima Donn'Anna:

JUAN: My friends, this poor young creature
For love of me, raves wildly:
Leave her to me, oh leave her
With her I'll reason mildly.

ELVIRA: Ah do not heed! his words are false!

JUAN: She's frantic; don't believe her.

ELVIRA: Stay, false one! nor deceive her.

ANNA AND OCTAVIO: Oh, which shall we believe?

ANNA, OCTAVIO AND JUAN: (I feel around my heart now stealing
Hopeless love, disdain, revealing
That this fair unhappy lady
Suffers more than words can tell.)

ELVIRA: (Despair around my heart now stealing
Hopeless love, disdain, revealing
That on earth I still shall ever
Suffer more than words can tell.)

OCTAVIO: Hence, I will not now depart,
Till I hear the truth of this.

ANNA: There's no madness in her manner,
And her words are not amiss.

JUAN: (If I go now, their blind anger
On me may suspicion turn.)

ELVIRA: From his face malign, now judge how
Justly does my fury burn.

OCTAVIO: (*to Juan*). This poor lady?

JUAN: Reason fails her.

ANNA: (*to Elvira*). This young signor?

ELVIRA: Is a traitor.

JUAN: Go, unhappy!

ELVIRA: Base deceiver!

ANNA AND OCTAVIO: Already I begin to doubt.

JUAN: Softly, softly, I beseech you!
People see who come this way;
Please have a little prudence—
Keep silence, and go away.

ELVIRA: Hope it not, you perjured traitor!
Prudence certainly has left me—
You have quite bereft me of that
I'll expose you, come what may.

ANNA AND OCTAVIO: Ah, how altered, see his manner!
What a change! what calm submission!
This, indeed, the truth disclosing,
Now to me does all betray.
(*Exit Elvira*).

JUAN: Unhappy lady! I must follow her
And watch her footsteps, lest in evil hour
Some desperate act she dare. Excuse me, then,

Se servirvi poss'io,
In mia casa v'aspetto. Amici, addio!
(*Parte*).

ANNA: Don Ottavio, son morta.

OTTAVIO: Cos'è stato?

ANNA: Per pietà soccorretemi!

OTTAVIO: Mio ben, fate coraggio.

ANNA: Oh, Dei! quegli è il carnefice del padre mio!

OTTAVIO: Che dite?

ANNA: Non dubitate più. Gli ultimi accenti
Che l'empio proferì, tutta la voce
Richiama nel cor mio di quell'indegno,
Che nel mio appartamento—

OTTAVIO: Oh, Ciel! possibile, Che sotto il sacro manto d'amicizia
Ma come fu?—Narratemi
Lo strano avvenimento.

ANNA: Era già alquanto
Avanzata la notte,
Quando nelle mie stanze, ove, soletta
Mi trovai per sventura, entrar io vidi
In un mantello avvolto
Un uom, ch'al primo istante
Avea preso per voi;
Ma riconobbi poi
Ch'un inganno era il mio.

OTTAVIO: Stelle! Seguite.

ANNA: Tacito a me s'appressa,
E mi vuol abbracciar; sciogliermi cerco,
Ei più mi stringe, io grido;
Non viene alcun; con una mano cerca
D'impedire la voce,
E coll'altra m'afferra
Stretta così, che già mi credo vinta.

OTTAVIO: Perfido! e alfin!

ANNA: Alfine il vuol, l'orrore
Dell'infame attentato accrebbe sì
La lena mia; che a forza
Di svincolarmi, torcermi, e piegarmi,
Da lui mi sciolsi.

OTTAVIO: Ohimè! respiro!

ANNA: Allora
Rinforzo i stridi miei, chiamo soccorso—
Fugge il fellon, arditamente il seguo
Fin nella strada per fermarlo; e sono
Assalitrice d'assalita. Il padre
V'accorre, vuol conoscerlo, e l'indegno;
Che del povero vecchio era più forte,
Compiè il misfatto suo col dargli morte.

---

Most charming Donna Anna:
If there is any service I can render,
I shall be found at home. My friends, farewell! (*Exit*).

ANNA: Don Octavio, I'm confounded.

OCTAVIO: What has happened?

ANNA: For pity's sake, support me!

OCTAVIO: My love, take courage.

ANNA: Oh, Heaven! he is the murderer of my father!

OCTAVIO: What is it you say?

ANNA: Yes, I can doubt no more.
His last few words—
His voice, form, accent, brought back to my mind
The image of the villain who had dared,
At night, in my apartment—

OCTAVIO: Heavens! can it be,
That, under friendship's sacred guise, the wretch—
But how was this? Relate to me
At once, the fearful tale.

ANNA: Already far advanced was then the night,
When, sitting in my room, and quite alone,
As chance would have it, lo! I saw then enter
Wrapped in a mantle,
A man, whom at the first moment
I took for you;
But soon perceived
That I'd made a mistake.

OCTAVIO: The wretch! Proceed.

ANNA: Silently he came nearer,
And clasped me in his arms: I shrieked
And tried to free myself, the more he pressed me;
But no one came; then with one hand
my voice he sought to stifle.
And with the other grasped me
So forcibly, I gave me up for lost.

OCTAVIO: Villain! and then!

ANNA: Grief and despair at last
Gave me new strength against
This infamous attempt; after a struggle
I disengaged myself,
And broke away.

OCTAVIO: Again I breathe!

ANNA: Then
My cries I still renewed, I called for help—
The villain fled, and instantly I followed,
Even to the street, to stop him; and I now
Became the assailant, who was once the assailed.
My father ran to aid me and detect him,
But the old man, being weaker than his foe,
Was overpowered, alas! and met his doom.

---

Or sai chi l'onore rapir a me volse,
Chi fu il traditore, ch'il padre mi tolse.
Vendetta ti chieggo—la chiede il tuo cor.
Rammenta la piaga del misero seno—
Rimira di sangue coperto il terreno,
Se 'l cor in te langue d'un giusto furor.
(*Parte*).

OTTAVIO: Come mai creder deggio
Di sì nero delitto
Capace un cavaliere!
Ah di scoprire il vero
Ogni mezzo si cerchi, io sento in petto
E di sposo, e d'amico
Il dover che mi parla,
Disingannarla voglio, o vendicarla.

Dalla sua pace la mia dipende—
Quel ch'a lei piace vita mi rende;
Quel che le incresce morte mi da;
S'ella sospira, sospiro anch'io;
E mia quell'ira, quel pianto è mio—
E non ho bene se non l'ha.
(*Parte*).

---

You know who it was that attempted mine honor,
And who was the traitor my father than slew
It is vengeance I ask for your heart claims it too.
Remember the earth stained with his sacred blood—
Remember his wound, for it calls from the tomb,
If thy zeal should relax; and let death be his doom.
(*Exit*).

OCTAVIO: Could I ever have believed
That a gallant cavalier
Should be the perpetrator
Of such a crime as now I heard?
Let me leave no means untried
To learn the truth; for, as her lover,
My heart now tells me that I ought
To undeceive or to avenge her.

For on her happiness mine is dependent—
Whatever delights her, to me gives joy;
Were her life misery, mine would destroy;
And to her every sigh mine does reply;
Mine is her vengeance, and mine are her tears—
I share her sorrows, her hopes, and her fears.
(*Exit*).

## SCENA XI

*Leporello; indi Don Giovanni.*

LEPORELLO: Io deggio ad ogni patto
Per sempre abbandonar questo bel matto.
Eccolo qui: guardate
Con quell'indifferenza se ne viene.

GIOVANNI: Leporellino mio, va tutto bene?

LEPORELLO: Don Giovannino mio, va tutto male.

GIOVANNI: Come? va tutto male?

LEPORELLO: Vado a casa
Come voi m'ordinaste
Con tutta quella gente.

GIOVANNI: Bravo!

LEPORELLO: A forza di chiacchere,—
Di vezzi, e di bugie,
Ch'ho imparato sì bene a star con voi,
Cerco d'intrattenerli.

GIOVANNI: Bravo!

LEPORELLO: Dico Mille cose a Masetto per placarlo.
Per trargli dal pensier la gelosia,

GIOVANNI: Ma bravo, in fede mia!

## SCENE XI

*Leporello; afterwards Don Juan.*

LEPORELLO: Whatever may be the consequence, I must
Leave this wild rake.
Yonder he comes: behold
With what a careless air be moves along.

JUAN: Well, my little Leporello, does all go well?

LEPORELLO: No, my little Don Juan, all goes ill.

JUAN: How? all goes ill?

LEPORELLO: I went to the house
As you directed me.
With all those people.

JUAN: Very well!

LEPORELLO: By chatting with them,—
By leading them to pastimes, and with fibs,
That I have learned so well in serving you,
I tried to amuse them.

JUAN: Very good!

LEPORELLO: I said A thousand things to pacify Masetto,
And lead him from the thought of jealousy.

JUAN: It is well, upon my word.

LEPORELLO: Faccio che bevano e gli uomini e le donne;
Son già mezzo ubbriachi:
Altri canta, altri scherza—
Altri seguita a ber; in sul più bello
Chi credete che capiti?

GIOVANNI: Zerlina.

LEPORELLO: Bravo! E con lei chi venne?

GIOVANNI: Donna Elvira.

LEPORELLO: Bravo! e disse di voi.

GIOVANNI: Tutto quel mal ch'in bocca le venia?

LEPORELLO: Ma bravo, in fede mia.

GIOVANNI: E tu cosa facesti?

LEPORELLO: Tacqui.

GIOVANNI: Ed ella—

LEPORELLO: Seguì a gridar.

GIOVANNI: E tu?

LEPORELLO: Quando mi parve,
Che già fosse sfogata, dolcemente
Fuor dell'orto la trassi, e con bell'arte
Chiusa la porta a chiave io me n'andai,
E sulla via soletta io la lasciai.

GIOVANNI: Bravo! Bravo! arcibravo!
L'affar non può andar meglio; incominciasti,
Io saprò terminar. Troppo mi premono
Queste contadinotte:
Le voglio divertir finchè vien notte.

GIOVANNI: Finch'han del vino
Calda la testa.
Una gran festa,
Fa preparar:
Se trovi in piazza,
Qualche ragazza,
Teco ancor quella
Cerca menar;
Senz'alcun ordine,
La danza sia,
Ch'il minuetto,
Che la follia
Chi l'Alemana,
Farai ballar;
Ed io frattanto,
Dall'altro canto,
Con questa e quella,
Vo' amoreggiar.
Ah la mia lista,
Doman mattina,
D'una decina deve aumentar.

LEPORELLO: I set both men and women drinking;
They were already half inebriate:
Some sung, and other sported—
The rest went drinking on: all was going well,
When, who do you think, arrived?

JUAN: Zerlina.

LEPORELLO: Right!
And with her, who came also?

JUAN: Donna Elvira.

LEPORELLO: Right! and she spoke of you.

JUAN: All the evil that her lips could utter?

LEPORELLO: True, upon my word.

JUAN: And what said you?

LEPORELLO: Nothing.

JUAN: And she—

LEPORELLO: Continued her abuse.

JUAN: While you?

LEPORELLO: When it appeared to me
That she was almost tired, I gently led her
Out of the garden, and then dexterously
I closed the door and locked it— stealing off,
I left her in the street, standing alone.

JUAN: Excellent! most excellent!
The affair could not go better; you have begun,
And I know how to finish.
These pretty country girls bewitch my heart:
I wish to entertain them till the night.

JUAN: Now that they're merry
With port or with sherry,
A feast, do not tarry,
Go and prepare;
If by-the-by, too
Nice girls you spy, too,
Quick, have an eye to
Let them be there;
Trumpets affrighting,
Waltzes inviting,
Minutes delighting,
Frolic and fun here,
French, English, German,
Bring far and near;
Minutes delighting
All who appear.
Frolics and feasting
All hearts to cheer.
While I go prying,
Pretty girls eyeing,
Tenderly sighing
Till they are won.
Many tomorrow,
Not to my sorrow,
You'll add to the list of ladies I've won.

## SCENA XII

*Campagna. Da un lato, il Palazzo di Don Giovanni; dall'altro, un Padiglione.*

*Zerlina e Masetto*

ZERLINA: Masetto, senti un pò! Masetto, dico!

MASETTO: Non mi toccar.

ZERLINA: Perchè?

MASETTO: Perfida! il tatto sopportar dovrei
D'una mano infedele?

ZERLINA: Ah, no! taci, crudele?
Io non merto da te tal trattamento.

MASETTO: Come! ed hai l'ardimento di scusarti?
Star sola con un uom? abbandonarmi
Il di delle mie nozze—porre in fronte
A nu villano d'onore
Questa marca d'infamia! Ah, se non fosse
Se non fosse lo scandalo, vorrei—

ZERLINA: Ma se colpa io non ho—ma se da lui
Ingannata rimasi? E poi che temi
Tranquillanti, mia, vita!
Non mi toccò la punta delle dita.
Non me lo credi, ingrato?
Vien qui, sfogati, ammazzami—
Fa pur tutto di me quel che ti piace,
Ma poi, Masetto poi, ma poi fa pace.

Batti, batti, o bel Masetto,
La tua povera Zerlina;
Starò qui come agnellina,
Le tue botte ad aspettar.
Lascerò stracciarmi il crine;
Lascerò stracciarmi gli occhi;
E le care tue manine
Lieta poi saprò baciar.
Ah! lo vedo, non hai core!
Pace, pace, o mia!
In contenti, ed allegria,
Notte e di vogliam passar.

MASETTO: Guarda un pò, come seppe
Questa strega sedurmi!
Siamo pure i deboli di testa.

## SCENA XIII

*I detti.—Don Giovanni, (di dentro) Servi.*

GIOVANNI: Sia preparato tutto a una gran festa.

## SCENE XII

*A Rural Prospect. On one side, the Palace of Don Juan; on the other, a Pavilion.*

*Zerlina and Masetto.*

ZERLINA: Masetto, listen a moment! Masetto, I say!

MASETTO: Do not come near me.

ZERLINA: And why?

MASETTO: Faithless! could I endure the touch
Of a false hand like yours?

ZERLINA: Ah, me! hush, cruel man!
From you I've not deserved such treatment.

MASETTO: How! are you bold enough to make excuses
To remain alone with a man? and to leave
Even on our wedding day—with infamy
To brand the forehead of an honest man,
And stain his name with shame! Ah, were not
That I consider what the world would say.

ZERLINA: But if I'm not in fault— if he deceived me?
And then what fear you? Nay,
Be calm, my life!
He did not touch me with a finger's tip.
Will you not now believe me, cruel man?
Come here, exhaust your rage, and take my life—
Do with me what you will; but then, Masetto,
Then, I entreat you, let's be friends again!

Beat me, beat me, dear Masetto,
Beat Zerlina at your will;
Like the patient lamb I'll suffer,
Meek and mute, and loving still.
Rend those locks you praised so highly;
From your arms Zerlina cast;
These fond eyes in rage extinguish
Fondly still they'll look their last.
Ah! I see, love, you're relenting—
Pardon, kneeling, I implore you!
Night and day, to you devoted,
here I vow to err no more.

MASETTO: This enchantress fair and shy
Soft persuasion now would try!
Men to be weak in mind have never ceased.

## SCENE XIII

*The same.—Don Juan (from without) and Servants.*

JUAN: Let all be now prepared for a grand feast.

**ZERLINA:** Ah, Masetto, Masetto!
odi la voce
Del monsù cavaliere!

**MASETTO:** Ebben, che c'è?

**ZERLINA:** Verrà.

**MASETTO:** Lascia che venga.

**ZERLINA:** Ah! se vi fosse
Un buco da fuggir—

**MASETTO:** Di cosa temi?
Perchè diventi pallida? Ah, capisco!
Capisco, bricconcella!
Hai timor, ch'io comprenda
Com'è tra voi passata la faccenda.

**MASETTO:** Presto, presto! pria
ch'ei venga
Por mi vò da qualche lato:
V'è una nicchia, qui celato
Cheto, cheto, mi vo' star.

**ZERLINA:** Senti, senti! dove vai!
Non t'ascondar, o Masetto!
Se ti trova, poveretto,
Tu non sai quel che può far?

**MASETTO:** Faccia, dica quel che
vuole.

**ZERLINA:** Ah! non giovan le parole!

**MASETTO:** Parla forte e qui
t'arresta.

**ZERLINA:** Che capriccio ha nella
testa?

**MASETTO:** (aparte). Capirò se
m'è fedele,
E in qual modo andò l'affar.

**ZERLINA:** Quell'ingrato, quel crudele
Oggi vuol precipitar.

**GIOVANNI:** (ai Contadini). Su
svegliatevi da bravi!
Su coraggio, o buona gente.
Vogliam star allegramente!
Vogliam ridere e scherzar.
Alla stanza della danza
Conducete tutti quante;
Ed a tutti in abbondanza
Gran rinfreschi fate dar.
(Partono i Contadini).

**CORO:** Su, svegliati, etc.

**ZERLINA:** Tra questi alberi celata,
Si può dar che non mi veda.

**GIOVANNI:** Zerlinetta mia garbata!
Ti ho già vista—non scappar!

**ZERLINA:** Ah! lasciatemi andar via!

**GIOVANNI:** No no resta gioja mia.

**ZERLINA:** Se pietade avete in core!

**GIOVANNI:** Si ben mio, son tutto
amore
Vieni un poco, in questo loco,
Fortunata io ti vò far.

**ZERLINA:** Ah, Masetto, Masetto!
that is the voice
Of my lord the cavalier!

**MASETTO:** Well, what of that?

**ZERLINA:** He will come here.

**MASETTO:** Well, let him come.

**ZERLINA:** Ah! had I but a loophole
To escape—

**MASETTO:** What do you fear?
Why do you turn pale? Ah, now I
know!
I understand, false girl!
You are afraid I should discover
The secrets that have passed between you.

**MASETTO:** Quick, oh quick! before he comes,
In this corner I will hide:
In this nook I'll stand concealed!—
Secret, silent, let me bide.

**ZERLINA:** Hear me, hear me! oh,
Masetto!
Do not hide yourself, but stay!
If he finds you, my poor fellow,
Who can tell what he may say?

**MASETTO:** Let him say or do his
worst.

**ZERLINA:** Ah! you heed not what I
say!

**MASETTO:** Speak aloud, and remain here.

**ZERLINA:** What folly now is in
your brain?

**MASETTO:** (aside). I shall know if
she is faithful,
And how went this strange affair.

**OCTAVIO:** Oh, how cruel and ungrateful!
Thus he tries what I can dare.

**JUAN:** (to the Country People).
Arise, enjoy yourselves like men!
Here we'll laugh and dance a measure.
Cast off coyness, oh sweet girls!
Here we live for joy and pleasure.
In the hall prepared for dancing,
Let the ball with joy be crowned;
And, amid the scene entrancing,
See the sparkling cup go round.
(Exeunt Peasants).

**CHORUS:** Arise, etc.

**ZERLINA:** Concealed among these
trees,
I, perhaps may pass unseen.

**JUAN:** My charming, my graceful
Zerlina!
I see you—you cannot escape!

**ZERLINA:** Ah! I entreat you, let me
go!

**JUAN:** No, my angel, pray remain.

**ZERLINA:** If you have one spark of
pity!

**JUAN:** Yes, my dearest, I'm all
love,
Come with me, then, to this bower
And I there will make you blessed.

**ZERLINA:** (aparte). Ah! s'ei vede
il sposo mio,
So ben io quel che può far.

**GIOVANNI:** Masetto!

**MASETTO:** Si, Masetto!

**GIOVANNI:** E chiuso là perchè?
La bella tua Zerlina—
Non può la poverina
Più star senza di te.

**MASETTO:** Capisco, si signore.

**GIOVANNI:** Adesso fate core;
I suonatori udite!
Venite omai con me.

**ZERLINA:** Si, si facciamo core,
Ed a ballar cogli altri
Andiamo tutti tre.

**MASETTO:** Si, si facciamo core,
etc.
(Partona).

## SCENA XIV

*Donna Anna, Donna Elvira, e
Don Ottavio.*

**ELVIRA:** Bisogna aver coraggio,
O cari amici miei;
E i suoi misfatti rei
Scoprir potremo allor.

**OTTAVIO:** L'amica dice bene—
Coraggio aver conviene,
(ad Anna).
Discaccia, o vita mia!
L'affanno ed il timor.

**ANNA:** Il passo e periglioso,
Può nascer qualche imbroglio;
Temo pel caro sposo—
E per noi temo ancor.

## SCENA XV

*Don Giovanni; Leporello. E detti.*

**LEPORELLO:** (dalla finestra).
Signor, guardate un poco!
Che maschere galanti!

**GIOVANNI:** Falle passar avanti,
Di che ci fanno onor.

**ANNA, ELVIRA E OTTAVIO:** Al
volto, ed alla voce
Si scopre il traditore.

**LEPORELLO:** Ps! ps! signore
maschere!

**ANNA E ELIVIRA:** Via rispondete.

**OTTAVIO:** Cosa chiedete?

**LEPORELLO:** Al ballo, se vi piace
V'invita il mio signor.

**OTTAVIO:** Grazie di tanto onore.
Andiam, compagne belle.

**ZERLINA:** (aside). Ah! if my jealous lover saw him
Well I know what he could do.

**JUAN:** Masetto!

**MASETTO:** Yes, Masetto.

**JUAN:** And why were you concealed there?
Your pretty girl, Zerlina—
She, poor maid, can no longer
Be happy without you.

**MASETTO:** My lord, I understand.

**JUAN:** Come, then, let us merry be;
Quickly! the musicians see!
Come, dance at once with me.

**ZERLINA:** Yes, let us all merry be,
And together go all three,
To join the rest, and dance.

**MASETTO:** Yes, let us all merry be,
etc. (Exeunt).

## SCENE XIV

*Donna Anna, Donna Elvira, and
Don Octavio.*

**ELVIRA:** Be firm, be firm, I pray
you—
My good friends, I implore you;
And soon the guilty traitor
Shall for his crimes atone.

**OCTAVIO:** Elvira counsels wisely—
We must have courage, truly,
(to Anna).
Then banish, oh my fair one!
Your fear and terror soon.

**ANNA:** The moments full of danger,
Some ill may yet befall;
I fear for you, beloved one—
I fear, indeed, for all.

## SCENE XV

*Don Giovanni; Leporello. The
same.*

**LEPORELLO:** (from the Window).
My lord, look out a moment!
See what gay masks are here!

**JUAN:** Invite them in, and beg
them
To come and share our cheer.

**ANNA, ELVIRA AND OCTAVIO:**
See, see, that look, that voice,
Betray the traitor there!

**LEPORELLO:** Hist! hist! oh, maskers, hist.

**ANNA AND ELVIRA:** Reply to him
for us.

**OCTAVIO:** What is your pleasure,
pray?

**LEPORELLO:** My lord entreats your
presence
To honor this his home.

**OCTAVIO:** We thank him for this
favor.
My fair companions, come.

LEPORELLO: (*aparte*). L'amico anche su quelle
Prova farà d'amor.

LEPORELLO: (*aside*). My lord will quickly prove
If these fair dames can love.

ANNA E OTTAVIO: Protegga il giusto Cielo
Il zelo del mio cor!

ANNA AND OCTAVIO: Just Heaven, our path protecting,
Oh, guide our steps aright!

ELVIRA: Vendichi il giusto Cielo
Il mio tradito amor!
(*Partono*).

ELVIRA: Just Heaven on him avenge me
Who all my hopes did blight!

## SCENA XVI

*Sala da Ballo net Palazzo di Don Giovanni.*
(*Zerlina, Don Giovanni, Leporello, Masetto, Contadini, Contadine; Servi con rinfreschi; Suonatori*).

## SCENE XVI

*A Ball-Room in the Palace of Don Juan.* (*Zerlina, Don Juan, Leporello, Masetto; Male and Female Peasants; Servants and Musicians.*)

GIOVANNI: Riposate, vezzose ragazze.

JUAN: Rest awhile, pretty maids, from your dancing.

LEPORELLO: Rinfrescatevi, bei giovinetti.

LEPORELLO: Come, refresh yourselves, gentlemen gay.

GIOVANNI E LEPORELLO:
Tornerete a far presto le pazze,
Tornerete a scherzar e ballar!

JUAN AND LEPORELLO: While around us bright eyes are thus glancing,
Who so happy, so happy as we!

GIOVANNI: Ehi caffè!

JUAN: Bring some coffee!

LEPORELLO: Cioccolatte!

LEPORELLO: Chocolate, here!

MASETTO: (*a Zerlina*). Ah, Zerlina, giudizio!

MASETTO: (*to Zerlina*). Ah, Zerlina, pray take care!

GIOVANNI: Sorbetti!

JUAN: Sherbet!

LEPORELLO: Confetti!

LEPORELLO: Some comfort!

MASETTO: (*a Zerlina*). Ah, Zerlina, giudizio!

MASETTO: (*to Zerlina*). Ah, Zerlina, pray beware!

MASETTO E ZERLINA: (*aparte*).
Troppo dolce comincia la scena;
In amaro potria terminar.

MASETTO AND ZERLINA: (*aside*). See, the scene has made us glad;
But its end may yet be sad.

GIOVANNI: Sei pur vaga, brillante Zerlina.

JUAN: You are indeed charming, lovely Zerlina!

ZERLINA: Sua bontà.

ZERLINA: Your lordship is very polite.

MASETTO: (*aparte*). La briccona fa festa!

MASETTO: (*aside*). The saucy girl makes holiday!

LEPORELLO: Sei pur cara, Giannotta, Sandrina!

LEPORELLO: How pretty you are, Giannotta, Sadrina!

MASETTO: (*aparte*). Tocca pur, che ti cada la testa!

MASETTO: (*aside*). Touch her, I'll knock your head off!

ZERLINA: (*aparte*). Quel Masetto mi par stralunato.
Brutto, brutto si fa quest'affar.

ZERLINA: (*aside*). This Masetto's gone out of his mind.
Sadly, I fear, this affair will end.

GIOVANNI E LEPORELLO:
(*aparte*). Quel Masetto mi par stralunato.
Qui bisogna cervello adoprar.

JUAN AND LEPORELLO: (*aside*). This Masetto's gone out of his mind.
And, to win her, I must use all my skill.

MASETTO: (*aparte*). La briccona mi fa disperar!

MASETTO: (*aside*). Despair and rage my bosom will fill.

## SCENA XVII

*Donna Anna, Donna Elvira, Don Ottavio.*

*I detti.*

LEPORELLO: Venite pur avanti,
Vezzose mascherette.

## SCENE XVII

*Donna Anna, Donna Elvira, Don Octavio.*

*The same.*

LEPORELLO: Fair maskers, I entreat you,
Enter and join our ball.

GIOVANNI: È aperto a tutti quanti,
Viva la libertà.

JUAN: My house to all is open,
And liberty for all.

ANNA, ELVIRA E OTTAVIO: Siam grati a tanti segni
Di generosità.

ANNA, ELVIRA AND OCTAVIO: We, my lord, most thankfully
Receive your hospitality.

GIOVANNI: (*a Leporello*). Ricominciate il suono!
Tu accoppia i ballerini,
Meco tu dei ballare,
Zerlina, vien pur quà.

JUAN: (*to Leporello*). Now, recommence the ball!
You marshal forth the dancing.
Come now, the gay throng joining,
Zerlina, dance with me.

LEPORELLO: Da bravi via! ballate.

LEPORELLO: Excellent! now for dancing.

ELVIRA: (*aparte*). Quell'è la contadina.

ELVIRA: (*aside*). That is the country girl.

ANNA: (*aparte*). Io moro!

ANNA: (*aside*). Ah, how I tremble!

OTTAVIO: (*aparte*). Simulate.

OCTAVIO: (*aside*). Conceal your alarm.

GIOVANNI E LEPORELLO:
(*aparte*). Va bene in verità!

JUAN AND LEPORELLO: (*aside*). Everything goes well!

MASETTO: (*aparte*). Va bene in verità.

MASETTO: (*aside*). Yes, everything goes well.

GIOVANNI: (*a Leporello*). A bada tien Masetto.

JUAN: (*to Leporello*). Take care of friend Masetto.

LEPORELLO: Non balla il poveretto.

LEPORELLO: He's jealous and won't dance.

GIOVANNI: Il tuo compagno io sono, Zerlina, vien pur quà.

JUAN: Zerlina, I'm your partner;
Come hither, come with me.

LEPORELLO: Vien quà, Masetto caro,
Facciam quel ch'altri fa,

LEPORELLO: Come here, my friend Masetto,
And let us do as they.

MASETTO: No, no ballar non voglio,

MASETTO: No, no, I will not dance.

LEPORELLO: Eh balla, amico mio.

LEPORELLO: Nay, listen to what I say.

MASETTO: No.

MASETTO: I tell you, never—no.

LEPORELLO: Si, caro Masetto.

LEPORELLO: Yes, dear Masetto, pray.

MASETTO: Ballare no, non voglio.

MASETTO: I will not dance today.

LEPORELLO: Eh Balla, amico mio:
Facciam quel ca'altri fa.

LEPORELLO: Yet, let us dance, my friend:
With me their joys partake.

ANNA: (*aparte*). Resister non poss'io.

ANNA: (*aside*). I'll pretend no longer.

OTTAVIO E ELVIRA: (*aparte*).
Fingete per pietà!

OCTAVIO AND ELVIRA: (*aside*). No, feign for pity's sake!

GIOVANNI: (*a Zerlina*). Vieni con me, mia vita!

JUAN: (*to Zerlina*). Come, come with me, my love!

MASETTO: (*a Leporello*). Lasciami. Ah no! Zerlina!

MASETTO: (*to Leporello*). Leave me alone. Zerlina!

GIOVANNI: Vieni, vieni.

JUAN: Come hither, quick, with me.

ZERLINA: Oh, Numi! son tradita!

ZERLINA: Oh, Heavens! I'm betrayed!

LEPORELLO: Qui nasce una rovina. (*Si nasconde*).

LEPORELLO: Some uproar sure will come. (*He hides himself*).

ANNA, ELVIRA E OTTAVIO:
(*aparte*). L'iniquo da se stesso,
Nel laccio se ne va.

ANNA, ELVIRA AND OCTAVIO: (*aside*). He leads her to her ruin,
And rushes to his doom.

ZERLINA: (*di dentro*). Gente! ajuto! ajuto gente!

ZERLINA: (*from within*). Help! help! Oh, aid me, aid me.

ANNA, ELVIRA E OTTAVIO: Soccorriamo l'innocente.

ANNA, ELVIRA AND OCTAVIO: Let us aid the helpless girl.

MASETTO: Ah, Zerlina!

MASETTO: Ah, Zerlina!

ZERLINA: (*di dentro*). Scelerato!

ZERLINA: (*from within*). Villain, leave me!

**ANNA E OTTAVIO:** Ora grida da quel lato.

**ZERLINA:** (*di dentro*). Scelerato!

**ANNA E OTTAVIO:** Ah gittiamo qui la porta!

**ZERLINA:** (*tornando*). Soccorretemi! Son morta!

**GLI ALTRI:** Siamo qui per tua difesa!

**GIOVANNI:** (*Tornando colla Spada straciata, e verso Leporello*). Ecco il birbo che t'ha offesa; (*Tenendolo*). Ma da me la pena avrà Mori iniquo!

**LEPORELLO:** Ah cosa fate?

**GIOVANNI:** Mori, dico!

**LEPORELLO:** Ah cosa fate?

**OTTAVIO:** (*a Giovanni*). Nol sperate, nol sperate

**ANNA, OTTAVIO E ELVIRA:** L'empio crede con tal frode Di nasconder l'empietà. (*Cavonsi le maschere*).

**GIOVANNI:** Donna Elvira!

**ELVIRA:** Si, malvagio!

**GIOVANNI:** Don Ottavio!

**OTTAVIO:** Si, signore!

**GIOVANNI:** Ah, credete—

**ANNA:** Traditore!

**ANNA, ELVIRA E OTTAVIO:** Traditore! traditore! Tutto, tutto già si sa! Trema, trema! scelerato!

**ZERLINA:** Saprà tosto il mondo intero Il misfatto orrendo e nero— La tua fiera crudeltà.

**GIOVANNI E LEPORELLO:** È confusa la mia testa: Non so più quel ch'io mi faccia, È un'orribile tempesta Minacciando, oh Dio, mi va! (*Si ode il tuono*).

**TUTTI:** (*eccetto Giovanni e Leporello*). Odi il tuon della vendetta, Che ti fischia intorno intorno, Sul tuo capo in questo giorno. Il suo fulmine cadrà.

**GIOVANNI E LEPORELLO:** Ma non manca in me coraggio, Non mi perdo, o mi confondo. Non si perde, o si confonde; Se cadesse ancora il mondo— Nulla mai temer mi fa!

*FINE DELL'ATTO PRIMO.*

---

**ANNA AND OCTAVIO:** Hark! from that side comes the voice.

**ZERLINA:** (*from within*). Villain!

**ANNA AND OCTAVIO:** Let us burst the door!

**ZERLINA:** (*Re-entering*). Help me, friends! I faint, I die!

**ALL:** Here we're ready to defend you!

**JUAN:** (*Re-entering with his Sword drawn, and turning to Leporello*). Here's the wretch that did the wrong But by my hand he shall die! (*Seizing him*). Villain, perish!

**LEPORELLO:** Why? oh why?

**JUAN:** You shall die!

**LEPORELLO:** Yet stay! why should I?

**OCTAVIO:** (*to Juan*). Hope not, hope not to escape.

**ANNA, ELVIRA AND OCTAVIO:** Vainly seeks he to deceive us— Hoping the truth to hide. (*They unmask*).

**JUAN:** Donna Elvira!

**ELVIRA:** Yes, you false one!

**JUAN:** Don Octavio!

**OCTAVIO:** Yes, Signor!

**JUAN:** Ah, believe me—

**ANNA:** Oh, you traitor.

**ANNA, ELVIRA AND OCTAVIO:** Traitor! traitor! Everything at length is known! Tremble, traitor! wrath is waking!

**ZERLINA:** Terror deep your conscience shaking, Sudden vengeance guilt overtaking. You, unheard, for aid shall cry.

**JUAN AND LEPORELLO:** Now my head is quite confounded: What to do I do not know; And by storms I am surrounded— Menacing some sudden blow. (*Thunder is heard*).

**ALL:** (*Except Juan and Leporello*). Dead to hope, unpityed falling, Wild remorse your heart appalling. You for mercy vainly calling, In despairing guilt shall die!

**JUAN AND LEPORELLO:** Though the lightning's round me flashing, Though the thunder's over me crashing, Fiery bolts may on me fall— Nothing shall appal my courage.

*END OF ACT I.*

---

## ■ ATTO II

*SCENA I*

*Piezza, come nel prim'Atto. A Lato la Casa di Elvira, con finestra, e Porta praticabile.*

*Don Giovanni; Leporello.*

**GIOVANNI:** Eh via, buffone, Non mi seccar.

**LEPORELLO:** No, no, padrone, Non vò restar.

**GIOVANNI:** Sentimi, amico.

**LEPORELLO:** Vò andar, vi dico.

**GIOVANNI:** Ma che ti ho fatto, Che vuoi lasciarmi?

**LEPORELLO:** Oh niente affatto! Quasi ammazzarmi, Ed io non burlo, Ma voglio andar.

**GIOVANNI:** Va, che sei matto.

**LEPORELLO:** Non vò restar.

**GIOVANNI:** Leporello!

**LEPORELLO:** Signore?

**GIOVANNI:** Vien qui, facciamo pace. (*Da una borsa*). Prendi.

**LEPORELLO:** Cosa?

**GIOVANNI:** Quattro doppie.

**LEPORELLO:** Oh sentite! Per questa volta ancora La ceremonia accetto; Ma non vi ci avvezzate—non credeste; Di sedurre i miei pari Come le donne, a forza di denari.

**GIOVANNI:** Non parliam più di ciò. Ti basta l'animo Di far quel ch'io ti dico?

**LEPORELLO:** Purchè lasciam le donne.

**GIOVANNI:** Lasciar le donne! Pazzo! Lasciar le donne! Sai ch'esse per me Son necessarie più del pan che mangio— Più dell'aria che spiro.

**LEPORELLO:** E avete core D'ingannarie poi tutte?

**GIOVANNI:** È tutto amore Chi a una sola è fedele Verso l'altra è crudele. Io, ch'in me serva Si esteso sentimento, Vo bene a tutte quante, Le donne poi, che calcolar non sanno, Il mio buon natural chiamano inganno.

**LEPORELLO:** Non ho veduto mai Naturale più benigno! Orsù cosa vorreste?

---

## ■ ACT II

*SCENE I*

*A Scene, as in Act 1. Elvira's House at the side, with practicable Window and Door.*

*Don Juan; Leporello.*

**JUAN:** Away, you buffoon, and Torment me no more.

**LEPORELLO:** I'll quit you now, sir. For thus I swore.

**JUAN:** Hear me, I pray you.

**LEPORELLO:** I'll go; but what say you?

**JUAN:** What have I done, now, That you will leave me?

**LEPORELLO:** Of course nothing! Only half-killed me; And I'm not joking, For now I will go.

**JUAN:** What are you thinking?

**LEPORELLO:** No; I will go.

**JUAN:** Leporello!

**LEPORELLO:** Signor?

**JUAN:** No more of this story. Come here, and take this. (*Gives him a purse*).

**LEPORELLO:** How much?

**JUAN:** Four guineas.

**LEPORELLO:** That's not amiss! For this once I permit— And to it must submit; But pray don't repeat it: It is really not fit To bribe my honor with money.

**JUAN:** Oh, speak of that no more. Have you the courage To do what I shall tell you?

**LEPORELLO:** Yes, if you'll leave the women.

**JUAN:** I leave the women! Fool! That shall I never do! Know that to me They're more delightful than the bread I eat— Yes, or the air I breathe.

**LEPORELLO:** And have you, then, the heart Thus to deceive them all?

**JUAN:** It is my love! He who is true to only one, Is harsh to all but her alone. This liberal view I still maintain, And I wish well to all I can. The ladies call my good intention Without considering, a deception.

**LEPORELLO:** Never have I seen, then, Benevolence more vast, nor more extensive! Now, what is it you want?

GIOVANNI: Odi! Vedesti tu la cameriera
Di Donna Elvira?

JUAN: Oh, listen! Have you seen the lady's maid
Of Donna Elvira?

LEPORELLO: Io no.

LEPORELLO: No.

GIOVANNI: Non hai veduto
Qualche cosa di bello!
Caro il mio Leporello: ora io con lei
Vò tentar la mia sorte; ed ho pensato,
Giacchè siam verso sera,
Per aguzzarle meglio l'appetito,
Di presentarmi a lei col tuo vestito.

JUAN: Then have you never
Seen person so charming!
Hear, my friend Leporello: when with her
To try my fortune hard I've been thinking,
Now that evening's drawing on
The more to heighten her enjoyment,
To show myself in this your vestment.

LEPORELLO: E perchè non poteste
Presentarvi col vostro?

LEPORELLO: And why could you not
Appear in yours?

GIOVANNI: Han poco credito
Con gente di tal rango
Gli abiti signorili
Sbrigati via!

JUAN: The dress of a noble
With people like her,
Would too fine appear.
Be quick!

LEPORELLO: Signor, per più ragioni—

LEPORELLO: My lord, hear me, I pray—

GIOVANNI: Finiscila, non soffro opposizioni.

JUAN: Be silent, for I'll have my way.

## SCENA II

*Donna Elvira, E detti.*

ELVIRA: (*alla finestra*). Ah taci, ingiusto core!
Non palpitarmi in seno!
È un empio, è un traditore
È colpa aver pietà.

LEPORELLO: Zitto! di Donna Elvira.
Signor, la voce io sento.

GIOVANNI: Cogliere io vò il momento!
Tu fermati un pò là.
Elvira, idolo mio!

ELVIRA: Non è costui l'ingrato?

GIOVANNI: Sì vita mia, son io,
E chieggo carità.

ELVIRA: Numi! che strano affetto
Mi si risveglia in petto!

LEPORELLO: (*aparte*). State a veder la pazza!
Ch'ancor gli crederà.

GIOVANNI: Discendi, o gioja bella!
Vedrai che tu sei quella,
Che adora l'alma mia,
Pentito io sono già!

ELVIRA: No! non ti credo, o barbaro.

GIOVANNI: Ah, credimi, o m'uccido!

LEPORELLO: (*aparte*). Se seguitate, io rido.

GIOVANNI: Idolo mio, vien quà!

A 3.

## SCENE II

*Donna Elvira. The same.*

ELVIRA: (*at the window*). Be silent, trembling heart!
Beat not, my breast within
He's impious, a deceiver;
To pity him is sin.

LEPORELLO: Hush! of Lady Elvira,
My lord, the voice I hear.

JUAN: Ah. let me seize the moment!
Remain an instant here.
Elvira, my adored one!

ELVIRA: Is that not the deceiver?

JUAN: Ah, yes, indeed. It is I, love,
Who once to you was dear.

ELVIRA: Heavens! what a strange confusion
Now agitates my heart!

LEPORELLO: (*aside*). Again see her delusion!
For she believes him still.

JUAN: Descend, oh beauteous lady!
And you again shall feel
How much my heart adores you,
And now repents its ill!

ELVIRA: Ah, cruel man! can I believe you?

JUAN: Slay me, my love, if I deceive you!

LEPORELLO: (*aside*). My laughter I must smother!

JUAN: My love, oh pray come here!

A 3.

ELVIRA: Dei! che cimento è questo?
Non so s'io vado, o resto!
Ah, proteggete voi
La mia credulità?

GIOVANNI: (*aparte*). Spero che cada presto—
Che bel colpetto è questo;
Più fertile talento
Del mio no non si da!

LEPORELLO: (*aparte*). Già quel mendace labbro
Torna a sedur costei;
Deh proteggete, o Dei!
La sua credulità!

GIOVANNI: Amico, che ti par!

LEPORELLO: Mi par ch'abbiate
Un'anima di bronzo.

GIOVANNI: Va là, che sè il gran gonzo! Ascolta bene;
Quando costei qui viene,
Tu corri ad abbracciarla—
Falle quattro carezze;
Fingi la voce mia; poi con bell'arte
Cerca teco condurla in altra parte.

LEPORELLO: Ma, signor—

GIOVANNI: Non più repliche!

LEPORELLO: E se poi mi conosce?

GIOVANNI: Non ti conoscerà, se tu non vuoi.
Zitto! ell'apre—ehi giudizio.

## SCENA III

*E detti.*

ELVIRA: Eccomi a voi!

GIOVANNI: (*aparte*). Vediamo che farà.

LEPORELLO: (*aparte*). Che bell'imbroglio!

ELVIRA: Dunque creder potrò, ch'i pianti miei
Abbian vinto quel cor! dunque pentito
L'amato Don Giovanni al suo dovere,
E all'amor mio ritorna?

LEPORELLO: Sì, carina!

ELVIRA: Crudele! se sapeste
Quante lagrime, e quanti
Sospiri voi mi costate!

LEPORELLO: Io, vita mia!

ELVIRA: Voi.

LEPORELLO: Poverina, quanto mi dispiace!

ELVIRA: Mi fuggirete più?

LEPORELLO: No, muso bello!

ELVIRA: Sarete sempre mio?

LEPORELLO: Sempre!

ELVIRA: Carissimo!

ELVIRA: Cruel one! can I believe you?
I am much too credulous
Pitying powers, protect me!
Now, shall I go or stay!

JUAN: (*aside*). It was well worth the trial—
There's none so much can say:
And I've a wonderous talent
For leading them astray!

LEPORELLO: (*aside*). Oh, what a smooth deceiver!
A second time he'll leave her:
Protect her, gracious Heaven!
And pity her, I pray!

JUAN: My friend, what think you of it.

LEPORELLO: A heart you have, I think
As hard as any bronze.

JUAN: Ah, what a simpleton are you! Now hear me:
When she comes hither,
Run and embrace her—
Caress her most tenderly—
Contrive to feign my voice; and then, with art
Seek to conduct her away with you.

LEPORELLO: But, sir—

JUAN: No reply!

LEPORELLO: If she should know me?

JUAN: She will not find you out, if you are prudent.
Peace! the door opens—now, take care!

## SCENE III

*The same.*

ELVIRA: Behold, I am here!

JUAN: (*aside*). Let us see what he'll do.

LEPORELLO: (*aside*). Here's a position!

ELVIRA: Then could I ever believe that my complaints
Would melt a heart like yours! and that, repentant,
Don Juan, my beloved, would to his faith,
And to my love, return!

LEPORELLO: Ah, yes, beloved!

ELVIRA: Oh, cruel! if you knew
How many sighs, and, ah! how many
A tear of sorrow, you've cost me!

LEPORELLO: I, my loved life!

ELVIRA: Yes, you.

LEPORELLO: Poor lady, ah, how much I grieve!

ELVIRA: Will you never leave me more?

LEPORELLO: No, angel dear!

ELVIRA: Will you be always mine?

LEPORELLO: Always!

ELVIRA: My dearest!

**LEPORELLO:** Carissima!
(*Aparte*).
La burla mi da gusto!

**ELVIRA:** Mio tesoro!

**LEPORELLO:** Mia venere!

**ELVIRA:** Son per voi tutta foco!

**LEPORELLO:** Io tutto cenere!

**GIOVANNI:** (*aparte*). Il birbo si riscalda.

**ELVIRA:** E non m'ingannerete?

**LEPORELLO:** No, sicuro.

**ELVIRA:** Giuratelo.

**LEPORELLO:** Lo giuro a questa mano,
Che bacio con trasporto, e a quei bei lumi!

**GIOVANNI:** Ih, eh, ah, ih! sei morto!

**ELVIRA:** Oh, Numi!
(*Fuggono Elvira e Leporello*).

**GIOVANNI:** Ih, eh, ah, ih! Par che la sorte
Mi secondi. Veggiamo;
Le finestre son queste: ora cantiamo.
Deh vieni alla finestra,
O mio tesoro;
Deh vieni a consolar,
Il pianto mio.
Se neghi a me di dar qualche ristoro;
Davanti agli occhi tuoi, morir vogl'io.
Tu ch'hai la bocca dolce,
Più del miele,
Tu che il zucchero posti in mezzo al core;
Non esser gioja mia con me crudele,
Lasciate almen veder mio bell'amore!

## SCENA IV

*Don Giovanni; Masetto, con seguito di Contadini armati.*

**GIOVANNI:** V'è gente alla finestra;
Forse è dessa. Ps! ps!

**MASETTO:** Non ci stanchiamo;—il cor mi dice
Che trovarlo dobbiamo.

**GIOVANNI:** (*aparte*). Qualcuno parla.

**MASETTO:** Fermatevi—mi pare
Ch'alcuno qui si mova.

**GIOVANNI:** (*aparte*). Se non fallo, è Masetto.

**MASETTO:** Chi va là? Non risponde?
Animo, schioppo al muso:
Chi va là?

**LEPORELLO:** Most loved!
(*Aside*).
The joke's delightful!

**ELVIRA:** My life's treasure!

**LEPORELLO:** Goddess of love!

**ELVIRA:** Love's soft flame, alas! consumes me!

**LEPORELLO:** My heart is scorched!

**JUAN:** (*aside*). The rogue grows warm.

**ELVIRA:** And you will not deceive me?

**LEPORELLO:** No, certainly.

**ELVIRA:** Swear it.

**LEPORELLO:** By this fair hand I swear,
That thus I kiss with joy, and by those eyes!

**JUAN:** Ah, ha, there wretch, you shall die!

**ELVIRA:** Oh, Heavens!
(*Elvira and Leporello run off*).

**JUAN:** Ah, ha, there, run! Fortune, it seems,
Would now befriend me. Let me see:
These are the windows: now, the serenade.
Come shining forth, my dearest,
With looks of warm delight;
Shed joy as you appear,
Like morning beams of light.
Mild shines your azure eye;
Your absence chilling night, love,
In which I droop and die.
O! let me hear that tongue, love,
Whose music thrills my heart.
Like notes by angels sung, love,
When souls in bliss depart;
And to your casement sing,
Illume my ravished sight,
Like day the world surprising
With morning's beam of light.

## SCENE IV

*Don Juan; Masetto, followed by a crowd of armed Peasants.*

**JUAN:** There's some on at the window:
Perhaps it's she. Hist! hist!

**MASETTO:** Let us not hesitate;—my heart now tells me
That we ought to find him here.

**JUAN:** (*aside*). Some one speaks.

**MASETTO:** Halt there a moment—listen:
I think that some one moves.

**JUAN:** (*aside*). If I mistake not it's Masetto.

**MASETTO:** Who goes there? Does no one answer?
Level your guns, my friends—be bold:
Who goes there?

**GIOVANNI:** (*aparte*). Non è solo,
Ci vuol giudizio. (*Forte*). Amici,
(*aparte*) Non mi voglio scoprir. Sei tu, Masetto!

**MASETTO:** Appunto quello; e tu?

**GIOVANNI:** Non mi conosci? Un servo
Son io di Don Giovanni—

**MASETTO:** Leporello! Servo di quell'indegno cavaliere?

**GIOVANNI:** Certo, di quel briccone.

**MASETTO:** Di quell'uom senz'onore, ah dimmi un poco,
Dove possiam trovarlo;
Lo cerco con costor per trucidarlo.

**GIOVANNI:** (*aparte*). Bagatelle!
(*Forte*). Bravissimo Masetto.
Anch'io con voi m'unisco
Per fargliela a quel birbo di padrone;
Ma udite un pò qual è la mia intenzione
Metà di qua metà là—in tal modo
Ei non potrà fuggir. S'a caso udite
Qualcuno amoreggiar sotto il balcone,
O se vedete passeggiar in piazza
Un damerino accanto a una ragazza,
Ferite pure, è desso; non tardate—
Partite, tutti, andate.
Tu sol resta con me,
Ed a te noto or or sarà il perchè.
(*I Contadini partono*).

## SCENA V

*Il Don Giovanni; Masetto.*

**GIOVANNI:** Zitto! lascia ch'io senta. Ottimanente!
Dunque dobbiamo ucciderlo?

**MASETTO:** Sicuro.

**GIOVANNI:** E non ti basteria rompergli l'ossa,
Fracassargli le spalle?

**MASETTO:** No, no! voglio ammazzarlo!
Vò farlo in cento brani.

**GIOVANNI:** Hai buone arme?

**MASETTO:** Cospetto!
Ho pria questo moschetto;
(*dandola a Giovanni*).
E poi questa pistola.
(*dandola*).

**GIOVANNI:** E poi?

**MASETTO:** Non basta?

**GIOVANNI:** Eh, basta certo. Or prendi
Questa per la pistola,
(*Battendolo*).
Questa per il moschetto.

**JUAN:** (*aside*). He's not alone; I must be cautious. (*Aloud.*) Here, my friends,
(*Aside.*) I wish not to betray myself. Masetto.

**MASETTO:** It is so; and you?

**JUAN:** Do you not know me? I am the servant of famed Don Juan—

**MASETTO:** Servant of that unworthy cavalier?

**JUAN:** Certainly, of that knave.

**MASETTO:** Of that man lost to honor, come, tell me now,
Where we may quickly find him:
I and my friends are seeking, and would kill him.

**JUAN:** (*aside*). A fine joke this!
(*Aloud.*) My brave Masetto,
I also will go with you
To help you catch this villain of a master;
But hear a moment what is my intention:
place half your numbers here, the others there—
Then he will not escape. If you should hear
Some person courting underneath the balcony,
Or should you chance to notice in the square
A lady walking with a well-dressed youth,
Strike hard, for that is he; do not delay—
Now, quickly, all begone.
Remain alone with me,
And shortly I'll explain the reason why.
(*Exeunt Peasants*).

## SCENE V

*Don Juan; Masetto.*

**JUAN:** Hush! let me listen. Excellent!
Then we must kill him?

**MASETTO:** Of course.

**JUAN:** But would it not suffice to break his bones,
And beat him black and blue?

**MASETTO:** No, no, sir! I will kill him!
I'll tear him all to pieces.

**JUAN:** Have you good weapons?

**MASETTO:** Have I not?
See, first I have this musket;
(*Giving it to Juan*).
And next, see here, this pistol.
(*Giving it*).

**JUAN:** And next?

**MASETTO:** It's not enough?

**JUAN:** Enough, of course. Now, take
This for your precious pistol,
(*Beating him*).
And this for your good musket.

**MASETTO:** Ahi! ahi! La testa mia—

**GIOVANNI:** Taci, o t'uccido.
(*Battendolo ancora*).
Questa per l'ammazzarlo,
Questa per farlo in brani;—
Villano, mascalzon, ceffo da cani!
(*Parte*).

## SCENA VI

*Masetto; indi Zerlina.*

**MASETTO:** (*Gridando forte*). Ahi,
ahi! La testa mia!
Ahi, ahi, le spalle! E il petto!

**ZERLINA:** M'è parso di sentire
La voce di Masetto.

**MASETTO:** Oh, Dio! Zerlina!
Zerlina mia, soccorso!

**ZERLINA:** Cose'è stato?

**MASETTO:** L'iniquo, il scelerato
Mi ruppe l'ossa, e i nervi

**ZERLINA:** O poveretta me! chi?

**MASETTO:** Leporello. O qualche
diavol che somiglia a lui.

**ZERLINA:** Crudel! non tel diss'io,
Che con questa tua pazza gelosia
Ti ridurresti a qualche brutto passo.
Dove ti duole?

**MASETTO:** Qui.

**ZERLINA:** E poi?

**MASETTO:** Qui, e ancora qui.

**ZERLINA:** E poi non ti duol altro?

**MASETTO:** Duolmi un poco
Questo piè, questo braccio, e questa mano.

**ZERLINA:** Via via, non è gran mal,
s'il resto è sano.
Vientene meco a casa.
Purchè tu mi prometta
D'essere men geloso.
Io, io ti guarirò, caro il mio sposo.
Vedrai carino,
Se, sei buonino,
Che bel rimedio,
Ti voglio dar.
È naturale,
Non da disgusto,
E lo speziale,
Non lo so far, nò.
È un certo balsamo,
Che porto addosso,
Dare tel posso,
S'il vuoi provar!
Saper vorresti?
Dove mi stà?
Sentilo battere
Toccami quà!

**MASETTO:** Alas! alas! Oh, my poor
head—

**JUAN:** Hush, or I'll kill you.
(*Beating him again*).
This is for going to kill him,
This is for tearing him up;—
You villain, you ruffian, you ugly-faced cur!

## SCENE VI

*Masetto; afterwards Zerlina.*

**MASETTO:** (*crying loudly*) Oh,
alas! Oh, my poor head!
Oh, oh, my shoulders! Oh, my back!

**ZERLINA:** I thought just now I
heard
The voice of my Masetto.

**MASETTO:** Oh, Heavens! Zerlina!
Zerlina, come and help me!

**ZERLINA:** What has happened?

**MASETTO:** The wretch, the
wicked villain
Has broken all my bones.

**ZERLINA:** Oh, dear me! who?

**MASETTO:** Leporello,
Or else some devil that resembles
him.

**ZERLINA:** How cruel! but I told
you,
That by your foolish senseless jealousy,
You'd bring yourself into some
dreadful harm.
Where are you hurt?

**MASETTO:** Here.

**ZERLINA:** Where else?

**MASETTO:** Here; and here, also.

**ZERLINA:** Are you hurt nowhere
else?

**MASETTO:** Ah, yes, a little.
Here in this foot, this arm, and in
this hand.

**ZERLINA:** Well, well, you're not
much hurt, if that is all.
Come with me to the house.
Only now make a promise.
Henceforth to be less jealous.
And I will heal you soon, my own
dear husband.
Listen, and I'll find, love,
If you are kind, love,
Balm for your mind, love,
Patient but be.
This balm so pure, love,
Simple and sure, love,
Sweet to endure, love,
None knew but me.
Thrilling and healing,
Over you stealing,
Exquisite feeling,
Meant but for you!
To your entreating
I'll yield it, dear,
Feel how it's beating!
Beating just here!

## SCENA VII

*Cortile interno delia casa di Elvira.*

*Leporello; Donna Elvira.*

**LEPORELLO:** Di molte fasi il lume
S'avvicina, o mio ben; stiamo qui
un poco,
Finchè da noi si scosta.

**ELVIRA:** Ma che temi,
Adorato mio sposo!

**LEPORELLO:** Nulla, nulla.
Certi riguardi—Io vò veder, s'il
lume
È già lontano. (*Aparte.*) Ah come
Da costei liberarmi?
(*forte*).
Rimanti, anima bella!

**ELVIRA:** Ah, non lasciarmi!

**ELVIRA:** Sola, sola, in bujo loco,
Palpitar il cor mi sento!
E m'assale un tal spavento,
Che mi sembra di morir.

**LEPORELLO:** Più che cerco men ritrovo
Questa porta sciagurata.
Piano, piano—l'ho trovata,
Ecco il tempo di fuggir.
(*Si nasconde*).

## SCENA VIII

*Don Ottavio; Donna Anna. E detti.*

**OTTAVIO:** Tergi il ciglio, o vita
mia!
E da calma al tuo dolore!
L'ombra omai del genitore
Pena avrà dè tuoi martir.

**ANNA:** Lascia almen alla mia pena
Questo piccolo ristoro,
Sol la morte, o mio tesoro—
Il mio pianto può finir!

**ELVIRA:** Ah, dov'è lo sposo mio?

**LEPORELLO:** (*aparte*). Se mi trova, son perduto.

**ELVIRA E LEPORELLO:** Una porta
là vegg'io
Cheta cheta io vò partir.

## SCENA IX

*Zerlina; Masetto, con lume. E detti.*

**MASETTO E ZELINA:** (*vedendo
Leporello*). Ferma briccone! dove
ten vai.

**ANNA E OTTAVIO:** Ecco il fellone! Com'era qua?

**ANNA, OTTAVIO, ZERLINA E
MASETTO:** Ah! mora il perfido,
Che m'ha tradito!

**ELVIRA:** È mio marito!
Pietà! pietà!

## SCENE VII

*An inner Court in the House of Elvira.*

*Leporello; Donna Elvira.*

**LEPORELLO:** The light of many
torches
Approaches, my beloved: let's stop
a moment
And give them time to pass.

**ELVIRA:** But what fear you,
My husband, my adored one?

**LEPORELLO:** Nothing, nothing;
Only I thought—I'll see now if the
light
Is gone yet. (*Aside.*) But how can I
Make my escape from her?
(*Aloud*). Wait here a moment,
love.

**ELVIRA:** Ah. leave me not!

**ELVIRA:** Here, alone, in this drear
darkness,
How my heart with fear trembles,
My alarm I can't dissemble—
I feel as if even death were near.

**LEPORELLO:** The more I search I
still am further
From this most infernal door.
Softly, softly—now I've found it,
And this is the time to fly.
(*He conceals himself*).

## SCENE VIII

*Don Octavio; Donna Anna. The
same.*

**OCTAVIO:** Dry those tears, they
wring my heart, love!
Could I comfort now impart, love!
Even the shade of your brave father
Will mourn at every deep-felt sigh.

**ANNA:** Yet amidst my desolation,
Still remains the consolation,
Death, my love, will end my suffering—
Would that now I here could die!

**ELVIRA:** Ah, where are you dearest
husband?

**LEPORELLO:** (*aside*). I am lost, if
they find me here!

**ELVIRA AND LEPORELLO:** Here's
a door;—now softly open it,
Let us try to escape them.

## SCENE IX

*Zerlina, Masetto, with lights. The
same.*

**MASETTO AND ZERLINA:** (*seeing Leporello*). Villain, stop! You
may not pass here!

**ANNA AND OCTAVIO:** See the
wretch! How did he come there?

**ANNA, OCTAVIO, ZERLINA AND
MASETTO:** Death to the traitor.
That has betrayed you!

**ELVIRA:** Ah, it is my husband!
Pity, I pray you.

## Act II, Scene IX

**ANNA, OTTAVIO, ZERLINA E MASETTO:** Donna Elvira
Quello ch'io vedo?
Appena il credo?
No; morirà!

**LEPORELLO:** Perdon, perdono!
Signori miei;
Quell'io non sono,
Sbaglia costei.
Viver lasciatemi
Per carità!

**ANNA, OTTAVIO, ZERLINA E MASETTO:** È Leporello!
Che inganno è questo!
Stupida resto.
Che mai sarà.

**LEPORELLO:** Mille torbidi pensieri
Mi s'aggiran per la testa;
Şe mi salvo in tal tempesta,
È un prodigio in verità!

**ANNA, OTTAVIO, ZERLINA E MASETTO:** Mille torbidi pensieri
Mi s'aggiran per la testa;
Che giornata, o stelle, è questa—
Che impensata novità?
(*Donna Anna e Leporello partono*).

**ELVIRA:** Ferma, perfido, ferma!

**MASETTO:** Il birbo ha l'ali ai piedi.

**ZERLINA:** Con qual arte
Si sottrasse l'iniquo!

**OTTAVIO:** Amici miei.
Dopo eccessi sì enormi,
Dubitar non possiam, che Don Giovanni
Non sia l'empio uccisore
Del padre di Donn'Anna. In questa casa
Per poche ore fermatevi: un ricorso
Vò far a chi si deve; e in pochi istanti
Vendicarvi prometto
Cosi vuole dover, pietade, affetto.
Il mio tesoro in canto
Andate, andate a consolar!
E del bel ciglio il pianto
Cercate di asciugar.
Ditele che i suoi torti
A vendicar io vado.
Che sol di stragi e morti
Nunzio vogl'io tornar.

### SCENA X

*Recinto murato, in mezzo al quale si vede la Statua del Commendatore.*

*Don Giovanni, salendo il muro; indi Leporello.*

**GIOVANNI:** Ah! ah! ah! questa è buona!
Or lasciala cercar. Che bella notte!
È più chiara del giorno; sembra fatta

---

**ANNA, OCTAVIO, ZERLINA AND MASETTO:** Is is Elvira
Whom I decry?
Can I believe it?
No; let him die!

**LEPORELLO:** Pardon, dear gentlemen!
She does mistake;
And she imagines
I am that rake.
Oh, pray don't kill me,
For mercy's sake!

**ANNA, OCTAVIO, ZERLINA AND MASETTO:** It is Leporello!
See, some new treachery!
Yet that is he
I cannot deny.

**LEPORELLO:** Like the roaring foaming ocean,
My brain is in a wild commotion;
If I escape in such a tempest,
It is a miracle indeed!

**ANNA, OCTAVIO, ZERLINA AND MASETTO:** Like the roaring foaming ocean,
Is my heart in wild commotion;
But just vengeance shall overtake him—
He shall perish, it's decreed!
(*Exeunt Donna Anna and Leporello*).

**ELVIRA:** Stay, traitor, stay!

**MASETTO:** The rogue has wings to his feet.

**ZERLINA:** How artfully
The wretch has slunk away!

**OCTAVIO:** My friends,
After offenses so enormous,
We can no longer doubt that this Don Juan
Was the impious murderer
Of Donna Anna's father. In this house,
For a few hours, remain: I'll have recourse
To those whose duty it is; and very soon
I promise to avenge you;
For honor, justice, love my efforts claim.
Fly, then, my love, entreating,
To clam, to calm her anxious fears;
Oh, still her heart's wild beating,
And wipe away her tears.
Tell her I'll take vengeance
On him who slew her sire;
This arm his grave shall make,
Or I'll by his expire.

### SCENE X

*A walled Cemetery, in the midst of which the Statue of the Commandant is seen.*

*Don Juan, who leaps over the wall; afterwards Leporello.*

**JUAN:** Ah! ah! ah! this is good!
Now let them seek me. What a lovely night!
It is clearer than the day; and seems to court me

---

Per gir a zonzo, a caccia di ragazze.
Vediam s'è tardi? Ah, no!
Ancor non son le due di notte. Avrei
Voglia un pò saper com'è finito
L'affar tra Leporello e Donna Elvira;
S'egli ha avuto giudizio.

**LEPORELLO:** (*Senz'alito, dietro il muro*). Alfin vuole ch'io faccia un precipizio!

**GIOVANNI:** È desso! Oh, Leporello!

**LEPORELLO:** Chi mi chiama?

**GIOVANNI:** Non conosci il padrone!

**LEPORELLO:** Così nol conoscessi!

**GIOVANNI:** Come? birbo!

**LEPORELLO:** Ah, siete voi? Scusate!

**GIOVANNI:** Cos'è stato?

**LEPORELLO:** Per cagion vostra io fui quasi accoppato.

**GIOVANNI:** Ebben, non era questo Un onore per te?

**LEPORELLO:** Signor, vel dono!

**GIOVANNI:** Via, via, vien qua:
Che belle cose ti deggio dir!

**LEPORELLO:** Ma cosa fate qui?

**GIOVANNI:** Vien dentro, e lo saprai.
Diverse istorielle,
Che accadute mi son dacchè partisti,
Ti dirò un'altra volta; or la più bella
Ti vò solo narrar.

**LEPORELLO:** Donnesca, al certo.

**GIOVANNI:** C'è dubbio! Una fanciulla,
Bella, giovin, galante,
Per la strada incontrai; le vado appresso,
La prendo per la man—figgir mi vuole;
Dico poche parole, ella mi piglia
Sai per chi?

**LEPORELLO:** Non lo so.

**GIOVANNI:** Per Leporello!

**LEPORELLO:** Per me!

**GIOVANNI:** Per te!

**LEPORELLO:** Va bene!

**GIOVANNI:** Per la mano
Essa allora mi prende.

**LEPORELLO:** Ancora meglio!

**GIOVANNI:** M'accarezza, m'abbraccia—
'Caro il mio Leporello!
Leporello, mio caro! Allor m'accorse
Ch'era qualche tua bella.

---

To rove about, and hunt for pretty girls.
Is it yet late? Oh no!
It is not two hours past midnight. I much wish
To know how that affair at length was finished.
Between Leporello and fair Donna Elvira;
And if he played his part discreetly.

**LEPORELLO:** (*Out of breath behind the wall*). Surely, he wishes to be death to me!

**JUAN:** It is he! Oh, Leporello!

**LEPORELLO:** Who calls me there?

**JUAN:** Do you not know your master?

**LEPORELLO:** Would I had never known him!

**JUAN:** How? you rogue!

**LEPORELLO:** Ah, is it you! Excuse me!

**JUAN:** What's the matter?

**LEPORELLO:** On your account, I've just been almost murdered.

**JUAN:** Well, and was not that An honor?

**LEPORELLO:** Sir, thank you!

**JUAN:** Come, come, this way:
I've some rare tales to tell you!

**LEPORELLO:** But what do you do here?

**JUAN:** Just jump over, and you shall know.
Some pleasant little affairs,
That have befallen me since you went away,
I'll tell you another time; the best of all
I'm going to tell you now.

**LEPORELLO:** Of the fair ones, I'm certain.

**JUAN:** You're right! A charming creature,
Beautiful, young, and gay.
I met in the street; and, accosting her,
I took her by the hand—she tried to avoid me:
But after a few words she took me for—
Whom do you think?

**LEPORELLO:** I know not.

**JUAN:** For Leporello!

**LEPORELLO:** For me!

**JUAN:** For you!

**LEPORELLO:** Very fine!

**JUAN:** She then, in turn, took me by the hand.

**LEPORELLO:** Still better!

**JUAN:** She smothered me with caresses—
Oh, my dearest Leporello!
Leporello, my dear! Then it struck me
She was some beauty of your's.

---

LEPORELLO: (aparte). Oh, maledetto!

GIOVANNI: Dell'inganno approfitto; non so come
Mi riconosce, grida, sento gente,—
A fuggire mi metto; e pronto pronto
Per quel muretto in questo loco io monto.

LEPORELLO: E mi dite la cosa
Con tal indifferenza—

GIOVANNI: Perchè no?

LEPORELLO: Ma se fosse costei stata mia moglie?

GIOVANNI: (Ridendo molto forte). Meglio ancora!
(Parla la Statua).

COMMENDATORE: Di rider finirai
Pria dell'Aurora!

GIOVANNI: Chi ha parlato?

LEPORELLO: Ah! qualch'anima
Sarà dall'altro mondo,
Che vi conosce a fondo.

GIOVANNI: Taci, sciocco! Chi va la?

COMMENDATORE: Ribaldo, audace!
Lascia ai morti la pace.

LEPORELLO: Ve l'ho detto.

GIOVANNI: Sarà qualcun di fuori,
Che si burla di noi.
(Con indifferenza e sprezzo).
Ehi! del Commendatore
Non è questa la statua! Leggi un poco
Quell'iscrizion.

LEPORELLO: Scusate:
Non ho imparato a leggere
A raggi della luce.

GIOVANNI: Leggi, dico!

LEPORELLO: (legge).
'Dell'empio, chi mi trasse al passo estreme,
'Qui attendo la vendetta.'
Udiste! io tremo!

GIOVANNI: O' vecchio buffonissimo
Digli che questa sera
L'attendo a cena meco.

LEPORELLO: Che pazzia!
Vi par! Oh, Dei! mirate
Che terribili occhiate
Egli ci da! Par vivo—par che senta—
E che voglia parlar.

GIOVANNI: Orsù va là
O qui t'ammazzo! E poi ti seppellisco!

LEPORELLO: Piano, piano, signore—ora ubbidisco.

LEPORELLO: O' statua gentilissima
Del gran Commendatore—
Pardon, mi trema il core;
Non posso terminar.

---

LEPORELLO: (aside). Oh, cursed chance!

JUAN: I profited by her mistake; unluckily,
She soon discovered me, and cried aloud,—
People approached and then it was time to run
And, quick as light, I jumped here over the wall.

LEPORELLO: And all this you tell me
As lightly and carelessly—

JUAN: Any why not?

LEPORELLO: Suppose that pretty girl should be my wife?

JUAN: (laughing loudly). Then, better still!
(The Statue speaks).

COMMANDANT: Your mirth shall have an end
Before the morning dawns!

JUAN: Who spoke there?

LEPORELLO: Ah! some spirit
Spoke from the other world,
Who knows your inmost soul.

JUAN: Silence, fool! Who goes there?

COMMANDANT: Audacious ribald, cease!
Let the dead sleep in peace.

LEPORELLO: Even so I told you.

JUAN: Some one must be outside,
Who scoffs at us.
(With indifference and contempt)
Ha! is not this the statue
Of the Commandant? Step forward
And read the inscription.

LEPORELLO: Excuse me:
I never learned to read
In light so pale.

JUAN: Read, I say!

LEPORELLO: (reads). On him
who slew me, Heaven's Revenge I here
Am now awaiting!
I shake with fear!

JUAN: Oh, venerable fool of fools!
Tell him that this evening
With me I hope he'll sup.

LEPORELLO: What madness!
See, see! Oh, Heaven's! behold
What an awful glance he cast
Upon us then! He is alive—he hears—
And is about to speak!

JUAN: At once go—speak,
Or else you die! Go quickly—speak I say!

LEPORELLO: Then softly, softly, master—I'll obey.

LEPORELLO: Oh, most gracious statue
Of the once great Commandant—
My lord, my courage fails me;
I can proceed no further.

---

GIOVANNI: Finiscila, o nel petto
Ti metto questo acciar.

LEPORELLO: (aparte). Che impiccio! che capriccio!
Io sentomi gelar!

GIOVANNI: (aparte). Che gusto, che spassetto!
Lo voglio far tremar.

LEPORELLO: O' statua gentilissima,
Benchè di marmo siate—
Ah, pardon mio! mirate
Che seguita a guardar.

GIOVANNI: Mori, mori!

LEPORELLO: No, attendete! (alla Statua). Signore, il padron mio—
Badate benn, non io—
Ah! ah! che scena è questa!
Oh, Ciel! chinò la testa!

GIOVANNI: Va là che sei un buffone—

LEPORELLO: Guardate ancor, padrone.

GIOVANNI: E che deggio guardar?

LEPORELLO: Colla marmorea testa
Ei fa così così.

GIOVANNI: Parlate, se potete,
Verrete a cena?

COMMENDATORE: Si!

LEPORELLO: Mover mi posso appena!
Mi manca, oh Dei, la lena!
Per carità partiamo:
Andiamo via di quà!

GIOVANNI: Bizzarra è inver la scena—
Verrà il buon vecchio a cena
A prepararla andiamo,
Partiamo via di quà.
(Partono).

## SCENA XII

*Camera.*

*Donna Anna; Don Ottavio.*

OTTAVIO: Calmatevi, idol mio, di quel ribaldo
Vedrem puniti in breve i gravi eccessi.
Vendicati sarem.

ANNA: Ma il padre, oh Dio!

OTTAVIO: Convien chinar il ciglio
Al volere del Ciel. Respira, o cara,
Di tua perdita amara
Fia domani, se vuoi, dolce compenso,
Questo cor, questa mano,
Ch'il mio tenero amor!

ANNA: Oh, Dei! che dite,
In sì tristi momenti?

OTTAVIO: E che vorresti
Con indugi novelli
Accrescer le mie pene?
Crudel!

---

JUAN: Go on, or you shall feel
The sharpness of this steel.

LEPORELLO: (aside). How horrid! his caprice how bold!
Now I feel my blood run cold!

JUAN: (aside). What a jest! oh, what delight!
Greatly I enjoy his fright.

LEPORELLO: Oh, most courteous statue,
Though you of marble be—
Ah, look, my lord! oh, see!
He turns his eyes on me.

JUAN: Perish, villain!

LEPORELLO: Stay, I entreat you! (To the Statue). My lord, my noble master—
My master, and not I—
Ah! ah! with fear I die!
Oh, Heaven! he bows his head!

JUAN: Away, or else this sword—

LEPORELLO: Oh, look again, my lord!

JUAN: And what should I behold?

LEPORELLO: My lord, the marble cold,
Even thus, inclines its head.

JUAN: Speak, if you are able:
To supper will you come?

COMMANDANT: Yes!

LEPORELLO: He has frightened me to death!
Scare can I draw my breath!
I really can't stay here:
For mercy's sake, begone!

JUAN: It ceases to be pleasant—
At supper he'll be present;
Then let us quick prepare,
And hence we will be gone. (Exeunt).

## SCENE XII

*A Room.*

*Donna Anna; Don Octavio.*

OCTAVIO: Be calm, my love, for soon this libertine
Shall punishment receive for his excesses,
And we shall be avenged.

ANNA: But yet, my father's death!

OCTAVIO: Still we must bow our heads
Before the will of the celestial powers.
For what you've lost, take comfort;
And, my beloved, to-morrow, if you please
Receive this hand and heart,
With my most tender love!

ANNA: Ah, me! what say you.
In moments of such sadness?

OCTAVIO: And why will you, With still-renewed delays
Increase my anxious cares!
It's cruel!

## Italian (left columns) / English (right columns)

ANNA: Crudele! ah no!
Mio ben, troppo mi spiace
Allontanarti un ben che lunga-
mente
La nostr'alma desia: ma il mondo!
oh Dio!
Non sedur la costanza
Del sensibil mio core
Abbastanza per te mi parla amore

ARIA: Non mi dir bell'idol mio,
Che son io crudel con te;
Tu ben sai quan'io t'amai,
Tu conosci la mia fè.
Calma, calma il tuo tormento!
Se di duol non vuoi ch'io mora
Forse un giorno il Cielo ancora
Sentirà pietà di me.
(*Parte*).

OTTAVIO: Ah! ci segua il suo pas-
so,
Io vo con lei dividere i martiri:
Saran meco men gravi i suoi sospiri.
(*Parte*).

ANNA: Cruel! ah, no!
My love, too much I grieve
Thus to delay a hope that long ago
Our hearts desired; and yet, what
will the world say?
Do not shake the constancy
Of my heart, so deeply grieved,
But yet love pleads for you too ear-
nestly.

AIR: Say not then, dear love, of me,
That I'm cruel to you;
Since you know my constancy,
And how faithfully I love.
Calm, ah! calm that anxious heart!
Unless with grief you'd see me die.
A day will come, no more to part,
And Heaven to us its grace will
prove.
(*Exit*).

OCTAVIO: Ah! Let me follow her
footsteps;
I'll share her griefs, and mingle
sighs with hers:
Her sorrow will be less, when
shared with mine
(*Exit*).

## SCENA XIII

*Gran Sala, illuminata, con Tavo-
la imbundita.*

*Don Giovanni, Leporello.*

GIOVANNI: Già la mensa è prepar-
ata—
Voi suonate, amici cari;
Già che spendo i miei danari,
Io mi voglio divertir
Leporello, presto in tavola.

LEPORELLO: Son prontissimo a
servir.

GIOVANNI: Che ti par del bel concerto?

LEPORELLO: È conforme al vostro
merto.

GIOVANNI: Ah che piatto saporí-
to!

LEPORELLO: Ah che barbaro ap-
petito!
Che bocconi di gigante.
Mi par proprio di svenir.

GIOVANNI: Nel veder i miei boc-
coni
Gli par proprio di svenir
Piatto!

LEPORELLO: Servo, 'Fra i due Liti-
ganti!'

GIOVANNI: Versa il vino. (*Beve*).
Eccellente marsimino!

LEPORELLO: (*aparte*). Questo
pezzo di fagiano,
Piano piano vò inghiottir.

GIOVANNI: Sta mangiando quel
marrano?
Fingerò di non capir.

LEPORELLO: (*udendo ancora la
musica*). Questa poi la canosco
pur troppo!

GIOVANNI: Leporello!

## SCENE XIII

*A large Hall, illuminated, with a
Table laid out.*

*Don Juan, Leporello.*

JUAN: All's prepared, the ban-
quet's ready—
Gaily let the music sound;
Here with mirth and joy abounding
Will we pass the night away.
Leporello, wait at table.

LEPORELLO: Sir, your orders I
obey.

JUAN: Is that melody not charming?

LEPORELLO: Yes, when wine the
heart is warming.

JUAN: And what delicious viands
these!

LEPORELLO: Bless me! how he
does enjoy it!
My poor mouth, I could employ it,
Very gladly, if he'd please.

JUAN: Ah! the hungry rascal's dy-
ing
Now to join in this good cheer,
Plates here!

LEPORELLO: Yes, sir.
Ah, I know that tune well!

JUAN: Bring me wine.
(*Drinks*). Excellent! the flavor's
fine!

LEPORELLO: (*aside*). Pheasant's
wing! just the thing!
It shall quickly disappear.

JUAN: Ah, the rascal! how he's
stuffing!
But I will not interfere.

LEPORELLO: (*again listening to
the music*). Ah, I know that also,
well!

JUAN: Leporello!

LEPORELLO: Pardon mio!

GIOVANNI: Parla schietto, mascalzone—

LEPORELLO: Non mi lascia una
flessione
Le parole preferir.

GIOVANNI: Mentre io mangio,
fischia un poco.

LEPORELLO: Non so far.

GIOVANNI: Cos'è?

LEPORELLO: Scusate! Sì eccellente è il vostro cuoco,
Che lo volli anch'io provar—

GIOVANNI: Si eccellente è il cuoco mio,
Che lo volle anch'ei provar.

LEPORELLO: Yes, good master!

JUAN: Plainly speak, you knave
and tell—

LEPORELLO: Ah, I've got a shocking cold, sir;
And my throat is not quite clear.

JUAN: You can whistle while I'm
eating.

LEPORELLO: I don't know how.

JUAN: What's that you say?

LEPORELLO: Pardon me!
But your cook's so very clever,
That I'm making an endeavor—

JUAN: Yes, my cook's so very clever,
You'll eat up everything that's
here.

## SCENA XIV

*Donna Elvira. E detti.*

ELVIRA: (*a Don Giovanni*).
L'ultima prova
Dell'amor mio
Ancor vogl'io
Fare con te:
(*s'inginocchia*)
Più non rammento
Gl'inganni tuoi,
Pietate io sento—

GIOVANNI E LEPORELLO:
(*aparte*). Cos'è? cose'è?

ELVIRA: Da te non chiede
Quest'alma oppressa
Della sua fede
Qualche mercè.

GIOVANNI: Mi maraviglio?
Cosa volete?
Se non sorgete—
Non resto in piè.

ELVIRA: Ah, non deridere
Gli affanni miei!

GIOVANNI: Io ti derido!
Cielo! perchè?

LEPORELLO: Quasi da piangere
Mi fa costei!

GIOVANNI: Che vuoi, mio bene?

ELVIRA: Che vita cangi!

GIOVANNI: Brava!

ELVIRA: Cor perfido!

GIOVANNI: Lascia ch'io mangi;
A se ti piace,
Mangia con me.

ELVIRA: Rimanti, barbaro,
Nel lezzo immondo,
Esempio orribile
D'iniquità.

LEPORELLO: (*aparte*). Se non si
muove
Al suo dolore,
Di sasso ha il core—
O cor non ha.

GIOVANNI: Vivan le femmine!
Viva il buon vino!
Sostegno e gloria
D'umanità.

## SCENE XIV

*Donna Elvira. The same.*

ELVIRA: (*to Don Juan*). The last
proof
Of my affection
Still I wish
To give to you:
(*She kneels*). For no longer
Your deception
Yet even pity—

JUAN AND LEPORELLO: (*aside*).
What's this to me?

ELVIRA: This injured heart
No more from you
Will claim your faith,
You now are free.

JUAN: What is it you ask?
I am surprised.
I can't permit—
Fair lady, rise.

ELVIRA: Ah, deride not
My misfortunes!

JUAN: I deride you
Heavens! for why?

LEPORELLO: Her sorrow almost
Makes me cry!

JUAN: What would you, fair lady?

ELVIRA: Ah, change your life!

JUAN: Very good!

ELVIRA: Oh, faithless heart!

JUAN: Let me be quiet;
Or, if you'll join me,
Sit here by me.

ELVIRA: Remains, then, barbarian,
In crime and despair—
A dreadful example
Of evil and care.

LEPORELLO: (*aside*). If by her sor-
row
She cannot move him,
His heart is of stone—
But heart he has none.

JUAN: Long live the women!
Here's to good wine!
Delight and support
Of all mankind.

ELVIRA: (*partendo*). Ah!
(*Parte*).

GIOVANNI: Che grido è questo
mai?
Va a veder che cos'è stato.

LEPORELLO: Ah!
(*Sorte Leporello, e ritorna spaventato*).

GIOVANNI: Che grido indiavolato?
Leporello, che cos'è?

LEPORELLO: Ah, signor, per carità,
Non andate fuor di quà!
L'uom di sasso, l'uomo bianco—
Ah, padrone, io gelo, io manco!
Se vedeste che figura,
Se sentiste come fa—
Ta, ta, ta, ta!

GIOVANNI: Non capisco niente affatto.

LEPORELLO: Ta, ta, ta, ta!
GIOVANNI: Tu sei matto in verità.
LEPORELLO: Ah sentite!
GIOVANNI: Qualcun batte:
Apri!
LEPORELLO: Io tremo!
GIOVANNI: Apri, dico!
LEPORELLO: Ah! ah!
GIOVANNI: Apri!
LEPORELLO: Ah! ah!
GIOVANNI: Matto!
Per togliermi d'intrico
Ad aprir io stesso andrò!
(*Parte*).

LEPORELLO: Non vò più veder
l'amico,
Pian pianin si m'asconderò.—
(*Si nasconde sotto la Tavola*)

## SCENA XV

*Il Commendatore. E detti.*

COMMENDATORE: Don Giovanni, a cenar teco
M'invitasti—e son venuto!

GIOVANNI: Non l'avrei giammai
creduto;
Ma farò quel che potrò.
Leporello, un'altra cena
Fa che subito si porti.

LEPORELLO: Ah, padron, siam tutti morti!

COMMENDATORE: Ferma un pò!
Non si pasce di cibo mortale
Chi si pasce di cibo celeste;
Altre cure più gravi di queste—
Altra brama quaggiù mi guidò!

LEPORELLO: La terzana d'avere mi
sembra.
E le membra fermar più non so!

ELVIRA: (*going*). Ah!
(*Exit*).

JUAN: What cry is that, Leporello?
Go see what has happened.

LEPORELLO: Ah!
(*Exit Leporello, and returns
affrighted*)

JUAN: What means that dreadful
cry?
Leporello, what is it?

LEPORELLO: Oh, my lord, for mercy's sake,
Not a step farther now!
The man of stone, the man in
white—
Ah, my lord, I'm fainting quite!
If you'd seen his dreadful figure,—
If you'd heard his footstep sound—
Ta, ta, ta, ta!

JUAN: This I do not understand.

LEPORELLO: Ta, ta, ta, ta!
JUAN: Certainly you are gone mad.
LEPORELLO: Listen! ah!
JUAN: It is some one knocking:
Open!
LEPORELLO: I tremble!
JUAN: Open, I say!
LEPORELLO: Ah! ah!
JUAN: Open!
LEPORELLO: Ah! ah!
JUAN: Madman!
So, this prodigy to witness,
I must myself open the door.
(*Exit*).

LEPORELLO: I do not wish to see
him more,
And I'll hide myself at once.
(*Hides himself under the Table*).

## SCENE XV

*The Commandant. The same.*

COMMANDANT: Don Juan, here,
at your request,
See, I am come—behold your
guest!

JUAN: Never could I have believed
it.
But I'll do the best I can.
Leporello, another supper
Order them at once to bring.

LEPORELLO: Ah my lord, I freeze
with horror!

COMMANDANT: Pause an instant!
We partake not earthly banquets
Who with Heavenly food are fed:
By other motives led here—
Other cares have brought me here!

LEPORELLO: My limbs are trembling as with fever,
And from head to foot I shake!

GIOVANNI: Parla dunque—che
chiedi? che vuoi?

COMMENDATORE: Parlo, ascolta!
più tempo non ho!

GIOVANNI: Parla, parla! ascoltandoti sto.

COMMENDATORE: Tu m'invitasti
a cena,
Il tuo dover or sai!
Rispondimi: verrai
Tu a cenar meco!

LEPORELLO: Oibò! oibò! tempo
non ha—scusate.

GIOVANNI: A torto di viltate
Tacciato mai sarò.

COMMENDATORE: Risolvi!
GIOVANNI: Ho già risolto.
COMMENDATORE: Verrai?
LEPORELLO: Dite di no!
GIOVANNI: Ho fermo il core in
petto;
Non ho timor: verrò!

COMMENDATORE: Dammi la
mano in pagno!

GIOVANNI: Eccola:—ohimè.
Che gelo è questo mai!

COMMENDATORE: Pentiti, cangia vita.
E l'ultimo momento!

GIOVANNI: No, no—ch'io non mi
pento,
Vanne lontan da me!

COMMENDATORE: Pentiti scelerato!

GIOVANNI: No, vecchio infatuato!

COMMENDATORE: Ah tempo più
non v'è: (*Parte*).

GIOVANNI: (*disperato*). Da qual
tremore insolito
Sento assalir gli spiriti!
Dond'escono quei vortici
Di foco pien d'orror?

CORO: Tutto a tue colpe è poco,
Vieni c'è un mal peggior!

GIOVANNI: Chi l'anima mi
lacera,—
Chi m'agita le viscere!
Che strazio ohimè! che smania
Che inferno! che terror!

LEPORELLO: Che ceffo disperato!
Che gesti di dannato!
Che gridi! che lamenti
Come mi fa terror!

CORO: Tutto a tue colpe è poco,
Vieni, v'è un mal peggior!

*FINE.*

JUAN: Speak—what would you? I
attend.

COMMANDANT: While I speak,
listen! my minutes are few!

JUAN: Speak, speak! I'm all attention.

COMMANDANT: You did invite
me here,
And now I invite you!
Reply: oh, will you come
To be a guest with me?

LEPORELLO: Alas! alas! we have no
time—excuse me.

JUAN: The stain of coward fear
Shall never spot my name.

COMMANDANT: Decide then!
JUAN: Already I've resolved.
COMMANDANT: You will come?
LEPORELLO: Say no!
JUAN: No doubt swells in my bosom;
I have no fear: I'll come!

COMMANDANT: Give me your
hand, in proof!

JUAN: Take it;—what sudden
chill,
That freezes thus my heart!

COMMANDANT: Repent, and
change your life,
Or your last hour is come!

JUAN: No, no—I'll not repent;
Far from here! away! begone!

COMMANDANT: Lost man! once
more, repent!

JUAN: No, obstinate old man!

COMMANDANT: Henceforth it
will be too late!
(*Exit*).

JUAN: (*seized with despair*).
Through every nerve I tremble,—
An icy chill overpowers me!
What mean these dreadful gulfs
That open to devour me?

CHORUS: Horror more dire awaits
you,
And dread is your dark doom!

JUAN: My heart bursts in my bosom,
The serpents gnaw my vitals!
What tortures! oh, what madness!
What horror! what despair!

LEPORELLO: Alas! what looks of
terror!
What agonizing gestures!
What cries, what lamentations!
They pierce my heart with woe!

CHORUS: Horror more dire awaits
you,
And dread is your dark doom!

*THE END.*

# Die Zauberflöte (1791)

## The Magic Flute

MUSIC BY WOLFGANG AMADEUS MOZART ■ LIBRETTO BY EMANUEL SCHIKANEDER

This two-act opera, set to a libretto by Emanuel Schikaneder, premiered at the Theater auf der Wieden in Vienna on September 30, 1791. Prince Tamino is saved from a huge serpent by Three Ladies. Papageno, the birdcatcher, enters and tells Tamino that he (Papageno) slew the serpent. The Queen of the Night bursts in and instructs Tamino to save her daughter Pamina from Sarastro's fortress in Egypt. Tamino, seeing Pamina's portrait, falls in love with her on sight. Tamino is given a magic flute to insure his safety; Papageno's mouth was padlocked for lying and is freed but, to his dismay, he must accompany Tamino on his mission. Papageno is given silver bells as his aid. Monostatos, Sarastro's slave, catches Pamina but is frightened by Papageno, who tells Pamina about Tamino's love and his plans to rescue her. Tamino and Papageno are guided by Three Boys to Sarastro's temple. Tamino tries to enter, and a High Priest warns him that it is the Queen who is evil. Pamina is safe, Monostatos and his helpers are stopped by Papageno's bells, the animals are charmed by Tamino's flute, and Sarastro promises Pamina her freedom. Sarastro proclaims that Tamino is a candidate for initiation to the temple but will have to undergo many trials, as will Papageno (though Papageno's are of quite a different nature, including the discovery of Papagena, for whom Papageno must become worthy!). Pamina is about to kill herself when she is saved by the Three Boys and brought to Tamino. At the caves of fire and water, they walk through together, protected by the magic flute. The opera ends as the crowd cheers Sarastro, Pamina and Tamino, repulsing an intended attack upon the temple by the Queen, Monostatos and the Three Ladies. This opera contains many symbols inherent in the Masonic Order, of which both Mozart and Schikaneder were members. It is said that Mozart was killed for revealing their secret rites.

---

## ■ ERSTER AUFZUG

*(Rauhe Felsengegend. Links vorn ein Felsenlager. Rechts und links vom Darsteller.)*
*(Tamino, mit einem Bogen aber ohne Pfeil, eilt herbei.)*

**TAMINO:** Zu Hilfe! zu Hilfe!
Sonst bin ich verloren, Der Listigen Schlange zum Opfer erkoren!
Barmherzige Götter!
Schon nahet sie sich!
*(Eine grosse Schlange verfolgt Tamino.)*
Ach rettet mich! ach schützet mich!
*(Er ist bis zu dem Felsenlager links vorn gelangt und sinkt darauf erschöpft und bewusstlos zusammen.)*
*(Tamino auf dem Felsenlager. Die drei Damen, mit silbernen Wurfspiessen, treten ein.)*

**DIE DREI DAMEN:** Stirb, Ungeheu'r, durch uns're Macht!
*(Sie durchbohren mit ihren Wurfspiessen die Schlange, die regungslos liegen bleibt.)*
Triumph!
Triumph!
Sie ist vollbracht, Die Heldenthat Er ist befreit durch unsers Armes Tapferkeit.

**ERSTE DAME:** *(Tamino betrachtend)* Ein holder Jüngling, sanft und schön!

## ■ ACT I

*(rugged cliffs. To the left in the foreground a cave.)*
*(Tamino rushes in with a bow but no arrow.)*

**TAMINO:** Help! oh help! or else I am lost, a certain victim of the cunning serpent.
Merciful Gods! it even now approaches.
*(A large serpent follows Tamino.)*
Oh save, oh protect me!
*(He reaches the cave and sinks down exhausted and unconscious.)*
*(Tamino at the cave. Three ladies, carrying silver darts, enter.)*

**THE LADIES:** Die! monster, by our hands.
*(They pierce the serpent with their darts, and it lies motionless.)*
Triumph!
Triumph! it is accomplished a heroic deed!
He is freed by the courage Of our arm.

**FIRST LADY:** *(looking at Tamino)* A noble youth, gentle and handsome!

**ZWEITE DAME:** So schön, als ich noch nie geseh'n!

**DRITTE DAME:** Ja, ja, gewiss zum Malen schön!

**ALLE DREI:** Würd' ich mein Herz der Liebe weih'n, So müsst es dieser Jüngling sein.
Lasst uns zu uns'rer Fürstin eilen, Ihr diese Nachricht zu erteilen.
Vielleicht, dass dieser schöne Mann Die vor'ge Ruhe ihr geben kann.

**ERSTE DAME:** So geht und sagt es ihr,
Ich bleib' indessen hier.

**ZWEITE DAME:** Nein, nein, geht ihr nur hin,
Ich wache hier für ihn!

**DRITTE DAME:** Nein, nein, das kann nicht sein,
Ich schütze ihn allein.

**ERSTE DAME:** Ich blieb indessen hier!

**ZWEITE DAME:** Ich wache hier für ihn!

**DRITTE DAME:** Ich schütze ihn allein!

**ERSTE DAME:** Ich bleibe!

**ZWEITE DAME:** Ich wache!

**DRITTE DAME:** Ich schütze!

**ALLE DREI:** Ich! ich! ich!

**SECOND LADY:** So handsome as I never have seen!

**THIRD LADY:** Yes, yes, handsome enough to be painted!

**ALL THREE:** Could I devote my heart to love
It would be to this fair youth.
Let us hasten to our princess, To impart this news to her.
Perhaps this young and handsome man
May bring her back her former calm.

**FIRST LADY:** Go then and tell the news
And I meanwhile will stay.

**SECOND LADY:** No, no, you go yourself,
I will watch over him.

**THIRD LADY:** No, no, that cannot be—
I will remain to guard him!

**FIRST LADY:** I meanwhile will stay.

**SECOND LADY:** I will watch over him!

**THIRD LADY:** I will remain to guard him!

**FIRST LADY:** I remain!

**SECOND LADY:** I watch!

**THIRD LADY:** I guard!

**ALL THREE:** I!
I!
I!

ALLE DREI: (*jede für sich.*) Ich sollte fort?
Ei, ei!
Wie fein!
Sie wären gern bei ihm allein.
Nein, nein, das kann nicht sein.
(*Eine nach der anderen und dann alle drei zugleich.*)
Was wollte ich darum nicht geben,
Könnt' ich mit diesem Jüngling leben!
Hätt' ich ihn doch so ganz allein!
Doch keine geht, es kann nicht sein.
Am besten ist es nun, ich geh'.—
Du Jüngling, schön und liebevoll!
Du trauter Jüngling, lebe wohl,
Bis ich dich wieder seh'.
(*Sie entfernen sich.*)
(*Papageno in einem Federkleid, auf dem Rücken einen grossen Vogelbauer, der sich hoch über seinen Kopf erhebt und verschiedene Vögel enthält, eilt von links herbei. In den Händen hält er ein Faunenflötchen.*)

ALL THREE: (*each to herself*) I should away? ha! ha! how good.
They'd gladly be with him alone.
No, no, that cannot be!
(*One after the other, then all three together.*)
What would I give
If I might live with this youth!
That is, all by myself.
It cannot be, they do not go.
It's best then that I go myself.
You handsome and beloved youth,
You gentle one, farewell,
Until I see you once again!
(*Exeunt.*)
(*Papageno in a dress of feathers, with a large bird cage on his back, which he raises high over his head, and which contains various birds, hastens in. In his hands he holds a fawn-flute.*)

PAPAGENO: Der Vogelfänger bin ich ja,
Stets lustig, heisa, hopsasa!
Der Vogelfänger ist bekannt
Bei Alt und Jung im ganzen Land.
Weiss mit dem Locken umzugehn
Und sich auf's Pfeifen zu verstehn.
Drum kann ich froh und lustig sein,
Denn alle Vögel sind ja mein.
(*Er pfeift und nimmt dann den Vogelbauer ab.*)
Der Vogelfänger bin ich ja,
Stets lustig, heisa, hopsasa!
Der Vogelfänger ist bekannt
Bei Alt und Jung im ganzen Land.
Ein Netz für Mädchen möchte ich,
Ich fing sie dutzendweis für mich;
Dann sperrte ich sie bei mir ein,
Und alle Mädchen wären mein,
Wenn alle mädchen wären mein.
Dann tauschte ich brav Zucker ein,
Die, welche mir am liebsten wär',
Der gäb' ich gleich den Zucker her.
Und küsste sie mich zärtlich dann,
Wär' sie mein Weib und ich ihr Mann.
Sie schlief an meiner Seite ein,
Ich wiegte wie ein Kind sie ein.
(*Er pfeift und wendet sich dann zum Abgang nach rechts.*)

PAPAGENO: The fowler merry and gay am I, Ever happy, heigh ho high!
The merry fowler too is known By young and old from zone to zone.
Knows how to whistle every sound, Knows the bird-calls all around.
Oh, none can be more blithe than I, For mine are the warblers of the sky.
(*He whistles and takes down the bird cage.*)
The fowler merry and gay am I, Ever happy, heigh ho high!
The merry fowler too is known, By young and old from zone to zone.
A net for maidens I should like, Would catch the pretty dears by dozens.
I'd shut them safely up at home And never from me would they roam.
Then I would some sugar buy, And to her who loved me, I Gladly would the sugar give, And if she kissed me tenderly, Man and wife we then would be.
At my side she then would lie, And I'd sing her a lullaby.
(*He pipes and goes to the right exit.*)

TAMINO, PAPAGENO:

TAMINO: (*er erwacht*) He da!

TAMINO AND PAPAGENO:

TAMINO: (*he awakes*) Holla!

PAPAGENO: Was da?

PAPAGENO: What's that?

TAMINO: Sag' mir, du lustiger Freund, wer du bist?

TAMINO: Tell me, jolly friend, who you are.

PAPAGENO: Wer ich bin?
(*Für sich.*)
Dumme Frage!
(*Laut.*)
Ein Mensch wie du.
—Wenn ich dich nun fragte, wer du bist?

PAPAGENO: Who I am?
(*Aside*)
Foolish question.
(*Aloud.*)
A man like you.—
And if I should ask who you are?

TAMINO: Mein Vater ist Fürst, der über viele Länder und Menschen herrscht; darum nennt man mich Prinz.

TAMINO: My father is a King who rules over many lands and peoples; therefore am I called Prince.

PAPAGENO: (*für sich*) Wie er mich so starr anblickt!
Bald fang' ich an, mich vor ihm zu fürchten.
Bleib zurück, sag' ich, und traue mir nicht, denn ich habe Riesenkraft.

PAPAGENO: (*aside*) How he stares at me!
I am beginning now to fear him.
Do not approach, tell you, and do not trust me, for I have gigantic strength.

TAMINO: Riesenkraft?
(*Er sieht auf die Schlange.*)
Also warst du wohl gar mein Erretter, der diese giftige Schlange bekämpfte?

TAMINO: Gigantic strength?
(*He looks at the serpent.*)
So you were my deliverer, who conquered this poisonous serpent?

PAPAGENO: Schlange?
(*Er sieht sich um, weicht zitternd einige Schritte zurück.*)
Ist sie tot oder lebendig?

PAPAGENO: Serpent?
(*He looks around and trembling, takes a few steps backward.*)
Is it dead or alive?

TAMINO: Aber um alles in der Welt, Freund, wie hast du dieses Ungeheuer bekämpft?
Du bist ohne Waffen!

TAMINO: How on earth have you conquered this monster?
You are without weapons!

PAPAGENO: Brauch' keine!
Bei mir ist ein starker Druck mit der Hand mehr als Waffen.

PAPAGENO: I need none!
My hands serve me better than weapons.

TAMINO: Du hast sie also erdrosselt?

TAMINO: Then you have strangled it?

PAPAGENO: Erdrosselt!
(*Für sich.*)
Bin in meinem Leben nicht so stark gewesen, als heute.
(*Die drei Damen erscheinen verschleiert von rechts; die erste Dame trägt ein Gefäss mit Wasser, die zweite Dame einen Stein, die dritte Dame ein Vorhängeschloss und ein Medaillonbildnis.*)

PAPAGENO: Strangled!
(*Aside.*)
Never have I been so strong as to-day!
(*The three ladies appear, veiled, from the right; the first lady carries a vase of water, the second a stone, the third a padlock and a protrait for a medallion.*)

DIE DREI DAMEN: (*halten sich noch zurück, drohen und rufen zugleich*) Papageno!

THE THREE LADIES: (*they still keep at a distance, threaten and shout all together.*) Papageno!

PAPAGENO: Aha!
Das geht mich an.
(*Halblaut zu Tamino.*)
Sieh dich um, Freund!

PAPAGENO: Aha! they call me!
(*To Tamino.*)
Look around, friend.

TAMINO: (*halblaut*) Wer sind diese Damen?

TAMINO: (*in a low tone*) Who are these ladies?

PAPAGENO: (*ebenso*) Wer sie eigentlich sind, weiss ich selbst nicht.

PAPAGENO: (*in a low tone*) I really do not know who they are.

TAMINO: (*ebenso*) Sie sind vermutlich sehr schön?

TAMINO: (*in a low tone*) They are doubtless very beautiful.

PAPAGENO: (*ebenso*) Ich denke nicht!
Denn wenn sie schön wären, würden sie ihre Gesichter nicht bedecken.

PAPAGENO: (*in a low tone*) I do not think so.
For were they beautiful they would not thus conceal their faces.

DIE DREI DAMEN: (*näher tretend, drohend*) Papageno!

THE THREE LADIES: (*drawing nearer, and threatening*) Papageno!

PAPAGENO: (*halblaut*) Sei still! sie drohen mir schon.
Hier, meine Schönen, übergeb' ich meine Vögel.
(*Die drei Damen nehmen die Mitte zwischen Tamino und Papageno*)

PAPAGENO: (*in a low tone*) Be still!
They chide me now.
Here, my fair ones, here are my birds!
(*The three Ladies stand between Tamino and Papageno*)

ERSTE DAME: (*reicht Papageno das Gefäss mit Wasser*) Dafür schickt dir unsere Fürstin heute zum erstenmal statt Wein reines, helles Wasser.

FIRST LADY: (*hands Papageno the vase with water*) In return our princess sends to-day clear water instead of wine.

# Act I

ZWEITE DAME: (*tritt an deren Stelle*) Und mir befahl sie, dass ich, statt Zuckerbrot, diesen Stein dir überbringen soll.
(*Sie überreicht Papageno den Stein.*)

DRITTE DAME: (*an die Stelle der zweiten Dame tretend*) Und statt der süssen Feigen hab' ich die Ehre, dir dies goldene Schloss vor den Mund zu legen.
(*Zu Tamino.*) Wir waren's, Jüngling, die dich befreiten. Hier, dies Gemälde überschickt dir die grosse Fürstin, es ist das Bildnis ihrer Tochter!
(*Sie überreicht es.*)
Auf Wiedersehen!

ZWEITE DAME: Adieu, Monsieur Papageno!
(*Die zweite und dritte Dame fassen den Vogelbauer und gehen damit rechts ab.*)

ERSTE DAME: Fein nicht so hastig getrunken!
(*Sie folgt lachend den beiden andern.*)
(*Papageno eilt in stummer Verlegenheit nach links ab.*)
(*Tamino hat gleich nach dem Empfang des Bildnisses seine Aufmerksamkeit nur diesem zugewendet.*)

TAMINO: Dies Bildnis ist bezaubernd schön, Wie noch kein Auge je gesehn!
Ich fühl' es, wie dies Götterbild Mein Herz mit neuer Regung füllt.
Dies Etwas kann ich zwar nicht nennen, Doch fühl' ich's hier wie Feuer brennen.
Soll die Empfindung Liebe sein? Ja, ja! die Liebe ist's allein.—
O, wenn ich sie nur finden könnte! O, wenn sie doch schon vor mir stände!
Ich würde—würde—warm und rein—
Was würde ich?
—Ich würde sie voll Entzücken An diesen heissen Busen drücken, Und ewig wäre sie dann mein.
(*Kurzer, starker Donner.*)
(*Es wird dunkel.*)

TAMINO: Ihr Götter! Was ist das?

DIE DREI DAMEN: Fasse dich!

ERSTE DAME: Es verkündet die Ankunft unserer Königin.
(*Donner.*)

DIE DREI DAMEN: Sie kommt!
(*Sehr starker Donner.*)

## OFFENE VERWANDLUNG

(*Die Berge teilen sich, man erblickt einen Sternenhimmel und in dessen Mitte den mit Sternen gezierten Thron der Königin der Nacht. Helles, blaues Mondlicht.*)

SECOND LADY: (*steps into her place*) And she commanded me to give you this stone instead of cake.
(*She gives him the stone.*)

THIRD LADY: (*steps into her place*) And instead of sweet figs I have the honor to put this golden padlock on your mouth.
(*To Tamino.*)
It was we, dear youth, who freed you.
Here, our great princess sends to you this picture.
It is the portrait of her daughter!
(*She presents it.*)
Farewell!

SECOND LADY: Adieu, sir Papageno!
(*The second and third take the bird-cage and go with it to the right.*)

FIRST LADY: He did not drink that so quickly.
(*She follows the two others, laughing.*)
(*Papageno hastens away in dumb astonishment to the left.*)
(*Tamino, immediately upon the receipt of the picture, gives his whole attention to it.*)

TAMINO: Oh, beautious form with semblance fair, No mortal may compare with you!
What rapture the sight imparts, What mingled feelings fill my heart.
I know not how to call this state, But it fills me all with its fire.
And is it love that wakes in me? It is only love that takes this form!
O could I but behold her now, Could she but now stand before me!
O, I would then be pure and true, What would I be? I would woo her, Press her fair form to my warm heart And she never would depart from me!
(*A short, loud clap of thunder.*)
(*It grows dark.*)

TAMINO: Great Gods, what is it?

THE THREE LADIES: Courage!

FIRST LADY: It announces the approach of our Queen.
(*Thunder.*)

THE THREE LADIES: She comes!
(*Very loud thunder.*)

## CHANGE OF SCENE

(*The mountains open up. A starry heaven appears, in the middle of which stands the star-covered throne of the Queen of the Night. Clear, bluish moonlight.*)

KÖNIGIN: O zitt're nicht, mein lieber Sohn!
Du bist unschuldig, weise, fromm;
Ein Jüngling, so wie du, vermag am besten,
Das tiefbetrübte Mutterherz zu trösten.
Zum Leiden bin ich auserkoren, Denn meine Tochter fehlet mir;
Durch sie ging all mein Glück verloren, Ein Bösewicht entfloh mit ihr.
Noch seh' ich ihr Zittern Mit bangem Erschüttern,
Ihr ängstliches Beben, Ihr schüchternes Streben.
Ich musste sie mir rauben sehen, Ach helft! war alles, was sie sprach;
Allein vergebens war ihr Flehen, Denn meine Hilfe war zu schwach.
Du wirst sie zu befreien gehen, Du wirst der Tochter Retter sein;
Und werd' ich dich als Sieger sehen, So sei sie dann auf ewig dein.
(*Sie tritt zurück.*)
(*Sehr starker Donner.*)
(*Tamino bleibt bewegt im Vordergrund stehen.*)

PAPAGENO: (*zeigt traurig auf das Schloss an seinem Mund*) Hm! hm! hm! hm! hm! hm! hm!

TAMINO: Der Arme kann von Strafe sagen, Denn seine Sprache ist dahin.

PAPAGENO: Hm! hm! hm! hm! hm! hm! hm!

TAMINO: Ich kann nichts thun, als dich beklagen, Weil ich zu schwach zu helfen bin.

PAPAGENO: Hm! hm! hm! hm! hm! hm! hm!
(*Die drei Damen erscheinen von rechts; die erste Dame trägt eine Flöte und ein Glockenspiel.*)
(*Die drei Damen treten zwischen Tamino und Papageno.*)

ERSTE DAME: (*zu Papageno*) Die Königin begnadet dich,
(*sie nimmt ihm das Schloss vom Mund und übergiebt es der zweiten Dame*)
Erlässt die Strafe dir durch mich.

PAPAGENO: Nun plaudert Papageno wieder.

ZWEITE DAME: Ja, plaud're! Lüge nur nicht wieder.

PAPAGENO: Ich lüge nimmermehr.
Nein! Nein!

DIE DREI DAMEN: Dies Schloss soll deine Warnung sein!

PAPAGENO: Dies Schloss soll meine Warnung sein!

QUEEN: O tremble not, beloved son!
You're innocent, devout and wise.
A youth like you does sure know best how to put a mother's heart at rest.
For I am doomed to mourn and sorrow.
My daughter left me in dismay.
With her my happiness has vanished, a scondrel bore my child away.
I still see her shiver, tremble and quiver, I still hear her shrieking, in vain seeking aid, I had to see her stolen from me, oh, help! was all the poor child said.
Alas in vain was all her pleading, too weak, oh Heaven, was my aid!
You, you alone, my friend, will free her, you will alone be her saviour, and if in your arms I shall see her, she shall be yours forever!
(*She steps back.*)
(*Very loud thunder.*)
(*Tamino stands in the foreground greatly moved.*)

PAPAGENO: (*points sadly at the lock on his mouth*) Hm, hm, hm, hm, hm, hm.

TAMINO: He was guilty of a falsehood and as penalty he's dumb.

PAPAGENO: Hm! hm! hm! hm! hm! hm!

TAMINO: I can do nothing, except sympathize with you, as I am powerless to help.

PAPAGENO: Hm! hm! hm! hm! hm! hm!
(*The three Ladies appear from the right. The first lady carries a flute and chimes.*)
(*The three ladies step between Tamino and Papageno.*)

THE FIRST LADY: (*to Papageno*)
The Queen is merciful
(*She takes the lock off from his mouth, and hands it to the second lady.*)
And remits your punishment through me.

PAPAGENO: Now Papageno will chatter again.

SECOND LADY: Yes, chatter, but never lie again.

PAPAGENO: I'll never lie again, no, never, never.

THREE THREE LADIES: Let this lock be your warning!

PAPAGENO: This lock shall be my warning.

ALLE: Bekämen doch die Lügner alle
Ein solches Schloss vor ihren Mund:
Statt Hass, Verleumdung, schwarzer Galle,
Bestünde Lieb' und Bruderbund.

ERSTE DAME: (*übergiebt Tamino die goldene Flöte*) O Prinz, nimm dies Geschenk von mir!
Dies sendet uns're Fürstin dir.
Die Zauberflöte wird dich schützen,
Im grössten Unglück unterstützen.

DIE DREI DAMEN: Hiermit kannst du allmächtig handeln,
Der Menschen Leidenschaft verwandeln.
Der Traurige wird freudig sein,
Den Hagestolz nimmt Liebe ein.

ALLE: O, so eine Flöte ist mehr als Gold und Kronen wert,
Denn durch sie wird Menschenglück und Zufriedenheit vermehrt.

PAPAGENO: Nun, ihr schönen Frauenzimmer,
Darf ich—so empfehl' ich mich.

DIE DREI DAMEN: Dich empfehlen kannst du immer,
Doch bestimmt die Fürstin dich,
Mit dem Prinzen ohn' Verweilen
Nach Sarastros Burg zu eilen.

PAPAGENO: Nein, dafür bedank' ich mich!
Von Euch selber hörte ich,
Dass er wie ein Tigertier!
Sicher liess ohn' alle Gnaden
Mich Sarastro rupfen, braten,
Setzte mich den Hunden für.

DIE DREI DAMEN: Dich schützt der Prinz, trau' ihm allein!
Dafür sollst du sein Diener sein.

PAPAGENO: (*für sich*) Dass doch der Priz beim Teufel wäre!
Mein Leben ist mir lieb;
Am Ende schleicht bei meiner Ehre,
Er von mir wie ein Dieb.

ERSTE DAME: (*übergiebt Papageno ein Kästchen mit einem Glockenspiel*)
Hier, nimm dies Kleinod, es ist dein.

PAPAGENO: Ei, ei! was mag darinnen sein?

DIE DREI DAMEN: Darinnen hörst du Glöckchen tönen.

PAPAGENO: Werd' ich sie auch wohl spielen können?

DIE DREI DAMEN: O ganz gewiss! ja, ja, gewiss!

DIE DREI DAMEN: Silberglöckchen, Zauberflöten
Sind zu eurem Schutz vonnöten.
Lebet wohl! wir wollen gehn,
Lebet wohl! auf Wiedersehn.

ALL: If every tongue when speaking falsehood,
Could have a lock to seal his lips,
Instead of seeking grief and scandal,
We all would feel love and friendship.

FIRST LADY: (*gives Tamino the golden flute*) O prince, take this rare gift from me
Which our fair princess sends to you!
This Magic Flute possesses power
To guide you safely in danger's hour!

THE THREE LADIES: The power lies now in your hand
All human passions to command.
The sad will ever be happy,
The loveless never be free from love.

ALL: O such a flute is worth its weight in gold,
Bringing both love and happiness untold.

PAPAGENO: And now ladies, With your leave I'll go.

THE THREE LADIES: You can freely go,
But the princess fair commands you
With the prince to take your way
To the castle of Sarastro.

PAPAGENO: No, I thank for the honor,
But myself I've heard you say
That he is a very tiger!
And he would without delay,
Have me plucked and quickly roasted,
A tasty prey for his dogs.

THE THREE LADIES: Trust the Prince, for he'll protect you,
You'll be his faithful servant.

PAPAGENO: (*aside*) The Prince may risk his royal being,
But I value mine more.
He may repent when all too late,
I'd rather now decline.

FIRST LADY: (*presents Papageno with a casket containing chimes.*)
Pray, take this treasure, it is yours.

PAPAGENO: Oh, oh, what can it be?

THE THREE LADIES: You can hear the bells ringing within.

PAPAGENO: And will I, too, have power to play them?

THE THREE LADIES: Why certainly, of course, you will.

THE THREE LADIES: Silver bells and magic flute are attuned to protect you,
Fare well, we must away,
Now we bid you both good day.

TAMINO UND PAPAGENO: Silberglöckchen, Zauberflöten
Sind zu userm Schutz vonnöten.
Lebet wohl! wir wollen gehn,
Lebet wohl! auf Wiedersehn.
(*Die drei Damen wenden sich nach rechts*)
(*Tamino und Papageno wenden sich gleichzeitig nach links; zurückkommend*)

TAMINO: Doch, schöne Damen, saget an:

PAPAGENO: Wie man die Burg wohl finden kann?

BEIDE: Wie man die Burg wohl finden kann?

DIE DREI DAMEN: (*ebenso*) Drei Knäbchen, jung, schön, hold und weise,
Umschweben euch auf eurer Reise;
Sie werden eure Führer sein,
Folgt ihrem Rate ganz allein.

TAMINO UND PAPAGENO: Drei Knäbchen, jung, schön, hold und weise,
Umschweben uns auf unsrer Reise.

ALLE: So lebet wohl! wir wollen gehn,
Lebt wohl, lebt wohl!
Auf Wiedersehn!
(*Die drei Damen ab nach rechts*)
(*Tamino und Papageno gleichzeitig ab nach links*)

PAPAGENO AND TAMINO: Silver bells and magic flute
Are attuned to protect.
Fare well, we must away,
Now we bid you all good day.
(*The three ladies go to the right.*)
(*Tamino and Papageno go at the same time to the left; coming back.*)

TAMINO: Fair ladies, will you tell us pray—

PAPAGENO: To this great castle the way?

BOTH: How to find the way to this great Castle?

THE THREE LADIES: Three handsome youths will fly before you,
And point you out the way;
Follow the counsel they may give,
Farewell, away, away!

TAMINO AND PAPAGENO: Three handsome youths will fly before us
And point us out the way.

ALL: Fare well, we must away,
Now we bid you both good day.
(*The three ladies go away to the right.*)
(*Tamino and Papageno go at the same time to the left.*)

## VERWANDLUNG

(*Reich ausgestattetes Zimmer der Pamina in Sarastros Palast.*)
(*Monostatos, Pamina, Sklaven treten ein*)

MONOSTATOS: (*Pamina an der Hand hereinschleudernd*) Du feines Täubchen, nur herein!

PAMINA: (*zu seiner Rechten*) O welche Marter!
Welche Pein!

MONOSTATOS: Verloren ist dein Leben.

PAMINA: Der Tod macht mich nicht beben,
Nur meine Mutter dauert mich;
Sie stirbt vor Gram ganz sicherlich.

MONOSTATOS: (*zu den im Hintergrund verweilenden Sklaven*)
He, Sklaven!
Legt ihr Fesseln an!
Mein Hass soll dich verderben.
(*Sklaven eilen hinzu, um Pamina zu fesseln*)

PAMINA: O lass mich lieber sterben,
Weil nichts, Barbar! dich rühren kann.
(*Sie sinkt ohnmächtig rechts vorn auf eine Ottomane.*)

MONOSTATOS: Nun fort! lasst mich bei ihr allein.
(*Sklaven eilen mit den Fesseln durch die Mitte ab*)
(*Papageno erscheint in der Mittel-*

## CHANGE OF SCENE

(*Sumptuously furnished room of Pamina in Sarastro's palace.*)
(*Monostatos, Pamina, Slaves enter*)

MONOSTATOS: (*patting Pamina's hand*) Come in, little dove!

PAMINA: Oh, wretched martyrdom, direful pain!

MONOSTATOS: Your life is lost.

PAMINA: I fear not the pains of death,
But my poor mother dies of grief,
With no one to bring her relief!

MONOSTATOS: (*to the slaves who are waiting in the back*) Hola slaves, let her straight be bound!
My hatred will be sated.
(*Slaves rush up to bind Pamina.*)

PAMINA: Oh let me, tyrant, rather die,
For nothing has abated your rage.
(*She sinks down unconscious on a couch.*)

MONOSTATOS: Away!
Let me alone with her!
(*The slaves withdraw with the chains.*)
(*Papageno appears in the middle*

# Act I

thür)
(Monostatos im Anschauen Paminas versunken, bemerkt das Erscheinen Papagenos nicht)

PAPAGENO: (noch in der Thür)
Wo bin ich wohl!
Wo mag ich sein?
Aha, da find' ich Leute!
Gewagt, ich geh' herein.
(Er tritt ein und nähert sich der Ottomane rechts vorn.)
Schön Mädchen, jung und fein,
Viel weisser noch als Kreide!
(Monostatos wendet sich.)
(Papageno steht bei Monostatos Anblick erstarrt; einer erschrickt über den andern.)

BEIDE: Hu! Das ist—der Teu—fel
si—cherlich!
Hab' Mitleid—und verschone mich!
Hu! hu! hu!
(Sie laufen, indem sie sich gegenseitig verstohlen über die Schulter zu beobachten trachten, nach der Mittelthür; dort stossen sie aufeinander und eilen mit einem Aufschrei durch die Mitte nach verschiedenen Seiten hin davon.)

PAMINA: (allein, erwachend, spricht wie im Traum) Mutter! Mutter!
Mutter!
(Sie erholt sich, sieht sich um.)
Wie!
Noch schlägt dieses Herz?
Zu neuen Qualen erwacht?
O, das ist hart, sehr hart—mir bitterer als der Tod!
(Papageno mit vorsichtigen Schritten beobachtend durch die Mitte)
Pamina. Papageno zu ihrer Linken.

PAPAGENO: Bin ich nicht ein Narr, dass ich mich schrecken liess?
Es giebt ja schwarze Vögel in der Welt, warum denn nicht auch schwarze Menschen?
(Er erblickt Pamina.)
Ach, sieh da!
Hier ist das schöne Mädchen noch.
(Zu Pamina.)
Du Tochter der nächtlichen Königin.

PAMINA: O, ich bin es.

PAPAGENO: Das will ich gleich erkennen.
(Er prüft das Porträt, welches der Prinz zuvor empfangen, und das Papageno nun an einem Band am Hals trägt.)
Die Augen blau (schwarz)—richtig blau (schwarz)—die Lippen rot—richtig rot—blonde (braune) Haare—blonde (braune) Haare.
Alles trifft ein.

PAMINA: Erlaube mir—
(Papageno zeigt ihr das Porträt.)

PAMINA: Ja, ich bin's.
Wie kam es in deine Hände?

door.)
(Monostatos absorbed in watching Pamina does not notice Papageno's arrival.)

PAPAGENO: (still in the door)
Where am I now?
Where can I be?
Aha, I see some people,
I'll venture in.
(He comes in and approaches the couch.)
A maiden greets me, pure and white as snow.
(Monostatos turns around.)
(Papageno is terrified by Monostatos's gaze; the one is frightened by the other.)

BOTH: That is the devil sure as fate,
Have mercy and commiserate!
Alas, alas, alas!
(They run away, looking back at each other cautiously over the shoulder. At the middle door they run into each other and rush with a cry through the middle door in different directions.)

PAMINA: (alone, awakening, speaks as in a dream) Mother! Mother!
Mother!
(She recovers and looks around.)
What?
Does my heart still beat?
Does it awake to new tortures?
O, it is so cruel, so cruel!
It is more bitter than death!
(Papageno with careful steps comes in and watches her.)

PAPAGENO: Am I not a fool that I allowed myself to be frightened?
There are black birds in this world, then why not black people?
(He notices Pamina.)
Ah, behold! here is the lovely maiden still!
(To Pamina.)
Oh daughter of the Queen of night!

PAMINA: I am she.

PAPAGENO: I'll know that right away.
(He examines the portrait which the Prince received and which Papageno now wears on a ribbon around his neck.)
Blue eyes (black)—very blue (black)—red lips—very red—blond (brown) hair—blond (brown) hair.
Everything tallies.

PAMINA: Permit me—
(Papageno shows her the portrait.)

PAMINA: Yes, it's I.
How did it come into your hands?

PAPAGENO: Ich muss dir das umständlicher erzählen.
Ich kam heute früh, wie gewöhnlich, zu deiner Mutter Palast meine Vögel abzugeben, dort sah ich einen Menschen vor mir, der sich Prinz nennen lässt.
Dieser Prinz hat deine Mutter so eingenommen, dass sie ihm dein Bildnis schenkte und ihm befahl, dich zu befreien.
Sein Entschluss war so schnell, als seine Liebe zu dir.

PAMINA: Liebe?
(Freudig.)
Er liebt mich also?
O sage mir das noch einmal, ich höre das Wort Liebe gar zu gern.

PAPAGENO: Das glaub' ich dir (ohne zu schwören), du bist ja ein Mädchen.—
Wo blieb ich denn?

PAMINA: Bei der Liebe.

PAPAGENO: Richtig, bei der Liebe.
(Das nenn' ich ein Gedächtnis haben.)
Nun sind wir hier, in den Palast deiner Mutter zu eilen.

PAMINA: Wohl denn, es sei gewagt!
Wenn dieser nun ein böser Geist von Sarastros Gefolge wäre?
(Sie sieht ihn bedenklich an.)

PAPAGENO: Ich ein böser Geist?
Wo denkst du hin. Ich bin der beste Geist von der Welt.

PAMINA: Freund, vergieb, vergieb, wenn ich dich beleidigte.
Du hast ein gefühlvolles Herz.

PAPAGENO: Ach, freilich hab' ich ein gefühlvolles Herz.
Aber was nützt mir das alles?
Ich möchte mir oft alle meine Federn ausrupfen, wenn ich bedenke, dass Papageno noch keine Papagena hat.

PAMINA: Armer Mann!
Du hast also noch kein Weib?

PAPAGENO: Noch nicht einmal ein Mädchen, viel weniger ein Weib!
Und unsereiner hat doch auch bisweilen seine lustigen Stunden, wo man gern gesellschaftliche Unterhaltungen haben möchte.

PAMINA: Geduld, Freund!
Der Himmel wird auch für dich sorgen; er wird dir eine Freundin schicken, ehe du dir's vermutest.

PAPAGENO: Wenn er sie nur bald schickte.

PAMINA: Bei Männern, welche Liebe fühlen, Fehlt auch ein gutes Herze nicht.

PAPAGENO: Die süssen Triebe mitzufühlen, Ist dann der Weiber erste l'flicht.

PAPAGENO: I must relate it to you in very great detail.
I came very early, as is my custom, to your mothers' palace to deliver my birds, when I saw a man before me who is called Prince.
This Prince so charmed your mother that she gave him your portrait, and ordered him to free you.
His resolution was as hasty as his love for you.

PAMINA: Love?
(Joyfully)
Then he loves me?
Tell it to me once again, for I rejoice at the sound of that word.

PAPAGENO: And I believe you (without swearing) for you are a maiden—

ALL THREE: Where was I?

PAMINA: At the word love.

PAPAGENO: Yes, you are right, at the word Love.
(I call that having a fine memory!)
Now we are here to hasten you to your mother's palace.

PAMINA: Well then, let us attempt it.
And if he be a villain in Sarastro's employ?
(She looks attentively at him.)

PAPAGENO: I a villain?
What are you thinking of?
I am the best man on earth.

PAMINA: Dear friend, forgive me if I have offended you.
You have a loving heart.

PAPAGENO: Ah, luckily I have a loving heart. But what is the good of it?
I sometimes want to pluck out all my feathers when I remember that Papageno has no loving mate.

PAMINA: Poor man!
So you have no wife?

PAPAGENO: Not even a fair maiden the less a wife.
And every one of us has his happy moments which he would like to spend in company.

PAMINA: Patience, my friend!
Heaven will reward you.
It will send you a companion before you know it.

PAPAGENO: Would that it did it soon!

PAMINA: The manly breast overflowing with love.
Will never lack a good heart.

PAPAGENO: And the sweet cares of love bestowing will ever be a woman's part.

**BEIDE:** Wir wollen uns der Liebe freun, Wir leben durch die Lieb' allein.

**PAMINA:** Die Lieb' versüsset jede Plage, Ihr opfert jede Kreatur.

**PAPAGENO:** Sie würzet uns're Lebenstage, Sie wirkt im Kreise der Natur.

**BEIDE:** Ihr hoher Zweck zeigt deutlich an,
Nichts edlers sei, als Weib und Mann.
Mann und Weib, und Weib und Mann,
Reichen an die Gottheit an.
(*Beide durch die Mitte ab.*)

## VERWANDLUNG

(*Hain, in dessen Mitte drei Tempel.*)
(*Die drei Knaben mit silbernen Palmzweigen in der Hand von links vorn kommend, geleiten Tamino, der seine Flöte umgehängt trägt.*)

**DIE DREI KNABEN:** Zum Ziele führt dich diese Bahn,
Doch musst du, Jüngling, männlich siegen.
Drum höre uns're Lehre an:
Sei standhaft, duldsam und verschwiegen.

**TAMINO:** Ihr holden Kleinen, sagt mir an,
Ob ich Pamina retten kann?

**DIE DREI KNABEN:** Dies kund zu thun, steht uns nicht an;
Sei standhaft, duldsam und verschwiegen.
Bedenke dies; kurz, sei ein Mann,
Dann, Jüngling, wirst du männlich siegen.
(*Sie gehen ab.*)
(*Tamino allein. Stimmen.*)

**TAMINO:** Die Weisheitslehre dieser Knaben
Sei ewig mir ins Herz gegraben.
Wo bin ich nun? Was wird mit mir?
Ist dies der Sitz der Götter hier?
Es zeigen die Pforten, es zeigen die Säulen,
Dass Klugheit und Arbeit und Künste hier weilen;
Wo Tätigkeit thronet und Müssiggang weicht,
Erhält seine Herrschaft das Laster nicht leicht.
(*Er zeigt nach rechts.*)
Ich wage mich mutig zur Pforte hinein,
Die Absicht ist edel und lauter und rein.
Erzitt're, feiger Bösewicht!
Pamina retten ist mir Pflicht.
(*Er nähert sich mit einigen Schritten der Tempelpforte rechts.*)

**STIMMEN:** (*Chor*) Zurück!

**BOTH:** It is Love alone that makes us happy,
It is Love alone makes life worth while!

**PAMINA:** It is Love that sweetens every care,
Every creature bends to her.

**PAPAGENO:** Love perfumes life with rare fragrance
And beauty leads to fair Nature.

**BOTH:** Nothing can prove dearer raptures
Than two fond hearts that truly love.
For man and woman, woman, man,
Complete Divinity's fair plan. (*Exeunt.*)

## CHANGE OF SCENE

(*Sacred grove in the middle of which are three temples.*)
(*The three youths with silver palm branches in their hands come out from the left accompanying Tamino. His flute hangs at his side.*)

**THE THREE YOUTHS:** To the goal this path will lead,
But you must be heroic!
Therefore to our counsel heed
And you'll set the captive free.

**TAMINO:** Fair youths, I crave an answer true—
Do you think I can save Pamina?

**THE THREE YOUTHS:** To make this known rests not with us
Be steadfast, patient and discreet!
Think of our words and be a man
And this will help you if anything can.
(*They go out.*)
(*Tamino (alone.) Voices.*)

**TAMINO:** The wisdom of these fair youths three,
May be engraved in my heart.
Where am I now? Where did I roam?
Is this perhaps the home of gods?
The portals and the gates impart,
That it is the home of work and art,
Where industry obtains full sway,
Vice no more can hold the reins.
(*He points to the right.*)
I'll boldly enter the temple door,
My purpose is noble and good and pure.
Tremble, villain bold.
Beware!
To save Pamina is my goal!
(*He approaches the temple door at the right.*)

**VOICES:** (*chorus*) Back!

**TAMINO:** Zurück?
So wag ich hier mein Glück!
(*Er wendet sich nach der Tempelpforte links.*)

**STIMMEN:** (*Chor*) Zurück!

**TAMINO:** Auch hier ruft man: zurück!
(*Er wendet sich nach der Tempelpforte in der mitte.*)
Da sehe ich noch eine Tür,
Vielleicht find' ich den Eingang hier.
(*Indem er sich der Mittelpforte nähert, öffnet sich diese und ein Priester in weissem Haar und Bart tritt heraus.*)

**PRIESTER:** Wo willst du, kühner Fremdling hin?
Was suchst du hier im Heiligtum?

**TAMINO:** Der Lieb' und Tugend Eigentum.

**PRIESTER:** Die Worte sind von hohem Sinn!
Allein wie willst du diese finden?
Dich leitet Lieb' und Tugend nicht,
Weil Tod und Rache dich entzünden.

**TAMINO:** Nur Rache für den Bösewicht.

**PRIESTER:** Den wirst du wohl bei uns nicht finden.

**TAMINO:** Sarastro herrscht in diesen Gründen?

**PRIESTER:** Ja, ja!
Sarastro herrschet hier!

**TAMINO:** Doch in dem Weisheitstempel nicht?

**PRIESTER:** Er herrscht im Weisheitstempel hier.

**TAMINO:** (*mit einigen Schritten nach links*) So ist denn alles Heuchelei!

**PRIESTER:** Willst du schon wieder gehn?

**TAMINO:** Ja, ich will gehn, froh und frei,
Nie euren Tempel sehn.

**PRIESTER:** Erklär' dich näher mir,
Dich täuschet ein Betrug.

**TAMINO:** Sarastro wohnet hier,
Das ist mir schon genug.

**PRIESTER:** Wenn du dein Leben liebst,
So rede, bleibe da!
Sarastro hassest du?

**TAMINO:** Ich hass' ihn ewig! Ja!

**PRIESTER:** Nur gieb mir deine Gründe an.

**TAMINO:** Er ist ein Unmensch, ein Tyrann.

**PRIESTER:** Ist das, was du gesagt, erwiesen?

**TAMINO:** Durch ein unglücklich' Weib bewiesen,
Das Gram und Jammer niederdrückt.

**TAMINO:** Back!
Here must I try my luck.
(*He goes to the temple door at the left.*)

**VOICES:** Back!

**TAMINO:** Here too they call: back!
(*He goes to the middle temple door.*)
There I see another door,
Perhaps I'll find one more entrance.
(*While he goes to the middle door it opens and a priest with white hair and beard comes out.*)

**PRIEST:** Where are you going, daring youth?
What do you seek in this sanctuary?

**TAMINO:** The home of virtue and of love.

**PRIEST:** Your words are certainly high sounding,
But where do you expect to find these?
Love and courage do not guide you,
Death and vengeance dire inflame you.

**TAMINO:** Only for vengeance on the villain.

**PRIEST:** You surely will not find him here.

**TAMINO:** Does Sarastro govern here?

**PRIEST:** Yes, Sarastro governs here.

**TAMINO:** But in the Temple of Wisdom?

**PRIEST:** Yes, in the Temple of Wisdom.

**TAMINO:** (*stepping to the left*) Then all is but hypocrisy.

**PRIEST:** Wilt you depart again, then?

**TAMINO:** Yes, I will gladly go from here,
And never again see your temple.

**PRIEST:** Explain yourself to me: a mistake deludes you.

**TAMINO:** Sarastro governs here,
That is enough for me.

**PRIEST:** If your life you prize,
Speak, and here remain!
Do you hate Sarastro?

**TAMINO:** I hate him, yes, and ever shall.

**PRIEST:** And pray, what are your reasons?

**TAMINO:** He is a tyrant and a brute.

**PRIEST:** Where is the proof of what you say?

**TAMINO:** By a luckless woman 'tis confessed,
Who by great sorrow is oppressed.

## Act I

PRIESTER: Ein Weib hat also dich berückt? Ein Weib tut wenig, plaudert viel. Du, Jüngling, glaubst dem Zungenspiel? O legte doch Sarastro klar Die Absicht seiner Handlung dar.

TAMINO: Die Absicht ist nur allzuklar; Riss nicht der Räuber ohn' Erbarmen Pamina aus der Mutter Armen?

PRIESTER: Ja, Jüngling! Was du sagst, ist wahr.

TAMINO: Wo ist sie, die er uns geraubt? Man opferte vielleicht sie schon?

PRIESTER: Dir dies zu sagen, teurer Sohn, Ist jetzt und mir noch nicht erlaubt.

TAMINO: Erklär' dies Rätsel, täusch' mich nicht.

PRIESTER: Die Zunge bindet Eid und Pflicht.

TAMINO: Wann also wird die Decke schwinden?

PRIESTER: Sobald dich führt der Freundschaft Hand Ins Heiligtum zum ew'gen Band. (*Er wendet sich und geht langsam durch die Mittelpforte ab.*)

TAMINO allein. STIMMEN.

TAMINO: O ewig Nacht! wann wirst du schwinden? Wann wird das Licht mein Auge finden?

STIMMEN: (*Chor hinter der Mittelpforte*) Bald, Jüngling, oder nie!

TAMINO: Bald, sagt ihr, oder nie? Ihr Unsichtbaren, saget mir, Lebt denn Pamina noch?

STIMMEN: (*Chor*) Pamina lebet noch!

TAMINO: (*freudig*) Sie lebt? Ich danke euch dafür. (*Er nimmt seine Flöte zur Hand.*) Wenn ich doch nur imstande wäre, Allmächtige, zu eurer Ehre, Mit jedem Tone meinen Dank Zu schildern, wie er hier (*aufs Herz zeigend*) entsprang! (*Er spielt auf seiner Flöte.*) (*Sogleich erscheinen wilde Tiere und Vögel aller Art. Er hört auf und sie fliehen.*) Wie stark ist nicht dein Zauberton, Weil, holde Flöte, durch dein Spielen Selbst wilde Tiere Freude fühlen. Doch nur Pamina bleibt davon. (*Er spielt.*) Pamina! höre, höre mich! Umsonst! (*Er spielt.*) Wo? Ach, wo find' ich dich?

PRIEST: 'Tis then a woman who beguiled you? Women do little and talk much. Do you give heed to empty talk? But still Sarastro has explained The motives of his actions.

TAMINO: His motives are alas too clear, Did not the robber without pity, Tear Pamina from her mother's arms?

PRIEST: Yes, youth, all you say is true.

TAMINO: Where is she whom he stole away? Perhaps by this time sacrificed?

PRIEST: To tell you this, dear friend, Is not yet permitted.

TAMINO: Explain this riddle—do not deceive me.

PRIEST: My tongue is bound by oath and duty.

TAMINO: When then will it be released?

PRIEST: As soon as friendship's hand shall lead you Into the sanctuary of immortal union. (*He turns around and goes out slowly through the middle door.*)

TAMINO: (*alone.*) VOICES:

TAMINO: Oh, endless night, how soon will you have vanished? When will the daylight greet my sight?

VOICES: (*chorus behind the middle door*) Soon, youth, or never!

TAMINO: Soon, say you, or never? Tell me, invisible ones, Does Pamina still live?

VOICES: Pamina still lives!

TAMINO: (*rejoicing*) She lives? I thank you all for that. (*He takes his flute in is hand.*) Oh, if I only had the power, Almighty ones, in praise of you, To express my thanks with each tone, To show the feelings in my heart! (*Points to his heart.*) (*He plays on his flute. Instantly wild animals and birds of every kind appear. He stops and they flee.*) How strong, flute, is your magic tune, That by your sweet, melodious playing, You moved beasts and hearts of stone, But where, oh where's Pamina staying? (*He plays.*) Pamina! hear, oh hear me!

(*Papageno antwortet von links hinten mit seinem Faunen flötchen*)

TAMINO: Ha, das ist Papagenos Ton! (*Er spielt.*) (*Papageno antwortet wie vorher*)

TAMINO: Vielleicht sah er Pamina schon, Vielleicht eilt sie mit ihm zu mir, Vielleicht führt mich der Ton zu ihr. (*Er eilt nach links hinten ab.*) (*Papageno und Pamina eilen, wenn Tamino verschwunden ist, ohne Fesseln von links vorn herbei*)

PAMINA UND PAPAGENO: Schnelle Füsse, rascher Mut, Schützt vor Feindes List und Wut. Fänden wir Tamino doch, Sonst erwischen sie uns noch.

PAMINA: (*mit einigen Schritten nach hinten, rufend*) Holder Jüngling!

PAPAGENO: Stille, stille, ich kann's besser. (*Er pfeift.*) (*Tamino antwortet links hinten mit seiner Flöte*)

BEIDE: Welche Freude ist wohl grösser? Freund Tamino hört uns schon; (*nach links hinten zeigend*) Hierher kam der Flötenton. Welch ein Glück, wenn ich ihn finde, Nur geschwinde! nur geschwinde! (*Sie wollen nach links hinten davoneilen.*) (*Monostatos tritt ihnen von dort her entgegen*)

MONOSTATOS: (*ihrer spottend*) Nur geschwinde! nur geschwinde! Ha, hab' ich euch noch erwischt? Nur herbei mit Stahl und Eisen; Wart, ich will euch Mores weisen. Den Monostatos berücken! (*Nach links hinten rufend.*) Nur herbei mit Band und Stricken, He, ihr Sklaven, kommt herbei! (*Sklaven kommen von links hinten mit Fesseln*)

PAMINA, PAPAGENO: Ach, nun ist's mit uns vorbei.

PAPAGENO: Wer viel wagt, gewinnt oft viel, Komm', du schönes Glockenspiel! Lass' die Glöckchen klingen, klingen, Dass die Ohren ihnen singen. (*Er spielt sein Glockenspiel.*)

MONOSTATOS UND DIE SKLAVEN: (*davon besänftigt, singen und tanzen nach dem Takt*) Das klinget so herrlich, das klinget so schön! Tralla lalala trallalalala! Nie hab' ich so etwas gehört und gesehn!

In vain! (*He plays.*) Where? Oh, where can I find you? (*Papageno answers with his fawn-flute.*)

TAMINO: Ah, that is Papageno's tone! (*He plays.*) (*Papageno answers as before.*)

TAMINO: Perhaps he has already seen Pamina, Perhaps with him she comes to me, Perhaps these tones will lead me to her. (*He goes out.*) (*Papageno and Pamina appear when Tamino has disappeared. They wear no chains.*)

PAMINA AND PAPAGENO: Nimble feet and dauntless courage may save us from the foe's dread rage. Could we but find Tamino! Now, they surely will surprise us.

PAMINA: (*takes a few steps back, calling*) Handsome youth!

PAPAGENO: Be still, I'll do it better. (*He whistles.*) (*Tamino answers with his flute from behind.*)

BOTH: Can there be a greater joy? Friend Tamino hears us now. (*Pointing to the left.*) From here came the sweet tones. Oh what joy when I shall find him! Quick, quick, let us hasten to him! (*They run to the left. Monostatos meets them.*)

MONOSTATOS: (*mocking her*) Quick, quick, let us hasten to him! Ha, ha, I have caught you then? Quickly, bind these daring ones! Wait, I'll teach you manners! You will never again deceive me! Slaves, come here and bind them! Take your ropes and bind them fast. (*Slaves come up with chains.*)

PAMINA AND PAPAGENO: Ah, it is all over with us!

PAPAGENO: Who ventures much, much ofttimes wins. Come, magic set of bells, Let your soft tones fill the air And resound in every ear! (*He plays.*)

MONOSTATOS AND THE SLAVES: (*they are subdued by the sound, sing and dance in time*) Its sound is so soothing, its sound is so sweet, Tralala, lalala, tralalalala! Oh, never, oh never, did I meet its equal!

Trallalala tralla lalala!
(*Sie entfernen sich singend und tanzend nach links hinten.*)

**PAPAGENO AND PAMINA:**
Könnte jeder brave Mann
Solche Glöckchen finden,
Seine Feinde würden dann
Ohne Mühe schwinden,
Und er lebte ohne sie
In der besten Harmonie.
Nur der Freundschaft Harmonie
Mildert die Beschwerden;
Ohne diese Sympathie
Ist kein Glück auf Erden!
(*Ein starker Marsch mit Trompeten und Pauken fällt ein.*)

**STIMMEN:** (*Chor von aussen*) Es lebe Sarastro!
Sarastro lebe!

**PAPAGENO:** (*mit einigen Schritten nach rechts*) Was soll das bedeuten?
Ich zittre, ich bebe!

**PAMINA:** (*ihm folgend*) O Freund, nun ist's um uns gethan!
Dies kündigt den Sarastro an.

**PAPAGENO:** O wär' ich eine Maus,
Wie wollt ich mich verstecken!
Wär' ich so klein wie Schnecken,
So kröch ich in mein Haus.
Mein Kind, was werden wir nun sprechen?

**PAMINA:** Die Wahrheit, sei sie auch Verbrechen.
(*Sarastro und Gefolge treten ein. Die Priester durch die Mittelpforte und von links ganz vorn; die Bewaffneten und das Volk von rechts; die Frauen hinter dem Wagen des Sarastro von rechts; die Sklaven von rechts und links.*)
(*Sarastro zuletzt von rechts auf einem Elefanten.*)

**CHOR:** Es lebe Sarastro!
Sarastro soll leben!
Er ist es, dem wir uns mit Freuden ergeben!
Stets mög' er des Lebens als Weiser sich freun,
Er ist unser Abgott, dem alle sich weihn.

**PAMINA:** (*kniet*) Herr, ich bin zwar Verbrecherin!
Ich wollte deiner Macht entfliehn,
Allein die Schuld ist nicht an mir—
Der böse Mohr verlangte Liebe;
Darum, o Herr! entfloh ich dir.

**SARASTRO:** Steh' auf, erheitere dich, o Liebe!
Denn ohne erst in dich zu dringen,
Weiss ich von deinem Herzen mehr:
Du liebest einen andern sehr.
Zur Liebe will ich dich nicht zwingen,
Doch geb' ich dir die Freiheit nicht.

**PAMINA:** Mich rufet ja die Kindespflicht,
Denn meine Mutter—

Tralalala, trala lalala!
(*they withdraw singing and dancing.*)

**PAPAGENO AND PAMINA:** If only every one could own
Bells of such melodious tone,
All our enemies would flee
And we would all be happy.
Without them each one can live
In the greatest harmony.
Only friendship's harmony
Softens every ill.
And without its sympathy, there can
Be no happiness on earth.
(*There is heard a loud march with trumpets and kettle-drums.*)

**VOICES:** (*from without*) Long live Sarastro! Long live Sarastro!

**PAPAGENO:** (*with a few steps to the right*) What can this mean? I tremble, I shudder.

**PAMINA:** (*following him*) O friend, we are lost forever!
The great Sarastro is announced.

**PAPAGENO:** O were I but a little mouse,
I would hide in some dark corner.
And were I as a snail,
I'd creep into my little house,
My child, what words will now avail?

**PAMINA:** Let's speak the truth, at any cost.
(*Enter Sarastro and his suite. The priest goes through the middle door to the left, the soldiers and the people to the right; the women behind the chariot of Sarastro at the right. The slaves at the right and left. Sarastro is borne in on an elephant.*)

**CHORUS:** Long live Sarastro, long live Sarastro!
It is he to whom we are all so devoted.
May he as a wise man enjoy life forever.
Our idol is he whom we worship and love!

**PAMINA:** (*kneels*) Oh Lord, it is true that I am guilty,
That I wished to flee from your power.
The guilt rests not only on me—
The wicked Moor desired my love,
Therefore, oh Sire, I fled from you.

**SARASTRO:** Arise, my love, and be happy.
For without further questioning you,
I know the secret of your heart.
For you already love another.
I never will compel you to love,
But I cannot give you freedom.

**PAMINA:** My filial duty calls me,
For my mother . . . .

**SARASTRO:** Steht in meiner Macht.
Du würdest um dein Glück gebracht,
Wenn ich dich ihren Händen liesse.

**PAMINA:** Mir klingt der Muttername süsse; Sie ist es—

**SARASTRO:** Und ein stolzes Weib.
Ein Mann muss eure Herzen leiten
Denn ohne ihn pflegt jedes Weib
Aus seinem Wirkungskreis zu schreiten.
(*Monostatos mit Tamino von links.*)

**MONOSTATOS:** Nun, stolzer Jüngling, nur hierher,
Hier ist Sarastro, unser Herr.

**PAMINA:** Er ist's!

**TAMINO:** Sie ist's!

**PAMINA:** Ich glaub' es kaum!

**TAMINO:** Sie ist's!

**PAMINA:** Er ist's!

**TAMINO:** Es ist kein Traum!
(*Sie nähern sich beiderseitig.*)

**PAMINA:** Es schling' mein Arm sich um ihn her!

**TAMINO:** Es schling' mein Arm sich um sie her!

**BEIDE:** Und wenn es auch mein Ende wär'!
(*Sie umarmen sich.*)

**ALLE:** Was soll das heissen?

**MONOSTATOS:** Welch' eine Dreistigkeit!
(*Indem er zwischen Pamina und Tamino tritt und sie trennt.*)
Gleich auseinander, das geht zu weit!
(*Er kniet vor Sarastro.*)
Dein Sklave liegt zu deinen Füssen,
Lass den vermess'nen Frevler büssen!
Bedenk', wie frech der Knabe ist:
Durch dieses selt'nen Vogels List
(*auf Papageno zeigend*)
Wollt' er Pamina dir entführen.
Allein ich wusst ihn auszuspüren!
Du kennst mich! Meine Wachsamkeit—

**SARASTRO:** (*winkt.*) Verdient, dass man ihr Lorbeer streut.
He! Gebt dem Ehrenmann sogleich—

**MONOSTATOS:** Schon deine Gnade macht mich reich.

**SARASTRO:** Nur siebenundsiebzig Sohlenstreich'.

**MONOSTATOS:** Ach Herr, den Lohn verhofft' ich nicht!

**SARASTRO:** Nicht Dank', es ist ja meine Pflicht!
(*Monostatos wird von einigen Sklaven, die vortreten, nach rechts abgeführt.*)

**SARASTRO:** Is in my power.
Your happiness would all be ended,
Were I to give you up to her.

**PAMINA:** The name of mother sounds so sweet,
It is she . . . .

**SARASTRO:** A haughty woman,
Only a man should guide your hearts,
Without him, woman is accustomed
To wend her way out of her sphere.
(*Monostatos and Tamino come from the left.*)

**MONOSTATOS:** Proud youth, come here—see
Sarastro, our dear lord.

**PAMINA:** It is he!

**TAMINO:** It is she!

**PAMINA:** I scarcely can believe it.

**TAMINO:** It is she!

**PAMINA:** It is he!

**TAMINO:** It is no dream.
(*They approach each other.*)

**PAMINA:** Oh, I would embrace him!

**TAMINO:** Oh, I would embrace her!

**BOTH:** Even if it brought death upon me. (*They embrace.*)

**ALL:** What does that mean?

**MONOSTATOS:** What strength!
(*He steps between Pamina and Tamino, and separates them.*)
Stop it at once. You go too far!
(*He kneels to Sarastro.*)
Your slave is kneeling at your feet,
Make the presumptuous youth do penance.
How impudent the bold youth is!
By the tricks of this rare bird
(*Pointing at Papageno*)
He sought to rob you of Pamina.
But I alone could track him.
You know me and my vigilance—

**SARASTRO:** (*beckons*). Deserves the laurel wreath.
Here!
Give to this gentleman at once—

**MONOSTATOS:** Alone your favor makes me rich.

**SARASTRO:** But seventy-seven bastinado stripes.

**MONOSTATOS:** Ah, sir, I did not merit such reward!

**SARASTRO:** Preserve your thanks, it's only my duty.
(*Monostatos is led away by slaves.*)

## Act I

**ALLE:** Es lebe Sarastro, der göttliche Weise!
Er lohnet und strafet in ähnlichem Kreise.

**SARASTRO:** Führt diese beiden Fremdlinge
In unsere Prüfungstempel ein;
Bedecket ihre Häupter dann,
Sie müssen erst gereinigt sein.
(*Zwei Priester gehn ab, kommen zurück mit Schleiern und bedecken damit die Häupter von Tamino und Papageno.*)

**SCHLUSSCHOR:** Wenn Tugend und Gerechtigkeit
Den grossen Pfad mit Ruhm bestreut,
Dann ist die Erd' ein Himmelreich,
Und Sterbliche den Göttern gleich.

**SARASTRO** (*reicht Pamina die Hand und geht mit ihr zur Mittelpforte*).
(*Tamino, Papageno wenden sich an der Hand der beiden Priester nach rechts.*)
(*Die Priester, die Bewaffneten, die Frauen, das Volk, die Sklaven wenden sich dem Hintergrunde zu.*)
(*Der Vorhang fällt.*)

**ALL:** Long live Sarastro, the divine sage!
He justly punishes and rewards

**SARASTRO:** Lead these two strangers
To our temple of probation.
Cover their heads,
For they must first be purified.
(*Two priests go out and come back with veils and cover the heads of Tamino and Papageno.*)

**CHORUS:** When virtue joined to justice
Strews the path with fame,
Then earth is indeed heaven,
And mortal men are like gods!
(*Sarastro takes Pamina's hand and goes with her to the middle door.*)
(*Tamino and Papageno go out with the two priests. The priests, soldiers, women, populace, slaves turn toward the background.*)
(*Curtain.*)

## ◼ ZWEITER AUFZUG

(*Unterirdischer Tempel.*)
(*Die Priester treten von rechts und links ein, schreiten nach vorn, begegnen sich in der Mitte; reichen sich die Hand, kreuzen sich, geben nach rechts und links. Sarastro erscheint zuletzt und nimmt die Mitte; vor ihm die beiden Sprecher, zu seiner Rechten und Linken die Priester.*)

**SARASTRO:** (*nach einer Pause*).
Ihr in dem Weisheitstempel eingeweihten Diener der grossen Götter Osiris und Isis!
Mit reiner Seele erklär' ich euch, dass unsere heutige Versammlung eine der wichtigsten unserer Zeit ist.
Tamino, ein Königssohn, wandelt an der nördlichen Pforte unseres Tempels.
Diesen Tugendhaften zu bewachen, ihm freundschaftlich die Hand zu bieten sei heute eine unserer wichtigsten Pflichten.
Haltet ihr ihn für würdig, so folgt meinem Beispiel.
(*Sarastro und die Priester blasen dreimal in die Hörner.*)

**SARASTRO:** Gerührt über die Einigkeit Eurer Herzen, dankt Sarastro euch im Namen der Menschheit.
Man führe Tamino mit seinem Reisegefährten im Vorhof des Tempels ein.
(*Zum Sprecher, der vor ihm niederkniet.*)

## ◼ ACT II

(*A Subterranean Temple.*)
(*The priest come in from the right and left, walk to the front and meet in the center. They shake hands, cross themselves, pass each other, go to the right and left. Sarastro appears and takes his place in the middle. In front of him the two Speakers; to his right and left the priests.*)

**SARASTRO:** (*after a pause*). You, ordained, in the Temple of Wisdom, servants of the great gods, Osiris and Isis!
With a pure heart I declare to you that our meeting of today is the most important of our time.
Tamino, the son of a king, waits before the north door of our temple. To protect this virtuous youth, to extend a friendly greeting to him, is one of our most urgent duties today. If you hold him worthy then follow my example.
(*Sarastro and the priests blow once into the horns.*)

**SARASTRO:** Moved by the unanimity of your hearts, Sarastro thanks you in the name of humanity.
Let Tamino and his companion be led to the vestibule of our temple.
(*To the Speaker who kneels before him.*)
And you, friend, fulfill your holy of-

Und du, Freund, vollziehe dein heiliges Amt und lehre sie die Macht der Götter erkennen
(*Die Priester bilden um Sarastro einen Halbkreis.*)

**SARASTRO:** O Isis und Osiris, schenket der Weisheit Geist dem neuen Paar! die ihr der Wand'rer Schritte lenket starkt mit Geduld sie in Gefahr, starkt mit Geduld sie in Gefahr,

**CHORUS:** Starkt mit Geduld sie in Gefahr

**SARASTRO:** Lasst sie der Prüfung Früchte sehen, doch sollten sie su Grabe gehen, so lohnt der Tugend kühnen Lauf, nehmt sie in euren Wohnsitz auf,—nehmt sie in euren Wohnsitz auf.

**CHORUS:** Nehmt sie in euren Wohnsitz auf.
(*Sarastro und die Priester entfernen sich in feierlicher Weise. Tamino rechts vorn, Sprecher zu seiner Linken, Papageno links vorn. Zweiter Priester zu seiner Rechten.*)

**SPRECHER:** Ihr Fremdlinge! was sucht oder fordert ihn von uns?

**TAMINO:** Freundschaft und Liebe.

**SPRECHER:** Bist du bereit, es mit deinem Leben zu erkämpfen?

**TAMINO:** Ja.

**SPRECHER:** Reiche mir deine Hand!
(*Sie reichen sich die Hände.*)
So!

**ZWEITER PRIESTER:** (*zu Papageno*). Willst auch du dir Weisheitsliebe erkämpfen?

**PAPAGENO:** Kämpfen ist meine Sache nicht.
Ich bin so ein Naturmensch, der sich mit Schlaf, Speis' und Trank begnügt; und wenn es ja sein könnte, dass ich nur einmal ein schönes Weibchen fänge.

**ZWEITER PRIESTER:** Die wirst du nie erhalten, wenn du dich nicht unseren Prüfungen unterziehst.

**PAPAGENO:** Worin besteht diese Prüfung?

**ZWEITER PRIESTER:** Dich allen unseren Gesetzen zu unterwerfen, selbst den Tod nicht zu scheuen.

**PAPAGENO:** Ich bleibe ledig.

**ZWEITER PRIESTER:** Wenn nun aber Sarastro dir ein Mädchen aufbewahrt hätte, das an Farbe und Kleidung dir ganz gleich wäre!

**PAPAGENO:** Mir gleich? Ist sie jung?

**ZWEITER PRIESTER:** Jung und schön.

**PAPAGENO:** Und heisst?

fice, and teach them to recognize the power of the gods.
(*The priests form a semi-circle around Sarastro.*)

**SARASTRO:** Oh Isis and Osiris, lead this faithful pair in wisdom's path! Concede your blessed protection, strengthen their hearts when danger's near, strengthen their hearts when danger's near.

**CHORUS:** Strengthen their hearts when danger's near.

**SARASTRO:** Grant that they bravely bear the trial, and that their prayers are not denied, But if you have fated that they succumb, grant them life beyond the tomb, O grant them life beyond the tomb.

**CHORUS:** Grant them life beyond the tomb.
(*Tamino, Speaker, Papageno, Second Priest.*)

**SPEAKER:** Stranger, what do you seek or ask from us?

**TAMINO:** Friendship and love.

**SPEAKER:** And are you prepared even if it costs you your life?

**TAMINO:** I am.

**SPEAKER:** Give me your hand!
(*They shake hands.*)
So!

**SECOND PRIEST:** (*to Papageno*). Will you, too, struggle for the love of wisdom?

**PAPAGENO:** Fighting is not my business
I am a son of nature content with sleep, food, and drink, and were it only possible, I should like to find a pretty little wife.

**SECOND PRIEST:** But you will never obtain one, if you do not submit to our probation.

**PAPAGENO:** Of what does it consist?

**SECOND PRIEST:** To follow all our laws, and not to shrink from death.

**PAPAGENO:** I'll remain single.

**SECOND PRIEST:** But if Sarastro has reserved for you a pretty maid who is just like you in dress and color?

**PAPAGENO:** Just like me? Is she young?

**SECOND PRIEST:** Young and beautiful.

**PAPAGENO:** And her name?

**ZWEITER PRIESTER:** Papagena.

**PAPAGENO:** Wie—Pa—?

**ZWEITER PRIESTER:** Papagena.

**PAPAGENO:** Papagena? Die möchte ich aus blosser Neugierde sehen.

**ZWEITER PRIESTER:** Sehen kannst du sie!

**PAPAGENO:** Aber wenn ich sie gesehen habe, hernach muss ich sterben? (*Zweiter Priester macht eine zweifelnde Bewegung.*) Ja?— Ich bleibe ledig.

**ZWEITER PRIESTER:** Sehen kannst du sie, aber bis zur verlaufenen Zeit kein Wort mit ihr sprechen.

**SPRECHER:** (*zu Tamino.*) Auch dir, Prinz, legen die Götter ein heilsames Stillschweigen auf. Du wirst Pamina sehen, aber nicht sie sprechen dürfen; dies ist der Anfang eurer Prüfungszeit.

**SPRECHER UND PRIESTER:** Bewahret euch vor Weibertücken: Dies ist des Bundes erste Pflicht! Manch' weiser Mann liess sich berücken, Er fehlte und versah sich's nicht. Verlassen sah er sich am Ende, Vergolten seine Treu mit Hohn! Vergebens rang er seine Hände, Tod und Verzweiflung war sein Lohn. (*Beide Priester ab nach rechts. Es wird dunkel.*)

**PAPAGENO:** He! Lichter her! Lichter her!

**TAMINO:** Ertrag' es mit Geduld und denke, es ist der Götter Wille. (*Die drei Damen eilen mit Fackeln von links berbei.*) (*Es wird heller.*)

**DIE DREI DAMEN:** Wie? Wie? Wie? Ihr an diesem Schreckensort? Nie, nie, nie, Kommt ihr wieder glücklich fort! Tamino, dir ist Tod geschworen! Du, Papageno, bist verloren!

**PAPAGENO:** Nein, nein, nein! Das wär' zu viel.

**TAMINO:** Papageno, schweig still! Willst du dein Gelübde brechen, Nichts mit Weibern hier zu sprechen!

**PAPAGENO:** Du hörst ja, wir sind beide hin.

**TAMINO:** Stille, sag' ich! schweige still!

**PAPAGENO:** Immer still und immer still!

**DIE DREI DAMEN:** Ganz nah' ist euch die Königin! Sie drang im Tempel heimlich ein.

**SECOND PRIEST:** Papagena.

**PAPAGENO:** What?—Pa—?

**SECOND PRIEST:** Papagena.

**PAPAGENO:** Papagena? I'd like to see her out of mere curiosity.

**SECOND PRIEST:** You can see her.

**PAPAGENO:** And when I have seen her, must I die? (*Second priest makes a sign of doubt.*) If so, then I'll remain single.

**SECOND PRIEST:** You can see her, but you must not speak to her until the appointed hour.

**FIRST SPEAKER:** (*to Tamino.*) And on you too, prince, the gods impose a holy silence. You shall see Pamina, but must not speak to her. The time of your probation now commences.

**FIRST SPEAKER AND PRIEST:** Beware of woman's treachery, It is the first duty to observe, Many a wise man was ensnared. He failed, and then was led astray. He saw himself at last forsaken, His faithfulness was met with scorn. Alas, he wrung his hands in vain, For his reward was death and pain (*Both Priests leave. It grows dark.*)

**PAPAGENO:** Here, let us have light! Light!

**TAMINO:** Come hear it patiently, it is the will of God! (*The three Ladies rush in with torches. It grows lighter.*)

**THE THREE LADIES:** What? what? what? You are in this place of terror? Never! never! never! Will you come out safely from here. Tamino, you are sworn to death! Papageno, you are lost!

**PAPAGENO:** No, no, no, that is too much!

**TAMINO:** Papageno, pray be still! Do you want to break your oath Never to speak to women?

**PAPAGENO:** You hear, we both are lost!

**TAMINO:** Still! I tell you, pray be still!

**PAPAGENO:** All you say is "still, still, still"!

**THE THREE LADIES:** The Queen is very near you. She stole secretly into the temple.

**PAPAGENO:** Wie? Was? Sie soll im Tempel sein?

**TAMINO:** Stille, sag' ich! schweige still! Wirst du immer so vermessen Deiner Eidespflicht vergessen?

**DIE DREI DAMEN:** Tamino, hör'! Du bist verloren! Gedenke an die Königin! Man zischelt viel sich in die Ohren Von dieser Priester falschem Sinn.

**TAMINO:** (*für sich.*) Ein Weiser prüft und achtet nicht, Was der gemeine Pöbel spricht.

**DIE DREI DAMEN:** Man sagt, wer ihrem Bunde schwört, Der ist verwünscht mit Haut und Haar.

**PAPAGENO:** Das wär' beim Teufel unerhört! Sag' an, Tamino, ist das wahr?

**TAMINO:** Geschwätz, von Weibern nachgesagt, Von Heuchlern aber ausgedacht.

**PAPAGENO:** Doch sagt es auch die Königin.

**TAMINO:** Sie ist ein Weib, hat Weibersinn, Sei still, mein Wort sei dir genug, Denk' deiner Pflicht und handle klug.

**DIE DREI DAMEN:** (*zu Tamino.*) Warum bist du mit uns so spröde? (*Tamino deutet bescheiden an, dass er nicht sprechen darf.*)

**DIE DREI DAMEN:** Auch Papageno schweigt—so rede!

**PAPAGENO:** (*heimlich zu den Damen.*) Ich möchte gern—wohl—

**TAMINO:** Still!

**PAPAGENO:** (*heimlich.*) Ihr seht, dass ich nicht soll.—

**TAMINO:** Still! Dass du nicht kannst das Plaudern lassen Ist wahrlich eine Schand für dich!

**PAPAGENO:** Dass ich nicht kann das Plaudern lassen, Ist wahrlich eine Schand' für mich!

**DIE DREI DAMEN:** Wir müssen sie mit Scham verlassen, Es plaudert keiner sicherlich; Von festem Geiste ist ein Mann, Er denket, was er sprechen kann.

**TAMINO, PAPAGENO:** Sie müssen uns mit Scham verlassen, Es plaudert keiner sicherlich; Vom festen Geiste ist ein Mann, Er denket, was er sprechen kann. (*Die drei Damen wollen sich nach links entfernen.*)

**CHOR DER PRIESTER:** (*von aussen.*) Entweiht ist die heilige Schwelle! Hinab mit den Weibern zur Hölle! (*Donner.*)

**PAPAGENO:** What? How? She is in the temple?

**TAMINO:** Silence, I tell you, silence! Will you ever be so bold And forget what you have sworn?

**THE THREE LADIES:** Tamino, listen! You are lost! Think of the wretched Queen. Much is whispered in these realms Of the priests' false nature.

**TAMINO:** (*aside*) A wise man heeds not What by the vulgar crowd has said.

**THE THREE LADIES:** They say who swears to their union Is doomed for all his life!

**PAPAGENO:** One would not even expect it of the devil! Tell me, Tamino, is it true?

**TAMINO:** But idle talk, that women have repeated And that bigots have invented!

**PAPAGENO:** Still our Queen has said it too.

**TAMINO:** She is a woman, has but woman's sense, Be silent, let my word be enough. Think of your duty and be prudent!

**THE THREE LADIES:** (*to Tamino*). Why are you so shy with us? (*Tamino intimates to them that he must not speak.*)

**THE THREE LADIES:** And Papageno too is silent—speak!

**PAPAGENO:** (*secretly to the Ladies*). I'd like to, but—

**TAMINO:** Be still!

**PAPAGENO:** (*aside*). You see I must not.

**TAMINO:** Still! That you cannot leave off talking Is really a disgrace!

**PAPAGENO:** That I cannot leave off talking Is really a disgrace!

**THE THREE LADIES:** We must leave you now with shame, No one speaks with surety, He is a man with judgment sound, Who's not afraid to speak his mind.

**TAMINO, PAPAGENO:** They must leave us now with shame, No one speaks with surety; He is a man with judgment sound Who's not afraid to speak his mind. (*The three Ladies are about to go.*)

**CHORUS OF PRIESTS:** (*from without*). The sacred threshold is defiled! Away, away with women! (*Thunder.*)

**DIE DREI DAMEN:** (*stürzen entsetzt nach links hinaus.*) O weh! o weh! o weh!

**PAPAGENO:** (*fällt vor Schrecken zu Boden.*) O weh! o weh! o weh!
(*Die drei Knaben kommen von links; der eine trägt die Flöte andere das Glockenspiel.*)

**DIE DREI KNABEN:** Seid uns zum zweitenmal willkommen,
Ihr Männer in Sarastros Reich.
Er schickt, was man euch abgenommen,
Die Flöte und die Glöckchen euch.
(*Ein goldener, mit Speisen und Getränken reich versehener Tisch kommt von rechts.*)
Wollt ihr die Speisen nicht verschmähan,
So esset, trinket froh davon.
Wenn wir zum drittenmal uns sehen,
Ist Freude eures Muthes Lohn!
Tamino, Muth! nah' ist das Ziel.
Du, Papageno, schweige still!
(*Während des Terzetts überreichen sie Tamino die Flöte, Papageno das Glockenspiel und entfernen sich dann nach links.*)

**PAPAGENO:** Tamino! wollen wir nicht speisen?
(*Tamino bläst auf seiner Flöte.*)

**PAPAGENO:** Blase du nur fort auf deiner Flöte, ich will meine Brocken blasen.
(*Er tritt hinter den Tisch und isst.*)
Herr Sarastro führt eine gute Küche.
Nun, ich will sehen, ob auch der Keller so gut bestellt ist.
(*Er schenkt sich ein und trinkt.*)
Ha, das ist Götterwein!
(*Tamino beendet sein Flötenspiel.*)
(*Pamina eilt von links herbei.*)
(*Tamino rechts vorn. Pamina zu seiner Linken. Papageno essend und trinkend hinter dem Mitteltisch.*)

**PAMINA:** (*freudig*). Du hier?
Gütige Götter!
Dank euch!
Aber du bist traurig?
Sprichst nicht eine
Silbe mit deiner Pamina?
Papageno, sage du mir, was ist meinem Freund?

**PAPAGENO:** (*winkt ihr mit gefülltem Mund, fortzugeben.*) Hm, hm, hm!

**PAMINA:** Wie?
Auch du?
O das ist mehr als Tod!
Ach, ich fühl's, es ist verschwunden,
Ewig hin der Liebe Glück!
Nimmer kommt ihr, Wonnestunden,
Meinem Herzen mehr zurück!
Sieh' Tamino, diese Thränen,

**THE THREE LADIES:** (*rush out in despair*). O woe, O woe, O woe!

**PAPAGENO:** (*falls down in fright*). O woe, O woe, O woe!
(*The three Youths come in. One carries the flute, the other the bells.*)

**THE THREE YOUTHS:** A second time be welcome here,
Dear friends, in Sarastro's kingdom,
He sends you what he's taken from you,
Your mellow flute and bells.
(*A golden table covered with food and drink appears.*)
If you do not scorn our table,
Drink and eat freely from it.
When we shall meet a third time,
You'll be rewarded with happiness.
Tamino, courage, your goal is near,
And Papageno, you be still!
(*They present the flute to Tamino, the bells to Papageno; exit.*)

**PAPAGENO:** Tamino, shall we eat?
(*Tamino plays his flute.*)

**PAPAGENO:** You blow on your flute and I will eat.
(*He goes to the table and eats.*)
Sir Sarastro has a fine kitchen!
Now I shall see if his cellar is just as good.
(*He fills his glass and drinks.*)
Ha, this is nectar!
(*Tamino stops playing his flute.*)
(*Pamina rushes in from the left.*)
(*Tamino, Pamina, Papageno eating and drinking at the table in the middle.*)

**PAMINA:** (*happily*). Are you here?
Good gods, I thank you!
But you are sad.
Won't you even say a word to your Pamina?
Pagageno, tell me what is the trouble with my friend.

**PAPAGENO:** (*motions to her, with full mouth, to go away*). Hm, hm, hm.

**PAMINA:** What? you too?
That is worse than death.
Oh, I feel that all has vanished,
The happiness of love has flown
From my heart; forever banished
Are the blissful hours I've known.
See my tears, Tamino,
Love, they flow alone for you,
If you do not feel love's longing,
Rest will be in death for me.

Fliessen, Trauter, dir allein.
Fühlst du nicht der Liebe Sehnen,
So wird Ruh' im Tode sein!
(*Sie geht traurig ab nach links.*)

**PAPAGENO:** (*isst hastig.*) Nicht wahr, Tamino, ich kann auch schweigen, wenn's sein muss?
(*Er trinkt.*)
Der Herr Koch und der Herr Kellermeister sollen leben!
(*Dreimaliger Posaunenton.*)
(*Tamino geht durch die Mitte ab.*)

**PAPAGENO:** Geh' du nur voraus, ich komm schon nach.
Jetzt will ich mir's erst recht wohl sein lassen.
Da ich in meinem besten Appetit bin, soll ich gehen?
Dass lass ich wohl bleiben.
(*Papageno, Stimmen, Sprecher.*)

**PAPAGENO:** (*von aussen rechts.*)
Tamino!
Tamino!
(*Er sucht von rechts herein*).
Wenn ich nur wenigstens wüsste, wo ich wäre?

**STIMME:** (*ruft ihm entgegen.*)
Zurück!
(*Donnerschlag, Feuer schlägt zur Thür hinaus.*)

**PAPAGENO:** Barmherzige Götter!
Wo wend' ich mich hin?
Wenn ich nur wüsste, wo ich hereinkam.
(*Er kommt zur Thür rechts vorn, durch die er hereinkam.*)

**STIMME:** (*ruft ihm entgegen.*)
Zurück!
(*Donner und Feuer, wie oben.*)

**PAPAGENO:** Nun kann ich weder zurück noch vorwärts,
(*er weint*) muss vielleicht am Ende gar verhungern!
Schon recht!
Warum bin ich mitgereist!

**SPRECHER:** Mensch, du hättest verdient, auf immer in finstern Klüften der Erde zu wandern.

**PAPAGENO:** Je nun, es giebt ja noch mehr Leute meinesgleichen.
Mir wäre jetzt ein gutes Glas Wein das grösste Vergnügen.

**SPRECHER:** Sonst hast du keinen Wunsch in die Welt?

**PAPAGENO:** Bis jetzt nicht.

**SPRECHER:** Man wird dich damit bedienen.
(*Ab nach links.*)
(*Ein grosser mit Wein gefüllter Becher kommt aus der Erde.*)

**PAPAGENO:** Juhe!
Da ist er schon!
(*Er trinkt.*)
Herrlich!—
Himmlisch!—
Göttlich!
Ha!
Mir wird ganz wunderlich ums Herz; ich möchte—ich wünschte—ja, was denn?
(*schlägt dazu das Glockenspiel.*)

(*She goes out sadly.*)

**PAPAGENO:** (*eats hastily*). Is it not true, Tamino, that I too can be silent if necessary?
(*Drinks.*)
Long live the cook and the butler!
(*Three trumpet calls.*)
(*Exit Tamino.*)

**PAPAGENO:** You go first, and I will follow.
Now I can really begin to enjoy it.
I should go when my appetite is at its best?
I'd like to see anyone get me away.
(*Papageno, Voices, Speaker.*)

**PAPAGENO:** (*from without*).
Tamino!
Tamino!
(*He looks about him.*)
If I only knew where I am!

**VOICE:** (*calls to him*). Go back!
(*Thunder clap. Fire darts out of the door.*)

**PAPAGENO:** Merciful gods!
Where shall I go?
If I only knew which way I came in!
(*Goes to the door through which he came.*)

**VOICE:** (*calls to him*). Back!
(*Thunder and fire as above.*)

**PAPAGENO:** Now I go neither forward nor backward,
(*he weeps*) and must perhaps die of hunger in the bargain!
Serves me right!
Why did I come along?

**SPEAKER:** Man, you deserve to wander forever in the dark recesses of the earth!

**PAPAGENO:** Perhaps; still there are many like me on this earth.
Now I'd enjoy a glass of wine better than anything!

**SPEAKER:** Have you no other wish at all?

**PAPAGENO:** So far none other.

**SPEAKER:** You will be served some.
(*Exit.*)
(*A large jug filled with wine comes up from the ground.*)

**PAPAGENO:** Hurrah! There it comes!
(*He drinks.*)
Great—
Heavenly!
Divine!
My heart feels quite strange; I'd like—I wish—now, what then?
(*Plays on the bells.*)
For why fair maidens should like me

Ein Mädchen oder Weibchen
Wünscht Papageno sich.
O so ein sanftes Täubchen
Wär' Seligkeit für mich!
Dann schmeckte mir Trinken und
Essen
Dann könnt ich mit Fürsten mich
messen
Des Lebens als Weiser mich freu'n,
Und wie im Elysium sein.
Ein Mädchen oder Weibchen
Wünscht Papageno sich.
O, so ein sanftes Täubchen
Wär' Seligkeit für mich.
Ach, kann ich denn keiner von al-
len
Den reizenden Mädchen gefallen?
Helf' eine mir nur aus der Noth,
Sonst gräm' ich mich wahrlich zu
Tod.
Ein Mädchen oder Weibchen
Wunscht Papageno sich.
O, so ein sanftes Täubchen
Wär' Seligkeit für mich.
Wird keine mir Liebe gewähren,
So muss mich die Flamme verzeh-
ren!
Doch küsst mich ein weiblicher
Mund,
So bin ich schon wieder gesund!
(*Das alte Weib, tanzend und sich
dabei auf einen Stock stützend,
kommt von rechts und tritt ihm
zur Linken.*)

**WEIB:** Da bin ich schon, mein Engel!

**PAPAGENO:** (*drecht sich un.*) Du
hast dich meiner erbarmt?

**WEIB:** Ja, mei Engel!
Komm, reich mir zum Pfand unseres Bundes deine Hand.

**PAPAGENO:** Nur nicht so hastig,
lieber Engel!

**WEIB:** Papageno, ich rathe dir, zau-
dre nicht.
Deine Hand, oder du bist auf immer
hier eingekerkert.

**PAPAGENO:** Eingekerkert?

**WEIB:** Wasser und Brod wird deine
tägliche Kost sein.

**PAPAGENO:** Wasser trinken?
Der Welt entsagen?
Nein, da will ich doch lieber eine
Alte nehmen, als gar keine.
Nun, da hast du meine Hand, mit
der Versicherung, dass ich dir immer getreu bleibe,
(*für sich*)
solange ich keine Schönere sehe.

**WEIB:** Das schwörst du?

**PAPAGENO:** Ja, das schwör' ich
dir!
(*Weib verwandelt sich in ein
junges Weib, welches ebenso gekleidet ist, wie Papageno.*)

**PAPAGENO:** Pa—pa Papagena!
(*Er will sie umarmen.*)
(*Sprecher tritt rasch von links ein
und zwischen beide.*)

Does Papageno sigh.
O such a gentle turtle-dove
Is a blessing from on high!
Then never while eating nor drink-
ing
Would I envy fair princes, I'm
thinking.
Like a wise man I'd find joy in life
If only I got me a wife!
For maiden fair, etc.
For my fair maidens should like me
Far less than others I can't see.
Help me in my misery.
Else I'll be praying for death!
For maiden fair, etc.
If no one grants her love to me,
I'll be consumed by flames of love!
Still if I should receive one kiss,
I would revive—this I believe!
(*The old Woman dancing and
leaning on her cane, comes to the
scene.*)

**WOMAN:** Here I am now, my fair
angel!

**PAPAGENO:** (*turns around*). Did
you take pity on me?

**WOMAN:** Yes, my angel!
Come, give me your hand as a
pledge of our union.

**PAPAGENO:** Not quite so hasty,
dear angel!

**WOMAN:** Papageno, I advise you,
do not hesitate.
Your hand or you will be imprisoned here forever.

**PAPAGENO:** Imprisoned?

**WOMAN:** Bread and water will be
your daily meal.

**PAPAGENO:** Bread and water?
To renounce the world?
If that is so, I'd rather take an old
one than none at all.
Here is my hand with the assurance
that I will always remain true to
you,
(*aside*)
as long as I see no fairer one.

**WOMAN:** Do you swear that?

**PAPAGENO:** Yes, I swear it to you.
(*The Woman changes into a
young woman, who is dressed like
Papageno.*)

**PAPAGENO:** Pa-Pa Papagena!
(*He tries to embrace her.*)
(*The Speaker comes in quickly be-
tween the two.*)

**SPRECHER:** (*nimmt sie hastig bei
der Hand.*) Fort mit dir, junges
Weib, er ist deiner noch nicht
würdig.
(*Er drängt sie nach links ab.*)

## VERWANDLUNG

(*Garten mit einem See im Hintergrund. Rechts ein von blühenden
Rosen überhangener Sitz. Heller
Mondschein überfluthet die Gegend.*)
(*Pamina schlafend auf dem Sitz
unter den Rosen. Monostatos von
links hinten.*)

**MONOSTATOS:** Ha!
Da find' ich ja die spröde Schöne!
Das Feuer, das in mir glimmt, wird
mich noch verzehren.
(*Es sieht sich um.*)
Wenn ich wüsste—dass ich so ganz
allein
und unbelauscht wäre!
Ein Küsschen, dächte ich, liesse
sich entschuldigen.
Alles fühlt der Liebe Freuden.
Schnäbelt, tändelt, herzt und küsst;
Und ich soll die Liebe meiden,
Weil ein Schwarzer hässlich ist!
Ist mir denn kein Herz gegeben?
Ich bin auch den Mädchen gut!
Immer ohne Weibchen leben,
Wäre wahrlich Höllengluth!
Drum so will ich, weil ich lebe,
Schnäbeln, küssen, zärtlich sein!
Lieber guter Mond. vergebe,
Eine Weisse nahm mich ein,
Weiss ist schön! ich muss sie
küssen;
Mond, verstecke dich dazu!
Sollt' es dich zu sehr verdriessen,
O so mach' die Augen zu!
(*Er schleicht langsam und leise zu
Pamina hin.*) (*Die Königin eilt
von rechts hinten herbei.*)

**KÖNIGIN:** (*gebietend zu Monostatos.*) Zurück!

**MONOSTATOS:** O weh!
(*Pamina rechts vorn schlafend,
die Königin mit drohender Geberde die Mitte nehmend. Monostatos zu ihrer Linken.*)

**KOCHT IN MEINEM HERZEN—:**
Air (*Queen*): Allegro assai

**KÖNIGIN DER NACHT:** Der Hölle
Rache kocht in meinem
Herzen, Tod und Verzweiflung,
Tod
und Verzweiflung, flammet um
mich her! Fühlt nicht, durch dich
Sarastro Todesschmerzen, Sarastro
Todesschmerzen, so bist du meine
Tochter nimmermehr, so bist du
mein', meine Tochter nimmermehr
meine Tochter nimmermehr, so
bist
du meine Tochter nimmermehr.
Verstossen sei auf ewig und verlas-
sen,
Zertrümmert alle Bande der Natur,
Wenn nicht durch dich Sarastro

**SPEAKER:** (*takes her quickly by
the hand*). Away with you, young
woman, he is not yet worthy of you!
(*He takes her away.*)

## CHANGE OF SCENE

(*Garden with a lake in the background. To the right a bench overhung with roses. Clear moonlight
floods the scene.*)
(*Pamina sleeping on the bench
under the roses. Monostatos in
the back.*)

**MONOSTATOS:** Ah, here I find the
timid maiden.
The flame which burns in me will
consume me.
(*He looks around.*)
If I only knew whether I am alone
and no one listening.
A little kiss, I should think would
be excusable.
Love is reigning in every heart,
Bills and coos, caresses and emb-
races,
But she is disdaining my love
Just because my skin is brown.
Have I not a heart within me?
Why should maidens frown at me?
Ever to dwell without wife,
Is worse than the fire of hell.
Therefore while I live I will.
Bill and kiss and be tender.
Dead good moon, forgive, forgive,
A white maid has enticed me.
White is lovely, I must kiss.
Moon, oh hide yourself the while,
And if it disturbs your bliss,
Close your eyes, and take it not
amiss.
(*He creeps up slowly and softly to
Pamina.*)

**QUEEN:** (*to Monostatos*). Back!

**MONOSTATOS:** Heavens!
(*Pamina, the Queen, Monostatos.*)

**THE PANGS OF HELL ARE RAG-
ING:** Air (*Queen*)

**QUEEN OF THE NIGHT:** The pangs
of hell are raging in my
bosom, Death and destruction,
Death and destruction, wildly
flame
around! Go forth, and bear my
vengeance to Sarastro, my
vengeance to Sarastro, or as my
daughter you shall be disowned, be
disowned, as my daughter be
disowned, as my daughter be
disowned, forever as my daughter
be disowned.
Be forever rejected and forlorn,
All the ties of nature torn to pieces,
If through you vile Sarastro dies not
now,

wird erblassen!
Hört!
Rachegötter!
Hört der Mutter Schwur!

**PAMINA:** (*sich erhebend*) Mutter!
Mutter!
Meine Mutter!
(*Sie fällt ihr in die Arme.*)

**KÖNIGIN:** (*zieht einen Dolch hervor.*) Siehst du hier diesen Stahl?
Er ist für Sarastro geschliffen.
Du wirst ihn tödten und den mächtigen Sonnenkreis mir überliefern.
(*Sie dringt ihr den Dolch auf.*)

**PAMINA:** Aber liebste Mutter!

**KÖNIGIN:** Kein Wort!
(*Donner. Sie verschwindet.*)

**PAMINA:** (*den Dolch in der Hand, mit einigen Schritten nach links.*) Morden soll ich?
Götter!
Das kann ich nicht.
Was soll ich thun?

**MONOSTATOS:** (*nimmt ihr den Dolch weg.*) Dich mir anvertrauen.

**PAMINA:** (*erschrickt.*) Ha!

**MONOSTATOS:** Warum zitterst du?
Vor meiner schwarzen Farbe oder vor dem ausgedachten Mord?

**PAMINA:** (*schüchtern.*) Du weisst also?

**MONOSTATOS:** Alles!
Du hast also nur einen Weg, dich und deine Mutter zu retten.

**PAMINA:** Der wäre?

**MONOSTATOS:** Mich zu lieben!

**PAMINA:** (*zitternd, für sich.*) Götter!

**MONOSTATOS:** Nun, Mädchen, ja oder nein!

**PAMINA:** (*entschlossen.*) Nein!

**MONOSTATOS:** (*voll Zorn.*)
Nein?
So fahr' hin!

**SARASTRO:** (*tritt gebietend zwischen beide, erhebt drohend den Arm und schleudert Monostatos zurück.*) Zurück!

**MONOSTATOS:** (*sich blitzschnell um sich selbst drehend und vor Sarastro auf die Knie fallend.*)
Herr, ich bin unschuldig!

**SARASTRO:** Ich weiss, dass deine Seele eben so schwarz als dein Gesicht ist.
Geh!
(*Er eilt nach rechts hinten ab.*)

**PAMINA:** Herr!
Strafe meine Mutter nicht!

**SARASTRO:** Ich weiss alles.
Du sollst sehen, wie ich mich an deiner Mutter räche.

Hear, gods of vengeance, hear a mother's vow!

**PAMINA:** (*arising*). Mother, mother, my mother!
(*She falls into her arms.*)

**QUEEN:** (*draws out a dagger*). Do you see this steel
It is sharpened for Sarastro.
You are to kill him and bring the powerful zodiac back to me.
(*She forces the dagger on her.*)

**PAMINA:** But, dearest mother!

**QUEEN:** Not a word!
(*Thunder. The Queen disappears.*)

**PAMINA:** (*with dagger in hand*). I must murder?
Gods!
That I cannot.
What shall I do?

**MONOSTATOS:** (*takes away her dagger*). Trust in me.

**PAMINA:** (*frightened*). Ha!

**MONOSTATOS:** Why do you tremble?
Is it because of my black skin or the intended murder?

**PAMINA:** (*timidly*). Then you know?

**MONOSTATOS:** All.
Only one way is left you now to save yourself and your mother.

**PAMINA:** Which is?

**MONOSTATOS:** To love me.

**PAMINA:** (*trembling, aside*). Heavens!

**MONOSTATOS:** Now, maiden, yes or no!

**PAMINA:** (*decidedly*). No!

**MONOSTATOS:** (*in anger*). No? then die!

**SARASTRO:** (*comes between them, raises a threatening arm, and hurls Monostatos back*). Back!

**MONOSTATOS:** (*turning around like a flash and falling at Sarastro's feet*). Sir, I am not guilty!

**SARASTRO:** I know that your soul is as black as your face.
Go!
(*Exit Monostatos.*)

**PAMINA:** Master, do not punish my mother!

**SARASTRO:** I know all.
You shall see how I shall take vengeance upon your mother.

**SARASTRO:** In diesen heil'gen Hallen kennt man
die Rache nicht, und ist ein Mensch gefallen, führt Liebe ihn zur Pflicht.
Dann wandelt er an Freundes Hand vergnügt und froh in's bess're Land, dann wandelt er an Freundes Hand vergnügt und froh in's bess're Land dann wandelt er an Freundes Hand vergnügt und froh in's bess're Land, in's bess're bess're Land.
In diesen heil'gen Mauern,
Wo Mensch den Menschen liebt,
Kann kein Verräther lauern,
Weil man dem Feind' vergibt.
Wen solche Lehren nicht erfreun,
Verdienet nicht ein Mensch zu sein.
(*Beide gehen nach links ab.*)

## VERWANDLUNG

(*Tempel der Götter Isis und Osiris.*)
(*Sprecher, Priester, Sarastro, die Mitte einnehmend*)

**CHOR DER PRIESTER:** (*Sarastro im Halbkreis umstehend.*) O Isis und Osiris, welche Wonne.
Die düstre Nacht verscheucht der Glanz der Sonne.
Bald fühlt der edle Jüngling neues Leben;
Bald ist er unserm Dienste ganz ergeben.
Sein Geist ist kühn, sein Herz ist rein,
Bald wird er unser würdig sein.

**SARASTRO:** Prinz!
Dein Betragen war bis hierher männlich und gelassen.
Deine Hand!
(*Er giebt einen Wink nach links hin.*)
Man bringe Pamina!
(*Zwei Priester entfernen sich nach links vorn und kommen sogleich mit Pamina zurück, welche mit dem Schleier der Eingeweihten bedeckt ist.*)

**PAMINA:** Wo bin ich?
Sagt, wo ist mein Jüngling?

**SARASTRO:** (*löst Taminos Schleier.*) Hier.

**PAMINA:** (*enzückt.*) Tamino!

**TAMINO:** (*sie von sich weisend.*) Zurück!

**PAMINA:** Soll ich dich, Theurer, nicht mehr sehn?

**SARASTRO:** Ihr werdet froh euch wieder sehn!

**PAMINA:** Dein warten tödliche Gefahren!

**TAMINO:** Die Götter mögen mich bewahren!

**PAMINA:** Dein warten tödliche Gefahren!

**SARASTRO:** Die Götter mögen ihn bewahren!

**SARASTRO:** Within this hallowed dwelling,
Revenge and Sorrow cease, Here troubled doubts dispelling The weary heart hath peace. If you have strayed a brother's hand shall guide you toward the better land, If you have strayed, a brothers hand shall guide you toward the better land, the better, the better land.
Within these holy walls
Where man loves brother man,
No traitor can lurk.
The enemy is forgiven.
He whom this teaching does not gladden,
Does not deserve to be a man.
(*Exit both.*)

## CHANGE OF SCENE

(*Temple of Isis and Osiris.*)
(*Speaker, Priests, Sarastro.*)

**CHORUS OF PRIESTS:** (*standing around Sarastro in semi-circle*).
O Isis and Osiris! O the ray Of rising Phoebus drives the night away.
The noble youth will soon feel joys of heaven,
When he is fully given to our service.
With courage bold, and heart that's free,
Of us he soon will worthy be.

**SARASTRO:** Prince, your behavior till now has been manly and composed.
Give me your hand!
(*He makes a sign.*)
Let Pamina be brought in.
(*Two priests go out and come back at once with Pamina, who is wrapped in the veil of the initiated.*)

**PAMINA:** Where am I?
Tell me where is my lover?

**SARASTRO:** (*removes the veil from Tamino*). Here!

**PAMINA:** (*in rapture*). Tamino!

**TAMINO:** (*beckoning to her*). Go back!

**PAMINA:** May I never see you again?

**SARASTRO:** You'll surely see each other again.

**PAMINA:** Deadly dangers await you!

**TAMINO:** May the gods protect me!

**PAMINA:** Deadly dangers await you!

**SARASTRO:** May the gods protect him!

TAMINO: Die Götter mögen mich bewahren!

TAMINO: May the gods protect me!

PAMINA: Du wirst dem Tode nicht entgehen;
Mir flüstert dieses Ahnung ein.

PAMINA: You cannot now escape from death,
My saddened heart forebodes it!

SARASTRO: Der Götter Wille mag geschehen,
Ihr Wink soll ihm Gesetze sein.

SARASTRO: May the will of the gods be done,
And their desire be law for him.

TAMINO: Der Götter Wille mag geschehen,
Ihr Wink soll mir Gesetze sein!

TAMINO: May the will of the gods be done,
And their desire be law for me.

PAMINA: O liebtest du, wie ich dich liebe,
Du würdest nicht so ruhig sein.

PAMINA: O if you were to love like me,
You surely would not be so calm!

SARASTRO: Glaub' mir, er fühlet gleiche Triebe,
Wird ewig dein Getreuer sein.

SARASTRO: Yes, he loves with equal passion,
And will be your lover forever!

TAMINO: Glaub' mir, ich fühle gleiche Triebe,
Werd' ewig dein Getreuer sein!

TAMINO: Yes, I love with equal passion,
And will be your lover forever!

SARASTRO: Die Stunde schlägt, nun müsst ihr scheiden!

SARASTRO: The hour has come when you must part!

TAMINO UND PAMINA: Wie bitter sind der Trennung Leiden!

TAMINO AND PAMINA: How bitter are the pains of parting!

SARASTRO: Die Stunde schlägt, nun müsst ihr scheiden!

SARASTRO: The hour has come when you must part!

TAMINO UND PAMINA: Wie bitter sind der Trennung Leiden!

TAMINO AND PAMINA: How bitter are the pains of parting!

SARASTRO: Tamino muss nun wieder fort.

SARASTRO: Tamino must at once depart!

TAMINO: Pamina, ich muss wirklich fort!

TAMINO: Yes, I must at once depart!

PAMINA: Tamino muss nun wirklich fort!

PAMINA: Tamino must at once depart!

SARASTRO: Nun muss er fort!

SARASTRO: He must depart!

TAMINO: Nun muss ich fort!

TAMINO: I must depart!

PAMINA: So musst du fort!

PAMINA: He must depart!

TAMINO: Pamina, lebe wohl!

TAMINO: Pamina, farewell!

PAMINA: Tamino, lebe wohl!

PAMINA: Tamino, farewell!

SARASTRO: Nun eile fort.
Dich ruft dein Wort.
Die Stunde schlägt, wir sehn uns wieder!

SARASTRO: Now hasten away,
Your promise calls you!
The time has come! We'll meet again!

TAMINO UND PAMINA: Ach, goldne Ruhe, kehre wieder!
(*Sie wird von zwei Priestern nach recht vorn abgeführt.*)
(*Sarastro entfernt sich mit Tamino an der Hand und allen Priester nach links vorn.*)

TAMINO AND PAMINA: O longed-for calm, return again.
(*She is led away by two priests.*)
(*Sarastro leaves with Tamino; exit the priests.*)

## VERWANDLUNG

## CHANGE OF SCENE

(*Kurzer Palmengarten. Halbdunkel. Es wird nach und nach ganz hell.*)
(*Die drei Knaben kommen von links.*)

(*Small palm garden. Twilight. It grows gradually lighter.*)
(*The three Youths come from the left.*)

DIE DREI KNABEN: Bald prangt, den Morgen zu verkünden,
Die Sonn' auf gold'ner Bahn!
Bald soll der Aberglaube schwinden,
Bald siegt der weise Mann.
O holde Ruhe, steig' hernieder.
Kehr' in der Menschen Herzen

THE THREE YOUTHS: The sun comes in to banish the night,
And beams upon earth brilliantly.
All superstition must soon vanish,
The wise man goes to victory.
O heavenly quiet, now descend,
Return to the heart of man.
Then the earth be as a heaven

wieder;
Dann wird die Erd' ein Himmelreich,
Und Sterbliche den Göttern gleich.

And mortals like Divinity.

ERSTER KNABE: Doch seht, Verzweiflung quält Paminen.

FIRST YOUTH: But see, Pamina's in despair.

ZWEITER UND DRITTER KNABE: Wo ist sie denn?

SECOND AND THIRD YOUTH: Where is she?

ERSTER KNABE: Sie ist von Sinnen.

FIRST YOUTH: She is out of her mind.

DIE DREI KNABEN: Sie quält verschmähter Liebe Leiden.
Lasst uns der Armen Trost bereiten!
Fürwahr, ihr Schicksal geht mir nah!
O wäre nur ihr Jüngling da!—
Sie kommt, lasst uns beiseite gehn,
Damit wir, was sie mache, sehn.
(*Sie ziehen sich nach links hinten zurück.*)
(*Pamina, halb wahnsinnig, mit dem Dolch, den sie von der Königin empfing, herbeistürzend.*)

THE THREE YOUTHS: She suffers pangs of disdained love,
Let us endeavor to console her,
Her fate indeed has greatly moved me,
Would that her lover here would be!
She comes, let us draw aside,
So, that we can observe her better!
(*They step to the back of the stage.*)
(*Pamina rushes in half insane, with the dagger given her by the Queen.*)

PAMINA: (*zu dem Dolch.*) Du also bist mein Bräutigam?
Durch dich vollend' ich meinen Gram!

PAMINA: (*to her dagger*). Now I see my bridegroom in you,
Through you my grief will be ended!

DIE KNABEN: (*beiseite.*) Welch' dunkle Worte sprach sie da?
Die Arme ist dem Wahnsinn nah'.

THE YOUTHS: (*aside*) Oh, woe! what did Pamina say!
And see, she is near to madness!

PAMINA: Geduld, mein Trauter, ich bin dein,
Bald werden wir vermählt sein.

PAMINA: Patience, beloved, I am yours.
Soon we shall be united.

DIE KNABEN: (*treten näher.*) Wahsinn tobt ihr im Gehirne;
Selbstmord steht ihr auf der Stirne.
(*Zu Pamina.*)
Holdes Mädchen, sieh uns an!

THE YOUTHS: (*draw nearer*).
Madness lurks in her poor brain,
She contemplates suicide.
(*To Pamina*)
Gracious maiden, behold us here!

PAMINA: Sterben will ich, weil der Mann,
Den ich nimmermehr kann hassen,
Seine Traute kann verlassen.
(*Den Dolch erhebend.*)
Dies gab meine Mutter mir.

PAMINA: I must die, since the man I can never hate
has forsaken the one he loves.
(*Raises the dagger.*)
My mother gave this to me.

DIE KNABEN: Selbstmord strafet Gott an dir.

THE THREE YOUTHS: Suicide by God is punished.

PAMINA: Lieber durch dies Eisen sterben.
Als durch Liebesgram verderben.
Mutter, durch dich leide ich.
Und dein Fluch verfolget mich.

PAMINA: Better to die by this steel,
Than to perish through grief and love,
Mother, alas, I suffer through you,
And your curse pursues me!

DIE KNABEN: Mädchen, willst du mit uns gehn?

THE THREE YOUTHS: Maiden, will you go with us?

PAMINA: Ha, des Jammers Mass ist voll!
Falscher Jüngling, lebe wohl!
Sieh, Pamina stirbt durch dich:
Dieses Eisen tödte mich.
(*Sie will sich erstechen.*)

PAMINA: The measure of my grief is full,
Faithless lover, farewell!
See, Pamina dies through you,
May this dagger destroy me!
(*She tries to stab herself.*)

DIE KNABEN: (*treten, zwei von rechts, einer von links, zu Pamina vor und entreissen ihr den Dolch.*) Ha, Unglückliche! halt ein!
Sollte dies dein Jüngling sehen,
Würde er vor Gram vergehen;
Denn er liebet dich allein.

THE THREE YOUTHS: (*come up and snatch the dagger from her*).
Hold, unhappy one, and hear.
Were your lover to see this,
He would expire with sorrow,
For he loves you alone.

PAMINA: (erholt sich.) Was?
Er fühlte Gegenliebe?
Und verbarg mir seine Triebe,
Wandte sein Gesicht von mir?
Warum sprach er nicht mit mir?

DIE KNABEN: Dieses müssen wir
verschweigen,
Doch, wir wollen dir ihn zeigen!
Und du wirst mit Staunen sehn,
Dass er dir sein Herz geweiht,
Und den Tod für dich nicht scheut.

PAMINA: Führt mich hin, ich
möcht' ihn sehen.

DIE KNABEN: Kommt, wir wollen
zu ihm gehen.

ALLE VIER: Zwei Herzen, die von
Liebe brennen,
Kann Menschenohnmacht niemals
trennen
Verloren ist der Feinde Müh',
Die Götter selbt beschützen sie.
(Sie gehen nach rechts ab.)

## VERWANDLUNG

(Wilde Felsengegend mit einem
eisernen Mittelthor. Rechts und
links eiserne Thore als Eingänge.
Im Hintergrund zu beiden Seiten
des Mittelthores Felsenhöhlen; in
der einen rechts sieht man durch
ein eisernes Gitter eine brausende
Wasserfluth, in der andern links
eine hellflammende Feuer-
gluth, — Es ist halbdunkel.)
(Tamino mit zwei Priestern von
links. Pamina's Stimme rechts
draussen.)

DIE ZWEI GEHARNISCHTEN:
Der, welcher wandert diese Strasse
voll Beschwerden.
Wird rein durch Feuer, Wasser, Luft
und Erden;
Wenn er des Todes Schrecken über-
winden kann,
Schwingt er sich aus der Erde him-
melan
Erleuchtet wird er dann imstande
sein,
Sich den Mysterien der Isis ganz zu
weihn.

TAMINO: Mich schreckt kein Tod,
als Mann zu handeln,
Den Weg der Tugend fortzuwan-
deln.
Schliesst mir die Schreckenspforten auf,
Ich wage froh den kühnen Lauf.

PAMINA: (von rechts draussen.)
Tamino, halt!
Ich muss dich sehen.

TAMINO: Was hör' ich?
Paminens Stimme?

DIE GEHARNISCHTEN: Ja, ja, das
ist Paminens Stimme.

PAMINA: (recovers herself).
What?
He, too, felt love?
And concealed his feelings for me?
He turned his face away.
Why did he not speak to me?

THE THREE YOUTHS: This, alas,
we must not tell,
But we will now show him to you.
And you will see with surprise,
That he gave his heart to you,
And for you he'd give his life!

PAMINA: Take me where I can see
him!

THE THREE YOUTHS: Come to
him, we will lead you.

ALL FOUR: Two hearts that are
burning with true love
Human weakness can never part.
Vain are the efforts of the enemy,
For they will be protected by the
gods!
(Exeunt.)

## CHANGE OF SCENE

(Wild mountain spot, with an
iron middle gate. To the right and
left, iron doors as entrances. In
the background, on both sides of
the middle door, small caves in
the rocks. Within the one to the
right, one sees through an iron
gate, a roaring stream. In the one
to the left, a brightly glowing fire.
Twilight.)
(Tamino with two priests. Pamina's voice heard without.)

MEN: He who pursues his path full
of dangers,
Becomes pure by fire, water, air and
earth
If he can overcome the pangs of
death,
From out of earth he rises unto
heaven.
Thus purified, he then will be able.
To devote himself to Isis' mystery.

TAMINO: I fear not death, for as a
man
I'll follow ever virtue's path,
Open the gates of horror wide,
I'll gladly risk the dangerous tide!

PAMINA: (from without). Tamino, wait! for I must see you!

TAMINO: What do I hear? Pamina's
voice?

MEN: Yes, yes, it is Pamina's voice.

TAMINO: Wohl mir, nun kann sie
mit mir gehn,
Nun trennet uns kein Schicksal
mehr,
Wenn auch der Tod beschieden
wär'!

DIE GEHARNISCHTEN: Wohl dir,
nun kann sie mit dir gehn,
Nun trennet euch kein Schicksal
mehr,
Wenn auch der Tod beschieden
wär'!

TAMINO: Ist mir erlaubt, mit ihr zu
sprechen?

DIE GEHARNISCHTEN: Dir sei erlaubt, mit ihr zu sprechen!
(Die zwei Priester gehen rechts
ab.)

TAMINO: Welch' Glück, wenn wir
uns wiedersehn.

DIE GEHARNISCHTEN: Welch'
Glück, wenn wir euch wiedersehn

TAMINO UND DIE GEHARNIS-
CHTEN: Froh Hand in Hand im
Tempel gehn.
Ein Weib, das Nacht und Tod nicht
scheut.
Ist würdig und wird eingeweiht.
(Die beiden Priester kommen mit
Pamina von rechts zurück.)
(Die Vorigen, Pamina.)

PAMINA: (Tamino unarmend.)
Tamino mein! o welch' ein Glück!

TAMINO: Pamina mein! o welch'
ein Glück!
(Er zeigt nach den beiden Felsen-
höhlen.)
Hier sind die Schreckenspforten,
Die Noth und Tod mir dräun.

PAMINA: Ich werd' an allen Orten
An deiner Seite sein.
Ich selber führe dich,
Die Liebe leite mich.
(Sie nimmt ihn bei der Hand.)
Sie mag den Weg mit Rosen streun,
Weil Rosen stets bei Dornen sein.
Spiel du die Zauberflöte an,
Sie schütze uns auf unsrer Bahn.
Es schnitt in einer Zauberstunde
Mein Vater sie aus tiefstem Grunde
Der tausendjähr'gen Eiche aus,
Bei Blitz und Donner, Sturm und
Braus,
Nun komm' und spiel' die Flöte an,
Sie leite uns auf grauser Bahn.

TAMINO, PAMINA: Wir wandeln
durch des Tones Macht,
Froh durch des Todes düst're
Nacht!

DIE GEHARNISCHTEN: Ihr wandelt durch des Tones Macht,
Froh durch des Todes düst're
Nacht.
(Tamino und Pamina wenden
sich, nach links zur Feuerhöhle,
die sie durchwandern, indem Pamina ihre Hand auf Tamino's
Schulter legt, wobei Tamino seine

TAMINO: Now she can surely go
with me,
Nothing can separate us,
Even if death should be our fate.

MEN: Now she can surely go with
you,
Nothing can separate you,
Even if death should be your fate.

TAMINO: Am I permitted to speak
to her?

MEN: You are permitted to speak to
her.
(The two priests exit.)

TAMINO: What happiness if we
should meet again!

MEN: What happiness if we should
meet again!

TAMINO AND MEN: Joyfully go
hand in hand to the temple,
A wife whom neither night nor
death dismay
Is worthy, and will be ordained.
(Priests come back with Pamina.)
(Above. Pamina.)

PAMINA: (embracing Tamino).
My Tamino! What happiness is this!

TAMINO: My Pamina! What happiness is this!
(He points to both mountain caverns.)
Here are the gates of horror,
They threaten danger dire and
death.

PAMINA: I will always.
Be your true companion.
I lead you myself,
And love guides me on:
(Takes him by the hand.)
Love will deck your thorny way,
And strew the path with roses,
Now you'll play your magic flute,
It will protect us on our way.
My father in a magic hour
Fashioned it himself
Out of a thousand-year old oak,
In thunder, lightning, storm and
gale,
Now you'll play your magic flute,
It will protect us on our way.

TAMINO, PAMINA: We wander by
the flute's sweet might,
Merrily into death and night.

MEN: They wander by the flute's
sweet might,
Merrily into death and night.
(Tamino and Pamina go toward
the cavern of fire, through which
they pass. Pamina keeping her
hand on Tamino's shoulder, and
Tamino playing his flute. As soon
as they emerge from the purgation

*Flöte bläst. Sobald sie aus der Feuerprobe heraus kommen, umarmen sie sich und bleiben in der Mitte.)*

**BEIDE:** Wir wandelten durch Feuergluthen,
Bekämpften muthig die Gefahr.
*(Zur Flöte)*
Dein Ton sei Schutz in Wasserfluthen, So wie er es im Feuer war.
*(Tamino und Pamina wenden sich nun ganz wie vorhin nach rechts zur Wasserhöhle. Sobald sie aus der Wasserprobe herauskommen:)*
*(Die Vorigen, Sarastro, die Priester hoch oben im Tempel.)*

**TAMINO, PAMINA:** Ihr Götter! Welch' ein Augenblick! Gewähret ist uns Isis Glück.

**CHOR DER PRIESTER:** Triumph! Triumph! du edles Paar! Besieget hast du die Gefahr, Der Isis Weihe ist nun dein, Kommt, tretet in den Tempel ein!
*(Tamino und Pamina wenden sich nach hinten zum Tempel.)*

## VERWANDLUNG

*(Kurze Gartendekoration; rechts ein Baum mit einem verdorrten Ast.—Es ist hell.)*
*(Papageno allein, mit einem Strick umgürtet.)*

**PAPEGENO:** *(ruft mit seinem Pfeifchen.)* Papagena! Papegena! Papegena!
Weibchen! Täubchen! Meine Schöne!
Vergebens! Ach, sie ist verloren!
Ich bin zum Unglück schon geboren.
Ich plauderte—und das war schlecht,
Darum geschieht es mir schon recht.
Seit ich gekostet diesen Wein.
Seit ich das schöne Weibchen sah,
So brennt's im Herzenskämmerlein,
So zwickt es hier, so zwickt es da.
Papagena! Herzenstäubchen!
Papagena! liebes Weibchen!
's ist umsonst! Es ist vergebens!
Müde bin ich meines Lebens!
Sterben macht der Lieb' ein End',
Wenn's im Herzen noch so brennt.
*(Er nimmt den Strick von seiner Mitte.)*
Diesen Baum da will ich zieren,
Mir an ihm den Hals zuschnüren,
Weil das Leben mir missfällt;
Gute Nacht, du falsche Welt.
Weil du böse an mir handelst,
Mir kein schönes Kind zubandelst:
So ist's aus, so sterbe ich,
Schöne Mädchen, denkt an mich.
Will sich eine um mich Armen,
Eh' ich hänge, noch erbarmen,
Wohl, so lass ich's diesmal sein!
Rufet nur, ja—oder nein.—
Keine hört mich, alles stille!

*by fire, they embrace.)*

**BOTH:** We wandered through the flames,
And bravely met the dangers.
*(To the flute.)*
May your tones protect us in the flood of waters,
As they did when fire was near.
*(Tamino and Pamina proceed into the cave of water. They soon come out of the purgation by water.)*
*(Above. Sarastro, Priests high up in the temple.)*

**TAMINO, PAMINA:** Oh gods, what a glorious sight! The joy of Isis is upon us!

**CHORUS OF PRIESTS:** Triumph, triumph, noble pair, You have overcome the danger. We consecrate you to Isis, Walk now within the temple gate.
*(Tamino and Pamina take their way to the temple.)*

## CHANGE OF SCENE

*(Small garden. To the right a tree with a dried up branch. It is daylight.)*
*(Papageno, alone, with a rope around his waist.)*

**PAPAGENO:** *(calls on his pipe).* Papagena, Papagena, Papagena!
Little darling, little dove!
In vain I sigh, she's lost to me.
Oh, I am born to misery!
I talked, I know, and that was wrong.
And so they'll say it served me right.
But since I tasted that wine,
And since her eyes had first met mine,
A constant fire burns in my heart,
And I am tortured day and night!
Papagena, light of life,
Papagena, darling wife!
In vain I sigh for you again,
So nothing is left me but to die!
I'm tired of life, so part from it,
To quench the flame that fires my heart!
*(He takes off the rope.)*
I will single out this tree,
And swing from its high branches,
For since life has lost its worth,
I will say farewell to earth.
Since you are so cruel to me,
And refuse to grant my prayer,
All is over, I shall die,
Since there's none to mourn or sigh,
Still if only one there be,
Who would love or pity me,
Then I will not end my woe.
Only tell me, yes or no—
No one hears me, all is still.
*(Looks around.)*
Tell me, then, is it your will?
Papageno, swing on high,

*(Er sieht sich um.)*
Also ist es euer Wille?
Papageno, frisch hinauf!
Ende deinen Lebenslauf.
*(Er sieht sich um.)*
Nun, ich warte noch, es sei,
Bis man zählet, eins, zwei, drei.
*(Er pfeift.)*
Eins!
*(Er sieht sich um und pfeift.)*
Zwei!
Zwei ist schon vorbei.
*(Er pfeift.)*
Drei!

*(Er sieht sich um.)*
Nun wohlan, es bleibt dabei!
Weil mich nichts zurücke hält!
Gute Nacht, du falsche Welt.
*(Er will sich aufhängen.)*
*(Die drei Knaben eilen von links herbei.)*

**DIE DREI KNABEN:** Halt ein, o Papageno, und sei klug;
Man lebt nur einmal, dies sei dir genug.

**PAPAGENO:** Ihr habt gut reden, habt gut scherzen.
Doch brennt es euch, wie mich im Herzen,
Ihr würdet auch nach Mädchen gehn.

**DIE DREI KNABEN:** So lasse deine Glöckchen klingen,
Dies wird dein Mädchen zu dir bringen.

**PAPAGENO:** Ich Narr vergass der Zauberdinge!
Erklinge, Glockenspiel, erklinge!
Ich muss mein liebes Mädchen sehn.
*(Er schlägt sein Glockenspiel.)*
Klinget, Glöckchen, klinget,
Schafft mein Mädchen her!
Klinget, Glöckchen, klinget,
Bringt mein Weibchen her!
*(Die drei Knaben eilen unter diesen Schlagen nach links ab und kehren sogleich mit Papagena zurück.)*
Nun, Papageno, sieh' dich um!
*(Sie entfernen sich nach links.)*
*(Papageno sieht sich um, komisches Spiel.)*
*(Papageno, Papagena zu seiner Linken.)*

**PAPAGENO:** *(sie umtanzend.)* Pa—Pa—Pa—Pa—Pa—Papagena!

**WEIB:** *(sie umtanzend.)* Pa–Pa–Pa—Pa—Pa—Papageno!

**BEIDE:** Pa—Pa—Pa—Pa—Pa—Papageno!
Papagena!

**PAPAGENO:** Bist du mir nun ganz gegeben?

**WEIB:** Nun bin ich dir ganz gegeben

**PAPAGENO:** Nun, so sei mein liebes Weibchen!

And nobly die like a hero!
*(He looks around.)*
Now I'm waiting, let it be
While I'm counting, one, two, three!
*(He whistles.)*
One!
*(He looks around and whistles.)*
Two!
Two's already past!
*(He whistles.)*
Three!
*(He looks around.)*
Now away, and let it be!
There is nothing to keep me!
Good night, false world, farewell!
*(He tries to hang himself.)*
*(The three Youths hurry in.)*

**THE THREE YOUTHS:** Stop, Papageno, and be prudent,
Man lives but once—let this be enough for you!

**PAPAGENO:** Your talk and joking's very fine,
Still, if your hearts would burn like mine,
You, too, would run after fair maids.

**THE THREE YOUTHS:** Then let your sweet bells ring,
They will bring your maiden to you.

**PAPAGENO:** Fool that I am, to forget the magic thing,
Ring, bells, ring, ring, ring!
My little wife I now would see.
*(Rings.)*
Ring, bells, ring, ring, ring!
My little maiden to me bring!
Ring, bells, ring, ring, ring!
My little maiden to me bring!
*(At the sound the three Youths go out and return with Papagena.)*
Now, Papageno, look about you!
*(Exit the Youths.)*
*(Papageno looks around—silly dumb show.)*
*(Papageno, Papagena at his left.)*

**PAPAGENO:** *(dancing around her).* Pa—Pa—Pa—Pa—Pa—Papagena!

**WOMAN:** *(dancing around him).* Pa–Pa—Pa—Pa—Pa—Papageno!

**BOTH:** Pa—Pa—Pa—Pa—Pa—Papageno!
Papagena!

**PAPAGENO:** Are you now all my own?

**WOMAN:** Now I am all your own.

**PAPAGENO:** Well, then be my little love!

**WEIB:** Nun, so sei mein Herzenstäubchen!

**BEIDE:** Welche Freude wird das sein!
Wenn die Götter uns bedenken,
Uns'rer Liebe Kinder schenken,
So liebe kleine Kinderlein!

**PAPAGENO:** Erst einen kleinen Papageno!

**WEIB:** Dann eine kleine Papagena!

**PAPAGENO:** Dann wieder einen Papageno!

**WEIB:** Dann wieder eine Papagena!

**BEIDE:** Papagena!
Papagena!
Papagena!
Es ist das höchste der Gefühle,
Wenn viele, viele, viele, viele
Pa—Pa—Pa—Pa—geno,
Pa—Pa—Pa—Pa—gena,
Der Segen froher Eltern sein.
(*Beide eilen Arm in Arm nach links ab.*)

## VERWANDLUNG

(*Kurze Felsengegend. Es ist Nacht.*)
(*Monostatos, Die Königin mit ihren drei Damen von rechts; sie tragen schwarze, brennende Fackeln in der Hand.*)

**MONOSTATOS:** (*der Königin zur Linken.*) Nur stille! stille! stille! stille!
Bald dringen wir im Tempel ein.

**ALLE DAMEN:** (*züruckstehend.*)
Nur stille! stille! stille! stille!
Bald dringen wir im Tempel ein.

**MONOSTATOS:** Doch Fürstin, halte Wort!
Erfülle—
Dein Kind muss meine Gattin sein.

**KÖNIGIN:** Ich halte Wort; es ist mein Wille.

**ALLE DAMEN:** Ihr Kind soll deine Gattin sein.
(*Man hört dumpfen Donner, Geräusch und Wasser.*)

**WOMAN:** Well, then be my turtle-dove!

**BOTH:** What a joy we now shall feel,
When the gods their gifts reveal,
Little boys and girls galore,
All we want and many more!

**PAPAGENO:** First a little Papageno.

**WOMAN:** Then a little Papagena.

**PAPAGENO:** Then another Papageno.

**WOMAN:** Then another Papagena.

**BOTH:** Papagena! Papagena! Papagena!
It is the greatest pleasure,
When many, many, many, many
Pa—Pa—Pa—Pa—geno,
Pa—Pa—Pa—Pa—gena,
Are the blessing of fond parents!
(*Both go out arm in arm.*)

## CHANGE OF SCENE

(*Rugged cliffs. It is dark.*)
(*Monostatos, the Queen with her three Ladies in Waiting; they carry lighted torches.*)

**MONOSTATOS:** (*at the left of the Queen*). Now silence, silence, silence!
Soon we will enter the temple.

**ALL THE LADIES:** Now silence, silence, silence!
Soon we will enter the temple.

**MONOSTATOS:** But, princess, you will keep your word—
Your child must be my wife.

**QUEEN:** I keep my word, it is my will!

**ALL THE LADIES:** Her child must be his wife.
(*Thunder, noise, rushing of water.*)

**MONOSTATOS:** Doch still! ich höre schrecklich Rauschen,
Wie Donnerton und Wasserfall.

**KÖNIGIN UND DAMEN:** Ja, fürchterlich ist dieses Rauschen,
Wie fernen Donners Wiederhall.

**MONOSTATOS:** Nun sind sie in des Tempels Hallen.

**ALLE:** Dort wollen wir sie überfallen—
Die Frömmler tilgen von der Erd'
Mit Feuersgluth und mächt'gem Schwert

**DIE DREI DAMEN UND MONOSTATOS:**
Dir grosse Königin der Nacht,
Sei unsrer Rache Opfer gebracht.
(*Sie versinken. Man hört starken Donner, Sturm.*)

**MONOSTATOS, KÖNIGIN UND DIE DAMEN:** Zerschmettert, vernichtet ist unsere Macht,
Wir alle gestürzet in ewige Nacht.
(*Exeunt.*)

## OFFENE VERWANDLUNG

(*Priester und Priesterinnen, Sarastro steht erhöht. Vor ihm Tamino und Pamina, beide in priesterlicher Kleidung, die Priester auf beiden. Seiten, die drei Knaben halten Blumen.*)

**SARASTRO:** Die Strahlen der Sonne vertreiben die Nacht,
Zernichten der Heuchler erschlichene Macht.

**CHOR DER PRIESTER:** Heil sei euch Geweihten! Ihr dranget durch Nacht,
Dank sei dir, Osiris und Isis, gebracht!
Es siegte die Stärke und krönet zum Lohn—
Die Schönheit und Weisheit mit ewiger Kron'!

*ENDE.*

**MONOSTATOS:** Be still!
I hear a horrid noise,
Like thunder and like water-fall.

**QUEEN AND LADIES:** Yes, a horrible noise,
Like thunder and like water-fall.

**MONOSTATOS:** Now we are in the temple hall.

**ALL:** There we will surprise them,
Remove the hypocrites from the earth,
Destroy them with sword and fire!

**LADIES AND MONOSTATOS:** To you, Queen of the Night,
We'll bring our sacrifice.
(*Thunder, lightning, storm.*)

**MONOSTATOS, QUEEN, LADIES:**
Our power is destroyed and demolished
We all will be hurled into darkness.
(*They sink into the earth.*)

## CHANGE OF SCENE

Temple of the Sun.
Priests and Priestesses. Sarastro, elevated, Tamino and Pamina before him, both in priestly garb. Priests on both sides. The Three Youths hold flowers in their hands.

**SARASTRO:** The rays of the sun chase away the night,
Destroy the sneaking power of the dissembler.

**CHORUS OF PRIESTS:** Glory to the consecrated!
You passed through darkness,
May thanks be given to you Isis and Osiris,
May the strong conquer!
And bring to wisdom and beauty
The crown eternal!

*THE END*

# Boris Godounov (1874)

MUSIC AND LIBRETTO BY MODESTE PETROVICH MOUSSORGSKY

Boris Godounov is in three acts with a prologue. The libretto, written by the composer, is based on Alexandre Pushkin's play and on Nikolay M. Karamzin's *History of the Russian Empire*. The opera premiered in Russian at the Maryinsky Theatre in St. Petersburg on February 8, 1874, but since has been performed more often in Italian. The year is 1598. Boris Godunov is in retreat at the monastery at Novodieuitchi, where a crowd of peasants gathers outside to pray. The Tsar Feodor is dead, his heir Dimitri died mysteriously many years before, and the people ask Boris to be the Tsar's successor. Boris' coronation takes place in Kremlin Square. In a cell at the Convent of Miracles, Grigori, a novice awakens and tells Pimenn, an old monk, about his dream, which Pimenn interprets to signify tremendous ambition. Pimenn advises Grigori not to yearn for life in the outside world, and he tells him the story of Dimitri's assassination, for which, we later learn, Boris was responsible. Grigori demands divine and human revenge. Two renegade friars Missail and Varlaam, burst into an inn on the Lithuanian border with Grigori on their heels. Grigori has left his order and, dressed in disguise, is trying to cross the border. At the Kremlin, Xenia, the daughter of Boris, cries over the death of her betrothed. Her old nurse tries to cheer her up. Boris enters and is filled with remorse for the murder he committed so long ago. Prince Chouïsky brings Boris news of an uprising invoked by a man who calls himself Dimitri. Boris, terrified, thinks Dimitri is alive. Chouïsky tries to calm him, but Boris has visions of the dead and collapses to the floor, sobbing. At the castle of Sandomir in Poland, Princess Marina intends to win over the pretender Dimitri (who is in fact Grigori) and marry him, thus becoming Tsarina of Russia. Ragoni, her confessor, agrees to this plan on the condition that she reinstates Catholicism in Russia. Dimitri (Grigori) awaits Marina in the garden. Father Rangoni assures him about the Princess' intentions as long as he does as suggested. Marina responds to Dimitri's passion coldly, and he is hurt by her attitude. However, she uses all of her charm to seduce him while Father Rangoni, invisible to Dimitri, enjoys his victory. The rebels capture a Boyar in the Kromy forest and taunt him, while an idiot is robbed of the little money he has as he prays. Missail and Varlaam join the crowd in vilifying Boris, and Dimitri is acclaimed as their new Tsar, promising them protection from oppression. The Duma meets at the Kremlin to discuss Dimitri's uprising. Boris has become delirious and asks for the monk, Pimenn. Close to death, Boris appoints his son, Teodoro, rightful successor and asks that he govern justly, after which he dies.

■ **ATTO I.**

■ **ACT I.**

*SCENA I*

*SCENE I.*

*Il muro del Convento di Novo-dievitchi, nei dintorni di Mosca. A destra, presso la ribalta, la gran porta del Monastero, riparata da una tettoia.*

*The wall of Novodievitchi Convent, in the environs of Moscow. To right, near front, the great door of the Monastery, with a shed over it.*

*All'alzarsi del sipario, il popolo, in piccoli gruppi, penetra nella corte del convento. Movimenti svogliati, forzati; andatura pigra ed indolente.*
*I boiardi attraversano la scena, ed hanno alla testa il Principe Chouisky. Si dirigono verso il convento e scambiano saluti col popolo. Allorquanda i boiardi sono entrati nel convento, i contadini si agitano. Gli uni, specialmente le donne, osservano attraverso la porta del conveto; gli altri parlano fra loro a bassa voce, grattandosi la nuca.*

*As the curtain goes up, the populace enter the courtyard of the convent in little groups. They move about reluctantly and with awkward, indolent gait. The Boyars cross the stage with Prince Shouisky at their head. They approach the convent and exchange greetings with the crowd. As soon as the Boyars have entered the Convent, the peasants bestir themselves; some, especially the women, peep through the door of the Convent; others converse in low tones, scratching their heads.*

*Entra l'Ufficiale di Polizia. Il popolo si agglomera e resta immobile. Le donne, col viso appoggiato nel cavo della mano; gli uomini colle mani incrociate alla cintura, facendo girare svogliatamente il berretto fra le loro mani.*

*Enter the Police Official. The crowd closes together and remains motionless; the women, resting their cheeks on the palms of their hands; the men, with their hands crossed at their waists, twirling their caps awkwardly.*

**L'UFFIZIALE DELLA POLIZIA:**
*(impugnando un grosso bastone, col quale minaccia il popolo).* Ebben!
Ma siete di stucco?! . . .
Via! . . . in ginocchio!
*(Minacciando)*
Presto . . . andiam! . . .
*(Il popolo striscia i piedi sul selciato, senza però muoversi dal suo posto.)*
Oh . . . qual razza diabolica!
*(Minacciando)*

**POLICE OFFICIAL:** *(Brandishing a big stick, with which he menaces the crowd).* Well! You are like stones!
On your knees!
*(Menacingly)*
Be quick!
*(The people shuffle their feet on the cobblestones, but do not move from their position.)*
Oh! A race of devils!
*(Menacingly)*

**IL POPOLO:** *(in ginocchio, col viso rivolto alla porta del convento).* Ma perchè tu ci abbandoni?
Oh, padre! . . . Oh, di', a chi affidi il popol tuo?
Buon padre!
Senza padre or noi restiam,
Orfani tristi!
Ah, noi t'imploriam . . .
O, padre.
Deh, vedi il nostro pianto . . .

**THE CROWD:** *(Kneeling, their faces towards the convent door).* But why do you abandon us?
Oh, Father! Say to whom have you entrusted your people?
Good Father! We now remain without a Father!
We are sad orphans!
Ah, we implore you . . .
Oh, Father!
Deign to see us weeping . . .

## Act I, Scene I

Senti i singhiozzi!
(*L'Uffiziale di Polizia, si dirige
verso il convento.*)
Grazia! grazia!
Grazia, buon padre!
O, padre . . .
Proteggici tu . . .
Ci dei vegliar!
Grazia!
(*Voci isolate nel coro. Il popolo ri-
mane in ginocchio.*)

**LE VOCI ISOLATE:** Mitioukhe, di',
Mitioukhe,
Perchè que' lai?

**MITIOUKHE:** Al diavol, s'io lo so!

**VOCI ISOLATE:** Noi diam uno zar
alla Russia!

**QUALCHE DONNA:** Non posso
più! non ho più fiato!
Vicina . . . per piacer,
Vuoi tu darmi da ber?

**SECONDA CONTADINA:** Oh, non
far la principessa!
Se ti piacque di vociar,
Puoi la lingua or tracannar!

**GLI UOMINI:** Ehi, laggi-
ù . . . tacete voi! . . .

**LE DONNE:** Credete spaventar? . . .
È inutil comandar!

**MITIOUKHE:** Oh, le
streghe! . . . non tacete?

**LE DONNE** (*con asprezza*). Ah,
briccon, non c'insultar!
Incredul! va' pel tuo cammin!
Oh, sta zitto, malandrin!
(*S'alzano.*)
Oh, Signor, che gente infame!
Via . . . via . . . partiam di
qui . . .
Ah, la sventura fuggiam! . . .
S'è possibil l'evitiam! . . .

**GLI UOMINI** (*ridendo*). Il nomig-
nolo non vi garba?
È piccante in verità!
V'offende e v'irrìta . . .
(*Ridono*)
Via di qui . . . su . . . vis . . . megère!
Ah, ah, ah, ah, ah, ah, ah!

**L'UFFIZIALE DI POLIZIA:** (*si pre-
senta sul limitare della porta del
convento. Le donne ricadono in
ginocchio e la folla resta immo-
bile.*) (*Alla folla*) Presto, su . . .
Strillate dunque! . . .
(*Minacciando col bastone.*)
Badate . . .
La vostra schiena, dimenticò il ba-
ston? . . .
(*Avanzandosi verso gli uomini.*)
Guardatelo . . . è qui!

**LE DONNE:** (*all'Uffiziale di Polizia*). Mio caro Antonia,
Deh, calma il furor . . .

**GLI UOMINI:** Ma lasciaci fiatar,
Se vuoi farci gridar!

**UOMINI E DONNE:** Noi vogliam fiatar, o mostro!

Hear our sobs!
(*The Police Official moves
towards the convent.*)
Mercy! Mercy!
Mercy, good Father!
Oh, Father . . .
Protect us . . .
Watch over us! Mercy!
(*Single voices in the Chorus. The
crowd remain kneeling.*)

**SINGLE VOICES:** Mitioukhe, say,
Mitioukhe!
Why these lamentations?

**MITIOUKHE:** The deuce I know!

**SINGLE VOICES:** We a Tzar give to
Russia!

**ONE OF THE WOMEN:** I can en-
dure no more!
My breath is gone!
Give me a drink, my neighbor!

**SECOND PEASANT WOMAN:** Oh!
Do not play the princess!
You did delight in shouting,
Now chew your tongue!

**THE MEN:** Hey, down
there . . . keep still!

**THE WOMEN:** You think to fright-
en us?
It is useless to command!

**MITIOUKHE:** Oh, the hags, will
you be quiet?

**THE WOMEN:** (*sharply*). Oh, ras-
cal! insult us not.
Cruel one, begone!
Keep silent, brigand!
(*They arise.*)
Oh, Lord, what knavish folks!
Away! away! Let us be gone from
here,
Flee the misfortune!
Let's avoid it, if we can.

**THE MEN:** (*laughing*). You dislike
the title?
Harshly it sounds, it is true!
Offends and vexes . . .
(*They laugh*)
Begone from here, witches!
Ah, ah, ah, ah, ah, ah, ah!

**THE POLICE OFFICIAL:** (*appear-
ing on the threshold of the con-
vent door. The women again fall
on their knees and the crowd re-
mains motionless.*)
(*To the crowd*)
Quick now . . .
Let's hear you shout!
(*Threatening them with his
stick.*) Beware!
Have your backs forgotten the
clout?
(*Advancing towards the men*)
Behold it . . . it is here!

**THE WOMEN:** (*to the Police Official*). My dear Anton,
Please calm your rage . . .

**THE MEN:** But let us breathe,
If you would have us shout!

**MEN AND WOMEN:** We want to
breathe, O monster!

**L'UFFIZIALE DI POLIZIA:** Orvia!
urlate e vi sgolate!

**IL POPOLO:** Sta ben!

**L'UFFIZIALE DI POLIZIA:** (*minacciando col bastone*).
Eh! . . .

**IL POPOLO:** (*gridando a squar-
ciagola*). Ma perchè tu ci abbandoni, O, padre?!
Oh, di', a chi affidi il popol
tuo? . . . Buon padre,
Noi qui t'imploriam! O, padre . . .
Deh, vedi il nostro pianto!
Senti i singhiozzi! . . .
Grazia! grazia, buon pa-
dre . . . O, padre! . . .
(*Agli ultimi gridi del Popolo, il
Segretario della Duma [Tchelka-
lov] appare sulla soglia della porta del convento.*)

**L'UFFIZIALE DI POLIZIA:** (*corre
verso il popolo*). Zitti . . . in
piè! sentite ben! . . . (*La folla si
alza.*)

**TCHELKALOV:** (*avanzandosi
verso il popolo. Si toglie il berretto
e saluta*). Moscoviti! Boris è infles-
sibil!
Il caldo appel dei boiardi, del patri-
arca,
Non bastò, e Boris non vuol il tron.
Grand'è il dolor del popol de la
Russia,
Moscoviti!
Tutt'il Regno soffre e piange!
Pregat'il Signor,
l'implorate . . .
Ch'Egli accordi
Alla Russia il favor,
E che rischiari di saggezza
Lo spirito del gran Boris!

**LE GUIDE DEI PELLEGRINI:** (*di
fanciulli, fra le quinte*). Grand'è
tua gloria su la terra, Dio creator!
Gloria! gloria! al celeste poter!
Gloria ai santi eletti! Gloria a la Russia!

**IL POPOLO:** (*mormorando*). Gli
eletti del Ciel, gli eletti del Ciel!

**I PELLEGRINI:** (*nelle quinte*).
L'angel di Dio lo proclamò!
Accorrete, o nubi nere
Verso la Santa Russia!
(*I Pellegrini entrano in scena, appoggiandosi alle spalle delle loro
guide. Hanno una lunga tonaca
con cappuccio, e sono carichi di
amuleti. S'appoggiano anche ad
un lungo bastone. Il popolo si divide, al loro passaggio, e li saluta
con devozione sincera.*)

**LE GUIDE ED I PELLEGRINI:** (*con
voce sonora*). Schiacciate il dragon,
L'idra a dodici teste, coll'ali . . .
Bestia difforme del disordin,
dell'iniquità!
Proclamatel nel gran regno,

**THE POLICE OFFICIAL:** Then,
shout yourselves hoarse!

**PEOPLE:** All right!

**THE POLICE OFFICIAL:** (*menacing with his stick*). Hey!

**THE CROWD:** (*shouting aloud*).
But why do you abandon us,
Oh, Father?
Say, to whom have you entrusted
your people?
Good Father!
Here, we implore you.
Oh Father!
Deign to see us weeping . . .
Hear our sobs!
Mercy! Mercy! Good Father . . .
Oh, Father!
(*At the last shouts of Crowd, the
Secretary of the Duma, Tchelka-
lov, appears on threshold of the
convent door.*)

**THE POLICE OFFICIAL:** (*running
towards the Crowd*). Si-
lence! . . . Arise! . . . Listen!
(*The Crowd arises*)

**TCHELKALOV:** (*advancing
towards the Crowd, removes his
cap in greeting*). Moscovians! Boris
remains inflexible.
In vain the earnest appeal of Boyars
and of the patriarch!
Boris the throne declines.
Great is the sorrow of Russia's peo-
ple, Moscovians!
The entire realm suffers and la-
ments!
The Lord beg, implore Him
That he grant
The favor sought to Russia—
Enlighten with wisdom
The mind of Boris the Great!

**GUIDES OF PILGRIMS:** (*Boys,
from behind the scenes*). On earth
great is your Glory, god Creator!
Glory! Glory! to the Heavenly Power!
Glory to the elect Saints! To Russia
Glory!

**THE CROWD:** (*murmuring*). The
elect of Heaven! The elect of Heav-
en!

**PILGRIMS:** (*from behind scenes*).
God's angel proclaimed it!
Draw up, black clouds,
From our Holy Russia!
(*The Pilgrims enter, leaning on
the shoulders of their guides. They
are attired in long cloaks, with
boods, and wear many amulets.
They also carry long staffs for support. The Crowd opens a passage
for them and greets them with
sincere devotion*).

**GUIDES AND PILGRIMS:** (*in so-
norous tones*). The dragon crush,
The twelve-headed hydra, with
wings
Shapeless beast of disorder and sin!
Through all the realm proclaim it
For his good!

Per il suo ben!
(*Distribuiscono amuleti al popolo.*)
Indossate abiti sacri . . .
Dei miracol, gli iconi portate
In procession, colle sante Vergini,
Per incontrar Boris!
(*Si dirigono verso il convento. Il canto s'estingue gradatamente.*)
Ed or cantiam la gloria al Dio possente!
Grand'è la gloria tua, Dio creator! . . .
(*Il sipario cala lentamente.*)

(*They distribute amulets among the crowd*)
Put on sacred garments . . .
These images, the icons wear
In procession with the Blessed Virgins,
To meet Boris!
(*They go towards the convent, the chant dying away gradually.*)
And now sing Glory to God Almighty!
Great is your Glory, God Creator!
(*The curtain descends slowly.*)

## SCENA II.

*Una cella, nel convento del Miracolo. Pimenn scrive all'incerto chiarore d'una lucerna. Grigori dorme.*

**PIMENN:** (*Interrompendo di scrivere*). Ancora un fatto . . . ancora una leggenda,
E la cronaca sarà finita.
Compiuta avrò quest'opra, che Dio legò
Al peccator!
(*Interrompendo di scrivere*)
Da molt'anni
Dio me rese testimon degli eventi . . .
Forse un dì, un monaco sapiente,
Troverà l'opra mia, umil, ignota,
E come me, al chiaror d'una lucerna,
Scuotendo la polver secolare,
Trascriverà i veritier miei detti!
Che la novella stirpe moscovita,
Impari così la storia del passato.
(*Rimane pensoso.*)
Carico d'anni, sento la primavera . . .
I dì passati in me tumultan
Come i marosi dell'oceàn! . . .
Jeri ancor, tutto vivea pieno d'eventi . . .
Ed oggi invece . . . calma e silenzio!
Il giorno sorge già, e la fiamma s'estingue.
(*Scrive.*)
Ancora un fatto . . . ancora una leggenda . . .

**CORO DI FRATI:** (*nell'interno*).
Dio potente e giusto,
Ascolta i servi tuoi,
Che qui t'imploran!
Scaccia, Signor lo spirito maligno
Lontan da' figli tuoi!

**GRIGORI:** (*svegliandosi*). Sempre quel sogno!
Tre volte il sogno istesso! . . .
M'atterrisce l'incubo orrendo!
E 'l vecchio
Non riposa, e senza tregua scrive . . .
Il sonno, gli occhi suoi, nemmen sfiorò!
Oh! come ammir quel monaco sì umil.

## SCENE II.

*A cell in the Convent of Miracles. Pimenn is writing by the uncertain light of a lamp. Gregory is asleep.*

**PIMENN:** (*ceasing to write*). One more fact . . . another legend,
And the chronicle is done.
This work completed then, which God bequeaths
to him who sins.
(*Ceasing to write*)
For many years
God made me witness these events . . .
Who knows? some day a learned monk
May find my humble work, unknown,
And, as I have done, by the light of a lamp,
Brushing the secular dust away,
My truthful sayings shall transcribe,
So the new Muscovite race may learn
The history of the past.
(*Remains thoughtful.*)
Burdened with years, I feel the spring . . .
The days long gone, stir within me,
Like billows of the ocean! . . .
But yesterday, a busy, bustling life,
Today, calm and silence!
The day already dawns and the flame sinks low!
(*He writes.*)
One more fact . . . another legend.

**CHORUS OF MONKS:** (*from within*). God, potent and just,
Hear your servants
Who here implore you.
Banish the evil spirit, Lord,
Far from your sons!

**GREGORY:** (*awaking*). Ever that dream!
Three times, the same vision!
It terrifies me, horrible nightmare . . .
And the aged man
Rests not, but writes unceasingly . . .
Sleep has not touched his eyes!
That humble monk, how admirable,
When surges through his mind the

Quand'il passato sorge nel suo spirto,
Calmo e sublime, egli registra i fatti.

**PIMENN:** Alzato gia?

**GRIGORI:** (*avvicinandosi a Pimenn e salutandolo profondamente*). O, padre amato, mi benedici.

**PIMENN:** (*se alza e lo benedice*).
Di Dio la santa benedizion,
Ti segua ovunque, ed anche in Ciel!

**I FRATI:** (*nell'interno*). Perchè, o Signore, ci abbandonasti Tu?
(*Pimenn siede. Grigori si alza esclamando.*)

**GRIGORI:** Tu scrivesti senza chiuder ciglio;
Ma 'l sonno mio fu ognor turbato
Da sogni diabolici, orrendi.
M'ascolta. Per una scala angusta
M'arrampicai e scorsi,
Da quell'altezza, Mosca! . . . Un formicaio . . .
Il popol giù, furente, m'oltraggiava,
E segnandomi a dito mi beffava! . . .
L'onta e 'l terror m'invaser . . .
Io caddi dalla torre . . . e mi svegliai! . . .

**PIMENN:** Arde il giovanil tuo sangue . . .
Dei digiunar . . . hai d'uopo di pregar . . .
I pensier, in corrotte vision
Si trasforman. Anch'io, quand'una sera
Lascio nel sonno addormentar lo spirto,
Senz'innalzar al Ciel la mia preghiera,
Perdo 'l riposo, e la notte è turbata
Vedo allor degli osceni convivi . . .
Le lotte, le battaglie,
E le follie commesse nella mia gioventù!

**GRIGORI:** Brillanti furon i tuoi prim'anni;
Ti battesti da eroe sotto Kazàn,
E le truppe nemiche respingesti.
Del Zar Terribil, lo splendore hai visto
Ma io, novizio dall'infanzia,
Vivo nella mia cella, frate umìl!
Oh . . . voglio anch'io gustar questi piacer . . .
L'ebbrezza di battaglie e dei festin! . . .

**PIMENN:** Non pianger, no! . . . s'abbandonasti
Il mondo! Oh, credi a me . . .
Da lungi ci seduce il suo fulgor,
E l'amor delle donne ci lusinga . . .
Oh, pensa, figlio, allo splendor dei Zar!
Son sì possenti e invece
Oh, ben sovente, essi abbandonan

past,
Sublime and calm, he chronicles his facts!

**PIMENN:** Awake already?

**GREGORY:** (*approaching Pimenn and bowing low*). Oh, beloved father, your blessings.

**PIMENN:** (*rising and blessing him*). God's holy blessing
Rest on you, even unto Heaven!

**THE MONKS:** (*within*). Why, Lord, did you abandon us?
(*Pimenn seats himself; Gregory rises exclaiming:*)

**GREGORY:** You did write, with eyes that rested not;
My sleep was ever troubled
By a diabolical dream—most terrible!
Hear me. On a narrow stair
I climbed and saw,
From a height, Moscow—as an ant's nest!
The raving crowd below abused me,
And, their fingers pointing, jeered me.
Shame and terror invading my soul,
I fell from the tower . . . and awoke.

**PIMENN:** Aflame is your youthful blood
From fasting . . . You need prayer.
Thoughts, in corrupted visions,
Transform themselves. So I—
When I allowed my mind to sink to slumber,
No prayer to Heaven raised,
My rest is lost, my night disturbed.
Then rise before me sinful scenes convivial,
And fights and battles,
The follies of my youth.

**GREGORY:** Brilliant your early years,
When under Kazàn you were hero
And you overcame the enemy's troops.
You have seen the terrible Tzar's splendor.
But I, at infancy a novice,
Live in my cell a humble monk!
Ah! . . . I, too, wish to taste these joys—
The thrilling scenes of battle and of banquets.

**PIMENN:** Lament not! . . . You gave up
The world! Oh, believe me . . .
From afar its dazzle tempts us,
And woman's love allures.
Think, my son, of the splendor of the Tzars,
So powerful they are, and yet,
Oh, often, they leave behind them,
The scepter and the royal purple,

## Act I, Scene II

Lo scettro e l'àurea porpora,
La fulgida corona,
Per l'aspro saio del frate,
Cercando in un convento
E pace e calma . . . In questa cella,
(Allor viveva qui Santo Cirillo
Il Giusto), io vidi qui lo Zar!
Pensoso e buon, Ivan, lo Zar Terribil,
Avea per noi parole di clemenza . . .
E vidi ne' suoi occhi ognor severi,
Per il rimorso le lagrime brillar.
Lo Zar piangea . . .
(è assorto in un profondo pensiero.)
Suo figlio, il Zar Teodoro,
Le sue stanze trasformò
In tristi celle . . . Un vero chiostro . . .
Il Ciel amò quel Zar amato e buon!
Sotto 'l suo Regno, la Russia intera
Visse taranquilla; e quand'anche per lui
L'ora suonò, un gran miracolo vidi compir.
La stanza sua s'empì d'un acre odor . . .
E 'l bianco volto come un sol splendè . . .
Oh, non avrem più mai, simile Zar!
Ed il Ciel ci punì! Come Signor
Noi ci siam dati, un regicida infame!

GRIGORI: (Siedendosi accanto al tavolo di Pimenn). Da molti . . . da molt'anni,
O, padre, io vo' saper,
L'età ch'avea lo Zarevic sgozzato.

PIMENN: Avrebbe l'età tua.
(Grigori, erge tutta la persona con fierezza, poi siede ancora umilmente, sullo sgabbello.)
Ei regnerebbe . . .
Ma Dio non l'ha voluto!
Coll'orrendo delitto di Boris lo Zar,
Il mio sunto stasera io vo' finir.
Frate Grigori!
Tu sei un dotto . . . ami la scienza . . .
Ebben, ti lego l'opra mia . . .
Scrivi senza indugiar; ma fedelmente,
Tutto quello che hai visto e che vedrai,
E guerra e pace è il regno degli Zar,
Le profezie del Ciel ed i presàgi . . .
(Alzandosi lentamente.)
Io, figliuol mio, di calma ho d'uopo!
(S'ode, in lontananza, il rintocco delle campane, che suonano il mattutino.)
Suona già il mattutin. Veglia, Signor,
Sui figli tuoi.
(A Grigori)
Dammi il baston.

---

The golden crown,
For the rough garb of monks,
Seeking in the privacy of a convent
Rest and peace . . . In this cell
When St. Cyril the Just lived here
I saw here that Tzar!
Thoughtful and good, Ivan the terrible Tzar,
For us had words of clemency;
And I saw in his stern eyes
The tears of remorse he felt.
That Tzar was weeping . . .
(He becomes absorbed in deep thought.)
His son, Tzar Theodore
Transformed his room
Into two dismal cells . . . a true cloister . . .
Heaven loved that Tzar, the good, the adored!
Under his rule all Russia
Lived in peace; and when for him too
The hour struck, a great miracle I saw accomplished.
His room was filled with a sharp, acrid odor,
But his pale face shone like the sun.
Oh, never shall we have such a Tzar!
Heaven has punished us! As Lord
We have now an infamous regicide!

GREGORY: (seating himself near Pimenn's table). For many . . . many years,
Oh, Father, I've longed to know
What age the butchered Tzarovitch was.

PIMENN: He would be your age.
(Gregory springs impetuously to his feet, and resumes his position on the stool humbly.)
And on the throne;
But God willed it otherwise!
With the horrible crime of Boris, the Tzar,
Before night shall end my theme.
Brother Gregory,
You are learned . . . . . . You love science . . .
Well, to you I bequeath my labors.
Write, delay not, but write truthfully
All that you have witnessed and shall see,
Both war and peace and the ruling of that Tzar,
Heaven's prophecies and presages.
(Rising slowly).
I, my son, need rest.
(In the distance the tolling of bells is heard, calling to matins.)
Matins already! Lord, watch
Over your sons.
(To Gregory)
Hand me the staff.

---

I FRATI: (coro interno). Accordaci la grazia,
Dio clemente,
O, buon Signor!
Padre che rengi su noi
Eterno e giusto!
(Pimenn s'allontana con raccoglimento. Grigori l'accompagna fino alla porta poi ritorna ed esclama.)

GRIGORI: (sulla soglia). Boris!
Boris! tutti a te s'inchinan . . .
Nessun osa lagnarsi
Della sorte crudel di quel fanciul . . .
Eppur qui, nella sua cella un frate,
Svela l'orrendo tuo misfatto . . .
E la giustizia dei mortal, quaggiù . . .
Ti colpirà . . . e il ciel ti punirà . . . . (Cala la tela.)

### SCENA III.

La piazza, fra le due cattedrali della Assunzione e degli Arcangeli. Il sacrato della prima è alla destra, quello della seconda si scorge in distanza, rimpetto agli spettatori. Sulla piazza, il popolo inginocchiato. Le campane suonano a distesa, in segno di festa. La Processione. Le Guardie. I figli dei Boiardi. Gli Streltzi. Tchelkalov, con bastone dello Zar, poi ancora degli Streltzi. Vengono poscia i Boiardi, i diaconi, ecc., ecc. La Processione attraversa la scena, passando fra la folla, ed entra nella Cattedrale dell'Assunzione. Gli streltzi si dispongono in fila sul sacrato.

IL PRINCIPE CHOUÏSKY: (dall'alto del Sacrato della Cattedrale dell'Assunzione). Salve a te, Zar Boris Theodorovich!

IL POPOLO: (alzandosi). Salute ed ogni ben al nostro Zar!

IL PRINCIPE CHOUÏSKY: Gloria!
(Entra nella Cattedrale.)

IL POPOLO: Gloria al bel sol del vasto ciel! Gloria!
Sia gloria al nostro Zar, a Zar Boris! Gloria!
(La processione ritorna dalla Cattedrale, preceduta dalle trombe degli Streltzi.)
Lungo regno al buon Zar!
Festa è per te, popol di Russia,
Glorifica il tuo buon Zar!

I BOIARDI: (dal Sacrato). Evviva lo Zar Boris Theodorovich.

IL POPOLO: (inchinandosi). Viva lo Zar!
(Tchelkalov e i boiardi seguono la processione, e si dispongono, descrivendo un mezzo cerchio, fra i sacrati delle due cattedrali.)

---

MONKS: (chorus within). Grant us grace,
Merciful God,
Oh, good Lord,
Father who rules over us,
Eternal and just!
(Pimenn walks away absorbed in thought. Gregory accompanies him to the door, then returns and exclaims:)

GREGORY: (on the threshold).
Boris! Boris! All bow before you,
None dares complain
Of that boy's sad fate . . .
But here, in his cell, a monk
Discloses your horrible misdeeds . . .
And the justice of mortals here below
Shall strike you . . . and Heaven shall punish! . . .

### SCENE III.

The Square between the two cathedrals of the Assumption and of the Archangels. The churchyard of the first is at right, that of the second in the distance facing the audience. In the Square the people are kneeling. The bells are ringing loudly. The procession. Guards. Sons of the Boyars. The Streltzi guards. Tchelkalov, with the staff of the Tzar, then more Streltzi. Then follow in order the Boyars, the deacons, etc. etc. etc. The Procession crosses the stage, passing through the crowd, and enters the Cathedral of the Assumption. The Streltzi arrange themselves in files in the churchyard.

PRINCE SHOUISKY: (from elevated ground of the Cathedral of the Assumption). Hail to you, Tzar Boris Theodorovich!

THE CROWD: (rising). Health and all good to our Tzar!

PRINCE SHOUISKY: Glory!
(He enters the Cathedral.)

THE CROWD: Glory to the fair son of the vast sky! Glory!
Glory be to our Tzar, our Tzar Boris! Glory!
(The procession returns from the Cathedral, preceded by the Trumpeters of the Streltzi.)
Long reign to the good Tzar!
This is a festal day for you, O people of Russia!
Glorify your good Tzar!

THE BOYARS: (from the Churchyard). Long live the Tzar, Boris Theodorovich!

THE CROWD: (bowing). Long live the Tzar!
(Tchelkalov and the Boyars follow the procession and arrange themselves, making a semicircle between the churchyards of the two Cathedrals.)

IL POPOLO: Sia gloria in Russia a Zar Boris!
Gloria, gloria al buon Zar!
Gloria! gloria! gloria!
(*Boris, appare sul sacrato. Chouisky è dietro lui, e fa segno al popolo di tacere.*)

BORIS: (*i figli suoi: Teodoro e Xenia, lo seguono*). Trist'è 'l mio cor!
La tema incessante
Dell'arcano nefasto,
Mi rode l'alma!
(*In estasi.*)
Santo defunto! O, mio avo regal!
Tu vedi dal Ciel le lagrime nostre . . .
Invia la tua santa benedizion
Su me, sul Regno . . .
Oh, rendimi buon e giusto come te,
E 'l mio tron felice sia!
(*Abbassa il capo.*)
Or salutiam i defunti Sovran
De la Russia!
(*con regale maestà.*)
Il mio popol avrà la sua festa!
Tutti! dal boiardo al povero mendico,
Tutti entreran; tutti è il Zar che invita!
(*Boris entra nella cattedrale.*)

IL POPOLO: Ogni ben! lunga vita al buon Zar,
E gloria al bel sol del vasto ciel!
Gloria! gloria!
Sia gloria in Russia a Zar Boris!
Gloria! gloria! gloria! ed ogni ben!
(*Fra le ovazioni entusiastiche, Boris esce dalla Cattedrale e si dirige ai suoi appartamenti. Il velario s'abbassa, fra le grida del popolo:*)
Gloria! Gloria! . . .
(*Le campane suonano a distesa.*)
(*Cala la tela.*)

*FINE DELL'ATTO I.*

# ■ ATTO II.

## SCENA I.

*Una locanda, alla frontiera della Lituania.*

L'OSTESSA: (*raccomoda una vecchia scarpa, cantarellando*).
Io presi un anitrotto blù e ner;
Anitrotto, tu sei bel
E t'ammiro con piacer.
L'anitrotto gentil voglio affidar
All'acqua dello stagno,
Degli alberi al ripar.
Vola, vola . . . amato augel
Deh, vola là . . . nel ciel . . .
Ma ritorna nell'ostel
Io vo' carezzar con tutt'il mister,
Le tue piume variopinte . . .
Piccol mio, blù e ner.
(*voci nelle quinte*)
Deh, vien, t'appressa. A me ti vo' vicin;

THE CROWD: Glory be in Russia to Tzar Boris!
Glory, glory to the good Tzar!
Glory! Glory! Glory!
(*Boris appears in the Churchyard. Shouisky is behind him and signals the people to be silent*).

BORIS: (*his son Theodore and his daughter Xenia following him*).
Sad my heart!
The unceasing fear
Of that heinous secret
Gnaws at my soul!
(*Ecstatically.*)
Saintly dead, Oh, royal ancestor,
You behold from Heaven our tears.
Send your blessing
On me and on my reign;
Oh, make me good and just as you,
And my throne make happy.
(*Bowing his head.*)
Now let us salute the dead sovereigns Of Russia.
(*With royal majesty.*)
My people shall have their feast!
All! from the Boyars to the beggar,
All shall enter; all!
It is the Tzar who invites!
(*Boris enters the Cathedral.*)

THE CROWD: All hail! Long life to the good Tzar,
And glory to the fair son of the vast sky! Glory! Glory!
Glory be in Russia to her Tzar Boris!
Glory! Glory! Glory! All hail!
(*Amid the enthusiastic ovation, Boris comes out of the Cathedral and takes his departure. The curtain descends amid the shouts of the populace.*)
Glory! Glory!
(*The bells ring jubilantly.*)
(*Curtain.*)

*END OF ACT I.*

# ■ ACT II

## SCENE I.

*An Inn on the frontier of Lithuania.*

INNKEEPER: (*a woman*).
(*Fixing an old shoe and singing to herself*). I caught a duckling all blue and black
Duckling you are fine,
I love you well.
The gentle duckling will I trust
To the water of the pond,
Under the shade of the trees.
Fly, fly . . . dear birdy,
Oh, fly away, there . . . to the sky . . .
But come back to your home again.
I wish to fondle your gaudy feathers,
My little one, blue and black.
(*Voices behind the scenes*)
Oh, come I pray you, come

Deh, baciami la bocca,
Bacia e mordimi, piccin!
(*Risa squillanti, ed il frastuono di conversazioni nelle quinte.*)
Chi va là?
(*guardando*)
Son de'viandanti! . . .
Qui entrar potete.
(*Le risa e le conversazioni cessono.*)
Olà! . . . Taccion? . . .
Nessun! Più nessun!
(*ritorna a cantarellare.*)
Oh ti vo' . . . mi bacia ancor,
Augel mio buono e gentil . . .
T'darò tutto 'l mio cor!
Deh, vienmi a rallegrar . . .
Ti vuol la vedovella . . .
Vien; non farla più penar!

MISSAIL E VARLAAM: (*nelle quinte*). Oh,
voi . . . cristiani
Buona gente . . . fedeli . . .
Oh dateci per innalzar,
Un tempio al buon Signor!
Dio dal ciel vi paghera! . . . .

L'OSTESSA: (*alzandosi*). Grazia, Signor! . . . .
Dei santi eremiti!
Che stolta sono stata;
Mi feci tentar dal peccato!
(*guardando dalla finestra*)
Son dessi . . . eccoli . . . qui
Gli inviati del Signor!
(*Apre la porta. Varlam a Missaïl entrano seguiti dal falso Dimitri sotto il nome di Gregori, vestito da contadino. L'Ostessa li saluta umilmente.*)

VARLAAM: All'ostel sia pace, o donna.

L'OSTESSA: In che posso io servir, Quei santi pellegrini?

MISSAIL: Offrir puoi ciò che tu hai.

VARLAAM: (*urtando Missaïl col gomito*). Un po' di vin . . .

L'OSTESSA: Con piacer, buon pellegrin!
Or or lo porterò
(*via*)

VARLAAM: (*osserva Grigori, che è seduto al tavolo pensoso*). Oh camerata, scaccia la tristezza.
Alfin raggiungi il grande tuo desir.
La frontiera potrai oggi varcar.

GRIGORI: Sicuro non sarò in Lituania.

VARLAAM: A che ti può servir la Lituania?
Noi due, il buon Missaïl e io, povero fratel,
Dopo la fuga dal monaster,
Ce la passiamo ben.

To me; I would have you near;
Oh, kiss me, please, upon the lips,
Kiss and bite me, little one!
(*A burst of laughter and conversation behind the scenes.*)
Who is there?
(*Looking*)
They are travellers!
Here, you may enter!
(*The laughter and conversation cease.*)
Hola! . . . they are silent.
No longer there!
(*Begins to sing again.*)
Oh, I want you to kiss me again,
My birdy, so good and gentle . . .
I shall give you all my heart,
Oh, come, gladden me,
The little widow wants you,
Come; make her suffer no more.

MISSAIL AND VARLAAM: (*from behind the scenes*).
Oh . . . Christians . . .
Good folks . . . faithful ones . . .
Oh, give us alms to raise
A temple to the Holy Lord!
God from Heaven shall repay you!

THE INNKEEPER: (*rising*). Mercy! O Lord,
They are saintly hermits!
How foolish I have been
In yielding to sin!
(*looking out of the window*)
It is they . . . here they are . . .
The messengers of the Lord!
(*She opens the door. Varlam and Missail enter, followed by the false Dimitri dressed as a peasant and under the name of Grigory.—The Innkeeper greets them humbly.*)

VARLAAM: To the inn be peace, O woman!

THE INNKEEPER: How can I serve These holy pilgrims?

MISSAIL: Offer what you have.

VARLAAM: (*nudging Missail*). A little wine.

THE INNKEEPER: Willingly, good pilgrims!
Anton, you shall have it. (*She goes out.*)

VARLAAM: (*observing Grigori who is seated at the table*). Oh, comrade, drive dull care away . . .
At last, you attain your earnest wish.
You shall cross the frontier today.

GRIGORY: Only in Lithuania shall I feel safe.

VARLAAM: How can Lithuania help you?
We two, good Missail and I, poor brother,
After our flight from the cloister.
We fare quite well.

O in Russia, o in Lituania,
Felice sempre son, quand'ho del vin.

L'OSTESSA: (*entra, e depone alcune bottiglie di vino sul tavolo*). A voi, fratelli, vi porto del buon vin.

VARLAAM: Ecco il buon vin!

VARLAAM E MISSAIL: Grazie, gentile ostessa, Che Dio ti colmi de'suoi favor!

VARLAAM: (*canta, con una bottiglia in mano*). Quand'ero a Kazàn la città bella, Il terribile Zar si trastullava ... Ma pei Tartari la stella, sul lor cielo non brillava. Ei li bruciò ... vadan al diavol! Nella notte il mio buon Zar, Circondò, strinse Kazàn ... E sotto il fiume la mina fe' saltar, Lo Zar Ivàn! I Tartari in città passeggian fieri Vorrebbero scacciar gli Zar alteri; I Tartari crudel! (*beve*) Allora il Zar terribil s'offuscò E, curvo 'l capo sulla spalla, gridò: "Miei cannonier or a voi tocca ... Mettete la miccia nella bocca Dei tremendi barril!" Con far spavaldo il cannonier marciò, Ed accese pian pian il cer sottil ... Il barril micidial su stesso girò ... Nelle, mine presto, ruzzolò E poi scoppiò! ... (*beve*) I Tartari gridaron dal dolore E fuggiron pel terrore! ... Zar Ivan domò tutti i ribelli ... La carne lor fu ridotta a brandelli! (*beve*) Quand'ero a Kazàn la città bella ... Eh! (*a Grigori*) Il tuo labbro è chiuso ancor? Per chi palpita il tuo cor?

GRIGORI: Mah! ... chi sa! ...

MISSAIL: Oh! è affar tuo! ...

VARLAAM: No certo il mio, buon camerata! Viva la nosta cara ostessa! (*beve*) (*a Grigori*) Ascolta ben ... Quand'io bevo i sobrï non mi piaccion. Ama l'ebbrezza e non la temperanza. Imitar mi vorrai? Vien qui ... m'abbraccia. Non vuoi? Sta ben! ... Al diavol va!

---

Either in Russia or Lithuania, I am always happy where there is wine.

INNKEEPER: (*entering and setting wine bottles on the table*). To you brethren, I bring good wine.

MISSAIL: Behold the good wine!

VARLAAM AND MISSAIL: Thanks, gentle hostess, God's wealth of favors be with you!

VARLAAM: (*singing with a bottle in his hand*). When I was in the fair City of Kazàn, The terrible Tzar passed his time in sport ... But the Tartar's star Illuminated not their sky. He burnt them ... to the devil let them go! At night my good Tzar Surrounded Kazàn, closing in ... And beneath the river sprang a mine, Tzar Ivan! The Tartars in the city proudly strutted, They would the haughty Tzars repel; The cruel Tartars! (*He drinks.*) Then frowned the terrible Tzar And shouted, cocking his head: "My gunners, it is your turn ... Apply the fuse to the mouth Of the terrible casks!" With boldish mien went forward the gunner. And with care the taper lighted ... Turned on itself the murderous cask ... And bounding into the mine There it burst! ... (*He drinks.*) With pain the Tartars shrieked ... And terror-stricken fled! ... Tzar Ivan subdued the rebels ... And tore their flesh to shreds! (*He drinks.*) When in Kazàn, that city fair ... Hey! ... (*To Grigory.*) Still shut are your lips? For whom throbs your heart?

GRIGORY: Well! ... who knows! ...

MISSAIL: Oh! it is your own concern! ...

VARLAAM: Not mine certainly, good comrade! Long live our hostess! (*He drinks; to Grigory.*) Listen carefully ... When I drink, the sober ones I like not. Love ebriety, not temperance. Would you copy me? Come ... embrace me. You will not? It is well! ... Go to the devil!

---

GRIGORI: Puoi ber, senza perder la ragion. Padre Varlaam ...

VARLAAM: La region? A che far? Non m'abbisogna, veh! (*incrocia le braccia sulla tavola, e s'addormenta cantarellando.*) È il buon uomo ... È il buon uomo ... Un gentiluomo! Un uomo! (*s'assopisce*)

GRIGORI: Ove conduce, ostessa, quel sentier?

OSTESSA: In Lituania.

VARLAAM: (*sonnecchiando*). Egli è un uomo ... Un gran buon'uomo È proprio un gentiluomo Un'uomo! ...

GRIGORI: Di, ostessa, ed è lontana?

OSTESSA: No, compar, essa è vicina; Oggi stesso vi sarai. Ma in guardia alle barriere

GRIGORI: Che barriere?

OSTESSA: Un colpevole fuggì, Ed arrestano i viandanti ... Per poi trafugarli.

GRIGORI: E che?! ... La mia speme Per sempre svanì? ...

VARLAAM: (*sonnecchiando*) È il meschin, Preso dal vin, E stiaccia un sonnellin ...

GRIGORI: Ma non sai chi cercan? ...

OSTESSA: Un mariuol ... non so ben ... od un brigante. Ma gli arcier non ci lascian più in pace!

GRIGORI: Sì?

OSTESSA: Ma credi tu ch'arrestino i ladron? Nemmen per sogno ... Poichè l'altro cammin posson varcar ... Ma senti ben ... Svoltar devi a sinistra, Per questo sentier. Va' verso la cappella di Tchekan, In riva al fiume; E di là sei nel Khlopino, Poscia a Zaitzevo. Allor anche una bimba Ti potria condur. Ma sai, questo spionaggio è una tal piaga Per l'infelice popol ... Ed anche più per noi, povere ostesse!

VARLAAM: (*stirandosi*). È il buon uomo E fa toc-toc ... (*Si batte alla porta.*)

---

GRIGORY: You may drink without losing your reason, Father Varlaam ...

VARLAAM: Reason? For what? I need it not, see! (*He crosses his arms over the table and goes to sleep, singing in low tones.*) It is the good man ... It is the good man ... A gentleman! A man! (*He falls asleep.*)

GRIGORY: Hostess, where leads that path?

INNKEEPER: Into Lithuania.

VARLAAM: (*drowsily*). He is a man ... A great good man And truly a gentleman! A man! ...

GRIGORY: Tell me, hostess, is it far?

INNKEEPER: No, my friend, near it is; Even today you can be there. But be careful at the barriers.

GRIGORY: What barriers?

INNKEEPER: A culprit has escaped, All travellers are arrested ... And then spirited away.

GRIGORY: Alas! ... So has my hope Forever vanished? ...

VARLAAM: (*drowsily*). So is the wretch, Caught by the wine, Snatching a little nap ...

GRIGORY: But do you know whom they seek?

INNKEEPER: A scoundrel ... I know not rightly ... or a brigand. But the bowmen leave us no peace!

GRIGORY: So?!

INNKEEPER: But do you think they will catch the thieves? Not even in their dreams ... For they can use the other road ... Now hear me carefully ... You must turn to the left, When following this path. Go to the chapel of Tchekan, Rising on the river's banks; And from there to Khlopin, Then on to Tzaitzevo. After that even a child Could lead you. But certainly this spying is indeed a plague For the unhappy people ... And for us, poor hostesses, much more so!

VARLAAM: (*stretching himself*). It is the good man Who goes: toc, toc ... (*A knock is heard at the door.*)

Più forte ancor . . . toc, toc, toc, toc!
(*i colpi si ripetono con maggior violenza.*)
OSTESSA: Ma cos'è quel rumor?
(*va verso la finestra e guarda al di fuori*)
Son proprio quegli infami!
Ancor dessi! . . . son gli arcier!
(*i poliziotti entrano tacitamente, ed osservano i vagabondi.*)

VARLAAM: È il buom uomo . . .
E il buon uomo!
Un gentiluomo!
(*i poliziotti si collocano dietro le spalle di Varlaam.*)
L'UFFIZIALE: Chi siete voi?
VARLAAM E MISSAIL: (*spaventati, rispondono umilmente*). Poveri frati ed umil religiosi . . . Facciam la quèstua, nelle città e nei borghi.
L'UFFIZIALE: (*a Grigori*). E tu? . . . Chi sei tu?
VARLAAM E MISSAIL: È un camerata.
GRIGORI: (*con studiata indifferenza*). Presso il gran borgo io vivo . . . I monaci accompagno . . . Dopo, io rincaso . . .
L'UFFIZIALE: (*agli arcieri*). Non c'è da far col giovin! Tentiam i frati . . . Hum! (*tossendo*) (*poi s'avvicina alla tavola.*) O, miei padri, e la questua come andò?

VARLAAM: Oh! . . . mal figliuol . . . mal! I fedeli amano l'or . . . Lo rinserran . . . lo nascondan . . . E più nulla pel Signor . . . E grande l'ingiustizia! Trionfa la nequizia . . . Chiedi e chiedi . . . prega e prega . . . Ma nulla ti von dar, O un misero copec! Noi, pel dolor, all'osteria veniam! Oh . . . sicur! . . . è del mondo la fin . . . Proprio la fin! . . .
OSTESSA: (*quasi supplicando l'uffiziale*). Signor, abbi pietà della tua serva.
VARLAAM: (*mentre l'uffiziale scruta il suo volto*). Oh, di' su . . . perchè su me fissi i tuo occhi?
L'UFFIZIALE: Ascolta, Aliokha, dammi l'editto, Sei tu che l'hai. (*prende la carta*) (*a Varlaam*)

Louder yet . . . toc, toc, toc, toc!
(*The knocks are repeated with greater force.*)
INNKEEPER: But what's all this racket?
(*goes to the window and looks out.*)
In very truth it is those rascals! They again! . . . It is the bowmen!
(*Soldiers enter in silence and observe the vagrants.*)

VARLAAM: It is the good man! . . .
It is the good man . . .
A gentleman!
(*The soldiers go and stand behind Varlaam.*)
THE OFFICER: Who are you?
VARLAAM AND MISSAIL: (*they are frightened and answer humbly*). Poor friars and humble churchmen . . . Collecting alms throughout the land.
THE OFFICER: (*to Grigory*). And you? . . . who are you?
VARLAAM AND MISSAIL: He is a comrade.
GRIGORY: (*with studied indifference*). I live near the great town . . . I accompany these monks . . . And shall return home after . . .
THE OFFICER: (*to the bowmen*). Nothing to be gained from the youth! We'll try the monks . . . Ahem! (*Coughing*) (*He approaches the table.*) Well, fathers, how did the begging fare?

VARLAAM: Oh! . . . Badly, my son . . . badly! The faithful love their gold . . . They hoard it . . . they hide it . . . And nothing for the Lord! . . . Great is the injustice! And iniquity triumphs . . . Beg and beg . . . pray and pray . . . But with nothing they part, Not even a paltry Kopek! We, in sorrow, seek the inn! Oh indeed! . . . it is the end of the world! Truly the end! . . .
INNKEEPER: (*almost imploring the officer*). Good sir, have pity on your servant.
VARLAAM: (*as the officer scrutinizes his face*). Oh, speak out . . . why inspect me so closely?
THE OFFICER: Here, Aliokha, give me the edict, you have it. (*He takes the paper. Then to Varlaam.*) Now read: A heretic has escaped from Moscow, Grishka Otre-

Or leggi.
Da Mosca un erètico fuggì, Grichka Otrepiev.
Di . . . non sei tu?
VARLAAM: (*umilmente*). Ignoro . . .
L'UFFIZIALE: Hum! Lo Zar ordinò d'arrestarlo Vivo o morto . . . Non comprendi ancor?
VARLAAM: No, figliuol.
L'UFFIZIALE: E sai tu legger?
VARLAAM: No, figliuol, Iddio non m'insegnò!
L'UFFIZIALE: Allor, i'editto guarda.
VARLAAM: (*respingendolo*). Ma che vuoi tu?
L'UFFIZIALE: Ebben . . . l'erètico, il ladron sei tu!
VARLAAM: Olà! quest'è un error, messer!
OSTESSA: (*a parte*). O, Signor! . . . imboscano persino gli eremiti.
L'UFFIZIALE: Eh? Chi di voi sa legger?
GRIGORI: (*avvicinandosi all'Uffiziale*). Io . . . se tu vuoi.
L'UFFIZIALE: Stà ben. Leggi allor lentamente. (*dandogli l'editto.*)
GRIGORI: (*leggendo*). "Dal convento del Miracolo, un indegno novizio, Grigori, detto Grichka Otrepiev, tentato dallo spirito maligno, osò turbar i santi religiosi, con sacrilegi ed empie seduzioni. Il brigante evase in Lituania. Lo zar ordina d'impadronirsi" . . .
L'UFFIZIALE: Ed impiccarlo!
GRIGORI: Ma non è scritto ciò . . .
L'UFFIZIALE: Tu menti. Il senso bisogna capir. Leggi: "arrestar e impiccarlo."
GRIGORI: "E impiccarlo . . . l'età sua . . . (*guardando Varlaam*) l'età sua . . . cinquant'anni . . . barba tutta bianca . . . ventre tondo . . . e naso rosso . . ."
L'UFFIZIALE: (*agli arcieri*). A voi . . . è lui! legatel bene!
VARLAAM: (*tutti si slanciano su Varlaam, che li respinge bruscamente*). Alt! (*stringe i pugni, pronto a baitersi*) Restate quieti . . . cattivi figliuoli . . . son tutte istorie . . . queste . . . Un ladro io? . . . io . . . Grichka?! Alt! No, basta la burla . . . bench'io legga appena . . . conosco ben le lettere . . . e leggerò . . . leggerò trattandosi della for ca . . . (*legge sillabando*) "E l'e . . . e

piev.
Are you he? . . . Answer! . . .
VARLAAM: I know not . . .
THE OFFICER: Humph! The Tzar orders his arrest Alive or dead . . . Do you not understand?
VARLAAM: No, my son.
THE OFFICER: Do you know how to read?
VARLAAM: No, son, God taught me not!
THE OFFICER: Then, look at the edict.
VARLAAM: (*repulsing him*). But what do you want?
THE OFFICER: Well . . . the heretic, the thief, it is you!
VARLAAM: Heydey! a mistake, master!
INNKEEPER: O, Lord! . . . they even entrap the hermits.
THE OFFICER: Hey? Which of you can read?
GRIGORY: (*approaching the officer*). I . . . if you wish.
THE OFFICER: (*handing him the edict*). It is well. Then read slowly.
GRIGORY: (*reading*). "In the convent of Miracles, a worthless novice, Grigory, by name Grishka Otrepiev, tempted by the evil spirit, dared perturb the holy men of God, with sacrilegious and wicked allurements. The brigand escaped into Lithuania . . . The Tzar orders that he be captured . . ."
THE OFFICER: And hung!
GRIGORY: But it does not say so here . . .
THE OFFICER: You lie . . . The sense must be understood. Read: "arrest him and hang him."
GRIGORY: "And hang him . . . his age . . . (*looking at Varlaam*) his age . . . fifty years . . . beard completely white . . . round of paunch . . . a red nose . . ."
THE OFFICER: (*to the bowmen*). Here you . . . it is he! bind him fast! (*All hurl themselves upon Varlaam who repulses them violently.*)
VARLAAM: Halt! (*he clinches his fists, prepared to fight*). Keep back . . . evil brood . . . these are all lies . . . these . . . I, a thief? . . . I . . . Grishka? Stand! Enough of this farce . . . even if I can scarcely read . . . letters I know well . . . and I will read . . . because of the gallows I will read . . . (*he reads by syllables*) "And his a . . . a . . age, his age . . . twenty years"—Twenty and

...tà...e l'età sua...vent'anni
..." Venti e non cinquanta?...
Vedi tu?!...(*Grigori rincula fino alla porta, colla mano destra sotto la giubba*) "di taglia media...capelli rossastri...sul naso...un porro...alla fronte idem...ed il braccio sinistro...più corto del destro..." (*avvicinandosi furtivamente a Grigorì*). Ma Grichka sei tu! (*Grigori agita il coltello e fugge dalla finestra.*)

**TUTTI:** (*colpiti, pietrificati dallo stupore*). E lui! fermate...arrestate!...
(*Passato il momento di stupore, corrono tutti alla porta e continuano a gridare nelle quinte.*)
Fermate il ladron! l'arrestate!...
(*Cala la tela.*)

## SCENA II.

*Gli appartamenti del Zar Boris al Kremlino a Mosca. A sinistra un globo terrestre su d'una piccola tavola, alla quale Teodoro è seduto, leggendo "Il Libro del Gran Disegno". A destra, un tavolo da lavoro, accanto al quale siede Xenia. Vicino ad essa, su d'uno sgabello, lavora la Nutrice. Verso il proscenio un'ampia poltrona. Di fronte un orologio a carillon e a figure movibili.*

**XENIA:** (*stringendo fra le mani un medaglione, col ritratto del suo fidanzato, piange*). Oh!...egli morì...
E là sotterra, riposa il mio ben...
Lontan dalla sua Xenia!...
Tu dormi dol, sotto la fredda pietra,
E non vedi 'l mio strazio...non odi i miei lai!
I lai di chi t'ama, e langue per te!
...

**LA NUTRICE:** Basta!...Cessa, mia graziosa Zarevna.
Non painger più...tergi le ciglia
...

**XENIA:** Il cor si spezza, e soffro tanto!...

**LA NUTRICE:** Ti calma, o cara.
Lagrime di fidanzati
Le asciuga il sol come la brina.
La terra è così vasta. Un bel garzon,
Snello e gentil, conoscerai,
E quello che morì tu scorderai!

**XENIA:** No, mia nutrice,
No! l'amo ancor, e sempre l'amerò.

**LA NUTRICE:** E che? L'hai visto appena, e vuoi morir per lui?
Languiva una donzella
Perchè amava un bel garzon...
Ma quel furbo si celò.
E anche lei si consolò.

---

not fifty?...Do you see?!...(*Grigory retreats to the door, his right hand under his blouse*); "of middle height...reddish hair...on the nose...on the nose...a wart...on the forehead ditto...and the left arm...shorter than the right..."
(*approaching Grigory stealthily*) You are Grishka! (*Grigory brandishing a knife escapes by the window.*)

**ALL:** (*stricken motionless by surprise*). It is he! stop him!...seize him!...
(*Recovering from their surprise all rush to the door and continue their shouts from behind the scenes.*)
Stop the thief! arrest him!...
(*Curtain.*)

## SCENE II.

*Apartments of the Tzar in the Kremlin at Moscow. At left a terrestrial globe, on a small table at which Theodore sits, reading "The Book of the Great Drawing." At right, a worktable, beside which Xenia is seated. Close by her, on a stool, the nurse is busy at work. Near front of stage a large arm-chair. At rear a musical clock, with automatic figures.*

**XENIA:** (*holding a medallion protrait of her betrothed; weeping*). Oh!...he died...
Beneath the sod rests my beloved
...
Far from his Xenia!...
You sleep alone, under the cold stone,
And do not see my pangs...nor hear my grieving!
The grief of her who loves you and who languishes for you!

**THE NURSE:** Enough!...Come, my graceful Tzarevna.
Weep no more...Dry your lashes
...

**XENIA:** My heart is breaking and I suffer.

**THE NURSE:** Calm yourself, dear one,
Tears of those betrothed
By the sun are dried like frost.
So vast the earth, some handsome youth,
Gentle and slender, you shall know,
And the one that died you shall forget!

**XENIA:** No, my nurse, No! I love him still and always shall.

**THE NURSE:** What? you scarcely saw him and will die for him!
Once a maiden languished
Because she loved a handsome lad.
But the artful rogue vanished.
Yet even she consoled herself.

---

O, colomba, scaccia la tristezza,
E non pensarci più.
Senti la mia canzon:
(*S'avvicina a Xenia.*)
Un moscon legna tagliava,
E pei re l'acqua tirava.
La pulce saltellante
Gli faceva da aiutante.
Plan! Guinge un farfallon,
Nel giardin del Pope Illon—
Ei comincia a svolazzar
Ed il fieno a mangiucchiar—
S'arrabbia il moscon
Con far da padron,
E prende un ramoscel
Per scacciare quel ribel.
Sventura pel moscon...
Lancia male il suo baston,
E le reni si spezzò,
Mentre l'altro via volò!
Ma in suo soccorso, lesta,
Corse la pulce mesta...
Sul dorso gli saltò
E con slancio l'aiutò.
La piccina si svenò
E al moscon si confessò
Che per lei ella spirò...
Ed in ciel se ne volò!

**TEODORO:** Oh, com'è strana la tua canzon...
Dopo le nozze, tu suoni a morto?
...

**LA NUTRICE:** Mio Zarevic,
Ne sai tu, dunque, delle più gaie?
Pazienza avrò con te. Ivan, lo Zar terribile,
Ce ne diede lezion quando regnò.
Canta—

**TEODORO:** O, cara, io t'assicuro ...tu canterai con me!
(*Teodoro incita la Nutrice a giuocare—Girano in tondo e, battendo le mani, cercano d'essere i primi a darsi un colpo.*)
Odi la fola: ò bella.
Una gallina fece una vitella...
E fece un uovo il porcellin.
Seria novella
Pe' sciocchi e pe' bambin.
(*si alza, si colloca rimpetto alla Nutrice e, mentre canta, batte le mani, un colpo per ogni battuta di musica.*)
Tu—ru, tu—ru, mio pulcin,
Dove porti tu quel gran?
Certamente ben lontan...
A Kieff te n'andrai
E sull'alber volerai...
Ma là un gufo troverai.

**TEODORO E LA NUTRICE:** S'ei fa l'occhiolin
Quì svolazza l'uccellin...
Zin zin, biricchin!
Facciam insiem zin zin...
Contenti danziam,
Orsù tutti invitiam,
Danzar noi vogliam.

---

O, dispel your sorrow, my dove,
And think no more of it.
Listen to my song!
(*Approaching Xenia.*)
A big fly was cutting wood
And drawing water for the king.
A jumping flea assisted him.
Then softly came a butterfly,
From out Pope Illon's garden.
Fluttering about he flew
And munched the hay as he did...
The big fly angry grows,
With lordly mien,
He takes a little twig
To chase the rebel.
Disaster for the big fly, though...
His stick he badly throws
And broken is his back,
While the other flew away!
But nimble to his succor
Ran the grieving little fly,
Jumped upon his back
And helped him ardently.
The little one bled soon to death,
Confessing to the bigger fly
That she died for him.
Then she flew away to heaven!

**THEODORE:** Oh, how funny is your song...
After the wedding you toll the bells.

**THE NURSE:** My Tzarovitch, you Know then some gayer ones?
Patience I shall have for you, Ivan the terrible Tzar
This lesson taught us when he ruled.
Sing—

**THEODORE:** Oh, I assure you, dear ...you shall sing with me!
(*Theodore urges the Nurse to play. They move around in a circle, clapping their hands, each trying to strike the other first.*)
Hear this fable; it is rich.
A hen bore a calf...
And the little pig laid an egg.
A serious novel
For children and ninnies.
(*He gets up, places himself before the nurse, and as he sings claps his hands, a stroke for every measure of the music.*)
Too — roo, too — roo, my chick,
Where do you take that grain,
To a distance surely...
To Kiev you shall go
And fly on the tree...
But there you will find an owl.

**THEODORE AND THE NURSE:** He winks his eye.
Here flutters the bird...
Zin, zin, urchin,
Let's say together: Zin, zin...
And contentedly dance,
Come now, all we invite,
We will dance!

TEODORO: Del diacon, nel cortil,
È rinchiuso un passerin . . .
Un nibbio ei non è; ma un uccellin
gentil . . .
Ha il becco lungo, bianco, ed è ca-
rin.—
Per visitar l'amico egli partì.

LA NUTRICE E TEODORO: (*si
congiungono a poco a poco*). E il
gufo gli disse pian pian:
"Il gran, falciato si batte ogni dì . . .
Il diacono e sua moglie, or or si bat-
teran!"
Il fuoco al grano s'appiccò
E 'l diacon s'arrabbiò.
Invaso dal terror
Nel granaio penetrò,
Con l'ansia in fondo al cor . . .
Ma le orecchia si scottò! . . .

TEODORO: Per il festin
I bei pasticcin.
Arrivano i signor;
Son già sul piatto d'or.
Gli arcier, giunti da lontan,
Mangion, bevon . . . con baccon!
Una vacca ed un bue si mangia
l'uffizial
E seicento fagian,
Per saziar l'epa infernal! Khliost!

(*Dà un colpo alla Nutrice.*)

LA NUTRICE: (*scorge Boris e lo
saluta a bassa voce.*) Ah!
Mio sovran, perdona.
Io vecchia son e tanto timorosa . . .

BORIS: (*a Xenia*). Mia Xenia! O,
povera colomba!
Appena fidanzata, e già vedova! . . .
Tu piangi sempre . . . senza tregua?

XENIA: O, Sovrano, che l'amar mio
pianto
Non ti rattristi.
Il mio dolor è ben sì poca cosa,
Di fronte al tuo soffrir.

BORIS: (*accarezzando i capelli di
sua figlia*). Oh, figlia mia! o, mia
colomba!
Raggiungi nel terem le tue com-
pagne.
Distrar ti dei . . . ti dei divertir.
(*Xenia e la Nutrice escono—
Boris segue sua figlia, affettuosa-
mente, collo sguardo triste.*)
Va, figlia mia!
(*A Teodoro.*)
E tu, figliuol che leggi?
Un atlante?

THEODORE: In the deacon's yard
A little sparrow is engaged.
Not a hawk he is; but a gentle fledg-
ling . . . With a long, white bill, and
he's a dear.
To visit a friend he went away.

THE NURSE AND THEODORE:
(*they come closer by degrees*).
And the owl said softly, softly:
"The great harvest is threshed every
day . . .
The deacon and his wife, each other
will thrash very soon."
The grain took fire,
The deacon grew angry,
Attacked by terror,
He went into the granary,
Rage deep in his heart.
But his ears got scorched.

THEODORE: To the banquet set
The lords arrive;
Nice little cakes
Are ready on golden plates.
The bowmen, who come from afar,
Eat and drink . . . with uproar!
A cow and an ox the officer eats,
And pheasants six hundred too,
To fill his great big paunch!
Khliost! . . .
(*He gives the Nurse a tap.*)

THE NURSE: (*catching sight of
Boris and greeting him in a low
voice*).
Ah!
My Sovereign, forgive me.
I am an old woman and timorous . . .

BORIS: (*to the Nurse*). What's
that? A great hawk threatens the little ones?

THE NURSE: My Sovereign, forgive
me.
I am an old woman and timorous
. . .

BORIS: (*to Xenia*). Oh, my daughter! my dove! . . .
Scarcely betrothed, and yet a widow!
You weep constantly . . . no truce
to your grief?

XENIA: Oh, my Sovereign, let not
my bitter weeping
Distress you.
So small a thing is my pain
Compared with your grief.

BORIS: (*stroking his daughter's
hair*). Oh, my daughter! my dove!
. . .
Go join your girlfriends in the ter-
em:
You must divert yourself . . . amuse
yourself.
(*Xenia and the Nurse go out.
Boris looks affectionately but sad-
ly at his daughter.*)
Go, my daughter!
(*to Theodore*)
And you, what are you reading, my
son —
An atlas?

TEODORO: La carta di Moscovia,
Da un punto all'altro il Regno.
Guarda: là Mosca e Novgorod,
Quì Kazàn, Astrakàn . . .
Ed il Mar Caspio.
Poi di Perm le folte boscaglie
E laggiù . . . la Siberia!

BORIS: Sì . . si . . . sta ben, figliuol.
D'un batter d'occhio, come
dall'alto,
Tu puoi contemplar l'intero regno.
Frontiere, fiumi e città . . .
Impara ben. Verrà un giorno . . .
Chi lo sa . . ., ben presto,
Un dì t'apparterrà tutto l'imper.
Studia, fanciul!
(*Si dirige verso la poltrona—
Prende delle pergamene, che si
trovano sulla tavola, e le scorre
distrattamente.*)
Ho il poter supremo!
Da cinque anni già, stringo lo scet-
tro,
E l'alma cerca ognor la dolce tre-
gua.
Invan tutti i maghi mi predisser,
Un regno lungo, savio e tranquil . . .
Ahimè! più nulla non mi seduce!
Nè gloria nè gli evviva . . .
Più nulla, mi può sedur!
(*Inclina il capo pensoso.*)
Nella famiglia, invan cercai la gioia
. . .
Io preparai le nozze di mia figlia,
Della mia Xenia, la pura colomba
. . .
Il suo fidanzato morì!
La man implacable di Dio pesò
Sull'alma mia nefanda,
E l'avvenir m'appar sì tetro,
Senza più traccia di speme!
Il cor si spezza e soffre . . .
L'anima mia s'esalta . . .
Io tremo . . . io fremo . . .
E pavento sventure! . . .
Per soffocar gli atroci rimorsi
Ai Santi innalzai le preci mie.
Nel fulgor del mio grande poter il-
limitato,
Io, Zar di Russia, mendicai il pianto
che consola!
Maledizione! Tutti cospiran . . .
Ovenque insidie . . . e mine mister-
iose . . .
Grandi flagel . . .e peste e carestia!
Come animal gli affamati accres-
con,
E 'l Regno inter piange e soffre!
Di questi mali orrendi, di cui il
Cielo
Pel mio delitto, su me pesò,
Il popol me solo accusa!
E 'l nome sacro di Boris
L'esecran tutti!
Da me 'l sonno sfuggì . . . e nelle
tenebre,
L'insanguinato fanciul chiede pie-
tà!
Gli occhi atterriti . . . colle manine
Invocar grazia . . .
Ma non ottenne grazia! . . .
Vedo ancor la piaga orrenda . . .
Sento 'l rantol d'agonia . . .
(*Cade accasciato sulla poltrona.*)

THEODORE: The map of Moscow,
From one end of the realm to the
other,
See: there Moscow and Novgorod,
Here Kazan, Astrakan . . .
And the Caspian Sea.
The Perm's thick woods . . .
And yonder . . . Siberia!

BORIS: Yes . . . yes . . . It is well, my
son.
At a glance, as from above,
The entire realm you may contemp-
late,
Frontiers, rivers and towns . . .
Note them well . . . It may happen
some day . . .
Who knows? . . . it may be soon,
All the Empire belongs to you!
Study, my boy.
(*He walks towards the armchair,
picks up some papers on the table
and scans them distractedly.*)
I have the supreme power!
For five years I have held the scep-
ter.
And my soul still seeks sweet
peace.
The magicians in vain foretold me:
"A long, wise and tranquil reign"
. . .
Alas! Nothing attracts me more!
Nor glory nor applause . . .
Nothing can seduce me now!
(*bowing his head thoughtfully*)
Within my family I've sought in
vain for joy . . .
I prepared my daughter's nuptials
. . .
My Xenia's, my pure dove . . .
Her lover died!
God's implacable hand weighed
Over this nefarious soul of mine,
And the future appears so dark,
With no trace of hope!
My heart is rent and grievous . . .
My soul is vexed . . .
I tremble . . . I fret . . .
And disasters fear! . . .
To smother my atrocious remorses
I raised my prayers to the Saints.
Amid the splendor of my boundless
power,
I, Tzar of Russia, for soothing tears
implored!
Curses! All conspire . . .
Plots everywhere . . . and mysteri-
ous mines . . .
Great scourges . . . and pest and fa-
mine!
Like beasts, the famished multiply,
And the whole realm weeps and
suffers!
These awful ills that Heaven,
For my crime, sends down on me,
My people ascribe to me alone!
And Boris's sacred name
Is loathed by all!
Sleep has flown from me . . . and in
the dark,
That bleeding boy cries out for pity!
With looks terrified . . . with his lit-
tle hands
He pleads for mercy . . .
But he obtained no mercy! . . .
I still see the ghastly wound . . .

Oh, dio! abbi pietà di me!

LE NUTRICI: (*nelle quinte*). Ei! Pst! Ei! Pst! Pst! Ei . . . Ei! . . .

BORIS: Qual frastuono! (*A suo figlio.*) Va a veder che cos'è ciò!

LE NUTRICI: (*nelle quinte*). Pst! Pst!

BORIS: (*al Boiardo della Corte, che entra.*) Ah: che rumor . . . Che vuoi tu?

LE NUTRICI: (*nelle quinte*). Pst! Pst! Pst! Ehi! . . . Ma fa mal! . . . Pst! Pst!

BORIS: Parla, alfin!

IL BOYARDO DELLA CORTE: Mio nobile Sovran, Verso te viene il Prence Chouïsky Tutt'umil . . .

BORIS: Chouïsky? Può entrar, (*Con ironia*) Felice io sono di vedere il Prence . . . M'alletta l'ascoltar . . .

IL BOIARDO DELLA CORTE: (*a bassa voce, all'orecchio di Boris*). Ier sera venne un servo di Pouchkine, Der denunziar Mstislawski, il Prence, Ed altri boiardi— Questa notte si videro in secreto . . . Da Cracovia giunse un corrier con . . .

BORIS: (*interrompendolo*). S'arresti! (*Il boiardo esce.*) Sì . . . Prence Chouïsky! (*A Teodoro che entra.*) Ebben?

TEODORO: O, padre mio, Sovran Io non so se deggio turbar Lo spirto tuo per una celia . . .

BORIS: Sì, sì, fanciul, racconta . . . dimmi tutto . . . (*Accarezza suo figlio.*)

TEODORO: (*si siede sulle ginocchia di Boris*). Il nostro pappagal Popignka, faceva il ciarlon Colle nutrici, che di lui ridevan, E dava a loro il picciol capo Chiedendo le carezze e i pasticcin

La nutrice Nastia gli rifiutò i suoi baci. Popignka s'irritò e "sciocca" la chiamò. La balia, arrabbiata, lo prese pel collo . . . Popignka, grindando, drizzò le sue piume . . . Le donne lo calman, gli danno de dolci, E poi, tutte in coro, gli chiedon perdon.

---

I still hear the death rattle of agony

(*He falls crushed into the armchair*) Oh, God! have pity on me!

THE NURSES: (*from behind the scenes*). Hey! Pst! Hey! Pst! Pst! Hey! Hey!

BORIS: (*to his son*). What an uproar! Go see what it is.

THE NURSES: (*from behind the scenes*). Pst! Pst!

BORIS: (*to the Court Boyar who enters*). Ah! what a noise! . . . What do you want?

THE NURSES: (*from behind the scenes*). Pst! Pst! Pst! Hey! . . . But he hurts! . . . Pst! Pst!

BORIS: Speak!

THE COURT BOYAR: My noble Sovereign, Prince Shouisky comes to you, Most humbly . . .

BORIS: Shouisky? Let him enter, (*with irony*) I am glad to see the Prince . . . I like to hear him . . .

THE COURT BOYAR: (*whispering in Boris's ear*). Came last night a servant of Pouchine, To denounce Prince Mstislawsky And other Boyars — Tonight they met secretly . . . A courier has arrived from Cracow with . . .

BORIS: (*interrupting*) Let him be arrested! (*The Boyar goes out.*) Yes . . . Prince Shouisky! (*To Theodore who enters.*) Well?

THEODORE: O, my father, my Sovereign . . . I know not if I should trouble Your mind with a trifling matter . . .

BORIS: Yes, yes, my boy, speak . . . tell me all . . . (*Fondles his son.*)

THEODORE: (*seating himself on Boris's knees*). Our parrot Popignka was chattering With the nurses, who made sport of him; He held out to them his little head Begging caresses and cakes . . . The nurse, Nastia, refused him her kisses. Popignka, much provoked, called her 'silly'. In anger the nurse caught him by the neck . . . Shrieking, Popignka bristled his feathers . . . Then the women to soothe him, gave him sweets, And all in chorus asked his pardon. But no . . . Popka is unrelenting . . .

---

Ma no . . . Popka non vuol . . . Imbronciato cela il becco sotto l'ala . . . Sgrida la nutrice, poi l'ingiuria, E a tradimento, piomba sulla donna . . . E si mette a beccar . . . e la vuol atterrar. S'allarmano le altre e, con paura, Gridan, cercando farlo entrar ne la gabbia. Popka più fier . . . volle tutte beccar. Sì, mio Sovran, da ciò venne il baccan! Fu Popka che turbò i gravi tuoi pensier. Sì . . . tutto dissi, o nobil padre mio!

BORIS: (*accarezza suo figlio con grande amore*). Oh, figlio! figliuol sì caro al mio cuor! con qual'arte e con qual grazia M'hai tutto raccontato. Oh, come tu sai bene, senz'orpel, Dettagliare un fatto sì banal. La tua saggezza appar ed i tuoi studï. La scienza coltiva. Oh, se avessi la gran gioia Di vederti regnar, Di saperti Zar di Russia! Oh, come tosto, Sdegnando il mondó inter, Per questo gaudio Ti darei lo scettro grave! . . .

CHOUÏSKY: (*entrando*). Salve! o, nobil Sovran!

BORIS: (*al Principe Chouïsky*). Ah, glorioso ciarlatan, Ed abil condottier d'insana folla . . . Capo ribel dei boiardi infedel, Nemico del trono, dello Zar, Vil mentitor, tre volte spergiur, Adulator, ipocrita, Fabbricator d'ostia, vestito da boiardo, . . . Buffon!

CHOUÏSKY: Zar, è grave . . . Apporto nuove che ti turberan . . .

BORIS: Parli delle azion d'antichi amici tuoi Tutti in disgrazia, Che il segreto corrier ti fe' conoscer?

CHOUÏSKY: Sì, Sovran. Un impostor si fa credere Zar. Il Re, il papa, credon tutti a lui.

BORIS: (*turbato, si solleva dalla poltrona*). Ma sotto qual nome, si cela il traditor? Qual nome assume l'impostor? Qual nome?! . . .

CHOUÏsky: Il tuo trono, Zar, è incrollabil. Pei tuoi favor, pel zel, per il tuo core,

---

Under his wing he sulkily hides his beak. He scolds the nurse, then abuses her, And swoops down treacherously on the woman . . . Pecking at her, bearing her down . . . The others in alarm, with frightened cries, Try to lure him to his cage. Popka, with increasing fury, tries all to bite. Yes, my Sovereign, this caused the bustle! Popka it was who disturbed your serious thoughts. Yes . . . that is all, my noble father!

BORIS: (*caressing his son with intense feeling*). Oh, son! my son, beloved of my heart! With what art and grace You have related all. How well you know, without artifice, To tell minutely this simple fact. Your wisdom is seen and your studies. Knowledge seek and cherish. Oh, could I but know the joy Of seeing you wisely rule, As Russia's Tzar! Oh, how readily, Scorning the entire world, For this one happiness I would yield to you the weighty scepter! . . .

SHOUIKY: (*entering*). Hail, noble Sovereign!

BORIS: (*to Prince Shouisky*). Ah, glorious charlatan, And able leader of a crazy crowd . . . Rebellious chief of faithless Boyars, Enemy of the throne and of the Tzar, Base liar, thrice a perjurer, Hypocritical flatterer; Baker of wafers, dressed-up Boyer . . . Buffoon!

SHOUISKY: Tzar, it is grave . . . I bear news that shall trouble you . . .

BORIS: The deeds of your old friends you mean . . . All in disgrace, Who did the secret messenger disclosed to you?

SHOUISKY: Yes, my Sovereign; An impostor claims to be the Tzar. The King, the Pope, all believe in him.

BORIS: (*disturbed, rises from the armchair*). But under what name does the traitor hide? What name assumes the impostor? What name? . . .

SHOUISKY: Your throne, Tzar, is unshaken. By your favors, your zeal and your heart

Conquidere sai tu l'alma di tutti,
E son devoti alla tua maestà!
Ma bench'io soffra, Zar, o nobil mio sovran,
Benchè tutt'il mio cor si schianti dal dolor,
Per certo io tacer non oserò,
Che se il mariuol, contando sull'audacia,
Arriva a penetrar nel Regno tuo,
Verso Dimitri il popol correrà,
Sedotto da quel nom, ch'egli risorge! . . .

**BORIS:** (*con terrore*). Dimitri!
(*A suo figlio*)
Ci lascia, zarevic . . .

**TEODORO:** O, Sovran, permettimi ch'io resti presso te.
Conoscer vo' il periglio che mina il tuo poter!

**BORIS:** Oh, no . . . no . . . mio figliuol! . . .
Zarevic, Zarevic, devi obbedir!
(*Boris conduce suo figlio, poi chiude la porta e ritorna a Chouïsky.*)
Noi tosto agirem—
Che il Regno sia cinto di barriere,
E sott'alcun pretesto, niun varcherà le mura.
Agisci.
(*Ferdinando Chouïsky, che stà per uscire.*)
No . . . attendi ancor . . . Chouïsky.
Hai tu, per caso, inteso dir
Che dei fanciulli uccisi, sorgan dal loro avel
Per conturbar gli Zar? Gli Zar leggittimi,
Eletti dal popolo?! . . .
Zar, consacrati dal gran patriarca?! . . .
(*Scoppia a ridere di un riso selvaggio*)
Ah, ah, ah, ah, ah, ah! . . .
Di . . . ridi?! . . .
(*Afferrando Chouïsky pel collo*). Ah! no ridi più . . . eh?! . . .

**CHOUÏSKY:** Perdona, Zar, potente sovran . . .

**BORIS:** Prence, dimmi: il dì che si compì
L'empio delitto; quand'il fanciul . . .
Perì tragicamente . . .
Dimmi: il fanciul . . . era ben . . . era Dimitri?

**CHOUÏSKY:** Sì!

**BORIS:** Vassili Ivanovitch,
Per il Cristo divin,
Io ti scongiuro, mi svela tutto quel che sai!
Io son buon . . . tu lo sai ben . . .
Ma se ti vuoi celar . . . oh, guai a te! . . .
Inventerò un martir così crudel
Ch'Ivan istesso, trasaliria d'orror
Ne la sua tomba! . . . Rispondi a me! . . .

**CHOUÏSKY:** La tua disgrazia io temo e non la morte!
Nel tempio d'Ouglitch, dinanzi al popol,

To conquer the soul of all you know;
All are devoted to your majesty!
But even should I suffer, Tzar, my sovereign,
Even should my heart burst with aching,
I dare not keep silent now.
If that knave set food within your realm,
Towards Dimitri all will hasten,
Led by that name which he revives.

**BORIS:** (*in terror*). Dimitri!
(*To his son*)
Leave us, Tzarevitch . . .

**THEODORE:** Oh, Sovereign, let me remain near you,
I would know the dangers which menace your power!

**BORIS:** Oh, no . . . no . . . my son!
. . .
Tzarevitch, Tzarevitch, you must obey me!
(*Boris leads away his son, then closing the door, he returns to Shouisky.*)
We shall act at once . . .
Let the entire realm be guarded,
Under no pretext must a single person pass the walls.
See to it.
(*Stopping Shouisky*)
No . . . wait . . . Shouisky.
Have you, perhaps, heard it said
That murdered boys from their graves would rise
To harass the Tzars? The rightful Tzars,
By the people elected?! . . .
Tzars anointed by the great Patriarch?! . . .
(*He bursts into wild laughter*)
Ah, ah, ah, ah, ah, ah! . . .
Say . . . . you laugh?! . . . .
(*Grasping Shouisky by the neck*)
Ah! you laugh no more . . . eh?! . . .

**SHOUISKY:** Pardon, Tzar, powerful Sovereign . . .

**BORIS:** Prince, tell me: the day which saw
That frightful crime committed; when the boy . . .
Perished so tragically . . .
Tell me: the boy . . . was surely . . . Dimitri?

**SHOUISKY:** Yes!

**BORIS:** Vassili Ivanovitch,
By Christ Divine,
I beg you, tell me all you know!
I am good . . . you know well . . .
But if you seek to conceal . . . Oh, woe to you!
I will invent a torment so cruel
That Ivan himself would shrink in horror
Within his grave! . . . Answer me!

**SHOUISKY:** I fear your displeasure, not death!
In the church of Uglitch, before the people,

A lungo contemplai quel piccol morto.
Intorno a lui giacean ben trenta corpi
Informi e orrendi . . . sangue e poltiglia . . .
E da quei corpi sprigionava il lezzo!
Ma il viso del figliuo! del Zar Ivan,
Era intatto . . .
Intorno al collo una piaga rossastra . . .
E su le labbra ancor si disegnava
Il sorriso gentil d'un cherubin . . .
Parea dormir placidamente,
Stanco, nella sua culla, le braccia in croce,
Stringendo nella man un ninnolo infantil!

**BORIS:** Oh! . . . oh . . . taci!
(*Fa segno a Chouisky di allontanarsi. Il Principe esce, gettando uno sguardo furtivo a Boris. Lo Zar ricade, accasciato, sulla poltrona.*)
Oh, soffocai! . . . il respir mi mancò
Com'onde agitate, il sangue
Battè le tempia, senza cessa . . .
Oh, fragil coscienza! tu vuoi l'espiazion! . . .
(*La scena s'oscura; la pendola suona.*)
Sì, basta . . . lo so . . . lo so . . . basta
Ch'una piccola macchia l'offuschi
E l'alma s'infiamma . . .
E 'l cor s'empie di pena!
Io soffro tutte le morti! . . .
Ed il rimorso, come un martel,
Ognor batte al mio cervel . . .
La strozza si serra . . . si serra . . .
La ragion perdo . . . vacilla . . .
Vedo il fanciul . . . di sangue intriso . . .
Là . . . laggiù . . . chi muovesi colà?!
. . .
Ei vien verso me . . . ancor . . .
Ei trasal . . . geme . . . ed implora . . .
Va . . . va . . . va via! . . .
(*Scaccia lo spettro*)
Non son'io . . . no . . . l'assassin! . . .
No, no, fanciul! . . . non io . . . non io . . .
Ma il popol fu . . .
Va . . . fanciul!
(*Nasconde il volto fra le mani e, affranto, cade in ginocchio innanzi alla poltrona, quasi biascicasse un'o razione.*)
O, Signor! . . . abbi tu pietà del peccator . . .
Proteggi di Boris l'alma colpevol!
(*Cala la tela.*)

*FINE DELL'ATTO SECONDO.*

Long I gazed upon that tiny corpse;
Around him lay fully thirty bodies,
Shapeless and ghastly . . . blood and mire . . .
And from those bodies the stench released itself!
But the face of Tzar Ivan's son
Was undisfigured . . .
Around the neck a reddish wound . . .
And the lips still bore
The gentle smile as of a cherub . . .
He seemed to slumber placidly,
tired out, in his cradle, his arms crossed,
Holding a childish toy in his hands!

**BORIS:** Oh! . . . oh . . . no more!
(*He bids Shouisky retire. The Prince goes out, casting a furtive glance at Boris. The Tzar drops again into the armchair, crushed.*)
Oh, I choked . . . breath failed me
As though the blood, like tossing waves,
Throbbed at my temples endlessly . . .
Oh, frail conscience! you claim atonement! . . .
(*The scene darkens, the clock strikes.*)
Yes, enough . . . I know it . . . I know enough!
For a little stain to tarnish it;
And my soul seethes within me . . .
And my heart is filled with pain! . . .
I suffer all deaths.
And remorse, like a hammer,
Beats ever on my brain . . .
The throttle closes . . . closes . . .
My reason I am losing . . . it totters . . .
I behold the boy . . . bathed in blood . . .
There . . . yonder . . . Who stirs there!? . . .
He approaches me . . . again
He shudders . . . groans . . . and implores . . .
Go . . . Go . . . get away from here!
(*Chasing the specter*)
I am not . . . not . . . the assassin!
No, no, boy . . . not I . . . not I . . .
But the people were . . . Go . . . boy!
(*He conceals his face in his hands and, broken, drops on his knees before the armchair, as if mumbling a prayer.*)
O Lord . . . have mercy on the sinner . . .
Protect the guilty soul of Boris!
(*Curtain.*)

*END OF ACT TWO.*

# ■ ATTO III.

## SCENA I.

*I castello di Mnichek. Un giardino. Una fontana. La scena è rischiarata dai raggi della luna.*

**IL FALSO DIMITRI:** (*esce dal Castello, quasi sognando*). "Stasera alla fontana". Voce divina! De qual delizia mi sogghioghi l'alma!
(*S'avvicina alla fontana*)
Verrai tu, al mio dolce appel? Ah! sei tu del mio cor tutta la speme! . . .
No . . . non scordar colui che tanto ti ama . . .
Tu vedi le sue pene, e 'l suo soffrir
. . .
Deh, vieni a consolar la mia tristezza,
Col tuo sorriso angelico e divino
. . .
Marina! Marina!
Rispondi . . . oh . . . rispondi!
Oh, vien . . . vien . . . io t'attendo!

T'attendo quì. Rispondi . . . Son'io che ti chiamo . . .
No . . . non v'è alcun! . . .

**RANGONI:** Zarevic!

**DIMITRI:** Ancor tu?!
L'ombra mia che mi persegue!

**RANGONI:** Augusto e valoroso Zarevic,
Son quì, perchè m'inviò mia figlia Marina.

**DIMITRI:** Marina?

**RANGONI:** La figlia spirituale che Dio mi diè.
Desidera sappiate
Che un malesser la tormenta,
Causato dall'amor che la strugge
. . .
E ch'ella quì verrà.

**DIMITRI:** Oh, se il vero tu dicessi
. . .
Oh, se Satàn non fosse,
Che t'inspira questi detti . . .
Con me io condurrei la mia colomba in Russia,
Con me l'innalzerei al tron dei Zar,
Offuscando il mondo inter col suo splendor.
Vil diavol!
Il fondo del mio cor tu vuoi certo penetrar,
E menti per strapparmi il grande arcan.
Marina non mi ama!

**RANGONI:** Io mento? . . . Mentire a te, Zarevic.
A te sol, notte e dì pensa Marina,
E soffre ognor per te.
Nella calma della notte
Ella sogna il tuo valor . . .
Se 'l tuo cor non vacillasse . . .
Se sapesse il suo martir . . .
Ciò che divora per l'ipocrita invidia,

Di color che la circondan,
E fanno allusion a segreti convegni,
A scambio di carezze!
Oh se ciò tu comprendessi . . .
Dubbio alcun più non avresti,
Nè per me, nè per Marina!

**DIMITRI:** Non più! Cessa il tuo biasmo!
A lungo io domai la fiamma ardente.
Dell'amor mio sublime! . . .
(*con tono cupo*)
Marina non ha più nulla a temer . . .
Piegherò il lor ardir . . .
Di quelle donne sventerò le trame,
E dei raggiri lor io riderò,
Poi, al cospetto, delle dame altere,
l'amor mio dischiarerò, Marina!
(*Con slancio*)
A' piedi suoi mi getterò implorando
D'ascoltar l'amor mio . . .
D'esser mia sposa e Zarina!

**RANGONI:** (*fra sè*). Che Sant'Ignazio ti protegga!

**DIMITRI:** Tu che il mondo diserti;
Tu che rifuggi le gioie della vita,
Esperto sei nell'arte di tentar . . .
Oh, ascoltami ben! Per tutto ciò che t'è sacro,
Per l'eterna salute, io ti scongiuro,
Da lei, deh mi conduci e lascia che l'ammiri . . .
Che le dica i miei strazï e le mie pene . . .
Poi, chiedi a me tutto quel che vuoi!

**RANGONI:** Umil frate che medita, prego per tutto,
E penso a Dio e agli orrendi castighi,
che 'l suo giusto furor ci serbò,
Per il dì del giudizio final!
Io son la tomba!
Che m'importa de' tesor che tu m'offri?
Però, se Dimitri a Dio s'inspira,
Se esaudisce il mio desir,
Ei vorrà che io lo segua,
Che non lo lasci mai,
Ch'io conosca i suoi pensier . . .
Che vegli su di lui . . . che lo protegga!

**DIMITRI:** Sì; starò sempre con te,
Se mi fai veder Marina!
Vo' ammirarla . . . vo' parlarle!

**RANGONI:** Ti cela, Zarevic.

**DIMITRI:** E perchè?

**RANGONI:** La folla dei magnati scorgerà la tua presenza.
Deh, va . . . Zarevic . . . ten prego; ti salva!

---

# ■ ACT III.

## SCENE I.

*The Castle of Michek. A Garden. A Fountain. The scene is lighted by the moon.*

**THE FALSE DIMITRI:** (*coming from the Castle, almost dreamily*). "Tonight at the fountain." Divine voice!
With what joy have you overcome the soul?
(*Approaching the fountain*)
Will you come at my sweet call?
Ah! you are my heart's one hope!
No! . . . forget not him who loves you . . .
You behold his pain and suffering
. . .
Oh! come, console my sadness,
With your smile divine and tender.
Marina! Marina!
Answer . . . Oh, answer!
Oh, come . . . come . . . I await you!
I await you here. Answer . . . it is I who call you.
No . . . no one is there! . . .

**RANGONI:** Tzarevitch!

**DIMITRI:** You again?!
My shadow pursuing me!

**RANGONI:** August and valiant Tzarevitch,
Here I am, sent by my daughter Marina.

**DIMITRI:** Marina?

**RANGONI:** The spiritual daughter whom God gave me.
She wishes you to know
How tormented she is by unrest,
Caused by the love which consumes her . . .
And that she shall come here.

**DIMITRI:** Oh, if you would speak the truth . . .
Oh, if it were not Satan who Inspires in you these words
I would take my dove with me to Russia,
To raise her with me to the throne of the Tzars,
To dazzle the entire world by her splendor.
Vile tempter!
You seek to enter into the depths of my heart,
And lie to snatch from me the great secret.
Marina does not love me!

**RANGONI:** I lie? . . . lie to you, Tzarevitch?
Of you alone, Marina thinks night and day,
And ever suffers for you.
In the quiet of the night
Of your valor she dreams . . .
If your heart would not waver . . .
If it would know her affliction . . .
And what she endures from the deceitful envy
Of those who surround her,
Who hint at secret meetings,
Of caresses there exchanged!
Oh, if you could understand . . .
Then never a doubt would you encourage,
Either of me or of Marina!

**DIMITRI:** No more! Cease your censure.
Full long I've smothered the flame
Of my love sublime! . . .
(*in a gloomy voice*)
Nothing more must Marina fear . . .
Their impudence I shall crush . . .
The plots of those women I shall expose,
And at their trickery I shall laugh.
Then, even before the haughty ladies,
I shall declare my love to Marina!
(*With heat*)
At her feet I shall fall imploring
That she listen to my love . . .
And be my spouse and Tzarina!

**RANGONI:** (*to himself*). May Saint Ignatius protect you!

**DIMITRI:** You who deserted the world;
You who fled the joys of life,
An expert in the tempter's art . . .
Oh, hear me well! By all that is sacred to you.
By your eternal salvation, I conjure you,
To lead me to her that I may admire
. . .
And tell her of my suffering and pains . . .
Then ask whatever you wish from me!

**RANGONI:** A humble, meditating friar, I pray for all:
I think of God and of the awful penance
That His just wrath reserves for us,
On the day of final judgement!
As the grave am I!
What care I for the treasure you offer?
But if Dimitri is inspired by God
And if he seeks to grant my wish,
Then he will need me as companion;
Never to leave him for an instant,
To know all his surging thoughts
. . .
To watch over him . . . to protect him!

**DIMITRI:** Yes; I shall always be with you,
If you show me Marina!
I must admire her . . . I must speak to her!

**RANGONI:** Conceal yourself, Tzarevitch.

**DIMITRI:** Why?

**RANGONI:** The approaching magnates would see you.
Pray, go . . . Tzarevitch . . . I beg you; save yourself.

DIMITRI: Che vengan. Li accoglierò
Secondo il lor rango ed il merto . . .

RANGONI: Stà in guardia, Zarevic;
se tu quì resti,
Tu rischi di perder Marina!
T'invola . . . m'ascolta! (*Una folla d'invitati esce, dal castello. Avanti a tutti è Marina, che dà il braccio ad un vecchio signore polacco. Gli invitati attraversano la scena, a coppie.*)

MARINA: (*al suo cavaliere*) Il vostro amor mi lascia indifferente;
I vostri giur, per me, son frasi vane;
E mai fede non avrò ne'vostri accenti.
(*passano nel giardino.*)

I CAVALIERI: Vincerem la Moscovia in un sol dì!
Faremo prigionier i Moscoviti,
E di Boris annienterem le truppe!

LE DAME: Su Mosca piombate d'un tratto;
Catturate quel perfido Zar! . . .
(*passano nel giardino.*)

I CAVALIERI: (*rientrando nel castello*). I vili Moscoviti
Pei Polacchi son oltraggio!

LE DAME: Marina è bella . . . ma forse
A noi, non può giovar!

MARINA: (*dall'alto della scalinata agli invitati*) Del vin! del vin! del vin! ospiti miei!

GLI OSPITI: In onor dei prodi Mnichek,
Beviam il vin, e viva la divina Mnichek!
Gloria a la corona di Marina!
(*nelle quinte*)
Viva! viva! viva!
(*Marina e gli ospiti entrano nel castello.*)

DIMITRI: (*entra in scena correndo*). Il vil gesuita m'ha sì fortemente
Stretto fra le grinfe,
Che appena potei, da lontano,
Gettar su Marina un sol guardo! . . .
Offuscato restai dal divino fulgor
Degli occhi suoi . . .
Il cor mio s'infrangeva,
E per elle sentiva il desir,
D'essere sol! Come bramava
D'allontanar quel frate falso ed ipocrita!
Declamò senza cessa dei discorsi,
Delle frasi imprudenti! . . .
Ed io . . . io scorsi nel giardin Marina
Che dava il braccio ad un nobil messere:
Vidi la bella prodigar sorrisi . . .
Sentii la frasi dolci ed amorose,
E che accettò di diventar sua sposa!
La sposa di colui . . . d'uno sventato . . .
Quand'il destin le offre l'amor mio;
La gloria . . . lo scettro . . .
La corona di Moscovia!

DIMITRI: Let them come. I shall receive them
As their merit and rank befit . . .

RANGONI: Be on guard, Tzarevitch: if you remain here,
You may lose Marina!
Fly now . . . Follow my advice!
(*A company of guests comes from the Castle. At their head walks Marina, leaning on the arm of an old Polish gentleman. The guests cross the stage in couples.*)

MARINA: (*to her escort*). Your love leaves me indifferent.
To me your oaths are vain expressions,
And never shall I trust in your tones.
(*Both pass into the garden.*)

THE KNIGHTS: We shall vanquish Moscow in a single day!
The Moscovites make prisoners
And the troups of Boris annihilate!

THE LADIES: Fall upon Moscow with a single stroke;
Capture that perfidious Tzar.
(*They enter the garden.*)

THE KNIGHTS: (*reentering the castle*). The vile Moscovites
Are hateful to the Poles!

THE LADIES: Marina is beautiful, but, perhaps,
She cannot be of use to us.

MARINA: (*from the top of the guest stairs*).
Some wine! some wine! My guests!

THE GUESTS: In honor of gallant Mnichek,
Let us quaff the wine, and long live his lady!
Glory to the crown of Marina!
(*From behind the scenes*)
Viva! Viva! Viva!
(*Marina and the Guests enter the Castle.*)

DIMITRI: (*rushing in*). The base Jesuit has
Kept me so securely within his clutches,
That scarcely could I throw from afar
Even a single glance at Marina! . . .
I was blinded by the divine splendor
Of her eyes . . .
My heart was bursting within me
And, for her, I felt the wish
To be alone! How I longed
To have that monk, false and deceitful, leave me!
Without rest he declaimed long speeches
And impudent phrases! . . .
And I . . . I in the garden Marina beheld,
Leaning on the arm of a noble lord;
The fair one I saw squandering her smiles . . .
I heard sweet and amorous phrases,
And her consent to be his spouse!
The spouse of him . . . a witling . . .
When fate offers her my love;

No .. non più! . . . Riprenderò
l'usbergo fulgido . . .
La spada ed il cimier!
Poi sul destrier . . . alla testa . . .
nell'accanita mischia!
Sì; alla testa con lor . . . con i miei prodi . . .
Contro lo Zar Boris,
E vittorioso avrò
Il tron degli avi miei!

MARINA: (*entrando*). Dimitri . . . Zarevic . . . Dimitri

DIMITRI: È lei Marina!
(*Va ad incontrarla*)
Tu, mia regina, o angel di beltà!
Oh, l'attesa fu lunga e tanto triste . . .
Quand'il cervel si trazia,
Da gelosia corroso,
Il cor, invaso dai tormenti, ottenebra il pensier,
Ed esecra l'amor . . . la sua regina!

MARINA: Stà ben . . . tutto io so!
Non dorme più! Notte e giorno
Sogna all'amor e vive per Marina!
No! . . . da te qui venni
Per parlarti di cose ben gravi e non d'amor
Sol, tu puoi, se ti piace,
Frèmere e spasimar d'amor per me!

DIMITRI: Marina!

MARINA: No! s'anco, per amor mio,
La vita tua tu m'offri,
Muto 'l mio cor sarà!
Quando a Mosca, entrerai come Zar?

DIMITRI: Io Zar? Marina, ho lo spavento in cor!
Di Zar il nome, del tron il fulgido splendor,
Di schiavi vili e adulator lo stuolo,
In te spensero l'amor . . .
E l'ardente desio d'abbandonarti
Alle dolce carezze,
Alla mia tenerezza,
E all'estasi adorata di questa mia passion?

MARINA: Or via, finiam!
Oh, degli innamorati, conosco ben l'adagio:
"Un tugurio ed il tuo cor, e felici noi sarem."
Ascolta ben, Zarèvic; pel tuo frivolo amor,
Potrai tu sceglier, fra tante Moscovite,
Una bella dagli occhi di foco! . . .

DIMITRI: Oh, no . . . sei tu! tu sol che desiro!
L'angelo mio sei tu! . . . tu, l'amor mio!
Abbi pietà del profondo dolor . . .
Non mi cacciar da te!

MARINA: Per te, Marina non è che un amante . . .
Un trastul!
Ebben no! Solo il tron dei Zar,
La lor corona sol, potran tentarmi!

And glory . . . the scepter . . .
The crown of Moscow!
No . . . enough! . . . I shall wear again the shining hauberk . . .
The sword and helmet!
Then on the charger . . . leading . . . in the savage tussle!
Yes! at the head . . . of my brave warriors . . .
Against the Tzar Boris,
And victorious I shall receive
The throne of my forefathers!

MARINA: (*entering*). Dimitri! . . . Tzarevitch . . . Dimitri

DIMITRI: It is she, Marina!
(*Moving to meet her*)
You, my queen, an angel of beauty!
Oh, how long the waiting and how sad!
When the mind is torn apart,
Corroded by jealousy, the heart,
tormented, dims the thought
And curses love . . . its queen!

MARINA: It is well . . . I know it all.
He sleeps no more! Night nor day
He dreams of love and lives but for Marina!
No I came to you
To speak of things the gravest, but not of love.
Alone, you may if it please you,
Rave and pine of love for me!

DIMITRI: Marina!

MARINA: No! Even if you gave your life
In love for me,
Heedless my heart shall be!
When shall you enter Moscow as its Tzar?

DIMITRI: I, a Tzar? Marina, fear fills my heart!
The name of Tzar, the throne's effulgent splendor,
Vile slaves and crowds of flatterers
Have slain all love in you . . .
And, with it, the ardent longing, yes, to yield yourself
To sweet caresses,
To my tender love for you
And to the raptures of my passion!

MARINA: Come, let's end this!
I know well the lovers' adage:
"A hut and you, and happy we shall be!"
Listen, Tzarevitch; for your foolish love
You shall choose among the many Moscovites
A fair one with eyes of fire!

DIMITRI: Oh, no! It is you!
I wish for you alone!
You are my angel,
You, my love!
Have pity on my sorrow,
Drive me not from you!

MARINA: For you Marina is but mistress . . .
A plaything!
No! Only the throne of the Tzars,
And their crown can tempt me!

## Act III, Scene I

**DIMITRI:** Tu ferisci 'l mio cor, cru-
del polacca . . .
Gli acerbi detti tuoi, lo fan penar!
Guarda . . . mi prostro ai tuoi piè
. . .
Umil imploro l'amor da te . . .
Deh! . . . alimenta questa fiamma!

**MARINA:** (*sarcastica*). No, mio
tenero amoroso . . .
Non ti prostrar . . . ti leva!
Povero martir! mi fai pietà!
Ti compiango perchè soffri . . .
Perchè d'amor, tu langui per Mari-
na . . .
Notte e dī sogni di lei . . .
E non pensi a la corona . . .
E non pensi più a Boris! . . .
Va . . . vagabondo!

**DIMITRI:** Marina! taci!

**MARINA:** Va, salariato! va . . . servo
vil!

**DIMITRI:** Oh, Marina!
Hai tu il diritto di rinfacciarmi
Tutto quel che soffersi nel passato?
Tu menti! sì, menti, polacca! . . .
Io son lo Zar!
Con me dei combattenti accorron
. . .
Domani all'alba io vo' partir con
essi,
E capo lor sarò!
Sul Kremlino da prodi piomberem,
Per conquistar il tron degli avi
miei,
Con qual gioia di te mi riderò!
Oh, in quel dì le lagrime di duol tu
verserai,
Per lo scettro perduto! Umile
Allor ti vedrò ed implorante,
Al piedi del mio trono nel Kremlin;
Ma tutti, al mio comando, della
stolta
Polacca rideran!

**MARINA:** Rideran! . . .
O, Zarevic, t'imploro!
Sii clemente . . . perdona i detti
miei!
Me l'inspirar non l'odio;
Ma la speme nel tuo fato!
Ti desiro la gloria e 'l poter . . .
Credi a me . . . ti seguirò
Io t'amo!
O, mio prode, Marina fedel ti sarà!
Ma pensa . . . pensa a te . . .
Il tron t'attende già . . .
Correr tu dei laggiù nel tuo Krem-
lin!

**DIMITRI:** Marina!
Cessa di fingere il santo amor . . .
Strazii indicibili mi fai soffrir!

**MARINA:** Oh, t'amo, prode guerrier,
Il mio signor sei tu!

**DIMITRI:** Oh, ripetimi, Marina,
Deh, repeti quegli accenti,
Solo il tuo fascin mi può inebbriar!

---

**DIMITRI:** You wound my heart,
cruel lady of Poland . . .
Your words are as shafts to my
heart!
See . . . I kneel at your feet,
Humbly before you I plead for your
love,
Oh, nourish this flame in my bosom!

**MARINA:** (*sarcastically*). No! my
tender love-swain!
Kneel not there . . . arise!
Poor martyr, you make me pity you!
Because you suffer so . . .
Because of love you languish for
Marina . . .
Night and day you dream of her . . .
And you think not of the crown,
Nor think of Boris!
Worthless one, leave!

**DIMITRI:** Marina! Say no more!

**MARINA:** Go, hireling! Leave! Vile
serf!

**DIMITRI:** Oh, Marina!
Have you right to reproach me thus
For all that I have suffered in the
past?
You lie, yes, lie, Lady of Poland!
I am that Tzar! . . .
Around me soldiers gather
And tomorrow, at dawn, I join
them,
And I'll be their chief!
We shall fall upon the Kremlin, like
heroes,
To conquer the throne of my forefa-
thers;
And the day that sees me Tzar
With what joy I shall laugh at you!
Oh, on that day your tears shall flow
For the lost scepter.
You'll be humble!
Then shall I see you there implor-
ing
At my throne in the Kremlin;
But at my command, all shall laugh
At the foolish Lady of Poland!

**MARINA:** They shall laugh!
Oh, Tzarevitch, I implore you!
Be merciful . . . forgive my speech!
Not hate inspired me
But my trust in your destiny!
I wish for you both glory and power
. . .
Believe me . . . I shall follow you
. . .
I love you!
Oh, my valiant, Marina shall be true
to you!
But think . . . think of yourself . . .
The throne awaits you;
Make haste to the Kremlin!

**DIMITRI:** Marina! Cease to feign a
holy love . . . You cause me indescribable pangs!

**MARINA:** Oh, I love you, brave
warrior.
You are my lord!

**DIMITRI:** Oh, repeat to me, Marina,
Do repeat those words!
Your charm alone can enrapture
me!

---

**MARINA:** (*si getta a' suoi ginocchi*). O, mio Zar!

**DIMITRI:** Vien, Marina, il mio per-
don ricevi,
Fra le braccia del tuo sposo!
Egli t'attende.

**MARINA:** Mio signor, tu mi rendi la
speme!
Son tua! conquistator!
(*s'abbracciano.*)
(*Rangoni attraversa la scena e, al
momento in cui s'abbracciano,
s'arresto soddisfatto della sua vittoria.*)

**GLI OSPITI:** (*nelle quinte*) Viva!
viva! viva!
(*Cala la tela*).

## SCENA II.

*La foresta di Kromy. A destra,
degli spettatori, un pendio da cui
comincia la strada, che attraversa la scena. In lontananza, si
scorgono le mura della città. Sulla vetta del pendio, un grosso
tronco d'albero. Rimpetto gli spettatori, la foresta. È notte.
All'alzarsi del sipario, nelle
quinte s'odono delle grida selvaggie di vagabondi. Essi sbucano, in
folla, dal pendio, e invadono la
scena. Conducono il boiardo
Khroutchov legato, colle vesti lacere, ed il capo scoperto.*

**I VAGABONDI:** Sia tratto qui, e
adagiatel sul tronco, fratelli!
Cosi.
(*fanno sedere il prigioniero sul
tronco*)
Piochè vuol urlar, curar noi dob-
biam
La nobil sua strozza!
L'imbavagliam!
(*Imbavagliano Khroutchov con
lembi di vesti, e lo legono al tron-
co con una cinghia.*)
Amen!
(*Accendono dei fuochi.*)

**GLI UOMINI:** Che, fratelli . . .
Senza scorta, quel boiardo vorreste
lasciar?
Noi protestiam! Egli è certo un
grand'uom!
Lo Zar Boris rubò 'l tron e la corona,
Ed ei rubò al ladron!
Eh! . . . rendiamogli gli onor,
Che meritò questo cialtron!
Eh! . . . vio . . . Fomka, Epihan, in
guardia là!
(*Due uomini armati di staffile, es-
cono dalla folla, e si mettono ac-
conte Khroutchov.*)

**LA FOLLA:** Amen!

**LE DONNE:** Ma che dite voi di ciò?
Si dice che 'l boiardo,
Una bella ancor non abbia . . .
Ma sarà ver?
Senz'un amante
Il boiardo è un alvear
Privo di miel—

---

**MARINA:** (*throwing herself at his
knees*). Oh, my Tzar!

**DIMITRI:** Come, Marina, my par-
don receive,
In the arms of your spouse.
He awaits you.

**MARINA:** My Lord, you give hope
again!
I am yours! O conqueror! (*They
embrace.*) (*Rangoni, crossing the
stage at the very moment they
embrace each other, stops, enjoying the triumph of his victory.*)

**THE GUESTS:** (*from behind the
scenes*). Viva! Viva! Viva!
(*Curtain.*)

## SCENE II.

*The Forest of Kromy. At right of
audience a slope, where starts a
road crossing the scene. In distance the walls of the city. At top of
slope, the large trunk of a tree.
Facing the audience, the forest. It
is night. As the curtain goes up,
from behind the scenes the wild
shouts of the Vagrants are heard.
They rush down the slope into the
scene, invading it. They bring the
Boyar Khroutchov with them,
bound, his dress torn and his head
bare.*

**VAGRANTS:** Bring him here, lay
him on the trunk, brothers! There!
(*They compel the prisoner to sit
on the trunk.*)
Since he wishes to shout, then we
must cure
The noble's throttle! Let us gag him!
(*They gag Khroutchov with bits of
torn clothing and bind him to the
trunk with a strap.*)
Amen!
(*They light fires.*)

**THE MEN:** What, brothers . . .
Without an escort would you leave
that Boyar?
We protest! Surely, a great man he!
The Tzar Boris stole the throne, the
crown
This one stole from the robber!
What say? . . . Let's render him hon-
ors
Deserved by the scoundrel!
Eh? . . . Here . . . Fomka, Epihan, on
guard here!
(*Two men carrying whips detach
themselves from the crown and
stand at the side of Khroutchov.*)

**THE CROWD:** Amen!

**THE WOMEN:** What do you think
of this?
It is said that the handsome Boyar
Has no lady love . . .
Shall this be true?
Without a mistress
The Boyar a beehive resembles

Afimia, colomba,
A quanto dicon,
Tra poco avrai cent'anni!
Sicura ne sei tu?
T'avanza, mio tesor, vers'il boiardo.
(*Una vecchia, gemendo e tossendo, si dirige verso Khroutchov.*)

**UOMINI E DONNE:** T'avanza! ah, ah, ah, ah, ah!
Amen! A lui rendiam gli onor!

**GLI UOMINI:** Eh, voi . . . donne; cominciate?!

**LE DONNE:** (*si dispongono in mezzo cerchio, attortorno al boiardo*). Il bel falco batte l'ali?
È un corsier che caracolla?
È il boiardo, gran messer,
Che pensa e che reflette notte e dì?

**TUTTI:** (*salutando il boiardo*). Gloria, Gloria al gran boiardo, Gloria al suo Zar Boris; gloria!

**VOCI DI UOMINI:** Eh, donne! il buon boiardo ha perduto 'l suo frustin!
Invece del baston . . . lo staffil!
(*metteno uno staffilo fra le mani del boiardo*)
Va ben . . . continuate . . .

**LE DONNE:** Il buon boiardo pensa notte e dì
Per contentar lo Zar,
Come potrà batter a morte,
La brava gente ed i cristian!

**TUTTI:** (*salutando*). Gloria a questo buon boiardo,
Gloria al suo Zar Boris!
Gloria!
(*si avvicinano tutti al boiardo*)
Ei sempre ci colmò de'suoi favor!
(*lo salutano*)
Per non sporcar di fango i tuoi calzar,
Ti facevi portar dai nostri figli!
(*lo salutano ancora*)
Ed a suon di staffil li commandavi!
Sia Gloria al gran boiardo, gloria al suo Zar Boris!
Gloria! gloria a te!
(*lo salutano profondamente.*)
(*A destra, sulla strada, accorre l'Innocente. Ha sul capo un elmo di latta. Egli è incatenato: i suoi peidi son nudi, ed ha in mano un sandalo di vimini.*)

**I BIRICCHINI:** Trrr . . . elmo di latta! elmo di latta!
Trrr . . . elmo di latta!
U—liù, liù, liù, liù, liù, liù . . . trrr . . .
(*Qualche uomo e qualche donna, minaccia i biricchini, che si tacciono*).

**L'INNOCENTE:** (*siede su di un sasso e canta, dondolandosi, ed accomodando il suo sandalo*).
Luna bianca
Il gatto piange!
Innocente sta tranquil . . .

Wanting in honey . . .
Afinia, my dove,
By what they say
Soon a hundred you shall be,
You know it well.
Approach, my treasure, come to the Boyar! (*An old woman, groaning and coughing, moves towards Khroutchov.*)

**MEN AND WOMEN:** Go on! ah, ah, ah, ah, ah,
Amen! Let's render him honors!

**THE MEN:** Hey, . . . women, begin!

**THE WOMEN:** (*disposing themselves in a semicircle around the Boyar*). The fine hawk beats its wings?
And a courser prances?
And the Boyar, mighty lord,
Thinks, and reflects, both night and day?

**ALL:** (*saluting the Boyar*). Glory, glory to the great Boyar,
Glory to his Tzar Boris; glory!

**MEN'S VOICES:** Hey, women! the good Boyar has lost his switch.
Instead of his stick . . . the whip!
(*Placing a whip in the Boyar's hands*)
Good! . . . now go on! . . .

**THE WOMAN:** The good Boyar thinks night and day
To please the Tzar,
How he may beat to death
Good folks and honest Christians.

**ALL:** (*saluting*). Glory to this good Boyar,
Glory to his Tzar Boris!
Glory!
(*All approach the Boyar*)
He always overwhelmed us with his favors!
(*Saluting*)
So as not to soil your boots
You forced our sons to carry you!
(*Again saluting*)
And you gave orders with the whip!
Glory to the great Boyar, Glory to his Tzar Boris,
Glory! Glory! to you!
(*Saluting profoundly*).
(*From right, on the road the Simpleton rushes in. He wears a tin helmet. He is in rags; his feet are bare and he carries a sandal of osier.*)

**THE URCHINS:** Trr . . . tin helmet! tin helmet!
Trr . . . tin helmet!
Oo . . . lyoo, lyoo, lyoo, lyoo, lyoo . . . trr . . .
(*Some of the men and women threaten the Urchins who become silent.*)

**THE SIMPLETON:** (*seats himself on a rock and sings, swaying from side to side and fixing his sandal*).
White moon
The cat is weeping!
Simpleton be tranquil . . .

Pensar devi all'orazion.
T'ador, mio Signor . . .
T'amo Gesù!
Notte serena . . .
Splende la luna!

**I BIRICCHINI:** (*con simulato rispetto*). Viva . . . viva! all'Innocente
Sion resi grandi onor!
Salutaci pian pian . . .
Ti leva l'elmo . . . egli è pesante!
(*dando dei colpi sull'elmo di latta*)
Zin! zin! zin! campanon!

**L'INNOCENTE:** Non sapete ch'ho un copec?

**I BIRICCHINI:** Fa veder . . . sei tu in error!

**L'INNOCENTE:** (*toglie dall'elmo un copec e lo mostro ai ragazzi*). Veh!
(*I Biricchini emettono un fischio di canzonatura, che imita il suono di "vuit"; gli strappono dalle mani il copec e fuggono.*)

**L'INNOCENTE:** (*piange, ed i suoi gridi si confondono col canto di Varlaam e Missaïl.*) Ah, ah, ah, han rubato all'innocente!
Ah, ah, ah! il pover mio copec! ah, ah, ah, ah!

**VARLAAM E MISSAIL:** (*nelle quinte*). Luna e sol non brillan più!
Tutti gli astri si son spenti . . .
Trema e sussulta o, terra,
Pel misfatto di Boris!
(*L'Innocente sistende sulla pietra e finge dormire. La folla ascolta il canto e si dirige da quel lato.*)
Strane bestie erran ovunque,
Inseguendo alati mostri,
Che i fanciul von divorar,
Per l'atroce delitto di Boris!
(*il canto s'avvicina*)
Di Zar Boris i servi,
Senza pietà torturan nè mercede,
Inspirati dai demoni impuri,
In onor del buon regno,
Del Sàtana Boris!

**LA FOLLA:** Quei vecchi giungon da la città,
Han dell'ardir, se canton le colpe dello Zar . . .
Le torture de' miser che langon.

**VARLAAM E MISSAIL:** Misero popol che geme e soffre,
E si contorce sotto la verga di quell'àpostata!
Dello staffil infam del regicida,
Alla gloria del suo mortal peccato!

**LA FOLLA:** Haïdà!
Nel popol s'accende l'ardir
Si ridesta 'l suo furor;
Il sangue cosacco s'infiamma nel cor!
Oh, da te noi siam invasi, o santa

You must think of prayer.
I adore you, my Lord . . .
I love you, Jesus!
Serene night . . .
The moon shines!

**THE URCHINS:** (*simulating respect*). Viva . . . viva! to the Simpleton.
Be paid great honors.
Salute us gently, gently . . .
Take off your helmet . . . it is heavy!
(*Striking on the tin helmet.*)
Zin! zin! zin! big bell!

**THE SIMPLETON:** Don't you know I have a kopeck?

**THE URCHINS:** Let's see . . . You are mistaken!

**THE SIMPLETON:** (*taking a kopeck from the helmet and showing it to the boys*).
See!
(*The Urchins whistle mockingly, imitating the sound 'vooit''. They snatch the kopeck from his hands and run away.*)

**THE SIMPLETON:** (*he weeps, and his cries become confused with the song of Varlaam and Missail.*)
Ah, ah, ah, they have robbed the Simpleton!
Ah, ah, ah! my poor kopeck! Ah, ah, ah!

**VARLAAM AND MISSAIL:** (*from behind the scene*). Sun and moon shine no more!
All the stars are spent . . .
Tremble and start, oh, earth,
At the misdeeds of Boris!
(*The Simpleton stretches himself on the rock and feigns sleep. The crowd listens to the song and moves toward it.*)
Strange beasts are roving everywhere,
Winged monsters pursuing,
Which seek the children to devour,
For Boris's atrocious crime!
(*The song draws near*)
Boris's minions unmercifully torture,
By the foul demons inspired,
In honor of the excellent reign
Of Boris the Devil.

**THE CROWD:** Those old men come from the city.
They are bold thus to sing the Tzar's guilt . . .
The tortures of wretches who languish . . .

**VARLAAM AND MISSAIL:** Wretched people who suffer and moan,
And squirm beneath that apostate's rod,
The infamous whip of the regicide,
To the glory of his mortal sin!

**THE CROWD:** Haida! The people are incited to boldness,
Their courage awakens again;
The Cossack blood in their hearts kindles,
Oh, blessed strength, by you we are

forza!
O, tu, forza vigorosa,
Forza immortal, possente, forza
vendicativa!
Forza terrificante!
I nostri fratel, non devi tradir . . .
Aiutali a lottar . . .
Aiutali a pugnar . . .
Con ardor a lottar . . . con ardor a
pugnar!
Tu li eccita a pugnar! . . .
Haïdà! . . .

**VARLAAM E MISSAIL:** Accettate,
buona gente,
Per vostro amato Zar,
Accettate colui che 'l Ciel salvò
Dalle man lorde dell'assassin!
Accetta, popol, come Zar,
Dimitri il figliuol, del zar Ivan!

**LA FOLLA:** Del popolo l'ardir già si
destò implacabil!
Invadici, forza, invadi il nostro cor!
Forza, che tutto fa espiar!
Notte e dì del zar Bòris i servi,
Torturan uomini giusti;
Li tagliano, li strazian . . .
Li assassinan con furor!
Morte! morte! morte a Boris . . .
Al regicida morte!

**LOVITZKI E TCHERNIAKOW-
SKY:** (*nelle quinte*). Domine, Do-
mine, salvum fac Regem,
Regem Demetrium Moscoviæ,
Salvum fac, salvum fac Regem
Demetrium
Omnis Russiæ . . . Salfum fac. Sal-
vum fac
Regem Demetrium!

**VOCI NELLA FOLLA:** Ancor costor! Che cosa voglion qui?
Son dei lupi gli ululati.
(*accorrono a sinistra, per affrontare i gesuiti*)
Sono neri quei demon!

**LOVITZKI E TCHERNIAKOW-
SKY:** Domine, Domine, salvum fac,
salvum fac!

**VARLAAM:** (*a Missaïl*). Dei corvi
la vil razza!
Vengon qui come noi per acclama-
no lo Zarevic!
Impedir lo dobbiam, Missaïl!

**MISSAIL:** Impediamol!

**LOVITZKI E TCHERNIAKOW-
SKY:** (*entrano*).Domine, Domine,
salvum fac Regem
Demetrium Moscoviæ.

**MISSAIL:** (*alla folla*). Morte alla
razza nera!

**LA FOLLA:** Haïdà! A morte!
Morte ai vampir!
Ai maghi! agli stregon!

**VARLAAM:** Dal pino si sprigiona
l'alma lor!
E cantino le lodi sulle foglie!
(*la folla si precipita sui gesuiti e li
lega*)

urged!
O vigorous strength,
Immortal strength, potent, aveng-
ing strength,
Strength terrifying!
You must not betray our brethren

Help them to struggle . . .
Help them to fight . . .
To struggle with ardor . . . with ar-
dor to fight.
You incite them to fight! . . .
Haida! . . .

**VARLAAM AND MISSAIL:** Good
folks, accept
As your beloved Tzar,
Accept whom Heaven saved
From the assassin's hands stained!
Accept, people, as your Tzar,
Dimitri, Tzar Ivan's son!

**THE CROWD:** Already the peo-
ple's boldness implacably wake!
O strength possess us, our hearts
possess
Strength to force atonement!
Night and day Tzar Boris's minions
Torture our righteous men;
They pinch, they tear them . . .
They slay them with fury!
Death! death! death to Boris . . .
To the regicide death!

**LOVITZKI AND TCHERNIAKOW-
SKY:** (*from behind the scene*). Do-
mine, Domine, salvum fac Regem,
Regem Demetrium Moscovæ,
Salvum fac, salvum Regem Deme-
trium
Omnis Russia . . .Salvum fac. Sal-
vum fac
Regem Demetrium!

**VOICES AMID THE CROWD:** Still
these! What do they seek here?
They howl like wolves.
(*They rush to the left to meet the
Jesuits.*)
They are black those demons!

**LOVITZKI AND TCHERNIAKOW-
SKY:** Domine, Domine, salvum fac,
salvum fac!

**VARLAAM:** (*to Missail*). The vile
tribe of ravens,
Here they come, like we, to acclaim
the Tzarevitch.
We must stop them, Missail!

**MISSAIL:** Let us do so!

**LOVITZKI AND TCHERNIAKOW-
SKY:** (*entering*) Domine, Domine,
salvum fac Regem
Demetrium Moscovæ.

**MISSAIL:** (*to the crowd*). Death to
the black brood!

**THE CROWD:** Haida! Death!
Death to the vampires!
The magicians, the sorcerers!

**VARLAAM:** In the pine tree let
their souls be unfettered!
Amid the foliage let them chant
their praises.
(*The crowd rushes at the Jesuits*

Stringete ancor!
Non si debbon muover più,
Nè indur gli altri in tentazion!

**LOVITZKI E TCHERNIAKOW-
SKY:** Sanctissima Virgo,
Juva, juva,
Servos tuos! (*3 volte di seguito.*)

**LA FOLLA:** Haïdà! la sul pino!

**LOVITZKI E TCHERNIAKOW-
SKY:** Sanctissima Virgo, juva servos
tuos, Servos tuos!
(*La folla trascina i gesuiti nella
foresta. S'odono i clamori delle
trombe, e compariscono sulla scena dei cavalieri, avvolti in candidi mantelli, che portano delle torcie. Processione di truppe di
Dimitri. I vagabondi invadono la
scena.*)

**VARLAAM E MISSAIL:** (*nelle
quinte*). Gloria allo Zarevic, figlio
d'Ivan
Che Dio i conservò!
(*bis!*)

**LA FOLLA:** Gloria allo Zarevic!
Dio per noi lo conservò!
Lo conservò per noi!
(*bis!*)
(*La folla, Varlaam, Missaïl e i gesuiti, si agitano sulla scena. Il falso Dimitri, entra montando un
cavallo, tenuto per la briglia, da
due guerrieri.*)

**LA FOLLA:** Viva e governi Dimitri
Ivanovìtch!
Gloria! gloria! gloria! gloria! gloria!

**IL FALSO DIMITRI:** (*a cavallo*).
Noi, Dimitri Ivanovìtch,
Per volontà di Dio, di Russia Zarev-
ic,
Forte dell'eredità degli avi,
Noi offriam al nostro, popol,
Straziato dal falsario,
Aiuto e libertà!

**KHROUTCHOV:** O Signor, nobil
Zarèvic!
Sia gloria a te!
(*salutandolo profondamente*)

**DIMITRI:** Vien, boiardo col tuo
Zar, il nemico ad affrontar . . .
Entrerem nella mia patria . . .
Là nel santo Kremelin!
(*Dimitri s'allontana, montando
il pendio a destra. Tutti, ad ecce-
zione dell'Innocente, lo seguono.*)

**LA FOLLA:** Gloria! gloria! gloria a
te!
Sia gloria ognor a Dimitri Iva-
nivitch!

**LOVITZKI E TCHERNIAKOW-
SKY:** (*seguono Dimitri*). Gloria
Deo! Gloria! (*Nelle quinte s'ode il
rintocco funebre delle campane.
Da lungi un bagliore d'incendio.
La scena si vuota.*)

and binds them.*)
Draw tighter the cords! They must
stir no more.
Nor lead others into temptation!

**LOVITZKI AND TCHERNIAKOW-
SKY:** Sanctissima Virgo,
Juva, juva,
Servos tuos!
(*3 times in succession.*)

**THE CROWD:** Haida! On the pine
tree over there!

**LOVITZKI AND TCHERNIAKOW-
SKY:** Sanctissima Virgo, juva servos
tuos,
Servos tuos!
(*The crowd drags the Jesuits into
the forest. Trumpets are heard
and horsemen appear, wrapped
in white cloaks and carrying
torches. Procession of troops of
Dimitri. The Vagrants invade the
stage.*)

**VARLAAM AND MISSAIL:** (*from
behind the scenes*). Glory to the
Tzarevitch, Ivan's son,
Whom God preserve!
(*Bis*)

**THE CROWD:** Glory to the Tzarev-
itch!
God kept him safe for us!
He guarded him for us!
(*Bis*)
(*The crowd, Varlaam, Missail and
the Jesuits move about the stage.
The false Dimitri enters riding a
horse whose bridle is held by two
soldiers.*)

**THE CROWD:** Long live and rule
Dimitri Ivanovitch!
Glory! glory! glory! glory!

**THE FALSE DIMITRI:** (*on horse-
back*). We, Dimitri Ivanovitch,
By God's will Tzarevitch of Russia,
Strength inheriting from his forefa-
thers,
Offer to you our people,
Tortured by the usurper,
Aid and liberty!

**KHROUTCHOV:** O Lord, noble
Tzarovitch!
Glory to you!
(*Saluting him profoundly.*)

**DIMITRI:** Come, Boyar, with your
Tzar, the enemy to meet . . .
We shall enter my fatherland . . .
There in the holy Kremlin!
(*Dimitri retires, climbing the
slope at right. All follow him, ex-
cept the Simpleton.*)

**THE CROWD:** Glory! glory! glory
to you!
Glory ever to Dimitri Ivanovitch!

**LOVITZKI AND TCHERNIAKOW-
SKY:** (*following Dimitri*). Gloria
Deo! Gloria!
(*From behind the scenes is heard
the mournful tolling of bells.
From afar the glow of a conflagra-
tion is seen. The stage is empty-
ing.*)

L'INNOCENTE: (*si guarda attorno, poi siede sui sasso e canta dondolandosi*) Scorga l'amaro pianto!
Piangi . . . piangi . . . alma infelice!
Il nemico qui verrà,
Tanto sangue colerà . . .
Ed il fuoco struggerà!
(*la tela cala lentamente*)
Oh, terror! oh . . . terror! . . .
Lascia sgorgar il pianto,
Misera plebe! . . .
(*Cala la tela*).

THE SIMPLETON: (*gazing around, then seating himself on the rock, he sings, swaying his body*) Let bitter tears flow.
Weep . . . weep . . . unhappy soul!
The enemy here shall come,
So much blood shall flow,
And the fire shall destroy . . .
(*The curtain is slowly lowered.*)
Oh, terror! oh, terror! . . .
Allow your tears to flow,
Wretched people!
(*Curtain.*)

## SCENA III.

(*Il palazzo angoloso del Kremlino. Banchi ad ogni lato. A destra una porta sul gran scalone. Alla sinistra gli appartamenti dello Zar. A destra, presso la rampa, una tavola coll'occorrente per scrivere. Verso sinistra, il posto dello Zar. Seduta straordinaria della Duma dei Boiardi.*)

I BOIARDI: (*una parte di essi*). Su, Boiardi, incominciam. Chi parla?

ALTRE VOCI: Voi pe' primi parlerete!

ALCUNI: Ma la nostr'opinion esposta è già!
(*a Tchelkalov*)
Scrivi: Andrea Mikhailovitch:
(*Tchelkalov siede alla tavola*.)

PRIME VOCI: Arso sia vivo lo scellerato!

TERZE VOCI: Ma pria bisogna arrestar quel maledetto!
Poi . . . l'arderete!

PRIME VOCI: Giusto!

QUARTE VOCI: Non totalmente ancor!
(*Man mano che espongono la loro opinione, i boiardi s'alzano, poi salutano e si rimettono a sedere*)

SECONDE VOCI: Calmatevi! dobbiam parlar!

PRIME VOCI: Pria di tutto si deve arrestarlo,
Poi sia appeso e flagellato!

SECONDE VOCI: Si giustizi e s'esponga il suo corpo
Al corvi famèlici!

TERZE VOCI: Indi bruciarlo, avanti al popol,
Sulla pubblica piazza, e maledir le sue ceneri
Per ben tre volte! . . .

QUARTE VOCI: E sparpagliar le sue ceneri,
Fuor delle mura, a' quattro venti!

TUTTI: Dello spergiur la traccia, sparisca sulla terra,
E s'alcun lo difende, anch'ei dovrà perir!
Il corpo suo sarà messo alla gogna

## SCENE III.

(*The angular palace of the Kremlin. Benches on every side. At right a door leading to the grand staircase. At left the Tzar's apartments. At right, near footlights, a table on which are writing materials. Towards left, the place set apart for the Tzar. Special session of the Duma of Boyars.*)

THE BOYARS: (*some of them*). Now, Boyars, let us begin. Who speaks?

OTHER VOICES: You first shall speak!

SOME ONE: But our opinion is already given!
(*To Tchelkalov.*)
Write: Andrey Mikailovitch.
(*Tchelkalov seats himself at the table.*)

FIRST VOICES: Let the scoundrel be burned alive!

THIRD VOICES: But first the villain must be arrested!
Then . . . you can burn him!

FIRST VOICES: Right!

FOURTH VOICES: Not exactly!
(*As they express their opinion in turns, the Boyars rise, salute and resume their seats.*)

SECOND VOICES: Be calm! We must speak!

FIRST VOICES: Before all, he must be arrested,
Then be hanged and scourged!

SECOND VOICES: Let him be executed and his body exposed
To famished ravens.

THIRD VOICES: Then burn him, before the people,
On the public square, and cursed be his ashes,
Three times accursed!

FOURTH VOICES: And scatter his ashes,
Outside the walls, to the four winds!

ALL: Let all trace of the perjurer be blotted from the earth,
And should one defend him, let him too perish!
His body shall be put into the pillo-

. . .
E dovunque sarà proclamato quest'editto:
"In tutti i borghi, in tutte le chiese, su tutti i borghi, in tutte le chiese, su tutti i crocevia e piazze . . .
(*lunga pa sa*)
che genuflesso il popol al Ciel innalzi le sue preghiere, a finchè risparmi la patria nostra . . ."

QUALCHE BOIARDO: Ma Chouïsky qui ci obliò! Benchè complotti,
Senza lui non possiam nulla finir.

CHOUISKY: (*entrando*). Degnate perdonarmi,
Se alquanto indugiai. Oh, scusate mio ritardo.

I BOIARDI: Ecco il Prence Chouïsky.

CHOUISKY: (*ai boiardi che lo circondono*). L'altra sera,
Mi congedai dal Zar col cuor straziato.
Perchè io mi tormento pel suo spirto . . .
Da uno spiraglio, allor, volli mirar . . .
Oh, boiardi! quale spettacol truce!
Pallido . . . la fronte di sudor intrisa . . .
Le man tremanti,
Lo Zar balbettaava frasi strane sconnesse . . .
Ed il suo sguardo incuteva terror!
Ròso da un arcano dolor,
Borìs, il martire, piangeva! . . .
Poi, livido, girò gli occhi a sinsitra . . .
Con orrendi gridi d'angoscia . . .
E all'ombra di Dimitri egli parlò,
Cacciando invan da lui l'orrido spettro.

I BOIARDI: No, tu menti!

ALTRI BOIARDI: Che?! . . .
(*Boris entra, cercando restare inosservato*)

CHOUISKY: (*continuando*). "Va, dicev'egli, va, va, va! va, fanciul!"

BORIS: Va, va, va, fanciul!

I BOIARDI: (*scorgono Boris*). O, Signor! . . . o, Dio del Ciel! che gli angel ci proteggan!

BORIS: (*avvicinandosi alla rampa*). Va! va!
Io l'uccisor? oh, no! no!
No . . . assassin! egli vive!
E Chouïsky che il falso guirò
Squartato sarà!

CHOUISKY: (*facendo il segno della croce su Boris*). Che la grazia del Ciel vegli su te!

BORIS: (*padroneggiandosi, si dirige verso il luogo riservato allo Zar e dice ai boiardi*). Vi feci qui venir, che ho d'uopo di vostri consigli.

ry.
And everywhere let this edict be proclaimed:
"In all towns, in all churches, in all squares and crossways . . .
(*Long pause.*)
that kneeling, the people may raise to Heaven their prayers that our country be spared . . ."

SOME OF THE BOYARS: But Shouisky has forgotten us. Although in the plot,
Nothing without him we can accomplish.

SCHOUISKY: (*entering*). Pray forgive me
If I delayed a while. Oh, excuse my lingering.

THE BOYARS: Behold, Prince Shouïsky!

SHOUISKY: (*to the Boyars who surround him*). The other night, I took leave of the Tzar with sorrowful heart,
For I was worried about his mind. I decided to look through a hole . . .
Oh, Boyars! what a harrowing sight I beheld!
Pallid . . . his brow bathed in sweat . . .
His hands trembling,
The Tzar stammered strange, disjointed phrases—
And his gaze inspired terror!
Assailed by some hidden grief,
Boris, the martyr, was weeping! . . .
Then livid, he turned his eyes to the left . . .
With agonizing cries,
And to Dimitri's ghost he spoke,
Vainly chasing the terrible specter.

THE BOYARS: No, you lie!

OTHER BOYARS: What?! . . .
(*Boris enters, seeking to remain unseen.*)

SHOUISKY (*continuing*). "Go," he said to him, "go, go, go, go, boy!"

BORIS: Go, go, go, boy!

THE BOYARS: (*perceiving Boris*). O, Lord! . . . O, God in Heaven! angels protect us!

BORIS: (*coming down front*). Go, Go!
I the murderer? oh, no! no!
No . . . assassin! he lives
And Shouisky who falsely swore
Shall be quartered!

SHOUISKY: (*making the sign of the cross over Boris*). Let Heaven's grace watch over you!

BORIS: (*assuming a lordly demeanor, moves towards the place reserved for the Tzar and addressing the Boyars*). Here I bade you assemble, for I need your counsel.

## Act III, Scene III

In tempo sinistro di disgrazia,
boiardi,
Da voi cerco rifugio.

CHOUISKY: Oh, mio sovran,
Fa che lo schiavo indegno
Pronunzi qualche accento!
Là, davanti al gran scalon,
Un vegliardo ti chiede il favor
Di essere introdotto al tuo cospetto!
Buon consiglier e giusto, di vita impeccabil,
Egli ti vuol svelar un gran mister!

BORIS: Sta ben. L'aspetto qui.
(a parte)
Questo santo, forse,
All'affranto spirto porterà
Un dolce riposo.
(Pimmen, entra — si ferma e guarda fissamente Boris.)

PIMMEN: Un frate umìl,
Che mai curò le discussion mondane,
Qui vien ad apportar la luce!

BORIS: (turbato). Oh, svelami,
buon vecchio
Quel mister . . .
Tutto puoi dir.

PIMMEN: Nel mister della notte
Da me venne un pastor, un venerando vecchio,
Che un arcano nefasto mi svelò:
"Dall'infanzia," fu questo 'l suo dir,
"Ero cieco, nè conobbi mai
La notte e 'l dì! Invan tutto provai
L'erbe, gli incanti, e i filtri!
Invan bagnai le mie pupille
Con l'acqua attinta alle sorgenti sante!
Nulla giovò . . . e m'ero rassegnato.
Ne' sogni miei non scorgevo alcun contorno,
Nè forme . . . ma sol i canti e i suon!
. . .
Una notte sognaai
Una voce infantil che mi chiamò
distintamente —
(Boris si turba sempre più)
Padre, lèvati . . . và . . .
Và nella città d'Ouglitch,
Visita la nostra cattedral,
E di sulla mia tomba un'orazion,
Perchè io son Dimitri, il Zarevic . . .
(Boris si dizza e si asciuga la fronte)
Dio m'accolse fra gli angeli
Ed or mi manda qui
Per compier de' miracol!"
Mi destai e lo volli obbedir;
E col mio nipotin là mi recai.
Orato avevo appena sulla tomba,
Che d'una santa gioia
L'anima mia s'invase . . .
Le mie spente pupille s'aprir . . .
Vid'il sol, la tomba . . . e il mio piccin! . . .

---

In sinister times, when misfortune
threatens,
I seek a refuge through you.

SHOUISKY: Oh, my Sovereign,
Permit your unworthy slave
To speak a word!
There waiting, at the great staircase,
An old man begs of you the favor
Of admission to your presence!
A counsellor, good and just, and of a blameless life,
He seeks to disclose to you some great mystery!

BORIS: It is well. I await him here.
(Aside)
This saint, who knows?
To my oppressed spirit may bring
Sweet repose.
(Pimenn enters, stops and gazes fixedly at Boris.)

PIMENN: A humble monk,
who cared never for worldly strife,
Here comes to shed the light!

BORIS: (troubled.). Oh, good old man, make known to me
that mystery . . .
All that you can say.

PIMENN: In the secret of the night
A shepherd came to me, a venerable man.
Who to me disclosed a heinous mystery:
"From childhood,"—thus he spoke,
"I have been blind, and know not
Night and day! All in vain I tried . . .
Herbs, charms and philters!
In vain I bathed my eyes
With water from the holy founts!
. . .
Nothing availed . . . I became resigned.
I perceived no outline in my dreams,
Nor shapes . . . but only sounds and songs! . . .
One night I dreamed
Of a childish voice that called me
distinctly—
(Boris becomes more and more troubled.)
Father, arise . . . go . . . .
Go into the city of Ouglitch,
visit our cathedral there,
And a pray offer at my tomb,
For I am Dimitri, the Tzarevitch . . .
(Boris sits up and wipes his brow.)
God among his angels took me
And now sends me here
To accomplish miracles!"
I awoke and decided to obey him;
And with my little nephew there went.
Hardly had I prayed over the tomb,
Than a saintly joy
Filled my soul . . .
My blind eyes were opened . . .
I beheld the sun, the tomb . . . my little one! . . .

---

BORIS: (mettendosi una mano sul cuore). Oh, manco . . . ahimè!
aiuto! . . .
(Cade nelle braccia dei boiardi, che si consultano. Gli uni, vanno a cercare dei soccorsi, altri si disperono. Boris sviene.)

BORIS: (riprendendo i sensi). Mio
figlio . . . l'erede! . . .
Al chiostro . . . Frate! . . .
(i Boiardi lo fanno sedere.)
(Chouisky, corre a cercare lo Zarevic. Una parte dei boiardi va a cercare il patriarco del Convento dei Miracoli. Soltanto cinque boiardi, rimangono attorno allo Zar. Teodoro entra correndo e si getta nelle braccia di Boris.)

BORIS: Lasciateci . . . sol vo' restar.
(i boiardi escono)
Addio mio figlio, io muoio . . .
E tu, ben presto, regnerai.
Non cercar come il trono acquistai

Non sei responsabil . . . tu sei lo Zar
leggittimo . . .
Erede mio, il mio primogenito.
Figliuol! caro figliuol amato!
Diffidaa de' consigli dei boiardi ribelli,
Segui accortamente il lor complotto in Lituania.
I traditor devi punir! punir senza pietà!
Rendi giustizia al popol tuo con probità . . .
Difendi sempre la nostra religion,
E onora tutti i santi protettor.
Difendi la mia Xenia o figlio mio!
. . .
L'aiuto suo devi essere tu sol!
Ama Xenia, la pura colomba . . .
(con unzione, di una voce che man mano s'affievolisce)
O, Signor, o mio Dio!
Vedi'il mio pianto.
O, grazia, grazia! . . . pel figlio del gran peccator!
La tua clemenza imploro—
(appoggia le mani sul capo di Teodoro e lo bendice)
Dalle celesti e angeliche vie
Oh, versa i tuoi favor sui figli miei,
Candidi, buon e dolci!
Angel del ciel custode, presso il trono divin . . .
Coll'ali vostre proteggete l'erede mio,
Da ogni tentazion . . . lo proteggete
. . .
(stringe suo figlio contro il suo petto e l'abraccia. S'ode il funebre rintocco delle camapane)
Dio è il suon funebre!

CORO: (interno). Deh! lagrimate tutti . . .
Egli si spegne!
Son chiuse le sue labbra.
Lo spirt s'invole
Piangete . . .
Alleluja!

BORIS: Funesti laì! Frate, un umil frate! Nel chiostro va lo Zar.

---

BORIS: (his hand on his heart)
Oh, I faint . . . ah me! help . . .
(He falls into the arms of the Boyars who take counsel. Some go in search of help, others are in despair. Boris faints.)

BORIS: (regaining his senses). My
son . . . the heir! . . .
to the cloister . . . Monk! . . .
(The Boyars persuade him to sit.)
(Shouisky rushes off for the Tzarevitch. Some of the Boyars go in search of the Patriarch of the Convent of Miracles. Only five Boyars remain around the Tzar. Theodore rushes in and throws himself into Boris' arms.)

BORIS: Leave us . . . I would be alone.
(The Boyars go out.)
Farewell my son, I die . . .
And you soon shall rule.
Seek not to learn how I gained the throne . . .
You are not accountable . . . you are the rightful Tzar . . .
My heir, my firstborn.
Son! dear son, beloved!
The advice of the rebel Boyars distrust,
Follow warily their plot in Lithuania.
You must punish the traitors! punish mercilessly!
Render strict justice to your people.
Defend ever our holy religion,
And honor all our patron saints
Shield my Xenia, O my son! . . .
You alone must protect her! . . .
Love Xenia, my pure dove . . .
(In tones that grow weaker by degrees.)
O Lord, O my God!
Behold my weeping.
Oh, mercy, mercy! . . . to the son of the great transgressor.
I implore your clemency
(He lays his hands on Theodore's head and blesses him.)
From celestial and angelic paths
Oh, pour your favors over my children,
Truthful, good and sweet!
Angel custodian of Heaven, near the divine throne . . .
With your wings protect my heir
From all temptation . . . protect him . . .
(He presses his son to his bosom. The mournful tolling of bells is heard.)
God! it is the funeral knell!

CHORUS: (within). Alas! weep all
. . .
His life is passing!
Closed are his lips.
The spirit wings its flight.
Weep . . .
Hallelujah!

BORIS: Mournful lamentations.
A monk, a humble monk!
To the cloister goes the Tzar.

TEODORO: (*piangendo*). Padre mio, ti calma!...
Il Ciel t'aiuterà...

BORIS: No, l'ora mia suona già...

CORO: (*interno*). Innanzi gli occhi miei, muore un fanciul...
Io singhiozzo... piango...
Ei sussulta... si dibatte...
Ed invoca il mio soccorso!
Per lui non c'è più speme!

BORIS: Signor! Signor... abbi pietà!
Pietà! oblia la colpa mia...
O, tetra morte, gli artigli tuoi son aspri!...
(*entrano i boiardi e la processione*)

THEODORE: (*crying*). My father, calm yourself!...
Heaven shall aid you...

BORIS: No, already my hour strikes...

CHORUS: (*within*). Before my eyes a boy is dying!
I sob... I weep...
He shudders... he quivers...
And invokes my aid!
For him there is no hope.

BORIS: Lord! Lord... have mercy!
Mercy! forgive this deed of mine...
O, frightful death, sharp are your claws!!...
(*The Boyars and the procession enter.*)

BORIS: (*alzandosi di soprassalto*). Ah, fermativi! son Zar ancor...
Io son lo Zar!
(*appoggia la mano sul cuore e ricade sulla poltrona*)
Oh muoio!... Dio... mi perdona!
...
(*ai boiardi, accennando il figlio*)
Lui!
È il vostro Zar!...
Oh, grazia... grazia!...
(*perde i sensi*)

I BOIARDI: (*col capo abbassato, come in un mormorio*). Ei muor!
(*Cala la tela.*)

FINE.

BORIS: (*getting up*). Ah, stop! I am still Tzar... I am the Tzar!
(*He places his hand on his heart and again drops into the arm-chair.*)
Oh, I die!... God... forgive me!
(*To the Boyars, pointing to his son.*)
He!
He is your Tzar!...
Oh, mercy... mercy!...
(*Boris dies.*)

THE BOYARS: (*with bowed heads, almost in a murmur*). He dies!
(*The curtain falls.*)

END.

# Contes D'Hoffmann (1881)

## Tales of Hoffmann

MUSIC BY JACQUES OFFENBACH ■ LIBRETTO BY JULES BARBIER & MICHEL CARRÉ

This three-act opera with a prologue and an epilogue, set to a libretto by Jules Barbier and Michel Carré (based on three stories by Ernst Theodor Amadeus Hoffmann), premiered at the Opére-Comique in Paris on February 10, 1881. The Prologue takes place in Master Luther's beer cellar in Nuremberg. Councillor Lindorf, who represents evil, intercepts a note sent to the poet Hoffman by a beautiful opera singer, Stella, requesting that they meet. The students in the beer-cellar ask the poet if he has ever experienced true love. He answers with the following stories encapsulating four different incarnations of evil. In the first, Hoffmann becomes the student of Spalanzani, a physicist, so that he may be close to Olympia, who he believes to be the physicist's daughter, although in actuality, she is a mechanical doll that was built by Spalanzani and Coppelius, his strange partner. Nicklausse, Hoffmann's friend, warns him of danger, but his attempt are useless. Hoffmann is smitten. During a ball he tells Olympia that he loves her. She sings and dances beautifully. But when she goes to her room we hear the sound of machinery splitting apart. Coppelius, one of Lindorf's incarnations, enters with the broken doll. Hoffmann realizes that he has been duped. In the next tale, we are in an exquisite gallery near the Grand Canal in Venice. Hoffmann is love with Giulietta this time, who is completely dominated by the evil Dapertutto, yet another of Lindorf's incarnations. Having captured the reflection of Schlemil, her lover, for Dapertutto, she is about to capture that of Hoffmann. Nicklausse tries once again to warn his friend, who remains deaf to his pleas. Schlemil possesses the key to Giulietta's room. Hoffman challenges him to a duel and kills him. He takes the key and goes to her, only to find that she has left with another lover. We are now in Munich at the house of Crespel, a lute-maker. Hoffmann is in love with his daughter, Antonia. She sings beautifully, but her father tells her that her singing could kill her, just as it did her mother. Dr. Miracle, the fourth incarnation of Lindorf, enters and conjures up the spirit of Antonia's mother, who encourages her to continue singing. He accompanies her on the violin; she is unable to resist and sings until she collapses, utterly spent, and dies. The epilogue takes place back in the beer cellar. Hoffmann has decided that Stella is deluding him. The opera ends as he drowns his memories of her in drink.

## ■ PREMIER ACTE

### SCÈNE PREMIÈRE

*Intérieur d'une taverne alle-
mande. Au fond, à droite, en pan
coupé, grande porte donnant sur
la rue. A gauche, en pan coupé,
une fenêtre à petits vitraux. Dans
le millieu un large enfoncement
rempli de tonneaux
symétriquement rangés autour
d'un tonneau colossal surmonté
d'un petit Bacchus tenant une
banderole qui porte cet exergue:
Au Tonneau de Nuremberg. Au-
dessus des tonneaux s'étagent des
rayons garnis de flacons de toutes
formes. Devant le grand tonneau,
un petit comptoir. Portes
latérales, sur le premier plan, à
gauche, un grand poêle; à droite,
une horloge de bois et une petite
porte cachée dans la boiserie.
Cette boiserie s'étend sur la muraille, tout autour de la salle à
hauteur d'homme. Çà et là, des tables et des bancs.*

## ■ ACT ONE

### SCENE I

*Lotharios' Tavern
Interior of a German Tavern. In
the back, to the right, a large door,
leading to the street. On the left, a
window with small panes. In the
middle a large recess filled with
casks symmetrically arranged
around a colossal cask with a
small Bacchus on the top, holding
a label with the inscription: A tonneau de Nuremberg. Above the
casks there are shelves with flasks
of every description. Before the
large cask, a small counter. Side
doors, in the foreground, to the
left a large stove; to the right a
wooden clock and a small door
hidden in the wainscoting. This
wainscoting extends all around
the room, the height of a man.
Here and there tables and
benches.*

*ESPRITS
Il fait nuit; la scène est éclairée par un
rayon de lune.*

**LES ESPRITS DE LA BIÈRE:** Glou!
glou! glou! glou! je suis la bière.
**LES ESPRITS DU VIN:** Glou! glou!
glou! glou! je suis le vin.
**TOUS LES ESPRITS ENSEMBLE:**
Glou! glou! glou! nous sommes
Les amis des hommes;
Nous chasson d'ici
Langueur et souci.
Glou!
**LINDORF:** (*entrant, suivi
d'Andrès*). Le conseiller Lindorf,
morbleu! C'est moi qui suis
Le conseiller Lindorf! . . . Ne
craine rien et me suis.
N'as-tu pas pour maitresse
La Stella, cette enchanteresse?

**ANDRÈS:** Oui.

**LINDORF:** Qui vient de Milan . . .

**ANDRÈS:** Oui.

**LINDORF:** Traînant sur ses pas
Nombre d'amoureux, n'est-ce pas!

**ANDRÈS:** Oui.

*SPIRITS.
(It is night. The stage is lighted by a
moon beam.)*

**THE SPIRITS OF BEER:** Glou,
glou, glou, glou, I am beer!
**THE SPIRITS OF WINE:** Glou,
glou, glou, glou, I am wine.
**ALL THE SPIRITS TOGETHER:**
Glou, glou, glou, we are
The friends of man;
We drive
Languor and care from here.
Glou!
**LINDORF:** (*enter, followed by An-
drés*) Counselor Lindorf, zounds, it
is I
Who am the counselor Lindorf! Fear
not and follow me.
You have, do you not, for your mis-
tress,
Stella—that enchantress?

**ANDRÉS:** Yes.

**LINDORF.:** Who comes from Milan . . .

**ANDRÉS:** Yes.

**LINDORF.:** Who always is followed
By numerous lovers?

**ANDRÉS:** Yes.

**LINDORF:** C'est à l'un d'eux, je gage,
Que tu portes ce message?

**ANDRÈS:** Oui.

**LINDORF:** Je te l'achète.

**ANDRÈS:** Bon.

**LINDORF:** Dix thalers!

**ANDRÈS:** Non!

**LINDORF:** Vingt! Trente! . . .
(*Andrès ne rèpond pas.—A part.*)
Parlons-lui sa langue.
(*Levant sa canne.*)
Quarante!

**ANDRÈS:** Oui! . . .

**LINDORF:** (*lui donnant de l'argent et prenant la lettre*).
Donne, et va-t'eu au diable.

**ANDRÈS:** Oui! oui!
(*Il sort.*)

**LINDORF:** (*regardant la suscription de la lettre*). Voyons: 'pour Hoffmann', bon . . . . . je m'en doutais! ô femmes
Voilà les maitres de vos coeurs!
Les heureux vainqueurs!
Un poète! . . . un ivrogne! . . . enfin! passons! . . .
(*Il ouvre la lettre, en tire une petite clef et lit.*)
'Je t'aime! . . .
'Si je t'ai fait souffrir, si tu m'aimes toi-même,
'Ami, pardonne-moi,
'Cette clef t'ouvrira ma loge, souviens-toi! . . . '
(*A lui-même.*)
Qui, l'on devient digne d'envie,
Quand, brisé par l'amour, on porte aux cabarets
Et ses espoirs et ses regrets!
Voilà ce qu'il vous faut! . . . Eh bien! non, sur ma vie!
(*Il regarde sa montre.*)
Deux heures devant moi! . . . Si j'ai bonne mémoire,
C'est dans ce cabaret, qu'avec de jeunes fous
Hoffmann vient deviser et boire!
Surveillons-le jusqu'au moment du rendez-vous!

**LUTHER:** (*entrant, suivi de ses garçons.*) Vite! vite! qu'on se remue!
Les brocs! les chopes, les quinquets!
Les toasts vont suivre les bouquets
Et souhaiter la bienvenue
A cet astre du firmament!
Vivement, garçons, vivement!
(*Les garçons achèvent de préparer la salle. La porte du fond s'ouvre: Nathanael, Hermann, Wolframm, Wilhelm et une troupe d'étudiants entrent gaiement en scène.*)

**LINDORF.:** I wager that to one of these
You are bringing this message!

**ANDRÉS:** Yes.

**LINDORF.:** I'll buy it!

**ANDRÉS:** Very well.

**LINDORF.:** Ten dollars!

**ANDRÉS:** No.

**LINDORF.:** Twenty! Thirty! . . .
(*André does not answer.—Aside.*)
I know what will get him.
(*Lifting his cane.*)
Forty!

**ANDRÉS:** Yes.

**LINDORF.:** (*giving him the letter and taking the money.*) Give it, and go to the devil!

**ANDRÉS:** Yes, yes! (*Exit.*)

**LINDORF.:** (*looking at the address of the letter*) 'For Hoffmann', very well . . . I thought as much! Oh, women
You are the masters of our hearts! And we
Are the fortunate winners of your souls!
A poet! a drunkard! but let us read on!
(*He opens the letter, takes out of it a little key and reads*)
'I love you!
If I made you suffer, if you love me, My friend, forgive me,
This key will open my house, remember!
(*Aside.*)
Yes, one is worth of envy,
When, broken by love, one brings to the wine-shop
One's hopes and regrets!
But such is one's lot! Still, that shall not be!
(*He looks at his watch.*)
Two hours before me! If I have a good memory,
It is in this tavern, that with some young scamps,
Hoffmann is coming to chat and to drink
Let's watch him till the time of his rendez-vous!

**LUTHER:** (*entering, followed by the waiters*) Lively, lively, get you busy!
The jugs, the glasses and the lamps!
The toasts will follow the bouquets,
And give a merry welcome,
To this star of heaven!
Waiters, lively, lively!
(*The waiters finish preparing the room. The door in the back opens. Nathanael, Hermann, Wolframm, William and a band of students enter gaily.*)

**CHOEUR DES ÉTUDIANTS:** Drig! drig! drig! maître Luther
Tison d'enfer,
Drig! drig! drig! à nous ta bière,
A nous ton vin,
Jusqu'au matin
Remplis mon verre,
Jusqu'au matin
Remplis les pots d'étain!

**NATHANAEL:** Luther est un brave homme;
Tire lan laire!
C'est demain qu'on l'assomme;
Tire lan la!

**LE CHOEUR:** Tire lan la!
(*Les étudiants frappent les gobelets sur le tables.*)

**LUTHER:** (*allant de table en table avec les garçons et servant les étudiants.*) Voilà, messieurs, voilá!

**HERMANN:** Sa cave est d'un bon drille;
Tire lan laire!
C'est demain qu'on la pille
Tire lan la!

**LE CHOEUR:** Tire lan la!
(*Bruit de gobelets.*)

**LUTHER:** Voilà, messieurs, voilá!

**WILHELM:** Sa femme est fille d'Ève;
Tire lan laire;
C'est demain qu'on l'enlève;
Tire lan la!

**LE CHOEUR:** Tire lan la!

**LUTHER:** Voilà, messieurs, voilá!

**LE CHOEUR:** Drig! drig! drig! maître Luther
Tison d'enfer!
Drig! drig! drig! à nous la bière,
A nous ton vin!
Jusqu'au matin
Remplis mon verre!
Jusqu'au matin
Remplis les pots d'étain!
(*Les étudiants s'assoient, boivent et fument dans tous les coins.*)

**LUTHER:** Eh bien! Stella?

**NATHANAEL:** Vive Dieu! mes amis, la belle créature!
Comme au chef-d'oeuvre de Mozart
Elle prête l'accent d'une voix ferme et sûre!
C'est la grâce de la nature,
Et c'est le triomphe de l'art!
Que mon premier toast soit pour elle!
Je bois à la Stella!

**TOUS:** Vivat! à la Stella!

**NATHANAEL:** Comment Hoffmann n'est-il pas là
Pour fêter avec nous cette étoile nouvelle!
Eh! Luther! . . . ma grosse tonne!
Qu'as-tu fait de notre Hoffmann.

**HERMANN:** C'est ton vin qui l'empoisonne!
Tu l'as tué, foi d'Hermann!
Rends-nous Hoffmann!

**CHORUS OF STUDENTS:** Drig, drig, drig, master Luther,
Spark of Hades,
Drig, drig, drig, for us more beer,
For us your wine,
Until morning,
Fill my glass,
Until morning,
Fill our pewter mugs!

**NATHANAEL:** Luther is a brave man,
Tire, lan, laire,
Tomorrow we'll crush him,
Tire, lan, la!

**CHORUS:** Tire, lan, la!
(*the students tap their glasses on the tables.*)

**LUTHER:** (*going from table to table with the waiters and serving the students*) Here, gentlemen, here.

**HERMANN:** His cellar is a goodly spot,
Tire, lan, la!
Tomorrow we'll devast it,
Tire, lan, la!

**CHORUS:** Tire, lan, la! (*knocking of glasses.*)

**LUTHER:** Here, gentlemen, here.

**WILHELM:** His wife is a daughter of Eve,
Tire, lan, laire,
Tomorrow we'll abduct her,
Tire, lan, la!

**CHORUS:** Tire, lan, la!

**LUTHER:** Here, gentlemen, here.

**CHORUS:** Drig, drig, drig, master Luther,
Spark of Hades!
Drig, drig, drig, for us more beer.
For us your wine
Until morning.
Fill my glass
Until morning.
Fill our pewter mugs!
(*Students sit drinking and smoking in all the corners.*)

**LUTHER:** What about Stella?

**NATHANAEL:** Long live the fair creature!
How
She lends the tone of a voice firm and sure to the master-pieces of Mozart!
She is grace itself,
She's the triumph part!
May my first toast be to her!
I drink to Stella.

**ALL:** Hurrah! for Stella!

**NATHANAEL:** And Hoffmann is not here
To drink to this new star?
Luther, my goodly vat,
What have you done with our Hoffmann?

**HERMANN:** Your wine poisoned him,
You've killed him, faith of Herrmann,
Give us back Hoffmann.

# Act I, Scene I

**TOUS:** Rends-nous Hoffmann!

**ALL:** Give us Hoffmann.

**LINDORF:** (*à part*). Au diable Hoffmann!

**LINDORF.:** (*aside*) To the devil, Hoffmann.

**NATHANAEL:** Morbleau! qu'on nous l'apporte
Ou ton dernier jour a lui!

**NATHANAEL:** Let them bring him to us
Or your last day has dawned.

**LUTHER:** Messieurs, il ouvre la porte,
Et Niklausse est avec lui!

**LUTHER:** Gentlemen, he comes. (*He opens the door, and Nicklausse is with him.*)

**TOUS:** Vivat! C'est lui!

**ALL:** Hurrah, it is he.

**LINDORF:** (*à part*). Veillons sur lui.

**LINDORF.:** (*aside*) Let's watch him.

**HERMANN:** (*d'un air sombre*). Bonjour, amis!

**HOFFMANN:** (*entering, with sombre voice*) Good day, friends.

**NICKLAUSSE:** Bonjour!

**NICKLAUSSE:** Good-day.

**HERMANN:** Un tabouret! un verre! Une pipe! . . .

**HOFFMANN:** A chair, a glass, A pipe . . .

**NICKLAUSSE:** (*railleur*). Pardon, seigneur! . . . sans vous déplaire,
Je bois, fume et m'assieds comme vous! . . . part à deux!

**NICKLAUSSE:** (*mocking*) Pardon, my lord, without displeasing, I drink, smoke and sit like you . . . . for two.

**LE CHOEUR:** C'est juste! . . . Place à tous les deux!

**CHORUS:** He's right . . . a place for both of them.

*Hoffmann et Nicklausse s'assoient; Hoffmann se prend la tête entre les mains.*

*Hoffmann and Nicklausse sit down, Hoffmann has head in his hands.*

**NICKLAUSSE:** (*fredonnant*). Notte a giorno mal dormire . . .

**NICKLAUSSE:** (*humming*) Notte a giorno mal dormire . . .

**HOFFMANN:** (*brusquement*). Tais-toi, par le diable! . . .

**HOFFMANN:** (*brusquely*) Shut up, in devil's name.

**NICKLAUSSE:** (*tranquillement*). Oui, mon maître.

**NICKLAUSSE:** (*quietly*) Yes, master.

**HERMANN:** (*À Hoffmann*). Oh! oh! d'où vient cet air fâché?

**HERRMANN:** (*to Hoffmann*) Oh, oh, from where comes this ill temper?

**NATHANAEL:** (*à Hoffmann*). C'est à ne pas te reconnaître.

**NATHANAEL:** (*to Hoffmann*) It's as if one did not know you.

**HERMANN:** Sur quelle herbe as-tu donc marché?

**HERMANN:** On what thorn have you trod?

**HOFFMANN:** Hélas! sur une herbe morte
Au souffle glacé du nord! . . .

**HOFFMANN:** Alas, on a dead herb With the iced breath of the north.

**NICKLAUSSE:** Et là, prés de cete porte,
Sur un ivrogne qui dort!

**NICKLAUSSE:** And there by this door, On a drunkard who sleeps.

**HOFFMANN:** C'est vrai! . . . Ce coquin-là, pardieu! m'a fait envie.
A boire! . . . et, comme lui, couchons dans le ruisseau.

**HOFFMANN:** True . . . that rascal, by Jove, I envy him. A drink. Like him, let's sleep in the gutter.

**HERMANN:** Sans oreiller?

**HERMANN:** Without pillow.

**HOFFMANN:** La pierre!

**HOFFMANN:** The flags.

**NATHANAEL:** Et sans rideau?

**NATHANAEL:** Without curtains.

**HOFFMANN:** Le ciel!

**HOFFMANN:** The sky.

**NATHANAEL:** Sans couvre-pied?

**NATHANAEL:** Without foot-covers?

**HOFFMANN:** La pluie!

**HOFFMANN:** The rain.

**HERMANN:** As-tu le cauchemar, Hoffmann?

**HERMANN:** Have you a nightmare, Hoffmann?

**HOFFMANN:** Non, mais ce soir Tout à l'heure, au théâtre . . .

**HOFFMANN:** No, but tonight, A while since, at the play . . .

**TOUS:** Eh bien?

**ALL:** Well?

**HOFFMANN:** J'ai cru revoir. Baste! . . . à quoi bon rouvrir une vieille blessure? La vie est courte! . . . Il faut l'égayer en chemin. Il faut boire, chanter et rire à l'aventure, Sauf à pleurer demain!

**HOFFMANN:** I thought to see again . . . The deuce . . . why reopen old wounds? Life is short. Enjoy it while we can. We must drink, sing, laugh, as we may, Leave the weeping for tomorrow!

**NATHANAEL:** Chante donc le premier, sans qu'on te le demande; Nous ferons chorus.

**NATHANAEL:** Then sing the first without asking, We'll be the chorus.

**HOFFMANN:** Soit!

**HOFFMANN:** Agreed!

**NATHANAEL:** Quelque chose de gai!

**NATHANAEL:** Something gay

**HERMANN:** La chanson du Rat!

**HERMANN:** The song of the Rat!

**NATHANAEL:** Non! moi, j'en suis fatigué. Ce qu'il nous faut, c'est la légende De Klein-Zach? . . .

**NATHANAEL:** No, for me, I'm tired of it. What we want is the legend Of Klein-Zach . . .

**TOUS:** C'est la légende de Klein-Zach!

**ALL:** It is the legend of Klein-Zach.

**HOFFMANN:** Va pour Klein-Zach! Il était une fois à la cour d'Eysenach Un petit avorton qui se nommait Klein-Zach! Il était coiffé d'un colbac, Et ses jambes faisaient clic, clac! Clic, clac! Voilà Klein-Zach!

**HOFFMANN:** Here goes for Klein-Zach! . . . Once at the court of Eysenach A little dwarf called Klein-Zach, Was covered with a colbac, And his legs they went clic, clac! Clic, clac, There's Klein-Zach.

**LE CHOEUR:** Clic, clac! . . . Voilà Klein-Zach!

**CHORUS:** Crick, crack, There's Klein-Zach.

**HOFFMANN:** Il avait une bosse en guise d'estomac; Ses pieds ramifiés semblaient sortir d'un sac, Son nez était noir de tabac, Et sa tête faisait cric, crac, Cric, crac, Voilà Kelin-Zach.

**HOFFMANN:** He had a hump in place of stomach, His webbed feet seemed to burst a sack, His nose was with tobacco black, And his head it went crick crack, Crick, crack. There's Klein-Zach.

**LE CHOEUR:** Cric, crac, Voilà Klein-Zach!

**CHORUS:** Crick, crack, There's Klein-Zach.

**HOFFMANN:** Quant aux traits de sa figure (*Il semble s'absorber peu à peu dans son rêve.*)

**HOFFMANN:** As for the features on his face. (*He becomes absorbed.*)

**LE CHOEUR:** Quant aux traits de sa figure? . . .

**CHORUS:** As for the features on his face.

**HOFFMANN:** (*très lentement*). Quant aux traits de sa figure . . . (*Il se lève*). Ah! sa figure était charmante! . . . Je la vois, Belle comme le jour où, courant après elle, Je quittais comme un fou la maison paternelle Et m'enfuis à travers les vallons et les bois! Ses cheveux en torsades sombres Sur son col élégant jetaient leurs chaudes ombres. Ses yeux, enveloppés d'asur, Promenaient autour d'elle un regard frais et pur Et, comme notre char emportait sans secousse Nos coeurs et nos amours, sa voix vibrante et douce

**HOFFMANN:** (*very slowly*) As for the features . . . (*He rises.*) Oh her face was charming . . . I see it, Fine as the day, running after her, I, like a fool, left the house paternal, And fled there on to woods and vales Her hair, in sombre rolls, On her neck threw warm shades, Her eyes of enveloping azure, Cast about glances fresh and pure. And as our car without shock or tremor Carried our loves and hearts, her vibrant voice and sweet, To the heavens that listened, threw the conquering cry, And the eternal echo resounded in

Aux cieux qui l'écoutaient jetait ce chant vainqueur
Dont l'éternel écho résonne dans mon coeur!

my heart.

NATHANAEL: O bizarre cervelle! Qui diable peins-tu là! Klein-Zach?..

NATHANAEL: Oh strangest brain! Who are you painting! Klein-Zach?

HOFFMANN: Je parle d'elle.

HOFFMANN: I speak of her . . .

NATHANAEL: (lui touchant l'épaule). Qui?

NATHANAEL: (tapping him on the shoulder) Who?

HOFFMANN: (sortant de son rêve). Non! personne! . . . rien! mon esprit se troublait!
Rien! . . . Et Klein-Zach vaut mieux, tout difforme qu'il est! . . .
Quand il avait trop bu de genièvre ou de rack
Il fallait voir flotter les deux pans de son frac,
Comme des herbes dans un lac! . . .
Et le monstre faisait flic, flac! . . .
Flic, flac!
Voilà Klein-Zach!

HOFFMANN: (coming out of his dream)
Nobody . . . nothing, my spirit is dullish.
Nothing. Klein-Zach is better, malformed as he is!
When he drank too much gin or arrack,
You should see his coat-tails flap,
Like grasses in a lake,
And the monster went flick, flack!

LE CHOEUR: Flic, flac!
Voilà Klein-Zach!

CHORUS: Flick, flack,
There's Klein-Zach.

HOFFMANN: (jetant son verre).
Peuh! . . . cette bière est détestable!
Allumons le punch! grisons nous!
Et que les plus fous
Roulent sous la table.

HOFFMANN: (throwing away his glass) Peuh! . . . this beer is detestable,
Let's light up the punch and drink;
And may the light-headed
Roll under the table.

LE CHOEUR: Et que les plus fous
Roulent sous la table!
(Mouvement général. On éteint les lumières. Luther allume un immense bol de punch; une lumière bleuâtre éclaire la scène.)
Luther est un brave homme,
Tire lan laire,
Tire lan la,
C'est demain qu'on l'assomme,
Tire lan laire,
Tire lan la,
Sa cave est d'un bon drille.
Tire lan laire,
Tire lan la,
C'est demain qu'on la pille,
Tire lan laire,
Tire lan la.

CHORUS: And may the light-headed
Roll under the table.
(General commotion.)
(The lights go out, Luther fires an immense punch bowl; a bluish light illuminates the stage.)
Luther is a brave man,
Tire lan laire,
Tire lan la.
Tomorrow we'll crush him,
Tire lan laire,
Tire lan la.
His cellar is a good spot,
Tire lan laire,
Tomorrow we will make it hot.
Tire lan laire,
Tire lan la.

NICKLAUSSE: A la bonne heure, au moins! voilà que l'on se pique
De raison et de sens pratique!
Peste soit des coeurs langoureux!

NICKLAUSSE: Very good, indeed.
At least we are pruned
With reason and practical sense!
Away with languorous hearts.

NATHANAEL: Gageons qu'Hoffmann est amoureux!

NATHANAEL: Let's wager that Hoffmann's in love.

HOFFMANN: Amoureux . . . Le diable m'emporte
Si jamais je le deviens! . . .

HOFFMANN: In love? May the devil take me
If ever I should fall in love.

LINDORF: (à mi-voix). Eh! eh! l'impertinence est forte;
Il ne faut jurer de rien!

LINDORF.: (softly) What! his impertinence is great;
One must never swear!

HOFFMANN: (se retournant).
Plaît-il?
(Reconnaissant Lindorf.)
Quand on parle du diable,
On en voit les cornes! . . .

HOFFMANN: (turning around) I beg your pardon?
(Recognizing Lindorf.)
Talk of an angel
And you hear its wings flutter.

NICKLAUSSE: Pardon,
La perruque! . . . chaste don
D'une épouse trop aimable!

NICKLAUSSE: Pardon me!
My wig! The kind gift
Of a too kind wife.

LE CHOEUR: Respect aux maris!
Ne les raillons pas!
Nous serons un jour dans le même cas!

CHORUS: Homage to husbands! Let us not mock them!
Some day we all will be in their boots.

NATHANAEL: Ta maîtresse est donc un trésor
Que tu méprises tant les nôtres?

NATHANAEL: Then your mistress is such a treasure
That you despise so much our own?

HOFFMANN: Ma maîtresse? . . . (A part.)
Oui, Stella!
Trois femmes dans la même femme!
Trois âmes dans une seule âme!
Artiste, jeune fille, et courtisane!
(Tendant la main vers la droite.)
Là! . . .
(Haut.)
Ma maîtresse? . . . . Non pas!
diets mieux, trois maîtresses,
Trio charmant d'enchanteresses
Qui se partagèrent mes jours!
Voulez-vous le récit de ces folles amours? . . .

HOFFMANN: My mistress?
(Aside.)
Yes. Stella!
Three women in one woman!
Three souls in a single soul!
Artist, unmarried, and courtesan!
(Pointing to the right.)
There!
(Aloud.)
My mistress, no, no, say rather three,
Charming trio of enchantresses.
Who are dividing my days.
Would you like the story of my crazy loves? . . .

LE CHOEUR: Oui, oui!

CHORUS: Yes, yes!

NICKLAUSSE: Que parles-tu de trois maîtresses?

NICKLAUSSE: What are you saying of three mistresses?

HOFFMANN: Fume! . . .
Avant que cette pipe éteinte se rallume
Tu m'auras sans doute compris,
O toi qui dans ce drame où mon coeur se consume
(Railleur.)
Du bon sens emportas le prix!
(Tous les étudiants vont reprendre leurs places.)

HOFFMANN: Smoke! . . .
Before this dead pipe is relighted
You will have comprehended,
You who in this play where my heart was consumed
(Jesting.)
In good sense took the first prize!
(All the students go to their places.)

LUTHER: (rentrant en scène).
Messieur, on va lever le rideau.

LUTHER: (coming in) Sire, the curtain is going to rise.

NATHANAEL: Qu'il se lève!
C'est là notre moindre souci!

NATHANAEL: Let it rise! We care least about that.

LINDORF. (à part). Avant que l'opéra s'achève,
J'ai le temps d'écouter aussi.
(Luther va reprendre sa place à son comptoir.)

LINDORF.: (aside) Before the opera is over,
I, too, have time to listen.
(Luther again takes his place at the counter.)

LE CHOEUR: Écoutons! il est doux de boire
Au récit d'une folle histoire,
En suivant le nuage clair
Que la pipe jette dans l'air!

CHORUS: Listen. It is nice to drink,
To the telling of a crazy tale,
While following the fragrant cloud,
That a pipe throws in the air.

HOFFMANN: (s'asseyant sur le coin d'une table). Je commence.

HOFFMANN: (sitting on corner of table) I begin.

LE CHOEUR: Silence!

CHORUS: Silence.

LINDORF: (à part). Dans une heure, j'espère, ils seront à quia!

LINDORF.: (aside) In an hour, I hope, they'll be nonplussed.

HOFFMANN: Le nom de la première était Olympia!
(Le rideau tombe, pendant qu'Hoffmann parle à tous les etudiants attentifs.)

HOFFMANN: The name of the first was Olympia
(The curtain falls as Hoffman is speaking to the attentive students.)

## SCÈNE DEUXIÈME

*Olympia*

## SCENE II

*Olympia*

## Act I, Scene II

*Un riche cabinet de physcien donnant sur une galerie dont les portes sont closes par des tapisseries; portes latérales fermées également par des portières. le théâtre est éclairé par des bougies.)*

SPALANZANI: (*seul, il tient la portière de droite soulevée.*) Là! dors en paix. Eh! Eh! . . . sage, modeste et belle,
Je rentrerai par elle
Dans les cinq cents ducats que la banqueroute
Du juif Elias me coûte!
Rests Coppélius dont la duplicité
Pour avoir de moi quelque somme,
Peut réclamer des droits à la paternité,
Diable d'homme! . . .
Il est loin, par bonheur!

*Spalanzani, Hoffmann, puis Cochenille et les Laqais*

SPALANZANI: (*voyant entrer Hoffmann*). Ah! bonjour . . . enchanté!

HOFFMANN: Je viens trop tôt, peut-être?

SPALANZANI: Comment donc, un élève . . .

HOFFMANN: Indigne de son maître.

SPALANZANI: Trop modeste, en vérité!
Plus de vers, plus de musique,
Et vous serez en physique
Professeur de faculté.
Vous connaîtrez ma fille, un sourire angélique,
Olympia vaut très cher! . . .

HOFFMANN: (*à part*). Quel rapport la physique a-t elle avec sa fille?

SPALANZANI: (*appelant*). Holà! hé! . . . Cochenille!
(*Cochenille paraît.*)
Fais allumer partout . . .

COCHENILLE: (*bégayant*)
Et . . . le champagne.

SPALANZANI: Attends!
Suis-moi.
(*A Hoffmann.*)
Pardon, mon cher, je reviens dans l'instant.
(*Ils sortent.*)

HOFFMANN: (*seul*). Allons! Courage et confiance
Je deviens un puits de science!
Il faut tourner selon le vent.
Pour mériter celle que j'aime,
Je saurai trouver en moi-même
L'étoffe d'un savant,
Elle est là . . . Si j'osais! . . .
(*Il soulève tout doucement la portière de droite.*)
C'est elle!
Elle sommeille! . . . Qu'elle est belle!
Ah! vivre deux! . . . N'avoir

---

*A richly furnished physicist's study, opening into a gallery, the doors of which are closed by portieres; side-doors likewise closed by portieres. The stage is lighted by candle-light.*

SPALANZANI: (*alone, raises the portiere on the right*) There, sleep in peace. Ah, ah, good, modest and beautiful,
Through her I will win
The five hundred ducats which the bankruptcy
Of the Jew Elias costs me!
There remains Coppelius, whose deceit,
In order to get a sum from me,
Can claim the rights of paternity,
The deuce of a man!
But luckily he is far away!

*Spalanzani, Hoffmann, then Cochenille and the lackeys*

SPALANZANI: (*seeing Hoffmann come in*) Ah, good day, charmed to see you!

HOFFMANN: I have come too early, perhaps?

SPALANZANI: Why, a pupil—

HOFFMANN: Unworthy of his master.

SPALANZANI: Too modest, indeed!
No more verse, and no more music,
And you will be
Professor of physics at the University.
You shall know my daughter, she has an angelic smile.
Physics is everything, my dear!
Olympia is worth a goodly price!

HOFFMANN: (*aside*) What relation has physics with his daughter?

SPALANZANI: (*calling*) Come here, Cochenille!
(*Cochenille appears*)
Turn on all the lights!

COCHENILLE: (*stammering*)
And—the champagne?

SPALANZANI: Wait!
Follow me!
(*To Hoffmann.*)
Pardon me, dear friend, I'll return in an instant.
(*Exit.*)

HOFFMANN: (*alone*) Come!
Courage and confidence;
I become a well of science.
I must turn with the wind that blows,
To deserve the one I love.
I shall know how to find in myself
The stuff of a learned man.
She is there . . . if I dared.
(*He softly lifts the portiere.*)
It is she!
She sleeps . . . how beautiful!
Ah! live together . . . both in the same hope,

---

qu'une même expérance,
Un même souvenir!
Partager le bonheur, partager la souffrance,
Partager l'avenir! . . .
Laisse, laisse ma flamme
Verser en toi le jour!
Laisse éclore ton âme
Aux rayons de l'Amour!
Foyer divin! . . . Soleil dont l'ardeur nous pénètre
Et nous vient embraser! . . .
Ineffable désir où l'on sent tout son être
Se fondre en un baiser.
Laisse, laisse ma flamme
Verser en toi le jour! . . .
Laisse éclore ton âme
Aux rayons de l'Amour!
(*Il soulève de nouveau la portière; Nicklausse paraît.*)

NICKLAUSSE: Pardieu! . . . J'étais bien sûr de te trouver ici! . . .

HOFFMANN: (*laissant brusquement retomber la portière*) Chut! . . .

NICKLAUSSE: Pourquoi? . . . C'est là que respire
La colombe qui fait ton amoureux souci,
La belle Olympia? . . . Va, mon enfant! Admire!

HOFFMANN: Oui, je l'adore!

NICKLAUSSE: Attends à la connaître mieux.

HOFFMANN: L'âme qu'on aime est aisée à connaître!

NICKLAUSSE: (*railleur*). Quoi? d'un regard? . . . par la fenêtre?

HOFFMANN: Il suffit d'un regard pour embrasser les cieux!

NICKLAUSSE: Quelle chaleur! . . . Au moins sait-elle que tu l'aimes?

HOFFMANN: Non!

NICKLAUSSE: Écris-lui!

HOFFMANN: Je n'ose pas.

NICKLAUSSE: Pauvre agneau! Parle-lui!

HOFFMANN: Les dangers sont les mêmes.

NICKLAUSSE: Alors, chante, morbleu! pour sortir d'un tel pas!

NICKLAUSSE: (*riant*). Oui, je sais!
Tout pour la physique! . . .
Une poupée aux yeux d'émail
Jouait au mieux de l'éventail
Auprès d'un petit coq en cuivre;
Tous deux chantaient à l'unisson
D'une merveilleuse façon,
Dansaient, caquetaient, semblaient vivre.

HOFFMANN: Plait-il? Pourquoi cette chanson?

---

The same remembrance
Divide our happiness and our sorrow,
And share the future.
Let, let my flame
Pour the light in you,
Let your soul open
To the rays of Love.
Divine hearth! Sun whose ardor penetrates
And comes to kiss us.
Ineffable desire where one's whole being
Melts in a single kiss.
Let, let my flame, etc., etc.
(*He again raises the portiere; Nicklausse appears.*)

NICKLAUSSE: By Jove, I felt sure you'd be here.

HOFFMANN: (*letting portiere fall*) Chut.

NICKLAUSSE: Why? It is there that breathes
The dove who's now your amorous care,
The beautiful Olympia? Go, my child, admire!

HOFFMANN: Yes, I adore her!

NICKLAUSSE: Wait to know her better.

HOFFMANN: The soul one loves is easy to know.

NICKLAUSSE: (*teasing*) What? by a look . . . through a window?

HOFFMANN: A look is enough to embrace the heavens.

NICKLAUSSE: What warmth! . . . At least she knows that you love her.

HOFFMANN: No.

NICKLAUSSE: Write her.

HOFFMANN: I don't dare.

NICKLAUSSE: Poor lamb! Speak to her.

HOFFMANN: The dangers are the same.

NICKLAUSSE: Then sing, to get out of the scrape.

HOFFMANN: Monsieur Spalanzani doesn't like music.

NICKLAUSSE: (*laughing*) Yes, I know, all for physics!
A doll with china eyes
Played cleverly with a fan,
Nearby a little cock in brass;
Both sang in unison
In a marvelous way,
Danced, gossiped, seemed to live.

HOFFMANN: Beg your pardon. Why this song?

NICKLAUSSE: Le petit coq, luisant et vif,
Avec un air rébarbatif,
Tournait par trois fois sur lui-même;
Par un rouage ingénieux,
La poupée, en roulant les yeux,
Soupirait et disait: Je t'aime!

NICKLAUSSE: The little cock, shining and smart,
With a very knowing air,
Turned three times on himself;
By some ingenious wheels,
The doll in rolling its eyes
Sighed and said: 'I love you.'

COPPÉLIUS: C'est moi, Coppélius! . . . doucement prenons garde!
(Apercevant Hoffmann.)
Quelqu'un . . .

COPPELIUS: It is I, Coppelius! Gently! Take care! (Noticing Hoffmann.)
Someone—

NICKLAUSSE: (se retournant). Hein! . . .

NICKLAUSSE: (turning around) What—

COPPÉLIUS: Qu'est-ce donc que ce monsieur regarde?
(Regardant par-dessus l'épaule d'Hoffmann.)
Notre Olympia! . . . fort bien . . .

COPPELIUS: What is the gentleman looking at? (Looking over Hoffmann's shoulder.)
Our Olympia! very well!

NICKLAUSSE: (à part). Leur Olympia?

NICKLAUSSE: (aside) Their Olympia?

COPPÉLIUS: (À Hoffmann).
Jeune homme, (Elevant la voix.)
Eh!. monsieur!
(voyant qu'Hoffmann ne répond pas, lui frappant sur l'épaule.)
Il n'entend rien!
Monsieur!

COPPELIUS: (to Hoffmann)
Young man,
(raising his voice.)
Eh, young man!
(Seeing that Hoffmann does not answer, strikes his shoulder.)
He does not hear!
Sir!

HOFFMANN: Plait-il?

HOFFMANN: I beg your pardon?

COPPÉLIUS: Je me nomme Coppélius, un ami
De monsieur Spalanzani.
(Hoffmann le salue.)
Voyez ces baromètres
Hygromètres,
Thermomètres,
Au rabais, mais au comptant.
Voyez, vous en serez content.
(Vidant à terre son sac rempli de lorgnons, lunettes et lorgnettes.)
Chacun de ces lorgnons rend noir comme le jais,
Ou blanc comme l'hermine,
Assombrit,
Illumine,
Éclaire, ou flétrit
Les objets.
J'ai des yeux, de vrais yeux,
Des yeux vivant, des yeux de flamme,
Des yeux merveilleux
Qui vont jusques au fond de l'âme
Et qui même dans bien des cas
Enpeuvent prêter une à ceux qui n'en ont pas.
J'ai des yeux, de vrais yeux vivants, des yeux de flamme.
J'ai des yeux,
De beaux yeux!
Oui!
Veux-tu voir le coeur d'une femme?
S'il est pur ou s'il est infâme!
Ou bien préfères-tu le voir
Le voir tout blanc quand il est noir?
Prends et tu verras
Ce que tu voudras.
Prenez mes yeux, mes yeux vivants,

COPPELIUS: My name
Is Coppelius, a friend
Of Mr. Spalanzani.
(Hoffmann bows to him.)
See these barometers,
Hydrometers,
Thermometers,
At a reduction, but for cash.
I'm sure you will like them.
(Emptying on the ground his bag filled with eyeglasses, spectacles, and opera glasses.)
Each one of these spectacles makes black as jet
Or white as ermine,
Darkens,
Brightens.
Lights up or dullens
Objects.
I have eyes, real eyes,
Bright eyes, eyes of flame,
Marvelous eyes,
Which go to the depth of the soul
And which even, in many cases
Can give one to those who have not any.
I have eyes, true living eyes, eyes of flame.
I have eyes,
Beautiful eyes!
Yes!
Do you wish to see the heart of a woman?
To see if it is pure or base?
Or else do you prefer to see,
To see it white when it is black?
Take and you shall see
All you wish to see.
Take my eyes, my living eyes, my

mes yeux de flamme,
Mes yeux qui percent l'âme.
Prenez mes yeux!

eyes of flame,
My eyes which pierce the soul.
Take my eyes!

HOFFMANN: Dis-tu vrai?

HOFFMANN: Are you telling the truth?

COPPÉLIUS: (lui présentant un lorgnon.) Voyez!

COPPELIUS: (giving him an eye glass) Look!

HOFFMANN: Donne!

HOFFMANN: Give it!

COPPÉLIUS: Trois ducats!

COPPELIUS: Three ducats!

HOFFMANN: (soulevant la portière et regardant). Dieu puissant! quelle grâce rayonne
Sur son front!

HOFFMANN: (raising the portiere and looking) God all powerful! what grace
Shines on her face!

COPPÉLIUS: Trois ducats.

COPPELIUS: Three ducats.

HOFFMANN: Cher ange, est-ce bien toi?

HOFFMANN: Dear angel, is it you?

COPPÉLIUS: (faisant retomber la portière). Trois ducats!

COPPELIUS: (letting the portiere drop) Three ducats!

HOFFMANN: Ah! pourquoi me ravir cette image
De bonheur et d'amour?
(Nicklausse donne les ducats à Coppélius.)

HOFFMANN: Ah, why to take from me
This image of happiness and love?
(Nicklausse gives the ducats to Coppelius.)

SPALANZANI: (entrant en se frottant les mains, puis apercevant Coppélius). Hein! Vous?

SPALANZANI: (enters, rubbing his hands, then noticing Coppelius) What, you?

COPPÉLIUS: Ce cher maître! . . .

COPPELIUS: Dear master!

SPALANZANI: Morbleu! Il était convenu . . .

SPALANZANI: Zounds! It was agreed—

COPPÉLIUS: Rien d'écrit . . .

COPPELIUS: Nothing was written—

SPALANZANI: Mais . . .

SPALANZANI: But—

COPPÉLIUS: Chimère! . . . L'argent sur vous pleuvra dans peu
Je veux tout partager.

COPPELIUS: Nonsense! Money will soon pour on you—
I want to share all.

SPALANZANI: Ne suis-je pas le père
D'Olympia?

SPALANZANI: Am I not
The father of Olympia?

COPPÉLIUS: Pardon, elle a mes yeux.

COPPELIUS: Pardon me, she has my eyes.

SPALANZANI: Plus bas! . . . (A part.)
Bien lui prend que j'ignore
Son secret. Mais j'y pense, oui! (Haut.)
Voulez-vous encore
Cinq cents ducats? qu'un écrit de vous m'abandonne
Ses yeux, ainsi que toute sa personne,
Et voici votre argent sur le juif Élias.

SPALANZANI: Not so loud!
(Aside.)
He thinks I don't know
His secret. But I certainly do!
(Aloud.)
Do you want
Five hundred ducats more? So that a written statement
Might give me her eyes, likewise the rest of her person,
And here is your money drawn on the Jew Elias.

COPPÉLIUS: Élias?

COPPELIUS: Elias?

SPALANZANI: Une maison sûre.

SPALANZANI: A very reliable house.

COPPÉLIUS: (écrit sur ses tablettes). Allons, c'est dit.

COPPELIUS: (writes in his notebook) Very well, that is agreed.

SPALANZANI: (Ils échangent leurs papiers). Donnant, donnant!
Ce cher ami!
(Ils s'embrassent.)

SPALANZANI: (They exchange papers.) A fair exchange!
My dear friend!
(They embrace.)

HOFFMANN: (bas, à Nicklausse). Quel marché peuvent-ils conclure?

HOFFMANN: (aside, to Nicklausse) What bargain are they making now?

COPPÉLIUS: Ce cher ami!

COPPELIUS: My dear friend!

**SPALANZANI:** (*à part*). Va, maintenant! Va te faire payer!

**COPPÉLIUS:** A propos, une idée, Mariez donc Olympia! (*Montrant Hoffmann.*) Le jeune fou que voilà, Ne vous l'a donc pas demandée? Quel nigaud!

**SPALANZANI:** C'est jeune!

**COPPÉLIUS:** Oui, vous l'avez endormi.

**SPALANZANI:** (*l'embrassant*). Ce cher ami!

**COPPÉLIUS:** (*même jeu*). Ce cher ami! (*Il sort en ricanant.*)

**SPALANZANI:** (*à Hoffmann*). La physique, mon cher! . . .

**HOFFMANN:** Ah! . . . c'est une manie.

**COCHENILLE:** (*paraissant au fond*). Monsieur, voilà toute la compagnie.

**LE CHOEUR DES INVITÉS:** Non, aucun hôte, vraiment, Ne recoit plus richement! Par le goût, sa maison brille! Tout s'y trouve réuni. Cà, monsieur Spalanzani, Présentez-nous votre fille. On la dit faite à ravir, Aimable, exempte de vices. Nous comptons nous rafraichir Après quelques exercices. Non, aucun hôte vraiment Ne recoit plus richement!

**SPALANZANI:** Vous serez satis faits, messieurs, dans un moment. (*Il fait signe à Cochenille de le suivre, et sort avec lui par la droite. Les invités se promènent par groupes en admirant la demeure de Spalanzani. Nicklausse s'approche d'Hoffmann.*)

**NICKLAUSSE:** (*à Hoffmann*). Enfin, nous allons voir de près cette merveille Sans pareille!

**HOFFMANN:** Silence! . . . la voici! . . .

*Entrée de Spalanzani conduisant Olympia. cochenille les suit Curiosité générale.*)

**SPALANZANI:** Mesdames et messieurs, Je vous présente Ma fille Olympia.

**LE CHOEUR:** Charmante! Elle a de très beaux yeux! Sa taille est fort bien prise! Voyez comme elle est mise! Il ne lui manque rien! Elle est très bien!

---

**SPALANZANI:** (*aside*) Go now! And get your money!

**COPPELIUS:** By the way, an idea, Marry off Olympia! (*Pointing to Hoffmann.*) Has not that young madman Asked you yet for her hand? What a fool!

**SPALANZANI:** He is young!

**COPPELIUS:** Yes, you have put him to sleep.

**SPALANZANI:** (*kissing him*) My dear friend!

**COPPELIUS:** (*does the same*) My dear friend! (*He goes out laughing.*)

**SPALANZANI:** (*to Hoffmann*) Physics, my dear!

**HOFFMANN:** Ah, that is a mania.

**COCHENILLE:** (*appearing in the rear of the room*) Sir, here is the whole company.

**CHORUS OF GUESTS:** No, no host, really, Receives more richly! Good taste shines through your house! Everything here matches. No, no host, really, Receives more richly. Now, Mister Spalanzani, Present your daughter to us. They say that she is charming, Lovable, free from all vices. We count upon refreshing ourselves After some exercise. No, no host, really, Receives more richly.

**SPALANZANI:** You will be satisfied, gentlemen, in a moment. (*He beckons to Cochenille to follow him, and goes out with him at the right. The guests walk about in groups admiring Spalanzani's home. Nicklausse approaches Hoffmann.*)

**NICKLAUSSE:** (*to Hoffmann*) At last we shall more nearly see this marvel Without equal!

**HOFFMANN:** Silence . . . she is here!

*Enter Spalanzani conducting Olympia. Cochenille follows them. General surprise.*

**SPALANZANI:** Ladies and gentlemen, I present to you My daughter Olympia.

**THE CHORUS:** Charming. She has beautiful eyes! Her shape is very good! See how well apparelled! Nothing is lacking! She does very well!

---

**HOFFMANN:** Ah! qu'elle est adorable!

**NICKLAUSSE:** Charmante, incomparable!

**SPALANZANI:** (*à Olympia*). Quel succès est le tien.

**NICKLAUSSE:** (*en la lorgnant*) Vraiment elle est très bien.

**LE CHOEUR:** Elle a de très beaux yeux Sa taille est fort bien prise Voyez comme elle est mise Il ne lui manque rien. Vraiment elle est très bien.

**SPALANZANI:** Mesdames et messieurs, fière de vos bravos, Et surtout impatiente D'en conquérir de nouveaux, Ma fille, obéissant à vos moindres caprices, Va, s'il vous plaît . . .

**NICKLAUSSE:** (*à part*). Passer à d'autres exercices.

**SPALANZANI:** Vous chanter un grand air, en suivant de la voix, Talent rare! Le clavecin, la guitare, Ou la harpe, à votre choix

**COCHENILLE:** (*au fond du théâtre, en voix de fausset*). La harpe! . . .

**UNE VOIX DE BASSE:** répondant dans la coulisse à la voix de Cochenille). La harpe! . . .

**SPALANZANI:** Fort bien! . . . Cochenille, Va vite nous chercher la harpe de ma fille! (*Cochenille entre dans l'appartement d'Olympia*).

**HOFFMANN:** (*à part*). Je vais l'entendre . . . ô joie!

**NICKLAUSSE:** (*à part*). O folle passion!

**SPALANZANI:** (*à Olympia*). Maîtrise ton émotion, Mon enfant!

**OLYMPIA:** Oui!

**COCHENILLE:** (*rentrant en scène avec une harpe*). Voilà!

**SPALANZANI:** (*s'asseyant auprès d'Olympia et plaçant sa harpe devant lui.*) Messieurs, attention!

**COCHENILLE:** A . . . attention!

**LE CHOEUR:** Attention.

**OLYMPIA:** (*accompagnée par Spalanzani.—De temps à autre sa voix faiblit, Cochenille lui touche l'épaule et l'on entend le bruit d'un ressort*). Les oi-seaux-dans-la-char-mille, Dans-les-cieux-l'astre-du-jour, Toute-parle-à-la-jeune-fil-le D'a-mour! D'a-mour! Voi-là

---

**HOFFMANN:** Ah, how adorable she is!

**NICKLAUSSE:** Charming, incomparable!

**SPALANZANI:** (*to Olympia*) What a success is yours!

**NICKLAUSSE:** (*taking her all in*) Really she is handsome.

**THE CHORUS:** She has beautiful eyes, Her shape is very good, See how well apparelled, Nothing is really lacking, She does very well.

**SPALANZANI:** Ladies and gentlemen, proud of your applause, And above all anxious To conquer more, My daughter obedient to your least caprice Will, if you please . . .

**NICKLAUSSE:** (*aside*) Pass to other exercises.

**SPALANZANI:** Sing to a grand air, following with the voice, Rare talent The clavichord, the guitar, Or the harp, at your choice!

**COCHENILLE:** (*at the rear*) The harp!

**BASS VOICE:** (*in the wings, answering Cochenille's voice*) The harp!

**SPALANZANI:** Very good, Cochenille! Go quickly and bring my daughter's harp! (*Cochenille enters Olympia's apartment.*)

**HOFFMANN:** (*aside*) I shall hear her . . . oh joy!

**NICKLAUSSE:** (*aside*) Oh, crazy passion!

**SPALANZANI:** (*to Olympia*) Master your emotion, my child!

**OLYMPIA:** Yes.

**COCHENILLE:** (*coming in, bringing a harp*) There!

**SPALANZANI:** (*sitting beside Olympia and putting the harp before him*) Gentlemen, attention!

**COCHENILLE:** Attention!

**THE CHORUS:** Attention!

**OLYMPIA:** (*accompanied by Spalanzani. From time to time her voice grows weak. Cochenille touches her shoulder and the sound of a spring is heard*) The birds in the bushes, In the heavens the orb of day, All speak to the young girl Of love, of love! There! The pretty song,

La-chan-son-gen-tille,
Voi-là
La-chan-son-d'O-lym-pia!
Ha!

**LE CHOEUR:** C'est la chanson d'Olympia!

**OLYMPIA:** Tout-ce-qui-chante-et-ré-sonne
Et-sou-pire-tour-à-tour-,
E-muet-son-coeur-qui-fris-sonne
D'a-mour!
Voi-la!
La-chan-son-mi-gnon-ne
Voi-là
Voi-là
La-chan-son-d'O-lym-pia.
Ha!

**LE CHOEUR:** C'est la chanson d'Olympia.

**HOFFMANN:** (à Nicklausse). Ah! mon ami! quel accent! . . .

**NICKLAUSSE:** Quelles gammes! . . .
(Cochenille a enlevè la harpe et tout le monde s'est empressé autour d'Olympia qui remercie tour à tour de la main droite et de la main gauche. Hoffmann la contemple avec ravissement. Un laquais vient dire quelques mots à Spalanzani.)

**SPALANZANI:** Allons, messieurs! . . . la main aux dames! . . .
Les souper nous attend! . . .

**LE CHOEUR:** Le souper! . . . Bon cela! . . .

**SPALANZANI:** A moins qu'on ne préfère
Danser d'abord! . . .

**LE CHOEUR:** (avec énergie). Non! . . . non! . . . le souper! . . . bonne affaire,
Ensuite on dansera.

**SPALANZANI:** Comme il vous plaira! . . .

**HOFFMANN:** (s'approchant d'Olympia). Oserai-je? . . .

**SPALANZANI:** (intervenant). Elle est un peu lasse;
Attendez le bal.
(Il touche l'épaule d'Olympia).

**OLYMPIA:** Oui.

**SPALANZANI:** Vous voyez, jusque-là
Voulez-vous me faire la grâce
De tenir compagnie à mon Olympia?

**HOFFMANN:** O bonheur!

**SPALANZANI:** (à part, en riant). Nous verrons ce qu'il lui chantera.

**NICKLAUSSE:** (À Spalanzani). Elle ne soupe pas?

**SPALANZANI:** Non!

**NICKLAUSSE:** (à part). Ame poétique!
(Spalanzani passe un moment derrière Olympia. On entend de

There!
The song of Olympia,
Ha!

**THE CHORUS:** It is the song of Olympia!

**OLYMPIA:** All that sings and resounds
Has its sighs in turn,
Moves its heart that trembles
With love,
There.
The little song,
There, there,
The song of Olympia,
Ha!

**THE CHORUS:** It is the song of Olympia.

**HOFFMANN:** (to Nicklausse) Ah, my friend, what an accent.

**NICKLAUSSE:** What runs!
(Cochenille has taken the harp and all surround Olympia who thanks them with the right hand and the left. Hoffmann looks at her with rapture. A servant speaks to Spalanzani.)

**SPALANZANI:** Come, gentlemen! your arms to the ladies,
Supper awaits you!

**THE CHORUS:** Supper! That's good . . .

**SPALANZANI:** Unless you would prefer
To dance first.

**THE CHORUS:** (with energy) No! no! the supper . . . good thing . . .
We'll dance after.

**SPALANZANI:** As you please . . .

**HOFFMANN:** (approaching Olympia) Might I dare . . .

**SPALANZANI:** (interrupting) She is a bit tired,
Wait for the ball.
(He touches Olympia's shoulder.)

**OLYMPIA:** Yes.

**SPALANZANI:** You see. Until then
Will you do me the favor
To keep company with my Olympia?

**HOFFMANN:** Oh happiness!

**SPALANZANI:** (aside, laughing) We'll see what kind of a story he'll give her.

**NICKLAUSSE:** (to Spalanzani) Won't she have supper?

**SPALANZANI:** No.

**NICKLAUSSE:** (aside) Poetic soul!
(Spalanzani goes behind Olympia for a moment. Noise of a spring is heard again. Nicklausse turns

nouveau le bruit d'un ressort qu'on remonte. Nicklausse se retourne).
Plaît-il?

**SPALANZANI:** Rien! la physique! . . . ah! monsieur! la physique.
(Il conduit Olympia à un fauteuil et l'y fait asseoir; puis il sort avec les invités.)

**COCHENILLE:** Le-e souper vou-ous attend.

**LE CHOEUR:** (avec un enthousiasme croissant). Le souper, le souper, le souper nous attend!
Non, aucun hôte vraiment,
Ne reçoit plus richement!

**HOFFMANN:** Ils se sont éloignés enfin! . . . Ah! je respire! . . . .
Seuls! seuls tous deux!
(S'approchant d'Olympia).
Que j'ai de choses à te dire,
O mon Olympia! . . . Laisse-moi t'admirer!
De ton regard charmant laisse-moi m'enivrer.
(Il touche légèrement l'épaule d'Olympia).

**OLYMPIA:** Oui.

**HOFFMANN:** N'est-ce pas un rêve enfanté par la fièvre?
J'ai cru voir un soupir s'échapper de ta lèvre!
(Il touche de nouveau l'épaule d'Olympia).

**OLYMPIA:** Oui.

**HOFFMANN:** Doux aveu, gage de nos amours,
Tu m'appartiens, nos coeurs sont unis pour toujours!
Ah! comprends-tu, dis-moi, cette joie éternelle
Des coeurs silencieux? . . .
Vivants, n'être qu'une âme, et du même coup d'aile
Nous élancer aux cieux!
Laisse, laisse ma flamme
Verser en toi le jour!
Laisse éclore ton âme
Aux rayons de l'amour!
(Il presse la main d'Olympia avec passion; celle-ci, comme si elle était mue par un ressort, se lève aussitôt, parcourt la scène en différents sens et sort enfin par une des portes du fond sans se servir de ses mains pour écarter la tapisserie. Hoffmann se lève et suit Olympia dans ses évolutions.)
Tu me fuis? . . . qu'ai-je fait? . . . Tu ne me réponds pas? . . .
Parle! . . . t'ai-je irritée? . . . Ah! . . . . je suivrai tes pas!
(Au moment où Hoffmann va s'éloigner à la suite d'Olympia, Nicklausse paraît à l'une des portes opposées et l'interpelle.)

around.)
What did you say?

**SPALANZANI:** Nothing, physics! ah, monsieur, physics!
(He conducts Olympia to a chair and seats her, then goes out with guests.)

**COCHENILLE:** The supper a-awaits you.

**THE CHORUS:** (with increasing enthusiasm) Supper, supper, supper awaits us!
No, really, no host
Receives more richly!

**HOFFMANN:** They are at last gone.
Ah, I breathe!
Alone, alone, the two of us!
(approaching Olympia)
I have so many things to say,
Oh my Olympia! Let me admire you!
With your charming looks let me intoxicate myself.
(He touches her shoulder.)

**OLYMPIA:** Yes.

**HOFFMANN:** Is it not a dream born of fever?
I thought I heard a sigh escape your lips!
(He again touches her shoulder.)

**OLYMPIA:** Yes.

**HOFFMANN:** Sweet avowal, pledge of our love,
You are mine, our hearts are united forever!
Ah! understand you, tell me, this eternal joy
Of silent hearts.
Living, with but one soul and with same stroke of wing,
Rush up to heaven!
Let, let, my flame
Show you the light of day!
Let your soul open
To the rays of love.
(He presses Olympia's hand with passion; she, as if she were moved by a spring, rises suddenly, rushes about the stage in every direction and finally goes out by one of the rear doors without using her hands to push aside the portieres. Hoffmann rises and follows Olympia in all her movements.)
You escape me? . . . What have I done?
You do not answer? . . .
Speak! Have I wounded you? Ah! I'll follow your steps!
(At the moment when Hoffmann goes out after Olympia, Nicklausse appears at one of the opposite doors and calls him.)

NICKLAUSSE: Eh! morbleu! modère ton zèle! Veux-tu qu'on se grise sans toi? . . .

HOFFMANN: (avec confusion). Nicklausse! . . . je sus aimé d'elie . . . Aimé, Dieu puissant! . . .

NICKLAUSSE: Par ma foi! Si tu savais ce qu'on dit de ta belle!

HOFFMANN: Qu'en peut-on dire? Quoi?

NICKLAUSSE: Qu'elle est morte.

HOFFMANN: Dieu juste! . . .

NICKLAUSSE: Ou ne fut pas en vie.

HOFFMANN: (avec ivresse). Ange que l'envie Suit en frémissant, Justice éternelle! Nicklausse! . . . Je suis aimé d'elle! . . . Aimé! . . . Dieu puissant! . . . (Il sort rapidement; Nicklausse le suit.)

COPPÉLIUS: (entrant, furieux, par la petite porte de gauche) Voleur! . . . brigand! . . . quelle déroute! . . . Elias a fait banqueroute! . . . Va, je saurai trouver le moment opportun Pour me venger . . . Volé! . . . moi! . . . je tuerai quelqu'un. (Les tapisseries du fond s'écartent. Coppélius se glisse dans la chambre d'Olympia, à droite.)

SPALANZANI: Voici les valseurs.

COCHENILLE: Voici la ritournelle!

HOFFMANN: C'est la valse qui nous appelle.

SPALANZANI: (À Olympia). Prends la main de monsieur, mon enfant . . . (Lui touchant l'épaule.) Allons! . . .

OLYMPIA: Oui.
(Hoffmann enlace la taille d'Olympia et ils commencent à valser. On leur fait place et ils disparaissent par la gauche. Le Chœur les suit des yeux. Spalanzani cause sur le devant de la scène avec Nicklausse.)

LE CHOEUR: Elle danse! En cadence! C'est merveilleux, Prodigieux! Place! place! Elle passe, Elle fend l'air Comme un éclair! (Pendant ce Chœur, Hoffmann et Olympia ont repassé en valsant dans le fond de la galerie et ont

NICKLAUSSE: Here, by Jove, moderate your zeal! Do you want us to drink without you?

HOFFMANN: (half crazy) Nicklausse, I am loved by her. Loved! By all the gods.

NICKLAUSSE: By my faith, If you knew what they are saying of your beauty!

HOFFMANN: What can they say? What?

NICKLAUSSE: That she is dead.

HOFFMANN: Great Heavens!

NICKLAUSSE: Or is not of this life.

HOFFMANN: (exalted) Angel whom envy Follows with trembling, Eternal justice! Nicklausse! I am beloved by her! Loved! By all the gods. (Exit hastily. Nicklausse follows him)

COPPELIUS: (enters, furious, by the small door on the left) Thief! brigand! what a tumble! Elias is bankrupt! But I shall find the opportunity To revenge myself . . . robbed! . . . Me! I'll kill somebody. (The portieres in the rear are drawn open. Coppelius slips into Olympia's room on the right.)

SPALANZANI: Here come the waltzers.

COCHENILLE: Here comes the round dance.

HOFFMANN: The waltz that calls us.

SPALANZANI: (to Olympia) Take the hand of the gentleman, my child. (Touching her shoulder.) Come.

OLYMPIA: Yes.
(Hoffmann puts his arm around Olympia's waist and they begin to waltz. Way is made for them and they disappear by the left. The chorus follows them with their gaze. Spalanzani talks in the foreground to Nicklausse.)

THE CHORUS: She dances! In cadence. It's marvelous, Prodigious, Room, room, She passes Through the air Like lightning. (During the chorus, Hoffmann and Olympia have passed, dancing, into the rear of the gallery

disparu par la droite. Le mouvement de la valse s'anime de plus en plus.)

LA VOIX D'HOFFMANN: (dans la coulisse). Olympia! . . .

SPALANZANI: (remontant la scène). Qu'on les arrête! . . .

LE CHOEUR: Qui de nous les arrêtera? . . .

NICKLAUSSE: Elle va lui casser la tête! . . .
(Hoffmann et Olympia reparaissent et redescendent en scène en valsant de plus en plus vite. Nicklausse s'élance pour les arrêter.) Eh! mille diables!
(Il est violemment bousculé et va tomber sur un faureuil en tournant plusieurs fois sur lui-même.)

LE CHOEUR: Patatra! . . .

SPALANZANI: (s'élançant à son tour). Halte là!
(Il touche Olympia à l'épaule. Elle s'arrête subitement. Hoffmann, étourdi, va tomber sur un canapé. Spalanzani continue en se retournant vers les invités.) Voilà.
(A Olympia.) Assez, assez, ma fille.

OLYMPIA: Oui.

SPALANZANI: Il ne faut plus valser.

OLYMPIA: Oui.

SPALANZANI: (à Cochenille). Toi, Cochenille Reconduis-la.
(Il touche Olympia qui se tourne vers la droite.)

COCHENILLE: (poussant Olympia). Va-a donc! . . . Va! . . .

OLYMPIA: Oui.
(En sortant, lentement poussée par Cochenille). Ha! ha! ha! ha! ha! ha! ah!

LE CHOEUR: Que voulez-vous qu'on dise? C'est une fille exquise! Il ne lui manque rien! Elle est très bien! (Olympia sort par la droite, suivie de Cochenille.)

NICKLAUSSE: (d'une voix dolente, en montrant Hoffmann). Est-il mort? . . .

SPALANZANI: (examinant Hoffmann). Non! en somme, Son lorgnon seul est en débris. Il reprend ses esprits.

LE CHOEUR: Pauvre jeune homme!

COCHENILLE: (dans la coulisse). Ah!
(Il entre en scène, la figure bouleversée.)

SPALANZANI: Quoi?

COCHENILLE: L'homme aux lunettes! . . . Là!

and disappeared by the right. The movement of the waltz becomes more and more animated.)

THE VOICE OF HOFFMANN: (outside) Olympia!

SPALANZANI: Stop them!

THE CHORUS: Who of us will do it?

NICKLAUSSE: She will break his head.
(Hoffmann and Olympia re-appear on the stage waltzing faster and faster. Nicklausse rushes to stop them.) A thousand devils!
(He is violently struck and falls in an arm chair turning around and around a few times.)

THE CHORUS: Patatra! . . .

SPALANZANI: (rushing in in turn) Halt!
(He touches Olympia on the shoulder. She stops suddenly. Hoffmann, exhausted, falls on a sofa. Spalanzani continues turning to the guests.) There!
(To Olympia.) Enough, enough, my child.

OLYMPIA: Yes.

SPALANZANI: No more waltzing.

OLYMPIA: Yes.

SPALANZANI: (to Cochenille) You, Cochenille, Take her back.
(He touches Olympia, who turns toward the right.)

COCHENILLE: (pushing Olympia) Go on, go!

OLYMPIA: Yes.
(Going out, slowly, pushed by Cochenille.) Ha, ha, ha, ha, ha, ha, ha!

THE CHORUS: What can we possibly say? She's an exquisite girl, She lacks nothing. She does very well! (Olympia goes out followed by Cochenille.)

NICKLAUSSE: (dolorous voice, pointing to Hoffmann.) Is he dead?

SPALANZANI: (examining Hoffmann) No! in fact His eye glass is broken. He is reviving.

THE CHORUS: Poor young man!

COCHENILLE: (outside) Ah!
(He enters, very agitated.)

SPALANZANI: What?

COCHENILLE: The man with the glasses . . . there!

SPALANZANI: Miséricorde! Olympia! . . .

HOFFMANN: Olympia!. (*Spalanzani va pour s'élancer. On entend dans la coulisse un bruit de ressorts qui se brisent avec fracas.*)

SPALANZANI: Ah! terre et cieux! Elle est cassée! . . .

HOFFMANN: (*se levant*). Cassée! . . .

COPPÉLIUS: (*entrant par la droite et éclatant de rie*). Ha! ha! ha! ha! oui . . . Fracassée! . . . (*Hoffmann s'élance et disparaît par la droite. Spalanzani et Coppélius se jettent l'un sur l'autre et se prennent au collet.*)

SPALANZANI: Gredin!

COPPÉLIUS: Voleur!

SPALANZANI: Brigand!

COPPÉLIUS: Païen!

SPALANZANI: Bandit!

COPPÉLIUS: Pirate!

HOFFMANN: (*apparaissant, pâle et épouvanté*). Un automate! un automate! (*Il se laisse tomber sur un fauteuil, Nicklausse cherche à le calmer. Eclat de rire général.*)

LE CHOEUR: Ha! ha! ha! la bombe éclate! Il aimat un automate!

SPALANZANI: (*avec désespoir*). Mon automate!

TOUS: Un automate!

LE CHOEUR: Ha! ha! ha! ha!

---

SPALANZANI: Mercy! Olympia! . . .

HOFFMANN: Olympia! . . . (*Spalanzani rushes out. Sound of breaking springs with much noise is heard in the wings.*)

SPALANZANI: Ah, heaven and earth, she is broken!

HOFFMANN: Broken!

COPPELIUS: (*entering by the right and bursting with laughter*) Ha, ha, ha, ha, yes. Smashed! (*Hoffmann rushes out and disappears by the right. Spalanzani and Coppelius go at each other, fighting, and seize each other by the collar.*)

SPALANZANI: Rascal!

COPPELIUS: Robber!

SPALANZANI: Brigand!

COPPELIUS: Pagan!

SPALANZANI: Bandit!

COPPELIUS: Pirate!

HOFFMANN: (*appearing, pale and terror stricken*) An automaton, an automaton. (*He falls into an armchair. Nicklausse tries to calm him. General laughter.*)

THE CHORUS: Ha, ha, ha, the bomb has burst, He loved an automaton.

SPALANZANI: (*despairingly*) My automaton.

ALL: An automaton.

THE CHORUS: Ha, ha, ha, ha!

---

# ▪ ACTE DEUXIÉME

*Giulietta*

A Venise. Galerie de fête dans un palais, donnant sur le grand canal. Eau praticable au fond pour les gondoles. Balustrade, escaliers, colonnes lampadaires, lustres, coussins, fleurs. Portes latérales sur le premier plan, plus loin de larges portes ou arcades en pans coupés, conduisant à d'autres galeries.

Hoffmann, Pitichinacchio, Jeunes Gens et Jeunes Femmes, Laquais, puis Giulietta et Nicklausse.

Les hôtes de Giulietta sont groupés debout ou étendus sur des coussins. Tableau brillant et animé.

GIULIETTA et NICKLAUSSE: (*Dans la coulisse*). Belle nuit, ô nuit d'amour, Souris à nos ivresses, Nuit plus douce que le jour, O belle nuit d'amour!

---

# ▪ ACT TWO

*Giulietta*

In Venice. A gallery, in festival attire, in a palace on the Grand Canal. In the rear, water accessible to gondolas. Balustrade, stair case, lamp-posts, chandeliers, cushions, flowers. Side doors in the foreground, further large doors or arcades opening out on other galleries.

Hoffmann, Pitichinaccio, young men and women, lackeys, then Giulietta and Nicklausse.

The guests of Giulietta are in groups, standing or reclining on cushions. Brilliant and gay picture.

GIULIETTA AND NICKLAUSSE: (*in the wings*) Oh soft night, oh night of love, Smile on our serene bliss, All the stars that shine above Surround the heaven's queen!

---

Le temps fuit et sans retour Emporte nos tendresses! Loin de cet heureux séjour, Le temps fuit sans retour Zéphyrs embrasés Versez-nous vos caresses; Zéphyrs embrasés. Donnez-nous vos baisers. Belle nuit, ô nuit d'amour, Souris à nos ivresses, Nuit plus douce que le jour, O belle nuit d'amour! (*Guiletta et Nicklausse entrant en scène, venant lentement de la galeries du fond.*)

HOFFMANN: Et moi, ce n'est pas là, pardieu! ce qui m'enchante! Aux pieds de la beauté qui nous vient enivrer Le plaisir doit-il soupirer? Non! . . . Le rire à la bouche, On boit, on rit, on chante. (*Les Mmes, Schlemil, puis Dapertutto.*)

SCHLEMIL: (*entrant en scène*). Je vois qu'on est en fête. A merveille, madame!

GIULIETTA: Comment! . . . Mais je vous ai pleure trois grands jours.

PITICHINACCHIO: Dame!

SCHLEMIL: (*à Pitichinacchio*). Avorton!

PITICHINACCHIO: Holà!

GIULIETTA: (*les calmant*). Calmez-vous! Nous avons un poète étranger parmi nous. (*Présentant Hoffmann.*) Hoffmann!

SCHLEMIL: (*de mauvaise grâce*). Monsieur!

HOFFMANN: (*ironique*). Monsieur!

GIULIETTA: (*à Schlemil*). Souriez-nous, de grâce. Et venez prendre place Au pharaon!

LE CHOEUR: Vivat! Au pharoan! (*Guiletta, après avoir invité du geste tout le monde à la suivre dans la salle de jeu, se dirige vers la sortie. Hoffmann va pour offrir sa main à Guiletta, Schlemil intervient vivement.*)

SCHLEMIL: (*prenant la main de Giulietta qui essaie de le calmer*). Morbleu!

GIULIETTA: (*aux invités*). Au jeu, messieurs, au jeu!

LE CHOEUR: Au jeu! au jeu! (*Tout le monde sort, moins Nicklausse et Hoffmann.*)

NICKLAUSSE: (*à Hoffmann*). Un mot! . . . J'ai deux chevaux sellés; au premier rêve Dont se laisse affoler mon Hoffmann, je l'enlève.

---

Time flies without return, Forgetting our tenderness! Far from I'll ever burn, In lonely strait and stress. Passioned zephyrs Soft are your kisses. O soft night, oh night of love, Smile on our bliss serene: All the stars that shine above Surround the heaven's queen. (*Giulietta and Nicklausse enter, coming slowly from the gallery in the rear.*)

HOFFMANN: For me, by Jove, that is not what's enchanting! Does pleasure sigh at the feet of the beauty who give us joy? No, with laughing mouth no sorrows are descanting. *The same; Schlemil, then Dapertutto*

SCHLEMIL: (*entering*) I see all is joy. Congratulations, madame.

GIULIETTA: What! Why, I've wept for you for three whole days.

PITICHINACCIO: Good.

SCHLEMIL: (*to Pitichinaccio*) Microbe!

PITICHINACCIO: Hola!

GIULIETTA: Calm yourselves! We have a strange poet among us. (*Presenting.*) Hoffmann!

SCHLEMIL: (*with bad grace*) Monsieur!

HOFFMANN: Monsieur!

GIULIETTA: (*to Schlemil*) Smile on us, I beg, And come take your place At pharoah!

THE CHORUS: Bravo! To pharoah! (*Giulietta after having invited by a gesture all to follow her, goes toward door. Hoffmann comes up to offer his hand to Giulietta. Schlemil comes between.*)

SCHLEMIL: (*taking Giulietta's hand and trying to calm her*) By heavens!

GIULIETTA: (*to the guests*) To the game, gentlemen, to the game!

THE CHORUS: To the game, the game! (*All go out except Hoffmann and Nicklausse.*)

NICKLAUSSE: (*to Hoffmann*) One word! I have two horses saddled. At the first dream That Hoffmann permits himself, I carry him off.

## Act I, Scene II

**HOFFMANN:** Et quels rêves, amais, pourraient être enfantés
Par de telles réalités?
Aime-t-on une courtisane? . . .

**NICKLAUSSE:** Ce Schlemil, cependant . . .

**HOFFMANN:** Je ne suis pas Schlemil.

**NICKLAUSSE:** Prends-y garde, le diable est malin.
(*Dapertutto paraît au fond.*)

**HOFFMANN:** Le fût-il,
S'il me la fait aimer, je consens qu'il me damne.
Allons!

**NICKLAUSSE:** Allons!
(*Il sortent.*)

**DAPERTUTTO:** (*seul*). Allez! . . . pour te livrer combat
Les yeux de Giulietta sont une arme certaine.
Il a fallu que Schlemil succombât . . .
Foi de diable et de capitaine!
Tu feras comme lui.
Je veux que Giulietta t'ensorcelle aujourd'hui.
(*Tirant de son doigt une bague où brille un gros diamant et le faisant scintiller.*)
CHANSON
Tourne, tourne, miroir où se prend l'alouette,
Scintille, diamant, fascine, attire-la.
L'alouette ou la femme
A cet appât vainqueur
Vont de l'aile ou du coeur;
L'une y laisse sa vie et l'autre y perd son âme.
Tourne, tourne, miroir où se prend l'alouette.
Scintille, diamant, fascine, attire-la.
(*Giulietta paraît et s'avance, comme fascinée, vers le diamant que Dapertutto tend vers elle.*)

**DAPERTUTTO:** (*passant la bague au doigt de Giulietta*). Cher ange!

**GIULIETTA:** Qu'attendez-vous de votre servante?

**DAPERTUTTO:** Bien, tu m'as deviné,
A séduire les couers entre toutes savante,
Tu m'as déjà donné
L'ombre de Schlemil! Je varie
Mes plaisirs et te prie
De m'avoir aujourd'hui
Le reflet d'Hoffmann!

**GIULIETTA:** Quoi! son reflet!

**DAPERTUTTO:** Oui!
Son reflet! . . . Tu doutes
De la puissance de tes yeux?

**GIULIETTA:** Non.

**DAPERTUTTO:** Qui sait? Ton Hoffmann rêve peutêtre mieux.
(*Avec dureté.*)
Oui, j'étais là, tout à l'heure, aux écoutes,
(*Avec ironie.*)
Il te défie . . .

**GIULIETTA:** Hoffmann? . . . C'est bien! . . . dès aujourd'hui J'en ferai mon jouet.
(*Hoffmann entre.*)

**DAPERTUTTO:** C'est lui!
(*Dapertutto sort après avoir baisé la main de Giulietta.*)
(*Hoffmann traverse le théâtre, salue Giulietta et fait mine de s'éloigner.*)

**GIULIETTA:** (*à Hoffmann*) Vous me quittez?

**HOFFMANN:** (*reilleur*) J'ai tout perdu . . .

**GIULIETTA:** Quoi! . . . vous aussi! . . .
Ah! vous me faites injure
Sans pitié, ni merci.
Partez! . . . Partez! . . .

**HOFFMANN:** Tes larmes t'ont trahie.
Ah! je t'aime . . . fût-ce au prix de ma vie.

**GIULIETTA:** Écoute, et ne ris pas de moi.
(*Elle enlace Hoffmann de ses bras et prend un miroir qui est sur la table*)
Ce que je veux, c'est ta fidèle image
Qui reproduit tes traits, ton regard, ton visage,
Le reflet que tu vois sur le mien se pencher.

**HOFFMANN:** Quoi! mon reflet? quelle folie!

**GIULIETTA:** Non! . . . car il peut se détacher
De la glace polie
Pour venir tout entier dans mon coeur se cacher.

**HOFFMANN:** Dans ton coeur?

**GIULIETTA:** Dans mon coeur.
C'est moi qui t'en supplie,
Hoffmann, comble mes voeux!

**HOFFMANN:** Mon reflet?

**GIULIETTA:** Ton reflet. Oui, sagesse ou folie,
Je l'attends, je le veux!

**HOFFMANN:** Extase! ivresse inassouvie,
Étrange et doux effroi!
Mon reflet, mon âme et ma vie A toi, toujours à toi!
A toi, toujours à toi!

**GIULIETTA:** Si ta présence m'est ravie,
Je veux garder de toi
Ton reflet, ton âme et ta vie,
Ami, donne-les-moi!
(*Les mêmes, Schlemil, Dapertutto, Nicklausse, Pitichinaccio.*)

**GIULIETTA:** (*vivement*) Schlemil!
(*Schlemil entre siuvi de Nicklausse, Dapertutto, Pitichinaccio et quelques autres invités.*)

---

**HOFFMANN:** And what dream ever could be born
By such relations?
Does one love a courtezan?

**NICKLAUSSE:** Yet this Schlemil, depends

**HOFFMANN:** I am not Schlemil.

**NICKLAUSSE:** Take care, the devil is clever.
(*Dapertutto appears at back.*)

**HOFFMANN:** Were it so,
If he makes me love her, may he damn me,
Come!

**NICKLAUSSE:** Let us go.
(*They go out.*)

**DAPERTUTTO:** (*alone*)
Yes! . . . to fight you.
The eyes of Giulietta are a sure weapon,
It needed that Schlemil fail,
Faith of captain and soldier,
You'll do like him.
I will that Giulietta shall use sorcery on you.
(*Drawing from his finger a ring with a big glittering diamond, and making it sparkle.*)
Turn, turn, mirror, where the lark is caught,
Sparkle, diamond, fascinate, draw her..
The lark or the woman
To this conquering bait
Comes with wing or with heart;
One leaves her life, the other her soul,
Turn, turn, mirror where the lark is caught.
Sparkle, diamond, fascinate, attract her.
(*Giulietta appears and advances fascinated toward the diamond that Dapertutto holds towards her.*)

**DAPERTUTTO:** (*placing the ring on Giulietta's finger*) Dear angel!

**GIULIETTA:** What do you await from your servant?

**DAPERTUTTO:** Good, you have divined
At seducing hearts above all others wise,
You have given me
The shade of Schlemil! I vary
My pleasures and I pray you
To get for me today
The reflection of Hoffmann!

**GIULIETTA:** What! his reflection!

**DAPERTUTTO:** Yes.
His reflection! You doubt
The power of your eyes?

**GIULIETTA:** No.

**DAPERTUTTO:** Who knows? Your Hoffmann dreams, perhaps better.
(*Severely.*)
Yes, I was there, a while back, listening.
(*With irony.*)
He defies you . . .

**GIULIETTA:** Hoffmann?
Well! . . . From this day forward, I'll make him my plaything.
(*Hoffmann enters.*)

**DAPERTUTTO:** It is he!
(*Dapertutto goes out after having kissed the hand of Giulietta.*)
(*Hoffmann crosses the stage, bows to Giulietta and pretends that he is leaving.*)

**GIULIETTA:** (*to Hoffmann*) You leave me?

**HOFFMANN:** (*mockingly*) I have lost everything.

**GIULIETTA:** What? you too . . .
Ah, you do me wrong.
Without pity, without mercy,
Go! . . . Go! . . .

**HOFFMANN:** Your tears betrayed you.
Ah! I love you . . . even at the price of my life.

**GIULIETTA:** Listen and don't laugh at me.
(*She takes Hoffmann in her arms and takes a mirror which is on the table.*)
What I want is your faithful image,
To reproduce your features, your look, your visage,
The reflection that I see above me bend.

**HOFFMANN:** My reflection? What folly!

**GIULIETTA:** No! for it can detach itself
From the polished glass
And come quite whole in my heart to hide.

**HOFFMANN:** In your heart?

**GIULIETTA:** In my heart. It is I who begs you
Hoffmann, give me my wish.

**HOFFMANN:** My reflection?

**GIULIETTA:** Your reflection. Yes, wisdom or folly,
I await, I demand.

**HOFFMANN:** Ecstasy, unappeased bliss,
Strange and soft terror,
My reflection, my soul, my life
To you, always to you!

**GIULIETTA:** If I lose your presence,
I would keep of you
Your reflection, your soul, your life;
Dear one, give them me.
(*Above. Schlemil, Dapertutto, Nicklausse, Pitichinaccio.*)

**GIULIETTA:** (*suddenly*) Schlemil!
(*Schlemil enters followed by Nicklausse, Dapertutto, Pitichinaccio and other guests.*)

SCHLEMIL: J'en étais sûr! Ensemble!
(*Il remonte, s'adressant aux invités.*)
Venez, messieurs, venez,
C'est pour Hoffmann, à ce qu'il semble,
Que nous sommes abandonné.
(*Rires ironiques.*)

HOFFMANN: (*presque parlé*)
Monsieur!

GIULIETTA: (*à Hoffmann*) Silence!
(*Bas.*)
Je t'aime, il a ma clef.

PITICHINACCHIO: (*à Schlemil*)
Tuons-le.

SCHLEMIL: Patience.

DAPERTUTTO: (*s'approchant d'Hoffmann*) Comme vous êtes pâle!

HOFFMANN: Moi!

DAPERTUTTO: (*lui présentant un miroir*) Voyez plutôt!

HOFFMANN: (*stupéfait, en regardant le miroir*) Ciel!

NICKLAUSSE: (*à Hoffmann*) Quoi?

HOFFMANN: (*avec une sorte d'effroi*) Mon reflet!
(*Courant à deux grandes glaces alternativement.*)
J'ai perdu mon reflet!

NICKLAUSSE: (*en montrant Giulietta ironiquement*) Pour madame.

TOUS: (*moins Hoffmann et Nicklausse, en riant, d'une voix étouffée*) Ha! ha! ha! voyez son effroi.

NICKLAUSSE: Ah! viens, fuyons ces lieux où tu perdras ton âme.

HOFFMANN: (*éperdu*) Non! non! je l'aime. Laisse-moi!

HOFFMANN: Hélas! mon coeur s'égare encore,
Mes sens se laissent embraser,
Maudit l'amour qui me dévore,
Ma raison ne peut s'apaiser.
Sous ce front clair comme une aurore
L'enfer même vient me griser.
Je la hais et je l'adore
Je veux mourir de son baiser.

GIULIETTA: Mon bel Hoffmann, je vous adore,
Mais n'ai point l'âme à refuser
Ce diamant aux feux d'aurore
Qui ne me coûte qu'un baiser.
Car je suis femme et j'adore
Ce qui me fait plus belle encore
Pour vous griser.
Poète, il faut vous apaiser.

DAPERTUTTO ET PITICHINACCIO: Pauvre Hoffmann, l'amour encore
Vainement vient t'embraser;
Ta belle au regard d'aurore
Nous a vendu son baiser.

SCHLEMIL: I was sure of it! Together!
(*He comes up addressing the guests.*)
Come, gentlemen, come,
It is Hoffmann, it seems to me
That we have abandoned.
(*Ironic laughter.*)

HOFFMANN: Monsieur!

GIULIETTA: (*to Hoffmann*) Silence!
(*Aside.*)
I love you, he has my key.

PITICHINACCIO: (*to Schlemil*)
Let us kill him.

SCHLEMIL: Patience!

DAPERTUTTO: (*approaching Hoffmann*) How pale you are!

HOFFMANN: I?

DAPERTUTTO: (*showing him a mirror*) Just look!

HOFFMANN: (*amazed*) Heavens!

NICKLAUSSE: (*to Hoffmann*) What?

HOFFMANN: (*somewhat terrified*) My reflection!
(*Running alternately to two mirrors.*)
I lost my reflection!

NICKLAUSSE: (*pointing ironically to Giulietta*) For madam.

ALL: (*except Hoffmann and Nicklausse, laughing in a choking voice*) Ha, ha, ha, behold his fright!

NICKLAUSSE: Ah, come, let us flee from this place
Where you will lose your soul.

HOFFMANN: (*in despair*) No! no! I love her, leave me!

HOFFMANN: Alas, my heart still wanders,
My senses are on fire.
Cursed be the love which consumes me,
My reason will not be calmed,
Hell itself intoxicates me.
I hate and adore her.
I wish to die of her kiss.

GIULIETTA: My beautiful Hoffmann, I adore you,
But have not the heart to refuse
This diamond bright as the dawn,
Which costs me but a kiss.
For I am a woman, and adore
That which makes me fairer still
To turn your head
Poet, you must calm yourself.

DAPERTUTTO AND PITICHINACCIO: Poor Hoffmann, love still
Vainly comes to consume you;
Your beauty fair as the dawn,
Has sold us her kiss
For the coquette adores herself;

Car la coquette s'adore;
Un bijou qui peut encore
L'embellir et nous griser
Vaut bien pour elle un baiser.

SCHLEMIL: (*en touchant la garde de son épée*) Ce poète j'abhorre
Aurait bientôt son baiser
Sans ce fer clair et sonore
Dont je sais fort bien user.
Un fol amour te dévore?
Je suis là pour t'apaiser.
Tu prétends qu'on t'adore,
C'est bon, nus allons causer.

NICKLAUSSE ET LE CHOEUR:
Hélas! son coeur s'enflamme encore!
Par elle il s'est laissé griser.
L'amour le brûle et le dévore.
Rien ne pourra l'apaiser.
La perfide qu'il adore
Prend les coeurs pour les briser.
Fuis la belle au front d'aurore,
Car on meurt de son baiser.
(*On entend un chant de gondoliers.*)

GIULIETTA: Écoutez, messieurs,
Voici les gondoles,
L'heure des barcarolles
Et celle des adieux!
(*Schlemil reconduit les invités jusqu'au fond de la scène. Giulietta sort par la gauche après avoir jeté un dernier regard à Hoffmann qui la suit des yeux. Dapertutto reste au fond de la scène. Nicklausse, voyant que Hoffmann ne le suit pas, revient à lui et lui touche l'épaule.*)

NICKLAUSSE: Viens-tu?

HOFFMANN: Pas encore.

NICKLAUSSE: Pourquoi?
Bien, je comprends! adieu!
(*A part.*)
Mais je veille sur toi.
(*Il salue Schlemil et sort.*)

SCHLEMIL: Qu'attendez-vous, monsieur?

HOFFMANN: Que vous me donniez certaine clef que j'ai juré d'avoir.

SCHLEMIL: Vous n'aurez cette clef, monsieur, qu'avec ma vie!

HOFFMANN: J'aurai donc l'une et l'autre.

SCHLEMIL: C'est ce qu'il faut voir! En garde!

DAPERTUTTO: Vous n'avez pas d'épée,
(*lui présentant son épée*)
Prenez la mienne!

HOFFMANN: (*prenant l'épée*)
Merci!

CHOEUR: (*dans la coulisse qui se termine au baisser du rideau*)
Belle nuit, ô nuit d'amour!
Souris à nos ivresses,
Nuit plus douce que le jour, O belle nuit d'amour!

A jewel which can still
Beautify her and turn our heads
Is sure worth a kiss to her.

SCHLEMIL: (*grasping the hilt of his sword*) This poet whom I detest,
Would soon have his kiss
Without this shining steel
Which I know how to wield.
Does a mad love consume you?
I am here to calm it.
You pretend you are adored,
That's good, we shall see.

NICKLAUSSE AND CHORUS:
Alas, his heart is still enflamed!
He let his head be turned by her.
Love burns and consumes him.
Nothing can calm him.
The false one whom he adores
Takes hearts to break them.
Flee from the beauty fair as dawn,
For one dies from her kiss.
(*The singing of gondoliers is heard.*)

GIULIETTA: Listen, gentlemen,
Here come the gondolas,
The hour of barcaroles
And of farewells!
(*Schlemil conducts the guests to the rear of the stage. Giulietta goes out at the left after having cast a last glance at Hoffmann who follows her with his gaze. Dapertutto remains at the rear of the stage. Nicklausse, seeing that Hoffmann does not follow him, comes back to him and taps him on the shoulder.*)

NICKLAUSSE: Are you coming?

HOFFMANN: Not yet.

NICKLAUSSE: Why? Very well. I understand, Good-bye. (*Aside.*)
But I'll watch over him.
(*He bows to Schlemil and goes out.*)

SCHLEMIL: What do you wait for?

HOFFMANN: That you give me a certain key
I've sworn to have.

SCHLEMIL: You shall have this key, sir,
Only with my life.

HOFFMANN: Then I shall have have one and the other.

SCHLEMIL: That remains to be seen. On guard!

DAPERTUTTO: You have no sword,
(*Presenting his sword.*)
Take mine!

HOFFMANN: (*taking the sword*)
Thank you.

CHORUS: (*in the wings, until the curtain falls*) O soft night, night of love,
Smile on our serene bliss,
When the stars that shine above
Greet the heavenly queen!

(Hoffmann et Schlemil se battent; après quelques passes, Schlemil est blessé à mort, et tombe. Hoffmann jette son épée, se penche sur le corps de Schlemil et lui prend une petite clef pendue à son cou. Hoffmann s'élance dans l'appartement de Giulietta, Pitichinaccio regarde Schlemil avec curiosité et s'assure qu'il est bien mort. Dapertutto ramasse tranquillement son épée et la remet au fourreau, puis il remonte vers la galerie . . . Giulietta paraît dans une gondole; au même moment rentre Hoffmann.)

HOFFMANN: Personne . . .

GIULIETTA: (riant) Ha! Ha! Ha!
(Hoffmann se retourne vers Giulietta et la regarde avec stupeur.)

DAPERTUTTO: (à Giulietta) Qu'en fais-tu maintenant?

GIULIETTA: Je te l'abandonne!

PITICHINACCHIO: (entre dans la gondole) Cher ange!
(Giulietta le prend dans ses bras.)

HOFFMANN: (comprenant toute l'infamie de Giulietta) Misérable!

NICKLAUSSE: Hoffmann! Hoffmann! Les sbires!
(Nicklausse entraîne Hoffmann. — Giulietta et Dapertutto rient.)

(Hoffmann and Schlemil cross swords. After several passes, Schlemil is mortally wounded and falls. Hoffmann throws away his sword, leans over the body of Schlemil and takes from it a small key which hung on the neck. Hoffmann rushes into the apartment of Giulietta. Pitichinaccio looks Schlemil over carefully and makes sure that he is dead. Dapertutto calmly picks up his sword and puts it into the scabbard, then he goes back to the gallery. Giulietta appears in a gondola. Hoffmann comes in at the same time.)

HOFFMANN: No one.

GIULIETTA: (laughing) Ha! ha! ha!
(Hoffmann comes up toward Giulietta and looks at her in a stupor.)

DAPERTUTTO: (to Giulietta) What will you do with him now?

GIULIETTA: I'll turn him over to you.

PITICHINACCIO: (entering the gondola) Dear angel.
(Giulietta takes him in her arms.)

HOFFMANN: (comprehending the infamy of Giulietta) Vile wretch!

NICKLAUSSE: Hoffmann! Hoffmann—the police!
(Nicklausse drags Hoffmann away. — Giulietta and Dapertutto laugh.)

# ■ ACTE TROISIÈME

### Antonia

A Munich chez Crespel. Une chambre bizarrement meublée. A droite, un clavecin. A gauche, canapé et fauteuil. Violons suspendus au mur. Au fond, deux portes en pan coupé. Sur le premier plan, à gauche, une fenêtre en pan coupé formant un enfoncement et donnant sur un balcon. Soleil couchant. Au fond, entre les deux portes, un grand portrait de femme accroché au mur.

ANTONIA: (seule. Elle est assise devant le clavecin et chante) Elle a fui, la tourterelle,
Elle a fui loin de toi!
(Elle s'arrête et se lève.)
Ah! souvenir trop doux! image trop cruelle! . . .
Hélas! à mes genoux, je l'entends, je le vois! . . .
(Elle descend sur le devant de la scène.)
Elle a fui, la tourterelle,
Elle a fui loin de toi! . . .
Mais elle est toujours fidèle
Et te garde sa foi.
Bien-aimé, ma voix t'appelle,

# ■ ACT THREE

### Antonia

At Munich, at the home of Crespel. A room furnished in a bizarre fashion. To the left a couch and arm-chair. Violins hung on the wall. In the rear two doors. In the fore-ground, at the left, a window forming a recess and opening out on a balcony. Sunset. In the rear, between two doors a large portrait of a woman hanging on the wall.

ANTONIA: (alone. She is seated at the clavichord) She has fled, the dove
She has fled far from you!
(She stops and rises.)
Ah, memory too sweet, image too cruel!
Alas at my knees I hear, I see him!
(She walks to the front of the stage.)
She has fled, the dove,
She has fled far from you;
She is faithful ever,
And she keeps her troth.
Beloved, my voice calls you,
All my heart is yours.

Tout mon coeur est à toi.
(Elle se rapproche du clavecin et continue debout, en feuilletant la musique.)
Chère fleur qui viens d'éclore, Par pitié, réponds-moi,
Toi qui sais s'il m'aime encore, S'il me garde sa foi! . . .
Bien-aimé, ma voix t'implore. Que ton coeur vienne à moi! . . .
(Elle se laisse tomber sur la chaise qui est devant le clavecin.)

CRESPEL: (entrant brusquement et courant à Antonia) Malheureuse enfant fille bien-aimée Tu m'avais promis de ne plus chanter.

ANTONIA: Ma mère s'était en moi ranimée;
Mon coeur en chantant croyait l'écouter.

CRESPEL: C'est là mon tourment. Ta mère chérie
T'a légué sa voix, regrets superflus! Par toi je l'entends.
Non . . . non . . . je t'en prie.

ANTONIA: (tristement) Votre Antonia ne chantera plus! . . .
(Elle sort lentement.)

CRESPEL: (seul)
Désespoir! . . . Tout à l'heure encore
Je voyais ces taches de feu Colorer son visage, Dieu! Perdrai-je l'enfant que j'adore? Ah! cet Hoffmann . . . C'est lui Qui jeta dans son coeur ces ivresses . . .
J'ai fui
Jusqu'à Munich . . .

CRESPEL: Toi, Frantz, n'ouvre à personne.

FRANTZ: Vous croyez . . .

CRESPEL: Où vas-tu? . . .

FRANTZ: Je vais voir si l'on sonne. Comme vous avez dit . . .

CRESPEL: J'ai dit: n'ouvre à personne!
(Criant.)
A personne! Entends-tu, cette fois!

FRANTZ: Eh! mon Dieu!
Je ne suis pas sourd!

CRESPEL: Bien! que le diable t'emporte!

FRANTZ: Oui, monsieur, la clef sur la porte.

CRESPEL: Bélître! Ane bâté!

FRANTZ: C'est convenu.

CRESPEL: Morbleu.
(Il sort vivement. Frantz va refermer la porte et redescend.)

FRANTZ: (seul) Eh bien! Quoi! toujours en colère!
Bizarre! quinteux! exigeant! Ah! l'on a du mal à lui plaire Pour son argent.
Bon si je chantais quel tapage, Je chante pitoyablement;

(She approaches the clavichord again, remains standing and fingers the music.)
Dear flower but now open,
In pity answer me,
You that knows if still he loves me, If he keeps his troth.
Beloved, my voice implores you. May your heart come to me.
(She falls in a chair which is in front of the clavichord.)

CRESPEL: (entering suddenly and rushing up to Antonia) Unhappy child, beloved daughter,
You promised to no longer sing.

ANTONIA: My mother in me lived again;
My heart while singing thought it heard her.

CRESPEL: There is my torment. Your loved mother
Left you her voice. Vain regrets! Through you I hear her. No, no, I beg . . . you

ANTONIA: (sadly) Your Antonia will sing no more!
(She goes out slowly.)

CRESPEL: (alone) Despair! A little while again
I saw those spots of fire
Mark her face. God!
Must I lose the one I adore?
Ah, that Hoffmann . . . It is he Who put this craze in her heart. I fled
Far as Munich . . .

CRESPEL: You, Frantz, open to nobody.

FRANTZ: (false exit) You think so . . .

CRESPEL: Where are you going?

FRANTZ: I'm going to see if anybody rang.
As you said . . .

CRESPEL: I said, Open to nobody. (Shouting) To nobody! This time do you hear?

FRANTZ: Good Heavens! we're not all of us deaf?

CRESPEL: All right! The devil take you!

FRANTZ: Yes, sir, the key is in the door.

CRESPEL: Idiot! donkey!

FRANTZ: It's agreed then

CRESPEL: Zounds!
(He exists quickly. Frantz goes to shut the door and comes back.)

FRANTZ: (alone) Well! What! angry always!
Strange, peevish, exacting!
One would think that one pleased him
For his money . . .
Of course, one can't have every-

Mais je danse agréablement,
Je me le dis sans compliment.
Corbleu! la danse est à mon avantage,
C'est là mon plus grand attrait,
Et danser n'est pas commode.
Tra la la! Tra la la!
(*Il danse. Il s'arrête.*)
Près des femmes le jarret
N'est pas ce qui me nuirait.
Tra la la! Tra la la!
(*Il tombe.*)
Non! c'est la méthode.
(*Hoffmann entre par le fond, suivi de Nicklausse.*)
FRANTZ, HOFFMANN, NICKLAUSSE.

**HOFFMANN:** (*paraît à la porte du fond*) Frantz! . . . C'est ici!
(*Il descend en scène, touchant l'épaule de Frantz.*)
Debout, l'ami.

**FRANTZ:** Hein! qui va là?
(*Il se relève surpris.*)
Monsieur Hoffmann!

**HOFFMANN:** Moi-même! Eh bien, Antonia?

**FRANTZ:** Il est sorti, monsieur.

**HOFFMANN:** (*riant*) Ha! ha! plus sourd encore
Que l'an passé? . . .

**FRANTZ:** Monsieur m'honore
Je me porte bien, grâce au ciel.

**HOFFMANN:** Antonia! . . . Va! . . . fais que je la voie!

**FRANTZ:** (*souriant*) Très bien! . . . Quell joie
Pour monsieur Crespel!
(*Il sort.*)

**HOFFMANN:** (*s'asseyant devant le clavecin et s'accompagnant*)
C'est une chanson d'amour
Qui s'envole,
Triste ou folle
Tour à tour! . . .

**ANTONIA:** (*entrant précipitamment en scène*) Hoffmann! . . .

**HOFFMANN:** (*se relevant et recevant Antonia dans ses bras*) Antonia! . . .

**NICKLAUSSE:** (*à part*) Je suis de trop; bonsoir.
(*Il s'esquive.*)

**ANTONIA:** Ah! je le savais bien que tu m'aimais encore!

**HOFFMANN:** Mon coeur m'avait bien dit que j'étais regretté!
Mais pourquoi nous a-t-on séparés?

**ANTONIA:** Je l'ignore.

**HOFFMANN:** Ah! j'ai le bonheur dans l'âme!
Demain tu seras ma femme.
Heureux époux,
L'avenir est à nous!
A l'amour soyons fidèles!
Que ses chaines éternelles
Gardent nos coeurs
Du temps même vainqueurs!

thing.
I sing pretty badly,
But dance agreeably,
And I do not flatter myself;
Dancing shows off my advantages.
It is my one great attraction,
But dancing isn't easy.
Tra la la, tra la la!
(*He dances and stops.*)
With women the shape of my leg
Would do me no harm,
Tra la la, tra la la!
(*He falls.*)
No, it is the method.
(*Hoffmann enters followed by Nicklausse.*)

**HOFFMANN:** (*appears in the rear door*) Frantz! This is it.
(*He comes to the front of the stage, tapping Frantz on the shoulder.*)
Up, my friend!

**FRANTZ:** Hey, who's there?
(*Rises, surprised.*)
Monsieur Hoffmann!

**HOFFMANN:** Myself. Well, Antonia?

**FRANTZ:** He's gone out, sir.

**HOFFMANN:** (*laughing*) Ha, ha, deafer yet
Than last year . . .

**FRANTZ:** Monsieur honors me,
I am very well, thanks to heaven.

**HOFFMANN:** Antonia! I must see her.

**FRANTZ:** (*smiling*) Very well! what a joy
For monsieur Crespel!
(*He goes out.*)

**HOFFMANN:** (*sitting before the clavichord and accompanying himself*) A song of love
Flies away,
Sad or gay;
It takes its turn . . .

**ANTONIA:** (*entering suddenly*) Hoffmann! . . .

**HOFFMANN:** (*standing up and receiving her in his arms.*) Antonia!

**NICKLAUSSE:** (*aside*) I am one too many, good night.
(*He exits.*)

**ANTONIA:** Ah, I well knew that you loved me still.

**HOFFMANN:** My heart told me that I was regretted,
But why were we separated?

**ANTONIA:** I do not know.

**HOFFMANN:** I have happiness in my heart;
Tomorrow you'll be my wife!
Happy couple.
The future shall be ours!
To love let's be faithful,
That her eternal chains,
Keep our hearts
Conquerors even against time!

**ANTONIA:** Ah! j'ai le bonheur dans l'âme!
Demain, je serai ta femme!
Heureux époux,
L'avenir est à nous!
Chaque jour, chansons nouvelles!
Ton génie ouvre ses ailes!
Mon chant vainqueur
Est l'écho de ton coeur!

**HOFFMANN:** (*souriant*) Pourtant, ô ma fiancée,
Te dirai-je une pensée
Qui me trouble malgré moi?
La musique m'inspire un peu de jalouise,
Tu l'aimes trop!

**ANTONIA:** (*souriant*) Voyez l'étrange fantaisie!
T'aimé-je donc pour elle, ou l'aimé-je pour toi?
Car toi tu ne vas sans doute me défendre
De chanter, comme a fait mon père?

**HOFFMANN:** Que dis-tu?

**ANTONIA:** Oui, mon père à présent, m'impose la vertu
Du silence.
(*Vivement.*)
Veux-tu m'entendre?

**HOFFMANN:** (*à part*) C'est étrange! . . . Est-ce donc . . .

**ANTONIA:** (*l'entraînant vers le clavecin*) Viens lá, comme autrefois.
Écoute, et tu verras si j'ai perdu ma voix.

**HOFFMANN:** Comme ton oeil s'anime et comme ta main tremble!

**ANTONIA:** (*le faisant s'asseoir devant le clavecin et se penchant sur son épaule*) Tiens, ce doux chant d'amour que nous chantions ensemble.
(*Elle chante, accompagné par Hoffmann.*)
C'est une chanson d'amour
Qui s'envole
Triste ou folle
Tour à tour;
C'est une chanson d'amour.
La rose nouvelle
Sourit au printemps.
Las! . . . combien de temps
Vivra-t-elle?

**ENSEMBLE:** C'est une chanson d'amour
Qui s'envole,
Triste ou folle
Tour à tour.
C'est une chanson d'amour.

**HOFFMANN:** Un rayon de flamme
Pare ta beauté.
Verras-tu l'été,
Fleur de l'âme?

**ENSEMBLE:** C'est une chanson d'amour
Qui s'envole
Triste ou folle
Tour à tour.
C'est une chanson d'amour.
(*Antonia porte la main à son coeur et semble prête à défaillir.*)

**ANTONIA:** I have joy in my heart!
Tomorrow I'll be your wife,
Happy couple,
The future is ours!
Each day new songs,
Your genius opens its wings,
My conquering song
Is the echo of your heart.

**HOFFMANN:** (*smiling*) Still, of my affianced,
Shall I speak my thought?
That, spite of myself, troubles me,
Music inspires a little jealousy,
You love it too much!

**ANTONIA:** (*smiling*) See the strange fantasy!
Did I love you for it, or it for you?
For you are not going to forbid me
To sing, as did my father.

**HOFFMANN:** What say you?

**ANTONIA:** Yes, my father at present imposes the virtue
Of silence.

**HOFFMANN:** (*aside.*) It is strange . . . can it be? . . .

**ANTONIA:** (*drawing him to the clavicord*) Come here as before;
Listen, and you'll see it I've lost my voice.

**HOFFMANN:** How your eye lights up, your hand trembles.

**ANTONIA:** (*making him sit down before the clavichord and leaning on his shoulder*) Here, the soft song of love we sang together.
(*She sings, accompanied by Hoffmann.*)
It is a song of love
That flies off
Sad or joyful,
Turn by turn,
It is a song of love,
The new rose
Smiles on the Spring.
Ah! how long will it be
That it lives?

**TOGETHER:** It is a song of love
That flies off, etc., etc.

**HOFFMANN:** A ray of flame
Matches your beauty.
Will you see the summer
Flower of the soul.

**TOGETHER:** It is a song of love,
That flies off
Sad or joyful,
Turn by turn.
It is a song of love.
(*Antonia puts her hand to her heart.*)

HOFFMANN: Qu'as-tu donc?

ANTONIA: (*mettant la main à son couer*) Rien.

HOFFMANN: (*écoutant*) Chut!

ANTONIA: Ciel! mon père! Viens! . . . viens! . . . (*Elle sort.*)

HOFFMANN: Non! je saurai le mot de ce mystère. (*Il se cache dans l'enfoncement de la fenêtre, Crespel paraît.*)

*CRESPEL, HOFFMANN caché, puis FRANTZ.*

CRESPEL: (*regardant autour de lui*) Non, rien! J'ai cru qu'Hoffmann étai ici. Puisse-t-il être au diable 1

HOFFMANN: (*à part*) Grand merci!

FRANTZ: (*entrant, à Crespel*) Monsieur!

CRESPEL: Quoi?

FRANTZ: Le docteur Miracle.

CRESPEL: Drôle! . . . infâme! Ferme vite la porte!

FRANTZ: Oui, monsieur, médecin . . .

CRESPEL: Lui! médecin? Non, sur mon âme, Un fossoyeur, un assassin! Qui me tuerait ma fille après ma femme. J'entends le cliquetis de ses flacons dans l'air. Loin de moi qu'on le chasse. (*Miracle paraît subitement. Frantz se sauve.*) (*Le mêmes, Miracle.*)

MIRACLE: Ha, ha, ha, ha!

CRESPEL: Enfin!

MIRACLE: Eh bien! me voilà! c'est moi-même, Ce bon monsieur Crespel, je l'aime! Où donc est-il?

CRESPEL: (*l'arrêtant*) Morbleu!

MIRACLE: Ha, ha, ha, ha! Je cherchais votre Antonia! Eh bien! ce mal qu'elle hérita De sa mère? Toujours en progrès? chère belle! Nous la guérirons. Menez-moi près d'elle.

CRESPEL: Pour l'assassiner! . . . Si tu fais un pas, Je te jette par la fenêtre.

MIRACLE: Eh! là! tout doux! Je ne veux pas Vous déplaire. (*Il avance un fauteuil.*)

CRESPEL: Que fais-tu, traître?

MIRACLE: Pour conjurer le danger, Il faut le connaître. Laissez-moi l'interroger.

---

HOFFMANN: Why, what is the matter?

ANTONIA: (*doing the same again*) Nothing.

HOFFMANN: (*listening*) Chut.

ANTONIA: Heavens, my father! Come, come . . . (*She goes out.*)

HOFFMANN: No! I must know the last word of this mystery. (*He hides in the recess of the window. Crespel appears.*)

*CRESPEL, HOFFMANN hidden, then FRANTZ*

CRESPEL: (*looking about him*) No, nothing. I thought Hoffmann was here. May he go to the devil!

HOFFMANN: (*aside*) Many thanks!

FRANTZ: (*entering, to Crespel*) Sir.

CRESPEL: What?

FRANTZ: Doctor Miracle.

CRESPEL: Infamous scoundrel, Quickly close the door.

FRANTZ: Yes, sir, the doctor.

CRESPEL: He, doctor? No, on my soul, A grave digger, an assassin! Who would kill my daughter after my wife. I hear the jingle of his golden vials, Let him be chased from me. (*Miracle suddenly appears. Frantz runs away.*) (*Above. Miracle.*)

MIRACLE: Ha, ha, ha, ha!

CRESPEL: At last!

MIRACLE: Well, here I am! It's myself, This good monsieur Crespel, I like him, But where is he?

CRESPEL: (*stopping him*) Morbleu!

MIRACLE: Ha, ha, ha, ha! I sought for your Antonia. Well, this trouble she inherited From her mother? Still progressing, dear girl. We'll cure her. Take me to her.

CRESPEL: To assassinate her . . . If you make one step I'll throw you out of the window.

MIRACLE: There now softly, I do not wish to Displease you. (*He advances a chair.*)

CRESPEL: What do you, traitor?

MIRACLE: To minimize the danger, One must know it. Let me question her.

---

CRESPEL ET HOFFMANN: L'effroi me pénètre.

MIRACLE: (*la main étendue vers la chambre d'-Antonia*) A mon pouvoir vainqueur Cède de bonne grâce! . . . Près de moi, sans terreur, Viens ici prendre place, Viens!

CRESPEL ET HOFFMANN: D'épouvante et d'horreur Tout mon être se glace. Une étrange terreur M'enchaine à cette place, J'ai peur.

CRESPEL: (*s'asseyant sur le tabouret du clavecin*) Allons, parle, et sois bref! (*Miracle continue ses passes magnétiques. La porte de la chambre d'Antonia s'ouvre lentement. Miracle indique par ses gestes qu'il prend la main d'Antonia invisible, qu'il la mène près de l'un des fauteuils et la fait s'asseoir.*)

MIRACLE: (*indiquant l'un des fauteuils et s'asseyant sur l'autre*) Veuillez vous asseoir là!

CRESPEL: Je suis assis!

MIRACLE: (*sans répoundre à Crespel*) Quel âge avez-vous, je vous prie?

CRESPEL: Qui? moi?

MIRACLE: Je parle à votre enfant.

HOFFMANN: (*à part*) Antonia?

MIRACLE: Quel âge? . . . (*Il écoute.*) Vingt ans!

CRESPEL: Hein?

MIRACLE: Le printemps de la vie! . . . (*Il fait le geste d'un homme qui tâte le pouls.*) Voyons la main! . . .

CRESPEL: La main? . . .

MIRACLE: (*tirant sa montre*) Chut! Laissez-moi compter.

HOFFMANN: (*à part*) Dieu! . . . suis-je le jouet d'un rêve? Est-ce un fantôme?

MIRACLE: Le pouls est inégal et vif, mauvais symptôme? Chantez! . . .

CRESPEL: (*se levant*) Non, non, tais-toi! . . . ne la fais pas chanter! (*La voix d'Antonia se fait entendre dans l'air.*)

MIRACLE: Voyez, son front s'anime et son regard flamboie; Elle porte la main à son coeur agité. (*Il semble suivre Antonia du gest, la porte de la chambre se referme brusquement.*)

CRESPEL: Que dit-il?

---

CRESPEL AND HOFFMANN: Terror penetrates me.

MIRACLE: (*his hand extended toward Antonia's room*) To my conquering power, Give way with good grace. Near me without terror Come take your place.

CRESPEL AND HOFFMANN: With fright and with horror All my being is cold; A strange terror Chains me to this place. I'm afraid.

CRESPEL: (*seating himself on the music-stool*) Come, speak and be brief. (*Miracle continues his magnetic passes. The door of Antonia's room opens slowly. Miracle indicates by gestures that he takes the hand of Antonia, invisible, and leads her to one of the arm chairs and makes her sit down.*)

MIRACLE: (*pointing out one of the chairs and sitting on another*) Please sit there.

CRESPEL: I am seated.

MIRACLE: (*paying no attention to Crespel*) How old are you, please?

CRESPEL: Who, I?

MIRACLE: I am speaking to your child.

HOFFMANN: (*aside*) Antonia.

MIRACLE: What age? (*He listens.*) Twenty!

CRESPEL: What?

MIRACLE: The Spring of life. (*He appears to feel the pulse.*) Let me see your hand! . . .

CRESPEL: The hand.

MIRACLE: (*pulling out his watch*) Chut! let me count.

HOFFMANN: (*aside*) God! am I the plaything of a dream? Is it a ghost?

MIRACLE: The pulse is unequal and fast, bad symptom. Sing.

CRESPEL: (*rising*) No, no, don't speak . . . don't have her sing. (*The voice of Antonia is heard.*)

MIRACLE: See her face brightens, her eyes are on fire; She carries her hand to her beating heart. (*He follows Antonia with his gestures. The door of her room closes quickly.*)

CRESPEL: What is he saying?

MIRACLE: (*se levant et remettant un des fauteuils en place*) Il serait dommage, en vérité, De laisser à la mort une si belle proie!

CRESPEL: Tais-toi! . . . (*Il repousse violemment l'autre fauteuil.*)

MIRACLE: Si vous voulez accepter mon secours, Si vous voulez, sauver ses jours, J'ai là certain flacons que je tiens en réserve. (*Il tire plusieurs flacons de sa poche et les fait sonner comme des castagnettes.*)

CRESPEL: Tais-toi! . . .

MIRACLE: Dont il faudrait . . .

CRESPEL: Tais-toi! Dieu me préserve D'écouter tes conseils, misérable assassin! . . .

MIRACLE: Dont il faudrait, chaque matin . . .

MIRACLE: Eh oui! je vous entends! Tout à l'heure! un instant! De flacons! pauvre père, Vous en serez, j'espèrre, Content!

CRESPEL: Va-t'en! va-t'en! va-t'en! Hors de chez moi, Satan! Redoute la colère Et la douleur d'un père! Va-t'en!

HOFFMANN: (*à part*) A la mort qui t'attend, Je saurai, pauvre enfant, T'arracher, je l'espère! Tu ris en vain d'un père, Satan!

MIRACLE: (*continuant toujours avec le même flegme*) Dont il faudrait . . .

CRESPEL: Va-t'en!

MIRACLE: Chaque matin . . .

CRESPEL: Va-t'en! . . . (*Il pousse Miracle debors, par la porte du fond et la referme sur lui*) Ah! le voilà dehors et ma porte est fermée! Nous sommes seuls enfin, Ma fille bien-aimée!

MIRACLE: (*rentrant par la muraille*) Dont il faudrait chaque matin . . .

CRESPEL: Ah! misérable! Viens! . . . viens! . . . Les flots puissent-ils t'engloutir Nous verrons si le diable T'en fera sortir! . . .

CRESPEL: Va-t'en! Va-t'en! Va-ten! Hors de chez moi, Satan! Redoute la colère Et la douleur d'un père, Va-t'en!

MIRACLE: (*rising and putting one of the chairs in its place*) It would be a pity truly To leave to death so fine a prey!

CRESPEL: Shut up! (*He violently pushes the other armchair.*)

MIRACLE: If you will accept my help, If you would save her days, I have there certain vials I keep in reserve. (*He takes vials from pocket which he makes sound like castanets.*)

CRESPEL: Shut up!

MIRACLE: Of which you should . . .

CRESPEL: Shut up! Heaven preserve me From listening to your advice, miserable assassin.

MIRACLE: Of which you should, each morning . . .

MIRACLE: Why, yes, I hear you. A while ago, an instant, These vials, poor father, You will be then, I hope, Satisfied.

CRESPEL: Be off, be off, be off! Out of this house, Satan, Beware of the anger And the sorrow of a father. Be off!

HOFFMANN: (*aside*) From the death that awaits you I shall know, poor child, How tear you away, I hope! Laugh in vain at a father, Satan!

MIRACLE: (*continuing with same coolness*) of which you should . . .

CRESPEL: Be off!

MIRACLE: Each morning . . .

CRESPEL: Be off! (*He pushes Miracle out through the back door and closes the door.*) Ah, he's outside and my door is closed! We are at last alone, My beloved girl!

MIRACLE: (*walking through the wall*) Of which you should each morning . . .

CRESPEL: Ah, wretch, Come, come, may the waves engulf you! We'll see if the devil Will get out.

CRESPEL: Be off, be off, be off! Out of this house, Satan! Beware of the anger And the sorrow of a father.

HOFFMANN: (*à part*) A la mort qui t'attend, Je saurai, pauvre enfant, T'arracher, je l'espère! Tu ris en vain d'un père, Satan!

MIRACLE: Dont il faudrait . . .

CRESPEL: Va-t'en!

MIRACLE: Chaque matin . . .

CRESPEL: Va-t'en! (*Il suit Miracle qui sort à reculons en faisant sonner ses flacons. Ils disparaissent ensemble.*) (*Hoffmann seul, puis Antonia.*)

HOFFMANN: (*redescend en scène*). Ne plus chanter! hélas! Comment obtenir d'elle Un pareil sacrifce?

ANTONIA: (*paraît*). Eh bien? Mon père, qu'a-t-il dit?

HOFFMANN: Ne me demande rien, Plus tard tu sauras tout; une route nouvelle S'ouvre ànous, mon Antonia! . . . Pour y suivre mes pas, chasse de ta mémoire Ces rêves d'avenir, de succès et de gloire Que ton coeur au mien confia.

ANTONIA: Mais toi-même?

HOFFMANN: L'amour tous les deux nour convie, Tout ce qui n'est pas toi n'est plus rien dans ma vie.

ANTONIA: Tiens donc! voici ma main!

HOFFMANN: Ah! chère Antonia! Pourrai-je reconaître Ce que tu fais pour moi? (*Il lui baise les mains.*) Ton père va peut-être Revenir, je te quitte . . . à demain!

ANTONIA: A demain! (*Hoffmann sort. Antonia le regarde s'éloigner. Après un moment, elle redescend en scène.*) (*Antonia, puis Miracle.*)

ANTONIA: (*allant ouvrir une des portes latérales*). De mon père aisément il s'est fait le complice! Allons, les pleurs sont superflus, Je l'ai promis, je ne chanterai plus. (*Elle se laisse tomber sur un fauteuil.*)

MIRACLE: (*surgissant tout à coup derrière elle et se penchant à son oreille*). Tu ne chanteras plus? Sais-tu quel sacrifice S'impose ta jeunesse, et l'as-tu mesuré? La grâce, la beauté, le talent, don sacré, Tous ces biens que le ciel t'a livrés en partage, Faut-il les enfouir dans l'ombre d'un ménage? N'as-tu pas entendu, dans un rêve

HOFFMANN: (*aside*) From the death that awaits thee I shall know, poor child, How tear thee away, I hope! Laugh in vain at a father, Satan!

MIRACLE: Of which you should . . .

CRESPEL: Get out!

MIRACLE: Each morning . . .

CRESPEL: Get out! (*He follows Miracle who goes out backwards making his bottles sound.*) (*Hoffmann, alone, then Antonia*)

HOFFMANN: (*coming down*) To sing no more! How obtain from her Such a sacrifice?

ANTONIA: (*appearing*) Well? What did my father say?

HOFFMANN: Ask me nothing; Later you'll know all; a new road Opens for us, my Antonia! . . . To follow my steps dismiss from your memory These dreams of future success and glory I have confided your heart to mine.

ANTONIA: But yourself?

HOFFMANN: Love calls to both of us, All that is not you is nothing in my life.

ANTONIA: Very well! Here is my hand!

HOFFMANN: Ah dear Antonia, shall I appreciate What you do for me? (*He kisses her hands.*) Your father will perhaps return. I leave you . . . until tomorrow.

ANTONIA: Until tomorrow. (*Hoffmann goes out. Antonia watches him depart. After a moment she comes back.*) (*Antonia, then Miracle.*)

ANTONIA: (*opening one of the doors*) He has easily become the accomplice of my father, But come, regrets are superfluous, I promised him. I shall sing no more. (*She falls in a chair.*)

MIRACLE: (*appearing suddenly behind her and leaning over her ear*) You will sing no more. Do you know what a sacrifice He imposes on your youth, and have you measured it? Grace, beauty, talent, sacred gift; All these blessings that heaven gave for your share, Must they be hid in the shadow of a household? Have you not heard, in a proud dream,

orgueilleux,
Ainsi qu'une forêt par le vent bal-
ancée,
Ce doux frémissement de la foule
pressée
Qui murmure ton nom et qui te suit
des yeux?
Voilà l'ardente joie et la fête
éternelle
Que tes vingt ans en fleur sont près
d'abandonner,
Pour les plaisirs bourgeois où l'on
veut t'enchaîner
Et des marmots d'enfants qui te rendront moins belle!

**ANTONIA:** (*sans se retourner*).
Ah! quelle est cette voix qui me
trouble l'esprit?
Est-ce l'enfer qui parle ou Dieu qui
m'avertit?
Non, non, ce n'est pas là le bonh-
eur, voix maudite,
Et contre mon orgueil mon amour
s'est armé;
La gloire ne vaut pas l'ombre heu-
reuse où m'invite
La maison de mon bien-aimé.

**MIRACLE:** Quelles amours sont
donc les vôtres
Hoffmann te sacrifie à sa brutalité;
Il n'aime en toi que ta beauté;
Et pour lui, comme pour les autres,
Viendra bientôt le temps de
l'infidélité! . . .
(*Il disparaît.*)

**ANTONIA:** (*se levant*). Non, ne
me tente plus! . . . Va-t'en,
Démon! . . . Je ne veux plus
t'entendre.
J'ai juré d'être à lui, mon bien-aime
m'attend.
Je ne m'appartiens plus et ne puis
me reprendre;
Et tout à l'heure encore, sur son coeur adoré.
Quel éternel amour ne m'a-t-il pas
juré! . . . Ah! qui me sauvera du
démon, de moi'même? . . .
(*regardant le portrait de sa
mère.*)
Ma mère! O, ma mère!
Je l'aime! Je l'aime!

**MIRACLE:** (*reparaît derrière Antonia.*) Ta mère? . . . Oses-tu
l'invoquer? . . .
Ta mère? Mais n'est-ce pas elle
Qui parle par ma voix, ingrate, et te
rappelle
La splendeur de son nom que tu
veux abdiquer?
(*Le portait s'éclaire et semble
s'animer. C'est le fantôme de la
mère qui apparît à la place de la
peinture.*)
Ecoute! . . .

**LA VOIX:** Antonia?

**ANTONIA:** Dieu! . . . ma mère!
ma mère!

Like unto a forest by the wind moving,
Like a soft shiver of the pressing
crowd,
That murmurs your name and follows you with its eyes?
There is the ardent joy and the eternal festival,
That the flower of your years is
about to abandon,
For the middle class pleasures
where they would enchain you,
And the squalling children who
will give you less beauty!

**ANTONIA:** (*without turning
round*) Ah, what is this voice that
troubles my spirit?
Is it Hell that speaks or Heaven that
warns me?
No! happiness is not there, oh
cursed voice,
And my love had armed me against
my pride;
Glory is not worth the happy shade
that
The house of my beloved offers me

**MIRACLE:** What loves can now be
yours,
Hoffmann sacrifices you to his bru-
tality,
He only loves in you your beauty,
And for him as for the others,
Soon will come the time of infideli-
ty.
(*He disappears.*)

**ANTONIA:** (*rising*) No, do not
tempt me! go away,
Demon! I will no longer listen.
I have sworn to be his, my beloved
awaits me,
I'm no longer my own and I can't
take myself back;
And a few moments since, on his
heart adored
What eternal love did he not pledge
me;
Who will save me from the demon,
from myself?
(*Looking at the portrait.*)
My mother, my mother, I love her.

**MIRACLE:** (*reappears behind Antonia*) Your mother? Dare you invoke her?
Your mother? But is it not she?
Who speaks by my voice, ingrate,
and recalls to you
The splendor of the name that you
would abdicate?
(*The portrait lights up and becomes animated. It is the ghost of
the mother which appears in the
place of the painting.*)
Listen.

**THE VOICE:** Antonia!

**ANTONIA:** Heavens! . . . my
mother, my mother!

**LE FANTOME:** Cher enfant que
j'appelle
Comme autrefois,
C'est ta mère, c'est elle,
Entends sa voix!

**ANTONIA:** Ma mère!

**MIRACLE:** Oui! oui! c'est sa voix,
l'entends-tu?
Sa voix, meilleure conseillère,
Qui te lègue un talent que le
monde a perdu!

**LE FANTOME:** Antonia!

**MIRACLE:** Écoute! Elle semble revivre
Et le public lointain de ses bravos
l'enivre!

**ANTONIA:** (*se levant*). Ma mère!

**LE FANTOME:** Antonia!

**MIRACLE:** Reprends donc avec
elle! . . .
(*Il saisit un violin et accompagne
avec une sorte de fureur.*)

**ANTONIA:** Oui, son âme
m'appelle
Comme autrefois!
C'est ma mère, c'est elle,
J'entends sa voix!

**LE FANTOME:** Cher enfant que
j'appelle
Comme autrefois,
C'est ta mère, c'est elle!
Entends sa voix!

**ANTONIA:** Non! assez! . . . Je
succombe!

**MIRACLE:** Encore!

**ANTONIA:** Je ne veux plus chanter.

**MIRACLE:** Encore!

**ANTONIA:** Quelle ardeur
m'entraîne et me dévore?

**MIRACLE:** Encore! Pourquoi
t'arrêter?

**ANTONIA:** (*baletante*). Je cède au
transport qui m'enivre!
Quelle flamme éblouit mes
yeux! . . .
Un seul moment encore à vivre,
Et mon âme s'envole aux cieux!

**LE FANTOME:** Cher enfant que
j'appelle etc.

**ANTONIA:** C'est ma mère, c'est
elle, etc.

**ANTONIA:** Ah!
(*Elle vient tomber mourante sur
le canapé. Miracle s'engloutit
dans la terre en poussant un éclat
de rire. le fantôme disparaît et le
portrait reprend son premier aspect.*)
(*Antonia, Crespel, puis Hoffmann, Nicklausse, Miracle et
Frantz.*)

**CRESPEL:** (*accourant*) Mon enfant! . . . ma fille! . . . Antonia!

**THE GHOST:** Dear child whom I
call,
As I used to do,
It is your mother, it is she,
Listen to her voice.

**ANTONIA:** Mother!

**MIRACLE:** Yes, yes, it is her voice,
do you hear?
Her voice, best counsellor,
Who leaves you a talent the world
has lost!

**THE GHOST:** Antonia!

**MIRACLE:** Listen! She seems to live
again,
And the distant public by its bravos
fills her bliss.

**ANTONIA:** Mother!

**THE GHOST:** Antonia!

**MIRACLE:** Join with her.
(*He seizes a violin and accompanies her with a sort of madness.*)

**ANTONIA:** Yes, her soul calls me
As before;
It is my mother, it is she
I hear her voice.

**THE GHOST:** Dear child whom I
call
As I used to do;
It is your mother, it is she;
Listen to her voice.

**ANTONIA:** No, enough, I cannot!

**MIRACLE:** Again.

**ANTONIA:** I will sing no more.

**MIRACLE:** Again! Why stop?

**ANTONIA:** What ardor draws and
devours me?

**MIRACLE:** Again! Why stop?

**ANTONIA:** (*out of breath*) I give
way to a transport that maddens,
What flame is it dazzles my eyes
A single moment to live,
And my soul flies to Heaven.

**THE GHOST:** Dear child whom I
call, etc., etc.

**ANTONIA:** It is my mother, it is
she, etc., etc.

**ANTONIA:** Ah!
(*She falls dying on the sofa. Miracle sinks in the earth uttering a
peal of laughter. The phantom disappears and the portrait takes on
again its former aspect.*)
(*Antonia, Crespel, then Hoffmann, Nicklausse, Miracle and
Frantz.*)

**CRESPEL:** (*running in*) My
child . . . my daughter . . .
Antonia! . . .

ANTONIA: (*expirante*). Mon père!
Ecoutez! c'est ma mère
Qui m'appelle! . . . Et
lui . . . de retour
C'est une chanson d'amour . . .
Qui s'envole . . .
Triste ou folle . . .
(*Elle meurt.*)

CRESPEL: Non! . . . un seul
mot! . . . un seul! . . . ma
fille . . . parle-moi.
Mais parle donc! . . . Mort
exécrable!
Non! . . . pitié! . . . gráce!
. . . Eloigne-toi.

HOFFMANN: (*entrant précipitamment*). Pourquoi ces cris?

CRESPEL: Hoffmann! . . . ah!
misérable!
C'est toi qui l'as tuée! . . .

HOFFMANN: (*courant à Antonia*). Antonia!.

CRESPEL: (*courant avec égarement*). Du sang!
Pour colorer sa joue! . . . Une arme, Un couteau! . . .
(*Il saisit un couteau sur une table et va pour s'élancer sur Hoffmann.*)

NICKLAUSSE: (*entrant en scène et arrêtant Crespel*). Malheureux! . . .

HOFFMANN: (*à Nicklausse*).
Vite! . . . donne
l'alarme! . . .
Un médecin! . . . un médecin! . . .

MIRACLE: (*paraissant*). Présent!
(*Il s'approche d'Antonia et lui tâte le pouls*)
Morte!

CRESPEL: (*éperdu*). Ah! Dieu,
mon enfant! ma fille!

HOFFMANN: (*avec désespoir*).
Antonia!
(*Frantz est entré le dernier et s'est agenouillé prè d'Antonia.*)

## EPILOGUE

### Stella

*Même décoration qu'au premier acte.*
*Hoffmann, Nicklausse, Lindorf, Nathanael, Hermann, Wilhelm, Wolframm, Luther. Les Étudiants. On retrouve tous les personnages dans la situation où on les a laissés à la fin du premier acte.*

HOFFMANN: Voilà quelle fut l'histoire
De mes amours
Dont la mémoire
En mon coeur restera toujours.

LUTHER: (*entrant*). Grand succès, on acclame
Notre prima donna.

---

ANTONIA: (*expiring*) My father!
Listen, it is my mother
Who calls me. And he . . . has returned . . .
It is your mother, it is she;
Flies away,
Sad or joyful . . .
(*She dies.*)

CRESPEL: No . . . a single
word . . . just one . . . my
child . . . speak!
Come, speak! Execrable death!
No! pity, mercy . . . go away!

HOFFMANN: (*coming hurriedly*)
Why these cries? . . .

CRESPEL: Hoffmann! . . . ah
wretch!
You killed her!.

HOFFMANN: (*rushing to Antonia*) Antonia!

CRESPEL: (*rushing up beside himself*) Blood to color her cheek.
A weapon, A knife! . . .
(*He seizes a knife on a table and attacks Hoffmann.*)

NICKLAUSSE: (*entering and stopping Crespel*) Unhappy man!

HOFFMANN: (*to Nicklausse*)
Quick! give the alarm;
A doctor . . . a doctor! . . .

MIRACLE: (*appearing*) Present!
(*He approaches Antonia and feels her pulse*) Dead!

CRESPEL: (*crazy*) Ah, God, my
child, my daughter!

HOFFMANN: (*despairingly*) Antonia!
(*Frantz is the last to enter and kneels near Antonia.*)

## EPILOGUE

### Stella

*The Tavern.*
*Hoffmann, Nicklausee, Lindorf, Nathanael, Hermann, Wilhelm, Wolfram, Luther, Students. The various personages are in the same position they were in at the end of First Scene First Act.*

HOFFMANN: There is the story
Of my loves,
And the memory
In my heart will always remain.

LUTHER: (*entering*) Great success, they applaud
Our prima donna.

---

LINDORF: (*à part*). Il n'est plus à
craindre . . . à moi la diva!
(*Il s'esquive.*)

NATHANAEL: Qu'a de commun
Stella?

NICKLAUSSE: (*se levant*). Ah! je
comprends! trois drames dans un drame
Olympia . . . Antonia . . . Giulietta
Ne sont qu'une même femme:
La Stella!

LE CHOEUR: La Stella!

NICKLAUSSE: Buvons à cette
honnête dame!

HOFFMANN: (*furieux, brisant son verre*). Un mot de plus et sur mon âme
Je te brise comme ceci! . . .

NICKLAUSSE: Moi, ton mentor?
Merci! . . .

HOFFMANN: Ah! je suis
fou! . . . A nous le vertige divin
Des esprits de l'alcool, de la bière et du vin!
A nous l'ivresse et la folie,
Le néant par qui l'on oublie

LE CHOEUR: Allumons le
punch! . . . grisons-nous!
Et que les plus fous
Roulent sous la table.
Luther est un brave homme,
Tire lan laire, tire lan la!
C'est demain qu'on l'assomme
Tire lan laire, tire lan la!
Sa cave est d'un bon drille,
Tire lan laire, tire lan la!
C'est demain qu'on la pille!
Tire lan laire, tire lan la!
Jusqu'au matin
Remplis mon verre,
Jusqu'au matin
Remplis les pots d'étain!
(*Les étudiants entrent en tumulte dans la salle voisine. Hoffmann reste comme frappé de stupeur.*)

LA MUSE: (*paraissant*). Et moi?
Moi, la fidèle amie
Dont la main essuya tes yeux?
Par qui la douleur endormie
S'exhale en rêve dans les cieux?
Ne suis-je rien? Que la tempête
Des passions s'apaise en toi!
L'homme n'est plus; renais poète!
Je t'aime, Hoffmann! appartiens-moi!
Des cendres de ton coeur rechauffe ton génie,
Dans la sérénité souris à tes douleurs,
La Muse adoucira ta souffrance bénie,
On est grand par l'amour et plus grand par les pleurs!
(*Elle disparaît.*)

HOFFMANN: (*seul*). O Dieu! de
quelle ivresse embrases-tu mon âme,
Comme un concert divin ta voix

---

LINDORF.: (*aside*) He is to be
feared no more. The singer for me!
(*Exit.*)

NATHANAEL: What does Stella
have to do with it?

NICKLAUSSE: (*rising*) Ah, I understand! Three dramas in one drama,
Olympia, Antonia, Giulietta are only one woman:
Stella!

THE CHORUS: Stella!

NICKLAUSSE: Let us drink to that
good lady!

HOFFMANN: (*furious, breaking his glass*) One word more and by my soul
I will break you like that!

NICKLAUSSE: I, your mentor?
Thank you!

HOFFMANN: Ah, I am mad. For us
the craze divine.
The spirits of alcohol, of beer and of wine,
For us intoxication,
Chaos where we forget.

THE CHORUS: Light up the punch,
we'll get drunk;
And may the weakest
Roll under the table;
Luther was a goodly man,
Tire lan laire, tire lan la,
Tomorrow we'll crush him!
Tire lan laire,
Tire lan la.
His cellar is a good spot,
Tire lan laire.
Tomorrow we will make it hot.
Tire lan laire.
Tire lan laire.
Until morning
Fill my glass,
Until morning
Fill our pewter mugs.
(*The students tumultuously go in the next room. Hoffmann remains as if in a stupor.*)

THE MUSE: (*appearing in an aureole of light*) And I? I, the faithful friend,
Whose hand wiped your tears?
By whom your latent sorrow
Exhales in heavenly dreams?
Am I nothing? May the tempest
Of passion pass away in you!
The man is no more; the poet revives!
I love you, Hoffmann! be mine!
Let the ashes of your heart fire your genius,
Whose serenity smiles on your sorrows,
The Muse will soften your blessed sufferings,
One is great by love but greater by tears.
(*She disappears.*)

HOFFMANN: (*alone*) Oh God!
what ecstasy embraces my soul,
Your voice has moved me like a concert divine,

## Act I, Scene II

m'a pénétré,
D'un feu doux et brûlant mon être
est dévoré,
Tes regards dans les miens ont
épanché leur flamme,
Comme des astres radieux,
Et je sens, ô Muse aimée,
Passer ton haleine embaumée
Sur mes lèvres et sur mes yeux!
(*Il tombe, le visage sur une table.*)

**STELLA:** (*allant vers Hoffmann*).
Hoffmann endormi! . . .

**NICKLAUSSE:** Non! . . . ivre-
more! . . . Trop tard, madame!

**LINDORF:** Corbleu!

**NICKLAUSSE:** Tenez, voilà le conseiller Lindorf qui vous attend.
(*Stella prend son manteau des
mains d'Andrès et le jette sur ses*

With soft and burning fire my being
is devoured,
Your glance has suffused its flame
in mine,
Like radiant stars.
And I feel, beloved Muse,
Your perfumed breath flutter
On my lips and on my eyes!
(*He falls face on table.*)

**STELLA:** (*approaching slowly*)
Hoffmann? asleep . . .

**NICKLAUSSE:** No, dead drunk.
Too late, madame.

**LINDORF.:** Corbleu!

**NICKLAUSSE:** Oh, here is the
counsellor, Lindorf, who awaits
you.
(*Stella takes his mantle from the*

épaules; puis elle s'eppuie sur le
bras de Lindorf, s'arrête au bout
de quelques pas pour regarder
Hoffmann, détache une fleur de
son bouquet et la jette à ses pieds.
Hoffmann la suit des yeux avec
une sorte de stupeur. Pendant
cette scène muette, les étudiants
chantent en frappant bruyamment des gobelets sur les table.*)

**LE CHOEUR:** Jusqu'au matin
Remplis mon verre!
Jusqu'au matin
Remplis les pots d'étain!

*FIN*

bands of Andrès and throws it
over his shoulders; then she leans
on Lindorf's arm, stops after several steps to look at Hoffmann,
takes a flower from her bouquet
and throws it at his feet. Hoffmann follows her with his gaze in
a sort of stupor. During this dumb
show, the students sing noisily,
clicking their glasses on the table.*)

**THE CHORUS:** Until morning
Fill my glass,
Until morning
Fill our pewter mugs!

*END*

# Manru (1901)

MUSIC BY I.J. PADEREWSKI ■ LIBRETTO BY ALFRED NOSSIG

This three-act romantic opera, set to a libretto by Alfred Nossig, premiered at the Court Theatre in Dresden on May 29, 1901. The story takes place in the Tatra Mountains, located between Hungary and Galicia. In a village set in the mountains, Hedwig is grieving over her daughter, Ulana, who has run away with Manru, a gypsy. Ulana appears in the village and comes to her mother's cottage in order to seek her forgiveness for running off. Hedwig promises that she will grant this if Ulana forsakes Manru forever, but Ulana steadfastly refuses to do this. Finally, her mother drives her away, cursing her as she goes. Ulana then asks Urok, a dwarf who is known to be a sorcerer, to assist her—Urok has often proclaimed his love for her. She is able to get a magic potion from him which will enable her to win back Manru's love, as Manru already desires to return to his previous life with the gypsies. Ulana is singing a lullaby to her baby in a hut located in the mountains. Manru is torn between his love for her and his desire to go back to his people. Urok enters, and Manru hears beautiful violin music in the distance. It is Jogu, the Gypsy fiddler, playing music which Manru recognizes. Hearing this music, he is overcome, and he runs from the hut and disappears into the forest. Jogu tries to persuade Manru to rejoin their band and become their chief, and he also tells him that Asa, the beautiful Gypsy maiden, is in love with him. In the middle of this Ulana enters and is able to persuade Manru to return with her to their hut, where she gives him a drink of the magic potion. The potion works temporarily, and Manru is once again in love with Ulana. Near a lake in the mountains, Manru is wandering in the moonlight. He hears voices he does not recognize and, becoming tired, falls sound asleep underneath the trees. He is discovered there by the band of Gypsies. Asa, who is amongst them, recognizes him at once and beseeches Oros, the chief of the Gypsies, to forgive him and welcome him back into the band. Oros refuses to do so and, as he discovers that his people are ready to forgive Manru, he leaves the Gypsies in a rage. Asa persuades Manru to become the Gypsy chief in Oros' place. Urok appears all of a sudden and begs Manru not to desert Ulana and their baby, but Manru finally caves in to Asa's charms and goes away into the mountains with the Gypsies. Ulana is told of this and becomes crazed with grief. She throws herself into the lake and is drowned. Manru and Asa are walking together arm-in-arm down a mountain path when they are suddenly confronted by Oros. Oros and Manru engage in a fight, during which Oros throws Manru in the abyss and regains his position as Gypsy chief.

## ■ ERSTER AUFZUG

*(Dorf im tatragebirge. Die Bühne stellt eine offene, von Stangen umgebene Tanzwiese dar. Rechts und links sind Bauernhütten angedeutet, darunter die Hedwig's mit einer Bank und einem kleinen Blumengärtchen. Hinter den Hütten Tannenwälder. Im Hintergrunde das Tatragebirge im Abendsonnenschein.)*

### ERSTE SCENE

HEDWIG EIN MÄDCHEN AUS DEM CHOR ERSTER UND ZWEITER CHOR DER LANDMÄDCHEN.
*(Die Mädchen treffen Vorbereitungen zum Erntefeste, indem sie aus Laub und Blumen Guirlanden winden und dieselben mit Bändern an die Stangen Knüpfen. Fröhliche Bewegung auf der Bühne; nur Hedwig sitzt traurig sinnend vor ihrer Hütte.)*

## ■ ACT I

*(A Village among the Tatra Mountains. A dancing-green surrounded by poles. Right and left, peasants' huts are indicated, among them that of HEDWIG; a bench in a small flower-garden. Back of the huts a pine forest. In the background, the Tatra Mountains. Sunset.)*

### SCENE I

HEDWIG. A MAIDEN OF THE CHORUS. FIRST AND SECOND CHORUSES OF COUNTRY MAIDENS.
*(The maidens adorn the green for the harvest festival, winding garlands and fastening them to the poles. Merry activity on the stage; HEDWIG sits lost in sad thought in front of her hut.)*

**HEDWIG:** Aus der Höh' Stürzt ein Habicht mit sich'rem Fall, Dunkel und jäh, Fasst ein Täubchen mit scharfer Krall';
Täubchen mein, Täubchen klein, Ach, sahst Du Dich nicht vor!

**ERSTER CHOR DER LANDMÄDCHEN:** Tra la la la!

**ZWEITER CHOR DER LANDMÄDCHEN:** Windet den Kranz, Schmücket die Wiese zum Tanz!

**HEDWIG:** Hatt' ein Kind, Ein Zigeuner, ein Zaub'rer kam; Mein Herzblut rinnt, Seit der Habicht mein Täubchen nahm.
Töchterlein, Täubchen mein, Ach, dass ich Dich verlor!

**ERSTER CHOR:** Tra la la la!

**ZWEITER CHOR:** *(indem er dem ersten die Guirlanden zuwirft).* Rasch und behend Fasst es am andern End'!
Ihr Faulen heran!
Greifet zu, bindet an!
Nur gewandt!

**ERSTER CHOR:** *(die Guirlanden auffangend und an die Stangen Knüpfend).* Jetzt ist es zierlich gespannt!

**HEDWIG:** From on high Darts a hawk with his hungry maw; Never a cry As he seizes with a cruel claw.
—
Pretty dove, Dainty love, Ah! why were you not on guard?

**FIRST CHORUS:** Tra la, la, la!

**SECOND CHORUS:** Maidens, advance, Garnish the green for the dance!

**HEDWIG:** The child was mine, But a conjuring Gypsy neared; Now I pine away, alone For my dove disappeared with the hawk!
Pretty love, Dainty dove, Why did you leave my ward?

**FIRST CHORUS:** Tra, la, la, la!

**SECOND CHORUS:** *(Throwing the garlands to the first.)* Bravo!
The end Now to the next pole extend!
You dawdlers, disband!
Up and work!
Lend a hand!
Deftly done!

**FIRST CHORUS:** *(Catching the garlands and fastening them to the poles.)* Lovelier garland there's none!

**ERSTER AND ZWEITER CHOR:** Tra la la la!

**HEDWIG:** Töchterlein, Säugte Dich dazu meine Brust, Dass Du in Pein Einem Heiden gehören musst!

**ZWEITER CHOR:** Wie einer Maid Macht ihr aus Blumen ein Kleid!

**ERSTER CHOR:** Tra la la la!

**HEDWIG:** Töchterlein, wärst Du heir, Freude käm' mit Dir!

**ERSTER CHOR:** Tra la la la! Rasch und behend! Bald ist die Arbeit zu End'!

**ZWEITER CHOR:** Bänder her! Von den rothen noch mehr! Rasch und behend, Bald ist die Arbeit zu End'!

**ZWEITER CHOR:** Wenn de Abendröthe Kömmt, den Himmel zu erhellen —

**ERSTER UND ZWEITER CHOR:** Weil der Sonne gold'ner Schild im dunklen Wald versinkt, Dann ertönt die Hirtenflöte und die Heerden Schellen, Ach, Freut Euch! Nach langer Pein kommt endlich Lust und Wonne! Tra la la la!

---

### ZWEITE SCENE

*DIE VORIGEN — UROK.*
*(Urok springt plötzlich auf die Bühne; ein zerlumpter, buckliger Wicht mit grossem, struppigem Kopf, und absichtlich angenommenem, blödem Gesichtsausdruck.)*

**UROK:** Ha, ha, ha, ha, ha!
*(Die Mädchen stieben erschrocken auseinander.)*

**ERSTER CHOR:** Ach, Urok!

**ZWEITER CHOR:** Uhu!

**ERSTER UND ZWEITER CHOR:** Drachenei!

**UROK:** Hi, hi! Ist mir einerlei!

**ERSTER CHOR:** Urok!

**ZWEITER CHOR:** Natter!

**ERSTER UND ZWEITER CHOR:** Teufelsbrei!

**UROK:** Hi, hi! Mir ist's einerlei!

**ERSTER UND ZWEITER CHOR:** Unhold!— Natter!

**EIN MÄDCHEN:** Waldswerg!

**ERSTER UND ZWEITER CHOR:** Kröte, Giftpilz!— Waldzwerg! Uhu!— Uhu!— Uhu.

**HEDWIG:** Was suchst Du da?

---

**FIRST AND SECOND CHORUS:** Tra, la, la, la!

**HEDWIG:** Oh Daughter Once you did lie upon my breast! What fate condign Let a pagan invest your heart?

**SECOND CHORUS:** With blossoms bright Now is the meadows bedlight!

**FIRST CHORUS:** Tra la la!

**HEDWIG:** Oh Daughter, If you where here, You'd bring Joy and cheer!

**FIRST CHORUS:** Scarcely begun, Soon will our labor be done!

**SECOND CHORUS:** Ribbons ho! Bring more ribbons of red! Scarcely begun, Soon will our labor be done!

**SECOND CHORUS:** When the setting sun, red-glowing, Fills the sky with blushes —

**FIRST AND SECOND CHORUS:** And his golden disk, still growing, Sinks behind the trees, — Cattle's lowing, Shepherds' piping, gushes over the landscape. Now list! the sound of vesper bells Comes floating on the breeze! Soon the harvesters will All seek their ease. Tra, la, la, la . . . . !

---

### SCENE II

*HEDWIG. MAIDENS. UROK.*
*(UROK rushes in on the scene; a ragged hunchback, with an abnormally large and frowsy head, and an assumed expression of idiocy.)*

**UROK:** Ha! ha! ha! ha! ha!

**FIRST CHORUS:** Ah, Urok!

**SECOND CHORUS:** Screech owl!

**BOTH CHORUSES:** Dragonspawn!

**UROK:** He! he! All is one to me!

**FIRST CHORUS:** Urok!

**SECOND CHORUS:** Viper!

**BOTH CHORUSES:** Devil's own!

**UROK:** He! he! All is one to me!

**BOTH CHORUSES:** Demon! Viper! Paddock! Screechhowl! Screechhowl!

**HEDWIG:** What do you seek here?

---

**UROK:** Ha, ha, ha, ha, ha! Alles singt und lacht!

**ERSTER UND ZWEITER CHOR:** Weil's uns Freude macht!

**UROK:** Selbst das Mütterlein Möchte lustig sein!

**ERSTER UND ZWEITER CHOR:** Darf heut' lustig sein!

**UROK:** Und Ulna dort Trauert und verdorrt!

**ZWEITER CHOR:** Ha, ha! Seht! Ulana's Bote!

**ERSTER CHOR:** Ha, ha, ha! Ulana's Bote!

**HEDWIG:** Für mich ist sie eine Todte!

**UROK:** Eine Todte—eine Todte . . . ! Eine Todte sah ich ziehn, Die fand keine Ruh'; Ich fragt' die arme Seel': Was jammersst du? Ach! stöhnt die Arme, Ach, dass sich Gott erbarme! Allzu lang' schon währt Der Verdammung Pein; Zu meiner Mutter Herd' Führt mich hinein!

**ZWEITER CHOR:** Ha, ha, ha!

**EIN MÄDCHEN:** Die arme Seel'!

**ERSTER UND ZWEITER CHOR:** Welch' Litanei!

**ERSTER UND ZWEITER CHOR:** Ha, ha, wie heisst, Sag's doch, der Geist? Wie heisst der Geist?

**UROK:** Ulana, Deine Todte Aechzt solch' Litanei! Doch mir, meiner Treu, Mir ist's einerlie!

**ERSTER UND ZWEITER CHOR:** Ha, ha, ha! Ulana heisst Der arme Geist! Ulana! Ha, ha, ha!

**HEDWIG:** Und wenn es mir auch das Herz zerreisst, Ich weiss meine Pflicht: So lang' sie die Frau des Zigeuners heisst, Kenn' ich sie nicht!

**UROK:** Mutter! Gieb nach!

**HEDWIG:** Nein, nie!
*(Ab in die Hütte.)*

---

### DRITTE SCENE

*DIE VORIGEN OHNE HEDWIG.*

**ERSTER UND ZWEITER CHOR:** Ha, ha, ha, ha!

**EIN MÄDCHEN:** Der kommt schön an! Das ist der Zigeunerin ihr Galan! Lässt Manru sie sitzen, so kommt er dran!

---

**UROK:** Ha! ha! Hear them laugh and sing!

**BOTH CHORUSES:** Now we have our fling!

**UROK:** Even our worthy Dame Must exclaim with joy!

**BOTH CHORUSES:** And with little blame!

**UROK:** While your child so far away. Keeps you from joy!

**SECOND CHORUS:** Ha! ha! Behold! Ulana's pleader.

**HEDWIG:** She's dead — idle interceder!

**UROK:** Interceder — for a spectre? Yet a ghost passed me while I was Vainly seeking rest. I asked the question. "What do you want? "Ah!" sighed the ghost, "Hear what I request: Long too long I'm kept From my hearth and home — Oper a haven to me, And I'd roam No more!"

**SECOND CHORUS:** Ha! ha! ha!

**A MAIDEN:** A solemn shade!

**BOTH CHORUSES:** A mournful Dame! Ha! ha! her name! Who was the jade? Out with her name!

**UROK:** Your daughter, dead to you, Breathed such doleful plaints! And yet by all the saints, 'Tis all one to me!

**BOTH CHORUS:** Ha! ha! ha! Ulana was the grievous ghost! Ulana! Ha! ha! ha!

**HEDWIG:** And though my heart is consumed with grief, I know my duty The while she remains in the home of the thief, May the pain and woe be Hers.

**UROK:** Mother, relent!

**HEDWIG:** Never! no! no!
*(HEDWIG enters the hut.)*

---

### SCENE III

*UROK. THE MAIDENS.*

**BOTH CHORUSES:** Ha! ha! ha! ha!

**A MAIDEN:** A pretty mess! He is the Romany bride's new beau! When Manru grows weary, Their love he'll bless!

ERSTER CHOR: Ihr Galan!

ZWEITER CHOR: Hahahaha!

UROK: Mit eurem Gethu!
Seid den Staub nicht werth Von Ulana's Schuh!

EIN MÄDCHEN: Weil sich die Burschen um sie nicht scheeren, Lässt sie sich von dem Waldzwerg verehren!

UROK: Wer Euch nicht passt, Verliert nicht viel, Doch Ulana lasst Mir aus dem Spiel!
Am Ende . . . es ist nichts dabei, Denn mir ist Alles einerlei!

EIN MACHEN: Alles einerlei!

UROK Welch' Aefferei!

ERSTER UND ZWEITER CHOR: Du bist der Galan!

ERSTER CHOR: Und bald kommst Du dran!

UROK: Du Papagei!

ZWEITER CHOR: Freu' Dich, Du Unhold!

ERSTÉR UND ZWEITER CHOR: Freu' Dich, Du Unhold!
Lang' wird's nicht dauern!

UROK: Dummes Geschrei!

ERSTER UND ZWEITER CHOR: Denn ein Zigeuner kann nicht verbauern!

ERSTER CHOR: Wie Schön!

ZWEITER CHOR: Uhu!

ERSTER CHOR: Wie fein!

ZWEITER CHOR: Uhu!

ERSTER CHOR: Wie lieb!

ZWEITER CHOR: Ach, wie fein!

ERSTER CHOR: Ach!

ERSTER UND ZWEITER CHOR: Wie fein!-Wie lieb!
Ein Herzensdieb Der Uhu!
Ist fort der Mann, Sogleich kommt dran Der Uhu!

UROK: Stets dieselbe Rederei!

ERSTER UND ZWEITER CHOR: Ach, zum Altar Mit dir, Fürwahr, Wie flög'sie!
Berückt, ach!

UROK: Dummer Singsang!-Blöd' Geschrei!
Rück mir nicht so auf den Leib!
Weg von mir, du ekles Weib!

ERSTER UND ZWEITER CHOR: Beglückt, ach!
(*ULANA erscheint in der Ferne.*)

EIN MÄDCHEN: Seht, da naht sie selbst, die Arme!

ERSTER CHOR: Wahrlich, eine Todte schier!

ZWEITER CHOR: Seht!-Seht!
In ihrem Harme Was sucht sie beim Feste hier?

---

FIRST CHORUS: Her beau!

SECOND CHORUS: Ha! ha! ha! ha!

UROK: Unworthy are you To loose the latchets Of Ulana's shoe!

A MAIDEN: Since our good fellows cast off the beauty, Happy is she in the forest-imp's duty.

UROK: Your favor lost, none will deplore, But do not mention Ulana any more! Yet why should I be angry? For is it not all the same to me?

A MAIDEN: "All the same to me!"

UROK: A poor cukoo!

BOTH CHORUSES: Her gallant new beau —

FIRST CHORUS: Shall soon have a show!

UROK: A parrot too!

SECOND CHORUS: Rejoice, sweet Paddock —

BOTH CHORUSES: Rejoice, sweet Paddock, Haste to your loving,

UROK: Trumpery trash!

BOTH CHORUSES: A gypsy never give up roving.

FIRST CHORUS: A bad!

SECOND CHORUS: Screech owl!

FIRST CHORUS: A mad!

SECOND CHORUS: Screech owl!

FIRST CHORUS: A bad!

SECOND CHORUS: Ah how mad —

FIRST CHORUS: Ah!

BOTH CHORUSES: A bad, a mad, A gallant lad — The screech owl!
When Manru grows weary He will their love bless!
The screech owl!

UROK: Rubbish!-Nonsense!-Puerile trash!

BOTH CHORUSES: Give up the search; Ah, hasten with me to church.
Caress me!

UROK: Silly sing-song, senseless chaff!
Out of my way!
Leave my sight!
Be off you hideous fright!

BOTH CHORUSES: Come, take me!
(*ULANA appears in the distance.*)

A MAIDEN: See it is she herself approaching!

FIRST CHORUS: Ghastly pale! she seems a ghost!

SECOND CHORUS: See!-See! On mirth encroaching: She is lost amid pleasure.

---

## VIERTE SCENE

*DIE VORIGEN — ULANA.*

ZWEITER CHOR: Frau Zigeunerin!

ULANA: Was höhnet Ihr Mich arme, unselige Frau?

UROK: 's ist Deine Schuld!

ULANA: Ach, weint mit mir Bitt're Thränen, Denn mein Schicksal ist zu rauh!

UROK: Trag's mit Geduld!

EIN MÄDCHEN: Wahrlich, glücklich bist Du nicht!

ERSTER CHOR: Ja, glücklich ist sie nicht!

EIN MÄDCHEN: Das frische Gesicht —

ERSTER CHOR: Ja, glücklich ist sie nicht!

EIN MÄDCHEN: Die ros'gen Wangen — Vergangen!

ERSTER CHOR: (*mitleidig*). Die ros'gen Wangen — Vergangen!

ZWEITER CHOR: (*spottend*). Vergangen!

UROK: Vergangen!

ULANA: Ihr Bösen, sagt, Hab'ich jemals Euch Leid's gethan?

ZWEITER CHOR: (*spottend*). Ha, ha, ha, ha!
Tralalala! - La

UROK: (*den ULANA hilfesuchend anblickt.*)

UROK: Mich geht's nichts an!

ULANA: Vergeblich klagt Die Verstossene, Und der arme, ach, der gemiedene Mann!

ZWEITER CHOR: (*spottend*). Tralalala!
Der arme Mann!
Der gemiedene Mann!

UROK: Der Herzensmann!

ZWEITER CHOR: Der arme Mann! —Ha, ha, ha, ha!

UROK: Ja, der süsse Mann!

ULANA: Und böhnt Ihr noch so sehr, Ich lieb'ihn immer mehr!

ERSTER CHOR: Wenn er nur lohnt die Liebe!

ZWEITER CHOR: Ach nein!

EIN MÄDCHEN: Wenn er nur treu Dir bliebe!

ZWEITER CHOR: Ach nein!

ULANA: Wer liebt, der kann nicht treulos sein!

ZWEITER CHOR: Ach nein!
Lang' wird's nicht dauern —

ERSTER CHOR: Denn ein Zigeuner kann nicht verbauern!

---

## SCENE IV

*AS BEFORE. ULANA.*

SECOND CHORUS: Gay Gitana!

ULANA: Why torture me, a heart-broken, poor outcast?

UROK: The fault was yours.

ULANA: I fear your hate!
Ah! hapless my fate!
My tears are falling fast.

UROK: Do not repine.

A MAIDEN: Hapless woman, wretched one!

FIRST CHORUS: Aye, hapless is her fate!

A MAIDEN: How sad her decline!

FIRST CHORUS: Aye, hapless is her fate!

A MAIDEN: The roses cherished, Have perished.

FIRST CHORUS: (*compassionately*). The roses cherished, Have perished!

SECOND CHORUS: (*mockingly*). Have perished!

UROK: Have perished!

ULANA: Oh wicked ones!
What evil have I done to you?

SECOND CHORUS: (*mockingly*). HA!ha!ha!ha!
Tra, la, la, la!
La, la, la, la!

UROK: (*to whom Ulana had cast a look for help*).

UROK: To me all's one!

ULANA: In vain the plaints of one desolate; Vain all her pleas for her vilified mate!

SECON CHORUS: (*mockingly*). Tra la, la, la!
The unhappy man! Thrice unhappy man!

UROK: The precious man!

SECOND CHORUS: The unhappy man!
HA, ha, ha, ha!

UROK: Yes, the precious man!

ULANA: You prove my constancy —
Your jeers awake my love a new.

FIRST CHORUS: Your love shall be requited.

SECOND CHORUS: Ah, no!

A MAIDEN: Never your heart be blighted!

SECOND CHORUS: Ah, no!

ULANA: A true love could not treat me so.

SECOND CHORUS: Ah, no!
It will soon be over.

FIRST CHORUS: Never a gypsy, but always a rover.

**ZWEITER CHOR:** (*umringt spottend ULANA*). Ist der Mond am Himmel voll Dann wird der Zigeuner toll!

**ERSTER CHOR:** Ha, ha, ha, ha!

**UROK:** Zu bunt wird die Geschicht'!

**ULANA:** (*beschützend*). Nein, nein, das duld' ich nicht!

**ZWEITER CHOR:** Schau, Schau!

**UROK:** Nein, nein, das duld' ich nicht!

**ZWEITER CHOR:** Ist der Mond am Himmel voll, Dann wird der Zigeuner toll. Lässt die Frau und lässt das Kind Und entläuft geschwind, geschwind!

**ULANA:** Haltet ein! Haltet ein! Ach, singet nicht, Ach, singet nicht, Was Herzen bricht!

**UROK:** Macht Ihr mir den Schädel heiss, Sag' ich Jeder, was ich weiss!

**ZWEITER CHOR:** Schau, schau, fürwahr, Ein Liebespaar!

**UROK:** Sag', was nächtlich winkt und grüsst, Was da flüstert, kost und küsst!

**ZWEITER CHOR:** Ach, seht den Schmerz! Welch' Ritterherz! Kennt keinen Scherz!

**ERSTER CHOR:** Lasst sein! Lasst sein!

**ZWEITER CHOR:** Wie leib, wie fein!

**ERSTER CHOR:** Lasst sien! Lasst sein! Genug der Pein!
(*Die MÄDCHEN entfernen sich, indem der*) (*ERSTE CHOR den ZWEITEN fortdrängt.*)
Tralalala . . .

**ZWEITER CHOR:** (*im Abgeben*). Ist der Mond am Himmel voll, Dan wird der Zigeuner toll! Hei, juchhei!
(*Die MÄDCHEN zerstreuen sich im Hintergrunde; manche knüpfen noch Guirlanden an die Stangen oder Hütten an.*)

## FUNFTE SCENE

*ULANA. UROK. (Im Hintergrunde der CHOR, sich allmälig verlierend.)*

**ULANA:** Weh mir, ach weh! Denn meine Qual Ist ihnen Spott!

**ERSTER CHOR:** Tralalala!

**ULANA:** Wohin ich geh', Folgt mir überall Der Hohn der Welt Wie eine Strafe von Gott!

**SECOND CHORUS:** (*forming a ring around ULANA, mockingly*). When the full moon floods the night Errant grows the gypsy wight.

**FIRST CHORUS:** Ha, ha, ha, ha!

**UROK:** (*protecting ULANA*). Their malice, manifest, is too cruel for jest.

**SECOND CHORUS:** Behold!

**UROK:** It is too cruel for jest.

**SECOND CHORUS:** When the full moon floods the night, Errant grows the gypsy wight. Burns his soul with longings wild, The forsakes he wife and child.

**ULANA:** Cease your song! Cease your song! Ah why should you prolong my grief?

**UROK:** Do not drive the game too far, Lest you unbar my malice.

**SECOND CHORUS:** Give heed! Beware! A loving pair!

**UROK:** Secrets many I might tell, — Meetings, kissing in the dell —

**SECOND CHORUS:** How sad the plight! What courteous knight Is not contrite?

**FIRST CHORUS:** Refrain! Refrain!

**SECOND CHORUS:** How sweetly kind!

**FIRST CHORUS:** Refrain! Refrain! Enough of pain.
(*The maidens leave the stage, the first chorus forced off by the second.*)
Tra, la, la, la!

**SECOND CHORUS:** (*while going*). When the full moon floods the night, Errant grows the gypsy wight! HA, hurrah! (*The maidens disperse in the background; some continue to fasten garlands to the poles and huts.*)

## SCENE V

*ULANA. UROK. (The chorus in the background gradually dispersing.)*

**ULANA:** Ah me! Alas! My dire sufferings turn to scorn!

**FIRST CHORUS:** Tra, la, la, la!

**ULANA:** Each fond desire Is a pricking thorn; All mankind jeers, Ah me! how God's vengeance sears!

**UROK:** Schau mich nur an! Bin auch nicht besser d'ran! Du hast's gewollt! Es ist Dein Lohn; Die Wahrheit sprachen sie, nicht Hohn!

**ULANA:** Zur Mutter wollt' ich still mich schleichen, Durch all' mein Leid ihr Herz erweichen; Vor uns'rer Hütte, ach, Trifft mich die Schmach!

**UROK:** Der Mutter Herz willst Du erweichen? Ha, ha! Eh' werden Deine Haare bleichen! Vor einer Weile sprach ich sie da.

**ULANA:** Und zürnt sie auch in ihrem Schmerz, Ich glaub' an's Mutterherz!

**UROK:** Ja, glaub' nur, glaub'!

**ULANA:** Voll Hoffnung klopf' ich an die Thür, Denn mir sagt Gott, dass ich sie rühr'!

**UROK:** Ja, klopf' nur, klopf'! (*ULANA klopft an die Thür HEDWIG'S.*)

## SECHSTE SCENE

*Die VORIGAN. An der Schwelle der Hütte erscheint HEDWIG. (Beim Anblick ULANA'S macht sie eine abwehrende Bewegung.)*

**ULANA:** Mutter! Meine Mutter! Siehst Du nicht Dein Kind?

**HEDWIG:** Ich hab' zu viel geweint — mein Aug' ist blind!

**ULANA:** Reich ware die Saat — ich kam zum frohen Fest, Um dir zu sagen —

**HEDWIG:** (*freudig*). Dass Du ihn verläss't?

**ULANA:** Dass Deine Kinder hungrig sind . . .

**HEDWIG:** Zigeuner leben von Luft und Wind!

**ULANA:** Mutter! So giebt es nichts, sag', das Dich rührt?

**UROK:** Rühr' lieber den, der Dich verführt!

**ULANA:** Einsam leb' ich und verlassen Mit dem Mann, den Alle hassen; Fern von dieser theuren Hütte, Fern von meiner Kindheit Sitte! Täglich schlaf' ich, Qual im Innern, Unter Thränen ein —

**UROK:** Wie süss muss Liebe sein!

**ULANA:** Täglich weekt des Kindes Wimmern Mich zu neuer Pein!

**UROK:** Du hast ja Dein Zigeunerlein!

**UROK:** But gaze on me! I suffer sorely with you! It was your wish—this your return, And truthful are those words that burn.

**ULANA:** A mother's heart would soon enfold me, If only her loving eyes could behold me! Before her gentle face I meet disgrace.

**UROK:** Your hope is in vain! She'll not receive you, Ha, ha! She will nevermore forgive you! Such were her words a moment since.

**ULANA:** Even though I must feel her rage, I may engage a mother's love.

**UROK:** Engage! Engage!

**ULANA:** With hopeful heart I'll near the door; A gracious God may restore love.

**UROK:** Go, stubborn one! in vain implore! (*ULANA knocks at the door of HEDWIG's hut.*)

## SCENE VI

*ULANA, UROK, HEDWIG. (The last appears at the door of her hut; seeing ULANA she makes a repelling gesture.)*

**ULANA:** Mother! Darling mother! Do you not See your child?

**HEDWIG:** Through grief my eyes are blind To her exiled!

**ULANA:** Rich were the fields— The joyous harvest-home Have lured me here.

**HEDWIG:** Have you come alone?

**ULANA:** Yes, faint with hunger, sick with care.

**HEDWIG:** Gypsies and vagabonds live on air!

**ULANA:** Mother! What word can move you? Great is my offense!

**UROK:** Turn to him Who stole you away!

**ULANA:** Lonely, sad, I sit in sorrow, I borrow nothing but grief and pain, Manru hunted by vile slander, I must wander from childhood's home; Nights are filled with bitter weeping, Nothing can bring me rest.

**UROK:** (A Gypsy's love is best!)

**ULANA:** Morning finds me keeping vigil By my babe's poor nest.

**UROK:** A Gypsy babe upon your breast!

**ULANA:** Mutter, ach, vergieb den Deinen, Lass Dein Kind nicht geh'n, Menschen bettelnd anzuweinen, Gott und den Tod zu fleh'n!

**UROK:** Glaub's nicht, Mütterlein!

**ULANA:** Sieh, Mutter, wie ich elend bin!

**HEDWIG:** (*nach innerm Kampfe, gerührt, zu ULANA*). Seh' ich Dich So in Elend und bitt'rer Pein, Fasst Mitleid mich, Es soll Alles vergessen sein. Töchterlein, Sei wieder mein! Lass den Zigeuner zieh'n!

**UROK:** Lass ihn zieh'n!

**ULANA:** Ich sollt' ihn verlassen, den theuren Mann?

**UROK:** Lass ihn zieh'n!

**ULANA:** Ich sollte flieh'n meines Kindes Vater? Zeigt mir die Frau, die dass kann!

**HEDWIG:** Bringe mir Auch Dein Kind — das Zigeunerkind!

**UROK:** Thu's für das Kind!

**ULANA:** Dank weiss ich Dir. Nur wenn wir mit Manru zusammen sind!

**HEDWIG:** Welch' starrer Sinn! Blick um Dich! Sieh Dein Vaterhaus! Deine Wiege steht d'rin. Zur Firmung gingest Du hier heraus! Sieh dor im Grün Die Rosen blüh'n, Die Du einst selbst gepflanzt!

**UROK:** Sieh den Platz, Wo Du so oft getanzt!

**HEDWIG:** Bleib bei mir, mein Herz, mein Kind!

**ULANA:** Nur wenn wir mit Manru zusammen sind!

**HEDWIG:** Ein Heide, ein Landstricher hier im Haus? Eh' tragt Ihr mich auf den Friedhof hinaus!

**ULANA:** Mutter, er liebt mich! Vergieb! Vergieb!

**HEDWIG:** Verblendete! Kurz währt Manru's Lieb'! Schon sah ich Zigeuner am Berge zieh'n — Manru wird flieh'n!

**ULANA:** Ist's wahr? Sie wollen ihn zwingen?

**UROK:** Ha, ha! Wenn sie nur vorübergingen, Fürwahr! Er liefe mit!

**HEDWIG:** Solang' es Zeit ist, kehr' zurück!

**UROK:** Folg' ihrem Ruf, es ist Dein Glück!

**ULANA:** Mother! Ah, forgive your children, Do not turn them away! Save them from the curse of begging, — God for death to pray!

**UROK:** Dame, believe her not!

**ULANA:** See, mother, see my misery.

**HEDWIG:** Sad the sight; Unhappy one, in bitter plight. I pity you— All your sins shall be forgiven Cease to pine— You are my daughter— Leave your gypsy mate.

**UROK:** Leave your mate!

**ULANA:** Abandon him, my lover, so gentle, mild?

**UROK:** Let him go!

**ULANA:** Take leave of him, the father of my child? There never was such wife— Nevermore!

**HEDWIG:** Bring to me, too, the child! The gypsy child.

**UROK:** Do it for the child.

**ULANA:** You shall earn thanks only. So long as Manru and I are one.

**HEDWIG:** O willful child! Glance around— this Is your childhood home. Here your cradle was found; To first communion you went from here; Here, in the close, There blooms your rose, Brightening all with its cheer.

**UROK:** See the green Where you were seen so often!

**HEDWIG:** Stay with me, my love, my own.

**ULANA:** No! Unless my Manru and I are one.

**HEDWIG:** A Pagan, a vagabond here at home! I would sooner be borne to the graveyard.

**ULANA:** Mother! He loves me! Forgive! Forgive!

**HEDWIG:** You'll find such love seldom lives The Gypsies are stirring, full soon they'll rove; Manru will flee.

**ULANA:** Is it true? And will they compel him?

**UROK:** In fleeing none will excel him— A chance is all he needs.

**HEDWIG:** The way is open. Come, return.

**UROK:** Be not deceived by fleeting joy.

**ULANA:** Vergebens! Er ist der Herr meines Lebens!

**HEDWIG:** So geh' von meiner Schwell, geh'!

**ULANA:** Mutter!

**UROK:** Ja, fleh' nur, fleh'!

**HEDWIG:** Für immer — höre wohl mein Wort — Sind wir geschieden!

**ULANA:** Mutter!

**HEDWIG:** (*an der Schwelle*). Geh! (*Ab in die Hütte.*)

**ULANA:** (*sich ihr auf den Knieen nachschleppend*). Mutter! — Mutter! — Mutter!

## SIEBENTE SCENE

*ULANA. UROK. (Gegen das Ende, MÄDCHENCHOR hinter der Bühne.)*

**ULANA:** (*sinkt vernichtet zusammen*). Ach! . . . Fort! . . . Fort! . . .

**UROK:** Auf mein Wort, Du hast es recht weit gebracht!

**ULANA:** Weh mir! Wohin ich blick', ist Nacht!

**UROK:** (*nähert sich, versucht sie aufzurichten*). Nur sacht! Nur sacht! Ich hab's Dir prophezeit: Nicht hier winkt Rettung Deinem Leid. Doch ist der wahre Freund nicht weit . . . Noch hast Du Alles nicht verloren!

**ULANA:** Weh mir! Mir flucht, die mich geboren! Ich darf der Hütte nicht mehr nah'n, Den Bäumen, die mich wachsen sah'n! . . . Und jene Hoffnung, die ich still gehegt —

**UROK:** Sie log! wie's zu geschehen pflegt! Doch sprich! Bist du denn ärmer wie zuvor? Hast ja den Fürst der dich erkor — Und mich!

**ULANA:** Manru! Ja! Manru ist mir geblieben, Hab alles geopfert für sein lieben! Ach! bliebe mir nur Seine Seele für ewig treu, Hielt er den Schwur, Gäb' ich freudig Heimath und Jugend Und kennte keine Reu'. Doch er, einst so gut mit mir, Er irrt nun für und für, Im Wald, am Weg.

## SCENE VII

*ULANA. UROK. (Toward the close CHORUS OF MAIDENS behind the scenes.)*

**ULANA:** Ah, go away!

**UROK:** Come, confess! You've cooked up a pretty mess.

**ULANA:** Woe's me—The way is pitiless!

**UROK:** (*approaches ULANA and attempts to raise her.*) Repress your grief I foretold the outcome: But there is still more to unfold! See! would you behold a true friend? You may still see in me none other!

**ULANA:** Woe's me! My mother's malediction! My childhood home I'll see no more Wander free within its garden; All hopes are faded; none remains, not one!

**UROK:** Hope lied again, as she so often has done. But speak! Are you more wretched than before? The prince is yours, what more do you want? And I!

**ULANA:** Manru! Yes, Manru still is my treasure! For him I gave my love's full measure! Ah! If I knew That he were constant, that he were true! If I could know, faithful ever he to his vow — Then no more would I feel rue! But he, once the soul of love, Now roves Through woods and meadows!

**ULANA:** In vain do you now employ your arts—

**HEDWIG:** Away, then, from my threshold! Go!

**ULANA:** Mother!

**HEDWIG:** Go!

**UROK:** Now plead your woe!

**HEDWIG:** Forever—mark before you go, you're banished from here!

**ULANA:** Mother!

**HEDWIG:** (*on the threshold*). Go! (*Exit into the hut.*)

**ULANA:** (*dragging herself on her knees after Hedwig*). Mother! Mother! Mother!

UROK: Nicht doch!
Er liebt dich ja, dein Mann, Und läuft er wie ein toller Hahn Zur Zeit auf allen Wegen, Und guckt sich blind, Wo die schwarzen Schönen sind.
Wen kann das erregen?
Ha, ha!
Das nenn ich Muth!
Sie glaubte dem Zigeunerblut!

ULANA: Zigeunerblut—

UROK: Zur Bande zieht es ihn zurück'!

ULANA: Wie rette ich mein Glück?

UROK: Ohn' Treu, ohn' Lieb' Gehorcht er blindlings seinem Trieb.

ULANA: Mein Gott!
Mein Gott!

UROK: Der Tagedieb, er stiehlt dein junges Leben.
Frau und Kind sind ihm nur Ketten.

ULANA: Nur Eines kann mich retten.

UROK: (der die letzten Worte ULANA's auf sich bezieht). Ulana!

ULANA: Ja, Nur Eine wird mich retten!

UROK: Ulana, hör'!
Wenn Manru Dein vergisst, Dann-siehst Du, wo die wahre Freundschaft ist!
Und wird Dir auch Dein Fürst dann fehlen—
Dir bleibt ein Knecht—mir hast Du zu befehlen!
Bis zum letzten Hauch wär' ich Dir treu—

ULANA: Ach, Urok!
Wärest Du mir treu!

UROK: (auf's neue Hoffnung schöpfend). Was willst Du?
Sag' es ohne Scheu!
Auf mich, ich schwör' es, kannst Du zählen!

ULANA: Du thätest's?

UROK: Alles! Du kannst wählen!

ULANA: Ich denk' an Manru.

UROK: Nun, was soll ich thun?
Soll ich ihn verjagen?
Soll ich ihm sagen, Du hätt'st genug der Plagen, Sie hätt' geschlagen, Des Zigeuners Uhr?

ULANA: Ach nein!
Was sprichst Du nur?
Es fiel mir ein, Um neu sein Herz zu finden, Um fester ihn an mich zu bidnen—

UROK: (enttäuscht, wüthend).
Um fester ihn zu binden —?

UROK: And yet in him you feel se-cure, Although he roves over field and groves, Over forest, mountain, meadow, — Fain to descry where the dark-skinned beauties lure.
Who should borrow trouble?
Upon my word, She trusted in her Gypsy lord!

ULANA: (listening, pondering).
Her Gypsy lord?

UROK: He will find his old companions!

ULANA: (heedless of UROK'S words; lost in her own thought).
Woe! gone is peace of mind!

UROK: His love has grown cool, Blind impulse is his only rule!
The Gypsy thief is stealing —
Your youth and charms
Wife and child arouse no feeling!

ULANA: Wait!
My brain is reeling!
In one thing only lies healing!

UROK: Ulana! Hear!
Should Manru prove faithless, In me you find a truer love.
In place of one, a prine unheeding, You'll have a slave, Who will do your bidding
My latest breath I'll give to you
And yet — all, all is one to me!

ULANA: Ah!
Urok! would you prove faithful —

UROK: Command me!
Charge me!
Prove my love!
No slave, I swear, shall be more willing.

ULANA: What would you do?

UROK: Stop not even at killing!

ULANA: I think of Manru — !

UROK: Well?
What's your hope?
Shall I not tell him That you've so far excelled him you now repell him —
You are his bride?

ULANA: Ah no!
That would not do!
It was my plan Again to awaken his love, Renew the vows which he has taken.

UROK: (disappointed, angry). To this, then, shall I help you?

ULANA: — Ein Mittel gäb' es wohl dazu, Doch dieses Mittel kennst — nur Du, Nur Du!

UROK: Ich selber soll da helfen, ich?
Dir Jenen wieder zu gewinnen?
Sprich.
Bist Du von Sinnen?
Ich?

ULANA: Ja, Du!
Du streifst im Wald herum, Kennst jedes Kraut—

UROK: Hi, hi!
Kenn' jedes Kraut!

ULANA: Du weisst, was klug macht und was dumm, Und wie man's braut . . .

UROK: Ha, ha!
Und wie man's braut!

ULANA: Du kennst den Trank auch, den man giebt, Wird man nicht mehr geliebt!

UROK: Ich kenn' den Trank? . . .

ULANA: Gieb mir den Trank!

UROK: Gäb's einen Trank, der Lieb' gewinnt, Dann hätt' ich selber längst schon Frau und Kind!

ULANA: Gieb mir den Trank!

UROK: Ich wüsste wohl, wem ich das Tränklein gäbe, So war ich lebe!

ULANA: Gieb mir den Trank!

UROK: Nein!
Mich lass' aus dem Spiel!

ULANA: Ach, Urok!
Hast Du kein Gefühl?

UROK: Ich macht' ihn lieber lahm und krank!

ULANA: Gieb mir den Trank!

UROK: Nein, nein!
Ich geb' ihn nicht!

ULANA: Nein, nein, Du musst den Trank mir geben, Denn Alles ruht, mein Heil, mein Leben, In ihm, der mir mein Herze nahm!
Du musst ihn geben!

UROK: Ich geb' ihn nicht!

ULANA: 's ist Deine Pflicht —

UROK: (blickt sie erstaunt an).
Hm?

ULANA: (nicht ohne Koketterie).
— hast Du mich lieb!

UROK: Was?

ULANA: (blickt ihm in's Auge).
Hast Du mich lieb?

UROK: Ulana!
So darfst Du nicht in's Aug' mir seh'n, Sonst ist's um mich gescheh'n!

ULANA: Verlass mich nicht in meiner Angst!

ULANA: I must on you depend, For all you are my good, my only friend.

UROK: I shall help regain him? restrain him from leaving you in peace?
You're mad! Mad! your wits are wandering!
I!
I?

ULANA: Yes, you!
You roam the wood,
And know every herb well!
You know what's baleful, harmless, good, — Can brew a spell!

UROK: Ha, ha! Can brew a spell!

ULANA: Can drew the potion, that will prove A cure for dying love!

UROK: A cure for love?

ULANA: Fetch me that drink.

UROK: Were there a drink That in-spired love, —

ULANA: Fetch me that drink!

UROK: By wife and child I'd long been admired!
I know full well Her for whom I'd play brewer, Nor long pursue her!

ULANA: Fetch me the drink!

UROK: No, no! it is not for you.

ULANA: Ah, Urok!
Can you be cruel?

UROK: I'd give him work direful of harm—

ULANA: Fetch me the charm.

UROK: No,
I'll fetch it not!

ULANA: Yes, yes!
You must provide me the charm.
Give protection lest woe betide me.
I'm his, to whom my heart belongs!
You can not chide me.

UROK: I'll fetch it not .

ULANA: Is all then forgot?

UROK: (astonished). H'm?

ULANA: (somewhat coquettishly). Have I your love?

UROK: What?

ULANA: Have I your love?

UROK: Ulana!
In pity turn your eyes away!
My wits will go astray!

ULANA: Oh, leave me not, see my terror!

UROK: Nein, zu viel ist's, was Du verlangst.
Bedenke!
Ich? . . .
Ich?

ULANA: Ach, thu's für mich, Mir ist so bang!

UROK: Mein Herz erbebt um ihre Noth, Ihr Schmerz mein Leid, ihr Glück mein Tod!

ULANA: Du giebst den Trank?

UROK: (*nach innerem Kampfe*). Es sei!

ULANA: Hab' Dank!
Hab' Dank!
Nun hab' ich Ruh'!

UROK: Meinst Du?
Hoffst Du für ewig ihn zu halten? Ich brau' den Trank,—doch bleibt's beim Alten; Lang' wird's nicht dauern, Denn ein Zigeuner—

MÄDCHENCHOR: (*hinter der Bühne*). Tralalala!

UROK: Kann nicht verbauern!

### ACHTE SCENE

*Die VORIGEN, MÄDCHENCHOR, hierauf CHOR DER BURSCHEN, BALLET, VOLK.*

**ERSTER MÄDCHENCHOR:** Ist der Mond am Himmel voll, Dann wird der Zigeuner toll!

UROK: Hörst Du?
Hörst Du?
Er wird toll!

MÄDCHENCHOR: Lässt die Frau und lässt das Kind Und läuft fort geschwind, geschwind!
Hei, juchhei!

CHOR DER BURSCHEN: (*hinter der Bühne*). Hei, juchhei!
(*Auf die Bühne kommen TÄNZER und TÄNZERINNEN gestürmt, zugleich erscheint der CHOR DER BURSCHEN; auf der Weise beginnt das Erntefest.*)

CHOR DER BURSCHEN: (*auf der Bühne*). Hei, juchhei!
Alle im Verein!
Lasst uns lustig sein!

CHOR DER MÄDCHEN: Hei, juchhei!
Lasst uns lustig sein, Alle im Verein!

BURSCHEN: Schliesset rasch den Kreis!—den Kreis!

MÄDCHEN: Rasch!
Den Kreis!

BURSCHEN: Stampft den Boden, heiss, heiss!

---

UROK: No, you ask too much of me.
Think a moment.

ULANA: I implore!
My heart is sore —

UROK: Were not my heart inclined to melt And you not enshrined in its fold —

ULANA: You'll fetch the drink?

UROK: (*after a struggle*). I will.

ULANA: Oh thanks!
Oh, thanks!
Now peace is mine.

UROK: What! yours?
Do you Hope forever to enchain him?
I'll brew the drink — you'll not regain him.
Haste to your loving!
Never yet gypsy —

CHORUS OF MAIDENS: (*behind the scenes*). Tra, la, la, la!

UROK: Gave up his roving.

### SCENE VIII

*THE SAME. CHORUS OF MAIDNES, AFTERWARD CHORUS OF YOUTHS, BALLET. PEOPLE.*

**FIRST CHORUS OF MAIDENS:** When the full moon floods the night, Errant grows the gypsy wight.

UROK: Do you hear aright?
Then mad grows each wight.

CHORUS OF MAIDENS: His soul burns with longings wild, Then foresakes he wife and child.
Ha!
Huzza!

CHORUS OF YOUTHS: (*Behind the scenes*). Ha!
Huzza!
(*Dancers, men and women, rush upon the stage simultaneously with the chorus of youths; the harvest festival begins upon the village green.*)

CHORUS OF YOUTHS: (*on the stage*). Ha!
Huzza!
Huzza!
Gaily now advance, Join the gladsome dance!

CHORUS OF MAIDENS: Ha!
Huzza!
Join the gladsome dance, Gaily now advances!

YOUTHS: Let us dance and sing—

MAIDENS: Dance and sing —

YOUTHS: Till we make the welkin ring!

---

MÄDCHEN: Juchhei!
Juchhei!
Juchhei!

BALLET: (*Der Tanz entwickelt sich in zwei gesonderten Gruppen, die Männer im Vordergrunde, die Mädchen im Hintergrunde.*)

BURSCHEN: Herbei, Ihr Schönen!
Hört Ihr's tönen?
Fliegt an unsere Brust!
Hoch in den Lüften Schwinget die Hüften!
Hop-ha!
Welche Lust!
Her zum Tanz, Jung und Alt!
Ruft im Kranz, Dass es schallt: Juchhei!
Ja, die ganze Welt soll erdröhnen, Hei!
Juchhei!
Bis zum Himmel soll ertönen Uns'res Tanzes Lust!
(*Nun tanzt nur ein Paar; die Tänzerin scheint vor dem Tänzer zu entfliehen, dieser setzt ihr nach. Die übrigen schauen mit lebhaften Bewegungen und den nun folgenden Ausrufen zu.*)

MÄDCHEN: Seht das Paar!
Schaut, seht's!
Die versteht's!
Ach, wie sie fliegt!
Sich schmiegt und wiegt!
Ach, so zu fliegen!
Sich so zu wiegen!

BURSCHEN: (*zum Tänzer*). Heda, Du!
Immer zu!
Brav, brav!
Gieb' nicht Ruh'!
Seht's, seht's!
Der versteht's!
Der versteht's
Rasch, rasch!
Greif', erhasch'!
Vorwärts!
Blind
Wie der Wind!

MÄDCHEN: (*da die Tänzerin wieder entflieht*). Ha, ha!

BURSCHEN: Nur zu!

MÄDCHEN: Ha, ha!

BURSCHEN: Schaut, schaut!
Fast erreicht, Wieder fleucht Die Windesbraut!
(*Schluss des Solotanzes. Tanz der Burschen.*)

GRUPPE ÄLTERER MÄNNER: Ist man frisch und jung, Macht man gern 'nen Sprung.
Lasst die Ziererei!
Mädchen, kommt herbei!

BURSCHEN: (*winken die Mädchen herbei*). Kommt herbei!
Herbei!
Herbei!
(*Die TÄNZERINNEN nahen, zugleich singt der CHOR der*)

---

MAIDENS: Huzza!
Huzza!
Huzza!

BALLET: (*The dance begins, the dancers divided into two groups — men in the foreground, maidens at the back.*)

CHORUS OF MEN: (*beckoning to the maidens*). Come here, you charmers!
Fair heart-warmers!
come to our arms.
While skirts are flying, Nothing denying, We feast on your charms!
Gaily whirl, Lad and lass, Pipes now skirl, Clangs the brass!
Ha!
Huzza!
Let the glad earth shake With our dancing, Till the skies above us glancing
in our joy partake.
(*Two dancers, male and female, come forward. The woman seems to seek to escape the man, who chases her. The others look on admiringly and comment on the dance.*)

MAIDENS: See the pair!
How fair!
Light as air!
See how she swings, As on light wings!
Would we were swinging, Thus freely winging!

YOUTHS: (*to the male dancer*).
Nimble blade, Catch the jade!
Bravo!
Keep her so!
You're not slow!
Like a flash Forward dash!
Haste!
Haste!
Clutch her waist!
Forward dash Like a flash!

MAIDENS: (*the female dancer having escaped*). Ha! ha!

YOUTHS: Bravo!

MAIDENS: Ha! Ha!

YOUTHS: O ho!
All but trapped, She proved apt, The lissome doe!
(*End of the solo dance. Dance of youths.*)

GROUP OF OLDER MEN: We are lusty and strong, Gladly join the throng!
Pretty maidens, fie!
Do not play so shy!

YOUTHS: (*Beckoning to the maidens.*) Maidens, fie!
Do not be shy!
(*The women dancers approach.*)

**MÄDCHEN:** Im Tanz sich finden Und entwinden, Das ist unsere Lust! Schon glaubt Ihr Blinden Uns zu binden, Zieht uns an die Brust — (*sich entwindend*). Das entrinnt, wie der Wind! Ei, ei, ei, wir sind frei! Hei, juchhei! Nimmer soll Euch das gelingen! Hei, juchhei! Nimmer sollt Ihr uns bezwingen, Nein, o nein!

**BURSCHEN:** (*nachsetzend*). Lauft, lauft! Fanget, greift! Ha, ha, ha! Wir sind nah! Hei, juchhei! Immer nach! (*sich endlich der Mädchen bemächtigend*). Und nun tanzen wir Dennoch im Verein. So muss es sein! Juchhei!

**BURSCHEN:** (*Zu ULANA*). Höre, Du! Komm' herzu! Tritt nur hier herein!

**ULANA:** (*will sich entwinden*). Lasst mich allein!

**BURSCHEN:** Hop, hop, hop! Sei nicht grob! Darfst Dich mit uns freu'n! Nur ein Tanz! Das kann keine reu'n. Hop, hop, hop! Rund herum!

**MÄDCHEN:** 's ist 'ne Frau von Stein, Die macht Ihr nicht heiss! Die wird nicht lustig sein. Lasst sie aus dem Kreis!

**UROK:** Wie dumm, wie dumm! O wärt Ihr Alle lahm und krumm! Zurück, zurück, verdammte Brut! Ein schwaches Weib — das nenn' ich Muth!

**ULANA:** (*will sich entwinden*). Höret mein Wort!

## NEUNTE SCENE

*Die VORIGEN. MANRU. (Am Waldesrand erscheint MANRU und blickt zornig auf die Tanzenden.)*

**MANRU:** Ulana!

**BURSCHEN:** Der Zigeuner! Der Zigeuner!

**MÄDCHEN:** Er hier?

**MANRU:** Lasst sie los!

**ULANA:** (*will zu MANRU*) Manru!

**MANRU:** Ihr Frechen, gebt sie frei! Lasst mich zu!

---

**MAIDENS:** To tread the mazes, Win your praises, This is all our joy. Would you embrace us, Deftly chase us, Employ your skill (*Escaping their pursuers.*) With a skip, Through we slip. Would you fain Try again? Ha! Huzza! Never shall the rapture be yours, Nevermore! Never we submit to capture, Nevermore!

**YOUTHS:** (*chasing*). Be spry! Be spry! We are near Ha, ha, ha! We are near! Ha, huzza! All be spry! (*Finally capturing the maidens.*) Now in couples free We'll reform the ring. This is the swing! Huzza! Huzza!

**YOUTHS:** (*to ULANA*). Do not be glum; Ulana come — Be one of our band!

**ULANA** (*seeking to escape*). Leave me in peace!

**YOUTHS:** Pretty prude, Be not rude, Mingle in the dance! One good fling, That's the thing that would enhance your mirth.

**MAIDENS:** An unfeeling jade, you never will warm her; An unfeeling jade, Will bring no merriment; Keep her from the ring!

**UROK:** Unkind! Unkind! O would you all were lame and blind! Fall back! Fall back! You craven pack! A woman she —

**ULANA:** Give me a word!

## SCENE IX

*THE SAME. MANRU. (MANRU appears at the edge of the forest and looks angrily at the dancers.)*

**MANRU:** Ulana!

**YOUTHS:** It is the gypsy! It is the gypsy!

**MAIDENS:** He here?

**MANRU:** Set her free!

**ULANA:** (*tries to go to MANRU*). Manru!

**MANRU:** Madmen! Set her free! Way for me!

---

**MÄDCHEN:** Ja, es muss enden! Tralalala!

**BURSCHEN:** (*zu Ulana*). Bleib! Ja, er muss fort aus unserm Ort!

**ANDERE BURSCHEN:** Hinweg, Zigan, Rühr' sie nicht an!

**ULANA:** Lasst los!

**UROK:** Ihr Tollen! Was wollen Die—

**BURSCHEN:** (*zu Ulana*). Nein! Bleib'! Genug der Schande! Wir jagen ihn fort zu seiner Bande!

**MÄDCHEN:** Genug der Schande!

**BURSCHEN:** Die Zigeunerhütte brennt nieder bald—

**MÄDCHEN:** Fort zu der Bande!

**BURSCHEN:** Auf! Auf! Brecht dürre Aeste im Wald!

**MÄDCHEN:** Die Zigeunerhütte brennt nieder bald!

**UROK:** Zurück!

**BURSCHEN UND MÄDCHEN:** Hin!

**UROK:** Zurück!

**BURSCHEN UND MÄDCHEN:** Hin, hin! Hin, hin!

**ULANA:** Erbarmen!

**UROK:** Zurück!

**MANRU:** Die Hütte nicht rühren, Wollt Ihr nicht meine Fäuste spüren!

**BURSCHEN:** Er wagt—er wagt es, uns zu droh'n? Uns zu droh'n? (*Stürzen sich auf MANRU.*) Zu Boden! Stirb, du Heidensohn! Ja, stirb!

**ULANA:** Manru!

## ZEHNTE SCENE

*DIE VORIGEN. HEDWIG (erscheint an der Schwelle ihrer hütte).*

**HEDWIG:** Halt! Lasst sie allein!

**BURSCHEN UND MÄDCHEN:** Ah! (*Alle blicken überrascht und voll Ehrfurcht auf HEDWIG und treten von MANRU und ULANA zurück.*)

**HEDWIG:** Wie die Verpesteten sollen sie sein! (*Während MANRU UND ULANA einander fest umarmen, entfernt sich das Volk immer mehr von dem Paar, so daas es ganz vereinsamt bleibt.*)

---

**MAIDENS:** It will soon be over! Tra, la, la, la!

**YOUTHS:** (*to ULANA*). Stay! We'll chase him from our place!

**OTHER YOUTHS:** Away you lout, Your threats we scout!

**UROK:** You madmen! What is it you do?

**YOUTHS:** (*to ULANA*) No! Stay! We'll end this babble! Away he must go to join his rabble!

**MAIDENS:** Yes, end the babble!

**YOUTHS:** The hut of the gypsy burn to the ground!

**MAIDENS:** Go, join your rabble!

**YOUTHS:** Up! Up! Easily kindling are found!

**MAIDENS:** The hut of the gypsy burn to the ground!

**UROK:** Fall back!

**YOUTHS AND MAIDENS:** Hence!

**UROK:** Fall back!

**YOUTHS AND MAIDENS:** Go! Go! Go!

**ULANA:** Have mercy!

**UROK:** Fall back!

**MANRU:** Fall back! Gather no kindling or heed not the wrath of a father!

**MEN:** What's this! He dares defy us? You Pagan vagabond, now die!

**ULANA:** Manru!

## SCENE X

*THE SAME. HEDWIG (appears at the door of her hut).*

**HEDWIG:** Touch not the lepers!

**YOUTHS AND MAIDENS:** Ah! (*All look with astonishment and awe at HEDWIG, and fall back from MANRU and ULANA*) Back from the pestilent, poisonous pair! (*While MANRU and ULANA are locked in each other's arms, the village folk draw back more and more from them until they stand quite alone.*)

**BURSCHEN UND MÄDCHEN:**
(*murmelnd*). Verpestete!—
Verpestete!—
Verpestete!

*Ende des ersten Aufzuges.*

# ■ ZWEITER AUFZUG

(*Das Gehöft MANRU'S. Im Hintergrunde ein finsterer Tannenwald. Links (vom Zuschauerraum) die Frontwand der Hütte. Rechts die Schmiede MANRU'S.*)

## ERSTE SCENE

MANRU. ULANA.
(*Anbrechender Abend. Beim Aufgeben des Vorhangs sieht man ULANA in der Thür der Hütte sitzen und mit dem Fusse die Wiege ihres Kindes bewegen. Sie ist mit dem Rücken zu MANRU gekehrt, welcher mit dem Hammer in der Hand bei seiner Schmiede steht.*)

**MANRU:** (*schlägt mit dem Hammer auf ein Eisenstück los, hierauflässt er den Hammer sinken. Mit einem Seitenblick auf ULANA.*) Da sitzt sie d'rin Und wiegt das Kind!
(*Hammerschläge.*)
Da sitzt sie d'rin Mit stillem Sinn,
Als wär' sie blind, Und wiegt das Kind!
Denn es vergisst Der herbsten Pein
Das Weib, das Mutter ist!
Ach!
Könnt' ich so sein!
(*Wieder hämmernd.*)
O nein!
Nein, nein!
Ich werd' in diesem Taubenschlag
Nie meines Lebens froh!
Ihr Brüder, hört!
Ich fluch' dem Tag, Da ich von
Euch entfloh!
Des Lagers Freiheit neid' ich Euch,
Das sturmdurchwehte Zelt, Ich
neid', die endlos liegt vor Euch, Die
grosse, freie Welt!
(*Vor der Hütte ertönt der Gesang ULANA'S.*)

**ULANA:** (*an der Wiege*). Schlaf
wohl, Theures Kind, Du mein
Schatz, meine Pracht!
Lüftchen lind, Komm geschwind,
Fächle süss mein einzig Kind!
Du mein Schatz, meine Pracht,
Schlaf wohl! Schlaf wohl!
Süss sei Dir Tag Nacht!
Schlaf wohl!

**MANRU:** Wie süss, wie gut, wie
liebevoll!
Und doch — mich macht es toll!
Wenn ich sie seh', bin ich bethört,
Denk' ihrer Lieb' und Treu'
Doch Treue, die lange währt, Ist
Sklaverei!
Sie ist so lieb, so weiss, so zart, So

**YOUTHS AND MAIDENS** (*murmuring*). The pestilent!
The pestilent!
The pestilent!

*END OF THE FIRST ACT.*

# ■ ACT II

(*The yard of MANRU'S hut. In the background a dark pine forest. To the left, as seen from the audienceroom, the front of a hut. To the right MANRU'S smithy.*)

## SCENE I

MANRU. ULANA.
(*Evening falls. On the rising of the curtain ULANA is seen seated in the doorway of her hut, rocking the cradle of her child. Her back is turned to MANRU, who is standing in his smithy with a hammer in his hand.*)

**MANRU:** (*He pounds upon the anvil, then lets the hammer sink. With a side glance at ULANA.*) She
sits within
And rocks her child!
(*Hammering*)
She sits within, whom care would
win, So meek, so mild, she rocks
her child.
No grief, no pain can cause to wane
A mother's matchless love.
Could I like her bestow such love!
(*Hammering renewed*).
Ah, no, no, no!
Within this dovecote I shall never
renew my former joys!
I curse the day I left the band and
followed love's decoys.
I envy them the windswept camp,
The canvas homes unfurled, I long
to stroll through forests damp And
roam through all the world!
(*ULANA'S lullaby sounds from the hut*)

**ULANA:** Sleep on, precious one,
Treasure mine, darling son; Come
quickly, zephyrs mild, Breath upon
my only child.
My treasure darling son, Sleep on!
Sleep on!
Happy though day is done, Sleep
on!
Sleep on!

**MANRU:** How sweet!
How good!
Her love how glad!
And yet — it drives me mad!
I look on her — my mind's awry; I
think — how true her love! —
But love that can all change defy is
servitude!

engelsmild . . .
Doch es giebt Frauen and'rer Art,
Feuring und Wild!

**ULANA:** Blumen Streu'ich Dir,
Jede Blum' sei ein Traum!
Engelstanz Voller Glanz Schilinge
sich im frohen Kranz Rund um den
gold'nen Baum Im Traum!
Im traun!
Schlaf sanft, du holdes Kind, Schlaf
sanft, mein kind

**MANRU** Nein, nein
Ich kann's nicht länger hören!
Viel schöner tönt des Hammers
Klang!
Und sollt' ich seinen Schlummer
stören —
(*In höchster Gereiztheit.*)
Ich schalage (*hämmert*) — ha!
Das ist ein Klang!
(*Lässt den Hammer geräuschvoll zu Boden fallen.*)

**ULANA:** (*aus der Hütte hervortretend*). Bist müde?

**MANRU:** Zum Sterben!

**ULANA:** (*reich ihm eine Schüssel dar*). So iss ruh' aus!

**MANRU:** Ich will kein Brod bei
dem Elend und Graus!

**ULANA:** (*die Schüssel niederstellend*). Was ist Dir?

**MANRU:** Ach, lass mich!

**ULANA:** Mir kannst Du's klagen!

**MANRU:** Du weisst's ja!
(*wild aufspringend*).
Wer kann solch ein Leben ertragen!
Zervissen hab'ich die heiligs en
Bande Und fand bei den Deinen nur
Schmach und Schande!
Mir zahlen die Leute für Arbeit mit
Hohn, Für alle liebe ist Hass mein
Lohn!

**ULANA:** Nur nicht verzagen!

**MANRU:** Stehlen und rauben, hexen, verfuhren —
Da hat der Zigeuner nichts zu verlieren!
Wenn er auch einst am Galgen
schwebt —
Er har gelebt!

**ULANA:** Wenn wir nur einander in
Liebe gehören!

**MANRU:** Ja freilich!
Wie lang' soll das Elend noch
währen?
Vereinsamt, vergrämt, verachtet,
vertrieben —
Ist das ein Lieben?

**ULANA** AD Manru, harr' aus!
Es wird besser werden!

**MANRU:** Nein, nein, für uns giebt
es kein "besser" auf Erden!

She is so gentle, patient, kind!
So wondrous mild —
But there are women filled with
fire, With passion wild!

**ULANA:** Flowers your canopy,
Each bears a dream for you Radiant,
an angel band Dances round you
hand in hand!
Plays round your golden bush,
Hush! hush! hush! hush!
sleep gently, darling son, Sleep on!
Sleep on!

**MANRU:** No, no!
Too long I'va been mistaken, More
music's in the hammer's sound;
And though I waken you from your
dreams.
I'll hammer!
I'll hammer!
I'll hammer!
Ha! thus I pound!
Ha! thus I pound!
Ha! thus I pound!
Ha!
(*He lets the hammer fall from his hand and sinks down upon the bench.*)

**ULANA:** (*coming from the but*).
Are you weary?

**MANRU:** Exhausted!

**ULANA:** (*bringing a dish*). Come,
eat; and then rest.

**MANRU:** I cannot eat When I've no
zest for food!

**ULANA:** What ails you?

**MANRU:** Don't question.

**ULANA:** Tell me your sorrow —

**MANRU:** You know it. —
Who can borrow joy from such living!
The holiest bonds I severed asunder, To find amongst yours only
shame for my plunder.
I'm paid for my labor with insult
and scorn; For love I get hatred, at
eve, noon and morn!

**ULANA:** O love, despair not!

**MANRU:** Falsehood, seduction,
theft, conjurations — These are the
Gypsy's true occupations; And
though the gallows comes at last,
He's had his fling!

**ULANA:** Enough, if we two remain
trully united.

**MANRU:** United!
it is that which has blighted my happines
Derided and spurned!
In exile!
A burden!
Is it love's guerdon?

**ULANA:** Patience, my love!
It will not las for ever!

**MANRU:** It is false!
Misfortunes like this will never
mend

## Act II, Scene I

Ulana: Ach, wär das nur Alles!
Entbehrung und Leiden, wie trüg'
ich sie gern!
Wo die Noth recht gross, da ist Gott
nicht fern! Ach, wär das nur Alles!.

MANRU: Was giebt es denn mehr?

ULANA: (*summt wehmüthig das
Lied*)! "Ist der Mon'd am Himmel
voll Dann wird der Zigeuner
toll . . . "

MANRU: (*stampft wüthend mit
dem fusse*). Zum Henker!
Verfolgt es mich bis hierher?
Auf Schritt und Tritt Hör' ich dieses
Lied!
Und nun gar zu Haus —
Das hält der Teufel aus!

ULANA: Manru!
Verzeih' mir!

MANRU: Hinweg!
Kam's so weit, Dann giebt es fürder
nur Hader und Streit!

ULANA: Vergieb!
Mir thut es in der Seele leid!

MANRU: Der zu klagen hat, bin
fürwahr nur ich!
Sah so Manchen, der um den hof
sich schlich!

ULANA: Ich bleib' Dir treu bis in
den Tod!

MANRU: Du bist's, die Haus und
kind verlässt, Dich zog es damals
zum Tanz zum Fest!

ULANA: Ich bat um Brot!

MANRU: Und holtest Dir nur der
Mutter Fluch —
Unheilbar mit Allen ist nun der
Bruch!

ULANA: Vergieb's!
Vergiss und gräme Dich nicht!

MANRU: So änd're erst Du Dein
verweintes Gesicht!

ULANA: O könnte ich lächeln, was
gäb'ich dafür
Ich blick' in Dein Aug', und das
Herzspringt mir schier!
Ich fühl es, ich fühl es, bin für Dich
todt —
So lass' mich denn sterben, barm-
herziger Gott!

MANRU: Das ist fürwahr eine
höllische Pein!
(*Erhebt die geballten Fäuste.*)

## ZWEITE SCENE

*DIE VORIGEN. UROK.*

UROK: (*tritt plötzlich hervor und
fällt MANRU in den Arm*). Grüss
Gott, Herr Nachbar!
Lasst das nur sein!

MANRU: Ach, Du bist's!

UROK: Ich selbst!

---

ULANA: Ah, if that were all!
want, exile and hunger Would never give me fear.
For where need is great God is ever
near!
Ah, if that were all!

MANRU: What more can befall?

ULANA: "When the full moon fills
the night, Errant grows the gypsy
wight".

MANRU Perdition!
That ditty to haunt me here!
Up hill and down dale, I have heard
this song! —
And now you, too dare —
It is more than hell can bear!

ULANA: Manru, forgive me!

MANRU: Away! Has it come to this?
Then discords and brawls Shall
drive away bliss!

ULANA: Forgive!
Dismiss sorrow from my heart!

MANRU: Shall one here accuse?
Then indeed it is I. —
Many skulkers have been seen hov-
ering nearby.

ULANA: I will be true to you till
death.

MANRU: You once did roam from
home and child, And hurried off to
the harvest home!

ULANA: I begged for bread!

MANRU: And bore away a mother's
curse!
The breach was then wide, but now
it is worse!

ULANA: Forgive me; forget the
disgrace.

MANRU: Then show not forever a
tear-furrowed face!

ULANA: If smiles could be purchased, What would I not pay!
I glance in your eyes, Which betray
my sentence.
I feel it, I feel it, You are mine no
more!
Be merciful, Heaven, Send death, I
implore!

MANRU: Must I endure all the torments of hell!
(*He raises his clenched fist.*)

## SCENE II

*The same. UROK.*

UROK: (*entering suddenly and
seizing MANRU's arm*). Forbear,
dear neighbor; This will not do!

MANRU: What, you here?

UROK: Myself.

---

MANRU: Die Teufelsbrut!
Der Einzige, der uns nichts Böses
thut!
(*Nähert sich weider dem Amboss.*)

UROK: Ja, die Leut' sind halt
bös . . . doch wir sind's auch; 's
ist so Brauch.
Dank' Gott, dass es so und nicht anders geschah —
Zigeunerlein, warst der Hölle nah!
Ha, ha!

MANRU: Oh!
Käm' ein lohendes Feuer vom Him-
mel herab Und brannte das Dorf
und das Erdenrund ab, Ohe!
Ohe!
Wie Jauchzt' ich da!

UROK: Mein Herzchen, die Welt
brennt nich ab Dir zu Lieb;
Doch vergieb:
Ist's auf der Welt Dir so unbequem,
So lass sie steh'n — Du kannst
geh'n
(*Deutet das Hängen an.*)

MANRU: (*in tiefer Niedergeschla-
genheit*). 's ist wahr, ich kann's
thun . . .
Und würd nach allen Qualen ruh'n!

ULANA: (*zu Urok*). Du Kobold
geh'!
Am Ende thut er sich ein Weh!

UROK: (*bei Seite*) Hi, hi!
Wenn's nur recht bald geschäh'!
(*Zu MANRU.*)
Die hütte ist Dir zu eng — eine
Gruft: Zieh' auf den Ast — da hast
Du Luft!
So steigst Du hoch und thronst über
Allen — Hier unten könntest zu
tief Du fallen!
(*Zu ULANA, ihre Stimme nacham-
end.*)
Und willst Du nicht hängen ihn
seh'n allein —
So hängt Euch zu Zwei'n!

ULANA: Herzloser Mensch, Du!

MANRU: Bösewicht!

UROK: Ich herzlos?
bös?
Das bin ich nicht!

UROK: Ich kenn' die Welt, mein
Aug' ist gut, Ich weiss, was tief im
Herzen ruht; Und nichts entgeht,
nichts, meinem Ohr:
Unheimlich wallt' ich hörs, Dein
Blut . . .
Was ich so lang' schon sah zuvor,
Das Unheil, das Euch droht, das
Leid, — 's ist nimmer weit!
(*Aus dem Walde ertönt eine
Geige.*)

ULANA: Ha!

---

MANRU: Imp of hell!
(The only one who seems to wish us
well.)
(*He approaches the anvil.*)

UROK: Yes?
Our neighbors are wroth, But so are
we —
We agree.
Thank God that I came in the nick
of time, Romanychal, that was al-
most crime.
Ha!
Ha!
Ha!

MANRU: Oh, that a torrent of fire-
rands would fall from on high, Consuming this place and all else beneath the sky!
What glad, what mad delight is
mine!

UROK: Old fellow, the world will
not burn for your sake.
But — a word:
Are you weary of life here below,
Spare us the world —
You can go!
(*He makes a gesture indicating
hanging.*)

MANRU: It is true!
Perhaps it would be best, At least, it
would give me peace and rest.

ULANA: Go, demon, go!
Nor seek to add to my woe!

UROK: (*aside*). Ha!
My wish ever so long ago!
(*To MANRU.*)
Your hut is too narrow and close, it
is a grave; Climb but on high, If air
you crave.
Thus might you rise, And rule over
all the humble —
Think to what depths here you may
yet tumble!
(*To ULANA, mimicking her
voice.*)
Should you feel sorrow to see him
hang alone —
Then mount, too, his throne!

ULANA: Infamous monster!

MANRU: Heartless one!

UROK: I heartless?
I!
You do me wrong.
I know the world, My eye is keen,
And human hearts Few secrets
screen.
No sound escapes My waking ear —
The pulsing of your blood I hear.
The bale I long, have known, fore-
seen, The evil blight in store Is even
now at your door!
(*A violin is heard from the forest.*)

ULANA: Ha!

UROK: Schau, schau, wie schön der spielt!
(*MANRU horcht in sichtbarer Ergriffenheit hin*)
Nur klingt's ein wenig wild!

MANRU: (*bewegt in innerem Kampfe*) ja, ja!
Der kann wohl zaubern, der so geigt!
Ob er sich zeigt?

UROK: Nicht wahr, das packt? — 's ist zum Vergeh'n?

ULANA: Warum erstarr' ich, Gott, mein Gott?

UROK: Hihi!
Jawohl, das Spierl ist schön!
Es lockt — es zieht — zum Paradies!
(*Zu ULANA*)
Versvhliess ihn, rath' ich Dir verschliess!

MANRU: O still, still — hört!

ULANA: Es ist mein Tod!

UROK: Und nun flog auch ein Vöglein aus, Das bringt ihr Lied Dir bis in's Haus!
Hör' hör . . . das Lied! —
Du hast's beschworen!

ULANA: Alles, Alles ist verloren!

MANRU: Nein, nein . . . nein, nein!
Sie sind es nich!
Ein Blinder ist's, ein Musikant . . .
(*Entfernt sich vom Amboss.*)

UROK: Warum erbleicht denn Dein Gesicht?
Kennst Du die Hand, Die aus den Saiten spricht?

ULANA: Du zitterst!

MANRU: Bei Gott!
So spielt nur der Erumanel!
(*will fortstürmen; UROK und ULANA halten ihn zurück.*)

ULANA: (*Was thust Du?
Mein Einz'ger, mein Liebster!*)

UROK: Halt, Halt! — — Bleib!

MANRU: O lasst mich, lasst!

ULANA: Geh' nicht von mir!
O Hör mein Fleh'n!

MANRU: Ich will ihn seh'n!
Nur seh'n!
Nur seh'n!

UROK: Halt, nicht so schnell!

MANRU: Ich will, ich will—

ULANA: Manru!

MANRU: Ich muss ihn seh'n!
(*Entwindet sich und stürmt in den Wald*).

UROK: Attend!
A clever chap!

MANRU: (*listens with obvious emotion.*) A trifle wild, mayhap.
(*inwardly disturbed.*) Aye, aye!
He's a magician, Who thus plays.
Is he in sight?

UROK: Beware!
He'll take you in his snare!

ULANA: My blood congeals!
God hear my prayer!

UROK: Hee Hee!
Now mark how in a trice He'll have his soul in Paradise.
(*To ULANA.*)
I pray you, quickly bar the door.

MANRU: O hush, hush!
Hear!

ULANA: I die with fear!

UROK: And now a bird is on the wing, It will bring its song up to your door.
Attend the song — you did invoke it!

ULANA: All's lost!
All's lost!
My doom is sealed!

MANRU: No, no, no, no!
They're not revealed; No gypsies these — a sightless bard.
(*He leaves the anvil.*)

UROK: Why are your cheeks so bloodless?
Do you know the voice that speaks in this music?

ULANA: You're trembling!

MANRU: A Romany alone con own such skill.
(*Seeks to rush off, but is detained by UROK and ULANA.*)

ULANA: O Manru, my husband!
My dear one!

UROK: Hold!
Hold!
Stay!

MANRU: Detain me not !

ULANA: O, leave me not!
O hear my prayer!

MANRU: I must see him!
I must!
I must!

UROK: Stay!
Not so fast!

MANRU: I will!
I will!

ULANA: Manru!

MANRU: I must see him!
(*Tears himself away and dashes into the forest.*)

## DRITTE SCENE

*Die Vorigen ohne Manru.*

UROK: Du lässt ihn geh'n? Ha, ha!

ULANA: (*rathlos, verzweifelt*).
Manru! Manru!

UROK: Da läuft es, dein Ziegeunerlein!

ULANA: (*mit plötzlichem Entschluss, MANRU nacheilend*). Ich hol' ihn ein!

UROK: (*hält sie zurück*). Lass sein, lass sein!

ULANA: (*will sich entwinden*).
Ich muss ihm nach!

UROK: (*wie oben*). Gemach, gemach!
Noch droht Dir nichts!

ULANA: (*händeringend*). Mein Glück!
Dahin! Dahin!

UROK: Es kommt zurück!
Da siehst Du, Thörin, wer ich bin:
Er rennt, der Schuft,
Wo ihn die Fiedel ruft,
Er plant Verrath, der Galgenstrick,
Indessen ich auf Rettung sinn'!
(*Zeigt ihr den Trank.*)

ULANA: Ach!

UROK: Schau! Mundet ihm das Tränklein da,
So hältst Du ihn!
Doch Eines, wiss'—

ULANA: (*ohne auf UROK'S Worten zu achten*).
Ja, ja, gewiss!
Nun fürcht' ich nichts mehr, Urok, Dank!
Ach, Dank!

UROK: Ich bleib ein Narr mein Leben lang!

ULANA: Mein Glück, mein Heil, mein Rettungstrank.

UROK: Frohlock' nicht!
Lieb', die man erzwang —

ULANA: Wie?
Dein Trank.
Er brächt' sie nicht zum Schweigen, Die Zaubergeigen?

UROK: Das wird sich zeigen!

ULANA: Ach!
Mir wird wieder bang!

## VIERTE SCENE

*Die VORIGEN. Am Waldesrand erscheint MANRU und JAGU, ein uralter Zigeuner.*
(*MANRU und JAGU bleiben während der ganzen Scene rechts, während ULANA und UROK — besonders im Beginne — links neben der Hütte verharren.*)

UROK: Ein Gast!
Ein lieber Gast!

## SCENE III

*ULANA. UROK.*

UROK: You let him go?
Ha!
Ha!

ULANA: (*in despair*). Manru!
Manru!

UROK: Your pretty one has gone away!

ULANA: (*with sudden determination, hurrying after MANRU*). I'll run to him!

UROK: (*holding her back*). Have done, have done!

ULANA: (*struggling to free herself*). I'm cold with dread!

UROK: Desist, desist! listen to me

ULANA: All joy is sped!

UROK: (*showing a phial*). He will return.
Now note your folly.
Look on me. —
He runs away, Soon as the devil-fiddles play —
false to his word, the gallows-bird,
And meanwhile I try to help you.

ULANA: Woe!

UROK: (*showing th phial*). See!
Give him but a drink of this He will return; but do not miss —

ULANA: (*sacrcely heeding UROK's word*). Yes, yes, I know.
Now hence, misgiving, go!
Urok, I bless you!

UROK: Still fool am I in my distress!

ULANA: You give me joy and happiness!

UROK: Rejoice not.
Love that is not free —

ULANA: What?
The drink?
Has then your art no power
Over gypsy strumming?

UROK: We'll test his thrumming!

ULANA: Ah!
All my fears return!

## SCENE IV

*THE SAME. MANRU and JAGU, a very old Gypsy, appear at the edge of the forest, During the entire scene MANRU and JAGU remain to the right, while UROK and ULANA, particularly st the beginning, remain to the left near the hut.*

UROK: A guest, a welcome guest!

ULANA: (*will auf JAGU zugehen, angstvoll*) Wer ist's?

UROK: (*hält sie zurück*). Gefasst!

ULANA: Wer ist's?

UROK: Der alte Jagu, der einst hier gehaust!

ULANA: Der Geiger ist's
Mir graust!

JAGU: (*Zu MANRU*). Einst rettet'st Du mich vor Galgen und Strick —

MANRU: Wer denkt an solche Dinge zurück?

ULANA: (*Zu UROK*). Was will er?

UROK: (*bedeutet ULANA zu schweigen und horcht auf das Gespräch MANRU'S und JAGU'S*). Stiller!

JAGU: Heut' will ich's vergelten.
Zum Fürsten wirst Du bald erwählt!

UROK: (*horchend, für sich*). Zum Fürsten!

JAGU: Du weisst, noch hat der Jagu' was zu sagen!

MANRU: Nein . . .

JAGU: Komm, komm!

MANRU: Nein, nein!
Sie Könnt's nicht tragen!

UROK: (*für sich*). Der Schuft!
Noch kann er es nicht wagen!

ULANA: O nein!
Ich lass' ihn nicht!

JAGU: Auf Deine Rückkehr hoffen sie Alle!

MANRU: Hoffen sie?

JAGU: Wir wollen nicht, dass ein Zigeuner verfalle!
Lass ab von der Fremden, lass ab!

MANRU: Nichts trennt mich ihr, als das Grab!

JAGU: Lass ab!
Lass ab!

ULANA: Er schickt ihn fort!

UROK: 's ist nur zum Spassen!

ULANA: Nein, Manru kann mich nicht verlassen —

JAGU: Denk' an Asa!

ULANA: Ich hab' den Trank!

UROK: (*wieder hinhorchend*). Welch' Name, der so seltsam klang!

JAGU: An Asa denk', an Asa!

MANRU: Sag', ist sie jetzt schön?

JAGU: Ein schön'res Mädchen hab' ich nie geseh'n
Das Feuraug!

MANRU: Das wunderbare!

JAGU: Sie blüht jetzt!

MANRU: Ach!
Der prächtige Gang!

ULANA: (*in fear, seeking to approach JAGU*). Who is it?

UROK: Be brave!

ULANA: Who is it?

UROK: Our friend, old Jagu, Who lived hard by.

ULANA: The fiddler!
I die!

JAGU: (*to MANRU*). You saved me once from gibbet and death —

MANRU: You are wasting your breath on things long past.

ULANA: What says he?

UROK: Silence!
(*He beckons to ULANA to remain in quiet while he listens to MANRU and JAGU.*)

JAGU: Now let me requite it.
You shall be before long our chieftain.

UROK: (*aside*). Their chieftain!

JAGU: You can rely on me , and I assure it.

MANRU: No.

JAGU: Come!
Come!

MANRU: No! no!
She'd not endure it!

UROK: (*aside*). The wretch!
As yet he's too faint-hearted!

ULANA: Ah no! He'll stay with me!

JAGU: To see you among them, kinsmen are hoping.

MANRU: Are hoping?

JAGU: We grieve to regard you a renegade gypsy.
Cast off the pale gentile, away!

MANRU: Death alone shall lead me astray!

JAGU: Away!
Away!

ULANA: He sends him away.

UROK: He will deceive you!

ULANA: No, Manru cannot, will not leave me —

JAGU: Think of Asa!

ULANA: I have the drink!

UROK: (*listening again*). How stangely sounds the name I hear!

JAGU: Asa calls!
Asa!

MANRU: Ha!
Is she still fair?

JAGU: A matchless beauty, fair beyond compare.
Her glowing eyes —

MANRU: I know their beauty.

JAGU: Are fire now.

MANRU: Ah, her lithesome gait!

JAGU: Nie gab's ein Weib, das schöner sang, So wahr ich Jagu bin!

UROK: Jetzt hat er ihn!

ULANA: Er zieht ihn fort!

UROK: Bleib'!

ULANA: Lass mich hin!

UROK: 's ist besser, glaub's, Du Hörst kein Wort!

MANRU: Und denkt sie mein?

JAGU: Du weisst, sie liebt nur Dich!
Manru ist ihr Lied, Manru ist ihr Leid!

MANRU: Die Herrliche!

JAGU: Ob nah, ob weit, Du weisst es, sie gehört nur Dir!

MANRU: Und ich verschmachte hier!

JAGU: Doch kommst Du nicht —

MANRU: Was dann — schnell, Alter, sprich!
(*Ergreift JAGU heftig beim Arm.*)

JAGU: Wird sie des Oros sich're Beute sein!

MANRU: Ah!
Oros? —
Nein!
Das duld' ich nicht!
(*Will forteilen, indem er JAGU nach sich zieht.*)

UROK: Ha, ha, ha, ha!

ULANA: Manru!

MANRU: (*ist im inneren Kampfe steben geblieben; blickt auf ULANA; resignirt*). Nein!
(*Entschlossen.*)
Nein!
Fort, Alter, fort!

UROK: Wie schad'!
Der Schuft will ehrlich sein!

JAGU: Komm!
Komm!

MANRU: (*da JAGU zaudert, — mit gebieteischer Handbewegung*). Du kennst mein Wort!

(*JAGU ab.*)

## FUNFTE SCENE

DIE VORIGEN ohne JAGU.

ULANA: (*zu MANRU*). Was wollt' der Alte von Dir, sag'?

MANRU:
Nichts, nichts!

JAGU: There never was a wench who sang so well, Upon old Jagu's word.

UROK: He's taken the bait!

ULANA: He'll draw him away!
(*Tries to cross over.*)

UROK: Stay!

ULANA: Let me go!

UROK: It were better far you had not heard.

MANRU: She thinks of me?

JAGU: She loves only you —
Manru all her song, She longs for Manru!

MANRU: The darling one!

JAGU: Though far you roam —
You know it —
She is yours alone.

MANRU: And here I sigh and groan!

JAGU: But stay away —

MANRU: What then?
Speak, quickly speak!
(*Vehemently seizing JAGU's arm.*)

JAGU: She will surely fall a prey to Oros!

MANRU: To Oros?
No!
Come, no delay!
(*Seeks to hurry away, dragging JAGU with him.*)

UROK: Ha!
Ha!
Ha!

ULANA: Manru!
Manru!
(*MANRU, who is struggling within himself, stops and gazes on ULANA.*)

MANRU: (*resignedly*). No!
No!
Away, tempter Away!

UROK: Too bad!
The wretch would be a saint.

JAGU: Come!
Come!

MANRU: (*with a gesture of command to the hesitating JAGU*). You know my will!

(*Exit JAGU.*)

## SCENE V

ULANA. MANRU. UROK.

ULANA: (*to MANRU*) What was it that old Gypsy sought?

MANRU: It was nothing.

UROK: Nichts?
Ich dacht', Er wollte viel.
Er soll wieder der ihre sein!

ULANA: Weh mir, willst Du wohl schweigen!

UROK: Packt ihn erst wieder der Wandertrieb, So ist es aus mit Weib und Lieb'!

ULANA: Ist's wahr!
Du gingest wieder in die Welt?

MANRU: Und wenn ich ging?
Und wenn wir Beide gingen?
Wer ist's, der mich zur Rede stellt?
Wer kann an diese Scholl' uns zwingen?

ULANA: Es liebt das Vögelchen sein Nest.
Es weint, wer je sein Heim verlässt:
Schlägt denn in Deiner Brust kein Herz?
Empfand'st Du nie der Trennung Schmerz? Ach sag', warum musst Du Stets wandern ohne Rast und Ruh?

MANRU: (an der Schmiede, mit dem Hammer in der Hand). Ich wand're nicht —
Mich zieht's dahin!
Ein Räthsel ist mir selbst mein Herz:
Urplötzlich zieht's mich anderwärts . . .
Warum? —
Wohin?
Ich weiss es nicht — doch muss ich zieh'n!
Uns fasst's mit wilder Frühlingslust, Unzähl'ge Stimmen singen, Und jauchzend spielt's in uns'rer Brust Als wollte sie zerspringen!
Es keimt, es sprosst, es schluchzt und lacht, Ein Sehnen, ungestillt, erwacht, Und trägt uns, hingerissen, blind, In's Weite fort mit Uebermacht!
So reisst ein Giesbach jäh sich los, Der wild, unhemmbar fällt, So rollt, gezeugt vom Erdenschloss, Der Strom der Lava durch die Welt, Vernichtend Alles, was ihn hält!
(Bleibt wie verzückt stehen.)

ULANA: Schau, schau!
Ein Zauber reisst ihn hin!

MANRU: So fliegt ein Blüthenstaub im Wind Zur fernen Blume hin!
So dringt, wenn er der Seel' entsprang, Zu den Sternen der Gesang!
Ihr nennt es Fluch —
Kein and'res Dasein giebt's für mich!
Geschrieben steht's im Schicksalsbuch: Dein Stamm muss alle Bande flieh'n Und irrèn, irren ewiglich!
Warum? —
Wohin?
Ich weiss es nicht — doch muss ich zieh'n!

UROK: Nothing
I thought He wanted much!
It was nothing less than your return.

ULANA: Woe's me!
Will you hold your peace?

UROK: When he again desires to rove.
It will be all day with wife and love!

ULANA: Is it true?
Would you become a wanderer?

MANRU: Suppose it were true?
And if we both should wander —
Who's he to whom I'd give account?
Who is it that can bind us to this clod?

ULANA: The bird is fond of its small home And grieves when it is forced to roam.
Have you no heart within your breast, That parting brings you no unrest?
O tell me, pray, why must you ever ramble?
Why has rest no charm?

MANRU: I ramble not.
I'm drawn afield.
Even my heart yields a riddle It is that tempts me far away.
But where, or why, it will not say.
I may not stay!
My soul is filled with longings.
Spring's voices shout within me;
Each fiber in my frame is thrilled.
With feelings that would win me.
In bush and brake The buds awake,
Of nature's joy the woods partake,
And bear me helpless, spent along,
Where freedom lives, far from the throng!
Thus pours the mountain torrent wild, That stubborn rocks would check; Thus rolls the molten lava-stream,
(As if in an ecstasy.)
Dispersing havoc dire, supreme,
Enfolding, whelming all in wreck!

ULANA: See, see!
He's in an ecstasy!

MANRU: Thus flies the pollen on the breeze, To meet its floral love;
The song, outgushing from the soul, Thus seeks the starry vault above.
It is a curse?
There is no other life for me.
It is written in the book of fate:
"Your race must abate every pledge, and wander, rove eternally!"
But why?
And where?
I know it not —
I must fare.
(He slowly approaches the anvil.)

ULANA: Irren . . . irren ewiglich . . . !
So wand're! — zieh'!
Für ewig ist mein Glück zerstört!

MANRU: Wer Dich so reden hört, Der glaubt fürwahr,
Schon wären die Zigeuner da Und frässen mich mit Haut und Haar!

UROK: Man sagt, man sagt, sie sind schon nah!
Auf Deine Rückkehr hoffen sie Alle!
Sie wollen nicht, dass ein Zigeuner verfalle!

MANRU: Das hörtest Du?

UROK: Ha, ha, ha, ha!
Das hört' ich — und ich selber sah Sogar tiefschwarzer Augen zwei —
Doch mir — hihi! — ist's einerlei!

ULANA: Ein Weib?

MANRU: Schweig, Du Höllenhund!

UROK: Ja, ja, ich sah — ja, ja, ich sah Die Perlenzähne, den Rosenmund . . .

MANRU: Schweig! Genug!

UROK: Ja, ja, das ist ein Weib! Ich sah!
Sie tanzte und drehte den Schlangenleib, Es rauschten die rothen Fetzen, Die Hölle hatt' ihr Ergötzen!

MANRU: Du Giftmaul, still!

ULANA: Sag', war sie schön?

UROK: Ha, ha!
Ein schön'res Mädchen hab' ich nie geseh'n!

MANRU: (geht mit erhobener Faust auf ihn los). Wirst Du nicht still?

UROK: (entschlüpft hinter den Amboss, wo er sich mit der Feuerzange gegen Manru wehrt). Ich will, ich will!
— Sie tanzte, sie tanzte und sang dabei —

ULANA: Sie sang?

MANRU: (wie oben). Still, sag' ich, still!

UROK: "Nie gab's ein Weib, das schöner sang, So wahr ich Jagu bin!"

MANRU: Ich stopf' Dir bald den Rachen!

ULANA: Sie ist's von der sie sprachen!

UROK: Und hei, wie klang das Tamburin!
Da, da, nicht wahr? — da zieht's Dich hin!

MANRU: Verruchter!

ULANA: (zu UROK). Schweig!

MANRU: Ich will dich lehren —

ULANA: "Wander, — rove eternally!"
Then ramble, roam!
My happiness is gone!

MANRU: (with an angry gesture).
To hear your maunderings, one might assume
The Gypsies have already come To steal me from my house and home!

UROK: It is said, it is said that they are near.
To see you amongst them they are hoping; They "grieve to think you a renegade gypsy."

MANRU: You heard the words?

UROK: Ha, ha!
Yes, truly, And indeed, I saw, besides, a pair of coal black eyes.
But yet — he, he! All is one to me!

ULANA: A lass?

MANRU: Peace, you imp of hell!

UROK: Aye, aye!
I saw the teeth so pearly, The rosebud mouth —

MANRU: Enough! Enough!

UROK: Yes, yes
There was a lass! I saw the jade, She danced and she capered, The sinuous maid.
Her ragged, red skirts were flying, All hell delighted in spying!

MANRU: You hell-hound, peace!

ULANA: Speak!
Was she fair?

UROK: Ha, ha!
A matchless beauty, Fair beyond compare.'

MANRU: (approaching UROK with raised fist). Will you hold your peace?

UROK: (taking refuge behind the anvil and arming himself with the tongs). I'll cease!
I'll cease!
She danced and she sang a song!

ULANA: She sang?

MANRU: Peace, I say, peace!

UROK: "Never was a wench who sang so well, Upon old Urok's word!"

MANRU: I'll end this wicked gabble!

ULANA: It is she of whom they babble!

UROK: Huzza!
How rings her tambourine! It is that which draws you here, I believe.

MANRU: You villain!

ULANA: (to UROK). Peace!

MANRU: An admonition —

# Act II, Scene V

ULANA: Schon' ihn!

UROK: Die Treu' zu brechen?

MANRU: Besser hören!

ULANA: Hinweg!
Hinweg!

MANRU: Ich schlag' dich todt!

UROK: Nur sachte, sachte!
Behut' Dich Gott!
(*Er lauft in den wald hinein.
MANRU will ihm nachfolgen, wird
aber VON ULANA
zurückgehalten.*)

MANRU: Mir kocht das Blut!

ULANA: Bleib'!
Bleib'!

MANRU: Längst hab ich ihm den
Tod geschworen!

ULANA: (*geht in die Hütte*). Nun
hilf mir, Trank, in meiner Noth!

MANRU: (*am Amboss*). Die Teufelsbrut, Von einer Hex' geboren!
Wer ihn hört, verdorrt, Denn Gift
ist jedes Wort!

ULANA: (*Kommt mit Blumen im
Haare zurück. Sie hält eine
Flasche und einen Becher in der
Hand*). Sei doch ruhig!
Sei doch gut!
Sag', möchtest Du ein Schlückchen
haben?

MANRU: Wie, Wein?

ULNA: Das wird Dich laben!

MANRU: Es ist wohl kaum ein edler
Trank!

ULANA: (*schenkt ein*). Versuch'
ihn nur, versuch'!

MANRU: Welch' würziger Geruch!

ULANA: Versuch'!
Du sagst mir Dank!

MANRU: Gefahr ist stets im Wein
—

ULANA: Trink', trink'! 's wiegt süss
in Traum Dich ein!

MANRU: Wenn du es willst —
Wenn Du mir selbst den Becher
füllst . . .

ULANA: Mit Freuden!

MANRU: Nun, so gieb!

ULANA: (*zögert*). Hast Du mich
lieb?

MANRU: (*ungeduldig*). Ach, Du
fragst?

ULANA: Liebst mich nicht mehr?

MANRU: Wie Du mich plagst!
Gieb her!

ULANA: So trink'!

MANRU: Ah, das thut gut!

ULANA: Trink', trink', das kühlt
das Blut!

ULANA: Spare him!

UROK: To prove unfaithful?

MANRU: Ha! Perdition!

ULANA: Away, Away!

MANRU: I'll have your live!

UROK: Ha!
Gently, gently!
Beware of strife! (*He runs into the
forest. MANRU attempts to follow
him, but is restrained by ULANA.*)

MANRU: I burn with rage!

ULANA: Stay, stay!

MANRU: I swore to kill him long
ago.

ULANA: Help, potion, now my
need is sore.
(*Goes into the hut.*)

MANRU: (*at the anvil*). The imp of
hell, Whom a foul beldame bore!
why should I refrain?
His every word is bane!
(*ULANA returns. Flowers are
twisted in her hair and she carries
a bottle and goblet.*)

ULANA: Patience, Manru!
Come, be kind!
See, see!
I offer a cooling drink.

MANRU: It is wine?

ULANA: Take what I offer.

MANRU: A soothing drink were
good for me.

ULANA: Try but a sip.

MANRU: It is sweet on the lip.

ULANA: You'll be grateful.

MANRU: There's treason in wine!

ULANA: Drink, drink!
It will incline you to sleep.

MANRU: It is your desire?
Then fill the cup you did inspire.

Ulana: Most gladly!

MANRU: Here, you dove!

ULANA: (*hesitates*) Have I your
love?

MANRU: (*impatiently*). Can you
ask?

ULANA: You love not!

MANRU: Is all forgot?
The cup!

ULANA: Here, drink!

MANRU: Ah!
That is good!

ULANA: Drink, drink!
It will cool your blood.

MANRU: 's giebt neuen Muth!
Wie Balsam rinnt es durch die
Kehle!

ULANA: (*für sich*). O Gott, Gott,
ändre seine Seele!

MANRU: (*für sich*). Ein guter
Trunk!

ULANA: (*für sich*). O wandle,
wandle seinen Sinn!

MANRU: (*für sich*). Wer gab ihr
ihn?
(*In Pausen, während deren aus
seinem stummen Spiel die Wir-
kung des Trankes ersichtlich
wird.*) . . .
Ja, ja . . .
Mir ist so leicht . . . zum Schweben!

ULANA: So trinke noch!

MANRU: Ach sieh, wie hübsch geschmückt!

ULANA: Nicht doch!

MANRU: Es ist doch schön, das Leben!

ULANA: (*für sich*). Ich seh's, ich
seh's Ein neues Herz ist ihm gegeben!

MANRU: Ulana!
Ich fühl's, es rollt in meinen Adern
Wie Honigseim und doch wie Flam-
mengluth!
Ich fühl's, ich lebe — ich fühl's,
ich liebe!

ULANA: Ach, dass es nur so bliebe!

MANRU: Ulana, ach, so lass das Ha-
dern!
Komm, komm . . . (*umfasst sie und
zieht sie an sich.*)
So, so . . .
Sei wieder gut!
Lächle mir froh!

ULANA: Mein Herz ist schwer!
Liebst mich nicht mehr!

MANRU: Ein böser Traum!
Ich denk' ihn kaum!

ULANA: Kalt war Dein Herz, Dein
Sinn mir fern!

MANRU: Verzeih', verzeih', Ulana,
hör'!

ULANA: Nur still, nur still!
Hast Du mich gern?

MANRU: Mein Lieb, mein Weib,
mein Stern!

ULANA: So sprich: hast Du mich
wirklich wieder gern?

MANRU: Wie im Sonnenscheine
Kühler Winde Kosen, Wie den Duft
der Rosen Lieb' ich Dich, Du Reine!
Wie der Lied-Erfinder Seiner Leier
Saiten, Wie die frommen Kinder
Heil'ger Glocken Läuten:
Heiss, wie Löwenherzen Die die
Lieb' beschlich, Voll ver-
schwieg'ner Schmerzen, Also lieb'
ich Dich!

MANRU: I feel new life.
All trace is gone of my dejection.

ULANA: O God!
Restore his affection!
Oh, fill his heart with love sincere!

MANRU: A potent drink.
(*Aside.*)
Who brought it here?
(*His actions indicate that the po-
tion is taking effect.*)
Up, up, light as the air I'm soaring.

ULANA: Then drink again!

MANRU: How fair!
Bedecked with flowers!

ULANA: It is nothing.

MANRU: Life's filled anew with
pleasure!

ULANA: It is true; God has restored
to me my treasure!

MANRU: Ulana!
A torrent throbbing through my
veins, Like a balsam sweet, yet like a
fire's fierce glow!
It is joy in living!
It is joy in loving!

ULANA: Were you but safe from
roving!

MANRU: Ulana!
Cease your sobbing.
Come, come!
(*Embracing her.*)
So, so!
Past is woe!
Grant me a smile, My heart beguile.
Show me your face!

ULANA: My heart is sad; your love
is dead!

MANRU: A wicked dream!
Away it is sped!

ULANA: Cold was your heart—
your thoughts did stray!

MANRU: Forgive, forgive, Ulana,
pray!

ULANA: And now, again have I
your love?

MANRU: My star!
My wife!
My dove!

ULANA: Oh, speak!
Do you truly love me?

MANRU: As the balmy zephyrs
Meet the sun's caresses,
Perfume from the roses Nature's
love confesses;—
As the ardent singer Loves his harp's
sweet measure, As the bells their
chiming,—
I love you, my treasure!
Fiercely as the lion, Filled with love
elate, Gently as the twilight, I love

Komm, schon sinkt der Schatten, Wonnig blüht der Flieder, Und ein hold Ermatten Löst die heissen Glieder! Horch wie in den Zweigen Webt ein Zauberreigen, Wie sie Küsse tauschen, Sich in Lieb' berauschen! Himmel, Erd' umschlingen Sich in Lieb' so weich, Alles scheint zu singen: Liebet, liebet euch! Zeig' mir Dein Gesicht! Warum schweigst Du? Sprich!

ULANA: Nein, ich kann's nicht denken, Dass Dein Herz erwacht!

MANRU: Süsse, zweifle nicht!

ULANA: Sag, willst Du mich kränken?

MANRU: Dich nur lieb' ich, Dich!

ULANA: Bin ich nur verlacht? War so ganz verlassen, Hab' an Tod gedacht —

MANRU: Liebste! Lass die Klagen, Sprich mir nicht von Tod!

ULANA: Wollte schon verzagen Ach, in meiner Noth! Nein, ich kann's nicht fassen, Dass Dein Herz erwacht!

MANRU: Hörst Du es nicht schlagen? Kann der Mund es sagen, Was im Herzen loht?

ULANA: O mein Gott! Ist's wahr? Sag, so hätt' Dein Blick Sich zu mir gewendet?

MANRU: War mein Aug' verblendet? Kannt' ich nicht mein Glück?

ULANA: Ach, wie gern vergäss' ich aller Noth und Pein, Wärst Du wieder mein!

MANRU: Welcher Stimme Klang trifft mein Herz so heiss? Wessen Stirn und Wang Ist so zart, so weiss? Wessen Herz so offen? Wessen Aug' so klar?

ULANA: Ach, so soll ich hoffen? Ist das Wunder wahr? In der Seele klingen Zarte Melodieen, Die von Liebe singen, Sternenaufwärts ziehen. Sehnsuchtsvolles Bangen, Sorgenschwüler Noth, Ist trostreich aufgegangen, Goldnes Morgenroth! Lass mich dich umwinden Küsse, Trauter, mich; Es soll mein Kuss dir künden Ewig lieb ich dich!

MANRU: Ja, ein neues Leben Fühl' ich in mir quellen, Fühl' mein Herz erbeben Und in Wonne schwellen!

you, my mate. Come, the night is darkling, Fragrant are the breezes, And a sweet emotion Seizes all my being Through the verdant branches Fairy folk are moving, And their myriad kisses Tell the bliss of loving. Heaven and earth embracing With the arms of love, Chant the tender passion Like the choirs above! Turn to me your cheek! Why so silent? Speak!

ULANA: No! It is past believing, That your heart is mine;

MANRU: Sweet one, banish fear!

ULANA: Lone was I, deserted, Thoughts of death were mine!

MANRU: Sweetheart, cease repining, Yield not to despair.

ULANA: Grief, entwining my heart, Had me in its snare; No! It is past believing, That your heart is mine!

MANRU: Listen only to its beating, Hear my voice repeating, I love you, my fair!

ULANA: O, my God! Is it true? Has indeed your heart Turned to me in kindness?

MANRU: Long I groped in blindness Feeling joy depart!

ULANA: Gladly would I banish Memories of pain, Having you again!

MANRU: Whose the voice that now Fills me with delight? Whose the cheek and brow, Gently fair and white? Whose the heart so tender? Whose the eye so clear?

ULANA: Gratitude I render, Knowing joy so near! Through my soul enraptured, Melodies are ringing; Love's and rapture's voices, To the skies are winging. All the pains of longing, All of sorrow's care, Through hope's touch have vanished Into viewless air! Let my arm enfold you! Let me feel your kiss! Each caress proclaiming Everlasting bliss!

MANRU: Life within me welling, Through my veins it is coursing; Every cloud dispelling, Enforcing happiness!

ULANA: Komm, mich zu erlösen Die in Dir nur lebt! Nimm mein ganzes Wesen, Das nach Dir nur strebt!

MANRU: Dir, der einzig Süssen, Lass aufs Neu' mich schwören: Dir bleib' ich zu Füssen, Dir will ich gehören!

ULANA: Ewig möcht ich's hören!

MANRU: O Du meine Sonne! Du mein ganzes Sein!

ULANA: Du mein Glück, Du Wonne!

MANRU. ULANA: Ewig, ewig Dein!

*(Ende des zweiten Aufzuges.)*

## ■ DRITTER AUFZUG

*Links (vom Zuschauer), mehr im Hintergrunde, ein See; dahinter gebirgige Landschaft mit mehreren gangbaren Bergpfaden. Links vorne eine kleine Erhöhung mit einem Steinblock. — Es ist Nacht. Im Beginne schwüle Gewitterstimmung, die sich jedoch allmählich aufheitert und dem klaren Vollmondlichte Platz macht.*

### ERSTE SCENE

*MANRU. Stimme hinter der Bühne.*

MANRU *(erscheint schwankend, wie schlaftrunken).* Luft! Luft! Ich ersticke! Der Hütte Schwüle . . . Der wüste Traum, der mich umwebt . . . Das Herz, das zum Zerspringen schwoll! *(Athmet tief.)* . . . Ah! Das thut wohl! — so wohl! . . . Die Nebel zieh'n, wohin ich blicke, Ich sehe nichts . . . jedoch ich fühle Den Mond, der hinter Wolken schwebt . . . *(Dämmernder Schein über dem Gebirge.).* Ah, das belebt! Vom See die Kühle! Und vom Gebrig' des Waldes Duft!

STIMME: *(in weiter Ferne).* Rasten, rasten wollen wir!

MANRU: Wer ruft? War's nicht ein ferner Schall? Nein, 's ist der Brandung Widerhall! . . . Unruhig wallt in mir das Blut, So wundersam ist heute mir zu Muth . .

.

Es ist, als ob man tief im See dort sänge Und von den Sternen fliessen Saitenklänge. Man gab mir wohl einen Zaubertrank? Gott soll mich strafen,

ULANA: Come, complete the capture, I am yours forever! Ah! Such heavenly rapture Does repay past grief!

MANRU: You are mine, mine only, I shall leave you never Sorrowful and lonely, — I am yours forever!

MANRU: You, are my sun, my treasure, You, are my bliss divine!

ULANA: Loving without measure,

BOTH: Ever I am yours!

*END OF ACT TWO.*

## ■ ACT III

*To the left, slightly in the background, a lake. Back of the lake a mountainous landscape with several practicable paths. In the left foreground a slight elevation and a rocky platform. It is night. In the beginning suggestions of a sultry summer storm, which are gradually dissipated and give place to the light of the full moon.*

### SCENE I

*MANRU: voices behind the scenes.*

MANRU: *(totters on the stage as if drunken with sleep).* Air! Air! I stifle! . . . Close was the cottage—wild was the dream that held me bound! My heart, I thought, would split in twain! *(Breathes deeply.)* Ah! Now I breathe again . . . The mists depart—wherever I look, nothing can be seen; and yet I feel the moon behind her cloudy veil! *(Light glimmers on the mountain peaks).* Ah! these refresh me! . . . the lake's cool breezes, and from the heights the forest's smell!

A VOICE FROM THE MOUNTAINS. *(Heard in the distance).* Here we'll rest and seek repose!

MANRU: Who calls? Was it not a distant cry? No! it was the echo's quivering sigh. The blood surges within my veins A nameless impulse urges me onward Methinks that voices from the lake are singing, And from the skies accordant harps are ringing. Mayhap I have drunk of a magic cup! It were God's vengeance were I be-

Ich bin behext!
Mir ist's, als wär' ich krank...
*(Die Kräfte scheinen ihn zu verlassen. Er schwankt und läst sich auf einen Stein block nieder.)*
Nein, nein, Der Vollmond ist's, der heut' begann.
Wild pocht mein Herz, die Unruh' wächst — Wohlan, wohlan, Ich will noch schlafen — schlafen!
*(Er schläft ein. Die Musik schildert seinen Traum, in welchem die Erinnerung an ULANA mit dem unruhigen Wandertrieb des Zigeuners Kämpft. Gleichzeitig spielt sich am Himmel zwischen dem Gewölk und dem Mond ein Kampf ab, in welchem der Mond schliesslich Sieger bleibt. So oft der Mond hindurchleuchtet, wirft sich MANRU unruhig auf seinem Lager herum; wenn er verschwindet, scheint er sich zu beruhigen. Schliesslich, als die volle Mondesscheibe hervortritt, beginnt MANRU mit zugemachten Augen, wie von einer magnetischen Kraft emporgezogen, sich zu erhebem).*

witched!
Alas!
I cannot think.
*(His strength seems to desert him. He staggers and sinks down upon a rock).*
No, no!
It is the moon now shining full!
How beats my heart!
My unrest grows!
It is well!
Let me slumber... slumber... slumber!
*(He falls asleep. The music delineates his dream in which memories of ULANA struggle with the gypsy desire to wander. Simultaneously a combat seems to be taking place in the sky between the clouds and the moon in which the latter comes out victor. Whenever the moon shines through the clouds MANRU tosses restlessly in his sleep: when it disappears he becomes quiet. At last when the full disk of the moon is disclosed, MANRU, his eyes closed, begins to rise to his feet as if drawn by the power of a magnet.)*

## *ZWEITE SCENE*

*MANRU. CHOR DER ZIGEUNER. (Der CHOR ertönt zunächst hinter der Bühne und scheint immer näher zu kommen. — Die Musik spielt den Zigeunermarsch.)*

**CHOR DER ZIGEUNER:** Lasst uns wallen!
Lasst uns wallen!

**MANRU:** *(Schreitet mit ausgestreckten Händen, die Augen immer geschlossen, den Bergen zu.)*

**CHOR DER ZIGEUNER:** Wie die Wellen wirbelnd wallen, Wie die Felsen widerhallen, Die Zigeunerlieder schallen!
*(Der Mond wird von schwerem Gewölk verdeckt, man hört Windstösse wie vor einem herannahenden Gewitter. — MANRU strauchelt und sinkt ohnmächtig zu Boden.)*

**CHOR DER ZIGEUNERINNEN:** In die Flammen starrt Unser Blick Und gewahrt Das Geschick!
*(Auf den Gebirgspfaden werden Zigeunergruppen sichtbar, welche von verschiedenen Seiten herabsteigen. In jeder Gruppe Musikanten, hauptsächlich mit Geigen und Bassgeigen. Malerische Kostüme.)*

**CHOR DER ZIGEUNER:** Wie Lawinen rollend fallen, Lasst uns wallen Von Ort zu Ort!

**CHOR DER ZIGEUNER-MÄDCHEN:** Wie die Flamme zehrt Unser Blick Und zerstört Manch' Geschick!
*(Ein Theil der Zigeuner betritt schon die Bühne, jedoch noch entfernt VON MANRU.)*

## *SCENE II*

*MANRU. CHORUS OF GYPSIES. (The chorus is first heard behind the scenes and seems to approach nearer and nearer. The orchestra plays a gypsy march.)*

**CHORUS OF GYPSIES:**
Onward, let us wander onward!

**MANRU:** *(with arms extended and closed eyes walks toward the mountain.)*

**CHORUS OF GYPSIES:** Like the restless billows curling, Gypsy songs now loud are skirling.
Hear the hills far echoes hurling—
*(The moon is veiled by dark clouds and gusts of wind heard, presaging an approaching storm, MANRU falls to the ground.)*

**CHORUS OF GYPSIES:** In the ruddy flame now we gaze, Reading fate in the blaze!
*(March music in the course of which groups of gypsies appear descending the paths on either side of the stage landscape. In each group there are musicians, principally violin and bass players. Picturesque costumes.)*

**CHORUS OF GYPSIES:** Like the landslip whirling downward!
Let us wander From place to place!

**CHORUS OF GYPSY MAIDENS:** Like the ruddy flame Blasts our gaze, Dealing fate Through the blaze!
*(Some of the gypsies appear upon the scene but at some distance from MANRU.)*

**CHOR DER ZIGEUNER:** Nur das Feuer, das wir schüren, Ist uns Heimath, Herd und Hort!

## *DRITTE SCENE*

*DIE VORIGEN. OROS, ASA, JAGU. (Auf dem See erscheint eine rohgezimmerte Barke, auf welcher man ASA bemerkt, au seiner Gruppe von Zigeunerinnen königlich hervorragend, ferner OROS, JAGU und andere ältere Zigeuner. Einige tragen Fackeln, welche die Gruppe roth beleuchten, ASA zeichnet sich durch ein malerisches, reichlich mit Goldflitter behängtes Zigeuner-kostüm aus; ihre schwarzen Haare sind aufgelöst, um ihren Nacken schlingt sich ein langes rothes Seidentuch. OROS ist durch sein Kostüm und einen hohen Beilstock, auf den er sich stützt, als der Stammesfürst gekennzeichnet.)*

**CHOR DER ZIGEUNER:** Lasst uns wallen!
Lasst uns wallen!

**CHOR DER ZIGEUNER-MÄDCHEN:** Zu verführen, zu gefallen —

**ALLE:** Wallen wir von Ort zu Ort!
*(Die vom Gebirge herabkommenden Zigeunermädchen stossen auf den am Boden liegenden MANRU. Gleichzeitig gelangt die Barks an's Ufer und ASA betritt als Erste den Boden.)*

**ZIGEUNERMÄDCHEN:** Ach!

**ASA:** Was giebt's denn?

**OROS:** Ein Mann liegt da!

**CHOR:** Ein Mann liegt da!

**ASA:** Wer ist's?

**CHOR:** Ein Erumanel.

**ASA:** Es ist Manru!

**ASA:** Wusst' ich's nicht?
Mit Zaubermacht Führt's in unsere Mitte ihn!
*(MANRU erwacht und stützt sich mühsam auf den Ellenbogen. Der Mond scheint wieder mit voller Klarheit).*

**ASA:** Ich hab' so stark an ihn gedacht Und zog ihn zu mir hin!

**MANRU:** Ein Traum war's....
Sagt, wo bin ich?

**ASA:** Unter Freunden! Nun—
*(reibt ihm die Hand und zieht ihn empor.)*
*—steh' auf!*
*Bleib bei uns!*

**OROS:** *(vortrentend).*
Nein, nie! Abtrünnig
Ward er seiner Väter Herd!

**CHORUS OF GYPSIES:** By the flames that we replenish Hearth and homes our foes may trace!

## *SCENE III*

*The same. OROS. ASA. JAGU. (A rude boat appears upon the lake, in which ASA is seen with queenly prominence, among a group of gypsy women; also OROS, JAGU and other elderly gypsies. A few carry torches which throw a red glow on the group. ASA is distinguished by a picturesque gypsy costume, richly bedecked with gilt spangles. Her black hair hangs loose and a red kerchief is knotted about her neck. OROS is recognized as the chief of the tribe by his costume and the staff upon which he leans.)*

**CHORUS OF GYPSIES:** Let us wander, let us wander!

**CHORUS OF GYPSY MAIDENS:** While we ponder new seductions —

**ALL:** Let us roam from place to place!
*(The gypsy women coming down from the mountain find MANRU lying on the ground. At the same moment the boat lands and ASA, first of the boat's company, steps ashore.)*

**A GYPSY MAIDEN:** Ah!

**ASA:** Why are you staying?

**OROS:** A man lies here!

**CHORUS:** A man lies here!

**ASA:** Who is it?

**CHORUS:** It is a Romany.

**ASA:** It is Manru!

**ASA:** Well I knew!
It was magic's thrill Led him to his kindred here.
*(MANRU revives and raises himself with an effort to his elbows. This moon shines in all its brightness.)*
It was my own resistless will Compelled him to appear!

**MANRU:** What ails me?
Where am I?

**ASA:** Among your kindred!
*(She offers her hand to him.)*
Now arise; stay with us.

**OROS:** No, no! He is a traitor A renegrade to us!

CHOR: Nein, nie! Abtrünnig Ward er seiner Väter Herd!

OROS: Du hast and're Brüder, Unser Zelt ist Dir verwehrt!

ASA: Oros! Nimm ihn auf! Ich will es!

OROS: Nein, nie, nie! Wer den eig'nen Stamm vergisst, Wem das Blut nicht heilig ist, Das in seinen Adern fliesst— Sei verflucht!

CHOR: Verflucht! Verflucht! Verflucht!

ASA: Nein! O nein!

OROS: Wessen Herz nicht uns umfasst, Wer nicht uns're Feinde hasst, Wem das Wandern ward zur Last— Sei verflucht!

CHOR: Verflucht! Verflucht! Verflucht!

ASA: Nein! O nein!

OROS: Wer ein festes Dach gewählt, Einer Fremden sich vermählt, Wer sich zu den Weissen zählt— Sei verflucht!

CHOR: Wer der Fremden sich vermählt, Sei verflucht, verflucht, verflucht!

ASA: (Manru umklammernd). Oros! Nimm Dein Wort zurück!

OROS: Bei Mroden-Oro! Es bleibt dabei!

CHOR: Es bleibt dabei!

ASA: (sich von MANRU entfernend, spöttisch). Nun wohl, wie Du willst!

CHOR: Es bleibt dabei!

ASA: Es sei! Ha, ha, es sei!

CHOR: Was soll's? Welcher Blick?

ASA: Dann hat er Glück—

CHOR: Was sinnt sie? Welcher Blick?

ASA: Ihm bleibt der Weg zu meinem Herzen frei! (Nähert sich wieder MANRU und lehnt sich zärtlich an ihn an).

OROS: (reisst sie leidenschaftlich zurück). Zurück! Du wirst ihn nie mehr schauen!

CHORUS: No, no! He is a traitor A renegade to us!

OROS: You have other kinsfolk — You must not invade our tents!

ASA: Oros! Take him back; for my sake!

OROS: No, no, no! Who deserts his father's race Seeks the black blood to debase, Which through his own veins chases, He be accurst!

CHORUS: Accurst! Accurst! Accurst!
ASA: No! Oh no!

OROS: He who does not hate our foes, In his heart our tribe enclose, He who gypsying foregoes, — He be accurst!

ASA: No, oh, no!

CHORUS: Accurst!

OROS: Who prefers a steadfast roof, Holds not from the whites aloof, Mingles with the Gentile woof — He be accurst!

CHORUS: Accurst! Accurst! Accurst!

ASA: No, oh, no!

CHORUS: He who does not hate our foes, etc.

ASA: Oros, your harsh words withdraw.

OROS: By Mro-den-Oro, that word is law!

CHORUS: His word is law!

ASA: (leaving MANRU, mockingly). It is well! As you please!

CHORUS: His word is law!

ASA: It is well! Ha, ha! It is well!

CHORUS: What means she? Strange her glance!

ASA: Twice happy he —

CHORUS: What means she? Strange her glance!

ASA: For him the pathway to my heart is free! (Approaches Manru and leans against him tenderly.)

OROS: (lifting his staff). Fall back! You must see him nevermore!

ASA: (lacht ihm spöttisch in's Gesicht). Ich frag' Dich viel! Ich sehe, wen ich will! (Schmiegt sich noch zärtlicher an MANRU.)

OROS: (erhebt drohend seinen Beilstock). Zurück, befehl' ich Zu der Frauen!

CHOR: Zurück! Zurück!

MANRU: (entwindet sich ASA und erfasst den erbobenen Arm OROS'). Sei ruhig, Oros! Ich kann nicht zieh'n! Weh mir, ich bin nicht mehr allein! Vergeblich wäre es zu flieh'n Mein Herz — ist nicht mehr mein!

ASA: Ha, ha!

OROS: (Zu ASA). Du hörst es, eitles Ding! Er liebt sie! Süss sind ihm die Ketten! Versuch's — ich gönn's Dir — ihn zu retten: Manru folgt nicht Deinem Wink!

ASA: (Zu MANRU). Du siehst, er höhnt!

OROS: (Zum CHOR). Bleibt eine Weil' an diesem Ort, Wir zieh'n gleich weiter fort!

CHOR: (zieht sich rechts in den Hintergrund zurück; während die Einen ein Feuer anrichten und sich zu lagern beginnen, murmeln die Anderen unwilling). Lasst uns wallen! Lasst uns wallen!

## VIERTE SCENE

OROS, JAGU und der CHOR rechts im Hintergrunde, um das Lagerfeuer geschaart, über welchem Kessel hängen. MANRU und ASA vorne, zunächst rechts; hierauf gehen sie nach links hinüber.

ASA: (mit Koketterie zu MANRU). Hast Dich nach uns, nach mir gesehnt?

CHOR: Lasst uns wallen! Lasst uns wallen! (Da sie MANRU mit gesenktem Kopfe dastehen sieht.)

ASA: Oder — hast Du Dich gewöhnt?

MANRU: Asa!

ASA (berührt ihn spöttisch an der Wange). O nein! Mich täuschest Du doch nicht! Glaubst Du denn, dass Dein Herz noch brennt?

ASA: A vain command! I see whomever I please!

OROS: Away! Back to the women! Dread my anger!

MANRU: (leaving ASA and grasping the arm of OROS.) Be quiet! Oros! I cannot go! Alas! I am no longer free. It is meet that you should know from me, No more, no more I'll roam with you!

ASA: Ha, ha, ha!

OROS: Do you mark him, vain coquette? He loves her — loves the chains that bind him! Now try; — you have my leave; perhaps you can blind him! Manru will not follow you!

ASA: You see — he taunts!

OROS: (turning to the CHORUS.) A moment more we'll tarry here, Then onward we will fare! (The CHORUS forms a group in the right background. A campfire is lighted. Part of the CHORUS seems to comply unwillingly.)

CHORUS: Onward, onward, let us wander!

## SCENE IV

(OROS, JAGU and CHORUS, in the right background, gathered around the campfire over which kettles are banging. MANRU and ASA in the foreground; first right, then they cross over to the left.)

ASA: (coquettishly to MANRU). Didst you feel no longing for us? (Seeing that MANRU stands with sunken head). Can you be leal to others?

MANRU: Asa!

ASA: (touching his cheek mockingly). Oh, no! My trust you'll not efface! Do you think you still have love in store?

Zu lang', mein Freund, schon sah'st
Du ihr Gesicht —
Es liebt der Mensch — was er nicht
kennt!

**MANRU:** Und doch — und doch!'s
giebt eine Kraft,
Die an die Hütte bindet...
Fest sind die Bande, die sie schafft,
Dass Niemand sich entwindet!

**ASA:** (*sich von Manru entfer-
nend*). Den Thoren bindet nicht
der Strick —
Ihn hält sein eig'ner Wille ...
Die Laune zahlt er mit dem Glück,
Und stirbt — in aller Stille!

**MANRU:** (*folgt ihr und will ihre
Hand fassen, die ihm ASA entzieht*). Ach ja! Dir will ich es gesteh'n: Wer einmal sich hat festgebannt, Hat keine Freude mehr
geseh'n, Hat lebend schon den Tod
erkannt!
Gleich schau'n ihm alle Stunden
aus.
Ein lahm' Gespann, so schleppen
sich die Tage, Was früher Lust, wird
Pein und Plage, Zum Sarg, zum
Grab wird ihm sein eigen Haus —
Niemand begreift ihn, ach, und
seine Klage!

**ASA:** (*nähert sich stürmisch
MANRU, umfasst ihn und presst
ihn an sich*). So komm mit uns, die
wir Dich lieben!
So komm mit mir, die Dich ver-
steht!
Manru!
Komm, ach komm mit mir!

**MANRU:** (*nach heftigem Kampfe,
indem er sich losmacht*). O lass
mich, lass mich!
Ach, ich bin verloren, Da ich nicht
mehr zu Euch gehör'!
(*Zur Seite, Für sich.*)
Und Jene, der ich Treu' geschwor-
en, Ach, dieses Weib — lieb' ich
nicht mehr!
Weh mir, ach, weh!

**ASA:** (*hat sich von ihm abgekehrt
und lässt sich links auf dem Stein-
block nieder, wo sie vom Mond-
licht hell beleuchtet wird. Sie
singt, wie für sich*): Seltsam ist das
Zigeunerkind, Mutter war ihm die
Lagerflamme,
Vater war ihm der rauhe Wind
Und der Thau war seine
Amme ...
Tra, la, la, la, la, la!
(*Sie schwingt das Tamburin.*)

**CHOR:** Tra, la, la, la, la, la ...
Lasst uns wallen von Ort zu Ort.

**ASA:** Irrend über Berg und Thal,
Träumt's von künft'ger Liebesqual,
Heiss wie die Flamme, rasend wie
der Wind, Süss wie der Thau, der
vom Himmel rinnt ...
Tra, la, la, la, la, la!
(*Tamburin.*)

Too long, my friend, you have
looked in her face —
It is the unknown that men adore!

**MANRU:** And yet there is a mystic
force Which with our homes ent-
wines us; Strong are the fetters it
creates, And hopelessly it binds us!

**ASA:** (*turning away*). Such fetters
do not bind the fool; His will's his
only jailer; He yields enjoyment for
a whim, And death's at last his bai-
lor!

**MANRU:** (*following her and seeking to grasp the hand which she
withdraws*). Ah, yes!
I'll confess all to you Who his freedom himself destroys Has seen the
last of happiness And, living, still
has tasted death!
The passing hours are one to him,
Decrepit, lame, the days their
lengths unwinding. Change what
were joys to plagues and torments
grinding!
His house — a grave which even he
dares not shun; None understands
him — none his plaint is minding!

**ASA:** (*throwing her arms impetuously around MANRU.*) Then
come with us who love you truly;
Then come with me who knows
your heart!

**MANRU:** (*freeing himself, after a
struggle*). Oh, spare me!
Spare!
My heart is blighted, Since I no
more may with you dwell; Against
her to whom my faith is plighted,
Against her even must my heart rebel!
Woe's me!

**ASA:** (*has turned away and seated herself on the rocky platform,
where the moonlight falls full
upon her. She sings as if to herself*). Nature's waif is the gypsy
child!
Born is he of the blazing fire, Fathered by the whirlwind, And
the dew gives him his nurture.
(*Striking her tambourine.*)
Tra la la!

**CHORUS:** (*moving softly about
the camp*). Onward, onward let us
wander, From place to place.

**ASA:** Wandering over hill and dale,
Early he dreams of love's travail.
Hot as the campfire, Furious as the
wind, Sweet as the dew In the buds
enshrined!

**CHOR:** Tra, la, la, la, la, la!
(*Die ZIGEUNERMÄDCHEN erhe-
ben sich, indem sie in das Lied
ASA's einstimmen.*)

**ASA:** Ahnt es wohl, wie Lieb' und
Leben Beim Zigeuner rasch Ver-
rinnt, Verraucht wie die Flamme,
verhaucht wie der Thau,
Verweht in's Leere wie der
Wind ...
Tra, la, la, la, la, la!
(*Tamburin.*)

**CHOR:** Tra, la, la, la, la, la ...
(*Der ganze CHOR greift ASA's
Lied auf.*)

**MANRU:** (*für sich, ergriffen*). Un-
ser Lied!
Die Jugendjahre
Seh'ich an mir
vorüberzieh'n ... Asa seh' ich
vor mir blüh'n Unser Feuer seh' ich
glüh'n!
Ach!
(*Zu ASA.*)
Brecht auf!

**ASA:** Tra, la, la, la, la, la!
(*ASA hat sich erhoben; sie bewegt
Körper und Arme nach art einer
Tänzerin, indem sie ihr Seiden-
tuch entrollt; dabei lächelt sie
MANRU verlockend an.*)

**MANRU:** Lass ab, lass ab!
O hör mein Fleh'n!
Ich fühl's, ich könnt nicht wider-
steh'n —
(*ASA schüttelt verneinend den
Kopf, ihre Bewegungen werden
zum feurigen Tanz; die Zigeuner-
mädchen betheiligen sich an dem
Tanz. Endlich nähert sich ASA
MANRU, umschlingt ihn leiden-
schaftlich und zieht ihn nach
rechts.*)

## FUNFTE SCENE

*Die VORIGEN. (MANRU und ASA
weider rechts mit den Uebrigen.)*

**OROS:** (*nähert sich zornig*). Halt
ein!
Was soll das Treiben?

**ASA:** (*indem sie MANRU trium-
phirend dem Zigeunerlager
zuführen will*).
Manru will mit uns bleiben!
(*Lebhafte Bewegung im Zigeunerlager*).

**CHOR:** Manru will bleiben?

**OROS:** (*reisst ASA von MANRU
weg*). Lass ab von ihn!
(*Zu MANRU.*)
Verräther, fort!

**ASA:** O lass ihn mir!

**OROS:** Ich änd're nie mein Wort!

**CHOR:** (*Manner*). Verräther, fort!
Gehorcht!
Gehorchet Oros' Wort!

**CHORUS:** Let us wander!

**ASA:** Haunted he by dread forebod-
ings, How both life and love depart.
Consumed like the kindling Dis-
pelled like the dew, Wafted like
breezes, Out of view!
(*Again shaking her tambourine*).
Tra la la!
Out of view!
(*At the last words of ASA the CHO-
RUS joins in the song*).

**CHORUS:** Tra la la!

**MANRU:** It is our song!
The days of childhood, Like pictures rise before my gaze; Asa dancing in the wildwood And the campfire's ruddy blaze.
Away!

**ASA:** (*smiling alluringly on MAN-
RU and swaying like a dancer*).
Tra la la!

**MANRU:** Desist, desist, I implore
you!
Have done and do not tempt me
more!
(*ASA shakes her tambourine, and
her movements develop into a
wild dance in which the other
maidens join. Finally she approaches MANRU, throws her
arms about him passionately,
and draws him off toward the
right*).

## SCENE V

*THE SAME. MANRU and ASA
again at the right with the others.*

**OROS:** (*approaching, angrily*).
Enough!
I'm burning with rage! (*ASA about
to lead MANRU triumphantly to
the camp*).

**CHORUS:** Manru returning?

**OROS:** Away from him!
You traitor, away!

**ASA:** He goes with me!

**OROS:** I'll hear of no defense!

**CHORUS OF MEN:** You traitor
away!
Endeavor no defense.

**OROS:** Ein Ende macht dem frechen Spiel!
Er ist in Acht — sein Urtheil fiel!

**CHOR:** Sein Urtheil fiel!
Sein Urtheil Fiel!

**OROS:** Die Frist, die ich vergönnt, verrann; Lass ab von ihm — er ist in Bann!

**CHOR:** (*Männer*). Er ist in Bann!

**ASA:** (*stellt sich OROS kühn entgegen*). Ich liebe ihn!
Was gilt nun Dein Verbot?

**OROS:** Du liebst ihn?

**ASA:** *Manru's Nacken umschlingend*. Sieh!

**OROS:** Das wagst Du mir zu sagen?

**ASA:** Mein Herz hat Oros nicht zu fragen!

**OROS:** Lass ab von ihm!
(*Stürzt auf ASA los.*)

**CHOR:** Lass ab von ihm!

**OROS:** Lass ab, sonst ist's Dein Tod!
(*Er schwingt den Beilstock gegen ASA.*)

**JAGU:** (*hält OROS am Arme zurück*). Halt!
(*OROS von JAGU und anderen Zigeunern an beiden Armen festgehalten, steht keuchend da*).

**JAGU:** Sie liebt den Jungen —'s ist ihr Recht;
Und Eifersucht steht Alten schlecht!

**CHOR:** (*Frauen*). 's ist Eifersucht!
's ist Eifersucht!
Der Alte!
Ha, ha, ha, ha, ha!

**OROS:** Habt Ihr vergessen, was er that?
Wer Manru liebt, der übt Verrath!

**CHOR:** (*Manner*). So ist's!
So ist's!

**ASA:** Welch' plumpe List!

**OROS:** Ihr müsset auseinandergehn.

**ASA:** Das woll'n wir seh'n!

**CHOR:** (*Männer*). Ihr müsst!
Ihr müsst!

**OROS:** Ihr müsst Euch meinem Urtheil beugen!
Ihr müsst dem Fürstenstab Euch neigen!

**ASA:** Das wird sich zeigen!

**CHOR:** (*Männer*). Ihr müsst!
Ihr müsst!

**CHOR:** (*Frauen*). Schweigen!
Schweigen!

**JAGU:** Hört mich!
Hört mich!

**CHOR:** Hört Jagu, Jagu!

---

**OROS:** No more I'll hear this idle jest —
He is proscribed . . the die is cast!

**CHORUS:** The die is cast!
The die is cast!

**OROS:** The respite that I gave is past —
Away from him, the accurst outcast!

**ASA:** (*boldly facing OROS*). My heart is his, what care I for your ban See!

**OROS:** You love him?

**ASA:** (*throwing her arms about MANRU'S neck*). See!

**OROS:** And you dare confess it to me?

**ASA:** I will express it to all the world!

**OROS:** Away from him!

**CHORUS:** (*rushing towards ASA*). Away from him!

**OROS:** Away!
It will be your death!
(*He raises his staff as if to strike ASA*).

**JAGU:** Hold!
(*JAGU and other Gypsies grasp OROS and hold him by the arms while he struggles and gasps*).
She loves the fellow — it is her right; No jealousy should that excite.

**CHORUS OF WOMEN:** It is jealousy!
Ha, ha!

**OROS:** Have you forgotten his offense?
Beware the fearful consequence!

**CHORUS OF MEN:** Beware!
Beware!
Ah weak device!

**OROS:** You shall never be united!

**ASA:** That we shall see!

**CHORUS OF MEN:** Respect his word!

**OROS:** My just decree must be respected!
Obey the chief whom you've elected!

**ASA:** That we shall see!

**CHORUS OF MEN:** Respect his word!

**CHORUS OF WOMEN:** Silence!
Silence.

**JAGU:** Hear me!
Hear me!

**CHORUS:** Hear Jagu!
Hear Jagu!

---

**JAGU:** Wollt Ihr nicht lieber mild Euch zeigen?

**CHOR:** Nein, nein!

**JAGU:** Will Manru wieder unser sein — 's ist uns're Pflicht, ihm zu verzeih'n!
(*JAGU's Worte scheinen auf die Versammelten Eindruck zu machen.*)

**CHOR:** (*Frauen*). Verzeih'n!
Verzeih'n!

**OROS:** Das duld ich nicht!

**CHOR:** (*Männer*). 's ist uns're Pflicht!

**JAGU:** Der Jugend kann es vergeben —

**CHOR:** (*Männer*). 's ist wahr!
's ist wahr!

**JAGU:** Man straft ja nicht für's ganze Leben!

**CHOR:** (*Männer*). 's ist wahr!
's ist wahr!

**JAGU:** Wozu kann solche Strenge führen?

**CHOR:** (*Männer*). Ganz recht!

**JAGU:** Wir wollen Manru nicht verlieren!

**CHOR:** (*Männer und Frauen*). Nein, nein!

**JAGU:** Wir woll'n nicht dass er uns verfalle!
Nicht wahr?
Wir Alle?

**CHOR und ASA:** Alle!
Alle!

**OROS:** Schweig', alter Thor!
Ich duld'es nicht!
Aufrührer Ihr!
Thut Eure Pflicht!
Lasst nicht gleich Hammeln Euch Führen!
Ich lehr' Dich, Aufruhr hier zu schüren!
Hier gilt nur Ein's — des Fürsten Wort!
Brecht auf! — (*Zu MANRU*). Und Du Verräther, fort!

**ASA:** Tra, la, la, la, la, la!
Ich lache Dein!
Ich Lach'!

**OROS:** Schamloses Weib Du!

**CHOR:** Er geht! Er geht mit uns!

**OROS:** (*Zu ASA*). Oh!
Verschlänge Dich die Erde!

**CHOR:** (*Zu MANRU*). Komm mit!
Komm mit!
(*Zu OROS*).
Wir schützen ihn!

---

**JAGU:** Should he not be protected by you?

**CHORUS:** No, no!

**JAGU:** Should Manru now rejoin our band, Forgiveness is the law's command!
(*JAGU'S words seem to make an impression on the Gypsies*).

**CHORUS OF WOMEN:** Forgive!
Forgive!

**OROS:** I'll not endure it!

**CHORUS OF MEN:** It is law's command!

**JAGU:** With striplings we have patience ever —

**CHORUS OF MEN:** It is true!

**JAGU:** Should punishment then last forever?

**CHORUS OF MEN:** No, no!

**JAGU:** If harsh, vengeful thoughts we smother, We shall regain a friend and brother.

**CHORUR:** It is true.

**JAGU:** A Romany should not be degraded.
He is — our kinsman!

**CHORUS:** Our kinsman!

**OROS:** Cease, mumbling fool!
Cease and obey!
Rebellious crew, no more delay.
Act not like sheep without reason.
(*To JAGU*).
I'll teach you how to foment treason!
The chief alone may dispense laws.
Break camp!
And you, you traitor, away!

**ASA:** Tra la, la!

OROS: Ihr Frechen, schweigt!

CHOR: Manru!
Manru!
Komm mit uns!

OROS: Meuterer! —
So seht!
(*Er wirft seinen Stab zu Boden und wendet sich zum Weggeben.*)
(*OROS Zu ASA und MANRU im Abgeben*).
Doch fürchtet meine Rache!
(*OROS ab.*)

CHOR: Er geht!
Er geht!
Er geht mit uns!
(*CHOR ein Theil bestürzt, der andere spöttisch*),
Er geht!
Er geht!
— Bleib,' Oros!
Bleib'!
Was liegt daran!
Es is gethan!
Das ist kein Mann!
Ein launisch Weib!

## SECHSTE SCENE

*Die VORIGEN ohne OROS.*
CHOR: (*verschiedene Stimmen*).
— Ja, ja, das ist kein Mann!
— 'st gut gethan!
— Bleib', Oros, Bleib'!
— Sind wir verkauft?
— Ihm nach!
Lauft
Lauft!
— Nein!
Nein!
— Ruft ihn zurück!
— Genug der Pein!
— Ruft ihn zurück!
— Dass er auf's Neue uns bedrückt?
Lasst sein!
Lasst sein!
— 's war ein Tyrann!
— Vorbei ist seine Zeit!
— Vorbei, vorbei
Die Sklaverei!
— Wir sind befreit!

EINIGE STIMMEN: Doch wer wird unser Führer sein?

CHOR: 's ist wahr!
Wer wird der Führer sein?
Wer wird es sein?

ASA und JAGU: Manru!

MANRU: Nein, nein!

CHOR: Manru!

MANRU: Nein! Den Führer wählt aus Eurer Mitte!

ASA: Du musst es sein!

CHOR: Du musst!
Du musst!
So will's die Sitte!

MANRU: Nein, überlasst mich dem Geschick!

---

OROS: You shameless creature!
If only the earth would swallow you!

CHORUS: He goes with us.
Come, come.
We'll hold you safe.
Tra la, la!

OROS: You babblers, peace!
Traitors, all!
Behold!
(*He throws down his staff of office*).
But dread my direful vegeance.
(*To ASA*).
(*He haughtily leaves the scene*)

CHORUS: He goes!
He goes!
Stay, Oros, stay!
(*Some in terror others in mockery*).
The deed is done; Now all is one.

## SCENE VI

(*THE SAME without OROS*).
CHORUS: He is no man!
What boots his ban?
A silly fool—
Why mind his rule?
Hurry!
Call him back!
Are we his pack!
We spurn his words!
Bid him return?
That he may again oppress us?
We'll acquiesce no more!
His time is past; have done!
Again we're free!
Our freedom we have won!
(*A few voices*).
But who shall now be our leader?

CHORUS: There!
Who shall now our chieftain be?
Who shall it be?

ASA AND JAGU: Manru!

MANRU: No, no!

CHORUS: Manru!

MANRU: No!
For chieftain choose one of your number.

ASA: You must consent.

CHORUS: You must consent; it is our custom.

MANRU:
Pray you leave me to my fate.

---

ASA: Du willst mich flieh'n?

MANRU: Nicht diesen Blick!

ASA: Er geht mit uns!
Ihn traf die Wahl!
Auf, Geigen, Spielt!
Erkling', Cymbal!
(*Auf ASA'S Zeichen treten die Musikanten zusammen; sie spielen unter JAGU'S Leitung, der das Geigensolo ausführt.*)

ASA: Hör', Manru!
Höre, ach, das Spiel!

CHOR: Hat er kein Herz mehr, kein Gefühl?
Bist Du Erumanel?

MANRU: Ach ja! mir schmilzt das Herz, hör' ich die Geigen!

ASA: Nicht wahr?

MANRU: Ach, lasst sie schweigen!

ASA: Es jauchzt, es klagt, es schluchzt und lacht!

MANRU: O lasst sie schweigen!
Ich darf es nicht!
Ich kann es nicht!

CHOR: Schaut, schaut!
Wie bleich wird sein Gesicht!

MANRU: Wie Wein ist's, der zu Kopfe stieg!

CHOR: Seht, ihn ergreift's mit Zaubermacht!
(*CHOR verschiedene Stimmen*).
— Schaut, schaut!
— Nein, hört!
— Seht Jagu —
Wie verklärt!
(*Auf MANRU deutend.*)
— Er träumt!
Er träumt!
Nun nicht gesäumt!
(*MANRU immer mehr hingerissen*). Wie Schwingen hebt's! . . . Mir ist's ich flieg'!

ASA: Es ist mein Sieg!

CHOR: (*nähert sich MANRU und umringt ihn, mit ausgestreckten Händen*). Komm mit uns!
Die Hand gegeben!
Komm, verleugne nicht Dein Blut!
Sieh, Dir winkt ein neues Leben!
Ach Komm mit uns in Freud' und Leiden, Komm, alter Freund!
In Dämmerung, in Morgenroth,
Ach, komm mit uns!
Durch blaue Berge, grüne Haiden!
Theil' uns're Lust und uns're Noth,
Theil mit uns Lust und Noth!
Ach komm, ach komm mit Deinen Brüdern!
Du musst der Liebe Gluth erwidern!

MANRU: (*Zu ASA*). Dein bin ich!
Ja, nimm mich hin!

CHOR: Vorwärts, Manru, Muth!

---

ASA: Do you wish to flee?

MANRU: My grief abate!

ASA: He'll go with us; he is our choice!
Plays, fiddles, play; and all rejoice.
(*The musicians come together. JAGU plays the solo*).

ASA: Listen, Manru.
Do you hear the strain?

CHORUS: Is he quite heartless,—
dull his brain?
(*To MANRU*).
Are you—Romanychal?

MANRU: Ah, yes!
How my heart leaps, I hear the viol!

ASA: It is true!

MANRU: Command their silence!

ASA: They laugh, complain,—
They sigh, exclaim!

MANRU: Command their silence!
I dare not hear!
I must not hear!

CHORUS: See, see!
His face grows white with fear!

MANRU: I'm reeling!
Earth holds me no more!
I'm borne on wings — I soar aloft!

CHORUS: See!
He is held by magic's thrall!
Transformed he dreams. —
Haste with our schemes.

ASA: At last he's mine!

CHORUS: (*the gypsies surround MANRU and hold out their hands*). Come with us!
Your hand as token; Come and do not shame your blood
Life anew for you bespoken.
Come, old-time friend, come with your kinsmen.
Share our joy, share our sorrow, At dawn of morn, at eventide, Over hill and dale we'll roam tomorrow;
Ah, come with us abide with us!
You must give answer to love's sweet call!
Courage, Manru, come!

MANRU: (*ecstatically, to ASA*).
Ah I am yours, take my soul!
Sweet, to you I yield control.
Take me from here; I will be free,
Still am I a Romany!

CHORUS: Come, Manru, come!

MANRU: Führ' mich, holde Zauberin!
Nehmt mich hin mit Leib und Seel'!
Ja, ich bleib' Erumanel!

CHOR: Muth, Manru, Muth!

MANRU: Ja, ich fühl' es wieder wallen, Manru's altes, tolles Blut! Mag die Welt in trümmer fallen, Lösch' ich meines Herzens Gluth: Dein bin jeh, Dein!

CHOR: Führt uns zu Zwei'n!

ASA. JAGU: Vergessen ist die Bauernmagd!

CHOR: Heil dem Fürsten! Heil!

ASA: Hinweg, es tagt!

MANRU: (sich abwendend). Mein Weib!
Mein Kind!
(Es beginnt zu dämmern.)

CHOR: (Männer). Es tagt, es tagt!

MANRU: (sich von den Uebrigen etwas abwendend, für sich). Gott weiss, es ist nicht meine Schuld! Ich fühlte Liebe, fühlte Geduld — Ulana, War ihr von ganzem Herzen gut ....
Es täuschte mich mein eigen Blut!

CHOR: Hinweg, es tagt!

MANRU: Willst Du von mir Leib' und Treue, Nimm das Aug' mir, das stets neue Lockende Gestalten sieht!

CHOR: Es tagt, es tagt!

MANRU: Willst Du, dass ich bei Dir bleibe, Reiss' das Herz mir aus dem Leibe, Das zur Andern mich zieht!

CHOR: Hinweg!
Es tagt!
Es tagt!
Es tagt!

MANRU: (mit Entschlossenheit). Asa!
Brüder!
Euch gehör ich an!
Die Freiheit winkt, die Kette springt, Ich geh' mit Euch, ein freier Mann!

CHOR: Hinweg mit aller Sklaverei! Die Welt ist unser, denn nur wir sind frei!
(Während der Zigeunermarsch mächtig erklingt, eilen MANRU und ASA, einander umschlingend, den Bergen zu; ihnen folgt der CHOR.)

### SIEBENTE SCENE

UROK. ULANA.

---

MANRU: Ah!
Anew my blood is gushing, Manru's fiery, fuming blood; Though it is to destruction rushing, I will float on passion's flood!
I am yours, Yours!

ASA: You are mine, mine!

CHORUS: Yes; lead our band!

ASA. JAGU: Forgotten is the peasant maid!

CHORUS: Hail to our chieftain! Hail!

ASA: Away!
Day dawns!

MANRU: (turning away). My wife!
My child!
(Morning breaks).

CHOURUS OF MEN: Day dawns! Day dawns!

MANRU: (turned from the others. Aside). As Heaven knows, I meant no wrong.
My love was ardent, my patience long; My heart was yours in every mood, I was deceived by my own blood!

CHORUS: Away!
Day dawns!

MANRU: You ask of me faithful duty Take away these eyes, which cannot see beauty without delight!

CHORUS: Day dawns!
Day dawns!

MANRU: Would you have me ever beside you, Take my heart; whatever betide me It takes its flight to others!

ASA: Away!
Day dawns!

MANRU: Asa!
Kinsmen!
I belong to you!
It is Freedom's call!
My fetters fall!
I'll rove with you!
No more a slave!

CHORUS: No more a slave!
Away with bonds and slavery! The world's our chattel, we alone are free!
(While the gypsy march resounds mightily MANRU and ASA, with their arms about each other, hurry towar the mountains followed by the CHORUS).

### SCENE VII

UROK. ULANA.

---

ULANA: (hinter der Bühne). Manru!
Wo bist Du?
Manru!
Bist Du dort?
Manru!
Manru!
(Auf der Bühne.)
O Jesus, Maria!
Er ist fort!

UROK: Der Höllensohn!

ULANA: Mein Gott!
Mein Gott!

UROK: Auf und davon!

ULANA: (wiederholt wie bewusstlos): Mein Gott ....
Mein Gott ....

UROK: Da hast Du Deiner Liebe Lohn!

ULANA: (die Hände zum Himmel emporhebend). Der Du im Himmel thronst, Erbarm' Dich meiner in dieser Noth, Allmächt'ger Gott!

UROK: Du Aermste!
Dir hilft kein Gott!

ULANA: Ich hab' ihn geliebt! — So geliebt!
Ich hab' ihm getraut! — So getraut!

UROK: Zigeunerbraut!

ULANA: (sich emporraffend, dem Gebirge zueilend). Manru!
Manru!
(In den Vordergrund zurückkehrend, mit rührender Klage.)
Verführt, berückt, Von den Meinen entrückt, bedrückt in Aengsten und Nöthen; Und nun geknickt, Verlassen, zerpflückt —
Zertreten, zertreten, zertreten!
(Sie fasst den Kopf mit beiden Händen; ihr Schmerz scheint an Wahnsinn zu grenzen.)

UROK: Ulana!

ULANA: Manru!
Manru!
Und bist Du nicht taub und blind, So hör:
Unser Kind!
Unser Kind!

UROK: Du sprichst in den Wind.

ULANA: So lauf'!
So lauf' und hol' ihn ein!

UROK: Gieb's auf!

ULANA: Lauf'!
Rett' uns Beibe!
Lauf'!

UROK: Ich thu's, ich hol' ihn Dir!
(Steigt, sichtbar unwillig, den Bergpfad empor,)

---

ULANA: (behind the scenes). Manru, where are you?
Manru are you here?
Manru!
Manru!
(she enters).
O holy virgin!
He is gone!

UROK: The son of hell!

ULANA: (breaking down). My God
My God!

UROK: Up and away!
It is thus he repays your love

ULANA: (lifting her hands toward heaven). O you, who rule on high!
Have pity on me
Oh be near, Almighty God!

UROK: You poor one!
He'll give no help!

ULANA: I gave him my love — all my love!
I gave my trust — all my trust!

UROK: To gypsy lust!

ULANA: (summoning all her strength and walking toward the mountain).
Oh, Manru! Manru! Manru! (returning to the foreground; pathetically).
Ensnared, deceived, Of my loved ones bereaved — Overwelmed with sorrow and anguish!
Cast aside, rejected and scorned —
Deserted!
Deserted!
Deserted!
(She clasps her head with her hands and seems maddened with grief).

UROK: Ulana!

ULANA: (turning again to the mountains). Manru you are not beguiled of sense, O hear, hear, hear our child!

UROK: Your ravings are wild!

ULANA: Then haste, oh, haste, overtake my love!

UROK: It is vain!

ULANA: Haste, be our savior, haste, oh, haste!

UROK: (ascends the path with obvious unwillingness). I hasten!
I hasten!

# Act III, Scene VII

ULANA: Manru!
Ach steh'!
Hörst du nicht, wie dein Weib dich fleht?
Manru!
Hör' mich!
Manru!

UROK: (*von den Bergen herab*).
Mir scheint es ist zu spät!
(*Er verschwindet an einer Biegung des Pfades.*)

## ACHTE SCENE

ULANA: Zu spät . . . .
Zu spät!
Mein Gott — verzeih' ihm seine Sünde!
Mein Gott — entgilt es nicht dem Kinde!
(*Sie wankt dem See zu.*)
Mein Gott . . . . o wie mein Kopf sich dreht
Mein Gott . . . . verlassen . . . .
verschmäht . . . . Ah!
(*Sie stürzt in den See.*)

## NEUNTE SCENE

UROK: (*wieder auftretend*). Halt!
Halt!
Was thust Du, Ulana?
Steh! —
Es ist aus! . . .
Verdammter!

---

ULANA: Manru, ah stay!
Do you hear
Hear your wife implore!

UROKD (*high up in the mountain*). Too late!
He's here no more!

## SCENE VIII

ULANA: Too late!
Too late!
O God, forgive him his transgression.
My child I leave in your possession.
My God!
My brain is in a whirl!
My God!
Deserted! (*In utter despair*).
Disdained!
Ah!
(*She throws herself into the lake*).

## SCENE IX

UROK: Hold!
Hold!
What have you done Ulana!
Hold! Ah!
Too late!
Accursed hellhound!

---

Mörder!
Bösewicht!
Du jubelst?
Frohlockst? —
Und sie hier?
(*Zeigt auf den See.*)
Dich pack' ich, Du entgehst mir nicht!
Ulana — wart, ich hol' ihn Dir!
(*Von einem plötzlichen Entschluss hingerissen sucht UROK den Felsblock zur Rechten zu erklimmen. Bei der ersten Stufe strauchelt er, stürzt zu Boden, erhebt sich aber sofort wieder und gewinnt unter mühsamem Klettern die Höhe des Bergpfades, wo er sich hinter einem Felsblock verbirgt. Oben auf dem Berg-pfade erscheinen die abziehenden Zigeuner. MANRU und ASA erscheinen, sich umschlungen haltend. Als sie am vordersten Punkte des Pfades angelangt sind, springt UROK plözlich hervor, wirft sich auf MANRU und stürzt ihn, nach kurzem Kampfe, den Abhang hinunter.*)

UROK: Da hast du ihn!
(*ASA sinkt mit einem lauten Schrei zu Boden Der Vorhang fällt schnell.*)

ENDE DES WERKES.

---

Murderer!
Do you rejoice?
Exult?
And she there?
(*Pointing to the lake*).
I'll have you!
Me, you'll not escape!
Ulana, wait!
I'll fetch him for you
(*Seized with a sudden determination UROK tries to climb the rocky heights to the right. At the first acclivity he stumbles and falls to the ground but recovers himself at once and by laborious climbing reaches the mountain path where he conceals himself behind a rock. The departing gypsies are seen on the path above. MANRU and ASA appear, their arms about each others waists. As they reach a point in the immediate foreground UROK leaps from his hiding place, throws himself on MANRU, and after a short struggle hurls him into the abyss*).

UROK: There you have him! (*ASA sinks to the ground with a loud cry. The curtain falls quickly*).

END OF THE OPERA.

# *Mona* (1912)

MUSIC BY HORATIO PARKER ■ POEM BY BRIAN HOOKER

---

This three-act opera, set to a libretto by Brian Hooker, premiered at the Metropolitan Opera House in New York in 1912. The story opens on a midsummer morning. At Arth's hut, Enya is doing her normal household chores as Nial lies next to the hearth. Mona and Gwynn stand nearby—he is begging her to marry him as she promised, but she tells him that while he was away she has been plotting to help the people overthrow the Romans, who rule their country. She shows him the sign of the druid which she wears. This sets her apart from other women to fulfill a holy task. She tells him that she has had a dream in which she walked between the sea and the trees with a sword that she used to force back the waves. A veiled being appeared and attempted to take the sword, but she killed this being and was then swamped by the trees and the waves. Arth comes in and throws a Roman sword at her feet. Gwynn is angry that he has broken the peace, but Arth argues against Roman rule. Gwynn gets Arth to quiet down and they bury the Roman soldier whom Arth has killed. Gwynn takes the sword; Mona tells him that he looks like a Roman and inadvertently cuts him when she grabs the sword. Arth and Caradoc, who has joined them, pledge themselves against the Romans and plan an uprising with Mona as the leader. Gwynn tries to stop her, but she agrees to lead the uprising. Gwynn vanishes into the forest and she drops the sword, crying out his name. A month later, Nial is celebrating in the forest. But the Roman Governor is there with a scouting expedition and takes him prisoner. He hopes to find out whether the Britons have met recently, but Nial doesn't answer him. Gwynn appears and is accused of treason against Rome, but he tells them that he hopes to quiet the uprising, using both his and Mona's influence. Nial is alone again as Gloom and Mona enter. Gloom declares that he loves Mona, but she says that she is fulfilling a holy task in which love is not a part, as he himself has told her. Mona, alone, prays as Gwynn enters; he is able to convince her to forget everything and everyone but him. He tells her about his birth and how their union can unite the Britons and the Romans once and for all. Realizing that he is the son of the Roman Governor and the enemy, she calls for help. The Britons come to her assistance and are about to tear Gwynn apart. Mona saves him and says he is a bard and thus can be taken prisoner but not killed. Then all prepare for the uprising. Just before dawn the next day, Enya and Nial are waiting for news. Mona is ashamed of the Britons' defeat, and she brings Gloom, mortally wounded, with her. A large Roman force has completely destroyed them. Arth is dead, and Mona blames herself for this terrible loss. Gloom says that their desire for power caused their defeat, but she thinks it is because she saved Gwynn's life. Gwynn, who has escaped from his guards, enters and tells her that he can negotiate with the Britons for peace. She doesn't believe him, nor does Gloom. She pretends to give in to him and stabs him to death as he embraces her. The Roman Governor arrives, and when he discovers his son's body he tells them they have destroyed their last chance. Mona confesses what she has done, and he tells her that she will mourn her action. She finally understands all of Gwynn's deeds and lays her sword across his body, bidding him farewell. She surrenders and is taken away as a prisoner.

---

NOTE: THE MUSIC FOR THIS OPERA WAS WRITTEN FOR THE FOLLOWING ENGLISH LIBRETTO AND THEREFORE HASN'T BEEN EDITED IN ANY WAY.

---

## ■ ACT I

*The scene represents Arth's hut in the forests of southwestern Britain: a rough, somber interior, so arranged as to appear smaller than the actual dimensions of the stage. Walls and roof are of unhewn logs; the floor is of earth, strewn with rushes and the skins of beasts. Other skins and various clumsy implements hang upon the walls and from the rafters; but there are no warlike weapons to be seen. The rear wall (which is the front of the hut) slants up stage from* ° *right to left, so that the left side of the set is considerably deeper than the right, and the*

*[° Right and Left mean throughout the right and left of a person on the stage, facing the audience;*

*Above and Below mean away from and toward the footlights.]*

*left wall clearly visible to the audience. Rather* ° *below the center of this left wall is a large hearth of rough stones, on which a fire is dying down to flickering flames and red embers; the faint wreaths of smoke from it rising through an opening in the roof overhead. Midway along the rear wall is a large doorway, framed with axe-hewn timbers; and on the lintel across the top of this doorway appears the Sign of the Unspeakable Name ⋀ burned deeply into the wood, and large enough to be clearly seen, indicating that a Druid has his dwelling here. Curtains of skins, drawn back from the doorway, show the sunlit summer forest without; the light from which, pouring inward through the doorway, makes a*

*moving brightness down the center of the stage. The right wall is a clay-and-osier partition, pierced near its upper end by a smaller doorway covered with a skin curtain, which leads into a dark inner room. A rude oaken bench stands diagonally above and to the right of the fireplace; bunks or settles are built out from the rear wall on either side of the door and from the right wall below the doorway there. To the left of this last, and as far down as possible, is a clumsy table with benches above and below it; and to the left of this again, at the edge of the lighted space, a low oaken stool.*

*The light appears to come wholly from the fire and through the doorway from the forest without; so that, although the whole stage is light enough to be clearly seen, and the central portion light*

*enough to distinguish facial expression, the general effect is that of gloom and shadow; deepening around the walls, reddened by the glow of the fire to the left, and contrasting with the brilliant sunshine of the green forest outside.*

*As the curtain rises, Mona is sitting on the stool, bent forward and gazing across into the fire, her white profile, the flame of coppery hair that falls back along her shoulders, and the gold rings about her brow and right arm thrown into relief against the pale gray of her loose robe. Gwynn, in the green robes of an Ovate, or scholar-bard, stands in the center of the stage, a little above her. Nial, in ragged deerskins with a wreath of flowers around his head, lies half asleep upon a bearskin before the fire, his back toward them and his head up*

*stage. Above the table, Enya, in dull brown, is busy removing horns, platters, etc., from the table to the inner room and to their places upon the wall. This action continues for some minutes; but at the curtain-rise she is motionless by the rear wall, her back to the audience. So that Mona and Gwynn, both by their positions in the light and by the coloring of their costumes, are made emphatic in the center of the opening picture.*

GWYNN: Not long now, till the end!

MONA: Until the end . . .

GWYNN: Not long until the end of all my doubt,
Not long until the end of all thy fear—
Kisses half-willing, half-reluctant arms,
And eyes that shirk their promise. I have made peace,
And brought down rest over this angry land
Whose trouble was thy trouble . . . Now I make
Mine own all I have known so long for mine,
All thy dear heart hath given.

MONA: (*still without moving*)
Have I all
To give thee, Gwynn?
(*Enya has come down to the table; she pauses there, watching Mona closely.*)

GWYNN: Still the old fear!

MONA: (*with more animation, turning to him*) Not fear . . .
Only . . . these many days I have not heard
Thy voice, nor seen thine eyes
. . . and the old dreams
Press closer, and thy face fades, lost among
A sea of raging faces, and a forest
Of white swords; and thy voice, murmuring joy,
Blows down a wind of war-cries
. . . What hath held thee
So long and far away?

GWYNN: Only the need
Of making all things ready for our love.

ENYA: (*to Gwynn, sharply*) Hast thou made the bride ready to be won?

GWYNN: It is this house: there is a shadow here.

MONA: (*touching her breast*)
There is a shadow here, Gwynn.
(*Enya starts, and moves forward as if about to speak; but as Gwynn goes on without noticing, she restrains herself.*)

GWYNN: Now I build
A house for us twain in the forest here,
Where sunlights laugh through moving leaves all day,
And the sweet blossoms brighten; where all night
Earth breathes joy and the moon makes mystery
Of silvern glamour—

MONA: (*heavily and sadly*) Thou shalt never build
That house, Gwynn.

GWYNN: What new change—?

ENYA: Trouble her not—
There is more in her than thy love can know.

GWYNN: Therefore I love her.

MONA: Dear, I am not changed—
That is our trouble, that I cannot change—
I cannot be like other women, loved
And loving, happy. I was never so;
Only, because of thy dear looks, I dreamed
Of love and thee a little—being young
And thrilled with May, a woman, feeling hands
Of little children touch me in the dark,
Unborn, crying to me to mother them . . .
I dreamed of them and thee. Waking, I know
That I am set apart.
(*She rises, and comes down a step. Nial stirs, and turns, half raising himself to watch them.*)

GWYNN: What fancy—

MONA: Dear, No fancy. Look—
(*She lays her hand upon the bosom of her gown, as if to draw it away from her throat. Enya springs forward in violent protest.*)

ENYA: Thou shalt not show him! No!

MONA: Look!
(*She draws the dress from her breast, and shows there the sign ⋀ red against the white skin like a brand or a birthmark. Enya wrings her hands. Gwynn starts back to the left side of the lighted space, so that the center of the stage, up to the doorway, is left open. Nial is on his feet, curious and wondering. All glance instinctively from Mona to the mark above the door.*)

GWYNN: The Name!

MONA: God's great Name.

ENYA: (*to Gwynn*) Better for thee
Not to have known.

GWYNN: The name that none may speak . . .
What means this, Mona?

MONA: I was born therewith.
I cannot read its meaning; but I know
Some great adventure waits for me, since God
Hath set His seal upon me. How shall I
Tarry for love?

NIAL: (*with a child's curiosity*) I cannot understand . . .
What is this great thing Mona has to do
That hinders loving? Does God write his name
On them that shall not love? I have it not . . .
I cannot love, because I have no soul.

MONA: I dare not love until my soul is free.

GWYNN: Thou *art* free! How should this great task divide
Thy fate and mine asunder? Being one
We shall be stronger for all good . . . Dear love,
What hinders the fulfillment of our dream?

MONA: I have had other dreams.

GWYNN: Love, thou hast been
Alone and listless, and the warm youth pent
Within thee, frustrate, like new wine that works
Close-covered, vapors up these visions. Come
With me, take life, and leave them! Come with me
Out of the shadows, out of the aimless days
And empty nights—find thou humanity
And God shall find thee greatness!

MONA: Listen, Gwynn—
And thou, Mother, in dream-lore deeply wise—
Three nights together have I dreamed this dream:
(*Nial has already settled back, uncomprehending, in his place by the fire; Enya seats herself upon the bench below the table, and Gwynn, a little later, on the right end of the bench above the fire. Only Mona is left standing and within the lighted space.*)
I walked upon a windy beach between
Dark forest and dim sea. Low-swollen clouds,
Heavy with storm, gloomed overhead and hung
Bellying against the tree-tops.
Close ashore
Towered one huge wave, curving over me
As a serpent curves to strike, crested with cloud
And foam, the hollow gulf beneath alive
With tremulous lights and angry glints of green,
High overhead looming: so that I seemed
To walk in a long cavern roofed with cloud
And walled with foam and forest.
And I bare
Upon my breast a naked sword, close held
As a mother holds her child. So when the surge
Poised to plunge down upon me, I thrust forth
The sword, shaking it seaward, and the sea
Bent backward and forebore. Meseemed one stood
Beside me, veiled in a white shroud, whose face
I could not see, that strove to snatch away
My sword. Therefore I smote and slew him. Then
The surge plunged, and the clouds burst, and the trees
Fell, thunder-rent, and whelmed me. And I woke
Trembling, and seeming still to see the sword
And the grim cloud and the green surge. And now
Three nights together have I dreamed this dream.

GWYNN: (*on his feet, but still in the shadow*) And the dream thrice beholden prophecies!—
I wonder . . .
(*He breaks off, pondering. Mona turns to Enya.*)

MONA: Mother . . . ?

ENYA: Dreaming of the sea
Foretells great happenings; dreaming of a sword,
Struggle . . . but then the forest, and the cloud,
And the white figure with no face
. . . Nay, child,
I cannot tell. I cannot read this dream.

GWYNN: God mocks us with a future half foreknown.

MONA: (*dropping back into her seat, and brooding there, her face resting upon her hands*) Nial, dost thou never dream?

NIAL: Always, I think—
Or never. Night by night, and day by day . . .
It must be all true, or else all a dream.

MONA: (*still pondering*) I alone
between surge and forest . . .
Gwynn,
What if the sea be—Rome!

GWYNN: (*startled and uneasy*)
Rome?—

MONA: The black flood
That whelms our miserable land!
(*As Gwynn is about to protest, Arth strides in at the central doorway—a lean, powerful old man with a bristle of grey hair and beard; bare-armed and bare-kneed, clad roughly in skins. He advances to the center of the stage, and hurls a short Roman sword, unsheathed, at Mona's feet.*)

**ARTH:** Here, child,
I bring thee a child's plaything!
(*The women have risen in surprise, and Nial also is upon his feet, peering curiously at the sword. Gwynn remains up left, in the shadow.*)

**MONA:** Father!

**ENYA:** Arth . . .
(*Mona has picked up the sword and is examining it. Suddenly she raises a drawn face of dreadful wonder.*)

**MONA:** It is the sword I dreamed of in my dream!

**GWYNN:** The sword of Rome . . . !

**MONA:** Father, whence came this?

**ARTH:** (*his grimness in sharp contrast with her wonder*) One
That was a Roman soldier gave it me
Yonder . . . These Romans are a weakly breed!

**ENYA:** Thou art a swordless man—
it is unlawful
For thee to fight, or to bear weapons . . .

**ARTH:** Bah!
I had no weapon—
(*He makes the action of strangling an enemy.*)
Only these bare hands
Of an old man.

**ENYA:** Blood! Blood! Ever more blood!

**ARTH:** (*disregarding her terror, and looking literally at his hands*)
Only a little, bitten from his lips
In dying.

**ENYA:** Thou hast roused the wolf!
Oh, now
We shall endure vengeance! Now, when our sleep
Was safe, and our days free—

**ARTH:** Free! Hear the woman!
Ay, free like dogs, free to the lash and the chain,
Licking the Wolf's feet lest we die—new stripes
Over old scars, one shame alike to sting
Surrender and rebellion,—tribute wrung
Out of dry hunger, swords taken away
From free hands, our shrines desolate, our Bards
Forbidden worship, our kings dead, our women
Shared with our lords—all men with blood in them
Hating the Wolf anew with each new day,
Eating and drinking hatred!
(*Gwynn has listened with growing displeasure, sharing neither Enya's terror nor Arth's rage. He now comes down, facing the furious old man with calm authority.*)

**GWYNN:** Thou art a fool,
Arth. Blood will follow this.

**ARTH:** (*noticing him for the first time, scornfully*) Gwynn
. . . the man of peace!
What dost *thou* here?

**GWYNN:** What I have ever done—
Guarded this house from trouble. Thou hast broke
The peace, wantonly slain a Roman. Fool,
What hope hath Britain save in Rome's goodwill?

**ARTH:** Rome's goodwill! The embrace of the soft scourge!
Kisses of the kindly spur! A fire's friendship,
A wolf's love!
(*Mona has been standing bright-eyed, the sword unconsciously clasped across her bosom, as a mother holds her child. As Arth finishes, she springs forward in a frenzy before the others, waving the sword at arm's length, and shouting.*)

**MONA:** Britain, old Britain! Ruin to Rome!

**ENYA:** (*catching the infection, with shrill fury*) Ruin to Rome!

**GWYNN:** Be still, women!
(*Their hysteria wilts before his confidence. He turns, facing Arth, and pointing steadily to the Sign above the doorway.*)
By that Sign,
I bid thee, peace. Now . . . thou hast slain a man—
Go bury him.
(*Their eyes fight. Arth bows his head.*)

**ARTH:** I will go bury him.
(*He goes out, slowly, into the forest. Mona crosses to Gwynn, and slides her left arm about his neck, the sword hanging loose in her right hand.*)

**MONA:** Thou art a man, Gwynn . . .

**NIAL:** I cannot understand—
What had he done, the Roman, wherefore Arth
Should slay him?

**MONA:** (*turning sharply*) Robbed us of our freedom.

**NIAL:** Nay,
Are we not free to breathe sweet breath, and sing
Under the sun, and laugh beside the fire,
And wonder at the world?

**MONA:** (*to Gwynn, examining the initials, S. P. Q. R. upon the hilt of the sword*) What mean these runes
Here graven?

**GWYNN:** Senate and Roman People.

**MONA:** (*swinging the sword*) See
How light it is! Even I have strength enough
To wield this. How can such women's weapons meet
The long sword and the British axe?

**GWYNN:** No so—
(*He takes the weapon from her, and illustrates his words with the easy precision of a trained man: at first quietly, then with increasing enthusiasm, until at the last he is vividly possessed by his patriotism.*)
Rome never strikes . . . Thus—
thrusting . . . The point kills
Quietly . . . The edge wastes power.
First the spears,
Hurled all together, bite and bend—then down
Swings the long legion, every man in turn
Guarded and guarding, shield by shield, and sword
By sword, closing the ranks above the slain—
The third line ready with new spears—not men
But one steel wall of manhood—
eagles borne
Forward, and trumpets clamoring victory—war!
Men die; but the living legion marches on
Conquering. Romans perish—
Rome abides,
Drinking the virtue of her dead strong sons,
Imperial, immortal!

**ENYA:** (*sourly, with half-suspicion*) Methinks thou knowest their warfare overwell!

**GWYNN:** I am a Bard . . . It is my work to learn . . .

**MONA:** (*eagerly*) Hast thou fought with them?

**GWYNN:** I have fought
. . . with them—
Before I was a Bard, I fought with them.

**MONA:** To have stood at sword's point with the very wolf . . . !
To have pierced flesh, and seen blood flow . . . to have slain
Romans—and now, to love Rome!

**GWYNN:** Now I love thee,
And dream of peace.
(*Mona turns listlessly away, and seats herself upon the stool, her head in her hands. Enya is above the table, and Nial back in his place by the fire, while Gwynn stands at the left of the lighted space, above the fire: so that the picture as well as the mood of the opening scene are reproduced.*)

**MONA:** I have had other dreams:
Fire, and a sound of battle, and a storm
Of hungry swords . . . our towns made strong once more,
Our shrines made holy as of old . . .
(*She rises nervously, and paces to and fro across the lower edge of the light like a caged creature, her hands clasped over the mark on her breast.*)
Great God,
What have I done with all this life of mine
To make life worthier? What have I done—
What can I do?

**NIAL:** (*innocently, with the air of having found the answer*) Thou art very beautiful.

**MONA:** Beautiful! Will my beauty break the chain?
—If I might make thereof a charm, to snare
The leader of our enemies—and then,
While he leaned down and loved me, strike one stroke
Into his wolf-heart, and leave Britain free . . .
I dream this; who shall make it more than dream?
(*Gwynn, standing motionless with the sword in his hand, has unconsciously stiffened into attention, the sword held vertically at his side. Mona turns upon him suddenly.*)
—Give me the sword.

**GWYNN:** Wherefore?

**MONA:** Give me the sword!
Thou art like a Roman soldier, standing so—
It is mine. Give it me!
(*She advances, and tries to take it from him. He resists; then, seeing that she is in earnest, lets go. Their position, at this instant, is exactly that of the previous line: "Thou art a man, Gwynn," on p. 18. But in snatching the sword, Mona has drawn its edge across Gwynn's bare right arm. She starts back to his right, dropping the sword, and catching his right hand: so that Gwynn's bleeding arm is outstretched in the center of the stage. Enya and Nial, at the same instant, spring forward and down stage to right and left, horrified at the omen. All this happens at once and in a moment.*)

**MONA:** —Gwynn!
(*At the moment of her cry, Gloom enters through the central doorway, releasing the leather curtain so that it falls behind him, cutting off the sunlight. The stage light darkens and reddens to firelight; and all eyes are turned upon Gloom standing motionless before the doorway in the white robes of a Druid, his arms*

*stretched outward and upward and his long white staff held vertically in his right hand. His black hair is crowned with oak-leaves, and his black beard flows down over his breast. After an instant, he brings his arms down, stretching them outward and downward, the staff still held vertically; then folds them inward upon his breast, so that the staff, held between his hands which are clasped at his throat, forms with his forearms the Sign of the Unspeakable Name. Then he comes down to Gwynn's left and just below him; picks up the sword, and looks from it to Gwynn's bleeding arm, speaking with a solemn relish at once prophetic and malicious.)*

**GWYNN:** *(as Gloom enters)* It is naught . . .

**GLOOM:** By that same blade it is thy doom to die.

**MONA:** Gloom . . . !

**GWYNN:** *(facing Gloom)* I shall not be slain by prophecies, Nor by ill-will.
*(Ignoring him, Gloom passes the sword to Mona, who takes it mechanically, and speaks to Enya.)*

**Gloom:** Mother, take Mona hence. Tell her . . . Thou knowest all she needs to know.
*(As Enya and Mona go out by the doorway to the right, Gwynn steps back below the table; and Gloom, crossing up to the central door, draws back the curtain and calls through.)*
Let the Bard enter, Father.
*(Arth appears in the doorway, ushering in Caradoc. He is very old, with a skin like wrinkled ivory, and hair and beard like spun glass; his costume is similar to those of Gwynn and Gloom, but deep blue in color. All his movements are deliberate and impressive; and he has an old saint's air of dreamy optimism. The others bear themselves toward him with reverence. He stands a moment under the doorway, going through the same ritual as Gloom had done, but with greater dignity and meaning. Arth and Gloom fall back to right and left of the door. Nial remains far to the left, below the fireplace; he takes no part in the ensuing scene, nor do the others notice his presence more than they would the presence of an animal.)*

**GWYNN:** *(as Caradoc enters)* Caradoc . . . !

**CARADOC:** The peace of the Great Name upon this house And all that dwell therein!

**ALL:** And with thee, peace.

**CARADOC:** *(coming down to the center of the stage)* Now let there be an oath between us.

**GWYNN:** Nay, I swear no blind oaths. What does Caradoc Here? What is this that Mona needs to know?
*(In answer, Caradoc throws back his gown. Gloom and Arth do likewise, showing that each is girt with a great sword. Together the three blades are drawn and held aloft, Caradoc's vertically, the other two slanting in toward its uplifted point.)*

**CARADOC:** The peace is broken: we have blessed the steel.

**GLOOM:** *(as the swords are sheathed again)* Thou shalt know all, being made one with us.

**GWYNN:** *(bitterly)* This is thy doing, Gloom. Thou hast undone Britain, and all our labor.

**ARTH:** Bah! He loves Rome overwell, prating of peace, peace, peace— Put thou no trust in him.

**GLOOM:** *(triumphantly)* If a man swear An oath, and bind his honor with a bond, He shall not break his word.

**GWYNN:** Have we not sworn An oath to keep the peace of the Great Name? I swear no oath to drown this land in war.

**CARADOC:** There is no peace that is not won by war.
*(Gwynn still hesitates. He must either swear disloyalty to Rome, or give up Mona, his influence among the Britons, and perhaps his life. To the others, of course, he appears merely driven from his known position as a peacemaker; and in this Gloom takes pleasure. After a moment Caradoc adds gravely:)*
Being a Bard, thou art made one with us.

**ARTH:** Being a Briton, thou art one with us!

**GLOOM:** Mona herself shall make thee one with us.
*(Gwynn still wavers, and Arth's temper gives way.)*

**ARTH:** Enough! Art thou a Roman?

**GWYNN:** *(bowing his head)* I will swear.

**CARADOC:** Then let there be an oath between us.
*(He drives his staff into the fire, causing it to blaze up. Then ceremonially draws forth a burning brand, which he elevates before the sign on the lintel, saying:)*
Now,
By the three circles round the Oak, whose names

Are Death and Life and Godhead . . . by the signs Of Earth and Air and Fire . . . ; and by the power Of the Great Name, . . . which made and maketh all . . . Our hearts are sealed forever to this trust; Our lips are sealed until the work be done.
*(At the pauses, he presents the brand in turn to Gloom, Arth, and Gwynn: each touches the fire, and carries his hand to breast and lips; then Caradoc breaks the brand in three, laying one fragment upon the earth, throwing another into the air, and returning the third to the fire.)*

**ALL:** By the Great Name; By Earth and Air and Fire.

**CARADOC:** The Gorsedd is declared!
*(He seats himself upon the bench above the fire, Arth and Gloom upon those to right and left of the doorway. Gwynn remains standing, near the table.)*

**GWYNN:** Caradoc, Thou art old, having seen generations, wise With love and sight and sorrow. Thou hast seen Boadicea, and the bloody fall Of that great uprising, and many wars Since then, lesser but not less vain. Say thou How Britain shall fight Rome!

**CARADOC:** Thou shalt know all— It is true, Gwynn, that all our wars were vain. They were but partial. Rome is Rome. Till now Britain was never Britain. We have found That leader long foretold who shall stamp down The Wolf, and save Britain—that leader sought Through many years and tears, whom all shall trust Even as a babe its mother, and obey As a young maid her love.

**GWYNN:** I know . . . but where Shall ye bring up one man all will receive As one foretold? Where find ye such a man?

**CARADOC:** No man.

**GWYNN:** *(logically triumphant)* What god, then?

**GLOOM:** Nor no god. We found A woman.

**GWYNN:** Woman . . . !

**CARADOC, GLOOM, ARTH:** *(confirming with some pleasure Gwynn's horrified anticipation)* Mona.

**GWYNN:** By God! No! Ye shall not make *her* your sacrifice! Ye shall not drown her in your surge of blood!
*(He raises his arms in the Sign, turning toward the doorway, and looking from Gloom to Caradoc.)* Is this the peace ye blessed this house withal?
*(The others have risen. Caradoc comes forward, facing him, his staff held before his breast.)*

**CARADOC:** There is no peace that is not won by war.
*(Then as Gwynn is about to protest further, he adds, pointing to the doorway.)*
We are thine elders, Gwynn. Be silent now.
*(He nods to Arth, glancing toward the door on the right; and Nial, obedient to Arth's gesture, goes out through it. There is a short pause. Then Mona enters alone, tall and pale, great-eyed with inspiration; dressed, like Gloom, in the white Druidic Robes, and with the sword still in her hand. She comes forward slowly, and kneels before Caradoc in the center of the stage. Gwynn is to the right, below the table, Arth above and to the right, Gloom below and to the left.)*

**CARADOC:** *(laying hands upon her head, quietly)* The peace of the Great Name upon thee, and the power Dwell with thee . . .

**MONA:** *(rising, tense with exultation)* It is all so wonderful. I to fulfill old prophecies . . . *(glancing toward Arth)* I not Thy daughter, but a daughter of strange names In an old tale . . . I to save Britain . . . Strange As birth . . .

**CARADOC:** Show me the sign, child.
*(She draws the robe away from her breast. The stage picture is the same, with different persons, as when she first showed it to Gwynn.)*
Twenty years Past, I beheld that sign, and saved the child For Britain.

**MONA:** Strange as love . . .

**CARADOC:** Sealed with God's great Name . . .

**MONA:** Strange as death . . .

**CARADOC:** Hear now the words of the Bard!
*(formally)*
Boadicea, dying, left her pledge (For dying eyes look through the veils of time) That one sprung of her seed should lead this land

In its great need against the Roman. Thee,
Last of her line, by that sign on thy breast,
And by Bard's insight, I receive and declare
For the one prophesied. Thee the Great Name
Shall guide where many thousand fighting men
Follow, to save Britain!

**MONA:** If I were sure . . .
(*She stands rigid, gazing before her into infinity, as one who sees a vision; her soul balancing between sainthood and humanity. Arth, up right, looks on with frowning impatience, and Caradoc, further down and to the left, patiently and with confidence. Gwynn and Gloom, to Mona's right and left and a little below her, watch tensely for the critical moment; it is they who are fighting for her.*)

**GLOOM:** Are not thy dreams fulfilled of other lives,—
Memorable of old wars?

**MONA:** How couldst thou know?—
Surely my dreams remember!
(*half to herself*)
The sea, Rome . . .
The forest, Britain . . . The sword, war . . . !

**GWYNN:** Remember
Also the veiled, white figure with no face—
God mocks us with a future half foreknown!
(*His tone softens, and he comes close to her, taking her passive hand. She looks past his eyes.*)
Thou art a woman, Mona. To be great,
First be a woman.

**MONA:** (*leaning toward him a little, but still not meeting his eyes*) I have had other dreams,
Of mating and of motherhood—not great,
But very dear. . . .
(*still gently, but hardening herself by an effort*)
Ah, Gwynn, I cannot be
A woman only!

**GLOOM:** (*venomously, catching at his opportunity*) Nor a pretty toy
For lover's lips to lap—

**GWYNN:** (*furiously, taking a step forward as if to strike him*)
Gloom!—

**ARTH:** (*sharply*) Enough words!
Dost thou accept thy task?

**MONA:** (*waveringly, almost in a whisper*) What shall I do . . . ?
(*The tide of inspiration flows over her. She throws herself erect, seeming to grow physically larger in her excitement, her face glorious, her arms thrown outward and upward, the sword shining in her hand. Her words are no longer a wail of hesitation, but a superb demand for use.*)
What shall I do?

**CARADOC:** The soul speaks! Child and Queen,
Come!

**MONA:** Yea, I come! Let the ravens follow me—
They shall be filled! Yea, let the wolves howl! Fire,—
Fire, and a sound of battle, and the whole
Manhood of Britain raging down to hurl
The wolf-born Roman back into the sea;—
Our towns made strong once more, our wasted shrines
Made holy, Druid and Bard called forth again
From lurking in forgotten dens, to fare
Once more in honor over a free land,
Singing and teaching freedom!
(*She is beside herself. Gwynn springs forward in an agony of desperate authority, pinions her arms, and by main force brings her to face him at arm's length.*)

**GWYNN:** Mona! Come down
Out of that frenzy. Mona
. . . Look at me!
This is I, Gwynn, a man, flesh and blood, I
Whose lips and eyes thou lovest . . .
(*The fire fades out of her under his eyes. She relaxes, and her head droops.*)
Now!—I say,
Thou shalt not ruin all we are, to feed
A fever and a folly.
(*He releases her, and steps back.*)
Love or war—
Choose!

**CARADOC:** (*slowly and gravely*)
Ay, choose well.

**GLOOM:** Vision or dream, that boy
Or Britain, lust or glory—

**GWYNN:** Let her be!
Thou art fain to madden her with words.

**GLOOM:** And thou
Art fain to eat her soul for thy desire,
To keep her wholly for thy pleasure; and so,
Holding her merry body in thine arms,
To laugh at Britain!
(*His profanation turns the struggle. Under the sting of it, Mona leaps back into her martyrdom. Gwynn is beaten.*)

**MONA:** Britain, old Britain, Ho!
(*The others join in the cry.*)

**ARTH:** Now let the traitor perish!

**GWYNN:** Mona!

**MONA:** (*turning upon Gwynn with bitter finality.*) Go!
I will not hear thy voice nor see thine eyes
For evermore!
(*As Gwynn turns away from her toward the door, Arth advances upon him, with clutching hands. Gwynn stops above center, facing him.*)

**ARTH:** Let me kill . . . !

**CARADOC:** Nay, we shed
No blood in Gorsedd. If a man swear an oath,
He shall not break his word.
(*They stand silent and motionless, while Gwynn draws back the curtain, letting in a momentary flood of pure sunlight, passes out slowly into the bright forest, and is gone. The curtain falls behind him across the light.*)

**GLOOM:** For evermore,
Thou shalt not see his face!
(*Mona stands motionless, with bowed head, down center, the sword clasped across her bosom. Caradoc crosses to her and kneels at her feet, drawing his sword and raising it aloft. Arth and Gloom, to right and left, Arth above her and Gloom below, do likewise.*)

**ALL:** Hail, Child and Queen! . . .

**MONA:** (*still in an inspiration*)
Fire . . . and a sound of battle, . . . and a dream
Reborn out of old years, and a new song,
Terrible with the joy of angry men
Gaining and guarding freedom—
(*The tension snaps. She drops her arms and wilts as if under a violent blow; turns half toward the door, and takes a step as though to follow.*)
—Gwynn! Ah, Gwynn!
For evermore, I shall not see his face . . .
(*The sword falls from her hand. She turns from the door again, buries her face in her hands, and shakes with sobbing, like a child.*)

The others have risen at her first giving way, and stand transfixed, their swords still raised aloft.)
(*The Curtain delays for a moment, to let the picture strike home; then falls quickly.*)

*END OF ACT I*

# ■ ACT II

*The scene represents a Cromlech, or Druidic open-air temple in the forest; so placed that its center is in the center of the stage, about ten feet above the footlights. At this point rises a huge oaktree, venerable with mistletoe and streaming moss; whose branches, spreading out on either side, extend the whole width of the proscenium, just under the arch. Immediately in front of the tree is a rude altar, composed of a single block of stone roughly rectangular in shape, about three feet high and four long. On its front is hewn the Sign ⋀ of the Name; and those branches of the tree which reach out toward the audience seem curiously to repeat this figure, bending downward and outward in three diverging lines. Behind the tree is a semicircular wall of large rough stones, whose diameter is a little less than the width of the stage. Directly behind the tree is an opening in this wall, six or eight feet wide; and the semicircle ends on each side about the same distance above the curtain, so as to give the impression of similar openings there—as if the other half of the circle were out in the audience. This wall is crumbling and irregular, nowhere more than four feet high: so that one looks over and through it, seeing beyond it and some distance back the huge standing stones of the outer circle, separated by about twice their own width; and between and beyond these again, green and mysterious forest as far as the eye can reach. Even now, the structure appears old and neglected; the forest is creeping in between the stones of the outer circle, and the space between it and the wall is dotted with bushes and young saplings. One or two of the great stones have fallen; the inner wall is crumbling here and there, and a few loose stones are lying about within; and the ground there is uneven, and covered with deep moss. Upon the altar are the charred remains of a small fire, some time extinct; and the moss thereabout is trodden as by many feet.*
*The light is that of a clear summer evening just after sunset and before dusk. Striking slantwise*

*across the scene from left to right, it marks the points of the compass (south being up stage) and the hour of the day. During the act, it grows darker so gradually that the advancing night is noticeable only as called attention to by the actors. And the end of the act takes place in bright moonlight.*

*As the curtain rises, Nial is seen within the inner circle, dancing with his shadow; at first to left of the altar, afterwards over the whole open space.*

**Nial:** (*still dancing*) Brother am I
to all the trees, and child
Of the warm-sweet earth and the
merry sun—
And all the birds and blossoms and
wild things
Of the forest, they are my brothers
too . . .
(*A bird begins to sing and flutter
among the branches above him.
He holds up his arms.*)
Come dance
With Nial, my brother!
(*The bird lights on his hand.*)
They are not afraid—
They know I have no soul.
(*Dancing again, the bird flutter-
ing about him.*)
Is it not brave
To breathe sweet breath, and sing
under the sun,
And laugh beside the fire, and have
no soul?
(*He pauses, to the right of the tree,
in a kind of dreaminess which is
his nearest approach to thought.*)
Mona and Gloom and Gwynn—all
my wise friends.
Surely their souls torment them.
They have strange
Hot joys called Love and Hate and
Fear, wherewith
To burn themselves . . . I cannot
understand . . .
(*Dancing again.*)
Nay, I had rather have my playfel-
low
To dance with. He must be my
brother too,
For the earth and the sunshine
made him. Brother, come,
Dance with Nial! Leap with Nial!
Ho!
(*Pausing again, before the altar.*)
Perhaps
He is my soul . . . I wonder
. . . and perhaps
*Their* souls are in their shadows;
. . . for their shadows
Gleam in the dark with strange
bright colors—green,
Purple, and crimson; . . . but
my shadow is gray,
And in the dark I have no shadow at
all . . .
Perhaps all souls are shad-
ows . . .
Nay, come dance
With me, my soul!

(*He is still dancing, to the left of
the altar, when The Governor, at
the head of a few light-armed Roman soldiers, enters up stage.
They push rapidly through the
trees and into the inner circle.*)

**THE GOVERNOR:** (*as they enter*)
Seize him . . . ! But slay him
not—
(*The Soldiers come down left and
surround Nial, who makes no attempt to escape. The Governor
comes down to right of the tree
and below it—a soldierly, vigorous man of fifty, thin-lipped and
quick-eyed, the black hair under
his helmet just beginning to be
threaded with gray; his manner
alert without hurry and decisive
without pomposity; dangerous
and efficient because he's free
from all doubts.*)

**NIAL:** How red your shadows are
. . . !
What would ye have
Of Nial?

**THE GOVERNOR:** Come hither.
Stand there.
(*Nial comes down beside the al-
tar.*)
(*to the soldiers*)
Guard him.
(*They close in around Nial with
leveled spears. Nial remains abso-
lutely unconcerned.*)
So . . .
(*Rapidly examining the altar and
the ground about it.*)
Footprints! A whole tribe hath been
gathered here—
Women, too . . .
Ashes! Ay, a sacrifice . . .
(*Finding a spearhead.*)
Spears!
(*to Nial*)
Listen, thou! What hath befallen
here?

**NIAL:** I have been dancing with my
soul.

**THE GOVERNOR:** Answer!
Who met here yesternight? How
many? Whence
And why came they?

**NIAL:** Gloom says I may not know.

**THE GOVERNOR:** Who is Gloom,
then?

**NIAL:** My brother. They are all
My brothers. They have souls, and
they are wise.
They say that ye are wolves that eat
this land;
Therefore, they say, ye shall all
surely die—
But how and when, Gloom says I
may not know . . .
(*curiously*)
What is it like to die?

**THE GOVERNOR:** (*grimly, but
without anger*) Thou shalt soon
learn—
A sword, there!
(*A Soldier draws his sword, and
presents it at Nial's throat. Nial remains utterly unimpressed.*)
Answer now!

**Nial:** I cannot answer—
Gloom says I may not know.
(*Looking naively at the sword,
and reaching out to touch it, as a
child might do.*)
That sword is like
The one that Mona dreamed of in
her dream . . .

**THE GOVERNOR:** Bind him!
. . . A bowstring round his temples, now—
Silence him!
(*Nial, still unresisting and uncomprehending, is bound and
gagged. A bowstring is knotted
about his forehead, and a stick
thrust through it to twist. Gwynn
enters suddenly from the right.*)

**GWYNN:** Father!—Hold!
(*The Governor turns to him with
the same matter-of-course for-
mality as if the meeting had been
expected and ordinary. Gwynn
kneels before him, and The Governor lays a hand upon his head.*)

**THE GOVERNOR:** Quintus, my
son,
I bless thee.

**GWYNN:** (*rising, to the soldiers*)
Let him go—unbind him!
(*They obey without waiting for
any confirmation of the order.
Gwynn turns to explain.*)
Nay,
Father, he would not speak: he is
one from whom,
Unborn, earth-daemons reft the
soul away—
The harmless, empty body of a man.

**NIAL:** (*feebly*) I give thanks; they
would have done me harm . . .
Surely these are not wolves—the
wolves are all
My brothers.

**GWYNN:** Nial—
(*Nial seats himself up to left of the
tree, interested but quite out of
the scene. The Soldiers draw up in
a rigid line at the left end of the
wall.*)
My father, ask of me.
(*He throws off his green robe,
disclosing beneath it the white
tunic, breastplate, and short
sword of a centurion.*)
I am a Roman soldier, and thy son.

**THE GOVERNOR:** Therefore I
came here. Many tongues have said
Thou art a Briton, and mine enemy.

**GWYNN:** Dost thou believe this,
Father?

**THE GOVERNOR:** Quintus, no.
I believe no dishonor of my blood
By hearsay. Answer therefore.
This whole land
Which late lay more at peace than
ever, now
Hums like a hive in swarm. Over
the length
And breadth of Britain, every camp
and town
Sends in the same tale—gatherings
by night,
Forbidden sacrifices in old shrines,
Forging of weapons, Druids
preaching war,
And here and there some lonely Ro-
man slain
Out in the forest. Southward, our
own towns
Return seditious rumors.
What hast thou
To say of this?

**GWYNN:** It is all true.

**THE GOVERNOR:** I have heard
Of one going about among the
tribes
To rouse revolt—a woman, beauti-
ful—
Her thou hast guarded and defend-
ed, held
Our garrisons from taking her, and
left
Her free to stir up trouble at her
will—
What of this?

**GWYNN:** (*As before, without the
least shame or embarrassment,
meeting his father's look fairly.*) It
is true . . . I love her.

**THE GOVERNOR:** (*Not shocked,
nor as a mentor, but as one who
hears quietly the confirming of a
shameful suspicion.*) Boy,
Man's honor hath no subtler enemy
Than longing for a woman.

**GWYNN:** She is more,
Father—she is their queen, even as
though
Boadicea came on earth again,
Whom they believe and follow;
(*emphatically*)
Winning her,
I win at once all Britain.

**THE GOVERNOR:** Take her, then!
I took thy mother captive even
so . . .
She, lying by my side, saved many
lives.

**GWYNN:** (*with premature triumph*) Mona and I together shall
save all—
Yet wherein should her body profit
me
But if I win her will?

**THE GOVERNOR:** (*impatiently
practical*) Play not with words—
A woman's heart is in her body,
Boy—
I had thought thee more a man!
Enough! Meanwhile,
What of this war?

GWYNN: There was to have been war;
There shall be peace.

THE GOVERNOR: Their plans, then—?

GWYNN: I have sworn
Not to betray—

THE GOVERNOR: (*losing patience*) Betray! Canst thou betray Enemies?
(*with infinite scorn*)
An oath to a Barbarian . . . !

GWYNN: An oath to their god, that is my god, too.

THE GOVERNOR: Gods! In these times, we make new gods each day! There is but one god for a man—his name
Is Duty. Speak!

GWYNN: Father, if a man swear, He shall not break his word . . .
(*The Governor's patience gives out altogether; he motions to The Soldiers, who spring forward.*)
Nay, hear me . . .
(*He stretches out his arms. The Governor hesitates an instant, then stops The Soldiers with a gesture, and paces frowningly to and fro before the altar while Gwynn continues; showing no sign of relenting, or even of being impressed.*)
All
These years of peace are mine—my work. I went
Among my mother's people, owned their god,
Became their Bard, knew them and
. . . honored them—
Do men love legions, or confide in foes?
They hate Rome; I have healed that hatred. Now,
Where the old scars ache shall we stab again
Till the whole body perish? True, our arms
Will crush them down. How long will they lie still?
Hearts, not swords, make our Roman provinces!—
Let peace make one conquest that shall endure!

THE GOVERNOR: (*pausing*)
Words again! When a sullen-snarling hound
Slinks close behind thy heel, dost thou delay
For parley? Strike the first blow, and be done!

GWYNN: These are no curs, to snarl and lick the lash—
These are they whom great Caesar could not quell!
(*The Governor faces him, impressed for the first time. Gwynn goes on with the authority and confidence of his ideal.*)
My way or thine—One peace or many wars—
Choose! Art thou general, or governor?

THE GOVERNOR: Thou hast failed thy duty; wilt thou teach me mine?

GWYNN: (*steadily*) Truth spoken by a traitor still is true.

THE GOVERNOR: (*pauses, for a moment of judgment; then delivers his ultimatum with deliberate emphasis.*) See now:
I hold these dogs in my two hands, And if they move, I break them.
(*with a gesture*)
Prove thy truth!
Save them! Thou art their fate. All hangs on thee.
Let them lie still and live, or strike and die!
I have spoken.

GWYNN: It is well; I ask no more—
Let them lie still and live, or strike and die!—
Mona and I shall hold them harmless.

THE GOVERNOR: (*with a last suspicion, looking keenly into Gwynn's eyes*) Boy,
Thou hast thy mother's blood
. . . If I could think
Thy double garment held a double heart—

GWYNN: (*not theatrically, but very quietly*) Two garments, Father, but one heart within;
Two nations, and one blood . . .
Nay, I confess
That I have let the weight of my great love
Hang round the neck of duty . . . I pray thee
Trust me . . . or trust me never.
(*He kneels, as at first. The Governor, with the first gentle emotion he has shown, repeats the gesture of blessing.*)

THE GOVERNOR: Be it so—
I trust thee then . . . my son!
(*Gwynn rises, and they grip hands.*)
If thy faith fail,
Let me die!

GWYNN: The dusk falls . . . Ye are too few
For safety. I will guide you to the town.
(*During the preceding scene, it has been growing darker so gradually, that only now does one realize that it is twilight. The Governor, motioning The Soldiers to follow, goes out center, Gwynn walking by his side. Nial, rising, follows them with his eyes until they disappear among the trees. When he can no longer hear them, he turns and comes slowly down.*)

NIAL: Red shadows, and the souls of angry men . . .
It must be all true, or else all a dream!
(*He lies down at full length before the altar, gazing into the dusk. The moon is just rising, shown by the direction of the stage light*
changing and the shadows falling from right to left; and her light increases as gradually as the daylight has waned, until by the time of Arth's entrance it is full moonlight.*)
Night, and cool winds . . . How still the forest is,
Now they are gone! My brothers are asleep
Already . . . Only the hushed owl drifts by,
Silently as a winged shadow . . . And there
The quick bat flutters past, a messenger
To wake the Little People—Nial knows!
Now the small voices under all the leaves
Are telling secrets . . .
(*As Nial pauses, Mona and Gloom enter slowly from the right. Mona is still in her white robe, with a spear and a short byrny over which the sword is girt from her shoulder; but she has neither helmet nor shield.*)

MONA: Nial! Art thou alone?

NIAL: My sister . . . !
(*He rises, and stands looking at her wonderingly.*)
Thou art very beautiful
And very far away—

GLOOM: Nial, what news?

NIAL: The Little People will be out; the bat
Has just gone—

GLOOM: (*impatiently*) Where is Arth?

NIAL: I know not.

GLOOM: Go
And seek him.
(*Nial goes out left, Gloom turns abruptly to Mona, who is standing with bowed head before the altar.*)
We have little space to dream.
Our war begins at midnight—before then,
Sacrifice and sword-giving. Presently
The Bards meet. Hast thou kept the tallies?

MONA: Here . . .
(*She hands him square wooden bars carved with runic signs. He seats himself on the rock, right, reading them and making additions with his knife.*)

GLOOM: Twelve myriad fighting men!
Rome has not half so many souls alive
In Britain! So our work ends—tonight, war—
To-morrow, victory!

MONA: (*turning from the altar, slowly*) If we ourselves
Fail not . . .

GLOOM: Dost thou fear failure?

MONA: (*Moving slowly away from him, to left of altar.*) Nay, not fear—
Only . . . all hangs on us.
(*pausing*)
If yonder town
Fall to-night, then from hill to hill our fires
Shall flash the tidings, till all Britain flares
Into one blaze ere dawn. But
. . . if we fail,
How then?
(*turning toward him*)
Were it not better all should strike
At one forechosen hour, waiting no sign?

GLOOM: What matter? We but prove our faith.
(*He thrusts the tallies into his girdle, and rises.*)
Nay, more—
Thou art here; Thou, the old Queen's self reborn,
Our leader and our strength. What fight can fail
Where thou art? All the hope of Britain waits
Thee, and thee only!

MONA: I to fight with men . . .
To pierce flesh . . . and see blood flow . . .
(*She is standing below him and to left, her head bent, her spear held slantwise across her body by the incongruous gesture of clasping her hands at her breast.*)

GLOOM: (*at his full height, magnificently*) Thou to save
And conquer!
(*advancing, in an ecstasy*)
Have no fear—thy womanhood
And the beauty of thee shall burn before us, fair
And terrible, a sweet white flame of war,
A light from old years, and a wonderful death,
And a dream plunging down eternity
To change the world.
(*He is close before her, aflame with an ardor which he struggles to color with patriotism. This at first she does not, and then will not, see.*)

MONA: (*impulsively*) Gloom, thou art glorious . . . !
If I were sure—

GLOOM: Thou and I throned above
Rejoicing freedom—Thou and I one power—

MONA: Brother and sister—

GLOOM: Priest and prophetess,—
One soul to be remembered when our bones
Blossom together—

MONA: Let my work not fail—
I ask no more. Take thou the glory.
(*She draws back from him. He throws off the mask.*)

# Act II

**GLOOM:** Child,
How have I any glory but in thee?
How have I borne thy beauty? How endured
These long dry years of brotherhood—
(*He stretches his arms to her. She springs back, turning so that the light falls upon her face, a frozen majesty in every line of her.*)

**MONA:** Gloom, Gloom,
I am not woman, but a sword; not flesh,
But steel. Who but thine own self taught me this?

**GLOOM:** It is true . . .
(*He draws back, conquered as much by reason as by her greater faith. Nial enters, from the left, followed by Enya and Arth.*)

**NIAL:** They are here, under the moon;
Their souls reach out before them.

**ENYA:** (*embracing Mona, with half-hysterical motherliness*) My little one
That loved me . . . !
(*They move across to the altar, then draw apart: Mona standing at the right lower corner of the altar, Enya a little above the altar, to left of the tree. Gloom and Arth are below them, to right and left. Nial remains near the left end of the inner wall.*)

**ARTH:** Gloom, how have ye fared?

**GLOOM:** We count
Twelve myriads now in arms.

**ARTH:** And the time?

**GLOOM:** To-morrow.
We ourselves move at midnight on the town.

**ARTH:** (*drunk with hate, brandishing his spear, and shouting*)
Ourselves first? I grow young again!
Ha, wolves
That feast and frolic yonder, sweet with oil
And glad with garlands—it shall not be long,
Not long, now, till the end!

**MONA:** (*Before the altar facing forward, her arms upraised, her face tense with inspiration.*) Until the end . . . !

**ENYA:** (*taking a step toward her, timidly*) Child, art thou that same child that pushed my breast
With baby hands, and wailed? Thou art glorified—
There is a light about thee, and a power—

**MONA:** (*rigid, her arms at her sides, looking into infinity*) I have remembered old years, and seen men
Fall down and worship me.

**ENYA:** Did they believe—
All those wild folk—?

**MONA:** (*half to herself*) It is as if these trees
Bowed themselves down before me—as if the sea
Obeyed me—yet not me, but what I am . . . A vision of swift journeyings by day,
Glimmering forests, windy crags, lone moors
Immeasurable where birds cry, and gray sands
Thunderous with the ever-changing sea—
Torches and shouts, wild gatherings by night,
And firelit circles of astonished eyes,
Men falling on their faces, oaths and prayers . . .
Strange as a dream's fulfillment of a dream!
I have heard voices in the dark, and seen
Visions of kings forgotten, bidding me
Go forward, and be strong, and have no fear—
I have dreamed of the White World, and God's love
Bathing me like sweet flame . . .

**ARTH:** Enough of dreams!
Come, let us feast before the battle. Come!
The time passes.

**MONA:** I have no need thereof.
Leave me here for a little while, to pray.

**ENYA:** Is there no danger?—

**ARTH:** Nay, with Nial at hand
No harm can fall. Come, then . . .
(*He leads the way out to the left. Enya hesitates, then follows. Gloom, going out last, pauses to look back at Mona standing to right of the altar and just below it.*)

**GLOOM:** (*slowly*) Foredoomed, ordained,
Prophesied . . .
(*He goes out. In the quietness Nial suddenly lifts his head and listens to something in the forest.*)

**NIAL:** Mona—Hark . . .

**MONA:** (*hearing nothing*) What is it, Nial?

**NIAL:** The Little People—They are calling me . . .

**MONA:** Go to them.
(*He goes out, up stage. Mona leans her spear against the tree; moves to the front of the altar, draws the sword, and lays it thereupon; then kneels before it, facing up stage.*)
Night and day, deed and dream, sight
And vision—all one faith, all one

desire—
Britain . . .
(*A pause. Gwynn enters quietly from the right. He stands a moment watching her, just inside the circle.*)

**GWYNN:** (*to himself, softly*) God help me now.
(*Another pause. Mona gradually becomes aware of his presence, and rises, facing him, her right hand on the sword, her left at her throat. When she speaks, her voice is tense and hollow, but unfaltering.*)

**MONA:** What dost thou here?

**GWYNN:** What I have ever done.

**MONA:** Thou art faithless. Go!
(*It is the same tone and manner that crushed Gloom a little while since; but this is not Gloom. He goes on quite evenly.*)

**GWYNN:** Why? Dost thou fear to look upon me, lest
Thine heart change?

**MONA:** (*stung out of her heroics, and struggling for self-possession*) Fear!
(*scornfully*)
I will not see thy face.
Get hence!

**GWYNN:** (*advancing upon her, while she shrinks away, the sword clasped to her breast*) Cry out then. Is one traitor's life
So great a matter? Thou that art to slay
Thousands ere dawn, canst thou not see me die?

**MONA:** (*desperately*) Go from me!

**GWYNN:** (*still nearer*) True, thou hast loved me. True, thine heart
Cries out for me—What matter?
Thou art not flesh
But steel. Summon thy swords!

**MONA:** (*recovering herself and rising into a martyrdom; facing him calmly, with the almost pitying tone of one who will not stoop to anger.*) Gwynn, presently
I must fight. It may be that I must die.
Canst thou not hush that little fleshly wail
Called love, and leave me here with God?

**GWYNN:** Canst *thou*?

**MONA:** (*with quiet finality, her hands pointing to the sign upon her breast*) I bear the Sign here of a greater thing,
Whereto I am reborn. I am not myself,
But Britain.
(*turning away to the altar as if he were not there*)
Go now.

**GWYNN:** Therefore I am here:
There is yet time to save Britain and thee . . .
—Now all things take one answer!
(*He takes her suddenly in his arms. She turns, writhing away from him, her body bent backward, and her head falling against his shoulder. Even at first, she cannot struggle with her full strength; and presently, as she overpowers herself, she grows more quiet, and at last quite still.*)
Struggle now—
Call to thy friends . . .
Look! Thou and I alone
In the whole great world, under the dim sky,
And the night's arms around us . . .

**MONA:** Let me go—

**GWYNN:** Night, and earth yearning upward to the moon,
And the shadows calling to us, and the winds
Dizzy with sweet, and the summer's huge heart, slow
Throbbing around us . . .
Thou and I close, close . . .

**MONA:** (*with closed eyes*) Be still—I will not hear thee . . .

**GWYNN:** Night, and thou
Near me amid the moonbeams, beautiful—
A lily on the gloom of a dim lake,
Thy golden heart wide open to the wind,
A freshness and a fragrance glimmering up
Out of cool depths—A wild bird with glad eyes—
A mystery beyond all dreaming dear,
Holier than the hope of pleasing God,
More to be hungered after than lost youth!
Now I make mine own all I have known so long for mine,
Arms and lips, life and glory, mine, mine, mine—
(*He stops suddenly, releasing her. She falls back a step below and to right of him, and stands half-stunned, her hands over her eyes. Gwynn catches the sword from the altar, and holds out the hilt to her, speaking with a sudden jarring sharpness.*)
Take thy sword. I shall die by that same blade.
So be it.
Strike now.
(*Her hands drop. She gazes at him blindly a moment; then the flood breaks.*)

**MONA:** Ah, Gwynn! . . . Oh, come to me!
(*She stretches forth her arms to him. He flings away the sword; they hold each other.*)

GWYNN: Mona . . . !
(*A short pause. He draws her down beside him on the rock, she half reclining below him and lower down, her head resting against his knee; he bending over her.*)
Night, and thou near me in the warm gloom . . .
And on thy lips a faintness and a flame—!
All the vain sorrow forgotten—all our dreams
New born, sweet with surrender—wonderful,
Holy . . .

MONA: There is a cloud over the moon—
I cannot see thy face . . . Only thine arms
Around me like strong sleep
. . . Only thy voice—
And all our children laughing in thine eyes . . . !
And it is good for me to put away Weariness, and the fever of high deeds,
And the dry hunger . . .

BOTH: Now earth sinks and swims
Falling, and the great river of joy flows down,—
Inevitable, tender, luminous,—
And whelms me, and I float under the moon
Quietly, toward the foam-bright sea . . . Down, down,
Where the glimmering shores grow faint, and darkness
Buries the sky, and the stars drown, and the deep
Rises over me, and I dream . . .

MONA: How soft
Thy hair is, Gwynn . . .
Far off in the dead void
Torches flare, and I hear a murmuring
Of old wars, and fierce multitudes that howl
For me to lead them, like some old ill dream.—
Ah, let me not remember . . . !

GWYNN: Dear, I bid thee
Remember, and rejoice in all. This night
Thou hast saved Britain.

MONA: Britain . . . Let me go!
(*The spell is broken. She shakes herself free and stands, dazed, between the rock and the altar. Gwynn, also on his feet, and not realizing the change in her, goes on confidently.*)
What have I done?

GWYNN: I would not speak till now—
I would not buy thy heart for promises—
Now it is finished! I must have thee first
Made queen over all Britain, then all mine,
Now all for peace.

"Let them lie still and live,
Or strike, and die!"
Mona, hear me—we two
Shall join in our firm love Britain and Rome
Forever!

MONA: Gwynn . . . I cannot see thy face . . .
It is all dark . . .

GWYNN: (*too full of his triumph to realize that she hardly hears him*) Dost thou need proof? What held
The Roman garrisons from taking thee?
Child, thou hadst been a prisoner twenty times
But for me.

MONA: (*harshly and dully*) What hast thou to do with Rome?

GWYNN: Not less than thou with Britain. My one voice
Answers for Rome here—

MONA: *What hast thou to do With Rome?*

GWYNN: I am Roman born—

MONA: Thou—Roman . . . ?

GWYNN: Yea,
Moreover—

MONA: Help, Ho!

GWYNN: (*utterly surprised*) Mona—

MONA: (*frantically*) Treason! Help, Ho!
(*She catches up the sword from the ground, and swings it at him, crying:*)
—By this same blade it is thy doom to die!
(*He catches her arm, and wrests the sword from her. As he does so, Arth rushes in center followed by a shouting crowd of Britons with torches and spears; and from the left, a throng of Bards and Druids, led by Gloom and Caradoc, pour in and across the stage. More and more keep pouring in, men and women, shouting and tossing their weapons. Mona springs back up stage and to the right to let them pass, pointing accusingly at Gwynn. Arth reaches him first, and strikes at him with his spear, Gloom attacking him from the left almost at the same instant.*)

ARTH: (*as he strikes*) Ha, Gwynn the Peacemaker!
(*Gwynn parries, and strikes him down with the hilt.*)

GLOOM: (*as he strikes*) At last!
(*Gwynn, his back against the rock, disarms him, and hurls him back among the crowd. But by this time the crowd has reached him, and still others, rushing in right, attack him from behind. He is instantly surrounded, disarmed, pinned down upon the rock, and threatened by many weapons. Mona stands above and*

to the right of Gwynn, upon a rising ground that makes her clearly visible above the heads of the crowd; Arth and Gloom are upon their feet again, and pushing forward, Arth to right of the tree and Gloom down stage to left of the altar; Caradoc is before the altar, and Enya up left, among the crowd. The stage is full of raging men, screaming women, and waving torches.*)

VOICES IN THE CROWD: (*as Gwynn is overpowered*) Who is he?

ENYA: Blood! Blood!

MONA: (*pointing to Gwynn with the sword*) He is—
(*The crowd suddenly quiets to listen; and in the momentary hush, Mona's rage looks upon itself. She could have killed Gwynn with her hands a moment since; but now, in cold blood, she cannot hand him over to be torn in pieces. She raises her arms in the sign of the Name; her tone changes.*)
He is a Bard!
(*The crow bears back from Gwynn, astonished and awed. Caradoc, Arth, and Gloom break through the shrinking circle of them and wave them on.*)

GLOOM: Heed her not!

CARADOC: He is not one of us!

ARTH: Kill! Kill!
(*The tumult rises afresh. Mona pushes forward in front of Gwynn, driving the Britons back.*)

MONA: Hold off,
On your lives! Back!
(*She turns, facing the three leaders.*)
Who am I . . . ? Answer me!
Who am I . . . ?

CARADOC: The Queen!
(*A short pause. No one moves or questions her will. She turns to the Britons who are holding Gwynn.*)

MONA: Bind him and lead him hence—
Do him no hurt . . .
(*As Gwynn is swallowed up in the crowd, she turns back to the others, once more an inspired Amazon.*)
Give out the swords! Wait not
For midnight—Call the warriors!

GLOOM, ARTH, CARADOC: It is not time—

MONA: I am the time—obey! Give out the swords!
Rouse the tribe! Sound the gathering! Bring hides,
Fagots and ladders—Give each man a torch—
To your work, Druids! Onward, by the Sign
Of the Name! Britain, Old Britain!
Ruin to Rome!
(*During these last lines, men have*

been hurrying about, bringing in torches, ladders, weapons, etc., until the stage is crowded and tumultuous with tossing lights and busy and disheveled figures. A fire is kindled on the altar, and Gloom and Caradoc take their places to right and left of it, with Druids and Bards grouped behind them, filling the space immediately about the tree. Mona stands upon the rock to the right, directing all; Arth and Enya up stage to the left of the tree; and the whole space above and around filled with confused preparation. As the Bards take their place they raise the following chant, the tribesmen joining in and brandishing their torches and weapons in time to it as they hurry about:*)

CHORUS:

**I:**
Out of the dim dens
Under the mountains,
Forth from the forest,
Far from the fenlands—
Summon the swordsmen,
Waken the warriors,
Gather the Druids
To battle for Britain—
(Long swords for old Britain—)
Ruin to Rome!
(*Three men come in left, bearing armfuls of long naked swords, which they lay before the altar. Mona descends from the rock, sheathing her sword, and places herself before it. As she sings, together with the Druids and Bards about the tree, the second stanza of the chant, she raises each sword in both hands high above her head, passes it from right to left in a circle around the fire, and hands it to Gloom and Caradoc, who present it to a Bard or Druid kneeling to receive it. As each receives his weapon, he rises and rushes out through the crowd, waving it aloft.*)

**MONA, GLOOM, CARADOC AND THE PRIESTS:**

**II:**
By the soul in the flame,
By the death in the earth,
By the life in the air—
By the sound of the Name
That no mortal may bear,
Bringing ages to birth—
For the freedom denied us,
For the shame of the slave—
Give swords to the swordless,
Bright blades to the Bards,
White Death to the Druids—
To guard us, to guide us,
To slay and to save!
(*With the singing of the third stanza, the tribesmen and their women begin to rush out and away into the forest in savage disorder, by twos and threes, still singing. The stage darkens gradually, as the torches more and more*

are carried away; and by the end of the stanza, only the altar-fire flickers against the moonlight. Arth follows the Britains. Mona, Gloom, and Caradoc are still in their places by the altar; and a moment after Arth's exit, Gloom draws his own sword and starts after, motioning the others on; Caradoc follows; Mona, catching up her spear from beside the tree, follows in turn, pausing to turn with a triumphant gesture as she passes through the inner wall.)

**CHORUS:**

**III:**

God is grown hungry
Watching our weakness—
Hungry, beholding us
Frail and faint-hearted.
Slay we a sacrifice,
Therefore, to feed Him—
Rouse the ravens,
Waken the lean wolves,
Onward for Britain!
(Broad spears for Old Britain—)
Ruin to Rome!

(The flame on the altar dies down. Only Enya remains on the stage. She runs to the opening in the wall up stage and stands a moment looking after the others, while the torches disappear and the sound of the singing grows fainter. Presently she reels down stage, wringing her hands, and throws herself full length upon her face before the altar, not sobbing but lying still.)

**CHORUS:** (outside, more and more faintly, but not slower)

**IV:**

The sword, the defender,
She is holy and human,
She is white like a woman—
And shapely and slender;
Demanding a master
To wield her and bend her—
Aflame for the foeman
Athirst for the Roman—
(Heart's blood of the Roman—)
Red life and disaster—
Revenge, and surrender!

(The singing dies out in the distance. There remains only darkness and stillness, and the old woman lying prone before the altar. The fire on the altar flickers and goes out, and Enya stirs a little, then lies still. Far away in the forest, a wolf howls. Then a moment of utter silence. And then the Curtain falls slowly.)

*END OF ACT II*

# ■ ACT III

The scene represents a small plateau on the southern edge of the forest, fronting the Roman Town. On the stage left, the edge of the forest extends diagonally back so that the left upper corner of the scene is hidden in thick woods, sloping upward to the left. The edge of this mass of trees, irregular and diversified with bushes and fallen tree-trunks, indicates that the open space is a natural glade and not a clearing. To the rear is the irregularly concave brow of a declivity at first sharp and steep (as shown by tree-tops just beyond its edge) then gradually sloping away across a shallow valley of meadow-land a mile or so in width; and beyond, on the corresponding rise of ground across this valley, the Roman Town appears: its apparent height being five or six feet above the stage-level, so that it may easily be seen from all parts of the house. Beyond and on both sides, open rolling country extends to the horizon. On the stage right, a high and craggy mass of rocks extends out onto the stage, in the shape, roughly, of the corner of a square obliquely placed. The wooded top of this is only a few feet below the proscenium arch; from thence the rock descends in a cliff to about the height of a man, then breaks to the level in a mass of boulders and rubble. The cliff is more broken toward its lower end, more precipitous toward its upper; so that near the footlights it may be scaled. Above this cliff, and between it and the edge of the plateau, a broad pathway runs diagonally off to the right, sloping down the hillside, and evidently the way to the plain and so across to the Town. Near the plateau's edge and about on a line with the foot of the cliffs to the right, lies a large fallen tree; and on the edge of the forest on the left is a seamed and broken boulder, lying half-way up stage. The ground in the center is fairly level and smooth, grass-grown and sloping a little upward at the edges. The whole effect is that of the mouth of a shallow gorge, open to the southward (up stage) and enclosed on the other three sides between rocky and wooded hills. In general appearance it is by far the most spacious of the three sets; and the only one in which the eye travels back into the extreme distance. At the beginning of the act, these details are invisible, for the time is about half after three in the morning of the same night as Act II; the moon has set, and there is not yet any sign of daybreak; the stage is as dark as is effectively possible—just light enough for the main outlines of the scene and actions of the characters to appear. The Roman Town is visible only by the tiny lights of the battle-fires on the walls and the moving sparks of torches all about, whose reflection glows dull red in the sky above it. And the roar of the battle is heard only as a faint, almost inaudible murmur.

Day breaks very gradually during the act; and the end takes place in brilliant sunlight, the brightest lighting of the entire play.

As the Curtain rises, the stage is empty and dark. It is at once apparent that the scene is the mouth of a hill-gorge ending in a steep slope with a valley and more hills opposite. But no more is to be seen and the eye is led from darkness to the Roman Town in the distance, aglow with the dim light of its own battle. Presently Nial and Enya come through the trees on the left. Nial crosses to the foot of the rocks; Enya goes up left to the edge of the slope.

**NIAL:** (as he enters) Here we can see, Mother.

**ENYA:** The town still holds—
I had hoped that red sky showed it all in flames . . .
And still no sign!
(She turns and gazes a moment up over the cliffs to the right, as if for a signal.)

**NIAL:** What are those tiny lights,
Gleaming like fireflies in the darkness there?
(Pointing toward the Town.)

**ENYA:** Torches.
How still the forest is—no wind,
Yet the trees move as if a storm were near . . .
(In the pause, the noise of distant battle is just audible.)
And listen! . . a dull murmur, like the sea . . .
(She moves back to the edge, and stands rigid with suspense.)
Fire . . . and a sound of battle.
Surely they
Have had full time by this . . . . !
How goes the night?

**NIAL:** (seated, unconcernedly, at the foot of the rocks) Not long now. In an hour it will be dawn.

**ENYA:** (moving about the stage uncontrollably, with wild gestures) Many there be shall never see that dawn—
God send our own be not among them . . . Yonder
Beneath that red glow, swords are swung, and shouts
Go up with groanings, and blood smokes and shines
In the flare of the battle-fires, and strong men fall,
And the press wavers—
(The black bulk of a raven flaps out of the forest and close over her head. She starts and cringes away, terrified, as the creature turns and flies straight toward the Town, growing smaller against the sky.)
—What was that?

**NIAL:** (quite unmoved) A raven—
Yet—it is strange:
(He rises, puzzled, and moves a little up stage, looking after it.)
He should not fly so soon,
Before the sun is risen . . .
Look! He flies
Southward, against the light . . . How red it is!—
As if all the battle had one angry soul . . .
(Casually, as he turns away; a little surprised that Enya pays no attention.)
Mother, the Little People are all gone
Under the hills. Our war drove them away;
They cannot live where there is hating.
(He seats himself as before. In the forest behind Enya a wolf howls, answered by another far away across the plain. She shrinks nervously toward Nial.)

**ENYA:** Hush!—
Listen . . . that sound there in the forest . . .

**NIAL:** (unconcerned, as before)
Wolves . . .
(without rising)
Yet—it is strange! They should not cry so late,
After the setting of the moon.

**ENYA:** (hysterically) And still,
No tidings! Can the dogs hold out so long,
Asleep, surprised, outnumbered . . .
Will the fight
Never be done . . . ?
How many, how many of us
Whose hearts are struggling yonder
watch and yearn
Through the void, endless hush, feeling their faith
Bleed away drop by drop and hour by hour!
Oh, I have waited many nights like this,
While flesh I bore spilled blood that came of me,
And the dawn brought the dead home!
(She drops, exhausted, at the foot of the boulder, to the left. The first suggestion of dawn appears: not light but a tinge of green in the blackness of the shadows, and a slight pallor of the sky. The red light fades above the battle, and at intervals the voices of birds are heard in the silences.)

NIAL: This is more
Than I can under-
stand . . . Somehow it seems
I should be wiser, seeing so much
pain . . .
(*He notices the change in the sky,
and tries to interest her in that.*)
Look! The light darkens.
(*Enya starts to her feet and
crosses up center, straining her
eyes across the dusk.*)
The stars fade. The dawn
Is coming . . .
There a bird wakes—Mother, hark!

ENYA: And still no tidings! Oh, if
Gloom were but here!
(*There is a crash in the brushwood down the path. A moment
later, a man appears, running
wildly up the slope—not Gloom,
but a skin-clad Briton breathless,
disheveled, and bloody. Enya
rushes across to him and catches
at his arm.*)
Oh, what news of the battle? What
news—
(*The man flings himself free without a word, and crosses down left,
at a staggering run. Then seeing
Nial, he turns back, and scram-
bles up the rocks out of sight.*)

NIAL: Fear!
His terror trails behind him like a
smoke—
He is mad-afraid.

ENYA: Woe! Woe!
(*An older man, wounded, draws
himself up the path. She stops
him.*)
What tidings? How
Went the battle?
(*She clutches at his arm.*)

THE OLD MAN: (*breathlessly*)
Nay, I know not—Let me go—
We were betrayed—They had been
warned of us—
The fight goes on still—Let me
pass—

ENYA: (*clinging to him*) Tell me,
What of Gloom? What of Arth?

THE OLD MAN: I know not—
dead,
Most like—they were among the
foremost—

ENYA: Mona,
The Queen, tell me of her—?

THE OLD MAN: I saw her last
Mounting a ladder, sword in hand,
her hair
Blown backward in the torchlight—
Let me go.
Woman!—I have told all—
(*He breaks from her, and stumbles away into the forest, up left.
All through the ensuing scene,
scattered fugitives, men mostly,
now and then a woman, scramble
up the path, and hurry across and
away either into the forest or up
the rocks down right. In the
pauses are heard the voices of
awakening birds. Very slowly the
sky pales to a dull flat gray, like
the skin of a corpse; and the
darkness fades into what is more
a sickly weakening of night than
any positive daybreak. It is light
enough to distinguish facial expression, but there is no sign yet of
sunrise, and the distance is still
blank and misty. The greenish
tinge of the light makes faces and
foliage look unnaturally colorless.*)

NIAL: It cannot be!
Gloom says, God promised us the
victory!

ENYA: Lost . . ! Lost . . !
(*Gloom stumbles in among the
fugitives, half dragging, half carrying Mona. He can use only his
left arm, for his right is broken
near the shoulder, and he is
wounded in the side. As he reaches
the clear space, he releases Mona,
who sinks dizzily upon the fallen
tree up right, her head droops forward almost between her knees,
and her arms reach limply outward and downward, the left
against her left knee, the right
hand, still grasping her sword, almost touching the ground: so that
the lines of her arms and of her
hair falling straight down over
her face, suggest the Sign of the
Name. Her scabbard is gone, her
byrny dented and broken and her
white robe stained with blood;
but she is unwounded. Gloom totters a pace or two down stage and
reels back against a sapling, his
right arm hanging useless and his
left hand pressed to his side. Enya
runs to him and clings about his
neck.*)

ENYA: Gloom!

GLOOM: (*flinging her savagely
away*) Off! . . . My arm!—
Hast thou no eyes? Fool!

ENYA: (*lamenting, not protesting*) Oh, my son, my son!

GLOOM: Broken. Let be. It is all
over.

ENYA: Arth—
Thy father?—

GLOOM: Dead.

ENYA: (*softly*) I knew it . . .

GLOOM: They were awake,
Under arms, waiting for us—their
garrison
Swelled to an army, sentries on the
plain,
Fires ready on the walls—what
could we do?
One traitor is more strong than
many swords—
Our Gwynn did his work well!

ENYA: (*trying, with grotesque
tenderness, to quiet him and lead
him away*) Gloom, thou art hurt—
Come thou home—let thy mother
bind thy wounds—
Nay, lean on me . . .

GLOOM: (*pushing her away, but
more gently than before*) Let be. I
have my death
Already—

ENYA: (*hysterical again*) All that
remained to me—my son,
My husband that was young with
me—

GLOOM: (*with a savage gesture*)
Be still!
Thou wilt have time enough for
wailing.
(*Mona raises herself wearily to a
sitting position, pushing back her
hair, and looking dully and steadily before her. Her grief is sharply
contrasted with Enya's hysterical
and noisy lamentation. It is the
quiet, stony pathos of a great nature crushed beyond the relief of
complaint: she seems rather to
wonder than to regret. Her manner is like the manner with which
she received the revelation of her
mission in Act I: a stroke of something too sudden and too great for
her to understand.*)

MONA: Gloom,
Why didst thou bring me here? I
might have died
Yonder, and not known.

GLOOM: Any place will serve
To die in.

MONA: (*rising, and coming
down slowly between Enya and
Gloom*) They all trusted me—the
women
Waiting for love, and the sweet-
eyed young men,
The mothers, and the merry children—all
Holding by me to make them happier—
And I . . . I trusted God.

GLOOM: Thou didst not well:
God smiles alone in the white
stillness, calm
Beyond all worlds, over all years,
beholding
All pain, remembering all death unmoved.
He mocks us with a future half
foreknown.

MONA: God forgive me!

GLOOM: (*sourly*) Bah!
Let us be honest! What has God to
do?—
I sicken at all these holy melancho-
lies—
Thou hadst a vanity, and a girl's
dream
Of huge deeds and high services;
for me,
I had a lust for lordship. I hated
Rome,
And hated more that sweet boy-lov-
er of thine—
His delicate heats and spirit-per-
fumes; then,
Too, I loved thy bright body. Good!
We strove,
As others do, after our own de-
sire—
We failed. Well, we shall die.

MONA: (*forcing herself still to believe in him*) This is thy pain
Speaking . . . It is not like thyself—

ENYA: Gloom, Gloom,
Thou art a priest!—

GLOOM: I *was*. I am a man
Now. Presently I shall be
less . . .
What, ashamed
At a soul's nakedness? We dress ourselves
In decencies of motive day by day,
Till our own hearts hide from us,
and we march
On proudly, leading God. Oh, we
believe
Our high words while we speak
them! No desire
for praise in Mona, nor in me for
her—
All was for Britain!
(*He sinks back, exhausted, on the
rocks to the right, overcome by his
own bitter violence and his increasing weakness. Enya rushes
to him and raises his head. Mona,
sickened by his blasphemy and
groping in her own conscience,
stands motionless down center.
Nial, as always utterly unconscious in the presence of emotion,
crosses up left, looking up into the
trees and out across the valley.
The tops of the distant hills are
touched with the first slant of sunlight, and the sky tinges with rose
and saffron toward the southeast.
On the stage, under the shade of
the cliffs, there is plenty of light to
see by, but the shadows are still
purplish, and the colors vague
and dull; there is no green in the
foliage yet, nor blue in the sky.*)

NIAL: Mona, see—the dawn
Is coming! All the birds waken.
(*Gloom groans and stirs. Mona
turns to Enya, a new horror of
self-distrust in her eyes.*)

MONA: Mother,
What if he spoke truth! What if I did
all
For myself, not for Britain . . .

ENYA: Child, who doubts thee?
He knew not what he said.

MONA: He is a Bard . . .
It was the voice of God that spoke
in him.
(*The sword clasped across her
breast.*)
I knew Gwynn faithless—why did I
save him?
His life meant death to Britain; but I
heard
My own blind heart crying for him.
God knows
There was a moment when I gave

up all—
All I was given life for, my whole use,
Britain, and many hopes, and my great dream—
Only to feel the glory of his arms
Around me in the night, only to see
His eyes between me and the stars, only
To know I could not struggle!

NIAL: Is it wrong
To love, then?

MONA: (*to herself, softly*)
One whose face I could not see,
Who strove to snatch away my sword . . .
(*Gwynn enters hurriedly down left in his Roman dress. At sight of them he pauses astonished.*)

GWYNN: Mona!—The fight is done, then.
—Art thou safe,
Unharmed . . . ?

GLOOM: What dost thou here, traitor?

GWYNN: (*too much concerned with what is to be done to grow excited on his own account: speaking rapidly.*) My guards
Fled with the rest . . . I am no traitor; all
This night's blood, if ye had but listened to me,
I had saved. Give thanks to God! I am in time
Even now to save your own.

GLOOM: I will yet spoil
Thy triumph!—Give me that sword—
(*He staggers forward, trying to take the sword from Mona; but his strength fails in spite of fury, and he falls back, half fainting. Enya and Nial support him. Mona turns upon Gwynn in a rage of scorn.*)

MONA: Roman, begone
Among thy kindred!—if perchance, even there
Among that carrion brood, any endure
Thy kinship unashamed! *Thou* save us!—who
Would owe thee life? Look on thyself! False friend,
False Bard, false lover. Thou hast done thy work—
Leave it! God sickens to hear thee speak his name,
And men take shame of thy humanity—
Why dost thou stand there breeding new lies? Go—
Leave us clean air to die in!

GWYNN: (*facing her*) Be silent now . . . !
There is more shame to thee saying these things
Than me to hear them. Look at me . . . Is this
Falsehood? If there were any reason in thy rage,
Could I endure to hear it—and from thee?

Answer me . . .
(*Their eyes fight; but he knows, and she is only certain. Hers fall first. Gwynn goes on slowly and emphatically.*)
Hear one word now that clears all:
The Governor of Britain is my own father—
I am his son—dost thou hear?
(*None of them believes. Mona, seeing instantly all that it would mean, sees also how clever a lie it might be; and her faith in Gwynn has been hurt to death. Enya doubts merely because it fits in with everything so perfectly—a weak mind's instinctive suspicion of finality. Gloom receives it with a sour howl of derision.*)

GLOOM: Only the son
Of the Governor? Only the son? Tell the whole truth! Say
The Governor himself—the Emperor
Come from Rome—hail, Caesar!

ENYA: Nay, it may be . . .

MONA: (*wearily, turning away from him*) Gwynn, thou hast lied already many times—
There is no need of other words.

GWYNN: My word
Speaks for Rome. Giving it for peace, I bind
The legions. Binding me, ye loosed them. Come
With me now to my father, make an end
Of this rebellion ere yet more be slain;
Give peace to Britain, and bind up her wounds.

MONA: (*monotonously*) The blood of all our slain cries out on thee,
The tears of all our women fall on thee,
The groans of all our captives answer thee,
Till thy life answer for their lives undone!
(*She stands looking blindly into space, the sword clasped to her breast, hearing nothing.*)

GWYNN: For their sake, wait no longer! Thou shalt learn
If I speak truth—

NIAL: I cannot understand
All this of truths and traitors; but I know
That Gwynn is good: I know that!

ENYA: It may be . . .
It may be . . .

GLOOM: Nay, go kiss thy lover, girl!
(*Mona does not seem to hear; and her next three lines are spoken as to herself. That which is rising up in her is the death of Gwynn; but the others, each from his own point of view, mistake it for hesitation.*)

GWYNN: Mona . . . come!

MONA: —One whose face I could not see . . .

GWYNN: Many shall die while we delay—Think not
Of me; save thine own people!

MONA: —One who strove
To snatch away my sword . . .

NIAL: There is a mist
About thy face, Gwynn—

MONA: —Therefore I smote . . .

GWYNN: Nay, then,
I dare not tarry longer, even for thee—
Guard her, Nial.
(*He turns away up stage, toward the path. Mona turns, and takes a step toward him, speaking mechanically in a dry voice: her tone and gesture are a ghastly parody of surrender.*)

MONA: Gwynn . . . I am very weary . . .

NIAL: (*springing forward, frightened for the first time in his life*)
Mona . . . !
Great God! . . thy shadow!
(*Gwynn turns back to her eagerly, and takes her in his arms. Her head droops forward upon his shoulder, and her left arm slips around his neck; her right hand, holding the sword, hangs at her side. The pose is precisely the same as when Gwynn was wounded ominously in Act I.*)

GWYNN: Love, now all is done
And we may yet save all!
(*She holds him close an instant, then suddenly brings the sword up with her free hand, and drives it into his throat. He falls limp in her arms, dying.*)

ENYA: What hast thou done—
O Child, what hast thou done—!
(*The body of Gwynn slips from Mona's hold, and falls at her feet, just below the rock on the left. She stands over him with the sword.*)

MONA: I have proved myself.
There lies my sacrifice.

NIAL: For evermore,
Thou shalt not see his face . . .

GWYNN: Mona . . . my father . . .
(*A slight struggle, and he is dead. There is a pause, through which are heard the joyous noises of the forest. The sunlight floods the valley, gleaming white upon the Roman Town, and strikes through the tree-tops from right to left. The stage itself is still in shadow, from the cliffs. Gloom gets to his feet, and totters over to where Mona stands motionless above the body, gazing into space.*)

GLOOM: Nay,
Now I believe all! . . . Let me look upon him . . .
At least, *he* cannot triumph over me . . . !
(*He turns back to his place, feebly.*)

NIAL: He cannot answer.

ENYA: Let him be; by this
He has paid all.

GLOOM: (*turning upon her, as he is about to sink upon the rocks to the right, with a last outburst of logical anger*) Paid? By his death? Aye, so—
Then for what evil must I pay with mine?
How should we two deserve alike, whose hearts
Opposed like East and West? The shame of one
Honors the other—See now our reward:
Both dead, both brought to shame, both overthrown—
Behold, O God, thy justice!
(*He raises his arms above his head in a furious gesture that travesties the Sign of the Name, reels, and falls back fainting upon the rocks. Mona neither sees nor hears. As Enya is bending over Gloom, Nial comes down a little, looking curiously at a point in the air seven or eight feet above the body of Gwynn.*)

NIAL: Mother, look—
Is Gwynn quite dead? He is not far away . . .

ENYA: (*turns, startled and glances at the body, then speaks with the irritation of fright*) Nial, have I not seen death enough to know—?
He is mere earth, I tell thee—

NIAL: Look—his shadow
Shines in the air above him, like a mist
Over the moon . . . See, close above us—there—
Bound to his body with a golden chain,
And shimmering like the wind above a fire—
He seems to listen and to wait . . .
(*The others, tense with horror, are gazing where he points, but seeing nothing. There is a short pause.*)
(*The body of Gwynn lies just below the rock on the left, Mona standing above and a little to left of it. Nial is up center, Gloom lying back against the rocks on the right, and Enya below and further to the right. In the hush, the rhythm of the Roman march, heard in Act II, begins to be heard: at first very softly, then gradually louder and nearer.*)

MONA: A murmur of many voices, like a storm
Over the sea . . .

ENYA: (*crossing up center, and looking over the cliff*) The legions!

MONA: —And a sound
Of men marching to battle, Romans marching
Steadily to battle.
(*She moves to the center of the stage, looking up left, to the head of the path. Nial goes up left. Gloom lies still upon the rocks. The Roman music grows louder and louder.*)

GLOOM: Save yourselves—
There is yet time. I wait here.

ENYA: Tell me, what
Have we to save?

NIAL: There is a cloud over the moon . . .
Cloud and storm.

MONA: Forest and cloud and a murmuring of the sea . . .
Surely my dreams remember . . .
(*The sunlight, which has darkened while she spoke, clears; and the light striking over the cliffs, fills the whole stage with a blaze of direct sunlight.*)

ENYA: (*with Mona and Nial*) I can see them
Winding up the long pathway from the plain,
A multitude of spears. Welcome, wolves!
(*A Briton, with an arrow through him, runs up the path, stumbles down right, and falls dead at the foot of the rocks, just above the curtain.*)

GLOOM: Welcome, wolves!
(*The stage fills with Roman Soldiers, entering by the path on the right. Most of them are legionaries in their panoply; a few archers. Gloom and Nial are surrounded and made prisoners at once. Enya retreats down right, as The Soldiers press forward. Mona remains left center. Among the last, The Governor enters, and steps up right. Gwynn's body, from where he stands, is hidden by the boulder. The Soldiers pay no attention to it; a corpse more or less does not concern them.*)

MONA: (*as the soldiers march in*) Now,
The end comes . . .

THE GOVERNOR: Guard that woman!
(*Mona is surrounded by soldiers. He looks from her to the others.*)
Where is he
Whom ye call Gwynn?

NIAL: Yonder—above himself . . .

GLOOM: (*relishingly*) There is a Roman spy here. He is dead.

THE GOVERNOR: Dead!—
(*Coming down center, he sees the body. The Soldiers turn the face upward. He stands looking.*)

GLOOM: Past rewarding!

THE GOVERNOR: It is he . . .
(*savagely*)
Who hath done
This thing?

MONA: It was I.

THE GOVERNOR: Thou! A woman . . .

MONA: One
That might have been a woman.

THE GOVERNOR: (*softly*) Be thou sure
Of paying for this blood . . .

GLOOM: Since *he* has paid,
What matter? He betrayed us. He is dead.
Thou hast thy triumph. Eat it.

THE GOVERNOR: (*with sudden fierceness*) Dogs, ye have slain
Your own last hope of mercy—the one soul
Roman-born that had care for you. These years
He hath made your peace with Rome, won back for you
Old liberties, given you the strength to dream
Of new conspiracy! But for his faith,
I should have broken you between my hands
In the beginning. Day by day, I spared
The sword, watching your fools' rebellion boil
Unpunished. He defended you; he died
Striving to save your miserable lives
From your own folly! I have said.
(*His grief breaking through his anger.*)
My son
My son . . . !

MONA: (*slowly, in a dry voice*)
Thy son!—Who art thou?
(*The Governor, still gazing at Gwynn's face and fighting for self-control, pays no heed; it is The Soldiers who answer in a fierce and gathering murmur.*)

THE SOLDIERS: Governor
Of Britain—Governor and lord for Rome!

ENYA: O Child, what hast thou done?

THE GOVERNOR: She shall have time
To learn—
(*A soldier gives him the sword, which has been taken from Mona. He takes it mechanically, and stands still gazing at Gwynn's body.*)

MONA: (*to herself*) So that was God's voice, after all!
That weakness, that strange fear of Gwynn's glad eyes,
That warm pain in my blood answering him,
That little, foolish whisper in my heart
All night long, that I put away from me,
Smothering it with huge dreams! That was all
God asked of me—only to drink my joy,
Only to be a woman, only to cease
From struggling, rest so, and be drowsy-glad
Like a child comforted! It was too slight
A service for great ends—too small, too sweet—
Any one could have done so much!
(*With gradually increasing passion, turning to the others.*)
Ah, Gloom!
And thou, Mother, in dream-lore deeply wise—
Thou who hast known a child's lips on thy breast
And life beginning in the dark
. . . and thou,
Nial, whose blind heart makes our wisdom vain—
Could ye not tell me how great dreams pass by
As a storm blows down the wind, while beauty grows
Day by day out of a thousand littlenesses,
As the rain swells the flood and fills the sea,
Till all things take one answer?—
(*Coming out of her inspiration—more quietly, awakening to the realities about her.*)
I might have died
Yonder, and not known.—See, how Earth holds up
Her freshness to the summer, and the light
Laughs over living green, and the birds are glad,
And the sweet blossoms brighten in the sun,
And all the bitter beauty of the day
Makes merry with my sorrow—And I go
To walk alive among dead hours, and see
Pitiless faces and the mirth of men
Whose eyes are evil, and be fawned upon
By strange hands . . . for I cannot even keep
My faith to him that died because of me,
Nor in a clean death lay my body down
Beside his body . . . I must bear my time,
Having done no good thing, remembering all—

And there will be so many other days,
So many other days . . .
(*She turns from Gwynn to The Governor, quietly.*)
Give me the sword—
It is mine. . . .
(*Misunderstanding her purpose, he steps back, motioning to The Soldiers to restrain her. She looks him in the face almost with a smile.*)
Dost thou think I can still fear?
I loved him . . . and I killed him . . .
Bear with me
A little.
(*She takes the sword, and kneels down by Gwynn's body, laying it across his breast.*)
Take the sword now. It is thine.
Thou hast done well for Britain.
For myself,
I have done only what I must have done,
Being myself, holding by mine own sight
And mine own blindness. I have sought beyond
Love, and above beauty, turning away
From God, to point what way the world should go,
Scorning my life because I found it fair,
Following the white fire of endeavor down
Under the last horizon, where stars fail
And the sea takes me, and the night ends all,
And the brave deeds I was too brave to do
Slumber, forgotten . . .
(*She lays her hands upon Gwynn's, bending over him.*)
Love, I could not be
A woman, loved and loving, could not bear
Motherhood and the wise ordinary joys
Of day by day . . . All that I had to give
I gave thee . . . I have known thy heart . . . Farewell.
(*She bends down and kisses him on the forehead.*)
Forgive
(*She rises, and stands among The Soldiers.*)
Do your will now.
(*They bind her hands.*)
I have had dreams—
Only great dreams . . .
A woman would have won.

# La Serva Padrona (1733)

## The Maid-Mistress

MUSIC BY GIOVANNI BATTISTA PERGOLESI ▪ LIBRETTO BY GENNARO ANTONIO FEDERICO

This intermezzo in two parts, set to a libretto by Gennaro Antonio Federico, was first performed between acts of Pergolesi's opera Il Prigionier Superbo. The premiere took place at the Teatro San Bartolomeo in Naples on August 28, 1733. The story concerns Uberto, an old bachelor whose household is managed by his maid, Serpina. He is tired of giving in to her every whim, and he decides to find a wife. He sends his servant, Vespone, off to search for a woman who will be submissive, never minding whether she is beautiful or ugly. Serpina knows very well how much Uberto secretly cares for her and decides that she will be the one to marry him. She announces that she plans to marry a man named Captain Tempesta and gives a description of this man to Uberto. But she draws such a terrifying picture of this man that Uberto, in his concern for her welfare, asks to meet him. Vespone, who is encouraging her in this matter, disguises himself as Captain Tempesta and presents himself to Uberto. Serpina then takes Uberto aside and tells him that Tempesta will marry her only if the old man pays him a stupendous dowry. If Uberto refuses, the captain will insist that Uberto himself marry her. Uberto happily agrees to the second suggestion, making Serpina the mistress of the house rather than a mere servant.

---

*Camera.*

*Uberto non interamente vestito, e Vespone di lui servo, poi Serpina.*

**UBERTO:** Aspettare e non venire,
Stare a letto e non dormire,
Ben servire e non gradire,
Son tre cose da morire,
Questa è per me disgrazia,
Son tre ore che aspetto,
E la mia serva
Portarmi il cioccolatte non fa grazia,
Ed io d'uscire ho fretta.
A flemma benedetta!
Or si, che vedo
Che per esser sì buono con costei,
La causa son di tutti i mali miei.
(*Chiama Serpina vicino alla scena.*)
Serpina . . .
Vien domani.
(*A Vespone.*)
E tu altro che fai?
A che qui te ne stai
Come un balocco?
Come? che dici? eh sciocco!
Vanne, rompiti presto il collo,
Sollecita;
Vedi che fa, Gran fatto!
Io m'ho cresciuta
Questa serva piccina,
L'ho fatta di carezze,
L'ho tenuta come mia figlia fosse!
Or elle ha preso perciò
Tanta arroganza,
Fatta è sì superbona
Che alfin di serva diverrà padrona.
Ma bisogna risolvermi in buon'ora . . .
E quest altro babbio ci è morto ancora.

*A Room.*

*Uberto, not fully dressed, and Vespone, his servant. Then Serpina.*

**UBERTO:** To wait and not to come,
To be in bed and not to sleep,
To serve well and not to please,
Are enough to make one die.
It is a disgrace to me.
I wait three hours
And my servant
Does not deign to bring my chocolate,
And I am in a hurry to go out.
O blessed patience
Now I know
That my being so good to her
Is the cause of all my troubles.
(*Calls Serpina near the stage.*)
Serpina—
She's coming tomorrow.
(*To Vespone.*)
And what are you doing?
Why are you standing here
Like a ninny?
How? What do you have to say?
Fool!
Go, break your neck,
Make haste;
See what she's doing. Fine work!
I have brought up
This little servant,
Have caressed her,
Have kept her as if she were my daughter!
But she has on that account
Assumed such arrogance,
Has become so haughty,
That at last the servant will become a mistress.
But I must soon make up my mind—
And that other fool is as good as dead, too.
Have you finished?

**SERPINA:** (*a Vespone*). L'hai finita?
Ho bisogno che tu mi sgridi?
E pure
Io non sto comoda, ti dissi.

**UBERTO:** Brava!

**SERPINA:** (*a Vespone*). E torna!
Se il padrone ha fretta, non l'ho
Il sai?

**UBERTO:** Bravissima.

**SERPINA:** (*a Vespone*). Di nuovo!
Oh tu da senno
Vai stuzzicando la pazienza mia,
E vuoi che un par dischiaffi alfin!
(*Batte Vespone*).

**UBERTO:** Olà, dove si stà? olà, Serpina!
Non ti vuoi fermare?

**SERPINA:** Lasciatemi insegnare
La creanza a quel birbo.

**UBERTO:** Ma in presenza del padrome?

**SERPINA:** Adunque
Perch'io son serva,
Ho da esser sopraffatta,
Ho da esser maltrattata? No signor
Voglio esser rispettata,
Voglio esser riverita
Come fossi padrona, arcipadrona
Padronissima.

**UBERTO:** Che diavol ha
Vossignoria illustrissima?
Sentiamo, che fu?

**SERPINA:** Cotesto impertinente . . .

**UBERTO:** (*accennando a Vespone*.) Questo? tu . . .

**SERPINA:** Venne a me . . .

**SERPINA:** (*to Vespone*). Must you scold me?
And yet you said
I am not useful.

**UBERTO:** Bravo!

**SERPINA:** (*to Vespone*). Come back!
Do you know it?
I'm not in a hurry even if the master is.

**UBERTO:** Bravo!

**SERPINA:** (*to Vespone*). Again!
You really vex me to the end of my patience.
You must want me to box your ears.
(*Hits Vespone.*)

**UBERTO:** Stop, what's the matter with you? Stop, Serpina!
Won't you ever stop?

**SERPINA:** Let me teach that rascal manners.

**UBERTO:** But in the master's presence?

**SERPINA:** Then,
Because I am a servant,
Must I be overburdened;
Must I be maltreated? No, sir.
I want to be respected,
I want to be revered,
As if I were mistress, head mistress,
The highest of mistresses.

**UBERTO:** What in the devil is the matter with you,
Your Excellence?
Let's hear, what was the trouble?

**SERPINA:** That impertinent fellow . . .

**UBERTO:** (*pointing at Vespone.*) He who? You!

**SERPINA:** Come to me—

UBERTO: Questo, t'ho detto?

SERPINA: E con modi si impro-
pri . . .

UBERTO: (a Vespone). Questo . . . Che tu sii maledetto.

SERPINA: Ma me la pagherai.

UBERTO: Io costui t'inviai . . .

SERPINA: Ed a che fare?

UBERTO: A che far?
Non ti ho chiesto il cioccolatte, io?

SERPINA: Ben, e per questo?

UBERTO: E m'ha da uscir l'anima
Aspettando che mi si porti?

SERPINA: E quando
Voi prenderlo dovete?

UBERTO: Adesso. Quando?

SERPINA: E vi par ora questa?
È tempo ormai di dover desinare.

UBERTO: Adunque?

SERPINA: Adunque?
Io già nol preparai.
Voi di men ne farete, pardon mio
bello,
E ve ne cheterete.

UBERTO: Vespone, ora che ho pre-
so il cioccolatte già,
Dimmi: buon pro vi faccia e sanità.
(Vespone ride.)

SERPINA: Di che ride quell'asino?

UBERTO: Di me,
Che ho più flemma d'una bestia.
Ma io bestia non sarò,
Più flemma non avrò,
Il giogo scuoterò,
E quel che non ho fatto alfin farò!
(A Serpina.)
Sempre in contrasti
Con te si stà.
E qua e là,
E su e giù,
E sì e nò.
Or questo basti,
Finir si può.
(A Vespone.)
Ma che ti pare?
Ho io a crepare?
Signor mio no.
(A Serpina.)
Però dovrai
Per sempre piangere
La tua disgrazia,
E allor dirai
Che ben ti stà.
(A Vespone.)
Che dici tu?
Non è così?
Ah! . . . che! . . . no! . . .
Ma così va!
Sempre in contrasti, ecc.

SERPINA: In somma delle somme
Per attender al vostro bene
Io mal ne ho da ricevere?

UBERTO: He, he said?

SERPINA: And in such an improper
way—

UBERTO: (to Vespone). He
who . . . Let there be curses on
you.

SERPINA: But he'll pay me for it.

UBERTO: I sent him to you—

SERPINA: What for?

UBERTO: What for?
Didn't I ask you for chocolate?

SERPINA: Well, and for this?

UBERTO: And must I die of impatience
Till you bring it to me?

SERPINA: And when
Must you take it?

UBERTO: Now. When?

SERPINA: And do you think now's
the time?
It's time to dine.

UBERTO: Then?

SERPINA: Then?
I'll not prepare it.
You can do without it, dear sir,
And you'll keep still about it, too.

UBERTO: Vespone, now that I have
already taken my chocolate,
Tell me: may you have health and
happiness.
(Vespone laughs.)

SERPINA: What is the fool laughing at?

UBERTO: At me,
Who has more patience than a
beast;
But I'll not be a beast,
I'll not be patient,
I'll shake off the yoke,
And I'll do what I have never done
before!
(To Serpina.)
I am ever quarrelling
With you
And here and there,
And up and down,
And yes and no.
Now it's enough.
Now it must end.
(To Vespone.)
But what do you think?
Must I die?
No, my sir, no.
(To Serpina.)
But you
Ought always weep
At your disgrace,
And then you'll say
That you're well off here.
(To Vespone.)
What do you say?
It is not so?
Ah! no!
But so goes it,
Ever quarrelling, etc.

SERPINA: In short,
Must I be insulted for waiting upon
you?

UBERTO: (a Vespone). Poveretta!
la senti?

SERPINA: Per aver di voi cura, io,
sventurata,
Debbo esser maltrattata?

UBERTO: Ma questo non va bene.

SERPINA: Burlate, sì!

UBERTO: Ma questo non conviene.

SERPINA: E pur?
Qualche rimorso aver dovreste
Di farmi e dirmi ciò che dite e fate.

UBERTO: Così è,
Da dottoressa voi parlate.

SERPINA: Voi mi state sui scherzi,
Ed io m'arrabbio.

UBERTO: Non v'arrabbiate,
Capperi, ha ragione.
(A Vespone.)
Tu non sai che dir?
Va dentro, prendimi il capello,
La spada ed il bastone, chè voglio
uscir.

SERPINA: Mirate. Non ne fate una
buona,
E poi Serpina è
Di poco giudizio.

UBERTO: Ma lei
Che diamine vuol mai dai fatti
miei?

SERPINA: Non vo' che usciate
adesso,
Gli è mezzodì.
Dove volete andare?
Andatevi a spogliare.

UBERTO: E il gran malanno
Che mi faresti . . .

SERPINA: Oibò, non occorre altro.
Io vo' così,
Non uscirete,
Io l'uscio a chiave chiuderò.

UBERTO: Ma parmi questa
Massima impertinenza.

SERPINA: Eh sì suonate.

UBERTO: Serpina,
Il sai, che rotta m'hai la testa?

SERPINA: Stizzoso, mio stizzoso,
Voi fate il borioso.
Ma non vi può giovare,
Bisogna al mio divieto
Star cheto, e non parlare.
Z . . . Serpina vuol così.
Cred'io che m'intendete,
Da che mi conoscete
Son molti e molti dì.
Stizzoso, mio stizzoso, ecc.

UBERTO: Benissimo.
(A Vespone.)
Ora al suo loco
Ogni cosa porrà vossignoria,
Chè la padrona mia
Vuol ch'io non esca.

UBERTO: (to Vespone). Poor
thing! Do you hear her?

SERPINA: For caring for you, unfortunate me,
Must I be maltreated?

UBERTO: But that is not right.

SERPINA: You are ridiculing me!

UBERTO: But that oughtn't to be
so.

SERPINA: And yet?
You must have some remorse,
For doing and telling me what you
have said and done.

UBERTO: You talk like a teacher.

SERPINA: You are making fun of
me,
And I grow furious.

UBERTO: Don't get angry,
She's right.
(To Vespone.) You don't know
what to say?
Go and get me my hat,
My sword and cane, for I want to go
out.

SERPINA: Look; you can't make
her good,
And besides, Serpina has little judgment.

UBERTO: But she,
Why in the devil does she interfere
with my business?

SERPINA: I don't want you to go
out now.
It is noon.
Where do you want to go?
Go and undress.

UBERTO: And the great wretchedness
You caused me—

SERPINA: Shame! That's all that
was wanting.
I want it so,
Do not go out,
I'll lock the door.

UBERTO: But this seems to me
The greatest impertinence.

SERPINA: Well, ring then.

UBERTO: Serpina,
Do you know you have made my
head split?

SERPINA: Irascible, you play the
proud one
But it can't help you any.
You must remain quiet
At my prohibition and not speak.
Serpina wants it so.
I believe you understand me,
For it is many, many days
That you know me.
Irascible, etc.

UBERTO: Very well.
(To Vespone.)
Did you understand?
Now you'll put everything
Back in its place,
For my mistress
Doesn't want me to go out.

|  |  |
|---|---|
| **SERPINA:** Così va bene. / Hai tu inteso? / (*A Vespone.*) / Andate, e non v'increasca. / (*Vespone vuol partire e poi si ferma.*) / Tu ti fermi? tu guardi? / Ti meravigli, e che vuol dir? | **SERPINA:** That's right. / (*To Vespone.*) / Go, and don't regret it. / (*Vespone wants to go and then stops.*) / You stop? You look? / You wonder what does it mean? |
| **UBERTO:** Si, fermati, guardami, / Meravigliati, / Fammi de' scherni, / Chiamami asinone, / Dammi anche un mascellone, / Ch'io cheto mi starò, / Anzi la man allor ti bacierò. / (*Uberto bacia la mano a Vespone.*) | **UBERTO:** Yes, stop, look at me. / Wonder, / Mock me, / Call me a donkey, / Give me a slap / So that I'll keep still / Or I'll kiss your hand. / (*Uberto kisses Vespone's hand.*) |
| **SERPINA:** Che fa . . . che fate? | **SERPINA:** What are you doing? |
| **UBERTO:** Scostati, malvagia, / Vattene insolentaccia, / In ogni conto vo' finirla. / Vespone, / In questo punto trovami una moglie, / E sia anche un'arpia, / A suo dispetto / Io mi voglio accasare. / Così non dovrò stare / A questa manigolda più soggetto. | **UBERTO:** Get away, you villain, / Go away, you insolent one. / I want to finish it at all cost. / Vespone, / Find me a wife this very moment, / And be she even a harpy, / In spite of her / I want to marry. / I must not remain / Thus governed by this rogue. |
| **SERPINA:** Oh! qui cade l'asino! / Casatevi, che fate ben; l'approvo. | **SERPINA:** Oh, the devil take him! / Marry and you do well; I approve of it. |
| **UBERTO:** L'approvate? / Manco mal, l'approvò, / Dunque io mi caserò. | **UBERTO:** You approve? / It only wanted your approval, / Therefore I'll marry. |
| **SERPINA:** E prenderete me? | **SERPINA:** And will you take me? |
| **UBERTO:** Te! | **UBERTO:** You? |
| **SERPINA:** Certo. | **SERPINA:** Certainly. |
| **UBERTO:** Affè. | **UBERTO:** Upon my faith. |
| **SERPINA:** Affè. | **SERPINA:** Upon my faith. |
| **UBERTO:** Io non so chi mi tien . . . / Dammi il bastone . . . / (*A Vespone.*) / Tanto ardir! | **UBERTO:** I don't know who holds me— / Give me a stick— / (*To Vespone*). Such impudence. |
| **SERPINA:** Oh! voi far e dir potrete / Che null'altra che me sposar dovrete. | **SERPINA:** Oh, you can say that / You must marry no one but me. |
| **UBERTO:** Vattene, figlia, mia. | **UBERTO:** Go, my daughter. |
| **SERPINA:** Voleste dir mia sposa. | **SERPINA:** You mean my wife. |
| **UBERTO:** O stelle! o sorte! / Questa è per me morte. | **UBERTO:** O stars! O fate! / This is death for me. |
| **SERPINA:** O morte o vita, / Così esser dee: / L'ho fisso nel pensiero. | **SERPINA:** Whether life or death, / Thus must it be: / I have it fixed in my mind. |
| **UBERTO:** Questo è un altro diavolo più nero. | **UBERTO:** Oh, she's a devil. |
| **UBERTO:** Lo conosco a quegli occhietti / Furbi, ladri, malignetti, / Che, sebben voi dite no, / Pur m'accennano di sì. | **SERPINA:** I know it by the little eyes, / Roguish, thievish, wicked, / Which, though you say no, / Really mean yes. |
| **UBERTO:** Signorina, v'ingannate, / Troppo in alto voi volate, / Gli occhi ed io vi dicon no, / Ed è un sogno questo, sì. | **UBERTO:** Young lady, you're mistaken. / You fly too high, / My eyes and I say no. / And this yes is but a dream. |
| **SERPINA:** Ma perchè? / Non son bella, / Graziosa / E spirotosa? / Su, mirate, / Leggiadria, / Ve' che brio, / Che maestà. | **SERPINA:** But why? / Am I not pretty, / Graceful, / And lovely? / Just look / What grace; / See what spirit, / What majesty. |
| **UBERTO:** (Ah! costei / Mi va tentando / Quanto val, che me la fa.) / Là, là, larà, là, là. | **UBERTO:** (Ah, she / Goes tempting me, / As much as she can, that I do it.) / Là, là, larà, là, là. |
| **SERPINA:** (Ei mi par / Che va calando.) / Via signore. | **SERPINA:** (It seems to me! / He's going to fall.) / Away, sir. |
| **UBERTO:** Eh! vanne via. | **UBERTO:** Ah, go away? |
| **SERPINA:** Risolvete. | **SERPINA:** Make up your mind. |
| **UBERTO:** Eh! matta sei. | **UBERTO:** You're mad. |
| **SERPINA:** Son per voi / Gli affetti miei / E dovrete sposar me. | **SERPINA:** My affections are for you, / And you must marry me. |
| **UBERTO:** Ah che imbroglio egli è per me! | **UBERTO:** Oh, what troubles I have! |
| *Camera.* / *Serpina e Vespone in abito da soldato, poi Uberto vestito per uscire.* | *Serpina, and Vespone (in soldier's uniform); then Uberto (dressed to go out).* |
| **SERPINA:** Or che fatto ti sei / Dalla mia parte, / Usa, Vespone, ogn'arte: / Se l'inganno ha il suo effetto; / Se del padrone io giungo ad esser sposa, / Tu da me chiedi, e avrai, / Di casa tu sarai / Il secondo padrone, io tel prometto. | **SERPINA:** Now that you have gone over / To my side, / Use all art, Vespone: / If deceit has an effect; / If I end by being the master's wife, / You ask of me and you shall have, / You'll be the second master, / I promise you. |
| **UBERTO:** Io crederei, che la mia serva adesso, / Anzi, per meglio dir, la mia padrona, / D'uscir di casa mi darà permesso. | **UBERTO:** I should believe that my servant, / Or rather, to say my mistress, / Will give me permission to go out. |
| **SERPINA:** Ecco, guardate: / Senza la mia licenza / Pur si volle vestir. | **SERPINA:** Look here; / Without my permission / You wanted to dress. |
| **UBERTO:** Or sì, che al sommo / Giunta è sua impertinenza. / Temeraria! / E di nozze richiedermi ebbe ardir. | **UBERTO:** Now her impertinence / Has reached the climax. / Rash one! / And she was bold enough to ask me in marriage. |
| **SERPINA:** (*a Vespone.*) / T'asconderai per ora in quella stanza. / E a suo tempo uscirai. | **SERPINA:** (*to Vespone.*) I'll hide you now in that room, / And you'll go out when it's time. |
| **UBERTO:** O qui sta ella. / Facciamo nostro dover. / Posso o non posso? / Vuole o non vuol la mia padrona bella? . . . | **UBERTO:** Now you stay here. / Let us to business. / May I or may I not? / Is my fair mistress willing, or not? |
| **SERPINA:** Eh, signor, già per me è finito il gioco, / E più tedio fra poco / Per me non sentirà. | **SERPINA:** Ah, sir, now all joking is over for me, / And soon you'll no longer be annoyed by me. |
| **UBERTO:** Cred'io che no. | **UBERTO:** I don't believe it. |
| **SERPINA:** Prenderà moglie già. | **SERPINA:** You'll take a wife. |
| **UBERTO:** Cred'io che sì, ma / Non prenderò te. | **UBERTO:** Yes, I will; but not you. |
| **SERPINA:** Cred'io che no. | **SERPINA:** I don't believe it. |

UBERTO: Oh! affatto così è.

SERPINA: Cred'io che sì:
Ma d'uopo è ancor ch'io pensi a' casi miei.

UBERTO: Pensaci, far lo dèi.

SERPINA: Io ci ho pensato.

UBERTO: E ben?

SERPINA: Per me un marito io m'ho trovato.

UBERTO: Buon pro vi faccia.
E lo trovaste a un tratto
Così già detto e fatto?

SERPINA: Più in un'ora venir suol che in cent'anni.

UBERTO: Alla buon'ora! Posso saper chi egli è?

SERPINA: L'è un militaire.

UBERTO: Ottimo affè. Come si fa chiamare?

SERPINA: Il capitan Tempesta.

UBERTO: Oh! brutto nome.

SERPINA: E al nome
Sono i fatti corrispondenti,
Egli è poco flemmatico.

UBERTO: Male.

SERPINA: Anzi è lunatico.

UBERTO: Peggio.

SERPINA: Va presto in collera.

UBERTO: Pessimo.

SERPINA: E quando poi è incollerito,
Fa ruina, scompigli,
Fracassi, un via, via.

UBERTO: Ci anderà mal la vostra signoria.

SERPINA: Perchè?

UBERTO: S'è lei così schiribizzosa meco,
Ed è serva: or pensa
Con lui essendo sposa.
Senza dubbio il capitan Tempesta
In collera andrà,
E lei di bastonate
Una tempesta avrà.

SERPINA: A questo poi Serpina penserà.

UBERTO: Me ne dispiacerebbe;
Alfin del bene io ti volli, e tu 'l sai.

SERPINA: Tanto obbligata.
Intanto attenda a conservarsi,
Goda colla sua sposa amata,
E di Serpina non si scordi affatto.

UBERTO: A te perdoni il ciel:
L'esser tu troppo boriosa,
Venir mi fe' a tal atto.

SERPINA: A Serpina
Penserete
Qualche volta.
In qualche dì,
E direte:
Ah! poverina,
Cara un tempo

---

UBERTO: Oh, but it's so.

SERPINA: Yes, I believe it.
But now I must think of my affairs.

UBERTO: Think of them, you must.

SERPINA: I have thought of them.

UBERTO: Well?

SERPINA: I have found a husband.

UBERTO: May you have good luck,
And did you find him
As quickly as you said it?

SERPINA: The sooner the better.

UBERTO: Well and good! May I know who he is?

SERPINA: He's a soldier.

UBERTO: That's fine. What's his name?

SERPINA: Captain Tempest.

UBERTO: What an ugly name.

SERPINA: And his other traits
Are as ugly as the name.
He is a little phlegmatic.

UBERTO: That's bad.

SERPINA: Or rather, he's a lunatic.

UBERTO: Still worse.

SERPINA: He gets angry very quickly.

UBERTO: That's dreadful.

SERPINA: And when he is angry
He ruins, he throws around,
He breaks without end.

UBERTO: You'll be having a wretched life.

SERPINA: Why?

UBERTO: If she is so tantalizing
When she's only my servant,
Imagine what'll happen when she's a wife.
Without doubt Captain Tempest
Will get angry
And there'll be a tempest
Of beatings.

SERPINA: Serpina'll think of this later.

UBERTO: To be displeased with it;
After I liked you so, and you know it.

SERPINA: I'm so obliged to you.
In the meantime take care of yourself,
Enjoy yourself with your beloved wife,
And don't forget Serpina.

UBERTO: May heaven forgive you:
For your having been too haughty,
You have driven me to such an act.

SERPINA: Think sometimes
Of Serpina.
Some day, sometimes
You will say,
She once was dear to me.
(It seems to me that gradually He begins to soften.)

---

Ella mi fu.
(Ei mi par che già pian piano
S'incomincia a intenerir.)
S'io poi fui
Impertinente,
Mi perdoni:
Malamente
Mi guidai:
Lo vedo, sì.
(Ei mi stringe per la mano, Meglio il fatto non può gir.)

UBERTO: (Ah! quanto mi sa male
Di tal risoluzione,
Ma n'ho colpa io.)

SERPINA: (Di' pur fra te che vuoi,
Che ha da ruiscir la cosa a modo mio.)

SERPINA: Orsù, non dubitare,
Che di te mai non mi saprò scordare.

SERPINA: Vuol vedere il mio sposo?

UBERTO: Sì, l'avrei caro.

SERPINA: Io mandero per lui.
Giù in strada ei si trattiene.

UBERTO: Va.

SERPINA: Con licenza.
(Serpina parte.)

UBERTO: Or indovina chi sarà costui!
Forse la penitenza farà cosi
Di quanto ella ha fatto al padrone.
S'è ver, come mi dice, un tal marito
La terrà fra la terra ed il bastone.
Ah! poveretta lei!
Per altro io penserei . . .
Ma . . . Ella è serva . . .
Ma . . . il primo non saresti . . .
Dunque, la sposaresti? . . . basta
Eh no, non, non sia.
Su, pensieri ribaldi, andate via.
Piano, io me l'ho allevata:
So poi com'ella è nata . . .
Eh! che sei matto!
Piano di grazia . . .
Eh . . . non pensarci affatto . . .
Ma . . . Io ci ho passione,
E pur . . . Quella meschina . . .
Eh torna . . . Oh Dio! . . .
Eh siam da capo . . .
Oh! che confusione.
Son imbrogliato io già,
Ho un certo che nel core
Che dir per me non so
S'è amore, o s'è pietà.
Sento un che, poi mi dice:
Uberto, pensa a te.
Io sto fra il sì e il no,
Fra il voglio e fra nol voglio,
E sempre più m'imbroglio.
Ah! misero, infelice,
Che mai sarà di me!
(Qui entra Serpina con Vespone in abito come sopra.)

SERPINA: Favorisca, signor . . . passi.

UBERTO: (a Serpina). Padrona. È questi?

---

And if I was
Impertinent,
Pardon me:
I behaved
Wickedly:
And now I see it.
(He clasps my hand, It couldn't be any better.)

UBERTO: (Ah, how sorry I am
For such a resolution,
But I am not to blame.)

UBERTO: (Say what you want,
And things will come out as I wish.)

UBERTO: Come now, don't doubt
That I will not forget you.

SERPINA: Do you want to see my husband?

UBERTO: Yes, I'd like to.

SERPINA: I'll send for him.
He's waiting on the street.

UBERTO: Go.

SERPINA: With your permission.
(Serpina leaves.)

UBERTO: Now guess who it will be!
Perhaps she'll repent
For what she has done to her master.
If it is true, as she says, such a husband
Will keep her in mortal fear of the stick.
Ah, poor she!
I thought otherwise;
But—she is a servant—
But—you'd not be the first—
Then, will you marry her?—
Ah no, no, it can't be.
Away, evil thought, away.
Gently have I brought her up:
I know how she was born—
Oh, you are crazy!
Softly, for heaven's sake!
Ah, better not to think of it—
But I have a passion for her.
And yet—that rascal—
Oh, she's coming back—Lord!
Here we are,
What confusion—
I am all perplexed.
I have something in my heart,
I don't know what,
Whether it's love, or pity,
I feel something that says:
Uberto, think of yourself.
I hesitate between yes and no,
Between wanting and not wanting,
And I grow more and more perplexed,
Ah, unhappy, wretched am I,
What will become of me!
(Serpina enters with Vespone dressed as a soldier.)

SERPINA: I beg your pardon, sir.

UBERTO: (to Serpina). Mistress. Is it he?

|  |  |
|---|---|
| SERPINA: Questi è desso. | SERPINA: It is he. |
| UBERTO: (Oh brutta cera! Veramente ha una faccia tempestosa.) E così, caro il capitan Tempesta, Si sposerà già questa mia ragazza, (*Vespone accenna di sì.*) O ben n'è già contento . . . (*Vespone come sopra.*) O ben non vi ha difficoltà? O ben . . . Egli mi pare che abbia poche parole. | UBERTO: (Oh, how hideous! He really has a tempestuous face!) And so, dear Captain Tempest, You will marry my girl, (*Vespone nods assent.*) Oh, are you happy . . . (*Vespone as above.*) Or is there some difficulty? Or— He seems to have very little to say. |
| SERPINA: Anzi pochissime. (*A Vespone.*) Vuol me? (*Ad Uberto.*) Con permissione. | SERPINA: Very little. (*To Vespone*). Does he want me? (*To Uberto.*) With your permission. |
| UBERTO: (E in braccio a quel brutto nibbiaccio Deve andar quella bella columbina?) | UBERTO: (And must my dove go To the arms of that hideous simpleton?) |
| SERPINA: Sapete cosa ha detto? | SERPINA: So you know what he said? |
| UBERTO: Di', Serpina. | UBERTO: Tell me, Serpina. |
| SERPINA: Che vuole che mi diate la dote mia. | SERPINA: That he wants you to give me my dowry. |
| UBERTO: La dote tua? Che dote! sei matta? | UBERTO: Your dowry? What dowry! Are you mad? |
| SERPINA: Non gridate, ch'egli in furia darà. | SERPINA: Don't scream or he'll get angry. |
| UBERTO: Può dar in furia Più d'Orlando Furioso, Che a me punto non preme. (*Vespone finge di andare in collera.*) | UBERTO: He can get more furious than Orlando Furioso For all I care. (*Vespone feigns at getting angry.*) |
| SERPINA: Oh! Dio! Vedete pur ch'egli già freme. | SERPINA: Oh, Lord! See, he is already raging! |
| UBERTO: (*A Serpina*). Oh! che guai! Va là tu, (Shatti a veder che costui mi farà . . . ) Ben, cosa dice? | UBERTO: Oh, what misfortune. (*To Serpina.*) Go. (Well, let's see what he'll do to me.) Well, what does he say? |
| SERPINA: Che vuole almeno quattromila scudi. | SERPINA: That he wants at least 4,000 crowns. |
| UBERTO: Canchero! Oh! questa è bella! Vuole una bagatella! Ah! padron mio . . . (*Vespone vuol metter mano alla spada.*) Non signor . . . Serpina . . . Che mal abbia . . . Vespone, dove sei? | UBERTO: The devil! Oh, that's fine! He wants a trifle! Ah, my sir— (*Vespone wants to take hold of his sword.*) No, sir—Serpina— The devil take her—Vespone, where are you? |
| SERPINA: Ma, padrone, Il vostro male Andate voi cercando. | SERPINA: But, sir, You are looking for trouble. |
| UBERTO: Senti un po'. Con costui Hai tu concluso? | UBERTO: Listen. Have you made any Agreement with him? |
| SERPINA: Io ho concluso e non concluso. (*Finge di parlare con Vespone.*) Adesso . . . | SERPINA: I have and I have not. (*Pretends to speak with Vespone.*) Now— |
| UBERTO: (Statti a veder, Che questo maledetto capitano Farà precipitarmi.) | UBERTO: (It remains to be seen How this accursed captain Will rush at me.) |
| SERPINA: Ha egli detto . . . | SERPINA: He said— |
| UBERTO: Cha cosa ha detto? (Ei parla per interprete.) | UBERTO: What did he say? (She acts as interpreter.) |
| SERPINA: Che, o mi date la dote Di quattromila scudi, O non mi sposerà. | SERPINA: That, either give me the dowry Of 4,000 crowns, Or he'll not marry me. |
| UBERTO: Ha detto? | UBERTO: Did he say so? |
| SERPINA: Ha detto. | SERPINA: He said so. |
| UBERTO: E s'egli non ti sposa a me ch'importa? | UBERTO: And what do I care if he doesn't marry you? |
| SERPINA: Ma che mi avete a sposar voi. | SERPINA: But that you'd have to marry me. |
| UBERTO: Ha detto? | UBERTO: He said so? |
| SERPINA: Ha detto, o che altrimenti In pezzi vi farà. | SERPINA: He said so, or else He'll cut you to pieces. |
| UBERTO: Oh! questo non l'ha detto! | UBERTO: Oh, he didn't say that! |
| SERPINA: E lo vedrà. | SERPINA: You'll see. |
| UBERTO: L'ha detto . . . Sì, signora. (*Vespone fa cenno di minacciare Uberto.*) Eh! non s'incomodi, Che già per me vuol così il destino. Or io lo sposerò. | UBERTO: He said it—yes, lady. (*Vespone makes a threatening sign to Uberto.*) And don't disturb yourself, For my destiny wills it so. I shall marry her. |
| UBERTO: Mi dia la destra in sua presenza. | SERPINA: Give me your right hand in his presence. |
| UBERTO: Sì. | UBERTO: Yes. |
| SERPINA: Viva il padrone. | SERPINA: Long live the master. |
| UBERTO: Va ben così? (*Vespone si leva i mustacchi.*) | UBERTO: Is that right? (*Vespone takes off his mustache.*) |
| SERPINA: E viva ancor Vespone. | SERPINA: And long live Vespone. |
| UBERTO: Ah! ribaldo! tu sei? E tal inganno . . . lasciami . . . | UBERTO: Ah, you rascal! Is it you? Oh, such deceit—let me— |
| SERPINA: Eh non occorre più strepitar, Ti son già sposa, il sai. | SERPINA: You needn't make such a fuss. I am already your wife and you know it. |
| UBERTO: È ver, fatta me l'hai: Ti venne buona. | UBERTO: It is true; you made me do it: Good luck to you. |
| SERPINA: E di serva divenni io già padrona. Per te ho io nel core Il martellin d'amore Che mi percote ognor. | SERPINA: And from servant I have become mistress. For you, I have in my heart The little hammer of love Which ever beats in me. |
| UBERTO: Mi sta per te nel core Con un tamburo amore, E batte forte ognor. | UBERTO: I have in my heart for you A little drum of love Which ever beats loud for you. |
| SERPINA: Deh! senti il tippiti. | SERPINA: Ah, listen to its hammering. |
| UBERTO: Lo sento, è vero, sì. Tu senti il tappatà. | UBERTO: I hear it, it's true. Listen to its drumming. |
| SERPINA: È vero, il sento già. | SERPINA: I hear it, it's true. |
| UBERTO: Ma questo ch'esser può? | UBERTO: But what may it be? |
| SERPINA: Io nol so. Caro sposo. | SERPINA: I do not know, Dear husband. |
| UBERTO: Cara sposa. | UBERTO: Dear wife! |
| UBERTO e SERPINA: Caro. Gioia. Oh Dio! Ben te lo puoi pensar. | UBERTO and SERPINA: Dear! Joy! Oh, God! May you think well of it. |
| SERPINA: Io per me non so dirlo. | SERPINA: I can't say it. |
| UBERTO: Per me non so capirlo. | UBERTO: I can't understand it. |

SERPINA: Sarà,
Ma non è questo.

UBERTO: Sarà,
Nè meno è questo.

SERPINA: Ah furbo, si t'intendo.

UBERTO: Ah! ladra, ti comprendo,
MI vuoi tu corbellar.

SERPINA: Contento tu sarai,
Avrai amor per me?

UBERTO: So che contento è il core,
E amore avrò per te.

---

SERPINA: It may be,
But not this.

UBERTO: It may be,
But not that.

SERPINA: Ah, rascal, I understand you.

UBERTO: Ah, thief, I understand you.
You want to question me.

SERPINA: Will you be happy,
Will you love me?

UBERTO: I know my heart is happy,
And I'll love you.

---

SERPINA: Di' pur la verità.

UBERTO: Quest'è la verità.

SERPINA: Oh Dio! mi par che no.

UBERTO: Non dubitar, oibò!

SERPINA: Oh sposo grazioso!

UBERTO: Diletta mia sposetta! . . .

SERPINA: Così mi fai goder.

UBERTO: Sol tu mi fai goder.

*FINE.*

---

SERPINA: Tell the truth.

UBERTO: That is the truth.

SERPINA: I don't think so.

UBERTO: Do not doubt it!

SERPINA: Oh, graceful husband!

UBERTO: Oh, my happy bride!

SERPINA: Now you make me happy.

UBERTO: You alone give me joy.

*END.*

# La Gioconda (1876)

MUSIC BY AMILCARE PONCHIELLI ■ LIBRETTO BY TOBIA GORRIO (ARRIGO BOITO)

This four-act *opera drammatica*, set to a libretto by Tobia Gorrio (an anagram of Arrigo Boito) is based on Victor Hugo's play *Angelo, tyran de padoue*. It premiered at La Scala in Milan on April 8, 1876. At the courtyard of the Venetian Ducal Palace, La Gioconda, a travelling singer, refuses the proposal of Barnaba, a spy. His revenge: he publicly accuses her mother, La Cieca, of practicing witchcraft. Enzo Grimaldi, a prince with whom La Gioconda is in love, stands up for La Cieca. Previously banished from Venice, Enzo returns to Laura Adorno, the Genoese wife of Alvise Badoero, an inquisition chief of the Venetian State. Alvise arrests La Cieca in spite of Enzo's efforts, but Laura obtains a pardon for her. La Cieca gives her a rosary in thanks. Barnaba, meanwhile tries to minimize the competition by promising to help Enzo elope with Laura. When La Gioconda discovers this plan as well as Barnaba's betrayal of her mother, she decides to kill Laura. She hides on the ship on which Enzo and Laura are about to escape; but when she sees La Cieca's rosary around Laura's neck, La Gioconda realizes that Laura helped save her mother. She decides to assist the lovers instead. Alvise arrives, Laura and La Gioconda run away; Enzo sets the ship ablaze and dives into the water. While a celebration is taking place in the reception rooms, Alvise confronts his wife and demands that she drink poison in punishment for her adultery. La Gioconda slips Laura a sleeping potion instead of the poison, telling her to drink it and feign death. Alvise raises a curtain to reveal Laura; seemingly dead, to the shock of the guests. Enzo is there, too, in disguise. Thinking his lover is dead, he surrenders to the authorities. La Gioconda knows that the only way to save him is to promise her love to Barnaba. Barnaba accepts her offer and takes La Cieca hostage. La Gioconda's men transport Laura to a ruined palace. In her grief over her mother's disappearance and her loss of Enzo; La Gioconda is contemplating suicide. With Barnaba's help Enzo escapes from jail, and he runs off with Laura despite all La Gioconda has done for him. Barnaba, however, expects her to fulfill the bargain; she stabs herself instead. Enraged, he screams that he has killed her mother; she doesn't hear him as she is already dead.

## ■ ATTO I

### LA BOCCA DEI LEONI

*Il cortile del Palazzo Ducale parato a festa. Nel fondo la Scala dei Giganti e il Portico della Carta colla porta che adduce nell' interno della chiesa di S. Marco. A sinistra lo scrittoio d' uno scrivano pubblico. Sopra una parete del cortile si vedrà una fra le storiche bocche dei leoni colla seguente scritta incisa sul marmo a caretteri neri:*
Denontie secrete per via d' inquisitione contra cada una persona con l'impunità segreteza et benefitii giusto alle legi.

*È uno splendido meriggio di primavera. La scena è ingombra di popolo festante. Barnabotti, Arsenalotti, Marinai, maschere d' ogni sorta, Arlecchini, Pantaloni, Bautte, e in mezzo a questa turba vivace alcuni Dalmati ed alcuni Mori. Barnaba, addossato ad una colonna, sta osservando il popolo; ba una piccola chitarra ad armacollo.*

## ■ ACT I

### THE LION'S MOUTH

*The Grand Courtyard of the Ducal Palace, decorated for festivities. At back, the Giant's Staircase, and the Portico della Carta, with doorway leading to the interior of the Church of St. Mark. On the left, the writing-table of a public letter-writer. On one side of the courtyard is seen one of the historical Lion's Mouths, with the following inscription cut in black letters into the wall:*
For secret denunciations to the inquisition against any person, with impunity, secrecy, and benefit to the state.

*It is a splendid afternoon in Spring. The stage is filled with holiday folks, Monks, Sailors, Shipwrights, Harlequins, Buffoons, Dominos, and amidst the busy crowd are seen some Dalmatians and Moors. Barnaba, leaning his back against a column, is watching the people. He has a small guitar, slung 'round his neck.*

**BARNABA, CORO DE MARINAI E POPOLO:** Feste e pane! la Repubblica domerà le schiatte umane
Finchè avran le ciurme e i popoli
Feste e pane.
L'allegria disarma i fulmini ed infrange le ritorte.
Noi cantiam! chi canta è libero, noi ridiam! chi ride è forte.
Quel sereno Iddio lo vuol che allegrò questa laguna
Coll' argento della luna e la porpora del sol.
(*Campane a distesa, squilli di trombe.*)
Feste e pane! a gioia suonano
Di San Marco le campane.
Viva il Doge e la Repubblica!
Feste e pane!

**BARNABA:** (*si muove dal posto*).
Compari! già le trombe
V' annuncian la regata.
(*Dominando il frastuono festosamente.*)

**BARNABA, CHORUS OF SAILORS AND PEOPLE:** Sports and feasting! Feasting and sports! Our Republic wise,
That rules the world from farthest East to West,
Provides us—galley-slaves and populace—Sports and feasts.
Joy disarms the angry thunderbolt, And breaks the fetters forged by sinners!
Let us sing! for free are they who sing:
Let us laugh! for they who laugh are winners!
Calmly, brightly, the heavens are shining;
Pouring joy over yon lagoon!
While rays, sent from the rising moon,
Blend with the sunset glow declining.
(*Pealing of bells in the distance, sound of trumpets.*)
But hark! the joyous bells of St. Mark are loudly pealing!
Cheers for our Republic and our Doge!

**BARNABA:** (*leaving his place, comes forward*). The Regatta now commences!
The trumpets loud are pealing.
(*Dominating the terrific noise with festive air.*)

MARINAI E POPOLO: Alla regata! (*Gridando e saltando, il popolo esce dal cortile, Il tumulto s' allontana.*)

BARNABA: (*accennando gli spiragli delle prigioni sotterranee*). E danzan su lor tombe! E la morte li guata! (*Cupamente.*) E mentre s' erge il ceppo o la cuccagna, Fra due colonne tesse la sua ragna, Barnaba, il cantastorie; e le sue file (*Guarda e tocca la sua chitarra.*) Sono le corde di questo apparecchio. Con lavorìo sottile E di mano e d' orecchio Colgo i tafàni al volo Per conto dello Stato. E mai non falla L' udito mio. Coglier potessi solo Per le mie brame e tosto Una certa vaghissima farfalla!. . . . (*Gioconda colla Cieca, entrando da destra. La Vecchia ha il volto coperto fin sotto gli occhi da un povero zendado.*)

GIOCONDA: (*conducendo per mano la madre e avviandosi alla chiesa lentamente*). Madre adorata, vieni.

BARNABA: (*scorge Gioconda e si ritrae accanto alla colonna*). Eccola! al posto.

CIECA: Figlia, che reggi il tremulo piè che all' avel già piega, Beata è questa tenebra che alla tua man mi lega. Tu canti agli uomini le tue canzoni, Io canto agli angeli le mie orazioni, Benedicendo l' ora e il destin, E sorridendo sul mio cammin. Io per la tua bell' anima prego chinata al suol, E tu per me coi vividi sguardi contempli il sol.

GIOCONDA: Vien! per securo tramite da me tu sei guidata. Vien! ricomincia il placido corso la tua giornata. Tu canti agli angeli le tue orazioni, Io canto agli uomini le mie canzoni, Benedicendo l' ora e il destin. E sorridendo sul mio cammin.

BARNABA: (*in disparte*). Sovr essa stendere la man grifagna! Amarla e coglierla nella mia ragna! Terribil estasi dell' alma mia! Sta in guardia! l' agile farfalla spia!

SAILORS AND PEOPLE: To the Regatta let us hasten. (*Screaming and dancing, the people leave the courtyard.*)

BARNABA: (*pointing to the gratings of the subterranean prisons*). Above their graves they're dancing! Death upon them is stealing! (*In a somber manner.*) And while the reckless victims seek their pleasure, Here will I weave my nets for them at leisure. (*He looks down on his guitar, accompanying himself.*) Stories, and songs, and legends, are attractions, Whose power no mortal ever thinks of denying! I watch the listening gadflies,— note all their actions, And catch them while they're flying. Woe to them thereafter!— My ear, unfailing, has worked their ruin! Ah! how I am longing to make my captive, At once and securely, The wayward Gioconda. (*Gioconda enters with Cieca (her blind mother) from the left. The old woman has her face half covered with an old veil.*)

GIOCONDA: (*leading her mother by the hand, and advancing slowly towards the church*). This way, dear mother!

BARNABA: (*perceiving Gioconda, retreats near the Colonnade*). She is here, I'll hide!

CIECA: Daughter my faltering steps Find guidance and protection in you; I gratefully bless my loss of sight, That heightens your affection! While you unto mankind are singing your songs, To Heaven my ceaseless prayers their flight are winging For you I pray, and thanks to Fate, That left me sightless, but not desolate.

GIOCONDA: Your steps are all guided by me To Heaven your ceaseless prayers their flight are winging. While I, unto mankind, my songs am singing, For you I pray and render thanks to Fate That you, though sightless, are not desolate. Ah! Mother, dear.

BARNABA: (*aside*). With joy my soul would be enraptured, If in my net she were captured; The wildest ecstasies within me waken! Beware, moth, if you're taken in my net!

GIOCONDA: L' ora non giunse ancor del vespro santo; Qui ti riposa appiè del tempio; intanto Io vado a rintracciar l'angelo mio

BARNABA: Derisïon!

GIOCONDA: Torno con Enzo.

CIECA: Iddio ti benedica. Addio, figliuola. (*Estrae da tasca un rosario.*)

BARNABA: (*sbucando e sbarrando la via a Gioconda, che fa per escire da destra*). Ferma.

GIOCONDA: Che?

BARNABA: Un uom che t' ama, e che la via ti sbarra.

GIOCONDA: (*vivacemente. Per andarsene*). Al diavol vanne colla tua chitarra! Già l' altra volta tel dissi: funesta M' è la tua faccia da mistero.

BARNABA: (*trattenendola e ironicamente*). Resta. Enzo attender potrà.

GIOCONDA: Va, ti disprezzo.

BARNABA: (*incalzando*). Ancor m' ascolterai.

GIOCONDA: Mi fai ribrezzo!

BARNABA: Resta. . . .t'adoro, o vaga creatura.

GIOCONDA: Vanne!

BARNABA: Non fuggirai! (*Slanciandosi su essa.*)

GIOCONDA: Mi fai paura! Ah! (*Fugge.*)

CIECA: (*alzandosi spaventata*). Qual grido! mia figlia! La voce sua!

BARNABA: La farfalla è scomparsa. . . .

CIECA: (*brancolando*). Figliuola! o raggio della mia pupilla, Dove sei? dove sei?

BARNABA: (*ridendo*). La Cieca strilla; Lasciamola strillar.

CIECA: (*lentamente e protendendo le palme ritorna a sedersi sui gradini*). Tenèbre orrende!

BARNABA: (*osservando la pensieroso*). Pur quella larva che la man protende, Potrebbe agevolar la meta mia. . . . Se la madre è in mia man. . . .

CIECA: (*rigirando con fervore le Ave Marie del suo rosario*). Ave Maria. . . .

BARNABA: (*sempre meditando*). Tengo il cor della figlia incatenato . . .

GIOCONDA: Before long the vesper chimes will be ringing; Here, rest near the sacred shrine, while—singing— I seek him I love tenderly and truly.

BARNABA: Silly fool!

GIOCONDA: I'll return with Enzo.

CIECA: Heaven duly will bless your footsteps! Adieu, my daughter! (*Takes rosary from her pocket.*)

BARNABA: (*draws from his hiding place and bars the way to Gioconda, who wants to go out to the right*). Stay!

GIOCONDA: How?

BARNABA: A man who loves you, and bars your onward progress.

GIOCONDA: (*vivaciously, wishing to go away*). Go to the devil, you and your guitar too! Stand aside from my pathway! Away! I love not faces full of mystery.

BARNABA: (*keeping her back, and with irony*). Stay! Enzo yonder can wait.

GIOCONDA: Go! go! I despise you.

BARNABA: (*pressing her*). Once more;—say, will you listen?

GIOCONDA: I shudder at you!

BARNABA: Stay, I adore you, angelic creature!

GIOCONDA: Quit me.

BARNABA: (*rushing towards her*). Ah no, you shall not fly me!

GIOCONDA: I hate and fear you. Ah! (*Escapes from the grasp of Barnaba.*)

CIECA: (*rising in great fright*). My daughter in danger. Help! No one hears me! It was her voice.

BARNABA: So, the moth has escaped me!

CIECA: (*groping about*). My daughter, sole ray beaming over my existence, Where are you? Where are you?

BARNABA: (*laughing*). La Cieca is screaming. Well, let her scream her best.

CIECA: (*slowly stretching out her hands, returns to sit upon the steps*). O darkness fearful!

BARNABA: (*thoughtfully observing her*). Yet may this spectral creature, weak and tearful, Aid me to conquer you, Gioconda mia! Once the mother is mine—

CIECA: (*repeating with fervor the Ave Maria on her rosary*). Ave Maria!

BARNABA: Then the daughter to foil me in vain will endeavor.

CIECA: Ave Maria. . . .

CIECA: Ave Maria!

BARNABA: . . . .con laccio inesorato.
L' angiol m' aiuti dell' amor materno,
E la Gioconda è mia! Giuro all' Averno!
(*Il Popolo porta in trionfo il Vincitore della Regata, il quale tien (la bandiera del premio). Donne, Marinai, Fanciulli con fiori e ghirlande, Zuane triste in disparte.*)

BARNABA: She's fettered forever!
Thanks to your aid, angel of love maternal,
She shall be mine; I swear it, powers infernal!
(*The people carry the hero of the regatta in triumph, who carries the prize-banner. Ladies, Sailors, Children with flowers and garlands; Zuane, sad, to the side.*)

CORO: Polso di cerro!
Occhio di lince!
Remo di ferro!
Gagliardo cor!
Gloria a chi vince il pallio verde!
Lieta brigata,
Per licto calle portiamo a spalle,
Il vincitor della regata,
Fra canti e fior. Gli sguardi avvince,
I flutti ei sperde. Gloria a chi vince!
Beffe a chi perde!
(*Quasi tutti affluiscono verso la Scala del Giganti, ove depongono il vincitore.*)

CHORUS: Hail to the victor!
Wrists that are oaken! Eyes of lynx!
Sinews of iron! Hail the victor!
Hail to the winner of the green banner!
Laugh at the losers! Why did they fail!
Merry, light hearted, onward we go,
With songs and with flowers to cheer our path;
Bearing the victor in the regatta
High on our shoulders—see him here!
All eyes beheld him the waves dispersing;
Hail to the winner of the green banner!
Laugh at the losers! Why did they fail?
(*Almost everybody rushes to the Giant's Staircase, where they depose the victor.*)

BARNABA: (*che già da qualche tempo avrà osservato Zuane, lo arresta*). Questi è l' uomo ch' io cerco. Non m' inganno.
Patron Zuanè, hai faccia da malanno.
Si direbbe davver che alla regata
Non hai fatto bandiera.

BARNABA: (*who since some time has been watching Zuane, stops him*). It is he whom I was seeking. I'm never mistaken.
How now, Zuane? by fortune you're forsaken,
If it is true as I'm told, that in the race
You never once were seen leading?

ZUANE: T' inforchi Satanasso!

ZUANE: May Satan send you torments!

BARNABA: E se la vera
Cagione io ti dicessi del tuo danno?

BARNABA: Suppose the case
That I explained what cause has hindered your succeeding?

ZUANE: Lo so, la prora ho greve ed arrembata.

ZUANE: I know; my boat was overweighted.

BARNABA: Baje!

BARNABA: Nonsense.

ZUANE: E che dunque?

ZUANE: What mean you?

BARNABA: (*con mistero*). T' avvicina.—O lasso!
(*Sottovoce.*)
Hai la barca stregata.

BARNABA: (*mysteriously*). It was the spell of a sorceress.
(*In a low tone.*)
Wherever you wander,
Witchcraft enfolds you.

ZUANE: (*inorridito*). Vergine Santa!

ZUANE: (*horrified*). Holy Virgin!

CORO: (*accanto alla Scalla dei Giganti*). Dadi e bambàra!
Cuccagne e corse!
Giuochiamo a zara
Le nostre borse!
(*Alcuni estraggono dei dadi molti si siedono sui gradini, e intavolano un giucco di zara.*)

CHORUS: (*near the Giant's Staircase*). Dice and bambara!
Races and frisking!
We'll play at zara,
Our purses risking.
(*A few of them sit upon the steps taking out their dice and begin to play at zara.*)

BARNABA: La vidi stamini gittar sul tuo legno
Un segno maliardo, un magico segno.
(*Continuando e sempre facendo fissare Cieca a Zuane.*)

BARNABA: I saw her this morning throw over your line
Some foul spell of her witchcraft—a magical sign.
(*Continuing, without ceasing to fix Zuane's attention upon the blind woman.*)

ZUANE: Orror!

ZUANE: Alas!

BARNABA: La tua barca sarà la tua bara.
Sta in guardia, fratello!

BARNABA: Lest your barque be your bier—through la cara,
Be watchful, Zuane.

CORO: Sei! Cinque! Tre! Zara!

CHORUS: Six! Five! Three! Zara!

CIECA: (*pregando*). Turris eburnea. . .
Mistica rosa. . . .

CIECA: (*praying*). Turris eburnea . . .
Mistica rosa. . . .

BARNABA: (*a Zuane*). La vidi tre volte scagliar su tuoi remi
Parole tremende—lùgubri anatèmi.
(*Isepo sarà mosso verso Barnaba e ascolterà curioso.*)

BARNABA: (*to Zuane*). I heard her three times curse your oars and your rudder,
In accents infernal, that made my soul shudder.
(*Isepo moves toward Barnaba and listens with curiosity.*)

ZUANE: Gran Dio!

ZUANE: Great Heaven!

BARNABA: La tua barca sarà la tua bara.
Sta in guardia, fratello. . . .

BARNABA: Lest your barque be your bier, through la cara,
Be watchful Zuane!

CORO: Sette! Otto! Tre! Zara!

CHORUS: Seven! Eight! Three! Zara!

CIECA: (*come sopra*). Turris Davidica. . . .
Mater gloriosa. . . .

CIECA: (*as before, praying*). Turris Davidica . . .
Mater gloriosa . . .

BARNABA: (*misterioso a Zuane e Isepo*). Suo covo è un tugurio—laggiù alla Giudeca,
Tien sempre quell' orrido zendado, ed è Cieca. . . .
Ha vuote le occhiaie eppure e chi il crede?!
Cieca ci guarda—Cieca ci vede!

BARNABA: (*to Zuane and Isepo*). Her den is a cabin, hard by the Giudeca;
And there, with the demons, her companions, dwells Cieca.
Her eye-sockets are empty, yet that will not free you,
Cieca is watchful, Cieca can see you.

QUATTRO MARINAI: (*che si saranno aggiunti al gruppo*). Ci vede!

FOUR SAILORS: (*who have drawn nigh*). Can see us!

ISEPO: Oh spavento!

ISEPO: Hateful monster!

TRE ARSENALOTTI: (*aggiunti anch' essi al gruppo*). Che avvenne?

THREE WORKMEN OF ARSENAL: (*who also have joined the group*). What has happened?

ZUANE: Oh maliarda!

ZUANE: Heaven free us!

QUATTRO BARNABOTTI: Che avvenne? che mormori?. . . .

FOUR MONKS: What has happened? What do these cries mean?

BARNABA, ZUANE E ISEPO: Cieca ci guarda!
(*Il gruppo si fa sempre più numeroso.*)

BARNABA, ZUANE, AND ISEPO: Cieca can see us!
(*The group becomes more numerous.*)

CORO: Addosso! accoppiamola!

CHORUS: Upon her! Let us bind her fast!

ZUANE: (*per avventarsi alla Cieca, poi retrocede*). Ho paura. . . .

ZUANE: (*venturing towards Cieca*). Now, courage! Ah! I fear her!

BARNABA: Badate, può cogliervi la sua jettatura.

BARNABA: Be careful! Lest she bewitches you, if you go near her.

CORO: Al rogo l' eretica!

CHORUS: We'll burn the old heretic!

ZUANE: Davver, più l' addocchio.
Più i rai le balenano.

ZUANE: The more I look at her,
More spiteful her glances seem!

BARNABA: (*ridendo*). Cieca ha il mal occhio.

BARNABA: (*laughing*). The evil-eyed Cieca!

CORO: Ah! ah! qual facezia!

CHORUS: The evil-eyed Cieca?—ha, ha!

BARNABA: (*ad Isepo che si sarà avvicinato pianemente alla Cieca, che gira sempre il rosario*). Già l'aure....s'annuvolavano.

ZUANE: Che brontola?

ISEPO: Prega.

CORO: Addosso alla strega! (*si scagliano sulla Cieca*).

BARNABA: Ah! ah! greggie umana! Scagliato ho il mio ciottolo, Or fuggo la frana!

CIECA: (*afferrata del popolo e trascinata in mezzo al palco*). Aiuto! Son cieca! Soccorso! soccorso!

BARNABA: Sgherrani, sia tratta nel carcere.

ZUANE, ISEPO E CORO: Addosso! Ai Piombi! Ai pozzi! Al rogo! A morte la strega! Martira! Al rogo. Sia tratta nel carcere. A morte la strega!

ENZO: (*vestito da marinaio dalmato, rompendo la calca con uno scoppio d'ira*). Assassini! Assassini! quel crin venerando Rispettate! o ch' io snudo il mio brando. Contro un' egra rejetta dal sole Generosa è la vostra tenzon! Vituperio! è cresciuta una prole Di codardi all' alato leon!

CORO: Iddio vuol cio che il popole vuole; No, la strega non merta perdon.

CIECA: Ah! su me si scatena l' averno!

CORO: A morte la strega.

ENZO: (*con impeto fa per togliere i ceppi alla Cieca, ma è impedito dal popolo*). Quel ceppo le strazia. Sciolta sia.

GIOCONDA: Ah! Madre mia.

ENZO: (*correndo all' ingresso della riva furiosamente ed esce*). La sciogliete, assassini Su, fratelli del mare! Alla lotta!

CORO: Al patibolo! (*Intanto sull' alto della scala saranno appars. Alvise e Laura, che avranno assistito al tumulto. Laura dall' alto della scala, scendendo. Il lembo della sua veste sarà sostenuto da due paggi. Ha una maschera di velluto nero sul volto*).

LAURA: Pietà.

---

BARNABA: (*to Isepo, drawing closer to the blind woman who is constantly praying over the rosary*). Already the clouds gather fast.

ZUANE: What's she about?

ISEPO: Praying.

CHORUS: Take hold of the witch. (*They fling themselves upon Cieca.*)

BARNABA: The fools yonder! The ball I've set rolling on, Now on let it roll.

CIECA: (*seized by the populace, and dragged to the middle of the stage*). Oh, help me! I'm sightless! Have mercy! Help!

BARNABA: Friends, there, lodge her in prison.

ZUANE, ISEPO AND CHORUS: Upon her, the irons! To the sewers! We'll burn her! The sorceress shall suffer. We'll kill her! To the stakes! To the prison! We'll burn her. Death to the witch!

ENZO: (*attired as a Dalmatian sailor, breaking through the crowd in an explosion of terrible anger*). Base assassins! Base assassins! these locks, gray and scattered, Harm no longer! My sword shall protect them! Against a woman, old, feeble, and sightless, It is noble and safe, to contend! You are monsters! Descendants of heroes! All are cowards, you winged lion disgracing.

CHORUS: No! Heaven wills what the populace wills! The sorceress' life now must end.

CIECA: Ah! on me hell's fury is lighting.

CHORUS: Death to the witch!

ENZO: (*in fury he trys to remove the fetters from Cieca, but is prevented by the multitude*). Let me free her! these fetters will kill her.

GIOCONDA: Mother, darling!

ENZO: (*running to the entrance of the sea, furious he rushes out*). Quick release her, base assassins! Rise, comrades, rise, for mercy meets denial. Now for fighting, for fighting!

CHORUS: Burn her! destroy her! (*Laura and Alvise, who have seen the tumult from the head of the stairs, are about to descend. Her skirt is carried by two pages and she is wearing a mask of black velvet.*)

LAURA: Mercy!

---

ALVISE: (*alteramente e con gravita*). Ribellion! che? la plebe or qui si arroga Fra le ducali mure I dritta della toga E della scure? (*Movimento di rispetto nella folla.*) (*A Cieca.*) Parla, o captiva! Perchè stai china là fra quelle squadre!

CORO: E una strega!

GIOCONDA: È mia madre!

LAURA: (*la Cieca alza la testa*). È Cieca! o mio signor! fa ch' essa viva!

ALVISE: (*freddamente a Barnaba*). Barnaba! è rea costel!

BARNABA: (*assai sottovoce all' orecchio è Alvise*). Di male fizio.

GIOCONDA: (*a Barnaba*). T' ho udito!....menti!

ALVISE: Sia tratta in giudizio.

GIOCONDA: (*gettasi ai piedi di Alvise*). Pietà....ch' io parli attendete....ora infrango Il gel che m' impietrave....e sgorga l' onda Del cor....Costei della mia infanzia bionda L'angelo fu....Sempre ho sorriso....or piango. Mi chiaman....la Gioconda. Viviam cantando ed io Canto a chi vuol le mie liete canzoni, Ed essa canta a Dio Le sue sante orazioni....

ENZO: (*che sarà ritornato da qualche tempo seguito dai marinai dalmati*). Salviamo l'innocente.

LAURA: (*scorgendo Enzo*). Qual volto!

GIOCONDA: (*alzandosi e trattenendo Enzo*). Ah! no! ti ferma! Quel possente La salverà!

BARNABA: (*osservando Laura, poi Enzo*). Come lo guardo fiso!

LAURA: (*ad Alvise in disparte*). Concedi, o mio signor, se non ti duole, Ch' io mi levi la maschera dal viso.

ALVISE: No, madonna, nemmen l' occhio del sole Non dee mirarti.

GIOCONDA: (*ad Alvise*). Dalle tue parole La vita attendo.

BARNABA: (*ad Alvise sottovoce*). E una strega, il nefario Suo silenzio tel dica.

---

ALVISE: (*imperiously, and with gravity*). Rebellion? What? The populace can venture here, Near our Ducal Palace— To claim to act as judges?— And as executioners? (*Movement of respect of the crowd.*) (*To Cieca.*) Answer me, captive. Why are you kneeling to yonder people?

CHORUS: She's a sorceress.

GIOCONDA: It is my mother.

LAURA: (*towards whom Cieca has turned her face*). She's sightless, see, signor! save her from outrage!

ALVISE: (*coldly to Barnaba*). Barnaba, has she been guilty?

BARNABA: (*whispering to Alvise*). Guilty of witchcraft.

GIOCONDA: (*to Barnaba*). I heard you! You lie!

ALVISE: Conduct her to trial.

GIOCONDA: (*throwing herself at Alvise's feet*). Mercy! ah, hear me one moment! I break The ice that was keeping my soul in fetters She has been the bright angel of my life; I once was ever smiling, now I'm weeping. They call me "La Gioconda." We are always singing; to all comers I sing my gay songs till day's ending; While gentle strains of pious rapture Are ascending from her pure lips.

ENZO: (*who has returned after a short time, followed by some Dalmatian sailors*). Let us save the innocent victim.

LAURA: (*observing him*). Those features?

GIOCONDA: (*rising up and restraining Enzo*). Ah no! have patience! The Duke will protect Cieca.

BARNABA: (*aside; watching Enzo and Laura*). His gaze is fixed upon her.

LAURA: (*to Alvise aside*). Permit me, sir, if it does not displease you. To take off my mask.

ALVISE: No, madame, not even the sun's rays Can touch your face.

GIOCONDA: (*to Alvise*). You alone have power to save my mother.

BARNABA: She is a sorceress! Her guilty silence betrays her.

LAURA: Essa ha un rosario!
No, l'inferno non è con quella pia.

ENZO: Qual voce!

BARNABA: Muoia!

LAURA: (ad Alvise supplichevole). La salva!

ALVISE: E salva sia.

GIOCONDA: Gioia!

BARNABA: Furore!

GIOCONDA: Oh, gioia!

CIECA: (liberta da Laura che l'allontana dagli Sgherri). Voce di donna o d'angelo
Le mie catene ha sciolto;
Mi vietan le mie tenebre
Di quella santa il volto,
Pure da me non partasi
Senza un pietoso don:
(Si toglie il rosario dalla cintola.)
A te questo rosario
Che le preghiere aduna.
Io te lo porgo, accettalo,
Ti porterà fortuna;
Sulla tua testa vigili
La mia benedizion.

GIOCONDA: O madre mia, ti guarda
Un angelo fedel.

CORO: Protegge la vegliarda
Visibilmente il ciel!
(Laura s'avvicina alla Cieca e prende il rosario, Cieca stende le mani come per benedirla, Laura fa per inginocchiarsi, Alvise, vede e afferra il braccio di Laura sforzandola a rialzarsi.)

ALVISE: (gettando una borsa a Gioconda). Che fai? vaneggi?
Bella cantatrice,
Quest'oro a te.

GIOCONDA: (raccoglie e s'inchina). Sia grazia a voi, Messere.
(A Laura.)
Acciò ch'io l'abbia nelle mie preghiere Dimmi il tuo nome, o ignota salvatrice.

LAURA: (guardando Enzo). Laura.

ENZO: (colpito). È dessa!

ALVISE: (a Laura, assorta). Ti scuoti! al tempio andiamo!

GIOCONDA: Madre!—Enzo adorato! Ah! come t'amo!
(Tutti si dirigono al tempio. Alvise e Laura primi, i due paggi dopo, indi tutto il Coro, e Gioconda fra la madre ed Enzo. Giunto alla porta della chiesa, Enzo s'arresta, e rimane indietro assorto profondamente ne' suoi pensieri. Barnaba lo sta fissando. La scena si vuota.)

BARNABA: (avvicinandosi ad Enzo). Enzo Grimaldo, Principe di Santafior, che pensi?

LAURA: She bears a rosary. Satan has nothing to do with this pious woman.

ENZO: (observing Laura). Those accents!

BARNABA: Burn her!

LAURA: (to Alvise, supplicating). O save her!

ALVISE: She is saved, and pardoned!

GIOCONDA: Ah joy!

BARNABA: They foil me!

GIOCONDA: What rapture!

CIECA: (liberated by Laura, who takes her away from the bailiffs). Thanks to you, angelic voice,
My fetters are broken asunder;
I cannot see the face of her
By whom those words were spoken.
(Takes the rosary from her belt.)
Yet, lady, you must not depart without a gift from me,
I offer this rosary—no richer boon possessing—
Deign to accept the humble gift, it will bring to you a blessing,
And on your head may bliss descend! I'll ever pray for you.

GIOCONDA: Ah, mother, it was an angel, sent down from yonder heaven!

CHORUS: It is evident unto her celestial aid is given.
(Laura approaches Cieca, and takes the rosary. Cieca extends her hands as if to bless Laura, who kneels before her. Alvise abruptly seizes the arm of Laura and compels her to rise.)

ALVISE: (throwing a purse to Gioconda). What now? It is folly.
Pretty singing maiden,
This gold is yours.

GIOCONDA: (picks it up and bows). Thanks, Signor!
(To Laura.)
That I may never in my prayers forget it,
Tell me your name, unknown, generous benefactress.

LAURA: (looking at Enzo). Laura.

ENZO: (struck). It is she!

ALVISE: (to Laura, who is absorbed). Arouse—Let us hasten to church.

GIOCONDA: Beloved mother!
Enzo, how I love you!
(All go into the church. Alvise and Laura first, followed by the two pages, then Gioconda, between her mother and Enzo, then the Chorus. At the door of the church, Enzo stops and remains behind profoundly absorbed in his thoughts. Barnaba looks at him fixedly).

BARNABA: (approaching Enzo). Enzo Grimaldo, Prince of Santa fior, you are pensive.

ENZO: Scoperto son.

BARNABA: Qual magico stupor t'invade i sensi?
Pensi a Madonna Laura d'Alvise Badoèro.

ENZO: (scosso). Chi sei?

BARNABA: So tutto: e penetro in fondo at tuo pensiero.
Avesti culla in Genova. . . .

ENZO: Prence non son, sui flutti
Guido un vascel, son dalmato: Enzo Giordan. . . .

BARNABA: Per tutti
Ma non per me. Venezia t'ha proscritto ma un forte
Disio qui ancor ti trasse ad affrontar la morte.
Amasti un dì una vergine—là, sul tuo mar beato,
A estranio imene vittima—la condannava il fato.

ENZO: Ho guirato fede a Gioconda.

BARNABA: La cantatrice errante
Ami come sorella, ma Laura come amante.
Già disperavi in terra di riveder quel volto,
E l'amor di Gioconda hai per pietà raccolto,
Ed or, sotto la maschera l'angelo tuo t'apparve. . . .
Ti riconobbe. . . .

ENZO: Oh giubilo!

BARNABA: L'amor passa le larve.
Badoer questa notte—veglia al dogale ostello
Col gran Consiglio, Laura sarà sul tub vascello.

ENZO: Dio di pietà!

BARNABA: Le angosce dell'amor tuo soccorro.

ENZO: O grido di quest'anima, scoppia dal gonfio core!
Ho ritrovato l'angelo del mio celeste amore.
A notte bruna sul brigantino aspetto Laura.

BARNABA: (inchinandosi e sogghignando.). Buona fortuna!

ENZO: E tu su maledetto!

BARNABA: Maledici? sta ben. . . .l'amor t'accieca.
Compiam l'opra bieca,
L'idolo di Gioconda sia distrutto.
S'annienti tutto.
(Va nel fondo, apre una porta accanto le prigioni, Isepo!)

ISEPO: (escendo). Padron Barnaba. . . .

ENZO: (aside). I am discovered.

BARNABA: What magic stupor steals away your senses?
It is of the Lady Laura, Alvise's wife, you're thinking.

ENZO: (moved). Who are you?

BARNABA: I know all; can penetrate your
Thoughts, however secret. Your birthplace was Genoa!

ENZO: I am not a Prince, but a sailor. Yonder's my ship.
I am Dalmatian, Enzo Giordan.

BARNABA: For others,
But not for me. Proscribed you were by Venice,
Yet here you are led, by chainless impulse.
Your life to peril. You did love a maiden
Yonder in your own Genoa, but she Became another's bride. Fate was cruel to you both.

ENZO: I have pledged my faith to Gioconda.

BARNABA: Poor wandering ballad singer!
You love her as a sister, but Laura as your mistress.
You had abandoned all hope, dreamed not to see her features,
But here, under her velvet mask, your beauteous angel saw you.
And recognized you.

ENZO: O happiness!

BARNABA: Love sees through disguises.
All this night will her husband stay at the Doge's palace,
With the Great Council. Laura shall be on board your vessel.

ENZO: Powers divine!

BARNABA: Love's sweetest consolations await you.

ENZO: Ah, with what joy my heart is filled,
Fortune at last is kind!
Soon shall I clasp the angel-form
In this fond heart enshrined.
When the dark night falls,
On board my ship I shall await my Laura.

BARNABA: (bowing low and sneeringly). Good luck attend you!

ENZO: And you—be accursed!

BARNABA: Accursed? We shall see. It is love that blinds you.
Should my dark plots be successful,
This idol of Gioconda's will be shattered,
And dashed to pieces.
(Goes to the rear, opens a door near the prisons and calls Isepo.)

ISEPO: (coming out). Padron Barnaba!

**BARNABA:** Scrivano,
L' anima m' hai venduto e la cotenna
Fin che tu vivi;
In son la mano
E tua la penna.
Scrivi.

**BARNABA:** (a Isepo). Al Capo occulto dell' Inquisizione.
(Isepo scrivi. Intanto alla porta del tempio appariscono Gioconda e Cieca.)

**GIOCONDA:** (a Cieca). Ti nascondi, c' è Barnaba.
(Alla madre ritraendola e sta spiando nascosta dal pilastro.)

**BARNABA:** La tua sposa con Enzo il Marinar.
Sta notte in mar
Ti fuggirà sul brigantino dalmato.

**GIOCONDA:** Ah!
(Disperatamente e scompare in chiesa.)

**BARNABA:** Più sotto:
"La Bocca del Leone."
Qua, porgi, taci, vanne.
(Prende il foglio, Isepo esce.)

**BARNABA:** (col piego in mano contemplando la scena). O monumento!
Regia e bolgia dogale! Atro portento!
Gloria di questa e delle età future;
Ergi fra due torture
Il porfido cruento.
Tua base i pozzi, tuo fastigio i piombi
Sulla tua fronte il volo dei palombi,
I marmi e l' ôr.
Gioia tu alterni e orror con vece occulta,
Quivi un popolo esulta,
Quivi un popolo muor.
Là il Doge, un vecchio scheletro
Coll' acidaro in testa,
Sovr' esso il gran Consiglio,
La Signoria funesta;
Sovra la Signoria
Più possente di tutti, un re; la spia.
O monumento! Apri le tue latèbre,
(Vicino alla bocca del leone.)
Spalanca la tua fauce di tenèbre,
S' anco il sangue giungesse a soffocarla!
Io son l' orecchio e tu la bocca: Parla!
(Getta il piego nella bocca del leone ed esce.)
(Entra nel cortile una Mascherata; la segue il popolo cantando e danzando. Poscia un Barna botto, Gioconda e Cieca.)

**BARNABA:** Now, penman, long since you did sell your soul to me;
Your skin also, to save your life.
I am the hand, and you are the pen.
Write.

**BARNABA:** (to Isepo). Unto the secret chief of the Inquisition—
(Isepo writes. In the meantime in the door of the church appear Gioconda and Cieca.)

**GIOCONDA:** (to Cieca). Quick conceal yourself. It is Barnaba.
(Drawing her mother behind a column, she hides and listens.)

**BARNABA:** Your wife will this night elope with Enzo, the young sailor, and will sail away from you,
On board his vessel.

**GIOCONDA:** Ah!
(Desperately she disappears in the church.)

**BARNABA:** Now lower down:
"The Mouth of the Lion."
Give it me. Silence! Go!
(Takes the paper, Isepo goes out.)

**BARNABA:** (with the letter in hand, he contemplates the scene).
O mighty monument, palace and den of the Doges!
Gloomy and wondrous, glory of this age,
And of the ages yet unborn,
Between twin tortures glistens
Your prairie ensanguined!
Below are the Pozzi beneath your roof the Piombi;
Your front is gay, with its fearless flocks of pigeons,
Its marble and gold,
Joy alternates with woe, in workings secret.
Here is a nation exulting; there a nation dies.
There the Doge, an ancient skeleton,
Sites in state, in his headdress quaint;
Above him, the Great Council—sinister oligarchy!
Over the oligarchs, far more powerful than they,
A King—the Spy!
O mighty monument, open your capacious jaws!
(Near the Lion's Mouth.)
Spread wide your throat, that waits in sullen darkness,
Until blood, poured in torrents, shall choke it forever!
I am the ear, and you the mouthpiece. Speak!
(Throws the letter into the Lion's Mouth, and goes out.)
(Enter Masquers and Populace, dancing and singing. Then a Barnabite, Gioconda and the blind woman.)

**CORO E DANZA:** Carneval! Baccanal!! Gaia turba popolana
Su! correte al torneamento! su! danzate la furlana!
(Si odono alcuni tocchi di campana.)

**CORO:** (dalla chiesa). Angelus Domini.

**CORO:** (sulla scena). Gloria à Dio!

**UN BARNABOTTO:** (schiundendo la tenda che copre la porta della basilica). Tramonta il sol.
Udite il canto
Del vespro santo
Prostrati al suol.

**CORO:** Angele Dei, qui custos es mei,
Me, tibi commissum, nocte illumina,
Rege, custodi et rege,
Rege et guberna, custodi,
Angele Dei, qui custos es mei.
(Tutti si prostrano rivolti verso il fondo. Gioconda e Cieca attradura l' orazione.)

**GIOCONDA:** Tradita!. . . . Ahimè!. . . . soccombo. . . . il fianco mio
Vacilla. . . .o madre. . . .mi sorreggi. O Dio!
Cuore! dono funesto!
Retaggio di dolor!
Il mio destino è questo:
O Morte o Amor!

**CIECA:** Dimmi dov' è il tuo cor! la man vi guida.
Ch' io lo posi sul mio!
Vieni e facciamo un sol di due dolor!
(Gioconda prendendo la mano della Cieca e portandosele ai cuore.)

**CORO:** (inginocchiata). Gloria al Signor
E pace agli uomini!
(Cala lentamente tela.)

**CHORUS AND BALLET:** Carnival! Bacchanal!
Day's last beams are glancing over us;
Let us pass our time in dancing La Furlana!
(Church bells are heard.)

**CHORUS:** (inside the church). Angelus domini.

**CHORUS:** (on the stage). Glory to God!

**MONK:** (to the people, drawing aside the curtain from before the door of the church). The sun sinks low, the vesper hymn is pealing;
Now listen to the holy strain, devoutly kneeling.

**CHORUS:** Angele Dei, qui custos es mei,
Me, tibi commissum, nocte illumina,
Rege, custodi et rege,
Rege et guberna, custodi,
Angele Dei, qui custos es mei.
(All are on their knees towards the rear. Gioconda and her mother pass through the crowd while the vesper prayer is being sung. Gioconda, vacillating and slow, is leaning on her mother.)

**GIOCONDA:** Forsaken! Betrayed!
All is over! In every limb
I am trembling. You must support me, dear mother.
O heart, gone is your gladness!
Your heritage is sadness!
My doom was framed by powers above:
To die! to die, if robbed of love!
Upon my heart, dear mother,
Place your hand, and you'll know,
The while it throbs so wildly,
How great, alas, my woe!

**CIECA:** Ah come, my child, my darling,
Hand in hand let us go,
One grief of two griefs making,
Sharing each other's woe!
(Gioconda puts her mother's hand on her heart.)

**CHORUS:** (kneeling). Angele Dei,
Qui custos es mei.
The curtain descends slowly.

# ■ ATTO II

## IL ROSARIO

Notte. Un brigantino visto di fianco. Sul davanti una riva deserta d' isola disabitata nelle acque Fusina. Nell' estremo fondo il cielo in qualche parte stellato, e la laguna; a destra la luna tramonta dietro una nube. Sul davanti un altarino della Vergine con una lampada rossa accesa. "Hecate," il nome del brigantino, sta scritto a prua. Alcune lanterne sul ponte.

# ■ ACT II

## THE ROSARY

Night. A brigantine, showing its starboard side. In front, the deserted bank of an uninhabited island in the Fusina lagoon. In the farthest distance, the sky and the lagoon. A few stars visible. On the right, a cloud, above which the moon is rising. In front, a small altar of the Virgin, lighted by a red lamp. The name of the brigantine— 'Hecate'—painted on the

# Act II

*All' alzarsi della tela alcuni Marinai sono seduti sulla tolda, altri in piedi aggruppati; tutti hanno un portavoce in mano; molti Mozzi sono arrampicati, o seduti, o sospesi alle sartie deglalberi e stanno cantando una marinaresca.*

**PRIMI MARINAI:** (*a destra sul ponte cantando attraverso il portavoce*). Ho! He! Ho! He! Ho!
Fissa il timone!

**SECONDI MARINAI:** (*a sinistra col portavoce*). Fissa!
Ho! He! Ho! He! Ho!

**MARINAI:** Siam qui sui culmini,
siam sulla borda,
Siam sulle tremule scale di corda,
Guardate gli agili mozzi saltar;
Noi gli scoiattoli siamo del mar.
Siam nel fondo più profondo della nave, della cala,
Dove il vento furibondo spreca i fischi e infrange l' ala.
Siam nel fondo più profondo della nave, della cala.

**PRIMI MARINAI:** Ha! Ho! Ha! Ho!
Vele a babordo!

**SECONDI MARINAI:** Issa!
Remi a tribordo!

**TUTTI:** Issa!
Il ciel tuonò!
Ha! Ho! Ha! Ho!

**MOZZI:** In mezzo ai fulmini delle tempesta,
Noi nuvole tuffiam la testa,
Come sugli alberi d' una foresta,
Osiam le pendule sartìe scalar.
Noi gli scoiattoli siamo del mar.
Sotto prora, sotto poppa è una placida dimora,
Qui vuotiam l' ardente coppa del liquor che inganna l' ora.
Sotto poppa, sotto prora.
Il mar mugghiante, il ciel furente,
Greco a Levante, bora a Ponente,
Scïoni e turbini sappiam sfidar.
Noi gli scoiattoli siamo del mar!
(*Una voce sola di dentro.*)

**BARNABA:** Pescator, affonda l' esca, e l' onda a te sia fedel,
Lieta sera e buona pesca ti promette il mare e il ciel.
(*Barnaba è vestito da pescatore con una rete in mano.*)

**PILOTA:** Chi va là?

**BARNABA:** La canzon ve lo dicea:
Un pescator che attende la marea.
Ho la barca laggiù nell' acqua bassa.
È tèmpora domani, e si digiuna,
Per mia fortuna,
La mensa magra il pescatore ingrassa.

---

*prow. Lanterns on deck. As the curtain rises Sailors are discovered; some seated on the deck, others standing in groups, each with a speaking trumpet. Several Midshipmen are seen; some clinging to the shrouds, some seated. Remaining thus grouped, they sing a Marinaresca.*

**FIRST SAILORS:** (*to the right of deck, singing through speaking trumpets*). Ho, he! ho, he!
Look to the rudder!

**SECOND SAILORS:** (*to the left, singing through speaking trumpets*). Look well! Look well!
Ho, he! ho, he!

**SAILORS:** We're here, some perched on the top,
Some on the edge, some on the tremulous ladders of rope.
Look at the agile midshipmen climb,
We are the squirrels of the sea.
We are in the most profound depths
Of the ship, of the hold,
Where the furious winds whistle
And tear the sails to tatters,
We are in the profound bottom
Of the ship, of the hold.

**FIRST SAILORS:** Look well!
Ho, he! ho, he!
Up with the mainsail!

**SECOND SAILORS:** Up with it!
Where are the rowers?

**ALL:** Ho, he! ho, he!
Rowers, reply!

**MIDSHIPMEN AND BOYS:** We're here; some perched aloft, some on the gunwale,
Some clinging to the tremulous rope ladders:
See how the nimble midshipmen can climb!
Behold in us the squirrels of the sea!
Here are we, in depths profoundest
Of the vessel; in the hold,
While angry winds, in fury howling,
Shriek, rending sails to tatters.
Here are we, in depths profoundest.
(*A voice alone from the hold.*)

**BARNABA:** (*from inside*). Fisher-boy, Now lower your bait;
May the waves prove true to you.
(*He enters.*)
Now good night! May luck attend you!

**A PILOT:** Who goes there?

**BARNABA:** My song itself will tell you.
I am a fisher; for the tide I am waiting,
And my boat waits for me
In yon deep waters.
Tomorrow is a fast day. When people fast,
They bring me good fortune;
And but for fast days fishermen never would fatten.

---

**MARINAI:** (*ridendo*). Ha! Ha! Ha! Ha!

**BARNABA:** (*ad Isepo*). Siam salvi!
Han riso. Sono ottanta
Fra marinari e mozzi. Han tre decine
Di remi e nulla più; due colubrine
Di piccolo calibro. Or va, con quanta
Lena ti resta, e disponi le scolte
Colà dove le macchie son più folte.
Io qui rimango a far l' ufficio mio.
Vanne con Dio. Ah!
(*Isepo esce.*)

**BARNABA:** Pescator, affonda l' esca
E l' onda a te sia fedel,
Lieta sera e buona pesca
Ti promette il mare e il ciel.
Va, tranquilla cantilena,
Per l' azzurra immensità;
Questa notte una sirena
Nella rete cascherà.

**CORO:** (*ridendo*). Ha! Ha! Ha! Ha!
Questa notte una sirena nella rete cascherà.

**BARNABA:** (*tra sè*). Spia coi fulminei tuoi sguardi accorti,
E fra le tenebre conta i tuoi morti.
Sì, da quest' isola deserta e bruna
Or deve sorgere la tua fortuna.
Sta in guardia! e il rapido sospetto svia,
E ridi e vigila e canta e spia.
(*Ripigliando la conzone.*)
Brilla Venere serena
In un ciel di voluttà.
Una fulgida sirena
Nella rete cascherà.

**CORO:** (*ripete ridendo*). Una fulgida sirena
Nella rete cascherà.
(*Barnaba esce all' entrare di Enzo.*)
(*Enzo, Marinai e Mozzi, il Nostromo, il Maestro delle vele, il Piloto. Enzo esce da sotto coperta con una lanterna in mano avanzandosi gaiamente, alla ciurma.*)

**ENZO:** Sia gloria ai canti
Dei naviganti!
Queste notte si salpa!

**MARINAI:** Evviva il nostro
Principe a capitano!

**ENZO:** (*esplorando il cielo*). Soffia grecale.
Vento buono per noi. . . .nella carena
(*Al Nos.*)
Tu, Nostromo, raccogli la gomèna.

---

**SAILORS:** (*laughing*). Ha! Ha! Ha! Ha!

**BARNABA:** (*to Isepo*). We are safe now! They're laughing. They, in all,
Number eighty, men and boys.
They have three ranks
Of ten oars each, and no more; only two culverins,
Both of small caliber. Now go, with all
The breath that is left to you, and place out the scouts
Down yonder where the bushes are thickest.
I remain here, till the moment comes for action.
Heaven go with you!
(*Isepo goes out.*)

**BARNABA:** Fisherman, Now lower your bait!
May the waves prove faithful to you.
Pleasant night and lucky fishing
Sea and sky both promise.
Go, your tranquil song outpouring
Beneath the azure boundless sky.
Lo! a gentle lovely siren
In your net this night shall fall.

**CHORUS:** (*laughing*). Lo! a gentle lovely siren
In your net this night shall fall.

**BARNABA:** (*to himself*). Spy, swift as lightning
Cast around your glances,
And in the darkness
Count your heedless victims.
Yes! from this islet
Deserted and barren
You shall see spring forth
Your harvest of fortune.
Be watchful, and evade swift-formed suspicions,
And gaily laugh, and sharply watch,
While singing still spying,
Laughing, singing.
(*Aloud as before, recommencing his song.*)
Ah! yonder Venus shines serenely
In a heaven of delight,
And a shining splendid siren
In your net shall fall tonight.

**CHORUS:** Tonight a lovely siren
In your net shall fall.
(*Barnaba goes out as Enzo comes in.*)
(*Enter Enzo, Sailors, Midshipmen, the boatswain, the Master of the Sails, the pilot. Enzo enters from below deck with a lantern in his hand, advancing gaily to the crew.*)

**ENZO:** Long live the songs
Of the sons of the sea!
We tonight will weigh anchor.

**SAILORS:** (*surrounding him*).
Long live our noble Prince!
Long live our captain.

**ENZO:** (*observing the sky*). Northeast the wind is.
It is a good wind for us. Down in the hold
(*To the Nostromo.*)
Do you, Nostromo, securely stow

Tu, Maestro delle vele, affiggi al rostro
Del brigantino il dalmato segnale
Che ci protesse in molte aspre fortune,
E al maggior pino inalbera il fanale.
(*Al Mozzi.*)
Voi siate pronti a distaccar la fune
D'amarra a un cenno mio. "Quest'erme onde
Più non vedremo all' ora mattutina.
Nocchier, l' abbrivio è verso Palestrina."
(*Alcuni uomini della ciurma eseguiscono gli ordini de Enzo; mentre gli altri ricantano la Marinaresca.*)

**ENZO:** (*a tutti*). Ed or scendete a riposarvi. Io vigilo
Solo sul ponte le inimiche flotte.
(*Guarda le stelle.*)
E tardi.

**CORO:** Buona guardia.

**ENZO:** Buona notte.
(*La ciurma scende sotto il ponte.*)
Cielo e mar!—l' etereo velo
Splende come un santo altar.
L' angiol mio verrà dal cielo?
L' angiol mio verrà dal mare?
Qui l' attendo, ardente spira
Oggi il vento dell' amore.
Ah! Quell' nom che vi sospira
Vi conquide, o sogni d' ôr!
Cielo e mar!—Per l' aura fonda
Non appar nè suol, nè monte,
L' orizzonte bacia l' onda,
L' onda bacia l' orrizzonte!
Qui nell' ombra ov' io mi giacio
Coll' anelito del cor,
Vieni, o donna, vieni al bacio
Della vita dell' amor.
(*Fissando il mare.*)
Machi vien? non è uno spettro
Del pensier! quella è una barca.
Odo già de' remi il metro,
Verso me volando varca. . . .

**LA VOCE DI BARNABA:** (*dietro il brigantino*). Capitano! a bordo!

**ENZO:** (*sclamando verso la direzione della voce di Barnaba*).
Avanti!!
Dio! sostieni ancor la piena
Della gioia! Naviganti,
Costeggiate la carena!
(*Prende una fune e la getta al di là della sponda.*)
Qua la fune . . . . aggrappa . . . . annoda
Un passo ancor. . . .
Non cadere! approda! approda!. . . .

**LAURA:** (*nelle braccia di Enzo*).
Enzo! Mio Enzo! Mio amor!

the cable.
You, master of the sails, upon the prow
Of our ship see hoisted the Dalmatian flag.
There it has floated through many sharp ordeals!
And on the mainmast at once hang out the lantern.
(*To the Midshipmen.*)
And you, be ready to let go the mooring cable
At my first signal.
(*Some of the crew execute Enzo's orders, while the others repeat the Marinaresca.*)

**ENZO:** (*to all*). Now go below; betake to slumber
While I alone upon deck
Watch the enemy's vessels.
It is late now. Good-night to all!

**CHORUS:** Heaven watch over you!

**ENZO:** Good-night.
(*The crew go below deck.*)
Heaven! and ocean! yon ethereal vail
Is radiant as a holy altar.
My angel, will she come from heaven?
My angel, will she come over ocean?
Here I await her; I breathe with rapture
The soft zephyrs filled with love.
Mortals often, when fondly sighing,
Find you a torment, O golden dreams!
In yon airy depths
There is seen neither shore nor mountain.
The horizon kisses the billows,
The billows kiss the horizon.
Here I am waiting in darkness,
My heart is wildly panting.
Come then, dearest! come, to the kisses
That can impart magic bliss.
(*Gazing at the sea.*)
But who comes? It is not a phantom
Of my brain? A boat approaches!
I already hear the rowers;
They towards me are swiftly steering

**VOICE OF BARNABA:** (*behind the brigantine*). Signor Captain, on board there?

**ENZO:** (*calling in the direction of the voice of Barnaba*). Come this way.
Heaven aid me to bear the fullness
Of this rapture! Now then, boatmen,
Keep on this side of the vessel.
(*Throws a rope over the side.*)
There! the guide rope, hold tightly.
Now tie it, mount quickly.
(*Enter Laura.*)

**LAURA:** (*in the arms of Enzo*).
Enzo, my Enzo! Ah, dearest, I am yours!

**ENZO:** Laura! Amore! Amor!

**LA VOCE DI BARNABA:** (*sinistramente, allontanandosi*). Buona fortuna.

**LAURA:** Oh! la sinistra voce!

**ENZO:** S' ei fu che ti salvò!. . . .

**LAURA:** Pur sorridea d'un infernal sorriso!. . . .

**ENZO:** È l' uomo che ci aperse il paradiso!
Deh! non turbare—con ree paure
Di questi istanti—le ebbrezze pure;
D' amor soltanto—con me ragiona,
È il cielo, o cara—che schiudi a me!

**LAURA:** Ah! del tuo bacio—nel dolce incanto
Celeste gioia—diventa il pianto,
A umano strazio—Dio non perdona,
Se perdonato—amor non è!

**ENZO:** Ma dimmi come—angelo mio,
Mi ravvisasti?

**LAURA:** Nel marinar
Enzo conobbi.

**ENZO:** Al pari anch' io
Te al primo suono—della parola. . . .

**LAURA:** Enzo adorato!—ma il tempo vola.
All' erta! all' erta!

**ENZO:** Deh, non tremar!
Siamo in un' isola—tutta deserta,
Fra mare e cielo—Fra cielo e mar!
Vedrem fra poco tramontar la luna. . . .
Quando sarà corcata, all' aura bruna
Noi salperem; cogli occhi al ìrmamento,
Coi baci in fronte e colle vele al vento!

**LAURA E ENZO:** Laggù nelle nebbie remote
Laggiù nelle tenebri ignote
Sta il segno del nostro cammin:
Nell' onde, nell' ombre, nei venti,
Fidenti ridenti, fuggenti,
Gitteam la vita e il destin.
La luna discende
Ricinta di rori de bende,
Siccome una sposa all' altar,
E asconde la spenta parvenza
Nell' ona, con lenta cadenza,
La luna è discesa nel mar.
(*La luna bassa si svolve dalle nuvole, il suo disce s' asconderà dietro il vascello.*)

**ENZO:** Laura! Laura! dearest, I am yours!

**VOICE OF BARNABA:** (*ominously, departing*). Good luck attend you!

**LAURA:** Ah! at that voice I shudder!

**ENZO:** It is by him you're saved.

**LAURA:** Yet, when he smiles, his smile appears infernal.

**ENZO:** It is he who for us opens Paradise.
Ah! cloud not, dearest, with fears and doubtings
The pure enjoyment of these blessed moments.
Of love, love only, let our discourse be!
Love is the heaven unvailed tonight.

**LAURA:** Ah, love your kisses, with sweet enchantment,
Change every sorrow to rapture celestial.
No human frailty will heaven pardon,
If it will not pardon love's delight.

**ENZO:** But tell me how, my angel,
You did recognize me?

**LAURA:** The sailor's dress hid not my Enzo.

**ENZO:** It was thus with me, love.
Soon as your voice
Blessed the air with its music.

**LAURA:** Enzo, beloved!
But time is flying—be watchful!

**ENZO:** Fear not, my love!
This is an island wholly deserted,
Amid sky and ocean, ocean and sky.
We soon shall see yonder the moon descending,
And when she sinks to slumber, favor by darkness,
We will set sail, with kisses on our foreheads,
And favoring winds our sails filling.

**LAURA AND ENZO:** Down yonder amid the dim, far-off mists,
Down yonder amid the dark, unknown clouds,
Our goal will be espied before long.
To the billows, the shadows, the breezes,
Both faithful, and smiling and flying
We confide our lives and our fate.
The moon is descending
Surrounded and veiled by the night dews,
Like bride attired for the altar.
And hiding her fast-fading lustre,
Sinks under the waves in slow cadence.
(*The moon disappears behind the clouds.*)

# Act II

ENZO: (*staccandosi*). E il tuo nocchiere
Or la fuga t' appresta—O amata donna,
Tu resta qui.
(*Scende sotto il ponte.*)

LAURA: Ho il cuor gonfio di lagrime
Quel lume! Ah! una Madonna!
(*Davanti all' immagine della Madonna orando con passione; mentre ch' essa prega, Gioconda mascherata escirà da un nascondiglio sotto prova, e s' avanzerà lenta.*)

GIOCONDA: È un anatèma!

LAURA: (*inorridita alzandosi*). Ah! chi sei?

GIOCONDA: Chi son, tu chiami?
Sono un' ombra che t'aspetta!
Il mio nome è la Vendetta.
Amo l' uomo che tu ami.

LAURA: Ciel!

GIOCONDA: (*accennando a prora*). Là attesi e il tempo colsi
Come belva nella tana,
Ah! la forza sovrumana,
Del furor m' invade i polsi!
Vuoi fuggire! d' amor ti struggi?
Vuoi fuggiere! lieta rivale?. . . .
Sì, l' antenna e il governale
Pronti son, sta ben, va, fuggi!
(*Ergendosi terribile.*)

LAURA: Furia orrenda!

GIOCONDA: Ah! mi paventi!
Ed ardisci amar d' amore
Quell' eroe?

LAURA: Sfido il tuo core,
O rival!

GIOCONDA: Bestemmi!

LAURA: Menti!
L' amo come il fulgor del creato!
Come l' aura che avviva il respir!
Come il sogno celeste e beato
Da cui venne il mio primo sospir.

GIOCONDA: Ed io l' amo siccome il leone
Ama il sangue, ed il turbine il vol
E la folgor le vette, e l' alcione
Le voragini, e l' aquila il sol!

LAURA: Pel suo bacio soave io disfido
Di morte l' orror!

GIOCONDA: Pel suo bacio soave t' uccido,
(*Ghermendo un pugnale.*)
Son più forte, più forte è il mio amor!
(*Afferrandola.*)
Il mio braccio t' afferra!
Vien ch' io ti scorga in viso! a terra! a terra!

ENZO: (*leaving Laura*). It is your pilot.
For flight now prepare yourself. O my beloved,
Rest here awhile.
(*Descends below deck.*)

LAURA: My heart is full of happy tears.
That light? Ah! It is a Madonna!
(*Throws herself at the foot of the altar, and prays earnestly. While she is praying, Gioconda, masked, comes from her hiding place, under the prow of the ship, and advances slowly towards Laura.*)

GIOCONDA: An anathema!

LAURA: (*frightened, she arises*). Ah! who art thou?

GIOCONDA: Who am I? ask you?
I am a shadow, waiting for you,
And my name is Vengeance!
I adore the man you love!

LAURA: Heaven!

GIOCONDA: (*pointing to the prow*). There, impatiently I waited,
Like a wild brute in its cavern.
Ah! the fury superhuman,
Of my wrath, invades my pulses!
You would fly? With love you are thrilling?
You would fly? say, joyous rival?
Yes, the sail yards and the rudder
Ready are, it is well. Go! I bid you.
(*Setting herself up as a judge, in a terrible manner.*)

LAURA: Rage appalling!

GIOCONDA: Ah! you fear me! Yet can you dare to speak
Of loving yonder hero.

LAURA: I love him with purer love than yours.

GIOCONDA: Blasphemer!

LAURA: Liar!
Him I love as the light of creation,
As the air that new life and strength brings me!
As the dream, that, celestial and blessed,
Brought me my first tender sigh.

GIOCONDA: Ah! and I love him, as the lion
Loves fresh blood; as the whirlwind its flight;
As the sunbeams love the hilltops; the sea bird
Yonder ocean depths; as eagles love the sun!

LAURA: While his sweet kisses greet me,
All the terrors of death I defy.

GIOCONDA: You shall die for those sweet kisses!
(*Seizing Laura's arm.*)
I am the stronger, and stronger is my love.
(*Taking hold of her.*)
Come, let me see your features!
Kneel down!
No escape for you now!

Or più scampo non hai!
Questo pagnale. . . .
Ma no. . . .
(*Star per darla un colpo ma si ferma subito.*)
Ti salvo! Olà, il mio palischermo!
(*Appariscondo due Marinai con una barca.*)
Fuggi! . . . a te. . . . questa maschera t'asconda!
(*Stacca la maschera e la pone sul volto a Laura.*)

LAURA: Ma mi dirai chi sei?

GIOCONDA: Son la Gioconda!
(*Gioconda spinge quasi a forza Laura nelle barca che si allontana rapidamente. Gioconda scomparisce un istante dietro al brigantino, come per assicurarsi della fuga di Laura.*)

BARNABA: (*dalla riva, asservando i movimenti della barca che porta Laura e scorgendo in distanza la gondola d' Alvise*). Maledizione! Ha preso il vol! Padron! Nel canal morto. . . .là. . . .forza di remi!. . . . (*Scomprisce.*)

GIOCONDA: E salva! O madre mia, quanto mi costi!. . . .

ENZO: (*scendendo dal ponte*). Laura, Laura! ove sei?

GIOCONDA: (*avanzandosi verso Enzo fieramente*). Laura è scomparsa!

ENZO: Gioconda! o ciel! che avvenne?

GIOCONDA: Invano a' rei
Baci sognati il tuo sospir la chiama. . . .

ENZO: Menti, menti, o crudel!

GIOCONDA: No! più t' ama!
(*Trascinandolo verso la riva.*)

MARINAI: Le galèe! le galèe! Salvi chi puo!

ENZO: (*strappando la fiaccola ad uno dei Marinai*). Sin ch' io sia vivo, no!
Al nemico darem cenere e brage! Incendio!
(*Da fuoco all' Hecate. La nave arde.*)

TUTTI: Incendio! Guerra! Morte! Strage!

ENZO: (*dalla tolda slanciandosi in mare*). O Laura, addio!

GIOCONDA: (*dalla riva*). E sempre Laura! ma almen poss' io con te morir.
(*La nave si sprofonda. Cade la tela.*)

Soon shall this poniard—
(*About to strike, stops suddenly.*)
But no!
(*A boat arrives with two Sailors.*)
I save you! Ho there! Bring my boat quickly!
(*Takes off the mask, which she puts on Laura's face.*)

LAURA: But tell me first, who are you?

GIOCONDA: I am La Gioconda.
(*Gioconda pushes her with great force into the boat, which goes away quickly. Gioconda disappears an instant behind the brigantine, assuring herself that Laura has escaped.*)

BARNABA: (*looking on all sides. observes the movements of the small boat which carries Laura and perceives the gondola of Alvise in the distance*). May they be cursed!
They have taken flight. Signor! By the canal, out there—(*pointing*) there!
Urge on the rowers, urge them!
(*He goes out.*)

GIOCONDA: (*entering again*). I've save her. Alas, dear mother, How much you cost me!

ENZO: (*entering from below deck*). Laura, Laura! where are you?

GIOCONDA: (*advancing haughtily towards Enzo*). Laura has vanished.

ENZO: Gioconda! oh heaven! what has happened?

GIOCONDA: In vain, to taste dreamy soft guilty kisses,
Your sighs may seek to recall her.

ENZO: Falsehood! cruel! it is false!

GIOCONDA: (*dragging him to the side of the boat*). No more she loves you!

SAILORS: No hope is left us. Ah, fly!

ENZO: (*taking a lighted torch from a Sailor*). While I'm living, no!
To the enemy we'll give ashes and embers!
We'll burn her!
(*He sets fire to the "Hecate," the ship burns.*)

ALL: We'll burn her! Fight them! kill them!

ENZO: (*throwing himself from the deck into the sea*). Adieu, my Laura!

GIOCONDA: (*aside*). It is ever Laura! Yet I, at least, may die with you!
(*The burning vessel sinks as the curtain falls.*)

## ■ ATTO III

### CÀ D'ORO

#### SCENA I

*Una camera nella Cà d'Oro. Sera; lampada accesa. Da un lato un' armatura antica.*

**ALVISE:** (*entrando in preda a violente aiitazione*). Sì! morir ella de'! Sul nome mio
Scritta l'infamia impunemente avrà?
Chi un Badoer tradì
Non può sperar pietà!....
Se ier non la ghermì
Nell' isola fatal questa mia mano,
L'espïazion non fia tremenda meno!
Ieri un pugnal le avria squarciato il seno,
Oggi....un ferro non è....sarà un veleno!
(*Accennando alle sale contigue.*)
Là turbini e farnetichi
La gaia baraonda,
Dell' agonia col gemito
La festa si confonda!
Ombre di mia prosapia
Non arrossite ancora!
Tutto la morte vendica,
Anche il tradito onor!
Là del patrizio veneto
S'adempia al largo invito,
Quivi il feral marito
Provveda al proprio onore!
Fremete, o danze, o cantici.
E un 'infedel che muor!

**LAURA:** (*entra en ricca veste da ballo, con perle e gemme: ad Alvise*). Qui chiamata m' avete?

**ALVISE:** (*con affettata cortesia*). Pur che vi piaccia. . . .

**LAURA:** Mio signor. . . .

**ALVISE:** Sedete!
(*Siedono ai due lati di un ampio tavolo.*)
Bella così, madonna,—io non v' ho mai veduta;
Pur il sorriso è languido;—perchè ristarvi muta?
Dite; un gentil mister—v' è grave a me svelar,
O un qualche velo nero—dovrò da me strappar?

## ■ ACT III

### THE HOUSE OF GOLD

#### SCENE I

*A Chamber in the House of Gold. Night; a lighted lamp. On one side of the stage, a suit of ancient armor.*

**ALVISE:** (*enters in violent agitation*). Yes, to die is her doom! My name, my honor,
Shall not with impunity be disgraced.
From Badoers, when betrayed,
It is vain to hope for pity.
Though yesterday upon the fatal isle
She escaped this vengeful hand,
She shall not escape a fearful expiation.
Last night, a sharp poniard should have pierced her bosom;
This night, I'll use no poniard! she dies by poison!
(*Pointing to the adjoining room.*)
While there the dancers sing and laugh,
In giddy movements flying,
Their mirthful tones shall blend with groans,
Breathed by a dying sinner:
Shades of my honored forefathers!
Soon shall your blushes disappear;
Soon shall a deadly vengeance prove
Honor to me is dear.
While dance the giddy crowd,
In mirthful movements flying,
Here shall be heard the bitter groans
The sinner breathes in dying.
Yonder, the nobles of the nation
Are gathered at my invitation;
Here, an insulted husband
For signal vengeance cries!
Exult, in dances and in songs,
While here a faithless one dies!

**LAURA:** (*enters in a ball dress of pearls and gems; to Alvise*). You have summoned me here?

**ALVISE:** (*with an affectation of courtesy*). Hoping to please you.

**LAURA:** My Lord—
(*Slowly seating herself.*)

**ALVISE:** Be seated.
(*They sit at opposite sides of large table.*)
Lovely as this, signora, I never yet have seen you;
Yet your smiles appear faint and languid,
Why do you sit speechless?
Tell me, is some gentle secret
About to be revealed?
Or will some vail of blackest dye
From me at once be torn?

**LAURA:** Dal vostro accento insolito—cruda ironia traspira,
Il labro a grazia atteggiasi—ma fuor ne scoppia l' ira. . . .
Mio nobile consorte,—non vi comprendo ancora!

**ALVISE:** (*concitato*). Pur d'abbassar la maschera—madonna, èquesta ora.
(*Alzandosi con violenza.*)
Giunta è l' ora!—ad altr' uomo rivolto,
Donna infame, è il tuo primo sospir. . . .

**LAURA:** Ad altr' uomo? Che dite? Che ascolto!
(*Fra sè.*)

**ALVISE:** Ieri quasi t' ho côlta in peccato,
Pur potesti salvarti e fuggir. . . .
Col mio guanto t' ho oggi afferrato,
Plù non fuggi,—t'e d'uopo morir!
(*La atterra violentemente. Laura getta un grido.*)

**LAURA:** (*a piedi di Alvise*). Morir! è troppo orribile!
Aver dinanzi il cielo
Discender nelle tenebre
D' un desolato avel!
Senti! di sangue tiepido
In seno mis corre un rivo. . . .
Perchè, se piango e vivo,
Dirmi: tu dêi morir?
La morte è pena infame
Anche a più gran fallir!

**ALVISE:** Invan tu piangi—invan tu speri,
Dio non ti può esaudir!
In lui raccogli—i tuoi pensieri:
Preparati a morir!
E già che ai nuovi imeni
L' anima tua sospira,
O indocil sposa, ten vieni
E mira!
(*Con forza sollevando la drapperia della camera attigua e indicando un catafalco. Si vedrà il riverbero dei ceri*).

**LAURA:** (*inorridita*). Ah! Ove m'adduci?

**ALVISE:** Vieni! Questo è il talamo tuo!
(*Entra Gioconda e s' appiatta in fondo. La serenata cessa per un momento.*)

**CORO:** Ten va serenata,
Per l' aura serena,
Ten va, cantilena,
Per l' onda incantata.

**ALVISE:** (*estraendo una fiala*). Prendi questo velen; e già che forte
Tanto mi sembri ne' tuoi detti audaci,
Con quelle labbra che succhiaro i baci,

**LAURA:** Throughout these accents unusual,
Irony still is breathing;
Your lips may kindness simulate,
Yet they are white with anger.
My noble lord and consort,
I do not understand you.

**ALVISE:** Well then, to tear away the mask,
The hour has come, signora;
(*Getting up in violence.*)
This is the moment. To another was given,
Shameless woman, your first loving sigh!

**LAURA:** To another? What mean you?

**ALVISE:** Yes, vilest of women.
I last night had nearly caught you when sinning
But you were able to fly from me!
In my grasp I today have enchained you,
Never to leave me, for now you must die. (*Throws her down violently.*)

**LAURA:** (*at the feet of Alvise*). To die! alas, it is a fate too horrible!
To quit a smiling sky,
And amid the deepest darkest gloom,
Die in desolation!
Lo! here, my lifeblood's rapid stream
Its onward course is keeping;
Yet life, for me, means weeping!
Why say you, I must die?
Death is the shameful punishment
For crimes of deepest dye!

**ALVISE:** In vain you weep, in vain you hope,
Heaven will not heed your prayer.
To yonder heaven your thoughts directing,
Prepare for death at once.
And now that for fresh nuptials
Fondly your soul is sighing,
Unfaithful consort, come here;
Admire this!
(*Violently uplifting the draperies of the adjoining chamber, and pointing to a funeral bier.*)

**LAURA:** (*horrified*). Ah! Where would you lead me?

**ALVISE:** Come! It is your bridal bed.
(*Serenade behind, far off on the Lagoon. Gioconda enters, the serenade ceases, she conceals herself.*)

**CHORUS:** Our gay songs are ending;
The soft echoes die,
And blithe careless laughter
Is changed to a sigh.

**ALVISE:** (*producing a flask*). You must take this poison. You have dared
To utter words that seem to me audacious,
Now let the lips that spoke them,

## Act III, Scene I

Suggi la morte.
Scampo non hai,
Odi questa canzon? Morir dovrai
Pria ch' essa giunga all' ultima sua
nota.
(*Esce.*)

CORO: La gaia canzon
Fa l' eco languir,
E l' ilare suon
Si muta in sospir.
Con vago miraggio
Riflette la luna
L' argenteo suo raggio
Sull' ampia laguna
E in quel si sublima
Riverbero pio,
Patetica rima
Creata da Dio.

GIOCONDA: (*accorrendo verso
Laura, afferra il veleno che Laura
ha tra le mani e le porge un' ampolla*). A me quel filtro! a te codesto! bevi!

LAURA: Gioconda, qui?

GIOCONDA: Previdi la tua sorte,
Per salvarti mi armai, ti rassicura.
Quel narcotico è tal, che della
morte
Finge il letargo i augosciasi e brevi
Sono gl' istanti. . . .bevi.

LAURA: Mi fai paura!

GIOCONDA: S' ei qui torna t' uccide.

LAURA: Atra agonia!

GIOCONDA: Prega per te quaggiù
la madre mia,
Nell' oratorio, i miei fidi cantori
Son presso. . . .ascolta.

LAURA: Orror!
Già la canzone muor!

CORO: Ten va, cantilena,
Per l' aura serena,
Ten va, serenata,
Per l' onda incantata
Udite le blande
Canzoni vagar.
Il remo ci scande
Gli accordi sul mar.
Ten va, serenata,
Sull' onda incantata.

GIOCONDA: Con essa muori!
La condanna t' è nota:
"Pria ch' essa giunga all' ultima suo
nota."

LAURA: Porgi! ho bevuto.
(*Prende la fiala dalle mani di Gioconda poi scompare dietro le cortine della camera mortuaria.*)

---

that drank kisses,
Drink in your death. No hope is left
for you.
Do you hear yonder song? Your life
must cease
Before the last note of that song has
sounded.
(*Alvise goes out.*)

CHORUS: Our gay songs are end-
ing,
The soft echoes die,
And blithe careless laughter
Is changed to a sigh.
The wavelets and moonbeams
Together are blending,
The bright rays of silver
On ocean descending.
Sublime is the message
By nature now given,
In tenderest cadence,
Created in Heaven!

GIOCONDA: (*runs to Laura,
seizes the poison that she has in
her hands and gives her a phial*).
Give me that flask, and take this
quickly!
Drink it.

LAURA: Gioconda here?

GIOCONDA: Your cruel doom
foreseeing,
I came here to save you. All fear
now banish.
This narcotic is such, that in a
trance
Like death, it will plunge you.
Drink it, drink it!
Full of anguish, yet brief
Are the moments now left for you.

LAURA: I am fearful of you.

GIOCONDA: He who returns here
will kill you.

LAURA: O dark despair!

GIOCONDA: For your safety my
mother in yon oratory
Is praying, and some staunch
friends are near
You hear their singing.

LAURA: Alas! slowly the song dies
out.

CHORUS: Our gay songs are end-
ing,
The soft echoes die,
And blithe careless laughter
Is changed to a sigh.
We listen to songs
Full of innocent glee,
Our oars keeping time
As we float over the sea.
Float on, serenade!
Heaven soft air is granting;
In harmony float
Over the waters enchanting.

GIOCONDA: Drink, then. With it,
your life was to cease!
This was the sentence:
"Before the last note of that song
has sounded."

LAURA: Give me. I have drained it.
(*Takes the phial from Gioconda
and rushes behind the curtains of
the funeral chamber.*)

---

GIOCONDA: La ìala a me!
(*Travasa il veleno d' Alvise nella
fiala del sonnifero e lascia l' am-
polla del veleno vuota ul travolo.*)
Gran Dio!
(*Esce precipitosa.*)

CORO: Il canto è la vita,
Di sogni si pasce,
Ai sogni c' invita,
Dai sogni rinasce,
D' un' anima ignota
E l' eco fedel;
L' estrema sua nota
Si perde del ciel.

ALVISE: (*mentre la cadenza della
serenata è alle ultime sue note, os-
serve l' ampolla vuoto sul tavolo*).
Tutto è compiuto!
Vuoto è il cristal.
(*Entra nella cella funeraria, vi ri-
mane un momento e torna in sce-
na.*)
Vola su lei la morte.
(*Esce lentamente.*)

GIOCONDA: (*ricomparisce dal
lato opposto a quello donde è uscito Alvise. Si guarda iutorno, solleva la cortina della cella, poi, vista-
si sola, esclama:*) O madre mia,
nell' isola fatale
Frenai per te la sanguinaria brama
Di rejetta rival. Or più tremendo
E il sacrifizio mio. . . .
Io la salvo per lui, per lui che l'
ama!
(*Esce precipitosamente.*)

---

GIOCONDA: Give me the flask.
(*Pours the poison into the phial
which had contained the narcotic, and leaves the empty flask on
the table.*)
Great heaven!
(*Leaves precipitately.*)

CHORUS: We listen to songs
Full of innocent glee;
Our oars keeping time
As we float over the sea.
From some unknown soul
Comes Echo's reply;
The last note, ascending,
Is lost in the sky!

ALVISE: (*alone during the end of
the serenade, he sees the empty
phial on the table*). All now is over!
Empty is the flask.
(*Enters the funeral chamber for a
moment, then re-enters.*)
Death has forever claim'd her!
(*He goes out slowly.*)

GIOCONDA: (*reappears from the
opposite side from which Alvise
has gone out, looks around, lifts
the curtain of the chamber, seeing
she is alone, exclaims:*) O dearest
mother, on yonder fatal island,
For your dear sake, I checked the
burning frenzy
Of a passion disdained. Now, more
tremendous
The sacrifice I'm making!
I save her; but for his sake, who
loves her.
(*Leaves precipitately.*)

---

## SCENA II

Sontuosissima sala attigua alla
cella funeraria, splendidamente
parata a festa. Ampio portone nel
fondo a sinistra, un consimile a
destra, ma questo tutto chiuso da
una drapperia. Una terza porta
nella parete a sinistra.

Entrano Cavalieri, Dame, Maschere. Alvise moverà loro incontro
ricevendo e complimentando chi
entra. Il Paggio gli sta accanto.
Gioconda.

ALVISE: Benvenuti messeri! An-
drea Sagredo!
Erizzo, Loredan! Venier! Chi vedo?
Isepo Barbarigo, a noi tornato
Cugino mio Partecipazio! O quanti
Bei cavalieri!. . . . Belle dame!
Avanti,
Avanti! e voi, vispi cantori e masch-
ere,
Presto sciogliete le carole e i canti

---

## SCENE II

A magnificent ball, adjoining the
funeral chamber, and splendidly
adorned for a festivity. At back,
wide entrance door. A similar
door to the left completely closed
by curtains. A third door, opening
from the right wall to the left.

(*Enter Cavaliers, Ladies, and
Masquers. Alvise advances to
meet them, and exchanges
compliments with all who arrive.
A page stands behind him. Gioconda enters unobserved.*)

ALVISE: Worthy friends, you are
welcome! Andrea Sagredo!
Erizzo, Loredan, Venier! Whom see
I?
Isepo Barbarigo, to us returning
From pale, far distant China?
And here my much loved cousin
comes, Partecipazio!
Of splendid knights what a
concourse!
Pass onward, charming ladies, pass
onward,
You, signors, too, are welcome,
cavaliers,

**CORO:** S' inneggi alla Cà d' Oro
Che intreccia ai rami d'oro
Dell virtù l'alloro
Col mirto dell' amor.

**ALVISE:** Grazie vi rendo per le vostre laudi.
Cortesi amici.
A più leggiadri guadi
Ora v' invito.
Ecco una mascherata
Di vaghe danzatrici.
Ognuna è ornata
Di bellezza e fulgore
E tutte in giro rappresentan l' oro.
S'incomincia la danza.

**DANZA DELLE ORÈ:** *Le Ore del Mattino.*
*Le Ore del Girono.*
*Le Ore della Sera.*
*Le Ore della Notte.*

**BARNABA:** (*trascinando Cieca che invano cerca svincolarsi dalle sue strette*). Vieni!

**CIECA:** Lasciami! Ohimè!

**CORO:** Cieca!

**GIOCONDA:** (*accorrendo*). O madre!

**ALVISE:** (*e Cieca*). Qui che fai tu?

**BARNABA:** Nelle vietate stanzo
Io la sorpresi al maleficio intenta!

**CIECA:** Pregavo per chi muor!
(*Si odono i lenti rintocchi della campana degli agonizzanti.*)

**CORO:** Per chi muor? che di' tu?
Qual suon funèbre!

**ENZO:** (*a Barnaba*). Un' agonìa! per chi?

**BARNABA:** (*sottovoce ad Enzo*). Per Laura!

**ENZO:** Orror!
Che più mi resta se quell' angiol muor?

**ALVISE:** (*avanzandosi tra la folla atterrita e confusa*). E che? la gioia sparve!
Se gaio è Badoreo,
Chi ha fra gli ospiti suoi dritto al dolore?

**ENZO:** Io l' ho più ch' altri.

**ALVISE:** Tu? ma tu chi sei?

**ENZO:** (*gettando la maschera*). Il tuo proscritto io sono, Enzo Grimaldo,
Prence di Santafior! Patria e amore
Tu m' hai rubato un dì. . . .
Or compi il tuo delitto!

And you merry young singers, and maskers, too.
Brighten the revelry with songs and dances!

**CHORUS:** We sing in praise of the House of Gold,
Where twine, in golden chaplets,
With virtue's laurel leaves,
The myrtles of true love.

**ALVISE:** Let me offer you thanks for these kind praises,
These accents courteous. And now let me invite you to gayer spectacles.
Here come the masqueraders,
A troop of lovely dancers. Each one is glowing
With beauty and ardor. In graceful movements
The Hours representing;
And their dance now commences.

**DANCE OF THE HOURS:** *The Hours of the Daybreak.*
*The Hours of the Day.*
*The Hours of the Evening.*
*The Hours of the Night.*

**BARNABA:** (*dragging in Cieca*). Come on!

**CIECA:** Let me go! Ah me!

**CHORUS:** Cieca.

**GIOCONDA:** (*running*). My mother!

**ALVISE:** (*to Cieca*). What do you want here?

**BARNABA:** In the forbidden chambers
I just now caught her, intent upon some malice.

**CIECA:** For her, just dead, I prayed. (*The passing bell for the dying is heard slowly tolling.*)

**CHORUS:** Her, just dead! What are you saying?
Ah! That sounds funereal!

**ENZO:** (*in an undertone to Barnaba*). The knell of death! For whom?

**BARNABA:** (*aside to Enzo*). For Laura.

**ENZO:** For Laura? O Heaven!
What now remains for me, if she is dead?

**ALVISE:** (*advancing through the crowd stunned and confused*).
What now? Joy is immortal!
If gay is Badoero,
Who, amongst all his guests, has the right to be gloomy?

**ENZO:** (*advancing*). I, of all others!

**ALVISE:** You! But who are you?

**ENZO:** (*unmasking*). By you proscribed; Enzo Grimaldo,
Prince of Santafior. My country, my beloved,
Were stolen from me by you.
Of crime you may now fill up the measure.

**ALVISE:** Audacia!

**CORO:** Audacia!

**ALVISE:** Sul capo tuo rispondi,
Barnaba, del codardo insultator!

**CORO:** D' un vampiro fatal,
L' ala fredda passè
E in teda funeral,
Ogni face mutò
Un sinistro baglior,
La man su noi passò,
No, gioia più regnar,
Nella festa non può!

**ENZO:** (*fra sè*). O mia stella d' amor,
O mio Nume fedel,
Se rapita a me sei,
Ti raggiungo nel ciel!

**GIOCONDA:** (*fra sè*). O tortura crudel!
Inaudito martir!
Quanto ei l' ama! è per lei,
Qui venuto a morir!

**CIECA:** (*a Barnaba*). O fatal delator,
Se trafitto alcun fu,
Riconosco la man,
L' assassino sei tu!

**BARNABA:** (*e Cieca*). Giuro al cielo, se ier,
Quella rea ti salvò!
La vendetta oggimai,
Più sfuggirmi non può!

**ENZO:** (*fra sè*). Già ti veggo immota e smorta
Tutta avvolta in bianco vel,
Tu su morta, tu sei morta,
Angiol mio dolce e fedel!
Su di me piombi la scure,
S' apra il baratro fatal,
E mi guidin le torture
All' imene celestial.

**GIOCONDA:** Scorre il pianto a stilla a stilla
Nel silenzio del dolore.
Piangi, o pupilla,
Mentre sanguina il mio cor.

**BARNABA:** (*a Gioconda*). Cedi alfin, della mia mano
Vedi qui l' opra fatale.

**GIOCONDA:** (*sottovoce a Barnaba*). Se lo salvi e adduci al lido,
Laggiù presso al Redentor,
Il mio corpo t' abbandono,
O terribile cantor.

**BARNABA:** (*a Gioconda*).
Disperato è questo dono,
Pur lo accetta il tuo cantor.
Al destin spietato irrido,
Pur d' averti sul mio cor.

**ALVISE:** Audacious!

**CHORUS:** Audacious! He dies!

**ALVISE:** Barnaba, your head shall answer for him,
Should the vile insulter escape.

**CHORUS:** As if over our brows a vampire's hand had passed,
A shudder takes the place of the smiles that each wore;
With a sinister gleam our foreheads are illumed,
And gay light-hearted joy at the feast reigns no more.

**ENZO:** (*aside*). O bright star of my soul, ever constant and sweet,
Though from me you are torn, we shall meet in Heaven!

**GIOCONDA:** (*aside*). Cruel tortures are mine, evil fated am I!
True love's martyr is he; he for her came to die!

**CIECA:** (*to Barnaba*). O vile hated spy! I too well know you, now!
If a death-wound was given, the assassin—it was you!

**BARNABA:** (*to Cieca*). Ah, hear me swear! If last night you were saved,
I'll today be revenged, too long I've been braved!

**ENZO:** (*aside*). I behold you motionless, pallid,
Shrouded in your snowy vail!
You are dead, love; you are dead, love!
Ah! my darling, hopeless I wail
The sharp axe is waiting for me,
Opens wide a dark abyss;
But to you shall torture guide me,
Soon we'll share celestial bliss!

**GIOCONDA:** Sadly fall the teardrops,
In the silence of despair;
Break, oh heart! sad eyes, rain torrents!
Fate, your sharpest doom prepare!

**BARNABA:** (*aside to Gioconda*).
Yield, yield! all around
See what power I have for ill!
Well may you fear me; powers infernal
Attract me still to ill deeds.

**GIOCONDA:** (*aside to Barnaba*).
Do you save him, bring him safe out there,
Close by the Redentor, and then
Myself I will surrender
To you, fearfulest of men.

**BARNABA:** (*to Gioconda*).
Though despair may prompt your offer,
I accept it for my part,
And the bitterest fate will welcome,
Once to press you to this heart.

**CIECA:** (*a Gioconda*). Le tue lagrime, o Gioconda,
Che non versi sul mio cor?
Un amor non ti circonda
Che sia pari a questo amor!

**CIECA:** (*to Gioconda*). You are weeping, O Gioconda,
Let me fold you to my breast.
Never love, like love maternal,
Can encounter every test.

**ALVISE:** Nel fulgor di questa festa
Mal venisti, o cavalier,
Par che sia per te funesta
L' allegria dei Badoer!
Ma già appresto a' tuoi sgomenti
Nuova scena di terror!
Tu saprai, se invan si attenti
Del mio nome al puro onor!

**ALVISE:** Amid the splendor this fête surrounding,
You are unwelcome, cavalier;
But before long, new scenes of horror
Shall claim attention from you.
You shall soon see if I am watchful
Of the honor of my name.

**CORO:** Tetri eventi! Audacie orrende!
Spaventevole festin!
Come rapida discende
La valanga del destin!

**CHORUS:** Mournful feasting, fearful horrors!
Mournful feast, soon desolate!
Ah! how rapidly descending,
Falls the avalanche of fate!

**ALVISE:** (*avanzandosi in mezzo della scena, con atto di suprema dignità*). Or tutti a me! La donna che fu mia
L' estremo oltraggio al nome mio recò!
(*Va verso la cella funeraria ed alza le cortine. Laura apparisce vestita di bianco stesa sul suo letto di morte. La cella è rischiarata da molti doppieri.*)
Miratela! Son io che spenta l' ho!

**ALVISE:** (*proudly glancing around*). Now, all draw near! A woman, once my wife,
The foulest outrage brought upon my name.
(*Opens the curtains and points to Laura all dressed in white on her death-bed, the chamber is lighted by many candles.*)
Behold her now! It was I who took her life!

**ENZO:** (*si slancia brandendo il pugnale ma è trattenuto dalle guardie*). Carnefice!

**ENZO:** (*brandishing a poniard, rushes on Alvise, but is seized by the guards*). Base murderer!

**GIOCONDA E CIECA:** Orror!

**GIOCONDA AND CIECA:** Horror!

**CORO:** Orror! orror!
(*Giocondo corre verso Enzo che viene trascinato dalle guardie. Barnaba afferra per la mano Cieca e, giovandosi della confusione la spinge entro una porta segreta. Alvise resta intinobile presso la cella funeraria, additando il cadavere di Laura. Gli invitati si attegiano ad espressioni di raccapriccio, di sdeggno è di pieta. Quadro. Cala la tela.*)

**CHORUS:** Horror! despair! woe!
(*Barnaba grabs Cieca and pushes her into a secret door. Alvise remains motionless near the funeral chamber pointing to the corpse of Laura. The guests compose themselves. Some show fear, some pity, others disdain. The curtain falls.*)

# ■ ATTO IV

## IL CANAL ORFANO

*L' atrio di un palazzo diroccato nell' isola della Giudecca. Nell' angolo di destra un paravento disteso, dietro il quale sta un letto. Un gran portone di riva nel fonda da cui si vedrà la laguna e la piazzetta di San Marco illuminata a festa. Una immagine della Madonna ed una croce appesa al muro. Un tavolo, un canapè, sul tavolo una lucerna ed una lanterna accese, un' ampolla di veleno, un pugnale. Sul canapè varii adornamenti scenici di Gioconda. A destra della scena una lunga e buia calle.*

# ■ ACT IV

## THE ORFANO CANAL

*The vestibule of a palace in ruins, on the island of Giudeca. In the right-hand corner an opened screen, behind which is a bed. Large porch at back, through which are seen the Lagoon and the square of St. Mark, brilliantly illuminated. A picture of the Virgin, and a crucifix, bang against the wall. Table and couch; on the table a lamp and a lighted lantern, a flask of poison, and a dagger; on the couch various scenic ornaments belonging to Gioconda. On the right of the scene, a long dimly-lighted street.*

*Gioconda sola, cupamente assorta ne' suoi pensieri, intanto dal fondo della calle si avanzano due uomini che portano in braccio Laura avvolta in un mantello nero. Battono all' uscio. Gioconda si scuote e va ad aprire. Entrano.*

**GIOCONDA:** Nessun v' ha visto?

**PRIMO CANTORE:** Nessuno.

**GIOCONDA:** Sul letto
La deponete.
(*Gioconda va al paravento. Laura è deposta sul letto.*)
I compagni
Verranno questa notte?

**CANTORE:** Sì.

**GIOCONDA:** Ecco l' oro
Che vi promisi.

**CANTORE:** Nol vogliam. . . .gli amici
Prestan opra da amici.

**GIOCONDA:** (*mutando accento e supplicando*). O pietosi,
Per quell' amor che v' ha creati, un altra
Grazia vi chiedo. Nella scorsa notte
Mi scomparve la mia cieca madre,
Già disperata la cercai, ma invano.
Deh! scorrete le vie, le piazze, e l' orme
Della mia vecchierella Iddio v' insegni
Doman, se la trovate, a Canareggio
V' aspetterò, Quest' antro di Giudecca
Fra brev' ora abbandono.

**CANTORI:** A noi t' affida.
(*Gioconda stringe ad essi la mano escono da dove son entrati. Gioconda presso il tavolo guarda il pugnale, la tocca, poi prende l' ampolla del veleno.*)

**GIOCONDA:** Suicidio!. . . .in questi
Fieri momenti
Tu sol mi resti,
E il cor mi tenti.
Ultima voce
Del mio destino,
Ultima croce
Del mio cammino.
E un dì leggiadre
Volavan l' ore;
Perdei la madre,
Perdei l' amore,
Vinsi l' infausta
Gelosa febbre!
Or piombo esausta
Fra le tenebre!. . . .
Tocco alla mèta. . . .
Domando al ciel
Di dormir queta
Dentro l' avel.
(*Guardando ancora l' ampolla.*)

*Gioconda, alone, gloomily buried in thought. From the end of the street two men advance, carrying in their arms Laura, who is enveloped in a black cloak. The two Cantori (street singers) knock at the door. Gioconda, startled, goes to open the door.*

**GIOCONDA:** No one has seen you?

**FIRST CANTORI:** No one.

**GIOCONDA:** Upon yonder bed
Now place her.
(*Gioconda walks to the screen and shows them where to carry Laura.*)
Our companions?
Will they be ready tonight?

**CANTORI:** Yes.

**GIOCONDA:** Here's the gold
That I promised to you.

**CANTORI:** Take it back; true friends
Willingly help one another.

**GIOCONDA:** (*changing accent and pleading*). O have pity! By the love of those who bore you,
For further aid I implore you. During yesternight
From my blind mother I was separated;
Since then despairingly have sought her but vainly.
Ah, then, search every highway and piazza!
To the traces of my blind angel mother
Kind heaven will guide you.
Tomorrow, if you find her at Canareggio
I shall be found.
I shall abandon this den, this foul Giudeca, before long.

**CANTORI:** Rely on us.
(*Gioconda clasps the hands of the singers, who depart through the porch by which they had entered. Gioconda approaches the table, and looks fixedly at the dagger, which she examines, and then takes up the flask of poison.*)

**GIOCONDA:** Yes, suicide! the sole
Resource now left me!
Stern Fate forever
Has bereft me of hope.
I the last accents
Of destiny hear,
Bear my last cross;
Know the end draws near.
Bright is the day,
The hours gaily flying!
Lost is my mother;
Love lies a-dying.
Conquered by jealousy's
Terrible fever,
I sink exhausted;
Sink down forever!
Near draws the end now!
If Heaven prove kind,
Before long in the grave
I may find repose.
(*Again contemplating the flask of poison.*)

Ecco, il velen di Laura, a un' altra vittima
Era serbato! io lo berrò!—Quand' esso
Questa notte qui giunga, io non vedrò
Il loro immenso amplesso;
Ma chi provvede alla lor fuga? ah! no!
(*Getta il veleno sul tavolo.*)
No, tentator, lungi da me! conforta,
Anima mia, le tue divine posse!
Laura è là. . . .là sul letto. . . .viva. . . .morta. . . .
Nol so. . . .se spenta fosse!!!
Io salvarla volea, mio Dio lo sai!
Pur, s' ella è spenta!?. . . .un indistinto raggio
Mi balena nel cor. . . .vediam. . . .coraggio.
(*Prende la lanterna, fa per avviarsi el letto e poi si pente.*)
Ah. . . .no. . . .giammai, giammai!
No, non mi sfugga questo dubbio arcano!
Ma s' ella vive? ebben. . . .Laura è in mia mano. . . .
(*Biecamente.*)
Siam sole—E notte—Nè persona alcuna
Saper potria. . . .profonda è la laguna. . . .

**UNA VOCE:** (*lontana sull' acqua*). Ehi! dalla gondola,
Che nuove porti?

**ALTRA VOCE:** (*piu lontana*). Nel Canal Orfano
Ci son dei morti.

**GIOCONDA:** Orrore! orrore!! orrore!!!
Sinistre voce! illuminata a festa
Splende Venezia nel lontano. . . .in core
Mi si ridesta
La mia tempesta
Immane! furibonda!
O amore! amore!!
Enzo! pietà!. . . .
(*Al culmine della disperazione si getta accanto al tavolo. Intanto si vedrà Enzo venir dalla calle, trova la porta socchiusa, entra.*)

**ENZO:** Gioconda!

**GIOCONDA:** Enzo!. . . .sei tu!

**ENZO:** (*cupamente*). Dal carcere
M' hai tratto; e i miei legami
Sciogliesti, e armato e libero
Qui son. Da me che brami?

**GIOCONDA:** (*con accento d' esaltazione straziante*). Da te che bramo? ahi! misera!
Ridarti il sol, la vita!
La libertà infinita!

The poison, meant for Laura, to another victim
Soon will be fatal. Let me drink it!
When *he*
Shall come tonight, I shall not see
How fervent their embraces.
But who will answer for their escape? Ah no!
(*Throwing the poison on the table.*)
Tempter away! out of my sight!
Take comfort,
O my soul, in your divine endurance!
(*With ferocious joy.*)
Laura is there! yonder lying: dead?—or living?
None knows. She's in my power—
I to save her endeavored, great Heaven you know!
Still, were she dead? An indistinct suggestion,
Like a lightning-flash comes. Let's see! Now, courage!
(*Takes up the lantern, and is about to approach the bed, but stops.*)
Ah no! no, never! No, never!
And yet—and yet the gloomy doubt still haunts me.
But—were she living? Well, then, we are alone—
Without witness; it is night, and no human being
Could know when it was over. And deep is yon Lagoon.

**A VOICE:** (*in the distance*). Ho! gondolier! have you any fresh tidings?

**OTHER VOICE:** (*in the distance*). In the Orfano Canal there are corpses.

**GIOCONDA:** Ah me! ah me! oh, horror!
O sinister voices! Illuminated brightly,
Resplendent Venice shines, out yonder! My heart
Is thus illumined
By flames of vengeance,
Relentless, unforgiving,
O love! O love!
Enzo, have pity! Have pity, love, on me!
(*In despair throws herself down, weeping and exhausted, near the table. In the meantime Enzo comes form the street, finds the door open and enters.*)

**ENZO:** Gioconda!

**GIOCONDA:** Enzo!—it is you!

**ENZO:** From prison
You have freed me: by you my chains
Have been unfastened, and armed and free
Behold me here. What would you do with me?

**GIOCONDA:** (*in accents heartrending exultation*). What would I do with you? Alas!
With smiles your life is surrounded,

La gioia e l' avvenir!
L' estatico sorriso,
L' estatico sospiro!
L' amore. . . .il paradiso!
Gran Dio! fammi morir!

**ENZO:** Donna! col tuo delirio
Tu irridi a un moribondo,
Per me non ha più balsami
L' amor, nè gioie il mondo.
Addio. . . .

**GIOCONDA:** Che fai?

**ENZO:** Non chiedere.

**GIOCONDA:** (*afferrandolo*). Resta . . . . M' ascolta.

**ENZO:** (*svincolandosi*). Cessa.

**GIOCONDA:** Tu vuoi morir per essa!

**ENZO:** Sì, sul suo santo avello
Baciare anco una volta
La pallida sepolta.

**GIOCONDA:** (*con possente ironia*). Ebben, corri al tuo voto,
Eroe mesto e fedel!
L' avel di Laura è vuoto;
Io l' ho rapita!

**ENZO:** (*con un grido*). Cielo!
(*Con un grido.*)

**GIOCONDA:** (*accennando alla croce appesa al muro*). Giuro,
Giuro su quella croce.

**ENZO:** No: la bestemmia atroce
Tergi dal labbro impuro!
Di' che hai mentito!

**GIOCONDA:** (*con fierezza, poi supplichevole*). No! No!
Io dissi il ver!

**ENZO:** Vedi! già brilla il fulmine
Del mio pugnal. . . .
(*Sguainando il suo pugnale e afferrando Gioconda.*)

**GIOCONDA:** No! io dissi il ver.

**ENZO:** Vedi! Già brilla il fulmine
Del mio pugna le.

**GIOCONDA:** Oh gioia!
M' uccide!

**ENZO:** Il tuo mister saprò.
Parla. . . .

**GIOCONDA:** No.

**ENZO:** Parla.

**GIOCONDA:** No.

**ENZO:** Ebben . . . . infame . . . . muori!
(*Per ferirla.*)

**LAURA:** (*dall' alcova*). Enzo!

**ENZO:** Chi è là!

**GIOCONDA:** (*atterrita*). Mio Dio!

Your liberty unbounded,
Bright joys lie in your pathway.
The smiles that speak love's yearning,
The sighs of rapture burning,
This earth to Eden turning!
(*Aside.*)
Great Heaven, now let me die!

**ENZO:** Woman, calm your frenzied passion;
My days will soon be over:
New life, new love, no balm can bring
A broken-hearted lover.
Adieu now!

**GIOCONDA:** What are you doing?

**ENZO:** Seek not to know.

**GIOCONDA:** (*seizing him*). Stay here, and listen!

**ENZO:** (*disengaging himself*). Cease!

**GIOCONDA:** You will then die for Laura?

**ENZO:** Yes, I go to Laura's tomb,
Once more to kiss, while dying,
My lost love, lying lifeless.

**GIOCONDA:** (*mockingly*). It is well; fulfill your purpose,
O faithful hero, but know,
The tomb of Laura is vacant.

**ENZO:** (*with a cry*). Heaven!

**GIOCONDA:** I have removed her.

**ENZO:** No! Falsehood! falsehood!

**GIOCONDA:** (*pointing to the crucifix on the wall*). I swear it.
Swear it by yon Redeemer.

**ENZO:** No! you are a blasphemer! Yon crucifix profaning.
No! you are perjured!
(*Takes out his dagger and seizes Gioconda.*)

**GIOCONDA:** No! I have sworn the truth.

**ENZO:** See! with gleam-like lightning-flash
Shines my keen poniard!

**GIOCONDA:** (*aside*). Oh joy!
He will kill me!

**ENZO:** Unfold your mystery!

**GIOCONDA:** No!

**ENZO:** Answer!

**GIOCONDA:** No!

**ENZO:** Then you shall forfeit your life.
(*About to stab her.*)

**LAURA:** (*from the alcove*). Enzo!

**ENZO:** Who's there?

**GIOCONDA:** (*terrified*). Great Heaven!

# Act IV

**LAURA:** (*comparendo*). Enzo! amor mio! Ah! il cor mi si ravviva. . . . Respiro all aura. . . .

**ENZO:** Non deliro.

**LAURA:** Enzo, vieni . . . . vieni . . . . son viva!

**ENZO:** (*slanciandosi, abbracciando Laura*). Laura! ciel! non deliro! Ah! Laura! Laura!

**GIOCONDA:** (*avviluppandosi la testa nel suo manto*). Nascondili, o tenèbra!

**LAURA:** (*guardando verso Gioconda*). Ahimè! quell' ombra Alvise. . . .fuggi. . . .

**ENZO:** No, il terror disgombra.

**LAURA:** (*avvicinandosi riconosce Gioconda che si sarà scoperta*). Sei tu?! costei salvò la vita a me.

**ENZO:** (*a Gioconda*). Fanciulla santa! Ch' io ti baci il piè! (*Laura ed Enzo cadono in ginocchio davanti a Gioconda.*)

**CORO:** (*nella distanza*). Ten va, serenata, Per l' aura serena, Ten va cantilena, Per l' onda incantata. Udite le blande Canzoni vagar, Il remo ci scande Gli accordi sul mar. Il canto è la vita, Di sogni si pasce, Ai sogni c' invita, Nei sogni rinasce, D' un' anima ignota E l' eco fedel, L' estrema sua nota Si perde nel ciel.

**GIOCONDA:** (*con calma dolcissima*). Questa canzone ti rammenti, o Laura? È la canzone della tua fortuna. Essa viene, per noi. Attenti udite, Fratelli miei, quei rematori in salvo Questa notte v' addurran. Per la fuga Tutto provvidi cautamente. Alzate Le vostre fronti, ch' io veda il sorriso Ch' io vi creai. No, d' attristar Gioconda Più non temete. . . .amatevi. . . . Ho il cuore rassegnato. Nessuno è qui colpevole, So che l' amore è un fato! (*Enzo e Laura al colmo della commozione.*) Basta! il tempo fugge! La barca s' avvicina. . . .i miei compagni Vi condurran prima dell' alba al lido Dei Tre Porti. . . . Verso Aquileja drizzerete il volo, E di là poco lunge il sol d' Illiria Vi splenderà liberamente in viso. (*A Laura.*)

**LAURA:** (*appearing*). Enzo! my beloved!— My strength is fast reviving— I breathe the pure balmy air—

**ENZO:** I'm not dreaming?—

**LAURA:** Enzo! Come love! I'm living!

**ENZO:** (*rushes forward, and embraces Laura*). I'm not dreaming!—Heaven!—Living!

**GIOCONDA:** (*covering her face with her mantle*). Let darkness hide them from me.

**LAURA:** (*looking towards Gioconda*). Ah me! yon shadow In mantle shrouded! Alvise! Fly!

**ENZO:** Dearest, have no fear!

**LAURA:** (*approaching and recognizing Gioconda, who has uncovered her face*). It is you! It is she by whose aid my life was saved!

**ENZO:** (*to Gioconda*). Angelic maiden, Ah, let me kiss your feet! (*Laura and Enzo kneel before Gioconda.*)

**CHORUS:** (*at a great distance off*). Float on, serenade! Heaven soft airs is granting; Float on, serenade, Over the waters enchanting! We listen to songs Full of innocent glee; With our oars keeping time As we float over the sea. A song is Existence, On dreams it has flourished. To dream we're invited, By dreams we are nourished. From some unknown soul, Comes echo's reply; The last note, ascending, Is lost in the sky.

**GIOCONDA:** (*with gentle calmness*). Do you remember that song, oh Laura? It is the song with which was linked your fortune. It is for us it is sung. Attentively listen! Dearest companions, yon rowers shall in safety Place you both, before morning dawns. For your flight All is provided, with due caution. (*Laura and Enzo at the height of their emotion.*) The barque is fast approaching: my companions Will arrive, just before daybreak, abreast Of the Three Gates: swiftly Towards Aquileja then your flight directing, You from thence (not far off) will see Illyria Smiling a welcome to the wandering lovers. Here are the boatmen. (*To Laura.*) O blessed one! Farewell! My cloak will serve to hide you.

Addio. . . . Ecco la barca. . . . il mio mantel v'asconda. (*Si vede la barca dei cantori che s' arresta alla riva. Gioconda si toglie il mantello di dosso e copre Laura; poi scorge al collo di Laura il rosario.*) Che vedo là! Il rosario! oh sommo Dio! Così dicea la profezia profonda: A te questo rosario Che le preghiere aduna, Io te lo porgo, accettalo, Ti porterà fortuna. . . . E così sia! quest' ultimo Bacio che il pianto inonda V' abbiate in fronte, è il povero Bacio del labbro mio. Talor nei vostri memori Pensieri alla Gioconda Date un ricordo. Amatevi. . . . Vivete liete siate felici. . . .Addio!

**ENZO E LAURA:** Sulle tue mani l' anima Tutta stempriamo in pianto. No, mai su queste lagrime Non scenderà l' oblio. Ricorderem la vittima Del sacrificio santo, Ti benedican gli angeli. Addio. . . .Gioconda. . . .Addio. (*Sull' ultimo verso Laura ed Enzo avranno già un piede sulla barca.—Quadro.—Partono.—Pausa.*)

**GIOCONDA:** (*afferra l' ampolla del veleno*). Ora posso morir. Tutto è compiuto. Ah no! mia madre! aiuto! Aiuto, o santa Vergine! Troppi dolori sovra un solo cuore! Vo' ricercar mia madre!. . . .Oh! mio terrore! (*Côlta da un pensiero improvviso.*) Il patto or mi rammento! Ah! la paura Di Barnaba m' agghiaccia! Qui riveder l' orribile sua faccia! (*Corre all' immagine della Madonna e si prostra.*) Vergine Santa, allontana il Demonio!!

**BARNABA:** (*viene dalla calle, si ferma alla porta socchiusa e sta spinado*). Il ciel s' oscura. (*Scompare la luna.*) Prega! ed essa non sa qual testimonio. Dell' orazion la guarda.

**GIOCONDA:** Vergine Santa, allontana il Demonio. . . . Ebben, perchè son così affranta e tarda, La fuga è il mio riscatto!

**BARNABA:** Ah! vuol fuggir. . . . (*Mentre Gioconda fa per fuggire s' incontra con Barnaba che spalanca l' uscio ed entra.*)

(*The barque of the Cantori arrives, and stops at the bank. Gioconda takes off her mantle, which she places on Laura, then sees the rosary on Laura's breast.*) What do I see? It is the rosary! Eternal Heaven! Thus did my mother speak in prophetic tones: This rosary I offer, Possessing no richer prize; Deign to accept the humble gift! It will bring to you a blessing. It brings you blessing: this last gentle kiss, By my tears inundated, I place on your forehead; the last kiss That my lips will proffer. Recall sometimes to memory Kind thoughts of ill-fated Gioconda! Keep me in memory, love each other: May you both be happy!

**ENZO AND LAURA:** Upon your hands, your generous soul Melting in grief is falling. These mournful parting tears of yours Shall never be forgotten. Your memory we'll cherish always, Your sacrifice recalling; May angels bring you bliss divine. Adieu, Gioconda, adieu! (*At the last verse Laura and Enzo have one foot in the small boat. They leave. Pause.*)

**GIOCONDA:** (*clutching the flask of poison*). Now I can die. All is over. Ah no!—my mother! Oh, aid me, Aid me, O Holy Virgin! Too heavy is for one sad heart this anguish I go to seek my mother. Oh woe is me! Ah! That compact I remember. (*Struck with a sudden thought.*) Ah me! the terror Of Barnaba overwhelms me; Here to behold again those hellish features! (*Flies to the image of the Virgin and kneels before it.*) O Holy Virgin! keep away the foul demon!

**BARNABA:** (*comes down the street, and stops at the half-opened door and looks around*). The sky is cloudy. (*The moon disappears.*) Praying! but she little knows what Witness to her prayers is listening.

**GIOCONDA:** O Holy Virgin, keep away the foul demon! And now, why am I thus exhausted and faltering? In flight is my only safety.

**BARNABA:** (*aside*). Ah! she would fly! (*Gioconda, when about to fly, meets Barnaba, who throws the door wide open, and enters.*)

**BARNABA:** (*terribilmente*). Così mantieni il patto?

**GIOCONDA:** (*prima atterrita, poi con coraggio suprema sino alle fine*). Si, il patto mantengo—lo abbiamo giurato,
Gioconda non deve—quel giuro tradir.
Che Iddio mi perdoni—l' immenso peccato
Che sto per compir.

**BARNABA:** (*fra sè*). Ebbrezza! delirio!—Sognata mia gioia
Ti colgo e repente—nell arido cuor
S' innonda di gioia!—Scompar l' atra noia
Coi rai dell' amor?

**GIOCONDA:** (*a Barnaba che fa per avvicinarsi*). T' arresta raffrena il selvaggio delirio!
Vo' farmi più gaia, ah! più fulgida ancora.
Per te voglio ornare—la bionda mia testa
Di porpora e d' ôr!
(*Va ad ornarsi.*)
Con tutti gli orpelli—sacrati alla scena

**BARNABA:** (*in terrible tones*). You keep your compact thus?

**GIOCONDA:** (*at first terrified, recovers her courage, and retains it to the end*). Yes, I keep to my compact; we both swore to keep it,
And never will Gioconda be false to her oath.
May Heaven in mercy withhold condemnation,
And pardon us both!

**BARNABA:** O rapture! O dream of Elysium!
You're mine now! and swift from this desolate heart,
Expelled by love's rays, somber shadows depart.

**GIOCONDA:** (*to Barnaba, who is approaching her*). No, stop! Restrain awhile your ardent passion!
You soon shall behold in splendor Gioconda,
For you, I am braiding my clustering tresses
With purple and gold. (*Begins to adorn herself.*)
With glittering jewels, the gay jew-

Dei pazzi teatri—coperta già son.
Ascolta di questa—sapiente sirena
La dolce canzon.
Ah! Ah! Mantengo il mio detto
Tradirti non vo'.
Volesti il mio corpo,—demon maledetto?
E il corpo ti do!
(*Si trafigge nel cuore col pugnale che avrà raccolto furtivamente nelle resti adornandosi e piomba a terra come fulminata.*)

**BARNABA:** Ah! ferma! irrisïon!
.... ebben .... or tu ....
M' odi.... e mori dannata:
(*Curvandosi sul cadavere di Gioconda e gridandogli al l' orecchio con voce furibonda*)
Ier tua madre m' ha offeso! Io l' ho affogata!
Non ode più!!
(*Esce precipitosamente a scompare nelle tenebri della calle.*)

*IL FINA.*

els worn nightly
By madcaps theatrical, I'll be covered;
Now listen to the song that this ardent young siren
Will sing to you!
I keep to my compact; no false oath was mine;
You claim my body? Now, demon accursed,
This body is yours!
(*Stabs herself to the heart with the dagger that she had furtively secreted while adorning herself, and falls dead, as if lightning-struck.*)

**BARNABA:** Ah stop! It is a jest! Well then, you
Shall hear this,
And die ever damned!
(*Bending over the corpse of Gioconda, and screaming furiously into her ear.*)
Last night, your mother did offend me;
I have strangled her!
She hears me not! Ah!!
(*With a cry of half-choked rage, rushes down the street.*)

*END OF THE OPERA.*

# L'Amour des Trois Oranges (1921)

## The Love of Three Oranges

MUSIC & LIBRETTO BY SERGEI PROKOFIEV ■ BASED ON A PLAY BY CARLO GOZZI

This four-act opera with ten scenes and a Prologue, set to a libretto by the composer from Carlo Gozzi's comedy, premiered at the Chicago Opera House on December 30, 1921. The curtain is down. An artistic discussion takes place among the Glooms, the Joys, the Emptyheads and the Jesters about what kind of play should be performed. Ten announcers shoo them off the stage, and a herald announces the start of the show. The King of Clubs is upset because his son, the Prince, suffers from depression that can only be cured if he is made to laugh. Pantaloon suggests that feasts and theatrical extravaganzas may work, and Truffaldino, the jester, promises to make all the arrangements. The King instructs Leandro, his Prime Minister, to organize the entertainment. This worries Pantaloon, who is aware that the Prime Minister is plotting against the Prince. The stage darkens to the rumble and flash of thunder and lightning. Tchelio, the magician, protector of the King, and Fata Morgana, Leandro's protector, appear. She beats Tchelio at a game of cards. Back at the King's palace, Leandro tells his partner-in-crime, Clarissa, the King's niece, how he expects to kill the Prince with boredom. They catch Smeraldina, a black slave, listening in on their conversation. She assures them that if Fata Morgana is at the planned festivities, they will be successful, since no one ever laughs when she appears. Truffaldino dresses the Prince for the festivities. The jester does everything he can to make everyone laugh, but Fata Morgana, disguised as an old beggarwoman, stops all laughter. Truffaldino picks a fight with her and knocks her over. The Prince finds this hilarious and bursts out laughing. As her revenge, she decrees that the Prince will go on a search for three oranges. He will be miserable until he finds them and falls in love with them. The Prince and Truffaldino travel through the desert to the castle of Creonte, the witch who owns the three oranges, with a magic ribbon for Creonte, given to them by Tchelio. Creonte, in the guise of a gigantic cook, theatens them with a ladle but is placated by their gift of the ribbon. The Prince sneaks into the kitchen and steals the three oranges. Back in the desert, it is nighttime, and the Prince is asleep. Truffaldino is thirsty and cuts open two of the three oranges, which are now enormous. Two beautiful Princesses, Linetta and Nicoletta, emerge, but they die of thirst as the oranges were not opened at the water's edge as Fata Morgana had originally decreed. The Prince wakes up and cuts open the third orange. The beautiful princess Ninetta steps out, and she is saved from dying of thirst with the help of the Jesters, who rush to her side with a bucket of water. The Prince and Princess undergo many more trials at the hand of Fata Morgana; the Princess is even changed into a rat at one point, but they finally overcome every tribulation. Fata Morgana, defeated at last, is captured and taken away. Without the protection of Fata Morgana's evil magic, Leandro and Clarissa are at the mercy of the King's wrath. The Prince and Princess marry, and there is much rejoicing.

---

## ■ PROLOGUE.

*(Le rideau est baissé, grande avant-scène. De chaque côté de l'avant-scène une tour avec des petits balcons et balustrades.)*

**LES TRAGIQUES:** *(Arrivent en courant de la Coulisse droite sur l'avant-scène en brandissant furieusement des parapluies.)* Donnez nous, donnez nous de grandes tragédies,
Tragédies mondiales et philosophiques!

**LES COMIQUES:** *(Se ruent sur l'avant-scène par la coulisse gauche brandissant des cravaches).* Donnez nous de vraies comédies,
Du rire joyeux, du rire sonore!

**LES TRAGIQUES:** Meurtres, douleurs, des âmes torturées!
*(Attaquant les Comiques.)* Assez de rire!

**LES COMIQUES:** Assez de tragique!

**LES TRAGIQUES:** *(Agitant les parapluies et refoulant les Comiques à gauche).* Non, des tragédies profondes!

**LES COMIQUES:** *(Reculant devant les Tragiques vers la coulisse gauche).* De la gaîté saine!

**LES TRAGIQUES:** Misérables!

**LES LYRIQUES:** *(Sortant de la coulisse droite avec des branches vertes).* Donnez de vrais drames lyriques . . .
*(Les Lyriques n'attaquent personne occupent le milieu de l'avant-scène.)*

**LES COMIQUES:** Bourreaux cruels!

## ■ PROLOGUE.

*(The curtain is lowered, large proscenium. On each side of the proscenium stands a tower with small balconies and balustrades.)*

**TRAGEDIANS:** *(Arrive running onto the proscenium from the right wing, vigorously waving umbrellas).* Give us, give us great tragedies,
Tragedies universal and philosophic!

**COMEDIANS:** *(Hurling themselves onto the proscenium from the left wing, snapping riding whips).* Give us true comedies,
Joyful laughter, loud laughter.

**TRAGEDIANS:** Murders, pain, tortured souls!
*(They attack the Comedians.)* Enough of laughter!

**COMEDIANS:** Enough tragedy!

**TRAGEDIANS:** *(Waving the umbrellas and pressing the Comedians to the left).* No, tragedies profound!

**COMEDIANS:** *(Retreating before the Tragedians toward the left wing).* Healthy joy!

**TRAGEDIANS:** You unhappy ones!

**LYRICISTS:** *(Enter from the right wing with green branches).* Give true lyric dramas . . .
*(The Lyricists attack nobody but occupy the center of the proscenium.)*

**COMEDIANS:** Cruel executioners!

LES TRAGIQUES: Tapageurs!

LES COMIQUES: (Se defendant près de la coulisse gauche). Perfides!

LES TRAGIQUES: Du tragique inextricable, Métaphysique!

LES LYRIQUES: Romantiques émotionnants, Des fleurs, la lune, des moments d'extase!

TÊTES VIDES: (Sortant de la coulisse droite avec de petites cannes attaquent de suite les Lyriques). Donnez, donnez des farces amusantes, Des mots d'esprit grivois!

LES COMIQUES: Assez! À-bas! À-bas!

TÊTES VIDES: (Ayant dispersé les Lyriques, attaquent les Tragiques). Donnez nous du luxe! (Aux Tragiques.) Au diable vieux croquemorts!

LES COMIQUES: Il faut de la joie et du rire, De la verve, de l'esprit Et des sujets complexes, Donnez nous du comique, De la comédie!

LES TRAGIQUES: (Se ruant sur les Têtes Vides). Fainéants! Débaucheurs! Têtes vides sortez d'ici! Parasites! Parasites! Parasites! Donnez nous de la tragédie! Du tragique!

LES LYRIQUES: L'amour rêveur et tendre! Des rêves, des songes lyriques.

TÊTES VIDES: À la porte vieux crétins! Ne pas penser, mais rire! Donnez des farces! (Dix Ridicules écartant le rideau au milieu se precipitent sur l'avant-scène et avec des pelles géantes dèblayent la scène des Combattants.)

LES RIDICULES: Eh! silence! Quittez la scène, allez-vous en! Allez dans la salle!

LES LYRIQUES: L'amour!

LES RIDICULES: (Ramassent avec les pelles les combattants, les refoulant dans les coulisses.) Voyez notre spectacle! C'est du bon théatre! C'est incomparable! C'est là qu'est le vrai chemin! (Enthousiasmés.) L'amour pour Trois Oranges! (Ayant chassé la foule les Ridicules, montent dans les tours, les tenors dans l'une, les basses dans l'autre.) Chut, silence! silence! Du calme! Pas de bruit! (Crient des tours dans la direction de la scène.) Vite, rideau! Et qu'on commence!

TRAGEDIANS: Disturbers!

COMEDIANS: (Defending themselves near the left wing). Traitors!

TRAGEDIANS: Tragedies unexplainable, Metaphysical!

LYRICISTS: Romantic, full of emotion, Flowers, the moon, Moments of ecstasy.

EMPTY HEADS: (Enter from the right wing with small sticks, and immediately attack the Lyricists). Give, give us amusing farces, Words of jovial humor.

COMEDIANS: Enough, down with you!

EMPTY HEADS: (Having dispersed the Lyricists, they attack the Tragedians.) Give us luxury. (To the Tragedians.) To the devil, you old dead heads!

COMEDIANS: Joy and laughter are needed, Verve and wit, And complex subjects, Give us the comic, Give us comedy!

TRAGEDIANS: (Hurling themselves at the Empty Heads). Lazy ones! Debauchers! Empty heads, away with you! Parasites! parasites! parasites! Give us tragedy! The tragic!

LYRICISTS: Love, dreamy and tender! Dreams and lyric imaginings!

EMPTY HEADS: Get out, you old idiots! Not to think, but to laugh! Give us farces. (Ten Absurdities open the curtain in the center and rush onto the proscenium scattering the fighters with giant shovels.)

ABSURDITIES: Hey! silence! Leave this stage, go away! Go into the hall!

LYRICISTS: Love!

ABSURDITIES: (Gathering up the fighters in their shovels and pushing them towards the wings). Watch our play! It is a good theatre! It is incomparable! There lies the true road! (Enthusiastically.) Love for the Three Oranges! (Having chased the crowd, the Absurdities enter the towers: the tenors in one, the basses in the other.) Sh! silence! silence! Be calm! No noise! (They shout from the towers in the direction of the stage.) Quickly, the curtain! Begin!

(Le Rideau s'ouvrant un peu au milieu laisse passer un bérault avec une trompette.)

LE HÉRAULT: (d'une manière imposante). Le roi de Trèfles est au désespoir, Car son fils, enfant chéri Et prince héritier, souffre D'un hypocondrie incurable.

LES RIDICULES: (Avec une agitation joyeuse). Ça çommence! ça commence! (Le Rideau se lève lentement.)

# ■ ACTE PREMIER.

## SCÈNE I.

(Le Palais du Roi. Le Roi. Près de lui Pantalon, devant eux des Médecins avec des instruments médicaux.)

LE ROI: (Avec sentiment.) Pauvre fils! (Aux médecins.) Je vous écoute. Qu'a-t'il au juste?

MÉDECINS: (Faisant leur rapport). Des douleurs au foie, des douleurs aux reins, L'asthme chronique. Des maux de tête, une apepsie, La faiblesse des artères, la tête ramolie, Une toux douloureuse, la vue affaiblie, Un corps anémique et maigre, Bien trop de bile, des étourdissements.

LE ROI: (Terrifié). Que faire?

MÉDECINS: Des terreurs sans motif évident De longues syncopes. De mauvais pressentiments, une indifférence Pour tout, des peurs inexplicables, Et la mélancolie profonde.

LE ROI: (Se bouchant les oreilles). Misère! Misère!

MÉDECINS: Et la mélancolie noire, Et la mélancolie aigue. (Faisant avec importance la Conclusion.) Un état d'hypocondrie Que nous jugeons inguérissable!

LE ROI: Quoi? quoi?

MÉDECINS: Un état d'hypocondrie Que nous jugeons inguérissable.

LE ROI: Et bien?

MÉDECINS: Incurable! (Le Roi renvoie par un mouvement tragique de la main les médecins qui s'en vont emportant leurs instruments avec désespoir.)

LE ROI: (Avec désespoir). Pauvre fils!

PANTALON: Pauvre prince!

(The curtain opens a little in the middle and permits the entry of a Herald with a trumpet.)

HERALD: (In an imposing manner). The King of Clubs is in despair, For his son, a beloved child, And heir, suffers From an incurable hypochondria.

ABSURDITIES: (With playful agitation). It is starting! it is starting! (The curtain rises slowly.)

# ■ ACT I.

## SCENE I.

(The Palace of the King. The King. Near him Pantaloon, and in front of them doctors with medical instruments.)

KING: (With feeling). Poor son. (To the doctors.) I am listening. What exactly has he?

DOCTORS: (Reporting). Pains in the liver, lumbago, Chronic asthma, Headaches, indigestion, Feeble arteries, softened head, Painful cough, enfeebled sight, An anemic and thin body, Biliousness and dizziness.

KING: (Terrified). What should be done?

DOCTORS: Fears without apparent reason, Prolonged swoons, Bad presentiments, an indifference To all things, inexplicable terrors, And profound melancholia.

KING: (Covering his ears). Misery! misery!

DOCTORS: And black melancholia, And acute melancholia, (Concluding impressively.) A condition of hypochondria We consider incurable!

KING: What? What?

DOCTORS: A condition of hypochondria We consider incurable!

KING: Well?

DOCTORS: Incurable! (The King dismisses the Doctors by a tragic motion of the hand and they leave in despair, taking their instruments with them.)

KING: (In despair). Poor son!

PANTALOON: Poor Prince!

## Act I, Scene I

LE ROI: Mon malheureux enfant!

LE ROI et PANTALON: (*Terrifiés, repetant la conclusion des Médecins*). Les docteurs ont constaté:
Un état d'hypocondrie incurable.

LE ROI: (*Répetant tristement les maladies de son fils*). Des douleurs au foie,
Des douleurs au reins,
Des maux de tête,
L'indigestion, des troubles nerveux
La faiblesse des artères,
De l'asthme chronique,
Une toux douloureuse,
Des syncopes profondes
Et la vue affaiblie.

PANTALON: (*Vivement*). Ah! grand Dieu! c'est ça la médecine!
Ils ne savent rien de rien,
Ils ne peuvent rien guérir.
(*Contrefaisant les Médecins*.)
Il a mal au foie! Que diable!
Soignez lui donc le foie!
Il a mal aux reins!
Que diable, soignez lui donc les reins.

LE ROI: Je suis si vieux!
Qui donc héritera de mon royaume?
Serait-ce ma nièce Clarice?
Si cruelle et ridicule!

PANTALON: Pauvre! Pauvre!
(*Sanglotant dans le manteau du Roi.*)

LE ROI: (*Sanglotant*). O pauvre moi! O pauvre fils!
Pauvre royaume!
(*Le Roi sanglotte.*)
(*Les Ridicules suivent tout le temps avec inquiètude la conduite du Roi craignant qu'il ne se soit rendu grotesque, par devant le public.*)

LES RIDICULES: Mais il perdra son prestige royal!
Son prestige . . . . .
Nous commes choqués!

PANTALON: (*Calmant le Roi*). Calmez vous! calmez vous!

LE ROI: (*Se calmant et comme en rêve*). J'ai dit, les docteurs ont dit:
Que seul le rire pouvait
Guérir mon pauvre fils.

PANTALON: (*d'un ton convaincu*). Alors qu'on le fasse rire!

LE ROI: Faible chance.
(*Pantalon de plus en plus agité.*)

PANTALON: Il faut le faire rire quand même.
La cour est bien trop triste.
Les gens se trainent la tête baissée et mornes!
Comment voulez vous que le prince puisse rire?
Tout! Tout doit être gai autour de lui.
(*Ayant trouvé le moyen de guérir le prince avec joie.*)

---

KING: My unhappy child!

KING AND PANTALOON: (*Terrified, repeat the Doctors' diagnosis*). The doctors have noted An incurable hypochondria.

KING: (*Repeats sadly his son's illnesses*). Pains in the liver,
Lumbago,
Headaches,
Indigestion, nervous troubles,
Feeble arteries,
Chronic asthma,
A painful cough,
Prolonged swoons,
And feeble sight.

PANTALOON: (*Vivaciously*). Ah! Dear me! that medicine!
They know nothing at all.
They can cure nothing.
(*Imitating the doctors.*)
He has liver trouble! What the devil!
Then take care of his liver!
He has kidney trouble!
Then take care of the kidneys!

KING: I am so old!
Who will inherit my kingdom!
Will it be my niece Clarisse?
So cruel and so ridiculous!

PANTALOON: Poor man! poor man!
(*Weeps in the King's robe.*)

KING: (*Weeping*). Oh poor me!
That poor son!
Poor kingdom!
(*The King weeps.*)
(*The Absurdities have been following The King's actions with anxiety, fearing that he might appear ridiculous to the public.*)

ABSURDITIES: But he will lose his royal prestige!
His prestige . . . . . .
We are shocked!

PANTALOON: (*Calming the King*). Be calm! be calm!

KING: (*Calming down and as in a dream*). I have said, the doctors said:
That only laughter can
Cure my poor son.

PANTALOON: (*With conviction*). Then make him laugh!

KING: Small chance of that.
(*Pantaloon becomes more and more agitated.*)

PANTALOON: He must be made to laugh nevertheless.
The court is much too sad,
People drag themselves around,
Heads bent and mournful!
How can the Prince laugh?
All! All should be gay around him!
(*Having found the means to cure the Prince, joyfully.*)

---

LE ROI: Non jamais le pauvre prince ne rira.

PANTALON: J'ai trouvé ce qu'il faut pour égayer
Le prince. Qu'on ordonne des spectacles,
Des tournois, des fêtes;
Qu'on appelle des gens qui peuvent le faire rire.
(*Pantalon se rappelant du nom dont il a besoin crie à tue tête dans la coulisse.*)
Trouffaldino! Trouffaldino!

LE ROI: Des fêtes? Des spectacles?
(*Faisant avec la main un signe désespéré.*)
Inutile!

PANTALON: Pourquoi ne pas le faire?
Si ça pouvait sauver le prince.
(*Criant vers la coulisse.*)
Trouffaldino!!!

TROUFFALDINO: (*Se précipite en courant vers Pantalon*). En quoi te suis-je utile?

PANTALON: (*Avec importance*). Pas à moi, à ton roi!
(*Trouffaldino se précipite a genoux devant Le Roi.*)

LE ROI: (*Pensif*). Dis-moi, Trouffaldino,
Je voudrais donner des fêtes,
Pour essayer de faire rire le pauvre prince.

TROUFFALDINO: Tout sera fait de suite,
Ça-y-est! je vais arranger des fêtes.
(*Il sort en courant.*)

LE ROI: (*Revolté par la conduite de Trouffaldino, tappe du pied*). Quoi donc! est-il fou?

PANTALON: (*Content*). Trouffaldino c'est vraiment parfait.
(*Le Roi frappe dans les mains.*)

PANTALON: (*à part*). O oui, c'est très bien!

LE ROI (*Aux serviteurs qui viennent d'entrer*). Nous voulons voir Léandre.
Notre premier ministre.

PANTALON: (*Tout bas en colère*). Ah! Léandre? je le déteste!
Il veut la mort du prince!
(*Entre Léandre qui salue profondément selon l'étiquette.*)

LE ROI: Léandre, qu'on ordonne de suite des fêtes joyeuses . . .
Des galas superbes; qu'on prépare des luttes,
De folles mascarades.

LES RIDICULES: (*Très contents de l'ordre du Roi répètent après lui*). Fêtes, galas superbes, des luttes.
Mascarades, mascarades, mascarades!
C'est maigre—il faut des bacchanales.

---

KING: No, the poor Prince will never laugh.

PANTALOON: I have found what is needed to cheer up
The Prince. Order performances,
Tournaments, festivals;
Call people who can make him laugh.
(*Pantaloon remembers the name he has been trying to recall and shouts loudly towards the wing.*)
Trouffaldino! Trouffaldino!

KING: Festivals! performances!
(*Expresses despair with his hand.*)
Useless!

PANTALOON: Why not do it?
If it can save the Prince.
(*Shouting toward the wings.*)
Trouffaldino!!!

TROUFFALDINO: (*Hastily runs towards Pantaloon*). What? Can I be of service to you?

PANTALOON: (*With dignity*). Not to me but to your King.
(*Trouffaldino throws himself on his knees before the King.*)

KING: (*Thoughtfully*). Tell me, Trouffaldino,
I would like to arrange festivals
To try to make the poor Prince laugh.

TROUFFALDINO: Everything will be done at once.
That is agreed. I will organize festivals.
(*He exits, running.*)

KING: (*Indignant at Trouffaldino's manner, stamps his foot*). What is it? Is he insane?

PANTALOON: (*With satisfaction*). Trouffaldino is really perfection.
(*The King claps his hands.*)

PANTALOON: (*Aside*). Oh yes, all is well!

KING: (*To servants who have entered*). We wish to see Leander, Our Prime Minister.

PANTALOON: (*Low but angrily*). Ah! Leander! I hate him!
He wants the Prince to die!
(*Enter Leander bowing low according to etiquette.*)

KING: Leander, give immediate orders for gay festivals . . . . . .
Superb feasts, organize combats,
Wild masquerades.

ABSURDITIES: (*Delighted with the King's orders, repeat his words*). Festivals, superb feasts, combats.
Masquerades! masquerades! masquerades!
It is not enough, there must be bacchanals.

LÉANDRE: (*Au Roi*). Oh! Mon Roi, ça fatiguera le pauvre prince, Cela est bien inutile.

PANTALON: (*En colère*). Ah!

LE ROI: Il faut toujours tenter la chance.
(*En ordonnant.*)
Des jeux, des spectacles,
(*Soulignant.*)
Des bacchanales.

RIDICULES: (*Contents*). Ah!

LÉANDRE: (*Cachant à peine sa colère*). Il en sera bien plus malade.

LE ROI: (*S'en allant ordonne avec autorité*). Des fêtes, des bacchanales.
(*Sort.*)

PANTALON: (*À Léandre avec rage*). Ah! traître.
(*Suit le Roi.*)

LÉANDRE: Bouffon!

## SCÈNE II.

( *La scène devient sombre. Un rideau cabalistique descend laissant seulement une petite partie de la scène pour l'action. Tout le tableau se joue dans l'obscurité. Il sort de la terre du feu et de la fumée. D'en bas paraît le magicien Tchélio suivi de tonnerres et d'éclairs.*)

RIDICULES: (*Bouleversés*). C'est Tchélio!
(*Le feu et la fumée apparaissent à un place de la scène près du magicien. Fata Morgana apparait avec tonnerres et éclairs.*)

LES RIDICULES: (*Encore plus bouleversés*). Fata Morgana.
(*La scène pullule de petits diables. Ils apportent une table, qu'ils placent entre Tchélio et Fata, des cartes et des immenses tableaux du roi de Trèfles et du roi de Pique, qu'ils posent: le primier derrière Tchélio et le second derrière Fata. Les deux tableaux sont lumineux et brillent dans l'obscurité.*)

LES PETITS DIABLES: (*Hurlent*). Hi hi hi hi hi!

LES RIDICULES: Ils jouent aux cartes!
(*Le jeu commence. Tchélio donne les cartes qui sont d'une dimension exagérée. Les petits diables commencent une danse infernale faisant une ronde autour de Tchélio et Fata Morgana.*)

TCHÉLIO: (*Ayant perdu, avec rage*). Oh!

FATA MORGANA: (*Ayant gagné, triomphant*). Ha!
(*Les Petits Diables tombent a genoux et se prostèrnent.*)

LEANDER: (*To the King*). Oh King, that will tire the poor Prince, It is quite unnecessary.

PANTALOON: (*Angrily*). Ah!

KING: One can always try.
(*Gives the order.*)
Games, plays,
(*Emphatically.*)
Bacchanals.

ABSURDITIES: (*With satisfaction*). Ah!

LEANDER: (*Barely able to conceal his anger*). He will only get worse.

KING: (*Exits and orders authoritatively*). Festivals, bacchanals.
(*Exit.*)

PANTALOON: (*Angrily to Leander*). Ah! Traitor!
(*Follows the King.*)

LEANDER: Clown!

## SCENE II.

(*The stage darkens. A cabalistic curtain is lowered leaving only a small part of the stage for the action. The entire scene is played in darkness. Fire and smoke rise from the ground. From below appears the magician Tchelio, followed by thunder and lighting.*)

ABSURDITIES: (*Upset*). It is Tchelio!
(*The fire and smoke appear in one section of the stage, near the magician. Fata Morgana appears in thunder and lightning.*)

ABSURDITIES: (*Still more upset*). Fata Morgana.
(*The stage is thronged with devilkins. They carry a table, which they place between Tchelio and Fata, and bring in cards and huge pictures of the Kings of Clubs and Spades. The first they place behind of Tchelio, the second behind Fata. The two pictures are luminous and shine in the darkness.*)

DEVILKINS: (*Yelling*). Hi, hi, hi, hi, hi!

ABSURDITIES: They are playing cards!
(*The game begins. Tchelio deals cards of an exaggerated size. The small devils start up an infernal dance, forming a circle around Tchelio and Fata Morgana.*)

TCHELIO: (*Having lost, angrily*). Oh!

FATA: (*Having won, triumphantly*). Ha!
(*The Devilkins fall on their knees in obeisance.*)

LES RIDICULES: Oh! Pauvre roi! La chance est à Léandre.
(*Fata Morgana a donné les cartes, les petits diables se lèvent brusquement et commencent une ronde infernale.*)

TCHÉLIO: (*Perdant de nouveau, avec fureur*). Oh!
(*Les Petits Diables tombent a genoux.*)

FATA: (*victorieusement*). Ha!
(*L'image du roi de Trèfles s'obscurcit encore plus. L'image du roi de Pique devient encore plus lumineuse.*)
(*Les Petits Diables se prosternent.*)

LES RIDICULES: Encore Léandre! O pauvre roi!
(*Le magicien Tchélio donne les cartes, les Petits Diables commencent une danse encore plus endiablée.*)
(*Fata Morgana lève en l'air très haut la dernière carte.*)

FATA MORGANA: (*Elle joue. D'un rire sardonique et victorieux.*) Ha-Ha-Ha-Ha-Ha-Ha!

TCHÉLIO: (*Perdant definitivement, agite les bras avec colère*). Maudite! sois maudite!

LES PETITS DIABLES: (*Servilement*). Fata Morgana! Fata Morgana!
(*Les Petits Diables remettent à Fata Morgana l'image du roi de Pique et à Tchélio celle du roi de Trèfles.*)

FATA MORGANA: Léandre!

LES PETITS DIABLES: Hi!

TCHÉLIO: Crève!
(*Fata Morgana s'enfonce dans la terre tenant dans ses bras l'image lumineuse du roi de Pique. Tchélio s'enfonce, tenant dans ses bras l'image obscure du roi de Trèfles. Les Diables disparaissent emportant la table de jeux.*)
(*La rideau cabalistique se l'eve. La Lumière.*)

## SCÈNE III.

(*Décor de la Ière. scène. Léandre est seule à la même place où il était.*)

LÉANDRE: (*Sombre, la tête baissée*). Tous mes désirs, n'ont rencontré
Que des obstacles,
De grands et lourds obstacles,
La chose n'est pas facile!
(*Entre Clarice revêche, décidée et extravagante.*)

CLARICE: Léandre, sachez ceci:
Si le prince meurt
Je suis héritière du trône de mon oncle
Et si nous perdons le prince.

ABSURDITIES: Oh, the poor King! Luck is with Leander.
(*Fata Morgana now deals. The devilkins rise quickly and start an infernal round dance.*)

TCHELIO: (*Losing again, with fury*). Oh!
(*The Devilkins fall on their knees.*)

FATA: (*victoriously*). Ha!
(*The picture of the King of Clubs becomes still darker. The picture of the King of Spades becomes more luminous.*)
(*The Devilkins prostrate themselves.*)

ABSURDITIES: Leander once more!
Oh poor King!
(*The magician Tchelio deals the cards. The Devilkins start an even more devilish dance.*)
(*Fata Morgana raises the last card high in the air.*)

FATA: (*Plays. With a sardonic and victorious laugh*). Ha-Ha-Ha!

TCHELIO: (*Losing definitely. Waves his arms in anger*). Be cursed! be cursed!

DEVILKINS: (*With servility*). Fata Morgana! Fata Morgana!
(*The Devilkins give the picture of the King of Spades to Fata Morgana and that of the King of Clubs to Tchelio.*)

FATA: Leander!

DEVILKINS: Hi!

TCHELIO: Die!
(*Fata Morgana disappears into the earth holding the luminous picture of the King of Spades. Tchelio disappears holding the dark picture of the King of Clubs. The Devilkins disappear carrying away the gaming table.*)
(*The cabalistic curtain rises. Light.*)

## SCENE III.

(*Same as Scene I. Leander stands alone in the same position.*)

LEANDER: (*Moodily, with bent head*). All my desires have met Nothing but obstacles,
Big and heavy obstacles,
It is not an easy matter!
(*Enter Clarisse, harsh, positive and extravagant.*)

CLARISSE: Leander, know this:
If the Prince dies
I am heiress to my uncle's throne.
And if we lose the Prince,
I will marry you, Leander.

Je vous épouse, Léandre.
(*Léandre s'incline pro-
fondément.*)
M'avez-vous bien comprise?

**LÉANDRE:** Oui princesse.

**CLARICE:** Comment pouvez vous
àgir
Avec autant de calme?
Je crains qu'il vivra plus
Que nous nonobstant
Sa maladie hypocondriaque.
Être si tranquille, lorsqu'il faut
oser?
Mais vous êtes indigne
Et de ma main et du trône.

**LÉANDRE:** Soyez un peu patiente.
Vous verrez j'atteins mon but.

**CLARICE:** (*Avec mépris*). Quel
flegme.
(*Léandre tendant le cou vers
l'oreille de Clarice lui chuchotte
méchamment.*)

**LÉANDRE:** Je le fais mourir de
prose extra tragique.
(*Les Ridicules tombent presque
des tours en se penchant pour entendre les paroles de Léandre.*)
Je le fais mourir avec des vers
martéliens.
Avec des vers martéliens.

**CLARICE:** (*Incrédule*). Pas possible.

**LÉANDRE:** C'est dans son pain que
je les glisse,
C'est dans sa soupe que je les
hâche,
Et il mourra d'une maladie hypocondriaque!

**LES TRAGIQUES:** (*Se ruant sur
l'avant scène*). Donnez nous de
grandes tragédies.

**LES RIDICULES:** (*Se tenant la
tête*). Encore ces types!
(*Se précipitent de leurs tours et
avec des pelles deblayent la scène
des Tragiques.*)

**LES TRAGIQUES:** Meurtres, souffrances,
Douleur des âmes torturées.
Des solutions profondes.
(*Les Ridicules repoussent les Tragiques dans la coulisse. Les Tragiques par un effort inattendu
pénètrent de nouveau sur la
scène.*)
Des souffrances mondiales.
(*Les Ridicules rentrent dans les
tours avec un air agacé.*)

**LES RIDICULES:** Ça fatigue vraiment.

**CLARICE:** Non Léandre, vos plans
me paraissent inéfficaces,
Il ne faut pas traîner les choses.
Donnez au prince de l'opium ou
une balle.
(*Au fond de la scène passe en sautillant Trouffaldino avec tous les
attirails d'un bouffon. Derrière
lui on porte les accessoires pour*

(*Leander bows profoundly.*)
Do you understand me?

**LEANDER:** Yes, Princess.

**CLARISSE:** How can you act
So calmly?
I fear he will live longer
Than we, in spite of
His hypochondria.
To be so calm when you should
dare!
You are unworthy
Both of my hand and throne.

**LEANDER:** Be a little patient.
You will see me gain my end.

**CLARISSE:** (*with disgust*). What
dullness!
(*Leander stretches his head
towards Clarisse's ear and whispers wickedly.*)

**LEANDER:** I feed him on super
tragic prose.
(*The Absurdities almost fall from
the towers in leaning down to
hear Leander's word.*)
I feed him harsh verses!
Harsh verses.

**CLARISSE:** (*Incredulously*). Is it
possible?

**LEANDER:** I slide them in his
bread,
I chop them in his soup,
And he will die of hypochondria!

**TRAGEDIANS:** (*Hurling themselves onto the proscenium*). Give
us great tragedies.

**ABSURDITIES:** (*Holding their
heads*). Those fellows again!
(*They hurl themselves from their
towers and clear the stage of the
Tragedians with the aid of shovels.*)

**TRAGEDIANS:** Murder, suffering,
The pain of tortured souls,
Solving profound problems.
(*The Absurdities push the Trage-
dians into the wings. The Traged-
ians reenter the stage by an unex-
pected move.*)
Universal suffering.
(*The Absurdities reenter the tow-
ers in an irritable mood.*)

**ABSURDITIES:** It is really tiring.

**CLARISSE:** Now, Leander, your
plans seem
Ineffectual to me,
Things cannot be postponed.
Give the Prince some opium or a
bullet.
(*Trouffaldino crosses back stage
jumping with all the allurement
of a clown. Accessories for a festi-*

*une fête et une mascarade. Tout
un défilé.*)
Qui est-ce? dites-moi.

**LÉANDRE:** Trouffaldino, un
homme qui fait rire.

**CLARICE:** Pourquoi vient-il?

**LÉANDRE:** Le roi l'a fait venir
Pour faire rire le prince
Dès demain on donnera de grandes
fêtes. (*Léandre d'un geste
coléreux agite le bras dans la di-
rection où a disparu Trouffaldi-
no.*)
Et ce polichinelle
Va priouetter même sur la tête!
(*Sarcastique.*)
Pourvu que le prince rigole!

**LES RIDICULES:** (*Gaîment et avec
verve*). Il va guérir, quand on pourra le faire rire:
On va bien rire quand on saura qu'il
va guérir.

**CLARICE:** (*Sombre comme avec
un mauvais pressentiment.*) Il va
guérir quand on pourra le faire rire.

**LÉANDRE:** Il va guérir quand on
pourra le faire rire.

**CLARICE:** Ce bouffon est drôle.

**LÉANDRE:** C'est vrai!

**CLARICE:** (*Reprochant
énergiquement à Léandre.*) Vous
êtes incorigible, Léandre!
Votre lenteur devient éxaspérante!
Donnez au prince de l'opium ou
une balle.
(*Un vase tombe de la table.
Léandre et Clarice reculent terri-
fiés.*)

**LÉANDRE:** Qu'est-ce?
(*Léandre renverse la table d'un
coup de pied. Sous laquelle
Sméraldine se trouve accroupie.*)
(*En colère.*)
Debout fille de serpent!
(*Sméraldine se lève.*)
Tu voulais surprendre
Une affair d'état secrète!
Je vais de suite te faire pendre!
(*Il veut appeler la garde.*)

**SMÉRALDINE:** (*Accourt vers
Léandre et lui parle d'un ton
sérieux*). Un instant, Léandre,
laisse moi vivre!
Il faut que je te sauve!
(*Tout bas.*)
Derrière le dos du prince se tient
Trouffaldino,
Et derrière Trouffaldino se tient le
mage.
Tchélio regarde.

**LÉANDRE:** Tchélio!
(*Obscurité au fond de la scène
passe. Tchélio est éclairé.*)
(*Sous l'impression de
l'apparition.*)
C'est étrange!

val and masquerade are carried
after him. There is a procession.*)
Who is that? Tell me.

**LEANDER:** Trouffaldino, the man
who creates laughter.

**CLARISSE:** Why has he come?

**LEANDER:** The King made him
come
To make the Prince laugh.
Great festivals will begin tomor-
row.
(*Leander waves his arm with an
angry gesture in the direction in
which Trouffaldino has disap-
peared.*)
And this clown
Will even pirouette on his head!
(*Sarcastically.*)
To make the Prince laugh!

**ABSURDITIES:** (*Calm but with
emphasis*). He will be cured when
he can be made to laugh:
Everybody will laugh when it is
known he will be cured.

**CLARISSE:** (*Dully as though with
an unpleasant presentiment*). He
will be cured when he can be made
to laugh.

**LEANDER:** He will be cured when
he can be made to laugh.

**CLARISSE:** That clown is funny.

**LEANDER:** That is true.

**CLARISSE:** (*Reproaching Leander
energetically*). You are incorrigi-
ble, Leander!
Your slowness is exasperating!
Give the Prince opium or a bullet.
(*A vase falls from the table. Leander and Clarisse step back in terror.*)

**LEANDER:** What is that?
(*Leander upsets the table with a
kick. Smeraldine is disclosed un-
derneath, squatting.*)
(*Angrily.*)
Rise, daughter of a serpent! (*Smer-
aldine rises.*)
You want to overhear
A state secret!
I will hang you immediately!
(*He is about to call the guards.*)

**SMERALDINE:** (*Approaches Lean-
der and speaks to him seriously*).
One moment, Leander, let me live!
I must save you!
(*Quite low.*)
Back of the Prince stands Trouffal-
dino,
And back of Trouffaldino stands the
Magician.
Tchelio watches.

**LEANDER:** Tchelio!
(*The darkness back stage lifts.
Tchelio is lighted.*)
(*Impressed by the apparition.*)
How strange!

CLARICE: (*Sur laquelle l'apparition de Tchêlio n'a produit aucune impression*). Eh bien voyez, Léandre.
Demain les fêtes commencement.
(*Dramatiquement.*)
Et il va rire!
(*Très énergiquement.*)
L'opium ou la balle.
(*Montrant Sméraldine.*)
L'esclave, il faut la tuer.

SMÉRALDINE: Princesse! Princesse on pourra empêcher le rire.
Léandre, tu as pour toi Fata Morganna
Elle va venir à cette fête . . . elle-même!
Près d'elle le prince ne peut pas rire.

LÉANDRE: (*émotionné*). Fata Morgana?

CLARICE: (*Saisie*). Fata Morgana?

LÉANDRE: Parles-tu pour elle?

SMÉRALDINE: Oui, Fata Morgana!
(*Ils font quelques pas en avant et étendant les bras appellent Fata Morgana.*)

TOUS: Ah! viens pour la fête!
Fais pour nous une fête,
Fata Morgana!

*FIN DE L'ACTE PREMIER.*

■ **ACTE DEUXIÈME.**

*SCÈNE I.*

(*La chambre du Prince hypocondriaque. Le Prince est asis dans un profond fauteuil, vélu d'un costume (caricatural) de malade. Il a sur la tête une compresse, près de lui une table chargée de flacons de pommades de crachoirs et d'autres objets correspondant à son état. Trouffaldino baletant est en train de finir une danse comique probablement très longue.*)

TROUFFALDINO: (*Haletant mais d'un air victorieux*). Est-ce drôle?

LE PRINCE: (*d'un voix malade*). Ah! Non! Non!

TROUFFALDINO: Est-ce possible que je ne sois pas drôle!

LE PRINCE: Non, non! Ma vue se brouille
J'ai la tête en feu!
Des douleurs aux reins
Et des douleurs au foie.

TROUFFALDINO: (*Compatissant*). Oh comme c'est pénible!

LE PRINCE: Tu dis que c'est pénible, c'est pire!
(*Gémissant.*)
O! O! O!

---

CLARISSE: (*Who is not impressed at all by the appearance of Tchelio*). Well, you see, Leander, Tomorrow the festivities begin.
(*Dramatically.*)
And he will laugh!
(*Very energetically.*)
Opium or the bullet.
(*Indicating Smeraldine.*)
The slave must be killed.

SMERALDINE: Princess! Princess, it is possible to prevent his laughing.
Leander, Fata Morgana supports you.
She will come to this festival . . . herself!
Beside her the Prince cannot laugh.

LEANDER: (*Moved*). Fata Morgana?

CLARISSE: (*Distressed*). Fata Morgana?

LEANDER: Are you speaking on her behalf?

SMERALDINE: Yes, Fata Morgana!
(*They take a few steps forward and stretch out their arms calling to Fata Morgana.*)

ALL: Ah, come to the festival!
Make it a festival for us,
Fata Morgana!

*END OF FIRST ACT.*

■ **ACT II.**

*SCENE I.*

(*Room of the hypochondriac Prince. The Prince is seated in a deep armchair, clothed in a caricatured costume of a patient. He has a compress on his head; near him a table covered with flasks of salve, spitoons and other objects necessary for his condition. Trouffaldino is haltingly finishing a very long undoubtedly comic dance.*)

TROUFFALDINO: (*Stopping but triumphant*). Is it funny?

PRINCE: (*In a sick voice*). Ah! no! no!

TROUFFALDINO: Is it possible that I am not funny?

PRINCE: No, no! My sight is blurred,
My head burns!
Pains in the kidneys
And pains in the liver.

TROUFFALDINO: (*With compassion*). How very sad!

PRINCE: You say it is sad, it is worse!
(*Groans.*)
Oh! Oh! Oh!

---

TROUFFALDINO: Qu'inventerais-je encore je dance,
Ça l'embête, je fais l'imbécile!
Il ne rit pas! Il pleure
Je suis à bout de mes ressources.
(*Les gémissements provoquent la toux.*)

TROUFFALDINO: Je crois que votre Altesse veut tousser?

LE PRINCE: Ah! Ah!
(*Faisant ressortir la machoire pleine de sang il montre du doigt le crachoir qu'il exige.*)

TROUFFALDINO: Je crois que votre Altesse veut cracher, faites!
(*Lui tend le crachoir.*)

LE PRINCE: (*Indiquant nerveusement le crachoir du doigt*). Ah!
(*Crache.*)
O!
(*Trouffaldino prend le crachoir, étudie son contenu, le renifle.*)

TROUFFALDINO: Ça sent des rimes puantes!
J'ai de suite reconnu l'odeur.

LES RIDICULES: Mais parbleux! Il le nourrit de vers martéliens!
Léandre. Canaille.

TROUFFALDINO: Prince, votre Altesse, on va donner
De si brillantes fêtes que vous rirez,
Prince, je vous jûre!
Souffrez qu'on vous habille,
Et partons sans retard.

LE PRINCE: M'habiller? Moi? C'est fou ce qu'il me dit.

TROUFFALDINO: Croyez Altesse c'est gai
On va nous faire rire.

LES COMIQUES: (*Survienent sur l'avant-scène*). Donnez-nous du rire, des vrais comédies,
Du rire joyeux, du rire sonore.

LES RIDICULES: Sortez d'ici, sortez plus vite.

LES COMIQUES: Des scènes vivifiantes.

LES RIDICULES: Laissez faire Trouffaldino
Il peut, sans vous, guérir
Le prince du diable!

LES COMIQUES: (*Avec fureur.*) Du rire.
(*Avec des pelles ils chassent les Comiques qui en se défendant sortent par la coulisse. Les Ridicules fatigués rentrent dans les tours. On entend de la coulisse la musique d'une marche gaie.*)

TROUFFALDINO: Attention! Que c'est beau!
On commence allons plus vite.

LE PRINCE: Non je reste.

TROUFFALDINO: Ah! à quel point . . .

---

TROUFFALDINO: What else can I invent. I dance,
And he is bored; I play the fool,
And he does not laugh; he weeps.
I am at the end of my resources.
(*The groans provoke a cough.*)

TROUFFALDINO: I think your Highness wants to cough?

PRINCE: Ah! Ah!
(*He shows a mouthful of blood and points his finger at the spitoon he needs.*)

TROUFFALDINO: I believe Your Highness needs to expectorate.
Here you are.
(*Passes him the spitoon.*)

PRINCE: (*Points nervously at the spitoon with his finger*). Ah!
(*Spits.*)
Oh!
(*Trouffaldino takes the spitoon, examines its contents and sniffs them.*)

TROUFFALDINO: I smell odorous rhymes!
I recognize the smell at once.

ABSURDITIES: Zounds! He feeds him harsh verses,
Leander, the scoundrel.

TROUFFALDINO: Prince, Your Highness, there are to be given Such brilliant festivals, that you will laugh.
Prince, I promise you!
Permit us to dress you,
And we will go without delay.

PRINCE: Dress myself! I! What he says is insane.

TROUFFALDINO: Believe me, Highness, it is gay,
And we will laugh.

COMEDIANS: (*Arrive on proscenium*). Give us laughter, true comedies,
Joyful laughter, loud laughter.

ABSURDITIES: Get out, leave quickly.

COMEDIANS: Invigorating scenes.

ABSURDITIES: Allow Trouffaldino to act,
He can, without you, cure The Prince of the devil!

COMEDIANS: (*With anger*). And laughter.
(*With shovels they chase the Comedians, who while defending themselves exit through the wings. The Absurdities, tired, re-enter the towers. The music of a gay march is heard back of the stage.*)

TROUFFALDINO: Listen! How beautiful it is!
It begins. Let us go quickly!

PRINCE: No, I will remain.

TROUFFALDINO. Ah! how . . .

**LE PRINCE:** (*l'interrompant*).
Donne-moi de cette médecine.

**TROUFFALDINO:** Oh! à quel point c'est amusant là-bàs!
Mettez ce grand manteau,
Mettez-le simplement sur la chemise.

**LE PRINCE:** (*Criant capricieusement*). Donne-mes ces gouttes!

**TROUFFALDINO:**
(*S'échauffant.*) Ce n'est pas la peine.

**LE PRINCE:** Vite, quinze
Gouttes!

**TROUFFALDINO:** (*Se fâchant comme avec un enfant capricieux*). Voilà ou vont partir les gouttes.
(*Il jette par la fenêtre tous les flacons et crachoirs.*)

**LE PRINCE:** Des gouttes!

**TROUFFALDINO:** (*Projettant les gouttes*). Voilà partez, partez.

**LE PRINCE:** (*Pleurant*). Quelle audace, canaille, infâme fripouille.

**TROUFFALDINO:** Encore voilà et puis en route.
(*En le couvrant avec le manteau il le saisit el l'emporte sur son épaule.*)

**LE PRINCE:** Ah! Ah! Ah!
(*Perdant sa compresse se défendant et pleurant.*)
Lache-moi, j'en mourrai.
(*Trouffaldino l'emporte.*)
Ah!
(*Le Prince crie à tue tête.*)
Ah!

## SCÈNE II.

(*La grande cour du Palais Royal. Sur une véranda le Roi, Clarice, le Prince enveloppé dans un manteau et des fourrures; sur des terraces des dames et des courtisans ainsi que Léandre et Pantalon.*)

**TROUFFALDINO:** (*Au milieu de la cour annonçant avec entrain*). Divertissement numéro un.
(*Par un mouvement large du bras il ordonne d'ouvrir les grandes portes. Apparaissent des monstres avec des têtes immenses.*)

**LES COURTISANS:** Bien bravo, bravo!

**TROUFFALDINO:** (*Il ordonne aux monstres*). Allez! allez!
(*On battaile avec des lances. Trouffaldino leur indique des mouvements terribles.—Un groupe de monstres est victorieux.*)

---

**PRINCE:** (*Interrupting him*).
Give me some of that medicine.

**TROUFFALDINO:** Oh, how interesting it is there!
Put on this big cape,
Put it over your shirt.

**PRINCE:** (*Shouting capriciously*).
Give me those drops!

**TROUFFALDINO:** (*Getting excited*). It is not worthwhile.

**PRINCE:** Quickly, fifteen
Drops.

**TROUFFALDINO:** (*Offended like a capricious child*). This is where the drops will go!
(*He throws the bottles and the cuspidor through the window.*)

**PRINCE:** Drops!

**TROUFFALDINO:** (*Contemplating the drops*). There, depart, depart.

**PRINCE:** (*crying*). What daring, you scoundrel, infamous cheat.

**TROUFFALDINO:** Some more and then we will start.
(*Covering him with a cape, he lifts him and carries him off on his shoulder.*)

**PRINCE:** Ah! Ah! Ah!
(*Losing his compress, he defends himself and cries.*)
Let me go! I shall die!
(*Trouffaldino carries him off.*)
Ah!
(*The Prince yells with full force.*)
Ah!

## SCENE II.

(*The courtyard of the Royal Palace. The King, Clarisse and the Prince, wrapped in a cape and furs, are standing on the veranda; on the terrace there are ladies and courtiers, also Leander and Pantaloon.*)

**TROUFFALDINO:** (*In the middle of the courtyard, making the announcements with animation*). Divertissement number one.
(*With a broad movement of the arm, he gives the signal for the large gates to open. Monsters with huge heads appear.*)

**COURTIERS:** Fine! Bravo!

**TROUFFALDINO:** (*Giving orders to the monsters*). Go on! go on!
(*They battle with lances. Trouffaldino makes grotesque movements. A group of monsters is victorious.*)

---

**LES COURTISANS:** (*Applaudissant*). Bien bravo, bravo, c'est incomparable!
C'est très gai, c'est vraiment parfait.
(*Trouffaldino montant sur les marches de la véranda royale.*)

**TROUFFALDINO:** Le prince a-t-il ri?

**LE ROI:** Non!

**LE PRINCE:** (*D'une voix pleurnicharde*). Ce bruit me fatigue la tête,
L'air est néfaste à mon pauvre coeur.

**LE ROI:** Ah! c'est mal!

**TROUFFALDINO:** (*Aux monstres*). Allez-vous en.
(*Il court très agité sur la scène préparant le divertissement suivant. Fata Morgana apparait sur l'avant-scène habillée en vieille femme. Léandre remarquant une apparition si étrange à la cour royale s'approche de Fata Morgana.*)

**LÉANDRE:** Qui es-tu? Qu'est-ce que tu cherches?

**FATA MORGANA:** Je suis Fata Morgana, quand je suis là
Il ne peut pas rire.
(*Elle sort dans le coulisse.*)
(*Léandre la suit des yeux joignant dévotement les mains.*)

**LÉANDRE:** Bienfaitrice! Oh! reine d'hypocondrie.

**TROUFFALDINO:** (*Déclarant avec entrain*). Divertissement numéro deux!
Ouvrez les fontaines
(*On ouvre la Ière. fontaine.*)
C'est de l'huile.

**LES COURTISANS:** Oh!

**TROUFFALDINO:** (*Il déclare pompeusement. On ouvre la 2ème. fontaine*). C'est du vin.

**LES COURTISANS:** (*en applaudissant*). Bien! Bien!
Oh! c'est admirable!

**TROUFFALDINO:** (*Aux gardes*). Amenez les ivrognes et les gloutons.

**LES COURTISANS:** C'est d'un goût remarquable!
(*Les gardes ouvrent les grandes portes, les ivrognes et gloutons avec des sceaux et d'autres récipients se précipitent en se bousculant vers les fontaines.*)

**TROUFFALDINO:** Eh! vous, bonnes gens, remplissez les sceaux
C'est à vous toutes les fontaines.
(*Il rit se réjouissant de la bousculade et de la querelle.*)
(*Montant les marches de la véranda royale.*)
Le prince a-t-il ri?

**LE ROI:** Non.

**LE PRINCE:** (*Pleurant*). Oh! Mettez-moi dans un lit bien douillet!

---

**COURTIERS:** (*Applauding*). Fine! Bravo! Incomparable!
It is most gay, really perfect.
(*Trouffaldino mounts the steps of the royal veranda.*)

**TROUFFALDINO:** Has the Prince laughed?

**KING:** No!

**PRINCE:** (*Tearfully*). The noise tires my head,
The air is bad for my poor heart.

**KING:** Ah! That is bad.

**TROUFFALDINO:** (*To the monsters*). Go away.
(*He runs around the stage in agitation preparing the next divertissement. Fata Morgana appears on the proscenium dressed as an old woman. Leander, noticing so strange an apparition at the royal court, approaches Fata Morgana.*)

**LEANDER:** Who are you? What do you seek?

**FATA MORGANA:** I am Fata Morgana. When I am here,
He cannot laugh.
(*Exit to the wing.*)
(*Leander's eyes follow her out and he stands with devoutly folded hands.*)

**LEANDER:** Benefactress! Oh, queen of hypochondria.

**TROUFFALDINO:** (*Announces with zest*). Divertissement number two!
Open the fountains!
(*The first fountain is opened.*)
That is oil.

**COURTIERS:** Oh!

**TROUFFALDINO:** (*Announcing pompously as the second fountain is opened*). That is wine.

**COURTIERS:** (*Applaud*). Good! good!
Oh, it is wonderful!

**TROUFFALDINO:** (*To the guards*). Bring the drunkards and gluttons.

**COURTIERS:** In wonderful taste!
(*The guards open the big gates. The drunkards and gluttons rush in towards the fountains pushing each other and holding pails and other receptacles.*)

**TROUFFALDINO:** Hey! good people, fill the pails,
The fountains belong to you.
(*He laughs with pleasure at the pushing and quarreling.*)
(*Mounting the stairs of the royal veranda.*)
Has the Prince laughed?

**KING:** No.

**PRINCE:** (*Crying*). Oh, put me in a nice soft bed.

LE ROI: Ah! c'est mal.

TROUFFALDINO: Je n'ai pas de chance! gardes,
Chassez tout ce monde,
Qu'ont-il à se battre?
(*Les gardes repoussent vers les portes les ivrognes et les gloutons*)
(*Trouffaldino contrarié s'avance sur le devant de la scène.*)
Que puis-je encore faire pour lui?
Il veut avoir un lit, douillet!
(*Fata Morgana arrive en titubant par la coulisse.*)
(*Contrarié par son echec s'en prend à Fata Morgana.*)
Qui est cette femme?

FATA MORGANA: Ça ne te re-garde pas.

TROUFFALDINO: Qui l'a fait entr-er ici?

FATA MORGANA: Quel droit as-tu de commander?

TROUFFALDINO: Ce n'est pas ta place.

FATA MORGANA: Laisse-moi!

TROUFFALDINO: Va t'en de suite!

FATA MORGANA: Qu'as-tu dit?

TROUFFALDINO: Une belle saleté comme toi,
Tu oses être ici à la porte?
Va-t'en, va plus vite!

FATA MORGANA: Ah! Quelle brute!
Assez, assez! Lâche-moi!

TROUFFALDINO: Fîche-moi la paix.
(*Elle tombe en relevant très haut les jambes.*)

FATA MORGANA: Ah!

TROUFFALDINO: (*La pousse*).
Ah, maudite.

LE PRINCE: (*Se soulevant du fau-teuil*). Ha ha ha ha . . . ha ha ha ha!
(*Le rire devient de plus en plus fort et joyeux.*)
Ha ha ha ha . . . ha ha ha ha!
(*Suffocant de rire.*)
Cette vieille! C'est si drôle!

LES RIDICULES: (*à demi-voix*). C'est le rire!

LE ROI: Ah, le rire!

LES COURTISANS: Oui, le rire!

TOUS: Il a ri, le prince!
Ha, ha, ha, ha, ha, ha!
(*Par près de joie tout le monde danse d'un façon saccadée. La cour est libérée d'un grand poids. Le Roi esquisse une danse restant assis sur son trône. Seuls Clarice et Léandre ne partagent pas la joie générale.*)
(*La danse s'arrête soudainement. Fata Morgana s'élève lentement d'une facon terrifiante, la lumière pâlit. Les Courtisans terri-fiés reculent vers la sortie.*)

KING: Ah! that is bad!

TROUFFALDINO: I have no luck! guards,
Chase those people away.
What are they fighting about?
(*The guards push the drunkards and gluttons towards the gates.*)
(*Trouffaldino, annoyed, ad-vances to the front of the stage.*)
What more can I do for him?
He wants a soft bed!
(*Fata Morgana stumbles in from the wings.*)
(*Irritated by his failure, he fastens on Fata Morgana.*)
Who is that woman?

FATA MORGANA: That is none of your business.

TROUFFALDINO: Who allowed her to come here?

FATA MORGANA: What right have you to give orders?

TROUFFALDINO: This is no place for you.

FATA MORGANA: Leave me be!

TROUFFALDINO: Get out at once!

FATA MORGANA: What did you say?

TROUFFALDINO: A filthy thing like you,
You dare to enter this gate?
Get out and go quickly!

FATA MORGANA: Ah! what a brute!
Enough, enough! Let me go!

TROUFFALDINO: Go to the dick-ens.
(*She falls with her legs in the air.*)

FATA MORGANA: Ah!

TROUFFALDINO: (*Shoves her*).
Cursed thing.

PRINCE: (*Rises in his armchair*).
Ha ha ha ha . . . ha ha ha ha!
(*The laugh stengthens and be-comes more and more gay.*)
Ha ha ha ha . . . ha ha ha ha!
(*Suffocating with laughter.*)
That old woman! It is so funny!

ABSURDITIES: (*Softly*). It is the laugh.

KING: Ah, the laugh!

COURTIERS: Yes, the laugh!

ALL: He has laughed, the Prince!
Ha, ha, ha, ha, ha, ha!
(*Carried away by joy, all the peo-ple begin dancing jerkily. The court has been freed of a great weight. The King dances, though still sitting on his throne. Only Clarisse and Leander do not share in this general merrymaking.*)
(*The dancing stops suddenly. Fata Morgana rises slowly in a ter-rifying manner, the lights turn pale. The terrified Courtiers crowd toward the exit.*)

FATA MORGANA: (*Férocement au Prince*). Monstre, écoute!
Ecoute mon anathème!
(*De toutes parts, de dessous les marches de la véranda apparais-sent des petits diables qui entur-ent Fata.*)

DIABLES: (*Hurlent*). Hi! hi! hi! hi!

FATA MORGANA: (*Prononce une malédiction*). Il faut que tu subisse
L'amour pour trois oranges.
A travers les plaintes et menaces
Jour et nuit tu marches.
Tu cherches, tu cherches les trois oranges désirées!
(*Fata Morgana disparait avec les petits diables. Les Courtisans et la garde fuient, il ne reste que le Roi, le Prince, Pantalon et Trouffaldi-no. La scène petit à petit redevient claire.*)

LES RIDICULES: Ah! quelle catas-trophe!
(*Commence à eprouver une agi-tation indescriptible.*)

LE PRINCE: Les trois oranges!
(*Le Prince se rue sur l'avant-scène. Pantalon et Trouffaldino tâchent de l'attraper.*)
Ah, trois oranges! Ah, trois oranges!

PANTALON: (*Tâchant d'attrapper le Prince*). Prince! Prince!

TROUFFALDINO: (*Tâchant d'attrapper le Prince*). Ah! ah! ah! Prince!

PANTALON: Ah! quelle histoire! Ah! Ah!

LE PRINCE: (*Étant attrappé es-saye de s'échapper*). . . . trois oranges!
Elles sont chez Gréonet, sans doute!

LES RIDICULES: (*Avec effroi*). Chez Gréonte la sorcière? Pauvre prince!

LE PRINCE: Venez m'aider, je pars de suite, mon casque! Vite l'épée!

PANTALON: Prince! Prince! Ah!

LE PRINCE: (*énergiquement*). Trouffaldino je t'enmène avec moi.

TROUFFALDINO: Pauvre moi!

LE PRINCE: Plus vite! plus vite!

TROUFFALDINO: Ça me trouble!

LE ROI: (*s'approchant du Prince*). De grâce prince?

LE PRINCE: (*Chaleureusement*).
Je veux les trois oranges—
Mon bonheur et mon seul amour.

LE ROI: Arrête-toi! Prince!

LE PRINCE: Elles sont captives chez Gréonte,
Je dois les prendre!

LE ROI: Ton sort m'angoisse!
Mon fils, tu cours des dangers,
Je vois des périls et la mort!

FATA MORGANA: (*Ferociously, to the Prince*). Listen, monster!
Hear my curse!
(*From all sides, from under the veranda steps, appear the devil-kins who surround Fata.*)

DEVILS: (*Yelling*). Hi! Hi! Hi! Hi!

FATA MORGANA: (*Utters a curse*). You must suffer
The love of the three oranges.
In spite of complaints and threats
You will move day and night.
You will seek, you will seek,
The three desired oranges.
(*Fata Morgana disappears with the devilkins. The Courtiers and the guards run away. There re-main only the King, the Prince, Pantaloon and Trouffaldino. Gradually the stage lightens.*)

ABSURDITIES: Ah, what a catastro-phe!
(*Begin to show an indescribable agitation.*)

PRINCE: The three oranges!
(*The Prince precipitates himself front stage. Pantaloon and Trouf-faldino try to catch him.*)
Ah, three oranges! Ah, three or-anges!

PANTALOON: (*Trying to catch the Prince*). Prince! Prince!

TROUFFALDINO: (*Trying to catch the Prince*). Ah! Ah! Ah! Prince!

PANTALOON: Ah, what an occur-rence! Ah! Ah!

PRINCE: (*Caught, tries to es-cape*). . . . three oranges!
Greonte has them without doubt!

ABSURDITIES: (*In terror*).
Greonte, the witch?
Poor Prince!

PRINCE: Help me. I am going at once! My helmet!
Quickly the sword!

PANTALOON: Prince! Prince! Ah!

PRINCE: (*Energetically*). Trouf-faldino, I will take you with me.

TROUFFALDINO: Poor me!

PRINCE: Quicker! quicker!

TROUFFALDINO: It worries me!

KING: (*Approaches the Prince*). Have pity, Prince!

PRINCE: (*Feverishly*). I want the three oranges.
My happiness and only love.

KING: Stop! Prince!

PRINCE: Greonte has them cap-tive,
I must take them!

KING: Your fate troubles me!
My son, you are in danger!
I see peril and death!

## Act II, Scene II

**TROUFFALDINO:** (*Tragiquement*). La mort!

**PANTALON:** (*tragiquement*). La mort!

**LE PRINCE:** (*Exalté*). J'adore, j'adore trois oranges! Plus vite! plus vite!

**LE ROI:** (*d'une voix plus ferme*). Non, je m'oppose, Pense au royame, Toi, l'héritier tu en es responsable.

**LE PRINCE:** J'adore, j'adore! Au diable le royame!

**LE ROI:** C'est impossible! Tu dois rester lorsque je l'éxige!

**LE PRINCE:** Pour rien au monde!

**LE ROI:** C'est moi qui ordonne!

**LE PRINCE:** (*Agitant les bras*). Non, non!

**LE ROI:** (*Bouleversé*). Quoi! tu as pu lever la main sur moi?

**LE PRINCE:** Plus vite Trouffaldino. (*Le Prince met sa cuirasse.*)

**LE ROI:** (*Tristement*). Un fils contre un père! A qui la faute? La faute est à ces sales farces!

**PANTALON:** (*Pathétique*). Ces farces vulgaires! (*Les Têtes Vides font irruption.*)

**TÊTES VIDES:** Donnez, donnez, des farces, amusantes, Des mots d'esprit grivois.

**LE ROI:** (*Il frappe du pied et crie contre les Têtes Vides*). Sortez de suite! A la porte.

**TÊTES VIDES:** Donnez-nous du luxe.

**LES RIDICULES:** (*Sautant des tours*). Silence!

**TÊTES VIDES:** Ne pas penser mais rire, rire!

**LES RIDICULES:** Silence, c'est bien assez pénible! (*Les chassent avec leurs pelles.*)

**TÊTES VIDES:** (*Reculant*). Farces! farces! (*Les Ridicules ayant chassé les Têtes Vides rentrent dans leurs tours.*)

**LE PRINCE:** (*Prêt pour le voyage*). Adieu mon père! Je crois que si je reste, Je redeviens mélancolique.

**LE ROI:** (*Effroyé*). Partez, partez de suite!

**TROUFFALDINO:** Oh, je tremble, je tremble. (*Apparait le diable Farfarello avec un soufflet et sautillant, souffle dans le dos du Prince et de Trouffaldino. Le Prince et Trouffaldino partent comme des flèches, Farfarello les poursuit.*)

**TROUFFALDINO:** (*Tragically*). Death!

**PANTALOON:** (*Tragically*). Death!

**PRINCE:** (*Exalted*). I adore, I adore the three oranges! Faster, faster!

**KING:** (*More firmly*). No, I oppose this. Think of the Kingdom. You, the heir, are responsible for it.

**PRINCE:** I adore, I adore! To the devil with the kingdom!

**KING:** It is impossible! You must stay when I demand it!

**PRINCE:** Not for the world!

**KING:** It is I who command!

**PRINCE:** (*Waving his arms*). No, no!

**KING:** (*Upset*). What? You can lift your hand against me?

**PRINCE:** Faster, Trouffaldino. (*The Prince puts on his cuirass.*)

**KING:** (*Sadly*). Son against father! And whom to blame? Those dirty farces are to blame!

**PANTALOON:** (*Pathetically*). Those vulgar farces! (*The Empty Heads come forward.*)

**EMPTY HEADS:** Give, give amusing farces, Words of joyous humor.

**KING:** (*Stamps his foot and shouts at the Empty Heads*). Get out at once! Get out!

**EMPTY HEADS:** Give us luxury.

**ABSURDITIES:** (*Leaving the towers*). Silence!

**EMPTY HEADS:** Not to think but to laugh, laugh!

**ABSURDITIES:** Silence! this is sufficiently painful! (*They chase them away with their shovels.*)

**EMPTY HEADS:** (*Falling back*). Farces! farces! (*Having chased away the Empty Heads, the Absurdities reenter the towers.*)

**PRINCE:** (*Ready for the voyage*). Farewell my father! I think that should I remain I would become melancholy again.

**KING:** (*Terrified*). Go, go at once!

**TROUFFALDINO:** I am shaking, I am shaking. (*The devil Farfarello appears with a bellows, and jumping, he blows at the back of the Prince and Trouffaldino. The Prince and Trouffaldino start off like arrows. Farfarello follows them.*)

**LE ROI:** (*Farouchement desespèré*). Tout s'écroule! (*Il tombe par terre évanoui.*)

**PANTALON:** (*Sincèrement malheureux*). Quel désastre pour la famille, Quel catastrophe! pour l'état!

*FIN DE L'ACTE DEUXIÈME.*

## ■ ACTE TROISIÈME.

### SCÈNE I.

(*Désert. Rideau. Le Magicien Tchélio trace des cercles pour forcer Farfarello à apparaître.*)

**TCHÉLIO:** (*invoquant*). Farfarello! Farfarello! Farfarello! (*Farfarello apparaît*).

**FARFARELLO:** Ho-là! Qui m'appelle ici Du fond des noirs ténèbres. Dis quel es ton vrai métier? Sorcier réel ou bien de théatre?

**TCHÉLIO:** (*reservé*). Oui, certes, de théatre! Quand même aussi un vrai sorcier! (*En élevant la voix.*) Je suis terrible! Je suis féroce! Et bien prends garde! Sois docile! Réponds-moi!

**FARFARELLO:** Bien! questionne!

**TCHÉLIO:** (*terrible*). Dis, de suite où sont-ils?

**FARFARELLO:** Couchés!

**TCHÉLIO:** Et pourquoi sont-ils couchés?

**FARFARELLO:** (*légèrement ironique*). J'ai soufflé, soufflé. (*Il souffle avec le soufflet.*) Mais à l'enfer j'ai du descendre, Et ils tombèrent.

**TCHÉLIO:** (*sombre*). Où mène ton souffle?

**FARFARELLO:** Chez la Gréonte.

**TCHÉLIO:** Mais tu ne sais pas Que ce sera leur perte?

**FARFARELLO:** C'est pour cela que je les souffle!

**TCHÉLIO:** (*faisant des gestes magiques impérieusement*). Je t'ordonne, arrête-toi!

**FARFARELLO:** (*moqueur*). Mon pauvre vieux, tu as perdu aux cartes, Et pour cela tes sortilèges sont inutiles! Adieu!

**KING:** (*In savage despair*). Everything is lost! (*He falls in a faint*).

**PANTALOON:** (*Sincerely unhappy*). What a family disaster, What a catastrophe for the country!

*END OF SECOND ACT.*

## ■ ACT III.

### SCENE I.

(*Dersert. Curtain. The magician Tchelio is drawing circles to force Farfarello's appearance.*)

**TCHELIO:** (*Invocation*). Farfarello! Farfarello! Farfarello! (*Farfarello appears*).

**FARFARELLO:** Hello! who calls me here. From the bottom of black shadows? Tell me your real profession? Are you a real sorcerer or a theatrical one?

**TCHELIO:** (*With reserve*). Yes, of course, a theatrical one! But also a true sorcerer! (*Raises his voice.*) I am terrible! I am ferocious! So take care! Be docile! Answer me!

**FARFARELLO:** All right! then put the question.

**TCHELIO:** (*Fearfully*). Tell me, where are they now?

**FARFARELLO:** Lying down.

**TCHELIO:** And why are they lying down?

**FARFARELLO:** (*With slight irony*). I blew, blew. (*He blows the bellows*). But I had to descend to hell, So they fell.

**TCHELIO:** (*Darkly*). Where does your blowing lead to?

**FARFARELLO:** To Greonte.

**TCHELIO:** But do you not know That they will be lost?

**FARFARELLO:** It is for that reason that I blow them.

**WTCHELIO:** (*With imperious magic gestures*). I order you to stop!

**FARFARELLO:** (*Scoffingly*). My poor old man, you lost at cards, So now your witchcraft is useless! Good bye! (*He disappears.*) (*Impotent rage on the part of*

*(Il disparaît.)*
*(Fureur stérile de Tchélio.—Le Prince et Trouffaldino entrent gaillardement.)*

**LE PRINCE:** Plus de vent c'est que les oranges sont proches.

**TROUFFALDINO:** A mon avis, c'était un cyclone.

**LE PRINCE:** Qu'importe!

**TROUFFALDINO:** Ou cela peut-être un mousson!

**LE PRINCE:** Qu'importe!

**TCHÉLIO:** *(les retenant)*. Arrêter où donc allez-vous?

**LE PRINCE:** Je cherche les trois Oranges.

**TCHÉLIO:** *(terrifié)*. Les trois Oranges?
Mais elles sont chez Gréonte!

**LE PRINCE:** Je ne crains pas gréonte!

**TCHÉLIO:** Elles sont gardées
Par une terrible cuisinière!

**LE PRINCE:** Une cuisinière! c'est drôle!
Plus vite Trouffaldino!

**TCHÉLIO:** *(ayant les yeux hors de la tête de frayeur)*. Avec une louche cette femme vous tuera sur place!

**LE PRINCE:** J'adore, j'adore! les trois Oranges!

**TCHÉLIO:** *(Faisant des gestes terrifiés)*. Avec une louche en cuivre, Par sa louche elle tue sur place!

**LE PRINCE:** Je dois avoir les trois Oranges.
Oh! je tremble, je tremble!

**TCHÉLIO:** Prenez garde! Cette louche est lourde!

**LE PRINCE:** *(Décidé)*. Moi! je ne crains pas la louche.
Plus vite Trouffaldino!
*(Tchélio constatant qu'il est impossible de retenir le Prince.)*

**TCHÉLIO:** Écoute, Trouffaldino!
*(Mystérieusement.)*
Emporte ce ruban magique,
Peut être ce ruban de soie
Pourrait bien ravir l'affreuse cuisinière!
Alors de suite sautez sur les oranges!

**TROUFFALDINO:** *(S'accrochant le ruban)*. Merci mon magicien!

**LE PRINCE:** *(Perdant patience)*. Plus vite Trouffaldino.

**TCHÉLIO:** Sachez encore, enfants téméraires,
Si les trois oranges vous appartiennent
Qu'elles soient ouvertes près d'une source d'eau
Si non je vois un drame.

**LE PRINCE:** Je rêve de mes chères oranges.

**TROUFFALDINO:** Merci mon magicien.

---

*Tchelio. The Prince and Trouffaldino enter jovially.)*

**PRINCE:** No more wind. It must be that the oranges are nearby.

**TROUFFALDINO:** It is my opinion that it was a cyclone.

**PRINCE:** What does it matter?

**TROUFFALDINO:** Or it might be a monsoon!

**PRINCE:** What does it matter?

**TCHELIO:** *(Stopping them)*. Stop! Where are you going?

**PRINCE:** I am looking for the three Oranges.

**TCHELIO:** *(With horror)*. The three Oranges?
But Greonte has them!

**PRINCE:** I do not fear Greonte.

**TCHELIO:** They are watched By a terrible cook!

**PRINCE:** A cook! how funny! Let us hurry, Trouffaldino!

**TCHELIO:** *(His eyes popping out of his head with terror)*. That woman will kill you on the spot with her ladle!

**PRINCE:** I adore! I adore the three Oranges!

**TCHELIO:** *(With gestures of terror)*. With a copper ladle, With her ladle she kills at once!

**PRINCE:** I must have the three Oranges.
Yes, I am trembling, trembling.

**TCHELIO:** Be careful! That ladle is heavy!

**PRINCE:** *(With determination)*. Me! I do not fear the ladle. Faster, Trouffaldino!
*(Tchelio realizes the impossibility of stopping the Prince.)*

**TCHELIO:** Listen, Trouffaldino!
*(Mysteriously.)*
Take this magic ribbon.
Perhaps this silk ribbon
May entice the fearful cook!
Then jump for the oranges at once!

**TROUFFALDINO:** *(Attaching the ribbon)*. Thank you, my magician!

**PRINCE:** *(Losing patience)*. Faster, Trouffaldino!

**TCHELIO:** Know also, daring children,
If the three oranges become yours
They must be opened near a spring.
Otherwise I foresee a tragedy.

**PRINCE:** I dream of my dear oranges.

**TROUFFALDINO:** Thank you, my magician.

---

**LE PRINCE:** Adieu!
*(Farfarello bondit sur la scène avec son soufflet, le Prince et Trouffaldino s'envolent, comme des flèches. Farfarello les poursuit.)*

**TCHÉLIO:** *(Faisant des incantations dans leur directions)*. Que le sort les garde contre la louche!
*(Rideau.)*

## SCÈNE II.

*(La cour du Chateau de Gréonte.—Farfarello souffle vers cette cour, le Prince et Trouffaldino qui courent à toute vitesse. Le Prince et Trouffaldino tombent par terre. Farfarello disparaît.)*

**LE PRINCE:** *(Se relevant)*. Qu'est-ce?

**TROUFFALDINO:** J'ai peur mon Prince.
*(Il voient une grande enseigne sur le château et lisent an épelant.)*

**LE PRINCE:** Gréonte! *(Ils se relèvent vivement pris d'une terreur folle.)*

**TROUFFALDINO:** Ah!

**LE PRINCE:** Ah! c'est effroyable!

**TROUFFALDINO:** C'est effroyable! La mort, arrive!

**LE PRINCE:** Cette fois c'est effroyable!

**TROUFFALDINO:** Partons mon Prince.

**LE PRINCE:** Attends!

**TROUFFALDINO:** Partons bien vite!

**LE PRINCE:** Non! Non! Nous devons avoir les trois Oranges!

**TROUFFALDINO:** C'est terrible!

**LE PRINCE:** Terrible!
Tchélio il me semble a dit qu'il faut Chercher les trois oranges dans la cuisine!

**TROUFFALDINO:** C'est juste!

**LE PRINCE:** Est-ce juste?

**TROUFFALDINO:** C'est juste!

**LE PRINCE:** Voilà la porte!
*(Ils se glissent vers la cuisine.)*

**TROUFFALDINO:** Prince! il dit, mífiez-vous de la louche.

**LE PRINCE:** Je rêve de mes chères oranges!

**TROUFFALDINO:** Prince! Prince! je crains la cuisinière.

**LE PRINCE:** *(Extasié)*. Les oranges!

**TROUFFALDINO:** Elle nous tuera avec sa grande louche.

**LE PRINCE:** Les oranges!
*(La cuisinière avec fracas secoue la porte du côté intérieur.)*

---

**PRINCE:** Goodbye!
*(Farfarello springs onto the stage with his bellows. The Prince and Trouffaldino fly away like arrows. Farfarello follows them.)*

**TCHELIO:** *(With incantations in their direction)*. May fate guard them from the ladle!
*(Curtain.)*

## SCENE II.

*(Courtyard of the Castle of Greonte. Farfarello blows the Prince and Trouffaldino, who are running full speed towards this courtyard. The Prince and Trouffaldino fall down. Farfarello disappears.)*

**PRINCE:** *(Rising)*. What is the matter?

**TROUFFALDINO:** I am frightened, Prince.
*(He sees a big sign on the castle and he spells it out.)*

**PRINCE:** Greonte!
*(They rise quickly under the impulse of insane terror.)*

**TROUFFALDINO:** Ah!

**PRINCE:** Ah! it is horrible!

**TROUFFALDINO:** It is horrible. Death has come.

**PRINCE:** This time it is horrible!

**TROUFFALDINO:** Let us leave, my Prince.

**PRINCE:** Wait!

**TROUFFALDINO:** Let us leave quickly!

**PRINCE:** No! No! we must have the three oranges!

**TROUFFALDINO:** It is horrible!

**PRINCE:** Horrible!
It seems to me that Tchelio said we must
Seek the three oranges in the kitchen!

**TROUFFALDINO:** That is so!

**PRINCE:** Is it so?

**TROUFFALDINO:** It is so.

**PRINCE:** Here is the door!
*(They glide towards the kitchen.)*

**TROUFFALDINO:** Prince! he said you should be careful of the ladle.

**PRINCE:** I am dreaming of my three dear oranges!

**TROUFFALDINO:** Prince! Prince! I fear the cook!

**PRINCE:** *(In ecstasy)*. The oranges!

**TROUFFALDINO:** She will kill us with her awful ladle!

**PRINCE:** The oranges!
*(The cook shakes the door noisily from inside.)*

LE PRINCE ET TROUFFALDINO: (*Ils reculent en bondissant*). Ah! Ah!
(*La porte est secouée de nouveau.*)
C'est elle!
(*Ils fuient éperdument la porte de la cuisine et se cachent dans des endroits différents. La porte s'ouvre toute grande, et la cuisinière apparait avec une énorme louche.*)

LA CUISINIÈRE: (*D'une voix de basse enrouée*). Qui piaille ici? Je veux savoir;
(*Regardant autour d'elle d'une voix plus forte.*)
Qui piaille ici?
(*Ne recevant pas de réponse elle s'avance inspectant de tous côtés.*)
Sortez, sortez, je trouverai sans faute! (*Elle découvre Trouffaldino.*)
Ah! toi! vaurien!

TROUFFALDINO: (*Perdant presque la conscience de frayeurs gémis*). Ah! ah! oh!

LA CUISINIÈRE: (*Révoltée*). Quel sale vaurien, une telle audace.

TROUFFALDINO: Ah! moi! Madame ma belle dame!

LA CUISINIÈRE: Attends voleur je te jette dans le fourneau!

TROUFFALDINO: Madame, ma noble dame.

LA CUISINIÈRE: Avec ma louche je t'écrase!
Et te flanque dans les ordures!

TROUFFALDINO: Je suis venu là par mégarde.
(*Il essaie de s'enfuir.*)
(*La Cuisinière brandit la louche et attrappant Trouffaldino au collet le secoue sans pitié.*)

LA CUISINIÈRE: Coquin tu fuis? Je te ferai rendre l'âme.
(*Révoltée.*)
Violer ma cuisine!
(*Tout à coup elle aperçoit le ruban magique et est immédiatement intéressée par lui.*)
Qu'est ce tu porte sur ton costume?

TROUFFALDINO: (*Qui n'est pas encore d'aplomb*). Un ruban.

LA CUISINIÈRE: (*d'une voix plus douce*). Fichtre! Mais il est adorable!

TROUFFALDINO: (*Timidement*). Adorable? Tu trouves?

LA CUISINIÈRE: Ce petit ruban fait perdre la tête!
Qui t'a donné ce ruban?

TROUFFALDINO: (*s'enhardissant*). Ça vois-tu . . . comment te dire?
C'est un secret!

---

PRINCE AND TROUFFALDINO: (*Jump back*). Ah! Ah!
(*The door is shaken once more.*)
It is she!
(*They run blindly from the kitchen door and hide in different places. The door opens wide and the cook appears with a huge ladle.*)

COOK: (*In a deep husky voice*). Who is bawling here? I must know.
(*She looks around and speaks louder.*)
Who is bawling here?
(*Receiving no answer she comes forward looking all around.*)
Come out! come out! I will find without fail!
(*She discovers Trouffaldino.*)
Ah! you! good for nothing!

TROUFFALDINO: (*Almost loses consciousness from fear. Groans*). Ah! ah! oh!

COOK: (*Disgusted*). What a dirty good-for-nothing. Such audacity!

TROUFFALDINO: Ah! I! Madam, my beautiful madam!

COOK: Wait, you thief. I will throw you into the stove!

TROUFFALDINO: Madam, my beautiful madam!

COOK: I will squelch you with my ladle!
And throw you in with the garbage!

TROUFFALDINO: I came by inadvertence.
(*He tries to escape.*)
(*The Cook brandishes the ladle and catching Trouffaldino by the collar, shakes him mercilessly.*)

COOK: Rascal! you want to escape? I will make you give up your soul!
(*Disgusted.*)
Violate my kitchen!
(*Suddenly she notices the magic ribbon and is immediately interested in it.*)
What is it you are wearing on your costume?

TROUFFALDINO: (*Who has not yet regained his audacity*). A ribbon.

COOK: (*In a softer voice*). My! but it is lovely!

TROUFFALDINO: (*Timidly*). Lovely? You think so?

COOK: That small ribbon makes me lose my head.
Who gave it to you?

TROUFFALDINO: (*Gaining courage*). You see . . . How can I explain?
It is a secret!

---

LA CUISINIÈRE: Tiens! tiens! Vraiment?
(*Le Prince par de grands bonds silencieux se dirige vers la cuisine et y disparaît.*)
J'amais je n'ai trouvé une telle merveille.
Ne voudrais tu pas m'en faire cadeaux.
(*Le Prince sort de la cuisine avec toris énormes oranges de la dimension d'une tête d'homme, et par de grands bonds, disparaît derrière la porte du château.*)
Eh?
(*Avec coquetterie.*)
Pour me plaier!

TROUFFALDINO: C'est pour te rappeler de moi que tu le veux, En es-tu bien sûre?

LA CUISINIÈRE: Ça me ferait plaisir.

LE PRINCE: (*Passant la tête par la porte*). Trouffaldino! Trouffaldino!

TROUFFALDINO: (*Lui remettant pompeusement le ruban*). Prends-le et sois contente.
(*Trouffaldino s'enfuit.*)

LA CUISINIÈRE: (*Charmée, regarde le ruban*). O ruban incomparable!
(*Fixant toujours le ruban cherche Trouffaldino en tâtonnant vers l'endroit où il était.*)
Où donc es-tu? Que fais-tu?
(*Caressante.*)
P'tit diable.

## SCÈNE III.

(*Un désert.—Le décor de la Ière. scène de ce même acte. C'est le soir. Le Prince et Trouffaldino entrent lentement du côte opposé à celui par lequel ils entrèrent à la Ière. scène. Ils traînent derrière eux avec une corde trois oranges qui ont grandi à tel point que chacune peut contenir une personne.*)

LE PRINCE: Comment marcher plus loin quand derrière Nous personne souffle.

TROUFFALDINO: Les oranges sont si grandes Que c'est a grand peine qu'on les traine.

LE PRINCE: Ah! quel sommeil!

TROUFFALDINO: Ah! quelle soif.

LES PRINCE: Je suis brisé!

TROUFFALDINO: J'ai soif prince!

LE PRINCE: Je voudrais m'étendre! Trouffaldino!

TROUFFALDINO: (*Agité*). Prince! Mais pendant que vous dormirez Je mourrai de soif!

---

COOK: Well, well! Really!
(*The Prince approaches the kitchen with large and silent jumps and disappears inside it.*)
Never have I seen such a marvel. Will you make me a gift of it?
(*The Prince comes out of the kitchen carrying three huge oranges, the size of a man's head. With big jumps he disappears back of the castle gate.*)
What?
(*Coquettishly.*)
To please me?

TROUFFALDINO: Do you want it as a souvenir of me? Are you sure of that?

COOK: It will give me so much pleasure.

PRINCE: (*Sticks his head through the door*).
Trouffaldino! Trouffaldino!

TROUFFALDINO: (*Presents her the ribbon with ceremony*). Take it and be happy.
(*Trouffaldino runs away.*)

COOK: (*Delighted, looks at the ribbon.*) Oh wonderful ribbon!
(*Still looking at the ribbon seeks Trouffaldino by groping for him where he had stood.*)
Where are you? What are you doing?
(*Caressingly.*)
You little devil!

## SCENE III.

(*A desert. Same settings as in the first scene of the same act. It is evening. The Prince and Trouffaldino enter slowly from the side opposite the one from which they entered in the first scene. They drag by strings three oranges, which have grown so that each can hold a human being.*)

PRINCE: How can we walk any further when behind Nobody blows?

TROUFFALDINO: The oranges are so big That it is difficult to drag them.

PRINCE: Ah! but how sleepy I am!

TROUFFALDINO: Ah! what an evening!

PRINCE: I am broken down.

TROUFFALDINO: I am thirsty, Prince!

PRINCE: I would like to lie down, Trouffaldino!

TROUFFALDINO: (*With agitation*). Prince! while you are sleeping I will die of thirst!

**LE PRINCE:** Ce n'est rien dors un peu
Le sommeil donnera des forces
Couche-toi bon Trouffaldino.
(*Il se couche et s'endort.*)

**TROUFFALDINO:** Il est drôle le prince!
Dormir quand j'ai une soif du diable!
Impossible de trouver une goutte d'eau
Donnez-moi à boire!
Donnez-moi de l'eau!
Donnez m'en de suite!
Prince! Prince! mon Prince!
Levez-vous Prince! Prince!
Il dort comme un sourd.
(*S'arrêtant devant les oranges.*)
Les oranges . . .
Mais si j'ouvrais ne fut-ce
Qu'une seule des trois?
Elles sont si belles et si juteuses!
(*Il saisit son glaive, mais immédiatement recule d'à côté des oranges.*)
Non! J'ai peur du Prince!
Et si j'allais mourir
De soif avant qu'on m'aide
Alors le Prince ne pourra
Jamais trainer tout seul!
Et tout s'écroule!
Les trois oranges!
Le Prince et moi!
C'est vraiment plus simple
Que j'en mange une.
(*Extasié il embrasse une orange.*)
Qu'elle est donc juteuse.
Ah! qu'elle est énorme!
(*Il scie l'orange en deux parties avec son glaive.*)
(*De l'orange sort une jeune fille.*)
(*Bouleversée.*)
Une jeune fille en blanc.

**VIOLETTE:** Je suis la princesse Violette.

**TROUFFALDINO:** Princesse! au lieu du jus frais d'une orange!

**VIOLETTE:** Donne à boire! à boire! de grâce!
Sinon je meurs de suite!
J'ai une soif affreuse
J'ai une soif mortelle!

**TROUFFALDINO:** (*Desemparé*).
Princesse! Princesse où trouver une source?
Tout est aride! oh! princesse!

**VIOLETTE:** De grâce! plus vite! . . .
Donne à boire ne sois pas sans pitié!

**TROUFFALDINO:** (*Essayant sans y parvenir de réveiller le Prince*).
Prince, mon prince!

**VIOLETTE:** Rien qu'une goutte!

**TROUFFALDINO:** Princesse! Princesse! Tout de suite
J'ouvrirai l'autre orange!
(*Il scie avec le glaive.*)

**VIOLETTE:** À boire.
(*De l'orange sort une seconde jeune fille en blanc.*)
À boire!

---

**PRINCE:** That is nothing. Sleep a little!
Sleep will give you strength.
Lie down comfortably, Trouffaldino.
(*He lies down, and goes to sleep.*)

**TROUFFALDINO:** He is quaint, this Prince!
To sleep when I have so devilish a thirst!
Impossible to find a drop of water!
Give me something to drink!
Give me water!
Give it to me at once!
Prince! Prince! my Prince!
He sleeps like a deaf man.
(*Stops in front of the oranges.*)
The oranges . . .
What if I should open
But one of the three?
They are so beautiful and juicy!
(*He grasps his sword, but immediately falls back from beside the oranges.*)
No! I fear the Prince!
But if I should die
Of thirst before aid could come?
Then the Prince could not
Drag them alone!
Then all would be lost!
The three oranges,
The Prince and I!
It really would be simpler
For me to eat one.
(*In ecstasy he kisses an orange.*)
How juicy it is.
How big it is!
(*He cuts the orange in two with his sword.*)
(*A young woman steps from the orange.*)
(*Upset.*)
A young woman in white!

**VIOLET:** I am the princess Violet.

**TROUFFALDINO:** Princess! instead of fresh orange juice!

**VIOLET:** Give me something to drink! drink! I beg of you!
If you do not, I will die at once!
I am terribly thirsty!
I am dying of thirst!

**TROUFFALDINO:** (*In despair*).
Princess, Princess, where can we find water?
All is arid! Oh! Princess!

**VIOLET:** I beg of you! quickly!
Give me a drink, do not be pitiless!

**TROUFFALDINO:** (*Trying vainly to wake the Prince*). Prince! my Prince!

**VIOLET:** Only a drop.

**TROUFFALDINO:** Princess! Princess! At once
I will open another orange!
(*He cuts with his sword.*)

**VIOLET:** A drink!
(*A second young woman in white steps from the orange.*) A drink!

---

**TROUFFALDINO:** Quoi encore une autre Princesse!

**VIOLETTE:** Une goutte . . .

**NICOLETTE:** Je me nomme Nicolette!

**TROUFFALDINO:** Quel miracle!

**NICOLETTE:** Donne à boire!

**VIOLETTE:** Une seule goutte!

**NICOLETTE:** À boire! de grâce si non je meurs de suite!
J'ai une soif affreuse, j'ai une soif mortelle!

**VIOLETTE:** Ma vue se trouble, Ah! sauve moi, pitié!

**TROUFFALDINO:** (*Effaré recule devant les deux princesses qui se tendent vers lui comme des ombres*). Princesses! patience! seulement quelques heures! Courage!
(*En aparté.*)
Ah! que c'est affreux tout ça!

**NICOLETTE:** Ma vue se trouble, pitié pour moi!

**VIOLETTE:** (*étant déjà par terre elle continue à se tendre vers Trouffaldino*). À boire, grâce! grâce! grâce!
(*Elle meurt.*)

**TROUFFALDINO:** Est-elle morte?

**NICOLETTE:** De l'eau.
(*Elle tombe.*)
Grâce! Grâce!
(*Murmurant.*)
Grâce!
(*Elle meurt.*)

**TROUFFALDINO:** Encore!!!
(*Pris d'une terreur superstitieuse.*)
Partir, partir, au plus vite.
(*Il s'enfuit.*)

**LE PRINCE:** (*Tout en dormant*).
Eh! Trouffaldino! Trouffaldino!
(*S'eveillant en sursaut.*)
Trouffaldino, nous partons,
Viens ici toujours tu traine!
(*Voyant les princesses mortes.*)
Mais qu'est-ce donc?
Deux jeunes filles blanches!
Deux jeunes filles mortes.
Dans ce désert aride, étrange destin.
(*Quatre soldats entrent en scène avec une allure militaire exagérée.*)
Halte!
(*Les soldats s'arrêtent comme fixés sur place.*)
Prenez ces deux cadavres
Et enterrez-les là-bas.
(*Les soldats avec des mouvements militaires brusques s'approchent des princesses et les relèvent de terre.—Portant les princesses ils partent par la coulisse opposée à celle par laquelle ils sont entrés.*)
Chère Orange! Enfin j'ai le bonheur
D'être seul avec toi
Rien que toi! et moi!
Je dois savoir ce que contient l'orange!

---

**TROUFFALDINO:** What? Another Princess?

**VIOLET:** A drop . . .

**NICOLETTE:** My name is Nicolette.

**TROUFFALDINO:** A miracle!

**NICOLETTE:** Give me something to drink!

**VIOLET:** One drop only!

**NICOLETTE:** A drink! Please! Otherwise I will die at once!
I am terribly thirsty, I will die of thirst!

**VIOLET:** My sight dims, Ah! same me! have pity!

**TROUFFALDINO:** (*Recoils from the two princesses with fear as each stretches towards him as a shadow*). Princesses! be patient! only a few hours! Courage!
(*Aside.*)
How terrible this is!

**NICOLETTE:** My sight dims! Pity me!

**VIOLET:** (*Already on the ground, she continues to stretch towards Trouffaldino*). A drink! I pray you!
(*She dies.*)

**TROUFFALDINO:** Is she dead?

**NICOLETTE:** Give me water.
(*She falls.*)
I pray you!
(*Murmurs.*)
I pray you!
(*Dies.*)

**TROUFFALDINO:** Also!!!
(*A superstitious terror grips him.*)
To go away, go away as quickly as possible.
(*He runs away.*)

**PRINCE:** (*Dreaming*). Hey! Trouffaldino! Trouffaldino!
(*Wakes up with a start.*)
Trouffaldino, we must go.
Come here, you are always lagging!
(*Sees the dead princesses.*)
But what is this?
Two white young women!
Two dead young women?
In this arid desert.
Strange destiny.
(*Four soldiers enter with an exaggerated military bearing.*)
Halt!
(*The soldiers stop as though fixed to the spot.*)
Take these two corpses
And bury them over there!
(*The soldiers approach the two princesses with snappy military movements and raise them from the ground. Carrying the princesses they exit through the wing opposite to the one by which they entered.*)
Dear Orange! At last I have the happiness
Of being alone with you!
Only you! and I!
I must know what the orange holds!

En elle je le sais se cache mon rêve
Chère orange! chère orange!
Donne-moi ce que je cherche.
(*D'un seul coup de glaive il par-
tage l'orange—Apparait une
3ème jeune fille.*)
Princesse?

NINETTE: Moi, je m'appelle Ninette!

LE PRINCE: (*Tombant à genoux*).
Princesse! Princesse! Je te cherche
depuis
Que je suis au monde!
Princesse! Princesse! Je t'adore bien
Plus que tout au monde!

NINETTE: Je t'attends depuis toujours.
(*Le Prince ivre d'amour lui embrasse les genoux.*)

LE PRINCE: Ah que je t'adore!

NINETTE: Donne à boire de grâce!
Si non je meurs de suite
J'ai une soif affreuse,
J'ai une soif mortelle.

LE PRINCE: Attends quelques instants, princesse!

NINETTE: À boire, ma vue se trouble!

LE PRINCE: C'est une désert terrible!
Mais nous partons tous de suite en
ville.

NINETTE: Je succombe!

LE PRINCE: Partons, Princesse!

NINETTE: Viens à mon aide!
(*Elle tombe dans les bras du
Prince.*)

LES RIDICULES: Eh! vous autres,
là,
N'auriez vous pas de l'eau?
C'est bien possible!

NINETTE: Ah! Ah!

LES RIDICULES: Mais! alors donnez donc,
Il faut qu'elle boive!
C'est bien grâce!
(*Les Ridicules apportent de la
tour un sceau d'eau et le place au
milieu de la scène.*)

LE PRINCE: Ah! c'est atroce!
(*Remarquant le sceau.*)
Tiens! de l'eau!
Bois ma douce princesse!
Bois, cette eau fraîche! (*Il lui
donne à boire dans le sceau.*)

NINETTE: (*Ayant bu*). Merci, mon
prince!
Tu m'as sauvé la vie!
Et tu m'as sortie de l'esclavage.
C'est toi que j'ai attendu depuis
toujours.

LE PRINCE: Non, rien ne pouvait
m'arrêter
Dans mon élan vers toi, bien aimée.
Je n'ai pas crains l'affreuse Gréonte
J'ai dominé l'atroce cuisinière!
J'ai bravé la louche mortelle!
J'ai passé l'enfer qu'est sa cuisine!
Oui mon amour est fort, plus fort
Que Gréonte, plus chaud que la

For in it is hidden my dream!
Dear orange! dear orange!
Give me what I seek!
(*With a single sword thrust, he
cuts the orange. A third young
woman appears.*)
Princess?

NINETTE: My name is Ninette.

PRINCE: (*Falling on his knees*).
Princess! Princess! I have sought
you
Since I have been on earth!
Princess! Princess! I adore you
More than anything in the world!

NINETTE: I have waited for you always.
(*The Prince, intoxicated with
love, kisses her knees.*)

PRINCE: Ah! I adore you!

NINETTE: Give me a drink please!
Otherwise I die at once.
I am terribly thirsty.
I am dying of thirst!

PRINCE: Wait a few seconds, princess.

NINETTE: A drink. My sight dims!

PRINCE: It is a terrible desert!
But we will go to town at once!

NINETTE: I fall!

PRINCE: Let us go, Princess!

NINETTE: Help me!
(*She falls into the arms of the
Prince.*)

ABSURDITIES: Hey! you others,
over there!
Have you no water?
Is it possible?

NINETTE: Ah! Ah!

ABSURDITIES: Then give it!
She must drink!
It is most serious!
(*The Absurdities bring a pail of
water from the tower and place it
in the middle of the stage.*)

PRINCE: Ah, it is atrocious!
(*Notices the pail.*)
Why! here is water!
Drink, my sweet Princess!
Drink this fresh water!
(*He lets her drink from the pail.*)

NINETTE: (*Having taken a
drink*). Thank you, my Prince!
You have saved me from slavery.
It is you I have awaited
Since long ago.

PRINCE: No, nothing could have
stopped me
In my attraction towards you, be-
loved.
I feared not the terrible Greonte,
I overcame the atrocious cook!
I dared the deathly ladle!
I passed through hell, her kitchen!
Yes, my love is strong, stronger

cuisine;
Devant l'amour s'inclinait la
louche
Et tremblait Gréonte.

NINETTE: (*Simplement*). O mon
prince c'est toi que j'attendais
À toi est mon amour
Je suis tellement heureuse par toi.

LES LYRIQUES: (*Sans bruit apparaissent sur scène*). Donnez de
vrais drames lyriques romantiques
Émotionnants, des fleurs, la lune!

LES RIDICULES: (*Des tours en
mettant les doigts sur les lèvres*).
Silence! silence!
Si vous aimez l'amour,
Ne troublez pas les amoreux!

LES LYRIQUES: Des moments
d'extase!

LES RIDICULES: Vite repartez sans
bruit.
(*Les Lyriques disparaissent sans
bruit.*)

LE PRINCE: (*Solennellement*).
Partons, princesse, dans mon palais!

NINETTE: Impossible en ce costume,
Que dirait le roi ton père?

LE PRINCE: (*d'un air décidé*).
Mon père n'a rien à dire!

NINETTE: Non! Prince! Pars
d'abord,
Va prévenir le roi
Tu m'apporteras aussi une robe ro-
yale!
Je t'attendrai là!

LE PRINCE: Si tu veux je t'obéis!
Le roi viendra ici lui même!

NINETTE: (*Tendrement*). Adieu!
Reviens, bien vite!

LE PRINCE: (*Tendrement*). Adieu
ma chère princesse!
(*Il s'en va.*)
(*Ninette est seule. Pensive elle
s'assoie sur une pierre.*)

NINETTE: (*Rêveuse*). Oh! que je
suis heureuse!
(*Il fait presque nuit. In voit la silhouette de Sméraldine qui se
glisse vers Ninette. Derrière
Sméraldine apparait la silhouette
de Fata Morgana.*)

LES RIDICULES: (*Inquièts*).
Sméraldine . . . Une
épingle
Fata Morgana . . . Ça devient
bien louche!
(*L'inquiétude des Ridicules atteint, une tel degré que sortant des
tours ils s'approchent de Ninette
sur la pointe des pieds, pour voir
ce qui se passera.*)
(*Sméraldine s'étant glissée
auprès de Ninette lui enfonce
dans la tête une grande épingle
magique.*)

Than Greonte; warmer than the
kitchen.
Before this love the ladle fell,
And Greonte trembled.

NINETTE: (*With simplicity*). Oh,
my Prince, it is you I awaited.
My love belongs to you.
Through you I am so happy.

LYRICISTS: (*Appear noiselessly
on the stage*). Give us true dramatic lyric dramas,
Full of emotion. Flowers, the
moon!

ABSURDITIES: (*From the towers,
placing their fingers on their lips*).
Silence! silence!
If you love love,
Then do not trouble the lovers!

LYRICISTS: Moments of ecstasy!

ABSURDITIES: Go away quickly,
without noise.
(*The Lyricists disappear noiselessly.*)

PRINCE: (*Solemnly*). Come, Princess, to my Palace!

NINETTE: Impossible in this costume,
What will the King, your father,
say?

PRINCE: (*With decision*). My father has nothing to say!

NINETTE: No, Prince! Go first,
Warn the King.
Then you can bring me a royal robe!
I will wait
For you here!

PRINCE: If you wish, I will obey!
The King himself will come!

NINETTE: (*Tenderly*). Goodbye.
Return quickly!

PRINCE: (*Tenderly*). Goodbye, my
dear princess!
(*He goes.*)
(*Ninette remains alone. She sits
down on a stone thoughtfully.*)

NINETTE: (*dreamily*). Oh! how
happy I am!
(*It is almost dark. The silhouette
of Smeraldine is seen gliding
toward Ninette. Behind Smeraldine appears the silhouette of Fata
Morgana.*)

ABSURDITIES: (*With agitation*).
Smeraldine . . . a hair
pin . . .
Fata Morgana . . . it looks bad!
(*The agitation of the Absurdities
reaches such a degree that they
leave their towers and approach
Ninette on tiptoes to observe more
closely the approaching event.*)
(*Smeraldine approaches Ninette
and stabs her in the head with a
big magic hairpin.*)

NINETTE: (*Gémissant longuement et plaintivement*). Ah! (*Ninette disparait s'étant transformée en rat. Le petit rat à travers toute la scène se précipite dans la coulisse.*)

LES RIDICULES: Aïe! diable! quel grand rat! (*Les Ridicules très effrayés par le rat se sauvent dans les tours.*) Pouah! c'est immonde un rat! Malheureuse Ninette! Devenir un rat immonde! (*Sméraldine reste à la place où elle a piqué Ninette. Fata Morgana est à une petite distance derrière elle.*)

FATA MORGANA: Et toi tu prends la place de Ninette Et dis que tu es la vraie Princesse! (*Disparaît.*) (*On entend une marche à la cantonnade.—Un cortège pompeux apparait avec des torches et des lanternes. Le Roi, Le Prince, Clarice, Léandre, Pantalon, des Courtisans, les gardes.*)

LE PRINCE: (*Joyeusement*). Quel bonheur! c'est ma belle princesse!

LE ROI: Cette femme? Princesse?

LE PRINCE: Mais ce n'est pas elle!

SMÉRALDINE: C'est bien moi! Je suis ta Ninette!

LE PRINCE: Non! non, quel affreux mensonge!

SMÉRALDINE: Prince, tu m'es lié par ta promesse.

LES PRINCE: T'épouser, non, jamais! Elle me dégoûte cette femme!

LE ROI: Prince!

LE PRINCE: Non, je refuse ce mariage!

LE ROI: (*Fermement*). Prince, tu sais qu'un prince royal N'a qu'une parole! Prince, tu es lié par ton honneur! (*Très autoritaire.*) Tu l'épousera j'ai dit!

LES COURTISANS: (*Surpris et épouvantés*). Oh!

LE PRINCE: Un négresse?

LE ROI: (*Terrible*). Je te l'ordonne!

LE PRINCE: (*Perplexe*). C'est terrible!

LE ROI: Je te l'ordonne Donne lui le bras, Le cortège, en marche! (*Le cortège rebrousse chemin. On force le Prince, qui est au désespoir, à donner le bras à Sméraldine—Léandre et Clarice restent derrière le cortège.*)

NINETTE: (*Groans deeply and plaintively*). Oh! (*Ninette disappears, having been transformed into a rat. The little rat crosses the entire stage and runs into the wings.*)

ABSURDITIES: Ah! the devil! what a big rat! (*Frightened by the rat, the Absurdities escape to their towers.*) Whew! a rat is foul! Unhappy Ninette! To become a foul rat! (*Smeraldine remains on the spot on which she stabbed Ninette. Fata Morgana stands a short distance behind.*)

FATA MORGANA: And you will replace Ninette And say you are the real Princess! (*Disappears.*) (*A march is heard back of the stage. A pompous procession appears with torches and lanterns. The King, the Prince, Clarisse, Leander, Pantaloon, Courtiers and Guards.*)

PRINCE: (*Joyously*). Happiness! There is my beautiful Princess!

KING: That woman? Princess?

PRINCE: But it is not she!

SMERALDINE: It is I! I am your Ninette!

PRINCE: No, no! what a fearful lie!

SMERALDINE: Prince, you are tied to me by your promise.

PRINCE: Marry you, never! She disgusts me, that woman!

KING: Prince!

PRINCE: No! I refuse to marry.

KING: (*Firmly*). Prince, you know that a royal prince Only has one word! Prince, you are bound by your honor! (*With authority.*) I say, you will marry her!

COURTIERS (*Surprised and horrified*). Oh!

PRINCE: A negress?

KING: (*Emphatically*). I command you!

PRINCE: (*Perplexed*). It is terrible!

KING: I command you! Offer her your arm. Procession! march! (*The procession retraces its steps. The Prince, who is in despair, is forced to offer his arm to Smeraldine. Leander and Clarisse remain behind.*)

LÉANDRE: (*Vénimeux*). L'orange est pourrie! Aussi la princesse en est sortie toute noire! (*Il tend le bras à Clarice et suit le cortège.*)

FIN DE L'ACTE TROISIÈME.

## ■ ACTE QUATRIÈME.

### SCÈNE I.

(*Après le lever du rideau, au lieu de décor, on voit un second rideau, cabalistique comme à la seconde scène du Ier. acte. Le Magicien Tchélio et Fata Morgana, hostile et farouches, se ruent l'un contre l'autre arrivant l'un de droite et l'autre de gauche.*)

TCHÉLIO: Ah! ignoble sorcière; ignoble sorcière! Lâche et misérable! Tu as été ratée par le diable! Lâche! Lâche!

FATA MORGANA: Oh! toi vieux sorcier prétentieux, Sorcier prétentieux sans force, Sans puissance Magicien auquel personne n'obéit jamais!

TCHÉLIO: Lâche créature! tu n'as pas honte De t'abaisser à te servir d'épingles de femmes, Viles épingles empoisonnées!

FATA MORGANA: Et toi! . . . Et toi! . . . Et toi sorcier sans gloire, Tu egrostes qu'avec tes p'tits rubans de soie magiques! Ha! Ha! Ha! Ha! C'est grotesque!

TCHÉLIO: Lâche! quelle honte!

FATA MORGANA: Ah quel imbécile tu n'es qu'un magicien, Bon à distraire des jeunes filles.

TCHÉLIO: (*D'un mouvement de main Tchélio provoque un éclair et un coup de tonnerre*). Vieille furie! Par couardise tu n'as même pas agi toi-même. (*D'un mouvement de main Fata Morgana provoque un éclair et un coup de tonnerre.*)

FATA MORGANA: Tu n'es qu'un malhonnête!

TCHÉLIO: Tu t'es servie d'une sale esclave noire.

FATA MORGANA: Car tu oublie que tu as perdu. (*Eclair et tonnerre provoqués par Tchélio.*) Aux cartes le destin du prince. (*Eclair et tonnerre provoqués par Fata Morgana.*) Il est à moi! (*Fata Morgana fait reculer*

LEANDER: (*With venom*). The orange was decayed! So the princess came out black! (*He offers his arm to Clarisse and they follow the procession.*)

END OF ACT THIRD.

## ■ ACT IV.

### SCENE I.

(*After the curtain has risen, instead of a stage setting there is seen a second curtain, cabalistic as in Scene II of the First Act. The magician Tchelio and Fata Morgana, hostile and furious, run into each other as they enter from opposite sides.*)

TCHELIO: Ah, ignoble witch! ignoble witch! Cowardly and wretched! The devil made you fail! Coward! coward!

FATA MORGANA: Oh! old pretentious sorcerer, Pretentious sorcerer without power, Powerless magician, Whom nobody ever obeys!

TCHELIO: Cowardly creature; you are not ashamed To lower yourself to the use of woman's hairpin, A vile poisoned hairpin!

FATA MORGANA: And you! . . . and you! You magician without glory. You are grotesque with your Small silk ribbons of magic! Ha! Ha! Ha! Ha! It is grotesque!

TCHELIO: Coward! what shame!

FATA MORGANA: Ha! what a fool! you are only a magician, Sufficient to distract young girls.

TCHELIO: (*With a movement of his arm he brings lightning and thunder*). Old fury! Through cowardice you did not even Act yourself! (*By a movement of the arm Fata Morgana brings lightning and thunder.*)

FATA MORGANA: You are nothing but an uncivil man!

TCHELIO: You made use of a dirty black slave.

FATA MORGANA: You forget that you lost (*Lightning and thunder brought on by Tchelio.*) The destiny of the Prince at cards. (*Lightning and thunder brought on by Fata.*) He is mine! (*Fata Morgana forces Tchelio to*

Tchélio.)
En les sauvant tu voles comme un
tricheur!
(*Éclair.*)
Tricheur!
(*Sortent des tours, se mettent en
deux rangs et avec une gravité
maligne, s'approchent de Fata
Morgana.*)

**LES RIDICULES:** Fata Morgana
nous venons parler d'affaires,
Fata Morgana!
Il faut que tu le sache,
Nous allons te dire
Une nouvelle curieuse.
Nous te chuchoterons à ton oreille!
Approche encore écoute c'est
grave!
Fata Morgana! Fata Morgana!
(*Brusquement ils la poussent
dans une des tours et l'enferment.
De la tour sort du feu et de la
fumée.*)
(*A Tchélio.*)
Va, maintenant, tu peux sauver
Ta cour royale!
(*La lumière eclaire le Magicien
Tchélio par en haut.*)

**TCHÉLIO:** (*Fait des gestes
d'incantation vers la tour où est
enfermée Fata Morgana*). Vois,
sorcière, quelle est ma puissance!

**LES RIDICULES:** Tiens, tiens!
(*Rentrant dans la cour avec une
bonhomie légèrement ironique.*)
Puissance!
(*Le Rideau Cabalistique se lève.*)

## SCÈNE II.

(*La salle au trône du palais royal
brillamment éclairée. A gauche sur
une grande estrade le trône du Roi
auprès duquel deux trônes l'un
pour le Prince, l'autre pour la future Princesse. Au dessus des trois
trônes un grand Baldaquin en velours qui peut se fermer. Le Maître
de Cérémonies, des serviteurs. La
salle se remplit de Courtisans.*)

**LÉANDRE:** (*Entrant hâtivement*). Est-ce en ordre?

**MAÎTRE DES CÉRÉMONIES:**
Certes!

**LÉANDRE:** Le trône aussi?

**MAÎTRE DES CÉRÉMONIES:** Oui,
seigneur!

**LÉANDRE:** Faites tomber le velours,
Le cortège arrive!
(*On ferme le baldaquin.*)
(*Une marche à la cantonnade.*)
(*Le cortège entre. Le Roi en tête,
après lui le Prince et Sméraldine,
puis Pantalon, Clarice, les Courtisans et les gardes.*)

**CHŒUR:** Gloire à notre Roi!
Le roi de Trèfles!
Et vive le Prince,
Qu'il règne brillant,
Monarque incomparable!

---

step back.)
In saving him you steal like a card
cheat!
(*Lightning.*)
Card cheat!
(*The Absurdities leave their towers, form a double file and approach Fata Morgana with a malign dignity.*)

**ABSURDITIES:** Fata Morgana! we
come to speak on business!
Fata Morgana!
You must know it.
We will tell you
Strange news.
We will whisper it in your ear!
Come closer! Listen! It is serious!
Fata Morgana! Fata Morgana!
(*They push her suddenly into one
of the towers and lock her in. Fire
and smoke rise from the tower.*)
(*To Tchelio.*)
Go! now you can save
Your royal court!
(*Light falls on the magician Tche-
lio from above.*)

**TCHELIO:** (*Makes gestures of incantation in the direction of the
tower in which Fata Morgana is
locked*). See, witch, my power!

**ABSURDITIES:** Why? that is good!
(*They re-enter the tower with
slightly ironical good humor.*)
My Power.
(*The cabalistic curtain rises.*)

## SCENE II.

(*The throne room of the royal palace, brilliantly lighted. To the left
stands the King's throne on a
large platform, beside it two other
thrones, one for the Prince, the
other for the future Princess.
Above the thrones a huge baldachin of velvet, which can be
drawn. Master of Ceremonies,
Servants. The room fills with
Courtiers.*)

**LEANDER:** (*Enters hastily*). Is everything ready?

**MASTER OF CEREMONIES:** Certainly!

**LEANDER:** The throne as well?

**MASTER OF CEREMONIES:** Yes,
sire!

**LEANDER:** Drop the velvet.
The procession is coming!
(*The baldachin is closed.*)
(*A march back stage.*)
(*The procession enters. The King
leads, after him the Prince and
Smeraldine; then Pantaloon,
Clarisse, the Courtiers and
Guards*).

**COURTIERS:** Glory to our King!
The King of Clubs!
And long live the Prince,
May he reign powerfully.
Matchless monarch!

---

**MAÎTRE DES CÉRÉMONIES:** (*Solennel*). Découvrez le trône!
(*Le rideau du Trône est levé. Sur le
trône de la princesse est assis un
rat, plus grand qu'un être humain, qui remue ses moustaches.
C'est la Princesse Ninette transformée en rat qui est accouru et
s'est assise sur sa place.*)
(*Tous en grand désarroi reculent
d'un pas. Plusieurs courtisans
saisissent leurs armes.*)

**TOUS:** Qu'est-ce? Qoui? Ah! c'est
terrible!

**LE ROI:** (*Desorienté*). Gardes!
Gardes!

**PANTALON:** Appelez les gardes!
(*Le Magicien Tchélio apparait,
éclairé. Il essaie de désenchanter
le rat par des gestes desespérés.*)

**TCHÉLIO:** (*Racontant*). Rat
j'exige que tu redevienne Princesse!

**LE ROI:** Aux armes!

**TCHÉLIO:** Je l'ordonne!
(*Les gardes tirent.*)
(*Le rat redevient la Princesse Ni-
nette. Le Magicien disparait.*)

**TOUS:** Quel miracle!

**LES RIDICULES:** (*Avec
étonnement joyeux*). Princesse
Ninette!

**LE PRINCE:** (*Se préipitant vers Ninette*). C'est elle, c'est ma princesse!
(*A genoux devant Ninette en lui
tenant les mains.*)
C'est mon amour, c'est mon orange!

**CHŒUR:** Grands Dieux, qu'elle
est belle la princesse!

**LE ROI:** Je suis surpris! Mais elle
n'est vraiment pas.

**LE PRINCE:** (*Tendrement*). Ninette!

**LE ROI:** (*En designant
Sméraldine*). Alors cette femme?

**TROUFFALDINO:** (*Arrivant on
ne sait d'où*). Mais c'est
Sméraldine!

**CLARICE et LÉANDRE:**
Sméraldine?

**LE ROI:** Sméraldine? N'est-elle pas
complice de Léandre.

**LÉANDRE** (*En faisant un pas en
avant*). Mon roi . . .

**LE ROI:** (*N'entendant pas
Léandre*). Oui, je commence à tout
comprendre.

**LÉANDRE:** Mon Roi . . .

**LE ROI:** (*En colère et avec
dédain*). Tais-toi, tu es un traître!

**LES COURTISANS:** Un
traître . . .

**CLARICE:** (*Emotionnée*). Oncle!

---

**MASTER OF CEREMONIES:** (*Solemnly*). Uncover the throne!
(*The curtain of the throne is lifted. A rat is seated on the throne of
the Princess. It is bigger than a human being and it is moving its
mustaches. It is the Princess Ninette, transformed into a rat, who
has come and seated herself on the
throne.*)
(*All fall back in confusion. Several Courtiers seize their weapons.*)

**ALL:** What is it? What! Ah! It is terrible!

**KING:** (*Lost*). Guards! Guards!

**PANTALOON:** Call the guards!
(*The magician Tchelio appears, illuminated. He tries to remove the
enchantment from the rat by desperate gestures.*)

**TCHELIO:** (*Narrates*). Rat, I demand that you turn back into the
Princess!

**KING:** To arms!

**TCHELIO:** I command it!
(*The guards fire.*)
(*The rat turns into the Princess
Ninette. The magician disap-
pears.*)

**ALL:** What a miracle!

**ABSURDITIES:** (*With happy
astonishment*). Princess Ninette!

**PRINCE:** (*Hurrying towards Ninette*). It is she! it is my Princess!
(*On his knees before Ninette,
holds her hands.*)
It is my love! it is my orange!

**COURTIERS:** How beautiful is the
Princess!

**KING:** I am surprised. But she is not
real!

**PRINCE:** (*Tenderly*). Ninette!

**KING:** (*Pointing to Smeraldine*).
And what about this woman?

**TROUFFALDINO:** (*Arrives from
no one knows where*). But that is
Smeraldine!

**CLARISSE AND LEANDER:** Smeraldine!

**KING:** Smeraldine? Is she not Leander's accomplice?

**LEANDER:** (*Taking a step forward*). My King . . .

**KING:** (*Does not hear Leander*).
Yes, I am beginning to understand.

**LEANDER:** My King . . .

**KING:** (*Angrily and with scorn*).
Be silent! you are a traitor!

**COURTIERS:** A traitor . . .

**CLARISSE:** (*with emotion*). Uncle!

**LES ROI:** Va-t'en, je sais que tu as trempé dans le crime!

**LES COURTISANS:** Crime!

(*Le Roi dans une colère solennelle monte vers le trône. Tous restent figés de peur.*)

Quel moment d'angoisse! Il décide.

**LE ROI:** (*Majesteusement*). J'ordonne que l'esclave Sméraldine,

(*Sméraldine terrifiée recule d'un pas.*)

Le traître Léandre,

(*Léandre recule d'un pas.*)

Et sa lâche complice ma nièce Clarice,

(*Clarice recule d'un pas.*)

Qu'on les pende!

(*Les Courtisans, les Gardes, Pantalon, Trouffaldino, le Maître des Cérémonies tombent à genoux.*)

(*Murmurant tragiquement.*)

Qu'on les pende!

**TROUFFALDINO:** (*D'un voix mielleuse*). O Roi, pardonne!

**PANTALON:** (*Le poussant*). Tais-toi!

**LE ROI:** (*Murmure tragiquement affirmant*). Qu'on les pende.

**LES COURTISANS:** (*Très impressionnées*). Les pendre!

**LE ROI:** (*Energiquement aux gardes*). Gardes, la corde!

(*Les gardes se dirigent vers eux, Sméraldine essaye de fuir, Clarice la suit, Léandre suit Clarice. Les gardes se jettent à leurs poursuite. Pantalon, Trouffaldino, Le Maître Des Cérémonies et tous les Courtisans se précipitent après les gardes. Il ne reste que le Roi sur les marches du trône, Ninette sur son trône et le prince toujours embrassant ses genoux.*)

**TROUFFALDINO, MAÎTRE DES CÉRÉMONIES et PANTALON:** À droite!

**LES COURTISANS:** À gauche! Tenez!

(*Tous en longues chaines courent vers l'avant-scène et dans la coulisse de gauche puis apparaissent au fond de la scène de la coulisse gauche et dans le même ordre courent à travers la scène dans la coulisse droite. Fata Morgana enfonce la porte de la tour. Fata Morgana court vers le milieu de la scène.*)

**FATA MORGANA:** Tonnerre! Venez à moi
Je vous protège!

(*Les poursuivis et les poursuivants réapparaissent sur scène de la coulisse droite et courent vers Fata Morgana. Devant elle s'ouvre une trappe. Sméraldine, Clarice et Léandre sautent dans la trappe, d'ou sort du feu et de la fumée. Fata Morgana s'y engouffre après eux. Les gardes et les Courtisans accourus, encerclent la place maintenant vide.*)

**CHOEUR:** Traître où êtez-vous donc.

**LES RIDICULES:** (*Entonnent*). Criez donc, Vive le Roi.

**LE ROI:** Non! Vive le Prince et la Princesse.

(*Les Ridicules sortis des tours se joignent à la foule.*)

**TOUS:** Bénis soit notre Roi, le Prince et la Princesse!

*FIN.*

**KING:** Go away. I know that you are deep in crime!

**COURTIERS:** Crime!

(*The King mounts the throne in solemn anger. All remain transfixed with fear.*)

What moments of anguish! He is deciding.

**KING:** (*Majestically*). I order that the slave Smeraldine,

(*Terrified, Smeraldine shrinks back.*)

The traitor Leander,

(*Leander shrinks back.*)

And his dastardly accomplice, my niece Clarisse,

(*Clarisse shrinks back.*)

That they be hanged!

(*The Courtiers, Guards, Pantaloon, Trouffaldino, Master of Ceremonies fall on their knees.*)

(*Tragic murmur.*)

That they be hanged!

**TROUFFALDINO:** (*In a soft voice*). Oh King! pardon!

**PANTALOON:** (*Pushing him*). Keep quiet!

**KING:** (*Murmurs tragically and positively*). Hang them!

**COURTIERS:** (*Impressed*). Hang them!

**KING:** (*Energetically to the Guards*). Guards, the rope!

(*The Guards approach them. Smeraldine tries to escape, and Clarisse follows her. Leander follows Clarisse. The Guards pursue them. Pantaloon, Trouffaldino, the Master of Ceremonies and all the Courtiers follow the Guards. Only the King remains on the steps of the throne. Ninette remains on her throne with the Prince kissing her knees.*)

**TROUFFALDINO, MASTER OF CEREMONIES AND PANTALOON:** To the right!

**COURTIERS:** To the left! There!

(*All run in a long file towards the proscenium and to the left wing, then appear back of the stage on the left and run in the same order to the right wing. Fata Morgana forces the door of the tower. She runs towards the center of the stage.*)

**FATA MORGANA:** Thunder! Come to me,
I will protect you!

(*The pursued and the pursuers appear on the stage from the right wing and run towards Fata Morgana. A trap door opens before her. Smeraldine, Clarisse and Leander jump into the trap, from which fire and smoke are rising. Fata Morgana follows them. The Guards and Courtiers surround the now empty spot.*)

**COURTIERS:** Traitors! Where are you?

**ABSURDITIES:** (*Astonished*). Shout: Long live the King!

**KING:** No! Long live the Prince and Princess!

(*The Absurdities leave their towers and join the crowd.*)

**ALL:** Blessings on our King, Prince and Princess!

*THE END.*

# Manon Lescaut (1893)

MUSIC BY GIACOMO PUCCINI ■ LIBRETTO BY RUGGERO LEONCAVALLO, MARCO PRAGA, DOMENICO OLIVA, LUIGI ILLICA AND GUISEPPE GIACOSA

Manon Lescaut, based on Abbé Prévost's novel and set to an "anonymous" libretto by Giuseppe Giacosa, Luigi Illica, Giulio Ricordi and others, premiered at the Teatro Regio in Turin on February 1, 1893. Manon Lescaut arrrives by stagecoach at the courtyard of an inn in Amiens with her brother, who is escorting her to a convent school. Manon and the chevalier des Grieux fall in love immediately. Edmondo tells des Grieux that the old official, Geronte de Ravoir, plans to kidnap Manon. The young lovers use his coach to elope. Manon's brother Lescaut tells Geronte that he's sure his sister will choose the old man's wealth over Grieux' poverty.

Manon does indeed choose Geronte over des Grieux, leaving her life with des Grieux to become the old man's mistress. She laments the loss of des Grieux for, even though she was poor, she was very happy. Lescaut brings Manon news of her former lover. He then tells des Grieux, who has now made a fortune from gambling, where he may find Manon. The lovers reunite. Geronte swears to seek vengeance. Manon and des Grieux prepare to depart, but Manon delays their escape to gather the jewels that Geronte gave her. The police arrest her, accusing her of being a thief and a common prostitute. At Le Havre, manon boards a ship—she is to be deported to New Orleans. Lescaut and des Grieux try to get her released. Des Grieux is granted permission to sail with her. Arrriving in North America, the lovers escape from New Orleans. They drag themselves along the road, hopelessly seeking an English colony. Thoroughly spent, Manon realizes she is going to die. Overwhelmed by grief, des Grieux collapses over her lifeless corpse.

---

## ■ ATTO I

*Ad Amiens.*

*Un vasto piazzale presso la Porta di Parigi.*

*Un viale a destra. A sinistra un'osteria con porticato sotto al quale sono disposte varie tuvole per gli avventori. Una scaletta esterna conduce al primo piano dell'osteria.*

*Studenti, Borghesi, Popolani, Donne, Fanciulle, Soldati passeggiano per la piazza e sotto il viale. Altri son fermi a gruppi chiacchierando. Altri seduti alle tavole, bevono e ginocano.—Edmondo, attorniato da altri Studenti, poi Des Grieux.*

**EDM:** (*tra il comico ed il sentimentale*) Ave, sera gentile, che discendi
col tuo corteo di zeffiri e di stelle;
Ave, cara ai poeti ed agli amanti.

**STUDENTI:** (*dopo averlo interrotto con una gran risata*) . . . e ai ladri ed ai brïachi!
Noi ti abbiamo spezzato il madrigale!

**EDM:** E vi ringrazio. Pel vïal giulive
vengono a frotte a frotte
fresche, ridenti e belle
le nostre artigianelle . . .

**STUDENTI:** Or s'anima il vïale.

## ■ ACT I

*At Amiens.*

*A spacious Square near the Paris Gate.*

*An Avenue, R. An Inn, L. Under its porch are tables for the customers. An outer staircase leads to the first floor of the Inn.*

*Students, Citizens, Villagers, Women, Girls and Soldiers stroll about in the square and the avenue. Some stand together talking, others are seated at the tables drinking and playing cards.—Edmondo with other Students, then Des Grieux.*

**EDM:** (*half in earnest, half in jest*)
Hail, beautiful night, advancing
With all your wondrous train of stars and zephyrs;—
Hail, night, so dear to bards and to all lovers . . .

**STUDENTS:** (*with a burst of laughter*) And to robbers and topers!
I fear that we have cut short your madrigal!

**EDM:** For that I thank you. Up the pleasant pathway
Come now in throngs so joyous,
Our merry, fresh and laughing
Fair young work-girls from their toiling.

**STUDENTS:** How gay the scene is growing.

**EDM:** Preparo un madrigale
furbesco, ardito e gaio;
e sia la musa mia
tutta galanteria!

**EDM. E GLI STUDENTI:** (*ad alcune fanciulle che si avanzano del viale*) Giovinezza è il nostro nome,
la speranza è nostra iddia
ci trascina per le chiome
indomabile virtù.
Santa ebbrezza! Or voi, ridenti,
amorose adolescenti,
date il labbro e date il core
alla balda gioventù.
Fanciulle (*avvicinandosi*) Vaga per l'aura
un'onda di profumi,
van le rondini a vol
e muore il sol.
È questa l'ora delle fantasie
che fra le spemi lottano
e le malinconie.
(*Entra Des Grieux vestito semplicemente come gli Studenti.*)

**STUDENTI:** Oh, Des Grieux!
(*Des G. li saluta senza accennare a volersi fermate.*)

**EDM:** (*chiamandolo*) Fra noi,
amico, vieni e ridi
e ti vinca la cura
di balzana avventura.
(*Des G., senza aver l'aspetto preoccupato, si mostra poco disposto ad unirsi alle schiere allegre dei suoi compagni.*)
Non rispondi? Perchè? Mesto tu sembri! Forse
di dama inaccessibile acuto amo, ti morse?

**EDM:** I'll fashion a madrigal
A rhyme of fun and frolic;
My muse shall be teeming
And rife with gallantry!

**EDM. and Students:** (*to some of the girls who come from the avenue*) Youth is ours with all its gladness,
Hope's the goddess of our creed,
And we dare the boldest deed
To win sweet favor from you.
Wondrous rapture! Rout all sadness
With the smile that love imparts;
Yield your lips and yield your hearts
To our youthful ardor true.
(*Girls approaching*) Soft waves of perfume
Are floating through the ether.
Home the swallows will fly,
Soon sunlight will die.
This is the hour of tender fantasy,
When hope or sorrow subtly strive for power.
(*Enter Des G. dressed as a student.*)

**STUDENTS:** Welcome, Des Grieux!
(*Des G. salutes them without stopping*)

**EDM:** (*calling him*) Now come and join us, friend, and gaily
We will wander in quest of amorous adventure.
(*Des G. shows no inclination to join the merry groups of students.*)
What, no answer? But why?
Haply for some unyielding fair one,
A hopeless flame consumes you?

**DES G:** (*lo interrompe, alzando le spalle*) L'amor! Questa tragedia, ovver commedia, io non conosco!
(*gli Studenti si dividono, alcuni restano a conversare con Des G. ed Edm. altri si danno a corteggiare le ragazze che passeggiano a braccetto sul piazzale e nel viale.*)

**ALCUNI STUDENTI:** (*a Des G.*) Baie!
Misteriose vittorie
cauto celi e felice;
fido il figliuol di Venere
ti guida e benedice.

**DES G:** Amici, troppo onore voi mi fate.

**EDM. E STUDENTI:** Per Bacco, indoviniam, amico . . . Ti crucci d'uno scacco . . .

**DES G:** No . . . non ancora . . . ma se vi talenta,
vo' compiacervi . . . e tosto!!
(*si avvicina ad alcune fanciulle che passano e con galanteria dice loro.*)
Tra voi, belle, brune e bionde
si nasconde
ritrosetta-giovenetta
vaga-vezzosa,
dal labbro rosa
che m'aspetta?
Sei tu quella-bionda stella?
Dillo a me!
Palesatemi il destino
e il divino
viso ardente
che m'innamori,
ch'io vegga e . . . adori
eternamente!
Sei tu quella-bruna snella?
Dillo a me!
(*le fanciulle comprendendo che egli scherza, si allontanano corrucciate da Des G. erollando le spalle. Gli Studenti ridono.*)

**GLI STUDENTI:** Ma bravo!

**EDM:** Guardate compagni,
di lui più nessuno si lagni!

**Tutti:** Festeggiam la serata,
com' è nostro costume,
suoni musica grata
nei brindisi il bicchier,
e noi rapisca il fascino
ardente del piacer!
Danze, brindisi, follie,
il corteo di voluttà
or s' avanza per le vie
e la notte regnerà;
E splendente ed irruente
è un poema di fulgor:
tutto vinca-tutto avvinca
la sua luce e il suo furor.
(*Squilla la cornetta del postiglione: dal fondo a destra arriva una diligenza: tutti si affollano per osservare chi arriva: la diligenza si arresta innanzi al portone dell' osteria. Scende subito Lescaut, poi Geronte, il quale galantemente aiuta a scendere Ma-*)

**DES G:** (*interrupts him, shrugging his shoulders*) What, love! what love! I have no notion of that sad tragedy
Or dismal farce.
(*the students separate, some remain to talk with Des G. and Edm. others court the girls who are strolling about arm-in-arm in the square and the avenue.*)

**STUDENTS:** (*to Des G.*) Nonsense!
You are secretly hiding.
Some glad and facile conquest
May the faithful son of Venus
Ever your fate be guiding.

**DES G:** No, friends, you do me too much honor.

**EDM. AND STUDENTS:** By Bacchus, then, we guess right . . .
You're crossed in love already!

**DES G:** Not yet, believe me, but if it so please you,
I will content you . . . directly!
(*approaches some of the girls and addresses them*)
Now among you, dark and fair ones,
Is there hiding
A sweet maiden coy and tender,
Whose lips so rosy will kisses render?
Are you my fair star, tell me, pray?
Does fate give me happy chances
And what promise yield your glances
That so enthrall me
To love's enchantment they ever recall me!
Are you my lodestar, tell me, pray?
(*the girls, seeing that he is joking, turn from him angrily, shrugging their shoulders. The Students laugh.*)

**STUDENT:** That's splendid!

**EDM:** Now note this well, comrades,
Let no one chaff him any more!

**CHORUS:** Let gay song and glad laughter,
With our wonted rejoicing,
Now resound, and thereafter
Let us quaff the purple wine;
And the spell that delights us
Shall be pleasure divine!
Dances, revels, wild enjoyment,
In the wake of pleasure stay.
Let us welcome the glad advent
Of night's sweet and dreamful sway.
All is wondrous and entrancing,
Like a dream of rapture bright
Ardor of all hearts enhancing,
Wreathed with song and crowned with light.
(*Postilion's horn heard without, a diligence comes on from the back, R.; all crowd together to see the arrivals; the diligence stops in front of the courtyard of the Inn.*)

non. Dall' osteria vengono frettolosamente alcuni garzoni i quali si affaccendano attorno a diversi viaggiatori, e dispongono per lo scarico dei bagagli.)
Giunge il cocchio d' Arras!
Discendono . . .
Vediam! . . . Viaggiatori eleganti-galanti!

**STUDENTI:** (*ammirando Man.*)
Chi non darebbe a quella
donnina bella
il gentile saluto
del benvenuto?

**LES:** Ehi! l' oste! (*a Ger.*) Cavalier,
siete un modello
di squisitezza . . .
(*chiamando*) Ehi! l' oste!

**L' OSTE:** (*accorrendo*) Eccomi qua!

**DES G:** (*guardando Man.*) Dio, quanto è bella!
(*la diligenza entra nel portone dell' osteria: la folla si allontana: parecchi Studenti tornano ai tavoli a bere e giuocare: Edm. si ferma da un lato ad osservare Man. e Des G.*)

**GER:** (*all' Oste*) Questa notte, amico,
(*all' Oste.*)
qui posero . . . (*a Les.*) Scusate!—
Ostiere, v' occupate
del mio bagaglio.

**L' OSTE:** Ubbidirò . . . (*dà qualche ordine*) Vi prego,
mi vogliate seguire.
(*preceduti dall' Oste salgono al primo piano Ger. e Les., che avrà fatto cenno a Man. d' attenderlo. Man. si siede.*)

**DES G:** (*che non avrà mai distolto gli occhi da Man. le si avvicina*)
Deh, se buona voi siete siccome siete bella,
mi dite il nome vostro, cortese damigella . . .

**MAN:** (*alzandosi, risponde modestamente*) Manon Lescaut mi chiamo.

**DES G:** Perdonate al dir mio, ma da un fascino arcano a voi spinto son io.
Persino il vostro volto parmi aver visto, e strani
moti ha il mio core. Quando partirete?

**MAN:** (*dolorosamente*) Domani all' alba io parto. Un chiostro m' attende.

**DES G:** E in voi l'aprile
nel volto si palesa e fiorisce! o gentile,
qual fato vi fa guerra?
(*Edm. cautamente si avvicina agli Studenti che sono all' osteria,*)

Lescaut gets down first, then Geronte, who assists Manon to alight. Servants run hurriedly from the Inn to attend to the passengers and take charge of the luggage.)
Here comes the coach from Arras!
Now they alight . . . Look there! . . .
Folk of some rank and station!
(*Man., Les., Ger. and the Innkeeper, Servants of the Inn.*)

**STUDENTS:** (*admiring Man.*)
Who would not to that maiden
With beauty laden,
A welcome tender
And cordial render?

**LES:** Ho! Landlord! (*to Ger.*) Honored Sir! you are a model of politeness (*calling*) Ho! Landlord!

**INNKEEPER:** (*running up*) I am here!

**DES G:** (*gazing at Man.*) How fair! how entrancing!
(*the diligence enters the courtyard of the Inn; the crowd disperses; some of the students sit down to drink and play cards; Edm. stands apart to watch Man. and Des. G.*)

**GER:** (*to the Innkeeper*) For this night, friend,
I will stay here (*to Les.*) Your pardon! (*to Innkeeper.*)
Now, landlord, please look after all my luggage.

**INNKEEPER:** I shall obey (*gives an order*) Be pleased, Sir, kindly to step this way.)
(*Ger. and Les., preceded by the Innkeeper, ascend to the first floor, Les, having signalled to Man. to wait for him. Man. sits down.*)

**DES G:** (*who has kept his eyes fixed on Man., approaches her*)
Fair lady, if your kindness can surpass your beauty,
Tell me your name, and take my homage as a duty.

**MAN:** (*rising, says with simplicity*) Manon Lescaut they call me.

**DES G:** Vouchsafe to hear me!
I am drawn toward you by some enthralling spell,
You come to me with wondrous grace, recalling
My heart's delight and devotion.
When are you going there?

**MAN:** (*mournfully*) I start tomorrow at dawn,
A convent awaits me.

**DES G:** The smiles of April adorn your glances
And linger there! O Fair enchantress!
What cruel fate pursues you?
(*Edm. cautiously approaches the*

## Act I

*ed indica loro furbescamente Des G. che è in stretto colloquio con Man.)*

**MAN:** Il mio fato si chiama: voler del padre mio.

**DES G:** Oh, come siete bella! Ah! no! non è un convento che sterile vi brama! No! sul vostro destino riluce un' altra stella.

**MAN:** La mia stella tramonta!

**DES G:** (*tristamente*) Or parlar non possiamo, Ritornate fra poco, e cospiranti contro il fato, vinceremo.

**MAN:** Tanta pietà traspare dalle vostre parole! Vo' ricordarvi! Il nome vostro?

**DES G:** Sono Renato Des Grieux . . .

**LES:** (*di dentro*) Manon!

**MAN:** (*subito*) Lasciarvi debbo. (*volgendosi verso l' albergo.*) Vengo? (*a Des G.*) Mio fratello m' ha chiamata.

**DES G:** (*supplichevole*) Qui tornate?

**MAN:** No! non posso. Mi lasciate!

**DES G:** O gentile, vi scongiuro . . .

**MAN:** (*commossa*) Mi vincete? Quando oscuro l'aere intorno a noi sarà! (*s'interrompe: vede Les. che sarà venuto sul balcone dell' osteria e frettolosamente lo raggiunge, entrando ambedue nelle camere.*)

**DES G:** (*che avrà seguito Man. collo sguardo, prorompe con accento appassionato*) Donna non vidi mai simile a questa! A dirle: io 'tamo, tutta si desta-l'anima. Manon Lescaut mi chiamo! Come queste parole mi vagan nello spirto e ascose fibre vanno a carezzare. O susurro gentil, deh! non cessare! (*Edm. e gli Studenti, che hanno sempre spiato Des G., lo circondano rumorosamente.*)

**STUDENTI:** La tua ventura ci rassicura. O di Cupido degno fedel, bella e divina ia pellegrina per tua delizia scese dal ciel! (*Des G. parte indispettito.*) Fugge: è dunque innamorato!

---

*students at the Inn, and slyly points out to them Des G. in close conversation with Man.)*

**MAN:** My sad fate is decided Alas! by paternal will.

**DES G:** Oh! how your face enchants me! Ah! no! It is not for you in convent grim to be repining, No, on your fate a more resplendent star is shining.

**MAN:** I fear my star is waning.

**DES G:** (*sadly*) Now we cannot speak further. Return then shortly, And We shall conquer warring fate bravely together!

**MAN:** Such pity betoken all your words for me, I would remember your name, as yet unspoken.

**DES G:** I am Renato Des Grieux.

**LES:** (*within*) Manon!

**MAN:** (*quickly*) I need to leave you (*turning towards the Inn*) I come! (*to Des G.*) My brother is calling for me.

**DES G:** (*entreatingly*) You'll return here?

**MAN:** No! I cannot, pray you leave me.

**DES G:** Oh! fair lady, I implore you—

**MAN:** (*much moved*) You persuade me. When it is darker grown and night is more advanced— (*Stops speaking as she sees Les. step on to the balcony of the Inn, and hurriedly joins him, they both retire.*)

**DES G:** (*who has intently watched Man., exclaims passionately*) Never did I behold so fair a maiden! To tell her: I love you, Awoke my heart and soul to life and rapture; "Manon Lescaut they call me," How those words seemed laden with fragrance, To charm me past recapture. What throbs of passion in my veins are dancing, O what music dwells in those tones entrancing. (*Edm. and Students who have kept their eyes fixed on Des G., surround him noisily.*)

**STUDENTS:** By your adventure You reassure us, You are in Cupid's favor, that's clear, Your heart's in danger From that fair stranger, An angel has sent you here. (*Exist Des G., vexed.*)

---

*(tutti gli Studenti si avviano allegramente al porticato dell' osteria: s' imbattono in alcune fanciulle e le invitano galantemente a seguirli. Intanto scendono dalla scaletta Les. e Ger., e parlano fra loro, passeggiando. Edm. si avvicina ad un fanciulla e le parla galantemente; sul finire del dialogo fra Les. e Ger. l' accompagna sino al viale a destra, ove le dà l'addio.)*

**STUDENTI:** Venite fanciulle! . . . Augurio ci siate di buona fortuna.

**FANCIULLE:** È bionda od è bruna la diva che guida la vostra tenzon?

**STUDENTI:** È calva la diva: ma morbida chioma voi fa desïar. Chi perde e chi vince, voi brama, o fanciulle, chi piange e chi ride; noi prostra ed irride la mala ventura: ma lieta proromope d' amore la folle, l'eterna canzon.

**FANCIULLE:** Amiche fedeli di un' ora, volete? Il riso chiedete, il bacio, il sospir? Orniam la vittoria, e il cope del vinto al tepido effluvio di molle carezza riposa, obliando, e l' onta e il martir. (*Studenti e Fanciulle prendono posto intorno alle tavole: alcuni ricominciano a giuocare, altri ordinano da bere.*)

**EDM:** (*ad una fanciulla*) Addio mia stella, addio mio fior, vaga sorella del Dio d'amor. A te d'intorno va il mio sospir, e per un giorno non mi tradir. (*saluta galantemente la fanciulla, la quale si allontana; poi vedendo Ger. e Les. in stretto colloquio, si ferma in disparte ad osservarli.*)

**GER:** (*a Les.*) Dunque vostra sorella il velo cingerà?

**LES:** Malo consiglio della gente mia.

**GER:** Diversa idea mi pare la vosta?

**LES:** Certo, certo, ho più sana la testa di quel che sembri, e benchè triste fama le giovanili mie gesta circondi. Ma la vita conosco,

---

He's off! Then he's downright in earnest. (*all the students hasten merrily to the porch of the Inn; they meet some girls coming from the opposite direction and invite them to join them. Meanwhile Les. and Ger. come down the staircase talking together. Edm. approaches one of the girls and pays her compliments. When Les. and Ger. finish speaking, Edm. goes with the girl as far as the avenue, R., and bids her good-bye.*)

**STUDENTS:** Come, join us fair damsels! And bring us good fortune And luck by your presence.

**GIRLS:** Are gold locks or raven, The boast of the goddess, For whom you contend?

**STUDENTS:** The dame's bald we fancy; but soft silken tresses Enhance all your charms. Who wins or who loses needs all your caresses, Who's laughing or weeping; It smites and derides us Ill luck to be reaping: But joyfully guides us The wild song of rapture And love without end.

**GIRLS:** For sweathearts you wish, only true for an hour, For laughter you wish, for a kiss and a sigh, Then crown we the victor; the vanquished we dower With rapturous fervor of tender endearments That quickly all shame and all sorrow outvie! (*Students and girls take their seats at the table; some play at cards, others order drinks.*)

**EDM:** (*to one of the girls*) Farewell, my flower, Farewell, my star, Fair child of Venus Indeed you are. Around you hover My sighs anew, To your fond lover This day be true. (*be salutes the girl, who goes off; then seeing Ger. and Les. in close conversation, he stands apart to watch them.*)

**GER:** (*to Les.*) Then your fair little sister Will shortly take the veil?

**LES:** Foolishly have her parents thus decided.

**GER:** Your own opinion I take it, must differ.

**LES:** Quite so! quite so; Oh! my head is more sober than doubtless appears, Though evil report has my actions maligned. But I know the world, bless you,

---

forse troppo. Parigi
è scuola grande assai.
di mia sorella guida, mormorando,
adempio il mio dovere,
come un vero soldato.
Solo, dico, che ingrato
evento al mondo non ci coglie, senza
qualche compenso: e voi conobbi
illustre
Signor?

**GER:** Geronte di Ravoir.

**LES:** Diporto vi conduce in vïaggio?

**GER:** No dovere;
l'affitto delle imposte a me fidato
dalla bontà del Re, dalla mia borsa.

**LES:** (Che sacco d'o).

**GER:** E non mi sembra lieta
neppur vostra sorella.

**LES:** Pensate! a diciott' anni.
Quanta festa di sogni e di speranze
in quella testolina . . .

**GER:** Comprendo . . . Poverina!
E d' uopo consolarla. Questa sera
meco verrete a cena?
Ci sian propizie l' ore.

**GER:** Quale onor! quale onore!
E intanto permettete . . .
(*gli fa un cenno d' offrirgli
qualche cosa all' osteria.*)

**GER:** (*che sulle prime aveva seguito Les., cambia subito di pensiero*) Scusate . . . m' attendete
per breve istante; qualche ordine io
debbo
all' ostiere impartir . . .
(*Les. s' inchina e Ger. s' allontana
verso il fondo: dall' interno dell'
osteria sono portate varie lampade e candele accese, che i garzoni dispongono sui tavoli dei giuocatori.*)

**GLI STUDENTI:** (*giuocando animatamente*) Un asso! Un fante! Un
tre!
Che gioco maledetto!

**LES:** (*attratto dalle voci si accosta
al porticalo e guarda con febbrile
interesse*) Giocano! Oh, se potessi
qualche colpo perfetto
tentare anch'io!

**GLI STUDENT:** Puntate!
Puntate! Carte! Un asso!

**LES:** (*si avvicina in modo deciso
agli Studenti, si pone alle spalle d'
un giuocatore, osserva il suo
giuoco, poi con aria di
rimprovero*) Un asso?! mio signore,
Un fante! Errore, errore!

**GLI STUDENTI:** (*a Les.*) È vero, un
fante; siete
un maestro?

only too well,
And Paris is a famous school.
Of my young sister, most unwilling
guardian,
I fulfil the duty
Like a true dauntless soldier.
Let me add, Sir, that in this life,
No sad event ever happens
Without some compensation,
And I met you, but your name—

**GER:** Geronte de Ravoir.

**LES:** It is pleasure that leads you to
travel?

**GER:** No, it is duty;
The high official charge, to me confided
By favor of the king, I have to pay
for.

**LES:** (*aside*) A mine of gold.

**GER:** To me she seems unhappy
Your pretty little sister.

**LES:** Just fancy! only eighteen, sir!
Full of dreams and illusions.

**GER:** Exactly—Sweet young creature!—
We should indeed console her.
Will you honor me, sir, tonight at
supper?

**LES:** We shall be too delighted!—
Meanwhile, will you allow me?—
(*inviting him with a gesture to
join in a drink.*)

**GER:** (*at first follows Les., but
suddenly changes his mind.*) Your
pardon—
Here wait me for a few moments,
I must some orders impart to the
landlord.
(*Les. bows and Ger. retires up
stage: it gets dark and from the
Inn lamps and candles are
brought on by the servants.*)

**STUDENTS:** (*intent on their
game*) An ace, sir! A knave, sir! A
three!
What wretched cards we're holding!

**LES:** (*at the sound of the voices
comes up to the porch and keenly
watches the players.*) They're at
cards! Oh, could I only
Attempt a coup and rook them of
their savings—

**STUDENTS:** Your deal, sir!
Cards!—An ace—

**LES:** (*approaches the Students,
and standing by the side of one of
the players, looks over his hand,
then says reproachfully*) An ace!
No, dear sire! a knave,
You're wrong, sir, you're wrong,
sir.

**STUDENTS:** (*to Lescaut*) That's
true—a knave.
You're a professor.

**LES:** Celiate!
Un dilettante . . .

**GLI STUDENTI:** A noi . . .
v' invito . . . banco!

**LES:** (*con aria fredda e sprezzante
sedendosi a giuocare*) Carte!
(*Ger., che da lontano bas osservato Les., vedendolo occupato al
giuoco, chiama l'Oste, che è sul limitare del portone; l' Oste accorre
premuroso; Ger. lo conduce in
disparte, mentre Edm., messo in
sospetto dagli andirivieni di Ger.,
cautamente si avvicina per sorve-
gliarlo*)

**GER:** (*all' Oste*) Amico, io pago
prima e poche ciarle!
Una carrozza e cavalli che volino
sì come il vento; fra un' ora!

**L'OSTE:** Signore!

**GER:** Dietro l'albergo, fra un' ora,
capite?!
Verranno un uomo e una fanciulla . . . e via
sì come il vento, via, verso Parigi!
E ricordate che il silenzio è d' or.

**L'OSTE:** L' oro . . . adoro.

**GER:** Bene, bene!
(*dandogli una borsa.*)
Adoratelo e ubbidite,
Or mi dite,
(*indicando il portone dell' osteria.*)
questa uscita ha l' osteria
solamente?

**L'OSTE:** Ve n' ha un' altra.

**GER:** Indicatemi la via.
(*partono dal fondo a sinistra.*)

**EDM:** (*che ha udito il colloquio
fra Ger. e l' Oste*)
Vecchietto amabile,
incipriato Pluton, sei tu!
La tua Proserpina
di resistere forse avrà virtù?
(*entra Des G. pensiero; Edm. gli si
avvicina: poi battendogli sulla
spalla.*)
Cavaliere, te la fanno!

**DES G:** (*con sorpresa*) Che vuoi
dir?

**EDM:** (*ironicamente*) Quel flor
dolcissimo
che olezzava poco fa
dal suo stel divelto, povero
flor, fra un' ora appassirà!
La tua fanciulla, la tua colomba
or vola, or vola:
Del postiglione suona la tromba . . .
Via, ti consola:
Un vecchio la rapisce!

**DES G:** (*grandemente turbato*)
Davvero?

**EDM:** Impallidisci?
Per Dio, la cosa è seria!

**LES:** You're jesting!
Quite a beginner.

**STUDENTS:** Come now—
I'll play you—banco!

**LES:** (*with nonchalance sits down
to play*) Cards!
(*Ger., who has watched Les. from
a distance, seeing him occupied
with the game, calls to the Innkeeper, who is standing at the
door, and he runs up obsequiously. Ger. takes him aside while
Edm., whose suspicion is aroused
by Ger.'s proceedings, cautiously
gets near him.*)

**GER:** (*to the Innkeeper*) Now
listen. I pay beforehand and do not
bargain!
In an hour I want a carriage and
horses
That fly like the wind.

**INNKEEPER:** As you wish, sir.

**GER:** Behind the tavern—in an
hour—you mark me.
A man will come there with a maid-
en—
Then, like the wind,
They'll gallop off en route to Paris.
Silence is golden, mind, remember.

**INNKEEPER:** I'll remember.

**GER:** Good, Good! Remember and
obey me.
(*gives him a purse.*)
And now tell me
(*points to the courtyard of the
inn.*)
To this inn is there any other egress?

**INNKEEPER:** There is another.

**GER:** Show me where it is directly.
(*Exeunt up stage L.*)

**EDM:** (*who has heard the conversation between Ger. and the Innkeeper*) Elderly charmer,
Indeed you are a wicked old Pluto!
Your Proserpine may yet
Your scheme have strength and
courage to resist.
(*Enter Des G. absorbed in
thought; Edm. goes up to him,
then taps him on the shoulder.*)
My dear friend, they would outwit
you!

**DES G:** (*surprised*) What do you
mean?

**EDM:** (*ironically*) That flower
sweet and fair
That shed lately fragrance rare;
From the stem so rudely torn
Poor flower will fade away forlorn.
Your lovely maiden, your snow-
white doveling,
Soon is flying here:
The post-boy's horn will blare out
loudly—
Come, friend, take comfort,
An old man takes her from you.

**DES G:** (*in great anxiety*) What say
you?

**EDM:** Your cheek grows paler!
By heaven! you're in earnest.

DES G: Que l' attendo, capisci?

EDM: Siamo a buon punto!?

DES G: Salvami!

EDM: Salvarti!? La partenza impedire? Tentiamo! Senti! Ti salvo, forse.
Del gioco all' amo morse
il soldato laggiù.

DES G: E il vecchio?

EDM: Il vecchio? Oh, il vecchio l'avrà da far con mei.
(*si avvicina ai compagni che giuocano, e parla all' orrecchio d' alcuni fra essi: poi esce e s' allontana a sinistra; si sospende il giuoco: Les. beve in compagnia degli Studenti: Man. comparisce sulla scaletta, guarda anisiosa intorno e visto Des G. scende e gli si avvicina.*)

MAN: Vedete? Io son fedele
alla parola mia. Voi mi chiedeste
con fervida preghiera,
che a voi tornassi un' altra volta. Meglio
non rivedervi, io credo, e al vostro prego
benignamente opporre il mio rifluto.

DES G: Oh come gravi le vostre parole!
Sì ragionar non suole
l' età gentile che v' infiora il viso;
mal s' addice al sorriso
che dall' occhio bellissimo traluce
questo severo ragionare e questo
disdegno melanconico!

MAN: Eppur lieta, assai lieta
un tempo io fui! La queta
casetta risonava
di mie folli risate,
e colle amiche gioconde ne andava
gioconda a danza!
Ma di gaiezza il bel tempo tuggi!

DES G: (*affascinato*) Nelle pupille
fulgide profonde
sfavilla il desiderio dell'
amore . . .
Amor ora vi parla! Date all' onde
del nuovo incanto e il dolce labbro
e il core
l' anima date a questo immenso invito
di baci e di carezze che ne è intorno!
V'amo! v' amo! Quest' attimo di giorno
deh! a me rendete eterno ed infinito!

MAN: Una fanciulla povera son io,
non ho sul volto luce de beltà,
regna tristezza sul destino
mio . . .

DES G: Shortly I await her here.

EDM: We're in good time then.

DES G: Help me, friend!

EDM: Assist you? Prevent their departure?
Let's try! Look here! Perhaps I'll do it.
The bait of play has hooked that brave soldier!

DES G: And the old one?

EDM: The old one? Oh! he'll have to deal with me!
(*goes up to the Students who are playing, and whispers to some of them, then goes off, L. The Students stop playing awhile; Les. drinks with the Students. Man. appears on the staircase, looks anxiously round, sees Des G. and comes down to him.*)

MAN: Behold me! I have been faithful
To my rash, thoughtless promise!
You did so urge me with passionate entreaty
To come again and meet you here.
It would have been wiser not to see you,
And your request, Sir, I ought most
Courteously to have rejected.

DES G: Oh! how your words sound grave and alarming!—
They jar with all the sweetness
And youth on your face so fondly beaming;
Blend them with rays of laughter
That from your eyes are streaming,
And rid your lovely lips of sad disdain!

MAN: And yet happy, ah! how happy once was I!
Our quiet dwelling ever resounded
With my gay peals of laughter,
And with my young and lively neighbors
Often I went dancing.
But soon, alas! these days of pleasure ceased.

DES G: (*enraptured*) In the pure depth and glamour of your glances,
How love's transcendent ecstacy is gleaning!
Let love unfold you all its wondrous trances.
I love you! love you! make this joy supernal,
A peerless realm of love and bliss eternal.

MAN: I'm but a lowly, modest little maiden,
No ray of beauty glows upon my face,
And all my future is with sadness laden.

DES G: Vinta tristezza dall' amor sarà!
La bellezza vi dona
il più vago avvenir,
o soave persona,
mio infinito sospir!
M' inonda soave delizia, o flore
dell' anima mia;
m' inonda profonda letizia,
e l' alma pei sogni s' avvia . . .
Oh! dove il tuo sguardo m' adduce
la vita comincia per me;
io sogno un futuro di luce,
la vita divisa con te.

MAN: No, non è vero! Troppo bello è il sogno!
Oh, non è inganno la vostra parola?

LES: (*alzandosi mezzo brillo, e picchiando sul tavolo*)
Non e' è più vino? E che? Vuota è la botte?
(*gli Studenti lo forzano a sedere e gli versano ancora del vino; all' udire la voce di Les., Man. e Des G. si ritraggono verso destra agitalissimi; Man. impaurita vorrebbe rientrare, ma viene trattenuta da Des G.*)

DES G: Deh! m' ascoltate, vi minaccia un vile
oltraggio; un rapimento!—Un libertino,
quel vecchio che con voi giunse,
una trama
a vostro danno ordi.

MAN: (*stupita*) Che dite?!

DES G: Il vero!

EDM: (*accorendo si avvicina a Des G. e Man. e dice loro, rapidamente*) Il colpo è fatto, la carrozza è pronta . . .
Che burla colossal! Presto! Partite . . .

MAN: (*sorpresa*) Fuggir? . . . Fuggir?

DES G: Fuggiamo! Concedete
che il vostro rapitor . . . un altro sia.

MAN: (*a Des G.*) Voi mi rapite?

DES G: Vi rapisce amore.

MAN: (*resistendo*) Ah! no!

DES G: (*con intensa preghiera*) V' imploro!

EDM.: Presto, via ragazzi!

DES G: (*insistendo*) Manon . . . Manon . . .

MAN: (*risoluta*) Andiam!

EDM: Oh! che bei pazzi!
(*Edm. dà a Des G. il proprio mantello, col quale può coprirsi il volto, poi tutti e tre fuggono dal fondo, dietro l' osteria. — Ger. viene dalla sinistra, da una rapida occhiata al tavalo; vedendovi Les. giuocare animatamente, lascia sfuggire un moto di soddisfa-*

DES G: We shall triumph over sadness by love's grace,
For your beauty assures you
The most jubilant fate.
In your sweetness and splendor
Fair dream of love,
Supremest joy to render.

LES: (*rising and rapping on the table*) More wine is wanted! Ho! there! Is the cask empty?
(*the Students oblige him to sit down; play goes on with greater animation. At the sound of Les.'s voice Man. and Des. G. retire, R., in dismay. Man. would go back to the Inn, but Des G. prevents her.*)

DES G: Hear me, I pray you!
You are threatened with an outrage.
An old audacious roúe,
You know, you arrived together;
A vile plot against you has planned.

MAN: (*astonished*) What say you?

DES G: The truth, love!

EDM: (*running up to Des G. and Man., says hurriedly*) The deed's accomplished, and the carriage ready;
Oh! what a splendid joke!
Make haste! Be off!—

MAN: (*surprised*) What!—
elope?—

DES G: With me, love,
Make me your captor and no other, dearest.

MAN: (*to Des G.*) You must not take me!

DES G: It is love that takes you.

MAN: (*resisting*) Ah! no!

DES G: (*imploringly*) I pray you!

EDM: Make haste, quick, be off now!

DES G: (*insisting*) Manon—Manon—

MAN: (*with decision*) I'll come!

EDM: Fine pair of madcaps!
(*Edm. takes off his cloak and gives it to Des G. to cover his face, then they all run off behind the Inn. Ger. enters from the L., catches sight of Les, intent on the game, and looks pleased. Then cautiously, so as not to attract anyone's attention, goes towards*

zione, e cautamente, in modo da non risvegliare l' attenzione di alcuno, va verso l' osteria, dove trova l' Oste.)

GER: Di sedur la sorellina
è il momento! - Via, ardimento,
che il sergente è al giuoco intento.
È bene ch' ei vi resti! Vi rimanga!
(*chiama sottovoce l' Oste.*)
Ehi, dico . . . (*l' Oste accorre.*)
È pronta la cena?

L' OSTE: Sì Eccellenza

GER: L'annunziate a quella signorina,
che . . .

EDM: (*che è ritornato e ha udito le ultime parole di Ger., gli si fa innanzi a grandi inchini*) Quella signorina?

GER: (*seccato*) Sì.

EDM: (*additando al fondo, lontano, verso la via che conduce a Parigi*) Eccellenza,
vedetela! Essa parte in compagnia d' un ardente-studente.
(*Edm. si avvicina agli Studenti.*)

GER: (*guarda sorpreso, poi nella massima confusione corre da Les. scuotendolo*) L' hanno rapita!

GER: (*giuocando*) Chi?

GER: Vosta sorella!

LES: Che?!—Mille e mille bombe!
(*butta le carte e corre fuori: l'Oste impaurito, fugge nell' osteria.*)

GER: L'inseguiamo!
È uno studente!

LES: (*vedendo la simulata indifferenza degli Studenti, crolla il capo*) È inutil!
(*e a Ger. che si lascia sfuggire un moto d'impazienza, dice calmo.*)
Riflettiamo!
Cavalli pronti avete?
(*Ger. accenna di no.*)
Il colpo è fatto!
È tardi il disperarsi ed è da matto!

GER: (*irritatissimo*) È ver.

LES: Vedo; Manon con sue grazie leggiadre
ha suscitato in voi . . . un affetto di padre!

GER: Non altrimenti!

LES: (*con dignitosa fierezza*) E a chi lo dite!Ed io da figlio rispettoso vi do un ottimo consiglio . . .
Parigi! E là Manon . . . Manon già non si perde!
Ma borsa di studente presto rimane al verde . . .

---

the Inn, where he finds the Innkeeper.)

GER: To allure that little sister
Now's the moment.
Come, take courage!
All absorbed in play is that soldier.
There let him stay!
(*calls softly to the Innkeeper.*)
Ho! landlord!
(*the Innkeeper runs in.*)
Is supper ready?

INNKEEPER: Yes, your Excellency.

GER: Straight announce it then to that young lady—
Who—
(*Edm., who has returned, and has heard the last words of Ger., approaches him, bowing profoundly.*)

EDM: That young lady!

GER: (*vexed*) Yes—

EDM: (*points to the background, far off, to the Paris road*) Will your Excellency just deign to look.
There she goes. She's off, you see,
With that young student.
(*Edm. goes up to the Students.*)

GER: (*looks surprised, then greatly agitated runs up to Les. and pulls him by the arm*) She is flying here?

LES: (*continuing to play*) Who?

GER: Your pretty sister?

LES: What!—Burst ten thousand bombshells!
(*throws down the cards and runs out of the porch; the Innkeeper, alarmed, retreats into the Inn.*)

GER: Follow fast!
It is a young student! Go!

LES: (*noticing the assumed indifference of the Students, shakes his head*) That's no good.
(*and calmly says to Ger., who shows signs of impatience*) Let me think.
Are any horses ready?
(*Ger. shakes his head.*)
The deed's accomplished,
To despair is most foolish.

GER: (*in a rage*) It is true.

LES: I see, Manon, with her graces and sweetness,
Has roused within your heart, sir,
A paternal affection—

GER: It is as you say, sir.

LES: (*with proud dignity*) Of that I'm certain—
Let me as a son devoted
Give you excellent advice, sir.
To Paris—she's there, Manon!
Manon, we shall not lose her!
The purse of a young student
Will soon be drained completely.

---

Manon non vuol miseria! Manon riconoscente accetterà
. . . un palazzo, per piantar lo studente!
Voi farete . . . da padre ad un' ottima figlia
ed io completerò, signore, la famiglia.
Che diamine! Ci vuole calma . . . filosofia . . .
(*Gli Studenti, tralasciato il giuoco ridono sottecchi dell' avventura di Des G. che sottovoce Edm. a loro narra; cauti però per la presenza del Sergente, prudentemente, in disparte, guardano ascoltano e si divertono.*)
Venticelli - ricciutelli che spirate
fra vermigli - fiori e gigli,
avventura
strana e dura,
deh, narrate,
Strana e dura - l'avventura
per mia fè!
Assetato labbro aveva
coppa piena;
ber voleva
e avidamente
già suggeva . . .
ma, repente,
bocca ignota - la fè vuota . . .
Dura è affè!
(*Ridono, ma allo squardo minaccioso di Les., frenano le risa e si ritirano verso il viale, ove ripigliano il loro motteggio.*)
(*vedendo a terra il tricorno che, in un momento d' ira era caduto a Ger. lo raccoglie e lo porge al vecchio ganimede ma, udendo ridere gli Studenti, si volge indispettito e minaccioso. - Poi dice a Ger.*)
Ecco il vostro tricorno!E domattina, in via!
Dunque, dicevo . . . A cena e il braccio a me!
(*preso a braccio Ger., si avvia verso l' osteria, parlando e gesticolando calmo e maestoso.*)
Degli eventi all' altezza esser convien!
Perchè . . . (*entrano nell' osteria.*)
(*Edm. e gli Studenti avanzandosi cautamente dal fondo sino alla porta dell' osteria, con malizia.*)
A volpe invecchiata
l' uva fresca e vellutata
sempre acerba rimarrà.
(*gli Studendi scoppiano in una gran risata; in quel mentre esce minaccioso Les.; gli Studenti fuggono ridendo.*)

*Fine Dell' Atto Primo.*

---

Manon cannot bear privation,
Manon will thankful be, sir,
To accept a palace and forsake her boyish lover.
You will act as a father to a dutiful daughter,
And I will complete the pleasant family party.
(*spoken*) Odd's life, sir! one must be calm—and philosophical—
(*The Students cease playing, and laugh amongst themselves at the adventure of Des G., which Edm. tells them in an undertone. The presence of Les. makes them cautious, and, keeping a little apart, they look on, listen and enjoy the fun.*)
Fragrant breezes, lightly wreathing
Mid the flowers,
Perfume sweet around us breathing;
Go, tell the story through the hours,
How cruel fate her victim sadly dowers.
Thirsty lips drew near a goblet,
Rich in measure
Of bliss and pleasure;
Love's lips quicker
Quaffed the liquor!
(*the Students laugh, but seeing that Les. looks at them menacingly, they restrain their laughter and go towards the avenue, where they continue their gibes.*)
(*seeing Ger.'s hat on the ground, which he had dropped in his rage, picks it up and hands it to him, but hearing the Students laugh, Les. turns round threateningly, then says to Ger.*)
Let me hand you your hat, sir,
And then we're off tomorrow.
As I was saying—to supper!
Give me your arm—
(*takes Ger.'s arm and walks towards the Inn, gesticulating as he talks.*)
One must ever rise to the occasion.
Because—
(*They enter the Inn.*)
(*Edm. and the Students, advancing cautiously from the background to the door of the Inn, say sarcastically*)
To fox old and hoary
Will the grapes in all its glory,
Always sour still remain.
(*the Students burst into loud laughter; Les. comes out and threatens them; the Students run off laughing.*)

*END OF THE FIRST ACT.*

# ■ ATTO II

*A Parigi.*

# ■ ACT II

*In Paris.*

# Act II

*Salotto elegantissimo in casa di Geronte.*
*Nel fondo due porte. A destra ricchissime e pesanti cortine nascondono l'alcova. A sinistra, presso alla finestra, una ricsa pettiniera. Sofà, sedili, poltrone, un tavolo.*

*Manon—Un Parrucchiere.*

*Manon è seduta avanti alla pettiniera: è coperta da un ampio accappatoio bianco che le avvolge tutta la persona. Il Parrucchiere le si affanna intorno. Due garzoni nel fondo stanno pronti ai cenni del Parrucchiere.*

MAN: (*guardandosi allo specchio*) Dispettosetto riccio questo! (*al Parrucchiere.*)
Il calamistro! . . . Presto! . . .
(*il Parrucchiere corre saltellando a prendere il ferro per arricciare e ritorce il riccio ribelle, quindi eseguisce premurosamente i vari ordini che gli da Man.*)
Or . . . la volandola!
Severe un po' le ciglia!
La cerussa!
(*soddisfatta.*)
Lo sguardo
vibri a guisa di dardo!
Qua la giunchiglia!
(*Lescaut e Detti.*)

LES: (*entrando*) Buon giorno, sorellina!

MAN: (*facendo attenzionne al Parrucchiere*) Il minio e la pomata!.

LES: Questa mattina mi sembri un po' imbronciata.

MAN: Imbronciata? Perche?

LES: No? Tanto meglio! (*sorridendo malizioso.*)
Geronte ov' é? Così presto ha lasciato . . . il gineceo?

MAN: (*al Parrucchiere*) Ed ora . . . un nèo!
(*il Parrucchiere porta a Man. la scatola di lacca giapponese contenente i nèi. Man. indecisa vi cerca dentro rovistandone i taffetà non decidendosi a scegliere.*)

LES: (*consigliando*) Lo Sfrontato! . . . Il Biricchino! . . . No? . . . il Galante!

MAN: (*ancora indecisa*) Non saprei . . . (*risolvendosi*) Ebben . . . due nèi! Al d'occhio l'Asassino! e al labbro il Voluttuoso!
(*il Parrucchiere pone i due nèi, poi graziosamente e con bravura toglie l'accappatoio a Man., che appare vestita, incipriata, pettinata; piega l'accappatoio, si inchino a Man. fa un cenno ai suoi garzoni e a grandi inchini esce.*)

---

*Handsome room in Geronte's house.—At the back two doors, Rich and heavy curtains shut in an alcove, R. A well-appointed toilet-table, L., near a window. Sofa, chairs, easy chairs, a table.*

*Manon and a hairdresser.*

*Manon is seated at the toilet-table, she is enveloped in a large combing-cloak. The hairdresser attends to her, and two assistants await his orders.*

MAN: (*looking at herself in the glass*) Really this curl is most unruly! (*to the hairdresser.*)
The curling tongs!—Bring quickly!
(*the hairdresser runs to get the curling-irons and curls the lock again, then he carries out the different orders given by Man.*)
Now powder carefully!
The eye-brows slightly darken!—
The cosmetic!—
(*pleased.*)
What flashing fire
Darts from my glances!
Here place the flower!
(*Lescaut and the same.*)

LES: (*enters*) Good-morrow, little sister!

MAN: (*goes on talking to the hairdresser*) The rouge and the pomatum!—

LES: You seem Upset this morning, dear, just a trifle.

MAN: Upset?—Oh! no!

LES: No! all the better— (*smiling slyly.*)
Geronte's out? What so early he's left your presence sweet?

MAN: (*to hairdresser*) And now— the patches!
(*the hairdresser offers Man. a box of Japanese lacquer containing the patches. Man. turns them over, hesitating which to choose.*)

LES: (*advisingly*) The Audacious—or the Roguish one!— No?—the Coquettish!—

MAN: (*still hesitating*) I don't know— I'll now—have two!— The eye will be most killing! The lip alluringly tempting! (*the hairdresser places the two patches, then skilfully removes the combing-cloak. Man. appears richly and tastefully dressed; the hairdresser folds the combing-cloak, bows to Man., beckons to his assistants and goes out bowing low.*)

---

LES: (*guarda attento Man. ed esclama ammirato*) Che insieme delizioso!
(*Lescaut—Manon, poi Musici.*)

LES: (*continuando ad ammirare Man.*) Sei splendida e lucente!
M'esalto! . . . En' ho il perchè!
È mia la gloria se
sei salva dall' amor d' uno studente.
Allor che sei fuggita . . . là, ad Amiens,
mai la speranza il cor m' abbandonò!
Là, la tua sorte vidi! . . . Laggiù il magico
fulgor di queste sale balenò.
T' ho ritrovata! Una casetta angusta era la tua dimora—possedevi innumerati baci e . . . niente scudi!
E un bravo giovinotto quel Des Grieux!
Ma . . . (*ahimè*) non è cassiere generale!
Dunque era naturale che un di Manon avesse abbandonato
per un palazzo aurato quell' umile dimora.

MAN: (*l' interrompe*) E . . . dimmi . . .

LES: Che vuoi dire?

MAN: Nulla!

LES: Nulla? Davver?

MAN: (*indifferente*) Volevo dimandar . . .

LES: Risponderò!

MAN: (*volgendosi con vivacità*) Risponderai?

LES: (*malizioso*) Ho inteso! . . . Ne' tuoi occhi io leggo un desiderio. (*guardando comicamente intorno.*) Se Geronte lo sospettasse!

MAN: (*allegra*) È ver! Hai côito!

LES: Brami nuovi di . . . Lui?

MAN: È ver! (*con tristezza*) L' ho abbcandonato senza un saluto . . . un bacio! (*si guarda intorno e si ferma cogli occhi all' alcova.*)
Ah . . . in quelle trine morbide
nell' alcova dorata v' è un silenzio
un freddo che m' agghiaccia! . . .
Ed io che m' ero avvezza
a una carezza
voluttuosa
di labbra ardenti e d' infuocate braccia
or ho . . . tutt' altra cosa!
(*pensierosa.*)
O mia dimora umile,
tu mi ritorni innanzi

---

LES: (*looks at Man. admiringly and exclaims*) How attractive and charming!
(*Lescaut, Manon, then the Singers.*)

LES: (*still admiring Man.*) You're resplendent with beauty! I'm proud—and with good cause! I saved you from the jaws Of danger through the love of that young student. When you eloped so rashly, there from Amiens, At heart I knew it would all come right in time. There I saw your fate, dear. The magic splendor of these rooms I even there beheld! At length I found you. A modest little cottage Was then your dwelling— Very rich in kisses, but short of money. He's a nice young fellow, that Des Grieux!— Alas! he's got no balance at his bankers, So it was right and proper That Manon should abandon That humble little dwelling, For this most gorgeous mansion.

MAN: (*interrupting him*) And— tell me—

LES: Speak out frankly!—

MAN: Nothing!—

LES: Nothing? Indeed?

MAN: (*as if carelessly*) I wanted just to ask—

LES: I'll answer you—

MAN: (*turning quickly round*) You'll answer me?—

LES: (*slyly*) I wonder! In your eyes I perceive a vague desire. (*with a comical look.*) If Geronte should but suspect it!—

MAN: (*gaily*) It's true!—you've guessed it!

LES: For his tidings you wish?—

MAN: I do indeed! (*sadly.*) Without a kiss or word of good-bye I left him. (*Looks round, fixes her eyes on the alcove.*) In those soft silken curtains— In that gilded alcove, there's a silence— There's a chill that freezes me. I who once knew The fervor Of fond caresses, And from dear lips to taste Love's ardent and most perfect kisses— And now—all that is over! (*pensively.*) My little humble dwelling,

gaia, isolata, bianca
come un sogno gentile
e di pace e d' amor!

**LES:** (*osservando inquieto Man.*)
Orben . . . poichè tu vuoi sa-
per . . . Des Grieux,
come Geronte, è un grande amico
mio.
Ei mi tortura sempre:
(*imitando Des G.*)
"Ov' è Manon?
Ove? . . . Con chi fuggi? Ad Est?
A Nord?
A Sud? . . . " Sempre io rispon-
do: "Non lo so! . . . "
E alfin l' ho persuaso!

**MAN:** (*sorpresa*) Ei m' ha scordata!?

**LES:** No! No! . . . Ma che vincendo pùo coll' oro
forse scoprir la via che mena a te!
(*con mistero e con gesti di giuocatore provetto.*)
Or . . . correggendo la fortuna
sta . . .
Io l' ho lanciato al gioco! . . .
Vincerà.—
E il vecchio tavolier (per noi) tal
quale
la cassa del danaro universale! . . .
Da me lanciato e istrutto
pelerà tutti e tutto!
Ma nel martirio delle lunghe lotte
intanto il dì e la notte
vive incosciente della sua follia,
e ognora chiede al giuoco ove tu
sia!

**MAN:** (*fra sè, dolorosamente*) Per
me tu lotti,
per me che, vile, ti lasciai:
che tanto duolo a te costai! . . .
Ah! vieni! Il passato mi rendi,
l' ore fugaci . . .
le tue carezze ardenti!
Rendimi i baci,
i baci tuoi cocenti . . .
l'ebbrezza che un dì mi bèo!
Vieni! . . . Son bella?
più bella ancor sarò!
(*rimane pensierosa, rattristata,
poi i suoi occhi si soffermano allo
specchio; la sua adorabile figura
vi si delinea; le mani quasi incon-
scenti aggiustano le pieghe della
veste; poi i pensieri si mutano, le
labbra sorridono, gli occhi sfavil-
lano nel trionfo di sua bellezza e
passando davanti allo specchio,
domanda a Les.*)
Davver che a maraviglia questa
veste
mi sta? . . .

**LES:** (*ammirando*) Ti sta a pennel-
la!

**MAN:** E il tupé? . . .

**LES:** Portentoso!

**MAN:** E il busto? . . .

I see you there before me
Secluded and enchanting,
Like a vision so peaceful
Of rest and love!

**LES:** (*watching Man. anxiously*)
Well—since you wish to know—
Des Grieux, just like Geronte,
Is my good friend and comrade.
And he is ever asking:
(*imitating Des G.*)
Where is Manon? Where has she
fled?
With whom? To North? or East? or
South?
I reply: "I don't know!—"
At last I've persuaded him—

**MAN:** (*surprised*) He has forgotten?

**LES:** No! No! But that in winning
heaps of money
He may find out the path that leads
to you!
(*mysteriously, and imitating a
card player.*)
Now—he'll improve his fortune
soon at play.
I've made him a gambler!—He
shall win.—
For him it will be a bank, the gaming table
Where he to fleece all players will
be able.
I've taught him how to swindle,
Their gains will quickly dwindle.
Amid all his life's excitement and
commotion
through day and night at play, dear,
One thought will ever stir his
heart's emotion,
Again to find his way beside you,
dear.

**MAN:** (*to herself, mournfully*) For
me you're striving,
Who, faithless, left you lonely,
Your life depriving of all joy.
Ah! come, love, the past restore me
only.
Hours so fleeting
Amid sweet caresses,
With lips fondly meeting
Each heart love confesses.
Let enchantment be ours once
more.
Come, love, I'm waiting,
Ah! come, all the past restore.
(*still pensive, turns to the looking
glass, sees the reflection of her
own beauty; her hands
unconsciously arrange the folds
of her gown; then her thoughts
change, a smile flits across her
face, her eyes sparkle with triumph, and passing before the
glass, she asks Les.*)
Tell me, does this gown not suit me
to perfection.

**LES:** (*admiringly*) Yes, to perfection.

**MAN:** My coiffure?

**LES:** It is most splendid!

**MAN:** My bodice!—

**LES:** Bello!!
(*entrano alcuni personaggi inci-
priati tenendo fra le mani dei fogli
di musica. Si avanzano ad inchini
e si schierano da un lato, avanti a
Man.*)

**LES:** (*sottovoce a Man.*) Che ceffi
son costoro? . . . Ciarlatani o
speziali?

**MAN:** (*annioata*) Son musici! . . . E Geronte che fa dei madrigali!

## IL MADRIGALE.

**I MUSICI:** Sulla vetta tu del monte
erri, o Clori:
hai per labbra due fiori:
l' occhio è una fonte.
Ohimè! Ohimè!
Filen spira ai tuoi piè!
Di tue chiome sciogli al vento
il portento,
ed è un giglio il tuo petto
bianco—ignudetto.
Clori sei tu, Manon,
ed in Filen, Geronte si mutò
Filen suonando sta;
la sua zampogna va
susurrando: pietà!
El l' eco sospira:—pietà
Piagne Filen:
"Cuor non hai Clori in sen?
Ve'. . . già . . . Filen . . . vien . . .
men!"
(*a bassa voce.*)
No! . . . Clori a zampogna che
soave plorò
non disse mai no!

**MAN:** (*seccata, dà una borsa a
Les.*) Paga costor!

**LES:** (*intasca la borsa*)
Oibò! . . . Offender
l'arte? . . .
(*ai Musici maestoso.*)
Ir v' accomiato in nome della Gloria!
(*I Musici escono inchinandosi.*)

## IL MINUETTO.

*Manon, Lescaut, Geronte, Vecchi
Signori, Abati, il Maestro di Ballo.
Suonatori.*

*Mentre da una porta escono i Mu-
sici, dall' altra si vedono sfilare
nell' anticamera alcuni amici di
Ger., vecchi signori, abati eleganti. Ger. li riceve. Intanto entrano
alcuni suonatori i quali si collocano nel fondo a sinistra*

**MAN:** (*mostrando quelli a Les.*) I
Madrigali! . . . E il bal-
lo! . . . E poi la musical . . .
Son tutte belle cose! Pur . . .
(*non pùo reprimere uno sbadi-
glio e sbadigliando esclama.*)
M' annoio! . . .
(*e va incontro a Ger. che entra seguito dal maestro di ballo ed altri.
Grandi inchini cerimoniosi.*)

**LES:** Charming!
(*enter singers with pieces of music in their bands. They advance
bowing low and take up their position opposite to Man.*)

**LES:** (*in an undertone to Man.*)
What sort of folk are these?
What curious mugs and noses!

**MAN:** (*bored*) They're singers—
Geronte composes madrigals.

## A MADRIGAL.

**THE SINGERS:** Speed over summit
of the mountain
Gentle Phyllis,
With your lips like fresh spring
flowers,
And eyes like crystal fountain.
Alas! fair sweet!
Phaon sighs at your feet!
All your hair its radiance showers.
Fair as lilies
Your bosom, O gentle Phyllis,
O gentle Phyllis.
You are Phyllis, Manon,
And Phaon now Geronte has be-
come.
Phaon through all the day
On his pipe will play.
Pity claims he alway;
Echo but answers his lay.
Phaon is weeping?
Without heart, you are Phyllis.
See—how Phaon faints now.
(*softly.*)
No! Phyllis to piping sweet and low
Has never said No!

**MAN:** (*bored, gives Les, a purse*)
Pay them with this!

**LES:** (*pockets the purse*) Not I!
How you insult them!—
(*to the singers with dignity.*)
Sirs, I bid you farewell
In the name of Glory!
(*exeunt singers bowing.*)

## THE MINUET.

*Manon, Lescaut, Geronte, old
beaus, Abbés, the dancing-master, musicians.*

*As the singers go out at one door,
several friends of Ger., old beaus
and foppish abbés come in at the
other. Ger. receives them. Musicians also enter and take up their
position L. C.*

**MAN:** (*pointing them out to Les.*)
The Madrigals!—The dances!—
And the music!
All these are very pretty!
(*Yawns.*)
But they bore me!
(*goes to meet Ger., who comes in
followed by the dancing-master
and others. They all salute cere-
moniously.*)

# Act II

(Les. osserva sorridendo quella scena di sdoleinature: suonatori accordano i loro istrumenti, mentre Ger. col maestro ai ballo sta organizzando e preparando il Minuetto.)

(Les looks on smiling: the musicians tune their instruments while Ger. arranges a lesson in the Minuet with the dancing-master.)

LES: (fra sè, filosoficamete riflettendo) Una donnina che s' annoia è cosa
da far paura! . . .
(dopo aver un po riflettuto.)
Andiam da Des Grieux!
È da maestro preparar gli eventi.
(esce.)
(Mentre il maestro di ballo riceve gli ordini da Ger., entrano altri personaggi, i quali si inchinano a Man., le baciano la mano, le offrono fiori, dolciumi, ecc. Il maestro di ballo si avanza, dà la mano a Man. per cominciare il Minuetto: Ger. fa cenno agli amici di tirarsi in disparte, e sedersi. Durante il ballo alcuni servi girano portando cioccolatta e rinfreschi.)

LES: (to himself, philosophizing) When a fair maiden's bored with pleasure
There's danger beyond measure!
(reflects a little.)
I'm off to Des Grieux,
And like a master
I'll arrange events.
(while Ger. gives instructions to the dancing-master, other visitors come in who salute Man. and kiss her hand, offering her flowers, bon-bons, &c. The dancing master then advances and takes Man.'s hand for the Minuet. Ger. beckons to his friends to sit down. During the dance servants pass round with refreshments.)

IL MAESTRO DI BALLO: (a Man.)
Vi prego, signorina,
un po' elevato il busto . . .
indi . . . Ma brava,
cosi mi piace! . . . Tutta
la vostra personcina
or s' avanzi . . . Cosi! . . .
Io vi scongiuro . . . a tempo!

THE DANCING-MASTER: (to Man.) I beg you fair young lady,
Now raise your head a little—that's it—
That's perfect, keep so, I pray you!
Now slightly bend and bring
Your body gently forward—Just so!
Now mind—I beg you, in time, please!

GER: (entusiasmato) Oh vago danzatrice!

GER: (enthusiastically) How sweet and fair a dancer!

MAN: (con falsa modestia) Un po'inesperta.

MAN: (with affected modesty) I'm but a novice.

IL MAESTRO: (impaziente) Vi prego . . . non badate
a lodi susurrate
E cosa seria il ballo! . . .

MASTER: (impatiently) I wish she would not heed you.
Their praise will but mislead you—
An art important, is dancing!—

SIGNORI ED ABATI: (a Gre.) Tacete! . . . Vi frenate,
come si fa da noi;
Ammirate in silenzio,
in silenzio adorate . . .
È cosa seria.

BEAUS AND ABBÉS: (to Ger.) Be silent!
An obedient example take from us;
Just admire in silence,
In silence adore her—
The art's important.

IL MAESTRO: (a Man.) A manca . . .!
Brava! . . . A destra! . . . Un saluto!
(figura dell' occhialetto.)
Attenta! L' occhialetto . . .

MASTER: (to Man.) To left, please!—
That's good!—To right, please!—
Now a curtsey!
(figure of the eye-glass.)
Attention! Use the eye-glass—

GER: Minuetto perfetto!
(Man. guarda qua e là nel gruppo dei suoi ammiratori, è provocantissima; i vecchi signori e gli abati guardano Man. cupidamente.)

GER: How delightful to watch you!
(Man. glances round at her admirers with the most coquettish grace. The old beaus and abbés gaze at Man. with eager admiration.)

SIGNORI ED ABATI: Che languore nello sguardo!
Che dolcezza!
Che carezza!
Troppo è bella!
Se sorride pare stella!
Che candori!
Che tesori!
Quella bocca!
baci scocca!
Se sorride stella pare!

BEAUS AND ABBÉS: How she sweetly
Charms completely!
She's too lovely,
Like star gleaming.
How alluring
Are her graces,
And how beautiful
Her face is.
See her smile
Like star-light gleaming.

MAN: Lodi aurate
mormorate
susurrate
or mi vibrano d' intorno;
Vostri cori
adulatori
su frenate!

MANON: All the golden praise you murmur
Floats delightfully around me.
Pray let not your lips so flatter,
Do not praise me!

ALCUNI SIGNORI ED ABATI: La deità siete del giorno!

SOME OF THE BEAUS AND ABBÉS: You are the dawn's fairest goddess!

ALTRI: Della notte ella è regina!

OTHERS: You are the queen of night's rapture!

GERONTE: Troppo è bella!
Si ribella
la parola e canta e vanta!
Voi mi fate
spasimare . . . delirare.
(il Maestro fa segni d' impazienza.)

GERONTE: She's too lovely!
I with wonder am dreaming.
How you charm and enchant me.
(The dancing-master shows signs of impatience.)

MAN: Il buon maestro non vuole parole . . .
Se m' adulate
non diverrò la diva danzatrice
ch' ora già si figura
la vostra fantasia troppo felice.

MAN: My kind good master dislikes this chatter—
If so you flatter
I never shall become the graceful dancer
That you already think me
With your too eager fancy,
Too kind indulgence.

IL MAESTRO: (impaziente) Un cavalier!

MASTER: (impatiently) A partner, please!

GER: (frettoloso) Son qua!

GER: (hurriedly) I'm here!

SIGNORI ED ABATI: Bravi! Che coppia!
(figura del saluto.)
(Ger. balla senza caricatura, marca appena i passi è superbamente allegro.)

BEAUS AND ABBÉS: Well done! What partners!
(figure of the salute.)
(Ger. dances without exaggeration, hardly marking the steps, he is supremely happy.)

SIGNORI ED ABATI: Evviva i fortunati-innamorati!
Ve' Mercurio e Ciprigna!
Oh! qui letizia
con amore e dovizia
leggiadramente alligna

BEAUS AND ABBÉS: Good luck attend that happy pair—of lovers!
Lo! Mercury and Venus!
Blessed with true love and riches
We find them both united.

MAN: (sull' aria del Minuetto, Ger.) L' ora, o Tirsi, è vaga e bella . . .
Ride il giorno—ride intorno
la tua fida pastorella
Te sospira—e per te spira.
Ma tu giungi e in un baleno
viva e lieta, è dessa allor!
Vedi il ciel com' è sereno
sul miracolo d' amor!

MAN: (to the air of the minuet, to Ger.) These are hours of joy's creating—
Daylight smiles so fair around you.
Faithful is your dear one, waiting;
Sighing for you, till she found you.
When you meet by love's sweet power,
Bliss thrills her being, sent from above.
Beauty all the world will dower
By the magic spell of love!

SIGNORI ED ABATI: (con grande ammirazione) Ah! voi siete il miracolo, ah! voi siete l' amore!

BEAUS AND ABBÉS: (with great admiration) You are truly magical, you really are Love!

GER: (frapponendosi mellifluo) Galanteria sta bene; ma obliate che è tardi . . .
Allegra folla ondeggia ora sui baluardi.

GER: (interposing) This flattery is pleasing, but time is rolling onward,
Gay crowds are now strolling upon the boulevard.

SIGNORI ED ABATI: Qui il tempo vola!

BEAUS AND ABBÉS: Here time is flying!

GER: È cosa ch' io so per prova. (a Man.) Voi,
mia fulgida letizia, esser compagna a noi
promette-te: di poco vi precediamo . . .

GER: (to Man.) That, sirs, there's no denying.
You, my radiant light of pleasure,
Promise to join us at your leisure.
We'll go on and there await you.

MAN: Un brevo
istante sol vi chiedo: attendermi fla
lieve
fra il bel mondo dorato.

SIGNORI ED ABATI: Grave
sempre è l' attesa.

GER: Dell' anima sospesa
non sian lunghe le pene.
(*tutti si muovono: saluti: baciamano.*)

GER: (*mentre bacia la mano a
Man.*) Ordino la lettiga . . .
Addio . . . bell' idol mio . . .
(*escono.*)

(*Manon sola, poi Des Grieux.*)
(*Man. si affretta ad acconciarsi,
ammirandosi soddisfatta nello
specchio.*)

MAN: Oh, sarò la più bella!
(*prende la mantiglia posata sopra una seggiola: sente che qualcuno s' avvicina: erede che sia il
servo.*)
Dunque questra lettiga?
(*Des G. appare alla porta; è pallidissimo: Man. gli corre incontro
in preda a grande emozione.*)
Tu amore? Tu? Sei tu,
mio immenso amore? . . . Dio!

DES G: (*con gesto di rimprovero*)
Ah, Manon!

MAN: Tu non m' ami?
Dunque non m' ami più?
Mi amavi tanto!
Oh, i lunghi baci! Oh, il lungo in-
canto!
La dolce amica d' un tempo aspetta
la tua vendetta . . .
Oh, non guardarmi cosi: non era
la tua pupilla
tanto severa!

DES G: (*violentemente*) Si, sciagurata, la mia vendetta . . .

MAN: Ah! La mia colpa! . . . È
vero! Io t'ho tradito!
Si, sciagurata dimmi!
Quando più nera scendeva su noi
la miseria, fuggendo,
volli che solo e libero
tu la fortuna
tentar potessi.

DES G: Taci . . . che il cor mi
frangi!
Tu non sai le giornate
che buie, desolate
son piombate su me!

MAN: Io voglio il tuo perdono . . .
Vedi! Son rieca! Questa
non ti sembra una reggia,
non ti sembra una festa
e d' ori—e di colori?
Tutto è per te: pensavo
a un avvenir di luce;
Amor qui ti conduce . . .
(*s' inginocchia.*)
Vedi, ai tuoi diedi io sono
e voglio il tuo perdono.

MAN: I soon will follow, sirs, believe me
Among the throng of fashion there
to linger
Surely will elate you.

BEAUS AND ABBÉS: Without you
there it will grieve me.

GER: Of those in suspense do not
lengthen the anguish.
(*all depart, salute, and kiss
Man. 's hand.*)

GER: (*as he kisses Man. 's hand*)
The sedan I will order—
Farewell—my heart's sweet idol—
(*exit.*)

(*Manon alone, then Des Grieux.*)
(*Man. hurriedly arranges her toilette, and admires herself in the
glass.*)

MAN: Oh! I shall be the fairest
(*takes her cloak which is on a
chair, hears somebody approaching, thinks it is a servant.*)
Has the sedan arrived yet?
(*Des G. appears at the door, he
looks very pale: Man, in the greatest agitation runs towards him.*)
You, you, my love, my love,
You, my own dear love, my own.
Oh! Heaven!

DES G: (*reproachfully*) Ah, Manon!

MAN: You love me then no
more?—
You once so loved me!
What sweet caresses,
What spell of rapture!
Your once loved sweetheart
With dread's awaiting
Your fatal vengeance!
No! do not gaze on me thus:
You never yet looked at me
With glance so cruel!

DES G: (*violently*) Yes, hapless
creature,
Await my vengeance—

MAN: Mine was the fault, love—I
own it!
I betrayed you!
You love me then no more.
Once how you loved me!

DES G: Silence! speak not! my heart
is breaking.
How my soul has suffered
Torture and desolation,
And what pangs of despair!

MAN: I pray you to forgive me—
Now, behold how rich I am!
Does not all this appear to you
A gorgeous dream of gold and col-
ors bright?
It is all for you. With you my own
love
I dreamt an ecstatic future;
To me it is love that led you—
(*kneels.*)
I betrayed you!
At your feet I kneel,

Non lo negar! . . . Son forse
della Manon d' un giorno
meno piacente e bella?

DES G: (*desolato*) O tentarice! È
questo
l' antico, maledetto e desïato
fascino che m' acciece!—

MAN: È fascino d' amor; cedi, son
tua!

DES G: Più non posso lottar! Son
vinto: io t'amo!

MAN: (*affascinante, si alza, cir-
condando colle braccia Des G.*)
Vieni! Colle tue braccia
stringi Manon che t' ama;
stretta al tuo sen m' allaccia!
Manon te solo brama.

DES G: Nell' occhio tuo profondo
io leggo il mio destino;
tutti i tesor del mondo
ha il tuo labbro diviuo.

MAN: Alle mie brame torna,
deh! torna ancor!
Alle mie ebbrezze, ai baci
lunghi, d'amor!

DES G: In te, Manon, s' inebria
l' anima ancor!
I baci tuoi son questi!
Questo è il tuo amor!
(*Man. si abbandona fra le braccia
di Des G., che dolcemente la fa
sedere sul sofà.*)

MAN: M'arde il tuo bacio!
Dolce tesor,
vivi e t' inebria
sovra il mio cor.

DES G: Nelle tue braccie care
v' è l' ebbrezza, l' oblio!

MAN: La mia bocca è un altare
dove il tuo bacio è Dio!
(*con immensa dolcezza mormorato.*)
Labbra adorate e care!

DES G: Manon, mi fai morire!

MAN: Labbra dolci a baciare!

DES G: Dolcissimo soffrire!

(*Geronte, Manon e Des Grieux.*)
(*Ger. si presenta improvviso alla
porta del fondo; si arresta stupito;
Man. e Des G. si alzano di scatto;
Des G. fa un passo verso Ger.;
Man. s' interpone.*)

Ah! let me gain your forgiveness.
Do not deny it me—
Perchance am I less fair and pleas-
ing
Than the Manon you cared for?

DES G: (*sadly*) O fatal temptress!
The old spell again comes over me
To bewitch me!—

MAN: It is love's own magic spell;
I'm yours forever!

DES G: I resist you no longer! I'm
vanquished.

MAN: (*rises and alluringly
throws her arms around Des G.*)
I'm yours for ever, ah! come, love,
Come enfold your Manon
In an enthralling embrace.
Close to your heart ever hold me,
Recalling Manon to joy.

DES G: Your eyes deep as the sea,
love,
Reveal me all my fate;
All joy and wealth for me, love,
Can your lips create.

MAN: Ah! Manon adores you only.
Come, for I need you near me
All else, yes, all else above.
Take my caresses,
My fervent kiss of love!

DES G: With your caresses thrill me
And with your love!
(*Man. falls into the arms of Des
G., who gently leads her to a
couch.*)

MAN: Dwell here forever
Close to my heart!

DES G: Never shall we sever,
Never shall we part.

MAN: Let my lips be your throne,
love,
You as King there I crown.

DES G: Your sweet solace alone,
love,
All my sorrows can drown.
MAN: (*with infinite tenderness*)
Lips that are freighted with love!

DES G: Manon with bliss you kill
me.

MAN: Lips for sweet love created.

DES G: Caress me still and thrill
me!

(*Geronte, Manon and Des
Grieux.*)
(*Ger. suddenly appears at the
door, C., and stands amazed;
Man. and Des G. rise hurriedly.
Des G moves a step towards Ger.;
Man. places herself between
them.*)

GER: (avanzandosi ironico ma dignitoso) Affè, madamigella, or comprendo il perchè di nostra attesa!
Giungo in mal punto. Errore involontario!
Chi non erra quaggiù?!
Anche voi, credo, ad esempio, obliaste
d' essere in casa mia.

DES G: Signore!

MAN: (a Des G.) Taci . . .

GER: Gratitudin, sia oggi il tuo dì di festa!
(a Man.)
Donde vi trassi
le prove che v' ho date
di un vero amore, come rammentate!

MAN: (prende lo specchio, lo pianta in viso a Ger. e coll' altra mano indica Des. G.; trattenendo le risa) Amore? Amore!
Mio buon signore,
ecco! . . . Guardatevi!
S' errai, leale
ditelo! . . . Or poi
guardate noi!

GER: (offeso, fa un gesto di minaccia: poi vincendosi, sogghignando) Io son leale, mia bella donnina
Conosco il mio dovere . . .
deggio partir di qui!
O gentil cavaliere,
o vaga signorina,
arrivederci . . . e presto!
(esce.)

MAN: (gaiamente spensierata)
Ah! ah! . . . Liberi! Liberi!
Liberi come l' aria!
Che gioia, cavaliere,
amor mio bello!

DES G: (mestamente preoccupato) Senti,
di qui partiamo: un solo
istante, questo tetto
del vecchio maledetto
non t'abbia più!

MAN: (quasi involontariamente)
Peccato!
Tutti questi splendori! . . .
Tutti questi tesori!
(sospirando.)
Ahimè! . . . Partir.dobbiamo!

DES G: (con immensu amarezza)
Ah! Manon, mi tradisce
il tuo folle pensiero:
Sempre la stessa! Trepida
divinamente,
nell' abbandono ardente . . .
Buona, gentile come la vaghezza
di quella tua carezza;
sempre novella ebbrezza;
indi, d' un tratto, vinta, abbacinata
dai raggi e dagli effluvi
della vita adorata! . . .
(con forza crescente.)
Io? Tuo schiavo e tua vittima discendo
la scala dell' infamia . . .
Fango nel fango io sono

GER: (ironically but with dignity) So ho! my fair young lady,
I clearly now perceive why you so tarried!
I'm an intruder. The error's accidental.
To err we all are prone!
Even you, methinks, perchance have forgotten
That you were beneath my roof.

DES G: Forbear, sir!

MAN: (to Des G.) Speak not!

GER: What gratitude! I marvel
That thus you should repay me.
(to Man.)
From where I took you,
And how have you remembered
The proofs of true affection that I gave you!

MAN: (takes a mirror and places it before Ger.'s face and then points to Des G., with suppressed laughter) What love, sir! You're jesting
Or much mistaken, look there—
Behold yourself!
If I am wrong, then tell me frankly,
And after glance at us.

GER: (offended, is moved to anger; then controlling himself, smiling sarcastically) I will be frank with you, my pretty lady,
Full well I know my duty—
From here I must depart!
I take my leave, sir gallant,
Adieu, my pretty lady;
We'll meet again—and quickly!

MAN: (with thoughtless gaiety)
Ah! ah! we are free
As the air, love.
What joy, love—
Free together—

DES G: (pensive and sad) Hear me!
we must away, love,
Not for a moment longer
Shall these accursed walls hold you
Not while I live!

MAN: (unconsciously) I'm sorry
To give up all this splendor,
All these jewels and treasures.
(sighing.)
Alas! we must depart!

DES G: (most bitterly) Tender
with an angelic grace,
Amid love's ardent passion,
Fair, kind, and gentle as the fond caresses
that you so sweetly lavish
With ever-thrilling rapture;
Then, on a sudden, overwhelmed and conquered
By splendor and allurements of pleasure!
(vehemently.)
I, your victim and your slave,
Am engulfed in the whirlpool
Of shame and dishonor.
Down the dark abyss I've fallen.
And of the gambling-hell

e turpe eroe da bisca
io m'insozzo, mi vendo . . .
L' onta più vile m' avvicina a te!
(sconfortato.)
Nell' oscuro futuro
dì, che farai di me?
(siede accasciato. Man. gli si avvicina amorosamente, e gli prende la mano.)

MAN: Un' altra volta, un' altra volta ancora,
deh!-mi perdona! . . .
Sarò fedele e buona,
lo giuro . . . lo giuro!
(Lescaut, Manon, Des Grieux, poi un Sergente cogli Arcieri indi Geronte.)
(entra Les. ansante, respirando a mala pena. Des G. e Man, sorpresi gli vanno incontro.)

DES G: Lescaut!

MAN: Tu? . . . Qui?
(Les. si laseia cadere su di una sedia sbuffando affannato.)

DES G: Che avvenne?

MAN: Di!
(Les. accenna cogli occhi e colle mani, e lascia capire che è accaduto qualche grave imbroglio.)

DES G. E MAN: (allibiti) O ciel! . . . Che è stato?!

LES: (balbettando) Ch' io . . . prenda . . . fiato . . . onde . . . parlar . . .

MAN: Ci fai tremar!

DES G: Ohimè! . . . Che è stato?

LES: V'ha . . . denunziato!

MAN: Chi

DES G: (iracondo) Il vecchio?

LES: (ripigliando fiato) Si!
Già vengon qui
e guardie e arcier!
Su, cavalier,
e, per le scale,
spiegate l' ale!
Da un granatiere
ch' era in quartiere
tutto ho saputo.

LES: Ah! . . . il vecchio astuto!

GER: Manon . . .

MAN: (impaurita) Ohime!

LES: Via . . . l' ali ai piè!
(a Des G.)
Ah, non sapete . . .
Voi la perdete . . .
La sciagurata
avrà spietata
crudele sorte:
L' esiglio' . . . .

MAN: (atterita) Ah! è morte!
(Les. continua, parlando sempre, ad affrettare, mentre Des G. preso d' ira impreca e Man. confusa si aggira turbata per la scena.)

Am I the vile degraded hero.
My shame and sorrow bring me back to you.
(despairingly.)
In the gloom that surrounds me
What will my fate decree?
(sits down disheartened. Man. lovingly approaches him, and presses his hand.)

MAN: Once more forgive me,
Only once more forgive me!
I do entreat you
I shall be true and faithful.
I swear it—I swear it!
(Lescaut, Manon Des Grieux, then a Sergeant of Archers and Geronte.)
(Les. enters breathless and panting. Des G. and Man. are surprised and run to him.)

DES G: Lescaut!

MAN: You here!
(Les, puffing and blowing drops into a chair.)

DES G: What has happened?

MAN: Speak!
(Les, signifies by his looks and by signs that something dreadful has happened.)

DES G AND MAN: (terrified)
What's happened?

LES: (stammeringly) I am—
quite—breathless—
I'll tell—you all—

MAN: I'm filled with dread!

DES G: Alas! what has befallen?

LES: He has—denounced you!—

MAN: Who?

DES G: (angrily) Geronte?

LES: (recovering his breath) Yes!
The guards and archers
Are at hand—
Make haste away.
Fly down the stair-case
At headlong speed!
By an old comrade
Down at the barracks
All the news was told me.

DES G: How I curse him—that old scoundrel.

LES: Manon—

MAN: (alarmed) Ah! me!

LES: Go—quickly fly!
(to Des G.)
Ah! Do not linger—
While there is danger—
What cruel doom
Will pursue her!
It is exile!—

MAN: (terrified) Ah! That doom—would kill me!
(Les. continues talking as he hurries them, while Des G. angrily curses and Man. in great agitation runs to and fro.)

**LES:** Or v' affrettate!
Non esitate!
Pochi minuti,
siete perduti!
Già dal quartier
uscìan gli arcier!
La compagnia
forse è per via! . . .
Ah, il vecchio vile
Morrà di bile,
se trova vuota
la gabbia e ignota
gli sia tuttora
l' altra dimora!
(*affrettando.*)
Manon! . . . Suvvia . . .
son già per via!
(*asservando.*)
Oh! il bel forzier!
Peccato inver!

**LES:** Now quickly hasten!
No hesitation!
Only a moment,
All will be over!
The guards must be
Now on their way!
That vile old scoundrel
Will die of venom,
On finding the cage
Left empty!
He never will trace us
To our new dwelling!
(*hurrying them.*)
Manon away!
They're close at hand!
(*looking round him.*)
This casket fine
It is hard to leave!

**DES G:** (*furibondo*) Ah, il maledetto vecchio!

**DES G:** (*furiously*) How I curse that scoundrel.

**MAN:** M' affretto!

**MAN:** At once, I come!

**DES G:** Manon!

**DES G:** Manon!—

**MAN:** Ohime!

**MAN:** Ah! me!

**DES G:** Sì! Bada a te, vecchio!

**DES G:** Beware of me Geronte!

**MAN:** Un istante . . . !
(*mostrando a Des G. un gioiello posto sulla pettiniera.*)
Questo smagliante smeraldo . . .

**MAN:** (*shows Des G. a jewel on the toilet-table*) Wait an instant.
I'll take this jewel
Rare and costly—

**DES G:** Andiamo!

**DES G:** Let's go!

**MAN:** Ma si!

**MAN:** Yes, yes—

**DES G:** Affrettiamo!

**DES G:** Haste, away!

**MAN:** Mio Dio! . . . Sì

**MAN:** Oh! heavens, yes!

**DES G:** Orsù . . .

**DES G:** Away!

**MAN:** Mi sbrigo! . . . E tu m' aiuta.

**MAN:** I'm coming!
Help me, assist me!

**DES G:** A fare?

**DES G:** But how?

**MAN:** Ad involtare codesti oggetti!
Vuota i cassetti!

**MAN:** To carry off
These precious trinkets!
Empty the cases!—

**LES:** (*affacendato*) Nostro cammino
sarà il giardino . . .
In un istante
de l' alte piante
sotto l' ombria,
siam sulla via . . .
Buon chi ci piglia!
(*gittandole la mantiglia.*)
La tua mantiglia
vesti, Manon . . .
(*corre ad una finestra.*)
Maledizion!

**LES:** (*busily*) We'll take the pathway
Down by the garden,
And in a moment
We shall be hidden
Under the shelter
Of those thick branches—
Let who can, catch us!
(*throws Manon's cloak to her.*)
Put on your cloak
quickly Manon.
(*looks out of window.*)
Plague seize the rogues!

**MAN:** (*con dolore*) E questo incanto
che adoro tanto
dovrò lasciare
e abbandonare?
Or via . . . pazienza! . . .
Saria imprudenza
lasciar quest' oro,
o mio tesoro!
(*apre affannosamente alcuni tiretti, ne estrae dei gioielli, e si serve della mantiglia per nasconderli.*)

**MAN:** (*mournfully*) All this great splendor
That I so cherish,
Now I must
For ever abandon.
To leave behind me
This gold were madness.
Here are my treasures!
(*opens hurriedly some of the drawers, takes out jewels and hides them in her cloak.*)

**DES G:** (*amoroso*) O mia diletta
Manon, t' affretta!
D' uopo è partire
tosto! . . . Fuggire . . .
Ah! torturare
mi vuoi ancor!!!
Con te portare
dèi solo il cor! . . .
Io vo' salvare
soli il tuo amor.
(*al grido di Les. succede una confusione indicibile. Man. imbarazzala si aggira di qua e di là, sempre tenendo i gioielli nascosti nella mantiglia. Les. corre dal balcone alla porta. Des G. corre per la stanza chiamando Manon.*)

**DES G:** (*lovingly*) O my beloved one!
Manon, make haste dear.
It is time to go,
Quickly away!
Do not torture
Me like this.
With you bring
Only your heart—
I only want
To have your love.
(*at Les.'s exclamation an indescribable confusion takes place. Man. well-nigh distraught rushes about the room still holding the jewels in her cloak. Les. runs from the balcony to the door. Des G. runs to and fro calling Manon.*)

**LES:** (*al balcone*) Eccoli! Accerchiano
la casa! . . . Il vecchio
ordina e sbraita.
Le guardie sfilano,
gli arcier's appostano!
(*alla porta.*)
Entran! Salgono!
(*atterrito, chiude la porta a chiave e corre presso Man. e Des G.*)

**LES:** (*at the balcony*) They are here—
The house surrounding!
Geronte angrily
Summons the guards
Now to enter.
The archers take their stand,
(*at the door.*)
Here they rush!
Up the stairs!
(*terrified, locks the door and hurriedly joins Man. and Des G.*)

**DES G:** Manon!

**DES G:** Manon!

**MAN:** Des Grieux . . .

**MAN:** Des Grieux!—

**DES G:** Fuggiam!

**DES G:** Let us fly!

**MAN:** Di qua?

**MAN:** This way?

**DES G:** No!

**DES G:** No!

**MAN:** Ebben?
(*accenna versa l' alcova.*)

**MAN:** Well then?—

**DES G:** Di là!

**DES G:** (*points to the alcove*) that way!

**MAN:** Presto . . .

**MAN:** Hurry!

**DES G:** (*a Man.*) Di': qui
v' ha uscita?

**DES G:** (*to Man.*) Is there a way out yonder?

**MAN:** (*indicando*) Sì . . .
Laggiù! All' alcova!

**MAN:** (*pointing*) Yes—
Behind the alcove—

**LES. E DES G:** Presto, all' alcova!
(*Les. spinge entro all' alcova Des G. e Man., seguendoli alla sua volta; ma quasi subito si sente dall' alcova un grido di Man. e questa ritorna ancora in scena fuggendo e dopo lei, lividi, Des G. e Les. Des G. vuol correre presso a Man . . . Les. lo trattiene . . . e dalle cortine dell' alcova schiuse appaiono un Sergente e due arcieri. Intanto la porta è buttata giù dal calcio dei fucili e nel suo vano si affaccia Ger. ghignando e dietro a lui alcuni Soldati.*)

**LES. AND DES G:** Quick to the alcove!—
(*Les. pushes Des G. and Man. into the alcove, and follows them; but almost immediately from within the alcove Man. is heard to scream, and she runs on to the stage attempting to escape, and after her come Des G. and Les, who are terror-stricken. Des G. tries to join Man.—but Les. holds him back—and from the open curtains of the alcove appear a sergeant and two archers. At the same time the door is burst open by the soldiers, with the butt end of their muskets, and Ger. stands in the doorway smiling sardonically, followed by soldiers.*)

**Sergente:** (*imperioso*) Nessun si muova!
(*a Man. sfugge nello spavento la mantiglia e i gioielli si spargono al suolo. Il Sergente con du soldati*)

**SERGEANT:** (*sternly*) Surrender at once!
(*Man. in her terror lets her cloak slip and the jewels all fall to the ground. The sergeant and two sol-*)

*a un cenno di Ger. afferrano Man.: Des G. furibondo sguaina la spada, ma vien disarmato da Les.)*

**LES:** Se vi arrestan, cavalier, chi potrà Manon salvar?
*(Man. è trascinato via.)*

**DES G:** *(disperato, vorrebbe slanciarsi dietro Man.; Les. lo trattiene a viva forza)* O Manon! O mia Manon!

## INTERMEZZO

*La prigionia.—Il viaggio all' Havre.*

**DES GRIEUX:** " . . . Gli è che io l' amo!—La mia passione è così forte che io mi sento la più sfortunata creatura che vive.—Quelle che non ho io tentato a Parigi per ottenere la sua libertà?! . . . Ilo implorato i potenti! . . . Ho picchiato e supplicato a tutte le porte! . . . Persino alla violenza ho ricorso! . . . Tutto fu inutile.—Una sol via mi rimaneva; seguirla! Ed io la seguo! Dovunque ella vada! . . . Fosse pure in capo al mondo! . . . "
*(Storia di Manon Lescaut e del cavalier Des Grieux dell' abate Prèvost.)*

*FINE DELL' ATTO SECONDO.*

## ■ ATTO III

*L'Havre.*

*Piazzale presso il porto.*

*Nel fondo, il porto: a sinistra l'angolo d' una caserma. Nel lato di faccia al pianterreno, una finestra con grossa feriata sporgente. Nella facciata verso la piazza il portone chiuso, innanzi al quale passeggia una sentinella.—Il mare occupa tutto il fondo della scena. Si vede la metà di una nave da guerra. A destra, una casa, poi un viottolo; all' angolo un fanale ad olio che rischiara debolmente. E l' ultima ora della notte; il cielo si andrà gradatamente rischiarando.*

*Des Grieux, Lescaut.*

*In disparte, dal lato opposto alla caserma.*

**DES G:** Ansia eterna . . . curdel . . .

**LES:** Pazianza ancora . . . La guardia là fra poco monterà l'arcier che ho compro . . .
*(indicandogli dove passeggia la scolta.)*

---

*diers, at a signal from Ger., seize Manon. Des G., in a fury, draws his sword, but Les. disarms him.)*

**LES:** If they now arrest you, sir, Who will try to save Manon?
*(Man. is dragged off.)*

**DES G:** *(in despair attempts to rush after Man., but Les. holds him back by force)* Oh, Manon! Oh, my Manon!

## INTERMEZZO

*The imprisonment—The journey to Havre.*

**DES GRIEUX:** " . . . How I love her! My passion is so ardent that I feel I am the most unhappy creature alive. What have I not tried in Paris to obtain her release!—I have implored the aid of the powerful! I have even resorted to force.—All was in vain.—Only one thing remains for me and that is to follow her! And I will follow her! Go where she may! Even to the end of the world!—"
*(The story of Manon Lescaut and of the Chevalier Des Grieux, by the Abbe Prèvost.)*

*END OF THE SECOND ACT.*

## ■ ACT III

*Havre.*

*A square near the Harbor.*

*In the background, the Harbor: the corner of the Barracks, L., with, on the side facing the audience, on the ground floor, a window, guarded by projecting iron bars. On the side looking towards the Square, the large Gate, which is closed, and a Sentinel is on guard. The Sea forms the background of the stage. A Man-of-War is partly visible. A house, R., then a narrow street, at the corner of which is an oil lamp, which gives a dim light. It is the last hour of the night; the sky gradually becomes lighter.*

*Des Grieux, Lescaut.*

*On the side opposite to the barracks.*

**DES G:** Racked with doubt and with fear—

**LES:** Be patient yet!—
Soon I will have bribed the archer
Take his turn on guard—
*(pointing to where the sentinel is on guard.)*

---

**DES G:** L'attesa m'accora!
*(con immenso slancio pieno di dolore.)* La vita mia . . . l'anima tutta è là!
*(accenna alla finestra della caserma.)*

**LES:** Manon sa già . . . e attende il mio segnale
e a noi verrà.—Io intanto tenterò il colpo cogli amici là nel viale . . .
Manon all'alba libera farò.
*(si avvolge fino agli occhi nel ferrajuolo e va cautamente nel fondo ad ossevare.)*

**DES G:** Dietro al destino così mi traggo livido, e notte e dì cammino.
E un miraggio m'angoscia e m' esalta! . . . Vicino or m' è poi fugge se l'avvinghio!
Parigi ed Havre . . . cupa, triste agonia! . . .
Oh! lungo strazio della vita mia! . . .
*(Manon, Des Grieux, Lescaut.)*

**LES:** *(avvicin indoglosi)* Eccoli!

**DES G:** Alfin! . . .
*(dalla caserma esce un picchetto guidato da un Sergente che viene a mutar la scolta.)*

**DES G:** *(che ha guardato attentamente i soldati)*
Ecco là l' uomo. È quello!
*(indicando uno.)*
*(il picchetto col Sergente rientrano in caserma.)*
*(Les., allegro, ponendo la mano sulla spalla a Des G.)*
E l' Havre addormenta! . . . L' ora è giunta!
*(si avvicina a la caserma, scambia un rapido cenno col soldato di guardia che passeggiando si allontana; poi si appressa alla finestra del pianterreno, piccha con precauzione alle sbarre di ferro. Des G. immobile, tremante, guarda; i vetri si aprono e appare Man. Des G. corre a lei.)*

**DES G:** *(con voce soffocata)* Manon! . . .
*(le sue mani si avvinghiano alle sbarre.)*

**MAN:** *(piano con immenso abbandono)* Des Grieux! . . .
*(Man. sporge le mani dalla ferriata; Des G. le bacia con febbrile trasporto.)*

**LES:** *(guardando Man.)* Manon, la mia miniera . . . il mio sostegno, lasciar partir? Al diavolo l' America!
No, il Nuovo Mondo non avrà Manon!
*(s' allontana da destra.)*
*(Manon, Des Grieux, Un Lampionaio.)*

---

**DES G:** I'm well near distraction!
*(with passionate grief.)*
My very soul and life are there with her!
*(points to the window of the barracks.)*

**LES:** Manon already knows and waits my signal
To come forth. Meantime, with trusty comrades,
Her rescue I'll attempt.
Manon, at dawn, shall be as free as air.
*(conceals his face with his cloak and goes cautiously up stage.)*

**DES G:** What fate pursues me, Dark and relentless,
Day by day and nightly for ever.
What dread phantoms dismay and allure me!
They seem so near, but vanish before I reach them.
Paris and Havre, both my doom have demanded;
How sadly, fatally, my hopes are stranded.
*(Manon, Des Grieux, Lescaut.)*

**LES:** *(approaching Des G.)* See, they come!—

**DES G:** At last!
*(a Sergeant with a picket comes to change the sentinel.)*

**LES:** *(looking attentively at the solders)* There is the archer—That soldier!
*(points him out. The picket returns to the barracks. Les. says gaily as he placed his hand on Des G.'s shoulder.)*
The town is wrapped in slumber!—Now is the moment.
*(approaches the barracks, hastily exchanges a sign with the sentinel, who retires; then walks to the window and taps cautiously on the bars. Des G. watches him anxiously. The window opens, Man. appears, Des G. runs towards her.)*

**DES G:** *(his voice trembling with emotion)* Manon!—
*(holds on to the bars of the window.)*

**MAN:** *(tenderly, in an ecstasy of joy)* Des Grieux!—
*(Man. stretches out her hands through the bars; Des G. kisses them passionately.)*

**LES:** *(intently gazing at Man.)* The devil take America!—
Manon shall never start!
*(goes off, R.)*
*(Manon, Des Grieux, A Lamplighter.)*

**MAN:** Tu . . . amore? E nell' estrema
onta non m'abbandoni?

**DES G:** Abbondonarti? Mai!
Se t' ho seguita per la lunga via
fu perchè fede mi regnava in core
onnipossente—indomita!
Ah! libera fra poco e mia sarai!

**MAN:** (*con mestizia*) Liberia! . . .
Tua . . . fra poco!

**DES G:** (*interrompendola impaurito*) Taci! taci!
(*un Lampionaio entra dal fondo a destra cantarellan lo, traversa la scena e va a spegnere il fanale.*)

**IL LAMPIONAIO:** Kate rispose al Re:
D' una zitella
Perchè tentare il cor?
Per un marito
mi fe' bella il Signor.
Rise il Re
Por le die'
gemme ed or
e un marito . . . è n' ebbe il cor.
(*si allontana dal viottolo: comincia ad albeggiare. Poco dopo nel fondo della scena passa una pattuglia, attraversa da sinistra a destra e scompare nel viottolo.*)

**DES G:** È l' alba! . . . O mia Manon,
pronta alla porta del cortil sii tu . . .
V' è là Lescaut con uomini dovoti . . .
Là vanne e tu sei salva!

**MAN:** Tremo per te! Tremo! . . . Pavento!
Tremo e m' angoscio . . . nè so il perchè
Ah! una minaccia funebre io sento!
Tremo a un periglio che ignoto m' è . . .

**DES G:** Ah! Manon, disperato
è il mio prego! . . . L' affanno
la parola mi spezza . . .
Vuoi che m' uccida qui?
Ti scongiuro, Manon.
Vieni! vieni! . . . Salviamoci!
(*addita il viottolo.*)

**MAN:** E sia! M' attendi amore . . .
Tutto chiedimi . . . tutto!
(*si ritira dalla finestra.*)
(*colpo di fuoco e grida di dentro di "All' armi!" Des G. corre verso il viottolo.*)
(*Lescaut, Des Grieux.*)

**LES:** (*entra fuggendo colla spada sguainata*) . . . Perduta è la partita!
Cavalier, salviam la vita!

**DES G:** Che avvenne?

**MAN:** You—my own love?
In my disgrace you do not forsake me?

**DES G:** Forsake you, dearest—never!
Love, I have followed you through toil and danger,
Because I bear at heart an enduring hope—
Soon you will be mine alone.

**MAN:** (*sadly*) Yes, free—and yours—for ever.

**DES G:** (*interrupting her and alarmed*) Silence! silence!
(*a Lamplighter enters, R. C., humming a tune, he crosses the stage and puts out the lamp.*)

**THE LAMPLIGHTER:** —And Katrine replied to the King:
Why tempt a maiden's coy tender little heart?
To snare a husband a heaven did my looks impart.
The King laughed, then he gave gems and gold
And a spouse—but her heart was sold.
(*he goes off by the street; day dawns. A patrol passes at the back of the stage, crossing from L. to R., and marches off by the street.*)

**DES G:** It is dawn, love! O my Manon,
Be ready at the entrance of your cell—
Lescaut is there with followers devoted—
They'll find you and give you freedom.

**MAN:** Fearful, I tremble for you—
I tremble—and do not know why!
Ah! portents of evil threaten and haunt me—
Fearful am I, and yet know not why.

**DES G:** Ah! Manon, in despair
I implore you—My words are broken by
My tears and signs—
Shall I seek death?
I beseech you, Manon. Ah! come, love,
We'll triumph yet.
(*pointing to the street.*)

**MAN:** You conquer! I'll do your bidding.
Your will is mine—my own love!
(*retires from the window.*)
(*sound of a shot heard and shouts of "To Arms!" Des G. runs towards the street.*)
(*Lescaut, Des Grieux.*)

**LES:** (*comes running from the street, sword in hand*) —The game is lost. We're routed—
Save your life, my friend, and quickly!

**DES G:** What happened?

**LES:** Udite come strillano!
(*nuove grida di "all' armi!"*)
Fallito è il colpo! . . . )

**DES G:** (*con impeto*) Ah! ben venga la morte!
Fuggir? Giammai!
(*fa per spada.*)

**LES:** (*impedendoglielo*) Ah! pazzo inver!

**MAN:** (*riappare alla finestra agitata; con immenso slancio a Des G.*) Se m' ami,
in nome di Dio
t' invola, amor mio!

**DES G:** Ah! Manon . . .

**LES:** (*trascinando via Des G., borbotta sfiduciato crollando il capo.*) Cattivo affare!
(*Man. abbandona la finestra e scompare.*)
(*Attratti dal colpo di fuoco e dai gridi d' allarme, accorrano da ogni parle borghesi, popolani, popolane e si domandano l' un l' altro che cosa è avvenuto: confusione generale: è giorno.*)

**BORGHESI, UOMINI E DONNE DEL POPOLO:** (*Poi il Sergente degli Arcieri, il Commandante della nave. In seguito Des Grieux e Lescaut Arcieri, Soldati di marina, Marinai.*)
—Udiste!
—Che avenne?
—Fu un ratto? Rivota?
—Figgiva una donna!
—Più d' una! La folta tenèbra protese laggiù i rapitori!
—Che audacia!
Che audacia!
—Vedete! Le guardie già sfilano.
(*rullo di tamburi: s' apre il portone della caserma, esce il Sergente con un picchetto di soldati, in mezzo al quale stanno parecchie donne incatenate: i soldati e le donne si arrestano avanti il portone: il Sergente s' avanza verso la folla, ordinandole di retrocedere.*)

**SERGENTE:** Il passo m' aprite.
(*dalla nave scende il Commandante: lo seque un drapello ai soldati di marina, il quale si schiera a destra. Sulla nave si schierano i marinai.*)

**COMMANDANTE:** (*al Sergente*) E pronta la nave. L' appello affrettate!

**BORGHESI, UOMINI E DONNE DEL POPOLO:** Silenzio! L' appello cominciano già.
(*la folla si è ritirata e guarda sfilare le cortigiane.*)

**IL SERGENTE:** (*con un foglio in mano fa l' appello: le donne, mano mano che sono chiamate, passano in diversi atteggiamenti da sinistra a destra presso al drappello dei marinai: il Comandante nota su di un libro.*)

**LES:** Just hear them, how they're shouting!
(*shouts of "To Arms!" are heard.*)
The game is over.

**DES G:** (*impetuously*) Ah! Death then is welcome!
What? escape? No! Never!
(*is about to draw his sword.*)

**LES:** (*prevents him*) You are mad indeed!

**MAN:** (*comes to the window greatly agitated: imploringly to Des G.*) Oh! dearest, if yet you love me
Escape now and leave me!

**DES G:** Ah! Manon—

**LES:** (*drags Des G. away and murmurs despondently*)
This time we've failed!
(*Man. retires from the window.*)
(*the sound of the shot and cries of alarm attract citizens and villagers from all sides, in the midst of the confusion they ask each other what has happened. It is daylight.*)

**CITIZENS AND PEOPLE:** (*The Sergeant of the Royal Archers, the Captain of the man-of-war. Afterwards Des Grieux and Lescaut, Archers, Marines, Sailors.*) —You heard then?
—What's happened?
—An escape? a revolt?
—A woman escaping!
—Was it then a revolt?
—Her attempt at flight, was favored by the night!
—What daring!
—What boldness!
—See! the soldiers are coming!
(*roll of drums heard, the gate of the barracks opens, and a sergeant with a picket of soldiers comes on in charge of an number of women, who are in chains; they all stop in front of the gate. The sergeant orders the crowd to stand back.*)

**SERGEANT:** Make way, there!
(*the Captain of the man-of-war lands, followed by a company of marines, which takes up its position, R., the sailors are drawn up on board the ship.*)

**CAPTAIN:** (*to the Sergeant*) The ship is ready. Hasten the roll-call!

**CITIZENS AND PEOPLE:** The roll-call already begins!
(*the crowd stands back and looks at the women as they pass.*)

**SERGEANT:** (*calls the roll; the women answer to their names by crossing over from left to right, close to the marines. The Captain marks their names in a book.*)

# Act III

Rosetta!
(*passa sfrontamente.*)

GIOVANOTTI: (*mormorando*) Eh! che aria!

ALTRI: E un amore!

Madelon!
(*indifferente, va al posto ridendo.*)

ALCUNI BORGHESI: (*con astio*) Ah! qui sei ridotta!

ALCUNE DONNE: (*indignate*) Che riso insolente!

Manon!
(*passa lentamente cogli occhi a terra.*)

ALCUNI VECCHI: Chissà? Una sedotta.

Ninetta!
(*altera fissando la folla.*)

DONNE: Madonna è dolente!

Caton!
(*con fare imponente.*)

GIOVANOTTI: Affè . . . che dolore!

Regina!
(*passa pavoneggiandosi.*)

ALTRI: Che incesso!

Claretta!
(*va al suo posto frettolosa.*)

ALTRI: E una dea!

Violetta!
(*traversa la piazza con modo procace.*)

ALTRI: Ah questa correi!

Nerina!
(*elegante.*)

ALTRA: Che bionda! . . .

Elisa!
(*se ne va tranquillamente.*)

ALTRI: Che bruna!

Ninon!
(*si copre il volto colle mani.*)

ALTRI: (*schernendole*) Che splendidi nèi!

Giorgetta!
(*civettuola.*)

ALTRI: Di vaghe nessuna!

ALTRI: Che gaia assemblea.
(*Aleuni Borghesi aggruppati sul davanti a sanistra—Lescaut indica Manon e purla loro sommessamente.*)

BORGHESI: È bello davvero.

LES: Costei? V' è un mistero!

BORGHESI: (*a Les.*) Sedotta? . . . Tradita?

LES: Costei fu rapita fanciulla all' amore d' un vago garzone!

BORGHESI: Che infamia, che orrore!

ALTRI: Ah! fa compassione.

---

Rosetta!
(*passes boldly with a defiant look.*)

YOUNG MEN: (*to each other*) What a look!

OTHERS: She's a charmer!

Madelon!
(*crosses unconcernedly and laughing.*)

SOME CITIZENS: (*spitefully*) How you have fallen!

SOME WOMEN: (*indignantly*) What insolent laughter!

Manon!
(*passes slowly, fixing her eyes on the ground.*)

OLD MEN: Who's that? Poor wretched woman.

Ninetta!
(*proudly, staring at the crowd.*)

WOMEN: My lady is doleful!

Caton!
(*with an air of importance.*)

YOUNG MEN: By faith, she's in sorrow!

Regina!
(*struts by conceitedly.*)

OTHERS: How proudly!

Claretta!
(*goes to her place hurriedly.*)

OTHERS: She's a queen.

Violetta!
(*crosses saucily.*)

OTHERS: I should like this one!

Nerina!
(*with an air of distinction.*)

OTHERS: The fair one!—

Elisa!
(*walks quietly.*)

OTHERS: The dark one!

Ninon!
(*covers her face with her hands.*)

OTHERS: What wonderful patches!

Giorgetta!
(*coquettishly.*)

OTHERS: Not one single beauty!

OTHERS: What a gay assembly!
(*A group of citizens, L.—Lescaut points out Manon to them and speaks to them in an undertone.*)

CITIZENS: Indeed she's lovely!

LES: This one? I know her story.

CITIZENS: (*to Les.*) Seduction? Betrayal?

LES: Manon was abducted from the love and devotion of her fond young lover.

CITIZENS: What baseness! what shame!

OTHERS: Ah! she wakens pity.

---

LES: Rapita alle nozze e all' orgia ed a sozze carezze gittata!

BORGHESI: (*indignati*) Ah! sempre così!

LES: (*eccitando gli ascoltatori*) Pel gaudio d' un di di vecchio signore . . . poi . . . sazio . . . cacciata!

BORGHESI: Che infamia, che orrore!

LES: (*additando Des G.*) Vedete quel pallido che presso le sta? Lo sposo è quel misero.

BORGHESI: Oh! inver fa pietà!

LES: Cosi, fra catene, nel fango e avvilita, rivede e rinviene la sposa rapita!
(*grida di sdegno.*)

(*Manon e Des Grieux.*)
(*Des G. è nel fondo perduto tra la folla.*)
(*Appena è passata Man., esso cautamente le si avvicina, cercando nascondersi dietro di lei. Man. se ne accorge ed a stento trattiene un grido ai riconoscenza: le loro mani si toccano e si stringono.*)

MAN: (*con passione ed angoscia*) Des Grieux, fra poco, lungi sarò . . . questo è il destino m o E te perduto per sempre avrò! Ultimo bene! . . . addio! Alla tua casa riedi! Un giorno potrai ancora amar! Ora a tuo padre dei far ritorno . . . devi Manon scordar! Forse abbastanza non fosti amato . . . questo è il rimorso mio? Ma tu perdona!
(*un disperato singhiozzo le tronca parola.*)
Mio desolato amore immenso . . . addio!

DES G: Guardami e vedi com' io soggiacio a questa angoscia amara, chè una tortura crudel m' è il bacio della tua bocca cara. Ogni pensiero si scioglie in pianto! E pianto anche il desio! . . . Ah! m'ho nell'animo l'odio soltanto degli nomini e di Dio!

SERGENTE: (*collacandosi di fronte alle cortigiane*) Presto! . . . In fila!
(*le cortigiane si mettono in fila.*) Marciate!
(*vedendo Man. ferma presso a Des G.*) Costui qui ancor? Finiamola.
(*va e prende brutalmente, Man.*

---

LES: Her wedding prevented, And lured amid orgies To wanton caresses.

CITIZENS: (*with indignation*) Ah! it is always the case!

LES: (*exciting their sympathy*) For the joy of a day, By a wicked old scoundrel, Who, sated, dismissed her.

CITIZENS: What baseness! what shame!

LES: (*pointing out Des G.*) You see that young fellow So pale, standing there? Poor lad, he's her husband.

CITIZENS: Oh! she wakes pity!

LES: It is thus, as a convict, Disgraced and dishonored, He comes to revisit The girl stolen from him!
(*with a cry of anger.*)

(*Manon and Des Grieux.*)
(*Des G. stands back in the midst of the crowd.*)
(*As soon as Man. has passed he cautiously approaches her, trying to conceal himself behind her. Man. sees him, and with difficulty suppresses a cry of joy; they clasp each other's hands.*)

MAN: (*with passionate anguish*) Dear love. It is time for us to part. To woe my fate is tending, Your loss will break my sorrowful heart. Farewell, my love's unending. Home to you dear ones, love, betake you, Some day you'll love again. Forget Manon; and then Will all your grief and pain be gone. You never knew how dear I held you, For this my heart grieves ever. Forgive me, love. My tears have quelled you—
(*a sob of despair checks her utterance.*)
Farewell, my love—we sever!

DES G: Look, love, how rudely I am shaken By this overwhelming sorrow. Your kisses but fresh torture waken For my sad lips to borrow. Each thought of you has tears for token; Sighs tell my heart's emotion. Ah! in my soul my grief unspoken Sobs at my vain devotion!

SERGEANT: (*marshalling the women*) Forward!—In line, there!—
(*the women advance in single file.*) Quick, March!—
(*seeing Manon standing close to Des G.*)
—What, you still here? No more of

*per un braccio e la spinge verso le altre.)*

DES G: (*non pùo trattenersi e d' un tratto strappa Man. dalle mani dal Sergente gridando.*) Indietro!

SERGENTE: (*a Des G.*) Via!

BORGHESI: (*aizzati da Les., a Des G.*) Coraggio!

DES G: (*furente, minaccioso*) Ah! guai a chi la tocca!
(*avvinghia stretta a sè Man. coprendola colla propria persona.*) Manon, ti stringi a me! . . .

BORGHESI: (*spinti da Les. accorrono in socorso di Des G., ed impediscono al Sergente di avvicinarsi a Man.*) Così! Bravo!

COMANDANTE: (*apparendo a un tratto in mezzo alla folla*) Che avvien?
(*la folla si ritira rispettosamente.*)

DES G: (*sempre coll' impeto della disperazione, guardando minaccioso intorno a sè.*)
Ah, non vi avvicinate!
Chè, vivo me, costei
nessun strappar potrà!
(*scorgendo il Comandante, vinto da profonda emozione, egli erompe in uno straziante singhiozzo; le sue braccia che stringevano Man. si sciolgono e Des G. cade ai piedi de Comandante dolorosamente implorando.*)
No! pazzo son! . . . Guardate.
como io piango ed imploro . . .
come io chiedo pietà!
Udite! M' accettate
qual mozzo od a più vile
mestiere . . . ad io verrò
felice! . . . Vi pigliate
il mio sangue . . . la vita!
Ah, ingrato non sarò!
(*intanto il Sergente avvia le cotigiane verso la nave, e spinge con esse Man., la quale lenta s' incammina e nasconde il volto fra le mani, disperatamente singhiozzando. La folla, cacciate ai lati dagli arcieri, guarda silenziosa con profonda sinso di pietà.*)

COMANDANTE: (*commosso, si piega verso Des G., gli sorride benignamente e gli dice col fare burbero del marinaio*) Ah! popolar le Americhe, giovanotto, desiate?
(*Des G. lo guarda con ansia terribile.*)
Ebbene . . . ebben sia pure!
(*battendogli sulle spalle.*)
Via, mozzo, v' affrettate!
(*Des G. gitta un grido di gioia e bacia la mano del Comandante. Man. si volge, vede comprende— e, il viso irradiato da una suprema gioia, dell' alto dell' imbarcatoio stende le braccia a Des G. che vi accorre, Les., in disparte, guar-*

this!
(*seizes Man. roughly by the arm and pushes her towards the others.*)

DES G: (*losing all control over himself, wrenches Man. from the grasp of the Sergeant, exclaiming*) Stand back, Sir!

SERGEANT: (*to Des G.*) Go!

CITIZENS: (*urged on by Les., to Des G.*) Take courage!

DES G: (*fiercely and threateningly*) He dies who dares to touch her!
(*clasps Manon close to him, protecting her.*)
Manon, cling fast to me!—

CITIZENS: (*urged by Les., run to help Des G. and prevent the Sergeant from approaching Man.*) That's it! That's right!

CAPTAIN: (*appears suddenly in the midst of the crowd*) What's this?
(*the crowd falls back respectfully.*)

DES G: (*in the desperation of the moment, threateningly*) Ah! do not dare approach her!
For while I live none shall
Tear her away from me!
(*sees the Captain, and overcome with emotion bursts into sobs; he loosens Manon from his grasp and falls at the feet of the Captain imploringly.*)
No! I am mad. Behold me—
I'm weeping and implore you.
Oh! I crave your mercy.
Then hear me. Take me as servant,
Or in meaner employment,
And I will come so gladly!
Take my life—if it please you.
For mercy's sake, I implore you.
(*meanwhile the Sergeant sends the women towards the ship, and Man. with them, who walks slowly, hiding her face with her hands, and sobbing bitterly. The crowd, driven back by the archers, looks on in silence and with deep compassion.*)

CAPTAIN: (*touched by his entreaties, looks kindly on Des G. and says to him in the bluff manner of sailors*)
Ah!
Young fellow, do you desire to populate America?
(*Des G. looks at him with the greatest anxiety.*)
Well, then, it shall be so.
(*patting him on the shoulder.*)
Quick, my lad, come, I'll take you!
(*Des G. utters a cry of joy and kisses the Captain's hand. Man. turns round and understands that Des G. will accompany her, and her face radiant with joy, stretches out her arms to Des G.,*

*da, crolla il capo e si allontana.*)

*FINE DELL' ATTO TERZO.*

## ATTO IV

*In America.*

*Una landa sterminata sui confini del territorio della Nuova Orleans.*

*Terreno brullo ed ondulato; orizzonte vastissimo; cielo annuvolato. Cade la sera.*

*Manon e Des Grieux s' avanzano lentamente dal fondo; sono poveramente vestiti; hanno aspetto di persone affrante; Manon pallida, estenuata, s' appoggia sopra Des Grieux, che la sostiene a fatica.*

DES G: (*procedendo*) Tutta su me ti posa,
o mia stanca diletta.
La strada polverosa,
la strada maledetta,
al termine s' avanza.

MAN: (*con voce fioca, oppressa*)
Innanzi, innanzi ancor! . . .
L' aria d' intorno
or si fa scura,
Erra la brezza nella gran pianura
e muore il giorno! . . .
Innanzi! . . . Innanzi! . . .
(*sfinita.*)
no . . . (*cade d' un tratto*)

DES G: (*con grido d' angoscia*)
Manon!

MAN: (*con voce sempre più debole*) Son vinta . . .
Son vinta! . . . Mi perdona!
Tu sei forte . . . t' invidio;
Donna, e debole, cedo!

DES G: (*ansiosamente*) Tu soffri?

MAN: (*subito*) Orribilmente!
(*Des. G., ferito da queste parole, dimostra collo sguardo e cogli alti uno spasimo profondo. Man. sforzandosi riprende.*)
No! che dissi! . . . una vana,
una stolta parola . . .
Deh ti consola!
Chieggo breve riposo . . .
Un solo istante . . .
Mio dolce amante
a me t' appressa . . . a me! . . .
(*sviene.*)

DES G: (*con intensa emozione*)
Manon . . . senti, amor
mio . . .
Non mi rispondi, amore?
Vedi, son io che piango . . .
vedi, son io che imploro . . .
io che carezzo e bacio . . .
i tuoi capelli d' oro!

*who rushes into them. Les., who has been watching them from a distance, shakes his head and goes off.*)

*END OF THE THIRD ACT.*

## ACT IV

*America.*

*A vast plain on the borders of the territory of New Orleans.*

*The country is bare and undulating, the horizon is far distant, the sky is overcast. Night falls.*

*Manon and Des Grieux advance slowly from the back; they are poorly clad; they seem worn out with fatigue; Manon is very pale and exhausted, she leans on Des Grieux, who supports her with difficulty.*

DES G: (*advancing*) Lean all your weight on me, love,
O sweetheart sad and weary,
How tired you must be, love!
The road so long and dreary
We soon will leave behind us.

MAN: (*with stifled voice*) Let's onward, still onward, love,
The air around us now grows darker,
Over the plain the wandering breeze is flying,
And daylight is dying!—
Let's onward, still onward—
(*completely overcome,*)
No!—
(*falls suddenly.*)

DES G: (*with a cry of anguish*) Manon!

MAN: (*her voice grows fainter*) I cannot!
Oh! forgive me!
I am only a woman . . .
But you, you are strong—I faint!

DES G: (*anxiously*) You suffer?

MAN: (*hastily*) Most cruel torture!
(*Des G. distressed at her sufferings, is deeply moved. Manon with an effort exclaims*)
No! what said I?—It is false,
I was jesting, believe me—
O love, take comfort!
I need rest for a moment—
Only a moment—
My heart's own treasure.
Come close, come near me—ah! come!
(*swoons.*)

DES G: (*with intense emotion*)
Manon—hear me, beloved—
You do not answer, my darling!
Look, dear, I am weeping—
Look, dear, I implore you,
My vigil here I'm keeping,
Ah! love, I who adore you!—
(*as he speaks his emotion be-*

MANON LESCAUT 783

# Act IV

*(a misura che parla l' emozione si fa più viva.)*
Rispondimi! . . . Mi guarda!
*(pausa.)*
Tace!? Maledizione! . . .
*(le tocca la fronte.)*
Crudel febbre l' avvince . . .
Disperato mi vince
un senso di sventura,
un senso di tenèbre e di paura!

MAN: *(si desta d' un tratto, guarda Des G. quasi sensa conoscerlo; Des G. si china e la solleva da terra)* Sei tu, sei tu che piangi? . . .
Sei tu, sei tu che implori? . . .
I tuoi singulti ascolto
e mi bagnano il volto
le tue lagrime ardenti . . .
La sete mi divora . . .
O amore, aita! Aita!

DES G: O amor, tutto il mio sangue
per la tua vita!
*(corre verso il fondo scrutando l' orizzonte lontano, poi sfiduciato ritorna.)*
E nulla! nulla!
Arida landa . . . non un filo d' acqua . . .
O immoto cielo! O Dio,
a cui fanciullo anch'io
levai la mia preghiera,
un soccorso . . . un soccorso!

MAN: Si . . . un soccorso! . . . Tu puoi
salvarmi! Senti,
qui poserò!
E tu scruta il mister dell' orizzonte,
e cerca, cerca, monte - o casolar;
Oltre ti spingi e con lieta favella
lieta novella—poi vieni a recar!
*(Des G. mentre parla Man. è compresa da grande ambascia; diversi e forli sentimenti lottano in lui; l' adagia sopra un rialzo di terreno; resta ancora irresoluto in preda a fiero contrasto; indi s' allontana a poco a poco; giunto nel fondo rimane di muovo dubbioso e fissa Man. con occhi disperati, poi d' un subito deciso, parte correndo.)*

MAN: *(sola; l' orizzonte s' oscura; l' ambascia vince Man.; è stravolta, impaurita, accasciata)*
Sola . . . perduta . . . abbandonata! . . . Sola!
Tutto dunque è finito. E nel profondo
deserto io cado, io la deserta donna!
Terra di pace mi sembrava questa . . .
Ah! mia belta funesta,
ire novelle accende . . .
Da lui strappar mi si voleva; or tutto
il mio passato orribile risorge
e vivo innanzi al guardo mio si posa.
Di sangue ei s' è macchiato . . .
A nova fuga spinta
e d' amarezze e di paura cinta
asil di pace ora la tomba invo-

*comes still more powerful.)*
Nay, answer me!—Look up, dear!—
*(pauses.)*
Silent!? Accursed fate!—
*(touches her forehead.)*
Her frame is racked with fever—

MAN: *(rising suddenly, gazes at Des G. as if she did not recognize him: Des G. stoops and raises her from the ground.)*
It is you, then, that are weeping?
And you that so implore me?
My heart your sigh is reaping!
Your tears fall softly over me!
Love, with your love, restore me!
A cruel thirst consumes me.
Oh! help me, dearest, help me.

DES G: Oh! love, a thousand deaths
I would die to save you.
*(runs up stage and scans the distant horizon, then returns despondently.)*
There's nothing!—nothing!
All arid waste land,—not a drop of water.
O heartless heaven! O God,
To whom I ever as a child
Would raise my prayer,
Now protect her—and defend her!

MAN: Yes,—help me, help me—
For you can save me!
Listen, I here will rest,
While you scan from afar the dim horizon,
And seek for shelter or a woodland hut,
Go swiftly onward, and then, with joyful accents,
All your glad tidings to me you'll convey.
*(While Manon is speaking Des G. looks at her with the greatest anxiety, he hesitates to leave her: he finds a resting place for her and remains awhile undecided; finally he walks away slowly and on reaching the background again stops to gaze at Manon, then with sudden resolve runs off.)*

MAN: *(the sky darkens, Man. is well nigh distraught with terror and fatigue)* Lonely—forsaken—and abandoned—
All my hope then is over.
And in the heart of this desert
I'm dying. O wretched hapless woman!
I sought this region as a peaceful haven.
Ah! through my fatal beauty
Torments afresh surround me—
They would have severed me from him;
How all my past does haunt me
With fearful pangs of anguish,
And rises straight before
My eyes to rend me.
New dangers come to threaten—
Only the tomb can release me from

co . . .
No . . . non voglio morire . . . amore . . . aita!
*(extra Des G. precipitosamente, Man. gli cade fra le braccia.)*

MAN: *(ridestandosi)* Fra le tue braccia . . . amore!
l' ultima volta!
*(si sforza; sorride, simula speranza.)*
Apporti
tu la novella lieta?

DES G: *(con immenza tristezza)*
Nulla rinvenni . . . l' orizzonte nulla
mi rivelò lontano
spinsi lo sguardo invano . . .

MAN: Muoio: scendon le tenebre:
Su me la notte scende.

DES G: Un funesto deliro
ti percuote, t' offende . . .
Posa qui dove palpito,
in tè ritorna ancor!

MAN: *(con passione infinita)* Oh!
t' amo tanto e muoio.
Già la parola . . . manca
al mio voler . . . ma posso
dirti che t' amo tanto!
Oh! amore! ultimo incanto!
*(cade lentamente, mentre Des G. cerca ancora di sostenerla fra le sue braccia.)*

DES G: *(le tocca il volto, poi fra sè atterrito)* Gelo di morte! Dio,
l' ultima speme infrangi

MAN: *(con voce sempre più debole)* Mio dolce amor tu piangi . . .
Ora non è di lagrime,
ora di baci è questa;
Il tempo vola . . . baciami!

DES G: E vivo ancora! *(imprecando)* Infamia!

MAN: Io vo' che sia una festa
di divine carezze
di novissime ebbrezze
per me la morte . . .

DES G: O immensa
delizia mia . . . tu flamma
d' amore eterna . . .

MAN: La flamma si spegne . . .
Parla, deh! parla . . . ahimè più
non t' ascolto . . .
Qui, qui, vicino a me, voglio il tuo volto . . .
Così . . . così . . . mi baci . . . ancor ti sento . . .

DES G: Senza di te perduto . . .
ti seguirò . . .

MAN: *(con ultimo sforzo, solennemente imperiosa)* Non voglio!
Addio . . . cupa è la notte . . . ho freddo . . . era amorosa
la tua Manon? Rammenti! dim-

my burden.
No!—let me not die—dearest—help me!
*(Des G. enters hurriedly, Manon falls into his arms.)*

MAN: *(recovering)* Enfold me in your arms, love,
For the last time!
*(with an effort, smiles and looks hopeful.)*
Do you bring back
Good tidings?

DES G: *(with the deepest grief)*
Alas! I found nothing—
The horizon revealed me nothing!
In vain I peered into the distance—

MAN: I die! Dark shadows fall around.
Night's gloom on me is falling.

DES G: Oh! what a terrible frenzy
Overcomes and distracts you—
Rest, dear love, on my beating heart
Until you revive once more.

MAN: *(with infinite tenderness)*
See, how my breath grows fainter—
I scarcely can speak—
But, I would tell you how fondly I love you!
My dearest, my only treasure!
*(sinks slowly to the ground, while Des G. endeavors to support her.)*

DES G: *(touches her cheek, and in the greatest alarm exclaims)* The chill of death is on her!
God, my last hope is shattered!

MAN: *(faintly)* My sweetest love, you're weeping!
For tears, it is not the hour;
Let lips fond troth be keeping
With kiss that love shall—dower!

DES G: And I still live!
*(vehemently)* Oh, horror!

MAN: Ah! rife be this moment,
With divinest caresses
Amid passion and fervor
Let death overtake me—

DES G: Supreme treasure and delight—
Flame of love eternal—

MAN: The flame is dying—
Speak, then, to me, love—Alas! no more I hear you—
Draw near—enfold me close—let your lips cling, love—
Ah! thus—Ah! thus—you kiss me—your touch thrills me!

DES G: I cannot live—without you—
I too shall die—

MAN: *(with a supreme effort, and in a solemn tone of command)*
You shall not!
Farewell, love!
The night grows darker. I shudder—
So truly loving was your Manon!—

mi . . . la luminosa
mia giovinezza? Il sole più non
vedrò . . .

DES G: Mio Dio!

MAN: Le mie colpe . . . sereno . . .
travolgerà l' oblio,
ma l' amor mio . . . non
muore . . .

Remember!
Tell me—the radiant happy dreams
of childhood—
To see the sunlight nevermore!

DES G: Oh! Heaven!

MAN: Time will obliterate my
faults—
But my love—will never die.
(*dies.*)

(*muore.*)
(*Des G. pazzo di dolore, scoppia
in un pianto convulso, poi cade
svenuto sul corpo di Manon.*)

FINE DELL' OPERA.

(*Des G., frantic with grief, bursts
into convulsive sobs, and falls
senseless upon Manon's body.*)

END OF THE OPERA.

# La Bohème (1896)

MUSIC BY GIACOMO PUCCINI ■ LIBRETTO BY GIUSEPPE GIACOSA AND LUIGI ILLICA

This four-act opera, set to a libretto by Giuseppe Giacosa and Luigi Illica (based on Henry Murger's novel *Scènes de la vie de Bohème*), premiered at the Teatro Regio in Turin on February 1, 1896. On Christmas Eve in Paris during the year 1830, Rodolfo, a poet, is gazing out of his attic at the snow-covered rooftops while his friend Marcello works on a painting. Rodolfo lights the stove with one of his manuscripts to lessen the cold. Two friends, Colline, a philosopher, and Schaunard, a musician, bring over food and wine. When Benoit, the landlord, interrupts their meal to claim the back rent the bohemians throw him out. Marcello, Colline and Schaunard go to the Café Momus. Rodolfo stays at home. His neighbor, Mimi, knocks on the door and asks him to light her candle. She is seized with a coughing fit and passes out. Rodolfo takes care of her and the two fall in love. In front of the Café Momus, Rodolfo buys Mimi a hat, Colline buys a second-hand overcoat, and Schaunard bargains over the cost of a horn. Musetta, formerly Marcello's mistress, arrives in the company of the elderly Alcindoro. Musetta entices Marcello to return to her. She sends Alcindoro off to buy some shoes, and as a military parade passes by the bohemians sneak off, leaving the old man with the bill.

On a February day, Rodolfo, after an argument with Mimi, moves to the inn where Marcello now resides. Mimi tells Marcello that Rodolfo is gone from her forever. She hides when Rodolfo appears, only to be given away by her cough. The lovers reunite. Musetta enters and fights with Marcello. Back in Rodolfo's attic, the two friends look back on the wonderful times with their lovers. Colline and Schaunard arrive and they all try to forget their troubles. Musetta enters; Mimi is at death's door. Musetta sends Marcello out to sell her earrings for money to buy medicine, and she goes out in search of a muff to warm her friend Mimi's freezing hands. Colline goes off to sell his coat. The two lovers, left by themselves, remember their first meeting. Their friends return to find Mimi dead. Grief-stricken, Rodolfo throws himself on top of her corpse.

---

## ■ ATTO PRIMO

*In soffitta*
*(Ampia finestra dalla quale si scorge una distesa di tetti coperti di neve. A destra un camino. Una tavola, un letto, quattro sedie, un cavalletto da pittore con una tela sbozzata: libri sparsi, molti fasci di carte. Rodolfo guarda meditabondo fuori della finestra. Marcello lavora al suo quadro "Il passaggio del Mar Rosso", colle mani intirizzite dal freddo e che egli riscalda alitandovi su di quando in quando.)*

**MARCELLO:** Questo "Mar Rosso" mi ammollisce
e assidera come se addosso
mi piovesse in stille.
Per vendicarmi affogo un Faraone.
*(a Rodolfo)*
Che fai?

**RODOLFO:** Nei cieli bigi
guardo fumar dai mille
comignoli Parigi,
e penso a quel poltrone
d'un vecchio caminetto ingannatore
che vive in ozio come un gran signor.

**MARCELLO:** Le sue rendite oneste
da un pezzo non riceve.

**RODOLFO:** Quelle sciocche foreste
che fan sotto la neve?

## ■ ACT I

*A garret*
*(A large window through which an expanse of snow-covered roofs is seen. At right, a stove. A table, a bed, four chairs, a painter's easel with half-finished canvas: books everywhere, manuscripts. Rodolfo is thoughtful, looking out the window. Marcello works at his painting "The Crossing of the Red Sea", his hands stiff with cold; he tries to warm them by blowing on them now and again.)*

**MARCELLO:** This "Red Sea" of mine
makes me feel cold and numb
as if it were pouring over me.
I'll drown a Pharaoh in revenge.
*(to Rodolfo)*
What are you doing?

**RODOLFO:** I'm looking at Paris,
seeing the skies gray with smoke
from a thousand chimneys,
and I think of that no-good,
hateful stove of ours that lives
a gentleman's life of idleness.

**MARCELLO:** It's been a long time since he received his just income.

**RODOLFO:** What are those stupid forests doing, all covered with snow?

**MARCELLO:** Rodolfo, io voglio dirti
un mio pensier profondo:
ho un freddo cane.

**RODOLFO:** Ed io, Marcel, non ti nascondo
che non credo al sudor della fronte.

**MARCELLO:** Ho ghiacciate le dita
quasi ancora le tenessi immollate
giù in quella gran ghiacciaia
che è il cuore di Musetta.
*(Lascia sfuggire un lungo, sospirone, e tralascia di dipingere.)*

**RODOLFO:** L'amore è caminetto che sciupa
troppo . . .

**MARCELLO:** E in fretta!

**RODOLFO:** Dove l'uomo è fascina.

**MARCELLO:** E la donna è l'alare . . .

**RODOLFO:** L'uno brucia in un soffio . . .

**MARCELLO:** E l'altro sta a guardare . . .

**RODOLFO:** Ma intanto qui si gela . . .

**MARCELLO:** E si muore d'inedia . . .

**RODOLFO:** Fuoco ci vuole . . .

**MARCELLO:** Rodolfo, I want to tell you
a profound thought I've had:
I'm cold as hell.

**RODOLFO:** As for me, Marcello, I'll be frank:
I'm not exactly sweating.

**MARCELLO:** And my fingers are frozen—
as if I still were holding them
in that enormous glacier,
Musetta's heart.
*(A sigh escapes him, and he leaves off painting.)*

**RODOLFO:** Love is a stove that burns too much . . .

**MARCELLO:** Too fast.

**RODOLFO:** Where the man is the fuel . . .

**MARCELLO:** And woman the spark . . .

**RODOLFO:** He burns in a moment . . .

**MARCELLO:** And she stands by, watching!

**RODOLFO:** Meanwhile, we're freezing in here!

**MARCELLO:** And dying from lack of food!

**RODOLFO:** We must have a fire . . .

MARCELLO: (afferando una sedia) Aspetta . . . sacrifichiam la sedia!
(Rodolfo impedisce l'atto di Marcello. Ad un tratto dà un grido di gioia.)

RODOLFO: Eureka!

MARCELLO: Trovasti?

RODOLFO: Sì. Aguzza l'ingegno. L'idea vampi in fiamma.

MARCELLO: (additando il suo quadro) Bruciamo il "Mar Rosso"?

RODOLFO: No. Puzza la tela dipinta.
Il mio dramma . . .
L'ardente mio dramma ci scaldi.

MARCELLO: Vuoi leggerlo forse? Mi geli.

RODOLFO: No, in cener la carta si sfaldi
e l'estro rivoli ai suoi cieli.
Al secol gran danno minaccia . . .
Ma Roma è in periglio . . .

MARCELLO: Gran cor!

RODOLFO: A te l'atto primo!

MARCELLO: Qua.

RODOLFO: Straccia.

MARCELLO: Accendi.
(Rodolfo accende quella parte dello scartafaccio buttato sul focolare. Poi i due amici prendono delle sedie e seggono, riscaldandosi voluttuosamente.)

RODOLFO E MARCELLO: Che lieto baglior.
(Si apre con fracasso la parta ed entra Colline, gelato, battendo i piedi. Getta sulla tavola un pacco di libri.)

COLLINE: Già dell'Apocalisse appariscono i segni.
In giorno di Vigilia non si accettano pegni!
(sorpreso)
Una fiammata!

RODOLFO: Zitto, si dà il mio dramma . . .

MARCELLO: . . . al fuoco.

COLLINE: Lo trove scintillante.

RODOLFO: Vivo.

MARCELLO: Ma dura poco.

RODOLFO: La brevità, gran pregio.

COLLINE: Autore, a me la sedia.

MARCELLO: Questi intermezzi fan morir d'inedia.
Presto!

RODOLFO: Atto secondo.

MARCELLO: Non far sussurro.

COLLINE: Pensier profondo!

MARCELLO: Giusto color!

RODOLFO: In quell'azzurro guizzo languente sfuma un'ardente scena d'amor.

---

MARCELLO: (seizing a chair) Wait . . . we'll sacrifice the chair!
(Rodolfo keeps Marcello from breaking the chair. Suddenly he shouts with joy.)

RODOLFO: Eureka!

MARCELLO: You've found it?

RODOLFO: Yes. Sharpen your wits.
Let Thought burst into flame.

MARCELLO: (pointing to his picture) Shall we burn the "Red Sea"?

RODOLFO: No. Painted canvas smells.
My play . . .
My burning drama will warm us.

MARCELLO: You mean to read it? I'll freeze.

RODOLFO: No, the paper will unfold in ash
and genius soar back to its heaven.
A serious loss to the age . . .
but Rome is in danger . . .

MARCELLO: What a noble heart!

RODOLFO: Here, take the first act!

MARCELLO: Here.

RODOLFO: Tear it up.

MARCELLO: Light it.
(Rodolfo lights the part of the manuscript thrown in the fire. Then the two friends draw up chairs and sit down, voluptuously warming themselves.)

RODOLFO AND MARCELLO: What blissful heat!
(The door opens and Colline enters, frozen, stamping his feet. He throws some books on the table.)

COLLINE: Signs of the Apocalypse begin to appear.
No pawning allowed on Christmas Eve.
(surprised)
A fire!

RODOLFO: Quiet, my play's being given . . .

MARCELLO: . . . to the stove.

COLLINE: I find it full of fire.

RODOLFO: Brilliant.

MARCELLO: But brief.

RODOLFO: Brevity, its great merit.

COLLINE: Your chair, please, Mr Author.

MARCELLO: These intermissions kill you with boredom.
Get on with it!

RODOLFO: Act two.

MARCELLO: No whispering.

COLLINE: What profundity!

MARCELLO: How colorful!

RODOLFO: In that dying blue flame
an ardent love-scene dies.

---

COLLINE: Scoppietta un foglio.

MARCELLO: Là c'eran baci!

RODOLFO: Tre atti or voglio d'un colpo udir.
(Getta al fuoco il resto del manoscritto.)

COLLINE: Tal degli audaci l'idea s'integra.

TUTTI: Bello in allegra vampa svanir.
(Applaudono. Poi la fiamma diminuisce.)

MARCELLO: Oh! Dio . . . già s'abbassa la fiamma.

COLLINE: Che vano, che fragile dramma!

MARCELLO: Già scricchiola, increspasi, muor.

COLLINE E MARCELLO: Abbasso, abbasso l'autore.
(Dalla porta entrano due garzoni, portando l'uno provviste di cibi, bottiglie di vino, sigari, e l'altro un fascio di legna. Al rumore i tre innanzi al camino si volgono e con grida di meraviglia si slanciano sulle provviste.)

RODOLFO: Legna!

MARCELLO: Sigari!

COLLINE: Bordò!

RODOLFO: Legna!

MARCELLO: Bordò!

TUTTI: Le dovizie d'una fiera il destin ci destinò
(I garzoni partono. Schaunard entra con aria di trionfo, gettando alcuni scudi a terra.)

SCHAUNARD: La Banca di Francia per voi si sbilancia.

COLLINE: (raccattando gli scudi insieme agli altri) Raccatta, raccatta!

MARCELLO: Son pezzi di latta!

SCHAUNARD: Sei sordo? . . . sei lippo?
(mostrando uno scudo) Quest'uomo chi è?

RODOLFO: Luigi Filippo! M'inchino al mio Re!

TUTTI: Sta Luigi Filippo ai nostri piè!
(Schaunard vorrebbe raccontare la sua fortuna, ma gli altri non lo ascoltano. Dispongono ogni cosa sulla tavola e la legna nel camino.)

SCHAUNARD: Or vi dirò: questo'oro,
o meglio, argento
ha la sua brava istoria . . .

RODOLFO: Riscaldiamo il camino!

COLLINE: Tanto freddo ha sofferto!

---

COLLINE: See that page crackle.

MARCELLO: There were the kisses!

RODOLFO: I want to hear three acts at once.
(He throws the rest of the manuscript on the fire.)

COLLINE: And so unified is your bold conception.

ALL: Beautiful death on the joyful flame.
(They applaud. Then the flame dies.)

MARCELLO: Oh Lord! The flame is dying.

COLLINE: So useless, so fragile a drama!

MARCELLO: Already curling up to die.

COLLINE AND MARCELLO: Down with the author!
((Two porters come in, one carrying food, bottles of wine and cigars; the other has a bundle of wood. At the sound, the three men in front of the fire turn around and with shouts of amazement fall upon the provisions.)

RODOLFO: Wood!

MARCELLO: Cigars!

COLLINE: Bordeaux!

RODOLFO: Firewood!

MARCELLO: Bordeaux!

ALL THREE: Destiny provides us with a feast of plenty!
(The porters leave. Schaunard enters triumphantly, throwing some coins on the floor.)

SCHAUNARD: The Bank of France has gone broke just for you.

COLLINE: (gathering up coins, with the others) Pick them up!

MARCELLO: They must be made of tin!

SCHAUNARD: Are you deaf? or blind?
(showing a crown) Who is this man?

RODOLFO: Louis Philippe! I bow to my King!

ALL: Louis Philippe is at our feet!
(Schaunard wants to tell his adventure, but the others won't listen to him. They set the provisions on the table and put wood in the stove.)

SCHAUNARD: Now I'll tell you: this gold,
this silver, rather,
has a noble history . . .

RODOLFO: Let's fire the stove!

COLLINE: It's hard to endure so much cold!

# Act I

SCHAUNARD: Un inglese . . . un signor . . . lord
o milord che sia, volea
un musicista . . .

MARCELLO: Via! Prepariamo la tavola!

SCHAUNARD: Io? Volo!

RODOLFO: L'esca dov'è?

COLLINE: Là.

MARCELLO: Qua.

SCHAUNARD: . . . e mi presento.
M'accetta, gli domando . . .

COLLINE: Arrosto freddo.

MARCELLO: Pasticcio dolce.

SCHAUNARD: . . . A quando le lezioni?
Mi presento, m'accetta,
gli domando: A quando le lezioni?
Risponde: "Incominciam . . .
guardare!" e un pappagallo
m'addita al primo pian.
Poi soggiunge: "Voi suonare
finchè quello morire!"

RODOLFO: Fulgida folgori la sala splendida!

MARCELLO: Ora le candele.

SCHAUNARD: E fu così:
suonai tre lunghi dì . . .
Allora usai l'incanto
di mia presenza bella . . .
Affascinai l'ancella . . .
Gli propinai prezzemolo . . .

MARCELLO: Mangiar senza tovaglia?

RODOLFO: No: un'idea!
(Prende un giornale dalla tasca.)

MARCELLO E COLLINE: Il Costituzional!

RODOLFO: Ottima carta . . .
Si mangia e si divora un'appendice!

SCHAUNARD: Lorito allargò l'ali,
Lorito il becco aprì,
un poco di prezzemolo;
da Socrate morì!

COLLINE: (a Schaunard)
Chi? . . .

SCHAUNARD: Il diavolo vi porti
tutti quanti . . .
Ed or che fate?
No! queste cibarie
sono la salmeria
pei dì futuri
tenebrosi e oscuri.
Pranzare in casa il dì della Vigilia
mentre il Quartier Latino le sue vie
addobba di salsicce e leccornie?
Quando un olezzo di fritelle imbalsama
le vecchie strade?
Là le ragazze cantano contente . . .

TUTTI: La vigilia di Natal!

---

SCHAUNARD: An Englishman . . . a gentleman . . .
A lord . . . was looking for
a musician . . .

MARCELLO: Come! Let's set the table!

SCHAUNARD: And I? I flew to him . . .

RODOLFO: Where are the matches?

COLLINE: There.

MARCELLO: Here.

SCHAUNARD: . . . I introduce myself.
He hires me. I ask him . . .

COLLINE: Cold roast beef.

MARCELLO: Sweet pastry.

SCHAUNARD: When do the lessons begin?
I introduce myself, he hires me,
I ask: When do the lessons begin?
He replies: "Let's start . . .
look!" and points to a parrot
on the first floor.
Then adds: "You play
until that bird dies!"

RODOLFO: The dining room's brilliant!

MARCELLO: Now the candles.

SCHAUNARD: And so it went:
I played for three long days . . .
Then I used my charm,
my handsome figure . . .
I won the serving-girl over . . .
We poisoned a little parsley . . .

MARCELLO: Eat without a tablecloth?

RODOLFO: No! I've an idea!
(He takes a newspaper from his pocket.)

MARCELLO AND COLLINE: The Constitutional!

RODOLFO: Excellent paper . . .
You eat and devour the news!

SCHAUNARD: Lorito spread his wings,
Lorito opened his beak,
took a peck of parsley,
and died like Socrates!

COLLINE: (to Schaunard) Who?

SCHAUNARD: Go to the devil, all of you . . .
Now what are you doing?
No! These delicacies
are the provender
for the dark and gloomy
days in the future.
Dine at home on Christmas Eve
when the Latin Quarter
has decked its streets with eatables?
When the perfume of fritters
is wafted through the ancient streets?
There the girls sing happily . . .

ALL: It's Christmas Eve!

---

SCHAUNARD: Ed han per eco, ognuna uno studente!
Un po' di religione, o miei signori:
si beva in casa, ma si pranzi fuor . . .
(Versano il vino. Poi bussano alla porta.)

BENOIT: (di fuori) Si può?

MARCELLO: Chi è là?

BENOIT: Benoit.

MARCELLO: Il padrone di casa!

SCHAUNARD: Uscio sul muso.

COLLINE: Non c'è nessuno.

SCHAUNARD: È chiuso.

BENOIT: Una parola.

SCHAUNARD: (dopo essersi consultato cogli altri, va ad aprire) Sola!
(Benoit entra.)

BENOIT: (mostrando una carta) Affitto.

MARCELLO: Olà. Date una sedia.

RODOLFO: Presto.

BENOIT: Non occorre, lo vorrei . . .

SCHAUNARD: Segga.

MARCELLO: Vuol bere?

BENOIT: Grazie.

RODOLFO E COLLINE: Tocchiamo.

SCHAUNARD: Beva.
(Benoit, posando il bicchiere, mostra la carta a Marcello.)

BENOIT: Questo
è l'ultimo trimestre . . .

MARCELLO: E n'ho piacere . . .

BENOIT: E quindi . . .

SCHAUNARD: Ancora un sorso.

BENOIT: Grazie.

I QUATTRO: Tocchiam. Alla sua salute!

BENOIT: (riprendendo con Marcello) A lei ne vengo
perchè il trimestre scorso
mi promise . . .

MARCELLO: Promisi ed or mantengo.
(Indica gli scudi sulla tavola.)

RODOLFO: (piano a Marcello) Che fai?

SCHAUNARD: Sei pazzo?

MARCELLO: (a Benoit, senza guardare gli altri)
Ha visto? Or via,
resti un momento in nostra compagnia.
Dica: quant'anni ha,
caro Signor Benoit?

BENOIT: Gli anni . . . Per carità!

RODOLFO: Su e giù la nostra età.

BENOIT: Di più, molto di più.
(Gli riempiono il bicchiere.)

---

SCHAUNARD: And each has a student echoing her!
Have some religion, gentlemen:
we drink at home, but we dine out.
(They pour the wine. A knock at the door.)

BENOIT: (outside) May I come in?

MARCELLO: Who's there?

BENOIT: Benoit.

MARCELLO: The landlord!

SCHAUNARD: Bolt the door.

COLLINE: Nobody's home.

SCHAUNARD: It's locked.

BENOIT: Just one word.

SCHAUNARD: (after consulting the others, open the door) Just one!
(Benoit enters.)

BENOIT: (showing a paper) Rent.

MARCELLO: Here! Give him a chair.

RODOLFO: At once.

BENOIT: Don't bother, I'd like . . .

SCHAUNARD: Be seated.

MARCELLO: Something to drink?

BENOIT: Thank you.

RODOLFO AND COLLINE: A toast.

SCHAUNARD: Drink.
(Benoit sets down his glass and shows the paper to Marcello.)

BENOIT: This is the bill
for three month's rent . . .

MARCELLO: That's fine . . .

BENOIT: Therefore

SCHAUNARD: Another drop.

BENOIT: Thank you.

THE FOUR: A toast. To your health!

BENOIT: (to Marcello again) I come to you
because last quarter
you promised me . . .

MARCELLO: I promised and I'll pay.
(He points to the money on the table.)

RODOLFO: (aside to Marcello) What are you doing?

SCHAUNARD: Are you crazy?

MARCELLO: (to Benoit, ignoring the others) You see? Now then
stay with us a moment.
Tell me: how old are you,
dear M. Benoit?

BENOIT: My age? . . . Spare me!

RODOLFO: Our age, more or less, I'd say.

BENOIT: More, much more.
(They refill his glass.)

COLLINE: Ha detto su e giù.

MARCELLO: L'altra sera al Mabil l'han colto in peccato d'amor.

BENOIT: Io?

MARCELLO: Al Mabil l'altra sera l'han colto . . . Neghi?

BENOIT: Un caso.

MARCELLO: Bella donna!

BENOIT: (mezzo brillo) Ah! molto!

SCHAUNARD poi RODOLFO: Briccone!

COLLINE: Seduttore! Una quercia . . . un cannone!

RODOLFO: L'uomo ha buon gusto.

MARCELLO: Il crin ricciuto e fulvo. Ei gongolava arzillo e pettoruto.

BENOIT: Son vecchio ma robusto.

COLLINE, SCHAUNARD E RODOLFO: Ei gongolava arzuto e pettorillo.

MARCELLO: A lui cedea la femminil virtù.

BENOIT: Timido in gioventù, ora me ne ripago. Si sa, è uno svago qualche donnetta allegra . . . e . . . un po' . . . non dico una balena o un mappamondo o un viso tondo da luna piena. Ma magra, proprio magra, no, poi no! Le donne magre son grattacapi e spesso . . . sopracapi . . . e son piene di doglie per esempio, mia moglie . . . (Marcello, fingendo indignazione, si alza; gli altri lo imitano.)

MARCELLO: Quest'uomo ha moglie e sconcie voglie ha nel cor!

GLI ALTRI: Orror!

RODOLFO: E ammorba, e appesta la nostra onesta magion.

GLI ALTRI: Fuor!

MARCELLO: Si abbruci dello zucchero!

COLLINE: Si discacci il reprobo.

SCHAUNARD: È la morale offesa che vi scaccia!

BENOIT: Io di . . . io di . . .

GLI ALTRI: Silenzio!

BENOIT: Miei signori . . .

GLI ALTRI: Silenzio . . . via signore . . . Via di qua! E buona sera a vostra signoria! Ah! Ah! Ah! (Benoit è cacciato fuori. Marcello chiude la porta.)

COLLINE: He said more or less.

MARCELLO: The other evening at the Mabille they caught him making love.

BENOIT: Me?

MARCELLO: They caught him at the Mabille the other evening . . . Deny it, then.

BENOIT: An accident.

MARCELLO: A lovely woman!

BENOIT: (half-drunk) Ah! Very!

SCHAUNARD, then RODOLFO: You rascal!

COLLINE: Seducer! He's an oak, a ball of fire!

RODOLFO: He's a man of taste.

MARCELLO: With that curly, tawny hair. How he swaggered, proud and happy!

BENOIT: I'm old but strong.

COLLINE, SCHAUNARD AND RODOLFO: How he swaggered, proud and happy!

MARCELLO: Feminine virtue gave in to him.

BENOIT: I'm paying myself back now for my shy youth . . . my pastime, you know, a lively woman . . . a bit . . . well, not a whale exactly or a relief-map of the world or a face like a full moon, but not thin, really thin. No! Thin women are worrisome and often . . . a nuisance . . . always full of complaints, for example—my wife . . . ! (Marcello rises, feigning moral indignation. The others do the same.)

MARCELLO: This man has a wife and foul desires in his heart!

THE OTHERS: Horrors!

RODOLFO: He corrupts and pollutes our respectable home.

THE OTHERS: Out with him!

MARCELLO: Burn some incense!

COLLINE: Throw out the scoundrel!

SCHAUNARD: Our offended morality expels you!

BENOIT: I say . . . I . . .

THE OTHERS: Silence!

BENOIT: My dear sirs . . .

THE OTHERS: Silence . . . Out, sir . . . Away with you! And good evening to your worship! Ha! Ha! Ha! (Benoit is thrown out. Marcello shuts the door.)

MARCELLO: Ho pagato il trimestre.

SCHAUNARD: Al Quartiere Latin ci attende Momus.

MARCELLO: Viva chi spende!

SCHAUNARD: Dividiamo il bottin!

GLI ALTRA: Dividiam! (Dividono gli scudi.)

MARCELLO: (presentando uno specchio a Colline) Là ci son beltà scese dal cielo. Or che sei ricco, bada alla decenza! Orso, ravviati il pelo.

COLLINE: Farò la conoscenza la prima volta d'un barbitonsore. Guidatemi al ridicolo oltraggio d'un rasoio.

TUTTI: Andiam.

RODOLFO: Io resto per terminar l'articolo di fondo del Castoro.

MARCELLO: Fa presto.

RODOLFO: Cinque minuti. Conosco il mestier.

COLLINE: T'aspetterem dabbasso dal portier.

MARCELLO: Se tardi udrai che coro.

RODOLFO: Cinque minuti.

SCHAUNARD: Taglia corta la coda al tuo Castoro. (Rodolfo prende un lume ed apre l'uscio. Gli altri escono e scendono la scala.)

MARCELLO: (di fuori) Occhio alla scala. Tieni alla ringhiera.

RODOLFO: (alzando il lume) Adagio.

COLLINE: È buio pesto.

SCHAUNARD: Maledetto portier!

COLLINE: Accidenti!

RODOLFO: Colline, sei morto?

COLLINE: (dal basso) Non ancor.

MARCELLO: Vien presto. (Rodolfo chiude l'uscio, pone il lume sulla tavola, e si mette a scrivere. Ma straccia il foglio e getta via la penna.)

RODOLFO: Non sono in vena. (Bussano timidamente alla porta.) Chi è là?

MIMÌ: (di fuori) Scusi.

RODOLFO: Una donna!

MIMÌ: Di grazia, mi si è spento il lume.

RODOLFO: (aprendo) Ecco.

MIMÌ: (sull'uscio, con un lume spento in mano ed una chiave) Vorrebbe . . . ?

MARCELLO: I've paid the rent.

SCHAUNARD: In the Latin Quarter Momus awaits us.

MARCELLO: Long life to him who pays!

SCHAUNARD: We'll divide my loot!

THE OTHERS: Let's divide! (They share the coins.)

MARCELLO: (giving Colline a mirror) Beauties are there, come from above. Now you're rich, you must look presentable. You bear! Trim your fur.

COLLINE: I'll make my first acquaintance of a beard-barber. Lead me to the absurd, outrageous razor.

ALL: Let's go.

RODOLFO: I must stay to finish my article for the paper, The Beaver.

MARCELLO: Hurry, then!

RODOLFO: Five minutes. I know my trade.

COLLINE: We'll wait for you downstairs.

MARCELLO: You'll hear us if you dawdle.

RODOLFO: Five minutes.

SCHAUNARD: Cut that Beaver's tail short. (Rodolfo takes a light and opens the door. The others start down the stairs.)

MARCELLO: (outside) Watch the stairs. Hold on to the railing.

RODOLFO: (raising the light) Careful.

COLLINE: It's pitch dark.

SCHAUNARD: That damn janitor!

COLLINE: Hell!

RODOLFO: Colline, are you killed?

COLLINE: (from below) Not yet.

MARCELLO: Come soon. (Rodolfo closes the door, sets his light on the table and tries to write. But he tears up the paper and throws the pen down.)

RODOLFO: I'm not in the mood. (There's a timid knock at the door.) Who's there?

MIMÌ: (outside) Excuse me.

RODOLFO: A woman!

MIMÌ: I'm sorry . . . my light has gone out.

RODOLFO: (opening the door) Here.

MIMÌ: (in the doorway, holding a candlestick and key) Would you . . . ?

# Act I

**RODOLFO:** S'accomodi un momento.

**MIMÌ:** Non occorre.

**RODOLFO:** La prego, entri.
(*Entrando, Mimì è presa da soffocazione.*)
Si sente male?

**MIMÌ:** No . . . nulla.

**RODOLFO:** Impallidisce!

**MIMÌ:** È il respir . . . quelle scale . . .
(*Sviene e Rodolfo è appena a tempo di sorreggerla ed adagiarla su una sedia, mentre dalle mani di Mimì cadono e candeliere e chiave.*)

**RODOLFO:** Ed ora come faccio?
(*Va a prendere dell'acqua e ne spruzza il viso di lei.*)
Così.
Che viso d'ammalata!
(*Mimì rinviene.*)
Si sente meglio?

**MIMÌ:** Sì.

**RODOLFO:** Qui c'è tanto freddo. Segga vicino
al fuoco.
(*La conduce a sedere presso al camino.*)
Aspetti . . . un po' di vino.

**MIMÌ:** Grazie.

**RODOLFO:** A lei.

**MIMÌ:** Poco, poco.

**RODOLFO:** Così.

**MIMÌ:** Grazie.

**RODOLFO:** (Che bella bambina!)

**MIMÌ:** (*alzandosi*) Ora permetta che accenda il lume.
Tutto è passato.

**RODOLFO:** Tanta fretta!

**MIMÌ:** Sì.
(*Rodolfo accende il lume e glielo dà.*)
Grazie. Buona sera.

**RODOLFO:** Buona sera.
(*Mimì, esce, poi riappare sull'uscio.*)

**MIMÌ:** Oh! sventata, sventata!
la chiave della stanza
dove l'ho lasciata?

**RODOLFO:** Non stia sull'uscio:
il lume vacilla al vento.
(*Il lume di Mimì si spegne.*)

**MIMÌ:** Oh Dio! Torni ad accenderlo.
(*Rodolfo accorre colla sua candela, ma avvicinandosi alla porta anche il suo lume si spegne e la camera rimane buia.*)

**RODOLFO:** Oh Dio! Anche il mio s'è spento.

**MIMÌ:** Ah! E la chiave ove sarà?

**RODOLFO:** Buio pesto!

**MIMÌ:** Disgraziata!

**RODOLFO:** Come in for a moment.

**MIMÌ:** There's no need.

**RODOLFO:** Please . . . come in.
(*Mimì enters, and has a fit of coughing.*)
You're not well?

**MIMÌ:** No . . . it's nothing.

**RODOLFO:** You're pale!

**MIMÌ:** I'm out of breath . . . the stairs . . .
(*She faints, and Rodolfo is just in time to support her and help her to a chair. The key and the candlestick fall from her hands.*)

**RODOLFO:** Now what shall I do?
(*He gets some water and sprinkles her face.*)
So.
How ill she looks!
(*Mimì come to.*)
Are you better now?

**MIMÌ:** Yes.

**RODOLFO:** It's so cold here. Come and sit
by the fire.
(*He helps her to a chair by the stove.*)
Wait . . . some wine.

**MIMÌ:** Thank you.

**RODOLFO:** Here.

**MIMÌ:** Just a little.

**RODOLFO:** There.

**MIMÌ:** Thank you.

**RODOLFO:** (What a lovely creature!)

**MIMÌ:** (*rising*) Now, please, relight my candle.
I'm better now.

**RODOLFO:** Such a hurry!

**MIMÌ:** Yes.
(*Rodolfo lights her candle for her.*)
Thank you. Good evening.

**RODOLFO:** Good evening.
(*Mimì goes out, then reappears at the door.*)

**MIMÌ:** Oh! foolish me!
Where have I left
the key to my room?

**RODOLFO:** Don't stand in the door:
the wind makes your light flicker.
(*Her candle goes out.*)

**MIMÌ:** Heavens! Will you relight it?
(*Rodolfo hastens to her with his light, but when he reaches the door, his candle goes out, too. The room is dark.*)

**RODOLFO:** There . . . Now mine's out, too.

**MIMÌ:** Ah! And where can my key be?

**RODOLFO:** Pitch dark!

**MIMÌ:** Unlucky me!

**RODOLFO:** Ove sarà?

**MIMÌ:** Importuna è la vicina . . .

**RODOLFO:** Ma le pare!

**MIMÌ:** Importuna è la vicina . . .

**RODOLFO:** Cosa dice? ma le pare!

**MIMÌ:** Cerchi.

**RODOLFO:** Cerco.
(*Cercano, tastando il pavimento colle mani.*)

**MIMÌ:** Ove sarà?

**RODOLFO:** Ah!
(*Trova la chiave, l'intasca.*)

**MIMÌ:** L'ha trovata?

**RODOLFO:** No.

**MIMÌ:** Mi parve . . .

**RODOLFO:** In verità!

**MIMÌ:** Cerca?

**RODOLFO:** Cerco.
(*Guidato dalla voce di Mimì, Rodolfo finge di cercare mentre si avvicina ad essa. Poi colla sua mano incontra quella di Mimì e l'afferra.*)

**MIMÌ:** (*sorpresa*) Ah!
(*Si alzano. Rodolfo tiene sempre la mano di Mimì.*)

**RODOLFO:** Che gelida manina!
Se la lasci riscaldar.
Cercar che giova?
Al buio non si trova.
Ma per fortuna
è una notte di luna,
e qui la luna l'abbiamo vicina.
Aspetti, signorina,
le dirò con due parole chi son,
chi son, e che faccio, come vivo.
Vuole?
(*Mimì tace.*)
Chi son? Chi son? Son un poeta.
Che cosa faccio? Scrivo.
E come vivo? Vivo.
In povertà mia lieta
scialo da gran signore
rime ed inni d'amore.
Per sogni e per chimere
e per castelli in aria
l'anima ho milionaria.
Talor dal mio forziere
ruban tutti i gioielli
due ladri: gli occhi belli,
V'entrar con voi pur ora
ed i miei sogni usati,
ed i bei sogni miei
tosto si dileguar!
Ma il furto non m'accora
poichè, poichè v'ha preso stanza
la speranza.
Or che mi conoscete
parlate voi. Deh parlate.
Chi siete? Vi piaccia dir?

**MIMÌ:** Sì. Mi chiamano Mimì,
ma il mio nome è Lucia.
La storia mia è breve.
A tela o a seta
ricamo in casa e fuori.
Son tranquilla e lieta,

**RODOLFO:** Where can it be?

**MIMÌ:** You've a bothersome neighbor . . .

**RODOLFO:** Not at all.

**MIMÌ:** You've a bothersome neighbor . . .

**RODOLFO:** What do you mean? Not at all!

**MIMÌ:** Search.

**RODOLFO:** I'm searching.
(*They hunt, touching the floor with their hands.*)

**MIMÌ:** Where can it be?

**RODOLFO:** Ah!
(*He finds the key and pockets it.*)

**MIMÌ:** Did you find it?

**RODOLFO:** No.

**MIMÌ:** I thought . . .

**RODOLFO:** Truthfully!

**MIMÌ:** Are you hunting?

**RODOLFO:** I'm hunting for it.
(*Guided by her voice, Rodolfo pretends to search as he draws closer to her. Then his hand meets hers, and he holds it.*)

**MIMÌ:** (*surprised*) Ah!
(*They rise. Rodolfo continues to hold Mimì's hand.*)

**RODOLFO:** How cold your little hand is!
Let me warm it for you.
What's the use of searching?
We'll never find it in the dark.
But luckily
there's a moon,
and she's our neighbor here.
Just wait, my dear young lady,
and meanwhile I'll tell you
in a word who and what I am.
Shall I?
(*Mimì is silent.*)
Who am I? I'm a poet.
My business? Writing.
How do I live? I live.
In my happy poverty
I squander like a prince
my poems and songs of love.
In hopes and dreams
and castles-in-air,
I'm a millionaire in spirit.
But sometimes my strong-box
is robbed of all its jewels
by two thieves: a pair of pretty eyes.
They came in now with you
and all my lovely dreams,
my dreams of the past,
were soon stolen away.
But the theft doesn't upset me,
since the empty place was filled
with hope.
Now that you know me,
it's your turn to speak.
Who are you? Will you tell me?

**MIMÌ:** Yes.
They call me Mimì,
but my real name's Lucia.
My story is brief.
I embroider silk and satin
at home or outside.

ed è mio svago
far gigli e rose.
Mi piaccion quelle cose
che han sì dolce malìa,
che parlano d'amor, di primavere,
che parlano di sogni e di chimere,
quelle cose che han nome poesia . . .
Lei m'intende?

**RODOLFO:** Sì.

**MIMÌ:** Mi chiamano Mimì.
Il perchè non so.
Sola, mi fo il pranzo
da me stessa.
Non vado sempre a messa,
ma prego assai il Signor.
Vivo sola, soletta,
là in una bianca cameretta;
guardo sui tetti e in cielo.
Ma quando vien lo sgelo
Il primo sole è mio,
Il primo bacio dell'aprile è mio!
Il primo sole è mio.
Germoglia in un vaso una rosa,
foglia a foglia l'aspiro.
Così gentil è il profumo d'un fior.
Ma i fior ch'io faccio, ahimè,
i fior ch'io faccio,
ahimè non hanno odore.
Altro di me non le saprei narrare.
Sono la sua vicina
che la vien fuori d'ora a importunare.

**SCHAUNARD:** (*dal cortile*) Ehi!
Rodolfo!

**COLLINE:** Rodolfo!

**MARCELLO:** Olà! Non senti?
Lumaca!

**COLLINE:** Poetucolo!

**SCHAUNARD:** Accidenti al pigro!
(*Rodolfo, impaziente, va alla finestra per rispondere. Dalla finestra aperta entrano i raggi lunari, rischiarando la camera.*)

**RODOLFO:** Scrivo ancora tre righi
a volo.

**MIMÌ:** Chi sono?

**RODOLFO:** Amici.

**SCHAUNARD:** Sentirai le tue.

**MARCELLO:** Che te ne fai lì solo?

**RODOLFO:** Non son solo. Siamo in due.
Andate da Momus, tenete il posto.
Ci saremo tosto.

**MARCELLO, SCHAUNARD E COLLINE:** Momus, Momus,
Momus,
zitti e discreti andiamocene via.
Momus, Momus.
Trovò la poesia.
(*Rodolfo volgendosi scorge Mimì avvolta come da un nimbo di luce, e la contempla, estatico.*)

I'm tranquil and happy,
and my pastime
is making lilies and roses.
I love all things
that have gentle magic,
that talk of love, of spring,
that talk of dreams and fancies—
the things called poetry . . .
Do you understand me?

**RODOLFO:** Yes.

**MIMÌ:** They call me Mimì
I don't know why.
I live all by myself
and I eat alone.
I don't often go to church,
but I like to pray.
I stay all alone
in my tiny white room,
I look at the roofs and the sky.
but when spring comes
the sun's first rays are mine.
April's first kiss is mine, is mine!
The sun's first rays are mine!
A rose blossoms in my vase,
I breathe its perfume, petal by petal.
So sweet is the flower's perfume.
But the flowers I make, alas,
the flowers I make, alas,
alas, have no scent.
What else can I say?
I'm your neighbor, disturbing you
at this impossible hour.

**SCHAUNARD:** (*from below*) Hey!
Rodolfo!

**COLLINE:** Rodolfo!

**MARCELLO:** Hey! Can't you hear?
You slow-coach!

**COLLINE:** You scribbler!

**SCHAUNARD:** To hell with that
lazy one!
(*Rodolfo, impatient, goes to the window to answer. When the window is opened, the moonlight comes in, lighting up the room.*)

**RODOLFO:** I've a few more words
to write.

**MIMÌ:** Who are they?

**RODOLFO:** Friends.

**SCHAUNARD:** You'll hear about
this.

**MARCELLO:** What are you doing
there alone?

**RODOLFO:** I'm not alone. There's
two of us.
Go to Momus and get a table.
We'll be there soon.

**MARCELLO, SCHAUNARD AND COLLINE:** Momus, Momus,
Momus.
Quietly, discreetly, we're off.
Momus, Momus.
He's found his poem at last.
(*Turning, Rodolfo sees Mimì wrapped in a halo of moonlight. He contemplates her, in ecstasy.*)

**RODOLFO:** O soave fanciulla, o dolce viso,
di mite circonfuso alba lunar,
in te ravviso il sogno
ch'io vorrei sempre sognar!

**MIMÌ:** (Ah, tu sol comandi, amor!)

**RODOLFO:** Fremon già nell'anima
le dolcezze estreme.

**MIMÌ:** (Tu sol comandi, amore!)

**RODOLFO:** Fremon nell'anima
dolcezze estreme, ecc.
Nel bacio freme amor!

**MIMÌ:** (Oh! come dolci scendono
le sue lusinghe al core . . .
Tu sol comandi, amor!)
(*Rodolfo la bacia.*)
No, per pietà!

**RODOLFO:** Sei mia!

**MIMÌ:** V'aspettan gli amici . . .

**RODOLFO:** Già mi mandi via?

**MIMÌ:** Vorrei dir . . . ma non oso.

**RODOLFO:** Di'.

**MIMÌ:** Se venissi con voi?

**RODOLFO:** Che? Mimì!
Sarebbe così dolce restar qui.
C'è freddo fuori.

**MIMÌ:** Vi starò vicina!

**RODOLFO:** E al ritorno?

**MIMÌ:** Curioso!

**RODOLFO:** Dammi il braccio, o
mia piccina . . .

**MIMÌ:** Obbedisco, signor!

**RODOLFO:** Che m'ami . . . di' . . .

**MIMÌ:** Io t'amo.

**RODOLFO E MIMÌ:** (*mentre escono*) Amor! Amor! Amor!

**RODOLFO:** Oh! lovely girl! Oh,
sweet face
bathed in the soft moonlight.
I see in you the dream
I'd dream forever!

**MIMÌ:** (Ah! Love, you rule alone!)

**RODOLFO:** Already I taste in spirit
the heights of tenderness!

**MIMÌ:** (You rule alone, o Love!)

**RODOLFO:** Already I taste in spirit
the heights of tenderness!
Love trembles in our kiss!

**MIMÌ:** (How sweet his praises
enter my heart . . .
Love, you alone rule!)
(*Rodolfo kisses her.*)
No, please!

**RODOLFO:** You're mine!

**MIMÌ:** Your friends are waiting.

**RODOLFO:** You send me away already?

**MIMÌ:** I daren't say what I'd
like . . .

**RODOLFO:** Tell me.

**MIMÌ:** If I came with you?

**RODOLFO:** What? Mimì!
It would be so fine to stay here.
Outside it's cold.

**MIMÌ:** I'd be near you!

**RODOLFO:** And when we come
back?

**MIMÌ:** Who knows?

**RODOLFO:** Give me your arm, my
dear . . .

**MIMÌ:** Your servant, sir . . .

**RODOLFO:** Tell me you love me!

**MIMÌ:** I love you.

**RODOLFO AND MIMÌ:** (*as they go out*) Beloved! My love! My love!

# ■ ATTO SECONDO

*Al Quartiere Latino
(Un piazzale con botteghe di ogni genere. Da un lato il Caffè Momus. Nella folla si aggirano Rodolfo e Mimì. Colline presso alla bottega di una rappezzatrice. Schaunard sta comprando una pipa e un corno. Marcello è spinto qua e là della gran folla. È sera. La Vigilia di Natale.)*

**I VENDITORI:** Aranci, datteri!
Caldi i marroni.
Ninnoli, croci.
Torroni e caramelle.
Fiori alle belle.
Oh! la crostata.
Panna montata.
Fringuelli, passeri.
Datteri! Trote!
Latte di cocco! Giubbe!
Carote!

**LA FOLLA:** Quanta folla! Che chiasso!
Stringiti a me, corriamo.
Lisa! Emma!

# ■ ACT II

*In the Latin Quarter
(A square with shops of all kinds. On one side is the Café Momus. Mimì and Rodolfo move about with the crowd. Colline is nearby at a rag-woman's stand. Schaunard is buying a pipe and a trumpet. Marcello is pushed here and there by the throng. It is evening. Christmas Eve.)*

**HAWKERS:** Oranges, dates!
Hot roasted chestnuts!
Crosses, knick-knacks!
Cookies and candies!
Flowers for the ladies!
Pies for sale!
With whipped cream!
Finches and larks!
Dates! Fresh fish!
Coconut milk! Skirts!
Carrots!

**THE CROWD:** What a throng! Such
noise!
Hold tight! Let's run!
Lisa! Emma!

Date il passo.
Emma, quando ti chiamo!
Ancora un altro giro . . .
Pigliam via Mazzarino.
Qui mi manca il respiro!
Vedi? Il Caffè è vicino.
Oh! Stupendi gioielli!
Son gli occhi assai più belli!
Pericolosi esempi
la folla oggi ci dà!
Era meglio ai miei tempi!
Viva la libertà!

**AL CAFFÈ:** Andiam. Qua, camerier!
Presto. Corri.
Vien qua. A me.
Birra! Un bicchier!
Vaniglia. Ratafià.
Dunque? Presto!
Da ber! Un caffè . . .
Presto. Olà . . .

**SCHAUNARD:** (*soffiando nel corno e cavandone note strane*) Falso questo Re!
Pipa e corno quant'è?

**COLLINE:** (*dalla rappezzatrice che gli sta cucendo un zimarrone usato che egli ha appena comprato*) È un poco usato . . .

**RODOLFO:** Andiam.

**MIMÌ:** Andiam per la cuffietta?

**COLLINE:** Ma è serio e a buon mercato . . .

**RODOLFO:** Tienti al mio braccio stretta . . .

**MIMÌ:** A te mi stringo.

**MIMÌ, RODOLFO:** Andiam!
(*Entrano dalla modista.*)

**MARCELLO:** Io pur mi sento in vena di gridar:
Chi cuol, donnine allegre, un po' d'amor?

**VENDITORI:** Datteri! Trote!
Prugne di Tours!

**MARCELLO:** Facciamo insieme a vendere e comprar:
Io do ad un soldo il vergine mio cuor.

**SCHAUNARD:** Fra spintoni e pestate accorrendo,
affretta la folla e si diletta
nel provar voglie matte—
insoddisfatte.

**VENDITORI:** Ninnoli, spillette! ecc.

**COLLINE:** (*mostrando un libro*) Copia rara, anzi unica:
la grammatica Runica.

**SCHAUNARD:** (Uomo onesto!)

**MARCELLO:** A cena!

**SCHAUNARD E COLLINE:** Rodolfo?

**MARCELLO:** Entrò da una modista.
(*Rodolfo e Mimì escono dalla bottega.*)

---

Make way there!
Emma. I'm calling you!
Once more around . . .
We'll take Rue Mazarin .
I can't breathe here . . .
See? The café's right here.
What wonderful jewels!
Your eyes are more wonderful!
This crowd tonight
sets a dangerous example!
Things were better in my day!
Long live freedom!

**AT THE CAFÉ:** Let's go, Here, waiter!
Hurry. On the run.
Come here. My turn.
Beer! A glass!
Vanilla. Liqueur!
Well? Hurry.
Drinks! Coffee . . .
Quickly. Hey, there . . .

**SCHAUNARD:** (*blowing on the trumpet, producing odd sounds*) This D is out of tune.
How much for the horn and pipe?

**COLLINE:** (*at the rag-woman's, who is sewing up an enormous overcoat he has just bought*) It's a little worn . . .

**RODOLFO:** Let's go.

**MIMÌ:** Are we going to buy the bonnet?

**COLLINE:** . . . But it's cheap and dignified.

**RODOLFO:** Hold tight to my arm.

**MIMÌ:** I'll hold you tight.

**MIMÌ, RODOLFO:** Let's go!
(*They go into the milliner's.*)

**MARCELLO:** I, too, feel like shouting:
which of you happy girls wants love?

**HAWKERS:** Dates! Trout! Plums from Tours!

**MARCELLO:** Let us make a bargain together—
for a penny I'll sell my virgin heart.

**SCHAUNARD:** Pushing and shoving and running,
the crowd hastens to its joys,
feeling insane desires—
unappeased.

**HAWKERS:** Trinkets! Brooches! etc.

**COLLINE:** (*showing a book*) A rare find, truly unique:
a Runic grammar.

**SCHAUNARD:** (What an honest fellow!)

**MARCELLO:** Let's eat!

**SCHAUNARD AND COLLINE:** And Rodolfo?

**MARCELLO:** He went into the milliner's.
(*Rodolfo and Mimì come out of the shop.*)

---

**RODOLFO:** Viene, gli amici aspettano.

**MIMÌ:** Mi sta ben questa cuffietta rosa?

**VENDITORI:** Panna montata! Latte di cocco!
Oh! la crostata! Panna montata!

**AL CAFFÈ:** Camerier! Un bicchier!
Presto. Olà . . .
Ratafia.

**RODOLFO:** Sei bruna
e quel color ti dona.

**MIMÌ:** (*guardando verso la bottega*) Bel vezzo di corallo.

**RODOLFO:** Ho uno zio milionario.
Se fa senno il buon Dio
voglio comprarti un vezzo
assai più bel! . . .

**MONELLI, SARTINE, STUDENTI:** Ah! ah! ah! ah! ecc.

**BORGHESI:** Facciam coda alla gente!
Ragazze, state attente!
Che chiasso! Quanta folla!
Pigliam via Mazzarino!
Io soffoco, partiamo!
Vedi il caffè è vicin!
Andiam là, da Momus!
Ah!

**VENDITORI:** Oh! la crostata! Panna montata!
Fiori alle belle!
Ninnoli, datteri, caldi i marron!
Fringuelli, passeri,
panna, torron!

**RODOLFO:** Chi guardi?

**COLLINE:** Odio il profano volgo al par d'Orazio.

**MIMÌ:** Sei geloso?

**RODOLFO:** All'uom felice sta il sospetto
accanto.

**SCHAUNARD:** Ed io quando mi sazio
vo' abbondanza di spazio.

**MIMÌ:** Sei felice?

**MARCELLO:** (*al cameriere*) Vogliamo una cena prelibata.

**RODOLFO:** Ah, sì. Tanto.

**MARCELLO:** Lesto.

**SCHAUNARD:** Per molti.

**RODOLFO:** E tu?

**MIMÌ:** Sì, tanto.
(*Marcello, Schaunard, e Colline si seggono ad una tavola davanti al caffè.*)

**STUDENTI:** Là, da Momus!

**SARTINE:** Andiam! Andiam!

**MARCELLO, COLLINE, SCHAUNARD:** Lesto.

**VOCE DI PARPIGNOL:** (*in lontananza*) Ecco i giocattoli di Parpignol!

---

**RODOLFO:** Come, my friends are waiting.

**MIMÌ:** Is my pink bonnet becoming?

**HAWKERS:** Whipped cream! Coconut milk!
Pies! Whipped cream!

**CAFÉ CUSTOMERS:** Waiter! A glass!
Quick. Hey there . . .
Liqueur.

**RODOLFO:** You're dark,
that color suits you.

**MIMÌ:** (*looking back at the shop*) That lovely coral necklace.

**RODOLFO:** I've a millionaire uncle.
If God acts wisely,
I'll buy you a necklace
much more beautiful . . .

**URCHINS, MIDINETTES, STUDENTS:** Ah! ah! ah! etc.

**TOWNSPEOPLE:** Let's follow these people!
Girls, watch out!
Such noise! What a throng!
We'll take the Rue Mazarin!
I'm stifling, let's go!
See, the cafe's right here!
Let's go there, to Momus!
Ah!

**HAWKERS:** Pies for sale! Whipped cream!
Flowers for the ladies!
Knick-Knacks, dates, hot roasted chestnuts.
Finches, larks!
Cream cakes!

**RODOLFO:** Whom are you looking at?

**COLLINE:** I hate the vulgar herd as Horace did.

**MIMÌ:** Are you jealous?

**RODOLFO:** The man who's happy must be
suspicious too.

**SCHAUNARD:** And when I'm stuffing myself
I want plenty of room about me.

**MIMÌ:** Are you happy then?

**MARCELLO:** (*to the waiter*) We want a prize dinner.

**RODOLFO:** Oh yes. Very.

**MARCELLO:** Quickly.

**SCHAUNARD:** And bring plenty.

**RODOLFO:** And you?

**MIMÌ:** Very.
(*Marcello, Schaunard and Colline sit at a table in front of the cafe.*)

**STUDENTS:** There, to Momus!

**MIDINETTES:** Let's go! Let's go!

**MARCELLO, COLLINE, SCHAUNARD:** Quickly!

**VOICE OF PARPIGNOL:** (*in the distance*) Here are the toys of Parpignol!

**RODOLFO:** Due posti!

**COLLINE:** Finalmente, eccoci qui!

**RODOLFO:** Questa è Mimì, gaia fioraia.
Il suo venir completa
la bella compagnia.
Perchè . . . perchè son io il poeta;
essa la poesia.
Dal mio cervel sbocciano i canti,
dalle sue dita sbocciano i fior—
dall'anime esultanti
sboccia l'amor.

**MARCELLO:** Dio che concetti rari!

**COLLINE:** *Digna est intrari.*

**SCHAUNARD:** *Ingrediat si necessit.*

**COLLINE:** Io non do che un *accessit.*

**VOCE DI PARPIGNOL:** (*più vicino*) Ecco i giocattoli di Parpignol!

**COLLINE:** Salame . . .
(*Arriva nel piazzale Parpignol, spingendo un carretto tutto a fronzoli e fiori.*)

**RAGAZZI E BAMBINE:** Parpignol!
Parpignol! Parpignol! . . .
Ecco Parpignol! Parpignol!
Col carretto tutto fior!
Ecco Parpignol!
Voglio la tromba, il cavallin!
Il tambur, tamburel . . .
voglio il cannon, voglio il frustin,
dei soldati i drappel.

**SCHAUNARD:** Cervo arrosto.

**MARCELLO:** Un tacchineo.

**SCHAUNARD:** Vin del Reno!

**COLLINE:** Vin da tavola!

**SCHAUNARD:** Aragosta senza crosta!

**MAMME:** Ah! che razza di furfanti indemoniati,
ché ci venite a fare in questo loco?
A casa, a letto! Via, brutti sguaiati,
gli scappellotti vi parranno poco!
A casa! A letto,
razza di furfanti, a letto!

**UN RAGAZZO:** Vo' la tromba, il cavallin . . .

**RODOLFO:** E tu Mimì, che vuoi?

**MIMÌ:** La crema.

**SCHAUNARD:** E gran sfarzo.
C'è una dama.

**RAGAZZI E BAMBINE:** Viva Parpignol!
Il tambur, tamburel . . .
Dei soldati il drappel.
(*Escono, seguendo il carretto di Parpignol.*)

**MARCELLO:** Signorina Mimì, che dono raro
le ha fatto il suo Rodolfo?

**RODOLFO:** Two places.

**COLLINE:** Here they are at last!

**RODOLFO:** This is Mimì, happy flower-girl.
Her presence alone
makes our company complete.
For . . . for I am a poet;
and she is poetry itself.
As songs flow from my brain,
the flowers bloom in her hands,
and in joyful spirits
love blossoms also.

**MARCELLO:** What rare imagery!

**COLLINE:** *Digna est intrari*

**SCHAUNARD:** *Ingrediat si necessit.*

**COLLINE:** I grant only one *accessit.*

**VOICE OF PARPIGNOL:** (*closer*) Here are the toys of Parpignol!

**COLLINE:** Salami . . .
(*Parpignol arrives in the square, pushing a barrow covered with frills and flowers.*)

**CHILDREN:** Parpignol! Parpignol!
Parpignol!
Here is Parpignol!
With his cart all decked with flowers!
Here is Parpignol!
I want the horn, the toy horse!
The drum! The tambourine!
I want the cannon; I want the whip,
I want the troop of soldiers.

**SCHAUNARD:** Roast venison.

**MARCELLO:** A turkey.

**SCHAUNARD:** Rhine wine!

**COLLINE:** Table wine!

**SCHAUNARD:** Shelled lobster!

**MOTHERS:** What a bunch of naughty rascals!
What are you doing here now?
Go home to bed, you noisy things.
Slaps will be the least you'll get . . .
go home to bed,
you bunch of rascals, to bed!

**A BOY:** I want the horn, the toy horse . . .

**RODOLFO:** What will you have, Mimì?

**MIMÌ:** Some custard.

**SCHAUNARD:** The best.
A lady's with us.

**CHILDREN:** Bravo Parpignol!
The drums! The tambourine!
A troop of soldiers!
(*They run off, following Parpignol.*)

**MARCELLO:** Tell me, Mimì, what rare gift
Rodolfo has given you?

**MIMÌ:** Una cuffietta a pizzi tutta rosa
ricamata. Coi miei capelli bruni
ben si fonde.
Da tanto tempo tal cuffietta
è cosa desiata . . . ed egli ha letto
quel che il core asconde . . .
Ora colui che legge dentro a un core
sa l'amore . . . ed è lettore.

**SCHAUNARD:** Esperto professore . . .

**COLLINE:** Che ha già diplomi e
non son armi prime le sue rime . . .

**SCHAUNARD:** Tanto che sembra
ver ciò che egli esprime!

**MARCELLO:** O bella età d'inganni e d'utopie!
Si crede, spera, e tutto
bello appare.

**RODOLFO:** La più divina delle poesie
è quella, amico, che c'insegna ad amare!

**MIMÌ:** Amare è dolce ancora più del miele!

**MARCELLO:** Secondo il palato è miele o fiele!

**MIMÌ:** O Dio, l'ho offeso!

**RODOLFO:** È in lutto, o mia Mimì.

**SCHAUNARD E COLLINE:** Allegri!
e un toast.

**MARCELLO:** Qua del liquor!

**TUTTI:** E via i pensier,
alti i bicchier. Beviam.

**MARCELLO:** (*vedendo Musetta che entra, ridendo*) Ch'io beva del tossico!

**SCHAUNARD, COLLINE E RODOLFO:** Oh! Musetta!

**MARCELLO:** Essa!

**LE BOTTEGAIE:** To'! Lei! Sì! To'! Lei!
Musetta!
Siamo in auge! Che toeletta!
(*Musetta si ferma, accompagnata dal vecchio, pomposo Alcindoro. Musetta prende posto ad un'altra tavola del Momus.*)

**ALCINDORO:** Come un facchino
correr di qua . . . di là . . .
No, no, non ci sta . . .

**MUSETTA:** (*chiamando Alcindoro come si chiama un cane*) Vien, Lulù!

**ALCINDORO:** Non ne posso più.

**MUSETTA:** Vien, Lulù.

**SCHAUNARD:** Quel brutto coso
mi par che sudi!

**ALCINDORO:** Come? qui fuori? qui?

**MUSETTA:** Siedi, Lulù.

**MIMÌ:** An embroidered pink bonnet, all
with lace. It goes well
with my dark hair.
I've longed for such a bonnet
for months . . . and he read
what was hidden in my heart . . .
Anyone who can read the heart's secret
knows love . . . he's such a reader.

**SCHAUNARD:** He's a professor in the subject.

**COLLINE:** With diplomas, and his verses
are not a beginner's . . .

**SCHAUNARD:** That's why what he says
seems to be true!

**MARCELLO:** Oh, sweet age of false utopias!
You hope and believe, and all seems beautiful.

**RODOLFO:** The poem most divine, my friend,
is what teaches us to love!

**MIMÌ:** Love is sweet, sweeter than honey.

**MARCELLO:** That depends: it's honey or gall!

**MIMÌ:** Heavens! I've offended him!

**RODOLFO:** He's mourning, Mimì!

**SCHAUNARD AND COLLINE:** Cheer up! A toast!

**MARCELLO:** Something to drink!

**ALL:** Away with brooding,
raise your glass. We'll drink.

**MARCELLO:** (*seeing Musetta enter, laughing*) I'll drink some poison!

**SCHAUNARD, COLLINE AND RODOLFO:** Oh! Musetta!

**MARCELLO:** Her!

**THE SHOPWOMEN:** What! Her!
Yes! Well! Her!
Musetta!
She's made it. What a dress!
(*Musetta stops, accompanied by the old and pompous Alcindoro. She sits at another table in front of the café.*)

**ALCINDORO:** Running like a porter
back and forth . . .
No, it's not proper.

**MUSETTA:** (*calling Alcindoro as if he were a dog*) Here, Lulu!

**ALCINDORO:** I can't take any more.

**MUSETTA:** Come, Lulu.

**SCHAUNARD:** That ugly old fool
all in a lather!

**ALCINDORO:** What? Outside? Here?

**MUSETTA:** Sit, Lulu.

# Act II

**ALCINDORO:** Tali nomignoli, prego, serbateli al tu per tu.

**ALCINDORO:** Please, save these little nicknames of yours for when we're alone.

**MUSETTA:** Non farmi il Barbablù!

**MUSETTA:** Don't act like Bluebeard!

**COLLINE:** È il vizio contegnoso!

**COLLINE:** He's evil behind that front!

**MARCELLO:** Colla casta Susanna.

**MARCELLO:** With the chaste Susanna.

**MIMÌ:** Essa è pur ben vestita.

**MIMÌ:** But she's beautifully dressed.

**RODOLFO:** Gil angeli vanno nudi.

**RODOLFO:** Angels go naked.

**MIMÌ:** La conosci? Chi è?

**MIMÌ:** You know her? Who is she?

**MARCELLO:** Domandatelo a me. Il suo nome è Musetta . . . Cognome—Tentazione! Per sua vocazione fa la rosa dei venti; gira e muta soventi d'amanti e d'amore . . . E come la civetta è uccello sanguinario; il suo cibo ordinario è il cuore . . . mangia il cuore! Per questo io non ne ho più.

**MARCELLO:** Ask me that question. Her first name's Musetta. Her last name's Temptation. Her occupation is being a leaf in the wind. Always turning, changing her lovers and her loves . . . Like the screech-owl she's a bird of prey. Her favorite food is the heart . . . she devours them! And so I have no heart.

**MUSETTA:** (Marcello è là . . . mi vide . . . E non mi guarda il vile! Quel Schaunard che ride! Mi fan tutti una bile! Se potessi picchiar, se potessi graffiar! Ma non ho sotto man che questo pellican. Aspetta!) Ehi! Camerier!

**MUSETTA:** (Marcello's there . . . he saw me . . . But the coward won't look at me. And that Schaunard's laughing! They all make me livid! If I could just hit them! Scratch their eyes out! But I've got this old pelican on my hands. Just wait!) Waiter!

**MARCELLO:** (*nascondendo la commozione*) Passatemi il ragù.

**MARCELLO:** (*hiding his emotion*) Pass me the stew.

**MUSETTA:** Ehi! Camerier! questo piatto ha una puzza di rifritto! (*Getta il ipatto a terra.*)

**MUSETTA:** Hey! Waiter! This plate smells dirty to me! (*throwing the plate on the ground*)

**ALCINDORO:** No, Musetta, zitto, zitto!

**ALCINDORO:** No, Musetta! Quiet, now!

**MUSETTA:** (Non si volta.)

**MUSETTA:** (He won't look.)

**ALCINDORO:** Zitto. Zitto. Modi. Garbo.

**ALCINDORO:** Quiet, now. Manners! Please!

**MUSETTA:** (Ah! Non si volta.)

**MUSETTA:** (He won't look.)

**ALCINDORO:** A chi parli?

**ALCINDORO:** To whom are you speaking?

**COLLINE:** Questo pollo è un poema!

**COLLINE:** This chicken is a poem!

**MUSETTA:** (Ora lo batto, lo batto!)

**MUSETTA:** (Now I'll hit him, I'll hit him!)

**ALCINDORO:** Con chi parli?

**ALCINDORO:** Who are you talking to?

**MUSETTA:** Al cameriere. Non seccar!

**MUSETTA:** To the waiter. Don't be a bore!

**SCHAUNARD:** Il vino è prelibato!

**SCHAUNARD:** The wine is excellent.

**MUSETTA:** Voglio fare il mio piacere . . .

**MUSETTA:** I want my own way!

**ALCINDORO:** Parla pian!

**ALCINDORO:** Lower your voice!

**MUSETTA:** Vo' far quel che mi pare!

**MUSETTA:** I'll do as I please!

**ALCINDORO:** Parla pian, parla pian!

**ALCINDORO:** Lower your voice!

**MUSETTA:** Non secc-a-a-ar!

**MUSETTA:** Don't be a bore!

**SARTINE E STUDENTI:** Guarda, guarda, chi si vede, proprio lei, Musetta! Con quel vecchio che balbetta, proprio lei, Musetta! Ah! ah! ah! ah!

**MIDINETTES AND STUDENTS:** Look, look who it is, Musetta herself! With that stuttering old man, it's Musetta herself! Ha ha ha ha ha!

**MUSETTA:** (Che sia geloso di questa mummia?)

**MUSETTA:** (But could he be jealous of this mummy?

**ALCINDORO:** La convenienza . . . il grado . . . la virtù!

**ALCINDORO:** Decorum . . . my rank . . . my reputation!

**MUSETTA:** (Vediamo se mi resta tanto poter so lui da farlo cedere.)

**MUSETTA:** (Let's see if I still have enough power over him to make him give in.)

**SCHAUNARD:** La commedia è stupenda!

**SCHAUNARD:** The play is stupendous!

**MUSETTA:** (*guardando Marcello*) Tu non mi guardi.

**MUSETTA:** (*looking at Marcello*) You aren't looking at me.

**ALCINDORO:** Vedi bene che ordino!

**ALCINDORO:** Can't you see I'm ordering?

**SCHAUNARD:** La commedia è stupenda!

**SCHAUNARD:** The play is stupendous!

**COLLINE:** Stupenda!

**COLLINE:** Stupendous!

**RODOLFO:** (*a Mimì*) Sappi per tuo governo che non darei perdono in sempiterno.

**RODOLFO:** (*to Mimì*) Let me tell you now: I'd never be forgiving.

**SCHAUNARD:** Essa all'un parla perchè l'altro intenda.

**SCHAUNARD:** She speaks to one for the other to hear.

**MIMÌ:** (*a Rodolfo*) Io t'amo tanto, e sono tutta tua . . . Che mi parli di perdono?

**MIMÌ:** (*to Rodolfo*) I love you so, and I'm all yours . . . Why speak of forgiveness?

**COLLINE:** (*a Schaunard*) E l'altro invan crudel finge di non capir, ma sugge miel.

**COLLINE:** (*to Schaunard*) And the other, cruel, in vain pretends he is deaf, but enjoys it all.

**MUSETTA:** Ma il tuo cuore martella.

**MUSETTA:** But your heart's like a hammer.

**ALCINDORO:** Parla piano.

**ALCINDORO:** Lower your voice!

**MUSETTA:** Ma il tuo cuore martella.

**MUSETTA:** But your heart's like a hammer.

**ALCINDORO:** Piano, piano!

**ALCINDORO:** Lower your voice.

**MUSETTA:** Quando men' vo soletta per la via, la gente sosta e mira, e la bellezza mia tutta ricerca in me, ricerca in me da capo a piè.

**MUSETTA:** As I walk alone through the streets, the people stop to look and inspect my beauty, examining me from head to toe.

**MARCELLO:** Legatemi alla seggiola!

**MARCELLO:** Tie me to the chair!

**ALCINDORO:** Quella gente che dirà?

**ALCINDORO:** What will people say?

**MUSETTA:** Ed assaporo allor la bramosia sottil che dagli occhi traspira e dai palesi vezzi intender sa alle occulte beltà. Così l'effluvio del desio tutta m'aggira. Felice mi fa, felice me fa.

**MUSETTA:** And then I savor the subtle longing in their eyes when, from my visible charms, they guess at the beauty concealed. This onrush of desire surrounds me. It delights me, it delights me.

**ALCINDORO:** (Quel canto scurrile mi muove la bile!)

**ALCINDORO:** (This scurrilous song infuriates me!)

**MUSETTA:** E tu che sai, che memori e ti struggi,
da me tanto rifuggi?
So ben: le angoscie tue
non le vuoi dir,
ma ti senti morir.

**MIMÌ:** Io vedo ben che quella poveretta
tutta invaghita di Marcello ell'è!

**ALCINDORO:** Quella gente che dirà?

**RODOLFO:** Marcello un dì l'amò . . .

**SCHAUNARD:** Ah! Marcello cederà!

**RODOLFO:** . . . La fraschetta l'abbandonò . . .

**COLLINE:** Chi sa mai quel che avverrà!

**RODOLFO:** . . . per poi darsi a miglior vita.

**SCHAUNARD:** Trovan dolce a pari il laccio
chi lo tende e chi ci dà.

**COLLINE:** Santi numi! in simil briga
mai Colline intopperà!

**MUSETTA:** (Ah! Marcello smania . . .
Marcello è vinto!)

**ALCINDORO:** Parla piano . . . Zitto, zitto!

**MIMÌ:** Quell'infelice mi muove a pietà.

**COLLINE:** Essa è bella—non son cieco . . .

**MIMÌ:** (stringendosi a Rodolfo) T'amo!

**SCHAUNARD:** (Quel bravaccio a momenti cederà!
Stupenda è la commedia!
Marcello cederà.)
(a Colline)
Se una tal vaga persona
ti trattasse a tu per tu,
la tua scienza brontolona
manderesti a Belzebù.

**RODOLFO:** Mimì!
È fiacco amore
quel che le offese vendicar non sa.
Spento amor non risorge, ecc.

**MIMÌ:** Quell'infelice mi muove a pietà.
L'amor ingeneroso è tristo amor!
Quell'infelice, ecc.

**COLLINE:** . . . ma piaccionmi assai più
una pipa e un testo greco.
Essa è bella, non son cieco, ecc.

**ALCINDORO:** Modi, garbo! Zitto, zitto!

**MUSETTA:** So ben: le angoscie tue
non le vuoi dir.
Ah! ma ti senti morir.
(ad Alcindoro)
Io voglio fare il mio piacere,
voglio far quel che mi par.
Non seccar, non seccar, non seccar!

**MUSETTA:** And you know, who remember and suffer
how can you escape?
I know: you won't admit
that you're in torment,
but it's killing you.

**MIMÌ:** I can tell that the poor girl
is head over heels in love with Marcello.

**ALCINDORO:** What will people say?

**RODOLFO:** Marcello loved her once . . .

**SCHAUNARD:** Ah! Marcello will give in!

**RODOLFO:** . . . The flirt ran off . . .

**COLLINE:** Who knows what'll happen!

**RODOLFO:** . . . to find a better life.

**SCHAUNARD:** The snare is equally sweet
to hunter and hunted.

**COLLINE:** Gods above! I'd never land myself
in such a situation!

**MUSETTA:** (Ah, Marcello's going mad!
Marcello is vanquished!)

**ALCINDORO:** Lower your voice! Be quiet!

**MIMÌ:** I feel so sorry for the poor girl.

**COLLINE:** She's lovely—I'm not blind . . .

**MIMÌ:** (nestling close to Rodolfo) I love you!

**SCHAUNARD:** (The braggart is about to yield!
The play is stupendous!
Marcello will give in!)
(to Colline)
If such a pretty creature
stopped and talked to you,
you'd gladly send to the devil
all your bearish philosophy.

**RODOLFO:** Mimì!
Love is weak
when it leaves wrongs unavenged.
Love, once dead, cannot be revived, etc.

**MIMÌ:** I feel so sorry for the poor girl.
Love is sad when it's unforgiving.
I feel so sorry, etc.

**COLLINE:** . . . but I'm much happier
with my pipe and a Greek text.
She's beautiful, I'm not blind, etc.

**ALCINDORO:** Mind your manners! Be quiet!

**MUSETTA:** I know: you won't admit your torment.
Ah! but you feel like dying!
(to Alcindoro)
I'll do as I please,
I'll do as I like,
don't be a bore, a bore, a bore!

(Or convience liberarsi del vecchio.)
(fingendo un dolore)
Ahi!

**ALCINDORO:** Che c'è?

**MUSETTA:** Qual dolore, qual bruciore!

**ALCINDORO:** Dove?

**MUSETTA:** Al piè!

**MARCELLO:** (Gioventù mia, tu non sei morta,
nè di te è morto il sovvenir . . .
Se tu battessi alla mia porta
t'andrebbe il mio core ad aprir!)

**MUSETTA:** Sciogli! slaccia! rompi! straccia!
Te ne imploro.
Laggiù c'è un calzolaio.
Corri presto! ne voglio un altro paio.
Ahi! che fitta, maledetta scarpa stretta!
Or la levo . . . eccola qua.
Corri, va, corri! Presto, va, va!

**MIMÌ:** (Io vedo ben: ell'è invaghita di Marcello.)

**RODOLFO:** (Io vedo ben: la commedia è stupenda!)

**ALCINDORO:** Imprudente!
Quella gente che dirà?
Ma il mio grado!
Vuoi ch'io comprometta?
Aspetta! Musetta! Vo'!
(Corre frettolosamente via.)

**COLLINE E SCHAUNARD:** (La commedia è stupenda!)

**MUSETTA:** Marcello!

**MARCELLO:** Sirena!
(Si abbracciano appassionatamente.)

**SCHAUNARD:** Siamo all'ultima scena!
(Il cameriere porta un conto.)

**TUTTI:** Il conto!

**SCHAUNARD:** Così presto?

**COLLINE:** Chi l'ha richiesto?

**SCHAUNARD:** Vediam.

**COLLINE E RODOLFO:** Caro!
(Si ode avviccinarsi un suon di tamburi.)

**RODOLFO, SCHAUNARD, COLLINE:** Fuori il danaro!

**SCHAUNARD:** Colline, Rodolfo e tu, Marcel?

**RAGAZZI:** La Ritirata!

**MARCELLO:** Siamo all'asciutto!

**SCHAUNARD:** Come?

**SARTINE, STUDENTI:** La Ritirata!

**RODOLFO:** Ho trenta soldi in tutto!

**BORGHESI:** La Ritirata!

**MARCELLO, SCHAUNARD, COLLINE:** Come? Non ce n'è più?

**SCHAUNARD:** Ma il mio tesoro ov'è?

Now to get rid of the old man.)
(pretending a pain)
Ouch!

**ALCINDORO:** What is it?

**MUSETTA:** The pain! The pain!

**ALCINDORO:** Where?

**MUSETTA:** My foot!

**MARCELLO:** (My youth, you're still alive,
your memory's not dead . . .
If you came to my door,
my heart would open it!)

**MUSETTA:** Loosen it! Untie it!
Break it! tear it!
Please!
There's a shoemaker nearby.
Run quickly! I want another pair!
Ah, how it pinches, this damn tight shoe!
I'll take it off . . . here it is.
Run, go on, run! Hurry, hurry!

**MIMÌ:** (I can see she's madly in love with Marcello.)

**RODOLFO:** (I can see: the play's stupendous!)

**ALCINDORO:** How unwise!
What will people say?
My reputation!
Do you want to ruin it?
Wait! Musetta! I'm going!
(He hurries off.)

**COLLINE AND SCHAUNARD:** (The play is stupendous!)

**MUSETTA:** Marcello!

**MARCELLO:** Siren!
(They embrace passionately.)

**SCHAUNARD:** Here's the finale!
(The waiter brings the bill.)

**ALL:** The bill!

**SCHAUNARD:** So soon?

**COLLINE:** Who asked for it?

**SCHAUNARD:** Let's see.

**COLLINE AND RODOLFO:** It's high!
(Drums are heard approaching.)

**RODOLFO, SCHAUNARD, COLLINE:** Out with the money!

**SCHAUNARD:** Colline, Rodolfo and you, Marcello?

**CHILDREN:** The Tattoo!

**MARCELLO:** We're broke!

**SCHAUNARD:** What?

**MIDINETTES, STUDENTS:** The Tattoo!

**RODOLFO:** I've only got thirty sous.

**TOWNSPEOPLE:** The Tattoo!

**MARCELLO, SCHAUNARD, COLLINE:** What? No more money?

**SCHAUNARD:** Where's my wealth?

## Act II

**MONELLI:** S'avvicinan per di qua?

**URCHINS:** Are they coming this way?

**MUSETTA:** (*al cameriere*) Il mio conto date a me.

**MUSETTA:** (*to the waiter*) Give me my bill.

**SARTINE, STUDENTI:** No! Di là!

**MIDINETTES, STUDENTS:** No! That way!

**MONELLI:** S'avvicinan per di là!

**URCHINS:** They're coming that way!

**SARTINE, STUDENTI:** Vien di qua!

**MIDINETTES, STUDENTS:** They're coming this way!

**MONELLI:** No! vien di là!

**URCHINS:** No, that way!

**MUSETTA:** Bene!

**MUSETTA:** Good!

**BORGHESI, VENDITORI:** Largo! largo!

**TOWNSPEOPLE:** Make way! Make way!

**RAGAZZI:** Voglio veder! voglio sentir!

**CHILDREN:** I want to see! I want to hear!

**MUSETTA:** Presto, sommate quello con questo! . . .
Paga il signor che stava qui con me.

**MUSETTA:** Quick, add these two bills together . . .
The gentleman who was with me will pay.

**MAMME:** Lisetta, vuoi tacere? Tonio, la vuoi finire?

**MOTHERS:** Lisetta, please be quiet.
Tonio, stop that at once!

**FANCIULLE:** Mamma, voglio vedere!
Papà, voglio sentire!

**GIRLS:** Mamma, I want to see.
Papa, I want to hear.

**RODOLFO, MARCELLO, SCHAUNARD, COLLINE:** Paga il signor!

**RODOLFO, MARCELLO, SCHAUNARD, COLLINE:** The gentleman will pay!

**RAGAZZI:** Vuò veder la Ritirata!

**CHILDREN:** I want to see the Tattoo!

**MAMME:** Vuoi tacer, la vuoi finir!

**MOTHERS:** Please be quiet! Stop that at once!

**SARTINE:** S'avvicinano di qua!

**MIDINETTES:** They're coming this way!

**BORGHESI:** S'avvicinano di là!

**TOWNSPEOPLE:** They're coming that way!

**BORGHESI, STUDENTI, VENDITORI:** Sì, di qua!

**TOWNSPEOPLE, STUDENTS, HAWKERS:** Yes, this way!

**MONELLI:** Come sarà arrivata, la seguiremo al passo.

**URCHINS:** When it comes by, we'll march with it!

**COLLINE, SCHAUNARD, MARCELLO:** Paga il signor!

**COLLINE, SCHAUNARD, MARCELLO:** The gentleman will pay!

**MUSETTA:** E dove s'è seduto, ritrovi il mio saluto!
(*mettendo il conto sulla sedia*)

**MUSETTA:** And here, at his place, he'll find my farewell!
(*putting the bill on the chair.*)

**BORGHESI:** In quel rulliò tu senti la patria maestà.

**TOWNSPEOPLE:** That drum-roll expresses
our country's glory.

**RODOLFO, COLLINE, SCHAUNARD, MARCELLO:** E dove s'è seduto, ritrovi il suo saluto!

**RODOLFO, COLLINE, SCHAUNARD, MARCELLO:** And here, at this place, he'll find her farewell!

**LA FOLLA:** Largo, largo, eccoli qua!

**THE CROWD:** Make way, make way, here they come!

**MONELLI:** Ohè! attenti, eccoli qua!

**URCHINS:** Hey! Look out, here they are!

**MARCELLO:** Giunge la Ritirata!

**MARCELLO:** Now the Guard is coming!

**LA FOLLA:** In fila!

**THE CROWD:** All in line!

**COLLINE, MARCELLO:** Che il vecchio non ci veda
fuggir colla sua preda.

**COLLINE, MARCELLO:** Don't let the old fool see us
make off with his prize.

**RODOLFO:** Giunge la Ritirata!

**RODOLFO:** The Guard is coming!

**MARCELLO, SCHAUNARD, COLLINE:** Quella folla serrata il nascondiglio appresti!

**MARCELLO, SCHAUNARD, COLLINE:** That crowded throng will be our hiding-place.

**LA FOLLA:** Ecco il tambur maggiore, più fiero d'un antico guerriero! Il tambur maggior!

**THE CROWD:** Here's the drum-major! Prouder than an ancient warrior! The drum-major!

**MIMÌ, MUSETTA, RODOLFO, MARCELLO, SCHAUNARD, COLLINE:** Lesti! lesti! lesti!

**MIMÌ, MUSETTA, RODOLFO, MARCELLO, SCHAUNARD, COLLINE:** Hurry! Let's run off!

**LA FOLLA:** I Zappatori! i Zappatori, olà!
Ecco il tambur maggior!
Pare un general!
La Ritirata è qua!
Eccola là! Il bel tambur maggior!
La canna d'or, tutto splendor!
Che guarda, passa, va!

**THE CROWD:** The Sappers! The Sappers, hooray!
Here's the drum-major!
Like a general!
The Tattoo is here!
Here he is, the handsome drum-major!
The golden baton, all a-glitter!
See, he looks at us as he goes past!

**RODOLFO, MARCELLO, SCHAUNARD, COLLINE:** Viva Musetta! Cuor biricchin!
Gloria ed onor, onor e gloria del Quartier Latin!

**RODOLFO, MARCELLO, SCHAUNARD, COLLINE:** Bravo Musetta! Artful minx!
Glory and honor, the glory and honor
of the Latin Quarter!

**LA FOLLA:** Tutto splendor!
Di Francia è il più bell'uom!
Il bel tambur maggior!
Eccola là! Che guarda, passa, va!
(*Musetta non potendo camminare con una scarpa sola, è alzata a braccia di Marcello e Colline. Tutti si mettono in coda alla ritirata e si allontanano. Alcindoro torna con un paio di scarpe; il cameriere gli presenta i conti. Vedendo la somma e non trovando più nessuno, Alcindoro cade su di una sedia, stupefatto.*)

**THE CROWD:** All a-glitter!
The handsomest man in France, the drum-major!
Here he is! See, he looks at us as he goes past!
(*Since Musetta cannot walk with only one shoe, Marcello and Colline carry her on their shoulders. They all follow the guards and disappear. Alcindoro comes back with a new pair of shoes, and the waiter hands him the bill. When he sees the amount and sees nobody around, Alcindoro falls, bewildered, onto a chair.*)

## ■ ATTO TERZO

*La Barriera d'Enfer*
(*Al di là della barriera il boulevard esterno, a sinistra un cabaret e un piccolo largo costeggiato da alcuni platani. Certi doganieri dormono avanti ad un braciere. Dal cabaret, ad intervalli, grida, risate. È un'alba di febbraio. La neve è dappertutto. Dietro la cancellata chiusa, battendo i piedi dal freddo stanno alcuni spazzini.*)

**SPAZZINI:** Ohè, là, le guardie . . . Aprite!
Quelli di Gentilly! Siam gli spazzini.
Fiocca la neve. Ohè, là! Qui s'agghiaccia!

**UN DOGANIERE:** (*sbadigliando*) Vengo.

**VOCI DAL CABARET:** Chi nel ber trovò il piacer
nel suo bicchier,
d'una bocca nell'ardor
trovò l'amor.

## ■ ACT III

*The Barrière d'Enfer*
(*Beyond the tollgate is the main highway. At left, a tavern. A small square flanked by plane trees. Some customs officers are asleep around a brazier. Shouts and laughter issue from the cabaret. Dawn. February. The snow is everywhere. Some street-sweepers are beyond the gate, stamping their feet in the cold.*)

**SWEEPERS:** Hey, there! Guards! Open up!
We're the sweepers from Gentilly.
It's snowing. Hey! We're freezing here.

**CUSTOMS OFFICER:** (*yawning*) I'm coming.

**VOICES FROM THE TAVERN:**
Some find pleasure
in their cups.
On ardent lips
some find love.

VOCE DI MUSETTA: Ah! Se nel bicchier sta il piacer,
in giovin bocca sta l'amor.

VOCI DAL CABARET: Trallerallè
Eva e Noè.

VOCI DAL BOULEVARD: Hopp-là! Hopp-là!

DOGANIERE: Son già le lattivendole!
(*Egli apre il cancello. Una fila di carretti con contadini entra assieme alle lattaie.*)

LE LATTIVENDOLE: Buon giorno!

LE CONTADINE: Burro e cacio!
Polli ed ova!
Voi da che parte andate?
A San Michele.
Ci troverem più tardi?
A mezzodì.
(*Si allontanano. Entra Mimì. Appena giunta al primo platano la coglie un accesso di tosse. Poi riavutasi dice al sergente:*)

MIMÌ: Sa dirmi, scusi, qual è l'osteria dove un pittor lavora?

SERGENTE: Eccola.

MIMÌ: Grazie.
(*Esce la fantesca dal cabaret. Mimì le si avvicina.*)
A buona donna, mi fate il favore di cercarmi il pittore
Marcello? Ho da parlargli.
Ho tanta fretta.
Ditegli, piano, che Mimì l'aspetta.

SERGENTE: (*ad uno che passa*)
Ehi, quel paniere!

DOGANIERE: Vuoto!

SERGENTE: Passi.
(*Marcello esce dal cabaret.*)

MARCELLO: Mimì?!

MIMÌ: Speravo di trovarvi qui.

MARCELLO: È ver, siam qui da un mese
di quell'oste alle spese.
Musetta insegna il canto
ai passeggieri.
Io pingo quei guerrieri
sulla facciata.
È freddo. Entrate.

MIMÌ: C'è Rodolfo?

MARCELLO: Sì.

MIMÌ: Non posso entrar. No! No!

MARCELLO: Perchè?

MIMÌ: O buon Marcello, aiuto! Aiuto!

MARCELLO: Cos'è avvenuto?

MIMÌ: Rodolfo m'ama e mi fugge.
Rodolfo si strugge per gelosia.
Un passo, un detto, un vezzo,
un fior lo mettono in sospetto . . .
Onde corucci ed ire.
Talor la notte fingo di dormire
e in me lo sento fisso

spiarmi i sogni in viso.
Mi grida ad ogni istante:
non fai per me, ti prendi
un altro amante,
non fai per me. Ahimè!
In lui parla il rovello, lo so;
ma che rispondergli, Marcello?

MARCELLO: Quando s'è come voi non si vive in compagnia.

MIMÌ: Dite bene. Lasciarci conviene.
Aiutateci, aiutateci voi.
Noi s'è provato
più volte, ma invano.

MARCELLO: Son lieve a Musetta,
ella è lieve a me,
perchè ci amiamo in allegria.
Canti e risa, ecco il fior
d'invariabile amor!

MIMÌ: Dite bene, dite bene.
Lasciarci conviene.
Fate voi per il meglio.

MARCELLO: Sta ben. Ora lo sveglio.

MIMÌ: Dorme?

MARCELLO: È piombato qui
un'ora avanti l'alba.
S'assopì sopra una panca.
Guardate.
(*Mimì tossisce.*)
Che tosse!

MIMÌ: Da ieri ho l'ossa rotte.
Fuggì da me stanotte
dicendomi: è finita.
A giorno sono uscita
e me ne venni a questa volta.

MARCELLO: (*osservando Rodolfo nell'interno*) Si desta . . . s'alza.
Mi cerca. Viene.

MIMÌ: Ch'ei non mi veda.

MARCELLO: Or rincasate, Mimì.
Per carità, non fate scene qua!
(*Mimì si nasconde dietro un platano. Rodolfo accorre dal cabaret.*)

RODOLFO: Marcello. Finalmente.
Qui niun ci sente.
Io voglio separarmi da Mimì.

MARCELLO: Sei volubil così?

RODOLFO: Già un'altra volta credetti
morto il mio cor.
Ma di quegli occhi azzurri
allo splendor esso è risorto.
Ora il tedio l'assale . . .

MARCELLO: E gli vuoi rinnovare il funeral?

RODOLFO: Per sempre!

---

VOICE OF MUSETTA: Ah! Pleasure is in the glass!
Love lies on your lips.

VOICES FROM THE TAVERN: Tra la la la
Eve and Noah.

VOICES FROM THE HIGHWAY: Houp-la! Giddap!

CUSTOMS OFFICER: Here come the milkmaids!
(*He opens the gate. The milkmaids enter together with a string of peasants' carts.*)

MILKMAIDS: Good morning!

PEASANT WOMEN: Butter and cheese!
Chickens and eggs!
Which way are you going?
To Saint Michel!
Shall we meet later?
Yes, at noon.
(*They go off. Enter Mimì. When she reaches the first tree, she has a fit of coughing. Then recovering herself, she says to the sergeant:*)

MIMÌ: Excuse me, where's the tavern
where a painter is working?

SERGEANT: There it is.

MIMÌ: Thank you.
(*A waitress comes out of the tavern. Mimì approaches her.*)
Oh, good woman, please . . .
Be good enough to find me
Marcello, the painter.
I must see him quickly.
Tell him Mimì's waiting.

SERGEANT: (*to someone coming in*) Hey! that basket!

CUSTOMS OFFICER: Empty!

SERGEANT: Let him through.
(*Marcello comes out of the tavern.*)

MARCELLO: Mimì?

MIMÌ: I hoped I'd find you here.

MARCELLO: That's right. We've been here
a month, at the host's expense.
Musetta teaches
the guests singing.
And I paint those warriors
by the door there.
It's cold. Come inside.

MIMÌ: Is Rodolfo there?

MARCELLO: Yes.

MIMÌ: I can't go in. No, no!

MARCELLO: Why not?

MIMÌ: Oh! help me, good Marcello!
Help me!

MARCELLO: What's happened?

MIMÌ: Rodolfo—he loves me
but flees from me, torn
by jealousy. A glance, a gesture,
a smile, a flower arouses
his suspicions, then anger,
rage . . .
Sometimes at night I pretend

to sleep, and I feel his eyes
trying to spy on my dreams.
He shouts at me all the time:
"You're not for me.
Find another.
You're not for me." Alas!
I know it's his jealousy speaking,
but what can I answer, Marcello?

MARCELLO: When two people are like you two,
they can't live together.

MIMÌ: You're right. We should separate.
Help us, Marcello, help us.
We've tried
again and again, but in vain.

MARCELLO: I take Musetta lightly,
and she behaves like me.
We love light-heartedly.
Laughter and song—that's the secret
of a lasting love.

MIMÌ: You're right, you're right.
We should separate.
Do your best for us.

MARCELLO: All right. I'll wake him up.

MIMÌ: Is he sleeping?

MARCELLO: He stumbled in here
an hour before dawn
and fell asleep on a bench.
Look at him . . .
(*Mimì coughs.*)
What a cough!

MIMÌ: I've been aching all over since
yesterday. He fled during the night,
saying
"It's all over." I set out
at dawn and came here
to find you.

MARCELLO: (*watching Rodolfo through the window*) He's waking up. He's looking
for me . . . Here he comes.

MIMÌ: He mustn't see me.

MARCELLO: Go home now, Mimì.
For God's sake, no scenes here.
(*Mimì hides behind a tree, Rodolfo hastens out of the tavern.*)

RODOLFO: Marcello! At last!
No one can hear us here.
I've got to leave Mimì.

MARCELLO: Are you as fickle as that?

RODOLFO: Already once before I thought
my heart was dead.
But it revived at the gleam
of her blue eyes.
Now boredom assails it . . .

MARCELLO: And you'll bury it again?

RODOLFO: Forever!

MARCELLO: Cambia metro.
Dei pazzi è l'amor tetro
che lacrime distilla.
Se non ride e sfavilla,
l'amore è fiacco e roco.
Tu sei geloso.

RODOLFO: Un poco.

MARCELLO: Collerico, lunatico,
imbevuto di pregiudizi,
noioso, cocciuto!

MIMÌ: (Or lo fa incollerire!
Me poveretta!)

RODOLFO: Mimì è una civetta
che frascheggia con tutti.
Un moscardino di Viscontino
le fa l'occhio di triglia.
Ella sgonnella e scopre la caviglia,
con un far promettente e lusinghier.

MARCELLO: Lo devo dir?
Che non mi sembri sincer.

RODOLFO: Ebbene, no. Non lo
son.
Invan, invan nascondo
la mia vera tortura.
Amo Mimì sovra ogni cosa
al mondo. Io l'amo! Ma ho paura.
Mimì è tanto malata!
Ogni dì più declina.
La povera piccina
è condannata . . .

MARCELLO: Mimì?

MIMÌ: (Che vuol dire?)

RODOLFO: Una terribil tosse
l'esil petto le scuote.
Già le smunte gote
di sangue ha rosse . . .

MARCELLO: Povera Mimì!

MIMÌ: (Ahimè, morire?)

RODOLFO: La mia stanza è una tana
squallida. Il fuoco è spento.
V'entra e l'aggira il vento
di tramontana.
Essa canta e sorride
e il rimorso m'assale.
Me, cagion del fatale
mal che l'uccide.

MARCELLO: Che far dunque?

MIMÌ: (O mia vita! È finita!
Ahimè! morir! ecc.)

RODOLFO: Mimì di serra è fiore.
Povertà l'ha sfiorita,
per richiamarla in vita
non basta amore.

MARCELLO: Poveretta. Povera
Mimì! Povera Mimì!
(Mimì singhiozza e tossisce.)

RODOLFO: Che! Mimì! Tu qui!
M'hai sentito?

MARCELLO: Ella dunque ascoltava.

RODOLFO: Facile alla paura,
per nulla io m'arrovello.
Vien là nel tepore.
(Vuol farla entrare nel cabaret.)

MARCELLO: Change your ways!
Gloomy love is madness
and brews only tears.
If it doesn't laugh and glow
love has no strength or voice.
You're jealous.

RODOLFO: A little.

MARCELLO: You're raving mad,
a mass of suspicions,
a boor, a mule!

MIMÌ: (He'll make him angry.
Poor me!)

RODOLFO: Mimì's just a flirt
toying with them all.
A foppish Viscount eyes her
with longing. She shows him
her ankles, promising,
luring him on.

MARCELLO: Must I tell you?
You aren't being honest.

RODOLFO: All right, then. I'm not.
I try in vain to hide
what really torments me.
I love Mimì more than the world.
I love her! But I'm afraid . . .
Mimì is terribly ill,
weaker every day.
The poor little thing
is doomed . . .

MARCELLO: Mimì?

MIMÌ: (What does he mean?)

RODOLFO: A horrible coughing
racks her fragile chest . . .
Her pale cheeks
are flushed . . .

MARCELLO: Poor Mimì!

MIMÌ: (Am I dying? Alas!)

RODOLFO: My room's like a cave.
The fire has gone out.
The wind, the winter wind
roars through it.
She laughs and sings;
I'm seized with remorse.
I'm the cause of the illness
that's killing her.

MARCELLO: What's to be done?

MIMÌ: (Oh! my life! It's over!
Alas! To die! etc.)

RODOLFO: Mimì's a hothouse
flower,
blighted by poverty.
To bring her back to life
love's not enough.

MARCELLO: Poor thing. Poor
Mimì!
(Mimì sobs and coughs)

RODOLFO: What, Mimì? You here!
You heard me?

MARCELLO: She was listening
then.

RODOLFO: I'm easily frightened,
worked up over nothing.
Come inside where it's warm.
(He tries to lead her inside.)

MIMÌ: No, quel tanfo mi soffoca.
(Dal cabaret s'ode Musetta che
ride.)

RODOLFO: Ah! Mimì!

MARCELLO: È Musetta che ride.
Con chi ride?
Ah la civetta! Imparerai.
(Corre nella taverna.)

MIMÌ: (a Rodolfo) Addio.

RODOLFO: Che! Vai?

MIMÌ: D'onde lieta uscì al tuo grido
d'amore torna sola Mimì.
Al solitario nido
ritorna un'altra volta
a intesser finti fior.
Addio senza rancor.
—Ascolta, ascolta.
Le poche robe aduna che lasciai
sparse. Nel mio cassetto
stan chiusi quel cerchietto
d'or e il libro di preghiere.
Involgi tutto quanto in un
grembiale
e manderò il portiere . . .
—Bada, sotto il guanciale
c'è la cuffietta rosa.
Se vuoi . . . serbarla a ricordo
d'amor.
Addio, senza rancor.

RODOLFO: Dunque è proprio finita.
Te ne vai, la mia piccina?
Addio, sogni d'amor!

MIMÌ: Addio dolce svegliare alla
mattina.

RODOLFO: Addio sognante vita!

MIMÌ: Addio rabuffi e gelosie . . .

RODOLFO: Che un tuo sorriso acqueta.

MIMÌ: Addio sospetti . . .

RODOLFO: Baci.

MIMÌ: Pungenti amarezze . . .

RODOLFO: Ch'io da vero poeta
rimavo con carezze.

RODOLFO E MIMÌ: Soli, l'inverno
è cosa da morire.

MIMÌ: Soli . . .

RODOLFO E MIMÌ: Mentre a primavera
c'è compagno il sol.

MIMÌ: C'è compagno il sol.
(Marcello e Musetta escono,
bisticciando.)

MARCELLO: Che facevi? Che dicevi?
Presso il foco a quel signore?

MUSETTA: Che vuoi dir? Che vuoi
dir?

MIMÌ: Niuno è solo l'april.

MARCELLO: Al mio venire
hai mutato di colore.

MIMÌ: No. It's so close. I'd suffocate.
(Musetta's laughter comes from
inside.)

RODOLFO: Ah, Mimì!

MARCELLO: That's Musetta laughing.
And with whom?
The flirt! I'll teach her.
(Marcello runs into the tavern.)

MIMÌ: (to Rodolfo) Goodbye.

RODOLFO: What? You're going?

MIMÌ: Back to the place I left
at the call of your love,
I'm going back alone
to my lonely nest
to make false flowers.
Goodbye . . . no hard feelings.
But listen.
Please gather up the few things
I've left behind. In the trunk
there's the little bracelet
and my prayer book. Wrap
them . . .
in an apron and I'll send
someone for them . . .
Wait! Under the pillow
there's my pink bonnet.
If you want . . . keep it in memory
of our love. Goodbye, no hard feelings.

RODOLFO: So it's really over.
You're leaving, my little one?
Goodbye to our dreams of love.

MIMÌ: Goodbye to our sweet wakening.

RODOLFO: Goodbye, life in a
dream.

MIMÌ: Goodbye, doubts and jealousies . . .

RODOLFO: That one smile of yours
could dispel.

MIMÌ: Goodbye, suspicions . . .

RODOLFO: Kisses . . .

MIMÌ: Poignant bitterness . . .

RODOLFO: That, like a poet,
I made rhyme with caress.

RODOLFO AND MIMÌ: But when
the spring comes
the sun is our companion.

MIMÌ: The sun is our companion.
(Marcello and Musetta come out,
quarrelling.)

MARCELLO: What were you doing
and saying
by the fire with that man?

MUSETTA: What do you mean?
What do you mean?

MIMÌ: Nobody's lonely in April.

MARCELLO: When I came in
you blushed suddenly.

MUSETTA: Quel signore mi deceva . . .
"Ama il balla, signorina?"

RODOLFO: Si parla coi gigli e le rose.

MIMÌ: Esce dai nidi un cinguettìo gentile.

MARCELLO: Vana, frivola civetta!

MUSETTA: Arrossendo io rispondevo:
"Ballerei sera e mattina."

MARCELLO: Quel discorso asconde mire
disoneste.

MUSETTA: Voglio piena libertà.

MARCELLO: Io t'acconcio per le feste . . .

RODOLFO E MIMÌ: Al fiorir di primavera
c'è compagno il sol.

MUSETTA: Che me canti?
Che mi gridi? Che mi canti?
All'altar non siamo uniti.

MARCELLO: . . . Se ti colgo a invicettire!
Bada, sotto il mio cappello
non ci stan certi ornamenti.

MUSETTA: Io detesto quegli amanti
che la fanno da mariti.

RODOLFO E MIMÌ: Chiacchieran le fontane,
la brezza della sera balsami
stende sulle doglie umane.

MARCELLO: Io non faccio da zimbello
ai novizi intraprendenti.
Vana, frivola civetta!
Ve ne andate? Vi ringrazio,
or son ricco divenuto.

MUSETTA: Fo all'amor con chi mi piace.
Non ti garba?
Fo all'amor con chi mi piace.
Musetta se ne va.

MARCELLO E MUSETTA: Vi saluto.

RODOLFO E MIMÌ: Vuoi che aspettiam
la primavera ancor?

MUSETTA: Signor, addio
vi dico con piacer!

MARCELLO: Son servo e me ne vo!

MUSETTA: (mentre ella se ne va)
Pittore da bottega!

MARCELLO: Vipera!

MUSETTA: Rospo!

MARCELLO: (ritornando nella taverna) Strega!

MIMÌ: Sempre tua . . . per la vita.

RODOLFO E MIMÌ: Ci lascieremo
alla stagion dei fior!

---

MUSETTA: The man was asking me . . .
"Do you like dancing, Miss?"

RODOLFO: One can speak to roses and lilies.

MIMÌ: Birds twitter softly in their nests.

MARCELLO: Vain, empty-headed flirt!

MUSETTA: I blushed and answered:
"I could dance day and night!"

MARCELLO: That speech conceals infamous desires.

MUSETTA: I want complete freedom.

MARCELLO: I'll teach you a thing or two . . .

RODOLFO AND MIMÌ: With the coming of spring,
the sun is our companion!

MUSETTA: What do you think you're saying?
We're not married, after all.

MARCELLO: . . . If I catch you flirting!
Keep in mind, no horns
will grow under my hat.

MUSETTA: I can't stand lovers who act just like husbands.

RODOLFO AND MIMÌ: The fountains whisper,
the evening breeze heals the pain of human creatures.

MARCELLO: I won't be laughed at by some young upstart.
Vain, empty-headed flirt!
You're leaving? I thank you,
I'll be a rich man then.

MUSETTA: I'll flirt with whom I please.
You don't like it?
I'll flirt with whom I please.
Musetta goes her way.

MARCELLO AND MUSETTA: Goodbye.

RODOLFO AND MIMÌ: Shall we wait
until spring comes again?

MUSETTA: I bid you, sir,
farewell—with pleasure!

MARCELLO: Your servant, and I'm off!

MUSETTA: (leaving) You housepainter!

MUSETTA: Viper!

MUSETTA: Toad!

MARCELLO: (re-entering the tavern) Witch!

MIMÌ: Always yours . . . all my life.

RODOLFO AND MIMÌ: We'll part when the flowers bloom!

---

MIMÌ: Vorrei che eterno
durasse il verno!

RODOLFO E MIMÌ: Ci lascierem
alla stagion dei fior!

# ■ ATTO QUARTO

*In soffitta*
*(Marcello di nuovo al cavalletto. Rodolfo al tavolo. Vorrebbero lavorare, ma non fanno che chiacchierare.)*

MARCELLO: In un coupè?

RODOLFO: Con pariglia e livree.
Mi salutò ridendo.
Tò Musetta —le dissi—
e il cuor?
"Non batte o non lo sento
grazie al velluto che il copre."

MARCELLO: Ci ho gusto davver.

RODOLFO: (Loiola va. Ti rodi e ridi.)

MARCELLO: Non batte? Bene.
Io pur vidi . . .

RODOLFO: Musetta?

MARCELLO: Mimì.

RODOLFO: L'hai vista?
*(fingendo noncuranza)*
Oh guarda!

MARCELLO: Era in carrozza
vestita come una regina.

RODOLFO: Evviva. Ne son contento.

MARCELLO: (Bugiardo. Si strugge d'amor.)

RODOLFO: Lavoriam.

MARCELLO: Lavoriam.
*(Si mettono al lavoro, ma subito gettano penna e pennello.)*

RODOLFO: Che penna infame!

MARCELLO: Che infame pennello!

RODOLFO: (O Mimì, tu più non torni.
O giorni belli,
piccole mani, odorosi capelli,
collo di neve! Ah! Mimì,
mia breve gioventù.)

MARCELLO: (Io non so come sia
che il mio pennello lavori
e impasti colori contro voglia mia.
Se pingere mi piace
o cielo o terre
o inverni o primavere,
egli mi traccia due pupille nere
e una bocca procace,
e n'esce di Musetta il viso ancor . . . )

RODOLFO: (E tu, cuffietta lieve,
che sotto il guancial partendo
ascose, tutta sai
la nostra felicità,

---

MIMÌ: I wish that winter
would last forever!

RODOLFO AND MIMÌ: We'll part
when flowers bloom!

# ■ ACT IV

*The garret*
*(Marcello once more at his easel, Rodolfo at his table. They try to work, but instead they are talking.)*

MARCELLO: In a coupé?

RODOLFO: With footmen and horses.
She greeted me, laughing.
"So, Musetta," I said,
"your heart?"
"It doesn't beat—at least I don't feel it.
Thanks to the velvet that covers it."

MARCELLO: I'm glad, really glad.

RODOLFO: (Faker, go on! You're laughing
and fretting inside).

MARCELLO: Not beating? Good.
I also saw . . .

RODOLFO: Musetta?

MARCELLO: Mimì.

RODOLFO: You saw her?
*(with pretended unconcern)*
Really?

MARCELLO: She was in a carriage
dressed like a queen.

RODOLFO: That's fine. I'm delighted.

MARCELLO: (The liar! Love's consuming him.)

RODOLFO: Let's get to work.

MARCELLO: Yes, to work.
*(They start working, but quickly throw down brush and pen.)*

RODOLFO: This pen is terrible!

MARCELLO: So is this brush!

RODOLFO: (O Mimì, you won't return!
O lovely days! Those tiny hands,
those sweet-smelling locks,
that snowy neck! Ah! Mimì!
My short-lived youth.)

MARCELLO: (I don't understand
how my brush
works and mixes colors
to spite me.
Whether I want to paint
earth or sky, spring
or winter, the brush
outlines two dark eyes
and inviting lips,
and Musetta's face comes
out . . . )

RODOLFO: (And you, little pink bonnet
that she hid under the pillow
as she left, you know

vien sul mio cor,
sul mio cor morto,
poichè è morto amor.)

MARCELLO: (E n'esce di Musetta il viso
tutto vezzi e tutto frode.
Musetta intanto gode
e il mio cuor vile
la chiama ed aspetta.)

RODOLFO: Che ora sia?

MARCELLO: L'ora del pranzo . . .
Di ieri.

RODOLFO: E Schaunard non torna.
(*Schaunard entra e posa quattro pagnotte sulla tavola. Colline è con lui.*)

SCHAUNARD: Eccoci.

RODOLFO E MARCELLO: Ebbene?

MARCELLO: Del pan?

COLLINE: È un piatto degno di Demostene;
un'aringa . . .

SCHAUNARD: . . . salata.

COLLINE: Il pranzo è in tavola.
(*Si seggono.*)

MARCELLO: Questa è cuccagna da Berlingaccio.

SCHAUNARD: (*Mette la bottiglia d'acqua nel cappello di Colline.*)
Ora lo sciampagna mettiamo in ghiaccio.

RODOLFO: Scelga, o Barone, trota o salmone?

MARCELLO: Duca, una lingua di pappagallo?

SCHAUNARD: Grazie, m'impingua,
stasera ho un ballo.
(*Colline si alza.*)

RODOLFO: Già sazio?

COLLINE: Ho fretta.
Il Re m'aspetta.

MARCELLO: C'è qualche trama?

RODOLFO, MARCELLO, SCHAUNARD: Qualche mister?

COLLINE: Il Re mi chiama al minister.

MARCELLO, RODOLFO, SCHAUNARD: Bene!

COLLINE: Però vedrò . . . Guizot!

SCHAUNARD: Porgimi il nappo.

MARCELLO: Sì, Bevi. Io pappo.

SCHAUNARD: Mi sia permesso . . .
al nobile consesso . . .

RODOLFO: Basta.

MARCELLO: Fiacco!

COLLINE: Che decotto!

MARCELLO: Leva il tacco.

all of our joy.
Come to my heart,
my heart that's dead
with our dead love.)

MARCELLO: (Her face comes forward then,
so lovely and so false.
Meanwhile Musetta is happy
and my cowardly heart
calls her, and waits for her.)

RODOLFO: What time is it?

MARCELLO: It's time for dinner . . .
Yesterday's dinner.

RODOLFO: And Schaunard's not back.
(*Schaunard comes in and sets four rolls on the table. Colline is with him.*)

SCHAUNARD: Here we are.

RODOLFO AND MARCELLO: Well?

MARCELLO: Just bread?

COLLINE: A dish worthy of Demosthenes:
A herring . . .

SCHAUNARD: . . . salted.

COLLINE: Dinner's on the table.
(*They sit down.*)

MARCELLO: This is like a feast day in wonderland.

SCHAUNARD: (*puts the water-bottle in Colline's hat*) Now let's put
the champagne on ice.

RODOLFO: Which do you choose, Baron,
salmon or trout?

MARCELLO: Well, Duke, how about
some parrot-tongue?

SCHAUNARD: Thanks, but it's fattening.
I must dance this evening.
(*Colline gets up.*)

RODOLFO: Full already?

COLLINE: I'm in a hurry.
The King is waiting for me.

MARCELLO: Is there some plot?

RODOLFO, MARCELLO, SCHAUNARD: Some mystery?

COLLINE: The King has asked me to join his Cabinet.

MARCELLO, RODOLFO, SCHAUNARD: Fine!

COLLINE: So . . . I'll see Guizot!

SCHAUNARD: Pass me the goblet.

MARCELLO: Here. Drink. I'll eat.

SCHAUNARD: By the leave . . .
of this noble company . . .

RODOLFO: Enough!

MARCELLO: Weakling!

COLLINE: What a concoction!

MARCELLO: Get out of here!

COLLINE: Dammi il gotto.

SCHAUNARD: M'ispira irresistibile
l'estro della romanza . . .

GLI ALTRI: No!

SCHAUNARD: Azione coreografica allora?

GLI ALTRI: Sì.

SCHAUNARD: La danza con musica vocale!

COLLINE: Si sgombrino le sale.
Gavotta.

MARCELLO: Minuetto.

RODOLFO: Pavanella.

SCHAUNARD: Fandango.

COLLINE: Propongo la quadriglia.

RODOLFO: Mano alle dame.

COLLINE: Io detto.

SCHAUNARD: La lera la lera la!

RODOLFO: (*galante a Marcello*)
Vezzosa damigella . . .

MARCELLO: Rispetti la modestia.
La prego.

COLLINE: *Balancez.*

SCHAUNARD: Prima c'è il *Rond.*

COLLINE: No, bestia.

SCHAUNARD: Che modi da lacchè!

COLLINE: Se non erro lei m'oltraggia.
Snudi il ferro.

SCHAUNARD: Pronti. Assaggia.
Il tuo sangue voglio ber.
(*Colline ha preso le molle, Schaunard la paletta. Si battono mentre gli altri cantano.*)

COLLINE: Un di noi qui si sbudella.

SCHAUNARD: Apprestate una barella.

COLLINE: Apprestate un cimiter.

RODOLFO E MARCELLO: Mentre incalza la tenzone
gira e balza Rigodone.
(*Entra Musetta.*)

MARCELLO: Musetta!

MUSETTA: C'è Mimì . . . c'è Mimì
che mi segue e che sta male.

RODOLFO: Ov'è?

MUSETTA: Nel far le scale
più non si resse.
(*Rodolfo si precipita verso Mimì, seduta sull'ultimo gradino. Poi la portano nella stanza e la stendono sul letto.*)

RODOLFO: Ah!

SCHAUNARD: Noi accostiamo quel lettuccio.

RODOLFO: Là. Da bere.

MIMÌ: Rodolfo.

COLLINE: The goblet, please!

SCHAUNARD: I'm irresistibly inspired
by the Muse of poetry . . .

THE OTHERS: No!

SCHAUNARD: Something choreographic then?

THE OTHERS: Yes.

SCHAUNARD: Dance with vocal accompaniment!

COLLINE: Let the hall be cleared.
A gavotte.

MARCELLO: Minuet.

RODOLFO: Pavane.

SCHAUNARD: Fandango.

COLLINE: I suggest the quadrille.

RODOLFO: Take your lady's arm.

COLLINE: I'll call the figures.

SCHAUNARD: La lera la lera la!

RODOLFO: (*gallantly, to Marcello*) Lovely maiden . . .

MARCELLO: Please, sir, respect my modesty.

COLLINE: *Balancez.*

SCHAUNARD: The *Rond* comes first.

COLLINE: No, damn it.

SCHAUNARD: What boorish manners!

COLLINE: You provoke me, I believe.
Draw you sword.

SCHAUNARD: Ready. Lay on.
I'll drink your blood.
(*Colline takes the fire-tongs and Schaunard the poker. They fight as the others sing.*)

COLLINE: One of us will be run through!

SCHAUNARD: Have a stretcher ready!

COLLINE: And a graveyard too!

RODOLFO AND MARCELLO:
While the battle rages,
the dancers circle and leap.
(*Musetta enters.*)

MARCELLO: Musetta!

MUSETTA: Mimì's here . . . she's coming
and she's ill.

RODOLFO: Where is she?

MUSETTA: She couldn't find strength
to climb all the stairs.
(*Rodolfo hastens out to Mimì, who is seated on the last step. Then they carry her into the room and place her on the bed.*)

RODOLFO: Ah!

SCHAUNARD: We'll move the bed closer.

RODOLFO: Here. Something to drink.

MIMÌ: Rodolfo.

**RODOLFO:** Zitta, Riposa.

**MIMÌ:** O mio Rodolfo, mi vuoi qui con te?

**RODOLFO:** Ah, mia Mimì! Sempre, sempre!

**MUSETTA:** (*agli altri, piano*) Intesi dire che Mimì, fuggita dal Viscontino, era in fin di vita. Dove stia? Cerca, cerca . . . la veggo passar per via, trascinandosi a stento. Mi dice, "Più non reggo . . . Muioi, lo sento . . . Voglio morir con lui . . . Forse m'aspetta . . . "

**MARCELLO:** Sst!

**MIMÌ:** Mi sento assai meglio . . .

**MUSETTA:** "M'accompagni, Musetta?"

**MIMÌ:** Lascia ch'io guardi intorno. Ah, come si sta bene qui. Si rinasce, si rinasce . . . Ancor sento la vita qui . . . No, tu non mi lasci più . . .

**RODOLFO:** Benedetta bocca, tu ancor mi parli.

**MUSETTA:** Che ci avete in casa?

**MARCELLO:** Nulla.

**MUSETTA:** Non caffè? Non vino?

**MARCELLO:** Nulla. Ah! Miseria.

**SCHAUNARD:** Fra mezz'ora è morta!

**MIMÌ:** Ho tanto freddo. Se avessi un manicotto! Queste mie mani riscaldare non si potranno mai?

**RODOLFO:** Qui, Nelle mia. Taci. Il parlar ti stanca.

**MIMÌ:** Ho un po' di tosse. Ci sono avvezza. Buon giorno, Marcello, Schaunard, Colline, buon giorno. Tutti qui, tutti qui sorridenti a Mimì.

**RODOLFO:** Non parlar, non parlar.

**MIMÌ:** Parlo pian. Non temere. Marcello date retta: è assai buona Musetta.

**MARCELLO:** (*porge la mano a Musetta*) Lo so. Lo so.

**MUSETTA:** (*dà gli orecchini a Marcello*) A te, vendi, riporta qualche cordial. Manda un dottore!

**RODOLFO:** Riposa.

**MIMÌ:** Tu non mi lasci?

**RODOLFO:** No, no!

**MUSETTA:** Ascolta! Forse è l'ultima volta che ha espresso un desiderio, poveretta! Pel manicotto io vo. Con te verrò.

---

**RODOLFO:** Rest now. Don't speak.

**MIMÌ:** O my Rodolfo! You want me here with you?

**RODOLFO:** Ah! My Mimì! Always, always!

**MUSETTA:** (*aside, to the others*) I heard Mimì had fled from the Viscount and was dying. Where was she? I sought her . . . Just now I saw her in the street stumbling along. She said; "I can't last long. I know I'm dying . . . But I want to die with him Perhaps he's waiting for me . . . "

**MARCELLO:** Sh!

**MIMÌ:** I feel much better . . .

**MUSETTA:** "Please take me, Musetta?"

**MIMÌ:** Let me look around. How wonderful it is here. I'll recover . . . I will . . . I feel life here again. You won't leave me ever . . .

**RODOLFO:** Beloved lips, you speak to me again.

**MUSETTA:** What is there in the house?

**MARCELLO:** Nothing.

**MUSETTA:** No coffee? No wine?

**MARCELLO:** Nothing. Poverty!

**SCHAUNARD:** She can't last an hour!

**MIMÌ:** I'm so cold. If I had a muff! Won't these hands of mine ever be warm?

**RODOLFO:** Here. In mine. Don't speak. You'll tire yourself.

**MIMÌ:** It's just a little cough. I'm used to it. Hello, Marcello, Schaunard, Colline . . . All of you are here, smiling at Mimì.

**RODOLFO:** Don't speak, don't . . .

**MIMÌ:** I'll speak softly. Don't fear. Marcello, believe me— Musetta is so good.

**MARCELLO:** (*holds Musetta's hand*) I know. I know.

**MUSETTA:** (*gives her earrings to Marcello*) Here. Sell them. Bring back some cordial and send the doctor!

**RODOLFO:** Rest now!

**MIMÌ:** You won't leave me?

**RODOLFO:** No! No!

**MUSETTA:** Listen! Perhaps it's the poor thing's last request. I'll get the muff. I'm coming with you.

---

**MARCELLO:** Sie buona, a mia Musetta.

(*Escono Musetta e Marcello.*)

**COLLINE:** (*levandosi il pastrano*) Vecchia zimarra, senti, io resto al pian, tu ascendere il sacro monte o devi. Le mie grazie recevi. Mai non curvasti il logoro dorso ai ricchi ed ai potenti. Passar nelle tue tasche come in antri tranquilli filosofi e poeti. Ora che i giorni lieti fuggir, ti dico addio, fedele amico mio. Addio. (*Mette l'involto sotto il braccio, poi dice sottovoce a Schaunard:*) Schaunard, ognuno per diversa via mettiamo insieme due atti di pietà; io . . . questo! . . . E tu . . . lasciali soli là . . .

**SCHAUNARD:** Filosofo, ragioni! Èver . . . Vo Via! (*Escono.*)

**MIMÌ:** Sono andati? Fingevo di dormire perchè volli con te sola restare. Ho tante cose che ti voglio fire, o una sola ma grande come il mare, come il mare profonda ed infinita . . . Sei il mio amor . . . e tutta la mia vita.

**RODOLFO:** Ah Mimì, mia bella Mimì!

**MIMÌ:** Son bella ancora?

**RODOLFO:** Bella come un'aurora.

**MIMÌ:** Hai sbagliato il raffronto. Volevi dir: bella come un tramonto. "Mi chiamano Mimì . . . il perchè non so."

**RODOLFO:** Tornò al nido la rondine e cinguetta. (*Leva la cuffietta di dove l'aveva riposta in sul cuore.*)

**MIMÌ:** La mia cuffietta! La mia cuffietta! Ah! te lo rammenti quando sono entrata la prima volta là?

**RODOLFO:** So lo rammento!

**MIMÌ:** Il lume s'era spento.

**RODOLFO:** Eri tanto turbata. Poi smarristi la chiave.

**MIMÌ:** E a cercarla tastoni ti sei messo!

**RODOLFO:** E cerca, cerca . . .

**MIMÌ:** Mio bel signorino, posso ben dirlo adesso, lei la trovò assai presto.

**RODOLFO:** Aiutavo il destino.

---

**MARCELLO:** How good you are, Musetta.

(*Marcello and Musetta go out.*)

**COLLINE:** (*taking off his greatcoat*) Listen, my venerable coat, I'm staying behind, you'll go on to greater heights. I give you my thanks. You never bowed your worn back to the rich or powerful. You held in your pockets poets and philosophers as if in tranquil grottoes . . . Now that those happy times have fled, I bid you farewell, faithful old friend. Farewell. (*He puts the bundle under his arm, then whispers to Schaunard:*) Schaunard, each separately, let's combine two kindly acts; mine is this . . . and you . . . leave the two of them alone.

**SCHAUNARD:** Philosopher, you're right! I'll go along. (*They leave.*)

**MIMÌ:** Have they gone? I pretended to sleep because I wanted to be alone with you. I've so many things to tell you, or one thing—huge as the sea, deep and infinite as the sea . . . I love you . . . you're all my life.

**RODOLFO:** Ah! my beautiful Mimì.

**MIMÌ:** Am I beautiful still?

**RODOLFO:** Beautiful as the dawn.

**MIMÌ:** You've mistaken the image: you should have said, beautiful as the sunset. "They call me Mimì . . . but I don't know why."

**RODOLFO:** The swallow comes back to her nest to twitter. (*He takes the bonnet from its place over his heart.*)

**MIMÌ:** My bonnet! My bonnet! Ah! do you remember when I came in here the first time?

**RODOLFO:** Do I remember!

**MIMÌ:** The light had gone out.

**RODOLFO:** You were so upset. Then you lost your key . . .

**MIMÌ:** And you knelt to hunt for it!

**RODOLFO:** I searched and searched . . .

**MIMÌ:** My dear sir, now I can tell you: you found it quick enough.

**RODOLFO:** I was helping Fate.

**MIMÌ:** Era buio e il mio rossor
non si vedeva . . .
"Che gelida manina . . .
Se la lasci riscaldar . . . "
Era buio e la man
tu mi prendevi . . .
(*Mimì è presa da uno spasimo di soffocazione.*)

**RODOLFO:** Oh Dio! Mimì!
(*Schaunard rientra in quel momento.*)

**SCHAUNARD:** Che avvien?

**MIMÌ:** Nulla. Sto bene.

**RODOLFO:** Zitta. Per carità.

**MIMÌ:** Sì, sì, perdona.
Or sarò buona.
(*Tornano Marcello e Musetta, poi Colline. Musetta pone un lume sulla tavola.*)

**MUSETTA:** Dorme?

**RODOLFO:** Riposa.

**MARCELLO:** Ho veduto il dottore.
Verrà. Gli ho fatto fretta.
Ecco il cordial.

**MIMÌ:** Chi parla?

**MUSETTA:** (*porgendo il manicotto*) Io, Musetta.

**MIMÌ:** O come è bello e morbido!
Non più, non più, le mani
allividite. Il tepore le abbellirà.
(*a Rodolfo*)
Sei tu che me lo doni?

**MUSETTA:** Sì.

**MIMÌ:** Tu! Spensierato!
Grazie. Ma costerà.
Piangi? Sto bene.
Pianger così perchè?
Qui . . . amor . . . sempre
con te!

**MIMÌ:** It was dark. You couldn't
see me blushing.
"How cold your little hand
is . . .
Let me warm it for you . . . "
It was dark. You took
my hand in yours . . .
(*Mimì has another spasm, a fit of choking.*)

**RODOLFO:** Good God! Mimì!
(*Schaunard enters at that moment.*)

**SCHAUNARD:** What's wrong?

**MIMÌ:** Nothing. I'm fine.

**RODOLFO:** Please . . . don't
talk.

**MIMÌ:** Yes, yes forgive me.
Now I'll be good.
(*Marcello and Musetta come back, then Colline. Musetta sets a candle on the table.*)

**MUSETTA:** Is she sleeping?

**RODOLFO:** She's resting.

**MARCELLO:** I saw the doctor.
He's coming. I made him hurry.
Here's the cordial.

**MIMÌ:** Who's speaking?

**MUSETTA:** (*handing her the muff*) Me. Musetta.

**MIMÌ:** Oh, how lovely and soft it is.
No more, no more . . . my hands
all
ugly and cold . . . The warmth
will heal them.
(*to Rodolfo*)
Did you give it to me?

**MUSETTA:** Yes, he did.

**MIMÌ:** You spendthrift!
Thank you . . . but the
cost . . .
You're crying? I'm well.
Why are you crying like this?
Here . . . beloved . . . with

Le mani . . . al caldo . . . e
dormire.
(*Silenzio.*)

**RODOLFO:** Che ha detto il medico?

**MARCELLO:** Verrà.

**MUSETTA:** (*pregando*) Madonna
benedetta,
fate la grazia a questa poveretta
che non debba morire.
(*interrompendosi, a Marcello*)
Qui ci vuole un riparo
perché la fiamma sventola.
(*Marcello mette un libro sulla tavola da paravento al lume.*)
Così.
E che possa guarire.
Madonna santa, io sono
indegna di perdono,
mentre invece Mimì
è un angelo del cielo.

**RODOLFO:** Io spero ancora. Vi
pare
che sia grave?

**MUSETTA:** Non credo.
(*Schaunard s'avvicina al letto.*)

**SCHAUNARD:** (*piano a Marcello*)
Marcello, è spirata.

**COLLINE:** (*entra e dà del danaro a Musetta*) Musetta, a voi.
Come va?

**RODOLFO:** Vedi, è tranquilla.
(*Rodolfo si accorge dello strano contegno degli altri.*)
Che vuol dire?
Quell'andare e venire . . .
Quel guardarmi così? . . .

**MARCELLO:** Coraggio.
(*Rodolfo accorre al lettucio.*)

**RODOLFO:** Mimì! . . . Mimì!

*FINE*

you always!
My hands . . . the warmth . . .
to sleep.
(*Silence.*)

**RODOLFO:** What did the doctor
say?

**MARCELLO:** He's coming.

**MUSETTA:** (*praying*) Oh blessed
Mother,
be merciful to this poor child
who doesn't deserve to die.
(*breaking off, to Marcello*)
We need a shade here;
the candle's flickering.
(*Marcello sets a book on the table which acts as a shade.*)
So.
Let her get well,
Holy Mother, I know
I'm unworthy of forgiveness,
but Mimì is an angel
come down from heaven.

**RODOLFO:** I still have hope.
You think it's serious?

**MUSETTA:** I don't think so.
(*Schaunard approaches the bed.*)

**SCHAUNARD:** (*softly to Marcello*) Marcello, she's dead.

**COLLINE:** (*enters, and gives money to Musetta*) Here, Musetta.
How is she?

**RODOLFO:** You see, she's resting.
(*Rodolfo becomes aware of the strange expression of the others.*)
What does this mean?
This going back and forth?
Why are you looking at me like this?

**MARCELLO:** Courage.
(*Rodolfo runs over to the bed.*)

**RODOLFO:** Mimì . . . Mimì

*THE END*

# Tosca (1900)

MUSIC BY GIACOMO PUCCINI ■ LIBRETTO BY LUIGI ILLICA, GIUSEPPE GIACOSA

---

Tosca premiered at the Teatro Costanzi in Rome on January 14, 1900. It is set to a libretto by Giuseppe Giacosa and Luigi Illica (based on Victorien Sardou's play). The time is June, 1800. Cesare Angelotti, a consul of the defeated Roman republic who has escaped from the Castel Sant'Angelo, hides in the church of Sant'Andrea della Valle. His sister, the Marchesa Attavanti, leaves clothes for him in the family chapel. Mario Cavaradossi is painting a portrait of the Madonna for the church and the sacristan comments on its resemblance to the woman who often visits—the Marchesa Attavanti. Angelotti discovers that the painter is his old friend and fellow Republican sympathizer. Floria Tosca, a famous opera singer and Cavaradossi's mistress, hears him whispering and thinks that he is deceiving her. He placates her with the promise of a rendezvous that night at his villa. Tosca recognizes the Marchesa Attavanti in the portrait and grows jealous. A cannon sounds the alarm for Angelotti's escape. Cavaradossi hides his friend at his villa outside Rome. The sacristan announces Napoleon's defeat. Scarpia, the chief of police, arrives. Marchesa Attavanti's fan is discovered; this leads Scarpia to believe that Cavaradossi has aided Angelotti. Tosca returns to change the evening's plans and finds that Cavaradossi has left. Scarpia uses the Marchesa's fan to arouse Tosca's jealousy, and she sets off for her lover's villa, where she intends to confront him. Spoletta, Scarpia's agent, follows her. Scarpia plans to hang Cavaradossi and win over Tosca. Tosca is singing in a concert at Farnese Palace while Scarpia dines in his room in another wing. Spoletta brings in Cavaradossi, who denies that he is aiding Angelotti. Tosca enters, having received a note from Scarpia. Before Cavaradossi can tell her to keep quiet, he is taken into the next room to be tortured. She cannot stand the sound of his screams and tells Scarpia where he may find Angelotti. Cavaradossi's anger at her betrayal is interrupted by news of Napoleon's victory at Marengo. Singing in praise of freedom, Cavaradossi is taken away by the guards to await execution. Tosca pleads with Scarpia to spare her lover—she will pay any price. Spoletta reports Angelotti's suicide; Scarpia demands that she be his mistress to save Cavaradossi, and she agrees. Scarpia pretends to order a mock execution for the painter and signs safe conducts for the lovers. He embraces Tosca, who stabs him with a dinner knife and grabs the safe conducts from him. At dawn Cavaradossi is escorted from his prison cell. His last thoughts are about Tosca, who tells him that his execution will be fake and that he should fall down as if he were dead. The shots are fired, and Tosca runs over to him. He is, in fact, dead. Scarpia's murder has been discovered and soldiers come to arrest Tosca. She jumps onto the parapet and throws herself down, crying out, "Scarpia, we will meet before God."

---

## ■ ATTO PRIMO

*La Chiesa di Sant'Andrea alla Valle.*

*A destra la Capella Attavanti. A sinistra un impaleato: su di esso un gran quadro coperto da tela. Attrezzi varí da pittore. Un paniere.*

**ANGELOTTI:** (*vestito da prigloniero, lacero, sfatto, tremante dalla paura, entra ansante, quasi correndo, dalla porta laterale. Dà una rapida occhiata intorno*)
Ah! . . . Finalmente! . . . Nel terror mio stolto
vedea ceffi di birro in ogni volto.
(*torna a guardare attentamente intorno a sè con più calma a riconoscere il luogo.—Dà un sospiro di sollievo vedendo la colonna colla pila dell'acqua santa e la Madonna*)
La pila . . . la colonna . . .
"A piè della Madonna"
mi serisse mia sorella . . .
(*vi si avvicina, cerca ai piedi della Madonna e ne ritira, con un soffocato grido di gioia, una chlave*)
Ecco la chiave . . . ed ecco la capella! . . .
(*addita ia Capella Attavanti; con gran precauzione introduce la chiave nella serratura, apre la cancellata, penetra nella Cappella, rinchiude . . . e scompare*).

## ■ ACT I

*Scene: The Church of Sant'Andrea alla Valle.*

*R.—The Attavanti Chapel. L.—Scaffolding, dáis, easel supporting a large picture covered by a cloth. Accessories of the painting craft. A basket.*
(*Enter Angelotti L., in prison garb, barassed, disheveled, panic-stricken, well-nigh breathless with fear and hurry. He casts a hasty glance around him*)

**ANGELOTTI:** Ah! I have stalled them . . . dread imagination
Made me quake with uncalled-for perturbation.
(*shuddering, he again looks around him, curiously and somewhat more calmly, heaving a sigh of relief as he recognizes a pillar-shrine containing an image of the Virgin and surmounting a receptacle for Holy Water*)
The pilar . . . and the column.
My sister wrote to tell me
"At the foot of the Madonna" . . .
(*he approaches the column and searches for the key beneath the feet of the Holy Virgin's image. Not finding it immediately, he appears discouraged, and renews his quest in a state of manifest agitation. Presently, stifling an exclamation of joy, he discovers the key*)
This is the key
(*quickly passing his hand over the portals of Attavanti Chapel*)
and this the Chapel entrance.
(*Stricken anew with alarm by the notion that he has been followed, he looks timorously about him, creeps up to the chapel-gates, carefully inserts the key in the keyhole, opens the folding-doors and passes through them, closing them behind him*)
(*Enter the Sacristan C., grasping in one hand a bundle of paint-brushes; he crosses from L. to R., and takes up his stand in the nave of the church, for a time, eventually moving towards the scaffolding while talking loudly, as though he were addressing some unseen person*)

# Act I

IL SAGRESTANO: (*entra dal fonde tenendo fra le mani un mazzo di pennelli e parlando ad alta voce come se rivolgesse la parola a qualcuno*) E frega e lava! . . . Ogni pennello è sozzo peggio che il collarin d'uno scagnozzo.
Signor pittore . . . Tò! . . . (*guarda verso l'Impalcato dove sta il quadro, e vedendolo deserto, esclama sorpreso*)
Nessuno.—Avrei giurato che fosse ritornato il cavalier Cavaradossi. (*depone i pennelli, sale sull'impalcato, guarda dentro il paniere e dice*)
No, sbaglio.—Il paniere è intatto. (*suona l'Angelus. Il Sagrestano si inginocchia e prega sommesso*).

CAVARADOSSI: (*dalla porta interale, vedendo il Sagrestano in ginocchio*) Che fai?

SAGRESTANO: (*alzandosi*) Recito l'Angelus.
(*Cavaradossi sale sull'impalcato e scopre il quadro. È una Maria Maddalena a grandi occhi azzurri con una gran pioggia di capelli dorati. Il pittore vi sta dinanzi muto attentamente osservando*).
(*Il Sagrestano volgendosi verso Cavaradossi per dirigergli la parola, vede il quadro scoperto e dà in un grido di meraviglia*)
O sante ampolle! Il suo ritratto! . . .

CAVARADOSSI: Di chi?

SAGRESTANO: Di quell'ignota che i dì passati a pregar qui venìa tutta devota—e pia.
(*e accenna verso la Madonna dalla quale Angelotti trasse la chiave*)

CAVARADOSSI: (*sorridendo*) È vero. E tanto ell'era infervorata nella sua preghiera ch'io ne pinsi, non visto, il bel sembiante.

SAGRESTANO: (*Fuori, Satana, fuori!*)

CAVARADOSSI: Dammi i colori!
(*Il Sagrestano eseguisce. Cavaradossi dipinge con rapidità e si sofferma spesso a riguardare: Il Sagrestano va e viene, portando una catinella entro la quale continua a lavare i pennelli*).
(*A un tratto Cavaradossi si ristà di dipingere; leva di tasca un medaglione contenente una miniatura e gli occhi suoi vanno dal medaglione al quadro*)
Recondita armonia di bellezze diverse! . . . È bruna

THE SACRISTAN: (*who has a nervous trick of twitching his neck and shoulders*) Vainly I soak them! They are dirty and sticky, Fouler than any slovenly choirboy's dickie . . .
Good sir, I pray you (*staring at the däis and amazed to see it vacant*) What! Nobody! I could have sworn I should have found Cavaradossi busily working at his easel.
(*He looks into the basket*) No, wrong again.
Nothing has been touched here.
(*he steps down from the däis. The Angelus is rung. He kneels, and intones the prayer. Bell. Enter Cavaradossi L. He sees the Sacristan kneeling*)

CAVARADOSSI: What now?

SACRISTAN: (*rising*) Only the Angelus.
(*Cavaradossi ascends the däis and uncovers the picture, which represents a Mary Magdalen with large blue eyes and masses of golden hair. The painter stands facing it, gazing upon it in silent and intent contemplation. Turning towards Cavaradossi to speak to him, the Sacristan catches sight of the uncovered picture and exclaims in great amazement:*)
SACRISTAN: Saints and Martyrs! It is the portrait . . .

CAVARADOSSI: (*turning towards the Sacristan*) Of whom?

SACRISTAN: Of that fair lady who, day by day, lately, came here to pray.
(*reverently bowing before the Virgin's image beneath which Angelotti had found the key*)
Deeply devout was her worship . . .

CAVARADOSSI: (*smiling*) Yes, truly! While absorbed in her devotions, plunged in dreamy rapture I, unseen, depicted her lovely semblance.

SACRISTAN: (*scandalized*) Get Satan, behind me!

CAVARADOSSI: (*to the Sacristan, who obeys him*) Give me the colors!
(*he begins to paint rapidly, often pausing to look at his own work, while the Sacristan fidgets backwards and forwards, eventually picking up the brushes and dabbling them in a bucket at the foot of the scaffolding. Cavaradossi suddenly stops painting, takes out of his breast-pocket a medallion containing a miniature, and compares the latter with the pic-*

Floria, l'ardente amante mia e te bel nobile fiore, cinga di chiome bionde! Tu azzuro hai l'occhio e Tosca sa l'occhio nero! L'arte nel suo mistero le diverse bellezze insiem confonde: ma nel ritrar costei il mio solo pensier, O il mio solo pensier, ser tu. Tosca ser tu.

SAGRESTANO: (*fra sè, brontolando*) (Scherza coi fanti e lascia stare i santi. Queste diverse gonne che fanno concorrenze alle Madonne mandan tanfo d'inferno. Ma con quei cani—de volterriani nemiei del santissimo governo non c'è da metter voce! . . . Facciam piuttosto il segno della croce).
(*a Cavaradossi*) Vado, Eccellenza?

CAVARADOSSI: Fa il tuo piacere! (*ritorna a dipingere*).

SAGRESTANO: (*indicando il cesto*) Pieno è il paniere . . . Fa penitenza?

CAVARADOSSI: Fame non ho.

SAGRESTANO: (*con ironia stropicciandosi le mani*) Oh! . . . mi rincresce! (*non può trattenere un gesto di gioia e uno sguardo di avidità verso il cesto che prende ponendolo un po' in disparte*) Badi, quand'esce chiuda.

CAVARADOSSI: Va!

*ture on the easel.*)
Strange harmony of contrasts, thus deliciously blending, My Floria's dusky glow with contending peach-like bloom.

SACRISTAN: (*grumbling under his breath*) He scorns the saints and jests with the ungodly. (*fetches water wherewith to cleanse the brushes*)

CAVARADOSSI: Oh fairest Queen of Heaven, Your tresses are gold and radiantly bright! Your eyes are blue—and Tosca's Dark as a moonless night.

SACRISTAN: (*returns up the stage, murmuring*) He scorns the saints and jests with the ungodly! (*The Sacristan recommences washing the brushes*)

CAVARADOSSI: Art, that potent magician, combines many beauties in one ideal; To me, beloved Tosca, when I paint your bright visage, you alone are real! (*he continues to paint*)

SACRISTAN: (*having dried the cleaned brushes, he goes on muttering*) These light of loves pernicious, So frivolously vicious, Delight in wiling human souls to perdition; And they, like heathenish unbelievers, Should all be hanged or burned as vile deceivers, By the Holy Inquisition. (*grumbles*)
He scoffs at saints, and jests with the ungodly!
(*He thrusts the basket under the scaffolding, and places the clean brushes in a jug near the painter*) (*aside*) (I may as well be off, with his permission.)
(*aloud*) Excellency, I'm going.

CAVARADOSSI: Do as you please, man. (*goes on painting*)

SACRISTAN: (*pointing to the basket*) Full is the pannier . . . Pray, are you fasting?

CAVARADOSSI: Nothing for me!

SACRISTAN: Oh! I am sorry! . . . (*rubs his hands ironically, but cannot repress a joyous gesture and a greedy glance at the basket, which he picks up and sets aside. He then takes two pinches of snuff*)
Please lock up, when leaving.

CAVARADOSSI: Go!

SAGRESTANO: Vo.
(s'allontana per il fondo)
(Cavaradossi volgendo le spalle alla Cappella lavora. Angelotti, credendo deserta la chiesa, appare dietro la cancellata e introduce la chiave per aprire).

CAVARADOSSI: (al cigolìo della serratura si volta) Gente là dentro!
(al movimento fatto da Cavaradossi, Angelotti, atterrito si arresta come per rifugiarsi ancora nella Cappella—ma—alzati gli occhi, un grido di gioia, che egli soffoca tosto timoroso, crompe dal suo petto. Egli ha riconosciuto il pittore e gli stende le braccia come ad un aiuto insperato)

ANGELOTTI: Voi! Cavaradossi!
Vi manda Iddio!

CAVARADOSSI: Ma . . .

ANGELOTTI: (va fin sotto l'impalcato) Non mi ravvisate?
Il carcere mi ha dunque assai mutato

CAVARADOSSI: Il carcere?
(Cavaradossi guarda fiso il volto di Angelotti, e finalmente lo ravvisa. Depone rapido tavolozza e pennelli, scende dall'impalcato verso Angelotti, guardandosi caute intorno)
Angelotti!

ANGELOTTI: Appunto.

CAVARADOSSI: Il Console della spenta repubblica romana.
(corre a chiudere la porta a destra)

ANGELOTTI: Fuggii pur ora da Castel Sant'Angelo . . .

CAVARADOSSI: Disponete di me.

VOCE di TOSCA: Mario!
(alla voce di Tosca, Cavaradossi fa un rapido cenno ad Angelotti di tacre)

CAVARADOSSI: Celatevi!
È una donna . . . gelosa. Un breve istante e la rimando.

VOCE DI TOSCA: Mario!

CAVARADOSSI: (verso la porta di dove viene la voce di Tosca) Eccomi!

ANGELOTTI: (colto da un accesso di debolezza si appoggia all'impalcato) Sono stremo di forze—non mi reggo.

SACRISTAN: I go. (Exit C.)
(Cavaradossi continues to work, turning his back to the Chapel. Angelotti, believing the Church to be empty, appears behind the railing, and uses the key to open it)

CAVARADOSSI: (hears the lock creak, and turns round) Someone is in there!
(Angelotti, alarmed by Cavaradossi's movement, is about to take refuge anew in the Chapel, but utters a half-stifled cry of gladness on recognizing the painter, towards whom he advances open-armed, as to an unhoped-for rescuer)

ANGELOTTI: You! Cavaradossi!
God sends you to me!
(Cavaradossi does not recognize Angelotti, and remains on the dais, petrified by amazement. Angelotti, craving recognition, approaches him)
Have you quite forgotten?
Has prison-life robbed me of all knowledge?

CAVARADOSSI: (recognizing Angelotti, hastily sets down his palette and brushes, and descends from the dais looking cautiously around him) Angelotti!
The Consul of the moribund Roman Republic!
(hastens to close the church-door L)

ANGELOTTI: (advancing towards Cavaradossi) I have escaped but now from Fort San Angelo . . .

CAVARADOSSI: (generously) Can I do anything to help you?

TOSCA: (from without) Mario!

CAVARADOSSI: (hearing Tosca's voice, makes a sign to Angelotti enjoining him to keep silence) Conceal yourself!
The most jealous of women . . .
I'll dismiss her within a minute.

TOSCA: Mario! (as before)

CAVARADOSSI: (in reply) Here I am!

ANGELOTTI: (overcome by weakness, leans against the scaffolding) I am hungry and weary and exhausted . . .

CAVARADOSSI: (rapidissimo, sale sull'impalcato, ne discende col paniere e incoraggiando Angelotti, lo spinge verso la Cappella) In questo panier vi è cibo e vino.

ANGELOTTI: Grazie!

CAVARADOSSI: Presto!
(Angelotti entra nella Cappella).

VOCE di TOSCA: (chiamando ripetutamente stizzita) Mario!

CAVARADOSSI: (apre) Son qui!

TOSCA: (entra con an specie di violenza, allontana bruscamente Mario che vuole abbracciaria e guarda sospettosa intorno a sè) Perchè chiuso?

CAVARADOSSI: Lo vuole il Sagrestano.

TOSCA: A chi parlavi?

CAVARADOSSI: A te!

TOSCA: Altre parole bisbigliavi. Ov'è? . . .

CAVARADOSSI: Chi?

TOSCA: Colei! . . . Quella donna!
Ho udito i lesti passi e un fruscìo di vesti . . .

CAVARADOSSI: Sogni!

TOSCA: Lo neghi?

CAVARADOSSI: Lo nego e t'amo!
(per baciaria)

TOSCA: (con dolce rimprovero) O! innanzi la madonna.
Lascia pria ch'io l'infiori e che la preghi.
(si avvicina alla Madonna, dispone con arte, intorno ad essa, i flori che ha portato con sè, si inginocchia e prega con molta devozione, poi s'alza)
(a Cavaradossi, che si è avviato per riprendere il lavoro)
Ora stammi a sentir—stassera canto,
ma è spettacolo breve. Tu mi aspetti sull'uscio della scena
e alla villa ne andiam soli e soletti.

CAVARADOSSI: (che fu sempre soprapensiero) Stassera?!

TOSCA: È luna piena ed il notturno effluvio floreale nebria il cor.—Non sei contento?

CAVARADOSSI: (ancora un po' distratto e peritoso) Tanto?

CAVARADOSSI: (produces the basket from under the scaffolding, and gives it to Angelotti) See, here is good store of food and liquor.

ANGELOTTI: Thank you!

CAVARADOSSI: (urging Angelotti forward, towards the Chapel) Hurry!
(Angelotti enters the Chapel)

TOSCA: (irritated) Mario! Mario! Mario!

CAVARADOSSI: (feigning calm, opens the door to Tosca) I am here!

TOSCA: (enters impetuously, looking suspiciously about her. Cavaradossi approaches her to embrace her; she repels him brusquely) Why lock the door?

CAVARADOSSI: (feigning indifference) By the Sacristan's order.

TOSCA: To whom were you speaking?

CAVARADOSSI: To you!

TOSCA: I heard you whispering to someone else.
Where is she?

CAVARADOSSI: Who?

TOSCA: Why, she! . . . Your fair lady!
I heard quite plainly
Her footsteps and the swish of her skirts . . .

CAVARADOSSI: Fancies!

TOSCA: Was it not so?

CAVARADOSSI: (passionately) It was not, beloved!
(he tries to embrace her)

TOSCA: (gently reproving him) Oh! before the good Madonna! No, Mario mine; let me pray to her first, and make my offering!
(she reverently adorns the Virgin's image with the flowers which she had brought with her for that purpose; then kneels down, prays devoutly, crosses herself, and arises. To Cavaradossi, who, meanwhile, has made preparations to resume work)
And now listen to me.
Tonight I'm singing, but the piece is a
short one. At the stage door await me
without fail, and we'll run off
to the villa by stealth together.

CAVARADOSSI: (absently) This evening?

TOSCA: The moon is full, and all the scents
that rise from fragrant flowers
perfume the night.
Will that please you?
(she sits down on the dais-step, close to Cavaradossi)

CAVARADOSSI: Surely!
(absently)

TOSCA: (*colpita da quell'accento*) Tornalo a dir!

CAVARADOSSI: Tanto!

TOSCA: Lo dici male:
(*va a sedere sulla gradinata presso a Cavaradossi*)
non la sospiri la nostra casetta
che tutta ascosa nel verde ci aspetta?
nido a noi sacro, ignoto al mondo inter.
pien d'amore e di mister?
Oh al tuo fianco sentire per le silenzïose stellate ombre, salire le voci delle cose!
Dai boschi, dai royeti, dall'arse erbe, dall'imo dei franti sepolcreti odorosi di timo,
la notte escon bisbigli di minuscoli amori e perfidi consigli che ammolliscono i cuori.
Fiorite, o campi immensi, palpitate aure marine nel lunare albor,
piovete voluttà, vôlte stellate!
Arde a Tosca nel sangue il folle amor!

CAVARADOSSI: (*vinto, ma vigilante*) Mi avvinci ne'tuoi lacci! . . .
Sì verrò mia sirena!
(*guarda verso la parte donde uscì Angelotti*)
Ma or lasciami al lavoro.

TOSCA: Mi discacci?

CAVARADOSSI: Urge l'opra, lo sai!

TOSCA: Vado! (*alza gli occhi e vede il quadro*)
Chi è quella
donna bionda lassu?

CAVARADOSSI: La Maddalena. Ti piace?

TOSCA: È troppo bella!

CAVARADOSSI: (*ridendo ed inchinandosi*) Prezioso elogio.

TOSCA: (*sospettosa*) Ridi?
Quegli occhi cilestrini io già li vidi . . .

CAVARADOSSI: (*con indifferenza*) Ce n'è tanti pel mondo!

---

TOSCA: (*struck with his indifference*) Say it again!

CAVARADOSSI: (*as before*) Surely.

TOSCA: (*vexed*) You say it badly.
Do you not long for our secluded cottage,
From which all cares and vexations are excluded?
Sweet, secret nest, in which we love-birds hide,
Safe and happy, side by side.
When the skies are calm and clear,
We'll listen to the voices
That only lovers hear
When Nature herself rejoices
From all the flowers that bloom in that earthly Eden,
Late breezes, laden with summer fragrance,
Cull perfumes that, blended, evoke a strange mysterious sensation,
Rife with subtle and sweet intoxication.
The babbling brooks, the rustling leaves and grasses,
The night-birds belated, the chirping red-breast and cooing turtle-dove
Murmur the story of the joy that surpasses all,
Tell the tale of ardent love.

CAVARADOSSI: You have caught me in your toils,
my fair enchantress.
Sweet siren, I will come!

TOSCA: My beloved!
(*leans her head against Cavaradossi's shoulder. Straightway he draws back a little fixing his gaze upon the Chapel-gates*)

CAVARADOSSI: Now leave me to my labors.

TOSCA: (*surprised*) You dismiss me?

CAVARADOSSI: I must work, child, as you know.

TOSCA: (*showing vexation, rises*) I am going!
(*moves away from Cavaradossi, but, looking back, perceives the picture, and returns to Cavaradossi, much agitated*)
Pray, who is that fair-haired woman there?

CAVARADOSSI: A Magdalen (*calmly*) Do you like her?

TOSCA: She is too handsome.

CAVARADOSSI: (*bowing and smiling*) A flattering judgment!

TOSCA: (*suspiciously*) You smile?
I fancy I have seen those blue eyes somewhere . . .

CAVARADOSSI: (*with indifference*) They're by no means uncommon! . . .

---

TOSCA: (*cercando ricordare*) Aspetta . . . Aspetta . . .
E l'Attavanti!

CAVARADOSSI: (*ridendo*) Brava!

TOSCA: (*cieca di gelosia*) La vedi?
Ti ama? Tu l'ami? Quei passi,
quel bisbiglio . . . Qui stava
pur ora! Ah la civetta!
A me!

CAVARADOSSI: (*serio*) La vidi
ieri—ma fu puro
caso. A pregar qui venne . . . e la ritrassi
non visto.

TOSCA: Giura!

CAVARADOSSI: (*serio*) Giuro!

TOSCA: (*sempre cogli occhi rivolti al quadro*) Come mi guarda fiso!

CAVARADOSSI: (*la spinge dolcemente a scendere dalla gradinata. Essa discende all'indietro tenendo alto le sue mani in quelle di Cavaradossi. Tosca scendendo ha sempre la faccia verso il quadro cui Mario dà le spalle*) Vien via

TOSCA: Di me, beffarda, ride. (*sona scesi*)

CAVARADOSSI: Follia! (*la Tiene presso di sè fissandola in viso*)

TOSCA: (*insistente*) Ah, quegli occhi . . . quegli occhi! . . .

CAVARADOSSI: Quale occhio al mondo mai può star di paro
al limpido ed ardente occhio tuo nero?
In quale mai dell'anima il mistero
si rivelò più subito e più chiaro?
È questo il desïato è questo il caro
occhio ove l'esser mio s'aflisa intero.
Occhio all'amor soave, all'ira fiero
quale altro al mondo ti può star di paro?

---

TOSCA: (*striving to remember*) A moment.
(*ascends the däis, and exclaims triumphantly*)
The Attavanti!

CAVARADOSSI: (*laughing*) Brava!

TOSCA: (*devoured by jealousy*)
You've seen her? She loves you?
You love her?

CAVARADOSSI: (*reassuringly*)
You are mistaken . . .

TOSCA: (*not listening to him, in her jealous rage*) Those footsteps . . . and all that whispering . . .
Ah! You have betrayed me for her . . .

CAVARADOSSI: What nonsense!

TOSCA: That hideous creature!
(*menacingly*) For her!

CAVARADOSSI: (*gravely*) I saw her yesterday by the merest chance.
She came here to pray, and—unseen—I sketched her features . . .

TOSCA: Swear it!

CAVARADOSSI: I swear it (*gravely*)

TOSCA: (*gazing steadfastly at the picture*) See how she stares, the harpy! . . .

CAVARADOSSI: Away, love!

TOSCA: As though she loathed and scorned me.

CAVARADOSSI: (*gently urging her to descend the steps*) What folly!
(*she comes down backwards, holding both Cavaradossi's hands, and never taking her eyes off the picture. Cavaradossi presses her to him fondly, looking lovingly into her eyes*)

TOSCA: (*softly reproaching him*) Ah! those eyes! . . .

CAVARADOSSI: No eyes on earth—not the brightest and clearest—
Are as lustrous as yours . . .
Why do you doubt me? What is it you fear?
Why would your jealous fancy fain discover
A faithless heart in the loyal breast of your own constant lover?

**TOSCA:** (*rapita, appoggiando la testa alla spalla di Cavaradossi*) Oh come la sai bene l'arte di farti amare! . . .
(*sempre insistendo nella sua idea*)
Ma . . . falle gli occhi neri!

**CAVARADOSSI:** Mia gelosa!

**TOSCA:** Sì, lo sento . . . ti tormento
senza posa.

**CAVARADOSSI:** Mia gelosa!

**TOSCA:** Certa sono—del perdono
se tu guardi al mio dolor!

**CAVARADOSSI:** Ogni cosa in te mi piace;
l'ira audace
e lo spasimo d'amor!

**TOSCA:** Dilla ancora
la parola che consola . . .
dilla ancora!

**CAVARADOSSI:** Sì, mia vita, amante inquieta,
dirò sempre: "Floria, t'amo!"
Se la dolce anima acquieta,
"T'amo!" sempre ti dirò!

**TOSCA:** (*sciogliendosi, pauro ad'esser vinta*) Dio, Dio! quante peccata!
M'hai tutta spettinata.

**CAVARADOSSI:** Or va—lasciami!

**TOSCA:** Tu fino a stassera
stai lì, fermo al lavoro. E mi prometti
che sia caso o fortuna,
sia treccia bionda o nera,
a pregar non verrà, donna nessuna?

**CAVARADOSSI:** Lo guiro, amore! . . . —Va!

**TOSCA:** Quanto mi affretti!

**CAVARADOSSI:** (*con dolce rimprovero vedendo rispuntare la gelosia*) Ancora?

**TOSCA:** (*cadendo nelle sue braccia e porgendogli la guancia*) No—perdona!

**CAVARADOSSI:** (*sorridendo*) Davanti la Madonna?

**TOSCA:** È tanto buona!
(*un bacio e Tosca esce correndo*).
(*Appena uscita Tosca, Cavaradossi sta ascoltandone i passi allontanarsi, poi con precauzione socchiude l'uscio e guarda fuori. Visto tutto tranquillo, corre alla Cappella. Angellotti appare subito dietro la cancellata*).

**TOSCA:** (*carried way, and resting her head on his bosom*) Whether you're false or faithful, Mario
I must believe you.
But (*maliciously*) let her eyes be black ones!

**CAVARADOSSI:** (*tenderly*) Jealous darling!

**TOSCA:** Yes, I feel that I torment you without reason

**CAVARADOSSI:** Jealous darling!

**TOSCA:** And I know you will forgive me,
for I hate to give you pain.

**CAVARADOSSI:** My Tosca, dear adored one,
every mood of yours is charming;
even your anger is an ecstasy of love!

**TOSCA:** Oh, repeat those words consoling.
If you love me, pray repeat them!

**CAVARADOSSI:** My own mistrustful angel,
I shall always love you dearly!
Yes, anxious spirit,
I shall love you till I die!

**TOSCA:** See! it is disgraceful!
My hair is quite dishevelled.

**CAVARADOSSI:** Now go; leave me.

**TOSCA:** Continue to work at your picture till nightfall
And you must promise that no pious lady,
no fair or dusky beauty,
shall be admitted here on any pretext!

**CAVARADOSSI:** I promise, beloved! . . . Go!

**TOSCA:** Why should I hurry?

**CAVARADOSSI:** (*reproachfully*) Again, love?

**TOSCA:** (*falls into his arms*) No! forgive me!
(*offers her cheek to his lips*)

**CAVARADOSSI:** (*jestingly*) Before the good Madonna?

**TOSCA:** (*saluting the image*) She won't be angry!
(*about to leave, she again gazes at the picture, and says maliciously*) But let her eyes be black ones!
(*exit hastily. Cavaradossi remains on the stage, plunged in thought. Remembering Angelotti, he listens to Tosca's retreating steps, opens the side-door and looks out. Seeing that all is quiet, he hurries back to the chapel. Angelotti appears behind the railings, which Cavaradossi opens, letting Angelotti out of the chapel. They shake hands affectionately*)

**CAVARADOSSI:** (*aprendo la cancellata ad Angelotti, che naturalment ha dovuto udire il dialogo precedente*) È buona la mia Tosca, ma credente
al confessore nulla tien celato,
ond'io mi tacqui. È cosa più prudente.

**ANGELOTTI:** Siam soli?

**CAVARADOSSI:** Sì. Qual'è il vostro disegno?

**ANGELOTTI:** A norma degli eventi, uscir di Stato
o star celato in Roma. Mia sorella . . .

**CAVARADOSSI:** L'Attavanti?

**ANGELOTTI:** Sì, . . . ascose un muliebre
abbigliamento là sotto l'altare . . .
vesti, velo, ventaglio. Appena imbruni
indosserò quei panni . . .

**CAVARADOSSI:** Ora comprendo!
Quel fare circospetto
e il pregante fervore
in giovin donna e bella
m'avean messo in sospetto
di qualche occulto amore! . . .
Era amor di sorella!

**ANGELOTTI:** Tutto ella ha osato
onde sottrarmi a Scarpia scellerato!

**CAVARADOSSI:** Scarpia?! Bigotto satiro che affina
celle devote pratiche—la foia
libertina—e strumento
al lascivo talento
fa il confessore e il boia!
Vi salverò, ne andasse della vita!
Ma indugiar fino a notte è mal sicuro.

**ANGELOTTI:** Temo del sole!

**CAVARADOSSI:** (*indicando*) La cappella mette
ad un oroto mal chiuso—indi un canneto
mena lungi pei campi a una mia villa.

**ANGELOTTI:** Mi è nota.

**CAVARADOSSI:** Ecco la chiave—innanzi sera
io vi raggiungo—portate con voi le vesti femminili.

**ANGELOTTI:** (*raccoglie in fascio le vestimenta sotto l'altare*) Ch'io le indossi?

**CAVARADOSSI:** Per or non monta, il sentiero è deserto.

**CAVARADOSSI:** (*to Angelotti, who, of course, has heard the preceding conversation*) My Tosca is true-hearted, but indiscreet.
She cannot keep a secret from her old Confessor.
So I deemed it were wiser
to keep your counsel strictly.

**ANGELOTTI:** Are we alone?

**CAVARADOSSI:** Yes. What plan have you concocted?

**ANGELOTTI:** As prudence shall dictate, I shall cross the frontier,
or lie hidden in the city . . . My sister . . .

**CAVARADOSSI:** The Attavanti?

**ANGELOTTI:** Yes . . .
Concealed a full suit of woman's garments,
there, under the altar . . .
The costume lacks nothing essential . . .
(*looks nervously around him*)
It will serve after dark as a disguise. What say you?

**CAVARADOSSI:** Let us hope so!
Such circumspect demeanor,
and devoutness so prayerful,
in such a youthful beauty; I fancied these
were symptoms of some subtle love intrigue! . . .
How I wronged her! She was trying to save you!

**ANGELOTTI:** Reckless of danger, she strove
to rescue me from Scarpia's clutches.

**CAVARADOSSI:** Scarpia?
A bigoted satyr and hypocrite,
secretly steeped in vice and most demonstratively
pious; sanctimonious, lascivious, and cruel;
a cross between confessor and hangman!
(*Indignantly*)—I'll save you,
should it cost even my life!
To delay until night is scarcely prudent . . .

**ANGELOTTI:** Daylight affrights me! . . .

**CAVARADOSSI:** (*pointing towards the chapel*) From the chapel-door you enter a garden.
There runs a roughish path, which, traversing some fields, leads to my villa . . .

**ANGELOTTI:** I know it.

**CAVARADOSSI:** Here is the door-key.
Before it is dark I will rejoin you.
Take with you
the clothes concealed here by your fair sister.

**ANGELOTTI:** (*picks up the garments hidden under the altar*) Must I wear them?

**CAVARADOSSI:** I think you need not, for the path is deserted.

ANGELOTTI: (*per uscire*) Addio!

ANGELOTTI: (*going out*) Farewell, then!

CAVARADOSSI: (*accorrendo verso Angelotti*) Se urgesse il periglio, correte
al pozzo del giardin. L'acqua è nel fondo,
ma a mezzo della canna (e sporgon pietre
ad agevol discesa) un picciol varco
guida ad un antro oscuro,
rifugio impenetrabile e sicuro!
(*un colpo di cannone; i due si guardano agitatissimi*)

CAVARADOSSI: (*follows him hurriedly*) Should danger be imminent, take refuge
in the garden well. Just half-way down
you will find a narrow passage connecting
the old well with a vast, dark cellar.
Hidden there, you will be in perfect safety.
(*A cannon-shot: they exchange glances of alarm*)

ANGELOTTI: Il cannon del castello!

ANGELOTTI: The cannon of the fortress!

CAVARADOSSI: Fu scoperta la fuga! Or Scarpia i suoi sbirri sguinzaglia!

CAVARADOSSI: Your escape has been discovered!
Now Scarpia is unleashing his hounds.

ANGELOTTI: Addio!

ANGELOTTI: Farewell, then!

CAVARADOSSI: (*con subita risoluzione*) Con voi verrò. Staremo all'erta!

CAVARADOSSI: (*resolutely*) I'll go with you. We will evade them!

ANGELOTTI: Odo qualcun!

ANGELOTTI: I hear a step!

CAVARADOSSI: (*con entusiasmo*) Se ci assalgon, battaglia!
(*escono rapidamente dalla Cappella*)

CAVARADOSSI: (*enthusiastically*) We'll fight if they follow!
(*Exeunt quickly through the chapel*)
(*Enter Sacristan hurriedly, well-nigh breathless, exclaiming:*)

SAGRESTANO: (*entra correndo, tutto scalmanato, gridando*) Sommo giubilo, Eccellenza! . . .
(*guarda verso l'impalcato e rimane sorpreso di non trovarvi neppure questa volta il pittore*)
Non c'è più! Ne son dolente!
Chi contrista un miscredente
si guadagna un'indulgenza!
(*accorrono da ogni parte chierici, confratelli, allievi e cantori della Cappella. Tutt costoro entrano tumultuosamente*)
Tutta qui la cantoria!
Presto!
(*altri allievi entrano in ritardo e alla fine si radunano tutti*)

SACRISTAN: Glorious news, your Excellency!
(*astounded at not seeing Cavaradossi seated before the easel*)
Now that's a pity!
He who grieves an unbeliever gains a plenary indulgence!
(*Boys rush in riotously from all the entrances. Enter Acolytes, Penitents, Choristers, and Pupils of the Chapel*)

SACRISTAN: Follow me, all the singing crew! This way, Quickly!

ALLIEVI: (*colla massima confusione*) Dove?

ALL: Where?

SAGRESTANO: In sagrestia.
(*spinge alcuni chièrici*)

SACRISTAN: This way . . .
(*pushing them towards the Sacristy*)

ALCUNI ALLIEVI: Ma che avvenne?

ALL: What has happened?

SAGRESTANO: Nol sapete?
Bonaparte . . . scellerato . . .
Bonaparte . . .

SACRISTAN: Don't you know?
Buonaparte . . .
the miscreant—Buonaparte . . .

ALTRI ALLIEVI: Ebben? Che fu?

ALL: Well, what of him?

SAGRESTANO: Fu spennato, sfracellato
e piombato a Belzebù!

SACRISTAN: Beaten, crushed, humiliated;
Satan has him on the hip!

ALLIEVI, CANTORI, ECC.: Chi lo dice?
—È sogno!
—E fola!

ALL: Who can prove it? What silly nonsense!

SAGRESTANO: È veridica parola
or ne giunse la notizia!
E questa sera
gran fiaccolata
veglia di gala a Palazzo Farnese,
ed un'apposita
nuova cantata
con Floria Tosca!
E nelle chiese
inni a Signore!
Presto a vestirvi,
non più clamore!

SACRISTAN: It's the truth, I assure you!
Soon the news will be made public.

ALL: It will be hailed with loud rejoicing!

SACRISTAN: This very evening
there will be great doings,
Gala performance and torchlight procession,
Also an apposite brand-new cantata
Sung by the Floria with appropriate expression
You singing boys
Put on your vestments, make no more noise.
Off! off, without delay!

TUTTI: (*ridendo e gridando gioiosamente*) Doppio soldo . . . Te Deum . . . Gloria!
Viva il Re! . . . Si festeggi l Vittoria! (*Le loro grida e le loro risa sono al colmo, allorchè una voce i onica tronca brusca- mente quella gazzara volgare di canti e risa. È Scarpia: dietro a lui Spoletta e alcuni sbirri*)

ALL: (*They burst out laughing and pay no attention to the SacristaN, who tries in vain to drive them into the sacristy*) Double wages! Te Deum, gloria!
Long live the King!
This very evening there will be great doings,
gala performance, torchlight procession,
a brand-new cantata sung by Tosca.
Long live the King!
Yes, this evening there will be great do—
(*enter Scarpia unexpectedly, he stands in the doorway; seeing him, all are stricken dumb and motionless, as though spellbound*)

SCARPIA: Un tal baccano in chiesa! Bel rispetto!

SCARPIA: (*imperiously*) Pray, why this great commotion?
In a church, too!
(*Spoletta and other police-agents follow Scarpia*)

SAGRESTANO: (*balbettando impaurito*) Eccellenza, il gran giubilo . . .

SACRISTAN: (*affrighted and stammering*) Excellency . . . We were overjoyed . . .

SCARPIA: Apprestate
per il Te Deum.
(*tutti si allontanano mogi: anche il Sagrestano fa per cavarsela, ma Scarpia bruscamente lo trattiene*)
Tu resta!

SCARPIA: Make ready, all, for the Te Deum.
(*They all sneak out, and the Sacristan is about to follow their example, when Scarpia bids him stay*)
Stay here!

SAGRESTANO: (*impaurito*) Non mi muovo!

SACRISTAN: (*alarmed*) I obey you!

SCARPIA: (*a Spoletta*) E tu va, fruga ogni angolo, raccogli ogni traccia!

SCARPIA: (*to Spoletta*) And go search every corner,
look sharply about you!

SPOLETTA: Sta bene!
(*fa cenno a due sbirri di seguirlo*)

SPOLETTA: I shall . . .

SCARPIA: (*ad altri sbirri*) Occhio alle porte,
ma senza dar sospetti!
(*al Sagrestano*) Ora a te. Pesa e tue risposte. Un prigionier di Stato
pur or fuggito di Castel Sant'Angelo s'è rifugiato qui.

SCARPIA: (*signals two agents to follow Spoletta*) Watch all the doorways.
(*to other agents of the party*)
Arouse no suspicion.
(*to the Sacristan*)
Now for you! Answer my questions truly.
A prisoner of State escaped, an hour ago,
from Fort San Angelo, and he is hidden here . . .

SAGRESTANO: Misericordia!

SACRISTAN: Misericordia!

SCARPIA: Forse c'è ancora. Dov'è la cappella
degli Attavanti?

SAGRESTANO: Eccola!
(*va al cancello e lo vede socchiuso*)
Aperta! Arcangeli!
E . . . un'altra chiave!

SCARPIA: Buon indizio. Entriamo.
(*entrano nella Cappella, poi ritornano: Scarpia, assai contrariato, ha fra le maui un ventaglio chiuso che agita nervosamente*)
Tardi! Fu grave sbaglio
quel colpo di cannone. Il mariolo
spiccato ha il volo, ma lasciò una presa . . .
prezïosa—un ventaglio.
Qual complice il misfatto preparò?
(*resta pensieroso, poi guarda attentamente il ventaglio; a un tratto egli vi scorge uno stemma*)
La marchesa
Attavanti! . . . Il suo stemma . . .
(*guarda intorno, scrutando ogni angolo della chiesa: i suoi occhi si arrestano sull'impalcato, sugli arnesi del pittore, sul quadro . . . e il note viso dell'Attavanti gli appare riprodotto nel volto della santa*)
Il suo ritratto!
(*a Sagrestano*)
Chi fe' quelle pitture?

SAGRESTANO: Il cavaliere
Cavaradossi.

SCARPIA: Lui!
(*uno dei birri che segui Scarpia, torna dalla Cappella portando il paniere che Cava radossi diede ad Angelotti*)

SAGRESTANO: (*vedendolo*)
Numi! Il paniere!

SCARPIA: (*seguitando le sue riflessioni*) Lui! L'amante di Tosca!
Un uom sospetto!
Un volterrian!

SAGRESTANO: (*che andò a guardare il paniere*) Vuoto? Vuoto!

SCARPIA: Che hai detto?
(*vede il birro col paniere*)
Che fu?

SAGRESTANO: (*prendendo il paniere*) Si ritrovò nella cappella
questo panier.

SCARPIA: Tu lo conosci?

SCARPIA: He must be here still. Which chapel bears the name of the Attavanti?

SACRISTAN: This is it.
(*goes up to the railing, and finds it unlocked*)
'Tis open! Archangels!
This key is a new one!
(*shows key*)

SCARPIA: That gives a clue . . . We shall see.
(*they enter the chapel and return promptly, Scarpia manifestly annoyed, holding in his hand a closed fan, which he flutters nervously*)
A stupid blunder (*aside*) that gunshot from
the fortress; it gave the criminal timely
warning, and he fled. But he left here
this bauble . . . (*waving the fan*) A love token.
What fair accomplice helped him to escape?
(*plunged in thought, carefully inspects the fan, and suddenly catching sight of a coat-of-arms, exclaims*)
'Twas the fair Attavanti! . . . These are her arms . . .
(*looks around, examining every nook and corner of the Church. His attention is caught by the scaffolding, the painter's easel, and the picture, which reproduces the well-known face of the Marchioness Attavanti in a counterfeit presentment of Mary Magdalen*)
It is her portrait.
(*to the Sacristan*)
Who painted that picture?

SACRISTAN: (*still terror-stricken*) Sir Mario Cavaradossi . . .

SCARPIA: He!

SACRISTAN: (*perceiving a police-agent, who issues from the Chapel, basket in hand*) Bless me! This is his basket!

SCARPIA: (*following up his train of thought*) He! The lover of Tosca!
A man suspected! An unbeliever!

SACRISTAN: (*having looked inside the basket, exclaims in great surprise*) Empty! . . . .

SCARPIA: (*catching sight of the agent and the basket*) What did you say? Speak up!

SACRISTAN: (*takes the basket from the agent*) It has been found inside the Chapel,
hidden away.

SCARPIA: Do you recognize it?

SAGRESTANO: Certo!
(*è esitante e pauroso*)
E il cesto del pittor . . . ma . . . nondimeno . . .

SCARPIA: Sputa quello che sai.

SAGRESTANO: Io lo lasciai
ripieno
di cibo prelibato . . .
il pranzo del pittore! . . .

SCARPIA: (*attento, inquirente per scoprir terreno*) Avrà pranzato!

SAGRESTANO: Nella cappella?
Non ne avea la chiave
nè contava pranzar . . . eisse egli stesso.
Ond'io già l'avea messo
qual mia spoglia al riparo.
(*mostra dove avea riposta il paniere e ve lo lascia*)

SCARPIA: (Tutto è chiaro . . .
la provvista—del sacrista
d'Angelotti fu la preda!)
(*scorgendo Tosca che entra frettoloso*)
Tosca? Che non mi veda.
(*ripara dietro la colonna dov'è la pila dell'acqua benedetta*)
(Per ridurre un geloso allo sbaraglio A Jago un fazzoletto—a me un ventaglio!)

TOSCA: (*corre al palco sicura di trovare Cavaradossi e sorpresa di non vederlo*) Mario?! Mario?!

SAGRESTANO: (*che si trova al piedi dell'impalcato*) Il pittore Cavaradossi?
Chi sa dove sia
l'eretico e con chi?
Sgattaiolò, svanì
per sua stregoneria. (*e se la svigna*)

TOSCA: Ingannata?
No . . . no . . .
tradirmi egli non può!

SCARPIA: (*ha girato la colonna e si presenta a Tosca, sorpresa del suo subito apparire. Intinge le dita nella pila e le offre l'acqua benedetta; fuori suonano le campane che invitano aila chiesa*).
Tosca divina
la mano mia

SACRISTAN: Doubtless! It is the painter's basket . . . .
(*stammering timidly*)
but . . . notwithstanding . . . .

SCARPIA: (*vehemently*) Spit out all that you know!

SACRISTAN: (*still affrighted, tearfully holds up the empty basket*) I brought it here,
filled wit the best of food and liquor . . .
The painter's mid-day meal . . .

SCARPIA: (*significantly*) Which he has eaten!

SACRISTAN: (*making a negative gesture*) Not in the Chapel!
for he did not have the key, nor did he
mean to eat at all . . . at least, so he told me.
So I had set it down there,
(*points to the place where he had left the full basket*)
beneath the easel.
(*Painfully impressed by Scarpia's stern and silent bearing*)
(Deliver us from temptation!) (*to himself*)

SCARPIA: (*aside*) It is clear as daylight . . . The provisions
of the Sacristan were devoured by Angelotti.
(*Enter Tosca nervously; she walkes straight up to the scaffolding. Not finding Cavaradossi there, in great agitation, she searches for him in the central nave of the church. Scarpia, as soon as he sees her come in, instantly hides behind the pillar to which the holy-water trough is affixed, imperatively signalling the Sacristan to stay where he is. The Sacristan trembling with confusion, stands near the painter's däis*)
Tosca! She must not see me!
It was a handkerchief that lit Othello's jealous fire,
Now shall this fragile fan rouse Tosca's ire!

TOSCA: (*returns to the däis, calling out loudly and impatiently*)
Mario! Mario!

SACRISTAN: (*approaching her*)
Do you mean Cavaradossi?
Where he is, who can say?
Obedient to some spell he vanished clean away.
(*exit furtively*)

TOSCA: Has he betrayed me? No!
To me he could not be untrue.

SCARPIA: (*turns round the pillar, dips his fingers in the trough, and offers holy water to Tosca. Bells ring to church*) Divinest Tosca,
(*gently and insinuatingly*)
your dainty hand, that milk-white wonder,
lend me for a moment, that I may

la vostra aspetta—piccola manina,
non per galanteria
ma per offrirvi l'acqua benedetta.

TOSCA: (*tocca le dita di Scarpia e si fa il segno della croce*) Grazie, signor!
(*Poco a poco entrano in chiesa, e vanno nella navata principale, popolani, borghesi, ciociare, trasteverine, soldati, pecorari, ciociari, mendicanti, ecc.: poi un Cardinale, col Capitolo, si reca all'altare maggiore; la folla, rivolta verso l'altare maggiore, si accalca nella navata principale*).

SCARPIA: Un nobile
esempio il vostro—al cielo
piena di santo zelo
attingete dell'arte il magistero
che la fede ravviva!

TOSCA: (*distratta e pensosa*) Bontà vostra.

SCARPIA: Le pie donne son rare . . .
Voi calcate la scena . . .
(*con intenzione*)
ma in chiesa ci venite per pregare.

TOSCA: (*sorpresa*) Che intendete?

SCARPIA: E non fate
Come certe sfrontate
che hanno di Maddalena (*indica il ritratto*)
viso e costumi . . . e vi trescan d'amore!

TOSCA: (*scatta pronta*) Che? D'amore? Le prove!

SCARPIA: (*mostra il ventaglio*) È arnese di pittore questo?

TOSCA: (*lo afferra*) Un ventaglio? Dove stava?

SCARPIA: Là su quel palco. Qualcun venne
certo a sturbar gli amanti
ed essa nel fuggir perdè le penne!

TOSCA: (*esaminando it ventaglio*) La corona! Lo stemma! È l'Attavanti!
Ah presago sospetto!

SCARPIA: (Ho sortito l'effetto!)

TOSCA: (*trattenendo a stento le lagrime, dimentica del luogo e di Scarpia*) Ed io venivo a lui tutta dogliosa
per dirgli: invan stassera
ai sospirosi amanti il ciel s'infosca
l'innamorata Tosca
dei regali tripudi è prigioniera!

---

lightly touch it
with my uncouth fingers dipped in holy water . . .

TOSCA: (*touches Scarpia's fingers, and crosses herself*) Thanks, many thanks!

SCARPIA: No woman alive does nobler work than you.
From heaven, teeming with fervid sanctity,
you conjure to earth the sacred raptures
that give life to religion.

TOSCA: (*thoughtful and inattentive*) Spare my blushes.
(*Several people enter the church and gather together up the stage*)

SCARPIA: Pious songsters are rare,
But you, the star of the lyric stage,
Come here to bend your knees in prayer.
(*Bells ring to church*)

TOSCA: (*surprised*) What do you mean?

SCARPIA: You are not like certain frivolous wantons;
(*points to the portrait*)
Magdalens they simulate profanely,
and come here to meet their lovers.
(*Emphatically.*)

TOSCA: (*starting*) How? Their lovers? What do you mean?

SCARPIA: (*showing her the fan*) Is this a painter's brush or mahlstick?

TOSCA: (*seizing it*) It's a fan! Where did you find it?

SCARPIA: There, on the easel. (*Enter the peasants*)
Some casual worshippers disturbed the lovers,
and in her hasty flight she dropped some feathers!

TOSCA: (*examining the fan*) A coronel! Her arms, too!
It is Attavanti's! Prophetic suspicion!

SCARPIA: (*aside*) My design has succeeded

TOSCA: (*sorrowfully, restraining her tears with difficulty, forgetful of the locality and of Scarpia*) And I who sought him here, oppressed with sorrow,
To say I could not meet him till tomorrow,
That Tosca, to her grief and consternation,
Would have to figure at this evening's celebration.

---

SCARPIA: (Già il veleno l'ha rosa.)
(*mellifluo a Tosca*)
O che v'offende,
dolce signora?
Una ribelle
lacrima scende
sovra le belle
guancie e le irrora;
dolce signora,
che mai v'accora?

TOSCA: Nulla!

SCARPIA: (*insinuante*) Io darei la vita
per asciugar quel pianto.

TOSCA: (*non ascoltandolo*) Io qui mi struggo e intanto
d'altra in braccio ci la mie smanie deride!

SCARPIA: (Morde il veleno.)

TOSCA: (*sempre più crucciosa*)
Dove son? Potessi
coglierli i traditori. O qual sospetto!
Ai doppi amori
è la villa recetto.
(*con immenso dolore*)
O mio bel nido insozzato di fango!
(*con pronta risoluzione*)
Vi piomberò inattesa.
(*rivolta al quadro minacciosa*)
Tu non l'avrai stanotte. Giuro!

SCARPIA: (*scandolezzato, quasi rimproverandola*) In chiesa!

TOSCA: Dio mi perdona. Egli vede ch'io piango!
(*parte in grande agitazione: Scarpia l'accompagna, fingendo di rassicuraria. Appens uscita Tosca, Scarpia ritorna presso la colonna e fa un cenno*).

SCARPIA: (*a Spoletta che sbuca di dietro la colonna*) Tre sbirri . . . Presto—seguila
dovunque vada . . . non visto . . . e provvedi!

SPOLETTA: Basta. Il convegno?

SCARPIA: A Palazzo Farnese!
(*Spoletta parte rapidamente con tre sbirri*)
Va, Tosca! Nel tuo cuor s'annida Scarpia.
Egli ti segue e ti sospinge. È Scarpia
che scioglie a volo il falco
della tua gelosia. Quanta promessa
nel tuo pronto sospetto! A doppia

---

SCARPIA: (*aside*) How the poison is working!
(*enter groups of peasants, carters, etc.*)
(*gently*) What has aggrieved you, Sweetest of creatures? . . .
Say, has some traitor basely deceived you,
That tears bedew those exquisite features?
Tell me, fair Tosca, what has aggrieved you?

TOSCA: Nothing!

SCARPIA: I'd give my life if I could mitigate your anguish.

TOSCA: (*not listening to him*) And here I must languish in grief,
While, embraced in other arms, he derides me!

SCARPIA: (Well works the poison!) (*aside*)

TOSCA: Where am I?
(*A few citizens stroll in*)
How could I think he would yield to temptation?
My pretty villa! (*angrily*)
Must I submit to its vile profanation?
Cruel Mario!
In mire my nest of love they have been steeping!
(*resolutely*)
I'll purge it of their vileness!
(*turns threateningly towards the picture*)
Tonight you shall not possess him!
(*desperately*)
I swear it!

SCARPIA: (*scandalized*) In church!

TOSCA: (*weeping*) God will forgive me, for He sees I am weeping!
(*sobs bitterly. Scarpia accompanies her to the door, pretending to reassure her. After her exit, the church becomes gradually fuller and fuller. Having escorted Tosca to the church-door, Scarpia returns to the chapel-gate and makes a sign, in obedience to which Spoletta issues from behind the pillar. The crowd withdraws to the back of the church, awaiting the Cardinal; some kneel down and pray*)

SCARPIA: Three agents, and a close carriage . . . Quickly . . . follow her whithersoever she may go . . . Be careful!

SPOLETTA: I will. Where shall I find you?

SCARPIA: At the Farnese Palace!
(*Exit Spoletta hurriedly. Scarpia smiles sardonically*)
Go, Tosca! There is room in your heart for Scarpia.
(*The Cardinal and his following advance to the high altar; the Swiss Guards divide the crowd, which ranges itself on either side*

mira tendo il voler, nè il capo del ribelle
è la più prezïosa. Ah di quegli occhi
vittorïosi vedere la fiamma
illanguidir nello spasmo d'amore!
La doppia preda avrò. L'uno al
capestro,
l'altra fra le mie braccia . . . me
ne affida
l'invincibil desïo . . .
(l santo sacro dal fondo della
chiesa lo scuote, come svegliando-
lo da un sogno. Si ri mette, fa il
segno della croce guardandosi intorno, e dice:)
Tosca, mi fai dimenticare Iddio!
(s'inginccchia e prega devota-
mente).

of the procession. Organ plays)
Go, Tosca! For Scarpia it is who has
fired
your soul and stirred up your jealous passion.
(Cannon fired)
Infinite promise lies in your hasty
suspicions.
There is room in your heart for Scarpia . . .
(ironically)
Go, Tosca!
(He bows reverently as the Cardinal passes by, blessing the kneeling throng)
(Fiercely) Twofold the purpose
now I entertain,
and the hanging of that rebel
is by no means my chief
desire . . .
It is in her gay, triumphant eyes that
I hope soon to kindle love's languid
flame,
when in my arms she is clasped,
mute with fond rapture, giddy with
amorous joy.
(Savagely) One to the scaffold, and
the other to my fond arms . . .
(The whole crowd turns towards
the high altar. Many kneel. Scarpia stands enwrapt in thought,
then starts, as in a dream)
Tosca! for you I could renounce
my hopes of heaven!
(With religious fervor, kneeling)
Te oeternum Patrem, etc.

*Quick Curtain*

# ■ ATTO SECONDO

*La camera di Scarpia al piano su-
periore del Palazzo Farnese.*

*Tavola imbandita. Un'ampia
finestra verso il cortile del Palazzo. È notte.*

SCARPIA: (*è seduto alla tavola e
vi cena. Interrompe a tratti la
cena per riflettere. Guarda
l'orologio: è smanioso e pensieroso*) Tosca è un buon falco! . . .
Certo a quest'ora
i miei segugi le due prede azzanna-
no!
Doman sul palco
vedrà l'aurora
Angelotti e il bel Mario al laccio
pendere.
(*suona—entra Sciarrone*)
Tosca è a palazzo?

SCIARRONE: Un ciambellan ne usciva
pur ora in traccia

# ■ ACT II

*Scene: The Farnese Palace.*

*Scarpia's apartments, on an up-
per floor. The table is laid for supper. A large window overlooks the
Palace Courtyard. Nightfall
(Scarpia is seated, supping and
breaking off at intervals to reflect.
From time to time he looks at his
watch, manifesting agitation and
disquietude.)*

SCARPIA: Tosca is a good decoy,
and, by this time,
my people have secured the two
conspirators.
Tomorrow's sunrise shall see them
hanging side by side like dogs,
upon my tallest gallows.
(*rings a hand-bell. Enter
Sciarrone.*)
Is Tosca in the Palace?

SCIARRONE: A page has been des-
patched
to fetch her here . . .

SCARPIA: (*accenna la finestra*)
Apri.—Tarda è la notte.
(*dal piano inferiore—que la Regina di Napoli, Maria Carolina, dà
una grande festa in onore di
Melas—si ode il suonare di
un'orchestra*)
Alla cantata ancor manca la Diva,
e strimpellan gavotte.
(*a Sciarrone*)
Tu attenderai la Tosca in
sull'entrata;
le dirai ch'io l'aspetto
finita la cantata . . .
o meglio . . .
(*si alza e va a scrivere in fretta un
biglietto*)
(*Sciarrone esce*) (*siede ancora a
tavola*) Ella verrà . . . per amor
del suo Mario!
Per amor del suo Mario al piacer
mio
s'arrenderà. Tal dei profondi amori
è la profonda miseria. IIa più forte
sapore la conquista vïolenta
che il mellifluo consenso. Io di sospiri
e di lattiginose albe lunari
poco mi appago. Non so trarre accordi
di chitarra, nè oròscopo di fiori,
nè far l'occhio di pesce, o tubar
come
tortora! (*alzandosi*)
Bramo.—La cosa bramata
persequo, me ne sazio e via la getto
volto a nuova esca. Dio creò diverse
beltà a vini diversi. Io vo' gustare
quauto più posso dell'opra divina!
(*beve*)

SCIARRONE: (*entrando*) Spoletta
è giunto.

SCARPIA: Entri. In buon punto.

SCARPIA: (*si siede e
tutt'occupato a cenare, interroga
intanto Spoletta senza guardano*)
O galantuomo, come andò la caccia?

SPOLETTA: (Sant'Ignazio mi aiuta!)
Della signora seguimmo la traccia.
Giunti a un'erma villetta
tra le fratte perduta
ella vi entrò. Ne uscì sola ben presto.
Io allor scavalco lesto
il muro del giardin co' miei cagnot-

SCARPIA: (*Sciarrone, pointing to
the window*) Open!
(*An orchestra is audible in a lower storey, where Queen Caroline is
giving an entertainment in honour of General Melas.*)
Late is the hour . . . For Tosca
they're waiting to commence the
Cantata,
and meanwhile they are dancing.
(*aside*)
(*to Sciarrone*)
You will await the Tosca at the entrance,
and will tell her I expect her
at the end of the Cantata . . .
(*He recalls Sciarrone, who is going, rises, crosses the stage to a
high desk, and hurriedly writes a
note, handing it to Sciarrone*)
Be sure you give her this letter
(*exit Sciarrone*)
She will come . . . for the sake of her
Mario!
For the sake of her Mario,
she will comply with my desire.
Such are the alterations of love's
deep joys and deep sorrows.
Keener far is the relish of a forcible
conquest
than of a passive surrender. Sighs of
entreaty
and sentimental rhapsodies by
moonlight
do not delight me. I am not skilled
in twanging the guitar, nor in
fortune-telling lore; I cannot leer
nor ogle,
nor coo like any turtle-dove (*disdainfully*)
(*he rises, but does not leave the table*)
Hence must I strive for the thing I
desire.
I possess it, and then discard it,
turning to other pleasures.
God created beauty and wine of various
merit; I choose to taste all that I can
of the heavenly produce.
(*enter Sciarrone*)

SCIARRONE: Here is Spoletta.

SCARPIA: (*loudly, in great excitement*) Bring him to me.

SCARPIA: (*resumes his seat. Exit
Sciarrone to summon Spoletta,
who returns with him and takes
up his stand near entrance C.
Busy with his supper, Scarpia in-
terrogates Spoletta without looking at him*) Well, my fine fellow.

SPOLETTA: (*coming forward
nervously*) Saint Ignatius protect
me! (*aside*)
(*aloud*) Quickly we followed the
track of the lady.
Soon we arrived at a villa almost
hidden by foliage;
Madam went in, and came out again
promptly.

ti
e piombo in casa . . .

SCARPIA: Quel bravo Spoletta!

SPOLETTA: (*esitando*) Fiuto! . . . Razzolo! . . . frugo!

SCARPIA: (*si avvede dell'indecisione di Spoletta e si leva ritto, pallido d'ira, le ciglia corrugate*) Ahi! l'Angelotti?

SPOLETTA: Non s'è trovato.

SCARPIA: (*furente*) Ah cane! Ah traditore!
Ceffo di basilisco,
alle forche!

SPOLETTA: Gesù!
(*cercando scongiurare la collera di Scarpia*)
C'era il pittore . . .

SCARPIA: Cavaradossi?

SPOLETTA: (*accenna di sì, ed aggiunge pronto*) Ei sa
dove l'altro s'asconde. Ogni suo gesto
ogni accento, tradìa
tal beffarda ironia,
ch'io lo trassi in arresto!

SCARPIA: (*con sospiro di soddisfazione*) Meno male!

SPOLETTA: (*accena all'anticamera*) Egli è là.
(*Scarpia passeggia meditando: a un tratto si arresta: dall'aperta finestra odesi la Cantata eseguita dai Cori nella sala della Regina.*)

SCARPIA: (*a Spoletta*) Introducete il Cavaliere. (*Spoletta esce*)
(*a Sciarrone*) A me
Roberti e il Giudice del Fisco.
(*Sciarrone esce; Scarpia siede di nuovo*)
(*Spoletta e quatro birri introducono Mario Cavaradossi. Poi Roberti, esecutore di Giustizia, il Giudice Del Fisco con uno Scrivano e Sciarrone.*)

CAVARADOSSI: (*alteramente*) Tale violenza! . . .

SCARPIA: (*con studiata cortesia*) Cavalier, vi piaccia accomodarvi.

CAVARADOSSI: Vo' saper . . .

SCARPIA: (*accennando una sedia al lato opposto della tavola*) Sedete.

Straightway I lightly scaled the coping of the wall
with my companions, and entered the garden . . .

SCARPIA: Well done, good Spoletta!

SPOLETTA: (*hesitantly*) Vainly we searched the house . . .

SCARPIA: (*perceiving Spoletta's embarrassment, arises, pale with anger, and frowning formidably*) Ah! Angelotti?

SPOLETTA: We could not find him!

SCARPIA: Base scoundrel! Vilest of traitors!
Spawn of the fiend incarnate!
to the gallows! (*furiously*)

SPOLETTA: Good Lord!
(*trying to assuage Scarpia's wrath, says timidly*)
The painter was there . . .

SCARPIA: (*interrupting him*) Cavaradossi?

SPOLETTA: (*nodding affirmatively*) He knows where the other one is hidden . . .
His scornful gestures, his contemptuous scoffings
aroused my suspicions; so I put him in irons . . .

SCARPIA: You did wisely.
(*Spoletta is evidently relieved. Scarpia walks about thoughtfully, then suddenly stands still, hearing through the open window the cantata executed by the choirs assembled in the Queen's reception-rooms. The singing proves that Tosca has returned and is actually in the Palace, on the storey beneath Scarpia's apartments*)

SPOLETTA: (*pointing towards the ante-room*) He is there!

SCARPIA: (*suddenly struck by an idea*) Bring the prisoner straightaway.
(*exit Spoletta*)
(*To Sciarrone*) Roberti and the Judge of the Exchequer.
(*resumes his seat. Spoletta and three police-agents bring in Cavaradossi. Enter Roberti the executioner, an Exchequer Judge with his clerk, and Sciarrone*)

CAVARADOSSI: (*angrily*) Why this outrage?

SCARPIA: (*with elaborate courtesy*) Noble sir, I beg you to be seated . . .

CAVARADOSSI: (*firmly*) I wish to know . . .

SCARPIA: (*pointing to a chair on the other side of the table*) Be seated . . .

CAVARADOSSI: (*riflutando*) Aspetto.

SCARPIA: E sia!—Vi è noto che un prigione . . .
(*odesi la voce di Tosca che Prende parte alla Cantata*)

CAVARADOSSI: La sua voce! . . .

SCARPIA: (*che si era interrotto all'udire la voce dì Tosca, riprende*) . . . vi è noto che un prigione
oggi è fuggito di Castel Sant'Angelo?

CAVARADOSSI: Ignoro.

SCARPIA: Eppur si pretende che voi
l'abbiate accolto in Sant'Andrea, provvisto
di cibo e vesti . . .

CAVARADOSSI: (*risoluto*) Menzogna!

SCARPIA: (*continuando a mantenersi calmo*) . . . e guidato ad un vostro podere suburbano.

CAVARADOSSI: Nego.—Le prove?

SCARPIA: (*mellifluo*)Un suddito fedele . . .

CAVARADOSSI: Al fatto. Chi mi accusa? I vostri birri
frugaro invan tutta la villa.

SCARPIA: Segno
che è ben celato

CAVARADOSSI: Sospetti di spia!

SPOLETTA: (*offeso, interviene*) Alle nostre ricerche egli sideva . . .

CAVARADOSSI: E rido ancor.

SCARPIA: (*con accento severo*) Questo è luogo di lacrime!
(*si aiza e chiude stizzito la finestra per non essere disturbate dai canti che banno luogo nel piano sottostante: poi si volge imperioso a Cavaradossi:*)
Ov'è Angelotti?

CAVARADOSSI: Non lo so.

SCARPIA: Negate
avergli dato cibo?

CAVARADOSSI: Nego!

SCARPIA: E vesti?

CAVARADOSSI: Nego!

SCARPIA: Ed asilo alla villa?

CAVARADOSSI: Nego!

CAVARADOSSI: (*refusing*) No thank you.

SCARPIA: As you please.
(*looks steadfastly at Cavaradossi before questioning him*)
Today escaped from prison—
(*breaking off at the sound of Tosca's voice singing in the cantata*)

CAVARADOSSI: It is her voice! . . . (*hearing Tosca*)

SCARPIA: (*resuming*) Today escaped from prison one whom you know to be a dangerous criminal.

CAVARADOSSI: I know nothing!

SCARPIA: And yet it is alleged that you concealed
him in the Church of Sant' Andrea, and
provided him with food and with raiment . . .

CAVARADOSSI: (*resolutely*) Mere falsehoods!

SCARPIA: (*preserving a calm demeanor*) Later on, you conveyed him to a
villa in the suburbs . . .

CAVARADOSSI: I deny it. Who says so?

SCARPIA: (*mildly*) A faithful, honest servant . . .

CAVARADOSSI: To the purpose. My accuser?
In vain (*ironically*) your myrmidons have
searched the villa.

SCARPIA: Proving he was well hidden.

CAVARADOSSI: Your spies could not find him!

SPOLETTA: (*interposes, offended*) Scoffing and sneering, he laughed at all
our endeavors . . .

CAVARADOSSI: And still he laughs.

SCARPIA: (*rising in anger*) This is no place for merriment! (*threateningly*)
I warn you! Enough now (*nervously*)
Answer truly!
(*disturbed and annoyed by the singing, he closes the window. Imperiously to Cavaradossi*)
Where is Angelotti?

CAVARADOSSI: I do not know.

SCARPIA: You never with food and drink supplied him?

CAVARADOSSI: Never!

SCARPIA: Nor with garments?

CAVARADOSSI: Never!

SCARPIA: Nor concealed him in your villa,
where he still lies hidden?

SCARPIA: E che là sia nascosto?

CAVARADOSSI: (*con forza*) Nego! nego!

SCARPIA: (*astutamente, ritornando calmo*) Via, Cavalier, pensateci: l'uom saggio
piega alla legge . . . armata. Una sollecita
confessìone può cansar dal vostro capo molte sciagure. Date retta: dov'è Angelotti?

CAVARADOSSI: Non lo so.

SCARPIA: Badate!
L'ultima volta. Dov'è?

CAVARADOSSI: Non lo so!

SPOLETTA: (O bei tratti di corda!)
(*Tosca, entra affannosa.*)

SCARPIA: (*vedendo Tosca*) (Eccola!)

TOSCA: (*vede Cavaradossi e corre ad abbracciarlo*) Mario, tu qui?!

CAVARADOSSI: (*sommessamente*) (Di quanto là vedesti, taci, o m'uccidi! . . . )
(*Tosca accenna che ha capito*)

SCARPIA: (*con solennità*) Mario Cavaradossi, qual testimonio il Giudice vi aspetta.
(*a Roberti*)
Pria le forme ordinarie.—
Indi . . . a miei cenni.
(*Sciarrone apre l'uscio che dà alla camera della tortura. Il Giudice vi entra e gli altri lo seguono, rimanendo Tosca e Scarpia. Spoletta si ritira presso alla porta in fondo alla sala*)
Ed or fra noi parliamo da buoni amici. Via
quell'aria sgomenta . . . (*accenna a Tosca di sedere*)

TOSCA: (*siede con calma studiata*) Sgomento alcun non ho.

SCARPIA: La storia del ventaglio?
(*passa dietro al canapè sul quale si è seduta Tosca e vi si appoggia, parlando sempre con galanteria*)

TOSCA: (*con simulata indifferenza*) Fu sciocca gelosia.

SCARPIA: L'Attavanti non era dunque alla villa?

TOSCA: No: egli era solo.

SCARPIA: Solo?—Ne siete ben sicura?

CAVARADOSSI: (*vehemently*) Never! Never!

SCARPIA: (*almost paternally*) I pray you, give my words attention; stubbornness such as yours is far from wise,
believe me. By frank confession you may avert the pain that else awaits you.
Let me advise you; tell me; where is Angelotti now?

CAVARADOSSI: I don't know.

SCARPIA: Once more, and for the last time.
Where is he?

CAVARADOSSI: I do not know!

SPOLETTA: (*aside*) (How he tightens his clutches!)
(*Enter Tosca in alarm; she runs up to Cavaradossi and embraces him*)

TOSCA: Mario! Are you here?

CAVARADOSSI: (*under his breath to Tosca, who makes sign that she understands*) Say nothing of what you have seen there, or you will kill me!

SCARPIA: Mario Cavaradossi, the judge is
waiting to take your deposition.
(*signals Sciarrone to open the entrance to the torture-chamber, and turns to Roberti*)
First the usual pressure; later, as I instruct you . . .
(*The judge passes into the torture-chamber, and other follow him, only Tosca and Scarpia remaining behind. Spoletta withdraws to the door situate C, at the back of the stage. Sciarrone closes the door L, greatly to Tosca's surprise. Scarpia reassures her with sedulous politeness*)
Now let us have a friendly talk together
(*signs to her to be seated*)
There is nothing to alarm you . . .

TOSCA: (*sits down with affected calm*) Nor do I feel alarmed . . .

SCARPIA: (*leans on the back of the sofa on which Tosca is seated*) The story of the fan?

TOSCA: (*with feigned indifference*) Was one of silly jealousy . . .

SCARPIA: The Attavanti, it seems, was not at the villa?

TOSCA: No. No one but he was there.

SCARPIA: No one? (*maliciously*) Of that you are quite certain?

TOSCA: Nulla, sfugge ai gelosi. Solo! solo!

SCARPIA: (*prende una sedia, la porta di fronte a Tosca, vi si siede e guarda fissamente Tosca*) Davver?

TOSCA: (*irritata*) Solo! sì!

SCARPIA: Quanto fuoco! Par che abbiate paura di tradirvi.
(*chiamando*) Sciarrone: che dice il Cavalier?

SCIARRONE: (*apparendo sul limitare dell'uscio*) Nega.

SCARPIA: (*a voce più alta verso lascio aperto*) Insistiamo.
(*Sciarrone rientra nella camera della tortura, chiudendone l'uscio*)

TOSCA: (*ridendi*) Oh, inutile.

SCARPIA: (*serlissimo, si alza e passeggia*) Lo vedremo, signora.

TOSCA: Dunque per compiacervi si dovrebbe mentir?

SCARPIA: No; ma il vero potrebbe abbreviargli un'ora
assai penosa . . .

TOSCA: (*sorpresa*) Un'ora penosa? Che vuol dir?
Che avviene in quella stauza?

SCARPIA: È forza che si adempia la legge.

TOSCA: Oh! Dio! . . . che avviene?

SCARPIA: Legato mani e piè
il vostro amante ha un cerchio uncinato alle tempia.
che a ogni niego ne sprizza sangue senza mercè.

TOSCA: (*balza in piedi*) Non è ver, non è vero! Sogghigno di demòne . . .
Quale orrendo silenzio! . . . Ah! un gemito . . . pietà . . .
(*ascolta ansiosamente*)

SCARPIA: Sta in voi salvarlo.

TOSCA: Ebbene . . . ma cessate!

SCARPIA: (*va presso all'uscio*) Sciarrone, sciogliete.

SCIARRONE: (*si presenta sul limitare*) Tutto?

SCARPIA: Tutto.
(*Sciarrone entra di nuovo nella camera aena tortu., chiudendo*)
(*a Tosca*) Ed or . . . la verità,

TOSCA: Ch'io lo veda!

SCARPIA: No!

TOSCA: I saw all that there was to see. (*insistently*) Alone!

SCARPIA: Indeed!

TOSCA: (*irritated*) Yes, alone!

SCARPIA: What excitement! Do you fear to commit some indiscretion?
(*turning towards the entrance to the torture-chamber*)
Sciarrone, what does the witness say?

SCIARRONE: (*appears in the door*) Nothing!

SCARPIA: (*still more loudly*) Be more urgent.
(*Sciarrone retires, closing the door*)

TOSCA: (*laughing*) Oh! It's useless!

SCARPIA: (*gravely, walking about the room*) We shall see, fairest lady.

TOSCA: (*slowly, smiling ironically*) So, if I wish to please you, I must tell you lies?

SCARPIA: No; by truthfulness only he may
be spared an hour of anguish . . .

TOSCA: An hour of anguish? (*surprised*)
What do you mean?
What is happening in that chamber?

SCARPIA: The laws are enforced, to the letter.

TOSCA: Oh, God! and how?

SCARPIA: (*with ferocious sternness*) Bound hand and foot, your lover there lies
prostrate, a fillet of steel encircling his temples
from which a jet of blood spurts out at every denial!

TOSCA: (*tottering to her feet*) It is not true! What a fiendish invention . . .
(*Cavaradossi groans deeply*)
A groan? Have mercy!

SCARPIA: Speak out and save him.

TOSCA: Yes, yes . . . but release him!

SCARPIA: (*turning towards the entrance L.*) Sciarrone, loosen him!

SCIARRONE: (*appearing at the threshold*) Quite?

SCARPIA: Quite.
(*Sciarrone re-enters the torture-chamber, closing the door*)
And now, tell me the truth.

TOSCA: Let me see him!

SCARPIA: No!

## Act II

TOSCA: (*riesce ad avvicinarsi all'uscio*) Mario!

LA VOCE DI CAVARADOSSI: Tosca!

TOSCA: Ti fanno male ancora?

LA VOCE DI CAVARADOSSI: No—corragio—Taci—Sprezzo il dolor.

SCARPIA: (*avvicinandosi a Tosca*) Orsù, Tosca, parlate.

TOSCA: (*rinfrancata dalle parole di Cavaradossi*) Non so nulla!

SCARPIA: Non vale la prova? . . . Ripigliamo . . .

TOSCA: (*si frappone fra l'uscio e Scarpia, per impedire che dia l'ordine*) Fermate! . . . no . . . che orror!

SCARPIA: Parlate!

TOSCA: No . . . mostro! lo strazi . . . l'uccidi!

SCARPIA: Lo strazia quel vostro silenzio assai più.

TOSCA: Tu ridi . . . tu ridi all'orrida pena?

SCARPIA: (*con feroce ironia*) Mai Tosca alla scena più tragica fu. (*con fermezza a Tosca, guardandola fissa negli occhi*) Qui pianti e rimbrotti son vani.

SCARPIA: Ov'è Angelotti? Rispondi, dov'è?

TOSCA: (*con voce soffocata*) Nol so.

SCARPIA: La vendetta su Mario cadrà. (*grida in tono di comando*) Sciarrone!

TOSCA: (*smarrita*) No . . . aspetta . . . (*vuol parlare, smania, resiste ancora*) Non posso . . . (*a mani giunte*) Pietà . . .

SCARPIA: (*per finirla*) Aprite le porte che n'oda i lamenti. (*Spoletta apre l'uscio e sta ritto sulla soglia*)

TOSCA: (*by degrees succeeds in approaching the door, and exclaims*) Mario!

CAVARADOSSI: (*from within, in pain*) Tosca!

TOSCA: Are they hurting you still?

CAVARADOSSI: No, take courage. Silence! I despise pain!

SCARPIA: And now speak out, fair Tosca.

TOSCA: (*firmly*) I know nothing!

SCARPIA: That test was not sufficient! If not, we can repeat it . . . (*walks towards the doorway*)

TOSCA: (*interposing herself between Scarpia and the door*) No! you shall not!

SCARPIA: Will you speak out, then?

TOSCA: No! No! Ah! monster, you have hurt him; you demon incarnate, you will kill him!

SCARPIA: Your obstinate silence hurts him worse than I do. (*laughs*)

TOSCA: You laugh, wretch . . . you laugh at his anguish!

SCARPIA: (*enthusiastically*) More tragic that Tosca was never on the stage! (*Tosca withdraws from Scarpia, who turns towards Spoletta in a transport of ferocity exclaiming loudly*) Throw open the doors! Let her hear him complaining! (*Spoletta opens the door and stands stiffly by the threshold*)

CAVARADOSSI: (*from within*) I defy you! . . .

SCARPIA: (*to Roberti*) Harder, still harder!

CAVARADOSSI: I defy you.

SCARPIA: (*to Tosca*) Say, where is Angelotti! Speak out, then!

TOSCA: What shall I say?

TOSCA: No! Ah! I know nothing! (*desperately*) Ah! must I tell lies . . . Ah! do not urge me! Ah! pray have pity!

LA VOCE DI CAVARADOSSI: Vi sfido.

SCARPIA: (*imperioso*) Più forte.

TOSCA: È troppo martir! (*si rivolge ancora supplichevole a Scarpia, il quale fa cenno a Spoletta di lasciare avvicinare Tosca: questa va presso all'uscio aperto ed esterrefatta alla vista dell'orribile scena, si rivolge a Cavaradossi col massimo dolore:*) O Mario, consenti ch'io parli? . . .

LA VOCE DI CAVARADOSSI: No.

TOSCA: (*con insistenza*) Ascolta, non posso più . . .

LA VOCE DI CAVARADOSSI: Stolta, che sai? . . . che puoi dir? . . .

SCARPIA: (*irritatissimo per le parole di Cavaradossi e temendo che da questa Tosca sia ancora incoraggiata a tacere, grida errible a Spoletta:*) Ma fatelo tacere! (*Spoletta entra nella camera della tortura e n'esce poco dopo, mentre Tosca, vinta dalla terribile commozione, cade prostrata sul canapè e con voce singhiozzante si rivolge a Scarpia che sta impassibile e silenzioso. Intanto Spoletta broutola preghiere sottovoce.*)

TOSCA: Io . . . son io che così torturate! . . . Torturate l'anima . . . (*scoppia in singhiozzi strazianti, mormorando:*) Sì, mi torturate l'anima! (*Scarpia, profittando dell'accasciamento di Tosca, va presso la camera della tortura e fa cenno di ricominclare il supplizio—un grido orribile si fa udire—Tosca si aiza di scatto e subito con voce soffocata dice rapidamente a Scarpia:*) nel pozzo . . . nel giardino . . .

SCARPIA: (*forte, a Spoletta*) Nel pozzo del giardin.—Va, Spoletta. (*Spoletta esce: Cavaradossi, che ha udito, si leva minaccioso contro Tosca; poi le forze l'abbandonano e si lascia cadere sul canapè, esclamando con rimprovero pieno e amarezza verso Tosca;*)

CAVARADOSSI: Ah! m'hai tradito!

TOSCA: (*supplichevole*) Mario!

SCARPIA: Speak! Linger no longer! Where is he?

TOSCA: Ah! torment me no longer! Have mercy, I pray, I can take no more! (*Mario groans*) (*At a sign from Scarpia, Spoletta allows Tosca to approach the open door; horror-stricken by what she sees, she advances toward Cavaradossi and, standing by the door of the torture-chamber, exclaims distractedly*) Mario! permit me to tell him!

CAVARADOSSI: (*his voice broken by pain*) No!

TOSCA: But hear me—I can take no more!

CAVARADOSSI: Woman, what do you know? What can you say?

SCARPIA: (*infuriated by Cavaradossi's utterances, and fearing that they may encourage Tosca to keep silence, exclaims aloud to Spoletta*) Compel him to be silent! (*Spoletta enters the torture-chamber, from which he promptly emerges, while Tosca, overcome by emotion, falls back on the sofa, and appeals in a tremulous voice to Scarpia, who stands by impassively and silently*)

TOSCA: Have I ever done you wrong? It is I who you torture so cruelly, whom you torture cruelly, yes, cruelly, cruelly torture! (*bursts into convulsive sobs*) (*Spoletta, kneeling, mutters a Latin prayer. Scarpia, profiting by Tosca's prostration, goes up to the door of the torture-chamber and signals Roberti to recommence operations. Cavaradossi utters a strident and prolonged cry of pain, whereupon Tosca rises from the sofa, and in a stifled voice says hurriedly to Scarpia*) The well . . . in the garden . . .

SCARPIA: (*loudly and authoritatively to Spoletta*) In the well of the garden—Go, Spoletta! (*Exit Spoletta*)

CAVARADOSSI: (*rises threateningly*) You have betrayed me! (*falls backwards, overcome*)

TOSCA: (*embracing him passionately*) Mario!

CAVARADOSSI: (*respingendo Tosca che si abbraccia stretta a lui*) Maledetta!
(*Sciarrone, a un tratto, irrompe tutto affannoso*)

SCIARRONE: Eccelenza . . . ah, quali nuove!

SCARPIA: (*sorpreso*) Che vuol dir quell'aria afflitta?

SCIARRONE: Un messaggio dì sconfitta . . .

SCARPIA: Qual sconfitta? Come? Dove?

SCIARRONE: A Marengo . . .

SCARPIA: (*impaziente*) Tartaruga!

SCIARRONE: Bonaparte è vincitor . . .

SCARPIA: Melas!

SCIARRONE: No. Melas è in fuga! . . .
(*Cavaradossi, che con ansia crescente ha udito le parole di Sciarrone, trova nel proprio entusiasmo la forza di alzarsi minaccioso in faccia a Scarpia*)

CAVARADOSSI: Ah c'è un Dio vendicator!
L'alba vindice appar che fa gli empi tremar!
Libertà sorge crollano tirannidi!
Del sofferto martir me vedrai qui gioir . . .
il tuo cuor trema, o livido carnefice!
(*Tosca, disperatamente aggrappandosi a Cavaradossi, tenta, con parole interrotte, di farlo tacere, mentre Scarpia risponde a Cavaradossi con sarcastico sorriso:*)

SCARPIA: Braveggia, urla!—T'affretta
a palesarmi il fondo dell'alma ria!
Va!—Moribondo,
il capestro t'aspetta!
(*ed irritato per le parole di Cavaradossi, grida agli sbirri:*)
Portatemelo via!
(*Sciarrone e gli sbirri s'impossessano di Cavaradossi, e lo trascinano verso la portam Tosca con un supremo sforzo tenta di tenersi stretta a Cavaradossi, ma invano: essa è brutalmente respinta*)

TOSCA: Mario . . . con te . . .
(*gli sbirri conducono via Cavaradossi; li seguono Spoletta e Sciarrone: Tosca si avventa per seguir Cavaradossi, ma Scarpia si colloca innanzi la porta e la chiude, respingendo Tosca*)

CAVARADOSSI: (*trying to push her away*) Be accursed!
(*enter Sciarrone, much perturbed*)

SCIARRONE: Excellency, dreadful tidings!

SCARPIA: (*surprised*) What has happened? Tell me quickly!

SCIARRONE: The Royal troops have been defeated . . .

SCARPIA: How defeated? When? Where?

SCIARRONE: At Marengo . . .

SCARPIA: (*impatiently*) Wretched dullard!

SCIARRONE: Bonaparte won the day!

SCARPIA: Melas!

SCIARRONE: No! Melas was routed!
(*With ever-increasing anxiety Cavaradossi, has listened to Sciarrone's announcements and in his exultation finds strength to arise and confront Scarpia menacingly*)

CAVARADOSSI: (*enthusiastically*) Victory! Victory!
Oh spirit of vengeance, awake!
Let tyrants and myrmidons quake!
Freedom, brandish your glaive and strike down your enemies!

TOSCA: (*in despair, endeavoring to quiet Cavaradossi*) Mario! Silence, in pity to me!

CAVARADOSSI: Raise your clarion voice!
Bid a sad world rejoice!
Tremble, Scarpia, you butcherly hypocrite!

SCARPIA: (*staring cynically at Cavaradossi and smiling sarcastically*) Bravado! Boaster! I hate you!
Your carcass soon shall swing,
a senseless lump of clay! Away,
doomed traitor, the hangman awaits you!
Now carry him away!
(*Sciarrone and the agents seize Cavaradossi and smilingly drag him towards the door*)

TOSCA: (*resisting with all her strength*) Mario, with you! . . .

SCARPIA: Go, dying traitor, go!

SCARPIA: Voi no!

TOSCA: (*con un gemito*) Salvatelo!

SCARPIA: Io? . . . Voi!
(*al avvicina alla tavola, vede la sua cena lasciata a mezzo e ritorna calmo e sorridente*)
La povera mia cena fu interrotta.
(*vedendo Tosca abbattuta, immobile, ancora presso la porta*)
Cosi accasciata? . . . Via, bella signora
sedete qui.—Volete che cerchiamo
insieme, Tosca, il modo di salvarlo?
(*Tosca si senote e lo guarda: Scarpia sorride sempre e si siede, accennando in pari tempo di sedere a Tosca*)
E allor sedete . . . e favelliamo . . . E intanto
un sorso. E vin di Spagna . . .
(*riemple il bicchiere e lo porge a Tosca*)
Un sorso per rincorarvi.

TOSCA: (*fissando sempre Scarpia si avvicina lentamente alla tavola, siede risoluta di fronte a Scarpia, poi coll'accento del più profondo dizprezzo gli chiede:*)
Quanto?

SCARPIA: (*imperturbabile, versandosi da bere*) Quanto? . . . (*ride*)

TOSCA: Il prezzo! . . .

SCARPIA: Già.—Mi dicon venal, ma a donna bella
io non mi vendo a prezzo di moneta.
Se la giurata fede
devo tradir, ne voglio altra mercede.
Quest'ora io l'attendea.
Già mi struggea
l'amore della diva! . . .
Ma poc'anzi la donna—io la mirai qual non la vidi mai
all'ire, al pianto ed all'amore più viva! . . .
Quel tuo pianto era lava
infocata a' miei sensi—ed il tuo sguardo,
che odio in me dardeggiava,
le selvaggie mie brame inferocia! . . .
Agil qual leopardo
ti avvinghiasti all'amante—in quell'istante
io t'ho giurata mia! . . .
Mia! . . . ruggente di collera e d'orgoglio!
A me! . . . Ti voglio!
(*si leva, stendendo le braccia ver-*

TOSCA: (*clinging to Mario, and brutally thrust back by the agents*) Mario! With you!
(*endeavors to force her way past Scarpia*)

SCARPIA: (*pushing her back and closing the door*) Not you!

TOSCA: (*gasping*) I conjure you, save him!

SCARPIA: I?—You!
(*approaches the table, as though to resume supping, but turns back, calm and smiling*)
My poor little supper was interrupted.
(*seeing Tosca downcast and motionless, still near the door*)
Why so disheartened? . . . Come, sweet sorrow-stricken lady, be seated here.
Devise with me some plan whereby we may contrive to save him,
and then . . . be seated . . .
(*sits down, motioning to Tosca to do the like*)
we'll talk it over.
(*polishes a wineglass with his napkin, and fills it with wine*)
Meanwhile, this cordial . . . it is wine of Spain . . .
pray taste it, it will raise your spirits.

TOSCA: (*seats herself opposite Scarpia, looking at him steadfastly, leaning her elbows on the table and shading face. Contemptuously she asks him:*) How much?

SCARPIA: (*imperturably, filling his glass*) How much?

TOSCA: Your price, man? . . .

SCARPIA: (*laughs*) Venal, my enemies call me, but to ladies fair
I do not sell myself for paltry sums of money.
No! if my plighted fealty I must betray
(*emphatically*) I'll choose some other payment.
This hour I've long awaited! . . .
(*excitedly*)
Goddess of song, you have scorned me and braved me.
It was your beauty that made me love you, It is your hatred
that has enslaved me;
When I saw your cheeks bedewed with tears of consternation,
Shed by lustrous eyes that fiercely sparkled with scorn and detestation,
When you clung to your lover like an amorous tigress,
Ah! it was at that hour I vowed you would be mine.
(*He approaches Tosca with open arms: she, who until now had listened to him without stirring, rises suddenly, horrified by his*

## Act II

*so Tosca: questa che aveva ascol-
tato immobile, le lascive parole di
Scarpia, s'alza di scatto e si rifu-
gia dietro il canapè)*

**TOSCA:** Tu? . . .

**SCARPIA:** Sì, e t'avrò!

**TOSCA:** *(correndo alla finestra)*
Pria giù mi avvento!

**SCARPIA:** *(freddamente)* In pegno il tuo Mario mi resta! . . .

**TOSCA:** L'orribile mercato! . . .
*(per subita idea)*
Ah!—la regina! . . .

**SCARPIA:** *(ironico)* Non ti tratten-
go.—Va.—Libera sei.
Ma è fallace speranza: la Regina
farebbe solo grazia ad un cadavere!
*(Tosca retrocede spaventata, e fis-
sando Scarpia si lascia cadere sul
canapè; poi staccad gli occhi da
Scarpia con un gesto di supremo
disgust e di odio)*
Come tu m'odii!

**TOSCA:** Ah! Dio! . . .

**SCARPIA:** *(avvicinandosele)* Così
ti voglio!

**TOSCA:** *(con ribrezzo)* Non toc-
carmi—demonio—t'odio, l'odio,
abbietto, vile!
*(fugge da Scarpia inorridita)*

**SCARPIA:** Che importa? Sei
mia . . .
Spasimi d'ira e spasimi d'amore!

**TOSCA:** Vile!!

**SCARPIA:** Mia!! *(cerca di afferrar-
la)*

**TOSCA:** Vile! *(si ripara dietro la
tavola)*

**SCARPIA:** *(inseguendola)*
Mia . . .

**TOSCA:** No—aiuto!
*(un lontano rullo di tamburi a
poco a poco si avvicina poi si di-
legna lontano)*

**SCARPIA:** *(fermandosi)* L'odi?
È il tamburo. S'avvia. Guida la scorta
ultima ai condannati. Il tempo passa!
*(Tosca, dopo aver ascoltato con
ausia terribile, si allontana dalla
finestra e si appoggia estenuata,
al canapè)*
Sai quale oscura opra laggiù si compia?

*audacious proposals, and rushes
behind the sofa. She screams.)*

**SCARPIA:** *(following her)* Mine,
wholly mine!

**TOSCA:** *(terrified, rushes to the
window and clings to it)* No! far
rather will I kill myself!

**SCARPIA:** *(coldly)* Your Mario's
life I'll hold in pawn for yours!

**TOSCA:** Think you that I will contract so hideous a bargain?
*(the idea of appealing to the
Queen occurs to her, and she hurries towards the door)*

**SCARPIA:** *(divining her
thoughts)* I will not force you to
stay,
*(draws aside)*
You are free to go, fair lady;
*(Tosca is joyfully leaving the
room when Scarpia, (laughing
ironically, stays her with a gesture)*
but your hope is fallacious . . .
It were vain to ask our gracious
Queen
to pardon a dead man!
*(Tosca turns back terror-stricken
and, staring at Scarpia, resumes
her seat on the sofa: then turns her
eyes away with a look of supreme
disgust and hatred)*
How you detest me!

**TOSCA:** *(with loathing and contempt)* I do!

**SCARPIA:** *(approaching her)* It is
thus, It is thus I love you!

**TOSCA:** *(exasperated)* Do not
touch me, you demon!
I hate you, you coward, you villain!

**SCARPIA:** *(approaching her still
nearer)* What matter? Hatred like
yours
and love are kindred passions!

**TOSCA:** Villain!
*(shrinking behind the table)*

**SCARPIA:** *(pursuing her)* Mine?

**TOSCA:** Help!
*(both are stayed by the sound of
distant drums)*

**SCARPIA:** Listen to the drums approaching;
leading the escort of men about to
die on the scaffold
And time is passing. Know you
what dismal
preparations my people are com-
pleting?
There . . . *(pointing to window)* they have
raised up a gallows-tree. *(Tosca*

Là si drizza un patibolo. Al tuo
Mario,
per tuo voler, resta un'ora di vita.
*freddamente si appoggia ad un
angolo della tavola continuando
a guardare Tosca)*

**TOSCA:** *(nel massimo dolore)*
Vissi d'arte vissi d'amore, non feci
mai.
male ad anima viva!
Con man furtiva
quante pene conobbi, allevïai.
Sempre con fè sincera
la mia preghiera
ai santi tabernacoli salì.
Diedi fiori agli altar
Nell'ora del dolore
perchè, perchè Signore,
perchè me ne rimuneri così? diedi
gioielli
della Madonna al manto,
e diedi il canto
agli astri, al ciel, che ne ridean più
belli.
Nell'ora del dolore
perchè, perchè Signore,
perchè me ne rimuneri così?

**SCARPIA:** *(avvicinandosi di nuovo a Tosca)* Risolvi?

**TOSCA:** No!

**SCARPIA:** Bada . . . il tempo è
veloce!

**TOSCA:** Mi vuoi supplice a tuoi
piedi?
*(inginocchiandosi innanzi a
Scarpia)*
Ecco—vedi—
le man giunte io stendo a te!
E mercè,
umiliata e vinta, aspetto
d'un tuo detto.

**SCARPIA:** Sei troppo bella, Tosca,
e troppo amante.
Cedo.—A misero prezzo
tu, a me una vita, io, a te chieggo un
istante!

**TOSCA:** *(alzandosi, con senso di
gran disprezzo)* Va—va—mi fai
ribrezzo!
*(bussano alla porta)*

**SCARPIA:** Chi è là?

**SPOLETTA:** *(entrando trafelato)*
Eccellenza, l'Angelotti al nostro giunger si uccise.

**SCARPIA:** Ebbene lo si appenda
morto alle forche, E l'altro prigioniero?

**SPOLETTA:** Il cavalier Cavaradossi? E tutto
pronto, eccellenza.

*shudders in terror and despair.
Scarpia approaches her)*
It is your will, then, that your fond
lover
should die in another brief hour?
*(Broken down by grief, Tosca falls
back on the sofa. Scarpia leans
against a corner of the table,
pours out coffee, and drinks it,
with his eyes fixed upon Tosca)*

**TOSCA:** *(mournfully)* Love and
music, I have lived for,
Never have harmed a living being . . .
The poor and distressful, times
without number,
by stealth, I have succored . . .
Ever a fervent believer, my humble
prayers
have been offered up sincerely to
the saints;
ever a fervent believer, I've laid
flowers on the altar . . .
In this, my hour of sorrow and bitter tribulation,
oh! Heavenly Father, why do you
forsake me?
Jewels I gave to bedeck Our Lady's
mantle;
I gave my songs to the starry hosts
in tribute to their
brightness . . .
In this, my hour of grief and bitter
tribulation,
why, Heavenly Father, why have
you forsaken me?

**SCARPIA:** What did you say?

**TOSCA:** *(resolutely)* No!

**SCARPIA:** Forget not that time flies
swiftly!

**TOSCA:** *(kneels before Scarpia)*
Must I, kneeling, beg for mercy?
Behold me, pleading here at your
feet for pity.
Hear me! Grant my entreaty!
Let me not implore you vainly!
*(desperately, yet humbly)*

**SCARPIA:** You are too lovely, Tosca, and too enchanting
to be resisted. I have the worst of
the bargain;
a life I barter against a minute of
your favor!

**TOSCA:** Go!
*(rising scornfully)*
You make me shudder! Go!
*(a knock at the door)*

**SCARPIA:** Who's there?
*(enter Spoletta in haste and much
agitated)*

**SPOLETTA:** Excellency, Angelotti
swallowed poison
when we seized him.

**SCARPIA:** It is well! Let them hand
up his corpse on the gibbet!
And how about the other?

**SPOLETTA:** You mean the painter,
Cavaradossi;
He awaits your decision!

TOSCA: (Dio! m'assisti! . . . )

SCARPIA: (a Spoletta) Aspetta. (a Tosca) Ebbene?
(Tosca accenna di sì col capo e dalla vergogna piangendo si nasconde il viso)
(a Spoletta) Odi . . .

TOSCA: (interrompendo, subito a Scarpia) Ma libero all'istante lo voglio . . .

SCARPIA: (a Tosca) Occorre simular. Non posso far grazia aperta. Bisogna che tutti abbian per morto il cavalier.
(accenna a Spoletta) Quest'uomo fido provvederà.

TOSCA: Chi mi assieura?

SCARPIA: L'ordin che gli darò voi qui presente.
(a Spoletta) Spoletta: chiudi.
(Spoletta chiude la porta, poi ritorna presso Scarpia)
Ho mutato d'avviso.
Il prigionier sia fucilato . . .
(Tosca scatta atterrita)
attendi . . .
(Assa con intenzione Spoletta che accenna replicatamente col capo di indovinare il pensiero di Scarpia)
Come facemmo del conte Palmieri.

SPOLETTA: Un'uccisione . . .

SCARPIA: (subito con marcata intenzione) . . . simulata! . . . Come avvenne del Palmieri! . . . Hai ben compreso?

SPOLETTA: Ho ben compreso.

SCARPIA: Va.

TOSCA: Voglio avvertirlo io stessa.

SCARPIA: E sia.
(a Spoletta) Le darai passo. Bada: all'ora quarta.

SPOLETTA: Sì. Come Palmiere.
(Spoletta parie. Scarpia, ritta presso la porta, ascolta Spoletta allontanarsi, poi trasformato nel viso e nei gesti si avvicina con grande passione a Tosca)

SCARPIA: Io tenni la promessa . . .

TOSCA: (arrestandolo) Non ancora.
Voglio un salvacondotto onde fuggire
dallo Stato con lui

SCARPIA: (con galanteria) Partir volete?

TOSCA: Sì, per sempre!

---

TOSCA: (aside) Heaven help me!

SCARPIA: (to Spoletta) A moment . . .
(to Tosca, softly) What say you?
(she nods consentingly; then, weeping for very shame, she buries her head in the sofa cushions)

SCARPIA: (to Spoletta) Listen . . .

TOSCA: (interrupting) But he must be set free on the instant!

SCARPIA: I fear that may not be. I dare not simply release him. It must be believed by everyone here that he is dead.
(points to Spoletta) This worthy fellow will arrange all . . .

TOSCA: Can he be trusted?

SCARPIA: Trust the orders I shall give him,
here, in your presence.
(turning to Spoletta) Spoletta! shut that door.
(Spoletta hastens to obey, and then returns to Scarpia, who looks fixedly at him. Spoletta repeatedly indicating by nods that he understands his master's meaning)
I have altered my purpose. Cavaradossi
will be shot . . . pay attention . . .
just as we did in the case of Palmieri . . .

SPOLETTA: An execution . . .

SCARPIA: (emphatically) Simulated! . . . As we did in the case of Palmieri!
Do you understand me?

SPOLETTA: I understand you.

SCARPIA: Go!

TOSCA: (who has listened eagerly, interrupting) And I in person will warn him.

SCARPIA: So be it.
(to Spoletta, pointing at Tosca) You will admit her.
Remember: (emphatically) at four o'clock . . .

SPOLETTA: (emphatically) Yes. Just like Palmieri . . .
(exit Spoletta. Scarpia, standing by the door, listens to Spoletta's retreating steps. Then, changing his manner and expression, he turns passionately to Tosca)

SCARPIA: I have fulfilled my promise.

TOSCA: Not entirely. I must have a safe-conduct
enabling me to quit the country with him.

SCARPIA: (politely remonstrating) You really mean to leave us?

TOSCA: (positively) Yes, for ever!

---

SCARPIA: Si adempia il voler vostro.
(va allo scrittoio: si mette a scrivere, interrompendosi per domandare a Tosca:)
Qual via scegliete?
(Mentre Scarpia scrive, Tosca si è avvicinata alla tavola e colla mano tremante prende il bicchieri di vino di Spagna versato da Scarpia; ma nel portare il bicchiere alle labbra, scorge, sulla tavola un coltello affilato ed a punta; da una rapida occhiata a Scarpia che in quel momento è occupato a scrivere—e con infinite precauzioni cerca di impossessarsi del coltello, rispondendo alle domande di Scarpia ch'essa sorveglia attentamente)

TOSCA: La più breve!

SCARPIA: Dunque Civitavecchia.
(scrivendo) Sta bene?

TOSCA: Sta bene.
(Finalmente ha potuto prendere il coltello, che dissimula dietro di è appogiandosi alla tavola e sempre servegliando Scarpia. Questi ha finito di scrivere il salvacondotto, vi mette il sigillo, ripiega il foglio: quindi aprendo le braccia si avvicina a Tosca per avvinceria a sè)

SCARPIA: Ed ora, Tosca, finalmente mia! . . .
(ma l'accento voluttuoso si cambia in un grido terribile.—Tosca io ha colpito in pieno petto)
Maledetta!!

TOSCA: Questo è il bacio di Tosca.
(Scarpia stende il braccio verso Tosca avvicinandosele barcollante in atto di aiuto. Tosca lo sfugge—ma ad un tratto ella si trova presa fra Scarpia e la tavola e vedendo che sta per essere toccata da Scarpia, lo aespinge inorridita. Scarpia cade, urlando colla voce suffocata dal sangue:)

---

SCARPIA: It shall be as you desire.
(goes to the desk and begins to write; breaks off in order to ask Tosca:)
By which road will you travel?

TOSCA: By the shortest!

SCARPIA: Civitavecchia?

TOSCA: Yes.
(while Scarpia is writing, Tosca approaches the table, and, with a trembling hand, takes up the glass filled with wine for her by Scarpia; and as she raises it to her lips, perceives a sharp-pointed knife lying on the table-cloth. She casts a rapid glance at Scarpia, still occupied at the desk, and with infinite caution takes possession of the knife, which she hides behind her, leaning on the table and carefully watching Scarpia, who, having finished writing the safe conduct, folds it up, and advances towards Tosca with open arms, intending to embrace her)

SCARPIA: Tosca, at last you are mine! . . .
(utters a terrible cry, as she stabs him full in the breast, and then groans deeply)
Accursed one!

TOSCA: (violently) It is thus that Tosca kisses!

SCARPIA: (hoarsely) Help me! I'm dying!
(strives to lay hold of Tosca's dress; she draws back horror-stricken)
Help!
(Tosca, between Scarpia and the table, and fearing that he will lay hold of her, thrusts him roughly from her. He falls, groaning and well nigh choked by blood)
Ah!

TOSCA: (pitilessly) Are you stifling with blood?

## Act II

SCARPIA: Aiuto . . . aiuto . . . muoio . . .

TOSCA: (*fissando Scarpai che si dibatte inutilmente e cerca di rialzarsi, aggrappandosi al canapè*) E ucciso da una donna . . . — M'hai tu assai torturato?! Su!—Parla!—Odi tu ancora? . . . Guardami! . . . Son la Tosca! Son la Diva! . . . Son Tosca, o Scarpia!

SCARPIA: (*fa un ultimo sforzo, poi cade riverso*) Soccorso! . . .

TOSCA: (*chinandosi verso Scarpia*) Ti soffoca il sangue? . . . il sangue? . . . Muori! muori!! muori!!! (*vedendolo immobile*) Ah! è morto! . . . Or gli perdono! E avanti a lui tremava tutta Roma! (*Senza abbandonare cogli, occhi il cadavere. Tosca va alla tavola, vi depone il coltello, prende una bottiglia d'acqua, inzuppa un tovagliolo e si lava le dita: poi va allo specchio e si ravvia i capelli. Quindi cerca il salvacondotto sullo scrittoio: non trovandolo, si volge e lo scorge nella mano raggrinzata del morto: ne toglie il foglio e lo nasconde in petto. Spegne il candelabro sulla tavola e va per uscire, ma si pente e colloca una candela a destra e l'altra a sinistra della testa di Scarpia. Alzandosi, cerca di nuovo intorno e scorgendo un crocifisso va a staccarlo dalla parete e portandolo religiosamente s'inginocchia pea posarlo sul petto di Scarpia—poi si alza e con grande precauzione esce rinchiudendo dietro a se la porta*).

## ■ ATTO TERZO

*La piattaforma di Castel Sant'Angelo.*

*A sinistra, una casamatta: vi è collocata una tavola, sulla quale stanno una lampada, un grosso registro e l'occorrente per scrivere: una panca, una sedia. Su di una parete della casamatta un crocifisso: davanti a questo è appesa una lampade. A destra, l'apertura di una piccola scala per la quale si ascende all'piattaforma Nel fondo il Vaticona e S. Pietro. È ancora notte: a poco a poco la luce incerta e grigia che precede*

SCARPIA: Help me! (*struggles ineffectually to rise, clutching at the sofa*) I'm dying!

TOSCA: And done to death by a woman! Say, what mercy did you show me? Can you still hear me? (*Scarpia makes a final effort, and falls backwards*) Answer! Look at me! Scarpia, I am Tosca!! Your victims' blood chokes you! (*bending over Scarpia's face*) Die, accursed one! Perish!

SCARPIA: (*all but voiceless*) Ah! (*expires*)

TOSCA: He is dead! Now I forgive him! (*without taking her eyes off Scarpia's corpse, she goes to the table, dips a napkin in the water-jug, and washes her fingers; then arranges her hair before the looking glass. Remembering the safe-conduct, she looks for it on the desk, and not finding it, searches elsewhere. At last she perceives it, clutched in the clenched fingers of Scarpia, and lifts up his arm, which she lets fall, stiff and stark, when she has possessed herself of the safe-conduct, which she hides in her bosom. She then constrains herself to contemplate Scarpia's dead body; she extinguishes the lights on the supper-table, and is about to leave when, seeing one of the candles on the desk still burning, she takes it, and with it lights the other candle*) And, yesterday, trembling Rome lay prostrate at his feet! (*Places one candle to the right of Scarpia's head, and the other to the left; again looks round her, and seeing a crucifix hanging on the wall, takes it down and, kneeling, places it reverently on the breast of the corpse. Roll of distant drums, and slow curtain. Tosca rises and departs cautiously, closing the door after her*)

## ■ ACT III

*Scene: A Platform of Castle Sant Angelo.*

*L.—A casemate, furnished with a table (on which stand a lantern, a huge register book, and writing materials), a bench and a stool. Suspended to one of the walls, a crucifix and votive lamp. R.—A trap-door opening on a flight of steps leading to the platform from below. The Vatican and St. Peter's are depicted on the back cloth. Night time. Clear sky, studded with stars. Sheep bells jangle afar off, then gradually nearer and nearer.*

*l'alba: le campane delle chiese suonano mattuttino. La voce d'un pastore che guida un armento.* (*Un Carceriere con una lanterna sale dalle scala, va alla casamatta e vi accende la lampada sospesa davanti al crocifisso, poi quella sulla tavola: siede ed aspetta mezzo assonnato. Più tardi un picchetto, comandato da un Sergente die guardia, sale sulla piattaforma accompagnando Cavaradossi: il picchetto si arresta ed il Sergente conduce Cavaradossi nella casamatta, consegnando un foglia al Carceriere.— Il Carceriere esamina il foglio, apre il registro e vi scrive mentre interroga*).

CARCERIERE: Mario Cavaradoss? (*Cavaradossi china il capo, assentendo. Il Carceriere porge la penna al Sergente*) A voi. (*il Sergente firma il registro, poi parte coi soldati, scendendo per la scala*) (*a Cavaradossi*) Vi resta un'ora. Un sacerdote i vostri cenni attende.

CAVARADOSSI: No. Ma di un'ultima grazia vi richiedo.

CARCERIERE: Se posso . . .

CAVARADOSSI: Io lascio al mondo una persona cara. Consentite ch'io le scriva un sol motto. (*togliendosi dal dito un anello*) Unico resto di mia recchezza è questo anel . . . Se promettete di consegnarle il mio ultimo addio, esso è vostro . . .

A SHEPHERD: (*in the distance*) Day is breaking now, The weary world awakening . . . (*the bells, still more distant, tinkle irregularly*) Lending new sorrow (*the tinkling of the bell dies away gradually*) If you could prize me, I might try to live, But if you despise me, I may as well die! (*a dim, grey light heralds the approach of dawn*) (*Afar off, the church bells begin ringing for matins. Enter Jailer, bearing a lantern. He emerges from the trap-door, enters the casemate, and lights, first the lamp suspended beneath the crucifix, and then the lantern standing on the table. Advancing to the parapet of the platform he leans over it and looks down into the courtyard to see if the firing party, told off to escort the condemned man, has arrived. Meeting a sentry, who is on guard within the precincts of the platform, and having exchanged a few words with him, the Jailer returns to the casemate, where he sits down and waits, half asleep. An infantry picket, commanded by a sergeant, and in charge of Cavaradossi, ascends the platform. The men are halted, and the sergeant conducts Cavaradossi to the casemate, which Cavaradossi enters. The Jailer, seeing the sergeant, rises and salutes, whereupon the sergeant hands him a paper, which the Jailer examines. Then, seating himself at the table, the Jailer opens the register book and writes in it while interrogating Cavaradossi*)

JAILER: Mario Cavaradossi? (*Cavaradossi nods affirmatively*) Please sign. (*to the sergeant, handing him the pen. The sergeant signs the register-book and descends the steps, followed by the picket. Bell*) You have an hour . . . (*to Cavaradossi*) A holy father is near, at your disposal . . .

CAVARADOSSI: No. But let me ask you to do me a favor . . .

JAILER: If possible . . .

CAVARADOSSI: I leave behind me one whom I cherish fondly. Can you grant me leave to write a few words to her? Nothing is left of all that I possessed but this little ring . . . (*takes a ring off his finger*) If you will pledge your word to convey my last farewell to her safely, it is yours . . .

CARCERIERE: (*tituba un poco, pol accetta e facendo cenno a Cavaradossi di sedere alla tavola, va sedere sulla panca*) Scrivete.

CAVARADOSSI: (*si mette a scrivere . . . ma dopo tracciate alcune linee è invaso dalle rimembranze*) E lucevan le stelle ed olezzava
la terra-e stridea l'uscio dell'orto—e un passo sfiorava la rena.
Entrava ella, fragrante,
mi cadea fra le braccia e mi narrava di sè; di me chiedea
con volubile impero.
Oh! dolci baci, o languide carezze,
mentr'io fremente
le belle forme disciogliea dai veli!
Svanì per sempre il bel sogno d'amore . . .
L'ora è fuggita
e muoio disperato! . . .
E non ho amato mai tanto la vita!
(*scoppia in singhiozzi*).
(*Dalla scala viene Spoletta accompagnato dal Sergente e seguito da Tosca: il Sergente porta una lanterna—Spoletta accenna a Tosca ove trovasi Cavaradossi, poi chiama a sè il Carceriere: con questi e col Sergente ridiscende, non senza avere prima dato ad una sentinella, che sta in fondo, l'ordine di sorvegliare il prigioniero*).
(*Tosca vede Cavaradossi piangente, colla testa fra le mani: gli si avvicina e gli solleva colle due mani la testa. Cavaradossi balza in piedi sorpreso. Tosca gli presenta convulsa un foglio, non potendo parlare per l'emozione*).
(*legge*) —Franchigia a Floria Tosca—
TOSCA: (*leggendo insieme con lui con voce affannosa e convulsa*) e al caviliere
che l'accompagna.—

TOSCA: (*a Cavaradossi con un grido d'esultanza*)
Sei libero!

CAVARADOSSI: (*guarda il foglio; ne legge la firma*) Scarpia! Scarpia benigno? A qual prezzo? la prima sua grazia è questa . . .

TOSCA: E l'ultima!
(*riprende il salvacondotto e lo ripone in una borsa*)

CAVARADOSSI: Che dici?

JAILER: (*after a little hesitation, accepts the ring, and signals Cavaradossi to be seated at the table*) Write your letter.
(*sits down on the bench. Cavaradossi is lost in thought, from which he rouses himself to write. After tracing a few lines, engrossed by memories of the past, he ceases writing*)

CAVARADOSSI: (*thinking aloud*) When the stars were brightly shining
And faint perfumes pervaded the air,
The gate of the garden creaked,
And a footstep invaded its precincts,
It was her's, the fragrant creature,
In her soft arms she clasped me
With sweetest kisses, tenderest caresses,
A thing of beauty, of matchless symmetry in form and feature!
My dream of love is now dispelled for ever;
I lived uncaring,
And now I die despairing!
Yet never was life so dear to me, no, never!
(*bursts into tears, covering his face with his hands. Enter Spoletta through the trap-door, accompanied by Tosca and followed by the sergeant, who carries a lantern. Spoletta points out to Tosca where she will find Cavaradossi, and then beckons to the Jailer, with whom and the sergeant he redescends the steps, not without having given orders to a sentry on guard at the back of the stage to keep close watch upon the prisoner. Tosca, who meanwhile has been manifestly in a state of violent agitation, sees Cavaradossi weeping, rushes to him, and—unable to speak for sheer emotion—lifts his head with both hands, showing him the safe-conduct. On perceiving her he starts to his feet in surprise, and then reads the document which she has handed to him*)
Ah! Safe-conduct to Floria Tosca and to the gentleman, her companion.
(*in unison with Tosca*)

TOSCA: (*enthusiastically*) You are free, my love!

CAVARADOSSI: (*perceiving the signature of the document*) Scarpia showed mercy!
(*looking intently at Tosca*)
Full surely his first concession!

TOSCA: (*puts away the safe-conduct in her bag*) And his last!

CAVARADOSSI: What are you saying?

TOSCA: Il tuo sangue o il mio amore
volea. Fur vani scongiuri e pianti.
Invan, pazza d'orrore,
alla Madonne mi volsi ed ai Santi . . .
Rideva—il mostro!—del mio martir!
Dicea: già negli oscuri
cieli il patibol le bracci leva!
Rullavano i tamburi . . .
Rideva, l'empio mostro . . . risdeva . . .
già la sua preda pronto a ghermir!
"Sei mia?"—Sì.—Alla sua brama mi promisi. Lì presso
luccicava una lama . . .
Ei scrisse il foglio liberator,
venne all'orrendo amplesso . . .
Io quella lama gli piantai nel cor.

CAVARADOSSI: Tu? . . . di tua man l'uccidesti!—tu pia, tu benigna—e per me!

TOSCA: N'ebbi le mani tutte lorde di sangue!

CAVARADOSSI: (*prendendo amorosamente fra le sue le mani di Tosca*) Oh! salvatrice!
O dolci mani mansuete e pure
o mani elette a belle opre e pietose,
a carezzar fanciulli, a coglier rose
a pregar, giunte, per l'altrui sventure,
dunque in voi, fatte dall'amor secure,
giustizia le sue sacre armi depose?
Voi deste morte, o man vittoriose,
o dolci mani mansuete e pure! . . .

TOSCA: (*svincolando le mani*)
Senti . . . l'ora è vicina; io già raccolsi
(*mostrando la borsa*)
ore e gioielli . . . una vettura è pronta.
Ma prima . . . ridi
amore . . . prema sarai
fucilato—per finta—ad armi scariche.
Simulato supplizio. Al colpo . . . cadi.
I soldata sen vanno—e noi siam salvi!
Poscia a Civitavecchia . . . una tartana
e via pel mar!

CAVARADOSSI ED TOSCA: Liberi!

TOSCA: He exacted your life or my love!
Entreaties and conjurations
Were vain. The saints above
Would pay no heed to my wild invocations.
He said, the impious monster,
"Now the
gallows tree is spreading its branches gaily!"
The muffled drums were sounding . . .
He laughed, the impious monster, laughed loudly,
hovering round his quivering prey! . . .
"Are you mine, then?" "Yes!"
Thus I avowed myself defeated.
He did not see the knife I had secreted . . .
He signed the permit that sets you free, and gives us license to depart . . .
I drove the glittering blade into his heart!

CAVARADOSSI: You?
With your own hand slay him?
You, most pious and merciful of souls!

TOSCA: Yes; both these hands were reeking with his hot blood!

CAVARADOSSI: (*taking her hands lovingly in his own*) Oh! gentle hands, so pitiful and tender;
Soft hands, designed to deck luxuriant tresses
With fragrant rosebuds, to bestow caresses,
And pray for Heaven's grace to the offender,
To you the Fates, grim ministers of death, surrender
The impassive steel that base injustice represses.
By you was dealt the blow that tyranny suppresses
Oh! gentle hands, so delicate and tender!

TOSCA: (*freeing her hands from his grasp*) Listen . . . all now is ready; (*shows a hand-bag*)
I have collected my jewels and money . . .
a carriage is in waiting . . . But first—smile,
dearest love—you must submit to be fired at . . .
In pretense, of course, and with blank
cartridges . . . a mere mimic execution.
When they fire, fall down. Then the soldiers
will retire . . . We shall be safe then!
Once in Civitavecchia—
about a lugger, and off to sea!

CAVARADOSSI AND TOSCA: We are free!

TOSCA: Chi si duole in terra più?
Senti effluvi di rose?
Non ti par che le cose
aspettan tutte innamorate il sole?

CAVARADOSSI: (*colla più tenera commozione*) Amaro sol per te
m'era il morire
Da te prende la vita ogni splendore,
all'esser mio la gioia ed il desire
nascon di te, come di fiamma ardore.
Io folgorare i cieli e scolorire
vedrò nell'occhio tuo rivelatore,
e la beltà delle cose più mire
avrà solo da te voce e colore.

TOSCA: Amor che seppe a te vita serbare
ci sarà guida in terra, in mar nocchiere
e vago farà il mondo a riguardare.
Finchè congiunti alle celesti sfere
dileguerem, siccome alte sul mare
a sol cadente, nuvole leggere!
(*rimangono commossi, silenziosi poi Tosca, chìamata dalla realtà delle cose, si guards attorno inquieta*)
E non giungono . . .
(*si volge a Cavaradossi con premurosa tenerezza*)
Bada! . . .
al colpo egli è mestiere
che tu subito cada
per morto.

CAVARADOSSI: (*la rassicura*)
Non temere
Che cadrò sul momento—e al naturale.

TOSCA: (*insistendo*) Ma stammi attento—di non farti male!
Con scenica seïenza
io saprei la movenza . . .

CAVARADOSSI: (*la interrompe, attirandola a sè*) Parlami ancor come dianzi parlavi,
è cosi dolce il suon della tua voce!

TOSCA: (*si abbandona quasi estasiata, quindi a poco a poco accalorandosi*) Uniti ed esulanti diffonderan pel mondo i nostri amori
armonie di colori.

CAVARADOSSI: (*esaltandosi*) ed armonie di canti!

TOSCA ED CAVARADOSSI: (*con grande entusiasmo*) Sparve il duol la sitibonda anima inonda celestiale crescente ardor. In armonicao vol l'anima sale all'estasi d'amor.

TOSCA: We shall be free and happy!
Do you smell the scent of roses?
Nature silently reposes
While dawn the secrets of night discloses.

CAVARADOSSI: The sting of death
I only felt for you, love;
From you my life took all its pride and pleasure
The world without you had been nothing to me, love,
You were my joy, my glory, and my treasure.
The brightening of the skies, and eke their darkening,
your refulgent eyes will be reflected,
Sweet sounds will reach my ears when you are hearkening,
Just as you are, so shall I be, joyous or dejected.

TOSCA: And Love, to whom is due your life's redemption,
Will be our guide on land, our pilot on the ocean
Peace shall be ours, from wordly cares exemption,
Until, united in some celestial sphere,
Fluttering like fleecy clouds ever in motion
(*she gazes fixedly, as though seeing a vision*)
We shall soar high above the globe terrestrial
(*recalled to the realities of the situation, she looks around uneasily*)
And they come not!
(*to Cavaradossi with anxious tenderness*)
Remember that you must fall on the instant at which the soldiers fire! . . .

CAVARADOSSI: (*sadly*) Do not fear, love. I shall fall at the right moment, and quite correctly.

TOSCA: (*insisting*) But pay attention; take care not to
hurt yourself! It is only a stage-trick;
I should know how to do it . . .

CAVARADOSSI: (*interrupting, draws her towards him*) Speak once again of yourself, of your lover, who listens to your dulcet accents with rapture!

TOSCA: (*ecstatically*) When once we shall be free, how joyously we will wander through a radiant world,
harmonious, sublime—the planet of love!

TOGETHER: (*in unison*) Farewell, pain!
Every feeling
Now is revealing
Heavenly bliss and perfect joy . . .
Our cares were idle and vain

TOSCA: La patria è là dove amor ci conduce.

CAVARADOSSI: Per tutto troverem l'orme latine
e il fantasma di Roma.

TOSCA: E s'io ti veda memorando guardar lungi ne' cieli, gli occhi ti chiuderò con mille baci e mille ti dirò nomi d'amore.
(*Frattanto dallo scaletta è salito un drappello di soldati: lo comanda un Ufficiale, quale schiera i soldati nel fondo: seguona Spoletta, il Sergente, Il Carceriere.— Spoletta dà le necessari istruzioni. Il cielo si fa più luminoso; è l'alba: suonano le 4 Il Carceriere si avvicina a Cavaradossi e togliendosi il berretto gli indica l'Ufficiale*)

CARCERIERE: L'ora!

CAVARADOSSI: Son pronto.
(*Il Carceriere prende il registro dei condannati e parte dalla scaletta*)

TOSCA: (*a Cavaradossi, con voce bassissima e ridendo di soppiatto*)
(Tieni a mente: al primo colpo, giù . . . )

CAVARADOSSI: (*sottovoce, ridendo esso pure*) (Giù).

TOSCA: (Nè rialzarti innanzi ch'io ti chiami).

CAVARADOSSI: (No, amore!)

TOSCA: (E cadi bene).

CAVARADOSSI: (Come la Tosca in teatro).

TOSCA: (Non ridere . . . )

CAVARADOSSI: (*facendosi cupo*) (Così?)

TOSCA: (Così).
(*Cavaradossi segue l'Ufficiale dopo aver salutato Tosca, la quale si colloca a sinistra nella casamatta, in modo però di poter spiare quanto succede sulla piattaforma. Essa vede l'Ufficiale ed il Sergente che conducono Cavaradossi presso al muro di faccia a lei: il Sergente vuol porre la benda*)

Now gladness is ours
Gladness without alloy!
(*Enter, through the trap-door, a firing party of soldiers, commanded by an officer, who parades it at the back of the stage, Spoletta, the sergeant, and the Jailer follow him. Spoletta imparts the necessary instructions. The sky brightens; day is dawning.*)

TOSCA: Your eyes I'll fondly close with countless kisses,
and loving words I'll whisper in your ears . . .

JAILER: Your time is come!
(*approaches Cavaradossi and points to the officer, taking off his cap; then picks up the register of condemned prisoners, and exit through the trap-door. The church clocks strike 4 a.m.*)

CAVARADOSSI: I'm ready!

TOSCA: (*in a low voice, suppressing her laughter*) Now remember . . . as soon as they fire . . . down!

CAVARADOSSI: (*speaking under his breath, and laughing*) Down!

TOSCA: On no account must you rise until I call you.

CAVARADOSSI: No, beloved.

TOSCA: And fall down lightly.

CAVARADOSSI: Just like La Tosca on the stage.

TOSCA: (*seeing him smile*) You must not laugh . . .

CAVARADOSSI: (*gravely*) Like this?

TOSCA: Like that.
(*Cavaradossi follows the officer after having taken leave of Tosca, who remains in the casemate, taking up a position L., from which she can see what takes place on the platform*)

*agli occhi di Cavaradossi: questi, sorridendo, rifiuta. — Tali lugubri preparativi stancano la pazienza di Tosca).*

**TOSCA:** Come'è lunga l'attesa!
Perchè indugiano ancor? . . . Già sorge il sole . . .
Perchè indugiano ancora? . . . è una commedia,
lo so . . . ma questa angoscia eterna pare!
*(l'Ufficiale e il Sergente dispongono il pelottone dei soldati, impartendo gli ordini relativi)*
Ecco! . . . apprestano l'armi . . . com'è bello il mio Mario!
*(redendo l'Ufficiale che sta per abbassare la sciabola, si porta le mani agli orecchi per non udire la detonazione; poi fa cenno colla testa a Cavaradossi di cadere, dicendo.)*
Là! muori!
*(vedendolo a terra gli invia colle mani un bacio)*
Ecco un artista!
*(Il Sergente si avvicinia al caduto e lo osserva attentamente: Spoletta pure si è avvicinato; allontana il Sergente impedendogli di dare il colpo di grazia, quindi copre Cavaradossi con un mantello. L'Ufficiale allinea i soldati il Sergente ritira la senti nella che sta in fondo, poi tutti, predecuti da Spoletta, scendono la scala. Tosca è agitatissima: essa sorveglia questi movimenti temendo che Cavaradossi, per impazienza, si muova o parli prima del momento opportuno).*
*(a voce repressa verso Cavaradossi)*
O Mario, non ti muovere . . .
Ma già s'avviano . . . taci! vanno . . . scendono.
*(vista deserta la piattaforma, va ad ascoltare presso l'imbocco della scaletta: vi si arresta trepidante, affannosa parendole ad un tratto che i soldati, anzichè allontanarsi ritornino sulla piattaforma — di nuovo sivolge a Cavaradossi, con voce bassa)*
Ancora non ti muovere . . .
ascolta — si sono tutti allontanati, va al parapetto e cautamente sporgendosi, osserve di sotto)*
Or varcano il cortile . . .
*(corre verso Cavaradossi)*
Mario, su, presto! Andiamo! . . . andiamo! . . . Su!
*(si china per alutare Cavaradossi a rialzarsi: a un tratto dà un grido suffocato di terrore, di sorpre-*

**TOSCA:** *(watching the officer and sergeant, who leads Cavaradossi up to the wall facing her)* This delay is frustrating!
What are they waiting for now?
The sun is now rising . . .
*(the sergeant offers to bandage Cavaradossi's eyes; smiling, Cavaradossi declines. These lugubrious preliminaries weary Tosca's patience)*
It's but a farce I know . . .
Yet this anxiety is dreadful!
*(The officer and sergeant draw up the firing-party in readiness for the word of command)*
At last! they are priming their muskets.
*(seeing that the officer is about to lower his sword, she stops her ears with her hands in order not to hear the explosion, and nods to Cavaradossi as a signal that he is to fall)*
How handsome is my Mario!
*(The officer lowers his sword, and the soldiers fire)*
There! Die now!
*(seeing Cavaradossi prostrate, she kisses her hand to him)*
How well he acts it!
*(The sergeant inspects the body carefully. Spoletta binders him from giving the customary coup de grace. The officer ranges his men in single file, the sergeant relieves the sentry C., and the whole party, preceded by Spoletta, passes through the trap-door and down the steps. Tosca has watched their every movement anxiously, fearing that Cavaradossi may lose patience, and move or speak prematurely)*
Oh! Mario, do not move yet . . .
lie quietly . . . silence!
*(when they had left the platform, she runs to the trap-door and stands by it listening in violent trepidation)*
They are going . . . going down . . . down!
*(fancying that she hears the soldiers returning to the platform, she turns again to Cavaradossi)*
Not yet, I pray . . . move not yet . . .
*(she leans cautiously over the parapet, looking downward)*
Now get up!
*(again approaching Cavaradossi)*

*sa e si guarda le mani colle quali ha sollevato il mantello)*
Del Sangue?!
*(si inginocchia, togli rapdiamente il mantello e balza in piedi livida, atterita)*
Morto! . . . Morto! . . .
*(con imposte parole, con sospiri, singhiozzi si butta sul corpo di Cavaradossi, quasi non credendo all'orribil destino)*
O Mario . . . morto? tu? così? Finire così? . . . cosè? . . . povera Floria tua!! *(autanto dal cortile al disotto del parapete e su dall'piccola scala arrivano prima confuse, poi sempre più vicine le voci di Sciarrone, di Spoletta e di alcuni soldati)*

**LA VOCE DI SCIARRONE:** Vi dico, pugnalato!

**VOCI CONFUSE:** Scarpia? . . .

**LA VOCE DI SCIARRONE:** Scarpia.

**LA VOCE DI SPOLETTA:** La donna è Tosca!

**VARIE VOCI PIU VICINE:** Che non sfugga!

**LA VOCE DI SPOLETTA:** *(più vicina)* Attenti là — allo sbocco delle scale . . .
*(Spoletta apparisce dalla scala, mentre Sciarrone dietro a lui gli grida additando Tosca.
È lei!*

**SPOLETTA:** *(gettandosi su Tosca)*
Ah! Tosca, pagherai ben cara la sua vita . . .
*(Tosca balza in piedi e invece di sfuggire Spoletta, lo respinge violentemente, rispo dendogli:)*

**TOSCA:** Colla mia!
*(all'urto inaspettato Spoletta dà addietro e Tosca rapida gli sfugge, passa avanti Sciarrone ancora sulla scala e correndo al parapetto si getta nei vuoto gridando:)*
O Scarpia, avanti a Dio! . . . Avanti a Dio!
*(Sciarrone ed alcuni soldati, saliti confusamente, corrono al parapetto e guardane giù. Spoletta rimane esterrefatto, allibito).*

*Finis.*

Mario! Up quickly! Away!
*(touching him)*
Blood?
*(uncovering the corpse)*
*(desperately)* Murdered! Dead!
*(sighing and sobbing)* Oh dead!
Oh Mario, how?
*(throwing herself upon the body)*
That you should end like this!
*(agonized by grief)*
What shall become of Floria?
Beloved Mario, what is life without you?
*(embracing the body)*
*(outcries of Spoletta, Sciarrone, Soldiers, &c., are heard afar off beneath the stage.)*

**SCIARRONE:** I tell you, stabbed to death!

**CONFUSED VOICES:** Scarpia?

**SCIARRONE:** Scarpia?

**SPOLETTA:** It was Tosca that killed him!
*(approaching closer and closer)*

**SCIARRONE AND CHORUS:** She must not escape!
Keep watch on the foot of the staircase!
*(Tosca, weeping bitterly, falls upon Cavaradossi's corpse. Great noise under the stage. Spoletta and Sciarrone issue from the trap-door)*

**SCIARRONE:** *(pointing out Tosca to Spoletta)* It is she!

**SPOLETTA:** Ah! Tosca, you shall pay full dearly for his life . . .
*(rushes at Tosca, who thrusts him back so violently that he all but falls prostrate. She then springs upon the parapet of the terrace)*

**TOSCA:** With my own! . . . Oh! Scarpia,
we shall meet on High!
*(throws herself into space. Sciarrone and the soldiers emerge from the staircase in confusion, rush to the parapet and lean over it, looking downward. Spoletta, horror-stricken, remains stationary.)*

*Quick Curtain.*

# Madam Butterfly (1904)

MUSIC BY GIACOMO PUCCINI ■ ITALIAN LIBRETTO BY LUIGI ILLICA AND GIUSEPPE GIACOSA

This three-act opera, set to a libretto by Giuseppe Giacosa and Luigi Illica (based on David Belasco's play from John Luther Long's story), premiered at the Teatro alla Scala in Milan on February 17, 1904. In Nagasaki, a Japanese wedding is planned between Pinkerton, a lieutenant in the United States Navy, and Cio-Cio-San, the geisha who is also called Madama Butterfly. Goro, the marriage-broker, shows the house to Pinkerton, who makes it clear that this marriage is not serious to him. Sharpless, the American consul, tells him that Butterfly plans to renounce her own religion. Her uncle, a Japanese priest, denounces her; the guests are horrified. Pinkerton dismisses them all and comforts the sobbing bride.

Three years later, she waits for Pinkerton to return. Sharpless receives a letter from Pinkerton telling him that he is married to an American wife and asking Sharpless to break the news to Butterfly. But before he can do this, Goro enters with Prince Yamadori, a wealthy gentleman who is eager to marry Butterfly. She rejects this offer outright, stating that she is married under United States law. Sharpless tries again to tell her about Pinkerton, but she doesn't listen. The harbor cannon announces the arrival of Pinkerton's ship. Butterfly and her maid Suzuki excitedly prepare the house for his return. Dawn comes, but Pinkerton does not. Suzuki finds out that Pinkerton arrived with his American wife, Kate. Pinkerton realizes that Butterfly has remained faithful to him; he has treated her most cruelly. Butterfly learns who the American lady is and wishes her all the happiness in the world. She agrees to give her child over to Pinkerton in half an hour's time. Alone, she stabs herself with her father's ceremonial hara-kiri dagger, inscribed with the words "Death with honor is better than life without honor." Before she dies, she crawls over to her child; Pinkerton enters a moment later.

## ■ ATTO I

*Colina presso Nagasaki*

*Casa giapponese, terrazza e giardino. In fondo, al basso, la rada, il porto, la città di Nagasaki.*

*Goro fa visitare la casa a Pinkerton, che passa di sorpresa in sorpresa.*

**PINKERTON:** E soffitto . . . e pareti . . .

**GORO:** (*godendo della sorprese*)
Vanno e vengono a prova
a norma che vi giova
nello stesso locale
alternar nuovi aspetti ai consueti,

**PINKERTON:** (*cercando intorno*)
Il nido nuziale
dov'è?

**GORO:** (*accennando a due locali*) Qui, o
là! . . . secondo . . .

**PINKERTON:** Anch'esso a doppio fondo!
La sala?

**GORO:** (*mostra la terrazza*) Ecco!

**PINKERTON:** (*stupito*)
All'aperto? . . .

**GORO:** (*mostrando il chiudersi d'una parete*) Un fianco scorre . . .

**PINKERTON:** Capisco! Un altro . . .

**GORO:** Scivola!

## ■ ACT I

*Hill Near Nagasaki*

*A Japanese house, terrace and garden. Below, in the background, the bay, the harbor and the town of Nagasaki.*

*Goro is showing Pinkerton over the house. Pinkerton passes from one surprise to another.*

**PINKERTON:** And the walls—and the ceiling—

**GORO:** (*enjoying his surprise*)
They will come and go,
Just as it may suit your fancy
To exchange or to vary
New and old in the same surroundings.

**PINKERTON:** (*looking around*)
The marriage-chamber,
Where is it?

**GORO:** (*pointing in two directions*) Here, or there!—according—

**PINKERTON:** A wonderful contrivance!
The hall?

**GORO:** (*showing the terrace*) Behold!

**PINKERTON:** (*amazed*) In the open?

**GORO:** (*making a partition slide out*) A wall slides outward—

**PINKERTON:** I see now! Another—

**GORO:** Runs along!

**PINKERTON:** E la dimora frivola . . .

**GORO:** (*protestando*) Salda come una torre
da terra, infino al tetto.

**PINKERTON:** È una casa a soffietto.

**GORO:** (*batte tre volte le mani palma a plama; entrano due uomini ed una donna e si genuflettono innanzi a Pinkerton*)
Questa è la cameriera
(*accennando*)
che della vostra sposa
fu già serva amorosa.
Il cuoco—il servitor. Sono confusi
del grande onore.

**PINKERTON:** I nomi?

**GORO:** (*presentando*) Miss Nuvola leggiera—
Raggio di sol nascente.—Esala aromi

**PINKERTON:** Nomi di scherno o scherzo.
Io li chiamerò: musi!
(*indicando*)
Muso primo, secondo, e muso terzo.

**SUZUKI:** (*fatta ardita*) Sorride
Vostro Onore?—
Il riso è frutto e fiore.
Disse il savio Ocunama:
dei crucci la trama
smaglia il sorriso. Schiude alla perla il guscio,
apre all'uom l'uscio
del Paradiso.
Profume degli Dei . . .
Fontana della vita . . .

**PINKERTON:** And so the fairy dwelling—

**GORO:** Springs like a tower from nowhere,
Complete from base to attic!—

**PINKERTON:** It comes and goes by magic!

**GORO:** (*claps his hand loudly twice; enter two men and a woman, who go down on their hands and knees in front of Pinkerton*)
This is the trusty handmaid,
Who waits upon your wife,
Faithful and devoted.
The cook—the servant. They're embarrassed
At such great honor.

**PINKERTON:** Their names?

**GORO:** (*introducing them*) "Miss Gentle-Breeze-of-Morning.—Ray-of-the-golden-sun.—Sweet-scented-pine-tree."

**PINKERTON:** Foolishly chosen nicknames!
I will call them: scarecrows!
(*pointing to them one by one*)
First scarecrow; second; and third!

**SUZUKI:** (*grown bolder*)
Your Honor deigns to smile?—
Your smile is like the fruit of a flower.
Thus spake the wise Ocunama:
A smile conquers all, and defies
Every trouble. Pearls may be won by smiling,
Smiles can open the portals
Of Paradise.
The Perfume of the Gods—

(*Goro accorgendosi che Pinkerton comincia ad essere infastidito dalla loquela di Suzuki batte le mani,—I tre si alzano e fuggono rapidamente rientrando in casa*).

(*Goro, perceiving that Pinkerton begins to be bored at Suzuki's loquacity, claps his hands thrice. The three rise and quickly disappear into the house*)

PINKERTON: A chiacchiere costei mi par cosmopolita.
(*a Goro andato in fondo ad osservare*)
Che guardi?

PINKERTON: When they begin to talk,
I find all women alike.
(*to Goro who has gone to the back to look out*)
At what are you looking?

GORO: Se non giunge ancor la posa.

SUZUKI: Watching for the bride's arrival.

PINKERTON: Tutto è pronto?

PINKERTON: All is ready?

GORO: Ogni cosa.

GORO: Every detail.

PINKERTON: Gran perla di sensale!

PINKERTON: You shining light of brokers!

GORO: (*ringrazia con profondo inchino*) Qui verran: l'Ufficiale del registro, i parenti, il vostro Console,
la fidanzata. Qui si firma l'atto e il matrimonio è fatto.

GORO: (*thanks with a deep bow*) They will come: the official registrar,
The relations, your country's Consul,
Your future wife. Here you'll sign the contract,
And solomnize the marriage.

PINKERTON: E son molti i parenti?

PINKERTON: Are there many relations?

GORO: La suocera, la nonna, lo zio Bonzo
(*che non ci degnerà di sua presenza*)
e cugini! e cugine . . .
Mettiam fra gli ascendenti
ed i collaterali, un due dozzine.
Quanto alla discendenza . . .
(*con malizia ossequiosa*)
provvederanno assai
Vostra Grazia e la bella Butterfly.
(*si ode la voce di Sharpless il Console, che sale il colle*)

GORO: Her mother, grandam, and the Bonze, her uncle,
(Who'll scarcely honor us with his appearance)
Her cousins, male and female—
Of ancestors I reckon, and other blood relations,
A round two dozen.
As to the descendants—
(*with obsequious presumption*)
That may be left, I reckon,
To your Honor and the fair Butterfly—
(*the voice of the Consul Sharpless, who is climbing the hill, is heard*)

LA VOCE DI SHARPLESS: (*un po' lontano*) E suda e arrampica!
e sbuffa e inciampica!
—Erta letale!

THE VOICE OF SHARPLESS: (*rather far off*) A plague on this steep ascent!
Stumbling, and spluttering—

GORO: (*che è accorso al fondo, annuncia a Pinkerton*) —il Consol sale.

GORO: (*who has run to the back, announces*) Here comes the Consul.

SHARPLESS: (*appare sbuffando: Goro si prosterna innanzi al Console*) Ah! . . . quei viottoli irti di ciottoli
m'hanno sfiaccato!

SHARPLESS: (*enters, quite out of breath. Goro bows low before him*) Ah! the scramble up
Has left me breathless!

PINKERTON: (*va incontro a Sharpless—i due si stringono la mano*) Bene arrivato.

PINKERTON: (*goes to meet the Consul: they shake hands*) Good-day, friend! Welcome!

SHARPLESS: Ouff!

SHARPLESS: Ough!

PINKERTON: Presto Goro qualche ristoro.
(*Goro entra in casa frettoloso*)

PINKERTON: Quickly, Goro, Fetch some refreshments.
(*Goro hurries into the house*)

SHARPLESS: (*guardando intorno*) Alto.

SHARPLESS: (*looking about*) Lofty!

PINKERTON: (*mostrandogli il panorama*) Ma bello!

PINKERTON: (*showing him the view*) But lovely!

SHARPLESS: (*contemplando il mare e la città sottoposti*) Nagasaki, il mare!
il porto . . .

SHARPLESS: (*looking at the sea and the town below*) Nagasaki—
the ocean—
The harbor—

PINKERTON: (*accennando alla casa*) e una casetta che obbedisce a bacchetta.

PINKERTON: (*pointing to the house*) This is a dwelling
Which is managed by magic.

SHARPLESS: Vostra?

SHARPLESS: Yours?

PINKERTON: La comperai per novecento novantanove anni,
con facoltà, ogni mese,
di rescindere i patti.
Sono in questo paese
elastici del par, case e contratti.

PINKERTON: I bought this house
For nine hundred and ninety-nine years,
But with the option, at every month,
To cancel the contract!
I must say, in this country
The houses and the contracts are elastic!

SHARPLESS: E l'uomo esperto ne profitta.
(*Goro viene frettoloso dalla casa, seguito dai due servi; portano bicchieri, bottiglie e due poltrone di vimini; depongono bicchieri e bottiglie su di un piccolo tavolo e tornano in casa*)

SHARPLESS: The man of business profits by it.
(*Goro comes bustling out of the house, followed by the two servants. They bring glasses, bottles and two wicker lounges; place the glasses and bottles on a small table, and return to the house*)

PINKERTON: (*Invitando à sedere*) Certo
Dovunque al mondo il yankee vagabondo
si gode e traffica
sprezzando i rischi.
Affonda l'àncora alla ventura
finchè una raffica . . .
(*Pinkerton's interrompe per offrire da bere a Sharpless*)
Milk-Punch, o Wiskey?
(*riprende*)
. . . scompigli nave, ormeggi, alberatura.
La vita ei non appaga
se non fa suo tesor
le stelle d'ogni cielo
i fiori d'ogni plaga,
d'ogni bella gli amor.

PINKERTON: (*inviting him to be seated*) Surely.
The whole world over,
On business and pleasure bent
The Yankee travels, scorning all dangers,
His anchor boldly he casts at random—
Until a sudden squall—
(*breaking off to offer Sharpless a drink*)
Milk punch or whisky?
(*resuming*)
Upsets his ship, then up go sails and rigging;
And life is not worth living
If he can't win the best
And fairest of each country,
The heart of each fair maid!

SHARPLESS: È un facile vangelo che fa la vita vaga
ma che intristisce il cuor.

SHARPLESS: That's an easy-going gospel
Which makes life very pleasant,
But is fatal in the end—

PINKERTON: (*continuando*) Vinto si tuffa e la sorte riacciuffa.
Il suo talento
fa in ogni dove.
Cosi mi sposo all'uso giapponese
per novecento novantanove
anni, Salvo a prosciogliermi ogni mese.
"America forever!"

PINKERTON: (*continuing*) Fate cannot crush him, he tries again undaunted,
No one and nothing
Breaks his plucky spirit.
And so I'm marrying in Japanese fashion,
Tied for nine hundred
And ninety-nine years,
Free, though, to annul the marriage monthly.
"America forever!"

SHARPLESS: Ed è bella la sposa?

SHARPLESS: Is the bride very pretty?

GORO: (*che ha udito, si avanza premuroso ed insinuante*) Una ghirlanda
di fior freschi, Una stella dai raggi d'oro.
E per nulla; sol cento yen.
(*al Console*)
Se la Grazia Vostra mi comanda ce n'ho un assortimento.
(*il Console ridendo, ringrazia*)

GORO: (*who has overheard, approaches the terrace officiously*) Fair as a garland
Of fragrant flowers! Brighter
Than a star in the heavens!
And for nothing: one hundred Yen.
(*to the Consul*)
If your Augustness will entrust me, I have a fine selection?
(*the Consul laughingly declines*)

# Act I

**PINKERTON:** (*con viva impazienza*)
Va, conducila Goro.
(*Goro corre in fondo e scompare discendendo il colle: i due servi rientrano in casa Pinkerton e Sharpless siedono*).

**SHARPLESS:** Quale smania vi prende!
Sareste addirittura cotto?

**PINKERTON:** Non so! Dipende. dal grado di cottura!
Amore o grillo—donna o gingilo
dir non saprei—Certo colei
m'ha colle ingenue—arti invescato.
Lieve qual tenue—vetro soffiato
alla statura—al portamento
sembra figura—da paravento
Ma dal suo lucido—fondo di lacca
come con subito—moto si stacca,
qual farfalletta—svolazza e posa
con tal grazietta—silenzioza
che di rincorrerla—furor m'assale
se pure infrangerne—dovessi l'ale.

**SHARPLESS:** (*seriamente e bonario*)
Ier l'altro, il Consolato
sen' venne a visitar!
Io non la vidi, ma l'udii parlar.
Di sua voce il mistero
L'anima mi colpi.
Certo quando è sincero
l'amor parla cosi.
Sarebbe gran peccato
le lievi ali strappar
e desolar forse un credulo cuor.
Quella—divina
mite—vocina
non dovrebbe dar note di dolor.

**PINKERTON:** Console mio garbato,
quetatevi! Si sa,
la vostra età è di flebile umor.
Non c'è gran male
s'io vo' quell'ale
dizzar ai dolci voli dell'amor!
(*offre di nuovo da bere*)
Wiskey?

**SHARPLESS:** Un altro bicchiere.
(*Pinkerton colma anche il proprio bicchiere*)
Bevo alla vostra famiglia lontana.

**PINKERTON:** (*very impatiently*)
Go and fetch her, Goro.
(*Goro runs to the back and disappears down the hill*)

**SHARPLESS:** What folly has seized you!
Do you think you are
Quite drunk?

**PINKERTON:** (*rises impatiently. Sharpless rises also*) May be! Depends
On what you call intoxication!
Is it love or fancy, maid or myth—
I cannot tell you—all that I know is
She, with her innocent charm, has entranced me.
Almost transparently fragile and slender,
Dainty in statute, quaint little figure,
Seems to have stepped down
Straight from a screen.—
But from her background of varnish and lacquer—
Suddenly, light as a feather she flutters,
And, like a butterfly, hovers and settles,
With so much charm and such seductive graces,
That to pursue her a wild wish seized me—
Though in the quest her frail wings should be broken.

**SHARPLESS:** (*seriously and kindly*) The other day, she came up
To call at the Consulate!
I did not see her, but I heard her speak.
And the mystery of her voice
Touched my very soul.
Surely love that is pure and true
speaks like that.
It would indeed be a sad pity
To tear those dainty wings,
And perchance to torment a trusting heart.
No cry of anguish should ever be uttered
By that gentle and trusting little voice.

**PINKERTON:** Dearly beloved Consul,
Allay your fears! We know
Men of your age look on life with mournful eyes.
No harm I reckon these wings to raise,
And guide them to the tender flights of love!
(*offers him more drink*)
Whisky?

**SHARPLESS:** Yes, mix me another.
(*Pinkerton fills up his own glass as well*)
Here's to your friends and relations at home.

**PINKERTON:** (*leva il calice*) E al giorno in cui mi sposerò con vere nozze, a una vera sposa . . . americana.

**GORO:** (*riappare correndo, venendo dal basso della collina*)
Ecco! Son giunte al sommo del pendìo.
(*accennando verso il sentiero*)
Già del femmineo sciame
qual di vento in fogliame
s'ode il brusìo.

**VOCE DI BUTTERFLY:** Ancora un passo or via.

**ALTRA VOCI:** Come sei tarda.
Ecco la vetta.—
—Aspetta.—
—Guarda, guarda.

**VOCE DI BUTTERFLY:**
Spira sul mare o sulla
terra un primaveril soffio giocondo.
Io sono la fanciulla
più lieta del Giappone, anzi del mondo.
Dalle vie, dalle ville
la città colle mille
sue voci mi saluta,
Amiche, io son venuta
al richiamo d'amor
nelle grandiose soglie
ove tutto s'accoglie
il bene di chi vive e di chi muor.

**LE AMICHE:** Gioia a te sia
dolce amica, ma pria
di varcare la soglia che ti attira
volgiti indietro e mira
le cose tutte che ti son sì care.
Quanti fior! Quanto cielo! Quanto mare!

**SHARPLESS:** O allegro cinguettar di gioventù!
(*Appaiono, superato il pendìo della collina. Butterfly colle amiche, tutte hanno grandi ombrelli aperti, a vivi colori*).

**BUTTERFLY:** Siam giunte.
(*vede il gruppo dei tre uomini e riconosce Pinkerton. Chiude subito l'ombrello e pronta addita Pinkerton alle amiche*)
B. F. Pinkerton. Giù.
(*si genuflette*)

**LE AMICHE:** (*chiudono gli ombrelli e si genuflettono*) Giù.
(*poi tutte si alzano e si avvicinano a Pinkerton, cerimoniosamente*)

**BUTTERFLY:** Gran ventura

**LE AMICHE:** Riverenza.

**PINKERTON:** (*raising his glass*)
And to the day on which I'll wed
In real marriage—a real American wife!

**GORO:** (*reappears running breathlessly up the hill*) See them! they've climbed the summit of the hill!
(*pointing towards the path*)
A crowd of women hustling,
Like the wind in branches rustling,
Here they come bustling!
(*The confused and lively hubbub of many voices is heard from the path. Pinkerton and Sharpless retire to the back of the garden, watching the path on the hill*)

**BUTTERFLY'S VOICE:** There's one step more to climb.

**OTHER VOICES:** How long you tarry—here is the summit—
One moment—look, oh look!

**BUTTERFLY'S VOICE:** Across the earth and over the ocean
Balmy breeze and scent of Spring are blowing—
I am the happiest maiden,
The happiest in Japan—
In all the world.
From every nook and corner
The city sends me greeting
With a thousand voices.
Friends, I have obeyed
The summons of love,
Upon the threshold standing,
Where all the glory awaits me,
That life or death can offer.

**HER GIRL FRIENDS:** The best of luck attend you,
Gentle maiden, but in case
You cross the threshold which invites you,
turn and admire the things you hold so dear.
What lovely flowers! what lovely sky, and lovely sea!

**SHARPLESS:** O happy prattle, careless days of youth!
(*Butterfly and her girl friends appear on the brow of the hill. They will carry large brightly coloured sunshades, open*)

**BUTTERFLY:** We're there now.
(*she sees the three men standing together and recognizes Pinkerton. She promptly closes her sunshade and introduces Pinkerton to her friends*)
B. F. Pinkerton. Down.
(*goes down on her knees*)

**THE GIRL FRIENDS:** (*close their sunshades and go on their knees*)
Down.
(*then they all rise and ceremoniously approach Pinkerton*)

**BUTTERFLY:** Augustly welcome—

**THE GIRL FRIENDS:** Hail, most mighty!

PINKERTON: (*sorridendo*) È un po' dura
la scalata?

PINKERTON: (*smiling*) The ascent
Is rather difficult?

BUTTERFLY: (*compassata*) A una sposa
costumata
più penosa
l' impazienza.

BUTTERFLY: (*measuredly*) Not so trying
To a bride
As are the weary hours
Of waiting.

PINKERTON: (*un po' derisorio*) Molto raro
complimento.

PINKERTON: (*rather sarcastically*) What a rare
Compliment!

BUTTERFLY: (*ingenua*) Dei più belli
ancor ne so

BUTTERFLY: (*ingenuously*) I know better ones
Than that—

PINKERTON: (*rincalzando*) Dei gioielli!

PINKERTON: (*good humouredly*)
Gems, I doubt not!

BUTTERFLY: (*volendo sfoggiare il suo repertorio di complimenti*) Se vi è caro
sul momento . . .

BUTTERFLY: (*anxious to show off her stock of compliments*) If you care for some
At this moment.

PINKERTON: Grazie—no.

PINKERTON: (*gently*) Thank you—no.

SHARPLESS: (*ha osservato prima curiosamente il gruppo delle fanciulle, poi si è avvicinato a Butterfly che lo ascolta con attenzione*) Miss Butterfly. Bel nome che vi sta a meraviglia.
Siete di Nagasaki?

SHARPLESS: (*after scanning the group of maidens with curiosity, approaches Butterfly, who listens to him attentively*) Miss "Butterfly"—How pretty!—Your name
Was well chosen. Are you from Nagasaki?

BUTTERFLY: Signor si. Di famiglia assai prospera un tempo.
(*alle amiche*)
Verità?

BUTTERFLY: Sir, I am. My people
Were formerly wealthy.
(*to her friends*) Say so!

LE AMICHE: (*approvando premurose*) Verità!

HER GIRL FRIENDS: (*assenting with alacrity*) It is so!

BUTTERFLY: Nessuno si confessa mai nato in povertà
e non c'è vagabondo che a sentirlo non sia
di gran prosapia. Eppure senza millanteria
conobbi la ricchezza. Ma il turbine rovescia
le quercie più robuste—e abbiam fatto la ghescia
per sostentarci.
(*alle amiche*)
Vero?

BUTTERFLY: There's no one cares to own he was born in poverty.
Is not every vagrant, when you listen to his tale,
Of ancient lineage? But yet indeed I have known riches. But the strongest oak
Must fall when the storm-wind wrecks the forest.
And we had to become geishas, to earn our living.
(*to her friends*) Say so!

LE AMICHE: (*confermano*) Vero!

THE FRIENDS: (*corroborating*) Truly!

BUTTERFLY: Non lo nascondo nè mi adonto.
(*vedendo che Sharpless sorride*) Ridete? Perchè? . . . Cose del mondo.

BUTTERFLY: I frankly own it,
And don't blush for it.
(*seeing that Sharpless smiles*) You're laughing? And why? That's how the world runs.

PINKERTON: (*ha ascoltato con interesse e si rivolge a Sharpless*) (*Con quel fare di bambola quando parla m'infiamma.*)

PINKERTON: (*has listened with interest and turns to Sharpless*) (With her innocent baby-face when she speaks, she sets my heart on fire.)

SHARPLESS: (*anch'esso interessato dalle chiacchiere di Butterfly, continua a interrogarla*) E ci aveta sorelle?

SHARPLESS: (*he also in interested in Butterfly's prattle, and continues to question her*) And have you no sisters?

BUTTERFLY: Non signore. Ho la mamma.

BUTTERFLY: None, Honorable sir, I've my mother.

GORO: (*con inportanza*) Una nobile dama.

GORO: (*importantly*) A most notable lady.

BUTTERFLY: Ma senza farle torto povera molto anch'essa.

BUTTERFLY: But through no fault whatever,
She is dreadfully poor.

SHARPLESS: E vostro padre?

SHARPLESS: And where's your father?

BUTTERFLY: (*si arresta sorpresa—poi secco secco risponde:*) Morto.

BUTTERFLY: (*stops short in surprise, then answers very shortly:*) Dead!

SHARPLESS: (*a Butterfly*) Quanti anni avete?

SHARPLESS: (*to Butterfly*) What might your age be?

BUTTERFLY: (*con civetteria quasi infantile*) Indovinate.

BUTTERFLY: (*with almost childish coquetry*) Now try to guess it!

PINKERTON: Dieci.

PINKERTON: Ten years.

BUTTERFLY: Crescete.

BUTTERFLY: Guess higher.

SHARPLESS: Venti.

SHARPLESS: Twenty.

BUTTERFLY: Calate.
Quindici, netti, netti;
sono vecchia diggià

BUTTERFLY: Guess lower.
Fifteen, exactly fifteen!
I am old, am I not?

SHARPLESS: Quindici anni! L'età dei giuochi . . .

SHARPLESS: Fifteen years old! The age
of playthings—

PINKERTON: e dei confetti
(*a Goro, che batte le mani, chiamando i tre servi, i quali accorrono dalla casa: Goro impartisce loro gli ordini, man mano che li riceve da Pinkerton*)
Qua i tre musi. Servite
ragni e mosche candite.
Nidi al giulebbe e quale
è licor più indigesto
e più nauseabonda leccornia
dell Nipponeria.
(*Goro nel seguire i servi che rientrano in casa si accorge che altre persone saigono il colle: osserva; poi corre ad annunciare a Pinkerton e a Sharpless:*)

PINKERTON: And of sweetmeats!
(*To Goro, who claps his hands, summoning the three servants, who come running from the house: Goro gives them the orders which he takes from Pinkerton*)
Call my scarecrows to hand round
Candied flies and spiders,
Preserves and pastry, and all
Sorts of curious liquors,
And such most peculiar delicacies
They fancy in Japan.
(*Goro is just about to follow the servants into the house, when he perceives movement climbing the hill; he goes to look then runs to announce the new arrivals to Pinkerton and to Sharpless:*)

GORO: (*con importanza*)
L'imperial Commissario e
l'Ufficiale
del registro—i congiunti.

GORO: (*importantly*) The imperial High Commissioner—
The official Registrar—the relations

PINKERTON: (*a Goro*) Fate presto.
(*Goro corre in casa*)

PINKERTON: (*to Goro*) Come now, hurry.
(*Goro runs into the house*)

ALCUNI PARENTI: (*con molta curiosità a Butterfly*) Dov'è?
Dove'è?

SOME OF THE RELATIONS: (*with great curiosity, to Butterfly*) Where is he? Where?

BUTTERFLY: (*indicando Pinkerton*) Eccola là!

BUTTERFLY: (*pointing to Pinkerton*) That is he—there!

I.A CUGINA: In verità
bello non è.—

FIRST COUSIN: To tell the truth,
Handsome he's not—

BUTTERFLY: (*offesa*) Bello è così
che non si può
sognar di più.

BUTTERFLY: (*offended*) Handsomer man
You never saw—
Not in your dreams.

LA MADRE DI BUTTERFLY: Mi pare un re!

BUTTERFLY'S MOTHER: I think he resembles a king.

LO ZIO: Vale un Perù.

THE UNCLE: He's worth a lot!

I.A CUGINA: Goro l'offri
pur anche a me.
Ma s'ebbe un no!

FIRST COUSIN: Why, Goro offered him to me,
But I said no!

BUTTERFLY: (*sdegnosa*) Si, giusto tu!

BUTTERFLY: (*contemptuously*) To you, my dear!

**ALCUNI AMICI AD ALCUNE AMICHE:** Ecco, perchè prescelta fu, vuol far con te la soprappiù.

**SOME MALE AND FEMALE FRIENDS:** Because on her His choice did fall, She would look down Upon us all!

**ALTRE AMICHE:** La sua beltà gia disfiorì.

**SOME OTHER GIRL FRIENDS:** I think her beauty's fading.

**CUGINI E CUGINE:** Divorzierà.

**MALE AND FEMALE COUSINS:** She'll be divorced.

**ALTRI:** Spero di sì.—

**OTHERS:** I hope so.

**GORO:** Per carità tacete un po' . . . chi v'insegnò la civiltà?

**GORO:** For goodness sake Be silent now— Where did you get Your manners?

**LA MADRE DI BUTTERFLY E ALCUNE CUGINE:** Oh quelli lì non smette più

**BUTTERFLY'S MOTHER AND A FEW COUSINS:** Why, that one there Won't let her be.

**GORO:** Stoltezza fu condurla qui.

**GORO:** You are fools To bring her here.

**LO ZIO:** Vino ce n'è?

**THE UNCLE:** Is there no wine?

**LA MADRE E LA ZIA:** Guardiamo un po'.

**THE MOTHER AND THE AUNT:** Let's look about.

**ALCUNE AMICHE:** Ne vidi già, color di thè, à chermisì!

**SOME FRIENDS:** I've just seen some, The hue of tea— And crimson too!

**LO ZIO:** Se ne berrò!

**THE UNCLE:** I'd like a drink!

**IL BAMBINO:** E chicche?

**THE CHILD:** And sweetmeats.

**SUA MADRE:** Sì.

**HIS MOTHER:** Yes.

**IL BAMBINO:** (gongolante) Curu-cucu!

**THE CHILD:** (capering for joy) Hurrah! Hurrah!

**BUTTERFLY:** (a sua madre) Mamma, vien qua. (agli altri) Badate a me: attenti, orsù, uno—due—tre e tutti giù. (e tutti si inchinano innazi a Pinkerton, tranne il Commissario e l'Ufficiale) (In tanto Goro ha fatto portare dia servi alcuni tavolini, sui quali dispongonsi varie confetture, pasticcietti, liquori, vini e servizi da thè; si portano alcuni cuscini e un tavolino a parte, coll' occorrente per scrivere. Parenti, amici guardano con molta soddisfazione i dulciani portati. Butterfly presenta i parenti à Pinkerton.)

**BUTTERFLY:** Mother, come here. (to the others) Listen to me: All of you, look, One—two—three— All of you: down! (They all bow low before Pinkerton) (Meanwhile, Goro has made the servants bring out some small tables, on which they lay a variety of cake, sweetmeats, liquors, wines and tea-sets. They set some cushions and a small table with writing-materials apart. The friends and relations evince great satisfaction at the refreshments. Butterfly presents her relations to Pinkerton)

**IL COMMISSARIO IMPERIALE:** (legge) E concesso al nominato Benjamin Franklin Pinkerton, Luogotenente nella cannoniera Lincoln, marina degli Stati Uniti America del Nord: ed alla damigella Butterfly del quartiere di Omara-Nagasaki, finor non maritata e in conseguenza non divorziata mai, di unirsi in matrimonio, per diritto il primo, della propria voluntà, . . . ed ella per consenso dei parenti qui testimoni all'atto. (porge l'atto per la firma)

**THE IMPERIAL COMMISSIONER:** (reads) Leave is given to the undersigned Benjamin Franklin Pinkerton, Lieutenant, serving on the gunboat Lincoln, of the United States Navy, Of North America; And to the spinster, known as Butterfly, Inhabitant of Omara-Nagasaki, Hitherto single, and in consequence Never divorced, To join in bonds of wedlock; to wit The former of his free accord and will, The latter with consent of her relations, Witnesses to the contract. (Hands the bond for signature)

**GORO:** (cerimonioso) Lo sposo. (Pinkerton firma) Poi la sposa. (Butterly firma) E tutto è fatto (circondano Butterfly festiggiandola)

**GORO:** (with much unction) The bridegroom. (Pinkerton signs) Now the bride. (Butterfly signs) And all is settled.

**LE AMICHI:** Madama Butterfly!

**THE GIRL FRIENDS:** (surround Butterfly, congratulating her) Dear Madam Butterfly.

**BUTTERFLY:** (le corregge) Madama B. F. Pinkerton. (L'Ufficiale della Stato Civile ritira l'atto e avverte il Commissario che tutto è finito.)

**BUTTERFLY:** (corrects them) No, Madam B. F. Pinkerton. (The Civil Registrar withdraws the bond and informs the Commissioner that the ceremony is over)

**IL COMMISSARIO IMPERIALE:** (congedandosi da Pinkerton) Auguri molti.

**THE COMMISSIONER:** (taking leave of Pinkerton) The best of wishes.

**PINKERTON:** I miei ringraziamenti.

**PINKERTON:** I thank you most sincerely.

**IL COMMISARIO IMPERIALE:** (al Console) Il signor Consol scende?

**THE COMMISSIONER:** (to the Consul) May I ask, are you going?

**SHARPLESS:** L'accompagno.

**SHARPLESS:** I'll go with you.

**UFFICIALE:** (congedandosi de Pinkerton) Posterità.

**THE REGISTRAR:** (taking leave of Pinkerton) The best of luck.

**PINKERTON:** Mi proverò.

**PINKERTON:** I'm much obliged.

**SHARPLESS:** (stringendo la mano a Pinkerton) Giudizio! Ci vedrem domattina.

**SHARPLESS:** (shaking hands with Pinkerton) We shall meet tomorrow! Be careful!

**PINKERTON:** A meraviglia. (Pinkerton accompagna i tre sino al sentiero che scende alla città e il saluta di nuovo quando già sono fuori di vista; sono passati prima fra due schiere di parenti e di amiche che li hanno salutati con molti cerimoniosi inchini. Butterfly si è recata presso sua madre. Pinkerton ritorna, e si capisce che è deliberato di sbarazzarsi dei parenti e delle amiche). (Ed eccoci in famiglia.) Sbrighiamoci al più presto—in modo onesto.) Qua, signor Zio.

**PINKERTON:** Tomorrow, surely. (Pinkerton accompanies the three as far as the path which leads down to the town and waves his hand to them as they vanish from sight. They had first to pass between two files of friends and relatives, who saluted them with many ceremonious bows. Butterfly has withdrawn close to her mother. Pinkerton returns and is naturally anxious to get rid of the wedding guests) (Now quickly to get rid Of this little family party! How shall I do it?) this way, good uncle.

**PINKERTON:** (al bambino) A te marmocchio; spalanca le tue maniche ed insacca chicche e pasticci a macca. (leva il proprio bicchiere) Ip! Ip!

**PINKERTON:** (to the child, giving him a lot of sweets) Your turn, young rascal; Spread out your hands, and stuff your sleeves With cakes and sweets and pastry. (raising his own glass) Hip! Hip!

**TUTTI:** (brindando) O Kami! O Kami!

**ALL:** (toasting) O Kami! O Kami!

**PINKERTON:** E beviamo ai novissimi legami.

**PINKERTON:** Let's drink to the newly-married couple.

**TUTTI:** O Kami! O Kami! (Grida terribili dal sentiero della collina interrompono i brindisi; ad un tratto appare dal fondo uno strano personaggio, la cui vista fa allibire tutti. E il Bonzo che si fa innanzi furibondo e vista Butter-

**ALL:** O Kami! O Kami! (The toasts are interrupted by strange cries from the hill; all of a sudden a weird figure appears in the background, at the sight of whom all are thunderstruck. It is the Bonze, who comes forward in

*fly, stende le mani minacciose verso di lei, gridando)*

*a towering rage, and, catching sight of Butterfly, stretches out threatening hands towards her, crying:)*

**IL BONZO:** Cio-cio-san! . . . Cio-cio-san! . . . Abbominazione!

**THE BONZE:** Cho-Cho-San! Cho-Cho-San! Abomination!

**GORO:** *(infastidito dalla venuta del Bonzo)* Un corno al guastafeste! Chi ci leva d'intorno le persone moleste?! . . . *(fa cenno ai servi di asportare tavoliui, sgabelli, suscini e prudentemente se ne parte adiratissimo, borbottando)*

**GORO:** *(annoyed at the Bonze's intrusion)* A plague on this intruder! What on earth brought him here Of all troublesome people? *(signs to the servants to remove the tables, cushions and stools; and then prudently retires himself, grumbling furiously)*

**TUTTI:** *(impauriti, si raccolgono in un angolo balbettando)* Lo zio Bonze! *(Pinkerton guarda la strana figura del Bonzo e ride)*

**ALL:** *(huddling together in a corner in terror)* The Bonze, her uncle! *(Pinkerton looks at the Bonze's weird figure and laughs)*

**IL BONZO:** *(a Butterfly, che s'è scostata da tutti)* Che hai tu fatto alla Missione?

**THE BONZE:** *(to Butterfly, who stands isolated from the rest)* What were You doing at the Mission?

**PINKERTON:** Che mi strilla quel matto?

**PINKERTON:** What is that madman shrieking?

**IL BONZO:** Rispondi, che hai tu fatto?

**THE BONZE:** Answer, what were you doing?

**TUTTI:** Rispondi Cio-cio-san!

**ALL:** Answer, Cho-Cho-San!

**IL BONZO:** Come, hai tu gli occhi asciutti? Son questi dunque i frutti? *(urlando)* Ci ha rinnegato tutti!

**THE BONZE:** How, then, don't you even falter? Are these the fruits of evil? *(shouting)* She has renounced us all!

**TUTTI:** Hou! Cio-cio-san!

**ALL:** Hou! Cho-Cho-San!

**IL BONZO:** Rinnegato, vi dico, degli avi il culto antico.

**THE BONZE:** She's renounced, let me tell you, Her true religion!

**TUTTI:** Hou! Cio-cio-san! *(Butterfly si copre il viso vergognosa)*

**ALL:** Hou! Cho-Cho-San! *(Butterfly, overcome with shame, hides her face in her hands)*

**IL BONZO:** *(gridando sul viso a Betterfly)* All'anima tua guasta qual supplizio sovrasta! *(La madre s'interpone per difendere Butterfly, ma il Bonzo la respinge brutalmente. Pinkerton infastidito, si alza e grida al Bonzo:)*

**THE BONZE:** *(shouting into her face)* In everlasting torment May your wicked soul perish! *(Butterfly's mother comes forward to protect her, but the Bonze roughly pushes her away. Pinkerton loses patience, rises and shouts to the Bonze:)*

**PINKERTON:** *(infastidito)* Ehi, dico: basta, basta! *(alla voce di Pinkerton il Bonzo si arresta stupefatto! . . . poi con subita risoluzione invita i parenti e la amiche a partire)*

**PINKERTON:** *(out of patience)* Be silent now, you hear me? *(At the sound of Pinkerton's voice, the Bonze stops short in amazement, then with a sudden resolve he invites his friends and relations to come away)*

**IL BONZO:** Venite tutti—Andiamo! *(a Butterfly)* Ci hai rinnegato e noi . . .

**THE BONZE:** Come with me, all. We'll leave her. *(to Butterfly)* You have renounced us all—and we—

**TUTTI:** Ti rinneghiamo!

**ALL:** Renounce you!

**PINKERTON:** *(autorevolmente)* Sbarazzate all'istante. In casa mia niente baccano e niente bonzeria. *(Tutti, parenti, amiche, il Bonzo, partono in gran fretta, scendendo la collina e continuando strilare imprecare contro Butterfly.—Le*

**PINKERTON:** *(authoritatively)* Leave this place on the instant! Here I am master— I'll have no turmoil and no disturbance here! *(All the guests, including the Bonze, depart in great haste, go-*

*voci a poco a poco si allontanano.—Butterfly ci stette sempre immobile e muta colla faccia nelle mani, scoppia in pianto infantile. Cominicia poco a poco a calare la sera: poi notte serena e stellata).*

*ing down the hillside and continuing to hurl threats and imprecations at Butterfly. By degrees the voices die away in the distance. Butterfly, who has been standing motionless and mute with her face buried in her hands, bursts into childish tears. Evening begins to draw in gradually, then night sets in, serene and starlit)*

**PINKERTON:** *(va presso Butterfly e con delicatezza le toglie le mani dal viso)* Bimba, Bimba, non piangere per gracchiar di ranocchi.

**PINKERTON:** *(goes up to Butterfly and gently draws her hands from her face)* Dearest, my dearest, weep no more! Let the frogs croak their loudest.

**BUTTERFLY:** *(udendo ancora le grida dei parenti, si tura colle mani le orecchie)* Urlano ancor!

**BUTTERFLY:** *(still hears the yells of her relations and holds her ears)* How they continue to yell!

**PINKERTON:** *(rincorandola)* Tutta la tua tribù e i Bonzi tutti del Giappon non valgono il pianto di quegli occhi cari e belli.

**PINKERTON:** *(cheering her)* All your respected tribe And all the Bonzes in Japan Are not worth a tear From those dear eyes of yours.

**BUTTERFLY:** *(sorridendo infantilmente)* Davver? Non piango più. E quasi del ripudio non mi duole per lo vostre parole che mi suonan così dolci nel cuor. *(si china per baciare la mano a Pinkerton)*

**BUTTERFLY:** *(smiling with childlike pleasure)* Indeed? I'll weep no more— And now I'm scarcely grieved at their desertion, So sweet are your words of comfort Which fall like gentle balm on my poor heart. *(stoops to kiss Pinkerton's hand)*

**PINKERTON:** *(sorpreso a quell' atto, dolcemente lo impedise)* Che fai? . . . la man?

**PINKERTON:** *(surprised at her action, gently stops her)* What's this?—My hand?

**BUTTERFLY:** Mi han detto che laggiù fra le gente costumata è questo il segno del maggior rispetto.

**BUTTERFLY:** They tell me That abroad, where the people are more cultured This is a token of the highest honour.

**PINKERTON:** *(sente un sordo bisbiglio)* Chi brontola lassù?

**PINKERTON:** *(hears a subdued murmuring)* Who's murmuring in there?

**BUTTERFLY:** É Suzuki che fa la sua preghiera seral.

**BUTTERFLY:** It is Suzuki who offers up Her evening prayer.

**PINKERTON:** *(attirandola)* Viene la sera . . .

**PINKERTON:** *(drawing her close to him)* Evening is falling—

**BUTTERFLY:** e l'ombra e la quiete.

**BUTTERFLY:** With shadows and quiet—

**PINKERTON:** E sei qui sola.

**PINKERTON:** You're here alone—

**BUTTERFLY:** Sola e rinnegata! Rinnegata e felice!

**BUTTERFLY:** Alone and renounced! They've renounced me, and yet I'm happy!

**PINKERTON:** *(ha battuto le mani, ed i servi sono accorsi)* A voi—chiudete.

**PINKERTON:** *(has clapped his hands and the servants have hastened in)* Come here—the shosi.

**BUTTERFLY:** *(i servi chiudono le pareti che danno sul terrazo poi si rittrano)* Sì, sì, noi tutti soli . . . E fuori il mondo.

**BUTTERFLY:** *(the servants close the partitions which run along the terrace, and then retire)* Yes, we are all alone— The world is yonder.

**PINKERTON:** *(ridendo)* E il Bonzo furibondo

**PINKERTON:** *(laughing)* And your uncle breathing thunder!

**BUTTERFLY:** *(a Suzuki, che è venuta coi servi e sta aspettando gli ordini)* Suzuki, le mie vesti. *(Suzuki fruga in un cofano di lac-*

**BUTTERFLY:** *(to Suzuki, who has come in with the servants and is awaiting orders)* Suzuki, bring my garments.

# Act I

*ca, mentre Pinkerton guarda i servi che stanno tramutando parte del terrazzo in una camera)*

**SUZUKI:** *(dopo di aver dato a Butterfly gli abiti per la notte ed un cofanetto coll' occorrente per la toeletta, si inchina innanzi a Pinkerton)* Buona notte. *(aiutata da Suzuki, Butterfly si reca in un angolo al fondo e fa cautelosamente la sua toeletta da notte, levendosi poi la veste nuziale ed indossandone una tutta bianca. Suzuke esce. Pinkerton dondolandosi sulla poltrona e prendendo una sigarette guarda Butterfly che è intenta ad acconciarsi)*

**BUTTERFLY:** Le sa. Forse dirle non vuole
per tema d'averne a morir!

**PINKERTON:** Stolta paura, l'amor non uccide
ma dà vita, e sorride
per gioie celestiali
come ora fa nei tuoi lunghi occhi ovali.
*(avvicinandosi a lei a prendendole la faccia)*

**BUTTERFLY:** Adesso voi
siete per me l'occhio del firmamento.
E mi piacceste dal primo momento
che vi ho veduto.—Siete
alto, forte.—Ridete
con modi sì palesi!
E dite cose che mai non intesi.
Or son contenta.—Vogliatemi bene,
un bene piccolino,
un bene da bambino
quale a me si conviene.
Noi siamo gente avvezza
alle piccole cose
umili e silenziose,
ad una tenerezza
sfiorante e pur profonda
come il ciel, come l'onda
lieve e forte del mare.

**PINKERTON:** Dammi ch'io baci le tue mani care.
*(prorompe con grande tenerezza)*
Mia Butterfly! . . . come t'han ben nomata
tenue farfalla . . .

**BUTTERFLY:** *(a queste parole si rattrista e ritira le mani)* Dicon che oltre mare
se cade in man dell'uom, ogni farfalla
da uno spillo e' trafitta
ed in tavola infitta!

**PINKERTON:** *(riprendendole dolcemente le mani e sorridendo)*
Un po' di vero c'è.
E lo sai tu perchè?
Perchè nen fugga più.
*(abbracciandola)*
Io t'ho ghermita . . .
Ti serro palpitante.
Sei mia.

*(Suzuki rummages in a lacquer trunk, whilst Pinkerton watches the servants who are changing part of the terrace into a room)*

**SUZUKI:** *(after having given Butterfly her night-attire and a small box with toilet necessaries, bows low to Pinkerton)* Good-night. *(Butterfly retires to a corner, and, assisted by Suzuki, carefully performs her toilet for the night, exchanging her wedding-garment for one of pure white. Suzuki goes out. Pinkerton, lolling on the wicker lounge, takes a cigarette and watches Butterfly, who is busy adorning herself)*

**BUTTERFLY:** She knows, but perhaps will not say them,
For fear she may die of her love!

**PINKERTON:** Fear not, my dearest, for love does not mean dying
But rather living; and it
Radiates celestial happiness.
I see it shine, as I am gazing in your eyes.
*(drawing close to her and taking her face in his hands)*

**BUTTERFLY:** But now, beloved!
You are all the world, more than the world to me.
Indeed, I liked you the very first moment
That I saw you.—You're so strong,
So handsome!—Your laugh
Is so open and so hearty!
the things you say are so fascinating.
Now I am happy.—Ah, love me a little,
Oh just a very little,
As you would love a baby,
That is all I ask for.
I come of a race
Accustomed to little;
Grateful for love that's silent,
Light as a blossom,
And yet everlasting
As the sky, as the fathomless ocean.

**PINKERTON:** Give me your darling hands, that I may kiss them!
*(bursts out very tenderly)* My Butterfly!—aptly your name was chosen.
Gossamer creation!—

**BUTTERFLY:** *(at these words her face clouds over and she draws away her hands)* They say that in your country
If a butterfly is caught by man,
He'll pierce its heart with a needle,
And then leave it to perish!

**PINKERTON:** *(gently taking her hands again and smiling)* There is some truth in that.
And can you tell me why?
That you may not escape.
*(embracing her)*
See I have caught you—
I hold you as you flutter—
Be mine.

**BUTTERFLY:** *(abbandonandosi)* Sì, per la vita.

**PINKERTON:** Vieni, vieni.

**PINKERTON:** Via dall'anima in pena
l'angoscia paurosa.
*(indicando a Butterfly il cielo stellato)*
Guarda: è notte serena!
Guarda: dorme ogni cosa!

**BUTTERFLY:** *(estatica)* Dolce notte! Quante stelle!
Non le vidi mai sì belle!
Trema, brilla, ogni favilla
col baglior d'una pupilla.
Oh! quanti occhi fisi, attenti
d'ogni parte a riguardare!
Lungi, via pei firmamenti,
via pei lidi, via pel mare
quanti fiammei sguardi pieni
d'ineffabile languor!
Tutto estatico d'amor
ride il cielo . . .

**PINKERTON:** *(con cupido amore)* Vieni, vieni! . . .
*(Butterfly e Pinkerton entrano nella camera nuziale.)*

# ■ ATTO II

*Interno della casetta di Butterfly*

*PARTE PRIMA*
*Suzuki prega, raggomitolata davanti all' immagine di Budda; suona di quando in quando la campanella della preghiera. Butterfly sta ritta ed immobile presso un paravento.*

**SUZUKI:** *(pregnado)* E Izaghi ed Izanami
Sarundazico e Kami . . .
*(interrompendosi)*
Oh! la mia testa!
*(suona la campanella per richiamare l'attenzione dei Numi)*
E tu
Ten-Sjoo-daj!
*(guardando Butterfly)*
Fate che Butterfly
non piango più, mai più, mai più, mai più.

**BUTTERFLY:** Pigri ed obesi
son gli Dei Giapponesi.
L'americano Iddio son persuasa
ben più presto risponde e chi l'implori.
Ma temo ch'egli ignori
che noi stiam qui di casa.
*(rimane pensierosa, poi si rivolge a Suzuki che si è alzata in piedi ed ha aperto la pareto verso il giardino)*
Suzuki, è lungi la miseria?

**SUZUKI:** *(apre un piccolo mobile e vi prende poche monete mostrandole a Butterfly)* Questo l'ultimo fondo.

**BUTTERFLY:** *(throwing herself in his arms)* Yes, yours for ever.

**PINKERTON:** Come then, come then—

**PINKERTON:** Love, while fear holds you trembling
Has done away with all misgivings.
*(pointing to the starlit sky)*
See, the night doth enfold us!
See, all the world lies sleeping!

**BUTTERFLY:** *(enraptured)* Ah!
Night of rapture! Stars unending!
Never have I seen such glory!
Throbbing, sparkling, each star in heaven
Like a fiery eye is flashing.
Oh! how kindly are the heavens!
Every star that shines afar
Is gazing on us, lighting our future for us
Ah! lovely night! Your perfect calm
Is breathing love near and far!—

**PINKERTON:** *(with passionate longing)* Come, then, come!—
*(They go into the marriage chamber)*

# ■ ACT II

*Inside Butterfly's Little House*

*Suzuki, coiled up in front of the image of Buddha, is praying; from time to time she rings the prayer-bell. Butterfly is standing rigid and motionless near the screen.*

**SUZUKI:** *(praying)* And Izaghi and Izanami
Sarundasico and Kami—
*(breaking off)*
My head is throbbing!
*(rings the prayer-bell to invoke the attention of the Gods)*
And thou
Ten-Sjoo-daj!
*(looking at Butterfly)*
Grant me that Butterfly
Shall weep no more, no more, no more.

**BUTTERFLY:** Lazy and idle
Are the Gods of Japan.
The God my husband prays to
Will give an answer far more quickly
To those who bow before Him.
But I'm afraid He knows not
That we are dwelling here.
*(remains pensive, then she turns to Suzuki, who has risen to her feet and has drawn back the partition leading to the garden)*
Suzuki, how soon shall we be starving?

**SUZUKI:** *(opens a small cabinet, and, taking a few coins from it, shows them to Butterfly)* This is all that is left us.

**BUTTERFLY:** Questo? Oh! Troppe spese!

**SUZUKI:** (*ripone il danaro e chiude il piccolo mobile, mentre sospirando dice:*) S'egli non torna e presto, siamo male in arnese.

**BUTTERFLY:** (*decisa*) Ma torna.

**SUZUKI:** (*crollando il capo*) Tornerà!

**BUTTERFLY:** (*indispettita a Suzuki*) Perchè dispone che il Console provveda alla pigione, rispondi, su! Perchè con tante cure la casa riforni di serrature, s'ei non volesse ritornar mai più?

**SUZUKI:** Non lo so.

**BUTTERFLY:** (*meravigliata a tanta ignoranza*) Non lo sai? (*con orgoglio*) Io te lo dico. Per tener ben fuorì le zanzare, i parenti ed i dolori e dentro, con gelosa custodia, la sua sposa che son io: Butterfly.

**SUZUKI:** (*poco convinta*) Mai non s'è udito di straniero marito che sia tornato al nido.

**BUTTERFLY:** (*furibonda*) Taci, o t'uccido. (*insistendo nel persuadere Suzuki*) Quell'ultima mattina: tornerete signor?—gli domandai. Egli, col cuore grosso, per celarmi la pena sorridendo rispose: (*cerca imitare Pinkerton*) —O Butterfly piccina mogliettina, tornerò colle rose alla stagion serena quando fa la nidiata il pettirosso. (*calma e convinta*) E tornerà.

**SUZUKI:** (*con indredulità*) Speriam.

**BUTTERFLY:** (*insistendo*) Dillo con me: Tornerà.

**SUZUKI:** (*per compiacerla ripete*) Tornerà . . . (*poi si mette pianger*)

**BUTTERFLY:** (*sorpresa*) Pinagi! Perchè? Ah la fede ti manca! (*poi continua fiduciosa e sorridente*) Senti—Un bel dì, vedremo levarsi un fil di fumo sull'estremo confin delmare. E poi la nave appare E poi la nave è bianca.

---

**BUTTERFLY:** No more? Oh, we've been spendthrifts!

**SUZUKI:** (*replaces the money in the cabinet, which she closes, saying with a sigh:*) Unless he comes, and quickly, Our plight is a bad one.

**BUTTERFLY:** (*with decision*) He'll come, though.

**SUZUKI:** (*shaking her head*) Will he come?

**BUTTERFLY:** (*vexed, to Suzuki*) Why did he order the Consul To provide this dwelling for us? Now answer that! And why was he so careful To have the house provided with safe locks If he did not intend to come again?

**SUZUKI:** I know not.

**BUTTERFLY:** (*surprised at such ignorance*) Know you not? (*with proud confidence*) Then I will tell you. It was to keep outside Those spiteful plagues, my own relations. And inside, it was to give me protection. Me, his beloved wife—his Butterfly.

**SUZUKI:** (*still far from convinced*) I never heard as yet Of foreign husband Who returned to his nest.

**BUTTERFLY:** (*furious*) Silence, or I'll kill you. (*still trying to persuade Suzuki*) Why, just before he went, I asked of him: "You'll come back again to me?" And with his heart so heavy, To conceal his trouble, With a smile he made answer: (*imitating Pinkerton*) O Butterfly, My tiny little child-wide, I'll return with the roses, The warm and sunny season When the red-breasted robins Are busy nesting. (*calm and convinced*) And he'll return.

**SUZUKI:** (*still incredulous*) We'll hope so.

**BUTTERFLY:** (*insisting*) Say it with me: He'll return!

**SUZUKI:** (*repeats, to please her*) He'll return! (*then she bursts out weeping*)

**BUTTERFLY:** (*surprised*) Weeping? and why? Ah, it is faith you are lacking! (*she then continues, full of faith, and smiling*) Hear me.—One fine day we'll notice A thread of smoke arising on the sea In the far horizon, And then the ship appearing;—

---

Entra nel porto, romba il suo saluto. Vedi? È venuto! Io non gli scendo incontro, Io no. Mi metto là sul ciglio del colle e aspetto, aspetto gran tempo e non mi pesa, la lunga attesa. E . . . uscito dalla folla cittadina un uomo, un picciol punto s'avvia per la collina. Chi sarà? chi sarà? E come sarà giunto che dirà? che dirà? Chiamerà Butterfly dalla lontana Io senza far risposta me ne starò nascosta un po' per celia, un po' per non morire al primo incontro, ed egli alquanto in pena chiamerà, chiamerà: 'Piccina—mogliettina olezzo di verbena'' i nomi che mi dava al suo venire. (*a Suzuki*) Tutto questo avverrà, te lo prometto Tienti la tua paura—io con sicura fede lo aspetto. (*congeda Suzuki*) (*Suzuki esce dalla porta di sinistra. Butterfly la segue mestamente collo sguardo*) (*Nel giardino campaiono Mr. Sharpless e Goro; Goro guarda entro le camera, scorge Butterfly e dice a Sharpless:*)

**GORO:** C'è.—Entrate. (*introduce Sharpless; poi torna subito fuori, e spia di quando in quando dal giardino*)

**SHARPLESS:** (*affacciandosi, bussa discretamente contro la porta di destra*) Chiedo scusa . . . (*vede Butterfly che udendo entrare alcuno si è mossa*) Madama Butterfly . . .

**BUTTERFLY:** (*senza volgersi, ma correggendo*) Madama Pinkerton Prego. (*si volge, riconosce il Console e giubilante batte le mani*) Oh il mio signor Console! (*Suzuki entra premurosa e prepara un tavolino coll'occorrente per fumare, alcuni cuscini ed uno sgabello*)

**SHARPLESS:** (*sorpreso*) Mi ravvisate?

**BUTTERFLY:** (*facendo gli onori di casa*) Benvenuto in casa americana.

**SHARPLESS:** Grazie.

---

Then the trim white vessel Glides into the harbour, her cannon thunders forth. You see? He is coming!— I do not go to meet him. Not I. I stay Upon the brow of the hill and wait, and wait For a long time, but never weary Of the long waiting. From out the crowded city, There is coming a man— A little speck in the distance, climbing the hill. Can you guess who it is? And when he's reached the summit Can you guess what he'll say? He will call "Butterfly" from the distance. I, without answering, Hold myself quietly concealed, A bit to tease him, and a bit so as not to die At our first meeting; and then, a little troubled, He will call, he will call: "Dear baby-wife of mine, dear little orange-blossom! The names he used to call me when he came here. (*to Suzuki*) This will all come to pass, just as I tell you. Banish your idle fears—for he'll return, I know it. (*dismisses Suzuki, who goes out of door on left. Butterfly looks after her, sadly*) (*Goro and Sharpless appear in the garden; Goro looks into the room, see Butterfly and says to Sharpless:*)

**GORO:** Come!—She's in here. (*brings Sharpless in; then goes outside again at once, and peeps in from the garden every now and then*)

**SHARPLESS:** (*knocks cautiously at the door on the right*) I am seeking— (*catches sight of Butterfly, who has risen on hearing him enter*) Madam Butterfly—

**BUTTERFLY:** (*corrects him, without turning round*) No, Madam Pinkerton, Excuse me. (*she turns round, recognizes the Consul, and claps her hands for joy*) Why here is the Consul; yes, the Consul! (*Suzuki enters eagerly and prepares a small table with smoking materials, some cushions and a stool*)

**SHARPLESS:** (*surprised*) What, you remember—?

**BUTTERFLY:** (*doing the honors of the house*) You are welcome; be seated, You are most honorably welcome.

**SHARPLESS:** Thank you.

BUTTERFLY: (*invita il Console a sedere presso il tavolino: Sharpless si lascia cadere grottescamente su di un cuscino: Butterfly si siede dall'altra parte e sorride con malizia dietro il ventaglio vedendo l'imbarazzo del Console; poi con molta grazia gli chiede:*) Avi-antenati
tutti bene?

SHARPLESS: (*sorride ringraziando*) Ma spero.

BUTTERFLY: (*fa cenno a Suzuki che prepari la pipa*) Fumate?

SHARPLESS: Grazie.
(*e desideroso di spiegare lo scopo per cui è venuto, cava una lettera di tasca*) Ho qui . . .

BUTTERFLY: (*gentilmente interrompendolo*) Signore—io vedo
il cielo azzurro.
(*dopo aver tirato una boccata dalla pipa che Suzuki ha preparata l'offre al Console*)

SHARPLESS: (*rifiutando*) Grazie . . .
(*e tenta riprendere il suo discorso*) Ho . . .

BUTTERFLY: (*depone la pipa sul tavolino e assai premurosa dice:*)
Preferite
forse le sigarette?
(*no offre*)
Americane.

SHARPLESS: (*ne prende una*) Ma grazie.
(*si alza e tenta continuare il discorso*)
Ho da mostrarvi . . .

BUTTERFLY: (*porge un fiammifero acceso*) A voi.

SHARPLESS: (*accende la sigarette, ma poi la depone subito e presentando la lettera si siede sullo sgabello*) Mi scrisse
Mr. B. F. Pinkerton . . .

BUTTERFLY: (*premurosissima*)
Davvero!
È in salute?

SHARPLESS: Perfetta.

BUTTERFLY: (*alzandosi, lietissima*) Io son la donna
più lieta del Giappone.—Potrei favri
una domanda?
(*Suzuki è in faccende per preparare il the*)

SHARPLESS: Certo.

BUTTERFLY: (*torna a sedere*)
Quando fanno
il lor nido in America
i pettirossi?

SHARPLESS: (*stupito*) Come dite?

BUTTERFLY: Sì,
prima o dopo di qui?

BUTTERFLY: (*invites the Consul to be seated near the table; Sharpless drops awkwardly on to a cushion. Butterfly sits down on the other side and slyly smiles behind her fan at his discomfort, then with much grace!*) And your honorable ancestors,
Is their health good?

SHARPLESS: (*thanks her, smiling*) I hope so.

BUTTERFLY: (*signs to Suzuki, who prepares the pipe*) You smoke?

SHARPLESS: Thank you.
(*he is anxious to explain the object of his visit, and draws a letter from his pocket*)
I've here—

BUTTERFLY: (*prettily interrupting him*) Honorable sir, the sky
Is quite unclouded.
(*after having taken a draw at the pipe, she offers it to the Consul*)

SHARPLESS: (*refusing*) Thank you.
(*trying again to resume the thread of his talk*)
I've—

BUTTERFLY: (*lays down the pipe on the table and says very pressingly:*) You prefer most likely
To smoke American cigarettes?
(*offers him some*)

SHARPLESS: (*taking one*) Well, thank you.
(*rises and tries to resume*)
I have to show you—

BUTTERFLY: (*hands him a lighted taper*) A light?

SHARPLESS: (*lights his cigarette, but then puts it down at once, and showing her the letter, sits down on the stool*) I've a letter from Mr. Pinkerton.

BUTTERFLY: (*with intense earnestness*) What? Really?
Is he in good health?

SHARPLESS: He's quite well.

BUTTERFLY: (*jumping up very joyfully*) Then I'm the happiest Woman in Japan. Would you
Answer me a question?
(*Suzuki is busy preparing tea*)

SHARPLESS: Gladly.

BUTTERFLY: (*sits down again*)
At what time of the year
Do robins nest in America?

SHARPLESS: (*amazed*) Are you serious?

BUTTERFLY: Yes.
Sooner or later than here?

SHARPLESS:
Ma . . . perchè? . . .
(*Goro sale dal terrazo del giardino ed escolta, non visto, quanto dice Butterfly*)

BUTTERFLY: Mio marito m' ha promesso
di ritornar nella stagion beata
che il pettirosso rifà la nidiata.
Qui l' ha rifatta ben tre volte, ma può darsi che di là
usi nidiar men spesso.
(*Goro scoppia in ridere*)

BUTTERFLY: Chi ride?
(*vede Goro*)
Oh, c' è il nakodo.
(*piano a Sharpless*)
Un uom cattivo.

GORO: (*ossequiso, inchinandosi*) Godo

BUTTERFLY: (*a Goro*) Zitto.
(*a Sharpless*)
Egli osò . . . No, prima rispondete
alla domanda mia.

SHARPLESS: (*imbarazzato*) Mi rincresce ma . . . ignoro . . .
Non ho studiato l'ornitologia.

BUTTERFLY: (*tentà di capire*) Ah!
l'orni . . .

SHARPLESS: . . . tologia.

BUTTERFLY: Non lo sapete
insomma.

SHARPLESS: No.
(*ritenta di tornare in argomento*)
Dicevamo . . .

BUTTERFLY: (*lo interrompte seguendo la sua idea*) Ah, sì—Goro, appena B. F. Pinkerton fu in mare
mi venne ad assediare
con ciarre e con presenti
per ridarmi ora questo, or quel marito.
Or promette tesori
per uno scimunito . . .

GORO: (*per giustificarsi, spiega la cosa a Sharpless*) Il ricco Yamadori.
Ella è povera in canna—I suoi parenti
l'han tutti rinnegata.
(*il Principe Yamadori attraversa il giardino seguito da due servi che portano fiori*)

BUTTERFLY: (*vede Yamadori e lo indica a Sharpless sorridendo*) Eccolo. Attenti.
(*Yamadori entra con grande imponenza, fa un graziosissimo inchino a Butterfly poi saluta il Console. I due servi consegnano i fiore a Suzuki e si ritirano nel fondu. Goro, servilissimo, porta uno sgabello a Yamadori, fra Sharpless e Butterfly, ed è dappertutto durante la conversazione. Sharpless e Yamadori siedono*) (*a Ya-*)

SHARPLESS: Tell me—why?
(*Goro comes up from the garden on to the terrace, and listens unseen by Butterfly*)

BUTTERFLY: My husband gave his promise
He would return in the joyous season,
When robin redbreasts rebuild their nests.
Here they have built them thrice already,
But I thought that over there
They might nest less often.
(*Goro bursts out laughing*)

BUTTERFLY: Who's laughing)
(*see Goro*)
Oh, the Nakodo.
(*softly to Sharpless*)
A wicked fellow.

GORO: (*bowing obsequiously*) I was—

BUTTERFLY: Silence.
(*to Sharpless*)
Why, he dared—No, first I'd like
An answer. Answer me what I asked you.

SHARPLESS: (*embarrassed*) I am sorry, but—I don't—
I never studied ornithology.

BUTTERFLY: (*trying to understand*) Ah! orni—

SHARPLESS: —thology.

BUTTERFLY: Ah, then
You cannot tell me?

SHARPLESS: No.
(*tries to return to his point*)
We were saying—

BUTTERFLY: (*interrupts him, pursuing her thoughts*) Ah, yes,
Scarcely was B. F. Pinkerton away,
Then Goro came here
And begged me,
With arguments and presents, to remarry.
He had half-a-dozen suitors.
Now he offers me riches
If I will wed an idiot—

GORO: (*to justify himself, tries to explain to Sharpless*) The wealthy Yamadori.
She's as poor as she can be—and her relations
Have cast her off completely.
(*Beyond the terrace the Prince Yamadori is seen, followed by two servants carrying flowers*)

BUTTERFLY: (*sees Yamadori, and points him out to Sharpless with a smile*) Here he is. Now listen.
(*Yamadori enters with much pomp, bows gracefully to Butterfly then salutes the Consul. The two servants deliver their flowers to Suzuki, and retire to the back. Goro, full of servility, brings a stool for Yamadori, between Sharpless and Butterfly, and is very much in evidence through-*)

madori)
Yamadori—ancor . . . le pene
dell'amor, non v'han deluso?
Vi tagliate ancor le vene
se il mio bacio vi ricuso?

YAMADORI: (*a Sharpless*) Tra le
cose più moleste
è l' inutil sospirar.

BUTTERFLY: (*con graziosa malizia*) Tante mogli omai toglieste,
vi doveste abituar.

YAMADORI: Le ho sposate tutte
quante
e il divorzio mi francò.

BUTTERFLY: Obbiigata.

YAMADORI: (*premuroso*) A voi
però
giurerei fede costante

SHARPLESS: (*sospirando, rimette in tasca la lettera*) (*Temo assai che il mio messaggio a tras-
metter non riesco.*)

GORO: (*con enfasi indicando Yamadori a Sharpless*) Ville, servi,
oro, ad Omura
un palazzo principesco.

BUTTERFLY: (*con serietà*) Già legata è la mia fede.

GORO E YAMADORI: (*a Sharpless*) Maritata ancor si crede.

BUTTERFLY: (*con forza*) Non mi
credo—sono—sono.

GORO: Ma la legge . . .

BUTTERFLY: (*interrompendolo*)
Io non la so.

GORO: (*continua*) . . . per la
moglie, l'abbandono
al divorzio equiparò.

BUTTERFLY: (*crollando vivamente il capo*) La legge giapponese . . .
non gia del mio paese.

GORO: Quale?

BUTTERFLY: (*con forza*) Gli Stati
Uniti.

SHARPLESS: (Oh, l' infelice!)

BUTTERFLY: (*nervosissima, accalorandosi*) Si sa che aprir la porta
e la moglie cacciar per la più corta
qui divorziar si dice.
Ma in America questo non si può.
(*a Sharpless*)
Vero?

SHARPLESS: (*inbarazzato*)
Vero, . . . Però

BUTTERFLY: (*lo interrompe rivolgendosi a Yamadori ed a Goro,
trionfante*) Là un bravo giudice
serio, impettito
dice al marito:

---

out the interview. Sharpless and
Yamadori sit down) (*to Yamado-
ri*)
Yamadori—and have the throes
Of unrequited love not yet released
you?
Do you still intend to die
If I withhold my kisses?

YAMADORI: (*to Sharpless*) There
is naught on earth more cruel
Than the pangs of hopeless love.

BUTTERFLY: (*with graceful raillery*) You have had so many consorts
Surely you must be inured!

YAMADORI: Every one of them I
married,
And divorce has set me free.

BUTTERFLY: Thank you kindly!

YAMADORI: (*eagerly*) But to you,
I would swear eternal faith.

SHARPLESS: (*sighing, replaces
the letter in his pocket*) (I am very
much afraid
My message will not be delivered.)

GORO: (*pointing out Yamadori
to Sharpless, with emphasis*)
Houses, servants, treasures, and
A regal palace at Omara!

BUTTERFLY: (*seriously*) But my
hand's bestowed already—

GORO AND YAMADORI: (*to
Sharpless*) She believes she still is
married—

BUTTERFLY: (*emphatically*) I
don't believe, for I know it.

GORO: But the law says—

BUTTERFLY: (*interrupting him*)
I know it not.

GORO: (*continues*) For the wife,
desertion
Gives the right of divorce.

BUTTERFLY: (*shaking her head*)
That may be Japanese law,
But not in my country.

GORO: Which one?

BUTTERFLY: (*with emphasis*)
The United States.

SHARPLESS: (Poor little creature!)

BUTTERFLY: (*strenuously, and
growing excited*) I know, of
course, to open the door
And to turn out your wife at any moment,
Here, constitutes divorce.
But in America, that cannot be
done.
(*to Sharpless*)
Correct?

SHARPLESS: (*embarrassed*) Yes,
yes—but yet—

BUTTERFLY: (*interrupts him,
turning to Yamadori and Goro in
triumph*) There, a true, honest
And unbiased judge
Says to the husband:

---

"Lei vuole andarsene?
"Sentiam perchè?—
"Sono seccato
"del coniugato!
E il magistrato:
"Ah, mascalzone,
"presto in prigione!
(*e per troncare si alza ed ordina:*)
Suzuki, il thè.
(*va anche lei presso Suzuki*)

YAMADORI: (*sottovoce a Sharpless, mentre Butterfly prepara il
thè*) L'udite?

SHARPLESS: Mi rattrista una si piena cecità.

GORO: (*sottovoce a Sharpless e
Yamadori*) Segnalata è già la nave
di Pinkerton.

YAMADORI: (*dispeato*)
Quand'essa lo riveda . . .

SHARPLESS: (*pure sottovoce ai
due*) Egli non vuol mostrarsi.—Io
venní appunto
per levarla d'inganno.—Ho qui
una lettera
di lui che la riflette . . .
(*vedendo Butterfly che si avvicina
per offrire il thè, tronca il discorso*)

BUTTERFLY: (*con grazia, servendo a Sharpless una tazza di thè*)
Vostra Grazia permette . . .
(*poi apre ventaglio e dietro a
questo accenna ai due, ridendo*)
Che persone moleste!
(*offre il thè a Yamadori, che rifiuta*)

YAMADORI: (*sospirando si alza
e si inchina a Butterfly, mettendo
la mano sul cuore*) Addio. Vi lascio il cuor pien di cordoglio:
ma spero ancor.

BUTTERFLY: Padrone.

YAMADORI: (*s'avvia, poi torna
presso Butterfly*) Ah! se voleste . . .

BUTTERFLY: Il guaio è che non
voglio . . .
(*Yamadori sospira di nuovo; saluta Sharpless, poi se ne va, seguito dal servi. Butterfly fa cenno a
Suzuki di sprepare il thè: Suzuki eseguisce, poi va in fondo
alla camera. Goro segue premurosamente Yamadori*)

SHARPLESS: (*continua*) "E forse
Butterfly
non mi rammenta più."

BUTTERFLY: (*sorpresa*) Non lo
rammento?
(*rivolgendosi a Suzuki*)
Auzuki, dillo tu.
(*ripete come scandolezzata le parole della lettera*)
"Non mi rammenta più!"
(*Suzuki accenna affermando, poi
entra nella stanza a sinistra*)

---

"You wish to free yourself?
"Let us hear why?—
"I am sick and tired
"Of conjugal fetters!"
Then the good judge says:
"Ah, wicked scoundrel,
"Clap him in prison!"
(*to put an end to the subject, she
orders Suzuki*)
Suzuki, tea.

YAMADORI: (*softly, to Sharpless,
whilst Butterfly makes tea*) You
hear her?

SHARPLESS: I am grieved at such
hopeless blindness.

GORO: (*whispers to Yamadori
and Sharpless*) Mr. Pinkerton's
ship is already
Signalled.

YAMADORI: (*in despair*) And
when they meet again—

SHARPLESS: (*whispers to both*)
He does not want to see her.—It is
for that I came
To try and prepare her.—I have
here a letter
From him, which—
(*seeing that Butterfly is approaching him with tea, he cuts short his
sentence*)

BUTTERFLY: (*charmingly, offering Sharpless a cup of tea*) Will
your Honor allow me—
(*opens her fan, and behind it
points to the two others, laughing*)
What troublesome people!
(*offers tea to Yamadori, who refuses*)

YAMADORI: (*rises with a sigh
and bows to Butterfly with hand
on heart*) Farewell, then. I go, my
heart heavy with sorrow,
But still I hope—

BUTTERFLY: So be it.

YAMADORI: (*is leaving, but returns to Butterfly*) Ah, if you
would but—

BUTTERFLY: The pity is: I will
not!—
(*Yamadori, after having bowed
to Sharpless, goes off sighing, followed by his servants. Butterfly
signs to Suzuki to remove the tea.
Suzuki obeys, then retires to the
back of the room. Goro promptly
follows Yamadori*)

SHARPLESS: (*continues*) "And
perhaps Butterfly
"Remembers me no more."

BUTTERFLY: (*surprised*) I not remember?
(*turning to Suzuki*)
Suzuki, tell him quickly.
(*repeats as though scandalized at
the words of the letter:*)
"Remembers me no more!"
(*Suzuki nods her head affirmatively, then goes into room on
left*)

# Act II

SHARPLESS: (fra sè) (Pazienza!)
(sguitaa a leggere)
"Se mi vuole
bene ancora, se mi aspetta . . ."

BUTTERFLY: (assai commossa)
Oh le dolci parole!
(prende la lettera e la bacia)
Tu, benedetta!

SHARPLESS: (riprende la lettera e seguita a leggere imperterrito, ma con voce commossa)
"A voi mi raccomando
perchè vogliate con circospezione
prepararla . . ."

BUTTERFLY: (ansiosa e raggiante) Ritorna

SHARPLESS: ("al colpa . . .")

BUTTERFLY: (salta di gioia e batte le mani) Quando?
Presto! presto!

BUTTERFLY: Ve ne prego,
già l'insistere non vale,
(congeda Suzuki, la quale va nel giardino)

SHARPLESS: (scusandosi) Fui brutale, non lo nego.

BUTTERFLY: (dolorosamente, portandosi la mano al cuore) Oh, mi fate tanto male,
tanto male, tanto, tanto!

SHARPLESS: (commosso) Poveretta! . . .
(Butterfly vacilla; Sharpless fa per sorreggerla)

BUTTERFLY: (subito dominandosi) Niente, niente!
Ho creduto morir.—Ma passa presto
come passan le nuvole sul mare . . .
Ah! . . . mi ha scordata?
(corre nella stanza di sinistra, rientra trionfalmente tenendo il suo bambino seduto sulla spalla e lo mostra a Sharpless gloriandosene)
E questo? . . . e questo? . . . e questo
dite che lo potrà pure scordare? . . .
(depone il bambino a terra e lo tiene stretto a sè)

SHARPLESS: (con emozione) Egli è suo?

BUTTERFLY: (indicando mano, mano) Chi mai vide
a bimbo del Giappone occhi azzurrini?
E il labbro? E i ricciolini
d'oro schietto?

SHARPLESS: (sempre più commosso) È palese.
E . . . Pinterton lo sa?

BUTTERFLY: No. E nato quando già
egli stava in quel suo grande paese.
(accarezza il suo bambino)
Ma voi gli scriverete che lo aspetta
un figlio senza pari!

SHARPLESS: (to himself) Oh, patience!
(continues reading)
"If she still
"Cares for me and expects me—"

BUTTERFLY: (deeply moved) Oh, what glorious tidings!
(takes the letter and kisses it)
You blessèd letter!

SHARPLESS: (takes the letter back and boldly resumes reading, though his voice is trembling with emotion) "On you I am relying
"To act discreetly, and with tact
"And caution to prepare her—"

BUTTERFLY: (anxiously, but radiant) He's coming—

SHARPLESS: "For the shock—"

BUTTERFLY: (jumping for joy and clapping her hands) Tell me quickly, quickly!

BUTTERFLY: I beseech you,
Let my words be quite forgotten.
(dismisses Suzuki, who goes into the garden)

SHARPLESS: (making excuses) I was brutal, I admit it.

BUTTERFLY: (sadly, laying her hand on her heart) Oh, you've wounded me so deeply
Wounded me so very deeply!

SHARPLESS: (with emotion) Poor little creature!
(Butterfly totters; Sharpless is about to support her, but she quickly rallies)

BUTTERFLY: It is nothing, nothing!
I felt ready to die!—but see, it passes,
Swift as shadows that flit across the ocean.
Ah! am I forgotten?
(runs into the room on the left, and comes back in triumph, carrying her baby on her shoulder, and shows him to Sharpless, full of pride)
Look here then! look here!
Can such as this well be forgotten?
(puts the child down on the ground and holds him close to her)

SHARPLESS: (deeply touched) Is it his?

BUTTERFLY: (pointing to his features one by one) What Japanese Baby was ever born with azure eyes?
Such lips too? and such a head
Of golden curls?

SHARPLESS: (more and more moved) It is his image.
Has Pinkerton been told?

BUTTERFLY: No, I bore him when he
Was far off in his big native country.
(caressing the child)
But you will write and tell him
There awaits him a son, who has no

e mi saprete dir s' ei non s' affretta
per le terre e pei mari!
(fa sedere il bimbo sul cuscino e lo bacia teneramente)
Sai tu cos' ebbe cuore
(gli indica Sharpless)
di pensar quel signore?
Che tua madre dovrà
prenderti in braccio ed alla pioggia e al vento
andar per la città
a guadagnarti il pane e il vestimento.
Ed alle impietosite
genti, ballando de' suoi canti al suon,
gridare:—Udite, udite,
udite la bellissima canzon
delle ottocentomila
divinità vestite di splendor.
E passerà una fila
di guerrïeri coll' Imperator,
cui dirò:—Sommo duce
ferma i tuoi servi e sosta a riguardar
(mostrando il bimbo e carezzandolo)
quest'occhi, ove la luce
dal cielo azzurro onde scendesti appar.
(si accoscia presso il bambino o continua con voce carezzante e lacrimosa)
E allor fermato il piè
l'Imperator d'ogni grazia degno,
(mette la sua guancia presso la guancia del bimbo)
forse farà di te
il principe più bello del suo regno.

SHARPLESS: (non può trattenere lagrime) (Quanta pietà!)
(poi, vincendo la propria emozione, dice:)
Vien sera. Io scendo al piano.
(Butterfly si alza in piedi e con atto gentile dà la mano a Sharpless che la stringe con ambe le mani con effusione)

SHARPLESS: Mi perdonate?

BUTTERFLY: (al bimbo) A te, dagli la mano.

SHARPLESS: (prende il bambino in braccio) I bei capelli biondi!
(lo bacia)
Caro: come ti chiamano?

equal!
And would you tell me then, that he won't hasten
Over land and over sea!
(seats the child on the cushion, and kisses him fondly)
Do you know, my sweet, what that bad man
(points to Sharpless)
Had heart to fancy?
That your mother should take you on her shoulder
And forth should wander in rain and tempest
Through the town, seeking to earn enough
For food and clothing.
And then, before the pitying people
to dance in measure to her song, and cry out:
"Oh, listen, good people,
"Listen for the love of all
"The eight hundred thousand gods and goddesses of Japan!"
And there will pass a band of valiant warriors
With their Emperor, to whom I'll say:
"Noble Ruler, tarry thy footsteps
"And deign to stop and look
(showing the child and caressing him)
"At these blue eyes, as blue as the azure heaven
Whence you, Most High, are come!"
(she crouches down beside the child, and continues in caressing and tearful tones)
And then, the noble King
Will stay his progress, full of gracious kindness,
(pressing her cheek next to the baby's cheek)
Who knows? he'll make you
The most exalted ruler of his kingdom.
(she strains the child to her heart, and crouching down on the ground, hugs him passionately)

SHARPLESS: (cannot restrain his tears) (Poor faithful soul!)
(then, conquering his emotion, he says:) It is evening. I must be going.
(Butterfly rises to her feet and with a charming gesture gives Sharpless her hand; he shakes it cordially with both of his) You will excuse me?

BUTTERFLY: (to the child) Now you—give him your hand, love.

SHARPLESS: (takes the child in his arms) What pretty golden ringlets!
(kisses him)
Darling, what do they call you?

BUTTERFLY: Rispondi:
Oggi il mio nome è: Dolore. Però
dite al babbo, scrivendogli, che il giorno
del suo ritorno
Gioia, mi chiamerò.

SHARPLESS: Tuo padre lo saprà, te lo prometto.
(*mette il bambino in terra, fa un saluto a Butterfly, ed esce rapidamento*)

BUTTERFLY: (*battendo le mani*) Suzuki.

SUZUKI: (*di fuori grida*) Vespa! Rospo maledetto!
(*poi entra trascinando con violenza Goro che tenta inutilmente di sfuggirle*)

BUTTERFLY: Che fu?

SUZUKI: Ci ronza intorno
il vampiro! e ogni giorno
ai quattro venti
spargendo va
che niuno sa
chi padre al bimbo sia!
(*Suzuki lascia Goro, il quale tenta di giustificarsi*)

GORO: Dicevo solo
che qui i vostri parenti
non han pietà;
che quel figliuolo
padre non ha.
Che stolto è lo sperare . . .
(*Butterfly, furente, corre al reliquiario e prende il coltello che servi per l' hari-kari—suicidio per condanna—di suo padrè, gridando:*)

BUTTERFLY: Ah! menti! menti!
(*afferra Goro, che cade a terra, e minaccia d' ucciderlo: Goro grida disperatamente*)
Dillo ancora e t'uccido! . . .

SUZUKI: (*Intromettendosi*) No!
(*spaventata a tale scena prende il bimbo e lo porta nella stanza a sinistra*)

BUTTERFLY: (*presa da disgusto, respinge Goro col piede*) Va via!
(*Goro fugge: poi Butterfly si scuote, va a riporre il coltello e volgendo il pensiero al sua bambino, esclama:*)
O mio piccolo amore,
mia pena e mio conforto,
il tuo vendicatore
ci porterà lontan nella sua terra
dove . . .
(*un colpo di cannone*)

SUZUKI: (*entrando affannosamente*) Il cannon del porto!
(*corre verso il terrazzo: Butterfly la seque*)
Una nave de guerra.

BUTTERFLY: Give answer:
Sir, to-day my name is Pain. But yet
Write and tell my father, on the day
Of his returning
Joy shall be my name.

SHARPLESS: Your father shall be told, that I will promise.
(*puts down the child, bows to Butterfly, and goes out quickly by door on the right*)

BUTTERFLY: (*clapping her hands*) Suzuki.

SUZUKI: (*shouting outside*) Scoundrel! Rascal! Wretched coward!
(*she then comes in, roughly dragging in Goro, who tries in vain to escape*)

BUTTERFLY: Who's that?

SUZUKI: He prowls around here,
Evil reptile! from morn to evening,
And tells this scandal
All through the town:
That no one knows
Who is this baby's father!
(*she releases Goro, who tries to justify himself*)

GORO: I only told her
That out in America
Whenever a baby
Is born in such conditions,
He will be shunned throughout his life
And treated as an outcast—
(*Butterfly, enraged, runs to the shrine, and takes down the sword which was used for the hara kiri—condemned suicide—of her father, crying:*)

BUTTERFLY: Ah, you're lying, lying!
(*seizes Goro, who falls down, and threatens to kill him: Goro utters desperate howls*)
Say it again and I'll kill you!

SUZUKI: (*thrusts herself between them*) No!
(*horrified at such a scene, she takes the baby and carries him into the room on the left*)

BUTTERFLY: (*seized with disgust, pushes him away with her foot*) Begone!
(*Goro makes his escape; Butterfly rouses herself and goes to put away the dagger, and her thoughts turning to her child, she exclaims:*)
Oh, you'll see, love of my heart,
My grief and yet my comfort,
That your avenger soon will be here
And take you and me to his own country,
Where—
(*a cannon-shot*)

SUZUKI: (*enters breathlessly*)
The harbor cannon!
(*runs toward the terrace—Butterfly follows her*)
Look, it's a man-of-war.

BUTTERFLY: (*giubilante, ansante*) Bianca . . . bianca . . . il vessillo americano
delle stelle . . . Or governa per ancorare.
(*prende sul tavolino un cannocchiale e corre sul terrazzo: tutta tremante per l' emozione, appunta il cannocchiale verso il porto e dice a Suzuki:*)
Reggimi la mano
ch'io ne discerna
il nome, il nome, il nome. Eccolo:
Abramo Lincoln
(*dà il cannocchiale a Suzuki, poi in preda a grande esaltazione scendendo dal terrazzo esclama:*)
Tutti han mentito!
tutti! . . . tutti! . . . sol io
lo sapevo—io—che l'amo.
(*a Suzuki*)
Vedi lo scimunito
tuo dubbio? È giunto! è giunto!
proprio nel punto
che mi diceva ognun: pinagi e dispera,
Trionfa il mio
amor, trionfa la mia fede intera.
Ei torna e m'ama,—
(*e in preda ad una esaltazione giubilante va al terrazzo, dicendo a Suzuki:*)
Scuoti quella fronda
e dei suoi fior m'innonda.—
Nella pioggia odorosa io vo' tuffare l'arsa fronte.
(*singhiozzando per tenerezza*)

SUZUKI: (*calmandola*) quetatevi; quel pianto . . .

BUTTERFLY: No: rido, rido! Quanto lo dovremo aspettare?
Che pensi? Un' ora?

SUZUKI: Di più.

BUTTERFLY: (*giudiziosa*) Certo di più Due ore forse. Tu va pei fiori.
Che qui tutto sia pieno di fior,
come la notte è di faville.
(*accenna a Suzuki di andare nel giardino*)

SUZUKI: (*dal terrazzo*) Tutti i fior? . . .

BUTTERFLY: Tutti. Pesco, vīola, gelsomino,
quanto di cespo, o d' erba, o d' albero fiorì.

SUZUKI: Uno squallor d' inverno sarà tutto il giardino.
(*scende nel giardino*)

BUTTERFLY: Tutta la primavera voglio che olezzi qui.

BUTTERFLY: (*breathless with excitement*) White—white—the American
Stars and stripes—it's putting
Into port to anchor.
(*takes a telescope from the table and runs on to the terrace; all trembling with excitement, she directs the telescope towards the harbor, and says to Suzuki:*)
Keep my hand steady
That I may read the name,
The name, the name. Here it is:
Abraham Lincoln!
(*gives the telescope to Suzuki, and goes down from the terrace in the greatest state of excitement*)
They all were liars!
Liars! liars! But I
Knew it always—I—who love him.
(*to Suzuki*)
Now do you see the folly of your doubting?
He's coming! He's coming!
Just at the moment you all were saying:
Weep and forget him. My love wins the day.
My love and faith have won completely—
He's here—he loves me!
(*a prey to the greatest excitement and joy, she goes on to the terrace, saying:*)
Shake that cherry-tree till every flower,
White as snow, flutters down—
His noble brow, in a sweet scented shower
I would smother.
(*sobbing for tenderness*)

SUZUKI: (*soothing her*) Sweet Madam,
Be calm, I pray: this weeping—

BUTTERFLY: No, laughing, laughing! When
May we expect him up here?
What do you think? In an hour?

SUZUKI: Too soon.

BUTTERFLY: (*thoughtfully*) Yes, it's too soon.
Two hours more likely. You
Go for flowers. Flowers be everywhere
As close together as stars are in the heavens.
(*signs to Suzuki to go into the garden*)

SUZUKI: (*from the terrace*) All the flowers?

BUTTERFLY: All—Peaches, violets, jessamine,
Every spray of gorse or grass or flowering tree.

SUZUKI: Desolate as in winter the garden will appear.
(*goes into the garden*)

BUTTERFLY: Ah! but the balmy breath of spring shall shed her sweetness here.

## Act II

SUZUKI: (*appare sul terrazzo e sporge un fascio di fiori e di fronde*) A voi signora.

BUTTERFLY: (*prendendo il fascio*) Cogline ancora.
(*Butterfly spàrge i fiori nella stanza, mentre Suzuki ritorna nel giardino*)

SUZUKI: (*dal giardino*) Soventi a questa siepe veniste a riguardare lungi, piangendo nella deserta immensità.

BUTTERFLY: Giunse l'atteso, nulla ormai più chiedo al mare; diedi pianto alla zolla, essa i suoi fior mi dà

SUZUKI: (*appare nuovamente sul terrazzo con un altro gran fascio de fiori*) Spoglio è l'orto.

BUTTERFLY: (*prendendo i fiori*) Qua il tuo carco.
Vien, m' aiuta.
(*spargono fiori ovunque*)

SUZUKI: Rose al varco della soglia.

BUTTERFLY: Il suo sedil di convolvi s' inghirlandi.

SUZUKI: Gigli? . . . viole? . . .

BUTTERFLY: intorno spandi.

BUTTERFLY E SUZUKI: Seminiamo intorno april.
(*con leggero ondulamento di danza spargono ovunque fiori*)
Gettiamo a mani piene mammole e tuberose, corolle di verbene petali d' ogni fior!
(*Butterfly, aiutata da Suzuki va a prendere il necessario per la toeletta*)

BUTTERFLY: (*a Suzuki*) Vienmi ad adornar . . .
No. Pria, portami il bimbo.
(*Suzuki va nella stanza a sinistra e porta il bambino che fa sedere vicino a Butterfly, fa quale, intanto, si guarda in un piccolo specchio e dice tristamente:*)
A'himè, non son più quella!
Troppi sospiri la bocca mandò, e l'occhio riguardò nel lontan troppo fisso.
(*si getta a terra, appoggiando la testa sui piedi di Suzuki*)
Suzuki, fammi bella, fammi bella!

SUZUKI: (*accarezzando la testa di Butterfly, per calmarla*) Gioia e riposo accrescono beltà.

GORO: (*appears on the terrace and holds out a large bunch of flowers and foliage to Butterfly*) Here's more, dear mistress.

BUTTERFLY: (*taking the bunch*) It's not enough yet.
(*Butterfly distributes the flowers about the room, while Suzuki goes back to the garden*)

SUZUKI: (*from the garden*) How often at this window you've stood and wept, and waited.
Gazing and gazing into the wide, wide world beyond.

BUTTERFLY: No more need I pray for, since the kind sea has brought him.
I gave my tears to the earth, and it returns me flowers!

SUZUKI: (*reappears on the terrace with another load of flowers*) Not a flower left.

BUTTERFLY: (*taking the flowers*) Give me your burden.
Come and help me.
(*they scatter flowers everywhere*)

SUZUKI: Roses shall adorn The threshold.

BUTTERFLY: Now round his seat Entwine convolvulus.

SUZUKI: Lillies?—Violets?

BUTTERFLY: Come, scatter flowers.

BUTTERFLY AND SUZUKI: Let us sow fair April here.
(*lightly swaying their bodies to a dance measure, they scatter flowers everywhere*)
In handfuls let us scatter Violets and roses white, Sprays of scented sweet verbena, And the petals of all flowers!
(*Butterfly, assisted by Suzuki, fetches out her toilet requirements*)

BUTTERFLY: (*to Suzuki*) Now, come and make me fine—
No, first bring me the baby.
(*Suzuki goes into the room on the left and brings the child, whom she seats near Butterfly who meanwhile looks at herself in a small hand-mirror, and says sadly:*)
Alas, how changed he'll find me!
Drawn, weary mouth from too much sighing,
And poor tired eyes from too much crying.
(*throws herself on the ground, laying her head on Suzuki's feet*)
Suzuki, make me pretty, make me pretty!

SUZUKI: (*stroking Butterfly's head, to sooth her*) Rest calm and happy, and you'll be fair once more.

BUTTERFLY: Chissà! Chissà!
(*si alza, torna alla toeletta e dice a Suzuki:*)
Dammi sul viso un tocco di carmino . . .
(*prende un pennello e mette del rosso sulle guancie del suo bimbo*)
ed anche a te piccino perchè la veglia non ti faccia vôte per pallore le gote.

SUZUKI: (*a Butterfly*) Ferma che v'ho i capelli a ravviare.

BUTTERFLY: (*seguendo una sua idea*) Che ne diranno ora i parenti!
E che dirà lo zio Bonzo? Qual cicallo faranno in coro le comari con Goro, già del mio danno tutti contenti!
E Yamadori coi suoi languori!
Beffati, scornati, spennati gl' ingrati!

SUZUKI: (*ha terminato la toeletta*) E fatto.

BUTTERFLY: L' obi che vestii da sposa.
(*Suzuki va ad un cassettone e vi cerca la veste, mentre Butterfly attira a sè il bambino*)

BUTTERFLY: (*depone il bimbo*) Qua ch'io lo vesta.
(*mentre indossa la veste, Suzuki mette l' altra al bambino, avvolgendolo quasi tutto nella pieghe ampia e leggiere*)
Vo' che mi veda indosso il vel del primo dì.
E un papavero rosso nei capelli . . .
(*Suzuki, che ha finito d'abbligliare il bambino, cerca il fiore e lo punta nei capelli di Butterfly che se ne compiace, guardandosi nello specchio*)
Così
(*poi fa cenno a Suzuki di abbassare lo shosi*)
Nello shosi o farem tre forellini per riguardar, e starem zitti come topolini ad aspettar.
(*Porta il bambino presso lo shosi, nel quale fa tre fori: uno alto per sè, uno più basso per Suzuki e il terzo ancor più basso pel bimbo, che fa sedere su di un cuscino, accennandogli di guardare attento fuori del foro preparatogli. Suzuki si accoscia e spia essa pure all'esterno. Butterfly si pone innanzi al foro più alto e spia da quello. Dopo qualche tempo Suzuki ed il bambino si addormentano. Intanto si è fatta notte ed i raggi lunari illuminano*)

BUTTERFLY: Who knows? who knows?
(*rises, resumes her toilet and says to Suzuki:*)
Put on each cheek A little touch of carmine— (*takes a paintbrush and puts a dab of rouge on the baby's cheeks*)
And also for my darling So that the watching may not make his face Heavy and pallid.

SUZUKI: Nay, but keep still, till I've finished arranging your hair.

BUTTERFLY: (*pursuing her thoughts*) What a surprise For all my relations!
And for the Bonze My uncle! How they Will prate and shout in chorus!
Oh what a hubbub I can hear The gossips make with Goro!
All of them sure and glad Of my downfall!
And Yamadori With his airs and graces!
My scorn and derision, My jeers and contempt For the wretches!

SUZUKI: (*has finished Butterfly's toilet*) I've finished.

BUTTERFLY: Bring me my wedding-garment.
(*Suzuki goes to a small coffer and brings out the obi and the white garment, returns with two garments, and gives one with the obi to Butterfly*)

BUTTERFLY: (*puts down the child*) Bring it hither quickly.
(*while she puts on her garment, Suzuki dresses the child in the other one, wrapping him up almost entirely in the ample and light draperies*)
I would have him see me in it As on my wedding-day.
In my hair we will put A scarlet poppy—
(*Suzuki, who has finished dressing the baby, fetches the flower and places it in Butterfly's hair. The latter looks at herself in the glass, and is pleased with the effect*)
Like this.
(*she then signs to Suzuki to lower the shosi*)
In the shosi we'll make three little holes that we can look out, And still as little mice we'll stay here To watch and wait.
(*She carries the child close to the shosi, in which she makes three holes; one high up for herself, one lower down for Suzuki, and a third one lower still for the baby, whom she seats on a cushion, showing him how to look out of his hole. Suzuki crouches down and also gazes out through her hole. Butterfly stands in front of*

*dall'esterno lo shosi. Butterfly rimane immobile, rigida come una statua.)*

■ **ATTO III**

*Passa la notte angosciosa.—Dal porto al basso della collina salgono voci confuse di maranai e rumori diversi.—All'alzarsi del sipario è già l'alba: Butterfly spia sempre al di fuori.*

**SUZUKI:** (*svegliandosi di soprassalto*) È l' alba.
(*si alza e batte docemente sulla spalla a Butterfly*)
Cio-Cio-San!

**BUTTERFLY:** (*si scuote e fidente dice:*) Verrà col pieno sole.
(*vede il bimbo addormentato e lo prende sulle braccia*).

**SUZUKI:** Salite a riposar, sì affranta e sì pallida sieta! Al suo venire testo vi chiamerò.

**BUTTERFLY:** (*cantando dolcemente s' avvia per la scaletta*)
Dormi amor mio
dormi sul mio cor.
Tu sei con Dio
ed io col mio dolor.
A te i rai
degli astri d' or:
dormi tesor!
(*entra nella camera superiore*)

**SUZUKI:** (*la guarda salire e dice con gran pietà:*) Povera Butterfly!
(*Suzuki si inginocchia innanzi al simulacro di Budda, poi va ad aprire lo shosi*)
Pinkerton e Sharpless picchiano lievemente all' uscio d' ingresso.

**SUZUKI:** Chi sia!
(*va ad aprire e rimane grandemente sorpresa*)
Oh! . . .

**SHARPLESS:** (*facendole cenno di non far rumore*) Zitta! zitta!
(*Pinkerton e Sharpless entrano cautamente in punta di piedi*)

**PINKERTON:** (*premurosamente a Suzuki:*) Dorme? Non la destare.

**SUZUKI:** Ell'era tanto stanca! Vi sette ad aspettare
tutta la notte col bimbo.

**PINKERTON:** Come sapea? . . .

---

*the top hole and gazes through it. After some time Suzuki and the child fall asleep. Meanwhile night has fallen, and the rays of the moon shed their lights from without the shosi. Butterfly remains motionless, rigid as a statue.*

■ **ACT III**

*(The weary night of watching passes. The clanging of chains and anchors and the distant voices of sailors rise from the harbor at the foot of the hill. At the rising of the curtain is already dawn; Butterfly, still motionless, is gazing out into the distance.)*

**SUZUKI:** (*awakening with a start*) It is daylight.
(*rises and taps Butterfly lightly on the shoulder*)
Cho-Cho-San!

**BUTTERFLY:** (*starts, and says confidently:*) He'll come; he'll come—I know he'll come.
(*sees that the child has fallen asleep, and takes him in her arms*)

**SUZUKI:** I pray you, go and rest, for you are weary,
And I will call you when he arrives.

**BUTTERFLY:** (*singing softly as she goes up the staircase*) My love, you are sleeping,
Cradled on my heart;
Safe in God's keeping,
While I must weep apart;
Around they head the moonbeams dart,
Sleep, my treasure!
(*goes into the room above*)

**SUZUKI:** (*watches her go, and says with deep pity:*) Poor Madam Butterfly!
(*Suzuki kneels before the image of Buddha, then goes to open the shosi*)
Pinkerton and Sharpless knock gently at the door

**SUZUKI:** Who is it?
(*goes to open the door, and stands greatly surprised*)
Oh!

**SHARPLESS:** (*signing her not to make a noise*) Hush! Hush!
(*Pinkerton and Sharpless enter cautiously on tiptoe*)

**PINKERTON:** (*anxiously, to Suzuki*) Is she asleep? Do not disturb her.

**SUZUKI:** She was so very weary!
She stood expecting you
All through the night, with the baby.

**PINKERTON:** How did she know?

---

**SUZUKI:** Non giunge
da tre anni una nave nel porto, che da lunge
Butterfly non ne scruti il color, la bandiera.

**SHARPLESS:** (*a Pinkerton*) Ve lo dissi? . . .

**SUZUKI:** (*per andare*) La chiamo . . .

**PINKERTON:** (*fermandola*) Non ancora

**SUZUKI:** Ier sera,
lo vedete, la stanza volle sparger di fiori.

**SHARPLESS:** (*commosso*) Ve lo dissi?

**PINKERTON:** (*turbato*) Che pena!

**SUZUKI:** (*sorpresa*) Pena!
(*sente rumore nel giardino*)
Chi c' è là fuori
nel giardino?
(*va a guardare fuori dalla shosi e con meraviglia esclama:*)
Una donna!! . . .

**PINKERTON:** (*la riconduce sul davanti*) Zitta!

**SUZUKI:** (*agitata*) Chi è? chi è?

**SHARPLESS:** Meglio dirle ogni cosa.

**PINKERTON:** (*imbarazzato*) È venuta con me.

**SHARPLESS:** (*deliberatamente*) Sua moglie.

**SUZUKI:** (*sbalordita, alza le braccia al cielo, poi si precipita in ginocchio colla faccia contro terra*)
Anime sante degli avi! . . . alla piccina s'è spento il sol!

**SHARPLESS:** (*calmando Suzuki e sollevandola da terra*) Scegliemmo quest'ora mattutina
per ritrovarti sola, Suzuki, e alla gran prova
un aiuto, un sostegno cercar con te.

**SUZUKI:** (*desolata*) Che giova?
(*Sharpless prende a parte Suzuki e cerca colla preghiera e colla persuasione di averno il consenso: Pinkerton, sempre più agitato, si aggira per la stanza ed osserva*)

**SHARPLESS:** (*a Suzuki*) Io so che alle sue pene
non ci sono conforti!
Ma del bimbo conviene
assicurar le sorti!
La pietosa
che entrar non osa
materna cura
del bimbo avrà.

**SUZUKI:** E volte ch'io chieda
a una madre . . .

**SHARPLESS:** (*insistendo*) Suvvia,
parla con quella pia
e conducila qui—s'anche la veda
Butterfly, non importa.

---

**SUZUKI:** No ship has crossed the harbor these three years
Whose flags and colours Butterfly has not
Eagerly examined.

**SHARPLESS:** (*to Pinkerton*) Did I not tell you?

**SUZUKI:** (*going*) I'll call her.

**PINKERTON:** (*stopping her*) No, not yet.

**SUZUKI:** Look around you,
Last night she had the room
Decorated with flowers.

**SHARPLESS:** (*deeply touched*)
Did I not tell you?

**PINKERTON:** (*distressed*) Oh, torment!

**SUZUKI:** (*distressed*) Torment?
(*hears sound from the garden*)
Who's that outside there
In the garden?
(*goes to look through the shosi and exclaims in surprise:*)
A lady!!—

**PINKERTON:** (*leading her forward again*) Hush!

**SUZUKI:** (*excitedly*) Who's that? Who's that?

**SHARPLESS:** Better tell her all.

**PINKERTON:** (*in confusion*) She came with me.—

**SHARPLESS:** (*deliberately*) She's his wife.

**SUZUKI:** (*stupified, raises her arms to Heaven, then falls on her knees with her face to the ground*)
Hallowed souls of my fathers!
The world is plunged in gloom!

**SHARPLESS:** (*calming her, and raising her from the ground*) We came here so early in the morning
To find you all alone, that you might give us
Your help and guidance in our plight.

**SUZUKI:** (*in despair*) How can I?
(*Sharpless takes her aside and tries with prayers and entreaties to get her consent, while Pinkerton, getting more and more agitated, wanders about the room, noting every detail*)

**SHARPLESS:** (*to Suzuki*) I know that for such a trouble
There is no consolation!
But the future of the baby
Must be our first and special thought!
This gentle lady
Who dare not enter
Will give the child a mother's care.

**SUZUKI:** Woe is me! do you ask me
To go and tell a mother—

**SHARPLESS:** (*persisting*) Delay not, call her,
Call in that gentle lady
And conduct her here—if even

# Act III

**Anzi—meglio se acorrta**
del vero si facesse alla sua vista.
Vieni, vieni! . . .

**SUZUKI:** Oh me trista! me trista!
(*spinta de Sharpless va nel giardino a raggiungere Mistress Pinkerton*)

**PINKERTON:** Oh! l'amara fragranza
di questi fiori
velenosa al cor mi va.
Immutata è la stanza
dei nostri amori . . .
ma un gel di morte vi sta.
(*vede il proprio ritratto, lo osserva*)
Il mio ritratto!—Svanita è
l'imagine
qual foglia in chiuse pagine.
(*lo depone*)
Tre anni son passati—e noverati
ella n'ha i giorni e l'ore
nell'immobile fede . . .
(*agitassimo a queste rimembranze si rivolge a Sharpless che è ritornato a lui vicino*)
Non posso rimaner.—Sharpless vi
aspetto
per via. Datele voi . . . qualche
soccorso . . .
(*consegna danari al Console*)
Mi struggo dal rimorso.

**SHARPLESS:** Non ve l'avevo detto?

**PINKERTON:** Sì. Tutto in un istante
vedo il mio fallo e sento
che di questo tormento
tregua mai non avrò.
Sempre il mite sembiante
vedrò, con strazio atroce,
sempre la dolce voce
lamentosa udrò.
Addio fiorito asil
di letizia e d'amor.
Non reggo al tuo squallor!
Fuggo, fuggo—son vil.

**SHARPLESS:** Vel dissi . . . vi ricorda?
quando la man vi diede:
Badate, ella ci crede
e fui profeta allor.
Sorda ai consigli, sorda
ai dubbi—vilipesa
nell'ostinata attesa
tutto raccolse il cor.
Ma ormai quel cor sincero
forse presago è già.
Andate—il triste vero
da sola apprenderà.
(*Pinkerton, strette le mani al Console, esce rapidamento, mentre Kate e Suzuki vengono dal giardino*)

**KATE:** (*a Suzuki*) Glielo dirai?

**SUZUKI:** Prometto.

**KATE:** E le darai consiglio di affidarmi? . . .

Butterfly should see her, no matter.
Then with her eyes she will learn
The cruel truth we dare not tell her.

**SUZUKI:** Oh, woe is me!
(*Sharpless pushes her into the garden, where she joins Mrs. Pinkerton*)

**PINKERTON:** Oh, the bitter fragrance
Of these flowers,
It is poison to my heart.
Unchanged is the chamber
Where once we loved—
But a deathly chill haunts the air.
(*sees his own likeness and takes it up*)
And here my portrait!
(*puts it down*)
Faded is the likeness,
Just like a leaf pressed between pages.
Three years have passed away,
And every day, every hour she counted—
(*agitated by these reminiscences he turns to Sharpless*)
I cannot remain,—Sharpless, I'll
wait for you
Outside. Give her this money, just
to support her—
(*gives the Consul some money*)
Remorse and anguish choke me.

**SHARPLESS:** Is it not as I told you!

**PINKERTON:** Yes. In one sudden moment
I see my heartless action,
And feel that I shall never free myself
From remorse.
Haunted for ever I shall be
By her reproachful eyes.
Farewell, O happy home!
Farewell, home of love!
I cannot bear to stay!
Like a coward let me fly—
Farewell!

**SHARPLESS:** I warned you—you remember?
When in your hand she laid hers:
"Be careful, for she believes you."
Alas, how true I spoke!
Deaf to doubting, humiliation,
Blindly trusting to your promise
Her heart will break.
But now this faithful heart
Has perhaps already divined.
Now go—the cruel truth
She should hear alone.
(*Pinkerton, wringing the Consul's hands, goes out quickly as Kate and Suzuki come in from the garden*)

**KATE:** (*to Suzuki*) Then you will tell her?

**SUZUKI:** I promise.

**KATE:** And you will counsel her
To trust me?

**SUZUKI:** Prometto.

**KATE:** Lo terrò come un figlio.

**SUZUKI:** Vi credo. Ma bisogna
ch'io le sia sola accanto . . .
Nella grande ora—sola!—Piangerà
tanto tanto!

**BUTTERFLY:** (*dall'interno della camera superiore*) Suzuki, dove
sie . . . parla . . .
(*appare in cima alla scaletta*)
Suzuki! . . .

**SUZUKI:** (*fa cenno agli altri di tacere, poi risponde:*) Son
qui . . . pregavo e rimettevo a
posto . . .
(*Butterly scende: Suzuki si precipita verso la scaletta per impedire a Butterfly di scendere*)
No . . . no . . . non discendete . . .

**BUTTERFLY:** (*discende precipitosa, svincolandosi da Suzuki che cerca invano di trattenerla, poi si aggira per la stanza con grande agitazione, ma giubilante*) E
qui . . . dov'è nascosto?
(*vede Sharpless*)
Ecco il Console . . . e . . . dove?
dove?
(*cerca dietro ai paraventi*)
Non c'è.
(*si volge a vede Madama Pinkerton*)
Chi siete?
Perchè veniste? Niuno parla! . . . Perchè piangete
No: non ditemi nulla . . . nulla—forse potrei
cader morta sull'attimo.—Tu Suzuki che sei
tanto buona—non piangere!—e
mi vuoi tanto bene
un Sì od un No—di'piano—Vive?

**SUZUKI:** Sì.

**BUTTERFLY:** Ma non viene
più. Te l'han detto! . . .
(*irritata al silenzio di Suzuki*)
Vespa! Voglio che tu risponda.

**SUZUKI:** Mai più.

**BUTTERFLY:** Ma è giunto ieri?

**SUZUKI:** Sì.

**BUTTERFLY:** (*guarda Kata, quasi affascinata*) Quella donna bionda
mi fa tanta paura! Mi fa tanta paura!

**SHARPLESS:** E la causa innocente
d'ogni vostra sciagura
Perdonatele.

**BUTTERFLY:** Ah! è sua moglie!
Tutto è morto per me!
Tutto è finito!

**SUZUKI:** I promise.

**KATE:** I will care for him like a son.

**SUZUKI:** I trust you! But I must be
alone beside her
In this cruel hour! She will weep so
sorely!

**BUTTERFLY:** (*calling from the room above*) Suzuki, Suzuki,
where are you?
(*appears at the head of the staircase*)

**SUZUKI:** (*signs to the others to keep quiet, then answers:*) I'm
here. I was praying, and going back
to watch—
(*Butterfly comes down. Suzuki rushes toward the staircase to prevent her from coming*)
No, no, do not come down.

**BUTTERFLY:** (*comes down quickly, freeing herself from Suzuki, who tries in vain to hold her back; then she paces the room in a state of great excitement but happiness*) He's here—where is he hidden?
(*see Sharpless*)
Here is the Consul—and where
is?—where is?—
(*looks behind the screens*)
Not here!
(*turns and sees Mrs. Pinkerton*)
Who are you?
Why have you come?—No one answers!—Why are you weeping?
No, no, tell me nothing—nothing—lest I fall dead
At your feet at the words I hear!
You, Suzuki,
Are always so faithful—do not
weep, I pray!
Since you love me so dearly, say
"yes" or "no" quite softly,
He lives?

**SUZUKI:** Yes.

**BUTTERFLY:** But he'll come
No more. They have told you!
(*angered at Suzuki's silence*)
Woman, I want you to reply.

**SUZUKI:** No more.

**BUTTERFLY:** He reached here yesterday?

**SUZUKI:** Yes.

**BUTTERFLY:** (*looks at Kate as though compelled*) Who is this
lady
That terrifies me—terrifies me?

**SHARPLESS:** Through no fault of her own
She's the cause of your trouble. Forgive her, pray.

**BUTTERFLY:** Ah! She is the wife
All is dead for me—
All is finished.

SHARPLESS: Corragio!

BUTTERFLY: Voglion prendermi tutto! il figlio mio.

SHARPLESS: Fatelo pel suo bene il sacrifizio.

BUTTERFLY: Ah! triste madre! Abbandonar mio figlio E sia! A lui devo obbedir!

KATE: (*dolcemente*) Potete perdonarmi, Butterfly?

BUTTERFLY: (*con aria grave*) Sotto il gran ponte del cielo non v' è donna di voi più felice. Siatelo sempre felice e non vi rattristate mai per me. Mi piacerebbe pur che gli diceste che pace io troverò.

KATE: (*stendendo la mano*) E la mano . . . la man . . . me la dareste?

BUTTERFLY: (*ritraendosi un poco ma rispondendo, con dolcezza*) Vi prego—questo . . . no . . . Andate adesso.

KATE: (*avviandosi, dice a Sharpless:*) Povera piccina!

SHARPLESS: (*assai commosso*) È un' immensa pietà!

KATE: (*sottovoce a Sharpless*) E il figlio lo darà?

BUTTERFLY: (*che ha udito*) A lui lo potrò dare se lo verrà a cercare. Fra mezz' ora salite la collina. (*Suzuki accompagna Kate e Sharpless che escono dalla porta di destra. Butterfly si regge a stento: Suzuki si affretta a sorreggeria*)

SUZUKI: (*mettendo una mano sul cuore a Butterfly*) Come una mosca prigioniera l' ali batte il piccolo cuor!

BUTTERFLY: (*si è riavuta e vedendo che è giorno fatto si scioglie de Suzuki dicendole:*) Troppo luce è di fuor, e troppa primavera. Chiudi. (*Suzuki chiude porte e tende: la camera rimane quasi in completa oscurita*) (*a Suzuki*) Il bimbo ove sia?

SUZUKI: Giuoca. Lo chiamo?

---

SHARPLESS: Courage!

BUTTERFLY: And you will take everything from me! He is my child.

SHARPLESS: Make the sacrifice for him.

BUTTERFLY: It's hard for me, very hard. Abandoned! ah! my son! To him I owe my duty.

KATE: (*gently*) Can you not forgive me, Butterfly?

BUTTERFLY: (*solemnly*) Beneath the blue vault of heaven There is no happier lady than you are— May you remain so Nor ever be saddened through me— Yet it would please me greatly That you should tell him That peace will come to me—

KATE: (*holding out her band*) Your hand—your hand, may I take it?

BUTTERFLY: (*drawing back, but replying kindly*) I pray you—no—not that! Now go and leave me.

KATE: (*going away, says to Sharpless*) Poor little lady!

SHARPLESS: (*deeply moved*) Oh, the pity of it all!

KATE: (*whispers to Sharpless*) And can he have his son?

BUTTERFLY: (*who has heard*) His son I will give him If he will come and fetch him. Climb this hill in half an hour from now. (*Suzuki escorts Kate and Sharpless, who go out by the door on the right; Butterfly is on the point of collapsing; Suzuki hastens to support her*)

SUZUKI: (*laying her hand on Butterfly's heart*) Like to a poor imprisoned bird Beats this little fluttering heart!

BUTTERFLY: (*gradually recovers; seeing that it is now broad daylight she disengages herself from Suzuki and says:*) Too much light shines outside, And too much smiling spring. Close them. (*pointing to the curtains*) (*Suzuki closes doors and curtains—the room is almost in total darkness*) Where is the child?

SUZUKI: Playing. Shall I call him!

---

BUTTERFLY: Lascialo giuocar. (*congedandola*) Va.—Fagli compagnia.

SUZUKI: Non vi voglio lasciar. (*si getta ai piedi di Butterfly piangendo*) Resto con voi.

BUTTERFLY: (*risolutamente batte le maui*) Va—va. Te lo comando. (*fa alzare Suzuki a la springe fuori dell'uscio di sinistra.—Poi Butterfly accende un lumedavanti al reliquiario, si inchina e rimane immobile assorta in doloroso pensiero: va allo stipo, ne leva un grau velo bianco che getta sul paravento; poi prende il coltelloehe chi, uso in un astuccio di lacca, sta appeso alla parete presso il simulacro di Budda, lo impugna e ne bacia religiosamente la lama tenendola colle due mani per la punta e per l'impugnature: quindl legge le parole che sono incise sulla lama:*) "Con onor muore Chi non può serbar vita con onore." (*si appunta il coltello alla gola; s'apre la porta di sinistra e si vede il braccio di Suzuki che spinge il bambino verso la madre; il bimbo entra correndo colle manine alzate; Butterfly lascia cadere il coltello, si precipita verso il bambino, lo abbraccia soffocandolo di baci.*) Tu, tu, piccolo Iddio! Amore, amore mio, fior di giglio e di rosa, qui la tua testa bionda qui, ch'io nasconda la fronte dolorosa ne' tuoi capelli. Non saperlo mai per te, per i tuoi puri occhi, muor Butterfly perchè tu possa andare di là dal mare senza che ti rimorda ai di maturi il materno abbandono. O a me, sceso dal trono dell' alto Paradiso, guarda ben fiso, fiso di tua madre là faccia! . . . che te'n resti una traccia, sia pur pallida e poca. Che non tutto consunto vada di mia beltà l'ultimo fior. (*guarda lungamente il suo bimbo e lo bacia ancora*) Addio! piccolo amor! Va. Gioca, gioca. (*Butterfly prende il bambino, lo mette su di una stuoia col viso voltato verso sinistra, guardà in mano una banderuola americana ed una puppattola e lo invita a trastullarsi mentre delicatamente gli benda gli occhi. Poi afferra il coltello, chiude la porta di sinistra e collo sguardo sempre fisso sul figlio, va dietro il paravento. Si ode cadera a terra il col-*

---

BUTTERFLY: Leave him at his play. (*dismissing her*) Go—go and play with him.

SUZUKI: I will not leave you alone. (*throws berself weeping at Butterfly's feet*) I stay with you.

BUTTERFLY: (*resolutely—clapping her hands*) Go—go—obey my orders. (*makes the weeping Suzuki rise, and pushes her outside the exit on the left. Then Butterfly goes in front of the image of Buddha, bows before it and remains motionless, lost in sad thought; she goes to the shrine and takes from it a large white veil which she throws across the screen; she takes the dagger which, in a waxen sheath, is leaning against the wall near the image of Buddha, and piously kisses the blade, holding it with both hands by the point and by the handle; then she reads the words inscribed on the blade:*) "To die with honor When one can no longer live with honor." (*she points the dagger at her throat; the door on the left opens and shows Suzuki's arm pushing in the child to his mother; the child runs to her with outstretched hands. Butterfly lets fall the dagger, darts towards the child and hugs and kisses him almost to suffocation*) You, you beloved idol! Adoréd being! Fairest Flower of beauty! Here on your dear fair head, Here let me bury My tortured brow Among your curls. though you must never know it It is for you I'm dying, I, poor Butterfly, That you may go away Beyond the ocean, Never to feel the torment when you are older That your mother forsook you! O my son, sent to me from Heaven, Straight from the throne of glory! Take one last careful look At your poor mother's face! That its memory may linger, Even though it may be dim and faint. Let not my beauty's lingering bloom Be faded! Farewell, beloved! Go—play—play. (*Butterfly takes the child, sets him on a stool with his face turned to the left, puts the American flag and a doll in his hands and motions him to play with them, while she gently bandages his eyes. Then she seizes a dagger, and her eyes still fixed on the child, goes behind the screen. The knife is heard*

tello, mentre il gran velo bianco sparisce come tirato da una mano invisibile. Butterfly scivola a terra, mezza fuori del paravento: il velo le circonda il collo. Con un debole sorriso saluta colla mano il bambino e si trascina presso di lui, avendo ancora forza sufficiente per abbracciarlo, poi gli cade vicino. In questo momento si ode fuori, a destra, la voce affannosa di Pinkerton che chiama ripetuta-

falling to the ground, and the large white veil disappears, as though drawn by an invisible hand. Butterfly emerges from behind the screen, the large white veil is round her neck. Tottering, she gropes her way towards the child, and, smiling feebly, has just enough strength to embrace him before she falls to the ground beside him. At this moment Pinkerton's voice is heard outside, on

mente:)
Butterfly! Butterfly!
(poi la porta di è violentemente scossa ed aperto: Pinkerton e Sharpless si precipitano nella stanza, accorrendo presso Butterfly che con debole gesto indica il bambino e muore. Pinkerton si inginocchia, mentre Sharpless prende il bimbo e lo bacia singhiozzando.)

the right, calling repeatedly: Butterfly! Butterfly! then the door on the right is violently burst open: Pinkerton and Sharpless rush into the room and up to Butterfly, who, with a feeble gesture, points to the child and dies. Pinkerton falls on his knees, while Sharpless takes the child and kisses him, sobbing.)

# La Fanciulla Del West (1910)

## The Girl of the Golden West

Music by Giacomo Puccini ■ Libretto by Carlo Zangarini & Guelfo Civinini ■ Based on the play by David Belasco

This three-act opera, set to a libretto by Carlo Zangarini and Guelfo Civinini (after David Belasco's play *The Girl of the Golden West*), premiered at the Metropolitan Opera House in New York on December 10, 1910. Minnie runs the Polka Saloon in the miners' camp at the foot of the Cloudy Mountains. It is the Gold Rush of 1849. Wallace sings a ballad about homesickness. An agent of the Wells Fargo Transport Company enters with the news that the infamous bandit Ramerrez and his thieves are nearby. Rance, the sheriff, declares his love for Minnie, inciting a barroom brawl. A letter from the bandit's mistress arrives, dispensing information about Ramerrez' movements. A stranger named Dick Johnson, who is really Ramerrez, enters. He and Minnie are immediately attracted to each other, making Rance jealous. Castro, one of Ramerrez' men, gives the sheriff and the miners false information as to the bandits' whereabouts. Alone with Ramerrez, Minnie tells him that the miners trust her with their gold and that she would rather die than betray them. She then invites him to her cabin. She tells Ramerrez how she ended up in the miners' camp and how much she loves her life. They confess their love for each other. The sheriff and his men come by to check on her safety, and she leads them to believe that she is alone. They tell her that Johnson and Ramerrez are the same man. She is furious at him for duping her. He tells her that his father, a bandit as well, left behind a large family to feed. She doesn't stop him from running out into the danger which awaits and he is shot. She hides him in her loft. Rance enters; a drop of blood falls from the loft, giving away Ramerrez' presence. Minnie suggests a game of poker, the outcome of which will determine Johnson's fate. If Rance wins, Johnson must pay for his crimes. If Minnie wins, Johnson will be freed. She cheats and wins. A manhunt continues in the Great Californian Forest. The miners capture Johnson. Minnie arrives on horseback, pistol in hand. She pleads with the miners to spare him, and despite Rance's objections, Johnson gains his freedom. He and Minnie go off together into the forest.

## ■ ATTO PRIMO

*L'interno Della "Polka"*
Uno stanzone costruito rozzamente in forma di triangolo, del quale due pareti costituiscono i lati, quello a destra più sviluppato. L'angolo nel fondo è smussato da una grande apertura che forma la porta, a due battenti, che si sprangano dall'interno. In una parete laterale una scaletta porta ad un pianerottolo che sporge sulla stanza come un ballatoio dal quale pendono pelli di cervo e ruvidi drappi di vivi colori. Sotto il ballatoio un breve passaggio immette nella "sala da ballo" come indica una scritta a caratteri rossi. Il passaggio è custodito da un orso impagliato. Presso la porta di fondo, è il banco con bicchieri, bottiglie, ecc.: dietro di esso, ad un lato, una credenzetta senza sportelli, con stoviglie, e dall'altro lato, un piccolo barile nel quale i minatori depositano la polvere d'oro. Dietro il banco, nel mezzo, una finestra rettangolare con telaio a dadi: in alto, sopra la finestra è scritto a grandi lettere: "A real home for the boys." Sulla stessa parete è affisso un avviso di taglia di 5000 dollari: si leggono

chiaro le cifre, il nome "Ramerrez," la firma "Wells-Fargo." Dal soffitto pende una varietà di caratteristici commestibili. Da una parte uno schermo di lamina di ferro, per riparare le persone dai colpi di pistola: dall'altro un largo camino. Verso il proscenio il tavolo del "faraone" con accessori pel giuoco—un altro tavolo verso il fondo—un altro ancora presso il banco.
(Dalla grande porta del fondo e attraverso la finestra si scorge la valle, con la sua vegetazione selvaggia di sambuchi, quercie, conifere basse, tutta avvolta nel fiammeggiare del tramonto. Lontano, le montagne nevose si sfumano di toni d'oro e di viola. La luce violeta dell'esterno, che va calando rapidamente, rende anche più oscuro l'interno della "Polka." Nel buio appena si scorgono i contorni delle cose. A sinistra, quasi al proscenio, presso il camino, si vede rosseggiare la bragia del sigaro di Jack Rance. Presso la scaletta a destra, su di una botte è seduto, con la testa fra le mani, Larkens. A un tratto si alza, si leva di tasca una lettera, la guarda con tristezza, va al banco, prende un francobollo, ve l'appiccica sopra, la depone nella cassetta e ri-

## ■ ACT I

*Interior Of The "Polka"*
A large room, roughly built in the shape of a triangle, of which two sides form the walls, with the right-hand wall further extended. The angle at the back is cut off by a large aperture forming the door—a folding door—which is barred from the inside. From a side-wall a small staircase leads to an upper landing projecting over the room like a balcony, from which hang deerskins and rough, bright-colored hangings. Underneath the balcony a short passage leads into the "Dancing Hall," as indicated by a placard in red letters. The passage is guarded by a stuffed bear. Near the door, at the back, is the bar, with glasses, bottles, etc. Behind it, on one side, is a cupboard without doors, full of kitchen utensils, and on the other side a small barrel in which the miners keep their gold dust. Behind the bar, in the middle, is a rectangular window, with diamond-shaped panes; above it, over the window, is written in big letters: "A real home for the boys." On the same wall is a reward notice of 5,000 dollars; the

figures, the name of "Ramerrez" and the firm "Wells-Fargo" are clearly legible from the front. From the ceiling a variety of characteristic dried fruits, etc., is hanging. On one side is a sheet-iron screen to protect a person from pistol-shots; on the other, a big chimney-piece. Towards the footlights is the faro table, with the paraphernalia of the game—another table further back—and still another near the bar.
(The big door in the background and the window both command a view of the valley with its wild vegetation of alders, oaks and dwarf pines all wrapped in sunset glow. In the distance the snow-mountains are tinted with gold and violet. The very strong light outside, which is rapidly fading, makes the inside of the "Polka" seem all the darker. In the gloom the outlines of things can scarcely be distinguished. On the left, close to the footlights, near the chimney-piece, the glimmer of Jack Rance's cigar is seen. Near the staircase on the right, Larkens is seated on a cask, his head in his hands. Suddenly he rises, takes a letter from his pocket, looks at it sadly, goes to the counter, takes a stamp, fixes it on the letter, which he puts

*torna a sedere. Fuori, nella lontananza, s'incrociano grida ed echi lamentosi di canti.)*

**VOCI LONTANE:** —Alla "Polka"!
—Alle "Palme"!
—Holla!
—Hello!
*(un ritornello lontanissimo)*
"Là, lontano,
Là, lontano,
quanto piangerà! . . . "
*(Nick, esce dal sottoscala con una candela che ha acceso al lumino ad olio. Accende le candele sparse qua e là: sale su uno sgabello e accende al lampada di mezzo: accende i lumi della sala da ballo, poi sale ad accendere quelli della saletta superiore. La "Polka" si anima ad un tratto. Cominciano ad entrare a gruppi i minatori di ritorno dal campo.)*

**HARRY, JOE, BELLO ED ALTRI:** *(entrando)* Hello, Nick!

**NICK:** Buona sera, ragazzi!

**SID E HAPPY, SEGUITI DA BILLY:** Hello!

**NICK:** Hello!

**JOE, BELLO E GLI ALTRI:** *(cantarellando un ritornello americano)* "Dooda, dooda, day . . . "

**HARRY:** *(sedendosi al tavolo del faraone)* Sigari, Nick!

**JOE:** *(battendo una mano sul tavolo)* E whisky!

**NICK:** Son qua.

**BELLO:** Minnie?

**NICK:** Sta bene.

**SID:** *(che si è seduto al tavolo del faraone, agli altri che sono intorno)* Ragazzi, un faraone! Chi ci sta?

**HARRY:** Io ci stò.

**HAPPY:** Anch'io ci stò.

**JOE:** Anch'io.

**BELLO:** "All right!" Chi è che tiene banco?

**HAPPY:** *(indicando Sid)* Sid.

**BELLO:** Brutto affare.

**SID:** *(gettando con sprezzo le carte sul tavolo)* Chi vuol mischiare, mischi.
*(Harry mischia le carte)*

**JOE:** *(battendo con la palma aperta sulla spalla di Sid)* Holla!
*(Entrano Sonora e Trin seguita da parècchi minatori [uomini del campo] con selle ed arnesi che vengono gettati rumorosamente a terra; alcuni poi salgono alle sale superiori, altri vanno nella sala da ballo e attorno ai tavolo di giuoco)*

---

*into the mail-box, and sits down on the cask again. Outside in the distance are heard mingled shouts and mournful strains of song.)*

**VOICES IN THE DISTANCE:**
To the "Polka!"
—To the "Palmeto!"
—Hello!
—Hello!
*(A refrain in the distance)*:
"In the homestead,
Far away,
How she'll weep for me!"...
*(Nick comes out from under the stairs with a candle which he has lighted at the oil lamp. He lights the candles placed here and there; climbs on a stool and lights the center lamp; lights the lights in the dancing hall, then goes to light up the upper room. The "Polka" suddenly becomes full of life. Groups of miners returning from camp begin to come in.)*

**HARRY, JOE, HANDSOME AND OTHERS:** *(entering)*: Hello, Nick!

**NICK:** Hello, boys, how goes it?

**SID AND HAPPY, FOLLOWED BY BILLY:** Hello!

**NICK:** Hello!

**JOE, HANDSOME AND OTHERS:** *(humming an American refrain)*: "Dooda, dooda, day"...

**HARRY:** *(sitting at the faro table)*: Bring the cigars, Nick!

**JOE:** *(banging the table with his hand)*: And whisky!

**NICK:** All right.

**HANDSOME:** How's Minnie?

**NICK:** She's jolly.

**SID:** *(who has sat down at the faro table, to those around him)*: You fellows, a game of faro? Who will play?

**HAPPY:** I for one.

**HARRY:** I'll take a hand.

**JOE:** And I.

**HANDSOME:** All right! Say boys—who's going to be banker?

**HAPPY:** Sid.

**HANDSOME:** Rotten business.

**SID:** *(throwing cards on table)*: Well, shuffle, if you want to.
*(Harry shuffles.)*

**JOE:** *(clapping Sid on the shoulder)*: Hello!
*(Other miners have come in and have gone straight to the dancing hall, humming the same refrain softly. Some have gone up to the upper room.)*

---

**SONORA E TRIN:** —Da cena, Nick!
—Che cosa c'è?

**NICK:** C'è poco. Ostriche sott'aceto . . .

**SONORA:** Quello che c'è.

**TRIN:** . . . Con whisky.

**SONORA:** Hello, Larkens! *(battendo sulle spalle di Larkens)*

**LARKENS:** *(con melanconia, senza alzare il capo dalle mani)* Hello!

**I MINATORI:** *(preparandosi al giuoco)* Andiamo! . . .

**SID:** Fate il ginoco.
*(Nick, affaccendato, va e viene con bottighe e bicchieri dalla saletta superiore alla sala da ballo. Apparecchia anche il tavolino di mezzo per Sonora e Trin)*

**JOE:** *(puntando)* Al "giardino"!

**HARRY:** *(c. s.)* Alle "piccole"!

**BELLO:** *(c. s.)* Alle "grandi"!

**I MINATORI:** *(dal ballatoio)* Nick, da bere!

**SONORA:** *(a Trin, sedendo al tavolino apparecchiato)* Ti aspetto?

**TRIN:** *(dal gruppo dei giuocatori, a Sonora)* Vengo . . .

**HAPPY:** Gettoni!

**SID:** Un re . . . Un asso.

**BELLO:** *(con rabbia)* Maledetto!

**RANCE:** *(a Nick che gli passa accanto, accennandogli Larkens, che ha chinato il capo sulle braccia)* Larkens che ha? Stà male?

**NICK:** Il suo solito male. Nostalgia. Mal di terra natìa! Ripensa la sua vecchia Cornovaglia e alla madre lontana che l'aspetta . . .

**RANCE:** *(riaccendendo il sigaro)* Che terra maledetta, quest'occidente d'oro!

**NICK:** Ha la malaria gialla. L'oro avvelena il sangue a chi lo guarda.

**RANCE:** E Minnie, come tarda!
*(Al tavolo del faraone il giuoco continua più intenso)*

**SID:** *(a Happy, indicando la puntata)* Quanti dollari?

**HAPPY:** Dieci.

**SID:** *(dandogli il resto)* E novanta, fan cento.
Fante . . .
Regina . . .

**JOE:** Holla!
Evviva!

**HAPPY:** *(con rabbia)* Sacramento!

**TRIN:** Australiano d'inferno!

---

**SONORA AND TRIN:** *(coming in)*: Some supper, Nick! Got any left?

**NICK:** Not much. Oysters in vinegar.

**SONORA:** *(clapping Larkens on the shoulder)*: Hello, Larkens!

**LARKENS:** *(in a melancholy tone, without raising his head from his hands)*: Hello!

**THE MINERS:** *(getting ready for the game)*: Come on, then!

**SID:** Put up your stakes.
*(Nick comes and goes very busily, with bottles and glasses from the upper room to the dancing hall. He also gets ready the table in the middle for Sonora and Trin.)*

**JOE:** *(staking)*: On the queen!

**HARRY:** *(staking)*: On the low!

**HANDSOME:** *(staking)*: On the high!

**THE MINERS:** *(from the balcony)*: Nick, some drinks!

**SONORA:** *(to Trin, seated ready at the table)*: I'm waiting.

**TRIN:** *(from the group of players, to Sonora)*: Coming.

**HAPPY:** Some chips!

**SID:** A king—An ace.

**HANDSOME:** Confound him!

**RANCE:** *(to Nick, who is passing by, points to Larkens sitting with his head in his hands)*: Look, what is wrong with Larkens?

**NICK:** Just his usual trouble. He is homesick; Sick for his native country! He's thinking of his dear old Cornwall And his mother who is waiting for him—

**RANCE:** *(lighting his cigar)*: This God-forsaken country, cursed with the lust of gold!

**NICK:** He's got the yellow fever; Once get the sight of gold and you are poisoned.

**RANCE:** But Minnie, what has kept her?
*(At the faro table the game becomes more exciting.)*

**SID:** *(to Happy, pointing to the score)*: How much?

**HAPPY:** Ten.

**SID:** *(giving him the rest)*: And ninety makes a hundred. Knave! Queen!

**JOE:** Hello! Hurrah!

**HAPPY:** Oh! damnation!

**TRIN:** Cursed Australian!

JOE: Il tre non vince mai.

TRIN: Tutto sul tre!

SID: Tre . . . Sette . . .
(*i giuocatori puntano con più accanimento, s'odono parole come bestemmie represse e tintinnio di monete*)

TRIN: Tutto perso.
"Good by!"
(*Si stacca dal tavolo del giuoco e siede a quello dove Sonora stà mangiando. Al tavolo del giuoco si acca, orano di più le discussioni e le proteste. Nick corre di qua e di là portando bibite, sigari, ecc. Alcuni minatori salgono al piano sūperiore, altri ne discendono; chi va al banco, chi si sofferma al tavolo del giuoco interessandosene. Entrano pure nuovi tipi di minatori. Billy si avvicina al banco furtivamente, ruba dei sigari ed esce. Nel cielo nuvoloso si vendono grandi squarci stellati*)

NICK: (*rientrando dalla sala da ballo, forte a tutti*) Nella sala, ragazzi, vi si vuole a ballare!

SONORA: A ballare?
Son pazzi!
Io non ballo uomini!
(*a Trin*)
Ti pare?

TRIN: È giusto.

SONORA: (*alzandosi, in disparte a Nick che torna dal banco con la cassetta dei sigari*) Minnie infine s'è decisa per me?

NICK: (*furbescamente, secondandolo*) Certo: ho capito che siete il preferito! . . .

SONORA: (*gongolando, forte ai compagni*) Sigari a tutti!

TUTTI: Hurrà!
(*Nick corre a prendere la cassetta degli sigari, distribuendo; discende; dalla sala da ballo escono due giovanotti danzando*)

TRIN: (*fermando Nick, in disparte, sotto voce*) Nick, che ti ha detto?

NICK: (*furbescamente anche a lui*) Mah!
Se ho ben capito siete voi il preferito.

TRIN: (*gongolando*) Whisky per tutti!

TUTTI: Hurrà!
(*Nick porta in giro bottiglie e bicchieri*)

JAKE WALLACE: (*di fuori cantando*) "Che faranno i vecchi miei là, lontano, là, lontano? . . . Tristi e soli i vecchi miei piangeranno, penseranno ch'io non ritorni più!"

---

JOE: The three will never win.

TRIN: All on the three!

SID: Three! seven!

TRIN: I'm cleared out.
Good-bye!
(*Leaves the card table and sits down at the table where Sonora is supping. The game goes on. Nick passes to and fro with trays and drinks. Billy furtively approaches the counter, steals some cigars and goes out. In the cloudy sky great patches of stars are seen.*)

NICK: (*coming back from the dancing room, aloud to all*): To the dance hall, you fellows, if you want to dance!

SONORA: Want to dance?
The idiots!
Not with men for my partners!
No, thank you!

TRIN: No, thank you!

SONORA: (*rising, aside to Nick who is coming back from the counter with a box of cigars*): Have you any news from Minnie for me?

NICK: (*slyly, humoring him*): Rather! I can tell you that you're the one she's chosen!

SONORA: (*jumping for joy, aloud*): Cigars all round!

ALL: Hurrah! (*Nick goes round with the cigars, distributing them; he goes down; two youths come dancing out of the dance-hall.*)

TRIN: (*taking Nick aside, sotto voce*): Nick, what of Minnie?

NICK: (*slyly to him also*): Well! Why, I can tell you you're the one she's chosen!

TRIN: (*jumping for joy*): Whisky all round!

ALL: Hurrah!
(*Nick hands round bottles and glasses.*)

JAKE: (*singing in the distance*): "I am thinking of my folk in the homestead, way back yonder, Are they sitting lone and sad, are they weeping?
Do they wonder when I'll come again?"

---

NICK: (*facendosi sulla porta*) Ragazzi, vi annunzio Jake Wallace il menestrel del campo!
(*Ma già la canzone nostalgica ha preso tutte quelle anime avide e rudi: le teste si sollevano, gli orecchi sono tesi: il giuoco langue. Quelli del piano superiore si affacciano ad osservare: nel silenzio, il tintinnio dei gettoni adagio adagio si spegne. Jake Wallace, il cantastorie, appare sulla porta cantando e accompagnandosi sul banjo*)

JAKE WALLACE: (*entrando*) "La mia mamma . . .
(*Si ferma stupito del silenzio che l'accoglie. Tutti i minatori, col viso proteso verso di lui, gli fanno cenno con le mani di continuare*).

JAKE: (*continuando*) . . . che farà s'io non torno, s'io non torno? Quanto, oh quanto piangerà!"

ALCUNI MINATORI: (*dal tavolo del giuoco*) "Al telaio tesserà lino e duolo pel lenzuolo che poi la ricoprirà . . ."

ALCUNI MINATORI: (*dal ballatoio della sala superiore*) "E il mio cane dopo tanto . . .

JAKE WALLACE: Il mio cane . . .

ALTRI MINATORI: (*di sopra*) Il mio cane mi ravviserà?"
(*Una nostalgia quasi disperata si impadronisce di tutti. Qualcuno, che ha cominciato ad accompagnare la canzone battendo col pugno dei colpi sordi sul tavolo, si interrompe*)

HARRY: (*prorompendo come in un singhiozzo*) "O mia casa, al rivo accanto . . .

I MINATORI: (*del tavolo*) "Là, lontano . . .

I MINATORI: (*di sopra*) "Là, lontano . . .

TUTTI:
(*sommessamente*) . . . Chi di noi ti rivedrà?
(*Il canto si spegne angosciosamente. Silenzio. Largens, al canto nostalgico, si è scosso dal suo sopore dolo*)

SID: (*supplichevole*) Per carità! . . .

JACK RANCE: (*avvicinandosi*) Che succede?

BELLO: Ha barato! Avrà ciò che gli spetta! . . .

VOCI: A laccio!

---

NICK: (*appearing in the doorway*): Here, boys, here he is! Jake Wallace, the camp minstrel! (*But the homesick refrain has caught hold of all these rough grasping souls: heads are raised, ears strained—they gradually leave off gambling. Those on the upper floor crowd out to hear better; in the silence the soft tinkling of the counters dies away; Jake Wallace, the minstrel, appears in the doorway singing and accompanying himself on his banjo.*)
Enter Jake Wallace.

JAKE: "My old mother—
(*He stops, amazed at the silence which greets him. All the miners, their faces turned towards him, sign to him to continue.*) —How she'll fret for her sonny, For her sonny, How she'll weep for him!"

SOME OF THE MINERS: (*from the card table*): I can see her at her loom Weaving linen For the winding sheet To cover her—

JAKE: How are my old folk out yonder? Do they wonder when I'll come again?

SOME OF THE MINER: (*from the balcony of the floor above*): And my dear old faithful dog.—

JAKE: Will he know me?

SOME OF THE MINERS: (*from above*): And my dog Tray, will he know me still?
(*A desperate homesickness overcomes them all. Someone who has started accompanying the song with muffled fist-thumps on the table, stops short.*)

HARRY: (*breaking into a despairing sort of sob*): Dear old home beside the river!

THE MINERS: (*at the table*): Far away, over yonder!

THE MINERS: (*from above*): Far away, over yonder!

ALL: (*softly*): Shall I ever see you more?
(*The song dies away in an anguished silence. Larkens, roused from his mournful lethargy by the homesick song, has risen. At the last words of the chorus he bursts out weeping aloud.*)

SID: (*wbining*): For pity's sake! Mercy, boys!—

JAKE RANCE: (*approaching*): What's the matter?

HANDSOME: He's been cheating! He'll get what he deserves!

VOICES: The gallows! Let's hang the wretch!

**RANCE:** (*sorride, si leva di tasca con flemma il fazzoletto, lo spiega con flemma, e si pulisce le scarpe appoggiando il piede ad una sedia.*) Andiamo, ragazzi!
Un po' di calma . . .
Qua . . . vediamo.

**VOCI:** —Al laccio, Sid!
—A morte!
(*Tutti si stringono di nuovo minacciosi attorno a Sid tremante*)

**RANCE:** (*trattenendoli, freddo*) Eh!
Cos'è poi la morte?
Un calcio dentro il buio e buona notte!
So un castigo più degno.
Datemi la sua carta . . .
(*dànno a Rance il due di picche; egli con une spillo lo appunta sul petto di Sid, sopra il cuore*)
Sopra il cuore, come si porta un fiore.
Non toccherà più carte.
È questo il segno.
Se si azzardasse a toglierlo, impiccatelo.
(*a Bello, con autorità*)
Domani al campo, tu spargi la voce.
(*a Sid*)
Va!

**SID:** (*piagnucoloso, raccomandandesi*) Ragazzi, siate buoni! . . .

**TUTTI:** (*sbertandolo e spingendolo fuori*) —Via di qua!
—Via!
—Fuori!
—Via di qua!
—Ladro!
—Uh!
—Uh!
(*lo cacciano a pedate: Billy, che teme anch'esso un calcio di Rance, scivola fuori, circospetto. Rance, come nulla fosse avvenuto, si siede al tavolo del faraone, invitando. Harry, Joe e un minatore si siedono al tavolo di destra, bevendo*)

**RANCE:** (*a Sonora e Trin*) Un poker!
(*a Nick*)
Nick, gettoni!
(*Nick porta; giuocano. Entra Ashby*)

**ASHBY:** Sceriffo, hello!

**RANCE:** (*ai minatori*) Ragazzi, fate largo!
Presento Mister Ashby, dell'Agenzia Wells-Fargo.
(*Ashby stringe la mano a Rance, a Sonora e a Trin e agli altri più vicini. Saluta con un cenno della mano i più lontani, che rispondono con lo stesso cenno*)

**ASHBY:** Nick, portami da bere.
(*ai vicini*)
Come stà la ragazza?

**RANCE:** (*smiles laconically, takes out his handkerchief, unfolds it, and polishes his boots with it, resting his foot on a chair.*) Look here, you boys; don't be hasty.—
Come; let's see!

**VOICES:** Let's hang the wretch!
He deserves death!
(*They all draw closer around the trembling Sid, and threaten him.*)

**RANCE:** (*restraining them coldly*): Is death so awful!
A sudden shock, a gasp, and all is over!
I know a much harder sentence.
Give me his card.
(*They hand Rance the two of spades; he pins it onto Sid's chest above his heart.*)
On his heart, just as he'd wear a flower.
He'll never touch a card again.
Let this be a warning.
If he dares to take it off, hang him!
(*To Handsome*):
To-morrow, pass the word in the camp.
(*To Sid*):
Go!

**SID:** (*entreating them, blubbering*): See here, boys, show some mercy!—

**ALL:** (*mocking him, and pushing him away*): Scoundrel!
Rascal!
You be off!
Out, rascal, out!
Ugh!
Ugh!
(*They kick him out; Billy, who fears another kick from Rance, slinks away furtively. Rance, as though nothing bad happened, sits down at the faro table, inviting them to join him. Harry, Joe and a miner sit down at a table on the right, drinking.*)

**RANCE:** (*To Sonora and Trin*): A poker!
(*To Nick*):
Nick, the chips!
(*While they settle to the game, enter Ashby.*)

**ASHBY:** The Sheriff, hello!

**RANCE:** (*to the miners*): Stand back, you boys, stand back!
This is Mister Ashby, agent of Wells-Fargo.
(*Ashby shakes hands with Rance, Sonora, Trin and others near him, and nods a greeting to those further off, who respond with a nod.*)

**ASHBY:** Nick, bring me some whisky.
(*To those near him*):
Tell me, how is the Girl?

**TUTTI:** (*lusingati*) Grazie, bene.
(*Nick porta quattro whisky al tavolo*)

**RANCE:** Che nuove del bandito?

**ASHBY:** Da tre mesi lo apposto: non è molto discosto . . .
(*Nick esce*)

**RANCE:** (*a Ashby*) Dicon che ruba come un gran signore!
È spagnuolo?

**ASHBY:** La banda di ladri, a cui comanda, è messicana: gentaccia gagliarda, astuta, pronta a tutto.
State in guardia.
Io mi sdraio.
Son stanco, ho l'ossa rotte.
A tutti, buona notte!
(*Prende un mantello sotto la scala: si adagia sui sacchi, senza curarsi di quanto gli succede intorno. Nick ritorna dentro con un vassoio pieno di bicchieri con whisky e limone*)

**TRIN:** (*a Nick*) Che cos'è?

**NICK:** Offre Minnie!

**TUTTI:** (*con sentimento d'affetto*) Viva Minnie!
Viva la nostra Minnie!

**RANCE:** (*con sussiego*) Signora Rance, fra poco.

**SONORA:** (*scattando*) No, faccia di cinese!
Minnie si prende giuoco di te!

**RANCE:** (*alzandosi, livido*) Ragazzo, è l' whisky che lavora.
Ti compatisco . . .
Di Jack Rance finora nessuno, intendi, s' è mai preso giuoco!
E buon per te ch'io non curi le offese degli ubriachi!

**SONORA:** (*estrae la pistola, ma è trattenuto dai compagni. Nick e qualche altro che sono rientrati si barricano dietro lo schermo di lamiera, come per evitare i colpi di pistola*) Vecchio biscazziere!
Minnie ti burla!

**RANCE:** (*avanzandosi d'un passo*) Provalo!

**SONORA:** (*svincolandosi*) Ti burla, muso giallo!

**RANCE:** Ah, miserabile! (*Gli si slancia contro; si azzuffano; gli altri cercano dividerli, ma non fanno a tempo: una donna è entrata d'un balzo, li ha, con fermo polso, divisi violentemente, strappando dalle mani di Sonora la pistola. È Minnie e Bello la segue, fermandosi al banco a guardare, ammirato. Un grido scoppia da tutte le parti: l'ira cade subita-*

**ALL:** All right, thank you. (*Nick brings four whiskies to the table.*)

**RANCE:** What news of the greaser?

**ASHBY:** After three months' tracking,
I am close on his heels. (*Nick goes out.*)

**RANCE:** (*to Ashby*): I've heard it said he robs you like a gentleman.
Is he Spanish?

**ASHBY:** I think not.
But he heads a band of Mexican greasers: A strong, wily rabble that sticks at nothing, keep a sharp look out.
I must rest now.
I am dead beat, my bones are aching.
Good-night, all you fellows!
(*Takes a cloak under the staircase—lies down comfortably without taking heed of what goes on around him.—Nick comes back with a jug of hot water and hands round glasses of whisky and lemons.*)

**TRIN:** (*to Nick*): What's this?

**NICK:** From Minnie!

**ALL:** Here's to Minnie!
Here's to our Minnie!

**RANCE:** (*impressively*): Missis Rance, quite shortly.

**SONORA:** (*bursting out*): No, you yellow-faced old Chinaman!
Minnie is making game of you!

**RANCE:** (*gets up, white with rage*): Sonora, your whisky is too strong.
I'll overlook it.
I'd have you remember
That nobody has ever dared to make game of Jack Rance!
It's well for you I take no notice of insults
From one who's tipsy!

**SONORA:** (*takes his pistol, but is held back by his mates. Nick and another hide behind the screen to get out of range of the pistol-shots*): Imbecile old gambler!
Minnie is fooling you!

**RANCE:** (*coming a step nearer*): Prove it!

**SONORA:** (*freeing himself*): Is fooling you, old yellow face!

**RANCE:** Ah, be damned to you!
(*He rushes upon him; they come to blows; the others try to separate them, but are too late; a woman has come in quite suddenly, has separated them with a strong arm, snatching Sonora's pistol from him and hiding it in a box on the counter. Handsome follows her and stops by the counter watching her, full of admiration.*

mente: solo Rance si apparta, tutto cupo, nella sua sedia di sinistra)

**TUTTI:** (con entusiasmo, agitando i cappelli) Hello, Minnie! Hello, Minnie!

**MINNIE:** (avanzandosi, con autorità) Che cos' è stato? . . . (severa, a Sonora) Sempre tu, Sonora?

**TRIN:** Nulla, Minnie; sciocchezze . . . Si scherzava!

**MINNIE:** (adirata) Voi manderete tutto alla malora! Vergogna! . . .

**JOE:** (presentandole un mazzolino di fiori) Minnie . . .

**MINNIE:** Non farò più scuola.

**TUTTI:** No, Minnie, no! . . .

**SONORA:** (imbarazzato) Sai, quando tu ritardi ci si annoia . . . Ed allora . . .

**MINNIE:** (scuote la testa e sorride rabbonita; avvicinandosi a banco; vede Bello in contemplazione) Bello, che fai? Che guardi?

**BELLO:** (si scuote, sorridendo impacciato) Nulla . . .

**ALCUNI:** (ridendo) Guardava . . . te!

**JOE:** (offrendole il mazzolino) Minnie, li ho colti lungo il "Torrente Nero". Al mio paese ce ne son tanti! I prati ne son folti . . .

**MINNIE:** Oh grazie, grazie, Joe!

**SONORA:** (levandosi di tasca un nastro ripiegato) È passato pel campo oggi un merciaio di San Francisco . . . Aveva trine e nastri. (svolgendo il nastro) Questo è per voi . . . Vedete, è color porpora come la vostra bocca . . .

**HARRY:** (spiegando un fazzoletto di seta) E questo è azzurro, come il vostro sguardo!

**MINNIE:** Grazie, grazie! . . .

**ASHBY:** (che si è rialzato e si è avvicinato al banco, alzando il bicchiere) Gli omaggi di Wells-Fargo!

**MINNIE:** (ridendo) Che confusione! . . . Siedi. (Harry siede confuso) A posto, Joe! Ora leggiamo. "Versetto secondo: Aspergimi d'issòpo e sarò mondo . . . "

They all give a shout; their anger dies away promptly. Rance alone moves away, gloomily, to his seat on the left.)

**ALL:** Hello, Minnie! Hello, Minnie!

**MINNIE:** What's the matter? (Severely to Sonora.) You again, Sonora?

**TRIN:** Nothing, Minnie, just nonsense. They were fooling!

**MINNIE:** You'll send the whole place to rack and ruin! Disgraceful!

**JOE:** (offers her a bunch of flowers): Minnie—

**MINNIE:** I'll give up the school.

**ALL:** No, Minnie, no!—

**SONORA:** (in confusion): Say, when you are late we get impatient— And then we—

**MINNIE:** (shakes her head and smiles; she goes up to the counter and sees Handsome lost in contemplation): Handsome, why are you staring?

**HANDSOME:** (starts, smiling, perplexed): Nothing.

**ALL:** (laughing): He stared at you!

**JOE:** (offering the flowers): Minnie, I picked these flowers by the Black Torrent. Lots of them grow in my country!

**MINNIE:** Oh, thank you, Joe!—

**SONORA:** (taking a folded ribbon from his pocket): This morning a trader came to the camp from San Francisco—. He had some lace and ribbons. (unfolding the ribbon): This is one for you—. Just look, bright crimson, The color of your lips—.

**HARRY:** (unfolding a silk handkerchief): And this is blue as blue, just like your eyes!

**MINNIE:** Thank you! Thank you!

**ASHBY:** (who has risen and gone to the counter, raising his glass): Regards of Wells-Fargo!

**MINNIE:** (laughing): O what a muddle— Sit down. (Harry sits down in confusion. To Joe, who has gotten up to sharpen a pencil with a huge knife.) Sit down, Joe! Now we'll have reading. The second verse: "Purge me with hyssop, and I shall be clean—"

**TRIN:** (ingenuo) Che cos' è quest' issòpo, Minnie?

**MINNIE:** È un'erba che fa in Oriente . . .

**JOE:** (dolcemente) E qui da noi non fa?

**MINNIE:** Si, Joe, nel cuore ognun di noi ne serba un cespuglietto . . .

**JOE:** (ridendo) Nel cuore?

**MINNIE:** (seria) Nel cuore. (continuando a leggere) "Lavami e sarò bianco come neve. Poni dentro al mio petto un puro cuore, e rinnovella in me uno spirito eletto . . . " (interrompendosi) Ciò vuol dire, ragazzi, che non v'è al mondo, preccatore cui non s'apra una via di redenzione . . . Sappia ognuno di voi chiudere in sè questa suprema verità d'amore. (Ashby e Rance si sono avvicinati e stanno anch'ess ad ascoltare. Billy entra col suo passo furtivo, si avvicina al banco e ingoia in fretta il fondo di due o tre bio chieri, leccandone l'orlo.)

**TRIN:** (ridendo) Guarda, Minnie!

**MINNIE:** Che c' è?

**JOE:** Billy lava i bicchieri!

**BILLY:** (ridendo con un riso sornione e battendosi una mano sul petto) Buono . . .

**MINNIE:** Billy!

**NICK:** (allungandogli una pedata) Va via di qua, briccone!

**BILLY:** (lo scansa, e si avvicina a Minnie, con umiltà ipocrita) Padrona . . .

**MINNIE:** Che fai qui? Sai la lezione?

**BILLY:** Lezione, Billy? . . . (ridendo ebete) He' . . .

**MINNIE:** Sentiamo: conta fino a dieci.

**BILLY:** . . . Uno . . . due . . . tre . . . quattro . . . cinque, sei, sette . . . fante, regina e re . . . (tutti scoppiano in una risata. Minnie si alza)

**MINNIE:** Che stupida marmotta! E Wowkle? L'hai sposata?

**BILLY:** (con aria sorniona) Ora tardi sposare . . . Abbiamo bimbo . . . (Un'altra risata accoglie quest'uscita. Minnie lo chiama. Egli si avvicina a malincuore. La fanciulla gli toglie di tasca i sigari rubati)

**JOE:** What is this hyssop, Minnie?

**MINNIE:** A plant that grows in the East.

**JOE:** And don't it grow out here?

**MINNIE:** Yes, Joe, in everybody's heart A little bit is growing—

**JOE:** (laughing): In the heart?

**MINNIE:** (gently): The heart. (Resumes the reading): "Wash me and I shall be whiter than snow. Create in me a clean heart, O God, renew a righteous spirit Within me—" (Breaking off): And that means, you boys, that all throughout The wide world there's no sinner Who can't find a way or means of redemption—. Don't we all of us know in our hearts That best and highest teaching of love? (Ashby and Rance have come closer and stand listening. Enter Billy with his usual stealthy steps; he goes to the counter and empties the dregs of two or three glasses, licking the brims.)

**TRIN:** (laughing): Look, Minnie!

**MINNIE:** What's up?

**JOE:** Billy's washing the glasses.

**BILLY:** (laughing slyly and smacking himself on the chest): Good—

**MINNIE:** Billy!

**NICK:** (giving him a kick): Get out of that, you rascal!

**BILLY:** (goes up to Minnie with feigned humility): Please, missis—

**MINNIE:** What d'you want? Know your lessons?

**BILLY:** (as before): Lessons, Billy? . . . (laughs drunkenly): He!—

**MINNIE:** Let's hear you; count up to seven.

**BILLY:** —One—two—three— four—five—six, seven—knave, queen and king— (All burst out laughing, Minnie gets up.)

**MINNIE:** You silly old idiot! And Wowkle—have you married her?

**BILLY:** (with a sly air): Too late to marry now!— We've got a baby— (Another burst of laughter greets this excuse. Minnie calls him and he goes up to her reluctantly. The girl takes the stolen cigars from his pocket.)

# Act I

MINNIE: Questo pezzente un giorno l'ha sedotta . . .
Furfante!
Ed hanno un bimbo di sei mesi!
Guai a te se domani non la sposi!
Ora, via!
(*Lo afferra per un orecchio e tra le risa di tutti lo mette alla porta. Ritorna al banco. Rance, che per tutto il tempo ha osservato le sue mosse, si avvicina al banco. A un tratto si sente il galoppo di un cavallo*)

NICK: (*accorrendo alla porta*) La posta!
POSTIGLIONE: (*fuori, apparendo sulla porta, a cavallo*) Hello, ragazzi!
(*dà le lettere a Nick, che le porta dentro*)
State attenti! s'è visto sul sentiero un ceffo di meticcio . . .
(*Nick distribuisce; un dispaccio per Ashby; tettere a Happy, Bello e Joe; a Harry un giornale. Ashby apre il dispaccio, lo legge con stupore*)

ASHBY: Postiglione!
(*Entra il Postiglione. Tutti gli sono intorno. Ashby lo interroga*)
ASHBY: Conosci certa Nina? Nina Micheltorena?

MINNIE: (*interponendosi, con aria di donna informata*) È una finta spagnuola
nativa di Cachuca, una sirena
che fa molto consumo
di nerofumo
per farsi l'occhio languido.
. . . Chiedetene ai ragazzi!
(*Trin e Sonora che sono li presso, imbarazzati, fan cenni di diniego. Il Postiglione esce con Nick. Minnie torna al banco. Happy, Bello, Joe ed altri, in varie pose, chi più indietro, chi più avanti scorrono le loro lettere. Harry legge il giornale. Ashby e Rance si avanzano verso il proscenio*)

ASHBY: Sceriffo, questa sera ho Ramerrez al laccio . . .
RANCE: Come?
ASHBY: (*mostrandogli il dispaccio ripiegato*) L'avventuriera
mi dice che sa il covo del bandito
e che stanotte a mezzanotte vada
alle "Palme."
RANCE: (*dubitoso*) Quella Micheltorena è una canaglia.
Ashby non vi fidate: è un brutto azzardo.
ASHBY: (*strizzando l'occhio*) Hum!
Vendette di donne innamorate . . .
Ad ogni modo, Rance, tengo

---

MINNIE: This thieving red-skin has betrayed her—
The rascal!
They've got a baby six months old!
There'll be trouble if you don't marry her tomorrow!
Off you go!
(*Takes him by the ear, and, amidst general laughter, puts him out of the door. Goes back to the counter. Rance, who has been watching her movements throughout, approaches the counter. The gallop of a horse is suddenly heard.*)

NICK: (*running to the door*): The post!
POST-BOY: (*outside, appears in the doorway on horseback*): Hello, you boys!
(*Gives Nick the letters, who carries them in.*)
Be on your guard! A greaser has been seen
Hanging round the district.
(*Nick distributes the post: a despatch for Ashby; letters for Happy, Handsome and Joe; a newspaper for Harry, Ashby opens his despatch, reads it with amazement.*)

ASHBY: Express! (*Enter the Post-Boy; all gather round him. Ashby questions him.*)
ASHBY: Do you know a certain Nina? Nina Micheltorena?

MINNIE: (*interposing, full of information*): She's a cute Spanish creature,
A native of Cachuca; we all know her;
A designing hussy,
Who spends her time ogling all the men—
You ask the boys about her!
(*Trin and Sonora who are near her, make embarrassed negative signs. The Post-Boy goes out with Nick; Minnie goes back to the counter. Happy, Handsome, Joe, and others, in various positions, some at the back, some more in front, peruse their letters. Harry reads his paper, Ashby and Rance advance towards the footlights.*)

ASHBY: Sheriff, tonight I'll have Ramerrez swinging—
RANCE: What's that?
ASHBY: (*showing him the folded despatch*): The adventuress, Nina, has betrayed his movements.
Tonight, at midnight, he'll be at the "Palmeto."
RANCE: (*doubting*): That Micheltorena is a wrong 'un.
Ashby, don't you trust her.
ASHBY: (*winking his eye*): Hum!
A love-lorn woman's revenge—
I've got him, Rance, absolutely.
(*Rance and Ashby move away again under the stairs and con-

---

l'invito.
(*Rance e Ashby si appartano di nuovo presso il sottoscala, continuando a parlare fra loro. Sparsi qua e là i minatori continuano a leggere le loro lettere; chi straccia con dispetto la lettera dopo averla letta, dicendo: maledetta! Altri bacia la lettera e la mette con grande cura nel portafoglio; altri leggono e ripongono le loro lettere dicendo: ve bene, Minnie, al banco, parla scherzosa con Sonora e Trin*)

BELLO: (*leggendo una lettera*)
Ketty sposa?
E chi sposa la mia Ketty?
Senti!
L'orologiaio suo vicino . . .
Quel vecchio sordo! . . .
Mah! . . .
(*sospiro di chi ricorda molte cose*)
Povera Ketty!

HAPPY: (*leggende, sotto voce*)
" . . . Perfino il pappagallo s'e avvilito; non grida più:
"Buongiorno, fratellino!" ma chiama:
"Happy" e poi dice:
"Partito!"

HARRY: (*leggendo il giornale*) Incendi, guerre, terremoti, piene . . .
Quante cose nel mondo!
E al mio paese, che faranno laggiù? Staranno bene?

JOE: (*leggendo*) "Pur troppo, Joe, ci son notizie tristi . . ."
(*continua a leggere sotto voce, poi dà un gran pugna sul tavolo e si butta di schianto sdraiato su una panca con la testa fra le mani, mugolando*)

TUTTI: (*facendoglisi attorno*)
—Joe, che c'è?
—Brutte nuove?
—Su, coraggio!

JOE: (*si alza, sbatte in terra il berretto, con ira dolorosa*) Ed anche nonna se n'è andata!
(*stà per dire altre parole, ma si trattiene, si morde un dito, asciuga gli occhi col dorso della mano e ordina, seccamente*)
Whisky!
(*va al banco dove è Minnie, beve ed esce*)
(*Nick è uscito. Ashby saluta Rance e Minnie stringendo loro la mano, e gli altri con un gesto ed esce. Rance rimane presso al banco e guarda Minnie*)

---

tinue their conversation. The miners, grouped about the stage, go on reading their letters. Minnie, at the counter, is joking with Sonora and Trin.*)

HANDSOME: (*reading a letter, sotto voce, but audibly*): Kitty married?
And who is marrying my Kitty? Fancy!
The clockmaker, her neighbor— That deaf old mummy!
Well!—
(*Sighing at the memory of many things*):
Poor little Kitty!

HAPPY: (*reading, sotto voce*): At last the poor old parrot is discouraged;
He no longer calls:
"Good morning, brother!"
But says:
"Happy," and then says:
"He's gone!"

HARRY: (*reading his paper*):
Great fires, wars, earthquakes, floods—
What awful disasters!—
In my own country,
How many things be there?
How are they faring?—

JOE: (*reads*): "Yes, truly, Joe, my news is sad"—
(*Continues reading sotto voce; suddenly he bangs the table with his fist, throws himself with a crash on a bench and howls, his head in his hands.*)

ALL: (*surrounding him*):—Joe, what's wrong?
Bad tidings?
Pluck up courage!

JOE: (*throwing his cap onto the ground in angry grief*):
(*Reads*):
"Your poor old granny is no more!"
(*Is about to say more, but restrains himself, bites his finger, wipes his eyes with the back of his hand, and dryly orders*):
Whisky!
(*Nick goes to the counter. Joe sits down again, motionless, head in hands; all round him look at him in silence. Harry folds up his newspaper, Happy and Handsome put their letters back in their pockets. Nick brings Joe the whisky and goes out with Ashby, who shakes hands with Rance and Minnie, and nods good-bye to the others. In the dancing hall the

NICK: (*reintrando*) C'è fuori uno straniero . . .

MINNIE: Chi è?

NICK: Non l'ho mai visto . . . Sembra di San Francisco. Mi ha chiesto un whisky ed acqua.

MINNIE: Whisky ed acqua? Che son questi pasticci?

NICK: È quello che gli ho detto: Alla ''Polka'' si beve l' whisky schietto.

MINNIE: Bene, venga. Gli aggiusteremo i ricci. (*Nick esce di nuovo. Intorno a un tavolo rimangono tre o quattro a giuocare ai dadi; dopo poco se ne vanno; tutti a poco a poco si squagliano, chi nella sala da ballo, chi esce, chi va sopra. Rimangono soli Minnie e Rance. Rance sì fa più dappresso a Minnie, parlandole con voce tremante di desiderio*)

RANCE: Ti voglio bene, Minnie . . .

MINNIE: (*sorridendo, indifferente*) Non lo dite . . .

RANCE: Mille dollari, qui, se tu mi baci!

MINNIE: (*nervosa, ridendo*) Rance, voi mi fate ridere . . . Su via, finitela!

RANCE: (*incalzandola*) Tu non puoi star qui sola! Ti sposo . . .

MINNIE: (*scansandolo, ironica*) E vostra moglie, che dirà?

RANCE: Se tu lo vuoi, mai più mi rivedrà!

MINNIE: (*con fierezza*) Rance, basta! M'offendete! Vivo sola così, vio lo sapete, perchè così mi piace . . . (*frugandosi in petto e facendo luccicare in faccia a Rance una pistola*) (*basso, sommesso, ma con forza*) con questa compagnia sicura e buona, che mai non m'abbandona . . . Rance, lasciatemi in pace. (*si ripone la pistola nel petto. Rance si allontana da banco in silenzio, siede al tavolo del faraone e nervosa mente mischia le carte.*)

MINNIE: (*lo guarda di sottecchi, poi gli si avvicina*) Siete in collera, Rance? Perchè? Vi ho detto il mio pensiero schietto . . .

*music starts a dance. All go over there. Joe drinks his whisky off at a gulp and goes out. Rance stays by the counter watching Minnie.*)

NICK: (*re-entering*): A stranger's just outside—

MINNIE: Who's he?

NICK: I've never seen him . . . Seems like a San Franciscan. He wants some whisky and water.

MINNIE: Whisky and water? What's all this nonsense?

NICK: Why, that's just what I told him: At the ''Polka'' we drink our whisky neat!

MINNIE: Fetch him in. We'll curl his hair for him. (*Nick goes out again. Rance draws near to Minnie, and speaks to her with a voice trembling with passion.*)

RANCE: I'm dead gone on you, Minnie . . .

MINNIE: (*smiling, indifferent*): You don't say so . . .

RANCE: A thousand dollars down if you will kiss me!

MINNIE: (*nervous, laughing*): Rance, you make me laugh at you . . . Be off, have done with it!

RANCE: (*edging up to her*): You can't stay here alone! I'll marry you . . .

MINNIE: (*dodging him ironically*): And your good wife? What of her?

RANCE: You've but to say so, she'll never see me more!

MINNIE: (*haughtily*): Rance, stop it! You annoy me! If I live like this, you know quite well It's because I like it . . . (*Feeling in her bodice and flashing a pistol before Rance's eyes*): I've got a sure and true protector by me, Who never will desert me. Rance, leave me in peace. (*Puts the pistol back in her bodice—Rance silently moves away from the counter, sits down at the faro table, and absentmindedly starts playing.—A pause.*)

MINNIE: (*looks at him surreptitiously, then goes up to him*): Are you cross with me, Rance? What for? I've told you straight what's in my mind.—

RANCE: (*getta le carte sul tavolo con un gesto violento, poi con voce aspra e tagliente*) Minnie, dalla mia casa son partito, ch'è là dai monti, sopra un altro mare: non un rimpianto, Minnie, m'ha seguito, non un rimpianto in me potea lasciare! Nessuno mai mi amò, nessuno ho amato, nessuna cosa mai mi diè piacere! Chiudo nel petto un cuor di biscazziere, amaro e avvelenato, che ride dell' amore e del destino: mi son messo in cammino attratto sol dal fascino dell'oro. È questo il solo che non m'ha ingannato. Or per un bacio tuo getto un tesoro!

MINNIE: (*sognando*) L'amore è un'altra cosa . . .

RANCE: (*beffardo*) Poesia!

MINNIE: Laggiù nel Soledad, ero piccina, avevo una stanzuccia affumicata nella taverna sopra la cucina. Ci vivevo con babbo e mamma mia. Tutti ricordo: vedo le persone entrare e uscire a sera. Mamma facea da cuoca e cantiniera, babbo dava le carte a faraone. Mamma era bella, aveva un bel piedino. Qualche volta giuocava anch'essa; ed io, che me ne stavo sotto al tavolino aspettando cader qualche moneta per comprarmi dei dolci, la vedevo serrar furtiva il piede al babbo mio . . . Si amavan tanto! . . . Anch'io così vorrei trovare un uomo: e forse l'amerei.

RANCE: (*guardandola fisso, minaccioso, poi reprimendosi*) Forse, Minnie, la perla è già trovata? (*Minnie stà per rispondere, quando Nick rientra. È con lui Dick Johnson. Ha sotto il braccio la sella del suo cavallo*)

JOHNSON: (*posando la sella in terra, fieramente*) Chi c'è, per farmi i ricci? . . .

MINNIE: (*ha uno scatto di sorpresa, come chi riconesce una persona. Ma si frena subito*) Salute allo straniero!

JOHNSON: (*anche lui, dopo un moto di stupore, con fare più dolce*) Io son quello che chiesi whisky ed acqua.

RANCE: (*throws down the cards with a violent gesture, then in a harsh and strident voice*): Minnie, when I left my little home Beyond the mountains, across the ocean: Nobody cared, Minnie, not a creature, Nor did I waste a tear at leaving! No one loved me, and I loved no one, And no one and nothing gave me pleasure! Deep in my breast I have a gambler's heart, Embittered, warped and poisoned, Which laughs at love, and mocks at destiny. I set forth on my journey, Attracted by nothing else but gold, And gold alone has not deceived me; Now for a kiss from you, I'll give a fortune!—

MINNIE: (*mockingly*): Real love is very different.

RANCE: (*mockingly*): Romantic!

MINNIE: Down home in Soledad, when I was little, I had a tiny, smoky little room above the kitchen, In my father's inn, And I lived there with father and mother. Ah!—I've not forgotten; Even now I see the men come in at sundown. Mother saw to the cooking and to the bar. Father dealt the cards for faro. Mother, she was lovely, her little feet were pretty; Sometimes she'd take a hand at faro, And I used to hide underneath the table, Hoping someone would drop some money; And sometimes I'd see her snuggle her feet close up to father's. Oh, how she loved him! Ah! So I don't want to take a husband Unless I really love him.

RANCE: (*sneeringly*): Perhaps you have found the treasure already? (*Minnie is about to reply, when Nick re-enters, and with him is Dick Johnson.*)

JOHNSON: (*throwing his saddle down, haughtily*): Who wanted to curl my hair?

MINNIE: (*gives a start of surprise, and recognition—but controls herself at once*): Good evening to you, stranger!

JOHNSON: (*also gives a start of surprise, then says more gently*): I'm the man who asked for water with his whisky.

# Act I

MINNIE: (*premurosa*) Davvero? Nick, il signore prende l' whisky come gli pare.
(*Controscena di meraviglia di Nick e Rance. Nick cerca sotto il banco la bottiglia di soda. Rance osserva, con le ciglie aggrottate*)

MINNIE: (*eagerly*): Not really? Nick, the stranger takes his whisky as he likes it.
(*Amazement on Nick's and Rance's part. Nick looks for a bottle of soda under the counter. Rance looks on, frowning.*)

MINNIE: (*indicando a Johnson una panca, un po' imbarazzata*) Sedetevi . . . Dovete essere stanco . . .

MINNIE: (*slightly embarrassed, points to a bench*): Be seated. I guess you're tired.

JOHNSON: (*con lo stesso imbarazzo, guardandola*) La ragazza del campo?

JOHNSON: (*equally embarrassed, looking at her*): The Girl of the camp?

MINNIE: (*arrossendo*) Si.

MINNIE: (*blushing*): Yes.

RANCE: (*provocante e canzonatorio, avvicinandosi a Johnson*) Nessun straniero può entrare al campo. Certo, voi sbagliaste sentiero, giovinotto. Per caso, andavate a trovare Nina Micheltorena?

RANCE: (*aggressively and rudely, goes up to Johnson*): We don't let strangers inside the camp. Don't you think you've struck the wrong turning? I fancy you set out to visit Nina Micheltorena?

RANCE: (*si è avvicinato al banco. Con un colpo rovescia il bicchiere di Johnson*) Mister Johnson, infine voi m'avete seccato! Sono Jack Rance, sceriffo. Non mi lascio burlare. Che venite a far qui?
(*Johnson si ritrae d'un passo e lo guarda sdegnosamente. Rance va alla porta della sala da ballo e chiama:*)
Ragazzi! Uno straniero ricusa confessare perchè si trova al campo!
(*Alcuni minatori escono dalla sala da ballo, investendo Johnson*)

RANCE: (*who has come up to the counter, knocks Johnson's glass off it with a blow*): Mister Johnson, your behavior's offensive; I am Rance, the Sheriff. I'm not here to be fooled. What's your business up here?
(*Johnson draws back a pace and looks at him contemptuously.*)
(*Rance goes to the door of the dance-hall and calls*): You fellows, come here a moment! This stranger won't explain His business in the camp!
(*Some miners come out of the dance-hall, clapping Johnson on the shoulder.*)

I MINATORI: Chi è? Dov' è? Lo faremo cantare!

MINERS: He won't? He won't? We'll make him speak up!

MINNIE: (*arrestandoli con un gesto imperioso*) Io lo conosco! Innanzi al campo intero stò garante per Johnson!
(*L'intervento di Minnie calma tutti i minatori, che si avvicinano a Johnson, salutando con fare cordiale*)

MINNIE: (*stopping them with an imperious gesture*): Wait a minute! I know him, boys, I know him— and I'll vouch for Johnson!
(*Minnie's intervention pacifies the miners, who go up to Johnson and welcome him with cordial faces.*)

SONORA: Buona sera, Mister Johnson!

SONORA: Well, good evening, Mister Johnson!

JOHNSON: (*con effusione, stringendo le mani che gli si tendone*) Ragazzi, buona sera!

JOHNSON: (*cordially, shaking the outstretched hands*): Good evening, good evening!

TRIN: (*indicando Rance, che si è ritirato indietro, più pallido del consueto*) Ho piacere per lui! Questo cialtrone smetterà quel suo fare da padrone!

TRIN: (*pointing to Rance, who has withdrawn into the background, paler than usual*) What a snub for old Rance! The fool will see at last He's not the master of the "Polka"!

HARRY: (*a Johnson, indicando la sala da ballo*) Mister Johnson, un valzer?

HARRY: (*to Johnson, pointing to the dancing hall*): Mister Johnson, you dancing?

JOHNSON: Accetto.
(*offrendo il braccio a Minnie*) Permettete?
(*Tutti guardano Minnie, fra lo stupore e la gioia, sorridendo come per incitare Minnie a ballare. Soltanto Rance ba l'aspetto accigliato*)

JOHNSON: With pleasure.
(*offering his arm to Minnie.*) Permit me!
(*All look at Minnie, with mingled surprise and pleasure, smiling as if to urge her to dance. Only Rance is frowning.*)

MINNIE: (*confusa, ridendo*) Io? Scusatemi, Johnson: voi non lo crederete, ma non ho mai ballato in vita mia . . .

MINNIE: (*laughing in confusion*): I? Excuse me, Sir! Perhaps you will not believe it, but I've never danced in all my life.

JOHNSON: (*sorridendo*) Andiamo . . .

JOHNSON: (*smiling*): Dance now, then—

TUTTI: Avanti, Minnie! Sarebbe scortesia!

ALL: Buck up, Minnie!

MINNIE: (*decidendosi, graziosamente*) E andiamo pure!
(*prende il braccio di Johnson*)

MINNIE: (*making up her mind graciously*): Well then, let's try it!
(*takes Johnson's arm.*)

TUTTI: Avanti! Musica! Hip! Hurrah!
(*Trin e Sonora tengono aperto l'uscio della sala: Harry ed altri minatori battono il tempo con le mani: Minnie e Johnson scompaiono nella sala, danzando, seguiti dagli uomini; restano Sonora, Trin, Bello, Harry, Rance*)

ALL: Strike up! Hip! Hurrah!
(*They all accompany the music: the first quarter by lightly stamping their feet on the floor; the others by lightly clapping their hands, thus following the two dancers. Trin and Sonora keep the door of the dance-room open. Sonora, Trin, Handsome, Harry and Rance remain on the stage.*)

NICK: (*rientrando*) Dov' è Minnie? A cavallo! A cavallo!
(*all'aprirsi della porta Castro ba guardato dentro; ba visto Johnson; Johnson lo ba notato*)

NICK: (*re-entering*): Where's Minnie? Get the horses! Get the horses! (*When the door is opened, Castro has looked in; has seen Johnson, and Johnson has seen him.*)

CASTRO: (*fra sè, lieto*) Non è preso! È nel ballo!

CASTRO: (*joyfully, to himself*): He's not taken! He is dancing!

UOMINI DEL CAMPO E DEL MONTE: (*uscendo dalla sala da ballo*) Dove si va?

MEN FROM THE CAMP AND THE MOUNTAIN: (*coming out of the dancing hall*): Where are you off to?

RANCE: S'insegue Ramerrez!

RANCE: We're tracking Ramerrez!

NICK: (*a Sonora, preoccupato per Minnie e il barile*) E l'oro?

NICK: (*anxious on account of Minnie and the gold barrel*): But the gold?

SONORA: (*con galanteria*) Gli occhi di Minnie bastano a guardare il tesoro!
(*Tutti escono. Fra essi il cantastorie Jake Wallace. Nick si trae dalla cintura la pistola e si mette sulla porta a fare la guardia. Poco appresso esce dalla sala Johnson: vede Castro, si domina: Castro finge di essere arso di sete*)

SONORA: (*gallantly*): Minnie's lovely eyes Will surely guard the treasure!
(*All go out; among them the minstrel, Jake Wallace. Nick takes his pistol from his belt and stands in the doorway on guard. Soon Johnson comes out of the dancing hall, sees Castro, controls himself. Castro pretends to be consumed with thirst.*)

CASTRO: (*a Nick*) Aguardiente!
(*Nick va dietro il banco a prendere l'acquavite: Johnson si avvicina a Castro senza farsi notare*)

CASTRO: (*to Nick*): Bring me some brandy!
(*Nick goes behind the counter and fetches the brandy.*)

CASTRO: (*pianissimo, rapido*) Mi son lasciato prendere per sviarli. Mi seguono nel bosco i nostri. Presto udrete un fischio; se c' è il colpo, col fischio rispondete.
(*Nick porta a Castro l'acquavite: Johnson si volge, indifferente:*)

CASTRO: (*to Johnson, very softly, quickly*): I let them take me to mislead them. Our men are close at hand, in hiding. Soon you'll hear a signal. If you're ready,

*Castro beve con avidità)*

NICK: (*a Johnson*) Quest'uomo sa la traccia di Ramerrez . . .
(*Dalla finestra, dietro il banco, si vedono apparire e sparire torce e lumi bianchi e rossi: si odono passi di cavalli: le teste dei cavalli appariscono all'altezza della finestra: si alternano voci. Rance entra con alcuni uomini*)

RANCE: (*indicando Castro*) Slegatelo!
(*Fissa Johnson, con dispetto, senza salutare; si morde di nascosto rabbiosamente una mano; ordina agli uomini di portare con sè Castro, che esce, guardando furtivamente Johnson*)
Ora via!
(*Partono: Nick, sulla porta, saluta*)

NICK: Buona fortuna!
(*Nick si dispone a chiudere la "Polka". Sale al piano superiore e spegne il lume: spegne, qua e là, lumi e candele; va alla sala da ballo; Minnie ne esce; Nick entra, spegne e ritorna*)

MINNIE: (*a Johnson*) Oh, Mister Johnson, siete rimasto indietro a farmi compagnia per custodir la casa?

JOHNSON: (*con un lieve turbamento*) Se volete . . .
(*siede presso al tavolo del giuoco. Minnie rimane in piedi dinnanzi a lui, appoggiata al tavolo. una pausa*)
Che strana cosa!
Ritrovarvi qui
dove ognuno può entrare
col tranquillo pretesto
di bere, e con l'intento
di rubare . . .

MINNIE: Vi dò la mia parola
che saprei tener fronte
a chiunque . . .

JOHNSON: (*osservandola, sorridendo*) Anche a chi
non volesse rubare
più che un bacio?

MINNIE: (*ridendo*) Anche!
Questo mi è accaduto, talvolta . . .
(*abbassando gli occhi con grazia*)
Ma il primo bacio debbo darlo ancora.

JOHNSON: (*guardandola con interesse crescente*) Davvero?
Ed abitate qui alla "Polka"?

MINNIE: Abito una capanna a mezzo il monte.

JOHNSON: Meritate di meglio.

---

You answer with a signal.
(*Nick brings Castro the brandy. Johnson turns away indifferently. Castro drinks greedily.*)

NICK: (*to Johnson*): This man can put us on the trail of Ramerrez.—
(*From the window, behind the counter, torches and red and white lights are seen flashing past; horses are heard stepping; and voices are heard. Rance comes in with some men.*)

RANCE: (*pointing to Castro*): Untie him!
(*Stares at Johnson, rudely, without nodding, biting his hand with rage; orders the men to take away Castro, who goes out, furtively looking at Johnson.*) Let's be off!
(*They go off. Nick nods to them from the door.*)

NICK: Good luck to you!
(*Nick starts closing the "Polka." He goes up to the floor above and puts out the light, puts out the lights here and there, and goes to the dancing hall. Minnie comes out of it. Nick enters, puts out the lights and comes back.*)

MINNIE: (*to Johnson*): Mister Johnson,
Have you been kind enough
To stay behind and keep me company?

JOHNSON: (*slightly perturbed*): If you're willing.
(*Sits down at the card table. Minnie remains standing in front of him, leaning against the table.*)
Curious thing!
To come across you here,
Where anyone can come
Who wants to drink—
Or to rob you.

MINNIE: You bet your bottom dollar
I should know what to do
With a fellow—

JOHNSON: (*watching her, smiling*): Even if he came
To rob you of a kiss?

MINNIE: (*laughing*): You're quite right there!
Not the first time it's happened;
(*lowering her eyes with charm*):
But I know what I'm about, and my first kiss;
Why, I've still to give it.

JOHNSON: (*looking at her with growing interest*): Not really?
D'you live here at the "Polka"?

MINNIE: No, in a cabin half-way up the mountain.

JOHNSON: You are worth something better.

---

MINNIE: Mi contento: a me basta;
credete.
Ci vivo sola sola, senza timore . . .
(*una pausa*)
Io sento che anche in voi mi fiderei,
ben ch'io non so chi siate . . .

JOHNSON: Non so ben neppur io
quello che sono.
Amai la vita, e l'amo,
e ancor bella mi appare.
Certo anche voi l'amate,
ma non avete tanto
vissuto per guardare fino in fondo
alle cose del mondo . . .

MINNIE: Non so, non vi comprendo.
Io non son che una povera fanciulla
oscura e buona a nulla:
mi dite delle cose tanto belle
che forse non intendo . . .
Non so che sia, ma sento
nel cuore uno scontento
d'esser così piccina,
e un desiderio d'innalzarmi a voi
su, su, come le stelle,
per esservi vicina,
per potervi parlare.

JOHNSON: Quello che tacete
me l'ha detto il cuore,
quando il braccio
v'offersi alla danza con me:
contro il mio petto
vi sentii tremare,
e provai una gioia strana,
una nuova pace,
che dir non so!

MINNIE: Come voi, leggermi
in cuor non so:
ma ho l'anima piena
di tanta allegrezza,
di tanta paura,
(*Nick è apparso sulla soglia, con aria preoccupata: Minnie resta contrariata*)
Che cosa c'è?

NICK: Guardatevi.
S'è visto qui attorno un altro ceffo messicano . . .

MINNIE: (*alzandosi, verso la porta*) Dove, Nick?

JOHNSON: (*trattenendola, con mistero*) Non andate!
(*Si ode un fischio acuto, nella notte. Johnson fra sè*)
Il segnale!

MINNIE: (*a un tratto timorosa, come rifugiandosi accanto a Johnson*) Ascoltate!
Che sarà questo fischio?
(*indica il barile*)
In quel barile, Johnson, c'è un tesoro.
Ci ripongono l'oro
i ragazzi . . .

JOHNSON: E vi lasciano così?

---

MINNIE: I don't want it.
This just suits me, I tell you.
I'm proud to live alone, and don't know
What fear is. Now I feel quite safe with you
And feel I can trust you,
Tho' you're a stranger to me.

JOHNSON: Really, I myself hardly know what I am.
I've lived my life, and enjoyed it.
I'm enjoying it now!
And so have you enjoyed your life;
But you have not yet lived it
For all its worth, and tasted
The very last drop in the cup.

MINNIE: Perhaps not, perhaps not—
I am only a common little creature,
Obscure and good for nothing.
You talk to me in new and lovely language
Beyond my understanding.
I can't explain it,
But down in my heart I feel discontented
That I should be so little,
And a longing to raise myself to you,
High as the stars.
A longing to be near you,
To be able to speak with you.

JOHNSON: What you cannot say
Has been revealed by your heart,
When my arm circled your waist
In the dance just now:
When against my heart
I could feel yours beat,
Mine was flooded with joy divine,
And a wondrous calm
I cannot describe.

MINNIE: Ah, that I could read
My heart like you!
(*Nick comes in trembling.*) All that I know is
That I'm full of joy,
And yet of fear . . .
(*Breaks off in annoyance, seeing Nick.*)
What do you want?

NICK: (*fearfully*): Take warning.
Another greaser is skulking round the camp.

MINNIE: (*rising, goes towards the door*): Oh, where?

JOHNSON: (*holding her back*):
Stay here!
(*A shrill whistle resounds through the darkness. Johnson to himself*):
The signal!

MINNIE: (*suddenly frightened, as if seeking protection with Johnson*): Just listen!
Whatever's that whistle?
(*Pointing to the barrel.*)
In that small keg, there, Johnson, there's a fortune.
This is where the boys
Leave their gold.

JOHNSON: And they leave you alone like this?

MINNIE: Ogni notte rimangon qui a vegliarlo
a turno, un po' per uno.
Stanotte son partiti sulle peste di quel dannato . . .
(*con impeto*)
Oh, ma, se qualcuno
vuole quell'oro, prima di toccarlo,
dovrà uccidermi qui!

JOHNSON: Minnie!
E potete correr tanto rischio per ciò che non è vostro?

MINNNIE: (*posa il piede sul barile come per custodirlo*) Oh, lo fareste anche voi!
Se sapeste quanta fatica costa, e com'è caro
questo denaro!
E una lotta superba!
l'alcali, il sasso, la creta, la zolla:
tutto è nemico! S'accoscian sull'erba
umida: il fango negli occhi, nell'ossa,
nel cuore! E un giorno, con l'anima frolla,
col dorso ricurvo, con arso il cervello,
sull'orlo a una fossa,
in riva a un ruscello
s'adagian: non sorgono più!
(*si sofferma, pensosa; si commove, a un ricordo; siede sul barile*)
Povera gente! Quanti son di loro
che han lasciato lontano una famiglia,
una sposa, dei bimbi,
e son venuti a morir come cani,
in mezzo alla fanghiglia,
per mandare un po' d'oro
ai cari vecchi, ed ai bimbi lontani!
(*risoluta, con semplicità*)
Ecco, Johnson, perchè
chi vuol quest'oro, prima
passerà su di me!

JOHNSON: (*con subito impeto*)
Oh, non temete, nessuno ardirà!
(*con un movimento appassionato*)
Come mi piace sentirvi parlare!
E me ne debbo andare . . .
Avrei voluto
salire a darvi l'ultimo saluto
nella vostra capanna . . .

MINNIE: (*malinconica*) Dovete proprio andare?
Che peccato!
(*si avvicina alla porta stà un momento in ascolto*)
I ragazzi saranno qui fra poco.
Quando saran tornati, io me ne andrò.
Se volete venirmi a salutare,
seguiremo la conversazione

MINNIE: Every night they stay here and sleep around it.
Taking turns to guard it.
To-night they're all gone off
On the track of that rascal. (*Impetuously.*)
Oh! whoever wants that gold,
Can only get it
If he kills me first!

JOHNSON: Minnie!
Do you mean that you would run such risks
For that which is another's?

MINNIE: (*places her foot on the keg as if to guard it*): Oh, but you'd do the same!
If you knew how hard they work to get it!
What all this dearly won gold means to them!
It's a desperate struggle!
Alkali, rocks, the clay, the earth:
All dead aginst 'em!
They squat on the damp and dirty ground:
Till the dirt fills their eyes,
Their bones and their hearts!
And then one day with back bent,
With spirit broken, with brain on fire,
On the edge of a sluice, on the bank of a stream,
They lie down, and they don't rise again!
(*She pauses, lost in thought, and moved by a reminiscence, sits down on the keg.*)
Poor, wretched fellows! Scarce a man among them
Who hasn't left some people far away.
A wife or some children;
While he has come out to die,
Like a dog or a packhorse in the mire,
Just to send home some money
To help his folk at home and his children
(*Determinedly*):
That's why the man
Who wants to take their gold
Will have to first kill me!

JOHNSON: (*on a sudden impulse*): Oh, have no fears, no one will dare!
(*With an impassioned movement*):
How much I like to hear you speak!
But I am bound to go now, I am bound to go:
Yet I wanted to say good-bye to you once more,
In your cabin on the hillside.

MINNIE: (*dejectedly*): Oh, must you really go now?
What a pity!
(*Goes to the door and listens for a moment.*)
The boys will be back quite soon now.
When they are back again, then I can go.
If you want to come and see my cab-

standoci accanto al fuoco . . .

JOHNSON: (*esita, poi decidendosi*) Grazie, Minnie . . .
Verrò.

MINNIE: (*scherzosa e triste*) Non vi aspettate molto!
Non ho che trenta dollari soli di educazione . . .
(*si sforza a ridere, ma gli occhi le si gonfiano di lacrime*)
Se studiavo di più, che avrei potuto essere?
Ci pensate?

JOHNSON: (*commosso, come fantasticando*) Ciò che avremmo potuto essere!
Io lo comprendo ora soltanto che vi guardo, Minnie!

MINNIE: (*asciugandosi una lacrima*) Davvero? . . .
Ma che vale!
(*risale la scena, appoggia le braccia al banco colla faccia nascosta, singhiozzando*)
Io non son che una povera fanciulla oscura, e buona a nulla . . .

JOHNSON: (*le si avvicina, con tenerezza*) No, Minnie, non piangete . . .
Voi non vi conoscete.
Siete una creatura
d'anima buona e pura . . .
e avete un viso d'angiolo!
(*Prende la sella, si avvia verso la porta con un gesto violento. Sta un momento in ascolto, poi apre, esce rapidamente. Nick accorre, cautamente abbassa i lumi intorno. Il silenzio è profondo. Nick si fa sulla porta e l'apre, aspettando che la padrona esca. Minnie come stordita, rimane ferma in mezzo alla stanza oscura, illuminata solo dai guizzi del lumicino del sottoscala. A un tratto, come perduta in un ricordo inebriante, mormora, piano:*)

MINNIE:
Ha detto . . .
Come ha detto?
(*raccogliendosi tutta in un sospiro e coprendosi il viso con le mani*)
Un viso d'angiolo! . . . .
(*Cala la tela lentamente*)

in,
We might go on with our conversation
Cosily by my fireside.

JOHNSON: Thank you, Minnie! I'll come.

MINNIE: Don't expect too much of me!
I've only thirty dollars' worth of education.
(*She attempts to laugh, but her eyes fill with tears.*)
If I'd studied more, you can't tell what I might have been!
Don't you think so?

JOHNSON: (*touched, half playfully*): When I think of what we might have been!
I understand it, Minnie,
When I look at you!

MINNIE: (*wiping away a tear*): D'you mean it?
But what good is it?
A useless, good-for-nothing—
(*Comes up the stage, leans her arms against the counter, sobbing, with her face hidden.*)
I'm only a poor, simple girl,
Who's no good for anything—

JOHNSON: (*goes up to her, tenderly*): No, do not cry, dear Minnie,
You don't know yourself.
Nothing really matters
When you've a good, pure nature.
And you've the face of an angel!
(*Takes his saddle, goes to the door with a violent gesture, stands listening a moment, then opens it and goes out quickly. Nick hastens in cautiously, lowers the lights. The silence is profound. Nick goes and opens the door, waiting for his mistress to go out. Minnie, half dazed, remains standing in the middle of the dark room, lighted only by the twinkling of the little lamp beneath the staircase.—Suddenly, as if lost in an intoxicating memory, she murmurs gently.*)

MINNIE: He said.—
What did he say?
(*Buries her face in her hands, giving vent to her feelings in a deep sigh.*)
The face of an angel!
(*The curtain falls slowly.*)

## ■ ATTO SECONDO

*L'Abitazione Di Minnie*
*È composta di una sola stanza, alla quale sovrasta un solaio, ove sono accatastati, con un certo ordine, bauli, casse vuote ed altri oggetti. La stanza è tappezzata nel gusto dell'epoca. Nel centro, in fondo, una porta che si apre sopra un breve vestibolo. A destra e a sinistra della porta, due finestre con tendine.*

## ■ ACT II

*Minnie's Dwelling*
*It consists of a single room, above which is a loft where trunks, empty boxes and various things are neatly piled up. The room is papered according to the taste of the period. In the center, at the back, is a door opening onto a short landing. On the right and left of the door, two windows with curtains.*

*Appoggiato ad una delle pareti il letto, con la testa spinta sotto la tettoia formata dal solaio, coperto fino a metà da un baldacchino di cretonne a fiorellini. Ai piedi del letto, un piccolo tavolo, con sopra una catinella e la brocca dell'acqua, ed un canterano sul quale stanno diversi oggetti destinati alla toilette femminile.*

*Da un lato, in fondo, un armadio di legno di pino, sullo sportello del quale è appeso un attaccapanni con una vestaglia, un cappellino ed uno scialletto. Accanto all'armadio, un focolare basso, sulla cui cappa stanno una vecchia pendola, un lume a petrolio senza campana, una bottiglia di whisky ed un bicchiere. Un'altra mensola a tre ripiani, accanto al focolare, con piatti, vasetti, oggetti di cucina. Dinanzi al focolare, una pelle di orso. Quasi dinanzi alla porta, un poco più verso il focolare, una tavola apparecchiata per uno. Della crema, dei biscotti, una torta, delle fette di carne, una zuccheriera. Lampada su la tavola. Fra la tavola e il focolare, una sedia a dondolo, fatta con un vecchio barile tagliato a metà e posto sopra due mezze lune di legno. Altre sedie di cuoio disposte qua e là. Alle pareti sono appese delle vecchie oleografie e molti altri bizzarri oggetti.*

*Non è passata un'ora dal primo atto. Fuori fischia il vento. I vetri sono appannati dal gelo.*

*(Quando si alza la tela Wowkle è accoccolata per terra, presso al fuoco, col bambino nella cuna portatile che ha appesa sul dorso. Con voce molle e monotona canta al bimbo una ninna nanna, cullandolo sul dorso)*

**WOWKLE:** "Il mio bimbo è grande e piccino,
è piccino e stà dentro la cuna,
è grande e tocca la luna,
tocca la luna col suo ditino.
Hao, wari! Hao, wari! . . . "
*(Billy batte all'uscio ed entra. Spesso, durante la scena, i due indiani emettono un mugolìo sordo, fra nasale e gutturale, molto simile ad un grugnito)*

**BILLY:** *(entrando, come un saluto)* Ugh . . . *(la stanza come a spiare che effetto farà la sua casa su Johnson: ha un mantello rosso*

*Running along on one of the walls is the bed, with its head underneath the room formed by the loft. It is half covered with a canopy of flowered cretonne. At the foot of the bed a small table, with handbasin and water-jug, also a bureau on which stand various feminine toilet accessories.*

*On one side, at the back, a pinewood wardrobe, on the door of which a dress, a hat and a shawl are hanging from a hook. Close by, a low fireplace, on the mantelshelf of which stand an old clock, an oil lamp without a globe, a bottle of whisky and a glass. Another three-shelved bracket close to the hearth holds plates, pots, kitchen utensils. In front of the hearth, a bear skin. Almost in front of the door, rather nearer the fireplace, is a table laid for one, with cream, biscuits, a tart, some slices of meat and a sugar basin, a lamp on the table. Between the table and the fireplace is a rocking-chair, made out of an old barrel cut in half, and set on two half-moon-shaped pieces of wood. Some other leather chairs about the room. The walls are hung with old oleographs and many other quaint objects.*

*Only one hour has elapsed since Act I. The wind is whistling outside; the panes are covered with frost.*

*(When the curtain rises Wowkle is squatting on the floor near the fire, her papoose on her back in a portable cradle. Her cape is open at the neck and turned down; it is tied round the waist with a red-fringed sash; buckskin moccasins; her hair parted in the middle, falling in two plaits tied with a ribbon. Round her neck she wears a number of strings of glass beads in various colors, also white and red striped; silver earrings and bracelets. She is young, sweet-faced, plump, supple and voluptuous; the regular type of an Indian squaw. Her eyes are small and beady. In a soft, monotonous voice she sings a lullaby to her baby, rocking it on her back.)*

**WOWKLE:** *(singing and rocking the baby)*: "Grant, O Sungod, grant thy protection,
Guard this innocent infant sleeping,
Starry guardian, ever joyful,
Faithful Moongod, ever watchful.
Hao, wari! Hao, wari!"
*(Billy knocks at the door and enters. At frequent intervals during this scene the two Indians utter a low growl, half nasal, half guttural, very like a grunt.)*

**BILLY:** *(coming in, grunts a greeting)*: Ugh!

*sopra il suo abito del primo atto. Ella appende la lanterna al chiodo di legno dell'uscio esterno. Wowkle alza la fiamma al lume della tavola)*

**MINNIE:** Billy, è fissato?

**BILLY:** Domani . . .

**MINNIE:** Sta bene. Va via.
*(Billy esce. A Wowkle)*
Stanotte, Wowkle, cena per due.

**WOWKLE:** Altro venire?
Ugh!
Mia prima d'ora.

**MINNIE:** *(appende il mantello all'attaccapanni)* Zitta, e pulisci!
Cio non ti riguarda.
Che ora è?
Sarà qui fra poco . . .
*(vede le calze stese, le strappa via, scuote Wowkle per una spalla)*
Guarda!
*(butta le calze in un cassetto. Wowkle mette i piatti sulla tavola. Minnie si guarda intorno)*
Dove hai messo le mie rose rosse?

**WOWKLE:** *(indicando il canterano, col solito grugnito)*
Ugh . . .

**MINNIE:** *(si trae dal petto la pistola e la ripone nel cassetto. Prende le rose e se la appunta fra i capelli guardandosi allo specchio)* Y bimbo come sta?
Billy davvero t'ha detto . . . ?

**WOWKLE:** Noi sposare.

**MINNIE:** *(gettandole un nastro)*
To', pel bimbo!
*(Wowkle ripone il nastro, continua ad apparecchiare. Minnie ha levato dal cassetto un paio di scarpette bianche)*
Vorrei mettermi queste.
Le scarpette di Monterey . . .
*(si siede in terra, scalzandosi rapidamente, e incomincia a infilarsene una)*
Purchè mi riesca d'infilarle . . .
Ahi!
Son strette!
*(La scarpetta, con grande sforzo è infilata. Poi anche l'altra scarpetta è calzata. Minnie si alza. Cammina un po' zoppicando)*
Guardami: credi che gli piaceranno?
*(va al canterano con aria contenta)*
Voglio vestirmi tutta
come un giorno di festa,
tutta, da capo a piedi.
*(si butta sulle spalle lo scialle e si guarda nello specchio)*
Non son poi tanto brutta . . .
*(si versa dell'acqua di Colonia nel fazzoletto)*
Anche il profumo . . .
Vedi?
*(si infila i guanti, stretti e troppo corti)*
E i guanti . . .

**MINNIE:** Billy, have you fixed it?

**BILLY:** Tomorrow . . .

**MINNIE:** That's right.
Now go.
*(Billy goes out. To Wowkle.)*
This evening, Wowkle, supper for two.

**WOWKLE:** Come another?
Ugh!
Never before.

**MINNIE:** *(hangs her cloak on the hook)*: You just get ready!
What's the time?
He's coming quite soon.
*(Sees the stockings hanging up and snatches them down, clapping Wowkle on the shoulder.)*
Look there!
*(Pops the stockings into a chest. Wowkle puts the plates on the table.)*
Where have you put my red roses?

**WOWKLE:** *(points to chest of drawers, with usual grunt)*:
Ugh . . .

**MINNIE:** *(takes the pistol from her bodice and puts it away in the chest. Fixes the roses in her hair, looking in the mirror as she does it)*: And baby, how is he?
Has Billy honestly told you?

**WOWKLE:** We get married.

**MINNIE:** *(throwing Wowkle a ribbon)*: Here!
For baby!
*(Wowkle folds the ribbon and goes on with her preparations. Minnie has taken a pair of white slippers from the chest.)*
Now I'm going to wear these—
These slippers from Monterey—
If only I'm able to get inside 'em.
Oh, they are tight! Oh, how tight!
Look at me: how do you think he'll like 'em?
I've got a fancy he'll like me in my best bib and tucker.
I'm going to wear all my finest!
*(Drapes the shawl over her shoulders and looks in the glass.)*
Well, I'm not so ugly!
*(Pours some Eau de Cologne on her handkerchief.)*
Now I'll scent it, see?
*(Puts on her gloves, tight and too short for her.)*
My gloves too, I haven't worn them for quite a year!
*(Looks at herself again, very pleased with the effect, and turns to Wowkle.)*
Think it looks a bit too dressy?

# Act II

È più d'un anno che non li metto!
*(guardandosi ancora, impacciata e contenta, e volgendosi a Wowkle)*
Dimmi, Wowkle, non gli farò l'effetto
d'essere poi troppo elegante?

WOWKLE: *(che ha assistito in piedi, immobile, alla toeletta della padrona)*
Ugh . . .
*(di fuori si bussa)*

MINNIE: *(ha un sussulto)*
Wowkle, è già qui!
*(si allaccia in fretta il corpetto, si tira su le calze, va ad aprire. Wowkle osserva di dietro alla cortina)*

JOHNSON: *(comparisce sulla porta con una lanterna in mano. E in pelliccia)* Hello!

MINNIE: *(presso il letto, imbarazzata, vergognosa)* Buona sera!

JOHNSON: *(osservandola)* Uscivate?

MINNIE: *(estremamente confusa)* Sì . . .
No . . .
Non so.
Entrate.

JOHNSON: *(posa la lanterna sul tavolo)* Come siete graziosa!
*(fa l'atto d'abbracciarla)*

WOWKLE: Ugh! . . . *(chiude la porta. Minnie si ritrae, aggrottando le sopracciglia)*

JOHNSON: *(si volge, vede Wowkle)* *(a Minnie)* Perdonate.
Non avevo osservato . . .

MINNIE: *(con aria offesa)* Basta così, signore:
non aggiungete scuse.

JOHNSON: *(continuando)* Mi siete apparsa così bella . . .

MINNIE: *(ancora un poco risentita, sedendosi alla tavola dalla parte del focolare)* È un andare un po' troppo per le corte.

JOHNSON: *(avvicinandosele)* Vi prego di scusare . . .

MINNIE: *(seria)* Siete pentito?

JOHNSON: *(scherzoso)* Affatto! . . .
*(Minnie, che stà a capo chino, lo guarda di sotto in su, incontra il suo sguardo ed arrossisce. Wowkle spegne la lanterna di Johnson a la posa in terra. Si toglie dalle spalle il bimbo e la posa sull'armadio)*

JOHNSON: *(accennando alla propriä pelliccia)* Mi tolgo?
*(Minnie risponde con un gesto di consenso. Egli si toglie la pelliccia, la depone col cappello sulla sedia accanto alla porta)*
Grazie.
*(si avvicina a Minnie, tendendole*

WOWKLE: *(who has been assisting her in stolid silence):*
Ugh . . .
*(A knock outside.)*

MINNIE: *(starting):* Wowkle, here he is!
*(Does up her bodice hastily; pulls up her stockings.)*

JOHNSON: *(appears in the doorway with a lantern in his hand. He is wearing a fur coat):* Hello!

MINNIE: *(by the bed, embarrassed and confused):* Good evening!

JOHNSON: *(looking at her dress):* Going out?

MINNIE: *(intensely confused):*
Yes . . .
No . . .
Dunno . . .
Come in.

JOHNSON: *(puts the lantern on the table):* Why, how pretty you're looking!
*(About to embrace her.)*

WOWKLE: Ugh! . . .
*(Shuts the door. Minnie draws back, frowning.)*

JOHNSON: *(turns and perceives Wowkle):* I beg your pardon.
I had not time to notice . . .

MINNIE: *(offended):* That's quite enough, Mr. Johnson:
No need for more excuses.

JOHNSON: I saw you standing there so lovely . . .

MINNIE: *(still rather huffy, sits on the table, near the fireplace):*
Aren't you going a little bit too quickly?

JOHNSON: *(going up to her):* I hope you'll forgive me . . .

MINNIE: *(seriously):* Are you sorry?

JOHNSON: *(playfully):* Not at all!
*(Minnie, with head bent down, looks at him from under her lashes, meets his glance and blushes. Wowkle has extinguished Johnson's lantern and puts it on the ground. She takes the baby from her shoulders and puts it in the cupboard.)*

JOHNSON: *(pointing to his overcoat):* May I?
*(Minnie makes a sign of assent. He takes off his fur coat, and puts it with his cap on the seat by the door.)*
Thank you.
*(He goes up to Minnie with out-*

la mano:)
Amici?
*(Minnie, vinta, sorride e gli stende la mano. Poi rimane in atteggiamento pensoso)*
Che pensate?

MINNIE: Un pensiero . . .
Questa notte alla "Polka" non veniste per me . . .
Che vi condusse, allora? Forse è vero
che smarriste il sentiero della Micheltorena?

JOHNSON: *(tenta ancora d'abbracciarla, come per sviare il discorso)* Minnie! . . .

MINNIE: *(scostandosi)* Wowkle, il caffè!

JOHNSON: *(guardandosi attorno)* Che graziosa stanzetta!

MINNIE: Vi piace?

JOHNSON: È tutta piena di voi . . .
Che cosa strana
la vostra vita, su questa montagna solitaria, lontana
dal mondo!

MINNIE: *(con gaiezza)* Oh, se sapeste come il vivere è allegro!
Ho un piccolo polledro
che mi porta a galoppo
laggiù per la campagna;
per prati di giunchiglie,
di garofani ardenti,
per riviere profonde
cui profuman le sponde
gelsomini e vainiglie!
Poi ritorno ai miei pini
ai monti della Sierra,
così al cielo vicini
che Iddio passando pare
la sua mano v'inclini.
lontani dalla terra
così, che vien la voglia
di battere alla soglia
del cielo, per entrare

JOHNSON: *(attento, sorpreso e interessato)* E quando infurian le tormente?

MINNIE: Oh, allora seno occupata. È aperta l'Accademia . . .

JOHNSON: L'Accademia?

MINNIE: *(ridendo)* È la scuola dei minatori.

JOHNSON: E la maestra?

MINNIE: Io stessa,
*(Johnson ta guarda ammirato. Minnie offrendogli il dolce)*
Del biscotto alla crema?

JOHNSON: *(servendosi)* Grazie . . .
Vi piace leggere?

MINNIE: Molto.

JOHNSON: Vi manderò dei libri.

stretched hand.)
Are we friends, Girl?
*(Minnie, vanquished, smiles and gives her hand, then she remains in a pensive attitude.)*
What are you thinking?

MINNIE: I've been thinking,
When you come to the "Polka,"
You weren't coming for me—
What took you there, then, this evening?
Was it perhaps true you mistook
The pathway that leads to Micheltorena?

JOHNSON: *(tries to embrace her again as if to change the subject):*
Minnie!

MINNIE: *(drawing back):* Wowkle, the coffee!

JOHNSON: *(looking about him):* What a nice, cosy room!

MINNIE: D'you like it?

JOHNSON: Everything in it is like you.
How curious
To live alone
Like you on the mountain,
Far away from all the world!

MINNIE: Oh, you've no notion
How exciting my life is!
You should see my little pinto—
See him carry me at a gallop,
Right down beyond the foothills—
Thro' meadows full of lilies,
All ablaze with golden jonquils.
Then I drift down the river,
Scented all along its banks
With jessamine and wild syringa.
When I'm tired I go back
To my mountains, my Sierras.
O my dearly-loved mountains,
They are so high,
The hand of God seems to touch them!
So far from earth,
And so near to God that you're longing
To let your soul drift upwards to Heaven,
To soar on high!

JOHNSON: *(struck, surprised, and interested):* But when the winter storms are raging?

MINNIE: Why then, I'm very busy.
Academy is open.

JOHNSON: What academy?

MINNIE: That's the school
I run for the miners.

JOHNSON: And who's the teacher?

MINNIE: Why, I am.
*(Johnson looks at her in admiration. Minnie offers him cakes.)*
Will you have some cream pastry?

JOHNSON: *(helping himself):*
Thank you.
You fond of reading?

MINNIE: Very.

JOHNSON: I'll send you up some books.

MINNIE: Oh, grazie, grazie!
Delle storie d'amore?

JOHNSON: Se volete.
Vi piacciono?

MINNIE: (*appassionatamente*)
Tanto!
Per me l'amore è una cosa infinita!
Non potrò mai capire
come si possa, amando una persona
desiderarla per un' ora sola.

JOHNSON: Credo che abbiate torto.
Vi sono delle donne
che si vorrebber nella nostra vita
per quell'ora soltanto . . .
E poi morire!

MINNIE: (*scherzosa, piegandosi su lui*) Davvero?
E . . . quante volte siete morto?
(*offrendogli un sigaro*)
Uno dei nostri avana?
(*a Wowkle*)
La candela!
(*Wowkle accende la candela e la porta a Johnson che accende il sigaro, poi Johnson va verso l'uscita, ritornando poi verso Minnie cercando di abbracciarla*)
(*sfuggendogli*)
Ah, le mie rose!
Me le sciuperete!

JOHNSON: Perchè non le togliete?
(*cercando di cingere Minnie*)
Un bacio, un bacio solo!

MINNIE: (*sciogliendosi con dolce violenza*) Mister Johnson, si chiede spesso la mano . . .
per avere il braccio!

JOHNSON: Il labbro
nega . . . quando il cuor concede!

MINNIE: (*a poco a poco affascinata, si toglie le rose, le ripone nel cassetto coi guanti*)
Wowkle, tu a casa!
(*Wowkle borbottando prende il bimbo dall' armadie, si lo mette sul dorso, c. si avvolge nella coperta avviandosi alla porta*)

JOHNSON: Anch'io? . . .

MINNIE: (*graziosa*)
Voi . . . potete restare
un'ora . . . o due, ancora.
(*Johnson ha un piccolo grido di gioia. Wowkle apre la porta*)

WOWKLE: Ugh . . . Neve!
(*Il vento turbina e fischia*)

MINNIE: (*nervosa*) Va! Riposati sul fieno.
(*Wowkle esce con un ultimo brantolio, chiudendo dietro a sè la porta*)

JOHNSON: (*a Minnie tendendole le braccia*) Un bacio, un bacio almeno, uno soltanto!

MINNIE: Oh, thank you, thank you!
Some stories of love?

JOHNSON: If you want them.
D'you like them best?

MINNIE: Yes, rather!
I think true love must last forever!
What I can't understand is how a person
Who loves another can wish to have her
Just for one short hour.

JOHNSON: There I think you're wrong.
There are some women with whom one longs to
Have one hour, just one short hour of rapture,
Then to die for them!

MINNIE: (*playfully, leaning towards him*): Indeed, I wonder how often you have died?
(*Offering him the cigars.*)
One of our real Havanas?
(*To Wowkle.*)
The candle!
(*Wowkle brings the candle. Johnson lights his cigar and then gets up laughing. He goes to the door, then comes back and tries once more to embrace Minnie.*)
(*Escaping him.*)
Ah, my roses, you'll crush them!

JOHNSON: Why don't you take them off?
(*Trying to embrace Minnie.*)
Just one kiss, one little kiss, dear!

MINNIE: Mister Johnson, if you give a man an inch
He'll take an ell!

JOHNSON: Your lips deny
me . . . while your heart is consenting!

MINNIE: (*takes off her roses and puts them in the chest with her gloves.*) Wowkle, go home now!
(*Wowkle, grumbling, takes the baby from the cupboard, puts it on her back, and wrapping herself up in the blanket, turns to the door.*)

JOHNSON: I, too?

MINNIE: (*graciously*): You may stay if you like—
An hour or two.
(*Johnson gives a little cry of pleasure. Wowkle opens the door.*)

WOWKLE: Ugh—Snowing!
(*The wind howls and whistles. As she opens the door, the bed and window curtains flutter and the lights flare up.*)

MINNIE: (*nervously*): Go and lie down on the hay then.
(*Wowkle goes out, shutting the door behind her.*)

JOHNSON: (*holding his arms out to Minnie*): A kiss—
I must have one!

MINNIE: (*si getta nelle sue braccia*) Eccolo!
È tuo!
(*S'apre la porta, che sbatte violèntemente a più riprese; tutto si agita al vento che entra furioso e raffiche di neve penetrano nella stanza. Minnie e Johnson abbracciandosi si baciano con grande emozione, dimentichi di tutto e di tutti.—La porta si chiude da sè; cessa il tumulto, tutto ritornando alla calma; dal di fuori si odono ancora raffiche di vento*)
(*S'apre la porta, che sbatte violèntemente a più riprese; tutto si agita al vento che entra furioso e raffiche di neve penetrano nella stanza. Minnie e Johnson abbracciandosi si baciano con grande emozione, dimentichi di tutto e di tutti.—La porta si chiude da sè; cessa il tumulto, tutto ritornando alla calma; dal di fuori si odono ancora raffiche di vento*)

JOHNSON: (*con grande emozione*) Minnie . . .
Che dolce nome!

MINNIE: Ti piace?

JOHNSON: Tanto!
T'amo da che t'ho vista . . .
(*Ha un improvviso movimento come di raccapriccio e si discosta da Minnie, come facendo forza a sè stesso*)
Ah, no, non mi guardare, non m'ascoltare!
Minnie, è un sogno vano!

MINNIE: (*non comprendendo, con voce umile*) Perchè questa parola?
Lo so, sono una povera figliuola . . .
(*riscotendo, senza ripulsa, dolcisimi*) Sognavo . . . Si stava tanto bene! . . . Ora conviene darci la buona notte . . . (*Johnson scuote il capo triste; si domina; Minnie gli accenna il letto*)
Ecco il tuo letto . . . (*trae presso il focolare la pelle d'orso; cerca della guardaroba una coperta e un cuscino*) Io presso il focolare . . .

JOHNSON: (*opponendosi*) Non vorrò mai! . . .

MINNIE: (*dolcissima*) Ci sono avvezza, sai? Quasi ogni notte, quando fa troppo freddo, mi rannicchio in quella pelle d'orso e m'addormento. (*Minnie posa la candela sul focolare; spegna il lume sul caminetto; abbassa un poco quello del cassettone abbassa quello sopra la tavola, salendo su una sedia per giungervi; va dietro la guardaroba: si sveste, rimsnendo con ia lunga camicia bianca, ricoperta da un ampio accappatoio di colore vivace; Johnson ha gettato sul letto il suo*

MINNIE: (*throws herself in his arms*): Well, if you must!
(*Johnson kisses her passionately on the mouth, bending over her as she abandons herself to his caresses*): I love you very dearly!
(*The snowstorm reaches the height of its violence. A great gust blows the door open, the snow drifts into the room, in the draught the other doors bang, the wind howls, the lights flicker, everything is disturbed. Johnson and Minnie remain in each other's arms, motionless and oblivious of everything in the midst of the turmoil. Suddenly the clock strikes two, and they spring apart, almost violently.—For one moment they stand gazing at each other, a few steps apart.—They are breathless.—Minnie's bosom is heaving.—She goes to the door, shuts it, goes back to the table, smoothes her disordered hair and sits down. Johnson goes up to her, takes her hand and kisses it.*)

JOHNSON: Minnie!
What a pretty name!

MINNIE: D'you like it?

JOHNSON: So much!
Right from the first I loved you.
(*Has a sudden movement as of horror, and moves away from Minnie.*)
Ah, no, don't look this way,
And don't you listen, Minnie, it's all no use!

MINNIE: (*not understanding, humbly*): What are you saying that for?
I know I'm very poor and humble.
I was dreaming!
I was so very happy!
But now, dear love,
We've got to say good-night.
(*Johnson shakes his head sadly, controls himself. Minnie points to the bed.*)
That is your bed.
(*Dragging her bearskin to the fireplace.*) And I will lie down here.

JOHNSON: I'd rather not!

MINNIE: (*promptly*): I really like it best.
How oft in winter, when it's too cold at night-time,
I lie sleeping all curled up
In my bearskin before the fire.
(*Minnie puts the candle on the hearth; puts out the light on the chimney-piece; lowers the one on the chest; lowers the one above the table, climbing on a chair to reach it; goes behind the wardrobe, undresses, keeping on a long white nightgown, covered with an ample, brightly colored*

# Act II

*mantello e il cappello. Minnie riappare; guarda a Johnson; rialza un poco la fiamma del lume di mezzo)*

JOHNSON: Benedetta! *(Minnie aggiusta i cuscini: calza le pianelle indiane: s'inginocchia a pregare: si ravvolge nella coperta e si corica. Vento e urli di fuori: Johnson fa per gettarsi sul letto; poi si avvicina all'uscio, origliando: parlano a bassa voce)* Che sarà?

MINNIE: Son folate di nevischio . . .

JOHNSON: Sembra gente che chiami . . . *(ritorna al lettuccio e vi si getta sopra)*

MINNIE: È il vento dentro i rami . . . *(sorgendo un poco)* Dimmi il tuo nome . . .

JOHNSON: Dick . . .

MINNIE: *(con sentimento)* Per sempre, Dick! Non conoscesti mai Nina Micheltorena?

JOHNSON: Per sempre!

JOHNSON: . . . Mai.

MINNIE: Buona notte!

JOHNSON: Buona notte!

MINNIE: *(con angoscia crescente, ribellandosi)* Ah! Non è vero! Io so che non è vero!

RANCE: *(sogghignando)* Bada di non fidarti troppo un'altra volta!

MINNIE: *(scattando)* Non è vero! Mentite!

ASHBY: Questa notte alla "Polka" è venuto a rubare . . .

MINNIE: Ma non rubò!

SONORA: *(riflettendo)* Non ha rubato, è vero . . . Pure, avrebbe potuto!

RANCE: Ha detto Nick che Sid l'ha veduto prender questo sentiero. È vero, Nick?

NICK: È vero . . . *(Minnie lo fissa, egli si turba)*

RANCE: Qui finisce la traccia. Tu non l'hai visto . . . *(guarda Minnie fissamente)* Dov'è dunque andato?

---

*cloak; Johnson has thrown his coat and cap on the bed. Minnie reappears, looks at Johnson, and turns up the center lamp a little again.)* Now you can talk to me a little from your bed
Ora mi puoi parlare là, dalla tua cuccetta . . .

JOHNSON: Best beloved! *(Minnie, after having arranged her pillows and put on her moccasins, kneels down to say her prayers. Johnson is about to throw himself on the bed—then he goes to the door listening. Minnie wraps herself in the bearskin and curls herself up. The wind howls outside.)* What is that?

MINNIE: The thud of falling snow.

JOHNSON: Sounds like people calling.

MINNIE: It's the wind against the branches.
*(Pause. Johnson goes back to the bed and throws himself on it. Minnie raises herself a little.)* Tell me your name.

JOHNSON: Dick.

MINNIE: Forever, Dick! Say, did you ever know Nina Micheltorena?

JOHNSON: Never.

MINNIE: Goodnight!

JOHNSON: Goodnight!

NICK: *(outside, knocking at the door)*: Hello! *(Minnie listens; Johnson draws open the bed-curtains and puts his pistols in his pocket.)*

MINNIE: *(with growing anguish, refusing to believe)*: Oh! It's not true, I know it's not true!

RANCE: *(sneering)*: Take care Not to be so trusting another time!

MINNIE: I don't believe it! No, you're lying!

ASHBY: To-night at the "Polka," He came to rob it.

MINNIE: But he did *not* rob it!

SONORA: *(reflecting)*: That's what puzzles me. He didn't, yet he easily could have!

RANCE: We heard from Nick That Sid had seen him head along this trail. You said so, Nick?

NICK: I said so. *(Minnie looks hard at Nick, who grows uneasy.)*

RANCE: But the trail ends here. You haven't seen him? *(Looks hard at Minnie.)* Then where can he be?

---

*(Nick, girando su e giù, ha scoperto in terra lo sigaro di Johnson, caduto dal tavolo. Passa d'accanto a Minnie: Minnie lo affisa, con intenzione)*

NICK: *(piano)* Uno dei nostri avana!
E qui!
*(correggendosi)*
Forse ho sbagliato . . .
Quel Sid è una linguaccia!

MINNIE: *(alteramente)* Ma chi vi ha detto, insomma, che il bandito sia Johnson?

RANCE: *(guardandola)* La sua donna.

MINNIE: *(scattando)* La sua donna?
Chi?

RANCE: *(sogghignando)* Nina.

MINNIE: Nina Micheltorena? Lo conosce?

RANCE: *(ironico)* È l'amante. Quando capimmo d'essere giocati, traemmo dietro Castro prigioniero, e prendemmo il sentiero verso le "Palme." Eravamo aspettati.
Nina era là. Ci ha fatto vedere il suo ritratto . . . *(si trae di petto la fotografia)* À te!

MINNIE: *(guarda il ritratto, profondamente commossa, poi lo restituisce con una piccola risata che vuol sembrare indifferente)* Ah! Ah! . . .

RANCE: Di che ridi?

MINNIE: Oh, di nulla . . . *(con grande ironia)* La compagnia gentile ch'egli si è scelto! Nina!

SONORA: Impara!

MINNIE: Ora, ragazzi, e tardi . . . Buona notte.

SONORA: *(cavalleresco)* Ti lasciamo dormire.

MINNIE: Grazie. Ora son calma.

ASHBY: Andiamo. *(si avviano: Nick ultimo)*

NICK: *(a Minnie, mostrando che ha capito)* Se lo volete . . . io resto.

MINNIE: No. Buona notte. *(escono: ella richiude; rimane immobile presso la porta. A Johnson, con freddo disprezzo)* Fuori! Vieni fuori! *(Johnson appare tra le cortine, vinto, disfatto)* Sei venuto a rubare . . .

JOHNSON: No . . .

---

*(Nick, walking up and down, has discovered Johnson's cigar on the ground, fallen from the table. He passes close to Minnie. She stares at him meaningly.)*

NICK: *(to himself)*: One of our best Havanas!
He's here—*(correcting himself.)*
Perhaps I'm mistaken—
That Sid is such a liar!

MINNIE: But who on earth has told you
That the road-agent's Johnson?

RANCE: *(looking at her)*: His woman!

MINNIE: *(bursts out)*: His woman? Who?

RANCE: *(sneering)*: Nina.

MINNIE: Nina Micheltorena? Does he know her?

RANCE: He's her lover. When we discovered we'd been fooled, We dragged Castro behind us And took the trail to the "Palmeto." We were expected there. Nina was there. She showed us her lover's photo— *(Takes Johnson's photograph from his pocket.)* See here!

MINNIE: *(looks at the photo, terribly upset—then gives it back to him with a little laugh, meant to seem indifferent)*: Ha! Ha!

RANCE: Why are you laughing?

MINNIE: Oh, nothing? *(disdainfully.)* What charming company He has been keeping! Nina!

RANCE: Take warning!

MINNIE: Now, boys, It's getting late, Good-night.

SONORA: *(gallantly)*: You must go back to bed now.

MINNIE: Thank you, I'm quite all right.

ASHBY: Come on! *(They all go off, Nick last.)*

NICK: *(to Minnie, showing he has understood)*: If you like—I'll stay.

MINNIE: No. Good-night; *(With deep contempt, turned towards Johnson.)* Come out, now, come out! *(Johnson appears between the curtains, wretched, broken down.)* You came to rob me!

JOHNSON: No!

MINNIE: Mentisci!

JOHNSON: No!

MINNIE: Sì!

JOHNSON: Tutto m'accusa . . . Ma . . .

MINNIE: Finisci! Dimmi perchè sei qui, se non che per rubare?

JOHNSON: (*deciso, avvicinandosi a Minnie*) Ma quando io v'ho veduta . . .

MINNIE: (*sempre aspra, trattenendolo con gesto secco*) Adagio, adagio! . . .
Non muovere un passo . . . o chiamo aiuto!
Un bandito! un bandito! . . .
(*con sorda ironia*)
Son fortunata!
Un bandito! un bandito!
Puoi andartene!
Va'! . . .
(*sta per piangere. La sua fierezza la trattiene*)

JOHNSON: (*prorompendo*) Una parola sola!
Non mi difenderò: sono un dannato!
Lo so, lo so!
Ma non vi avrei rubato!
Sono Ramerrez: nacqui vagabondo: era ladro il mio nome da quando venni al mondo.
Ma fino a che fu vivo mio padre, io non sapevo.
Ora sono sei mesi che mio padre mori . . .
E tutto appresi!
Sola ricchezza mia, mio solo pane per la madre e i fratelli, alla dimane, l'eredità paterna: una masnada di banditi da strada!
L'accettai.
Era quello il destino mio!
Ma un giorno v'ho incontrata . . .
Ho sognato d'andarmene con voi tanto lontano, per redimermi tutto in una vita di lavoro e d'amore . . .
E il labbro mio mormorò una preghiera ardente:
Oh Dio! ch'ella non sappia mai la mia vergogna!
Il sogno è stato vano!
Ora ho finito . . .

MINNIE: (*commossa, senza asprezzo*) Che voi siate un bandito . . . ve lo perdoni Iddio.
(*con grande amarezza*)
Ma il primo bacio mio vi siete preso, chè vi credevo mio, soltanto mio! . . .
Andate, andate!
Addio! . . .
V'uccideranno . . .
Che m'importa? . . .
(*dice queste parole macchinalmente, disfatta, cercando di farsi forza*)

MINNIE: You lie!

JOHNSON: No!

MINNIE: Yes!

JOHNSON: Things look against me—But—

MINNIE: Oh, stop it!
Why are you here, then,
If not to rob me?

JOHNSON: (*after a pause*): It's true—yes—but when I saw 'twas you—
(*Takes a step towards her.*)

MINNIE: (*stopping him with an abrupt gesture*): No nearer, no nearer!
No, not any nearer.
Or I'll call the sheriff!
You a thief!
You a robber!
(*With bitter irony.*)
I'm truly lucky!
A thief, a robber!
(*Disdainfully and violently.*)
But now you can go!
(*Her pride alone prevents her from crying.*)

JOHNSON: (*bursts out*): Let me just say one word,
But not in self-defense:
I am accursed. I know! I know!
But I would not have robbed you!
I am Ramerrez, vagabond by birth:
From the day I was born I was reared on stolen money.
But while my father was living I didn't know it.
My father died just six months ago,
And then I knew!
The only heritage for my mother,
For my brothers, to face the future,
The only thing he left us,
Was a gang of road-agents and robbers!
I took the road. . . .
It was Fate, and had to be!
But then one day I saw you—.
From that moment I longed to take you with me far, far away,
And to start a fresh life of honest work,
Honest work and love—
And all the while in my heart
I was uttering a prayer:
O God, grant that she may never know what I am!
My prayer has not been answered!—
Now I've finished.

MINNIE: (*moved, without harshness*): I could even forgive you
For being a road-agent—
(*Very bitterly.*)
But what I can't forgive is
That you have taken my first, first kiss,
And I trusted you—So leave me, go!
Let them kill you—What's it matter?
(*She says these words mechanically, but is spent, trying to steel herself.*)

JOHNSON: (*disperato, deciso, senz'armi, apre la porta, pronto al sacrificio, come a un suicidio ed esce precipitosamente*) Addio!

MINNIE: (*rasciugandosi le lagrime*) È finita . . .
Finita!
(*un colpo d'arma da fuoco, vicinissimo. Essa trasalisce*)
L'han ferito . . .
(*con uno sforzo supremo su sè stessa*)
Che importa?
(*si sente di fuori il rumore di un corpo che cade rovescio contro la porta. Minnie non resiste più, apre. Johnson si è rialzato, barcolla, sta per cadere ancora. Minnie lo sorregge, cerca di tirarlo dentro a di chiudere. Johnson è ferito al fianco; pallidissimo si preme la ferita con un fazzoletto*)

JOHNSON: (*con voce soffocata, resistendole*) Non chiudete la porta . . .
Debbo uscire . . .

MINNIE: Entra!

JOHNSON: No . . .

MINNIE: Entra!

JOHNSON: No, non chiudete!
Voglio uscire!

MINNIE: (*trascinandolo, disperata*) Sta qui . . .
Sei ferito! . . .
Nasconditi!
(*chiude la porta*)

JOHNSON: Aprite la porta . . .
Voglio uscire!

MINNIE: (*vinta, perduta*) Resta!
T'amo!
Deh, resta!
Sei l'uomo che baciai la prima volta . . .
Non puoi morire!
(*con fatica sorreggendo ancora Johnson, ha appoggiata la scala al solaio e lo sospinge a salire*)
Sali su . . .
Presto! . . .
(*Rance bussa alla porta. Johnson sospinto da Minnie ha già salito i primi scalini*)
Salvati . . .
Poi verrai con me . . . lontano!

JOHNSON: (*Quasi mancando*)
Non posso più . . .

JOHNSON: (*desperate, resolutely, unarmed, he opens the door ready for sacrifice, like a suicide, and goes out*): Good-bye!

MINNIE: (*wipes away her tears, trying to convince herself of her indifference*): That's all over—
All over.
(*A shot outside, quite near. She starts.*)
They have shot him—
(*With supreme self-control.*)
No matter!
(*The sound of a body falling with a thud against the door is heard outside. Minnie resists no longer and opens it. Johnson has risen, staggers, and is about to fall again. Minnie supports him, tries to draw him into the cabin and to shut the door. Johnson is wounded in the side; he is livid, and tries to staunch his wound with his handkerchief.*)

JOHNSON: (*in faint tones of resistance*): Don't shut the door—I am going—No!

MINNIE: Come!—

JOHNSON: No—

MINNIE: Come in!

JOHNSON: Don't shut the door.
I must go out!—

MINNIE: (*drags him in, in despair*): Stay here—
You're wounded!—
(*Shuts the door.*)
Hide yourself.

JOHNSON: Open the door.
I want to go!

MINNIE: Hurry!
This way!
Hurry!

JOHNSON: No!
No!
No!

MINNIE: I love you; this way, hurry.
Ah!
Aren't you the man I kissed for the first time?
You shall not die!
(*Supporting Johnson with difficulty, has placed the ladder against the loft and helps him to go up it.*) Just a step, quickly!

JOHNSON: (*his strength failing him*): No!
I can't!
I can't!

MINNIE: Just one step.
Then you'll come with me far away.
A step!
Just one more step!

MINNIE: (*aiutandolo ancora*)
Cosi . . .
Lo puoi, lo devi . . .
Coraggio . . .
T'amo!
(*Johnson è già sul solaio, Minnie discende, leva in fretta la scala e poi corre ad aprire. Rance entra cautamente colla pistola spianata, esplorando ogni angolo*)

MINNIE: Che c'è di nuovo, Jack?

RANCE: (*volgendosi, severo, imperioso*) Non sono Jack . . .
Son lo Sceriffo, a caccia del tuo Johnson d'inferno.
N'ho seguito la traccia.
Dev'esser qui.
Dov'è?

MINNIE: (*aspramente*) Ah, mi avete seccato con questo vostro Ramerrez!

RANCE: (*spianando la pistola verso il letto e avanzi nao*) E la!
Non c'è . . .
(*impazientito*)
Ma l'ho ferito, perdio, ne sono certo!
Non può esser fuggito!
Non può esser che qua.

MINNIE: (*sempre più aspra*) E cercatelo, dunque!
Rovistate dove vi pare . . .
E poi levatevi dai piedi una volta per sempre!

RANCE: (*con un sussulto, abbassando la pistola*) Mi giuri che non c'è?

MINNIE: (*beffarda*) Perchè non seguitate a cercarlo?

RANCE: (*si guarda attorno, guarda Minnie, poi con un moto d'ira rattenuto*) E sarà L'avrò sbagliato . . .
(*volgendosi a Minnie con impeto improvviso*)
Ma dimmi che non l'ami!

MINNIE: (*sprezzante*) Siete pazzo!

RANCE: (*avvicinandosi, pallido, tremante*) Lo vedi!
Sono pazzo di te!
T'amo e ti voglio!
(*l'abbraccia violentemente e la bacia*)

MINNIE: (*svincolandosi*) Ah, vigliacco! . . .
(*si libera e fugge*)

---

JOHNSON: I can't!
I can't!

MINNIE: (*helping him again*):
That's right!
You can!
You must!
Take heart!
Come!
I love you!
(*Loud knocking at the door.*)
(*Johnson is already in the loft and falls down exhausted behind the boxes. Minnie draws the Indian curtain, comes down, takes away the ladder. Rance knocks again, more excitedly. Minnie runs to open, feigning surprise. Rance comes in cautiously, his pistol in his hand, and searches every corner.*)

MINNIE: Why, what's the matter, Jack?

RANCE: (*turning round, severe and imperious*): No more "Jack."
I am the Sheriff,
After your infernal Johnson.
I have followed his trail.
He must be here!
But where?

MINNIE: (*harshly*): Ah, I'm sick and tired of hearing
About your Ramerrez!

RANCE: (*going towards the bed with aimed pistol*): He's there!
No, he's not.
(*Impatiently*):
But he is wounded,
I'm certain.
I hit him!
He can't have escaped!
He can only be here.

MINNIE: (*still more roughly*):
Well, look for him then!
Search the place wherever you please;
But then be off, and take yourself
Out of my sight forever!

RANCE: (*starts and lowers his pistol*): Do you swear he isn't here?

MINNIE: (*mocking*): You'd really better go on looking!

RANCE: (*looks about; looks at Minnie, then with a gesture of suppressed anger*): Well, all right! I was mistaken.
(*Turning to Minnie on a sudden impulse.*)
Just tell me you don't love him!

MINNIE: (*contemptuously*):
You're a madman!

RANCE: (*approaches her, pale and trembling*): You know it!
I'm mad about you!
(*Embraces her violently, kisses her.*)

MINNIE: (*struggling, and wrenching herself free*): Ah, you coward!
(*She throws him off and escapes.*)

---

RANCE: (*rincorrendola, al parossismo dell'eccitazione*) Ti voglio! . . .

MINNIE: (*afferra una bottiglia e lo minaccia sulla testa*) Via di qua, vigliacco! . . .
Esci!
(*incalza Rance verso l'uscita*)

RANCE: (*con atto minaccioso, fermandosi sotto il ballatoio*) Sei fiera . . . L'ami!
Vuoi serbarti a lui . . .
Si, vado.
Ma ti giuro . . .
(*stende una mano verso Minnie*)
che non ti avrà! . . .
(*una stilla di sangue, gocciando dal solaio, gli cade sulla mano. Egli si sofferma stupito*)
Oh, strano!
Del sangue sulla mano . . .

MINNIE: (*avvicinandosi, con voce meno aspra, un po' tremante, per sviare il sospetto*) Forse v'avrò graffiato!

RANCE: (*si pulisce la mano col fazzoletto*) No, non c'è graffio . . .
Guarda!
(*uno stillicidio insistente cade sul fazzoletto, arrossandolo*)
Ah!
Sangue ancora!
(*guarda il solaio, poi con un grido di gioia e d'odio, come avventandosi*)
E là!

MINNIE: (*disperata, opponendosi a Rance con tutte le sue forze*) Ah, no . . . non voglio!

RANCE: (*cercando sciogliersi dalla stretta di Minnie*) Lasciami!
(*imperioso, rivolto verso il solaio*)
Mister Johnson, scendete!
(*vede la scala, l'appoggia al solaio*)

MINNIE: (*supplichevole*) Aspettate . . .
Vedete!
Non può, non può!
(*Johnson con uno sforzo supremo si aiza, comincia a discendere pallido e sofferente, ma con volto fiero*)

RANCE: (*impaziente*) Scendete!
O, perdio . . .
(*spianando la pistola verso Johnson*)

MINNIE: (*smarrita, sempre più implorante*) Un sol minuto, Rance!
Un minuto ancora!

RANCE: Un minuto?
E perchè?
Ah, ah, che mutamento! . . .
(*Johnson, aiutato da Minnie, ha disceso gli ultimi scalini, si trascina verso il tavolo*)
Volete ancor giuocare la partita con me, signor di Sacramento?

---

RANCE: (*runs after her in a paroxysm of excitement*): I want you!

MINNIE: (*seizes a whisky bottle, and swings it up in self-defense—Rance stops, steps back*): Go away, you coward!
Leave me!

RANCE: (*backing, he has nearly reached the door—with a wicked sneer on his distorted features*): I thought so.
You love him!
You're waiting here for him . . .
Yes, I'll go.
But I swear
(*Stretches out a hand to Minnie.*)
He shall never have you! . . .
(*A drop of blood dropping from the ceiling, falls on his hand—He stops short, in amazement.*)
Why, look!
Some blood on my hand!

MINNIE: (*approaching, her voice trembling and less harsh, to dispel suspicion*): Just now . . .
I must have scratched you!

RANCE: (*wipes his hand with his handkerchief*): No, there's no scratch . . .
Look!
(*A steady drip on the handkerchief dyes it red.*)
Ah!
Blood again!
(*Looking at the ceiling, then with a cry of joy and hate.*)
He's there!

MINNIE: (*desperate, holds him back*): Ah, no!
He's not!

RANCE: (*roughly freeing himself from Minnie's grip*): Let go!
(*Imperiously calling up to the loft.*)
Mister Johnson, come down!
(*sees the ladder and leans it against the trap door.*)

MINNIE: (*entreatingly*): Wait a minute—
He can't!
You see he can't come!—
(*Johnson with a supreme effort, gets up and begins to come down the ladder, pallid and suffering, but with haughty expression.*)

RANCE: Come down!
Or by Heaven—
(*Levelling his pistol at him.*)

MINNIE: (*in anguish, entreatingly*): Wait a minute, Rance!
Wait another minute!

RANCE: A minute?
What for?
Ha ha! what a change!—
(*Johnson, helped by Minnie, has come down the last few steps and drags himself to the table.*)
You still inclined to play a
Game of poker with me,

---

Lascio la scelta a voi: a corda od a pistola!
(*Johnson si siede di peso sulla sedia, appoggia i gomiti sul tavolo, vi abbandona sopra il capo. È svenuto*)

MINNIE: (*violentissima*) Basta, uomo d'inferno!
Vedetelo: è svenuto.
Non può darvi più ascolto . . .
(*disperata si preme le tempie con le mani, come per cercare un'ispirazione, poi si avvicina a Rance, lo guarda con gli occhi negli occhi, parlandogli con voce secca e concitata*)
Parliamoci fra noi . . .
E si finisca!
Chi siete voi, Jack Rance?
Un biscazziere.
E Johnson?
Un bandito.
Io?
Padrona di bettola e di bisca vivo sul whisky e l'oro.
Tutti siam pari!
Tutti banditi e bari!
Stanotte avete chiesto una risposta alla vostra passione . . .
Eccovi la mia posta!

RANCE: (*studiandola*) Che vuoi dire?

MINNIE: (*affannosamente*) Ch'io v'offro quest'uomo e la mia vita! . . .
Una partita a poker!
Se vincete, prendetevi questo ferito e me . . .
Ma se vinco, parola di Jack Rance gentiluomo, è mio, è mio quest'uomo! . . .

RANCE: Come l'ami!
Accetto, sì!
T'avrò!

MINNIE: La parola?

RANCE: So perdere come un signore . . .
Ma perdio! son tutto della sete di te arso e distrutto . . . ma se vinco, t'avrò . . .
(*Minnie si ritrae con un senso di ripulsione, va verso l'armadio e vi si indugia. Si vede che furtivamente si nasconde qualche cosa in una calza*)

MINNIE: Abbassate la lampada . . .

RANCE: (*impaziente*) Che aspetti?

MINNIE: (*indugiando*) Cercavo un mazzo nuovo . . .
(*si avvicina al tavola, preoccupata*)
Son nervosa; scusatemi.
È una cosa terribile pensar che una partita decide d'una vita.
(*si siede al tavolo in faccia a Rance*)
Siete pronto?

---

Fine mister of Sacramento?
Well, you can choose:
The gallows or the pistol!
(*Johnson sits down heavily on the chair, rests his elbows on the table, and drops his head down on his arms. He has fainted.*)

MINNIE: (*roughly*): Stop it, wretch that you are!
Can't you see he's fainted?
Can't you see he can't hear you?
(*Desperately pressing her hands on her temples, she tries to find an inspiration. Suddenly she goes up to Rance, looks him straight in the eyes, and says in a dry, excited voice*):
We'll settle it between us—and make it final!
What are you, Jack Rance?
You're just a gambler, and Johnson is a thief.
And I?
I run a gambling-house and tavern,
Living on whisky and gold;
We're all three the same!
All three are thieves and gamblers!
You ask me if the answer
I gave you this evening was final—
Now I make you this offer!

RANCE: (*staring at her*): What d'you mean?

MINNIE: My stakes in the game
Are my life and Johnson's!
We'll play a game of poker!
If you're lucky,
You take this wounded man and me—
But if I win, your word of honor, Jack,
This man is mine!

RANCE: How she loves him!
I'll take you on!
I'll win!

MINNIE: Word of honor?

RANCE: And if I lose, I lose like a gentleman—
But, my God!
I'm just consumed with hunger and longing
Till I get you.
If I'm lucky, you're mine!
(*Minnie retires behind the open door of the cupboard to gain time—one can see her hiding something furtively in her stocking.*)

MINNIE: Turn the lamp down—

RANCE: (*impatiently*): What's that?

MINNIE: (*procrastinating*): A fresh pack of cards.
(*Coming to the table—preoccupied.*)
I'm nervous;
Have patience. It's an awful thing
To think a game of poker decides
Two people's lives.
(*Sits at the table: Rance is opposite her: Johnson, unconscious,*

---

RANCE: Son pronto.
Taglia.
A te.

MINNIE: Due mani sopra tre.

RANCE: (*dà le carte*) Quante?

MINNIE: Due . . .

RANCE: Ma cos'ha che l'adori?

MINNIE: (*scartando le carte*) Voi che trovate in me?
Che avete?

RANCE: Io re.

MINNIE: Io re.

RANCE: Fante.

MINNIE: Regina.

RANCE: Hai vinto.
Alla mano seguente!
(*giocano*)
Due assi e un paio . . .

MINNIE: (*mostrando il suo gioco*) Niente!

RANCE: (*con gioia*) Pari!
Siam pari!
Evviva!

MINNIE: (*preoccupata*) Ora è la decisiva?

RANCE: Sì. Taglia.

MINNIE: (*cercando raddolcirlo*) Rance, mi duole delle amare parole . . .

---

*La Grande Selva California
Lembo estremo della selva sul digradare lento di un contrafforte della Sierra. Uno spiazzo circondato dai tronchi enormi, diritti e nudi, delle conifere secolari, che formano intorno come un colonnato gigantesco. Nel fondo, dove la selva s'infoltisce sempre più, s'apre un sentiero, che s'interna fra i tronchi: qua e là appaiono picchi nevosi altissimi di montagne. Per lo spiazzo, che è come un bivacco dei minatori, visono stesi dei grandi tronchi di alberi tagliati alla base, che servono da sedile, accanto ad uno di questi arde un fuoco alimentato da grossi rami. Nella luce incerta della prim'alba la grandiosa fuga dei tronchi rossigni muore in un velo folto di nebbia. Da un lato, nell'ampio tronco d'un albero colossale, è scavato un ripostiglio d'arnesi da minatore—da un altro lato, tra felci ed arbusti, legato ad un ramo, un cavallo insellato.
(Rance è seduto a sinistra, presso il fuoco, con gli abiti in disordine, il viso stanco e sconvolto, i capelli arruffati; Nick, pensieroso, è seduto in faccia a Rance. Ashby e*

---

between the two. Rance, who has got out his own pack, puts it back and takes Minnie's instead.)
Are you ready?

RANCE: I'm ready, cut; your turn.

MINNIE: The best two out of three.
(*Dealing.*)

RANCE: What?

MINNIE: Two. . .

RANCE: What do you see in him?

MINNIE: (*discarding*): What do you see in me?
What've you got?

RANCE: King High.

MINNIE: King High.

RANCE: Jack.

MINNIE: Queen.

RANCE: You've got it.
Now for the next hand!
(*They play.*)
Two aces and a pair.

MINNIE: (*showing her hand*): Nothing!

RANCE: (*joyfully*): Even!
We're even!
Hurrah!

MINNIE: Now it's the next; that's final?

RANCE: Yes. Cut.

MINNIE: (*trying to soften him*):
Rance, I'm sorry
I spoke bitterly to you.

---

*The Great California Forest
The extreme edge of the great Californian forest, where it gradually slopes downward on a ridge of the Sierras. An open space surrounded by enormous, straight and bare pine trees which form a gigantic colonnade round it. In the background, where the wood is still denser a trail is seen winding between the trees; here and there the snowy peaks of the highest mountains are visible. Large felled tree trunks lie scattered about the clearing, which is used as a sort of camp by the miners. These trunks serve as seats; near one of them a big log-fire is burning.
In the indistinct light of the early dawn, the lofty mass of reddish trunks is wrapt in a thick mist. On one side the trunk of an enormous tree has been hollowed out to form a depository for the miners' utensils; on the other side, among the ferns and bushes, a saddle-horse is tied to a branch.
(Rance is seated on the left, near the fire, looking tired and perturbed, his clothes untidy, his hair disordered. Nick, worried, is*

# Act III

*sdraiato in terra presso al cavallo, in ascolto. Indossano tutti e tre pesanti cappotti. Nessun rumore turba il silenzio dell'alba invernale)*

NICK: *(attizzando il fuoco con la punta dello stivale, sotto voce, cupamente)* Ve lo giuro, sceriffo: darei tutte le mance di dieci settimane pur di tornare indietro d'una sola, quando questo dannato Johnson della malora non ci s'era cacciato ancor fra i piedi!

RANCE: *(con rabbia, cupamente)* Maledetto cane! Parea ferito a morte . . . E pensar che da allora, mentre noi si gelava fra la neve, è stato là, scaldato dal respiro di Minnie, accarezzato, baciato . . .

NICK: *(con uno scatto di protesta)* Oh, Rance! . . .

RANCE: Un ladro del suo stampo! Avrei voluto a tutti gridar quel che sapevo . . .

NICK: *(con approvazione un po' canzonatoria)* E non l'avete fatto. È stato proprio un tratto cavalleresco . . .

RANCE: *(sogghignando amaramente, fra sè)* Ah, sì! *(a Nick, con rancore sostenuto)* Ma che ci vede, dimmi, ma che ci trova la nostra bella Minnie in quel fantoccio?

NICK: *(sorridendo, con fare accorte)* Mah! Qualcosa ci vedrà . . . *(con comica filosofia)* Amore, amore! Paradíso ed inferno, è quel chè: tutto il dannato mondo s'innamora! Anche per Minnie è giunta oggi quell'ora. *(A poco a poco la luce del giorno va rischiarando la scena. A un tratto un clamore lontano, vago e confuso, giunge dalla montagna. Ashby balza in piedi di scatto scioglie il cavallo, lo afferra alla briglia, si fa in mezzo allo spiazzo, nel fondo, verso il sentiero; anche Rance e Nick si alzano)*

VOCI LONTANE: Ah! . . .

ASHBY: *(all'udire le voci grida)* Urrah, ragazzi! . . . Urrah! . . . *(rivolto a Rance)* Sceriffo, avete udito? N'ero certo! Han trovato il bandito! . . . Una buona giornata per Wells-Fargo!

---

*walking up and down. Ashby is lying on the ground near his horse, listening. They all three wear heavy cloaks. No noise breaks the silence of the winter dawn.)*

NICK: *(going to the fire, and stirring it with the toe of his boot)*: Word of honor, Sheriff: I'd gladly give the whole of My tips for seven weeks, If only we could put back The clock for one; Before that rascal Johnson,— Curses on his head,— In an evil hour had crossed our path!

RANCE: *(grimly)*: Curses on the dog! I thought his wound was fatal! And to think that while we've been freezing Out in the snow upon the mountain, He's been in there, Basking in the smiles of our Minnie, Her caresses, her kisses!

NICK: *(bursts out in protest)*: Oh, Rance!

RANCE: A common thief like him! I simply ached to shout out loud Where he was hiding.

NICK: *(with rather quizzical approval)*: And yet you didn't; You acted like a perfect gentleman!

RANCE: *(sneering bitterly, aside)*: Oh, yes! *(To Nick.)* But what on earth, I ask you, Can our Minnie find To love in that puppy?

NICK: *(smiling in a worldly wise way)*: Well! There's something, I suppose! *(With droll philosophy.)* Oh, love! Oh, love! Now it's heaven, now it's hell on earth! You and I and the whole damn world must catch it! And now our Minnie has caught it, very badly! *(By degrees the daylight lights up the stage. Suddenly a distant noise, vague and confused, is heard from the mountain. Ashby leaps to this feet with one bound, unties his horse, seizes it by the bridle and goes off in the center background towards the path. Rance and Nick get up also.)*

DISTANT VOICES: Ah!

ASHBY: *(hearing the voices, shouts)*: Hurrah, you fellows! Hurrah! *(Turning to Rance.)* Well, Sheriff, do you hear that? I knew it! They've captured the villain! It is a lucky day for Wells-Fargo!

---

VOCI PIÙ VICINE: *(da vari punti)* Hollà! Hollà! *(le grida si ripetono più distinte. Rance si alza)*

ASHBY: *(a Rance)* Non udite! Ah, questa volta non mi stuggi, brigante!

RANCE: *(amaro)* Siete più fortunato di me . . .

ASHBY: *(osservandolo, stringendo gli occhi con uno sguardo indagatore)* Da quella notte là, alla "Polka" non vi ho capito più, Sceriffo . . . *(Rance alza le spalle e non risponde)*

VOCI VICINISSIME: Hollà! *(Un gruppo di uomini sbucano correndo da destra, traversando la scena nel fondo con un movimento aggirante. Alcuni hanno in pugno coltellacci e pistole altri delle vanghe e dei bastoni. Gridano tutti che fusamente, come cani che inseguano un selvatico)*

ASHBY: *(lanciandosi verso di loro)* Hollà! . . . Fermi tutti, perdio! *(La folla degli inseguitori si ferma un istante, volgendosi alle grida)* Giù le armi! Egli dev'esser preso vivo! *(Alcuni corrono fuori di scena gridando: "hollà, hollà." Sopraggiungono altri cinque o sei minatori che sono affrontati da Ashby e si fermano, affannati dalla corsa)* Dov'è?

ALCUNI MINATORI: S'insegue . . .

ALTRI: *(indicando la direzione)* Per di qua . . .

ASHBY: Dove?

ALTRI MINATORI: Di là dal monte!

ALTRI: Il bosco fino a valle è già tutto in allarme!

ALTRI: Ashby, a fra poco! Addio!

ASHBY: *(balzando in sella al cavallo)* Vengo con voi!

TUTTI: Urrah! . . . *(Ashby saluta con la mano Rance e Nick e si allontana al trotto preceduto dai minatori)*

ALCUNI MINATORI: *(indicando la direzione)* Per di qua! Per di qua! *(Il gruppo scompare fra gli alberi. Nick e Rance rimangono soli)*

RANCE: *(levando le braccia, come per rivolgersi verso la casa di Minnie, in uno scatto di gioia crudele)* Minnie, ora piangi tu! Per te soltanto attanagliato dalla gelosia mi son disfatto per notti di pianto, e tu ridevi alla miseria mia!

---

VOICES: *(nearer, from different directions)*: Hallo! hallo! *(The shouts are renewed more distinctly. Rance gets up.)*

ASHBY: *(to Rance)*: D'you hear them? Ah, this time he shan't escape me, the scoundrel!

RANCE: *(bitterly)*: You seem to be more lucky than I!

ASHBY: *(looks hard at him with a searching glance)*: Ever since that night at the "Polka," I've not understood you, Sheriff. *(Rance shrugs his shoulders, but does not answer.)*

VOICES: *(very near)*: Hallo! *(A number of men come running on from the right, crossing the stage at the back in a straggling manner. Some carry knives and pistols, others have spades and cudgels. They all yell in confusion, like dogs on the track of a wild animal.)*

ASHBY: *(rushing up to them)*: Hallo! Stop, you fellows! D'you hear? Arms down! He must be taken alive! *(Some run off the stage shouting: "Hallo, hallo." Five or six others come on, who are stopped by Ashby, and pause, breathless from running.)* Where is he?

SOME MINERS: We're on him.

OTHERS: *(pointing the direction)*: Over there.

OTHER MINERS: Beyond the mountain.

OTHERS: The forest, to the valley, Is alive with pursuers!

OTHERS: Back again soon, Ashby! So long!

ASHBY: *(jumps into the saddle)*: I'm coming with you!

ALL: Hurrah! *(Ashby waves his hand to Rance and Nick and goes off at a trot, preceded by the miners.)*

SOME MINERS: *(pointing)*: Over there! Over there! *(The party disappears among the trees. Nick and Rance remain alone.)*

RANCE: *(throwing up his arms towards Minnie's cabin, in a burst of cruel joy)*: It is your turn now, O Minnie, to weep in vain! For you alone, I've spent so many nights awake and weeping, While you with laughter mocked at

---

Ora quel pianto mi trabocca in riso!
Quegli che amasti non ritornerà:
Minnie, ora piangi tu, che m'hai deriso!
La corda è pronta che l'impiccherà!
(*Si getta a sedere sul tronco riverso, serbando sul viso il suo riso cattivo. Nick in disparte passeggia e si ferma a guardare lontano, in atteggiamento ansioso ed incerto. Alcuni minatori entrano in scena correndo*)

**NICK:** (*ai più prossimi, interrogandoli*) Dite! . . .

**ALCUNI MINATORI:** (*seguitando la corsa*) È rinchiuso!

**ALTRI MINATORI:** (*dal fondo a quelli che li seguono*) Avanti!

**ALTRI:** (*a Nick, senza fermarsi*) Fra poco!

**ALTRI:** (*che sopraggiungono, incitando gli altri alla corsa*) Avanti!
Avanti!
(*La muta furiosa si è allontanata. Nick riprende la sua passeggiata, cogitabondo, poi si ferma vicino a Rance, che è ancora seduto, chiuso e torvo*)

**VOCI INTERNE:** Urrah!

**NICK:** Sceriffo, avete udito?

**RANCE:** (*senza rispondergli, con ira sorda, guardando in terra*) Johnson di Sacramento, un demonio t'assiste!
Ma, perdio! . . . se ti prendono al laccio e non ti faccio scontare ogni tormento, puoi sputarmi sul viso! . . .
(*Giunge un'altra turba urlante d'uomini a cavallo e a piedi. Vedendo Rance e Nick si fermano. Harry e Bello sono avanti a tutti*)

**VOCI:** (*confuse*) Fugge!
Fugge!

**RANCE:** (*scattando in piedi e slanciandosi verso Harry*) Ah, perdio!

**HARRY:** È montato a cavallo!

**RANCE:** (*facendosi in mezzo alla turba in clamore, gridando*) Come?
Dove?

**BELLO:** (*ansando*) Alla Bota già un uomo gli era sopra . . .

**HARRY:** Sembrava ormai spacciato!

**UN MINATORE:** Non gli restava scampo!

**UN ALTRO:** Già l'aveva acciuffato pei capelli . . .

my love and misery!
My weeping now will soon be turned to laughter!
Now, Minnie, weep in vain,
'Tis your turn now, you who used to mock me!
He whom you loved will not return to you.
The rope is ready from which he will swing!
(*Sits down on a fallen trunk, his evil smile still on his face. Nick, lost in anxious thought, keeps aloof, and resumes his pacing up and down, looking out in the distance. Some miners come rushing on.*)

**NICK:** (*to the nearest, questioning them*): What news?

**SOME MINERS:** (*following on*): He's surrounded!

**OTHERS:** (*from the back, to those behind them*): Come on!

**OTHERS:** (*to Nick, without stopping*): Back again soon!

**OTHERS:** (*who come on, encouraging the rest*): Come on!
Come on!
(*The angry band has rushed off. Nick resumes his walk, lost in thought, then he stops close to Rance, who is still seated, surly and reserved.*)

**VOICES BEHIND:** Hurrah!

**NICK:** Sheriff, did you hear them?

**RANCE:** (*without answering him, looking down at the ground in dull anger*): Johnson of Sacramento,
The devil's fighting on your side!
But by heaven,
If they take you alive,
And I don't make you pay
For all I have suffered,
You may spit in my face!
(*Another yelling band of men on horse and foot rush on; seeing Nick and Rance, they stop. Harry and Handsome are in front of the rest.*)

**VOICES:** (*confusedly*): Bolted!
Bolted!

**RANCE:** (*bounding to his feet and rushing up to Harry*): By the Lord!

**HARRY:** He has jumped on a horse!

**RANCE:** (*pushing his way into the midst of the noisy crowd, shouts*): How?
Where?

**HANDSOME:** (*out of breath*): At the Bota,
A man was right upon him.

**HARRY:** We thought him done for, that time!

**A MINER:** And no escape was possible!

**ANOTHER:** Tight by his hair,
The man had got him—

**UN TERZO:** Quand'ecco . . .

**RANCE:** Racconta . . . avanti . . . avanti . . .

**BELLO:** Quand'ecco il maledetto con un colpo lo sbalza giù d'arcioni, s'afferra ai crini, balza in sella, sprona, e . . . via come un lampo!
(*Alcuni accompagnano il racconto con un concerto di esclamazioni irose; altri lo continuano con un grande agitare delle braccia in gesti violenti*)

**VOCI:** (*varie*) Gli uomini di Wells-Fargo l'inseguono a cavallo!
—Ashby è con la sua gente!
—Gli son tutti alle spalle!
—Han passato il torrente!
—Corron giù per la valle!
—È un turbine che passa! . . .
(*Un urlo formidabile, selvaggio, echeggia in distanza. Tutti tacciono, si volgono, restano un attimo sospesi. L'urlo si ripete. La turba scoppia in un grido:*)
—Urrah!
—Via, ragazzi!
—Alla caccia!
—Via!
Via tutti . . .
—Alla valle!
(*Stanno per lanciarsi nuovamente, quando il galoppo lontano di un cavallo a corsa sfrenata li arresta*)

**JOE:** (*indicando in direzione degli aiberi, a destre*) È Sonora, guardate!

**SONORA:** (*dà lontano*) Hollà!

**JOE ED ALTRI:** Hollà!
Hollà!
(*Sonora entra a galoppo. Rance afferra per la briglia il cavallo e lo ferma. Sonora scende da cavallo*)

**RANCE:** (*afferrando Sonora per un braccio*) Racconta!

**SONORA:** (*con un grido strozzato*) È preso!

**TUTTI:** (*in un solo grido*) Urrah!
(*Arrivano altri gruppi di uomini correndo. Tutti si stringono attorno a Sonora chiedendo notizie. Billy sbuca di fra gli alberi. Ha in mano una lunga corda che va gettando qua e là attraverso i rami, per trovarne uno adatto al capestro*)

**VOCI:** (*confuse*)
—Come fu? . . .
—Dov'è stato?
—L'hai visto? —L'han legato?
—Di' su, presto!

**RANCE:** Racconta!

**A THIRD:** When suddenly—

**RANCE:** Go on—Go on—

**HANDSOME:** When suddenly the ruffian, with a blow,
Knocks him clean off the saddle,
And seizing the horse's mane,
Leaps into the saddle,
Spurs, and is off like lightning!
(*Some accompany his words with a chorus of angry ejaculations; others brandish their arms in intense excitement.*)

**VOICES:** (*mixed*): All the men of Wells-Fargo
Are chasing him on horseback!
Ashby and all his men
Are very close on his heels!
They've got across the water!
Now they're close on his heels!
They're flying like a whirlwind!
(*A formidable savage yell resounds from the distance. All are silent, turn around and remain in suspense for a moment. The yell is heard once more. The crowd then bursts out shouting also.*)
Hurrah!
Come on, boys!
Join the chase!
Come on!
To the valley!
(*They are about to rush off again, when the sound of a galloping horse in the distance makes them pause.*)

**JOE:** (*pointing right, towards the trees*): It's Sonora—d'you see?

**SONORA:** (*from afar*): Hallo!

**JOE AND OTHERS:** Hallo!
Hallo!
(*Sonora comes galloping on. Rance seizes the horse by the bridle and stops it. Sonora dismounts.*)

**RANCE:** (*catching hold of Sonora's arm*): Tell us, what news?

**SONORA:** (*with a hoarse shout*): We've got him!

**ALL:** (*shout*): Hurrah!
(*Other groups of men come running on. All press round Sonora, clamoring for news. Billy emerges from among the trees. He has a long rope in his hand, which he slings now and again over a branch, looking for a suitable one from which to hang it.*)

**VOICES:** (*in confusion*): Tell us, how? . . .
Tell us, where? . . .
Did you see him? . . .
Come on, hurry!

**RANCE:** Do hurry!

# Act III

SONORA: (*fa cenno d'essere affannato dalla corsa*) L'ho veduto!
Perdio!
Pareva un lupo stretto dai can!
Fra poco sarà qui.

ALCUNI MINATORI: Maledetto
spagnuol!
Che ne faremo? . . .

ALTRI: (*indicando l'albero dove Billy prepara il laccio*): Un ottimo
pendaglio!
Lo faremo ballare appena arriva.
E quando ballerà
Pam!
Pam!
Pam!
Pam!
tireremo al bersaglio!
(*si muovono tutti in massa, gridando e cantando il ritornello:
"Dooda, dooda, day!"*)

RANCE: Minnie, Minnie, è finita!
Io non fui, non parlai!
tenni fede al divieto!
A che ti valse, a che ti vale,
ormai!
Il tuo bel vagheggino dondolerà da
un albero al rovaio!
(*si siede affronto*)
(*Rimangono soli Rance, Nick e
Billy, ancora occupato indifferentemente nelle sue prove crudeli.
Silenzio grave, rotto soltanto da
un vago clamore lontano. La luce
del giorno è ormai chiarissima. Le
vette nevose scintillano al sole fra
gli alberi*).

NICK: (*portando con violenza
Billy sul davanti della scena e
dandogli una manciata d'oro*)
(*rapidamente, sotto voce*) Questo
è per te.
Ritarda a fare il laccio . . .
Ma guai se mi tradisci!
(*puntandogli la pistola in faccia*)
In parola di Nick, bada, t'ammazzo!
(*Nick fugge precipitosamente.
Un'orda precede l'arrivo di Johnson*)
(*Appare Johnson in mezzo a uomini a cavallo e alla folla dei minatori e degli uomini del campo; è
sconvolto, pallido, col viso graffiato e gli abiti stracciati, ha una
spalla nuda*)

TUTTI: (*entrando in scena con
gesti di minaccia*) A morte!
Al laccio!
Al laccio lo spagnuolo!

ASHBY: (*a Rance*) Sceriffo Rance!
Consegno a voi quest'uomo perchè
sia dato alla comunità.
Faccia essa giustizia!
(*monta a cavallo*)

TUTTI: La farà!

ASHBY: (*a Johnson, da lontano,
mentre se ne va*) Buona fortuna,
mio bel gentiluomo!
(*Tutti si dispongono a gruppi a

SONORA: (*out of breath still*):
Yes, I've seen him!
By heaven! 'twas like a wolf
Set upon by dogs!
In a minute he'll be here!

SOME MINERS: To hell with the
Spaniard!
What shall we give him? . . .

SOME: (*Pointing to the tree where
Billy is preparing the noose*): The
very finest hanging!
We'll teach him how to dance
When we have caught him!
And while he does his dance,
Pom!
Pom!
Pom!
Pom!
He'll be sport for our rifles!
(*The miners all run off in a body,
shouting and singing the refrain:
"Dooda, dooda, day!"*)

RANCE: Minnie, Minnie, it's all
over!
'Twas not I that told!
I kept my word of honor!
What has it helped you,
What will it help you now?
Your fascinating swell has got to
swing
From a tree in the North wind!
(*Sits down wearily.*)
(*Only Rance, Nick and Billy remain, the latter still lackadasically busy with his cruel experiments. Intense silence, only
broken by a confused din in the
distance. Broad daylight now. Between the trees the snow-peaks
glitter in the sun.*)

NICK: (*roughly drags Billy to the
front and giving him a handful of
gold, says quickly, sotto voce*):
This is for you,
Don't make the noose until I tell
you.
If you play me false, upon my word,
look out,
I'll kill you!
(*Levels pistol at him.*)
(*Nick goes off hurriedly. A crowd
precedes Johnson's arrival.*)
(*Johnson appears in the midst of a
crowd of horsemen, miners and
camp followers; he is defeated,
ashy pale, his face scratched, his
clothes torn, one shoulder bare.*)

ALL: (*coming on with threatening gestures*): We'll hang him!
The scoundrel!
String up the cursed Spaniard!

ASHBY: (*to Rance*): Sheriff Rance,
I give this man into your charge.
Deliver him at once to the community.
Justice must be done.
(*Mounts his horse.*)

ALL: So it shall!

ASHBY: (*to Johnson, as he is riding off*): I wish you luck, my fine
gentleman!
(*They all arrange themselves in

guisa di un tribunale, i cavalli nel
fondo, abbrigliati agli alberi.
Johnson è nel mezzo, solo*)

RANCE: (*dopo aver acceso un sigaro, si avvicina a Johnson e gli
getta una lunga boccata di fumo
in viso. Con ironia:* ) E così, Mister
Johnson, come va?
Scusate se vi abbiamo disturbato . . .

JOHNSON: (*sdegnoso, guardandolo fisso*) Purchè facciate presto!

RANCE: Oh, quanto a questo
basteranno a sbrigarci
pochi minuti . . .

JOHNSON: (*indifferente*) E quello
che desidero.

RANCE: (*con cortesia affettata*) E
che desideran tutti, vero?
(*La turba dei minatori si stringe
atterno ai due uomini con un
brontolìo iroso e impaziente*)
(*Il brontolìo sordo che corre fra i
minatori scoppio ad un tratto in
un tumulto rabbioso,
vio'entissimo Tutti sono intorno
a Johnson, che li fronteggia colla
sua fierezza sdegnosa, il busto eretto, la fronte aggrottata, e lo investono con gesti e voci minacciose. Anele gli uomini a cavallo
sono scesi di sella, lasciando i cavalli nel fondo e si sono uniti alla
turba*)

VOCI VARIE: (*con violenza*)—Al
laccio!
—A morte!
—Cane!
Figlio di cane!
—Ladro!

HARRY: (*con accanimento,
avanzandosi verso Johnson*) Hai
saccheggiato tutto il paese!

BELLO: (*c. s.*) La tua banda ladra ha
rubato ed ucciso!

JOHNSON: (*scattando*) No!

TRIN: (*con accanimento avanzandosi verso Johnson*) La squadra di Monterey, bandito,
fu massacrata dalle faccie gialle
(*avvicinando la faccia a Johnson*)
di quelle tue canaglie messicane!

HARRY: Pugnalasti alle spalle
il nostro Tommy!

JOHNSON: (*pallidissimo*) Non è
vero!

HAPPY ED ALTRI: Sì!

VOCI: A morte!
A morte!

HARRY: Non è un mese, alla valle
fu ucciso un postiglione!

BELLO: Tu lo uccidesti!

VOCI: A morte!
A morte!

groups in the manner of a tribunal; the horses at the back, fastened to trees. Johnson in the middle, alone.*)

RANCE: (*lights a cigar, goes up to
Johnson, and deliberately puffs
the smoke into his face. Ironically*): And now, Mr. Johnson, how are
you?
Do pray excuse us if we have disturbed you!

JOHNSON: (*contemptuously,
looking him straight in the face*):
Only get it over quickly!

RANCE: Oh, as for that,
Two minutes will be quite enough
To despatch you!

JOHNSON: (*indifferently*): That's
all I'm asking for.

RANCE: (*with mock courtesy*):
And all that everyone's asking for,
Isn't it?
(*The crowd of miners closes in
round the two men with angry
and impatient mutterings.*)
(*The subdued mutterings of the
miners suddenly burst out in a rabid and most violent tumult. They
are all round Johnson, who confronts them with defiant pride, erect, with raised eyebrows. They
close in upon him with threatening gestures and cries. The horsemen have got off their saddles and
joined the crowd, leaving their
horses in the background.*)

DIFFERENT VOICES: (*violently*):
To death with him!
Dog!
Son of a Dog!
Robber!

HARRY: (*furiously, going
towards Johnson*): You've sacked
The whole of the country!

HANDSOME: (*as above*): Your
gang of robbers
Has plundered and murdered!

JOHNSON: (*bursts out*): No!

TRIN: (*furiously, going up to
Johnson*): The squadron of Monterey was murdered,
Massacred foully, wiped out altogether!
By your accursed gang of Mexican
butchers!

HAPPY: It was your vile hand
That stabbed poor Tommy!

JOHNSON: (*ashy pale*): No!
It's not true!

HAPPY AND OTHERS: Yes!

HARRY: In this valley quite lately
A post-boy was killed!

HANDSOME: 'Twas you that killed
him!

VOICES: Let's hang him!
Let's hang him!

JOHNSON: (*fierissimo, alzando il capo, con gli occhi sfavillanti sotto le sopracciglia corrugate*) No! Maledizione a me! Fui ladro, ma assassino mai!

JOE ED ALTRI: Non è vero!

HARRY: Se pure, fu la sorte che ti aiutò!

TRIN: (*sommessamente, con accento drammatico*) Alla "Polka" quella notte venisti per rubare . . .

SONORA: Furon gli occhi e il sorriso di Minnie, a disarmarti!

BELLO: Anche lei ci hai rubato!

SONORA: Ladro! L'hai stregata.

HARRY: Ladro! ladro!

BELLO: Ladro d'oro e di ragazze!

VOCI VARIE: —Al laccio lo spagnuolo!
—A morte!
—A morte!
—Billy ha la mano maestra!
E sarai fatto re della foresta!
(*coro di risa feroci*)

TRIN—HARRY—JOE: Ti faremo ballare l'ultima contraddanza . . .

SONORA—BELLO—HAPPY: Ti faremo scontare le carezze di Minnie . . .

BELLO: Ti faremo cantare da Wallace la romanza della "Bella fanciulla"!
(*Spingono brutalmente Johnson verso l'albero dove sta Billy col laccio*)

RANCE: (*battendo sulla spalla a Johnson, ridendo*) Non vi preoccupate, caballero!
È una cosa da nulla . .

JOHNSON: (*freddamente, poi esaltandosi*) Risparmiate lo scherno . .
Della morte non mi metto pensiero: e ben voi tutti lo sapete!
(*con sprezzo altezzoso*)
Pistola o laccio è uguale . . .
Se mi sciogliete un braccio, mi sgozzo di mia mano!
D'altro voglio parlarvi:
(*con grande sentimento*) della donna che amo . . .
(*Un mormorio di sorpresa serpeggia fra la folla dei minatori*)

RANCE: (*ha uno scatto, fa come per avventarsi su Johnson, poi si frena e gli dice con freddezza guardando l'orologio*) Hai due minuti per amarla ancora . . .
(*Il brontolio dei minatori si muta in uno scoppio di voci irose*)

JOHNSON: (*very haughtily, raising his head, his eyes flashing beneath his frowning brows*): No! It's true I've been a thief, But never stooped to murder!

JOE AND OTHERS: That's a lie!

HARRY: Or, if it's true, 'Twas only a chance that stopped you!

TRIN: (*in low-pitched, dramatic accents*): At the "Polka" that night You came to rob it!

SONORA: It was Minnie's eyes And smiles that stopped you!

HANDSOME: And of those you have robbed us!

HARRY: Robber! Robber!

HANDSOME: Thief of gold and of women!

DIFFERENT VOICES: Let's hang the dirty Spaniard! We'll hang him! Billy has the master-hand! Now we will make you king of the forest!
(*Chorus of fierce laughter.*)

TRIN, HARRY, JOE: We'll teach you to dance, Teach you the very latest dance!

SONORA, HANDSOME, HAPPY: We'll make you pay most dear For Minnie's caresses!

HANDSOME: We'll make you sing The famous ballad of The "Fair and Lovely Lady"!
(*They roughly push Johnson towards the tree where Billy is standing with the noose.*)

RANCE: (*clapping Johnson on the shoulder, laughing*): Pray don't let it agitate your lordship! It's a mere nothing . .

JOHNSON: (*coldly, then growing excited*): At least spare me your mocking. As to death, I don't care when I meet it: I've run the risk of death too often!
(*With supreme contempt.*)
I care not how or when. Untie my arm and I'll cut my throat With my own hand! It is of something else I must speak—
(*With deep feeling.*)
Of the girl whom I love.
(*A murmur of surprise runs through the crowd of miners.*)

RANCE: (*has a sudden movement as if about to throw himself on Johnson; then he restrains himself, and looking at his watch, says coldly*): You've just two more minutes left to love her.
(*The miners' mutterings change into a burst of angry voices.*)

VOCI VARIE: (*con accento represso d'ira*)—Basta!
—Alla corda!
—Fatelo star zitto!
—Parlerà da quel ramo!

SONORA: (*dominando il tumulto*) Lasciatelo parlare! E nel suo dritto!
(*Si fa accanto a Johnson e lo guarda fisso, combattuto fra l'odio, l'ammirazione e la gelosia. Tutti tacciono*)

JOHNSON: (*sorpreso*) Ti ringrazio, Sonora!
(*rivolto a tutti*)
Per lei, per lei soltanto, che tutti amate, a voi chiedo una grazia e una promessa . .
Ch'ella non sappia mai come son morto!
(*mormorii sommessi in vario senso*)

RANCE: (*guardando l'orologio, nervoso*) Un minuto . . . sii breve.

JOHNSON: (*con grande espressione, esaltandosi, col viso quasi sorridente*) Ch'ella mi creda libero e lontano, sopra una nuova via di redenzione!
Aspetterà ch'io torni . . .
E passeranno i giorni, ed io non tornerò . . .
Minnie, della mia vita unico fiore, Minnie, che m'hai voluto tanto bene!

RANCE: (*si slancia su Johnson, lo colpisce con un pugno sul viso*) Ah, sfacciato!
(*tutti disapprovano l'atto di Rance*)
Hai null'altro da dire? . . .

JOHNSON: (*con alterigia*) Nulla. Andiamo!
(*Si avvia con passo sicuro verso l'albero, al cui piede Billy attende immobile, reggendo il laccio. La folla lo segue in un silenzio quasi rispettoso. Sei uomini con le pistole in pugno si dispongono ai due lati del tronco. Rance rimane fermo a guardare con le braccia incrociate*)
(*Un grido ucutissimo giunge da destra col rumore sordo di un galoppo. Tutti si fermano e si volgono*)

VOCI VARIE: —È Minnie! È Minnie! E Minnie!
(*Scena confusa. Tutti guardano verso il fondo da dove apparirà Minnie a cavallo seguita da Nick pure a cavallo.*)

RANCE: (*slanciandosi verso Johnson e gridando come un forsennato*) Impiccatelo!
(*Nessuno più bada a Rance. Tutti guardano verso il fondo e si agitano per l'arrivo di Minnie*).

DIFFERENT VOICES: (*with restrained anger*): Enough! Get the rope ready! Make him shut up! He can speak from that branch!

SONORA: (*dominating the crowd*): No, let him have his say! It is his right!
(*He goes up to Johnson and looks at him, torn between hatred, admiration and jealousy. All are silent.*)

JOHNSON: (*surprised*): I thank you, Sonora!
(*Turning to all.*)
For her, for her alone Whom you all love. I now ask a kindness and your promise; That she may never know how I have died!
(*Subdued murmurs for and against.*)

RANCE: (*looking at his watch, nervously*): One more minute. Look sharp.

JOHNSON: (*with intense expression, growing excited and almost smiling*): Let her believe that I have gained my freedom, Living the better life that she has taught me! Let her await my coming. The days will pass away, And I shall not return. Minnie, star of my wasted life, that lights my journey. Minnie, true heart, that loved me so very dearly!

RANCE: (*rushes up to Johnson and hits him in the face*): How dare you?
(*They all disapprove of Rance's action.*)
Have you no more to say?

JOHNSON: (*haughtily*): Nothing! Come on!
(*He goes with a firm step towards the tree, at the foot of which Billy is waiting motionless, holding the noose. The crowd follows him in silence which is almost respectful. Six men with pistols draw themselves up on either side of the tree. Rance stands still, with folded arms, watching them.*)
(*A piercing cry is heard from the right, and the sound of a galloping horse. All pause and turn around.*)

DIFFERENT VOICES: It's Minnie! It's Minnie!
(*Scene of confusion. All look towards the background whence Minnie will appear on horseback, followed by Nick, also on horseback.*)

RANCE: (*rushing towards Johnson and shouting like a madman*): Hang him, I tell you!
(*No one pays any more heed to Rance. They all gaze towards the background and grow excited at

# Act III

(*Minnie arriva in scena a cavallo, discinta, i capelli al vento, stringendo fra i denti una pistola. Nick la segue, scende e corre verso il gruppo che circonda Johnson*).
(*La folla dei minatori si ritrae, Johnson rimane immobile in mezzo ai sei uomini armati*).

**MINNIE:** (*balza in terra abbandonando il cavallo. Con un grido disperato:*) Ah, no!
Chi l'oserà?

**RANCE:** (*facendolesi innanzi*) La giustizia lo vuole!

**MINNIE:** (*fronteggiandolo*) Di quale gíustizia parli tu
Che sei la frode istessa?
Vecchio bandito?

**RANCE:** (*fa segno di minaccia e s'avvicina a Minnie*) Bada, donna, alle tue parole!

**MINNIE:** (*guardandolo negli occhi*) Che puoi tu farmi?
Non ti temo!

**RANCE:** (*scostandola violentemente, ai minatori con voce imperiosa:*)
Orsù!
Impiccate quest'uomo!
(*Qualcuno dei minatori risolutamente si avvicina a Johnson*)

**MINNIE:** (*d'un balzo si pone dinanzi a Johnson spianando la pistola*) Non lo farete!
No.
Nessuno l'oserà . . .
(*La turba indietreggia mormorando alla minaccia di Minnie*)

**RANCE:** (*incitando la folla*) Strappatela di là!
Nessun di voi ha sangue nelle vene?
Una gonna vi fa sbiancare il viso?
(*La turba non si muove, come affascianta dallo sguardo di Minnie*)

**MINNIE:** Osate!
Osate!
(*si stringe più accanto a Johnson, appoggia il viso sulla sua spalla continuando a fissare lo turba con uno sguardo di sfida, sempre spianando la pistola*)

**RANCE:** (*come pazzo di rabbia*)
Orsù!
Finiamola!
Bisogna che giustizia sia fatta!

**VOCI VARIE:** Basta!
Al laccio!
(*La turba esaltandosi a poco a poco si stringe attorno a Minnie e a Johnson*).
(*La turba ripresa dal suo furore d'odio e di gelosia si avanza più minacciosa. Due degli uomini armati che fiancheggiano l'albero*

*Minnie's arrival.*)
(*Minnie—followed by Nick—comes on, on horseback, dishevelled, her hair flying in the wind, a pistol between her teeth; she gets down and runs to the group of men surrounding Johnson.*)
(*The crowd of miners draws back. Johnson remains motionless in the middle of the six armed men.*)

**MINNIE:** (*jumps down from her horse with a desperate shriek*): Ah no!
Who will dare?

**RANCE:** (*going up to her*): Justice demands it.

**MINNIE:** (*confronting him*):
And who are you
To talk of justice?
Rascal yourself!

**RANCE:** (*goes up to Minnie threateningly*): Best take care
What you say to me!

**MINNIE:** (*looking him straight in the face*): What can you do?
I don't fear you!

**RANCE:** (*pushing her away roughly—to the miners in imperious tones*): Now then!
Make haste and hang this fellow!
(*Some of the miners resolutely approach Johnson.*)

**MINNIE:** (*with one bound places herself in front of Johnson and levels the pistol at the crowd*): Oh, no, you won't!
Not a man of you will dare!
(*The crowd draws back, muttering at Minnie's threats.*)

**RANCE:** (*urging on the crowd*):
Tear her away from there!
Is there not one of you that has an ounce of courage?
Does a petticoat make your faces grow white?
(*The crowd remains motionless, as if spell-bound by Minnie's look.*)

**MINNIE:** I dare you! I dare you!
(*She presses close to Johnson, leans her face on his shoulder, and continues to gaze on the crowd with defiance, keeping the pistol levelled at them.*)

**RANCE:** (*half mad with rage*):
Now then!
Now make an end!
You know that justice must be done!
Enough!

**DIFFERENT VOICES:** Stop it!
Let's hang him!
Stop it!
(*The crowd, growing gradually more excited, presses close around Minnie and Johnson. Then succumbing again to its rage of hatred and jealousy, it advances more threateningly. Two*

*afferrano Minnie alle spalle; essa si svincola e si aggrappa a Johnson alzando rapidamente la pistola*)

**MINNIE:** Lasciatemi, o l'uccido, e m'uccido!

**SONORA:** (*con un grido, gettandosi fra lei e la turba*) Lasciatela!
(*Tutti si ritraggono. Rance, pallido e torvo, si discosta e si siede nel cavo dell'albero dov'era il fuoco. Sonora rimane in piedi presso Minnie e Johnson minaccioso*)

**MINNIE:** (*pallidissima, tremante di sdegno, la voce sibilante*) Non vi fu mai chi disse
"Basta!"
Quando per voi davo i miei giovani anni . . . quando, perduta fra bestemmie e risse, dividevo gli affanni e i disagi con voi . . .
Nessuno ha detto allora "Basta!"
(*La turba tace colpita. Molti abbassano il capo*)
Ora quest'uomo è mio com'è di Dio!
Dio nel cielo l'aveva benedetto!
Se ne andava lontano,
verso nuovi orizzonti!
Il bandito che fu
è già morto lassù, sotto il mio tetto,
Voi non potete ucciderlo!
(*Una commozione rude comincia ad impadronirsi di tutti gli animi. Nessuno più protesta*)

**SONORA:** (*con un grido che pare un singhiozzo*) Ah, Minnie, più dell'oro ci ha rubato, un tesoro . . . il tuo cuore!

**MINNIE:** (*rivolgendoglisi, fatta d'un subito affettuosa*) Oh il mio Sonora buono, sarà primo al perdono . . .

**SONORA:** (*soggiogato, commosso, abbassa gli occhi*) Minnie!

**MINNIE:** Perdonerai come perdonerete tutti . . .

**VOCI:** (*commossi e a testa bassa*) No!
Non possiamo!

**MINNIE:** Si può ciò che si vuole!
(*va verso Joe*)
E anche tu lo vorrai,
Joe . . .
Non sei tu quei che m'offeriva i fiori, colti per me lungo il torrente azzurro, simili a quelli delle tue brughiere?
(*rivolgendosi a Harry, accarezzandogli la mano*)
Harry, e tu, quante sere
t'ho vegliato morente . . .
e nel delirio credevi in me vedere la tua piccola Maud,

*of the armed men beside the tree seize Minnie by the shoulders; she wrenches herself free and clings to Johnson again, swiftly raising her pistol.*)

**MINNIE:** Stand off, or I'll kill him and myself, too!

**SONORA:** (*with a shout, throwing himself between Minnie and the crowd*): Oh, let her go!
(*All draw back. Rance, ashy pale and grim, goes apart and sits down in the hollow of the tree near the fire. Sonora remains standing in a threatening attitude near Minnie and Johnson.*)

**MINNIE:** (*white as death, trembling with disdain, in strident tones*): Was ever one of you who said "Stop it,"
When I gave up the best of my days to you?
When in the midst of oaths and quarrels I used to
Share your worries and your want with you
Like a comrade?
Not one of you did ever then say "Stop it!"
(*The crowd is guiltily silent. Many lower their heads.*)
I claim this man as mine,
Mine from God!
God in his heaven above had blessed him;
He was going away, going to start a new life;
And the robber that was,
Died a week ago in my cabin;
You cannot kill him!
(*A rough feeling of emotion steals into their hearts. No one offers any further protest.*)

**SONORA:** (*with a cry which is almost a sob*): Ah, Minnie, the gold wouldn't matter,
But he's robbed us of your heart!

**MINNIE:** (*turning round, suddenly affectionate*): My good old Sonora,
Always the first to forgive.

**SONORA:** (*conquered, moved, lowers his eyes*): Minnie!

**MINNIE:** You will forgive,
As you will all forgive . . .

**VOICES:** (*moved, with bent heads*): No!
We can't!

**MINNIE:** You can do what you want!
(*Goes up to Joe.*)
And surely you will want it,
Joe . . .
Wasn't it you that would bring me flowers
You picked by the Torrent, like the ones
That grow in your country?
(*Turns to Harry, stroking his hand.*)
Harry, how many evenings,
When we thought you were dying,

la sorella che adori,
venuta di lontano . . .
(*a Trin con dolcezza*)
E tu mio Trin, a cui ressi la mano
quando scrivevi
le prime incerte lettere,
che partivan di qui per San Domingo . . .
(*rivolgendosi a Happy, poi a Bello, accarezzandolo alla guancia*)
E tu, buon Happy, e tu,
Bello, che hai gli occhi ceruli d'un bimbo,
(*rivolgendosi a tutti*)
e voi tutti, fratelli del mio cuore,
anime rudi e buone,
(*gettando via la pistola*)
ecco, getto quest'arma!
Torno quella
che fui per voi, l'amica, la sorella
che un giorno v'insegnò
una suprema verità d'amore:
fratelli, non v'è al mondo peccatore
cui non s'apra una via di redenzione!

**SONORA:** (*ad un gruppo di minatori*) —E necessario . . .
—Troppo le dobbiamo!
(*ad uno*)
—Deciditi anche tu!

**UN MINATORE:** No, non possiamo!

**SONORA:** (*ad Happy*) Tu taci!
E il suo diritto!

**ALCUNI MINATORI:** E che deá Ashby?

**SONORA:** Quel che vorrà!
I padroni siam noi!
(*investendone uno*)
Non t'opporre, tu!
(*ad altri*) Andiamo!
(*ad altro gruppo*)
E necessario alfin . . .
(*ad un altro*)
Deciditi anche tu.

**I MINATORI:** (*stringendosi nelle spalle*) E se' tu che lo vuoi . . .

**SONORA:** (*ad uno*) Anche tu, via!

**HAPPY:** (*allo stesso*) Anche tu . . .

**TRIN:** (*asciugandosi una lagrima*) Sì, tu m'hai fatto piangere!
Guardate come l'ama!

**HAPPY:** E com'è dolce è bella!

**I MINATORI:** È una viltà!
Rideranno di noi!

And you tossed on your bed in delirium,
Have I watched by your side,
While you thought I was Maud,
Your little sister come from home.
(*To Trin, very gently.*)
And you, my Trin, whose big hand I have guided,
When you scrawled the first
Unsteady letters that we sent from here
To San Domingo.
(*Turning to Happy, then to Handsome, stroking his cheek.*)
And you, dear old Happy,
And you, Handsome, with big blue eyes like a baby . . .
(*Turning to all.*)
And you all, who are dear to me as brothers,
Honest and faithful souls . . .
(*Throws away her pistol.*)
Look, I throw away my pistol!
Once again let me be as before,
Your loving friend, your sister,
Who once, not long ago, taught you
The best and highest teaching of Love:
That the very worst of sinners
May be redeemed and shall find the way to Paradise!

**SONORA:** We must . . .
We owe her too much!
(*To one of the men.*)
You surely will agree!

**A MINER:** No, we can't!

**SONORA:** (*to Happy*): You're silent!
It is her right!

**SOME MINERS:** And what will Ashby say?

**SONORA:** Who cares what he will say?
We are the masters here!
(*Going up to one.*)
You must give in, too!
(*To others.*)
Come on!
(*To others.*)
I say we must!
(*To another.*)
You surely will agree!

**SOME MINERS:** (*shrugging their shoulders*): If you say so . . .

**SONORA:** (*to one*): You, too, come on!

**HAPPY:** (*to the same one*): You, too!

**TRIN:** (*wiping away a tear*): Yes, you have made me cry!
See how she loves him!

**HAPPY:** And how sweet and kind she is!

**THE MINERS:** It's a shame—
We'll be a laughing stock.

**JOE, HARRY, SONORA E BELLO:** Minnie merita tutto!

**SONORA:** (*rivolto a tutti*) Per lei per me, lo fate!
(*i minatori con moti espressivi assentono*)
(*Johnson s'inginocchia commosso, bacia il lembo della veste di Minnie mentre essa pone la mano sulla testa di lui quasi benedicendolo*)

**SONORA:** (*stringe ad alcuni le mani e si avanza verso Minnie che lo guarda ansiosa, sorridendogli fra le lacrime*)
(*a Minnie*) Le tue parole sono di Dio.
Tu l'ami come nessuno al mondo!
(*Sonora rialza Johnson; con un coltello taglia rapidamente la corda che gli lega le mani*) In nome di tutti, io te lo dono.
(*piangendo*)
Va, Minnie, addio!
(*Le sue parole finiscono in un singhiozzo. Minnie bacia Sonora, poi, con un grido di gioia, si avvinghia a Johnson nascondendo nel di lui petto il suo pianto di felicità*)

**JOHNSON:** (*sorreggendola e guardando la turba silenziosa dalla quale si elevano singhiozzi sommessi*) Grazie, fratelli!

**MINNIE:** (*commossa*) Addio!

**TUTTI:** (*sommessamente, commossi*) Mai, mai più!
(*Minnie stringe le mani a Nick, accarezzandolo, e ad altri vicini a lei; poi ritorna verso Johnson*)
(*Nick commosso piange*)

**JOHNSON E MINNIE:** (*Minnie e Johnson, abbracciati, si avviano*)
Addio, mia dolce terra, addio, mia California!
Bei monti della Sierra, o nevi, addio!
(*escono di scena*)
(*La turba è accasciata. Alcuni sono a terra e piangono, altri appoggiati ai loro cavalli, altri agli alberi, si abbandonano al dolore—altri ancora, tristamente, fanno cenni di addio a Minnie che va allontanandosi*)

**LE VOCI DI MINNIE E DI JOHNSON:** (*interne, allontanandosi*) Addio, mia California, addio!

**LA TURBA:** (*sotto voce, singhiozzando*) Mai più ritornerai . . . mai più . . . mai più!

(*Sipario lentissimo*)

**JOE, HARRY, SONORA AND HANDSOME:** Minnie is worth it all!

**SONORA:** (*turning to all*): For her, for my sake, do it!
(*The miners signify their assent.*)
(*Johnson kneels down deeply touched; he kisses the hem of Minnie's gown while she places her hand on his head as if blessing him.*)

**SONORA:** (*shakes hands with some of them and goes up to Minnie*):
(*To Minnie.*):
O, Girl,
Your words must come from God,
Your love is something high and holy!
(*Sonora raises Johnson from the ground; with his knife he quickly cuts the rope which binds his hands.*)
In the name of all
I give him to you!
(*Crying.*)
Go, Minnie, good-bye!
(*His words end in a sob. Minnie kisses Sonora, then with a cry of joy she clings to Johnson, crying with joy, her face buried on his shoulder.*)

**JOHNSON:** (*supporting her and looking at the silent crowd from which subdued sobs are heard*): You shall not regret it!

**MINNIE:** (*touched*): Good-bye!

**ALL:** (*in low tones, very moved*): Good-bye!
(*Minnie wrings Nick's hands very affectionately, and shakes hands with others near her; then she goes up to Johnson.*)
(*Nick, deeply touched, is crying.*)

**JOHNSON AND MINNIE:** (*Johnson, his arm round Minnie, goes off with her*): Good-bye, beloved country; good-bye, my California, My mountains, my Sierra Mountains—Good-bye!
(*They go off the stage.*)
(*The crowd is in a state of dejection. Some are on the ground, crying; others, leaning against their horses or the trees, give way to their grief, others again wave good-bye, sadly, to Minnie, as she disappears.*)

**THE VOICES OF MINNIE AND JOHNSON:** (*behind in the distance*): Good-bye, my California, good-bye!

**THE CROWD:** (*sotto voce, weeping*): You'll never come again! Good-bye! Good-bye!

(*THE CURTAIN FALLS SLOWLY.*)

# La Rondine (1917)

## The Swallow

### MUSIC BY GIACOMO PUCCINI ■ LIBRETTO BY GIUSEPPE ADAMI

La Rondine, set to a libretto by Giuseppe Adami, premiered at the Théâtre du Casino in Monte Carlo on March 27, 1917. Magda de Civry, mistress of the banker Rambaldo, is giving a party at her beautiful Parisian home. Prunier, a poet and living-room philosopher, speaks derisively about romantic love. Prunier, who also claims to be a palm-reader, reads Magda's hand, pronouncing that she will fly away to the sea like a sparrow. A new guest arrives—Ruggero Lastouc, an old friend of Rambaldo's father. This is his first time in Paris, and Magda's maid, Lisette, suggests that he go to Bullier's cafe. Magda decides to go as well—dressed in Lisette's clothes. At Bullier's cafe, Magda sits down at a table already occupied by Ruggero, who does not recognize his hostess from earlier. Overwhelmed by memories of her earlier life, when she was poor and dreamed of passionate love, she gives in to her growing attachment to Ruggero. She leaves behind her Parisian comforts, flying to the sea like a sparrow, and lives with Ruggero in a little house on the Côte d'Azur. He wants to marry her and writes to his mother for her consent, which she grants—if his intended is virtuous. Magda knows that her past life deems her fit only to be Ruggero's mistress. She tells him who she really is. Desperately unhappy, she realizes that the swallow must fly back. She returns to her life in Paris with Rambaldo.

---

## ■ ATTO PRIMO

*Un salone elegantissimo in casa di Magda, A Parigi.*
*Nell'angolo di destra una serra-veranda a grandi vetrate, oltre le quali si vede una parte delle Tuilleries in pieno crepuscolo.*
*La porta d'entrata, assai grande e decorata da un ricco cortinaggio, è un poco a sinistra, nella parete di fondo.*
*A sinistra—in primo piano—una piccola porta conduce al boudoir. Vi si accede per una scaletta di pochi gradini, con ringhiera di legno.*
*Nel fondo, a destra—primo piano—un caminetto di marmo sormontato da un grande specchio. Presso il caminetto due poltrone e un piccolo tavolo basso.*
*Molti altri piccoli tavoli, poltrone, sedie, divani, son distribuiti qua e là con arte e con gusto.*
*Presso la veranda, un paravento.*
*Sulle pareti arazzi e stampe preziose. Sui mobili ninnoli e fiori.*
*A destra—a metà sala—un pianoforte a coda ricoperto da un ricco broccato. Sul piano un vaso di rose rosse. Vicino al pianoforte una lampada a stelo con grande abat-jour. Altre piccole lampade velate da abat-jour a diversi colori, sui tavoli, diffondono una luce intima e sobria.*
*Quando si schiude il velario i riflessi rossastri del tramonto illanguidiscono.*
*Rambaldo Fernandez è a destra, verso il fondo, e insieme con lui sono gli amici Perichaud, Gobin, Crebillon.*
*Yvette, Bianca e Suzy si sono avvicinate a Prunier, il quale appoggiato al pianoforte, le intrattiene con sottile vivacità. Magda sta versando il caffè che Lisette serve, scodinzolando rapidissima e petulante da un gruppo all'altro. Poi ritirerà le tazze che raccoglierà in un vassoio d'argento posato sul piccolo tavolo.*

**YVETTE:** (*con una risata*) Ah! no! no!

**BIANCA:** Non dite questo!

**PRUNIER:** Signore! Vi contesto il diritto di ridere! . . .

**YVETTE:** E noi quello di parlare sul serio!

**PRUNIER:** È pura verità!

**MAGDA:** (*avvicinandosi*) La verità sarebbe?

**PRUNIER:** Una cosa assai grave:
A Parigi si ama!
Imperversa una moda
nel gran mondo elegante:
L'Amor sentimentale!

**LISETTE:** (*interrompendolo vivacemente*) Amor sentimentale?
. . .
Ma non dategli retta!
Storie! . . .
Si vive in fretta:
"Mi vuoi? . . ."
"Ti voglio . . ."
È fatto!

## ■ ACT I

*An elegant salon in Magda's house in Paris.*
*In a corner, at the right, a covered veranda with large windows, from which the Tuilleries are seen in the twilight.*
*The entrance door is large and draped with a rich portière—It is a little to the left of the rear wall.*
*To the left—on the first floor—a small door leads to the boudoir. It is reached by a stairway of a few steps with a wooden banister.*
*To the rear, at the right,—on the first floor—a marble mantelpiece surmounted by a large mirror.*
*Near the fireplace two armchairs, and a small low table. Scattered around artistically and in good taste are more small tables, armchairs, chairs and divans. Near the veranda, a screen. On the walls hang tapestries and priceless prints. On the tables, nick-nacks and flowers.*
*To the right—halfway—a grand piano covered with rich brocade. On the piano a vase full of red roses. Near the piano a pedestal lamp with a large shade. Other smaller lamps, shaded in various colors, on the tables, shed a subdued light.*
*At the rising of the curtain, the reddish reflexes of the sunset linger on the scene.*
*Rambaldo Fernandez is seen to the right, towards the rear, and with him are his friends, Perichaud, Gobin, Crebillon.*
*Yvette, Bianca and Suzy are near Prunier, who, leaning against the piano, is entertaining them in a very lively manner. Magda is pouring out coffee and Lisette is handing it round, turning quickly and saucily from one group to the other. She then gathers up the cups and puts them on a silver tray, on a small table.*

**YVETTE:** (*with a burst of laughter*) Ah! no! no!

**BIANCA:** Don't say that!

**PRUNIER:** Ladies, I challenge your right to laugh!

**YVETTE:** And we, yours to talk seriously!

**PRUNIER:** And yet, I tell you it is true!

**MAGDA:** (*approaching*) What is true?

**PRUNIER:** A very serious matter;
Love has broken out in Paris!
The fashion of sentimental Love
Rages in the highest places!

**LISETTE:** (*interrupting with vivacity*) Sentimental Love? . . .
Don't listen to him!
Rubbish! . . . !
We all live in a hurry:
"Do you want me?"
"All right!"
. . . It is done!

PRUNIER: (con esagerato risentimento si rivolge a Magda accennando a Lisette) Scacciatela! . . .
Il contatto
con una cameriera . . . mi ripugna!

PRUNIER: (with exaggerated resentment to Magda, pointing at Lisette) I wish you would discharge her! . . .
Contact with a maid . . . is repugnant to me!

MAGDA: (intervenendo benevolmente) Poeta, perdonate! . . .
In casa mia
L'anormale è una regola . . .
(a Lisette)
Tu via!

MAGDA: (interrupting, kindly)
Forgive her, Poet! . . .
Abnormality is the Rule in my house . . .
(to Lisette)
You can go!

LISETTE: (con un inchino) Io ritorno al mio servizio
se del mio giudizio
non si sa che far!
(esce rapida)

LISETTE: (with a curtsy) I'll go back to my work, since you are not
Able to appreciate my wit!
(hurries out)

MAGDA: (sedendo presso a Prunier) Unque . . . raccontavate? . . .

MAGDA: (seating herself near Prunier) Well . . . you were saying? . . .

PRUNIER: Che la moda è romantica:
Sguardi amorosi,
streete furtive,
baci, sospiri,
ma niente più

PRUNIER: Romance is the fashion:
Loving glances,
Hands meeting stealthily,
Kisses, sighs . . .
And that's all!

YVETTE—BIANCA—SUZY: (giocando comicamente intorno a Prunier)
—Amore!
—O cielo!
—Svengo! . . . !
—Io struggo!
—Cedo! . . .
—Muoio! . . .
—Illanguidisco tutta!
—Consolami, Poeta!
—Assistimi fortuna!
—Dammi un chiaro di luna . . .
E un verso del Musset!

YVETTE—BIANCA—SUZY
(playing around Prunier for the fun of it)
—Love!
Ye Heavens!
I'm fainting!
I'm consumed!
I surrender!
I'm dying!
I'm languishing! Poet, console me!
Ye Fates help me!
Ah! for a moonbeam!
For a verse by Musset!

MAGDA: (interrompendo il gioco delle amiche)
Non scherzate!

MAGDA: (interrupting her friends' game)
Don't laugh!

PRUNIER: (colpito dal gesto di Magda)
Che c'è?
La moda v'interessa?

PRUNIER: (struck by Magda's behavior)
What do you say?
The fashion interests your?

MAGDA: Può darsi! . . .
Continuate.
(Nel frattempo Crebillon che sfogliava un giornale, pare colpito da una notizia che s'affretta a indicare agli altri. Tutti si aggruppano vicino a lui leggendo, poi sembrano discutere animatamente.)

MAGDA: Perhaps! . . . Go on.
(Meanwhile, Crebillon, who is reading the paper, seems to be struck by some item of news, which he is anxious to impart to the others. They all gather around him while he reads. They discuss the matter with animation.)

PRUNIER: La malattia . . .
diciamo epidemia . . .
meglio è dire follia,
fa grande strage
nel mondo femminile! . . .
(Tutte gli si avvicinano attente)
È un microbo sottile
che turbina nell'aria . . .
Vi prende di sorpresa
E il cuor non ha difesa!

PRUNIER: This sickness . . .
Or rather epidemic . . .
Better still, this madness,
Is making terrible inroads
In the feminine world!
(all draw near and listen attentively)
It is a tiny microbe
Which gyrates in the air . . .
It takes you by surprise
And no heart is proof against it!

TUTTE: (con comica preoccupazione) È un microbo sottile
Che turbina nell'aria? . . .
Ci prende di sorpresa
E il cuor non ha difesa? . . .

ALL: (with comic earnestness) A tiny microbe
Which gyrates in the air . . .
It takes you by surprise
And no heart is proof against it! . . .

PRUNIER: Nessuno può salvarsi
tanto è oscura l'insidia! . . .

PRUNIER: No one can save himself,
So subtle is the snare!

TUTTE: (a bassa voce, quasi con terrore) Nessuna?

ALL: (in low tones, almost in terror) No one?

PRUNIER: Nessuna!

PRUNIER: No one!

TUTTE: (c. s.) Nessuna! . . .

ALL: (same as above) No one!

PRUNIER: (gravemente ripete)
Nessuna! . . .
Anche Doretta . . .

PRUNIER: (repeats gravely) No one! . . .
Not even Doretta . . .

TUTTE: Doretta?
E chi sarebbe?

ALL: Pray, who may Doretta be?

PRUNIER: La mia nuova eroina:
una cara donnina
che fu presa dal male
e immortalai tal quale
nell'ultima canzone . . .

PRUNIER: My new heroine:
A charming little lady
Who was struck with the evil.
I have immortalized her
In my latest song . . .

TUTTE: La vogliamo sentire!

ALL: Let's hear it!

PRUNIER: (con comica ironia)
Ne potreste soffrire!

PRUNIER: (with comic sarcasm)
It might cause you pain!

TUTTE: Non fatevi pregare!

ALL: Don't let us have to ask you twice!

MAGDA: Vi impongo di cantare!
(e voltandosi dal gruppo degli uomini)
E voi laggiù, silenzio!
(con esagerata solennità)
Il poeta Prunier, gloria della nazione,
Degna le nostre orecchie d'una nuova canzone!

MAGDA: I command you to sing!
(turning from the group of men)
Silence, over there!
(with exaggerated solemnity)
Prunier, the Poet, the Glory of the Nation,
Will condescend to honor our ears with a new song!

RAMBALDO: (alzandosi) Argomento?

RAMBALDO: (rising) The subject?

PRUNIER: L'Amore!

PRUNIER: Love!

RAMBALDO: (sedendo) Il tema è un po' appassito!
(Perichaud, Gobin, Crebillon annuiscono)

RAMBALDO: (taking his seat again) That subject is a little bit off color!
(Perichaud, Gobin, Crebillon assent)

MAGDA: L'amore è sempre nuovo!
(a Prunier, invitandolo al piano)
Su, Poeta!

MAGDA: Love is always new!
(to Prunier, motioning him to the piano)
Begin, Poet!

PRUNIER: Mi provo!
(Egli accende la lampada a stelo vicino al pianoforte, poi siede e abbozza i primi accordi. Nella sala si fa un grande silenzio)
Chi il bel sogno di Doretta
potè indovinar!
Il suo mistero nessuno mai scoprì!
Un bel giorno il re la bimba volle avvicinar:
—"Se tu a me credi,
se tu a me cedi,
ti farò ricca!
Ah! cretura!
Dolce incanto!
La vana tua paura,
il trepido tuo pianto
ora sparirà!"
—"No! mio sire!
No, no piango!
Ma come son, rimango,
chè l'oro non può dare
la felicità!"
(poco a poco Magda s'avvicina)
(Pruiner si alza)

PRUNIER: Let's see, if I can!
(He lights the lamp near the piano, sits down, and strikes a few chords. Silence in the room)
Who can guess Doretta's dream?
Who can solve her mystery?
The King approached the Maid one day:
"Put your trust in me;
Be mine and riches shall be yours
Ah! creature of enchantment sweet,
Your fears and weeping soon will cease!
"No Sir! I am not shedding tears!
I will remain just as I am, for
No gold can buy me happiness!"
(Magda approaches slowly)
(Prunier rises)

MAGDA: Perchè non continuate?

MAGDA: Why don't you go on?

## Act I

PRUNIER: Il seguito mi manca:
Se voi l'indovinate
Vi cedo la mia gloria!

MAGDA: La conquista mi tenta,
e la semplice istoria! . . .
(*Siede al pianoforte. L'attenzione si far ancor più viva*)
Chi il bel sogno di Doretta
potè indovinar?
Il suo mistero come mai finì?
Ahimè! un giorno uno studente
in bocca in baciò
e fu quel bacio
rivelazione:
Fu la passione!
Folle amore!
Folle ebbrezza!
Chi la sottile carezza
D'un bacio così ardente
mai ridir, potrà?

TUTTI: (*sussurando sommessamente*)—Deliziosa!

MAGDA: (*con crescente calore*)
Ah! mio sogno!
Ah! . . . mia vita!

TUTTI: —È squisita! . . .
—È squisita! . . .

MAGDA: —Che importa la ricchezza
Se alfine è rifiorita
la felicità!
(*Non appena il suo canto è finito, Prunier prende dal vaso che è sul pianoforte le rose rosse e le sparge lentamente ai piedi di Magda*)

PRUNIER: Ai vostri piedi
Tutte le grazie della Primavera!

MAGDA: (*alzandosi sorridente e stringendo le mani che gli amici le tendono*)—No . . . Adesso non burlatemi . . .

PERICHAUD: Vi ripeto: squisita!

CREBILLION: Che arte!

GOBIN: Che finezza!

RAMBALDO: Che calore!

MAGDA: (*stupita, a Rambaldo*)
Come? . . . voi . . . l'uomo "pratico"? . . .

RAMBALDO: (*allargando le braccia, con rassegnazione*) La corrente trascina!

MAGDA: (*ironica*) Merito di Prunier, nostra rovina!

PRUNIER: Non sono io! . . .
Nel fondo
d'ogni anima c'è
un diavolo romantico
ch'è più forte di me,
di voi, di tutti!

RAMBALDO: —No!
Il mio diavolo dorme!

YVETTE: (*ingenuamente*) Che peccato!
Perchè?

PRUNIER: I don't seem to get the end:
If you have guessed it,
I cede my glory to you!

MAGDA: The conquest tempts me,
It is a simple story! . . .
(*she seats herself at the piano*)
(*attention is still more eager*)
Who can guess Doretta's dream?
What was the solution of the mystery?
Woe is me! One day a student
Kissed her lips and that kiss revealed to her
Passion!
Love's madness!
And wild exuberance!
For who can recount
The subtle caress
Of so ardent a kiss?

ALL: (*in a low voice*) Delightful!

MAGDA: (*with increasing passion*) O! dream of mine!
O Life!

ALL: Exquisite! . . .
Exquisite!

MAGDA: —What matter riches
If happiness returns at last!
(*She has hardly come to the end of her song, when Prunier, taking the vase of red roses from the piano, slowly scatters them at the feet of Magda*)

PRUNIER: At your feet all the gifts of Spring!

MAGDA: (*rising with a smile and clasping the hands of her friends*)
No . . . Now, don't laugh at me . . .

PERICHAUD: I assure you: exquisite!

CREBILLON: What art!

GOBIN: What finesse!

RAMBALDO: What passion!

MAGDA: (*stupified, to Rambaldo*) What? . . . you . . . the "practical" man? . . .

RAMBALDO: (*spreading his arms, with resignation*) The current drags me under!

MAGDA: (*with irony*) Prunier's merit is our ruin!

PRUNIER: It is not I! . . .
In the depths of each
Soul there lurks a devil of romance,
Which is stronger than I, you, or anyone!

RAMBALDO: —No!
My devil is asleep!

YVETTE: (*innocently*) What a pity!
Why? . . .

RAMBALDO: Mi armo di acqua santa e lo sconfiggo.
Lo volete vedere?
(*leva dal taschino un astuccio contenente una collana di perle e l'offre a Magda*)
Ecco!

MAGDA: (*prendendo il gioiello, un po' meravigliata*)—A me?

RAMBALDO: Certo! . . . la mia intenzione
era di offrirvelo prima di pranzo . . .
me ne dimenticai . . . ma l'occasione
sembra inventata apposta!

MAGDA: Ho una sola risposta:
Non cambio d'opinione . . .

RAMBALDO: Non lo esigo! . . .
(*S'allontana mentre gli altri si raggruppano intorno a Magda. Gobin, Perichaud, Crebillon, dopo essersi passati l'uno all'altro il gioiello, quasi per valutarne il prezzo, e dopo aver espressa la loro ammirazione, si staccano dal gruppo avviandosi verso la veranda, dove si fume*)

PRUNIER: —La Doretta
della mia fantasia
non si turba . . .
ma, in verità,
mi pare che vacilli
quella della realtà!

LISETTE: (*Entra rapidissima da destra, si dirige verso Rambaldo e trascinandolo in disparte gli sussurra con incredibile velocità*) Un momento: scusi, ecco:
quel signore giunse ancora.
Gli risposi: "Calma! Aspetti!"
Mi rispose: "Già da un'ora
Sto in istrada passeggiando
In attesa d'un comando!
Che mi dica se non può! . . ."

RAMBALDO: (*parlato*) Non ho capito una parola!

LISETTE: (*come prima*) Auff!
Quel signore che le dissi
La cercava poco fa . . .

RAMBALDO: Ebbene?

LISETTE: Non si muove,
non la smette,
sette volte
già tornò!

RAMBALDO: Sette volte?

LISETTE: Sette!
Sette!
Le ripeto: non la smette . . .
fra un minuto tornerà.

RAMBALDO: (*avvicinandosi a Magda*) Scusate, Magda:
Mi permettete
di ricevere qui il figlio
d'un mio amico d'infanzia?
Da due ore m'aspetta . . .

MAGDA: Ma fate pure!
Siete in casa vostra.

RAMBALDO: I arm myself with Holy Water and cast him out.
Do you want to see him?
(*He takes from his pocket a jewel case containing a pearl necklace and offers it to Magda*)
—There!

MAGDA: (*takes the necklace somewhat surprised*)—For me?

RAMBALDO: For you! . . .
—It was my intention to give it to you
Before dinner . . . but I forgot . . .
however, the
Moment seems very well chosen!

MAGDA: I have just one reply:
I adhere to my opinion . . .

RAMBALDO: I do not expect the contrary!
(*He goes off while the others group around Magda. Gobin, Perichaud, Crebillon, after having passed the jewel to each other, as if to place a valuation on it, and after having expressed their admiration, leave the group and pass on to the veranda to have a smoke*)

PRUNIER: —The Doretta
Of my fantasy is adamant . . .
But it seems to me that the
One in the flesh is surrendering!

LISETTE: (*Enters in a hurry, on the right, she goes to Rambaldo and drawing him aside whispers to him with incredible velocity*)
One moment: excuse me:
That man has come again.
I told him: "Calm yourself! Wait!"
He replied: "I have been walking
Around the streets already for an hour . . .
Awaiting a sign! . . .
Let him tell me, if he can't . . ."

RAMBALDO: (*spoken*) I haven't understood a word!

LISETTE: (*flustered as before*) Oh, dear! The man I told you about,
The one who was looking for you a little while ago . . .

RAMBALDO: Well?

LISETTE: He won't budge,
He just keeps on,
He has returned seven times!

RAMBALDO: Seven times?

LISETTE: Yes, seven! Seven!
And I tell you: he just keeps on . . .
He will be back again in a minute.

RAMBALDO: (*going up to Magda*) Excuse me, Magda:
Will you allow me to receive here
The son of a friend of my childhood?
He has already been waiting for me two hours . . .

MAGDA: Do as you like!
You are in your own house.

RAMBALDO: Razie.
(*a Lisette*)
Ditegli allora
Che passi pure qui.
(*Lisette esce rapida*)
(*Rambaldo si avvia verso la serra*)

PRUNIER: (*a Magda, accennando a Lisette*) Come fate a sopportarla?
È un mulinello!

MAGDA: (*bonariamente*) No. E una brava ragazza . . .
Forse invadente,
ma divertente . . .
Un po' di sole
nella mia vita!

BIANCA: La tua vita è invidiabile!

YVETTE: Rambaldo generoso!

BIANCA: Credi a me che nessuna ebbe la tua fortuna

MAGDA: Che importa la fortuna!
(*Prunier nel frattempo ha raggiunto gli altri nella veranda*)

SUZY: La vita è assai difficile!

BIANCA: Costa tanto il denaro!

MAGDA: Denaro . . . denaro . . .
Nient'altro che denaro! . . .
Ma via! Siate sincere!
Son sicura che voi m'assomigliate
e spesso rimpiangete
la piccola "grisette"
ch'è felice col suo innamorato!

BIANCA: Sono sogni!

MAGDA: Può darsi! . . .
Ma che non si dimenticano più! . . .
Ah, quella sera
che son scappata alla mia vecchia zia!
Mi pare ieri! . . .
E perchè non potrebbe
essere anacora domani? . . .
Perchè? . . .
(*assorta nella visione lontana*)
Ore dolci e divine
di lieta baraonda
fra studenti e sartine
d'una notte a Bullier! . . .
Come andai? Non lo so!
Come uscii? . . . No lo so!
Cantava una lenta canzone
la musica strana
e una voce lontana
mi diceva così:
"Fanciulla, è sbocciato l'amore!
Difendi, difendi il tuo cuore!
Dei baci e sorrisi l'incanto
Si paga con stille di pianto! . . ."
. . . Quando ci sedemmo,
stanchi, estenuati
dalla danza, la gola
arsa, ma 'lanima
piena d'allegrezza,
mi parve che si schiudesse
tutta una nuova esistenza! . . .
Due bocks—egli disse—al garzone!
Stupita fissavo quel grande scial-

RAMBALDO: Thanks.
(*to Lisette*)
Tell him to come in.
(*Lisette goes out hurriedly*)
(*Rambaldo goes to the covered veranda*)

PRUNIER: (*to Magda, pointing to Lisette*) How can you put up with her?
A regular idiot!

MAGDA: (*good humoredly*) No.
She is a good girl . . .
Perhaps officious,
But amusing . . .
A little sunshine
In my life!

BIANCA: Your life is to be envied!

YVETTE: With Rambaldo, so generous!

BIANCA: Believe me, no one has had your good luck.

MAGDA: What is the use of good luck!
(*meanwhile Prunier has rejoined the others*)

SUZY: Life is hard enough!

BIANCA: Money costs so much!

MAGDA: Money . . .
Money . . .
Nothing but money! . . .
Get along with you!
Be sincere!
I am sure that you are just as I am,
And many a time you regret the little "grisette"
So happy with her lover!

BIANCA: Those are only dreams!

MAGDA: Maybe! . . .
But they are unforgettable! . . .
Oh that night, when I ran away from my old aunt!
It seems like only yesterday! . . .
And why should the same tomorrow not be? . . .
Why? . . .
(*absorbed in a far away vision*)
What hours of sweetness divine,
Of joyful revelry,
Between students and seamstresses,
A night at Bullier! . . .
How I went? I cannot say!
How I left? I do not know!
Strange music droned in a slow rhythm
And a distant voice said:
Child, love has awakened!
Defend, defend your heart!
The incantation of kisses and smiles
Must be repaid with tears and anguish . . .
When we rested
Tired and extenuated
From the dance, our throats parched,
But our souls alive with joy,
It seemed to me as if a new existence
Had sprung into being . . .
Two bocks—he said—to the waiter!
Stupified I stared at that spendthrift

one!
Gettò venti soldi. Aggiunse: Tenete! . . .

YVETTE: Che gesto da Creso!
(*le amiche ridono*)

SUZY—BIANCA: Che nobile gesto!
Che lusso!—Che sfarzo!

YVETTE: —C'è tutto compreso?

BIANCA—SUZY: —La birra ed il resto?

BIANCA—SUZY—YVETTE: Vogliamo la chiusa!
Vogliamo la fine!

MAGDA: (*riprendendo*)
—"Piccola adorata mia
il tuo nome vuoi dir?"
Io non glielo dissi
Ma sul marmo scrissi:
Ed egli accanto
Il nome suo tracciò . . .
E là fra la mattana
di tutta quella gente,
ci siamo guardati
ma senza dir niente . . .

YVETTE: Oh! strano! . . . senza dir niente?

BIANCA: E allora?

MAGDA: M'impaurii? . . . Non lo so!
Poi fuggii! . . . Più non so!
Cantava una triste canzone
la musica strana,
E una voce lontana
mi diceva così:
"Fanciulla è sbocciato l'amore!
Difendi, difendi il tuo cuore!
Dei baci e sorrisi l'incanto
Si paga con stille di pianto! . . ."
(*alzandosi*)
Potessi rivivere ancora
la gioia di un'ora!

YVETTE: E poi?

MAGDA: Basta . . . È finito . . .

BIANCA: (*con delusione*) Finito così?

MAGDA: Il profumo squisito
della strana avventura,
amiche, è tutto qui.

BIANCA: (*a Prunier che resale dal fondo*) Poeta, un argomento!

YVETTE—BIANCA—SUZY: (*alternandosi*) "Storia d'un puro amore
fra Magda giovinetta
E un ignoto signore . . .
Incontro ed abbandono
In meno di due ore . . ."

PRUNIER: Due ore? . . .
È quanto basta!

BIANCA: No: l'avventura è casta.

PRUNIER: Date i particolari!

As he flung him twenty sous, adding:
Keep it! . . .

YVETTE: The act of a Croesus!
(*the friends laugh*)

SUZY—BIANCA: What a noble act!
What luxury!
What extravagance!

YVETTE: —And was everything comprised?

BIANCA—SUZY: The beer and the rest?

BIANCA—SUZY—YVETTE: We want to hear the rest!
We want the end!

MAGDA: (*continuing*)
—"Little adored one
Tell me your name?"
I would not tell him
But on the marble table wrote:
And he, next to mine, traced his . . .
And there, amongst that seething crowd,
We gazed into each other's eyes
Without a word . . .

YVETTE: How funny! Without a word?

BIANCA: And then?

MAGDA: I felt frightened! . . . I know not why!
And I fled! . . . I know no more!
Strange music droned in a slow rhythm
And a distant voice said:
"Child, love has awakened!
Defend, defend your heart!
The incantation of kisses and smiles
Must be repaid with tears and anguish . . ."
(*she rises*)
Could I but live once more
The joy of that one hour!

YVETTE: And then?

MAGDA: That's all . . . It is finished . . .

BIANCA: (*disappointed*) Finished in that way?

MAGDA: The exquisite perfume
Of that strange adventure
Still lingers.

BIANCA: (*to Prunier who approaches from the rear*) Poet, a subject!

YVETTE—BIANCA—SUZY: "The story of a pure love
Between Magda, as a young girl,
And an unknown man . . .
Meeting and desertion
In less than two hours . . ."

PRUNIER: Two hours? . . .
Well, isn't that enough?

BIANCA: No: the adventure is chaste!

PRUNIER: Let's hear the particulars!

# Act I

BIANCA: Una fuga, una festa,
un po' di birra . . .

YVETTE: A casa, tutta sola,
la vecchia zia che aspetta,

BIANCA: E due baffetti bruni
che fan girar la testa!

PRUNIER: (equivocando per gioco) La zia coi baffi bruni
che beve della birra?
Curiosa! . . .
Non m'attira!

MAGDA: (sorridendo) V'attira la
nipote?

PRUNIER: Può darsi . . . ma qualora
essa risponda ai miei gusti d'artista!
La donna che conquista
dev'essere raffinata,
elegante, perversa . . .
Degna insomma di me:
Galatea, Berenice,
Francesca, Salomè! . . .

YVETTE: (impressionata) O che
uomo difficile!

BIANCA: (c. s.) Che nomo complicato!

PRUNIER: Non ne ho colpa: son nato
per le grandi avventure!

MAGDA: Ma come le scoprite
tante virtù: Poeta?

PRUNIER: È semplice: la mèta
d'ogni donna è segnata
nel palmo della mano . . .

MAGDA: Davvero?

BIANCA: —O strano!

YVETTE: —Strano!

PRUNIER: Se volete provare . . .
Ma esigo un gran mistero.
(indicando)
Il paravento!

BIANCA: Presto!
(Corre al fondo e aiutana da Suzy
e Yvette transporta il paravento
che è collocato dopo molte prove
in modo da formare un piccolo
recesso vicino al pianoforte. Le
donne vi si raccolgono sedendo
intorno a Prunier)

PRUNIER: Un angolo appartato . . .
(allundendo agli uomini che
sono nella veranda)
Laggiù il volgo profano! . . .
E qui, bellezza e . . .
Scienza! . . .
(le donne ridono)

MAGDA: (alle amiche, con comico rimprovero) Serietà, ve ne prego!

PRUNIER: Incomincio?

MAGDA: (tendendo la destra)
Son pronta!
Dite!

BIANCA: —Svelateci!

YVETTE: —Scoprite!

---

BIANCA: A flight, a feast.
A little beer.—

YVETTE: At home, all alone,
An old aunt waiting.

BIANCA: And a pair of side whiskers
Send a head a' spinning!

PRUNIER: (misinterpreting for fun) What, an aunt with side whiskers,
Drinking beer?
Strange! . . .
That doesn't attract me!

MAGDA: (smiling) But the niece does?

PRUNIER: Maybe . . . providing she measures up
To my artistic taste!
The woman who conquers
Must be refined,
Elegant, perverse . . .
In short, worthy of me:
A Galatea, Bernice,
Francesca, Salomé . . .

YVETTE: (very much impressed)
What a fastidious man!

BIANCA: (the same) What a complicated creature!

PRUNIER: It isn't my fault. I was born for great adventures!

MAGDA: But how can you find out all these virtues, Poet?

PRUNIER: It is quite simple: the fate of every woman
Is marked within the palm of her hand.

MAGDA: Really?

BIANCA: How strange!

YVETTE: How strange!

PRUNIER: Do you want to know . . .
But I require the greatest secrecy.
(indicating)
The screen!

BIANCA: Quickly!
(She runs to the rear and with the
help of Suzy and Yvette carries the
screen near the piano, where, after many trials, it is adjusted to
form a small recess. The ladies
seat themselves around Prunier)

PRUNIER: A select angle . . .
(alluding to the men who are on
the veranda)
Over there vulgar profanity! . . .
Here, Beauty and . . . Science!
(the women laugh)

MAGDA: (to her friends, scolding them for fun) Can't you be serious, please!

PRUNIER: I'm starting!

MAGDA: (presenting her right hand)—I'm ready!
Go ahead!

BIANCA: Unfold our lives!

YVETTE: Disclose!

---

SUZY: Anch'io voglio sapere!
(Lisette entra da destra recante su
un vassoio una carta che porge a
Rambaldo)

RAMBALDO: (dropo aver letto)
Ah! Ruggero Lastouc . . .
Fate passare . . .
(Lisette solleva la portiera, entra
Ruggero)

RAMBALDO: (movendogli incontro) O mio giovine amico . . .
Dovete perdonare . . .

RUGGERO: (impacciato e timido) Son io che chiedo scusa . . .
ecco . . . con questa lettera
mio padre mi presenta . . .
Vi scrive . . . leggerete . . .

RAMBALDO: (prendendo la lettera e disponendosi a leggere) Ma
vi prego . . . sedete.

PRUNIER: (dopo aver scrutata la
mano di Magda) Vi siete rivelata!
L'avvenire
è grave e misterioso . . .

TUTTI: —Sentiamolo!

PRUNIER: —Non oso!
È troppo sibillino . . .

MAGDA: Non turbatevi . . . Osate
. . .

PRUNIER: (grave) Vi trascina il
Destino! . . .
Forse, come la rondine,
migrerete oltre il mare,
verso un chiaro paese
di sogno . . . Verso il sole,
verso l'Amore . . .
E forse . . .

MAGDA: (interrompendolo) Un
cattivo presagio?

PRUNIER: —No. Il Destino
Ha in suo duplice viso:
Un sorriso o un'angoscia? . . .
Mistero!

RAMBALDO: (deponendo la lettera—a Ruggero) . . . Ed è la prima
volta
Che venite a Parigi?

RUGGERO: La prima . . .

PRUNIER: (dopo aver esaminato
la mano di Bianca)—A voi la folta
contorsione dei segni
suggerisce un "Et ultra!"

BIANCA: Significa?

PRUNIER: —Più avanti!
Chi più offre la vince
su tutti gli aspiranti . . .
(Lisette entra e reca una coppa di
champagne che colloca sul tavolo
davanti a Ruggero. Questi fa un
cenno di ringraziamento e vi accosta appena le labbra. Lisette
sorride e si avvicina al gruppo di
sinistra)

---

SUZY: I also want to know!
(Lisette enters to the right with a
visiting card on a tray, which she
hands to Rambaldo)

RAMBALDO: (after glancing at
the card) Ah!
Ruggero Lastouc . . .
Tell him to come in . . .
(Lisette raises the portière—
Ruggero enters)

RAMBALDO: (going to meet him)
My dear young friend . . .
You must forgive . . .

RUGGERO: (embarrassed and
timid) I ought to excuse myself . . .
Well . . . with this letter
My father introduces me . . .
He writes to you . . . read it . . .

RAMBALDO: (taking the letter,
starts reading) Please be seated.

PRUNIER: (after having scrutinized Magda's hand) You have revealed yourself!
The future is serious and mysterious . . .

ALL: —Let's hear what it all is
about!

PRUNIER: I hardly dare!
It is too sibylic . . .

MAGDA: Don't be confused . . .
start . . .

PRUNIER: (gravely) Fate is drawing you! . . .
Perhaps, like a swallow,
To migrate beyond the seas,
Into a sunny land of dreams . . .
Towards the sun, towards Love . . .
And perhaps . . .

MAGDA: (interrupting) A bad
omen?

PRUNIER: —No, fate is double
faced:
A smile or anguish? . . .
Mystery!

RAMBALDO: (lays down the letter)—(to Ruggero) . . . Is it the
first time you are in Paris?

RUGGERO: The first time . . .

PRUNIER: (after having examined Bianca's hand)—There is
obstruction;—
Confusion of the signs
Suggests an "Et ultra"!

BIANCA: What does that mean?

PRUNIER: —Forward!
He who offers most
Wins over all other aspirants . . .
(Lisette enters with a cup of champagne, which she places on the table in front of Ruggero. The latter thanks her and hardly touches it with his lips. Lisette smiles and joins the group on the left)

**RAMBALDO:** (*chiamando Prunier*) Poeta raffinato, dite un po', dove si può mandare un giovinotto che vuol passar la sera allegramente?

**PRUNIER:** (*interrompe il gioco, si alza, e movendo verso Rambaldo*)—A letto!

**RAMBALDO:** —Non scherzate.

**PRUNIER:** È verità.
(*avvicinandosi a Ruggero, con superiorità*)
La prima serata a Parigi
Non è che una vana leggenda
È tempo oramai di sfatarla!

**LISETTE:** (*prorompendo fra lo stupore di tutti*)—No! no! mille volte no!
Non è vero! . . .
Io sono parigina
nell'anima e difendo
il regno della donna!
(*Le donne incuriosite, spiano nel frattempo il nuovo arrivato. Quando Lisette prorompe, s'avvicinano tutte, meno Magda che si tiene sempre in disparte conversando con Perichaud. —Gobin e Crebillon invece attratti dal proromper di Lisette si avvicinano ridendo*)

**PRUNIER:** (*interrompendola*)
Storie!
Ma che!

**LISETTE:** Non ascoltatelo!
Parigi è piena
di fascini, sorprese e melaviglie!

**TUTTI:** Brava . . .

**PRUNIER:** (*sbracciandosi*) Esigo un contegno!

**LISETTE:** (*senza badargli con crescente calore*) La prima sera a Parigi
è come vedere il mare
per la prima volta!
Mai si è immaginato niente
di più grande e di più bello!

**PRUNIER:** Basta!
Basta!
Mettetela alla porta!

**LISETTE:** (*agli altri, accennando a Prunier*) Lasciatelo ai suoi sdegni!
Aiutatemi voi!

**PRUNIER:** (*che ba razgiunto Magda dalla parte opposta*) Essa è troppo insolente!

**MAGDA:** Compatite, poeta!
(*E segue Prunier cercando di calmarlo e avviandosi con lui verso la veranda dove resteranno appartati*)

**RAMBALDO:** (*a Lisette*) Avanti, dunque!
Indica tu la mèta!

**RUGGERO:** (*a Rambaldo*) Vi ringrazio!

**LISETTE:** (*agli altri*) Dove lo mandiamo?

**YVETTE:** Ora penseremo . . .

**RAMBALDO:** (*calling to Prunier*)
Astute Poet, tell me,
Where can I send a youth
Who wants to spend a happy evening?

**PRUNIER:** (*interrupting the game, rising and going over to Rambaldo*)—To bed!

**RAMBALDO:** No joking.

**PRUNIER:** That's the truth.
(*going over to Ruggero, in a superior manner*)
The first night in Paris
Is but a vain legend,
Which it is time to destroy!

**LISETTE:** (*interrupting to the discomfort of all*) No! no! a thousand times no!
It is not true! . . .
I am a Parisian
And with all my soul I will defend woman's kingdom!
(*The women, in the meanwhile, drawn by curiosity, join the new arrival. At Lisette's interruption, they all draw near, with the exception of Magda, who remained at a distance talking with Perichaud. —Gobin and Crebillon attracted by Lisette's remark, draw near laughing*)

**PRUNIER:** (*interrupting*) Rubbish!
Nothing but rubbish!

**LISETTE:** Don't listen to him!
Paris is full of fascination, surprises and wonders!

**ALL:** That's right . . .

**PRUNIER:** (*infuriated*) What behavior!

**LISETTE:** (*without noticing him, with increased vivacity*) The first night in Paris
Is like the first sight of the sea!
Nothing greater or more beautiful could be imagined!

**PRUNIER:** That's enough!
That's enough!
Turn her out!

**LISETTE:** (*to the others, pointing to Prunier*) Leave him to his anger!
And all of you help me!

**PRUNIER:** (*who has rejoined Magda on the other side of the room*) She is too insolent!

**MAGDA:** Be lenient, Poet!
(*She follows Prunier, trying to calm him and walks with him to the veranda where they remain*)

**RAMBALDO:** (*to Lisette*) Go on!
Let's hear the means!

**RUGGERO:** (*to Rambaldo*) I thank you!

**LISETTE:** (*to the others*) Where shall we send him?

**YVETTE:** Let us think . . .

**BIANCA:** Ci vuole una trovatta che sia degna di noi!

**YVETTE:** Lisette, tocca a voi!

**BIANCA:** Tocca a voi!

**LISETTE:** Tocca a me? . . .
(*va a prendere dal tavolo una matita e un foglio*)
Prendete nota, mio signor! . . .
(*gli porge carta e matita*)
Scrivete qua . . .
(*gli indica il tavolo*)
. . . Presto! Orsù!
(*Ora tutti sono intorno a Ruggero, suggerendogli scherzosamente i più noti ritrovi notturni*)

**LE DONNE:** (*l'una dopo l'altra*)
Le Bal Musard!
Prè Catelan!
A Frascati!
Meglio Cadet! . . .
Tutta Parigi scintilla!
Tutta Parigi sfavilla! . . .

**LISETTE:** (*dopo aver nel frattempo riflettuto, dominando il piccolo tumulto*) No! . . .
Da Bullier!

**TUTTI:** (*approvando*) Sì! Da Bullier!! . . .
Bullier!
È questa la scelta miglior!

**LISETTE:** (*indicando a Ruggero di prenderne nota*) Qua!
Segnate! . . .
E andate! . . .
(*E mentre Ruggero si alza, s'accomiata da Rambaldo e si avvia, Lisette, tenendo sollevata la portiera, dice:*)
Amore è là, gioia e piacer . . .
Scegliete il cuor che vi convien . . .
Ma ricordate che da Bullier
Tra risa, luci e fior
Canta più ardente Amor! . . .
(*Ruggero esce. Lisette lo segue. Gli altri prorompono in una risata Magda e Prunier che dal limitare della veranda hanno assistito alla scena, ora si avanzano. Magda tiene in manto la collana di perle e ne fa mulinello per gioco, con noncuranza*)

**MAGDA:** No . . . povero figliolo!
Un poco di pietà . . .
Me l'avete intontito.

**RAMBALDO:** Laggiù si sveglierà!

**BIANCA:** Bullier fa dei miracoli!

**MAGDA:** (*vagamente*) Bullier! . . .
(*considera la collana un momento e la getta con noncuranza su un tavolo*)

**PRUNIER:** Avea tutto il profumo della sua gioventù.
L'aria è pregna di lavanda . . .
(*annusando comicamente*)
Non sentite?

**BIANCA:** We must find someplace worthy of us!

**YVETTE:** Lisette, it is your turn!

**BIANCA:** It's your turn!

**LISETTE:** My turn?
(*she picks up a pencil and paper from the table*)
Just make a note of this, Sir! . . .
(*she hands him the paper and pencil*)
Write . . .
(*and tells him to draw near the table*)
Quickly!
Now!
(*All stand around Ruggero, laughingly suggesting the most notorious night resorts*)

**THE WOMEN:** (*each in her turn*)
Le Bal Musard!
Pré Catalan!
Frascati!
Or better . . . Cadet! . . .
All Paris is aflame!
All Paris is a'glitter! . . .

**LISETTE:** (*after having reflected awhile, dominating the tumult*)
No! . . . To Bullier!

**ALL:** (*approvingly*) Yes!
To Bullier!! . . .
Bullier!
That's the best choice!

**LISETTE:** (*telling Ruggero to make a note of it*) There!
Write it down! . . .
And go! . . .
(*And while Ruggero rises and takes leave of Rambaldo, Lisette holding back the portière, says:*)
Love is there, joy and pleasure . . .
Choose the heart that appeals to you . . .
But remember that at Bullier's
Between laughter, light and flowers;
Love sings most ardently of all! . . .
(*Ruggero goes. Lisette follows him. The others burst out laughing. Magda and Prunier, who, from the veranda have witnessed the scene, now join the others, Magda playing with her pearl necklace and whirling it around carelessly*)

**MAGDA:** No . . . the poor boy!
You should have shown a little mercy . . .
You quite bewildered him.

**RAMBALDO:** He'll wake up over there!

**BIANCA:** Bullier works miracles!

**MAGDA:** (*vaguely*) Bullier! . . .
(*She looks at the pearl necklace for an instant and then throws it carelessly on the table*)

**PRUNIER:** He was in the full bloom of his youth.
The air is full of lavender . . .
(*sniffing comically*)
Can't you smell it?

# Act I

RAMBALDO: (*accomiatandosi*) Sento . . . e scappo! Buona sera. (*gli ospiti tutti seguono il suo esempio e salutano Magda*)

MAGDA: Buona sera . . .

PERICHAUD: Vi ringrazio . . .

BIANCA E YVETTE: A domani . . .

PRUNIER: Buona sera . . . (*tutti escone*) (*Magda ritorna lentamente sui suoi passi. Va alla parete di sinistra, suona il campanello. Poi si abbatte sulla poltrona, aspettando. Entra Lisette*)

MAGDA: La carrozza.

LISETTE: Va bene. (*fa per avviarsi*)

MAGDA: (*d'improvviso richiamandela*) No, Lisette. Non esco. Accendete di là! . . . (*Lisette va verso il boudoir, accende la luce*)

LISETTE: Ricordo alla signora che più tardi non mi troverà: è serata d'uscita.

MAGDA: Andate pure.

LISETTE: Grazie. (*Esce rapida, spegnendo le luci della sala. Dalla serra soltanto viene una debole luce*)

MAGDA: (*resta un momento assorta, ripetendo a sè stessa l'enigmatica profezia di Prunier*) . . . Forse, come la rondine migrerò verso il mare, verso un chiaro paese di sogno . . . Verso il sole! (*Fa qualche passo verso destra vicino al posto che era occupato da Ruggero. Il foglio da lui dimenticato, sul quale poco prima aveva segnato i nomi dei ritrovi notturni, la colpisce. Lo prende lo lascia cadere come se una risoluzione improvvisa la decidesse*)

MAGDA: Bullier! . . . (*Il suo viso s'illumina di un sorriso, e corre rapida verso il boudoir richiudendone la porta*) (*La scena resta per un momento deserta. Poi Lisette a passettini svelti appare dalla serra. Reca in mano un vistoso cappello e sul braccio un mantello di seta. Attraversa in punta di piedi la sala, si ferma ad origliare dietro l'uscio del boudoir, risale tutta rassicurata incontrandosi con Prunier che, in soprabito col bavero rialzato e cilindro, le si avvicina e la bacia*)

PRUNIER: (*con esagerato slancio*) T'amo! . . .

LISETTE: (*scostandosi violentemente*) Menti!

RAMBALDO: (*taking leave*) I can smell it . . . and escape! Good night. (*all the guests follow his example and take leave of Magda*)

MAGDA: Good night . . .

PERICHAUD: I thank you . . .

BIANCA AND YVETTE: Till tomorrow . . .

PRUNIER: Good night . . . (*all leave*) (*Magda turns back slowly. She goes towards the wall to the left and touches the bell. She then drops into an armchair and waits. Enter Lisette*).

MAGDA: The carriage.

LISETTE: All right. (*she is on the point of leaving*)

MAGDA: (*recalling her suddenly*) No, Lisette. Don't go. Turn the light on in there! . . . (*Lisette goes into the boudoir and turns on the light*)

LISETTE: I would like to remind you That you will not find me in later, As it is my evening out.

MAGDA: You can go, Lisette.

LISETTE: Thank you. (*She goes out hurriedly, after turning the lights out in the drawing room. From the covered veranda a feeble light flickers*).

MAGDA: (*remains absorbed for a moment, repeating to herself the enigmatic prophesy of Prunier*) . . . perhaps, like a swallow, To migrate beyond the seas, Into a sunny land of dreams . . . Towards the sun! . . . (*She takes a few steps to the right, near the seat which had been occupied by Ruggero. The sheet forgotten by him, on which a little while ago he had marked down the names of the night resorts, is noticed by her. She picks it up, then drops it, as if decided by a sudden resolution*)

MAGDA: Bullier! . . . (*Her face lights up in a smile. She runs hurriedly to the boudoir and closes the door behind her*). (*The scene remains deserted for a while. Then Lisette, with hurried short steps, appears on the veranda. She carries a very showy hat in her hand and on her arm a silk wrap. She hurries through the room on tip-toe; stops at the boudoir door and listens; reassured she turns back—meets Prunier who, in his overcoat with upturned collar and wearing a top hat, approaches and kisses her*)

PRUNIER: (*in exaggerated tone*) I love you! . . .

LISETTE: (*violently struggling to be free*) You lie!

PRUNIER: (*con comica enfasi*) No! Tu sapessi a quale prezzo ti disprezzo! . . . Tu non sai che la mia gloria vuole orpello e falsità? Non può amar che donne ricche un poeta come me! Io lo dico, c'è chi crede, ed invece son per te! . . .

LISETTE: (*avvicinandosi a lui dolcemente*) Che silenzio!

PRUNIER: Che mistero!

LISETTE: M'ami!

PRUNIER: T'amo!

LISETTE: T'avvilisce?

PRUNIER: Ne son fiero! (*Lisette mette il cappello*)

LISETTE: Ora andiamo! . . . Tutto tace! . . .

PRUNIER: No! Il cappello non mi piace!

LISETTE: Non ti piace? . . . È il suo migliore!

PRUNIER: Non s'intona con il resto!

LISETTE: Cambio?

PRUNIER: Cambia? . . . Ma fa presto! (*Lisette esce di corsa lasciando cadere la borsetta*) Nove Muse, a voi perdono Se discendo così in basso! L'amo, l'amo . . . e non ragiono! Nove Muse a voi perdono!

LISETTE: (*rientrando con un nuovo cappello*) Questo è meglio?

PRUNIER: È originale!

LISETTE: E il mantello?

PRUNIER: Non è tale da strapparmi un'ovazione.

LISETTE: Vuoi che metta quella cappa che indossavo l'altra sera?

PRUNIER: Si: la cappa in seta nera! . . . (*Lisette esce ancora di corsa*) Nove Muse, a voi perdona Se mi abbasso a consigliarla, Ma da esteta quale sono, No, non posso abbandonarla!

LISETTE: (*rientrando con il nuovo mantello e girando intorno a Prunier*) Son completa?

PRUNIER: Sei squisita!

LISETTE: La borsetta?

PRUNIER: (*raccogliendola da terra*) Eccola qua.

LISETTE: (*aprendo la borsetta e disponendosi a un rapido "maquillage"*) Vuoi rossetto sulle labbra?

PRUNIER: Si. Il tuo labbro fiorirà!

LISETTE: (*eseguendo*) Sulle gote?

PRUNIER: (*with comic emphasis*) No! You know little of how I despise you! You don't seem to understand that my glory requires tinsel and deceit! A poet, such as I, can only love wealthy women! And yet, believe it or not, I am yours! . . .

LISETTE: (*approaching him sweetly*) What silence!

PRUNIER: What mystery!

LISETTE: You love me?

PRUNIER: I love you!

LISETTE: You lower yourself?

PRUNIER: I pride myself on it! (*Lisette puts on her hat*)

LISETTE: Let's go! . . . There is silence everywhere! . . .

PRUNIER: No! I cannot stand that hat!

LISETTE: You don't like it? It's her best!

PRUNIER: It doesn't harmonize with the rest!

LISETTE: Shall I change it?

PRUNIER: Change it! . . . Make haste! (*Lisette runs off and drops her purse*) O, you nine Muses, I crave your pardon, If I fall so low! I love her, I love her . . . I no further reason! Forgive me, you nine Muses!

LISETTE: (*returning with a new hat*) Do you like this better?

PRUNIER: It's original!

LISETTE: And the wrap?

PRUNIER: It is not such as to draw from me an ovation.

LISETTE: Would you rather I put on the coat she wore the other evening?

PRUNIER: Yes, the black silk wrap . . . (*Lisette runs out again*) Oh nine Muses, forgive me, If I fall so low as to guide her; But aesthetic as I am, I would willingly forsake her!

LISETTE: (*returning with the new wrap and walking around Prunier*) Now, I am complete!

PRUNIER: You are exquisite!

LISETTE: My purse?

PRUNIER: (*picking it up*) Here it is.

LISETTE: (*opening her pocketbook and starting to paint herself quickly*) Shall I rouge my lips?

PRUNIER: Yes, let your lips bloom!

LISETTE: (*rouging*) My cheeks?

PRUNIER: (*annuendo*) Sian due rose!

LISETTE: Nero agli occhi?

PRUNIER: Pochi tocchi!

LISETTE: Ecco!

PRUNIER: Fatto?

LISETTE: Fatto!

PRUNIER: (*con un sospiro di soddisfazione*) Là!
(*si avviano lentamente*)

LISETTE: Che silenzio!

PRUNIER: Che mistero!
(*la recinge con un braccio*)

LISETTE: (*con abbandono*) Chi ci chiama?

PRUNIER: Il nostro amore!

LISETTE: Chi mi ama?

PRUNIER: Questo cuore!

LISETTE: Chi mi bacia?

PRUNIER: (*baciandola*) Il labbro mio!

LISETTE: (*con un fil di voce*) Perchè bacia? . . .
Di'? . . .
Perchè? . . .

PRUNIER: Per ridirti: io sono te!
(*un nuovo bacio ed escono*)

MAGDA: (*Ora, lentamente, la porticina del boudoir si apre. Appare Magda vestita assai semplicemente da "grisette," e pettinata diversamente in modo da esser quasi irriconoscibile. S'accosta a un vaso di fiori, ne toglie una rosa rossa, va a uno specchio, punta il fiore fra i capelli, sussurrando*)
Chi mi riconoscerebbe? . . .
(*poi si drappeggia sulle spalle uno scialle e s'avvia, canterellando*)
"Chi il mistero di Doretta potè indovinar? . . ."
(*Giunta sulla soglia ha una breve esitazione. Ritorna allo specchio, si considera, ripete*)
Ma sì! . . . Chi mi riconoscerebbe?
(*ed esce rapida*)

*SIPARIO*

# ■ ATTO SECONDO

*Da Bullier.—Si scende nella sala da una ricca scala a sinistra. Nella sala è un grande audirivieni di folla una folla mista di studenti, di artisti, di "grisettes," di mondane, di avventori, di curiosi. Alcuni sono seduti qua e là ai tavoli variamente disposti. Altri a gruppi o soli, entrano scendendo la gradinata. Altri ancora salgono quella che conduce alle loggie. Nel fondo il giardino, illuminato da piccole lampade bianche ed opache.*
*Nella parete di sinistra sono due grandi finestroni ad arco coperti*

PRUNIER: (*consenting*) Let them be two roses!

LISETTE: Black for my eyes?

PRUNIER: A few touches!

LISETTE: There!

PRUNIER: That's done!

LISETTE: That's done!

PRUNIER: (*with a satisfied sigh*) There!
(*they go off slowly*)

LISETTE: What silence!

PRUNIER: What mystery!
(*puts his arm around her*)

LISETTE: Who calls us?

PRUNIER: Our Love!

LISETTE: Who loves me?

PRUNIER: This heart!

LISETTE: Who'll kiss me?

PRUNIER: (*kissing her*) My lips!

LISETTE: (*in a whisper*) Why do you kiss me? . . .
Tell me?
Why? . . .

PRUNIER: To tell you: I am yours!
(*they kiss again and go*)

MAGDA: (*Slowly the door of the boudoir is opened and Magda appears, dressed with simplicity, like a "grisette," her hair done in a way that changes her appearance. She takes from a flower vase a red rose, goes over to the looking glass, fixes it in her hair, and whispers*)
Who can recognize me now?
(*she drapes a shawl around her shoulders and goes off humming*)
"Who can guess Doretta's mystery? . . ."
(*at the door, she hesitates somewhat. Returns to the looking glass, and repeats*)
Well!
Who can recognize me now?
(*and goes out quickly*)

*CURTAIN*

# ■ ACT II

*At Bullier.—A sumptuous stairway, to the left, leads to the Amusement Hall. In the Hall a dense crowd of students, artists, "grisettes," adventurers and curiosity seekers.*
*Groups are seen here and there at tables, disposed in various ways. Other groups or people alone are seen entering and descending the stairs. While others again ascend the stairs to the balcony.*
*In the background, the garden illuminated with small opaline lamps.*
*The wall on the left has two arched*

*di tende, oltre i quali è la strada che sale.*
*Sui tavoli, nella sala, nella loggia vasi di fiori in grande profusione. Alcune fioraie si aggirano tra la folla che entra, esce, siede, si alza, chiama, dà ordini, confusamente.*
*I camerieri vanno e vengono da un tavolo all'altro.*

UN GRUPPO DI BEVITORI: Via, su! Presto!
Cameriere!
Qua da bere!
(*il cameriere accorre e serve*)

LE FIORAIE: Fiori freschi! . . .

UN AVVENTORE: (*alzandosi*) Cameriere: Dammi il resto!
(*paga e se ne va*)

UN GIOVANE: (*offrendo*) Vuoi, tu, bionda?
(*la bionda accetta i fiori e s'allontana*)

UN BORGHESE: (*ad un altro*) Oh! La strana baraonda!

LE FIORAIE: (*offrendo*)—Le violette?
—Belle rose?

TRE UOMINI E TRE DONNINE:
Via, non fate le ritrose!
Sulla loggia o nel giardino?
(*salgono verso la loggia*)

UN AVVENTORE E ALCUNE "GRISETTES": —Paghi!
—Pago!
—Birra!
—Grazie!

DUE AMANTI: (*litigando in disparte*)—Non far scene!
—Sono stanca!
—Mi vuoi dir quel che ti manca?
—Vieni!
—Resto!
—No, ti prego!
—(*l'amante trascina la ritrosa—Si confondono nella folla*)

DUE DONNE E UN GIOVINE: —Scegli!
—È grave!
—Su! . . . Coraggio!
—Io son grassa!
—Sono magra!
—Sono oca!
—Sono scaltra!
—Per avere l'equilibrio
Io vi scelgo l'una e l'altra!

ALCUNE DONNE AD ALCUNE ALTRE: —In giardino già si balla!
—Voi restate?
—Vi seguiamo.

*and curtained windows, beyond which is seen the street sloping upward.*
*Everywhere, on the tables, in the hall, on the balcony, a profusion of flowers in vases.*
*Several flower girls accost the entering crowds, who come, go, seat themselves, rise, call to each other and give their orders in confusion.*
*The waiters come and go from one table to the other.*

A GROUP OF DRINKERS: Hi there!
Waiter!
Let's have something to drink!
(*the waiter runs up and serves them*)

FLOWER GIRLS: Fresh flowers!

A CUSTOMER: (*getting up*) Waiter: Let me have my change!
(*he pays and goes*)

A YOUNG MAN: Do you want them, blondie?
(*the blonde woman accepts the flowers and goes*)

ONE BOURGEOIS: (*to the other*) What a motley crowd!

FLOWER GIRLS: (*offering flowers*)
Violets?
Beautiful roses!

THREE MEN AND THREE WOMEN: Come along, don't make a fuss!
On the balcony or in the garden?
(*they go up to the balcony*)

A CUSTOMER AND SEVERAL GRISETTES: —You pay?
—I pay!
—Beer!
Thank you!

TWO LOVERS: (*quarreling—aside*)—Now, don't make a scene!
—I'm tired!
What's the matter with you?
—Come!
—I shan't!
—No, please!
(*the lover drags his stubborn sweetheart away—They disappear in the crowd*).

TWO WOMEN AND A YOUNG MAN: —Choose!
—That's dangerous!
—Come along! . . .
Courage!
—I'm fat!
—I'm slim!
—I'm a goose!
—I'm smart!
To keep my balance, I'll choose you both!

SEVERAL WOMEN TO SEVERAL OTHERS: —They are already dancing in the garden!
—Are you going to stay here?
—We will follow later.

## Act II

UN GRUPPO D'UOMINI: (*ad alcune donne impazienti*)—Un momento che veniamo.

A GROUP OF MEN: (*to several women who show signs of impatience*)—Wait a moment, we are coming.

LE DONNE IMPAZIENTI: Gia la danza ferve e snoda
Il suo ritmo e la sua grazia.

THE WOMEN: —This air with its rhythm and grace
Sways me and sets me dancing.

GLI UOMINI: (*battendo sui tavoli*) Cameriere!
Presto! . . .
Il conto!

THE MEN: (*knocking on the table*) Waiter!
Quick! . . .
The bill!

UN GRUPPO: (*attorniando una mondana*)—Senza te la vita era troppo amara.

A GROUP: (*around a cocotte*)—Without you
Life was too sad.

ALTRI: (*sopraggiungono e completano*)—Ma con te la vita costa troppo cara.

OTHERS: (*arriving and finishing the sentence*)—But with you
Life is too dear.

LA FOLLA: —Qui si trinca!
—Là si balla!

THE CROWD: —Here they drink!
—There they dance!

UN GRUPPO DI STUDENTI: (*che ha imprigienata una modella, passandosela dall'uno all'altro e baciandola*)—A chi tocca tocca!
—Dammi la tua bocca!
—Dammi la tua bocca! . . .

A GROUP OF STUDENTS: (*who have captured an artist's model, passing her along to each other and kissing her*) Your turn!
My turn!
Right on the lips . . .

UN GRUPPO DI BEVITORI: (*seduti a un tavolo*) Fino a che non spunta il giorno
Guai a chi farà ritorno!
Nel bicchiere è l'ideal!
(*entra il vecchio Edoardo. I pittori lo circondano subito*)

A GROUP OF DRINKERS: Woe to him that talks about leaving before dawn!
The Ideal is only to be found at the bottom of one's cup!
(*Old Edward enters and is immediately surrounded by artists*)

I PITTORI: —Siete voi dei nostri? Sì!
—Siete voi che paga? . . .
Sì!
—Scorra a fiumi lo champagne!
(*chaimando*)
—Qua, ragazze!
—Cose pazze!
(*il gruppo con le donnette si avvia verso il giardino cantando e saltando*)
—Su, beviamo! Su, danziamo! . . .
Giovinezza, eterno riso,
fresco fiore che incorona
delle donne il dolce viso! . . .
Sol tu illumini e incateni
le illusioni degli amanti! . . .
(*sfollano*)
(*Entrano dal giardino, diretti verso l'uscita, un Giovine elegante che tiene strette al braccio due belle donnine*)

THE ARTISTS: Are you one of us?
Yes!
You'll do the paying! . . .
Yes!
Let champagne run in torrents!
(*calling*)
Here, girls!
The sky is the limit!
(*the group with their women go towards the garden, dancing and singing*)
Let's sing!
Let's dance! . . .
Youth, eternal joy,
Flowers which engarland
Woman's countenance fair!
Sun which lightens and retains
The lover's illusions . . .
(*they disappear in the crowd*)
(*From the garden a smart youth and two beautiful women trend their way toward the door*)

PRIMA DONNINA: (*puntando l'indice sullo sparto del giovine*) Questa è una perla vera?

FIRST WOMAN: (*pointing to the youth's shirt front*) Is that a real pearl?

IL GIOVINE: Vera come il Vangelo!

THE YOUTH: Real like the Gospel!

SECONDA DONNINA: Siete ricco?

SECOND WOMAN: Are you rich?

IL GIOVINE: (*enigmatico*) Talvolta!

THE YOUTH: (*enigmatically*) Sometimes!

PRIMA DONNINA: (*conciliante*) A noi basta stasera!
(*escono*)
(*Alcune "grisettes" poco disoste dal tavolo al quale è seduto Ruggero che è là tutto solo e silenzioso. Altre "grisettes" si avvicinano alle amiche e chiedono*)
—Che guardate? . . .

FIRST WOMAN: (*in a conciliatory tone*) It would only be for tonight!
(*they go out*)
(*Several "grisettes" near the table at which Ruggero is sitting watch the young man alone and silent. Other "grisettes" go up to their friends and ask*)
—What are you looking at?

V'attira la conquista?
(*le "grisettes" di prima, rispondono*)
—Che pena! . . .
Così solo! . . .
È funebre! . . .
Rattrista! . . .
(*poco a poco s'avvicinano al tavolo*)
—È un solitario . . . un timido . . .
Un giglio . . . Una mimosa . . .
—Non degna d'un sorriso, d'uno sguardo!
(*Reggero le guarda, fra seccato e stupito. E allora le ragazze sempre più vicine, lo interrogano chiassosamente*)
—Suvvià! Come ti chiami?
—Armando? . . . No? . . . Abelardo?
—Marcello? Enrico? Alberto?
—Tommaso? Ernesto? Dario?
—Domenico? Giovanni?
—Carlo? Luigi? Mario?
—Santi del calendario,
fornite l'inventario.
Se trovato non fu,
il nome dillo tu!
(*Ma Ruggero ha un gesto dispetto e le ragazze, canzonandolo, con risatine sommesse, e allontanandosi, commentano*)
—È un principe che viaggia
in incognito stretto!
Vien da remota spiaggia!
Rifiuta il nostra letto! . . .

Does that conquest draw you?
(*the former "grisettes" reply*)
—What misery! . . .
What loneliness! . . .
—A funeral! Piteous!
(*little by little they draw near to the table*)
—He is a hermit . . . shy . . . a lily . . . a mimosa . . .
—He does not deign to smile or to look!
(*Ruggero gives them a look of annoyance and surprise. The girls draw nearer and question him noisily*)
Wake up, now!
What's your name?
Armando? . . .
No? . . .
Abelardo?
Marcello?
Enrico?
Alberto?
Tommaso?
Ernesto?
Dario?
Domenico?
Giovanni?
Carlo?
Luigi?
Mario?
Oh saints of the calendar,
Furnish the inventory . . .
If we cannot guess it,
Tell us your name yourself!
(*But Ruggero only makes a gesture of annoyance and the girls, laughing at him, turn away saying*)
It is a Prince traveling
In strictest incognito!
He comes from distant shores!
And has no use for us!

UNA GRISETTE: (*ad un'amica*) Non avresti per caso
Un po' di cipria?
Ho rosso il naso!
(*L'amica leva dalla borsetta la cipria. L'altra, sporgendo il visetto insolente, fa un rapido col piumino*)
(*Magda è apparsa sulla gradinata. Guarda interno incerta, titubante. Scende un altro gradino, si ferma, torna a guardare. Alcuni giovanotti si avvedono di lei, notamo la sua invertezza, le muovono incontro*)

A GRISETTE: (*to a friend*) Do you happen to have a little powder?
My nose is all red!
(*The friend takes her powder out of her bag. The other girl jerks her face forward insolently and touches it up with the powder puff*)
(*Magda appears on the staircase. She looks around hesitating and timid. She walks down a few steps, stops and looks around. Several young men notice her hesitation and approach her*)

I GIOVANI: (*sommessamente, accennando a Magda*)—Chi è?
—Mai vista!
—Esita!
—Una donna per bene?
—Dimessa, ma graziosa!
—Nuova per queste scene!

THE YOUNG MEN: (*whispering, and looking at Magda*)—Who is she?
—Never seen her before!
—She is hesitating!
—She seems well bred!
—Poorly dressed, but charming!
—New to these surroundings!

UN GIOVINE: (*più audacemente degli altri, salendo la scala incontro a Magda*) Posso offrirvi il mio braccio?

A YOUTH: (*bolder than the others, going up the stairs to meet Magda*) Can I offer you my arm?

MAGDA: (*con grande imbarazzo*) No . . . grazie . . .

MAGDA: (*very much embarrassed*) No . . . thank you . . .

GLI ALTRI: (*incoraggiati dall'esempio circondano Magda*)
—Siamo studenti . . .
—Artisti . . .
—Gaudenti . . .
—Un poco audaci . . .
—Molto loquaci . . .
—Ricchi di gioia!
—Prodighi in baci!
—Molto più rari
Sono i denari!
—Siamo studenti . . .
—Se non trova di meglio,
Non faccia complimenti!

THE OTHERS: (*encouraged by the example, surrounded Magda*) We are students . . .
—Artists . . .
—Pleasure seekers . . .
—Somewhat audacious . . .
—Free of speech . . .
—Rich in humor!
—Prodigal in kisses!
—Scarce of funds!
—We are students!
—If you can't find anything better, Don't stop for compliments!

MAGDA: (*è venuta scendendo la scala sempre più stretta fra il gruppo*) Grazie . . . grazie . . . non posso . . .

MAGDA: (*Magda has walked to the bottom of the stairway—the group closing around her*) Thanks . . . thanks . . . I cannot . . .

UN GIOVINE: C'è già un impegno?

A YOUTH: You already have an appointment?

MAGDA: (*approfittando dell'occasione offertale con questa domanda per sbarazzarsi degli importuni*) Ecco . . . Precisamente . . .

MAGDA: (*takes advantage of the opportunity offered her with this question to rid herself of the annoyance*) That's it . . . Precisely . . .

UN GIOVINE: E il luogo del convegno?

A YOUTH: And the place of meeting?

MAGDA: Siete troppo curiosi!

MAGDA: You are by far too curious!

UN GIOVINE: Siamo gelosi!

A YOUTH: We are jealous!

MAGDA: Di già?

MAGDA: Already?

PERICHAUD: Noi si fa presto!

A YOUTH: We don't lose any time!

UN ALTRO: Indicate l'eletto!

ANOTHER: Show us the elect one!

MAGDA: (*smarrita*) Non so . . . non so . . . vi ho detto . . .

MAGDA: (*bewildered*) I don't know . . . I don't know . . . I have already told you . . .

IL GIOVINE DI PRIMA: Se il mistero ci svelate
alla mèta vi guidiamo!

FIRST YOUTH: Unveil the mystery to us
And we will guide you to the goal!

MAGDA: (*a sè*) Che dire? . . .
(*Gia intorno lo sguardo smarrito. I suoi occhi si posano istintivamente su Ruggero che la guarda. I Giovani se ne avvedono e dicono*)
—Eccolo . . . È là!
(*Con molto grazia trascinano Magda riluttante verso il tavolo di Ruggero che stupefatto senza capire, guarda ora Magda, ora i Giovani*)

MAGDA: (*to herself*) What shall I say? . . .
(*She looks around bewildered, and her eyes fall instinctively on Ruggero, who is watching her. The youths notice this and say*)
Oh! There he is!
(*They drag Magda gently towards Ruggero's table, who surprised, and not understanding, looks first at Magda and then at the youths*)

I GIOVANI: Amanti godete
la giovine vita!
(*e si allontanano, ridendo*)

THE YOUTHS: Lovers, enjoy
Your young lives!
(*they depart, laughing*)

MAGDA: (*a Ruggero, con esitazione e semplicità*) Scusatemi . . . scusate . . .
Ma fu per liberarmi
Di loro, che volevano invitarmi
A danzare . . . Risposi: "Sono attesa . . ."
Han creduto che voi mi aspettavate . . .
Ora, quando non vedono, vi lascio . . .

MAGDA: (*to Ruggero, with hesitation and simplicity*) Excuse me . . . excuse me . . .
But I had to get rid of them,
As they wanted to invite me to dance . . .
I told them you were waiting for me . . .
As soon as they have turned their backs, I will leave you . . .

RUGGERO: (*colpito dalla sincerità della giovane e facendole cenno di sedere*) No . . . Restate . . . Restate

RUGGERO: (*struck by the sincerity of the young woman, motions her to sit near him*) No . . . stay . . . stay . . .

Siete tanto graziosa e mi sembrate
Cosi diversa
da tutte . . .

You are so charming and seem to me
So different than the others . . .

MAGDA: (*sedendo*) Veramente?

MAGDA: (*seating herself*) Is that true?

RUGGERO: Veramente.

RUGGERO: Quite true.

MAGDA: (*sorridendo*) Perchè?

MAGDA: (*smiling*) Why?

RUGGERO: Così timida e sola assomigliate
Alle ragazze di Montauban,
Quando vanno a ballare, alla carezza
D'una musica vecchia,
Tutte sorriso e tutte giovinezza.

RUGGERO: So timid and lonely, you resemble
The girls of Montauban,
When they dance to the strain
Of an old air . . .
All smiles, all youth.

MAGDA: (*con piccola ironia*) Ne sono lusingata!

MAGDA: (*somewhat ironically*) I am deeply flattered!

RUGGERO: (*un poco confuso*) Cercate di capirmi . . .
Le ragazze, laggiù, son molto belle
E semplici, e modeste . . .
Non sono come queste:
Basta al loro ornamento
Un fiore nei capelli . . .
Come voi . . .

RUGGERO: (*confused*) Try and understand me . . .
The girls over there are very beautiful,
Simple and modest . . .
Not like the girls here.
All they need as ornament
Is a flower in their hair . . .
Just like you . . .

MAGDA: . . . Se sapessi ballare
Come si balla a Montauban! . . .

MAGDA: . . . If only I could dance as they do
In Montauban! . . .

RUGGERO: (*offrendole il braccio*) Volete che proviamo?

RUGGERO: (*offering her his arm*) Shall we try?

MAGDA: Proviamo . . .
Ma se poi
Vi mancassi alla prova?

MAGDA: Let's try . . .
But should I fail
At the lesson?

RUGGERO: No, no . . .
Ne sono certo:
Ballate meglio voi!
(*Porge il braccio. Magda vi si appoggia languidamente*)

RUGGERO: No, no . . . I am certain.
You dance better than I do!
(*he offers her his arm. Magda leans on it languidly*)

MAGDA: (*quasi a sè*) Oh! . . .
L'avventura strana . . .
Come nei dì lontani . . .

MAGDA: (*to herself*) O! . . . What a strange adventure . . .
Just like old times . . .

RUGGERO: Che dite?

RUGGERO: What did you say?

MAGDA: Son contenta
D'essere al braccio vostro! . . .
Nella dolce carezza della danza
Chiudo gli occhi per sognar.
Tutto è ornamai lontano,
Niente mi può turbar . . .
E il passato
Sembrami dileguar! . . .
(*si confondono colla folla*)

MAGDA: I am happy to be in your arms!
In the sweet caressing melody of the dance
I can close my eyes to dream.
Everything seems far, far away . . .
Nothing can disturb me . . .
And the past seems to be vanishing . . .
(*they are lost in the crowd*)

LA FOLLA: (*danzando*) "Vuoi tu dirmi che cosa più ti tormenta
quando ride giocondo amor?
Quando lo stesso petto
chiude lo stesso cuor,
Quando un bacio
Brucia d'unguale ardor!
Baci lievi e tremanti,
Baci folli e vibranti,
Sono vita per gli amanti! . . .
Dammi nel bacio la vita
E vivi per baciar! . . . ."
(*la danza prende movimento e calore. Grida allegre e gioiose della folla*)

THE CROWD: (*dancing*) "Can you tell me what causes you torment
When love mirthfully smiles?
When the same bosom enfolds the same heart.
When a kiss burns with ardor intensive!
Kisses trembling on your lips,
Kisses mad and burning;
They are life's breath to the lover!
Let your kiss be life to me
And let me live to kiss you . . ."
(*the dance gets more lively and colorful. Cries of joy arise from the crowd*)

## Act II

**LE VOCI DI MAGDA E RUGGERO:** (*dal giardino*)—Dolcezza! . . .
—Ebbrezza! . . .
—Incanto!
—Sogno! . . .
—Per sempre!
—Per sempre!
—Eternamente! . . .
(*le voci si perdono*)
(*entrano le coppie delle danzatrici raffiguranti la Primavera*)

**THE VOICES OF MAGDA AND RUGGERO:** (*in the garden*)—
What sweetness!
—Inebriation!
—Enchantment!
—A dream! . . .
—Forever!
—And forever!
—Eternally!
(*the voices fade away*)
(*enter dancing couples representing Spring*)

**CORO A DANZA:** O profumo sottil
D'una notte d'April!
L'aria è tutta piena
di primavera e languor! . . .
Sboccian fiori ed amor
di Primavera al tepor! . . .

**CHORUS AND DANCE:** O subtle perfume
Of an April night!
The languor of Spring
Is in the air! . . .
The breath of Spring
Brings forth flowers and love!

**LE VOCI DI MAGDA E RUGGERO:** (*lontane*) Come batte il tuo cuor!
O primavera d'amor! . . .

**THE VOICES OF MAGDA AND RUGGERO:** (*from a distance*)
How your heart throbs!
O Spring of Love . . .

**IL CORO:** "Vuoi tu dirmi che cosa
più ti tormenta
Quando ride giocondo amor?
Quando lo stesso petto
Chiude lo stesso cuor,
Quando un bacio
Brucia d'uguale ardor! . . .
(*Nel frattempo, mentre la folla ritorna verso il giardino, entrano Prunier e Lissete*)

**CHORUS:** "Can you tell me what causes you torment
When love mirthfully smiles?
When the same bosom enfolds the same heart?
When a kiss burns with ardor intensive . . .
(*Meanwhile, while the crowd returns to the garden, Prunier and Lisette are seen entering*)

**PRUNIER:** (*con esagerate compostezza*) Ti prego: dignità, grazia, contegno! . . .

**PRUNIER:** (*with exaggerated composure*) Please!
Be dignified, gracious and composed! . . .

**LISETTE:** (*alzando le spalle un po' seccata*) Ti voglio bene,
Anche ti ammiro,
Ma se mi agito,
Se guardo, giro,
Ballo, scodinzolo,
Rido, saluto,
Canto, sternuto,
Ecco il tuo monito
Come una morsa
Prendermi, stringermi
Nella mia corsa! . . . .

**LISETTE:** (*shrugging her shoulders and somewhat annoyed*) I like you,
And even admire you,
But the least thing I do—
Whether I look around,
Dance, jest,
Laugh, nod,
Sing, sneeze,
You immediately call me to order—
You tighten the rein,
You pull me up and
Stop me in my course! . . .

**PRUNIER:** Se mi confondo
A dar lezione
È per rifarti
L'educazione!
Questo è il mio còmpito,
Sarà un miracolo,
Solo chi ama
Non guarda ostacolo:
Ti rifarò! . . .
(*essi hanno attraversata la scena e si sono uniti alla folla, ballando*)
(*Durante le scene che seguono, di tratto in tratto nuovi arrivi di tipi e di coppie diverse, dalla scala d'entrata*)
(*Magda e Ruggero rientrano, accaldati, stanchi di danzare, pieni di allegrezza, e si precipitano al tavolo occupato prima, abbandonandosi sulle sedie*)

**PRUNIER:** If I take the trouble
Of giving you lessons,
I am trying to
Mend your education!
I've set myself the task,
And it will be short of miraculous,
But he who loves
Knows of no impediment:
I'll remake you! . . .
(*They walk across the stage and join the dancing crowd. During the scene which follows, new arrivals of individuals and couples are seen on the stairway*)
(*Magda and Ruggero reenter, tired from dancing and in buoyant spirits, they rush to the table which they had occupied before and drop into their seats*)

**MAGDA:** (*agitando un piccolo fazzoletto*) Ah!
Che caldo!
Che sete!

**MAGDA:** Oh!
The heat!
I'm so thirsty!

**RUGGERO:** (*subito, ad un cameriere che passa*) Due bocks!

**RUGGERO:** (*immediately, to a passing waiter*) Two bocks!

**MAGDA:** (*con gioia, quasi rivivesse un ricordo*) Presto! . . .
Presto! . . .
(*poi a Ruggero*)
Posso chiedervi una grazia?

**MAGDA:** (*full of joy, as if she were reliving the past*) Quick! . . .
Quick! . . .
(*then to Ruggero*)
May I ask you a favor?

**RUGGERO:** Tutto quello che volete!

**RUGGERO:** Anything you wish!

**MAGDA:** (*accennando al cameriere*) . . . . Dategli venti coldi,
E lasciategli il resto!

**MAGDA:** (*including the waiter*)
. . . Give him twenty sous,
And let him keep the change!

**RUGGERO:** (*sorridendo, senza capire*) Tutto qui? . . .
Che idea strana! . . . .

**RUGGERO:** (*smiling, without understanding*) Is that all?
What a strange idea!

**MAGDA:** (*con molta grazia, vagamente*)
È un piccolo ricordo
D'una mia zia lontana . . .
"Una fuga, una festa,
Un po' di birra! . . .
A casa, tutta sola,
La vecchia zia che aspetta,
E due baffetti bruni
Che fan girar la testa! . . . "

**MAGDA:** (*gracefully and vaguely*) A little remembrance
Of an aunt far away . . .
"A flight, a feast,
A little beer,
At home, all alone,
An old aunt waiting,
And a pair of side whiskers
Sending a head a'spinning!"

**RUGGERO:** Cosa andate dicendo?

**RUGGERO:** What are you talking about?

**MAGDA:** Fantasie! . . .
Fantasie!
(*il cameriere reca la birra*)

**MAGDA:** Fantasies, fantasies! . . .
(*the waiter brings the beer*)

**RUGGERO:** (*alzando il bicchiere*)
Alla vostra salute!

**RUGGERO:** (*raising his glass*)
Your health!

**MAGDA:** (*imitandolo*) Ai vostri amori!

**MAGDA:** (*imitating him*) To your loves!

**RUGGERO:** (*colpito, con gesto di dispetto depone improvvisamente il bicchiere*) Non ditelo!

**RUGGERO:** (*struck by her manner, puts his glass down with a contemptuous gesture*) Do not say that!

**MAGDA:** Perchè

**MAGDA:** Why not?

**RUGGERO:** (*seriamente*) Perchè
se amassi . . . allora . . .
Sarebbe quella sola,
E per tutta la vita!

**RUGGERO:** (*seriously*) Because if
I did love . . .
It would be she alone
Throughout life!

**MAGDA:** (*colpita dalla sincerità della sue parole, ripete quasi a sè stessa*) Ah! Per tutta la vita! . . .
(*un silenzio*)

**MAGDA:** (*struck by the sincerity of his words, repeats almost inaudibly*) Ah! Throughout life! . . .
(*silence*)

**RUGGERO:** (*fissando Magda e notando il suo cambiamento, con molta dolcezza*) Siamo amici . . . e non so ancora
il vostro nome . . .
Qual'è? . . .

**RUGGERO:** (*looking at Magda and noting the change in her, with much tenderness*) We are friends and yet I don't even
Know your name . . .
What is it . . .

**MAGDA:** Volete che lo scriva?
(*Ruggero le offre una piccola matita. Essa segna sul marmo del tavolo*)

**MAGDA:** Shall I write it down?
(*Ruggero offers her a small pencil. She writes on the marble table*)

**RUGGERO:** (*leggendo mentre Magda scrive*) "Paulette . . ."
mi piace . . .

**RUGGERO:** (*reading while Magda writes*) "Paulette . . ."
I like that name . . .

**MAGDA:** E il vostro? . . .

**MAGDA:** And yours? . . .

**RUGGERO:** (*segnando il suo nome vicino all'altro*) Io mi chiamo Ruggero!

**RUGGERO:** (*writing his next to hers*) My name is Ruggero!

**MAGDA:** (*puntando l'indice sul tavolo*) Qualche cosa di noi che resta qui!

**RUGGERO:** No . . . Questo si cancella . . .
In me resta ben altro! . . .
Resta il vostro mistero.

**MAGDA:** (*fissandolo con tenerezza*) Perchè mai cercare di saper
Chi'io sia e quale il mio mister? . . .
Non vi struggete
E m'accogliete
Come il destino mi portò!

**RUGGERO:** (*predendole le mani che essa gli tende*) Io non so chi siate voi, perchè
Per qual via, giungeste fino a me.
Ma pure sento
Strano un tormento
Dolce, infinito, nè so dir qual'è! . . .
(*con crescente commozione*)
Sento che tu non sei un'ignota,
Ma sei la creatura
Attesa dal mio cuor! . . .

**MAGDA:** (*con abbandono, chiudendo gli occhi, come cullata da un fascino travolgente*) Parlami ancora . . .
Lascia ch'io sogni . . .

**RUGGERO:** No!
Questa è vita,
Questa è realtà! . . .
(*insieme*)
Mio amor! . . . (*un lungo bacio spezza la parola*)
(*I giovani di prima rientrano dal giardino. Vedendo i due innamorati sostano additandoseli l'un l'altro, silenziosamente*)

**UN GIOVANE:** Zitti!
Non disturbiamoli!

**UN ALTRO:** Due cuori che si fondono! . . .

**UN TERZO:** (*ad alcuni che ridono*) Non facciomo umorre!

**ALCUNI ALTRI:** (*sommessamente*) Rispettiamo l'amore! . . .
(*Lisette e Prunier si sono avanzati più degli altri che ora alla spicciolata s'allontanano. Lisette fissa Magda, indietreggia quasi con un grido di stupore*)

**LISETTE:** Dio!
Lei!

**PRUNIER:** (*stupito*) Chi?

**LISETTE:** Guardala! . . .
La padrona!
(*Magda e Ruggero, al grido di Lisette, si sono staccati. Magda voltandosi si incontra con lo sguardo di Prunier che la fissa. Essa gli fa un rapido cenno di tacere. Prunier risponde con un altro segno: "ho capito" e voltandosi a Lisette dice*)

**PRUNIER:** È il vino che ti ha dato un po' alla testa!

**LISETTE:** Eppure . . . è tutta lei . . .

**MAGDA:** (*pointing with her finger on the table*) Something of ourselves which will remain here!

**RUGGERO:** No . . . This will be blotted out . . .
But more than that will remain within me . . .
Your mystery will linger.

**MAGDA:** (*looking at him tenderly*) Why should you try and fathom
My being or my mystery? . . .
Do not long to know.
Take me as I am,
Since fate has brought us together!

**RUGGERO:** (*clasping her hand*) I know not who you are and
Why you came to me as you did.
But I feel within me a torment, sweet
And infinite, which I cannot define!
(*with increased emotion*)
I feel that you are no stranger to me,
But the creature of my heart's desire . . .

**MAGDA:** (*passionately, closing her eyes, as if culled by incantation*) Speak to me again . . .
Let me dream . . .

**RUGGERO:** No! This is life,
This is reality! . . .
(*together*)
My love! . . .
(*their words are lost in a long embrace*)
(*The same youths return from the garden and seeing the lovers, nudge each other, silently*)

**A YOUTH:** Silence! Don't disturb them!

**ANOTHER:** Two hearts are overflowing!

**A THIRD:** (*to others who are laughing*) Don't be too funny!

**OTHERS:** (*softly*) All honor to love!
(*Lisette and Prunier, who have drawn nearer than the others, now hurry away. Lisette staring at Magda and walking backwards with a stiffled cry of astonishment*)

**LISETTE:** Heavens!
She!

**PRUNIER:** (*stupified*) Who?

**LISETTE:** Look at her! . . .
My Mistress!
(*Magda and Ruggero draw away from each other at Lisette's cry. On turning round Magda catches Prunier's eye. She makes a quick sign to him to be silent*)

**PRUNIER:** The wine has got into your head!

**LISETTE:** And yet . . . It is exactly like her . . .

**PRUNIER:** Ne vuoi la prova?
(*trascina Lisette verso Ruggero e Magda*)

**LISETTE:** (*riconoscendo Ruggero, sempre più stupefatta*) E l'altro è lui . . . non sbaglio!

**PRUNIER:** (*salutando Ruggero*) Buona sera!
(*poi a Lisette*)
Sì . . . lui te lo concedo, ma l'altra che par lei,
Non è lei, guardala bene.

**LISETTE:** (*quasi a sè stessa senza più capire*) Sono o non sono la sua cameriera?

**PRUNIER:** Lo sei—ma non di lei—
Che non è lei
Ma sembra lei . . .
E ubbriaca tu sei!
(*a Ruggero*)
La mia amica Lisette vuole sapere
Se il suo consiglia vi portò fortuna
. . .

**RUGGERO:** (*indicando Magda*) Lo vedete!

**PRUNIER:** È carina!
Volete presentarla?

**RUGGERO:** (*presentando*) La mia amica Paulette!

**PRUNIER:** (*a Lisette*) Sei convinta, Lisette?

**RUGGERO:** (*presentando Prunier*) Il signore è un poeta . . .
Amico d'un amico di mio padre . . .

**PRUNIER:** (*completando*) E quindi amico vostro! . . .

**RUGGERO:** Ne son proprio onorato! . . .

**MAGDA:** (*a Lisette*) Che cosa v'ha turbato? . . .
Continuate a guardami . . .

**LISETTE:** (*a sè*) Non so raccapezzarmi . . .
(*poi, sedendo vicino a Magda, confidenzialmente*)
Strano! . . . c'è una persona
Che pare il vostro ritratto!

**MAGDA:** (*divertendosi al gioco e provocandolo*) E chi sarebbe?

**PRUNIER:** (*facendo cenno a Lisette di tacere*) Ma no!

**LISETTE:** (*senza curarsene*) La mia padrona!

**PRUNIER:** È una sua fissazione!

**RUGGERO:** (*interessato*) La padrona è carina?

**LISETTE:** (*indicando Magda*) Come lei . . . se lei fosse elegante!

**MAGDA:** (*ridendo*) Se io fossi elegante!
(*poi considerando le vesti di Lisette, con comica ammirazione*)
Voi elegante lo siete!

**PRUNIER:** Do you want a proof?
(*he draws Lisette towards Ruggero and Magda*)

**LISETTE:** (*recognizes Ruggero, still more surprised*) And the other one is he . . . I'm making no mistake!

**PRUNIER:** (*taking his hat off to Ruggero*) Good evening!
(*then turning to Lisette*)
Yes . . . I'll grant you it is he, but the other one is not Magda,
It isn't, look at her well.

**LISETTE:** (*almost inaudibly to herself*) Am I or am I not her maid?

**PRUNIER:** You are—but not hers—
As this isn't her . . .
It only looks like her . . .
You are drunk! . . .
(*to Ruggero*)
My friend Lisette wants to know
Whether her advice has brought you luck . . .

**RUGGERO:** (*indicating Magda*) You can see for yourself!

**PRUNIER:** She's charming!
Please, introduce her?

**RUGGERO:** (*introducing her*) My friend Paulette!

**PRUNIER:** (*to Lisette*) Now, are you convinced, Lisette?

**RUGGERO:** (*introducing Prunier*) The gentleman is a poet . . .
A friend of my father . . .

**PRUNIER:** (*finishing the sentence*) And consequently a friend of yours . . .

**RUGGERO:** I am very much honored . . .

**MAGDA:** (*to Lisette*) What is worrying you? . . .
You keep on staring at me . . .

**LISETTE:** (*to herself*) I don't seem to remember . . .
(*then seating herself near Magda, confidentially*)
It's strange! . . . but there's someone
Who seems the image of you.

**MAGDA:** (*enjoying the fun and trying to draw her*) And who could that be?

**PRUNIER:** (*making a sign to Lisette to stop*) But no!

**LISETTE:** (*without taking the slightest notice*) My mistress!

**PRUNIER:** It's an obsession with her!

**RUGGERO:** (*interested*) Is your mistress nice?

**LISETTE:** (*indicating Magda*) Just like her, . . . if she were elegant!

**MAGDA:** (*laughingly*) If I were elegant!
(*after having examined Lisette's attire, with comic admiration*)
But how elegant you are!

LISETTE: (*ridendo*) Oh! Non mi costa fatica!

MAGDA: Che bel cappelo!

LISETTE: (*battendo confidenzialmente su un ginocchio di Magda*) E il suo!

MAGDA: (*con finto stupore*) Ma davvero?

LISETTE: Tutto ciò che ammirate L'ho sottratto abilmente!

MAGDA: (*con grazioso gesto di ammonimento*) Non lo dite, che è troppo imprudente!
(*Prunier scoppia in una risata*)

LISETTE: (*rivoltandosi, offesa*) No! Prunier non ridete!
(*Ruggero chiama un cameriere e gli dà ordini a voce bassa. Il cameriere esce*)

PRUNIER: Rido, non so di che cosa!

MAGDA: (*piano a Prunier, accennando a Lisette*) È Salomè o Berenice?

PRUNIER: (*umiliato*) Siate pietosa!

MAGDA: (*ridendo*) Può Lisette L'una o l'altra a sua scelta imitar!
(*il cameriere reca lo champagne*)

RUGGERO: Già che il caso ci unisce inneggiamo all'amore!

TUTTI: Inneggiamo alla vita Che ci donò l'amor!

RUGGERO: (*alzando il calice e guardando Magda*) Bevo al tuo fresco sorriso,
Bevo al tuo sguardo profondo,
Alla tua bocca che disse il mio nome!

MAGDA: Il mio cuore è conquiso!

RUGGERO: T'ho donato il mio cuore,
O mio tenero, dolce mio amore!
Custodisci gelosa il mio dono perchè viva sempre in te!

MAGDA: È il mio sogno che si avvera! . . .
Ah! se potessi sperare che questo istante non muore,
che il mio rifugio saran le tue braccia,
la salvezza il tuo amore,
Sarei troppo felice nè più altro vorrei dalla vita!
Oh! godere la gioia infinita che soltanto il tuo bacio può dar!

RUGGERO: Piccola ignota t'arresta!
No, questo istante non muore!
A me ti porta il clamor d'una festa ch'è una festa d'amore,
ch'è una festa di baci!
Nè più altro domando alla vita che godere l'ebbrezza infinita che soltanto il tuo bacio può dar!

LISETTE: (*laughingly*) Oh! It does not cost me much!

MAGDA: What a delightful hat!

LISETTE: (*touching Magda's knee confidentially*) It is hers!

MAGDA: (*with feigned surprise*) Really?

LISETTE: Everything you have admired I have cleverly sneaked from her!

MAGDA: (*with a charming gesture of reproach*) Do you really mean it—that's awfully impudent!
(*Prunier bursts out laughing*)

LISETTE: (*turns round, offended*) Please, Prunier, don't laugh!
(*Ruggero calls a waiter and gives his order in a low voice. The waiter goes off*)

PRUNIER: I don't know what I am laughing at.

MAGDA: (*in a whisper to Prunier, and indicating Lisette*) Is that Salomé or Bernice?

PRUNIER: (*humiliated*) Be merciful!

MAGDA: (*laughing*) Let Lisette play at being either one or the other at her choice.
(*the waiter brings the champagne*)

RUGGERO: Since fate has united us, let us Raise our glasses to Love!

TOGETHER: Let us toast Life Which gives us Love!

RUGGERO: (*raising his cup and looking at Magda*) I drink to your inebriating smile,
And to your eyes so deep—
To your mouth which spoke my name!

MAGDA: My heart is conquered!

RUGGERO: I have given you my heart,
O dearest and sweetest love!
Jealously guard my gift That it may live in you forever!

MAGDA: My dream is coming true!
Ah! If I could but hope for This moment never to pass!
Let my refuge be in your arms,
My redemption in your love,
It would be too much happiness;
Nothing more could I hope from life!
To live in the infinite joy That only your kiss can give!

RUGGERO: Little unknown one, it shall linger—
This moment cannot die!
Has it not brought us the clamor of a feast?
A Feast of Love and a Feast of Kisses!
I ask no more of life than to enjoy The infinite inebriation Which only your kiss can give!

LISETTE: Dimmi le dolci parole che la divina tua musa ricama per colorire di grazia la trama di gioconde canzoni.
Le tue ardenti fantasie io raccoglier saprò nel mio cuor.
E saranno poesie tutte mie,
che, gelosa, asconderò.

PRUNIER: Ogni tuo bacio è una strofa Ogni tuo sguardo è una facile rima.
Tu sei la sola—perchè sei la prima—
che ha parlato al mio cuore.
Inspirato dal tuo amore,
le canzoni dirò sol per te.
E saran tutte tue,
le poesie! . . .
Tutte tue! . . .

LISETTE: (*con grande dolcezza*) Tutte mie!

MAGDA: Fa che quest'ora si eterni!
vedi io son tutta tua.
e per sempre! . . . Per sempre con te!

RUGGERO: Deve ques'ora segnare un avvenire d'amore!
E per sempre! Per sempre con me!

LISETTE: Le mie virtù sono poche,
ma, se le vuoi, te le dono,
e felice, per sempre sarò!

PRUNIER: Le tue virtù le raccolgo,
l'anima mia ne ravvolge,
più poeta sarò . . .

LA FOLLA: (*Che nel frattempo si è avvicinata con cautela, commenta sommessamente, invadendo a poco la sala e la loggia*) Guardo!
Fermo!
Vedi la!
È l'amor che non ragiona!
E l'amor che non nasconde!
Fate piano! . . .
Fate piano! . . .
State attenti!
Non lasciamoci scoprire!
Sull'amore fiori e fronde!
Per le Muse una ghirlanda!
Al poeta una corona!
Sian sorpresi nel momento del più dolce giuramento!
Intercciamo i quattro cuori con i fiori! . . .
Soffochiamo i quattro amori con i fiori!
(*E così: mentre un duplice bacio unisce gli amanti, dai lati, dal fondo, dall'alto, la folla getta fiori sulle due coppie*)
(*Alcune ragazze hanno intessuta una corona e ne recingono a testa del Poeta; poi tutti tornano a sbandarsi*)
(*Lo stupore dei quattro sorpresi è*)

LISETTE: Repeat to me the sweet words Which your divine muse spins To give color and grace to the plot Of joyous songs.
Your ardent fantasy shall flood my heart With poetry all mine own,
Which I will jealously guard.

PRUNIER: Your every kiss is a verse Your every look an easy rhyme.
You are the only one—because the very first—
To speak to my heart.
Inspired by your love,
My songs will be for you alone,
My verses will be yours . . .
All yours . . . . . .

LISETTE: (*with deep tenderness*) All mine!

MAGDA: Make this hour to last into eternity!
I am yours forever . . .
To be with you always

RUGGERO: This hour is the forerunner Of a future full of love!
And forever and ever with me!

LISETTE: My virtues are but few,
But, if you want them,
Take them, and I will be Happy forevermore.

PRUNIER: I will enfold your virtues And enclose them within my heart,
To blossom into poetry!

THE CROWD: (*Which meanwhile has gathered around cautiously, whispers softly, invading little by little both hall and balcony*) Look!
Stop!
Watch them!
Love which knows no reasoning!
Love which has no hiding place!
Softly! . . . Softly! . . .
Take care!
Don't let us be caught watching!
Scatter flowers and leaves on Love!
And garlands for the Muses!
For the poet a crown!
Let us surprise them in their moment Of sweetest troth!
Let us bind these four hearts With flowers! . . .
Let us stifle these four loves With flowers!
(*While the lovers embrace, the crowd scatters flowers on them.
Girls make a garland and crown the poet. The crowd then retires*)
(*The surprise of the four at being thus caught is interrupted by Prunier, who has seen Rambaldo on the stairs watching Magda and Ruggero*)

*subito rotto da Prunier Egli ha visto Rambaldo fermo sulla scala dala quale allora allora è disceso, fissare Magda e Ruggero)*

PRUNIER: (*rapido, a voce bassa, a Magda*) Rambaldo!

MAGDA: (*Soffocando un grido*) Ah! M'aiutate! Ruggero allontanate!

PRUNIER: Ci penso io! (*forte*) Lisette! Attenta! C'è il padrone!

LISETTE: (*sconvolta*) Dov'è? Dov'è?

PRUNIER: Sta ferma! (*La folla comincia ad andarsene ridendo e parlando sommessamente. Chi si indugia. Chi si avvia verso l'uscita. Altri aiutati dai servi indossano il soprabito. Altri si trattengono a pagare, ecc. ecc.*)

PRUNIER: (*a Ruggero concitatamente*) Ve l'affido, Ruggero, Portatela laggiù!

RUGGERO: (*premurosamente*) Fidatevi di me, non dubitate! (*Una grisette ha levato di testa il cilindro a un signore grave, e cacciatoselo in capo s'avvia. Questi appena se ne accorge la insegue, smettendo di pagare il conto. Il cameriere dopo un attimo di sorpresa li insegue*)

PRUNIER: (*Chiamando con doppio giucco in disparte Lisette, rapido e sommesso*) Tu trattienlo laggiù, mi raccomando. (*Ora il cameriere ritorna soddisfatto, e a un gruppetto che lo interroga, mostra il danaro ricevuto*) (*Ruggero prende sottobraccio Lisette e la trascina rapido verso il giardino dove si confonde con la gente che esce*)

ALCUNE RAGAZZE E ALCUNI UOMINI: Via ci intenderem, Se ci accompagnate! (*a un recalcitrante*) Perchè non vuoi venir? (*Altri insistono. Egli segue il gruppetto che esce*)

MAGDA: (*che è rimasta ferma al suo posto*) M'ha vista?

PRUNIER: (*scrutando i movimenti di Rambaldo*) S'avvicina! Io resto. Voi andate!

TRE STUDENTI: Che aspettate ancor?

MAGDA: (*risoluta*) Non mi muovo di qua!

TRE SARTINE: Sol voialtri tre!

PRUNIER: (*in a low voice to Magda*) Rambaldo!

MAGDA: (*stifling a cry*) O! Help me! Ruggero, go!

PRUNIER: Leave it to me! (*aloud*) Lisette! Look out! There's the master!

LISETTE: (*upset*) Where? Where?

PRUNIER: Keep still! (*The crowd disperses laughing and speaking softly. Some stay on. Some leave the hall. Others are helped into their coats by the ushers, or stop to pay, etc., etc.*)

PRUNIER: (*excitedly to Ruggero*) I leave her to you, take her over there!

RUGGERO: (*earnestly*) Come with me, have faith in me! (*A grisette has taken the top hat from the head of a very serious gentleman and has put it on her own. As soon as he finds this out, he runs after her, leaving the account unpaid. The waiter, after recovering from his surprise, runs after them*)

PRUNIER: (*Calling Lisette, and motioning the others aside, quickly and excitedly*) You stay over there, Now, don't fail me. (*The waiter now returns satisfied, a group starts questioning him, and he shows them the money he has just received*) (*Ruggero, taking Lisette by the arm, drags her quickly towards the garden, where they are lost in the crowd*)

SEVERAL GIRLS AND MEN: We'll arrive at some kind of an understanding, If you will come with us (*to one resisting*) Why won't you come with us? (*Others press him and he follows the group as they go out*)

MAGDA: (*who has remained where she was*) Did he see me?

PRUNIER: (*watching Rambaldo's movements*) He's coming! I'll remain here. You go away.

THREE STUDENTS: What are you waiting for?

MAGDA: (*resolutely*) I won't move from here!

THREE DRESSMAKERS: You three, of course!

PRUNIER: Incauta! Non pensate

QUATTRO DONNE: (*Dopo essersi aiutate a infilarsi il mantello*) È tardi, quasi l'alba . . . (*al cameriere che accorre*) Pagherem doman! . . . (*escono*)

MAGDA: (*subito*) No! Chi ama non pensa! (*E resta immobile, quasi rigida, appoggiata al tavolo*)

PRUNIER: (*Non sapendo che altro fare muove incontro a Rambaldo cercando di coprire Magda al suo sguardo*) Buona sera, Rambaldo! (*Rambaldo senza rispondergli gli tende la mano*)

PRUNIER: (*Tenendo fra le sue la mano di Rambaldo e considerando i suoi anelli*) Oh! che grosso smeraldo!

RAMBALDO: (*bruscamente*) Lasciatemi, vi prego! . . . (*Il suo tono è tale da non ammettere repliche. Prunier fa un gesto come per dire "Sarà quel che sarà" e s'avvia verso il giardino. Sparisce. Rambaldo resta fermo dinnanzi a Magda che alza francamente su di lui gli occhi aspettando ch'egli parli. Un breve silenzio*)

RAMBALDO: (*serio, grave, contegnoso*) Che significa questo? Mi volete piegare?

MAGDA: (*freddamente*) Non ho niente da aggiungere ciò che avete visto.

RAMBALDO: (*più dolce, quasi conciliante*) Dunque, niente di grave . . . Una scappata . . . Andiamo! . . .

UN GRUPPO: (*sbadigliando*) Che sonno, ahimè! . . . non mi reggo più! . . . (*escono*) (*Ora la sala e il giardino sono quasi completamente sfollati. Non resta che qualche piccolo gruppo di ritardatari*)

MAGDA: (*recisa*) Inutile! Rimango!

RAMBALDO: (*stupito*) Restate?

MAGDA: (*prorompendo*) L'amo! . . . L'amo!

RAMBALDO: Che follia vi travolge?

UN ULTIMO GRUPPO (*sfollando*) Ah! Viva Bullier! Qui soltanto regna la felicità! (*le loro voci si perdono*)

PRUNIER: Don't be so foolish! Think . . .

FOUR WOMEN: (*After having helped each other into their coats*) It's late, almost dawn . . . (*to the waiter who comes up quickly*) We'll pay tomorrow! . . . (*they leave*)

MAGDA: No! He who loves does not think! (*She remains stubbornly, leaning against the table*)

PRUNIER: (*Not knowing what to do, goes to meet Rambaldo, meanwhile, trying to hide Magda from his sight*) Good evening, Rambaldo! (*Rambaldo without replying takes his hand*)

PRUNIER: (*Holding Rambaldo's hand in his and looking at his rings*) Oh! What a big emerald!

RAMBALDO: (*roughly*) Let me go, please! (*The tone of his voice is such as not to admit of any reply. Prunier's gesture seems to indicate the words "Let it come to the worst!" He goes off towards the garden. Rambaldo remains standing in front of Magda, who raises her eyes frankly towards him and waits for him to speak. A short pause*)

RAMBALDO: (*serious, grave and dignified*) What is the meaning of this? Do you want to break me?

MAGDA: (*coldly*) I have nothing to add to What you have seen.

RAMBALDO: (*in a more conciliatory tone*) Well then, nothing much . . . An escapade . . . Let's go!

A GROUP: (*yawning*) I'm dead beat . . . Oh dear I can't move! (*they go off*) (*The hall and the garden are now almost deserted. Only here and there are seen small groups of stragglers*)

MAGDA: (*resolutely*) It's no use! I'll stay!

RAMBALDO: (*astounded*) You want to stay?

MAGDA: (*interrupting*) I love him! . . . I love him!

RAMBALDO: What madness possesses you?

THE LAST GROUP: (*dispersing*) Hurrah for Bullier! Here happiness only reigns! (*their voices are lost*)

## Act II

**MAGDA:** Ma voi non lo sapete cosa sia
aver sete d'amore
e trovare l'amore,
aver voglia di vivera
e trovare la vita?
Lasciatemi seguire il mio destino
Lasciatemi!...
È finita!...
(*Rambaldo la fissa intontito, quasi non credendo a ciò che ascolta. E alora la donna, turbata e pentita, gli tende la mano dolcemente, susurrando*)

**MAGDA:** Perdonate, Rambaldo,
Se vi reco un dolore...
Ma non posso... non posso...
È più forte il mio amore!

**RAMBALDO:** (*dopo un breve silenzio*) Possiate non pentirvene!
(*s'inchina, s'avvia senza più voltarsi, unendosi agli ultimi che escono*)
(*Magda s'abbatte sfibranta su una sedia, guardando innanzi a sè fissamente, come se interrogasse il suo stesso destino*)
(*Ora la sala è deserta. Nel giardino si sono spente le luci. I primi chiarori freddi dell'alba non illuminano che tavoli in disordine, fiori sparsi e sfogliati per terra, bicchieri rovesciati. Tutta l'infinita tristezza d'una festa passata è in queste prime luci mattutine. Dalla strada una voce che canta. Attraverso le vetrate, nella strada, i primi indizi del risveglio della città. Carretti che passano, finestre che s'aprono, ecc.*)

**LA VOCE LONTANA:** Nella trepida luce d'un mattin
M'apparisti ricinta di rose...
E ti vidi leggera camminar
Seminando di petali il ciel.
—Mi vuoi dir
Chi sei tu?
—Son l'aurora che nasce per fugar
Ogni incanto di notte lunar!
—Nell'amor
Non fidar!
(*dal fondo appare Ruggero che reca lo scialle di Magda*)

**RUGGERO:** (*avvicinandosi*) Paulette!...
(*Magda trasalisce, si risolleva, si volta. Ruggero non s'avvede del suo pallore mortale e Pavverte*)

**RUGGERO:** I nostri amici
Son già partiti...
Sai, è l'alba...
Vuoi che andiamo?

**MAGDA:** (*con voce spenta*) Un momento!...

**RUGGERO:** (*accorrendo presso di lei, con ansia*) Che hai?
(*Magda sembra svegliarsi improvvisamente da un sogno. Tutta la sua energia la riprende essa tende le braccia verso l'amato,*)

**MAGDA:** How little you know
what it means
To be thirsting for love
And to find love,
To long to live and
To find life!
Leave me to my fate!
Leave me!...
It is finished!
(*Rambaldo looks at her astounded and cannot believe her words. The woman, then feeling compassion and remorse, takes his hand and whispers gently*)

**MAGDA:** Forgive me, Rambaldo,
If I give you so much pain...
But, I cannot... I cannot
My love is too great!

**RAMBALDO:** (*after a short silence*) May you not regret it!
(*He bows to her, and goes without once turning round, following the last stragglers out*)
(*Magda drops into a chair unnerved, her eyes fixed into the distance, as if she were interrogating her own destiny*)
(*The hall is empty. The lights are out in the garden. The first cold rays of dawn faintly illuminate a disorderly scene of tables, faded flowers littering the floor and overturned glasses. The whole sadness of a consummated feast is reflected in the cold light of dawn. From the street a voice is heard singing. From the windows of the hall, the first signs of a waking city are visible. Vehicles are passing, windows are being opened, etc.*)

**A DISTANT VOICE:** In the early dawn of the morn
You appear to me wreathed in roses...
And I watch you glibly following your course
Strewing petals all over the skies.
—O, tell me who you are?
—I am the Dawn, born but to dispel
The enchantment wrought by the beams of the moon!
Beware of Love and do not trust it!
(*Ruggero enters from the rear and brings Magda her shawl*)

**RUGGERO:** Paulette!...
(*Magda starts, rises and turns around. Ruggero does not seem to notice her deathly pallor and says*)

**RUGGERO:** Our friends have already left...
The day is dawning...
Shall we go?

**MAGDA:** (*in a colorless voice*) One moment...

**RUGGERO:** (*going to her, anxiously*) What is it?
(*Magda seems to suddenly awaken as from a dream. Her energy returns. She extends her arms towards her lover, as if anxious to*)

come se si aggrappasse alla sua stessa speranza) Niente... niente...
Ti amo!...
Ma tu non sai...
Tu non sai!...
Vedi, ho tanta paura!...
Sono troppo felice!
È il mio sogno, capisci?
Tremo e piango... mia vita... mio amore!...

*SIPARIO*

## ■ ATTO TERZO

Un piccolo padiglione sopra un'altura che degrada su uno spiazzo erboso. Dinanzi al padiglione una piccola terrazza ove sono un tavolo e alcune sedie da giardino. Attraversa tortuosamente un ruscelletto tagliato da un ponticello di legno. Qua e là alberi sottili e in fiore. Nel fondo è un muro aperto nel mezzo: sul muro edera e rose rampicanti. Al di là le chiome rade degli ulivi attraverso le quali si vede un lembo della Costa Azzurra. Da questa apertura si scende verso il mare. E il pomeriggio avanzato d'una magnifica giornata di primavera. Voli di rondini nel cielo lontano. Magda a Ruggero, presso il tavolo sul quale è stato portato il tè, sembrano assaporare la dolcezza intima dell'ora e del paesaggio.

**MAGDA:** Senti?...
Anche il mare respira sommesso...
L'aria beve il profumo dei fiori!...
(*Lentamente si alza. Porge all'amante la tazza nella quale ha versato il tè. S'avvicina a lui con grazia e gli sussurra con mistero*)
So l'arte strana
di comporre un filtro
che possa rendere vana
ogni tua stanchezza...
(*e come Ruggero la guarda sorridendo, riprende*)
Dimmi che ancora, che sempre ti piaccio!

**RUGGERO:** Tutto, mio amore, mi piace di te!

**MAGDA:** La solitudine, di, non ti tedia?

**RUGGERO:** Non son più solo con l'amor tuo
che si risveglia ogni giorno più ardente,
più intenso, più santo!...
(*Magda, piena di riconoscenza commossa, lo cinge con le sue braccio. E Ruggero le sussurra*)
Ecco, il tuo braccio
lieve mi circonda
come un dolcissimo laccio
che nessuno spezza!...

cling to her one hope) Nothing...
Nothing...
I love you!
But you don't know,
You can't understand!
I am so frightened!...
I am too happy!
This is my dream, can you realize it!
I tremble and weep... my life...
my love...

*CURTAIN*

## ■ ACT III

A little cottage on a hillock and fields beyond. The frontage has a small terrace, on which are a table and a few garden chairs.
A winding rivulet with a small rustic bridge. Here and there trees and flowers. At the rear is seen a wall with an opening in the middle. On the wall, climbing roses and ivy. Further still an olive grove, through the scant foliage of which is seen the Azure Coast; from there a path leading to the sea.
It is the afternoon of a glorious Spring day. Flights of swallows against the distant sky.
Magda and Ruggero are seated at a table on which tea has been served; they seem imbued with the sweetness of the hour and the beauty of the scenery.

**MAGDA:** Don't you have the sensation of the sea breathing softly?...
The air absorbs the scent of the flowers!
(*Rises slowly. She hands her lover the cup of tea she has just poured out and going up close to him whispers as if divulging a secret*)
I know of a strange art;
The composition of a filter
Which will make your lassitude vain...
(*and while Ruggero gazes at her smiling, she continues*)
Tell me once more that I still please you!

**RUGGERO:** Everything, my love, pleases me in you!

**MAGDA:** This loneliness does not annoy you, does it?

**RUGGERO:** How can I be lonely when your love
Grows more ardent each day,
More intense, more sacred!...
(*Magda, deeply moved and thankful, embraces him. Ruggero whispers to her*)
Your arm encircles
And enfolds me
In so tender an embrace
That nothing could divide us...

MAGDA: (*tutta stretta a lui*) Ah! ti ricordi ancora
il nostro incontro laggiù?
T'ho visto, e ho sognato l'Amore!

MAGDA: (*nestling close to him*) Do you remember our meeting there?
I saw you and Love entered my heart!

RUGGERO: E siam fuggiti qui per nasconderlo!

RUGGERO: And we fled to hide it away!

MAGDA: Il nostro amore nato tra i fiori!

MAGDA: That love of ours born among the roses!

RUGGERO: Tra i fiori vivo!

RUGGERO: I live with the flowers!

MAGDA: Inghirlandato di canti e danze!

MAGDA: Engarlanded by songs and dances!

RUGGERO: Di primavera!...
(*Magda corre a raccogliere delle rose*)

RUGGERO: Of Spring!
(*Magda runs to gather roses*)

MAGDA: (*con languoroso abbandono gettando con grazia delle foglie di rose su Ruggero*) Oggi lascia che ancora
il nostro amore inghirlandi!
Lascia che ti avvolga
Tutta la mia tenerezza!...
Senti la mia carezza
Trepida come il mio cuore?

MAGDA: (*with languorous abandonment and grace she strews rose petals on Ruggero*) Let this day still be the witness
Of our love amid the roses!
Let me encircle you with
All my tenderness...
Feel how my caresses flutter,
Like the beating of my heart!

RUGGERO: Benedetto l'amore
e benedetta la vita!
La tua grazia squisita,
la tua fiorente beltà!...

RUGGERO: Blessed by Love—
And blessed be Life!
Your exquisite grace
And your beauty so fair!...

MAGDA: Taci... Non parlare...
Stringimi, stringimi a te!...
(*i due amanti restano per un momento così, assorti e avvinti*)

MAGDA: Silence... Do not speak...
Just hold me tightly, tightly to you...
(*the lovers remain a few instants lost in silence*)

RUGGERO: Oggi meriti molto!

RUGGERO: Today you deserve a great lot!

MAGDA: Un premio?

MAGDA: A prize?

RUGGERO: No. Un segreto.

RUGGERO: No. A secret.

MAGDA: Un segreto?

MAGDA: A secret?

RUGGERO: Nascosto con ogni precauzione.
Non volevo parlartene se prima non giungeva la risposta paterna...
Ma la risposta tarda.

RUGGERO: Hidden with the greatest precaution.
I did not want to tell you about it Before receiving my parent's reply...
However, the reply has been delayed.

MAGDA: (*transalendo*) Hai scritto?

MAGDA: (*starting*) Have you written?

RUGGERO: Son tre giorni... Domandavo il denaro
(*leva di tasca alcune carte*)
per levarci d'impiccio. In ogni tasca guarda,
c'è una richiesta, un conto...

RUGGERO: Three days ago... I asked for money
(*he draws from his pocket several letters*)
To get us out of this muddle. Look, in each pocket I have
Demands for money or bills...

MAGDA: (*tristemente*) Per colpa mia!...

MAGDA: (*sadly*) All my fault...

RUGGERO: (*sorridendo*) La colpa va divisa!...
È una pioggia insistente...
Anche l'albergatore ha la faccia un po' scura...

RUGGERO: (*smiling*) The fault is divided...
It just rains bills...
Even the hotel proprietor is making a sour face...

MAGDA: Povero mio Ruggero!

MAGDA: My poor dear Ruggero!

RUGGERO: (*ridendo allegramente*) Andremo a mendicare:
"Chi vuole aprir le porte
a due amanti spiantati?..."

RUGGERO: (*laughingly*) We had better go out and beg.
"Who'll open the door
To two lovers dead broke?..."

MAGDA: (*con pena*) on dire!...

MAGDA: (*sadly*) Don't!...

RUGGERO: Ma che importa!...
Che m'importa di questo!
Il segreto è più grande!

RUGGERO: What does it matter...
What do I care!
The secret is of more importance!

MAGDA: Parla, dimmi, fa presto!

MAGDA: Tell me, tell me, quickly!

RUGGERO: Non l'hai indovinato?

RUGGERO: Haven't you guessed it yet?

MAGDA: Che posso dirti?

MAGDA: How could I?

RUGGERO: Ho scritto per avere il consenso al nostro matrimonio!

RUGGERO: I have written to obtain permission for our marriage!

MAGDA: (*arretrando, colpita*) Ruggero, hai fatto questo?

MAGDA: (*drawing back as if stung*) Ruggero, you did that?

RUGGERO: Perchè?... non vuoi?

RUGGERO: Why?... don't you want to?

MAGDA: Che dirti?...
Non so, non m'aspettavo...
Non sapevo... pensavo...

MAGDA: What can I say?...
I don't know... I never expected...
I didn't know... I thought...

RUGGERO: Che io non lo facessi?

RUGGERO: That I would not do it?

MAGDA: No... Non so... dimmi tutto!

MAGDA: No... I don't know... tell my everything!

RUGGERO: Non c'è altro di più.
Se ti amo e mi ami, voglio che sia per sempre!

RUGGERO: There is nothing more to be said.
If I love you and you love me, I want it to be for always!

MAGDA: "Per sempre!..."
Mi ricordo... Lo dicesti laggiù!...

MAGDA: "For always..." I remember... Back there you said the same.

RUGGERO: E laggiù non sapevo ancora chi tu fossi,
Tu che non sei l'Amante, ma l'Amore!
(*attirando a sè Magda, così vicina che le sue parole possano sfiorarla sul viso*)
Dimmi che vuoi seguirmi alla mia casa
Che intorno ha un orto e in faccia la collina
Che si risveglia al sole, la mattina ed è piena, alla sera, d'ombre strane!...
Il nostro amore troverà in quell'ombra
la sua luce più e più serena...
la santa protezione di mia madre
sopra ogni angoscia e fuori d'ogni pena!
E chi sa che a quel sole mattutino
un giorno non si tenda lietamente
la piccola manina d'un bambino...
E chi sa che quell'ombra misteriosa
non protegga i giocondi sogni d'oro
della nostra creatura che riposa...
(*Magda singhiozzando sommessamente, a poco a poco si è tutta ripiegata su di lui*)
(*Ruggero, dolcemente staccandosi la bacia teneramente sui capelli ed esce rapido. Magda lo segue con lo sguardo fin che può, intensamente. Poi uno smarrimento, un terrore quasi, pare stringa la sua anima in tumulto. E guardando inanzi a sè, fissamente, come scrutasse l'oscurità del futuro, sussurra*)

RUGGERO: And back there I did not yet know who you were,
That you were not a lover, but Love!
(*drawing Magda towards him, so near to him that his words seem to caress her face*)
Tell me that you will follow me to my house,
Surrounded by an orchard and facing the hill,
Which awakens to the rays of the sun in the morning
And at night is full of strange shadows!...
Our life will find in those shadows
A purer light and more serenity...
The sacred protection of my mother
Against all anguish and all pain!
And who knows but that to the morning sun
Some day in joy and pleasure
A little child's hand may not be outstretched!
And who knows whether those mysterious shadows
Do not hide the joyous golden dream
Of a dormant hope...
(*Magda sobs softly in his arms*)
(*Ruggero, rising slowly, kisses her tenderly and goes*)
(*Magda follows him with her eyes as long as she can. Then a terror seizes and oppresses her and she gazes fixedly into the distance, as if scrutinizing her unfathomable destiny, whispering*)

MAGDA: Che più dirgli?...
Che fare?...
Continuar a tacere... O confessare,
Ma come to potrei?...
Con un solo mio gesto far crollare

MAGDA: What more can I say to him?...
What can I do?...
Continue in silence... or confess?,
But, how can I?...

## Act III

Sogni, felicità, passione, amore! . . .
No!
Non devo parlare! . . .
(*poi come stupita della sua stessa affermazione*)
Nè tacere io posso! . . .
Contnuare l'inganno
per conservarmi a lui?
O mio povero cuore!
Quanta angoscia!
Che pena!
(*lenta, tutta ripiegata nel suo dolore, s'avvia verso il padiglione, entra le voci di Prunier e di Lisette da destra*)

**LISETTE:** —E' qui?

**PRUNIER:** —Non so!

**LISETTE:** —La rivedrò?

**PRUNIER:** —Speriam
(*Prunier entra. Lisette lo segue. Essa appare in preda a un vivo, a un esagerato terrore*)

**PRUNIER:** Avanti, vile!
Vieni!
Fa presto!
Il padiglione? . . .
Eccolo: è questo.
Che fai?
Che temi?
Esagerata!
Non c'è nessuno!

**LISETTE:** M'hai rovinata!

**PRUNIER:** Non mi stupisce la ricompensa!
Volli innalzare la mia conquista improvvisandoti canzonettista.
Ma non appena scoperto, l'astro morì, si spense!

**LISETTE:** Dio!
Che disastro!
Sempre mi pare di risentire
il sibilare di quella gente!

**PRUNIER:** Che conta un fischio?
Che vale?
Niente!
Ora dimentica: qui tutto tace.

**LISETTE:** Dammi, ti prego, dami la pace!

**PRUNIER:** La gloria, o donna, volevo darti!

**LISETTE:** No, no.
Ti supplico: non esaltarti.

**PRUNIER:** Io m'illudevo, in una sera,
di soffocare la cameriera!

**LISETTE:** Pur di non essere così fischiata
Anche la vita l'avrei donata!
(*con improvviso terrore*)
Guarda! non vedi? . . .
Laggiù . . . qualcuno! . . .

**PRUNIER:** Ma no, vaneggi!
Non c'è nessuno!

**LISETTE:** Di proseguire più non m'arrishcio!
(*sobbalzando, livida*)
Ahimè!
Non senti?

With one single word destroy
Dreams, happiness, passion, love?
No! I must not speak! . . .
(*then, as if surprised at her own decision*)
And yet I cannot remain silent . . .
And continue this deception
To keep him for myself? . . .
O my poor heart? . . .
What anguish! . . .
What pain!
(*slowly, bowed down by grief, walks towards the cottage and enters; the voices of Prunier and Lisette are heard from the left*)

**LISETTE:** —Is it here?

**PRUNIER:** —I don't know!

**LISETTE:** —I wonder, if I'll find her?

**PRUNIER:** —Let's hope so! (*Prunier enters. Lisette follows. She seems to be the prey of a wild and exaggerated terror*)

**PRUNIER:** Go on, coward!
Come along!
Make haste!
The cottage? . . .
Why, there it is.
What are you doing?
What are you afraid of?
Don't be so exaggerated!
There's no one!

**LISETTE:** You've ruined me!

**PRUNIER:** I am not surprised at the reward!
I wanted to raise my conquest
In making you a diseuse.
But hardly had I discovered the star
When it faded, and vanished.

**LISETTE:** Oh heavens!
What a disaster!
I am still haunted by the hisses of those people!

**PRUNIER:** What does a hiss mean?
What is it worth?
Nothing!
Now, forget it all: everything is still here.

**LISETTE:** Leave me alone, please; leave me in peace!

**PRUNIER:** It is glory, oh woman, I would give you!

**LISETTE:** No, no.
I beg of you: don't get excited.

**PRUNIER:** And I who dreamed, in one evening,
To stamp out the servant!

**LISETTE:** I would rather have died
Than be hissed in that way!
(*with sudden terror*)
Look!
Don't you see?
There's some one over there! . . .

**PRUNIER:** False alarm!
There's no one!

**LISETTE:** I'm afraid of going any further!
(*starting, deathly pale*)
O, dear! Don't you hear?

**PRUNIER:** Che cosa?

**LISETTE:** Un fischio!

**PRUNIER:** Decisamente vittima sei dei nobilissimi consigli miei!

**LISETTE:** Dimmi, dovremo girare ancora
per ritrovare la mia signora?

**PRUNIER:** E se ciò fosse?

**LISETTE:** Non lo potrei!

**PRUNIER:** Bisogna vincersi!

**LISETTE:** Prima vorrei
frugare ogni angolo, esser sicura
che qui nessuno può far paura.

**PRUNIER:** Ti riconduco alla tua mèta!
In questa placida oasi segreta
Gli amanti tubano fuori del mondo!
La solitudine, vedi, è completa!
Nizza è lontana, Nizza è là in fondo!

**LISETTE:** (*ripresa dal terrore*) No!
Non m'inganno! . . .
Laggiù c'è un uomo.

**PRUNIER:** (*dopo aver guardato*)
Lo riconosco, è il maggiordomo.
(*Infatti a destra s'avanza il maître d'hôtel recando alcune lettere su un vassoio. Vedendo Prunier gli si avvicina ossequiente*)

**IL MAGGIORDOMO:** Desidera che avverta la signora?

**PRUNIER:** Le direte soltanto cosi:
Un amico e un'amica di Parigi l'aspettano qui.
(*il maggiordomo s'inchina, entra nel padiglione*)

**LISETTE:** (*a Prunier*) Hai fatto male!
Io non sono sua amica!

**PRUNIER:** Che cosa sei?

**LISETTE:** (*vagamente*) Vedrai prima di sera!

**PRUNIER:** Quali stolte intenzioni ti passan per la testa?

**LISETTE:** (*con uno scatto ribelle*)
Alla fine m'hai seccata!
Troppe, troppe osservazioni!
Non mi sono ribellata
Ma tramontan le illusioni!
Sono stanca di tutto!

**PRUNIER:** (*freddo e ironico*) Quali sono i tuoi sogni?

**LISETTE:** I miei sogni?
Che t'importa!
So ben io quello che sogno!
Ho bisogno di calma!
Di star sola ho bisogno!

**PRUNIER:** La gratitudine non è il tuo forte!

**LISETTE:** Non intrometterti nella mia sorte!

**PRUNIER:** What?

**LISETTE:** A hiss!

**PRUNIER:** There is no further doubt, you are the victim
Of my noble endeavors!

**LISETTE:** Do we have to run around much longer
To find my mistress?

**PRUNIER:** Well, supposing we had to?

**LISETTE:** I couldn't do it!

**PRUNIER:** You must control yourself!

**LISETTE:** First of all, let me look into every corner,
I want to make sure there's no one to frighten me.

**PRUNIER:** I'll return you to your own calling!
In this peaceful and secret oasis
Lovers retire from the maddening crowd!
Solitude here, as you see, is complete!
Nice is far away; Nice is right in the distance over there!

**LISETTE:** (*again in sudden terror*) No! I'm not mistaken! There's a man over there.

**PRUNIER:** (*after looking around*)
I recognize him, it is the steward.
(*In fact, the Maitre d'Hôtel is seen approaching from the left. He carries a few letters on a tray. Prunier goes to meet him*)

**THE STEWARD:** Do you wish me to call the lady?

**PRUNIER:** You will only tell her that:
Two friends from Paris
Await her here.
(*the Steward bows and goes into the cottage*)

**LISETTE:** (*to Prunier*) You did wrong!
I'm not her friend!

**PRUNIER:** What are you then?

**LISETTE:** (*vaguely*) You'll see that on the first night!

**PRUNIER:** What foolish ideas are now passing through your head?

**LISETTE:** (*in sudden rebellion*)
I've had enough of you now!
With all your remonstrances!
I did not revolt;
But my illusions have faded
And I am sick of everything!

**PRUNIER:** (*coolly and with irony*) Let's hear your dreams?

**LISETTE:** My dreams?
What business are they of yours?
My dreams are my affair!
I want peace!
I want to be left alone!

**PRUNIER:** Gratitude is not your chief virtue!

**LISETTE:** Don't interfere with my fate!

PRUNIER: (*sdegnoso*) Misera
sorte!
Povera mèta!

LISETTE: (*con gesto di disprezzo*)
Ah! lo so bene!
Grande poeta!

PRUNIER: (*offeso*) M'insulti?

LISETTE: (*soffiandogli le parole
sui viso*) Ti spezzo!
(*Appare Magda seguita dal maggiordomo che si inchina ed esce
Prunier e Lisette si ricompongono
subito. Movendole incontro*)

MAGDA: Ma come?
Voi, che ricordate ancora
la vecchia parigina? . . .

LISETTE: (*con tenerezza*) Mia signora!

PRUNIER: Siam venuti a turbare il
vostro nido . . .
Siete dunque felice?

MAGDA: (*con un velo di tristezza*) Interamente.

PRUNIER: Se ne parla, a Parigi! . . .
Si ricorda! . . .
E . . . devo dirvi tutto? . . .
Non si crede.

MAGDA: Non si crede? . . .
Perchè? . . .

PRUNIER: Perchè la vostra vita non
è questa,
tra piccole rinuncie e nostalgie,
con la visione d'una casa onesta
che chiude l'amor vostro in una
tomba!

MAGDA: (*interrompendolo vivamente*) No, Prunier!
Non sapete
quanto male mi fate a dir così! . . .
(*poi per sviare*)
Or parliamo di voi . . . che fate qui?

PRUNIER: Il teatro di Nizza iersera
decretò
che Lisette non ha stoffa
per la gloria, e perciò
io che vedo e capisco
ve la restituisco!
L'artista di una sera
tornerà cameriera!

LISETTE: (*a Magda*) Sarò quella
d'allora, se volete!

MAGDA: Ma certo!

LISETTE: (*con un gran sospiro*)
Finalmente!

PRUNIER: (*a Magda, accennando
a Lisette*) È una donna felice: lo
vedete?
Torna l'anima antica a palpitare.
Anche voi, come lei, Magda, dovrete
Se non oggi, domani abbandonare
una illusione che credete vita . . .

MAGDA: (*subito*) Tacete.

PRUNIER: È mio dovere.
Ho avuto questo incarico e lo compio!

PRUNIER: (*scornfully*) Such a
fate! A miserable existence!

LISETTE: (*with a gesture of
scorn*) I know it only too well!
Great Poet!

PRUNIER: (*offended*) You insult
me?

LISETTE: (*throws the words directly into his face*) I despise you!
(*Magda appears followed by the
Steward, who bows to her and
goes. Prunier and Lisette compose
themselves and go to meet her*)

MAGDA: What, you?
So you still remember the old Parisienne? . . .

LISETTE: (*with tenderness*) My
mistress!

PRUNIER: We have come to disturb you in your nest . . .
Are you really happy?

MAGDA: (*with a tinge of sadness*)
Absolutely.

PRUNIER: It is the talk of Paris . . .
Do you remember? . . .
And . . . if I am to tell the truth?
Nobody believes it.

MAGDA: Nobody believes it? . . .
But why? . . .

PRUNIER: Because you are not
made for such a life,
Of petty tribulations and longings,
With the vision of an honest home
That buries your love as in a tomb!

MAGDA: (*interrupting*) No, Prunier!
You don't know how you hurt me
Speaking thus! . . .
(*to broach another subject*)
Tell me about yourselves . . . what
are you doing here?

PRUNIER: The Theatre in Nice de-
creed yesterday
That Lisette is not made of the stuff
That reaps glory; therefore,
Seeing and understanding, as I do,
I return her to you!
The artist of one evening
Will return to her maid's service!

LISETTE: (*to Magda*) I shall be
what I was formerly, if you wish it!

MAGDA: I certainly do!

LISETTE: (*with a deep sigh*) At
last!

PRUNIER: (*to Magda, pointing to
Lisette*) She is a happy woman: you
see?
She has found herself back into her
place.
You likewise, Magda, will have
to—
Be it today or tomorrow—give up
An illusion which you believe real.

MAGDA: (*suddenly*) Stop.

PRUNIER: It is my duty.
I was given this message
And I have delivered it!

MAGDA: Da chi?

PRUNIER: Da chi vi aspetta,
Sa dei vostri imbarazzi,
ed è pronto a salvarvi in ogni modo!

MAGDA: (*vivamente*) Non più!
. . .
Non più! . . .

PRUNIER: Mi basta: ho detto!
(*poi volgendosi verso Lisette*)
Addio per sempre.

MAGDA: Ve ne andate?

PRUNIER: (*accennando Lisette*)
Parto: Con certa gente non ho più a
che fare . . . (*bacia la mano a Magda*)

LISETTE: (*a Prunier con un inchino*) Ne son felice!

PRUNIER: (*a Lisette*) Solo una preghiera . . .

LISETTE: (*con comica conces-
sione*) Dite pure: vi ascolto.

PRUNIER: (*a Magda*) Permettete
signora?
(*Magda ha un piccolo gesto di ac-
consentimento. E allora il poeta
sussurra a Lisette*)
A che ora sei libera stasera?

LISETTE: Alle dieci.

PRUNIER: Ti aspetto! (*ed esce con
molta dignità*)

LISETTE: (*gettando vivamente
mantello e cappello*) Mi dia da fare
subito!
Chi sa quanto disordine
ci sarà senza di me!

MAGDA: (*distrattamente*) Davvero t'ho rimpianta!

LISETTE: La scena è un precipizio!
ma la follia passò!
Ora, immediatamente
vedrà, rimedierò.
(*ed esce rapida*)
(*dopo un attimo riappare in aspetto di cameriera*)
Un grembiulino bianco,
e riprendo servizio!
(*fa un inchino e rientra*)

RUGGERO: (*entra di corsa da des-
tra tenendo in mano una lettera*)
Amore mio!
Mia madre!
È mia madre che scrive!

MAGDA: (*vacillando, terribilmente pallida*) Tua madre?

RUGGERO: (*sostenendola e riani-
mandola*) Perchè tremi?
Non lo sai che acconsente? . . .
(*porgendole gioiosamente la lettera*)
Guarda!
Leggi tu stessa!
(*la fa sedere, le siede vicino*)

MAGDA: By whom?

PRUNIER: By one who awaits you,
Who knows of your embarrassment,
And is ready to save you at whatever
cost!

MAGDA: (*quickly*) Never! . . .
Never! . . .

PRUNIER: That's enough: I have
spoken!
(*then turning to Lisette*)
Goodbye forever.

MAGDA: What, you are going?

PRUNIER: (*pointing to Lisette*) I
go:
I will have nothing to do with certain persons . . .
(*he kisses Magda's hand*)

LISETTE: (*to Prunier with a curtsy*) I am delighted!

PRUNIER: (*to Lisette*) Only one favor . . .

LISETTE: (*with comic concession*) Speak: I am listening.

PRUNIER: (*to Magda*) With your
permission, Madame?
(*Magda makes a gesture of assent.
And the poet whispers to Lisette*)
At what time will you be free to-
night?

LISETTE: At ten o'clock.

PRUNIER: I will meet you?
(*he goes off with great dignity*)

LISETTE: (*quickly throwing her
coat and hat aside*) Give me something to do, immediately!
Goodness only knows how untidy
everything is
Since I am not there!

MAGDA: (*hardly heeding*) Yes, I
have missed you!

LISETTE: The theatre is a regular
pitfall!
But I have recovered from my
madness!
I'll get back to work, immediately,
You'll see, everything will be in order.
(*she goes off quickly*)
(*reappears immediately after in
her maid's dress*)
My white apron,
And I begin service again!
(*she curtsies and reenters*)

RUGGERO: (*enters running,
holding a letter in his hand*) Dear
heart!
My mother!
My mother writes!

MAGDA: (*staggering, deathly
pale*) Your mother?

RUGGERO: (*assisting and reviving her*) Why do you tremble?
She is consenting . . .
(*handing her the letter joyously*)
Look! Read it yourself!
(*he makes her sit down near him*)
Come . . . quite close to me . . . No,
closer,

# Act III

Così . . .
Vicina a me . . .
No, più vicina,
che il tuo viso mi sfiori!

**MAGDA:** (*come intontita, ripete*)
Tua madre!

**RUGGERO:** Leggi!
Leggi!

**MAGDA:** (*Compiendo un grande sforzo su sè stessa, comincia a leggere con voce lenta e tremante*)
"Figliuolo, tu mi dici
che una dolce creatura
ha toccato il tuo cuore . . .
Essa sia benedetta
Se la manda il Signore . . ."
(*piega la testa, commossa*)

**RUGGERO:** Continua . . .
Leggi!
Leggi!

**MAGDA:** "Penso con occhi umidi
di pianto
Ch'essa sarà la madre dei tuoi figli

È la maternità che rende santo
l'amore . . ."

**RUGGERO:** Amore mio!

**MAGDA:** "Se tu sai ch'essa è buona, mite, pura,
Che ha tutte le virtù, sia benedetta
Mentre attendo con ansia il tuo ritorno,
la vecchia casa onesta dei tuoi vecchi
Si rischiara di gioia
per accoglier l'eletta . . .
Donale il bacio mio!"

**RUGGERO:** Il bacio di mia madre!
(*attira a sè Magda per baciarla in fronte*)

**MAGDA:** (*scostandosi vivamente*) No! non posso riceverlo!

**RUGGERO:** Non puoi?

**MAGDA:** No! Non devo ingannarti!

**RUGGERO:** Tu?

**MAGDA:** Ruggero!
Il mio passato non si può scordare
. . .
Nella tua casa io non posso entrare!

**RUGGERO:** Perchè?
Chi se?
Che hai fatto?

**MAGDA:** Sono venuta a te contaminata!

**RUGGERO:** Che m'importa!

**MAGDA:** (*incalzando perdutamente*) Tu non sai tutto!

**RUGGERO:** So che sei mia!

**MAGDA:** Trionfando son passata
tra la vergogna e l'oro!

**RUGGERO:** No! Non dirmi! . . .
Non voglio! . . .

---

I want to feel your face near mine!

**MAGDA:** (*stupefied, repeats*)
Your mother!

**RUGGERO:** Read! Read!

**MAGDA:** (*making a great effort, begins reading in a stifled and slow voice*) "My son, you tell me
That a dear sweet woman
Has entered your heart . . .
May she be blessed,
If it is the will of the Lord . . ."
(*she bows her head, very much affected*)

**RUGGERO:** Continue . . . Read!
Read!

**MAGDA:** "My eyes are stained with tears
When I think that she will be
The mother of your children . . .
Motherhood sanctifies Love . . ."

**RUGGERO:** My love!

**MAGDA:** "If you feel that she is good, meek and pure,
And possesses all the virtues, she is blessed . . .
I await with anxiety your return.
The old home of your fathers
Will be full of joy
To receive your bride . . .
Give her a kiss from me!"

**RUGGERO:** My mother's kiss!
(*he draws Magda towards him to kiss her forehead*)

**MAGDA:** (*tearing herself away*)
No! I cannot receive it!

**RUGGERO:** You cannot?

**MAGDA:** No! I cannot deceive you!

**RUGGERO:** You?

**MAGDA:** Ruggero!
My past life cannot be forgotten . . .
I cannot enter your home!

**RUGGERO:** Why?
Who are you?
What have you done?

**MAGDA:** I came to you contaminated!

**RUGGERO:** What does it matter!

**MAGDA:** (*continuing, in despair*) You do not know all!

**RUGGERO:** I only know that you are mine!

**MAGDA:** In triumph I lived
Between shame and money!

**RUGGERO:** No! Not that! . . .
Don't . . .

---

**MAGDA:** Tu m'hai dato un tesoro
. . .
la tua fede, il tuo amore,
ma non devo ingannarti!

**RUGGERO:** Quale inganno?

**MAGDA:** Posso esser l'amante, non la sposa,
la sposa che tua madre vuole e crede!

**RUGGERO:** (*disperatamente*)
Taci! Le tue parole
son la mia perdizione!
Che farò senza te che m'hai svelato
quanto si possa amare? . . .
Ma non sai che distruggi la mia vita?

**MAGDA:** E non sai che il mio strazio è così grande
che mi par di morire? . . .
Ma non devo,
non devo più esitare:
nella tua casa io non posso entrare!

**RUGGERO:** No!
Non dir questo!
Guarda il mio tormento!

**MAGDA:** Tua madre oggi ti chiama!
e devo abbandonarti
perchè t'amo e non voglio rovinarti!

**RUGGERO:** No!
Non lasciarmi solo!
No!
Non lasciarmi solo!
(*e aggrappandosi a lei, intensamente*)
Ma come puoi lasciarmi
se mi struggo in pianto,
se disperatamente io m'aggrappo a te!
O mia divina amante
o vita di mia vita
non spezzare il mio cuor!

**MAGDA:** Non disperare, ascolta:
Se il destino vuole
che tutto sia finito pensa ancora a me!
Pensa che il sacrificio
che compio in questo istante
io lo compio per te!

**RUGGERO:** No!
Rimani!
rimani!
Non lasciarmi!

**MAGDA:** Non voglio rovinarti!

**RUGGERO:** No! Rimani!

**MAGDA:** (*Afferrando fra le sue mani il volto di Ruggero, e fissandolo intensamente come se volesse imprimersi negli occhi la visione ultima di questo dolore*)
L'anima mia che solo tu conosci,
l'anima mia è con te, con te per sempre!
(*Ruggero reclina la testa, abban-*

---

**MAGDA:** You gave me a treasure
. . .
Your faith and your love,
I cannot deceive you!

**RUGGERO:** What, deception?

**MAGDA:** I can be the lover, but not the wife,
The wife your mother wishes and hopes for!

**RUGGERO:** (*desperately*) Stop!
Your words
Are my undoing!
What shall I do without you
Who have revealed to me
How much I can love? . . .
But, don't you realize that you are destroying my life?

**MAGDA:** And don't you know that my misery is such
That I would welcome death? . . .
No, I must not,
I must hesitate no longer:
I cannot enter your home!

**RUGGERO:** No! Do not say that!
See what torment you cause me.

**MAGDA:** This day your mother calls you!
And I must leave you.
Because I love you and do not wish for your ruin.

**RUGGERO:** No! Do not leave me!
Do not leave me!
(*clinging to her with all intensity*)
How can you leave me when
I am consumed in misery, when
I cling to you in despair!
O my divine love,
Life of my life,
Do not break my heart!

**MAGDA:** Do not despair, listen:
If destiny ordains
That all be finished,
Think of me still.
Think that the sacrifice
I now make, is made for you!

**RUGGERO:** No! Remain! Remain!
Do not leave me!

**MAGDA:** I do not want to ruin you!

**RUGGERO:** No! Stay!

**MAGDA:** (*Taking Ruggero's face in her hands, looks at him intently as if she wanted the last vision of this anguish to remain unforgettable in her mind*) My soul
which only you know—
My soul is with you forever!
(*Ruggero drops his head in despair*)

*dono, senza speranza)*
Lascia che io ti parli
Come una madre al suo figiuolo
caro . . .
*(accarezzandolo dolcemente sui capelli)*
Quando sarai guarito, te ne ricorderai . . .
Tu ritorni alla casa tua serena . . .
io riprendo il mio volo e la mia pena . . .

RUGGERO: Amore . . .

MAGDA: Non dir niente . . .
più niente . . . che sia mio questo dolore . . .
*(Ruggero s'abbatte singhiozzando)*
*(Ora Lisette appare dal padiglione. Vede. Intuisce. Avanza lentamente, s'avvicina a Magda, la sorregge. Magda ha un ultimo, lungo, tenerissimo sguardo verso Ruggero accasciato, il viso tra le mani. Poi, appoggiandosi tutta a Lisette—che con il suo fazzolettino le asciuga le lagrime—s'avvia per il declivio, nel silenzio, fra i richiami delle campane, le ombre della prima sera, e il sommesso singhiozzare dell'amnate)*

*SIPARIO*

Let me talk to you
As a mother would to her child . . .
*(fondling his hair quietly)*
When you will have got over this, it will be but a memory.
You will return to your people
And I to my life and my sorrow . . .

RUGGERO: My love . . .

MAGDA: Say no more . . . no more . . .
Let this sorrow be mine alone . . .
*(Ruggero falls prostrate weeping)*
*(Lisette now appears from the cottage. Looks around. Understands. Advances slowly towards Magda and assists her. Magda looks at Ruggero for the last time long and tenderly, then buries her face in her hands. Leaning on Lisette—who dries her tears with her handkerchief—she walks down the incline, in silence, amid the calls of the woods, the shadows of the twilight, and the sobs of her lover)*

*CURTAIN*

# Gianni Schicchi (1918)

MUSIC BY GIACOMO PUCCINI ■ LIBRETTO BY GIOVACCHINO FORZANO

This one-act opera is set to a libretto by Giovacchino Forzano from an episode in Dante's Inferno. In Florence during the year 1299, Buoso Donati has just died, surrounded by his family. There is a rumor that he has bequeathed his entire fortune to the monks of Signa in atonement for his sins. The family is very upset by this. They search the house for a will. Rinuccio, Zita's nephew, discovers the all-important piece of paper, but before he will give it to his aunt he demands that she consent to his marriage to Lauretta, whose father, Gianni Schicchi, is of humble birth. The will confirms the rumor. Rinuccio urges his family to send for Gianni Schicchi, as he may be able to help them. He arrives with Lauretta and receives such an unfriendly greeting that he prepares to depart at once. But Lauretta threatens to throw herself into the Arno if she is not permitted to purchase a wedding ring. Schicchi gives in and devises a plan in which he will pretend to be the dying Donati and dictate his will to a notary. The family greets this plan with great enthusiasm, and each member privately attempts to bribe Schicchi in order to receive the greatest share of the inheritance. Attired in Donati's clothes and lying in his bed, Schicchi dictates a will that leaves the lion's share of the inheritance to him. The family is totally shocked but cannot say anything because under Florentine law the penalty for fraud—in which they are all implicated—is exile and the loss of one hand. When the notary departs, Schicchi throws Donati's family out of the house. Rinuccio and Lauretta embrace, and Schicchi bids his audience farewell, saying that for this plan he will go to hell. But if the audience enjoyed it as much as he did, then these were "extenuating circumstances."

---

## ■ ATTO UNICO

*Ai lati del letto quattro condelabri con quattro ceri accesi.*

*Davanti al letto, un candelabro a tre candele, spento.*
*Luce di sole e luce di candele: sono le nove del mattino.*

*Le sarge del letto, semichiuse, lasciano intravedere un drappo rosso che ricopre un corpo.*

*I parenti di Buoso sono in ginocchio, con le mani si coprono il volfo e stanno molto curvati verso terra.*
*Gherardino è a sinistra vicino alla parete; è seduto in terra, volta le spalle ai parenti e si diverte a far ruzzolare delle palline.*
*I parenti sono disposti in semicerchio; a sinistra del letto la prima è la vecchia, poi Rinuccio, Gherardo e Nella, quindi Betto di Signa, nel centro resta un po' isolato perchè essendo povero, mal vestito e fangoso è riguardato con disprezzo dagli altri parenti; a destra, la Ciesca Marco e Simone che sarà davanti alla vecchia.*

*Da questo gruppo parte il sordo brontolio di una preghiera. Il brontolio è interrotto da singhiozzi, evidentemente fabbricati tirando su il fiato a strozzo. Quando Betto di Signa si azzarda a singhiozzare, gli altri si sollevano un po', alzano il viso dalle mani e danno a Betto una guardataccia. Durante il brontolio si sentono esclamazioni soffocate di questo genere:*

**LA VECCHIA:** Povero Buoso!

**SIMONE:** Povero cugino!

**RINUCCIO:** Povero zio!

**MARCO E LA CIESCA:** Oh! Buoso!

**GHERARDO E NELLA:** Buoso!

**BETTO:** O cognato! Cognà . . . .
*(È interrotto perchè Gherardino butta in terra una sedia e i parenti, con la scusa di zittire Gherardino, fanno un formidable sciiii sul viso a Betto.)*

**GHERARDO:** Io piangerò per giorni e giorni.
*(a Gherardino che si è alzato e lo tira per la veste dicendogli qualche cosa:)*
Sciò!

**NELLA:** Giorni? Per mesi! . . . .
*(come sopra):*
Sciò!
*(Gherardino va dalla vecchia):*

**LA CIESCA:** Mesi? Per anni ed anni!

**LA VECCHIA:** Ti piangerò tutta la vita mia! . . . .
*(allontanando Gherardino, seccata si volge a Nella e a Gherardo):*
Portatecelo voi; Gherardo, via!
*(Gherardo si alza, prende il fi-*

## ■ ACT I

*At the four corners of the bed, four tall candlesticks with four lighted candles.*

*In front of the bed, a three-branch candelabrum—unlighted. There is sunshine and the glow of candles. It is nine o'clock in the morning.*

*Through the half open bed-curtains can be seen a red silk drapery covering a body.*

*Buoso's relatives, kneeling, with their faces buried in their hands, bend down close to the ground. Gherardino, seated on the floor, to the left and near the wall, turns his back to the other relatives, intent at playing with marbles. The relatives form a semi-circle; on the left side of the bed, first of all can be seen the old woman, then Rinuccio, Gherardo and Nella; Betto of Signa remains somewhat isolated in the center because his poverty and his shabby appearance make the other relatives look upon him with contempt. To the right, Ciesca, Marco and Simone are facing the old woman.*

*From this group rises the customary mumbling sound of prayers. This mumbling is interrupted by sobs, plainly forced and fabricated by a drawing of the breath through the throat. Each time that Betto of Signa takes a chance at a sob, the other relatives raise their faces from between their hands and frown upon Betto. During the mumbled prayers the following exclamations are heard:*

**THE OLD WOMAN:** My poor, poor Buoso!

**SIMONE:** Poor, poor, poor dear cousin!

**RINUCCIO:** Poor, poor dear Uncle!

**MARCO AND CIESCA:** Oh! Buoso!

**GHERARDO AND NELLA:** Buoso!

**BETTO:** My good brother-in-law! . . . .
*(He is interrupted by Gherardino letting a chair drop to the floor with a crash, and the relatives, with the excuse of quieting Gherardino throw a formidable "hush" in Betto's face.)*

**GHERARDO:** For days and days I'll shed bitter tears.
*(To Gherardino who is pulling at this coat tails, saying something):*
Hush!

**NELLA:** Days, you said? Months! . . . . ('s above):
Hush! *(Gherardino goes to the old woman.)*

**CIESCA:** Months! Why, for years and years!

**THE OLD WOMAN:** I know I'll weep all my life!
*(She pushes Gherardino away, annoyed. She turns to Nella and Gherardo):*
Don't bother! Can't you send that child away?

gliolo per un braccio e, a stratto-
ni, lo porta via dalla porticina di
sinistra.)

**TUTTI:** Oh! Buoso, Buoso,
Tutta la vita
Piangeremo la tua dipartita!

**NELLA:** (*Betto, curvandosi a sinistra, mormora qualcosa
all'orecchio di Nella*): Ma come?
Davvero?

**BETTO:** Lo dicono a Signa.

**RINUCCIO:** (*curvandosi fino a
Nella, con voce piangente*): Che
dicono a Signa?

**NELLA:** Si dice che . . . .
(*Gli mormora qualcosa
all'orecchio.*)

**RINUCCIO:** (*con voce naturale*):
Giaaaaa?!

**BETTO:** Lo dicono a Signa.

**LA CIESCA:** (*curvandosi fino a
Betto, con voce piangente*): Che
dicono a Signa?

**BETTO:** Si dice che . . . .
(*Le mormora qualcosa
all'orecchio.*)

**CIESCA:** (*con voce naturale*):
Nooooo!?
O Marco, lo senti
che dicono a Signa? Si dice
che . . . . (*Gli mormora
all'orecchio.*)

**MARCO:** Eeeeeh?!

**BETTO:** Lo dicono a Signa.

**LA VECCHIA:** (*con voce piagnucoloso*): Ma insomma possiamo . . . .
sapere che diami—
— . . . .ne dicono a Signa?

**BETTO:** Ci son delle voci . . . .
. . . .Dei mezzi discorsi . . . .
Dicevan iersera
dal Cisti fornaio: 'Se Buoso crepa,
per i frati è manna!
Diranno; pancia mia, fatti capanna! . . . .''
E un altro: "si, si, si, nel testamento
ha lasciato ogni cosa ad un convento! . . . .''

**SIMONE:** (*A metà di questo discorso si è sollevato anche lui ed ha
ascoltato*): Ma che?!?! Chi lo dice?

**BETTO:** Lo dicono a Signa.

**SIMONE:** Lo dicono a Signa????

**TUTTI:** Lo dicono a Signa!
(*Un silenzio. Ora i parenti sono,
si, sempre in ginocchio, ma bene
eretti sul busto.*)

**GHERARDO:** O Simone?

**LA CIESCA:** Simone?

(*Gherardo gets up, takes the boy
by the hand, and dragging him
along, takes him away through
the small door at left.*)

**ALL:** Oh! Buoso, Buoso,
From Paradise
See how we mourn for you in your
demise!

**NELLA:** (*Betto bending to his left
whispers a few words into Nella's
ear*): Impossible! . . . . Truly?

**BETTO:** It is rumored in Signa.

**RINUCCIO:** (*bending towards
Nella, in a lamenting tone*):
What's rumored in Signa?

**NELLA:** They're saying
that . . . .
(*She whispers into his ear.*)

**RINUCCIO:** (*in a natural voice*):
No..o,.o..o..!

**BETTO:** It is rumored in Signa!

**CIESCA:** (*bending towards Betto,
in a lamenting tone*): What's rumored in Signa?

**BETTO:** They're saying
that . . . .
(*He whispers into her ear.*)

**CIESCA:** (*in her natural voice*):
No..o..o..!
Marco, you know
What's rumored in Signa?
They're saying that . . . .
(*She whispers into his ear.*)

**MARCO:** What-a-at? . . . .

**BETTO:** It is rumored in Signâ.

**THE OLD WOMAN:** (*in a lament-
ing tone*): Can't we all know now
Whatever may be
That's rumored in Signa?

**BETTO:** There are many ru-
mors . . .
. . . . Half words here and
there . . . .
For instance, somewhere
Someone did declare:
"If old man Buoso now gives up his
ghost
The convent and the monks will get
the most" . . . .
Another said . . . . "I know that
in his will
He has left to the monks even his
mill' . . . .!

**SIMONE:** (*in the middle of this
narrative has also gotten up to listen with the others*): Indeed? . . . . And who said it?

**BETTO:** It is rumored in Signa.

**SIMONE:** It is rumored in Signa? . . . .

**ALL:** It is rumored in Signa!
(*A pause. Though still kneeling,
the relatives now keep their bodies
erect.*)

**GHERARDO:** Oh! Simone!

**CIESCA:** Simone!

**LA VECCHIA:** Parla, tu se' il più
vecchio . . . .

**MARCO:** Tu che sei stato podestà a
Fucecchio . . . .

**LA VECCHIA:** Cosa ne pensi?

**SIMONE:** (*Riflette un istante, poi,
gravemente*): Se il testamento è in
mano d'un notaio,
chi lo sa? . . . . Forse è un guaio!
Se però ce l'avesse
lasciato in questa stanza,
guaio pe' frati, ma per noi: speranza!

**TUTTI:** Se il testamento fosse in
questa stanza . . . .
guaio pe' frati, ma per noi: speranza!
(*Tutti istintivamente si alzano di
scatto. Simone e Nella si dirigono
allo stipo nel fondo. La Vecchia,
Marco, Ciesca allo stipo che è sul
davanti alla parete di destra.
Gherardo torna ora in scena senza il ragazzo e raggiunge Simone
e Nella. Rinuccio si dirige verso lo
stipo che è in cima alla scala.*)

**RINUCCIO:** (O Lauretta, Lauretta,
amore mio,
speriam nel testamento dello zio!)
(*È una ricerca febbrile. Fruscio di
pergamene buttate alll' aria. Betto, scacciato da tutti, vagando per
la stanza adocchia sul tavolo il
piatto d'argento col sigillo
d'argento e le forbici pure
d'argento. Cautamente allunga
una mano. Ma dal fondo si ode un
falso allarme di Simone che crede
di aver trovato il testamento.*)

**SIMONE:** Ah!
(*Tutti si voltano. Betto fa il distratto. simone guarda meglio una
pergamena*):
No. Non è!
(*Si riprende la ricerca. Betto ag-
guanta le forbici e il sigillo; li
striscia al panno della manica
dopo averli rapidamente appannati col fiato, li guarda e li mette
in tasca. Ora tira al piatto. Ma un
falso allarme de La Vecchia fa vol-
tare tutti.*)

**LA VECCHIA:** Ah!
(*Guarda meglio*):
No. Non è!
(*Si riprende la ricerca. Betto ag-
guanta anche il piatto e lo mette
sotto il vestito temendolo assicu-
rato col braccio.*)

**THE OLD WOMAN:** Speak! You are
the oldest here . . . .

**MARCO:** You who have been town
sheriff all this year! . . . .

**THE OLD WOMAN:** What's your
opinion?

**SIMONE:** (*thinks a while, then
with an air of gravity*): If Buoso's
will was filed in the town hall
There is no hope for us, at all!
But if by mere good luck
The will is in this room
The flower of our hopes again
might bloom!

**ALL:** If Buoso's will is hidden in
this room
The flower of our hopes again
might bloom!
(*Instinctively, they all jump to
their feet. Simone and Nella move
towards the chest of drawers up
stage. The old woman, Ciesca and
Marco rush to the coffer down
front, along right hand wall.
Gherardo, who returns without
the boy, joins Simone and Nella.
Rinuccio goes towards the chest
on top of the stairs.*)

**RINUCCIO:** Oh Lauretta, Lauretta,
my sweetheart
Let's hope from now on we'll never
part!
(*A feverish search for the will.
Rustling of parchments being
thrown in haste and confusion.
Betto, chased away by everybody,
wanders about the room, when,
suddenly, his glance falls upon
the silver tray bearing on top a silver seal and silver scissors. Cautiously, he stretches his hand
towards the tray. But from up
stage at this moment comes a
false alarm from Simone who
thinks he has found the will.*)

**SIMONE:** Ah! . . . .
(*All turn around. Betto has an innocent look upon his face. Simone, scanning a parchment
more closely*):
No! . . . . I'm wrong!
(*The search starts again. Betto
grabs the seal and scissors; he
rubs them hard on the cloth of his
sleeve after first breathing hard
upon them several times. He examines them critically and puts
them in his pocket. He is now
slowly pulling the tray towards
himself; but an exclamation from
the Old Woman makes all turn
around.*)

**THE OLD WOMAN:** Ah! . . . .
(*She scans a parchment more
closely*):
No. I'm wrong!
(*The search starts again. Betto
grabs the tray and puts it under
his coat, holding it tight in place
with his arm.*)

RINUCCIO: Salvàti!
(*Legge sul rotolo di pergamena.*)
"Testamento di Buoso Donati."
(*Tutti accorrono con le mani protese per prendere il testamento. Ma Rinuccio mette il rotolo di pergamena nella sinistra, protende la destra come per fermare lo slancio dei parenti e, mentre tutti sono in un'ansia spasmodica*):
Zia, l'ho trovato io! . . . .
Come compenso, dimmi . . . .
Ah! dimmi, se lo zio
—povero zio!—m'avesse lasciato bene bene,
se tra poco si fosse tutti ricchi . . . .
in un giorno di festa come questo,
mi daresti il consenso di sposare la Lauretta figliola dello Schicchi?
Mi sembrerà più dolce il mio redaggio . . . .
potrei sposarla per Calendimaggio!

TUTTI TRANNE LA VECCHIA: —
Ma sì!
—Ma sì!
—C'e tempo a riparlarne!
—Qua, presto il testamento!
—Non lo vedi
che si sta con le spine sotto i piedi?

RINUCCIO: Zia! . . . .

LA VECCHIA: Se tutto andrà come si spera,
sposa chi vuoi, magari . . . . la versiera!

RINUCCIO: Ah! lo zio mi voleva tanto bene,
m'avrà lasciato con le tasche piene!
(*a Gherardino che torna ora in scena*)
Corri da Gianni Schicchi,
digli che venga qui con la Lauretta;
c'è Rinuccio di Buoso che l'aspetta!
(*Gli dà due monete*)
A te, due popolini:
comprati i confortini!
(*Gherardino corre via.*)
(*Rinuccio dà a Zita il testamento: tutti seguono Zita che va al tavolo. Cerca le forbici per tagliare i nastri del rotolo, non trova nè forbici nè piatto. Guardaintorno i parenti; Betto fa una fisionomia incredibile. Zita strappa il nastro con le mani. Apre Appare una seconda pergamena che avvolge ancora il testamento. Zita vi legge sopra.*)

LA VECCHIA: "Ai miei cugini
Zita e Simone!"

SIMONE: Povero Buoso!

LA VECCHIA: Povero Buoso!

---

RINUCCIO: We're saved!
(*Reading from a roll of parchment*):
"The last will of Buoso Donati."
(*All rush towards him with outstretched hands to grab the will, but Rinuccio, holding the parchment tightly in his left hand, raises his right to stop the avalanche of relatives who, burning with impatience, cannot keep still.*)
Aunt, I found the will! . . . .
As a recompense, tell me . . . .
Ah, tell me if Uncle Buoso—poor Uncle!
Has made me legatee;
If we find all of us suddenly rich,
On this joyous occasion
Would you consent that I should marry
Lauretta, Schicchi's fair daughter?
That thought would make me happier on this day
And I could make her mine the first of May!

ALL: (*except the Old Woman*): All right!
All right!
There's time to talk it over!
Come, come, show us the will!
What do you fear?
We're all on pins and needles waiting here!

RINUCCIO: Aunt!

THE OLD WOMAN: If in that will there be no hitch
I leave you free to wed even a witch!

RINUCCIO: Uncle Buoso who cared so much for me
No doubt has left me there enough for three!
(*to Gherardino who comes back*):
Run, run to Gianni Schicchi
Tell him to come right over with his girl
As Rinuccio's poor head is in a whirl!
(*Giving him two coins*):
These pennies will be handy
For you to buy some candy!
(*Gherardino rushes out.*)
(*Rinuccio hands the will to Zita; all follow Zita who moves toward the table. She looks for the scissors to cut the ribbons around the roll, but she finds neither the scissors nor the tray. She looks around, scanning the faces of the other relatives. Betto's expression is incredible! Zita tears the ribbon off with her fingers. She unrolls the parchment from which a second roll appears—the one containing the will.*)

THE OLD WOMAN: (*reading*):
"To my dear cousins
Zita and Simone!"

SIMONE: Dear, dearest Buoso!

THE OLD WOMAN: Dear, dearest Buoso!

---

SIMONE: (*In un impeto di riconoscenza accende anche le tre candele del candelabro spento*):
Tutti la cera
tu devi avere!
Insino in fondo
si deve struggere!
Sì! godi, godi!
Povero Buoso!

TUTTI: (*mormorano*): Povero Buoso!
—Se m'avesse lasciato questa casa!
—I mulini di Signa!—
—E poi la mula!
—Se m'avesse lasciato . . . .

LA VECCHIA: Zitti! È aperto!
(*La vecchia col testamento, in mano; vicino al tavolo ha dietro a si un grappolo umano. Marco e Betto sono saliti sopra una sedia. Si vedranno bene tutti i visi assorti nella lettura. Le bocche si muoveranno come quelle di chi legga senza emettere voce. A un tratto i visi si cominciano a rannuvolare . . . . arrivano ad una espressione tragica . . . . finchè la Vecchia si lascia cadere seduta sullo sgabello davanti alla scrivania. Simone è il primo, del gruppo impietrito, che si muove; si volta, si vede davanti le tre candele testè accese, vi soffia su e le spegne; cala le sarge del letto completamente; spegne poi tutti i candelabri. Gli altri parenti lentamente vanno ciascuno a cercare una sedia e vi seggono. Sono come impietriti con gli occhi sbarrati fissi; chi qua, chi là.*)

SIMONE: Dunque era vero! Noi vedremo i frati
ingrassare alla barba dei Donati!

LA CIESCA: Tutti queri bei fiorini accumulati
finire nelle tonache dei frati! . . . .

GHERARDO: Privare tutti noi
d'una sostanza,
e i frati far sguazzar
nell'abbondanza!

BETTO: Io dovrò misurarmi il bere a Signa,
e i frati beveranno il vin di vigna! . . . .

NELLA: Si faranno slargar spesso la cappa,
noi schianterem di bile, e loro . . . . pappa!

RINUCCIO: La mia felicità sarà rubata
dall' "Opera di Santa Resparata!"

---

SIMONE: (*In an impulse of gratitude lights the three candles on the candelabrum*): All these three candles
Will burn for you!
Melting 'till ended
Inside the lee!
Rest in peace
Dear, dearest Buoso!

ALL: (*whispering*): Dear, dearest Buoso!
—I hope he has bequeathed me this house!
—The old saw-mills of Signa!
—And then his mule!
—I hope he has bequeathed . . . .

THE OLD WOMAN: Hush! it's open!
(*Behind the old woman standing close to the table, the relatives press on top of each other as tight as they can. Marco and Betto have climbed on a chair. All their faces can plainly be seen, absorbed in the reading of the will. All mouths can be seen moving as when people read without emitting actual sounds. Suddenly, a cloud overshadows all faces . . . . until they take a tragic look . . . . till the old woman fairly drops on the stool placed in front of the desk. Simone is the first of the petrified group to move; he turns around and seeing the three candles he had lighted a few moments before, blows on them and puts them out; he drops the bed curtains completely, then he puts all the candles out. Slowly, the other relatives move towards different chairs and sit down. There they stay, like graven images, eyes wide open and staring straight ahead.*)

SIMONE: So it was true! The convent and the priest
Will fatten on the wealth of that old beast!

CIESCA: All the good florins made by theft and lurch
Are now to fill the coffers of the church!

GHERARDO: Fine trick to cut us off without a thought
To let the monks and nuns feast at will!

BETTO: I will have to restrain my constant thirst
While the monks drink to the fill!

NELLA: They will feast in full joy, ever content
And we'll pine in distress without a cent!

RINUCCIO: All happiness is stolen thus from me
To fully satisfy the Holy See!

MARCO: Aprite le dispense dei conventi!
Allegri frati, ed arrotate i denti!

LA VECCHIA: (*feroce*): Eccovi le primizie di mercato!
Fate schioccar la lingua col palato!
A voi, poveri frati: tordi grassi!

SIMONE: Quagliè pinate!

NELLA: Lodole!

MARCO: Ortolani!!

BETTO: E galletti!

TUTTI: Galletti?? Gallettini!! . . . .

RINUCCIO: Gallettini di canto teneriiini!

LA VECCHIA: E con le facce rosse e ben pasciute,
schizzando dalle gote la salute,
ridetevi di noi: ah! ah! ah! ah!
Eccolo là un Donati, eccolo là!
E la voleva lui l'eredità . . . .

TUTTI: (*Con un riso che avvelena si alzano accennandosi l'un l'altro*): —Ah! ah! ah! ah! ah! ah! ah! ah! ah! ah!
—Eccolo là un Donati!
—Eccolo là
—E la voleva lui l'eredità! . . . .
—Ah! ah! ah! ah!
—Ah! ah! ah! ah!
(*erompendo a pugni stretti*): Si, si, ridete! Si, ridete, o frati!
Ingrassati alla barba dei Donati!
(*Cadono anchora a sedere. Pausa. Ora c'è piange sul serio.*)

LA VECCHIA: Chi l'avrebbe mai detto . . . .
che quando Buoso andava al cimitero,
noi . . . . si sarebbe . . . .
pianto . . . . per davvero!

VOCI: —E non c'è nessun mezzo . . . .
—Per cambiarlo . . . .
—Per girarlo . . . .
Addolcirlo . . . .
—O Simone? Simone? . . . .

LA VECCHIA: Tu se' anche il più vecchio! . . . .

MARCO: Tu che sei stato podestà a Fucecchio! . . . .

SIMONE: (*Fa un gesto come per dire: impossibile!*)

RINUCCIO: C'è una persona sola che ci può consigliare . . . .
forse salvare . . . .

TUTTI: Chi?

---

MARCO: What cheer in the cellars of the convent!
Raise up, ye monks, your heads in prayer bent!

THE OLD WOMAN: The fat of the whole land will be for you
While we will have to live on watery stew!
Fat squabs and juicy steaks will be your fare!

SIMONE: Thick mutton chops!

NELLA: And pork loin . . .

MARCO: Fresh-killed hare!

BETTO: And fat pheasants!

ALL: Yes, pheasants and spring chickens!

RINUCCIO: Of course, who could forget that tasty bite!

THE OLD WOMAN: And with your cheeks so rubicund and bloated
Full of health by Donati's gold promoted
You will laugh in our faces: ah! ah! ah!
They thought they would inherit! ah! ah! ah!
Those fool Donati geese! ah! ah! ah!

ALL: (*all rise, pointing at each other. With poisoned laughter*): Ah! ah! ah! ah! ah! ah! ah! ah! ah!
See, there goes a Donati!
—See him down there?
He thought he'd be his Uncle's heir for sure!
Ah! ah! ah! ah!
Ah! ah! ah! ah!
(*Bursting with anger, with clenched fists*):
Yes, yes, we know you smile amid your prayers
At the wonderful joke on Buoso's heirs!
(*Again they sit down with a thump. A pause. A few are now really weeping.*)

THE OLD WOMAN: Who would ever have thought
When Buoso would be taking his last journey,
We would be crying and sobbing without faking!

VOICES: Couldn't we find any scheme . . . .
—To change that will . . . .
To upset it . . . .
—To alter it!
Oh! Simone! Simone!

THE OLD WOMAN: You are the oldest here!

MARCO: You who have been town-sheriff all this year!

SIMONE: (*makes a gesture as if to say: Impossible!*)

RINUCCIO: I know there's but one man
Who could advise this clan . . . .
And who might save us . . . .

ALL: Who? . . . .

---

RINUCCIO: Gianni Schicchi!
(*Tutti gesto di disillusione*).

LA VECCHIA: (*furibonda*): Di Gianni Schicchi,
della figliola,
non vo' sentirne
parlar mai più!
E intendi bene! . . . .

GHERARDINO: (*Entra di corsa urlando*): È qui che viene!

TUTTI: Chi?

GHERARDINO: Gianni Schicchi!

LA VECCHIA: Chi l'ha chiamato?

RINUCCIO: (*accennando il ragazzo*): Io; I' l'ho mandato
Perchè speravo . . . .

ALCUNI: È proprio il momento d'aver Gianni Schicchi tra' piedi!

LA VECCHIA: (*interrompendolo*) Ah! bada! se sale gli fo ruzzolare le scale!

GHERARDO: (*a Gherardino*) Tu devi obbedire soltanto a tuo padre: là! là!
(*Sculaccia Gherardino e lo butta nella stanza a destra in cima alla scala.*)

SIMONE: Un Donati sposare la figlia d'un villano!

LA VECCHIA: D'uno sceso a Firenze da! contado!
Imparentarsi colla gente nova! . . . .
Io non voglio che venga!

RINUCCIO: Avete torto!
È fine! . . . . astuto . . . .
Ogni malizia
di leggi e codici
conosce e sa.
Motteggiatore! . . . . Beffeggiatore! . . . .
Ç'è da fare una beffa nuova e rara?
È Gianni Schicchi che la prepara!
Gli occhi furbi gli illuminan di riso
lo strano viso,
ombreggiato da quel suo gran nasone
che pare un torracchione
per così!
Vien dal contado? Ebbene? E che vuol dire?
Basta con queste ubbie grette e piccine!
Firenze è come un albero fiorito,
che in piazza dei Signori ha tronco e fronde,
ma le radici forze nuove apportano
dalle convalli limpide e feconde;
e Firenze germoglia ed alle stelle
salgon palagi saldi e torri snelle!
L'Arno prima di correre alla foce
canta, baciando piazza Santa Croce
e il suo canto è sì dolce e sì sonoro
chè a lui son scesi i ruscelletti in coro! . . . .
Così scendano i dotti in arti e

---

RINUCCIO: Gianni Schicchi!
(*They all make a gesture of disappointment.*)

THE OLD WOMAN: You will do well to speak no more of Gianni Schicchi And his fair daughter!
No more I say! . . . .

GHERARDINO: (*rushing in out of breath, yells at the top of his voice*): He's on his way!

ALL: Who? . . . .

GHERARDINO: Gianni Schicchi!

THE OLD WOMAN: Who sent for him?

RINUCCIO: I sent for him Because I hoped . . . .

A FEW: This is not the moment to have Gianni Schicchi come here and bother us!

THE OLD WOMAN: (*stopping him short*) Look here! if he comes! I will surely kick him down-stairs!

GHERARDO: (*to Gherardino*) You are to take orders from no one but your father! There! there!
(*He spanks Gherardino and throws him into the room to the right on top of the stairs.*)

SIMONE: A Donati can't marry the daughter of a peasant!

THE OLD WOMAN: One who came into Florence from the back-woods!
It's always wrong to mix with the new rich!
I don't want him to come!

RINUCCIO: You are all wrong!
He's smart . . . . and keen-eyed . . . .
He knows the law
And all the tricks
That lawyers practice.
Always good-humored, and full of fun!
At all parties, when looking for some jest
Gianni Schicchi finds the best!
His bright brown eyes light up with charm and grace
That strangest face
Upon which his big nose projects a shade
That never seems to fade.
Just like that!
What matters one's ancestors' wondrous fame?
Deeds count nowadays and not your name!
Our Florence is a great, big, robust tree
That covers with its shade Signoria Square;
But its roots get more strength and longer life
From the new streams that flow from everywhere;
And our Florence grows large, and broad and high

scienze
a far più ricca e splendida Firenze!
E di Val d'Elsa giù dalle castella
ben venga Arnolfo a far la torre bella!
E venga Giotto del Mugel selvoso
e il Medici mercante coraggio-
so! . . . .
Basta con gli odi gretti e coi ripic-
chi!
Viva la gente nuova e Gianni Schicchi!
(Si bussa alla porta)
E lui! lo faccio entrare?
(I parenti fanno un gesto che non
significa niente. Rinuccio apre;
entrano):

**GIANNI SCHICCHI E LAURETTA:**

**GIANNI:** (Si sofferma sull'uscio:
dà un'occhiata ai parenti): (Quale aspetto sgomento e desolato! . . . .
Buoso Donati, certo, è migliorato!)

**RINUCCIO:** (a Lauretta, fra il
pianerottolo e la porta) (Lauret-
ta!—
—Rino!
—Amore mio!
—Perchè si pallido? . . . .
—Ahimè, lo zio
—Ebbene, parla . . . .
—O Amore! Amore!
Quanto dolore!
Quanto dolore! . . . .)
(Gianni lentamente avanza verso
la Vecchia che gli volta le spalle;
avanzando vede i candelabri in-
torno al letto.)

**GIANNI:** Ah! . . . .
Andato??
(E perchè stanno a lacrimare?
ti recitano meglio d'un giullare!)
(falso, forte)
Ah! comprendo il dolor di tanta
perdita . . .
Ne ho l'anima commossa . . . .

**GHERARDO:** Eh! la perdita è stata
proprio grossa!

**GIANNI:** (come chi dica parole
studie di circostanza):
Eh! . . . . Sono cose . . . .
Mah! . . . . Come si fa!
In questo mondo
una cosa si perde . . . . .

---

While new towers and domes rise
to the sky!
Before reaching its mouth the Arno
river
Doth send through Santa Croce a
joyous quiver
With its singing so sweet, so full of
fire
That brooks and torrents join with
their full choir!
Thus do come men of skill in art and
science
To make more rich and splendid
our Florence!
Let from Val d'Elsa's hills come every year
One more Astolfo, builder without
peer!
And let come Giotto from the Mugel forest
And the Medicis, merchants fair
and honest!
Dismiss all thoughts derived from
snobbish lore
And welcome be Gianni Schicchi
to our door.
(A knock is heard at the door):
It is he! May he come in?
(The relatives make a meaningless gesture. Rinuccio opens the
door and Gianni Schicchi enters
with Lauretta.)

**Gianni Schicchi and Lauretta**

**GIANNI:** (stops on the threshold
and looks around at the relatives): (To judge from their air so
grave and sad
Buoso Donati's state can't be so
bad!)

**RINUCCIO:** (to Lauretta, between
the landing and the door) Lauret-
ta!
Rino!
—My dear sweetheart!
—Why pale and haggard?
—What piercing dart!
—Do speak, I beg you!
—My dear sweetheart
—What cruel dart!
—What cruel dart!
(Gianni slowly moves towards
the Old Woman, who turns her
back on him. Coming further
front he notices the candelabra
around the bed!)

**GIANNI:** Ah!
He's dead!
Why this air of solemn vesper?
(aside):
They are all better actors than a jes-
ter!
(low, falsely)
I comprehend your grief at such a
loss!
I feel it heart and soul!

**GHERARDO:** It wasn't a partial
loss, it was the whole!

**GIANNI:** (like a person saying
anything coming to his mind):
Well! . . . . in these matters! . . . . Well, what can you
do? . . . .
In this old world, so vain,

---

una si trova
(seccato che facciano la commedia con lui):
si perde Buoso,
e c'è l'eredità . . . .

**LA VECCHIA:** (Gli si avventa
come una bestia feroce): Sicuro!
Ai frati!

**GIANNI:** Ah! Diseredati?

**LA VECCHIA:** Diseredati! Si! Diseredati! E perciò ve lo canto:
pigliate la figliola,
levatevi di torno,
io non do mio nipote
ad una senza—dote!

**RINUCCIO:** O Zia! io l'amo, l'amo.

**LA VECCHIA:** Non me ne importa
un corno!

**LAURETTA:** Babbo! Babbo! Lo voglio!

**GIANNI:** Figliola, un po' d'orgolio!

**GIANNI:** (erompe): Brava la vecchia; Brava! Pel la dote
sacrifichi mia figlia e tuo nipote!
Vecchia taccagna!

**LAURETTA:** (tendendosi il braccio libero): Rìnuccio, non lasciarmi!
Ah! tu me l'hai giurato
sotto la luna a Fiesole
quando tu m'hai baciato!

**RINUCCIO:** Lauretta mia, ricordati!
tu m'hai giurato amore!
E quella sera Fiesole
sembrava tutto un fiore!
(a due)

**LAURETTA, RINUCCIO:** Addio,
speranza bella,
s'è spento ogni tuo raggio;
non ci potrem sposare
per il Calendimaggio!

**LAURETTA:** (Gli sfugge e corre a
Rino.) Babbo, lo voglio!
Babbo, lo voglio!
Amore!

**RINUCCIO:** (Le sfugge e corre a
Lauretta.) O Zia, la voglio!
O Zia, la voglio!
Amore!

**GIANNI:** (tirando Lauretta verso
la porta) Vecchia taccagna!
Stillina!
Spilorcia! Gretta!
Vieni, Lauretta,
rasciuga gli occhi,
sarebbe un parentado
di pitocchi!
Ah! vieni, vieni!
(Riprende la figlia.)
Un po' d'orgoglio,
un po' d'orgoglio!
Via, via di qua!

---

If you lose on one side
You still may gain . . . .
(Annoyed at seeing them playing
their part in front of him):
You lose your Buoso
And find his hoarded money!

**THE OLD WOMAN:** (rushing
towards him like a wild beast): All
for the convent!

**GIANNI:** Oh, what a portent!

**THE OLD WOMAN:** It is a portent,
yes it is a portent!
That's why I tell you now;
Go home with your fair daughter
Go away, go away from here
For I won't let my nephew
Get married to a pauper!

**RINUCCIO:** My aunt I am in love!

**THE OLD WOMAN:** Well, I don't
give a rap!

**LAURETTA:** Father, father, I love
him!

**GIANNI:** More pride, my little
dove!

**GIANNI:** (bursting with indiga-
tion): So for the greed that stills
your vile old heart!
Your nephew from my girl would
tear apart!
You mean old wretch!

**LAURETTA:** (each stretching
towards the other the arm they
have free): Rinuccio, do not leave
me!
Remember our great bliss!
When one bright night in Fiesole
I did consent to a kiss!

**RINUCCIO:** Lauretta, dear, remem-
ber!
You promised to be true
And that bright night, all Fiesole
Was singing, dear, of you!
(Together:)

**LAURETTA, RINUCCIO:** Farewell,
oh fondest hope,
Extinguished is thy ray;
We can't be joined together
Upon the first of May!

**LAURETTA:** (escapes and rushes
to him) Papa, I want him!
Papa, I want him!
Sweetheart!

**RINUCCIO:** (escapes and rushes
to Lauretta) My aunt, I want her!
My aunt, I want her!
Sweetheart!

**GIANNI:** (pulling his daughter
towards the door) Miserly woman!
Mean, avaricious!
You greedy wench!
Come, come, Lauretta
Dry quick your dearest eyes,
This match would surely cost you
Far more sighs!
Come on, child, come!
(taking back his daughter)
More pride, my dove!
More pride, my dove!
Come, I say, we must go!

ZITA: (*tirando Rino a destra*)
Anche m'insulta!
Senza la dote
non do il nipote,
non do il nipote!
Rinuccio, vieni,
lasciali andare,
ah! sarebbe un volerti
rovinare!
Ma vieni, vieni! . . . .
(*Riprende Rinuccio.*)
Ed io non voglio,
ed io non voglio!
Via, via di qua!
(*I parenti restano neutrali e si limitano ad esclamare di tanto in tanto.*)

I PARENTI: —Anche le dispute fra innamorati!
—Proprio il momento! —Pensate al testamento!
(*Gianni, quasi sulla porta, è per portar via Lauretta.*)

RINUCCIO: (*liberandosi*): Signor Giovanni!
Rimanete un momento!
(*alla Vecchia*):
Invece di sbraitare,
dategli il testamento!
(*a Gianni*):
Cercate di salvarci!
A voi non può mancare
un'idea portentosa, una trovata,
un rimedio, un ripiego, un espediente! . . . .

GIANNI: (*accennando ai parenti*): A pro di quella gente? Niente! Niente!

LAURETTA: (*Gli si inginocchia davanti*): O mio babbino, caro,
mi piace, è bello bello,
vo'andare in Porta Rossa
a comperar l'anello!
Si, si, ci voglio andare!
E se l'amassi indarno,
andrei sul Ponte Vecchio
ma per buttarmi in Arno!
Mi struggo e mi tormento,
oh! Dio vorrei morir!
(*Piange; una pausa.*)

GIANNI: (*come chi è costretto ad accondiscendere.*) Datemi il testamento!
(*Rinuccio glielo dà. Gianni legge e cammina. I parenti lo seguono con gli occhi poi inconsciamente finiscono per andargli dietro come i pulcini alla chioccia, tranne Simone che siede sulla cassapanca a destra, e, incredulo, scrolla il capo. Ansia.*)

GIANNI: Niente da fare!
(*I parenti lasciano Schicchi e si avviano verso il fondo della scana.*)

---

ZITA: (*pulling Rinuccio to the right*) Stop your cheap insults!
Without a dowry
I will say no!
I will say no!
Rinuccio, come
Stop all that nonsense!
I'm sure you cannot love her!
Nonsense! Nonsense!
Come, Rino, come!
(*taking back Rinuccio*)
You're not in love!
You're not in love!
Come, I say, we must go!
(*The relatives remain neutral and content themselves with a few exclamations now and then.*)

THE RELATIVES: —Who cares to listen to quarrels of lovers!
—Oh! what a pill!—Let's see about the will!
(*Gianni, almost at the door, moves to drag Laurette away.*)

RINUCCIO: (*freeing his hand from his aunt's grasp*): Master Giovanni!
Will you please wait a moment?
(*To the old woman*):
Instead of losing your temper
Show him that testament!
(*To Gianni*):
Do see if you can help us!
I know you will invent
Some device, a new scheme, a trap, a plot
A way out of this mess: I know you can!

GIANNI: (*pointing to the relatives*): To help that crowd? No sir, I'm not the man!

LAURETTA: (*kneeling in front of him*): Oh, my beloved Daddy
He's handsome as a King
I'm going to Porta Rossa
To buy our wedding-ring!
Yes, father, I do mean it!
And if you still say no
I swear from Ponte Vecchio
I'll throw myself below!
What shivers! What a chill!
Poor me, I want to die!
(*She weeps.—A pause.*)

GIANNI: (*in the tone of a man who feels constrained to condescend*): Give me Donati's will!
(*Rinuccio hands it to him. Gianni reads it as he paces up and down the room. The relatives first follow him with their eyes, then, unconsciously, start walking in his footsteps, like chicks after a hen, with the exception of Simone who remains seated on the bench to the right and shakes his head doubtfully. Great anxiety prevails.*)

GIANNI: It can't be done!
(*The relatives leave Schicchi and move up stage.*)

---

RINUCCIO, LAURETTA: Addio, speranza bella,
s'è spento ogni tuo raggio,
non ci potrem sposare
per il Calendimaggio!

GIANNI: (*Riprende a leggere e a camminare*): Niente da fare!
(*I parenti si lasciano cadere sulle sedie.*)

RINUCCIO, LAURETTA: Addio, speranza bella,
s'è spento ogni tuo raggio . . . .

GIANNI: (*tonante*): Però!
(*Tutti i parenti si alzano di scatto e corrono a Gianni.*)

RINUCCIO, LAURETTA: (Forse ci sposeremo
per il Calendimaggio!)

GIANNI: (*Si ferma nel mezzo della scena col viso aggrottato come perseguendo un suo pensiero gesticola parcamente guardando avanti a sè. Tutti sono intorno a lui; ora, anche Simone; più bassi di lui, con i visi voltati verso il suo viso come uccellini che aspettino l'imbeccata. Gianni a poco a poco si rischiara, sorride, guarda tutta quella gente . . . . alto, dominante; troneggiante.*)

TUTTI: (*con un filo di voce*): Ebbene?

GIANNI: (*infantiel*): Laurettina!
Vai là sul terrazzino,
port i minuzzolini all'uccellino.
(*e perchè Rinuccio la vorrebbe seguire, egli la ferma*):
Sola.—
(*Lauretta va sul terrazzino a sinistra, Gianni la segue con gli occhi; appena la figlia è fuori di scena egli si volge al gruppo dei parenti sempre intorno a lui*):
Nessuno sa
che Buoso ha reso il fiato? . . . .

TUTTI: Nessuno!

GIANNI: Bene! Ancora
Nessun deve saperlo!

TUTTI: Nessuno lo saprà!

GIANNI: (*assalito da un dubbio*): Ma i servi?

LA VECCHIA: (*con intenzione*): Dopo l'aggravamento . . . .
in camera . . . ., nessuno!

GIANNI: (*a Marco e Gherardo; tranquillizzato, deciso*): Voi due partate il morto e i candelabri
(*accenna al sottoscala*):
là dentro nella stanza di rimpetto!
(*a Ciesca e Nella*): Donne! Rifate il letto!

LE DONNE: Ma . . . .

---

RINUCCIO AND LAURETTA:
Farewell, oh fondest hope
Extinguished is your ray
We cannot be united
Upon the first of May!

GIANNI: It can't be done!
(*At this, all the relatives drop again upon their chairs with a thud.*)

RINUCCIO AND LAURETTA:
Farewell, oh fondest hope,
Extinguished is your ray . . . .

GIANNI: (*in a thundering voice*): And yet! . . . .
(*All the relatives jump to their feet and rush towards Gianni.*)

RINUCCIO AND LAURETTA: Perhaps we will be wedded
Upon the first of May!

GIANNI: (*stops in the center of stage a frown upon his face, as if in hot pursuit of an idea. He makes quiet gestures, looking straight ahead. All the relatives crowd around him, Simone included. As Gianni towers above them, the relatives keep their faces upturned to him, like chicks awaiting their food. Slowly, Gianni's face becomes severe, he smiles and looks down at the crowd around him . . . .He stands tall, dominating, imposing.*)

ALL: (*almost in a whisper*): Do tell us!

GIANNI: (*in a child-like voice*): Laurettina!
Go out, my darling daughter
And bring the little birdie bread and water!
(*As Rinuccio moves to follow her, Gianni stops him*):
Alone.—
(*Lauretta goes out onto the terrace on the left. Gianni follows her with his eyes, and, as soon as the girl has disappeared, he turns to the group of relatives crowding around him*):
Who knows outside
That he gave up his ghost?

ALL: No one!

GIANNI: Good! Again I say
No one is to be told!

ALL: No one will know a thing.

GIANNI: (*seized by a doubt*): And the servants?

THE OLD WOMAN: (*in a meaning tone*): Since he became unconscious
No one has entered here!

GIANNI: (*to Marco and Gherardo, his mind now at ease and fully made up*): You two will bring the dead man with those candles.
(*Pointing to the stairs*):
In yonder room overlooking Buoso's shed!
(*to Ciesca and Nella*):
And you will make the bed!

THE WOMEN: But . . . .

GIANNI: Zitte. Obbedite!
(*Marco e Gherardo scompaiono fra le sarge del letto e ricompaiono con un fardello rosso che portano a destra ne la stanza sotto la scala, Simone, Betto e Rinuccio portano via i candelabri. Ciesca e Nella ravviano il letto.*)
(*Si bussa alla porta.*)

GIANNI: (*contrariatissimo, con voce soffocata*): Chi può essere? Ah! . . . .

LA VECCHIA: (*a bassa voce*): Maestro Spinelloccio il dottore! . . . .

GIANNI: Guardate che non passi! Ditegli qualche cosa . . . . che Buoso è migliorato . . . . che riposa . . . .
(*Betto va a chiudere le impannate e rende semioscura la stanza. Tutti si affollano intorno alla porta e la schiudono appena.*)

MAESTRO SPINELLOCCIO: (*accento bolognese*): L'è permesso? . . . .

TUTTI: Buon giorno, Maestro Spinelloccio! Va meglio?
—Meglio!
—Meglio! . . . .

MAESTRO SPINELLOCCIO: Ha avuto il benefissio? . . . .

TUTTI: Altro che! Altro che! . . . .

MAESTRO SPINELLOCCIO: A che potensa l'e arrivata la sciensa! Be', vediamo, vediamo . . . .
(*per entrare.*)

TUTTI: (*fermandolo*): No! riposa!

MAESTRO SPINELLOCCIO: Ma io . . . .

GIANNI: (*seminascosto fra le sarge del letto, contraffacendo la voce di Buoso, tremolante*): No! No! Maestro Spinelloccio! . . . .
(*Alla voce del morto i parenti danno un trabballone, poi si accorgono che è Gianni che contraffa la voce di Buoso. Ma nel trabballone a Betto è scivolato il piatto, d'argento e gli è caduto.*)

MAESTRO SPINELLOCCIO: Oh! Messer Buoso!

GIANNI: Ho tanta voglia di riposare potreste ripassare questa sera? Son quasi addormentato . . . .

MAESTRO SPINELLOCCIO: Sì, Messer Buoso! . . . . Ma va meglio? . . . .

GIANNI: Da morto, son rinato!

GIANNI: Hush! Do what I say!
(*Marco and Gherardo disappear under the bed-curtains and come out again carrying a long red bundle which they bring to the right to the room under the stairs. Simone, Betto and Rinuccio carry the candelabra away. Ciesca and Nella re-arrange the bed. There is a knock at the door.*)

GIANNI: (*very much put out, in a stifled voice*): What's that? . . . . Who might it be?

THE OLD WOMAN: (*in a whisper*): It is Master Spinelloccio The physician! . . . .

GIANNI: Don't let him get in here! Give him some excuse . . . . Tell him Buoso's now taking a quiet rest . . . .
(*Betto goes to the window, and by closing the shutter makes the room almost dark. All crowd around the door and hold it barely ajar.*)

MASTER SPINELLOCCIO: (*with a foreign accent*): May I come in?

ALL: Good morning, Good Master Spinelloccio! He's better!
—Better!
—Better!

MASTER SPINELLOCCIO: Did he get full relief? . . . .

ALL: You bet he did! You bet! . . . .

MASTER SPINELLOCCIO: What wondrous height Has now reached Science's light! Well, let's see him, let's see him!
(*He moves to enter.*)

ALL: (*stopping him*): No! he's sleeping!

MASTER SPINELLOCCIO: (*insisting*): But I . . . .

GIANNI: (*half hidden behind the bed-curtains and imitating Buoso's quavering voice*): No! no! no! Master Spinelloccio!
(*At the sound of the dead man's voice, all the relatives start with fright, but they soon realize it is Gianni imitating Buoso's voice. However, in his fright, Betto has let the silver tray fall to the floor.*)

MASTER SPINELLOCCIO: Oh! Master Buoso!

GIANNI: Doctor, I feel so tired and sleepy . . . . Couldn't you return to see me some time tonight? Yes, as late as you can . . . .

MASTER SPINELLOCCIO: So, Master Buoso . . . . You feel better?

GIANNI: I feel like a new man! Until tonight!

MAESTRO SPINELLOCCIO: A stasera!
(*al parenti*)
Anche alla voce sento: è migliorato! Eh! a me non è mai morto un ammalato! Non ho delle pretese, il merito l'è tutto della scuola bolognese! A questa sefa.
—Schicchi!!!!
—Schicchi!!!!
—Schicchi!!!!
—Schicchi!!!!

LA VECCHIA: (*a Rinuccio*): Va corri dal notaio!
(*Via Rinuccio*):

I PARENTI: (*Si abbracciano, si baciano con grande effusione*):
—Caro Gherardo!
—O Marco!
—O Ciesca!
—O Nella!
—Zita, Zita!
—Simone!

GIANNI: (O quale commozione!)

TUTTI: Oh! giorno d'allegrezza! La burla ai frati è bella! Ah! felici e contenti! Com'è bello l'amore fra i parenti!

SIMONE: O Gianni, ora pensiamo un po' alla divisione: i fiorini in contanti . . . .

TUTTI: In parti eguali!
(*Gianni dice sempre di sì con la testa.*)

SIMONE: A me i poderi di Fucecchio.

LA VECCHIA: A me quelli di Figline.

BETTO: A me quelli di Prato.

GHERARDO: A noi le terre d'Empoli.

MARCO: A noi quelle di Quintole.

LA VECCHIA: Resterebbero ancora: la mula, questa casa, e i mulini di Signa!

MARCO: Son le cose migliori.
(*Pausa; i parenti cominciano a guardarsi in cagnesco.*)

SIMONE: (*falsamente ingenuo*): Ah! capisco! capisco! perchè sono il più vecchio e sono stato potestà a Fucecchio, volete darli a me! Io vi ringrazio!

LA VECCHIA: No, no, no, no! Un momento! Se tu se' vecchio, peggio per te!

MASTER SPINELLOCCIO: Until tonight
(*To the relatives*):
Even his voice now seems clearer and high! It is a fact, my patients never die! Praise I am not begging here All credit must be given To our school which has no peer! Until tonight!
—Schicchi!!!!
—Schicchi!!!!
—Schicchi!!!!
—Schicchi!!!!
-Schicchi!!!!

THE OLD WOMAN: (*to Rinuccio*): You run and fetch the notary!
(*Exit Rinuccio in haste.*)

THE RELATIVES: (*kissing and embracing each other with great effusion*):
—Dearest Gherardo!
—Oh Marco!
—Oh Ciesca!
—Oh Nella
—Zita! Zita!
—Simone!

GIANNI: How much they love each other!

ALL: Oh! happiest of our born days! The joke is on the convent! We couldn't be more content! How beautiful is love among relations!

SIMONE: Now Gianni, let us settle The question of division: All cash will go in hand . . . .

ALL: In equal shares!
(*Gianni keeps on nodding assent.*)

SIMONE: To me the farmlands Of Fucecchio.

THE OLD WOMAN: For me those of Figline.

BETTO: For me the farm of Prato.

GHERARDO: For us the lands of Empoli.

MARCO: For us all those of Quintole.

THE OLD WOMAN: That would leave undivided: The mule, this ancient palace And the saw mills of Signa!

MARCO: The best of the whole lot!
(*A pause. The relatives begin to eye each other askance.*)

SIMONE: (*simulating ignorance*): Oh! I see now! I see now! Being the oldest here And having been town-sheriff for a year You say they'll be for me! Thank you! Thank you!

THE OLD WOMAN: No, no, no, wait a moment! If you are old, so much worse for you!

**MARCO E GLI ALTRI:** Sentilo, sentilo il potestà!
Vorrebbe il meglio dell'eredità!

**GIANNI:** (*da una parte*) (Quanto dura l'amore tra' parenti!
(*ride.*)

**TUTTI:** La casa la mula i mulini di Signa
La mula i mulini di Signa la casa
La mula la casa i mulini di Signa
Di Signa i mulini la mula la casa
La mula i mulini di Signa la casa
toccano a me.
toccano a noi.
toccano a noi.
toccano a me.
La casa . . .
di Signa . . . .
la mula . . . .
i mulini . . . .
(*Si odono i rintocchi di una campana che suona a morto. Tutti cessano di gridare ed esclamano*):
L'hanno saputo!
(*ascoltando la campana, con voce soffocata*)?
Hanno saputo che Buoso è crepato!
(*Gherardo corre alla porta e scende le scale a precipizio.*)

**GIANNI:** Tutto crollato!

**LAURETTA:** (*affacciandosi da sinistra*): Babbo, si può sapere? . . . .
L'uccellino non vuole più minuzzoli . . . .

**GIANNI:** (*nervoso*): Ora dagli da bere!
(*Lauretta rientra.*)

**GHERARDO:** (*Risale affannoso, non può parlare. Fa segno di no*): . . . È preso un accidente al moro battezzato
del signor capitano!

**TUTTI:** (*allegramente*): Requiescat in pace!

**SIMONE:** (*con autorita*): Per la casa, la mula ed i mulini propongo di rimetterci alla giustizia, all'onestà di Schicchi.

**TUTTI:** Rimettiamoci a Schicchi.

**GIANNI:** Come volete!
Datemi i panni per vestirmi, presto!
(*La Vecchia e Nella prendono dall'armadio e dalla cassapanca, che è in fondo al letto la cappelina, la pezzolina e la camicia.*)

**MARCO AND OTHERS:** With his modesty he gives us a thrill!
He'd claim the fattest share in the new will!

**GIANNI:** (*aside*) How lasting is love among relatives.
(*he laughs*)

**ALL:** The palace, the mule, the saw mills of Signa
The mule, the saw mills of Signa, the palace
The mule, the palace, the saw mills of Signa
Of Signa the saw mills, the mule, the palace
The mule, the saw mills of Signa, the palace
are all for me
are all for us
are all for us
are all for me
The palace . . . .
of Signa . . . .
the mule . . . .
the saw mills . . . .
(*The slow and mournful pealing of a bell announces that someone is dead. All stop shouting and exclaim*):
How did they know?
(*With stifled voices*):
How did they learn he'd given up his ghost?
(*Gherardo rushes out of the room and rushes down-stairs.*)

**GIANNI:** The game is lost!

**LAURETTA:** (*peeping in from left*): Papa, what do you think
Of the bird. He now refuses to eat!

**GIANNI:** (*nervously*): Well, give him a drink!
(*Lauretta goes out again.*)

**GHERARDO:** (*comes again panting and out of breath. He cannot speak, but motions "no" with his head.*)
. . . A stroke has just brought down
The moorish major-domo
Of the mayor of the town!

**ALL:** (*gaily*): Requiescat in pace!

**SIMONE:** (*with an air of authority*): As to the house, the mule and the saw mills
I move to leave that matter
To the high sense of fairness of Gianni Schicchi!

**ALL:** We leave it all to Schicchi.

**GIANNI:** Just as you say!
Give me the clothes! I must get ready quick!
(*The old woman and Nella take from the wardrobe and the chest, on the other side of the bed, a nightcap, a lace handkerchief and a night-gown.*)

**LA VECCHIA:** Ecco la cappellina!
(*a bassa voce a Schicchi*):
(Se mi lasci la mula
questa casa e i mulini
di Signa,
ti do trenta fiorini!)

**SCHICCHI:** (Sta bene).
(*Via la Vecchia verso l'armadio, fregandosi le mani.*)

**SIMONE:** (*avvicinandosi con fare distratto a Schicchi; a bassa voce*): (Se lasci a me la casa
la mula e i mulini
di Signa,
ti do cento fiorini!)

**GIANNI:** (Sta bene!)

**BETTO:** (*furtivo, a Schicchi*): (Gianni, se tu mi lasci
questa casa la mula ed i mulini
di Signa, ti fo gonfio di quattrini!)
(*Nella parla a parte con Gherardo.*)

**GIANNI:** (Sta bene!)
(*La Ciesca parla a parte con Marco.*)

**NELLA:** (*lasciando Gherardo che ora la sta a osservare, mentre essa parla a Gianni*): Ecco la pezzolina!
(Se lasci a noi la mula
i mulini di Signa e questa casa,
a furia di fiorini ti s'intasa!)

**GIANNI:** (Sta bene!)
(*Nella va da Gherardo, gli parla all'orecchio e tutti e due si fregano le mani.*)

**LA CIESCA:** Ed ecco la camicia!
(Se ci lasci la mula
i mulini di Signa e questra casa,
per te mille fiorini!)

**GIANNI:** (Sta bene!)
(*La Ciesca va da Marco, gli parla all'orecchio; si fregano le mani.
—Tutti si fregano le mani.*)
(*Si infila la camicia. Quindi con lo specchio in mano si accomoda la pezzolina e la cappellina cambiando l'espressione del viso come per trovare l'atteggiamento giusto. Simone è alla finestra per vedere se arriva il notaio. Gherardo sbarazza il tavolo a cui dovrà sedere il notaio. Marco e Betto tirano le sarge del letto e ravviano la stanza.*)

**ZITA—NELLA—CIESCA:** (*Guardano Gianni comicamente, quindi*):

**NELLA:** Spogliati, bambolino,
chè ti mettiamo a letto,
e non aver dispetto
se cambi il camicino!
Si spiuma il canarino,

**THE OLD WOMAN:** Here is the night cap for you!
(*aside to Schicchi*):
If you leave me the mule
The palace and the mills
Of Signa
You will get thirty florins!

**SCHICCHI:** You'll get them!
(*The old woman moves towards the wardrobe rubbing her hands.*)

**SIMONE:** (*drawing near Gianni, with an air of nonchalance*): If you leave me this house
The mule and the saw mills
Of Signa
You'll get a hundred florins!

**GIANNI:** (You'll get them!)

**BETTO:** (*to Schicchi, afraid of being noticed*): Gianni, if you leave me
This palace with the mule and all the saw mills
I'll fill with gold your pocket until it spills!
(*Meanwhile, Nella is talking aside to Gherardo.*)

**GIANNI:** You'll get them!
(*Ciesca is now talking aside to Marco.*)

**NELLA:** (*moving away from Gherardo who follows her with his eyes while she speaks to Schicchi*): Here is a bit of old lace!
If you leave us the mule
We'll make you as rich and fat as the old miller!
All the saw mills of Signa and this villa

**GIANNI:** You'll get them!
(*Nella returns near Gherardo and whispers something in his ear. All are rubbing their hands gleefully.*)

**CIESCA:** And here is the nightgown!
If you leave us the mule
The saw mills of Signa and this villa
For you there is a thousand florins!

**GIANNI:** Good! You'll have them!
(*Ciesca goes near to Marco, whispers in his ear and they rub their hands gleefully, as do all the others.*)
(*Gianni puts on the night-gown. Then, mirror in hand, he arranges the night-cap and chin band, his face changing expression as if to find the right adjustment. Simone is at the window watching for the notary. Gherardo clears up the table for the notary to write on. Marco and Betto pull the bed-curtains and put the room in order.*)

**ZITA—NELLA—CIESCA:** (*first look at Gianni comically, then*):

**NELLA:** Undress, dear little tot
For it is now bed-time
Don't think it is a crime
To change and wash a lot
All birds do change their plumage

la volpe cambia pelo,
il ragno ragnatelo,
il cane cambia cuccia,
la serpe cambia buccia . . . .

**LA CIESCA:** Fa' presto, bambolino,
chè devi andare a letto,
se va bene il giuochetto
ti diamo un confortino!
L'uovo divien pulcino,
il fior diventa frutto
e i frati mangian tutto,
ma il frate impoverisce,
la Ciesca s'arricchisce . . . .

**LA VECCHIA:** È bello! Portentoso!
chi vuoi che non s'inganni?
è Gianni che fa Buoso . . . .
o Buoso che fa Gianni?
Un testamento è odioso?
Un camicion maestoso,
il viso dormiglioso,
il naso poderoso,
l'accento lamentoso . . . .
e il buon Gianni
cambia panni,
cambia viso,
muso e naso,
cambia accento
e testamento
per poterci servir! . . . .

**GIANNI:** Vi servirò a dovere! . . . .
Contenti vi farò!

**LE DONNE:** O Gianni, Schicchi,
nostro salvator!
È preciso?

**GLI UOMINI:** —Perfetto!

**TUTTI:** —A letto! A letto!
(*Spingono Gianni verso il letto,
ma egli il ferma con un gesto quasi solenne.*)

**GIANNI:** Prima un avvertimento!
O messeri, giudizio!
Voi lo sapete il bando?
"Per chi sostituisce
se stesso in luogo d'altri
in testamenti e lasciti,
per lui e per i complici
c'è il taglio della mano e poi
l'esilio!"
Ricordàtelo bene! Se fossimo scoperti:
la vedete Firenze?
(*accennando la torre di Arnolfo
che appare dalla finestra aperta*):
Addio Firenze, addio cielo divino,
ti saluto con questo moncherino,
e vo' randagio come un Ghibellino! . . . .

**TUTTI:** (*soggiogati, impauriti, ripetono*): Addio Firenze, addio,
cielo divino,
ti saluto con questo moncherino
e vo' randagio come un Ghibellino! . . . .
(*Si bussa. Gianni schizza a letto; i
parenti rendono la stanza semioscura; mettono una candela sul tavolo dove il notaio deve scrivere;*

The foxes shed their fur,
The spider spins his web,
The dog seeks a new layer
And snakes cast their skin

**CIESCA:** Undress, dear little mite
For it is now bed-time
If this game comes out right
You'll get a gingerbread
An egg becomes a chick
For flowers become fruit
Monks eat and grow fat
But monks will grow poor
While Ciesca rich for sure!

**THE OLD WOMAN:** It is wondrous! Portentous!
One must fall in this trap!
For who could tell that Buoso
Is not this other chap?
You hate a fellow's will,
A long white gown with frill
A face hard like a mill
A nose just like a bill
A voice so weak and still..
. . . .Gianni express
Change dress
Changes face
Nose and mug
Changes voice
Will and choice
To aid us in this pass!

**GIANNI:** I'll fix you up all right
And happy you will be!

**THE WOMEN:** O Gianni Schicchi,
our saviour you are!
Does he look the part?

**THE MEN:** Great!

**ALL:** To bed, it's late!
(*They push Gianni towards the
bed, but he stops them with a solemn gesture.*)

**GIANNI:** First, you must heed my warning!
My dear friends, do be careful!
And keep in mind this law!
"Whoever substitutes
Himself in place of others
To falsify a will
Will lose, with his accomplices,
One hand, and all will have to leave the State."
So do keep well in mind! In case we are found out
Do you see there our Florence?
(*pointing to Arnolfo's tower
which is plainly visible through
the open window*):
Florence, farewell, farewell, city of charm!
I wave good-bye with this poor, handless arm!
My fate is now to beg from farm to farm!

**ALL:** Florence, farewell, farewell, city of charm!
I wave good-bye with this poor, handless arm!
My fate is now to beg from farm to farm!
(*A knock is heard at the door. Gianni jumps into the bed, the relatives close the shutters so as to
darken the room and place a can-*

buttano un mucchio di roba sul
letto; aprono.*)

**RINUCCIO:** Ecco il notaro ed ecco i
testimoni.

**MESSER AMANTIO, PINELLINO,
GUCCIO**

**I TRE:** (*mestamente*): Messer Buoso, buon giorno!

**GIANNI:** Oh! siete qui?
Grazie, messer Amantio!
O pinellino calzolaio, grazie!
Grazie, Guccio tintore, troppo buoni
di venirmi a servir da testimoni!

**PINELLINO:** (*commosso, fra sè è
sè*): Povero Buoso! . . . .
il l'ho sempre calzato . . . .
verderlo in quello stato . . . .
vien da piangere!

**GIANNI:** Il testamento avrei voluto
scriverlo
con la scrittura mia,
me lo impedisce la paralisia . . . .
perciò volli un notaio
solempne et leale . . . .
(*In questo tempo il notaio ha preso dalla sua cassetta le pergamene, i bolli, ecc., e mette tutto
sul tavolo.*)

**MESSER AMANTIO:** O messer
Buoso, grazie!
Dunque tu soffri di paralisia?
(*Gianni allunga in alto le mani
agitandole tremolanti. Gesto di
compassione di tutti, —voci:
Povero Buoso!*)
Oh! poveretto! basta! I testi videro,
testes viderunt!
Possiamo incominciare . . . .
Ma . . . . . i parenti? . . . .

**GIANNI:** Che restina presenti!

**MESSER AMANTIO:** Dunque incomincio:
In Dei nomini, anno D. N. J. C. ab
eius salutifera incarnatione millesimo, ducentesimo nonagesimo
nono, die prima septembris, indictione undecima, ego notaro Amantio di Nicolao, civis Florentiae, per
voluntatem Buosi Donati scribo
hunc testamentum

**GIANNI:** (*con intenzione, scandendo ogni parola*): Annullans, revocans
et irritans omne aliud testamentum!

**I PARENTI:** —Che previdenza!
—Che previdenza!

dle on the table at which the notary is to sit to write out the will.
They throw all sorts of things in a
heap on the bed and then open the
door.*)

**RINUCCIO:** Here is the notary and
here the witnesses!

**Masters Amantio, Pinellino,
Guccio**

**THE THREE:** (*sadly*): Master Buoso, good day!

**GIANNI:** Oh! are you here?
Thank you, Master Amantio!
O Pinellino, the shoemaker, thank you!
Thank you, Guccio, the dyer, you
are too good
To come and act as witnesses for
me!

**PINELLINO:** (*very much moved,
aside*): Poor Master Buoso! . . . .
I have served him for years
And the state he appears
To be in, makes me cry!

**GIANNI:** It was my firm intention
to write out
My own will with my hand
Paralysis forbids me! . . . . understand
Therefore I want a notary.
Solempne et leale . . . .
(*In the meantime the notary has
taken from his box parchments,
seals, etc., disposing them all on
the table.*)

**MASTER AMANTIO:** Thank you,
good Master Buoso!
Are you sure it's paralysis that ails
you?
(*Gianni raises his trembling
hands from under the covers. A
movement of general pity. Several
are heard to mutter: "Poor Buoso."*)
Oh! that will do! both witnesses
have seen!
"Testes viderunt!"
Let's begin! Do you want these folks
to hear?

**GIANNI:** Yes, yes, they can stay
here!

**MASTER AMANTIO:** Then I'll
commence!
In Dei nomini, anno D. N. J. C., al
eius salutifera incarnatione millesimo, ducentesimo monagesimo
nono, die prima septembris indictione undecima, ego notaro Amantio di Nicolao, civis Florentiae, per
voluntatem Buosi Donati scribe
hunc testamentum . . . .

**GIANNI:** (*with intention and emphasizing each word*): Annullans,
revocans
Et irritans aliud testamentum!

**THE RELATIVES:** Wonderful foresight!
—Wonderful foresight!

**MESSER AMANTIO:** Un preambolo: dimmi, i funerali, (il più tardi possibile) il vuoi ricchi? Fastosi? Dispendosi? . . . .

**GIANNI:** No, no, pochi quattrini! Non si spendano più di due fiorini!

**I PARENTI:** —Oh! che modestia! Oh! che modestia! —Povero zio! che animo! —che cuore! . . . . —Gli torna a onore!

**GIANNI:** Lascio ai frati minori e all'opera di Santa Reparata . . . . (*I parenti, leggermente turbati, si alzano lentamente*): . . . .cinque lire!

**I PARENTI:** (*tranquillizzati*): —Bravo! —Bravo!— —Bisogna sempre pensare alla beneficenza!

**MESSER AMANTIO:** Non ti sembra un po' poco? . . . .

**GIANNI:** Chi crepa e lascia molto alle congreghe e ai frati fa dire a chi rimane: eran quattrin rubati!

**I PARENTI:** —Che massime! —Che mente! —che saggezza!

**MESSER AMANTIO:** Che lucidezza!

**GIANNI:** I fiorini in contanti il lascio in parti eguali fra i parenti.

**I PARENTI:** —Oh! Grazie, zio! —Grazie! Grazie, cugino!

**GIANNI:** Lascio a Simone i beni di Fucecchio.

**SIMONE:** Grazie!

**GIANNI:** Alla Zita i poderi di Figline.

**LA VECCHIA:** Grazie!

**GIANNI:** A Betto i campi a Prato.

**BETTO:** Grazie, cognato!

**GIANNI:** A Nella ed a Gherardo i beni d'Empoli.

**NELLA E GHERARDO:** Grazie, grazie!

**GIANNI:** All Ciesca ed a Marco i beni a Quintole!

**LACIESCA E MARCO:** Grazie!

**TUTTI:** (*fra i denti*): (Ora siamo alla mula, alla casa e a' mulini.)

**GIANNI:** Lascio la mula mia, quella che costa 300 fiorini, ch'è la migliore mula di Toscana . . .

**MASTER AMANTIO:** First of all, do tell me: about your funeral (I hope as late as possible) Must it be grand? Expensive? Impressive?

**GIANNI:** I haven't that kind of pride! You may spend two florins at the most

**THE RELATIVES:** Oh! what modesty! Oh! what modesty! Wonderful man! What soul! —Generous heart! He's good and smart!

**GIANNI:** I leave to the monastery And the order of Santa Reparata . . . . (*The relatives, somewhat worried, slowly get up*): Say . . . .five liras!

**THE RELATIVES:** (*now easy in their minds*): Splendid! Splendid! —It is fair To keep in mind our duty towards the poor!

**MASTER AMANTIO:** Methinks it's a small sum!

**GIANNI:** Who leaves a lot of money For poverty's relief Will make the people say "He must have been a thief!"

**THE RELATIVES:** What principles! —What mind! —What great wisdom!

**MASTER AMANTIO:** Wonderful keenness!

**GIANNI:** All bonds and cash in hand I leave in equal shares to my relations!

**THE RELATIVES:** Oh! Thank you, uncle! —Thank you! Thank you, dear cousin!

**GIANNI:** To Simone the farm lands of Fucecchio.

**SIMONE:** Thank you!

**GIANNI:** And to Zita my corn fields of Figline!

**THE OLD WOMAN:** Thank you!

**GIANNI:** To Betto, Prato's meadows.

**BETTO:** Thank you! Thank you!

**GIANNI:** To Nella and to Gherardo, Empoli's lands!

**NELLA and GHERARDO:** Thank you! Thank you!

**GIANNI:** To Ciesca and to Marco all in Quintole.

**CIESCA AND MARCO:** Thank you!

**ALL:** (*with clenched teeth*): Now we get to the mule, To the house and to the saw mills.

**GIANNI:** I leave my own young mule, For which I paid three hundred florins

al mio devoto amico . . . . Gianni Schicchi.

**TUTTI I PARENTI:** (*scattando*): Come? Come? —Com'è? . . . .

**NOTAIO:** Mulam relinquit eius amico devoto Joanni Schichi.

**TUTTI:** Ma . . . .

**SIMONE:** Cosa vuoi che gl'importi a Gianni Schicchi di quella mula? . . . .

**GIANNI:** Tienti bono, Simone! Lo so io quel che vuole Gianni Schicchi! Lascio la casa di Firenze al mio caro devoto affezionato amico Gianni Schicchi!

**I PARENTI:** (*erompono*) —Ah questo no! —Un accidente a Gianni Schicchi! —A quel furfante! —Ci ribelliamo! —Ci rebelliamo! —Sì, sì, piuttosto . . . . — Ci . . . ri . . . be . . . Ah! Ah! Ah! Ah! . . . .

**GIANNI:** Addio, Firenze . . . . Addio, cielo divino . . . . Io ti saluto . . . . (*A questa vocina si calmano fremendo.*)

**NOTAIO:** Non si disturbi del testatore la volontà!

**GIANNI:** Messer Amantio, io lascio a chi mi pare! Ho in mente un testamento e sarà quello, se gridano sto calmo . . . . e canterello! . . . .

**GUCCIO — PINELLINO:** Oh! Che uomo! Che uomo!

**GIANNI:** (*continuando a testare*): E i mulini di Signa . . . .

**I PARENTI:** I mulini di Signa? . . . .

**GIANNI:** I mulini di Signa (addio, Firenze) li lascio al caro (addio, cielo divino) affezionato amico . . . . Gianni Schicchi! (Ti saluto con questo moncherino! . . . .) Ecco fatto! (*I test ed il notaio sono un po' sorpresi*): Zita, di vostra borsa date 100 fiorini al buon notaio! e 20 ai testimoni!

And which is the best mule of Tuscany . . . . To my devoted friend . . . .Gianni Schicchi.

**THE RELATIVES:** (*all jumping up at once*): What's that? What's that?—What's that?

**THE NOTARY:** Mulan relinquit eius amico devoto Joanni Schicchi.

**ALL:** But . . . .

**SIMONE:** What use do you suppose Could be that mule To Gianni Schicchi? . . . .

**GIANNI:** Do please keep quiet, Simone! I know what things our Gianni Schicchi likes best! I leave my house in Florence to my dear Most affectionte and devoted friend, Gianni Schicchi!

**THE RELATIVES:** (*in an outburst of rage*)—That is too much! —Not on your life! —To Gianni Schicchi! —That cursed rascal! —We all rebel! —We all rebel! —Rather we would — We . . . .all . . . .re . . . Ah! —Ah! Ah! Ah!

**GIANNI:** Florence, farewell! Farewell, city of charm . . . . I wave good-bye (*At the sound of Gianni's thin, little voice, all relatives calm down, fuming.*)

**THE NOTARY:** Don't you disturb The final will Of Master Buoso!

**GIANNI:** Master Amantio, I leave to whom I choose! That is my will and such it must remain. If they yell . . . . I will sing the old refrain! . . . .

**GUCCIO AND PINELLINO:** What a wonderful man!

**GIANNI:** (*continuing his dictation*): And the saw mills of Signa . . . .

**THE RELATIVES:** Yes, the saw mills of Signa?

**GIANNI:** And the saw mills of Signa (farewell, Florence) Go to my dear . . . (farewell, city of charm) And most devoted friend . . . . Gianni Schicchi! (I wave good-bye with this poor, handless arm!).. And that is all! (*The witnesses and the notary seem rather surprised.*) Zita, from your own purse You'll give one hundred florins to the notary And twenty to the witnesses!

**MESSER AMANTIO — PINELLINO — GUCCIO:** (*Non sono più sorpresi*): O Messer Buoso! Grazie! . . . .
(*Fanno per avviarsi verso il letto.*)

**GIANNI:** (*arrestandoli con un gesto della mano tremolante*): Niente saluti! Nienti. Andate, andate . . . . Siamo forti! . . . .

**MESSER AMANTIO — GUCCIO — PINELLINO:** (*commossi, avviandosi verso la porta*): —Ah! che uomo! . . . . —Che uomo! —Che peccato! Che perdita! . . . . —Che perdita! . . . .
(*ai parenti*): Coraggio!
(*Escono.*)
(*Appena usciti il notaio e i testi, i parenti restano un istante in ascolto fichè i tre si sono allontanati, quindi tutti, tranne Rinuccio che è corso a raggiungere Lauretta, sul terrazzino.*)

**I PARENTI:** (*a voce suffocata da prima, poi urlando feroci contro Gianni*): —Ladro! Ladro! Furfante! —Traditore! Birbante! —Iniquo! Ladro! Ladro!
(*Si slanciano contro Gianni che, ritto sul letto, si difende come può; gli riducono la camicia in brandelli.*)

**GIANNI:** Gente taccagna! Senza la dote
non do il nipote! . . . .
non do il nipote! . . . .
Ora la dote c'è!
ora la dote c'è! . . . .
(*Afferrando il bastone di Buoso, che e a capo del letto, dispensa colpi . . . .*)
Vi caccio via!
È casa mia!
È casa mia!

**TUTTI:** —Saccheggia! Saccheggia!
—Bottino! Bottino!
—La roba d'argento! . . . .
—Le pezze di tela! . . . .
—Saccheggio! Saccheggio!
—Bottino! Bottino!
—Ah! Ah! Ah! . . . .
(*I parenti corrono qua e là rincorsi da Gianni. Rubano. Gherardo e Nella salgono a destra e ne tornano carichi con Gherardino carico. Gianni tenta difendere la roba. Tutti, mano a mano che son carichi, si affollano alla porta,*)

**AMANTIO, PINELLINO, GUCCIO:** (*no longer surprised*): O Master Buoso! Thank you!
(*They move towards the bed.*)

**GIANNI:** (*stopping them with a wave of his trembling hand*): Kind friends! No farewells! Please be going! Let's be brave! . . . .

**AMANTIO, GUCCIO, PINELLINO:** (*very much upset move towards the door*): What a wonderful man! . . . . It's a real pity! What a loss! . . . . What a loss!
(*To the relatives*): Take heart, good people!
(*exeunt.*)
(*As soon as the notary and his witnesses have gone out, the relatives at first remain quiet a moment listening to the vanishing footsteps of the three men. Then, all, with the exception of Rinuccio, who has rushed out to join Lauretta on the terrace.*)

**THE RELATIVES:** (*with hissing voices at first, then with ferocious yells*): Robber! Robber! Vile scoundrel!
Traitor! Traitor! Cheap counsel! Imposter! Robber! Robber!
(*They all rush in a mass towards Gianni, who, standing on the bed, defends himself as best he can. They tear his night-gown to shreds.*)

**GIANNI:** You miserly lot! Without a good dowry
I won't consent!
I won't consent!
There is a dowry now!
There is a dowry now!
(*Grabbing Buoso's stick hanging from a bed post, he wields it around with wonderful effect*):
Get out, swine!
This house is mine!
This house is mine!

**ALL:** —Let's rummage! Yes, let's pillage!
—Let's grab all we can!
—The fine silverware!
—Silk, velvets and linen!
—Let's rummage! Come, let's pillage!
—Let's grab all we can!
Ah! ah! ah!
(*The relatives run around here and there pursued by Gianni. They steal all that comes under their hands. Gherardo and Nella go up stairs and come back laden*)

*scendono le scale — Gianni li rincorre — La scena resta vuota.*)

**RINUCCIO:** (*Dal fondo apre di dentro le impanute del finestrone; appare Firenze inondata dal sole; i due innamorati restano sul terrazzo*): Lauretta, mia Lauretta! Staremo sempre qui! Guarda! Firenze è d'oro! Fiesole e bella!

**LAURETTA:** Là mi giurasti amore!

**RINUCCIO:** Ti chiesi un bacio;

**LAURETTA:** Il primo bacio!

**RINUCCIO:** Tremante e bianca —Volgesti il viso . . . .
(*a due*):

**RINUCCIO, LAURETTA:** Firenze da lontano
Ci parve il Paradiso! . . . .
(*Si abbracciano e restauo mel fondo abbracciati.*)

**GIANNI:** (*Torna risalendo le scale, carico di roba che butta al suolo*): La masnada fuggi!
(*Di colpo s'arrest—vede i due— si pente di aver fatto rumore—ma i due non si turbano—Gianni sorride—è commosso—vienne alla ribalta e accennando gli innamorati . . . . con la berretta in mano*):
(*Licenziando senza cantare*)
Ditemi voi, Signori,
se i quattrini di Boso
potevan finir meglio di cosi!
Per questa bizzarria
m'han cacciato all'Inferno . . . .
e cosi sia;
ma, con licenza del gran padre Dante,
Se stasera vi siete divertiti . . . .
concedetemi voi . . . .
(*Fa il gesto di applaudire*):
l'attenuante!—
(*si inchina graziosamente.*)

**VELARIO.**

with loot. Gianni does all he can to prevent the relatives from carrying away too much. All, as they have their arms full crowd around the door and rush downstairs. Gianni runs after them. The stage remains empty.)

**RINUCCIO:** (*way up stage, opens the large window. Florence appears, bathed in glorious sunshine. The two lovers remain on the terrace*): Lauretta, my dear Lauretta!
This house will be our own! Behold our radiant Florence! Fiesole is beautiful!

**LAURETTA:** You promised love eternal!

**RINUCCIO:** I begged a kiss!

**LAURETTA:** Yes, my first kiss!

**RINUCCIO:** All white and trembling
You turned your face . . . .
(*together*):

**RINUCCIO, LAURETTA:** And Florence in the valley,
Looked like a Paradise!
(*They embrace and remain upstage clasped in each other's arms.*)

**GIANNI:** (*returns, laden with bundles which he throws on the floor*): That pack of thieves have fled!
(*Suddenly he stops. Seeing the two lovers, he is sorry for having been noisy, but the young people do not seem to mind. Gianni's face is smiling. Very much moved, he comes to the footlights, cap in hand, and pointing to the lovers.*)
(*Taking leave of the audience, without singing*)
Tell me, Ladies and Gentlemen, Whether you could imagine A better use for Buoso's hoarded money!
For my trick, those good men Have sent my soul to Hades . . . . well, amen!
But, giving Dante credit for this plot
If a good time has been tonight your lot
I hope to learn your verdict is . . . .
(*Makes motion of applause*):
. . . not guilty!
(*He bows gracefully to the audience.*)

**CURTAIN**

# Il Tabarro (1918)

## The Cloak

MUSIC BY GIACOMO PUCCINI ■ LIBRETTO BY GIUSEPPE ADAMI

This one-act opera is set to a libretto by Giuseppe Adami from Didier Gold's play La Houppelande. Michele, Giorgetta's husband, gazes at the sunset from the helm of his barge, which is moored in the Seine. An organ-grinder plays a waltz. Michele expresses his sympathy to Giorgetta for Luigi, a young, penniless stevedore. A song-seller's voice is heard from the distance. Luigi, Giorgetta's lover, is tired of his miserable existence and unable to stand his secret love any longer. He tells Michele that he is going to leave his employ as soon as the barge reaches Rouen. While Michele is below, Giorgetta and Luigi sing about their guilty love and their desire for one last hour of bliss. They agree to Giorgetta's usual all-clear signal—the striking of a match. Luigi departs and Michele returns. He reminds her of how, in the days when they were happy together, he would wrap his cloak around her. He knows she no longer loves him and this makes him sad. She is uncomfortable with him and he wonders if she has a lover. He considers three possibilities—Talpa, who is too old; Tinca, who is too drunk; and Luigi, who is leaving. Michele lights his pipe and Luigi, watching from the riverbank, rushes onto the barge. Michele now realizes the truth. He forces a confession from Luigi and strangles him, hiding the dead man under his cloak. Giorgetta, frightened by the noise, approaches Michele. She pretends that she regrets her earlier discomfort with him and asks him to wrap his cloak around her like he used to. Michele opens the cloak, revealing Luigi's dead face.

*Quando si apre il velario, Michele—il padrone del barcone—è seduto presso il timone, gli occhi fissi a contemplare il tramonto. La pipa gli pende dalle labbra, spenta.*

*Dalla stiva al molo vanno e vengono gli scaricatori trasportando faticosamente i sacchi, e cantando questa loro canzone:*

Oh! Issa! oh!
Un giro ancor!
Se lavoriam senza ardore,
si resterà ad ormeggiare,
e Margot
con altri ne andrà.
*(Sulla Senna, di tratto in tratto, la sirena d'un rimorchiatore lancia il suo grido lugubre. Qualche cornetta d'automobile lontano.)*

Oh! Issa! oh!
Un giro ancor!
Non ti stancar, battelliere,
dopo potrai riposare,
e Margot
felice sarà!
Oh! Issa! oh!
Un giro ancor!
Ora la stiva è vuotata,
chiusa è la lunga giornata,
e Margot
l'amor ti darà! . . . .
*(Giorgetta esce dalla cabina senza avvedersi di Michele. Accudisce alle sue faccende; ritira alcuni panni stesi ad asciugare; cava una secchia d'acqua dal fiume e innaffia i suoi fiori; ripulisce la gabbia dei canarini.)
Finalmente si accorge che il suo*

*As the curtain rises, Michele, the skipper, seated close to the tiller, can be seen steadily gazing at the wondrous sunset. His unlighted pipe is hanging from his lips.*

*From the hold to the wharf, long-shoremen come and go, backs bent under heavy bags, and singing their customary song:*

Oh! hoist! hoist! oh!
Another trip to go!
If we labor without zest,
We'll remain at anchor forever!
And Margot will go
With others!
*(Now and then there comes from the river the whistle of the passing tugs. Automobile horns are heard in the distance.)*

Oh! hoist! hoist! oh!
Another trip remains!
Don't grow weary, sailor boy
Leisure and rest will come later
And Margot
Will be full of glee!
Oh! hoist! hoist! oh!
Another trip remains!
The hold is now empty and clean
You can fold your weary arms
And
Margot will go with you!
*(Giorgetta emerges from the cabin, not noticing Michele. She takes her wash down from the line. She draws up a bucket of water from the river and waters her flowers; then she cleans the bird cage. She finally sees her husband still seated motionless near the tiller, and,*

*uomo è laggiù, e facendo schermo con la mano agli occhi, tanto è vivo il riflesso del sole che tramonta, lo chiama:)*

**GIORGETTA:** O Michele? . . . .
Michele? . . . . Non sei stanco d'abbacinarti al sole che tramonta?
Ti sembra un gran spettacolo?

**MICHELE:** Sicuro!

**GIORGETTA:** Lo vedo bene: dalla tua pipa
il fumo bianco non sbuffa più!

**MICHELE:** *(accennando agli scaricatori)* Han finito laggiù?

**GIORGETTA:** Vuoi che discenda?

**MICHELE:** No. Resta, Andrò io stesso.

**GIORGETTA:** Han lavorato tanto! . . . .
Come avevan promesso,
La stiva sarà sgombra, e per domani si potrà caricare.
Bisognerebbe, ora, compensare questa loro fatica; un buon bicchiere.

**MICHELE:** Ma certa. Pensi a tutto, cuore d'oro!
Puoi portare da bere.

**GIORGETTA:** Sono alla fine: prenderanno forza.

*shading her eyes with her hand to protect them from the glare, she calls out):*

**GIORGETTA:** O Michele? . . . .
Michele? . . . . Are you not tired
Of blankly gazing there at that bright sunset?
Is it truly a wondrous sight?

**MICHELE:** Truly it is!

**GIORGETTA:** Indeed it must be so;
I knew it was
For your pipe, Michele, now smokes no more!

**MICHELE:** *(pointing to the stevedores)* Are they all through down there?

**GIORGETTA:** Shall I go and see?

**MICHELE:** No; stay. I will go myself.

**GIORGETTA:** The men toiled hard all day!
And they fulfilled their promise
The hold will sure be emptied, and tomorrow
We can take in new cargo.
As a fair token of your appreciation
For their efforts, I think a glass of wine . . . .

**MICHELE:** Of course! You have a heart of gold!
Never forgetting anyone! Fetch the wine!

**GIORGETTA:** They're almost through. A drink will give them courage.

**MICHELE:** Il mio vinello smorza la sete, e li ristora.
E a me, non hai pensato?

**GIORGETTA:** A te? . . . . Che cosa?

**MICHELE:** (*cingendola con un braccio*) Al vino ho rinunciato, ma, se la pipa è spenta, mon è spento il mio ardore . . . . Un tuo bacio, o mio amore . . . .
(*La bacia; essa si scansa voltando il viso. Michele un po' contrariato s'avvia, verso la stiva e discende.*)

**LUIGI:** (*passando dallo scalo al battello*) Si soffoca, padrona!

**GIORGETTA:** Lo pensavo.
Ma ho io quel che ci vuole.
Sentirete che vino!
(*Si avvia verso la cabina, dopo aver lanciata un'occhiata espressiva a Luigi.*)

**TINCA:** (*salendo dalla stive*) Sacchi dannati! . . . .
Mondo birbone! . . . .
Spicciati, Talpa!
Si va a mangiare!

**TALPA:** Non aver fretta! non mi seccare!
Ah! questo sacco spacca il groppone!
(*Scotendo la testa e tergendosi il sudore col rovescio della mano.*)
Dio! che caldo! . . . . O Luigi, ancora una passata.

**LUIGI:** (*indicando Giorgetta che reca la brocca del vino e i bicchieri*) Eccola la passata! . . . . Ragazzi, si beve!
Qui, tutti insieme, lesti!
(*Tutti accorrono alla chiamata, facendosi intorno a Giorgetta che distribuisce bicchieri e versa mescendo.*)
Ecco! Pronti!
Nel vino troverem l'energia per finir!
(*e beve.*)

**GIORGETTA:** (*ridendo*) Come parla difficile! . . . . Ma certo: vino alla compagnia!
Qua, Talpa!
Al Tinca! . . . . A voi! Prendete! . . . .

**IL TALPA:** Alla salute vostra il vino si beva!
S'alzi il bicchiere lieti
Tanta felicità
per la gioia che dà!
(*e s'asciuga la bocca con il dorso dalla mano.*)

**GIORGETTA:** Se ne volete ancora! . . . .

**MICHELE:** My wine helps in quenching
Thirst, and lightens their labor.
But, didn't you think of me?

**GIORGETTA:** Of you? . . . .
What can I? . . . .

**MICHELE:** (*gently putting an arm around her waist*)
No wine touches my lips now,
But, if my pipe is out,
My desire is aflame . . .
Just one little kiss, sweetheart . . . .
(*Michele kisses Giorgetta, who turns her face away. Disappointed, Michele walks off and goes down into the hold.*)

**LUIGI:** (*coming from the wharf to the barge*) Oh! what heat! It's awful!

**GIORGETTA:** I am sorry!
But I have what will bring coolness!
Wait, and taste our new wine!
(*Giorgetta walks towards the cabin after exchanging an expressive glance with Luigi.*)

**TINCA:** (*coming up from the hold*) Some weight to carry! . . . .
A life all burdens! . . . .
Hurry, Talpa,
It is time for supper!

**TALPA:** Why should I hurry? Just stop your shouting!
More yet to hoist and my back is breaking!
(*He shakes his head and wipes the perspiration from his brow with the back of his hand.*)
Heavens! What heat! Oh, Luigi, We have another trip to make!

**LUIGI:** (*pointing to Giorgetta who appears with a pitcher of wine and glasses*) There comes our other trip! Now come and be merry!
Here, all together,
Quick! Quick!
(*They all rush around Giorgetta who distributes glasses and pours out the wine.*)
Now then! Ready!
This wine will give us strength
For the rest of our work!
(*He gulps down his wine.*)

**GIORGETTA:** (*laughing*) Your words are hard indeed! . . . . But anyway
Wine, wine, for the whole party!
Here, Talpa!
You, Tinca! . . . . Now then!
Drink, boys! . . . .

**TALPA:** To your good health we drink with all our hearts!
Friends, lift your glasses!
Drink on!
And thank with all your heart
Our hospitable hostess!
(*He wipes his mouth with the back of his hand.*)

**GIORGETTA:** Come forth, come with your glasses!

**IL TALPA:** Non si rifiuta mai!
(*e porge ancora il bicchiere.*)

**GIORGETTA:** (*agli altri*) Avanti coi bicchieri!

**LUIGI:** (*indicando un suonatore di organetto che passa sulla panchina*) Guarda là l'organetto!
È arrivato in buon punto.

**IL TINCA:** (*alzando il bicchiere*) In questo vino affogo i tristi pensieri.
Bevo al padrone!
Viva!
(*Beve. Giorgetta torna a mescere.*)
Grazie! Grazie!
L'unico mio piacer
sta qui in fondo al bicchier!

**LUIGI:** (*al suonatore*) Ei, là! Professore! Attacca!
(*agli amici.*)
Sentirete che artista!

**GIORGETTA:** Io capisco una musica sola:
quella che fa ballare.

**IL TINCA:** (*offrendosi*) Ma sicuro! Ai suoi ordini sempre, e gamba buona!

**GIORGETTA:** (*ridendo*) To'! Vi prendo in parola!

**IL TINCA:** (*lusingatissimo*) Ballo con la padrona!
(*Si ride. Ma si ride anche di più perchè il Tinca non riesce a prendere il passo e a mettersi d'accordo con Giorgetta.*)

**LUIGI:** La musica e la danza van d'accordo.
(*al Tinca*)
Sembra che tu pulisca il pavimento!

**GIORGETTA:** Ahi! mi hai pestato un piede!

**LUIGI:** (*allontanando il Tinca con una spinta e sostituendolo*) Va! Lascia! Son qua io!
(*E serra Giorgetta fra le braccia. Essa s'abbandona languidamente. La danza continua mentre dalla stiva appare Michele.*)

**IL TALPA:** (*con rapida mossa*) Ragazzi, c'è il padrone!
(*Luigi e Giorgetta si staccano. Luigi getta qualche moneta al suonatore, poi assieme agli altri s'avvia verso la stiva, mentre Michele procede verso Giorgetta.*)

**GIORGETTA:** (*dopo essersi ricomposta e ravviati i capelli, s'avvicina a Michele, con stentata naturalezza*) Dunque, che cosa credi? Partiremo la settimana prossima?

**MICHELE:** (*vagamente*) Vedremo.
(*da lontano il sibilo d'una sirena.*)

**TALPA:** We never will say no! (*He extends his glass.*)

**GIORGETTA:** (*to the others*) Come on! There is still more!

**LUIGI:** (*pointing to an organ-grinder who is passing along the wharf*) Look at the organ-grinder! . . . .
He comes at the right moment.

**TINCA:** (*raising his glass*) In this good wine we drown all thoughts of sadness.
To our kind master!
Good health!
(*He drinks. Giorgetta pours out more wine.*)
Thanks, ma'am! Thanks, ma'am!
The only good of life
Lies at the bottom of my glass!

**LUIGI:** (*to the organ-grinder*) Say, there! Professor! Music!
(*to the men*)
You will hear a great artist!

**GIORGETTA:** I understand only one sort of music:
The kind that's good for dancing.

**TINCA:** (*approaching her*) Very good and I am here at your orders . . . . I love dancing!

**GIORGETTA:** (*laughing*) I'll take you at your word!

**TINCA:** (*highly flattered*) I dance with our fair mistress!
(*They all laugh, and the merriment increases because, in spite of all his efforts, Tinca does not succeed in keeping step with Giorgetta.*)

**LUIGI:** (*to Tinca*) Say, Tinca, what's the matter with your dancing?
What are you trying to do? Polish the floor?

**GIORGETTA:** Ouch! You stepped on my foot, Tinca!

**LUIGI:** (*shoving Tinca aside and taking his place*) Stop it! You don't know how!
(*He takes Giorgetta into his arms and holds her tightly. She abandons herself languidly. They are still dancing as Michele emerges from the hold.*)

**TALPA:** (*quickly*) Oh, boys, the boss is coming!
(*Luigi and Giorgetta stop dancing. Luigi throws a few coins to the organ-grinder; then, together with the other men, proceeds towards the hold, while Michele approaches his wife.*)

**GIORGETTA:** (*after putting her disheveled hair in order, with forced composure*) Tell me, Michele! Are we going to sail Away from here next week?

**MICHELE:** (*vaguely*) We'll see!
(*From afar is heard the shrill whistle of a tug.*)

GIORGETTA: Il Talpa e il Tinca restano?

MICHELE: Resterà anche Luigi.

GIORGETTA: Ieri non lo pensavi.

MICHELE: Ed oggi, penso.

UN VENDITORE DI CANZONETTE: (*lontano*) Chi la vuole l'ultima canzonetta? . . . Chi la vuole? . . . .

GIORGETTA: (*avvicinandosi*) Perchè?

MICHELE: Perchè non voglio ch'egli crepi di fame.

GIORGETTA: Quello s'arrangia sempre.

MICHELE: Lo so: s'arrangia, è vero. Ed è per questo che non conclude nulla.

GIORGETTA: (*seccata*) Con te non si sa mai chi fa male o fa bene!

MICHELE: (*semplicemente*) Chi lavora si tiene.

GIORGETTA: Già discende la sera . . . . Oh che rosso tramonto di settembre! Che brivido d'autunno!

IL VENDITORE: (*più vicino*) Con musica e parole, chi la vuole?

GIORGETTA: Non sembra un grosso arancio questo sole che muore nella Senna? (*indicando al di là della Senna.*) Guarda laggiù la Frugola! La vedi? Cerca di suo marito. Non lo lascia! . . . .

MICHELE: È giusto. Beve troppo!

GIORGETTA: Non lo sai ch'è gelosa?

MICHELE: (*non risponde.*) (*N'el frattempo il cantasterie è apparso sulla strada, al di là della Senna, seguito da un gruppo di midienttes che escono da una casa di mode e che si fermano ad ascoltarlo.*)

IL VENDITORE DI CANZONETTE: Chi vuole la canzone?

LE MIDINETTES: Bene! bene! sì! sì!

IL VENDITORE: 'Primavera, primavera, non cercare più i due amanti là fra l'ombre della sera. Chi ha vissuto per amore per amore si morì . . . . È la storia di Mimi . . . .

GIORGETTA: Will Tinca work with Talpa?

MICHELE: And with them also Luigi!

GIORGETTA: You didn't think so before . . . .

MICHELE: But now I think . . . .

A SONG PEDDLER: (*in the distance*) Who will buy the latest and newest song? Who will buy? . . . .

GIORGETTA: (*drawing near Michele*) Why?

MICHELE: Because I fear He might die of starvation!

GIORGETTA: He always gets around.

MICHELE: I know he does: that's true! And for that reason He'll never get ahead!

GIORGETTA: (*annoyed*) With you one never can tell If one is right or wrong!

MICHELE: (*simply*) He who works gets along.

GIORGETTA: Night already descends What a clear crimson sunset of September! How chilly is the air!

THE SONG PEDDLER: (*coming nearer*) The music and the words . . . . who wants my ballad?

GIORGETTA: Oh! look at the huge sun, as red as blood Fast dying out in the Seine! (*She points beyond the river*) Oh! see who comes! . . . . it is Frugola in quest Of her fool husband. She is like his shadow . . . .

MICHELE: She's right. He drinks too much!

GIORGETTA: Why! Don't you know she is jealous?

(*Michele does not answer. In the meanwhile the song peddler has appeared on the street beyond the Seine, followed by a group of milliners who have rushed out of a near-by shop and stop to listen.*)

THE SONG PEDDLER: Who wants to hear my ballad?

THE MILLINERS: Go on! Go on! Quick! Quick!

THE SONG PEDDLER: Spring, beloved! Spring, beloved! No longer are the youthful lovers sitting In the dark and lonely corners. Those who love with fervid passion No more will see their dear ones . . . . It is the story of Mimi! . . . .

GIORGETTA: (*che ha sempre scrutato Michele*) O mio uomo, non sei di buon umore! Perchè? . . . . che hai? . . . . Che guardi? . . . . E perchè taci? . . . .

MICHELE: T'ho mai fatto scenate?

GIORGETTA: Lo so bene: tu non mi batti!

MICHELE: Forse lo vorresti?

GIORGETTA: Ai silenzi talvolta, si, preferirei lividi di percosse!

MICHELE: (*senza rispondere risale il barcone.*)

GIORGETTA: (*seguendolo con insistenza.*) Dimmi almeno che hai!

MICHELE: Ma nulla! . . . . Nulla! . . . .

IL VENDITORE: 'Chi aspettando sa che muore conta ad ore le giornate con i battiti del cuore. Ma l'amante non tornò, e i suoi battiti finì anche il cuore di Mimì!' (*Il cantore si allontana. Le ragazze, leggendo le parole sui foglietti comperati, sciamano ripetendo la strofa. Le loro voci si perdono.*)

GIORGETTA: Quando siamo a Parigi io mi sento felice.

MICHELE: Si capisce.

GIORGETTA: Perchè? (*La Frugola è apparsa sul molo; attraversa la passerella e sale sul barcone. È una figura cenciosa e caratteristica. Ha sulle spalle una vecchia sacca gonfia di agni sorta di roba raccattata.*)

LA FRUGOLA: Eterni innamorati, buona sera.

GIORGETTA: O buonasera, Frugola! (*Michele, dopo di avere salutato con un gesto la Frugola, entra nella cabina.*)

LA FRUGOLA: Il mio uomo ha finito il lavoro? Stamattina non ne poteva più dal mal di reni. Faceva proprio pena. Ma l'ho curato io: una buona frizione e il mio rum l'ha bevuto la sua schiena! (*ride rumorosamente, poi getta a*

GIORGETTA: (*who has been watching Michele*) Oh, Michele, you seem so strange this evening Say why! Do tell! What ails you? Why so silent?

MICHELE: I treat you well, Giorgetta.

GIORGETTA: Yes, Michele, I get no abuse.

MICHELE: Have you lacked attention?

GIORGETTA: No, but to your dull silence I would fain prefer Bruises, blows and rough handling! (*Not replying, Michele walks to the other end of the barge. Giorgetta follows him, with insistence.*) Michele! Tell me what ails you!

MICHELE: Why, nothing! . . . . Nothing!

THE SONG PEDDLER: 'He who knows he soon must die By the hour his days will reckon With his heart's quickening pulsation. But her beau did not return And The heart of poor Mimi is as still as still can be. (*The peddler disappears in the distance. The girls, reading the words on the sheets they have purchased, rush away, repeating the verse. Their voices grow fainter and fainter.*)

GIORGETTA: When we linger in Paris I am full of contentment!

MICHELE: Yes, of course!

GIORGETTA: Why so? (*Frugola appears on the wharf; she comes up the gang plank and jumps onto the barge. She is a dirty, ragged woman, but still presents a characteristic figure. Frugola carries on her shoulder a large knapsack filled with the rubbish she has picked up.*)

FRUGOLA: Oh, perennial lovers! Good evening!

GIORGETTA: How do you do, dear Frugola? (*Michele greets Frugola with a gesture, then enters the cabin.*)

FRUGOLA: Is my husband Through with his work yet? You know this morning He was all pains and aches, my poor old man! Worse than ever, Giorgetta. I patched him up all right, though! Rubbed and rubbed and rubbed Until his back had sponged up all

terra la sacca e vi fruga dentro
con voluttà cavandone vari oggetti.)
Giorgetta, guarda: pettine fiam-
mante!
Se lo vuoi, te lo dono.
E quanto di più buono
ho raccolto in giornata.

**GIORGETTA:** (*prendendo il pettine*) Ilanno ragione di chiamarti
Frugola:
tu rovisti ogni angolo ed hai la sacca
piena.

**LA FRUGOLA:** Qui dentro è un po'
di tutto!
(*mostrando di mano in mano le
cose che nomina.*)
Se tu sapessi—gli oggetti strani
che in questa sacca—sono racchi-
usi!
Ciuffi di piume—velluti e trine,
stracci, barattoli—vechie scar-
pine.
Vi son confusi—strane reliquie,
i documenti—di mille amori.
Gioie e tormenti—quivi raccolgo
senza distinguere—fra il ricco e il
volgo!

**GIORGETTA:** E in quel cartoccio?

**LA FRUGOLA:** Qui c'è una cena!
(*e ridendo dello stupore di Giorgetta, spiega*)
Cuore di manzo per Caporale,
il mio soriano
dal pelo fulvo,
da l'occhio strano,
che non ha uguale!

**GIORGETTA:** (*ridendo*) Gode di
privilegi il tuo soriano!

**LA FRUGOLA:** Li merita! Vedessi!
È il più bel gatto e il mio più bel romanzo
Quando il mio Talpa è fuori,
il soriano mi tiene compagnia.
Insieme noi filiamo i nostri amori
senza puntigli e senza gelosia.
Vuoi saperla la sua filosofia?
Ron ron: meglio padrone
in una catapecchia
che servo in un palazzo.
Ron ron: meglio cibarsi
con due fette di cuore
che logorare il proprio nell'amore!
(*Il Talpa appare dalla stiva, seguito da Luigi*)

**IL TALPA:** To'! guarda la mia vecchia! . . . . Che narravi?

**LA FRUGOLA:** Parlavo con Giorgetta del soriano.

my good rum!
(*She laughs boisterously, then
throws her bag down on the floor,
and greedily rummages through
it, bringing forth several objects.*)
Giorgetta, look! A comb, brand new
and shining!
If you want it, dear, take it!
It is the best result
Of all my work today!

**GIORGETTA:** (*accepting the
comb*) Our friends were right in
calling you Frugola . . . .
For you search every corner to daily
fill your bag.

**FRUGOLA:** A thousand and one
quaint objects . . . .
(*She shows Giorgetta the various
articles as she goes on naming
them.*)
. . . .of every order. Things rare
and common huddle together—
In this, my grab bag!
Laces and feathers—silk scarves
and velvets,
Cream pots and ruffles—old silver
bracelets
Here in confusion—quaint and
strange memories,
Documents true of love and deep
passion—
Pleasures and torments, are kept
here in jumble
Making no caste line between rich
and humble . . . .

**GIORGETTA:** And in that bundle?

**FRUGOLA:** This is the supper
(*And laughing at Giorgetta's
amazement, she explains*)
Beef-heart for dearest old Caporale
My fine Angora
With snow-white fur
And deep blue eyes!
Most rare, I tell you!

**GIORGETTA:** (*laughing*) A real
privileged beast, your white Angora . . . .

**FRUGOLA:** He truly is deserving.
The dearest cat and my most fond
romance;
When my husband is out
Caporale, good boy, stays home
with me.
Together, we two dream of a new
life
Without distrust, or jealousy or
strife!
Do you want me to tell you his phi-
losophy?
Purr! Purr! Better be master
In your own little shanty
Than servant in a mansion.
Purr! Purr! You're better off
Eating heart, hard as stone
Thank in a fruitless love wearing
out your own.
(*At this moment Talpa emerges
from the hold.*)

**TALPA:** Well, see there my old girl!
What's all about?

**FRUGOLA:** I was telling Giorgetta
of our Angora.

**MICHELE:** (*uscendo dalla cabina,
si avvicina a Luigi*) O Luigi, domani
si carica del ferro.
Vieni a darci una mano?

**LUIGI:** Verrò, padrone.

**IL TINCA:** (*venendo dalla stiva seguito dagli altri scaricatori che se
ne vanno pel molo dopo di avere
salutato Michele*) Buona notte a
tutti.

**IL TALPA:** Hai tanta fretta?

**LA FRUGOLA:** Corri già a ubbria-
carti?
Ah! se fossi tua moglie!

**IL TINCA:** Che fareste?

**LA FRUGOLA:** Ti pesterei finchè
non la smettessi
di passare le notti all'osteria.
Non ti vergogni?

**IL TINCA:** No. Fa bene il vino!
S'affogano i pensieri di rivolta:
chè se bevo non penso,
e se penso non rido!
(*Michele discende nella stiva.*)

**LUIGI:** Hai ben ragione; meglio
non pensare,
piegare il capo ed incurvar la schiena.
Per noi la vita non ha più valore
ed ogni gioia si converte in pena.
I sacchi in groppa e giù la testa a terra.
Se guardi in alto, bada alla frustata.
(*con amarezza*)
Il pane lo guadagni col sudore,
e l'ora dell'amore va rubata . . . .
Va rubata fra spasimi e paure
che offuscano l'ebbrezza più divina.
Tutto è conteso, tutto ci è rapito . . . .
la giornata è già buia alla mattina.
Hai ben ragione: meglio non pensare.

**IL TINCA:** Segui il mio esempio:
bevi.

**GIORGETTA:** Basta!

**IL TINCA:** Non parlo più!
A domani, ragazzi, e state bene!
s'incammina e scompare su per il
molo.)

**IL TALPA:** (*alla Frugola*) Ce ne
andiamo anche noi? Son stanco
morto.

**LA FRUGOLA:** (*stancamente*) Ah!
quando mai potremo
comprarci una bicocca?
Là ci riposeremo.

**GIORGETTA:** È la tua fissazione la
campagna!

**MICHELE:** (*steps out of the cabin
and approaches Luigi*) Oh, Luigi,
tomorrow
We take in heavy steel bars.
Will you come too and help?

**LUIGI:** I certainly will!

**TINCA:** (*comes up from the hold,
followed by the other stevedores,
who scatter off on the wharf after
saluting Michele*) Good-night! Until tomorrow.

**TALPA:** Why such a hurry?

**FRUGOLA:** Bound for the saloon, I
suppose?
If you were my husband . . . .

**TINCA:** What would you do?

**FRUGOLA:** I'd keep on beating you
until you'd give up
Consuming all your nights in the
wine shop.
Don't you know better?

**TINCA:** No. Wine's the spice of
life!
In wine we drown all thoughts of
revolution,
When I drink, I don't think!
And when I think, I'm gloomy!
(*Michele descends into the hold.*)

**LUIGI:** Quite right you are. It is
vain for us to ponder;
With bended heads and backs we
will fare better
In this cruel world where life is
nothing but hard toil,
Where every joy soon turns into a
new fetter!
Down with your heads and backs,
herd of the soil,
Heads down, or you will bend un-
der the lash!
(*With bitter resentment.*)
To earn our bread, we work year af-
ter year,
Our hour of love is stolen with
trembling fear,
The hour we steal is fraught with
mortal anguish
And on our face is slammed love's
blissful portal.
All is forbidden us, all is a crime,
Our hours of dawn are dark, more
than night-time.
Quite right you are . . . . It is
vain for us to ponder!

**TINCA:** Then follow my example:
Drink!

**GIORGETTA:** Enough!

**TINCA:** I say no more! . . . .
Until tomorrow, friends! God be
with you!
(*He walks away and disappears
on the wharf.*)

**TALPA:** (*to Frugola*) Shall we go
home? I am too tired to stay.

**FRUGOLA:** (*with lassitude*) I wish
were here the day
When we can buy a shanty
Where we can rest at last!

**GIORGETTA:** Always you've
dreamt of living in the woods!

LA FRUGOLA: (*cantilenando*) Ho sognato una casetta con un piccolo orticello. Quattro muri, stretta stretta, e due pini per ombrello. Il mio vecchio steso al sole, ai miei piedi Caporale, e aspettar così la morte ch'e il rimedio d'ogni male!

FRUGOLA: (*with rythmical cadence*) I have dreamt of a small house With a garden filled with roses Just four walls, under fine old trees A dear home of my own . . . . My old man stretched in the sun, At my feet old Caporale Quietly waiting for Death's call Which is cure for every ill!

GIORGETTA: (*vivamente*) È ben altro il mio sogno! Son nata nel sobborgo e solo l'aria di Parigi m'esalta e mi nutrisce! Oh! se Michele, un giorno, abbandonasse questa logora vita vagabonda! Non si vive là dentro, fra il letto ed il fornello! Tu avessi visto la mia stanza, un tempo!

GIORGETTA: (*with excitement*) Oh! My dream is quite different! I was born in the suburbs, and the air Of my Paris is life and joy to me! Oh! If we could some day give up forever Our vagarious and stupid, bleak, existence! It is no life for a woman, in that dark, dingy cabin . . . . You should have seen the room of my young days!

LA FRUGOLA: Dove abitavi?

FRUGOLA: Where did you live, then?

GIORGETTA: Non lo sai?

GIORGETTA: Don't you know?

LUIGI: (*avanzando d'improvviso*) Belleville!

LUIGI: (*suddenly*) Belleville!

GIORGETTA: Luigi lo conosce!

GIORGETTA: Luigi knows the village!

LUIGI: Anch'io ci sono nato!

LUIGI: The place where I was born!

GIORGETTA: Come me, l'ha nel sangue!

GIORGETTA: Like me, he loves it still.

LUIGI: Non ci si può staccare!

LUIGI: I can't forget that town!

GIORGETTA: Bisogna aver provato! (*con crescente entusiasmo*) Belleville è il nostro suolo e il nostro mondo! Noi non possiamo vivere sull'acqua! Bisogna calpestare il marciapiede! Là c'è una casa, là ci sono amici, festosi incontri, piene confidenze . . . .

GIORGETTA: Yes, it's all in the knowing . . . . (*with growing enthusiasm*) Belleville is our own soil and all our world! We cannot live forever on the water! We want to hear our footsteps on the flag-stones! Our home is there, and our best friends live there With joyous meetings of fond and true hearts!

LUIGI: Ci si conosce tutti! S'è tutti una famiglia!

LUIGI: There we all know each other! There we are all related!

GIORGETTA: (*continuando*) Al mattino, il lavoro che ci aspetta. Alla sera i ritorni in comitiva . . . . Botteghe che s'accendono di luci e di lusinghe . . . . vetture che s'incrociano, domeniche chiassose, piccole gite in due al Bosco di Boulogne! Balli all' aperto ę intimità amorose!? . . . . È difficile dire cosa sia quest'ansia, questa strana nostalgia . . . .

GIORGETTA: (*continuing*) In the morning, there's work awaiting us. And at night we come back home all together; The shops in their bright splendor Of light, and things attractive! . . . . And carriages rushing forth, The merriment of Sundays, Excursions two by two To the Bois de Boulogne! Feasts in the open And amorous intimacy! It is hard to comprehend; unless you witness This frenzy of ours, this impelling home sickness!

LUIGI e GIORGETTA: (*con esaltazione*) Ma chi lascia il sobborgo vuol tornare, e chi ritorna non si può staccare. C'è là in fondo Parigi che ci grida con mille voci il fascino immortale! . . . . (*I due amanti restano per un attimo assorti, la mano nella mano, come se lo stesso pensiero e la stessa anima li trascinasse. Poi, riprendono instantaneamenta la coscienza che gli altri li guardano, e si staccano.*)

LUIGI AND GIORGETTA: (*with excitement*) But all those who depart crave to return, Their hearts constantly burn with boundless love. Down yonder rises Paris, ever calling Her children with undying fascination! (*The two lovers remain a while as if transfigured, hand in hand, as if spellbound by the same thought, one soul. Then, realizing that others are present, they drop each other's hands.*)

LA FRUGOLA: (*dopo un breve silenzio*) Adesso ti capisco: qui la vita è diversa . . . .

FRUGOLA: (*after a brief pause*) Oh! Now I understand. Life is different on board!

IL TALPA: (*che s'è poco interesato dello sfogo di Giorgetta*) Se s'andasse a mangiare? . . . . (*a Luigi*) Che ne dici?

TALPA: (*who is not interested in Giorgetta's outburst*) What about my supper? (*to Luigi*) Won't you join us?

LUIGI: Io resto: ho da parlare col padrone.

LUIGI: No, thanks! I've got to wait and see Michele.

IL TALPA: Quand'è così, a domani.

TALPA: Well, then, until tomorrow!

GIORGETTA: Miei vecchi, buona notte! (*Il Talpa e la Frugola s'incamminano canterellando: 'Ho sognata una casetta' . . . . Le loro voci si perdono.*)

GIORGETTA: My friends, goodnight! (*Talpa and Frugola walk off, singing . . . . 'I dream of a small house' . . . . Their voices are lost in the distance.*)

GIORGETTA: (*sommessa, ma con ardore*) O Luigi! Luigi! (*e come Luigi fa l'atto di avvicinarsi, essa con un gesto lo ferma.*) Bada a te! Può salir fra un momento! Resta pur là, lontano!

GIORGETTA: (*low, but fervidly*) O Luigi! Luigi! . . . . (*But as Luigi rushes towards her, she stops him with a gesture.*) Do take care! He'll return here any moment! Stay where you are! Remain!

LUIGI: Perchè dunque inasprisci il tormento? Perchè mi chiami invano?

LUIGI: Why, then, embitter my dreadful torment? Why call me here in vain?

GIORGETTA: Vibro tutta se penso a iersera, all'ardor dei tuoi baci! . . . .

GIORGETTA: A new thrill pervades my whole body At the thought of your kisses last night!

LUIGI: In quei baci tu sai cosa c'era . . . .

LUIGI: And your kisses felt like burning blades!

GIORGETTA: Sì, mio amore . . . . Ma taci!

GIORGETTA: Oh, my love! . . . . But hush! . . . . Hush!

LUIGI: Quale folle paura ti prende?

LUIGI: By what sudden new fear are you seized?

GIORGETTA: Se ci scopre, è la morte!

GIORGETTA: If he knew, he would kill us!

LUIGI: Preferisco morire, alla sorte. che ti tiene legata!

LUIGI: Death is better than living at the cost Of constant separation!

GIORGETTA: Ah! se fossimo soli, lontani . . . .

GIORGETTA: Ah! To be alone with you, far away . . . .

LUIGI: E sempre uniti!

LUIGI: With you, forever! . . . .

GIORGETTA: E sempre innamorati . . . . Dimmi che non mi manchi! . . . .

GIORGETTA: Ever loving and true . . . . Swear that you are true, Luigi!

LUIGI: Mai! (*e fa l'atto di correre a lei.*)

LUIGI: True! (*He rushes towards her.*)

GIORGETTA: (*bruscamente*) Sta attento! (*Infatti Michele risale dalla stiva.*)

GIORGETTA: (*hastily*) Be careful! (*In fact, Michele comes up out of the hold.*)

MICHELE: (*a Luigi*) Come? Non sei andato? . . . .

MICHELE: (*to Luigi*) Still here? What made you stay? . . . .

LUIGI: Padrone, v'ho aspettato,
perchè volevo dirvi
quattro sole parole:
intanto ringraziarvi
per avermi tenuto . . . .
Poi volevo pregarvi,
se lo potete fare,
di portarmi a Rouen
e là farmi sbarcare . . . .

MICHELE: A Rouen? Ma sei matto?
Là non c'è che miseria:
ti troveresti peggio.

LUIGI: Sta bene. Allora resto.

MICHELE: (*senza rispondere
s'avvia verso la cabina.*)

GIORGETTA: (*a Michele*) E adesso
dove vai?

MICHELE: A preparare i lumi

LUIGI: Buona notte, pa-
drone . . . .

MICHELE: Buona notte.
(*entra nella cabina.*)
(*Luigi è quasi presso la passerella.
Giorgetta lo raggiunge rapidamente—Il dialogo che segue è rapido, concitato, sommesso, ma
pieno di intensità amorosa.*)

GIORGETTA: Dimmi: perchè gli
hai chiesto
di sbarcarti a Rouen?

LUIGI: Perchè non posso
dividerti con lui! . . . .

GIORGETTA: Hai ragione: è un tormento . . . .
Anch'io ne sono presa, anch'io la
sento
ben più forte di te questa catena! . . . .
È un'angoscia, è una pena,
ma quando tu mi prendi,
è più grande il compenso!

LUIGI: Par di rubare insieme
qualche cosa alla vita!

GIORGETTA: La voluttà è più intensa!

LUIGI: È la gioia rapita
fra spasimi e paure . . . .

GIORGETTA: In una stretta ansiosa

LUIGI: Fra grida soffocate . . . .

GIORGETTA: E parole som-
messe . . . .

LUIGI: E baci senza fine!

GIORGETTA: Giuramenti, promesse

LUIGI: D'essere soli noi . . . .

GIORGETTA: Noi, soli, via, lontani!

LUIGI: Noi tutti soli, lontani dal
mondo!
(*poi sussultando come se avesse
sentito dei passi*) È lui? . . . .

LUIGI: Kind sir, I thought I'd wait
Until you came up again
To speak with you alone.
I wanted first to thank you
For keeping me at work . . . .
Then I wished to ask you,
If such a thing be possible,
To take me to Rouen
And let me off down there!

MICHELE: To Rouen? Are you cra-
zy?
There's no work for you there!
You'd be worse off, by far!

LUIGI: All right. I'll have to stay,
then!
(*Michele moves towards the
hold.*)

GIORGETTA: (*to Michele*) And
now, where are you going?

MICHELE: I go to light the lanterns.

LUIGI: Good-night, sir!

MICHELE: Good-night!
(*He enters the cabin. Luigi is almost on the gangplank when
Giorgetta rushes up to him. The
ensuing dialogue is quick, in an
undertone full of amorous intensity.*)

GIORGETTA: Tell me, why did you
ask him
To take you to Rouen?

LUIGI: Because I cannot
Share you with him, Giorgetta!

GIORGETTA: You are right: It is a
torment
It gnaws . . . . it preys on me,
and I lament
The cruel chain that binds mine to
his fate!
It is far harder than hate!
But then your ardent kisses
Well reward my deep anguish!

LUIGI: As if we two were stealing
keener raptures from life!

GIORGETTA: A more intense delight!

LUIGI: An enchantment with strife
Amid ecstasy and fear . . . .

GIORGETTA: We two, clasped together . . . .

LUIGI: With stifled sobs and
cries . . . .

GIORGETTA: And low voiced,
burning words . . . .

LUIGI: And kisses without end!

GIORGETTA: Solemn oaths, sincere promises

LUIGI: To be joined for-
ever

GIORGETTA: We two, in distant
lands!

LUIGI: We two, together, away
from the world
(*He starts as if he heard footsteps.*)
Is it he?

GIORGETTA: (*rassicurandolo*)
No . . . . non ancora . . . .
(*con ardore*)
Dimmi che tornerai
più tardi . . . .

LUIGI: Sì . . . . fra
un'ora . . . .

GIORGETTA: Ascolta: come ieri
lascerò la passerella . . . .
Sono io che la tolgo . . . .
Hai le scarpe di corda?

LUIGI: (*alzando il piede*)
Sì . . . .
Fai lo stesso segnale?

GIORGETTA: Sì . . . . il fiammifero acceso!
Come tremava sul mio braccio teso
la piccola fiammella!
Mi pareva d'accendere una stella,
fiamma del nostro amore,
stella senza tramonto! . . . .

LUIGI: Io voglio la tua bocca,
voglio le tue carezze!

GIORGETTA: Dunque anche tu lo
senti
il folle desiderio! . . . .

LUIGI: (*con grande intensità*)
Folle di gelosia!
Vorrei tenerti stretta
come una cosa mia!
Vorrei non più soffrire
che un altro ti toccasse,
e per sottrarre a tutti
il corpo tuo divino,
te lo giuro, non tremo
a vibrare il coltello
e con gocce di sangue
fabbricarti un gioiello!

GIORGETTA: (*con improvviso
scatto lo spinge via. Poi, sola risalendo lentamente e passandosi
una mano sulla fronte*) Come è
difficile esser felici!
(*Ora l'oscurità è completa. Michele, recando i fanali accesi,
viene dalla cabina.*)

MICHELE: Perchè non vai a letto?

GIORGETTA: E tu?

MICHELE: No . . . . Non ancora . . . (*Un silenzio.—Michele ha collocato i fanali sul barcone.*)

GIORGETTA: Penso che hai fatto
bene a trattenerlo.

MICHELE: Chi mai?

GIORGETTA: (*semplicemente*)
Luigi.

MICHELE: Forse ho fatto male.
Basteranno due uomini: non c'è
molto lavoro.

GIORGETTA: (*soothingly*) No,
not yet, darling!
(*with passion*)
Tell me you will return . . . .
Won't you?

LUIGI: In an hour . . . .

GIORGETTA: Now, listen! as last
night,
I shall leave the gang-plank
there . . . .
That's a nightly task of mine.
Have you on corded shoes?

LUIGI: (*showing his feet*)
See?
What signal will you give?

GIORGETTA: You know . . . . I
will light a match.
It shook and trembled in my hand
last night
That tiny wooden bar . . . .
I thought I had set fire to a new star,
Flame of our ardent love,
A star that will never set!

LUIGI: I crave your dear, sweet
lips,
And your bewitching kisses!

GIORGETTA: So then, you also are
held
By that immense attraction?

LUIGI: (*with great intensity*)
Burning with jealous fire,
I want to hold you entwined
Like ivy on a spire!
I will no longer suffer
Another to approach you . . . .
And to forbid to all men
Sight of your divine form
I would kill without fear
And with drops of red blood
Make you a rare jewel!

GIORGETTA: (*startled, suddenly
pushes him away; then, alone and
walking up stage, she wearily passes her hand over her forehead*) It
is hard indeed to find real joy on
earth!
(*Now darkness is complete; Michele emerges from the cabin carrying the lighted lanterns.*)

MICHELE: Why don't you go to
bed?

GIORGETTA: And you?

MICHELE: No . . . . not just
yet . . . .
(*A deep pause. Michele sets the
lanterns in place.*)

GIORGETTA: You were quite right
in keeping him at work.

MICHELE: Him? . . . .
Who? . . . .

GIORGETTA: (*negligently*) Luigi.

MICHELE: Perhaps I was
wrong . . . .
As two hands would suffice . . . .
Our work will not be heavy.

GIORGETTA: Il Tinca lo potresti
licenziare . . . .
beve sempre . . . .

MICHELE: S'ubriaca
per calmare i suoi dolori . . . .
Ha per moglie una bagascia . . . .
Beve per non ucciderla . . . .
(*Giorgetta non risponde. Ma appare turbata e nervosa.*)

MICHELE: Che hai?

GIORGETTA: Son tutte queste storie . . . .
A me non interessano . . . .

MICHELE: (*improvvisamente avvicinandosi a lei con angoscia e con commozione*) Perchè non
m'ami più? . . . . Perchè non
m'ami? . . . .

GIORGETTA: Ti sbagli . . . .
T'amo . . . . Tu sei buono, onesto . . .
(*poi, per troncare*)
Ora andiamo a dormire . . . .

MICHELE: (*fissandola*) Tu non
dormi! . . . .

GIORGETTA: Lo sai perchè non
dormo . . . .
E poi . . . . là dentro soffoco . . . . Non posso!

MICHELE: Ora le notti sono tanto
fresche
E l'anno scorso là in quel nero guscio
eravamo pur tre . . . . c'era il lettuccio
del nostro bimbo . . . .

GIORGETTA: (*sconvolta*) Il nostro bimbo! . . . . Taci! . . . .

MICHELE: (*insistendo, commosso*) Tu sporgevi la mano, e lo cullavi
dolcemente,
lentamente!
e poi sul braccio mio
t'addormentavi

GIORGETTA: (*c. s.*) Ti supplico,
Michele: non dir niente . . . .

MICHELE: (*c. s.*) Erano sere come
queste . . . .
Se spirava la brezza,
vi raccoglievo insieme nel tabarro,
come in una carezza . . . .
Sento sulle mie spalle
le vostre teste bionde . . . .
Sento le vostre bocche
vicino alla mia bocca . . . .
Ero tanto felice! . . . .
Ora che non c'è più,
i miei capelli grigi
mi sembrano un insulto
alla tua gioventù!

GIORGETTA: Well, then, why not
dismiss that fellow Tinca?
He's always drunk . . . .

MICHELE: Yes, he drinks
To forget his fearful sorrows . . . .
For his wife was never faithful . . . .
He drinks so as not to kill
her . . . .
(*Giorgetta does not answer, but
she seems troubled and nervous.*)

MICHELE: What ails you?

GIORGETTA: Why all this foolish
gossip?
I really don't care to hear . . . .

MICHELE: (*close to her, with anguish*) Why don't you love me,
dear? Why can't you love me?

GIORGETTA: You're
wrong! . . . . I love you . . . .
you are kind and honest!
(*Then, to cut the conversation
short*)
It's time to go to sleep!

MICHELE: (*staring at her*) You
don't sleep!

GIORGETTA: You know the reason
why . . . .
And then I stifle in there . . . .
It's suffocating!

MICHELE: But now the nights are
cool and so refreshing
It was just last year that there, in our
dark cabin
We lived happy, all three . . . .
there was the cradle
Of our dear child . . . .

GIORGETTA: (*painfully*) My little
baby! Darling!

MICHELE: (*insisting, deeply
moved*) You would put out your
hand and would rock him
So tenderly . . . .
Gently, softly . . . .
And then you'd fall asleep quietly
on my arm.

GIORGETTA: (*as above*) I beg of
you, Michele . . . . do keep silent!

MICHELE: (*as above*) Evenings
were they, like this clear
night . . . .
If the breeze was too brisk
I would wrap you both tightly in my
old cloak,
As in one fond embrace . . . .
I felt upon my shoulder
Your two beloved heads . . . .
I felt your fragrant lips
There, close to my own!
I was so warm and happy!
Now that he is no more
My gray and scanty hairs
Seem like a gross insult
That I bring to your door!

GIORGETTA: No . . . . calmati,
Michele . . . . Sono stanca . . .
Non reggo . . . . Vieni . . . .

MICHELE: (*aspro*) Ma non puoi
dormire!
Sai pure che non devi addormentarti!

GIORGETTA: (*atterrita*) Perchè
mi dici questo?

MICHELE: Non so bene . . . .
Ma so che è molto tempo che non
dormi!
(*Poi ancora dominandosi e cercando di attirare Giorgetta fra le
sue braccia*)
Resta vicino a me! . . . . Non ti ricordi
altre notti, altri cieli ed altre
lune? . . . .
Perchè chiudi il tuo cuore?
Rammentati le ore
che volavano via su questa barca
trascinate dall'onda! . . . .

GIORGETTA: Meglio non ricordare . . . .
Oggi è malinconia . . . .

MICHELE: Ritorna come allora
ritorna ancora mia!
quando anche tu m'amavi
ardentemente,
e mi cercavi,
e mi baciavi,
ed i primi chiarori del mattino
risvegliavan due corpi ancora stretti
nell'amplesso divino!
Resta vicino a me! La notte è bella!

GIORGETTA: Che vuoi!
S'invecchia! Non son più la stessa.
Tu pure sei cambiato . . . . Diffidi . . . . Ma chè credi?

MICHELE: Non so nemmeno io!

GIORGETTA: (*per tagliar corto*)
Buona notte, Michele . . . . Ho
tanto sonno . . . .

MICHELE: (*con un sospiro*) E allor
va pure . . . . Ti raggiungo . . . .

GIORGETTA: Buona notte!

MICHELE: (*cerca di baciarla, ma
Giorgetta si schermisce e s'avvia.
Michele, guardandola allontanarsi, mormora cupamente*)
Sgualdrina!
(*Sulla strada due ombre
d'amanti passano*)
—Bocca di rosa fresca . . . .
—E baci di rugiada . . . .
—O labbra profumate . . . .
—O profumata sera . . . .
—C'è la luna che illumina la strada . . . .
—La luna che ci spia . . . .
—A domani, mio amore . . . .
—Domani, amante mia! . . . .

GIORGETTA: Hush! Hush! . . . .
Keep quiet, Michele . . . . I am
weary
So weary . . . . Come, dear!

MICHELE: And yet you can't sleep!
You know that you won't sleep at
all tonight!

GIORGETTA: (*frightened*) Oh,
tell me why you say so?

MICHELE: I'm not sure . . . .
But I do know it's long since you
could sleep!
(*Then, mastering himself and trying to draw Giorgetta into his
arms.*)
Stay here . . . . here, close to
me! . . . . don't you remember
Other nights, other skies and other
moonlights?
Why do you close your dear heart?
Remember the sweet hours,
The fleeting hours we spent happily together,
Swept away by the tide!

GIORGETTA: I'd rather not remember . . . .
It is cruel to make me pine.

MICHELE: Oh, love me, love me
again
And be forever mine!
Remember how you loved me
With ardent passion . . . .
Ever sealing my lips
With burning kisses . . . .
And the first crimson fires of the
new sun
Would then gild our two bodies,
still entwined . . . .
Two souls merged into one!
Stay here! Keep close to me! The
night is divine!

GIORGETTA: We're growing
old . . . . I no longer feel the
same . . . .
You also seem another . . . . You
doubt me? What's on your mind?

MICHELE: Truly, I don't know myself!

GIORGETTA: (*to cut short*) Well,
good-night now, Michele! I am
sleepy . . . .

MICHELE: (*with a sigh*) Yes, yes,
good-night . . . . I'll soon be
over!

GIORGETTA: Good-night!

MICHELE: (*tries to kiss her, but
Giorgetta escapes him and runs
away.*)
(*As he follows her with his eyes, he
savagely mutters*) Vile wench,
you!
(*On the boulevard, the shadows
of two lovers, entwined, pass by.
They sing*)
'Mouth like vermillion roses
And kisses fresh as dew—
O lips so sweet and pungent—
O night, so clear and starlit!
See the moon shining brightly upon
our path

(*Da una caserma suona il silenzio.*)
(*Michele ha preso il suo tabarro, se n'è avvolte le spalle, e, appoggiato al timone del barcone, contempla fissamente la Senna che scorre silenziosamente.*)

**MICHELE:** Scorri, fiume eterno! Scorri!
Come il tuo mistero è fondo!
Ah! l'ansia che mi strugge non ha fine!
Passa, fiume eterno; passa!
E me pure travolgi!
Quante son le rovine
che calmò la tua onda!
Tu della miseria
hai segnata la fine! . . . .
E sempre calmo passi, e non ti ferma
dolore nè paura nè tormento
nè volgere di anni!
Continui la tua corsa,
continui il tuo lamento! . . . .
Sono i lamenti, forse, dei tuoi morti?
Di migliaia di morti che portasti
l'un dopo l'altro verso il gran destino
sulle tue braccia lugubri ma forti!
Sono i dolori che tu soffocasti
chiudendo l'urlo estremo in un gorgoglio?
Acqua misteriosa e cupa,
passa sul mio triste cuore!
Lava via la pena e il mio dolore,
fa pur tua la mia sorte! . . . .
E se non puoi la pace,
allor dammi la morte!
(*S'accascia sfibrato. Macchinalmente leva di tasca la pipa e l'accende. Alla luce del fiammifero Luigi cautamente attraversa la passerella e balza sul barcone. Michele vede l'ombra, sussulta, si mette in agguato, riconosce Luigi e di colpo si precipita afferrandolo per la gola.*)

**MICHELE:** T'ho colto!

**LUIGI:** (*dibattendosi*) Sangue di Dio! Son preso!

**MICHELE:** (*con voce roca e sommessa*) Non gridare!
Che venivi a cercare?
Volevi la tua amante?

**LUIGI:** Non è vero!

**MICHELE:** Mentisci! Confessa! La tua amante!

**LUIGI:** (*tentando di levare il coltello*) Ah! perdio!

---

The moon so sweetly smiling,
Until tomorrow, sweetheart
Good-night, my own beloved!
(*From a near-by barracks taps are sounded. Michele, taking his big, black cloak, throws it upon his shoulders, and leaning upon the tiller of the barge, he steadily gazes upon the still river.*)

**MICHELE:** Flow on, eternal river!
Flow, deep and mysterious waters!
The anguish that pervades my soul is endless!
Pass on, pass, eternal river!
Drag me on, engulf me!
How many profound sorrows
Were soothed by the waves?
Of many dire distresses
You have marked the vile end!
Forever calm, you flow, never halted
By laments, nor sorrows, nor cringing fear
Nor lapsing of long years!
Forever flowing on
Moaning on your way!
Are those perhaps the moans of icy corpses
The thousands of dead men that you carried
In quick succession towards their fatal goal,
Upon your slimy arms, nor did you tarry?
Are those perhaps the sorrows that you quelled
By choking in your vortex their last yell?
O mysterious, silent waters
Flow on, pass over my broken heart!
Wash away my tears and my bitter sorrow!
Dispose of my fate too,
And if peace you cannot give me
Then let me die with you!
(*At these words he collapses entirely. Mechanically he takes his pipe from his pocket and lights it. At the flaring of the match, Luigi cautiously moves towards the gang-plank and jumps onto the barge. Michele, seeing the shadow, is startled; he hides, then recognizing Luigi, he throws himself upon him and catches him by the throat.*)

**MICHELE:** I've got you!

**LUIGI:** (*struggling to free himself*) By all the Saints! I'm caught!

**MICHELE:** (*hoarsely and almost voiceless*) Don't scream now!
How and why did you return?
Are you looking for your mistress?

**LUIGI:** I am not!

**MICHELE:** You are lying! Confess! You seek your mistress!

**LUIGI:** (*trying to get at his knife*) By all angels!

---

**MICHELE:** (*serrandogli il braccio*) Giù il coltello!
Non mi sfuggi, canaglia!
Anima di forzato! . . . . Verme!
Volevi andar giù, a Rouen, non è vero?
Morto ci andrai! Nel fiume!

**LUIGI:** Assassino! Assassino!

**MICHELE:** Confessami che l'ami!

**LUIGI:** Lasciami!

**MICHELE:** No! Confessa!
Infame! Infame! . . . . Infami! . . . .
Se confessi, ti lascio!

**LUIGI:** Si . . . .

**MICHELE:** Ripetì!

**LUIGI:** Si L'amo!

**MICHELE:** Ripeti!

**LUIGI:** L'amo!

**MICHELE:** (*stringendolo furiosamente*) Ancora!

**LUIGI:** (*rantolando*)
L'amo . . . . Ah! . . . .
(*e resta aggrappato a Michele in una contorsione di morte.*)
(*Dall'interno della cabina la voce di Giorgetta chiama: 'Michele?.. Un silenzio. Michele sente, e rapidissimo siede e ravvolge il tabarro sopra il cadavere aggrappato a lui.*)
(*Giorgetta appare sulla porta, indagando con lo sguardo smarrito.*)

**GIORGETTA:** (*a mezza voce*) Ho paura, Michele!
(*poi, vedendo il marito seduto e calmo, rassicurata, soggiunge*)
No . . . . Ho avuto paura . . . .
(*S'avvicina lentamente a Michele, sempre guardando intorno con ansia.*)

**MICHELE:** (*calmissimo*) Avevo ben ragione: non dovevi dormire . . . .

**GIORGETTA:** (*con sottomissione*) Son presa dal rimorso d'averti dato pena . . . .

**MICHELE:** Non è nulla . . . . i tuoi nervi . . . .

**GIORGETTA:** Ecco . . . . è questo . . . . hai ragione . . . .
Dimmi che mi perdoni . . . .
(*insinuante*)
Non mi vuoi più vicina? . . . .

**MICHELE:** Dove? . . . . Nel mio tabarro?

---

**MICHELE:** (*pinioning his arms*)
Drop your knife!
No escape for you, scoundrel!
Vile beast, fit for the gallows! Monster!
You would have me take you to Rouen? . . . . True?
Dead you'll go . . . . there's the river!

**LUIGI:** Help! Assassin! Assassin!

**MICHELE:** Confess now that you love her!

**LUIGI:** Let me go!

**MICHELE:** No. Confess!
You rascal! Scoundrel! Scoundrels! . . . .
Confess, and I'll let you go!

**LUIGI:** Yes . . . .

**MICHELE:** Repeat it!

**LUIGI:** I love her!

**MICHELE:** Repeat it!

**LUIGI:** I love her!

**MICHELE:** (*tightening his hold of Luigi's throat*) Once more!

**LUIGI:** (*with a raucous cry*) I love her . . . . Ah!
(*And he remains holding on to Michele in a death-like contortion.*)
(*From inside the cabin, Giorgetta's voice is heard calling: Michele? A deep pause. Hearing her voice, Michele quickly sits down throwing his cloak over the corpse still clinging to him. Giorgetta appears on the threshold and looks about her, frightened.*)

**GIORGETTA:** (*in a low voice*) I'm afraid, Michele!
(*Then, as she sees her husband quietly seated, she is calmer and continues*)
No . . . I did feel afraid . . . .
(*She draws near Michele always looking around anxiously.*)

**MICHELE:** (*very calm*) Didn't I tell you before that you were not to sleep?

**GIORGETTA:** (*meekly*) I am sorry, Michele,
For having been so horrid!

**MICHELE:** Don't worry . . . .
You are nervous . . . .

**GIORGETTA:** Yes, I know . . . . you are right.
Tell me that you forgive me!
(*coquettishly*)
Don't you want me near you?

**MICHELE:** Where? . . . .
Where? . . . . Under my cloak?

**GIORGETTA:** Sì . . . . vicina . . . . vicina . . . .
(*con voce tremante*)
Sì . . . . mi dicevi un tempo:
'Tutti quanti portiamo
un tabarro che asconde
qualche volta una gioia
qualche volta un dolore . . . .''

**MICHELE:** (*selvaggiamente*) Ma
talvolta un delitto!
Vieni nel mio tabarro! . . . .
Vieni! . . . . Vieni! . . . .

**GIORGETTA:** Yes, quite
close . . . . very close . . . .
(*with trembling voice*)
You know, you used to tell
me . . . .
'Every man needs to carry
Some great cloak, where he hides
Sometimes a wondrous joy
Sometimes a profound sorrow.''

**MICHELE:** (*savagely*) Sometimes a
crime . . . . a murder . . . .
Come, hide beneath my cloak!
Come here! Come here! . . . .

(*Si erge terribile, apre il tabarro;
il cadavere di Luigi rotola ai piedi
di Giorgetta che lancia un grido
terribile e indietreggia con orrore. Ma Michele le è sopra,
l'afferra, e la trascina, e la piega
violentemente contro il volto
dell'amante morto.*)

*VELARIO*

(*He rises, throws open the cloak.
Luigi's dead body falls at Giorgetta's feet. With a great cry she
draws back, horror stricken. But
Michele rushes upon her and violently throws her upon the body of
her dead lover.*)

*CURTAIN*

# Suor Angelica (1918)

## Sister Angelica

MUSIC BY GIACOMO PUCCINI ■ LIBRETTO BY GIOVACCHINO FORZANO

This one-act opera is set to a libretto by Giovacchino Forzano. The time is the end of the seventeenth century. Angelica's noble family forces her to retire to a convent because of an illicit relationsip that produced an illegitimate son seven years earlier. Sister Genovieffa shows the sisters the rays of the setting sun which, three times a year, cause the fountain to glow as if the water was pure gold. The sisters sprinkle this water on the tomb of one of their members. They speak of earthly desires. Sister Genovieffa says she longs to hold a lamb, as she used to be a sheperdess. Sister Angelica says she desires nothing. But the others know she is unhappy because she hasn't heard from her family since she arrived. A grand carriage arrives. It is her aunt, the Princess, who has come to request that she sign away her inheritance and to tell Angelica that her young son has died. Angelica is filled with unhappiness; when darkness falls, she signs the document. After the Princess departs, she cries over the death of her child. The sisters try to comfort her, but she has already decided that she will poison herself. As she prays for forgiveness for this sin, a heavenly choir sings to her. The Virgin appears, bathed in light, leading a child to Angelica. She raises her arms to the child, who comes to her, and as the voices sing of her salvation, she collapses to the ground in death.

## ■ ATTP UNICO

### LA PREGHIERA

*Si apre il velario. Tramonto di primavera. Un raggio di sole batte al di sopra del getto della fonte. La scena è vuota. Le suore sono in chiesa e cantano.*

*Due Converse, in ritardo per la preghiera, traversano la scena; si soffermano un istante ad ascoltare un cinguettio che scende dai cipressi, quindi entrano in chiesa.*

*Suor Angelica, anch'essa in ritardo, esce da destra e si avvia in chiesa, apre la porta e fa l'atto di penitenza delle ritardatarie che le due converse non hanno fatto, ossia si inginocchia e bacia la terra; quindi richiude la porta. La preghiera termina. Le monache escono dalla chiesa a due per due. La Badessa si sofferma devanti alla croce. Le monache, passandole innanzi, fanno atto di reverenza. La Badessa le benedice, quindi si ritira a sinistra.*

*(Le suore restano unite formando, a piccoli gruppi, una specie di semicerchio. La Sorella zelatrice viene nel mezzo.)*

### LE PUNIZIONI

**LA SORELLA ZELATRICE:** *(alle due converse)*: Sorelle in umiltà mancaste alla quindéa, ed anche Suor Angelica,

## ■ ACT I

### THE PRAYER

*The curtain rises. A clear spring sunset. A ray of sunshine strikes above the spout on the fount. The stage is empty. The sisters are in the church, singing.*

*Two postulants, late for prayers, cross the stage. They pause an instant to listen to the chirping of birds, coming from atop the cypresses, then enter the church.*

*Sister Angelica, also late, enters from right and moves towards the church. She opens the door, and makes the act of penance customary with late-comers (which was not done by the two postulants) that is to say, she kneels down and kisses the ground; then she closes the door. The sisters come out of the church two by two. The Abbess stops in front of the Cross. The sisters, as they file past the Abbess, bow reverently. The Abbess blesses them, then withdraws to the left.*

*The sisters remain together, forming, in small groups, a semi-circle. The Monitor comes forward to the center.*

### THE PENANCES

**THE MONITOR:** *(to the two postulants)*. My sisters in the Lord You missed one tridual day; So did Sister Angelica

che però fece contrizione piena. Invece voi, sorelle, peccaste in distrazione e avete perso un giorno di quindéna!

**LA CONVERSE:** M'accuso della colpa e invoco una gran pena, e più grave sarà, più grazie vi dirò. sorella in umiltà. *(Restano in attesa della penitenza mentre la zelatrice medita.)*

**LA MAESTRA DELLE NOVIZIE:** *(alle due novizie)*: (Chi arriva tardi in coro, si prostri e baci terra.)

**LA SORELLA ZELATRICE:** *(alle converse)*: Farete venti volte la preghiera mentale per gli affitti, gli schiavi e per quelli che stanno in peccato mortale.

**LA CONVERSE:** Con gioia e con fervore! Cristo Signore, Sposo d'Amore, io voglio sol piacerti, ora e nell'ora della mia morte. Amen. *(Si ritirano compunte sotto gli archi di destra.)*

**LA SORELLA ZELATRICE:** *(a Suor Lucilla)*: Suor Lucilla, il lavoro. Ritiratevi e osservate il silenzio.

Who, however, did not forget to pray. Instead, you both, my sisters, Omitted a plain duty And thus you both have lost one tridual day!

**THE POSTULANTS:** I own that I am guilty And beg for a harsh penance! Let it be in accord With my base, foolish sin My sister in the Lord! *(They await their penance, while the Monitor remains absorbed in deep meditation.)*

**THE MISTRESS OF NOVICES:** Late comers to church service Must kneel and kiss the threshold.

**THE MONITOR:** *(to the postulants)*. For twenty times repeat Our usual mental prayer For the slaves, for the needy, For, all men and all women who are In need of absolution.

**THE POSTULANTS:** With joy and with true fervor! Christ, Blessed Saviour, And loving Spouse I will serve you only In life and in the hour Of my last breath. Amen! *(They withdraw, full of compunction, under the right hand arcade.)*

**THE MONITOR:** *(to Sister Lucilla)*. You, Lucilla, to work now. Please withdraw And observe strictest silence.

(*Suor Lucilla si avvia sotto gli archi di destra, prende la rocca che è sopra una panca e si mette a filare.*)

(*Sister Lucilla goes under the arch on the right and taking down a spinning-wheel, begins to spin.*)

**LA MAESTRA DELLE NOVIZIE:**
(*alle novizie*): (Perchè stasera in coro
ha riso e fatto ridere.)

**THE MISTRESS OF NOVICES:** (*to the Novices*). Because today at psalms
She caused outbursts of laughter!

**LA SORELLA ZELATRICE:** (*a Suor Osmina*): Voi, Suor Osmina, in chiesa
tenevate nascoste nelle maniche
due rose scarlattine.

**THE MONITOR:** (*to Sister Osmina*). Sister Osmina, in church
You had hidden today into your sleeves
A bunch of scarlet roses!

**SUOR OSMINA:** (*indocile*): Non è vero!

**SISTER OSMINA:** (*restive*). Not so!

**LA SORELLA ZELATRICE:** (*severa ma senza asprezza*): Sorella, entrate in cella.
(*Suor Osmina scuote le spalle*): Non tardate! La Vergine vi guarda!
(*Suor Osmina si avvia sensa far parola. Le suore la seguono con lo sguardo fino a che non è scomparsa nella sua cella e mormorano: Regina virginum, ora pro ea.*)

**THE MONITOR:** (*severely, but not harshly*). My sister, to your cell!
(*Sister Osmina shrugs her shoulders.*)
Do not tarry! The Virgin is there watching!
(*Sister Osmina starts out without saying another word. The sisters follow her with their eyes until she disappears, and murmur: Regina virginium ora pro ea, etc.*)

## LA RICREAZIONE

## THE RECREATION

**LA SORELLA ZELATRICE:** Ed or, sorelle in gioia,
poichè piace al Signore
e per tornare
più allegramente
a faticare
per amor Suo,
ricreatevil!

**THE MONITOR:** And now, beloved sisters
Since that is our Lord's pleasure
And that we may
With more contentment
Return to work
To please our Master,
Relax and play!

**LE SUORE:** Amen!
(*Le figure binache delle suore si sparpagliano per il chiostro e oltre gli archi. Suor Angelica sappetia la terra e innaffia l'erbe e i fiori.*)

**THE SISTERS:** Amen!
(*The white silhouettes of the sisters scatter through the cloister and beyond the arches. Sister Angelica is busy hoeing and watering the grass and flowers.*)

**SUOR GENOVIEFFA:**
(*gaiamente*): Oh sorelle! Sorelle!
Poichè il Signore vuole,
io voglio rivelarvi
che una spera di sole
è entrata in clausura!
Guardate dove batte,
là, là fra la versura!
Il sole è sull'acoro!
Comincian le tre sere
della fontana d'oro!

**SISTER GENEVIEVE:** Oh, my sisters! My sisters!
Since that is our Lord's way
I'm going now to tell you
That a bright, golden sun ray
As silent as a mouse
Has stealthily entered here.
See, there amongst the boughs!
So that we may now count
The first of our three evenings
Of the fair golden fount!

**ALCUNE SUORE:** —È vero, fra un istante
vedrem l'acqua dorata!
—E per due sere ancora!
—È Maggio! È Maggio!
—E il bel sorriso di Nostra Signora
che viene con quel raggio.
—Regina di Clemenza, grazie!

**A FEW SISTERS:** It is true, within an instant
The water will be golden,
Resplendent as a fairy!
It is May! It is May!
The smiling face of our beloved Mary
Comes to us with that sun ray.
Oh Queen who is so merciful, we thank you!

**UNA NOVIZIA:** Maestra, vi domando
licenza di parlare.

**A NOVICE:** My teacher, with your leave
I wish to speak a word.

**LA MAESTRA DELLE NOVIZIE:**
Sempre per laudare
le cose sante e belle.

**THE MISTRESS OF NOVICES:** Provided it is in praise
Of matters holy and choice.

**LA NOVIZIA:** Qual grazia della Vergine
rallegra le sorelle?

**THE NOVICES:** About what special grace do
My sisters now rejoice?

**LA MAESTRA DELLE NOVIZIE:**
Un segno risplendente
della bontà di Dio!
Per tre sere dell'anno solamente,
all'uscire dal coro,
Dio ci concede di vedere il sole
che batte sulla fonte e la fà d'oro!

**THE MISTRESS OF NOVICES:** A splendid, wondrous sign
Of God's unbounded mercy!
For three nights every year our Lord benign
When our work is all done,
Grants us the grace, as we return from prayers
To see the fount made golden by the sun!

**LA NOVIZIA:** E le altre sere?

**THE NOVICE:** And other evenings?

**LA MASESTRA DELLE NOVIZIE:**
O usciamo troppo presto e il sole è alto
o troppo tardi e il sole è tramontato.

**THE MISTRESS OF NOVICES:** We leave either too soon in full daylight
Or much too late, long after shadows fall!

**ALCUNE SUORE:** (*con un accento di grande malinconia*): —Un altr'anno è passato! . . . .
—E passato un altr'anno! . . . .
—E una sorella manca! . . . .
(*Le suore, assorie, sembrano rievocare l'immagine della sorella che non è più.*)

**A FEW SISTERS:** (*with great melancholy*). Another year has gone! . . . .
Another year has gone! . . . .
One sister dear is missing! . . . .
(*The sisters, absorbed in thought, seem to make an effort to bring back to their eyes the image of the dead sister.*)

**SUOR GENOVIEFFA:** (*improvvisamente, con accento ingenuo e quasi lieto*): O sorelle in pio lavoro,
quando il getto s'è indorato,
non sarebbe ben portato
un secchiello d'acqua d'oro
sulla tomba a Bianca Rosa?

**SISTER GENEVIEVE:** (*suddenly, with simplicity and almost gaily*). My dear sisters, I propose
When the fount is all aglow
That we carry, in a row,
A few drops of golden water
On the tomb of Sister Rose.

**LE SUORE:** Si, la suora che riposa
lo desidera di certo!

**THE SISTERS:** Our dear friend, in her repose
Must be wishing that, for sure!

**SUOR ANGELICA:** I desideri sono i fior dei vivi,
non fioriscon nel regno delie morte,
perchè la Madre Vergine soccorre,
e in Sua benignità
liberamente al desiar precorre;
prima che un desiderio sia fiorito
la Madre delle Madri l'ha esaudito.
O sorella, la morte è vita bella!

**SISTER ANGELICA:** Wishes are buds adorning living bodies
Never blooming where death holds her calm sway
Because the Virgin Mother's watchful eye
Is always fixed on her flock
Anticipating wishes from on high.
Before one lone desire is born in you,
The Mother of all Mothers makes it true!
Oh, my sister, we die to live anew!

**LA SORELLA ZELATRICE:** Noi non possiamo
nemmen da vive avere desideri.

**THE MONITOR:** We're not allowed
Even in life, to nurture vain desires.

**SUOR GENOVIEFFA:** Se son leggieri e candidi perchè?
Voi non avete un desiderio?

**SISTER GENEVIEVE:** Even though light, and candid and unselfish?
Do you not ever wish for things?

**LA SORELLA ZELATRICE:** Io no!

**THE MONITOR:** Not I.

**UN'ALTRA:** Ed io nemmeno!

**ANOTHER SISTER:** The same with me.

**UN'ALTRA:** Io no!

**ANOTHER SISTER:** Nor I.

**UNA NOVIZIA:** (*timorosa*): Io no!

**A NOVICE:** (*timidly*). Nor I.

**SUOR GENOVIEFFA:** Io si.
E lo confesso:
(*Volge lo sguardo in alto*):
Soave Signor mio,
tu sai che prima d'ora
nel mondo ero pastora . . . .
Da cinqu'anni non vedo un agnellino;

**SISTER GENEVIEVE:** I do.
I will confess in love . . . .
(*with uplifted eyes*):
Oh, sweetest Lord and Master,
You know I used to be
A shepherdess . . . .
It has been five years since I've seen a little lamb!

Signore, ti rincresco
se dico che desidero
vederne uno piccino,
poterlo carezzare,
toccargli il muso fresco
e sentirlo belare?
Se è colpa t'offerisco
il Miserere mei.
Perdonami, Signore,
Tu che sei l'Agnus Dei.

Oh, Lord, am I capricious
For wishing I might see
One lamb all white and small
To hold and hug a while
Its darling, fuzzy head
And hear its tender call? . . . .
If wrong, I beg to offer
The "Miserere mei,"
Forgive me, oh Master
You are "Agnus Dei."

**SUOR DOLCINA:** (*grassottella e rubiconda*): Ho un desiderio anch'io!

**SISTER DOLCINA:** (*rosy cheeked and rather stoutish*). I have a wish to make!

**LE SUORE:** —Sorella, li sappiamo i vostri desideri! . . . .
—Qualche boccone buono!
—Della frutta gustosa!
—La gola è colpa grave! . . . .
(*alle novizie*):
(È golosa! È golosa! . . . .)
(*Suor Dolcina resta mortificata e interdetta.*)

**THE SISTERS:** Oh, Sister, we all know
What are your fond desires! . . . .
—Something really good to eat!
—Candy and the best of meat!
—A sin among the blackest!
(*to the novices*):
A gourmande! A gourmande!
(*Sister Dolcina looks highly mortified and dejected.*)

**SUOR GENOVIEFFA:** (*a Sour Angelica che sta annaffiando i fiori*): Suor Angelica, e voi avete desideri?

**SISTER GENEVIEVE:** Angelica, do tell . . . .
Have you had wishes, ever?

**SUOR ANGELICA:** (*volgendosi verso le suore*): . . . .Io . . . . no, sorella mia.
(*si volge ancora ai fiori*):

**SISTER ANGELICA:** (*turning towards the sisters*). I . . . . no . . . . my sister . . . . never . . . .
(*She again turns towards the flowers.*)

**LE SUORE:** (*facendo gruppo dalla parte opposta a Suor Angelica. A bassa voce*): -Che Gesù la perdoni, ha detto una bugia!
—Ha detto una bugia!

**THE SISTERS:** (*grouping themselves on the side opposite to Sister Angelica, whispering*). Pray that Jesus forgive her!
She told a fearful lie!
She told a fearful lie!

**UNA NOVIZIA:** (*avvicinandosi, curiosa*): Perchè?

**A NOVICE:** (*drawing near, full of curiosity*). Why?

**ALCUNE SUORE:** (*piano*):—Noi lo sappiamo,
ha un grande desiderio!
—Vorrebbe aver notizie della famiglia sua!
—Sono più di sett'anni, da quando è in monasterio, che non ha avuto nuove!
—E sembra rassegnata, ma è tanto tormentata!
—Nel mondo era ricchissims, lo disse la Badessa.
—Era nobile!
—Nobile!
—Nobile? Principessa!
—La vollero far monaca sembra . . . . per punizione!
—Perchè? . . . .
—Perchè? . . . .
—Mah!?
—Mah!?

**A FEW SISTERS:** (*in low tone*). Because we know!
She wishes more than ever
To hear what has become
Of all her kin and friends!
—It's been over seven years
Since she entered here
And has not heard from home!
—She seems to be resigned,
In truth she pines away!
—She comes of wealthy family
So said our Mother Abbess,
—She was noble!
—Rich and noble!
—Noble? She was a Princess!
—She had to make her vows
Forcibly . . . . and in punishment!
—Why? . . . .
—Why? . . . .
—Oh!
—Oh!

**LA SORELLA INFERMIERA:** (*Accorre affannata*): Suor Angelica, sentite! . . . .

**THE SISTER NURSE:** (*rushing in, out of breath*). Oh, Angelica, do help me!

**SUOR ANGELICA:** O sorella infermiera,
che cosa accadde, dite!

**SISTER ANGELICA:** Oh, my sister, my dear nurse,
What has happened, do tell me!

**LA SORELLA INFERMIERA:** Suora Chiara, là nell'orto,
assettava la spalliera delle rose; all'improvviso tante vespe sono uscite,
i'han pinzata qui nel viso!
Ora è in cella e si lamenta.
Ah! calmatele, sorella,
il dolor che la tormenta!

**THE SISTER NURSE:** Sister Chiara, in the garden
Went on trimming a new rose-bush
When a swarm of frantic wasps
Stung her on the head!
She's bemoaning in her cell!
Her distress is hard to tell!
Do help her, beloved sister!

**ALCUNE SUORE:** Poveretta! Poveretta!

**A FEW SISTERS:** Oh, poor Chiara!
Oh, poor Chiara!

**SUOR ANGELICA:** Aspettate, ho un'erba e un fiore!
(*Corre cercando fra i fiori e l'erbe.*)

**SISTER ANGELICA:** Wait, I have fine herbs and flowers!
(*She rushes about in search of herbs and flowers.*)

**LA SORELLA INFERMIERA:** Suor Angelica ha sempre una ricetta buona, fatta coi fiori,
sa trovar sempre un'erba benedetta per calmare i dolori!

**THE SISTER NURSE:** Sister Angelica has always a good recipe made with flowers
She will find a blessed herb to sooth and cure all pain.

**SUOR ANGELICA:** (*alla Suora infermicra porgendole alcune erbe*): Ecco, questa è calenzólà:
col latticcio che ne cola le bagate l'enfiagione;
e con questa, una pozione.
Dite a sorella Chiara che sarà molto amara
ma che le farà bene.
E le direte ancora che punture di vespe
sono piccole pene;
e che non si lamenti,
chè a lamentarsi crescono i tormenti.

**SISTER ANGELICA:** (*to the Sister Nurse, handing her some herbs*).
Now this herb is something fine!
Aromatic more than pine!
It will help, used as a lotion,
And with this you'll make a potion.
Please tell our dear sister
To drink it, although bitter
It will help her a whole lot . . . .
And also please tell Chiara
That a sting in the main
Means just a little pain;
That if she laments
More severe will be her torments.

**LA SORELLA INFERMIERA:** Le saprò riferire.
Grazie, sorella, grazie.

**THE SISTER NURSE:** Your directions I'll observe
Thanks, my dear sister, thanks!

**SUOR ANGELICA:** Sono qui per servire.

**SISTER ANGELICA:** I am here, glad to serve.

## IL RITORNO DALLA CERCA

## THE RETURN FROM THE QUEST

(*Dal fondo a sinistra entrano due Suore cercatrici conducendo un ciuchino carico di roba.*)

(*From rear, left, enter two Questuants leading a little donkey loaded with all sorts of things.*)

**LE CERCATRICI:** Laudata Maria.

**THE QUESTUANTS:** God bless the Virgin Mary!

**TUTTE:** E sempre sia!

**ALL:** Amen!

**LE CERCATRICI:** Buona cerca stasera,
sorella dispensiera!
(*Le Suore si fanno intorno al ciuchino; le cercatrici scaricano e consegnano le limosine alla Sorella dispensiera.*)

**THE QUESTUANTS:** Our quest has been successful
As all of you can see!
(*The sisters crowd around the donkey; the Questuants unload, and turn the gifts over to the sister housekeeper.*)

**UNA CERCATRICE:** Un otre d'olio.

**A QUESTUANT:** Ten gallons of oil.

**SUOR DOLCINA:** (*che non può stare*): Uh! buono!

**SISTER DOLCINA:** (*who cannot resist her craving for good things*). Oh, fine!

**L'ALTRA CERCATRICE:** Nocciòle, sei collane.

**OTHER QUESTUANT:** New filberts, fifty pounds.

**UNA CERCATRICE:** Un panierin di noci.

**A QUESTUANT:** A basket full of walnuts.

**SUOR DOLCINA:** Buone con sale e pane!

**SISTER DOLCINA:** So good with salt and biscuits!

**LA ZELATRICE:** (*riprendendola*): Sorella!

**THE MONITOR:** (*reproachfully*). Now, sister!

**UNA CERCATRICE:** Qui farina,
e qui una caciottella
che suda ancora latte,
bona come una pasta!
Un sacchetto di lenti,
dell'uova, burro e basta.

**ALCUNE SUORE:** Buona cerca stasera,
sorella dispensiera!
(*Una cercatrice porta via il ciuchino.*)

**L'ALTRA CERCATRICE:** Per voi
sorella ghiotta . . . .

**SUOR DOLCINA:** (*felice*): Un tralcetto di ribes!
(*vedendo che le altre si scandalizzano*):
Degnatene, sorelle!

**UNA SUORA:** (*scherzosamente*):
Uh! Se ne prendo un chicco la martorio!

**SUOR DOLCINA:** No, no, prendete!

**ALCUNE SUORE:** Grazie!
(*Formano un gruppetto a desira e beccano il ribes, fra risatine discrete.*)

**LA CERCATRICE:** Che è venuto
stasera in parlatorio?

**ALCUNE SUORE:** —Nessuno.
—Nessuno.
—Perchè?

**LA CERCATRICE:** Fuor del portone c'è
fermata una ricca berlina.

**SUOR ANGELICA:** (*volgendosi, come assalita da una improvvisa inquietudine.*) Come, sorella?
Come avete detto?
Una berlina è fuori? . . . .
Ricca? . . . . Ricca? . . . . Ricca? . . . .

**LA CERCATRICE:** Da gran signori.
Certo aspetta qualcuno
che è entrato nel convento
e forse fra un momento
suonerà la campana a parlatorio.

**SUOR ANGELICA:** (*conansia crescente*): Ah! ditemi sorella,
com'era la berlina?
Non aveva uno stemma?
Uno stemma d'avorio? . . . .
E dentro tappezzata
d'una seta turchina
ricamata in argento? . . . .

**LA CERCATRICE:** (*interdetta*): Io
non lo so, sorella;
ho veduto soltanto
una berlina . . . . bella!

**LA SUORE:** (*osservando suor Angelica*):—E diventata bianca . . . .
—Ora è tutta vermiglia! . . . .
—Poverina!
—È commossa!

**A QUESTUANT:** Lots of flour!
See here this fine pot-cheese
As fresh as morning dew
The best I can recall!
A small bag of new lentils,
Eggs, butter, and that's all!

**A FEW SISTERS:** The quest has
been successful
As all of us can see.
(*One of the Questuants leads the donkey away.*)

**OTHER QUESTUANT:** For you
who like good cheer . . . .

**SISTER DOLCINA:** (*happy*). A
whole branch of raspberries!
(*Noticing the other sisters' teasing attitude*):
Oh, sisters, do have some!

**A SISTER:** (*teasingly*). I'd be afraid
to take one! Thank you, no!

**SISTER DOLCINA:** No, no, do take
some!

**A FEW SISTERS:** Thanks, dear!
(*They form a group to the right, picking berries from the branch. There is subdued laughter.*)

**THE QUESTUANT:** Who is now at
the convent? Do you know?

**A FEW SISTERS:** —No one.
—Yes, no one
—Tell us why.

**THE QUESTUANT:** Outside the
gate
A gorgeous, magnificent coach is
standing.

**SISTER ANGELICA:** (*turning
around as if seized by a sudden fear*). What is it, sister? Just what
did you say?
You said a coach outside? . . . .
Gorgeous? . . . . Gorgeous? . . . . Gorgeous?

**THE QUESTUANT:** Truly imposing.
It is waiting for someone.
Who has come to the convent,
And maybe in a moment
The great bell will announce the
visitor.

**SISTER ANGELICA:** (*with growing trepidation*). Oh do tell me,
my sister,
What did that coach look like?
Did you notice its blazon?
A blazon made of ivory? . . . .
And inside all upholstered
With a rare azure damask
And embroidered with silver? . . . .

**THE QUESTUANT:** (*somewhat
confused*). I really couldn't tell,
my sister;
All I know is I saw
A splendid coach . . . . my sister!

**THE SISTERS:** (*all watching Sister
Angelica*).—She was as white as
snow . . . .
—And now is red as fire! . . . .
—The poor darling!
—She is trembling!

—Supra che sien persone di famiglia!
(*Una campanella rintocca; le
suore accorrono da ogni parte.*)

**LE SUORE:** —Vien gente in parlatorio!
—Una visita viene!
—Per chi?
—Per chi sarà?
—Fosse per me!
—Per me!
—Fosse mia madre
che ci porta le tortorine bianche!
—Fosse la mia cugina di campagna
che porta il seme di lavanda buono! . . . .
(*Suor Genovieffa si avvicina alle
compagne e quasi interrompe
queste esclamazioni indicando
con un gesto pietoso Suor Angelica.*)

**SUOR ANGELICA:** (*volgendo gli
occhi al cielo, mormora*): O Madre
eletta, leggimi nel cuore,
volgi per me un sorriso al Salvatore . . . .
(*Il gruppo delle suore si avvicina
in silenzio a Suor Anelica. —Suor
Genovieffa esce dal gruppo e con
grande dolcezza*):

**SUOR GENOVIEFFA:** (*a Suor
Angelica*): O sorella in amore,
noi preghiamo la Stella delle Stelle
che la visita, adesso, sia per voi.

**SUOR ANGELICA:** (*commossa*):
Buone sorelle, grazie!
(*Da sinistra entra la Badessa per
chiamare la suora che dovrà audare al parlatorio.—L'attesa è
viva.—In quell'attimo di silenzio
tutte le suore fanno il sacrificio
del loro desiderio a pro della sorella in gran pena.—Suor Angelica
ha sempre gli occhi volti al cielo,
immobile come se tutta la sua vita
fosse sospesa.*)

**LA BADESSA:** (*chiamando*): Suor
Angelica!
(*Fa cenno che le suore si ritirino.*)

**LE SUORE:** (*come respirando, finalmente*): Ah! . . . .
(*Il getto della fonte si è indorato,
le suore riempiono un secchiello
d'acqua, si avviano, serso il cimitero e scompaiono.*)

**SUOR ANGELICA:** Madre, Madre,
parlate!
chi è, Madre . . . . chi è?
Son sett'anni che aspetto! . . . .
Son sett'anni che aspetto una parola . . . .
una nuova, uno scritto . . . .

—She hopes someone has come to
inquire for her!
(*The bell rings; the sisters rush in
from all sides.*)

**THE SISTERS:** —The bell announcing strangers!
—A visitor is coming!
—For whom?
—For whom will it be?
—Maybe for me!
—For me!
—Perhaps my mother
Is bringing us a pair of dear, white
doves!
—I wish it were my cousin from
the mountains
Who brings us lavender and other
seeds! . . . .
(*Sister Genevieve draws near her
companions and almost interrupts their exclamations by pointing to Sister Angelica with a gesture of pity.*)

**SISTER ANGELICA:** (*with uplifted
eyes, whispers*). Oh! Blessed Mother, read within my mind
And smile for me to Jesus, pure and
kind!
(*The group of sisters silently approaches Sister Angelica.—Sister
Genevieve comes out of the group
and addresses Sister Angelica
with exquisite sweetness.*)

**SISTER GENEVIEVE:** (*to Angelica*). Oh! sister, kind and true!
We shall implore the Star of all the
Stars
That the visit announced be for
you.

**SISTER ANGELICA:** (*with great
emotion*). Good sister, I thank you!
(*From the left enters the Abbess
who is to announce for which sister is the visit. Expectancy is very
high. In that moment of silence,
all the sisters offer their desire in
sacrifice in favor of the afflicted
sister. Sister Angelica, her eyes
still uplifted, remains motionless,
as if her whole being were being
held in suspense.*)

**THE ABBESS:** (*calling*). Sister
Angelica!
(*With a wave of her hand she directs the other sisters to withdraw.*)

**THE SISTERS:** (*as if breathing at
last*). Ah! . . . .
(*The spout of the fount is now the
color of purest gold. The sisters fill
a small watering pot with the
golden water, they move away in
the direction of the cemetery and
disappear.*)

**SISTER ANGELICA:** Mother, Mother, oh, tell me
Who came, Mother? . . . . who
came?
Seven years I've been waiting
Seven years, spent without a single
word

Tutto ho offerto alla Vergine
in piena espiazione . . . .
che adesso vi scompone!

**LA BADESSA:** Offritele anche
l'ansia
che adesso vi scompone!
(*Suor Angelica, affranta, si curva
lentamente in ginocchio e si raccoglie.*)
(*De voci delle suore arrivano dal
cimitero.*)

**LE VOCI DELLE SUORE:** Requiem
aeternam
dona ei, domine,
et lux perpetua
luceat ei—Requiescat in pace—
Amen.

**SUOR ANGELICA:** (*alzando gli
occhi*): Madre, sono serena e sot-
tomessa.

**LA BADESSA:** È venuta a trovarvi
vostra zia Principessa.

**SUOR ANGELICA:** Ah! . . . .

**LA BADESSA:** In parlatorio
si dica quanto
vuole ubbidienza,
necessità.
Ogni parola è udita
dalla Vergine Pia.

**SUOR ANGELICA:** La Vergine
m'ascolti e così sia.

## LA ZIA PRINCIPESSA

(*La Badessa si avvia e scompare a
sinistra. Suor Angelica si avvia
verso gli archi del parlatorio.
Guarda ansiosamente verso la
porticina. Si ode un rumore di
chiavi. La porta viene aperta in
dentro dalla Suora clavaria che
rimarrà a finaco della porta, nella penombra della stanza. Quindi
si vedrà la Badessa che si sofferma
davanti alla Suora clavaria. La
due Suore fanno ala e fra le due
figure bianche, che si curvano
lievemente in atto di ossequio,
passa una figura nera, severamente composta in un naturale
atteggiamento di grande dignità
aristocratica; la zia Principessa.
Entra. Cammina lentamente appoggiandosi ad un bastoncino di
ebano. Si sofferma: getta per un
attimo lo sguardo sulla nipote,
freddamente e senza tradire nessuna emozione; Suor Angelica invece alla vista della zia è presa da
grande commozione, ma si frena
perchè la figura della clavaria e
della Badessa si profilano ancora
nell'ombra. La porticina si richiude. Suor Angelica, commossa;
quasi vacillante va incontro alla
zia, ma la vecchia protende la sinistra come per consentire soltanto
all'atto sottomesso del baciamano. Suor Angelica prende la mano
che le viene tesa, la porta alle labbra e, mentre la siede, ella cade in
ginocchio, senza porter parlare.*)

Or a letter, or news . . . .
All have I offered to the Virgin
In fullest expiation . . . .

**THE ABBESS:** To the Virgin offer
also
Your present exaltation!
(*Sister Angelica, crushed, slowly
bends her knees and concentrates
in prayer. The voices of the sisters
are heard from the cemetery.*)

**THE VOICES OF THE SISTERS:** Re-
quiem aeternam
Don ei, domine,
Et lux perpetua
Luceat ei—Requiescat in pace—
Amen!

**SISTER ANGELICA:** (*raising her
eyes*). Mother, I am serene and
blessed by God.

**THE ABBESS:** I announce a visit
From your aunt, the Princess!

**SISTER ANGELICA:** Ah! . . . .

**THE ABBESS:** Your words will be
Full of humility
And all submission!
On this occasion! . . . .
All you say will be known
To the Virgin, in Heaven!

**SISTER ANGELICA:** I pray the
Blessed Virgin to hear, Amen!

## THE PRINCESS

(*The Abbess moves away towards
left of stage and disappears. Sister
Angelica walks towards the reception arcade and anxiously looks
in the direction of the little door. A
noise of keys. The door is opened
outwardly by the sister portress
who remains standing alongside
the door in the shadow of the
room. Then appears the Abbess
who stops next to the sister portress. The two sisters stand one on
each side of the door, and, between the two white figures, bending in a deferential attitude, passes a dark figure severely
composed in a deportment of aris-
tocratic dignity. Enter the Princess, who walks rather slowly, leaning on a thin ebony stick. She
stops and throws a glance at her
niece, coldly and without a trace
of emotion. Sister Angelica, at
sight of her aunt, is very much
moved, but controls herself because the figures of the Abbess
and the sister portress are seen at
the door. The little door is closed
again. Sister Angelica, full of emotion, and almost staggering,
moves towards her aunt, but the
old lady merely stretches out her
left hand as if to indicate that she
will only consent to Sister Angelica kissing it. Sister Angelica seizes
the outstretched hand, raises it to
her lips, and while the Princess
sits down, she falls upon her*)

*Un attimo di silenzio. Suor Ange-
lica, con gli occhi pieni di lacrime,
non ha mai tolto lo sguardo dal
volto della zia, uno sguardo pietoso, implorante. La vecchia invece
ostentatamente guarda avanti a
sè.*)

**LA ZIA PRINCIPESSA:** Il Principe
Gualtiero vostro padre,
la Principessa Clara vostra madre,
quando venti anni or sono
vennero a morte . . . .
(*La vecchia si interrompe per farsi
il segno della croce*):
mi affidarono i figli ancor fanciulli
e tutto il patrimonio di famiglia.
Io dovevo dividerlo
quando ciò ritenessi conveniente,
e con giustizia piena.
È quanto ho fatto. Ecco la pergamena.
Voi potete osservarla, discuterla,
firmarla.

**SUOR ANGELICA:** Dopo
sett'anni . . . . son davanti a
voi . . . .
Ispiratevi a questo luogo santo . . . .
È luogo di clemenza
È luogo di pietà . . . .

**LA ZIA PRINCIPESSA:** Di penitenza.
Io debbo rivelarvi la ragione
perchè addivenni a questa divisione:
vostra sorella
Anna Viola
anderà sposa.

**SUOR ANGELICA:** Sposa?!
Sposa la piccola
Anna Viola?
Sposa la sorellina,
la piccina?
(*Si interrompe; pensa un attimo*):
piccina?! . . . . Ah! . . . . Son
sett'anni! . . . .
Son passati sett'anni!
O sorellina bionda che vai sposa,
o sorellina mia, tu sia felice!
E chi la ingemma?

**LA ZIA PRINCIPESSA:** Chi per
amore condonò la colpa
di cui macchiaste il nostro bianco
stemma.

**SUOR ANGELICA:** Sorella di mia
madre,
voi siete inesorabile!

**LA ZIA PRINCIPESSA:** Che dite? E
che pensate?
Implacata son io? Inesorabile?
Vostra madre invocate
quasi contro di me?
Di frequente, la sera,
là, nel nostro oratorio,
io mi raccolgo

knees, unable to utter a single
word. A moment of silence. Sister
Angelica, with tears streaming
down her cheeks, imploringly
keeps her eyes upon her aunt's
face. But the old lady ostentatiously stares straight ahead.*)

**THE PRINCESS:** Your father, the
all powerful, Prince Gualtiero
And your beloved mother, Princess
Clara,
Upon their death
Twenty years ago . . . .
(*The old lady stops to cross her-
self*):
Entrusted to my care their little
children
Together with their ample patrimo-
ny:
I was to subdivide it
With wisdom and all fairness
In case I should have deemed it op-
portune.
This I have done.
Here is the document.
You may have it, examine and sign
it.

**SISTER ANGELICA:** After seven
years . . . . I am before you
May this blessed ground touch your
heart, my aunt . . . .
This place ought to entrance
Your clemency and pity . . . .

**THE PRINCESS:** And also your pen-
ance.
I must, however, tell you now the
reason
That made imperative this subdivi-
sion;
Your little sister,
Anna Viola,
Will soon be married.

**SISTER ANGELICA:** Mar-
ried? . . . .
Married, my little
Anna Viola?
My darling little sister
Still so young!
(*She stops and thinks a moment*):
Why so young? . . . . Seven
years! . . . .
Seven years have gone by!
Oh! sister blond and fair, you will
be married,
My darling little pet, may you be
happy!
Who is the bridegroom?

**THE PRINCESS:** A man who has
forgiven the black stain
Cast upon our unblemished blazon.

**SISTER ANGELICA:** Oh, sister of
my mother
You are so hard and merciless.

**THE PRINCESS:** How dare you
speak that way?
You call me hard? . . . . You dare
call me merciless?
Your mother you would sway
Almost against your aunt?
Very often at night
In our chapel at home

Nel silenzio di quei raccoglimenti,
il mio spirito par che s'allontani
e s'incontri con quel di vostra madre
in colloqui eterei e arcani!
Come è penoso
udire i morti dolorare e piangere!
Quando l'estasi mistica scompare
per voi serbata ho una parola sola:
espiare! Espiare! . . . .
Offritela alla Vergine
la mia giustizia!

**SUOR ANGELICA:** Tutto ho offerto
alla Vergine . . . . sì . . . . tutto!
Ma v'è un'offerta che non posso
fare!
Alla Madre soave della Madri
non posso offrire di scordar . . . . mio figlio,
mio figlio! Il figlio mio
La creatura che mi fu strappata,
che ho veduto e baciato una sol volta!
Creatura mia! Creatura mia lontana!
È questa la parola
che imploro da sett'anni!
Parlatemi di lui!
Com'è, com'è mio figlio?
Com'è dolce il suo volto?
Come sono i suoi occhi?
Parlatemi di lui,
di mio figlio . . . . mio figlio!
(Un silenzio; la vecchia tace,
guardando la madre in angoscia):
Perchè tacete?
Perchè tacete?
Un altro instante di questo silenzio
e vi dannate per l'eternità!
La Vergine vi ascolta e Lei vi giudica!

**LA ZIA PRINCIPESSA:** Or son due
anni
venne colpito
da fiero morbo . . . .
Tutto fu fatto per salvarlo.

**SUOR ANGELICA:** È morto?
(La zia curva il capo e tace): Ah!
(Suor Angelica, con un grido,
cade di schianto in terra, in avanti, col volto sulle mani. La zia si
alza come per soccorrerla credendola svenuta; ma, al singhiozzare
di Suor Angelica, frena il suo
movimento di pietà; in piedi si
volge verso un'immagine sacra
che è al muro, alla sua destra, e
con le due mani appoggiate al
bastoncino di ebano, con la testa
curva, in silenzio, prega. Il pianto
di Suor Angelica continua suffocato e straziante.—Nel parlatorio

I kneel in prayer
In the stillness of that religious solitude
I feel my spirit sallying forth from
me
To encounter the spirit of your
mother!
In ethereal and lofty reverie!
It is sad and painful
To hear the dead's long sighs when
they bemoan!
When the mystical vision fades
away
Of you remains in me one thought
alone:
She must pay for her sin! . . .
Now offer to the Virgin
My sternest justice!

**SISTER ANGELICA:** All have I offered her . . . . yes . . . . all I
had!
But there's an offer I can never
make!
To that Mother, the sweetest of all
Mothers
I cannot offer to forget . . . . my
son.
My son! . . . . my darling son!
The sweet, dear baby torn away
from me
Whom I have seen and kissed but
once!
My darling child! My darling child
so distant!
This is the word I've expected
For seven years!
Do speak to me of him!
Tell me what he looks like!
Hasn't he the sweetest face?
Are his eyes like stars?
Do speak to me of him
Of my son . . . . of my son!
(A pause. The old lady does not
answer while gazing at the distracted mother):
Why don't you speak?
Why don't you speak?
Another instant of this gruesome silence
And for all time you'll damn your
cruel soul!
The Virgin, is there listening. She
will judge!

**THE PRINCESS:** It has been two
years since
The child was stricken
By fatal sickness . . . .
No care was spared to save his life.

**SISTER ANGELICA:** He's
dead? . . . .
(The aunt silently bends her
head):
Ah!
(Sister Angelica, with a heartbreaking cry, drops to the ground
face downwards. Her aunt gets up
to aid her, thinking she has fainted; but, hearing Sister Angelica's
sobs, she controls her movement
of pity. Standing up, she turns
towards a sacred image on the
wall to her right and, leaning with
both hands on the ebony stick,
with bent head, she prays in si-

è già la semioscurità della sera.—
Si ode la porta aprirsi. Suor Angelica si solleva restando sempre in
ginocchio e col volto coperto. Entra la Suora clavaria con una lucernina accesa che pone sul tavolo. La zia Principessa parla alla
Suora. La Suora esce e ritorna con
la Badessa recando in mano una
tavoletta, un calamaio e una penna. Suor Angelica ode entrare le
due Suore si volge, vede, comprende; in silenzio si trascina verso il tavolo e con mano tremante
firma la pergamena. Quindi si allontana di nuovo e si ricopre il
volto con le mani. Le due Suore escono. La zia Principessa prende la
pergamena, fa per andare verso la
nipote, ma al suo avvicinarsi
Suor Angelica fa un leggiero movimento con tutta la persona come
per ritrarsi. Allora la zia procede
verso la porta, batte col bastoncino, la clavaria apre, prende il
lume, va avanti. La zia Principessa la segue. Di sulla soglia volge
uno sguardo alla nipote. Esce.
Scompare. La porta si richiude.—
La sera è calata; nel cimitero le
Suore vanno accendendo i lumini
sulle tombe.)

## LA GRAZIA

**SUOR ANGELICA:** (rimasta
sola): Senza mamma,
bimbo, tu sei morto!
Le tue labbra
senza i baci miei,
scoloriron
fredde, fredde!
E chiudesti,
bimbo, gli occhi belli!
Non potendo
carezzarmi,
le manine
componesti in croce!
E tu sei morto
senza sapere
quanto t'amava
questa tua mamma!
Ora che sei un angelo del cielo,
ora tu puoi vederla la tua mamma,
tu puoi scendere giù pel firmamento
ed aleggiare intorno a me ti sento.
Sei qui, baci e m'accarezzi.
Ah! dimmi, quando in ciel potrò
vederti?
Quando potro baciarti?
O dolce fine d'ogni mio dolore,
quando in cielo con te potro salire?
Quando potrò morire?
Dillo alla mamma, creatura bella,
con un leggero scintillar di stella.
Parlami, amore, amor!

lence. Sister Angelica's sobs continue, stifled and heartrending.
Darkness now begins to pervade
the entire scene. The door opens.
Sister Angelica raises herself from
the ground, but remains kneeling
with both hands covering her
face. The portress enters with a
small light which she places on the
little table. The Princess speaks to
the portress, who leaves only to return immediately with the Abbess
carrying in her hand a tablet, and
ink-well and a quill. Sister Angelica hears the sisters approaching,
turns around and understands.
In silence, she drags herself up to
the table and with trembling
hand affixes her signature to the
parchment. Then she moves
away, and, again, she covers her
face with both hands. The two sisters leave. The Princess takes the
parchment, then moves towards
her niece; but, as she draws near,
Sister Angelica shrinks away from
her with a slight movement of her
whole body. Then the Princess
proceeds towards the door, strikes
it with her cane, the portress
opens, takes up the lantern and
shows the Princess her way out.
The Princess follows her. From the
threshhold she again glances back
to her niece. She goes out and disappears. The door is again closed.
Night has fallen. In the cemetery
the sisters are lighting the small
lanterns on the various tombstones.)

## THE GRACE

**SISTER ANGELICA:** (alone).
Without your mother,
Dearest, you died!
Your sweet lips
Without my fond kisses
Grew white and
Cold as snow!
And your eyes
You did close, my darling!
Then, unable
To caress me,
Your tiny hands
Were crossed on your chest!
And you died
Without ever knowing
With what wild passion
Your mother loved you!
Now that you are an angel of the
heavens
You will at last behold your mother's face.
You can descend to me from up
above
And I seem to hear your flight
through the space.
I feel your kisses and caresses!
Oh tell me, when may I see you in
heaven?
When will I know your kisses?
Oh sweetest end of all my bitter sorrows,
Tell me when I may hope to fly to

(*I lumi del cimitero sono tutti accesi: il chiostro è ormai quasi oscuro. Le Suore escono dal cimitero e si avviano verso Suor Angelica che è come in estasi. Il gruppo delle Suore si avvicina in silenzio. Nella semioscurità sembra che le figure bianche, camminando, non tocchino terra.*)

**LE SUORE:** Sarete contenta, sorella,
la Vergine ha accolto la prece.
Sarete contenta, sorella,
la Vergine ha fatto la grazia.
(*Suor Angelica si leva come in preda ad un'esaltazione mistica.*)

**SUOR ANGELICA:** La grazia è discesa, dal cielo
già tutta già tutta m'accende,
risplende! risplende! risplende!
Già vedo, sorelle, la meta . . . .
Sorelle, son lieta! son lieta!
Cantiamo! Già in cielo si canta
Lodiamo la Vergine santa!

**TUTTE:** Lodiamo la Vergine santa!
(*Si ode dal fondo a destra il segnale delle tavolette. Le Suore si avviano verso l'arcata di destra e la teoria bianca scompare nelle celle.*)

**LA VOCE DI ANGELICA:** La grazia è discesa dal ciel! . . . .
(*La notte avvolge il chiostro. Sulla chiesetta si va illuminando a poco a poco una scintillante cupola di stelle. La luna dà sui cipressi—Si apre una cella: esce Suor Angelica.*)

**SUOR ANGELICA:** (*Ha in mano una ciotola di terracotta che posa a piè di un cipresso; raccoglie un fastelletto di sterpi e rami, raduna dei sassi a mo' d'alari e vi depone il fastelletto; va alla fonte e riempie la ciotola d'acqua: accende con l'acciarino il fuoco e vi mette su la ciotola. Quindi si avvia verso la fiorita.*)
Amici fiori, voi mi compensate
di tutte le premure mie amorose!
(*come chiamando per nome il fiore e l'erba che coglie.*)
Vieni, oleandro.
Pruno lauro, ove sei? . . . .
Atropo bello, vieni! . . . .
Ed ora a te, cicuta viperina! . . . .
Mi dici: "Non scordarmi!"
No, non ti scordo, vieni ad aiutarmi!

you
When will death overtake me?
Do tell your mother, sweetest of all children,
With the bright light of yonder flickering stars,
Speak, oh speak, my sweetheart!
(*The lanterns are all lighted in the cemetery; the cloister is now shrouded in almost complete darkness. The sisters come out of the graveyard two by two and draw near Sister Angelica, now absorbed in ecstasy. The group of the sisters draws closer, in silence. In the penumbra it seems as if the white-clad shadows scarcely touch the ground as they walk along.*)

**THE SISTERS:** Your wish will be granted, dear sister,
The Virgin has heard your heart's prayer.
Your wish will be granted, dear sister,
The Virgin takes you in her care!
(*Sister Angelica rises as if under the spell of a mystic exaltation.*)

**SISTER ANGELICA:** Her blessing has come down from Heaven
And pours in my soul new delight,
Resplendent, so brilliant, so bright!
I see now, dear sisters, my goal
And filled with great joy is my soul!
Sing, sisters, the angels are singing . . . .
Our souls to the Virgin are clinging!

**ALL:** Our souls to the Virgin are clinging!
(*From back stage, to the right, is heard the rattle. The sisters move in the direction of the arcade and the white theory vanishes into the cells.*)

**ANGELICA'S VOICE:** Her blessing has come down from Heaven!
(*The cloister is now submerged in complete darkness. Upon the little church, gradually, is lighted a shining cupola of stars. The moon rises above the cypresses—A cell-door opens. Sister Angelica appears.*)

**SISTER ANGELICA:** (*carries in her hand an earthen jar which she puts down at the foot of a cypress; she makes a small bunch of brambles and branches, heaps up a few stones in the fashion of andirons and places the bunch upon them. She goes to the fount and fills the jar with water. She lights the fire with a piece of flint and puts the jar on the fire. Then she walks towards the shrubbery*): Oh, friendly flowers, you are fair compensation
For all the sorrows flung on me by love!
(*As if calling by name the flowers and herbs she is picking*):
Come, oleander.
Where are you, darkest laurel? . . . .

(*volgendosi e stringendo i fiori al petto*):
E siate benedetti, amici fiori,
che consolate tutti i miei dolori!
(*Fa un pugnello delle erbe e dei fiori colti e li getta nella ciotola fumante, guarda un attimo il formarsi del veleno, prende la ciotola e la posa a piè della croce; quindi si volge a destra verso le cellette.*)
Addio, buone sorelle, addio, addio!
Io vi lascio per sempre.
M'ha chiamata mio figlio!
Dentro un raggio di stelle
m'è apparso il suo sorriso,
m'ha detto: Mamma, vieni in Paradiso!
Addio! Addio!
Addio, chiesetta! In te quanto ho pregato!
Buona accoglievi preghiere e pianti.
È discesa la grazia benedetta!
Muoio per lui e in ciel lo rivedrò!
(*Esaltata, abbraccia la croce, la bacia, si curva rapidamente, prende la ciotola, si volge verso la chiesa e guardando al cielo beve il veleno. Quindi si appoggia ad un cipresso e comprimendosi il petto con la sinistra e abbandonando lentamente il braccio destro lascia cadere la ciotola a terra. L'atto del suicidio ormai compiuto sembra la tolga dalla esaltazione a cui era in preda e la riconduca alla verità. Un rapido silenzio. Il suo volto prima sereno e sorridente si atteggia in una espressione angosciosa come se una rivelazione improvvisa e tremenda le fosse apparsa.*)
(*Le nubi coprono adesso la luna e le stelle; la scena è oscura.*)
(*Si leva un grido disperato*):

Beautiful nightshade, come! . . . .
It is now your turn, oh powerful, bitter hemlock!
You say: "Forget me not!"
How could I! Come, I have fought enough!
(*Turning around and pressing the flowers to her breast*):
And you be blessed all, oh fragrant flowers,
You who will quench the pain of my last hours!
(*She takes a handful of the herbs and flowers she has picked and throws them into the boiling water, looks a while at the poison being formed, takes the jar and places it at the foot of the cross; then turns to the right, toward the cell*):
My dear sisters, farewell, farewell, farewell!
I am leaving for ever.
My son is calling!
Among the flickering stars
I saw his smile so dear!
He said from Heaven:
"Mother, come, come here!"
Farewell! farewell!
Farewell, dear church! Wherein I prayed so much!
Friendly shelter for my sobs and my prayers.
From Heaven did descend the Virgin's blessing!
I die for him and rush into his arms!
(*In an impulse of irresistible exaltation she embraces and kisses the cross, then, bending rapidly, she picks up the jar, turns towards the church and with her eyes fixed in the heavens, drinks the poison. Then she leans against a cypress and, pressing her chest with her left hand and slowly dropping her right arm, she lets the jar fall to the ground.*
*The act of suicide she has committed seems to free Sister Angelica from the exaltation that had seized her, bringing her back to reality. A brief pause. Her face, so serene and smiling before, now takes an expression of intense anguish, as if a sudden and terrible revelation had come upon her.*)
(*Clouds now cover the moon and the stars; the stage is very dark. A desperate cry is heard.*)

## IL MIRACOLO

Ah! Son dannata!
Mi son data la morte!
Io muoio in peccato mortale!
(*Si getta disperatamente in ginocchio.*)
O Madonna, Madonna,
per amor di mio figlio
smarrita ho la ragione!
non mi fare morire in dannazione!
Dammi un segno di grazia! grazia!
Dammi un segno di grazia! grazia!
O Madonna, salvami!

## THE MIRACLE

Ah, I am lost!
I have taken my life!
I die with the blackest of sins!
(*In despair, she throws herself to the ground*):
Oh! Madonna, Madonna!
It was the love of my child
That made me lose my reason.
Don't let me die, Madonna, in disgrace!
Give me a sign of your mercy!
Give me a sign of your mercy!

Una madre ti prega,
una madre t'implora . . . .
O Madonna, salvami!
(*Già le sembra udire ie voci degli angeli imploranti per lei la Madre delle Madri.*)

**GLI ANGELI:** O gloriosa virginum
Sublimis inter sidera,
Qui te creavit, parvulum
Lactente nutris ubere.
Quod Heva tristis abstulit
Tu reddis almo germine:
Intrent ut astra flebiles,
Coeli recludis cardines.
(*Suor Angelica vede il miracolo*

Oh, Madonna, save me!
It is a mother that prays to you!
It is a mother imploring . . . .
Oh, Madonna, save me!
(*She seems to hear the voice of angels imploring for her, the Mother of all Mothers.*)

**THE ANGELS:** O gloriosa Virginum
Sublimis inter sidera,
Qui te crevait, parvulum
Lacente nutris ubere.
Quod Heva tristis abstulit
Tu reddis almo germine:
Intrent ut astra flebiles,
Coeli recludis cardines.
(*Sister Angelica sees the miracle*

compiersi: la chiesetta Sfolgora di mistica luce, la porta si apre: apparisce la Regina del conforto, solenne, dolcissima e, avanti a Lei, un bimbo biondo, tutto bianco.*)

**SUOR ANGELICA:** Ah! . . . .
(*La Vergine sospinge, con dolce geto, il bimbo verso la moribonda*)

**SUOR ANGELICA:** Ah!
(*Muore.*)

Velario.

taking place. The little church suddenly becomes resplendent with mystic light. The door opens and the Queen of comfort appears, solemn, with a su eet expression on her face and, in front of her, a blond child, all white, is seen.*)

**SISTER ANGELICA:** Ah!
(*The Virgin gently, with the kindest of gestures, pushes the child towards the dying mother*)

**SISTER ANGELICA:** Ah!
(*she dies.*)

CURTAIN.

# Dido and Æneas <small>(1689)</small>

MUSIC BY HENRY PURCELL ■ LIBRETTO BY NAHUM TATE

This three-act opera, set to a libretto by Nahum Tate based upon the fourth book of the *Aeneid* by Virgil, was premiered at Hosiah Priest's Boarding School for Girls, London in October or December, 1689. The opera begins at the royal palace at Carthage, where Belinda pleads with Dido to be calm. But Dido has fallen in love with Aeneas, who has recently come from overseas. Belinda reassures Dido that Aeneas is in love with her, and the chorus urges Dido to marry him. Aeneas indeed confesses his love to Dido, who begs him to follow his destiny. Belinda calls upon the goddess of Love to assist in their union. In the cave of the witches, a Sorceress tells of her plan to separate the lovers and ruin Carthage. She sends her elf, disguised as Mercury, to Aeneas, instructing him with a fake message from Jupiter to leave Dido and Carthage behind. Aeneas, Dido and Belinda are out hunting with their retainers when the Sorceress raises a storm, forcing them to leave the woods. Aeneas is told by the elf to leave Carthage that very night. Aeneas' sailors prepare to depart. The sorceress and the witches enter, delighted about Dido's soon-to-be-ruin and the fleet's destruction. Aeneas is about to leave, and Dido laments to Belinda about her loss. Aeneas, caught between obeying the orders of Love and Jupiter, chooses Jove. Grief-stricken, Dido orders him to go and, left alone with Belinda, prays that her mistakes will not cause Aeneas harm. She dies, and the chorus asks Love to scatter rose petals upon her body.

NOTE: THE MUSIC FOR THIS OPERA WAS WRITTEN FOR THE FOLLOWING ORIGINAL ENGLISH LIBRETTO AND THEREFORE HAS NOT BEEN EDITED IN ANY WAY.

## ■ ACT I

### Scene the Plaza

*(Enter Dido and Belinda, and Train.)*

**BEL:** Shake the Cloud from off your Brow,
Fate your wishes doth Allow.
Empire Growing,
Pleasures Flowing,
Fortune Smiles and so should you,
Shake the Cloud from off your Brow,

**CHO:** Banish Sorrow, Banish Care,
Grief should ne'er approach the Fair.

**DIDO:** Ah! Belinda I am prest,
With Torment not to be Confest,
Peace and I are Strangers grown,
I Languish till my Grief is known,
Yet wou'd not have it Guest.

**BEL:** Grief Encreasing, by Concealing,

**DIDO:** Mine admits of no Revealing.

**BEL:** Then let me Speak the Trojan guest,
Into your tender Thoughts has prest.

**2 WOMEN:** The greatest blessing Fate can give,
Our Carthage to secure, and Troy revive.

**CHO:** When Monarchs unite how happy their State,
They Triumph at once on their Foes and their Fate.

**DIDO:** Whence could so much Virtue Spring,
What Stormes, what Battels did he Sing.
Anchises Valour mixt with Venus's Charmes,
How soft in Peace, and yet how fierce in Armes.

**BEL:** A Tale so strong and full of wo,
Might melt the Rocks as well as you.

**2 WOMEN:** What stubborn Heart unmoved could see,
Such Distress, such piety.

**DIDO:** Mine with Stormes of Care opprest,
Is Taught to pity the Distrest.
Mean wretches grief can Touch,
So soft so sensible my Breast,
But Ah! I fear, I pity him too much.

**BEL and ATTENDANT:** Fear no danger to Ensue,
The Hero Loves as well as you.
Ever Gentle, ever Smiling,
And the Cares of Life beguiling.
Cupid Strew your path with Flowers,
Gathered from Elizian Bowers.
*(AEneas Enters.)*

**BEL:** See your Royal Guest appears,
How God like is the Form he bears.

**AEN:** When Royal Fair shall I be blest,
With cares of Love, and State distrest.

**DIDO:** Fate forbids what you pursue,

**AEN:** Æneas has no Fate but, you.
Let Dido Smile, and I'le defie,
The Feeble stroke of Destiny.

**CHO:** Cupid only throws the Dart.
That's Dreadful to a Warriour's Heart.
And she that Wounds can only cure the Smart.

**AEN:** If not for mine, for Empire's sake,
Some pity on your Lover take.
Ah! Make not in a hopeless Fire,
A Hero fall, and Troy once more Expire.

**BEL:** Pursue they Conquest,
Love—her Eyes,
Confess the Flame her Tongue Denyes.

**CHO:** To the Hills and the Vales, to the Rocks and the Mountains
To the Musical Groves, and the cool Shady Fountains.
Let the Triumphs of Love and of Beauty be Shown,
Go Revel ye Cupids, the day is your own.

## ■ Act II

### Scene the Cave.

*(Enter Sorcerer.)*

**SORC:** Weyward Sisters you that Fright,
The Lonely Traveller by Night.
Who like dismal Ravens Crying,
Beat the Windows of the Dying.
Appear at my call, and share in the Fame,
Of a Mischief shall make all Carthage Flame.
*(Enter Inchanteresses.)*

**INCHA:** Say Master what's thy will,
Harms our Delight and Mischief all our Skill,

**SORC:** The Queen of Carthage whom we hate,
As we do all in prosperous State.
E're Sun set shall most wretched prove,
Deprived of Fame, of Life and Love.

**CHO:** Ho, ho, ho, ho, ho, ho, &c.

**INCHA:** Ruin'd e're the Set of Sun.
Tell us how shall this be done.

**SORC:** The Trojan Prince you know is bound
By Fate to seek Italian Ground,
The Queen and He are now in Chase,
Hark, how the cry comes on apace.
But when they've done, my trusty Elf
In form of Mercury himself.
As sent from Jove shall chide his stay,
And Charge him Sail to Night with all his Fleet away.
Ho, ho, ho, ho, &c.

**SORC:** But e're we, we this perform.
We'l Conjure for a Storm
To Mar their Hunting Sport,
And drive 'em back to Court.

**CHO:** In our deep-Vaulted Cell the Charm wee'l prepare,
Too dreadful a Practice for this open Air,
*(Inchanteresses and Fairees.)*
*(Enter AEneas, Dido and Belinda, and their Train.)*

## Scene the Grove.

**BEL:** Thanks to these Lonesome Vailes,

**CHO:** These desert Hills and Dales.
So fair the Game, so rich the Sport.
Diana's self might to these Woods Resort.

**2D. WOM:** Oft she Visits this Loved Mountain,
Oft she bathes her in this Fountain.
Here Acteon met his Fate,
Pursued by his own Hounds,
And after Mortal Wounds.
Discovered, discovered too late.

**AENEAS:** Behold upon my bending Spear,
A Monsters Head stands bleeding.
With Tushes far exceeding,
These did Venus Huntsmen Tear.

**DIDO:** The Skies are Clouded, heark how Thunder
Rends the Mountain Oaks asunder.

**BEL. AND CHORUS:** Hast, hast, to Town this open Field,
No Shelter from the Storm can yield.

(*The Spirit of the Sorceress descends to AEneas in likeness of Mercury.*)

**SPIR:** Stay Prince and hear great Joves Command,
He summons thee this Night away.

**AEN:** To Night.

**SPIR:** To Night thou must forsake this Land,
The Angry God will brook no longer stay,
Joves Commands thee wast no more,
In Loves delights those precious Hours,
Allowed by the Almighty Powers.
To gain th' Hesperian Shore,
And Ruined Troy restore.

**AEN:** Joves Commands shall be Obey'd,
To Night our Anchors shall be weighed,
But ah! what Language can I try,
My Injured Queen to pacify.
No sooner she resignes her Heart,
But from her Armes I'm forc't to part.
How can so hard a Fate be took,
On Night enjoy'd, the next forsook.
Your be the blame, ye Gods, for I
Obey your will—but with more
Ease cou'd dye.

## ■ Act III

### Scene the Ships.

(*Enter the Saylors.*)

(*The Sorceress and her Inchanteress.*)

**CHO:** Come away fellow Saylors, your Anchors be weighing,
Time and Tide will admit no delaying.
Take a Bouze short leave of your Nymphs on the Shore,
And Silence their Morning,
With vows of returning.
But never intending to Visit them more.

**SORC:** See the Flags and Streamers Curling,
Anchors weighing, Sails unfurling,
Phoebus pale deluding Beames,
Guilding more deceitful Streams.
Our Plot has took,
The Queen forsook, ho, ho, ho.
Elisas ruin'd, ho, ho, ho,
Our next motion

Must be to storme her Lover on the Ocean.
From the Ruines of others our pleasure we borrow,
Elisas bleeds to Night, and Carthage Flames tomorrow.

**CHO:** Destruction our delight, delight our greatest Sorrow,
Elisas dyes to Night, and Carthage Flames to Morrow.

(*Enter Dido, Belinda, and Train.*)

**DIDO:** Your Councel all is urged in vain,
To Earth and Heaven I will Complain.
To Earth and Heaven why do I call,
Earth and Heaven conspire my Fall.
To Fate I Sue, of other means bereft,
The only refuge for the wretched left.

**BEL:** See Madam where the Prince appears,
Such Sorrow in his Looks he bears,
As you'd convince you still he's true,

*Æneas Enters.*

**AEN:** What shall lost Æneas do.
How Royal fair shall I impart,
The Gods decree and tell you we must part.

**DIDO:** Thus on the fatal Banks of Nile,
Weeps the deceitful Crocodile.
Thus Hypocrites that Murder Act,
Make Heavens and Gods the Authors of the Fact.

**AEN:** By all that's good,

**DIDO:** By all that's good no more,
All that's good you have Forsworn.
To your promised Empire fly,
And let forsaken Dido dye.

**AEN:** In spite of Joves Command I stay,
Offend the Gods, and Love obey.

**DIDO:** No faithless Man thy course pursue,
I'm now resolved as well as you.
No Repentance shall reclaim,
The Injured Dido's lighted Flame.
For 'tis enough what e're you now decree,
That you had once a thought of leaving me.

**AEN:** Let Jove say what he will I'le stay.

**DIDO:** Away.

(*Exit Aen.*)

To Death I'le fly, if longer you delay.
But Death, alas? I cannot Shun,
Death must come when he is gone.

**CHO:** Great minds against themselves Conspire,
And shun the Cure they most desire.

**DIDO:** Thy Hand Belinda—darkness shades me,
On thy Bosom let me rest,
More I wou'd but Death invades me.
Death is now a Welcom Guest,
When I am laid in Earth may my wrongs Create,
No trouble in thy Breast,
Remember me, but ah! forget my Fate.

**CHO:** With drooping Wings you Cupids come,
To scatter Roses on her Tomb.
Soft and Gentle as her Heart,
Keep here your Watch and never part.

*Finis.*

# L'Heure Espagnole (1911)
## The Spanish Hour

MUSIC BY MAURICE RAVEL ■ LIBRETTO BY FRANC-NOHAIN

This one-act *comédie musicale*, set to a libretto by Maurice Etienne (written under Etienne's pen name, Franc-Nohain), premiered at the Opéra-Comique in Paris on May 19, 1911. The story is set in eighteenth-century Toledo at the shop of Torquemada, the clock-maker. Ramiro, a muleteer, brings an old watch to Torquemada for repair. Concepción, Torquemada's wife, reminds her husband to check all of the town clocks as he does every Thursday. Torquemada leaves and asks Ramiro to wait for him to return. This angers Concepción, who is waiting for her liaison with Gonzalve, her young lover. She asks Ramiro to carry a heavy Catalan clock upstairs for her. Gonzalve enters and recites poems to her. She tells him how much she has looked forward to seeing him again. When Ramiro returns, she asks him to go back upstairs, bring the first clock down and take a second one upstairs in its place. When Ramiro leaves the room, she hides her lover inside the second clock. The situation becomes further complicated when Inigo Gomez, an influential banker, arrives. He is also an admirer of hers, but she is very upset by his arrival on the scene. Ramiro enters with the first clock and puts the second clock, with Gonzalve hiding inside, on his shoulder with no effort. This time Concepción goes upstairs with him as Gomez hides inside the first clock in order to trick her. Ramiro comes back with Concepción, who is annoyed that her lover is all talk and no action. She tells Ramiro that the clock in her bedroom is too noisy and asks him to bring it downstairs once more. Gomez decides to tell Concepción that he loves her. Once the clock he is in has been carried to the bedroom, he finds himself too fat to get out from the clock! Concepción, thoroughly disgusted by her two lovers, decides to leave them shut in their respective clocks and retires with Ramiro, whom she has grown to admire immensely. Her erstwhile lovers escape their clocks at last, but they stay in the shop too long and are discovered by Torquemada. They pretend that they are customers; he pretends to believe their story and sells them the two clocks, though he of course knows the truth. The story ends as Torquemada informs his wife that they no longer have the two clocks. She answers that it doesn't matter because Ramiro will come by every day to tell the time!

---

*La boutique d'un horloger espagnol, port au fond a gauche, large fenêtre au fond au milieu, a gauche escalier menant a l'appartement de CONCEPCION, a droite au premier plan deux grandes horloges catalanes c'est a dire normandes, ça et là des automates: un oiseau des îles, un petit coq, des marionettes a musiques—Au lever du rideau, TORQUEMADA, le dos tourné au public, est assis devant son établi. On entend les balanciers qui s'agitent, et toutes les pendules de la boutique sonnent des heures différentes.*

*The shop of a spanish clockmaker; a door at the back left, a large window at the back center, at the left a staircase leading to the apartment of Concepcion; to the right on the first floor two large Catalan clocks, i, e., Norman, here and there some automatics; a bird of passage, a little rooster, some musical marionettes —. At the rising of the curtain. Torquemada, his back to the audience, is seated before his store. The movement of pendulums is heard, and all the clocks in the shop strike different hours.*

## SCENE I

**RAMIRO** (*entrant*). Senor Torquemada, horloger de Tolède.

**TORQUEMADA:** Torquemada, c'est moi, Monsieur.

**RAMIRO:** Ma montre, à chaque instant s'arrête.

**TORQUEMADA:** Voilà qui va des mieux, voilà qui va des mieux.

**RAMIRO:** Or, je suis à votre service,
Muletier du gouvernement
Connaitre l'heure exactement
En conséquence est mon office

## SCENE I

**RAMIRO:** (*entering*). Señor Torquemada, clockmaker of Toledo!

**TORQUEMADA:** Torquemada, that's me, Monsieur!

**RAMIRO:** My watch stops every second.

**TORQUEMADA:** Here is one that will go better.

**RAMIRO:** I'm at your service,
A muleteer in government employ,
Consequently, it behooves me to know
Always the exact time;

Car chaque jour, a heure fixe
Mes mulete doivent, sur leur dos,
Emporter les colis postaux.

**TORQUEMADA:** Voyons la montre
(*Il la prend et l'examine*).
Elle est de style!

**RAMIRO:** (*gravement*). Oui c'est un bijou de famille,
Mon oncle, le toréador,
Par elle fut sauvè des cornes de la mort.
Aux arènes de Barcelone
Alors que le taureau fonçait,
Cette montre en son gousset,
Le prèserva du coup de corne;
Mais si le monstre par la montre fut arrêté
C'est a présent la montre qui s'arrête.

**TORQUEMEDA:** Nous allons donc la démonter

**CONCEPCION:** (*Dans la coulisse*). Totor!

**TORQUEMEDA:** On m'appelle...ma femme...Totor est de Torquemeda,
Le diminutif plein de charme

For each day at a set hour,
My mules must carry, on their backs,
The parcels of mail.

**TORQUEMADA:** Let us see the watch.
(*He takes it and examines it*).
Quite stylish.

**RAMIRO:** (*gravely*).
Yes, it is a family treasure.
My uncle, the toreador,
Was saved by it from the horns of death.
In the arena of Barcelona
While the bull was rushing upon him,
This watch, in the gusset of his shirt,
Saved him from the thrust of the horn;
But if the beast was then stopped by the watch,
It is now the watch which stops itself.

**TORQUEMADA:** Now we'll take it apart.

**CONCEPCION:** (*Behind the scenes*). Totor!

**TORQUEMADA:** My wife . . . calls me . . .
'Totor' is the charming pet name
Formed from Torquemada.

## SCENE II

CONCEPCION: (*entrant*). Eh!
quoi! vous n'êtes point parti?
L'étourderie est sans égale!
Vous souvient il plus
qu'aujourd'hui
Il faut aller régler comme chaque
jeudi
Les horloges municipales?

TORQUEMADA: Mais quelle
heure est il done?

RAMIRO: Comment?

TORQUEMADA: Que voulez vous!
Les horloges, Monsieur, on
n'entend plus leurs coups:
Ce serait a devenir fou!

CONCEPCION: (*Montrant les
horloges*). Pourquoi, depuis que je
vous en réclame une pour ma
chambre a coucher
Garder ici ces deux horloges catalanes!

TORQUEMADA: Si vous croyez
que c'est léger,
Une horloge, et facile a prendre!

CONCEPCION: (*Avec un mépris
très significatif et a mi-voix*). De
force musculaire, oui, vous avez sujet
De vous montrer avare, ou du
moins. ménager:
Vous n'en avez pas a revendre!
(*Haut*).
Mais plus longtemps ne faites pas
attendre
Les balanciers municipaux.

TORQUEMADA: (*S'apprêtant a
sortir*). J'ai mes outils? J'ai mon
chapeau?

RAMIRO: (*intervenant*). Pardon
. . . Monsieur. . . pardon. . . ma montre? . . .

TORQUEMADA: Je cours, mon
cher Monsieur, je cours
Demeurez jusqu'a mon retour!

CONCEPCION: (*àpart*). Voilà qui
ne fait pas mon compte!

TORQUEMADA: Excusez moi. Je
reviens de ce pas:
L'heure officielle n'attend pas.
(*Il sort*).

## SCENE III

CONCEPCION: Il reste, voilà bien
ma chance!
Le jour de la semaine où mon époux
est loin,
Mon unique jour de vacances,
Me sera t'il gâté par ce fâcheux
tèmoin?

RAMIRO: (*a part*). Il faut pourtant
qu'avec la senora je cause.
Mais . . . de quoi diable lui parler?
J'aurais mieux fait de m'en aller,
Car je n'ai jamais su dire aux
femmes des choses . . .

## SCENE II

CONCEPCION: (*entering*).
Eh! What, not yet gone?
This carelessness passes belief!
Have you forgotten that today,
Like every Thursday, it is necessary
to go
To regulate the municipal clocks?

TORQUEMADA: What time is it
then?

RAMIRO: Pardon?

TORQUEMADA: The clocks, Monsieur, their strokes are no longer audible.
It will drive me mad.

CONCEPCION: (*Pointing to the
clocks*). Why should you keep here
those two Catalan clocks,
After I have already asked for one
for my bedroom?

TORQUEMADA: Perhaps you
think it is light,
Perhaps you think it is easy to carry
a clock.

CONCEPCION: (*With very signifi-
cant and half-expressed scorn*).
Ay, you have reason to show your
miserliness
Of your muscles, or at least, to hus-
band them;
You've none to spare!
(*Aloud*).
But do not keep waiting any longer
The municipal pendulums.

TORQUEMADA: (*Getting ready
to go out*). Have I my tools, my hat?

RAMIRO: (*Interrupting*). Pardon,
Monsieur, my watch.

TORQUEMADA: I am in haste,
Monsieur, I run,
And you wait here till I return!

CONCEPCION: (*aside*). This did
not enter in my calculation.

TORQUEMADA: Excuse me, I'll
return directly
The official clock must not wait.
(*Exit*)

## SCENE III

CONCEPTION: He remains, Now's
my chance.
My husband's day away from home.
My only day of liberty.
Will it be ruined by this annoying
witness?

RAMIRO: (*aside*). I ought to speak
with this woman.
But what the devil can I speak
about?
I had done better had I gone away.
For I never did know how to talk to
women . . .

CONCEPCION: (*Hésitante, mon-
trant a RAMIRO une des deux
Horloges*). Cette horloge, Mon-
sieur, la jugez vous d'un poids
Tel, pour la déplacer, qu'il faille
L'effort de deux hommes ou trois?

RAMIRO: Ca, Madame?
C'est une paille,
C'est une coquille de noix,
On lève ça avec un doigt,
C'est de la très petite ouvrage.
Votre chambre?

CONCEPCION: Au premier
étage . . . Mais.

RAMIRO: Je vais l'y porter!

CONCEPCION: Quoi! vous consen-
tiriez?

RAMIRO: C'est dit, senora , je m'en
charge!

CONCEPCION: Je n'osais pas vous
en prier!

RAMIRO: Il fallait oser au con-
traire!
Tout muletier a dans son coeur
Un déménageur amateur
Et voilà qui va me distraire
En attendant votre mari.

CONCEPCION: Je suis confuse!

RAMIRO: Celà m'amuse!

CONCEPCION: (*a art*). Tout
s'arrange fort bien ainsi!
(*Haut*).
L'escalier est au fonds du couloir
que voici . . .
Vraiment, Monsieur, vraiment,
j'abuse!

RAMIRO: C'est moi, senora qui
m'excuse:
Je fais si piètre mine, Hélas! dans un
salon! . . .
Les muletiers n'ont pas de conversation
(*On entend vocaliser GONZALVE
dans la coulisse, RAMIRO sort,
emportant l'horloge sur son
épaule*).

## SCENE IV

CONCEPCION: (*Qui quette a la
fenêtre*). Il était temps voici Gonzalve!

GONZALVE: Enfin revient le jour
si doux
Harpes, chantez, éclatez salves!
Enfin revient le jour si doux,
Le jour où d'un époux jaloux,
Ma maitresse n'est plus l'esclave.

CONCEPCION: (*passionément*).
Gonzalve! Gonzalve! Gonzalve!

GONZALVE: Enfin revient le jour
si doux . . .

CONCEPCION: Oui mon
ami . . . Dépêchons nous,
Ne perdons pas, à de vaines paroles
L'heure qui s'envole,
Et qu'il faut cueillir.

CONCEPTION: (*hesitating, showing RAMIRO one of the two
clocks*). This clock, Monsieur, do
you think it has such a weight
That, to move it, would require
The labor of two or three men?

RAMIRO: This Madame?
Why it is a straw.
It is a nutshell,
One could lift it with a finger.
A trifling bit of work.
Your room?

CONCEPTION: On the first floor.
But . . .

RAMIRO: I'll carry it.

CONCEPTION: How! Would you
do it?

RAMIRO: It is said, señora, I'll do
it.

CONCEPTION: I never dared to ask
you.

RAMIRO: It would be necessary to
dare the contrary.
Every muleteer is in his heart
An amateur mover of household
goods.
With that I'll occupy myself, while
I await your husband.

CONCEPTION: I am confused.

RAMIRO: This amuses me.

CONCEPTION: (*aside*). Everything works well this way.
(*Aloud*).
The staircase is at the end of the passageway.
Indeed, Monsieur, I am imposing
upon you.

RAMIRO: It is I, señora, I beg your
pardon
For making so pitiful a face. Alas! In
a parlor
Muleteers are a crude lot.
(*GONZALVE is heard singing in
the passageway*).
(*Exit RAMIRO carrying the clock
up on his shoulder*).

## SCENE IV

CONCEPTION: (*Who is watching
at the window*) It was time, there is
Gonzalve!

GONZALVE: At last the sweet day
returns,
Sing, harps, burst into praise!
At last the sweet day returns,
The day that my mistress is no long-
er
The slave to a jealous husband.

CONCEPTION: (*passionately*).
Gonzalve! Gonzalve! Gonzalve!

GONZALVE: At last the sweet day
returns!

CONCEPTION: Ay my friend. Let
us make haste
Let us not lose, to vain words,
The fleeting hour.
The hour which must be plucked,

# Scene IV

GONZALVE: (*déclamant*).
L'email de ces cadrans dont s'orne ta demeure,
C'est le jardin de mon bonheur émaillé d'heures,
Que l'on voit éclore et fleurir . . .

CONCEPCION: (*impatiente*).
Oui, mon ami . . .
(*At part*).
Le muletier va revenir . . .

GONZALVE: Cette image est trè poétique.
J'en veux faire un sonnet et le mettre en musique
"Le Jardin des Heures . . ." sonnet!

CONCEPCION: (*àpart*). Si le muletier revenait! . . .
(*Haut*).
Oui, mon ami, mais profitons de l'heure unique . . .
Tiens, sens, comme battait mon coeur en l'attendant!

GONZALVE: (*déclamant*). Horloge, c'est ton coeur, le rythme en est le même.
Ton coeur ballant, ton coeur battant,
Que, mélancolique, on entend . . .
"Le Coeur de l'Horloge . . ." poème!

CONCEPCION: (*àpart*). Le muletier va revenir dans un instant!
(*Haut*).
Oui mon, ami, mais vois, le temps s'achève,
Où réaliser le doux rêve.

GONZALVE: (*distrait*). La, la, la, la, . . . La, la, la, la.

CONCEPCION: Après lequel nous soupirons.

GONZALVE: Les baisers qu'appellent tes lèvres
Egrèneront leurs carillons!

CONCEPCION: (*excédée*). Oh!
(*À mi-voix*).
Mon ami . . . Oui, mon ami,
Mais l'heure fuit, prends garde.
Le temps nous est mesuré sans pitié!

GONZALVE: "Le Carillon des Armours" . . . sérénade.

CONCEPCION: (*Avec dépit, apercevant RAMIRO qui revient*). Et puis, voici le muletier.

## SCENE V

RAMIRO: C'est fait! l'horloge est a sa place,

CONCEPCION: Déjà? Ah! Monsieur, que de grâces!
(*À part*).
Il n'y a pas à dire, il faut
Que' à nouveau
Je m'en débarrasse!
(*Haut*).
Vous allez me trouver bien folle,

---

GONZALVE: (*pompously*). The enamel of these dials, gracing your home,
Is the garden of my happiness enamelled with hours,
Blooming and bursting into flower.

CONCEPTION: (*impatiently*). Ay, my friend . . .
(*Aside*)
The muleteer will return.

GONZALVE: This image is very poetic.
I will make of it a sonnet, and set it to music
"The Garden of Hours', a sonnet!

CONCEPTION: (*aside*). If the Muleteer returned! . . .
(*Aloud*)
Ay, my friend, but let us profit by the single hour —
Come, feel the impatient beating of my heart.

GONZALVE: (*pompously*). The clock, that is your heart, its rhythm is the same,
Your dancing heart, your beating heart,
Which, melancholy, is heard —
"The Heart of the Clock." A poem . . .

CONCEPTION: (*Aside*). The muleteer will return in an instant —
(*Aloud*).
Ay, my friend, but see, the time is here,
To realize the sweet dream . . .

GONZALVE: (*distracted*). La, la, la, la, — La, la, la, la, —

CONCEPTION: For which we are sighing, longing.

GONZALVE: The kisses which your lips call forth,
Will evoke their chimes!

CONCEPTION: (*Beside herself*).
Oh . . .
(*In a low voice*)
Oh, my friend . . . Yes, my friend,
But the hour is passing, take care,
Time is doled out to us pitilessly!

GONZALVE: "The Chime of Loves" . . . A serenade

CONCEPTION: (*With vexation, perceiving the returning RAMIRO*). And now, here's the muleteer.

## SCENE V

RAMIRO: It is done. The clock is in its place.

CONCEPTION: Already? Ah! Monsieur, I thank you
(*Aside*).
There is nothing left to say,
I must
Rid myself of him! (*Aloud*). I fear,
Monsieur, you'll think me silly,
I know not how to confess it to you.

---

cher Monsieur,
Comment vous faire cet aveu?
Donc, à peine étiez vous parti
Avec l'horloge vers ma chambre,
(*Montrant l'autre horloge*).
J'ai réfléchi
Que celle ci
Y serait mieux . . .
Que vous en semble?

RAMIRO: Senora, c'est votre plaisir?
Je suis tout a votre service!

CONCEPCION: Tant d'indulgence à mon caprice!
Ah! Monsieur, je me sens rougir!

RAMIRO: Voilà
C'est celle ci, à l'instant que j'emporte . . .

CONCEPCION: (*vivement*)
Quand vous aurez remporté l'autre! . . .
Quelle courtoisie est la votre! . . .
Vous êtes un vrai paladin.

GONZALVE: C'est ainsi que ton coeur, éternel féminin,
Apparait plus mouvant que les plis d'une jupe!
"Caprice de Femme" . . . Chanson!

RAMIRO: (*s'éloignant*). Moi, ca m'est égal ça m'occupe.

GONZALVE: (*Lui lancant un regard dédaigneux*). Le muletiers n'ont pas de conversation.

## SCENE VI

CONCEPCION: (*Ouvrant précipitamment le coffre de Phorlage*). Maintenant, pas de temps a perde!
Là dedans, vite, il faut entrer!

GONZALVE: (*tragique*).
Dans cette boite de cyprés,
De sapin, de chêne, ou de cêdre?

CONCEPCION: Oui, c'est fou je te le concéde,
Mais céde!
Songe donc, ici de nous voir
En tête-a-tête, nul espoir!
Car le muletier à l'oeil noir
Se dresse entre nous, et je tremble!
Au contraire, sans le savoir,
L'horloge et toi, tous deux ensemble,
Il vous emporte dans ma chambre!

GONZALVE: Il me plait de franchir ton seuil,
Entre ces planches clos, comme dans un cercueil . . .
J'y goterai des sensations neuves,
(*Il s'installe dans l'horloge*).
Et cette horloge ou m'enferme le sort,
O mon amante, est-ce pas une épreuve
De l'amour plus fort
Que la mort?

---

For, hardly had you left
With the clock for my room
(*Pointing to the other clock*).
When I thought
That this one would be better.
What think you of it?

RAMIRO: Señora. That is your pleasure?
I am entirely at your service!

CONCEPTION: So much patience with my whims!
Ah, Monsieur, I feel that I am blushing.

RAMIRO: There
This one here, when I bring the other one . . .

CONCEPTION: (*vivaciously*).
When you will have brought the other one! . . .
How courteous you are!
Indeed you are a Paladin.

GONZALVE: Such always is your heart, eternal feminine,
More ephemeral than the folds of a skirt!
"Capriciousness of Women." A Song!

RAMIRO: (*moving away*). To me it is all the same, it keeps me busy . . .

GONZALVE: (*Throwing after him a disdainful glance*). Muleteers are a dumb lot!

## SCENE VI

CONCEPTION: (*Suddenly opening the chest of the clock*). Now we've no time to lose!
Quick, you must go in there!

GONZALVE: (*tragically*). In this box of cypress,
Pine, oak, or cedar?

CONCEPTION: It is silly, I admit,
But yield to me!
For think, were we to be seen here, all alone,
Then we were hopeless!
For the black-eyed muleteer,
Stands between us, and I tremble!
On the contrary, without knowing it,
He'll carry the clock and you, both together, into my room.

GONZALVE: It pleases me to cross your threshold,
Between closed boards, as in a coffin,
There I shall taste new sensations
(*He gets into the clock*).
And this clock, in which I am enclosed by Fate,
Oh, my beloved, is this a test of love,
Stronger than death?

CONCEPCION: (*Sombre et tragique*). Oui, mon ami . . .
(*A part*).
Il exagère!

## SCENE VII

DON INIGO GOMEZ: (*Passant devant la fenêtre*). Salut à la belle horlogère!

CONCEPCION: (*Fermant brusquement l'horloge*). Don Inigo Gomez!
Qui peut ici lui plaire?

INIGO: Sournoise qui le demanda!
Eh! le seigneur Torquemada
Ne serait il pas chez l'Alcade?

CONCEPCION: Vous voulez le voir?

INIGO: Dieu m'en garde!
Aurais je s'il n'était parti,
Pris le chemin de sa boutique?
Moi qui, précisément, usai de mon crédit
Pour faire confier á cet heureux mari
Le soin des horloges publiques?
Car il est raisonnable, il est juste, il est bon
Que l'époux ait dehors une occupation
Régulière et périodique

CONCEPCION: Don Inigo Gomez est un seigneur puissant!

INIGO: Que ma puissance apparait vaine,
Si, quand son mari est absent,
Certaine belle me consent
A se montrer un peu moins inhumaine
Vous seule pouvez tout!
(*Il veut lui prendre la main*).

CONCEPCION: (*se dégageant*).
Excusez moi, seigneur!
(*Avec un regard inquiet sur l'horloge où se cache GONZALVE*).
Parlez plus bas . . . les horloges ont des oreilles!

INIGO: (*plaintif*). J'attends de votre arrêt l'excès de mon malheur . . .
(*Résolu*).
Ou félicité sans pareille!
(*Il la presse, elle se dégage encore. On voit poindre l'extrémité de l'horloge que RAMIRO rapporte sur son epaule*).

CONCEPCION: (*Dans la plus grande agitation*). Seigneur, excusez moi!
J'ai les déménageurs!

## SCENE VIII

RAMORI: (*posant l'horloge*). Voilà!
Et maintenant à l'autre!
(*Il va pour prendre la 2ème horloge dans laquelle est enfermé GONZALVE*).

---

CONCEPTION: (*Somber and tragic*). Ay, my friend.
(*Aside*).
He exaggerates.

## SCENE VII

DON INIGO GOMAZ: (*Passing before, the window*). Hail to the beautiful wife of the clockmaker!

CONCEPTION: (*Closing brusquely the clock*). Don Inigo Gomez! Who can be here of service?

INIGO: Sly woman, that you ask! Eh! Signor Torquemada, Is he not at the Alcada?

CONCEPTION: You want to see him?

INIGO: God forbid! Would I have taken the road to his shop, Had he not gone? I, who used my influence, To secure for this happy husband the care Of the public clocks? For it is reasonable, it is just, it is good, That the husband have an outside occupation, That is regular and constant.

CONCEPTION: Don Inigo Gomez is a powerful gentleman.

INIGO: How useless would my power appear If, in the absence of her husband, A certain beautiful woman did not consent To show herself, a bit more human. You alone can do all! (*He tries to take her hand*).

CONCEPTION: (*Disengaging herself*). Excuse me, seigneur! (*With an anxious look at the clock wherein GONZALVE is hiding*). Speak lower . . . Clocks have ears.

INIGO: (*pleadingly*). I expect from your decision a great misfortune. (*Resolutely*). Or matchless happiness! (*He presses her, she again disengages herself. The end of the clock, which RAMIRO carries on his shoulder, is seen to break*).

CONCEPTION: (*With great agitation*). Excuse me, signor! Today I have the movers of furniture!

## SCENE VIII

RAMIRO: (*Setting down the clock*). There! And now for the other one! (*He goes to fetch the second clock in which GONZALVE is enclosed*).

---

CONCEPCION: Celle ci est peut être un peu . . .
Je vous préviens . . . un peu plus lourde . . .

RAMIRO: (*Chargeant la 2ème horloge sur son épaule*). Peuh!
C'est seulement que l'on dirait que ça ballette . . .
Mais ça n'en est pas plus ardu . . .
C'est moins le poids, ces objets là que le volume,
Car, pour le poids, c'est un fétu,
C'est une plume! . . .
(*Il fait passer l'horloge d'une épaule à l'autre avec une aisance prodigieuse*).
On porte ça, les bras tendus,
Des combles jusqu'à la cave . . .

CONCEPCION: (*à part*). Cet homme a des muscles de fer!
Mais s'il secoue ainsi Gonzalve,
Il finira par lui donner le mal de mer . . .
Je vous accompagne . . .

RAMIRO: (*s'eloignant*). Inutile!

INIGO: Quoi! faut il que vous me quittiez?

CONCEPCION: (*à INIGO*). Le mécanisme est très fragile,
Et notamment le balancier . . .
J'en demande pardon a votre Seigneurie! . . .
(*Elle s'éloigne*).

## SCENE IX

INIGO: Evidemment, elle me congédie,
Et s'il me fallait écouter
Les conseils de ma dignité,
J'abandonnerais la partie . . .
Cependant je n'ai qu'une envie,
Et cette envie est de rester!
Dans ces conjonctures extrêmes
Un amant, pensèje, avec art
S'introduirait dans un placard:
Tant pis, ma foi, si je déroge!
Je conçois à l'instant le fantasque projet
De me cacher
Dans cette horloge
Ces horloges sont les placards des horlogers.
(*Il s'introduit avec effort dans l'horloge trop étroit pour sa corpulence*).
Ma mine imposante et sévère
A la pauvrette faisait pour.
Montrons un autre caractère
Conforme a sa galante humeur,
Et que nous sommes, au contraire,
Dans le fond, un petit farceur!
(*Il entend des pas*).
Elle revient . . . coucou
(*RAMIRO parait. INIGO referme brusquement l'horloge*).

---

CONCEPTION: This one is perhaps a little bit . . .
I warn you . . . a little bit heavier . . .

RAMIRO: (*Taking the second clock up on his shoulder*). Pheu! It is only, as one would say, that it is not steady,
But it is no heavier . . .
It is less their weight, these objects, than their size,
For, as for the weight, it is a trifle.
It is a feather! . . .
(*He shifts the clock from one shoulder to the other with a tremendous nonchalance*).
It is thus, with outstretched arms, one carries,
Heaps of goods to the cellars.

CONCEPTION: (*Aside*). This man has iron muscles!
But if thus he tosses Gonzalve,
He'll end by making him so dizzy,
I'll go with you . . .

RAMIRO: (*moving off*). It is not necessary.

INIGO: How? Must you leave me?

CONCEPTION: (*To INIGO*). The mechanism is very fragile,
Especially the pendulum . . .
I beg your Highness' pardon! . . .
(*She goes off*).

## SCENE IX

INIGO: Evidently, I am dismissed,
And if I were to heed the Counsels of my dignity,
I should abandon the business . . .
Meanwhile, I have but one desire And that is to remain.
In these extreme positions,
A lover would, artfully,
Conceal himself in a cupboard:
So much the worse, my soul, if I demean myself.
I conceive this instant the fantastic scheme
Of hiding myself
In this clock.
These clocks are the cupboards of the clockmakers.
(*He squeezes himself, with great effort, into the clock, which is too narrow for his corpulence*).
My stern and pompous bearing Scared the poor little woman.
I'll assume another manner,
More suited to her passionate temper
And show her that I am, at bottom Something of a wag.
(*He hears a step*).
She is returning . . . coucou . . .
(*RAMIRO appears. INIGO closes the clock brusquely*).

## SCENE X

*(RAMIRO seul, INIGO dans l'horloge).*

RAMIRO: Voilà ce que j'appelle une femme charmante!
Maintenant elle me demande
De venir garder la boutique
Voilà qui est bien compris et pratique,
Et c'est ainsi qu'une maitresse de maison
A chaque visiteur doit assigner un rôle
En rapport avec ses facons,
Moi, ma facon . . . c'est mes épaules!
Quand je vois ici rassemblés
Toutes ces machines subtiles.
Tous ces ressorts menus, â plaisir embroillés,
Je songe au mécanisme qu'est
La femme mécanisme autrement compliqué
S'y reconnaitre est difficile!
A Dieu ne plaise aussi que je m'arroge
Le soin minutieux d'en toucher les resserts.
Tout le talent que m'a donné le sort
Se borne a porter des horloges . . .

## SCENE XI

CONCEPCION: *(Accourant vers RAMIRO).* Monsieur! Ah! Monsieur!
*(A part).*
Dans ma gorge
Les mots s'arrêtent de dépit
*(Haut).*
Traitez moi de folle, tant pis
Mais comment voulez vous qu'en ma chambre je garde
Une horloge qui va, Monsieur, tout de travers,
*(Douloureusement).*
Quel martyre affreux pour mes nerfs!

RAMIRO: La rapporter, ca me regarde . . .
A tout à l'heure!

## SCENE XII

INIGO: *(Entrouvant l'horloge, à mi-voix).*
Enfin, il part!
Dieu! que ces muletiers sont de fâcheux bavards! . . .
*(Haut).*
Coucou . . .
*(A part).*
Amusons cette belle! . . .
*(Haut).*
Coucou . . .

CONCEPCION: *(Se retournant vers l'horloge dont INIGO a refermé aussitôt la porte sur lui).* Tiens, l'horloge . . .

## SCENE X

*(RAMIRO alone, INIGO in the clock).*

RAMIRO: That's what I call a charming woman!
Now she asks me to watch the shop;
A good and practical woman,
And besides a capable manager,
To assign to each visitor a role
Conforming to his talents.
I . . . my talents . . . are my shoulders!
When I see here assembled
All these subtle machines,
All these slender springs, wound for pleasure,
I think of the mechanism which is
Woman, a mechanism far more complex,
To know which were difficult!
It would displease God mightily
Were I to tamper
In the slightest with those springs.
All the talent that Fate has given me
Is limited to the carrying of clocks . . .

## SCENE XI

CONCEPTION: *(Running toward RAMIRO).* Monsieur! Ah! Monsieur!
*(Aside).*
The words are stopped in my throat
From vexation.
*(Aloud).*
Treat me as a fool,
So much the worse, but how do you expect me
To keep in my room a clock in which, Monsieur,
Everything goes wrong?
*(Mournfully).*
What a terrible trial for my nerves!

RAMIRO: To carry it again, that means me . . .
Presently . . .

## SCENE XII

INIGO: *(Slightly opening the clock, in an undertone).* At last, he's gone.
God! What nuisances these muleteers are!
*(Aloud).*
Coucou . . .
*(Aside).*
Let's have some fun with this beauty.
*(Aloud).*
Coucou . . .

CONCEPTION: *(Returning toward the clock in which INIGO has closed the door).* Ah, the clock . . .

INIGO: *(Même jou).* Coucou . . .

CONCEPCION: *(rageuse).* L'allusion est de haut goût, par Saint Jacques de Compostelle!
Et le moment est bien choisi
Pour parler de coucou ici! . . .

INIGO: *(Même jou).* Coucou . . .

CONCEPCION: *(apercevant INIGO).* Don Inigo!

INIGO: Coucou! . . . Coucou! . . .
*(Noblement).*
Oui dà vous avez devant vous
Don Inigo Gomez, roi de la haute banque!
Et même y serais-je à genoux,
Si ce n'était que la place me manque..

CONCEPCION: Cessez ce jou, Don Inigo, vous êtes. fou!

INIGO: Oui, fou de toi, ô ma jolie.
Fou a faire mille folies!
Ceci n'est qu'un commencement,
Un tout petit exercice d'entrainment!

CONCEPCION: Mais je n'en veux point davantage!
Tenez vous en là simplement!
Et sortez, je vous y engage,
De ce bizarre logement!

INIGO: Eh quoi! lorsque j'eus de peine,
Tant de peine à entrer, faut il déjà sortir?
Où il y eut beaucoup de gêne,
On mérite un peu de plaisr!
Manqué je à votre fantaisie,
De jeunesse, de poésie?
Trop de jeunesse aussi a son mauvais côté,
Un jeune homme est souvent inexpérimenté!

CONCEPCION: *(nostalgique).* En vérité! . . . en vérité!

INIGO: Un rien l'arrête et l'embarasse!
Et les poètes, affairés
A poursuivre un rêve éthéré,
Oublient que la réalité sous leur nez passe . . .

CONCEPCION: *(Avec une conviction navrée).* Si vous saviez combien vous dites vrai! . . .

INIGO: Un amant comme moi offre plus de surface!

## SCENE XIII

RAMIRO: *(entrant avec l'horloge où est enfermé GONZALVE).* Voilà l'objet! Que faut il que j'en fasse?

CONCEPCION: *(indifférente).* Ah! l'horloge! . . .
C'est bon! . . . Merci! . . . mettez ça là . . .

INIGO: *(Still in fun).* Coucou . . .

CONCEPTION: *(Raging).* The allusion is in good taste, by St. Jacques de Compostelle!
And the moment is well chosen
To speak here of cuckoos!

INIGO: *(Still in fun).* Coucou . . .

CONCEPTION: *(perceiving INIGO).* Don Inigo!

INIGO: Coucou! Coucou!
*(Nobly).*
Yes, you have before you,
Don Inigo Gomez, king of the upper bench!
I would be there, even on my knees,
If it were not that there were no room.

CONCEPTION: Quit this fooling, Don Inigo, you are crazy!

INIGO: Crazy for you my pretty one.
Enough to commit a thousand follies.
This is but a beginning,
Just a little exercise . . .

CONCEPTION: But I want no more of it!
Be satisfied with that!
and leave, I beseech you,
This strange prison.

INIGO: And how? After I had gone to so much pain,
Such trouble to go in, must I go out already?
After so much uneasiness,
One deserves a bit of pleasure!
Do I lack, for your fancy,
Youth, poetry?
Too much of youth has too its evil side,
A young man is often inexperienced.

CONCEPTION: *(Despairingly).* True . . . true . . .

INIGO: A trifle halts him and confuses him . . .
And the poets, occupied
In pursuing a flimsy dream,
Forget that reality is beneath their nose.

CONCEPTION: *(With broken-hearted desperation).* If you knew how true you spoke!

INIGO: A lover like me offers more breadth!

## SCENE XIII

RAMIRO: *(Entering with the clock in which GONZALVE is enclosed).* Here it is. Now what must I do with it?

CONCEPTION: *(Indifferently).*
Ah! The clock!
Well! Thanks! Place it there.

**RAMIRO:** (*après avoir posé l'horloge, montrant celle d'''INIGO*). Et maintenant, c'est celle là
Que dans votre chambre l'on place?

**CONCEPCION:** (*troublée*). Dans ma chambre? . . .

**INIGO:** (*par l'horloge entr'ouverte*). Dans votre chambre!

**RAMIRO:** Vous n'avez qu'un mot a dire et je l'enlève!

**CONCEPCION:** (*bas à INIGO*). C'est un guet apens!

**INIGO:** (*bas à CONCEPCION en lui baisant la main*). C'est un rêve! . . .

**RAMIRO:** Est ce dit, senora?

**INIGO:** O ivresse! . . .

**CONCEPCION:** (*se décidant brusquement*). Enlevez! . . .
Mais n'est ce pas plus lourd?

**RAMIRO:** (*chargeant l'horloge sur son épaule*). Goutte d'eau, grain de sable.

**CONCEPCION:** (*le regardant pleine d'admiration, cependant qu'il emporte l'horloge, et INIGO dans cette horloge, avec la plus grande facilité*). A coup sûr cet homme est doué.

## SCENE XIV

**CONCEPCION:** (*ouvrant l'horloge où est GONZALVE*). Ah! vous, n'est ce pas, preste! leste! Trêve aux poèmes étoilés! Vous aller, j'espère filer, Et sans demander votre reste.

**GONZALVE:** (*exstatique*). O impérieuse maîtresse, Laisse!

**CONCEPCION:** (*évasive et rageuse, entre ses dents*). La, la, la, la, la, la, la, la, la.

**GONZALVE:** Je veux graver ici nos chiffres enlacés
Au tour d'un coeur, de flèches transpersé
Comme font emmi les sites sylvestres
Où l'amour complaisant égara leurs baisers.

**CONCEPCION:** (*excédée*). Ah! . . .

**GONZALVE:** Comme font deux amants sur l'écorce des trembles . . .

**CONCEPCION:** Demeurez donc, si bon vous semble,
Mais n'attendez pas, s'il vous plait,
Que j'écoute encore les couplets
De la romance
Qui recommence
Vous avez de l'esprit, mais manquez d'à-propos . . .
J'en ai assez, de vos pipeaux!
(*Elle sort*).

---

**RAMIRO:** (*After having placed it in position, pointing to that in which INIGO is*). And now, that one there Goes into your room?

**CONCEPTION:** (*troubled*). In my room?

**INIGO:** (*Through the slight opening in the clock*). In your room!

**RAMIRO:** You have but to speak, and it shall be done.

**CONCEPTION:** (*Softly, to INIGO*). This is a bad fix.

**INIGO:** (*Low, to CONCEPTION, kissing her hand*). It is a dream.

**RAMIRO:** Well, signora?

**INIGO:** Oh, joy!

**CONCEPTION:** (*Making up her mind brusquely*). Lift it up! But is it not heavier?

**RAMIRO:** (*Placing the clock upon his shoulder*). A drop of water, a grain of sand.

**CONCEPTION:** (*Looking at him, admiringly, while he carries the clock, and INIGO, in this clock, with the greatest ease*). This man is gifted, indeed.

## SCENE XIV

**CONCEPTION:** (*Opening the clock in which GONZALVE is*) Ah, You no? Quick, quick. A truce to starry poems! Quick, let us not lose time, Nor wait.

**GONZALVE:** (*Ecstatically*). O imperious mistress, Leave me!

**CONCEPTION:** (*Evasively and angrily, between her teeth*). La, la, la, la, la, la, la, la.

**GONZALVE:** I am going to cut our monogram,
Around a heart, pierced with arrows.
As the interwined verdure of wild landscapes do,
Wheather passionate love drives their kisses.

**CONCEPTION:** (*Beside herself*). Ah!

**GONZALVE:** As two lovers do on the aspen barks.

**CONCEPTION:** Then stay, if you like it better,
But please do not expect me
To hear more of your couplets,
Of endless romance.
You have enough of spirit, but lack timeliness . . .
I have enough of your bird-calls.
(*Exit*).

---

## SCENE XV

**GONZALVE:** (*seul, dans l'horloge*). En dèpit de cette inhumaine,
Je ne veux pas quitter l'enveloppe de chêne
Où le destin me fit entrer,
Sans évoquer les nymphes des forêts
Qu'emprisonnait une semblable gaîne.
On n'a pas toujours un motif
Pour traiter ce sujet au vif:
"Impressions d'Hamadryade" . . .
(*Il entend revenir RAMIRO*).
Mais prenons garde
Car le muletier revient:
Ces gens là goûtent peu les symboles paiens! . . .

## SCENE XVI

(*GONZALVE, enfermé dans l'horloge, RAMIRO, puis CONCEPCION*).

**RAMIRO:** Voilà ce que j'appelle une femme charmante!
M'avoir si gentiment ce labeur ménagé,
Tantôt emménager, tantôt déménager!
Voilà ce que j'appelle une femme charmante!
Et puis cette boutique est un plaisant séjour;
Entre chaque montée, après chaque descente,
Nul importun, par ses discours,
N'y vient troubler ma quiétude nonchalante
Rien à dire, rien à penser;
On n'a qu'à se laisser bercer
Au tic tac régulier de tous ces balanciers!
Et les timbres de ces pendules
Joyeusement tintinnabulent
Tout ainsi que, par les sentiers Muletiers
Sonnent les grolots de mes mules . . .
Si je devais mon sort changer,
N'étais-je muletier, je serais horloger,
Dans cette horlogerie, avec cette horlogère.

**CONCEPCION:** (*entrant brusquement à RAMIRO*). Monsieur!

**RAMIRO:** L'horloge encor ne fait pas votre affaire?
Bon! Bien! laissez, laissez! je la vais rechercher! . . .
(*Il sort*).

## SCENE XVII

**CONCEPCION:** Oh! la pitoyable aventure!
Et faut il que, de deux amants, L'un manque de tempérament,
Et l'autre, à ce point de nature!
Oh! la pitoyable aventure!
Et ces gens là se disent Espagnols

---

## SCENE XV

**GONZALVE:** (*Alone, in the clock*). Despite this inhuman woman,
I do not want to leave this oaken envelope.
Into which Destiny has ordered me,
Without calling the forest nymphs,
Imprisoned by a similar fate.
There is not always an opportunity
For handling this subject realistically:
"Impressions of Hamadryade . . .
(*He hears RAMIRO returning*).
But let us beware,
For the muleteer is returning:
Those people have little taste for pastoral symbols.

## SCENE XVI

(*GONZALVE in the clock; RAMIRO, then CONCEPTION*).

**RAMIRO:** That's what I call a charming woman!
To have managed so gently this labor,
No sooner planned than moved!
That's what I call a charming woman!
Then this shop is a pleasant place;
After each step, after each trip,
No word of impatience in her speech
Came to trouble my careless quietude.
Nothing to say, nothing to think;
Nothing to do but sleep in peace,
To the regular tictac of the pendulums!
And the sounds of these pendulums
Joyously jingling,
Just as the muleteers,
On the highway, sound the little bells on the mules.
If I could change my fate,
I should not be a muleteer,
I should be a clockmaker,
In this clock-shop, with this women as wife.

**CONCEPTION:** (*Entering brusquely, to RAMIRO*). Monsieur!

**RAMIRO:** The clock does not yet suit?
Well. I'll go see to it. (*Exit*)

## SCENE XVII

**CONCEPTION:** Oh, pitiful adventure!
And is it necessary that of two lovers,
One lacks temperament,
And the other, this natural essential.

## Scene XVII

Dans le pays de dona Sol,
A deux pas de
l'Estramadure! . . .
Le temps me dure, dure,
dure . . .
Oh! la pitoyable aventure!
L'un ne veut mettre ses efforts,
Qu'à composer des vers baroques,
Et l'autre, plus grotesque encor,
De l'horloge n'a pu sortir rien qu'à
mi corps,
Avec son ventre empêtré de brolo-
quez! . . .
Maintenant, le jour va finir.
Et mon époux va revenir:
Et je reste fidèle et pure . . .
A deux pas de l'Estramadure
Au pays du Guadalquivir! . . .
Le temps me dure, dure,
dure! . . .
Ah! pour ma colère passer,
Avoir quelque chose a casser,
A mettre en bouillie, en salade!
(*Elle frappe du poing l'horloge où
est GONZALVE*).

**GONZALVE:** (*entr'ouvrant
l'horloge*). "Impressions
d'Hamadryade" . . .

*Oh, pitiful adventure!
And these people call themselves
Spaniards
In the country of the Sun,
Two steps from Extramadura
Time hangs heavy upon my hands.
Oh, pitiful adventure!
One does not want to take pains,
Except of compose florid verses,
And the other, still more grotesque,
Could come only halfway out of the
clock,
With his belly entangled with trin-
kets,
Now, the day nears its end.
And my husband will return,
And I remain faithful and pure.
Two steps from the Extramadura
In the country of the Guadalquivir!
Time hangs heavy upon my hands.
Ah! To end my anger,
To have something to break,
To smash, to shatter . . .*
(*She smashes her fist into the
clock wherein is GONZALVE*)

**GONZALVE:** (*Slightly opening the
clock*). "Impressions of Hama-
dryad."

## SCENE XVIII

**RAMIRO:** (*rapportant sur son
épaule l'horloge qui renferme INI-
GO*) Voilà! . . .
Et maintenant, senora, je suis prêt à
rementer dans votre chambre
L'autre horloge, si bon vous sem-
ble,
Voire même les deux ensem-
ble . . .
Ce sera comme vous voudrez!

**CONCEPCION:** (*à part*). Quelle
sérénité, quelle aisance il conserve,
Et comme il jongle avec les poids!
Il les soulève, les enlève . . .

**RAMIRO:** Senora, faites votre
choix!

**CONCEPCION:** (*à part*). Et touj-
ours le sourire aux lèvres! . . .
Vraiment cet homme a des biceps
Qui dépassent tous mes con-
cepts . . .
Avec lui, pas de propos mièvres!
(*Haut, très aimable*).
Dans ma chambre, Monsieur, il
vous plait romenter?

**RAMIRO:** Mais laquelle y dois je
porter
De ces horloges?

**CONCEPCION:** (*Simple et nette*).
Sans horloge!
(*Elle sort précédée de RAMIRO*).

## SCENE XVIII

**RAMIRO:** (*Bearing upon his
shoulder the clock enclosing INI-
GO*). There!
And now, senora, I am ready to go
up again to your room.
The other clock
If it suits you,
To see both together,
It will be as you desire.

**CONCEPTION:** (*Aside*). What serenity, what nonchalance,
And, like the juggler with his
weights,
He throws them up, and drops
them..

**RAMIRO:** Senora, make your
choice!

**CONCEPTION:** (*Aside*) And al-
ways with a smile upon his
lips . . .
Truly that man has biceps
Surpassing my conception . . .
His lips frame no sly words.
(*Loud, very amiably*).
Into my room, Monsieur,
Does it please you to go up?

**RAMIRO:** But which of these
clocks
Shall I bring up?

**CONCEPTION:** (*Simply and innocently*). Without the clocks!
(*Exit with RAMIRO leading*).

## SCENE XIX

(*INIGO et GONZALVE chacun
dans son horloge*).

## SCENE XIX

(*INIGO and GONZALVE each in
his clock*).

(*INIGO entr'ouvre la porte de
l'horloge, un coucou chante, il referme précipitamment la porte,
puis la rouvre, une horloge sonne,
il rentre, puis reparait*).

**INIGO:** Mon oeil anxieux inter-
roge,
Mélancolique, l'horizon.
Amour! Amour! méchant garçon,
A quelle enseigne tu me
loges! . . .
Comme on doit être bien chez soi,
Dans un large fauteuil, les pieds
dans ses pantoufles!
Quand je languis ici, tellement à
l'étroit,
Que celà me coupe le souf-
fle! . . .
Et personne pour me haler! . . .
Personne! . . .
Cordon, s'il vous plaît!
La porte! la porte! la porte!
(*Il la referme sur lui, au bruit que
fait GONZALVE entr'ouvrant à
son tour l'horloge*).

**GONZALVE:** Il m'a semblé qu'on
appellait? . . .
Aussi bien, il est, je crois, sage
D'abandonner notre ermitage.
Adieu, cellule, adieu, donjon!
Adieu, cuirasse et morion
Qu'au chevalier fit revêtir sa dame!
Adieu, tables du violon
Dont, poète amant, je fus l'âme.
Adieu cage pour ma chanson.
Cheminée aussi pour ma
flamme . . .
Adieu!
(*Apercevant TORQUEMADA qui
rentre*).
Sacrebleu!
Voilà le mari!
Pour nous éviter le souci
D'explications sans charme,
Regagnons au plus vite un asile op-
portun . . .
Dépêchons!
(*Il se trompe d'horloge*).

**INIGO:** (*apparaissant dans
l'horloge*). Il y a quelqu'un!

## SCENE XX

(*TORQUEMADA, GONZALVE, IN-
IGO que l'on voit blotti dans
l'horloge*).

**TORQUEMADA:** (*entrant*). Il
n'est, pour l'horloger, de joie égale
à celle
De trouver au logis nombreuse
clientèle!
Messieurs, soyez les bienvenus,
Et veuillez m'excuser: vous avez attendu?

**INIGO:** (*dans l'horloge, un peu
embarrassé*). Mais comment donc,
je vous en prie!

**GONZALVE:** (*avec un enthousiasme feint*). Vos montres sent de
purs bijoux . . .

(*INIGO slightly opens the doors of
the clock; a cuckoo sings, he suddenly closes the door, then re-
opens it, one clock sounds, then
returns, then reappears*).

**INIGO:** My anxious eye
Scans sadly over the horizon.
Love, love, wicked boy,
In what a fix you place me!
Just when I ought to be comfortable
at home,
In a large armchair, feet in slippers,
I languish here, thus cramped.
How it cuts off my breath.
And nobody to haul me out!
No one!
A rope, please, somebody
The door the door, the door!
(*He closes it upon himself, to the
noise made by GONZALVE in his
turn, opening the clock*).

**GONZALVE:** Did someone call?
Well enough, methinks, and wise,
To abandon our retreat.
Adieu, my cell, adieu, dungeon!
Adieu, breast-plate and morion,
With which the lady fits her cava-
lier!
Adieu, violin, of which I,
The loving poet, was the soul,
Goodbye, cage of my song.
Outlet, for my flame . . .
Adieu!
(*Perceiving TORQUEMADA re-en-
tering*).
Sacrebleu!
There's the husband!
Let us avoid the trouble
Of painful explanations,
By returning at once to some handy
hiding-place . . .
Let us make haste
(*He gets the wrong clock*).

**INIGO:** (*Appearing in the clock*).
There's someone!

## SCENE XX

(*TORQUEMADA, GONZALVE, IN-
IGO cowering in the clock*).

**TORQUEMADA:** (*entering*).
There is no joy, for a clockmaker,
Like finding a large clientele wait-
ing for him!
Welcome, gentlemen.
And I crave your pardon. Have you
waited long?

**INIGO:** (*In the clock, a little embarrassed*). How, what, I beg you?

**GONZALVE:** (*With feigned enthusiasm*). Your clocks are jewels!

TORQUEMADA: (*le ramenant à l'horloge où se tient INIGO*). C'est de cette horloge, surtout,
Que vous me direz des nouvelles.

INIGO: Devant que vous veniez, je la considérais,
Précisément avec tant d'intérê . . .

TORQUEMADA: La curiosité est toute naturelle!

INIGO: Qu'à l'intérieur j'ai voulu pénétrer.
Pour examiner de plus près
Le fonctionnement merveilleux du pendule . . .

TORQUEMADA: Quais!
Mais je ne trouve pas celà si ridicule!
Et croyez moi, vous en aurez pour votre argent!
Car vous prenez, bien entendu, l'horloge?

INIGO: Certes!

TORQUEMADA: (*à GONZALVE*).
Allons, ne soyez pas jaloux!
(*Montrant l'autre horloge*).
J'ai la pareille au même prix: elle est à vous:
C'est une chance!

GONZALVE: Mais . . . sans doute . . .
(*A part*).
Impossible de dire non,
Il faut endormir ses soupçons;
Mais que ce trafiquant âpre au gain me dégoûte!

TORQUEMADA: Eh bien! nous voilà tous d'accord!

INIGO:
Je voudrais seulement vous demander encor
De me tirer de cette boîte:
Car, soit dit sans reproche,
Elle est un peu étroite . . .

TORQUEMADA: (*tirant INIGO et prenant GONZALVE par la main*).
Vouillez seconder mes efforts, Monsieur . . .
(*Tous deux tirent*).
Hé là donc . . . je t'en souhaite! . . .
(*Cependant que TORQUEMADA et GONZALVE s'efforcent, INIGO aperçoit RAMIRO qui revient, suivi de CONCEPCION*).

## SCENE XXI

INIGO: (*appelant RAMIRO*). Pardieu, déménageur, vous venez à propos!

TORQUEMADA: (*apercevant RAMIRO*). Je l'avais oublié: où avais je la tête?
(*A CONCEPCION*).
Ma femme, vous non plus, vous n'êtes pas de trop! . . .
(*TORQUEMADA, GONZALVE, CONCEPCION font la chaine et tirent INIGO, mais la chaine se romp et INIGO est toujours dans l'horloge. RAMIRO prend INIGO à bras le corps et l'enlève de l'horloge le plus naturellement du monde*).

RAMIRO: Voilà.

INIGO: Sacrebelu, quelle peigne!

CONCEPCION: De sa vigueur chacun témoigne!

TORQUEMADA: (*à CONCEPCION*). Vous n'aurez pas encor d'horloge, chère amie . . .

CONCEPCION: (*montrant RAMIRO*). Régulier comme un chronomètre,
Monsieur passe, avec ses mulets
Chaque matin, sous ma fenêtre . . .

TORQUEMADA: (*à RAMIRO*).
Chaque matin, donc, s'il vous plait,
Vous lui direz l'heure qu'il est.
(*Les acteurs viennent avec intention se placer sur le devant de la scène, après s'être offert mutuellement, en des cérémonies affectées, l'honneur de commencer l'addresse au public*).

## QUINTETTE FINAL

GONZALVE: Un financier . . .

INIGO: Et un poète . . .

CONCEPCION: (*pouffant de rire*). Un époux ridicule . . .

TORQUEMADA: Une femme coquette . . .
(*Ensemble*).

GONZALVE: Qui se servent, dans leurs discours,
De vers tantôt longs, tantôt courts
Au rythme qui se casse, à la rime cocasse.
(*Tous approuvent*).

RAMIRO: Avec un peu d'Espagne autour.

CONCEPCION: C'est la morale de Boccace:
Entre tous les amants, seul amant efficace.

RAMIRO: Il arrive un moment, dans les déduits d'amour

CONCEPCION: Où le muletier a son tour.

TOUS: Il arrive un moment dans les déduits d'amour
Où le muletier a son tour.

*RIDEAU.*

TORQUEMADA: (*Leading him to the clock in which INIGO is hiding*). Above all, tell me some news About that clock.

INIGO: Before you came, I was considering,
With so much interest . . .

TORQUEMADA: Curiosity is very natural!

INIGO: That I wanted to penetrate into the interior.
To examine from as near as possible
The marvellous operation of the pendulum . . .

TORQUEMADA: I see.
But that's not so ridiculous.
And believe me, you will get enough for your money!
For, of course, you will take the clock?

INIGO: Certainly!

TORQUEMADA: (*To GONZALVE*). Come, do not be jealous!
(*Pointing to the other clock*).
I have a similar one at the same price.
It is at your disposal.
It is a bargain.

GONZALVE: But . . . Without doubt . . .
(*Aside*).
Impossible to say No,
I must lull his suspicions:
How this vile trafficker disgusts me!

TORQUEMADA: Well, now, we are agreed!

INIGO: I would only ask you, in addition,
To pull me out of this box,
For, faultless though it is,
It is a little narrow.

TORQUEMADA: (*Pulling Inigo and taking Gonzalve by the hand*). Please help me, gentlemen . . .
(*Both pull*).
He . . . la! There! I'll help you out of it!
(*Meanwhile, while Torquemada and Gonzalve are striving, Inigo perceives Ramiro returning, followed by Conception.*)

## SCENE XXI

INIGO: (*calling Ramiro*). By God, mover of furniture, you come just in time!

TORQUEMADA: (*perceiving Ramiro*). I had forgotten him; where was my head?
(*To Conception*).
My wife, you too, all can help!

(*Torquemada, Gonzalve, Conception make a chain and pull INIGO. But the chain breaks and Inigo is still in the clock. Ramiro takes Inigo around the body and pulls him out of the clock just as naturally as you please*).

RAMIRO: There!

INIGO: Sacrebleu, what a fix!

CONCEPTION: Each one bears witness to his strength!

TORQUEMADA: (*To Conception*) You still want a clock from me, dear friend?

CONCEPTION: (*Pointing to Ramiro*). Regular as a chronometer,
Monsieur passes, with his mules,
Each morning, beneath my window . . .

TURQUEMADA: (*to Ramiro*).
Each morning, then if you please,
You will tell her what time it is.
(*The actors come with the intention of placing themselves before the fore-scene, after having mutually paid their respects to one another, in affected ceremonies, and offering each other the opportunity to commence the address to the public*).

## FINAL QUINTETTE

GONZALVE: A financier—

INIGO: And poet—

CONCEPTION: (*Bursting into laughter*). A ridiculous husband . . .

TURQUEMADA: A coquettish wife . . .
(*Together*).

GONZALVE: Who use, in their speech,
Verses now long, now short . . .
In broken rhythm, in ridiculous rhyme . . .

RAMIRO: With a bit of Spain around.

CONCEPTION: This is the moral of Boccaccio;
Among all lovers, the only efficient lover . . .

RAMIRO: There arrives a time, in the occupations of love.

CONCEPTION: When the muleteer has his turn.

ALL: There arrives a moment, in the occupations of love,
When the muleteer has his turn.

*CURTAIN.*

# *Salammbo* (1890)

MUSIC BY ERNEST REYER ▪ LIBRETTO BY CAMILLE DU LOCLE ▪ BASED ON A NOVEL BY GUSTAVE FLAUBERT

This five-act opera, set to a libretto by Camille du Locle (based on Flaubert's novel), premiered at the Théâtre de la Monnaie in Brussels on February 10, 1890. The story takes place in Carthage in 240 BC. Salammbo, daughter of Hamilcar, walks into the gardens of Hamilear at Megara, and reprimands the mercenaries who are drinking a toast to their gods and celebrating their victories. Matho, one of the barbarian chiefs, offers her a glass of wine as Narr'Havas, a king of Numidia, looks on with jealousy. When Salammbo departs, Spendius tells Matho that he can win Salammbo if he will lead a revolt of the mercenaries. Matho's task is to steal Zaimph, a sacred veil of tanit, which is the symbol of Carthage's greatness and security.

Salammbo comes to the high priest and begs him to let her keep the sacred veil as she is afraid for the welfare of her city, but the priest considers this a sacrilege. Matho comes in from his hiding place in the shadows with Spendius, and he gives her the veil. She thinks that he is a god and prepares to worship him. When he tells her he loves her and proves his mortality, she is angry. Her cries are heard by the priests, who enter—but Matho makes his escape, wrapped in the Zaimph.

Hamilcar is dismayed when told about the revolt of the mercenaries, the disappearance of the holy veil and Salammbo's love for Matho. Meanwhile, Salammbo, reproaching herself for the disappearance of the veil, is convinced by Shahabarin to go to the barbarian camp in order to retrieve it. She meets Matho who refuses to give her the sacred veil until they both give in to their love, and he wraps the veil around her. They are exchanging vows when Hamilcar and his generals interrupt them. Salammbo shows the sacred veil in triumph, and Matho, defeated by Narr'Havas, is sentenced to be sacrificed on the alter of Tanit by Hamilcar. It is Salammbo's wedding day to Narr'Havas, and a happy throng gathers in the forum of Carthage. Matho is brought forth to be sacrificed, and Salammbo is given the honor of executing him as she is the rescuer of the sacred veil. Instead, the crowd watches in horror as she stabs herself and Matho, taking the same sword, kills himself.

---

## ▪ ACTE PREMIER

*Le festin des mercenaires.*
*Les jardins d'Hamilcar, à Mégara,*
*près de Carthage. Au fond, une*
*grande terrasse d'où l'on descend*
*par un large escalier. Au-dessus*
*de la terrasse, le palais. A gauche,*
*les logements des esclaves. A*
*droite, au loin, la mer et les*
*édifices de Carthage.*

### SCÈNE PREMIÈRE

*Matho, Autharite. Les Merce-*
*naires assir au festin.*

**LE CHOEUR:** Héos victorieux,
Aux jardins d'Hamilcar,
Sur des lits de brocart,
Buvons, pareils aux dieux!

**QUATRE CHEFS DES MERCE-
NAIRES:** Carthage est riche et ne
sait pas la guerre!
Grâce à nos bras vaillants, elle est
debout encor
Que les festins, les voluptés et l'or
Payent sa dette au soldat merce-
naire!

**LE CHOEUR:** Héos victorieux,
Aux jardins d'Hamilcar,
Sur des lits de brocart,
Buvons, pareils aux dieux!

## ▪ ACT I

*(Gardens of Hamilcar at Megara,*
*near Carthage. Back a terrace and*
*extensive stairs. Above, the*
*palace. Left, the slaves' lodgings.*
*Right, in distance, the sea and*
*buildings of Carthage).*

### SCENE I

**MATHO, AUTHARITE and MER-
CENARY SOLDIERS:** (*seated at*
*festival*). Victorious heroes, in the
gardens of Hamilcar, let us drink to
the gods on brocaded seats.

**FOUR CHIEFS:** Carthage is rich,
knows nothing of war; and thanks
to our arms is proud as ever. So let
feats, pleasure and gold, give the
price to the mercenary.

**CHORUS:** (*Repeat*). Victorious heroes in the gardens of Hamilcar,
etc.

**LES GRECS:** (*élevant leurs*
*coupes*). A toi, dieu rayonnant cher
à notre patrie,
Jupiter, qu'on adore au temple
d'Olympie!

**LES ÉGYPTIENS:** (*de même*). O
vierge qu'on adore en notre doux
pays,
A toi, reine du Nil.

**LES GAULOIS:** (*de même*). Teutates, dont la voix dans les orages
gronde,
A toi, dieu dont le temple est la
forêt profonde! . . . .

**LES SYRIENS:** (*de même*). A toi,
reine d'amour, reine de volupté,
O Vénus Syrienne, ô brillante Astarté!

**LA VOIX DES ESCLAVES:** (*dans*
*l'ergastule*). O fils d'une terre
étrangère,
Heureux qui jouit ici-bas
De l'air divin, de la lumière!
O Liberté! Soleil! ô biens perdus!
hélas!

**DEMI-CHOEUR:** Ecoutez!
Qui gémit dans cette voix plaintive?

**DEMI-CHOEUR:** Le vent dans les
palmiers ou le flot sur la rive!

**LE CHOEUR:** Héros victorieux,
Aux jardins d'Hamilcar
Sur des lits de brocart,
Buvons, pareils aux dieux!

**THE GREEKS:** (*raising their*
*cups*). To you, shining god of our
soil, to Jupiter, whom we worship
on Olympus.

**EGYPTIANS:** (*same action.*) Oh,
virgin, we adore in our own sweet
land. To you, queen of Nile, goodly
Isis.

**GAULS:** (*same action*). Teutates
to you, whose voice is in the storm
and also in darkest forest.

**SYRIANS:** (*same action*). To you,
Queen of Love, Queen of Pleasure,
to you, Syrian Venus, brilliant
Astarte.

**VOICES OF SLAVES:** (*outside*).
Oh; sons of foreign countries, happy are those who breathe the air of
liberty, see light. Oh, beneficent
sun, lost forever alas!

**CHORUS:** Listen who speak in such
plaintive tone.

**OTHERS:** The sighing of the palms
or the lapping on the shore.

**ALL:** (*Repeat*). To victorious heroes in gardens of Hamilcar, etc.
(*Enter Narr'Havas*).

AUTHARITE: (*désignant les Numides qui entrent*). Ces cavaliers hardis, alliés de Carthage, Comme nous, ont, par leur courage, Soutenu sa fortune et sauvé son destin! Offrons-leur prés de nous une place au festin! (*Les Mercenaires accueillent les Numides.*)

NARR'HAVAS: (*á Matho*). Guerrier, quel est ton nom, et quelle est to patrie? Je t'ai vu combattre avec nous, Et parmi les vaillants, le plus vaillant de tous!

MATHO: (*á Narr'Havas*). Guerrier, quel est ton nom? où reçus-tu la vie? Oui, tu combattis près de moi. Nul parmi les vaillants n'est plus vaillant que toi!

NARR'HAVAS: Mon nom est Narr'Havas, et la plaine numide Mon pays!

MATHO: Je suis né dans la Lybie aride, Et mon nom est Matho.

NARR'HAVAS: Parmi les bataillons J'ai grandi.

MATHO: J'ai grandi, moi, chassant les lions. Je suis fils d'un berger.

NARR'HAVAS: Moi, je suis roi! Soyons Amis . . . .

MATHO: Asseyons-nous côte à côte . . . .

NARR'HAVAS: Et buvons!

LA VOIX DES ESCLAVES: (*dans l'ergastule*). O fils d'une terre étrangère, Heureux qui jouit ici-bas De l'air divin, de la lumière! O Liberté! Soleil! ô biens perdus!.. helas! . . . .

LA CHOEUR: Quoi? ce chant douloureux Dans les airs monte encore?.

MATHO: Qui sont ces malheureux Dont la voix nous implore?

NARR'HAVAS: Ne prenous d'eux aucun souci.

MATHO: (*se levant*). Dans ce jour triomphant, qui nous invoque ainsi?

NARR'HAVAS: (*l'arretant*). Garde en paix ton épée, et laisse sans scrupule, Se plaindre au fond de l'ergastule Les esclaves d'Hamilcar. Ce qui les fait fèmir, ces pâles misérables, C'est l'odeur du festin qui fait ployer nos tables E le parfum de ce nectar!

AUTHARITE: (*pointing at Numidians*). These hardy horsemen allied to Carthage have, like us, by their courage, saved her destiny. So let us offer them a place at our table. (*All fraternize.*)

NARR'HAVAS: (*to Matho*). Warrior, what is your country and what is your name. I have seen you fight, and among the bold, you are the boldest of all.

MATHO: And your name, the place of your birth. You struggled by my side, nor one more bold than you.

NARR: My name is Narr'havas, and the Numid land my country.

MATHO: My place of birth was arid Lybia. My name is Matho.

NARR: I grew among soldiers.

MATHO: And I hunting the lion; yet son of a shepherd.

NARR: I am a king, but let us be friends.

MATHO: And sit side by side.

NARR: A drink and a toast.

THE SLAVES: (*outside, repeating*). Oh, sons of foreign countries, happy are those who breathe the air of liberty, etc.

CHORUS: What! this plaintive chant breaks again upon our hearing.

MATHO: Who are these unfortunates whose voices implore us?

NARR: Let's give them little worry.

MATHO: On this triumphal day who calls upon us?

NARR: (*stopping him*). In peace keep your sword and have no scruple in leaving Hamilcar's slaves in their dungeon. What makes them cry out is the odor of the meats they smell from afar and the perfume of the wine.

MATHO: Des esclaves, dis-tu? Non! par tout où nous sommes Il n'est plus d'esclaves! (*Aux Lybiens.*) Allons! (*Matho sort à la tête des Lybiens.*)

NARR'HAVAS: (*riant*) Des esclaves sont ils des hommes? . . . . Eh quoi? quitter pour eux la table où nous buvons?

AUTHARITE: (*aux Mercenaires qui l'entourent*). Amis! celui qui va délivrer ces esclaves Il est fort, il est juste, et brave entres les braves. Si Carthage, encore aujourd'hui Manquant à la foi solennelle, Retient l'or, prix du sang par nous versé pour elle; S'il faut pour nous venger un chef, que ce soit lui!

MATHO: (*rentrant avec ses compagnons et ramenant les esclaves delivres*). Calmez vos cris, séchez vos larmes, Saluez un meilleur destin. Melez-vous parmi nous, prenez part au festin, Demandez à la fois une coupe et des armes!

SPENDIUS: Salut à mes libérateurs! Salut á vous, dieux protecteurs, Dieux d'Ionie! Salut, riant éclt des cieux, Astre d'or au char radieux, Splendeur bénie! Salut, sylvains, fils des forêts, Et nous nymphes des autres frais, Et des fontaines! Salut, hommes fiers et vaillants Dont l'épée aux éclairs brillants Brisa mes chaînes!

MATHO: Prends cette coup et bois!

SPENDIUS: Pourquoi ne vois-je pas Entre vos mains victorieuses Étinceler les coupes glorieuses Ou l'on boit à Carthage, au retour des combats?. Je me souviens! La légion sacrée Boit seule aux coupes d'or relique vénérée Que le Sénat, jaloux, conserve en son trésor!.

LE CHOEUR: Nous voulons boire aux coupes d'or!.

NARR'HAVAS: Non,..craignez les Baals! c'est un voeu sacrilège!

SPENDIUS: En Grèce, mon pays, il n'est nul privilège Qu'un dieu jaloux dispute à des soldats vainqueurs!

LE CHOEUR: Les coupes!.

NARR'HAVAS: Giscon vient, au nom des sénateurs.

SPENDIUS: La légion sacrée a formé son cortège. (*Entrèe de Giscon, avec sa suite.*)

MATHO: Slaves, you say? I know no slaves wherever I may be. (*To his men,*) Come. (*He heads his followers and exits.*)

NARR: (*laughing*). Slaves are not men, and why leave the table for them.

AUTHARITE: (*to the Mercenaries*). Friends, the one who delivers these slaves is strong, he is just and bravest of all, and if Carthage today abjuring her vow, keeps our gold, the price of blood spent for her, if for vengeance, a chief we must have, let it be be.

MATHO: (*returning with his companions and bringing with him the delivered slaves*). Calm yourselves. Dry your tears. Bow to a happier fate. Join us; take part in the feast. Ask at once to drink and to fight.

SPENDIUS: Joy to my liberators. Joy to the protecting gods, gods of Ionio. Joy, light and air, oh, sun, in your splendor. Joy to the sylvan glades, to the nymphs of the forest and of the fountains. Homage to the proud and valiant men whose shining swords broke my chains.

MATHO: Take this cup and drink.

SPENDIUS: Why do I not see in your victorious hands bristle the glorious cups they drink from in Carthage after a fight. I remember. Alone the Senate drinks from these venerated and sacred cups of gold. The Senate, jealous, keeps its treasure.

CHORUS: Let us all drink from the golden cups.

NARR: No! Fear Baal, this is an impious thing.

SPENDIUS: Greece is my country, and there is nothing a conquerer may not have.

CHORUS: The cups—the wine.

NARR: Giscon, in the name of the senate, now comes.

SPENDIUS: The sacred legion has formed itself in line. (*Formal entry of Giscon, escorted*).

LE CHŒUR: Nous voulons boire aux coupes d'or!.
L'ingrate cité nous outrage
Elle tombait, sans notre effort!
Nous avons pour sauver Carthage,
Bravé le feu, le fer, la mort!
Nous voulons boire aus coupes d'or.

CHORUS: We wish to drink in golden cups, for Carthage has insulted us. Without us she would have fallen. To save Carthage we've met fire, iron, death, and now we'll drink in cups of gold.

GISCON: O sauvers de Carthage! ô fils de la victoire!
Nul honneur n'est pour vous trop haut, trop plein de gloire!

GISCON: Saviors of Carthage, oh, sons of victory. No honor is too great for you or any too great glory.

LE CHŒUR: C'est vrai! vivat!

CHORUS: It is true. Hurrah!

GISCON: Mais de nos dieux jaloux, Ne nous demandez pas d'éveiller le courroux!

GISCON: But do not arouse the rancor.

SPENDIUS: Plaisants dieux, pour troubler coeur vaillant d'un homme
Que ces dieux qui, sans vous, partaient captifs pour Rome! . . .

SPENDIUS: Pleasant gods that would trouble valiant men, and these gods without you would depart captive for Rome.

LE CHŒUR: Vengeance!.

CHORUS: Vengeance!

MATHO: Apportes-tu l'or
Qu'on nous doit encor
Pour prix de notre sang versé dans vingt batailles?

MATHO: Do you bring us the gold won by our blood in twenty battles?

LE CHŒUR: Notre solde . . .

CHORUS: Our pay.

GISCON: Allez tous camper hors des murailles
Et vous serez payés..

GISCON: All go camp outside the walls and you'll be paid.

DEMI-CHŒUR: Non!
Carthage est à nous!

HALF CHORUS: No, Carthage belongs to us.

DEMI-CHŒUR: C'est un piège!

OTHER HALF: It is a trick.

DEMI-CHŒUR: On nous chasse!

HALF CHORUS: We're dismissed.

DEMI-CHŒUR: On ment!

OTHER HALF: And he lies.

MATHO: On nous outrage!
Qu'elle tremble Carthage!

MATHO: They outrage us. Let Carthage tremble.

LE CHŒUR: Des haches! des torches! courez!

CHORUS: Axes, torches—anything.

GISCON: Par Tanit et Moloch, vous tous repentirez!

GISCON: By Tanit and Moloch, you'll all repent.

MERCENAIRES: Dans mes mains la foudre résonne!
Mon glaive laboure et moissonne!
Le maître du monde, c'est moi.
Tous tremblant devant ma colère;
Tous, prosternés dans la poussière,
M'appellent seigneur et grand roi!
(Giscon est sorti avec son escorte. Les jardins sont mis au pillage. les tables sont enversées. L'incendie commence à luire au millieu des arbres.)
(Les Prêtres de Tanit apparaissent au sommet de l'escalier du palais, puis Salammbô.)

MERCENARIES: (and all Chorus join.) It is in our hands the thunder growls. It is in our hands the harvest grows. The Master of Earth is ourself, and bend before choler. All humbly in the dust speak of us only as lord and great king. Enough.
(GISCON leaves with escort. The gardens are put to pillage, table thrown about. Fires begin to burn.)
(The Priests of Tanit appear at head of stairs then Salammbo.)

LES PRÊTRES: Tanit, déesse austère,
Qui verses sur la terre,
Ton lait et ta lumière!
Tanit, astre changeant
Dans l'azur dirigeant
Ta nacelle d'argent!
Tanit, ô bonté sage,
Qui vis dans ton image
Aux autels de Carthage!
Tanit, verse su nous

PRIESTS: (chant). Tanit, austere goddess that our earth gives milk and light, Tanit, in the milky way, direct your silver ship, Tanit, oh, wise and good, who lives in your image on the altars of Carthage, Tanit pour upon us in peaceful fashion your looks without anger (Salammbo appears at steps of palace).

Dans des rayons plus doux
Des regards sans courroux!
(Salammbô parait au scull du palais.)

LE CHŒUR: Voyez! dans sa beauté suprême
Est-ce la déesse elle-même?

CHORUS: See in her splendid beauty—she is the goddess herself.

NARR'HAVAS: Le regard
De Tanit est moins pur et moins beau,
Et c'est la fille d'Hamilcar,
C'est Salammbô!

NARR'HAVAS: The mere look of Tanit is less and no more. This is the daughter of Hamilcar. It is Salammbo.

SALAMMBÔ: Qu'avez-vous fait O cité lamentable!
O Carthage!
Où sont-ils tes défenseurs, tes fils,
Qui t'avaient faite et grande et redoutable!
Où sont-ils tes guerriers qui labouraient jadis
Les flots, par qui les flots se couronnaient d'épis?
Carthage! ôsol sacré dont se sépare:
Cite sainte qui insulte une horde barbare!

SALAMMBO: What have you done? oh, lamentable city. Oh, Carthage, where are your defenders, your sons. Those who made you great and redoutable. Where are your seamen, who a short while ago ploughed the sea and brought grain in abundance? Carthage! Oh, Carthage! Tanit is aghast, for now you are ploughed by a barbarian horde.

LE CHŒUR: Un éclair surhuman a brillé dans ses yeux!
On entend dans sa voix quelque chose des dieux!

CHORUS: Great heaven, we see the supernatural in her eyes. We hear something in her voice.

SALAMMBÔ: Des glaives, des flambeaux, courage!
Livrez au feu ce toitsacré.
Hamilcar est loin de Carthage,
Je suis seule et je m'enfuirai!
Sur ces murs de cédre et d'ivoire
Portez vos sacrilèges mains;
Tout y raconte notre gloire
Et les défaites des Romains!
Un serpent noir, vivant mystère,
Dort là-haut, parmi les lotos
Pour me suivre dans ma galère.
A ma voix il fendra les flots!
O ciel, où naissent les étoiles,
Cache ton azur obscurci,
Tanit, cache-toi dans tes voiles,
Un autre va regner ici!

SALAMMBO: I want swords, torches, courage. Give this sacred roof to the flammes. Hamilcar is now far from Carthage I am alone, and I shall fly. Upon these walls of cedar and ivory bring at once your sacrilegious hands. All here accounts our glory and the routs of the Roman bands, A serpent black, a living mystery lives above among the lotos. Let to follow me in my galère—he will defy the sea. Oh heaven, where stars are born, hide your blue azure. Oh Tanit, get behind your veil for another will reign in your precinct.

LES PRÊTRES: Tanit, déese austère
Qui verses sur la terre
Ton lait et ta lumière!

PRIESTS: Tanit, austere goddess, that to our earth gives light and strength, have mercy for our wrongs.

SALAMMBÔ: Déese, exauce-moi!

LES PRÊTRES: Tanit, verse sur nous,
Dans des rayons plus doux,
Des regards sans courroux . . . !

SALAMMBÔ: Déese, apaise-toi!

SALAMMBO: Oh, Goddess forgive us.

NARR'HAVAS: Non! ne redoute rien, ô vierge, de leurs armes!
Qui voudrait de tes yeux faire couler des larmes?
Chacun de nous frappe de respect transporte
D'amour, en toi, grâce exquise, ô beauté,
Voit la divinité
Qui régne en sa patrie!

NARR'HAVAS: No, fear nothing; oh, virgin, from their arms. Who would wish to cause your alarms. Every one and all of us with respect and joy welcome your beauty. It is with love we look upon a divinity who reigns in her native country.

LES ÉGYPTIENS: (s'inclinant). Isis!

EGYPTIANS: (bowing). Isis!

LES ITALIOTES: (de méme). Vesta!

ITALIANS: (bowing). Vesta!

LES SPARTIATES: (*de méme*). Pallas!

LES SYRIENS: (*de méme*). O Venus Astarté!

LES IONIENS: (*de méme*). O Venus Uranie

MATHO: (*s'agenouillant devant Salammbô*).
Oui devant toi, qui de nous
Ne sent fléchir ses genoux?

SALAMMBÔ: (*a Matho*). Comme gage de paix et d'heuseuse espérance,
Soldat, prends cette coupe, où de mes mains versés
Les flots de ce vin pur scellent no alliance.
Bois, soldat!Soix heureux!

AUTHARITE: Salut aux fiancés!

MATHO et NARR'HAVAS: Que dit-il?

SPENDIUS: (*riant*). Il dit vrai! verser dans un cratère.

MATHO et NARR'HAVAS: Que il?
Le vin pur, et l'offrir à quelqu'homme de guerre,
Aux pays des Gaulois, c'est offrir son amour!

MATHO: (*vidant la coupe*). Je bois à Salammbô!
J'accepte cet augure!

NARR'HAVAS: (*à Matho*). Je l'aime, et depuis plus d'un jour, Entends-tu bien?

MATHO: Je l'aime, et pour jamais!
(*Narr'Havas se precipite sur Matho*).
(*blessé*). Parjure!
(*Il prend une table et la jette à Narr'havas Salammbô et les Prêtres ont disparu.*)
(*Matho s'assied. Spendius s'approche de lui.*)

MATHO: Va-t'en!

SPENDIUS: Non! . . . Spendius par tes mains delivre
T'appartient!
Commande et j'obiérai! . . .
Laisse-moi panser ta blessure! . . .
(*Matho le repousse.*)

SPENDIUS: Ecoute . . . je connais
Chaque détour de ce palais
Splendide,
Je serai, si tu veux,
Vers des tresors prodigieux,
Ton guide . . .
De vertige surpris,
Le coeur devant ces biens sans prix
Palpite.
Viens et tout est a toi,
Or, perles, diamants, suis-moi,
Viens vite!

GREEKS: (*bowing*). Pallas!

SYRIANS: (*bowing*). Oh, Venus Astarté.

IONIANS: (*bowing*). No, Venus Urania!

MATHO: (*on his knees*). Let who would not bow before you—on his knees.

SALAMMBO: (*to Matho*). As a gage of peace and happy hope— soldier take this cup by my own hand filled. May the toast seal the alliance between us.
Soldier drink, and be happy.

AUTHARITE: To the bride and bridegroom.

MATHO and NARR: What does he say?

SPENDIUS: (*laughing*). He say that to drink pure wine from a glàss together to a man of war means among the Gauls to offer your love.

MATHO: (*emptying his glass*). I drink to Salammbo and accept the augury.

NARR: (*to Matho*). I have loved her for a day and more. Understand me well.

MATHO: I love her and for her always. (*Narr'Havas throws himself on Matho, who is wounded. Matho seizes a table, which he dashes at Narr. crying "coward!"* (*Salammbo and the Priests are gone. Matho, wounded, seats himself. Spendius comes near.*)

MATHO: Go away.

SPENDIUS: (*throwing himself at his feet*). No—Spendius, by your hands delivered, belongs to you. Command, and I obey.
Let me bathe your wound. (*Matho repulses him.*)

SPENDIUS: Listen! I know every detour of this splendid palace. I shall be your guide to enormous treasures. The heart beats at the thought of such priceless things. Come, all is for you—gold, pearls, diamonds—come now.

MATHO: (*à part*). Ah!
Moloeh m'a maudit!
Le feu
Dans mes veines circule
La colere ardente du dieu
Embrase mon coeur et me brúle!

SPENDIUS: Tu ne me responds pai?tu méprises cet or?
Vois!
Je puis t'offrir plus encor . . .
(*Montrant la cité lointaine.*)
Veuxta mettre demain cette ville au pillage?

MATHO: (*le repoussant*). Non!

SPENDIUS: A son fier Sénat veux-tu dicter des lois?

MATHO: Non.

SPENDIUS: Veux-tu voir trembler a tous genoux Carthage?

MATHO: Non.

SPENDIUS: Veux-tu pour ton front le bandeau d'or des rois?

MATHO: Non.

SPENDIUS: Quel demon, l'agite?

MATHO: (*comme dans un rêve*). Où donc est-elle?

SPENDIUS: (*indiquant le bras blessé de Matho.*) Tu souffres?

MATHO: (*frappant sa poitrine*). Elle est là, la blessure mortelle!

MATHO: Ah! Moloch m'a maudit!
Le feu
Dans mes veines circule
La colere ardente du Dieu
Embrase mon coeur et ma brûle!

SPENDIUS: (*à part*). Tel sous sa tunique de feu
Se plaignait le divin Hercule;
Eros des pleurs se fait un jeu
Et d'un trait vainqueur il le brûle!
(*Autharite, les Mercenaires entrant*).

AUTHARITE: Le clairon retentit dans l'aire!
La cite jette au loin comme un grand bruit de houle,
De sinistres clameurs s'elèvent de la foule . . .

SPENDIUS: On prépare pour vous, non de l'or, mais du fer!

LE CHOEUR: Oui! c'est la guerre!Allons choisissons le plus brave
Pour notre chef!

AUTHARITE: Matho!

LE CHOEUR: Matho nous conduira! . . .
Oui! donnons-lui la pourpre! . . .
(*Matho refuse du geste.*)

SPENDIUS: (*à Matho.*) Ah! crois-en ton esclave.
Accepte, et je le jure, elle t'appartiendra!
(*On jette sur les épaules de Matho un manteau de pourpre, les enseignes se rangent autour de lui, etc., etc.*)

MATHO: Moloch has cursed me. I feel now in my veins that the warm anger of the god has taken hold of my heart annd burns me.

SPENDIUS: You do not answer— you despise this gold. Look, I can offer even more.
(*Showing the distant city*). Would you wish to pillage it?

MATHO: (*pushing him aside*). No.

SPENDIUS: Dictate its laws to the proud Senate?

MATHO: No.

SPENDIUS: Wuold you like to see at your knees—Carthage?

MATHO: No.

SPENDIUS: Would you wish for your forehead the gold circle of the kings?

MATHO: No.

SPENDIUS: What devil seizes him?

MATHO: (*as in a dream*). Where can she be?

SPENDIUS(*touching his arm*). You suffer.

MATHO: (*striking his breast*). The wound is here and mortal.

MATHO: Yes, Moloch has cursed me. The fire in my veins runs wild. The anger of the deity burns my heart and all.

SPENDIUS: Thus under his tunic of fire found divine Hercules.
Thus Eros makes play of tears and in a second burns him to death.
(*Autharite and the Mercenaries enter.*)

AUTHARITE: The trumpet resounds in the air. The distant city is in great clamor and sinister clamors arise from the crowd.

SPENDIUS: They prepare not gold, but the sword.

CHORUS: Yes, it is war; let us choose the most valiant for our chief.

AUTHARITE: Matho.

CHORUS: Yes, Matho now shall lead us—we'll place the purple on him (*Matho makes gesture of refusal.*)

SPENDIUS: (*to Matho*). Believe in your slave. Accept, and I swear that she shall belong to you.
(*They throw over Matho's shoulders a purple mantle and the troops align round him*).

## Act I, Scene I

LE CHOEUR: (*Chant de Mercenaires.*) Dans mos mains la foudre résonne!
Mon glaive laboure et moissonne!
Le maître du monde, c'est moi!
Tous tremblant devant ma colere,
Tous prosternés dans la poussierre,
M'appellent Seigneur et grand Roi!
(*Salammbo fuyant vers Carthage apparait dans un char, sur la terasse supérieure. Matho et les Mercenaires se précipitent vers elle. Elle les arrete d'un ste et poursuit son chemin.*)

CHORUS: (*Repeat*). It is in our hands the thunder sounds. It is in our hands the harvest grows. The Master of Earth is ourself, and bend before our anger. All buried in the dust proclaim you Lord and Great King.
(*Salammbo flying toward Carthage, appears in a chariot on the terrace above. Matho and the Mercenaires make a dash toward and are stopped by a motion of her hand. She moves on.*)

## ■ ACTE DEUXIÈME

*Tanit.*
(*L'enciente sacrée du temple de Tanit. Les Prêtres prosternes attendent, en invoquant Tanit, Shahabarim est debout prés d'un trepied.*)

LES PRÊTRES ET LES PRÊTRESSES: Anaîtis, Derceto, Mylitta,
O Rabbetna, Baalet, Tyratha, Tanit, parais!

SHAHABARIM: Sors des flots, déesse éclante,
Et sur Carthage, où tu te plais,
Verse de tes rayons la splendeur bienfaisante!
Viens, et recois de nous ô maîtresse du ciel,
Avec l'encens, le vin mêlé de miel!
(*Dans des Courtisanes Sacrées.*)

LES PRÊTRES ET LES PRÊTRESSES: Anaîtis, Derceto, Mylitta,
O Rabbetna, Baalet, Tyratha, Tanit, parais!
(*La lune, brille un disque d'argent.*)

LE CHOEUR: Tanit, Salut!
Carthage te bénit!
Retentissez, cris d'allégresse!
Sonnesz, clairons sacrés! hymnes religieux,
Elancez-vous aux cieux,
Saluez la déesse!
La lune descend lentement.
(*Pendant que la lumière decend,*)
O Tanit, blanche déité,
Beinfaitrice féconde,
O clair miroir, ô pureté,
Vers dans ta sérénité
Tes rayons sur le monde!
Elle fuit ton char radieux,
L'horreur de la nuit sombre;
Et les monstres mystérieux,
Sitôt que tu parais aux cieux,
Rentrent au sein de l'ombre.
Que tu glisses légèrement
Dan les vapeurs humides!
Les astres d'or au firmament
Comme un troupeau, docilement
S'en vont où tu les guides!
Tu règnes sur les profondeurs
Où la vague déferle,
Tu remplis l'air de tes splendeurs
Semant sur la terre les fleurs,
Au sein des mers la perle!

## ■ ACT II

*Tanit.*
(*The surroundings of the Temple of Tanit. Priests are worshipping. Shahabarim stands by a censer.*)

PRIESTS AND PRIESTESSES: Anaitio, Derceto, Mylitta, oh, Rabetna, Baalet, Tyratha. Tanit appear!

SHAHABARIM: From the deep, magnificent deity. On Carthage, the town you love. Throw down your sunbeams in splendid fashion. Come and receive, oh, Mistress of Heaven, with incense the honey mixed with the wine.
(*Dance of the sacred women.*)

PRIESTS AND WOMEN: (*they repeat first refrain, ending as Tanit appears. While the moon slowly rises and illuminates the scene.*)

CHORUS: Tanit, we bow, Carthage loves you. Ring again shouts of joy. Bray again you sacred brasses. Sound high to heaven—sound for the deity.
(*The moon gradually descends.*)
Oh Tanit, white deity, goodness fecund, oh mirror of purity, send in severity your beams on the world. Your radiant chariot is in horror of somber night. So mysterious monsters, as soon as you appear, return to the desolate gloom. How lightly you slip through the clouds moist and clear. The golden stars in the firmament, like a flock docilely go where you guide them. You reign on the ocean where the wave mounts on high; fill the air with your splendor, carpeting earth with flowers, at the bottom of the sea the pearl. The crowd madly in love follows you enchantress. You take them in your course, changing as you do every day, only more youthful tomorrow. Oh, Tanit, white goddess, goodness fecund, oh, mirror of purity, send your beams on the world in severity.

La foule ardente des amours
Te suit, enchanteresse!
Tu les entraînes dans ton cours
Changeant comme toi tous les jours
Pour rajeunir sans cesse!
O Tanit, blanche déité,
Bienfaitrice féconde,
O clair miroir, ô pureté,
Vers dans ta sérénité
Tes rayons sur le monde

LE CHOEUR: Tanit, Salut!
Carthage te bénit!
Retentissez, cris d'allégresse,
Sonnez, clairons sacrés, hymnes religieux,
Elancez-vous aux cieux!
Saluez la déesse
(*Danse des Courtisanes Sacrées,*)

SHAHABARIM: La déesse a rempli tout l'azur de sa gloire!
Ouvrons donc les portes d'ivoire
Du sanctuaire redouté,
Adorons le manteau que Tanit a jeté
Sur sa mystérieuse image,
Le Zamïph qui, gardien des destins de Carthage,
Est une part de la divinité!
(*Marche. Shahavarim entre dans le sanctuaire. Spendius et Matho entrent furtivement.*)

SPENDIUS: (*à Matho*). Suis-moi!

MATHO: Par cette route sombre,
En franchissant les murs et nous glissant dans l'ombre,
Ou donc m'as-tu conduit?

SPENDIUS: Au temple de Tanit!
Veux-tu voir tes soldats vainqueurs, Carthage en flamme?
Veux-tu voir à tes pieds cette orgueilleuse femme
Qui torture ton coeur, qui t'a vole ton âme?

MATHO: Ah! revoir Salammbô, puis s'il le faut, mourir!

SPENDIUS: Il est un voile saint qu'en ce temple on vénère.
Il couvre la déesse au fond du sanctuaire.
Qui le posséderait serait un dieu sur terre!

MATHO: Eh bien?

SPENDIUS: Jet'ai conduit ici pour le ravir!

MATHO: (*épouvanté*). O sacrilège!

SHAHABARIM: (*paraissant au seuil du sanctuaire, portant le Zaïmph*). Priez!
Adorez ce voile
Où frémit l'âme des dieux,
Le Zaïmph mystérieux
Tissu des feux d'une etoile!

LE CHOEUR: O Rabbetna, Baalet, Tyratha!

SPENDIUS: (*à Matho*). Que le Zaïmph dans tes mains resplendisse!

CHORUS: Tanit, Carthage, salutes you. Sound sacred cymbals, religious tones—let them be heard up even to heaven.
(*Dance of the Sacred Women.*)

SHAHABARIM: The goddess has filled the heavens with her glory. Then let us open the ivory gates of the dreaded sanctuary. Let us adore the mantle that Tanit threw upon her mysterious symbol. The Zaimph, which guardian of Carthage is part of her divinity.
(*March. Shahabarim enters the sanctuary while Spendius and Matho come in furtively.*)

SPENDIUS: (*to Matho*). Follow me!

MATHO: By this roundabout way, climbing ditches and walls, where have you brought me?

SPENDIUS: To the Temple of Tanit. Would you see your soldiers victorious, Carthage in flame? Would you see at your feet this imperious woman who has tortured your heart, who has stolen your soul?

MATHO: See Salammbo once more? Yes, perhaps, then die.

SPENDIUS: There is in this temple a sacred veil, that covers the goddess in the depths of the sanctuary. Who possesses it is a god on this earth.

MATHO: Well?

SPENDIUS: I brought you here to ravish it.

MATHO: (*frightened*). A sacrilege!

SHAHABARIM: (*appearing on steps*). Pray all adore this veil, wherein is the soul of the gods, the mysterious Zaimph made from a fiery star.

CHORUS: Oh, Rabetna, Baalat, Tyratha!

SPENDIUS: (*to Matho*). May the Zaimph in your hands be resplendent.

**MATHO:** Pour ce forfait, cherche un autre complice!

**LE CHOEUR:** Anaïtis, Dercéto, Mylitta!

**SHAHABARIM:** Priez! ce voile est un gage
De victore et de splendeur!
Il est le gardien, l'honneur,
La fortune de Carthage!

**LE CHOEUR:** O Rabbetna, Baalet, Tyratha!

**SPENDIUS** (à Matho). Vois! c'est pour toi la foudre vengeresse!

**MATHO:** Non! ce serait te braver, ô déesse!

**LE CHOEUR:** Anaïtis, Dercéto, Mylitta!

**SHAHABARIM:** Priez!ce voile est terrible!
Celui qui le toucerait,
Maudit des dieux, tomberait
Frappé d'un fer invisible!

**LE CHOEUR:** O Rabbetna, Baalet, Tyratha!

**SPENDIUS:** (à Matho). Crains-tu la mort? tu tardes encore?

**MATHO:** Je crains les dieux et mon coeur les honore!

**LE CHOEUR:** Anaïtis, Dercéto, Mylitta!
(Shahabarim rentre dans le sanctuaire où il dépose le Zaïmph, puis il en sort en en laissant les portes ouvertes.)

**SHAHABARIM, LE CHOEUR:** Tanit, reine immortelle,
Nous te glorifions,
Astre dont étincelle
Le front ceint des rayons!

**SPENDIUS:** (à Matho). Où donc est ton amour?
Ta force où donc est-elle?

**MATHO:** Je crains les dieux! fuyons!
(Spendius et Matho se sont écartes. On frappe aux portes du temple.)

**SHAHABARIM:** Qui donc, frappant au sanctuaire
Ose troubler ce saint mystère?

**UN PRÊTRE:** C'est Salammbô!

**MATHO:** Salammbô!
Justes dieux!

**SPENDIUS:** (à Matho). Elle est pour toi, la fortune prospere!
(Spendius disparait. Matho reste caché dans l'ombre. Salammbô entre.)

**SHAHABARIM:** O fille d'Hamilcar, que veux-tu donc?

**SALAMMBÔ:** O pére!
Toi qui dans les choses des cieux
Daignas instruire ma jeunesse,
Toi dont l'esprit est plein de l'antique sagesse,
Prends en pitié ma douleur, mon ef-

**MATHO:** For this crime find some other accomplice.

**CHORUS:** Anaitis, Derceto, Mylitta.

**SHAHABARIM:** Pray all for this veil is the symbol of victory and splendor. It is the keeper of the honor and fortune of Carthage.

**CHORUS:** Oh Rabetna, Baalet, Tyratha!

**SPENDIUS:** See for you it is a vengeful thunder.

**MATHO:** No, I dare not outrage the deity.

**CHORUS:** Anaitis, Derceto, Mylitta.

**SHAHABARIM:** Pray all, this veil is terrible—whoever should touch, cursed by the gods would fall stricken by invisible arm.

**CHROUS:** Oh, Rabetna, Baalet, Tyratha!

**SPENDIUS:** (to Matho). Do you fear death?—Why you still wait?

**MATHO:** I fear the gods, whom in my heart I honor.

**CHORUS:** Anaitis, Derceto, Mylitta!
(Shahabarim re-enters the sanctuary, where he deposits the Zaimph, leaving open the doors.)

**SHAHABARIM AND CHORUS:** Tanit, immortal queen, we glorify you, star whose light makes the whole world white.

**SPENDIUS:** (to Matho). Where is your love? Your strength, where does it lie?

**MATHO:** I fear the gods; let's fly.
(Spendius and Matho part. Knocking at door of temple.)

**SHAHABARIM:** Who knocks at the sanctuary; who dares disturb the sacred mystery.

**A PRIEST:** It is Salammbo!

**MATHO:** Salammbo, great gods!

**SPENDIUS:** (to Matho). She belongs to you, fortune favors you.
(Spendius disappears, Matho remains hidden; Salammbo enters.)

**SHAHABARIM:** Oh, daughter of Hamilcar, what would you do?

**SALAMMBO:** Oh, father, you who in the things of heaven deigned to instruct my youth. You whose mind is full of ancient wisdom, take pity on my weakness, my fear. Blest pontiff soften the heart of the goddess.

froi.
Pontife saint apaise la déesse . . .
Son courroux pése sur moi!

**SHAHABARIM:** Parmi les parfums, parmi les prières
Jusqu'ici tes jours coulaient purs et doux.
Dans les rites saints dont ils sont jaloux
As-tu donc blessé nos dieux tutélaires?

**SALAMMBÔ:** Je nes sais.
Tout m'accable et le repos me fuit!
J'ai supplié les Baals redoutables,
Eschmoun qui se déroule aux astres de la nuit,
Khamon etincelant aux flèches implacables!
J'ai conjure les dieux ancêtres d'Hamilcar;
Les Kabyres, caches dans les feux de la terre;
J'ai dormi, pâle et solitaire,
Sous l'olivier d'or de Melkarth.
C'est en vain!

**SHAHABARIM:** Je sais ta grande âme!
Jamais dans le sein d'une femme
N'a battu coeur plus fier, plus digne d'un héros.
Ce coeur saigne des maux
Dont Carthage est la proie!

**SALAMMBÔ:** Peut-être!
Qui connaît le repos et la joie?
Le barbare insolent sous nos murs est campé!
Pourtant, si mon espoir, prêtre, n'est point trompé
Tu peux rendre le calme à mon âme blessée!

**SHAHABARIM:** Parle . . . as-tu peur de ta pensée?

**SALAMMBÔ:** Au sein des ombres de la nuit,
Dans l'extase de la priere,
Des voix qui n'ont rien de la terre
Me répètent ces mots dont l'horreur me poursuit . . .
"Salammbô, le voile bénit
"C'est le salut de ta patrie.
"Donne ton coeur, ton sang, ta vie
"Sauve le voile de Tanit!

**SHAHABARIM:** (á part). Etrange illusion!

**SALAMMBÔ:** Ce voile saint, ô père,
Je veux le voir, apaiser
Mon trouble en le pressant sur mon sein le baiser
L'adorer! viens . . . montons au sanctuaire.
Marchons!

**SHAHABARIM:** Impie et téméraire Sacrilège!où veux-tu courir?
Je sais tu pas que nul profane ne contemple?
Le voile de Tanit; mystère de son temple?
Que le pontife seul le touche sans mourir?

**SALAMMBÔ:** Viens! guide-moi!

Her anger weighs upon me.

**SHAHABARIM:** Amid the perfumes, amid the prayers—until now your days were simple and pure. In the holy rites of which they're so jealous, how did you wound the gods of your land?

**SALAMMBO:** You know not. Everything weighs upon me and oppresses. I have to the fearsome Baals, Eschmoun, who waits in the watches of the night; Khamon, whose quivers never, never fail. I have begged of the gods, ancestors of Hamilcar, to the Kabyles hidden in the center of the earth. I have slept sick and solitary under the golden olive tree of Melkarth. All in vain!

**SHAHABARIM:** I follow your great soul. Never in bosom of woman beat a heart more proud, more worthy of hero. This heart beats the agonies of which Carthage is the victim.

**SALAMMBO:** It may be! You who know quietude and happiness. But the insolent barbarian is camped beneath our walls. Still if my hope is not mistaken, you can give some balm to my wounded soul.

**SHAHABARIM:** Speak—do you fear your own thought?

**SALAMMBO:** In the midst of the shadows of night—in the ecstacy of prayer, voices that nothing terrestrial, spoke words of horriful vent—
"Salammbo, the sacred veil, it is the saving of your land. Give your heart, your blood, your life. But save the veil of Tanit."

**SHAHABARIM:** (aside). Strange illusion.

**SALAMMBO:** This sacred veil, oh, father, I would see it, calm my trouble and pressing it to my bosom, kiss it, adore it. Come to the sanctuary—come!

**SHAHABARIM:** Impious and audacious—a sacrilege—where would you go? Know you not that no one profane can contemplate Tanit's veil, the mystery of her temple, that only the archpriest can touch it without death.

**SALAMMBO:** Come, guide me!

SHAHABARIM: C'est marcher à l'abîme!

SALAMMBÔ: Viens! par pitié!

SHAHABARIM: Tu mourrais sur le seuil!

SALAMMBÔ: Je veux le voir!

SHAHABARIM: Ces mots seuls sont un crime.

SALAMMBÔ: Tanit, m'appelle!

SHAHABARIM: Illusion! Orgueil!
Le sanctuaire est là! rien n'en défend l'entrée.
Monte, et brave Tanit jusqu'au fond du saint lieu,
Ou déplore a genoux ton audace abhorée.
Sois, a ton gré, pieuse ou sacrilège.
Adieu!

SALAMMBÔ: 'O ceil! me voilà seule en ce lieu redoubtable.
La déesse est presente et sous sa majesté
Qui m'accable
Mon coeur frémit épouvanté!
Qu'exiges-tu, Tanit, de l'esclave tremblante
Qui t'implore et t'adjure, embrassant ton autel?
Que me veulent ces voix, dans un doute cruel
Plongeant mon âme éperdue, hesitante?
Que ne puis-je au sein de la nuit
Et dans les flots purs des fontaines,
Dans le rayon qui passe et fuit,
Dans la brise aux tiédes haleines,
M'anéantir, glisser, couler,
Et jusqu'à toi, mère adorable,
Parfum, rayon, souffle impalpable,
Dans l'éther, dans l'azur, voler!
Voeux superflus! mon âme est liée à la terre!
Tanit, malgré ta volonté,
La prêtre a repoussé mon ardente prière,
Je n'ose le franchir, le seuil du sanctuaire
Et je ne verrai rien de ta divinité!

MATHO: Que tes voeux soient comblés!
(Il monte au sanctuaire.)

SALAMMBÔ: (Épouvantée, sans voir Matho). Qu'entends-je? quel mystère?

CHOEUR INVISIBLE: Salammbô, le voile bénit
C'est le salut de ta patrie.
Donne ton coeur, ton sang, ta vie!
Sauve le voile de Tanit!

SALAMMBÔ: Les voix parlent encore! ô
Tanit, tu m'appelles!
J'obéis!
(Elle se dirige vers le sanctuaire.)

MATHO: (paraissant couvert du Zaïmph). Salammbô!
(Salammbô tombant à genoux).
Puissances éternelles!

---

SHAHABARIM: You go to an abyss.

SALAMMBO: In pity's name, guide me.

SHAHABARIM: Would you die upon the threshold?

SALAMMBO: I must see it.

SHAHABARIM: The wish alone is a crime.

SALAMMBO: Tanit calls upon me.

SHAHABARIM: It is illusion, pride. The sanctuary is there. Naught prevents your entrance. Go and brave Tanit in the depths of her sainted home or on your knees deplore your awful audacity. Be as you wish, either pious or bold—farewell!

SALAMMBO: Great heaven, alone in this dreaded place—the goddess is here and in her majestic presence that overwhelms me; my heart almost stops beating. What would you Tanit from your trembling slave, who implores you, adjures you, kisses your altar?
What say the voices in such cruel doubt, thus making my soul unable to speak.
Why cannot I in the night, in the pure waters of fountains, in the ray that flits and passes, in the breeze that softly blows—reach chaos to live and yet die, to join you, adorable mother, and have my own place in the sky. A riffle, a thought, a mere zephyr, but fly to you now in the sky.
Vain thoughts; no, I am bound to earth, alas, and Tanit, in spite of your will, the priest has denied my prayer. I dare not cross your sacred precinct. I shall not see you, nor dare.

MATHO: (walking to the sanctuary). Your wish shall be accomplished.

SALAMMBO: (frightened, not seeing Matho). What do I hear—what new mystery?

INVISIBLE CHORUS: Salammbo, the sacred veil is the emblem of your country. Give your heart, your blood, your life, but save the veil of Tanit.

SALAMMBO: The voices speak again.
Oh, Tanit, you call me—I obey.
(She goes toward the sanctuary.)

MATHO: (appearing, covered with the Zaïmph). Salammbo!
(Salammbo falling on her knees.)

---

MATHO: Le voilà, ce voile sacré,
Le voilà, ce voile adoré.
Que l'on vénère dans la poudre . . .
D'éclat divin et de splendeur
Enivre tes yeux et ton coeur,
Et que sur moi tombe la foudre!

SALAMMBÔ: Toi qui m'aparais au seuil du saint lieu,
Parmi les rayons, dans l'éclat d'un dieu,
Vêtu des splendeurs de l'aurore;
Toi, qui viens vers moi pieux et clément
O consolateur, dieu jeune et charmant
Dis-moi sous quel nom l'on t'adore?

MATHO: Je t'aime?

SALAMMBÔ: Ah! daigne t'approcher
De ce coeur qui frémit d'ivresse!

MATHO: Je t'aime!

SALAMMBÔ: Ah! si j'osais toucher
Le voile saint de la déesse!

MATHO: Je t'aime . . .

SALAMMBÔ: Ah! Je la sentirais
Ainsi, se répandre en moi-même!

MATHO: Je t'aime!

SALAMMBÔ: Ah! viens! plus près! plus près!
O divine extase!

MATHO: (prêt à prendre Salammbô dans ses bras). Je t'aime!

SALAMMBÔ: O consolateur, dieu jeune et charmant,
Dis-moi sous quel nom l'on t'implore.

MATHO: Celui que tu crois quelque dieu clément
Ce n'est qu'un mortel qui t'adore!

SALAMMBÔ: (reculant, effrayée)
Qui donc es-tu, si tu n'es pas un dieu?
J'ai déjà vu, peut-être en un rêve, le feu
Terrible et doux dont ton regard S'eclaire?

MATHO: Je suis le mercenaire
Dont tu remplis la coupe aux jardins d'Hamilcar,
Je suis un soldat, un barbare,
Au camp barbare on m'obéit!
Vainqueur de tes dieux, je m'empare
Du voile sacre de Tanit,
Son pouvoir me fait plus qu'un homme.
Je puis braver Carthage ou Rome, Et ceindre le bandeau royal.
Viens!
Je t'aime à perdre la vie!
Vierge dont mon âme est ravie,
Veux-tu ce manteau nuptial?

SALAMMBÔ: O terreur! tout mon sang se glace!
Ah Tanit! a puni mon désir insultant!

MATHO: Salammbô! par grâce.

---

MATHO: Here is the sacred veil, the veil you all adore, that is venerated in the dust, of divine beauty and splendor. Let this sight rejoice you. Upon my head the anger of the gods.

SALAMMBO: You who appear in this sacred place, amid the rays in the garb of a god, clothed in the splendors of the dawn. You who greet me pious and forgiving, consoler, young and graceful god. Under what name shall I worship you?

MATHO: I love you.

SALAMMBO: Would you deign to approach this heart, now wild with joy?

MATHO: I love you.

SALAMMBO: If I only dared touch the sacred veil of the goddess.

MATHO: I love you.

SALAMMBO: The delight would permeate my being.

MATHO: I love you.

SALAMMBO: Oh, come nearer, yes nearer—divine ecstasy.

MATHO: (about to take her in his arms). I love you.

SALAMMBO: Great consoler, god young and charming. Tell me by what name they worship you.

MATHO: The one you think is some forgiving god is only a mortal who adores you.

SALAMMBO: (drawing back terrified). Who are you then, if not a god. I have already seen as in a dream the fire of your eyes, terrible, yet gentle. Speak.

MATHO: I am the mercenary whose cup you did fill in the gardens of Hamilcar; a soldier, a barbarian. In the camp they obey me. Conquerer of your gods, I hereby hold the sacred veil of Tanit. Its power makes me more than man. I can dare both Carthage and Rome, and assume the royal bandelet. Come to me, I love you more than life. Virgin who melts my soul. Take this nuptial garment.

SALAMMBO: Oh, horror, my blood freezes in my veins. Oh, Tanit has punished my impious desire.

MATHO: Salammbo, I beg you.

**SALAMMBÔ:** Va-t'en!
Va, sacrilège exécrable,
Va, monstre infâme et maudit!
Tombe et péris, misérable,
Sous les flèches de Tanit,
Va, que le dieu des batailles
Ouvre tes flancs douloureux:
Que le dieu des funérailles
T'étouffe en ses bras affreux!
Quel'horreur en toi circule,
Et que prompt à s'enflammer
Celui qu'on n'ose nommer
Te brûle . . .

**MATHO:** Salammbô! par pitié!
Tais-toi!
Je sens ma poitrine frappée
Comme par le fer d'une épée,
Epargne-moi!!
(*La lune s'est éteinte peu à peu.*)

**SALAMMBÔ:** O forfait inouï! dans
la voûte étoilée,
Tu le vois, Tanit s'est voilée!
Accorez! venez tous! un infâme! un
maudit!
Un sacrilège a dérobé Tanit!
(*Les Prêtres, accourant.*)

**LE CHOEUR:** O terreur! ô mortelle
offense!
Accourez tous!
Vengeance!

**MATHO:** (*tirant son épée*).
Malheur à qui m'ose approcher!
Craignez cette arme
vengeresse!
(*Remettant son épée au four-
reau.*)
Mais qui donc oserait toucher
Au voile saint de la déesse?

**LE CHOEUR:** (*menacant Matho*).
Sois maudit! sois brûle! que Moloch
te torture!
Que ta chair aux lions soit jetée en
pâture!
Tombe sous les traits de Tanit,
Sacrilège!
Infâme!
Maudit!
(*Matho se dirige vers la porte,
Shahabarim apparait.*)

**SHAHABARIM:** Outragée en sainte
image,
Dans sa juste indignation
Tanit abandonne Carthage!

**SALAMMBÔ:** (*désespérée*). Tanit
abandonne Carthage!

**TOUS:** O malédition!
(*Matho sort couvert du Zaïmph.*)

---

**SALAMMBO:** Go! Vanish! Sacrilegious wretch! Go, infamous and
cursed monster. Miserable wretch,
fall and perish. Go may the god of
battles open your wounds afresh.
May the god of death stifle you in
his horrible arms. Let horror be
your lot. Burn in a hell where
flames are everlasting.

**MATHO:** Salammbo, in pity spare
me. I feel myself hurt as by stroke of
steel.
Spare me!
(*The moon is growing dim.*)

**SALAMMBO:** Oh, inconceivable
sin in the starry vault, look, Tanit
hides her face. Come one, come all!
Infamous one, accursed. A sacrilege has come upon Tanit!
(*The priests rush in.*)

**CHORUS:** Oh, terror! Oh, mortal
offense. Come all; we cry for vengeance.

**MATHO:** (*drawing his sword*). He
who dares approach me may be unhappy. Be fearful of this vengeful
arm. (*Putting back his sword.*)
But who would dare place hands on
the sacred veil of the goddess.

**CHORUS:** (*threatening Matho*).
Be accursed! burn! May Moloch torture you. Fall under the ban of Tanit. Horror of horrors. Perish accursed!
(*Matho directs his steps toward
the gate.*)
(*Shahabraim appears.*)

**SHAHABARIM:** Outraged in her
sacred image Tanit in her indignation leaves Carthage.

**ALL:** Malediction!
(*Matho exits, covered by the
Zaïmph.*)

---

**LES ANCIENS:** Hélas!
hélas!
le courroux des dieux
S'est appesanti sur Carthage!
Hélas!
les Baals, soutiens des aeïux,
Ont de ce rivage
Detourne les yeux!

**UN GRAND PRÊTRE:** Khamon!
dieu du soleil splendide,
Souviens-toi de nous!

**LE GRAND PRÊTRE
D'ESCHMOUN:** Eschmoun!
dieu de la nuit limpide
Souviens-toi-de nous!

**LE GRAND PRÊTRE DE MOLOCH:**
Moloch!
dieu de larmes avide
Calme ton courroux!

**LES ANCIENS:** (*à Shahabarim*).
Toi, prêtre de Tanit, quel noir penser t'ègare?
Ne peux-tu te lever á ton tour, et
prier?

**SHAHABARIM:** (*avec désespoir*).
Qui m'entendrait?qui supplier?
La déesse irritée est au camp du bar-
bare!

**LES ANCIENS:** Hélas!
hélas!
Le courroux des dieux
S'est appesanti sur Carthage
Helas!
les Baals, soutiens des aeïux,
Ont de ce rivage
Détourne les yeux!

**CHOEUR:** (*lointain*). C'est le salut!
c'est la victoire!
Notre bouclier et notre rempart,
Fortune et gloire
Eu suffète Hamilcar!
(*Un esclave est entre et a remis à
Giscon des tablettes.*)

**GISCON:** Hamilcar débarque au ri-
vage,
Le peuple l'acclame au passage,
Il va parmi nous arriver . . .

**DES ANCIENS:** Pour parler en
tyran!

**D'AUTRES ANCIENS:** Non!
non!
pour nous sauver!

**LE CHOEUR:** (*au dehors, rap-
proché*). C'est le salut!
c'est la victoire!
Notre bouclier et notre rempart,
Fortune et gloire
Au suffète Hamilcar!
(*Les mêmes, Hamilcar.*)

**HAMILCAR:** Salut à vous d'abord,
ô dieux de la patrie;
Vous par qui je revois cette terre
bénie,
Où dorment mes aïeux!
Salut, pontifes saints, interprètes
des dieux!
Anciens . . . Sénat auguste et
sage . . .
Gardiens, défenseurs de Carthage,
Salut à vous!

---

**THE ANCIENS:** Alas! Alas! The anger of the gods has fallen upon Carthage. Alas, great Baal, god of our
ancestors, has withdrawn his aid
from our shores.

**ONE HIGH PRIEST:** Khamon! god
of the splendid sun—take pity on
us.

**SECOND HIGH PRIEST:** Eschmoun! god of the liquid night, take
pity on us.

**THIRD HIGH PRIEST:** Moloch!
god of tears and anger, avert that
your vengeance.

**ANCIENTS:** (*to Shahabarim*).
And you, Priest of Tanit, what black
thoughts take your mind. Can you
not also rise and pray?

**SHAHABARIM:** Who would hear
me—who to pray to? Our outraged
goddess is now in the barbarian's
camp.

**CHORUS:** Alas! Alas! the anger of
the gods has fallen upon Carthage.
Alas! great Baal, god of our ancestors, has withdrawn his aid from
our shores.

**CHORUS:** (*in distance*). It is salva-
tion!
It is victory! our shield is our pro-
tection. Honor and glory to great
Hamilcar.
(*Slave enters and hands tablets to
Giscon.*)

**GISCON:** Hamilcar debarks on the
shore.
The people acclaim his presence.
He will soon arrive among us.

**THE ANCIENTS:** To order as a
tyrant.

**OTHER ANCIENTS:** No, No! To
save us.

**CHORUS:** (*outside, but nearer*). It
is salvation! His victory! our shield
is our protection. Honor and glory
to great Hamilcar.
(*Enter Hamilcar*).

**HAMILCAR:** First, thanks to you,
oh gods of our country. To you
thanks for seeing once more this
blessed land, where my fathers
sleep. Ancients, Senate, just and
strong keepers and guardians of
Carthage, long life to you!

---

# ■ ACTE TROISIÈME

## *SCÈNE I*

*Le Conseil des Anciens.*
(*Le sanctuaire du temple de Mol-
och avec la statue du dieu, élevée
sur un piedestal.*)
(*Les anciens de Carthage, Giscon,
Shahabarim, les Grands Prêtres.*)

# ■ ACT III

## *SCENE I*

*Council of the Ancients.*
(*Sanctuary of the Temple of Moloch with the statue of the god on a
pedestal.*)
(*The ancients of Carthage, Giscon, Shahabarim and High Priests.*)

## Act III, Scene I

**LES PONTIFES ET LES ANCIENS:** Suffète de la mer, prends place parmi nous!

**HAMILCAR:** (*prenant place*). Et maintenant, veuillez me dire Quels sont ces crimes, ces malheurs Dont le bruit monte à moi dans de vagues rumeurs?

**LES ANCIENS:** Giscon, parle pour l'en instruire!

**GISCON:** Les Mercenaires révolté Assiègent les murs de Carthage, Livrant à la flamme, au pillage Nos faubourgs èpouvantes.

**HAMILCAR:** Quels griefs sont les leurs? Voulant le ciel propice, Avez-vous avec vous le droit et la justice?

**DES ANCIENS:** La justice?

**DES ANCIENS:** Il dit bien.

**DES ANCIENS:** Il trahit!

**DES ANCIENS:** Respectons Hamilcar!

**DES ANCIENS:** Paix!

**LES PONTIFES:** Il prend leur défense!

**LES PONTIFES:** Écoutons!

**HAMILCAR:** Avez-vous payé leur service? Leur solde?

**GISCON:** (*avec embaras*). On n'a pu l'acquitter encore.

**DES ANCIENS:** (*hypocritement*). Où trouverait-on tout cet or?

**HAMILCAR:** Vous faites détester partout la foi punique! Pour briser notre République, Le monde s'unira dans un immense effort; Des peuples accourront jusque des Atlantides! Les Lybiens viendront de leurs deserts arides, On verra d'Occident descendre les Numides, Les nomades du Sud, et les Romains du Nord; Tu tomberas, Carthage!

**LES ANCIENS:** (*se voilant de leurs manteaux*). Horreur!

**LES PONTIFES:** Dieux! détournez ce funeste présage!

**DES ANCIENS:** (*entre eux*). Lui seul peut nous sauver . . . parle-lui, toi, Giscon.

**GISCON:** Suffète, acceptes-tu le commandement?

**HAMILCAR:** Non! Qui peut vaincre avec vous?

**DES ANCIENS:** Il a peur!

**DES ANCIENS:** Il ménage Les barbares.

**DES ANCIENS:** Non! non!

**PRIESTS AND ANCIENTS:** Commander of the seas, take your place among us.

**HAMILCAR:** (*taking his seat*). And now, pray tell me, what crimes and misfortunes I vaguely hear have happened in this land.

**ANCIENTS:** Giscon, speak, that he may know.

**GISCON:** Revolted mercenaries besiege the walls of Carthage, giving to flame and pillage our homes without the walls.

**HAMILCAR:** What wrongs are theirs? Wishing heaven's blessing, have you in fact the right upon your side?

**ANCIENTS:** The right.

**OTHER ANCIENTS:** He speaks justly.

**ANCIENTS:** He talks treason.

**OTHER ANCIENTS:** Hamilcar! Respect him.

**STILL OTHERS:** Peace!

**HIGH PRIESTS:** He undertakes their defense.

**OTHER PRIESTS:** Let us listen!

**HAMILCAR:** Have you paid their service, their wage?

**GISCON:** (*embarrassed*). We have not been able to do it.

**ANCIENTS:** (*hypocritically*). Where could we find all this gold?

**HAMILCAR:** You make all detest the Punic war. To kill our republic the world will join in one immense effort. The people invade us even from the Atlantic coast. The Lybians from their aird deserts. We shall see the Occident send their Numidians and the Nomads of the South, and the Romans on the North. You will fall, poor Carthage!

**ANCIENTS:** (*covering their faces*). Oh, horror!

**HIGH PRIESTS:** Oh gods, do not allow such a thing to occur!

**ANCIENTS:** (*among themselves*). He alone can save us—speak to him, Giscon.

**GISCON:** Great chief, will you accept the command?

**HAMILCAR:** No! Who can win with you?

**ANCIENTS:** He's afraid.

**OTHER ANCIENTS:** He is in league with the barbarians.

**OTHER ANCIENTS:** No—no!

**DES ANCIENS:** Il veut se faire roi! (*Une partie des anciens se précipite du côté d'Hamilcar en brandissant des poignards. D'autres cherchent a les arrêter.*)

**HAMILCAR:** (*défiant ses agresseurs*). Osez porter la main sur moi, Courage! Et répandez ce sang Verse vingt fois pour la patrie!

**LES PONTIFES:** (*s'interposant*). Carthage vous supplie, Songez au peril menaçant! (*Les anciens reprennent leurs places.*)

**HAMILCAR:** (*aux Pontifes*). Avez-vous Tanit favorable? (*Un silence.*) Vous vous taisez? Vous baissez tous les yeux? (*À Shahabarim.*) Parle, pontif vénérable, Gardien du voile saint ou vit l'ame des dieux!

**SHAHABARIM:** Le manteau de Tanit est au camp du barbare!

**HAMILCAR:** O juste ciel!

**SHAHABARIM:** Leur chef audacieux Est venu le ravir.

**DES ANCIENS:** (*ironiquement à Hamilcar*). Un homme vigoureux, Alerte!

**DES ANCIENS:** (*aux autres*). Taisez-vous!

**DES ANCIENS:** Oui! d'une force rare. Plus grand que toi, suffète, et de plus amoureux De Salammbô qui l'aime. Ah! c'est un homme heureux!

**HAMILCAR:** Par tout ce qui brûle et devore! Par le feu des volcans, par la soif des deserts, Par l'abîme sale des mers. Par la foudre grondante et par le meteore, Devant Moloch a tête de taureau, Je le jure, Ma fille est sans reproche et pure! Tous avez menti tous, accusant Salambô! (*Un silence*) (*toujours menaçant*). Vous me choisissez tous pour chef, et sans partage?

**LES ANCIENS:** (*terrifies*). Oui!

**HAMILCAR:** De votre or, de vous, pouvant tout exiger?

**LES ANCIENS:** Oui!

**HAMILCAR:** Commandant à tous, dans l'armèe, á Carthage?

**LES ANCIENS:** Oui!

**HAMILCAR:** J'accepte!

**LES PONTIFES:** Les dieux puissent te protéger!

**ANCIENTS:** He wants to be king. (*One section of the ancients goes to side of Hamilcar, shaking their daggers. Others try to stop them*).

**HAMILCAR:** Dare to put a hand upon me! Have courage and let the blood flow, spent twenty times for our country.

**PRIESTS:** (*interposing*). Carthage supplicates you; think of the dire peril that greets us.

**HAMILCAR:** (*to Priests*). Is Tanit favorable? (*Silence*). You wait, you are silent, drop your eyes. (*To Shahabarim*) Speak, venerable pontiff, keeper of the sainted veil, the soul of the gods.

**SHAHABARIM:** The mantle of Tanit is in the barbarian camp.

**HAMILCAR:** Great god!

**SHAHABARIM:** Their audacious chief came here to ravish it.

**ANCIENTS:** (*ironically*). Yes, a strong man, vigorous, alert!

**OTHER ANCIENTS:** Keep quiet!

**ANCIENTS:** Yes, with marvelous force. Larger than you, Commander, and besides in love with Salammbo, who loves him. Oh, a happy man.

**HAMILCAR:** By all that burns and devours. By the fire of volcanoes; by the thirst of the desert; by the salted abysm of the seas; by the grinding thunder, and all the meteors. Before Moloch, with his head of a bull, I swear to you, my daughter is pure, without reproach. You have lied, all accusing Salammbo! (*General silence. Hamilcar, still menacing*). You choose me all for chief, and now without a partner.

**ANCIENTS:** (*terrified*). Yes!

**HAMILCAR:** Of your gold, of you, everything exacting?

**ANCIENTS:** Yes!

**HAMILCAR:** Mind you, commanding all the army of Carthage?

**ANCIENTS:** Yes, yes!

**HAMILCAR:** Then I accept.

**HIGH PRIESTS:** May the gods all protect you.

HAMILCAR: (*terrible*). Puissent-ils aussi me venger!
(*Montant à la statue de Moloch.*)
Pour que Moloch cruel et sanglant soit propice.
Je lui voue un cruel et sanglant sacrifice.

LES ANCIENS: (*suppliant*). Non! non!
Oh par pitié! grâce!
Ne parle pas!

HAMILCAR: Qui!
que Moloch en feu reçoive entre ses bras Vingt de vos fils, rançon du succès de nos armes!

LES ANCIENS: (*épouvantés*).
Dieux!

LES PONTIFES: Sois content, Moloch!
Enivre-toi de larmes!

LES ANCIENS: Horreur!
Effroi mortel!
Nos fils!
O dieux!
Héas!
(*Les anciens, désespérés, tombent prosternés autour de Moloch, devant qui Hamilcar est debout.*)

(*Rideau de manoeuvre.*)

## SCENE II

(*La terrasse de Salammbô, d'où l'on voit l'acropole de Carthage.*)

SALLAMBÔ: (*perdue dans ses pensées*). Oui de ce sacrilège affreux je suis coupable!
Oui je sens de Tanit le courroux redoubtable
Peser sur Carthage et sur moi.
Et toujours, toujours je le vois
Lui . . . ce ravisseur exécrable
Dans les splendeurs de ce voile de feu
Descendant vers moi tel qu'un dieu!
Tout m'épouvante et m'accable . . . Mon père,
Quand les bras ouverts je marchais vers lui,
A détourné son front sévère
Et son regard glacé m'a fui!
(*Douloureusement.*)
Mon père!
(*Salammbô, Shahabarim.*) (*Shahabarim à paru.*)

SHAHABARIM: (*s'approchant de Salammbô.*) Il est parti pour commander l'armée!
Dans un cercle de fer Carthage est en fer fermée;
Il va le briser ou mourir!

SALAMMBÔ: Heureux qui comme lui peut vous donner sa vie,
Q foyers, ô tombeaux des aïeux!
O patrie,
Désespérer de toi, c'est te trahir!

SALAMMBÔ: Les barbares sont là, campés devant nos portes?

---

HAMILCAR: (*angry*). May they also revenge me.
(*Going up to statue of Moloch.*)
To that Moloch, cruel and propitious, I vow to him a cruel and bloody sacrifice.

ANCIENTS: (*supplicating*). No, no, for pity's sake do not speak.

HAMILCAR: Yes, holding his embrace in fire, may take twenty of your sons; of his success, a ransom to our arms.

ANCIENTS: (*in terror*). Great gods!

HIGH PRIESTS: (*praying*). Be Moloch, happy, be happy with our tears.

ANCIENTS: Horror, mortal terror, our sons; oh, gods, alas!
(*The ancients in despair fall prone before Moloch, while Hamilcar stands defiant.*)

CURTAIN.

## SCENE II

(*The terrace of Salammbo looking upon the Carthaginian Acropolis.*)

SALAMMBO: (*alone*). Yes, in this sacrilege I feel myself guilty; I feel more of Tanit the angry, fierce vengeance that weighs on Carthage and on me. Yet always, always I see—He! the execrable one, who ravished, in the splendors of this veil of fire, coming down to me like a god. Everything frightens and unmoves me. Even my father, when I walked, open armed, toward him, turned away his severe face, and his icy glance froze my veins (*dolorously.*)
Oh, father!

SHAHABARIM: (*who has appeared*). He has departed to command the army. Carthage is incerned in a circle of iron. He will break it or die.

SALAMMBO: Happy like he who can give you his life. Oh, homes! oh, tombs of my ancestors; oh, country, to despair of you would be treason.

Salammbo: Barbarians are there before our very doors.

---

SHAHABARIM: Oui.

SALAMMBÔ: Leur chef?

SHAHABARIM: C'est Matho.

SALAMMBÔ: C'est bien.
De leurs cohortes
Sait-on le nombre?
De combien
De soldats sont-elles formées?

SHAHABARIM: Cent mille soldats . . . trois armées!

SALAMMBO: C'est bien . . .
(*Shahabarim observe toujours Salammbô. Au loin, une clarté rouge est apparue.*)

SALAMMBÔ: Là bas quel feu s'eleve?

SHAHABARIM: A Moloch on prépare
Un cruel sacrifice.

SALAMMBÔ: O terreur!
Et c'est moi! c'est mon crime!
Horreur!
Ah! j'irai dans le camp barbare!
Je ne veux pas mourir
Laissant un nom maudit.
Je veux reconquérir
Le voile de Tanit!

SHAHABARIM: Tu le pourrais peut-être!

SALAMMBÔ: Oui . . . du camp de Matho je prendrai le chemin.
Je saurai m'y glisser une arme dans la main.

SHAHABARIM: (*l'interrompant*). Non, ce n'est point ainsi . . .

SALAMMBÔ: Comment donc? parle, prêtre!
Tu te tais? ton regard
Se trouble!
Ah! je ne crains la mort ni la torture.

SHAHABARIM: Il est une arme plus sûre,
Plus têrrible que le poignard!
Va, souriante, avec ta plus riche parure.
Si tu dois mourir . . . ce sera plus tard.

SALAMMBÔ: Aller ainsi vers lui!
Tu me l'as dit, ô père,
L'âme des dieux parfois s'incarne sur la terre;
Et Matho, c'est Moloch peut-être!
Dans le feu De son regard, oui, j'ai senti le dieu!

SHAHABARIM: Delivre donc Tanit de Moloch prisonnière!
Va sauver Hamilcar, va sauver ton pays!

SALAMMBÔ: Tanit m'appelle et j'obéis!
Ordonne . . .

SHAHABARIM: En parure de fête,
Dès que viendra la nuit, sois prête.
Un homme sûr te guidera.

SALAMMBÔ: Toi, prêtre?

---

SHAHABARIM: It is true.

SALAMMBO: Who is their chief?

SHAHABARIM: One Matho.

SALAMMBO: It is well.
Do they know the number of their cohorts? Of how many soldiers are they formed?

SHAHBARIM: One hundred thousand—three armies!

SALAMMBO: Good.
(*Shahabarim continues to observe Salammbo. Far away a red light appears.*)

SALAMMBO: Beyond there what light appears?

SHAHABRIM: To Moloch they prepare a cruel sacrifice.

SALAMMBO: And it is me. It is my crime! Horror, I shall go in the barbarians' camp. I do not wish to die, leaving a cursed name. I wish to reconquer the Veil of Tanit.

SHAHABARIM: Perchance you might do it.

SALAMMBO: Yes, to the camp of Matho I might find the road and do it with a dagger in my hand.

SHAHABARIM: (*interrupting*). No, it cannot be thus.

SALAMMBO: What do you mean, speak, Priest—you are silent, you look away. I do not fear either death or torture.

SHAHABARIM: There is an arm more sure, more terrible than the poignard—go smiling in your richest dress, then if you must die—well it will be later.

SALAMMBO: Go thus to him—you told so, oh, father, sometimes the souls of gods are incarnated on the earth. Perhaps Matho is Moloch. In the fire of his eyes I felt the real god.

SHAHABARIM: Then deliver from Moloch the prisoner, Tanit—go, save our Hamilcar and our country.

SALAMMBO: Tanit calls and I shall obey. Command.

SHAHBARIM: In costume of feast, as soon as night comes, be ready. A trusty man shall guide you.

SALAMMBO: You, oh Priest?

**SHAHABARIM:** Un homme sur au camp te conduira.
(*Shahabarim sort. Taanach parait.*)

**SHAHBARIM:** He will be sure and to the camp will take you.
(*Shabaharim exits, Taanach appears.*)

**SALAMMBÔ:** Taanach, prends dans le coffre aux clous de diamant Ma parure, d'or pâle et de perles brodée

**SALAMMBO:** Taanach, take from the coffer with nails of diamonds my parure of pale gold and embroidered with pearls.

**TAANACH:** (*avec joie*). Celle pour tes noces gardée? Maîtresse, se peut-il?

**TAANACH:** (*joyfully*). Those selected for your wedding—good mistress is it possible?

**SALAMMBÔ:** Obéis seulement!
(*Toilette de Salammbô.*)

**SALAMMBO:** Simply obey.

**TAANACH:** Admire en ce miroir fidèle
Ta parure splendide, aux brillantes couleurs,
A ses noces bientôt, sous l'or et sous les fleurs,
La fille d'Hamilcar ne sera pas plus belle!

**TAANACH:** Admire in this faithful mirror the splendid jewels of brilliant colors. At her wedding under gold and with flowers, the daughter of Hamilcar could not be more beautiful.

**SALAMMBÔ:** Mes noces!

**SALAMMBO:** My wedding!

**TAANACH:** Quoi! Tes yeux se remplissent de pleurs?

**TAANACH:** What! Why do your eyes fill with tears?

**SALAMMBÔ:** (*à Taanach*). Vois là-haut dans le ciel passer ce blanc nuage . . .
Nous sommes dans ces tristes jours
Où les colombes de Carthage
Partent pour abriter loin d'elle leurs amours . . .
Regarde . . . elles vont disparaître,
Avec elles l'amour fuit ces bords délaissés.

**SALAMMBO:** (*to Taanach*). Do you see that fleecy cloud pass n the heavens. We are in the saddest days when the doves of Carthage go far away to make love and be loved Look—see—they will disappear and with them love leaves these wretched shores.

**TAANACH:** Mais elles reviendront, maîtresse.

**TAANACH:** But, mistress, they will come back.

**SALAMMBÔ:** Je le sais.

**SALAMMBO:** I know it.

**TANNACH:** Et tu les reverras . . .

**TAANACH:** And you will see them.

**SALAMMBÔ:** Peut-être!
(*Taanach sort. La nuit vient lentement.*)

**SALAMMBO:** Perhaps.
(*Taanach exits, Night comes slowly.*)

**SALAMMBO:** (*seule*). Qui me donnera, comme à la colombe,
Des ailes pour fuir dans le soir qui tombe?
Qui m'emportera libre de tourments, D'angoisses mortelles,
Vers de dieux plus doux, des cieux plus cléments?
Qui me donnera, colombes, vos ailes?
Pareille à la victime enchaînée à l'autel,
Qui tremblante et parée attend le coup mortel,
J'attends! je frémis! quel abîme
Devant mes pas va s'ouvrir?
Je ne sais rien sinon que je suis la victime,
Et que bientôt je dois mourir.
Qui me donnera, comme à la colombe, Des ailes pour fuir dans le soir qui tombe?
Qui m'emportera libre de tourments, D'angoisses mortelles,
Vers des dieux plus doux, des cieux plus cléments?
Qui me donnera, colombes, vos ailes?

**SALAMMBO:** (*alone*). Who would give me as the dove wings to fly in the twilight that falls. Who would take me away free from torment and mortal misery. Toward gods more good, toward heavens more sweet, give me, oh, dove, your wings to fly. Like the victim enchained to the altar—which appareled and trembling waits the fatal stroke, I wait—I tremble—what abyss before my steps will disclose. I know nothing beyond I'm the victim and that soon I must die. Who will give me wings as the dove has to fly away and on high. In the twilight, etc.
(*repeat*)
(*Night has come, Trumpets in Temple of Tanit.*)
Oh gods, already the sacred brass. The east already shows the color of dawn. The hour has come. What mortal terror has frozen my veins—what exact you from me? Oh hide me beneath your shadow, gates of this somber palace, gods fearful of human beings, place me beneath your portals—save me paternal

(*La nuit est presque venue. Fanfares au loin dans le temple de Tanit.*)
Dieux . . . Déjà retentit la trompette sacrée.
L'Orient se remplit d'une lueur nacrée.
C'est l'heure! Ah! quel mortel effroi
M'a glacée!
O Tanit! qu'exiges-tu de moi?
Ah! dérobez-moi sous votre ombre,
Portiques de ce palais sombre.
Dieux pitoyables aux mortels,
Sauves-moi; gardez-moi, doux foyers paternals!
(*La lune apparait sur la mer.*)

home.
(*The moon comes up.*)

**CHOEUR:** (*au loin dans le temple de Tanit*). Retentissez, cris d'allégresse,
Sonnez, clairons sacrés, hymnes religieux,
Saluez la déesse,
Elancez-vous aux cieux!

**CHORUS:** (*in Tanit's temple*). Ring out songs of joy, Resound your sacred brasses and religious hymns, Sing now to the goddess, sound to the heavens!

**SALAMMBÔ:** O Tanit, pardonne!
A toi je me devoue, a toi je m'abandonne!
(*Shahabarim déguise, suivi d'un autre homme, parait Salammbô va vers eux.*)

**SALAMMBO:** Oh, Tanit, forgive—to you I vow my life; to you my soul, my all.
(*Shahabarim disguised followed by another, appears. Salammbo goes toward them.*)

CURTAIN.

# ■ ACTE QUATRIÈME

# ■ ACT IV

## SCÈNE I

## SCENE I

Le Camp.
La tente de Matho, trophèes d'armes au milieu duquel le Zaïmph est caché sous un peau de lion; au fond, le camp des Mercenaires. Effect de soleil couchant.
(*Spendius, Autharite, Mercenaires, Soldats, Danseuses jouent aux dés. On entend le bruit joyeux du camp.*)
(*A la fin du ballet, les clarions se font entendre au dehors.*)

The Camp.
(*The tent of Matho. A trophy of arms in the midst of which is the Zaimph hidden under a lion's skin. At back the camp of the Mercenaries. Effect of setting sun.*)
(*Spendius, Autharite, Mercenaries, Soldiers, Female dancers. They are playing dice. The joyful sounds of the camp are heard.*)
(*At end of ballet the bugles are heard outside.*)

**NARR'HAVAS:** (*à Matho*). Terreur et fléau de Carthage,
Toi, que le voile saint dont tu t'es emparé
A fait de tous ceux qu'elle outrage
Le chef superbe et vénéré;
Matho, je viens à toi t'offrant mon alliance,
J'ai des élephants, de l'or, je suis roi!
Dix mille cavaliers, combattent avec moi!
Contre Carthage, unis dans la meme vengeance,
Nous pourrons la briser comme un faible roseau!
Comme je brise cette lance!
(*A part, à Matho.*)
Pardonne un jour d'ivresse folle . . .

**NARR'HAVAS:** (*to Matho*). Terror and curse of Carthage, who has taken the sacred veil has made you the superb and venerated chief by all whom it outrages! Matho, I come to you offering my alliance. I have elephants and gold. I am king. Ten thousand horsemen combat with me. Against Carthage united in the same vengeance, we can break its power like a feeble reed-just as I break this lance!
(*Aside to Matho.*) Forgive a day of silly folly—Salammbo. None will see her again. She has fled from the palace of her father this night.

Salammbô.
Nul ne doit la revoir.
Du palais de son père
Cette nuit a fui . . .

**MATHO:** Grands dieux.

**NARR'HAVAS:** Une galère
Sans doute la conduit à quelque bord lointain.

**MATHO:** J'accepte, ô roi, voici ma main!

**AUTHARITE:** Qui trahit aujourd'hui pourra trahir demain!

**MATHO:** Vous chefs, et vous Soldats, jurez tous avec nous!
(*Matho, Narr'Havas, Spendius, Autharite, les chefs numides mettent l'épée à la main et les reunissent sur le meme bouclier, les Mercenaires les entourent l'épée haute.*)

**MATHO, NARR'HAVAS, SPENDIUS, AUTHARITE ET COEUR:**
Soyes témoins, dieux des batailles,
Soyez témoins, dieux infernaux!
Nous jurons de combattre en frères, en héros!
Nous jurons de braver les mêmes funérailles!
Nous jurons de mêler notre sang et nos os!
Soyez témions, dieux des batailles!
Soyez témions, dieux infernaux!
(*La nuit est venue.*)

**MATHO:** Voici la nuit!
Interrompez les jeux . . .
Rentrez au camp sans tarder davantage
Et que partout étincellent les feux.
(*Salammbô voilée, conduite par Shahabarim déguise, parait au dehors de la tente.*)

**AUTHARITE:** Deux transfuges sont là qui viennent de Carthage
Et demandant à voir le chef très valeureux.

**MATHO:** Sur-le-champ, dans ma tente, introduis-les tous deux.

**NARR'HAVAS:** (*à part*). Si c'était, Salammbô qui parût en ces lieux
Esclave d'un amour sacrilège, odieux,
Pour la reconquérir, pour venger mon injure
Rein ne me coûterait, pas même le parjure.
(*Il s'élance vers Salammbô, mais Shahabarim se place entre elle et lui et se jetant a ses pieds, découvre son visage. Narr'Havas reconnait Shahabarim qui lui fait un geste de silence et l'entraine vers le camp. La tente se referme.*)

**SALAMMBÔ:** (*jetant son voile*).
La voix des dieux à moi s'est fait entendre, Je viens vers toi, soldat, pour te reprendre, Le voile divin!
Je n'ai tremblé de la nuit, ni des piques
Ni d'être ici, soldat, les dieux puniques Me donnaient la main!
Je viens sans arme et pourtant vengeresse,

**MATHO:** Great gods!

**NARR'HAVAS:** A vessel, no doubt, took her to foreign shores.

**MATHO:** I accept, oh, king; here is my hand.

**AUTHARITE:** Who betrays today may betray tomorrow.

**MATHO:** Chiefs, all of you, and soldiers too, swear with us.

**PRINCIPALS AND CHORUS:** Be witness, gods fo battles. Be witness, gods of the inferno. We swear to fight as brothers, as heroes. We swear to confront the same deaths on the field. We swear to mingle our bones and our blood. Be witness, gods of battle—be witness, gods of war.
(*Night has come*).

**MATHO:** Night has come, stop your playing. Go back to your camps without further murmur, and at once put out the fires that flame.
(*Salammbo veiled, guided by Shahabarim disguised, appears outside the tent.*)

**AUTHARITE:** Here come two refugees from Carthage who ask to see our valorous chieftain.

**MATHO:** On the spot in my tent, introduce them—would see them.

**NARR'HAVAS:** (*aside*). If it were Salammbo who appeared in this place, slave of a sacrilegious and odious love. Now to regain her, to revenge wrong done to me; nothing would cost me, not even perjury.
(*He leaps toward Salammbo, but Shahabarim places himself between the two, throws himself at his feet, discovers his face. Narr. recognizes Shahabarim, who makes a move of silence and drags him toward the camp. The tent closes.*)

**SALAMMBO:** (*opening her veil*). The voices of the gods have come to me. I come to you, soldier, to take back from you the divine veil. I have not trembled of the night, nor from anger, nor even to be here. Soldier, the punic gods would give me their aid. I come without arms and still an avenger, to deliver, soldier, our goddess, and save my

Pour déliverer, soldat, notre déesse, Sauver mon pays.
Rends-moi le voile, âme de ma patrie,
Ou frappe-moi, soldat, et prends ma vie.
J'ordonne! obéis!

**MATHO:** O charme cruel et supreme, Maudis-moi, mais ne me fuis pas!
Ah! je voudrais mourir entre tes bras . . .
Je suis à toi, tout à toi!
je t'aime!

**VOIX DES SENTINELLES:** Des feux ont brillé là-bas!
Soldats, veillez! Veillez, soldats!
(*Sur un geste de Salammbô, Matho s'approche du trophée et decouvre le Zaïmph qui apparaît resplendissant.*)

**MATHO:** Le voilà, ce voile sacré
Le voilà, ce voile adoré
Vois, son tissu divin rayonne!
De son éclat, de sa splendeur
Enivre tes yeux et ton coeur.
Il est à toi, je te le donne!

**SALAMMBÔ:** (*s'agenouillant*).
Anaïtis,
Dercéto, Mylitta,
O Rabettna, Baalet, Tyratha!

**LES VOIX DES SENTINELLES:** (*au dehors*). Soldats, veillez!
Veillez, soldats!
Des feux ont brillè là-bas!
(*Salammbô se releve s'approche du Zaïmph et va pour le prendre.*)

**MATHO:** (*l'arrêtant*). Que fais-tu?

**SALAMMBO:** Je retourne à Carthage!

**MATHO:** (*prennant son épée*). Ah! tu viens
Reprendre le Zaïmph pour me livrer aux tiens.
Désarme, ma force abattue?
N'essaye pas de t'enfuir! Je te tue!
Vierge insolente, aux fiers regards, tu m'appartiens!
Je suis le maître et toi l'esclave et la servante!
Tes temples, tes palais, dans les cris, l'épouvante
S'écrouleront en feu sous le ciel rougissant!
Tes vaisseaux flotteront sur des vagues de sang!
Pas un palmier sur ce rivage, Pas une pierre ne dira:
Elle était là, Carthage!

**SALAMMBÔ:** (*se jetant a lui*). Frappe-moi donc la première!

**MATHO:** (*laissant tomber son épée*). Ah! pardon!
Pitié! j'ai perdu la raison!

**SALAMMBÔ:** (*à part*). Ah! garde-moi, bonté supreme!
Tanit, sauve-moi di moi-même!

country. Give me back the veil, soul of my land, or strike me here, soldier, and take my life. I order! Obey!

**MATHO:** Oh, cruel and supreme charm! Curse me, but do not go away. Ah, that I could die in your arms. I am yours, yes all yours. I love you!

**VOICES OF SENTINELS:** Fires have burned on the ramparts. Be watchful, be careful! Watch!
(*On a motion of Salammbo, Matho approaches the trophy and uncovers the Zaimph, which appears resplendeut.*)

**MATHO:** It is there, the mystic veil. It is there, this veil so adored. See its exquisite tissue divinely shines. From its beauty, its splendor, make glad your eyes and your heart. It is yours, it is my gift.

**SALAMMBO:** (*kneeling*). Anaitis, Deceto, Mylitta; oh, Rabettna, Baalet, Tryatha!

**VOICES OF SENTINELS:** Be watchful, be careful! Watch! Fires have burned on the ramparts.
(*Salammbo rises and goes to take the Zaimph.*)

**MATHO:** (*stopping her*). What would you do?

**SALAMMBO:** Why! Return to Carthage!

**MATHO:** (*taking his sword*). Ah, then, you come to take the Zaimph so as to deliver me to your people. Disarmed, my strength gone and finished. Do not try to escape, I'd kill you. Insolent virgin, in spite of your haughty look, you now belong to me. I'm now the master, you the servant and slave. Your temples, your palaces, amid the shrieks and the terror, will die out in flames under a reddening sky. Your vessels shall float on a sea of blood! Not a palm tree on this shore, not a stone erect shall say, Here was Carthage.

**SALAMMBO:** (*throwing herself at him*). Then let me be the first one stricken!

**MATHO:** (*letting fall his sword*). Oh, pardon; have pity; I've lost my reason.

**SALAMMBO:** (*aside*). Oh keep me, great gods on high. Tanit, save me even from myself!

**MATHO:** Ne les détourne pas, ces regards radieux,
Profonds comme la mer et purs comme l'aurore.
Je m'abandonne à toi!
Tes dieux seront mes dieux,
O Salammbô, mon bien, mon âme, je t'adore!

**SALAMMBÔ:** (*à part*). Dieux! Quel trouble s'éveille en mon coeur éperdu!
Quel feu divin en moi s'est répandu?

**MATHO:** (*suppliant*). O Salammbô, mon bien, mon âme, je t'adore!

**SALAMMBÔ:** Ah! l'univers est oublié quand il m'implore!
(*Matho va prendre le Zaïmph: a ce moment l'orage. Appels de clairons se repandant.*)

**VOIX:** (*au dehors*). Alerte compagnons!
Aux armes! les clairons!
C'est l'ennemi! les soldats de Carthage
L'ennemi vient pendant l'orage,
Alerte, compagnons!

**SALAMMBÔ:** (*repoussant le Zaïmph que Matho lui offre*). Non! garde ton présent et laisse-moi partir!
C'en est fait!
Laisse-moi suivre ma destinée.
Va! nos dieux m'ont abandonnée.
Matho . . . Je ne puis te haïr!

**MATHO:** Salammbô!

**VOIX:** (*au dehors*). Trahison! les perfides!
Aux armes! les Numides!

**SALAMMBÔ:** On t'appelle au combat! adieu, va, laisse-moi Partir!

**MATHO:** Non, non! ma vie et ma glorie, c'est toi! (*Jetant le Zaïmph sur les épaules de Salammbô.*)
Ah! Je t'aime à perdre la vie!
Vierge dont mon âme est ravie,
Violà ton manteau nuptial!

**SALAMMBÔ:** (*faiblissant*) A quel pouvoir fatal
Tu me livres déesse!

**MATHO:** Viens sur ce coeur
Que tu remplis d'ivresse!

**SALAMBÔ:** O souffrance adorable ineffable langueur!
Un ordre des Baals m'entraíne et me soulève
Dans des nuages d'or m'emportant comme un rêve!
La force m'abandonne et mes yeux pleins de pleurs
Se violent! dans l'effroi, dans l'extase je meurs!

**MATHO:** Sois à moi pour jamais!

**SALAMMBO:** Ah! voile ton flambeau, Tanit! . . . Ah! Moloch! tu me brûles!

**MATHO:** Do not turn from me those radiant glances. Deep as the sea and pure as the dawn, I give myself to you. Your gods shall be my gods. On Salammbo, my own, my soul, I adore you.

**SALAMMBO** Oh gods what strange feeling has come in my heart. What divine fire has captured my whole being.

**MATHO:** (*supplicating*). Oh Salammbo, my own, my soul, I adore you!

**SALAMMBO:** Oh, the world is forgotten when thus he implores. (*Matho goes to take the Zaimph, and at the moment a storm bursts, and then bugle calls are heard.*)

**VOICE:** (*outside*). To arms! companions, to arms! Sound trumpets. The enemy is here, the soldiers of Carthage! They come, thinking the storm will protect them, on foot!

**SALAMMBO:** (*giving back the veil Matho offers her*). No keep your present and let me go. It is done! Let me meet my fate. Go! Our gods have abandoned me. But Matho, I should, but I cannot hate you.

**MATHO:** Salammbo.

**SHOUTS:** (*outside*). Treason, oh, treason; the Numids to arms!

**SALAMMBO:** They call you to arms. Farewell! Go, let me leave.

**MATHO:** No, no, my life, my glory, it is you. (*Throwing the Zaimph on her shoulders*). Ah, I love you enough to forfeit my life. Virgin, of whom my soul is in flame, here is your nuptial mantle!

**SALAMMBO:** (*weak and aflame*). To what fatal power do you give me up, oh, goddess.

**MATHO:** Come to my heart, you fill me with ecstacy.

**SALAMMBO:** Oh, adorable suffering, oh, ineffable languor. An order of the gods carries me and lifts me into golden clouds appearing like a dream. My strength gives way, my eyes, so full of tears—are blind . . . in terror and ecstacy I die!

**MATHO:** Be mine forever.

**SALAMMBO:** Put out your torch, Tanit, oh, Moloch, do not burn me.

**MATHO:** (*la prenant dans ses bras*).Salammbô!
(*Violent coup de tonnerre. Le fond de la la tente gagnée par les flammes, s'écroule et laisse voir le camp tout en feu.*)

**VOIX:** (*au dehors*). Matho! Matho!

**MATHO;** (*comme s'éveillant*). Ciel!
Quelles voix m'appellent?
Tout le camp est en feu!
Des armes étincellent
Au combat! au combat!
(*S'arrachant à Salammbô, éperdué*)
Adieu!
(*Il prend son épée et s'élance.*)

**SALAMBÔ:** (*seule*). Le voile saint est reconquis.
Mais que la foudre me dévore,
O dieux cruels, je vous abhorre
Et vous maudis!!!
(*Elle va pour sortir couverte du Zaïmph*)

## SCÈNE II

Le champ de Bataille.
(*Decouvre le champ de bataille jonché de ruines et de morts. Au fond le camp barbare détruit dont les ruines fument encore. A l'extreme lointain, Carthage.*)

**HAMILCAR, NARR'HAVAS, LE CHOEUR DES CARTHAGINOIS ET DES NUMIDES:** Triomphe! gloire!
Victorie!

**HAMILCAR:** Carthage est libre et ses farouches ennemis Sont dispersés, anéantis!
Du bataillon sacré la valeur était vaine,
Déjà nos éléphants s'enfuyaient dans la plaine,
Mais un secours du ciel est sur nous descendu.
Oui, Tanit apaisée, oubliant sa colère,
A répandu sur nous sa force tutélaire . . .
Tanit pour nous a combattu!

**SHAHABARIM:** Que partout l'encens fume
Sur les autels de la cité!
O Tanit, que le feu consume
Un holocauste offert à ta divinité!

**CHOEUR:** Triomphe!
Glorie!
Victorie!

**NARR'HAVAS:** Hamilcar, tu le sais, dans un jour de folie,
Aux ennemis de ta patrie
J'avais promis mon appui . . .
Ces liens
Je les ai détestés, ma colère anvolée,
Et suis venu vers toi: dans le mêlée
Mes cavaliers se sont unis aux tiens!

**MATHO:** (*holding her in his arms*). Salammbo!
(*Violent stroke of thunder; tent in flames falls, giving view of camp alight.*)

**VOICES:** Matho! Matho!

**MATHO:** (*as if awakening*). Heavens, what voices call me. All the camp is afire. The men are all in arms. To the fight, to the fight (*tearing himself away from Salammbo*). Farewell! (*He seizes his sword and rushes out.*)

**SALAMMBO:** (*alone*). The sacred veil is recovered. But let the lightning devour me. Oh, cruel gods, I abhor and detest you.
(*She exits, covered with the Zaimph*).

## SCENE II

The Battle.
(*The scene shows the ruins and the dead. The destroyed Barbarian camp and the smoking tents. In the distance—Carthage.*)

**HAMILCAR, NARR'HAVAS, CARTHAGINIANS and NUMIDIANS:** (*on stage.*) Triumph, glory and victory.

**HAMILCAR:** Carthage is free and her ferocious enemies are dispersed and at an end. Of the sacred battalion the valor was in vain. Already our elephants were flying in the plain, when from heaven a sudden succor came. Yes, Tanit, appeased, forgetting her anger, spread over us her tutelary strength. Tanit spoke and fought for us!

**SHAHABARIM:** That everywhere incense burns, on the altars of the city. Oh Tanit may the fire consume a holocaust offering to your divinity.

**CHORUS:** Triumph, glory and victory!

**NARR'HAVAS:** Hamilcar, you know upon a day of folly, to the enemies of your country I promised help and aid. These bonds I detested once my anger gone, and thus came back to you. In the battle my horsemen quickly joined your own.

**HAMILCAR:** (*froidement*). J'ignore, ô roi, quel prix t'offriront les anciens, Mais Hamilcar n'est point ingrat . . .

**HAMILCAR:** (*coldly*). I know not, oh, king, what price they will offer you, but Hamilcar is not ungrateful.

**NARR'HAVAS:** La récompense La plus charmante et le prix le plus beau, Hamilcar, sont en ta puissance. (*Montrant Salammbô qui paraît.*) Ta fille!

**NARR'HAVAS:** The recompense, most charming, and the prize most rich, Hamilcar, are in your power. (*Showing Salammbô, who appears*).

**HAMILCAR, SHAHABARIM ET LE CHOEUR:** Salammbô! (*Salammbô, couverte d'un long manteau noir, descend lentement.*)

**HAMILCAR, SHAHABARIM and CHORUS:** Salammbo! (*Salammbo, covered with black, comes slowly.*)

**LE CHOEUR:** Quelle pâleur mortelle! Qu'elle est touchante et belle, Marchant ainsi d'un pas religieux Et sans lever sur nous les yeux!

**CHORUS:** What mortal pallor, how touching and how lovely; coming thus with religious mien, not even lifting her eyes.

**SALAMMBÔ:** (*encore au fond*). Le gage à qui vous devez la victoire, Le manteau de Tanit rayonnant de sa glorie, Il est reconquist! Le voilà! (*Elle écarte son manteau, et l'on voit le Zaïmph.*)

**SALAMMBO:** (*still at back*). The prize to which you owe the victory, the great veil of Tanit, splendid in its glory, is reconquered—here it is. (*She pulls back her mantle and the Zaïmph is seen.*)

**LE CHOEUR:** O joie! espoir! orgueil! c'est notre bon génie! Salammbô, sois bénie!

**CHORUS:** Oh, joy, hope and pride our good genius has returned. Salammbo, you're blessed.

**LE CHOEUR ET SHAHABARIM:** (*adorant le Zaïmph*). Anaïtis! Dercéto! Mylitte! O Rabbetna, Baalet, Tyratha!

**SHAHABARIM AND CHORUS:** (*adoring the Zaïmph*). Anaitis! Derceto! Mylitta! Oh Rabetna, Baalet, Tyratha!

**NARR'HAVAS:** (*à part*). Matho sans doute est'mort en trompant ma colère!

**NARR'HAVAS:** (*aside*). Matho no doubt is dead while deserving my anger!

**HAMILCAR:** (*à Salammbô.*) Qu'as-tu fait?

**HAMILCAR:** (*to Salammbo*). What did you do?

**SALAMMBÔ:** J'ai sauvé ma patrie et mon père! (*Shahabarim, suivi des prêtres, sort en emportant le Zaïmph.*)

**SALAMMBO:** Saved my country and my father! (*Shahabarim, followed by priests, exits with the Zaïmph, as on come Spendius, Autharite, barbarian chiefs and prisoners.*)

**LE CHOEUR:** Des chefs prisonniers! (*Les mêmes, Spendius, Autharite, chefs, barbares, prisonniers.*)

**CHORUS:** (no text)

**LE CHOEUR:** Maudits! Sacrilèges! bandits! Scélérats! détestable engeance! La croix, la torture! Vengenace!

**CHORUS:** Be accursed, sacrilegious bandits. Scoundrels detestable wretches—to the cross, to the torture! vengeance!

**AUTHARITE ET LES PRISONNIERS:** Nous saurons subir notre sort. Nous ne demandons point de grâce Nous serions sans pitié, vainqueurs a votre place. Envoyez-nous donc à la mort!

**AUTHARITE AND PRISONERS:** We know how to meet our fate and ask no sort of mercy. Without pity, had we been the conquerers, so send us now to death!

**SPENDIUS:** (*aux pieds d'Hamilcar*). Noble Hamilcar, sauve moi! Ce lambeau De pourpre, je l'arrache et redeviens esclave!

**SPENDIUS:** (*at the feet of Hamilcar*). Noble Hamilcar, save me! These rags of purple I'll tear away, become again a slave. Oh, pallor of death, let some other than myself now mock you. Save me,

O pâle mort, qu'un autre et t'appelle et te brave! Sauve-moi; Narr'Havas! Sauve-moi, Salammbô!

Narr'Havas—save me, Salammbo.

**AUTHARITE:** O honte! devant un maître Lâchement s'humilier, Et lâchement supplier Jusqu'a Narr'Havas, ce traître!

**AUTHARITE:** Oh, shame! Before a master, cowardly humiliant, and cowardly begging even to the traitor Narr'Havas.

**HAMILCAR ET SHAHABARIM:** Tous á la mort! Que l'on dresse leurs croix! (*Pendant la scène suivante, on voit des croix, s'élevant lentement, se détacher sur le ciel au lointain.*)

**HAMILCAR AND SHAHABARIM:** All to the death—let the crosses be raised. (*During the following scene crosses are seen slowly erected in the distancee*).

**MATHO:** (*s'élançant, son épée brisée à la main*). Et la mienne aussi.

**MATHO:** (*rushing on, sword in hand*). Give me also mine.

**SALAMMBÔ:** Grands dieux! . . . je le revoi!

**SALAMMBO:** Great gods! I see him once more!

**TOUS:** Matho! Dans l'agonie horrible Le lion est encore terrible!

**ALL:** Matho! Even in his horrible agony the lion still is terrible.

**MATHO:** Pourquoi ces cris et cet effroi? Quoi! vous reculez tous? aves-vous peur de moi? Ne craignez rien! ma force est épuisée. (*Il jette son épée.*) Mon épée brisée! Mon coeur aussi!

**MATHO:** Why these cries and this fright? What, you all fall back? Are you afraid of me? Fear nothing, for my strength is gone. (*Throws away his sword.*) My word is broken, also my heart.

**SALAMMBÔ** (*à part*). Dieux! faites-moi mourir! Votre victime est lasse de souffrir!

**SALAMMBO:** (*aside*). Oh, gods, let me die; your victim is tired of suffering.

**MATHO:** (*à Hamilcar*) Toi qui n'as pas rogi de souiller tant de gloire En achetant ce misérable roi! (*A Narr'Havas.*) Toi qui vas lâchement où s'en va la victoire, Courtisan couronné qui hier étais à moi! (*A Salammbô.*) Toi, plus que le destin, et fatale et cruelle, O Salammbô, si perfide et si belle! (*S'attendrissant*). Salammbô! Salammbô! (*Avec force.*) Je vous déteste tous! O dieux vengeurs, tenez vos foudres prêtes! Dieux infernaux, épousez mon courroux, Semez le désespoir et la mort sur leurs têtes!

**MATHO:** (*to Hamilcar*). You who have not blushed to soil glory so great in buying this miserable king. (*To Narr'Havas*). You! you coward, who at the moment of victory, deserted, Crowned courtesan who but yesterday belonged to me. (*To Salammbo*). You, more than destiny fatal and cruel; oh, Salammbo, so false and so beautiful. (*Weeping*). Salammbo! Salammbo! (*With force*). I detest you all, oh avenging gods, keep your thunders ready. Gods of infernal depths, join in my anger, let only death and despair fall on their heads.

**TOUS:** (*moins Salammbô et les captifs*). Dieux infernaux, épargnez-nous! Au supplice!

**ALL:** (*excepting Salammbo and captives*). Gods infernal, spare us. To the torture.

**SALAMMBÔ:** (*épouvantée*). Au supplice!

**SALAMMBO:** (*fearful*). To the torture!

**HAMILCAR:** Non! Matho doit vivre un jour encore, Et son sang doit rougir l'autel où l'on t'adore, Tanit!

**HAMILCAR:** No! Matho shall live one day longer. His blood shall redden the altar where you adore—Tanit!

## Act IV, Scene II

LE CHOEUR: Quels cris de joie aux cieux s'éleveront!

HAMILCAR: Expirant, il verra Carthage triomphante,
Narr'Havas épousant dans la pompe éclatante
Celle qui délivra le voile de Tanit.

SALAMMBÔ: Grand Dieux!

NARR'HAVAS: Demain tu mourras!

MATHO: Délivrance!

HAMILCAR: C'est ainsi qu'Hamilcar récompense
Et punit!
(*On sépare Matho des autres captifs, Matho est emmens chargé de chaines. Hamilcar arrête Salammbô qui fait un mouvement vers Matho.*)

(*Rideau.*)

CHORUS: What shouts of joy will go up to heaven.

HAMILCAR: Expiring, he will see Carthage triumphant and Narr'Havas' wedding in splendor and in pomp, the one who rescued the veil of Tanit.

SALAMMBO: Great gods!

NARR'HAVAS: Tomorrow you die.

MATHO: Good deliverance.

HAMILCAR: Thus it is that Hamilcar punishes and awards.
(*They take Matho away from the other captives. Matho is put in chains. Hamilcar stops Salammbo, who wants to run to Matho.*)

CURTAIN.

## ■ ACTE CINQUIÈME

*Les noces de Salammbô.*
(*Le forum de Carthage. La foule couvre les terrasses. Tout est en fête.*)
(*Au lever du rideau, les cinq pontifes sont debout au pied de la statue de Tanit.*)

CHOEUR: O fête! ô triomphe! ô joie! ô délire!
Carthage ton sol sacré
Du barbare est délivre!
Brûlez pour les dieux l'encens et la myrrhe!
Salammbô va devant nous
S'unir à son jeune époux!
Mêlez à vos chants la flûte et la lyre!
Voile saint, trésor sans prix,
Salammbô t'a reconquis!
O fête! ô triomphe! ô joie! ô délire!

SHAHABARIM: Peuple, tes dieux
Partageant ton ivresse,
Frémissent d'allégresse Au sein des cieux!
Quittant sa demeure étoilée
Pour se livrer à ton amour,
Devant toi Tanit pour un jour S'est dévoilée.

LES PONTIFES ET LES PRÊTRES:
Peuple, tes dieux
Partageant ton ivresse
Frémissent d'allégresse
Au sein des cieux!

LE CHOEUR: O fête! ô triomphe! ô joie! ô délire!
Carthage, ton sol sacré
Du barbare est délivre!
Brûlez pour les dieux l'encens et la myrrhe
Salammbô va devant nous
S'unir à son jeune époux.
Mêlez à vos chants la flûte et la lyre!
Voile saint, trésor sans prix,
Salammbô t'a reconquis . . .
O fête! ô triomphe! ô joie! ô délire!

## ■ ACT V

*Wedding of Salammbo.*
(*The forum of Carthage. The crowd swarms about the terraces. All is noise and joy.*)
(*At rise of curtain the High Priests stand at the foot of the statue of Tanit.*)

CHORUS: Oh, let us feast on triumph, on joy, on a craze. Sacred land of Carthage, is delivered from barbarians. Burn the incense and the myrrh for the gods. Salammbo goes before us to join her youthful spouse. Join in your songs both flute and lyre. Sainted veil, priceless treasure, Salammbo has reconquered you. Oh, triumph, let's feast; oh, joy, let us feast!

SHAHABARIM: People, your gods join in your happiness; they tremble with joy beyond bounds to the very heaven. Giving up her starry abode to deliver herself to your love. Before you for a day Tanit is uncovered.

HIGH PRIESTS AND OTHERS:
Oh, people, your gods partaking in your joy would feast with you in heaven itself.

CHORUS: Let us feast on triumph, on joy, on a craze. Your sacred soil, oh, Carthage, is delivered from the Nomad. Burn for the gods the incense and the myrrh. Salammbo goes before to join her young spouse. Join your songs the flute and the lyre. Sacred veil, priceless treasure, Salammbo has reconquered it. Let's feast and drink and celebrate the day.

CHOEUR: Voyez! entendez! l'air résonne
Des saintes clameurs des clairons . . .
Les dieux marchent vers nous!
Salammbô qu'environne
Leur gloire, vient parmi l'encens et les rayons!
(*Marche triomphale.*)
(*Le cortège des prêtres. Les Anciens, Trophées des victoires d'Hamilcar. Enfin Narr'Havas, puis, sur un char de triomphe, Hamilcar et Salammbô.*)

CHOEUR: (*a l'apparition de Salammbô*). Salut! et sois bénie
Au nom de la patrie,
Des vieillards, des enfants!
Salut! et sois heureuse,
Fortune radieuse,
Suis ses pas triomphants!
(*Des prêtres apportent l'appareil des sacrifices.*)

LES PONTIFES: (*à Salammbô et à Narr'Havas*). Avant que le ciel vous unisse, Roi Narr'Havas, et toi notre orgueil, Salammbô!
Nous devons à Tanit un sanglant sacrifice.

HAMILCAR: Amenez la victime!

SALAMMBÔ: O dieux sauvers!
(*Grand mouvement dans le peuple. Matho amene par des gardes est jete devant la statue de Tanit; il vient tomber devant Salammbô, auprès de l'autel.*)

TOUS: Matho!

LE CHOEUR: Eh bien? pourquoi tarder!à l'autel!le couteau!
Sacrilège! bandit! ravisseur! lâche! traître!

SHAHABARIM: (*prenant une épée*). Accepte donc ce sang, Tanit!

LE CHOEUR: Non, pas le prêtre!!
Celle qui délivra le voile!
Salammbô!!

HAMILCAR, NARR'HAVAS, MATHO, SHAHABARIM, LES PONTIFS, LES PRÊTRES DE TANIT: Salammbô!dieux!

SALAMMBÔ: (*s'avançant*). J'entends ce que le peuple ordonne!

HAMILCAR: Quoi! tu veux obéir!

NARR'HAVAS: (*voulant l'arreter*). Salammbô!

SALAMMBÔ: Prêtre, donne!
(*Elle prend l'épée et descend près de Matho agenouillé a l'autel. Matho lève vers elle des regards pleins d'amour. Salammbô fait un effort surhumain pour soulever l'épée. Son bras retombe.*)

TOUS: Quoi?
De sa main le glaive échappe!
Venge Tanit, Salammbô, frappe!

MATHO: Frappe!

OTHERS: Oh, hear, oh hear, the very air resounds with sacred clamors of the brass. The gods come near us. In the midst of their glory Salammbo comes amid perfume and incense.
(*Triumphal march. Procession of Priests, people and ancients and trophies of Hamilcar, and last Narr'Havas, and on a triumphal chariot Hamilcar and Salammbo.*)

CHORUS: (*as Salammbo appears*). In the name of our country be blessed and be happy; the vow of old and young, we bend the knee, be happy. May radiant fortune follow her radiant course.

PRIESTS: (*bringing the sacrificial altar*). Before heaven joins you together with King Narr'Havas, and you, our pride, Salammbo, we owe to Tanit a bloody sacrifice.

HAMILCAR:Bring forth the victim.

SALAMMBO: Oh, protecting gods.
(*Great emotion among the people. Matho dragged in by the guards in thrown before the statue of Tanit. He falls in front of Salammbo by the altar.*)

ALL: Matho.

CHORUS: Well, why wait—to the altar, to the knife. Sacrilegious bandit! ravisher! coward traitor!

SHAHABARIM: (*taking the sword*). Accept this blood, oh Tanit.

CHORUS: No—not the priest! The one who rescued the veil—Salammbo!

HAMILCAR AND THE REST: Salammbo! oh gods on high.

SALAMMBO: (*coming forward*) I hear what the people ordain.

HAMILCAR: What, and you would obey?

NARR'HAVAS: (*trying to stop her*) Saslammbo!

SALAMMBO: Priest, give me the knife.
(*She takes the sword and goes toward Matho, who is kneeling by the altar. He looks toward her, his eyes full of love. Salammbo makes a superhuman effort to lift the sword. Her arm falls.*)

ALL: What? the sword escapes from her hand Revenge Tanit, Salammbo, strike!

MATHO: Strike!

**SALAMMBÔ:** (*levant l'épée*). Accepte donc, Tanit,
Le sange qui va couler!
Que par cette rosée, Ta vengeance soit apaisée!
Quiconque ta toucha, voile saint et bénit,
Doit mourir!
(*Elle se frappe.*)

**TOUS:** O dieux! ô jour lamentable!

**MATHO:** (*brisant ses liens, s'armant de l'épée et pregnant Salammbô dans ses bras.*) N'approchez pas! elle est à moi!

**SALAMMBO:** (*raising the sword*). Then Tanit accept the blood that now will run. Thus by this dew let your vengeance be appeased—whoever touched your saintly and blessed veil—must die.
(*She strikes herself.*)

**ALL:** Oh gods, lamentable day!

**MATHO:** (*breaking his bonds, taking the sword and holding Salammbo in his arms*). Do not approach, for she is mine. Salammbo,

Salammbô, je t'adore et je m'en vais à toi!
(*Il se frappe et tombe tenant entre ses bras Salammbô expirante.*)

**TOUS:** Quiconque aura touché ton voile vénérable
Devra mourir, ô déesse implacable!

**LES PONTIFES ET LES PRÊTRES:** Anaïtis, Dercéto, Mylitta, O Rabbetna, Baalet, Tyratha!
(*Rideau.*)

*FIN.*

I adore you and with you I die.
(*He delivers the fatal stroke, holding the dying Salammbo.*)

**ALL:** Whoever shall hold this awful veil must die, unforgiving goddess.

**HIGH PRIESTS AND OTHERS:** Anaïtis, Derceto, Mylitta, oh Rabetna, Baalet; Tyratha.

*CURTAIN.*

# Snégurotchka (1882)

## The Snow Maiden

MUSIC BY NIKOLAI ANDREEVICH RIMSKY-KORSAKOFF ■ LIBRETTO BY ALEXANDRE OSTROVSKY

This four-act opera (a spring fairy tale) with a prologue is set to a libretto by the composer (based upon Alexander N. Ostrovsky's comedy). It premiered at the Maryinski Theatre in St. Petersburg on February 10, 1882. The opera opens with the Spring fairy, who does not want to end the winter, telling the birds that she doesn't want to leave her daughter, Snégurotchka, whose father is Old Winter. The birds know that Snégurotchka will die if Yarilo, the sun, ever sees her. Winter is afraid that Yarilo will make his daughter fall in love with him, causing her heart (which is made of ice) to melt. He places her in the care of the Spirit of the Woods, and she is adopted by Bobil and Bobilicka, a peasant couple who live at the entrance to Tsar Berendey's village. Snégurotchka is not happy there, and Kupava, her closest friend, invites her to her wedding and introduces her to Mizgir, her fiancé. He falls in love with Snégurotchka at once and leaves Kupava, who appeals to Tsar Berendey for assistance. Berendey questions Snégurotchka, who answers that she loves no one, and he invites the two friends to the a ball celebrating the end of winter as a way of reconciling them. Snégurotchka remains immobile throughout the ball, but Kupava accepts the love of a shepherd, Lehl, who wants to marry her. Mizgir tells Snégurotchka that evening that he is in love with her. She returns to the woods and pleads with her mother to give her the ability to love. The Spring fairy comes, bearing flowers for her. Snégurotchka feels a deep new emotion as she goes to meet her beloved, and she accepts his marriage proposal. Just before the wedding, Mizgir asks the Tsar for his blessing, but a sun ray melts Snégurotchka completely away. Mizgir, deeply grieved, throws himself into the lake and drowns. As soon as Snégurotchka has melted, the sun shines once more.

---

*PROLOGUE.*

*Commencement du printemps; il fait nuit; la Montagne Rouge est couverte de neige. A droite, des buissons, un bouquet de bouleaux clairsemés et sans feuilles. A gauche, une épaisse forêt de pins et de sapins. Les branches plient sous le poids de la neige. Au fond, au pied de la montagne, un fleuve; les trous dans la glace sont entourés de petits sapins. De l'autre côté du fleuve le bourg de Berendeyeff, capitale du tzar Berendey; les palais, les maisons et les izbas sont en bois ornés de découpures peintes en différentes couleurs. Les fenêtres sont éclairées. La pleine lune argente tout le terrain découvert. Au*

*loin, les coqs chantent.*

*PROLOGUE.*

*It is at the beginning of spring; night has fallen, and the Red Mountain is covered with snow. To the right, bushes, a scattered cluster of leafless birches. To the left, a thick forest of pine and fir trees, their branches bending beneath the weight of the snow. At the back, at the foot of the mountain, a river; holes in the ice are surrounded by small firs. On the other side of the river, the town of Berendeyeff, the capital of the Tzar Berendey. Its palaces, houses and izbas are of wood, ornamented with carvings painted in various colors. Lights shine in the windows. A full moon silvers the open country. In the distance the cocks are crowing.*

## SCÈNE I.

LE FAUNE, LA FÉE PRINTEMPS et les OISEAUX.

*Le Faune est assis sur un souche déssechée. Le ciel tout entier se couvre peu à peu d'oiseaux arrivés d'au-delà des mers.*

**LE FAUNE:** Adieu l'hiver! Les coqs ont chanté,
La Fée Printemps va naître avec l'aurore,
Voici le temps, où finit ma garde.

## SCENE I.

THE FAUN, FAIRY SPRING and the BIRDS.

*The Faun is seated in a hollow tree. Little by little, the entire sky is covered with birds arriving from beyond the seas.*

**THE FAUN:** Farewell winter! The cocks have crowed,
And Fairy Spring will come to earth with dawn.
The time's at hand when my long vi-

Je puis dormir en paix.
*(Il disparaît dans le creux de l'arbre).*
*(Les oiseaux arrivent de plus en plus nombreux.)*
*(La Fée Printemps, portée par les cigognes, les cygnes et les oies, et entourée d'une suite d'oiseaux, descend sur la Colline Rouge.)*

**LA FÉE PRINTEMPS:** A l'heure dite, au jour marqué dans l'ordre
Des temps, je viens au pays des Berendeys,
Pays du froid, pays des long hivers,
Pays muet, pays de triste accueil.
Où sont, hélas! les pays,
Les beaux pays du soleil?
Le pays toujours heureux
Au bord des flots d'azur?
Là-bas, les prés fleuris,
Les sombres bois de myrtes
Et les jardins de roses
Embaument l'air des soirs;
Un tiède et doux parfum
S'exhale de la terre.
Là-bas, la lune d'argent,
La lune tendre et calme,
Caresse de ses rayons
Les arbres tout en fleurs;
Dans l'âme des hommes
J'éveille l'amour,
Dans l'ombre immense et morne
des bois en deuil,
Je fais du sol glacé jaillir des fleurs.
*(S'adressant aux oiseaux qui grelottent de froid.)*

gil is over,
I'll once more sleep in peace.
*(He disappears in the hollow of the tree.)*
*(The birds continue to arrive in increasing numbers.)*
*(Fairy Spring, borne through the air by storks, swans and geese, and surrounded by a retinue of birds, alights on the Red Mountain.)*

**FAIRY SPRING:** At the hour given, the day is marked in the calends
Of time, I seek the country of the Berendeys;
A land of cold, a land of winters long,
A silent land, whose welcome does not cheer.
Where are, alas, those lands,
Those lovely lands of sunshine?
The land whose joy endures,
Beside the azure waves?
Yonder, the flowering meads,
The somber myrtle thickets,
And gardens full of roses
Scent all the evening air.
A fragrance warm and sweet
Is breathed forth by the earth.
Yonder, a silver moon,
A tender moon and calm,
Caresses with its rays
The blossom-laden trees,
And in men's souls
I waken love.
Now in the very shadow, vast and chill, of woods that mourn,
I bid the flowers spring up from the

Mes chers oiseaux, vous mes commères pies
Voilà seize ans déjà, par pur caprice,
J'ai voulu faire la coquette avec l'hiver,
Galant au coeur gelé. Depuis ce jour
C'est moi qui suis esclave. Une fille
Nous est née; en son pouvoir
Il garde mon enfant chérie
Snégourotchka.
Dans ces forêts où l'ombre est éternelle,
Au plus profond des bois toujours glacés,
Le père en son palais retient ma fille,
Je la voudrais heureuse et je l'adore;
Il faut pour l'amour d'elle me soumettre
Au vieux Bonhomme Hiver, tyran morose
De ce pays et de moi-même.
Il ne veut pas au doux printemps céder la place,
Vite, vite, dansez en rond, dansez pour vous chauffer,
Dansez, dansez, ainsi que font les hommes!
(*Quelques oiseaux prennent leurs instruments, d'autres commencent à chanter, d'autres encore dansent.*)

CHOEUR DES OISEAUX: D'un bout à l'autre
Du vaste monde
Les oiseaux accourent;
Devant leur reine,
Sujets fidèles,
Les oiseaux s'assemblent.
Qui dans notre peuple
Sont les forts, les maîtres?
Les petits, les faibles?
Qui dans notre peuple
Sont les forts, les maîtres?
Les petits, les faibles?
(*Le givre, puis des flocons de neige commencent à tomber sur les oiseaux qui dansent; le vent se lève, le ciel se voile de nuages qui couvrent la lune; le brouillard s'étend sur le lointain.*)

LES OISEAUX: (*se pressant, en criant, autour de la Fée Printemps*). Ah! Ah! Il neige! Il neige à gros flocons!

LA FÉE PRINTEMPS: Bein vite, entrez sous bois,
Voici venir le vieil Hiver!
(*Les oiseaux se cachent dans les buissons. Le Bonhomme Hiver sort de la forêt.*)

## SCÈNE II.

LA FÉE PRINTEMPS, LE BONHOMME HIVER.

---

frozen sod.
(*Speaking to the birds, who are trembling with cold.*)
Dear birds of mine, you gossips dear to me,
It was sixteen years ago, moved by mere caprice,
That I coquetted with old Winter here,
Galant with heart of ice. And since that day,
I am his slave. A girl
Was born to us, and is in his power.
He keeps my child, my cherished Snegurotchka,
In these vast forests of eternal shade,
Deep in the heart of woods that never thaw,
Her father in his place guards my child;
I, who adore her, willingly would see her happy,
For love of her I must submit
To my old husband Winter, despot morose,
Ruling this land and me.
He will not, does not wish to yield his place to gentle Spring!
Come, come, dance a round, dance to warm yourselves,
Dance, dance, as dance the sons of men!
(*Some birds seize their instruments, others begin to sing, while still others dance.*)

CHORUS OF BIRDS: From one end to the other
Of this vast world,
The birds come hastening;
To their queen's presence,
Subjects loyal,
The birds assemble.
Who among our folk
Are the strong, the masters?
Who are the small and weak?
(*Hail, followed by snowflakes, commences to fall on the dancing birds; the wind begins to blow, the sky is veiled in clouds which hide the moon; the storm spreads afar.*)

THE BIRDS: (*crowding around Fairy Spring, cry out*). Ah, ah! It is snowing! The big flakes are falling!

FAIRY SPRING: Quick! Into the woods!
King Winter himself is coming!
(*The birds hide in the bushes. King Winter comes out of the forest.*)

## SCENE II.

FAIRY SPRING, KING WINTER.

---

LE BONHOMME HIVER: Quand le froid fait craquer la charpente
Et les murs des maisons,
Quand le froid fait grincer sur leurs gonds
Les grand' portes des cours,
La fumée qui s'élève au-dessus des maisons,
La légère fumée qui s'envole et s'enfuit
Sous le souffle du vent,
Je la gèle soudain
Je la gèle et la tiens
Suspendue—
Sur la plaine, sur les arbres;
Suspendue
Quel plaisir pour moi,
Quel plaisir!

LA FÉE PRINTEMPS: La fête a bien assez duré. Allons,
Sois raisonnable, et pars! En route!

LE BONHOMME HIVER: Laisse donc,
Je vais partir—mais tu ne m'aimes plus.
Il ne te souvient pas du temps passé.

LA FÉE PRINTEMPS: Mais à qui
Veux-tu laisser ta fille?

LE BONHOMME HIVER: La voilà
Déjà grande et sage, et d'âge à se conduire;
Sa retraite est sûre, nul chemin n'y mène:
Elle peut y demeurer en paix.

LA FÉE PRINTEMPS: Folie!
Non, c'est la liberté qu'il faut aux filles.

LE BONHOMME HIVER: Je sais que le soleil
Veut la mort de notre enfant chérie,
Que le soleil brûlant veut embraser et fondre
Au feu du ciel, au feu d'amour le coeur
De notre enfant Snégourotchka.
Mais elle,
Tant qu'elle restera candide et pure,
N'a rien à craindre du soleil. Ecoute!
Jamais fille n'est trop bien gardée.
Bobyl, le pauvre diable, est sans enfants,
Donnons-la-lui, et qu'elle soit sa fille!

LA FÉE PRINTEMPS: J'accepte.
LE BONHOMME HIVER: Petite Snégourotchka, viens vite ici!
SNÉGOUROTCHKA: (*met la tête à la lisière du bois*). Holà! Holà!
(*Entre en scène en courant et s'approche de son père.*)

## SCÈNE III.

SNÉGOUROTCHKA, LE BONHOMME HIVER et LA FÉE PRINTEMPS, plus tard le FAUNE.

---

KING WINTER: When the cold cracks the timbers,
And the walls of the houses;
When the frost makes the great courtyard gates
Creak on their hinges,
Then the smoke rising over the dwellings,
The smoke floating upward to vanish
Beneath the breath of the wind,
I freeze of a sudden.
Aye, I freeze it and hold it Suspended;
Over the plain, above the trees Suspended
What pleasure it gives me,
How I enjoy it!

FAIRY SPRING: Your holiday has lasted long enough. Come,
Be reasonable, and go! Off with you!

KING WINTER: Let be!
I'm going—You no longer love me, though.
No longer do you recall the days gone by.

FAIRY SPRING: Now to whom
Will you trust your daughter?

KING WINTER: She is here,
Already grown up, steady, old enough to behave;
No road leads to her refuge safe:
There she can stay all undisturbed.

FAIRY SPRING: Madness!
No, liberty is what a young girl needs.

KING WINTER: Well do I know the sun
Would gladly slay our darling child,
I know the burning sun would clasp and melt
In the sky's fire, in passion's flame the heart
Of our child Snegurotchka. She, however,
As long as she is pure and innocent,
Need never fear the burning sun. Listen!
No girl can ever be too virtuously guarded.
Bobyl, the poor devil, he is childless,
We'll give her to him, she shall be his daughter!

FAIRY SPRING: I am willing.
KING WINTER: Little Snegurotchka, come here quickly!
SNEGUROTCHKA: (*peering out from the edge of the forest*). Hallo! Hallo!
(*She runs out on the stage and goes up to her father.*)

## SCENE III.

SNEGUROTCHKA, KING WINTER and FAIRY SPRING, afterward the FAUN.

## Scene III

**LA FÉE PRINTEMPS:** Pauvre petite neige, fleur sauvage,
Vien vite près de moi que je t'embrasse!
(*Caressant Snégourotchka.*)
Ma belle, veux-tu vivre seule et libre
Chez les humains?

**SNÉGOUROTCHKA:** Oh oui, oh oui, ma mère!
Aller au bois cueillir la framboise,
Répondre aux voix joyeuses des compagnes,
A-ou, A-ou!
Chanter en choeur, redire après Lel
Les chants joyeux qui fêtent le printemps,
Oi, Lado Lel!
Voilà mon rêve et mon bonheur;
Je ne puis vivre sans chansons.
Consens, mon père, et quand tu reviendras
Avec l'hiver, dans les grands bois épais,
Le soir, le soir, je chanterai, je chanterai,
Pour égayer la solitude,
Les plus gais de mes refrains.
Le beau Lel me les apprendra,
Je les saurai bien vite.

**LE BONHOMME HIVER:** Ce beau Lel qui te l'a fait connaître?

**SNÉGOUROTCHKA:** De ma cachette
Je l'ai vu passer, j'ai vu les jeunes filles
Venir à lui, promettre à ce berger
Le plus doux baisers, s'il veut chanter pour elles,
Lui dire des noms tendres; gentil Lel.
O Lel charmant, o Lel chéri!

**LA FÉE PRINTEMPS:** Ce Lel
Chante-t-il donc si bien, mignonne?

**SNÉGOUROTCHKA:** Mère! Je connais,
Je connais, ma mère, tous les chants les plus beaux,
Le chant de l'alouette qui monte et rit au ciel d'été,
Et le plaintif appel du cygne sur l'eau dormante de l'étang.
Et je connais, oui, je connais
La voix sublime et pure du rossignol,
Charmeur divin des nuits profondes: j'aime mieux les chants de Lel,
Oui, j'aime mieux les chants de Lel; le jour, la nuit,
Sans trève et sans repos
J'écoute, j'écoute
Et sens mon coeur se fondre.

**LE BONHOMME HIVER:** Fondre! fondre!
Mot redoutable, mot d'affreux présage!
Snégourotchka, fuis Lel, ma fille,
Crains ses chansons et ses paroles.

**FAIRY SPRING:** Poor little flower, poor wild flower,
Come to me quickly, come into my arms!
(*Caressing her.*)
My sweet, would you live alone and free
Among mere men?

**SNEGUROTCHKA:** Oh yes, oh yes, dear mother!
To go strawberrying in the woods,
Replying to merry-voiced companions,
A-ou, A-ou!
To sing in chorus, after Lel repeat
The joyous songs that celebrate the spring,
Oi, Lado Lel!
Such is my dream, were my delight;
For without song I cannot live.
Consent, dear father, and when you return,
With winter to deep forest fastnesses,
At fall of night when I will sing, I'll sing,
To lend our loneliness a needed cheer,
The gayest of the songs I know.
It is handsome Lel who'll teach me them,
And I'll be quick to learn.

**KING WINTER:** This handsome Lel, who made him known to you?

**SNEGUROTCHKA:** From out of my hiding place
I've seen him passing. I have seen the girls
Go to him, promising the shepherd boy
The sweetest kisses if he'd sing for them,
And call him tender names: You handsome Lel!
You charming Lel, Oh Lel beloved!

**FAIRY SPRING:** This Lel,
Say, does he sing so well, my pet?

**SNEGUROTCHKA:** Mother! I know
I know, dear mother mine, all of the loveliest songs,
The lark's which rises laughing to the skies,
And the swan's plaintive call,
sounding over lakes adream.
Yes, and I know, I know
The nightingale's pure voice, her song sublime,
Enchantress of profoundest night;
but I love Lel's songs best of all.
Yes, I love best the songs of Lel, and day and night,
Without rest or repose
I hark and listen;
And feel my whole heart melt.

**KING WINTER:** Melt! Melt!
O dreaded word! Word filled with evil omen!
Snegurotchka, avoid Lel, my daughter,
Mistrust his song and pleasant words!

**LA FÉE PRINTEMPS:** O ma fille,
Ta mère t'aime et veillera sur toi!

**SNÉGOUROTCHKA:** Je suis enfant soumise et sage, mais je
Ne crains vraiment ni Lel, ni ses chansons.

**LA FÉE PRINTEMPS:** Snégourotchka, si tu dois être
Un jour dans l'angoisse et la douleur,
Viens me trouver dans le val du dieu Yarilo,
Appelle-moi et quoi que tu demandes
Je le ferai pour toi!

**SNÉGOUROTCHKA:** Merci, ma mere.

**VOIX DANS LA FORÊT:** A-ou! A-ou!
(*Le Faune sort du creux d'un arbre desséché, s'étirant et baillant.*)

**LE BONHOMME HIVER:** Faune, écoute:
Si Lel où si quelque autre de ces hommes
Poursuit jamais la fille de neige,
De leur coupable atteinte défends-la;
Egare-les, attire-les au fond des fourrés sombres,
Embourbe-les dans les tourbières!

**LE FAUNE:** Bien, mon maître!
(*Croise ses bras au-dessus de la tête et disparaît dans sons creux d'arbre.*)
(*Les Berendeys conduisent le carnaval derrière la scène.*)

**CHOEUR:** Oï, oï, oï,
Oï! beau carnaval, carnaval,
Oï! beau carnaval, carnaval!

**LE FÉE PRINTEMPS:** Ce sont les chants joyeux des Berendeys.
Partons, bonhomme!
Snégourotchka, adieu,
Et sois heureuse, ô mon enfant!

**SNÉGOUROTCHKA:** O ma mère
Qu'on puisse ou non trouver le bonheur, je veux le chercher!

**LE BONHOMME HIVER:** Adieu, ma fille si chérie!

**LA FÉE PRINTEMPS:** Allons, que l'hiver cesse!
Plus de brouillards, plus de frimas.
Pars vite et
N'attriste pas ainsi le gai cortège du carnaval!

**LE BONHOMME HIVER:** Fini le froid, fini l'hiver!
(*Sort en faisant signe de son bonnet.*)
(*La chasse-neige cesse, les nuages s'en vont. Le temps redevient serein comme au début de l'acte. Foule des Berendeys. Les uns poussent vers la forêt le traîneau portant le mannequin du carnaval (Ier choeur), d'autres restent un peu plus loin (IIe choeur).*)

**FAIRY SPRING:** O my daughter,
Your mother loves you, and will watch over you!

**SNEGUROTCHKA:** I am a child both prudent and discreet, but I
Fear neither Lel, nor yet the songs he sings.

**FAIRY SPRING:** Snegurotchka, if it should chance that you
Some day are filled with anguish and with grief,
Come seek me in the vale of the god Yarilo,
Call on my name, and whatever you demand,
That will I do for you!

**SNEGUROTCHKA:** Thanks, mother of mine.

**VOICES IN THE FOREST:** A-ou! A-ou!
(*The Faun comes out of the hollow tree trunk, stretching and yawning.*)

**KING WINTER:** Hark to me, Faun:
If Lel, or any other of these men,
Ever pursues the daughter of the snow,
Against their culpable attempts, defend her;
Lead them astray amid the tangled thickets,
And set them floundering in the water bogs!

**THE FAUN:** I shall, my master!
(*Crossing his arms above his head he disappears in the hollow trunk.*)
(*The Berendeys are celebrating the carnival, off stage.*)

**CHORUS:** Oi, Oi, Oi,
Oi, fair carnival, carnival!
Oi, fair carnival, carnival!

**FAIRY SPRING:** They are the joyous songs sung by the Berendeys.
King Winter, let us be off! Snegurotchka, farewell!
Be happy now, O child of mine!

**SNEGUROTCHKA:** O mother of mine,
Whether or not I may find happiness, at least I'll seek it!

**KING WINTER:** So long, my so beloved daugther.

**FAIRY SPRING:** Come now, let winter cease!
A truce to hailstorms and to frosts!
Go swiftly,
Do not sadden the merry carnival cortege!

**KING WINTER:** A truce to cold, the winter's over!
(*Off, making a sign with his cap.*)
(*The snowfall ceases, the clouds disappear. The weather becomes clear as at the beginning of the act. A crowd of the Berendeys. Some are pushing the sleigh bearing the mannikin representing the Carnival toward the forest (Chorus I.); others remain somewhat further to the rear (Chorus*

*Snégourotchka se tient derrière les buissons, près du creux d'arbre.)*

## SCENE IV.

*SNÉGOUROTCHKA, BOBYL, BO-BYLICKA, BERENDEYS.*

**II. CHŒUR:** *(entrant en scène).*
Oï, Oï, Oï!
Oï! beau carnaval, Oï! beau carnaval!
*(Conduite du Carnaval.)*

**I. CHŒUR:** Les coqs chantent depuis l'aurore
Annonçant le doux printemps,
Adieu, adieu, carnaval, adieu!
Tu nous as gorgés de bonne chère,
Enivrés d'hydromel et de bière,
Adieu, adieu, carnaval, adieu!
Le bon vin coulait comme un fleuve,
Le bon vin coulait à flots,
Adieu, adieu, carnaval, adieu!
Te voilà debout glorieux et fier,
Bourré de foin, vêtu de mousse,
Adieu, adieu, carnaval, adieu!
On te rend ici des honneurs royaux,
On te mène aux bois dans un beau traîneau,
Adieu, adieu, carnaval, adieu!
Nous allons te quitter tout à l'heure
Et nos yeux ne te verront plus,
Adieu, adieu, carnaval, adieu!
*(Le Ier chœur pousse le traîneau vers la forêt et se met à l'écart.)*

**II. CHŒUR:** Oï, Oï, Oï!
Oï, beau carnaval, Oï! beau carnaval, oï!
Pendant un an tu dormiras,
Et l'an prochain t'éveilleras, Adieu!

**CARNAVAL:** L'été qui vient bientôt fuira,
Adieu, soleil de flamme et d'or!
Après l'été fuira l'automne,
Adieu, moissons, adieu, vendange!
Voici les mois aux longues nuits!
Voici l'hiver tout blanc de neige.
Mais déjà le jour s'allonge et le
Soleil devient plus chaud, quand le
Dégel viendra, quand les oiseaux
Boiront l'eau vive des ruisseaux,
Alors vous reverrez Carnaval!
*(Il disparaît. Bobyl s'accroche au train vide, sa femme s'accroche à lui.)*

---

*II.). Snegurotchka remains behind the bushes, near the hollow tree.)*

## SCENE IV.

*SNEGUROTCHKA, BOBYL, BO-BYLICKA, BERENDEYS.*

**CHORUS II:** *(entering upon the stage).* Oi, Oi, Oi!
Oi, fair carnival! Oi, fair carnival!
*(Carnival procession.)*

**CHORUS I:** The cocks have crowed since dawn began,
Announcing merry carnival,
Farewell, farewell, Carnival, farewell!
You have gorged us with good food,
Made us tipsy with hydromel and beer,
Farewell, farewell, Carnival, farewell!
Good wine has been running in streams,
Good wine has been running like water,
Farewell, farewell, Carnival, farewell!
There you stand, so haughty and proud,
Stuffed with straw, dressed in moss,
Farewell, farewell, Carnival, farewell!
Royal honors have been paid you here,
We lead you to the woods in a handsome sleigh,
Farewell, farewell, Carnival, farewell!
We shall leave you in a moment or so,
And our eyes shall see you no more,
Farewell, farewell, Carnival, farewell!
*(Chorus I pushes the sleigh toward the forest and steps aside.)*

**CHORUS II:** Oi, Oi, Oi!
Oi, fair Carnival, Oi, fair Carnival, oi!
A whole year long there you shall sleep,
And when next year comes awake again. Farewell!

**CARNIVAL:** The coming summer soon will fly,
Farewell, sun of gold and flame!
Fall will take flight when summer's gone,
Farewell, crops, harvests farewell!
Then come the months whose nights are long,
The winter white with fallen snows.
Already, though, the day grows long, the
Sun grows hotter. When
The thaw sets in, and when the birds once more
Drink running water from the brooks,

---

**BOBYLICKA:** Allons, rentrons!

**BOBYL:** Arrête!
Quoi! ma femme, c'est donc fini déjà,
Fini de rire? on ne va plus
Manger ni boire aux frais des autres?
Il va falloir peiner et se serrer le ventre?
Merci, merci, vraiment, ce n'est pas mon compte.
Bobyl, que faire, hélas!
Mon pauvre ami, comment rester sans boire?
*(Il danse.)*
Le plus gueux de tous les gueux,
C'est Bobyl—la Misère.
Il n'a rien sur la terre,
Sou ni maille, feu ni bien.

**BOBYLICKA:** Veux-tu rentrer, ivrogne!

**CHŒUR DES BERENDEYS:** Bah, laisse donc!
*(Bobyl se dirige vers la forêt. Snégrourotchka se montre. Tout le monde s'approche du creux d'arbre.)*

**BOBYL:** Bonnes gens, venez et voyez tous cette merveille!

**CŒUR DES BERENDEYS:** Une princesse! Vivante! Vivante!
Avec ses gants, ses bottes, sa pelisse!

**BOBYL:** Princesse, dites-nous où vous allez,
Comment vous vous nommez! Parlez, princesse!

**SNÉGOUROTCHKA:**
Snégourotchka! où je vais, qu'en sais-je?
Mais si vous êtes bons, soyez mes hôtes,
Je veux vous suivre en votre bourg.
Celui qui m'a su trouver
Qu'il me prenne pour fille.

**BOBYL:** Eh bien, je suis à présent grand seigneur,
Venez vous tous, venez dans mon palais,
Dans mon palais aux sept piliers de marbre,
Venez, boyards et princes, venez tous!
Apportez-moi vos dons les plus superbes
Et moi, pas fier, je vous ferai risette.

**SNÉGOUROTCHKA:** Adieu, mon père, adieu, adieu, ma mère!
O forêt, adieu, adieu!

**VOIX DANS LA FORÊT:** Adieu, adieu, adieu!
*(Les arbres et les buissons saluent Snégourotchka en s'inclinant.)*

---

You will see Carnival again!
*(He disappears. Bobyl catches hold of the empty sleigh, his wife clings to him.)*

**BOBYLICKA:** Come, let us go back!

**BOBYL:** Now wait!
What, wife of mine, is it already over?
Our laughter done? Are we no more
To eat and drink at the expense of others?
Must we now toil and tighten up the belt?
Thanks, thanks! In truth, that will not do for me.
Bobyl, what shall we do, alas!
Poor dear, how can we manage without drink?
*(He dances.)*
Most beggarly of all beggars
Is Bobyl!—named wretchedness.
He has nothing here on earth,
To spend or wear, no goods nor chattels.

**BOBYLICKA:** Will you come back here, drunkard!

**CHORUS OF BERENDEYS:** Bah, let him be!
*(Bobyl moves off toward the forest. Snegurotchka shows herself. Everybody draws near the tree-trunk.)*

**BOBYL:** Good people, come and see this wondrous miracle!

**CHORUS OF BERENDEYS:** A princess! A live one, a real one!
With her gloves, her boots and her pelisse!

**BOBYL:** Princess, tell us where you're going!
What shall we call you? Speak, Princess!

**SNEGUROTCHKA:** Snegurotchka!
Where I go how can I tell?
Yet if you be kind, then be my hosts,
And I will follow you into your town.
He who had the wit to discover me
Let him take me for his daughter.

**BOBYL:** Ah well, then I'm a great lord this moment.
Come all of you, come step into my palace,
Enter my palace with its seven marble pillars.
Come, boyars and princes, come one and all!
Bring to me all your most splendid gifts
And I, who am not proud, will smile on you.

**SNEGUROTCHKA:** Farewell, father, farewell, farewell, my mother!
Oh forest, farewell, farewell!

**VOICES IN THE FOREST:** Farewell, farewell, farewell, farewell!
*(The trees and bushes salute Snegurotchka, bending down before her.)*

# Scene IV

**CHOEUR DES BERENDEYS:** A-ou, a-ou! quelle épouvante!
Aie, aie, aie, aie, aie!
(*La foule se disperse épouvantée.*)

*RIDEAU.*

**CHORUS OF BERENDEYS:** A-ou, a-ou! How terrifying!
Aie, aie, aie, aie, aie!
(*The crowd disperses in a panic.*)

*CURTAIN.*

# ■ IER ACTE.

*Faubourg de Berendey, au-delà du fleuve. A droite, la pauvre maison de Bobyl avec sa façade croulante; devant la maison un banc; à gauche, la maison peinte en différentes couleurs de Koupava; au fond, une rue; de l'autre côté de la rue une houblonnière et un rucher. Entre eux, un sentier, menant à la rivière.—C'est le soir; on entend les cors des bergers. Les habitants du faubourg se réunissent, parmi eux Bobyl.*

## SCÈNE I.

*BOBYL, LEL, SNÉGOUROTCHKA, plus tard plusieurs JEUNES FILLES.*

**LEL:** (*Entre en jouant de son chalumeau. Bobyl l'invite par un geste à entrer chez lui*). Pour un aimable accueil
Le pauvre Lel ne peut rien t'offrir,
Il n'a que sa musique et ses chansons,
Ami, veux-tu qu'il chante?

**BOBYL:** La musique, je ne l'aime guère,
Chante plutôt pour Snégourotchka;
Mais prends garde de perdre tes chansons,
Elle est avare de ses faveurs
Et froide comme neige,
Tu n'auras d'elle qu'un merci et qu'un adieu.
(*Il sort.*)

**SNÉGOUROTCHKA:** Bonjour, beau Lel, bonjour, viens près de moi.

**LEL:** Faut-il chanter?

**SNÉGOUROTCHKA:** Ah! Lel, j'osais à peine t'en faire la prière.

**LEL:** Fillette, il est un prix
Que je préfère pour mes chansons.
Fillette, par un peu de tendresse,
Le berger, le pauvre Lel,
Serait mieux payé, ou bien par un baiser.

**SNÉGOUROTCHKA:** Vraiment, c'est là ta récompense?
Un baiser vaut-il si cher?
En échange un baiser est peu de chose
Et je ne t'embrasserai pas, Lel!

**LEL:** Cueille une fleur dans l'herbe,
Offre-la-moi pour ma chanson!

# ■ ACT I.

*A suburb of Berendey, across the river. To the right, Bobyl's wretched hut, with its crumbling front; before it, a bench. To the left, Koupava's house, painted with various colors. At the back, a street; at the other end of the street a hop garden and a beehive. Between them, a path leading to the river. It is evening; the horns of the shepherds are heard. The inhabitants of the suburb gather together, among them Bobyl.*

## SCENE I.

*BOBYL, LEL, SNEGUROTCHKA, somewhat later, YOUNG GIRLS.*

**LEL:** (*He enters, playing his shepherd pipe. Bobyl signs to him to enter his hut*). For your kindly greeting
Poor Lel has nothing to offer you,
He has only his music and his songs.
Say, friend, would you have him sing?

**BOBYL:** For music I have no great liking,
Sing for Snegurotchka rather than for me;
But watch out for fear that your songs be sung in vain.
She is sparing with her favors,
And cold as the snow,
You'll get but a word of thanks and—farewell!
(*Off.*)

**SNEGUROTCHKA:** Good day, handsome Lel, good day!
Come closer!

**LEL:** Shall I sing?

**SNEGUROTCHKA:** Ah, Lel, I hardly dared to beg you to.

**LEL:** Little maid, there is a price
Which I prefer to others for my songs.
Little maid, with a little kindness
Poor Lel, the shepherd
Rather would be paid, or with a kiss.

**SNEGUROTCHKA:** In truth, is that the price you ask?
A kiss is it so dear?
A kiss is not enough to pay your songs,
And therefore I'll not kiss you, Lel!

**LEL:** Then pick a flower amid the grass,
And offer me it for my song!

**SNÉGOUROTCHKA:** (*cueillant une fleur*). Voici, prends-la!

**LEL:** Si l'on demande
Qui me l'offrit, je répondrai: c'est toi!
(*Snégourotchka pose, presque en pleurant, sa main sur l'épaule de Lel.*)
La forêt gaîment s'éveille
Et là-bas le pâtre chante;
Ah! que vivre est doux!
Le soleil rayonne et luit,
Parmi les branches, les bouleaux d'argent
Frissonnent sous la brise,
Ah! que vivre est doux!
A travers les buissons, au loin,
Par l'étroit sentier du bois,
Une fille accourt à pas pressés;
Elle court et court toujours plus vite,
Elle porte deux bouquets de fleurs,
Pour elle et pour son ami.

**CHOEUR DES JEUNES FILLES:**
Lel, Lel, Lel, beau Lel,
Loeli, Loeli, Lel si doux, si joli,
Notre Lelionka, Lel, notre Lel, beau Lel,
Viens donc vite, Lelionka.
(*Lel jette la fleur donnée par Snégourotchka et veut aller vers les jeunes filles.*)

**SNÉGOUROTCHKA:** Où cours-tu donc? Ma fleur, tu la rejettes?

**LEL:** Que puis-je en faire? Elle est déjà fanée!
Où je m'en vais? Tu vois sur cette branche
L'oiseau posé. Il va chanter un peu
Et puis s'envoler. Peux-tu le retenir?

## SCÈNE II.

**SNÉGOUROTCHKA:** (*seule*). Ah! que j'ai mal! et que mon coeur a de peine!
Comme une lourde pierre cette fleur
Que Lel a rejettée a meurtri mon coeur.
Les autres filles savent le charmer,
Leur rire est plus ardent, plus chaude est leur voix.
Hélas! ici je reste seule et je pleure,
Car Lel me dédaigne et fuit loin de moi!
Mon père Hiver, quel mal m'as-tu donc fait!
Maman Printemps, sois bonne, et donne-moi
Un peu d'ardente flamme et de soleil,
Pour réchauffer enfin mon pauvre coeur!

## SCÈNE III.

*SNÉGOUROTCHKA, KOUPAVA.*

**SNEGUROTCHKA:** (*picking a flower*). Here, take it then!

**LEL:** If any ask
Who offered it to me I shall say it was you!
(*Snegurotchka stands, nearly in tears, her hand resting on Lel's shoulder.*)
The forest gaily awakens
And yonder the herdsman sings;
Ah, how sweet it is to live!
The sun shines radiantly
Among the branches, the silver birches
Quiver when blows the breeze.
Ah, how sweet it is to live!
Amid the bushes, in the distance,
By the narrow woodland path,
A maid comes running hurriedly;
She runs and runs, fast and ever faster,
She bears two bouquets of flowers,
For her lover and herself!

**CHORUS OF YOUNG MAIDENS:**
Lel, Lel, Lel, handsome Lel.
Loeli, Loeli, Lel, so kind, so graceful!
Our Lelionka, Lel, our Lel, handsome Lel,
Come join us quickly, Lelionka!
(*Lel casts away the flower given him by Snegurotchka, and is about to go toward the Young Maidens.*)

**SNEGUROTCHKA:** To where are you going? Do you reject my flower?

**LEL:** What shall I do with it? It has already faded!
Where do I go? Behold, on yonder branch,
That perching bird. He'll pipe a snatch of song
Then fly away. Say, can you hold him?

## SCENE II.

**SNEGUROTCHKA:** (*alone*). Ah, how ill I feel, and how my poor heart suffers!
Like some heavy stone the flower Lel cast aside has bruised this heart of mine!
The other girls know how to charm him,
With laugh more kindling, and with warmer voices,
Alas, I stay alone here and I weep,
For Lel disdains me, flees afar from me!
O Father Winter, what evil you have done me?
O Mother Spring, be kind, and give to me
A bit of ardent sunshine and of flame,
To warm again this poor cold heart of mine!

## SCENE III.

*SNEGUROTCHKA, KOUPAVA.*

KOUPAVA: Snégourotchka, je suis heureuse,
Je suis heureuse et je voudrais jeter mes bras
Au cou de tout venant et lui crier ma joie.
Ecoute-moi, Snégourotchka, et prends ta part de mon bonheur!
A l'aube je cueillais des fleurs sur la colline
Ensoleillée; auprès de moi parut
Un beau jeune homme aux longs cheveux bouclés,
Au doux regard; tu sais toi-même,
On ne peut vivre sans amitié,
Un jour où l'autre il faut aimer.
D'un coeur sincère, il m'a juré
Qu'à l'aube, au jour sacré du dieu Yarilo
Devant le tzar il me mettrait des fleurs au front,
Et qu'il ferait de moi sa femme.
Snégourotchka, bientôt mon cher Mizguir
Ici viendra chercher sa fiancée
Parmi les autres filles. Mais le voici!
*(Au loin se montre Mizguir avec deux serviteurs. Les Jeunes filles et Lel rentrent en scène.)*

KOUPAVA: Snegurotchka, I am happy,
I'm happy, and would like to throw my arms around
The neck of every passerby, and shout my joy.
Listen, Snegurotchka, and share with me the joy I feel!
At dawn I gathered flowers on the hill
In the sunshine; when I saw appear
A handsome youth with long and curly hair,
His glance was kind; and well you know yourself,
That without friendship it is vain to live.
Some one day or another we must love . . . .
He swore and meant it honestly,
At dawn, the day held holy to god Yarilo,
Before the tzar he'd crown my brow with flowers,
And make me his wife.
Snegurotchka, soon my dear Mizguir
Will hasten here, seeking his betrothed
Among the other maids. Look, here he comes!
*(Mizguir makes his appearance in the distance, with two servitors. The young maidens and Lel reenter.)*

## SCÈNE IV.

*SNÉGOUROTCHKA, KOUPAVA, MIZGUIR, LEL, des SERVITEURS, JEUNES FILLES et JEUNES HOMMES.*

*(Mizguir et ses deux serviteurs entrent, ils portent des sacs.)*

*(Koupava court se cacher au milieu des jeunes filles.)*

KOUPAVA: Jeunes filles, o mes compagnes,
Hélas voici venir l'amant qui veut me prendre
A mes parents chéris, à mon village.
Ne livrez pas votre soeur, ô mes compagnes!
Ou s'il le faut, ne la livrez pas sans rançon!

MIZGUIR: O belles jeunes filles, plus qu'à vous
Koupava m'est utile. Je n'ai personne
Pour prendre soin de moi, de ma demeure,
Et pour orner mes longs cheveux bouclés.

CHOEUR DES JEUNES FILLES: Il faut payer rançon pour conquérir la beauté
Que parmi nous tu viens chercher.
Donne-nous bien vite un rouble, un demi rouble
Et Koupava t'appartient.

## SCENE IV.

*SNEGUROTCHKA, KOUPAVA, MIZGUIR, LEL, SERVITORS, YOUNG MAIDENS and YOUNG MEN.*

*(Mizguir and his two servitors enter bearing bags.)*

*(Koupava hastens to hide among the young maidens.)*

KOUPAVA: Young maidens, my comrades dear,
Ah, here comes the lover who would bear me off
From my loving parents and my village home!
Do not yield up your sister, comrades!
Or if it must be, let there be ransom paid!

MIZGUIR: O fair young maidens, of more use than to you
Koupava is to me. I have no one
To care for me and for my dwelling-place
No one to comb my long and curling hair.

CHORUS OF YOUNG MAIDENS: He must pay ransom who would gain the beauty
Whom you come seeking in our midst.
Give us a rouble, a half a rouble, quickly,
And you shall have Koupava.

MIZGUIR: *(prend de l'argent dans un sac que tient un serviteur et le donne aux jeunes filles)*. Voici de l'or, prenez, mes belles filles,
Je suis joyeux de vous payer rançon.
*(Il leur donne un sac plein de noix et de pains d'épice.)* Voici pour vous des sacs remplis d'épices,
Prenez encore!
*(Les jeunes filles commencent une chanson de mariage, les jeunes gens entourent Koupava.)*

CHOEUR DES JEUNES FILLES:
Dans sa gloire, il marche superbe
Comme un paon, lorsqu'il fait la roue;
Mais les plumes qu'il perd sont en or.
C'est l'époux qu'a choisi Koupava.
Pour le suivre, pour le suivre
Elle est prête à fuir ses compagnes.

CHOEUR DES JEUNES GENS: Tu n'auras pas Koupava, gardons-la bien,
Défendons-la, ne la donnous pas pour rien;
Ou bien chacun croira qu'il peut venir nous prendre
A son plaisir les belles filles du village.
*(Ils présentent leurs chapeaux.)*

MIZGUIR: *(vers les jeunes gens)*. A vous, je veux parler d'un autre ton!

KOUPAVA: Mon doux ami, mon doux ami,
Je quitte mon village et mes parents,
Je quitte tout pour toi, mon bien aimé.
N'afflige pas Koupava, ne brise pas son coeur fidèle et tendre.
Mes chères soeurs, chantons un chant de fête
Et dans le pré dansons joyeusement!

CHOEUR DES JEUNES FILLES:
Ah, dans la plaine, ah dans la plaine
Est un tilleul;
Sous le tilleul, sous le tilleul
Est une tente.
*(Mizguir et Koupava s'approchent de Snégourotchka.)*

KOUPAVA: Snégourotchka, fais-moi plaisir encore;
Pour la dernière fois menons la danse!

SNÉGOUROTCHKA: Allez danser, quel Lel nous suive!
Je range mon fuseau et vous rejoins en hâte.
*(Rentre dans son izba.)*

KOUPAVA: Mon doux ami, partons, ils vont nous suivre.

MIZGUIR: Arrête! Arrête!

MIZGUIR: *(taking money from a bag which a servitor holds, and giving it to the maidens)*. Here, take this gold, you handsome maidens,
It gladdens me to pay the ransom to you.
*(He hands them a bag full of walnuts and gingerbread.)*
Here are some bags of spiced cake for you,
Accept them, pray!
*(The young maidens begin to sing a wedding chorus, while the young men surround Koupava.)*

CHORUS OF YOUNG MAIDENS:
Filled with pride, he struts superbly,
Just like a peacock when he spreads his tail;
Yet golden are the feathers he is molting.
It is the bridegroom by Koupava chosen,
Him to follow, him to follow
She is ready to desert her comrades!

CHORUS OF YOUNG MEN: You shall not have Koupava, we'll protect her!
We'll defend her, nor yield her up for nothing,
Or everyone may think that they can come and take
Our loveliest village maids if so inclined.
*(They hold out their hats.)*

MIZGUIR: *(to the young men.)* To you, I'll speak in quite another tone!

KOUPAVA: O my dear love, my dearest love,
I leave my parents and my village home,
I leave them both for you, my well-beloved.
Bid not Koupava sorrow, nor break her heart so faithful and tender.
My dear sisters, now sing a festive chorus
And let us dance gaily in the meadow!

CHORUS OF YOUNG MAIDENS:
Ah, in the plain, ah, in the plain,
Stands a linden tree;
Beneath the linden, beneath, the linden tree
Is a tent.
*(Mizguir and Koupava draw near to Snegurotchka.)*

KOUPAVA: Snegurotchka, to please me, once again;
For the last time come dance with us!

SNEGUROTCHKA: Go dance then, let Lel follow us!
I'll lay my spindle down and quickly join you.
*(She goes into her izba.)*

KOUPAVA: My dear love, let us go, and they will follow!

MIZGUIR: O wait! Do wait!

## Act I, Scene IV

**KOUPAVA:** Les filles du pays nous attendant làbas.
(*Snégourotchka revient, derrière elle sortent Bobyl, et sa femme.*)

**MIZGUIR:** Cette fillette est Snégourotchka; mais Lel,
Qui donc est-il?

### SCÈNE V.

*SNÉGOUROTCHKA, KOUPAVA, MIZGUIR, LEL, BOBYL, BOBYLICKA.*

**KOUPAVA:** Snégourotchka, sans Lel, serait bien triste.

**MIZGUIR:** Crois-tu vraiment? Avec Mizguir, je pense,
Elle aurait plus de joie encore.

**KOUPAVA:** Mais moi, Mizguir?

**MIZGUIR:** Eh bien, que Lel te prenne!

**KOUPAVA:** Mon bien aimé, je suis à toi,
La tombe seule peut nous séparer.

**MIZGUIR:** Va-t-en où tu voudras!
Pour moi, je reste ici.

**BOBYL:** Je te salue!

**KOUPAVA:** D'un flot de lave ardente
Aveugle mes deux yeux,
Et sous la lourde meule
Écrase-moi le coeur.
Alors, aime une autre femme, car mes yeux
Ne pourront plus voir ton crime,
Et mon coeur ne pourra sentir sa peine!
Oh! rends-moi, Snégourotchka cruelle,
Rends-moi mon bien aimé!

**SNÉGOUROTCHKA:** Koupava, ma pauvre âme, et toi, son fol ami,
Allez en paix, Snégourotchka ne veut plus vous connaître.
(*Elle vent s'en aller.*)

**MIZGUIR:** (*la retenant*). Oh non!
Snégourotchka, demeure,
Dis, quel est ton heureux amant?

**SNÉGOUROTCHKA:** Personne!

**MIZGUIR:** Alors ce sera moi!
(*À Koupava.*)
Vois-tu là-bas, Koupava, le soleil
Qui déjà descend dans l'ombre et va s'éteindre?
Peut-il se rallumer au ciel?

**KOUPAVA:** Soleil couché n'a plus de flamme!

**MIZGUIR:** Amour défunt ne peut renaître!
En vain tu veux le ranimer, Koupava!

**KOUPAVA:** Malheureuse, malheureuse!

---

**KOUPAVA:** The village girls are waiting for us yonder.
(*Snegurotchka returns, Bobyl, and Bobylicka coming behind her.*)

**MIZGUIR:** This little maid is Snegurotchka; but Lel,
Say, who is he?

### SCENE V.

*SNEGUROTCHKA, KOUPAVA, MIZGUIR, LEL, BOBYL, BOBYLICKA.*

**KOUPAVA:** Without Lel, Snegurotchka will be very sad.

**MIZGUIR:** You think, so, eh? With Mizguir, I am sure
That she would be far happier.

**KOUPAVA:** But Mizguir, what of me?

**MIZGUIR:** O well, then Lel shall have you!

**KOUPAVA:** My well-beloved, I am your own;
The grave alone can part us.

**MIZGUIR:** Go where you choose! For my part, here I stay.

**BOBYL:** I greet you!

**KOUPAVA:** A flood of burning tears
Now blinds my eyes,
The mill-stone of his scorn
Crushes this heart of mine.
Go, love another woman, since my eyes
No longer can behold the wrong you do;
Nor my heart feel the agony you cause!
Oh, Snegurotchka, cruel one,
Return to me my well-beloved!

**SNEGUROTCHKA:** Koupava, hapless friend, and you, mad love of hers,
Depart in peace, Snegurotchka would no longer know you.
(*She endeavors to leave them.*)

**MIZGUIR:** (*holding her back*).
Ah, no! Snegurotchka, remain.
Tell me what is your happy lover's name?

**SNEGUROTCHKA:** I have none!

**MIZGUIR:** Then I shall be your lover!
(*To Koupava.*)
Look yonder, Koupava, do you see the sun
Already seek the shadows, soon to vanish?
Will he again illumine the skies?

**KOUPAVA:** Suns that have set have lost their flame!

**MIZGUIR:** A dead love is not born again!
Vainly you would rekindle it, Koupava!

**KOUPAVA:** Misfortune is my fate!

---

### SCÈNE VI.

*SNÉGOUROTCHKA, MIZGUIR, BOBYL, LEL, KOUPAVA, BERENDEYS et FEMMES DES BERENDEYS.*

**KOUPAVA:** (*revenant*). Aidez-moi dans ma détresse!

**CHOEUR DU PEUPLE:** O malheureuse amie, comme il t'outrage!
Ah! quel indigne outrage, quel indigne outrage!
Ah! quel affront pour nos jeunes filles!

**KOUPAVA:** Dis-moi, cruel, devant tout notre peuple,
Ton coeur trahissait-il la foi jurée
Dans le temps même où tu disais m'aimer?
Ou ce seul jour t'a-t-il rendu parjure?
Réponds!

**MIZGUIR:** J'ai pu t'aimer jadis, j'en aime une autre:
Snégourotchka.

**CHOEUR DU PEUPLE:** Sa lâche trahison nous offense toutes,
O honte pour nous toutes!
Jamais chez nous n'advint malheur semblable!

**MIZGUIR:** Tes yeux au fond des miens plongeaient
Sans crainte; ta voix était ardente,
Et je pensais en te voyant si libre
Qu'un jour quelque autre amant
Prendrait ma place.

**KOUPAVA:** Ah! mon père, Ah! mon père!
Qui donc voudra défendre moi?

**CHOEUR DU PEUPLE:** Le juste protecteur de ceux qui souffrent
C'est notre tzar. Va voir le tzar, Koupava!

**KOUPAVA:** Mizguir! ô désespoir! ô désespoir!
(*Elle tombe évanouie, Lel la soutient.*)

*FIN DE L'ACTE PREMIER.*

### ■ IIE ACTE.

*Une antichambre ouverte dans le palais de Berendey. Au fond, derrière la balustrade de la galerie, on voit les sommets des arbres, ainsi que des tours et des balcons en bois, ornés de découpures.*

---

### SCENE VI.

*SNEGUROTCHKA, MIZGUIR, BOBYL, LEL, KOUPAVA, BERENDEYS and WIVES of the BERENDEYS.*

**KOUPAVA:** (*reenters*). Aid me in my distress!

**CHORUS OF THE PEOPLE:** O hapless friend, how he has outraged you!
What an unworthy insult, what an unworthy insult!
What an affront for our young maidens!

**KOUPAVA:** Tell me, cruel one, before all the people,
Did your heart then betray the faith you pledged
At the same time when you declared you loved me?
Or this one day, has it made you a perjurer?
Answer!

**MIZGUIR:** I might have loved you always, now
I love another;
Snegurotchka!

**CHORUS OF THE PEOPLE:** His cowardly betrayal insults us all!
O shame we all must suffer!
We have not yet suffered such a misfortune!

**MIZGUIR:** Your eyes plunged into my eyes' very depths,
All unafraid, you voice was ardent;
And I thought, seeing you thus lack restraint.
Some day some other lover
Might take my place!

**KOUPAVA:** Ah, my father, ah, my father!
Who will defend me?

**CHORUS OF THE PEOPLE:** The just protector of all those who suffer
Is our tzar. Go see the tzar, Koupava!

**KOUPAVA:** Mizguir! O wretched fate! My heart despairs!
(*She loses consciousness, Lel supporting her.*)

*END OF ACT ONE.*

### ■ ACT II.

*An open anteroom in the palace of Berendey. At the back, behind the balustrade of the gallery, treetops as well as towers and wooden balconies, ornamented with carvings, are visible.*

---

## SCÈNE I.

*Le Tzar Berendey est assis sur une chaise dorée et s'occupe à peindre en couleurs une des colonnes. Un peu plus loin on voit des aveugles joueurs de gousli avec leurs instruments; aux portes de la galerie se tiennent les pages du tzar.*

**CHOEUR DES AVEUGLES:** La voix prophétique et vibrante des guzzlas
Chante, ô notre tzar, ta grandeur et ta gloire.
Nos yeux éteints sont baissés vers la terre,
Dans la nuit sans aurore, ils sont clos pour toujours.
Gloire, gloire à jamais au sage tzar,
Au protecteur de la paix!
Nous chanterons sans cesse sur nos guzzlas,
O père et tzar, ta grandeur et ta gloire!
*(Le Tzar remercie les aveugles d'un signe, on les emmène.)*

## SCÈNE II.

*LE TZAR, BERMIATE, UN PAGE, puis KOUPAVA.*

**UN PAGE:** *(entrant)*. Une fillette demande
En pleurant qu'on lui
Donne audience.

**LE TZAR:** Pour les enfants
De mon peuple, ma porte
Jamais n'est fermée!

## SCÈNE III.

*LE TZAR, BERMIATE, KOUPAVA, DES PAGES.*
*(Le Page introduit Koupava.)*

**KOUPAVA:** O tzar, mon père.

**LE TZAR:** *(la relevant avec bonté)*. Parle, j'écoute.

**KOUPAVA:** Puis-je tout dire?

**LE TZAR:** Il faut tout dire!

**KOUPAVA:** Daigne répondre:
Quand un garçon vous regarde et vous parle d'amour,
Quand on croit avec lui vivre heureuse,
Et quand on l'aime enfin, est-on coupable?

**LE TZAR:** Non, chère fille.

**KOUPAVA:** C'est mon seul crime!
Puis-je tout dire?

**LE TZAR:** Il faut tout dire!

**KOUPAVA:** Pour lui j'avais oublié tout l'univers,
L'amour le plus tendre emplissait ma vie et mon âme.
Dans la forêt profonde nos coeurs

étaient heureux,
Les yeux dans les yeux, nous restions en extase.

**LE TZAR:** Mon coeur est ému de ta peine sincère.

**KOUPAVA:** Grand tzar, mon père, dis-moi,
Le bonheur n'est-il donc qu'un vain rêve?

**LE TZAR:** O simple et pauvre enfant!

**KOUPAVA:** O grand tzar, mon père, dans la prairie . . .

**LE TZAR:** Parle, j'écoute.

**KOUPAVA:** J'étais allée, emmenant mes compagnes,
Dès que Mizguir parmi nous aperçoit
La perfide Snégourotchka.

**LE TZAR:** Achève, achève!

**KOUPAVA:** Auprès de cette voleuse de coeurs il s'élance;
Il m'oublie, il me raille, il m'insulte;
La force abandonne mon corps, qui se glace;
Soudain comme tombe une gerbe de blé
Je chancelle; ah! regarde, et je tombe,
Je tombe, je tombe sans vie . . .
*(Elle veut tomber, le Tzar la soutient.)*

**LE TZAR:** Allez que l'on saisisse dans sa demeure
Ce vil félon, sur l'heure amenez-le
Devant son tzar. Et puis que l'on appelle
Du haut des tours mon peuple bien aimé,
Sans plus tarder qu'il vienne au tribunal.
*(Il s'en va dans ses appartements.)*
*(Deux hérauts montent sur les pignons.)*

**2E HÉRAUT:** *(d'une voix sonore)*. Ecoutez ma parole!
Boyards très vaillants,
Très puissants et très nobles,
Boyards majestueux,
Aux longues barbes fleuries,
Seigneurs de beaux châteaux
Et de serfs aux pieds nus!

**IER HÉRAUT:** Tous entendez l'appel de votre tzar,
Connaissez sa volonté souveraine!

**LES DEUX HÉRAUTS:** Venez vers le trône magnifique,
Venez vers le trône sublime
Du palais où votre tzar vous appelle,
Venez à la justice du tzar,
Venez tous au tribunal de sa justice,
A la justice!
*(Ils descendent des pignons.)*
*(Des appartements intérieurs sortent des courtisans, des femmes de boyards, des pages; par la porte*

## SCENE I.

*The Tzar Berendey is seated in a gilded chair, occupied with painting one of the columns in colors. Somewhat further on may be seen blind gusli-players with their instruments; the Tzar's pages stand at the doors opening on the gallery.*

**CHORUS OF BLIND GUSLI-PLAYERS:** The vibrant and prophetic voice of the gusli
Sings, O tzar of ours, your grandeur and your glory!
Our sightless eyes are turned toward the earth,
They are closed forever in a night that knows no dawn.
Glory, glory through the ages, to the wise tzar,
To the protector of the peace!
Ceaselessly upon our guslis we will sing,
O sire and tzar, your grandeur and your glory!
*(The Tzar thanks the blind men with a gesture, and they are led off.)*

## SCENE II.

*THE TZAR, BERMIATE, A PAGE, later KOUPAVA*

**A PAGE:** *(entering)*.
A young girl prays
In tears, that she
Be given an audience.

**THE TZAR:** To the children
Of my people, my door
Is never closed!

## SCENE III.

*THE TZAR, BERMIATE, KOUPAVA, PAGES.*
*(The Page introduces Koupava.)*

**KOUPAVA:** O tzar, my father!

**THE TZAR:** *(raising her, kindly)*. Speak, I am listening.

**KOUPAVA:** May I tell all?

**THE TZAR:** You must tell all!

**KOUPAVA:** Condescend to reply:
When a youth looks at one and speaks to one of love,
When one believes that one could live with him happily,
When, finally, one loves him, is one at fault?

**THE TZAR:** No, my dear daughter.

**KOUPAVA:** It is my sole crime.
May I tell all?

**THE TZAR:** You must tell all!

**KOUPAVA:** For him I had forgotten all the universe,
The tenderest love possessed me, life and soul.
In the deep forest our two hearts

were happy,
Lost in each other's gaze, we were in ecstasy.

**THE TZAR:** My heart is moved by this your honest grief.

**KOUPAVA:** Great tzar, my father, tell me,
Happiness, is it nothing but an empty dream?

**THE TZAR:** O simple, unfortunate child!

**KOUPAVA:** O great tzar, to the meadow . . . .

**THE TZAR:** Speak, I am listening.

**KOUPAVA:** I had gone, taking my comrades with me,
And there no sooner had Mizguir seen among us
Treacherous Snegurotchka . . .

**THE TZAR:** Go on, go on!

**KOUPAVA:** Than he rushed up to this fair thief of hearts;
Forgets me, mocks me and insults me, too!
All strength forsakes my body, which grows cold;
Suddenly, as falls a sheaf of grain
I totter; ah, look at me, I fall,
I fall, I fall, my senses flee . . . .
*(She is about to fall, the Tzar supports her.)*

**THE TZAR:** Go, and straightway seize within his home
This felon vile! Let him be brought at once
Before his tzar. And then let there be called
From all the towers my people well-beloved,
That they make haste to come to the tribunal.
*(He goes off into his own apartments.)*
*(Two heralds mount the gables.)*

**SECOND HERALD:** *(sonorously)*.
Hark to my words!
Most valiant boyars,
Most powerful and noble,
Majestic boyars,
With your long, flowering beards,
Lords of fair castles
And of barefoot serfs!

**FIRST HERALD:** Hear the summons of your tzar,
Know the expression of his sovereign will!

**THE TWO HERALDS:** Draw near this magnificent throne,
Draw near that throne sublime
Of the palace where your tzar summons you!
Come to the courtyard of the tzar,
Come all unto his tribunal of justice,
Where he gives judgement!
*(They descend from the gables.)*
*(From the inner rooms of the palace issue forth courtiers, wives of*

extérieure et l'escalier pénètre le peuple, entre autres Lel. On amène Mizguir. Bermiate place les courtisans. A la fin de la procession paraît le Tzar Berendey lui-même.)

## SCÈNE V.

LE TZAR, BERMIATE, LEL, KOUPAVA, MIZGUIR, femmes des boyards, hérauts, pages, peuple.

LE TZAR: Enfants, merci! où donc est le coupable?

BERMIATE: Grand tzar, Mizguir attend ton jugement.

LE TZAR: Son crime est-il connu de tous?

CHOEUR DU PEUPLE: Oui, certes!

LE TZAR: Et toi, reconnais-tu ta faute?

MIZGUIR: Oui, tzar!

LE TZAR: Parlez, à quoi faut-il fixer sa peine?

BERMIATE: Commande-lui de prendre Koupava pour femme!

CHOEUR DU PEUPLE: O tzar, qu'il lui demande sa grâce Ou bien qu'il soit puni!

LE TZAR: Mizguir, veux-tu lui demander ta grâce? Veux-tu qu'elle soit ta femme?

MIZGUIR: Mizguir n'a plus qu'un seul amour dans l'âme, Snégourotchka.

KOUPAVA: Sublime tzar, Mon coeur n'a plus que du mépris pour lui.

LE TZAR: Nous laissons Aux augustes dieux le soin de la vengeance. Et c'est pourquoi, moi juge, je condamne Mizguir à s'exiler de sa patrie, Qu'il vive dans les bois déserts avec les loups Aussi cruels que lui; leur coeur sauvage Comprendra ton coeur, Mizguir!

MIZGUIR: Je n'aurai pas un mot pour me défendre. Pourtant, ô tzar, si tu voyais jamais Snégourotchka paraître— (*Entrent Snégourotchka, Bobyl et sa femme.*)

CHOEUR DU PEUPLE: Voilà Snégourotchka avec Bobyl et Bobylicka!

## SCÈNE VI.

LE TZAR, BERMIATE, KOUPAVA, LEL, MIZGUIR, SNÉGOUROTCHKA, BOBYL, sa femme, femmes des boyards, pages, peuple.

---

the boyars, pages; through the outer door and by way of the staircase the people enter, Lel among them. Bermiate orders the ranks of the Courtiers. At the end of the procession appears Tzar Berendey himself.)

## SCENE V.

THE TZAR, BERMIATE, LEL, KOUPAVA, MIZGUIR, wives of the boyards, heralds, pages, the people.

THE TZAR: I thank you, children! The culprit, where is he?

BERMIATE: Great tzar, Mizguir awaits your judgment.

THE TZAR: And is his crime known unto all?

CHORUS OF THE PEOPLE: Yes, it is known!

THE TZAR: And you, do you admit your fault?

MIZGUIR: Yes, tzar!

THE TZAR: Speak, how shall he be punished?

BERMIATE: Command he take Koupava for his wife!

CHORUS OF THE PEOPLE: O tzar, let him implore her to forgive, Or else let him be punished!

THE TZAR: Mizguir, would you ask her to forgive you? Do you wish her for wife?

MIZGUIR: Mizguir has but one love within his soul, Snegurotchka.

KOUPAVA: O tzar sublime, There is nothing but scorn for him now in my heart!

THE TZAR: Then we will leave The task of vengeance to the august gods. Therefore do I, his judge, condemn Mizguir to exile from his native land; Let him live with the wolves in forest wastes, Wolves cruel as himself; their savage hearts Will understand your own, Mizguir!

MIZGUIR: I have no word to say in my defense; And yet, O tzar, if you had ever seen Snegurotchka appear— (*Enter Snegurotchka, Bobyl and his wfe.*)

CHORUS OF THE PEOPLE: There comes Snegurotchka, with Bobyl and Bobylicka!

## SCENE VI.

THE TZAR, BERMIATE, KOUPAVA, LEL, MIZGUIR, SNEGUROTCHKA, BOBYL, BOBYLICKA, wives of the boyards, pages, the people.

---

SNÉGOUROTCHKA: (*regardant le palais*). Quel beau palais! Combien tout est splendide! Regarde, mère, tout brille, tout rayonne, regarde! (*S'assied par terre et examine la fleur peinte sur une colonne.*)

BOBYLICKA: N'ai-je pas la mine d'une dame? Voit-on mon beau bonnet?

LES FEMMES DES BOYARDS: Bobylicka! voyez-la! regardez son beau bonnet! Un bonnet avec des cornes de rubans et une perle!

SNÉGOUROTCHKA: On t'admire, on te regarde.

LE TZAR: Cette beauté nous peut servir, Bermiate, Pour apaiser Yarilo.

BOBYLICKA: Dis donc bonjour!

SNÉGOUROTCHKA: Pardon! je vous en prie! (*Elle salue.*) Bonjour, mes bons amis, à tous bonjour!

BOBYLICKA: Les femmes des boyards sont toutes là, Mais mon bonnet est le plus beau.

SNÉGOUROTCHKA: Le tien est plus beau! Qui donc est la? Là-bas Avec sa robe et sa ceinture d'or, Et cette longue barbe toute blanche?

BOBYL: Mais c'est le tzar! Vers lui va-t'en sans crainte, Incline-toi, mignonne.

SNÉGOUROTCHKA: Salut, ô tzar!

LE TZAR: Nature auguste et douce, pouvoir sacré, divin mystère, Mon coeur joyeux adore les dons charmants que tu nous fais Et tes secrets desseins et ta bonté. Loin de tous les yeux Au fond du bois sauvage pour nous tu fais éclore Cette humble et fraîche fleur, ce blanc muguet; Tu fais pleuvoir sur elle les pleurs d'argent de l'aube, Et la fleur exhale un si subtil et si profond parfum Qu'il charme tous les sens et trouble l'âme. Snégourotchka, voici le temps venu, Choisis l'époux que tu désires!

SNÉGOUROTCHKA: Qui donc choisir, ô tzar! Je l'ignore!

LE TZAR: Ton coeur te parle!

SNÉGOUROTCHKA: Mon coeur n'a pas parlé!

---

SNEGUROTCHKA: (*looking about the palace*). How fair a palace! How splendid all things are! Look, mother of mine, all shines and sparkles, look! (*She crouches on the ground to examine a flower painted on a column.*)

BOBYLICKA: Do I not look like a lady? Do they see my handsome bonnet?

WIVES OF THE BOYARS: Bobylicka, see her! Look at her handsome bonnet! It is one with horns of ribbon and a pearl!

SNEGUROTCHKA: They admire and look at you.

THE TZAR: This beauty could be useful to us, Bermiate, To appease Yarilo.

BOBYLICKA: Come, say 'good day!'

SNEGUROTCHKA: Forgive me, I beg of you! (*She bows.*) Good day, dear friends, good day to all!

BOBYLICKA: The wives of the boyars all are here; Yet my bonnet is of all the most handsome.

SNEGUROTCHKA: Yours is the handsomest! Yet who is that? Over there, In a robe with golden girdle, And that long beard of white?

BOBYL: Why that's the tzar! Go to him withour fear, Bow to him, little one!

SNEGUROTCHKA: Greetings, O tzar!

THE TZAR: Solemn and kindly nature, O holy power and mystery divine, My heart rejoicing worships all the wondrous gifts you give to us; Your hidden purposes and goodness. Far from the sight of all, Deep in the savage woods you bade for us unfold This fresh and humble flower, this little white mayflower. You made dawn weep over her his silvery tears of dew; So subtle and profound a perfume this flower exhales, It charms each sense and stirs the very soul! Snegurotchka, the time has come, So choose the bridegroom whom you may desire!

SNEGUROTCHKA: Whom shall I choose, O tzar! I know not!

THE TZAR: Your heart will tell you!

SNEGUROTCHKA: But my heart has not spoken.

**LE TZAR:** Sois sans crainte, Car l'âge enfant, rapproche le vieillard De la jeune fille. Pourquoi rougirai-telle Devant des yeux éteint et paternels? Dis-moi donc tout, quel est celui que tu attends Le soir, devant le seuil, et frémissante? Celui qui vient toujours trop tard, celui Que tu reçois avec un cri de joie, Avec des rires et des pleurs et des baisers? Qui donc? dis-moi, ma fille!

**SNÉGOUROTCHKA:** Mais personne.

**BERMIATE:** Son coeur candide ignore encore l'amour.

**LE TZAR:** Ignorer l'armour alors qu'on est si belle? C'est une offense au grand Yarilo, Et c'est pourquoi le dieu s'irrite contre nous. Celui qui fera naître avant l'aurore L'amour au coeur glacé de cette enfant— Je le jure ici—avec un don royal La prendra pour femme!

**BERMIATE:** Pas un qui dise mot!

**LES FEMMES DES BOYARDS:** O notre tzar! Parmi les jeunes hommes D'ici, il n'en est qu'un qui sache Troubler, d'un mot un coeur de femme Et l'émouvoir d'amour, c'est Lel!

**LE TZAR:** Quel grand honneur pour toi, berger!

**LEL:** J'embraserai son âme de mes ardeurs, Et grâce au Dieu Soleil, au maître tout puissant, Elle aimera.

**MIZGUIR:** Illustre tzar! Surseois à mon exil, Et, je t'en fais serment, c'est moi Qui gagnerai l'amour de ce coeur vierge.

**LE TZAR:** Mizguir et Lel, j'accepte vos promesses; Je prends espoir et j'attendrai sans crainte L'arrêt du sort. Dans la forêt sacrée Allons ce soir tous ensemble; vos chants Et votre danse charmeront les heures. La douce nuit de printemps passera comme un songe. Et demain, quand paraîtra la pâle aurore, Demain, avec le peuple entier j'irai A ta rencontre, soleil, ô dieu de flamme!

**THE TZAR:** Be not afraid, For age, my child, it brings the old man near To the young maiden. Why should you blush Before these faded and paternal eyes? At night, upon the doorstep, tremblingly, The one who ever, ever comes too late, the one Whom your lips welcome with a cry of joy, With laughter and with kisses and with tears? Who is it? Tell me, daughter!

**SNEGUROTCHKA:** There is no one.

**BERMIATE:** Her candid heart as yet knows nothing of love.

**THE TZAR:** She knows nothing of love when one is fair as she? It is an offense to Yarilo the great! Because of that the god is angry with us. He who before another dawn will wake Love in the frozen heart of this fair child I vow and swear—with a most royal gift Shall take her for his wife!

**BERMIATE:** There's no one says a word!

**WIVES OF THE BOYARDS:** O lord and tzar! Among the youths Of this place there's only one who knows With but a word to move a woman's heart, And waken it to love, it is Lel!

**THE TZAR:** How great an honor waits you, shepherd!

**LEL:** My ardent passion shall embrace her soul, And thanks to the sun-god, our lord omnipotent, She too shall love!

**MIZGUIR:** Illustrious tzar! Recall my banishment, And this I swear to you, I will gain the love of that young virgin heart!

**THE TZAR:** Mizguir and Lel, your promise I accept; Hopeful am I, and without fear will wait for What fate decrees. Into the sacred wood This evening we shall all together go; your songs And dances shall while away the hours. The sweet spring night will pass as does a dream, And on the morrow, when the first dawn pales, Tomorrow, with the people, I myself Shall go to meet you, O sun-god, lord of flame!

**CHOEUR DU PEUPLE:** Honneur et gloire à toi, Très puissant et sage tzar, O père de ton peuple! Maître bienfaisant, O très sage tzar, Pour nous rendre heureux, Règne à tout jamais, Très puissant et sage tzar!

*FIN DE L'ACTE DEUXIÈME.*

## ■ IIIE ACTE.

*Vaste clairière dans la forêt; à gauche et à droite, une épaisse futaie qui forme comme un mur derrière les buissons. Au loin, entre les arbustes, on voit de riches tentes. Le soleil achève de se coucher.*

### SCÈNE I.

*Les jeunes Berendeys font des rondes. Les juenes gens et les jeunes filles ont des couronnes de fleurs sur leurs têtes. Les vieux et les vieilles sont assis par groupes sous les buissons, buvant la cervoise et mangeant des pains d'épice. Dans la première ronde se trouve Koupava, au centre de cette ronde Lel et Snégourotchka. Mizguir ne prenant aucune part aux jeux tantôt se montre parmi la foule, tantôt s'en va dans la forêt. Bobyl danse en jouant de la musette. Sa femme et quelques voisins sont assis autour et boivent de la bière. Le Tzar et sa suite regardent de loin le peuple qui s'amuse.*

**JEUNES GENS ET JEUNES FILLES, SNÉGOUROTCHKA, LEL:** Ah, dans la plaine est un tilleul! Sous le tilleul se dresse une blanche tente, Et sous la tente est une fille. Dans la prairie, Ah! la belle A cueilli des fleurs, en a fait une couronne. Pour qui la couronne? heureux qui la portera! La couronne est pour l'aimé! (*Elle met la couronne sur la tête de Lel.*)

**BOBYL:** (*danse et imite le castor*). Un castor Dans l'eau se baigne Et barbote, Aï! Loeli, Loeli, Loeli! Puis hors du ruisseau Faisant sa toilette, Monte sur un rocher. Aï! Loeli, Loeli, Loeli! Du haut du rocher Partout il regarde, S'il ne vient personne. Aï! Loeli, Loeli, Loeli! Les chasseurs joyeux Et leurs chiens rapides

**CHORUS OF THE PEOPLE:** Honor and glory be yours, Most mighty and sagacious tzar! O father of your people! Master beneficent! O tzar most wise! That we may be happy. O live forever, Most mighty and sagacious tzar!

*END OF ACT SECOND.*

## ■ ACT III.

*A vast glade in the forest; to the left and to the right a thick growth of timber which rises like a wall behind the brush. In the distance, among the bushes, may be seen splendid tents. The sun is about to set.*

### SCENE I.

*The young Berendeys are dancing their rounds. The youths and maidens wear crowns of flowers upon their heads. The old men and women are seated in groups among the bushes, drinking beer and eating gingerbread. Among the first group of dancers is Koupava, in the middle of the group Lel and Snegurotchka, Mizguir, who takes no part in the merriment, now shows himself amid the crowd, now moves off toward the forest. Bobyl plays the shepherd pipe while he dances. Bobylicka and some of her neighbors are seated nearby, drinking beer. The Tzar and his suite watch from a distance as the people amuse themselves.*

**YOUNG MEN and YOUNG WOMEN, SNEGUROTCHKA, LEL:** Ah, a linden tree grows on the plain! Beneath the linden tree a white tent rises, Beneath the tent stands a girl. In the prairie, ah, the fair one Has gathered flowers and made a crown of them. For whom is the crown? Happy the youth who wears it! The crown is for her well-beloved! (*Snegurotchka places the crown on the head of Lel.*)

**BOBYL:** (*dancing and imitating a beaver*). A beaver Bathes in the water, And ducks about, Ai, Loeli, Loeli, Loeli! Then leaves the stream And climbs a rock, And dried himself. Ai, Loeli, Loeli, Loeli! From the top of the rock He looks all around. To see if anyone is coming. Ai, Loeli, Loeli, Loeli! The merry huntsmen And their swift hounds

## Act III, Scene I

Traquent le castor
Aï! Loeli, Loeli, Loeli!
Ah, ah, ah, ah, ah! Loeli, Loeli, Loeli, Aï!

Are trailing the beaver.
Ai, Loeli, Loeli, Loeli!
Ah, ah, ah, ah, ah, Loeli, Loeli, Ai!

**LE TZAR:** (*entrant avec sa suite dans l'avant-scène*). Salut à vous, ô mes enfants. Je dis à tous merci, Merci de vos chansons, merci de votre danse.
Et j'ai le coeur joyeux de votre joie!
Mais nous voulons encore un peu rire,
Bouffons, dansez et faites tous vos tours!
(*Les bouffons accourent, ils dansent.*)

**THE TZAR:** (*entering the foreground with his suite*). I greet you, O my children! I give thanks to all, Thanks for your songs, and for your merry dance.
My heart rejoices in the joy you feel!
Yet you would like to laugh a little longer,
Buffoons, now dance and show the tricks you know!
(*The Buffoons hurry up, they dance.*)

**LEL:** (*jouant de sa corne*). Le nuage a dit un jour au tonnerre: Gronde! Gronde! Moi je verse la pluie
Et la terre sera rafraîchit;
Et les fleurs seront heureuses par nous.
Les fillettes cueilleront la framboise,
Et les jeunes hommes les suivront.
Lel, mon Lel, mon Loeli, Loeli, Loeli! Lel!
Dans le bois vient à passer un vieillard
Qui voyant les jeunes filles leur dit: Mes enfants, que faites-vous à tant pleurer?
La méchante qui se cache là-bas
Ne voundra jamais répondre à vos cris?
Voyez-la qui rit de vous dans les buissons!
O mon Lel, mon Lel, Loeli, Loeli, Lel!

**LEL:** (*blowing his horn*). One day the cloud said to the thunder: Growl, growl. It is I who pour down rain
That the earth may be refreshed;
And the flowers may be happy, thanks to us.
And the young men shall follow them.
Lel, my Lel, my Loeli, Loeli, Loeli, Lel!
Through the woods an old man slowly passes
Who, seeing the young maidens says to them:
My children, tell me why so hard you're weeping?
The naughty girl now hiding from you yonder,
Will she not answer to the calls you utter?
Behold her laughing at you amid the bushes!
O my Lel, my Lel, Loeli, Loeli, Loeli, Lel!

**LE TZAR:** Merci, beau Lel! Enfants, cette histoire,
Je n'en crois rien! Parmi ces jeunes filles
Choisis la plus charmante à ton avis,
Conduis-la-moi, et que sur l'heure même
Elle te donne devant le peuple entier
Par un baiser le prix de ta chanson!
(*Lel se dirige vers les jeunes filles. Snégourotchka met sa parure en ordre. En passant devant elle, Lel s'arrête un instant comme indécis.*)

**THE TZAR:** Thanks, handsome Lel! Children, this story
I disbelieve! Among the fair young maidens
Pick out the one you think most charming,
Lead her before me, and this very moment
Let her, before the people here assembled
Give a kiss to pay you for your song!
(*Lel moves toward the young girls. Snegurotchka arranges her hair. In passing before her, Lel stops a moment as though undecided.*)

**SNÉGOUROTCHKA:** Prends-moi, beau Lel! prends-moi, prends-moi, cher Lel!
(*Lel passe et va plus loin vers Koupava. Snégourotchka, en larmes, se sauve dans les buissons. Lel choisit Koupava, la conduit à travers toute la scène vers le Tzar Berendey et s'approchant d'elle l'embrasse.*)

**SNEGUROTCHKA:** Take me, handsome Lel! Take me, take me, dear Lel!
(*Lel passes her by and goes on to Koupava. Snegurotchka, in tears, conceals herself in the bushes. Lel chooses Koupava, and leads her across the entire stage to the Tzar Berendey; then drawing her to him, embraces her.*)

**LE TZAR:** Allons, amis, la nuit s'avance:
Venez prendre place au festin, Et tous ensemble attendons le dieu Yarilo.
Hâtons-nous.

**THE TZAR:** Come, my friends, night closes around us;
Come, take your part now in the festival,
While together we wait for the god Yarilo.

Mes chers enfants, je fais des voeux pour votre joie!
(*Il sort avec sa suite.*)

Let us make haste!
My children dear, I pray that joy attend you!
(*Off, with his suite.*)

**CHOEUR DU PEUPLE:** Et que la joie emplisse aussi ton âme! Allons, allons voir le festin du tzar! (*Tous sortent peu à peu. Nuit. La scène est vide.*)

**CHORUS OF THE PEOPLE:** May joy fill your soul as well! Come, we will see our kind tzar's festival!
(*Little by little, they go off. It is night. The stage is empty.*)

## SCÈNE II.

## SCENE II.

*SNÉGOUROTCHKA et MIZGUIR, puis le FAUNE.*

*SNEGUROTCHKA and MIZGUIR, then the FAUN.*

**SNÉGOUROTCHKA:** (*entre*). Comment, cher Lel, as-tu le coeur si dur
Pour Snégourotchka, la pauvre orpheline?
N'est-elle pas jolie? Oui, certes! Et toi, tu prends Koupava, tu la mènes au tzar,
Tu l'embrasse! Elle est donc plus belle,
Elle est donc plus belle, hélas! que moi?
Mon gentil Lel, écoute-moi!
Et la fille de neige un jour aussi te chérira.
Viens, donne-moi la main, allons ensemble
Voir le soleil levant surgir de l'ombre!
(*Elle ôte sa couronne.*)
Et je suis seule et Lel déjà m'oublie, Il me délaisse, il est auprès d'une autre.
(*Commence à chanter, pensive.*)
Et ce n'est pas pour me plaire, Non, ce n'est pas pour me plaire, Hélas, qu'il chantera ses chansons.

**SNEGUROTCHKA:** (*enters*). How is it, dear Lel, your heart is so cold To Snegurotchka, the poor orphan girl?
Is she not pretty? Yes, indeed! Yet you, you choose Koupava, lead her to the tzar,
And kiss her. She must be handsomer,
She must be handsomer, alas, than I?
My handsome Lel, listen to me! The daughter of the snow will love you too, someday!
Come, give me your hand, and let us go together
To see the rising sun break from the shades!
(*She takes off her crown.*)
But I am alone, by Lel already I'm forgotten,
He abandons me, he is with another.
(*She begins to sing, pensively.*)
Ah, it is not to please me, No, it is not to please me, that he sings his songs.

**MIZGUIR:** (*entre*). Snégourotchka, je t'ai longtemps cherchée!
(*Il la prend par la main.*)

**MIZGUIR:** (*entering*). Snegurotchka, long have I looked for you!
(*He seizes her hand.*)

**SNÉGOUROTCHKA:** (*avec effroi*). Non, non, va-t'en!

**SNEGUROTCHKA:** (*terrified*). No, no, go away!

**MIZGUIR:** Ah! dis-moi le mot d'espoir qui fait revivre!
A genoux, tu vois, je t'en supplie encore,
Ah! serai-je un jour aimé de toi? Réponds!

**MIZGUIR:** Ah, speak the word which will rekindle my hope! Upon my knees, look at me, I beg that you will say it!
Ah, shall I be loved by you someday? Reply!

**SNÉGOUROTCHKA:** 'Joyaux et richesses tu peux les garder pour toi, Mon pauvre coeur ne vaut pas tant de choses,
Mais il n'est pas à vendre, pour lui Je ne veux rien qu'un peu d'amour, Mais non le tien, Mizguir!

**SNEGUROTCHKA:** Your jewels and your wealth keep for yourself, For my poor heart is not worth so much treasure;
Yet it is not for sale, my heart, It only craves a little bit of love, But not your love, Mizguir!

**MIZGUIR:** Je suis ton maître!

**MIZGUIR:** I am your master!

**SNÉGOUROTCHKA:** Pitié, pitié! A moi, à moi, beau Lel! Accoure me sauver, beau Lel!

**SNEGUROTCHKA:** Mercy, mercy! O save me, my handsome Lel! Hasten to save me, Handome Lel!

**MIZGUIR:** Si Lel t'entend, qu'il vienne! Mais il viendra trop tard pour te sauver.
(*Snégourotchka s'efforce de se dégager. Le faune apparaît.*)

**MIZGUIR:** If Lel should hear you, let him come! Yet he would come too late to save you now.
(*Snegurotchka struggles to release herself. The Faun appears.*)

LE FAUNE: (*enserrant Mizguir par derrière*). Arrête! arrête! attends un peu, Mizguir!
(*Snégourotchka se dégage et court à travers la clairière pour se cacher dans la forêt.*)
(*Le faune se transforme en une souche desséchée. Mizguir veut courir à la poursuite de Snégourotchka, une forêt surgit de terre et l'arrête. Il s'efforce de traverser l'épaisseur des arbres.*)

LE FAUNE: (*apparaît de nouveau*). Au fond du bois poursuis encor son ombre!
(*La vision de Snégourotchka apparaît de l'autre côté et appelle Mizguir.*)

MIZGUIR: C'est toi, c'est toi, je t'ai revue,
C'est toi, partout je veux te suivre.

LE FAUNE: Le clair soleil peut seul chasser ton rêve.
(*Il disparaît sous terre.*)
(*La clairière reprend son aspect premier. Lel entre.*)

## SCÈNE IV.

LEL, puis KOUPAVA, plus tard SNÉGOUROTCHKA.

KOUPAVA: (*en voyant Lel se jette vers lui*). Enfin je te retrouve, toi que j'aime,
Mon doux ami, mon Lel, ma seule joie!
Je sens mon coeur renaître, tu m'as sauvée
Du plus cruel affront et de la honte,
Tu m'as rendu le droit de vivre fière,
Tu m'as faite par ton baiser l'égale des heureuses!

LEL: Je savais bien quel coeur m'allait soumettre
Ce doux baiser, ma belle, bien aimée;
Sur tes doux yeux mes yeux ravis se posent,
Enfin mon âme trouve son refuge!
(*Snégourotchka se montre entre les buissons et observe Lel et Koupava.*)

SNÉGOUROTCHKA: (*avec désespoir*). O mère, on m'a trompée!
O mère, Ô Fée Printemps,
Je pleure et je supplie;
Je veux aimer!
O donne-moi, ma mère,
Un coeur comme aux autres filles!
Je veux aimer! Je veux aimer!
O mère, ô Fée Printemps!
Je veux aimer ou bien je veux mourir!
(*Elle sort en courant.*)

*FIN DE L'ACTE TROISIÈME.*

---

THE FAUN: (*clasping Mizguir from behind*). Wait, wait, now wait a bit, Mizguir!
(*Snegurotchka disengages herself, and runs across the glade to hide in the forest.*)
(*The faun changes himself into a dead tree. Mizguir attempts to pursue Snegurotchka, but a forest springs up from out of the ground and stops him. He endeavors to make his way through the thickset trees.*)

THE FAUN: (*reappears*). In woodland depths pursue her shadow still!
(*A vision of Snegurotchka appears beyond the trees, beckoning to Mizguir.*)

MIZGUIR: It is you, it is you I see once more!
It is you, whom I will follow everywhere!

THE FAUN: The clear sunlight alone can drive away his dream.
(*He disappears underground.*)
(*The glade resumes its previous aspect. Lel enters.*)

## SCENE IV.

LEL, then KOUPAVA, later SNEGUROTCHKA.

KOUPAVA: (*seeing Lel, she hurries to him*). At last once more I find you, whom I love,
My dearest friend, my Lel, my only joy!
My heart once more can feel, for you have saved me
From insult cruel, and from deepest shame.
You have restored to me my pride in life,
And with your kiss made me the equal of the happiest!

LEL: Well did I know which heart would overcome me!
In your sweet eyes my ravished glance is lost;
At last my soul its place of refuge finds!
(*Snegurotchka shows herself among the bushes, watching Lel and Koupava.*)

SNEGUROTCHKA: (*in despair*). O mother, they've deceived me!
O mother, O Fairy Spring,
I weep and I implore you;
I want to love!
O give me, mother,
A heart like other maidens have!
I want to love! I want to love!
O mother, O Fairy Spring!
I want to love, or else I want to die!
(*Off, running.*)

*END OF ACT THIRD.*

---

## ■ IVE ACTE

La vallée de Yarilo: au fond, un lac couvert de plantes aquatiques et de fleurs; au bord, des arbustes fleuris dont les branches pendent sur l'eau; à droite du lac, la montagne de Yarilo, nue, au sommet pointu. Le lever du soleil.

## SCÈNE I.

SNÉGOUROTCHKA (*descendant de la Montagne*), puis la FÉE PRINTEMPS suivie des fleurs.

SNÉGOUROTCHKA: O mère, mes yeux sont pleins de larmes,
Mon coeur est lourd d'angoisse et de douleur!
A mon appel surgis du fond des ondes,
Entends ma plainte et prends pitié de moi!
(*Du fond du lac sort la Fée Printemps entourée de fleurs.*)

LA FÉE PRINTEMPS:
Snégourotchka, ô mon enfant, qu'implores-tu de moi?
Dis-moi quelle est ta peine?
Pour l'apaiser un seul instant me reste.

SNÉGOUROTCHKA: Oh donne moi l'amour! Je veux aimer ou bien mourir!

LA FÉE PRINTEMPS: O mon enfant, sois exaucée!

LA FÉE PRINTEMPS et le CHOEUR DES FLEURS: Fleur de l'aube printanière,
Blanc muguet du bois profond,
Illumine son visage
De ton tendre et doux reflet.
Fleur des songes, noir pavot,
Magique fleur,
Endors et charme sa raison;
Houblon d'or, que ton ivresse
Se répande dans son coeur!
(*Elle met la couronne sur la tête de Snégourotchka.*)

SNÉGOUROTCHKA: (*en extase*). Ah mère, quel prodige et quel bonheur!
Quel charme sur la terre et dans le ciel!
Quel doux reflet sur l'eau! quelle ombre heureuse
Et calme dans les bois! Que l'aube est pure et belle!

LA FÉE PRINTEMPS: Chère fille, dérobe ton amour au dieu Yarilo;
Rentre au logis, ma fille, en toute hâte
Sans t'arrêter à voir au ciel surgir l'aurore.
Adieu, ma fille, et sois fidèle

---

## ■ ACT IV.

The valley of the god Yarilo: at the back a lake covered with aquatic plants and flowers; along its border, flowering shrubs whose branches overhang the water to the right of the lake, with pointed summit. The sun is rising.

## SCENE I.

SNEGUROTCHKA (*coming down from the mountain*), then FAIRY SPRING, followed by FLOWER-SPIRITS.

SNEGUROTCHKA: O mother, my eyes are full of tears,
My heart weighed down with anguish and with sorrow!
You, whom my call brought from beneath the waves,
Listen to my lamentation and take pity on me!
(*Fairy Spring rises from the lake, surrounded by Flower-Spirits.*)

FAIRY SPRING: Snegurotchka, oh my child, what do you ask of me?
Tell me what sorrow moves you?
I have a single moment only to appease it.

SNEGUROTCHKA: Oh grant me the gift of love, for I would love or die!

FAIRY SPRING: O my child, your wish is granted!

FAIRY SPRING and CHORUS OF FLOWER SPIRITS: Flower of the springtime dawn,
White lily of the somber woods,
Her face illumine
With your reflection kind and sweet!
Flower of dreams, black poppy-bloom,
You magic flower,
Lull her, and enchant her thoughts!
Golden flower of the hop, your exaltation
Spread through her heart!
(*She places the crown upon Snegurotchka'S forehead.*)

SNEGUROTCHKA: (*in ecstasy*). Ah, mother, what a miracle, how great my joy!
How lovely all on earth and in the skies,
What soft reflections of the waves, what kindly shadows!
How calm the forests! How pure and fair the dawn!

FAIRY SPRING: Dear daughter, hide your love from Yarilo the god;
Back to your dwelling, child, now quickly hasten,
Nor pause to watch the dawn suffuse the sky.
Farewell, my daughter, and be

A cet aveu suprême!
(*Elle disparaît dans le lac en même temps que les fleurs*).

## SCÈNE II.

*SNÉGOUROTCHKA et MIZGUIR.*

**MIZGUIR:** (*en courant*). Attends, attends, Snégourotchka!

**SNÉGOUROTCHKA:** Ah! que vois-je?

**MIZGUIR:** Snégourotchka, en vain je t'ai cherchée
La nuit dans la forêt; te fais-je peur?

**SNÉGOUROTCHKA:** Non, mon coeur ne sait plus la peur,
Laisse-moi regarder ton visage!
Ce n'est plus l'effroi qui trouble et saisit mon âme,
L'éclair de ton regard, l'accent de ta voix ardente!
Doux ami, je suis à toi,
Prends-moi dans tes bras, emporte-moi!
Je veux t'aimer, n'avoir pour lois
Que tes désirs. Pour toujours je suis à toi!
Sous le bois profond abrite-moi
Des feux mortels du dieu soleil!
(*Snégourotchka et Mizguir se mettent à l'ombre d'un buisson. La foule descend de la montagne à travers la forêt; en avant marchent les joueurs de gousli jouant de leurs instruments, et les bergers jouant de leurs cors; derrière eux vient le Tzar avec sa suite. Derrière le Tzar marchent par couples les jeunes gens et les jeunes filles fiancés, en vêtements de fête; plus loin viennent les autres Berendeys; arrivée dans la vallée, la foule se divise en deux parties.*)

## SCÈNE III.

*SNÉGOUROTCHKA, MIZGUIR, le TZAR, LEL et tout le peuple. Tous dans l'attente regardent vers l'Orient; aux premiers rayons du soleil, ils entonnent le choeur.*

**CHOEUR GÉNÉRAL:**

**IÈRE PARTIE:** Nous avons semé le millet dans la plaine,
Oï did Lado, nous l'avons semé.

**IIÈME PARTIE:** Nous écraserons le millet sur l'aire,
Oï did Lado, nous l'écraserons.

**IÈRE PARTIE:** Et comment écraserez-vous le millet?
Oï, did Lado.

**IIÈME PARTIE:** Les chevaux nous y mettrons,
Oï, did Lado.

faithful now
To your great vow supreme!
(*She disappears in the lake, together with the flower spirits.*)

## SCENE II.

*SNEGUROTCHKA and MIZGUIR.*

**MIZGUIR:** (*enters running*).
Wait, wait for me, Snegurotchka!

**SNEGUROTCHKA:** Ah, who do I see?

**MIZGUIR:** Snegurotchka, in vain I sought you
Last night in the forest; say, do you fear me?

**SNEGUROTCHKA:** No, my heart knows fear no longer.
Let me look into your eyes!
No longer terror troubles and vexes my soul,
I see your open glance, I hear your ardent voice!
Dear one, I am your own!
Take me in your arms and carry me away!
I want to love you, know no other law
Than your own wish! Forever I am yours!
Hide me where deepest woodland shadows lie,
From Yarilo, the sun-god's mortal fires!
(*Snegurotchka and Mizguir place themselves in the shade of a bush. The crowd descends from the mountain, moving across the forest. In the van come the gusli-players playing upon their instruments, and the shepherds blowing their horns; behind them the Tzar and his suite. Following the Tzar, in pairs, come the young men and young maidens who are betrothed, in holiday attire; further on, the rest of the Berendeys. Reaching the valley, the crowd separates into two groups.*)

## SCENE III.

*SNEGUROTCHKA, MIZGUIR, the TZAR, LEL and the PEOPLE. All in attendance look to the Orient; at the first sparkle of sun, they begin to sing as a chorus.*

**GENERAL CHORUS:**

**I:** We have sown the millet in the plain.
Oi, did Lado, we have sown it.

**II:** We will thresh the millet on the floor,
Oi, did Lado, we will thresh it.

**I:** And how will you thresh the millet?
Oi, did Lado.

**II:** We will put the horses to it,
Oi, did Lado.

**IÈRE PARTIE:** Les chevaux, nous les prendrons,
Oï, did Lado.

**IIÈME PARTIE:** Nous vous en paierons la rançon sans peine,
Oï, did Lado.

**IÈRE PARTIE:** Quelle est la rançon qui nous est offerte?
Oï, did Lado.

**IIÈME PARTIE:** Nous vous donnerons une jeune fille,
Oï, did Lado.

**IÈRE PARTIE:** Et nous serons un de plus,
Oï, did Lado.

**IIÈME PARTIE:** Et nous serons un de moins.
Oï, did Lado.
(*Pendant le chant les deux parties se rapprochent lentement en suivant le rythme de la chanson. Le chant fini les jeunes gens prennent leurs fiancées et saluent le Tzar.*)

**LE TZAR:** Que votre mariage soit béni!
Vivez dans la tendresse, vivez dans la joie
Et l'abondance, achevez
Entourés d'enfants le cours de votre vie!

**MIZGUIR:** (*Amenant Snégourotchka devant le Tzar*).
Auguste tzar, tu m'as commandé
De gagner ce coeur, j'ai fait selon ton ordre;
Je te demande ici de nous bénir!

**LE TZAR:** Veux-tu de ton plein gré te confier
A son amour? Avec ta main, ma fille,
Lui donne-tu ton coeur!

**SNÉGOUROTCHKA:** O notre tzar,
Je te dirai cent fois, si tu le veux,
Qu'il est mon bien aimé. Avant l'aurore,
J'ai fait à mon ami le cher aveu
De mon amour, je lui donne ma vie!
(*Un rayon éclatant perce le brouillard et tombe sur Snégourotchka.*)
Quel trouble en moi! L'extase ou bien la mort?
Quel feu profond pénètre tous mes sens!
Maman Printemps, je te bénis pour cette ivresse,
Pour ce divin bonheur d'avoir connu l'amour!
Mon coeur, mon sang, mon être tout entier
S'embrase et brûle! Je meurs et me fonds
D'amour et de bonheur. Adieu, vous toutes
Mes compagnes, adieu, adieu mon bien aimé!
O mon ami, je suis à toi,
Dans ce regard reçois mon âme!
(*Elle fond.*)

**I:** The horses, we will take them,
Oi, did Lado.

**II:** We will pay the ransom for them easily,
Oi, did Lado.

**I:** What is the ransom offered us?
Oi, did Lado.

**II:** We will give you a young maiden,
Oi, did Lado.

**I:** And there will be one more of us,
Oi, did Lado.

**II:** And there will be one less of us,
Oi, did Lado.
(*During this song the two groups have slowly drawn nearer each other, moving in cadence to the rhythm of their singing. When the song is ended, the young men take their sweethearts and bow to the Tzar.*)

**THE TZAR:** May your marriage be blessed!
Live lovingly, live happily,
And in abundance. And at last,
Surrounded by your children end your days!

**MIZGUIR:** (*Leading Snegurotchka before the Tzar*). O tzar august,
you have commanded me
To win this heart, and I have done your bidding;
And now I ask that you will bless us here!

**THE TZAR:** Is it by your own wish that you confide
In Mizguir's love? My daughter, with your hand
Do you give him your heart?

**SNEGUROTCHKA:** O Lord tzar,
A hundred times I'll tell you, if you wish
He is my well-beloved! Before the dawn,
I fondly had confessed to him
The love I feel, and given him my life!
(*A dazzling ray pierces the clouds and alights on Snegurotchka.*)
How I am moved! It is ecstasy or death?
What profound fire penetrates all my being!
O Mother Spring, thanks for this exaltation,
This joy divine given me, to know love!
My heart, my blood, the fiber of my being
Takes fire and burns! I die and melt away
In love and happiness! Farewell, all of you
Companions! Farewell, farewell, my well-beloved!
Oh love of mine, I am all yours,
In this last glance receive my soul!
(*She melts.*)

**CHOEUR GÉNÉRAL:** Ah! quel prodige étrange et quel mystère!
Ainsi que fond la neige au feu du clair soleil,
Elle a péri—Snégourotchka n'est plus!

**LEL:** O soleil, lumière et force,
Soleil, splendeur du monde,
Gloire à toi, dieu Yarilo!

**CHORUS:** Ah, marvel strange and most mysterious!
Thus, as the snow melts in the sun's clear fire,
She has perished—Snegurotchka is no more!

**LEL:** O sun, radiance and power,
Sun, splendor of the world,
Glory to you, god Yarilo!

**CHOEUR GÉNÉRAL:** Gloire à toi!
(*Sur un signe du Tzar, les serviteurs apportent des boeufs et des moutons aux cornes dorées, des barils d'hydromel, de la vaisselle et tout ce qu'il faut pour un festin.*)

*FIN.*

**CHORUS:** Glory to you!
(*At a sign from the Tzar, servitors lead in cattle and sheep with gilded horns, barrels of hydromel, plates and dishes and all the paraphernalia of a banquet.*)

*THE END.*

# Le Coq D'Or (1909)
## The Golden Cockerel

MUSIC BY NIKOLAI ANDREEVICH RIMSKY-KORSAKOV ■ LIBRETTO BY VLADIMIR IVANOVICH BIELSKY

---

Set to a libretto by Vladimir Bielsky (based on Alexander Pushkin's story), this three-act opera premiered at the Solodovnikov Theatre in Moscow on October 7, 1909. A prologue, sung by an astrologer (a counter-tenor), sets the stage for the story. An enemy lies in wait on the borders of Dodon's kingdom; the King and his ministers meet to discuss this dilemma. The astrologer enters with a golden cockerel that he says will crow in warning whenever danger threatens the kingdom. Dodon promises to give the astrologer whatever he asks for in return. The astrologer requests that the King put this in writing so that he may take him up on it at a later date. Dodon goes to sleep with the cockerel, which soon awakens him with crowing. The princes depart with their armies, accompanied by a reluctant Dodon. On a narrow mountain pass, Dodon is beside himself; the princes and many of the soldiers are already dead. General Polkan catches sight of a tent; he is about to open fire when the Queen of Shemakha emerges. She admits that she is responsible for the princes' deaths. She succeeds in seducing the old King, who dances and sings at her will. Back in the capital, the people await the King's return. He arrives in a splendid chariot, accompanied by the Queen. The astrologer asks for the Queen as his reward. The King refuses, killing him with a stroke of his scepter. The golden cockerel attacks the King and pecks him to death. The Queen disappears, and the people are left in mourning. The astrologer sings a brief epilogue which states that the opera is only a fairy tale, and that the only real people in it are the Queen and the astrologer himself.

---

## PROLOGUE

*(Devant le rideau apparaît L'Astrologue, une clef à la main.)*

**L'ASTROLOGUE:** *(au public).* Par mon art cabalistique,
Par les lois que je pratique,
On va voir renaître ici
Le héros d'un vieux récit.
Pour vous d'un conte tous les masques
Revivront, joyeux, fantasques.
Certes ce n'est qu'une fable,
Mais la morale en este louable.
*(Il disparaît.)*

## ■ ACTE PREMIER

*(Avant le lever du rideau, on present qu'il va se passer quelque chose de grave et de solennel. En effet, on voit une vaste salle, dans le palais du Roi Dodôn, qui fut jadis maître de tous les steppes de la Russie méridionale. Le conseil royal est en séance. La salle est richement ornée de peintures, de sculptures, de dorures. Le vert, le bleu, le jaune, couleurs favorites des sujets du Roi Dodôn, prédominent, sur des bancs recouverts de brocart, siègent des seigneurs graves et barbus. Au milieu, sur un trône richement orné de plumes de paon, est Dodôn, couronne en tête et vétu d'un habit d'apparat, jaune. Près de lui sont assis ses deux fils, Aphrôn et Gvidôn. Parmi les conseillers le général Polkan, vieux soldat brutal.)*

**LE ROI DODÔN:** *(qui paraît accablé de soucis).* Chers sujets, le coeur troublé,
Je vous ai tous rassemblés
Pour vous apprendre, en personne,
Combien lourde est ma couronne.
Mon sort est triste! écoutez:
Jeune, j'étais redouté
Sans scrupule l'âme fière,
Je portais au loin la guerre.
Maintenant, je suis bien vieux;
Les combats sont périlleux.
Or, mes ennemis se lèvent.
Ils m'attaquent tous, sans trêve
On dirait qu'ils font exprès!
Sans répit, nous restons prêts
A combattre.
*(Avec désespoir.)*
Nous veillons au Nord: du tout,
C'est du Sud qu'il fond sur nous!
On est là: tous ces sauvages
Viennent par la mar.
J'enrage: On n'a plus aucun répit,
J'en sanglote de dépit.
A ces maux est-il un remède?
Qu'un de vous me vienne en aide.
Un conseil!

## PROLOGUE

*(The Astrologer appears before the curtain with a magic key in his hand.)*

**THE ASTROLOGER:** *(to the audience).* I am a magician. By the occult sciences I am endowed with the extraordinary gift of evoking the shades, and in dead bodies breathing an enchanted life. Here before you will live again the droll masks of an old fairy tale. The tale's not true, but there's a hint in it; a lesson to all of you, good people. *(Disappears.)*

## ■ ACT I

*(Before the curtain rises there is a feeling that something extraordinarily important and solemn is to be presented. And in fact one sees a vast hall in the palace of the famous King Dodon during the sitting of the Council of Boyars. The hall is richly ornamented with Russian carving, gilded and painted, by which it is clearly evident that green, blue, and yellow are the favorite colors of King Dodon's people. On benches covered with brocade, the Boyars are seated in a semi-circle,—grave and bearded men. Upon a throne in the middle, magnificently decorated with peacock feathers, is seated King Dodon himself, wearing a golden crown and in royal vestments of yellow. On either side of him are the impatient Princes—his sons Afron and Guidon. Amongst the Boyars is the old and rude Voevoda Polkan.)*

**KING DODON:** *(appears overwhelmed with cares).* I have summoned you here, so that everyone
In the kingdom should know, what a burden it is
To the mighty Dodon to wear a crown.
So, listen, my friends!
From my youth up I have been redoubtable,
And time and time again I have daringly affronted
My neighbors.
But now I wish to rest from warlike deeds.
And seek repose.
As if on purpose a neighbor now is disturbing me
By unceasingly doing evil deeds.
In order to defend
The frontiers of my kingdom from attack
I must maintain a large Army.
We expect invasion from the North, and lo!
A force is coming from the South.
We have mastered these, but evil guests
Are coming from the sea,
So that I, Dodon, weep from anger
And cannot sleep.
My life is so anxious. I desire advice and help.
Counsel me!

**UN SEIGNEUR:** (*avec hésitation*). Autrefois une vieille, par les fèves, Savait expliquer les rêves.

**SECONDE SEIGNEUR:** Allons donc! Cette autre était Bien meilleure, qui savait lire, Dans le marc, et tout prédire.

**GVIDÔN:** Dans le ciel on peut trouver Le sens de ce qu'on a rêvé.

**TOUS:** Par le marc, oui! On explique par les fèves . . . . Tous les reves.

**AMELFA:** (*empressée et avec une infinie sollicitude*). Mais bien sûr! Voici les hommes Qui t'apportent ton grand lit. (*Sur un signe d'elle, les serviteurs se précipitent dans le palais et reparaissent, portant un grand lit d'ivoire, couvert de fourrures; ils le dressent au soleil. Amelfa s'approche de Dodôn; elle apporte un grand plateau chargé de sucreries.*) N'astu pas quelque appetit? Mange donc ces confitures, Quelques noix, ou bien des mûres! Bois le cidre: il est tout frais, Parfumé, mousseux, sucré. Ces fruits plein de miel, d'amandes, Et bien cuits au vin, t'attendent. Chasse donc tous les soucis, Tâte des pruneaux farcis.

**LE ROI DODÔN:** (*bâille et s'installe à portée du plateau.*) Hum . . . . J'accepte . . . . Mais prends garde, Mon aimable babillarde, Qu'un pesant sommeil soudain N'interrompe mon festin. (*Le Roi a fini sa collation, et regarde du côté du lit. Amelfa arrange les oreillers et rabat les couvertures.*)

**AMELFA:** Dors un peu sur cette couche Viens, je chasserai les mouches Loin de ton august front.

**LA VOIX DU COQ:** Cocori! Cocori-co! Règne et dors en ton lit clos! (*Dodôn ne plut plus résister au sommeil. Il se couche et s'endort sans plus, avec · autant d'insouciance qu'un enfant. L'intendante, penchée au dessus du lit, chasse les mouches.*)
**DES GARDIENS:** (*dans les coulisses.*) Règne et dors en ton lit clos! (*Les Gardiens, font l'appel, d'une voix somnolente, mais bientôt ils succombent à la douceur enchanteresse du sommeil de midi. Tous dorment profondement, sauf Amelfa. La capitale en-*

**ONE BOYAR:** (*besitatingly*). It is a pity our fortune-teller is dead. She would have unravelled the question By means of beans . . . .

**SECOND BOYAR:** Beans? We had—it's a pity it was some time ago— A better witch. She divined by dregs.

**GUIDON:** There was also one who knew How to foretell things by the stars.

**CHORUS OF BOYARS:** Dregs are better. The beans are more to be believed in.

**AMELFA:** (*clasping her hands in boundless devotion*). Bàtyushka! If you wish We shall turn the whole capital into a bed! (*At a sign from her the servants rush to the palace and carry out into the sun a bed of ivory with fur coverings. Amelfa herself comes to him with a large tray filled with delicacies.*) See that you have an empty tummy. Taste a little of these Turkish pods; Or some walnuts in honey. Drink some cold kvass, With mint, hops, ginger. Or will it please the royal taste To have some prunes stuffed with raisins And dipped in wine? Try and see if they are tasty. (*Dodon, yawning, sits down before the dishes.*)

**KING DODON:** Oh well! All right! And while I dally with the dishes, amuse me So that I shall not fall asleep. (*Having finished the delicacies, he glances at the bed.*)

**AMELFA:** (*Shakes up the pillow and arranges the bed.*) Lie down! I shall Drive off the annoying flies from the royal face.

**VOICE OF THE BIRD:** Cock-a-doo-dle-do! Sleep in thy regal bed! (*Dodon lies down, and instantly goes to sleep, as free from care as a child. Amelfa drives away the flies, bending over the bed. At first the guards sleepily call out to one another the words: "Reign, lying at ease." Then the sweet charm of the mid-day nap overcomes them. All except Amelfa indulge in a long, sweet sleep. Silence reigns throughout the capital. The indefatigable flies alone buzz about Dodon, and the everlasting sun shines as before with his steady*

tiere est possible. Seules les mouchés infatigables bourdonnent autour du lit royal, que le soleil continue d'éclairer d'une lumière égale et douce.*)

**AMELFA:** Tous s'endorment, tous sommeillent. Cher printemps! paix sans pareille! (*Elle s'accounde au lit du Roi et s'endort à son tour. Dodôn, dans son rêve, sourit comme à une belle inconnue.*)

**LA VOIX DU COQ:** Cocori! Cocori-cou! Ouvrez l'oeil et garde à vous! (*Trompettes dans la coulisse.— Bruit. Des gens courent. Des trompettes sonnent de divers côtés. Des chevaux henissent. La foule se précipite autour du palais. Sur les visages interloqués se lit une terreur profonde.*)

**LA FOULE:** (*dans la rue*). Le coq a donné l'alarme. Courez tous, prenez les armes! Oh! Malheur, calamité! Le royaume est dévasté.

**POLKAN:** (*accourant*). Roi puissant, ma voix t'appelle! Vois ton général fidèle! Ah! Réveille toi! Malheur! (*Amelfa va se cacher prèpitamment.*)

**LE ROI DODÔN:** (*encore à moitié endormi*). Quel est donc ce bruit, Seigneur!

**POLKAN:** L'ennemi sur nous s'avance!

**LE ROI DODÔN:** (*se lève en bâillant*). Hein? Quoi donc? Quelle démence . . . . Est-ce le feu dans mon palais?

**POLKAN:** Foin du vieux niais! Notre coq a chanté, il tourne et s'agite . . . . Tous nos gens ont fui. Viens vite!

**LA VOIX DU COQ:** Cocori! Cocori-cou! Ouvrez l'oeil et garde â vous! (*Dodôn regarde le Coq.*)

**LE ROI DODÔN:** (*au peuple*). Bien! Va pour la guerre, enfants! Hâtez vous, courez aux camps. Faites vite, qu'on s'empresse! Mais d'abord, ouvrez les caisses.

**LE PEUPLE:** (*docilement*). Nous serons obéissants! (*Dodôn s'assied sur son trône. Des chambres intérieures du palais sortent précipitamment Aphrôn et les Seigneurs, tous armés. Gvidôn arrive et, tout en courant, boucle le ceinturon de son épée.— Il embrasse trois fois chacun de ses fils, qui partent, maussades, suivis des Seigneurs.— On entend le bruit de l'armée qui s'ébranle:*)

and welcome light.*)

**AMELFA:** All are asleep! All are weary! All tired by the breath of Spring! (*She leans her elbows on the royal bed, and falls asleep beside Dodon, who smiles in his sleep, dreaming of some wonderful beauty who never existed.*)

**VOICE OF THE BIRD:** Cock-a-doo-dle-do! Beware! (*Uproar, and running to and fro. Horses neigh. Sound of trumpets—sometimes here, sometimes there. People appear on the street. Terrible fear is depicted upon their pitiful faces.*)

**PEOPLE ON THE STREET:** The bird is crowing! Get up! Saddle your fleet horses! Quickly! The enemy does not wait. He will trample down the cornfields And burn the villages.

**POLKAN:** (*running in*). Our King! Father of the people! I am your Voevoda. Sire! Awake! A calamity is upon us. (*The Housekeeper jumps up and hurriedly disappears.*)

**KING DODON:** (*not quite awake*). What is it?

**POLKAN:** It must be that a strange foe is advancing.

**KING DODON:** (*getting up and yawning*). Eh! What? What calamity? Is my palace burning?

**POLKAN:** Devil take him! The bird is crowing, turning about on the spire. Noise and hubbub throughout the capital.

**VOICE OF THE BIRD:** Cock-a-doo-dle-do! Open your eyes and beware! (*His own eyes assure Dodon of the restlessness of the bird.*)

**KING DODON:** (*to the people*). Well! My children. It is war. We must have assistance. No delay! Make haste! Unlock your coffers quickly.

**PEOPLE ON THE STREET:** (*abasing themselves*). We are yours, body and soul. (*Dodon sits on his throne. Afron and the Boyars rush in, armed. Guidon runs in, buckling his sword belt. Dodon kisses each of his sons thrice.*) (*The sons much cast down, go out with The Boyars. The noise of the departing army is heard, then all is silent.*)

**LA VOIX DU COQ:** (*Lorsque tout s'est calmé on entend la voix du Coq*). Cocoricou! Règne et dors en ton lit clos!

**VOICE OF THE BIRD:** Cock-a-doo-dle-do! Reign, taking your ease.

**LE ROI DODÔN:** Joli Coq, je te rends grâce.
(*Le Roi Dodôn, Amelfa les gardes s'endorment d'endorment d'un sommeil calme et profond.*)

**KING DODON:** (*yawning*). Dear bird! Many thanks.
(*Dodon falls asleep; also Amelfa and the Guards. His dreams about the wonderful beauty become more definite and insistent.*)

**GARDES:** (*dans la coulisse*). Règne e dors, en ton lit clos!
(*Le rêve de Dodôn se précise.*)

**LA VOIX DU COQ:** Cocori! Cocoricou!
Ouvrez l'oeil, et garde à vous!
(*De nouveau s'entendent des cris, des pas précipités. Des trampettes sonnent. La foule, en grand désordre, se rassemble dans la rue, devant le palais. Trompettes dans la coulisse.*)

**VOICE OF THE BIRD:** Cock-a-doo-dle-do! Beware!
(*Again noise and running to and fro. Trumpets. A terrified crowd of people assemble at the Palace, not daring to awake Dodon.*)

**LE PEUPLE:** (*dans la rue*). Ah, tout est perdu! Alerte!
(*Ils restent tous indécis, n'osant réveiller le roi.—Trompettes dans la coulisse.*)
Notre roi qui dort!
Oui, certes! Quel malheur!
Vite à genoux!
Comment faire? Sauvons nous!
Et Polkân reste introuvable!

**PEOPLE ON THE STREET:** O!
What misfortune! O, brothers, what evils!
Our King is fast asleep. All is quiet In the palace.. It is impossible to wake them.
What shall we do? What will become of us?
Where is Polkan, our Voevoda?
(*Polkan rushes in with armed Boyars. Amelfa runs away.*)

**POLKAN:** (*se précipite, suivi de seigneurs en armes. Amelfa va se dacher précipitament*). Un destin cruel nous accable,
Sors enfin, oui, sors de ce doux repos!

**POLKAN:** Sire! Father of your people!
Sire! Another calamity!

**LE ROI DODÔN:** (*réveillé en sursaut*). Ah! toujours mal à propos!

**KING DODON:** (*leaping from the bed*). Always at the wrong time!

**POLKAN:** Dans la ville tous s'irritent
Et là haut, ton coq s'agite,
Clame à pleine voix son chant
Et regarde le levant.
Nous ne sommes pas en nombre;
L'avenir me parait sombre.
Fais donner les vétérans!

**POLKAN:** Noise and hubbub in all the capital,
And again the bird high up
On the spire is playing tricks,
Turning towards the East.
It seems the Army has not been successful.
I suppose it would be the thing
To call out the old men!

**LE ROI DODÔN:** (*se frotte les yeux et bâille*). Oui! Je vais venir, attends.
(*Il s'approche de la balustrade et regarde en l'air.*)

**KING DODON:** (*rubbing his eyes and yawning*). Wait! I shall look for myself.
(*Goes to the balustrade and looks up at the roof.*)

**LA VOIX DU COQ:** Cocori! Cocoricou!
Ouvrez l'oeil et garde à vous!

**VOICE OF THE BIRD:** Cock-a-doo-dle-do! Beware!

**LE ROI DODÔN:** (*d'un ton plaintif*). Le coq d'or nous met en garde.
En avant! Que nul ne tarde.
Chers amis marchons, vaillants.
Au secours de nos enfants!
(*Il se prépare sans empressement; les domestiques apportent en hâte son équipement couvert de poussière et de rouille. Amelfa regarde le Roi avec tristesse.*)
Mon armet! Puis, ma cuirasse.
Ouf! L'étroite carapace!
Cherchez moi mon bouclier,

**KING DODON:** (*plaintively*). The golden cock is flapping its wings not in vain;
A dangerous journey is before us.
Now, old man, we shall arise quickly
And go to help our children.
(*He gets ready without any animation.*)
Where is my helmet? Bring my armour.
(*The servants quickly fetch the dusty and rusty arms and invest*

Le beau rouge; un baudrier . . . .

My armour is too tight!
Look where my favourite red shield is hanging.
(*They fetch the shield.*)

**LA VOIX DU COQ:** Cocoricou! Ouvrez l'oeil et garde à vous!

**VOICE OF THE BIRD:** Cock-a-doo-dle-do! Beware!

## ■ DEUXIÈME ACTE

## ■ ACT II

(*Nuit obscure. Les troubles rayons de la lune éclairent de lueurs sanglantes un défilé étroit, parsemé de petits buissons, et les roches escarpées. Le brouillard de montagne remplit toutes les cavités d'un voile blanc. Parmi les buissons ou sur les pentes nues des collines, gisent les cadavres des guerriers: on las dirait pétrifiés au milieu de leur dernière bataille. Des aigles et d'autres rapaces, en bandes, se sont abattus sur les corps; à chaque coup de vent, ils s'envolent, effarés. Deux chevaux se tiennent immobiles, la tête inclinée sur les cadavres de leurs maitres, les fils de Dodôn. Tout est calme, silencieux et menaçant.*)
(*On entend au loin un bruit de pas. C'est l'armée de Dodôn qui avance, craintivement. Des guerriers paraissent, suivant le défilé. Ils vont deux par deux, s'arrêtent, se retournent.*)

(*A dark night. A dim moon casts a ruddy glow over a narrow gorge covered with small bushes and hemmed in by cliffs. The mountain mist, slightly stirred by the wind, fills all the hollows with a milky shroud. In the midst of the bushes, and on the bare hillocks, wherever one looks, lie in heaps the bodies of dead warriors killed in battle. Eagles and other birds of prey sit on the corpses in flocks, flying away in fright at every gust of wind. Two horses stand motionless with heads lowered over the bodies of their masters. All is quiet, silent, and ominous. There is heard in the distance the sound of the unsteady footsteps of the discouraged army of King Dodon. In the gorge, looking about and stopping, the warriors come down in a file, two abreast.*)

**LES SOLDATS:** Nuit épouvantable et sombre!
Tout est calme: seuls, dans l'ombre,
Les vautours veillent nos morts.
La lune pourpre sur leurs corps
Brille comme un cierge funèbre.
Hou! Le vent, dans les ténèbres,
Fait entendre un chant de deuil
Sur les cadavres sans cercueil.
Triste, il pleure; il geint sans trêve . . . .
Sa voix retombe et puis s'élève.
Il agite doucement
Leurs cheveux, leurs vêtements.
(*Le Roi Dodôn, tourmente par de sombres pensées, arrive au pas avec son vieux général. Ils trébuchent contre les corps des deux princes.*)

**WARRIORS:** The silent night is whispering fearful things.
All is waste; only a flock of birds
Guard the bodies of the fallen.
The pallid disc of the moon
Has risen, and is like a funeral taper.
A mournful and dreary wind
Steals through the darkness;
Stumbling on the bodies,
It blows moaning over the dead.
At times it is silent; and again dejectedly
It presses close to the faces of the fallen,
And plucks at their sleeves.
(*Enter, riding their horses at a walk, King Dodon with his old Voevoda, plunged in gloomy thoughts, and stumble against the bodies of both the Princes.*)

**LE ROI DODÔN:** (*se précipitant sur les corps de ses fils*). Quel spectacle abominable!
Mes deux fils! . . . . Le sort m'accable . . .
Désarmés, sanglants et froids,
Leurs yeux fixes pleine d'effroi . . . .
Ils se sont tués l'un à l'autre!
Leurs vaillants coursiers arpentent
Le gazon souillé, les pentes
Que rougit le sang des nôtres . . . .
Ah, douleur cruelle!
Mes fils! Mon espoir!
Quelle erreur mortelle
Put ainsi vous décevoir?

**KING DODON:** (*throwing himself upon the bodies of his sons*). What terrible sight is this?
It is my sons! My own sons!
Without their helmets and their armor.
And both lie dead,—
The sword of each piercing the other.
Their horses wander over the meadows
Upon the grass trampled down
And red with blood,
Oh! Our support! My children!
Woe is me! Caught in a net
Are both my falcons.
O grief! My death is here.

Hélas, je n'ai plus qu'à mourir:
Coulez, coulez mes larmes amères!
Que le steppe solitaire
Nous entende tous gémir.
Les rochers, les bois, la plaine
Compatiront à notre peine.
Ah! Ah! Ah!

CHOEUR: (tous sanglotent). Ah! Ah! Ah!

LE ROI DODÔN: (plaintivement). Désormais
Je vous conduirai moi-même:
C'est pitié que ceux au'on aime
Tombent ainsi, décimés!
Ah!
(Il pleure de nouveau.)

POLKAN: (a Dodôn). Adieu paniers, vendanges sont faites!
(Il se tourne vers l'armée.)
Votre maître est opprime:
Vos epées sont-elles prêtes?

CHOEUR: L'ennemi sera chassé!
Mais où diable est-il passé?
(Rien ne répond. Le jour commence à poindre. Le brouillard se disperse graduellement, et l'on aperçoit, sortant de terre une tente. Les rayons de l'aurore se jouent sur les arabesques de ses parois de brocart bigarré. — Consternation générale.)

LE ROI DODÔN: Voyez donc, la belle tente!
(Les premiers rayons du soleil paraissent; on voit remuer les parois de la tente.)
(Les canonniers s'enfuient en débandade, abandonnant leur pièce.)
(De la tente sort une belle jeune femme à la démarche legère, mais majestueuse. Elle est suivie de quatre esclaves qui portent des instruments de musique: goussli (psalterions), goudok (viole), chalumeau et tambour. Sa longue robe de soie rouge est richement brodée d'or. Elle porte un turban blanc, orne d'une haute plume. Elle paraît ne rien voir, et, les bras levés comme pour la prière, chante en s'adressant au soleil qui brille.)

LA REINE DE CHÉMAKHA: Salut à toi, soleil de flamme!
Nous reviens-tu de l'Orient,
Du doux pays cher à mon âme,
De ses paysages souriants?
Ah! Parle-moi des fraiches roses
Et des buissons ardents des lys;
Des beaux oiseaux qui se reposent,
Auprès des lacs bordés d'iris!
Qui chantent auprès des lacs bordés d'iris!
Dis moi: le soir, près des fontaines,
Quand chaque belle entonne un chant
D'extase ou d'amoureuse peine
Qui monte au rouge firmament,
Voit-on toujours, sous leurs grands voiles,
Leurs yeux sourire au beau galant,
Qui, dans la nuit semée d'étoiles,

Weep all, as Dodon does.
Let the deepest valleys groan
And the highest mountains shake with
Grief.
(All sob.)

KING DODON: (pitifully). From now on I shall lead my army everywhere myself.
The young men enough have been
Exposed to the misfortunes of a martial life.
(Renewed sobbing.)

POLKAN: (to Dodon). Whatever has happened, it is past and done.
(To the army.)
Friends! Let us stand up for Dodon;
Let us give the enemy a lesson!

WARRIORS: We shall! That we shall!
If only we can find the enemy.
(No answer. It begins to grow light. The mist rises a little, and the outline of a tent is seen. The rosy reflection of the dawn falls upon the bright, many coloured patterns of the brocade flaps of the tent. All are amazed.)

KING DODON: Good heavens! A tent!
All in patterns.
(The first rays of the rising sun.)
(The flaps of the tent move. The warriors hastily disperse, leaving the cannon. From the tent emerges with an easy but imposing gait a beautiful, bright-eyed woman, accompanied by four female slaves with dulcimer, rebec, reed, and a drum. She wears a long silk garment of raspberry color, plentifully adorned with pearls and gold. On her head a white turban with a high feather. The beautiful woman, as if she had noticed nothing, turns towards the bright sun, raising her hands to it in prayer.)

QUEEN OF SHEMAKHAN: Answer me, bright orb of day!
You come to us from the East—
Have you visited my native land,
The country of fairy dreams?
Are the roses still glowing there
And the bushes of burning lilies?
Do the turquoise dragon-flies
Kiss the gorgeous leaves?
In the evening by the waters,
In the shy songs of the women and the maidens
Is there still that same intoxicating faintness,
The passionate dream of forbidden love?
Is the unexpected guest still welcomed—
Are there gifts prepared for him—
A modest feast—a secret look

Viendra d'un pas furtif et lent?
Vient-on l'attendre à la fenêtre,
L'oeil attentif, le coeur tremblant?
A peine l'a-t-on vu paraître,
Saint-on charmer l'heureux amant,
Le coeur en flamme,
Saint-on charmer l'armant,
l'heureux amant?
(Avant fini de chanter, elle se retourne vers le roi, et le regarde longtemps sans rien dire.)

LE ROI DODÔN: (a voix basse, et poussant Polkan du coude.)
Comme elle chante!
Qui peut-elle être?

POLKAN: (de même). Si dès qu'elle nous voit paraître
Son accueil est si charmant,
Allons-y pour un moment!
(Dodôn s'approche gravement ae la reine. Polkan le suit. Les autres n'osent point s'approcher.)

LE ROI DODÔN: N'ais pas peur de nous, ma belle!
Dis moi comment tu t'appelles,
Quel est ton pays.
Dis-moi, Viens-tu seule ici?
Pourquoi?

LA REINE DE CHÉMAKHA: (Timide, et les yeux baissés). Je suis libre, et seule ici.
I Chémakha je suis la reine,
Et je viens de mes domaines
Pour soumettre ton pays!

LE ROI DODÔN: (avec stupéfaction). Nous soumettre, sans vergogne?
Tu vas bien vite en besogne!
Sans armée tu nous vaincras,
Par la force de ton bras?

LA REINE DE CHÉMAKHA: (toujours avec timidité). Ma pensée n'est point si folle:
Mon sourire, mes paroles,
Ma beauté me suffiront
Pour faire courber les fronts.
(Elle frappe dans ses mains. De la tente sortent deux esclaves qui portent des vaisseaux d'argent, et remplissent de vin des coupes.)
Pardonnez à mon audace,
Mes chers hôtes: prenez place:
Par faveur, daignez gouter de ce vin.
(Elle s'incline et offre une coupe pleine au Roi Dodôn, qui recule avec méfiance.)
A vos santés!

LE ROI DODÔN: Bois d'abord, que nul mécompte N'en résulte.

LA REINE DE CHÉMAKHA: N'as tu pas honte?
Tiens, regarde dans mes yeux,
D'un dessein si ténébreux
Peux-tu m'estimer capable?
Suis-je donc si haissable?
(Elle lève les yeux, en souriant. Dodôn, troublé, boit, et Polkan suit son exemple. Les esclaves reviennent; elles étendent un tapis

Through the interfering veils?
When the blue night darkens,
Does the young mistress hasten to him
With a sweet avowal on her lips,
Having forgotten both fear and shame!
(The song being ended The Queen turns towards The King and looks for a long time at him in silence.)

KING DODON: (quietly poking Polkan with his elbow). That's a song for you!

POLKAN: (with a wink). If the young mistress wishes to entertain us
It is possible for us to pass a little time here.
(Dodon gravely goes nearer to the Queen. Polkan follows him. The others remain at a distance, not daring to approach.)

KING DODON: Fair lady! Fear us not.
Be open with us in everything.
What is your name? Who are you?
And where is your land?

QUEEN OF SHEMAKHAN: (modestly lowering her eyes). By your leave I am the
Virgin Queen of Shemakhan.
I am stealing like a thief
To conquer your city.

KING DODON: (in astonishment, almost roughly). You are an amusing jester,
Wilful maiden.
To wage war, an army is necessary;
Without it, it's a sorry business.

QUEEN OF SHEMAKHAN: In this you are mistaken.
An army is not needed for a victory.
Beauty alone makes all bend low
Before her.
(Claps her hands. Two more slaves come out of the tent with silver pitchers and pour wine into goblets.)
I am glad of unexpected guests.
The goblets are full of the fiery juice of the vine;
They are frothing to the rim.
(She bows and strikes the face of Dodon who recoils in distrust.)
Your Health!

KING DODON: You shall drink first,—
We after.

QUEEN OF SHEMAKHAN: I did not expect this.
Look in my eyes, which glow
Brighter than the dawn itself.
How could I, with such a heavenly look.
Regale the stranger with poison?
(Smilingly she raises her eyelashes. Dodon, in confusion, drinks the wine. Polkan does the

## Act II

*au milieu de la scène, et disposent autour trois coussins en guise de sièges. Sur un signe de Polkan, les soldats, au fond de la scène, s'installent commodément. On enlève les cadavres. Dodôn, Polkan et la reine s'assoient. Les deux hommes sont tout décontenancés. La reine a un sourire énigmatique.*)

**POLKAN:** (*Reprenant courage, et se penchant brusquement vers la reine, avec l'intention d'être aimable*). Avez-vous la nuit dernière Bien dormi?

**LA REINE:** Merci! Hum guère . . . .
Pas trop mal . . . .
Mais, au matin,
Je me réveillai soudain
L'air plus chaud et plus languide
Vint troubler mes sens timides;
Un parfum d'étranges fleurs
Enivra mon pauvre coeur . . . .
A travers la nuit obscure,
J'entendis un lent murmure . . . .
Toi, qu'appelle mon amour,
Viens! oh, viens, oh!

**POLKAN:** (*jovial*). Il viendra un de ces jours.

**LA REINE:** (*bondissant de son siège*). Sire, chasse ce vieil homme Ses propos grossiers m'assomment. (*Polkan paraît déconcerté.*)

**LE ROI DODÔN:** Tu me pousseras à bout!
Tu es là comme un hibou,
Et tous tes discours stupides
Gênent cette enfant timide.
N'as tu pas compris?
Va-t-en dans un coin, et puis attends!
(*Polkan se lève, docile, et va derrière la tente, d'où à chaque moment il sort un peu son nez et sa longue barbe. La reine rapproche son coussin de celui de Dodôn.*)

**LA REINE:** (*presque à l'oreille de Dodôn*). Viens me dire quelque chose.

**LE ROI DODÔN:** (*plus décontenancé que jamais*). Quoi donc? parle!

**LA REINE:** Mais je n'ose . . . . !
Bah! Réponds la vérité:
On me vante ma beauté,
On m'accable de fadaises;
(*Elle regarde Dodôn bien dans les yeux.*)
Qu'en dis-tu?

**LE ROI DODÔN:** (*bégayant*).
Hein. Oui . . . vraiment . . . .
Certes . . .

*same. The slaves who brought the pitchers again appear, spread out a carpet in their midst, and arrange pillows for them to sit on. At a sign given by the Voevoda, the warriors withdraw to a distance, for a prolonged rest and to gather the bodies of the slain. Dodon, Polkan, and The Queen seat themselves. The first two are perplexed and silent. The Queen smiles enigmatically.*)

**POLKAN:** (*making an effort, suddenly bows to The Queen, trying to be easy in manner and agreeable.*) How has the Queen been pleased to Pass the night?

**QUEEN OF SHEMAKHAN:** I thank you I slept not badly.
But at dawn something happened to me;
The air became intoxicating—
Moist, heavy, and spicy—
Like the aroma of night flowers,
Like the play of tangled dreams.
Someone unseen was breathing,
Oppressed by secret passion.
I heard a voice, tender as the air of Spring.
Teasing the ear with the words:
"Dearest! Let me go."
Louder—softer—farther—nearer.

**POLKAN:** (*with a smile*). They will come. Do not grieve.
(*The Queen arises in great emotion.*)

**QUEEN OF SHEMAKHAN:** King! Drive away this monster!
I do not love your Voevoda.
(*Polkan is put out of countenance.*)

**KING DODON:** Why, indeed, old dotard,
Do you stare like an owl?
You see the damsel is put to shame—
Still fears us men,
Away with you. Go!
Behind the tent.
(*Polkan gets up hurriedly and goes behind the tent, from where his long beard is seen sticking out from time to time. The Queen moves her pillow close to Dodon.*)

**QUEEN OF SHEMAKHAN:** (*almost in Dodon's ear*). My business is with you.

**KING DODON:** (*still more confused by the danger of propinquity*). Well, what is it?

**QUEEN OF SHEMAKHAN:** I should like to know for certain If the virgin beauty of the Queen Is really so brilliant; Or is it empty talk. (*Looks straight into Dodon's eyes.*) What sayest thou?

**KING DODON:** (*hesitating*).
I . . . . that is . . . . in truth . . . .

**LA REINE:** Quel beau compliment!
Tu me vois sous mes parures:
Je suis belle, j'en suis sûre,
Par moi même.
Et tous les soirs
Je le vois dans mon miroir,
(*Comme éprise d'elle même, et avec une animation croissante.*)
Quand j'ai fait tomber ces robes
Dont l'étoffe te dérobe
La splendeur de mes attraits,
Quand mon corps d'argent paraît . . . .
Au milieu de cette tente
Je me vois, resplendissante . . . .
Je dénoue mes longs cheveux,
Dont le flot tumultueux,
Comme un noir torrent, s'épanche
Sur le marbre de mes hanches,
Et me fait un lourd manteau
Pour rafraîchir la peau
Je m'asperge de rosée,
Dont les perles irisées
Se répandent sur mes seins.
Que n'en vois-tu le pur dessin!
Ils sont frais comme la rose,
Fermes, tendres, blancs et roses.
Si doux, si clairs si transparents . . . .
Tu parais peu souffrant?
Aurais tu mal à la tête?

**LE ROI DODÔN:** (*avec effort*).
Non . . . . C'est au foie . . . .
Ca s'arrête!

**LA REINE:** Ce n'est rien. Je vais chanter:
Tu n'auras qu'à m'écouter.
(*Fais silence.*)
(*D'un coup d'oeil elle ordonne aux esclaves d'accompagner son chant.*)
"Viens dans l'ombre, viens l'ombre
De ma tente aux rideaux lourds.
Marche, glisse, marche, glisse
Sur mes ta pis de velours!"
Veux tu venir sous ma tente,
Beau vieillard?

**LE ROI DODÔN:** Tu ris, méchante!
Beau vieillard?
Je n'ai pourtant
Que tout au plus . . . .

**LA REINE:** Ah! pourquoi me souvenir?
Mon malheur ne peut finir
Un destin cruel m'accable,
Vivre m'est insupportable.
(*A travers ses larmes.*)
Où trouver quelqu'un qui ose
Me contredire en toute chose,
(*Encore comme en rêve.*)
Me soumettre à son désir,
Me dominer?

**QUEEN OF SHEMAKHAN:** Is that all?
You are to be pitied knowing
The Queen only in her garments.
I am not so bad without them.
When I go to sleep, I look a long time in the mirror.
(*Thoughtfully admiring herself. Becomes more and more carried away.*)
I throw off my garments,
And as a ray of sunlight in the mist
Falling on a silver statue
I shine within the tent.
I look and see if
There is a mole or any blemish anywhere on my body.
I remove the pearly fastenings, and
Wanton masses of hair,
Not embarrassed with any headdress,
Pour forth in black torrent
Over my supple marble thighs . . . .
So that my sleep may be fresh and sweet
For the night, I sprinkle myself with dew.
On my breasts fall drops of liquid fire—
And I have breasts indeed!
They vie with glory of the southern roses—
Magnificent and firm—and they are
As white, light, and transparent as a dream . . . .
What is the matter, my friend? Are you not
Yourself? Is your little head turned?

**KING DODON:** (*controlling himself*). There is something the matter with my liver.

**QUEEN OF SHEMAKHAN:** Rubbish! I shall sing.
Listen to my song!
(*With a look commands her slaves to accompany her.*)
"Dark and narrow
Is my gaily-decked tent;
Warm and soft is the carpet in it . . . ."
Do you wish, old man, to see
What is within?

**KING DODON:** Why do you wish to offend us? You know
I am not old. These are not wrinkles, but—

**QUEEN OF SHEMAKHAN:** Ah!
Why do I think of it—
Only to open the wound afresh?
My grief is as boundless
As the wide expanse of the blue sea.
O! Take my life!
(*through her tears*).
Where shall I find someone who will be able
To contradict me in everything;
(*as in a dream.*)
Who will place a limit to my desires,
Firmly and masterfully?

LE ROI DODÔN: (*solonnel*). Que! plaisir de te contenter, ma belle! Celui que tes voeux appallent Est ici, devant tes yeux. Tu auras des jours joyeux. Je veux être despotique, Et te tourner en bourrique . . . . En un mot, je suis tout prêt, Tu n'auras aucun regret!

LA REINE: (*abasourdie*.) En bourrique? Ha, ha, ha, ha, ha, ha, ha, ha, ha! (*D'un ton gai.*) Quel délice! O, le merveilleux service! (*Dans l'excès de sa joie, elle saisit les deux mains de Dodôn.*) Crois a ma reconnaissance! J'en suis folle! Saute, Danse!

LE ROI DODÔN: (*effrayé*). Mais je ne sais plus danser!

LA REINE: Danse comme en ton jeune age.

LE ROI DODÔN: (*fâché*). Non! tous ces gens-là m'agacent.

LA REINE: Bien: Polkân prendra ta-place. Hé, Polkân! Danse avec moi! (*Polkan avance la tête, mais n'ose point bouger de sa cachette.*)

LE ROI DODÔN: (*conciliateur*). Non! pardonne à mon émoi. Quoique gauche pour la danse, Je veux bien, par complaisance . . . .

LA REINE: Commençons! Allons, venez! Dodôn va vous fasciner. (*Timidement, Polkan et les guerriers s'approchent du tapis et forment le cercle; ils s'efforcent de ne point regarder Dodôn. Les esclaves entament un air de danse lente. Un tambourin à la main, la reine avance, gracieuse et legere.*)

LA REINE: (*Elle danse*). Sous mon voile, je m'avance, Je te fais la révérence, Fort timidement. Puis à toi: Viens ici, d'un pas courtois, Mais sans crainte, l'air bravache, Et retrousse en vainqueur tes moustaches. Puis, encore trois pas en avant. (*Dodôn danse selon ces indications et arrive auprès de la reine.*) Bien! Tu viens la, me suivant. Je m'échappe, vagabonde, Comme un poisson d'or, sous les ondes, Fuit le venimeux crapaud Qui lui court après. (*Dodôn danse de nouveau.—Se fachant.*) Mauvais travail! Rentre les talons, de grâce! Cambre-toi, la tête en place!

KING DODON: (*solemnly*). Cease weeping, and rejoice, Maiden Queen of Shemakhan. Thou hast sought and found. Thy life will now be bright. I shall thwart thee and Contradict thee in everything; In fine—without unnecessary words— I am ready to do all for thee.

QUEEN OF SHEMAKHAN: (*in amazement*). Me? Thwart? I am very glad (*joyfully*) Such happiness! Such bliss! (*Takes Dodon by both hands, who is unutterably happy.*) And for this occasion let us dance, Forgetting our exalted rank.

KING DODON: (*in fear*). I no longer know how to dance.

QUEEN OF SHEMAKHAN: Well! Be a child once more.

KING DODON: (*gloomily*). I am not going to dance in the presence of people.

QUEEN OF SHEMAKHAN: Then, Polkan must be with me. Here, Polkan! Come here, my friend! (*Polkan sticks his head out from behind the tent, but dares not to approach.*)

KING DODON: (*seeks a reconciliation*). Do not get angry, darling! Although I do not know how to dance. I shall not spare myself.

QUEEN OF SHEMAKHAN: Well, let us begin. People, come hither! Our Dodon is going to dance. (*Polkan and the Warriors cautiously draw near to the carpet, stand in a circle and try not to look at Dodon. The female slaves begin a measured and graceful dance; The Queen with a tambourine joins in, slowly and light as air.*)

QUEEN OF SHEMAKHAN: (*dancing*). At first I shall dance. Having lowered my veil, Modestly, languidly.—Now it is Your turn, Dodon. Come! Step in front Like a turkey, full of conceit, And sideways, as if by accident, Knock up against me. (*Dodon dances as commanded and awkwardly jostles the Queen.*) Good! I, striking my tambourine, Shall fly away from you, Silently, supple as a little fish. And then you, a loathsome old crab, Must try and catch me. (*Dodon dances again.*) (*angrily*). Not that way! You have the ways of a camel. Don't keep your heels out. (*Dance becomes livelier.*) And now, wave your hand,

Agite ton éventail, Et montre-toi plus dispos! (*La danse devient plus animée.*) Je m'assieds; rien ne te gêne: Tourne jusqu'à perdre haleine! (*Dodôn, agitant les bras avec désespoir, commence une danse frénétique. La reine s'est assise à un bout du tapis; elle rit aux éclats en voyant les pirouettes de Dodôn.—De petite nègres sortent de la tente et se rangent autour de Dodôn.—Exténué. Dodôn se laisse tomber sur le tapis. Les musiciens cessent de jouer. Les petits nègres s'enfuient.*)

LE ROI DODÔN: (*se dressant sur les genoux*). C'est assez! Je veux souffler! (*Debout.*) Belle enfant, si je te plais, Viens régner sur mon empire: Tous mes biens pour ton sourire! Prends mon royaume; Prends, je t'en fais don!

LA REINE: (*avec dédain*). Bah! mais qu'y ferais je donc?

LE ROI DODÔN: Quoi? Hé bien: manger et boire, Dormir, écouter des histoires, Obtenir de ton amant Tout . . . . . oui, tout sauf le merle bland! Tu verras: l'on s'y goberge.

LA REINE: Ça partons, et faisons hâte Je veux voir des ciels nouveaux. Vite, en marche! (*De la tente sortent des esclaves qui portent des miroirs, des éventails, des bijoux, des tapis. Ils aident la reine à se préparer pour le voyage. Dans le camp de Dodôn, même agitation.*)

LE ROI DODÔN: Mes chevaux! Mon char doré! Prenez les rênes! Viens près de moi, ma souveraine.

LA REINE: (*se plaçant à côté de Dodôn*). Je suis prête. Avancez! Chantez ta gloire du fiancé!

LES ESCLAVES DE LA REINE: O, mes soeurs, l'etrange histoire! Notre reine, qui l'escorte? Un vieillard aux jambes tortes! La couronne d'or qu'il porte Cache mal son front d'esclave. O, cet air pédant et grave! Il est tout pareil à l'âne, Lourd d'esprit, et dur de crâne. Comme un singe il gesticule. Mon Dieu, qu'il est ridicule! Son aspect hideux effare.

Turn around, take mincing steps; Stamp your feet until you are ready to fall down; While I sit down here. (*The Queen sits to one side and laughs continually, amused at Dodon. Dodon waves his hand despairingly and starts the mad dance. Black boys run out from the tent and form a circle around Dodon. His strength exhausted, he falls down on the carpet. The dance ends, and the black boys re-enter the tent.*)

KING DODON: (*on his knees*). Stop! I have no more strength. (*Gets up.*) If I am so dear to you Take me and all my Kingdom; For all I have is yours, and likewise I myself.

QUEEN OF SHEMAKHAN: (*disdainfully*). What shall I do with you?

KING DODON: What shall you do? Eat sweetmeats— Rest, and listen to fairy tales . . . . Everything will be provided for my little darling; I shall spare nothing.

QUEEN OF SHEMAKHAN: There is no reason to linger; My preparations are made quickly. Let us be on our way at once! (*Out of the tent there come in an endless file, every time moving apart the flaps of the tent, the slaves of The Queen, carrying looking-glasses, fans, coffers of precious things, pitchers, carpets, etc. They array The Queen. The army also get ready to move.*)

KING DODON: Ho! A horse! A golden chariot To carry the Queen!

QUEEN OF SHEMAKHAN: (*standing beside Dodon*). I am ready. Ha, ha! (*To her slaves.*) Sing the praises of the Bridegroom.

SLAVES: Sisters! Who limps beside The resplendent beauty? He is a King by rank and dress— But a slave—by body and soul. With what shall we compare him Because of his rolling gait, he is like a camel. Because of his wry face and odd ways, He is like a real ape! He is like a spectre! (*They bring in the chariot.*)

## Act II

LE ROI DODÔN: (*ne se contenant plus*). Hé, Polkàn! Sonnez, fanfares! Je suis fancé: victoire!
(*Fanfares; les soldats crient. Le cortège s'ebranle.*)

LES SOLDATS: Hourra! Hourra! Hourra! Hourra!

*RIDEAU.*

## ■ TROISIÈME ACTE

(*Journée chaude et ensoleillée: mais à l'est, un lours nuage noir avance lentement: l'air est chargé d'orage. De temps en temps arrivent des messagers essoufflés. qui apportent les dernières nouvelles. Ils montent l'escalier et disparaissent a l'intérieur. Tout le monde attend anxieusement l'arrivée du roi.*)

LE PEUPLE: J'ai grand peur amis! Pourquoi? Je l'ignore! tiens-toi coi! Nul malheur ne nous menace: Voyez! Le coq d'or reste en place. Il se prélasse au soleil. Il ne donne point l'eveil. Et le coq est de bon conseil! Un nuage lourd d'orage Apparaît à l'orient, Noir, obscur, terrifiant! Il pleuvra! A Grêlera! Voici venir la tempête! Oui, la tempête!
(*Au haut de l'escalier apparaît l'intendante Amelfa; tous se précipitent vers elle.*)

LE PEUPLE: (*avec de grands saluts*). Viens-tu rassurer nos coeurs? Nos soldats sont ils vainqueurs? Ont ils chassé les rebelles? De l'armée quelles nouvelles?

AMELFA: (*d'une voix saccadée*). Ca ne vous regarde pas! Détournez d'ici vos pas.

LE PEUPLE: Grà! l'attente est cruelle!
(*Plusieurs assistants s'approchent D'Amelfa et s'efforcent de baiser le bas de sa robe. Elle les repousse.*)

AMELFA: He bien!
(*Pour se defaire d'eux.*)
Voici les nouvelles: Quatre rois sont restés sur le carreau: Trefle, pique, coeur, carreau. Notre armée triomphe seule. Dodôn sauva de la gueu le D'un dragon la jeune reine Qu'en triomphe il vous ramène

## ■ ACT III

KING DODON: (*beside himself with joy*). Ho! Polkan! Sound the trumpets for A victory! I am going home with a bride!
(*Trumpets, and cries of the army.*)

SOLDIERS: Hurrah! Hurrah! Hurrah!

*CURTAIN.*

(*Stifling heat. Although the sun is shining, a heavy black cloud is creeping from the East and the air is charged with a presentiment of a dreadful thunderstorm. From time to time runners, out of breath, enter, ascend the staircase and disappear within the palace. All await the royal cortege in vague alarm.*)

PEOPLE: (*amongst themselves*). It is dreadful! What is? I don't know myself. There's nothing to fear; Nothing bad will happen to us. You see the golden cock is not beating his wings, And is sticking up in the sun! He warms his back and keeps silent. If there was any misfortune he would awaken. Look at that sullen, heavy cloud Coming up from the East. It carries evil in its dark depths. There will be rain in the city; Yes, and with thunder, even hail as well.
(*The Royal Housekeeper, Amelfa, appears on the upper steps of the stairway. All rush towards her.*)

PEOPLE: (*bowing*). Be kind! Honored mother, And tell us if the Army is safe. Are we to have peace, or misfortune? You know. There were runners.

AMELFA: (*curtly*). There were. Only it is no affair of yours. Away with you! That is all I have to say.

PEOPLE: Be merciful! Our hearts are sore.
(*Many of them run to Amelfa and try to kiss the hem of her dress. She pushes them away.*)

AMELFA: Go away!
(*Wishing to get rid of them.*)
Here's the news! You see, there are four Kings— Hearts, Spades, Clubs, and Diamonds; Our King has conquered them. He has saved A Royal Maiden from the Dragon's jaws. She will be our Queen!

LE PEUPLE: (*sans beaucoup de joie*). Allégresse! Mais les princes? Il serait temps qu'ils revinssent!

AMELFA: Ils ne vont pas revenir: Notre roi les fit mourir.

LE PEUPLE: (*avec effroi*). Sa justice est implacable! Etaient ils donc bien coupables?

AMELFA: (*avec indifférence*). Ils sont mal tombés, voilà!
(*Sur un ton de menace.*)
Votre tour bientôt viendra!

LE PEUPLE: (*Ils se grattent la nuque et sourient stupidement*). Notre roi est seul le Maître! Nous devons tous nous soumettre!
(*On entend le son des trompettes.*)

AMELFA: Ils viennent. Tournoyez, sautez! Montrez votre loyauté Par des bonds et des grimaces, Mais n'espérez point de grâces!
(*Les menaçant du doigt, elle rentre dans le palais. Dans la rue commence le cortège triomphal. D'abord, les miliciens du roi, avec des airs importants et fanfarons; puis, la suite de la Reine De Chémakha, bariolé et bizarre, comme sortie d'un conte oriental: certains personnages n'ont qu'un oeil, au milieu du front; d'autres ont des cornes, d'autres des têtes de chiens. Géants, nains. Ethiopiens grands et petits, esclaves voilées portant des cassettes et des vaisseaux precieux. Cette pompe insolite dissipe pour un instant l'anxiété du peuple. Tous s'amusent comme des enfants. —Le cortège de la reine.*)
(*Le Roi et La Reine apparaissent sur leur char doré. Le Roi paraît vieilli. Il a perdu sa prestance majestueuse. Son air est soucieux. Il regarde continuellement, avec tendresse, La Reine. Celle-ci s'est capricieusement tournée de côté et trahit de temps en temps par ses gestes brusques, un énervement caché. La foule se trémousse, saute, tournoie, pousse de joyeuses acclamations.*)

LE PEUPLE: Soyez bienvenus! Hourra! Longue vie à notre roi! Hourra! Hourra! Vois tes serviteurs fidèles, Dévoués et pleins de zèle, Prêts à t'obéir toujours, Afin d'embellir tes jours. Nous nous mettrons à quatre pattes Pour te dilater la rate. Nous nous flanquerons des coups. Le spectacle sera doux. Nous ne sommes sur la terre Que pour t'obéir, te plaire,

PEOPLE: (*without any special joy*). Well! We shall have a holiday! But where are our hope—the Princes?

AMELFA: The King has put them in chains And has punished them with a cruel death.

PEOPLE: (*shuddering*). Ah! Heavy is the Royal hand! What did they do?

AMELFA: (*indifferently*). They had bad luck. Something awaits you, too!
(*threateningly.*)

PEOPLE: (*scratching their heads and stupidly smiling*). We are yours, body and soul; If we are beaten we have deserved it.
(*A sound of trumpets is heard.*)

AMELFA: They are coming! Jump like goats— Turn somersaults for very joy. Greet the King loudly— But do not expect mercy.
(*Threatening them once again with her finger, Amelfa enters the palace. The triumphant procession begins to pass by. First come the Royal Warriors, on foot and mounted, with faces puffed up with pride. Then the suite of The Queen of Shemakban, of as many colors and as fantastic as those in Eastern fairy tales. There are giants and dwarfs, people with one eye in the middle of their forehead, people with borns, with heads like a dog, negros and negro boys, female slaves covered with veils carrying coffers and precious plate. The curious splendour of the procession disperses for a time the weight of expectation. All become as gay as children.*)
(*The golden chariot appears with the King and Queen. The King has aged somewhat, has become restless, has lost his majestic carriage, and all the time looks fondly into the eyes of the haughty Queen. The Queen capriciously turns away, expressing her secret impatient irritation by jerky movements. The People move about, jump, turn somersaults, and shout a joyful welcome.*)

PEOPLE: (*shouting*). Long life to you! Hurrah! May you have every good thing!
(*Begin to sing.*)
We are your faithful servants, Who kiss the Royal feet. We are glad to serve you, To amuse you with our foolishness, To box for you upon a holiday, To bark, to crawl on all fours, So that your hours may flow quickly And may bring sweet sleep. Without you we should have no Reason for existing;

Que pour être tes jouets,
Tes esclaves dévoués!
(*Sur le perron d'une des maisons apparaît L'Astrologue, toujours vêtu de sa robe bleue et la tête couverte de son bonnet.—Ayant aperçu L'Astrologue, La Reine l'examine longuement et avec attention.—Le Roi s'apprête a descendre, mais La Reine le retient, et, designant du doigt L'Astrologue.*)

**LA REINE:** (*d'un ton inquiet*). Quel est donc ce personnage? Il a l'air fort grave et sage. (*La foule reculé devant L'Astrologue et attend, silencieuse. La Reine observe toujours L'Astrologue. Coup de tonnerre lointain.*)

**LE ROI DODÔN:** (*joyeux de reconnaître son vieil ami*). Hé, bonjour, devin prudent, Mon ami, mon confident! Dis-nous, en ce jour propice, Tes désirs, qu'ils s'accomplissent. (*L'Astrologue traverse la foule et s'approche du char royal. Il ne quitte point des yeux La Reine.*)

**L'ASTROLOGUE:** Roi sublime, j'obéis! Liquidons en bons amis. Hier, en ta reconnaissance, Tu promis sans réticence D'exaucer mon premier voeu: Voici donc ce que je veux: Sans tarder tiens ta promesse, Fais moi don de la princesse

**LE ROI DODÔN:** Par le diable! C'est ainsi? Ma réponse, la voici: L'insolence est par trop grande, Polisson! je te commande De vider sans plus ces lieux. Chassez-moi d'ici ce vieux! (*Les gardes entraînent le vieillard, qui se débat.*)

**L'ASTROLOGUE:** C'est donc la . . . .

**LE ROI DODÔN:** (*furieux.*) Quoi, tu discutes? Tu veux entamer la lutte? (*Il lui applique un coup de sceptre sur la tête. L'Astrologue tombe inanimé et rend l'esprit. Frémissement dans l'assistance. Des nuages voilent le soleil; le tonnerre gronde.*)

**LA REINE:** (*à part, éclate de rice*). Hihihi! Hahahaha! Que c'est drôle, tout celà! (*Dodôn est fort troublé, mais il continue de regarder La Reine en souriant.*)

**LE ROI DODÔN:** (*avec une terreur superstitieuse*). Juste avant le mariage! C'est un bien mauvais présage . . . . . Ce sang . . . Un malheur s'ensuivra . . .

We were born for you
And for you we have had children.
(*The Astrologer appears in the portico of one of the houses, in the same blue garment and high hat. Having observed the Astrologer, the Queen looks at him long and steadfastly. The King, wishing to descend, is stopped by the Queen, who points out the Astrologer to him.*)

**QUEEN OF SHEMAKHAN:** (*uneasily*). Who is that standing there in the white hat And with hair as white as a swan? (*The crowd parts before the Astrologer, and is dumb with expectation. The Queen follows his movements.*)

**KING DODON:** (*delighted to see his old acquaintance*). Ah! It's you, my wise man, My benefactor and father! What have you to say to us on this festal occasion? Come nearer! What do you ask of us? (*The Astrologer wends his way through the crowd to the chariot, not taking his eyes off the Queen.*)

**ASTROLOGER:** Great King! It is I. Let us settle matters as friends. Do you remember that in return for an obligation You did swear, in transports of delight, to fulfil My first wish as if it were your own? Give the maiden to me— The Queen of Shemakhan.

**KING DODON:** (*trying to bring The Astrologer to his senses*). What! Has the devil got into you? Or have you lost your senses? What has got into your head? Away with you, before I injure you! Drag the old man away! (*The guards drag The Astrologer away. He resists.*)

**ASTROLOGER:** Is it to be thus?

**KING DODON:** (*raging*). Are you going to argue again? I shall show you how to argue with me! (*Strikes him on the forehead with his sceptre. He falls down dead. All the people shudder. The sun goes behind a cloud and a clap of thunder is heard.*)

**QUEEN OF SHEMAKHAN:** (*laughing to herself*). Ha! Ha! Ha! I am not afraid of sin. (*Dodon very agitated, but still smiles fondly upon The Queen.*)

**KING DODON:** (*superstitiously*). I hope it will not bring misfortune On the eve of marriage It is not good to shed blood upon a wedding day!

**LA REINE:** (*sèchement*). Hé bien, qui vivra vera, Voilà tout!

**LE ROI DODÔN:** (*tranquillisé et avec ivresse*). Par nos caresses Célébrons notre allégresse. (*Il vent embrasser La Reine, mais elle le repousse avec fureur et dégoût*).

**LA REINE:** Disparais, monstre hideux, Toi et ton peuple odieux! C'est assez! ton âme immonde Trop longtemps souilla le monde. Tu souris, vieux scélérat, Mais ton châtiment viendra!

**LE ROI DODÔN:** (*avec un sourire contraint*). Ma princesse, tu plaisantes . . .

**LA REINE:** Non, plus à l'heure présente. (*Ils montent l'escalier.*)

**LA VOIX DU COQ:** Cocoricocou! Je te percerai d'un coup.

**CHOEUR:** Kchi! Kchi! Kchi! Kchi! (*Subitement, Le Coq s'envole de sa flèche et voltige au-dessus de la foule. Tous, épouvantés, agitent les bras pour le chasser.—Le Coq donne un grand coup de bec sur la tête du Roi, qui tombe mort. Epouvante générale; violent coup de tonnerre.—Une obscurité complète se fait pour un moment, durant lequel on entend le rire tranquille de La Reine*).

**LA VOIX DE LA REINE:** Hihihihi! Hahahaha! (*Quand la nuit s'est dissipée, on ne voit plus La Reine, ni Le Coq.*)

**LE PEUPLE:** (*avec stupéfaction*). Où donc est la reine? Envolée! Ah! notre âme est affollée . . . . (*avec espoir.*) Mais le roi? (*Tristement.*) Il est bien mort. Quel invraisemblable sort. (*Ecrasé de douleur, Le Peuple entier entonne une lamentation funèbre.*) Il est mort . . . O peine àmere! Notre prince! Notre père! Notre seigneur sans pareil, Qui brillait comme un soleil! Il était prudent, sagace, Parresseux, rêveur, bonasse! Sa colère était terrible, Sa fureur incoercible. Il nous frappait comme un sourd Plus souvent qu'à notre tour. Mais l'orage enfin passé, L'on pouvait se prélasser Sous son ombre tutélaire; Il était pour nous un père.

**QUEEN OF SHEMAKHAN:** (*curtly*). There will be a scuffle at the banquet— That is all.

**KING DODON:** (*tranquilly, in a caressing tone*). Let us kiss each other— To drive away the evil omen! (*Dodon tries to embrace and kiss The Queen. She, with anger and aversion, pushes him away.*)

**QUEEN OF SHEMAKHAN:** May you perish, wicked monster! And your people! How can the earth endure such as you? Wait! Grey-headed babbler! Your death is not far off!

**KING DODON:** (*smiling pitifully*). You are still joking, my dear!

**QUEEN OF SHEMAKHAN:** No! Already we have had a sorry jest. (*They ascend the staircase. Suddenly the cock begins to fly and circles above their heads. All wave him off with their hands.*)

**VOICE OF THE BIRD:** Cock-a-doodle-do! I shall peck the old man on the crown of his head!

**CHORUS:** Sh! Sh! Sh! Sh! (*The Cock pecks Dodon on the head, and he falls dead. A clap of thunder. All struck dumb. For a moment total darkness, in which is heard the quiet laugh of The Queen. When it grows light again neither Queen nor the bird is seen.*)

**PEOPLE:** (*to each other, in astonishment*). Where is the Queen? She has vanished As if she had never been at all! (*Hopefully.*) Is the King groaning? (*Sadly.*) No! He is dead—if it is not all a dream! (*Crushed by despair, the people finally break into mournful sobbing.*) The King is dead! Our dear one is killed! Our happy, our debonnair, and Never-to-be-forgotten King! Lord of Lords! He was most wise, And ruled the Kingdom with his Hands folded, lying at his ease It's true! Our King in anger Was like a thunderbolt from the heaven, Which strikes at random, Carrying destruction right and left,

## Act III

(avec un profond désespoir.)
Quel terrible désarroi!
Qui va nous donner un roi?
(Ils s'écroulent par terre et
sanglotent.)

RIDEAU.

## CONCLUSION

(L'Astrologue, écartant le rideau,
si présente.)

---

But when the cloud is passed
The heavy air is fresher,
And the King, like the golden
dawn,
Lightens all without distinction.
(In perplexity.)
What will a new dawn bring?
How shall we live without a King?
(They fall on their faces and weep
inconsolably.)

CURTAIN.

## EPILOGUE

(Moving apart the folds of the curtain, The Astrologer looks out.)

---

L'ASTROLOGUE: (aux spectat-
eurs). Nobles spectateurs, mes
frères,
Ce dénouement sanguinaire
Ne doit point vous émouvoir.
Ceux que vous venez de voir
N'étaient que de vains fantômes.
Sachez que dans le royaume
De Dodôn, la reine et moi.
Etions seuls humains . . . voilà!
(Il salue et disparaît.)

FIN

---

ASTROLOGER: (to the audience).
There! My story's ended;
But the bloody conclusion,
However sad it may be,
Need not disturb you.
Perhaps the Queen and I
Were the only living people in it;
The rest were—a delirium, a
dream:
A pale spectre, nothing
more . . . .
(Disappears.)

END

# Il Barbiere Di Siviglia (1816)

## The Barber of Seville

Music by Gioacchino Antonio Rossini ■ Libretto by Cesare Sterbini ■ Based on the comedy by Pierre Augustin Caron de Beaumarchais

This two-act melodramma buffo, set to a libretto by Cesare Sterbini (based on the comedy by Beaumarchais) was first performed at the Teatro Argentina in Rome on February 20, 1816. Count Almaviva is in love with Rosina, Dr. Bartolo's ward, and he serenades her to no reply. Figaro, barber and jack-of-all-trades, promises to assist him. The two men overhear Bartolo's plan to marry Rosina as soon as possible. The count, advised by Figaro, sings another serenade to Rosina disguised as Lindoro—so as to win her love for the man and not the title. This time she replies. Rosina's music teacher, Basilio, enters, telling of Count Almaviva's arrival in Seville. Rosina gives Figaro a note for Lindoro. The count, disguised as a tipsy soldier, tells Rosina that he is actually Lindoro. Bartolo intercepts the note. When he sees that it is a laundry list (!), he demands that the "soldier" be arrested. The soldier presents his card to the arresting officer and is freed at once. Bartolo is now very suspicious; the Count arrives again, disguised as the music teacher Don Alonso. Bartolo mistrusts him, and Don Alonso hands him the note from Rosina, pretending he intercepted it before Count Almaviva received it. While Bartolo naps, Don Alonso and Rosina have a "music lesson." While shaving Bartolo, Figaro takes his key to the balcony window so that the count and Rosina may escape that night. Basilio arrives unexpectedly; the count bribes him to fake an illness. Bartolo realizes that he is being fooled. Berta, the housekeeper, comments on all of the ridiculous goings-on. Bartolo sends Basilio to find a notary to witness his marriage to Rosina. He shows her the note from Lindoro, convincing her that Lindoro is not in love with her but is acting as a go-between for Count Almaviva. She falls for this and confesses her plan to escape. Figaro and Lindoro enter through the balcony window, and Lindoro tells Rosina his true identity. They declare their love and try to escape, but their ladder has been removed. Basilio enters with the notary, and Figaro brings the count and Rosina forward as the intended couple. Bartolo comes in with the police, but the marriage has already taken place. The count reveals his true identity to Bartolo, who is allowed to keep Rosina's dowry. All rejoice, and the opera ends.

---

## ■ ATTO I

### SCENA PRIMA

*Il momento dell'azione è sul termine della Notte.—La Scena rappresenta una Strada in Siviglia.*

*Fiorello, con lanterna nelle mani, introducendo vari Suonatori; indi il Conte Almaviva avvolto in un mantello.*

**FIORELLO:** Piano, pianissimo, senza parlar
Tutti con me venite quà.

**CORO:** Piano, pianissimo, eccoci quà
Piano, venite quà.

**FIORELLO:** Tutto è silenzio, nessun qui c'è;
Che i nostri canti possa turbar.

**CONTE:** Fiorello—olà!
(*Sotto voce.*)

**FIORELLO:** Signor, son quà.

**CONTE:** Ebben; gl'amici?

**FIORELLO:** Son pronti già.

**CONTE:** Bravi, bravissimi;
Fate silenzio.

## ■ ACT I

### SCENE I

*A Street in Seville.—Dawn of Morning.*

*Fiorello, with a lantern in his hand, introducing various Musicians; the Count Almaviva, wrapped up in a mantle.*

**FIORELLO:** Piano, pianissimo, in tender sound,
Let love's light airs now float around.

**CHORUS:** Piano, pianissimo,
Love's music sound.

**FIORELLO:** All wrapped in silence, no soul is near;
No wandering footstep falls on the ear.

**COUNT:** Fiorello—ho!
(*In a low voice.*)

**FIORELLO:** Sir, I am here.

**COUNT:** Well; and our friends?

**FIORELLO:** They are all ready.

**COUNT:** All's well;
Keep silence.

**FIORELLO:** Piano, pianissimo!
Senza parlar.
O, istante d'amor!
Felice momento!
O, dolce contento
Ch'eguale non ha.
Ei, Fiorello!
(*Accordano gl'instrumenti, e il Conte canta accompagnato da essi.*)

**FIORELLO:** Mio signore?

**CONTE:** Dì, la vedi?

**FIORELLO:** Signor, nò.

**CONTE:** Ah, che è vana ogni speranza!

**FIORELLO:** Signor Conte, il giorno avanza.

**CONTE:** Ah, che penso—che farò?
Tutto è vano. Buona gente?

**CORO:** Mio signore?
(*Sotto voce.*)

**CONTE:** Avanti, avanti;
Più di suoni più di canti
Io bisogno ormai non ho.
(*Dà una borsa a Fiorello, il quale distribuisce devari a tutti.*)

**CONTE:** Ecco ridente il cielo,
Spunta la bella aurora, E tu non sorgiancora E puoi dormir così? Ah!
Sòrgi mia dolce speme, Vieni bell'I

**FIORELLO:** Softly, softly!
Utter not a word.
Oh, moment full of rapture!
Oh, bliss almost divine!
Such beauty well may capture
A heart already yours.
Ho, Fiorello!
(*They tune their instruments, and the Count sings, accompanied by them.*)

**FIORELLO:** Sir?

**COUNT:** Say, have you seen her?

**FIORELLO:** No, sir.

**COUNT:** Ah, how vain is every hope!

**FIORELLO:** Behold, sir, the dawn advances.

**COUNT:** Ah, what am I to think—what shall I do?
All is vain. Well, my friends?

**CHORUS:** Sir?
(*Softly.*)

**COUNT:** Retire, retire;
I no longer need
Your songs or your music.
(*He gives a purse to Fiorello, who distributes money to all.*)

**COUNT:** Lo! smiling in the orient sky, Morn in her beauty breaking, Canst thou, my love, inactive lie My life, art thou not waking? Arise, my

dol mio, Rendimen crudo, o Dio!
Lo stral, lo stral che mi ferì; lo stral
che mi, ferì. Oh, sorte! gia veggo?
Quei caro sembiante; Quest' anima
amante otten ne pietà?

heart's own treasure, All that my
soul holds dear; Oh! turn my grief
to pleasure! Awake, my love, my
love, appear; awake, my love, appear. Oh, joy! and do I see thee? My
doubts all disappear; Those eyes
are heaven to me! What have I now
to fear?

**FIORELLO:** Buona notte a tutti
quanti;
Più di voi che far non so.
(*Gli Suonatori circondano il
Conte, ringraziandolo, e bacian-
dogli la mano. Egli, indispettito
per lo strepito che fanno li và cacciando. Lo stesso fa anchè Fiorello.*)

**FIORELLO:** Good night to all;
I have nothing farther for you to do.
(*The Musicians surround the
Count, thanking him and kissing
his hand. Annoyed by the noise
they make, he tries to drive them
away. Fiorello does the same.*)

**CORO:** Mille grazie, mio Signore;
Del favore, dell'onore,
Ah! di tanta cortesìa,
Obbligati in verità!
Q che incontro fortunato
È un signor di qualità!

**CHORUS:** Many thanks, sir, for this
favor;
Better master, nor a braver,
Ever did we sing a stave for.
Pray, good sir, command our
throats!
We will ever sing and pray for
One who gives us gold for notes!

**CONTE:** Basta! basta! non parlate,
Ma non serve, non gridate,
Maledetti, andate via,
Ah, canaglia, via di quà!
Tutto quanto il vicinato
Questo chiasso sveglierà.

**COUNT:** Silence! silence! cease
your bawling,
Nor like cats with caterwauling
Wake the neighbors—stop your
squalling,
Rascals, or I'll dust your coats!
If you still keep making this noise,
You'll be waking all the neighbors.

**FIORELLO:** Zitti! zitti! che rumore!
Ma che onore—che favore!
(*Con ironia.*)
Maledetti, andate via—
Ah, canaglia, via di quà!
Veh, che chiasso indiavolato!
Ah, che rabbia che mi fa?
(*Il Coro parte.*)

**FIORELLO:** Silence! silence! what
an uproar!
For these favors—for such honor!
(*Mocking them.*)
Rascals, hence, away—
Scoundrels, quit the spot!
Eh, what a devilish uproar!
Are you mad, or not?
(*Exit Chorus.*)

**CONTE:** Gente indiscreta! Ah qua-
si,
Con quel chiasso importuno,
Tutto quanto il quartier han risve-
gliato.
Alfin sono partiti! E non si vede.
(*Guardando verso la Ringhiera.*)
E inutile sperar; eppur qui voglio
(*Passeggia riflettendo.*)
Aspettar di vederla. Ogni mattina
Ella su quel balcone
A prender fresco viene in sull'Au-
rora.
Proviamo.—Olà, tu ancora
Ritirati, Fiorello!

**COUNT:** The indiscreet rabble!
They had nearly,
Awakened the whole neighbor-
hood with their importunate cla-
mors.
At last they're gone! But she does
not appear.
(*Looking towards the balcony.*)
It is in vain to hope; yet I will
(*He paces pensively up and
down.*)
Wait here till I behold her. Every
morning
She comes into this balcony
To breathe the fresh air at early
dawn.
Here will I wait.—Ho, Fiorello!
Do you also retire.

**FIORELLO:** Vado. Là in fondo
Attenderò suoi ordini.
(*si ritira.*)

**FIORELLO:** I go. Yonder
I will await your commands.
(*He withdraws.*)

## SCENA II

*Figaro, con Chitarra appesa al
collo, e detti.*

**FIGARO:** Largo al factotum della
città largo, La,la, la,la,la,la,la,la, la,
la. Presto a botte gache l'albaè già
presto, la,la, la,la,la,la,,la,la la, la.

## SCENE II

*Figaro, with his Guitar round his
neck, and the preceding.*

**FIGARO:** Room for the city's factotum, here, La,la la,la,la,la,la,la, la,
la. I must be off to my shop, for the
dawn is near, la,la,

Ah, che bel vivere, che bel pìacere,
che bel piacere, Per un barbiere, di
qualità, di qualità. Ah, bravo, Figaro; bravo, bravissimo bravo. La, la,
la, la, la, la, la, la, la la; Fortunatissimo, per verità, bravo, la,la,
la,la,la,la,la,la la, la; fortunatissimo, per verità, fortunatissimo per
verità, la,la,la, la, la,la,la
la,la,la,la,la,la, la,la la la,la,la, la.

**FIGARO:** La ran la lera,
La ran la la!
Pronto a far tutto
La notte e il giorno—
Sempre d'intorno
In giro stà.
Miglior cuccagna,
Per un barbiere
Vita più nobile,
Nò non si dà.
La ran la lera,
La ran la la!
Rasori, e pettini,
Lancette, e forbici—
Al mio comando
Tutto quì stà! Vi è la risorsa
Poi del mestiere
Colla donnetta,
Col cavaliere
La ran la lera,
La ran la la!
Tutti mi chiedono,
Tutti mi vogliono—
Donne, ragazze,
Vecchi, fanciulle:
Quà la parucca!
Presto la barba!
Quà la sanguigna:
Figaro! Figaro!
Son quà, son quà.
Figaro sù, Figaro giù!
Figaro quà, Figaro la!
Pronto prontissimo—
Son come un fulmine—
Sono il factotum
Della città.
Ah, bravo, Figaro!
Bravo, bravissimo!
Fortunatissimo
Per verità!
La ran la la!
Ah! ah! che bella vita!
Faticar poco, e divertirsi assai;
E in tasca sempre aver qualche dob-
lone,
Gran frutto della mia reputazione.
Ecco quà: senza Figaro
Non si accasa in Siviglia una ragaz-
za;
A me la vedovella
Ricorre per marito: io, colla scusa
Del pettine di giorno,
Della chitarra col favor la notte,
A tutti onestamente—
Non fo per dir—m'adatto a far pia-
cere,
Oh, che vita, che vita! oh, che mes-
tiere!
Orsù, presto a bottega—

la,la,la,la,la,la,la, la, What a merry
life, what gay pleasure, what gay
pleasure, Awaits a barber of quality, of quality. Ah, bravo, Figaro;
bravo, bravissimo bravo. La,la,
la,la,la,la,la, la, la; You are surely
the happiest of men, bravo. la,la,
la,la,la,la,la,la la, la; The happiest
of men, surely you are. The happiest of men, surely, la,la,la, la,
la,la,la, la,la,la,la,la,la,
la,la,la,la,la,la, la.

**FIGARO:** La ran la lera,
La ran la la!
Ready to do everything
Both by night and by day—
Perpetually in bustle
And in motion.
What happier lot,
What nobler life
For a barber,
Than my own!
La ran la lera,
La ran la la!
Razors and combs,
Lancets and scissors—
Everything is
Ready at command!
Then there are the snug
Perquisites of business
With gay damsels,
With cavaliers.
La ran la lera,
La ran la la!
All call for me,
All want me—
Dames, maidens,
Old and young:
My peruke! cries one;
Quick, my beard! another;
Here, bleed me! a third:
Figaro! Figaro!
I am here, I am here.
Figaro up, Figaro down!
Figaro here, Figaro there!
I am activity itself—
I'm quick as lightning—
I'm the factotum
Of the city.
Ah, bravo, Figaro!
Bravo, bravissimo!
Most fortunate of men
In every truth.
La ran la lera,
La ran la la!
Ah! ah! what a happy life!
But little fatigue, and abundant
amusement;
Always with some doubloons in my
pocket,
The noble fruit of my reputation.
So it is: without Figaro
There's not a girl in Seville will
marry;
To me the little widows
Have recourse for a husband: I, un-
der excuse
Of my comb by day,
And under favor of my guitar by
night,
Endeavor—though I don't do it for
the sake of saying so—
To please all in an honest way.
Oh, what a life, what a life! Oh,
what business!
Now, away to the shop—

**CONTE:** (È desso, o pur m'inganno.)

**FIGARO:** (Chi sarà mai costui?)

**CONTE:** Oh, è lui senz' altro. Figaro!

**FIGARO:** Mio padrone! Oh, chi veggo?—Eccellenza—

**CONTE:** Zitto! zittoù prudenza: Qui non son conosciuto, Nè vò farmi conoscere—per questo Ho le mie gran ragioni.

**FIGARO:** Intendo, intendo— La lascio in libertà.

**CONTE:** No!

**FIGARO:** Che serve?

**CONTE:** No, dico—resta quà: Ora mi spiego. Al Prado Vidi un fior di bellezza—una fanciulla, Figlia di un certo medico barbogio, Che quà da pochi dì s'è stabilito. Io di questa invaghito Lasciai patria e parenti; e quà men venni, Col nome di Lindoro; E quà la notte e il giorno, Passo girando a quei balconi intorno.

**FIGARO:** A quei balconi?—un medico? Oh, cospetto! Siete ben fortunato: Sui maccheroni il cacio v'è cascato.

**CONTE:** Come!

**FIGARO:** Certo.—Là dentro Io son barbiere, parucchier, chirurgo, Botanico, spezial, veterinario— Il faccendier di casa.

**CONTE:** Ah, bella sorte!

**FIGARO:** Non basta: la ragazza Figlia non è del medico—e soltanto La sua pupilla.

**CONTE:** Ah, che consolazione!

**FIGARO:** Perciò? zitto!

**CONTE:** Cos'è?

**FIGARO:** S'apre il balcone! (*Si ritirano sotto il Portico.*)

## SCENA III

*Rosina; e poi Bartolo, sul Balcone; e detti in Strada.*

**ROSINA:** Non è venuto ancora?—forse—

**CONTE:** Oh, mia vita! mio nume! mio tesoro! Vi veggo al fine—al fine—

**ROSINA:** (Ah, che vergogna! Vorrei dargli il biglietto.)

---

**COUNT:** (It is he, or I am much deceived.)

**FIGARO:** (Who may this be?)

**COUNT:** It is no less than himself. Figaro!

**FIGARO:** Good master! Oh, whom do I see?—your Excellency—

**COUNT:** Hush! hush! be prudent; I am not known here, Nor do I wish to be—for this I have the best of reasons.

**FIGARO:** I understand, I understand— I'll not interrupt you.

**COUNT:** Stop!

**FIGARO:** For what purpose?

**COUNT:** No, I tell you—stop here: I will explain myself. On the Prado I beheld a flower of beauty—a maiden, The daughter of a certain silly old physician, who Has established himself here within these few days. Enamored of this damsel, I have left My country and relatives; and come here, Under the name of Lindor: Night and day, I watch and wander near this balcony.

**FIGARO:** Near this balcony?—a physician? Zounds! You are very fortunate: And must make hay while the sun shines.

**COUNT:** Explain!

**FIGARO:** Certainly.—In this house I am a barber, perruquier, surgeon, Botanist, apothecary, veterinary— The major-domo of the house.

**COUNT:** Oh, how fortunate!

**FIGARO:** But this is not all: the girl is not The daughter of the physician— she is only his ward.

**COUNT:** Oh, what a consolation!

**FIGARO:** How so? but hush!

**COUNT:** What is it?

**FIGARO:** See, the balcony opens. (*They retire under the Portico.*)

## SCENE III

*Rosina; afterwards Bartolo, on the Balcony; and the preceding, in the Street.*

**ROSINA:** Has he not come yet? Perhaps—

**COUNT:** Oh, my life! my angel! my treasure! At length do I behold you—at length—

**ROSINA:** (Oh, how provoking! I wished to give him this note.)

---

**BARTOLO:** Ebben, ragazza, Il tempo è buono. cos'è questa carta?

**ROSINA:** Nulla, signore: sono le parole Dell'aria dell' "Inutil Precauzione."

**CONTE:** Ma brava!—dell' "Inutil Precauzione."

**ROSINA:** Ah me meschina! l'aria mi è caduta: Raccoglietela presto.

**BARTOLO:** Vado, vado. (*Scende.*)

**ROSINA:** Pst! pst!—

**CONTE:** Ho inteso—

**ROSINA:** Presto!

**CONTE:** Non temete.

**BARTOLO:** Son quà. Dov'è? (*Uscendo in Strada.*)

**ROSINA:** Ah, il vento Se l'ha portato via— Guardate.

**BARTOLO:** Io non la veggo;—ehi, signorina? Io non vorrei. (Cospetto! Costei m'avesse preso!) In casa! in casa! Animo, sù! A chi dico? In casa, presto!

**ROSINA:** Vado, vado;—che furia!

**BARTOLO:** Quel balcone lo voglio far murare. Dentro, dico!

**ROSINA:** A che vita da crepare! (*Entrando.*)

**CONTE:** Povera disgraziata! Il suo stato infelice Sempre più m'interessa.

**FIGARO:** Presto, presto— Vediamo cosa scrive.

**CONTE:** Appunto, leggi.

**FIGARO:** "Le vostre assidue premure hanno eccitato la mia curiosità. Il mio tutore è per uscir di casa: appena si sarà allontanato, procurate con qualche mezzo ingegnoso di indicarmi il vostro nome, il vostro stato, e le vostre intenzioni. Io non posso giammai comparire al balcone senza l'indivisibile compagnia del mio tiranno. Siate però certo che tutto à disposto a fare per rompere le sue catene, la sventurata Rosina."

**CONTE:** Sì, sì le romperò;—su, dimmi un poco Che razza d'uomo è questo suo tutore?

**FIGARO:** Un vecchio indemoniato! Avaro, sospettoso, brontolone; Ajuto, ajuto!

**CONTE:** Che?

---

**BARTOLO:** Well, daughter, It is fine weather. Pray, what letter is that?

**ROSINA:** Nothing, sir: only the words Of an air in the "Useless Precaution."

**COUNT:** Well and good!—of the "Useless Precaution!"

**ROSINA:** Unfortunate that I am! I have let the air drop. Make haste and pick it up.

**BARTOLO:** I go, I go. (*He goes down.*)

**ROSINA:** Pst! Pst!

**COUNT:** I understand—

**ROSINA:** Make haste!

**COUNT:** Never fear.

**BARTOLO:** Here I am. What is it? (*Coming into the Street.*)

**ROSINA:** Oh, the wind Has carried it away— Look again.

**BARTOLO:** I can't see it;—where, young lady? I'll search no more. (Zounds! She may have tricked me!) In! into the house! Come, come! Do you mind what I say? Quick, into the house!

**ROSINA:** Well, I am going;—what a fury!

**BARTOLO:** I will surely have that balcony walled up. In, I say!

**ROSINA:** Oh, what a scolding life I lead! (*Entering.*)

**COUNT:** Poor unhappy maid! Her wretched situation Still more interests me in her behalf.

**FIGARO:** Come, come— Let us see what she has written.

**COUNT:** Well, read.

**FIGARO:** "Your assiduous attentions have excited my curiosity. My guardian is shortly going out: as soon as you see him leave the house, devise some ingenious method of acquainting me with your name, circumstances, and intentions. I can never appear at the balcony without being haunted by the inseparable attendance of my tyrant. Be, therefore, assured, that entirely disposed to break her chains, is the unhappy—Rosina."

**COUNT:** Yes, yes, she shall break them;—but tell me, What kind of fellow is this guardian of hers?

**FIGARO:** Oh, a very demon! All avarice and suspicion, a terrible blusterer, But have a care, have a care!

**COUNT:** Oh what?

## Act I, Scene III

**FIGARO:** S'apre la porta.

**FIGARO:** The door opens.

**BARTOLO:** Ehi; fra momenti io torno.
(*Uscendo dalla porta, e parlando verso le quinte.*)
Non aprite a nessun. Se Don Basilio
Venisse a ricercarmi, che m'aspetti.
(*Chiude la porta di casa.*)
Le mie nozze con lei voglio affrettare.
Sì, dentr'oggi finir vò quest'affare.
(*Parte.*)

**BARTOLO:** So; I shall return in a few minutes.
(*Coming out of the door, and speaking towards the side.*)
Don't let any one in. If Don Basilio
Should come to inquire for me, let him wait.
(*He shuts the door cautiously.*)
I wish to hurry on my marriage with her.
Yes, this very day I am going to conclude the affair.
(*Exit.*)

**CONTE:** Dentr'oggi le sue nezze con Rosina.
Ah vecchio rimbambito!
Ma dimmi or tu, chi è questo Don Basilio?

**COUNT:** This very day conclude his marriage with Rosina?
Oh, the foolish old dotard!
But tell me, who is this Don Basilio?

**FIGARO:** È un solenne imbroglion di matrimonj—
Un collo torto, un vero disperato.
Sempre senza un quattrino.
Già è maestro di musica,
Insegna alla ragazza.

**FIGARO:** A famous intriguing matchmaker—
A hypocrite, a desperate fellow,
With never a farthing in his pocket.
He has lately turned music-master.
And teaches this girl.

**CONTE:** Bene, bene!
Tutto giova saper; di tue fatiche
Largo compenso avrai.

**COUNT:** Well and good!
It is right to know all these things;
And you shall be well rewarded for your trouble.

**FIGARO:** Davver!

**FIGARO:** Indeed!

**CONTE:** Parola.

**COUNT:** On my word.

**FIGARO:** Dunque oro a discrezione?

**FIGARO:** Then, shall I touch the gold handsomely?

**CONTE:** Oro a bizzeffe.
Animo, via.

**COUNT:** To your heart's content.
Come, be active.

**FIGARO:** Son pronto. Ah, non sapete
I simpatici effetti prodigiosi;
Che ad appagare il mio Signore Lindoro
Produce in me la dolce idea dell'oro.

**FIGARO:** I'm all readiness. You cannot imagine
What a prodigious effect the idea of a
Reward has produced on me; and what sympathy
I feel in the success of Signor Lindor.

**FIGARO:** All' idea di quel metallo,
Portentoso onnipossente, Un vulcano, un vulcano, la mia mente. Già comincia, gia comincia a diventar;
Sì all' idea di quel metallo un vulcano, La mia mente già comincia a diventar, Sì, sì, all' idea di quel metallo un vulcano, La mia mente già comincia a diventar, a diventar, a diventar, Un vulcano incomincia a diventar.

**FIGARO:** Mighty Jove, in golden shower, Once, who fell on Danae's breast, Give to me, oh! give to me gold's dazzling power. Every maid would make me blessed, would make me blessed; Yes, give to me, give to me gold's dazzling power, Every maid would make me blessed, would make me blessed, Yes, yes, give to me, give to me gold's dazzling power, Every maid would make me blessed, would make me blessed would make me blessed, would make me blessed. Every maid would make me blessed.

**CONTE:** Su vendiamo, su vediam di quel metallo, Qual che effetto, qual che effetto sorprendente: Del vulcan, del vulcan della tua mente, Qual che mostro, qualche mostro, singolar, sì, Del vulcan della tua mente, Qual che mostro, singolar, sì, sì, Del vulcan della tua mente, Qual che mostro singolar, sì, singolar, sì, singolar; Qual che mostro

**COUNT:** Hold your pompous, hold your pompous silly railing, Gold but wins, gold but wins the meaner part: True love's song is more prevailing, more prevailing, Dearest, give me, dearest, give me heart for heart; Ah, true love's song is more prevailing, Dearest, give me, dearest, give me heart for heart, True love's song is more prevailing Dear-

est, give me, dearest, give me heart for heart, oh, give me heart for heart; Dearest, give me heart for heart.

**FIGARO:** Voi dovreste travestirri, per esempio da soldato

**FIGARO:** You must disguise yourself—
For example, as a soldier.

**CONTE:** Da soldato?

**COUNT:** As a soldier?

**FIGARO:** Sì, signore.

**FIGARO:** Even so, sir.

**CONTE:** Da soldato!—e che si fà?

**COUNT:** As a soldier!—and for what purpose?

**FIGARO:** Oggi arriva un reggimento.

**FIGARO:** Today a regiment is expected here.

**CONTE:** Sì, m'e amico il Colonello.

**COUNT:** Yes; the Colonel is a friend of mine.

**FIGARO:** Va benon!

**FIGARO:** Excellent!

**CONTE:** Ma, e poi?

**COUNT:** Why so?

**FIGARO:** Cospetto!
Dell' alloggio col biglietto,
Quella porta si aprirà.
Che ne dite, mio signore?
L'invenzione è naturale.

**FIGARO:** Zounds!
By means of a billet, yonder door
Will soon open to you.
What say you to this, my good sir?
The invention is not amiss.

**CONTE:** Oh, che testa universale!
Bravo! bravo in verità!

**COUNT:** What an original genius.
Excellent! excellent in truth!

**FIGARO:** Oh, che testa universale!
Bella—bella in verità!
Piano, piano—un altra idea.
Veda l'oro cosa fà!
Ubriaco!—si ubriaco,
Mio signor, si fingerà.

**FIGARO:** What a capacious head I have
Excellent! excellent, in truth!
Softly, softly—another thought.
See the power of your gold!
Drunk!—yes, my good sir,
You must pretend to be drunk.

**CONTE:** Ubriaco?

**COUNT:** Drunk?

**FIGARO:** Sì, signore.

**FIGARO:** Even so, sir?

**CONTE:** Ubriaco!—ma perchè?

**COUNT:** Drunk!—but for what purpose?

**FIGARO:** Perchè d'un che poco è in se—
Che dal vino casca già
(*Imitando i moti di Ubriaco.*)
Il tutor credete a me,
Il tutor si fiderà.

**FIGARO:** Because the guardian, believe me—
The guardian would less distrust
(*Imitating the movements of a drunken man.*)
A man not quite himself
But overcome with wine.

**ASSIEME:** Questa è bella per mia fè.
Bravo! bravo! in verità!

**BOTH:** This is excellent, by my faith.
Bravo! bravo! excellent truly!

**CONTE:** Dunque?

**COUNT:** Well, then?

**FIGARO:** All' opra.

**FIGARO:** To business.

**CONTE:** Andiam.

**COUNT:** Let us to it.

**FIGARO:** Da bravo.

**FIGARO:** With spirit.

**CONTE:** Vado.—Oh, il meglio mi scordavo:
Dimmi un po, la tua bottega?
Per trovarti dove stà.

**COUNT:** I go.—Oh, I had forgotten the important part of the business:
Tell me, where is your shop?
That I may not miss finding you.

**FIGARO:** La bottega?—non si sbaglia.
Guardi bene, eccola là.
(*Additando fra le quinte.*)
Numero quindici, a mano manca, bianca—
Quattro grandini, facciata bianca
Cinque parrucche nella vetrina;
Sopra un cartello, "Pommata Fina;"
Mostra in azzurro alla moderna
V'è per insegna una lanterna.
Là senza fallo mi troverà.

**FIGARO:** My shop?—you cannot mistake it.
Look yonder, there it is:
(*Pointing to the side.*)
Number fifteen, on the left hand,
With four steps, a white front—there,
Five wigs in the window;
On a placard, "Pomade Divine;"
A show-glass, too, of the latest fashion,
And my sign is a lantern.
There, without fail, you will find me.

**CONTE:** Ho ben capito.

**COUNT:** Do you be upon the alert.

FIGARO: Or, vado presto.
CONTE: Tu guarda bene.
FIGARO: Io penso al resto.
CONTE: Di te mi fido.
FIGARO: Cola l'attendo.

CONTE: Mio caro Figaro!
FIGARO: Intendo, intendo.

CONTE: Porterò meco—
FIGARO: La borsa piena?
CONTE: Si quel che vuoi.

FIGARO: Ma il resto poi—
Oh, non si dubiti che bene andrà.

CONTE: Ah, che d'amore, La fiammaio sento, Nunzia di giubilo E di contento! D'ardor insolito, Quest'alma accende E di me stesso, Maggior mi fà. Ah che d'amore. La fiamma sento, Nunzia di giù billo E di contento! Ecco propizia, Che in sen mi scende

FIGARO: Delle monete, Il suon già sento, Delle monete, il suon già sento, Delle monete, Il suon già sento, Il suon già sento, Già viene l'e ro; Già viene l'oro, Viene l'argento, Già viene l'oro, Viene l'argento; Già viene loro Già viene l'oro, eccolo; Eccolo già vien' l'argento, Già' vien' l'argento, eccolo; Eccolo in tasca scende, Eccolo quà; D'ardor insolito, Que st'almaaccende.
(Figaro entra in Casa.—Il Conte parte.)

FIGARO: Leave the rest to me.
COUNT: I perfectly understand.
FIGARO: Haste, no delay!
COUNT: I trust in you.
FIGARO: I shall wait for you yonder.

COUNT: My dear Figaro!
FIGARO: I understand, I understand.

COUNT: I will bring with me—
FIGARO: A purse well filled?
COUNT: Yes, to your heart's content.

FIGARO: And as for the rest—
Oh, doubt not of our complete success.

COUNT: When song is flowing, When love is glowing, Over fancy throwing Her light divine! Thoughts bright and beaming, As sunbeams, streaming, Over maidens dreaming, Then, then, are mine. When song is flowing. When love is glowing, Over fancy throwing Her light, her light divine. Over maidens dreaming, Then, then, are mine.

FIGARO: When cups are clinking, When gold is chinking, Those to my thinking Are more divine! Thoughts bright and beaming, as guineas streaming, Over misers dreaming, Then, then, are mine; Thoughts bright and beaming, As guineas streaming, Over misers dreaming, Then, then, are mine; As guineas streaming, Then, then, are mine, then are mine; Thoughts bright and beaming, As guineas streaming, then are mine; Over misers streaming, Then, then, are mine; Over misers dreaming, Then, then are mine.
(Figaro enters the House.—Exit the Count.)

## SCENA IV

Camera nella Casa di Don Bartolo.

Rosina, con lettera in mano.

ROSINA: Una voce poco fà:
Qui' nel cor mi risuonò!
Il mio cor ferito è già;
E Lindor fu che il piagò.
Sì, Lindoro mio sarà!
Lo giurai, la vincerò.
Il tutor ricuserà;
Io l'ingengno aguzzerò:
Alla fin s'acchetterà,
E contenta io resterò,
Sì, Lindoro mio sarà!
Lo giurai—la vincerò.
Sì, sì, la vincerò. Potessi almeno
Mandargli questa lettera!—ma come?
Di nessun quì mi fido:
Il tutor ha cent'occhi.—Basta, basta,
Sigilliamo intanto.

## SCENE IV

A Chamber in Don Bartolo's House.

Rosina, with a letter in her hand.

ROSINA: I heard a little voice just now:
Oh, it has thrilled my very heart!
I feel that I am wounded sore;
And it was Lindor who hurled the dart.
Yes, Lindor, dearest, shall be mine!
I've sworn it, and we'll never part.
My guardian sure will never consent;
But I must sharpen all my wit:
Content at last, he will relent,
And we, oh, joy! be wedded yet,
Yes, Lindor I have sworn to love!
And, loving, we'll our cares forget.
Yes, yes, he shall triumph. Could I but
Send him this letter!—but how?
There is no one here I can trust:

Con Figaro il barbiere dalla finestra
Discorrer l'ho veduto più d'un ora;—

ROSINA: Io sono docile, Sonrispettosa, Sono obbediente Dolceamorosa; Mi lascio reggere, Mi lascio reggere Mi fò guidar, mi fo guidar, Ma se mi toccano doveil mio debole, Saròuna vipera, sarò, E cento trappole Prima dicedere, farò giocar, farò giocar, E cento trappole, Prima dicedere, farò giocar, farò giocar;
Figaro è un galantuomo,
Un giovin di buon cuore:
Chi sà ch'ei non protegga il nostro amore?

My guardian has a hundred eyes.—
Well, well,
At least I will seal it.
From my window I beheld him conversing
For more than an hour with Figaro the barber;—

ROSINA: With mild and docile air, And playful as a lamb, never was gentler fair Than all confess I am; Doves not more meek appear, if none provoke or chide, If none provoke or chide; But if with tyrant sway My mind they seek to fix, My mind they seek to fix, I'd die to have my way: A thousand wayward tricks, and subtle wiles, I'd play, before they should guide my will, Before they should guide my will, Before they should guide my will; Figaro is an honest fellow, A good-hearted lad: Who knows: he may favor our love?

## SCENA V

Rosina e Figaro.

FIGARO: Oh, buon dì! Signorina.

ROSINA: Buon giorno! signor Figaro.

FIGARO: Ebbene, che si fa?

ROSINA: Si muor di noja.

FIGARO: Oh, diavolo! possibile!
Una ragazza bella e spiritosa.

ROSINA: Ah, ah, mi fate ridere
Che mi serve lo spirito,—
Che giova la bellezza,
Se chiusa io sempre sto fra quattro mura,
Che mi par d'esser proprio in sepoltura?

FIGARO: In sepoltura! oibò!
(Chaimandola a parte.)
Sentite, io voglio—

ROSINA: Ecco il tutor!

FIGARO: Davvero!

ROSINA: Certo, certo! la sua voce!

FIGARO: Salva! salva! fra poco
(Parte.)
Ci rivedremo—ho a dirvi qualche cosa.

ROSINA: E ancor io, Signor Figaro.

FIGARO: Bravissima, vado!

ROSINA: Quanto è garbato.
(Parte.)

## SCENE V

Rosina and Figaro.

FIGARO: Oh, good day! Signorina.

ROSINA: Good day! Signor Figaro.

FIGARO: Well, what are you doing?

ROSINA: I am dying with ennui.

FIGARO: Oh, the deuce! impossible!
For one so handsome, so full of spirit.

ROSINA: You make me smile, Figaro:
Of what use is my spirit,
What avails my beauty,
If forever shut up between four walls,
Which appear as dreary as a sepulchre?

FIGARO: A sepulchre! good Heavens!
(Taking her aside.)
I wish to know—

ROSINA: See! see! my guardian!

FIGARO: Indeed!

ROSINA: Certainly, certainly! There is his voice!

FIGARO: Adieu! adieu! in a few moments
(Exit.)
I will see you again—I have something to tell you.

ROSINA: And so have I, Signor Figaro.

FIGARO: Adieu, fair lady!

ROSINA: A civil fellow this.
(Exit.)

## SCENA VI

Bartolo e Don Basilio.

## SCENE VI

Bartolo and Don Basilio.

**BARTOLO:** Don Basilio,
Venite a tempo. Oh io voglio
Per forza, oh per amor, dentro do-
mani
Sposar la mia Rosina.—Avete inte-
so?

**BASILIO:** Eh, voi dite benissimo;
E appunto io quì veniva ad avvisar-
vi.
(*Chiamandola a parte.*)
Ma segretezza!—è giunto
Il Conte d'Almaviva.

**BARTOLO:** Chi! l'incognito amante
Della Rosina?

**BASILIO:** Appunto quello.

**BARTOLO:** Oh, diavolo!
Ah quì ci vuol riparo.

**BASILIO:** Certo; ma, alla sordina—

**BARTOLO:** Sarebbe a dir—

**BASILIO:** Così con buona grazia
Bisogna principiare
A inventar qualche favola
Che al pubblico lo metta in mala
vista.

**BARTOLO:** E vorreste?—Ma una
calunnia—

**BASILIO:** Ah, dunque,
La calunnia cos'è voi non sapete?

**BARTOLO:** No, davvero.

**BASILIO:** No?—Uditemi, e tacete.
La calunnia è un venticello
Un'auretta assai gentile;
Che insensibile, sottile,
Leggermente, dolcemente
Incomincia a susurrar
Piano piano, terra terra,
Sotto voce sibillando,
Và scorrendo, và ronzando
Nelle orecchie della gente,—
S'introduce destramente,
E le teste ed i cervelli,
Fà stordire, e fa gonfiar.
Dalla bocca fuori uscendo,
Lo schiamazzo và crescendo;
Prende forza a poco a poco,
Scorre già di loco in loco,
Sembra il tuono, la tempesta,
Che nel sen della foresta,
Va fischiando, brontolando,
E ti fa d'orror gelar.
Alla fin trabocca, e scoppia,
Si propaga, e si raddoppia,
E produce un'esplosione
Come un colpo di cannone.
Un tremoto, un temporale,
Un tremoto generale,
Che fa l'aria rimbombar.
E il meschino, calunniato,
Avvilito, calpestato,
Sotto il pubblico flagello,
Per gran sorte và a crepar.
(*Partono.*)

**BARTOLO:** Don Basilio,
You come just in time. I wish
Tomorrow, either by force or love,
To marry my Rosina.—Do you un-
derstand?

**BASILIO:** Ah! you speak wisely;
And I was just coming myself to ad-
vise with you.
(*Taking him aside.*)
But be secret!—The Count Almavi-
va has arrived.

**BARTOLO:** What! the unknown
lover
Of Rosina?

**BASILIO:** The very same.

**BARTOLO:** Oh, the devil
Something must be done here.

**BASILIO:** Certainly; but, between
ourselves—

**BARTOLO:** That is to say—

**BASILIO:** We must boldly
Begin by inventing
Some plausible story, that may
Disgrace him in the eyes of the pub-
lic.

**BARTOLO:** And would you? But a
calumny—

**BASILIO:** Oh, then,
You don't know what a calumny is?

**BARTOLO:** No, indeed.

**BASILIO:** No?—Then hear, and be
silent.
Oh! calumny is like the sigh
Of gentlest zephyrs breathing by;
How softly sweet, along the
ground,
Its first shrill voice is heard around:
So soft, that, sighing amid the bow-
ers,
It scarcely fans the drooping flow-
ers.
Thus will the voice of calumny,
More subtle than the plaintive sigh,
In many a serpent-wreathing, find
Its secret passage to the mind,—
The heart's most inmost feelings
gain,
Bedim the sense, and fire the brain.
Then passing on from tongue to
tongue,
It gains new strength, it sweeps
along
In giddier whirl from place to
place,
And gains fresh vigor in its race;
Till, like the sounds of tempests
deep,
That sweep through the woods in
murmurs
And howl amid their caverns,
It shakes the trembling soul with
fear.
At length the fury of the storm
Assumes its wildest, fiercest
form,—
In one loud crash of thunder
And, like an earthquake, rocks the
shores.
While all the frowning vault of
heaven.
Is riven with many a fiery bolt

Thus calumny, a simple breath,
Engenders rain, wreck, and death;
And sinks the wretched man for-
lorn,
Beneath the lash of slander torn,
The victim of the public scorn.
(*Exeunt.*)

## SCENA VII

*Figaro, uscendo con precauzione;
indi Rosina.*

**FIGARO:** Ma bravi! ma benone!
Ho inteso tutto. Evviva il buon dot-
tore!
Povero babbuino!
Tua sposa!—eh via. Pulisciti il boc-
chino
Or che stanno là chiusi,
Procuriam di parlare alla ragazza;
Eccola appunto.

**ROSINA:** Ebbene, Signor Figaro?

**FIGARO:** Gran cose Sigorina

**ROSINA:** Si, davver!

**FIGARO:** Mangerem dei confetti.

**ROSINA:** Come sarebbe a dir?

**FIGARO:** Sarebbe a dire
Che il vostro bel tutore ha stabilito
Esser dentro doman vostro marito.

**ROSINA:** Eh, via!

**FIGARO:** Oh, ve lo giuro;
A stendere il contratto
Col maestro di musica,
Là dentro si è serrato.

**ROSINA:** Si! L'ha sbagliata affè!
Povero sciocco! l'avrà da far con
me.
Ma dite, Signor Figaro,
Voi poco fa sotto le mie finestre,
Parlavate a un signore—

**FIGARO:** Ah! un mio cugino—
E' un bravo giovinotto; buona testa,
Ottimo cuor! quì venne
I suoi studj a compire, e il poveri-
no,
Cerca di far fortuna.

**ROSINA:** Fortuna?—eh, la farà.

**FIGARO:** Oh, ne dubito assai; in
confidenza,
Ha un gran difetto addosso.

**ROSINA:** Un gran difetto?

**FIGARO:** Ah, grande;
E'innamorato morto.

**ROSINA:** Sì, davvero?
Quel giovine, vedete
M'interessa moltissimo.

**FIGARO:** Per Bacco!

**ROSINA:** Non ci credete?

**FIGARO:** Oh sì.

## SCENE VII

*Figaro, coming forth with precau-
tion; then Rosina.*

**FIGARO:** Bravo! all goes on well!
I have overheard everything.
So, so, good Mr. Doctor!
Your spouse!—a good joke. The
grapes are sour.
While they remain shut up yonder,
I will endeavor to speak to the girl;
But here she is, à propos.

**ROSINA:** Well, Signor Figaro?

**FIGARO:** I have great things to tell
you, Signorina.

**ROSINA:** Indeed!

**FIGARO:** We shall eat wedding
cake shortly.

**ROSINA:** What do you mean?

**FIGARO:** I mean
That this fine guardian of yours has
settled
That tomorrow he is to be your husband.

**ROSINA:** Oh, pooh!

**FIGARO:** Yes, I swear it:
Even now he is closeted
With your music-master,
Drawing up the contract.

**ROSINA:** Indeed! In truth he is
much mistaken!
Poor fellow! he shall find with
whom he has to do.
But tell me, Mr. Figaro,
Just now, below my window,
You were speaking to a gentle-
man—

**FIGARO:** Oh, a cousin of mine—
An excellent young man, with a
good head,
And the best of hearts; he has come
here
To finish his studies, and to try,
poor fellow,
To make his fortune.

**ROSINA:** His fortune?—Oh, he
will make it.

**FIGARO:** Aha, I doubt it much; in
confidence,
I tell you he has one great failing.

**ROSINA:** A great failing, said you?

**FIGARO:** Yes, a great one;
He is dying in love.

**ROSINA:** Ah, indeed?
Do you know that this young man
Interests me extremely.

**FIGARO:** Good Lord!

**ROSINA:** Don't you believe it?

**FIGARO:** Oh, certainly.

ROSINA: Ma la sua bella
Dite, abita lontano?

FIGARO: Oh nò!—cioè!
Quì a due passi—

ROSINA: Ma è bella?

FIGARO: Oh, bella assai—eccovi
il suo ritratto,
Che vi fo in due parole:
Svelta, gentil, vezzosa,
Capelli neri, guancia porporina,
Occhio che parla, mano che inna-
mora.

ROSINA: E il nome?

FIGARO: Ah, il nome ancora?
Il nome?—Ah, che bel nome!—
Si chiama—

ROSINA: Ebben? si chiama?

FIGARO: Poverina!
Si chiama Ro-ro-ro-si-na—Rosina.

ROSINA: Dunque io son, tu non
m'inganni? Dunqeu io son, la fortunata? (Già l'ero immaginata, Lo sapevo pria dite;) Dunque io sono, tu
non m'inganni; Già l'ero immaginata, Lo sapevo pria di te, già lo sapevo pria di te; Lo sapevo pria dite.

FIGARO: Di Lindoro il vago oggetto; Siete voi, bella Rosina, siete voi,
siete voi, bellà Rosina (Oh che
volpe sopraffina, ah! che volpe sopraffina Mà l'a vrà da far con me;)
Si, mà l'a vrà da far con me.

ROSINA: Senti, senti, ma a Lindoro,
Per parlar come si fà.

FIGARO: Zitto, zitto, quì Lindoro
Per parlarvi or sarà.

ROSINA: Per parlarmi? bravo! bra-
vo!
Vengo pur, ma con prudenza;
Io già moro d' impazienza!
Ah che tarda? cosa fa?

FIGARO: Egli attende qualche seg-
no
Poverin del vostro affetto
Sol due righe di biglietto,
Gli mandate, e quì verrà.
Che ne dite?

ROSINA: Non saprei.

FIGARO: Su coraggio!

ROSINA: Non vorrei–

FIGARO: Sol due righe.

ROSINA: Mi vergogno.

FIGARO: Ma di che?—di che?—si
sa?
Presto, presto, quà un biglietto.
(*Andando allo scrittojo.*)

ROSINA: Un biglietto! eccolo quà.
(*Richiamandolo; cava dal seno il
biglietto, e glie lo da.*)

ROSINA: But tell me, does this fair
one
Live far from this place?

FIGARO: Oh no!—that is—
But two paces from here—

ROSINA: Is she handsome?

FIGARO: Oh, very much so—be-
hold her portrait,
Which I give you in two words:
A handsome, graceful figure,
Jetty locks, a rosy cheek,
An eye that speaks, a hand whose
touch thrills one.

ROSINA: And her name?

FIGARO: Ah, her name too?
Her name?—Ah, what a sweet
name!—
She's called—

ROSINA: Well, what is she called?

FIGARO: Sweet creature!
She's called Ro-ro-ro-si-na—Rosina.

ROSINA: What am I, or do you
mock me? Am I, then, the happy being? (But I foreseeing all the
scheme, Knew it, sir, before yourself;) What am I then, or do you
mock me? But I, foreseeing all the
scheme, Knew it, sir, before you
did, I knew it, sir, before you did;
Knew it, sir before you did.

FIGARO: Yes, Lindoro loves you,
lady; he sighs for his Rosina, softly
sighing, softly sighing for his Rosina She seems cunning as a fox ah!
She seems cunning as a fox, Ah! by
my faith, she sees through all;) Yes,
by my faith she sees through all.

ROSINA: Still one word, Sir, to my
Lindor.
How shall I contrive to speak.

FIGARO: Patience, patience, and
your lover
Soon will seek your presence here

ROSINA: Will seek me here? Oh,
joy supreme!
Let him come with caution.
I die to know how he will scheme!
Where can he linger?

FIGARO: Poor man, he awaits some
sign
Of your affection and assent:
A little note, a single line,
And he will soon present himself.
To this, what say you?

ROSINA: I do not know.

FIGARO: Take courage, pray you.

ROSINA: I could not so—

FIGARO: A few lines merely.

ROSINA: I blush to write.

FIGARO: At what?—why really—
may I indite?
Haste, haste, invite your lover
quick.
(*Going to the desk.*)

ROSINA: A letter! Oh, here it is.
(*Calling him; she takes a note
from her bosom, which she gives
him.*)

FIGARO: Già era scritto!—oh ve'
che bestia!
(*Attonito.*)
E il maestro io faccio a lei!
Ah, che in cattedra costei
Di malizia può dettar.
Donne, donne! eterni dei,
Chi vi arriva a indovinar?

ROSINA: Fortunati affetti miei,
Io comincio a respirar;
Ah tu solo, amor tu sei,
Che mi devi consolar.
(*Figaro parte.*)

## SCENA VIII

*Rosina, indi Bartolo.*

ROSINA: Ora mi sento meglio.
Questo Figaro è un bravo giovinotto!

BARTOLO: In somma, colle
buone,
Potrei sapere dalla mia Rosina
Che venne a far colui questa mattina?

ROSINA: Figaro?—Non so nulla.

BARTOLO: Ti parlò?

ROSINA: Mi parlò.

BARTOLO: Che ti diceva?

ROSINA: Oh, mi parlò di certe ba-
gatelle:
Del figurin di Francia,—
Del mal della sua figlia, Marcellina.

BARTOLO: Davvero! ed io scomet-
to
Che protò la risposta al tuo biglietto.

ROSINA: Qual biglietto?

BARTOLO: Che serve!
quell'arietta.
Del dramma del' "Inutil Precau-
zione,"
Che ti cadde staman giù dal bal-
cone.
Vi fate rossa—(l'avrei indovinato!)
Che vuol dir questo dito
Così sporco d'inchiostro?

ROSINA: Sporco!—Oh, nulla:
Io me l'avea scottato,
E con l'inchiostro or l'ho medicato.

BARTOLO: (Diavolo!) E questi fogli?
Or son cinque—eran sei.

ROSINA: Quei fogli? E vero:
D' uno mi son servito
A mandar de' confetti a Marcellina.

BARTOLO: Bravissima! E la penna—
Perchè fu temperata?

ROSINA: (Maledetto!) La penna?
Per disegnare un fiore sul tamburo.

BARTOLO: Un fiore?

FIGARO: Already written!—what a
fool I was.
(*Astonished.*)
To think to be her master!
Much fitter, that she should school
me.
Her wits can flow much faster than
mine.
Oh, woman, woman! who can find,
Or fathom, all that's in your mind?

ROSINA: Upon my young desires,
See love propitious shine;
It is he, with his soft fires,
Must ease a heart like mine.
(*Exit Figaro.*)

## SCENE VIII

*Rosina, then Bartolo.*

ROSINA: Now I feel relieved.
This Figaro is a kind creature!

BARTOLO: With fair words,
May I know from my Rosina what
this
Fellow came to do here this morning?

ROSINA: Who? Figaro?—Oh, I
know not.

BARTOLO: Didn't he speak to you?

ROSINA: Yes, he spoke to me.

BARTOLO: What said he?

ROSINA: Oh, he told me a hundred
trifles:
Of the fashions of France,—
Of the ill health of the child, Marcellina.

BARTOLO: Indeed! now I would
venture to wager
That he brought an answer to your
note.

ROSINA: What note?

BARTOLO: Oh, come, come! that
air
From the drama of the "Useless Pre-
caution,"
Which you dropped this morning
from the balcony.
You blush—(I have guessed it!)
How came that finger
To be so marked with ink?

ROSINA: With ink!—Oh, nothing:
I had hurt myself,
And used this ink by way of a cure.

BARTOLO: (The devil!) But these
sheets of paper?
There are now only five—there
were six.

ROSINA: Those sheets? Oh, true:
I made use of one of them
To send some sweetmeats to Mar-
cellina.

BARTOLO: Most excellent! And
the pen—
For what purpose has that been cut?

ROSINA: (Confound him!) That
pen?
To design a flower on my tambour.

BARTOLO: A flower?

ROSINA: Un fiore.

BARTOLO: Un fiore!
Ah, fraschetta!

ROSINA: Davver.

BARTOLO: Zitto!

ROSINA: Credete.

BARTOLO: Basta così

ROSINA: Signor—

BARTOLO: Non più—tacete.
A un dottor della mia sorte,
Queste scuse, Signorina,
Vi consiglio mia carina
Un pò meglio a impostur ar.
I confetti alla ragazza!
Il ricamo sul tamburo!
Vi scostate, e via!
Ci vuol altra figlia mia
Per potermi corbellar?
Perchè manca là quel foglio?
Vo' saper cotesto imbroglio.
Sono inutili le smorfie—
Ferma là, non mi toccate.
Signorina, un altra volta
Quando Bartolo andrà fuori,
La consegna ai servitori
A suo modo dar saprà.
Ah, non servono le smorfie,
Faccia pur la gatta morta!
Cospetton per quella porta
Nemmen l'aria entrar potrà
E Rosina, innocentina,
Sconsolata, disperata:
In sua camera serrata,
Fin ch'io voglio star dovrà.
(Partono.)

## SCENA IX

*Berta, sola.*

BERTA: Finora in questa camera
Mi parve di sentir un mormorio;
Sarà stato il tutor colla pupilla;
Non ha un'ora di ben. queste ragazze
No la voglion capir;—battono.
(Si ode picchiare.)

CONTE: Aprite!
(Di dentro.)

BERTA: Alla fine farà qualche stortura?
O anderà dalla noja in sepoltura.
(Apre e parte.)

## SCENA X

*Il Conte travestito da Soldato contrafacendo i moti d'ubriaco; indi Bartolo.*

CONTE: Ehi di casa!—buona gente!
Ehi di casa!—niun mi sente!

BARTOLO: Chi è costui?—Che brutta faccia!
E ubriaco, chi sarà!

---

ROSINA: A flower.

BARTOLO: A flower!
Ah, you cunning minx!

ROSINA: It's true.

BARTOLO: Silence!

ROSINA: Believe me.

BARTOLO: Enough of this.

ROSINA: Sir—

BARTOLO: No more—be silent.
To a doctor of my rank,
These excuses, Signorina,
I advise
That you better should invent another time,
The sweetmeats for the girl!
The embroidery on the tambour!
Out of my sight! begone!
And is it thus my more than daughter
Dares to trifle with me?
Why is the paper missing?
That I would wish to know.
Useless, ma'am, are all your airs—
Be still, nor interrupt me so.
Another time, sweet Signorina,
When the doctor quits his house,
He will carefully provide
For keeping you inside.
Useless now are your grimaces,
No one heeds your affectation!
A vow I make that no one now
Shall come within my habitation.
And poor innocent Rosina,
Disappointed, then may pout:
In her room shall she be locked,
Till I choose to let her out.
(Exeunt.)

## SCENE IX

*Bertha, alone.*

BERTHA: I thought just now
I heard a noise within this chamber,
It perhaps was the guardian with his ward;
He never has an hour's peace.
These girls
Will not hear;—some one knocks.
(A knocking is heard.)

COUNT: Open the door!
(Within.)

BERTHA: Poor girl! she will be driven to some rash act,
If she be longer confined in this sepulchral place.
(Bertha opens the door, and exits.)

## SCENE X

*The Count, disguised as a Soldier, and pretending to be drunk; then Bartolo.*

COUNT: Hallo! house there!—Hey! good people!
Hallo! house there!—Faith, you'll sleep ill.

BARTOLO: Who can this be?—Ugly fellow!
Drunken rascal, thus to bellow!

---

CONTE: Ehi di casa!—maledetti!

BARTOLO: Cosa vuol, Signor Soldato?

CONTE: Ah! sì, sì!—Ben obbligato?
(Vedendolo, cerca in tasca.)

BARTOLO: Quì costui!—che mai vorrà?

CONTE: Siete voi—aspetta un poco!
Siete voi—Dottor Balordo?

BARTOLO: Che Balordo?

CONTE: Ah, ah! Bertoldo—
(Leggendo.)

BARTOLO: Che Bertoldo.
Eh, andate al diavolo!
Dottor Bartolo!

CONTE: Ah, bravissimo!
Dottor Barbaro; benissimo;
Già c'è poca differenza.
(Non si vede! che impazienza!
Quanto tarda!—dove stà?)

BARTOLO: Io già perdo la pazienza.
Qui prudenza ci vorrà.

CONTE: Dunque voi siete Dottore?

BARTOLO: Son Dottore—si, Signore.

CONTE: Ah, benissimo!
un'abbraccio—
Quà collega.

BARTOLO: Indietro.

CONTE: Quà!
(Lo abbraccia per forza.)
Sono anch' io Dottor perfetto,
Marescalco al reggimento:
Dell' alloggio sul biglietto:
(Presentando il biglietto.)
Osservate, eccolo quà.

BARTOLO: (Dalla rabbia—dal dispetto
Io già crepo in verità;
Ah ch'io fo se mi ci metto
Qualche gran bestialità!
(Legge il biglietto.)

CONTE: (Ah, venisse il caro oggetto—
Della mia felicità;
Vieni, vieni; il tuo diletto,
Pien d'amor, t'attende quà.)

## SCENA XI

*Rosina, e detti.*

ROSINA: D'ascoltar quà m'è sembrato,
Un'insolito rumore.
Un soldato!—ed il tutore!—
Cosa mai faranno quà?
(Si avanza piano piano.)

CONTE: E' Rosina! Or son contento.

---

COUNT: Hallo! house there!—All are still here!

BARTOLO: Signor Whiskers, what's your will here?

COUNT: Hey! oh, oh!—Pray, how d'ye do, sir?
(Seeing him, he searches in his pocket.)

BARTOLO: Stupid puppy!—Who are you sir?

COUNT: Are not you, sir—but steady—order!
Doctor Balordo?

BARTOLO: What, Balordo?

COUNT: Ah, ah! Bertoldo—
(Reading.)

BARTOLO: Pooh! pooh! Bertoldo!
No such person.—Hear me, fool, do!
Doctor Bartolo!

COUNT: Ah, bravissimo!
Doctor Barbaro; well and good;
The difference, after all, is trifling.
(She appears not! what impatience I feel!
How long she delays!—where can she be?)

BARTOLO: I am already out of all patience.
Prudence is necessary here.

COUNT: You, then—are a doctor?

BARTOLO: I am a doctor—yes, sir.

COUNT: Ah, how fortunate! let me embrace—
Here, fellow collegian.

BARTOLO: Stand off.

COUNT: Here!
(Embracing him by force.)
I also am a doctor of full degree,
And marshal of the regiment:
Here on the billet for my lodgings.
(Presenting a billet.)
Look, here it is.

BARTOLO: (With rage and vexation
I'm ready to burst in good earnest;
Ah, let me be cautious
Not to commit some rash act!)
(Reads the billet.)

COUNT: (Ah, would my heart's dear idol come—
Sole object of my love, appear;
Haste, oh, haste; your fond adorer,
Full of love, awaits you here.)

## SCENE XI

*Rosina, and the preceding.*

ROSINA: I thought I overheard just now,
A most unusual clamor here.
A soldier!—and my guardian!—
What can they be doing here?
(She advances softly.)

COUNT: It is Rosina!—I now am content.

ROSINA: Ei mi guarda, e s'avvicina!

CONTE: Son Lindoro.
(*Piano, a Rosina.*)

ROSINA: Oh, ciel che sento?
Ah, giudizio, per peità!

BARTOLO: Signorina che cercate?
Presto, presto, andate via.
(*Vedendo Rosina.*)

ROSINA: Vado, vado, non gridate.

BARTOLO: Presto, presto, via di
quà.

CONTE: Ehi ragazza vengo anch'io.

BARTOLO: Dove, dove, Signor
mio?

CONTE: In caserma: oh, questa è
bella!

BARTOLO: In caserma? bagatella!

CONTE: Cara!

ROSINA: Ajuto!

BARTOLO: Olà! cospetto!

CONTE: Via, gettate il fazzoletto;
Fate presto per pietà!
(*A Rosina mostrandola furtiva-
mente un biglietto.*)

ROSINA: Ah, ci guarda!
(*Al Conte.*)
Maledetto!
Ah, giudizio, per pietà.
(*Guardando Bartolo.*)

BARTOLO: Ubriaco maledetto!
Ah costui crepar mi fa.

CONTE: Dunque vado—

BARTOLO: O no: Signore!
(*Trattenendolo.*)
Qui d'alloggio star non può.

CONTE: Come, come?

BARTOLO: Eh, non v'è replica;
Ho il brevetto d'esenzione.

CONTE: Che brevetto?
(*Adirato.*)

BARTOLO: Oh mio padrone,
Un momento, e il mostrerò.
(*Và allo scrittojo.*)

CONTE: Ah, se qui restar non posso,
Deh, prendete—
(*Accennandolo di prendere un biglietto.*)

ROSINA: Ahimè! ci guarda.

ROSINA E CONTE: Cento smanie
io sento addosso!
Ah, più reggere non so.

BARTOLO: Ah trovarlo ancor non
posso,
Mà sì, sì, lo troverò.
(*Cercando nello scrittojo.*)
Ecco quì.
(*Legge.*)
"Colla presente,
(*Venendo avanti con una per-
gamena.*)
Il dottor Bartolo, et cetera.
Essentiamo"—

CONTE: Eh, andate al diavolo!
(*Con un rovescio di mano manda
in aria la pergamena.*)

BARTOLO: Cosa fa, Signor mio
caro?

CONTE: Zitto là, Dottor Lomaro!
Il mio alloggio è quì fissato,
E in alloggio quì vo star.

BARTOLO: Vuol restar!

CONTE: Restar, sicuro.

BARTOLO: Ah, son stufo, mio pa-
drone:
Presto fuori, o un buon bastone
Lo farà di quà sloggiar.
(*Minacciandolo.*)

CONTE: Dunque lei—lei vuol bat-
taglia?
Ben, battaglia le vuò dar.
(*Tirandosi indietro.*)
Bella cosa una battaglia!
(*Ridendo.*)
Ve la voglio or quì mostrar.
(*Avvicinandosi, amichevolmente
a Bartolo.*)
Osservate! questo è il fosso,
L'inimico voi sarete.
(*Gli da una spinta.*)
Attenzion! (Giù fazzoletto.)
(*Piano, a Rosina.*)
E gli amici stan di quà—
Attenzione!
(*Cogli il momento in cui Bartolo
l'osserva meno attentamente, e
lascia il biglietto, e Rosina vi fa
cadere sopra il fazzoletto.*)

BARTOLO: Ferma! ferma!

CONTE: Che cos' e?—ah!

BARTOLO: Vo' vedere.

CONTE: Sì, se fosse una ricetta;
Mi dovete perdonar.
(*Fa una riverenza a Rosina, e le
da il biglietto, e il fazzoletto.*)

ROSINA: Grazie, grazie!

BARTOLO: Grazie, come!
Vo saper cotesto imbroglio!

CONTE: Qualche intrigo di fanciulla.
(*Tirandolo a parte; intanto, Rosina cambia la lettera.*)

ROSINA: Ah, cambiar potessi il
foglio!

BARTOLO: Vuò veder.

ROSINA: Ma non è nulla.

BARTOLO: Quì quel foglio, presto
quà!
(*Escono da una parte Basilio; e
dall'altra, Berta.*)

BASILIO: Ecco quà!—oh, cosa
vedo?

BERTA: Il barbiere! Oh, quanta
gente!

---

ROSINA: He looks at me, he approaches me!

COUNT: I am Lindor.
(*Softly, to Rosina.*)

ROSINA: Heavens! what do I hear?
Prudence, for mercy's sake!

BARTOLO: The Signorina here?
Quick, quick, make your exit.
(*Pushing Rosina.*)

ROSINA: I am going; don't holler
so.

BARTOLO: Quick, quick, away, I
tell you.

COUNT: Well, sweetheart, and I'll
follow you.

BARTOLO: Follow! where sir?

COUNT: To my quarters: oh, this is
excellent!

BARTOLO: To your quarters? a
pretty joke!

COUNT: Dearest!

ROSINA: Help!

BARTOLO: Hold! zounds!

COUNT: Quick, let drop your
handkerchief;
Quick, for goodness' sake!
(*To Rosina, showing her a note by
stealth.*)

ROSINA: Ah, he's looking!
(*To the Count.*)
How unlucky!
Ah, discretion, for goodness' sake!
(*Eyeing Bartolo.*)

BARTOLO: A curse on this drunk-
en fellow!
I am ready to burst with vexation

COUNT: Then I go—

BARTOLO: Oh no; stop, sir!
(*Retaining him.*)
You can have no lodging here.

COUNT: How say you?

BARTOLO: Oh, it is in vain to re-
monstrate;
I am exempt from lodging troops.

COUNT: How are you exempt?
(*In a rage.*)

BARTOLO: Oh, my good sir,
A moment, and I will show you.
(*Goes to his desk.*)

COUNT: Ah, if I cannot remain
here,
Quick, take it—
(*Making signs to her to take the
note.*)

ROSINA: He looks at me again.

ROSINA AND COUNT: Oh, this
heart is filled with pain!
No more can I contain myself.

BARTOLO: At present I have
searched in vain,
But soon I hope to find it.
(*Searching in the desk.*)
Oh, here it is.
(*Reads.*)
"By these presents,
(*He comes forward with a parch-
ment.*)
The Doctor Bartolo, etc., etc.
We exempt"—

COUNT: Oh, go to the devil!
(*With a dash of his hand he sends
the parchment into the air.*)

BARTOLO: My dear sir, what
would you?

COUNT: Silence, Mr. Doctor Loma-
ro!
My lodging is fixed here,
And here will I remain.

BARTOLO: Will remain!

COUNT: Yes, will remain.

BARTOLO: My good sir, I have
something else to do:
I beg you will begone, or a cudgel
Shall dislodge you.
(*Threatening him.*)

COUNT: Then you—you wish to
fight with me?
Well, you shall have your way.
(*Drawing back.*)
A battle is a fine thing, truly!
(*Laughing.*)
I'll show you a specimen.
(*Advances, pretending to fight.*)
This is the trench, observe,
And you are the enemy.
(*Makes a pass at him.*)
Now, mark! (Drop your handker-
chief.)
(*Aside, to Rosina.*)
Our friends are stationed here—
Now mark!
(*He seizes the moment when Bar-
tolo is less attentive, and lets fall
the note; Rosina drops her hand-
kerchief upon it.*)

BARTOLO: Hold! hold!

COUNT: What is it?—ah!

BARTOLO: Let me see it.

COUNT: Prescriptions only are for
you;
But letters go where they are due.
I ask your pardon. (*He bows to Rosina, and gives her the note and
the handkerchief.*)

ROSINA: Charming, charming,
how delightful!

BARTOLO: Charming, truly!
Oh, it is frightful.

COUNT: Some little girlish love af-
fair.
(*Drawing him aside; meanwhile,
Rosina changes the letter.*)

ROSINA: Could I but change the
letter there!

BARTOLO: I wish to see it.

ROSINA: There is nothing to see.

BARTOLO: Quick, give the paper—give it to me.
(*Enter Basilio on one side; Bertha
on the other.*)

BASILIO: Look here!—what do I
see?

BERTHA: The barber! Eh, what stir
is here!

## Act I, Scene XI

**BARTOLO:** Quà quel foglio, impertinente!
(*A Rosina.*)
A chi dico?—presto quà!

**ROSINA:** Ma quel foglio che chiedete,
Per azzardo m'e cascato,
E la lista del bucato.

**BARTOLO:** Ah, fraschetta presto quà!
(*Lo strappa con violenza a legge.*)
Ah, che vedo?—ho preso sbaglio!
E la lista, son di stucco!
Ah, son proprio un mamalucco!
Ah, che gran bestialita!

**ROSINA E CONTE:** Bravo! bravo! il mamalucco
Che nel sacco entrato e già.

**BASILIO E BERTA:** Non capisco, son di stucco:
Qualche imbroglio qui ci stà.

**ROSINA:** Ecco quà sempre un istoria,
(*Piangendo.*)
Sempre oppressa, e maltrattata;
Ah, che vita disperata—
Non la so più sopportar.

**BARTOLO:** Ah, Rosina! poverina!

**CONTE:** Via quà tu! cosa l'hai fatto?
(*Minacciando, e afferrandolo per un braccio.*)

**BARTOLO:** Gente, ajuto! soccorretemi!

**ROSINA:** Ma chetatevi.

**CONTE:** Lasciatemi!

**TUTTI:** Gente, ajuto per pietà!

## SCENA XII

*Figaro, entrando con bacile sotto il braccio; e detti.*

**FIGARO:** Alto là! Alto là!
Che cosa accadde?—Signori miei!
Che chiasso è questo? Eterni Dei!
Già sulla piazza a questo strepito
S'e radunata mezza città.
(*Piano, al Conte.*)
(Signor, prudenza, per carità!)

**BARTOLO:** Questo è un birbante!
(*Additando il Conte.*)

**CONTE:** Questo è un briccone!

**BARTOLO:** Ah disgraziato!—

**CONTE:** Ah maledetto!
(*Minacciandolo con la sciabola.*)

**FIGARO:** Signor Soldato, porti respetto,
(*Alzando il bacile, e minacciando il Conte.*)
O questo fusto, corpo del diavolo,
Or le creanze le insegnera.

**CONTE:** Brutto scimiotto—
(*Al Bartolo.*)

---

**BARTOLO:** Give here the paper, impertinence!
(*To Rosina.*)
Do you mind what I say—quick!

**ROSINA:** The paper, sir, you wish to have,
Which slipped by chance out of my hand,
Is just a list of linen.

**BARTOLO:** Quick, give it here, wench!
(*He seizes it violently.*)
What do I see?—I am mistaken!
The list I'd taken for a letter.
Oh, what a fool, indeed, am I!
Oh, what immense stupidity!

**ROSINA AND COUNT:** Bravo! bravo! the old fool
At last is caught in his own snare.

**BASILIO AND BERTHA:** What it means I cannot tell:
Confusion here has wrought some work.

**ROSINA:** It is ever thus you rate and school
(*Weeping.*)
Me.
And rule me with rod of iron;
But I no more this life will lead—
I'll be freed from such tyranny.

**BARTOLO:** Ah, Rosina! poor young lady!

**COUNT:** Leave her, sir! What have you done?
(*Threatening him, and pushing him away by the arm.*)

**BARTOLO:** Holloa! help, there!

**ROSINA:** No, be quiet.

**COUNT:** Unhand me, sir!

**ALL:** What's all this riot?

## SCENE XII

*Enter Figaro, with a basin under his arm and the preceding.*

**FIGARO:** Holloa here!
What has happened?—my good people,
What clamor's this? Great gods!
This tumult has together drawn
Half the city into the street.
(*Softly to the Count.*)
(Prudence, sir, in pity!)

**BARTOLO:** This is a rogue!
(*Pointing to the Count.*)

**COUNT:** This is a knave!

**BARTOLO:** Ah, the scoundrel!

**COUNT:** Ah, the rascal!
(*Threatening him with his sword.*)

**FIGARO:** Mr. Soldier, take care,
(*Raising his basin and threatening the Count.*)
Or this basin soon shall teach you
Of your manners to beware.

**COUNT:** You ugly savage—
(*To Bartolo.*)

---

**BARTOLO:** Birbo malnato—

**TUTTI:** Zitto, Dottore—

**BARTOLO:** Voglio gridare—

**TUTTI:** Fermo, signore!
(*Al Conte.*)

**CONTE:** Voglio ammazzarlo.

**TUTTI:** Fate silenzio!
Per carità!
Si ode bussare con violenza alla porta di strada.)
Zitti, che battono?
Chi mai sarà?

**BARTOLO:** Chi è?

**CORO:** La forza. Aprite quà!
(*Di dentro.*)

**TUTTI:** La forza!—Oh diavolo!

**FIGARO:** L' avete fatta!
(*Al Conte, Rosina, e Bartolo.*)

**CONTE:** Niente paura.

**BARTOLO:** Vengan pur quà.

**TUTTI:** Questa avventura
Ah, come diavolo
Mai finirà!

## SCENA ULTIMA

*Un Uffiziale; con Soldati; e detti.*

**UFFIZIALE:** Fermi tutti! Niun si muova.
Miei Signori che si fa?
Questo chiasso donde è nato?
La cagione presto quà.

**CONTE:** La cagione—

**BARTOLO:** Non è vero.

**CONTE:** Si, Signore.

**BARTOLO:** Signor nò.

**CONTE:** E un birbante.

**BARTOLO:** E un impostore.

**UFFIZIALE:** Un per volta.

**BARTOLO:** Io parlerò!
Questo soldato,
M' ha maltrattato.

**ROSINA:** Il poverino,
Cotto è dal vino.

**BARTOLO:** Cava la sciabola!
Parla d'uccidere.

**FIGARO:** Io son venuto
Quì per dividere.

**UFFIZIALE:** Fate silenzio!
Che intesi già,
(*Al Conte.*)
Siete in arresto,—
Fuori di quà!
(*I Soldati si muovano per circondarlo.*)

---

**BARTOLO:** You low-born scoundrel—

**ALL:** Peace, Doctor—

**BARTOLO:** I'll not hold my peace—

**ALL:** Hold, sir!
(*To the Count.*)

**COUNT:** I am determined to kill him.

**ALL:** Silence, silence!
For goodness' sake!
(*A knocking at the street door.*)
Silence! Who is it that knocks?
Who can it be?

**BARTOLO:** Who is it?

**CHORUS:** Open, and you soon shall see.
(*Within.*)

**ALL:** The police!—Oh, the devil!—

**FIGARO:** You have done it now!
(*To the Count, Rosina, and Bartolo.*)

**COUNT:** Fear not.

**BARTOLO:** Let them come in.

**ALL:** I wonder
How the devil
Will terminate this adventure!

## SCENE THE LAST

*An Officer, with Soldiers; and the preceding.*

**OFFICER:** Hold, here! Let no one stir.
Good Sirs, what is the matter?
What's the cause of this disturbance?
What's the reason for this clatter?

**COUNT:** The reason—

**BARTOLO:** It is not true.

**COUNT:** Yes, sir.

**BARTOLO:** No, sir.

**COUNT:** He is a rascal.

**BARTOLO:** He is an impostor.

**OFFICER:** One at a time.

**BARTOLO:** But I will speak!
Sir, this soldier has abused me,
Has used me like a dog.

**ROSINA:** Pray, sir, pity the poor fellow,
Wine has made him rather mellow.

**BARTOLO:** Pity! he drew his sabre!
The villain spoke of murder, too.

**FIGARO:** Sir, I came to hear the clatter,
But know nothing of the matter.

**OFFICER:** Silence! silence!
Listen, fellow,
(*To the Count.*)
You're our prisoner,—
Quick, away!
(*The Soldiers are about to surround him.*)

CONTE: Io in arresto?—
Io, fermi, ola?
(*Con gesto autorevole trattiene i Soldati; chiama a se l'Uffiziale, gli mostra segretamente l'ordine di Grande di Spagna, che ha sotto l'uniforme, e gli dice all'orecchio suo nome. L'Uffiziale sorpreso, fa cenna ai Soldati che si ritirino, e anch'egli fa lo stesso. Tutti restono attoniti.*)

ROSINA: Fredda ed immobile
Come una statua, Fiato non estami
Da respirar, Fiato non restami Da respirar, Fiato non restami Da respirar; Fiato non restami Da respirar, Fiato non restami Da respirar.

CONTE: Freda ed immobile Come una statua, Fiato non restagli Da respirar, Fiato non restagli Da respirar; Fiato non restagli da respirar.

BARTOLO: Freddaed immobile Come una statua, Fiato non restami Da respirar.

FIGARO: Guarda Don Bartolo Sembra una statua, Ah, che dal ridere Sto per crepar.

BARTOLO: Ma, Signore—
(*All' Uffiziale.*)

CORO: Zitto tu!

BARTOLO: Ma un dottore—

CORO: Oh non più.

BARTOLO: Ma se lei—

CORO: Non parlar.

BARTOLO: La vorrai—

CORO: Non gridar.

A 3: Ma se noi—

CORO: Zitti voi.

A 3: Ma so poi—

CORO: Pensiam noi.
Vada ognun pe' fatti suoi.
Si finisca d'altercar.

BARTOLO AND CHORUS: Mi par d'esser colla testa! In un orrida facina! Par mi d'esser colla testa! In un orrida facina! Dove crescee mai non resta, e mai non resta, Dell' incudini sonora L'importuno strepitar!

CORO: Alternando questo e quello,
Pesantissimo martello,
Fà con barbara armonìa
Muri e volte rimbombar.
E il cervello poverello,
Già stordito, sbalordito,
Non ragiona, si confonde,
Si riduce ad impazzar!

---

COUNT: I, your prisoner? hold awhile—
Now what is it you please to say?
(*Repulsing the Soldiers with an air of authority, he calls the Officer towards him, privately shows him the order of the Grandees of Spain, which he has under his uniform, and whispers to him his name. The Officer surprised, makes a sign to the Soldiers, who retire, and he does the same. All remain astonished.*)

ROSINA: Cold and immovable as sculptured fear, All power has left me to see or hear; All power has left me to see or hear; All power has left me to see or hear; All power has left me to see or hear.

COUNT: Cold and immovable as sculptured fear, All power has left him to see or hear, All power has left him to see or hear; All power has left him to see or hear.

BARTOLO: Cold and immovable as sculptured fear, All power has left me to see or hear.

FIGARO: To see the doctor's Frantic fear, I'm laughing so hard I scarcely can hear.

BARTOLO: But, sir—
(*To the Officer.*)

CHORUS: Silence!

BARTOLO: For a doctor—

CHORUS: I have done!

BARTOLO: But if she—

CHORUS: Hold your tongue.

BARTOLO: She wished—

CHORUS: How you bawl.

ALL THREE: But if we—

CHORUS: Silence, all.

ALL THREE: But if—

CHORUS: We'll think of it, Let every one now quit the house. Let this altercation cease.

BARTOLO AND CHORUS: What confusion! with the dinning, Round my (his) giddy head is spinning! What confusion with the dinning! Round my (his) giddy head is spinning! No one ending, each beginning, each beginning, What confusion! with the dinning, Round my (his) giddy head is spinning!

CHORUS: Like hammers ringing on the anvil,
Till, echoing with the horrid sound,
The walls and vaulted roofs rebound.
Thus does your outrage stun the brain,
That seeks for quiet here in vain,
Where furious tongues confound the senses,
Till reason's drowned in the clamor,
And madness seems to rage around!

---

*FINE DELL' ATTO PRIMO.*

## ■ ATTO II

### SCENA I

*Camera in Casa di Bartolo.*

BARTOLO: (*Solo.*) Ma vedi il mio destino! Quel Soldato Per quanto abbia cercato, Niun lo conosce in tutto il reggimento.
Io dubito—oh cospetto!
Che dubitar?—scommetto
Che dal Conte Almaviva,
E stato quà spedito quel Signore,
Ad esplorar della Rosina il core.
Nemmeno in casa propria
Sicura si può star! ma io—
(*Battone.*)
Chi batte?
Ehi! chì è di la? battono,
Non senitite?
In casa io son, non ho timore?
Aprite.
(*Verso le quinte.*)

### SCENA II

*Il Conte, travestito da Maestro di Musica; e detto.*

CONTE: Pace e gioja il ciel vi dia!

BARTOLO: Mille grazie! non s'incommoda.

CONTE: Gioja e pace per mille anni!

BARTOLO: Obbligato in verità.
(Questo volto non m'è ignoto;
Non ravviso—non ricordo—
Ma quel volto—ma quell' abito—
Non capisco chi sara.)

CONTE: (Ah, se un colpo è andato a vuoto
A gabbar questo balordo,
La mia nuova metamorfosi
Più propizia a me sarà.)
Gioja, e pace; pace a gioja.

BARTOLO: Ho capito—(oh ciel che noja!)

CONTE: Gioja e pace, ben di cuore.

BARTOLO: Basta, basta! per pietà.
(Ma che perfido destino:
Tutti quanti a me davanti!
Che crudel fatalità.)

---

*END OF ACT I.*

## ■ ACT II

### SCENE I

*A Room in Bartolo's Home.*

BARTOLO: (*Alone.*) Do but see my ill-fortune! That soldier, As far as I can learn, Is known by no one in the regiment.
I doubt—zounds!
Doubt, did I say?—I would venture to wager
That this fellow was sent here
By the Count Almaviva,
To sound the heart of Rosina.
Not even in one's own house
Can one be secure! but I—
(*A knocking is heard.*)
Who knocks?
Holloa! who's there? they knock again,
Don't you hear?
I am in my own house, why should I be afraid?
Open the door.
(*Speaking to the side.*)

### SCENE II

*The Count, dressed as a Music-master, and the preceding.*

COUNT: May heaven send you peace and joy!

BARTOLO: A thousand thanks! no more, good sir.

COUNT: Joy and peace for thousands of years!

BARTOLO: In truth I'm very much obliged.
(That face is not unknown to me,
I don't recollect—I can't remember—
But that countenance—that dress—
I can't recall who it can be.)

COUNT: (Ah, if before I was unsuccessful
In deceiving this simpleton.
My new metamorphosis
May prove more propitious to me.)
Joy and peace; peace and joy.

BARTOLO: Enough—(Heavens! what an annoyance!)

COUNT: Joy and peace from my very heart.

BARTOLO: Enough, enough! for mercy's sake.
(What a wretched fate is mine:
Every knave conspires against me!
What a cruel destiny.)

# Act II, Scene II

**CONTE:** (Il vecchion non mi conosce:
Oh mia sorte fortunata!
Ah! mio ben, fra pochi instanti,
Parlerem con libertà.)

**BARTOLO:** In somma, mio Signore,
Chi è lei, si può sapere?

**CONTE:** Don Alonzo,
Professore di Musica, ed allievo
Di Don Basilio.

**BARTOLO:** Ebbene?

**CONTE:** Don Basilio,
Sta male il poverino, ed in sua
vece—

**BARTOLO:** Sta mal?—Corro a vederlo.
(In atto di partire.)

**CONTE:** Piano, piano.
(Trattenendolo.)
Non è un mal così grave.

**BARTOLO:** (Di costui non mi
fido.) Andiamo, andiamo.

**CONTE:** Ma, signore!

**BARTOLO:** Che c'è?

**CONTE:** Voleva dirvi.
(Tirandolo a parte, e sotto voce.)

**BARTOLO:** Parlate forte.

**CONTE:** Ma—

**BARTOLO:** Forte, vi dico.

**CONTE:** Ebben, come volete.
(Alzando la voce.)
Ma chi sia Don Alonzo apprenderete.
Vo dal Conte Almaviva—
(In atto di partire.)

**BARTOLO:** Piano, piano—
(Trattenendolo con dolcezza.)
Dite, dite, v'ascolto.

**CONTE:** Il Conte—
(A voce alta.)

**BARTOLO:** Piano, per carità.

**CONTE:** Stamane,
(Calmandosi.)
Nella stesa locanda
Era meco d'alloggio, ed in mie
mani
Per caso capitò questo biglietto
Dalla vostra pupilla a lui diretto.

**BARTOLO:** Che vedo? È sua scrittura!

**CONTE:** Don Basilio occupato col
curiale,
Nulla sà di quel foglio, ed io per lui
Venendo a dar lezione alla ragazza,
Volea farmene un merito con voi;
Perchè, con quel biglietto, si potrebbe—

**BARTOLO:** Che cosa?

---

**COUNT:** (The old fellow knows me
not:
How fortunate for me!
A few short moments, my love,
And we shall speak without restraint.)

**BARTOLO:** In a word, sir,
Who are you? may I know?

**COUNT:** Don Alonzo,
Professor of music, and pupil
Of Don Basilio.

**BARTOLO:** Well?

**COUNT:** Don Basilio,
Poor man, has taken ill; and in his
stead—

**BARTOLO:** Taken ill, say you?—
I'll run and see him.
(About to depart.)

**COUNT:** Gently, gently,
(Detaining him.)
His illness is not so serious.

**BARTOLO:** (I do distrust this fellow.) Come, let us go.

**COUNT:** But, sir!

**BARTOLO:** Well, what?

**COUNT:** I wished to say—
(Taking him aside, and in a whisper.)

**BARTOLO:** Well, speak out.

**COUNT:** But—

**BARTOLO:** Speak out, I say!

**COUNT:** Well, as you wish:
(Raising his voice.)
Then you shall know who Don Alonzo is.
I came from the Count Almaviva—
(Going.)

**BARTOLO:** Softly, softly—
(Gently restraining him.)
Speak, speak, I can hear you.

**COUNT:** The Count—
(Raising his voice.)

**BARTOLO:** Softly, for goodness'
sake.

**COUNT:** This morning he came by
chance
To the same inn! and by accident
I took up this note, which I found
Directed to him by your ward.

**BARTOLO:** What do I see? It is indeed her writing!

**COUNT:** Don Basilio being engaged with the lawyer,
Knows nothing of this letter, and I,
being sent
To give lessons to your ward, in his
stead,
Wished to make a merit of the thing
with you;
Because, by means of this letter I
might—

**BARTOLO:** You might what?

---

**CONTE:** Vi dirò,
S' io potessi parlare alla ragazza,
Io creder, verbigrazia le farei
Che me lo diè del Conte un' altra
amante:
Prova significante,
Che il Conte di Rosina si fa gioco,
E perciò—

**BARTOLO:** Piano un poco;—una
calunnia!
Or sì vi riconosco
Bravo e degno scolar di Don Basilio!
Io saprò come merita
(La abbraccia e mette in tasca il
biglietto.)
Ricompensar sì bel suggerimento;
Vò a chiamar la ragazza.
Poichè tanto per me v'interessate,
Mi raccommando a voi.
(Entra nella camera di Rosina.)

**CONTE:** Non dubitate
L'affare del biglietto
Dalla bocca mi è uscito non volendo.
Ma come far? Senza di un tal ripiego
Mi toccava andar via come un bagiano,
Il mio disegno a lei
Ora paleserò: s'ella consente,
Io son felice appieno.
Eccola! Ah, il cor sento balzarmi in
seno!

## SCENA III

Bartolo, conducendo Rosina; e
detti; indi Figaro.

**BARTOLO:** Venite, Signorina: Don
Alonzo, Che quì vedete, o vi darà
lezione.

**ROSINA:** Ah!

**BARTOLO:** Cos'è stato?

**ROSINA:** È un granchio al piede.

**CONTE:** Oh, nulla.
Sedete a me vicin, bella fanciulla;
Se non vi spiace, un poco di lezione
Di Don Basilio invece io vi darò.

**ROSINA:** Oh! col più gran piacer la
prendero.

**CONTE:** Che vuol cantare?

**ROSINA:** Quel che lei aggrada.

**BARTOLO:** Or ben, dunque sentiamo.

**ROSINA:** Eccola quì.

**CONTE:** Da brava incominciamo.
(Rosina canta qualche Aria, scelta, ad libitum, per l occasione.)

---

**COUNT:** I will tell you,
If I could just speak a few words
with her,
I think, with deference be it said,
that I could
Make her believe that it was given
to me by a mistress of the Count's:
A tolerable good proof to Rosina,
That she is only made a fool of by
the Count,
And therefore—

**BARTOLO:** Softly, softly;—a calumny this!
Oh, I see very well that you are
A scholar worthy of Don Basilio!
I shall know how to reward
(Embraces him and puts the note
in his pocket.)
So happy a suggestion;
I will go and call the girl.
And as you interest yourself so
much about me,
I recommend myself to your good
offices.
(He goes into Rosina's apartment.)

**COUNT:** Never doubt me.
This affair of the note
Slipped from my tongue against my
will.
But what was I to do? Without some
strategem
I should have gone away like a simpleton
I must now acquaint her
With my plan: if she consents,
I shall be completely happy.
She comes! How my heart beats in
my bosom!

## SCENE III

Bartolo, bringing in Rosina; and
the preceding then Figaro.

**BARTOLO:** Come, Signorina; Don
Alonzo,
Whom you see here, will give you
your lesson.

**ROSINA:** Ah!
(Starting.)

**BARTOLO:** What's the matter?

**ROSINA:** It is a cramp in my foot.

**COUNT:** Oh, nothing at all.
Seat yourself by my side, fair lady;
And, if not disagreeable, I will give
you
A little lesson in place of Don Basilio.

**ROSINA:** Oh, sir! with the greatest
pleasure.

**COUNT:** What will you sing?

**ROSINA:** Whatever you please.

**BARTOLO:** Well, let us hear, then.

**ROSINA:** Here it is.

**COUNT:** Now let us begin with
spirit.
(Rosina sings an Air, chosen, ad
libitum, for the occasion.)

|  |  |
|---|---|
| **CONTE:** Bela voce! bravissma! | **COUNT:** Bravissimo! a fine voice, truly! |
| **ROSINA:** Oh, mille grazie! | **ROSINA:** A thousand thanks! |
| **BARTOLO:** Certo, bella voce; / Ma quest' aria, cospetto! è assai no-josa. / La musica a miei tempi era altra cosa: / Oh! quando, per esempio, cantava Cafariello / Quel' aria portentosa—'Là, là, là!' / Sentite, Don Alonzo, eccola quà. / Quando mi sei vicina, / Amabile Rosina, / L' aria dicèa Giannina, / Ma io dico Rosina; / Il cor mi balza in petto, / Mi balla il minuetto. / (*A Figaro, che entra contra fiecondolo.*) / Bravo! Signore Barbiere! | **BARTOLO:** Yes, truly, a fine voice; / But, then, good Lord! that air is very tiresome. / In my time music was another thing: / Oh! when, for instance, / Cafariello sung that wondrous air— / "La, la, la!" / List, Don Alonzo, I will give it you. / With that bewitching mein, ah! / Oh, come to me, Rosina! / And on my arm, oh, lean, ah! / There let me chant my lay; / Or, if you more incline, ah! / To dancing, so divine, ah! / Then thus in grace we'll twine, ah! / With minuetto sway. / (*To Figaro, who enters, mimicking him.*) / Bravo! Mr. Barber. |
| **FIGARO:** Eh niente affatto. / Scusi sue debolezze. | **FIGARO:** Oh! no harm, sir; / Excuse my folly. |
| **BARTOLO:** Ebben, gridone, / Che vieni a far? | **BARTOLO:** Well, rogue, / And what have you come here for? |
| **FIGARO:** O bella! / Veggo a farvi la barba—oggi vi tocca. | **FIGARO:** Here for! / Why, I have come to shave you— / this is your day. |
| **BARTOLO:** Oggi non voglio. | **BARTOLO:** Oh, not today—I don't wish it. |
| **FIGARO:** Oggi non vuol? domani / Non potrò io. | **FIGARO:** Not today? but / Tomorrow I can't come. |
| **BARTOLO:** Perchè? | **BARTOLO:** And why not? |
| **FIGARO:** Perchè ho da fare. / E poi—e poi—che serve? / Doman non posso. | **FIGARO:** Because I am otherwise engaged. / And then—and then—what does it matter? / I cannot come tomorrow. |
| **BARTOLO:** Orsù, meno parole: / Oggi non vo' far barba. | **BARTOLO:** Come, less chattering; / I'll not be shaved today. |
| **FIGARO:** Ma? che mi avete preso / Per un qualche barbier da contadino? / Chiamate pur un altro;—io me ne vado. | **FIGARO:** What? Do you treat me / As you would some country barber? / Then find some other person;—I am off. |
| **BARTOLO:** Che serve?—a modo suo— / (Vedi che fantasia!) / Và in camera a pigliar la biancheria. / No; vado io stesso. | **BARTOLO:** Well, what signifies it?—this is his way— / What a whimsical dog! / Quick! into my room, and bring the cloth. / No; I'll go myself. |
| **FIGARO:** (Ah, se mi dava in mano / Il mazzo delle chiavi, ero a cavallo.) / Dite, non è fra quelle / (*A Rosina.*) / La chiave, che apre quella gelosía? | **FIGARO:** (Oh, if he would hand me / That bunch of keys, all would be right.) / Tell me, is not the key / (*To Rosina.*) / Which opens that lattice among them? |
| **ROSINA:** Sì certo; è la più nuova. | **ROSINA:** Yes; and it is the newest. |
| **BARTOLO:** (Ah son per buono / A lasciar quì quel diavolo di barbiere!) / Animo, va tu stesso: / (*Dando le chiavi a Figaro.*) / Passato il corridor, sopra l' armario / Il tutto troverai. / Bada non toccar nulla. | **BARTOLO:** (Oh, I'm mighty wise / To leave that devil of a barber here!) / Here, go yourself: / (*Giving the keys to Figaro.*) / Pass yonder corridor, and on the shelf / You will find everything. / Have a care, but touch nothing. |
| **FIGARO:** Ah, non son matto. / (Allegri!) Vado e torno. / (Il colpo è fatto!) / (*Entra.*) | **FIGARO:** Eh, I am no fool. / O be joyful! I'll be back in an instant. / (The trick is done!) / (*He goes in.*) |
| **BARTOLO:** E quel briccon, che al Conte / (*Al Conte.*) / Ha portato il biglietto di Rosina. | **BARTOLO:** That's the rascal, sir, who brought / (*To the Count.*) / The Count's letter to Rosina. |
| **CONTE:** Mi sembra un imbroglion di prima sfera. | **COUNT:** He seems a very adept in intrigue. |
| **BARTOLO:** Eh, a me non me la fic-ca— / (*Si scente di dentro rumore come di vasellonne che al spezza.*) / Ah, disgraziato me. | **BARTOLO:** Ah, he'll not trick me— / (*A noise within, as of some earthen vessels breaking.*) / Oh, I'm undone. |
| **ROSINA:** Ah, che rumore? | **ROSINA:** What noise was that? |
| **BARTOLO:** Ah, che briccon! me lo diceva il core. / (*Entra.*) / Tutto mi ha rotto, tutto; / Sei piatti, otto bicchieri, una terri-na. | **BARTOLO:** Oh, the rascal! I felt my heart misgive me. / (*Goes in.*) / He has broken everything, / Six plates, eight basins, one tureen. |
| **FIGARO:** Vedete che gran cosa! ad una chiave / Se mai non m'attaccava per fortuna. / (*Mostrando al Conte la chiave della golosia.*) / Per qual maledettissimo / Corridor, così oscúro, / Spezzato mi sarei la testa al muro. / Tiene ogni stanza al bujo; e poi—e poi— | **FIGARO:** A might matter, truly! had I not hit / Upon the key by good fortune, / (*Showing the Count the key of the veranda.*) / In that same cursed / Corridor, I should have broken / My head against the wall. / He keeps every room so dark; and then— |
| **BARTOLO:** Oh, non più. | **BARTOLO:** No more of this! |
| **FIGARO:** Dunque, andiam. (Giudizio.) / (*Al Conte, e Rosina.*) | **FIGARO:** Come, then. (Be prudent.) / (*To the Count and Rosina.*) |
| **BARTOLO:** A noi. / (*Si siede a farsi radere.—Entra Basilio.*) | **BARTOLO:** Proceed to business. / (*He seats himself to be shaved; at this moment enter Basilio.*) |

## SCENA IV

*Don Basilio, e detti.*

## SCENE IV

*Don Basilio, and the preceding.*

|  |  |
|---|---|
| **ROSINA:** (Don Basilio!) | **ROSINA:** (Don Basilio!) |
| **CONTE:** (Cosa veggo?) | **COUNT:** (What do I see?) |
| **FIGARO:** (Quale intoppo!) | **FIGARO:** (What an unfortunate encounter!) |
| **BARTOLO:** Come quà? | **BARTOLO:** How is this? |
| **BASILIO:** Servitor di tutti quanti. | **BASILIO:** Good day to you all. |
| **BARTOLO:** (Che vuol dir tal novità!) | **BARTOLO:** (What an unexpected visit!) |
| **FIGARO E CONTE:** (Qui franchez-za ci vorrà.) | **FIGARO AND COUNT:** (Some courage is necessary here. |
| **ROSINA:** (Ah, di noi che mai sarà!) | **ROSINA:** (Alas! what will become of us!) |
| **BARTOLO:** Don Basilio, come state? | **BARTOLO:** Basilio, how do you find yourself? |
| **BASILIO:** Come sto! | **BASILIO:** Find myself! |
| **FIGARO:** Or che s'aspetta? / (*Interrompendolo.*) / Questa barba benedetta! / La facciamo sì, o nò? | **FIGARO:** Who is to wait here? / (*Interrupting him.*) / That blessed beard of yours! / Shall I operate on it or no? |

# Act II, Scene IV

**BARTOLO:** Ora vengo. / I'll be with you directly.
*(A Figaro.)* / *(To Figaro.)*
E là il curiale— / And the lawyer—
*(A Basilio.)* / *(To Basilio.)*

**BASILIO:** Il curiale!— / The lawyer!—

**CONTE / COUNT:** Io gli ho narrato / I have already told him
Che già tutto è combinato; / That everything is arranged;
Non è ver? / Is it not true?

**BARTOLO:** Sì; tutto io sò. / Yes; I know it all

**BASILIO:** Ma, Don Bartolo spiegatemi— / But, Don Bartolo, explain to me—

**CONTE / COUNT:** (Ehi, dottore, una parola—) / Doctor, a word with you—
*(Interrorapendolo.)* / *(Interrupting him.)*
Don Basilio, son da voi. / Don Basilio, I shall be with you immediately.
*(A Bartolo.)* / *(To Bartolo.)*
Ascoltate un poco quà. / Listen to me a moment.
*(A Figaro.)* / *(To Figaro.)*
(Fate un pò ch'ie vada via, / (Try and get him off,
Ch'ei ci scopra ho gran timore.) / Else I fear he will discover us.)
*(Piano, a Bartolo.)* / *(Softly, to Bartolo.)*
(Della lettera, Signore, / (Of the affair, sir, of the letter,
Ei l'affare ancor non sà.) / Recollect, he knows nothing.)

**BARTOLO:** Colla febbre, Don Basilio, / With this fever, Don Basilio,
Chi v'insegna a passeggiare? / Who taught you to walk abroad?
*(Figaro, ascoltando con attenzione, si prepara a secondare il Conte.)* / *(Figaro, listening with attention, prepares to second the Count.)*

**BASILIO:** Colla febbre! / With a fever!
*(Attonito.)* / *(Astonished.)*

**FIGARO:** E chi vi pare? / Why, what think you?
Siete giallo come un morto. / You are as yellow as a corpse.

**BASILIO:** Come un morto? / As a corpse, say what?

**FIGARO:** Bagatella! / Heavens, man!
*(Tastandogli il polso.)* / *(Feeling his pulse.)*
Cospetton che tremarella! / Zounds, what a galloping pulse!
Questa è febbre scarlatina. / It's certainly the scarlet fever.

**FIGARO E CONTE / FIGARO AND COUNT:** Via, predete medicina. / Go home, take medicine.
*(Il Conte da a Basilio una borsa di soppiatto.)* / *(The Count secretly gives a purse to Basilio.)*

**FIGARO:** Presto, presto andate a letto— / Quick, quick, home to bed—

**CONTE / COUNT:** Voi paura in ver mi fate— / I am quite alarmed for you—

**BARTOLO E ROSINA / BARTOLO AND ROSINA:** Dice bene, andate a letto— / He says well; go home to bed—

**TUTTI / ALL:** Presto andate a riposar. / Quick, retire, and rest yourself.

**BASILIO:** (Una borsa!—Andate a letto!— / (A purse!—Go to bed!—
Ma che tutti sian d'accordo.) / They all seem of the same mind.)

**TUTTI / ALL:** Presto a letto. / Quick, home to bed.

**BASILIO:** Eh, non son sordo, / Eh, I'm not deaf;
Non mi faccio più pregar. / Pray cease your entreaties.

**FIGARO:** Che color—eh! / What a color—eh!

**CONTE / COUNT:** Che brutta cera! / Oh! what a rueful visage!

**BARTOLO:** Brutta cera! / 

**FIGARO:** / Rueful visage!

**FIGARO E CONTE / FIGARO AND COUNT:** Oh, brutta assai. / Rueful, truly.

**BASILIO:** Dunque vado. / Well, I'm going.

**TUTTI / ALL:** Andate, andate. / Go, go!

**ROSINA E CONTE / ROSINA AND COUNT:** Buona sera, buona sera; Buona sera, mio Signore; Buona sera, mio Signore; Presto andate via di quà. / Fare you well, then, good Signore; Fare well, then, good Signore; Fare well, then, good Signore; Peace and joy and better health.

**ROSINA:** (Maledetto seccatore!) / (Plague upon you, can't you stir, ah!)
Presto, andate via di quà. / Quick, begone, and nurse yourself.

**BASILIO:** Buona sera—ben di cuore— / Oh, good night, I quite agree—
Obligato—in verità. / I really am much obliged.
(An, che in saco va il tutore!) / (Guardy's in the trap I see!)
Non gridate, intesi già. / Cease your noise, I go, good man.
*(Parte.)* / *(Exit.)*

**BARTOLO:** Son quà. / I am here.
*(Bartolo siede, e Figaro disponesi a fargli la barba; durante l'operazione va comprendo i due amanti.)* / *(Bartolo seats himself, and Figaro prepares to shave him, during the operation he conceals the two lovers.)*
Stringi bravissimo. / Now work away.

**CONTE / COUNT:** Rosina, deh ascoltatemi. / Rosina, now attend to me.

**ROSINA:** V'ascolto, eccomi quà. / I'm all attention, sir.
*(Siedono fingendo studiar la musica.)* / *(They sit down, pretending to be at their musical studies.)*

**CONTE / COUNT:** (A mezza notte in punto, / At midnight precisely,
*(A Rosina con cautela.)* / *(Cautiously, to Rosina.)*
A prendervi quì siamo; / We'll wait for you here;
Or che la chiave abbiamo. / For since we've the keys
Non v'e da dubitar.) / We have nothing to fear.

**FIGARO:** Ahi! ahi! / Ahi! ahi!
*(Distrando Bartolo.)* / *(Calling off Bartolo's attention.)*

**BARTOLO:** Che cosa è stato? / What's the matter?

**FIGARO:** Un non sò che nell' occhio! / Something flew in my eye,
Guardate, non toccate— / Look, but don't touch it:
Soffiate per pietà. / Blow, for pity's sake.

**ROSINA:** A mezza notte in punto, / At midnight, precisely,
Anima mia, t'aspetto; / My love, I'll await you;
Io già l'istante affretto, / May the moments be fleeting
Che teco m' unirà. / That remain before we are united.

**BARTOLO:** Ma lasciami vedere! / No, let me look!

**FIGARO:** Vedete, chi vi tiene? / Well, look; who hinders you?

**ROSINA E CONTE / ROSINA AND COUNT:** Do, re, mi, fa, sol, la. / Do, re, mi, fa, sol, la.

**CONTE / COUNT:** Ora avvertirvi voglio, / But now I tell you,
*(Bartolo si alza. e si avvicina agli amanti.)* / *(Bartolo rises, and draws near the lovers.)*
Cara che il vostro foglio, / That I showed your letter,
Perchè non fosse inutile / In order that I might disguise
Il mio travestimento. / Myself much better.

**BARTOLO:** Ma bravi, ma bravissimi! / Oh, excellent, forsooth!
Ma bravi, in verità! / Excellent, in very truth!
Bricconi! birbanti! / Rascals! scoundrels!
Ah, voi tutti quanti / I see you've all
Avete giurato / Conspired this day
Di farmi crepar. / To haste my fall.
Uscite furfanti! / Avaunt!
Vi voglio accoppar! / Or I shall slay you all!
Di rabbia, di sdegno / I'm nearly like to die with rage.
Mi sento crepar.

**CONTE, ROSINA E FIGARO / COUNT, ROSINA AND FIGARO:** L'amico delira; / Your friend is delirious:
La testa gli gira. / His head is oppressed.
Dottore, tacete, / Be silent, good doctor,
Vi fate burlar. / It is only a joke.
Tacete, partiamo; / Peace, peace, let's away;
Non serve a gridar. / We've been overheard.

Intesi ci siamo—
Non v'è a replicar.
(*Partono.*)

This clamor is useless—
He'll not hear a word.
(*Exeunt.*)

## SCENA V

*Berta, sola.*

**BERTA:** Sempre gridi e tumulti in questa casa;
Si litiga, si piange, si minaccia.
Non v'è un'ora di pace
Con questo vecchio avaro e brontolone.
Oh, che casa! oh, che casa di confusione!
Il vecchietto cerca moglie,
Vuol marito la ragazza:
Quello freme questa è pazza—
Tutti e due son da legar.
Ma che cosa è questo amore
Che fà tutti delirar?
Egli è un male, universale,
Una smania, un pizzicore,
Un solletico, un tormento;
Poverina! anch'io lo sento,
Nè so come remediar.
Ah, vecchiaia maledetta!
Son da tutti disprezzata,
E arrabiate—disperata,
Mi convien così crepar!
(*Parte.*)

## SCENA VI

*Don Bartolo, introducendo Don Basilio.*

**BARTOLO:** Dunque voi Don Alonzo
Non conoscete affatto?

**BASILIO:** Affatto.

**BARTOLO:** Ah, certo
Il Conte lo mandò. Qualche gran trama
Quì si prepara.

**BASILIO:** Io dico
Che quel garbato amico,
Era il Conte in persona.

**BARTOLO:** Il Conte?

**BASILIO:** Il Conte!
(*La borsa parla chiaro.*)

**BARTOLO:** Sia che si vuole—amico, al notaro
Vo' in questo punto andare, in questa sera
Stipular di mie nozze io vo' il contratto.

**BASILIO:** Il notar! siete matto?
Piove a torrenti; e poi,
Questa sera il notaro
E impegnato con Figaro; il barbiere
Marita una nipote.

**BARTOLO:** Una nipote!
Che nipote?—Il barbiere
Non ha nipoti. Ah, quì v'è qualche imbroglio,
Questa notte i bricconi
Me la voglion far. Presto, il notaro
Quà venga sull' istante;

## SCENE V

*Bertha, alone.*

**BERTHA:** There is nothing but noise and clamor in this house;
Nothing but disputing, weeping, and threatening.
There's not an hour's peace
With this avaricious old wrangler.
Oh, what a house! what a house of confusion!
The fond old dotard seeks a wife,
The merest girls for husbands pine
The one a fool, the other mad—
In jacket straight I'd all confine.
What can this love be
That drives the folks mad?
Some all happiness seem,
While other are sad.
It is something that teases,
That plagues and inspires;
Even I am its prey,
And am scorched by Love's fires.
But because I am old.
I am passed by all;—
Ah, I expire with rage!
With vexation I die!
(*Exit.*)

## SCENE VI

*Don Bartolo, introducing Don Basilio.*

**BARTOLO:** Then you don't know Don Alonzo at all?

**BASILIO:** Not at all.

**BARTOLO:** Ah, surely
He was sent by the Count! Some great scheme
Is, no doubt, in agitation.

**BASILIO:** I tell you
That this friend
Was no other than the Count himself.

**BARTOLO:** The Count himself?

**BASILIO:** The Count!
(*This purse clearly bespeaks it.*)

**BARTOLO:** Let him be what he may—
I will hasten this moment to the notary,
And settle the marriage contract.

**BASILIO:** To the notary! are you mad?
It rains in torrents; and, besides,
This evening the notary is to be
with Figaro: the barber
Gives his niece in marriage.

**BARTOLO:** His niece?
What niece?—The barber
Has no nieces. Ah, there must be some plot here.
This very night the scoundrels will
Lie in wait to betray me. Haste, and call

Ecco la chiave del portone—andate,
Presto, per carità.
(*Gli dà una chiave.*)

**BASILIO:** Non temete; in due salti io torno quà.
(*Parte.*)

## SCENA VII

*Bartolo, indi Rosina.*

**BARTOLO:** Per forza, o per amore,
Rosina avrà da cedere, cospetto!—
Mi viene un altra idea. Questo biglietto,
(*Cava dalla tasca il biglietto datogli dal Conte.*)
Che scrisse la ragazza al Conte Almaviva,
Potria servir—Che colpo da maestro!
Don Alonzo, il briccone,
Senza volerlo mi diè l' armi in mano.
Ehi, Rosina! Rosina!
(*Rosina dalla sue camere esce senza parlare.*)
Avanti, avanti;
Del vostro amante io vi vo' dar la novella.
Povera sciagurata in verità,
Collocaste assai bene il vostro affetto!
Del vostro amor, sappiate,
Ch'ei si fa gioco in sen d'un altro amante;
Ecco la prova.
(*Le dà il biglietto.*)

**ROSINA:** Oh cielo! il mio biglietto!

**BARTOLO:** Don Alonzo, e il barbiere
Congiuran contro voi; non vi fidate.
In potere del Conte d' Almaviva
Vi vogliono condurre—

**ROSINA:** (In braccio a un'altro!
Che mai sento?—Ah Lindoro!—Ah traditore!
Ah sì!—vendetta! e vegga
Quell'empio chi è Rosina.)
Signore, sposarmi,
Voi bramavate?

**BARTOLO:** E il voglio.

**ROSINA:** Ebben, si faccia!
Io son contenta—ma all'istante.
Udite:
A mezza notte quì barbier;—con lui fuggire,
Per sposarlo io voleva.

**BARTOLO:** Ah, scellerati!
Corro a sbarar la porta.

**ROSINA:** Ah, mio Signore!
Entran par la finestra: hanno la chiave.

**BARTOLO:** Non mi muovo di quì!
Ma—e se fossero armati?—Figlia mia,
Poichè ti sei si bene illuminata,

The notary, instantly;
Here is the key to the door—go,
Make haste, for goodness' sake.
(*Gives him a key.*)

**BASILIO:** Don't be alarmed; in two minutes I will be here again.
(*Exit.*)

## SCENE VII

*Bartolo, then Rosina.*

**BARTOLO:** Either by force, or love,
Rosina shall yield, I am determined!—
I have another thought. The note,
(*Takes from his pocket the note given him by the Count.*)
Which the girl wrote to Almaviva,
May serve—Oh, what a masterly thought!
That rascal, Don Alonzo,
Has undesignedly put weapons into my hands.
Eh, Rosina! Rosina!
(*Rosina comes from her room without speaking.*)
Come here, come here;
I have some news to give you from your lover
Poor unhappy girl! in truth,
You have placed your affections on a noble object!
Know that, in the arms of another,
He makes a joke of your affections;
Behold the proof.
(*He gives her a note.*)

**ROSINA:** Oh, heaven! my note!

**BARTOLO:** Don Alonzo and the barber
Are conspiring against you: do not trust them.
They wish to give you up
Into the arms of Count Almaviva—

**ROSINA:** (Into the arms of another!
What do I hear?—Oh, Lindor!—
Oh, betrayer!
Ah, yes!—vengeance—I will teach the wretch,
Who is Rosina,
Tell me, sir, do you
Wish to marry me?

**BARTOLO:** I do.

**ROSINA:** Well, let it be done!
I am content—let it be instantly.
Listen:
At midnight the wretch will be here,
With Figaro, the barber;—and it was settled,
That I should fly and marry him.

**BARTOLO:** Oh, wretches!
I hasten to bar the door.

**ROSINA:** Oh, my dear sir!
They are to enter by the window: they have the key.

**BARTOLO:** I will not stir from this spot!
But suppose they should be armed?
My dear child,

Facciam così. Ti chiudi a chiave in camera,
Io vo a chiamar la forza.
Dirò che son due ladri, e come tali,
Corpo di Bacco! l' avremo da vedere!
Figlia, chiuditi presto: io vado via.
(*Parte.*)

**ROSINA:** Quanto, quanto è crudel la sorte mia!
(*Parte.*)
(*Un temporale. Si vede aprire le gelosia, ed entrare un dopo l'altro Figaro, ed il Conte avvolti in mantelli.*)

## SCENA VIII

*Conte, Figaro, indi Rosina.*

**FIGARO:** Al fine eccoci quà.

**CONTE:** Figaro, dammi man. Poter del mondo!
Che tempo indiavolato!

**FIGARO:** Tempo da innamorati!
(*Figaro accendde i lumi spiando.*)

**CONTE:** Ehi, fammi lume,
Dove sarà Rosina?

**FIGARO:** Ora vedremo—
Eccola appunto.

**CONTE:** Ah mio tesore—
(*Con trasporta.*)

**ROSINA:** Indietro,
(*Respingendolo.*)
Anima scellerata! Io quì di mia
Stolta credulità venni soltanto
A riparar lo scorno; a dimostrarti
Qual io sono, e quale amante
Perdesti, anima indegna, e sconoscento!

**CONTE:** Io son di sasso!

**FIGARO:** Io non capisco niente.

**CONTE:** Ma per pietà!—

**ROSINA:** Taci! Fingesti amore,
Sol per sagrificarmi
A quel tuo vil Conte Almaviva—

**CONTE:** Al Conte?—
Ah, sei delusa. Ah me felice! adunque!
Tu di verace amore.
Ami Lindor!—rispondi—

**ROSINA:** Ah, sì! t'amai pur troppo!

**CONTE:** Ah, non è tempo
Di più celarsi. anima mia! ravvisa,
(*S'inginocchia, gettando il mantello.*)
Colui che sì gran tempo:
Seguì tue traccie; e che per te sospira:

Since you are now so awake to your situation,
Let us act thus. Shut yourself up in your room,
While I go and see for assistance.
I will declare they are two thieves, and as such,
By Bacchus! we shall see what the consequence will be!
Child, shut yourself up immediately: I go.
(*Exit.*)

**ROSINA:** How cruel! how cruel is my fate!
(*Exit.*)
(*A storm. The veranda is seen to open, and one after the other, Figaro and the Count enter, wrapped up in mantles.*)

## SCENE VIII

*The Count, Figaro, then Rosina.*

**FIGARO:** At last, here we are.

**COUNT:** Figaro, your hand. By the powers!
What a tempestuous night!

**FIGARO:** Truly, a lover's night!
(*Figaro lights the candles, and looks around.*)

**COUNT:** Eh, show a light.
Where can Rosina be?

**FIGARO:** We soon shall see—
There she is.

**COUNT:** Ah! treasure of my soul—
(*With transport.*)

**ROSINA:** Stand off,
(*Repulsing him.*)
Wretch that you are! I have come here
To repair the fault of my
Too foolish credulity; to show you
What I am, and what a mistress
You have lost, unworthy and thoughtless man.

**COUNT:** I am petrified!

**FIGARO:** I know not what this can mean.

**COUNT:** But, for mercy's sake!—

**ROSINA:** Peace! You have pretended love,
In order to sacrifice me to the wishes
Of the vile Count Almaviva—

**COUNT:** To the Count?—
Ah, you are deceived. Happy that I am!
Then you return with truth
The affections of Lindor!—answer—

**ROSINA:** Ah, yes! I loved him but too well!

**COUNT:** This, then, is the moment
At which to reveal myself. My sweetest life,
(*He kneels, throwing aside his mantle.*)
Behold one who
Has followed your steps for so long;

Che suo ti vuol. Mirami, o mio tesoro!
Almaviva son io: non son Lindoro.

**ROSINA:** Ah, qual colpo inaspettato,
Egli stesso! oh ciel! che sento!
Di sorpresa, di contento,
Son vicina a delirar!

**CONTE:** Qual trionfo inaspettato!
Me felice! oh bel momento!
Ah, d'amore, di contento,
Son vicina a delirar!

**FIGARO:** Son rimasti senza fiato!
Ora muojon dal contento;
Guarda, guarda il mio talento,
Che bel colpo seppe far!

**ROSINA:** Mio Signore—ma voi—ma io—

**CONTE:** Ah, non più, non più, ben mio!
Il bel nome di mia sposa
Idol mio! t'attende già.

**ROSINA:** Il bel nome di tua sposa;
Ah, qual gioja al cor mi dà.

**ROSINA E CONTE:** Dolce nodo avventurato,
Che fai paghi i miei desiri!
Alla fin de' miei martiri,
Tu sentisti Amor, pietà.

**FIGARO:** Presto, andiamo: vi sbrigate,
Via, lasciate quei sospiri;
Se si tarda, i miei raggiri,
Fanno fiasco in verità.

**ROSINA E CONTE:** Dolce nodo avventurato!
Che fai paghi i miei desiri;
Alla fin de' miei martiri,
Tu sentisti, Amor, pietà.
(*Figaro va al balcone.*)

**FIGARO:** Ah, cospetto! che ho veduto?
Alla porta—una lanterna—
Due persone—che si fa?

**CONTE, ROSINA E FIGARO:** Zitti, zitti, piano, piano, Non faciam più confusione, Per la scala del balcone Presto andiamo via di quà! Non facciamo confusione. Presto, andiamo via di quà! Non facciamo confusione, Presto, andiamo, via di quà! Per la scala dal balcone, Presto andiamo, via di quà! Piano, piano! Per la scala dal balcone, Presto andiamo via di quà!

**CONTE:** Che avvenne mai?
(*Vanno per partire.*)

**FIGARO:** La scala—

**CONTE:** Ebben—

**FIGARO:** La scala non v'è più.

who sighs for you:
Who hopes to possess you. See,
treasure of my kind
I am Almaviva: I am not Lindor.

**ROSINA:** What unexpected bliss,
What peace without alloy!
Oh, heavens! It is he indeed,
I'm almost mad with joy!

**COUNT:** My triumph is complete
No more shall doubt annoy!
This moment all repays,
I'm almost mad with joy!

**FIGARO:** One moment all was grief!
The next they kiss and toy;
But thanks to my designs,
Their hearts are filled with joy!

**ROSINA:** Dear sir—but you—but I.

**COUNT:** No, never fear, my love!
The blessed name of wife!
Awaits you from above.

**ROSINA:** The blessed name of wife!
What joy it gives my heart.

**ROSINA AND COUNT:** Oh, happy bond of love, We'll never, never part!
The fates proved propitious,
And gave us heart for heart.

**FIGARO:** Quick, let us hence: have done with sighs,
All difficulty's passed;
But often, acts too long delayed,
To nothing come at last.

**ROSINA AND COUNT:** Oh, happy bond of love!
We'll never, never part!
The fates propitious proved,
And gave us heart for heart.
(*Figaro runs to the balcony.*)

**FIGARO:** Ah, zounds! what do I see?
At the door—a lantern—
Two persons—what is to be done?

**COUNT, ROSINA AND FIGARO:** Step as soft as zephyrs dying, Through the window gently hieing, Down the ladder quickly flying, Trip it lightly and away!

**COUNT:** Through the window gently hieing. Trip it lightly and away! Through the window gently hieing, Trip it lightly, and away! Down the ladder quickly flying, Trip it lightly and away! Piano, piano! Down the ladder quickly flying, Trip it lightly and away!

**COUNT:** What has happened?
(*About to depart.*)

**FIGARO:** The ladder—

**COUNT:** Well—

**FIGARO:** The ladder is gone.

CONTE: Che dici?

FIGARO: Chi mai l'avrà levata?

CONTE: Quale inciampo crudel!

ROSINA: Me sventurata!

FIGARO: Ah, zitti! sento gente,
(ora ci siamo.)
Signor mio, che si fa?

CONTE: Mia Rosina, coraggio.
(Si ravvoglie nel mantello.)

FIGARO: Eccoli quà.
(Si ritirano verso le quinte.)

## SCENA IX

*Don Basilio con lanterna, introducendo un Notajo con carta in mano.*

BASILIO: Entrate qui Don Bartolo.

FIGARO: Don Basilio!
(*Chiamando dalla quinta apposta, accennando al Conte.*)

CONTE: E quell'altro?

FIGARO: Ve', ve', nostro notajo.
Allegramente!
Lasciate fare a me. Signor Notajo.
(*Basilio e il Notajo si rivolgono, e restano sorpresi. Il Notajo si avvicina a Figaro.*)
Dovevate in mia casa
Stipular questa sera
Un contratto di nozze
Fra il Conte d' Imaviva e mia nipote
Gli sposi, eccoli quà! Avete indosso
La scrittura? Benissimo!
(*Il Notajo cava una scrittura.*)

BASILIO: Ma, piano;
Don Bartolo dov'è?

CONTE: Ehi, Don Basilio,
(*Chiamande a parte Basilio e cavandosi un'anello dal dito, e gli addita di tacere.*)
Quest'anello è per voi.

BASILIO: Ma io—

CONTE: Per voi
Vi sono ancor due palle nel cervello
Se v'opponete.

BASILIO: Oibo prendo l'anello.
Chi firma?

ROSINA E CONTE: Eccoci quà.
(*Sottescrivone.*)

CONTE: Son testimonj
Figaro e Don Basilio;—essa è mia sposa.

FIGARO E BASILIO: Evviva!

CONTE: Oh mio contento!

ROSINA: Oh, sospirata mia felicità!

TUTTI: Evviva!
(*Nell' atto che il Conte bacia la mano a Rosina. e Figaro abbraccia Basilio, entra Bartolo come appresso.*)

---

COUNT: What did you say?

FIGARO: Who could have taken it away?

COUNT: What a cruel obstacle!

ROSINA: I am so unhappy!

FIGARO: Ah, hush! somebody is coming, and here we are.
What is to be done?

COUNT: Courage, my dear Rosina.
(*Wraps himself in his mantle.*)

FIGARO: Here they are.
(*They retire to the side.*)

## SCENE IX

*Don Basilio with a lantern, introducing a Notary with a paper in his hand.*

BASILIO: Come in, Don Bartolo.

FIGARO: Don Basilio!
(*Calling to the opposite side, beckoning to the Count.*)

COUNT: And that other?

FIGARO: Oh, oh, our notary. Delightful!
Leave the affair to me. Mr. Notary.
(*Basilio and the Notary turn round, and remain surprised. The Notary approaches Figaro.*)
This evening
You were to settle in my house,
The marriage contract between
The Count Almaviva and my niece
Here are the parties! Have you indorsed
The papers? Oh, very well!
(*The Notary takes out a paper.*)

BASILIO: But softly;
Where is Don Bartolo?

COUNT: Here, Don Basilio,
(*Calling Basilio aside, and taking a ring from his finger, beckons him to be silent.*)
This ring is for you.

BASILIO: But I—

COUNT: You
(*Taking out a pistol.*)
Will have two balls in your head
If you offer any opposition.

BASILIO: O Lord! I take the ring.
Who signs?

ROSINA AND COUNT: Here we are.
(*They sign.*)

COUNT: Figaro and Don Basilio
Are witnesses;—this is my wife.

FIGARO AND BASILIO: Viva!

COUNT: How am I blessed!

ROSINA: Oh, long-sighed-for happiness!

ALL: Viva!
(*While the Count is kissing the hand of Rosina, and Figaro is embracing Basilio, enter Bartolo in haste.*)

---

## SCENA ULTIMA

*Don Bartolo, un Alcalde, Alguazils, Soldati, e detti.*

BARTOLO: Fermi tutti. Eccoli quà.
(*Additando Figaro e il Conte all' Alcade, e slanciandosi contro Figaro.*)

FIGARO: Colle buone, Signor.

BARTOLO: Signor, son ladri;
Arrestate, arrestate!

UFFIZIALE: Signore,
(*Al Conte.*)
Il suo nome.

CONTE: Il mio nome? Egli è quel
d'un nom d'onore;
Lo sposo io son di questa—

BARTOLO: Eh, andate al diavolo!
Rosina esser dève mia sposa, non e vero?

ROSINA: Come debbo esser sua?
Oh nemmen per pensiero.

BARTOLO: Come, come, fraschetta! ah, son tradito.
Arrestate, vi dico:
E un ladro!

FIGARO: Or, or l'accoppo.

BARTOLO: E un birbante, è un briccone.

UFFIZIALE: Signore?
(*Al Conte.*)

CONTE: Indietro!

UFFIZIALE: Il nome—

CONTE: Indietro, dico; indietro!

UFFIZIALE: Ehi, mio Signor, abbassi quel tuono;—
E chi è lei?

CONTE: D' Almaviva il Conte io sono.
(*Scoprendosi.*)

BARTOLO: Insomma, io ho tutti i torti.

FIGARO: Pur troppo è così.

BARTOLO: Ma tu briccone—
Tu pur tradirmi, e far da testimonio!

BASILIO: Ah Dottore Bartolo mio,
Quei Signor Conte certe ragioni
Ha in tasca; certi argomenti
A cui non si risponde.

BARTOLO: Sì, sì, ho capito tutto.

CONTE: Ebben, Dottore?

BARTOLO: Sì, sì, che serve? quel
ch'è fatto è fatto.
Andate pur; che il Ciel vi benedica!

FIGARO: Bravo, bravo,
un'abbraccio!
Venite quà, Dottore.

ROSINA: Ah, noi felici!

CONTE: Oh, fortunato amore!

---

## SCENE THE LAST

*Don Bartolo; an Alcalde, Alguazils, Soldiers; and the preceding.*

BARTOLO: Hold, all of you. There they are.
(*Pointing out Figaro and the Count to the Alcalde, and rushing towards Figaro.*)

FIGARO: Softly, sir, softly.

BARTOLO: Sir, they are thieves;
Arrest them, arrest them.

OFFICER: Sir, your name.
(*To the Count.*)

COUNT: My name? It is that of a man of honor;
I am husband to this lady—

BARTOLO: Eh! go to the devil!
Rosina is to be mine;—is it not true?

ROSINA: How! yours!
No; not even in thought.

BARTOLO: How now, wench! Ah, I have been betrayed!
Arrest him, I tell you:
He is a thief!
(*Pointing to the Count.*)

FIGARO: I shall be the death of him.

BARTOLO: He is a rogue—a scoundrel!

OFFICER: Sir?
(*To the Count.*)

COUNT: Stand off!

OFFICER: Your name—

COUNT: Stand off, I say; stand off.

OFFICER: Eh, my good sir, lower that tone;—
Who are you?

COUNT: I am the Count Almaviva!
(*Discovering himself.*)

BARTOLO: The fact is, I bear all the blame.

FIGARO: Ay, and justly, too.

BARTOLO: But you, you rascal—
Even you to betray me, and turn witness!

BASILIO: Ah, doctor,
The Count has certain persuasives
And certain arguments in his pocket,
Which there is no withstanding.

BARTOLO: Ay, ay! I understand you.

COUNT: Well, Doctor?

BARTOLO: Well, well, what matters it? what's done is done.
Go, and may Heaven bless you!

FIGARO: Bravo, bravo, Doctor!
Let me embrace you.

ROSINA: Oh, how happy we are!

COUNT: Oh, propitious love!

## Act II, Last Scene

**FIGARO:** Di si felice innesto,
Serbiam memoria eterna,
Io smorzo la lanterna,
Quì più non ho che far!

**BARTOLO:** Amore e fede eterna,
Si vegga in voi regnar.

**ROSINA:** Costò sospiri e pene,
Un sì felice istante
Alfin quest'alma amante,
Comincia a respirar!

**FIGARO:** Young Love, triumphant smiling,
All harsher thoughts exiling,
All quarrels reconciling.
Now waves his torch on high!

**BARTOLO:** Young Love, our hearts beguiling,
Bids care and sorrow fly.

**ROSINA:** May all our lot now viewing,
Find every hour renewing
The joys of youth's first wooing,
And happy prove as I.

**CONTE:** Dell' umile Lindoro,
La fiamma a te fu accetta
Più bel destin t'aspetta,
Sù, vieni a giubilar.

**CORO:** Amore e fede eterna,
Si vegga in voi regnar!

*END OF THE OPERA.*

**COUNT:** The humble Lindor wooed you,
And kind was your reply;
A brighter fate pursued you—
No more, then, heave a sigh.

**CHORUS:** May love, our hearts beguiling,
Bid care and sorrow fly!

*END OF THE OPERA.*

# William Tell (1829)

MUSIC BY GIOVACCHINO ROSSINI ■ LIBRETTO BY ÉTIENNE DE JOUY & HIPPOLYTE BIS ■ BASED ON FRIEDRICH SCHILLER

This four-act opera premiered at the Paris Opéra on August 3, 1829. It is set to a libretto by Etienne de Jouy and Hippolyte Bis (from Friedrich Schiller). In an Alpine village, William Tell is thinking about Austria's domination over Switzerland. Edwidge, Tell's wife, and Jemmy, his son, are working. Melchthal berates his son, Arnold, because he is not married. Arnold tells him that he is in love with Mathilde, the daughter of the Austrian governor Gessler. Tell helps a shepherd, Leuthold, escape from Gessler's troops after he killed a soldier who tried to kidnap his daughter. The soldiers set the village on fire and take Melchthal hostage. In a valley near Lake Lucerne, Arnold and Mathilde tell each other of their love. Mathilde implores Arnold to join the Austrians so that he may gain glory so that they can wed. Tell then arrives with the news of Melchthal's death. Arnold swears to fight on the side of the Swiss patriots, and Tell rouses them with a call to arms. Arnold tells Mathilde of his intentions and she promises to be loyal to him. Near Gessler's castle, the governor calls upon the people to bow before a pole which he has erected, bearing his hat on top. Tell and his son refuse to do this and are accused of assisting in Leuthold's escape. Tell is ordered to shoot an apple off Jemmy's head, which he hesitates to do. Jemmy assures him that he will stand still, and Tell shoots his arrow straight at the target. He tells the cheering crowd that he would have shot Gessler if he had missed the apple and injured his son. Gessler arrests them, but Jemmy is spared and placed in Mathilde's custody. Arnold and the Swiss patriots prepare for war. Mathilde and Jemmy arrive with news that Tell has escaped. Jemmy gives the signal for battle to begin. A storm breaks out; Gessler manages to reach safety in his boat, but is killed by an arrow shot by Tell. The patriots celebrate Switzerland's freedom from tyranny.

---

## ■ ATTO I

### SCENA I

*Il Teatro representa una specie di Villaggio in mezzo alle Montagne—A destra dell' attore un Torrente, che va a perdersi sulla sinistra in mezzo alle Recce—In lontano le alte Montagne della Svizzera—Sopra una Roccia a sinistra la Casa di Guglielmo Tell—Sul davanti altre tre capanne.*

*Guglielmo Tell, pensoso, appoggiato alla sua vanga—Eduige e Jemmy intenti a vari lavori rustici—Un Pescatore nella sua barca sul torrente.*

**CHORUS:** E il ciel seren, sereno e il giorno, Tutto d'intorno parla d'amor, L'ecogiuliva di questa riva ripeta il giubbilo de nostri cor, di nostri cor, ripeta il giubbilo de nostri cor! Coll'opre ognuno, poi presti omaggio. del mondo ognor, del mondo ognor, Al Creator! E il ciel seren, sereno e il giorno, Tutto d'intorno parla d'amor! Coll'opre ognuno poi presti omaggio, del mondo ognor al Creator!

**PESCATORE:** Deh vieni, o mia diletta,
In sen di mia barchetta;
Deh! vieni, ove t' aspetta

Il tenero mio cor.
Io lascio il lido, o Lisa,
Non sii da me divisa;—
Il ciel sereno ê pegno
A noi d'un grato di.

**GUG:** (Dolce è per lui la cura
Del foco ond' arde in seno,
Nè prova il rio veleno
Che mi divora il cor.
Perchè vivere ancora
Or che il destin ci umilia?
Ei canta; e Elvezia intanto
Ahi quanto-piangerà!).

**PES:** Gentil come la rosa
D' un bel mattin nascente,
Potrai d' un ciel fremente
Plascar, ben mio, l' orror.
Ed al tuo fianco assiso
Novella vita io spero,
Proteggerà il mistero
Le gioie dell' amor.

**EDU. E JEM:** Felice nell' orgoglio
D' un tenero abbandono,
Delle tempeste il suono
Non desta in lui timor.
Ma se al temuto scoglio
Lo tragge avversa sorte,
L'inno unirà di morte
A' canti dell' amor.
(*Odonsi in poca distanza suoni e grida di gioja.*)

**TATTI:** Oh! quale altra d'intorno
Dolce armonia risuna!
Di festa il lieto giorno
Ne viene ad annunziar.
Del sol siccome il raggio

## ■ ACT I

### SCENE I

*The scene represents a Village in the midst of Mountains—From the right descends a Torrent, which disappears among the Rocks below—The high Mountains of Switzerland bound the distance—On a Rock to the left is seen the House of William Tell—In the foreground are three Huts.*

*At the rising of the curtain, William Tell is discovered, leaning on his hoe—Edwidge and Jemmy engaged in rural occupations—A Fisherman seated in his boat, which is fastened to the shore.*

**CHORUS:** Fair is the morning, shining upon the mountains, Light from the eastern skies, joy from above, From cliffs rebounding, sweet echo sounding, Joyful repeats our song; fervent and pure and strong, Praising the Maker of day and of night! The Great Creator, Loudly we praise you, Father of all, Maker of all, Maker of all! Fair is the morning, shining on the mountains, Light from the eastern skies, joy from above! All things we're praising anthems upraising, singing to praise the God of love!

**FISHERMAN:** Come here, my dearest love!
In my little boat embark;
Ah! come here and rejoice

My loving heart with your smile.
Though I must leave, Eliza dear,
Do not let me depart alone.
See how the shining sky above predicts
A brilliant day

**WIL:** (Of love he lightly sings,
In his heart so lately kindled;
For the cares he hath no feeling
Which now my heart oppress.
For me what blandishments has life
While my country thus is humbled?
He sings; and yet Switzerland
In lamentation languishes!)

**FISH:** Gentle as the bending rosebud,
Born in the morning's early dew,
Heaven's threatened tempests wild
Will love, appease your presence;
When I'm seated by your side,
What new life my soul receives!
There's a Providence above us that will protect
Our hearts' affections

**EDW & JEM:** In the full conviction happy,
Of affection fond requited,
The sound of the tempest raging
Awakens no fear in him.
But if on the treacherous rock
Should adverse fate propel him,
With hymns of death he'll mingle
His present songs of love.
(*Sounds of rejoicing heard in the distance*)

**ALL:** Oh! what harmony enchanting
All around salutes us!
Of a coming festival
It is the glad announcement.

# Act I, Scene I

Risplende a' flor' sereno,
La gioja in ogni seno
Rivive, e sente amor.

As do the sun's bright rays
The budding flowers expand;
So joy revives the heart
And ignites the bosom with love!

*Entre Melchtal, dalla collina, seguite da altri suizzeri, Arnoldo e detti.*

*Enter Melchtal, descending the hill, followed by Arnold and Swiss Peasants.*

**TUTTI:** Salute, onore, omaggio
Al saggio-tra i pastor'.

**ALL:** Health, honor, and happiness
To the wisest of our shepherds.

**EDU:** Il rito si rinnovi
Di tempi men funesti,
E premio alfin ritrovi
La fedeltà, l' amor.

**EDW:** Let us renew the rites
Of less unhappy times;
And may meet reward attend
On fidelity and love.

**ARN:** (L' amore—oh, Dio!—
l'amore!—
Oh, qual pensier!—io gelo!)

**ARN:** (Love!—Oh, heavens!—who
speaks of love?
I shudder at the painful thought.)

**EDU:** (*Pregandolo a voler celebrare le nozze de' Pastors.*) Per te fien lieti.

**EDW:** (*To Melchtal, requesting him to complete the nuptials of the Peasants.*) Their happiness complete.

**MEL:** (Oh, cielo!)

**MEL:** (Oh, great Heaven!)

**EDU:** E ognuno il fia per te.

**EDW:** Let all be made happy by you.

**GUG:** Della virtù, degli anni
Il privilegio è questo
Cedi, e giammai funesto
Il ciel per noi sarà.

**WIL:** Such is the privilege of virtue
and old age;
Comply with their wishes,
And Heaven will smile on us.

**MEL:** (*Cedendo alle istanze che gli vengano fatte.*) Alzate insieme il canto,
E celebrate in sì bel giorno
Le pure gioje d' imene e amor.

**MEL:** (*Yielding to the solicitations of the Shepherds.*) Now raise on high your voices,
And celebrate, this festive day,
The joys of Hymen and of love!

**TUTTI:** Alziamo, alziamo insieme il canto,
Celebriamo in sì bel giorno
Le pure gioje d' imene e amor.
Al fremer del torrente
S' alzi di gioja il grido,
E l eco-dolcemente
Da questo ameno lido
A' monti, al bosco, al piano
Il suon ripeterà.
(*Il Coro parte.*)

**ALL:** We'll raise on high our voices
and celebrate, this festive day,
The joys of Hymen and of love.
Above the torrent's crashing roar
Let our joyous songs be heard,
And Echo, in her sweetest tones,
From these shores, over the mountains,
Through the forests, through the plains,
Will the glad sound repeat.
(*Exeunt Chorus.*)

**GUG:** Contro l' ardor del giorno
Il solingo mio tetto
V' offre sicuro ed ospital ricetto.
Ivi, nel sen di pace,
Vissero gli avi miei;
Ivi io fuggo i nemici,
E a' sguardi loro ascondo
Che, padre essendo, io son felice al mondo.
(*Abbracciando il figlio.*)

**WIL:** Against the meridian heat
My lonely habitation
Offers you a shelter safe and hospitable.
There, in peaceful serenity,
Have my ancestors long lived;
I fly from my foes,
And there I conceal from them
The happiness I have in being a father.
(*Embracing his Son.*)

**MEL:** Egli è padre, e felice—
(*Ad Arnoldo.*)
Udisti, figlio mio?
Questo è il maggior de' beni. E vorrai sempre
Della mia lunga età schernire i voti?
La festa de pastori
Con un duplice nodo
Consacra in questo giorno di contento
I giuri dell' imen—ma il tuo non sento
(*Partono tutti fuorchè Arnoldo.*)

**MEL:** A father, and a happy one, is he!
(*To Arnold*)
Did you not hear him, my son?
Of all the blessings the greatest!
And will you neglect
The hopes of my old age—
The festival of the shepherds
On this day consecrates
A double Hymeneal vow;
But I have not heart of your's!
(*Exeunt all but Arnold.*)

**ARN:** (*Solo.*) Il mio giuro, egli disse!
Il mio giuro!—Giammai. Perchè a me stesso
Tacer non posso in qual fatale oggetto
Son rapiti i miei sensi?
O tu, di Gessler aura, eppur si umana,
O mia Matilde, io t' amo,
T' adoro, e l' onor mio
Per te il dover, l' Elvezia, il padre obblio.
Contro la micidial valanga io fui
Di scudo a' giorni tuoi;
Illustre donna, io te salvai da morte,
Te che destina altroi l' empia mia sorte.
(*Odesi un suono di caccia.*)
Ma quel suon!—Del superbo i rei seguaci
Scendon dal monte—Oh, Dio!
Ivi è Gessler, e seco è l' idol mio!—
Veder, udire io voglio
Colei che m' innamora—
Se reo son io, sia almen, felice ancora.
(*Per partire.*)

**ARN:** (*Solus.*) My promise, said he?
My promise!—Ah, never!—Why can't I conceal
The fatal object from myself
Which my whole soul enthrals?
O you, of Gessler the sister, and yet so fair!
O, my Matilda, how I love you!
I adore you!—and for you I neglect
My honor, my country, and my father!
With this arm I snatched you from the deadly avalanche.
Ah! noble lady, from death I saved you
And cruel fate yields you to another
(*The sound of a horn heard.*)
What sound is that!—The minions of the tyrant
Descend the mountain heights!—
Oh, God!
Gessler is there, and with him comes my idol.
I must see her, and once more hear
The voice that my soul enchants!
And, if it is a crime, still there's bliss in it!
(*Going.*)

*Entra Guglielmo.*

*Enter William.*

**GUG:** Non fuggire! qual mai dolor ti preme?
D' amico l' appressar
A fermarti non vale?

**WIL:** Fly not! what trouble ails you?
Can a friend's approach detain you
For a while?

**ARN:** No, no!

**ARN:** No, no!

**GUG:** Perchè tremar?

**WIL:** Why do you tremble?

**ARN:** (Ah, che finger tento invano.)
Mentre opprime il fiero strano
Ogni cor or prova il duol.

**ARN:** (Ah! vain is all dissembling.)
While the tyrant's yoke continues,
My heart is overwhelmed with grief.

**GUG:** Io provo un duol più ch' altri vero
(Arnoldo il suo non svela già.)

**WIL:** My grief surpasses all other
(The cause of his Arnold tells not.)

**ARN:** Altra sciagura v' ha!

**ARN:** Other miseries await us!

**GUG:** Che dì tu? qual mister? perchè tacer?

**WIL:** What did you say? What mystery? Why are you silent?

**ARN:** Che speri tu?

**ARN:** What do you desire?

**GUG:** Il tuo dover membrarti, e tua virtù,
Arnoldo.

**WIL:** To recall you, Arnold, to your duty
And honor.

**ARN:** Ah, Matilde, io t' amo, e amore
Spegner debbo nel mio core,
Ma se il chiede il patrio onore
In me tregua abbia il dolor.

**ARN:** Ah! Matilde, dearly do I love you;
But from my heart the passion I must root,—
If my country and my honor so demand
The sacrifice I must cease to mourn.

**GUG:** Leggo appieno nel suo core,
Della colpa ei sente orror,
Serve è vero all' oppressore
Ma se pur fu traditore,
Mostra almeno il suo dolore
Che detesta un tanto error.
Per noi dubbio, taccia, e tema
Se v' è ardir si vincerà.

**WIL:** The remorse of his heart I clearly read
In the blanched aspect of his countenance;
That the tyrant he has served is true,
But if he has been unfaithful to us,
His grief attests to his repentance
And that his error he now regrets.
We have no need for doubt or fear—
If true to ourselves, we shall conquer.

**ARN:** In noi possa tanta v' ha?

**ARN:** What power do we possess?

GUG: Possa immensa ha chi non trema.

ARN: Contro all' armi, l' oppressor, In voi forza ov' è?

GUG: Nel cor Se non manca in noi valor. Si cadrà l' empio stranier.

ARN: Quanto perdi ohimè!

GUG: Non calmi.

ARN: Gloria speri trarne or tu?

GUG: Ancor non so che sia cotesta gloria, Ma ben io so che sia la schiavitu.

ARN: La tua speranza?

GUG: E la vittoria! In te giova sperarla.

ARN: Si vincerà.

GUG: Dubbio non v' ha.

ARN: Vinti, qual è il nostro asil?

GUG: Las tomba.

ARN: E il nostro gran vendicator?

GUG: Il ciel.

ARN: Quando è l' ora del periglio, Io son presto fido amico.

GUG: Attendi.
(*Odesi un suono di caccia.*)

ARN: Oh, momento fatal!

GUG: Melchtal, Melchtal! che sento, è Gessler, come? Mentre ei ne sprezza Vorresti tu piegar l' umil cervice Il bene a mendicar d' un bieco sguardo?

ARN: Ah! quei severi accenti Per me son duro oltraggio. Io volo al suo passaggio, Gessler a minacciar.

GUG: Lungi da noi precipitata impresa: Pensa al padre ed il proteggi; Della patria alla vendetta.

ARN: Mio padre!

GUG: (Ei dubita.)

ARN: La patria!

GUG: (E pallido.)

ARN: E l' amor mio.

GUG: (E qual è il suo mistero?)

ARN: Che penso? Ciel pietoso tu lo sai, Se Matilde è a me diletta, Ma virtù mi chiama e aspetta, Odio e morte all' oppressor.

GUG: Delle nozze da lungi odo il canto. Non s' attristi la gioja ai pastor, Il piacer non sia misto col pianto, Ed un sol di non segni il dolor.

---

WIL: Strength enough has he who does not doubt

ARN: What force have we to meet the army of the tyrant?

WIL: In our hearts. If our doesn't valor fail us, The tyrant will surely fall.

ARN: Think, should defeat await you?—

WIL: I care not.

ARN: Do you hope for glory to win?

WIL: What this glory is I know not— But too much I know of bondage.

ARN: Then what do you hope for?

WIL: Victory!—and victory I hope to win through you!

ARN: You expect to conquer.

WIL: I have no doubt of it.

ARN: But, if conquered, where our refuge?

WIL: In the tomb.

ARN: And who will avenge our fall?

WIL: Heaven!

ARN: When the hour of danger comes, Faithfully I will stand by you.

WIL: Listen!
(*The sound of a horn heard*)

ARN: Oh, perilous moment!

WIL: Melchtal, Melchtal! what do I hear? 'Tis Gessler While we are condemned by him, Would you, coward like, bend to him, And supplicate his scornful favour?

ARN: Ah! these words sarcastic and unkind Put an insult on my honor;— On his passing, I will cross him, And bid defiance to this Gessler.

WIL: Let us do nothing rashly: First let your father be made safe, And then let us free our country.

ARN: O, my father!

WIL: (He hesitates.)

ARN: And my country!

WIL: (He turns pale.)

ARN: And my love!

WIL: (He has thoughts that he will not reveal.)

ARN: What shall I do? Heaven, you know my thoughts. How dear to me Matilda is! But to my country I yield my love, Till death the oppressor shall lay low.

WIL: Afar I hear the nuptial hymns. Let us not abridge the shepherds' joy, Let not their mirth be mingled with grief, Let this one day be free from care.

---

*Entrano Jemmy, Eduige, Il Pescatore, Melchtal, Svizzeri, due Fidanzante, ed i loro Sposi.*

ARN: (Oh, smania!)

MEL: (*Agli sposi.*) Allor che il cielo La vostra fede accoglie, Bendirvi degg' io.

GUG: Chi d' onorar s'assume La molta età, suol riverire il Nume.

ARN: (Il lor contento m' è al cor velen. Oh, mio tormento!—fatale amore!)

CORO: Ciel, che del mondo sei l' ornamento, Splendi secondo, al lor contento. Puio è l' affetto nel loro petto, Come la luce d' un dì seren.
(*A' due sposi.*)

MEL: Delle antiche virtudi L' esempio rinnovate; O figli miei, pensate Che il suolo ove nasceste, al vostro imene Domanda degli appoggi e de' custodi. E voi, gentili a lor fide compagne, Chiusa e nel vostro petto La lor posteritarde. I figli vostri, Degli avi lor fian degni: Da voi l' Elvezia attende i suoi sostegni.
(*Odesi il suono della caccia.*)

GUG: (Gessler di nuovi!)

ARN: Andiamo.
(*Partono.*)

GUG: (Gessler proscrive i voti!)

EDU: Quai t' agitan trasporti?
(*A Guglielmo.*)
Perchè liberamente sian palesi IL dì sorgea—

GUG: Lo spero; Ma più Arnoldo non vedo.

EDU: E ne lascia.

GUG: Ei mi fugge. Pur cela indarno il turbamento suo. Volo ad interrogarlo; E tu ravvia i giuochi.
(*A Eduge.*)

EDU: M' agghiaccia di spavento, E mi parli di festa?

GUG: Cela il fragore a' rei della tempesta, Può soffocarla della gioja il canto. Fia chi l' odano i erudi Quando le prische avrem nostre virtudi.
(*Parte.*)

CORO: Cinto il crine—di bei fiori, Tra gli amori—scendi Imen. Teco alfine—pace scenda E ne renda—lieti appien.

---

*Enter Jemmy, Edwidge, Fisherman, Melchtal, and Peasants, ushering two Brides and Bridegrooms.*

ARN: (Oh, vengeance!)

MEL: (*To the Brides and Bridegrooms.*) Now that your vows are recorded, in heaven, I must give you my blessing.

WIL: He who reveres old age Will himself be blessed in heaven.

ARN: (Their merriment to my heart but sorrow brings.) Oh, agony!—oh! love most fatal!

CHORUS: Oh, Heaven! of earthly bliss the source, On their loves propitious deign to look;— Pure as the celestial light above Are the affections which unite them.
(*To the Bridegrooms*)

MEL: You'll now endeavor to emulate the bright example of your ancestors; Remember, O my children dear, That your country, from this your union, For guardians and protectors looks; And you, their companions, gentle and fair, On whose fond care our early youth depends will imbue, The minds of their offspring With sentiments worthy of their ancestors;— On you Helvetia rests for succour.
(*The sound of the chase heard.*)

WIL: (Gessler is here again!)

ARN: Let us begone.
(*Exit.*)

WIL: Gessler will thwart your wishes.

EDW: What is it that agitates you?
(*To William.*)
Already your anger dawns the day To give vent to.

WIL: I hope so; But I no longer see Arnold.

EDW: He has left us.

WIL: He avoids me. But the troubles he ill conceals which afflict him. I will go, and interrogate him, While you keep up the merriment.
(*To Edw.*)

EDW: Your words alarm me, And yet of merriment you speak!

WIL: Thus may the roar of the coming tempest Be masked in sounds of revelry;— Such sounds shall assail our tyrant's ears, When we have regained our liberties!
(*Exit.*)

CHORUS: Your brow adorned with sweet flowers. Descend, O Hymen, by Cupids guarded;

---

Per te solo—tace il duolo;
Per te lieto vive il cor,
Muta resta—la tempesta
Nelle gioje dell' amor.

JEM: Ecco colà, tremante,
E reggendosi appena,
Madre; un pastor s' inoltra—

PES: Egli è il buon Leutoldo.
Qual frangente lo guida?

*Entra Leutoldo*

LEU: Salvatemi!
(*Appoggiandosi sopra una scure insanguinata.*)
EDU: Che temi?
LEU: Il loro sdegno.
EDU: Parla.—Chi ti minnaccia?

LEU: Quell' empio, che giammai
Perdona; il più crudele,
Di tutti il più funesto—
Deh! mi salvate, o tro voi spento io resto.

MEL: Che festi?
LEU: Il mio dovere!
Solo di mia famiglia
Lasciammi il cielo un' adorata figlia
Un vil seguaco del governatore
Rapirla osava al mio paterno amore—
Quest' arma mia l' oppresse—
Ah! lo vedete voi: quest' è il suo sangue.

MEL: Cielo!—chi lo sostiene?
Tutto pe' giorni suoi temer conviene.

LEU: Sopra l' opposta sponda
Un certo asil m' avrei—Deh! mi vi guida.
(*Pregando il Pescatore.*)

PES: Il torrente e la rocca
Vietano avvicinarsi ove tu brami,
E l' affrontarli, o misero,
E darsi a certa morte.

LEU: Oh, quanto ingiuste
Sei meco! all' ultim' ora
Non oda i tuoi rimorsi il sommo nume.

*Entra Guglielmo.*

GUG: (Egli spar), nè a rinvenirlo io giunsi.)
Sciagurato Leutoldo!
(*Voci di dentro.*)

LEU: Gran Dio! tu sol mi puoi salvar.

---

Joyous Plenty bring here with you;
And happy henceforth render us.
Through you alone our sorrows cease;
Through you alone our hearts rejoice;
In silence hushed, the tempest sleeps
Amid the sweet delights of love.

JEM: See! a trembling shepherd advances,
Who scarcely can sustain himself,
Mother, behold—he comes this way.

FISHERMAN: It surely is the worthy Leuthold!
What sad event can bring him here?

*Enter Leuthold.*

LEU: O, pray save me! (*Supporting himself upon a hatchet still reeking with blood.*)
EDW: What fear you?
LEU: Their vengeance.
EDW: Speak—Who has threatened you?

LEU: That monster impious and cruel,—
Who never pardons—shows no mercy—
Amongst the most unrelenting tyrants;—
Save me;—or on this spot they'll slay me!

MEL: What have you done!
LEU: My duty!
Of all my once large family Heaven left me;
An only daughter
One of the minions of the governor dared to steal her
From her father's bosom;—
And by this weapon he has fallen!—
Ah! behold—here streams the wretch's blood!

MEL: O, heavens! who will dare protect him!
His life is now in direst peril!

LEU: To the opposite shore bear me;
There a safe asylum I shall find.
(*Soliciting the Fisherman.*)

FISH: Between the torrent and the rocks,
That shore to reach would be impossible;—
The mere attempt, unhappy man,
Would certain death be to us both.

LEU: Oh! can you refuse me?
In your last moments may the Almighty
Your prayers reject.

*Enter William.*

WIL: (He escaped, and I could no where find him.)
O, unhappy Leuthold!
(*Voices within*)

LEU: Great God! you alone can save me now.

---

GUG: Io sento minacciar e dolersi—

LEU: Oh mio Guglielmo!
Crudo destin m' opprime—
Mi si persegue: non son reo, mel credi,
E per sottrarmi al mio crudel destino,
Quello mi resta solo arduo cammino.

GUG: Tu l' doi, pescator? salvarlo.

LEU: E vano:
Come il tristo Gessler egli è crudele.

GUG: Sventurato!—che apprendo?
Ma s' ei lo nega, io di salvarti intendo.

VOCI DI DENTRO: Chiede sangue l' assassinio,
E Leutoldo il verserà!

GUG: Vieni, vieni, t' affretta—
(*A Leutoldo.*)

EDU: A morte vai.

GUG: Non temer, Eduige;
Trova sicura guida
L' nom che nel cielo interamente affido.
(*Scende in un battello, e vogando parte con Leutoldo.*)

*Entrano Rodolfo e Coro di Soldati.*

CORO DI SVIZZERI: Nume pietoso, Dio di bontà!
Salvar clemente tu puoi, Signor,
Dell innocente il difensor.

ROD E SOL: Di morte e scempio e giuta l' ora.
Sciagura all' empio! convien che mora.

JEM: Egli è salvo.

ROD: Oh, mio furor!

SVIZ: Superato ha il rischio omai.

EDU: (Non invano il ciel pregai.)

JEM. E MEL: (Ah! perchè, perchè, l' etade
Non risponde al mio desir!)

ROD: (M' è d' oltraggio il lor goder.)

SVIZ: (Mugge il tuon sul nostro capo:
Di tempesta egli è forier.
Fuggiam—fuggiam.)

ROD: Restate,
E tosto a me svelate
Chi l' assassino ha salvo,
Chi l' trasse in securità.
Tosto obbedite.
O, chi tace cadrà.
(*I Soldati circondano gli Svizzeri.*)

SOL: (Treman tutti di già.)

JEM: (Che sento?—oimè!)

---

WIL: Threats and wailing my ears, assail.

LEU: Oh, my dear William,
A fearful fate awaits me;
I am pursued—but I am not guilty,
Believe me!—From danger free me:
This dreadful passage alone remains.
(*Pointing to the opposite shore.*)

WIL: You hear him, fisherman;—you'll save him?

LEU: It is in vain;—
He is cruel as Gessler is wicked.

WIL: Poltroon! what do I hear?
But if he denies you, I will yet save you.

VOICES WITHIN: Murder must be expiated by blood,
And that of Leuthold shall be shed!

WIL: Come—quickly come—delay not.

EDW: On death you rush.

WIL: Fear not, Edwidge;—
A sure protection will he find
Who puts his trust in Heaven.
(*He springs into the boat and rows off with Leuthold.*)

*Enter Rodolf, and a Chorus of Soldiers*

CHORUS OF SWISS PEASANTS:
Pitying Heaven, God of mercy,
You alone, in your clemency,
Can now preserve the innocent.

ROD & SOL: For death and vengeance the hour is come;
Seize the murderer—he must die!

JEM: He is safe!

ROD: Oh, I'm furious!

SWISS: He is beyond the reach of danger.

EDW: (Not in vain have I prayed to heaven.)

JEM E MEL: (Ah! why—oh, why
does my strength not respond now
To my wishes!)

ROD: (Their joy is an insult to my pride.)

SWISS: (The thunder roars above our heads;
A coming storm it forebodes—
Let us fly—let us fly.)

ROD: Remain here,
And quickly disclose to me
Who the assassin has saved—
Who has conveyed him to a place of safety?
Obey! or you shall die!
(*The Soldiers surround the Swiss Peasantry.*)

SOL: (Fear now overwhelms them.)

JEM: (What do I hear?—Alas!)

**EDU:** (Già m' ingombra il terrore!)

**EDW:** I am now overcome with fear!)

**SVIZ:** (Pietoso cielo accogli
Il voto, il priego nostro!
Dall' ira di quel mostro
Ne salva per pietà!
Di noi che mai sarà?)

**SWISS:** (Merciful Heaven! kindly listen
To our wishes—to our prayers!
From the vengence of this monster
Graciously relieve us;
Or what will become of us?)

**MEL:** Ciò ch' ei fece; ognun di noi
L' oserebbe. Ardir, amici.

**MEL:** What he has done, so would each of us
Have done.—Take courage, friends.

**ROD:** Ah! tremate—Il reo svelate.

**ROD:** Ah! tremble, or give up the guilty one.

**MEL:** Sciagurato! questo suolo.

**MEL:** Miscreant!—this fair land
Is not the seat of treachery!

**ROD:** Quel ribaldo circondate;
(A Soldati, che afferrano Melchtal.)
E sia tratto al mio signor.
Su, via, struggete; tutto incendete:
Orma non resti d' abitator.
Strage e ruina sia la lor sorte.
Lampo di morte è il mio furor.

**ROD:** Surround and seize that villain;
(To the Soldiers, who surround Melchtal)
And let him be taken before my lord.
Approach—destroy or burn all things
Leave no trace of living habitation;
Let slaughter and ruin of all be the lot;
My fury shall be like the breath of death!

**SOL:** Lampo di morte è il suo furor.

**SOL:** His fury shall be like the breath of death!

**JEM:** Sì, sì, struggete; tutto incendete;
Ma in ciel v' ha un Nume vendicator.
Te forse un giorno farà perduto
L' arco temuto del genitor.

**JEM:** Yes, yes,—destroy or burn all our chattels;
But above there is a God avenging,—
Justice may perhaps one day overtake you,
Through the trusty bow of my father!

**EDA MEL PES. E SVIZ:** Sì, sì, struggete, tutto incendete;
Ma in ciel v' ha un Nume vendicator.
Verrà un gagliardo, il di cui dardo
Saprà punire un oppressor.
(Malgrado l' opposizione de' suoi Compagns, Melchtal è circondato e trascinato da' Soldati di Rodolfo.)

**EDW. MEL. FISH. & SWISS:** Yes, yes, all our chattels destroy or burn;
But above there is a God avenging!
A man will arise whose arrow true
shall carry punishment
To the tyrant.
(Notwithstanding the opposition of his companions, Melchtal is surrounded by the Soldiers of Rodolf, and made Prisoner.)

*Fine Dell' Atto Primo.*

*END OF THE FIRST ACT.*

# ■ ATTO II

## SCENA I

*Valle profonda tra le Montagne del Rutli—A sinistra si scorge parte del Lago de' Quattro Cantoni.—Crepuscole.*

*Entrano Cacciatori—Pastori sono scopriti in dietro recando le uccise belve.*

**CORO DI CACCIATORI:** Qual silvestre metro intorno
Si congiunge al nostro corno?
Mesce il daino il suon morente
Al fragore del torrente;
Ed allor ch' estinto resta,

# ■ ACT II

## SCENE I

*A deep Valley among the lofty Mountains of Rutli—On the left is seen part of the Lake of the Four Cantons—Twilight.*

*Enter Huntsmen—Shepherds discovered in background carrying slain wild animals.*

**CHORUS OF HUNTSMEN:** Hark! the rural sounds around us
Are blending with our mellow horns,
The death-cry of the gentle deer rings

Chi il gioja può imitar?
Il furor della tempesta
Può quel giubbilo uguagliar.

With the torrent's roar
Yet, when the chamois dies
The hunter rends the skies with shouts
The raging of the tempest
Alone can equal this joy!

**CORO DI PASTORI:** Dal raggiante lago intorno
Cade il giorno;
Il suo placido sereno
Sparve intorno;
La'campagna del villaggio
Di partenza è a noi messaggio.
Già cade il dì.
(Partono.)

**CHORUS OF SHEPHERDS:** From the placid lake above us
The day is departing;
The mild rays of the setting sun
Are disappearing;
The village evening bell reminds us
That the hour of repose is nigh;—
Fast fades the day.
(Exeunt.)

**CORO DI CACCIATORI:** La molesta voce è questa
Del monotono pastor.
Di Gessler risuona il corno;
Ciascum riede al suo soggiorno
Già cade il dì.
(Partono.)

**CHORUS OF HUNTSMEN:** These are the tedious hymnings
Of the shepherd so monotonous;
The stirring blasts of Gessler's horns
Should summon Huntsmen to their homes;
Let us depart.
(Exeunt.)

*Entra Matilde, distaccandosi furtivamente da' Cacciatori.*

*Enter Matilda, furtively, as they go off*

**MAT:** S' allontanano alfine!
Io spero rivederlo,
E il cor non m' ha ingannato;
Ei mi seguia—Esser non dee lontano—
Io tremo!—Oimè!—Se qui venisse mai!
Che fia quel sentimento
Profondo, misterioso,
Di che nutro l' ardor, che amar pur oso?
Arnoldo amato, ah! vieni!
Te sol desia quest' alma!
Da te lontana non ritrovo calma!
Vieni, a spegner l' ardor,
Che mi accendesti in seno!
Dal dì che il braccio tuo
A me salvò la vita,
L' immagin tua scolpita
Nel core mi restò.
Ah! vieni; l' amor mio
Nasconder più non so.

**MAT:** At last they have departed!
To see him once more, I trusted,
And my heart cannot have deceived me;
He followed me—far off he cannot be.
How I tremble!—Alas!—should he hither come!
What means that inward sentiment,
So deeply felt, so incomprehensible,
With which my love I feed and cherish!
Arnold, my beloved, oh! hither speed!
My heart fondly pants for thee
Away from you I feel no joy!
Come, and appease the burning flame
That you've kindled in my breast!
Since the day your arm so lusty
Nobly snatched me from destruction,
The image of your form so manly
On my heart has been engraven.
Ah! come;—no longer can my fondness languish
In hopeless concealment.

**MATILDA:** Selva opaco, deserta brughiera, Qual piacer vostra vista mi da; Sovra monti ove il turbine impera, Alla calma, alla calma il mio cor s'aprira. Eco sol . . . .
Eco sole . . . . . mie pene udira, le . . . . mie . . . . pene udira. Tu bell'astro al cui dolce riflesso, Il mio . . . passo vagando sen va, Tu mi addita ove Arnoldo s'aggira, A lui solo, a lui so lo, il mio cor s'aprira. Eco sol . . . Eco sol le mie pene udira. Eco sol le mie pene udira, udira. Eco sol le mie pene udira, . . . . udira.
Eco . . . .sol, eco . . . . sol.
*Entra Arnoldo*

**MATILDE:** Wild shady wood, whose deep shadow surrounds me, I prize you more than the pomp of a throne; here midst the storm that beats wildly around you, with the man that I love . . . . I would make you my home.
Echo, . . . .echo . . . . .Alone you hear;
Echo . . . alone . . . . you hear these words I say. May some bright star, with a holy influence, Guide and direct me wherever I roam; Tell me, I ask in spirit so lowly, How . . . . I may reveal to him this heart's love? Echo . . . .
Echo, alone you hear me. Echo al-

**ARN:** Perdona il mio venir,
I passi miei,
Incauto, sino a te spingere osai.

**MAT:** A mutua colpe è facile il perdono.
Arnoldo, io t' attenda.

**ARN:** Comandami, Matilde;
Fuggir dagli occhi tuoi;
Che abbandoni l' Elvezia, il padre mio;—
Morte trovar sopra straniera terra
Sceglier per tomba inospital foresta;—
Parla,—pronunzia un solo accento.

**MAT:** Arresta.
Tutto apprendi, sventurato,
Il segreto del mio cor.
Per te solo fu piagato,
Per te palpita d' amor.

**ARN:** Se il tuo foco è uguale al mio,
Se per me ti parla amor,
Al piacer ch' io sento, oh Dio!
Non può reggere il mio cor.
Ma tra noi qual mai distanza,
Quali ostacoli vi sono!

**MAT:** Ah! non perder la speranza;
Tutto il ciel ti dette in dono.

**ARN:** Dolci affetti! grati accenti!
Di piacer colmate il cor.

**MAT:** (Posso amarlo!—Quai momenti
Proverò di gioja e amor!)
Riedi al campo della gloria
Nuovi allori a conquistar.
Potrai sol colla vittoria
La mia destra meritar.

**ARN:** Riedo al campo della gloria
Nuovi allori a meritar,
Quanto in premio di vittoria
Cesserò di palpitar!

**A 2:** Il core che t' ama
Sol cerca, sol brama
Di viver con te.
Ah! questa speranza,
Che sola m avanza
Fia sempre con me!
(*S' ode un calpestio.*)

**MAT:** Alcun vien—Separiamci.

**ARN:** Potrò vederti ancora?

**MAT:** Al nuovo giorno,
Quando sorga l' aurora,
Nell' antico tempietto,
Al cospetto di Dio,
Da te riceverò l' ultimo addio.

**ARN:** Oh! sorpresa bonta!
(*Cadendole a pied i bacia la mano.*)

one, you hear me, you hear
me, . . . . you hear me.
Echo . . . . alone, echo alone.
*Arnold enters.*

**ARN:** Pardon my coming, I pray,
If my presence offend you;—
My steps have wended here unconsciously.

**MAT:** A mutual fault is easily pardoned.
Arnold, I have been expecting you,

**ARN:** Your commands, Matilda, give,
Thought they be to fly your presence
To abandon Helvetia, and my father dear;
In a strange land to meet an ignoble death,
Or in a forest to fill a nameless grave;—
Speak,—in one word my doom pronounce.

**MAT:** Stay,
And learn from me, unhappy man,
The secret of my trusting heart.
For you alone it grieves,
For you alone with love it beats.

**ARN:** If your love with mine be equal,
If for me your heart pleads,
The joy which I shall feel—oh, heaven!
My happy heart will scarce sustain!
But in our states what difference!
Think of the obstacle thus raised.

**MAT:** Ah! do not abandon hope—;
Heaven will favor our wishes.

**ARN:** Sweet avowal! welcome accents!
They suffuse my heart with delight.

**MAT:** (Then I may love him!—
What sweet hours
Shall I now have of joy and love!)
Now return to the field of glory,
Fresh laurels there to win and wear;
Returning victorious,
My hand will command your merit.

**ARN:** To the field of glory I'll return,
To win and wear fresh laurels there,
Returning victorious,
My merit may command your hand.

**TOGETHER:** Of this heart so loving
The great, the longing hope
Is to live with you.
Ah! that hope so cheering,
The only one fate yields me,
Will ever be with me.
(*A footstep heard.*)

**MAT:** Some one is coming—we must part.

**ARN:** When may I see you again?

**MAT:** At the earliest dawn
Of tomorrow's opening morn,
In the ancient tabernacle,
And in the Almighty presence,
I will receive your last adieu.

**ARN:** Oh! happiness unlooked for!
(*Kneeling at Matilda's feet, and kissing her hand.*)

**MAT:** Forza e lasiarti!

**ARN:** Ciel-Guglielmo!—Gualteno!—oh parti, parti.
(*Matilde s'allont*)

*Entra Guglielmo Tell e Valter.*

**GUG:** So o non eri in questo luogo.

**ARN:** Ebbene!

**GUG:** Un colloquio ben grato
A sturbar giunsi.

**ARN:** Eppure io non vi chiedo
A che mirate.

**VAL:** E forse,
Più che a ciascun, è a te mestieri
udirlo.

**GUG:** No. Ad Arnoldo che importa
S' egli abbandona i suoi,
S' egli in segreto aspira
A servir quell' indegno?

**ARN:** E donde il sai?

**GUG:** Dal fuggir di Matilde e dal tuo stato.

**ARN:** E tu mi vegli?

**GUG:** In questo cor lasciasti
Sin da jeri il sospetto.

**ARN:** Ma se amassi?

**VAL:** Gran Dio!

**ARN:** Se amato fossi,
I supposti sarian—

**GUG:** Veri.

**ARN:** E il mio amore—

**VAL:** Empio saria.

**ARN:** Matilde—

**GUG:** Ella è nostra nemica.

**VAL:** Ha nelle vene un abborrito
sangue.

**GUG:** E vilmente egli cade a' piedi
suoi.

**ARN:** Ma di qual dritto il cieco furor vostro—

**GUG:** Un solo accento, e ti sarà palese.
Schietto, Arnoldo, rispondi:—
Ami l' Elvezia tu?

**ARN:** Voi parlate d' Elvezia?
Ah! più non v' è per noi.
Io lascio queste rive
Abitate dall' odio,
Dalla discordia, dal timor—fantasmi
Che le rendono orrende:
In arene men triste onor m'attende.

**GUG:** Allor che scorre—de' forti il
sangue
Che tutto langue,—che tutto è orror,
La spada impugna,—Gessler difendi,
La vita spendi—pel traditor!

**MAT:** It is time I departed.

**ARN:** Heavens! William Tell! Walter!—Depart—oh, depart!
(*Exit Matilda.*)

*Enter William Tell and Walter.*

**WIL:** You have not been alone in
your seclusion.

**ARN:** Well, what then?

**WIL:** I fear I have disturbed an
agreeable tête-a-tète.

**ARN:** I ask no explanation
Of this intrusion.

**WAL:** Yet, perhaps,
More than any other you should ask
it.

**WIL:** No. To Arnold what can it import
That he abandons his friends,
If in secret he aspires to serve
That unworthy man?

**ARN:** How do you know that?

**WIL:** By Matilda's flight and your
confusion.

**ARN:** Then you have watched me?

**WIL:** In my bosom,
Suspicion has been excited since
last night.

**ARN:** But suppose I love?

**WAL:** Great Heaven!

**ARN:** If my love should be returned,
Your supposition then would—

**WIL:** Be true.

**ARN:** And my attachment—

**WAL:** Would be ill placed.

**ARN:** Matilda—

**WIL:** She is our bitter enemy.

**WAL:** Abhorent the very blood that
runs in her veins.

**WIL:** At her feet he meanly cast
himself.

**ARN:** By what right does your fury
blind—

**WIL:** One single question will explain all;
Truthfully now, Arnold, reply:—
Do you still love Helvetia?

**ARN:** Do you speak of Helvetia?
Ah! it no longer exists for us;
I am about to leave the land,
The abiding-place of hatred,
Discord, and cowardice—phantoms
Which to me make it odious;
Honor calls me to a less unhappy
land.

**WIL:** When the blood of the brave
is flowing freely,
When all is yielded to ruin,
The tyrant will defend your recreant sword;
You will risk your life for Gessler

ARN: Al campo solo—onor m' attende,
Ardir m' accende,—m' accende amor
Desio di gloria—m' invita all' armi,
E di vittoria—ardente il cor.

VAL: Estinto un vecchio—Gessler facea;
Quell' alma rea—svenar lo fe'.
Da noi vendetta—l' estinto aspetta,
E la domanda,—la vuol da te.

ARN: O, qual mistero!—
Un vecchio ei spense!—O, Dio!

VAL: Per te moria piangendo—

ARN: Ed è?—

VAL: Tacer, degg' io?

GUG: S' ei parla, il cor ti squarcia.

ARN: Mio padre!—

VAL: Sciagurato!
Ei stesso fu svenato,
Ei stesso cadde spento
Per man del traditor.

ARN: Ah, che sento!—O, delitto!—oimè—io moro—
Troncar suoi dì quell' empio ardiva,
Ed il mio acciar non si snudo?
Il padre, oimè! Mi mediva!
Ed io l' Elvezia allor tradiva!—
Cielo! mai più lo rivedro?

GUG: (Quali smanie! egli appena respira.
Il rimorso che il cor gli martira
Dell' amore ogni nodo spezzo.)

VAL: (A quel duolo già cede e delira,
Già la benda fatale strappò.)

ARN: E dunque vero?

VAL: Vidi il delitto,
Il derelito vidi spirar.

ARN: Che far?—Gran Dio!

GUG: Il tuo dover.

ARN: Morir degg' io—

GUG: Viver dei tu.

ARN: Quell' empio al suole cadrà svenato;
Io l' ho giurato pel genitor.

GUG: Deh! frenz i tuei trasporti
Calma quell' ira omai.

VAL: E vendicar potrai
L' Elvezia, il genitor

ARN: E a che tardiam?

ARN: To the camp my honor summons me,
Valor and love divides my heart;
The hope of glory invites me to arms.
My heart now pants for victory.

WAL: An aged man has been murdered by Gessler;
Ruthlessly has his life been taken.
On all of us his blood calls for vengeance—
From you it more than all demands it.

ARN: What mystery is this?
He put an old man to death!—Oh, Heaven!

WAL: He expired while weeping for you.

ARN: Name him.

WAL: Shall I disclose his name?

WIL: If he speaks your heart will break with grief.

ARN: It was my father!

WAL: Unhappy man!
He was the victim;
He was put to death
By the hand of the traitor.

ARN: Ah! what do I hear! What iniquity! I shall die!
The tyrant wickedly has taken his life;
And yet my sabre reposes in its sheath!
Alas! my father was needing his son's aid,
While I was even then betraying Helvetia,
Heavens! never again shall I behold him!

WIL: (What agony! scarcely can he draw his breath!
The remorse which his breast now lacerates
Has broken the shackles of his mad love.)

WIL: (Grief has driven him to delirium!
And has torn the fatal band from his eyes!)

ARN: Oh! can it be true?

WAL: I saw the deed done!
I saw the unhappy old man expire.

ARN: What shall I do?—Oh, God!

WIL: Do your duty.

ARN: Would you have me die?

WIL: No: you must live.

ARN: The miscreant shall fall by my own hand;—
His son will avenge a father's murder.

WIL: Ah! restrain this burst of passion—
Your troubled mind to calm surrender.

WAL: You shall have revenge
For Helvetia and your murdered father.

ARN: Why should we delay?

GUG: La notte,
A' voti nostri amica,
Già già distende un' ombra protettrice
E tu vedrai tra poco
Qui giunger cauti i generosi amici,
Che udranno i pianti tuoi:
E il vomere e la falce,
Cangiati in brandi ed aste,
Tentar con miglior sorte
Alla vendetta o morte.

TRIO: La gloria infiammi—i nostri petti;
Il ciel propizio—con noi cospira.
L' ombra del padre—il cor e' ispira.
Chiede vendetta—e non dolor.
Nel suo destino—ei fortunato,
Con la sua morte—par che ci dica
Che del martirio—il serto è dato
A coronare—tanta virtù.

VAL: Confuso de quel bosco
Sembrami udir fragor—
Ascoltaimo.

ARN: Silenzio.

GUG: Si ascoltiamo.
Di numerosi passi
Risuona la foresta.

ARN: Piu lo strepito appressa.

GUG: Chi s' avanza!

*Entrano abitanti d' Unterval.*

CORO: Amici del Elvezia.

VAL: O, sorte!

GUG: O, sorte!

ARN: O, mia vendetta!
Onore al cor del forte.

CORO: Con ardor—richiese il cor
Di sfidar—di superar
Ls distanza ed i perigli,
E ogni core con ardor
Brama vincere o morir.
Il vigor de' tuoi consigli
Nuovo in noi destava ardir

GUG: O d' Unterval voi generosi figli!
Questo nobile ardor non ne sorprende.

VAL: Imitarlo sapremo.
*(Si ode una tromba.)*
Degli amici di Svitz
Odo la tromba risuonar d'intorno.
E surto, o Elvezia, di tua gloria il giorno!

*Entrano Abitanti di Switz.*

WIL: The night,
Our designs kindly favoring,
Her shades already spreads over us;
And here speedily will you see
Our noble friends cautiously approach to claim,
Vengeance for your wrongs;—
The ploughshare and the peaceful scythe converted
Into spears and swords,
In surer hope to make the attempt,
Vowing to conquer or to die.

TRIO: May glory exalt our hearts with courage
Propitious Heaven will aid our cause
The shade of your father will inspire our souls!
It calls for vengeance and not lamentation;
Although departed, he seems to say, he has been
Happy in his destiny;
His remains shall hallow a martyr's tomb,
Of virtue such as his the fit recompense.

WAL: What noise is that I hear,
Proceeding from the wood!
Listen, all of you.

ARN: Silence.

WIL: Yes, let us all listen.
The forest resounds with the footsteps of many persons.

ARN: Nearer to us the sound approaches.

WIL: Who comes there?

*Enter Inhabitants of the Unterwald.*

CHO: The friends of Helvetia.

WAL: Good fortune

WIL: Oh, welcome

ARN: Oh, vengeance is at hand!
Honor to the bold of heart!

CHORUS: Our bosoms now throb with courage;
With one accord we come to brave
The march and its dangers dire;
Every man, burning with ardor,
Longs for death or victory;—
The wisdom of your councillings renovate
Our hopes within us.

WIL: O, valiant sons of Unterwald,
Your noble ardor does not surprise me.

WAL: We shall know how to imitate it
*(The sound of a trumpet heard.)*
Our honored friends of Switzerland!
I hear the trumpets sound around us!
Now, Helvetia, the day of your glory arises!

*Enter Swiss Inhabitants.*

CORO: Domo, O ciel! da un vil straniero.
A' suoi mali il forte indura,
E celandosi all' altero,
E qui tratto a lagrimar.

GUG: E scusabil la tema
In chi qual noi si vive.
Alla mia speme v' affidate: amica
Ne airriderà la sorte.

TUTTI: Onore al cor del forte!

VAL: D' Urì mancan soltanto
I magnanimi amici.

GUG: Onde le tracce
Nasconder de' lor passi,
E per meglio celar la nostra impressa,
S' apron co' remi loro
Sul mobil elemento,
Il sol sentier che non tradisce mai.

VAL: De' prodi, ascolto, è già compito il patto.
Non odi tu?

GUG: Chi vien?

*Entrano Abitanti d' Uri, dalla parte del lago, a detti.*

CORO: Amici dell' Elvezia.

TUTTI: Onore, onor
D' Elvezia a' difensor.

CORO: Guglielmo, sol per te
Tre popoli s' ùnir.
Il barbaro a punir
Ciascuno è presto.
Parla, e il tuo dir sarà
Di stimolo al codardo;
E, come acceso dardo,
Il come infiammerà.

GUG: Mostriamci degni alfine
Del sangue onde sortiamo;
Senza frapporre indugio.
S' armino i tre Canton' di lancia e spada
Domani fia che sorga
Il giorno di vendetta.
Ne reggerete voi?

CORE: Non lo temer. Sì, tutti.

GUG: Presti a vincer?

CORO: Sì, tutti.

GUG: Presti a morir?

CORO: Sù, tutti.

GUG: Ebben, serbate
Vigore ed ardimento.
Sia fermo il patto, e saldo il giuramento.

GUG. POI TUTTI: Giuriam, giuriamo pel nostro onor,
Pe' nostro dormi, per gli avi nostri,
pe' nostri afanni
Al ciel ch' è giusto vendicator,
Di tosto abbattere l' empio oppressor.
Se qualche vile V' ha qui tra noi,
Lo privi il Sole de' raggi suoi,

CHA: Subdued by a vile foreigner,
The brave submits to his fate,
Patiently awaiting his day,
Bewailing his fortune in his tears.

WIL: Fear is excusable
In those who live as we have,
But, friends, like me repose in hope,
And Fate will smile upon us yet.

ALL: Honor to the brave of heart!

WAL: Our noble-hearted friends of Uri
Now alone are parted from us.

WIL: To conceal their track,
As also the enterprise embarked in—
Their scheme favoring night's darkness,
They are crossing the turbid lake,
By a path known but to themselves—
The only one which never can betray.

WAL: The compact of the brave is now completed.
Do you not hear?

WIL: Who comes there?

*Enter Inhabitants of the Uri, from the Lake.*

CHO: Friends of Helvetia.

ALL: Honor all honor
To the defenders of Helvetia.

CHO: William Tell, under you alone
Have three cantons united here;
The barbarian to punish,
Each and all are now prepared
Speak, and the words you utter
Will arouse the timid into action;
And, as with a burning arrow,
Their manly bosoms will be pierced.

WIL: Let us at least show ourselves
Worthy of the blood of our fathers.
Without a moment's more delay,
Let the three cantons be armed with sword and spear;
The long-sought day of vengeance
Will tomorrow dawn on us.
You will not then desert us?

CHO: Do not doubt us. We swear!

WIL: Prepared to conquer?

CHO: Yes, all of us!

WIL: Or ready to die?

CHO: Yes, all of us!

WIL: Well! keep up
Your courage and resolution.
Let our compact now be consecrated by oath.
Let us swear—let us all swear—
By our honor—by our wrongs—
By our forefathers—by our progeny—
By the avenging heaven above to

Non oda il cielo la sua preghiera;
E giunto al fine di sua carriera,
Gli neghi tomba la terra ancor.

ARN: Già sorge il di.

VAL: Segnal per noi dell' armi.

GUG: Di vittoria.

VAL: Qual grido
Corrisponder le deve?

GUG: All' armi!

TUTTI: All' armi!
(*Partono.*)

*Fine Dell Atto Secondo.*

destroy,
This vile oppressor.
If there be a recreant among us
May he be shut out from heaven's light.
May God refuse to hear his prayers
May the end of his career be near,
And the earth deny a tomb to him.

ARN: Already the day is breaking

WAL: The signal of war for us.

WIL: And of victory.

WAL: What shall be
The watchword of our party?

WIL: To arms!

ALL: To arms!
(*Exeunt.*)

*END OF THE SECOND ACT.*

# ■ ATTO III

## SCENA I

*Passaggio tra le Montagne.*

*Entrane Matilde e Arnoldo.*

MAT: O ciel! sì torbido e perchè? E questo
Il dolce addio che tu mi dài ben mio?
Non temer:—al mio seno
Presto ti stringerò.

ARN: No, io resto. Onore
Me ne impone il dover, chè vendicare
Vo' il padre mio.

MAT: Che parli tu?

ARN: Vogl' io
Sangue e vendetta: è questo
L' unieo mio pensiero.
Alla gloria rinuncio,
Agli onori, all' amor, a te Matilde.

MAT: A me! Melchtal!

ARN: Che vuoi di più? mio padre
Empi cicarii han spento.
E sai chi lor giudò la man?

MAT: Io gelo!

ARN: Te lo dice il terror, Gessler.

MAT: O! cielo!
Pel nostro amor non v' ha più speme;
Ci aspettan solo affanni e pene
A noi la sorte è avversa ognor.
Oh! Matilde sventurata
Per te pace più non v' è.
Sdegnata l' ombra del padre tuo
S' oppone al nostro infausto amor,
Un gran dover crudel t' aspetta,
Arnoldo compi il tuo dover.
Oh! giorno di sciagure!
In odio io sono al ciel!
Ora che il padre tu dei vendicar,

# ■ ACT III

## SCENE I

*An open Space among the Mountains.*

*Enter Matilda and Arnold.*

MAT: Oh, heavens! why are you so excited?
Is this the fond adieu you give me?
Doubt me not,—shortly
I'll take you lovingly to my bosom.

ARN: No, I must decline.
Honor and duty alike call on me to avenge.
My father's death.

MAT: What are you saying?

ARN: I pant
For blood and vengeance—the only passion
Which now may occupy my heart;
I renounce all glory and all honor—
Love, even—and you Matilda.

MAT: Me, Melchtal!

ARN: Ay—would you hear yet more?
My father has been slain by assassins,
And know you by whose orders?

MAT: I tremble.

ARN: Your terror plainly tells it was Gessler.

MAT: Oh! heavens
No hope remains now for our love so fond;
Sorrow and misery alone are left us;
Adverse Fate for ever waits on us!
Oh, most unhappy Matilda
For ever fled from this peace,
The angry shade of your sire departed
Our ill-assorted love interdicts
A duty stern and cruel calls on you,
My Arnold, and you must obey the call,
Oh! wretchedness unlooked for!

Più non ti lice a Matilde pensar.
Da te mio ben lontano
Traendo mesti i di
Farò le piagge invano
Del nome tuo suonar.
L' immago tua scolpita
Nel cor io porterò.
Chi mi salvò la vita.
Giammai scordar saprò.

**ARN:** Quai grida? qual rumor si sente?
Qual suon? che fia.

**MAT:** Gessler si sveglia.

**ARN:** Delitti nuovi ad eseguir.

**MAT:** No: d' una festa or militare
La gioia annuncia questo rumor
O! non t' esponi ai guardi lor.
Arnoldo, ah! credi all' amor mio,
Fuggi, o tremar per te degg' io.
Ah! se cara a te son' io,
Non tardar di più, ben mio,
Mi farai dal duol morir.
Ovunque ti trarrà la sorte
Ti seguiranno i miei sospir.

**ARN:** Invan tu tenti allontanarmi,
Quei canti m' empion d' alto furor.

**MAT:** Ah! per pietà, deh! non tardar.
Fuggi, o degg' io per te tremar.
Ah! se cara a te son 'io, etc.

**MAT & ARN:** O! quale istante di rio dolor!
Straziar mi sento in seno il cor.
Giammai scordar non ti saprò.
A te mai sempre io penserò.
(*Partono.*)

## SCENA II

*Gran Piazza d' Altorf—nel fondo scorgesi, il Castello di Gessler—Da una parte evvi un palco destinato al Governatore—Omano le Piazza alcuni alberi di tigli, melice—Nel mezzo sarà piantato un palo, al quale è sovrapposto un berretto, innanzi a cui tutti dovranno inchinare.*

*Gessler, Rodolfo, Guardie, Soldati, Svizzeri d' ambo i sessi, e Popolo.*

**CORO:** Gloria a Gessler si renda, gloria,
Temasi Gessler
Del mondo il terror;
Si, si, nella rabbia estrema,
Ei lancia l' anatema,
Sul popolo e il guerrier.

---

I seem deserted by Heaven!
Now that you have your father to avenge,
No longer must you think of Matilda.
Transported far away from you,
My days passing in melancholy,
In vain regrets the wilds and shores
I'll make resound,
With your name.
Your image, engraven on my heart
Henceforth I shall for ever bear;
He who so nobly saved my life,
Must live ever in my memory!

**ARN:** Those cries! what tumult is it that I hear?
Those sounds—what mean they?

**MAT:** Gessler approaches

**ARN:** Some new crime to perpetrate.

**MAT:** No: of some military pageant
These are the joyous announcements;—
Oh, do not expose your dear life!
Arnold, depending on my fond love,
Fly, or for your safety I shall tremble.
Ah! if ever I was dear to you
Do not longer tarry, love,
Or I of grief shall perish;
Wherever fate your steps may guide, My sorrows will follow there.

**ARN:** In vain do you incite me to flight;—
Those cries with fury fell inspire me.

**MAT:** Ah! for pity's sake, do not delay
Fly, or I shall fear for your safety
Ah, if ever, &c.

**MAT & ARN:** Oh! the agony I now endure!
What conflict within my bosom rages!
Never can I forget my fond love
To my thoughts ever be present
(*Exeunt.*)

## SCENE II

*The Grand Square of Altorf—The Castle of Gessler in the background—On one side is erected a Throne for the Governor—Apple and Limetrees border the Square—Among them is a Pole erected, surmounted by a Cap, to which the Populace are required to bow.*

*Gessler, Rodolf, Guards, Soldiers, Swiss, and the Populace, Male and Female.*

**CHO:** Glory to Gessler singing, glory,
We bow down to him,
Whose power we obey;
Yes, yes fearing this dread anger,
With awe his presence nearing,
We pay homage to him.

---

**CORI DI SVIZZERS FRA LORO:**
Ben altre leggi avremo,
O Nume, un dì per te.
Fa' che il poter supremo
Sei tutto amor a fè.

**GES:** No, l' orgoglio invan pretende
Di sfidar la mia vendetta,
Le mie leggi trasgredir.
Dee ciascun, come me stesso,
D' ogni grado, d' ogni sesso,
Quest' insegna riverir.
(*Va a sedorss sul palco.*)
Ch' io, reggitor d' Elvezia, oggi riceva
Dalla vostra obbedienza il scaro pegno—
co' canti e in un co' giuochi
Di questo dì l' orgoglio
S' esalti. Udiste? Il voglio.

**CORI:** Quell'agil pie Ch'egual; non ha, Invan l'augel Seguir potra. Non ha l'aprile, Un fior piu gentile Che sia simile a tua belta, Quell'agil pie, Ch'egual non ha- invan l'angel Seguir potra, Egual non ha, Equal non ha, L'augell'in van Seguir po- tra, Non ha l'aprile, Un fior piu gentile, Che sia simile A tua belta.

*Entrano Guglielmo e Jemmi, trascinats sul proscenio da Rodolfo e alcuni Soldati.*

**ROD:** (*A Guglielmo.*) Inchinati, superbo!

**GUG:** Nella fiacchezza sua
Solo potrai tu, armato,
Questa gente avvilir; me no, che sprezzo,
Qualunque cenno che à viltà mi spinge.

**ROD:** (*A Gessler.*) Avvi chi tenta
Infranger le tue leggi.

**GES:** Qual' è, qual' è l' audace?

**ROD:** Quell' ardire, signor, me lo palesa:
Egli è guglielmo Tell, è quell' iniquo,
Che Leutoldo sottrasse all' ira tua.

**GES:** S' arresti, olà!
(*Vien tolta la balestra e la faretra a Guglielmo.*)

**CORO DI SOLDATI:** Egli è quello.
L' arcier temuto tanto,
L' ardito nuotator.

**GES:** Per lui non v' ha pietade:
Ei cadde in poter mio.

**GUG:** L' ultimo almen foss' io
Scherno del tuo furor!
(*Di nascosto a il figlio.*)
Corri alla madre, e fa' che tosto incenda

---

**CHORUS OF SWISS:** Wiser laws we shall yet have,
Oh God! through you some day;—
Then will the power supreme
Be better loved and trusted.

**GES:** No: vainly this insolence dares to provoke,
My vengeance,
And my sovereign laws transgress:
Each and all of you, as you bow to me,
Of whatever grade, shall reverence make
To this, of my authority the symbol.
(*Pointing to the cap on the pole.*)
Here, of Helvetia the lawful governor,
Will I receive upon my throne,
This sacred pledge of your allegiance;
And then in song, and dance, and merry sport,
Shall pass the day.—Hear you all?—This is my will!

**TYROLEAN CHORUS:** In vain we strive to reach unequalled heights, April has no flower sweeter or even similar to your beauty. In vain we strive to reach unequalled heights. There is no equal, no equal to the heights that we strive to reach, and April has no flower sweeter or even similar to your beauty.

*Enter William and his Son, who are dragged forward by Rodolf and some Soldiers.*

**ROD:** (*To William.*) Bow your head, proud man!

**WIL:** Your arms enable you
Upon the known weakness of the people
To perpetrate this wrong. You make them fear,
But not me;—the base order I despise,
As I despise all that can a man abase.

**ROD:** (*To Gessler.*) There is one here
Who dares infringe your laws.

**GES:** Who is the audacious man?

**ROD:** His audacity, my lord, betrays him:
He is William Tell, the miscreant
Who snatched Leuthold from your fury.

**GES:** Arrest him at once!
(*Soldiers seize him, and take his bow and arrows.*)

**CHORUS OF SOLDIERS:** Unarmed we have him!
The archer so feared by all,
The boldest of all swimmers!

**GES:** There shall be no mercy for him
He shall now feel my power!

**WIL:** I wish it were my lot to be
The last victim of your malice.
(*In a low tone to this son.*)
Quickly run to your mother,
And bid her raise a lighted torch

In sulla estrema cima
Colà de' nostri monti
La fiamma che segnale a' tre canton;
Sia di battaglia.

**GES:** (*A Jemmi, che si allontana.*)
Arresta:
(La loro tenerezza
La mia vendetta infiamma.) A te:
rispondi,
D' questi il figlio tuo?

**GUG:** I! solo.

**GES:** Ebben, salvarlo vuoi?
(*Scenaendo dal palco.*)

**GUG:** Salvarlo!
Qual è il suo fallo mai?

**GES:** L' esserti figlio—
Il tuo parlar, l' incauto orgoglio
tuo—

**GUG:** Me solo, io sol t' offesi:
Me solo, punir dei.

**GES:** Del suo perdono or tu l' arbi-
tro sei.
Siccome abile arciero
Ti tiene ognun de' tuoi,
Sul capo di tuo figlio
Pongasi questo pomo, e d' un tuo
dardo
Involarglielo dei sotto il mio sguar-
do.

**GUG:** Che chiedi mai!

**GES:** Lo voglio.

**GUG:** Qual orribil decreto!
Sul figlio mio!—mi perdo!
E tu, crudel, puoi domandarlo!
Ah, mai!—Troppo grande, è il del-
itto.

**GES:** Obbedisci.

**GUG:** Ma tu figli non hai?
V' è un Dio, Gessler: egli ne ascolta.

**GES:** Assai dicesti; cedi alfin.

**GUG:** Non posso.

**GES:** (*A Soldati.*) Pera,
Pera il suo figlio.

**JEM:** Ah! padre,
Pensa alla tua destrezza

**GUG:** Temo il troppo amor mio.

**JEM:** Dammi la mano,
Posala sul mio core;
Senti: di tema, no, batte d' amore.

**GUG:** Ti benedico, figlio mio, pian-
gendo,
E il prisco ardir sul petto tuo ripren-
do.
La calma del tuo core
Ritorna in me il vigore.
(Affetti miei, tacete.)
A me l' armi porgete,—
Io son Guglielmo Tell.
(*Gli vien ristituita la balestra e la*

On the top of yonder mountain;—
By the three cantons' will be known
As the battle-signal.

**GES:** (*To Jemmy, who is going.*)
Stay here!
(By their tenderness so plain
I am the more incensed.) Answer
me, you:
Is that a son of yours?

**WIL:** My only one.

**GES:** Well, would you wish to save
him?
(*Glancing at the pole*)

**WIL:** Save him!
Why, what wrong can he have
done?

**GES:** In being your son—
Your haughty words—your pride
incautious—

**WIL:** In that I only have offended:
And I only must be punished.

**GES:** Of his fate the arbiter you
shall be.
The most able archer you are reck-
oned
Amongst all your countrymen:
On the head of your son this apple
place,
And with an arrow, before my eyes,
You shall strike if off.—This is my
pleasure!

**WIL:** What do you ask?

**GES:** I will so have it.

**WIL:** What a horrible decree!
On my own son's head!—I am lost!
Oh, can you, cruel man, demand
this deed!
Ah, never!—It is too great a crime!

**GES:** Obey at once.

**WIL:** But have you no children!
There is a God above who knows all
things.

**GES:** You have already spoken too
much: desist.

**WIL:** I cannot do it!

**GES:** (*To the Soldiers.*) Death,
then:
I sentence to death his son.

**JEM:** Ah! father,
Remember your matchless skill.

**WIL:** My love will cause my skill to
fail.

**JEM:** Give me your hand—.
Place it upon my heart: listen
Not with terror, but with love, it
throbs.

**WIL:** With weeping eyes I bless
you, my only son;
On your bosom I feel my nerve re-
newed.
The calm about your little heart
Brings my usual courage to me.
(Paternal love, be silent.)
Bring my bow and arrows here.—
I once again am William Tell.
(*They restore him his bow and ar-*

faretra, che vuota a terra, sceglie
uno strale, e ne cela un altro sotto
la sua vesta.*)

**GES:** S' annodi il figlio suo.

**JEM:** Annodarmi!—Che ingiuria!
Ah! no, che almeno
Libero io mora. Espongo,
Senza tremare il capo al colpo or-
rendo.
E senza impallidir fermo l' attendo.

**CORO DI SVIZZERI:** (Ah! nemmeno l' innocenza
Può calmar la sua vendetta.)

**JEM:** Coraggio, padre mio!

**GUG:** Alla sua voce, dalla man mi
cadono
Quest' armi abbominate,
E le luci ho di pianto ottenebrate.
Ah! figlio! ch' io t' abbracci,
Un altra voltra ancora.
(*Al cenno di Gessler, Jemmi ritor-
na presse il padre.*)

**GUG:** Resto immobile, e ver la terra
Inchina un ginocchio a pregar.
Invoca Iddio, Invoca Iddio.
Che, sol pel suo favore,
Il figlio può salvare il genitore;
Fermo così; ma volgiti al ciel.
Fermo così; ma volgiti al ciel.
Nel periglio d' un capo a me sì caro;
Questa punta d' acciar può tradir la
mia speme;
Al minor movimento, al minor
movimento.
Jemmi, Jemmi, pensa a tua madre,
chi ci attende
Insiem, Jemmi, Jemmi,
Pensa a tua madre,
che ci attende insiem.
(*Vien posto il pomo sul capo a
Jemmi, ch' è tornato in fretta al
suo luogo— Guglielmo con torbi-
di squardi scorre intorno la piaz-
za, guarda Gessler e porta la
mano dove ha colato il secondo
strale—prende la mira, scocca, e
coglie il pomo.*

**SVIS:** Vittoria!

**JEM:** O, padre!

**SVIZ:** Sua vita è salva.

**GES:** (Il pomo, O, rabbia!
Close!—O furor!)

**SVIS:** Dal capo glielo tolse,
Guglielmo trionfò!

rows—he empties the quiver on
the ground, and selects two arrows, one of which he hides in his
bosom.*)

**GES:** Now let the son be bound and
placed.

**JEM:** Bind me!—What indignity!
Ah, no—to that I'll not submit.
Let me die unshackled!—Daunt-
lessly
To the fearful ordeal I will sub-
mit;—
The result without trembling I'll
abide

**CHORUS OF SWISS:** (Ah! that even
innocence like this
Will not mitigate his fury

**JEM:** Have courage, my dearest father!

**WIL:** At hearing his sweet voice,
within my hands
Scarcely can I hold the hated weapons;
And my sight grows dim with weeping!
Ah! my son, again let me embrace
you,—
Once more—and yet again once
more!
(*At a signal from Gessler, Jemmy
goes to his father.*)

**WIL:** Firmly remaining, courage
sustaining.
On bended knee raise your prayer!
In heaven above place your
trust,—
Your only hope is there.
Be firm, my child; remember one
beholds you,
Whose aid may save and protect
you,
Whose aid may save and protect
you from pain,
Ah! Your eyes should be uplifted to
him;
His pity yet may set you free, free
again;
Set you free, set you free,—yes,
again set you free,
My child, my child, think of your
mother dear, my child!
Oh! think of her, my child!
Bravely sustain you,
Heaven may yet befriend you.
(*They place an apple on Jemmy's
head, and he promptly takes his
place— William casts a wild look
around, gazing fiercely on Gessler, and feels for the second arrow, where he has concealed it—
he then takes his aim, shoots, and
strikes the apple from the boy's
head.*)

**SWISS:** Victory!

**JEM:** Oh, father!

**SWISS:** His life is saved!

**GES:** (He truly hit the apple!
Oh, rage!—Oh, fury!)

**SWISS:** He truly struck it from his
head;
William has triumphant proved,

**JEM:** Ei mi salvò la vita.
Un padre potea mai
Spregnere un figlio? O ciel!

**GUG:** Io più non reggo!
Io mi sostengo appena!
Sei tu, mio caro figlio?
Io soccombo alla gioja!
(*Sviene, abbracciando il figlio, e gli cade lo strale che avea nascosto.*)

**JEM:** Ah! soccorrete il padre.

**GES:** (Ei sfugge all' ira mia.)
Che vedo!
(*Osservande il dardo caduto.*)

**GUG:** O cielo! il sol mio ben salvai.

**GES:** Quel dardo a che?

**GUG:** Per te, s' egli era setinto.

**GES:** Trema!

**GUG:** Io tremar?

**GES:** Sia di catene avvinto.
(*I Soldati esequiscono.*)

*Entrano Matilde, Rodolfo, e Damigelle.*

**MAT:** Fia ver? Delitto orrendo!

**SOL:** Entrambi den morir.

**SVIZ:** (E ancor dobbiam soffrir?)

**GES:** Che tosto sien troncati
Lor giorni sciagurati.
Io lo giurai; ma i rei
Sfidaro i sdegni miei.
Attendam quindi in ceppi
L' ora del lor morir.

**MAT:** Che! il figlio?—Ah, no!—t' arrests.
Fiera sentenza è questa.

**GES:** Dato fu il segno e basti;
Meco tu invan contrasti.
Il figlio ancor.

**MAT:** Giammai!
Giammai, finchè vivrò.
In nome del sovrano,
Suo figlio a me sia dato.
Un popol vedi, insano,
(*A Gessler.*)
Contro di te sdegnato,
E tu resisti ancor.

**ROD:** Cedila; il padre almen ne resta.
(*Sotto voce a Gessler.*)

**SVIZ:** Ah! sì, bontade del cielo è questa
Guglielmo!—O, sorte!
(*Vedendole incatenanto fra' sol-*

**JEM:** And he has preserved my life.
Could a father kill his own son!
Oh, heaven!

**WIL:** I can scarcely see!
My trembling limbs my form can scarce support;
My heart, from excess of joy, fails me!
(*He faints while embracing his son, and the arrow which he had concealed in his vest falls to the ground.*)

**JEM:** Ah! to my father bring succour

**GES:** (From my vengeance he will escape.)
What do I see?
(*Observing the dropped arrow.*)

**WIL:** (*Recovering.*) Oh, heavens! my dearest treasure I have saved!

**GES:** Why had you this other arrow?

**WIL:** For you, if I had slain my child.

**GES:** Tremble!

**WIL:** I tremble!

**GES:** Bind him with fetters.

*Enter Matilda, Rodolf, and Attendants.*

**MAT:** Can it be true? Horrid barbarity!

**SOL:** Both will now be put to death.

**SWISS:** (Shall we look on and suffer this?)

**GES:** To their traitorous existence
A speedier termination
I had intended: but my rage
The wretches have ventured to brave
Therefore, in chains let them await
The hour of their approaching death.

**MAT:** And the son, too?—Ah, no!—recall;—
You will revoke that cruel sentence.

**GES:** My orders are already given,
And their fulfilment none shall prevent.
The son, too, shall die.

**MAT:** He shall not!
He shall not, while there's life in me.
In the name of our sovereign,
That boy I here demand of you.
You perceive a people enraged,
(*To Gessler.*)
Against you incensed one and all,
And yet you resist their wishes.

**ROD:** Give up the boy: the father still remains.
(*In an undertone to Gessler.*)

**SWISS:** Ah! yes! it was a merciful interposition!
William!—Oh, sad fate!
(*On seeing him chained and

*dati.*)
Atra! funesta!
Tal premio ottiene la sua virtù?

**ROD:** Mormoran essi;
(*Sotto voce a Gessler*)
Non l' odi tu?

**GES:** L' audacia dell' infido
Nell' odio lor rivive.
Verso Kusnacht il guido;
Pel lago il condurrò.

**ROD:** Sul lago la bufera—deh! pensa.

**GES:** Vanor timor!
Chi, mai, chi mai dispersa dall' abil nuotator?
(*Deridendo Guglielmo.*)
A nuovo il traggo orribile
Supplizio entro Kusnacht a cui fa cinta il lago.

**SVIZ:** Grazia!

**GES:** Si: or or vedrete
Come ciascun fo pago,
Io l' abbandono a' rettili;
La lor vorace fame
gli schiuderà l' avello.

**JEM:** Ah, padre!

**GUG:** O, figlio!

**SVIZ:** Grazia! Grazia!

**GES:** Giammai no, no!

**GES, ROD & SOLDATI:** L' ira solo
che m' accende l' accende
Il lor sanguè può placar.

**MAT:** (E il suo destin segnato;
Ma fia per me salvato
Il figlio e il genitor.)

**JEM:** Quando mi vuol l' ingrato
Da un padre separato,
In voi sol spera il cor.
(*A Matilde*)

**GUG:** Compi il crudel mio fate;
(*A Gessler*)
Ma almeno il figlio amato
Sia tolto a tant' orror.

**SVIZ:** (Misero! a qual mai fato
Serbato, è il suo valor!)

**GES:** Si sgombri olà recinto,
O a' piedi vostri estinto
Faccio costui cader.

**ROD E SOL:** Il cenno ognun rispetta—
Temon la tua vendetta.

**CORO DI SVIZ:** Silenzio!—E forza ancora
Coprirsi nel mister.

**GUG:** Anatèma a Gessler!

**JEM:** Udite la sentenza?

**ROD:** E noi tanta insolenza
Dovrem soffrir? tacer?

*guarded.*)
Oh, sad spectacle!
Is this the fitting reward of heroism?

**ROD:** The people murmur;
(*Aside to Gessler.*)
Do you not hear?

**GES:** The audacity of the traitor
Their rancour encourages;
I will have him taken to Kusnacht,—
He shall be borne across the lake.

**ROD:** The lake is impracticable—pray pause.

**GES:** Needless fear.
The best of swimmers he is thought—he shall now exhibit his skill.
(*Derisively to Wil.*)
Kusnacht is surrounded by the water,
A fine feat, it will be for him to reach it.

**SWISS:** Mercy!

**GES:** Yes: speedily shall you see
How I will fulfill your wishes
I will abandon him to the beasts of prey,
And trust to their voracity
To make a fitting grave for him.

**JEM:** Ah, father!

**WIL:** Oh, my son!

**SWISS:** Mercy! Mercy!

**GES:** Never!—No, never!

**GES, ROD & SOLDIERS:** The wrath which rages in my/his breast
By his blood alone can be appeased.

**MAT:** (His death he now thinks settled;
But both of them will I yet save—
The young son and his brave father.)

**JEM:** Since the tyrant
Harshly separates me from my father,
In you alone I place my hopes.
(*To Matilda*)

**WIL:** My cruel fate may be fixed
(*To Gessler.*)
But my son you'll surely spare
An early death so terrible.

**SWISS:** Unhappy man, how sad a fate
Has his valor brought on him!

**GES:** Let every one at once depart,
Or, in the presence of you all,
Forthwith he shall be put to death.

**ROD. & SOL:** Your orders are obeyed by all—
They all tremble at your vengeance.

**CHORUS OF SWISS:** Silence! the appointed hour
Has not yet arrived!

**WIL:** May perdition fall on Gessler!

**JEM:** Did you hear the sentence?

**ROD:** And insolence such as this
Shall we suffer in silence?

## Act III, Scene II

**GES:** Se alcun di loro inoltrasi,
Si faccia al suol cader.

**MAT:** Ah! vieni meco,—affrettati:
Fuggiamo da Gessler.

**JEM: GUG:** O, padre! Oh! qual supplizio!, O, figlio! Oh! qual supplizio! Anàtema a Gessler.

**CORO DI SOLDATI:** Ah! viva ognor Gessler.

**CORO DI SVIZ:** Anàtema a Gessler.
(*Gessler, Rodolfo, ed i Soldati si schiudone cella forza un vassaggio fra il popolo, trascinando Guglielmo.*)

*Fine Dell' Atto Tereo.*

# ■ ATTO IV

## SCENA I

*Esterno di una rustica Abitazione.*

*Arnoldo solo.*

**ARN:** Ah! non m' abbandonare,
O speme di vendetta—
Guglielmo è fra catene—Impaziente
L' istante aspetto di pugnar—In questo
Caro asil—qual silenzio!
Do mente—e de' miei passi odo soltanto
Il suono—O!—vada in bando
Il segreto terror—entriam!—Gran Dio!—
(*Fermandosi dopo di aver fatto alcuni passi onde penetrare nelle stanza interne.*)
Sul limitar, malgrado mio mi arreato,
Entrar colà non vo:—mio padre è morto.

**ARNOLDO:** O, muto asil del pianto, dove io sortiva il di. Iere felice, ahi quanto felice, Oggi fatal, fatal cosi. Il padre io chiamo, ahi sventurato, il padre io chiamo ahi sventurato, Invan, egli non m'ode piu, invan, egli non m'ode piu. Cari luoghi vi l'escie lestremo addio vido! Vi lascio, si vi lascio, si l'estremo addio vido. o muto asil del pianto, dove io sortiva il di. Cari luoghi cari luoghi, vi lascio l'estremo addio oggi vido l'estremo addio, si vi do l'estremo addio vido.

**CORO:** (*Di dentro.*) Vendetta!—

**ARN:** Oh! mia sperenza!
D' allarme io sento i gridi—
Che mai li guida a me?

*Entra Coro di Svizzeri.*

---

**GES:** If any one advances a foot here
Consign him to death on the instant.

**MAT:** Ah! come with me! Let us hasten from here,
From Gessler let us fly!

**JEM. WIL:** Oh father! Oh my son! Oh! what a state of woe! May perdition fall on Gessler!

**CHORUS OF SOLDIERS:** Ah! long life to Gessler!

**CHORUS OF SWISS:** May perdition fall on Gessler!
(*Gessler, Rodolf, and Soldiers force a passage through the populace, dragging William with them.*)

*END OF THE THIRD ACT.*

# ■ ACT IV

## SCENE I

*Exterior of a Rustic Habitation.*

*Arnold discovered, alone.*

**ARN:** Ah! I will never abandon
My heart's thirsting for revenge!
William is imprisoned in chains!
I wait impatiently the hour of battle
What silence reigns!
I listen, I hear my own steps alone.
Oh! begone, all idle apprehensions
And secret terrors. I will enter.—
Great God!
(*He advances some steps towards an adjoining room, and then stops suddenly.*)
In spite of my boasted resolution,
I dare not enter!—My father is dead!

**ARNOLDO:** Oh! Blessed abode, within whose walls my eyes first saw light, Once so beloved, yet now your halls bring misery, misery to my aching sight, I call in vain: no father's greeting, which now is repeating to me, will ever again these meet ears. Then home once loved for ever more, ever more, farewell! Home once loved, yes home once loved, for ever more farewell! Oh! Blessed abode, once beloved now brings misery, misery to my aching sight, my aching sight, my aching sight.

**CHORUS:** (*Within.*) Vengeance!

**ARN:** Oh! my forebodings!
Cries of distress now meet my ear—
What brings these people after me?

*Enter Chorus of Swiss.*

---

**CORO:** Guglielmo è prigioniero.
E ognun ferro è privo.
Di farlo salvo è un vivo
In noi grande desir;—
Dell' armi aver vogliamo, e poi morir.

**ARN:** Dal pianto omai si resti!
L' ira al pensier si desti
Di mia fatalita.
Su chi mio padre ha spento,
Chi d' ogni mi priva,
La morte or scenderà.

**CORO:** Non temere in noi t' affida;
Già sul reo la morte sta.

**ARN:** Corriam, voliam, s' affretti
Lo scempio di quel vile
che su noi trionfò.
Si vendetta dell' empio facciamo
Il sentiero addittarvi saprò.
Sì, venite; delusa la speme
Renderem di chi vili ne brama.
Gloria, onore, vendetta ci chiama,
E Guglielmo per noi non morrà.

**CORO:** Sì, vendetta!—Delusa la speme
D' ogni tristo per noi resterà.
(*Partono tutti.*)

## SCENA II

*Il Lago de' Quattro Cantoni.—Denso nubi foriere di procella.*

*Entrano Eduige, a Donne Sviezzeri.*

**CORO:** Resta omai; ti perde il duolo;
Vedi in ciel qual nembo freme.

**EDU:** Io Gessler veder vo' solo

**CORO:** Ma da lui che puoi sperar? Morte? morte?

**EDU:** Io la bramo;
Chè qui trovarmi, e priva
D' ogni maggior mio ben non fia ch' io viva.

*Entrano Matilde e Jemmi.*

**JEM:** Ah, madre!—
(*Di dentro.*)

**EDU:** Chi parlo?—Questa soave
Voce a me cara?

**JEM:** (*Di dentro.*) Madre!

**EDU:** (*escone Matilde e Jemmi.*)
Udirlo parmi,
E desso! E desso.—Oh, sorte! Il figlio mio!
Ma, oimè—tuo padre, i passi tuoi non segue?

---

**CHO:** William has been made a prisoner;
Without assistance he must perish;
We have determined to set him free;
And we put our greatest hope in you!
With these arms we'll save him, or we'll die!

**ARN:** All present grief be now suspended,
And all my angry thoughts
Give way to this great enterprise.
He who murdered my father,
And did cause this grief to my heart,
Shall by me die, or I by him!

**CHO:** Do you rashly rush into danger,
Or your own life may be the forfeit!

**ARN:** Let us rush to the rescue,
And boldly seize on the tyrant
Who seeks our liberties to crush.
If you but fearlessly follow,
I will boldly lead you forward.
Yes, come;—delusive is all hope
Of justice from what vile tyrant.
Glory, honor, vengeance, alike demand,
That William may be saved by our prowess.

**CHO:** Yes, revenge! Of our foes the hopes delusive
Will be frustrated by our courage.
(*Exeunt.*)

## SCENE II

*The Lake of the Four Cantons—The sky denotes a coming storm*

*Enter Edwidge and Swiss Peasants.*

**CHO:** Rest awhile, or you'll meet certain death;—
A storm in the heavens is gathering.

**EDW:** Alone would I encounter Gessler.

**CHO:** What do you hope to obtain from him?
Death? certain death?

**EDW:** That I wish for;
If all that is dear to me be lost,
Death for me can have no terrors.

*Enter Matilda and Jemmy.*

**JEM:** Ah, mother!
(*Within*)

**EDW:** Who speaks?—What sweet voice is that
Which thus salutes my ear?

**JEM:** (*Within.*) Mother!

**EDW:** (*Seeing Matilda and Jemmy*) I thought I heard his voice,
Oh, yes! It is he—
My own dear son is here.—Ah, happy lot!
But your father—why is he not with you?

**JEM:** Ai ferri ond' egli è cinto
Togliersi alfin saprà, che da Matilde
Tutto aspettar dobbiamo.

**EDU:** Tu, d' ogni ben capace,
Esser l' angiol per noi potrai di
pace?

**MAT:** A te ritorno il figlio,
Sottratto a orribil nembo.
Di bella pace in grembo,
Nol giungerà il periglio.
Matilde a voi predice
Un termine al dolor.
Con me la speme il dice,
La speme ond' arde il cor.

**EDU E JEM:** Vivrem di pace in
grembo,
N' è il labbro suo presago.
Del ciel cessato il nembo,
Essa è per noi l' imago;
Se a noi lieta predice
Un termine al dolor.
La speme in essa il dice,
col suono dell' amor.

*Entrano Guglielmo e Arnold.*

**JEM:** He will soon be freed from
captivity;
Matilda's good heart so watches
over him
That our hopes cannot be disappointed.

**EDW:** You were as a blessing given
to us—
You have ever been our guardian
angel!

**MAT:** To you your son now returns
Escaped from the frightful storm,
Restored to peace and quietness,
No longer threatened by danger,
Matilda predicates for you both.
To your grief this happy ending;
The same hope arises in me,
A hope which my heart enlivens.

**EDW. & JEM:** We may yet hope to
live in peace
Her lips as much for us presage.
The clouds now are breaking above
us,
Her good genius watches over us;
And she predicts to us
A happy ending to our griefs
Hope, blended with the voice of
love,
Sweetly speaks from her bright
face.

*Enter William followed by Arnol-
do*

**SVIZ:** (*Di dentro.*) Vittoria e libertà!

**GUG:** Eduige!

**EDW:** O, mio Guglielmo!

**GUG:** Gessler alfin soccombe. Eccoti il dardo
Che gli trafisse il cor, e là in quel
lago
Egli trovò la tomba.

**TUTTI:** Onore al forte!
Gloria al liberator!

**ARN:** Vei qui, Matilde?

**MAT:** Per sempre!

**ARN:** Oh, qual contento!
Ahi! che manchi tu solo, O genitore!
All' Elvezia, a tuo figlio, al nostro
amore!

**TUTTI:** I boschi, i monti, e la città,
Alzin tonante un grido solo;
Pe' cieli è tu spiegasti il volo.
Vittoria e libertà!

**GUG:** Gloria ed onor al popol vincitor!

**DONNE:** Bello s' intrecci a lor
Serte di mirto e allor!

*The End*

**SWISS:** (*Within.*) Victory and liberty!

**WIL:** Edwidge!

**EDW:** O, my beloved William!

**WIL:** Gessler has fallen at last. Behold the arrow
With which I've pierced his heart
and the lake has
Proved his burying-place

**ALL:** All honor to the brave!
Glory to our liberator!

**ARN:** You here, Matilda?

**MAT:** And for ever!

**ARN:** Oh, what joy!—But my father—
Alas! you are yet wanting
To Helvetia—to your son—his
love to bless.

**ALL:** Through the forest wild—
over the mountains high
Through the glad city, let the cry re-
sound—
Even to heaven above be exalted—
Of victory and liberty!

**WIL:** Glory and honor to the conquering people.

**LADIES:** Now let us crown the victor's brow,
With myrtle and laurel enwreathed!

*The End*

# Samson et Dalila (1877)

## Sampson and Delilah

MUSIC BY CAMILLE SAINT-SAËNS ■ LIBRETTO BY FERDINAND LEMAIRE

This three-act opera with four tableaux, set to a libretto by Ferdinand Lemaire (inspired by the Biblical chapter), premiered at the Hoftheater in Weimar on December 2, 1877. The curtain opens on a public square in Gaza, Palestine; it is 1115 BC, and the Israelites are cruelly oppressed by the Philistines. Sampson, an Israelite, tries to raise their spirits by recounting the story of the Red Sea crossing. He persuades them to have faith in God's mercy. Abimelech, satrap of Gaza, declares that belief in God will accomplish little. Sampson, inspired by God, grabs Abimelech's sword and kills him with it. He warns the Philistines that their end is near and leads a rebellion against them. In spite of the curse the High Priest of Dagon pronounces on the Israelites, Sampson and his followers take Gaza by nightfall.

Delila, a beautiful Philistine maiden, performs a dance, enticing Sampson. At the valley of Sorek, Delila agrees to help the High Priest overcome Sampson. She seduces Sampson, and he tells her his secret—his hair is the source of his strength. Delila cuts off his hair as he sleeps. The Philistines capture Sampson, now harmless, and blind him. They tie him to a mill wheel, which he turns with other Jewish prisoners who chide him for betraying them to a woman. Sampson pleads for God's forgiveness. In the temple of Dagon the High Priest is surrounded by Philistine princes. Delila mocks Sampson and challenges him to participate in their holy orgy. In the center of the temple he is forced to his knees and made to humiliate himself before Dagon. He is led between two pillars that support the roof of the temple; the High Priest commands him to make a sacrifice to Dagon. He prays to God that his strength be renewed, if only for a moment; his prayer is answered and he pushes the pillars apart. The temple collapses, killing everyone, including Sampson.

---

## ■ ACTE 1

*Une place publique dans la ville de Gaza en Palestine. A gauche le portique du Temple de Dagon. Au lever du rideau une foule d'Hebreux, hommes et femmes, sont rèunis sur la place dans l'attitude de la douleur et de la priére. Samson est parmi eux.*

### SCENE I

**CHOEUR:** (*Derriere la toile.*)
Dieu! Dieu d'Israël!!
Dieu d'Israel!
Ecoute la prière de tes enfants,
De tes enfants t'implorant à genoux,
T'implorant à genoux!
Prends en pitié ton peuple
Et sa misère!
Que sa douleur désarme ton courroux!
Un jour, de nous tu détournas ta face,
Et de ce jour ton peuple fut vaincu!
Quoi! veux tu donc qu'à jamais on efface
Des nations, celle qui t'a connu!
Mais vainement tout le jour
Je l'imment tou le jour l'implore;
Sourd à ma voix, il ne me répond pas!
Et cependant, du soir jusqu'à l'aurore,
J'implore ici le secours de son bras!

## ■ ACT I

*A public square in the city of Gaza, in Palestine. At the left the portico of the Temple of Dagon. When the curtain rises, a crowd of Hebrews, men and women, are assembled in attitudes of grief and prayer. Samson is among them.*

### SCENE I

**CHORUS:** (*Behind the scenes.*) Oh God! gracious God of Israel,
O, listen we implore you!
Your children cry, your children cry,
"Save us from our dark fate,
Save us from foes that hate!"
O, pity grant to us who kneel before you!
May our deep grief disarm your wrath on high!
When you turned your face from us, your people,
From that sad day our victory was lost!
Would you behold us, your people, now vanquished,
The only nation that you might have known?
Shall we in vain forever beseech thee?
(*Deaf to our voice He heeds not our alarm!*)
Does our united prayer, then, fail to

reach you,
Our hearts sore cry for the aid of your arm?
We have beheld our cities' destruction,
And Gentile foes your blest altars profane.
Beneath their yoke our tribes are scattered widely;
O Israel, does your name not remain!
Are you no more the God of our salvation,
Who saved from Egypt our tribes long ago?
Lord! Did you forget your word, pledged to our nation
In those sad days when Israel mourned in woe?

Nous avons vu nos cités renversées,
Et les Gentils profanant ton autel;
Et sous leur joug nos tribus dispersées
Ont tout perdu, jusqu'au nom d'Israel!
Ne's tu donc plus ce Dieu delivrance
Qui de l'Egypte arrachait nos tribus?
Dieu! Astu rompu cette sainte alliance
Divins serments par nos aïeux recus?

**SAMSON:** (*Sortant, de la foule, à droite.*) Arrêtez, ô mes frères!
Et benissez le nom du Dieu saint de nos pères!
Car l'heure du pardon est peu être arrivée!
Oui, j'entends dans mon coeur une élevée!
C'est la voix du Seigneur, qui parle ma bouche
Ce Dieu plein de bonté, que la prière touche,
Promet la liberte!
Frères! brisons nos chaines
Et revelons l'autel du seul Dieu d'Israel!

**SAMPSON:** (*Coming out from the throng. R.*)
Stop, O my brothers,
And bless the holy name of the God of our fathers!
For now the hour is here when pardon shall be spoken.
Yes, a voice in my heart of this hope is the token.
'Tis the voice of the Lord, who by my mouth thus speaks.
On us his goodness showers.
Our prayers to him have risen,
And liberty is ours.
Brothers! we'll break from bondage!
Our altars raise once more
To our God, as before!

CHOEUR: Hélas! paroles vaines!
Pour marches aux combats
Où donc trouver des armes?
Comment armer nos bras?
Nous n'avons que nos larmes!

SAMSON: L'astu donc oublié,
Celui dont la puisance
Se fit toi: allié?
Lui qui, plein de clèmence,
A si souvent pour toi
Fait parler ses oracles,
Et rallumé ta foi
Au feu de ses miracles?
Lui, qui dans l'Océan
Sut frayer un passage
A nos pères fuyant
Un honteux esclavage?

CHOEUR: Ils ne sont plus, ces
temps
Où le Dieu de nos pères
Protégeait ses enfants.
Entendait leurs prières!

SAMSON: Malheureux, taisez vous!
Le doute est un blasphème!
Implorons à genoux
Le Segigneur qui nos aime!
Remettons dans ses mains
Le soin de notre gloire,
Et puis ceignons nos reins,
Certains de la victoire!
C'est le Dieu des combats!
C'est le Dieu des armées!
Il armera vos bras d'invincibles
épées!

CHOEUR: Ah! le souffle du Seign-
eur a passé dans sone âme!
Ah! chassons de notre coeur
Une terreur infame!
Et marchons avec lui
Pour notre délivrance!
Jéhovah le conduit
Et nous trend l'esperance!

## SCENE II

Les memes. Abimélech, satrape de
Gaza. Il entre par la gauche, suivé
de plausieurs guerriors et soldats
Philistins.

ABIMÉLECH: Qui donc élÈve ici la
voix?
Encor ce vil troupeau d'esclaves,
Osant toujours braver nos lois
Et voulant briser leures entraves!
Cachez vos soupirs vos pleurs
Qui lassent notre patience;
Invoquez plutôt la clémence
De ceux qui furent vos vainqueurs!
Ce Dieu que votre voix implore
Est demuré sound à vos cris,
Et vous l'osez prier encore,
Quand il vous livre à nos mépris?
Si sa puissance n'est pas vaine,
Qu'il montre sa divinité!
Qu'il vienne briser votre chaîne;
Qu'il vous rende la liberté!
Croyez vous ce Dieu comparable à
Dagon,
Le plus grand des Dieux,
Guidant de son bras redoutable
Nos guerriers victorieux?

CHORUS: Alas! You speak vainly,
For marching into combat,
Where are our weapons?
How will we arm ourselves?
We have nothing but our tears!

SAMPSON: In the Lord still abide.
Have you so soon forgotten
That to us he's allied,
Whatsoever may betide?
His blessed help divine
Has to us been plighted.
In wonder of his might
Our faith has been re-lighted.
When we came through the sea,
Then a passage he made,
So that safely might flee
All our fathers from bondage.

CHORUS: Those wondrous days are
past.
Now our God has ceased heeding
Tears or cries from our hearts,
Or his children's sore pleading.

SAMPSON: Wretched ones, silence
keep!
Nor doubt that God loves you!
Contrite fall on your knees,
For the Lord reigns above you.
Leave your glory to him.
His might will uphold you.
To him yield up the reins;
His mercy will enfold you.
He's the god of combat!
He's the god of armies!
He will endow you with
invincible swords!

CHORUS: Ah! his words are from
the Lord!
With might divine they bless us.
Ah! we'll chase from our hearts
All fear that doth possess us!
We'll march at his side,
For he is our salvation,
And our God is his guide;
He will save our whole nation!

## SCENE II

(The same. Abimelech, satrap of
Gaza, enters at the left, followed
by many warriors and Philistine
soldiers.)

ABIMELECH: Ah! who that's here
dares raise his voice?
In this vile troop who dares to defy
us?
Who dares against our rigid laws
Strive for freedom, and vainly try
us?
Conceal all your groans and your
tears.
We are your conquerors forever,
And compassion we'll never show
you,
We shall not heed your grief nor
fears.
That God whom you are now imp-
loring
Is deaf to your pains and your cries.
For beneath our scorn he lets you
languish,
Paying no heed to all your sighs.
Ah! vain is all his boasted power!
That he's divine, then let him show.

Votre divinité craintive,
Tremblante fuyait devant lui,
Comme la colombe plaintive
Fuit le vautour qui la poursuit!

SAMSON: (Inspiré.) C'est toi que
sa bouche invective,
Et la terre n'a point tremble?
O Seigneur, l'abime est comblé!
Je vois aux mains des anges
Briller l'arme de feu,
Et du ciel les phalanges
Accourent venger Dieu! Oui, l'ange
des ténèbres,
En passant devant eux,
Pousse des cris funèbres
Que font frémir les cieux!
Enfin l'heure est venue,
L'heure du Dieu vengeur,
Et j'eutends dans la nue
Eclater sa fureur.
Oui, devant sa colère
Tout s'épouvante et fuit!
On sent trembler la terre,
Aux cieux la foudre luit!

CHOEUR: Oui, devant sa colère
Tout s'épouvante et fuit!
On sent trembler la terre,
Aux cieux la foudre luit!

ABIMÉLECH: Arrête! Insensé
téméraire,
Ou crains d'exciter ma colère!

SAMSON: Israël! romps ta chaîne!
O peuple, lève toi! Viens assouvir
haîne! le Seigneur est en moi! O toi,
Dieu de lumière, Comme jours
d'autre fois. Exance ma prière, Et
combats pour tes lois! Oui, devant
sa colère, Tout s'é pouvante et fuit,
On sent trembler terre; Aux cieux
la foudre luit! Il déchaîne l'orage,
commande a le gan; On voit sur son
passage Reculer l'Ondes.
(Abimélech se précipite sur Samson l'épée à la main pour le frapper; Samson loi arrache l'épée des
mains et le frappe. Abimélech en
tombant, "A moi!" Les Philistins
qui accompagnant le Satrape veulent le secourir; Samson brandissant son épée, les èloigne. Ils occupent la droit de la scene, la plus
grande confusion règne parmi
eux. Samson et les Hebreux sortent à droite.)
(Les Portes du temple de Dagon
s'ouvrent, le Grand Prêtre suivi de
nombreaux serviteurs et gardes
descend les degrés du portique; il

If he will but free you from bond-
age
Then his might and glory we'll
know.
Can your God compare with Da-
gon,
Who's greater than all your powers,
Who guides so bravely in battle
Till all glorious victory is ours?
Your Jehovah, so weak and fearful,
Flies when he sees our leader
Trembling like the dove so timid,
When it flees from the vulture.

SAMPSON: (Inspired.) It is you, O
my God, he defames!
Let the earth tremble beneath his
feet!
Make his fall and destruction com-
plete!
I see in hands of angels
Sharp swords gleaming with fire.
All the brave ranks of heaven
Sound forth their righteous ire.
And even the souls of darkness,
As the foe they pass by,
Howl forth such cries of anger
As rise to vaulted sky.
At last now is the hour
When God's just wrath is nigh,
And I hear in the clouds
Thunder-claps from on high.
Yes, resounds his vengeance;
Pallid with fear they fly!
The earth trembles in anger,
Bright flashes light the sky!

CHORUS: Yes, resounds his ven-
geance
Pallid with fear they fly!
The earth trembles in anger,
Bright flashes light the sky.

ABIMELECH: But hold! in your
course rushing madly,
For I would avenge me, most gladly.

SAMPSON: Israel! break thy chain!
O people arise! Nourish thy righteous vengeance, For the Lord is
with me! O thou God of light, us
uphold with thy might, As in the
days gone by, When we fought for
the right!
Yes, resounds his vengeance, In
cringing fear they fly, The earth
now quakes in anger, Bright flashes
light the skies. He the tempest com-
mandeth, And holdeth storms and
the tide. His hand, if He but pass it
Makes the waves stand aside.
(Abimelech, sword in hand, attacks Samson. Samson wrests his
sword from him and stabs him.
Abimelech, falling, cries for help.
The Philistines rush to help him.
Samson brandishes his sword and
keeps them off. They fill the stage
at the right. Great confusion
reigns among them. Samson and
the Hebrews pass off.)
(The gates of Dagon's Temple
open. The High Priest, followed by
a throng of attendants and

*s'arrête devant le cadavre d'Abimélech's; les Philistins s'ecartent devant lui.)*

*guards, descends the steps of the portico; he pauses before Abimelech's body. The Philistines draw back from him.)*

## SCENE III

**LE GRAND PRÊTRE:** Que vois-je?
Abimelech! Frappe par des esclaves!
Pourquoi les laisser fuir?
Courons! courons, mes braves!
Pour venger votre Prince, écrasez sous vos coups
Ce peuple révolté bravant votre courroux!

**IER PHILISTIN:** J'ai senti dans mes veines
Tout mon sang se glacer;
Il semble que des chaines
Soudain vont m'enlacer.

**2E PHILISTIN:** Je cherche en vain mes armes,
Mes bras sont impuissants,
Mon coeur est plein d'alarmes,
Mes genoux sont tremblants!

**GRAND PRÊTRE:** Lâches! plus lâches que des femmes!
Vous fuyez devant des combats!
De leur Dieu eraignez vous les flammes,
Qui doivent deséchér vos bras!

## SCENE IV

**UN MESSAGER PHILISTIN:** Seigneur! la troupe furiese
Que conduit et guide Samson,
Dans sa révolte audacieuse,
Accourt ravageant la moisson.

**IER ET 2E PHILISTINS ET MESSAGER:** Fuyons un danger inutile!
Quittons au plus vite ces lieux.
Seigneur, abandonnons la ville,
Et cachons honte aux yeux.

**GRAND PRÊTRE:** Maudite à jamais soit la race
Des enfants d'Israël!
Je veux en effacer la trace,
Les abreuver de fiel!
Maudit soit celui qui les guide
J'écraserai du pied
Ses os brisés, sa gorge aride,
Sans frémir de pitié!
Maudit soit le sein de la femme
Qui lui donna le jour!
Qu'enfin une compagne infâme
Trahisse son amour!
Maudit soit le Dieu qu'il adore,
Ce Dieu, son seul espoir!
Et dont ma haine insulte encore
L'autel et le pouvoir!

**IER AND 2E PHILISTINS ET MESSAGER:** Fuyons dans les montagnes,
Abandonnons ces lieux,
Nos maisons, nos compagnes,
Et jusques à nos Dieux!

## SCENE III

**HIGH PRIEST:** What see I? Abimelech!
Struck down and low before me!
Let not the slaves escape!
But, fly, I implore you,
To avenge your prince!
Now in haste cut them down,
These rebels in revolt,
Who brave your very crown!

**1ST PHILISTINE:** Then with horror seemed frozen
All the blood in my veins;
My limbs seemed as heavy
As they were bound in chains.

**2D PHILISTINE:** My weapon sought I vainly,
My arm no power lent;
My heart fainted within me,
And my knees trembling bent.

**HIGH PRIEST:** Cowards! More cowardly than women!
You have fled in your vain alarms!
From their god you fear that anger
Would scorch and wither you arms!

## SCENE IV

**A PHILISTINE MESSENGER:** My Lord, the band, in their fury,
With Samson strong at their head,
Are all revolting and audacious,
Ravaging where they are led.

**1ST AND SECOND PHILISTINES:** We'll flee, then, exposure that's useless,
We'll leave to more fleet ones this place;
My lord, we'll leave this fearful village,
Concealing our face with shame.

**HIGH PRIEST:** Cursed be your nation forever!
O Israel's hated band!
Fall! and leave no trace behind;
Be swept from off the land!
Cursed, also, he who guides you!
I will grind him beneath my heel;
His anguish keen could I behold
And no remorse would I feel!
Cursed ever be the woman
Who brought him forth to light!
On all who may in love adore him
Now let there fall a blight!
Cursed be the God that he worships,
That God, his hope and delight!
My hate would sweep away his nation,
His altar and his might!

**IST AND 2ND PHILISTINE AND MESSENGER:** We'll fly to yonder mountains,
Nor leave behind a track;
To our homes and companions,
And gods, we will go back.

---

*(Ils sortent par la gauche, emportant le cadavre d'Abimélech, suivis, le Grand Prêtre. Entrent les Hébreux, viellards et femmes, droit.)*

## SCENE V

*Les femmes et les vieillards Hébreux. Puis Samson suivi des Hébreux victorieux.*

**VIEILLARDS HÉBREAUX:** Hymne de joie, hymne de délivrance,
Montez vers l'eternal!
Il a daigné dans sa toute puissance
Secourir Israël!
Par lui le faible est devenu le maitre,
Du fort qui l'opprimait!
Il a vaincu l'orgueil lieux et le traître
Dont la voix l'insultait!
*(Les Hébreux, conduits par Samson, entrent à droite.)*

**UN VIEILLARD HÉBREU:** Il nous frappait dans sa colère,
Car nous avions bravé ses lois.
Plus tard, le front dans la poussière,
Vers lui nous élevions la voix.
Il dit à ses tribus aimées:
Levez vous marchez aux combats!
Je suis le Seigneur des armées,
Je suis la force de vos bras!

**VIEILLARDS HÉBREUX:** Il est venu vers nous dans la détresse,
Car ses fils lui sont chers.
Que l'univers tressaille d'allégresse!
Il a rompu nos fers!
Hymne de joie, etc.

## SCENE VI

*Les portes du temple de Dagon s'ouvrent. Dalila entre suivie des femmes Philistins tenant dans leurs mains des guirlandes de fleurs.*

**CHOEUR DES FEMMES:** Voici le printemps portant des fleurs
Pour orner le front des guerriers vainqueurs!
Mêlons nos accents au parfum des roses,
A peine écloses!
Avec l'oiseau chantons, mes soeurs!
Beauté, don du ciel, printemps de nos jours,
Doux charme des yeux, espoir des amours,
Pénètre les coeurs verse dans les âmes,
Tes douces flammes!
Aimons, mes soeurs, aimons toujours.

---

*(They go off at left, bearing the body of Abimelech, followed by High Priest. At the same time the Hebrews, old men and women, enter at right. Sun rises)*

## SCENE V

*(Hebrews, women and old men. Afterwards, Samson and victorious Hebrews.)*

**OLD HEBREW MEN:** Rise, hymn of joy, hymn of deep thanksgiving,
And tell our eternal truths!
For he who reigns is deliverer all powerful,
He aids Israel.
By him the weak have become so mighty
Against tyranny strong:
He overcomes the pride of the traitor,
Who does battle for the wrong.
*(The victorious Hebrews, led by Samson, enter at the right.)*

**AN AGED HEBREW:** He censured us in rage and anger,
For we his righteous laws had braved.
When bowed before him we entreated
That from his wrath we might be saved.
He said to all his tribe beloved,
"Rise in arms! to combat now fly!
For I, your God, will bless your weapons,
And in the strife be at your side."

**OLD HEBREW MEN:** He came to save his sons, who else had perished.
Now no sorrow remains;
Let all the universe sound his praises!
He hath broken our chains!
Hymn of joy, etc.

## SCENE VI

*(The gates of Dagon's Temple open. Delilah enters, followed by Philistine women with garlands of flowers in their hands.)*

**CHORUS OF WOMEN:** With flowers the spring comes forth gladly now,
Bright garlands to make for brave conqueror's brow.
And cheerful our tones as the glow of roses that spring discloses,
We sing our glad triumphant song,
As sing the birds that round us throng.
The springtime of youth—a gift from above,
Imparts a grace to our early love.
All soft as the breeze in its lightest motion is our devotion.
Then let us love while all is bright,
While nature sports in delight.

**DALILA:** (*À Samson*) Ja viens célébrer la victoire
De celui qui règne en mon coeur.
Dalila veut pour son vainqueur
Encor plus d'amour que de gloire!
O mon bien aimé, suis mes pas
Vers Soreck la douce vallée,
Dans cette demeure isolée
Où Dalila t'ouvre ses bras!

**DELILAH:** (*To Samson.*) I come to resound the brave story
Of the one who reigns in my heart,
And to whom I would joy impart,
Giving more of love than glory.
My beloved one, follow me!
Unto fair Soreck will I guide you,
And there with sweet comfort provide you.
With open arms I'll welcome you.

**SAMSON:** O, Dieu! toi qui vois ma faiblesse,
Prends pitié de ton serviteur!
Ferme mes yeux, ferme mon coeur
A la douce voix qui me presse!

**SAMSON:** (*Apart.*) O God! in your might all sufficing,
Grace to your poor servant impart!
Close my eyes, close my heart
Against that dear voice so enticing!

**DALILA:** Pour toi j'ai couronné mon front
Des grappes noires du troëne,
Et mis des roses de Saron
Dans ma chevelure d'ébène!

**DELILAH:** For you I have crowned my own brow
With the fairest springtime possesses.
The rose of Sharon I have culled
And twined among my dark tresses.

**VIEILLARD HEBREU:** Détour netoi, mon fils, de son chemin!
Evite et crains celle fille étrangère;
Ferme l'oreille a'sa voix mensongère,
Et du serpent évite le venin.

**OLD HEBREW MAN:** O turn, my son, from dark temptation's harm;
Avoid and fear the wiles of this stranger.
Close now your eyes and avoid this great danger,
Flee in terror from the serpent's charm.

**SAMSON:** Voile ses traits dont la beautié
Trouble mes sens, trouble mon âme
Et de ses yeux éteins la flamme
Qui me ravit la liberté!

**SAMSON:** O, veil those eyes whose faintest ray
My sense doth blind, my soul possessing;
Conceal that face so all obsessing
That now my freedom takes away.

**DALILA:** Doux est le muguet parfumé;
Mes baisers le sont plus encore:
Et le suc de la mandragore
Est moins suave ô bien aimé!
Ouvre tes bras à ton amante
Et dèposela sur ton coeur
Comme un sachet de douce odeur,
Dont la senteur est enivrante!
Ah! viens!

**DELILAH:** Sweet the lilies' soft, grateful breath,
But far sweeter the fond caresses
Of the one whom your heart possesses—
Of she who loves you unto death.
Then open your arms, for I adore you.
And let me rest on your heart—
Joy of the angels thus impart.
List to my prayer, I now implore you!
Ah! come!

**SAMSON:** Flamme ardente qui me dévore,
Et qu'elle ravive en ce lieu,
Apaise toi, apaise toi devant mon Dieu,
Pitié, Seigneur, pour celui qui l'implore!

**SAMSON:** O ardent flame that does devour,
Of which this place revives the zest,
Appease my pain, appease my pain,
And ease my breast!
Have pity, Lord, now in my trial's hour!
O Lord!

**VIEILLARD HEBREU:** Jamais tes yeux n'auron assez de larmes
Pour desamer la colère du ciel!
(*Danse des Prêtresses de Dagon.*)
(*Les jeunes filles qui ont accompagné Dalila dansent en agitant des guirlandes de fleurs, et semblent provoquer les guerriers Hébreux qui accompagnent Samson. Ce dernier, profondément trouble, cherche en vain à éviter les regards de Dalila; ses yeux, malgré lui, suivent au milieu des jeunes Philistins, prenant part à leurs poses et à leurs gestes voluptueux.*)

**OLD HEBREW MAN:** A curse on you if heed her pleading,
Or by that voice so strangely sweet be led,
Those eyes could never wash away with weeping
All heaven's rage that would fall on your head!
(*Dance of the Priestesses of Dagon.*)
(*The young girls accompanying Delilah dance, waving garlands of flowers; and try to entice the Hebrew warriors that are with Samson. He tries, but in vain, to avoid Delilah's glances. In spite of him his eyes follow the movements of the enchantress, as she takes part in the voluptuous poses and gestures of the young Philistine maidens.*)

**DALILA:** Printemps qui commence,
Portant l'espérance,
Aux coeurs amoureux,
Ton souffle qui passe.
De terre efface
Les jours malheureux.
Tout brûle en notre âme,
Et ta douce flamme
Vient se cher nos pleurs;
Tu rends à la terre,
Par un doux mystère,
Les fruits et les fleurs.
Et vain je suis belle!
Mon coeur plein d'amour,
Pleurant l'infidèl.
Attend son retour!
Vivant d'espérance,
Mon coeur desolé
Garde souvenance
Du bonheur passé!
A la nuit tombante
J'irai, triste amante,
M'asseoir autorent.
L'attendre en pleurant!
Chassant ma tristesse,
S'il revient un jour,
A lui ma tendresse
Et la douce ivresse
Qu'un brûlant amour.
Garde à son retour!

**DELILAH:** Spring voices are singing,
Bright hope they are bringing,
All hearts making glad.
And gone sorrow's traces,
The soft air effaces
All days that are sad.
Our hearts warm are glowing,
When sweet winds are blowing
They dry our every tear.
The earth glad and beaming,
With freshness is teeming,
While fruits and flowers are here.
In vain all my beauty:
I weep my poor fate.
My heart filled with love,
The faithless wait.
In vain am I striving?
Can hope never last?
I must then remember
Only joys now past.
When night is descending,
With love all unending,
Bewailing my fate,
For him will I wait.
I'll banish all sadness,
Though deeply I may yearn,
When fond love returning,
In his bosom burning
May enforce his return.

**LE VIEILLARD HEBREU:** L'esprit du mal a conduit cette femme
Sur ton chemin pour troubler ton repos.
De ses regards fuis la brûlante flamme!
C'est un poison qui consume les os!

**OLD HEBREW MAN:** This woman, guided by some evil power
Comes in his path to beguile him to shame.
Oh, let him fly from her enticing glances!
For only poison does consume his frame.

**DALILA:** Chassant ma tristesse, etc.
(*Dalila regague en chantant les degrés du temple, et provoque Samson du regard. Il hésite, il lutte, et trahit le trouble de son âme.*)

**DELILAH:** I'll banish all sadness, etc. (*Delilah continues her song on the steps of the Temple. She succeeds in securing Samson's regard by enticing glances. He hesitates and otherwise betrays his trouble and emotion.*)

# ■ ACTE II

Le théâtre représente la vallée de Soreck en Palestine. A gauche, la demeure de Dalila, précédée d'un léger portique et entourée de plantes Asiatiques et de lianes luxuriantes.
Au lever du Rideau la nuit commence et se fait plus complète pendant toute lu durée de l'acte.

## SCENE I

(*Dalila, seule. Elle est plus parée qu'au premier acte. Au lever du rideau elle est assise sur une roche près du portique de sa maison, et semble rêveuse.*)

# ■ ACT II

(*The theatre represents the valley of Soreck in Palestine. At the left Delilah's dwelling, which has a graceful portico, surrounded with Asiatic plants and luxuriant vines.*)
(*At the rising of the curtain night begins and wholly comes on during the course of the act.*)

## SCENE I

(*Delilah, alone. She is more richly attired than in Act I. At the rising of the curtain she is seated on a rock near the entrance of her dwelling, and seems in a reverie.*)

DALILA: Samson, recherchant ma présence,
Ce soir doit venir en ces lieux.
Voici l'heure de la vengeance
Qui doit satisfaire nos dieux!
Amour! viens aider ma faiblesse!
Verse le poison dans son sein!
Fais que, vaincu par mon adresse,
Samson soit enchaîné demain!
Il voudrait en vain de son âme
Pouvoir me chasser, me bannir!
Pourraitil éteindre la flamme
Qu'alimente le souvenir?
Il est à moi! c'est mon esclave!
Mes frères craignent son courroux,
Moi, seule entre tous, je le brave,
Et le retiens à mes genoux!
Amour! viens aider, etc.
Contre l'amour sa force est vaine;
Et lui, le fort parmi les forts,
Lui, qui d'un peuple rompt la chaîne,
Sucombera sous mes efforts!
(*Eclairs lointains*)

## SCENE II

*Dalila et le Grand Prêtre de Dagon.*

LE GRAND PRÊTRE: J'ai gravi la montagne
Pour venir jusqu'à toi;
Dagon qui m'accompagne
M'a guidé vers ton toit.

DALILA: Salut à vous, mon père!
Soyez le bienvenu,
Vous qu'ici l'one revère!

LE GRAND PRÊTRE: Notre sort t'est connu,
La victoire facile
Des eclaves Hébreux
Leur a livré la ville,
Nos soldats devant eux
Ont fui, pleins d'epouvante
Au seul nom de Samson,
Dont l'audace effrayante
A troublé leur raison.
Fatal à notre race,
Il recut de son Dieu
La force avec l'audace,
Enchaîné par un voeu,
Samson, dès sa naissance,
Fut marqué par le ciel
Pour rendre la puissance
Au peuple d'Israël.

DALILA: Je sais que son courage
Brave votre courroux,
Et qu'il n'est pas d'outrage
Qu'il ne garde pour vous.

GRAND PRÊTRE: A tes genoux sa force un jou l'abandonna;
Mais depuis, il s'efforce d'oublier Dalila.

---

DELILAH: To-night Samson comes to greet me;
He'll hasten my sorrows to ease.
For behold, strikes the hour of vengeance
When we blessed gods shall appease.
O Love! in my weakness give power!
Poison Samson's brave heart for me!
Beneath my soft sway may he be vanquished;
To-morrow let him captive be!
Every thought of me he would banish,
And from his tribe he would swerve,
Could he only drive out the passion
That remembrance does now preserve.
But he is under my dominion;
In vain his people may entreat.
I alone can hold him—
I'll have him captive at my feet.
O love, in my weakness, give power, etc.
Against his deep love he battles vainly,
And he, the strongest of the strong!
He'll break the tie to his own nation,
And to my people he'll belong.
(*Distant flashes of lightning.*)

## SCENE II

*(Delilah and the High Priest of Dagon.)*

HIGH PRIEST: I have climbed lofty mountains,
And I have safely reached you.
Good Dagon came to guide me,
Till your roof we might see.

DELILAH: I now salute you, father,
Be welcome, though it's late;
Even here you have honor.

HIGH PRIEST: Known to you is our fate.
And the victory was easy,
For, by treachery led,
Our slaves gave up our cities,
And our brave soldiers fled.
In terror they were scattered;
At Samson's name they fly;
For of his deeds they know—
They to madness were nigh.
It was fatal to our nation.
He received from his God
The force and skill to conquer—
he but serves his Lord.
On him at birth, from heaven
This most holy mission fell,
To aid his chosen people,
The tribe of Israel.

DELILAH: I know his mighty courage
Braves even your direst hate,
And that he deems no outrage
Can for you be too great.

HIGH PRIEST: His courage and his mighty force
Vanished away
At the feet of Delilah,

---

On dit que, dans son âme
Oubliant ton amour,
Il se rit de la flamme
Qui ne dura qu'un jour!

DALILA: Je sais que de ses frères
Ecoutant les discours,
Et les plaintes amères
Que consent nos amours,
Samson, malgré lui-même,
Combat lutte en vain;
Je sais combien il m'aime,
Et mon coeur ne craint rien.
C'est en vain qu'il me brave;
Il est fort aux combats,
Mais il est mon esclave
Et tremble dans mes bras.

GRAND PRÊTRE: Sers-nous de ta puissance,
Prête-nous ton appui!
Que, surpris dans défense,
Il succombe aujourd'hui!
Vends-moi ton esclave Samson!
Et pour te payer sa rancon,
je ne ferai point de promesses;
Tu peux choisir dans mes richesses.

DALILA: Qu'importe à Dalila ton or!
Et que pourrait tout un trésor,
Si je ne rèvais la vengeance!
Je t'ai trompé par cet amour.
Samson sut vous dompter un jour;
Mais il n'a pu mé vaincre encore,
Car, autant que toi, je l'abhorre!

GRAND PRÊTRE: J'aurais dû deviner ta haine
Et ton dessein!
Mon coeur en t'ecoutant tressaille d'allegresse,
Mais sur son coeur dé ja n'aurais tu en vain
Mesuré ta puissance, essayé ton adresse?

DALILA: Oui, déjà, par trois fois deguisant mon projet,
J'ai voulu de sa force éclaircir le secret.
J'allumai cet amour, espérant qu'à sa flamme
Je lirais l'inconnu dans le fond de son âme.
Mais, par trois fois aussi déjouant mon espoir,
Il ne s'est point livré, ne m'a rien laissé voir.
En vain d'un fol amour j'imitai les tendresses!
Espérant amollir son coeur par mes caresses
J'ai vu ce fier captif. enlacé dans mes bras
S'arracher de ma couche et courir combats!
Aujour d'hui cependant il subit ma puissance
Car je l'ai vu pâlir, trembler en ma presence;

---

Where he fell, on that day.
They say, within his bosom
Love for you now is past,
And he laughs at a passion
That but a day can last.

DELILAH: I know that his near kindred
Bitterly all discourse
On his ardent emotion,
And would destroy its force.
But Samson will not fail me,
He combats all in vain;
My fearless heart assures me
That his love will remain.
He is powerful in battle,
And can brave fortune's chance;
But a slave, when I am near him,
And trembles beneath my glance.

HIGH PRIEST: For us employ your power,
And to us lend your aid!
Unto you shall a ransom
For the captive be paid.
This Samson, your slave, sell to me,
And, high though the price may be,
Only name to what you aspire
I'll grant you whatever you desire.

DELILAH: What value to me your gold,
If my vengeance had I sold?
Though you gave me your richest treasure,
With hatred it never could measure!
You are deceived; you know not me.
Though you by him may vanquished be,
He yields to me—I've long possessed him,
Yet more than you I detest him.

HIGH PRIEST: Your design and your hatred I might well have read;
For words but make my trembling heart now thrill with pleasure.
Though counting on his love, do not in vain be led;
Try as you might to ensnare him, but your powers ever measure.

DELILAH: Yes, disguising my motive I've thrice made appeal
That the secret of strength he to me might reveal.
I have kindled his love so, that with its confession,
Of the knowledge I seek he might give me possession.
Thus three times I have hoped; but, alas! all in vain,
For closed within his breast does his secret remain.
In vain with all the ardor my tried art possesses
His proud heart I've tried to render soft by my caresses
I've seen this haughty slave from my arms break away,
And with zeal only warlike rush to thickest of the fray.
This day he will fall;
I need no more dissemble;
He now again will blanche
And in my presence tremble.

Et je sais qu'à cette heure abandonn-
nant les siens,
Il revient en ces lieux resserrer nos
liens.
Pour ce dernier combat j'ai préparé
mes armes:
Samson ne pourra pas résister à mes
larmes.

**GRAND PRÊTRE:** Que Dagon, notre Dieu, daigne étendre son bras!
Tu combats pour sa gloire et par lui
tu vaincras!

**DALILA:** Il faut, pour assouvir ma
haine,
Il faut que mon pouvoir l'enchaîne!
Je veux que, vaincu par l'amour,
Il courbe le front a son tour!

**GRAND PRÊTRE:** Je veux, pour as-
souvir ma haîne,
Je veux que Dalila l'enchaîne;
Il faut que, vaincu par l'amour,
I courbe le front à son tour!
En toi seule est mon espérance,
A toi l'honneur de la vengeance!

**DALILA:** A moi l'honneur de la
vengeance
A moi l'honneur! A moi!

**GRAND PRÊTRE ET DALILA:** Je
veux, pour assouvir ma heine, etc.
Unissons nous tous deux!
Mort au chef des Hébreux!

**GRAND PRÊTRE:** Samson, me di-
sais-tu, dans ces lieux doit se rendre?
Je m'éloigne, il pourrait nous surprendre.
Bientôt je reviendrai par de secrets
chemins.
Les destin de mon peuple, ô
femme, est dans tes mains!
Dechire de son coeur l'invenèrable
écorce,
Et surprends le secret qui nous
cache au force.
(*Il sort.*)
(*Dalila se rapproche de la gauche
de le scène vers le portique de sa
maison, et s'appuie rêveuse à un
des piliers.*)

**DALILA:** Se pourrait-il, que sur son
coeur
L'amour eut perdu sa puissance?
La nuit est sombre et sans lueur
Rien ne peut trahir sa présence.
Helas! Il ne vient pas!
(*Samson arrive par la droit; il
semble emu, troublé, hésitant; il
regarde autour de lui. La nuit
s'assombrit de plus en plus.*)

## SCENE III

(*Éclairs lointains.*)

**SAMSON:** En ces lieux, malgré
moi, m'ont ramené mes pas
Je voudrais fuir, hélas. et ne puis
pas!
Je maudis mon amour et pourtant

Yes, I know he will leave his very
own, and fly
To this most hallow'd place, to renew our blest tie.
For this last combat my surest
weapons I'm keeping,
For he can ne'er withstand my
feign'd grief and weeping.

**HIGH PRIEST:** Oh, may Dagon, our
god, ever sustain thee in right!
You fight for his glory, and conquer
by his might!

**DELILAH:** Let hatred in disguise
now gain him!
Let love with gilded links enchain
him!
May passion his reason enthrall,
That lowly his proud head may fall!

**HIGH PRIEST:** Let hatred in dis-
guise now gain him!
Let love with gilded links enchain
him?
May passion his reason enthrall,
That lowly his proud head may fall?
Thou ever shall be with honor in-
vested.

**DELILAH:** On me alone his hope is
rested,
On me alone!

**BOTH:** Let hatred in disguise, etc.
Our forces we'll unite!
Death to that Israelite!

**HIGH PRIEST:** We'll see that the
brave Hebrew no more defies us;
I'll depart, lest he come and surprise us.
I'll soon return, and by a secret pas-
sage-way:
You hold in your hand my people's
fate this day.
Employ your arts till Samson, all his
soul revealed,
Tear out from his heart the secret he
concealed.
(*Exit High Priest.*)
(*Delilah goes slowly to the entrance of her house, where she remains leaning against one of the
pillars, in pensive attitude.*)

**DELILAH:** Can it be true, that in his
heart
My love no longer has power?
His presence can betray nothing
For the dark night is lowering on
all.
Alas! he is not coming.
(*Samson enters from right, hesi-
tatingly and troubled. The night
grows darker.*)

## SCENE III

(*Lightning in distance.*)

**SAMSON:** To this place I am led,
Vanquished again am I!
To fly from here, alas!
I fain would try.
Yet, when I would depart—

j'aime encore,
Fuyons, fuyons ces lieux que ma
faiblesse adore!

**DALILA:** (*S'élance vers Samson.*)
C'est toi!
C'est toi, mon bien aimé!
J'attendais ta présence!
J'oubie, en te voyant,
Des heures de souffrance!
Salut! salut! ô mon doux maitre!

**SAMSON:** Arrètes ces transports!
Je ne puis t'écouter sans honte et
sans remords!

**DALILA:** Samson! ô toi! mon bien
aimé,
Pourquoi, repousser ma tendresse?
Pour-quoi, de mon front parfumé,
Pour-quoi détourner tes caresses?

**SAMSON:** Tu fus toujours chère à
mon coeur,
Et tu n'en peux être bannie!
J'aurais voulu donner ma vie
A l'amour qui fit mon bonheur!

**DALILA:** Près de moi, pres de moi
pour-quoi ces alarmes?
Auraistu douté de mon coeur?
N'estu pas mon maître et seigneur?
L'amour at-il perdu ses charmes?

**SAMSON:** Hélas! esclave de mon
Dieu,
Je subis sa volonté sainte;
Il faut, par un dernier adieu,
Rompre sans murmure et sans
crainte
Le doux lien de notre amour,
D'Israël renaît l'espérance,
Le Seigneur a marqué le jour
Qui verra notre délivrance!
Il a dit à sone serviteur:
"Je t'ai chois parmi tes frères,
Pour les guider vers le Seigneur
Et mettre un terme à leurs miseres!"

**DALILA:** Qu'importe à mon coeur
désole
Le sort d'Israël et sa gloire!
Pour moi le bonheur envolé
Est le seul fruit de la victoire.
L'amour égarait ma raison
Quand je coyais à tes promesses,
Et je n'ai bu que le poison
En m'enivrant de tes caresses!

**SAMSON:** Ah! ces se d'affliger mon
coeur!
Je subis une loi suprême,
Tes pleurs ravient ma douleur!
Dalila! Dalila! Je t'aime!
(*Eclairs lointains.*)

Would haste from before her,
Then more and ever more
In weakness I adore her.

**DELILAH:** (*Coming to him quick-
ly.*) It's you!
It's you, my best beloved!
Long for thee have I waited.
I now forget my woes;
To happiness we're fated!
To you a welcome sweet from me!

**SAMSON:** Oh, cease your transports wild!
For without deep remorse my heart
is not beguiled!

**DELILAH:** O Samson, my own! my
best beloved!
Your heart your fond love now represses.
Why do you turn away your dear
face?
Ah! why withhold from me your
caresses?

**SAMSON:** My fatal love I can never
destroy.
From out my heart you will never
be banished,
Or happiness would all be vanished.
In my ardent love is my joy!

**DELILAH:** By my side why do you
fear?
Ah, why so faint-hearted?
Is it doubt that seizes your heart?
You ever are the Lord of my life.
Have all love's charms for you de-
parted?

**SAMSON:** Alas! I'm pledged to my
own God.
To his will do I yield me gladly.
I'll tell you a last sad farewell,
And loose the tie that binds me
madly.
I'll break the bond of our false
love—
Love that on Israel's freedom en-
croaches
For the day of release is nigh,
Our deliverance even now ap-
proaches.
Our blessed Lord to his servant said,
"I've chosen you from out your na-
tion
To guide your people unto me,
To lead in working their salvation."

**DELILAH:** What joy to my desolate
heart,
Though Israel's' fate may be glori-
ous?
From me would all gladness depart,
Should your own people be victori-
ous.
By love is my reason dethroned,
For lost the hope the soul possesses!
All vain your promises to me;
Like poison all your fond caresses!

**SAMSON:** Ah! cease to wound my
anguished heart!
I but yield to the powers above you!
Thy tears increase my bitter grief—
Woe is me! woe is me! I love you!
(*Lightning.*)

# Act II, Scene III

**DALILA:** Un dieu plus puissant que le tien,
Ami, te parle par ma bouche;
C'est le dieu d'amour, c'est le mien!
Et, si ce souvenir te touche,
Rapelle à ton coeur beaux jours
Passés aux genoux d'une amante
Que tu devais aimer toujours,
Et qui seule, hélas! est constante!

**SAMSON:** Insensée! oser m'accuser!
Quand pour toi tout parle à mon âme,
Oui! dût la foudre m'écraser!
Dussé je perir de sa flamme!
*(Éclairs plus rapprochés.)*
Pour toi si grand est mon amour,
Que j'ose aimer malgré Dieu même!
Oui! dussé-je en mourir un jour,
Dalila! Dalila! je t'aime!

**DALILA:** Mon coeur d'ouvre à ta voix Comme s'ouvrent les fleurs, Aux baisers de l'aurore! Mais, ô mon bien ai mé Pom mieux secher mes pleurs Avec ta voix parle encore! Dis mon qu'à Dalila Tu reviens pour jamais, Redis à ma tendresse Les serments d'autre fois, Ces serments que j'ai mais! Ah! réponds a ma tendresse, Ver se moi, ver se moi, l'i vres se! Réponds à ma tendresse, Réponds à ma tendresse! Ah! ver se moi, ver se moi l'i vres se!

**SAMSON:** Dalila! Dalila! Je t'aime.

**DALILA:** Ainsi qu'on voit des blés Les é pis enduler Sous la brise légère, Ainsi frémit mon coeur, Prêt à se consoloer. A ta voix qui m'est chè re! La flèche est moins rapide À parter le trépes, Que ne l'est tou a mau te À voler dans tes bras, A voler dans tes bras. Ah! réponds à ma tendresse, Ver se moi, ver se moi lédresse! Reponds à ma tendresse, Réponds à ma tendresse, ah! Ver se moi, Ver se moi l'i vres se

**SAMSON:** Par mes baisers Je veux sècher tes larmes Et de ton coeur Eloigner les a larmes, Je veux sè cher tes larmes, Je veux sècher tes larmes Dalila! Dalila! Je t'aime!
*(Éclairs.)*
*(Violent coup de tonnerre.)*

**DALILA:** Mais! non! que disje, hélas!
La triste Dalila doute de tes paroles!
Egarant ma raison, tu me trompas déja
Par des serments frivoles!

**DELILAH:** A god more despotic than yours
By my own lips to you is speaking,
It is the god of Love, that is mine;
He brings the bliss all are seeking!
Recall I the joys that are past,
When you at my feet then were kneeling,
Vowing to love me evermore!
Now, alas! it is I who has feeling!

**SAMSON:** You ingrate! You dare accuse!
Only you alone do I cherish,
or strike me, bolts from on high,
Or let me in fierce flames now perish!
So mighty is my love for you,
I brave the God that reigns above me,
Though his vengeance may strike me down!
Woe is me! woe is me! I love you!

**DELILAH:** My heart at your dear voice Does unfold and rejoice, Like a flower when dawn is smiling. You can my weeping stay. My sadness charm away With your tones so beguiling Then, oh! to me but say you have returned for always Repeat your vows so tender, your vows of the past, That I dreamed ever would last! Ah! once more your vows so tender, And your heart, and your heart surrender, Once more your vows so tender, Once more your vows so tender, Ah! and your heart, and your heart, surrender!

**SAMSON:** Woe is me! woe is me! I love you!

**DELILAH:** As when a field of grain, Like the waves on the main, In the breeze is swaying, bounding, So all my heart is swayed, In deepest chords are played, When your voice is resounding. The arrow in its flight, Though so soon gone from sight, Moves more slowly than I, If, to you I may fly! Yes, if to your I fly. Ah! once more your vows so tender, And your heart and your heart surrender Once more your vows so tender, Once more your vows so tender, ah! and your heart, and your heart surrender

**SAMSON:** Fondly my kiss Each tear of thine represses I in thy heart Joy restore with caresses Though smite the God above you Though smite the God above thee Woe is me! woe is me! I love you
*(Lightning and violent crash of thunder.)*

**DELILAH:** But no! I speak in vain!
Delilah is distraught,
My sad heart is bereaving
You've struck me down in despair!
You've ensnared my soul!
With your traitorous vows.

**SAMSON:** Quand pour toi j'ose oublier Dieu,
Sa gloire, mon peuple et mon voeu!
Ce Dieu qui marqua ma naissance
Du sceau divin de sa puissance!

**DALILA:** Eh bien! connais donc mon amour!
C'est ton Dieu même que j'envie!
Ce Dieu qui te donna le jour,
Ce Dieu qui consacra ta vie!
Le voeu qui t'enchaîne à ce Dieu
Et qui fait ton bras redoutable,
A mon amour faisen l'aveu,
Chasse le doute qui m'accable!

**SAMSON:** Dalila! que veux tu de moi?
Crains que je ne doute de toi!

**DALILA:** Si j'ai conservé ma puissance,
Je veux l'essayer en ce jour!
Je veux éprouver ton amour,
En réclamant ta confiance!
*(Éclairs et tonnerre plu en plus rapprochés.)*

**SAMSON:** Hélas! qu'impore à ton bonheur
Le lien sacré qui m'enchaîne?
Ce secret que garde mon coeur—

**DALILA:** Par cet aveu soulage ma doleur.

**SAMSON:** Pour le ravir ta force est vaine!

**DALILA:** Oui! vain est mon pouvoir,
Car vaine est ta tendresse!
Quand je veux le savoir,
Ce secret qui me blesse,
Dont je veux la moitié,
O sestu, ans ton âme
Sans honte et sans pitié,
M'accuser d'être inflâme!

**SAMSON:** D'un immense douleur
Ma pauvre âme accablée
Implore le Seigneur
D'une voix désolée!

**DALILA:** J'avais paré pour lui
Ma jeunesse et mes charmes!
Je n'ai plus au jour d'hui
Qu'à répandre des larmes!

**SAMSON:** Dieu tout-puissant, j'invoque te m'appui!

**DALILA:** Pour ces derniers adieux
Ma voix est impuissante!
Fuis! Samson, fuis ces lieux
Où mourra ton amante!

**SAMSON:** Laisse moi!

**DALILA:** Ton secret!

**SAMSON:** Je ne puis!

**DALILA:** Ton secret? ce secret qui cause mes alarmes!

**SAMSON:** L'orage sur ces monts
Déchaîne sa colère!
Le Seigneur sur nos fronts
Fait gronder son tonnerre!

**SAMSON:** Now I bow to you in worship,
Forgetting my people and vow!
Forgetting my God and his dower,
The seal that marked me with his power!

**DELILAH:** Alas! You've forgotten my love!
I envy him whom I have hated,
Your God who has given you birth,
To whom you, consecrated your life.
The vow that has chained you to him,
Making you victorious in battle,
Oh, give to me and my poor heart!
Your love's reward will then be glorious!

**SAMSON:** Delilah, what would you do with me?
Do you doubt my mad love for you?

**DELILAH:** If I'm presiding over your heart,
I'd prove it a truth on this day.
A ray of your love then betray
In secrets dark to me confiding.
*(Thunder and lightning nearer.)*

**SAMSON:** Alas! What do sacred ties, or
power vested in me, matter to you?
That great secret closed in my heart—

**DELILAH:** Open your heart, and impart joy to me—

**SAMSON:** By your vain might never can be wrested!

**DELILAH:** Oh, vain all my sad strife!
In vain your love surrounds me,
If I can never divine
That dark secret that wounds me.
When your thoughts I would share
Do you dare to refuse me?
and pitiless, cold,
Would in your heart accuse me?

**SAMSON:** Great the anguish I feel!
O, my God, be near me!
My soul is rent with pain—
I implore you to hear me!

**DELILAH:** For him have I displayed
All my beauty, nothing reaping!
To me only is left
Sorrow and anguished weeping!

**SAMSON:** All powerful God!
Oh, hear me, my Lord!

**DELILAH:** To try to speak farewell
Is vain; my soul defies me!
Samson, fly! fly from here
Where your own love now dies!

**SAMSON:** Leave me!

**DELILAH:** Tell me, then!

**SAMSON:** Ask me not!

**DELILAH:** Tell to me the secret
For which my heart now dies!

**SAMSON:** O tempest, on these heights
Let loose, on us descending,
All the wrath of the Lord
Our guilty souls now rending!

DALILA: Je le brave avec toi! Viens!

SAMSON: Non!

DALILA: Viens!

SAMSON: Laisse Mois!

DALILA: Que m'importe la foudre!

SAMSON: Je ne puis m'y résoudre—
C'est la voix de mon Dieu!

DALILA: Lâche! coeur sans amour!
Je te meprise! Adieu!
(Eclairs et tonnerre.)
(Dalila court vers sa demeure;
l'orage est dans toute sa feurer.
Samson levant les bras au ciel,
semble invoquer Dieu. Il s'élance
à suite Dalila, hésite, et entre en-
fin dans sa demeure.)
(Par la droite arrivent des soldats
Philistins, qui s'approchent de la
demeure.)
(Violent coup de tonnerre.)
(Dalila paraissant à sa feuêtre.)

DALILA: A moi! Philistins! à moi!

SAMSON: Trahison!
(Les soldats se précipitent dans la
demeure de Dalila. Rideau.)

# ■ ACTE III

La prison de Gaza. Samson enchaine avengle, les cheveux
coupes tourne la meule. Dans la
coulisse, choeur des Hebreux captifs.

SAMSON: Vois ma misère, hélas!
vois ma détresse!
Pitié, Seigneur! pitié pour ma faib-
lesse!
J'ai détourné mes pas de ton che-
min:
Beintôt de moi tu retiras ta main.
Je t'offre, ô Dieu, ma pauvre âme
brisée!
Je ne suis plus qu'un objet de risée!
Ils m'ont ravi la lumière du ciel;
Ils m'ont versé l'amertume et le
fiel!

CHOEUR: Samson, qu'astu fait de
tes frères?

SAMSON: Hélas! Israël dans les
fers,
Du ciel allirant la vengeance,
A perdu jusqu'à l'espérance
Par tous lex maux qu'il a soufferts!
Que nos tribus tes jeux trouvent
grâce!
Daigne à ton peuple èpargner la
douler!
Apaise toi devant leurs maux,
Seigneur!
Toi, dont jamais la pitié ne se lasse!

DELILAH: I will brave all with you!
Come!

SAMSON: No!

DELILAH: Come!

SAMSON: Leave me!

DELILAH: I care nothing for what
awaits me!

SAMSON: I can never settle myself!
It's the voice of my God!

DELILAH: Coward! Loveless heart,
I despise you! Farewell!
(Thunder and lightning.)
(Delilah hastens to her house; the
storm breaks furiously. Samson
raises his arms, as if to call upon
God; then hastily follows Delilah—hesitates, but finally enters
the dwelling.)
(Philistine soldiers are seen at
right, approaching the house.)
(Music of the scene continues. Finally a violent crash of thunder.
Delilah re-appears, on the terrace.)

DELILAH: Philistines! your aid!

SAMSON: (Within.) I am betrayed!
(The soldiers rush into Delilah's
house.)
(Curtain.)

# ■ ACT III

(A prison at Gaza. Samson, in
chains, blinded and shorn, is
grinding at a mill.)
(Chorus of Hebrew captives behind the scenes.)

SAMSON: Sore my distress, alas! my
guilt and anguish!
Have pity, Lord, in misery I lan-
guish.
Away from your most righteous
laws I've gone,
And now is your protecting hand
withdrawn.
I offer you a heart that is broken;
Of my most bitter repentance the
token.
From me all light they have taken
away.
To gall is turned every hour of day.

CHORUS: Ah! why have you, Samson, taken false pledges?

SAMSON: Behold! Israel now in
chains!
God's wrath from high heaven de-
scends,
And our hearts, all deserted, rend.
Not even a ray of hope remains.
To our grief, O gracious Sovereign,
awaken!
Deign to hear when we cry unto
you!
Your ire appeasing, your grace we
would see.
Have pity! let not our tribe be for-
saken!

CHOEUR: Dieu nous confiait à ton
bras
Pour nous guider dans les combats;
Samson! qu'astu fait de tes frères?

SAMSON: Frères! votre chant do-
loureux
Pénétrant dans ma nuit profonde,
D'une angoisse mortelle inonde
Mon coeur coupable et malheu-
reux!
Dieu! prends ma vie en sacrifice
Pour satisfaire ton courroux.
D'Israël détourne tes coups,
Et je proclame ta justice!

CHOEUR: Pour une femme il nous
vendait,
De Dalila payant les charmes.
Fils de Manoah, qu'astu fait
De notre sang et de nos larmes?

SAMSON: A tes pieds brisé, mais
soumis,
Je bénis la main qui me frappe.
Fais, Seigneur, que ton peuple
échappe
A la fureur des enemis!

CHOEUR: Samson! qu'astu fait de
tes frères?
Qu'astu fait du Dieu de tes pères?
(Les Philistins entrent dans la
prison. Ils entraines Samson.
Changement.)

## SCENE II

Interieur du Temple de Dagon.
Statue du Dieu. Table des sacrifices. Au milieu du sanctuaire
deux colonnes de marbre semblant supporter l'edifice.

La Grande Prêtre de Dagon entouré des princes Philistins. Dalila, suivie des jeunes femmes Philistins, couronnées de fleurs, des
cóupes à la main. Une foule de
peuple remplit le Temple. Le jour
se lève.

CHOEUR: L'aube qui blanchit déjà
les coteaux,
D'une nuit si belle étaint les flam-
beaux;
Prolongeons la fête, et malgré
l'aurore,
Aimons encore;
L'amour verse au coeur l'oubli de
nos maux.
Au vent du matin, l'ombre de la
nuit
Comme un léger voile à l'horizon
fuit.
L'orient s'empourpre, et sur les
montagnes
Le soleil luit,

CHORUS: Be once again at our side
In danger's strife, and combat
guide!
Why, Samson, has taken false
pledges,
Or let our blessed tribe be forsaken?

SAMSON: Brothers! your sad
strains, like a dart
Penetrate through the night that is
over me.
Bring not all my guilt before me,
Or rend still more my anguished
heart!
My life in sacrifice I offer, O God,
your holy wrath to stay;
Turn not your face from Israel
away!

CHORUS: He sold us for a woman's
charms,
With only love's false pleasure
reaping!
You, Manoah's son, what will you
do
With blood that's shed and bitter
weeping?

SAMSON: Take this atonement that
I offer!
At your feet I fall in despair,
But I bless the hand that's oppress-
ing.
Gracious Lord, give my tribe your
blessing—
My gloomy fate let them not share!

CHORUS: Ah! Why have you taken
false pledges?
(The Philistines enter the prison
and take Samson out. Change of
scene.)

## SCENE II

(Interior of the Temple of Dagon.
Statue of the idol; altars, etc. Two
marble pillars which seem to support the building.)

(The High Priest stands surrounded by the chief Philistines. Delilah
appears, followed by young wom-
en bearing wine-cups in their
hands. Day is dawning; a great
throng is in the Temple.)

CHORUS: Dawn now on the hill-
top sheds rosy light,
And before its gleam stars vanish
from sight.
We'll rejoice although now comes
the morning,
And day is dawning.
Sorrows of the heart vanish with the
night.
Fast before the odorous morning
breeze,
Like a fleecy veil gloomy darkness
flees.
In the east the sun its clear face is
showing,
In splendor's might, over all the

## Act III, Scene II

Dardant ses rayons au sein des cam-
pagnes,
Au sein des campagnes.
(*Danse.*)

land its bright rays are glowing.
(*Dance.*)

## SCENE III

*Samson—conduit par un enfant.*

**LE GRAND PRÊTRE:** Salut! Salut au
juge d'Israël,
Qui vient par sa presence égayer
notre fête!
Dalila! par tes soins qu'une coups
soit prête;
Verse à ton amant l'hydromel!
Il videre sa coupe en chantant sa
maitresse
Et sa puissance enchanteresse!

**CHOEUR:** Samson! nous buvons
avec toi!
A Dalila ta souveraine!
Vide la coupe san effroi:
L'iversse dissipe la peine.

**SAMSON:** (*À part.*) L'ame triste
jusqu'a la mort,
Devant toi, Seigneur, je m'incline;
Que par ta volonté divine
Ici s'accomplisse mon sort!

**DALILA:** (*S'approchant de Sam-
son une coupe a la main.*) Laisse
moi prendre ta main
Et te montrer le chemin,
Comme dans la sombre allée
Qui conduit à la vallée,
Le jour où suivant mes pas
Tu m'enlacais de tes bras!
Tu gravissais les montagnes
Pour arriver jusqu'à moi,
Et je fuyais mes compagnes
Pour ètre seule avec toi.
Souviens-toi de nos ivresses!
Souviens-toi de mes caresses!
L'amour servait mon projet!
Pour assouvir ma vengeance
Je t'arrachai ton secret:
Je l'avais vendu d'avance!
Tu croyais à cet amour,
C'est lui qui riva ta chaine!
Dalila venge en ce jour
Son dieu, son peuple et sa haine!

**CHOEUR:** Dalila venge en ce jour
Son dieu, son peuple, et sa haine.

**SAMSON:** (*À part.*) Quand tu par-
lais, je restais sourd;
Et dans le trouble de mon âme,
Hélas! j'ai profané l'amour,
En le donnant à cette femme.

**GRAND PRÊTRE:** Allons, Samson,
divertis nous,
En redisant à ton amante
Les doux propos, les chants si doux
Dont la passion s'alimente.

## SCENE III

*(Samson enters,—led by a child.)*

**HIGH PRIEST:** All hail! the judge of
Israel,
Who by his presence, lends joy to
our festival!
Hail to you whom Delilah in love
ever tends!
The cup we'll fill with hydromel!
We'll let him drink to her glory and
power,
And on her name his praises show-
er.

**CHORUS:** We'll drink, Samson,
we'll drink with you!
Drink, and leave care until tomor-
row!
Drink to Delilah with all joy
For the cup drowns every sorrow.

**SAMSON:** (*Aside.*) All my soul is
sad unto death,
At your throne your servant kneel!
Your holy will your law reveals.
Here you will receive my last
breath!

**DELILAH:** (*Approaching Samson
with a wine-cup in her hand.*)
Give me your hand, come by my
side,
I will your uncertain footsteps
guide
As, upon that day, soon ended,
To the vale our steps we wended,
And you, free from love's alarms,
Did twine around me your arms.
You did ascend lofty mountains,
Only to fly to me,
And I deserted companions
To be alone with you.
Your past love your heart con-
fesses.
Do you recall your fond caresses?
Your passion furthered my plan
My vengeance your love impelling;
I tore your secret from you,
In my hate the knowledge selling!
You, all trustful, did confide
In her who now enchains you.
Yes, Delilah's vengeance comes,
And her god, her people, now ar-
raign you.

**CHORUS:** On this day her vengeance comes,
Her God, her people, arraign you.

**SAMSON:** (*Aside.*) When you did
speak, I heard you not,
Transgressing law when well did I
know it.
Alas! your servant loved profaned—
On this false woman did bestow it!

**HIGH PRIEST:** Oh, cease your
strain, and turn to her,
And tell again the oft-told story.
Rehearse your love in sweetest
strain,

Que Jéhovah compatissant
A les yeux rende la lumière!
Je servirai ce Dieu puissant,
S'il peut exaucer ta prière!
Mais incapable à servir,
Ce Dieu, que tu nommes ton père.
Je puis l'outrager, le haïr,
En me riant de sa colère!

**SAMSON:** Tu permets, ô Dieu
d'Israël!
Que ce prêtre imposteur outrage,
Dans sa fureur dans sa rage,
Ton nom, à la face du ciel!
Que ne puis je venger ta gloire,
Et par un prodige éclatant
Retrouver pour un seul instant
Les yeux, la force et la victoire!

**CHOEUR:** Ha! ha! ha! Rions de sa
fureur!
Dans ta rage impuissante, Samson
tu s'y vois pas!
Prends garde à tes pas! Samson!
Sa colère est plaisante!
Ha! ha! ha!

**GRAND PRÊTRE:** Viens, Dalila,
rendre grâce à nos dieux
Qui font trembler Jéhovah dans les
cieux!
Du grand Dagon consultons les aus-
pices:
Versons pour lui le vin des sacrifices.
*(Dalila, et le Grand Prêtre se di-
rigent vers à la table des sacrifices, sur laguelle se trouvenet les
coupes sacres. Un feu brûle sur
l'autel qui est orne des fleurs. Dalila et le Grand Prêtre, prenant les
coupes, font une libatium sur le
feu sacré qui s'active, puis disparait, pour repartire au 3e couplet
d l'invocation.)*
*(Samson est resté au milieu de la
scène, ayant prés de lui l'enfant
qui le conduit; it est accablé par la
doleur ensemble prier.)*

**GRAND PRÊTRE:** Gloire à Dagon
vainqueur!
Il aidait ta faiblesse,
Inspirant à ton coeur
Et la force et l'adresse.
O toi! le plus grand entre tous!
Toi qui fis la terre où nous sommes,
Qui ton esprit soit avec nous,
O maître des dieux et des hommes!

**DALILA:** Gloire à Dagon vainqu-
eur!
Il aidait ma fablesse,
Inspirant a mon coeur
Et la force et l'adresse.
O toi! le plus grand entre tous!

Softly chant her praises and glory!
Let Jehovah show his might,
And in his mercy cure your
blindness.
I will adore your boasted god,
If he will show you his kindness!
But if he fail in this extreme,
His mercy on you now to shower,
He merits but hatred and scorn—
I laugh at all his might and power!

**SAMSON:** Ah! do you permit this,
my God?
This false priest in revenge engag-
ing,
Who in his fury and his raging
Blasphemes even your name, O, my
Lord?
To avenge you, my Father glorious,
Grant me but one proof of your
might,
For a moment give me back my
sight!
Hear my cry—make me victorious!

**CHORUS:** Ah! ah! ah! Your rage
does vain appear!
You can not rouse our fear,
Even though your words are fright-
ful,
For never will you see!
Well guarded then be!
Your anger is delightful!
Ah! ah! ah!

**HIGH PRIEST:** Thank you Delilah,
our gods upon high,
Who shake Jehovah's weak throne
in the sky!
We'll now consult the agents of Dagon;
For Samson we'll pour wine from
every flagon.
*(Delilah and High Priest ap-
proach the table on which are
placed the sacred bowls. On the altar which is ornamented with
flowers, a fire burns. Delilah and
High Priest take up the bowls and
pour the libation upon the sacred
flame, which flashes up, then disappears, but again flames up at
the third couplet of the invocation.)*
*(Samson stands in the center of
the scene, with the child who led
him. He is grief-striken, and appears to be devoutly praying.)*

**HIGH PRIEST:** (*To Delilah.*) Glory
forever more to Dagon the victori-
ous,
Who inspired your weak heart with
his might so all-glorious!
(*To Dagon.*)
O greatest of all the great,
Who the heavens and earth have
created!
Ruler of gods as well as men,
With your spirit we'd be inflated!

**DELILAH:** Glory for evermore
To Dagon the victorious,
Who inspired my weak heart
With his might so all-glorious!
O greatest of all the great,
Who the heavens and earth have

Toi qui fis la terre où nous sommes,
Que ton esprit soit avec nous,
O maître des dieux et des hommes!

**CHOEUR:** Marque d'un signe
Nos longs troupeaux;
Mûris la vigne
Sur nos coteaux;
Rends à la plaine
Notre moisson
Que, dans sa haine,
Brûla Samson!

**DALILA ET GRAND PRÊTRE:** Reçois sur nos auteis
Le sang de nos victimes,
Qu't'offrent des mortels
Pour expier leurs crimes.
Aux yeux de tes prêtres divins,
Pouvant seuls contempler ta face,
Montre l'avenir qui se cache
Aux regards des autres humains!

**CHOEUR:** Dieu, sois propice
A nos destins!
Que ta justice
Aux Philistins
Donne la gloire
Dans les combats;
Que la victoire
Suive nos pas!

**DALILA ET GRAND PRÊTRE:** Dagon se révèle
La flamme nouvelle
Sur l'autel
Renaît de la cendre:
L'immortel
Pour nous va descendre!
C'est le dieu
Qui par sa présence
Montre sa puissance!
Ah!
L'immortel, pour nous va descendre!
C'est le dieu qui par sa presence
Montre sa puissance.
En ce lieu.
Sur l'autel, renaît de la cendre!
Dagon se révèle!

**CHOEUR:** C'est le dieu qui par sa
présence
Montre sa puissance
En ce lieu.

**GRAND PRÊTRE:** (A Samson.)
Pour que le sort soit favorable
Allons, Samson, viens avec nous
A Dagon, le dieu redoutable,

created!
Ruler of gods as well as men,
With your spirit we'd be inflated!

**CHORUS:** Mark with your blessing
our flock and field;
Make our vineyards with richness
yield!
Give, in our harvest, good unalloyed,
For all our substance foes have destroyed!

**DELILAH AND HIGH PRIEST:**
Upon your altar blessed
A victim's blood we offer;
To expiate our sins
Our gifts in love we proffer.
May thy priests who all humbly
kneel,
See your face so divinely lighted;
Even though we are not so clearsighted,
To their eyes our future reveal!

**CHORUS:** O listen, our god, when
thus we cry!
May your blessed aid be ever near!
You are so mighty; gird us with
power,
Make us victorious in combat's
hour!

**DELILAH AND HIGH PRIEST:** Dagon's might surprising!
Flames anew are rising
From the ashes of the sacred altar!
God makes the flames upward tower.
Thus he shows his power.
Ah!
From the ashes of the sacred altar!
God makes the flames upward tower.
Thus he shows his power.
Bless his name!

**CHORUS:** Let our hearts with fear
never falter!
Dagon's might surprising!
Ah! God makes the flames upward
tower;
Thus he shows his power,
In this flame.

**HIGH PRIEST:** (To Samson.) O
may our fate be all propitious!
Come, Samson, come, our gods to
please!

Offrir ta coupe à deux genoux!
(A l'enfant.)
Guidez ses pas vers le milieu du
temple,
Pour que de loin le peuple le contemple.

**SAMSON:** Seigneur, inspire moi,
ne m'abandonne pas!
Vers les piliers de marbre, enfant,
guide mes pas!
(L'enfant conduit Samson.)

**CHOEUR:** Dagon se révèle,
La flamme nouvelle,
Sur l'autel renaît de la cendre;
C'est le dieu,
Qui par sa presence
Montre sa puissance
Ence lieu!
Dieu, sois propice
A nos destins!
Que ta justice
Aux Philistins
Donne la gloire
Dans les combats!
Que la victoire
Suive nos pas!
Devant toi d'Israël
Disparaît l'insolence!
Nos bras guidés par ton esprit
Dans les combats.
Ou par tes charmes.
Ont vaincu ce peuple maudit,
Bravant ta colère et tes armes
A nos destins
Dieu, sois propice, etc.
Gloire à Dagon!
Gloire à Dagon!
(Samson placé entre les deux piliers et charchant a les ébranler.)

**SAMSON:** Souviens-toi de ton serviteur!
Qu'ils ont privé de la lumière!
Daigne pour un instant, Seigneur,
Me rendre ma force première!
Qu'avec toi je me venge, O Dieu!
En les écrasant en ce lieu!
(Le Temple s'écroule au milieu
des cris.)
(Rideau.)

And to Dagon mighty and direful
Present your offering on your
knees!
(To the child.)
Out to the middle of the temple
guide him,
That all beholding may in scorn
deride him!

**SAMSON:** Inspire me with your
might,
With me, O Lord, abide!
On to the marble pillars,
My child, my footsteps guide.
(The child leads Samson between
the two pillars.)

**CHORUS:** Dagon's might surprising!
Flames anew are rising!
From the ashes of the sacred altar
God makes the flames upward tower:
Thus he shows his power.
Bless his name!
O listen, our God, when thus we
cry!
May your blessed aid be ever near
You are so mighty! Gird us with
power!
Make us victorious in combat's
hour!
Before you Israel is all bereft of
power!
Guide our arm; gird us with power.
Make us victorious; give us victory
in combat's hour!
May this cursed tribe in this hour
Feel your direful anger and power.
O listen, our god, etc.
Glory! glory!
(Samson has placed himself between the pillars and attempts to
remove them.)

**SAMSON:** Lord, your servant remember now!
You made him blind your just
wrath showing.
For one sole moment make him
strong,
His power of old on him bestowing!
To avenge me, O lend your might!
Let the foe be destroyed in your
sight!
(The Temple falls.)
(Cries and shrieks of the people.)

(Curtain descends.)

# The Bartered Bride (1866)

Music by Bedrich Smetana ■ Libretto by Karel Salbina

The Bartered Bride is a comic opera in three acts. Set to a libretto by Karel Sabina, it was first performed at the Provisional Theatre in Prague on May 30, 1866. In a Czech village during a spring holiday, Marenka and Jeník are unhappy because her parents want her to marry a wealthy man instead of Jeník. No one knows anything about Jeník's parentage. The village marriage broker, Kecal, convinces her parents that Vasek, the younger son of Tobias Mícha, a rich landlord, would make a suitable son-in-law. Marenka refuses Vasek. When he arrives in the village, Marenka tells him terrible things about his intended. She suggests that he marry someone much prettier and nicer. Kecal asks Jeník to give up Marenka for money and Jeník agrees on the condition that her groom be Vasek. Kecal gathers the villagers to witness Jeník's signing of the agreement; everyone is horrified that Marenka has been bartered! Vasek cannot find the strange young woman he has met, but he comes upon a traveling circus and falls for Esmeralda, a ballerina. He dresses up as a dancing bear when the real performer is too drunk to go on. Marenka, deeply upset by Jeník's arrangement, agrees to marry Vasek, who is delighted when he discovers who she really is. Tobias Mícha arrives and recognizes Jeník as his long-lost eldest son. Jeník shows him the document containing Kecal's promise to give him 700 florins when Marenka marries Mícha's son. Everyone is highly amused, especially when a dangerous roaming bear is discovered to be Vasek, still in costume!

## ■ ERSTER ACT

*(Der Hauptplatz des Dorfes mit Wirthshaus zur Zeit des Kirchweihfestes in Frühling.)*

### ERSTE SCENE

*Chor der Landleute. MARIE und HANS.*

**CHORUS OF VILLAGERS**
Seht am Strauch die Knospen springen, Hört die munter'n Vögel singen! Glanz und Jubel weit und breit, weit und breit! O du schöne Frühlingszeit, Frühlingszeit! O du schöne Frühlingszeit, Frühlingszeit!
Jeder leicht ein Schätzlein findet In der Jugend heissen Jahren, Doch bevor man fest sich bindet, Soll man keine Vorsicht sparen.

**CHOR:** Ehe, Wehe
Sind gar nah' verwandt!
Mög' uns Gott bewahren!
Mancher hat's erfahren.
Liebe lockt uns in die Falle,
Das ist leider weltbekannt!
Darum nehmt in Acht Euch Alle,
Ihr Verliebten rings im Land!

**HANS:** Sprich, mein liebes Herz, warum
Du so schweigsam bist und traurig!

## ■ ACT I

*(Main square in the village, with an inn at the side, at the time of the church fair in spring.)*

### SCENE I

*Marie and Hans. Chorus of Villagers.*

**CHORUS OF VILLAGERS:**
1. Why should we not be rejoicing? Why should we not be rejoicing When we have the best of health, best of health, When we have the best of health, best of health? Those who married should have tarried, For to them all joys are ended. Husband out to seek his pleasure, Wife at home, no moment's leisure. 2. Only he is truly happy, Who possesses this great wealth, this great wealth, Who possesses this great wealth. Those who married should have tarried, For to them all joys are ended. Husband out to seek his pleasure, Wife at home, no moment's leisure.

**CHORUS:** Woe is me!
Woe is me!
Pleasure at an end;
Cares their bosom rend,
Troubles and vexations.
Why should we not be rejoicing
When we have the best of health?
Only he is truly happy
Who possesses this great wealth.

**HANS:** Why are you so downcast
And so sad, my darling?

**MARIE:** Wie auch sollte ich's nicht sein!?
Hat die Mutter doch gesagt,
Dass er, der für mich Erwählte,
Heute zu uns kommen würde!
Weisst Du keine Hilfe?

**HANS:** Höre!
Wenn der Freier Dir verhasst,
Mög' er immer kommen nur.
Bleibe standhaft! Glaube mir:
Niemand zwingt ein starkes Herz!

**CHOR:** Nur nicht klagen, nicht verzagen!
Liebe lehrt uns Leid ertragen,
Alles, Alles darf sie wagen!
Seht am Strauch die Knospen springen,
Hört die munter'n Vögel singen!
Glanz und Jubel weit und breit!
O, du schöne Frühlingszeit!
Aber nehmt in Acht Euch Alle,
Ihr Verliebten, rings im Land:
Liebe lockt uns in die Falle,
Das ist leider weltbekannt!
Nun zum Tanze! Rührt die Glieder!
Lustig geht es auf und nieder!
Hei, da zeige Jedermann,
Was er kann!
*(Chor ab.)*

### ZWEITE SCENE

*MARIE und HANS.*

**MARIE:** Zum Tanze rufen sie mich heut' umsonst....
O, mir ist weh' um's Herz.

**HANS:** Mein Liebchen, wie? Noch immer trübe Augen?
Was kann es helfen?

**MARIE:** Sadness is my fate!
My dear mother told me
That the man chosen to be my husband
Is to meet me here to-day.
O God! How will all this end?

**HANS:** Listen!
Have no fear, and trust in me;
Then all will be well. If your will
Is strong and firm, to their wishes
You'll not incline. Then you'll be mine.

**CHORUS:** Stop your sighing, stop complaining.
Your true love will sure be gaining
Its reward for ever remaining.
Why should we not be rejoicing
If we have the best of health?
Why should we not be rejoicing
If we have the best of health?
Only he is truly happy
Who possesses this great wealth.
Only he is truly happy
Who possesses this great wealth.
O come with us, dance and warble;
Do not let anger fill your bosom.
Come then! To music lightly step.
Sing and dance.
*(Exit Chorus.)*

### SCENE II

*Marie and Hans.*

**MARIE:** Then is it really all to happen?...
Unhappy me!

**HANS:** Why! my darling! What makes you so very sad?
What has happened?

**MARIE:** Kaum zu denken wag' ich's!
Bald werden kommen sie zur Braut-schau Micha,
Vater und Sohn, und um mich wer-ben!

**HANS:** Nun gut. . .
Was willst Du thun?

**MARIE:** Was soll ich thun? Ja, wollte
Gott, dass ich etwas wüsste! Eins nur weiss ich,
Dass ich für alle Zeiten bin die Deine!
Wenn nur die Eltern mich nicht zwingen werden!

**HANS:** Das wäre freilich traurig.

**MARIE:** Doch Dich scheint
Es wenig zu bekümmern. . . Gar so ruhig, Freund? . . .
Wenn Dir der widrige Fall gelegen käme? . . .
Ich bin verzweifelt, voller Angst und Sorgen,
Und Dich berührt dies Alles kaum! . . . Ach, wenn
Mein treues Herz Du hintergingest, wenn heimlich
Du eine Andere geliebt!?

**HANS:** O niemals!

**MARIE:** Gern ja will ich Dir ver-trauen,
Gläubig blicken auf zu Dir!
Ach, worauf noch könnt' ich bauen,
Wärst Du, Liebster, untreu mir!
Der von fern Du hergekommen,
Wer Du bist, ich weiss es nicht,
Habe Dich zum Schatz genommen
Auf Dein ehrliches Gesicht!
O sage, was Dich fort von Hause in
Die Fremde trieb? Von Deiner frühen Jugend
Sprachst Du noch nie zu mir!

**HANS:** Nur ungern red' ich
Davon, es ist zu schmerzlich! . . .
Wohl bin ich
Aus einem reichen Hause, doch es starb
Mir die geliebte Mutter. Bald darauf
Nahm sich der Vater eine zweite Frau.
Voll Falschheit hat sie mir des Va-ters Herz
Entwendet, . . . aus dem Hause jagt' er mich!
Bei fremden Leuten dien' ich nun um's Brot.
Mit der Mutter sank zu Grabe
Meiner Jugend ganzes Glück,
Was ich früh verloren habe,
Bringt kein Sehnen mir zurück!

**MARIE:** O Du guter, armer Knabe,
Wie beklag' ich Dein Geschick!
Doch getrost nur: freundlich labe
Dich ein warmer Liebesblick.

**HANS:** Nun wirst Du länger wohl nicht zweifeln Heimath
Und Vaterhaus ist Deine Liebe für
Den Frühverwaisten!

**MARIE:** Do not be surprised!
Today Micha and his son are to visit us
And ask for my hand.

**HANS:** And you!
What will be your answer?

**MARIE:** What will be my answer?
How can you ask me such a ques-tion?
Can I belong to any one but you,
Hans, my darling? But my father is under obligations.

**HANS:** That is really awful.

**MARIE:** You seem timid, Hans! or even bashful,
As if you were afraid of something, or somebody,
Swear to me, Hans, that you have no other love,
Nor obligation, that binds you. Be-lieve me,
More than once I had an idea
That you had another sweetheart.

**HANS:** No, never!

**MARIE:** If I ever should find out
That such a thing is really so,
I would turn against you,
Hatred take the place of love's pure glow.
Tell me now, my dearest lover,
How came you to such a pass,
As to leave your home in anger,
And perhaps give up a lass?
Tell me now, as your past is shroud-ed in deep mystery,
So that my father even noticed it, and spoke of it.

**HANS:** My! history is really a pain-ful subject.
I am a son of comfortably well off parents.
But I lost my mother very early.
Unfortunately my father married a second time,
And my stepmother soon drove me out of the house.
I went out into the world,
And made my living among strang-ers.
A mother is a sweetest blessing,
A curse who takes her place!
With no feeling for another,
But only hatred in her face.

**MARIE:** A mother is sweetest bless-ing,
A curse who takes her place,
With no feeling for another
And only hatred in her face.

**HANS:** There may happen what will,
True and pure affection
Will resist all force
To bring about defection.

**MARIE:** Nun in Lust und Leide,
Nun in Schmerz und Freude sind vereint wir Beide! Wollen mitei-nand' durch's Leben Wie ein Schwalbenpärchen schweben, Hof-fen und vertrauen, und uns ein Nestchen bau'n. Heimlich, und leise nur unser Glück verkünden, hoffen und ver trau'n, uns ein Nest-chen bau'n . . . Beide Beide wollen wir vertrau'n! Beide, beide, beide, beide vertrau'n, wollen wir ver-trau'n,

**HANS:** Nun in Lust und Leide, Nun in Schmerz und Freude sind vereint wir Beide! Wollen mit ei-nand' durch's Leben Wie ein Schwalben-pärchen schweben, Hoffen und vertrauen uns ein Nestchen bauen, Hoffen und vertrauen, uns ein Nest-chen bau'n, Heimlich uns, ver-stohl'ner Weise Unser Glück ver-künden leise! Hoffen und vertrauen, Uns ein Nestchen bauen, Hoffen und vertrauen, Uns ein Nestchen bau'n, Sind vereint wir Beide, nun in Lust und Leide Beide, beide, beide vertrau'n, wollen wir vertrau'n,

**MARIE:** Doch still! Man kommt! O, grosser Gott, der Vater!
Man sucht mich schon!

**HANS:** Dann ist's Zeit wohl, dass ich geh'!
Scheiden! Scheiden! Das thut weh.
Lebwohl, bis ich Dich wiederseh'! (Ab.)
(Marie verbirgt sich.)

## DRITTE SCENE

*Kruschina, Kathinka und Kezal.*

**KEZAL:** Alles ist so gut wie richtig,
Und das Eine nur ist wichtig:
Euer Wort gabt Ihr zum Pfande.
Und somit ist Alles gut.
Ja, was glücklich ist im Lande,
Bracht' ich Alles unter'n Hut.
Denn auf Scharfblick und Ver-stande
Der Erfolg allein beruht.
Kommt das Pärchen erst zusam-men,
Ei, so soll mich Gott verdammen,
Stehen beide nicht in Flammen,
Lodern beide nicht in Gluth!

**KRUSCHINA:** (*zu Kathinka.*)
Nun, so sag', was meinst Du, Alte?
Steh' ich doch schon halb im Wort!

**KATHINKA:** Eines ich mir vorbe-halte:
Soll es sein, dann nicht sofort!
Ohne uns'rer Tochter Beirath
Kommt zu Stande keine Heirath;
Bin zu fragen gern erbötig,
Ob sie schon entschlossen sei!

**KEZAL:** Gar nicht nöthig, gar nicht nöthig!
Euer Wort . . . es bleibt dabei.

**KATHINKA:** Doch erst seh'n muss sie den Freier

**MARIE:** True and pure affection
Will resist all force To bring about defection. We have sworn eternal love, And our word shall be above All time and change. We will be faithful forever Love, love, And our word is, is above all time and change. We will be faithful forever, ever, Faithful forever. We will be ever faithful, faithful, Faithful, we will be faithful for ever.

**HANS:** True and pure affection
Will resist all force To bring about defection We have sworn eternal love, And our word is above All time and change. We will, we will, We will be faithful for ever. We have sworn eternal love, And our word is above All time and change. We will, we will, We will be faith-ful for ever, Faithful for ever, Faith-ful for ever

**MARIE:** Here they are! Father is coming with them.
They are looking for me.

**HANS:** They must not see me.
Farewell, my love
Think often of me.
(*Hans exits.*)
(*Marie hides.*)

## SCENE III

*Krushina, Kathinka, and Ketsal.*

**KETSAL:** Now I say, with great as-surance,
You gave your word and promise
To uphold your pact and bargain,
Then everything is done.
Only trust to my experience
And my great wisdom.
For many a doubtful case,
Which to others was a problem,
I brought to a happy close.
And perhaps if your dear daughter
Should refuse to marry,
Then you'll see how I'll teach her to yield and to obey you. So trust me.

**KRUSHINA:** (*To Kathinka*). Well!
what do you think, mother?
I—I am satisfied.

**KATHINKA:** This is so sudden, and too much for one day,
For we must stop to consider, and ask the bride,
If there is no impediment
Or some other objection in the way.

**KETSAL:** What objection! What ob-jection!
Your decision and my craft
Will overcome every obstacle.

**KATHINKA:** It depends on who is the bridegroom.

KEZAL: Auch noch sehen? Ei, zum
Geier!
Nichts da giebt es zu bekritteln!
Würd' ich sonst wohl hier vermit-
teln?
Bin ich denn zum Spasse da?
Micha's lieber Sohn wird Allen,
Gleich dem Vater, wohlgefallen!
Nun, Ihr kennt ihn ja!
Hochgeehrt!
Sein Besitz ist unter Brüdern
Volle dreissig Tausend werth.
Alles ist so gut wie richtig,
Und das Eine nur ist wichtig:
Euer Wort gabt Ihr zum Pfande,
Und somit ist Alles gut.

KATHINKA: Doch man will erst
wissen, was man thut.

KRUSCHINA: (für sich). Ihr zu
widersprechen, fehlt der Muth.

KEZAL: Ja, was glücklich ist im
Lande,
Bracht' ich Alles unter'n Hut.

KRUSCHINA: Nun freilich! Den
Tobias Micha kannte
Als Kind ich schon, doch wenig
habe ich
Erfahren noch von seinen beiden
Söhnen,
Kaum, dass ich ihrer Namen mich
erinn're

KEZAL: Wie seltsam! Denn vor
wenig Jahren habt
Ihr ihm versprochen Euer
Töchterlein
Dem Sohn zur Frau zu geben!

KATHINKA: Sagt doch, sagt:
Für welchen von den beiden denn
bewerbt
Ihr Euch?

KEZAL: Könnt Ihr noch fragen? Hat
er ja
Nur Einen, der heisst Wenzel. Denn
der Sohn
Von seiner ersten Frau ist längst ver-
schollen,
Ja, wie man glaubt, gestorben.

KRUSCHINA: Und was ist
Mit unserm Wenzel? Wohl nicht
ohne Grund
Hält er sich fern, versteckt?

KEZAL: Gekommen wär'er mit,
wie gerne!
Doch zarte Rücksicht hält ihn
ferne,
Er sieht auf Anstand, feinen Ton.
Ja, seine Tugenden und Sitten,
Sie machen überall ihn wohlgelit-
ten,
Wohl jede Mutter wünscht sich sol-
chen Sohn
's ist kein Schlemmer und kein
Säufer,
Spätausgeher, Kneipenläufer,
Auch kein Prahler und kein Prach-
er,
Kartenspieler, Schuldenmacher,
Kein verweg'ner Messerträger,
Pascher, Schwärzer, wilder Jäger,
Auch kein Zänker
Und kein Stänker,

KETSAL: Who the bridegroom?
In vain is such a question.
You can see that he is proper,
If security go I.
Tobias Micha you know surely.
But perhaps not. Then I say,
For his farm and buildings
I'll give forty thousand cash.
Now I say with great assurance,
You gave your word and promise,
To uphold your pact and bargain,
Then everything is done.

KATHINKA: This is so sudden, and
too much for one day.

KRUSHINA: (to himself). I—I am
satisfied.

KETSAL: Only trust to my experience
And my great wisdom, . . . happy
close.

KRUSHINA: Surely! I knew Tobias
Micha when he was a child.
He had two sons,
Hans by the first wife
And Wenzel by the second.
Of these, I know neither one nor
the other.

KETSAL: That is true. Many years
ago,
Before witnesses, you promised
To give your daughter
To his son for a wife.

KATHINKA: But say! for which of
the sons are you speaking?

KETSAL: For which one? He has
only one,
And his name is Wenzel.
The other one, by the first
Wife, is a tramp and good for
Nothing. Nobody knows where he
is.

KRUSHINA: Well, what kind of a
fellow is this Wenzel?
Why didn't you bring him with you
at once?

KETSAL: He did not come now be-
cause he is bashful.
He is not flighty but thoroughly in
earnest.
He is as gentle as gentlest lamb,
though of high condition.
Faults he has not any, nor vices.
Every mother would be proud to
have a son
With such a lovely disposition.
He is neither tall nor little,
Nor's his health so very brittle.
Neither proud, nor very naughty,
Neither loud, nor rough, nor
haughty,
Neither lavish, nor too stingy,
Well, in short, he is as normal
As a human being can be.
With a farm worth thirty thousand.
Well then! Well then!

Läst'rer, Flucher,
Händelsucher!
Er ist wohlabgeschliffen,
Er ist leicht von Begriffen,
Nüchtern,
Schüchtern,
Fein im Ton . . .
Doch, das sagt' ich schon.

KRUSCHINA und KATHINKA:
Wär' er nur gleich mitgekommen!
Staunend haben wir's vernommen,
Und sind sehr erstaunt davon.

## VIERTE SCENE

*Marie und die Vorigen.*

KEZAL: Seht, da kommt sie sonder
Ahnung!
Zeit jetzt wär 'es zur Vermahnung!

MARIE: Lieber Vater, liebe Mutter,
Was wollt Ihr mir sagen?

KEZAL: Darf ich, schönstes Kind-
chen,
Dich wohl fragen:
Hast Du nicht daran gedacht,
Dass ich Dir was mitgebracht?
Rathe schnell, wer rathen kann!
Einen jungen Mann.

MARIE: Was geht mich an
Ein fremder Mann?

KRUSCHINA: Sollst sein Weibchen sein,
Liebes Töchterlein!

KATHINKA: (leise zu Marie).
Willst Du aber ihn nicht haben.
Nun, so sagst Du nein!

MARIE: Ich sein Weibchen sein?
Ei, was fällt Euch ein!?
Er mag ruhig weiter traben
Und wo anders frei'n!

KATHINKA: Sollst sein Weibchen
sein,
Liebes Töchterlein!
Willst Du aber ihn nicht haben,
Nun, so sagst Du nein!

KRUSCHINA und KEZAL: Sollst
sein Weibchen sein,
Liebes Töchterlein!
Diesem feinen jungen Knaben
Deine Liebe weih'n!

KEZAL: Nicht lange mehr sich zier-
en!
Nur keine Zeit verlieren!
Ein fröhlich Ja gesprochen,
Und Hochzeit giebt es in vier
Wochen!

MARIE: Fein langsam! Denn es eilt
nicht sehr
Ein Umstand ist dagegen
Gewichtig, voll und schwer.

KEZAL: Umstand hin . . . Umstand
her . . .
Was ist daran gelegen!
Nein, Hindernisse giebt's nicht
mehr,
Wo meine Kräfte sich regen!

MARIE: So muss ich bekennen?
Muss meinen Liebsten nennen?

Who can ask for more!
He did not come now because he is
bashful.
He is not flighty but thoroughly in
earnest.
He is as gentle as gentlest lamb,
Though of high condition.

KRUSHINA AND KATHINKA:
Your description is sufficient,
Your description is sufficient.
We trust your honesty.

## SCENE IV

*Marie and the preceding.*

KETSAL: Now we have her, now
we have her.
Seriously, we now can take her.

MARIE: My dear father, my dear
mother!
Are you looking for me?

KETSAL: I just asked them if you
love somebody,
If you have not any swain
Who to your love would attain.
I can bring you a young man
Who will be to your gain.

MARIE: What! who will be to my
gain?

KRUSHINA: You will see him
And can judge for yourself.

KATHINKA: (whispers to Marie).
If you do not like him,
Why, he can go by himself.

MARIE: I shall see him,
And can judge for myself.
If I do not like him,
Why, he can go by himself.

KATHINKA: You will see him,
And can judge for yourself,
If you do not like him,
Why, he can go by himself.

KRUSHINA AND KETSAL: You
will see him,
And can judge for yourself.
If you do not like him,
Why, he can go by himself.

KETSAL: Then let us at once
The contract put together.
Let Marie give her consent now,
And all will be fixed forever.

MARIE: That—that cannot be done
as quickly as you think. No, really
not,
For there is a something which will
prevent it.

KETSAL: Something this, some-
thing that,
No obstacle can ever stop me.
To whatever I put my mind
A complete success will surely be.

MARIE: I love another
More than a brother.

KEZAL: Pah! Von solchen Kinder-
eien
Will ich Dich gar bald befreien!

MARIE: Treue hab' ich ihm geschworen ...

KEZAL: Damit ist noch nichts verloren!

MARIE: Der zur Gattin mich erkoren!

KEZAL: Laufen lass den armen Thoren!

MARIE: Ihm gehören Herz und
Hand.

KEZAL: Das war eitel Spiel und
Tand!
Wozu hätte ich Verstand?
Dafür bin ich ja bekannt!
Und zum Ziele wird gelangen,
Wer die rechte Strasse fand.

MARIE, KRUSCHINA, KATHIN-
KA: Ja, zum Ziele wird gelangen,
Wer die rechte Strasse fand.

MARIE: Mit Hans bin ich vereinigt,
denn wir haben
Uns ew'ge Treue heute noch gelobt!

KRUSCHINA: (mit gewaltsamer
Energie). Was? Ohne Vorspruch
und Bewilligung?
Ich, als der Vater, sage: Nein! Ich
steh'
Dem Micha doch im Wort, sie sein-
em Sohn
Zu geben.

KATHINKA: O, wie ungeschickt
von Dir,
Dass Du's versprochen hast!

KEZAL: (zieht ein Papier hervor).
Ja, schwarz auf weiss!
Hier steht es Alles deutlich, unter-
schrieben
Von den Parteien und den Zeugen
auch.

MARIE: Nur bin ich nicht dabei!
(Schlägt ihm das Papier aus der
Hand.)
Und also gilt
Es nichts! Was ich gesagt, ist meine
Meinung
Und soll es bleiben!
(Ab.)

KEZAL: Darauf war ich nicht gefasst!

KRUSCHINA: Von Euch war es ein
grosser Fehler,
Allein zu kommen! Warum habt Ihr
uns
Den Wenzel nicht gleich mitgebracht? Er hätte
Bei seiner Braut sich vorgestellt
zum Mind'sten.

KEZAL: Ja freilich! Doch er war
nicht zu bewegen.
Er ist verzagt und schüchtern, des
Verkehres
Mit Weibern gänzlich ungewohnt.

KRUSCHINA: Dann wird es
schwerlich etwas werden.

KETSAL: Give him up as you'll be
no pair,
Let him seek his fortune elsewhere.

MARIE: My word I gave him, and
my troth.

KETSAL: Word and troth are of no
value.

MARIE: Our contract also has been
signed.

KETSAL: We shall tear it into
pieces.

MARIE: Just you try, just you try.

KETSAL: Trust all to my ready wit.
All will be well if you have grit.
And my massive brain,
My mind, my mind,
Will soon conquer the whole
world.
What no one can unravel
That my great mind can achieve.

MARIE, KRUSHINA, KATHINKA:
What no one can unravel
That his great mind can achieve.

MARIE: My Hans will never give
me up,
I can stake my life on it.

KRUSHINA: (with forceful ener-
gy). Give you up, or not give you
up,
That is not the question.
I put myself under obligation
To Tobias Micha before witnesses.

KATHINKA: But pray, dear husband!
What obligation?

KETSAL: (drawing out a paper).
Here it is! Black on white!
Signed by Micha, Krushina, and wit-
nesses.

MARIE: What does that amount to?
(Knocks the paper out of his
hand.)
That is of no value.
Hans and I know nothing of it, and
we never can yield.
(Exit.)

KETSAL: Oh, what a perverted
world this is.

KRUSHINA: Where did you leave
Micha, and his son, that honored
and respected bridegroom?
It would have been proper for him
to speak to Marie.

KETSAL: Oh well! of course he is
not accustomed to speak to women.
He is a bashful as a country maiden.

KRUSHINA: Then the courting
will be hard.

KEZAL: Hört, Was ich Euch rathen
will: Das Beste wäre,
Ihr sprächet Euch jetzt einmal
gründlich aus.
Mit Vater Micha in dem Wirthshaus
dort!
Man stört Euch nicht, denn Alles
läuft zum Tanze.
Mit Hans will ich inzwischen re-
den, ich
Krieg' ihn herum!
(Sie gehen nach verschiedenen
Seiten ab.)

## FÜNFTE SCENE

(Das Landvolk versammelt sich
vor dem Wirthshause, die
ältlichen setzen sich an die Tische
und trinken; die Jüngeren bereit-
en sich zum Tanz vor.)

CHOR: Durch die Reihen
Hinzufliegen!
Sich zu Zweien
Anzuschmiegen!
Herz am Herzen
Fühlt man schlagen.
Unter Scherzen.
Fortgetragen!
Frohe Weise,
Laut und leise,
Sollst Du geben
Neues Leben!
Ging'es, wie es uns gefällt,
Tanze mit die ganze Welt!
Violin' und Clarinette
Jauchzen trillernd am die Wette
Selbst dem alten Rumpelbass
Macht das tolle Wesen Spass.

*ENDE DES ERSTEN ACTES.*

# ■ ZWEITER ACT

*Wirthsstube.*

## ERSTE SCENE

(Hans, mit jungen Landleuten,
sitzt am Tisch auf der einen, Kezal
auf der anderen Seite der Stube.
Sie trinken Bier.)

CHOR: Wie schäumst Du in den
Gläsern, edler Gerstensaft!
An Dir trinkt sich ein Jeder Feuer
und Kraft!
Dich preisen die Jungen und Alten.
Heissassa!
Wenn wir bei'm Biere sitzen, Mann
gereiht an Mann,
Was geht uns das Andere weiter
noch an?
In Gnaden wird uns Gott erhalten!
Heissassa!

HANS: (steht auf). Ihr Freunde,
wohl stimm' ich von Herzen mit
ein;
Doch denk' ich dabei auch an das
Liebchen mein.
Denn das allein ist Himmelslust auf
Erden:
Zu lieben und geliebt zu werden!

KETSAL: And, now, my dear sir, I
think it best for you to go over
To the other inn, and meet Micha
and his son as if by chance.
It will be noisy here;
They are going to dance.
Meanwhile, I'll look up Hans and
convince him
That it's for the best
(They go off in different direc-
tions.)

## SCENE V

(The villagers come in. The older
ones seat themselves at the tables
and drink. The younger ones prepare to dance.)

CHORUS: Come, my darling!
Start the bounding
While the Polka
Still is sounding.
Hands entwining,
Eyes in trance,
Let the whole world
Join the dance.
Hear the basses
Set in motion,
All the band
In great commotion.
All the earth
Is moving fast.
Let us dance
While life does last.

*End of Act I.*

# ■ ACT II

*Interior of the inn.*

## SCENE I

(Hans, with young villagers, sits
at a table on the one side and Ketsal on the other side of the room.
They drink beer.)

CHORUS: Oh, beer a blessing real-
ly is to all;
For troubles and worries it drives to
the wall,
And gives us the strength to bear
our fate. Hurrah!
A man who does not drink is a sol-
emn guest.
The world full of troubles is even at
its best.
So let us partake and not come late.
Hurrah!

HANS: (gets up). Well, boys, believe me, I say it from my heart,
That love really is above all wine
and beer
The only thing that makes life
worth living.
And makes us hopefully look to the
future.

## Act II, Scene I

CHOR: (*Tenöre.*) Aus Liebe verlierst Du den Kopf noch, Du Thor!
(*Basse.*) (*auf Kezal anspielend*).
Sich' lieber beizeiten vor Dem da Dich vor!

KEZAL: (*steht ebenfalls auf*). Was hilft die Liebe Dem, der Hab' und Gut verlor'!?
Zuverlässig ist nur Eines,
Und das ist das baare Geld!
Armer Schlucker, hast Du keines
Dann verlacht Dich alle Welt!
(*Erhebt das Glas.*)
Hoch das baare Geld!

HANS: (*erhebt das Glas*). Mein Mädchen ist's die mir gefällt!
(*Mädchen treten nach und nach herein und betheiligen sich an dem Tanze nach dem Trinkliede.*)

CHOR: Wie schäumst Du in den Gläsern, edler Gerstensaft,
An Dir trinkt sich ein Jeder Feuer und Kraft!
Dich preisen die Jungen und Alten.
Heissassa!
(*Tanz Furiant*). (*Nach dem Tanze ziehen die Mädchen die jungen Leute aus dem Wirthsstube. Alle ab.*)

CHORUS: (*Tenors*). Hans, you are in love, we see with half an eye.
(*Basses*) (*alluding to Ketsal*).
Look, that one his finger may put in your pie!

KETSAL: (*also stands up*). No, if it should be so, he thereby will be no loser.
Good advice and real sound money
Are the greatest powers in this world.
He who uses them with wisdom
Cannot, cannot ever go astray.
(*Raises his glass.*)
Here's to sound money.

HANS: (*raises his glass*). Here's to love the best of all.
(*Girls enter one by one, and take part in the dance, after the drinking song.*)

CHORUS: Oh, beer a blessing really is unto us all;
For troubles and worries it drives to the wall,
And gives us strength to bear our fate. Hurrah!
(*Dance Furiant, a Bohemian national dance. After the dance the girls drag the young men out of the room.*)
(*Exeunt.*)

## ZWEITE SCENE

WENZEL: (*schüchtern eintretend*). Theu'...theurer Sohn,
Sprach Mütterlein,
Zeit ist es schon
Für Dich zu frei'n!
Fa...fass' Dir Muth
Und sei ein Mann:
Was Jeder thut,
Ist wohlgethan.
Si...sicherlich,
Kehrt' ich nach Haus,
La...lachte mich.
A...alles aus.

## SCENE II

WENZEL: (*enters timidly*) Mo-mother dear Said to me
That she would like soon to see
Me get happily Married.
So long had I tarried
That they all Round about,
Do think me A great big lout.

## DRITTE SCENE

*MARIE und WENZEL.*

(*Beide lachen laut, wie sie sich erblicken.*)

MARIE: Seid der Verlobte Ihr von Kruschina's Mariechen nicht?

WENZEL: (*erst erschreckt, dann zutraulicher*). A...allerdings, mein schö...
Schö...schönes Kind, der bin ich.

MARIE: Hab' ich's Euch Doch angesehen...Nein, wie hübsch Ihr seid!
Die Mädchen alle hier im Dorfe schon
Beklagen Euch.

WENZEL: (*ängstlich*). Beklagen mich? Warum?

MARIE: Euere Braut-ich sag's Euch-meint's nicht ehrlich.
'nen Andern liebt sie!

## SCENE III

*Marie and Wenzel*

(*Both begin to laugh, when they catch sight of one another.*)

MARIE: Are you not the one chosen to become
Marie Krushina's husband?

WENZEL: (*first afraid, then more trustingly*). Ye-ye-yes, of course.
But ho-how did you know it?

MARIE: Why! Cannot every one see it?
How dressed up you are!
The whole town is talking about you
And is sorry for you.

WENZEL: (*anxiously*). So-so-sorry for me! and why?

MARIE: Because she will deceive you.
She loves another.

WENZEL: (*einfältig*). Ka...ka...kann sie lieben
Denn einen Anderen? Ich bin ja da!

MARIE: (*lacht*). Haha! Kennt sie Euch denn, und kennt Ihr sie?

WENZEL: Ke...kennen? Nein. Do...doch sie weiss, dass ich Ihr Ga...Ga...Gatte werde!

MARIE: Mag wohl sein,
Und eben d'rum lacht sie Euch aus! Sie wird
Euch schmäh'n, Euch hintergeh'n,
Euch quälen bis
Zu Tode.

WENZEL: (*entsetzt*). Wa...was sagst Du da? Doch wenn
Die Mutter haben will, dass ich sie nehme!
Heirathen mu...mu...muss ich nun einmal!

MARIE: Ei, freilich, warum nicht?
Das sollt Ihr auch!
(*Kokett.*)
Es giebt ja hier noch and're
Mädchen! –Sucht
Euch eine aus!

WENZEL: (*erleichtert*). Ich will's.

MARIE: Ich weiss Euch einen lieben Schatz,
Den Mancher schon begehrt,
Ein schönes Mädchen, hier am Platz,
Die lange Euch verehrt.

WENZEL: (*froh*).
Wär's möglich wohl? Versteh' ich recht?
Ein schönes Kind? Das wär' nicht schlecht!
Jedoch Mariechen wird sich grämen.

MARIE: (*immer überlegen und doppelsinnig*). Die wird sich schon den Andern nehmen.

WENZEL: Doch mein Mütterlein,
Das wird Zeter schrei'n.

MARIE: Sie wird mit Eurer Wahl zufrieden sein.

WENZEL: Ist schön die Andre?

MARIE: Gerade wie Mariechen.

WENZEL: Und jung an Jahren?

MARIE: Gerade wie Mariechen.

WENZEL: Doch will sie mich denn auch zum Mann?

MARIE: Wenn ohn' Euch sie nicht leben kann!
Verzichtet auf Marie,
Sonst geht zu Grunde sie,
Die Tag und Nacht
An Euch gedacht!
(*Sie thut, als ob sie weine.*)

WENZEL: (*gerührt*). Wei...wei...weinen seh' ich Dich?

MARIE: Ach, ihr Loos bekümmert mich!

WENZEL: (*schwankend*). Ich darf es ja nicht,
Mich bindet die Pflicht!

WENZEL: (*stupidly*). Ho-how can she love another
If she's to have me?

MARIE: (*laughs*). Ha ha! You?
Does she know you? Or you her?

WENZEL: She-she does not. But she knows
That I am to be her hu-hu-husband.

MARIE: Of course she does,
And that is why she enjoys the prospect of teasing you, deceiving
You, and worrying you to death.

WENZEL: (*horrified*). Wh-why, that's awful!
Bu-but my mo-mother told me
That I must marry,
So-so marry I must.

MARIE: Of course! Why not? Such a fine fellow!
(*Coquettishly.*)
There are lots of fine girls here.
Pick one out yourself!

WENZEL: (*relieved*). I will

MARIE: I know a charming maiden
Wants you with all her might.
With love her heart is laden,
Without you all is night.

WENZEL: (*joyously*). Oh, oh, what ecstasy!
When such a girl really loves me.
Oh, oh, what ecstasy!
Bu-but, Marie! What will she say?

MARIE: (*decidedly*). Nothing! For surely
After marrying you
She'll run away.

WENZEL: Bu-but my mother! She will raise a row.

MARIE: As soon as she'll see the bride
A smile will light her brow.

WENZEL: Is she then so lovely?

MARIE: Just the same as Marie.

WENZEL: A-and is she young, too?

MARIE: Just the same as Marie.

WENZEL: A-a-and that one would really take me?

MARIE: If you would not want her
Grief sure would make her rave,
and water be her grave.
Charcoal would end her days and she would weep always, if she
could not get you.
(*She pretends to be crying.*)

WENZEL: (*touched.*) Wh-why do you weep?

MARIE: Oh, because you do not want her.

WENZEL: (*undecided*). I, I do not dare.
My mother is there.

**MARIE:** (*vorwurfsvoll*). So grausam fand ich Keinen!
Vor Gram um Euch zehrt sie sich auf,
Ihr aber lasst sie weinen.

**WENZEL:** (*ratblos*). Wer sagt mir, was ich thu'?
(*schüchtern.*)
Ja, wäre sie wie Du,
Dann...
(*entschlossen.*)
nur immerzu

**MARIE:** (*kokettirend*). So wie ich? Wollt Ihr sie so?

**WENZEL:** Ja, Ja, gerade so.

**MARIE:** Macht' Euch meine Liebe froh?

**WENZEL:** Ja, sie macht mich froh.

**MARIE:** (*Innig*). Dem halt' ich Treue bis an's Grab, Den ich in's Herz geschlossen hab'!
(*bestimmt.*)
Was ich jetzt Euch sage, höret:
Ihr beschwöret,
Dass Ihr fest entschlossen seid,
Von Marie Euch loszusagen,
Jetzt und alle Zeit!

**WENZEL:** (*misstrauisch*). Nu... nu... nur nicht schwören!
Da... das geht zu weit!

**MARIE:** (*scheinbar gekränkt*). Ihr wollt nicht? Gut, lasst es sein!
Eure Lieb' ist wahrlich klein.
Möget Ihr es nie bereuen,
An Marien's Seite Euch
Eures Lebens freuen!
(*Thut, als wollte sie gehen.*)

**WENZEL:** (*sie zurückrufend*). Ha ... ha ... halt! Ich schwöre ja!

**MARIE:** (*den Schwur vorsprechend*). "Was geschieht und was geschah,"

**WENZEL:** (*nachstammelnd*). Ge... geschieht und ge... geschah..

**MARIE:** "Niemals komm' ich mehr ihr nah,"

**WENZEL:** Me... mehr ihr na... na... nah...

**MARIE:** "Und für mich ist sie nicht da!"

**WENZEL:** Sie... sie... sie nicht da... da... da.

**MARIE:** Ich weiss Euch einen lieben Schatz,
Den Mancher schon begehrt,
Ein schönes Mädchen hier am Platz,
Die lange Euch verehrt!

**WENZEL:** Wär's möglich, und versteh' ich recht?
Du ha... ha... hast mein Herz bekehrt.
(*Er will sie umarmen; sie entzieht sich ihm und läuft lachend davon. Wenzel hinter ihr her.*)

**MARIE:** (*reproachfully*). You only make excuses,
And she who loves you dearly
You let grieve so sorely.

**WENZEL:** (*puzzled*). No, no, no. I do not.
(*Timidly.*)
If she is just like you, then,
(*Decidedly.*)
I'll love her.

**MARIE:** (*coquettishly*). You would love me all your life?

**WENZEL:** My-my life.

**MARIE:** Make me your own darling wife?

**WENZEL:** My-my wife.

**MARIE:** (*affectionately*). Then you I'll love with all my heart,
And from you never part.
(*Determinedly.*)
Put your hand in mine, here.
You must swear now.
You must swear you are in earnest and sincere,
To resign and give up Marie
From now, for evermore.
You must swear that.

**WENZEL:** (*suspiciously*). Must I swear? That makes me sore.

**MARIE:** (*apparently grieved.*)
Well, I see you are a fool.
You will only be her tool,
And she'll treat you awfully.
So for the worst prepare,
Unless you will now swear.
(*Pretends to go away.*)

**WENZEL:** (*holds her back.*) Wa-wait. I'll swear.

**MARIE:** "I solemnly give up Marie."

**WENZEL:** I-I gi-give up.

**MARIE:** Never hope to see her again.

**WENZEL:** S-s-see her again.

**MARIE:** Never hope to hear of her, then.

**WENZEL:** He-he-hear of her, then. I'll give her up for evermore.

**MARIE:** I know a charming maiden
Wants you with all her might.
With love her heart is laden,
Without you all is night.

**WENZEL:** O-oh, ecstasy and joy!
You have fully conquered this boy!
(*He tries to embrace her, but she dodges him, and laughing runs away; he after her.*)

## VIERTE SCENE

*Hans und Kezal.*

**KEZAL:** (*zieht Hans herein*). Komm', mein Söhnchen, auf ein Wort
Will Dir was vertrauen!

**HANS:** (*sträubt sich*). Lasst mich gehen, ich muss fort,
Auf die Felder schauen!

**KEZAL:** Weisst Du denn nicht, wer ich bin?

**HANS:** Ja, man sagt' es mir vorhin;
Und wonach steht Euer Sinn?

**KEZAL:** Bist gescheidt, flink und gewandt,
Magst zu Vielem taugen,
Einem Mädchen, wie bekannt,
Stachst Du in die Augen.
Hast Du auch Vermögen?

**HANS:** Meinetwegen Sorgen gar?
Steht in Gottes Segen
Doch ein jedes treue Paar!

**KEZAL:** Thorheit! Das lieget auf der Hand;
Dass Dein Glück nicht von Bestand!
Ohne Geld ist alles Tand.
Drum ein Sümmchen sparen!...
Hab' es selbst erfahren
Einst in jungen Jahren.
(*Verlegenheitspause.*)
Eines noch
Sag' mir doch:
Gern hätt' ich vernommen,
Wo Du hergekommen?

**HANS:** Weit von hier
Wohnen wir.
Von der Moldau Wogen
Bin ich hergezogen.

**KEZAL:** Dort sollst Du Dein Weibchen finden!
In der Fremde sich zu binden,
Thut nicht gut, das glaube mir!

**HANS:** Was ich in der Fremde fand,
Bietet mir kein Heimathland.
Einen Engel nenn' ich mein,
Und der soll mein Weibchen sein!

**KEZAL:** Wer in Lieb' entbrannt,
Hält aus Unverstand
Weiber für Engel,
Meint in Schwärmerei
Dass sein Mädchen sei.
Ganz ohne Mängel.
Ja, so manches Schätzchen,
Ist ein Schmeichelkätzchen,
Das mit Sammetpfötchen Dich umspielt;
Aber, wie entsetzlich,
Wenn man später plötzlich
Ihre scharfen Tigerkrallen fühlt!
Einer sorgt und sinnt
Um ein schönes Kind,
Bis er sie gewinnt,
Und das Glück ist gross;
Leider hinterher
Seufzt er bang und schwer:
Du, mein Gott und Herr,
Wär' ich sie erst los!
Doch ein Praktikus

## SCENE IV

*Hans and Ketsal*

**KETSAL:** (*drags Hans in*). Come, my friend, don't make a row!
I'll tell you something good.

**HANS:** (*struggling*). Let me go, I'm busy now,
Else I'd not repel you.

**KETSAL:** Don't you know then who I am?

**HANS:** I have not that honor, sir!
Neither do you, who I am.

**KETSAL:** You are quick, and smart and bright;
They tell me you're a wonder.
But beyond this, you're beloved
By a maiden yonder.
Have you enough of money?

**HANS:** No, but many a happy pair
So got along, it seems.
Honest maidens, blithe and fair,
Love men and not their means.

**KETSAL:** Believe me, I have knowledge great
And tell you that to shun.
Without cash, marriage is only confusion.
Tell me now whence you come,
And perhaps something you'll hear
To your advantage.

**HANS:** I come from afar,
From a distant country.
My childhood's home is
Where the Moldau rolls

**KETSAL:** Then at once to it return.
To love a stranger our
Maidens never learn.

**HANS:** All may think that way but one.
That one I have surely won.
She to me is all my life,
And her I'll make my wife.

**KETSAL:** Every one like you
Thinks his love is true;
In her only
Goodness he believes.
But how dreadful
When she him deceives!
Then he sighs and weeps,
And so quietly reaps
When he cannot cure.
Then he sighs and weeps,
And so quietly reaps
What he must endure.
But a man of sense
Will well prepare,
And before the time
All things weigh with care.
He will count
The profit
All the same.
And if none,
Why he will
Quit the game.

Stets sich wohl bewahrt;
Vielerlei Verdruss
Bleibt ihm dann erspart.
Nichts schlägt ihn darnieder,
Weil das Für und Wider
Er zuvor sich weislich überlegt.
Der kann heiter scherzen,
Der nicht blos in Herzen
Seinen Schatz, nein, auch im Beutel trägt
Was ist Dir geblieben?
Freund, hab' Acht!
Froher Sinn und Lieben
Gute Nacht!

**HANS:** (*unwirsch*). Bin ich dafür
Dank Euch schuldig?
Treibt mit Andern Euren Spass!

**KEZAL:** Freundchen, nur nicht ungeduldig
Dir zu bieten hab' ich 'was.

**HANS:** Weiss er doch eine die hat
Dukaten, hat Dukaten. Wer die
kleine nennt die Seine der ist gut
berathen. Nicht zu verschweigen,
Was noch ihr Eigen, was ihr Eigen.
Jedes hoffen er sagt's offen willes
übersteigen. Häuschen und Garten,
Vieh aller Arten! Milchende Kühe
lohnender Mühe, Schweinchen im
Koben, hoch zu loben! Hühner,
Tauben kaum zu glauben! Tröge,
Wannen, Krüge, Kannen, in der
Truhe Kleider Schuhe, und ein nagelneuer Schrank. Ich seh' es ein,
doch sag ich nein, ich seh' es ein
doch sag ich nein, Ich seh' es ein
doch sag ich nein, Ich seh' es ein
doch sag ich nein. Ja, ich ech' es
ein, doch sag ich nein . . . ja, ja, ich
seh' es ein doch sag ich nein.

**KEZAL:** Weiss ich doch eine die
hat Dukaten, hat Dukaten! Wer die
kleine nennt die Seine, der ist gut
berathen. Nicht zu verschweigen,
was noch ihr Eigen, was ihr Eigen,
Jedes hoffen, ich sag's offen willes
übersteigen, Häuschen und Garten
Vieh aller Arten! Milchende Kühe,
lohnender Mühe Schweinchen im
Koben hoch zu loben, Hühner,
Tauben kaum zu glauben, Tröge,
Wannen, Krüge, Kannen, in der
Truhe Kleider, Schuhe! Häuschen
und Garten, Vieh aller Arten! Milchende Kühe lohnender Mühe,
Schweinchen im Koben, hoch zu
loben! Hühner, Tauben kaum zu
glauben! Tröge, Wannen, Krüger,
Kannen, in der Truhe Kleider,
Schuhe, obendrein ein nagelneuer
Schrank. Dürfte kein Prinz sich
schämen, hörst Du! sondern sich
bald bequemen, hörst Du! solch
eine Braut zu nehmen würde wohl
gar mit ihr zufrieden sein, dürfte
sich ein Prinz nicht schämen, hörst
Du! sondern sich gleich bequemen,
hörst Du, solch eine Braut zu nehmen würde gar wohl mit ihr zufrieden sein Weiss ich doch eine
die hat Dukaten, und wer sie nimmt
der ist gut berathen, wird gar wohl

**HANS:** (*impatiently*). What do
you mean with all this?
I do not understand you.

**KETSAL:** That I know a better
bride, for you, my
dear boy.

**HANS:** He knows a maiden, She has
the money, has the money, she will
also get a house from pa, you bet,
my honey. He knows a maiden, she
has the money, has the money. She
will also get a house from Pa, you
bet, my honey. She has two cows,
And one calf to match them. fowls
by the dozen, Pigs you can't watch
them, A great big farm, And well
filled, well filled brand new till,
and well filled, well filled brand
new till; A great big farm, a great
big farm, A great big farm, and well
filled, well filled brand new till.
Too well I know, still I say no, Too
well I know, still I say no, He
knows, he knows a maiden, She has,
she has the money, Yes, too well I
know, still I say no,
Yes, yes, too well I know, still I say
no!

**KETSAL:** I know a maiden, She has
the money, has the money! She will
also get a house from pa, you bet,
my honey. I know a maiden, She has
the money, has the money. She will
also get a house from Pa, you bet,
my honey, She has two cows, And
one calf to match them; fowls by
the dozen, pigs you can't watch
them; A great big farm and well
filled brand new till, a well filled,
well filled brand new till, A great
big farm, a great big farm. And well
filled, well filled brand new till.
She has two cows, And one calf to
match them. Fowls by the dozen,
Pigs you can't watch them, A great
big farm, And well filled brand new
till. And well filled, well filled
brand new till. A great big farm,
And well filled, well filled brand
new till, A great big farm, And well
filled, well filled brand new till.
Now that would be a something,
something, Now that would be a
something, something, that would
be a something, something, something, Now that would be a something, something, Now that would
be a something, Now that would be
a something which would thrill, I
know a maiden, She has the money,

mit ihr zufrieden sein, . . . der wird
gar wohl mit ihr zufrieden sein, zufrieden sein.

**KEZAL:** Gieb doch die dumme
Liebschaft auf! Es soll
Dich nicht gereuen! . . . Willst Du? .
. . Ohne Faxen:
Ich lass' es hundert Gulden kosten
mich.

**HANS:** Nur hundert Gulden? So
viel also gälte
Ein solches Opfer Euch!? Nein, lieber Herr,
Das nehm' ich nicht!

**KEZAL:** (*eifrig*). Mein'thalb' das
Doppelte!

**HANS:** Was Euch nicht einfällt!

**KEZAL:** Na, dreihundert Gulden!
Doch eilig zugegriffen, dass die
Sache
Einmal zum Ende kommt! . . . Wie?
Du zögerst
Noch immer?
(*Drohend.*)
Hüte Dich! Ich habe hier
Sehr gute Freunde; sag' ich nur ein
Wort,
Bringt man Dich weg von hier der
Schub! Sodann
Hast weder eine Braut Du,
noch'nen Kreuzer!

**HANS:** Und wer giebt die ver-
sproch'ne Summe her?

**KEZAL:** Ich! Ich!

**HANS:** (*stellt sich erstaunt und
ungläubig*). Ihr? Etwa für Euch
selbst? Euch liess' ich
Das Mädchen nicht, um keine Million!

**KEZAL:** Was für ein Einfall! Ich bin
längst versehen,
Hab' an der Meinen auch genug
schon!–Weisst
Du nicht, dass ich vermittele für
den Sohn
Tobias Micha's nur? Wir setzen auf
Ein kleines Schriftstück, Du be-
kommst Dein Geld . . .
Dann aber, mach' Dich auf den
Weg!

**HANS:** Nun, also,
Sei's d'rum! Es ist ein schönes Geld
Habt Ihr.
Gezahlt. dann ist in Ordnung Alles.
(*Zögernd.*)
Doch noch Eins beding' ich aus:
Kein Anderer
Darf sie bekommen, die Marie, als
Der Sohn Tobias Micha's! Andern-
falls
Gilt der Vertrag für nichts!

**KEZAL:** Ganz selbstverständlich!
Das will ja ich! Kein And'rer soll sie
haben
Als Micha's Sohn.

I know a maiden, She has the money, that would be a something
which would thrill, Which would
thrill.

**KETSAL:** If you will stop this flirta-
tion,
I shall pay you something.
Will you? Here I give you my prom-
ise,
A hundred florins,
If you'll give up your love.

**HANS:** One hundred only?
That is little money for such an
Amount of love;
I cannot sell it so cheaply.

**KETSAL:** (*eagerly*). I will give you
twice as much.

**HANS:** Even that is too little.

**KETSAL:** then, three hundred flo-
rins.
I do it only because I want the thing
over with.
But if you do not consent now,
(*Threateningly.*)
I will do my very, very best to have
You finally sent away from
Here in disgrace. And then
You will neither have the girl
Nor the three hundred florins.

**HANS:** Well, well! but who is going
to give me the promised sum?

**KETSAL:** I! I!

**HANS:** (*surprised and distrust-
ful*). You? Surely not for yourself?
I would not give her to you for a
million!

**KETSAL:** Don't be silly! I don't
want her for myself. I have one of
My own, up to the neck. Don't
You know that I am arranging
This for the son of Tobias Micha?
As soon as the contract is
Signed, you will get your
Money, and then away with you!

**HANS:** Well, then, I consent.
Money is money!
Put down the cash, and all
Will be settled.
(*Hesitatingly.*)
Under one condition,
That nobody else will get
My Marie, but the son of
Tobias Micha! Otherwise,
This contract will be null and void.

**KETSAL:** Why, of course, most assuredly!
That nobody else gets her, or
Will be allowed to take her, but Micha's son.

HANS: Nur unter der Bedingung
Setz' ich den Namen hin; denn keinem Andern
Tret' ich sie ab. So laut' es deutlich im Vertrage!

KEZAL: Gleich will ich schreiben den Vertrag und auch
Die Zeugen schnell beschaffen!

HANS: Ferner bitt' ich,
Ausdrücklich sei vermerkt: sobald
Als meine früh're Braut und Micha's Sohn
Die Hände sich gereicht zum Ehebunde,
Darf Micha von Mariens Vater nicht
Des Geldes Rückbezahlung mehr verlangen.
Er trägt des Kaufes Preis allein!

KEZAL: Das ist Sehr klug und wohlbemerkt.
(*Er geht vergnügt ab.*)

## FÜNFTE SCENE

HANS: (*allein*). Armer Narr, Du glaubtest mich zu fangen?
Bist nun selber in das Netz gegangen! Es muss gelingen! Alles soll
Nach Wunsch und Willen gehen! So feine Schlingen,
Kann Liebeslust nur drehen. Schlau und toll,
Dir, Treue, Süsse, Viel tausend Grüsse'
In wenig Stunden
Ist es gescheh'n,
Dass wir, verbunden,
Uns wiederseh'n!
Nach Wetterschlägen,
Nach Angst und Pein,
Nach Sturm und Regen
Lacht Sonnenschein,
Himmlischer Segen,
Bald bist Du mein!

## SECHSTE SCENE

*Hans, Kezal, Kruschina und Volk.*

KEZAL: (*die Neugierigen abwehrend*). Nicht zu hitzig! Ihr werdet hören
Alles, was wir abgemacht!
Den Verlauf der Sache nicht zu stören
Haltet Ruhe, gebet Acht!

CHOR: Ja, wir wollen's endlich hören!

KEZAL: Denkt daran: Ihr müsst beschwören
Ob es richtig zu Papier gebracht!
Was hier steht, lasst mich berichten;
(*Liest.*)
"Auf die Braut will ich verzichten"

CHOR: (*sich um Kezal drängend*). Ja, so steht's! Was für Geschichten!?
Auf die Braut will er verzichten!?

HANS: And I shall leave her to no
Other than Micha's son.
That must specially be stated
When you draw up the contract.

KETSAL: I shall write out the contract at once and
call the witnesses together.

HANS: Still another word.
It shall also be stated, that
As soon as Marie and Micha's son
have joined hands
In wedlock, then shall
The elder Micha cease from
Insisting on the payment of Krushina's debt.
It shall be regarded as wiped out.

KETSAL: Yes, I agree to that.
(*Exit, contented.*)

## SCENE V

HANS: (*alone*). When you'll see
who by the bargain has profited,
You'll return quite discomforted.
Who could believe
That I'd sell
My darling Marie!
The angel of my life,
My crowning glory when
She'll be my wife.
Not for a thousand would I her exchange.
In the whole world
There's none like her, I know.
She loves but me, and I too love her so.

## SCENE VI

*Hans, Ketsal, Krushina and people.*

KETSAL: (*holding off the curious ones*). Not so wildly there
Without tension!
Follow the contract
With attention.

CHORUS: We'll follow that contract with attention.

KETSAL: Bear in mind that this document
Is of the whole transaction a record true.
All therein let me know proclaim,
(*Reads.*)
"To my bride I give up all claim."

CHORUS: (*crowding in around him*). All therein let him, now proclaim,
To his bride he gives up all claim.

HANS: (*zeigt auf das Papier und liest*). "Doch zu Gunsten keines Andern,
Als der Sohns des hochverehrten,
Wackeren Tobias Micha!"

KEZAL: Ja, des Sohns Tobias Micha's.

HANS: (*wie oben*). "Wenn er sie von Herzen liebt,
Wenn er treu sich ihr ergiebt,
Wenn vor Zeugen er beschwört,
Dass nur ihr sein Herz gehört."

KEZAL: Ganz genau so steht's geschrieben,
Ueberzeugt Euch, meine Lieben!
(*Er lässt die Umstehenden in den Vertrag sehen*).

CHOR: Nicht versteh'n wir, was geschehen!

KRUSCHINA: (*zu Hans*). Dankbar sollst Du stets mich sehen!
Gott sei Lob, wir sind so weit!
Weg ist jede Schwierigkeit.

KEZAL: Ja, Gottlob, wir sind im Reinen! Etwas noch will wichtig scheinen!
(*Zu Kruschina.*)
Braucht ihm weiter keinen Dank zu schulden,
Denn ich zahl'ihm baar dreihundert Gulden
Um diesen Preis, so steht's allhier,
Verkauft er die Marie!

CHOR: Ha, wie schändlich, zu verschachern seine Braut!

KRUSCHINA: Dass er auf das Geld nur schaut–
Frei will ich es Euch gestehen,–
Hätt'ich ihm nicht zugetraut!

KEZAL: Punctum, satis. So geschehen Nach Gesetzeslaut.
Unterschreibt nun!
(*Zu Hans.*)
Du zuerst.
Hier, mein Lieber! Dann die Zeugen!

HANS: Hier mein Nam';
(*unterschreibt.*)
Hans Ehrentraut.

CHOR: Er verkaufte seine Braut!
O Schande!

*ENDE DES ZWEITEN ACTES.*

## DRITTER ACT

(*Dekoration wie im ersten Act.*)

## ERSTE SCENE

WENZEL: (*allein. Sehr niedergeschlagen*). Wa . . . was ich mich betrübe!
Schwie . . . schwierig ist die Liebe!
Kä . . . Kämpfe mich bedrohen!
Mä . . . Mädchen ist entflohen!
Sche . . . Schelten wird die Mutter!

HANS: (*points to the paper and reads*). "But to none other than the honorable and honored son of Sir Tobias Micha."

KETSAL: Yes, son of sir Tobias Micha.

HANS: (*as above*). If indeed he truly loves,
And to her devotes his life,
And before the people swears
That he freely makes her his wife.

KETSAL: Here it's written, as he said it.
See, it's all here.

CHORUS: We cannot grasp now what has happened.

KRUSHINA: (*to Hans*). I would never have believed
That you have such a noble heart,
And so quickly us relieved
Of great trouble, on your part.

KETSAL: This affair is almost ended,
But with other matter blended.
(*To Krushina.*)
You to him are under no great obligations.
I agreed to pay three hundred florins.
And for this price you here behold,
His Marie he has sold.

CHORUS: What a shame. Oh, what a shame.
To sell his bride, to sell his bride.

KRUSHINA: What! Have you been guilty of such an act?
Then I must say you are a rascal for a fact.

KETSAL: Punctum, satis. Let all things go on as in the pact.
Now affix your names.
(*To Hans.*)
First of all you, Hans,
Then the witnesses.

HANS: Here it is written.
(*Signs.*)
Hans Ehrentraut.

CHORUS: He has sold his bride,
Oh, what a shame!

*END OF ACT II.*

## ACT III

(*Stage setting the same as for Act II.*)

## SCENE I

WENZEL: (*alone. Very downhearted.*) It wo-won't go out of my head,
Tha-that I soon may be dead!
She wi-will worry me; I'll die;
The-then will bury me, oh, my!
She wi-will tease me, she says,

# Act III, Scene I

He . . . Herz ist weich wie Butter!
We . . . Wenzel, weh Dir, Armer!
Hi . . . hilf, Du, mein Erbarmer!

## ZWEITE SCENE

*Wenzel, Springer und Esmerelda, Statisten.*

**SPRINGER:** (*ruft aus*). Dem nie genug verehrten Publikum
Wird unterthänigst bekannt gemacht,
Dass heut' Nachmittag eine Vorstellung
Zwei-und vierbeiniger Celebritäten
Von seltener Niedagewesenheit
Schlag drei Uhr pünktlich vor sich gehen wird,
Theils auf der Erde, theils auch in der Luft.
Besond're Zierden der Gesellschaft sind:
(*Fanfare.*)
Vorerst die wunderschöne Esmeralda,
Gebor'ne Spanierin aus Napagedos,
"Die Königin des Drahtseils,"
"Tochter der Luft"–
Springt auf Verlangen über ihren Schatten.
(*Fanfare.*)
Sodann der Indianerhäuptling Murru,
Gefangen auf der Insel Bummerang,
Die hunderttausend Meilen weit entfernt
Waschecht und braun bei Sonnenschein und Regen,
Von Haus aus Kannibal' und Menschenfresser.–
Er thut Euch nichts!–Jetzt frisst er nur noch Hühner
Und Tauben–die man mitzubringen hat!–
Mit Haut und Haar und schluckt nebstbei auch Gabeln.
(*Fanfare.*)
Doch das Erstaunlichste von Allem kommt
Zuletzt, "Das Wunder der Dressur!" Ein grosser
Lebend'ger Landbär aus Amerika,
Den ich mir selbat gezähmt. Mit Esmeralda
Tanzt er ein Pas de deux wie im Ballet,
Geht auf den Zeh'n und hüpft auf einem Bein.
Damit man sehe, dass ich nicht zuviel
Gesagt, so finde gleich die Probe statt.
Das Weit're folgt dann . . . He! Hollah. Fangt an!
(*Tanz und Production der Komödianten, die dann abziehen, das Volk hinter ihnen her.*)

**WENZEL:** (*der Esmeralda mit Entzücken bewundert hat*). Ei, ei, ei, ei, wie rei . . . rei . . . reizend! Was
Die Spa . . . pa . . . panierin für Füsschen hat!

---

And de-deceive me, I guess.
It wo-won't go out of my head,
Tha-that I soon may be dead!

## SCENE II

*Wenzel, Ringmaster and Esmeralda, Acrobats*

**RINGMASTER:** (*announces*). We hereby announce to the
Honored audience here assembled,
That we shall give them a performance
In the air and on the ground,
Never before witnessed by mortal eyes.
First of all we present
(*Flare of trumpets.*)
Senorita Esmeralda Salamanka,
The celebrated Spanish dancer,
Queen of the tight-rope,
Daughter of the air, who will
Perform numerous graceful,
Daring and hazardous feats.
Then will appear
(*Flare of trumpets.*)
A real Indian from the Fiji
Islands, especially brought over at an enormous
Expense of money and trouble.
Although he must now
Content himself with ordinary
Fare, he is really a man-eating cannibal.
He will swallow wives—I mean
Knives and swords with great alacrity.
Then will appear the most wonderful number of the whole programme.
(*Flare of trumpets.*)
A real American Grizzly Bear,
Whom I tamed myself.
After performing many astonishing
Feats, such as walking and hopping
On his hind legs and front paws,
He will dance a Ballet with
Esmeralda in the most approved
Graceful and artistic manner.
That you may not think that
I too highly praised this collection,
I will give you a small production.
But more hereafter.
And now! Let's begin.
(*Dance and performance of acrobats, who then retire, and the people after them.*)

**WENZEL:** (*casting admiring glances at Esmeralda*). Oh my, oh my! How lovely!
And that Spanish dancer, what beautiful legs she has!

---

**ESMERALDA:** (*zu Wenzel*).
Kommt wohl der schöne Herr heut'
Mittag auch?

**WENZEL:** Versteht sich! Wenn Ihr
auf dem Seile tanzt,
So will ich kommen!

**MUFF, DER INDIANER:** (*kommt eilig und erschreckt*). Direktor!
Herr Direktor!
Sagt' ich es doch: ein Unglück
giebt's! Der Michel
Hat sich betrunken, vollständig betrunken!
Im Wirthshaus liegt er unterm
Tische da
Und rührt sich nicht! Und Keinen
sonst der uns
Den Bären spielt, besitzen wir!

**SPRINGER:** Den Teufel! 's ist unsre
beste Nummer!
(*Für sich.*)
Was zu thun?
Nein, ohne Bären geht's nun einmal
nicht.
Sonst prügeln uns am End' die Bauern durch . . .
Mein Künstlerruf steht auf dem
Spiel dabei.
(*Laut.*)
Lauf' nur und such' mir einen Andern Irgend
Ein Bursche find't sich schon.

**MUFF:** Es ist vergebens,
Besehen hab' ich Alles. Keiner ist,
Der passte: Der zu dick und der zu
dünn,
Einer zu gross, ein Anderer zu
klein!
In's Fell will Niemand auch hinein,
und Zeit
Ist weiter nicht mehr zu verlieren,
sollen
Wir fertig sein!

**SPRINGER:** Was meinst Du, Esmeralda?

**WENZEL:** (*der die ganze Zeit über
Esmeralda mit verliebten Blicken
betrachtet hat*). Das wär' ein
Mädchen, die . . . die mir gefällt,
So schön! We . . . wenn ich die zur
Frau bekäme!
Beneiden sollte mich das ganze
Dorf!

**ESMERALDA:** (*ihn ermuthigend*). Was seht Ihr mich so an?
Gelt ja, Ihr habt
Noch eine Frage?

**WENZEL:** (*verschämt*). Kö . . . kö .
. . könntet Ihr
Mich lieben wohl?

**MUFF:** (*der den Wenzel mit Kennerblicken gemustert hat, zu
Springer*.) Ei, seht mir doch: dem
sässe
Das Bärenfell so trefflich, dass man
schwört'
Es sei für ihn gemacht!

**SPRINGER:** So geh' und ruf' die
Vorstellung aus! Und Den da nehm'
ich gleich
Hier in die Arbeit.
(*Der Indianer ab.*)

---

**ESMERALDA:** (*to Wenzel*). And is
this fine gentleman coming to our
show?

**WENZEL:** Why, of course. I would
love
To see you dance on the tight-rope.

**MUFF, THE INDIAN:** (*rushes in
excitedly*). Ringmaster! Ringmaster!
A great misfortune has happened.
Mike got drunk in the other
Inn, and there he lies under
The table, and I cannot
Induce him to play the bear,
Try as I may.

**RINGMASTER:** The deuce! the
deuce! It is our best number.
(*Aside.*)
If the bear cannot appear, we cannot perform
The celebrated ballet. No, no, no,
that cannot be! That must not be!
(*Aloud.*)
We will have to look for somebody
else—
Any old youngster out of the town.

**MUFF:** He would give it away,
And the people would ridicule us.
Where could we find somebody?
He must be fully grown;
Otherwise the bear's skin will not
fit him.
The people are coming in, and
We really have no time left to look
around.

**RINGMASTER:** What can we do,
Esmeralda?

**WENZEL:** (*who during all this
time has been casting loving
glances at Esmeralda*). What a fine
girl she is!
Her I like! Well, well, if
She should become my wife,
The whole town would admire, and
envy me.

**ESMERALDA:** (*encouraging
him*). I like you very much, and
would like to marry you.

**WENZEL:** (*bashfully.*) Ma-marry
me?

**MUFF:** (*who took Wenzel in with
the eye of a connoisseur, to Ringmaster.*) That one the bear's skin
would fit like a glove,
As if expressly made for him.

**RINGMASTER:** Well, then, go and
announce the performance!
This young man I will look after myself.
(*Exit Muff.*)

(*Zu Wenzel.*)
He, mein Theuerster!
Liebt Ihr sie, meine Esmeralda,
dann
Den Segen geb' ich Euch! Ihr tretet
gleich
Bei meiner Truppe ein; mit Esmer-
alda
Sollt Ihr noch heute tanzen!

WENZEL: (*froh bestürzt*). Ta . . . ta
. . . tanzen!?
(*Traurig.*)
Ach, tanzen ka . . . ka . . . kann ich
nicht!

ESMERALDA: Lehrt Euch die
Liebe, was Euch etwa fehlt.

WENZEL: (*beglückt*). Die Liebe!
Lasst doch hören!

SPRINGER: Euch erwartet
Vergnügtes Leben: immer frisch
und lustig!
Von früh bis Abends singen, scher-
zen, springen!
Heut' hier und morgen dort! Und
angeseh'n
Sind allenthalben wir als Künstler!
Ja,
Den Stand der Komödianten nennt
man wohl
Den Stand der Stände auch, malum
malorum,
So heisst es auf Lateinisch!
Komödie wird
Gespielt allüberall, nicht im The-
ater nur,
Ja, manchmal besser noch und
täuschender
Im Leben, aber nicht so heiter,
harmlos,
Als wie bei uns.

ESMERALDA: Wie? Ihr bedenkt
Euch noch?
Fasst Euch ein Herz! Die Liebe
reiche Euch
Den ersten Lorbeer!

SPRINGER: Was kann Euch
geschehen?
Ihr seid ja nicht gebunden! Eine
Probe
Und heute nur!

ESMERALDA: Lasst Ihr umsonst
mich bitten?
Ach, mein Geliebter, thätet Ihr's, ja
dann
Wär' ich die Eure!

WENZEL: (*bekommt Lust*). Wa . . .
was soll ich machen?

ESMERALDA: Tanzen!

WENZEL: Ta . . . tanzen, kann ich's
denn?

ESMERALDA: Ich will's Euch zeig-
en: beide tanzen wir zusammen.

WENZEL: Doch die Mu . . . Mutter!

ESMERALDA: Die erkennt Euch
nicht.

ESMERALDA und SPRINGER:
Alles geht am Schnürchen,
Da man Dich nicht quält,
Hab' ein hübsches Thierchen
Für Dich ausgewählt,

---

(*To Wenzel.*)
Well, my dear sir! If you really love
Esmeralda, then you
Can easily get her.
Become one of the members of my
troupe,
And you shall yet dance to-day with
Esmeralda.

WENZEL: (*joyfully*). I da-dance?
(*Sadly.*)
I do not know how!

ESMERALDA: My love will teach
you how to do everything.

WENZEL: (*happily*). Love! Well,
that's worth hearing.

RINGMASTER: You will always
have a happy time with us.
Bright and lively,
Late and early,
Dancing, singing,
Joking, springing,
Here to-day and gone to-morrow.
Well, as you see, we are honored as
actors,
Yes, the profession of actor is
called the art of all arts;
Malum malorum, as they call it in
Latin.
We know all the world is a stage;
And the people actors more or less.
Only their play is important and
more serious,
But not as entertaining as ours,
Nor as gay.

ESMERALDA: Well, then, my dear!
Come and join us.
My love shall be to you the sweetest
of rewards.

RINGMASTER: What can happen
to you!
You are not bound as yet.
Try it for once,
You can now.

ESMERALDA: Yes, to-day you can
try it.
Come, my darling, only once!
And then
I shall be yours forever.

WENZEL: What must I do?

ESMERALDA: Dance the ballet.

WENZEL: Dance the ballet?
What it that?

ESMERALDA: We are to dance together;
You with me, and I with you.

WENZEL: Bu-but my mother!

ESMERALDA: She will not know
you.

ESMERALDA AND RINGMAS-
TER: A most charming creature
We will make of you.
It will be a feature
Only known to few.

---

Prinz im Märchen,
Braunes Bärchen
Sollst Du sein!
Das verstehst Du,
Artig gehst Du,
Schmuck und fein!
Freundlich musst Du nicken,
Denn Du bist in mich verliebt!
Hold und zärtlich blicken . . .
's wird ein Spass, wie's keinen
giebt!
Alles geht am Schnürchen,
Da man Dich nicht quält,
Hab' ein hübsches Thierchen
Für Dich ausgewählt.
(*Esmeralda und Springer ab
(weil sie die neu Auftretenden
von Weitem sehen). Sie winken
Wenzel nachzukommen.*)

### DRITTE SCENE

*Wenzel. Gleich darauf Micha,
Agnes und Kezal.*

WENZEL: A . . . ach, wie wird es
mir ergehen? Alle
Die schönen Mädchen, sie entbe . . .
be . . . brennen
Für mich in Liebe.
(*Er übt sich im Tanzen.*)

AGNES: Endlich sieht man Dich!
Was treibst Du denn? Bist Du von
Sinnen? Komm'
Jetzt mit uns, damit wir zu dem
niedlichsten
Bräutchen des Dorfs Dich führen!

WENZEL: Lasst mich gehen!

AGNES: Nimm doch Vernunft an!
Vater und ich wir haben
Geordnet Alles. Zeit wird es nun
endlich,
Dir 'ne verständ'ge Frau zu geben!

KEZAL: Wenzel Wird das hier un-
terschreiben, abgethan
Ist dann die Sache.

WENZEL: Wo . . . wozu verpflichtet
Mich das Papier?

MICHA: Dass Du Maria Kruschina
Zum Weibe nehmen wirst!

WENZEL: Nei . . . nein! Die will
Ich gar nicht haben.

AGNES, MICHA und KEZAL: Ha,
das trifft wie ein Donnerschlag!
Ich weiss nicht, trau' ich meinen
Ohren!
So sage mir doch, Wenzel, sag',
Wo hast Du den Verstand verloren?

WENZEL: Das Schicksal kenn' ich,
das mir droht;
Sie will mich quälen bis zum Tod!

AGNES, MICHA und KEZAL:
Woher stammt diese Kunde?
O sprich, aus wessen Munde?

WENZEL: Je . . . jemand, der sein
Herz mit bot . . .

---

### SCENE III

*Wenzel, then Micha, Agnes and
Ketsal.*

WENZEL: (*sadly*). Oh, poor unfortunate me!
All the girls want to marry me, and
then kill me.
(*He practices dancing.*)

AGNES: O why are you so sad, my
dear boy!
Brace up and be joyful!
You get married and all
Your troubles and sorrows will
Quickly be ended.

WENZEL: I-I am afraid.

AGNES: What are you afraid of, my
darling?
Nothing bad can ever happen to
you.
You will get a wife,
And that is the finest thing in the
world.

KETSAL: Yes, just so! Wenzel will
here sign the contract.
And everything will be settled.

WENZEL: What-what kind of a contract is this?

MICHA: That you promise to make
Marie Krushina your wife.

WENZEL: I-I do not want her!

AGNES, MICHA AND KETSAL:
What, really, not want her!
What can it be that makes him wa-
ver?
Speak, speak, Wenzel!
What nonsense were you led
To take into your head?

WENZEL: I'm-I'm afraid she'll
tease me all my life,
And will deceive me, and worry me
to death.

AGNES, MICHA AND KETSAL:
Oh, what a foolish notion!
Speak, where did you get it?

WENZEL: Someone told me and
warned me to-day.

---

We will put a lovely mask over face
and nose,
And the softest shoes upon your
feet and toes.
You will be a cherub
Who will all entrance,
And the people
Will hasten to see you dance,
A most charming creature
We will make of you.
It will be a feature
Only known to few.
(*Esmeralda and Ringmaster go
because they see the people ap-
proaching. They motion to Wen-
zel to follow.*)

**AGNES, MICHA und KEZAL:** Der feindlich Deinem Bunde.

**AGNES, MICHA AND KETSAL:** Who was that villainous person?

**WENZEL:** O nein, O nein! Ein rei... rei... reizend Mägdelein.

**WENZEL:** A beautiful girl.

**AGNES, MICHA und KEZAL:** Was machte Dir das Mädchen weis?

**AGNES, MICHA AND KETSAL:** And what did she say to you?

**WENZEL:** Sie sagt' es mir, sie liebt mich heiss!

**WENZEL:** She said to me, she loves me so!

**AGNES:** Und kennst Du sie?

**AGNES:** And do you know her?

**WENZEL:** Ach nein! (*Läuft davon.*)

**WENZEL:** No, not I! (*He runs away.*)

**AGNES, MICHA und KEZAL:** Das sind verwünschte Dinge! Man legt' ihm eine Schlinge! Drum, wie ich zur Vernunft ihn bringe, Soll meine Sorge sein.

**AGNES, MICHA AND KETSAL:** This is a pesky matter. Someone has spoken to him, And turned his trusting mind. I'll the culprit find.

## VIERTE SCENE

## SCENE IV

*Marie, Kruschina, Kathinka und die Vorigen. Später Wenzel.*

*Marie, Krushina, Kathinka, and the foregoing, later Wenzel*

**MARIE:** (*stürzt herein, Kruschina und Kathinka hinter ihr her*). Nein, nein, nein! Es ist erlogen! Sie lästern, schreien, Uns zu entzweien! Sie lästern, schreien, Mein Liebster habe mich betrogen.

**MARIE:** (*rushes in, followed by Krushina and Kathinka*). No, no, no! I cannot believe that! It is a mere trick put up to deceive me. My love can never be a rascal.

**KRUSCHINA:** Die Arme zweifelt noch!

**KRUSHINA:** And still it is the truth.

**KEZAL:** Komm' her und schaue doch.

**KETSAL:** What, is she still in doubt?

**KRUSCHINA:** Er gab Dich schämlos preis.

**KRUSHINA:** Hans gave you up!

**KEZAL:** Hier steht es schwarz auf weiss! (*Zeigt das Papier.*) Ja, um dreihundert Gulden Verkauft' er seine Braut.

**KETSAL:** Here it is in black and white! (*Shows her the paper.*) For three hundred florins Hans sold to us his bride.

**MARIE:** Wer hätte das ihm zugetraut!? (*Weinend.*) Gott mög' es ihm verzeih'n! Hab' ich verdient so tiefe Schmach? Noch immer klingt es in mir nach: "Ja, Dein bin ich allein!"

**MARIE:** Oh, what an awful blow this is! (*Weeping.*) O men, you are deceitful! His solemn word he gave to me, That all the world he'd brave for me.

**KRUSCHINA:** Sei ruhig, armes Kind, Vergiss den Sausewind! Nimm einen Besser'n Dir, Der rein und treu gesinnt!

**KRUSHINA:** Take comfort, my dear child. Though you on him relied, You will now another find, who will be always kind.

**KEZAL:** Hier unterschreib' geschwind! (*Wenzel ist im Hintergrunde wieder sichtbar.*) Nun, Wenzel, schnell herbei!

**KETSAL:** Now you will sign, my hearty! (*Wenzel appears in the background.*) And our Wenzel, where is he?

**KATHINKA:** Mein Kind, Du musst Dich fassen, Es sei nun, wie es sei!

**KATHINKA:** Just see him on the common. What is he staring at?

**MARIE:** Und hat er mich verlassen, Ich bleibe dennoch frei! Vertrauern will ich meine Zeit In stiller Einsamkeit!

**MARIE:** I'll never sign this contract, For Wenzel I'll not take! I'd rather, rather live alone and all my friends forsake.

**DIE ANDERN:** Wohl in Vergessenheit Wird Dir entschwinden bald Dein Leid.

**THE OTHERS:** You cannot do that now! The moments hasten! You must decide.

**KEZAL:** (*erblickt Wenzel und ruft*). He, Wenzel! He, mein Wenzelchen! Lass fahren Deine Blödigkeit!

**KETSAL:** (*catches sight of Wenzel and calls him*). Hey, Wenzel, hey, Wenzel dear! Come and drop your bashfulness.

**WENZEL:** (*kommt hervor, ärgerlich*). Was giebt es denn schon wieder? (*Erblickt Marie, freudig erstaunt.*) Die-die-die sprach ich heute Morgen! Nu... nun ist nichts mehr zu besorgen.

**WENZEL:** (*comes up angrily*). Well, what is now the matter? (*Notices Marie, agreeably surprised.*) She-she-she spoke to me this morning.

**KATHINKA, AGNES, KRUSCHINA, MICHA, KEZAL:** Weiss ich doch nicht wo und wie? Sprach er wirklich mit Marie?

**KATHINKA, AGNES, KRUSHINA, MICHA, KETSAL:** Was it really Marie then Who did scare him thus?

**WENZEL:** Ja, heut' Morgen in der Früh'! Ich gefiel ihr, sagte sie.

**WENZEL:** She told me that all apart, Me she loved with all her heart.

**KATHINKA, AGNES, KRUSCHINA, MICHA, KEZAL:** Das ist ja das Bräutchen, Das Dir zugedacht!

**KATHINKA, AGNES, KRUSHINA, MICHA, KETSAL:** Well, this is the lady we picked to be your wife.

**WENZEL:** Dann ist's abgemacht!

**WENZEL:** Yes, yes, her do I like

**KEZAL:** Nicht lange mehr geplaudert, Gezweifelt und gezaudert, Jetzt sind am Ziele wir!

**KETSAL:** Then let us not wait longer, For that won't make it stronger, But sign the contract now.

**MARIE:** Ich bitte, nur ein Weilchen Lasst noch allein mich hier!

**MARIE:** Leave me here a moment all alone to think.

**KATHINKA, KRUSCHINA, KEZAL; AGNES, MICHA, KEZAL:** (*then all together.*): Noch ein Weilchen, Marie, bedenk es dir, Noch ein Weilchen, Marie, bedenk es dir, Aber bald dann kommen wieder wir! Deinen Willen zu erfüllen lassen wir dich hier. Bleibt doch dein Lebensglück in deiner Hand, Bleibt doch dein Lebensglück in deiner Hand, O weis' es, weis' es nicht zurück wenn du's erkannt. O weis' es nicht zurück wenn du's erkannt. noch ein Weilchen Marie bedenk' es dir! Deinen willen zu erfüllen lassen wir dich hier, Deinen willen zu erfüllen, lassen wir Dich hier, wir Dich hier...

**KATHINKA, KRUSHINA, AND KETSAL** (*repeat*) **AGNES, MICHA, AND KETSAL:** (*then all together*) Think it over, Marie dear, yes, think it over, Think it over, Marie dear, yes, think it over; It is for your good we you implore, It is for your good, is for your good, we you implore. You will gain happiness to us it's plain, You will gain happiness to us it's plain, Do not, O do not miss your chance, nor give us pain. O do not miss your chance nor give us pain. Think it over, Marie dear, oh think it over, It is for your good, is for your good we you implore, It is for your good, is for your good we you implore, you implore.

**MARIE:** Ja, es bleibt in meiner Hand, bleibt... in meiner Hand ja, es bleibt in meiner Hand, meiner Hand... (*All exeunt but MARIE.*)

**Marie:** Fully I will think it over, I will think it over fully, fully think it over, think it over .. (*All exeunt but Marie.*)

## FÜNFTE SCENE

## SCENE V

**MARIE:** (*allein*). Endlich allein! Allein mit mir, mit meinem Grame! Noch immer kann ich es nicht glauben, Steht auch dabei sein Name!... Was hier noch leise für ihn spricht, Ich darf es hören nicht. War seine Liebe nur ein Wahn? Wehe mir Armen! Was hab' ich ihm gethan?

**MARIE:** (*alone*). What shall I do? Deserted now, and weighed down by my sorrow. Still I cannot understand it. His name is there most plainly. How can he countermand it? Perhaps, I doubt him vainly! Would to God that out of all This confusion no harm my love befall.

(Träumerisch.)
Wie fremd und todt ist Alles umher,
Und war so traut, voll Leben!
Die Welt hat keine Freuden mehr,
Ich muss mich d'rein ergeben.
O Lenz, Dein buntes Blumenkleid,
Wie welk ist es geworden!
Der böse Herbst kam vor der Zeit
Einhergeweht von Norden . . .
(Wie erwachend.)
Nein! Alles ist noch, wie es war
Und will nur anders scheinen,
Weil trübe ward mein Augenpaar
Vom Weinen.
Du Maienzeit, wie warst Du schön
Mit Deinen frischen Trieben!
Ade nun, helles Lustgetön!
Ade, Du junges Lieben!

## SECHSTE SCENE

*MARIE und HANS.*

**HANS:** (*stürmt fröhlich herein*).
So find 'ich Dich, Feinsliebchen, hier,
Mein Sehnen, mein Verlangen?
O sprich, erzähle, wie es Dir
Inzwischen ist ergangen!

**MARIE:** Hinweg! Nicht bin ich mehr Dein Lieb
Lass' Deinen schlechten Scherz!
Erst stahlst Du mir, ehrloser Dieb,
Und dann verkauftest Du mein Herz!
Sag', ist es Wahrheit oder nicht?
Ein Wort allein:
Ja oder nein!

**HANS:** (*übermüthig*). So einfach
geht es schwerlich an!

**MARIE:** Ich will nur Antwort, falscher Mann
Sag', war's Du so abscheulich?

**HANS:** (*wie vorher*). Nun ja doch, freilich, freilich

**MARIE:** Von Reue zeigst Du keine Spur,
Genug hab' ich vernommen!

**HANS:** (*zärtlich, schalkhaft*). O
Du Geliebte, lass' mich nur
Einmal zu Worte kommen!

**MARIE:** Mit uns'rer Liebe
Ist's aus nun, merk Dir das!
Ich nehme mir den Wenzel!

**HANS:** (*lacht*). Ha, ha, ha, ha!
Das ist wahrhaftig
Ein höchst gelung'ner Spass!

**MARIE:** (*zornig*). Ha, Spott ist meiner Liebe Lohn?

**HANS:** (*immer lachend*). Ich muss Dir was erzählen,
Zwar stimmt's nicht zu dem Trauerton.

**MARIE:** (*unterbricht*). Ich lass' mich nimmer quälen.

**HANS:** Mein lieber Schatz, nun aufgepasst.
Ich geb' Dir was zu hören!
Nur gönne mir ein wenig Rast

Und wolle mich nicht stören!
Mein lieber Schatz, nun aufgepasst,
Ich geb' Dir was zu hören!

**MARIE:** Ein Märchen wohl, von Dir verfasst,
Um Dich herauszuschwören?
Ich weiss, was Du verbrochen hast
Du wirst mich nicht bethören
Ein Märchen wohl, von Dir verfasst
Um Dich herauszuschwören?

## SIEBENTE SCENE

*Kezal und die Vorigen.*

**KEZAL:** He, Hans? Du möchtest wohl Dein Geld schon haben?
Warte nur noch ein Bischen hier!
Giebt die Marie mir ihre Unterschrift,
Erhälst Du, was Dir zukommt!

**MARIE:** Ha! Der glatte Heuchler!

**KEZAL:** (*zu Marie.*) Nun, und Du?
Nimmst Du
Dafür zu Deinem Mann des Micha Sohn?

**HANS:** Ja, das verbürg' ich Euch!
Sie wird ihn nehmen.
Kein Anderer als er soll sie bekommen.
So ward es abgemacht!

**KEZAL:** (*scherzend*). Und so ist's recht.
Du Heirathsmittler!

**MARIE:** Nichts da! Er lügt Euch an!
Nein, sag' ich, nein, nein! Nun und nimmermehr!
Und stürb' ich d'rum hier auf der Stelle!

**HANS:** Was wollt Ihr wetten, dass sie's dennoch thut?
Wenn ich es will, so nimmt sie Micha's Sohn!

**MARIE:** Wie? Hans? Und dazu wolltest Du
Im Ernst mich bringen? Solch' ein' Ungeheuer
Hab's auf der Welt noch nie! Du Teufel, Du!

**HANS:** Gesegnet, wer da liebt und auch vertraut!
Kein Zweifel trübt sein Glück.
Bald kehret Dir, verkaufte Braut,
Was Du verlorst, zurück!
Es liebt Dich jenes Micha Sohn
Wie keiner sonst auf Erden,
Für Deine Treue Dank und Lohn
Kann Dir von ihm nur werden!

**MARIE:** Ein Schmeichler und ein Heuchler
Macht hier sein Meisterstück!

**KEZAL:** Das ist ein zweiter Salomo!
(*Für sich.*)
Oder ein Galgenstrick!
Jetzt rufen wir die Eltern her,
Dazu die andern Zeugen!
Nun kommt mir nichts mehr in die

---

(Dreamily.)
My dream of love how fair it was,
So full of rapture and hope.
It shone so brightly in my heart
It seemed we would never part.
What happy life I pictured here
With Hans, to live together;
But love is killed, I greatly fear
It's killed by wintry weather.
(As if awakening.)
No, can there happen such deceit,
Can love live on unfulfilled?
The world would shed a tear, indeed,
Over love that's so cruelly killed.
My dream of love how fair it was,
It shone so brightly in my heart;
It seemed we would never part.
My dream of love, how fair it was!

## SCENE VI

*Marie and Hans*

**HANS:** (*rushes in joyfully*). How I sought you,
My darling Marie!
Star of my being!
O speak, do you still know of anything,
That might prevent our marriage?

**MARIE:** Away! I am your star no more,
Our dream of love is over.
You stole my heart and lowered yourself
By selling it for worthless pelf.
Speak, is it true, or is it not?
But yes or no, one word alone!

**HANS:** (*teasingly*). So simply—
that cannot be done!

**MARIE:** I want no explanations, now!
Speak, is it true as written?

**HANS:** (*the same*). Yes, then, yes, then, yes, then!

**MARIE:** Now go away, and never more
Let me behold your features.

**HANS:** (*affectionately, playfully*).
O let me all explain before
I go, you loveliest of creatures!

**MARIE:** Our love is ended, bear in mind,
And I am going to marry Wenzel.

**HANS:** (*laughs*). Ha, ha, ha, that would truly be
A stupendous joke!

**MARIE:** (*angrily*). What, is this all so very gay?

**HANS:** (*still laughing*). I want to tell you something,
Then listen, only let me say—

**MARIE:** No, you can tell me nothing.

**HANS:** You are an awful stubborn case
For you'll not let me tell you.
How could I look into your face

If really I did sell you.
You are an awful stubborn case
For you'll not let me tell you.

**MARIE:** You are an awful wicked case,
The devil cannot beat you.
I'll never look into your face,
And never want to meet you,
You are an awful wicked case,
The devil cannot beat you.

## SCENE VII

*Ketsal and the foregoing.*

**KETSAL:** Here, Hans! You, I suppose, wait for your money?
Well, have a little patience!
As soon as Marie signs the contract
You will get every penny.

**MARIE:** Ha, how disgraceful!

**KETSAL:** Well, and you? Will you take for your husband Micha's son?

**HANS:** Of course she will, I say!
That he will get her and nobody else, is fixed by the contract,
And to that, I swear.

**KETSAL:** You're a good boy, with good understanding.

**MARIE:** You're a villainous liar!
No, no, now surely not!
I will not take him
If I die on the spot for it.

**HANS:** What will you give if I induce her
That she will take Tobias Micha's son?

**MARIE:** What! Hans, you want to induce
Me to do such a thing!
No, such a bold proceeding
The world never did see nor ever hear.

**HANS:** Have patience, and do not give up hope,
But trust to me as you did never before.
You hardly know what happiness
For you there is in store.
He loves you more than anything
In this wide world of ours,
and Micha's son will brighten your life
With bliss and all its powers.

**MARIE:** O heavens, O heavens, how these
Words are racking my poor heart!

**KETSAL:** I never heard a wiser word.
(*Aside.*)
He is indeed a glorious bird.
(*Aloud.*)
Now let us call the parents here

Quer
Der Himmel hängt voll Geigen.
(*Geht ab.*)

MARIE: (*ergeben*). Ich habe keine
Wünsche mehr
Und will in's Joch mich beugen,
Mein Sinn ist trüb', mein Herz ist
schwer
Was kann ich thun als schweigen?

HANS: Die Alten, ja, das freut mich
sehr!
Willkommen sind die Zeugen,
Und käme gleich ein ganzes Heer
Was mein ist, bleibt mein Eigen!
(*Zu Marie.*) Des Micha Sohn wird
doch Dein Mann!

MARIE: Nur fort! Ich schaue Dich
nicht an!

## ACHTE SCENE

Agnes, Kathinka, Kruschina, Micha, Kezal, Chor und die Vorigen.

CHOR: Kommen wir gerne, so
kommen wir gleich
Aber Mariechen, weshalb so
bleich?

MARIE: (*für sich*). So räch' ich
mich für den Verrath!
Er soll mich nimmer äffen!
Um was er höhnisch erst mich bat,
Ich thu's, um ihn zu treffen!
(*Laut, mit Anstrengung.*)
Was Ihr gewollt, das thu' ich gern!

CHOR: Das Brautpaar soll leben!
Mariechen kriegt nun einen Herrn!
Der Tag der Hochzeit ist nicht fern!

HANS: (*vortretend*). Ja, lustig
wird es werden da,
Denn solch' ein Paar noch Keiner
sah!

AGNES und MICHA: Was seh' ich?
Das ist ja der Hans!

HANS: Herr Vater und Frau Mutter
auch,
Da bin ich wieder, heil und ganz!
Bin aus der Fremde heimgekehrt,
Zu gründen einen eig'nen Herd!

KEZAL: Ei! Soll ich's glauben oder
nicht,
Was dieser Flausenmacher spricht?
Er wäre, Micha, Euer Sohn?
Der ist ja wohl gestorben schon!

HANS: Erkannten mich die Eltern
doch!
Und schätzt mich auch nicht jeder
hoch.
(*mit Beziehung auf Kezal und die
Stiefmutter.*)
Das Beste ist: ich lebe noch!

AGNES: Hier bist Du nicht am
rechten Ort
Mit Deinen alten Ränken!

---

And witnesses together,
As nothing more will interfere
To end this joyous matter.
(*Exit.*)

MARIE: (*resigned*). Now I will call
my parents here
And all my friends together,
As nothing more will interfere
To end this painful matter.

HANS: Yes, you may call the par-
ents here
And witnesses together,
As nothing more will interfere
To end this ludicrous matter.
(*To Marie.*)
What, do you still not understand?

MARIE: Go! What do you want
here?

## SCENE VIII

Agnes, Kathinka, Krushina, Micha, Ketsal, Chorus and the preceding.

CHORUS: Have you decided and
thought out with care,—
Speak—what you shall do in this
mixed up affair?

MARIE: (*aside*). I'll have revenge,
and I shall do,
What he is trying to prevent.
O sadly and mournfully
He'll be eyeing me.
(*Aloud with exertion.*)
I shall do all that you desire.

CHORUS: Good luck, to you, Mar-
ie!
All discontent must emigrate.
The marriage feast we'll celebrate.

HANS: (*stepping to the front*). The
marriage feast we'll celebrate,
And all the world will think it great.

AGNES AND MICHA: What do I
see? Is this really Hans?

HANS: Yes, father! Many a long and
weary day
From you I've been away.
I have no wish again to roam,
And so shall found my own sweet
home.

KETSAL: What, is it truth or only
fun?
That simple chap, old Micha's son,
The elder, is that truly so?
I thought he'd gone to fight the foe.

HANS: I am truly old Micha's son,
From foreign part; and not for fun
But no real earnest battles fought,
(*Referring to Agnes and Ketsal.*)
Against adverse foes my fortune
sought.

AGNES: And you have time enough
on hand
To do it more! You understand?

---

HANS: Ich kann es mir wohl denk-
en,
Gern schicktet Ihr mich wieder
fort!
Doch wenn ich geh', dann nicht al-
lein!
Mit Micha's Sohn die Liebste sein
Marie, die nun für ewig mein!

AGNES: Das gilt nicht, weil Betrug
es ist!

HANS: Betrug nicht, nein, nur eine
List;
Geschrieben ist geschrieben!
Ihr bleibt die Wahl: Den Wenzel
oder mich!
(*Zu Marie.*)
Triff die Entscheidung nun und
sprich:
Wen von uns willst Du lieben?

MARIE: Hab' ich doch längst
entschieden!
(*Eilt Hans in die Arme.*)
Ja, Dein bin ich, ja, Dein bin ich!

KEZAL: Wer hätte das von ihm ge-
dacht!
Mir schwillt vor Zorn die Galle!
Um Einfluss, um Gewicht und
Macht
Hat der Hallunke mich gebracht,
Ich ging ihm in die Falle!

MICHA: (*höhnisch zu Kezal*).
Lasst Euch bewundern! Ja, das habt
Ihr wirklich gut gemacht!

AGNES: (*ebenso*). Der Wichtig-
thuer, hochbegabt
Nun wird er ausgelacht.

MARIE, HANS, KATHINKA,
KRUSCHINA: Lasst Euch bewun-
dern! Ja, das habt
Ihr wirklich gut gemacht!

CHOR: Ha, ha, ha, ha! Er wird verlacht!
(*KEZAL läuft wüthend fort.*)

## LETZTE SCENE

(*Grosser Lärm hinter der Bühne.
Knaben rennen über die Bühne.
Ein Knabe schreit: "Rettet Euch,
der Bär ist los!" Ein Anderer, "Es
rennt geradenwegs hierher!"*)

Wenzel und die Vorigen.

WENZEL: (*als Bär verkleidet*).
Seid ohne Furcht! Ich bin kein
Landbär, nur
Der We ... We ... Wenzel!

AGNES: (*erbost*). Du Gimpel, was
hast Du gethan? O Schande!
Schere, Du Narr, Dich weg von
hier! Denn man
Verlacht uns und verspottet uns!
(*Sie zieht Wenzel mit sich fort.*)

KRUSCHINA: Gevatter Micha wer-
det selbst begreifen
Wohl, dass sein Kind man ihm ver-
weigert Ja,
Da ist der Hans mir lieber!
(*Begütigend.*)
's ist Euer Blut
Ihr seid der Vater!

---

HANS: I know, that goes without
saying,
I am not a welcome guest.
But never mind we'll pass the rest,
Since to my love I have a claim,
I, Micha's son by blood and name.

AGNES: That is not fair, that's
cheating quick!

HANS: Not cheating, but only a
trick.
It's written here, it's written.
See, we are two, put it to her.
Let her say whom she'll prefer!
(*To Marie.*)
Whom do you want to marry?

MARIE: Now, at last, I understand.
(*Throws herself into Hans' arms.*)
You my darling Hans!
I'm yours, I'm yours!

KETSAL: This fellow is a tricky
scamp,
He's beaten me all over.
A great big blot upon my name,
My reputation gone, my fame,
How can I them ever again recover?

MICHA: (*sarcastically to Ketsal*).
Your wisdom has just left you,
Truly and for a fact.

AGNES: (*the same*). And may we
mention, made you
Do and perform a very stupid act.

MARIE, HANS, KATHINKA, AND
KRUSHINA: Your wisdom has just
left you,
Truly and for a fact.

CHORUS: Ha, ha, ha, ha, a stupid
act.
(*Ketsal runs away.*)

## LAST SCENE

(*A loud noise behind the scenes.
Boys run across the stage. One
boy cries: "Run for your life! The
bear got loose." Another, "He's
coming this way, run!"*)

Wenzel and Foregoing.

WENZEL: (*disguised as a bear*)
Don't be afraid! I am not a wild
bear! I am Wenzel!

AGNES: (*enraged*). You donkey,
what are you doing?
Oh, what a disgrace! Get away from
here, You ninny, and get out of that
rank disguise.
(*She drags Wenzel away.*)

KRUSHINA: Now, my dear friend
Micha, you
Yourself must acknowledge that
There can be no talk of Wenzel.
Why, he hasn't his reason yet.
(*Coaxingly.*)
But bear in mind that Hans is, too,
Your son and you're his father.

**KATHINKA:** Ja, Gnade hat Euch Gott verlieh'n,
Dass Ihr ihn noch bekommen,
An Eurer Stelle hätt' ich ihn
Mit Freuden aufgenommen!

**MICHA:** Nun meinetwegen, meinetwegen!
Da habt Ihr meinen Vatersegen!
(*Er segnet das vor ihm niederknieende Paar.*)

**KATHINKA:** You should be glad that your son
Has returned from a foreign land.
Receive him joyfully with love,
And extend to him your hand.

**MICHA:** Well, well, so be it, so be it!
I'll give you now my blessing.
(*He blesses the pair kneeling before him.*)

**ALLE UND CHOR:** So ist's recht, es freut uns Alle!
Stimmet ein mit Jubelschalle!
Und von Herzen tön' es laut:
Vivat die "verkaufte Braut"!

*ENDE DER OPER.*

**ALL AND CHORUS:** Let us sing and shout and rattle,
For true love has won the battle.
We now wish with joy and pride
Happiness to the "Bartered Bride."

*END OF THE OPERA*

# La Vestale (1807)

## The Vestal

MUSIC BY GASPARE SPONTINI ■ LIBRETTO BY ÉTIENNE DE JOUY

This three-act *tragédie lyrique*, set to a libretto by Victor Joseph Étienne de Jouy, premiered at the Paris Opéra on December 16, 1807. The story opens in Rome, at the forum near the temple of Vesta. The Romans are preparing for the triumphant return of the young general Licinio, who has been the winner in battle against Gaul. Licinio tells his friend Cinna that he is in love with Giulia. However, Giulia has obeyed the wishes of her dying father and is now a priestess of Vesta and sworn to remain a virgin. The chief priestess persuades Giulia to resist physical love and chooses her to crown Licinio with the symbolic laurel wreath. As he is crowned, Licinio tells Sappho that he loves her. Giulia, alone at the temple of Vesta, is guarding the sacred flame which must never go out. She prays for the strength to resist Licinio, but when he comes they sing of their passionate love. While doing so they forget about the holy flame, which goes out. Cinna warns them that the priests and Vestals are coming. Licinio escapes in order to get help, and Giulia refuses to tell the pontifex maximus who her lover is. She prays that he will be spared the fate which awaits her—she is to be stripped of her priesthood and buried alive. Licinio, near the tomb where her burial is about to take place, confesses his culpability to the pontifex maximus, but to no avail. Giulia's black veil, a symbol of her shame, is put on the altar as she says good-bye to life. The sky suddenly darkens and lightning strikes the altar upon which Giulia's scarf rests. The sacred flame is ablaze once again, a sign that the goddess Vesta has granted Giulia forgiveness. The lovers are now free to marry, and a chorus of Vestals welcome them in a grove of roses before the temple of Venus Erycina.

## ■ ATTO PRIMO

*(Foro.)*

*A destra l'atrio del tempio di Vesta che comunica, per mezzo d'un intercolonnio, col soggiorno delle Vestali. In fondo, e dal medesimo lato, il palazzo di Numa e parte del Bosco sacro che lo circonda. In lontano il Monte Palatino.—Si vedono sulla piazza i preparativi di un trionfo.—Il giorno spunta appena.*

LICINIO E CINNA: (*Durante il ritornello, Licinio è appoggiato ad una delle colonne dell'atrio. Cinna esce dal bosco.*)

CINNA: Presso il sublime tempio a Vesta sacro,
A che Licinio mai previene il giorno?
D'ambascia e di languore
Divorato è il tuo cuore. All' amistade,
Quel segreto che ignora, deh! confida.
(*Licinio vuole allontanarsi.*)
Ivan fuggir mi vuoi:
Io seguo i passi tuoi.

LICINIO: (*accennando l'atrio*).
Queste mura perchè sul capo mio
Or crollar non vegg'io? Tanto infelice
Sarò!
E che giovano a me gli onori vani
D'importune grandezze
E di sterili allori? A me che giova
Roma tutta, la gloria e la mia vita?

CINNA: Quali voti, o Licinio,
Puoi tu formare ancora?
La trïonfal tua pompa
Forse non vedo? e d' oro
Cingerti al crin l' alloro
La giovane Vestal non vedo omai?

LICINIO: Taci: dicesti assai . . .

CINNA: perchè fremi? Onde han fonte
Il trasporto e l'affanno
Che la ragione abbandonar ti fanno?
Tu nascondi a un fido core
La cagion del tuo dolore . . .
Il vedermi a te dispiace . . .
Qual compenso alla mia fè!
Soffrirei l'oltraggio in pace
Se vedessi il tuo contento:
Ma l'affanno, ma il tormento
Vo' dividere con te.

LICINIO: Ebbene, il mio delitto, il mio furore
Meco adunque dividi:
L'estreme vïolenza
Della fiamma che m' arede
Partecipa con me; quella Vestale

## ■ ACT I

*(The Forum.)*

*To the right the atrium of the Temple of Vesta, communicating by means of a colonnaded passage with the house of the Vestals. At the back, on the same side, King Numa's palace and part of the Sacred Wood surrounding it. The Palatine Hill in the distance. On the piazza preparations for the celebration of a triumph are in evidence. It is the grey dawn of day.*

LICINIUS AND CINNA: (*During the instrumental prelude Licinius leans against one of the columns of the atrium. Cinna issues from the Wood.*)

CINNA: Here, near this noble temple, Vesta's shrine,
Why does Licinius await the dawn?
Is by some gnawing grief or anguish
His heart devoured? To friendship's ear
The secret which it does not know confide!
(*Licinius makes as though to disappear.*)
In vain you would elude me;
Your footsteps I will follow!

LICINIUS: (*nodding toward the atrium*). These walls, how is it they refuse to fall
And crush me? Would I then be more wretched
Than I am?
Ah, what are they to me, those empty honors
Importunate grandeur gives?
What mean the useless laurels? Of what avail to me
Are Rome, glory and life itself?

CINNA: What wish, O my Licinius,
What wish is left for you to make?
Do you not see the splendors of your coming triumph?
The wreath of gold
Which soon will bind your hair
Will not the youthful Vestal see it, say?

LICINIUS: Silence! You have said enough.

CINNA: Why do you tremble? From where spring
These transports, and this anguish
Which threatens to deprive you of your reason?
Something you're hiding from this heart so faithful.
The reason of your preying sorrow . . .
Even the sight of me annoys you . . .
What a return for my fidelity.
I have shared contentment with you;
And your anguish and your suffering
I would also share with you.

LICINIUS: So be it then, my rage, like my delight
I will divide with you.
The violence exalted
Of the flame within me burning
I will reveal to you. The Vestal

Ch' amo, contendi al cielo.
T'e noto il mio destin.

CINNA: D'orrore io gelo!
LICINIO: Giulia . . . sì, quest'oggetto
Di terrore e d'affetto.
Fu dalla madre un tempo
Promesso alla mia fè. Ma il Capo altero,
D' un' illustre famiglia
A donarmi la figlia, allor che gloria
La mia stirpe ignorava e il nome mio.
Poteva indursi mai?
Al campo alfin volai.
Nobile ambizïone,
Col mezzo de' felici miei sudori,
Segnalò la mia vita. Dopo un lustro
Vincitore alla patria io fo ritorno,
E la speranza di quel ben che attendo
Il cor m' inebria . . . Ahi barbara sciagura!
Terribil Fato! Giulia
Agli altari obbligata,
Ohimè! dal moribondo genitore,
Tradito i giuramenti ha dell'amore.

CINNA: Io ti compiango.
LICINIO: È poco
Il compiangermi.
CINNA: E speri?
LICINIO: Nulla; ma stanco di temer son io.
CINNA: Ad un fatal trasporto
Non darti in preda; pensa
Alle leggi, agli Dei
Che offende l'amor tuo: tremende in loro
Son l'ira e la vendetta.
LICINIO: La vïolenza
Di questa fiamma rea
È tale, che de' Numi il poter tutto
Oppor solo potrebbe all' amor mio
Il mio morir.

CINNA: Vogl' io
Indicarti i perigli a cui t'espone
Il furor che t'invade.
Amor vuole affrontarli:
Amistade saprà parteciparli.

LICINIO: Quando amistà seconda il mio ardimento
Di quai perigli io proverò l' orror?
Sgombra da te sì rio presentimento:
Amato io son: felice è questo cor.

CINNA: Ah! sgombri il ciel sì rio presentimento,
Che fa penar quest'agitato cor.

---

whom
I love I will defy the heavens to gain.
Mark me, it is my fate!

CINNA: Now horror chills me!
LICINIUS: Julia, yes, she is aim and end
Of all my fears and fondness.
Once on a time her mother
Blessed our betrothal, yet could I hope
The lordly head of an illustrious family
Would give the girl to me the while
My race and name to fame were quite unknown?
He was intractable.
At last I sought the camp
Urged by high ambitions.
Through mine own efforts, to command I rose
And made my name illustrious. Five years have passed;
I came back to my native land a victor,
But that fond hope on which so long I'd waited
With heart exalted . . . Ah, barbarous disaster!
Terrible fate! Julia
Bound to the Vestal altar,
Alas, by mandate of her dying father,
She had betrayed our love's most solemn vows!

CINNA: I sympathize with you.
LICINIUS: It is little,
To sympathize with me.
CINNA: And still you hope?
LICINIUS: I do not hope, yet weary of my fears.
CINNA: See that you do not yield
To some wild burst of passion.
Think of the laws, the gods
Whom your mad love offends.
They are all powerful in wrath and vengeance.
LICINIUS: The violence
Of this my lawless passion
Is such the power of all the gods above
Could not extinguish it. My love
Yields only to death.
CINNA: Would that I
Could make you see the perils you invite
With this mad love that sways you.
Yet if your love dares to brave them
My friendship shall share these dangers.

LICINIUS: Should your friendship second the ardor I am feeling,
And in the perils it provokes take part,
Renounce presentiments of guilt that may be stealing over you,
I am beloved. Joy dwells within my heart.

CINNA: Ah, heaven bid fly forebodings that are stealing
To carry suffering to your throbbing heart.

---

LICINIO: No, del mio colpevol foco
Nulla può smorzar l'ardor.
A te che nel periglio
Compagno esser ti piace,
Nel mio disegno audace
Soccorso io chiederò.
Teco è quest' alma unita
In un eterno nodo:
Da chi poteva aita,
Senza di te, sperar?

CINNA: Se del tuo colpevol foco
Nulla può smorzar l'ardor,
In sì fatal periglio
Compagno esser mi piace:
Nel tuo disegno audace
Soccorso io ti darò.
Teco è quest' alma unita
In un eterno nodo
In me potevi aìta
Soltanto ritrovar.
Oggi sopporta almen che la prudenza
Ti rammenti la gloria,
E l'onor che t'attende.
Mi sequi, poichè l'ora
In cui tu devi trionfar s'avanza.

LICINIO: Invigorisce amor la mia costanza.
(Partono. Durante questa scena si è fatto giorno.)
(La Gran Vestale, Giulia, Le Vestali escono dall' atrio e cantano l' inno seguente prima di condursi al Tempio. Inno mattutino.)

LA GRAN VESTALE: Alma Vesta del ciel pura figlia,
Splendon qui le divine tue faci,
E conserva a noi fide seguaci
Quella fiamma destata da te.

VESTALI: Alma Vesta, ecc.
(Durante quest' inno, Giulia mostrasi nella più profonda meditazione, e non si scuote che per appropriare a sè stessa le minaccie che l'inno contiene contro le Sacerdotesse infedeli.)

GIULIA: Fremo al nome di Vesta, e le ciglia,
Di reo pianto mi sento inondar!

LA GRAN VESTALE: Casto nume, alla sola innocenza
Degli altari affidasti il pensier;
Vota impuri, tua diva presenza,
Rei desiri non san sostener.

---

LICINIUS: No, these guilty fires within me
I cannot quench their mounting flame.
To you, who now in danger's hour
Would be my comrade, bravely sharing
With me my projects mad and daring,
I turn to you for aid.
With your soul mine own united,
Forms friendship's deathless chain,
On your assistance counting,
Without you were hope not vain?

CINNA: I know those guilty fires within you,
You cannot quench their mounting flame.
And I will now, in danger's hour,
Be your true comrade, bravely sharing
With you the perils you are daring.
With your soul mine own united,
Forms friendship's deathless chain,
And my assistance count on
To restore your hopes again.
Today at least, yield to what prudence counsels.
The claims of glory seek not to deny,
And all those honors which await you.
Follow me, for the hour is near
When you must appear in the triumph.

LICINIUS: Faith makes my love more strong and dear.
(Exeunt. During the scene day has fully dawned.)
(The Chief of the Vestals, Julia and other Vestals, passing from the atrium, sing the following hymn before entering the Temple.)

CHIEF OF THE VESTALS: Vesta, divine, pure daughter of the heavens,
Your torches in the sky, burning in splendor
On your adorers refrain from turning,
The flame which you irradiate.

VESTALS: Vesta divine, pure daughter of the heavens, etc.
(While the hymn is sung Julia is absorbed in profoundest meditation which she shakes off only to apply to herself the menaces which the hymn voices with regard to the priestess faithless to her trust.)

JULIA: I tremble at Vesta's name. My eyes
With guilty tears I now feel overflow!

CHIEF OF THE VESTALS: Virgin goddess, chaste innocence shall ever
In thought and deed your altars here attend;
Impure longings in your presence never
Nor base desires offend your cult divine.

# Act I

**VESTALI:** Alma Vesta, ecc.

**VESTALS:** Vesta divine, pure daughter of the heavens, etc.

**LA GRAN VESTALE:** Quel delubro ove il mondo t'adora
L'empia Vergine accoglier ricusa;
La smorzata tua fiamma l'accusa
Poi la terra la chiude nel sen.

**CHIEF OF THE VESTALS:** Within your temple, where the world adores you,
The impious Vestal, faithless to duty found,
Who lets your sacred fire die on the altar
She shall be buried, living, underground!

**VESTALI:** Alma Vesta, ecc.

**VESTALS:** Vesta, divine, pure daughter of the heavens, etc.

**LA GRAN VESTALE:** Vestali, in questo giorno
Roma vittorïosa
Al Prode suo presenta
Il premio del valore;
A voi spetta l'onore
D'ornar di lauro il glorioso crine.
Vedrete al vostro piede,
Sotto quest' archi di trïonfo, tutto
Il popol di Quirino radunato,
E lo stesso Senato
La maestà suprema
Dei Consoli prostrarsi anche vedrete
Innanzi a' vostri fasci. Ite nel tempio,
E i vostri sagrifizi
Rendan Giano ed Astrea numi propozi.
Giulia, rimanti.
(*Le Vestali vanno al tempio per via dell' intercolonnio che ivi conduce.*)

**CHIEF OF THE VESTALS:** Vestals, this very day
Victorious Rome
Awards the conquering hero
The premium of valor.
And yours shall be the honor
To deck his glorious brow with laurels.
You shall see at your feet
Beneath the great triumphal arch
The people of the Quirinal assembled,
With the whole Senate
The majesty supreme
Of the Consuls you shall see bow down
Before the fasces. While in the temple
Your sacrifices shall be made
In Janus and Astrea's the propitious names,
Julia, do you remain.
(*The Vestals proceed to the Temple by way of the colonnaded passage leading to it.*)

**LA GRAN VESTALE:** È questa
L'ultima volta che de' tuoi perigli
L'immagin ti presento, che ravvivo
Il tuo coraggio, e del dover la voce
Udir ti fo. Ti nuoce
La catena che cingi,
E fino a piè dell'Ara
Quegli sguardi piangenti
Provano il grave duol che in petto senti.
Di Vesta il culto e i sacri suoi misteri
Non ponno dileguar l'orror che provi.
Ne' sensi tuoi smarriti un' altra furia
Di sacrilega brama
Il veleno versò, che a' lumi tuoi
Cela l'abisso in cui piombar tu vuoi.

**CHIEF OF THE VESTALS:** This is
The last time I shall call up before you
The image of your danger, bid you steel
Your heart, and lend an ear
To duty's voice. Do not forget
The chain that binds you
Is welded to the altar's foot;
For your sorrowful glances
Prove the deep grief which you hide in your breast.
The worship of Vesta and her holy mysteries
Have not dispelled dread thoughts you harbor,
Your senses throb with other ardors,
With sacrilegious desires.
The venom poured with which you flame
Hides the abyss wherein I see you falling.

**GIULIA:** Che si vuole da me? Le vostre leggi
Vittima sventurata
Dalla forza obbligata,
Obbedisco, piangendo il mio destino.

**JULIA:** What do you ask of me? Of your laws
The unfortunate victim,
Compelled by main force
I obey while I am lamenting my fate.

**LA GRAN VESTALE:** Forse d'invidia degno
Maggior ve n' ha sopra la Terra?
Roma
Del sacro suo Palladio a noi confida

**CHIEF OF THE VESTALS:** Even envy is forced to admit it,
Has earth ever seen an empire that is greater? Rome
Its sacred Palladium* leaves in our

Il prezïoso arredo: omaggio, onori
Di nostra vita fan lieta la sorte.

keeping,
Its most precious jewel. Homage and honors
To our lives their glory are lending.

**GIULIA:** E un istante d'error ci danna a morte.

**JULIA:** (*aside*). Death ending a moment of error!

**LA GRAN VESTALE:** In vera pace immerse,
E nel sen del soggiorno il più felice,
I tributi del mondo riceviamo,
E i perigli d'amor sprezzar possiamo.
(*Giulia sospira.*)
E l'Amore un mostro, un barbaro;
E nemico a Vesta Amor:
Gli diè vita un di Tisifone
Dell' Averno fra l'orror.
Per lui sol di colpe e lagrime
L'empia terra s'innondò;
Sugli abissi il trono orribile,
Sulle tombe egli piantò.
Il tuo cor si perde, o figlia,
E per te tremar dovrò.

**CHIEF OF THE VESTALS:** A great peace us surrounding,
In an abode beyond others delightful;
The world's tribute borne to us,
We may look at love's perils with scorn.
(*Julia sighs.*)
Ah, love is a brute and a monster,
The foe of chaste Vesta. In error
Conceived by Tisiphone from Avernus
He rose, spreading terror.
He has called forth the tears and the anguish
That flood earth with woes unavailing,
He rules deep abysses of horror
And the tombs where his poor victims wail.
You will lose your heart, O my daughter,
And I shudder lest you, too, may fail!

**GIULIA:** (*spaventata*). In nome degli Dei
E di Vesta che adoro,
Quella grazia che imploro a me concedi;
Soffri che in queste mura
Celata a ognum, senza di me disposta
La cerimonia del trïonfo sia.

**JULIA:** (*terrified*). In the name of the gods
And of Vesta whom I adore,
Grant me the favor that I ask of you:
Let me within these walls,
Hidden from all, now be excused
From taking part in this day's triumph.

**LA GRAN VESTALE:** Invan sottrarti vuoi
Alle cure devote
Che la legge t'impone. Tu sei quella
Che viglia fra l'ombre della notte
L'eterna fiamma; l'immortal corona
Oggi ricever deve a' piedi tuoi
Il vincitor; invan sottrarti puoi.
(*La Gran Vestale entra nel tempio.*)

**CHIEF OF THE VESTALS:** In vain you seek to escape
From the sacrosant duties
Our law imposes. You are the one
Who shall keep vigil when night's shadows fall,
Over the deathless flame. The crown of glory
Today the victor kneels at your feet
To receive! It is your place to obey!
(*The Chief of the Vestals enters the Temple.*)

**GIULIA:** O di funesta possa
Invincibil comando!
Speme non v'è; da' Numi
Mi veggo abbandonata.
Ribelle all' amor mio, volli, ma invano,
Al mio fato sottrarmi
Non solo, ma privarmi
Di mia sorte maggiore,
Licinio vincitore
Rimirando al mio piè: di compier seco
Dell' impero il dovere . . . Oh Diva! questo
Sforzo dell' alma mia
Bastante al tuo rigore esser dovria.
Ti vedrò fra momenti o mio bene!
La soave tua voce udirò!
Ravvivar la primiera mia speme,
Al tuo sguardo, nel petto saprò.
D'una misera vita,
Condannata da' Numi,
quell'istante

**JULIA:** Ah, dread and fateful power!
Mandate I dare not resist!
I see no hope. The gods themselves
Now have abandoned me.
Rebelling against my love I sought,
Not only to escape fate's spell,
But also rob myself as well
Of my last chance of happiness.
Licinius, victor in the battle's press,
To see him at my feet, see his perfection
At duty's strict behest. Oh, goddess,
Where is the strength of soul
That will suffice to carry out your stern command?
A moment I'll see you, O my beloved,
My ear caressed by your sweet voice!
It will recall the hopes that once I cherished,
When first I saw you, hidden in my

Potrò almen consecrare al caro amante.
Ove mai l'error fatale
Ti trasporta, empia Vestale?
Ahi! qual nome a te sfuggì!
Grazia, clementi Dei . . .

breast.
To lead a wretched life
The gods condemn me. That moment, swiftly flying,
To loves's dear memory vainly were I denying.
Where will this fatal error
Lead you, poor impious Vestal?
Alas, what infamy will weight your name!
Have mercy, gracious gods!

**VESTALI:** (*sui gradini del tempio*). Ministra vieni;
L'assenza tua sospende il sagrifizio.
A questa volta il cocchio
Del trïonfante Duce
Seque il corteggio, il qual qui si conduce.

**VESTALS:** (*on the steps of the Temple*). Behold, he draws near.
Your absence retards the sacrifice.
This very moment the chariot
Of the triumphant leader
Follows the cortège whose steps are turning here.

**CORO:** (*di dentro*). Pace richiama alfine
Or de' Romani il vindice,
De' Galli il domator.

**CHORUS:** (*within*). Now peace at last has crowned our hopes
Won by the avenging Roman sword,
The dominator of the Gauls!

**GIULIA:** O affanno! . . . ahi! che terrore!
Oh! di funesta possa
Invincibil comando!
Gelare il cor mi sento.
Di me che fia in sì fatal momento.
(*entra ne tempio.*)
(*Da varie parti si avanza sulla piazza il corteggio preceduto dal popolo che riempie il fondo della scena, vengono quindi i Sacerdoti di varii templi, alla cui testa sono il Sommo Sacerdote, il Capo degli Aruspici, il Senato, i consoli, le Matrone ed i Guerrieri. Dopo che questa prima parte del corteggio ha pigliato posto, escono dal tempio le Vestali: la Gran Vestale porta il Palladio. Vien recata innanzi a Giulia (come Vestale addetta alla custodia del fuoco) un' Ara accesa. Le Vestali passano davanti alle schiere che loro fanno gli onori supremi, il Popolo s' inginocchia, il Senato s' inclina, i fasci de' Consoli si abbassano innanzi a quelli delle Vestali, portati da quattro Littori: elleno vanno a situarsi in cima ad un palco eretto vicino all' atrio; e sotto il medesimo si fermano i Consoli ed il Senato. Comparisce il carro del Trionfatore, preceduto da suonatori e tirato dagli schiavi in catene. Alcuni duci, nemici e prigionieri, seguono il cocchio. Licinio è in abito trionfale e tiene il bastone del comando. Cinna è alla testa delle schiere.*)

**JULIA:** Oh, grief and woe! Alas, I tremble!
Ah, dread and fateful power!
Mandate I dare not resist!
My heart is chill with terror.
What, when the fateful moment comes, will happen to me?
(*Julia enters the Temple.*)
(*The triumphal processional enters the piazza from various points, preceded by the populace which fills the background of the stage, and followed by the priests of the different temples, the Pontifex Maximus at their head, the Chief of the Augurs, Senators, Consuls, Matrons and Soldiers. When this first section of the processional has taken its place the Vestals enter, coming from the Temple, the Chief of the Vestals bearing the Palladium. Immediately after Julia, the custodian of the sacred fire, is carried a portable altar on which it flames. The Vestals pass before the ranks of the legionaries, who pay them the supreme military salute, while the populace kneels, the Senate bows and the fasces of the Consuls are inclined before those of the Vestals, borne by four lictors. The Vestals take their places on a scaffold erected near the atrium, and the Consuls and Senators establish themselves below them. The chariot of the triumphator appears, preceded by trumpeters and drawn by slaves in chains. Various enemy leaders, prisoners, follow the chariot. Licinius is arrayed in the robes of a triumphator and holds the baton of command in his hand. Cinna is at the head of the legionaries.*)

**CORO GENERALE:** Di lauri il suol spargiamo
Di Vesta il tempio orniamo;
Pace richiama alfine

**GENERAL CHORUS:** Let victory's laurels deck the ground.
Let Vesta's temple be adorned.
Now peace at last our hopes has

Nelle latine mura
Or de' Romani il vindice,
De' Galli il domator.

crowned,
Within the walls of Latium,
Won by the avenging Roman sword
The dominator of the Gauls!

**POPOLO:** La morte,—le ritorte
Già di Quirino ai figli
Il fato minacciò.
Ma da un Eroe guidata,
L'aquila i feri artigli
A danni altrui spiegò.

**THE PEOPLE:** With death, death and chains
Fate's menace once disheartened
The Quirinal's sons;
Yet by a Roman hero led,
The eagle its talons spread,
And on the foe darted!

**CORO GENERALE:** Di lauri il suol spargiamo, ecc.

**GENERAL CHORUS:** Let victory's laurels deck the ground, etc.

**POPOLO:** Arbitro egli è di guerra,
A lui si presti onor.

**THE PEOPLE:** Arbiter of glorious war
To him is honor due!

**DONNE:** Riposo ottien la Terra
Per lui; si adori ancor.

**WOMEN:** Through him the earth once more knows peace
Acclaim him then anew!

**LICINIO:** Trïonfan le armi nostre.
Marte guidar ci volle
Al campo di vittoria;
E, figli della gloria,
Tuttor noi siam dei popoli l' onore,
De' nemici il terrore. A' sommi Numi
Grazie rendiam di quanto
La mano lor concede,
E di riconoscenza ognun prepari
Puri incensi votivi sugli altar
(*I Consoli assistono Licinio mentre scende dal cocchio, e lo conducono sotto un trofeo innalzato a destra del proscenio.*)

**LICINIUS:** Our arms in battle triumphed,
Mars their fierce onset guiding
To the goal of victory;
And, sons of glory, we
Whom all the people honor
Are the terror of the foe. The gods,
With thanks we praise their name
For what their hand has given,
To show the gratitude they claim,
Let us cast incense in the altar-flame!
(*The Consuls aid Licinius as he descends from the chariot and lead him under a trophy erected at the right side of the proscenium.*)

**LA GRAN VESTALE:** (*a Giulia*).
Tu dell' immortal face
Vigil custode, in la solenne notte
Che annunzia al mondo un giorno glorïoso,
Consacra, o Giulia, il serto prezïoso.
(*Le dà il lauro d' oro.*)

**CHIEF OF THE VESTALS:** (*to Julia*). You, who are the immortal light's
Custodian and attendant, through the solemn night
Heralding the dawn of glory's day elate,
O Julia, this garland to the victor consecrate!
(*Gives her the golden laurel wreath.*)

**LICINIO:** (*piano a Cinna*). Ascolti? . . . questa notte . . . ella . . . nel tempio.

**LICINIUS:** (*softly, to Cinna*). What do I hear? tonight . . . She? . . . In the temple?

**CINNA:** (*piano a Licinio*). Taci: ciascun osserva i nostri moti.

**CINNA:** (*softly to Licinius*). Silence! All observe our movements.

**LA GRAN VESTALE:** (*a Giulia*).
All'Ero dei Romani il guiderdone
Porgi della vittoria, e sia per lui,
Mentre è d'onore il pegno,
Dell' amor nostro un segno.

**CHIEF OF THE VESTALS:** Give to the hero of the Roman people
The guerdon of this victory, now his due;
For it is honor's noble token,
A pledge in which our love is spoken.

**GIULIA:** (*prendendo la corona e passandola sul fuoco sacro*).
Sostenetemi, o Numi!

**JULIA:** (*taking the wreath and passing it above the altar-flame*). Aid and support me, O ye gods!

**LICINIO:** È dessa . . . Al cor mi sento
L' ebbrezza del contento.
(*Durante le cerimonie, alle quali Giulia presiede, il popolo canta il seguente.*)

**LICINIUS:** Yes, it is she. Over my heart I feel
Joy's mad intoxication slowly steal.
(*During the ceremony, over which Julia presides, the People chant the following hymn.*)

**CORO GENERALE:** Della dea pura, seguace,
Cingi a lui l'illustre fronte,
Mentre il cantico di pace

**GENERAL CHORUS:** Priestess of the pure, chaste goddess,
With laurel crown his noble head;
While canticles of peace resound-

# Act I

Il suo nome innalza al ciel.

ing, His name in glory's echoes spread.
(*During the preceding chorus Julia crosses the stage and ascends with wavering steps to the place where Licinius is waiting. He bows before her and she places the laurel crown on his head, singing with an agitated voice.*)

**GIULIA:** (*Durante il precedente coro attraversa la scena, e con piede vacillante ascende dov'è Licinio; questi s'inginocchia innanzi a lei, che nel porgli in capo la coronoa, canta con voce alterata.*) Giovin prode, in sì bel giorno Prendi il pegno della gloria; Monumento è di vittoria, E lo sia del nostro amor.

**JULIA:** Youthful hero, on this day so glorious, Accept the token that bespeaks your fame; An emblem of your deeds of might victorious, And of the love you have a right to claim.

**CORO:** Giovin prode, in si bel giorno, ecc.

**CHORUS:** Youthful hero, on this day so glorious, etc.

**LICINIO:** (*piano a Giulia*). Ascolta . . . Giulia . . . ascolta . . . Qui . . . sotto questa volta . . .

**LICINIUS:** (*aside, to Julia*). Listen! . . . Julia . . . listen! Here . . . from beneath this roof! . . .

**LA GRAN VESTALE:** (*osservando Giulia*). Quanto agitato ha il cor! Sopra quel mesto ciglio I segni del dolor, Veder si fanno.

**CHIEF OF THE VESTALS:** (*watching Julia*). How wildly her heart now beats! I know that in her eyes Soon sorrow's tears will meet And show themselves.

**CINNA:** (*piano a Licinio*). Tradisce il tuo pensier Quello smarrito ciglio Che puote esser forier Di duol, d'affanno.

**CINNA:** (*aside, to Licinius*). Your every thought you show In your unhappy glances; Harbingers of the woe That you are feeling!

**IL SOMMO SACERDOTE:** (*in tuono profetico fissando gli occhi sull' altare dell libazioni*). Nel seno di splendor Qual nube tetra appare! Di fosca luce ancor Langue l'altare.

**PONTIFEX MAXIMUS:** (*in prophetic tones, fixing his eyes on the sacrificial altar*). In the fire's heart of light What dark cloud now appears! A blackness veils the flame so bright, It dies upon the altar.

**GIULIA:** (*con ismarrimento*). Oh! istante che temer Tanto mi fece e tanto! Altro non so veder Che lutto e pianto.

**JULIA:** (*in consternation*). Ah, moment which I dread! Almost beyond all bearing. Non can suspect the strife My soul with anguish tearing.

**GIULIA:** (*piano a Giulia*). Ascolta . . . o Giulia . . . ascolta . . . Qui . . . sotto questa volta . . . Della vicina notte Intra gli orrori amici, T'involerò.

**LICINIUS:** (*aside, to Julia*). Listen, O Julia! . . . listen! Here . . . from beneath this roof . . . This coming night, From among your horrified friends, I shall carry you off!

**GIULIA:** (*spaventata*). Che dici? . . .

**JULIA:** (*alarmed*). What do you say?

**UNO DE' CONSOLI:** (*approssimandosi a Licinio*). La pace in questo giorno E il frutto del valor; Godi del tuo sudor A lei nel seno. E qual presiedi al fato De' cittadini ognor, Al giubilo di lor Presiedi appieno.

**A CONSUL:** (*approaching Licinius*). We gain the peace this day, Valor's fruit is the best; Due to your heroic toil It fills our breasts with joy. Whatever fate in time May betide this people, You share their jubilee, And preside over their joy.

**CORO:** La pace in questo giorno, ecc.
(*Giulia va a riprendere il suo luogo presso il fuoco sacro, E licinio fra' due Consoli. I giuochi, le danze, i combattimenti de' lottatori seguono successivamente.*)

**CHORUS:** We gain the peace this day, etc.
(*Julia reoccupies her place beside the sacred fire, and Licinius his before the two Consuls. Games, dances and gladiatorial combats now take place in succession.*)

**IL SOMMO SACERDOTE:** (*terminati i giuochi*). Omai cessi il tripudio: al sommo Giove Nel Campidoglio andiamo Le vittime a immolar. D'opime spoglie spoglie Adorni il vincitor le sacre soglie.
(*Il corteggio va al Campidoglio nell' ordine con cui è venuto.*)

**PONTIFEX MAXIMUS:** (*when the games are concluded*). And now let cease the dance. To Jove supreme, Throned in the Capitol our footsteps turn, To slay the victims. The victor shall dower with rich spoils The altars in the godhead's seat of power.
(*The triumphal processional moves off toward the Capitol in the order of its entrance on the stage.*)

**CORO GENERALE:** Di lauri il suol spargiamo, ecc.

**GENERAL CHORUS:** Let victory's laurels deck the ground, etc.

# ■ ATTO SECONDO

*Interno del tempio di Vesta in forma circolare. Sovra un vasto altare di marmo, eretto nel centro del santuario, arde il fuoco sacro. Sedile per la Vestale.*

# ■ ACT II

*Interior of the Temple of Vesta, circular in form. Upon a vast marble altar rising in the middle of the shrine burns the sacred fire. There are seats for the Vestals.*

**VESTALI:** (*cantano l' Inno della Sera intorno all' altare*). Divin foco, alma del mondo, Della vita immortal segno, Il tuo ardor,—vivo e fecondo, Splenda ognor, su questo altar.

**VESTALS:** (*singing the Evening Hymn around the altar*). Divine fire, soul of all things terrestrial, Symbol of life's immortal yearning, May your bright flame, radiant celestial, Ever be burning upon your altar.

**LA GRAN VESTALE:** (*consegnando a Giulia la verga d'oro che serve ad attizzare il fuoco*). Del più gran ministero Il venerato segno, Che depongo in tua mano, in questa notte Te fa custode del favor de' Numi, E della sorte de' Romani ancora. O Giulia, è questa l' ora Solenne, augusta, che de' sommi Dei T'espone alla presenza, deh! rifletti. Che un infedel sospiro Punir da lor vedrai, Eh che ciechi non son questi archi mai.

**CHIEF OF THE VESTALS:** (*delivering to Julia the rod of gold used to stir the fire*). Of this, greatest of ministries, The venerated symbol, Which I lay in your hand, throughout the night Makes you custodian of the great gods' favor, And of the fate of Rome and every Roman! O Julia, this is the hour, The solemn hour when the fire-priestess elect Stands in the gods' presence! Ah, reflects, That but a single faithless sigh May call forth punishment, That no roof bars Vesta's all-seeing eye!

**VESTALI:** (*nel ritrarsi*). Divin foco, alma del mondo, ecc.

**VESTALS:** (*as they withdraw*). Fire divine, soul of all things terrestrial, etc.
(*Julia kneels on the altar steps in an attitude of the profoundest dejection, and remains prostrate there for some moments.*)

**GIULIA:** (*In atto del più profondo abbattimento s'inginocchia sui gradini dell'altare, dove per un istante rimane prosternata.*) Tu che invoco con orrore, Dea tremenda, alfin m'ascolta; Questo misero mio core

**JULIA:** You whom I invoke with terror, O fearsome goddess, deign to hear me. Each breath of mine is effort claiming. Since wretchedness so fills my

Fa che possa respirar.
Or che vedi il mio tormento,
Le mie smanie, i miei contrasti,
Deh! ti basti—In me l'ardore
Puoi tu sola dissipar.
(*Si alza, ascende sull'altare e vi attizza il fuoco.*)
Su questo sacro altare,
Che oltraggia il mio dolor, fremendo io porto
La sacrilega mano. L'odïoso
Aspetto mio pallida rende questa
Immortal fiamma: Vesta
Ricusa i voti miei;
E m'urta il braccio suo lungi da lei.
(*Smarrita si aggira per la scena.*)
Amor, tu il vuoi, m'arrendo . . .
Ma dove io porto il piè?
E qual delirio, ohimè!
Miei sensi invade?
Invincibil potere
A' danni miei cospira;
Mi stringe, mi trasporta . . .
T'arresta: hai tempo ancor; sotto i tuoi passi
La morte, o Giulia, stassi,
La folgor sul tuo capo . . .
(*Delirando.*)
Ma Licinio è colà . . . posso mirarlo,
Favellargli, ascoltarlo,
E il timor mi trattiene? . . .
Non più; del mio delitto
Furore, amor, la pena han già prescritto,
Sospendete qualche istante
La vendetta, o crudi Numi,
Finchè possa il caro amante
Coll'aspetto e i vaghi lumi
Queste soglie consolar.
Poi sommessa alla vostra possanza
Quella vita fatal che m'avanza
Sia l'oggetto del vostro furor.
La mia sorte è decisa.
La carriera ho compita:
Vieni, amato mortal, t'offro la vita.
(*Apre la porta del tempio, e va ad appoggiarsi all'altare.*)

heart!
Now that you see me suffering torture,
The mad desires that rend and sear me,
Ah it is enough!—my ardor flaming
You only, you, can bid depart!
(*She rises, ascends the altar steps and feeds the flame.*)
Your sacred altar,
Outraged by my woe, trembling I touch
With sacrilegious hand. Ah, such
A guilty pallor, such a face of shame
I show in the accusing flame! Vesta,
Reject the vow that made me thine,
And cast me out, far from your holy shrine!
(*She strays across the stage as though dazed.*)
Love, you have willed it, I yield;
Yet where, ah, where shall I go?
What fell delirium, ah, woe,
Invades all my senses?
O power invincible,
Vainly against you I conspire,
Vainly rebel and flout you!
Stop, for there is still time! Underfoot, as you stray,
O Julia, death's way lies open.
May lightnings blast you!
But Licinius will come . . . and I would see him,
Talk to him and listen to him.
Is it fear that stays my hand?
I cannot from my own offense win free,
Nor flee the punishment the fates decree.
Hold in abeyance for another hour
Your vengeance, gods so merciless;
Until my dear love's sight,
Here in the temple's shadowy light,
Solaces my distress,
Then, yielding to your power,
That fated life you gave me
Shall be subject to your rage.
My fate is now determined,
I am through with fear.
Come, mortal lover, I offer you my life!
(*She opens the temple door, then returns and rests against the altar.*)

**LICINIO:** (*in fondo alla scena*). Giulia!

**LICINIUS:** (*at the back of the stage*). Julia!

**GIULIA:** È la voce sua . . .

**JULIA:** It is his voice!

**LICINIO:** Giulia!

**LICINIUS:** Julia!

**GIULIA:** Trema l'altar!

**JULIA:** The altar trembles!

**LICINIO:** Pur ti rivedo!

**LICINIUS:** Once more I behold you!

**GIULIA:** In qual tempo, in qual loco!

**JULIA:** At what a time, in what a place!

**LICINIO:** Quel Dio che ci riunisce,
Or vigila d'intorno a queste mura,
E de' tuoi giorni ha cura.

**LICINIUS:** Which god brings us together here.
And over these walls broods in the air,
And has your passing days in care?

**GIULIA:** Io tremo sol per te . . .

**JULIA:** I tremble only for you!

**LICINIO:** De' tuoi perigli
L'immagin disprezzai.
Da sforzo sì terribile, conosci
Il mio coraggio.

**LICINIUS:** These perils
Whose picture dread you paint, I scorn
Their power terrific, for I know
The courage that is mine.

**GIULIA:** Ah, Licinio!

**JULIA:** Ah, Licinius!

**LICINIO:** (*avanzandosi*). Ricevi
Il giuramento mio:
Vivere sol vogl' io
Per amarti, difenderti, servirti.

**LICINIUS:** (*coming forward*).
Bear witness to
This solemn oath I swear:
That I will only live
To love, defend and serve you.

**GIULIA:** Posso aspirare almeno
D'un istante al piacer?

**JULIA:** And may I look forward
To such a joyous moment?

**LICINIO:** Forse non hanno
Asilo le foreste,
Sotto altro cielo, in qualche antro selvaggio?
Parla: da un rio servaggio
Involarti saprò.

**LICINIUS:** Can we not find
A refuge in the forests,
Beneath another sky, in some great wilderness?
Speak, tell me I may bear you,
Far from servitude's distress.

**GIULIA:** No, mai non fia.
Di questa vita mia, caro, disponi:
La sacrifico a te; ma della tua
Son debitrice a Roma ed agli Dei,
E tra' perigli miei,
Che m'è dolce affrontare,
Penso alla gloria tua; la vo' serbare.

**JULIA:** No, for I cannot
Dispose of my life, my beloved.
I can die for you, but your own life
Is dedicated to Rome and the gods.
Amid dangers to dare which I am fated
And which I take joy in defying,
Your glory to save I am trying.

**LICINIO:** Avran pietà gli Dei
Di tante nostre pene;
Un raggio vibran già d'amica spene.
Figlia del cielo, idolo del cor mio!
Arbitra te vogl' io—della mia vita;
Fan quegli sguardi tuoi
La mia felicitade. Invidi i Numi
Fian del nostro destino.
La Dea d'amor che invoco
Uni giorno ci unirà.

**LICINIUS:** The gods, taking on us pity
Because of the torments that rend us,
A ray of encouraging hope will send us.
Daughter of heaven, dear idol of my heart,
You shall decide my life for me.
And with the glance of your dark eyes
Make my felicity! The gods are jealous,
But revoking the ills of fate
Love's goddess, whom I am invoking,
Will unite us some day.

**GIULIA:** Cielo! . . . da questo
Altar, per noi funesto,—
t'allontana;
Langua la fiamma.
(*Giulia accorre all'altare e vi attizza il fuoco. Licinio, atterrito, ritirasi in fondo al tempio.*)

**JULIA:** Ye gods! From yonder
Altar, for us so fateful, withdraw.
The flame burns dimly.
(*Julia hastens to the altar and stirs the fire while Licinius, alarmed, withdraws to the rear of the Temple.*)

**LICINIO:** Oh casta Diva! sgombra
Il funesto presagio.
La mia colpa è d'amar chi ti somiglia,
E nasce il nostro amore
Tutto dal tuo candore.

**LICINIUS:** O goddess chaste, recall
Your dread and fateful omen!
My crime has been the love you're now confronting,
This love by which we are torn,
Of your own purity was born.

**GIULIA:** Di Saturno la figlia
I nostri prieghi ascolta;
Dell' infocato altar la viva fiamma
Il celeste favor chiaro ci mostra.

**JULIA:** Stern Saturn's glorious daughter
Ah, listen to our prayers!
Let a bright flame upon your burning altar
Show that you accord us your grace!

**LICINIO:** Chi dubitar potea
Del favor della Dea?
Qual Dio, se tu l'implori,
Ascoltarti potria,
E non impietosirsi, anima mia!

**LICINIUS:** Who can doubt that the goddess
Her favor will concede you?
What god when you implore
Would ever refuse to heed you,
Not take pity on you, soul of mine?

# Act II

GIULIA: Ah! ch' io ritorno in vita!
Del passato a me resta
Una debol memoria; un fosco velo
Sull'avvenir si stende,
E un punto tutto l'esser mio comprende.
Che smania!

LICINIO: Quai trasporti!

GIULIA: Son teco, mio tesor!

LICINIO: Di quegli sguardi teneri
S'inebra questo cor.
Vieni: colà sull'ara
Ricevi la mia fè.

GIULIA: Brillar mi sento l'anima!
Vieni: colà sull'ara
Ricevi la mia fè.
Nell'eccesso del contento
Terra e Numi—a un tratto obblio,
In quei lumi—idolo mio,
Tutto accolto è il ciel per me.

LICINIO: All'amore io
m'abbandono:
Altro ben per me non v'è.

LUCINIO E GIULIA: Sol per te viver vogl' io.
Voglio vivere per te.
Vieni: colà sull'ara
Ricevi la mia fè.
(Mentre i due amanti si avviano all'altare, il fuoco, che a grado a grado si è indebolito, in un tratto si smorza, e la scena non rimane illuminata che da un barlume, supponendosi che venga di fuori.)

GIULIA: Qual notte!

LICINIO: Giusti Dei!

GIULIA: (sull'altare). Perduta io sono!
Ah! più non v'è speranza!
La fiamma si smorzò; vissi abbastanza.

LICINIO: Che dici?

GIULIA: Io morirò . . .

LICINIO: Gelar mi fia.

CINNA: (entra precipitosamente). Licinio!

GIULIA: Ciel, qual voce!

CINNA: Il tempo vola:
Là, nel primo recinto,
Strepito s'ode. Andiamo:
Involarci possiamo

LICINIO: (con voce smarrita). Ebben seguimi . . . andiam . . .

CINNA: Ferma: al suo fato
Così schiudi la via.

LICINIO: Ah! disperato io son. Giulia! . . .

CINNA: Oh follia!

GIULIA: Se ti son cara, senti
Pietà di te, mio bene!
Quest'anima ha presenti
Solo i perigli tuoi . . .
Tel chiedo per l'amore
Che ad ambo avvinse il core:

JULIA: Ah, a new life let me be gaining!
Of the past all that is remaining
Is a faint memory. A veil of shadows
The future is hiding from me,
In one hope all my soul is abiding,
What madness!

LICINIUS: Ah, what emotions!

JULIA: You motive them, my treasure!

LICINIUS: With your tender, ardent glances
Fill my heart with rapture,
Come, here before the altar,
You shall receive my vow.
(Together).

JULIA: With joy my soul is leaping!
Come, here before the altar
My vow you shall receive.
In the excess of our rapture
Heaven and earth a moment forgot,
With joy's glory, beloved, this spot
Irradiate, the gods will favor me.

LICINIUS: To love all my soul I abandon
No treasure but love can I see!

LICINIUS AND JULIA: For you,
you alone I would live.
For you my own life I would give.
Come, here at this altar,
Receive my vow of love.
(While the two lovers approach the altar the fire which, little by little, has been dying down, suddenly goes out, and the stage is illuminated only by a glimmer of light which seems to come from without.)

JULIA: What a night!

LICINIUS: Ye gods divine!

JULIA: (at the altar). I am undone!
Ah, no gleam of hope is left me!
The fire has gone out, and of life has bereft me!

LICINIUS: What do you say?

JULIA: That I must die.

LICINIUS: You chill my blood!

CINNA: (entering precipitately).
Licinius!

JULIA: Ye gods, who speaks?

CINNA: Time's on the wing!
From yonder, in the first courtyard
Now voices echo. Let us go,
We can bear her off with us.

LICINIUS: (in a discouraged tone). Then follow me. We will go.

CINNA: Be steadfast. Perhaps your fate
Will protect you from death.

LICINIUS: Ah, desperation fills me! Julia!

CINNA: What madness!

JULIA: I am dear to you, I know, and riven
By pity for you, my beloved!
My soul thought alone has given
To the dangers which threaten you.
I plead because of the fondness

Se tu salvarmi vuoi
T'invola per pietà.

LICINIO: Finir tra questo orrore
La vita mia dovrà.

CINNA: Fuggi da questo orrore
E cedi all'amistà.
Vieni . . .
(Lo prende per mano.)

LICINIO: Lasciarla! . . . oh Dio!

CINNA: È d' uopo.

LICINIO: Nol poss' io.

CINNA: Se tardi un solo istante
La perdi.

LICINIO: (con furore, a Cinna).
Andiam. La voce
Sol dell'ardir m'invita.
Se l'amor mio ti nuoce
(a Giulia.)
Proteggerti saprà.
Licinio alla tuo sorte
T'involerà, mia vita;
O teco almen da forte
Ei la dividerà.
(Odonsi le grida del Popolo al di fuori.)

CORO: (di dentro). Il ciel vendetta grida
Contro la Coppia infida,
Che coll'indegno aspetto
L'are contaminò.

CINNA: (tendendo l'orecchio).
Lontane grida
Udir si fanno . . .
Affretta il piè.

LICINIO: In tanto affanno
Che farmi? ohimè!

GIULIA: Fuggite . . .

CINNA: Fuggasi.

LICINIO: (a Giulia). Di te che fia!

GIULIA: Pel nostro amore,
Anima mia! . . .
(Si odono nuovamente le grida del Popolo.)
Odo ripetere
Le grida orribili . . .

GIULIA: Vanne a difendermi . . .

CINNA: Vieni a difenderla . . .

LICINIO: Vado a difenderti;
Morrò per te.
(Parte con Cinna.)

CORO: (di dentro). Il ciel vendetta grida
Contro la Coppia infida,
Che coll' indegno aspetto
L'are contaminò.

Which binds our two hearts together:
If it is your wish to save me,
Out of compassion I follow.

LICINIUS: Let it end, this dread oppressing us,
Your life now is mine by right.

CINNA: Fly from this horror obsessing,
With confidence friendship requite.
Come! . . .
(Seizing his hand.)

LICINIUS: Leave her! O ye gods!

CINNA: To what purpose?

LICINIUS: No, I cannot.

CINNA: If you wait a moment longer
She is lost.

LICINIUS: (furiously, to Cinna).
Let us go! Now is tearing
At my heart-strings the voice of my yearning.
And if you endanger my love
(To Julia.)
I'll know how to protect you!
Licinius, his fate with you sharing,
Will bear you off, danger spurning,
And whatever betide us
Together with you he will dare.
(The cries of the People are heard without.)

CHORUS: (within). The vengeful heavens clamor,
Decry the faithless lovers,
Whose face their guilt uncovers
By the desecrated shrine!

CINNA: (listening). Cries
Makes themselves heard in the distance.
Let us hasten to go!

LICINIUS: Grief is hounding us.
What to do? Woe is me!

JULIA: Do you flee!

CINNA: We must flee!

LICINIUS: (to Julia). Now make your will known.

JULIA: I trust in our love,
My lover, my own!
(The cries of the People are heard again.)

JULIA, LICINIUS, CINNA: Once again lend your ear
To the terrible cry!

JULIA: Hasten and defend me!

CINNA: Hasten to defend her!

LICINIUS: I hasten to defend you,
For you to die!
(He leaves with Cinna.)

CHORUS: (within). The vengeful heavens clamor,
Denounce the faithless lovers,
Whose face their guilt discovers
By the desecrated shrine!

IL SOMMO SACERDOTE: Oh delitto! oh sventura!
Oh colmo di sciagura!
Il divin foco estinto . . .
La Ministra spirante . . . i sommi Dei
Immergono di nuovo,
Per segnalar lo sgegno lor severo,
Nel càos primo l' Universo intero!
*(Alcune Vestali si affollano intorno a Giulia.)*

GIULIA: Che! . . . vivo ancora? . . .

VESTALI: Misera donzella!

IL SOMMO SACERDOTE: Il tempio è profanato,
I Numi, e insiem le genti,
Il misfatto perseguitan; reclamasi
La vittima da lor. Forse sei quella
*(A Giulia.)*
Ch' espiar deve la colpa? Olà, favella.

GIULIA: Mi si rechi la morte: io già l'aspetto,
Io la voglio, ed è questa
La speme che mi resta.
De' lunghi affanni miei
Orribil ricompensa. Almen mi toglie
Dei vostri lacci al peso.
Sacerdote di Giove, amo: il paleso.

IL SOMMO SACERDOTE: In questo sacro asilo, oh! quale ascolto
Esecranda bestemmia!
Nell'oltraggiare i dritti
Del tempio augusto, la più santa legge
Tradisti, infida a' voti,
A tuoi giuri spergiura.

GIULIA: Fui colpevole, è ver, vinse natura.

CORO DI SACERDOTI: Pronunziato—ha l'indegna—il suo fat:
Abbia morte condegna—all'error.

GIULIA: O Nume tutelar degli infelici,
Latona; odi i miei prieghi;
L'ultimo voto mio ti mova. Pria
Che al destino io soccomba,
Fa che dalla mia tomba
S'allontani l'oggetto
Per cui morte m'attende.

IL SOMMO SACERDOTE: A noi svela l'indegno,
Che, di Vesta lo sdegno
Per attirarti, in questo sacro albergo
Osò portare il piede:
Il suo nome palesa.

GIULIA: Invan si chiede.

---

PONTIFEX MAXIMUS: O fatal crime! O mischance vaster
Than any other dread disaster!
Extinguished is the fire divine,
Its priestess dying . . . gods supreme,
To show your scorn and rigor
Once more immerse
In chaos primeval the entire universe!
*(Some of the Vestals crowd about Julia.)*

JULIA: What! Am I still alive?

VESTALS: Wretched maiden!

PONTIFEX MAXIMUS: The Temple has been desecrated,
And gods and mortals offended
The evil done will punish, will claim
The victim due them. Can it be that she
*(To Julia.)*
Whom here I see is guilty?
Hearken to my words!

JULIA: I am prepared for death and I await it,
I crave it. Of all else fate bereaves me,
This hope alone is left me!
Of all my lasting sorrows
The dreadful recompense. Now free from the distress
Of those deceits which weighed me,
Highpriest of Jove, freely I confess my love.

PONTIFEX MAXIMUS: Within this holy shrine, alas, what must I hear!
Accursed blasphemy!
Outraging its sacred rights,
This temple revered, its law most holy
You have flouted. Faithless to your vow,
You have foresworn your solemn oath!

JULIA: I am guilty, it is true, betrayed by Nature!

CHORUS OF PRIESTS: This maid judges her own case unworthy.
Death and death only can efface her fault.

JULIA: O tutelary god of those unhappy,
Latona, hear the prayer I offer:
May the last plea I utter move you. I pray
When I succumb to fate,
When I have vanished from earth,
Far from my tomb be banished
The one to whom my death is due.

PONTIFEX MAXIMUS: Name the scoundrel unworthy
Who, chaste Vesta's anger compelling,
To snare you in this sacred dwelling
Dared to set foot.
Reveal his name to us!

JULIA: In vain you ask it.

---

IL SOMMO SACERDOTE: Interprete supremo
Dell'ira degli Dei,
L'anatema terribile
Vibro sopra di te.

GIULIA: Non v'è più speme!
Son tronchi i giorni miei,
E la gelida mano della morte
Mi sento in fronte.

IL SOMMO SACERDOTE: Perfida Ministra,
Ti prepara ad uscir da queste mura:
Va nel sen della Terra;
Le tue colpe esecrande ivi rinserra.
Da quel fronte—che ha l'onte—scolpite
*(Alle Vestali.)*
Le togliete le bende avvilite,
Dei littori alle mani cruente
L'empia testa dovete lasciar.
*(Si tolgono a Giulia gli ornamenti di Vestale, e le vengono fatti baciare.)*

CORO GENERALE: Da quel fronte—che ha l'onte—scolpite,
Le togliamo le bende avvilite;
Dei littori alle mani cruente
L'empia testa dobbiamo lasciar.
*(Il Sommo Sacerdote getta un velo nero sul capo a Giulia, la quale è condotta dai littori fuori del tempio. Le Vestali ed i Sacerdoti si ritirano.)*

■ **ATTO TERZO**

*(Campo scellerato.)*

*Confinante a sinistra colla porta Collina, sulla quale sta scritto: Scelleratus Ager. Si vedono tre tombe in forma piramidale: due delle quali son chiuse da nera pietra, su cui si legge il nome della Vestale ivi rinchiusa, e l'epoca della sua morte. La terza, destinata a Giulia, è aperta: una scala introduce nella parte interna.)*

LICINIO: *(solo e nel massimo disordine).* Ohimè! quale apparato! . . .
Spettacolo d'orrore!
L'alma mia s'abbandona al suo furore.
Cieco sdegno mi guida . . . freme il suolo
*(Andando verso la tomba aperta.)*
Sotto i miei passi, e pronto è già l'avello
A ingoiar quanto il mondo ha di più bello.
Giulia fia ver che mora! . . .
Ah! no, s' io vivo ancora;

---

PONTIFEX MAXIMUS: As the supreme interpreter
Of the ire of the offended gods,
I duly lay upon you,
Their dread and awful curse.

JULIA: No hope is left to me!
My days cut short in their flower,
I feel death's chilly hand this hour
Upon my brow!

PONTIFEX MAXIMUS: Priestess foresworn,
Make ready then to leave these holy walls!
Within the earth's dark bosom
Your crime accursed we'll hide away,
From your brow, dishonored now, by guilt defaced
*(To the Vestals.)*
Be it removed the veil she has defiled!
The lictors' hands shall tear from impious head
That veil it is not fit to wear.
*(Julia is stripped of her Vestal insignia, which are saluted and carried away.)*

GENERAL CHORUS: From that brow, dishonored now, defaced by guilt,
Be it removed, the veil she has defiled!
The lictors' hands from impious head shall tear
The Vestal veil it is not fit to wear!
*(The Pontifex Maximus casts a black veil over Julia's head and when two lictors have led her from the Temple, the Vestals and Priests withdraw.)*

■ **ACT III**

*(The Field of Infamy.)*

*On the left it is bordered by the Colline Gate, on which are inscribed the words: Scelleratus Ager (The Field of Infamy). It reveals three pyramidal tombs chiseled in black stone, on two of which may be read the names of the Vestals reposing within them, and the date of their interment. The third tomb, meant for Julia, is open and a flight of steps lead down into it.)*

LICINIUS: *(alone, with greatest agitation).* Woe is me! What preparations!
What a spectacle of horror!
My soul now itself abandons to its rage.
Blind anger is my guide. Let the earth tremble!
*(Approaching the open tomb.)*
Already the grave is yawning under my very feet
To swallow the loveliest flower of beauty's dawning.
Julia, must I behold her dying!
Ah, no, my chance awaiting,
Of her dear life and beauty

## Act III

Di così bella vita
Vo' farmi difensor.
Contro il destin severo
Che invan placare io spero,
Dovrà prestarmi aita
Un disperato amor.
(*Cinna e detto.*)

LICINIO: Cinna, l'arme che fan?

CINNA: Speriamo invano;
Geme ognun; ti compiange,
Ma non osa difenderti.

LICINIO: Codardi!

CINNA: Le schiere tutte lo spavento agghiaccia;
Ma per morirti al fianco
Di amici e di guerrier numero scelto
Seguita i passi miei, e là celati
Stansi sul Quirinal, gli ordini tuoi
Seco attenderò.

LICINIO: Fido nell'amico.

CINNA: Fida nell'ardir mio;
Ma pria d'avventurar l'inegual pugna
Del Supremo Pontefice il potere
Da te s'invochi.

LICINIO: Ogni speranza esclude
Del Grande Sacerdote
La fatal cecità.

CINNA: L'ira de'Numi
Ei sol può deviàre,
La Vestale involando al suo destino.

LICINIO: Qui giacer deve.

CINNA: Alla Collina porta
Appunto eccolo innanti
Fra questi orrori ei vien, seco rimanti.
(*Parte.*)

LICINIO: D'un sacrifizio orrendo
Disposto è l'apparato,
Vittima d'altra legge la beltade,
La giovinezza in preda
De' carnefici, viva nella tomba
Discenderà?

IL SOMMO SACERDOTE: Tal' è il voler de' Numi.

LICINIO: Per disarmare l'ira
A te pur lascia i modi
La somma lor clemenza:
Vengo per Giulia a chiederti assistenza.

IL SOMMO SACERDOTE: Che ardisci domandar, mentre lo Stato,
La salvezza di Roma
D'una vittima han d'uopo?
Giulia deve morir.

LICINIO: Da un delitto
Il bene degli Stati non dipende.

IL SOMMO SACERDOTE: Que' tetri monumenti assai ti mostrano
Che mai tali orror mai perdonò la Dea.

I shall be the defender!
Against a fate so cruel,
Beyond hope of placating,
I shall be seeking support
In a love born of despair!
(*Cinna enters.*)

LICINIUS: Cinna, what of the legionaires?

CINNA: Vain to rely on them
Some sigh and others pity,
They dare not try to defend you!

LICINIUS: The cowards!

CINNA: The soldiers are all congealed with terror;
Yet at your side, prepared to die,
A chosen group of friends and legionaries
Have followed my steps, and are hidden
Nearby, on the Quirinal.
They now are waiting for your commands.

LICINIUS: My trust is in my friend!

CINNA: Trust in the ardor that fills me,
Yet until you dare the unequal struggle,
Invoke the power of the Supreme Pontiff
In your behalf.

LICINIUS: Every hope is excluded
By the Pontifex Maximus's
Immovable blindness.

CINNA: Yet the ire of the gods
He alone can assuage,
The Vestal maiden rescue from her dread fate.

LICINIUS: He must avert that fate.

CINNA: At the Colline Gate,
They assemble to keep death's tryst
Stay with her amid these horrors that make us tremble!
(*Exeunt.*)

LICINIUS: The preparations have been made for a repellant sacrifice
A victim of cruel laws, must beauty
And youth, the executioners'
Unhappy spoil, alive into the tomb
Descend?

PONTIFEX MAXIMUS: It is the will of the gods.

LICINIUS: Their anger to disarm
To you I leave the methods
Their mercy best commanding.
For Julia your aid I am demanding.

PONTIFEX MAXIMUS: What dare you ask of me, when for the State,
For Rome's salvation,
The victim must meet her fate?
Julia will have to die!

LICINIUS: There is no state
That from a crime derives advantage.

PONTIFEX MAXIMUS: Yon monuments funereal to you should prove
Such horrid guilt the goddess never pardons.

LICINIO: Romolo deridea allor che nacque
La tua legge fatal: d'una Vestale
Gli diede in sen Marte la vita.

IL SOMMO SACERDOTE: Giulia
Deve morir . . .

LICINIO: No, no . . . non fia mai vero! . . .
Suo complice son io.
O salvarla, o morir con lei desìo.

IL SOMMO SACERDOTE: Morrai senza salvarla.
Contro il divin poter, che insultar osi,
Debole scudo è il tuo valore istesso;
La Tarpèa Rupe è al Campidoglio appresso.

LICINIO: Tu sol dovrai tremare
In fra gli sdegni e l'ira;
Il tuo crudele Altare
Col brando scuoterò.

IL SOMMO SACERDOTE: La folgore piombare
Sopra di te vedrò.

LICINIO: Provar dovrai il mio sdegno
Se Giulia perirà.

IL SOMMO SACERDOTE: L'iniquo tuo disegno
Il ciel confonderà.

LICINIO: Co' miei fidi, chi' io sproni al furore,
Coprirò questi campi d'orrori,
E la vittima illesa sarà.

IL SOMMO SACERDOTE: Trema, trema, son vani i furori,
E la vittima estinta cadrà.
(*Licinio parte.*)

ARUSPICE: Differir vi consiglio il sacrifizio;
È vittima possente.

IL SOMMO SACERDOTE: Venerabile Aruspice,
Non temete di lui;
Sarà mia cura gl'impeti arrestar
D'un giovin folle.

ARUSPICE: De' soldati e del popolo se la turba
Sdegnata . . .

IL SOMMO SACERDOTE: Degli altari è la gloria sicura;
Or si compia il dover nostro, e del resto
Si lasci al ciel la cura.
(*Giulia, condotta di' littori, è circondata da' suoi congiunti e da un numero di Donzelle. Innanzi a lei viene portata un'ara spenta. Le Vestali recano gli ornamenti della Vestale condannata.*)

CORO DI POPOLO: (*durante la marcia della comitiva*). La Vestale infida mora,
Che in orrore è degli Dei:

LICINIUS: Romulus laughed to scorn at very birth
Your fateful law. To a Vestal
He granted life upon the Martian Field.

PONTIFEX MAXIMUS: Julia
Will have to die.

LICINIUS: No, no, this cannot be the truth!
I am the sharer of her guilt, even I!
O save her or else let me die with her!

PONTIFEX MAXIMUS: She shall die and nothing can save her.
Against the powers divine which you have dared insult
Vainly your feeble valor strives. Remember
Near Campidoglio's field towers the Tarpeian Rock.

LICINIUS: The sun himself must tremble
At these fierce scorns and hatreds;
Your sanguinary altar
Beneath its brand should quake.

PONTIFEX MAXIMUS: The lightning's bolt shall strike you
Before my waiting eyes.

LICINIUS: My just wrath I shall prove anon,
If hapless Julia dies.

PONTIFEX MAXIMUS: The wickedness you have in mind
The heavens will frustrate.

LICINIUS: The faithful followers
I'll rouse to fury
Will turn these fields into a place of horror,
The victim rescue from her fate.

PONTIFEX MAXIMUS: Tremble, tremble, your rage is useless,
It is too late to save the victim!
(*Licinius off.*)

AN AUGUR: Do you advise that we defer the sacrifice;
The victim's friend has power.

PONTIFEX MAXIMUS: Venerable Augur,
Be not afraid of him;
Mine is the task to curb the ardor
Of a mad youth.

AUGUR: I know we are defying
The soldiers and the people . . .

PONTIFEX MAXIMUS: Upon our altars and their sanctity relying,
With our stern duty let us be complying,
All else we'll trust to heaven's care!
(*Julia, conducted by lictors, is surrounded by her colleagues and a group of Maidens. Before her is carried an altar on which the fire has been extinguished. The other Vestals carry the ornaments of the condemned Vestal.*)

CHORUS OF THE PEOPLE: (*sung during the processional march*).
The recreant Vestal must perish,
Outraged gods have decreed her

E la morte serva a lei
Il misfatto ad espiar.

And death will serve its purpose to expiate
Her error.

**CORO DI DONZELLE E DI VESTALI:** Sul fior degli anni—tanta beltade,
Tra crudi affanni—perir dovrà!
Numi, perdono, se la pietade
Amare lagrime spander ci fa!

**CHORUS OF MAIDENS AND VESTALS:** In her youth's flower this maid so lovely,
Who such grief has suffered, must seek death's bed!
Ye gods forgive her, have mercy on her.
Behold the bitter tears we shed for her!

**GIULIA:** (*alle Vestali*). Tenere suore addio!
(*Alla Gran Vestale.*)
E tu, che ancor degg' io
Venerar, tu disarma
Per me l'ira del ciel; d'essermi madre
In questi estremi istanti
Non isdegnar; la figlia
Benedici o che abbraccia
Le tue ginocchia.
(*Le cade ai piedi.*)

**JULIA:** (*to the Vestals*). Beloved sisters, farewell!
(*To the Chief of the Vestals.*) And you, you whom I still
Must venerate, do you disarm
Heaven's rage against me! Do not disdain
In these last moments of my life, to be
A mother to me; your daughter
Blessing, and granting her parting plea,
That she may clasp your knee!
(*She falls at her feet.*)

**GIULIA:** Oh! clemenza del ciel! La spenta face
De' miei dì si riaccende,
Ed a novella vita amor mi rende.
(*Il Sommo Sacerdote, la Gran Vestale, e seco loro i littori partono, portando seco il fuoco sacro.*)
(*A Licinio.*)
Per amarti io vivrò.
(*La scena si cambia e rappresenta il tempio di Venere in mezzo al bosco di rose.—Da un lato la statua di Flora.*)

**JULIA:** O divine grace! The dying spark
Of life takes fire and soars in me again.
Love restores a new existence to me!
(*The Pontifex Maximus, the Chief of the Vestals, followed by their attendants and lictors, depart, carrying the sacred fire.*)
(*To Licinius.*)
I will live to love you!
(*A change of scene represents the Temple of Venus, rising amid a garden of roses. At one side is a statue of Flora.*)

**CORO DI VESTALI:** Lieti concenti,
Dolci momenti,
Regnar fra noi
Possiate ognor.

**CHORUS OF VESTALS:** Sweet hours of pleasure,
To music's measure,
May their joy nevermore
Pass you by!

**LICINIO E GIULIA:** Vieni: colà sull' ara
Ricevi la mia fè.
Viver per te, ben mio,
Morir vogl' io per te.
Lieti concenti, ecc.

**LICINIUS AND JULIA:** Come, at the altar here,
Now I will make my vow,
To live for you alone
To die for you!
Sweet hours of pleasure, etc.

*FINE.*

*THE END.*

# Salome (1905)

## MUSIC AND LIBRETTO BY RICHARD STRAUSS

This one-act musical drama, set to a text by Hedwig Lachmann (based on Oscar Wilde's play), was first performed at the Königliches Opernhaus in Dresden on December 9, 1905. Herod, Tetrarch of Judea, is celebrating at a banquet at his palace in Tiberias, next to the Sea of Galilee. Narraboth, the Captain of the Guard, moons over Herod's beautiful stepdaughter, Salome. He is in love with her despite his friend the Page's warnings. When Salome goes outside to get away from the banquet she hears the voice of John the Baptist, who is being held prisoner by Herod. He speaks of the coming of the Messiah. She requests permission to visit him, but the guards are afraid of Herod's wrath. She promises to give her love to Narraboth if he will grant her this wish. John the Baptist is brought up from his dungeon; he denounces not only Herod but also Herodias, Salome's mother, for marrying her dead husband's brother. Salome thinks that John the Baptist is beautiful and sings of her wish to kiss him on the mouth. Finding this unbearable, Narraboth commits suicide. Salome barely notices. John the Baptist curses her too when he realizes that she is Herodias' daughter. Herod and Herodias quarrel over Herod's desire for Salome, and Herodias demands that John the Baptist die for having insulted her. But Herod, who is in awe of the holy man, refuses to harm him. Herod asks Salome to dance for him. But she will fulfill his wish only if he promises to give her whatever she wants when she is done. He gives in, and she performs the dance of the seven veils. She demands the head of John the Baptist as fulfillment of Herod's promise. The executioner hands her the head on a silver platter, and she grabs it in mad joy. She may now kiss him on the mouth as many times as, and for as long as, she wants. Herod is disgusted by her behavior and calls for his guards to kill her. They crush her to death with their shields.

## ■ ACTE PREMIER

### SCÈNE I

*Une grande terrasse dans le palais d'Hérode donnant sur la salle de festin. Des soldats sont accoudés sur le balcon. A droite, il y a un énorme escalier. A gauche, au fond une ancienne citerne entourée d'un mur de bronze vert. Clair de lune.*

**NARRABOTH:** Comme la princesse Salomé est belle ce soir!

**LE PAGE D'HÉRODIAS:** Regardez la lune. La lune a l'aire très étrange. On dirait une femme qui sort d'un tombeau.

**NARRABOTH:** Elle a l'aire très étrange. Elle ressemble à une princesse, qui a des pieds comme des petites colombes blanches . . . On dirait qu'elle danse.

**LE PAGE D'HÉRODIAS:** Elle est comme une femme morte. Elle va très lentement. (*Bruit dans la salle de festin.*)

**PREMIER SOLDAT:** Quel vacarme! Qui sont ces bêtes fauves qui hurlent?

**SECOND SOLDAT:** Les Juifs. Ils sont toujours ainsi. C'est sur leur religion qu'ils discutent.

## ■ ACT I

### SCENE I

*A great terrace in the palace of Herod, set above the banqueting-hall. Some soldiers are leaning over the balcony. To the right there is a gigantic staircase, to the left, at the back, an old cistern surrounded by a wall of green bronze. The moon is shining very brightly.*

**THE YOUNG SYRIAN:** How beautiful is the Princess Salome tonight!

**THE PAGE OF HERODIAS:** Look at the moon. How strange the moon seems! She is like a woman rising from a tomb. She is like a dead woman. One might fancy she was looking for dead things.

**THE YOUNG SYRIAN:** She has a strange look. She is like a little princess who wears a yellow veil, and whose feet are of silver. She is like a princess who has white doves for feet. One might fancy she was dancing.

**THE PAGE OF HERODIAS:** She is like a woman who is dead. She moves very slowly. (*Noise in the banqueting-hall.*)

**FIRST SOLDIER:** What an uproar! Who are those wild beasts howling?

**SECOND SOLDIER:** The Jews. They are always like that. They are disputing about their religion.

**NARRABOTH:** Qu'elle est belle, la princesse Salomé, ce soir! Qu'elle est belle!

**LE PAGE D'HÉRODIAS:** Vous la regardez toujours. Vous la regardez trop! Il ne faut pas regarder les gens de cette façon . . . . Il peut arriver un malheur.

**NARRABOTH:** Elle est très belle ce soir.

**PREMIER SOLDAT:** Le tétrarque a l'air très sombre.

**SECOND SOLDAT:** Oui, il a l'aire sombre.

**PREMIER SOLDAT:** Qui regarde-t-il?

**SECOND SOLDAT:** Je ne sais pas.

**NARRABOTH:** Comme la princesse est pâle! Jamais je ne l'ai vue si pâle. Elle ressemble au reflet d'une rose blanche dans un miroir d'argent.

**LE PAGE D'HÉRODIAS:** Il ne faut pas la regarder. Vous la regardez trop! Je vous prie de ne pas la regarder.

**LA VOIX D'IOKANAAN:** (*dans la citerne*). Après moi viendra un autre encore plus puissant que moi. Je ne suis pas digne même de délier la courroi de ses sandales. Quand il viendra, la terre déserte se réjouira. Quand il viendra, les yeux des aveugles verront le jour. Quand il viendra, les oreilles des sourds ser-

**THE YOUNG SYRIAN:** How beautiful is the princess Salome tonight!

**THE PAGE OF HERODIAS:** You are always looking at her. You look at her too much. It is dangerous to look at people in such fashion. Something terrible may happen.

**THE YOUNG SYRIAN:** She is very beautiful tonight.

**FIRST SOLDIER:** The Tetrarch has a sombre aspect.

**SECOND SOLDIER:** Yes; he has a sombre aspect.

**FIRST SOLDIER:** At whom is he looking?

**SECOND SOLDIER:** I cannot tell.

**THE YOUNG SYRIAN:** How pale the Princess is. Never have I seen her so pale. She is like the shadow of a white rose in a mirror of silver.

**THE PAGE OF HERODIAS:** You must not look at her. You look too much at her.

**THE VOICE OF IOKANAAN:** (*from the cistern.*) After me shall come another mightier than I. I am not worthy so much as to unloose the latchet of his shoes. When he comes the solitary places shall be glad. They shall blossom like the rose. The eyes of the blind shall see the day, and the ears of the deaf

ont ouvertes.

SECOND SOLDAT: Faites-le taire. Il dit toujours des choses absurdes.

PREMIER SOLDAT: Mains non: c'est un saint homme. Il est très doux. Chaque jour, je lui donne à manger; il me remercie toujours.

UN CAPPADOCIEN: Qui est-ce?

PREMIER SOLDAT: C'est un prophète.

UN CAPPADOCIEN: Quel est son nom?

PREMIER SOLDAT: Iokanaan.

UN CAPPADOCIEN: D'où vient-il?

PREMIER SOLDAT: Du désert. Une grande foule de disciples le suivait.

UN CAPPADOCIEN: De quoi parle-t-il?

PREMIER SOLDAT: Il est impossible de le comprendre.

UN CAPPADOCIEN: Peut-on le voir?

PREMIER SOLDAT: Non. Le tétrarque ne le permet pas.

NARRABOTH: Mais la princesse se lève! Elle quitte la table! Elle a l'air très ennuyée. Elle vient par ici.

LE PAGE D'HÉRODIAS: Ne la regardez pas.

NARRABOTH: Ah! Elle vient par ici, vers nous!

LE PAGE D'HÉRODIAS: Je vous prie, ne la regardez trop.

NARRABOTH: Elle est comme une colombe qui s'est égarée.

## SCÈNE II

*Entre Salomé.*

SALOMÉ: Je ne resterai pas. Je ne peux pas rester. Pourquoi le tétrarque me regarde-t-il toujours avec ses yeux de taupe sous ses paupières tremblantes?..C'est étrange que le mari de ma mère me regarde comme cela. Comme l'air est frais ici! Enfin, ici on respire! Là dedans, il y a des Juifs de Jérusalem qui se déchirent à cause de leurs ridicules cérémonies, des Egyptiens, subtils,

---

shall be opened. The suckling child shall put his hand upon the dragon's lair, he shall lead the lions by their manes.

SECOND SOLDIER: Make him be silent. He is always saying ridiculous things.

FIRST SOLDIER: No, no. He is a holy man. He is very gentle, too. Every day when I give him food to eat he thanks me.

THE CAPPADOCIAN: Who is he?

FIRST SOLDIER: A prophet.

THE CAPPADOCIAN: What is his name?

FIRST SOLDIER: Iokanaan.

THE CAPPADOCIAN: Where does he come from?

FIRST SOLDIER: From the desert where he fed on locusts and wild honey. He was clothed in camel's hair and round his loins he had a leather belt. He was very terrible to look upon. A great multitude used to follow him. He even had disciples.

THE CAPPADOCIAN: What is he talking of?

FIRST SOLDIER: We can never tell. Sometimes he says things that make one afraid, but it is impossible to understand what he says.

THE CAPPADOCIAN: May one see him?

FIRST SOLDIER: No. The Tetrarch has forbidden it.

THE YOUNG SYRIAN: The Princess is getting up! She is leaving the table! She looks very troubled. Ah, she is coming this way.

THE PAGE OF HERODIAS: Do not look at her!

THE YOUNG SYRIAN: Ah, she is coming towards us.

THE PAGE OF HERODIAS: I pray you not to look at her.

THE YOUNG SYRIAN: She is like a dove that has strayed . . . She is like a narcissus trembling in the wind . . . She is like a silver flower.

## SCENE II

*(Enter SALOME.)*

SALOME: I will not stay. I cannot stay. Why does the Tetrarch look at me all the while with his mole's eyes under his shaking eyelids? It is strange that the husband of my mother looks at me like that. How sweet the air is here! I can breathe here! Within there are Jews from Jerusalem who are tearing each other to pieces over their foolish ceremonies, and Egyptians si-

---

silencieux, des Romains avec leur lourdeur, leur brutalité, leurs gros mots. Ah! que je déteste les Romains!

LE PAGE D'HÉRODIAS: Oh! Il va arriver un malheur. Pourquoi le regarder?

SALOMÉ: Que c'est bon de voir la lune. On dirait une toute petite fleur d'argent, froide et chaste. Elle a la beauté d'une vierge . . . Je suis sûre, qu'elle est vierge.

LA VOIX D'IOKANAAN: Il est venu, le Seigneur! Il est venu le fils de l'Homme.

SALOMÉ: Qui a crié cela?

SECOND SOLDAT: C'est le prophète, princesse.

SALOMÉ: Ah! le prophète . . . celui dont le tétrarque a peur?

SECOND SOLDAT: Nous ne savons rien de cela, princesse. C'est le prophéte Iokanaan.

NARRABOTH: Voulez-vous que je commande votre litière, princesse? Il fait très beau dans le jardin.

SALOMÉ: Il dit des choses monstrueuses, à propos de ma mère, n'est-ce pas?

SECOND SOLDAT: Nous ne comprenons jamais ce qu'il dit, princesse.

SALOMÉ: Oui, il dit des choses monstrueuses d'elle.

UN ESCLAVE: (*Entrant.*). Princesse, le tétrarque vous prie de retourner au festin.

SALOMÉ: Je n'y retournerai pas. (*L'esclave sort.*) Est-ce un vieillard, le prophète?

NARRABOTH: (*toujours plus insistant*). Princess il vaudrait mieux retourner. Permettez-moi de vous reconduire.

SALOMÉ: Le prophète . . . est-ce un vieillard?

PREMIER SOLDAT: Non, princesse, c'est un tout jeune homme.

LA VOIX C'IOKANAAN: Ne te réjouis point, terre de Palestine, parce que la verge de celui qui te frappait a été brisée. Car de la race du serpent il sortira un basilic, et ce qui en naîtra dévorera les oiseaux.

SALOMÉ: Quelle étrange voix! Je voudrais bien lui parler.

---

lent and subtle, and Romans brutal and coarse, with the uncouth jargon. Ah! how I loathe the Romans!

THE PAGE OF HERODIAS: Why do you speak to her? Oh! something terrible will happen. Why do you look at her?

SALOME: How good to see the moon! She is like a little piece of money, a little silver flower. She is cold and chaste. I am sure she is a virgin. She has the beauty of a virgin. Yes, she is a virgin. She has never defiled herself. She has never abandoned herself to men, like the other goddesses.

THE VOICE OF IOKANAAN: Behold! the Lord has come. The Son of Man is at hand.

SALOME: Who was that who cried out?

SECOND SOLDIER: The prophet, Princess.

SALOME: Ah, the prophet! He of whom the Tetrarch is afraid?

SECOND SOLDIER: We know nothing of that, Princess. It was the prophet, Iokanaan, who cried out.

THE YOUNG SYRIAN: Is it your pleasure that I bid them bring you litter. Princess? The night is fair in the garden.

SALOME: He says terrible things about my mother, does he not?

SECOND SOLDIER: We never understand what he says, Princess.

SALOME: Yes; he says terrible things about her.
(*Enter a slave.*)

THE SLAVE: Princess, the Tetrarch prays you to return to the feast.

SALOME: I will not return.
(*The slave goes out.*)
Is he an old man, this prophet?

THE YOUNG SYRIAN: (*insisting.*) Princess, it were better to return. Suffer me to lead you in.

SALOME: This prophet . . . is he an old man?

FIRST SOLDIER: No, Princes, he is quite young.

THE VOICE OF IOKANAAN: Rejoice not, O land of Palestine, because the rod that smote you is broken. For from the seed of the serpent shall come a basilisk, and that which is born of it shall devour the birds.

SALOME: What a strange voice! I would speak with him.

## Act I, Scene II

SECOND SOLDAT: Princesse, le tétrarque ne veut pas qu'on lui parle. Il a même défendu au grand prêtre de lui parler.

SALOMÉ: Je veux lui parler.

SECOND SOLDAT: C'est impossible, princesse!

SALOMÉ: (toujours plus violente). Je le veux. Faites sortir le prophète.

SECOND SOLDAT: Nous n'osons pas, princesse.

SALOMÉ: (s'approchant de la citerne et y regardent). Comme il fait noir, là-dedans! Cela doit être terrible d'être dans un trou si noir! Cela ressemble à une tombe . . . (aux soldats, féroce). Vous ne m'avez pas entendue? Faites-le sortir. Je veux le voir.

PREMIER SOLDAT: Je vous prie, princesse, de ne pas nous demander cela.

SALOMÉ: (regardant le jeune Syrien). Ah!

LE PAGE D'HÉRODIAS: Oh! qu'est ce qui va arriver? Je suis sûr qu'il va arriver un malheur.

SALOMÉ: (s'approchant du jeune Syrien.) Vous ferez cela pour moi, n'est-ce pas, Narraboth? Pour vous, j'ai toujours été très douce. Vous ferez cela pour moi? Je veux seulement le regarder, cet étrange prophète. On a tant parlé de lui. Je pense qu'il a peur de lui, le tétrarque.

NARRABOTH: Le tétrarque a formellement défendu qu'on lève le couvercle de ce puits.

SALOMÉ: Vous ferez cela pour moi, Narraboth; et demain quand je passerai dans ma litière sous la porte des vendeurs d'idoles, je laisserai tomber pour vous une petite fleur, une petite fleur verte.

NARRABOTH: Princesse, je ne peux pas, je ne peux pas.

SALOMÉ: Vous ferez cela pour moi, Narraboth (plus décidément) Vous savez bien, que vous ferez cela pour moi. Et demain je vous regarderai à travers les voiles de mousseline, Narraboth, je vous regarderai, peut-être je vous sourirai. Narraboth, regardez-moi! Ah! vous savez vien que vous allez faire ce que je vous demande. Vous le savez bien . . . Moi je le sais bien.

NARRABOTH: (faisant un signe au second soldat). Faites sortir le prophète . . . La princesse Salomé veut le voir.

---

SECOND SOLDIER: I fear it may not be, Princess. The Tetrarch does not allow any one to speak with him. He has even forbidden the high priest to speak with him.

SALOME: I desire to speak with him.

SECOND SOLDIER: It is impossible, Princess.

SALOME: (violently). I will speak with him.

SECOND SOLDIER: We dare not, Princess.

SALOME: (Approaching the cistern and looking down into it.) How black it is down there! It must be terrible to be in so black a hole! It is like a tomb . . . (To the soldiers.) Did you not hear me? Bring out the prophet. I would look on him.

FIRST SOLDIER: Princess, I beg you, do not require this of us.

SALOME: (Looking at the young Syrian.) Ah!

THE PAGE OF HERODIAS: Oh! what is going to happen? I am sure that something terrible will happen.

SALOME: (Going up to the young Syrian.) You will do this thing for me, will you not, Narraboth? You will do this thing for me. I have ever been kind towards you. You will do it for me. I would but look at him, this strange prophet. Men have talked so much of him. Often I have heard Tetrarch talk of him. I think he is afraid of him, the Tetrarch.

THE YOUNG SYRIAN: The Tetrarch has formally forbidden that any man should raise the cover of this well.

SALOME: You will do this thing for me, Narraboth, and tomorrow when I pass in my litter beneath the gateway of the idol-sellers I will let fall for you a little flower, a little green flower.

THE YOUNG SYRIAN: Princess, I cannot, I cannot.

SALOME: (smiling). You will do this thing for me, Narraboth. You know that you will do this thing for me. And tomorrow when I shall pass in my litter by the bridge of the idol-buyers, I will look at you through the muslin veils, I will look at you Narraboth, it may be I will smile at you. Look at me, Narraboth, look at me. Ah! You know that you will do what I ask of you. You know . . . I know that you will do this thing.

THE YOUNG SYRIAN: (To the third Soldier.) Let the prophet come forth . . . The Princess Salome desires to see him.

---

SALOMÉ: Ah! (Le prophète sort de la citerne.)

### SCÈNE III

(Salomé le regarde et recule.)

IOKANAAN: Où est celui, dont la coupe d'abominations est déjà pleine? Où est celui qui en robe d'argent mourra un jour devant tout le peuple? Dites-lui de venir afin qu'il puisse entendre la voix de celui qui a crié dans les déserts et dans les palais des rois.

SALOMÉ: De qui parle-t-il?

NARRABOTH: On ne sait jamais, princesse.

IOKANAAN: Où est celle ayant vu des hommes peints sur la muraille, qui s'est laissée emporter à la concupiscence de ses yeux, et a envoyé des ambassadeurs en Chaldée?

SALOMÉ: C'est de ma mère qu'il parle.

NARRABOTH: Mais non, princesse.

SALOMÉ: Si, c'est de ma mère.

IOKANAAN: Où est celle qui s'est abandonnée aux capitaines des Assyriens? Où est celle qui s'est abandonée aux jeunes hommes d'Egypte qui sont vêtus de lin et d'hyacinthe, et portent des boucliers d'or et des casques d'argent, et qui ont de grands corps. Dites-lui de se lever de la couche de son impudicité, de sa couche incestueuse, afin qu'elle puisse entendre les paroles de celui qui prépare la voie du Seigneur; afin qu'elle se répente de ses péchés. Quoiqu'elle ne se repentira jamais, dites-lui de venir, car le Seigneur a son fléau dans la main.

SALOMÉ: Mais il est terrible, il est terrible.

NARRABOTH: Ne restez pas ici, princesse, je vous en prie.

SALOMÉ: Ce sont les yeux surtout qui sont terribles. On dirait des cavernes noides lunes fantastiques . . . Pensezres où demeurent des dragons. On dirait des lacs noirs troublés par vous qu'il parlera encore?

NARRABOTH: Ne restez pas ici, princesse! je vous prie de ne pas rester ici.

SALOMÉ: Comme il est maigre aussi! Il ressemble à une mince image d'ivoire. Je suis sûre qu'il est chaste, autant que la lune. Sa chair

---

SALOME: Ah! (The prophet comes out of the cistern.)

### SCENE III

(Salome looks at him and steps slowly back.)

IOKANAAN: Where is he whose cup of abominations is now full? Where is he, who in a robe of silver shall one day die in the face of all the people? Bid him come forth, that he may hear the voice of him who has cried in the waste places and in the houses of kings.

SALOME: Of whom is he speaking?

THE YOUNG SYRIAN: No one can tell, Princess.

IOKANAAN: Where is she who saw the images of men painted on the walls, even the images of the Chaldaens painted with colors, and gave herself up to the lust of her eyes, and sent ambassadors into the land of Chaldaea?

SALOME: It is of my mother that he is speaking.

THE YOUNG SYRIAN: Oh no, Princess.

SALOME: Yes: it is of my mother that he is speaking.

IOKANAAN: Where is she who gave herself unto the Captains of Assyria? Where is she who has given herself to the young men of the Egyptians, who are clothed in fine linen and hyacinth, whose shields are of gold, whose helmets are of silver, whose bodies are mighty? Go, bid her rise up from the bed of her abominations, from the bed of her incestuousness, that she may hear the words of him who prepares the way of the Lord, that she may repent of her iniquities. Though she will not repent, but will stick fast in her abominations, go bid her come, for the fan of the Lord is in His hand.

SALOME: Ah, but he is terrible, he is terrible!

THE YOUNG SYRIAN: Do not stay here, Princess, I beseech you.

SALOME: It is his eyes above all that are terrible. They are like the black caverns where dragons live, the black caverns of Egypt in which the dragons make their lairs. They are like black lakes troubled by fantastic moons . . . Do you think he will speak again?

THE YOUNG SYRIAN: Do not stay here, Princess. I pray you do not stay here.

SALOME: How wasted he is! He is like a thin ivory statue. He is like an image of silver. I am sure he is chaste, as the moon is. He is like a

doit tre très froide . . . froide comme l'ivoire . . . Je veux le regarder de près.

**NARRABOTH:** Non, non, princesse!

**SALOMÉ:** Il faut que je le regarde de près.

**NARRABOTH:** Princesse! Princesse!

**IOKANAAN:** Qui est cette femme qui me regarde? Je ne veux pas qu'elle me regarde. Pourquoi me regarde-t-elle avec ses yeux d'or sous ses paupières dorées? Je ne sais pas qui c'est. Je ne veux pas le savoir. Dites-lui de s'en aller. Ce n'est pas à elle que je veux parler.

**SALOMÉ:** Je suis Salomé, fille d'Hérodias, princesse de Judée.

**IOKANAAN:** Arrière! Fille de Babylone! N'approchez pas d l'élu du Seigneur. Ta mère a rempli la terre du vin de ses iniquités, et le cri de ses péchés est arrivé aux oreilles de Dieu.

**SALOMÉ:** Parle encore Iokanaan. Ta voix m'enivre.

**NARRABOTH:** Princesse! Princesse! Princesse!

**SALOMÉ:** Mais parle encore, Iokanaan, et dis-moi ce qu'il faut que je fasse.

**IOKANAAN:** Fille de Sodome, ne m'approchez pas! Mais couvrez votre visage avec un voile, mettez des cendres sur votre tête, et allez dans le désert chercher le fils de l'Homme.

**SALOMÉ:** Qui est-ce, le fils de l'Homme? Est-il aussi beau que toi, Iokanaan?

**IOKANAAN:** Arrière! Arrière! J'entends dans le palais le battement des ailes d l'ange de la mort.

**SALOMÉ:** Iokanaan!

**NARRABOTH:** Princesse, je vous supplie de rentrer!

**SALOMÉ:** Iokanaan! Je suis amoureuse de ton corps, Iokanaan. Ton corps est blanc comme le lis d'un prè que le faucheur n'a jamais fauché. Ton corps est blanc comme les neiges sur les montagnes de Judée. Les roses du jardin de la reine d'Arabie ne sont pas aussi blanches que ton corps. Ni les roses de la reine d'Arabie, ni les pieds de l'aurore sur les feuilles, ni le sein de la lune quand elle couche sure le sein de la mer . . . Il n'y reint au monde d'aussi blanc que ton corps . . . Laisse-moi toucher ton corps!

moonbeam, like a shaft of silver. His flesh must be very cold, cold as ivory . . . I would look closer at him.

**THE YOUNG SYRIAN:** No, no Princess!

**SALOME:** I must look at him closer.

**THE YOUNG SYRIAN:** Princess! Princess!

**IOKANAAN:** Who is this woman who is looking at me? I will not have her look at me. Why does she look at me, with her golden eyes, under her gilded eyelids? I do not know who she is. I do not desire to know who she is. Bid her begone. It is not to her that I would speak.

**SALOME:** I am Salome, daughter of Herodias, Princess of Judaea.

**IOKANAAN:** Back! daughter of Babylon! Do not come near the chosen of the Lord. Your mother has filled the earth with the wine of her iniquities, and the cry of her sinning has come up even to the ears of God.

**SALOME:** Speak again, Iokanaan. Your voice is as music to my ear.

**THE YOUNG SYRIAN:** Princess! Princess! Princess!

**SALOME:** Speak again! Speak again, Iokanaan, and tell me what I must do.

**IOKANAAN:** Daughter of Sodom. Do not come near me! But cover your face with a veil, and scatter ashes upon your head, and get to the desert, and seek out the Son of Man.

**SALOME:** Who is he, the Son of Man? Is he as beautiful as you are, Iokanaan?

**IOKANAAN:** Get behind me! I hear in the palace the beating of the wings of the angel of death.

**SALOME:** Iokanaan!

**THE YOUNG SYRIAN:** Princess, I beseech you to go within.

**SALOME:** I am amorous of your body, Iokanaan! Your body is white, like the lilies of the field that the mower has never mowed. Your body is white like the snows that lie on the mountains of Judaea, and come down into the valleys. The roses in the garden of the Queen of Arabia are not so white as your body. Neither the roses of the garden of the Queen of Arabia, the garden of spices of the Queen of Arabia, nor the feet of the dawn when they light on the leaves, nor the breast of the moon when she lies on the breast of the sea . . . There is nothing in the world so white as your body. Allow me to touch your body.

**IOKANAAN:** Arrière, fille de Babylone! C'est par la femme que le mal est entré dans le monde. Ne me parlez pas. Je ne veux pas t'écouter. Je n'écoute que les paroles du Seigneur Dieu.

**SALOMÉ:** Ton corps est hideux. Il est comme le corps d'un lépreux. Il est comme un mur de plâtre où les scorpions ont fait leur nid. Il est comme un sépulcre blanchi, qui est plein de choses dégoûtantes. Il est horrible, il est horrible ton corps! . . . C'est de tes cheveux que je suis amoureuse, Iokanaan. Tes cheveux ressemblent à des grappes de raisins, des raisins noirs qui pendent des vignes d'Edom dans le pays des Edomites. Tes cheveux sont comme les cèdres, les grands cèdres du Liban; les cèdres qui donnent de l'ombre aux lions et aux voleurs. Les longues nuits noires, les nuits où la lune ne se montre pas, où les étoiles ont peur, ne sont pas aussi noires, ni le silence dans les forêts. Il n'est rien au monde d'aussi noir que tes cheveux . . . Laisse-moi toucher tes cheveux.

**IOKANAAN:** Arrière, fille de Sodome! Ne me touchez pas. Il ne faut pas profaner le temple du Seigneur Dieu.

**SALOMÉ:** Tes cheveux sont horribles. Ils sont couverts de boue et de poussière. On dirait une couronne d'épines qu'on a placée sur ton front. On dirait un noeud de serpents noirs qui se tordent autour de ton cou. Je n'aime pas tes cheveux . . . C'est de ta bouche que je suis amoureuse, Iokanaan. Ta bouche est comme une bande d'écarlate sur une tour d'ivoire. Elle est comme une pomme de grenade coupée par un couteau d'ivoire. Les fleurs de grenade dans les jardins de Tyr, plus rouges que les roses, ne sont pas aussi rouges. Les cris rouges des trompettes qui annoncent l'arrivée des rois et font peur à l'ennemi, ne sont pas aussi rouges que ta bouche. Ta bouche est plus rouge que les pieds de ceux qui foulent le vin dans les pressoirs. Elle est plus rouge que les pieds des colombes qui demeurent dans les temples. Ta bouche est comme une branche de corail dans le crépuscule de la mer. Le vermillon que les rois prennent dans les mines de Moab . . . Il n'y a rien d'aussi rouge que ta bouche. Ta bouche, laisse-moi la baiser.

**IOKANAAN:** Back! daughter of Babylon! By woman came evil into the world. Speak not to me. I will not listen to you. I listen but to the voice of the Lord God.

**SALOME:** Your body is hideous. It is like the body of a leper. It is like a plastered wall, where vipers have crawled; like a plastered wall where the scorpions have made their nest. It is like a whited sepulchre, full of loathsome things. It is horrible, your body is horrible. It is of your hair that I am enamoured, Iokanaan. Your hair is like clusters of grapes, like the clusters of black grapes that hang from the vine-trees of Edom in the land of the Edomites. Your hair is like the cedars of Lebanon, like the great cedars of Lebanon that gave their shade to the lions and to the robbers who would hide them by day. The long black nights, when the moon hides her face, when the stars are afraid, are not so black as your hair. The silence that dwells in the forest is not so black. There is nothing in the world that is so black as your hair . . . Allow me to touch your hair.

**IOKANAAN:** Back, daughter of Sodom! Touch me not. Do not profane the temple of the Lord God.

**SALOME:** Your hair is horrible. It is covered with mire and dust. It is like a crown of thorns placed on your head. It is like a knot of serpents coiled round your neck. I do not love your hair . . . It is your mouth that I desire, Iokanaan. Your mouth is like a bank of scarlet on a tower of ivory. It is like a pomegranate cut in twain with a knife of ivory. The pomegranate flowers that blossom in the gardens of Tyre, and are redder than roses, are not so red. The red blasts of trumpets that herald the approach of kings, and make afraid the enemy, are not so red. Your mouth is redder than the feet of those who tread the wine in the wine-press. It is redder than the feet of the doves who inhabit the temples and are fed by the priests. It is redder than the feet of he, who comes from a forest where he has slain a lion, and seen gilded tigers. Your mouth is like a branch of coral that fishers have found in the twilight of the sea, the coral that they keep for the kings! . . . It is like the vermilion that the Moabites find in the mines of Moab, the vermilion that the kings take from them. It is like the bow of the King of the Persians, that is painted with vermilion, and is tipped with coral. There is nothing in the world so red as your mouth . . . Allow me to kiss your mouth.

IOKANAAN: Jamais! fille de Babylone! Fille de Sodome, jamais!

SALOMÉ: Je baiserai ta bouche, Iokanaan. Je baiserai ta bouche.

NARRABOTH: Princesse, princesse, toi qui es comme un bouquet de myrrhe, toi qui es la colombe des colombes, ne regarde pas cet homme. Ne lui dis pas de telles choses. Je ne peux pas les souffrir.

SALOMÉ: Je baiserai ta bouche, Iokanaan. Je baiserai ta bouche . . .

NARRABOTH: Ah!
(*Il se tue et tombe entre Salomé et Iokanaan.*)

SALOMÉ: Je baiserai ta bouche, Iokanaan.

IOKANAAN: N'avez-vous pas peur, fille d'Hérodias?

SALOMÉ: Laisse-moi baiser ta bouche, Iokanaan.

IOKANAAN: Fille d'adultère, il n'y a qu'un homme qui puisse te sauver. Allez le chercher. C'est celui dont je t'ai parlé, il est dans un bateau sur la mer de Galilée, et il parle à ses disciples. Agenouillez-vous au bord de la mer, et appelez-le par son nom. Quand il viendra vers vous, et il vient vers tous ceux qui l'appellent, prosternez-vous à sés pièds et demandez lui la rémission de vos péchés.

SALOMÉ: Je baiserai ta bouche, Iokanaan.

IOKANAAN: Soyez maudite, fille d'une mère incestueuse, soyez maudite.

SALOMÉ: Je baiserai ta bouche, Iokanaan.

IOKANAAN: Je ne te regarderai pas. Tu es maudite, Salomé. Tu es maudite.
(*Il descend dans la citerne.*)

## SCÈNE IV

*Entré D'Hérode, D'Hérodias et de toute la cour.*

HÉRODE: Où est Salomé? Où est la princesse? Pourquoi n'est-elle pas retournée au festin, comme je le lui avais commandé? Ah! la voilà!

HÉRODIAS: Il ne faut pas la regarder. Vous la regardez toujours!

HÉRODE: La lune a l'air très étrange, ce soir. N'est-ce pas, très étrange? On dirait une femme hystérique, qui va chercher des amants partout. N'est-ce pas, qu'elle chancelle comme une femme ivre?

IOKANAAN: Never! daughter of Babylon! Daughter of Sodom! never!

SALOME: I will kiss your mouth, Iokanaan. I will kiss your mouth.

THE YOUNG SYRIAN: Princess, Princess, You who are like a garden of myrrh, you who are the dove of all doves. Do not look at this man, do not look at him! I cannot endure it . . . Princess, do not speak these things.

SALOME: I will kiss your mouth, Iokanaan.

THE YOUNG SYRIAN: Ah!
(*He kills himself, and falls between Salome and Iokanaan.*)

SALOME: Allow me to kiss your mouth, Iokanaan.

IOKANAAN: Are you not afraid, daughter of Herodias? Did I tell you that I had heard in the palace the beatings of the wings of the angel of death, and hasn't it come, the angel of death?

SALOME: Allow me to kiss your mouth.

IOKANAAN: Daughter of adultery, there is but one who can save you. It is He of whom I spake. Go seek Him. He is in a boat on the sea of Galilee, and He talks with His disciples. Kneel down on the shore of the sea, and call to Him by His name. When He comes to you and to all who call on Him He comes, bow at His feet and ask of Him the remission of your sins.

SALOME: Allow me to kiss your mouth.

IOKANAAN: Be accursed, daughter of an incestuous mother, be accursed!

SALOME: I will kiss your mouth, Iokanaan.

IOKANAAN: I will not look at you. You are accursed, Salome, you are accursed.
(*He goes down into the cistern.*)

## SCENE IV

*(Enter Herod, Herodias, and all the Court.)*

HEROD: Where is Salome? Where is the Princess? Why did she not return to the banquet as I commanded her? Ah! there she is!

HERODIAS: You must not look at her! You are always looking at her!

HEROD: The moon has a strange look tonight. Has she not a strange look? She is like a mad woman, a mad woman who is seeking everywhere for lovers. She is naked too. The clouds are seeking to clothe her nakedness, but she will not let them. She shows

HÉRODIAS: Non. La lune ressemble à la lune, c'est tout. Rentrons.

HÉRODE: Je resterai! Manassé, mettez des tapis là. Allumez des flambeaux. Je boirai encore du vin avec mes hôtes. Ah! j'ai glissé! j'ai glissé dans le sang! C'est un mauvais présage. Pourquoi y a-t-il du sang ici? . . . Et ce cadavre? Que fait ici ce cadavre? Enfin qui est-ce? Je ne veux pas le regarder.

PREMIER SOLDAT: C'est notre capitaine, Seigneur.

HÉRODE: Je n'ai donné aucun ordre de le tuer.

PREMIER SOLDAT: Il s'est tué lui-même, Seigneur.

HÉRODE: Cela me semble étrange. Le jeune Syrien, il était beau. Je me rappelle que je l'ai vu regardant Salomé d'une façon langoureuse . . . Emportez-le . . .
(*On emporte le cadavre.*)

HÉRODE: Il fait froid icic. Il y a du vent ici. N'est-ce pas qu'il y a du vent?

HÉRODIAS: (*sèchement*). Mais non. Il n'y a pas de vent.

HÉRODE: Mais si, il y du vent . . . Et j'entends dans l'air quelque chose comme un battement d'ailes, d'ailes gigantesques. Ne l'entendez-vous pas?

HÉRODIAS: Je n'entends rien.

HÉRODE: Je ne l'entends plus moi-même. Mais je l'ai entendu. C'était le vent sans doute. C'est passé. Mais non, je l'entends encore. Ne l'entendez-vous pas? C'est tout à fait comme un battement d'ailes . . .

HÉRODIAS: Vous êtes malade. Rentrons.

HÉRODE: Je ne suis pas malade. C'est votre fille qui a l'air très malade. Jamais je ne l'ai vue si pâle.

HÉRODIAS: Je vous ai dit de ne pas la regarder.

HÉRODE: Versez du vin. (*On apporte du vin*) Salomé, venez boire un peu de vin avec moi: un vin très exquis. C'est César lui-même qui me l'a envoyé. Trempez là dedans vos petites lèvres, vos petites lèvres rouges et ensuite je viderai la coupe.

SALOMÉ: Je n'ai pas soif, tétrarque.

HÉRODE: Vous entendez comme elle me répond, votre fille.

herself naked in the sky. She reels through the clouds like a drunken woman . . . I am sure she is looking for lovers. Does she not reel like a drunken woman? She is like a mad woman, is she not?

HERODIAS: No; the moon is like the moon, that is all. Let us go within . . . We have nothing to do here.

HEROD: Yes; the air is very sweet. Come, Herodias, our guests await us. Ah! I have slipped! I have slipped in blood! It is an ill omen. It is a very ill omen. Why is there blood here? . . . and this body, what does this body here? Do you think I am like the King of Egypt, who gives no feast to his guests but that he shows them a corpse? Whose is it? I will not look on it.

FIRST SOLDIER: It is the captain, sire.

HEROD: I issued no orders that he should be slain.

FIRST SOLDIER: He slew himself, sire.

HEROD: That seems strange to me. I had thought it was but Roman philosophers who slew themselves. Is it not true, Tigellinus, that the philosophers at Rome slay themselves. (*They take away the body.*)

HEROD: It is cold here. There is a wind blowing. Is there a wind blowing?

HERODIAS: No; there is no wind.

HEROD: I tell you there is a wind that blows . . . And I hear in the air something that is like the beating of wings, like the beating of vast wings. Do you not hear it?

HERODIAS: I hear nothing.

HEROD: I hear it no longer. But I heard it. It has passed away. But no, I hear it again. Do you not hear it? It is just like a beating of wings.

HERODIAS: I tell you there is nothing. You are ill. Let us go inside.

HEROD: I am not ill. It is your daughter who is sick to death. Never have I seen her so pale.

HERODIAS: I have told you not to look at her.

HEROD: Pour me some wine.
(*Wine is brought.*) Salome, come drink a little wine with me. I have here a wine that is exquisite. Caesar himself sent it to me. Dip into it thy little red lips, that I may drain the cup.

SALOME: I am not thirsty, Tetrarch.

HEROD: You hear how she answers me, this daughter of yours?

HÉRODIAS: Je trouve qu'elle a bien raison. Pourquoi la regardez-vous toujours?

HÉRODE: Apportez des fruits. (*On apporte des fruits.*) Salomé, venez manger des fruits avec moi. J'aime beaucoup voir dans un fruit la morsure de tes petites dents. Mordez un tout petit morceau de ce fruit, un tout petit morceau, et ensuite je mangerai ce qui reste.

SALOMÉ: Je n'ai pas faim, tétrarque.

HÉRODE: (*à Hérodias*). Voilà comme vous l'avez élevée, votre fille.

HÉRODIAS: Ma fille et moi, nous descendons d'une race royale. Quant à toi, ton grand père gardait des chameaux! Aussi, c'était un voleur!

HÉRODE: Salomé, viens t'asseoir près de moi. Je te donnerai le trône de ta mère.

SALOMÉ: Je ne suis pas fatiguée, tétrarque.

HÉRODIAS: Vous voyez bien ce qu'elle pense de vous.

HÉRODE: Apportez . . . Qu'est-ce que je veux? Je ne sais pas. Ah! Ah! je m'en souviens . . .

LA VOIX D'IOKANAAN: Ce que j'ai prédit est arrivé. Voici le jour dont j'avais parlé.

HÉRODIAS: Faites-le taire. Cet homme vomit toujours des injures contre moi.

HÉRODE: Il n'a rien dit contre vous. Aussi, c'est un très grand prophète.

HÉRODIAS: Je ne crois pas aux prophètes. Je sais bien que vous avez peur de lui.

HÉRODE: Moi, je n'ai peur de personne.

HÉRODIAS: Si, vous avez peur de lui. Pourquoi ne pas le liver aux Juifs qui depuis six mois vous le demandent?

PREMIER JUIF: En effet, Seigneur, il serait mieux de nous le livrer.

HÉRODE: Assez sur ce point. Je ne veux pas vous le livrer. C'est un saint homme. C'est un homme qui a vu Dieu.

PREMIER JUIF: Cela, c'est impossible. Personne n'a vu Dieu depuis le prophète Elie. Lui, c'est le dernier qui ait vu Dieu. En ce temps-ci, Dieu ne se montre pas. Il se cache. Et par conséquent il y a de grands malheurs dans le pays, de grands malheurs.

HERODIAS: She does right. Why are you always gazing at her?

HEROD: Bring me ripe fruits. (*Fruits are brought.*) Salome, come and eat fruits with me. I love to see in a fruit the mark of your little teeth. Bite but a little of this fruit, that I may eat what is left.

SALOME: I am not hungry, Tetrarch.

HEROD: (*to Herodias*). You see how you have brought up this daughter of yours.

HERODIAS: My daughter and I come of a royal race. As for you, your father was a camel driver! He was a thief and a robber to boot.

HEROD: Salome, come and sit next to me. I will give you your mother's throne.

SALOME: I am not tired, Tetrarch.

HERODIAS: You see in what high regard she holds you.

HEROD: Bring me——What is it that I desire? I forget. Ah! ha! I remember.

THE VOICE OF IOKANAAN: Behold the time is come! That which I foretold has come to pass. The day that I speak of is at hand.

HERODIAS: Bid him be silent. I will not listen to his voice. This man is for ever hurling insults against me.

HEROD: He has said nothing against you. Besides, he is a very great prophet.

HERODIAS: I do not believe in prophets. I know well that you are afraid of him.

HEROD: I am not afraid of him. I am afraid of no man.

HERODIAS: I tell you, you are afraid of him. If you are not afraid of him why do you not deliver him to the Jews who for these six months past have been clamouring for him?

FIRST JEW: Truly, my lord, it were better to deliver him into our hands.

HEROD: Enough on this subject. I have already given you my answer. I will not deliver him into your hands. He is a holy man. He is a man who has seen God.

FIRST JEW: That cannot be. There is no man who has seen God since the prophet Elias. He is the last man who saw God face to face. In these days God does not show Himself. God hides Himself. Therefore great evils have come upon the land.

SECOND JUIF: Enfin, on ne sait pas si le prophète Elie a réellement vu Dieu. C'était plutôt l'ombre de Dieu qu'il a vue.

TROISIÈME JUIF: Dieu ne se cache jamais. Il se montre toujours et dans toute chose. Dieu est dans le mal comme dans le bien.

QUATRIÈME JUIF: Il ne faut pas dire cela. C'est une idèe très dangereuse d'Alexandrie. Et les Grecs sont des gentils.

CINQUIÈME JUIF: On ne peut pas savoir comment Dieu agit, ses voies sont très mystérieuses. Le nécessaire c'est de se soumettre à tout. Dieu est très fort.

PREMIER JUIF: C'est vrai cela. Dieu est terrible. Mais cet homme, cet homme n'a jamais vu Dieu Personne n'a vu Dieu depuis le prophète Elie. C'est le dernier, qui ait vu Dieu. En ce temps ci, Dieu ne se montre pas. Dieu se cache. Il y a de grands malheurs dans le pays. C'est le dernier, qui ait vu Dieu.

HÉRODIAS: (*à Hérode*). Faites les taire. Ils m'ennuient.

HÉRODE: Mais j'ai entendu dire qu'Iokanaan lui-même est votre prophète Elie.

PREMIER JUIF: Cela ne se peut pas. Depuis le temps du prophète Elie, il y a plus de trois cents ans.

PREMIER NAZARÉEN: Moi, je suis sûr que c'est le prophète Élie.

PREMIER JUIF: Ca ne se peut pas. Depuis le temps du prophète Elie, il y a plus de trois cents ans.

SECOND, TROISIÈME, QUATRIÈME, ET CINQUIÈME JUIF: Mais non, ce n'est pas le prophète Élie.

HÉRODIAS: Faites les taire.

LA VOIX D'IOKANAAN: Le jour est venu, le jour du Seigneur, et j'entends sur les montagnes les pieds de celui qui sera le Sauveur du monde.

HÉRODE: Qu'est ce que cela veut dire? Le Sauveur du monde?

PREMIER NAZARÉEN: Le Messie est venu.

PREMIER JUIF: (*criant*). Le Messie n'est pas venu.

PREMIER NAZARÉEN: Il est venu, et fait des miracles partout. A l'occasion d'un mariage qui a eu lieu dans une ville de Galilée, il a changé de l'eau en vin. Il a guéri des aveugles. On l'a vu sur une

SECOND JEW: Verily, no man knows if Elias the prophet did indeed see God. Perhaps it was just the shadow of God that he saw.

THIRD JEW: God is at no time hidden. He shows Himself at all times and in all places. God is in what is evil even as He is in what is good.

FOURTH JEW: You should not say that. It is a very dangerous doctrine. It is a doctrine that comes from Alexandria, where men teach the philosophy of the Greeks. And the Greeks are Gentiles. They are not even circumcised.

FIFTH JEW: No man can tell how God works. His ways are very dark. It may be that the things which we call evil are good and that the things which we call good are evil. There is no knowledge of anything. We can only bow our heads to His will, for God is very strong. He breaks in pieces the strong together with the weak, for He regards no one.

FIRST JEW: You speak truly. Verily, God is terrible. He breaks in pieces the strong and the weak as men break corn in a mortar. But as for this man, he has never seen God. No man has seen God since the prophet Elias.

HERODIAS: (*to Herod*). Make them be silent. They tire me.

HEROD: But I have heard it said that Iokanaan is in very truth your prophet Elias.

FIRST JEW: That cannot be. It has been more than three hundred years since the days of the prophet Elias.

FIRST NAZARENE: I am sure that he is Elias the prophet.

FIRST JEW: No, but he is not Elias the prophet.

SECOND, THIRD, FOURTH, AND FIFTH JEWS: No, he is not Elias, the prophet.

HERODIAS: Make them be silent.

THE VOICE OF IOKANAAN: Behold the day is at hand, the day of the Lord, and I hear upon the mountains the feet of Him who shall be the Savior of the world.

HEROD: What does that mean? The Savior of the world?

FIRST NAZARENE: Concerning Messiah, who has come.

FIRST JEW: Messiah has not come.

FIRST NAZARENE: He has come, and everywhere He works miracles! This Man works true miracles. Thus, at a marriage which took place in a little town of Galilee, a town of some importance, He

montagne parlant avec des anges.

SECOND NAZARÉEN: Aussi il a guéri deux lépreux, seulement en les touchant.

HÉRODIAS: Oh! Oh! Je ne crois pas aux miracles. J'en ai vu trop.

PREMIER NAZARÉEN: La fille de Jaïre était morte. Il l'a ressuscitée.

HÉRODE: (effrayé) Ah! Il ressuscite les morts?

PREMIER ET SECOND NAZARÉEN: Oui, Seigneur. Il ressuscite les morts.

HÉRODE: Je ne veux pas qu'il fasse cela. Ce serait terrible, si les morts revenaient. Où est-il à présent cet homme?

PREMIER NAZARÉEN: Il est partout, Seigneur, mais est il très difficile de le trouver.

HÉRODE: Mais il faut le trouver.

SECOND NAZARÉEN: On dit qu'il est à Samarie à présent.

PREMIER NAZARÉEN: Il a quitté Samarie il y a quelques jours. Moi, je crois qu'en ce moment-ci il est dans les environs de Jérusalem.

HÉRODE: Enfin, je ne permets pas qu'il ressuscite les morts . . . Ce serait terrible, si les morts reviennent.

LA VOIX D'IOKANAAN: Ah! l'impudique!—la prostituée! La fille de Babylone! Voici ce que dit le Seigneur. Faites venir contre elle une multitude d'hommes. Que le peuple prenne des pierres et la lapide . . .

HÉRODIAS: (furieuse). Mais c'est infâme. Faites-le taire! C'est infâme.

LA VOIX D'IOKANAAN: Que les capitaines de guerre la percent de leurs épées, qu'ils l'écrasent sous leurs boucliers!

HÉRODE: Faites le taire!

LA VOIX D'IOKANAAN: C'est ainsi que j'abolirai les crimes de dessus la terre, et que toutes les femmes apprendront à ne pas imiter les abominations de celle-là.

HÉRODIAS: Vous entendez ce qu'il dit contre moi? Vous le laissez insulter votre épouse?

HÉRODE: Mais il n'a pas dit votre nom.

changed water into wine. Certain persons who were present related it to me. Also He healed two lepers that were seated before the Gate of Capernaum simply by touching them.

SECOND NAZARENE: No, they were lepers. But He has healed blind people also, and He was seen on a mountain talking with angels.

HERODIAS: Ho! ho! miracles! I do not believe in miracles. I have seen too many.

FIRST NAZARENE: The daughter of Jarius was dead. This Man raised her from the dead.

HEROD: How! He raises people from the dead?

FIRST AND SECOND NAZARENE: Yea, sire; He raises the dead.

HEROD: I do not wish Him to do that. I forbid Him to do that. I suffer no man to raise the dead. This man must be found and told that I forbid Him to raise the dead. Where is this man at present?

FIRST NAZARENE: He is in every place, my Lord, but it is hard to find Him.

HEROD: But He must be found!

SECOND NAZARENE: It is said that He is now in Samaria.

FIRST NAZARENE: He left Samaria a few days since. I think that at the present moment He is in the neighborhood of Jerusalem.

HEROD: No matter! But let them find Him, and tell Him, said Herod the King, 'I will not suffer you to raise the dead.'

THE VOICE OF IOKANAAN: Ah! The wanton one! The harlot! Ah! the daughter of Babylon with her golden eyes and he: gilded eyelids! Thus said the Lord God, Let there come up against her a multitude of men. Let the people take stones and stone her . . .

HERODIAS: Command him to be silent!

THE VOICE OF IOKANAAN: Let the captains of the hosts pierce her with their swords, let them crush her beneath their shields.

HERODIAS: Nay, but it is infamous.

THE VOICE OF IOKANAAN: It is like this that I will wipe out all wickedness from the earth, and that all women shall learn not to imitate her abominations.

HERODIAS: You hear what he says against me? You allow him to revile your wife!

HEROD: He did not speak your name.

LA VOIX D'IOKANAAN: (solennel). En ce jour là, le soleil deviendra noir comme un sac de poil, et la lune deviendra comme du sang, et les étoiles du ciel tomberont sur la terre comme les figures vertes tombent d'un figuier. En ce jour là, les rois de la terre auront peur.

HÉRODIAS: Ah! Ah! Ce prophète parle comme un homme ivre . . . Mais je ne peux pas souffrir le son de sa voix. Je déteste sa voix. Ordonnez qu'il se taise.

HÉRODE: Salomé, dansez pour moi.

HÉRODIAS: (violent). Je ne veux pas qu'elle danse.

SALOMÉ: (tranquille). Je n'ai aucune envie de danser, tétrarque.

HÉRODE: Salomé, fille d'Hérodias, dansez pour moi.

SALOMÉ: Je ne danserai pas, tétrarque.

HÉRODIAS: (riant). Voilà comme elle vous obéit.

LA VOIX D'IOKANAAN: Il sera assis sur son trône. Il sera vêtu de pourpre et d'écarlate. Et l'ange du Seigneur Dieu le frappera. Il sera mangé des vers.

HÉRODE: Salomé, Salomé, dansez pour moi. Je suis triste ce soir. Ainsi, dansez pour moi, Salomé. Je vous supplie. Si vous dansez pour moi, vous pourrez me demander tout ce que vous voudrez et je vous le donnerai.

SALOMÉ: (se levant). Vous me donnerez tout ce que je demanderai, tétrarque?

HÉRODIAS: Ne dansez pas, ma fille.

HÉRODE: Tout, tout ce que vous voudrez je vous le donnerai, fût-ce la moitié de mon royaume.

SALOMÉ: Vous le jurez, tétrarque?

HÉRODE: Je le jure, Salomé.

SALOMÉ: Sur quoi jurez-vous, tétrarque?

HÉRODE: Sur ma vie, sur ma couronne, sur mes dieux. Oh Salomé, Salomé, dansez pour moi.

HÉRODIAS: Ne dansez pas, ma fille.

SALOMÉ: Vous avez juré, tétrarque.

HÉRODE: J'ai juré, Salomé.

HÉRODIAS: Ne dansez pas, ma fille.

THE VOICE OF IOKANAAN: In that day the sun shall become black like sackcloth of hair, and the moon shall become like blood, and the stars of the heaven shall fall upon the earth like unripe figs that fall from the fig-tree, and the kings of the earth shall be afraid.

HERODIAS: Ah! ha! I should like to see that day of which he speaks, when the moon shall become like blood, and when the stars shall fall upon the earth like unripe figs. This prophet talks like a drunken man . . . but I cannot stand the sound of his voice. I hate his voice. Command him to be silent.

HEROD: Dance for me, Salome.

HERODIAS: I will not have her dance.

SALOME: I have no desire to dance, Tetrarch.

HERODIAS: Salome, daughter of Herodias, dance for me.

SALOME: I will not dance, Tetrarch.

HERODIAS: (Laughing). You see how she obeys you.

THE VOICE OF IOKANAAN: He shall be seated on his throne. He shall be clothed in scarlet and purple. In his hand he shall bear a golden cup full of his blasphemies. And the angel of the Lord shall smite him. He shall be eaten by worms.

HEROD: Salome, Salome, dance for me. I pray you, dance for me. I am sad tonight. Yes, I am passing sad tonight. Dance for me, Salome, I beseech you. If you dance for me, you may ask of me what you will, and I will give it to you. Yes, dance for me, Salome, and whatever you shall ask of me I will give to you even up to the half of my kingdom.

SALOME: (Rising). Will you indeed give me whatever I shall ask of you, Tetrarch?

HERODIAS: Do not dance, my daughter.

HEROD: Whatever you shall ask of me, even up to the half of my kingdom.

SALOME: You swear it, Tetrarch?

HEROD: I swear it, Salome.

SALOME: By what will you swear this thing, Tetrarch?

HEROD: By my life, by my crown, by my gods O Salome, Salome, dance for me!

HERODIAS: My daughter, do not dance.

SALOME: You have sworn an oath, Tetrarch.

HEROD: I have sworn an oath, Salome.

HERODIAS: My daughter, do not dance.

**HÉRODE:** Fût-ce la moitié de mon royaume. Comme reine, comme reine, tu serais très belle. (*frémissant*), Ah! il fait froid ici! il y a un vent, très froid, et j'entends . . . pourquoi est-ce que j'entends dans l'air ce battement d'ailes? Oh! On dirait qu'il y a un oiseau, un grand oiseau noir qui plane sur la terrasse. Pourquoi est-ce que je ne peux pa le voir, cet oiseau? Le battement de ses ailes est terrible. C'est un vent froid . . . Mais non, il ne fait pas froid du tout. Il fait trop chaud. Versez-moi de l'eau sur les mains. Donnez-moi de la neige á manger. Dégrafez mon manteau. Vite! Vite! Non. Laissez-le. C'est ma couronne qui me fait mal. Ces fleurs sont faites de feu. (*Il arrache de sa tête la couronne et la jette sur la table.*) Ah! enfin, je respire. Maintenant je suis heureux. N'est-ce pas que vous allez danser pour moi, Salomé?

**HÉRODIAS:** Je ne veux pas qu'elle danse.

**SALOMÉ:** Je danserai pour vous, tétrarque.

**LA VOIX D'IOKANAAN:** Qui est celui qui vient d'Edom, qui est celui qui vient de Bosra avec sa robe teinte de pourpre qui éclate dans la beauté de ces vêtements, et qui marche avec une force toute puissante? Pourquoi vos vêtements sont ils teints d'écarlate?

**HÉRODIAS:** Rentrons. La voix de cet homme m'exaspère. Je ne veux pas que ma fille danse pendant qu'il crie comme cela. Je ne veux pas qu'elle danse pendant que vous la regardez comme cela. Enfin, je ne veux pas qu'elle danse.

**HÉRODE:** Ne te lève pas, mon épouse, ma reine, c'est inutile. Je ne rentrerai pas avant qu'elle ait dansé: Dansez, Salomé, dansez pour moi.

**HÉRODIAS:** Ne dansez pas, ma fille.

**SALOMÉ:** Je suis prête, tétrarque.

## LA DANSE DE SALOMÉ

*Les musiciens commencent à jouer une danse effrénée. Salomé, d'abord immobile, se redresse et fait un signe aux musiciens, qui par une transition rapide changent le rythme impétueux en une mélodie doucement berçante. Salomé exécute "la danse des sept voiles."*

**HEROD:** Even to the half of my kingdom. You will be passing fair as a queen, Salome, if it pleases you to ask for the half of my kingdom. Will she not be fair as a queen? Ah! it is cold here! There is an icy wind, and I hear . . . wherefore do I hear in the air this beating of wings? Ah! one might fancy a huge black bird that hovers over the terrace. Why can I not see this bird? The beating of its wings is terrible. The breath of the wind of its wings is terrible. It is a chill wind. No, but it is not cold, it is hot. I am choking. Pour water on my hands. Give me snow to eat. Loosen my mantle. Quick! quick! loosen my mantle. Nay. but leave it. It is my garland that hurts me, my garland of roses. The flowers are like fire. They have burned my forehead. (*He tears the wreath from his head, and throws it on the table.*) Ah! I can breathe now. How red those petals are! They are like stains of blood on the cloth. That does not matter. Now I am happy. I am passing happy. Have I not the right to be happy? Your daughter is going to dance for me. Salome? You have promised to dance for me.

**HERODIAS:** I will not have her dance.

**SALOME:** I will dance for you, Tetrarch.

**THE VOICE OF IOKANAAN:** Who is this who comes from Edom, who is this who comes from Bozra, whose raiment is dyed with purple, who shines in the beauty of his garments, who walks mightily in his greatness? Wherefore is your raiment stained with scarlet?

**HERODIAS:** Let us go within. The voice of that man maddens me. I will not have my daughter dance while he is continually crying out. I will not have her dance while you look at her in this fashion. In a word, I will not have her dance.

**HEROD:** Do not rise, my wife, my queen, it will avail you nothing. I will not go within till she has danced. Dance, Salome, dance for me.

**HERODIAS:** Do not dance, my daughter.

**SALOME:** I am ready Tetrarch.

## THE DANCE OF SALOME

*The musicians begin to play a furious dance. Salome, at first motionless, straightens herself and makes a sign to the musicians who, by a rapid transition, change the impetuous rythm to a sweetly lulling melody. Salome executes the 'Dance of the seven veils.'*

*Elle semble affaiblir un moment, puis recommence avec une fougue nouvelle. Elle reste un moment comme en extase au bord de la citerne dans laquelle Iokanaan est emprisonné, puis elle se précipite en avant aux pieds d'Hérode.*

**HÉRODE:** Ah! Ah! C'est magnifique, c'est magnifigue! (*à Hérodias*) Vous voyez qu'elle a dansé pour moi, votre fille. Approchez, Salomé! Approchez, afin que je puisse vous donner votre salaire. Toi, je te paierai bien. Je te donnerai tout ce que tu voudras . . . Que veux-tu, dis?

**SALOMÉ:** (*doux*) Présentement, dans un bassin d'argent . . .

**HÉRODE:** (*riant*) Dans un bassin d'argent? mais oui, . . . dans un bassin d'argent . . . certainement. Elle est charmante, n'est-ce pas? Qu'est-ce que voulez qu'on vous apporte dans un bassin d'argent, ma chère et belle Salomé, vous qui êtes la plus belle de toutes les filles de Judée? Qu'est-ce que vous voulez qu'on vous apporte dans un bassin d'argent? Dites-moi. Quoi que cela puisse être, on vous le donnera. Mes trésors vous appartiennent. Qu'est-ce que c'est, Salomé?

**SALOMÉ:** (*se levant*). La tête d'Iokanaan.

**HÉRODE:** Non, non.

**HÉRODIAS:** Ah! c'est bien dit, ma fille. C'est bien dit.

**HÉRODE:** Non, non. Salomé. Vous ne me demandez pas cella. N'écoutez pas votre mère. Elle vous donne toujours de mauvais conseils. Il ne faut pas l'écouter.

**SALOMÉ:** Je n'écoute pas ma mére. C'est pour mon propre plaisir que je demande la tête d'Iokanaan dans un bassin d'argent. Vous avez juré, Hérode. N'oubliez pas que vous avez juré.

**HÉRODE:** Je le sais. J'ai juré par mes dieux. Je le sais bien. Mais je vous supplie, Salomé, de me demander autre chose. Demandez-moi la moitié de mon royaume, et je vous la donnerai. Mais ne me demandez pas ce que vous m'avez demandé.

**SALOMÉ:** Je vous demande la tête d'Iokanaan.

**HÉRODE:** Non, non je ne veux pas.

**SALOMÉ:** Si! Vous avez juré, Hérode.

**HÉRODIAS:** Oui, vous avez juré. Tout le monde vous a entendu.

**HÉRODE:** Taisez-vous. Ce n'est pas à vous que je parle.

*She appears to weaken for a moment, then begins again with renewed passion. She remains for an instant as in ecstacy at the edge of the cistern in which Iokanaan is imprisoned, then rushes forward to Herod's feet.*

**HEROD:** Ah! wonderful! wonderful! You see that she has danced for me, your daughter. Come near, Salome, come near, that I may give you your fee. Ah! I pay a royal price to those who dance for my pleasure. I will pay you royally. I will give you whatever your soul desires. What would you have? Speak.

**SALOME:** (*Kneeling*) I would like that they presently bring me in a silver charger . . .

**HEROD:** (*Laughing*) In a silver charger? Surely yes, in a silver charger. She is charming, is she not? What is it you would have in the silver charger, O sweet and fair Salome. you that are fairer than all the daughters of Judaea? What would you have them bring you in a silver charger? Tell me. Whatever it may be. You shall receive it. My treasures belong to you. What is it that you would have, Salome?

**SALOME:** (*Rising*). The head of Iokanaan.

**HEROD:** No, no!

**HERODIAS:** That is well said, my daughter.

**HEROD:** No, no Salome. It is not that you desire. Do not listen to your mother's voice. She is ever giving you evil counsel. Do not heed her.

**SALOME:** It is not my mother's voice that I heed. It is for my own pleasure that I ask the head of Iokanaan in a silver charger. You have sworn an oath, Herod. Forget not that you have sworn an oath.

**HEROD:** I know it. I have taken an oath by my gods. I know it well. But I pray you, Salome. ask of me something else. Ask of me the half of my kingdom, and I will give it to you. But do not of me what your lips have asked.

**SALOME:** I ask you for the head of Iokanaan.

**HEROD:** No, no, I will not give it to you.

**SALOME:** You have sworn an oath, Herod.

**HERODIAS:** Yes, you have sworn an oath. Everybody heard you. You swore it before everybody.

**HEROD:** Peace, woman! I do not speak to you!

**HÉRODIAS:** Ma fille a bien raison de demander la tête de cet homme. Il a vomi des insultes contre moi. On voit qu'elle aime beaucoup sa mère. Ne cédez pas, ma fille, ne cédez pas. Il a juré, il a juré.

**HÉRODE:** Taisez vous. Ne me parlez pas . . . Voyons, Salomé, il faut être raisonnable, n'est-ce pas? Salomé, je vous ai toujours aimée . . . Peut-être je vous ai trop aimée. Ainsi, ne me demandez pas cela. La tête d'un homme décapité, n'est-ce pas, c'est une chose laide? Écoutez-moi un instant. J'ai une émeraude. C'est la plus grande émeraude du monde. N'est-ce pas que vous la voulez? Demandez-moi cela et je vous la donnerai, la plus grande émeraude.

**SALOMÉ:** Je demande la tête d'Iokanaan.

**HÉRODE:** Vous ne m'écoutez pas, vous ne m'écoutez pas. Enfin, laissez-moi parler, Salomé.

**SALOMÉ:** La tête d'Iokanaan.

**HÉRODE:** Vous me dites cela seulement pour me faire de la peine, parce que je vous ai regardée toute la soirée. Votre beauté m'a terriblement troublé. Oh oh! du vin! j'ai soif. Salomé, Salomé, soyons amis. Enfin, voyez . . . Ah! qu'est-ce que je voulais dire? Qu'est-ce c'était? Ah! je m'en souviens! . . . Salomé, vous connaissez mes paons blancs, mes beaux paons blancs qui se promènent dans le jardin entre les myrtes. Il n'y a pas dans le monde d'oiseaux si merveilleux. Il n'y a aucun roi du monde qui possède des oiseaux aussi merveilleux. Je n'en ai que cent. Je vous les donnerai tous.

**SALOMÉ:** Donnez-moi la tête d'Iokanaan.

**HÉRODIAS:** C'est bien dit, ma fille! Vous, vous êtes ridicule avec vos paons.

**HÉRODE:** Taisez-vous. Vous criez toujours comme une bête de proie. Votre voix m'ennuie. Taisez-vous, je vous dis . . . Salomé, pensez à ce que vous faites. Cet homme vient peut-être de Dieu. Je suis sûr; c'est un saint homme. Le doigt de Dieu l'a touché. Eh bien! Salomé, vous ne voulez pas qu'un malheur m'arrive? Enfin, écoutez-moi.

**SALOMÉ:** Donnez-moi la tête d'Iokanaan.

**HÉRODE:** Ah! vous voyez, vous ne m'écoutez pas. Soyez calme. Moi, je suis tres calme. Écoutez: J'ai des bijoux cachés ici que même votre mère n'a jamais vus, des bijoux tout

**HERODIAS:** My daughter has done well to ask for the head of Iokanaan. He has covered me with insults. He has said unspeakable things against me. One can see that she loves her mother well. Do not yield, my daughter. He has sworn an oath, he has sworn an oath.

**HEROD:** Peace! Do not Speak to me! . . . Salome. I pray you don't be stubborn. I have ever been kind toward you. Therefore, do not ask this thing of me. The head of a man that is cut from the body is ill to look upon, is it not? No, no, it is not that that you desire. Listen to me. I have an emerald, a great emerald and round, that the minion of Caesar has sent to me. When you look through this emerald you can see that which happens far away. It is the largest emerald in the whole world. Ask it of me and I will give it to you.

**SALOME:** I demand the head of Iokanaan.

**HEROD:** You are not listening. You are not listening. Allow me to speak, Salome.

**SALOME:** The head of Iokanaan!

**HEROD:** No, no, you would not have that. You say that to trouble me, because I have looked at you and not ceased this night. Your beauty has grievously troubled me, and I have looked at you too much. Oh! oh! bring wine! I thirst . . . Salome, Salome, let us be friends. Just think, Salome, you know my beautiful white peacocks, that walk in the garden between the myrtles and the tall cypress trees . . . I have got a hundred. But I will give them all to you Only you must loose me from my oath, and must not ask of me that which your lips have asked me.

**SALOME:** Give me the head of Iokanaan!

**HERODIAS:** Well said, my daughter! As for you, you are ridiculous with your peacocks.

**HEROD:** Peace! You cry like a beast of prey. Your voice wearies me. Peace, I tell you! . . . Salome, think on what you are doing. It may be that this man comes from God. He is a holy man. The finger of God has touched him. God has put terrible words into his mouth. If he dies also, perhaps some evil may befall me. You would not that some evil should befall me, Salome? Listen to me again.

**SALOME:** Give me the head of Iokanaan!

**HEROD:** Ah! You are not listening to me. Be calm. As for me, am I not calm? Listen. I have jewels hidden in this place—jewels that your mother even has never seen; jewels

à fait extraordinaires. J'ai un collier de perles à quatre rangs. J'ai des topazes jaunes commes les yeux des tigres, des topazes roses comme les yeux des pigeons, des topazes vertes comme les yeux des chats. J'ai des opales qui brûlent toujours avec une flamme qui est très froide. Je vous les donnerai tous, mais tous (*toujours plus excité*) Moi, j'ai des chrysolithes et des béryls, j'ai des chrysoprases et des rubis. J'ai des sardonyx et des hyacinthes, et des calcédoines. Je vous les donnerai tous, mais tous, et j'ajouterai d'autres choses. J'ai un cristal qu'il n'est pas permis aux femmes de voir. Dans un coffret de nacre j'ai trois turquoises merveilleuses. Quand on les porte sur le front, on peut imaginer des choses qui n'existent pas. Ce sont des trésors de grande valeur. Enfin, que veux-tu, Salomé? Je te donnerai tout ce que tu demanderas, sauf une chose. Je te donnerai tout ce que je possède, sauf une vie. Je te donnerai le manteau du grand prêtre. Je te donnerai le voile du sanctuaire.

**LES JUIFS:** Oh! oh! oh!

**SALOMÉ:** (*féroce*). Donnez-moi la tête d'Iokanaan.

**HÉRODE:** (*épuisé s'affaissant sur son siège.*) Qu'on lui donne ce qu'elle demande! C'est bien la fille de sa mère! (*Hérodias prend de la main du tétrarque la bague de la mort et la donne au premier soldat qui l'apporte immédiatement au bourreau.*) Qui a pris ma bague? (*Le bourreau descend dans la citerne*) Il y avait une bague à ma main droite. Qui a bu mon vin? Il y avait du vin dans ma coupe. Elle était pleine de vin. Quelqu'un l'a bu? Oh! je suis sûr qu'il va arriver un malheur à quelqu'un.

**HÉRODIAS:** Je trouve que ma fille a bien fait.

**HÉRODE:** Je suis sûr qu'il va arriver un malheur.

**SALOMÉ:** (*elle se penche sur la citerne et écoute.*) Il n'y a pas de bruit. Je n'entends rien. Pourquoi ne crie-t-il pas cet homme? Ah! si quelqu'un cherchait à me tuer, je crierais, je me débattrais, je ne voudrais pas souffrir . . . Frappe, frappe, Naaman. Frappe, je te dis . . . Non, je n'entends rien. Il y a un silence affreux. Ah! quelque chose est tombé par terre. J'ai entendu quelque chose tomber. C'était l'épée du bourreau. Il a peur, cet esclave! Il a laissé tomber son épée. Il n'ose pas le tuer. C'est

that are marvellous to look at. I have a collar of pearls, set in four rows. I have topazes yellow as the eyes of tigers, and topazes that are pink as the eyes of a wood-pigeon, and green topazes that are like the eyes of cats. I have opals that burn always, with a flame that is cold as ice, opals that make sad men's minds, and are afraid of the shadows. I have chrysolites and beryls, and chrysophrases and rubies; I have sardonyx and hyacinth stones, and stones of chalcedony, and I will give them all to you all, and other things I will add to them. I have a crystal, into which it is not lawful for a woman to look, nor may young men behold it until they have been beaten with rods. In a coffer of nacre I have three wondrous turquoises. He who wears them on his forehead can imagine things which are not, and he who carries them in his hand can turn the fruitful woman into a woman that is barren. These are great treasures above all price. What do you desire more than this, Salome! Tell me the thing that you desire and I will give it to you. I will give you all that is mine, save only the life of one man. I will give you the mantle of the high priest. I will give you the veil of the sanctuary.

**THE JEWS:** Oh! oh!

**SALOME:** Give me the head of Iokanaan!

**HEROD:** (*Sinking in his seat.*) Let her be given what she asks! She is her mother's child! (*The first soldier approaches. HERODIAS draws from the hand of the Tetrarch the ring of death, and gives it to the Soldier, who straightway bears it to the Executioner. The Executioner looks scared.*) Who has taken my ring? There was a ring on my right hand. Who has drunk my wine? There was wine in my cup. It was full of wine. Some one has drunk it. Oh! surely some evil will befall some one. (*The executioner goes down in the cistern.*)

**HERODIAS:** My daughter has done well.

**HEROD:** I am sure that misfortune will happen.

**SALOME:** (*She leans over the cistern and listens.*) There is no sound. I hear nothing. Why does he not cry out, this man? Ah! if any man sought to to kill me, I would cry out, I would struggle, I would not suffer . . . Strike, strike, Naaman. No, I hear silence, a terrible silence. Ah! something has fallen upon the ground. I heard something fall. It was the sword of the executioner. He is afraid, this slave. He has dropped his sword. He is a coward, this slave! Let soldiers be sent. (*She sees the Page of Hero-*

un lâche, cet esclave! Il faut envoyer des soldats. (*Elle voit le page d'Hérodias et s'adresse à lui.*) Viens ici. Tu as été l'ami de celui qui est mort, n'est-ce pas? Eh bien, il n'y a pas eu assez de morts. Dites aux soldats qu'ils descendent et m'apportent ce que je demande, ce que le tétrarque m'a promis, ce qui m'appartient. (*Le page recule. Elle s'adresse aux soldats.*) Venez ici, soldats. Descendez dans cette citerne, et apportez-moi la tête de cet homme. (*Les soldats reculent.*) Tétrarque, tétrarque, commandez à vos soldats d'apporter la tête d'Iokanaan. (*Un grand bras noir, le bras du bourreau, sort de la citerne portant sur un bouclier d'argent la tête d'Iokanaan. Hérode se cache le visage avec son manteau . . . Hérodias sourit et s'évente. Les Nazaréens s'agenouillent et commencent à prier. Salomé saisit la tête.*)

Ah! tu n'as pas voulu me laisser baiser ta bouche, Iokanaan. Eh bien! je la baiserai maintenant. Je la mordrai avec mes dents. Je la mordrai avec mes dents comme on mord un fruit mûr. Oui, je baiserai ta bouche, Iokanaan. Je te l'ai dit, n'est-ce pas? je te l'ai dit? Ah! Ah! Je la baiserai maintenant . . . Mais pourquoi ne me regardes-tu pas, Iokanaan? Tes yeux si terribles, si pleins de colère et de mépris, ils sont fermés maintenant. Pourquoi sont-ils fermés? Ouvre tes yeux! Soulève tes paupières, Iokanaan. Pourquoi ne me regards-tu pas? As-tu peur de moi, Iokanaan, que tu ne veux pas me regarder? . . . Et ta langue, elle ne remue plus, Iokanaan, cette vipère rouge qui a vomi son venin sur moi. C'est étrange, n'est-ce pas? Comment se fait-il que la vipère rouge ne remue plus? Tu m'as traitée comme une courtisane, moi, Salomé, la fille d'Hérodias, Princesse de Judée! Eh bien, Iokanaan, moi je vis encore, mais toi tu es mort et ta tête, ta tête m'appartient. Je puis en faire ce que je veux. Je puis la jeter aux chiens et aux oiseaux de l'air. Ce que laisseront les chiens, les oiseaux de l'air le mangeront.. Ah! Ah! Iokanaan, Iokanaan, tu étais beau. Ton corps était une colonne d'ivoire sur un socle d'argent. C'était un jardin plein de colombes et de lis, de lis d'argent. Riend' aussi blanc que ton corps, rien n'était aussi noir que tes cheveux. Dans le monde tout entier il n'y avait rien d'aussi rouge que ta bouche. Ta

dias and addresses him.*) Come here you were a friend of the dead man weren't you? Well, I tell you, there are not dead men enough. Go to the soldiers and bid them go down and bring me the thing I ask, the thing the Tetrarch has promised me, the thing that is mine. (*The Page recoils, She turns to the soldiers.*) Come here, soldiers. Go down into this cistern and bring me the head of this man. Tetrarch, Tetrarch, command your soldiers that they bring me the head of Iokanaan. (*A huge black arm, the arm of the Executioner comes forth from the cistern, bearing on a silver shield the head of Iokanaan. Salome seizes it. Herod hides his face with his cloak. Herodias smiles and fans herself. The Nazarenes fall on their knees and begin to pray.*)

Ah! You would not allow me to kiss your mouth, Iokanaan. Well! I will kiss it now. But why do you not look at me, Iokanaan? Your eyes that rage and scorn, are shut now. Are you afraid of me, Iokanaan, that you will not look at me? . . . And your tongue, that was like a red snake darting poison, it moves no more, it speaks no words, Iokanaan, that scarlet viper that spat its venom upon me. It is strange, is it not? you did bear yourself toward me as to a harlot, as to a woman that is a wanton, to me, Salome, daughter of Herodias, Princess of Judaea! Well, I still live, but you are dead, and your head belongs to me. I can do with it what I will. I can throw it to the dogs and to the birds of the air . . . Ah, Iokanaan, Iokanaan, you were the man that I loved alone among men! Your body was a column of ivory set upon feet of silver. It was a garden full of doves and lilies of silver. It was a tower of silver decked with shields of ivory. There was nothing in the world so white as your body. There was nothing in the world so black as your hair. In the whole world there was nothing so red as your mouth. Your voice was a censer that scattered strange perfumes, and when I looked on you I heard a strange music. Ah! why didn't you look at me, Iokanaan? You put on your eyes the covering of him who would see his God. Well, you have seen your God, Iokanaan, but me, me, you did never see. If you had seen me you had loved me. I saw you, and I

voix était un encensoir qui répandait d'étranges parfums, et quand je te regardais, j'entendais une musique étrange! Oh! pourquoi ne m'as-tu pas regardée, Iokanaan? Tu as mis sur tes yeux le bandeau de celui qui veut voir son Dieu. Eh bien! tu l'as vu, ton Dieu, Iokanaan, mais moi, moi . . . tu ne m'as jamais vue. Si tu m'avais vue, tu m'aurais aimée. J'ai soif de ta beauté. J'ai faim de ton corps. Et ni le vin, ni les fruits ne peuvent apaiser mon désir. Que ferai-je, maintenant, Iokanaan? . . . Ni les fleuves ni les grandes eaux, ne pourraient éteindre ma passion. Ah! pourquoi ne m'as-tu pas regardée? Si tu m'aurais regardée, tu m'aurais aimée. Je sais bien que tu m'aurais aimée, et le mystère de l'amour est plus grand que le mystère de la mort.

**HÉRODE:** (*à voix basse à Hérodias.*) Elle est monstrueuse, ta fille, elle est tout à fait monstrueuse.

**HÉRODIAS:** J'approuve ce que ma fille a fait, et je veux rester ici maintenant.

**HÉRODE:** Ah! l'épouse incestueuse qui parle! Viens! Je ne veux pas rester ici. (*Violent.*) Viens, je te dis. Je suis sûr qu'il va arriver un malheur. Cachons-nous dans notre palais, Hérodias. Je commence à avoir peur.
(*Un grand nuage noir passe sur la lune et la cache complètement.*) Manassé, Issachar, Ozias, éteignez les flambeaux. Cachez la lune, cachez les étoiles. (*La scène devient tout à fait sombre.*) Il va arriver un malheur.

**SALOMÉ:** (*épuisée.*) Ah! j'ai baisé ta bouche, Iokanaan. Ah! j'ai baisé ta bouche. Il y avait une âcre saveur sur tes lèvres. Etait-ce la saveur du sang? . . . Mais peut-être, est-ce la saveur de l'amour. On dit que l'amour a une âcre saveur . . . Mais qu'importe? Qu'importe? J'ai baisé ta bouche, Iokanaan. J'ai baisé ta bouche, Iokannan.
(*Un rayon de lune tombe sur Salomé et l'éclaire.*)

**HÉRODE:** (*se retournane et voyant Salomé*). Tuez cette femme!
(*Les soldats s'élancent et écrasent Salomé sus leurs boucliers.*)

*FIN.*

loved you . . . I am thirsty for your beauty; I am hungry for your body; and neither wine nor apples can appease my desire. What shall I do now, Iokanaan? Neither the floods nor the great waters can quench my passion. Ah! ah! Why didn't you look at me? If you had looked at me you had loved me. Well I know that you would have loved me, and the mystery of Love is greater than the mystery of Death.

**HEROD:** (*in a low voice to Herodias.*) She is monstrous, your daughter! I tell you; she is monstrous.

**HERODIAS:** I am well pleased with my daughter. She has done well. And I would stay here now.

**HEROD:** (*Rising*). Ah! There speaks my brother's wife! Come! I will not stay in this place. Come, I tell you. Surely some terrible thing will befall. (*A great cloud crosses the moon and conceals it completely.*) Manasseh, Issachar, Ozias, put out the torches. Hide the moon. Hide the stars! Let us hide ourselves in our palace, Herodias. I begin to be afraid.

**SALOME:** (*exhausted*). Ah! I have kissed your mouth, Iokanaan, I have kissed your mouth. There was a bitter taste on your lips. Was it the taste of blood? No; but perchance it was the taste of love . . . They say that love has a bitter taste. But what does it matter? I have kissed your mouth, Iokanaan. I have kissed your mouth.
(*A ray of moonlight falls on SALOME and illumines her.*)

**HEROD:** (*Turning around and seeing SALOME.*) Kill that woman!
(*The soldiers rush forward and crush beneath their shields SALOME, daughter of HERODIAS, Princess of Judaea.*)

*THE END.*

# Elektra (1909)

MUSIC BY RICHARD STRAUSS ■ LIBRETTO BY HUGO VON HOFMANNSTHAL

A tragedy in one act, Elektra is set to a libretto by Hugo von Hofmannsthal after Sophocles. It was first performed at the Königliches Opernhaus in Dresden on January 25, 1909. In the courtyard of the palace of the Atridae in Mycenae, serving women make fun of Elektra, disgraced daughter of King Agamemnon. Elektra remembers her father's murder—her mother, Klytaimnestra, helped her lover, Aegisth, stab him. Klytaimnestra herself delivered the fatal blow with an ax. Dreaming of revenge, Elektra calls upon her deceased father for help. Chrysothemis, her sister, comes to tell her that their mother and Aegisth are planning to imprison her.

Klytaimnestra is preparing for a sacrifice. She will ask the gods to free her from nightmares that plague her sleep. On seeing Elektra, she lashes out at her, then speaks calmly, thinking she can obtain a cure for her nightmares once and for all. She will sacrifice whatever or whomever is demanded. Elektra takes Klytaimnestra to see Orest, her son—the spirit in Klytaimnestra's dreams that is seeking vengeance. But Klytaimnestra threatens to imprison Elektra unless Elektra tells her what the offering is to be. Elektra answers that Klytaimnestra herself is the chosen sacrifice. The Queen's confidante enters with news that Orest is dead. Elektra asks her sister to help, but Chrysothemis, horrified, runs off. Elektra digs for a hidden ax, chastising the messenger for surviving his master's death. The messenger, Orest, tells his sister that Orest lives. Although the servants recognize him at once, Elektra refuses to accept him until he makes a statement that undeniable identifies him. Blessing him, she mourns her lost beauty in the quest for revenge. Orest, eager for vengeance, enters the palace with his tutor; Elektra waits in front. From inside, Klytaimnestra screams. Aegisth tries to go to her but Elektra detains him. Orest succeeds in avenging Agamemnon's death. Elektra and Chrysothemis sing a duet in celebration of their freedom. Elektra dances on her father's grave in triumph, then collapses lifeless on the ground.

---

*(Une cour intérieure jormée par l'ardière-palais et les communs où logent les serviteurs.—Des servantes sont groupées autour du puits, sur le devant et la côte gauche de la scène. Parmi elles La Surveillante.)*

**PREMIÈRE SERVANTE:** *(soulevant sa cruche).* Où est Elektra?

**DEUXIÈME SERVANTE:** C'est pourtant son heure,
C'est l'heure où le nom
De son père hurlant,
Elle en ébranle les murs.
*(Elektra sort en courant d'une galerie déjà pleine d'ombre. Toutes se tournent vers elle.— Elektra, le bras levé devant sa figure, fait un saut en arrière, comme un animal regagnant son terrier.)*

**PREMIÈRE SERVANTE:** Avez-vous vu? quels regards sur nous?

**DEUXIÈME SERVANTE:** Telle une sauvage chatte.

**TROISIÈME SERVANTE:** Là, je l'ai vue hier, geignante …

**PREMIÈRE SERVANTE:** Toujours, au soleil couchant, là, prostrée, elle geint.

**TROISIÈME SERVANTE:** A deux nous l'approchâmes,
Peut-être de trop près …

*(An interior court formed by the rear of the palace and the servants' quarters.—The maids are grouped around the well, which is at the left side of stage, near front.—Among them is the Surveillante.)*

**FIRST MAID:** *(lifting her jug)* Where is she Elektra?

**SECOND MAID:** It is now the hour when
She shouts aloud her father's name,
The walls echoing her noise.
*(Elektra rushes from a gallery hidden in shadow.—All turn towards her.—Elektra, her arm raised before her face, springs backwards, like an animal regaining its burrow.)*

**FIRST MAID:** Did you see?
Oh, how she looks at us!

**SECOND MAID:** Like a wild cat, no less.

**THIRD MAID:** I saw her there yesterday, moaning …

**FIRST MAID:** At sunset there she always kneels and moans.

**THIRD MAID:** We both approached her,
Perhaps too closely.

**PREMIÈRE SERVANTE:** Elle a horreur qu'on la regarde.

**TROISIÈME SERVANTE:** Oui, nous vinmes un peu près;
Soufflant alors comme une chatte vers nous:
"Hou! mouches" fit-elle "Hou!"

**QUATRIÈME SERVANTE:** "Hou! mouches, hou!"

**TROISIÈME SERVANTE:** "Fuyez loin de mes plaines!"
Et son balai de loin menace.

**QUATRIÈME SERVANTE:** "Hou! mouches, hou!"

**TROISIÈME SERVANTE:** "Ne venez pas ici vous gaver de mes pleurs.
Ne pompez pas l'écume de ma bouche amère."

**QUATRIÈME SERVANTE:** "Fuyez, cachez-vous," nous cria-t-elle;
"Mangez gras, et bouvez doux,
Allez au lit avec vos hommes, allez!"
Mais elle …

**TROISIÈME SERVANTE:** J'eus bientôt fait …

**QUATRIÈME SERVANTE:** … sût lui répondre!

**TROISIÈME SERVANTE:** "Mais, lorsque tu as faim,"
Lui répondis-je, 'tu mang' aussi!'
Elle bondit, darda quels affreux regards,

**FIRST MAID:** She dislikes to be watched.

**THIRD MAID:** Yes, we came too near;
Breathing like a cat towards us:
"Shoo! flies," she cried, "Shoo!"

**FOURTH MAID:** "Shoo! flies, shoo!"

**THIRD MAID:** "Far from my plains begone!"
And with her broom menaced us.

**FOURTH MAID:** "Shoo! flies, shoo!"

**THIRD MAID:** "Don't come here to mock my tears,
"Don't suck the foam from my bitter mouth."

**FOURTH MAID:** "Go, hide yourself," she cried to us:
"Eat meat, and drink but little,
Go to bed—begone!"
But she …

**THIRD MAID:** I would soon …

**FOURTH MAID:** Know how to answer her!

**THIRD MAID:** "But when you are hungry,"
I told her, "you also eat!"
She sprang at me, her eyes ablaze,
Her fingers clawing, and she shout-

Et, comme des griffes, crispa ses doigts vers nous, criant:
"C'est un vautour qui de moi même ai nourit!"

**DEUXIÈME SERVANTE:** Et toi?

**TROISIÈME SERVANTE:** "Tu aimes t'accroupir," dis-je, "Où t'attire l'odeur de pourriture, Tu grattes après un vieux cadavre."

**DEUXIÈME SERVANTE:** Alors qu'a-t-elle dit?

**TROISIÈME SERVANTE:** Hurlante, dans son coin elle s'est rejetée.

**PREMIÈRE SERVANTE:** Pourquoi donc la Reine Laisse-t-elle pareil demon aller, Venir, dans la maison?

**DEUXIÈME SERVANTE:** Sa propre enfant!

**PREMIÈRE SERVANTE:** Ah! fut-elle ma fille, Moi, par dieu! Je la mettrais sous grilles!

**QUATRIÈME SERVANTE:** Sont-ils pas pour elle assez barbares? Son émelle, sa pâtée, voisinent avec celles des bêtes! *(Soupirant:)* N'as-tu pas vu le Maitre la frapper?

**CINQUIÈME SERVANTE:** *(toute jeune, avec une voix tremblante et émue).* Je veux me jeter à genoux devant Elle et baisser ses pieds nus! Na'a-t-elle pas un Roi pour père, Celle qui souffre tels outrages? Ses pieds je veux les oindre, Et que mes cheveux les sèchent.

**LA SURVEILLANTE:** *(la poussant)* Veux-tu rentrer!

**CINQUIÈME SERVANTE:** Il n'est rien, sachez-le, De royal autant qu'elle en ce monde Elle git en haillons devant la porte, Mais personne, personne ici n'oserait N'oserait braver son regard.

**LA SURVEILLANTE:** *(la poussant du côté de la porte basse, ouverte, à gauche de la scène).* Allons!

**CINQUIÈME SERVANTE:** *(s'accrochant la porte).* Comment osez-vous respirer Cet air qu'elle même respire! Toutes, puisse-je un jour, Toutes, vous voir pendues Dans une grange obscure, Oui, pendues, juste salaire Des maux par Elektra soufferts!

**LA SURVEILLANTE:** *(ferme la porte sur elle).* L'entends-tu? Nous, nous qu'Elektra, Dès qu'on l'invite à notre propre table. Ose insulter insolemment; Elle crache vers nous, de chiennes nous traite.

---

ed: "It is a vulture whom I nourished!"

**SECOND MAID:** And you?

**THIRD MAID:** "You love to squat," I said, "Where the odor of dust attracts you, You scratch at graves!"

**SECOND MAID:** What did she say then?

**THIRD MAID:** Yelling, she fled to her corner.

**FIRST MAID:** Why does the Queen Allow a demon such as she, To come and go about the house?

**SECOND MAID:** Her own child!

**FIRST MAID:** Ah! were she my daughter, Rest assured, I'd place her Well behind the bars!

**FOURTH MAID:** Are they not cruel enough to her? Feeding her with food for beasts! *(Sighing):* Have you not seen the Master beat her?

**FIFTH MAID:** *(very young, in a trembling voice).* I fain would kneel before her, And kiss her naked feet! Has she not a King as father, She who suffers these insults? Her feet, I would anoint them, And dry them with my hair.

**THE SURVEILLANTE:** *(pushing her away).* Will you go in!

**FIFTH MAID:** There is nothing, you know, As royal as she in this world. She lies in rags before the door, But no one here would dare to face her.

**THE SURVEILLANTE:** *(pushing her towards the low door, which is open, at the left of stage).* Go!

**FIFTH MAID:** *(laying hold of the door).* How dare you breathe This air she breathes! May I see you all some day Hung in a darksome barn, Ah, hung, and justly, too. For the evils Elektra suffers!

**THE SURVEILLANTE:** *(closing the door upon her).* Do you hear her? We, who Elektra dares insult. When to our own table she is asked, We are treated, well, like dogs.

---

**PREMIÈRE SERVANTE:** Oui, elle a dit:
Pas un chien ne veut s'abaisser À cet ouvrage qui est le vôtre: En vain vous voulez effacer Avec de l'eau l'eneffaçable sang du meurtre Qui toujours suinte."

**TROISIÈME SERVANTE:** "Mais opprobre," ajouta-t-elle, "L'opprobre, qui nuit et jour se renouvelle, Quelle eau l'efface?"

**PREMIÈRE SERVANTE:** "Votre corps semble raidi par la crasse Dont il est l'esclave!" *(Les servantes portent les cruches dans la maison, à gauche.)*

**LA SURVEILLANTE:** *(qui leur a ouvert la porte).* Quand elle nous voit avec nos enfants, elle s'écrie:—
"Rien n'est plus immonde, rien, que ces enfants, qu'en chiennes, Sur les marches de sang glissantes, là, dans la maison, Vous avez conçus et enfantés." Oui ou non, le dit-elle?

**PREMIÈRE SERVANTE:** Le dit-elle, oui ou non? *(La Surveillante rentre, la porte se ferme.)*

**DEUXIÈME SERVANTE:** *(s'en allant).* Oui, oui.

**TOUTES:** *(l'intérieur).* Oui, oui.

**TROISIÈME et QUATRIÈME SERVANTE:** Oui, oui, oui, oui.

**LA CINQUIÈME SERVANTE:** Oui, oui.
*(De l'intérieur:)*
On m'a battue!
*(Elektra sort de la maison.)*

**ELEKTRA:** Toute seule! Ah! toute seule! Le père mort, roulé au fond du noir et froid abîme . . .
*(Tout contre le sol:)*
Agamemnon! Agamemnon! O mon père! N'as tu pas la force de trainer Jusqu'à moi ton cher visage?
*(A voix basse:)*
C'est juste l'heure, c'est notre heure, Oui, c'est l'heure où jadis ils te frappèrent, Ta femme et Lui, celui qui, dans ta couche, Dans ta royale couche, avec elle dort. Ils te frappèrent nu dans ton bain, ton sang Giola sur tes paupières, Et le bain fut rouge de sang fumant. Il te prit, lui, lui le lâche, aux épaules, Te tirant ainsi hors de la chambre! tête en avant; Tes jambes balayaient la tèrre. Tes yeux paraissaient béants, regardaient la maison. Tu reviendras de même, pas à pas,

---

**FIRST MAID:** Yes, she has often said:
A dog wouldn't stoop To work like yours; In vain you seek with water to efface The ineffaceable blood of murder, Which always oozes and remains.

**THIRD MAID:** "But the sin," she added, "The sin which night and day renews itself, What water shall efface?"

**FIRST MAID:** "Your body seems stiff with dirt, Of which it is the slave." *(The maids carry the jugs into the house, at left.)*

**THE SURVEILLANTE:** *(who has opened the door for them).* When she sees us with our children, Then she cries:—
"Nothing is more unclean than these children, who like dogs, Upon the slippery, bloodstained steps of yonder house, You have conceived and nursed." Yes or no, this did she say?

**FIRST MAID:** Did she say this, yes or no? *(The Surveillante goes in, the door is closed.)*

**SECOND MAID:** *(going).* Yes, yes.

**ALL:** *(within).* Yes, yes.

**THIRD and FOURTH MAIDS:** Yes, yes, yes, yes.

**THE FIFTH MAID:** Yes, yes.
*(From within:)*
They have beaten me,
*(Elektra comes out of the house.)*

**ELEKTRA:** All alone! Ah! All alone! The father dead, consigned to the dark, cold, desolate depths . . . Agamemnon! Agamemnon! O my father! Can't I behold again Your countenance so dear to me?
*(In a low voice:)*
It is the hour, yours and mine, Yes, it is the hour when they struck you, Your wife and he who in thy couch, Your royal couch, sleeps with her. They struck you naked in your bath, That bath was red with foaming blood. He took you, he the coward, by the shoulders, And dragged you thus, head foremost, from the room; Your feet trailing the ground. Your eyes, wide open, looked around you. You shall return like this, step by step, and suddenly. And your eyes shall be wide open staring. And the royal circlet shall again adorn thy brow—

Là, tout à coup, debout,
Et tes deux yeux seront grands ouverts,
Et le bandeau royal ciendra de nouveau ton front
Le pourpre bandeau de ta plaie.
Agamemnon! Père!
Je veux te voir, aujourd'hui parais encor!
Comme tu fis hier, comme une ombre,
La, dans l'ombre,
Viens vers ton enfant!
Père! Agamemnon, que ton jour vienne.
Comme tombe des astres une pluie de feu,
Qu'ainsi le sang, jailli des gorges tombe sur la tombe!
Et comme d'urnes renversées
Puisse-t-il s'écouler du flanc des meurtriers;
Ainsi qu'un ruisseau gonflé qu'um fleuve qui se précipite,
Tu vas sortir, ô vie des défuntes vies
...
(*Solonnellement pathétique.*)
Et tes cheveaux de guerre, ô mon Père,
Tous, seront trainés vers ta tombe.
Dans l'air ils hennirout, pressentant leur sort,
Et que c'est l'heure où il faut qu'il meurent.
Nous t'immolerons tes chiens,
Ceux qui léchaient les pieds
Qui suivaient tes chasses, que te mains aimaient repaître,
Leur sang coulera vers toi, pour to servir encor,
Et nous, nous, ton sang, ton fils Orest.
Et des deux filles, tous trois, la tâche accomplie,
Sous la voûte empourprée des vapeurs,
De sang pareilles à celles que traine le soleil
Nous danserons, tous trois autour de ta tombe.
(*Encore plus inspiré et pathétique.*)
Et les genoux levés, bondissant, haut,
Je franchirai les morts,
Et tous ceux-là qui me verront,
Pareille a quelqu'ombre dansante,
Ainsi ceux-là me voyant pourront se dire:
"C'est un grand, un grand roi,
Qu'en ces lieux aujourd'hui célèbrent
Sa propre chair, son sang,
Heureux le père de tels enfants qui près
De sa haute tombe dansent si gaiement
Ces royales danses.
Agamemnon! Agamemnon!"

**CHRYSOTHÉMIS:** (*sa soeur, plus jeune, debout devant la porte.—A voix basse*). Elektra!
(*Elektra sursaute de frayeur, et comme sourtant d'un rêve, regarde du côté de Chrysothémis.*)

The purple circlet of your wound
Agamemnon! O my father!
I would see you once again today!
And yesterday you came like a shadow.
In the shadow yonder,
Approach your child!
O my father! O my father!
Agamemnon! May your day be born,
As a rain of fire descends from the stars.
And may the blood from severed throats fall upon your tomb!
And like urns upturned,
May it flow from out the assassin's side;
Like a swollen brook or like a river in flood,
You shall come forth, O life of dead lives ...
(*Solemnly pathetic:*)
And your war horses, O my father,
They also shall be led to your tomb.
They shall neigh aloud, foreseeing their fate,
And knowing their hour of death has come.
We shall offer up to you your dogs,
The dogs that licked your feet,
That went with you to hunt, that your hands caressed,
Their blood shall be before you to save you again.
And we, your offspring, your son Orestes
And your two daughters, their duty done,
Under the purple vault of vapors,
Like those of the sun when it burns red,
We three shall dance around your tomb.
(*More inspired and pathetic:*)
Skipping high, I shall leap over the dead,
And all who there behold me,
Dancing like a shade, shall say:
"It is a mighty monarch
Who is here extolled today
By those who are his kin and offspring.
Ah! happy parent, whose children thus
Do honor at his tomb, and dance the royal dances.
Agamemnon! Agamemnon!"

**CHRYSOTHEMIS:** (*her younger sister, standing before the door; in a low voice*). Elektra!
(*Elektra, frightened, and as if awaking suddenly from a dream, looks towards Chrysothemis.*)

**ELEKTRA:** Ah! ce visage!

**CHRYSOTHÉMIS:** (*toujours sur le pas de la porte*). Est-il pour toi si haïssable?

**ELEKTRA:** (*brusquement*). Que veux-tu?
Parle, dis explique toi, puis va, va-t-en, va!
(*Chrysothémis lève ses mains comme pour se défendre.*)

**ELEKTRA:** Que veut dire ce geste?
Ainsi le Père levait ses mains le jour
Que la hache horrible s'abbattit sur sa chair.
Que veux-tu?
Fille de ma mère,
Fille de Klytaimnestra?

**CHRYSOTHÉMIS:** (*à voix basse*).
Ils trament une affreuse trahison!

**ELEKTRA:** Les deux femelles?

**CHRYSOTHÉMIS:** Qui?

**ELEKTRA:** Qui, notre mère avec cette autre femme,
Le lâche, cet Aegisth, cet assassin si brave,
Dont le coeur, l'audace ne se voient qu'au lit.
Et quel est leur dessein?

**CHRYSOTHÉMIS:** De te jeter dans une tour,
Où sans voir lune ni soleil, tu gémiras.
(*Elektra rit.*)
C'est vrai, te dis-je, l'entendis.

**ELEKTRA:** Comment fis-tu pour les entendre?

**CHRYSOTHÉMIS:** (*à voix basse*).
A la porte, Elektra!

**ELEKTRA:** (*éclatant*). Il ne faut pas ouvrir de porte ici!
Des râles rauques, oui, des plaintes qu'on étrangle,
S'exhalent sans cesse de ces murailles,
Il ne faut pas ouvrir!
Mais, immobile, à mes côtés t'assceoir,
En appelant à haute voix la'mort sur elle et lui.

**CHRYSOTHÉMIS:** Rester assise, immobile, dans l'ombre?
Non, non! Car j'ai du feu dans ma poitrine;
Et c'est pour quoi toujours je vais et viens;
Pas une chambre où rester, de l'une a l'autre
Jerre course folle ah! monter, descendre ...
Na'a-t-on pas dit mon nom?
J'accours bien vite
C'est une chambre vide qui me regarde!
Et mon angeoisse est telle,
Que mes genoux tremblent jour et nuit;

**ELEKTRA:** Ah! that countenance!

**CHRYSOTHEMIS:** (*still at the door.*) Is it so hateful to you?

**ELEKTRA:** (*sharply*). What do you wish?
Speak, explain yourself, then go!
(*Chrysothemis raises her hands as if to defend herself.*)

**ELEKTRA:** What does that gesture mean?
Thus my father raised his hands that day
When the terrible axe felled him dead.
What do you wish?
Daughter of my mother,
Daughter of Klytaimnestra?

**CHRYSOTHEMIS:** (*in a low voice*). They plot treason!

**ELEKTRA:** The two?

**CHRYSOTHEMIS:** Who?

**ELEKTRA:** Who but our mother and that other,
The wicked Aegisthes, the daring assassin,
Whose heart, whose audacity are but seen in private.
And what is their design?

**CHRYSOTHEMIS:** To throw you into a dark tower,
Where you shall moan, deprived of sun and moon.
(*Elektra laughs.*)
It is true—I heard them.

**ELEKTRA:** How did you learn this?

**CHRYSOTHEMIS:** (*in low tones*). At the door, Elektra.

**ELEKTRA:** (*blazing up*). There is no need to open a door here!
The hoarse death rattles, ah, and they stifle their cries,
All re-echo ceaselessly from these walls,
There is no need to open!
But, motionless, beside me sit
And call aloud for death to strike her and him.

**CHRYSOTHEMIS:** In the shadow remain motionless?
No, no! there's fire in my breast;
This is why I always come and go;
In no chamber can I rest, now here, now there,
I wander madly, up and down ...
Did they not call my name?
I hasten there, but, alas!
I see nothing more than an empty chamber,
And my anguish is such
That my strength forsakes me;
And my breath seems choked
So no tears can flow,
All turned to stone!
My sister, I beseech you!

Cela m'étreint la gorge si fort
Que je n'ai plus de larmes,
Tout est de pierre!
Soeur, je t'en prie!

**ELEKTRA:** Hé bien?

**CHRYSOTHÉMIS:** Toi c'est toi qui
me riv-au sol
Avec des crampons de fer!
Je pourrais, sans toi m'évader.
N'était ta haine que rien n'endort,
Que rien ne dompte et qu'ils re-
doutent,
Ah! Ah! ils nous laisseraient sortir
De notre geôle, Soeur!
Je veux sortir!
Je ne veux pas, ici,
Jusqu'au trépas dormir!
Que je meure mais d'abord vivre!
Avant d'être vieille,
Je veux de doux enfants,
Chers petits êtres dussé-je même
Les enfanter d'un rustre;
Des enfants que mes bras,
Sur mon sein réchauffe raient
Quand l'orage gronde
Et secoue les portes.
Me comprends-tu?
Réponds moi . . . Soeur!

**ELEKTRA:** Corps misérable!

**CHRYSOTHÉMIS:** (*toujours ex-
cessivement exaltée*). Ah! grâce,
pour toi-même et pour moi!
A qui sert ce tourment?
Le Père, il est mort.
Le Frère, ne vient pas!
Telles deux oiseaux sur la branche,
Nous attendons inquiètes;
Regardant de tous côtés . . .
Personne ne vient . . . ni Frère . . .
Ni même un message, ni l'annonce
De ces message . . . rien . . .
Avec son stylet le temps s'en vient
sur nous
Creuser nos traits; dehors le ciel
rayonne
Ou s'éteint, des femmes hier en-
core sveltes,
De viennent grosses, à la fontaine
lourdement
Se trainent, puis soudain de leur
fardeau délivrées,
Puisent joyeuses l'eau claire
Et d'elles même s'épanche un breu-
vage ivrant;
Une autre vie à leur sein est suspen-
due,
Et l'enfant va grandissant.
Non, non, je suis femme et veux le
sort des femmes!
Plutôt la mort que vivre hors la vie!
(*Elle éclate en profonds sanglots.*)

**ELEKTRA:** Tu hurles?
Va! rentre! C'est là ta place!
Mais quel tumulte?
(*Ironiquement:*)
Est-ce qu'on prépare déjà tes noces?
J' entends courir.
Et là-dedans on crie.
On tue, ou l'on enfante!
Pour oreiller s'il manque un ca-
davre,
Il faut bien qu'on tue!

**ELEKTRA:** Well?

**CHRYSOTHEMIS:** It is you who
bound your sister to the earth
As with bands of steel!
But for you, I could escape.
Were it not your hate which never
sleeps,
Which nothing lessens, which they
all suspect,
Ah! they would let us leave our jail,
my sister!
I wish to go!
I would not stay here, perhaps to
die!
Let me die, but let me, ah! live first!
Before age approaches me,
I would know a child's caress,
I would clasp it in my arms,
I would hold it against my breast
Laughing, while the tempest roars
around us,
And shakes the doors in rage!
Do you understand, my sister?
Answer then, I pray . . .

**ELEKTRA:** Most miserable body!

**CHRYSOTHEMIS:** (*still greatly
exalted*). Ah, mercy, for you and
for myself!
What use this torment?
Our father is dead,
Our brother is absent!
Like two birds upon a branch,
We anxiously await;
On all sides we look . . .
But no one comes . . . nor brother . .
.
Nor message even, nor the hint of a
message . . .
Nothing!
Time with its brush draws near to
us,
To line our features; outside, the
skies are bright
Or overcast, the women still slen-
der yesterday,
Are grown stout, to the fountain
they drag
Wearily their steps, then suddenly
of their burden freed,
Draw joyously the sparkling wa-
ter—
Another life is nestling at their
breasts.
And the child begins to grow in stat-
ure.
No, no, I am a woman, I crave a
woman's lot!
Better death than mere existence!
(*She sobs bitterly.*)

**ELEKTRA:** You howl?
Go in! Your place is there!
What tumult is this?
(*With irony:*)
Do they prepare for your wedding?
I hear steps running,
And within they shout.
It is death, or else a child is born!
If for a pillow they are short a
corpse,
Then it is necessary that they kill!

**CHRYSOTHÉMIS:** Va-t'en, bien
vite! qu'elle ne te voie.
Ne te mets pas sur son chemin:
La mort vieille en ses regards!
Elle a revé.
(*Le bruit de nombreux arrivants,
a l'intérieur, se rapproche.*)
Va-t'en d'ici!
On marche dans l'entrée . . .
On va passer ici.
Elle a rêvé.
Elle a rêvé, je ne sais quoi
Je l'ai entendu dire aux servantes:
Ou dit qu'elle a rêve d'Orest,
Oui, l'Orest lui-même,
Elle a crié cette nuit en rêve
Comme quelqu'un que l'on
étrangle.
(*Des torches et des ombres rem-
plissent l'entrée, à gauche de la
porte.*)
Les voici tous,
Voici le long troupeau des por-
teuses de torches,
Poussant des bêtes, portant des
glaives.
Soeur l'épouvante la rend terrible!
(*Pressante:*)
Eloigne toi, ne reste pas au travers
de sa route!

**ELEKTRA:** J'ai le très-vif désir de
lui parler à ma mère, aujourd'hui.

**CHRYSOTHÉMIS:** J'ai peur
d'entendre!
(*Chrysothémis s'enfuit par la
porte de la cour.—Devant les
baies, violemment illuminées, un
cortège tumultueux passe rapidement; bruit d'animaux que l'on
traîne et que l'on fouaille,
grondements sourds, cris aussitôt
réprimés, claqument d'un
fouet.—Klytaimnestra parait
dans l'encadrement de la large
baie. Son visage blême et bouffi
est plus pâle encore, à cause du
feu des torches et de la couleur
pourpre de sa tunique. Elle
s'appuie d'un côté sur une confidente vêtue de violet foncé, de
l'autre sur une canne d'ivoire in-
crustée de pierres précieuses. Une
forme jaune, dont la figure aux
cheveux noirs rejetés en arrière
semble celle d'une Egyptienne, et
dont l'allure semble celle d'un serpent qui se dresse, porte la traîne.
La Reine est couverte de pierres
précieuses et de talismans, ses
brus disparaissent sous les bracelets, ses doigts sont raidis par les
bagues. Les paupières de ses yeux
sont extrêmement grandes et elle
parait ne pouvoir, sans effort, les
tenir ouvertes.—Elektra se dresse
de tout son haut.*)

**KLYTAIMNESTRA:** (*ouvre tout à
coup les yeux, et tremblants de
colère, se penche en dehors de la
baie, en menaçant Elektra de sa
canne*). Que veux-tu?
Voyez, la!
Mais voyez done!
Quelle attitude ce long coutendu,

**CHRYSOTHEMIS:** Go, go quickly!
she must not see you.
Do not cross her path!
Death watches through her eyes!
She had a dream.
(*The noise of many footsteps ap-
proaching is heard within.*)
Come here!
They are marching this way.
She has dreamed,
I do not know of what.
I heard her tell the servants:
They say she dreamed of Orestes,
Yes, Orestes himself,
She cried aloud in her dream,
As though she were being stran-
gled.
(*Torches and shadows fill the en-
trance, at right of door.*)
Behold them all!
Behold the long line of torch bear-
ers!
Driving beasts before them, bearing
spears.
Sister, fear has made her terrible.
(*Urging:*)
Go, remain not in her path.

**ELEKTRA:** I must speak to my
mother today.

**CHRYSOTHEMIS:** I fear to wait.
(*Chrysothemis makes her escape
through the door of the court.—
Before the windows, brilliantly illuminated, a noisy procession
passes rapidly; sounds of animals
which are being led and driven,
harsh cries that are immediately
suppressed, the cracking of a
whip.—Klytaimnestra appears in
the large bay window. Her sallow,
bloated countenance is paler on
account of the fire of the torches
and the purple color of her tunic.
She leans on one side upon the
arm of a companion dressed in
dark violet, on the other upon an
ivory cane encrusted with precious stones. A yellow figure,
whose black hair, drawn back
from the face, suggests an Egyptian, and whose posture recalls
that of a serpent raising itself, supports her train. The Queen is covered with precious stones and talismans, her arms are hidden
under bracelets, her fingers sparkle with rings. Her eyelids are un-
usually large and she seems unable to keep them open without
effort.—Elektra raises herself to
her full height.*)

**KLYTAIMNESTRA:** (*suddenly
opens her eyes, and trembling
with anger, leans out of the window, threatening Elektra with her
cane.*) What do you wish?
Behold her, there!
That neck extended,
That pointed tongue,

Cette langue qui pointe!
Et dire que ça librement,
Chez moi circule!
(*Respirant avec peine:*)
De ses yeux que ne peut-elle me de-
truire!
O Dieux, d'où vient que sa vue
m'oppresse;
Pourquoi vous même m'accabler?
Pourquoi faut-il que ma force soit
brisée?
Pourquoi? Pourquoi mon corps,
bien qu'il vive.
N'est-il plus qu'un desert.
Et cette partie, qui naquit de lui,
Pourquoi ne l'ai-je pas sarclée?
D'ou vient ce qui m'arrive.
Dieux vénérables?

ELEKTRA: (*très calme*). Les
Dieux!
Mais toi-même, n'es-tu pas Déesse,
Oui tout comme eux!

KLYTAIMNESTRA: (*à ses suivantes*). Qu'a-t-elle dit?
Avez-vous compris ses paroles?

LA CONFIDENTE: Que tu es de
souche divine aussi.

LA PORTEUSE DE TRAINE:
(*d'une voix sifflante*). Elle se mo-
que!
(*Klytaimnestra laisse retomber
ses lourdes paupières.*)

KLYTAIMNESTRA:
(*doucement*). O douce voix per-
due,
De qui le timbre resonne loin si
loin.
Elle lit en moi.
Mais qui pourrait savoir sa vraie
pensée.
(*La Confidente et La Porteuse de
Traine chuchotent ensemble.*)

ELEKTRA: (*s'approche lentement
de Klytaimnestra*). Toi, tu n'es
plus la même.
La vermine se suspend à toi!
A ton oreille elle siffle,
Et partage en deux ta pensée,
Violà pourquoi tu es toujours
Dans l'ivresse et dans le rève.

KLYTAIMNESTRA: Je veux descendre,
Seule, seule pour qu'elle me parle.
(*Elle quitte la baie et parait avec
ses suivantes sur le pas de la
porte.*)

KLYTAIMNESTRA: (*du seuil*).
Aujourd'hui elle est moins far-
ouche
Et parle comme un mage.

LA CONFIDENTE: (*à voix basse*).
Elle ne dit pas sa pensée.

LA PORTEUSE DE TRAINE: Ses
mots sont tous mensonges.

KLYTAIMNESTRA:
(*s'emportant*). Vous deux, si-
lence!
Ce qui sort de vous toutes
N'est que l'haleine d'Egisthe.
Quand je m'eveille la nuit,
Etes-vous d'accord sur mes souf-

And say that she is free
To live beside me!
(*Breathing with difficulty:*)
With her eyes she would destroy
me!
O Gods, why does her look oppress
me so,
Why overwhelm me, why rob me of
my strength?
Why is my body, though it is living,
Like unto a desert place,
And this one here, begot of him,
Why have I not removed her?
From where comes this affliction,
most venerable Gods?

ELEKTRA: (*very calm*). The Gods!
But are you, too, not a Goddess,
Yes, like unto them?

KLYTAIMNESTRA: (*to her
maids*). What did she say?
Did you understand her words?

THE COMPANION: That you also
are of divine origin.

THE TRAIN BEARER: (*in a hissing voice*). She mocks!
(*Klytaimnestra closes her heavy
eyelids.*)

KLYTAIMNESTRA: (*softly*). O
lost sweet voice,
Whose tones resound so far, so far.
She reads my thoughts,
But who could know her own?
(*The Companion and the Train
Bearer whisper together.*)

ELEKTRA: (*slowly approaching
Klytaimnestra*). You who are not
still the same,
The vermin hangs on to you!
At your ear it hisses,
And shares with you your thoughts.
Hence you are always
Either drunk or dreaming!

KLYTAIMNESTRA: I would descend,
That she may speak to me, alone.
(*She leaves the window and appears with her maids at the door.*)

KLYTAIMNESTRA: (*from the
threshold*). Today she is less ferocious.
She speaks, too, like a sage.

THE COMPANION: (*smiling maliciously*). She does not speak her
thoughts.

THE TRAIN BEARER: Her words
are lies.

KLYTAIMNESTRA: (*flying into a
passion*). You two, be silent.
You are but the breath of Aegisthes.
When I am awake at night,
Are you agreed as to my suffering?
You cry:
That my eyelids are too heavy,

frances?
Toi tu cris:
Que mes paupières sont par trop
pesantes,
Et que mon foie gonfle.
Tu me susurres, toi, à l'autre or-
eille:
Que tu as vu des demons affreux,
Avec des becs en pointe.
Qui viennent sucer mes veines.
Et ne m'as-tu pas montré.
Sur moi, leurs traces?
Et sur tes conseils je frappe,
Frappe, frappe, tant de victimes.
Voulez vous donc me harceler
De vos avis contraires jusqu'à la
mort?
Je suis lasse d'entendre:
"Je dis vrai et l'antre trompe.
Ou es-tu, Vérité?
Pas un homme ne te commit.
Quand elle me parle
(*Toujours très oppressée.*)
De ce que j'aime entendre.
Je suis heureuse et je l'écoute . . .
Devant qui sait me dire ce qui
m'agrée.
Fut-ce même ma fille, oui, même
elle,
Ah! qu'il m'est doux de mettre
A nu mon torturée,
De laisser la brise tiède,
D'ou qu'elle vienne, souffler
Sur elle.
Les malades, quand vient le soir,
Assis au bord des ondes, offrent
leurs ulcères
Et leurs affreuses plaies aux
fraiches caresss
Des brises nocturnes . . .
Et tous ne pensent qu'à ceci:
Ne plus souffrir!
Laissez-moi seule près d'elle!
(*D'un geste impérieux de sa
canne, elle fait rentrer dans la
maison La Confidante et La Por-
teuse de Traine. En hésitant,
celles-ci franchissent la porte. Les
torches s'éclipsent aussi, et c'est
seulement une faible lueur, venue
de la maison, qui éclare les visages des deux femmes, dans la
cour.—Klytaimnestra s'avance.*)

KLYTAIMNESTRA: (*à voix
basse*). Mes nuits ne sont plus jamais bonnes.
A tous rèves, quel remède?

ELEKTRA: (*se rapprochant*).
Rèves-tu, Mère?

KLYTAIMNESTRA: Lorsqu'on
vieillit, l'on rève.
On peut trouver un remède.
Il existe.
Il est pour chaque mal un remède
juste.
Tu vois, je me suis couverte de
pierres,
En chacune d'elles réside une
force.
Ce qu'on ignore, c'est leur exact
emploi.
Mais toi si tu voulais,
Toi, en ceci tu peux m'être utile.

ELEKTRA: Moi, Mère, moi?

And that my liver is swollen.
You whisper at the other ear:
That you have seen awful demons,
With pointed beaks,
That suck my veins.
And have you not shown me
The marks it left behind?
And by your counsel I struck them
down,
Struck, yes, struck those num-
berless victims.
Will you still torment me,
And cross me even to death?
I am weary of hearing:
"It is the truth I speak, the other
lies."
Where are you, O Truth?
No one knows you
When it speaks to me—
(*Still much oppressed:*)
Of what I love to hear,
I am happy and I listen . . .
To what is pleasing to me,
Were it even my daughter, yes,
even she,
Ah! How sweet to free my tortured
soul,
That the warm breeze, from where-
ever it comes
May blow upon it.
The sick, when evening falls,
Seated by the shore, their sores ex-
pose,
And their grievous wounds,
To the sweet caresses
Of the evening breezes . . .
And they think of this alone:
To suffer no longer.
Leave me alone with her.
(*With an imperious gesture of her
cane, she sends The Companion
and The Train Bearer into the
house. They go in reluctantly. The
torches also go out, and but a
faint light remains, coming from
the house, which lights up the
faces of the two women in the
court. Klytaimnestra comes forward.*)

KLYTAIMNESTRA: (*in a low
voice*). No longer happy are my
nights.
What remedy is there to all dreams?

ELEKTRA: (*approaching*). You
dream, my mother?

KLYTAIMNESTRA: When one is
wakeful, one dreams.
There is a remedy—it exists.
For every evil, there's a remedy.
I am covered with precious stones;
In each one resides a force.
We are only ignorant of how to use
them.
But you, if you wish,
May serve me in this matter.

ELEKTRA: I, my mother?

KLYTAIMNESTRA: (avec éclat).
Oui, oui.
Tu es lucide.
Tu as la tête très solide.
En tout ceci tu peux m'être utile.
Si rien qu'un mot est peu de chose.
..
Qu'est-ce donc qu'un souffle?
Apprends done que du crépuscule à l'aube,
Quand je m'agite sur mon lit un rien rampe sur moi.
Pas même un mot, pas même un mal c'est quelque chose
D'impondérable; rien dis-je ...
Pas même un cauchemar, et pourtant,
C'est si terrible que mon âme.
A cette approche, aimerait se pendre.
Que chaque membre en moi hurle à la mort!
Et je puis vivre, sans même être malade:
Regarde moi: semblai-je être malade?
Peut-on dissoudre vivante,
Comme pourriture?
Et s'écrouler, lors qu'on n'est pas malade,
Semblable à quelque robe qui s'emiette,
Rongée par les mites?
Si je dors, je rève, rève,
Que toute la moelle de mes os s'enfuit,
Et lorsque je me lève, rien qu'un dixième,
A peine, coula de la lente clepsydre.
Derrière le rideau un réilet.
Mais ce n'est pas la bleme aurore,
Non, c'est encor la torche de la porte qui frissonne.
Et qui semblable à quelqu'eyre vivant, m'epie.
Tous ces rèves, il faut qu'ils finissent il faut ...
Qui me les apporte, l'étrange Démon.
Va s'enfuir dès que le juste sang aura coulé.

ELEKTRA: Etrange!

KLYTAIMNESTRA: (sauvage).
Quand je devrais à tout ce qui rampe.
Et vole ouvrir les veines,
Dans la rouge vapeur du sang marcher
Et puis dormir,
Comme font les enfants de Thule aux brumes pourpres:
Je veux ne plus rèver.

ELEKTRA: Quand le juste sang sous la hache jailira,
Mourront tous tes rèves!

KLYTAIMNESTRA: (vivement).
Quel est-il, ce sang, et de quel animal pur?

ELEKTRA: (riant mystérieusement). Sang d'une bête impure.

---

KLYTAIMNESTRA: (with fervor).
Yes, yes.
You are sensible,
You understand readily.
In all this you may be useful to me.
A word is but a little thing ...
It is only a breath!
Learn then that from sunset to dawn,
When I toss restless on my bed,
A trifle keeps me wakeful.
Not even a word, nor yet an ill, is a thing impondarable;
A trifle, did I say? ...
Not even a nightmare, and yet it is so terrible,
That my soul, at its approach, is terrified,
And my being is paralyzed with dread!
And I can live despite this;
Behold me, am I ill?
Can one yet live and rot,
Like dirt?
Can one decay, and yet be not ill,
Like a robe worm-eaten?
If I sleep, I dream, ah! dream,
That the marrow in my bones has melted;
And when I awake (the hour glass scarcely indicating ten),
Behind the curtain I behold a reflection,
But not the golden dawn of day,
No, it is still the torch that flares,
Like a human eye watching me.
All these dreams must end—they must ...
The strange demon shall flee from where they come.
So soon as the right blood shall flow.

ELEKTRA: Strange!

KLYTAIMNESTRA: (savagely).
When I shall open the veins of a body
To all that creep about me
In the red vapor of blood, I shall march
And then sleep,
As do the children of Thule in the purple mist:
I wish to dream no more.

ELEKTRA: When the right blood flows under the hatchet
All your dreams shall end.

KLYTAIMNESTRA: (quickly).
What is this blood, of what pure animal?

ELEKTRA: (laughing mysteriously). The blood of an impure animal.

---

KLYTAIMNESTRA: D'un de mes prisonnièrs?
ELEKTRA: Non, un homme libre.
KLYTAIMNESTRA: Et quels remèdes?
ELEKTRA: Merveilleux remèdes qu'il faut strictement prendre.
KLYTAIMNESTRA: (impatientée). Parle donc!
ELEKTRA: Ne peux-tu me comprendre?
KLYTAIMNESTRA: Non, vite éxplique.
(Elle adjure solemnellement Elektra).
Dis-moi le nom de l'holcauste!
ELEKTRA: Une femme!
KLYTAIMNESTRA: (avec ampatience). Est-elle au nombre de mes suivantes,
Enfant? Est-elle vierge encore?
Ou femme, ayant connu le mâle?
ELEKTRA: (tranquillement). Oui, connu, c'est ça!
KLYTAIMNESTRA: (pressante). Ce sacrifice, dis-m'en donc l'heure, le lieu!
ELEKTRA: (avec calme). Qu'importe le lieu, qu'importe l'heure, le jour ou la nuit.
KLYTAIMNESTRA: Dis-moi le rite!
Que dois-je faire?
Faut-il moi-même ...
ELEKTRA: Non, non tu n'iras pas cette fois à la chasse filet, hache au poing.
KLYTAIMNESTRA: Qui donc? Qui doit agir?
ELEKTRA: Un homme!
KLYTAIMNESTRA: Aegisth?
ELEKTRA: (riant). J'ai dit pourtant: un homme!
KLYTAIMNESTRA: Qui? Mais réponds vite.
Quelqu'un des nòtres?
Ou bien sera-ce un étranger?
ELEKTRA: (fixant le sol, l'esprit ailleurs). Oui, oui, étrange,
Et malgré tout de la maison.
KLYTAIMNESTRA: Explique-moi l'enigme.
Elektra, continue.
Je suis heureuse, pour cette fois,
De te trouver moins rude ...
ELEKTRA: Vas-tu laisser rentrer le Frère, Mère?
KLYTAIMNESTRA: J'ai fait defense que de lui l'on parle.
ELEKTRA: As-tu donc peur de lui?
KLYTAIMNESTRA: Qui l'a dit?
ELEKTRA: Mère, pourquoi trembler?
KLYTAIMNESTRA: Qui aurait peur d'un misérable insensé!

---

KLYTAIMNESTRA: One of my prisoners?
ELEKTRA: No, a free man.
KLYTAIMNESTRA: And what remedies?
ELEKTRA: Marvelous remedies that must be strictly taken.
KLYTAIMNESTRA: (impatiently). Then speak!
ELEKTRA: Can you not understand me?
KLYTAIMNESTRA: No, explain quickly.
(She solemnly adjures Elektra.)
Tell me the name of this holocaust!
ELEKTRA: A woman.
KLYTAIMNESTRA: (with impatience). Is she among my servants?
Is she still a virgin?
Or a woman who has mated?
ELEKTRA: (quietly). Ah! has mated—that is it!
KLYTAIMNESTRA: (urging). Tell me the place and hour of this sacrifice!
ELEKTRA: (calmly). What does time or place matter, day or night?
KLYTAIMNESTRA: Tell me the rites!
What must I do?
Shall I myself ...
ELEKTRA: No, you shall not go to the chase, net and axe in hand—Not on this occasion.
KLYTAIMNESTRA: Who then shall act?
ELEKTRA: A man!
KLYTAIMNESTRA: Aegisthes?
ELEKTRA: (laughing). I said—a man!
KLYTAIMNESTRA: Who? Answer quickly.
Is he one of ours?
Or must he be a stranger?
ELEKTRA: (her eyes on the ground, her thoughts elsewhere). Ah, a stranger.
And yet of this house.
KLYTAIMNESTRA: Explain your enigma.
Go on, Elektra.
I am pleased to see you Less rude than usual ...
ELEKTRA: Will you allow my brother to return here, my mother?
KLYTAIMNESTRA: I have forbidden that his name be mentioned.
ELEKTRA: Are you, then, afraid of him?
KLYTAIMNESTRA: Who said so?
ELEKTRA: Why tremble, my mother?
KLYTAIMNESTRA: Who could be afraid of a poor fool!

ELEKTRA: Quoi?

KLYTAIMNESTRA: Le pauvre, bégaie, couche auprès des chiens de garde, Et confond la bête et l'homme, âme chétive.

ELEKTRA: L'enfant était très sain.

KLYTAIMNESTRA: C'est que, on lui donna mauvais gite Et les chiens de la cour pour companie.

ELEKTRA: Ah!

KLYTAIMNESTRA: (*baissant ses paupieres*). En vain j'envoyai de l'or, de l'or. Pour qu'on le traitât comme doit l'etre un fils de Roi!

ELEKTRA: Tu mens! L'or envoyé, c'était pourqu'on l'étrangle.

KLYTAIMNESTRA: Qui te l'a dit?

ELEKTRA: Je le vois dans tes yeux. Et à ton tremblement je dévine qu'il vit encor. Et que le jour, la nuit, sans cesse tu pense à lui. Et que ton coeur se sèche de peur quand tu te dis: il vient!

KLYTAIMNESTRA: Ceux du dehors je n'en ai curé. Je suis ici la souveraine. J'ai des servants assez qui veillent à ma porte, Et, s'il me plait, je place jour et nuit, Devant ma chambre, trois guetteurs Armés et qui, l'oeil ouvert, me gardent. Quelque jour, de facon ou bien d'autre je saurai te faire parler. Déjà tu l'avouas que tu connais la victime juste, Et le remède que je cherche. Si tu te tais, libre, Tu parleras enchaînée. On fait parler ceux qu'on affame. Rêves sont choses qu'on supprime. Qui les souffre, sans en jamais trouver Le vrai remède, n'est rien qu'un sot! Mais je saurai qui doit saigner et mourir Ici pour qu'enfin, moi, je dorme!

(*Elektra fait un bond hors de l'ombre, vers Klytaimnestra, dont elle se rapproche de plus en plus. Elle lui parle avec une exaltation croissante.*)

ELEKTRA: Qui doit saigner? Ta gorge elle même quand le chasseur t'aura prise! J'entends qu'il entre dans ta chambre. J'entends les rideaux de ton lit qu'il tire: Mais qui tuerait la victime endormie. Il te reveille, hurlante tu t'en fuis, Sur tes pas il s'élance, te traque en ta maison!

ELEKTRA: What?

KLYTAIMNESTRA: The poor wretch lies with the watch dogs, And, mean soul, confounds the beast with man.

ELEKTRA: The child was very healthy.

KLYTAIMNESTRA: It is why they gave him a sorry lodging, And the dogs for company.

ELEKTRA: Ah!

KLYTAIMNESTRA: (*lowering her eyelids*). In vain I sent them gold, That they might treat him as befits a king's son!

ELEKTRA: You lie! The gold was sent to tempt his death.

KLYTAIMNESTRA: Who told you so?

ELEKTRA: I see it in your eyes. And by your trembling I divine he lives. And that you think of him day and night. And that your heart stands still When they say: he comes!

KLYTAIMNESTRA: I have no fear of those outside. I am mistress here. I have servants, too, who watch, And, if it please me, I can set Night and day before my door three sentries armed, Who shall guard me with watchful eye. Some day I'll find the means to make you speak. You have already owned, you know the proper victim And the remedy I need. If you keep silent, free, Then you shall speak in chains. Those who starve shall speak. Dreams can be suppressed. Those who suffer them, never finding The true remedy, are simply fools! But I shall know who must bleed and die, So I may sleep at last!

(*Elektra springs out of the shadow toward Klytaimnestra, whom she approaches gradually. She speaks to her with increasing exaltation.*)

ELEKTRA: Who must bleed? Your throat, when the hunter has taken you I hear him entering your chamber, I hear the curtain of your bed drawn back: But who would slay the sleeping victim! He awakens you. Screaming, you flee He follows after, tracking your footsteps through your house!

Cours-tu à droite, là est le lit! A gauche, là fume le bain sanglant, Et l'ombre et les torches t'enveloppent De leur filet noirâtre et rouge...

(*Klytaimnestra est secouée d'un frisson muet.*)

Au bas des marches, sous des voutes. Des voutes et des voutes il te poursuit...

Et moi, moi, moi, moi, moi, qui te l'en voyai, Moi, je suis le chien forçant la bête Si tu veux te terrer; d'un saut je te relance. Et-nous irons ainsi, jusqu'à un mur qui nous arrête, et là...

Dans les ténèbres, vois-tu pas déjà une ombre, Oui, là, une forme vague où le blanc des yeux reluit? Ah! c'est le Pere, indifférent, Sachant que cela doit être; C'est à ses pieds que tu t'écrouleras. Tu voudrais crier mais l'air étrangle alors ton cri Et il retombe, muet, par tèrre. Inconsciente, tu tends déjà le cou, Et le froid du fer te semble attaque déjà ta vie. Mais non, il convient d'attendre. Le rite doit être observé. Tout se tait, tu n'entends que ton coeur en ta poitrine battre; Cet instant se creuse sous toi comme un grand trou noir d'années Cet instant on te l'accorde pour ceci: Que tu souffres l'angoissante horreur Des naufragés dont les clameurs s'éfforcent En vain de traverser la tempête. Cet instant on te l'accorde ce que tu envies Tous ceux qu'on a rivés aux murs des geolés, Ceux qui du fond des puits, invoquent le trépas, Et comme un sauveur l'appellent...

O toi, toi qui en toi même est encagée Ainsi qu'au ventre ardent d'un animal d'airain, Tu ne pourras, toi non plus, crier! Je suis devant toi, tu peux lire de tes yeux Hagards l'horrible mot qui sur mon visage Est écrit: Aux lacs posés par toi-même ton âme s'étrangle. Elle tombe la hache, et je suis là, Je te vois, je te vois morte! Finis tous tes rèves, et ceux qu'on m'obligerait à faire; Et qui lors vivra, gaiment pourra jouir de sa vie!

(*Elles se tiennent l'une devant l'autre, les yeux dans les yeux. Elektra pleine d'une farouche ivresse, Klytaimnestra haletante de peur.*)

You run to the right, there stands the bed! To the left, there foams the bath of blood, And the shadow and the torches envelope you In their black and scarlet net...

(*Klytaimnestra shivers as with a chill.*)

Down the stairs, below the arches, From arch to arch, he chases you...

And I, I, I, I, who sent him to you, I shall be the dog hunting the beast; If you seek cover, I hurl myself on you. And we shall go thus to the wall before us, and there...

In the darkness, do you see already a shadow, Ah, a vague form whose eyes are brilliant? It is my father, heedless, indifferent, Knowing that this must be; 'Tis at his feet that you shall fall. You seek to call aloud, But the air shall choke your breath And your voice shall sink, soundless, to the earth. Unconscious, you already stretch your neck, And fancy the cold steel that already attacks your life. But no, the time is not, The rite must be observed. You are silent, you await me, your heart beating wildly; Before you yawns a pit, black with age, May you suffer the most awful horrors, Like shipwrecked sailors whose shouts In vain are raised against the tempest. Now you are granted what you seek. As those who have been bound in jails, Who from the depths of wells, invoke the end, And see in it their savior... O you who are encaged in yourself, You, too, shall have no power to cry! I am before you, you can read in your haggard eyes The awful word which is written on your face: In the lakes you dug yourself, your soul is strangled, The axe falls and I am there, I see you, I see you die! Ended are your dreams, and those that were forced on me; And he who then shall live shall know the joy of life!

(*They stand facing each other, gazing into each other's eyes— Elektra, filled with an intense anger; Klytaimnestra, breathing with difficulty.—At this instant*

(A ce moment le vestibule s'illumine.)
(La Confidante accourt. — Elle chuchotte quelque chose à L'oreille de Klytaimnestra. — Celle-ci semble d'abord ne pas comprendre.)
(Petit a petit elle revient à elle. — Elle fait un signe: "De la lumière." — Des servantes avec des torches arrivent en courant et se placent derrière Klytaimnestra. — Klytaimnestra fait encore signe: "Plus de lumière." — La Porteuse de traine. — Maintenant ses traits se detendent peu à peu, et une expression mauvaise, de triomphe vient remplacer son air d'angoisse. — Des servantes arrivent, de plus en plus nombreuses, et se placent derrière Klytaimnestra. — Maintenant la cour est toute plaine de lumières et de lueurs rougeâtres courent sur les murs. — Sans perdre Elektra de vue un seul instant, Klytaimnestra se fait redire la nouvelle.)
(Et saturée d'une joie sauvage, dans un geste de menace, elle étend ses deux mains vers Elektra. — La Confidente lui ramasse sa canne, et s'appuyant sur l'une et l'autre, vivement, voracement, retroussant sa robe pour franchir les marches, elle rentre en courant dans la maison. — Les servantes avec les lumières la suivent, comme si on les poursuivait.)

the vestibule is illumined. — The Companion hastens in. She whispers something in Klytaimnestra's ear. The latter seems at first not to understand. Suddenly she recovers herself. She makes a sign for light. The servants enter, running, with torches, and place themselves behind Klytaimnestra. — Klytaimnestra makes another sign for more light. The Train Bearer enters. Her features now relax gradually, and an evil expression of triumph replaces her looks of anguish. Servants continue to enter in larger numbers and stand behind Klytaimnestra. The court is now brilliantly illumined and the lurid light is reflected from the walls. Without losing sight of Elektra for an instant, Klytaimnestra has the news repeated. Then, permeated with a savage joy, she extends both her hands menacingly towards Elektra. — The Companion picks up her cane and, supporting herself on both, she quickly gathers up her robe to mount the steps. She enters the house running. The servants, carrying the lights, follow her, as though they were pursued.)

**ELEKTRA:** Que lui ont elles dit? D'ou vient sa joie? Ma tête! Rien ne me dit ce qui égaye cette femme!
(Chrysothémis hurlant comme une bête blessée, arrive en courant par la porte de la cour.)

**ELEKTRA:** What did they tell her? From where came her joy? My head! Nothing tells me what has pleased that woman!
(Chrysothemis, screaming like a wounded animal, rushes in by the door of the court.)

**CHRYSOTHÉMIS:** (en criant). Orest! Orest est mort!
(Elektra, tout à ses pensées, lui fait signe de s'éloigner.)

**CHRYSOTHEMIS:** (crying). Orestes! Orestes is dead!
(Elektra, engrossed in thought, signs her to go.)

**ELEKTRA:** Tais-toi!

**ELEKTRA:** Be silent!

**CHRYSOTHÉMIS:** Orest est mort.
(Elektra rémue les lèvres.)
Quand je sortais, tous savaient déjà! Tous, en cercle, parlaient . . . Oui, tous déjà le savaient, tous sauf nous.

**CHRYSOTHEMIS:** Orestes is dead!
(Elektra moves her lips.)
When I came out, they all knew already! All were speaking of it . . . Yes, all knew it, save we two.

**ELEKTRA:** (sourdement). Nul ne sait ça!

**ELEKTRA:** (in a hollow voice). No one knows that!

**CHRYSOTHÉMIS:** Tous le savent.

**CHRYSOTHEMIS:** They all know.

**ELEKTRA:** Nul ne peut savoir. Car ce n'est pas vrai.
(Chrysothémis, désésperée, se jette à tèrre.)

**ELEKTRA:** No one can know, For it is not true.
(Chrysothemis, despairingly, casts herself on the ground.)

**ELEKTRA:** (relevant de force Chrysothémis). Ce n'est pas vrai! Ce n'est pas vrai. Je te le dis, ce n'est pas vrai!

**ELEKTRA:** (raising Chrysothemis by force). It is not true! It is not true, I tell you, it is not true!

**CHRYSOTHÉMIS:** Les hôtes, les deux étrangers. Les hôtes envoyés pour porter la nouvelle: Deux, un vieux et un jeune, Se tenaient dans l'entrée debout Et tout le monde, en cercle, Les écoutait, et tous et tous, Savaient déjà.

**CHRYSOTHEMIS:** The guests, the two strangers, Sent to bring the news: An old man and a youth, Are standing in the entrance, All around them gathered, Listening, and all, yes all, now know.

**ELEKTRA:** (avec la plus grande énergie). Cê n'est pas vrai!

**ELEKTRA:** (with the greatest energy). It is not true!

**CHRYSOTHÉMIS:** A nous deux nul ne pense. Mort, Elektra, mort! En tèrre étrangère! Mort! très distant, Tout là-bas. Par ses chevaux, Qui s'emportèrent, écrase.
(En proie à un désespoir sauvage, elle s'écroule sur le seuil de la maison, aux côtés d'Elektra.)
(Un jeunne serviteur sort précipitamment de la maison, et bute contre celles qui sont étendues devant le seuil.)

**CHRYSOTHEMIS:** No one thinks of us. Dead, Elektra, dead! In a strange country! Dead! so far away, Down yonder. His horses ran away, they trampled on him.
(Overcome by savage despair, she falls prone upon the threshold of the house, beside Elektra. — A young servant comes hurriedly out of the house, and collides with the two girls, who are lying before the threshold.)

**LE JEUNE SERVITEUR:** Place! qui done épie, devant le seuil? Ah! Encore elle! Hé quelqu'en! hô!

**YOUNG SERVANT:** Give place! Who spies on the threshold? Ah! She again! Eh! Some one! Eh!

**VIEUX SERVITEUR:** (à la figure triste, se montre à la porte de la cour). Qu'est-ce donc? Que veux tu?

**OLD SERVANT:** (sad of countenance, appearing at the door of the court). What is it? What do you wish?

**LE JEUNE SERVITEUR:** Qu'on selle bien vite aussi vite que possible, Cheval, ou mule, ou bien même s'il le faut, une vâche, vite!

**YOUNG SERVANT:** Let a horse be saddled at once, Or a mule, or if necessary a cow— make haste.

**VIEUX SERVITEUR:** Pour qui?

**OLD SERVANT:** For whom?

**LE JEUNE SERVITEUR:** Pour qui te le commande. M'entends-tu? Vite, pour moi! Oui, oui, pour moi! Hop! hop! Il me faut joindre, aux champs, Le Maitre même, c'est un message que je lui porte Un message qui mérite que pour le porter vite Je crève une bête!
(Le Vieux sort aussi.)

**YOUNG SERVANT:** For him who commands you. Do you hear me? Quick, for me! Yes, yes, for me! Make haste, I must join the master at once, I bear a message to him— A message to be carried quickly, And on horseback.
(The old man also goes out.)

**ELEKTRA:** (à elle même, d'une voix basse, mais avec beaucoup d'énergie). C'est donc à nous d'agir ici.

**ELEKTRA:** (to herself in a low voice, but with great energy). It's for us to act here now.

**CHRYSOTHÉMIS:** (l'intèrrogeant, anxieuse). Elektra?

**CHRYSOTHEMIS:** (questioning her anxiously). Elektra?

**ELEKTRA:** (à voix précipitée). Nous, c'est nous qui devons le faire.

**ELEKTRA:** (precipitately). Yes, we must act.

**CHRYSOTHÉMIS:** Quoi, Elektra?

**CHRYSOTHEMIS:** What is it, Elektra?

**ELEKTRA:** (à voix basse). Aujourd'hui même, Ce sera mieux ce soir.

**ELEKTRA:** (in a low voice). Even today, Later this evening.

**CHRYSOTHÉMIS:** Quoi, Soeur?

**CHRYSOTHEMIS:** What is it, sister?

**ELEKTRA:** Quoi? La tâche Qui nous échoit à toutes deux, (Très douloureusement.) Puisque hélas il ne peut venir!

**ELEKTRA:** What? The task Which falls to us, (Very mournfully:) Since, alas! he cannot come.

CHRYSOTHÉMIS: (de plus en plus angoissée). Quelle est cette tâche?

ELEKTRA: Il nous faut toi et moi, aller, abattre
Et la femme et son homme!

CHRYSOTHÉMIS: (d'une voix basse et frissonante). Soeur, parles-tu de la Mère.

ELEKTRA: (farouche). D'elle et de lui.
Sans hésiter il nous faut agir.
Tais-toi. Parler n'est rien.
Nous ne devons songer qu'à ceci:
Comment ferons nous.

CHRYSOTHÉMIS: Moi?

ELEKTRA: Oui, toi et moi.
Quel autre?

CHRYSOTHÉMIS: (épouvantée).
Nous, nous deux tenter la chose
Nous, nous deux, avec ces mains-là?

ELEKTRA: Répose toi sur moi seule.
(Mystérieusement.)
La hache ...
(plus fort).
La hache dont le Père ...

CHRYSOTHÉMIS: Toi, c'est toi qui l'as!
Toi, ma soeur.

ELEKTRA: Je la gardais pour le Frère.
Mais que nos bras la lèvent.

CHRYSOTHÉMIS: Toi?
Se peut-il que tu frappes cet Aegisth?

ELEKTRA: (sauvage). Ou elle, puis lui, ou lui,
Puis elle, qu'importe!

CHRYSOTHÉMIS: Ah! que j'ai peur!

ELEKTRA: Nul ne veille devant sa porte.

CHRYSOTHÉMIS: Frapper qui dort!

ELEKTRA: Qui dort est la victime liée.
S'ils ne dormaient tous deux ensemble seule j'irais.
Mais j'ai besoin de toi.

CHRYSOTHÉMIS: (se défendant).
Elektra!

ELEKTRA: De toi!
De toi! car tu es forte.
Si forte tu es!
Ah! combien tes nuits
Virginales t'out faite robuste.
Tout ton etre plein de vigueur frémit.
Vive comme une pouliche,
Svelte est ta démarche.
Flexible ta taille et si souples
Tes deux frèles hanches.
Tu peux glisser par chaque fente,
Passer par les fenêtres!
Et combien tes tras que je tate sont frais
Et forts ma soeur.
Quand tu te débats, ah!
Quelle force est dans tes bras!

CHRYSOTHEMIS: (more and more distressed). What is this task?

ELEKTRA: We, you and I, must overcome
The woman and that man!

CHRYSOTHEMIS: (in a low voice and shuddering). Sister, do you speak of our mother?

ELEKTRA: (fiercely). Of her and of him.
Without hesitating we must act.
Be silent. Words are useless.
We must think of this alone:
How shall we act?

CHRYSOTHEMIS: I?

ELEKTRA: Yes, you and I.
What other?

CHRYSOTHEMIS: (frightened).
We, we two, to attempt this thing?
We, we two, with these hands of our?

ELEKTRA: Trust in me alone.
(Mysteriously:)
The axe ...
(Louder:)
The axe with which my father ...

CHRYSOTHEMIS: You, you have it!
You, my sister!

ELEKTRA: I kept it for my brother.
But let us grasp it now!

CHRYSOTHEMIS: You?
Do you mean to strike this man Aegisthes?

ELEKTRA: (savagely) Or her, then him, or him,
Then her, what matters it!

CHRYSOTHEMIS: Ah! I am afraid.

ELEKTRA: No one watches at the door.

CHRYSOTHEMIS: To strike the sleeper!

ELEKTRA: Who sleeps is the victim bound,
If they sleep not together, alone I'll go,
But should I need you—

CHRYSOTHEMIS: (in self defence). Elektra!

ELEKTRA: Should I need you.
For you are strong—
(Approaching Chrysothemis:)
You are so strong
Ah! How your peaceful nights have made you robust.
All your being is full of vigor.
Your spirit is like a young colt
Your limbs so slender
Your body so flexible and so supple
You can slip
Your two frail hips through any opening
Or enter by the window!
And how strong, my sister, are your arms
Whey you struggle, ah! What force is in your arms—

Et ce qu'ils étreignent,
Ils l'étoufféraient.
Oui tu pourrais, moi-même ou un homme,
Nous étouffer d'une etreinte,
Ton être plein de vigueur frémit.
Ainsi qu'une eau jaillissante coule d'un rocher,
Ainsi coule la force en tes longs cheveux denouées.
A travers la fraicheur ta chair ton jeune sang me brule.
Avec ma joue je sens le duvet Si fin des bras robustes.
Ah! que tu es forte, forte et belle,
Pareille à quelque fruit que l'été murit.

CHRYSOTHÉMIS: Laisse-moi!

ELEKTRA: Non je te garde à moi!
Avec mes tristes bras, mes bras si frèles,
J'entoure ton corps, plus tu résistes,
Plus je te serre et me noue,
Et je te lierai aprement,
Je plongerai mes racines en toi
Pour que mon vouloir s'infiltre en ton sang.

CHRYSOTHÉMIS: Laisse-moi!
(Elle s'écarte de quelques pas.)

ELEKTRA: (poursuit sauvagement et la rétient par sa robe).
Non, n'y compte pas.

CHRYSOTHÉMIS: Elektra, grace!
O toi, si sage,
Tache que nous fuyions.
Ah! fais nous libres!
Elektra, grace,
Ah! fais-nous libres ...

ELEKTRA: C'est maintenant que je veux être ta soeur,
Mais une soeur que je fus jamais!
Je veux, à tes côtés assise dan ta chambre,
Attendre ton fiancé.
Pour lui j'oindrai ton corps
Et mes mains dans un bain parfume te longeront, doux cygne,
Et c'est la tête sur mon sem cachée.
Qu'émue tremblante, tu recevras l'hommage de l'époux,
Avant qu'au lit des noces ses bras robustes t'attirent.

CHRYSOTHÉMIS: (fermant les yeux). Non, Soeur, non!
De telles choses, ici, ne les dis pas.

ELEKTRA: Oh! oui, bien mieux.
Bien mieux qu'une soeur serai-je pour toi désormais:
Je veux, pour toi être une esclave!
Quand viendront tes couches, prés de toi
Je serai sans tréve jour et nuit,
Chassant les mouches, te versant l'eau fraiche
Et lorsque, tout à coup de ton flane,
Qui saigne un être vivant sortira,
Si frèle et nu, je veux l'éléve bien haut.
Pour que son sourire qui rayonne
Doucement jusqu'au plus profond de ton âme tombe.

What they seize, they crush.
Yes, you could crush me or a man
With but little effort,
Your being is so full of vigor.
Like a foaming stream falling from a rock,
So flows the strength in your long hair untied.
Through your fresh skin, your young blood boils.
I feel it, with my cheek I feel
The velvet texture of your robust arms.
Ah! How strong you are strong and beautiful,
Like some fruit which ripens in summer.

CHRYSOTHEMIS: Leave me!

ELEKTRA: No; I keep you here!
With my poor weak arms
I hold your body, and if you resist
I clasp you closer, linking you to me.
I'll even root myself in you
So my will may reach your blood.

CHRYSOTHEMIS: Leave me!
(She moves away a few paces.)

ELEKTRA: (following her, and seizing hold of her dress). No; think not of it.

CHRYSOTHEMIS: Elektra, please!
Oh you are so wise,
Let us escape.
Ah! Let us be free!

ELEKTRA: It is now I wish to be your sister,
But such a sister as I never was before!
I wish to sit beside you in your chamber.
To await your lover,
To anoint your body for him,
And plunge my hands in a perfumed bath, sweet swan,
And, your head upon your breast, trembling,
You will receive the homage of your spouse.

CHRYSOTHEMIS: (closing her eyes). No, sister, no!
Such things do not here.

ELEKTRA: Oh! Yes, even more than a sister
I shall be to you from now on:
I wish to be your slave
To wait upon you night and day,
Pouring your water,
And when your child is born,
I would raise it in my arms
So that its smile should reach you
And your soul be filled with joy.
Then, your anguish banished by this new light,
O, my sister, your happy tears would flow.

Alors, sentant l'ancienne angoisse
par ce soleil chassée.
O ma soeur, en claires larmes fon-
dront tes yeux.

**CHRYSOTHÉMIS:** Emporte-moi!
Je meurs entre ces murs!

**ELEKTRA:** (*aux genoux de Chry-
sothémis*). Ta bouche est belle lo-
rsqu'elle
S'ouvre et crie avec colère!
De cette bouche forte un cri terri-
ble,
Un cri devra sortir, terrible,
Ainsi qu'un cri de Thanato;
C'est quand, à tes pieds ils giront là
où je gis.

**CHRYSOTHÉMIS:** Que veux-tu
dire?

**ELEKTRA:** (*se relevant*). Avant de
fuir et la maison et moi,
Il fant que tu agisses.
(*Chrysothémis vent parler, Elektra lui ferme la bouche.*)

**ELEKTRA:** Voici le seul chemin
qui mène hors d'ici.
Si tu veux qu'il te soit ouvert jure
moi que tu vas agir.

**CHRYSOTHÉMIS:** (*se détachant*).
Laisse moi!

**ELEKTRA:** (*la saisissant de nou-
veau*). Jure de venir,
Cette nuit même,
Au pied des marches.

**CHRYSOTHÉMIS:** Laisse-moi!

**ELEKTRA:** (*la tenant par sa
robe*). Ne crains pas, enfant,
De conserver la moindre tache de
sang.
Vite, au sortir des vètements rougis,
Tu vétiras le voile nuptial!

**CHRYSOTHÉMIS:** Laiss-moi!

**ELEKTRA:** (*toujours plus
préssante*). Ne sois pas lâche!
Et surmonte l'horreur de cet instant
Que paieront tant de joies durant
de longues nuits.

**CHRYSOTHÉMIS:** N'y compte pas!

**ELEKTRA:** Dis que tu vas venir!

**CHRYSOTHÉMIS:** N'y compte pas!

**ELEKTRA:** Vois, je sus couchée à
tes pieds que j'embrasse!

**CHRYSOTHÉMIS:** N'y compte pas!
(*S'enfuyant par la porte de la maison.*)

**ELEKTRA:** Je te hais!
(*Avec une résolution sauvage.*)
Allons à toute seule!
(*Silencieusement, à la façon
d'une bête, elle va creuser le long
du mur de la maison, à côté du
seuil de la porte.—Elektra
s'arrête de creuser, regardant autour d'elle.—Elle creuse de nouveau.—Une nouvelle fois Elektra
regarde autour d'elle et écoute.—
Elektra se remet à creuser.—Or-

**CHRYSOTHEMIS:** Take me away, I
die between these walls.

**ELEKTRA:** (*at the knees of Chrysothemis*). Your mouth is beautiful
when it opens,
And it cries with anger.
From that strong mouth a cry most
terrible
Shall be heard, as terrible as Thanato's cry!
It is when they lie at your feet, as I
do now.

**CHRYSOTHEMIS:** What do you
mean?

**ELEKTRA:** (*rising*). Before you
leave the house and me,
You must act.
(*Chrysothemis tries to speak.—
Elektra closes her mouth.*)

**ELEKTRA:** Behold, just one road
leads here.
If you find it open, swear that you
will act.

**CHRYSOTHEMIS:** (*freeing herself*). Leave me!

**ELEKTRA:** (*seizing her again*).
Swear that you will come,
This very night,
To the foot of the stairs.

**CHRYSOTHEMIS:** Leave me!

**ELEKTRA:** (*holding her dress*).
Fear not, child,
To keep the least spot of blood,
When you lay aside the reddened
garments,
You shall put on the nuptial veil.

**CHRYSOTHEMIS:** Leave me!

**ELEKTRA:** (*still more urgently*).
Don't be a coward!
Overcome the horror of this mo-
ment.
Long nights of pleasure shall repay
you.

**CHRYSOTHEMIS:** Don't count on
it!

**ELEKTRA:** Say that you will come!

**CHRYSOTHEMIS:** Don't count on
it!

**ELEKTRA:** See, I am at your feet,
which I embrace!

**CHRYSOTHEMIS:** Don't count on
it!
(*Escaping through the door of the
house.*)

**ELEKTRA:** I hate you!
(*With savage resolution:*)
Let us go alone!
(*Silently, in the manner of a wild
animal, she creeps along the wall
of the house, to the threshold of
the door.—Elektra stops creeping, looking around her.—She
creeps forward again.—Again
she looks around her and listens.—Elektra begins to creep forward again.—Orestes appears in

est se dresse dans l'encadrement
de la porte de la cour, et sa silhouette se découpe en noir sur les dernières clartés du jour—Orest
s'avance.—Elektra lève les yeux
sur lui, il se tourne lentement de
son côté, et son regard tombe sur
elle.—Elektra se redresse vivement.*)

**ELEKTRA:** (*tremblante*). Que
veux-tu done, étranger?
Que cherches-tu ô noir rodeur de
l'ombre,
Pourquoi m'epier ainsi?
Je fais ici ma tâche.
Et que t'importe?
Laisse-moi seule!

**OREST:** Je dois attendre.

**ELEKTRA:** Attendre?

**OREST:** Mais, n'es-tu pas du logis?
Serais-tu pas servante en ce logis?

**ELEKTRA:** Oui, je sers en ce logis.
Toi meme, qu'ici rien n'appele,
sois heureux, va-t'en!

**OREST:** Je te l'ai dit:
Je dois attendre que l'on m'appele.

**ELEKTRA:** Qu'on t'appelle? Tu
mens.
Je sais bien que le Maitre est absent.
Et elle, que pourrait-el-te vouloir?

**OREST:** Moi, et un autre qui
m'accompagne,
Nous portons un message à la
Reine.
Vers elle on nous envoie pour tem-
oigner ensemble
Que son fils Orest à succombe à no-
tre vue,
Ecrase par ses coursiers eux-
mêmes.
J'étais de son âge, et son ami de cha-
que instant.

**ELEKTRA:** Oses-tu paraitre, ramper devant moi
En ma lugubre retraite, Heraut funeste!
Ton affreux message va le trompeter la où l'on s'égaye!
Si ta paupiere luit la sienne n'est
close.
Ta bouche à toi se meut, la sienne
est immobile, emplie de tèrre.
Tu vis, et lui, cent fois meilleur que
toi,
Cent fois plus noble aussi,
Et qui pour cent raisons aurait du
vivre, il est mort!

**OREST:** (*avec calme*). Laisse Orest
Il se rejouissait par trop de vivre.
Les Dieux, la-haut n'aiment guère
le cris de l'humaine joie.
Il meritait la tombe.

the doorway of the court, and his
silhouette is clearly defined in
black by the dying light of the
day.—Orestes comes forward.—
Elektra raises her eyes and sees
him; he turns slowly towards her,
and his eyes fall upon her.—Elektra gets up quickly.*)

**ELEKTRA:** (*trembling*). What do
you wish, stranger?
What do you seek, oh, shadow,
Why spy on me like this?
I here accomplish my task.
And what is it to you?
Leave me alone!

**ORESTES:** I must wait.

**ELEKTRA:** Wait?

**ORESTES:** But are you not of the
house?
Perhaps a servant here?

**ELEKTRA:** Yes, I serve in this
house.
Be happy that nothing calls you
here.
Begone!

**ORESTES:** I have told you.
I must wait here until they call me.

**ELEKTRA:** Till they call you? You
lie.
I know full well that the Master is
absent.
And she, what could she want of
you?

**ORESTES:** I and another who ac-
companied me,
We bring a message to the Queen.
They send us to her as witnesses
That her son Orestes died before
our eyes,
Crushed by his chargers,
I was the same age as he and his
dearest friend.

**ELEKTRA:** Do you dare appear be-
fore me
In my dark retreat, sad Herald!
Your awful message, go announce
it
To those who now divert them-
selves!
If your eyelid shines hers is not
closed.
Your mouth is silent, hers is mo-
tionless, filled with earth.
You live, and he, a hundred times
better than you,
A hundred times more noble also,
And who for a hundred reasons
would have lived, is dead!

**ORESTES:** (*calmly*). Let Orestes
be.
He loved to live.
The gods above love not the shouts
of human joy.
He deserved the tomb.

# Act I, Scene IV

**ELEKTRA:** Mais moi!
Etre là, et me dire que l'enfant
Ne reviendra pas, jamais, plus jamais
Que l'enfant, là-bas, dans les ombre du Styx se traine . . .
Tandis que ces gens-la vivent se réjouissent,
Que leur engeance en cette bauge vit et mange et boit et dort . . .
Et moi-même, plus misérable que bête dans les bois,
Moi je vis seule, toujours!

**OREST:** Qui donc es-tu?

**ELEKTRA:** Et que t'importe qui je suis?

**OREST:** Tu dois être d'un sang très-proche de ces morts:
Agamemnon et Orest.

**ELEKTRA:** Très-proche? Je suis ce sang.
Je suis le propre sang du roi des roi Agamemnon.
Elektra même.

**OREST:** Non.

**ELEKTRA:** Il me dément.
Il souffle sur moi et veut me prendre mon nom.

**OREST:** Elektra!

**ELEKTRA:** Enfant sans père . . .

**OREST:** Elektra!

**ELEKTRA:** Sans Frère, et ce gamin me raille!

**OREST:** Elektra! Elektra!
Vous, je vous vois?
Je vous vois vraiment, toi?
Est-ce ainsi que l'on t'a traitée?
Peut-être . . . ils out osé te battre?

**ELEKTRA:** Laisse-moi!
Des yeux ne fouille pas ma robe.

**OREST:** Ah! qu'on ils donc fait de tes nuits, les traitres?
Oh! tes regards terribles!

**ELEKTRA:** Laisse-moi!

**OREST:** Oh! tes pauvres joues!

**ELEKTRA:** Entre là, tu verras ma soeur qui se garde
Pour de joyeuses fêtes!

**OREST:** Ecoute, Elektra!

**ELEKTRA:** Que m'importe qui tu es?
Qu'on me laisse en paix!

**OREST:** Le Temps presse, écoute moi, écoute!
(à voix basse.)
Orest vit!
(Elektra se retourne vivement.)
Tais-toi, ou sinon tu le trahis!

**ELEKTRA:** N'est-il pas libre? Où est-il?

**OREST:** Il est sain et sauf comme moi.

**ELEKTRA:** Sauve-le donc avant qu'ils ne l'étranglent.

---

**ELEKTRA:** But I!
To be there and say the child
Will not come, never, never again.
That the child, below, amid the shadow of Styx is drawn . . .
While these people live rejoicing,
May their brood, in this lair, live and eat and drink and sleep . . .
Ah, more miserable than the forest beasts,
I live alone, always!

**ORESTES:** Who, then, are you?

**ELEKTRA:** What does it matter to you who I am?

**ORESTES:** You must be of kinship with the dead—Agamemnon and Orestes.

**ELEKTRA:** Kinship? I am of their blood. I am the true blood of the king of kings, Agamemnon.
Elektra, even.

**ORESTES:** No.

**ELEKTRA:** He contradicts me.
He breathes upon me and would take away my name.

**ORESTES:** Elektra!

**ELEKTRA:** A child without a father . . .

**ORESTES:** Elektra!

**ELEKTRA:** Without a brother, and this boy jeers at me!

**ORESTES:** Elektra! Elektra!
Do I see you?
Do I really see you, yourself?
Have they, then, treated you like this?
Perhaps . . . they have dared to beat you?

**ELEKTRA:** Leave me!
Remove your gaze from off my dress.

**ORESTES:** Ah! what have they made your nights, the traitors?
Oh! Your terrible looks!

**ELEKTRA:** Leave me!

**ORESTES:** Oh! Your poor cheeks!

**ELEKTRA:** Go in there, you will see my sister who prepares
For a joyous festival!

**ORESTES:** Listen, Elektra!

**ELEKTRA:** What is it to me who you are?
Let me be in peace!

**ORESTES:** Time presses, listen to me, listen!
(In a low voice:)
Orestes lives!
(Elektra turns round quickly.)
Hush, or you betray him!

**ELEKTRA:** Is he not free? Where is he?

**ORESTES:** He is safe and sound, as I.

**ELEKTRA:** Save him, then, before they slay him.

---

**OREST:** Par le corps de mon Père,
Pour cela je viens!

**ELEKTRA:** (frappée de son accent). Mais, qui donc es-tu?
(Le vieux serviteur à la figure triste, suivi de trois autres serviteurs, sort silencieusement de la cour. Il se prosterne devant Orest, dont il baise les pieds, tandis que les autres embrassent et les mains et le bas de la robe d'Orest.)

**ELEKTRA:** (se maitrisant avec peine).
Qui donc, qui donc es-tu?
Ah! j'ai peur!

**OREST:** (doucement). Les chiens du logis me reconnaissent . . .
(plus haut.)
Mais non ma propre soeur!

**ELEKTRA:** (dans un cri). Orest!
(Tout bas, tremblant.)
Orest! Orest! Orest!
Non, rien ne bouge.
Oh! ton chèr regard que je le voie.
Vision retrouvée, plus douce encor.
Que le plus doux rève.
Adorable, adoré visage d'un frère,
C'est bien toi!
Ah! ne va pas t'évanouir,
Ah! reste devant mes yeux,
Ne t'enfuis pas si ce n'est pour m'emportes.
Avec toi ou pour me dire qu'il me faut mourir:
La mort je l'aime, venant par toi!
Orest! Orest! Orest!
(Orest se penche vers Elektra, et ils s'embrassent.)

**ELEKTRA:** (avec violence). Non, tu ne dois pas m'étreindre!
Va-t'en!
J'ai honte devant toi.
Que vois-tu quand tu me fixes?
Je suis l'affreux cadavre de ta soeur,
Mon pauvre enfant.
Je sais tu trembles devant moi,
Pourtant d'un très grand Roi j'étais fille.
Je crois que j'étais belle:
Quand je jetais le yeux sur mon miroir,
Quelque chose me le disait tout bas.
De même, lorsque, sur la blancheur de mon corps nu
Se réflétaient les froids rayons nocturnes,
Ainsi qu'en un lac pale.
Mes cheveux étajent de ceux.
Devant qui l'homme tremble.
Ceux-ci, mélés, souillés, informes,
Me comprends-tu, Frère?
Ce que j'avais, jadis, il fallut
Que je l'abandonne.
Ma pudeur fut immolée, vertu
Meilleure que tout au monde, vertu
Enveloppante et frèle, qui tisse autour
Des femmes un rayonnant manteau d'argent
Et protège leur âme chaste des

---

**ORESTES:** By my father's body,
It is that brings me here!

**ELEKTRA:** (struck by the accent).
But who, then, are you?
(The old servant with the sad countenance, followed by three other servants, comes silently from the court. He prostrates himself before Orestes, whose feet he kisses, while the others embrace the hands and the skirts of Orestes' robe.)

**ELEKTRA:** (recovering herself with difficulty). Who, then, are you?
Ah! I am afraid!

**ORESTES:** (softly). The dogs of the house knew me—
(Louder:)
But not my own sister!

**ELEKTRA:** (with a cry). Orestes!
(Very low, trembling:)
Orestes! Orestes! Orestes!
No, nothing moves.
Ah! Your dear countenance which I behold,
Your looks of old, sweeter than the sweetest dream.
Beloved, adored countenance of a brother,
It is you indeed!
Ah! vanish not from me,
Ah! remain before my eyes,
Go not unless it is to take me
With you or to tell me that I must die:
I love death, coming to me through you!
Orestes! Orestes! Orestes!
(Orestes stoops towards Elektra, and they embrace.)

**ELEKTRA:** (violently). No, you must not embrace me! Go!
I am ashamed before you.
What do you behold in me?
I am the awful shadow of your sister,
My poor child.
I know you tremble before me,
Although I was the daughter of a mighty king.
I believe that I was beautiful:
When I look now within my mirror,
What does it whisper to me?
So, too, when the cold night rays upon the whiteness of my naked body reflect,
As in a pale, calm lake.
My hair was once like those
Before whom all men tremble.
These, knotted, soiled, disordered,
Do you understand, my brother?
What was mine I had to leave behind.
My modesty was sacrificed,
Virtue, better than all else, virtue
Enveloping yet frail, which clothes
All womanhood as with a silver mantle
And protects their pure, white souls from stain,
Do you understand, my brother?
This sweet thing, I had to offer up in homage to my father.

souillures,
Comprends-tu, non Frère?
Cette douce chose, j'ai dû, au Père
en faire hommage.
Crois-tu donc, qu'au temps ou mon
corps
Enchantait mes yeux que ses plaintifs soupirs
Que ses gémissements ne troublaient pas mes nuits?
Ils sont jaloux les trépassés, et lui,
A la seule haine, la haine aux yeux
creux il m'a fiancée.
De moi il fit prophétesse toujours
inspirée,
Et rien n'est plus sorti de moi-
même.
Non, plus rien que cris de vengeance.
Pourquoi tressailles-tu donc?
Parle-moi! Parle!
Pourquoi trembler de tout ton
corps?

**OREST:** Il tremble tout ce corps,
Sachant quel chemin je le mène.

**ELEKTRA:** Tu vas agir? Tout seul?
Toi, pauvre enfant?

**OREST:** Ceux qui la veulent cette
action ...

**ELEKTRA:** Tu veux agir!

**OREST:** ... Les Dieux viendront en
aide à ma faiblesse.

**ELEKTRA:** Bien heureux qui peut
agir!

**OREST:** Je veux agir, et je le veux
sur l'heure.

**ELEKTRA:** L'action est comme un
lit sur lequel l'âme repose.

**OREST:** Je veux, je veux agir!

**ELEKTRA:** Comme un lit de
baume,
Ou notre àme repose,
Elle qui est la plaie,
Le brandon, la purulence et la
flamme!

**OREST:** Je veux agir!

**ELEKTRA:** Bienheureux qui vient
parfaire l'oeuvre,
Bienheureux qui l'attendit,
Bienheureux qui l'aperçoit!
Bienheureux qui connait l'homme,
Bienheureux qui l'approche.
Bienheureux qui lui déterre la
hache
Bienheureux qui lui tient la torche;
Bienheureux, bienheureux qui lui
ouvre la porte.
(Le Précepteur, d'Orest, vieillard
robuste, aux veux étinceiants, pa-
rait sur le seuil de la porte de la
cour.)

**LE PRÉCEPTEUR:** (courant vive-
ment à eux). Insensés, dont la
bouche bavarde,
Quand un souffle, un cri, un rien
Peuvent nous briser, nous et notre
oeuvre?
(À Orest, avec précipitation:)
Elle t'attend.

Do you believe that when my body
My eyes enchanted, his plaintive
sighs
His groans did not disturb my
nights.
The dead are jealous, and he
To a single hate—the hate with hol-
low eyes—affianced me.
He made me prophetess inspired,
And nothing else was heard from
me,
But cries of vengeance—nothing
else.
Why shudder, then, my brother?
Speak! Speak to me!
Why does your body tremble so?

**ORESTES:** It trembles, every member,
Knowing well the path before it.

**ELEKTRA:** You will act? You
alone?
Poor child?

**ORESTES:** Those who wish this action ...

**ELEKTRA:** You wish to act!

**ORESTES:** ... The gods shall aid my
weakness.

**ELEKTRA:** Thrice happy he who
can act!

**ORESTES:** I wish to act and now.

**ELEKTRA:** Action is like a bed on
which the soul reposes.

**ORESTES:** I wish, I wish to act.

**ELEKTRA:** Like a bed of balm,
Where our soul reposes,
She who is the sore,
The purulence, and the flame!

**ORESTES:** I wish to act!

**ELEKTRA:** Happy he who comes to
end the work,
Happy he who awaited it,
Happy he who saw it!
Happy he who knows the man,
Happy he who approaches him.
Happy he who unearths the axe,
Happy he who hands him the torch;
Happy, thrice happy he who opens
for him the door!
(Orestes' Preceptor, a robust old
man, with keen eyes, appears
upon the threshold of the door of
the court.)

**THE PRECEPTOR:** (running
quickly to them).
You are fools to chatter like this,
When a breath, a cry, a trifle,
May undo us, ah, and our work!
(To Orestes, precipitately:)
She awaits you.
Her servants are seeking you, Or-

Ses servantes sont à ta recherche.
Pas un homme au logis.
Orest!
(Orest se redresse, réprimant, un
frisson.—La porte de la maison
s'éclaire. Une servante parait, une
torche à la main, derrière elle La
Confidente. Elektra qui s'est rejetée en arrière, se tient dans
l'ombre.—La Confidente
s'incline devant les deux
étrangers, et leur fait signe de la
suivre, Orest et Le Précepteur vont
pour entrer.—La servante fixe la
torche à un anneau de fer, dans le
montant de la porte.—Orest, pris
d'un etourdissement, ferme un
instant les yeux, Le Précepteur est
tout contre lui, ils échangent un
regard rapide, la porte se ferme
sur eux.—Elektra seule, dans une
horrible attente. Tête baissée, pareille à une bête fauve dans sa cage,
elle passe et repasse devant la
porte.)

**ELEKTRA:** (s'arrétant tout à
coup) Je n'ai pas eu le temps de
donner la hache!
Ils sont partis et je n'ai pas en le
temps
De donner la hache
Il n'est pas de Dieux au ciel!
(Encore un terrible moment
d'attente.—Du loin, dans le palais, un cri aigu de Klytaimnestra.)

**ELEKTRA:** (hurlant comme un
Demon). Frappe, frappe encor!
(Second cri dans le palais.—Elektra se place devant le seuil,
adossée à la porte.—Chry-
sothémis et une foule de suivantes, sortent du corps de bati-
ment de gauche.)

**CHRYSOTHÉMIS:** Quelque chose
a du se passer?

**PREMIÈRE SERVANTE:** Elle crie
comme en dormant.

**DEUXIÈME SERVANTE:** Il est entré des hommes.

**TROISIÈME SERVANTE:** Toutes
les portes sont verrouillées!

**DEUXIÈME SERVANTE:** J'ai vu
entrer des hommes, certes.

**QUATRIÈME SERVANTE:**
(criant). Des assassins! Des assassins sont la!

**PREMIÈRE SERVANTE:** (criant).
Oh!

**DEUXIÈME ET TROISIÈME SER-
VANTE:** Quoi donc?

**PREMIÈRE SERVANTE:** Voyez-
vous pas, là, quelqu'un se tient à la
porte!

**CHRYSOTHÉMIS:** Mais c'est Elek-
tra!
Oui, c'est bien Elektra! Elektra,
Pourquoi ne parles tu pas?

estes!
(Orestes gets up, repressing a
shudder.—The door of the house
is illumined. A maid appears, a
torch in her hand, behind her The
Companion.—Elektra, who has
shrunk back, keeps in the shadow.—The Companion bows low
before the two strangers, and
makes a sign to them to follow
her.—Orestes and The Preceptor
move forward to enter.—The
Maid fastens the torch in an iron
ring in the facing of the door.—
Orestes, suddenly seized with dizziness, closes his eyes for an instant.—The Preceptor is opposite
him, they exchange a rapid
glance, the door closes upon
them.—Elektra, alone, waits in
terrible anxiety. Her head lowered, like a wild beast in its cage,
she walks up and down before the
door.)

**ELEKTRA:** (stopping suddenly) I
did not have the time to give him
the axe!
They have gone and I did not have
the time
To give him that axe,
There are no gods in heaven!
(Another moment of terrible,
anxious waiting.)
(In the distance, within the pal-
ace, a sharp, piercing cry from
Klytaimnestra.)

**ELEKTRA:** (screaming like a demon). Strike, strike again!
(Another cry within the palace.)
(Elektra places herself before the
threshold, leaning against the
door.)
(Chrysothemis and a crowd of
servants come out of the building
at left.)

**CHRYSOTHEMIS:** What is happening?

**FIRST MAID:** She screams as in her
sleep.

**SECOND MAID:** Men have gone in.

**THIRD MAID:** All the doors are
locked!

**SECOND MAID:** I saw men go in,
believe me.

**FOURTH MAID:** (shouting). Assassins! Assassins are there!

**FIRST MAID:** (crying). Oh!

**SECOND AND THIRD MAID:**
What then?

**FIRST MAID:** Look! there's some
one at the door!

**CHRYSOTHEMIS:** It's Elektra.
Yes, Elektra! Elektra!
Why do you not speak?

## Act I, Scene IV

**PREMIÈRE et DEUXIÈME SERVANTES:** Elektra! Elektra! Pourquoi ne parles tu pas?

**FIRST AND SECOND MAID:** Elektra! Elektra! Why do you not speak?

**TROISIÈME et QUATRIÈME SERVANTES:** Elektra! Elektra!

**THIRD AND FOURTH MAID:** Elektra! Elektra!

**QUATRIÈME SERVANTE:** (*seule*). Je veux dehors chercher des hommes! (*Elle sort en courant par la droite.*)

**FOURTH MAID:** (*alone*). I must go and look for men! (*She runs out at right.*)

**CHRYSOTHÉMIS:** Ouvre nous la porte, Elektra!

**CHRYSOTHEMIS:** Open the door for us, Elektra!

**SIX SERVANTES:** Elektra, ouvra la porte!

**SIX MAIDS:** Elektra, open the door!

**CHRYSOTHÉMIS:** Elektra!

**CHRYSOTHEMIS:** Elektra!

**QUATRIÈME SERVANTE:** (*revenant*). Arrière! Aegisth! Arrière! Vite, en nos chambres, vite! Aegisth viene par ici.

**FOURTH MAID:** (*returning*). Stand Back! Aegisthes! Back! Quick, to your rooms! Here Aegisthes comes.

**SIX SERVANTES:** Aegisth!

**SIX MAIDS:** Aegisthes!

**I, I, III, SERVANTE:** Aegisth!

**FIRST, SECOND AND THIRD MAID:** Aegisthes!

**QUATRIÈME SERVANTE:** Et s'il nous trouve, si quelque chose s'est passé dedans, il nous tueras!

**FOURTH MAID:** And if he finds us here, if anything has happened He will slay us.

**CHRYSOTHÉMIS:** Arrière!

**CHRYSOTHEMIS:** Get back!

**I, II, III SERVANTE:** Arrière!

**FIRST, SECOND AND THIRD MAID:** Back!

**SIX SERVANTES:** Arrière! (*Elles disparaissent dans le maison, à gauche.*)

**SIX MAIDS:** Back! (*They disappear into the house, at left.*)

**I, II, III SERVANTE:** Arrière! (*Aegisth entre, de droite, par la porte de la cour.*)

**FIRST, SECOND AND THIRD MAID:** Back! (*Aegisthes enters, at right, through the door of the court.*)

**AEGISTH:** (*s'arrêtant sur la seuil*). Des torches! Des torches! Pour m'éclairer, personne? Pas un seul coquin ici ne remue? Est-ce là comme on sert, canailles? (*Elektra sort la torche de l'anneau, déscend à sa rencontre en courant, et s'incline devant lui.—Aegisth recule, éffrayé par cette apparition confuse qu'il entrevoit à la lueur tremblante de la torche.*)

**AEGISTHES:** (*stopping short on the threshold*). Torches there! Torches! To light me! Not even a varlet stirs! Is that how they serve, the rascals! (*Elektra takes the torch from the ring, descends to meet him running, and bows low before him.*) (*Aegisthes shirks back, startled by the confused apparition which he discerns by the trembling light of the torch.*)

**AEGISTH:** Ah! quelle est donc cette éffrayante femme? J'ai fait defense à tout étranger, Quel qu'il soit, de s'approcher de moi! (*Il la reconnait:*) Toi! Toi! Qui donc à ma rencontre t'envoie?

**AEGISTHES:** Ah! who is this frightful woman? I forbade them to admit a stranger, Whoever you are, do not approach! (*he recognizes her.*) You! You? Who sent you to meet me?

**ELEKTRA:** Faut-il que j'éclaire?

**ELEKTRA:** Shall I light you?

**AEGISTH:** Mais, j'y pense la nouvelle t'intéresse fort. Où sont-ils donc ces étrangers Qui disent qu'Orest ést mort?

**AEGISTHES:** But, I think the news must greatly interest you. Who are these two strangers Who say Orestes is dead?

**ELEKTRA:** Entre. Une aimable hotesse les a reçus Ils se divertissent avec elle.

**ELEKTRA:** Enter. An aimable hostess has received them, They are now engaged with her.

**AEGISTH:** Est-il vrai qu'ils annoncent, Qu'Orest est mort, bien mort? Et de façon qu'on n'en saurait douter?

**AEGISTHES:** Is it true what they announce, That Orestes is really dead? In such a way that no doubt remains?

**ELEKTRA:** O Maitre ce n'est pas qu'en paroles, Qu'ils affirment ce qu'ils disent, Devant leur preuves nul doute n'est possible.

**ELEKTRA:** O Master, it is not by word alone That they affirm their speech, With such proofs as theirs no doubt is possible.

**AEGISTH:** Qu'y a-t-il dans ta voix? Et que t'arrive-t-il pour me parler ainsi? Pourquoi chancelles-tu ainsi avec la torche?

**AEGISTHES:** What is there in your voice? What has happened that makes you speak like this? Why do you waver with the torch?

**ELEKTRA:** C'est facile à comprendre, C'est qu'à présent plus sage, plus prudente, Au parti du plus fort je me range. Permets que j'éclaire ici ta marche.

**ELEKTRA:** It is easy to understand, Simply that, being now wiser and more prudent, I take the side of the strongest party. Allow me to light thy steps.

**AEGISTH:** (*un peu hésitant*). Jusqu'à la porte. (*Elektra, l'enveloppe d'une danse inquietante, puis s'incline profondement tout à coup.*) Que danses-tu? Prends garde!

**AEGISTHES:** (*hesitating a little*). To the door. (*Elektra envelopes him with a disquieting dance, then suddenly bows low before him.*) Why do you dance? Take care!

**ELEKTRA:** Voici les marches, ne tombe pas!

**ELEKTRA:** Here's the stairs, don't fall!

**AEGISTH:** (*sur le pas de la porte*). D'où vient que tout est sombre? Et qui sont ces gens?

**AEGISTHES:** (*on the threshold*). Why is it so dark? And who are these people?

**ELEKTRA:** Ceux-là mêmes qui en personne de sirent te saluer, Maitre. Et moi, qui souvent par mon importune présence t'exasperai, je saurai bien cette fois. Quand il le faudra, Maitre, rentre dans l'ombre. (*Aegisth entre dans la maison. Silence.—Bruit à l'intérieur.*)

**ELEKTRA:** Those who wish to salute you in person, Master. And I, who often by my awkward presence, exasperated you, now know When the Master must enter within the shadow. (*Aegisthes enters the house.—Silence.—Noise within.*)

**AEGISTH:** (*apparait à une petite fenêtre dont il arrache le rideau*). A l'aide! Au meurtre! Au meurtre! À moi! à moi! N'est-il personne qui m'entende? (*On l'enlève.*)

**AEGISTHES:** (*appearing at a small window, the curtain of which he tears down*). Help! Murder! Murder! Help! Help! Does no one hear me? (*He is dragged away.*)

**ELEKTRA:** (*haut dressée*). Agamemnon t'entend! (*Le visage d'Aegisth apparait encore une fois à la fenêtre.*)

**ELEKTRA:** (*raising herself high*). Agamemnon hears you. (*Aegisthes' face appears again at the window.*)

**AEGISTH:** Ah! malheur! (*Il est emporté.—Elektra, debout face à la maison, halète horriblement—Les femmes accourent de gauche, Chrysothémis est au milieu d'ellès. Comme inconscientes, elles se précipitent vers la porte de la cour, et la, soudain s'arrêtent, et se retournent.*)

**AEGISTHES:** Ah! misfortune! (*He is borne away.—Elektra, standing facing the door, pants horribly.—Women rush in from the left, Chrysothemis amongst them.—As if bewildered, they hurl themselves towards the door of the court, then suddenly they stop and turn around.*)

**CHRYSOTHÉMIS:** Elektra, Soeur! Viens avec nous! Oh! viens avec nous! C'est notre Frère qui est là! Oui, c'est Orest qui nous delivre!

**CHRYSOTHEMIS:** Elektra! Sister! Come with us! It is our brother who is there! Yes, it is Orestes who delivers us!

**HOMMES:** (*dans la maison*). Orest! Orest!

**MEN:** (*in the house*). Orestes! Orestes!

DEX VOIX DERRIÈRE LA SCENE: Orest!
(*Tumulte dans la maison, éclats de voix parmi lesquels on distingue de loin l'appel des chœurs: "Orest!"*)

CHRYSOTHÉMIS: Viens! Il est dans la salle,
Tous autour de lui sont là,
Et baisent ses genoux,
Ceux qui pour Aegisth cachaient leur haine,
Ont assailli les partisans du traitre,
Et partout, dans chaque cour, gisent des cadavres,
Même ceux qui vivent sont couverts de sang,
Et criblés de blessures.
(*Le tumulte de la bataille, de la bataille mortelle entre les esclaves partisans d'Orest et les tenants d'Aegisth s'est etendu peu à peu aux cours intérieures, avec lesquelles, à droite, communique la porte de la cour.*)

CHOEUR: (*derrière la scène.— Femmes et hommes*). Orest! Orest!

CHRYSOTHÉMIS: Mais ils sont en joie! en joie!
Tous s'embrassent, crient de joie.
(*Tumulte croissant au dehors, qui lorsqu'Elektra commencera, s'éteignant de plus en plus, à droite et au fond, du côté des cours éxtérieures. Les femmes sont sorties en courant.*)

CHRYSOTHÉMIS: Mille torches, s'embrasent et brillent,
Entends-tu? Entends-tu?
(*Chrysothémis seule est restée, lumière vient du dehors.*)
Ah! n'entends-tu pas?

FEMMES et HOMMES: (*plus loin*). Orest! Orest!

ELEKTRA: (*accroupie sur le scull*). Si je n'entends pas?
Si je n'entends pas la musique!
Elle sort de moi-même.
Ces mille porteurs de torches dont j'entends les pas dont j'entends sonner par myriades les pas.
Tout outour de moi, oh! douce harmonie,
Tous, je le sais, m'attendent;
Je sais bien ce que tous attendent.
Et que je dois mener leur danse.
Et je ne puis; un Océan, un prodigieux
Un incommensurable Océan enlize tous mes membres
En ses ondes, me lever m'est impossible!

CHRYSOTHÉMIS: N'entends-tu donc pas?
Ils le portent tous, le portent sur leurs mains tromphantes!
(*Elle se lève.*)

VOICES BEHIND THE SCENES: Orestes!
(*Tumult in the house; noise of voices, amongst which is distinguished the distant call of the Chorus: "Orestes!"*)

CHRYSOTHEMIS: Come! He is in the hall,
All around him are gathered,
Embracing his knees.
Those who hid their hate of Aegisthes,
Have attacked the traitor's partisans,
And everywhere, in each court, lie corpses,
Even those who live are covered with blood
And marked by many wounds.
(*The tumult of battle, a mortal struggle between the slaves who side with Orestes and those who remain faithful to Aegisthes, has gradually spread to the interior courts, with which, at right, the door of the court communicates.*)

CHORUS: (*behind the scenes— men and women*). Orestes! Orestes!

CHRYSOTHEMIS: Their joy is supreme!
They all embrace each other, shouting with joy.
(*Increasing tumult within, which, when Elektra begins, grows gradually fainter, to right and at rear, on the side of the exterior courts.— The women have rushed out.*)

CHRYSOTHEMIS: A thousand torches burn and intermingle;
Do you hear? Do you hear?
(*Chrysothemis, alone, remains.— Light comes from without.*)
Ah! do you not hear?

WOMEN and MEN: (*farther away*). Orestes! Orestes!

ELEKTRA: (*crouched on the threshold*). If I do not hear?
If I do not hear the music,
It comes from me, myself.
These thousand torch bearers whose steps I hear,
Whose myriad steps I hear re-echoing
All around me, O sweet harmony,
All, I know await me;
Full well I know why they await me:
I must lead them in the dance.
And I cannot. A vast ocean,
Immeasurable, surrounds my body,
I cannot rise from it!

CHRYSOTHEMIS: Do you not hear?
They all bear him in their triumphant arms!
(*She rises.*)

ELEKTRA: (*elle se parle à elle-même, sans preter attention à Chrysothémis*). Nous sommes chez les Dieux,
Nous, les tacherons.
(*Avec enthousiasme:*)
Nos corps sont transpercés par la glaive d'or des Dieux,
Mias toute leur gloire ce n'est pas trop pour nous!

CHRYSOTHÉMIS: Toutes figures sont transformés.
On voit briller dans les yeux
Sur les joues, de douces larmes.
Tout le monde pleure.
N'entends-tu pas?

ELEKTRA: Ce sont les ténèbres que j'ai semées, je récolte joie sur joie.

CHRYSOTHÉMIS: Ah! que les Dieux sont bons!

ELEKTRA: J'étais un noir cadavre parmi les vivants,
Et à cette heure je suis le feu de la vie
Et ma flamme dévore les noires ténèbres du monde.

CHRYSOTHÉMIS: Une autre vie commence pour nous,
Pour tous les hommes.
Ce sont les Dieux dans leur bonté infinie qui nous l'accordent.

ELEKTRA: Mon visage semble pale plus que le pale visage de la lune.

CHRYSOTHÉMIS: Qui nous a jamais aimées?

ELEKTRA: Celui qui me regarde on doit mourir soudain
Ou si-non defaille de joie.

CHRYSOTHÉMIS: Qui nous a jamais aimées?

ELEKTRA: Voit-on pas mon visage? Voit-on pas la flamme qui des moi s'exhale?

CHRYSOTHÉMIS: Notre cher Frère est là, et l'Amour
Coule sur nous comme l'huile et la myrrhe.
C'est notre Maitre! Qui peut vivre sans l'Amour?

ELEKTRA: Ah! L'Amour nous tue,
Mais personne ne s'en va sans connaitre l'Amour!

CHRYSOTHÉMIS: Elektra, je veux au-près du Frère aller!
(*Elektra descend du seuil, Elle rejeté sa tête en arrière comme une menace. Elle plie les genoux, étend les bras, et ses pas sont ceux d'une danse sans nom.— Chrysothémis reparait à la porte, derrière elle des torches, la foule, visages l'hommes et de femmes.*)

CHRYSOTHÉMIS: Elektra!
(*Elektra s'arrête, la regarde fixement.*)

ELEKTRA: (*speaking to herself, without paying attention to Chrysothemis*). We are with the Gods.
(*With enthusiasm:*)
Our bodies are transfixed by the golden sword of the Gods,
But all their glory is not too much for us!

CHRYSOTHEMIS: All faces are transformed.
In each eye, upon each cheek,
The happy tears we see.
All weep with joy.
Do you hear?

ELEKTRA: Shadows I have sown, I reap now joy upon joy.

CHRYSOTHEMIS: Ah! how good the Gods are!

ELEKTRA: I was a corpse amid the living,
And now I am the fire of life,
And my flame devours the blackness of the world.

CHRYSOTHEMIS: Another life begins for us,
For all men here.
It is the Gods in their infinite goodness,
Who have granted it to us.

ELEKTRA: My countenance seems paler than the pale face of the moon.

CHRYSOTHEMIS: Who has always loved us?

ELEKTRA: He who sees me must either die suddenly
Or if not, faint with joy.

CHRYSOTHEMIS: Who has always loved us?

ELEKTRA: Don't you see my countenance?
Don't you see the flame which I exhale?

CHRYSOTHEMIS: Our dear brother is there, and love
Flows over us as oil and myrrh.
He is our Lord! Who can live without love?

ELEKTRA: Ah! Love kills us,
But none can live without knowing love!

CHRYSOTHEMIS: Elektra, I must go to our brother!
(*Elektra descends from the threshold. She has thrown back her head like a bachanal. She bends her knees, extends her arms and her steps are those of some unknown dance.— Chrysothemis re-appears at the door; behind her are torch bearers, a crowd of men and women.*)

CHRYSOTHEMIS: Elektra!
(*Elektra stops, looks at her fixedly.*)

## Act I, Scene IV

**ELEKTRA:** Tais toi et danse!
Tous, que tous ici viennent!
Formez la ronde!
Le porte le faix du bonheur
Et je danse devant vous.
Qui est heureux autant que nous
m'imite:
Se taise et danse . . .
(*Elle fait encore quelque pas
d'une danse triomphale. — Elek-*

**ELEKTRA:** Be silent and dance!
All who come here!
Form the ring!
I bear the burden of happiness,
And I dance before you.
Let he who is as happy as we are, im-
itate me:
Be silent and dance!
(*She again dances a few steps in a
triumphant dance. — Elektra falls*

*tra s'écroule. — Chrysothémis
court vers elle. — Elektra est
couchée, toute raide.*)

**CHRYSOTHÉMIS:** (*court à la
porte de la maison et frappe*). Orest! Orest!
(*Un silence.*)

FIN.

*prone. — Chrysothemis runs to
her. — Elektra lies, prostrate and
rigid.*)

**CHRYSOTHEMIS:** (*rushing to the
door of the house and knocking*).
Orestes! Orestes!
(*Silence.*)

END.

# Der Rosenkavalier (1911)

## The Rose-Bearer

MUSIC BY RICHARD STRAUSS ■ LIBRETTO BY HUGO VON HOFMANNSTHAL

This three-act "comedy for music," set to a libretto by Hugo von Hofmannsthal, premiered at the Königliches Opernhaus in Dresden on January 26, 1911. The place is Vienna during the reign of the Empress Maria Theresa. The Feldmarschallin, Princess of Werdenberg, trysts with her young lover, Count Octavian Rofrano (performed by a mezzo-soprano), while her husband is away. Her cousin Baron Ochs von Lerchenau pays an unexpected visit to ask her help with his betrothal to Sophie, Herr von Faninal's daughter. Ochs enters the bedroom before Octavian, dressed in some the Marschallin's clothes, can get away. The Baron flirts with "her" while asking the Marschallin if she can recommend someone to carry the traditional silver rose to his beloved. The Marschallin names Count Octavian and shows the Baron his picture. Though the chambermaid resembles the portrait, Ochs decides that she must be a bastard sister. The Marschallin's retainers enter. Ochs discusses his wedding plans with the notary and hires Valzacchi and Annina to find out whatever they can about Sophie. Finally alone, the Marschallin bemoans her age and that Octavian will leave her for someone younger. Octavian assures her of his love, but after he leaves she realizes they haven't even kissed good-bye. At Herr von Faninal's palace, Sophie eagerly awaits the Rosenkavalier, with whom she immediately falls in love. Ochs and Sophie's father, Faninal, negotiates the marriage contract; Octavian swears that the marriage will never happen. Ochs' two spies come upon Octavian and Sophie. Octavian challenges Ochs to a duel and wounds him. Sophie refuses to marry him, and Octavian decides to hire Valzacchi and Annina himself. Sophie gives Ochs a note from the Marschallin's chambermaid, "Mariandel," which says that she will meet him on the following night. In a private room in a tavern, the spies are laying a trap for Ochs. Octavian, dressed in women's clothing, pays them and leaves, returning arm-in-arm with Ochs, who settles in for an evening to remember. But "Mariandel" still reminds him of Octavian. Annina, dressed and veiled in mourning attire, appears, claiming that Ochs is her husband and has deserted her. Valzacchi, the innkeeper and the waiters shout their encouragement as children run in yelling "Papa." A police commissar investigates the noise. Ochs protests that he is merely trying to enjoy dinner with Sophie, his betrothed. Faninal and Sophie, who have been notified by Valzacchi, arrive and are shocked to find the Baron with "Mariandel." The Marschallin enters and sends the commissar, a former employee of her husband, away, saying that the affair is "just a farce and nothing more." On hearing this, Sophie wonders if this is how Octavian feels about her. The Marschallin brings Sophie and Octavian together; they sing of their love for each other as she adds her voice to theirs in a magnificent trio. At last she accepts that her youth is gone forever. She takes Faninal's arm and invites everyone to return to Vienna in her coach.

## ■ ERSTER AUFZUG

*Das Schlafzimmer der Feldmarschallin. Links im Alkoven das grosse zeltförmige Himmelbett. Neben dem Bett ein dreiteiliger chinesischer Wandschirm, hinter dem Kleider liegen. Ferner ein kleines Tischchen und ein paar Sitzmöbel. Auf einem Fauteuil links liegt ein Degen in der Scheide. Rechts grosse Flügeltüren in das Vorzimme. In der Mitte kaum sichtbar kleine Türe in die Wand eingelassen. Sonst keine Türen. In dem Alkoven rechts steht ein Frisiertisch und ein paar Sessel an der Wand. Fauteuils und zwei kleine Sofas. Die Vorhänge des Bettes sind zurückgeschlagen. Octavian kniet auf einem Schemel vor dem Sofa links und hält die Feldmarschallin, die in der Sofaecke liegt, halb umschlungen. Man sieht ihr Gesicht nicht, sondern nur ihre sehr schöne Hand*

## ■ ACT I

*The bedroom of the Princess. In the alcove to the left the large, tent-shaped fourposter. Next the bed a threefold screen, behind which clothes are scattered to the ground. A small table, chairs, etc. To the right, folding doors leading to the bedchamber. In the center, scarcely visible, a little door let into the wall. No other doors. Between the alcove and the small door, a toilet table and some armchairs against the wall. The curtains of the bed are half drawn. Through the half-open window the morning sun streams in. From the garden sounds the song of birds. Octavian kneels on a footstool, half embracing the princess who is reclining in the bed. Her face is hidden, only her beautiful hand is seen, and her arm peeping from out the sleeve of her night gown of lace.*

*und den Arm, von dem das Spitzenhemd abfällt. Durch das halbgeöffnete Fenster strömt die helle Morgensonne herein. Man hört im Garten Vöglein singen.*

OCTAVIAN: Wie du warst!
Wie du bist!
Das weiss niemand, das ahnt keiner!

MARSCHALLIN: (*richtet sich in den Kissen auf*): Beklagt Er sich über das, Quinquin?
Möcht' Er, dass viele das wüssten?

OCTAVIAN: (*feurig*): Engel! Nein!
Selig bin ich,
Dass ich der Einzige bin, der weiss, wie du bist.
Keiner ahnt es! Niemand weiss es!
Du, du—was heisst das "Du"? Was "du und ich"?
Hat denn das einen Sinn?
Das sind Wörter, blosse Wörter, nicht? Du sag'!
Aber dennoch: Es ist etwas in ihnen,

OCTAVIAN: (*rapturously*): All your soul, all your heart— Who can measure their perfections?

PRINCESS: Why grieve so sorely at that, Mignon, Should they be known on the housetops?

OCTAVIAN: (*passionately*): Angel!
No!
Blessed am I that it is I, I alone who know their secrets.
Who can measure such perfection? You, You, You! What does this mean, "You'?
That "You and I,"
Have they meaning or sense?— They are merely empty nothings. What? O say.

ein Schwindeln, ein Ziehen, ein
Sehnen und Drängen,
ein Schmachten und Brennen:
Wie jetzt meine Hand zu deiner
Hand kommt,
Das Zudirwollen, das Dichumklam-
mern,
das bin ich, das will zu dir;
aber das Ich vergeht in dem Du . . .
Ich bin dein Bub', aber wenn mir
dann Hören und Sehen vergeht—
wo ist dann dein Bub?

**MARSCHALLIN:** (*leise*): Du bist
mein Bub', du bist mein Schatz!
(*Sehr innig*).
Ich hab' dich ieb!

**OCTAVIAN:** (*fährt auf*): Warum
ist Tag?
Ich will nicht den Tag!
Für was ist der Tag?
Da haben dich alle!
Finster soll sein!
(*Er stürzt ans Fenster, schliesst es
und zieht die Vorhänge zu. Man
hört von fern ein leises Klingeln.
Marschallin lacht leise*).
Lachst du mich aus?

**MARSCHALLIN:** (*zärtlich*): Lach'
ich dich aus?

**OCTAVIAN:** Engel!

**MARSCHALLIN:** Schatz du, mein
junger Schatz! ..
(*Wieder ein Leises Klingeln*.)
Horch!

**OCTAVIAN:** Ich will nicht.

**MARSCHALLIN:** Still, pass auf!

**OCTAVIAN:** Ich will nichts hören!
Was wird's denn sein?
(*Das Klingeln näher*.)
Sind's leicht Laufer mit Briefen und
Komplimenten?
Vom Saurau, vom Hartig, vom por-
tugieser Envoyé?
Hier kommt mir keiner herein. Hier
bin ich der Herr!
(*Die kleine Tür in der Mitte geht
auf und ein kleiner Neger in Gelb,
behängt mit silbernen Schellen,
ein Präsentierbrett mit der Schokolade tragend, trippelt über die
Schwelle. Die Tür hinter dem Neger wird von unsichtbaren Händen
geschlossen.*)

**MARSCHALLIN:** Schnell, da versteck' Er sich! Das Frühstück ist's.
(*Octavian gleitet hinter den vorderen Wandschirm*.)

**MARSCHALLIN:** Schmeiss' Er
doch Seinen Degen hinters Bett.
(*Octavian fährt nach dem Degen
und versteckt ihn*):
(*Marschallin: verschwindet hinter den Battvorbängen, die sie fall-
en lässt.*)
(*Der Kleine Neger stellt das Servierbrett auf das kleine Tischchen, schiebt dieses nach vorne,
neben das linksstehende Sofa, verneigt sich dann tief gegen das
Bett, die kleinen Arme über die*

Yet have they something,
Yet a something is in them
That craved, that urged, strived,
That fainted and yearned.
To yours my hand thus has found:
And this quest for you and this
clinging—
That am I, who seek you out
Mingling with you and lost in that
"You."
I am your Boy; but when reft of all
senses I lie in your arms.
Where then is your Boy?

**PRINCESS:** You are my Boy.
You are my love.
I love you so.

**OCTAVIAN:** Why dawns the day?
How hateful is day.
What avails the day?
Then all men can see you. Let it be
dark.
(*He rushes to the window and
closes it. A bell is heard ringing
softly in the distance. The Princess
smiles to herself.*)
Are you smiling at me?

**PRINCESS:** I smile at you?

**OCTAVIAN:** Angel!

**PRINCESS:** Dearest, my dearest
Boy!
(*Bell again.*)
Listen!

**OCTAVIAN:** I will not!

**PRINCESS:** Hush, beloved!

**OCTAVIAN:** I am deaf and blind.
What can it be?
(*The tinkling grows more distinct.*)
Is it couriers with letters and decla-
rations?
From Sauvan and Hartig or the Portuguese Ambassador?
I hold the door against the world. I
am master here.
(*The little door in the center is
opened and a small black boy in
yellow, with silver bells, carrying
a silver salver with chocolate, enters with mincing steps. The door
is closed behind him by unseen
bands. Octavian slips behind the
screen.*)

**PRINCESS:** Quick!
Go conceal yourself.
My chocolate!

**PRINCESS:** Foolish Boy!
Hide your sword and do not stir!
(*Octavian reaches after the sword
and hides it.*)
(*The boy puts the salver on one of
the small tables, moves it to the
front of the stage and places the
sofa next to it, bows to the Princess with his hands crossed over
his breast, then dances away
backward with his face always
towards his mistress; at the door
be bows again and disappears.*)

Brust gekreutzt. Dann tanzt er zi-
erlich nach rückwärts, immer das
Gesicht dem Bette zugewandt. An
der Tür verneigt er sich nochmals
und verschwindet*).
(*Marschallin tritt swischen den
Bettivorbängen hervor. Sie hat ei-
nen leichten mit Pelz verbrämten
Mantel umgeschlagen*).
(*Octavian kommt zwischen der
Mauer und dem Wandschirm her-
vor*).

**MARSCHALLIN:** Er Katzenkopf, Er
Unvorsichtiger!
Lässt man in einer Dame Schlafzim-
mer seinen Degen herumliegen?
Hat Er keine besseren Gepfogen-
heiten?

**OCTAVIAN:** Wenn Ihr zu dumm
ist, wie ich mich benehm',
und wenn Ihr abgeht, dass ich kein
Geübter in solchem Sachen bin,
dann weiss ich überhaupt nicht,
was Sie an mir hat!

**MARSCHALLIN:** (*zärtlich, auf
dem Sofa*): Philosophier' Er nicht,
Herr Schatz, und komm Er her.
Jetzt wird gefrühstückt. Jedes Ding
hat seine Zeit.

**OCTAVIAN:** (*setzt sich dicht neben sie. Sie frühstücken sehr
zärtlich. Octavian legt sein Gesicht auf ihr Knie. Sie streichelt
sein Haar. Er blickt zu ihr auf.
Leise*): Marie Theres'!

**MARSCHALLIN:** Octavian!

**OCTAVIAN:** Bichette!

**MARSCHALLIN:** Quinquin!

**OCTAVIAN:** Mein Schatz!

**MARSCHALLIN:** Mein Bub'! (*Sie
früstücken weiter.*)

**OCTAVIAN:** (*lustig*): Der Feld-
marschall sitzt im krowatischen
Wald
und jagt auf Bären und Luchsen.
Und ich, ich setz' hier, ich junges
Blut, und jag' auf was?
Ich hab' ein Glück, ich hab' ein
Glück!

**MARSCHALLIN:** (*indem ein
Schatten über ihr Gesicht fliegt*):
Lass Er den Feldmarschall in Ruh'!
Mir hat von ihm geträumt.

**OCTAVIAN:** Heut nacht hat dir von
ihm deträumt? Heut Nacht?

**MARSCHALLIN:** Ich schaff' mir
meine Träume nicht an.

**OCTAVIAN:** Heut Nacht hat dir
von deinem Mann geträumt?
Heut Nacht?

**MARSCHALLIN:** Mach' Er nicht
solche Augen.
Ich kann nichts dafür.
Er war auf einmal wieder zu Haus.

(*The Princess appears from behind the curtains of the bed. She
has wrapped round her a light
dressing gown edged with fur.*)
(*Octavian reappears from behind
the screen.*)

**PRINCESS:** You featherhead!
You careless Good for nothing!
Is it allowed to leave a sword lying
in the room of a lady of fashion?
Where have you learned to show
such lack of breeding?

**OCTAVIAN:** Well, if my breeding
be not to your taste,
If it displeases you that in scenes
like this my skill is far to seek
Then truly it were better to bid you
farewell.

**PRINCESS:** (*tenderly from the
sofa*): Cease your philosophizing,
Sir, and come to me.
Now let us eat breakfast.
Everything in its own time.
(*Octavian seats himself close to
her. They breakfast. He puts his
head on her lap; she strokes his
hair.*)

**OCTAVIAN:** Marie Theres'!

**PRINCESS:** Octavian!

**OCTAVIAN:** Bichette!

**PRINCESS:** Mignon!

**OCTAVIAN:** Beloved.

**PRINCESS:** My Boy!

**OCTAVIAN:** The Field Marshal
stays in far Croatian wilds, hunting
for brown bears and black boars,
And I in the flower of my youth, stay
here, hunting for what?
I am happy! I am happy!

**PRINCESS:** (*a shadow passing
over her face*): But, let the Marshal
be in peace.
I dreamed a dream of him this
night.

**OCTAVIAN:** This night you
dreamed a dream of him?
This night?

**PRINCESS:** My dreams are not mine
to command.

**OCTAVIAN:** You dreamed a dream
this very night of him?
The Prince?

**PRINCESS:** Why look so sad and an-
gry?
It is no fault of mine . . .
My husband was at home again.

OCTAVIAN: (*leise*): Der Feldmarschall?

MARSCHALLIN: Es war ein Lärm im Hof von Pferd' und Leut' und er war da,
Vor Schreck war ich auf einmal wach, nein, schau' nur,
schau' nur, wie kindisch ich bin: ich hör' noch immer den Rumor im Hof.
Ich bring's nicht aus dem Ohr.
Hörst du leicht auch was?

OCTAVIAN: Ja freilich hör' ich was, aber muss es denn dein Mann sein!?
Denk' dir doch, wo der ist: im Raitzenland, noch hinterwärts von Esseg.

MARSCHALLIN: Ist das sicher sehr weit?
Na, dann wird's halt was anders sein.
Dann ist's ja gut.

OCTAVIAN: Du schaust so ängstlich drein, Theres!

MARSCHALLIN: Weiss Er, Quinquin—wenn es auch weit ist—Der Feldmarschall ist halt sehr geschwind.
Einmal—
(*Sie stockt.*)

OCTAVIAN: (*eifersüchtig*): Was war einmal?
Was war einmal?
Was war einmal?
Bichette!
Bichette!
Was war einmal?

MARSCHALLIN: Ach sei Er gut, Er muss nicht alles wissen.

OCTAVIAN: (*wirft sich verzweifelt aufs Sofa rechts*): So spielt Sie sich mit mir!
Ich bin ein unglücklicher Mensch!

MARSCHALLIN: (*horcht*): Jetzt trotz' Er nicht. Jetzt gilt's: es ist der Feldmarschall.
Wenn es ein Fremder wär', so wär der Lärm da draussen in meinen Vorzimmer.
Es muss mein Mann sein, der durch die Garderob' herein will
Und mit den Lakaien disputiert.
Quinquin, es ist mein Mann!
(*Octavian fährt nach seinem Degen und läuft gegen rechts*).
Nicht dort, dort ist das Vorzimmer.
Da sitzen meine Lieferanten und ein halbes Dutzend Lakaien.
Da!
(*Octavian läuft hinüber zur kleinen Türe*).
Zu spä! Sie sind schon in der Garderob'!
Jetzt bleibt nur eins!
Versteck' Er sich!
(*Nacht einer kurzen Pause der*

OCTAVIAN: Your husband here?

PRINCESS: There was a noise outside of horse and man—and he was here.
For fright I started up in haste—Now look you,
Now look what a child I am—still I can hear it, all the noise without.
It is a ringing in my ears, do you not hear it?

OCTAVIAN: Yes, truly, I hear sounds: but why think it must be your husband?
Think just of where he's hunting—far away,
At Esseg or a score of leagues beyond.

PRINCESS: Is he so far, do you think?

OCTAVIAN: Then it is something else we hear, and all is well,
You look so full of fear, Theres'.

PRINCESS: But see, Mignon, though it be distant,
The Prince at times can travel wondrous fast; for once—

OCTAVIAN: What did he, once?
What did he, once?
Bichette, Bichette!
What did he, once?

PRINCESS: Oh, let him be—why should I tell you all things?

OCTAVIAN: See how she flouts my love!
(*Throws himself in despair on to the sofa.*)
Why will you drive me to despair?

PRINCESS: Command yourself.
It is true.
It is the Prince indeed.
For were a stranger here, the noise would surely be there in the antechamber.
It is my husband.
I hear his footsteps in the closet.
In vain the lackeys bar his way.
Mignon, it is the Prince.
(*Octavian draws his sword and runs to the right.*)
Not there, there is the antechamber.
There, sure, a crowd with wares to offer, and a score of lackeys are in waiting.
There!
(*Points to the small door. Octavian runs in that direction.*)
Too late!
I hear them in the closet now.
There's but one chance.

*Ratlosigkeit.*)
Dort!

OCTAVIAN: Ich spring' ihm in den Weg! Ich bleib' bei dir.

MARSCHALLIN: Dort hinters Bett!
Dort in der Vorhäng!
Und rühr' dich nicht!

OCTAVIAN: (*zögernd*): Wenn er mich dort erwischt, was wird aus dir, Theres'?

MARSCHALLIN: (*flehend*): Versteck' Er sich, mein Schatz.

OCTAVIAN: (*beim Wandschirm*): Theres!
(*Er verschwindet zwischen dem Wandschirm und der Alkovenwand.*)

MARSCHALLIN: (*ungeduldig aufstampfend*): Sei Er ganz still!
(*Mit blitzenden Augen.*)
Das möcht' ich sehn,
Ob einer sich dort hinüber traut, wenn ich hier steh'.
Ich bin kein napolitanischer General: wo ich steh', steh' ich.
Sind brave Kerl'n, meine Lakaien, wollen ihn nich herein lassen, sagen, dass ich schlaf'.
Sehr brave Kerl'n!
(*Aufhorchend.*)
Die Stimm'!
Das ist ja gar nicht die Stimm' vom Feldmarschall!
Sie sagen "Herr Baron" zu ihm!
Das ist ein Fremder.
(*Lustig.*)
Quinquin, es ist ein Besuch.
(*Sie lacht.*)
Fahr' Er schnell in seine Kleider, aber bleib' Er versteckt,
dass die Lakaien Ihn nicht seh'n.
Die blöde grosse Stimm' müsste ich doch kennen.
Wer ist denn das? Herrgott, das ist der Ochs.
Das ist mein Vetter, der Lerchenau, der Ochs auf Lerchenau,
Was will denn der?
Jesus Maria!
(*Sie muss lachen.*)
Quinquin, hört Er,
Quinquin, erinnert Er sich nicht?
Vor fünf oder sechs Tagen—den Brief—
Wir sind im Wagen gesessen, und einen Brief haben sie mir an den Wagenschlag gebracht.
Das war der Brief vom Ochs.
Und ich hab' keine Ahnung, was drin gestanden ist.
(*Lacht.*)
Daran ist Er allein schuld, Quinquin!

Conceal yourself!
(*After a brief pause of helplessness.*)
There!

OCTAVIAN: I will not let him pass: I stay with you!

PRINCESS: There—by the bed—there in the curtains!
And do not move!

OCTAVIAN: (*hesitating*): Should I be caught, what a fate is yours, Theres'!

PRINCESS: (*pleading*): Conceal yourself, beloved.
(*Stamping her foot impatiently.*)

OCTAVIAN: (*by the screen*): Theres'—

PRINCESS: Quick now, be still!
Now let me see who dares to stir one inch towards the door
While I am here.
I'm no faint-hearted Italian brigadier.
Where I stand, stand I.
(*She walks energetically towards the little door and listens.*)
They're worthy fellows, keeping guard outside, vowing they'll not make way for him,
Vowing I sleep—most worthy fellows—
(*The noise in the anteroom grows louder.*)
That voice
(*Listens.*)
That is not, truly, no, it is not my husband's voice.
It is Baron that they're calling him: It is a stranger!
(*Laughing.*)
Mignon, it is someone else.
Now escape will be quite easy.
But remain in hiding,
That the footmen do not see you.
That loutish, foolish voice, surely I know it too well—
Mon Dieu! It is Ochs, I do protest, my cousin of Lerchenau.
It is Ochs of Lerchenau.
What can he seek?
But stay:
I have it—
(*Bursts into a laugh.*)
Listen, Mignon, you cannot have forgot
(*Going a few steps towards the left.*)
The league-long letter that they brought
When I was in my coach (you were with me)—
Some five days since, starting for Court, and I scarcely looked at it.
That letter came from Ochs.
And now I have no inkling what my Cousin said.
See to what evil ways, Mignon, you lead me!

**STIMME DES HAUSHOFMEISTERS:** (*draussen*): Belieben Euer Gnaden in der Galerie zu warten! (*Die kleine rückwärtige Türe wird während des Folgenden mehrmals bis zum Spalt geöffnet und wieder geschlossen, als wollte von aussen jemand eindringen, dem von anderen der Eintritt verwehrt wird.*)

**STIMME DES BARONS:** (*draussen*): Wo hat Er seine Manieren galernt? Der Baron Lerchenau antichambrieret nicht.

**MARSCHALLIN:** Quinquin, was treibt Er denn? Wo steckt Er denn?

**OCTAVIAN:** (*in einen Frauenrock und Jäkchen, das Haar mit einem Schnupftuch und einem Bande wie in einem Häubchen tritt hervor und knickst*): Befehl'n fürstli' Gnad'n i bin halt noch nit recht lang in fürstli'n Dienst.

**MARSCHALLIN:** Du, Schatz! Und nicht einmal mehr als ein Busserl kann ich dir geben. (*Küsst ihn schnell. Neuer Lärm draussen.*) Er bricht mir ja die Tür ein, der Herr Vetter. Mach' Er, dass Er hinauskomm'. Schleich Er frech durch die Lakaien durch. Er ist ein blitzgescheiter Lump! Und komm' Er wieder, Schatz, aber in Mannskleidern und durch die vordre Tür, wenn's Ihm beliebt. (*Setzt sich auf das Sofa links mit dem Rücken gegen die Tür und beginnt ihre Schokolade zu trinken. Octavian geht schnell gegen die kleine Tür und will hinaus. Im gleichen Augenblick wird die Tür aufgerissen, und Baron Ochs, den die Lakaien vergeblich abzuhalten suchen, tritt ein. Octavian, der mit gesenktem Kopf rasch entwischen wollte, stösst mit ihm zusammen. Dann drückt er sich verlegen an die Wand links von der Tür. Drei Lakaien sind gleichzeitig mit dem Baron eingetreten, stehen ratlos.*)

**BARON:** (*mit Grandezza zu den Lakaien*): Selbstverständlich empfängt mich Ihre Gnaden. (*Er geht nach vorn, die Lakaien zu seiner Linken suchen ihm den Weg zu vertreten.*) (*zu Octavian mit Interesse*). Pardon, mein hübsches Kind! (*Octavian dreht sich verlegen gegen die Wand*). (*mit Grazie und Herablassung*) Ich sag': Pardon, mein hübsches Kind. (*Marschallin sieht über die Schulter, steht dann auf und kommt dem Baron entgegen*). (*galant zu Octavian*). Ich hab' Ihr doch nicht ernstlich weh getan?

**VOICE OF THE MAJOR-DOMO:** (*without*): Will your Lordship be pleased to attend in the gallery?

**VOICE OF THE BARON:** (*without*): Where did you learn to treat a nobleman like this? A Baron Lerchenau cannot be waiting.

**PRINCESS:** Mignon, where are you hid? What tricks are these?

**OCTAVIAN:** (*in a skirt and a short jacket, with his hair tied with a kerchief and ribbon to look like a cap, comes from behind the screen and curtseys*): An't please you, your Highness, I've not long been of your Highness' household here.

**PRINCESS:** Sweetheart, and only one kiss may I give you, One only, my dearest. (*Kisses him quickly.*) My noble kinsman's battering all the doors down. Now as quickly as may be March boldly past the footman there. It is sport for brazen rogues like you! And come back soon, beloved, In your own habit, and through the main door, as a gentleman should. (*The Princess sits down with her back to the door and begins to sip her chocolate. Octavian goes quickly towards the little door and tries to go out, but at that moment the door is flung open, and Baron Ochs, whom the footmen vainly try to keep back, forces his way in. Octavian, who attempts to escape, hiding his face, runs into him. Then, in confusion, he stands aside against the wall, to the left of the door. Three footmen enter with the Baron and stand hesitating what to do.*)

**BARON:** (*pompously to the footmen*): Why, never doubt her Highness will receive me. (*To Octavian, who in confusion turns his face to the wall.*) Forgive, my pretty child. (*With gracious condescending.*) I said, forgive, my pretty child. (*The Princess looks over her shoulder, rises and goes to meet the Baron.*) (*gallantly to Octavian*). I hope I did not incommode you much.

**LAKAIEN:** (*zupfen den Baron, leise*): Ihre fürstlichen Gnaden! (*Sie rangieren sich beim Nahen der Marschallin zu einer dichtgeschlossenen Front hart vor der kleinen Türe.*) (*Baron macht die französische Reverenz mit zwei Wiederholungen*).

**MARSCHALLIN:** Euer Liebden sehen vortrefflich aus.

**BARON:** (*verneigt sich nochmals, dann zu den Lakaien*): Sieht Er jetzt wohl, dass Ihre Gnaden entzückt ist, mich zu sehn. (*Auf die Marschallin zu, mit weltmännischer Leichtigkeit, indem er ihr die Hand reicht und sie vorführt.*) Und wie sollten Euer Gnaden nicht! Was tut die frühe Stunde unter Personen von Stand? Hab' ich nicht seinerzeit wahrhaftig Tag für Tag unserer Fürstin Brioche meine Aufwartung gemacht, da sie im Bad gesessen ist, mit nichts als einem kleinen Wandschirm zwischen ihr und mir. Ich muss mich wundern, (*zornig umschauend*) Wenn Euer Gnaden Livree— (*Octavian wäre währenddessen gern hinausgeschlüpft; die befremdeten Blicke und Gesichter der Lakaien nötigen ihn zur äussersten Vorsicht, und er zieht sich mit gespielter Unbefangenheit an der Wand gegen dem Alkoven hin zurück*).

**MARSCHALLIN:** Verzeihen Sie! Man hat sich betragen, wie es befohlen war. Ich hatte diesen Morgen die Migräne. (*Auf einen Wink der Marschallin haben die Lakaien die beiden kleinen Sofas mehr nach vorn gebracht und sind abgegangen.*) (*Baron sieht öfters nach rückwärts*). (*Octavian macht sich möglichst unsichtbar beim Bett zu schaffen*). (*Marschallin setzt sich auf das Sofa rechts, nachdem sie dem Baron den Platz auf dem Sofa links angeboten hat*).

**BARON:** (*versucht sich zu setzen, äusserst okkupiert von der Anwesenheit der hübschen Kammerzofe. Für sich*): Ein hübsches Ding! Ein gutes saub'res Kinder!! (*Marschallin aufstehend, ihm zeremoniös aufs neue seinen Platz anbietend*).

**MARSCHALLIN:** Ich bin auch jetzt noch nicht ganz wohl. Der Vetter wird darum vielleicht die Gnade haben— (*Baron setzt sich zögernd und bemüht sich, der hübschen Zofe nicht völlig den Rücken zu kehren. Im folgenden wendet er sich*

**THE FOOTMEN:** (*nudging the Baron*): Yonder, Sir, is her Highness. (*The Baron makes an obeisance in the French manner and repeats it twice.*)

**PRINCESS:** Faith, my dear cousin, you're in looks today.

**BARON:** (*to the footmen*): Did I not say to you, her Highness would most surely welcome me? (*Goes to the Princess with the grace of a man of the world, offers her his hand and leads her to her chair.*) You will not deny yourself to me? Of early hours, we take no account of the quality. Did I not, every morning without fail, repair To the Princess you wot of? Did I not pay my respects As she took her ease in her bath, And there was nothing to divide us but a tiny screen? (*Octavian has made his way along the wall towards the alcove and is busying himself, trying to escape observation, by the bed. In obedience to a sign from the Princess, the footmen carry a little sofa and an armchair to the front and retire.*) Indeed I wonder (*Looking around angrily.*) That any lackey should have dared.

**PRINCESS:** Forgive them, Coz. They did but obey me—for it was I that bade them, (*Seats herself on the sofa, after offering the Baron the armchair.*) I suffered much this morning from the vapors. (*The Baron tries to sit and is much distracted by the presence of the pretty waiting maid.*)

**BARON:** (*to himself*): A pretty wench, egad! She's vastly pleasing.

**PRINCESS:** (*rising and again ceremoniously offering a seat to the Baron*): And even now I'm not quite well. (*The Baron takes his seat with hesitation and tries his utmost not to turn his back to the pretty waiting maid.*)

*bald nach der Marschallin, also nach seiner Linken, bald nach Octavian, also nach seiner Rechten).*

BARON: Natürlich.
*(Er dreht sich nach seiner Rechten um, um Octavian zu sehen.)*

MARSCHALLIN: Meine Kammerzofe, ein junges Ding vom Land. Ich muss fürchten, sie inkommodiert Euer Liebden.

BARON: *(nach seiner Rechten)*: Ganz allerliebst!
*(Nach seiner Linken.)*
Wie?
Nicht im geringsten!
Mich?
Im Gegenteil!
*(Er winkt Octavian mit der Hand, dann zur Marschallin.)*
Euer Gnaden werden vielleicht verwundert sein, dass ich als Bräutigam.
*(sieht sich nach seiner Linken um.)*
indes—inzwischen—

MARSCHALLIN: Als Bräutigam?

BARON: *(nach seiner Linken)*: Ja, wie Euer Gnaden denn doch wohl aus meinem Brief genugsam—
*(Nach seiner Rechten.)*
Ein Grasaff', appetitlich, keine fünfzehn Jahr!

MARSCHALLIN: *(erleichtert)*: Der Brief, natürlich, ja, der Brief, wer ist denn nur die Glückliche? Ich hab' den Namen auf der Zunge.

BARON: *(nach seiner Linken)*: Wie?
*(Nach rückwärts.)*
Pudeljung!
Gesund!
Gewaschen!
Allerliebst!

MARSCHALLIN: Wer ist nur schnell die Braut!?

BARON: Das Fräulein Faninal. Ich habe Euer Gnaden den Namen nicht verheimlicht.

MARSCHALLIN: Natürlich! Wo hab' ich meinen Kopf? Bloss die Famili ist mir nicht bekannt. Sind's keine Hiesigen?
*(Octavian macht sich mit dem Servierbrett zu tun, wodurch er mehr hinter den Rücken des Barons kommt).*

BARON: Jawohl, Euer Gnaden, es sind Hiesige. Ein durch die Gnade Ihrer Majestät Geadelter. Er hat die Lieferung für die Armee, die in den Niederlanden steht.
*(Marschallin bedeutet Octavian ungeduldig mit den Augen, er solle sich fortmachen).*
*(missversteht ihre Miene durchaus). Ich seh', Euer Gnaden runzeln Dero schöne Stirn ob der Mes-*

And so, dear Cousin, Bear me no ill will that I do deny myself ...

BARON: No, truly
*(He turns round, so as to look at Octavian.)*

PRINCESS: My own waiting-woman ... come freshly from the country, And I fear that her untaught ways cause you displeasure.

BARON: Charming, I vow Displeasure? Do not think it, I like such ways.
*(Makes a sign to Octavian, then says to the Princess):* But your Highness may have felt surprise to learn that I design to take a wife.
*(Turns round.)*
But yet, the reason ...

PRINCESS: To take a wife?

BARON: As your Highness knows without a doubt, for in my recent letter ... A novice ... how enticing—barely fifteen years!

PRINCESS: *(relieved)*: You wrote, why surely ... And who has been so fortunate? The name was on my tongue this instant.

BARON: How? And how fresh! egad! how dainty! What a waist!

PRINCESS: Pray tell me who's the bride?

BARON: Young Mistress Faninal.
*(With slight vexation.)*
Yet of her name and mercy I made no secret.

PRINCESS: Forgive, I beg, my memory plays me false. What of her family, pray, is it native here?
*(Octavian busies himself with the tray and gradually tries to get behind the baron.)*

BARON: Indeed, your Highness, it is native here— One which Her Majesty of late has raised to the nobility. The whole provisioning of the armies in the Netherlands is in his hands.
*(The Princess impatiently makes signs to Octavian that he should withdraw.)*
I see your Highness' pretty lips express disdain at such a misalliance.

alliance.
Allein dass ich sag', das Mädchen ist für einen Engel hübsch genug. Kommt frischweg aus dem Kloster. Ist das einzige Kind.
*(Stärker.)*
Dem Mann gehören zwölf Häuser auf der Wied'n nebst dem Palais am Hof. Und seine Gesundheit
*(schmunzelnd)*
soll nicht die beste sein.

MARSCHALLIN: Mein lieber Vetter, ich kapier' schon, wieviel's geschlagen hat.
*(Winkt Octavian, den Rückzug zu nehmen.)*
*(Octavian will mit dem Servierbrett rückwärts zur Tür hin).*

BARON: Warum hinaus die Schokolade? Geruhen nur! Da! Pst, wieso denn!
*(Octavian steht unschlüssig, das Gesicht abgewendet):*

MARSCHALLIN: Fort, geh' Sie nur!

BARON: Wenn ich Euer Gnaden gesteh', dass ich noch so gut wie nüchtern bin.

MARSCHALLIN: *(resigniert)*: Mariandel, komm' Sie her. Servier' Sie Seiner Liebden.
*(Octavian kommt, serviert an der Rechten des Barons, so dass dieser sich wieder zwischen der Marschallin und Octavian befindet.)*

BARON: *(nimmt eine Tasse, bedient sich)*: So gut wie nüchtern, Euer Gnaden. Sitz' im Reisewagen seit fünf Uhr früh. Recht ein gestelltes Ding!
*(Zu Octavian.)* Bleib' Sie dahier, mein Herz. Ich hab' Ihr was zu sagen.
*(Zur Marschallin, laut.)*
Meine ganze Livree, Stallpagen, Jäger, alles—
*(Er frisst.)*
Alles unten im Hof zusamt meinen Almosenier.

MARSCHALLIN: *(zu Octavian)*: Geh' Sie nur.

BARON: *(zu Octavian)*: Hat Sie noch ein Biskoterl? Bleib' Sie doch!
*(Leise.)*
Sie ist ein süsser Engelsschatz, ein saubrer.
*(Zur Marschallin.)*
Sind auf dem Wege zum "Weissen Ross", wo wir logieren, heisst bis übermorgen—
*(Halblaut zu Octavian.)*
Ich gäb' was Schönes drum, mit Ihr—
*(zur Marschallin, sehr laut.)*
bis übermorgen—
*(schnell zu Octavian.)*
unter vier Augen zu scharmutzier-

But then, although I say it, the girl is pretty as an angel and as good, Comes straight from out a convent, is an only child. The man has half a score of houses in the city and has a mansion too. His health is failing too.
*(Chuckles.)*
So the physicians say.

PRINCESS: It needs no glasses to discover what hour of day it is.
*(Repeats her signs to Octavian to retire.)*
*(Octavian tries to back to the door with the tray.)*

BARON: Why leave the chocolate unfinished?
*(To Octavian, who stands undecided with averted face.)*
Hey! Pst! Pst! What ails you?

PRINCESS: Quick, get you gone!

BARON: Grant me permission, your Highness, To say that I am faint for food.

PRINCESS: *(resigned)*: Mariandel, bring it back and wait upon his Lordship.

BARON: As good as fasting, my dear cousin—sitting in my post-chaise since the early dawn
*(Octavian brings the tray to the Baron, who takes a cup and fills it.)*
Gad, what a strapping wench!
*(To Octavian.)*
Do not go yet, my child, There's something I would tell you.
*(To the Princess.)*
All my suite I have brought—footmen and grooms and couriers— They are all down below together with my almoner.

PRINCESS: *(to Octavian)*: You may go.

BARON: *(to Octavian)*: Have you another biscuit? Do not go— It is the daintiest morsel, sweet and adorable.
*(To the Princess.)*
I halted here, but we are lodging at an inn, the White Horse,
*(Softly to Octavian.)*
I'd pay a heavy price to court you ...
*(To the Princess, very loud.)*
But till tomorrow.
*(To Octavian.)*
Where there is no one by to mar our pleasure.
*(The Princess cannot refrain from*

en!
Wie?
(*Marschallin muss lachen über Octavians freches Komödienspiel.*)
Dann ziehn wir ins Palais von Faninal.
Natürlich muss ich vorher den Bräutigamsaufführer—
(*wütend zu Octavian.*)
will Sie denn nicht warten?—
an die wohlgeborne Jungfer Braut deputieren,
Der die silberne Rosen überbringt nach der hochadeligen Gepflogenheit.

MARSCHALLIN: Und wen von der Verwandtschaft haben Euer Liebden
für dieses Ehrenamt ausersehn?
wen denn nur?
den Vetter Jörger?
Wie?
Den Vetter Lamberg?
Ich werde—

BARON: Dies liegt in Euer Gnaden allerschönsten Händen.

MARSCHALLIN: Ganz gut.
Will Er mit mir zu Abend essen, Vetter?
Sagen wir morgen, will Er?
Dann proponier' ich Ihm einen.

BARON: Euer Gnaden sind die Herablassung selber.

MARSCHALLIN: (*will aufstehen*): Indes—

BARON: (*halblaut*): Das Sie mir wiederkommt!
Ich geh' nicht eher fort!

MARSCHALLIN: (*für sich*): Oho!
(*Laut.*)
Bleib' Sie nur da!
Kann ich dem Vetter
für jetzt noch dienlich sein?

BARON: Ich shäme mich bereits:
An Euer Gnaden Notari eine Rekommandation
wär mir lieb.
Es handelt sich um den Eh'vertrag.

MARSCHALLIN: Mein Notari
kommt öfters des Morgens.
Schau' Sie doch, Mariandel,
ob er nicht in der Antichambre ist
und wartet.

BARON: Wozu das Kammerzofel?
Euer Gnaden beraubt sich der Bedienung
um meinetweillen.
(*Hält zie auf.*)

MARSCHALLIN: Lass Er doch, Vetter, Sie mag ruhig gehn.

BARON: (*lebhaft*): Das geb' ich nicht zu, bleib' Sie dahier zu Ihrer Gnaden Wink.
Es kommt gleich wer von der Livree herein.
Ich liess ein solches Goldkind, meiner Seel',

laughing at Octavian's impudent by-play.)
Then I and mine will be the guest of Faninal.
But first, I must despatch the bridegroom's Ambassador,
(*Angrily to Octavian.*)
Will you not have patience?
To my highly-born and beauteous bride, one who shall bring to her
As a pledge of love a silver Rose,
As is the custom in all noble families.

PRINCESS: On whom of all our kinsmen has your Lordship's choice
Fallen for this grave Embassy?
Who is fit? Our cousin Preysing? Or Kinsman Lambert . . .
I'll tell you . . .

BARON: All this I gladly leave in your sweet hands, your Highness.

PRINCESS: It is well.
Will you not sup with me tonight, dear kinsman?
Or else tomorrow?
I'll not fail then with proposals.

BARON: No, your Highness' condescension overwhelms me.

PRINCESS: (*rising*): But yet . . .

BARON: (*aside*): You must come back again.
I stay till you are here!

PRINCESS: (*aside*): Oho!
(*To Octavian.*)
Stay where you are. Will you command me
dear Cousin, now?

BARON: No, truly, I'm ashamed
A word or two to commend me to your Highness's attorney
I would crave.
A conference, touching settlements.

PRINCESS: My man of law is often here early.
Go to seek Mariandel,
(*To Octavian.*)
If he's by chance yet waiting in the anteroom.

BARON: Why send your waiting-woman?
Your Highness might be needing her help—
It is too much kindness.
(*Holds Octavian back.*)

PRINCESS: Let her be, Cousin, she's not needed here.

BARON: (*eagerly*): That will I not allow.
(*To Octavian.*)
Stay you here, at her Highness's beck and call,
It will not be long before a footman comes.

nicht unter das infame Lakaienvolk.

MARSCHALLIN: Euer Liebden sind allzu besorgt.
(*Haushofmeister tritt ein*).

BARON: Da, hab' ich's nicht gesagt?
Er wird Euer Gnaden zu melden haben.

MARSCHALLIN: (*zum Haushofmeister*): Struhan, hab' ich meinen Notari in der Vorkammen warten?

HAUSHOFMEISTER: Fürstliche Gnaden haben den Notari,
dann den Verwalter, dann den Kuchelchef,
dann von Excellenz Silva hegeschickt
ein Sänger mit einem Flötisten.
(*Trocken.*)
Ansonsten das gewöhnliche Bagagi.

BARON: (*hat sein Sofa hinter den breiten Rücken des Haushofmeisters geschoben, ergreift zätlich die Hand der vermeintlichen Zofe*):
Hat sie schon einmal
mit einem Kavalier im tête-à-tête zu Abend g'essen?
(*Octavian tut sehr verlegen*).
Nein?
Da wird Sie Augen machen.
Will Sie?

OCTAVIAN: (*leise, verschämt*): I weiss halt nit, i dös derf.
(*Marschallin dem Haushofmeister unaufmerksam zuhörend, beobachtet die beiden, muss leise lachen*).
(*Haushofmeister verneigt sich, tritt zurück, wodurch die Gruppe für den Blick der Marschallin frei wird*).

MARSCHALLIN: (*lachend zum Haushofmeister*): Warten lassen.
(*Haushofmeister ab.*)
(*Baron setzt sich möglichst unbefangen zurecht und nimmt eine gravitätische Miene an*):
Der Vetter ist, ich seh' kein Kostverächter.

BARON: (*erleichtert*): Mit Euer Gnaden
(*aufatmend*) ist man frei daran.
Da gibt's keine Flausen, keine Etikette,
keine spanische Tuerei!
(*Er küsst der Marschallin die Hand.*)

MARSCHALLIN: (*amusiert*): Aber wo Er doch ein Bräutgam ist?

BARON: (*halb aufstehend, ihr genähert*): Macht das einen lahmen Esel aus mir?
Bin ich da nicht wie ein guter Hund auf einer guten Fährte?
Und doppelt scharf auf jedes Wild: nach links nach rechts?

I should not let this sweet child, on my soul,
Go mix with all the scurvy men below.
(*Stroking Octavian's hands.*)

PRINCESS: There's no need for such fear, my dear Coz.
(*Enter the Major-Domo.*)

BARON: There, is it not as I said?
He comes with some news that concerns your Highness.

PRINCESS: Struban, tell me, is my attorney waiting in the antechamber?

MAJOR-DOMO: Yes, the attorney waits without, your Highness,
Then there's the Steward, next to Head Cook—
Then, the Duke of Silva commends
To your Highness a singer and a flute-player,
(*Drily.*)
And lastly all the usual petitioners.

BARON: (*to Octavian*): Say, have you ever, with any gentleman
Been tête-à-tête to supper, Mariandel?
(*Octavian simulates embarrassment.*)
No?
It will make you stare, I warrant.

OCTAVIAN: (*softly, confused*): Her Highness won't let me, I'm sure.
(*The Princess listens inattentively to the Major-Domo, while watching the Baron and Octavian with much amusement.*)

PRINCESS: (*to the Major-Domo*): Let them wait then.
(*Exit Major-Domo.*)
(*To the Baron, who tries to regain his composure.*)
My cousin takes, I notice, pleasure where he finds it.

BARON: (*relieved*): Your Highness puts me at my ease at once.
With you we have no nonsense and no Spanish affectations.
(*Kissing her hand.*)
No airs, no buckram, and no compliments.

PRINCESS: (*amused*): But a man of birth, who's just betrothed. . .

BARON: (*approaching her*): Must I, because of that, live like a monk?
Do I not well, like a hound of breed, keen on the quarry ever.
To follow hot-foot every scent to right or left?

MARSCHALLIN: Ich seh', Euer Liebden betreiben es als Profession.

BARON: Das will ich meinen. Wüsste nicht, welche mir besser behagen könnte. Ich muss Euer Gnaden sehr bedauern, dass Euer Gnaden nur—wie drück' ich mich aus— die verteidigenden Erfahrungen besitzen. Parole d'honneur! Es geht nichts über die von der anderen Seite.

MARSCHALLIN: (lacht): Ich glaube Ihm, dass die sehr mannigfaltig sind.

BARON: Soviel Zeiten das Jahr, soviel Stunden der Tag, da ist keine—

MARSCHALLIN: Keine?

BARON: Wo nicht—

MARSCHALLIN: Wo nicht—

BARON: Wo nicht dem Knaben Cupido ein Geschenkerl abzulisten wär!

BARON: (lässt von Octavian ab und nimmt wieder würdevolle Haltung an): Geben mir Euer Gnaben den Grasaff' da zu meiner künftigen Frau Gemahlin Bedienung.

MARSCHALLIN: Wie, meine Kleine da? Was sollte die? Die Fräulein Braut wird schon versehen sein und nicht anstehn auf Euer Liebden Auswahl.

BARON: Das ist ein feines Ding! Kreuzsakerlot! Da ist ein Tropfen guten Bluts dabei!

OCTAVIAN: (für sich): Ein Tropfen guten Bluts!

MARSCHALLIN: Euer Liebden haben ein scharfes Auge!

BARON: Geziemt sich. (Vertraulich.) Find' in der Ordnung, dass Personen von Stand in solcher Weise von adeligem Blut bedient werden. Führ' selbst ein Kind meiner Laune mit mir.

OCTAVIAN: Ein Kind Seiner Laune?

MARSCHALLIN: Wie? Gar ein Mädel? Das will ich nicht hoffen.

---

PRINCESS: I see now that my cousin pursues his sport quite seriously.

BARON: And why deny it? For what sport more becomes a man of birth and breeding? I vow, I do condole with you sincerely That you can only know—it is hard to express— From experience the sensations of defenders— Parole d'honneur—nothing can equal those which inspire the attacking party.

PRINCESS: I doubt not they are vastly various.

BARON: Though the months of the year, though the hours and the minutes by many . . .

PRINCESS: Many?

BARON: There's none . . .

PRINCESS: There's none?

BARON: In which sly Master Cupido Will not smile upon him who woos him aright.

BARON: (suddenly resumes his dignified bearing): Pray will your Highness permit me to take this wench To be my Baroness's chosen attendant!

PRINCESS: What, my favorite girl? What could you gain? And sure, your bride will have no need of her, Such a choice she would wish to make unaided.

BARON: That is a splendid wench, Gadzooks, she is! I dare be sworn, she has blue blood in her.

OCTAVIAN: (aside): Yes, blue blood indeed.

PRINCESS: What a keen discernment is yours, my cousin.

BARON: It is needful. (Confidentially.) Is it not right, that a man of birth Should have those about his person Who also are of pedigree unblemished? I have a lackey as well-born as I.

OCTAVIAN: (still much amused): As well-born as he is!

PRINCESS: What? I am curious. How vastly diverting!

BARON: Son of a Prince . . .

PRINCESS AND OCTAVIAN: Of a Prince?

BARON: So like, that none can mistake him, are the two. He is my body-servant.

PRINCESS AND OCTAVIAN: (laughing): His body-servant!

---

BARON: Nein, einen Sohn. Trägt lerchenauisches Gespräge im Gesicht. Halt' ihn als Leiblakai. Wenn Euer Gnaden dann werden befehlen, dass ich die silberne Rosen darf Dero Händen übergeben, wird er es sein, der sie herauf bringt.

MARSCHALLIN: Soll mich recht freuen. Aber wart' Er einmal. (Octavian winkend.)

BARON: Geben mir Euer Gnaden das Zofel! Ich lass nicht locker.

MARSCHALLIN: Ei! Geh' Sie und bring' Sie das Medaillon her.

OCTAVIAN: (leise): Theres! Theres, gib acht!

MARSCHALLIN: (ebenso): Bring's nur schnell! Ich weiss schon, was ich tu.

BARON: (Octavian nachsehend): Könnt' eine junge Fürstin sein. (Dann, im Konversationston.) Hab' vor, meiner Braut eine getreue Kopie meines Stammbaumes zu spendieren— nebst einer Locke vom Ahnherrn Lerchenau, der ein grosser Klosterstifter war und Oberst-Erblandhofmeister in Kärnten und in der winischen Mark. (Octavian bringt das Medaillon aus dem Bettalkoven).

MARSCHALLIN: Wollen Euer Gnaden leicht den jungen Herrn da als Braüutigamsaufführer haben?

BARON: Bin ungeschauter einverstanden!

MARSCHALLIN: (etwas zögernd): Mein junger Vetter, der Graf Octavian.

BARON: Wüsste keinen vornehmeren zu wünschen! Wär in Devotion dem jungen Herrn sehr verbunden!

MARSCHALLIN: (schnell): Seh' ihn an! (Hält ihm das Medaillon hin.)

BARON: (sieht bald auf das Medaillon, bald auf die Zofe): Die Aehnlichkeit!

MARSCHALLIN: Ja, ja.

BARON: Aus dem Gesicht geschnitten!

---

BARON: Whenever your Highness shall deign to command me To give to your keeping the Rose of Silver (He is without now—in the courtyard) It will be from him I shall receive it.

PRINCESS: I understand—but one instant, I beg, (Beckoning to Octavian.) Mariandel!

BARON: Once more I beg your Highness—the waiting maid for My Lady!

PRINCESS: Ah! (To Octavian.) Go bring the miniature set in jewels

OCTAVIAN: (softly): Therese, Therese, beware!

BARON: (looking after him): Gad, she might be a young Princess. (To the Princess.) Do you think it would be well if I gave to my bride My pedigree, fairly copied— Or even a lock of the first of the Lerchenaus—a pious founder of convents he And First Hereditary Grand Warden Of the Karinthian Domains? (Octavian brings the medallion.)

PRINCESS: Would your Lordship choose to have this gentleman To take the Rose of Silver to your mistress? (All in an easy tone of conversation.)

BARON: Without a glance I trust your Highness.

PRINCESS: (hesitating): It is my young cousin, Count Octavian—

BARON: (still very courteous): Who could wish for a nobler or more gallant? And vastly to your kinsman should I be indebted.

PRINCESS: (quickly): Look at him well. (Shows him the miniature.)

BARON: It is wonderful. (Looking first at the portrait, then at Octavian.) Like two copies from one model!

**MARSCHALLIN:** Hab' mir auch schon Gedanken gemacht.
(*Auf das medaillon deutend.*) Rofrano, des Herrn Marchese zweiter Bruder.

**BARON:** Octavian Rofrano! Da ist man wer, wenn man aus solchem Haus,
(*mit Beziehung auf die Zofe.*) Und wär's auch bei der Domestikentür!

**MARSCHALLIN:** Darum halt' ich sie auch wie was Besonderes.

**BARON:** Geziemt sich.

**MARSCHALLIN:** Immer um meine Person.

**BARON:** Sehr wohl.

**MARSCHALLIN:** Jetzt aber geh' Sie, Mariandel, mach' Sie fort.

**BARON:** Wie denn? Sit kommt doch wieder.

**MARSCHALLIN:** (*überhört den Baron absichtlich*): Und lass Sie die Antichambre herein.
(*Octavian geht gegen die Flügelthür rechts*).

**BARON:** (*ihm nach*): Mein schönstes Kind!

**OCTAVIAN:** (*an der Tür rechts*): Derft's eina geh'!
(*Läuft nach der andern Tür.*)

**BARON:** (*ihm nach*): Ich bin Ihr Serviteur! Geb' Sie doch einen Augenblick Audienz!

**OCTAVIAN:** (*schlägt ihm die klein Tür vor der Nase zu*): I komm' glei.
(*In diesem Augenblick tritt eine alte Kammerfrau, die Waschbecken, Kanne und Handtuch trägt, durch die gleiche Türe ein. Der Baron zieht sich enttäuscht zurück. Zwei Lakaien kommen von rechts herein, bringen einen Wandschirm aus dem Alkoven, die alte kammerfrau, mit ihr, zwei Lakaien tragen den Sessel und den Frisiertisch nach vorne in die Mitte. Zwei Lakaien öffnen die Flügeltüren rechts. Es treten ein der Notar, der Küchenchef, hinter diesen ein Küchenjunge, der das Menübuch trägt. Dann die Modistin, ein Gelehrter mit einem Folianten und der Tierhändler mit winzig kleinen Hunden und einen Aeffchen. Valzacchi und Annina, hinter diesen rasch gleitend, nehmen den vordersten Platz links ein, die adelige Mutter mit ihren drei Töchtern, alle in Trauer, stellen sich in den rechten Flügel. Der Haushofmeister führt den Tenor und den Flötisten nach vorne. Baron rückwärts winkt einen Lakaien zu sich, gibt ihm den Auftrag, zeigt: "Hier durch die Hintertür.")*

**PRINCESS:** It has caused me myself no small surprise.
(*Pointing to the portrait.*) Rofrano, the younger brother of the Marquis.

**BARON:** Octavian? Rofrano? It is no small thing, such a relationship,
(*Pointing to Octavian.*) Even if it be not quite . . . canonical.

**PRINCESS:** For that same cause have I advanced her over all the rest.

**BARON:** It is fitting—

**PRINCESS:** Always in waiting on myself.

**BARON:** It is well.

**PRINCESS:** Now get you gone, you, Mariandel.
(*Octavian goes towards the folding door on the right.*)

**BARON:** (*following him*): My sweetest child!

**OCTAVIAN:** La! Naughty man!
(*At the door.*)

**BARON:** I am your most obedient servant—Only let me speak.

**OCTAVIAN:** (*slams the door in the Baron's face*): Yes, shortly.
(*At this moment an old tirewoman enters by the same door. The Baron starts back disappointed. Two Footmen enter from the right and bring a screen from the recess. The Princess steps behind the screen, attended by her tirewoman. The toilet table is moved to the center. The footmen open the folding doors through which enter the Attorney, the Head Cook, followed by an assistant, carrying the book of Menus. Then a Milliner, a Scholar, carrying a ponderous folio, and the Vendor of Animals with tiny lap-dogs and a small monkey. Valzacchi and Annina slipping in behind the last-named, take their places on the extreme left. The noble Mother with her three Daughters all in deepest mourning take position on the right wing. The Major-Domo leads the Tenor and the Flute Player to the front. The Baron, in the background beckons to a footman, gives him an order, pointing "Here through the small door."*)

**DIE DREI ADELIGEN TÖCHTER:** (*schreiend*): Drei arme adelige Waisen—
(*Die Adelige Mutter bedeutet ihnen, nicht so zu schreien und niederzuknien*).

**DIE DREI WAISEN:** (*niederkniend*): Drei arme adelige Waisen erflehen Dero hohen Schutz!

**MODISTIN:** (*laut*): Le chapeau Paméla! La poudre à la reine de Golconde!

**DER TIERHÄNDLER:** Schöne Affen, wenn Durchlaucht schaffen, auch Vögel hab' ich da aus Afrika.

**DIE DREI WAISEN:** Der Vater ist jung auf dem Felde der Ehre gefallen, ihm dieses nachzutun, ist unser Herzensziel.

**MODISTIN:** La chapeau Paméla! C'est la merveille du monde!

**DIE TIERHÄNDLER:** Papageien hätt' ich da, aus Indien und Afrika. Hunderln, so klein und schon zimmerrein.
(*Marschallin tritt hervor, alles verneigt sich. Baron ist links vorgekommen.*)

**MARSCHALLIN:** (*zum Baron*): Ich präsentier' Euer Liebden hier den Notar.
(*Notar tritt mit Verneigung gegen den Frisiertisch, wo sich die Marschallin niedergelassen, zum Baron links. Marschallin winkt die jüngste der drei Waisen zu sich, lässt sich vom Haushofmeister einen Geldbeutel reichen, gibt ihn dem Mädchen, indem sie es auf die Stirne küsst. Gelehrter will vortreten, seine Folianten überreichen, Valzacchi springt vor, drängt ihn zur Seite.*)

**VALZACCHI:** (*ein schwarzgerändertes Zeitungsblatt hervorziehend*): Die swarze Seitung! Fürstlike Gnade: Alles 'ier ge'eim gesrieben! Nur für 'ohe Persönlikeite. Die swarze Seitung! Eine Leikname in 'Interkammer von eine gräflike Palais! Eine Bürgersfrau mit der amante vergiften der Hehemann diese Nackt um dreie Huhr!

**MARSCHALLIN:** Lass er mich mit dem Tratsch in Ruh'!

**VALZACCHI:** In Gnaden: tutte quante Vertraulikeite aus die grosse Welt!

**THE THREE NOBLE ORPHANS:** (*shrilly*): Three poor and high-born orphan children . . .
(*Their Mother makes signs to them to kneel and not to sing so loudly.*)

**THE THREE ORPHANS:** (*kneeling*): Three poor and high-born orphan children, Implore your Grace to grant our prayer.

**THE MILLINER:** (*loudly*): Le Chapeau Pamèla—La Poudre à la Reine de Golconda!

**THE VENDOR OF ANIMALS:** For your pleasure In hours of leisure Of tricksy apes a score From Afric's shore.

**THE THREE ORPHANS:** My father dies in youth a glorious death for his country, It is my heart's one desire to be his worthy child.

**THE MILLINER:** Le Chapeau Pamèla! C'est la merveille du monde!

**THE VENDOR:** Parrots too of plumage gay From India and Africay. Lap-dogs so wise Very small in size.
(*The Princess appears. All bow low. The Baron, on the left, steps forward.*)

**PRINCESS:** (*to the Baron*): I here make known to you, dear Kinsman, my attorney.
(*The Attorney, with many obeisances towards the toilet table at which the Princess has seated herself, advances to the Baron on the right. The Princess signs to the youngest of the three Orphans to approach her, and takes a purse from the Major-Domo and gives it to the girl, whom she kisses on the forehead. The Scholar attempts to approach the Princess and hand her his volumes, but Valzacchi rushes forward and pushes him aside.*)

**VALZACCHI:** (*drawing from his pocket a black-edged news sheet*): Ze latest scandals! True news, your 'Ighness! Learnt from secret information! Meant only for ze Quality! Ze newest Scandals! A dead body in a secret chamber In ze town 'ouse of a Count! A rich merchant's wife poisons 'er 'usband Viz ze 'elp of her lover Soon after sree o'clock zis night.

**PRINCESS:** Fudge! Let me hear no more of it!

**VALZACCHI:** Your pardon, your 'Ighness Tutte quante. Ze hidden secrets Of ze elegant world!

**MARSCHALLIN:** Ich will nix wissen!
Lass er mich mit dem Tratsch in Ruh'!
(*Valzacchi mit bedauernder Verbeugung springt zurück*).

**DIE DREI WAISEN:** (*zuletzt auch die Mutter, haben der Marschallin die Hand geküsst*): Glück und Segen allerwegen Euer Gnaden hohem Sinn!
Eingegraben steht erhaben er in unsern Herzen drin.
(*Geben ab samt der Mutter.*)
(*Der Friseur tritt hastig auf, der Gehilfe stürzt ihm mit fliegenden Rockschössen nach. Der Friseur fasst die Marschallin ins Auge verdüstert sich, tritt zurück, er studiert ihr heutiges Aussehen. Der Gehilft indessen packt aus am Frisiertisch. Der Friseur schiebt einige Personen zurück, sich Spielraum zu schaffen. Nach einer kurzen Ueberlegung ist sein Plan gefasst, er eilt mit Entschlossenheit auf die Marschallin zu, beginnt zu frisieren. Ein Läuffer in rosa, schwarz und Silber tritt auf, überbringt ein Billet. Haushofmeister mit Silbertablett ist schnell zur Hand, präsentiert es der Marschallin. Friseur hält inne, sie lesen zu lassen. Gehilfe reicht ihm ein neues Eisen. Friseur schwenkt es: ist zu heiss. Gehilfe reicht ihm nach fragendem Blick auf die Marschallin das Billet, die nickt, worauf er es lächelnd verwendet, um das Eisen zu kühlen. Gleichzeitig hat sich der Sänger in Position gestellt, hält das Notenblatt. Flötist sieht ihm, begleitend, über die Schultern. Die Lakaien haben rechts ganz vorne Stellung genommen, andere stehen im Hintergrund.*)

**DER TENOR:** Di rigori armato il seno
Contro amor mi ribellai
Ma fui vinto in un baleno
In mirar due vaghi rai.
Ahi! che resiste puoco
Cor di gelo astral di fuoco.
(*Der Friseur übergibt dem Gehilfen das Eisen und applaudiert dem Sänger. Dann fährt er im Arrangement des Lockenbaues fort. Ein Bedienter hat indessen bei der kleinen Tür den Kammerdiener des Barons, den Almosenier und den Jäger eingelassen. Es sind drei bedenkliche Gestalten. Der Kammerdiener ist ein junger grosser Lümmel, der dumm und frech aussieht. Er trägt unterm Arm ein Futteral aus rotem Saffian. Der Almosenier ist ein verwilderter Dorfkooperator, ein vier Schuh hoher, aber stark und verwegen*

**PRINCESS:** What is that to me?
Let me be with your vicious talk!
(*Valzacchi retires with a deprecatory bow. The three Orphans prepare to withdraw, after they and their Mother have kissed the Princess's hand.*)

**THE THREE ORPHANS:**
(*whining*): May Heaven joy send you, may bliss attend you
Wherever you may be.
We shall praise ever, forgetting never
Your great generosity!
(*Exeunt with their Mother.*)
(*The Hairdresser hurriedly steps forward, his assistant follows him with flying coat-tails. The Hairdresser gazes at the Princess, looks solemn and steps back a few paces, the better to study her appearance. In the meantime the assistant unpacks his paraphernalia at the toilet table. The Hairdresser pushes several persons back, so as to make more room for himself.*)
(*The Flute Player now steps forward and begins his Cadenza. Some Footmen have taken up positions at the front to the right. Others remain in the background.*)
(*After brief deliberation, the Hairdresser has made up his mind and with an air of determination goes to the Princess and begins to dress her hair. A Courier in a livery of pink, black and silver, enters carrying a note. The Major-Domo is quickly at hand with a silver salver and presents it to the Princess. The Hairdresser pauses to allow her to read. The assistant hands him a fresh pair of curling tongs. The Hairdresser swings it: it is too hot. The assistant gives him, after a questioning glance at the Princess, who nods assent, the note, which he smilingly uses for cooling the tongs. The Singer has taken up his position.*)

**THE TENOR:** (*reading from a sheet of music*): Di rigori armeto il seno
Contro amor mi ribellai
Ma fui vinto in un baleno
In mirar due vaghi rai
Ahi! Che resiste poco
Cor di gelo a stral di fuoco!
(*The Hairdresser hands the tongs to his assistant and applauds the singer. Then he continues to work at the coiffure of the Princess. In the meantime a Footman has admitted through the small door the Body Servant, the Almoner and the Chasseur of the Baron. They are three strange apparitions. The Body Servant is a tall young fellow of foolish insolent mien. He carries under his arm a leather jewel case. The Almoner is an unkempt village councillor, a stunted but strong and bold-looking imp.*

aussehender Gnom. Der Leibjäger mag, bevor er in die schlechtsitzende Livree gesteckt wurde, Mist geführt haben. Der Almosenier und der kammerdiener scheinen sich um den Vortritt zu streiten und steigen einander auf die Füsse. Sie steuern längs der linken Seite auf ihren Herrn zu, in dessen Nähe sie Halt machen.*)

**BARON:** (*auf dem Faninal links ganz vorne zum Notar, der vor ihm steht, seine Weisungen entgegennimmt. Halblaut*): Als Morgengabe—ganz separatim jedoch—
und vor der Mitgift—bin ich verstanden, Herr Notar?—
kehrt Schloss und Herrschaft Gaunersdorf an mich zurück!
Von Lasten frei und ungemindert an Privilegien,
so wie mein Vater selig sie besessen hat.

**NOTAR:** (*kurzatmig*): Gestatten hochfreiherrliche Gnaden die submisseste Belehrung,
dass eine Morgengabe wohl vom Gatten an die Gattin,
nicht aber von der Gattin an den Gatten
(*tief aufatmend.*)
bestellet oder stipuliert zu werden, fähig ist.

**BARON:** Das mag wohl sein.

**NOTAR:** Dem ist so—

**BARON:** Aber im besondern Fall—

**NOTAR:** Die Formen und die Präskriptionen kennen keinen Unterschied.

**BARON:** (*schreit*): Haben ihn aber zu kennen:

**NOTAR:** (*erschrocken*): In Gnaden!

**BARON:** (*wieder leise, aber eindringlich und voll hohen Selbstgefühles*): Wenn eines hochadeligen Blutes blühender Spross sich herablässt
im Ehebette einer so gut als bürgerlichen Mamsell Faninal
—bin ich verstanden?—acte de présence zu machen
vor Gott und der Welt und sozusagen
angesichts kaiserlicher Majestät—
(*Flötist beginnt wieder zu präludieren*).
Da wird, corpo di Bacco! von Morgengabe
als geziemendem Geschenk dankbarer Devotion
für die Hingab' so hohen Blutes sehr wohl die Rede sein!
(*Sänger macht miene wieder anzufangen, wartet noch, bis der Baron still wird.*)

**NOTAR:** (*zum Baron, leise*): Vielleicht, dass man die Sache separatim—

The Chasseur looks as if, before being thrust into his ill-fitting livery, he had worked in the farm. The Almoner and the Body Servant seem to be fighting for precedence, and trip each other up. They steer a course to the left, towards their master, in whose vicinity they come to a halt.*)

**BARON:** (*seated, to the Attorney, who stands before him, taking his instructions*): As compensation, as a separate gift,
Before the dowry, Master Attorney, understand,
I shall receive the title-deeds of Gaunersdorf,
Released from all encumbrances and all claims whatsoever.
With privileges intact, just as my father held them.

**ATTORNEY:** (*asthmatic*): Your Lordship—with dutiful submission—has not been pleased to remember
That a donatio ante nuptias may be given by the husband
But cannot ever come from wife to husband—
(*Fetching a deep breath.*)
Such contracts are unprecedented quite.

**BARON:** That may be so.

**ATTORNEY:** It is so.

**BARON:** But in this special case—

**ATTORNEY:** That statutes are precise, no way is known of circumventing them.

**BARON:** (*shouts*): But I insist that you shall know one.

**ATTORNEY:** (*alarmed*): Your pardon.

**BARON:** But, do you see, when a noble race's chief condescends to a union
With a young person, a Mistress Faninal,
Whose father has no pedigree—
upon whose patent of nobility
The ink is scarcely dry—if then I choose in face of Heaven
And of the Empress thus to honor her.
(*The Flautist begins another Prelude.*)
I think, corpo di Bacco, that such is clearly
A case where an exception can be made, and that the bride
Should have full leave to show her gratitude
For the honor done to her.

**ATTORNEY:** (*to the Baron, softly*): Perhaps by means of purchase and conveyance . . .

## Act I

**BARON:** (*leise*): Er ist ein schmählicher Pedant: als Morgengabe will ich das Gütel!

**NOTAR:** (*ebenso*): Als einen wohl verklausulierten Teil der Mitgift—

**BARON:** (*halblaut*): Als Morgengabe!
Geht das nicht in Seinen Schädel!

**NOTAR:** (*ebenso*): Als eine Schenkung inter vivos oder—

**BARON:** (*schlägt wütend auf den Tisch, schreiend*): Als Morgengabe!

**DER SÄNGER:** (*während des Gesprächs der beiden*): Ma si caro è'l mio tormento
Dolce è si la piaga mia,
Ch' il penare è mio contento
E'l sanarmi è tirannia
Ahi! Che resiste puoco—
Cor . . . . . . .
(*Hier erhebt der Baron seine Stimme so, dass der Sänger jäh abbricht, desgleichen die Flöte.*)
(*Notar zieht sich erschrocken in die Ecke zurück*).
(*Marschallin winkt den Sänger zu sich, reicht ihm die Hand zum Kuss*).
(*Sänger Nebst Flötist ziehen sich unter tiefen Verbeugungen zurück*).
(*Baron tut, als ob nichts geschehen wäre, winkt dem Sänger leutselig zu, tritt dann zu seiner Dienerschaft, streicht dem Leiblakai die bäurisch in die Stirn gekämmten Haare hinaus; gebt dann, als suchte er jemand, zur kleinen Tür, öffnet sie, spioniert hinaus, argert sich, dass die Zofe nicht zurückkommt; schnüffelt gegen's Bett, schüttelt den Kopf, kommt dann wieder vor*).

**MARSCHALLIN:** (*sieht sich in dem Handspiegel, halblaut*): Mein lieber Hippolyte,
Heut haben Sie ein altes Weib aus mir gemacht:
(*Der Friseur mit Bestürzung wirft sich, fieberhaft auf den Lockenbau der Marschallin und verändert ihn aufs neue. Das Gesicht der Marschallin bleibt traurig.*)
(*über die Schulter zum Hausho-meister*): Abtreten die Leut'!
(*Die Lakaien, eine Kette bildend schieben die aufwartenden Personen zur Tür hinaus, die sie dann verschliessen. Nur der Gelehrte, vom Hausbofmeister ihr zugeführt bleibt noch im Gespräch mit der Marschallin, bis zum Schluss des Intermezzos zwischen Valzacchi, Annina und dem Baron. Valzacchi, hinter ihm Annina, haben sich im Rücken aller rings um die Bühne zum Baron hinübergeschlichen und präsentieren sich ihm mit übertriebener Devotion*).

**BARON:** (*to himself*): The wretched pettifogging fool!
As compensation I must have it!

**ATTORNEY:** Or in the marriage settlement, with special clauses . . .

**BARON:** No—compensation. Can you not get that into your thick skull?

**ATTORNEY:** Or as donatio inter vivos—or else.

**BARON:** (*in a fury, thumping the table, shouts*): No, compensation.

**THE TENOR:** (*during this conversation*): Ma si caro è il mio tormento
Dolce è si la piaga mia,
Che il penare è mio contento
E'l sanarmi è tirannia
Ahi che resiste poco
Cor . . . . .
(*At this point the Baron raises his voice so that the Singer ends abruptly, likewise the Flute Player.*)
(*The Princess beckons the Singer and gives him her hand to kiss. The Singer and the Flute Player retire with deep obeisances. The Attorney withdraws into a corner in alarm. The Baron does as if nothing had happened, and makes a sign of condescending approval to the Singer, then goes across to his servants; straightens the towzled hair of his body servant; then goes, as if looking for somebody, to the small door, opens it, peers out, is annoyed, looks by the bed, shakes his head and comes forward again.*)

**PRINCESS:** (*looking at herself in a hand mirror, aside*): My good friend Hippolyte, this will not do,
You've made me look a very fright.
(*The Hairdresser in consternation falls on the Princess's headdress with feverish energy and changes it again. The Princess continues to wear a pensive expression. Valzacchi, followed by Annina, has, behind the back of everybody else, slunk to the other side of the stage, and they present themselves to the Baron with exaggerated obsequiousness.*)
(*over her shoulder to the Major-Domo*): They are all dismissed.
(*The Footmen, taking hands, push them all out by the door, which they then close. Only the Scholar, whom the Major-Domo presents to the Princess, remains in conversation with her till the close of the episode between the Baron, Valzacchi and Annina.*)

**VALZACCHI:** (*zum Baron*): Ihre Gnade sukt etwas. Ik seh, Ihr Gnade at eine Bedürfnis. Ik kann dienen. Ik kann besorgen.

**BARON:** (*tritt zurück*): Wer ist Er, was weiss Er

**VALZACCHI:** Ihr Gnade Gesikt sprikt ohne Sunge.
Wie ein Hantike: come statua do Giove.

**BARON:** Das ist ein besserer Mensch.

**VALZACCHI:** Erlaukte Gnade, attachieren uns an Sein Gefolge
(*Fällt auf die Knie, desgleichen Annina*)

**BARON:** Euch?

**VALZACCHI:** Onkel und Nikte. Su sweien maken alles besser. Per esempio: Ihre Gnade at eine junge Frau—

**BARON:** Woher weiss Er denn das, Er Teufel Er?

**VALZACCHI:** (*eifrig*): Ihre Gnade ist in Eifersukt: dico per dire Eut oder morgen könnte sein. Affare nostro!
Jede Sritt die Dame sie tut, jede Wagen die Dame steigt, jede Brief die Dame bekommt—wir sind da!
An die Ecke, in die Kamin, 'inter die Bette—
in eine Schranke, unter die Dache, wir sind da!

**ANNINA:** Ihre Gnaden wird nicht bedauern
(*Halten ihm die Hände hin, Geld heischend, er tut, als bemerke er es nicht.*)

**BARON:** (*halblaut*): Hm: Was es alles gibt in diesem Wien?
Zur Probe nur: kennt Sie die Jungfer Mariandel?

**ANNINA:** (*ebenso*): Mariandel?

**BARON:** (*ebenso*): Das Zofel hier im Haus bei Ihrer Gnaden?

**VALZACCHI:** (*leise zu Annina*): Sai tu, cosa vuole?

**ANNINA:** (*ebenso*): Niente!

**VALZACCHI:** (*zum Baron*): Sicker! Sicker!
Mein nickte wird besorgen. Seien sicker, Ihre Gnade? Wir sind da!
(*Hält abermals die Hand hin, Bar-*

**VALZACCHI:** (*to the Baron*): Is your Lords'ip lacking aught? I see zat your Lords'ip is looking for somezing.
I can help you, I can be useful.

**BARON:** (*drawing back*): And who may you be, pray?

**VALZACCHI:** Zough your Lords'ip say nozzing
Ve understand from your Lords'ip expression.

**ANNINA:** Vat your Lords'ip wishes . . .

**VALZACCHI:** Come statua di Giove.

**BARON:** He might be useful, I think.

**VALZACCHI AND ANNINA:** (*kneeling*): May't please your Lords'ip we declare ourselves your 'umble servants.

**BARON:** You?

**VALZACCHI AND ANNINA:** Uncle and niece
In couples our vork is easier. Per esempio?
'As your Lords'ip married a youzful bride . . .

**BARON:** How come you to know so much, you dog?

**VALZACCHIE AND ANNINA:** (*eagerly*): 'As your Lords'ip cause for jealousy?
Dico per dire.
Now or tomorrow?
Who can tell?
Affare nostro!
Every step ze lady may take, Every coach zat ze lady 'ires, Every billet doux zat she 'as—Ve are zere
At ze corner, or by ze fire Or in a cupboard, or in ze attic, Or by ze bedside, under ze table, Ve are zere!

**ANNINA:** Sure your Lords'ip vill not regret it.
(*They hold out their hands as if for money. The Baron pretends not to notice them.*)

**BARON:** (*aside*): Hm! What things we see and hear in this great town! To try your skill, do you perchance know Mariandel?

**VALZACCHI:** Mariandel?

**BARON:** Her Highness's waiting maid that's always with her!

**VALZACCHI:** (*aside to Annina*): Sai tu? cosa vuole?

**ANNINA:** Niente.

**VALZACCHI:** (*to the Baron*): Trust us, trust us: ve vill soon 'ave information—
Put your trust in us, your Lords'ip—
Ve are zere!

*on tut, als sähe er es nicht. Marschallin ist aufgestanden. Friseur nach tiefer Verbeugung eilt ab. Gehilfe hinter ihm.)*

**BARON:** *(die beiden Italiener steben lassend, auf die Marschallin zu):* Darf ich das Gegenstück. *(diskret.)* zu Dero sauberm Kammerzofel präsentieren? *(Selbstgefällig.)* Die Ahnlichgeit soll, hör ich, unverkennbar sein. *(Marschallin nickt):* Leupold, das Futteral. *(Der jung Kammerlakai präsentiert linkisch das Futteral.)*

**MARSCHALLIN:** *(ein bischen lachend):* Ich gratulier' Euer Liebden sehr.

**BARON:** *(nimmt dem Burschen das Futteral aus der Hand und winkt ihm zurückzutreten).* Und da ist nun die silberne Rosen! *(Will's aufmachen.)*

**MARSCHALLIN:** Lassen nur drinnen. Haben die Gnad' und stellen's dort hin.

**BARON:** Vielleicht das Zofel soll's übernehmen? Ruft man ihr?

**MARSCHALLIN:** Nein, lassen nur. Die hat jetzt keine Zeit. Doch sei Er sicher: den Grafen Octavian bitt' ich ihm auf, er wird's mir zulieb schon tun und als Euer Liebden Kavalier vorfahren mit der Rosen bei der Jungfer Braut. *(Leichthin.)* Stellen indes nur hin. Und jetzt, Herr Vetter, sag' ich Ihm Adieu. Man retiriert sich jetzt von hier: Ich werd' jetzt in die Kirchen gehn. *(Lakaien öffnen die Flügeltür.)*

**BARON:** Euer Gnaden haben heut durch unversiegte Huld mich tiefst beschämt. *(Macht die Reverenz; entfernt sich unter Zeremoniell. Der Notar hinter ihm, auf seinen Wink. Seine drei Leute hinter diesem, in mangelhafter Haltung. Die beiden Italiener lautlos und geschmeidig, schlissen sich unbemerkt an. Lakaien schliessen die Tür. Haushofmeister tritt ab. Marschallin allein.)*

**MARSCHALLIN:** *(allein):* Da geht er hin, der aufgeblasene schlechte Kerl, und kriegt das hübsche junge Ding und einen Pinkel Geld dazu. *(Seufzend.)* Als muss's so sein. Und bildet sich noch ein, dass er es ist, der sich was vergibt.

**BARON:** *(leaving the two Italians, to the Princess):* May I now introduce, in all discretion, The counterpart of your young servant to your Highness? The likeness is wonderful, my friends all tell me. *(Princess nods.)* Leopold, the jewel-case!

**PRINCESS:** *(smiling):* He does great honor to his ancestry. *(The young body servant awkwardly hands over the jewel-case.)*

**BARON:** *(taking his seat and signing to the young man to withdraw):* The Silver Rose is here, in this casket. *(Opening it.)*

**PRINCESS:** Do not disturb it. Pray, place it yonder, I'll be obliged.

**BARON:** Or shall I call your waiting-maid And give it to her—

**PRINCESS:** Not to her. She is now occupied. But this I promise—I will at once make known your wishes to the Count, For me he will consent, I know— And all proper usage observing, Duly to your bride the Rose of Silver bear, Meanwhile I'll keep it here. And now, your Lordship, I bid you adieu— It is high time that I should go Else I shall be too late for church— *(The Footmen open the folding door.)*

**BARON:** The most gracious courtesy your Highness renders me Overwhelms me quite— *(He makes an obeisance and ceremoniously withdraws. At a sign from him, the Attorney follows; and after him the Baron's three servants shuffle out awkwardly. The two Italians silently and obsequiously join the train without his observing them. The Major-Domo withdraws. The Footmen close the door. The Princess is left alone.)*

**PRINCESS:** Now go your ways.— Go, vain pretentious profligate! And what is your reward? An ample dowry and a pretty bride— He takes it all, thinking it is but his due— And boasts that he has greatly honored her.

Was erzürn' ich mich denn? Ist doch der Lauf der Welt. Kann mich auch an ein Mädel erinnern, die frisch aus dem Kloster ist in den heiligen Ehestand kommandiert word'n. *(Nimmt den Handspiegel.)* Wo ist die jetzt? Ja, *(seufzend.)* such' dir den Schnee vom vergangenen Jahr! Das sag' ich so: *(Ruhig.)* Aber wie kann das wirklich sein, dass ich die kleine Resi war und dass ich auch einmal die alte Frau sein werd'. Die alte Frau, die alte Marschallin! "Siegst es, da geht's die alte Fürstin Resi!" Wie kann denn das geschehen? Wie macht denn das der liebe Gott? Wo ich doch immer die gleiche bin. Und wenn er's schon so machen muss, warum lasst er mich denn zuschaun dabei mit gar so klarem Sinn! Warum versteckt er's nicht vor mir? Das alles ist geheim, so viel geheim. Und man ist dazu da, *(seufzend)* dass man's erträgt. Und in dem "Wie" *(sehr ruhig.)* da liegt der ganze Unterschied— *(Octavian tritt von rechts ein, in einem Morgananzug mit Reitstiefeln).*

**MARSCHALLIN:** *(ruhig, mit halbem Lächeln):* Ach, du bist wieder da!

**OCTAVIAN:** *(zärtlich):* Und du bist traurig!

**MARSCHALLIN:** Es is ja schon vorbei. Du weisst ja, wie ich bin. Ein halb Mal lustig, ein halb Mal traurig. Ich kann halt meinen Gedanken nicht kommandier'n.

**OCTAVIAN:** Ich weiss, warum du traurig bist, du Schatz. Weil du erschrocken bist und Angst gehabt hast. Hab' ich nicht recht? Gesteh' mir nur: du hast Angst gehabt, du Süsse, du Liebe, um mich, um mich!

**MARSCHALLIN:** Ein bissel vielleicht, aber ich hab' mich erfangen und hab' mir vorgesagt: Es wird schon nicht dafür stehn. Und wär's dafür gestanden?

**OCTAVIAN:** *(heiter):* Und es war kein Feldmarschall, nur ein spassiger Herr Vetter, und du gehörst mir, du gehörst mir:

*(Sighs.)* But why trouble myself? The world will have its way Did I not know a girl, just like to this one, Who straight from out her convent was marched off Into the Holy Estate of Wedlock? Where is she now! *(Sighs.)* Go seek the snows of yesteryear! But can it be—can it be—though I say it so, That I was that young Tess of long ago And that I shall be called, ere lone, "the old Princess," "The Old Field Marshal's lady."— "Look you There goes the old Princess Theresia"— How can it come to pass? How can the Powers decree it so? For I am I, and never change. *(Gaily.)* And if indeed it must be so, Why then must I sit here, a looker on, And see it all and grieve? Were it not better we were blind? These things are still a mystery—a mystery— And we are here below to bear it all. *(Sighs.)* But how? But how? *(Very quietly.)* In that lies all the difference. *(Enter Octavian, from the right, in riding dress with riding boots.)*

**PRINCESS:** *(quietly, smiling):* Ah! You are back again—

**OCTAVIAN:** And you are pensive!

**PRINCESS:** The mood has flown again. You know me, how I am— A brief awhile merry—a brief while mournful— My thoughts fly here and there, I know not how.

**OCTAVIAN:** I know why you have been so sad, beloved, You were beside yourself with fear for us both. Is it not so? Confess to me. You were sore afraid, My angel, my dearest, For me—for me!

**PRINCESS:** A little at first, But soon my courage had come back, and to myself I said— "It cannot be—It is not yet." And if it had been fated?

**OCTAVIAN:** *(gaily):* And it was not the prince at all, It was only your comical kinsman. And you are mine own! You are mine own.

# Act I

MARSCHALLIN: (*erhebt sich, ihn abwehrend*): Taverl, umarm' Er nicht zu viel.
Wer allzuviel umarmt, der hält nichts fest.

OCTAVIAN: (*leidenschaftlich*): Sag' dass du mir gehörst! Mir!

MARSCHALLIN: Oh, sei Er jetzt sanft, sei Er gescheit und sanft und gut.
(*Octavian will lebhaft erwidern*). Nein, bitt' schön, sei Er nicht, wie alle Männer sind!

OCTAVIAN: (*misstrauisch auffahrend*): Wie alle Männer?

MARSCHALLIN: (*schnell gefasst*): Wie der Feldmarschall und der Vetter Ochs.

OCTAVIAN: (*nicht dabei beruhigt*): Bichette!

MARSCHALLIN: (*mit Nachdruck*): Sei Er nur nicht, wie alle Männer sind.

OCTAVIAN: (*zornig*): Ich weiss nicht, wie alle Männer sind.
(*Plötzlich sanft.*)
Weiss nur, dass ich dich lieb hab', Bichette, sie haben mir dich ausgetauscht.
Bichette, wo ist Sie denn!

MARSCHALLIN: (*ruhig*): sie ist wohl da, Herr Schatz.

OCTAVIAN: Ja, ist Sie da? Dann will ich Sie halten, dass Sie mir nicht wieder entkommt!
(*Leidenschaftlich.*)
Packen will ich Sie, packen, dass Sie es spürt, zu wem Sie gehört—zu mir: Denn ich bin Ihr und Sie ist mein!

MARSCHALLIN: (*sich ihm entwindend*): Oh, sei Er gut, Quinquin.
Mir ist zumut, dass ich die Schwäche von allem Zeitlichen recht spüren muss, bis in mein Herz hinein, wie man nichts halten soll, wie man nichts packen kann, wie alles zerlauft zwischen den Fingern, alles sich auflöst, wonach wir greifen, alles zergeht wie Dunst und Traum.

OCTAVIAN: Mein Gott, wie Sie das sagt.
Sie will mir doch nur zeigen, dass Sie nicht an mir hängt.
(*Die Tränen kommen ihm.*)

MARSCHALLIN: Sei Er doch gut, Quinquin!
(*Octavian weint stärker*):
Jetzt muss ich noch den Buben dafür trösten,
Dass er mich über kurz oder lang

PRINCESS: (*pushing him aside*): Dearest, embrace me not so much! Who tries to grasp too much, holds nothing fast.

OCTAVIAN: (*passionately*): Tell me that you are mine—mine!

PRINCESS: Oh, be not so wild! Be gentle and tender and kind. No, pray you now—
(*Octavian is about to answer excitedly.*)
Do you not be like all the other men.

OCTAVIAN: (*suspiciously*): Like all the others?

PRINCESS: (*quickly recovering herself*): As the Marshal is, and as my kinsman Ochs.

OCTAVIAN: (*still dissatisfied*): Bichette!

PRINCESS: (*emphatically*): No—do not be like all the other men.

OCTAVIAN: (*angrily*): The others?
How can I know what they are—
(*With sudden tenderness.*)
Only I know I love you.
Bichette, there surely is some changeling here.
Bichette, it is not you.

PRINCESS: No, it is I, my dear.

OCTAVIAN: Yes, it is you?
I will clasp you closer,
That you'll never, never escape me,
I will cling to you tightly,
That in truth you will know whose you are.

PRINCESS: (*freeing herself from him*): Command yourself, Mignon.
I feel I know
That all things earthly are but vanity, but empty dreams.
Deep in my heart I know
How we should grasp at nothing,
How we can cling to nothing
How the world's joys cheat and elude us—
How empty all things are that we deem precious,
All things must pass, like mists—like dreams.

OCTAVIAN: Oh Heaven!
Why so distraught,
You do but want to tell me that your love is dead.
(*Weeps.*)

PRINCESS: Be not so sad, Mignon.
(*Octavian weeps more passionately.*)
(*Quietly.*)
And now must I for him find consolation—

wird sitzen lassen.
(*Sie streichelt ihn.*)

OCTAVIAN: Ueber kurz oder lang?
(*Heftig.*)
Wer legt Ihr heut die Wörter in den Mund, Bichette?

MARSCHALLIN: Das Ihn das Wort so kränkt!
(*Octavian hält sich die Ohren zu*).

MARSCHALLIN: Die Zeit im Grund, Quinquin,
Die Zeit, die ändert doch nichts an den Sachen.
Die Zeit, die ist ein sonderbar Ding.
Wenn man so hinlebt, ist sie rein gar nichts.
Aber dann auf einmal, da spürt man nichts als sie.
Sie ist um uns herum, sie ist auch in uns drinnen.
In den Gesichtern rieselt sie, im Spiegel da rieselt sie, in meinen Schläfen fliesst sie.
Und zwischen mir und dir da fliesst sie wieder, lautlos, wie eine Sanduhr.
(*Warm.*)
Oh, Quinquin!
Manchmal hör' ich sie fliessen—unaufhaltsam.
Manchmal steh' ich auf mitten in der Nacht
und lass die Uhren alle, alle stehn.
Allein man muss sich auch vor ihr nicht fürchten.
Auch sie ist ein Geschöpf des Vaters, der uns alle erschaffen hat.

OCTAVIAN: (*mit ruhiger Zärtlichkeit*): Mein schöner Schatz, will Sie sich traurig machen mit Gewalt?
wo Sie mich da hat.
wo ich meine Finger in Ihre Finger schlinge,
wo ich mit meinen Augen Ihre Augen suche,
Wo sie mich hat—
gerade da ist Ihr so zumut?

MARSCHALLIN: (*sehr ernst*): Quinquin, heut oder morgen geht Er hin
und gibt mich auf um einer andern willen,
(*etwas zögernd.*)
die schöner oder jünger ist als ich.

OCTAVIAN: Willst du mit Worten mich von dir stossen,
weil dir die Hände den Dienst nicht tun?

MARSCHALLIN: (*ruhig*): Der Tag kommt ganz von selber.
Heut oder morgen kommt der Tag, Octavian.

And for what?
Because—sooner or later—one day he'll leave me.
(*Strokes his hair.*)

OCTAVIAN: I will leave you one day?
(*Angrily.*)
Who is it prompted you to talk of this?

PRINCESS: Do my words hurt you so?

OCTAVIAN: Bichette!

PRINCESS: What fate decrees must come, Mignon.
(*Octavian stops his ears.*)
And time—how strangely does it go its ways—
First we are heedless—Lo! It is as nothing!
Then a sudden waking, and we feel nothing else but it,
All the world tells of it, all our souls are filled with it,
No face but shows the maker of it,
No mirror but shows it us—
All my veins feel its throbbing,
And there—between you and me—
It flows in silence,
Trickling—like sands in the hourglass—
(*Earnestly.*)
Oh! Mignon!
But sometimes I hear it flowing Ceaselessly.
(*Softly.*)
Sometimes I arise at the dead of night
And take the clocks and stop them every one—
And yet—to be afraid of it—what boots it?
For, mindful of its creatures all.
Heaven in its own wisdom has ordained it so.

OCTAVIAN: (*quietly and tenderly*): And why let such dark forebodings cloud your soul, beloved?
Now that I am here,
With my fingers like tendrils round your fingers twining,
Now that mine eyes are plunged in yours and blaze with rapture,
Now that I am here,
At such time can you think of grief?

PRINCESS: (*very serious*): Mignon, now or tomorrow, surely,
You will go from me, leave me and choose another.
(*Hesitates.*)
A younger or a prettier than I.

OCTAVIAN: Is it with words with which you would drive me,
Thinking your hands will not serve your turn?

PRINCESS: (*quietly*): The day will come unbidden—
Now or tomorrow it must come, Octavian.

OCTAVIAN: Nicht heut, nicht morgen! ich hab dich lieb.
Nicht heut, nicht morgen!
Wenn's so einen Tag geben muss, i denk' ihn nicht!
So einen hässlichen Tag!
Ich will den Tag nicht sehn
Ich will den Tag nicht denken.
Was quälst du dich und mich, Theres'?

MARSCHALLIN: Heut oder morgen oder den übernächsten Tag.
Nicht quälen will ich dich, mein Schatz.
Ich sag' was wahr ist, sag's zu mir so gut als zu dir.
Leicht will ich's machen dir und mir.
Leicht muss man sein,
mit leichtem Herz und leichten Händen
halten und nehmen, halten und lassen . . .
Die nicht so sind, die straft das Leben, und Gott erbarn sich ihrer nicht.

OCTAVIAN: Sie spricht ja heute wie ein Pater.
soll dass heissen, dass ich Sie nie mehr
werd' küssen dürfen, bis Ihr der Atem ausgeht?

MARSCHALLIN: (sanft): Quinquin, Er soll jetzt gehn, Er soll mich lassen.
Ich werd' jetzt in die Kirchen gehn, und später fahr' ich zum Onkel Greifenklau,
der alt und gelähmt ist, und ess' mit ihm: das freut den alten Mann.
Und Nachmittag werd' ich Ihm einen Laufer schicken,
Quinquin, und sagen lassen, ob ich in' Prater fahr'.
Und wenn ich fahr'
und Er hat Lust,
so wird Er auch in' Prater kommen und neben meinem Wagen reiten.
Jetzt sei Er gut und folg' Er mir.

OCTAVIAN: (leise): Wie Sie befiehlt, Bichette.
(Er geht. Eine Pause.)

MARSCHALLIN: (allein, fährt leidenschaftlich auf): Ich hab' Ihn nicht einmal geküsst.
(Sie klingelt heftig. Lakaien kommen von rechts.)
Lauit's dem Herrn Grafen nach und bittet's ihn noch auf ein Wort herauf.
(Lakaien schnell ab).
Ich hab' ihn fortgehn lassen und ihn nicht einmal geküsst.
(Sie sinkt auf den Sessel am Frisiertisch. Die Lakaien kommen zurück ausser Atem.)

ERSTER LAKAI: Der Herr Graf sind auf und davon.

ZWEITER LAKAI: Gleich beim Tor sind aufgesess.

OCTAVIAN: Not now, not tomorrow—it will never come,
Though Fate have decreed it must come, I will not think
Nor see such a day,
I will not think such a day,
(With growing passion.)
I will not see nor think it!
Why torture me and yourself, Thérèse?

PRINCESS: Now or tomorrow—if not tomorrow, very soon—
It is not to torture you, my dearest,
It is truth that I'm speaking—to myself no less than to you.
Let us then lightly meet our fate.
Light must we be,
With spirits light and grasp lightfingered,
Hold all our pleasures—hold them and leave them.
If not, much pain and grief await us, and none in earth or heaven will pity us.

OCTAVIAN: You speak today like a confessor—
Does it mean that never again—no, never,
I shall kiss you—kiss you in endless rapture?

PRINCESS: Mignon, now you must go. It is time to leave me.
I now must go to Church, and then It may be, visit my dear uncle Greifenklau,
Who's old and bedridden,
And dine with him: It will please the old man much.
Then to your house I'll send a courier,
Mignon, and he will tell you Whether I shall take the air;
And if I drive,
And if you please,
You will meet me in the Prater, riding,
And stay awhile beside my carriage.
Do what I ask—and be not rash.

OCTAVIAN: (softly): As you command, Bichette.
(He goes. A pause.)
(The Princess starts up violently.)

PRINCESS: And he has gone, and not one kiss!
(She rings violently. Footmen enter hurriedly from the right.)
Run and overtake the Count
And say I beg a word with him.
(Exeunt Footmen quickly.)
I have let him go from me. No farewell—not one kiss!
(The four Footmen enter breathless.)

FIRST FOOTMAN: The young Count is off and away.

SECOND FOOTMAN: At the door he mounted quickly.

DRITTER LAKAI: Reitknecht hat gewartet.

VIERTER LAKAI: Gleich beim Tor sind aufgesessen wie der Wind.

ERSTER LAKAI: Waren um die Ecken wie der Wind.

ZWEITER LAKAI: Sind nachgelaufen.

DRITTER LAKAI: Wie haben wir geschrien.

VIERTER LAKAI: War umsonst.

ERSTER LAKAI: Waren um die Ecken wie der Wind.

MARSCHALLIN: Es ist gut, geht's nur wieder.
(Die Lakaien ziehen sich zurück.)

MARSCHALLIN: (ruft nach): Den Mohammed!
(Der kleine Neger herein, klingelnd, verneigt sich.)

MARSCHALLIN: Das da trag'.
(Neger nimmt eifrig das Saffianfutteral).
Weisst ja nicht wohin. Zum Grafen Octavian.
Gib's ab und sag':
Da drin ist die silberne Ros'n.
Der Herr Graf weiss ohnehin.
(Der Neger läft ab.)
(Marschallin stützt den Kopf auf die Hand und bleibt so während des ganzen Nachspiels).

*End of Act I.*

## ■ ZWEITER AUFZUG

*Saal bei Herrn von Faninal. Mitteltüre nach dem Vorsaal. Tür links. Rechts ein grosses Fenster. Stüble an der Wand. In den Ecken jederseits grosse Kamine. Zu beiden Seiten der Mitteltüre je ein Lakai.*

FANINAL: (im Begriffe, von Sophie Abschied zu nehmen): Ein ernster Tag, ein grosser Tag!
Ein Ehrentag, ein heiliger Tag!
(Sophie küsst ihm die Hand).

MARIANNE: Der Josef fahrt vor mit der neuen Kaross',
hat himmelblaue Vorhäng',
vier Apfelschimmel sind dran.

HAUSHOFMEISTER: (nicht ohne Vertraulichkeit zu Faninal): Ist höchste Zeit, dass Euer Gnaden fahren.
Der hochadelige Bräutigamsvater, sagt die Schicklichkeit,
muss ausgefahren sein
bevor der silberne Rosenkavalier vorfahrt.
Wär nicht geziemend,
das sie sich vor der Tür begegneten.

THIRD FOOTMAN: Servants had been in waiting—

FOURTH FOOTMAN: At the gate he mounted like the wind—

FIRST FOOTMAN: Galloped round the corner like the wind—

SECOND FOOTMAN: We all ran after—

THIRD FOOTMAN: We cried ourselves hoarse—

FOURTH FOOTMAN: It was too late.

FIRST FOOTMAN: Galloped round the corner like the wind—

PRINCESS: Very well.
You may leave me.
(The Footmen withdraw.)

PRINCESS: (calling after them): Send Mahomet.
(Enter the Black Boy, with tinkling bells. Bows.)

PRINCESS: Carry that—
(The Boy quickly takes the jewel case.)
Stop till I say where—To Count Octavian
And say he'll find
Within it the Silver Rose
It is enough—the Count will know.
(The Black Boy runs off. The Princess bows her head on her hand and remains so—deep in thought—till the curtain falls.)

*END OF ACT I.*

## ■ ACT II

*A room in the house of Herr von Faninal. Center door leading to the antechamber. Doors right and left. To the right a large window. At either side of the center door chairs against the wall. In the rounded corners at either side large fireplaces.*

HERR VON FANINAL: (in the act of saying goodbye to Sophia): A solemn day, a day of no
A festal day, a sacred day
(Sophia kisses his hand.)

MARIANNE: There's Joseph at the door with the new equipage,
With curtains of blue satin.
And four fine greys to draw it.

MAJOR-DOMO: (a little confidentially to Faninal): Now by your leave, Sir, it is high time for starting,
For the most noble father of the bride,—
So etiquette prescribes—
Must not be found within,
When the bridegroom's messenger appears who brings the Silver Rose.
Well then, so be it.

# Act II

(*Lakaien öffnen die Tür.*)

(*Footmen open the doors.*)
It would be unseemly
If at the door you should encounter
him.

FANINAL: In Gottes Namen. Wenn ich wiederkomm',
so führ' ich deinen Herrn
Zukünftigen bei der Hand.

FANINAL: When I return again,
I bring your bridegroom with me,
holding him by the hand.

MARIANNE: Den edlen und gestrengen Herrn von Lerchenau!
(*Faninal geht*).
(*Sophie vorgehend, allein, indessen Marianne am Fenster*).

MARIANNE: The virtuous and noble Lord of Lerchenau.
(*Exit Faninal.*)
(*Sophia advances to the front by herself, while Marianne is at the window.*)

MARIANNE: Jetzt steigt er ein. Der zaver und der Anton springen hinten auf.
Der Stallpag' reicht dem Josef seine Peitsch'n.
Alle, Fenster sind voller Leut'.

MARIANNE: Now he's got in. Now Antony and Francis have climbed up behind,
And Joseph cracks his whip and now they've started,
And all the windows are filled full of folk.

SOPHIE: (*am Fenster*): In dieser feierlichen Stunde der Prüfung,
da du mich, o mein Schöpfer, über mein Verdienst erhöhen
und in den heiligen Ehestand führen willst,
(*sie hat grosse Mühe, gesammelt zu bleiben*)
opfere ich dir in Demut, mein Herz in Demut auf.
Die Demut in mir zu erwecken,
muss ich mich demütigen.

SOPHIA: In this most sacred hour, my God, O my Creator,
When Thy great blessings lift me high above my worth, I thank you,
That I am led to the Holy Estate by your will.
(*She controls herself with difficulty.*)
A contrite heart unto your Throne—Your Throne—I bring.
Oh! Grant that the sin of vainglory
May ever be far from my soul.

MARIANNE: Die halbe Stadt ist auf die Füss'.
Aus dem Seminari schaun die Hochwürdigen von die Balkoner
Ein alter Mann sitzt oben auf der Latern'.

MARIANNE: (*very excited*): Half the Town is now afoot!
From the Seminary all the reverend men look on dumb founded,
And high up on a lantern there is one old man.

SOPHIE: (*sammelt sich mühsam*): Demütigen und recht bedenken: die Sünde, die
Schuld, die Niedrigkeit, die Verlassenheit, die Anfechtung!
Die Mutter ist tot und ich bin ganz allein.
Für mich selbst steh' ich ein.
Aber die Ehe ist ein heiliger Stand.

SOPHIA: (*collects her thoughts with difficulty*): Be far from my soul . . .
From all temptations, Lord, preserve me of the pomps and vanities
Of this world here below, by your great mercy—
My Mother, she is dead and all alone am I,
For me there's none to plead but I alone,
But wedlock is in truth a holy estate.

MARIANNE: (*wie oben*): Er kommt, er kommt in zwei Karossen.
Die erste ist vierspännig, die ist leer.
In der zweiten, sechsspännigen, sitzt er selber, der Rosenkavalier.

MARIANNE: (*at the window*): He is here! He's here! I see two coaches.
The first one has four horses—it is empty. In the second,
(Six horses it has)
I see him, the bridegroom's messenger.

SOPHIE: (*wie oben*): Ich will mich niemals meines neuen Standes überheben—
(*die Stimmen der Läufer zu dreien vor Octavians Wagen unten auf der Gasse: Rofrano, Rofrano!*)
—mich überheben.
(*Sie hält es nicht aus.*)
Was rufen denn die?

SOPHIA: (*as above*): Let me not be puffed up with pride unduly by the honors,
(*The servants followed by three couriers, who are running after Octavian's carriage, cry in the street below "Rofrano! Rofrano!"*)
(*She loses her self-control.*)
Of my new station.
What is it they cry?

MARIANNE: Den Namen vom Rosenkavalier und alle Namen
von deiner neuen fürstlich'n und gräflich'n Verwandtschaft rufen's aus.
Jetzt rangieren sich die Bedienten.
Die Lakaien springen rückwärts ab!
(*Die Stimmen der Läufer zu dreinen näher: Rofrano, Rofrano!*)

MARIANNE: They're shouting the name of him that's come and all the titles
Of this your high-born new relation, and his noble name.
(*With excited gestures.*)
Look! Now our footmen take position,
And all his servants have alighted now!
(*The voices of the couriers, drawing nearer: "Rofrano! Rofrano!"*)

SOPHIE: Werden sie mein' Bräutigam sein Namen
auch so ausrufen, wenn er angefahren kommt!?
(*Die Stimmen der Läufer dicht unter dem Fenster: Rofrano, Rofrano!*)

SOPHIA: And when my future husband comes, pray tell me,
Will they call out then?
Will his name be shouted too?
(*The voices of the couriers immediately under the window: 'Rofrano! Rofrano!'*)

MARIANNE: Sie reissen den Schlag auf!
Er steigt aus!
Ganz in Silberstück' ist er angelegt, von Kopf zu Fuss.
Wie ein heil'ger Engel schaut er aus.
(*Sie schliesst eilig das Fenster. Zwei Faninalsche Lakaien haben schnell die Mitteltür aufgetan.*)

MARIANNE: (*enthusiastically*):
They open the door now! He alights!
All in silver he glitters from head to foot,
A holy angel might he be—

SOPHIE: Herrgott im Himmel!
Ich weiss, der stolz ist eine schwere Sünd'.
Aber jetzt kann ich mich nicht demütigen.
Jetzt seht's halt nicht!
Denn das ist ja so schön, so schön!
(*Währenddem ist Octavians Dienerschaft in seinen Farben; weis. mit blassgrün rasch eingetreten. Die Lakaien, die Haiducken mit kurmmen ungarischen Säbeln an der Seite, die Läufer in weissem sämischem Leder mit grünen Straussenfedern. Dicht hinter diesen ein Neger, der Octavians Hut, und ein anderer Lakai. der das Saffianfutteral für die silberne Rose in beiden Händen trägt. Dann Octavian, die Rose in der Rechten. Er geht mit adeligem Anstand auf Sophie zu, aber sein Knabengesicht ist von seiner Schüchternheit gespannt und gerötet. Sophie ist vor Aufregnung über seine Erscheinung und die Zeremonie leichenblass. Sie stehen einander gegenüber, und machen sich wechselweise durch ihre Verlegenheit und Schönheit noch verwirrter.*)

SOPHIA: Oh Saints in Heaven, I know that pride is a most deadly sin;
But this day all my prayers are vain—I cannot
Be duly meek—
For it is all so fair! so fair!
(*The Footmen quickly open the center door. Enter Octavian bareheaded, dressed all in white and silver, carrying the Silver Rose in his hand. Behind him his servants in his colours—white and pale green, the Footmen, the Heyducks, with their crooked Hungarian swords at their side; the Couriers in white leather with green ostrich plumes. Immediately behind Octavian a black servant carrying his hat, and another Footman carrying the case of the Silver Rose in both hands. Behind these, Faninal's servants. Octavian taking the Rose in his right hand, advances with highborn grace towards Sophia; but his youthful features bear traces of embarrassment and he blushes. Sophia turns pale with excitement at his splendid appearance. They stand opposite each other—each disconcerted by the confusion and beauty of the other.*)

OCTAVIAN: (*etwas stockend*):
Mir ist die Ehre widerfahren,
dass ich der hoch- und wohlgeborenen Jungfer Braut,
in meines Herrn Vetters Namen,
dessen zu Lerchenau,
die Rose seiner Liebe überreichen darf.

OCTAVIAN: (*with slight hesitation*): I am much honored by my mission
To say to you, most noble lady, high-born bride,
That my dear kinsman, whose ambassador I am,
Baron Lerchenau, begs you
To take from me, as token of his love, this Rose.

SOPHIE: (*nimmt die Rose*)
Ich bin Ener Liebden sehr verbunden.
Ich bin Ener Liebden in aller Ewigkeit verbunden.
(*Einer pause der verwirrung.*)
(*Sophie indem sie an der Rose riecht*). Hat einen starken Geruch.
Wie Rosen, wie lebendige.

OCTAVIAN: Ja, ist ein Tropfen persischen Rosenöls darein getan.

SOPHIE: Wie himmelische, nicht irdische, wie Rosen
vom hochheiligen Paradies.
Ist Ihm nicht auch?
(*Octavian neight sich über die Rose, die sie ihm hinhält; dann richtet er sich auf und sieht auf ihren Mund*).
Ist wie ein Gruss vom Himmel.
Ist bereits zu stark, als dass man's ertragen kann.
Zieht einen nach, als lägen Stricke um das Herz.
(*Leise.*)
Wo war ich schon einmal
und war so selig?

OCTAVIAN: (*zugleich mit ihr wie unbewusst und noch leiser*). Wo war ich schon einmal
und war so selig?

SOPHIE: (*mit Ausdruck*): Dahin muss ich zurück! und müsst ich völlig sterben auf dem Weg!
Allein ich sterb' ja nicht.
Das ist ja weit. Ist Zeit und Ewigkeit in einem sel'gen Augenblick,
den will ich nie vergessen bis an meinen Tod.

OCTAVIAN: (*zugleich mit ihr*):
Ich war ein Bub',
da hab ich' die noch nicht gekannt.
Wer bin denn ich?
Wie komm' denn ich zu ihr?
Wie kommt denn sie zu mir?
Wär' ich kein Mann, die Sinne möchten mir vergehn.
Das ist ein seliger Augenblick,
den will ich nie vergessen bis an meinen Tod.
(*Indessen stand die Livree Octavians rückwärts regungslos. Ebenso die Faninalschen Bedienten mit dem Haushofmeister. Der Lakai Octavians übergibt jetzt das Futteral an Marianne. Sophie schüttelt ihre Versunkenheit ab und reicht die Rose der Marianne, die sie ins Futteral schliesst. Der Lakai mit dem Hut tritt von rückwärts an Octavian heran und reicht ihm den Hut. Die Livree Octavians tritt ab, während gleichzeitig die Faninalschen Bedienten drei Stüble in die Mitte tragen, zwei für Octavian und Sophie, einen rück- und seitwärts für die Duenna. Zugleich trägt der Faninalsche Haushofmeister das Futteral mit der Rose durch die Tür links ab. Sofort treten auch die Faninalschen Bedienten durch die Mitteltür ab. Sophie*)

SOPHIA: (*taking the Rose*): I am to your Honor much indebted—
I am to your Honor to all eternity indebted—
(*A short pause of confusion.*)
(*Sophia smelling the rose*). It is a fragrance entrancing—like roses—yes, like living ones. . . .

OCTAVIAN: Yes—some few drops of Persian attar have been poured thereon.

SOPHIA: A celestial flower, it seems not of earth.
A blossom from the sacred groves of Paradise.
Think you not so?
(*Octavian bends over the Rose, which she holds out to him; then raises his head and gazes at her lips.*)
It is like a heavenly message.—Oh! how strong the scent
I scarcely can suffer it,
(*softly.*)
Drawing me on—like something tugging at my heart.

OCTAVIAN: (*Together with her—as in a reverie—still more softly*): Where did I taste of old
Such rapture celestial?

SOPHIA: Though death await me there, to that fair scene I must betake me once again.
But yet, why think of death?
It is far from here!
In one blest moment dwells all life and all eternity—
Never may its memory fade!

OCTAVIAN: I was a child
Till her fair face I saw this day!
But who am I?
What fate brings her to me?
What fate brings me to her?
Feeling and sense would leave me,
Were I not a man.
Day blest to all eternity—
Never may its blessing fade.
(*During this, Octavian's servants have taken up their position on the left at the back, Faninal's with the Major-Domo to the right. Octavian's footman hands the jewel case to Marianne. Sophia wakes from her reverie and gives the Rose to Marianne, who encloses it in the case. The Footman with the hat approaches Octavian and gives it to him. Octavian's servants then withdraw, and at the same time Faninal's servants carry three chairs to the center, two for Sophia and Octavian, and one for Marianne further back, at the side. Faninal's Major-Domo carries the jewel-case with the Rose through the door to the right. The other servants immediately withdraw through the center door.*)
(*Sophia and Octavian stand opposite each other almost restored to the every day world—but still a little embarrassed. At a sign from*)

und Octavian steben einander gegenüber, einigermassen zur gemeinen Welt zurückgekehrt, aber befangen. Auf einer Handbewegung Sophies nehmen sie beide Platz, desgleichen die Duenna, im gleichen Augenblick, wo der Haushofmeister unsichtbar die Tür links von aussen zuschliesst.)

SOPHIE: Ich kenn' Ihn schon recht wohl, mon cousin!

OCTAVIAN: Sie kennt mich, ma cousine?

SOPHIE: Ja, aus dem Buch, wo die Stammerbäume drin sind,
Dem Ehrenspiegel Oesterreichs.
Das nehm' ich immer abends mit ins Bett
und such' mir meine künftige Verwandtschaft drin zusammen.

OCTAVIAN: Tut Sie das, ma cousine?

SOPHIE: Ich weiss, wie alt Euer Liebden sind:
Siebzehn Jahr' und zwei Monat'.
Ich weiss all Ihre Taufnamen: Octavian, Maria, Ehrenreich, Bonaventura, Ferdinand, Hyacinth.

OCTAVIAN: So gut weiss ich sie selber nicht einmal.

SOPHIE: Ich weiss noch was.
(*Errötet.*)

OCTAVIAN: Was weiss Sie noch, sag' Sie mir's, ma cousine.

SOPHIE: (*ohne ihn anzusehen*): Quinquin.

OCTAVIAN: (*lacht*) Weiss Sie den Namen auch?

SOPHIE: So nennen Ihn halt seine guten Freund'
und schöne Damen, denk' ich mir, mit denen er recht gut ist.
(*Kleine Pause.*)
(*mit Naivität*)
Ich freu' mich aufs heiraten!
Freut er sich auch darauf?
Oder hat Er leicht noch gar nicht dran gedacht, mon cousin?
Denk' Er: Ist doch was andres als der ledige Stand.

OCTAVIAN: (*Leise, während sie spricht*): Wie schön sie ist!

SOPHIE: Freilich, Er ist ein Mann, da ist Er, was Er bleibt.
Ich aber brauch' erst einen Mann, dass ich was bin.
Dafür bin ich dem Mann dann auch gar sehr verschuldet.

OCTAVIAN: (*wie oben*): Mein Gott, wie schön und gut sie ist.
Sie macht mich ganz verwirrt.

SOPHIE: Und werd' ihm keine Schand nicht machen
und meinen Rang und Vortritt.
Tät' eine, die sich besser dünkt als ich,
ihn mir bestreiten
bei einer Kindstauf' oder Leich',

Sophia, both seat themselves, and the Duenna does likewise at the same moment as the door on the right is locked from without.)

SOPHIA: You're quite well known to me, mon cher Cousin.

OCTAVIAN: You know me, ma Cousine?

SOPHIA: Yes, your great House I have read of in a book,
"The Mirror of Nobility."
I take it of an evening to my room,
And seek for all the Princes, Dukes and Counts
Who are to be my kinsfolk.

OCTAVIAN: Is it so, ma Cousine?

SOPHIA: I know how old, to a week, you are—
Seventeen years and a quarter—
I know all your baptismal names—
Octavian—Maria—Ehrenreich—Bonaventura—Fernand—Hyacinth.

OCTAVIAN: Faith, I have never known them half as well.

SOPHIA: I know also—

OCTAVIAN: And what is it you know besides, ma Cousine?

SOPHIA: (*without looking at him*): Mignon—

OCTAVIAN: (*Laughing*): Do you know that name too?

SOPHIA: So all your best friends are allowed to call you,
Court beauties also, more than one,
Who are with you most friendly
(*A short pause.*)
(*Naively.*)
It pleases me that I shall marry soon.
Will you not like it too
When you shall find a bride? Have you not thought of it, mon Cousin?
But think, how lonely all you bachelors are!

OCTAVIAN: (*softly*) Oh heaven! How fair and good she is!

SOPHIA: Truly, you are a man, and men are what they are.
But, till a husband is her guide, a woman's naught.
I'll be much indebted to my husband for these things.

OCTAVIAN: (*deeply moved—softly*): How good and fair she is. She confuses me quite.

SOPHIA: I never will, for sure, disgrace him—
And as for due precedence
(*very eagerly*)
If haply another woman ever should
Dare to dispute it—

so will ich, wenn es sein muss,
meiner Seel' ihr beweisen,
dass ich die Vornehmere bin
und lieber alles hinnehme
wie Kränkung oder Ungebühr.

OCTAVIAN: (*lebhaft*). Wie kann
Sie denn nur denken,
dass man Ihr mit Ungebühr begegnen wird,
da Sie doch immer die Schönste,
die Allerschönste sein wird.

SOPHIE: Lacht er mich aus, mon
cousin?

OCTAVIAN: Wie, glaubt Sie das
von mir?

SOPHIE: Er darf mich auslachen,
wenn er will.
Von Ihm lass ich alles mir gerne
geschehen,
weil mir nie noch ein junger Kavalier . . . .
von Nähen oder Weitem also wohlgefallen hat wie Er.
Jetzt aber kommt mein Herr
Zukünftiger.
(*Die Tür rückwärts geht auf. Alle
drei erheben sich. Sophie und
Marianne treten nach rechts. Octavian nach links vorne. Faninal
führt den Baron zeremoniös über
die Schwelle und auf Sophie zu indem or ihm den Vortritt lässt. Die
Lerchenausche Livree folgt auf
Schritt und Tritt: zuerst der Almosenier mit dem Sohn und Leib-
kammerdie er. Dann folgt der Leibjäger mit einem ähnlichen
Lümmel, der ein Pflaster über der
eingeschlagenen Nase trägt, und
noch zwei von der gleichen Sorte
vom Rübenacker her in die Livree
gesteckt. Alle tragen wie ihr Herr
Myrthensträusschen. Die zwei
Fanalischen Boten bleiben im
Hintergrunde.*)

FANINAL: Ich präsentiere Euer
Gnaden Dero Zukünftige.

BARON: (*macht die Reverenz,
dann zu Faninal*): Deliziös!
Mach' Ihm mein Kompliment.
(*Er ki_sst Sophie die Hand, gleich-
sam prüfend.*)
Ein feines Handgelenk. Darauf halt'
ich gar viel.
Ist unter Bürgerlichen eine seltne
Distinktion.

OCTAVIAN: (*halblaut*): Es wird
mir heiss und kalt.

FANINAL: Gestatten dass ich die
getreue Jungfer
Marianne Leitmetzerin—
(*Mariannen präsentierend, die
dreimal tief knickst.*)

BARON: (*indem er unwillig ab-
winkt*): Lass Er das weg.
Begrüss Er jetzt mit mir meinen
Herrn Rosenkavalier.
(*Er tritt mit Faninal auf Octavian
zu, unter Reverenz, die Octavian
erwiedert. Das Lerchenausche Ge-*

---

At christenings or funerals—
I'll shower very quickly,
If needs must, with a slapping,
That I am better bred than she,
And rather will bear anything
Than such overweening impu-
dence.

OCTAVIAN: (*eagerly*): No, do not
think there's anyone
So graceless who would put a slight
on you.
For you will still be the fairest, always the crown you will bear.

SOPHIA: Mock me not so, mon
Cousin—

OCTAVIAN: What, think you thus
of me?

SOPHIA: You are allowed such
freedom, if you will,
From you I gladly take all that you
choose.
For, truthfully, no gentleman I've
seen
Or met with, has been able yet to
please me half as well as you.
Now I must cease, for look, the Baron's here.
(*The door at the back is thrown
open. All three rise and step to the
right. Faninal ceremoniously
conducts the Baron over the
threshold towards Sophia, giving
him the precedence. The servants
of Lerchenau follow in his footsteps, first the Almoner, then the
Body Servant. Next follows the
Chasseuz, with a clown of the
same kidney, who has a plaster
over his battered nose, and two
others no less uncouth, looking as
if they had stepped straight from
the fields into their liveries. All,
like their master, carry sprigs of
myrtle. The servants of Faninal remain in the background.*)

FANINAL: I have the honor to your
Lordship to present your bride.

BARON: (*bows—then to Faninal*): Delicieuse! I compliment
you, Sir.
(*He kisses Sophia's hand as
though examining it.*)
A hand so delicate is a thing I much
admire.
It is an attraction rarely found
among the bourgeoisie.

OCTAVIAN: (*To himself*): Can I
command myself?

FANINAL: Permit me my most
faithful friend and servant—
(*Presenting Marianne, who
makes three deep curtseys.*)

BARON: (*with a gesture of vexation*): Pray, spare me that.
(*After having almost knocked
Sophia over, Lerchenau's servants
come to a standstill, and then
withdraw a few paces.*)
Now greet the Count, and thank

---

*folge kommt endlich zum Still-
stand, nachdem es Sophie fast
umgestossen, und retiriert sich
um ein paar Schritte nach rechts
rückwärts.*)

SOPHIE: (*mit Marianne re-
chsstehend, halblaut*): Was sind
das für Manieren? Ist er leicht ein
Rosstauscher
und kommt ihm vor, er hätt' mich
eingekauft?

MARIANNE: (*ebenso*): Ein Kavalier hat halt ein ungezwungenes,
leutseliges Betragen.
Sag' dir vor, wer er ist
und zu was er dich macht,
so werden dir die Faxen gleich vergehn.

BARON: (*während des Auf-
führens zu Faninal*): Ist gar zum
Staunen, wie der junge Herr jemand
Gewissem ähnlich sieht.
Hat ein Bastardl, recht ein saubres,
zur Schwester.
Ist kein Geheimnis unter Personen
von Stand.
Hab's aus der Fürstin eignem Mund,
und weil der Faninal sozusagen jetzo
zu der Verwandtschaft gehört!
Mach' dir kein Depit, darum Rofrano,
dass dein Vater ein Streichmacher
war,
befindet sich dabei in guter Kom-
pagnie, der selige Marchese.
Ich selber exkludier' mich nicht.
(*Zu Octavian.*)
Seh', Liebden, schau' dir dort den
Langen an,
den Blonden, hinten dort.
Ich will ihn nicht mit Fingern weis-
en,
aber er sticht wohl hervor
durch eine adelige Kontenance.
Ist auch er ein ganz besondrer Kerl.
Sag's nicht, weil ich der Vater bin,
hat's aber faustdick hinter den Ohren.

SOPHIE: (*während dessen*): Jetzt
lässt er mich so stehn, der grobe
Ding!
Und das ist mein Zukünftiger.
Und blattersteppig ist er auch, o
mein Gott!
(*Der Haushofmeister tritt ver-
bindlich auf die Lerchenauschen
Leute zu und führt sie ab. Desglei-
chen tritt die Faninalsche Livree
ab bis auf zwei, welche Wein und
Süssigkeiten servieren.*)

FANINAL: (*zum Baron*): Belieben
jetzt vielleicht?—ist ein alter Tokaier.
(*Octavian und Baron bedienen
sich.*)

---

him for being my ambassador.
(*They go towards Octavian, bowing. He returns the compliment.*)

SOPHIA: (*standing at the back
with Marianne*): How vulgar his
behaviour.
Like some low horse-dealer
Who thinks he's bought me like a
yearling colt.

MARIANNE: Oh what an air! How
free from affectation,
How full of grace is his behaviour!
Tell yourself who he is,
What he helps you to be
And soon your silly whimsies will
be gone.

BARON: (*To Faninal*): I can but
wonder, when I see his face,
How like he is to someone else.
Has a sister—most bewitching
young baggage.
(*Coarsely confidential.*)
These are no secrets among persons
of our rank,
It was her Highness who did tell me
so,
(*Genially.*)
And now you, Faninal, may be ac-
counted almost as being one of us.
There is no need to be ashamed, Ro-
frano,
That once your father chose to sow
wild oats—
I warrant you he was in noble com-
pany,
(*Laughing.*)
The late lamented Marquis—I
count my self among it, too.
(*To Faninal.*)
Look well now at that long-legged
rascal there,
The fair one at the back.
I cannot point my finger at him,
But at a glance you will pick out
His high-born features from among
the rest.
And see he bears himself like any
courtier.
He has a noble pedigree, but he's
the greatest fool of all my house-
hold.

SOPHIA: What breeding's this, to
leave me here alone!
And he my husband that's to be,
And pock-marked also is his face, I
do protest.
(*The Major-Domo approaches the
servants of Lerchenau most politely and conducts them out of the
room. At the same time Faninal's
servants withdraw—all but two,
who offer wine and comforts.*)

FANINAL: (*To the Baron*): Perhaps you would partake . . .
It is Tokay, an old vintage.

BARON: Brav, Faninal, er weiss, was sich gehört.
Serviert einen alten Tokaier zu einem jungen Mädel.
Ich bin mit Ihm zufrieden.
(*Zu Octavian.*)
Musst denen Bagatelladeligen immer zeigen,
dass nicht für unsersgleichen sich ansehen dürfen,
muss immer was von Herablassung dabei sein.

OCTAVIAN: (*spitzig*): Ich muss deine Liebden sehr bewundern.
Hast wahrhaft grosse Weltmanieren.
Könntst einen Ambassadeur vorstellen heut wie morgen.

BARON: (*derb*): Ich hol' mir jetzt das Mädl her.
Soll uns jetzt Konversation vormachen,
damit ich seh', wie sie beschlagen ist.
(*Geht hinüber, nimmt Sophie bei der Hand, führt sie mit sich.*)
Eh bien: Nun plauder' Sie uns eins, mir und dem Vetter Taverl.
Sag' Sie heraus, auf was Sie sich halt in der Eh' am meisten freut.
(*Setzt sich, will sie halb auf seinen Schoss ziehen.*)

SOPHIE: (*entzieht sich ihm*): Wo denkt Er hin?

BARON: (*behaglich*): Pah! Wo ich hindenk'!
Komm' Sie da ganz nah zu mir, dann will ich Ihr ersählen, wo ich hindenk'.
(*Gleiches Spiel, Sophie entzieht sich ihm heftiger.*)
(*behaglich*)
Wär Ihr leicht präferabel, dass man wegen Ihrer
den Zeremonienmeister sollt' hervortun
Mit "mille pardons" und "devotion"
und "Geh da weg" und "hab' Respekt"?

SOPHIE: Wahrhaftig und ja gefiele mir das besser!

BARON: (*lachend*): Mir auch night!
Das sieht Sie!
Mir auch ganz und gar nicht!
Bin einer biedern offenherzigen Galanterie recht zugetan.
(*Er macht Anstalt, sie zu küssen, sie wehrt sich energisch.*)

FANINAL: (*nachdem er Octavian den zweiten Stuhl angeboten hat, den dieser ablehnt*): Wie ist mir denn!
Da sitzt ein Lerchenau
und karessiert in Ehrbarkeit mein Sopherl, als wär' sie ihm schon angetraut.
Und da steht ein Rofrano, sonsten nix—
der Bruder vom Marchese Obersttruchsess.

BARON: Good, Faninal, you know what's right and fitting
To serve a mellow wine of an old vintage to drink a young bride's health,
You have my commendation.
(*To Octavian*).
It is not amiss to show some condescension
In talking to gimcrack nobility,
And show them clearly,
They must not deem themselves equal to such as us.

OCTAVIAN: (*Pointedly*): I vow, I do admire your Lordship's wisdom,
You have mastered the great world's manners,
Like an Ambassador or Chancellor you bear yourself.

BARON: (*roughly*): I'll bring the wench now to my side,
That I may see if her talk pleases me,
(*Crosses over, takes Sophia by the hand and leads her back with him.*)
That of her points and paces I may judge.
Eh bien! Now let us hear you talk, me and you cousin Tavy,
Tell me now, what will, do you think, please you most about marriage?

SOPHIA: (*withdrawing from him*): What mean these ways?

BARON: (*at his ease*): Pooh! Why this pother?
Now come here quite close to me
And I will tell you quickly all my meaning.
(*Same by-play. Sophia tries to withdraw still more angrily.*)
Would you la'ship perhaps prefer it, if one came
Like a dancing master, bowing and congeeing,
With "Mille pardons" and "Devotion"
And "By your leave" and "My respects."

SOPHIA: Most surely yes, it would please me better!

BARON: I think not—All flimflam, fudge and silly nonsense—
My taste is all for free and easy ways, and open-hearted gallantry.
(*He tries to kiss her. She resists energetically.*)

FANINAL: (*offering a chair to Octavian, who refuses.*): What!
Can it be?
There sits a Lerchenau
A-paying his addresses to my Sophy,
as if they had been wed and all,
And there stands a Rofrano, just as natural!
A Count Rofrano, nothing less—
A brother to the Empress' Lord High Steward.

OCTAVIAN: (*zornig für sich*): Das ist ein Kerl, dem möcht' ich wo begegnen
mit meinem Degen da,
wo ihn kein Wächter schreien hört.
Ja, das ist alles, was ich möcht'.

SOPHIE: (*zum Baron*): Ei, lass Er doch, wir sind nicht so vertraut!

BARON: (*zu Sophie*): Geniert Sie sich leicht vor dem Vetter Taverl?
Da hat Sie unrecht.
In der grossen Welt,
wo doch die hohe Schul' ist für Manieren,
da gibt's fret nichts,
was man nit willig pardonnieren tat',
wenn's nur mit einer adligen Noblesse
und richtigen Galanterie vollführt wird.
(*Er wird immer zärtlicher, sie weiss sich kaum zu helfen.*)

FANINAL: (*für sich*): Wär' nur die Mauer da von Glas,
dass alle bürgerlichen Neidhammeln von Wien uns könnten
so en famille beisammen so sitzen sehn!
Dafür wollt' ich mein Lerchenfelder Eckhaus geben, meiner Seel'!

OCTAVIAN: (*wütend*): Dass ich das Mannsbild sehen muss,
so frech, so unverschämt mit ihr.
Ich büss' all meine Sünden ab!
Könnt' ich hinaus und fort von hier!

BARON: (*zu Sophie*): Lass Sie die Flausen nur!
Gehört doch jetzo mir!
(*Halb für sich, sie kajolierend.*)
Ganz meine Massen!
Schultern wie ein Henderl!
Geht all's recht!
Sei Sie gut!
Geht alles so wie am Schnürl!
Hundsmager noch—das macht nichts, aber weiss
mit einem Glanz darauf, wie ich ihn ästimier'!
Ich hab' halt ja ein lerchenauisch Glück!
(*Sophie reisst sich los und stampft auf*).
(*vergnügt*)
Ist Sie ein rechter Kapricenschädel!
(*Auf und ihr nach.*)
Steigt Ihr das Blut gar in die Wangen,
dass man sich die Hand verbrennt?

SOPHIE: (*rot und blass von Zorn*): Lass Er die Hand davon!
(*Octavian in stummer Wut, verdrückt das Glas, das er in der Hand hält, und schmeisst die Scherben zu Boden*).

OCTAVIAN: Faugh! What a boor!
How I should like to meet him
Alone with my good sword—
No watch to hear him shout for help—
Yes, nothing better I should wish.

SOPHIA: (*To Baron*): I pray you cease, we are but strangers yet!

BARON: (*To Sophia*): Is it my cousin Octavian that makes you bashful?
That's out of reason.
In the highest ranks
Where surely they know most about good manners
There's nothing
That will not be allowed, and freely pardoned,
If but it be done rightly with a courtly grace,
Befitting folk of birth and breeding.
(*The Baron grows more and more importunate—she is at her wit's end.*)

FANINAL: (*To himself*): Would that the walls could be of glass . . .
If but the townsfolk all could see them sitting there,
Quite en famille, how green would they turn with envy!
Gladly for that I'd give the best of all my houses, on my soul!

OCTAVIAN: (*furious*): Oh, that I must stand here and see him thus,
So course and so unmannerly.
If I could only up and flee from here!

BARON: (*To Sophia*): Put your airs aside, for I have got you now!
All goes well!
Never fear!
It is all just as I wish it!
(*Half to himself, fondling her.*)
Just as I wish it! Tender as a pullet!
Not very plump—no matter—but so white,
White—and what a bloom—there's nothing I like more!
I have the luck of all the Lerchenaus!
(*Sophia tears herself away and stamps her feet.*)
Gad, what a mettlesome little filly!
(*Rises and runs after her.*)
And see how hot her cheeks are burning—
Full hot enough to burn one's hands!

SOPHIA: (*pale with anger*): Hands off, I say!
Be gone!
(*Octavian in silent anger, crushes the glass he holds in his hand and throws the pieces to the ground.*)
(*Marianne runs with affected grace towards Octavian, picks up the pieces and confides her delight to him.*)

DUENNA: (*läuft mit Grazie zu Octavian hinüber, hebt die Scherben auf und raunt ihm mit Entzücken zu*): Ist recht ein familiärer Mann, der Herr Baron! Man delektiert sich, was er all's für Einfäll' hat!

BARON: (*dicht bei Sophie*): Geht mir nichts drüber! Konnt' mich mit Schmachterei und Zärtlichkeit nicht halb so glücklich machen, meiner Seel'!

MARIANNE: (*scharf, ihm ins Gesicht*): Ich denk' nicht dran, dass ich Ihn glücklich mach'! (*Indessen ist der Notar mit dem Schreiber eingetreten, eingeführt durch Faninals Haushofmeister. Dieser meldet ihn dem Herrn von Faninal leise; Faninal geht zum Notar nach rückwärts hin, spricht mit ihm und sieht einen vom Schreiber vorgehaltenen Aktenfaszikel durch.*)

SOPHIE: (*zwischen den Zähnen*): Hat nie kein Mann dergleichen Reden nicht zu mir geführt! Möcht wissen, was ihm dünkt von mir und Ihm? Was ist Er denn zu mir?

BARON: (*gemütlich*): Wird kommen über Nacht, dass Sie ganz sanft wird wissen, was ich bin zu Ihr. Ganz wie's im liedel heisst—kennt Sie das Liedel? Lalalalala— (*Recht gefühlvoll.*) Wie ich dein alles werde sein! Mit mir, mit mir keine Kammer dir zu klein, ohne mich, ohne mich jeder Tag dir so bang, (*frech und plump*) mit mir, mit mir keine Nacht dir zu lang? (*Sophie da er sie fester an sich drückt, reisst sich los und stösst ihn beftig zurück.*)

DUENNA: (*zu ihr eilend*): Ist recht ein familiärer Mann, der Herr Baron! Man delektiert sich, was er all's für Eihnfäll' hat! (*Krampfhaft in Sophie hineinredend.*) Nein, was er all's für Einfäll' hat, der Herr Baron!

OCTAVIAN: (*ohne hinzusehen, und doch sieht er alles, was vorgeht*): Ich steh' auf glüh'nden Kohlen! Ich fahr' aus meiner Haut! Ich büss in dieser einen Stund' all meine Sünden ab!

BARON: (*für sich, sehr vergnügt*): Wahrhaftig und ja, ich hab' halt ein lerchenauisch Glück! Gibt gar nichts auf der Welt, was mich so enflammiert und also vehement verjüngt als wie

MARIANNE: His Lordship has most uncommon easy ways, The jests he thinks of, la, they make me laugh till I could cry. (*In the meantime the Attorney has entered with his clerk, introduced by Faninal's Major-Domo. He announces them in a whisper to Faninal: Faninal goes to the back to the Attorney, speaks with him and looks through a bundle of documents presented to him by the Clerk.*)

SOPHIA: (*with clenched teeth*): There is no man has ever dared to speak to me like this! What can you think of me and of yourself? What are you, pray, to me?

BARON: (*contentedly*): One day you'll wake and find That you have just Discovered what I am to you. Just as the ballad says—Do you not know it? La la la la la. (*Very sentimentally.*) How to you I'll be all in all! With me, with me no attic seems too small, Without me, without me slowly will pass all the days, (*Impudently and coarsely.*) With me, with me time will seem short always! (*Sophia, as he tries to draw her still closer to him, frees herself and violently pushes him back.*)

MARIANNE: (*now hurrying to Sophia*): It is most uncommon easy way his Lordship has, The jests he thinks of make me laugh till I could cry; (*Speaking to Sophia with feverish energy.*) They make me laugh till I could cry, his Lordship's jests.

OCTAVIAN: (*without looking at the Baron, and yet aware of all that is passing*): I'm standing on coals of fire! It is more than I can bear! In this one hour before Heaven I do Penance for all my sins!

BARON: (*To himself, very contented*): I always did say, I have all the luck of all the Lerchenaus! Nothing else in the world does so renew my youth Or whet my appetite so well as a

ein rechter Trotz! (*Faninal und der Notar, hinter ihnen der Schreiber, sind an der linken Seite nach varne gekommen.*)

BARON: (*sowie er den Notar erblickt, eifrig zu Sophie, ohne zu ahnen, was in ihr vorgeht*): Dort gibt's Geschäften jetzt, muss mich dispensieren: bin dort von Wichtigkeit. Indessen der Vetter Taverl leistet Ihr Gesellschaft!

FANINAL: Wenn's jetzt belieben tät', Herr Schwiegersohn!

BARON: (*eifrig*): Natürlich wird's belieben. (*Im Vorbeigehen zum Octavian, denn er vertraulich anfasst.*) Hab' nichts dawider, wenn du ihr möchtest Augerln machen, Vetter, jetzt oder künftighin. Ist noch ein rechter Rühr-nicht-an. Betracht's als förderlich, je mehr sie degourdiert wird. Ist wie bei einem jungen ungerittenen Pferd. Kommt all's dem Angetrauten letzterdings zugut. wofern er sein eh'lich Privilegium zunutz zu machen weiss. (*Er geht nach links. Der Diener, der den Notar einliess, hat indessen die Türe links geöffnet. Faninal und der Notar schicken sich an, hineinzugehen. Der Baron misst Faninal mit dem Blick und bedeutet ihm, drei Schritte Distanz zu nehmen. Faninal tritt devot zurück. Der Baron nimmt den Vortritt, vergewissert sich, dass Faninal drei Schritte Abstand hat und geht gravitätisch durch die Tür links ab. Faninal hinter ihm, dann der Notar, dann der Schreiber. Der Bediente schliesst die Türe links und geht ab, lässt aber die Flügeltüre nach dem Vorsaal offen. Der servierende Diener ist schon früher abgegangen.*) (*Sophie rechts, steht verwirrt und beschämt*). (*Duenna neben ihr knickst nach der Türe hin, bis sie sich schliesst*).

OCTAVIAN: (*mit einem Blick hinter sich, gewiss zu sein, dass die anderen abgegangen sind, tritt schnell zu sophie hinüber, bebend vor Aufregung*): Wird Sie das Mannsbild da heiraten, ma cousine?

SOPHIE: (*einen Schritt auf ihr zu, leise*): Nicht um die Welt! (*Mit einem Blick auf die Duenna.*) Mein Gott, wär' ich allein mit Ihm, dass ich Ihn bitten könnt'! dass ich Ihn bitten könnt'!

real spitfire can. (*Faninal and the Attorney, followed by the Clerk, have advanced to the front, on the left.*)

BARON: (*as soon as he sees the Attorney, eagerly to Sophia, without the smallest idea what she is thinking*): But now there's work to do, so for a while forgive me: They need my presence there. And meanwhile There's Cousin Tavy, he will entertain you!

FANINAL: May I beg the honor now, dear Son-in-law!

BARON: (*eagerly*): Of course you'll have the honor. (*In passing to Octavian, whom he touches familiarly.*) It would not displease me If you should cast some sheep's eyes at her, Cousin, Now or at any time: You're still content with looks alone. The more she learns from you, the better I shall like it For a girl, do you see, is just like an unbroken foal: The husband in the end gets all the benefit, Provided he has but sense enough to use His opportunities. (*He goes to the left. The servant who had admitted the Attorney, has in the meantime opened the door on the left. Faninal and the Notary make for the door. The Baron fixes his eyes on Faninal and signifies to him he must keep a distance of three paces. Faninal obsequiously retreats. The Baron takes precedence, assures himself that Faninal is three paces behind him, and walks solemnly through the door on the left. Faninal follows, and after him come the Attorney and his Clerk. The Footman closes the door to the left, and goes out, leaving the door which leads to the ante-room open. The Footman who was serving refreshments has already left the room.*) (*Sophia on the right, stands confused and humiliated. The Duenna curtseys in the direction of the door till it closes.*)

OCTAVIAN: (*quivering with excitement, hurries towards Sophia, after glancing backwards so as to be sure that the others have gone.*) And do you marry that thing there, ma Cousine?

SOPHIA: (*moving one step towards him, in a whisper*): Not for the world! (*With a look to the Duenna.*) Oh Heaven! Could we but be alone, That I might beg of you! That I might beg of you!

OCTAVIAN: (*halblaut, schnell*): Was ist's, das Die mich bitten möcht'? Sag' Sie mir's schnell!

OCTAVIAN: (*quickly below his breath*): What is it you would beg of me? Tell me now, quick!

SOPHIE: (*noch einen Schritt näher zu ihm*): O mein Gott, dass Er mir halt hilft! Und Er wird mir nicht helfen wollen, weil Er halt sein Vetter ist!

SOPHIA: (*coming another step nearer to him*): O, gracious Heaven, befriend me in my need! But since he is your friend and cousin, You will not wish to succour me!

OCTAVIAN: (*heftig*): Nenn' ihn Vetter aus Höflichkeit; Gott sei Lob und Dank, hab' ihn im Leben vor dem gestrigen Tag nie gesehn! (*Quer durch den Vorsaal flüchten einige von den Mädgen des Hauses. denen die Lerchenauischen Bedienten auf den Fersen sind. Der Leiblakai und der mit dem Pflaster auf der Nase jagen einem hübschen jungen Mädchen nach und bringen sie fast an der Schwelle zum Salon bedenklich in die Enge.*)

OCTAVIAN: (*vehemently*): I am his cousin but by courtesy; Thanks be to all my stars, I had not ever seen his hateful face till yesterday! (*Some of the servant girls rush headlong across the anteroom, hotly pursued by Lerchenau's attendants. The Body Servant and the one with the plaster on his nose are at the heels of a pretty young girl and bring her to bay close to the door of the salon.*) (*Faninal's Major-Domo runs in much perturbed, to call the Duenna to help him.*)

DER FANINALSCHE HAUSHOFMEISTER: (*kommt verstört hereingelaufen die Duenna zu Hilfe zu holen*): Die Lerchenauischen sind voller Branntwein gesoffen und gehn aufs Gesindel los zwanzigmal ärger als Türken und Krowaten!

MAJOR-DOMO: The Baron's menfolk, with our good wine quite besotted; Run after all the girls, worse than an army From Turkey, or Croatians!

MARIANNE: Hol' Er unsere Leut', wo sind denn die? (*Läuft ab mit dem Haushofmeister, sie entreissen den beiden Zudringlichen ihre Beute und führen das Mädchen ab; alles vertiert sich, der Vorsaal bleibt leer●●●*

MARIANNE: Fetch our men, quick, to help you. Where can they be hid? (*She runs off with the Major-Domo. They rescue the girl from her assailants and lead her away. All disappear. The anteroom remains empty.*)

SOPHIE: (*nun, da sie unbeobachtet ist, mit freier Stimme*): Zu Ihm hätt' ich ein Zutrau'n, mon cousin, so wie zu niemand auf der Welt, dass Er mir könnte helfen, wenn Er nur den guten Willen hätt'!

SOPHIA: (*speaking freely, now that she is unobserved*): In you I place my trust, mon Cousin, Knowing that you, like no one else, Could be my help, my savior, Would you but bend your will to it!

OCTAVIAN: Erst muss Sie sich selber helfen, dann hilf ich Ihr auch. Tu' Sie das Erste für mich, dann tu' ich was für Sie!

OCTAVIAN: First must you for yourself take courage, Then I too will help. Till you have helped yourself, I can do nothing for you!

SOPHIE: (*zutraulich, fast zärtlich*): Was ist denn das, was ich zuerst tun muss?

SOPHIA: (*confidingly, almost tenderly*): What is it then, I for myself must do?

OCTAVIAN: (*leise*): Das wird Sie wohl wissen!

OCTAVIAN: (*softly*) Surely you know it!

SOPHIE: (*den Blickt unverwandt auf ihn*): Und was ist das, was Er für mich will tun? O sag' Er mir's!

SOPHIA: (*looking at him undismayed*): And what is it that you will do for me, Now tell me that!

OCTAVIAN: (*entschlossen*): Nun muss Sie ganz alleinig für uns zwei einstehn!

OCTAVIAN: (*decidedly*): Now must you strike a blow alone—you for us twain!

SOPHIE: Wie? Für uns zwei? O sag Er's noch einmal.

SOPHIA: What, for us twain? O say it once again!

OCTAVIAN: (*leise*): Für uns zwei!

OCTAVIAN: (*softly*): For us twain!

SOPHIE: (*mit hingegebenem Entzücken*): Ich hab' im Leben so was Schönes nicht gehört!

SOPHIA: (*rapturously*): O words of rapture! I've heard nothing so sweet till now.

OCTAVIAN: (*stärker*): Für sich und mich muss Sie sich wehren und bleiben—was Sie ist. (*Sophie nimmt sein Hand, er küsst sie schnell auf den Mund*).

OCTAVIAN: (*loudly*): To save us both must you be steadfast, And still be—

SOPHIA: Still be?

OCTAVIAN: What you are. (*Sophia seizes his hand, bends over it, kisses it quickly before he can withdraw it. He kisses her on the lips.*)

OCTAVIAN: (*indem er sie, die sich an ihn schmiegt, in den Armen, habt zärtlich*): Mit Ihren Augen voller Tränen kommt Sie zu mir, damit Sie sich beklagt. Vor Angst muss Sie an mich sich lehnen, Ihr armes Herz ist ganz verzagt. Und ich muss jetzt als Ihren Freund mich zeigen und weiss noch gar nicht, wie! Mir ist so selig, so eigen, dass ich dich halten darf: Gib antwort, aber gib sie nur mit Schweigen: Bist du won selber so zu mir gekommen? Ja oder nein? Ja oder nein? Du musst es nicht mit Worten sagen— Hast du es gern getan? Sag', oder nur aus Not? Aus Not so alles zu mir hergetragen, dein Herz, dein liebliches Gesicht? Sag', ist dir nicht, dass irgendwo in irgendeinem schönen Traum das einmal schon so war? Spürst du's wie ich? Sag', spürst du's so wie ich?

OCTAVIAN: (*holding her in his arms as she nestles closely to him*): With tear-dimmed eyes, all affrighted, My aid you seek, telling your sorrows all, Fear nothing, henceforth to me united, Fear nothing, whatever may befall! To save you now must be my one endeavor, And yet I know not how. Rapture like this, you never Grant to a mortal, gods! Give me answer, but with eloquent silence,— Did your free will guide you here to me? Say yea or nay—say yea or nay! No words could tell me all your meaning. Was your free will your guide? Say, or your direful need? Why brought you here these gifts so lavish? Your loving heart, your face so fair? Say, seems it not that once in days Far off, in some dear magic dream We loved each other thus? Think you not so? Dreamed you never thus, as I? My heart, my soul, Will always be with you? Wherever you be, For all eternity.

SOPHIE: Ich möchte mich bei Ihm verstecken und nichts mehr wissen von der Welt. Wenn Er mich so in Seinen Armen hält, kann mich nichts Hässliches erschrecken. Da bleiben möcht' ich, da! Und schweigen, und was mir auch gescheh', geborgen wie der Vogel in den Zweigen, stillstehn und spüren: Er ist in der Näh'! Mir müsste angst und bang im Herzen sein, statt dessen fühl' ich Freud und Seligkeit und keine Pein, ich könnt' es nicht mit Worten sagen! Hab' ich was Unrechtes getan? Ich war halt in der Not! Da war Er mir nah!

SOPHIA: What rapture, thus with you to hale me And hear no whisper of the world, When thus contented in your arms I be, I fear nothing, ill can never betide me. There fain I'd linger, there, for ever Secure from grief and fear, And know that our fond union naught can sever. Naught now can harm me, You, you are always near. My pulse should cease to beat for shame and dread. But lo! I feel an endless joy and happiness. All pain is fled, No words can tell you all my meaning, Haply it was sinful what I did? But direful was my need, And lo! you were near— I saw your face so fair— Your eyes, your valiant air—

# Act II

Da war es Sein Gesicht,
Sein' Augen jung und licht,
auf das ich mich gericht,
Sein liebes Gesicht—
Er muss mir Seinen Schutz vergonnen,
Was Er will, werd' ich können;
Bleib' Er nur bei mir!
Er muss mir Seinen Schutz vergönnen—
Bleib Er nur bei mir!
*(Aus den Kaminen in den rückwärtigen Ecken sind links Valzacchi, rechts Annina lautlos spähend herausgeglitten. Lautlos schleichen sie, langsam, auf den Zehen, näher. Octavian zieht Sophie an sich, küsst sie auf den Mund; in diesem Augenblick sind die Italiener dicht hinter ihnen, ducken sich hinter den Lehnsesseln: jetzt springen sie vor, Annina packt Sophie, Valzacchi fasst Octavian.)*

**VALZACCHI UND ANNINA:** *(zu zweien schreiend)*: Herr Baron von Lerchenau!—
Herr Baron von Lerchenau!—
*(Octavian springt zur Seite nach links).*

**VALZACCHI:** *(der Mühe hat, ihn zu halten, atemlos zu Annina)*: Lauf und 'ole Seine Gnade!
Snell, nur snell, ik muss 'alten diese 'err!

**ANNINA:** Lass ich die Fräulein aus, läuft sie mir weg!

**ZU ZWEIEN:** Herr Baron von Lerchenau,
Herr Baron von Lerchenau!
Komm' zu sehn die Fräulein Braut!
Mit eine junge Kavalier!
Kommen eilig, kommen hier! Ecco!
*(Baron tritt aus der Tür links. Die Italiener lassen ihre Opfer los, springen zur Seite, verneigen sich vor dem Baron mit vielsagender Gebärde.)*
*(Sophie schmiegt sich ängstlich an Octavian).*
*(Baron die Arme über die Brust gekreuzt, betrachtet sich die Gruppe, Unheilsschwangere Pause, endlich)*: Eh bien, Mamsell, was hat Sie mir zu sagen?
*(Sophie schweigt).*

**BARON:** *(der durchaus nicht ausser Fassung ist)*: Nun, resolvier' Sie sich!

**SOPHIE:** Mein Gott, was soll ich sagen,
Er wird mich nicht verstehn!

**BARON:** *(gemütlich)*: Das werden wir ja sehn!

**OCTAVIAN:** *(einen Schritt auf den Baron zu)*: Eu'r Liebden muss ich halt vermelden,
dass sich in Seiner Angelenheit was Wichtiges verändert hat!

And healed was my despair.
And thenceforth nothing I know,
Nothing more of myself—
O stay now with me—
Protect me, save me, stay beside me,
I follow wherever you guide me.
Save me, leave me not—
*(From the fireplaces to the left and right respectively come Valzacchi and Annina noiselessly and watch the lovers. They approach silently on tiptoe. Octavian draws Sophia to him and kisses her on the lips. At this moment the two Italians are close behind them. They duck behind the armchairs. Then they jump forward, Annina seizes Sophia, Valzacchi takes hold of Octavian.)*

**VALZACCHI AND ANNINA:** *(screaming together)*: Quick, Baron Lerchenau, quick, Baron Lerchenau!
*(Octavian leaps aside to the right.)*

**VALZACCHI:** *(holding him with difficulty, breathless to Annina)*: Run, bring 'izzer 'is Lords'ip—
Quick, make 'aste: I must 'old zis young man.

**ANNINA:** If I not 'old zis lady, she escape me!

**VALZACCHI AND ANNINA:**
Quick! Baron Lerchenau!
Quick! Baron Lerchenau!
Come to see your future wife
Discovered viz a gentleman,
Pray come quickly!
Pray come 'ere!
*(The Baron enters through the door on the left and with folded arms contemplates the group. Ominous pause. Sophia nestles timidly close to Octavian.)*
Ecco!

**BARON:** Eh bien, Ma'mselle!
What would you wish to tell me?
*(Sophia remains silent. The Baron retains his composure.)*
Well, do not hesitate.

**SOPHIA:** Alas!
What could I tell you?
You would not understand—

**BARON:** *(quickly)*: Ecod, I think I will.

**OCTAVIAN:** *(moving a step nearer the Baron)*: It is my duty to inform your Lordship
That most important changes have been wrought
In matters that concern you nearly.

**BARON:** *(gemütlich)*: Verändert?
Ei, nicht dass ich wüsst'!

**OCTAVIAN:** Darum soll Er es jetzt erfahren!
Die Fräulein—

**BARON:** Ei, Er ist nicht faul!
Er weiss zu profitieren,
mit Sein siebzehn Jahr'!
Ich muss Ihm gratulieren!
*(halb zu sich)*
Ist mir ordentlich, ich seh' mich selber!
Muss lachen über den Filou, den pudeljungen.

**OCTAVIAN:** Die Fräulein—

**BARON:** Ei! Sie ist wohl stumm und hat Ihn angestellt für Ihren Advokaten!

**OCTAVIAN:** Die Fräulein—
*(Er hält abermals inne, wie um Sophie sprechen zu lassen.)*

**SOPHIE:** *(angstvoll)*: Nein!
Nein!
Nein!
Ich bring' den Mund nicht auf.
Sprech' Er für mich!

**OCTAVIAN:** *(entschlossen)*: Die Fräulein—

**BARON:** *(ihm nachstotternd)*: Die Fräulein, die Fräulein!
Die Fräulein!
Die Fräulein!
Ist eine Kreuzerkomödi wahrhaftig!
Jetzt echappier' Er sich, sonst reisst mir die Geduld.

**OCTAVIAN:** *(sehr Bestimmt)*: Die Fräulein, kurz und gut,
die Fräulein mag Ihn nicht.

**BARON:** *(gemütlich)*: Sei Er da ausser Sorg'.
Wird schon lernen mich mögen.
*(Auf Sophie zu.)*
Komm' Sie da jetzt hinein: wird gleich an Ihrer sein,
die Unterschrift zu geben.

**SOPHIE:** *(zurucktretend)*: Um keinen Preis geh' ich an seiner Hand hinein!
Wie kann einn Kavalier so ohne Zartheit sein!

**OCTAVIAN:** *(der jetzt zwischen den beiden anderen und der Tür links)*: Versteht Er deutsch?
Die Fräulein hat sich resolviert.
Sie will Euer Gnaden ungeheirat' lassen
in Zeit und Ewigkeit!

**BARON:** *(mit der Miene eines Mannes, der es eilig hat)*: Mancari!
Jungfernred' ist nicht gehaun und nicht gestochen!
Verlaub' Sie jetzt!
*(Nimmt sie bei der Hand.)*
*(Er macht Miene, Sophie mit scheinbarer Unbefangenheit gegen die Mitteltür zu führen, nachdem ihm die Italiener lebhafte Zeichen gegeben haben, diesen*

**BARON:** *(genially)*: Important?
Changed?
Not that I know!

**OCTAVIAN:** And therefore I now have to tell you,
This lady—

**BARON:** Well, you lose no time,
And take the best advantage
For all your seventeen years—I must congratulate you!
This lady—
'Gad, I like you well. Was I not just so?
The rascal! I must laugh, egad!
To start so early?

**OCTAVIAN:** This lady—

**BARON:** Ah! She's dumb, I presume, and is employing you
To plead as her attorney.

**OCTAVIAN:** This lady—
*(He pauses again, as though to let Sophia speak.)*

**SOPHIA:** *(timidly)*: No, no!
I cannot speak the word—
Speak you for me—

**OCTAVIAN:** *(with determination)*: This lady—

**BARON:** *(mimicking him)*: This lady, this lady, this lady, this lady!
This is jack-pudding foolery, by heaven!
And you had best depart, I've borne with you too long.

**OCTAVIAN:** *(very determined)*: This lady, once for all now, will have none of you.

**BARON:** As for that, have no fear—
She will soon enough have me.
*(To Sophia)*:
Come with me now in there—you will be needed soon to sign the marriage contract.

**SOPHIA:** *(retreating)*: No, not for all the world I'll let you lead me in!
How can a gentleman be so indelicate!

**OCTAVIAN:** *(who has now taken his place between them and the door on the left)*: Please understand.
The lady has determined finally
That she will let your Lordship stay unmarried
For now and evermore!

**BARON:** Baby-talk!
By hard words never a bone is broken!
And time is short.
*(Takes her by the hand.)*
*(He attempts, with feigned unconcern, to lead Sophia towards the center door, after the Italians have signified to him by lively gestures to take that way.)*
Come, now! Go to your father, who

Weg zu nehmen.) Komm' Sie!
Gehn zum Herrn Vater dort
hinüber!
Ist bereits der nähere Weg!

OCTAVIAN: (*ihm nach, dicht an ihr*): Ich hoff', er kommt vielmehr jetzt mit mir hinters Haus, ist dort recht ein bequemer Garten. (*Baron setzt seinen Weg fort, mit gespielter Unbefangenheit Sophie an der Hand nach jener Richtung zu führen bestrebt, über die Schulte: zurück*):

BARON: Bewahre.
Wär mir jetzo nicht genehm.
Lass um all's den Notari nicht warten.
Wär' gar ein Affront für die Jungfer Braut!

OCTAVIAN: (*fasst ihn an Aermel*): Beim Satan, Er hat eine dicke Haut!
Auch dort die Tür passiert Er mir nicht!
Ich schrei's Ihm jetzt in Sein Gesicht:
Ich schrei's Ihn für einen Filou, einen Mitgiftjäger, einen durchtriebenen Lügner und schmutzigen Bauer, einen Kerl ohne Anstand und Ehr'!
Und wenn's sein muss, geb' ich ihm auf dem Fleck die Lehr'!
(*Sophie hat sich vom Baron losgerissen und ist hinter Octavian zurückgesprungen. Sie stehen links, ziemlich vor der Tür*).

BARON: (*steckt zwei Finger in den Mund und tut einen gellenden Pfiff Dann*): Was so ein Bub' in Wien mit siebzehn Jahr schon für ein vorlaut Mundwerk hat!
(*Er sieht sich nach der Mitteltür um.*)
Doch Gott sei Lob, mann kennt in hiesiger Stadt den Mann, der vor ihm steht, halt bis hinauf zu kaiserlicher Majestät!
Man ist halt was man ist, und braucht's nicht zu beweisen.
Das lass Er sich gesagt sein und geb' mir den Weg da frei.
(*Die Lerchenausche Livree ist vollzählig in der Mitteltür aufmarschiert; er vergewissert sich dessen durch einen Blick nach rückwärts. Er rückt jetzt gegen die beiden vor, entschlossen, sich Sophiens und des Ausgangs zu bemächtigen.*)
Wär mir wahrhaftig leid, wenn meine Leut' da hinten—

OCTAVIAN: (*wütend*): Ah, untersteht Er sich, Seine Bedienten hineinzumischen in unsern Streit!
Jetzt zieh Er oder gnad' ihm Gott!
(*Er zieht.*)
(*Die Lerchenauschen, die schon einige Schritte vorgerückt waren, werden durch diesen Anblick eini-*

awaits us.
By this door is the speedier way.

OCTAVIAN: (*following them, close to her*): I beg you rather come with me—
At the back of the house
I know a most convenient garden.
(*The Baron continues in the same direction still with simulated unconcern, trying to lead away Sophia, whom he still holds by the hand, and speaks over his shoulder.*)

BARON: Enough of this. Your jests are most ill-timed—
We must not keep the Notary waiting,
It would be an insult to this lady here.

OCTAVIAN: (*seizing him by the sleeve*): By heaven!
I never knew so tough a hide!
And by this door I swear you will not pass—
That you may know it, to your face
I say that you are but a cheat,
And dowry-hunter,
Nothing but a rascally, lying, unmannerly clown, Sir,
But a boor, unclean in thought and in deed,
And with my sword I'll give you the sharp lesson you need.
(*Sophia has freed herself from the Baron and takes refuge behind Octavian. They stand to the left, almost in front of the door.*)

BARON: (*putting two fingers into his mouth and giving a shrill whistle*): How soon these boys do learn in Vienna here,
To set their tongues a-wagging.
(*Looking towards the center door.*)
But, heaven be praised, the Court and all the Town
Know him that you affront,
Even to the throne of her Imperial Majesty!
We all are what we are, and there's no need to prove it.
Now, young Sir, I have said my say, and get you from my path—
(*Lerchenau's servants, in full numbers, have appeared at the center door. The Baron, by a backward glance, assures himself of their presence. He now approaches Sophia and Octavian, determined to secure Sophia and his retreat.*)
Truly I should regret it if my people yonder—

OCTAVIAN: Now, as you prize your life, Sir, do not dare
To drag your grooms and lackeys into our quarrel.
Draw, Sir, or Heaven protect your soul!
(*The Baron's servants, who had already approached a few steps,*

germassen unschlüssig und stellen ihren Vormarsch ein.)
(*Baron tut einen Schritt, sich Sophiens zu bemächtigen*):
(*schreit ihn an*)
Zum Satan, zieh' Er oder ich stech' Ihn nieder!

SOPHIE: O Gott, was wird denn jetzt geschehn?

BARON: (*retiriert etwas*): Vor einer Dame, pfui!
so sei Er doch gescheit!
(*Octavian fährt wütend auf ihn los*).
(*Baron zieht, fällt ungeschickt aus und hat schon die Spitze von Octavians Degen im Oberarm. Die Lerchenauschen stürzen vor*).

BARON: (*indem er den Degen fallen lässt*). Mord! Mord! Mein Blut! Zu Hilfe! Mörder! Mörder! Mörder!
(*Die Diener stürzen alle zugleich auf Octavian los. Dieser springt nach rechts hinüber und hält sie sich vom Leib, indem er seinen Degen blitzschnell um sich kreisen lässt. Der Almosenier, Valzacchi und Annina eilen auf den Baron zu, den sie stützen und auf einem der Stühle in der Mitte niederlassen*)

BARON: (*von ihnen umgeben und dem Publikum verstellt*): Ich hab' ein hitzig' Blut!
Um Aerzt', um Leinwand!
Verband her!
Ich verblut' mich auf eins, zwei!
Aufhalten den!
Um Polizei! Um Polizei!

DIE LERCHENAUSCHEN: (*indem sie mit mehr Ostentation als Entschlossenheit auf Octavian eindringen*): Spinnweb' her!
Feuerschwamm!
Reisst's ihn den Spadi weg!
Schlagt's ihn tot auf'm Fleck!
(*Die sämtliche Faninalsche Dienerschaft, auch das weibliche Hausgesinde, Küchenpersonal, Stallpagen sind zur Mitteltür hereingeströmt.*)
(*Valzacchi und der Almosenier ziehen dem Baron, der fortwährend stöbnt, seinen Rock aus.*)

DIE FANINALISCHE DIENERSCHAFT: Schaut's nur die Fräulein an,
Schaut's, wie sie blass is'!

OCTAVIAN: (*Sophie verzweifelt zurufend*): Liebste!
(*Die Lerchenauschen machen Miene, sich zu diesem Zweck der Hemden der jüngeren und hübscheren Mägde zu bemächtigen. Handgemenge, bis Faninal beginnt. In diesem Augenblick kommt die Duena, die fortgestürzt war, zurück, atemlos, beladen mit Leinwand; hinter*

hesitate as they see what is happening and pause in their advance. The Baron takes a step forward in order to secure Sophia.)
Draw, ruffian, draw!
Or on my sword I'll split you.

SOPHIA: Oh! Heaven!
Oh, what will happen now!

BARON: (*withdraws a step*): What!
In a lady's presence!
Is the boy possessed?
(*Octavian rushes at him furiously, the Baron draws and lunging clumsily receives the point of Octavian's sword in his upper arm. Lerchenau's servants rush forward.*)

BARON: (*dropping his sword*): Help! Help! I bleed! A surgeon! Murder! Murder! Murder!
(*All the servants rush towards Octavian. He springs to the right and keeps them at arm's length whirling his sword about him. The Almoner, Valzacchi and Annina hurry to the Baron, and supporting him, lead him to one of the chairs in the middle of the room.*)

BARON: (*surrounded by his servants and the Italians, who conceal him from the public.*) I have most fiery blood! A doctor! Linen! A bandage!
Call the watch! I bleed to death before you can count to three!
Don't let him go! And call the watch! And call the watch!

LERCHENAU'S SERVANTS: (*closing round Octavian with more swagger than courage*): Break his crown!
Cobwebs here!
Sponge him down!
Take his sword, break his head
Who's afraid?
Kill him dead!
(*All Faninal's Servants, the female domestics, the kitchen staff and the stable hands, have streamed in by the center door.*)
(*Valzacchi and the Almoner divest the Baron, who groans uninterruptedly, of his coat.*)

FANINAL'S SERVANTS: Look at the brazen thing,
How dared she do it?

OCTAVIAN: (*calling to Sophia, in despair*): Dearest!
(*Lerchenau's Servants make as if to tear up the clothes of the younger and prettier servant maids. Mêlée till Faninal comes. At this moment the Duenna, who had rushed out, returns, breathless, bringing linen for bandages, behind her two maids with sponges and basins. They surround the*

# Act II

*ihr zwei Mägde mit Schwamm und Wasserbecken. Sie umgeben den Baron mit eifriger Hilfeleistung. Faninal kommt zur Türe links hereingestürzt, hinter ihm der Notar und der Schreiber, die in der Türe ängstlich stehen bleiben.)*

BARON: *(man hört seine Stimme, ohne viel von ihm zu sehen)*: Ich kann ein jedes Blut mit Ruhe fliessen sehn,
nur bloss das meinig' nicht! Oh! Oh!
*(Die Duenna anschreiend.)*
So tu' Sie doch was G'scheidt's, so rett' Sie doch mein Leben!
Oh! Oh!
*(Sophie ist, wie sie ihres Vaters ansichtig wird, nach rechts vorne hingelaufen, steht neben Octavian, der nun seinen Degen einsteckt).*

ANNINA: *(knicksend und eifrig zu Faninal links vorne)*: Der junge Kavalier
und die Fräulein Braut, Gnaden,
waren im Geheimen
schon recht vertraut, Gnaden!
Wir voller Eifer
Für'n Herrn Baron, Gnaden,
haben sie betreten
in aller Devotion, Gnaden!

DUENNA: *(um den Baron beschäftigt)*: So ein fescher Herr!
So ein gross' Malheur,
so ein schwerer Schlag, so ein Unglückstag!

FANINAL: *(anfangs sprachlos, schlägt nun die Häde überm Kopf zusammen und bricht aus)*: Herr Schwiegersohn!
Wie ist Ihm denn?
mein Herr und Heiland!
Dass Ihm in mein' Palais das hat passieren müssen!
Gelaufen um den Medikus!
Geflogen!
Meine zehn teuren Pferd' zu Tod gehetzt!
Ja hat denn niemand von meiner Livree
daswischen fahren mögen!
Füttr' ich dafür
ein Schock baumlanger Lackeln,
dass mir solche Schand'
passieren mus in meinem neuchen Stadtpalais!
*(Gegn Octavian hin.)*
Wär wohl von Euer Liebden
hochgräfliche Gegenwart allhier
Warhaftig einer anderen Freud'
gewärtig!

OCTAVIAN: *(höflich)*: Er muss mich pardonieren
Bin ausser Massen sehr betrübt über den Vorfall.
Bin aber ausser Schuld.
Zu einer mehr gelegenen Zeit

*Baron and busy themselves about him. Faninal rushes in by the door to the left followed by the Attorney and his Clerk, who remain standing, in great alarm, in the doorway.)*

BARON: *(his voice is heard, but he is scarcely visible)*: I can look on other people's blood unmoved, But my own makes me faint.
Oh! Oh!
*(Shouting to the Duenna.)*
Stop whining!
Stir yourself!
Don't stand and watch
His lifeless corpse will be your bridegroom!
Me dying!
Oh! Oh!
*(Sophia, as soon as she has seen her father, has run across the front of the stage to the right, and stands by Octavian, who sheaths his sword.)*

ANNINA: *(curtseying and crossing over to Faninal, eargerly)*: Ze gentleman 'ere
And Mistress Sophia zere, yes, Sir,
Secretly were intimate,
I declare, yes Sir,
Ve, full of zeal
For his Lords'ip's sake, yes Sir,
Kept a watch and found zem,
And zere was not mistake, yes Sir.
Kept a watch and found zem,
And zere was no mistake, yes Sir.

MARIANNE: *(busied about the Baron)*: Such a high-born Lord!
Such a cruel sword!
Such a heavy blow!
Such a day of woe!

FANINAL: *(at first speechless, wrings his hands and breaks out)*: Dear Son-in-law, how is't with you?
The Saints preserve us!
That such a brawling boy should so disgrace my Palace!
Send some one for a surgeon, quick!
Delay not!
Ride all my costly thoroughbreds to death.
How is it none of my men had the sense,
To interfere between them? Do I feed whole troops
Of long-legged good-for-nothings,
just that such disgrace
Should fall on me in my new Palace here in Town?
*(Going to Octavian, with suppressed fury.)*
Indeed from your Lordship.
I ventured to expect for other pleasures.

OCTAVIAN: *(courteously)*: I beg you, Sir, forgive me;
I too am grieved beyond all measure for this accident;
But I am free from blame.
At some more fitting time and place

erfahren Euer Liebden wohl den Hergang
aus Ihrer Fräulein Tochter Mund.

FANINAL: *(sich mühsam beherrschend)*: Da möcht' ich recht sehr bitten!

SOPHIE: *(entschlossen)*: Wie Sie befehlen, Vater.
Werd' Ihnen alles sagen.
Der Herr dort hat sich nich so, wie er sollt', betragen.

FANINAL: *(zornig)*: Ei, von wem red't Sie da?
Von Ihrem Herrn Zukünft'gen?
Ich will nicht hoffen, wär mir keine Manier.

SOPHIE: *(ruhig)*: Ist nicht der Fall.
Seh' ihn mit nichten an dafür.
*(Der Arzt kommt, wird sogleich zum Baron geführt.)*

FANINAL: *(immer zorniger)*: Sieht ihn nicht an?

SOPHIE: Nicht mehr.
Bitt' Sie dafür um gnädigen Pardon.

FANINAL: *(zuerst dumpf vor sich hin, dann in helle Wut ausbrechend)*.
Sieht ihn nicht an.
Nicht mehr.
Mich um Pardon.
Liegt dort gestochen.
Steht bei ihr.
Der Junge.
*(Ausbrechend.)*
Blamage.
Mir auseinander meine Eh',
Alle Neidhammeln von der Wieden und der Leimgrub'n auf! in der Höh!
Der Medikus!
Stirbt mir womöglich.
*(Auf Sophie zu, in höchster Wut.)*
Sie heirat' ihn!
*(Auf Octavian, indem der Respekt vor dem Grafen Rofrano seine Grobheit zu einer knirschenden Höflichkeit herabdämpft)*:
Möchte Euer Liebden recht in aller Devotion
gebeten haben, schleunig sich von hier zu retirieren
und nimmer wieder zu erscheinen!
*(Zu Sophie.)*
Hör Sie mich!
Sie heirat' ihn!
Und wenn er sich verbluten tät',
so heirat' Sie ihn als Toter!
*(Der Arzt zeigt durch eine beruhigende Gebärde, dass der Verwundete sich in keiner Gefahr befindet. Octavian sucht nach seinem Hut, der unter die Füsse der Dienerschaft geraten war. Eine Magd überreicht ihm knicksend den Hut. Faninal macht Octavian eine Verbeugung, übertrieben höflich, aber unzweideutig. Octavian muss wohl gehen, möchte aber gar zu gerne Sophie noch ein Wort*

Your Lordship from your daughter will discover
How these mischances came to pass.

FANINAL: *(controlling himself with difficulty)*: It would please me—nothing better.

SOPHIA: *(determined)*: As you command me, father, I will relate all truly:
His Lordship did not treat me as a man of honor.

FANINAL: *(angrily)*: What?
Of whom do you speak?
Of my future son-in-law?
I hope it is not so: I should think it a sin—

SOPHIA: *(quietly)*: No, it is not so—I do not look on him as such.

FANINAL: *(still more angry)*: What?
Not as such?

SOPHIA: No more.—I ask your gracious pardon, if I err.
*(The Doctor arrives and at once goes to the Baron.)*

FANINAL: *(at first muttering to himself)*: Looks not on him?
No more?
Pardon she asks?
And he lies wounded.—
By her side the Schoolboy!
*(Breaking out.)*
A scandal!
What?
This splendid marriage broken off!
All the jealous fools of the quarter and the streets around,
How they will laugh!
The surgeon quick!
What if it were fatal?
*(To Sophia, in utmost fury.)*
You marry him!
*(To Octavian, subduing his rudeness, out of respect to Rofrano's rank to obsequious civility.)* And may I now, in all humility, request Your Lordship to retire as speedily from hence as may be
And never again to darken these doors!
*(To Sophia.)*
Mark my words—
You marry him, and if he now should bleed to death,
His lifeless corpse will be your bridegroom!
*(The Doctor indicates by a reassuring gesture that the wounded man is in no danger. Octavian looks for his hat, which had fallen under the feet of the servants. A maid hands it to him with a curtsey. Faninal makes an obeisance of exaggerated civility, but unmistakable significance to Octavian. Octavian realizes that he must go, but is longing to speak one more word to Sophia. He replies to Faninal's obeisance by an equally ceremonious bow. Sophia*

sagen. Er erwidert zunächst Faninals Verbeugung durch ein gleich tiefes Kompliment.)

**SOPHIE:** (beeilt sich das Folgende noch zu sagen, solange Octavian es hören kann. Mit einer Reverenz): Heirat' den Herrn dort nicht lebendig und nicht tot! Sperr' mich zuvor in meine Kammer ein!

**FANINAL:** (in Wut, und nachdem er abermals eine wütende Verbeugung gegen Octavian gemacht hat, die Octavian prompt erwidert): Ah! Sperrst dich ein. Sind Leut' genug im Haus, die dich in Wagen tragen werden.

**SOPHIE:** (mit einem neuen Knicks): Spring' aus dem Wagen noch, der mich zur Kirch'n führt!

**FANINAL:** (mit dem gleichen Spiel zwischen ihr und Octavian, der immer einen Schritt gegen den Ausgang tut, aber von Sophie in diesem Augenblick nicht los kann): Ah! Springst noch aus dem Wagen! Na, ich sitz' neben dir, werd' dich schon halten!

**SOPHIE:** (mit einem neuen Knicks): Geb halt dem Pfarrer am Altar Nein anstatt Ja zur Antwort! (Der Haushofmeister indessen macht die Leute abtreten. Die Bühne leert sich. Nur die Lerschenauschen Leute bleiben bei ihrem Herrn zurück.)

**FANINAL:** (mit gleichem Spiel): Ah! Bigst Nein statt Ja zur Antwort. Ich steck' dich in ein Kloster stante pede! Marsch! Mir aus meinen Augen! Lieber heut als morgen! Auf Lebenszeit!

**SOPHIE:** (erschrocken): Ich bitt' Sie um Pardon! Bin doch kein schlechtes Kind! Vergeben Sie mir nur dies eine Mal!

**FANINAL:** (hält sich in Wut die Obren zu): Auf Lebenszeit! Auf Lebenszeit!

**OCTAVIAN:** (schnell, halblaut): Sei Sie nur ruhig, Liebste, um alles! Sie hört von ir! (Duenna stösst Octavian, sich zu entfernen.)

**FANINAL:** Auf Lebenszeit!

**DUENNA:** (zieht Sophie mit sich nach links): So geh' doch nur dem Vater aus den Augen! (Sieht sie zur Türe links hinaus, schliesst die Tür. Octavian ist zur Mitteltür abgegangen. Baron, umgeben von seiner Dienerschaft, Duenna, zwei Mägden, den Italienern und dem Arzt, wird auf einem aus Sitzmöbeln improvisierten Rubebett jetzt in ganzer Gestalt sichtbar.)

**FANINAL:** (schreit nochmals durch die Türe links, durch die Sophie abgegangen ist): Auf Lebenszeit! (Eilt dann dem Baron entegegen.) Bin überglücklich! Muss Eu'r Liebden embrassieren!

**BARON:** (dem bei der Umarmung der Arm webgetan): Oh! Oh! Jesus Maria!

**FANINAL:** (nach rechts hin in neuer Wut): Luderei! (Nach der Mitteltür.) Ein Gefängnis! Auf Lebenszeit!

**BARON:** Is gut! Is gut! Ein Schluck von was zu trinken!

**FANINAL:** Ein Wein? Ein Bier? Ein Hippokras mit Ingwer? (Der Arzt macht eine ängstlich abwehrende Bewegung).

**FANINAL:** (jammernd): So einen Herrn zurichten miserabel! In meinem Stadtpalais! Sie heirat' ihn um desto früher! Bin Manns genug!

**BARON:** (matt): Is gut, is gut!

**FANINAL:** (nach der Tür links, in aufflammender Wut): Bin Manns genug! (Zum Baron.) Küss Ihm die Hand für Seine Güt und Nachsicht. Gehört alles Ihm im Haus. Ich lauf' — ich bring' Ihm — (Nach links.) Ein Kloster ist zu gut! (Zum Baron.) Sei'n ausser Sorg'. (Sehr devot.) Weiss, was ich Satisfaktion Ihm schuldig bin. (Stürzt ab. Desgleichen gehen Duenna und Mägde ab. Die beiden Italiener sind schon während des Obigen fortgeschlichen.)

**BARON:** (halb aufgerichtet): Dalieg' ich was ei'm Kavalier mit all's passieren Kann in Dieser Wienerstadt! Wär nicht mein Gusto hier, — da ist eins gar zu sehr in Gottes Hand, Wär lieber schon daheim! (Ein Diener ist aufgetreten, eine Kanne Weines z servieren.)

---

bastens to speak the following words ere Octavian is out of earshot. With a curtsey.)

**SOPHIA:** That man I will not marry living, and not dead First will I lock me in my chamber and starve!

**FANINAL:** (furious, after he has again made an angry bow to Octavian, to which he promptly responds): Ah! Lock yourself in—I've men enough to drag you To a coach if I command them.

**SOPHIA:** (curtseying again): Then on the way to church from out the coach I jump!

**FANINAL:** (with similar by-play between himself and Octavian, who each time takes a step towards the door, but cannot tear himself from Sophia at such a moment): From the coach you'll jump, Miss! Well, I'll be by your side, And I'll know how to hold you.

**SOPHIA:** (Curtseys again): Then at the altar I shall say, "No," and not "Yes."—No, never! (The Major-Domo has in the meantime made the servants leave. The stage is gradually cleared. Only Lerchenau's servants remain with their master.)

**FANINAL:** (with similar by-play). Ah! Say No and never Yes at the altar! I send you to a convent on the instant! March! Out of my sight! Hussy! Better now than tomorrow. For all of your life!

**SOPHIA:** (alarmed): Pray pardon, I implore! I am your loving child— Forgive me, father, but this once, this once.

**FANINAL:** (furious, closing his ears): For all of your life! For all of your life!

**OCTAVIAN:** (whispers): Do not speak so rashly, dearest, for my sake! You'll hear from me. (The Duenna pushes Octavian towards the door.)

**FANINAL:** For all your life! (The Duenna takes Sophia with her to the left.)

**DUENNA:** Go, be gone from out your father's sight now. (Takes her out by the door to the left—closes the door. Octavian goes out by the center door. The Baron, surrounded by his servants, the Duenna, two Maids, the Italians and the Doctor, is now discovered lying on a couch improvized out of several chairs.)

**FANINAL:** (shouts once more through the door after Sophia): For all your life! (Hurries towards the Baron.) What joy unbounded! I must embrace you, my dear Baron!

**BARON:** (whose arm has been burt by the embrace): Oh! Oh! Jesus Maria!

**FANINAL:** (turning to the right, his anger rising again): You hussy! A convent! (Turning to the center.) A prison cell! For all your life!

**BARON:** Let be! Let be! Some drink, for I am thirsty.

**FANINAL:** Some wine? Some beer? Some hippicras with ginger? (The Doctor makes a nervous deprecating gesture.)

**FANINAL:** (plaintively): So nobly born, so nobly born, so mauled and so insulted! And in my Palace too! You'll marry him but all the sooner. I'm master here!

**BARON:** (wearily): Let be! Let be!

**FANINAL:** (towards the door on the left, his anger rising): I'm master here! (To the Baron.) I kiss your hand. My thanks for such indulgence. Command all that is in this house! I run—I bring you . . . (To the left.) A convent is too good. (To the Baron.) Pray have no fear. (Very obsequious.) I know what satisfaction, is your due from me. (Faninal rushes off. The Duenna and the Maids follow. The two Italians had already slunk off during the preceding scene.)

**BARON:** (half sitting up): Here am I! Now! What curious adventures may befall a man In this Metropolis. Not all are to my taste— Here is one far too much the sport of fate! It is better at home. (A Footman enters and serves wine. The Baron tries to drink and makes a movement which causes him pain.)

BARON: (*will trinken, da macht er eine Bewegung, die ihm Schmerzen verursacht*): Oh! Oh!
Der Satan!
Oh!
Oh!
Sakramentsverfluchter Bub',
nit trocken hinterm Ohr und fuchtelt mit 'n Spadi!
(*In immer grösserer Wut.*)
Wällischer Hundsbub' das!
Dich sollt' ich nur erwischen.
In Hundezwinger sperr' ich dich,
bei meiner Seel,' in Hühnerstall!
In Schweinekofen!
Tät' dich kuranzen!
Solltest alle Engel singen hör'n!
(*Zu dem Faninalschen Diener.*)
Schenk' Er nur ein da, schnell!

DIE LERCHENAUISCHEN:
(*gedämpft*): Wenn ich dich erwisch',
Du liegst unter'm Tisch.
Wart', dich hau' i z'samm,
dass dich Gott verdamm'!

BARON: (*zum Arzt gewandt*):
Herr Medicus, verfüg' Er sich voraus!
Mach' Er das Bett aus lauter Federbetten.
Ich komm'.
Erst aber trink' ich noch.
Marschier' Er nur indessen.
(*Der Arzt geht ab mit dem Leiblakai. Annina ist durch den Vorsaal hereingekommen und schleicht sich verstohlen heran, einen Brief in der Hand*).

BARON: (*vor sich leise, den zweiten Becher leerend*): Ein Federbett.
Zwei Stunden noch zu Tisch.
Werd' Zeitlang haben.
"Ohne mich, ohne mich, jeder Tag dir so bang,
mit mir, mit mir, keine Nacht dir zu lang."
(*Annina stellt sich so, dass der Baron sie sehen muss und winkt ihm geheimnisvoll mit dem Brief.*)
Für mich?

ANNINA: (*näher*): Von der Bewussten.

BARON: Wer soll da gemeint sein?

ANNINA: (*ganz nahe*): Nur eigenhändig, insgeheim zu übergeben.

BARON: Luft da!
(*Die Diener treten zurück, nehmen den Faninalschen ohne weiteres die Weinkanne ab und trinken sie leer.*)
Zeig' Sie den Wisch!
(*Reisst mit der Linken den Brief auf. Versucht ihn zu lesen, indem er ihn sehr weit von sich weghält.*)
Such' Sie in meiner Taschen meine Brillen.
(*Misstrauisch, da sie sich dazu anschickt.*)
Nein! Such' Sie nicht!
Kann Sie Geschriebnes lesen?
Da.

ANNINA: (*nimmt und liest*):
"Herr Kavalier!
Den morgigen Abend hätt' i frei.
Sie ham mir schon g'fall'n, nur g'schamt
hab' i mi von der fürstil'n Gnad'n,
weil i noch gar so jung bin. Das bewusste Mariandel,
Kammerzofel und Verliebte.
Wenn der Herr Kavalier den Nam'
nit schon vergessen hat.
I wart' auf Antwort."

BARON: (*entzückt*): Sie wart' auf Antwort!
Geht all's recht am Schnürl so wie z' Haus
und hat noch einen andern Schick dazu.
Ich hab' halt schon einmal ein lerchenauisch Glück.
Komm' Sie nach Tisch, geb' Ihr die Antwort nachher schriftlich.

ANNINA: Ganz zu Befehl, Herr Kavalier.
Vergessen nich der Botin?

BARON: (*sie überhörend, vor sich*): "Ohne mich, ohne mich jeder Tag dir so bang."

ANNINA: (*dringlicher*): Vergessen nicht der Botin, Euer Gnad'n?

BARON: Schon gut.
"Mit mir, mit mir kein Nacht dir zu lang."
(*Annina macht nochmals eine Gebärde des Geldforderns*).
Das später.
Alls auf einmal.
Dann zum Schluss.
Sie wart' auf Antwort!
Tret' Sie ab indessen.
Schaff' Sie ein Schreibzeug in mein Zimmer, bin dort drüben,
dass ich die Antwort dann diktier'.
(*Annina geht ab, nicht ohne mit einer drohenden Gebärde hinter des Barons Rücken angezeigt zu haben, dass sie sich bald für seinen Geiz rächen werde*).
(*tut noch einen letzten Schluck, er geht, von seinen Leuten begleitet, seinem Zimmer zu*): "Mit mir, mit mir keine Nacht dir zu lang!"

*End of Act II.*

BARON: Oh! Oh!
The Devil!
Oh! Oh! Oh, a plague upon that boy!
A baby, scarcely breeched, and plays with swords already.
(*With growing passion.*)
Cursed Italian hound!
Wait till I catch your Lordship!
In my kennel, I'll teach you to fight, upon my soul!
With cocks and hens I'll house you.
Egad, I'll trounce you!
Make you hear the angels sing!
(*To Faninal's Footman.*)
Give me some wine there, quick!

LERCHENAU'S SERVANTS: (*with hollow voices*): We will towzle you!
Beat you black and blue!
We will do for you,
Beat you black and blue!

BARON: (*to the Doctor*): And now, my friend, precede me to my room,
And make my bed, and let it be all feathers.
I come, but first, another draught
Remember what I told you.
(*The Doctor goes out with the Body Servant. Annina has entered through the ante-room and comes up to him mysteriously with a letter in her hand.*)

BARON: (*to himself softly, emptying the second cup*): A feather bed!
Two hours yet till I dine, and no distraction.
"Without me, without me, slowly pass all the days,
With me, with me, time will seem short always."
(*Annina places herself so that the Baron must see her and makes mysterious signs to him with her letter.*)
For me?

ANNINA: (*nearer*): From her you know of!

BARON: And whom may you mean, pray!

ANNINA: (*coming quite close*): Into your own hands I must give it, and in secret.

BARON: Room there!
(*His servants retire without more ado, take the wine-can from Faninal's servant and empty it.*)
Show me the thing!
(*Tears the letter open with this left hand. Tries to read it, holding it as far as possible from him.*)
Look in my pocket for my glasses.
(*Suspiciously, as she is searching.*)
No! Do not look.
Are you a scholar? Read it
There—

ANNINA: (*takes the letter and reads*): "Worshipful Sir! Tomorrow at nightfall I am free!
You pleased me, but I felt it shame,
Ven 'er 'ighness was looking, to say it,
For I am still a young thing,
She you know of, Mariandel,
Tirewoman, and your sweetheart,
And I hope that your Lords'ip's
'onor 'as not forgotten me.
I wait an answer."

BARON: (*delighted*): She waits an answer!
It all goes on wheels—as at home
And, look you, what an air of fashion it has.
(*Very merry.*)
I have all the luck of the Lerchenaus—
Come when I've dined—I'll give the answer then in writing.

ANNINA: Your most obedient servant, my Lord.
Your Lords'ip v'on't forget me?

BARON: (*not noticing her—to himself*): "Without me, without me, slowly pass all the days."

ANNINA: (*importunately*): Your Lords'ip 'has forgotten ze bearer

BARON: Enough—
"With me, with me, time will seem short always—
(*Annina makes another begging gesture.*)
Afterward—all together—at the end.
"I wait an answer." In the meantime leave me,
Bring to my room soon all that you need for writing,
And I'll dictate you my reply.
(*Annina goes out, not without indicating by a threatening gesture behind the Baron's back, that she will be even with him for his niggardliness. The Baron takes a last sip of wine, and goes toward his room, accompanied by his people.*)
"With me, with me, time shall seem short always!"

*END OF ACT TWO.*

# ■ DRITTER AUFZUG

*Ein Extrazimmer in einem Gasthaus. Im Hintergrund links ein Alkoven, darin ein Bett. Der Alkoven durch einen Vorhang verschliessbar, der sich auf- und zuziehn lässt. Vorne rechts Türe ins Nebenzimmer. Rechts steht ein für zwei Personen gedeckter Tisch, auf diesem ein grosser vielarmiger Leuchter. In der Mitte rückwärts Ture auf den Korridor.*

# ■ ACT III

*A private room in an inn. At the back to the left a recess (in it a bed.) the recess is separated from the room by a curtain, which can be drawn.
At the center, towards the left, a fire-place with a fire, over it a mirror. In front on the left, a door leading to a side room. Opposite the fire-place is a table laid for two, on which stands a large,*

*Daneben links ein Büfett. Rechts rückwärts ein blindes Fenster, vorne links ein Fenster auf die Gasse. Armleuchter mit Kerzen auf den Seitentischen, sowie an den Wänden. Es brennt nur je eine Kerze in den Leuchtern und auf den Seitentischen. Das Zimmer halbdunkel.*

*Annina steht da, als Dame in Trauer gekleidet. Valzacchi richtet ihr den Schleier, zupft da und dort das Kleid zurecht, tritt zurück, mustert sie, zieht einen Crayon aus der Tasche, untermalt ihr die Augen. Die Türe rechts wird vorsichtig geöffnet, ein Kopf erscheint, verschwindet wieder, dann kommt eine nicht ganz unbedenklich aussehende, aber ehrbar gekleidete Alte hereingeschlüpft, öffnet lautlos die Tür und lässt respektvoll Octavian eintreten, in Frauenkleidern, mit einem Häubchen, wie es die Bürgermädchen tragen.*

*Octavian, hinter ihm die Alte, gehen auf die beiden anderen zu, werden sogleich von Valzacchi bemerkt, der in seiner Arbeit innehält und sich vor Octavian verneigt. Annina erkennt nicht sofort den Verkleideten, sie kann sich vor Staunen nicht fassen, knickst dann tief. Octavian greift in die Tasche ( nicht wie eine Dame sondern wie ein Herr und man sieht, dass er unter dem Reifrock Männerkleider und Reitstiefel anhat, aber ohne Sporen ) und wirft Valzacchi eine Börse zu. Valzacchi und Annina küssen ihm die Hände, Annina richtet noch an Octavians Brusttuch. Indessen sind fünf verdächtige Herren unter Vorsichtsmassregeln eingetreten. Valzacchi bedeutet sie mit einem Wink zu warten. Sie stehen nahe der Türe.*

*Eine Uhr schlägt halb. Valzacchi zieht seine Uhr, zeigt Octavian: es ist hohe Zeit. Octavian geht eilig ab, gefolgt von der Alten, die als seine Begleiterin fungiert. Annina geht zum Spiegel (alles mit Vorsicht, jedes Geräusch vermeidend) arrangiert sich noch, zieht dann einen Zettel hervor, woraus sie ihre Rolle zu lernen scheint. Valzacchi nimmt indessen die Verdächtigen nach vorne, indem er mit jeder Gebärde die Notwendigkeit höchster Vorsicht andeutet. Die Verdächtigen folgen ihm auf den Zehen nach der Mitte. Er bedeutet ihrer einem, ihm zu folgen: lautlos, ganz lautlos. Führt ihn an die Wand rechts, öffnet lautlos eine Falltür unfern des gedeckten Tisches, lässt den Mann hinabsteigen, schliesst wieder die Falltür. Dann winkt er zwei zu*

*many-branched candlestick. At the back, in the center, a door leading to the corridor. Next to it, on the right, a sideboard. At the back, on the right, a blind window; in front, on the right, a window looking on the street. Candelabra with candles on the sideboard and on the chimney piece, and sconces on the walls. Only one candle is burning in each candlestick on the chimney-piece. The room is in semi-darkness.*

*Annina discovered, dressed as a lady in mourning. Valzacchi is arranging her veil, putting her dress to right, takes a step backwards, surveys her, takes a crayon from his pocket and paints her eyes. The door on the left is opened cautiously, a head appears, and vanishes. Then a not unsuspicious-looking but decently dressed old woman slips in, opens the door silently and respectfully introduces Octavian, in female clothes, with a cap such as girls of the middle classes wear. Octavian, followed by the old woman, moves towards the others. Valzacchi is at once aware of them, stops in his occupation, and bows to Octavian. Annina does not at once recognize him in his disguise. She cannot restrain her astonishment, and curtseys low. Octavian feels in his pocket (not like a woman, but like a man, and one sees that under his skirt he is wearing riding boots without spurs) and throws a purse to Valzacchi; Valzacchi and Annina kiss his hands. Annina puts a finishing touch to his kerchief.*

*Five suspicious looking men enter very cautiously from the left. Valzacchi makes them a sign to wait. They stand at the left, near the door.*

*A clock strikes the half-hour. Valzacchi takes out his watch; shows it to Octavian; it is high time. Octavian hurries out to the left, followed by the old woman, who acts as his duenna. Valzacchi leads the suspicious looking men to the front, impressing on them with every gesture the necessity of extreme caution. Annina goes to the mirror (all the while cautiously avoiding every noise) completes her disguise; then draws from a pocket a piece of paper, from which she seems to be learning a part. The suspicious looking men follow Valzacchi on tiptoe to the center. He signs to one of them to follow him noiselessly, quite noiselessly, leads him to the wall on the right, noiselessly opens a trapdoor not far from the table, makes the man descend, closes the*

*sich, schleicht ihnen voran bis an die Eingangstüre, steckt den Kopf heraus, vergewissert sich, dass niemand zusieht, winkt die zwei zu sich, lässt sie dort hinaus. Dann schliesst er die Tür, führt die beiden letzten leise an die Türe zum Nebenzimmer voran, schiebt sie hinaus. Winkt Annina zu sich, geht mit ihr leise links ab, die Türe lautlos hinter sich schliessend. Er kommt wieder herein, klatscht in die Hände. Der eine Verstechkte hebt sich mit halbem Leib aus dem Boden hervor. Zugleich erscheinen über dem Bett und andern Stellen Köpfe. Auf Valzacchis Wink verschwinden dieselben ebenso plötzlich, die geheimen Schiebtüren schliessen sich ohne Geräusch. Valzacchi sieht abermals nach der Uhr, geht nach rückwärts, öffnet die Eingangstür, dann zieht er ein Feuerzeug hervor und beginnt eifrig die Kerzen auf dem Tisch anzuzünden. Ein Kellner und ein Kellnerjunge kommen gelaufen mit zwei Stöcken zum Kerzenanzünden. Entzünden die Leuchter auf dem Kamin, auf dem Büfett, dann die zahlreichen Wandarme. Sie haben die Tür hinter sich offen gelassen, man hört aus dem Vorsaal (im Hintergrunde) Tanzmusik spielen. Valzacchi eilt zur Mitteltür, öffnet dienstbeflissen auch den zweiten Flügel, springt unter Verneigung zur Seite.*

*Baron Ochs erscheint, den Arm in der Schlinge. Octavian an der Linken führend, hinter ihm der Leiblakai. Baron mustert den Raum. Octavian sieht herum, läuft an den Spiegel, richtet sein Haar. Baron bemerkt den kellner und Kellnerjungen, die noch mehr Kerzen anzünden wollen, winkt ihnen, sie sollten es sein lassen. In ihrem Eifer bemerken sie es nicht. ( Baron ungeduldig, reisst den Kellnerjungen vom Stuhl, auf den er gestigen war, löscht einige ihm zunächst brennende Kerzen mit der Hand aus. Valzacchi zeigt dem Baron diskret den Alkoven und durch eine Spalte des Vorhanges das Bett. Der Wirt mit mehrerer Kellnern eilt herbei, den vornehmen Gast zu begrüssen).*

**WIRT:** Haben Euer Gnaden noch weitere Befehle?

**KELLNER:** Befehl'n mehr Lichter?

**WIRT:** Ein grösseres Zimmer?

**KELLNER:** Befehlen mehr Silber auf den Tisch?

*trapdoor; then he summons the others to his side, slinks in front of them to the door of the room, puts his head out, assures himself that they are not observed, makes a sign to the two to come to him, and lets them out. Then he closes the door, directs the two remaining men to precede him to the door which leads to the side room, pushes them out, signs to Annina to come to him, goes out with her silently to the left, and noiselessly closes the door behind him. He returns—claps his hands. The man who is hidden rises to his waist from the trapdoor. At the same moment heads appear above the bed and in other places. At a sign from Valzacchi they disappear as suddenly—the secret panels close without a sound. Valazacchi again looks at his watch, goes to the back, opens the door. Then he produces a tinder-box and busily lights the candles on the table.*

*A Waiter and a Boy run in with tapers for lighting candles, and light the candles on the chimney, on the sideboard, and the numerous sconces. They have left the door open behind them, dance music is heard from the anteroom at the back.*

*Valzacchi hurries to the center door, opens it respectfully (both wings) and bowing low springs aside.*

*Baron Ochs appears, his arm in a sling, leading Octavian by his left, followed by his Body Servant. The Baron surveys the room. Octavian looks round, runs to the mirror and arranges his hair. The Baron notices the Waiter and the Boy, who are about to light more candles, and signs to them to stop. In their preoccupation they do not notice him. The Baron, in his impatience, pulls the Boy from the chair on to which he has climbed, and extinguishes some of the candles nearest him with his hand. Valzacchi discreetly points out the recess to him (and through an opening of the curtains the bed). (Enter the Landlord.)*

**LANDLORD:** (*hurrying forward to greet the noble guest*): Has your Lordship any further wishes?

**WAITERS:** D'you lack more candles?

**LANDLORD:** A larger apartment?

**WAITERS:** We'll bring your Lordship more lights if you wish— More silver—

# Act III

BARON: (*eifrig beschäftig mit einer Serviette, die er vom Tisch genommen und entfaltet hat, alle ihm erreichbaren Kerzen auszulöschen*): Verschwindt's!
Macht mir das Madel net verruckt
Was will die Musik?
Hab' sie nicht bestellt.
(*Löscht weitere Kerzen aus.*)

WIRT: Schaffen vielleicht, dass man sie näher hört
Im Vorsaal da als Tafelmusik.

BARON: Lass Er die Musick, wo sie ist.
(*Bemerkt das Fenster rechts rückwärts im Rücken des gedeckten Tisches.*)
Was ist da für ein Fenster da?
(*Probiert, ob es hereinzieht.*)

WIRT: Ein blindes Fenster nur.
(*Verneigt sich.*)
Darf aufgetragen werd'n?
(*Alle fünf Kellner wollen abeilen.*)

BARON: Halt, was woll'n die Maikäfer da?

KELLNER: (*an der Tür*): Servier'n, Euer Gnaden.

BARON: (*winkt ab*): Brauch' niemand nicht.
(*Als sie nicht gehen, heftig.*)
Packt's Euch!
Servieren wird mein Kammerdiener da.
Einschenken tu' ich kelber.
Versteht Er?
(*Valzacchi bedeutet sie, den Willen seiner Gnaden wortlos zu respektieren. Schiebt alle zur Tür hinaus.*)

BARON: (*löscht aufs neue eine Anzahl Kerzen aus, darunter mit einigen Mühe die hoch an der Wand brennenden, zu Valzacchi*): Er ist ein braver Kerl.
Wenn er mir hilft, die Rechnung 'runterdrucken,
Dann fallt was ab für Ihn.
Kost' sicher hier ein Martergeld.
(*Valzacchi unter Verneigung ab.—Octavian ist nun fertig.*)
(*Baron führt ihn zu Tisch, sie setzen sich*).
(*Der Lakai am Büffet sieht mit unverschämter Neugierde der Entwicklung des tete-a-tete entgegen, stellt Karaffen mit Wein vom Büffet auf den Esstisch. Baron schenkt ein. Octavian nippt. Baron küsst Octavian die Hand. Octavian entzieht ihm die Hand. Baron winkt dem lakaien abzugeben, muss es mehrmals wiederholen, bis die Lakaien endlich gehen.*)

OCTAVIAN: (*schiebt sein Glas zurück*): Nein, nein, nien, nein!
I trink' kein Wein.

BARON: (*busily engaged in extinguishing all the candles in his reach with a napkin which he has taken from the table and unfolded.*) Be off!
Such talk will turn the hussy's brain.
(*Extinguishes more candles.*)
What is that music?
I commanded none.

LANDLORD: They can come near it it is your Lordship's wish—
To play to you in yonder anteroom.

BARON: Best let them stay there, as they are.
(*Notices the blind window to the right behind the table.*)
Tell me, what means that window there?
(*Tries it.*)

LANDLORD: That window?
That is blind.
(*Bows.*)
Can supper now begin?
(*All five waiters make as if to hurry off.*)

BARON: Stop!
What mean those grinning apes?

WAITERS: To wait upon your Lordship.

BARON: (*makes a sign to them to go*): I need no help.
Be off!
My man there will serve all the meats to us.
Myself I'll fill the glasses. Now leave us
(*Valzacchi signing to them to respect his Lordship's wishes without demur, pushes them all out of the door. The Baron continues to extinguish the candles, among them some high on the walls which he reaches with difficulty.*)

BARON: You are an honest fellow.
If you can help me reduce the reckoning,
There will be vails for you.
It is surely very costly here.
(*Exit Valzacchi, bowing.*)
(*Octavian has now finished arranging his hair. The Baron leads him to the table. The Body Servant at the sideboard contemplates the developments of the tête-à-tête with impudent curiosity. He places bottles of wine from the sideboard on the table. The Baron pours out wine. Octavian takes a sip. The Baron kisses Octavian's hand. Octavian withdraws his hand. The Baron signs to the lackey to withdraw, but he has to repeat the signal several times before he goes.*)

OCTAVIAN: (*pushing back his glass*): What do you think?
I drink no wine.

BARON: Geh, Herzel, was denn?
Mach' doch keine Faxen.

OCTAVIAN: Nein, nein, i bleib' net da.
(*Springt auf, tut, als wenn er fort wollte.*)

BARON: (*packt sie mit seiner Linken*): Jetzt komm' Sie.
Setz' Sie sich schön.
Kommt gleich wer mit'n Essen
Hat Sie denn kein' Hunger nicht?
(*Legt ihr die Hand um die Taille.*)

OCTAVIAN: (*wirft dem Baron schmachtende Blicke zu*): O weh, wo Sie doch ein Bräutigam tun sein.
(*Wehrt ihn ab.*)

BARON: Ach, lass Sie schon einmal das fade Wort!
Sie hat doch einen Kavalier vor sich und keinen Seifensieder:
Ein Kavalier lässt alles, was ihn nicht konveniert, da draussen vor der Tür. Hier sitzt kein Bräutigam und keine Kammerjungfer nicht:
Hier sitzt mit seiner Allerschönsten ein Verliebter beim Souper.
(*Zieht sie an sich.*)
(*Octavian lehnt sich kokett in den Sessel zurück, mit halbgeschlossenen Augen*).
(*erhebt sich, der Moment für den ersten Kuss scheint ihm gekommen. Wie sein Gesicht dem der Partnerin ganz nahe ist, durchzuckt ihn jäh die Aehnlichkeit mit Octavian. Er fährt zurück und greift unwillkürlich nach dem verwundeten Arm*): Ist ein Gesicht!
Verfluchter Bub'!
Verfolgt mich alser wacher und im Traum!

OCTAVIAN: (*öffnet die Augen und blickt ihn frech und kokett an*): Was meint Er denn?

BARON: Sieht einem ähnlich, einem gottverfluchten Kerl!

OCTAVIAN: Ah geh'!
Das hab' i no net g'hört! (*Baron nun wieder versichert, dass es die Zofe ist, zwingt sich zu einem Lächeln. Aber der Schreck ist ihm nicht ganz aus den Gliedern. Er mus Luft schöpfen und der Kuss bleibt aufgeschoben. Der Mann unter der Falltür öffnet zu früh und kommt zum Vorschein*).
(*Octavian der ihm gegenübersitzt, winkt ihm eifrig zu verschwinden. Der Mann verschwindet sofort. Baron, der, um den unangenehmen Eindruck von sich abzuschütteln, ein paar Schritte getan hat und sie von*

BARON: Come, sweetheart, why not?
Now let's have no flim-flams.

OCTAVIAN: No, no, no,no, I will not stay.
(*Jumps up as if he would go away.*)

BARON: (*seizing him with his left hand*): Sit down now, take your place, here.
They'll soon bring supper . . .
Then we'll fall to with appetite.
(*Put his arm round his waist. Octavian casts languid glances at him.*)

OCTAVIAN: Oh dear! Oh! to think you're promised and all!
(*Keeping him off.*)

BARON: Have done with such old wives' tales once for all.
You see here nothing but a gentleman,
None of your common fellows—
A gentleman forgets
And leaves behind him everything
That is not to his taste. Here sits no promised man,
Here at my side no waiting-maid—
Here sit we two and sup, a lover and his lass.
That merely,—nothing more.
(*Draws him to his side. Octavian leans back coquettishly in his chair, with half-closed eyes. The Baron rises. The moment for the first kiss seems to have come. As his face is close to that of his companion, the resemblance to Octavian strikes him like a blow. He starts back and half unconsciously feels his wounded arm.*)

BARON: One face, I swear,
Accursèd boy . . .
Pursues me when I'm waking and all night.

OCTAVIAN: (*opening his eyes and looking at him with impudent coquetry*): Lawk! How you talk!

BARON: You're like to some one—an accursèd scurvy boy—

OCTAVIAN: Have done! Who can it be I'm like?
(*The Baron has once again assured himself that it is the waiting-maid, and forces a smile. But he is not quite rid of his fright. He must take breath, and the kiss is postponed. The man under the trapdoor opens it too soon and appears. Octavian who is sitting opposite to him makes violent signs to him to get out of sight. He vanishes at once. The Baron, who to shake off the unpleasant impression, has taken a few steps and is on the point of embracing Octavian from behind, just*

*rückwärts umschlingen und küssen will, sieht gerade noch den Mann. Er erschrickt heftig, zeigt hin).*

OCTAVIAN: (*als verstände er nicht*): Was ist mit Ihm?

BARON: (*auf die Stelle deutend, wo die Erscheinung verschwunden ist*): Was war den das? Hat Sie den nicht gesehn?

OCTAVIAN: Da is ja nix.

BARON: Da is nix? (*Nun wieder ihr Gesicht angstvoll musternd.*) So? Und da ist auch nix? (*Fährt mit der Hand über ihr Gesicht.*)

OCTAVIAN: Da is mei' G'sicht.

BARON: (*atmet schwer, schenkt sich ein Glas Wein ein*): Da is Ihr G'sicht—und da is nix—mir scheint, ich hab' die Kongestion. (*Setzt sich schwer, es ist ihm ängstlich zumute. Die Tür geht auf, man hört draussen wieder die Musik. Der Lakai kommt und serviert.*)

OCTAVIAN: (*sehr weich*): Die schöne Musik!

BARON: (*wieder sehr laut*): Is mei Leiblied, weiss Sie das?

OCTAVIAN: (*horcht auf die Musik*): Da muss ma weinen.

BARON: Was?

OCTAVIAN: Weil's gar so schön is.

BARON: Was, weinen? Wär nicht schlecht. Kreuzlustig muss Sie sein, die Musik geht ins Blut. (*Sentimental.*) G'spürt Sie's jetzt— (*Winkt dem Lakaien abzugehen.*) Auf die letzt, g'spürt Sie's dahier, Dass Sie aus mir Kann machen alles frei, was Sie nur will. (*Der Lakai geht zögernd ab, öffnet nochmals die Tür, schaut mit frecher Neugierde herein und verschwindet erst auf einen neuen heftigen Wink des Barons gänzlich*).

OCTAVIAN: (*zurückgelehnt, wie zu sich selbst sprechend, mit unmässiger Traurigkeit*): Es is ja eh als eins, es is ja eh als eins, Was ein Herz noch so gach begehrt. (*Indes der Baron ihre Hand fasst.*) Geh', es is ja all's net drumi wert.

BARON: (*lässt ihre Hand fahren*): Ei, was denn? Is sehr wohl der Müh wert.

*catches a last glimpse of him. He is violently alarmed and points to the spot.*)

OCTAVIAN: (*does as if he did not understand.*) What's wrong with you?

BARON: Gad! What was that? (*Points to the spot where the apparition has vanished.*) Did you see that man there?

OCTAVIAN: There's nothing there.

BARON: Nothing there? (*Again anxiously scanning Octavian's face.*) No? (*Passing his hand over his face.*) Nothing there, neither?

OCTAVIAN: That is my face.

BARON: (*breathing heavily, pours out a glass of wine*): There is your face, and nothing there. It seems I have a feverish brain— (*The door opens. The music from outside is heard again. The Body Servant comes and serves.*)

OCTAVIAN: (*very sweetly*): The pretty music!

BARON: It is the song that I like best.

OCTAVIAN: It sets me weeping—

BARON: What?

OCTAVIAN: It is that pretty—

BARON: What? Weeping? Why, what next? It is merry you should be. The music fires the blood. (*Sentimentally.*) Do you still doubt, my dear? (*Signs to the Lackey to go.*) Do you not see how it is with me? You now can make of me Your willing slave. (*The Lackey goes reluctantly— then opens the door again, and looks in with insolent curiosity and does not go till the Baron has made an angry sign.*)

OCTAVIAN: It is all one—it is all one— All our joys, and all our bitter pain, In the end are they not all in vain? (*Leaning back in his chair as though to himself with exaggerated melancholy. The Baron takes his hand.*)

BARON: (*dropping his hand*): Why? What's this? No, sweetheart, not in vain. (*Octavian casts languishing glances at him.*)

OCTAVIAN: (*immer gleich melancholisch, wirft dem Baron schmachtende Blicke zu*): Wie die Stund hingeht, wie der Wind verweht, So sind wir bald alle zwei dahin. Menschen ein' ma halt. (*Schmachtender Blick auf den Baron.*) Richtn's nichts mit G'walt, Weint uns niemand nach, net dir net und net mir.

BARON: Macht Sie der Wein leicht immer so? Is ganz gewiss Ihr Mieder, das aufs Herzer! Ihr druckt. (*Octavian mit geschlossenen Augen, gibt keine Antwort*). (*steht auf und will ihr das Mieder aufschnüren*): Jetzt wird's frei mir a bisserl heiss. (*Schnell entschlossen nimmt er seine Perücke ab und sucht sich einen Platz, sie abzulegen. Indem erblickt er ein Gesicht, das sich wieder im Alkoven zeigt und ihn anstarrt. Das Gesicht verschwindet gleich wieder. Er sagt sich: Kongestionen! und verscheucht den Schrecken, muss sich aber doch die Stirne abwischen. Sieht nun wieder die Zofe willenlos wie mit gelösten Gliedern dasitzen. Das ist stärker als alles, und er nähert sich ihr zärtlich. Da meint er wieder das Gesicht Octavians ganz nahe dem seinigen zu erkennen, und er fährt abermals zurück. Mariandl rührt sich kaum. Abermals verscheucht der Baron sich den Schreck, zwingt Munterkeit in sein Gesicht zurück, da fällt sein Auge abermals auf einen fremden Kopf, welcher aus der Wand hervorstarrt. .Nun ist er masslos geängstigt, er schreit dumpf auf, ergreift die Tischglocke und schwingt sie wie rasend*): Da und da und da und da! (*Plötzlich springt das angeblich blinde Fenster auf. Annina in schwarzer Trauerkleidung erscheint und zeigt mit ausgestreckten Armen auf den Baron*).

BARON: (*ausser sich vor Angst*): Da und da und da und da! (*Sucht sich den Rücken zu decken.*)

ANNINA: Er ist es! Es ist mein Mann! Er ist's! (*Verschwindet.*)

BARON: (*angstvoll*): Was ist denn das?

OCTAVIAN: Das Zimmer ist verhext. (*Schlägt ein Kreuz.*)

ANNINA: (*gefolgt von dem Intriganten, der sie scheinbar anzuhalten sucht, vom Wirt und von drei Kellnern, stürzt zur Mitteltür herein; sie bedient sich des böhmisch-deutschen Akzentes, aber gebildeter Sprechweise*): Es ist mein Mann, ich leg' Beschlag auf

OCTAVIAN: (*still very melancholy*): As the hours that go, as the winds that blow, So we twain will pass away; Flesh and blood are we, ruled by Fate's decree. (*With another languishing glance.*) When we die there's none to cry for us—not for you and not for me.

BARON: Does wine make you so sad always? It is surely your stomacher, that is pressing on your heart. (*Octavian with closed eyes does not answer. The Baron rises and tries to open his dress.*) It grows warm—I will take my ease. (*Without ado he takes off his wig, and seeks a place to deposit it. At this moment he espies a face which shows itself in the recess and glares at him. The face vanishes in a trice. He says to himself "Brainsick" and struggles with his fright, but has to mop his forehead. His eyes fall once again on the waiting-maid, sitting there helpless with relaxed limbs. That decides him, and he approaches tenderly. Then again he sees Octavian's face close to his own. He starts back again. "Mariandel" scarcely stirs. Once more the Baron fights with his terror, and forces himself to take a cheerful mien. Then his eyes alight once again on a strange face, staring at him from the wall. Now he is beside himself with fright—he gives a muffled scream, seizes the handbell from the table and swings it distractedly.*) There! and there! and there! and there! (*Suddenly the presumed blind window is torn open. Annina in mourning appears and with outstretched arms points to the Baron.*)

BARON: (*beside himself with fear*): There! and there! and there! and there!

ANNINA: My husband! Yes, it is he! it is he! it is he! (*Vanishes.*)

BARON: Zounds, what was that?

OCTAVIAN: (*crosses himself*): The room is bewitched!

ANNINA: (*followed by Valzacchi who makes pretence of holding her back, the Landlord, and three Waiters, rushes in at the center door; speaking with a Bohemian accent, but like a woman of education*): I am his wife! I make a claim to him!

ihn!
Gott ist mein Zerge, Sie sind meine Zeugen!
Gerichte!
Hohe Obrigkeit! Die Kaiserin muss ihn mir wiedergeben!

BARON: (*zum Wirt*): Was will das Weibsbild da von mir, Herr Wirt! Was will der dort und der und der und der?
(*Zeigt nach allen Richtungen.*)
Der Teufel frequentier' sein gottverfluchtes Extrazimmer!
(*Baron hat sich eine kalte Kompresse auf den Kopf gelegt, hält sie mit der Linken fest, geht dann dicht auf die Kellner, den Wirt, zuletzt auf Annina zu, mustert sie ganz scharf, um sich über ihre Realität klar zu werden*)

ANNINA: Leupold bedenk': Anton von Lerchenau, dort oben richtet dich ein Höherer!
(*Erschrickt zuerst heftig, dass sie in ihrer Anrede unterbrochen wird, fasst sich aber schnell.*)

BARON: (*starrt sie fassungslos an*): Kommt mir bekannt vor.
(*Sieht wieder auf Octavian.*)
Hab'n doppelte Gesichter alle miteinander.

WIRT: Die arme Frau Baronin!

KELLNER: Die arme Frau, die arme Frau Baronin!

VIER KINDER: (*zwischen vier und zehn Jahren stürzen zu früh herein und auf den Baron zu*): Papa! Papa! Papa!

ANNINA: Hörst du die Stimme deines Blutes! Kinder, hebt eure Hände auf zu ihm!

BARON: (*schlägt wütend mit einer Serviette, die er vom Tisch reisst, nach den Kindern; zum Wirt*): Debarassier' Er mich von denen da, Von der, von dem, von dem!
(*Zeigt nach allen Richtungen. Valzacchi indessen zu Octavian leise.*)

OCTAVIAN: (*zu Valzacchi*): Ist gleich wer fort, den Faninal zu holen?

VALZACCHI: (*leise*): Sogleich in Anfang. Wird sogleich zur Stelle sein.

Heaven is my witness—you shall be my witness!
The Law, the Ministers, Her Majesty Must restore him to my arms!

BARON: (*to the Landlord*): Landlord, what does this female want of me? What does he want? and he? and that one there?
(*Pointing all round the room.*)
Hell is let lose in this foul den of thieves.
(*The Baron has put a cold compress on his head, holds it in its place with his left hand, then goes close up to the Landlord, the Waiters and Annina in turn, and scans them closely, as if to convince himself that they are real.*)

ANNINA: Leopold, reflect! Anton of Lerchenau, Above us dwells a Judge that knoweth all!

LANDLORD AND WAITERS: Poor ill-used lady! Oh wretched, ill-used lady!

BARON: (*stares in amazement at Annina*): Surely I know you!
(*Looks towards Octavian again.*)
They all have double faces! All of them together!
(*Four children between the ages of ten and four, entering too soon, rush towards the Baron.*)

THE FOUR CHILDREN: Papa! Papa! Papa!
(*Annina at first starts violently, so that her speech is interrupted, but soon regains her composure.*)

ANNINA: Hear you the voices of your offspring? My children, raise your hands to him in prayer!
(*The Baron hits out at the children with a napkin which he takes from the table.*)

BARON: (*to the Landlord*): Take all this crew away from here at once— Take her, take him, and him, and him!

OCTAVIAN: (*aside to Valzacchie*): Have messengers been sent for Faninal?

VALZACCHI: Before you 'ad come 'ere: in a moment you vill see 'im.

WIRT: (*im Rücken des Barons, leise*): Halten zu Gnaden, gehen nit zu weit. könnten recht böse Folgen g'spüren! Bitterböse!

BARON: Was? ich was g'spür'n? Von dem Möbel da? Hab's nie nicht angerührt, nicht mit der Feuer zang'!

ANNINA: (*schreit laut auf*): Aah!

WIRT: (*wie oben*): Die Bigamie ist halt kein G'spass, Is gar ein Kapitalverbrechen!

VALZACCHI: (*zum Baron leise*): Ik rat' Euer Gnaden, sei'n vorsiktig, Die Sittenpolizei sein gar nicht tolerant!

BARON: Die Bigamie? Die Sittenpolizei?
(*Die Stimmen der Kinder nachahmend.*)
Papa, Papa, Papa?
(*Greift sich wie verloren an den Kopf, dann wütend.*)
Schmeiss' Er hinaus das Trauerpferd! Wer? Was? Er will nicht? Was? Polizei! Die Lackln woll'n nicht? Spielt das Gelichter Leicht alles unter einem Leder? Sein wir in Frankreich? Sein wir unter Kurutzen? Oder in kaiserlicher Hauptstadt?
(*Reisst das Gassenfenster auf.*)
Polizei! Herauf da, Polizei: Gilt Ordnung herzustellen Und einer Stand'sperson zu Hilf' zu eilen!
(*Man hört auf der Gasse laute Rufe nach der Polizei.*)

WIRT: (*jammernd*): Mein renommiertes Haus! Das muss mein Haus erleben.

DIE KINDER: (*plärrend*): Papa! Papa! Papa
(*Kommissarius mit zwei Wächtern treten auf. Alles rangiert sich, ihnen Platz zu machen.*)

VALZACCHI: (*zu Octavian*): Oh weh, was maken wir?

OCTAVIAN: Verlass' Er sich auf mich und lass' Er's gehen, wie's geht.

VALZACCHI: Zu Euer Excellenz Befehl!

KOMMISSARIUS: (*scharf*): Halt! Keiner rührt sich! Was ist los? Wer hat um Hilf' geschrien? Wer hat skandal gemacht?

BARON: (*auf ihn zu, mit der Sicherheit des grossen Herrn*): Is all's in Ordnung jetzt. Bin mit Ihm wohl zufrieden. Hab' gleich verhofft, das in Wein

LANDLORD: (*behind the Baron*): Asking your pardon, venture not too far, Else might it end in harm for you— in harm most serious.

BARON: What? Harm to me from that old beldam there? Never have I touched her—no, not with a pitchfork's end

ANNINA: (*screams shrilly*): Ah!

LANDLORD: For bigamy is not a trifle, It is a hanging matter—

VALZACCHI: I counsel zat your Lords'ip 'ave a care, Ze police in zis town, it 'ave no mercy, Sir!

BARON: Bigamy! Pooh! A fig for your police!
(*Mimicking the voices of the children.*) Papa! Papa! Papa!
(*Striking his head as if in despair, then furiously.*)
Turn out that whining Jezebel! Who? What? You will not? What? The Watch here! The rascals will not stir! Is all this scurvy crew Plotted to do me mischief? Are we among heathens? Or in France, or Turkey? Or in this Empire's foremost city.
(*Tears open the window that looks on to the street.*)
The Watch! The Watch, here! Hurry! Here! Quick, here, to quell a riot! Here is a man of quality in danger!
(*Loud cries of "The Watch" are heard from the street.*)

LANDLORD: Oh! my old inn disgraced! Oh, my fair reputation!

THE CHILDREN: (*whining*): Papa! Papa!
(*A Commissary of Police enters with two Constables. All stand back to make way for them.*)

VALZACCHI: Alas! Vat can ve do?

OCTAVIAN: Put all your trust in me and happy chance.

VALZACCHI: Your humble servant to command.

COMMISSARY: (*roughly*): Stop! No one stirs now! What's amiss? Who was it called for help? Who was it broke the peace?

BARON: (*going towards him with the self-confidence of a great gentleman*): The trouble now is passed. Right well done!

all's so wie am Schnürl geht.
(*Vergnügt.*)
Schaff' Er mir da das Pack vom Hals.
Ich will in Ruh' soupieren.

I commend you,
I knew at once that there's no danger in Vienna.
(*Relieved.*)
Drive me this crowd from out the room.
I wish to sup unhindered.

**KOMMISSARIUS:** Wer ist der Herr?
Was gibt dem Herrn Befugnis?
Ist Er der Wirt?
(*Baron sperrt den Mund auf.*)
(*scharf*): Dann hal' Er sich gefällig still
Und wart' Er, bis man ihn vernehmen wird.
(*Baron retiriert sie etwas, perplex, begiunt nach seinen Perücke su suchen, die in dem Tumult abbanden gekommen ist und unauffindbar bleibt*).
(*Kommissarius setzt sich, die zwei Wächter nehmen hinter ihm Stellung*).
Wo ist der Wirt?

**COMMISSARY:** Who are you, pray?
By what right do you meddle?
Is this your house?
(*The Baron stands open-mouthed.*)
Then hold your peace, withdraw,
And wait in patience till I need your evidence.
(*The Baron retires in perplexity, begins to look for his wig, which had disappeared in the confusion and is not to be found. The Commissary seats himself. The two Constables take up their position behind him.*)
The Landlord first.

**WIRT:** (*devot*): Mich dem Herrn Oberkommissarius schönstens zu rekom mandieren.

**LANDLORD:** By your leave.
Report myself.
I'm landlord here, very much at your service.

**KOMMISSARIUS:** Die Wirtschaft da rekommandiert Ihn schlecht.
Bericht' Er jetzt!
Von Anfang!

**COMMISSARY:** These goings-on do not speak well for you.
Now your report—
The whole truth!

**WIRT:** Herr Kommissar!
Der Herr Baron—-

**LANDLORD:** It happened thus—
His Lordship there . . .

**KOMMISSARIUS:** Der grosse Dicke da?
Wo hat er sein Paruckl?

**COMMISSARY:** That very fat man there?
Where have you put your wig, Sir?

**BARON:** (*der die ganze Zeit gesucht hat*): Das frag' ich Ihn!

**BARON:** (*who has been searching all the time*): That I would from you.

**WIRT:** Das ist der Herr Baron von Lerchenau!

**LANDLORD:** That is his Lordship, Baron Lerchenau—

**KOMMISSARIUS:** Genügt nicht.

**COMMISSARY:** First prove it.

**BARON:** Was?

**BARON:** What?

**KOMMISSARIUS:** Hat Er Personen nahebei,
Die für Ihn Zeugnis geben?

**COMMISSARY:** Is any person near at hand
Whom you can call as witness?

**BARON:** Gleich bei der Hand!
Da hier mein Sekretär, ein Italiener.

**BARON:** Yes, close at hand.
There!
My secretary, an Italian.

**VALZACCHI:** (*wechselt mit Octavian einen Blick des Einverständnisses*): Ik exkusier' mik.
Ik weiss nix.
Die Herr kann sein Baron, kann sein auch nit.
Ik weiss von nix.

**VALZACCHI:** (*exchanges glances of intelligence with Octavian*): I can say nozzing!
I not know.
'E may
Be Lerchenau—'e may be not.
I do not know.

**BARON:** (*ausser sich*): Das ist doch stark, wällisches Luder, falsches!
(*Geht mit erhobener Linken auf ihn los.*)

**BARON:** (*beside himself*): That is too much.
Lying Italian scum, you!
(*Goes toward him with raised fist.*)

**KOMMISSARIUS:** (*zum Baron, scharf*): Fürs erste moderier' Er sich.

**COMMISSARY:** It would be best for you keep a civil tongue.
(*Octavian, who up to now has stood quiet, now does as if, running about in despair, he could not find the way out, and mistook the window for the door.*)

**OCTAVIAN:** (*der bis jetzt ruhig rechts gestanden, tut nun, als ob er, in Verzweiflung hin und her irrend, den Ausweg nicht fände und das Fenster für eine Ausgangstür hält*): Oh mein Gott in die Erd'n möcht' ich sinken!
Heilige Mutter von Maria Taferl!

**OCTAVIAN:** Oh! I pray that the earth may start open
Under my feet and swallow me up!
(*The Body Servant, who is much alarmed at the situation, suddenly has a hopeful inspiration and hastily rushes out by the center door.*)

**KOMMISSARIUS:** Wer ist dort die junge Person?

**COMMISSARY:** And that young woman there, who is she?

**BARON:** Die?
Niemand.
Sie steht unter meiner Protektion!

**OCTAVIAN:** That?
No one—she stands under my protection here—

**KOMMISSARIUS:** Er selber wird bald eine Protektion sehr nötig haben.
Wer ist das jung Ding, was macht Sie hier?
(*Blickt um sich.*)

**COMMISSARY:** Yourself will find protection needful soon.
Who is that girl, I say.
Why is she here?
(*Looks round.*)

**BARON:** Ist die Jungfer Faninal
Sophia Anna Barbara, eheliche Tochter
des wohlgeborenen Herrn von Faninal.
Wohnhaft am "Hof" im eignenPalais.
(*An der Tür haben sich Gasthofpersonal, andere Gäste, auch einige der Musiker aus dem andern Zimmer neugierig angesammelt. Herr von Faninal drängt sich durch sie durch, eilig aufgeregt in Hut und Mantel.*)

**BARON:** It is young Mistress Faninal,
Sophia Anna Barbara, heiress and daughter
In lawful wedlock born to the most noble Lord
Faninal, domiciled here in the Hof.
(*The servants of the inn, other guests, also some of the musicians from the next room have crowded around the door and look in curiously. Herr von Faninal forces his way through the crowd, much perturbed, in hat and cloak.*)

**FANINAL:** Zur Stell'!
Was wird von mir gewünscht?
(*Auf den Baron zu.*)
Wie sieht Er aus?
War mir vermutend nicht zu dieser Stunde,
in ein gemeines Beisl depeschiert zu werden!

**FANINAL:** The same, Sir.
What might you desire of me?
(*Goes to the Baron.*)
Why, how you look,
I scarce expected you would need my presence
At this untimely hour, here in a common pot-house.

**BARON:** (*sehr erstaunt und unangenehm berührt*): Wer hat Ihn hierher depeschiert?
In des Dreiteufels Namen?

**BARON:** (*very much surprised and annoyed*): And who asked you to meddle, in the name of mischief?

**FANINAL:** (*halblaut zu ihm*): Was soll mir die saudumme Frag',
Herr Schwiegersohn?
Wo Er mir schier die Tür einrennen lässt mit Botschaft.
Ich soll sehr schnell
Herbei und Ihn in einer üblen Lage soutenieren,
In die Er unverschuldter Weise geraten ist!
(*Baron greift sich an den Kopf*).

**FANINAL:** Why ask such questions, like a fool, Sir son-in-law,
When messengers from you came batt'ring at my house-door
And shouting I must come in hottest haste to rescue you from gravest danger,
Which by no fault of yours was threatening your liberty.
(*The Baron seizes his head in his hand.*)

**KOMMISSARIUS:** Wer ist der Herr?
Was schafft der Herr mit Ihm?

**COMMISSARY:** Whom have we here?
What is your talk with him?

**BARON:** Nichts von Bedeutung.
Ist bloss ein Bekannter, hält sich per Zufall hier im Gasthaus auf.

**BARON:** It is nothing—nothing.
We are scarce acquainted—
It is but a chance that he is staying here.

**KOMMISSARIUS:** Der Herr geb' seinen Namen an!

**COMMISSARY:** (*to Faninal*): Your name—and tell me why you're here.

**FANINAL:** Ich bin der Edle von Faninal.

**FANINAL:** I am the Baron of Faninal.

**KOMMISSARIUS:** Ja, ja, genügt schon.
(*Zu Faninal.*)
Er erkennt demnach in diesem Herrn hier Seinen Schwiegersohn?

**FANINAL:** Sehr wohl!
Wie sollt' ich Ihn nicht erkennen? Leicht, weil Er keine Haar nicht hat?

**KOMMISSARIUS:** (*zum Baron*): Und Er erkennt nunmehr wohl auch in diesem Herrn Wohl oder übel Seinen Schwiegervater?

**BARON:** (*nimmt den Leuchter vom Tisch, beleuchtet sich Faninal genau*): So so, la la! Ja, ja, wird schon derselbe sein. War heut den ganzen Abend gar nicht recht beinand, Kann meinen Augen heut nicht traun. Muss Ihm sagen, Liegt hier was in der Luft, man kriegt die Kongestion davon

**KOMMISSARIUS:** (*zum Faninal*): Dagegen wird von Ihm die Vaterschaft zu dieser Ihm verbatim zugeschobenen Tochter Geleugnet.

**FANINAL:** (*bemerkt jetzt erst Octavian*): Meine Tochter? Meine Tochter soll herauf! Sitzt unten in der Tragchaise. Im Galopp herauf!
(*Wieder auf den Baron losstürzend.*)
Das zahlt Er teuer! Bring' Ihn vors Gericht!
(*Baron im Wilden Herumfahren, um die Perücke zu suchen, fasst er einige der Kinder an und stösst sie zur Seite*).

**BARON:** (*im Suchen findet wenigstens seinen Hut, schlägt mit dem Hut nach den Kindern*): Gar nix, ein Schwindel! Kenn' nit das Bagagi! Sie sagt, dass sie verheirat' war mit mir. Käm' zu der Schand', so wie der Pontius ins credo!
(*Sophie kommt im Mantel eilig herein, man macht ihr Platz. An der Tür sieht man die Faninal-*

**COMMISSARY:** Yes, yes, I follow. Then you recognize This gentleman for your son-in-law?

**FANINAL:** For sure; how should I fail to recognize him? Maybe because his pate is bald?

**COMMISSARY:** (*to the Baron*): And you now recognize this gentleman to be For good or evil, the young lady's father?

**BARON:** (*taking the candlestick from the table and holding it up to Faninal's face*). So, so! La, la! Yes, yes! Maybe that it is he— My head today has been quite giddy and confused— I can no longer trust my eyes. I feel There's here a something in the air that gives a man a fevered brain.

**COMMISSARY:** (*to Faninal*): You on the other hand deny you are The father of this girl here who is said To be your daughter?

**FANINAL:** (*now for the first time noticing Octavian*): That my daughter? Summon my daughter here. She waits in her sedan-chair— Bid her come up at once.
(*Again going to the Baron.*)
You'll pay this dearly! I will go to law!

**BARON:** What mighty pother you are making About a little thing—To be your son-in-law a man must have The patience of an ass, parole d'honneur! Now bring my wig here!
(*Shakes the Landlord.*)
Find my wig! Find me my wig!
(*In his wild hunt for his wig, he seizes some of the children and pushes them aside.*)

**THE FOUR CHILDREN:** (*automatically*): Papa! Papa! Papa!

**FANINAL:** (*starts back*): What brats are those?

**BARON:** (*in his wild search he has come across his hat and hits out at the children with it*): Nothing! A lie! Till now I never saw her! She says that she's my lawful wedded wife! Heaven only knows why things like this are sent to try us!
(*At the door appear servants of Faninal, each one holding the pole of a sedan-chair. Sophia*

schen Bedienten, jeder eine Tragstange der Sänfte haltend. Baron sucht die Kahlheit seines Kopfs vor Sophie mit dem Hut zu beschatten*).

**VIELE STIMMEN:** (*indes Sophie auf ihren Vater zugeht, dumpf*): Da ist die Braut. Oh was für ein Skandal!

**DUMPFE STIMMEN:** Der Skandal! Der Skandal! Fürn Herrn von Faninal!

**FANINAL:** Da! Aus dem Keller! Aus der Luft! Die ganze Wienerstadt!
(*Auf den Baron zu, mit geballter Faust.*)
Oh, Er Filou! Mir wird nicht gut! Ein' Sessel!
(*Bediente springen hinzu, fangen ihn auf. Zwei desgleichen haben vorher ihre Stange einem der Hinterstehenden zugeworfen. Sophie ist angstvoll um iln bemüht. Wirt springt gleichfalls hinzu. Sie nehmen ihn auf und tragen ihn ins Nebenzimmer. Mehrere Kellner den Weg weisend, die Türe öffnend voran. Baron wird diesen Augenblick seiner Perücke ansichtig, die wie durch Zauberhand wieder zum Vorschein gekommen ist, stürzt darauflos, stülpt sie sich auf und gibt ihr vor dem Spiegel den richtigen Sitz. Mit dieser Veränderung gewinnt er seine Haltung so ziemlich wieder, begnügt sich aber, Annina und den Kindern, deren Rücken zu kehren. Hinte, Herrn von Faninal und s einer Begleigtung hat sich die Türe links geschlossen. Wirt und Kellner kommen bald darauf leise wieder heraus, holen Medikamente, Karaffen mit Wasser und anderes, das in die Tür getragen und von Sophie in der Türspalte übernommen wird.*)

**BARON:** (*nunmehr mit dem alten Selbstgefühl auf den Kommissarius zu*): Sind desto ehr im Klaren. Ich zahl', ich geh'!
(*Zu Octavian.*)
Ich führ' Sie jetzt nach Haus.

**KOMMISSARIUS:** Da irrt Er sich. Mit Ihm jetzt weiter im Verhör!
(*Auf den Wink des Kommissarius entfernen die beiden Wächter alle übrigen Personen aus dem Zimmer, nur Annina mit den Kindern bleibt an der linken Wand stehen.*)

**OCTAVIAN:** Kerr Kommissar, i geb' was zu Protokoll, Aber der Herr Baron darf nicht zuhörn dabei.
(*Auf den Wink des Kommissarius drängen die beiden Wächter den Baron nach vorne rechts. Octavian scheint dem Kommissarius*

comes in in hat and cloak. All make room for her. The Baron tries to conceal his bald pate from Sophia with his hat, while Sophia goes towards her father.*)

**CHORUS:** The bride! Oh, what a sad disgrace!

**MUFFLED VOICES FROM ALL SIDES:** A disgrace! A disgrace! For him and all his race!

**FANINAL:** From the cellar! From the air! I dare not show my face—
(*Going towards the Baron with clenched fist.*)
The villain! I am not well! An armchair!
(*His servants run forward and save him from falling. Two of them had already given their poles to the onlookers. Sophia hurries to his aid. They lift him up and carry him to the next room. Several waiters precede them, showing the way and opening the door. At this moment the Baron is aware of his wig, which has reappeared, as if by magic, darts towards it, clasps it on his pate and, going to a mirror, sets it straight. With this change he regains some of his lost self-confidence, but satisfies himself with turning his back on Annina and the Children, whose presence, after all, he regards with uneasiness.*)
(*The door to the left is closed behind Herr von Faninal and his following. The waiters and the Landlord after a time emerge quietly and go to fetch drugs, bottles with water and other things, which they carry as far as the door and hand to Sophia through the opening.*)

**BARON:** (*going towards the Commissary with self-confidence now fully restored*): This clears our path but the sooner. I pay, and go.
(*To Octavian.*)
And you I'll now take home.

**COMMISSARY:** Pray, not so fast. A few more questions before you go—
(*At a sign from the Commissary, the Constables remove from the room everybody except Annina and the Children, who remain standing by the wall to the left.*)

**OCTAVIAN:** (*speaking*): I have something that I would say to the Officer Gentleman, but the Baron must not listen.
(*At a sign from the Commissary the two Constables shepherd the Baron to the front of the stage to*

**DIE KINDER:** (*automatisch*): Papa! Papa! Papa!

**FANINAL:** (*fährt zurück*): Was ist denn das?

*etwas zu melden, was diesen sehr überrascht.)*

BARON: *(zu den Wächtern, familiär, halblaut, auf Annina hindeutend)*: Kenn' nicht das Weibsbild dort, auf Ehr'.
War grad' beim Essen!
Hab' keine Ahnung, was sie will.
Hätt' sonst nicht selber um die Polizei—
*(Der Kommissarius begleitet Octavian bis an den Alkoven. Octavian verschwindet hinter dem Vorhang. Der Kommissarius scheint sich zu amüsieren und ist den Spalten des Vorhangs ungenierterweise nahe.)*
*(bemerkt die Heiterkeit des Kommissarius, plötzlich sehr aufgeregt über den unerklärlichen Vorfall)*: Was g'schieht denn dort?
Is wohl nich möglich das?
Der Lackl!
Das heisst Ihr Sittenpolizei?
Ist eine Jungfer!
*(Er ist schwer zu halten.)*
Steht unter meiner Protektion!
Beschwer' mich!
Hab' da ein Wörtel drein zu reden!
*(Reisst sich los, will gegen das Bett hin. Sie fangen und halten ihn wieder. Aus dem Alkoven erscheinen Stück für Stück die Kleider der Mariandel. Der Kommissarius macht ein Bündel daraus.)*
*(immer aufgeregt, ringt, seine beiden Wächter los zu werden)*: Muss jetzt partout zu ihr!
*(Sie halten ihn mühsam, während Octavians Kopf aus einer Spalte des Vorhangs hervorsieht.)*

WIRT: *(hereinstürmend)*: Ihre hochfürstliche Gnaden, die Frau Fürstin Feldmarschallin!
*(Kellner herein, reissen die Türe auf. Zuerst werden einige Menschen in der Marschallin Livree sichtbar, sie rangieren sich, Marschallin tritt ein, der kleine Neger trägt ihre Schleppe.)*

BARON: *(hat sich von den Wächtern losgerissen, wischt sich den Schweiss von der Stirne, eilt auf die Marschallin zu)*: Bin glücklich über Massen, hab' die Gnad' kaum meritiert,
Schätz' Dero Gegenwart hier als ein Freundstück ohnegleichen.

OCTAVIAN: *(streckt den Kopf zwischen dem Vorhang hervor)*: Marie Theres', wie kommt Sie her?
*(Marschallin regungslos, antwortet nicht, sieht sich fragend um.)*

*the right. Octavian says something to the Commissary which seems to surprise him very much. The Commissary accompanies him to the recess and he disappears behind the curtain.)*

BARON: *(familiarly to the Constables, pointing to Annina)*: I never did see that slut till now.
We were at supper—
I have no inkling what she seeks.
*(The Commissary seems to be vastly entertained and unconcernedly approaches the open curtain.)*
Else would I surely not have asked your aid.
*(Suddenly much perturbed at the inexplicable proceeding.)*
What is happening there?
Can I believe my eyes?
The scoundrel!
Look!
He too, who dared to threaten me!
It is an outrage, yes, an outrage!
*(They have difficulty in holding him back.)*
She's under my protection. I warn you,
You'll smart for this behavior.
*(He makes himself free and goes towards the recess; they pursue him and seize him again. From the recess are thrown Mariandel's clothes, piece by piece. The Commissary makes a bundle of them. The Baron struggles with his captors. They hold him with difficulty, while Octavian puts his head out of the opening of the curtains.)*

LANDLORD: *(rushes in)*: The Princess, her Highness the Princess of Werdenberg.
*(First some men in the Princess's livery appear, then the Baron's Body Servant. They form a line. Then the Princess enters, the Little Black Boy carrying her train. The Baron has shaken off his captors, mops his forehead and hurries towards the Princess.)*

BARON: Your Highness overwhelms me.
This is more than I deserve.
Your presence, here, your Highness, does betoken truest friendship.

OCTAVIAN: *(his head appearing behind the curtain)*: Marie Theres'!
How have you come here?
*(The Princess stands motionless and does not answer. She looks round with a questioning glance.)*

KOMMISSARIUS: *(auf die Fürstin zu, in dienstlicher Haltung)*: Fürstliche Gnaden, melde mich gehorsamst
Als vorstädtischer Unterkommissarius.

BARON: *(gleichzeitig)*: Er sieht, Herr Kommissar, die Durchlaucht haben selber sich bemüht.
Ich denk', Er weiss, woran Er ist.
*(Leiblakai auf den Baron zu, stolz und selbstzufrieden. Baron winkt ihn als Zeichen seiner Zufriedenheit.)*

MARSCHALLIN: *(zum Kommissar, ohne den Baron zu beachten)*: Er kennt mich?
Kenn' ich Ihn nicht auch?
Mir scheint beinah'.

KOMMISSARIUS: Sehr wohl.

MARSCHALLIN: Dem Herrn Feldmarschall seine brave Ordonanz gewest?

KOMMISSARIUS: Fürstliche Gnaden, zu Befehl!
*(Octavian steckt abermals den Kopf zwischen den Vorhängen hervor.)*

BARON: *(winkt ihm heftig, zu verschwinden, ist zugleich ängstlich bemüht, dass die Marschallin nichts merkte. Halblaut)*: Bleib' Sie. zum Sakra, hinten dort!
*(Dann hört er, wie sich Schritte der Tür links vorne nähern; stürzt hin, stellt sich mit dem Rücken gegen die Türe, durch verbindliche Gebärden gegen die Marschallin bestrebt, seinem Gebaren den Schein völliger Unbefangenheit zu geben.)*
*(Marschallin kommt gegen links, mit zuwartender Miene den Baron anblickend).*

OCTAVIAN: *(in Männerkleidung tritt zwischen den Vorhängen hervor, sobald der Baron ihm den Rücken kehrt; halblaut)*: War anders abgemacht!
Marie Theres', ich wunder' mich!
*(Marschallin als hörte sie ihn nicht, hat fortwährend den verbindlich erwartungsvollen Blick auf den Baron gerichtet, der in äusserst Verlegenheit zwischen der Tür und der Marschallin seine merksamkeit teilt. Die Tür links wird mit Kraft geöffung dass der Baron der vergebens versucht hatte, sich dagegen stemmen, wütend zurückzutreten genötigt ist. Zwei Faninal Diener lassen jetzt Sophie eintreten).*

*(The Body Servant, proud and pleased with himself, goes towards the Baron. The Baron gives him signs of his satisfaction.)*

COMMISSARY: *(going towards the Princess, at attention)*: May it please your Highness, my most humble duty.
The Commissary of this district.

BARON: Her Highness, as you see, has deigned to come in person to my aid.
And now perhaps you'll know the man I am.

PRINCESS: You know me?
Do I know you too?
I almost think—

COMMISSARY: Right well.

PRINCESS: Were you not long ago the Prince Field Marshal's orderly?

COMMISSARY: It is so, your highness, to command.
*(Octavian again puts his head through the curtains.)*

BARON: *(makes a sign to Octavian to vanish, and is at the same time in great anxiety lest the Princess should observe him.)* Plague on you, stay there!
Hide yourself.
*(The Baron hears steps approaching the door on the left to the front, rushes there and places himself with his back to the door, trying by means of gestures in the direction of the Princess to appear quite at his ease. The Princess steps towards the left and looks at the Baron expectantly. Octavian comes from behind the curtain, in male clothes, as soon as the Baron has turned his back.)*

OCTAVIAN: It was not this we hoped!
Marie Theres', I wonder much!
*(The Princess, as though not hearing Octavian, fixes a courteous expectant look on the Baron, who in the utmost perplexity is dividing his attention between the Princess and the door. The door on the left is opened violently, so that the Baron, who has been leaning against it in a vain attempt to keep it closed, is pushed forward. Two of Faninal's servants now stand aside to let Sophia pass.)*

# Act III

SOPHIE: (*ohne die Marschallin zu sehen, die ihr durch den Baron verdeckt ist*): Hab' ihm von mei'm Herrn Vater zu vermelden!

BARON: (*ihr ins Wort fallend, halblaut*): Is jetzo nicht die Zeit, Kreuzelement! Kann Sie nicht warten, bis dass man Ihr rufen wird? Meint Sie, dass ich Sie hier im Beisl präsentieren werd'?

OCTAVIAN: (*ist leise hervorgetreten, zur Marschallin, halblaut*): Das ist die Fräulein—die—um derentwillen—

MARSCHALLIN: (*über die Schulter zu Octavian halblaut*): Find' Ihn ein bissl empressiert, Rofrano. Kamm mir wohl denken, wer sie ist. Find' sie scharmant. (*Octavian schlüpft zwischen die Vorhänge zurück.*)

SOPHIE: (*den Rücken gegen die Türe, so scharf, dass der Baron unwillkürlich einen Schritt zurückweicht*): Er wird mich keinem Menschen auf der Welt nicht präsentieren, Dieweilen ich mit Ihm auch nicht so viel zu schaffen hab. (*Die Marschallin spricht leise mit dem Kommissar.*) Und mein Herr Vater lasst Ihm sagen: wenn Er alsoweit Die Freichheit sollte treiben, dass man seine Nasen nur Erblicken tät' auf hundert Schritt von unserm Stadtpalais, So hätt' Er sich die bösen Folgen selber zuzuschreiben, Das ist, was mein Herr Vater Ihm vermelden lässt.

BARON: (*zornig*): Corpo di bacco! Was ist das für eine ungezogene Sprach'!

SOPHIE: Die Ihm gebührt.

BARON: (*ausser sich, will an ihr vorbei, zur Tür hinein*): He, Faninal, ich muss—

SOPHIE: Er untersteh' sich nicht! (*Die zwei Faninalschen Diener treten hervor, halten ihn auf, schieben ihn zurück. Sophie Tritt in die Tür, die sich hinter ihr schliesst.*)

BARON: (*gegen die Tür brüllend*): Bin willes, alles Vorgefall'ne Vergeben und vergessen sein zu lassen!

MARSCHALLIN: (*ist von rückwärts an den Baron herangetreten und klopft ihm auf die Schulter*): Lass' Er nur gut sein und verschwind' Er auf eins zwei!

SOPHIA: (*without seeing the Princess, who is hidden from her by the Baron*): I have to bring you a message from my father ...

BARON: (*interrupting her, in an undertone*): It is most untimely now, can you not wait! Can you not wait until the proper time has come? Think you this pothouse here is fitting for an introduction?

OCTAVIAN: (*who now comes quietly from the recess, aside to the Princess*): That is the lady—who—to whom you sent me—

PRINCESS: (*aside to Octavian, over her shoulder*): Surely there's here a little haste, Rofrano. It is easy guessing who she is. Your taste is good. (*Octavian slips back behind the curtain.*)

SOPHIA: (*her back to the door, so angrily that the Baron instinctively starts back a step*): You will not here, nor anywhere, to anyone present me, Know that from henceforth I have done with you once and for all. (*The Princess converses in a low voice with the Commissary.*) And this my father bids me tell you: should you ever So far carry your presumption, as to dare to let your face Be seen within a hundred yards of where our mansion is, You'll have yourself alone to thank for all that may befall you. That is the message that my father sends to you.

BARON: (*very angrily*): Corpo di Bacco! What impertinence is this, what ill-bred language?

SOPHIA: It is your desert.

BARON: (*beside himself, tries to pass her and reach the door*): Ha, Faninal, I must—

SOPHIA: Stand back, Sir! Do not dare! (*The two footmen of Faninal come forward, bar his passage and push him back. Sophia passes out. The door is closed behind her.*)

BARON: (*shouting against the door*): I am content that all that's happened Shall henceforth be forgiven and forgotten. (*The Princess approaches the Baron from behind and taps him on the shoulder.*)

PRINCESS: Leave well alone, and before I count to three, withdraw! (*The Baron turns round and stares at her.*)

BARON: (*dreht sich um, starrt sie an*): Wieso denn?

MARSCHALLIN: (*munter, überlegen*): Wahr' Er sein Dignité und fahr' Er ab!

BARON: (*sprachlos*): Ich? Was?

MARSCHALLIN: Mach Er bonne mine a mauvais jeu: So bleibt Er quasi doch noch eine Standsperson. (*Baron starrt sie stumm an*). (*Sophie tritt leise wieder heraus. Ihre Augen suchen Octavian.*)

MARSCHALLIN: (*zum Kommissar, der hinten rechts steht, desgleichen seine Wächter*): Er sieht, Herr Kommissar: das Ganze war halt eine Farce und weiter nichts.

KOMMISSARIUS: Genügt mir! Retirier' mich ganz gehorsamst. (*Tritt ab, die beiden Wächter hinter ihm.*)

SOPHIE: (*vor sich, erschrocken*): Das Ganze war halt eine Farce und weiter nichts (*Die Blicke der beiden Frauen begegnen sich; Sophie macht der Marschallin einen verlegnen Knicks.*)

BARON: (*zwischen Sophie und der Marschallin stehend*): Bin gar nicht willens!

MARSCHALLIN: (*ungeduldig, stampft auf*): Mon Cousin, bedeut' Er Ihm! (*Kehrt dem Baron den Rücken.*)

OCTAVIAN: (*geht von rückwärts auf den Baron zu, sehr männlich*): Möcht Ihn sehr bitten!

BARON: (*fährt herum*): Wer? Was?

MARSCHALLIN: (*von rechts, wo sie nun steht*): Sein' Gnaden, der Herr Graf Rofrano, wer denn sonst?

BARON: (*nachdem er sich Octavians Gesicht scharf und in der Nähe betrachtet, mit Resignation*): Is schon a so! (*Vor sich.*) Hab' g'nug von dem Gesicht, Sind doch nicht meine Augen schuld. Is schon ein Mandl. (*Octavian steht frech und hochmütig da.*)

MARSCHALLIN: (*einen Schritt näher tretend*): Ist eine wienerische Maskerad' und weiter nichts.

SOPHIE: (*halb traurig, halb höhnisch für sich*): Ist eine wienerische Maskerad' und weiter nichts.

BARON: What mean you?

PRINCESS: (*gaily, sure of victory*): Think of your dignity and take your leave!

BARON: (*speechless*): I? How?

PRINCESS: If you would still preserve your name As gentleman, make virtue of necessity (*The Baron stares at her in speechless amazement. Sophia comes quietly out of the other room. Her eyes seek Octavian.*)

PRINCESS: (*to the Commissary, who is standing at the back on the right with the two Constables*): And now, it is all quite clear; It all has been just a diversion—nothing more.

COMMISSARY: Enough! I humbly beg leave to withdraw. (*Exit, followed by the two Constables.*)

SOPHIA: (*aside, afraid*): The whole has been just a diversion—nothing more. (*The eyes of the two women meet; Sophia makes an embarrassed curtsey.*)

BARON: (*standing between Sophia and the Princess*): Not so, your Highness!

PRINCESS: (*impatiently, stamping her foot*): Mon cousin, explain to him! (*Turns her back on the Baron.*)

OCTAVIAN: (*approaches the Baron from behind. Very mannish*): Will you permit me?

BARON: (*turns on him sharply*): Who? What?

PRINCESS: (*on the right, where she now takes up her position*): The Count Rofrano, my dear kinsman, who but he?

BARON: (*resignedly, after careful scrutiny of Octavian's face*): I thought as much! (*To himself.*) That face, I'm sick of it, My eyes did not mislead me then. For sure, 'twas he. (*Octavian stands there, arrogant and defiant.*)

PRINCESS: (*approaching a step nearer*): A masquerade, as we in Vienna practise,—nothing more.

SOPHIA: (*half sadly, half ironically to herself*): A masquerade, as we in Vienna practise,—nothing more.

BARON: (*sehr vor den Kopf geschlagen*): Aha!
(*Für sich.*)
Spiel'n alle unter einem Leder gegen meiner!

MARSCHALLIN: (*von oben herab*): Ich hätt' Ihm nicht gewunschen,
Dass Er mein Mariandl in der Wirklichkeit mir hätte debauchiert!
(*Baron wie oben, vor sich hin sinnierend*).

MARSCHALLIN: (*wie oben und ohne Octavian anzusehen*): Hab' jetzt einen montierten Kopf gegen die Männer—
so ganz im allgemeinen!

BARON: (*allmählich der Situation beikommend*): Kreuzelement!
Komm' aus dem Staunen nicht heraus!
Der Feldmarschall—Octavian—Mariandl—die Marschallin—Octavian.
(*Mit einem ausgiebigen Blick, der von Marschallin zu Octavian, von Octavian wieder zurück zur Marschallin wandert.*)
Weiss bereits nicht, was ich von diesem ganzen qui-pro-quo mir denken soll!

MARSCHALLIN: (*mit einem langen Blick, dann mit grosser Sicherheit*): Er ist, mein' ich, ein Kavalier?
Da wird Er sich halt gar nichts denken.
Das ist's, was ich von Ihm erwart'.
(*Pause.*)

BARON: (*mit Verneigung und weltmännisch*): Bin von so viel Finesse scharmiert, kann gar nicht sagen wie.
Ein Lerchenauer war noch nie kein Spielverderber nicht.
(*Einen Schritt an sie herantretend.*)
Find' deliziös das ganze qui-pro-quo,
bedarf aber dafür nunmehro Ihrer Protektion.
Bin willens, alles Vorgefallene vergeben und vergessen sein zu lassen.
(*Pause.*)
Eh bien, darf ich den Faninal—
(*Er macht Miene, an die Türe links zu gehen.*)

MARSCHALLIN: Er darf—Er darf in aller Still' sich retirieren.
(*Baron aus allen Himmeln gefallen*).

MARSCHALLIN: Versteht Er nicht, wenn eine Sach' ein End' hat?
Die ganze Brautschaft und Affär' und alles sonst.
Was drum und dran hängt,
(*sehr bestimmt*)
Ist mit dieser Stund' vorbei.

SOPHIE: (*sehr betreten, für sich*): Was drum und dran hängt, ist mit dieser Stund vorbei!

BARON: (*greatly amazed*): Aha!
(*To himself.*)
I see now they are all conspiring to befool me!

PRINCESS: (*haughtily*): It is well for you it was not
Really my Mariandel whom you villainous persuasions have misled!
(*Baron as before deep in thought.*)

PRINCESS: (*as before and without looking at Octavian*): I feel just now a bitter grudge, a deep resentment
Against all men in general!

BARON: (*gradually realizing the situation*): God bless my soul!
I'm in a maze without a clue!
(*With a comprehensive glance which wanders from the Princess to Octavian and from Octavian back to the Princess.*)
In all this crazy comedy I'm at a loss to know
What I should think.

PRINCESS: (*looking at him fixedly, then emphatically*): It best befits a gentleman in such case to refrain from thinking.
That is what I expect of you.

BARON: (*with a bow and the manner of a man of the world*):
Sure, sentiments so exquisite with admiration fill me quite.
And none could ever say of any Lerchenau that he would spoil good sport.
(*Approaching the Princess.*)
I find this whole diversion vastly droll,
But in return I need your Highness's help and interest.
I am content to let these incidents
And all that's passed from henceforth be forgotten.
(*Pause.*)
Eh bien, may I tell Faninal—
(*Approaching the door to the left.*)

PRINCESS: You may—you may say nothing, and so leave us.
(*The Baron is thunderstruck with surprise.*)

PRINCESS: Do you not know when you can go no further?
Your great alliance and whatever it means both now
And in the future
(*Emphatically.*)
From this hour you must renounce.

SOPHIA: (*in great astonishment, aside*): His great alliance from this hour he must renounce.

BARON: (*für sich, empört, halblaut*): Mit dieser Stund' vorbei!
Mit dieser Stund' vorbei

MARSCHALLIN: (*scheint sich nach einem Stuhl umzusehen, Octavian springt hin, gibt ihr einen Stuhl. Marschallin setzt sich rechts, mit Bedeutung für sich*): Ist halt vorbei.

SOPHIE: (*links vor sich, blass*): Ist halt vorbei!
(*Baron findet sich durchaus nicht in diese wendung, rollt verleges und aufgebracht die Augen. In diesem Augenblick kommt der Mann aus der Falltür hervor. Von links tritt Valzacchi ein, die Verdächtigen in bescheidener Haltung hinter ihm. Annina nimm Witwenhaube und Schleier ab, wischt sich die Schminke weg und zeigt ihr gewöhnliches Gesicht. Dies alles zu immer gesteigertem Staunen des Barons. Der Wirt, eine lange Rechnung in der Hand, tritt zur Mitteltüre herein, hinter ihm Kellner, Musikanten Hausknechte, Kutshcer.*)

BARON: (*wie er sie alle erblickt, gibt er sein Spiel verloren. Ruft schnell entschlossen*): Leupold, wir gehn!
(*Macht der Marschallin ein tiefes, aber zorniges Kompliment. Keiblakai ergreift einen Leuchter vom Tisch und will seinem Herrn voran.*)

ANNINA: (*stellt sich frech dem Baron in den Weg*): "Ich hab' halt schon einmal ein Lerchanauisch Glück."
(*Auf die Rechnung des Wirtes deutend.*)
"Komm' Sie nach Tisch, geb' Ihr die Antwort nachher schriftlich!"
(*Die Kinder kommen dem Baron unter die Füsse. Er schlägt mit dem Hut unter sie.*)

DIE KINDER: Papa! Papa! Papa!

KELLNER: (*sich zuerst an den Baron drängend*): Entschuld'gen Euer Gnaden!
Uns gehen die Kerzen an!

WIRT: (*sich mit der Rechnung vordrängend*): Entschuld'gen Euer Gnaden!

ANNINA: (*vor dem Baron her nach rückwärts tanzend*): "Ich hab' halt schon einmal ein Lerchenauisch Glück!"

VALZACCHI: (*höhnisch*): "Ich hab' halt schon einmal ein Lerchenauisch Glück!"

DIE MUSIKANTEN: (*sich dem Baron in dem Weg stellend*): Tafelmusik über zwei Stunden!
(*Leiblakai bahnt sich den Weg gegen die Tür hin*).
(*Baron will hinter ihm durch*).

BARON: (*aside, indignantly, softly*); From now I must renounce! From now I must renounce!

PRINCESS: (*seems to look for a chair. Octavian hurries forward and gives her one. The Princess takes a seat to the right and says significantly, aside*): I must renounce!

SOPHIA: (*on the left, pale*): He must renounce.
(*The Baron finds it difficult to realize the new developments and rolls his eyes in anger and perplexity. In this moment the man emerges from the trap-door. Valzacchi enters from the left, his suspicious accomplices following him. Annina takes off her widow's cap and veil, wipes off the paint and shows her natural face. The Baron watches this in growing astonishment. The Landlord carrying a long bill in his hand enters by the center door, followed by the Waiters, Musicians, Boots and Coachmen.*)

BARON: (*when he sees this knows that his game is lost, calls out quickly and decidedly*): Leopold, we go!
(*Makes a deep but angry bow to the Princess. His Body Servant takes a candle from the table and precedes his master.*)

ANNINA: (*insolently bars the Baron's passage*): "For sure I have the luck of all the Lerchenaus."
(*Pointing to the Landlord with his bill.*)
"Come when I've dined, I'll give the answer then in writing."
(*The Children run between the Baron's legs. He hits out at them with his hat.*)

CHILDREN: Papa! Papa! Papa!

WAITERS: (*pressing round the Baron*): May it please you, your Lordship,
Item, the candlelight!

LANDLORD: (*pressing forward with his bill*): May it please you your Lordship.

ANNINA: (*dancing backwards in front of the Baron*): "I surely have the luck of all the Lerchenaus!"

VALZACCHI: (*ironically*): "I surely have the luck of all the Luchenaus!"

MUSICIANS: (*coming in front of the Baron*): Item, music two hours and over.
(*The Body Servant forces a passage to the door. The Baron tries to follow him.*)

**DIE KUTSCHER:** (*auf den Baron eindringend*): Für die Fuhr', für die Fuhr', Rösser g'schund'n ham ma gnua!

**HAUSKNECHT:** (*den Baron grob anrempelnd*): Sö fürs Aufsperrn, Sö, Herr Baron!

**WIRT:** (*immer die Rechnung präsentierend*): Entschuld'gen Euer Gnaden.

**KELLNER:** Zwei Schock Kerzen, uns gehen die Kerzen an.

**BARON:** (*im Gedränge*): Platz da, zurück da, Kreuzmillion.

**DIE KINDER:** Papa! Papa! Papa! (*Alle schreien wild durcheinander*). (*Baron drängt sich mit Macht durch gegen die Ausgangstür, alle dicht um ihn in einem Knäuel*).

**HAUSKNECHT:** Führa g'fahr'n, aussa g'ruckt, Sö. Herr Baron! (*Alle sind schon in der Tür, dem Lakai wird der Armleuchter entwunden*). (*Baron stürzt ab*). (*Alle stürmen ihm nach, der Lärm verhallt. Die zwei Faninalschen Diener sind indessen links abgetreten. Es bleiben allein zurück: Sophie, die Marschallin und Octavian*).

**SOPHIE:** (*links stehend, blass*): Mein Gott, es war nicht mehr als eine Farce. Mein Gott, mein Gott! Wie Er bei ihr steht und ich bin die leere Luft für Ihn.

**OCTAVIAN:** (*hinter dem Stuhl der Marschallin verlegen*): War anders abgemacht, Marie Theres', ich wunder' mich. (*In höchster Verlegenheit*.) Befiehlt Sie, dass ich—soll ich nicht—die Jungfer—der Vater—

**MARSCHALLIN:** Geh' Er doch schnell und tu' Er, was sein Herz Ihm sagt.

**SOPHIE:** (*verzweifelt*): Die leere Luft. O mein Gott, o mein Gott!

**OCTAVIAN:** Theres', ich weiss gar nicht—

**MARSCHALLIN:** Geh' Er und mach' Er seinen Hof.

**OCTAVIAN:** Ich schwör Ihr—

**MARSCHALLIN:** Lass Er's gut sein.

**OCTAVIAN:** Ich begreif' nicht, was Sie hat.

**MARSCHALLIN:** (*lacht zornig*): Er ist ein rechtes Mannsbild, geh' Er hin.

**OCTAVIAN:** Was Sie befiehlt. (*Geht hinüber*.) (*Sofphie wortlos*). (*Octavian bei ihr*): Eh bien, hat Sie

**COACHMEN:** (*pressing round the Baron*): Coach hire, coach hire! Our poor horses whipped to death!

**BOOTS:** (*insolently shouting at the Baron*): For opening the doors, your Lordship!

**LANDLORD:** (*still presenting his bill*): May it please you, your Lordship.

**WAITERS:** Two score candles, item, the candlelight!

**BARON:** (*in the middle of the crowd*): Make room, make room, deuce take you all!

**CHILDREN:** Papa! Papa! Papa! (*The Baron struggles violently towards the door, all follow him in confusion*.)

**BOOTS:** I am the boots, that opened the doors, may it please your Lordship! (*The whole crowd is in the doorway, someone wrests the candlestick from the Body Servant. The Baron rushes off. All tear after him. The noise grows fainter. Faninal's two Footmen have in the meanwhile gone through the door on the left. Sophia, Princess and Octavian are left alone*.)

**SOPHIA:** (*standing on left, pale*): The whole affair has been a mere diversion And nothing more— How he leans over her, and I am but as empty air for him.

**OCTAVIAN:** (*behind the Princess's chair, embarrassed*): It was not thus we hoped, Marie Theres'—I stand amazed— (*In extreme perplexity*.) Perchance you wish it.... Shall I not.... The lady.... Her father...

**PRINCESS:** Go quickly, go, and do all that your heart commands.

**SOPHIA:** (*in despair*): But empty air! O help me, gracious Heaven!

**OCTAVIAN:** Theres', I have no words!

**PRINCESS:** Woo her and win her love—

**OCTAVIAN:** I wonder—

**PRINCESS:** It is no matter—

**OCTAVIAN:** On my honor, what you mean—

**PRINCESS:** (*laughs angrily*): How like the rest! How manlike! Go to her!

**OCTAVIAN:** As you command! (*Crosses to Sophia, who stands silent*.) Eh bien, have you no kindly word

kein freundlich Wort für mich? Nicht einen Blick, nicht einen lieben Gruss?

**SOPHIE:** (*stockend*); War mir von Euer Gnaden Freundschaft und Behilflichkeit Wahrhaftig einer andern Freud' gewärtig.

**OCTAVIAN:** (*lebhaft*): Wie—freut Sie sich denn nicht?

**SOPHIE:** (*unmutig*): Hab' wirklich keinen Anlass nicht.

**OCTAVIAN:** Hat man Ihr nicht den Bräutigam vom Hals geschafft?

**SOPHIE:** Wär' all's recht schön, wenn's anders abgegangen wär'. Schäm mich in Grund und Boden. Versteh' sehr wohl, Mit was für einen Blick Ihre fürstliche Gnaden mich betracht'.

**OCTAVIAN:** Ich schwör Ihr, meiner Seel' und Seligkeit.

**SOPHIE:** Lass Er mich gehn.

**OCTAVIAN:** Ich lass Sie nicht. (*Fasst ihre Hand*.)

**SOPHIE:** Der Vater braucht mich drin.

**OCTAVIAN:** Ich brauch' Sie nötiger.

**SOPHIE:** Das sagt sich leicht.

**OCTAVIAN:** Ich hab' Sie übermässig lieb.

**SOPHIE:** Das ist nicht wahr, Er hat mich nicht so lieb, als wie Er spricht. Vergess' Er mich!

**OCTAVIAN:** Ist mir um Sie und nur um Sie.

**SOPHIE:** Vergess' Er mich!

**OCTAVIAN:** (*heftig*): Mag alles drunter oder drüber gehn!

**SOPHIE:** (*leidenschaftlich*): Vergess' Er mich!

**OCTAVIAN:** Hab' keinen andern Gedanken nicht. Seh' alleweil Ihr lieb Gesicht. (*Fasst mit beiden Händen ihre Beiden*.)

**SOPHIE:** (*schwach abwehrend*): Vergess' Er mich!

**MARSCHALLIN:** (*ist indessen aufgestanden, bezwingt sich aber und setzt sich wieder, vor sich, getragen, gleichzeitig mit Octavian und Sophie*): Heut oder morgen oder den übernächsten Tag. Hab' ich mir's denn nicht vorgesagt? Das alles kommt halt über jede Frau. Hab' ich's den nicht gewusst? Hab' ich nicht ein Gelübde tan, Dass ich's mit einem gans gefassten Herzen Ertragen werd' ...

for me? No smile, no look, no greeting, not one sign?

**SOPHIA:** I had hoped, truly, that your Lordship would quite otherwise Befriend me, and would bring me help and comfort—

**OCTAVIAN:** What, are you then not glad?

**SOPHIA:** (*angrily*): And tell me, pray, what cause I have?

**OCTAVIAN:** Is it not cause enough that you are rid of him?

**SOPHIA:** Had it been done quite otherwise, it would have been well. I am angered and shamed—I feel the smart Of every glance of scorn and pity that her Highness casts at me.

**OCTAVIAN:** You wrong her, on my soul, by such a thought!

**SOPHIA:** Leave me in peace!

**OCTAVIAN:** That cannot be! (*Seizes her hand*.)

**SOPHIA:** My father needs my help—

**OCTAVIAN:** My need is greater far—

**SOPHIA:** It is lightly said—

**OCTAVIAN:** I love you with a mighty love—

**SOPHIA:** No—it is not so Your love is not as great as you declare— Forget me quite—

**OCTAVIAN:** You are my all—you are my all.

**SOPHIA:** Forget me quite—

**OCTAVIAN:** (*vehemently*): Beside you, the whole world is nothing worth!

**SOPHIA:** (*passionately*): Forget me quite—

**OCTAVIAN:** My thoughts are ever of you alone! Nothing but you I see. (*Seizes both her hands in his*.)

**SOPHIA:** (*defending herself weakly*): Forget me quite—

**PRINCESS:** "Now or tomorrow: if not tomorrow, very soon"— Did I not say the words myself? There is no woman can escape her fate! Did I not know the truth? Did I not swear by all the Saints That I with chastened heart and tranquil spirit Would bear the blow . . . "Now or tomorrow: if not tomorrow, very soon"— (*Wipes her eyes and rises*.)

**SOPHIE:** (*leise*): Die Fürstin da!
Sie ruft Ihn hin!
So geh' Er doch.
(*Octavian ist ein paar Schritte gegen die Marschallin hingegangen, steht jetzt zwischen beiden, verlegen. Pause*).
(*Sophie in der Tür, unschlüssig, ob sie gehen oder bleiben soll*).
(*Octavian in der Mitte, dreht den Kopf von einer zur andern*).
(*Marschallin sieht seine Verlegenheit; ein trauriges Lächeln huscht über ihr Gesicht*).

**SOPHIE:** (*an der Tür*): Ich muss hinein und fragen, wie's dem Vater geht.

**OCTAVIAN:** Ich muss jetzt was reden, und mir verschlagt's die Red'.

**MARSCHALLIN:** Der Bub', wie er velegen da in der Mitten steht.

**OCTAVIAN:** (*zu Sophie*): Bleib' Sie um alles hier.
(*Zur Marschallin.*)
Wie, hat Sie was gesagt?
(*Marschallin geht, ohne Octavian zu beachten hinüber zu Sophie*).
(*Octavian tritt einen Schritt zurück*).
(*Marschallin steht vor Sophie, sieht sie prüfend, aber gütig an*).
(*Sophie in Verlegenheit, knickst*).

**MARSCHALLIN:** So schnell hat Sie ihn gar so lieb?

**SOPHIE:** (*sehr schnell*): Ich weiss nicht, was Euer Gnaden meinen mit der Frag'.

**MARSCHALLIN:** Ihr blass Gesicht gibt schon die rechte Antwort drauf.

**SOPHIE:** (*in grosser Schüchternheit und Verlegenheit, immer sehr schnell*): War gar kein Wunder, wenn ich blass bin, Euer Gnaden.
Hab' einen grossen Schreck erlebt mit dem Herrn Vater.
Gar nicht zu reden von gerechtem Emportement
gegen den skandalösen Herrn Baron.
Bin Euer Gnaden recht in Ewigkeit verpflichtet,
Dass mit Dero Hilf' und Aufsicht—

**MARSCHALLIN:** (*abwehrend*): Red' Sie nur nicht zu viel, Sie ist ja hübsch genug!
Und gegen den Herrn Papa sein Uebel weiss ich etwa eine Medizin.
Ich geh' jetzt da hinein zu ihm und lad' ihn ein.
Mit mir und Ihr und dem Herrn Grafen da
In meinem Wagen heimzufahren—meint Sie nicht—
Das ihn das rekreieren wird und all-

**SOPHIA:** (*softly*): Her Highness!
Look!
She calls to you!
Then go to her!
(*Octavian, after advancing a few steps towards the Princess, now stands undecided between the two.*)
(*Sophia in the doorway, hesitating whether to go or to remain.*)
(*Octavian, between them, turns his head from one to the other. The Princess notices his perplexity and a melancholy smile flits over her countenance.*)

**SOPHIA:** (*by the door*): I must go in and ask how my dear father does.

**OCTAVIAN:** Much fain would I tell her, but thought and language fail.

**PRINCESS:** The boy, look how he stands beside her there, perplexed and pale.

**OCTAVIAN:** (*to Sophia*): Stay here, by all you love.
(*To the Princess.*)
How? did you speak to me?
(*The Princess, paying no heed to Octavian, crosses to Sophia and looks at her, critically but kindly. Sophia, much embarrassed, makes a curtsey. Octavian retreats a step.*)

**PRINCESS:** So quickly did you learn to love him?

**SOPHIA:** (*very quickly*): Indeed, Madam, your question I can hardly understand.

**PRINCESS:** Your cheek so pale gives me the answer plain enough.

**SOPHIA:** (*very timid and embarrassed. Still very quickly*): It is small wonder too your Highness, if I am pale.
But I was sorely frightened by my dear father's sickness.
Did not that monster the Baron, too, give me just cause
For great offense by all that he has said and done?
And to your Highness I shall be most grateful always
Because your timely intervention—

**PRINCESS:** (*deprecatorily*): Waste not your words on me, your're pretty, that's enough!
And for your worthy father's humours, a most sovereign cure I think I know.
I'll go, say a word to him, and bid him come
With me and you and Count Octavian,
In my own coach, and bring him homeward—

bereits
ein wenig munter machen?

**SOPHIE:** Euer Gnaden sind die Güte selbst.

**MARSCHALLIN:** Und für die Blässe weiss vielleicht mein Vetter da die Medizin

**OCTAVIAN:** (*innig*) Marie Theres', wie gut Sie ist.
Marie Theres', ich weiss gar nicht.—

**MARSCHALLIN:** (*mit einem undefinier baren Ausdruck leise*): Ich weiss auch nix.
(*Ganz tonlos.*)
Gar nix.
(*Winkit ihm zurückzubleiben.*)

**OCTAVIAN:** (*unschlüssig, als wollte er ihr nach*): Marie Theres'!
(*Marschallin bleibt in der Tür stehen. Octavian steht ihr zunächst, Sophie weiter rechts.*)

**MARSCHALLIN:** (*vor sich, zugleich mit Octavian und Sophie*): Hab' mir's gelobt, Ihn lieb zu haben in der richtigen Weis'.
Dass ich selbst Sein Lieb' zu einer andern
noch lieb hab! Hab' mir freilich nicht gedacht,
dass es so bald mir auferlegt sollt' werden!
(*Seufzend.*)
Es sind die mehrenen Dinge auf der Welt,
So dass sie ein's nicht glauben tät'.
Wenn man sie möcht' erzählen hör'n.
Alleinig wer's erlebt, der glaubt daran und weiss nicht wie—
Da steht der Bub' und da steh' ich,
und mit dem fremden Mädel dort
Wird Er so glücklich sein, als wie halt Männer
Das Glücklichsein verstehen. In Gottes Namen.

**OCTAVIAN:** (*zugleich mit der Marschallin und Sophie, erst vor sich, dann Aug' in Aug' mit Sophie*): Es ist was kommen und ist was g'schehn,
Ich möcht' Sie fragen: darf's denn sein?
und grad' die Frag',
die spür ich, dass sie mir verboten ist.
Ich möcht' Sie fragen: warum zittert was in mir?—
Ist denn ein grosses Unrecht geschehn? Und grad' an Sie
Darf ich die Frag' nicht tun—und dann seh' ich dich an,
Sopie, und seh' nur dich und spür nur dich,
Sophie, und weiss von nichts als nur: dich hab' ich lieb.

Will that not,
Think you, soon to his wonted health restore him quite,
And cheer his drooping spirits?

**SOPHIA:** Such graciousness puts me to shame.

**PRINCESS:** And for your poor pale cheeks I think my cousin there will know the cure.

**OCTAVIAN:** (*with deep feeling*): Marie Theres', how good are you,
Marie Theres', I do not know—

**PRINCESS:** (*with an enigmatical expression, softly*): And I know nothing.
(*Quite toneless.*)
Nothing—
(*She makes a sign to him to remain.*)

**OCTAVIAN:** (*uncertain, as if he wished to follow her*): Marie Theres'!
(*The Princess remains standing in the door. Octavian stands next to her, Sophia further to the right.*)

**PRINCESS:** (*to herself*): I made a vow to love him rightly as a good woman should,
No, even to love the love he bore another
I promised! But in truth I did not think
That all so soon my vow would claim fulfilment.
(*sighing.*)
Full many a thing is ordained in this world,
Which we should scarce believe could be,
If we heard others tell of them ...
But soon he whom they wound believes in them, and knows not how—
There stands the boy, and here stand I, and with his love, new found this day,
He will have happiness,
After the manner of men, who think they know it all. It is done—so be it.

**OCTAVIAN:** (*together with the Princess and Octavian, first aside, then gazing into Sophia's eyes*): What has come over me, what has come to pass?
I fain would ask her. Can it be? And just that question,
I know I cannot ask of her.
I fain would ask her: oh, why trembles all my soul?—
Has bitter wrong, a sinful deed been done?
And just of her
I may not ask the question—and then on your dear face
I gaze, and see but you, and know but you,
Sophia, and I know only this:
You, you I love!

# Act III

**SOPHIE:** (*zugleich mit der Marschallin und Octavian, erst vor sich, dann Aug' in Aug' mit Octavian*): Mir ist wie in der Kirch'n, heilig ist mir und so bang. Und doch ist mir unheilig auch! Ich weiss nicht, wie mir ist. (*Ausdrucksvoll.*) Ich möcht mich niederknien dort vor der Frau und möcht ihr was antun, denn ich spür', sie gibt mir ihn und nimmt mir was von ihm zugleich. Weiss gar nicht, wie mir ist! Möcht' all's verstehen und möcht' auch nichts verstehen Möcht fragen und nicht fragen, wird mir heiss und kalt. Und spür nur dich und weiss nur eins: dich hab' ich lieb! (*Marschallin geht leise links hinein, die beiden bemerken es gar nicht. Octavian ist dicht an Sophie herangetreten, einen Augenblick später liegt sie in seinen Armen.*)

**OCTAVIAN:** (*zugleich mit Sophie*): Spür nur dich, spür nur dich allein und dass wir beieinander sein! Geht all's sonst wie ein Traum dahin vor meinem Sinn!

**SOPHIE:** (*zugleich mit Octavian*): Ist ein Traum, kann nicht wirklich sein, dass wir zwei beieinander sein, beieinand' für alle Zeit und Ewigkeit!

**OCTAVIAN:** (*ebenso*): War ein Haus wo, da warst du drein, und die Leut' schicken mich hinein, mich gradaus in die Seligkeit! die waren g'scheit!

**SOPHIE:** (*ebenso*): Kannst du lachen? Mir ist zur Stell' bang wie an der himmlischen Schwell'! Halt' mich, ein schwach Ding, wie ich bin, sink' dir dahin! (*Sie muss sich an ihn lehnen. In diesem Augenblick öffnen die Faninalschen Lakaien die Tür und treten herein, jeder mit einem Leuchter. Durch die Tür kommt*

---

**SOPHIA:** (*together with the Princess and Octavian first aside, then gazing into Octavian's eyes*): As one at worship, thoughts most holy fill my soul, And yet thoughts most unholy too posses me: I'm distraught. (*With much expression.*) At yonder lady's feet I fain would kneel, yet would I too Fain harm her, for I feel that she gives him to me And yet robs me of part of him. So strangely I'm perplexed! I would know all things, yet I fear to know the truth. Now longing to ask, all now fearing, hot am I and cold. And know but you and know but this one thing, that I love you! (*The Princess goes quickly into the room on the left; the two others do not notice her. Octavian has come quite near to Sophia. A moment later she is clasped in his arms.*)

**OCTAVIAN:** (*together with Sophia*): You alone I know, only you That you love me and I love you— All besides like a vision seems Of fleeting dreams.

**SOPHIA:** (*together with Octavian*): It is a dream of heaven: is it true, That you love me and I love you? Never in this world to part, One soul, one heart!

**OCTAVIAN:** (*louder*): In a great house was your bower, They sent me there in a happy hour Straight to you and paradise, Oh, they were wise.

**SOPHIA:** Dare you laugh so? I fear my fate, As a soul that trembles at Heaven's own gate! Clasp me closer, friendless and weak, I seek your arms. (*She leans on him for support. At this moment Faninal's footmen open the door and enter, each carrying a candlestick. Faninal,*

---

*Faninal, die Marschallin an der Hand führend. Die beiden jungen stehen einen Augenblick verwirrt, dann machen sie ein tiefes Kompliment, das Faninal und die Marschallin erwidern. Faninal tupft Sophie väterlich gutmütig auf die Wange.*)

**FANINAL:** Sind halt aso, die jungen Leut'!

**MARSCHALLIN:** Ja, ja. (*Faninal reicht der Marschallin die Hand, führt sie zur Mitteltür, die zugleich durch die Livree der Marschallin, darunter der kleine Neger, geöffnet wurde. Draussen hell, herinnen halbdunkel, da die beiden Diener mit den Leuchtern der Marschallin voraustreten. Octavian und Sophie, allein im halbdunklen Zimmer, wiederholen leise.*)

**OCTAVIAN:** (*zugleich mit Sophie*): Spür nur dich, spür nur dich allein und dass wir beieinander sein! Geht all's sonst wie ein Traum dahin vor meinem Sinn!

**SOPHIE:** (*zugleich mit Octavian*): Ist ein Traum, kann nicht wirklich sein, dass wir zwei beieinander sein, beieinand' für alle Zeit und Ewigkeit!

(*Sie sinkt an ihn hin, er küsst sie schnell. Ihr fällt, ohne dass sie es merkt, ihr Taschentuch aus der Hand. Dann laufen sie schnell. Hand in Hand, hinaus, Die Bühne bleibt leer, dann geht nochmals die Mitteltür auf. Herein kommt der kleine Neger, mit einer Kerze in der Hand, sucht das Taschentuch, findet es, hebt es auf, trippelt hinaus.*)

---

*leading the Princess by the hand, enters through the door. The two young people stand for a moment confused, then they make a deep bow, which Faninal and the Princess return. Faninal pats Sophia with paternal benevolence on the cheek.*)

**FANINAL:** It is just their way,— youth will be young! (*Faninal gives his hand to the Princess, conducts her to the center door which the suite of the Princess, among them the little Black Boy, at that moment throw open.*)

**PRINCESS:** Yes, yes. (*Bright light outside, within a half-light, as the two Footmen with the candlesticks precede the Princess.*)

**OCTAVIAN:** (*dreamily*): You alone I know, only you, That you love me and I love you! All besides like a vision seems Of fleeting dreams.

**SOPHIA:** (*dreamily*): It is a dream, of heaven: is it true, That you love me and I love you? Never in this world to part— One soul, one heart.

**OCTAVIAN AND SOPHIA:** I know you alone! (*She sinks into his arms. He kisses her quickly. Without her noticing it, her handkerchief drops from her hand. Then they run off quickly, hand in hand. The stage remains empty. Then the center door is opened again. Through it comes the little Black Boy with a taper in his hand. Looks for the handkerchief—finds it—picks it up—trips out.*)

*The End*
(*THE CURTAIN FALLS QUICKLY.*)

# Eugenio Oneghin (1879)

## Eugene Onegin

MUSIC BY PYOTR ILYICH TCHAIKOVSKY ■ LIBRETTO BY K. S. SHILOVSKY ■ BASED ON THE POEM BY ALEXANDRE PUSHKIN

This three-act opera, set to a libretto by K.S. Shilovsky and the composer himself (based on Pushkin's poem), was first performed by students at the Imperial College of Music in Moscow on March 29, 1879. It received its first official performance at the Bolshoi Theatre on April 23, 1881. The story takes place in Russia during the early nineteenth century. Madame Larina and her nurse, Filipevna, are conversing in her garden. They can hear Tatiana and Olga, her daughters, singing to celebrate the end of the harvest. Olga is happy and outgoing, in contrast to Tatiana, who is more shy and romantic. Lenski, Olga's fiancé, arrives with his friend, Eugene Oneghin, to visit. Oneghin is a well-brought-up young man but egotistical and dandy-ish, bored by everything. Tatiana falls head over heels for him. In her room later that night, she writes him a long love-letter, pleading that they should meet. Although he comes to see her, he is polite but unresponsive. He is unreliable and she should forget all about him. At a ball held at Madame Larina's house in honor of Tatiana's birthday, Monsieur Triquet, the dancing master, sings a song for her. Oneghin overhears some gossip regarding his dancing with Tatiana and decides to flirt with Olga, making Lenski jealous. They argue; Lenski challenges Oneghin to a duel to be fought the next morning at dawn. Hesitant at first because of their long-standing friendship, neither man makes a move. The seconds load the pistols and measure the distances; the duel takes place and Lenski dies as a result of Oneghin's first shot. Six years later at a ball held at the palace of Prince Gremin in St. Petersburg, Oneghin is among the guests; he has recently returned from long journeys to faraway places, which he took to try and forget his friend's death. He encounters Tatiana once again, now married to the Prince, and falls deeply in love with her. She receives him in her drawing room as he requests. He beseeches her with his love, but she remains loyal to her husband, sending Oneghin away forever.

---

## ■ ATTO PRIMO

### SCENA I

(*Giardino nella proprietà Larinto. A sinistra, casa con terrazza, a destra un albero e aiuole fiorite. In fondo alla scena una grata di legno, al di là della quale, fra gli alberi, si vede un villaggio. Comincia ad imbrunire. La signora Larina seduta sotto l'albero, intenta a confezionar confettura, presta l'orecchio al canto delle figlie, la balia le stavicino. Alla seconda strofa del duetta di Tatiana e Olga le due vecchie entrano in conversazione. Dalla casa si sente cantare. Le porte sulla terrazza sono aperte*).

**TATIANA:** Udiste voi il dolce gorgheggiar del rossignol Che canta amore a duolo al queto albor; Nei campi ancor sopiti il mesto suon del semplice pastor. L'udiste voi? l'udiste voi? L'udiste voi la flebile canzon del semplice pastor?

**OLGA:** Udiste voi il gorgheggiar di vin del rossignol che canta duolo! Nei queti campi ancor sopiti il mesto suon del semplice pastor?

## ■ ACT I

### SCENE I

(*Garden on the estate of Larino. To the left, house with terrace; to the right a tree and path of flowers. In the rear of the stage a wooden gate, through which a village is seen. It is dusk. The signora Larina, seated under the tree, busy making candy, is listening to the song of the little girls, the nurse standing nearby. At the second stanza of the duet between Tatiana and Olga the two old women begin a conversation. From the house singing is heard. The doors on the terrace are open*).

**TATIANA:** Do you hear the sweet trilling Of the nightingale, Singing of love and grief In the quiet light; In the still silent fields The sad sound of the simple shepherd, Do you hear it? Do you hear it? Do you hear the sad song Of the simple shepherd?

**OLGA:** Do you hear the divine trill Of the nightingale's sad song; In the still quiet fields, Do you hear the sad sounds Of the simple shepherd?

**LARINA E FILIPIEVNA:** Dal ciel la quete a noi si dà in luogo di felicità. Ah, sì, davver. (*Dietro la scena si ode un coro di contadini che vengono appressandosi*).

### SCENA II

**CORO:** Il veloce piè più non vuole andar! La man soffre ahimè, del gran lavorar! Ahimè il mesto mio cor si strugge Il mio cor per il gran penar!

**UNO DEL CORO:** Che mai deggio far l'amor mio per obliar!

**CORO:** Il buon giorno, signora, a te Di gran cuore auguriamo noi! Noi ti rechiam come l'uso vuol, Le spighe ornate di nastri e fior! L'opera nostra finì.

**LARINA:** Grata vi sono! Or gioite, contenta io son. Cantate una canzon che lieta sia!

**CORO:** Felici noi sarem Noi liete canterem, Il cerchio orsù formate, Fanciulle vi fermate!

**LARINA and FILIPIEVNA:** Heaven sends us quiet In place of happiness. Ah, yes, truly (*Behind the scene is heard a chorus of peasants approaching*).

### SCENE II

**CHORUS:** The swift foot no longer Wants to move; Alas! the hand suffers, overworked; Alas! my sad heart is wasted In endless suffering!

**ONE OF CHORUS:** May I never have to make love to forget!

**CHORUS:** Good day, signora, to you, We wish you good day With all our heart. We greet you, as custom decrees, With ears adorned with ribbons And with flowers our work.

**LARINA:** I thank you! Now rejoice, I am content! Sing a song, a happy song.

**CHORUS:** We will be happy We will sing gaily. Come, form a ring, Maidens, join hands.

UNO DEL CORO: Sia lieta la canzon,
Il cerchio sù formate,
Via venite!
(*Durante il coro le contadine ballano intorno al covone.*)

ONE OF CHORUS: Let the song be gay!
Come, form a ring.
Come away!
(*During the chorus the peasants dance around the sheaf*).

CORO: Sopra il ponte ponticello,
Pass'ardito un garzoncello, Vainu, vainu, vainu,
Passa e canta la mattina
Non c'è rosa senza spina,
Canta, tace, si riposa.
Chi mai sia tu l'indovina
Quel che canta la mattina.
(*Durante il canto Tatiana e Olga escono sulla terrazza.*)
Sparve il sol, tu dormi omai,
Qui mandar dame potrai
Daria, Nina, Caterina, O la bionda bella Irina,
Vainu, vainu, vainu.
Venne Nina la gioconda
Delle belle la seconda.
Disse, tu sei garzoncello
Che traversi il ponticello
E che canti ogni mattina.
Non c'è rosa senza spina.

CHORUS: Under the pontifical bridge
Passes boldly a little boy,
Vainu, vainu, vainu,
Passes, and sings the morning song,
There is no rose without thorns
Sings, is silent, and rests.
You be the prophet, and say
Who is he that sings the morning song.
(*During the song Tatiana and Olga go out on the terrace*).
The sun has disappeared,
You are sleeping now,
You will be able to send ladies here,
Daria, Nina, Caterina,
Or the beautiful blond Irene,
Vainu, Vainu, Vainu.
There came Nina the joyous one,
The second of the beautiful ones.
Who said, you are a little boy,
Who crosses the pontifical bridge,
And who sings every morning:
There is no rose without thorns.

## SCENA III

(*Durante il coro precedente Tatiana e Olga sono uscite sulla terrazza*).

## SCENE III

(*During the preceding chorus Tatiana and Olga have gone out on the terrace*).

TATIANA: (*con un libro in mano*) Ei m'è pur grato al suon di quelle voci
Lasciar libero corso ai miei pensier che vagan,
Che vagan là, lontan.

TATIANA: (*with a book in her hand*) More than ever grateful am I
For the sound of those voices,
Leaving my wandering thoughts
Free to roam,
Far, far from here.

OLGA: Ah, Tania, Tania! sei lì sempre a sognar.
Davver pari non siam no!
Quel cantar mi rende lieto il core.
(*Ballando.*)
Sopra il ponte ponticello
Pass'ardito un garzoncello!
(*Filipievna e Tatiana s'allontanano dagli altri.*)

OLGA: Ah, Tania, Tania!
Art always dreaming.
Indeed, we two are not alike.
Yon singing makes my heart happy.
(*Dancing*).
"Under the pontifical bridge
Passes boldly a little boy".
(*Filipievna and Tatiana move away from the others*).

## SCENA IV

LARINA: Al par d'un augellino sei viva e lieta mia buona fanciulla.
(*Al Coro.*)
Dei vostri dolci canti io vi son grata!
(*Tatiana siede sulla scala della terrazza e s'immerge nella lettura d'un libro. Filipievna esce coi contadini.*)
Ed ora andatene, Filipievna,
Io vo' che a lor si dia del vin.
Addio, miei cari.

## SCENE IV

LARINA: Little child of mine,
you are lively and happy
like a little bird.
(*to the chorus*).
I am grateful to you for your sweet songs.
(*Tatiana sits on the steps of the terrace and loses herself in the reading of a book. Filipievna goes out with the peasants*).
And now leave us, Filipievna,
And then let us have some wine.
Addio, my beloved ones.

CORO: Vi benedica il ciel!
(*I contadini escono.*)

CHORUS: Heaven bless you! (*The peasants go out*).

OLGA: Mammina, non vi par che soffre Tania?

OLGA: Mother dear, does it not seem to you
That Tatiana is suffering?

LARINA: E che? Davver, davver sei tutta smorta.

LARINA: How? indeed, indeed, you're deathly pale

TATIANA: Sempre tale io sono.
Non v'allarmate, mamma.
Leggo un'avventura che mi commuove.

TATIANA: I am always like this.
Do not alarm yourself
I am reading a tale
That moves me greatly.

LARINA: E triste sei sol per ciò?
(*Ride.*)

LARINA: Are you sad only because of this?
(*smiles*).

TATIANA: Ma certo, mamma.
Narra la novella le pene
Acerbe di due cuori
Che l'amor tormenta.
Dio! triste è il loro fato.

TATIANA: Indeed, Mamma.
The story relates
The bitter sufferings
Of two hearts
Tortured by love.
God, what a fate was theirs.

LARINA: Eh via! Tania. Rammento pur anch'io
I miei sospir per gl'infelici eroi;
Son tutte larve, sì. Pasaro i dì,
Ed ora certa son che sogno son gli eroi.
Or queta io son.

LARINA: Come, come, I too remember
How I did sigh
For the unhappy heroes;
Phantoms all. Those days are over;
And now I know that heroes
Are but dreams.
And now peace fills my mind.

OLGA: Invan cotanta quete, mirate,
Il grembiale non toglieste.
(*Larina si toglie in fretta is grembiale*).
Or or qui verrà Lenski, che dirà?
(*Ride*).
Oh! Odi alcun s'appressa . . .
Certo è lui.

OLGA: In vain to complain. Look you
Have not removed your apron.
(*Larina hastily removes her apron.*)
What will Lenski say, to see you like this?
(*Laughs*).
Ah! I hear some one approaching.
Certainly it is he.

LARINA: Sì, sì, Davvero!

LARINA: Yes, yes indeed!

TATIANA: (*Guardando dalla terrazza*). Ei non è sol . . .

TATIANA: (*Looking down from the terrace*). And he is not alone . . .

LARINA: Che mai sarà?
(*Entrano frettolosi la balia ed il servo*).

LARINA: And who might it be?
(*Enter hastily the nurse and the servant*).

FILIPIEVNA: Padrona mia, il nobil Lenski giunse
Con un signor, Oneghin!
(*Tatiana vuol andarsene, ma Larina la trattiene*).

FILIPIEVNA: Mistress, the noble Lenski has arrived
With one Signor Oneghin!
(*Tatiana wishes to withdraw, but Larina restrains her*)

TATIANA: Ah! sù presto io men vo'.

TATIANA: Ah! quick, I faint!

LARINA: Ei Tania, Tania, ciò non conviene.
Dio, che orror!
La cuffia a sghembo mi stà.
(*Il servo esce correndo. Tutti, in grande emozione, aspettano le visite.*)

LARINA: Ah! Tania, Tania!
This does not become you!
God, how dreadful!
My bonnet is awry!
(*The servant runs out. All, in great commotion, await the visitors*).

## SCENA V

(*Entrano Oneghin e Lenski.*)

## SCENE V

(*Enter Oneghin and Lenski*).

LENSKI: Mesdames! La vostra cortesia
Mi rese ardito.
Io raccomando a voi
Oneghin, mio vicin.

LENSKI: Mesdames. Your courtesy
Has emboldened me.
Permit me to present
My neighbor, Oneghin.

ONEGHIN: E' un grand'onore.

ONEGHIN: This a great honor. .

LARINA: (*confusa*). Ma che signor . . .
Per noi l'onor.
Sedete. Le figlie mie, signor!

LARINA: (*confused*). Ah, no, signor . . .
The honor is ours.
Be seated. My daughter, signor!

ONEGHIN: Ben fortunato inver.

ONEGHIN: How fortunate!

**LARINA:** Accomodatevi; o forse
v'è più caro
Goder del bel sereno cielo?
Sta bene! Di cure ha d'uopo ancor la
casa; io vi corro.
Voi gli ospiti ono-
rate . . . Tornerò . . .
(*Esce facendo segno a Tatiana
d'essere amabile. — Lenski e Oneghin passano a destra. Tatiana e
Olga restano dalla parte opposta*).

**LARINA:** Make yourselves comfort-
able. Or perhaps you'd rather
Enjoy the serenity of our lovely sky?
As you please! I am needed within
the house.
I will go. You entertain our guests.
I shall return.
(*Exit, making a sign to Tatiana to
be amiable. Lenski and Oneghin
pass to the right, Tatiana and
Olga remain opposite*).

**TATIANA:** Non fu il mio sogno una
chimera!
E' desso, il cor non m'ingannò!
Il guardo suo mi dice 'spera''
Scordarlo, ahimè, no non saprò.
Sarà la vita mia beata
Da quell'immagine desiata,
Sarà signore del mio cor
In cui s'accese ardente amor!
Sarà signore del mio cor
Che accese un potente amor.

**TATIANA:** My dream was not a
chimera!
It is he himself. My heart does not
decieve me.
His glance says to me "Hope!"
Alas to forget him were impossible!
Blessed were my life,
To be desired of yon figure
She in whom ardent love will wak-
en
Will be the mistress of my heart;
He that will kindle overpowering
love,
Will be the master of my heart.

**OLGA:** Era già noto a me ch'il giov-
in sere Oneghin
Parria strano signor d'assai strane
maniere,
Ma di geniale e lieto umor.
Assai diversa è l'opinione.
Ognun adduce a sua ragione,
Nessun poi sa la verità
A Tania per fidanzato si darà!

**OLGA:** I have already noticed that
young Oneghin
Is an unusual man, of uncommon
manner,
Withal of genial and lively humor.
Different are our opinions,
Each with its own reasons,
But none knows the truth.
He'll pretend to be betrothed to Ta-
nia.

**LENSKI:** E' lei che triste se ne sta
E silenziosa qual Svetlana.
E chè?
Amico mio, l'alpe il ruscello,
La prosa il verso, fiamma e gelo
Non son dissimili fra lor.
Per quanto vari i nostri cor.

**LENSKI:** And she, why so sad
Why so silent, yon Svetlana.
And why?
My friend, Alps from the brooklet,
Pros from verse, flame from ice,
Do not so much from each other dif-
fer.
As do our hearts from one another.

**ONEGHIN:** Or dimmi tu, qual'è Ta-
tiana?
Favella orsù, lo vuò saper.
E tu l'altra fanciulla adori?
Io l'altra avrei prescelta
Se delle muse foss'io cultor.
La vita in lei non ha tepor.
Siccome classica Madonna.
Purpurea tonda, per mia fè
Come l'idiota luna ell'è che
splende
Su nel firmamento!
Son vari i nostri cori.
(*Lenski s'avvicina ad Olga. One-
ghin senza cerimonie considera
Tatiana che sta cogi occhi bassi,
poi s'avvicina a lei e le parla*).

**ONEGHIN:** Now tell me which is
Tatiana?
Come speak, I yearn to know.
Do you adore the other girl?
I would have chosen the other one,
Were I a patron of the arts.
Her being does not possess the luke
warmness
Of the classical Madonna.
Deep purple, by my soul,
Shining like the stupid moon,
Over the firmament.
Indeed our hearts are different.
(*Lenski approaches Olga. One-
ghin rudely stares at Tatiana,
who stands with downcast eyes;
then he comes closer and speaks
to her*).

## SCENA VI

**LENSKI:** (*con vivacità*). Felice,
felice io son,
Io vi rivedo ancora!

**OLGA:** Eppur voi foste ieri qui, mi
par!

## SCENE VI

**LENSKI:** (*with animation*). Happy, I am happy.
That I see you again!

**OLGA:** I thought you were here
yesterday.

**LENSKI:** Ahimè! un di passava,
Triste di da voi lontano,
E fu eterno!

**LENSKI:** Alas! One day passed,
And I have been saddened by you
absence.
It has been an eternity.

**OLGA:** Eterno! E' strano affè! strano
davver,
Eterno un sol di!

**OLGA:** Eternal faith! strange indeed,
One day of eternity!

**LENSKI:** Vi sembra strano, si,
Miei detti l'ispira amor!
(*Lenski ed Olga escono.*)

**LENSKI:** Does it seems strange to
you? yes,
Do my words not inspire love!
(*Exit Lenski and Olga*)

**ONEGHIN:** (*A Tatiana con fred-
dezza*). Or dite a me,
Io penso che la noja a voi
Compagna esser de' qui!
Ridente é il loco, ma lontano.

**ONEGHIN:** (*To Tatiana, coldly*).
Now tell me,
Methinks that you
Are lonesome here;
There are livelier places but they
are far away.

**TATIANA:** Talvolta sogno errando
pel giardino.

**TATIANA:** At times
I wander dreaming in the garden.

**ONEGHIN:** Quai sono i vostri sogni
allor?

**ONEGHIN:** What do you dream
then?

**TATIANA:** Sognar fu mia più dolce
cura Fin dalla prima gioventù.

**TATIANA:** Dreaming has always
been
My most soothing cure
Since my childhood days.

**ONEGHIN:** Vagar v'è grato per le
nubi d'oro
Ed io, confesso, fui pur tal.
(*Oneghin passa dall'altra parte
del giardino, Lenski ed Olga ritornano.*)

**ONEGHIN:** To roam through the
golden clouds is pleasant
And, I confess,
That I have felt the same:
(*Oneghin crosses to the other side
of the garden. Lenski and Olga appear*).

**LENSKI:** (*Con calore e passione*).
T'amo tanto Olga, tanto io t'amo
Che si strugge sola l'alma
D'un poeta di sì possente e puro
amor.
Nei sogni sempre una visione
Nei cor impera una passione
Che non dà pace e notte e dì.
Fin dall'estrema giovinezza
Rapisti a me l'ingenuo cor
Ed invidiai pur la carezza
Che al labbro tuo faceano i fior!
L'oscuro ciel, la dolce aurora
Contemplavam fanciulli ancora,
ah!
(*Con grande espressione*).
Io t'adoro, io t'adoro quanto l'alma
D'un poeta amor puote;
Sola imperi sul mio core;
Da te sola, o mia diletta,
gioie e duol la vita aspetta,
O mio dolce amor,
Il pensier mio sarà fedel
Compagno al tuo pensier,
Nei di felici e nei tristi,
Teco pur sarà quest'alma
Che consuma un santo amor divin!

**LENSKI:** (*with warmth and pas-
sion*).
I love you so much Olga, so much
That only a poet's soul.
Could feel such pure love as mine.
In my dreams I see your vision.
In my heart a strong passion rules
That I do not rest day, or night.
Since my youth,
You have wrested away my heart,
I have envied the caresses
Of the flowers upon your lips!
The obscure sky,
And the sweet aurora
Yet contemplated our childhood,
ah!
(*With great expression*).
I adore you, I adore you as only
A poet's soul can love;
You rule supreme in my heart,
From you alone, Oh my beloved,
Joy and sorrow my life awaits,
Oh, my sweet love, my thoughts
will
Be loyal to your thoughts,
In happy and gloomy days
With you rests my soul
That consumes a divine love!

**OLGA:** Quei dolci dì te ne sovvien,
Di nostra prima e cara età!

**OLGA:** You have not forgotten
The sweet memories
Of your childhood days!

**LENSKI:** O mio dolce amor!

**LENSKI:** Oh, my dear love!

**OLGA:** Noi celavam gelosi in sen la
speme
E la felicità nei nostri cor!

**OLGA:** We were jealously conceal-
ing
Our hopes in each other's bosom,
And the happiness of out heart!

**LENSKI:** O mio dolce amor!
(*Escono sulla terrazza Larina e Filipievna. Comincia a far notte; alla fine notte completa*).

## SCENA VII

(*La scena rappresenta la camera di Tatiana, mobiliata con semplicità e decoro. Sedie bianche di vecchia forma, tese di cotonina. Tenede simili alle finestre. Un letto con mensola per libri. Una comode coperta di tovaglia; sulla comode uno specchio e vasi di fiori. Presso la finestra, una scrivania—Sipario—Tatiana, pensierosa, siede allo specchio. Filipievna le sta vicino. Tatiana è in vesta da camera bianca*).

**FILIPIEVNA:** Via, non vò più ciarlar!
E' tempo, Tania, dei tu destarti
All'alba per la messa,
Or dei dormir!

**TATIANA:** Dormir non posso, non respiro,
Aprir convien; poi siedi qui!
(*Aperta la finestra la balia siede presso Tatiana.*)

**FILIPIEVNA:** Di! Tania di! che hai?

**TATIANA:** M'annojo; mi narra dell'antichità!

**FILIPIEVNA:** Ma non m'ascolti tu, perchè?

**TATIANA:** (*Abbraccia la balia con passione.*) Ah, balia, balia, soffro tanto,
Io mi struggo, io soffro,
Si, diletta mia, si pianger,
Singhiozzar vorrei!

**FILIPIEVNA:** Fanciulla mia, malata sei!
Signor ci salva per pietà!
La fronte segnerò coll'acqua santa,
Ardente sei.

**TATIANA:** (*indecisa*). Non è dolor.
M'ascolta, balia, no! soffre il cor . . .
Mi lascia or tu, mi lascia or tu,
Mi strugge amor!

**FILIPIEVNA:** Che dici?

**TATIANA:** Va via, mi lascia sola qui.
Ma pria, diletta, porgi un foglio.
Io scriverò; formir non voglio.
Addio!

**FILIPIEVNA:** Ti benedica il cielo!
(*Esce*).

## SCENA VIII

(*Tatiana resta a lungo pensierosa, poi s'alza agitatissima, ma decisa.*)

---

**LENSKI:** Oh, my dear heart!
(*Exit on the terrace Larina and Filipievna. It is late in the evening, near midnight*).

## SCENE VII

(*The scene represents the room of Tatiana, furnished with simplicity and dignity. Chairs are white, of old style, upholstered in calico, similar curtains for the windows. A bed with a bracket for books. A dresser covered with a cloth scarf, and on it a mirror and flower vases. Near the window a desk.—Curtain.—Tatiana sitting thoughtfully by the mirror with Filipievna near by. Tatiana wears a white boudoir negligee*).

**FILIPIEVNA:** Come, let us not talk!
Or you, Tania, will not awake at daybreak for mass,
Let us sleep now!

**TATIANA:** I cannot sleep, I cannot breathe,
It is better to open the window;
Come sit by me!
(*The nurse opens the window, and sits besides Tatiana*).

**FILIPIEVNA:** Tell me! Tell me Tania!
What is the matter?

**TATIANA:** I am weary; I am bored by every thing!

**FILIPIEVNA:** But you do not listen to me, why?

**TATIANA:** (*Embraces the nurse affectionately*).
Ah! nurse, I suffer much,
I worry, I suffer,
Yes, my dear, I would like to cry, and sob!

**FILIPIEVNA:** My girl, you are sick!
God have pity on us!
I will mark your forehead with holy water.
For you are feverish.

**TATIANA:** (*in doubt*). It is not pain,
Listen, nurse, no.
It is my heart that suffers . . .
Leave me alone,
I want to be alone,
Love consumes me!

**FILIPIEVNA:** What do you say?

**TATIANA:** Leave me, I wish to be alone,
But, before you go dear,
Hand me that sheet,
I will write; I cannot sleep.
Farewell!

**FILIPIEVNA:** God bless you, dear!
(*Exit*).

## SCENE VIII

(*Tatiana remains in a thoughtful mood, she bestirs herself, much agitated, but resolved*).

---

**TATIANA:** (*con vivacità, forza e passione*). Sia poi quel che sarà,
Ma prima abbandonata alla speranza
Ignoto gaudio invocherò,
Delizia arcana in core avrò.
M'inebbria il tossico desiato,
Un grato sogno arride a me!
Rapit'io son, l'acuto stral
Del guardo suo dolce e fatal,
Si fe' signore del mio core!
(*Siede alla'scrivania. Scrive un poco, poi si ferma*).
No, non è ciò! Orsù da capo!
(*Straccia la lettera*).
Dio, non so più! Ah, quale ardor!
Che dire . . . io non so!
Perchè, perchè moveste il passo voi
A questo nostro asil beato!
Io non sapea che fosse io duol;
Qui pura l'alma avea sognato
Il dolce nido desiato
E forse un dì, signor, chi sa?
Avria trovato un cor amante.
Del focolar le gioie sante
Io conosciuto avrei allor!
(*Balzando in piedi.*)
A un altro!
No! no! su questa terra
Ad altri non darei il mio cor!
Ciò che il d'estino ha stabilito
Si dee compire, io son tua!
Dal dì che nel pensier di Dio
Fui creata vissi sol per te;
Lo sento, Dio ti fece mio
Per la vita, per l'eternità!
(*S'avvicina alla tavola e 'scrive; cessa di scrivere e resta pensierosa*).
Chi sa? La speme sconsigliata,
Chimera vana sogno fu!
Tutt'altra sorte m'è serbata!
(*S'alza e cammina pensierosa*).
Sia pur così!
Il mio destin in tuo potere
Omai confidando.
Il pianto mio ti muova alfin,
M'affido a te ben mio m'affido,
Si m'affido!
(*Con forza e passione*).
Mistero a tutti è il io soffrir,
Il mio pensier da me s'invola!
(*Animandosi sempre più*).
Son qui straziata, sola
E sola alfin dovrò perir!
Deh! vieni a me
Tu mi consola.
Di speme un raggio arreca a me,
Oppur distruggi il sogno,
Ahimè, ansiosa attendo omai,
Attendo omai la tua parola!
(*S'avvicina con impeto alla scrivania e finisce di scrivere la lettera—Alzandosi e sigillando la lettera*).
E' fatto! Ciel! Che scrissi mai!
Timor, vergogna ho nel core,
Omai l'indugio saria van;
Confido sol nell'onor suo!

---

**TATIANA:** (*With liveliness and strong passion*). Whatever shall come to be,
I have given all my hopes, to you,
I shall invoke the unknown joy,
With its mysterious delight
Which breeds a poison in my heart.
Like a beautiful dream
Which smile down upon me!
I behold you with the sweet,
And yet fatal look,
Which has wrested my heart away
like a pointed arrow.
(*Sits at the desk. Writes a little, then stops*).
No, No, it is not so!
Cheer up! begin over again!
(*Tears the letter*).
God, I do not know!
Ah, such ardor!
What can I say . . .
I do not know!
Why, why did I start all this
In our blessed refuge,
I did not know our souls
Would come to grief
Over the happy days
We had longed for.
Perhaps! a day will come, sir,
Who knows?
When I shall have found a heart to love,
And then I would know
How to speak of our joys by the hearth!
(*Then leaping to her feet*).
To someone else!
No, no, I'll not on this earth
give my love to another.
Whatever part fate may decree,
I am yours!
Since the day that in the thought
Of God I came to life,
I've lived only for you!
I feel that God has made you mine
For life, and for eternity!
(*She sits at the table and writes, stops writing and remains thoughtful*).
Who knows? That hope
Has been like a chimera
As empty as a dream!
Perhaps some other fate awaits me!
(*Arises and walks about in a thoughtful mood*).
So be it!
My fate is within your power,
And everything depends on you.
My cry will move you to an end,
I trust myself to you, my dear,
Yes, I trust in you.
(*Passionately*).
My suffering has been
A mystery to everyone,
It has been my thoughts
That have carried me off secretly.
(*With strong emotion*).
Here I am tortured, alone!
And alone to the end, I shall die!
Oh! come to me.
You will comfort me.
You will be like a ray of hope to me,
Or you will destroy my dream.
Alas! I am anxiously waiting,
Awaiting anxiously your word!

*(With a sudden impulse she seats herself at the desk, and ends her letter. Arises and closes the letter).*
It is done! Oh God,
What have I written!
Fear and shame possess my heart,
It is too late, I've done it,
I trust only in his honor.

## SCENA IX

*(Tatiana s'avvicina alla finestra e tira la tenda. La luce irrompe nella camera).*

TATIANA: Ah! Ecco il giorno, sereno il ciel,
Il sole spunta già!
*(Siede presso la finestra).*
Il pastor suona la sua canzon . . .
*(Pensierosa).*
Ed io! . . . Io . . .
*(Entra la balia, aprendo la porta con precauzione).*

FILIPIEVNA: *(Non vedendo ancora Tatiana).* Tatiana, è tempo omai. Suvvia!
*(Vede Tatiana).*
Che vedo, già tu sei levata?!
O dolce labor degli occhi miei.
Ieri per te quant'io temei! . . .
Sien grazie al cielo,
Tu non sei malata.
Sveniro i sogni ed i terror,
*(Tatiana s'allontana dalla finestra e prende la lettera).*
Il dolce viso sembra un fiòr!

TATIANA: Ah! balia, d'un servizio ho d'uopo.

FILIPIEVNA: Il ciel m'è testimonio . . .

TATIANA: Il tuo garzon rechi in segreto
Cotesta lettera ad . . . a quel . . .
Quel signor, ma sappia il bambin
Che non de' profferir parola eppoi
Che favellar di me non de'! . . .

FILIPIEVNA: A chi? diletta dimmi orsù?
L'età m'ha ottusa la ragione.
Non era tale in altra età.
Un detto, un detto sol bastava . . .

TATIANA: Ah! balia, balia cess'alfine,
Di vecchie storie parli invan.
Non odi? Della lettera parliam!

FILIPIEVNA: Ho inteso, inteso, basta, mia diletta,
Non t'adirar! La mente mia non sa pensar.

TATIANA: Di vecchie storie, balia, parli invan.
Dovrà ricevere codesto foglio, balia!

## SCENE IX

*(Tatiana goes to the window and draws the curtains. The light streams into the room).*

TATIANA: Ah! it is daylight, with a clear sky.
The sun is coming out!
*(Sits by the window).*
The shepherd sings his song . . .
And I! . . . I . . .
*(Pensively).*
*(The nurse enter, opening the door softly).*

FILIPIEVNA: *(Who has not yet seen Tatiana).* Tatiana, it is time.
Come! Come!
*(Sees Tatiana).*
What do I see?
Are you already awake?
I see the brightness in your eyes.
Yesterday I was fearing for you,
But thank heavens, you are not ill.
And now my dreams of terror have vanished.
*(Tatiana withdraws from the window, and takes the letter).*
Your sweet face is like a flower!

TATIANA: Ah! nurse,
I would ask a favor of you . . .

FILIPIEVNA: Heaven bear me witness!

TATIANA: That your boy should take this letter
Secretly to . . . to that . . .
That gentlemen, but tell the boy,
Not to say a word,
And not to talk about me! . . .

FILIPIEVNA: To whom, my dear,
Who would I tell?
Age has obtused my reasoning.
It was not so in younger years,
For once a thing was said,
Once was sufficient . . .

TATIANA: Ah! nurse, nurse, please stop.
You speak in vain of old stories,
Do you hear me?
Let us speak of the letter!

FILIPIEVNA: I have heard, I have heard,
It is sufficient, my dear.
Pray do no get angry.
I have no mind to think.

TATIANA: Do not speak in vain of old stories, nurse.
Speak of Oneghin! . . .
Will he recieve this letter, nurse?

FILIPIEVNA: Su, via fanciulla, mia, non t'adirar,
La mente mia non sa pensar.
Ma tu do nuovo impallidisci?

TATIANA: T'inganni, balia, in verità!
Non rifiutarmi per pietà!
*(La balia, presa la lettera, rimane indecisa. Tatiana le fa cenno di uscire. La balia 'si avvia, si ferma sulla porta, pensierosa, poi torna indietro. Finalmente fa intendere con cenni, che ha capito ed esce. Tatiana siede al tavolo e resta pensieorsa, la fronte nella palma.).*

## SCENA X

*(Tatiana entra correndo e cade seduta sul banco).*

TATIANA: Ei qui! qui! Eugenio! . . . Mio Dio!
Che pensato avrà? Che mai dirà?
Ah! perchè mai a tal s'indusse il triste cor!
Mi spinse sconsigliato amor.
Or le mie pene a lui son note!
Ed ei, chi sa? Forse, crudele,
In riso volge il mio dolor!
O mio fatale tentator!
Ahimè, Signor! me sventurata!
O mio soffrir!
Qualcun s'appressa . . .
Al certo egli è . . .
Si, è lui!
*(Entra Oneghin. Tatiana balza in piedi. Oneghin le si avvicina. Essa abbassa il capo).*

ONEGHIN: *(Dignitoso, calmo e freddo).* Voi mi scrivete . . .
Negar non vale.
Or io so il senso arcan del vostro core.
E' puro e santo ingenuo amore!
Io la franchezza so apprezzar.
I vostri accenti ravvivar
Nell'alma un senso già scordato,
Ma pur lodarvi non poss'io.
E senz'ambagi il pensier mio
A voi sarà qui rivelato.
Io mi confesso al vostro piè,
Il vostro cor decider de'.

TATIANA: O cielo, quale offesa!
Quant'io soffro.
*(Si lascia andare sul banco).*

ONEGHIN: Se dell'imen la dolce cura
Empisse d'estasi il mio cor,
Se la ribelle mia natura
Piegasse ai palpiti d'amor,
Fedel compagna per mia fe',
Sareste sola voi per me.
Ma non m'arride il gaio sole.
Non v'ha per me felicità,
Imene, amor son vane fole
Che l'indoman fanno pietà.

FILIPIEVNA: Come, my dear, do not get angry.
My mind cannot think clearly,
Why, you are getting pale again?

TATIANA: You are truly deceiving yourself, nurse!
For pity sake do not refuse me!
*(The nurse hesitates to take the letter, Tatiana motioins to her to go. The nurse stops short at the door, and in a thoughtful mood comes back again. Finally she motions that she has understood and departs. Tatiana sits at the table, and remains pensive, with her forehead resting in her palms.)*

## SCENE X

*(Tatiana comes in running, and sits down on the bench).*

TATIANA: Here! Here! Eugene!..
Oh, my God!
What will he think?
What ever will he say? . . .
Ah! why did my sad heart ever
Induce me to do such a deed?
It has been the unreasoning love
that has moved me.
Now my troubles are known to him!
And he, who knows?
Perhaps shall mock my grief!
Oh, what fatal temptation!
Alas! God, I am unfortunate!
Oh! I shall suffer for this!
Some one is approaching
I am almost certian that it is he . . .
Yes, it is he! . . .
*(Enter Oneghin. Tatiana jumps to her feet. Oneghin comes close to her. She stands meekly).*

ONEGHIN: *(With dignity and calmness).* You have written to me . . .
Can you deny it?
Now I know the mysterious feeling in your heart.
A pure and holy love!
I know how to appreciate your frankness,
And your hopes I revive.
No, I cannot praise you,
I will reveal to you my thoughts
Without subterfuges.
At your feet I will confess myself . . .
And your heart will then decide!

TATIANA: Oh heavens, what an offense!
Must I endure all this? . . .
*(She falls on the bench).*

ONEGHIN: If wedlock were a cure,
And would fill my heart with rapture,
Then my nature would rebel,
And yield to the throbs of love.
And then you alone would be
The only loyal companion of my faith.
But the gay sun do not smile upon me
And brings me no happiness

## Act I, Scene X

A che cercar sì grave cura?
L'imen per noi saria sventura.
L'amor dell'oggi saria van;
Non v'amerei già più doman!
Or voi sapete le delizie
Che l'imeneo ci arrecherà
E forse per l'eternità.
(*Esaltandosi*).
L'età felice s'è involata,
Ah! s'è involata,
Mutarsi l'alma no non può,
Ogni altra sorte m'è negata
D'amor fraterno io v'amerò!
E forse ancor . . . d'un più pos-
sente amor
Il mio parlar non dia livore,
Fanciulla vaga al vostro core!
Amore, amore caccia un altro amor!
Il detto mio guida vi sia,
Un passo falso, ahimè!
Ancor potria piombarvi nel dolor!

Love is like an empty tale,
That on the morrow it wakes pity.
And why look for such a
cure? . . .
Wedlock would mean misfortune
for us,
The love of today is all in vain;
Tomorrow I could no longer love
you!
Now, you know the delight,
That the world will render us,
And perhaps to eternity!
(*He becomes exalted*)
The happy age has flown by,
Ah, it has passed!
We cannot change our souls,
I have been denied of any chance.
I shall love with a brotherly love!
And perhaps with a more powerful
love!
If I have spoken thus,
Do not let hatred fill your heart.
For love will always hunt for love!
Let my words be a guide to you,
For if you should take a false step,
Alas! . . . You would sink for-
ever
Into the abyss of suffering!

**CORO DIETRO LE QUINTE:** Foro-
sette amabili, vaghe e desiabili
Intrecciar dovete or voi
Danze, giochi e canti orsù!
(*Il coro s'allontana poco a poco*).
Se il garzon ci apparirà,
Ei non de' fuggir da noi.
Accorrete tutte voi,
Lo colpite dritto al cor
Sei curioso bel garzon!
Ed avrà di te ragion,
La purpurea bocca in fe'!
(*Oneghin offre il braccio a Tatia-
na. Essa lo guarda lungamente in
atto di silenziosa preghiera, poi si
alza macchinalmente, s'appoggia
al braccio di Oneghin ed esce len-
tamente*).

**CHORUS IN BACK OF THE
STAGE:** Amiable countrywomen,
charming and desirous,
Come, let us all indulge
In dancing, games and singing.
(*The chorus withdraws slowly*).
And when the boy will come back,
Let us all run to meet him,
And with our looks
We shall pierce his heart like an ar-
row.
Then we shall learn the truth.
Come! Come! Hurry up!..
(*Oneghin offers his arm to Tatia-
na. She looks at him meekly and
in action of prayer, then she rises,
mechanically supporting herself
on Oneghin's arm, and departs
slowly*).

*SIPARIO.*

*CURTAIN.*

# ■ ATTO SECONDO

# ■ ACT II

## *SCENA I*

## *SCENE I*

**CORO:** Brillante idea davver inas-
pettata!
Che bella musica e gaia si davver!
Brillante assai, sì è la serata
Ed il festin giocondo, miei signor!
Bravo! Bravo! Genial sorpresa!
Brillante assai è davver la festa!
Il festino giocondo, in verità!

**CHORUS:** Clever idea, indeed, and
so unexpected!
What lovely music and so merry!
Lovely indeed is the evening.
What merriment, my gentlemen!
Bravo! bravo! such a genial surprise!
It has been a clever idea,
And such gay merriment!

**VECCHI SIGNORI:** Solo cacciando
noi ci dilettiamo
Al bosco, al piano sol moviam il piè

**OLD GENTLEMEN:** Hunting from
woods to woods is
Our only amusement.

**VECCHIE SIGNORE:** Altro che
danze! Per valli, per piani,
Per boschi si corre, ai campi si va!
Poi stanchi ritornano al sonno si
danno
E noi che facciamo, Dio solo lo sa!
(*Le giovani circondano il capita-
no*).

**OLD LADIES:** What of the dances!
From the fields
Into the woods, and up and down
hills we go!
Then we come home all tired out,
and fall asleep!
(*The maidens surround the cap-
tain*).

Ah! Trifon Petrovic sien grazie a
voi,
Davver noi vi siamo grati assai!
Danziamo, danziamo or noi!

Ah! Trifon Petrovitch, we are thank-
ful to you,
Very very thankful indeed!
Let us dance, let us dance!

**IL CAPITANO:** Nossignor! Io grato
vi sono.
Anch'io son disposto,
Si prenda a danzar.
(*Oneghin balla con Tatiana. Tutti
si fermano per vederli ballare*).

**THE CAPTAIN:** I am grateful to
you all,
I, too, feel inclined to dance,
Then let us dance.
(*Oneghin dances with Tatiana.
All stop to look at them*).

**LE VECCHIE SIGNORE:** Danzano!
Danzano! le dolci colombe.
Convien che si spieghi . . .
Bel tipo inver.
Sua sposa la farà.
O povera Tania!
Tiranno sarà!
(*Oneghin passa sbadatamente
presso le vecchie signore, cercan-
do di sorprendente le loro conver-
sazioni*).

**THE OLD LADIES:** The sweet
doves are dancing! dancing!
It is almost time for him to ex-
plain.
Fine specimen indeed.
Will he make her his own?
Ah! poor Tania!
What a tyrant he will be!
(*Oneghin carelessly passes in
front of the old ladies, trying to
listen to their conversation*).

**CORO:** E' un vero orrore, un villa-
no,
Ei non s'appressa al baciamano,
E' un framasson, vizioso egli è.
E la bottiglia amica gli è.

**CHORUS:** He is abominable, he is
rude,
We do not want him near us,
He is a freemason, full of vices,
With the bottle as his best friend.

**ONEGHIN:** Bell'opinione! Benissi-
mo.
Or basta di lor giudizi abbietti.
Son piene di veleno!
A che venut'io son?
Davver, davver non so perchè!
Vendetta avrò sensibile per tal ser-
viglio!
Ecco farò il galante a Olga.
(*Passa Olga seguita da Lenski*).
Va là!.. sarai contento.
Essa è qui. Vi prego . . .
(*Olga indecisa*).

**ONEGHIN:** Fine opinion! Very
well.
It is time to stop such vile opinions.
They are full of poison to me!
What place have I come to?
Indeed, indeed, I know not why I
came!
I shall avenge myself for such treat-
ment!
Now, I am going to make love to
Olga.
(*Olga passes, followed by Lenski*).
You will be happy now . . .
She is here. I pray you . . .
(*Olga is undecided*).

**LENSKI:** La danza concedete a me!

**LENSKI:** You promised me the
dance!

**ONEGHIN:** Al certo sei in error!
(*Oneghin e Olga balleno*).

**ONEGHIN:** You are mistaken!
(*Oneghin and Olga dance*).

**LENSKI:** O ciel, che avvenne?
Io non comprendo . . .
Olga! Dio! Mi manca il cor.

**LENSKI:** Oh heavens! What is hap-
pening?
I do not understand . . .
Olga, God! My heart is failing.

**CORO:** Brillante idea, brillante in-
ver!
Brillante è la festa,
E gaia, si davver.
Il festino!
Brillante idea, davver, inaspettata,
Che bella musica e gaia,
E lieta la serata, il festino,
Bravo! Bravo! Genial sorpresa!
La festa e dèliziosa,
Si, la bella musica!
O qual divario! o che piacer.
Il festino è divino!

**CHORUS:** Clever idea! clever idea!
And so unexpected!
It is gay indeed!
What lovely music, so lively,
Gay indeed is the evening and the
feast!
Bravo! bravo! such a genial surprise!
Yes, the feast is delightful!
The music is lovely!
Oh so much variety!
Oh such pleasure!

## *SCENE II*

## *SCENE II*

**LENSKI:** (*Avvicinandosi ad Olga
che ha appena finito di ballare*).
Perchè, perchè mi fate triste e scon-
solato?
Ah! Olga! siete meco assai crudel!
Che fec'io mai?

**LENSKI:** (*Approaching Olga, who
has just stopped dancing*). Why,
why do you make me feel so sad?
Ah! Olga! you are cruel to me!
What have I ever done?

OLGA: Che dir vogliate, no, io capir non so!

LENSKI: Voi con Oneghin danzaste,
E con lui sol!
Io non comprendo . . .
Io v'invitai pur ma rifiutaste.

OLGA: Davver mi meraviglio.
Non so di che parlar vuoi tu!

LENSKI: Che! Non intendi ancor?
E non si spezza il core
Al sol veder lo sguardo
Tuo gentil fissato
Agli occhi suoi,
Sommesso ti parlava
E ti stringeva a sè!
O mio dolor!

OLGA: Comprenderti non so davver!
Invan tu sei geloso!
M'è grato il suo parlar,
E' assai gentil.

LENSKI: Ah! gentil!
Ah! Olga, Olga, tu non m'ami!

OLGA: Che stravagante!

LENSKI: (Oneghin s'avvicina).
Olga, tu non m'ami!
Meco il cotillon danzar vuoi tu?

ONEGHIN: No! con me! A me voi
deste la parola.

OLGA: Certo si, vi seguo!
Punir così voglio il mal pensier!

LENSKI: Olga!

OLGA: (Dal fondo viene Triquet
circondato dalle fanciulle). No
davver! Le damigelle amabili
Qui vengon con Triquet.

ONEGHIN: Chi è?

OLGA: Di Francia venne, qui maestro.

CORO: Monsieur Triquet non lo
dirà!
Chantez de grâce un couplet!

TRIQUET: Un madrigal ho pronto
già!
Ma dove sta Mademoiselle?
(Tutti formano cerchio intorno a
Tatiana che vuole schivarsi, ma
viene trattenuta).
Monsieur Triquet non lo dirà!
Car le couplet est fait pour elle!

CORO: Essa è qui! Essa è qui!

TRIQUET: Ah! Ah! Mademoiselle,
je vous en prie!
Mesdames, voi state ad ascoltar.
E' tempo omai di cominciar.
(Con molta espressione).
In questo bel felice dì
La fanciulla piena di beltà,
Spira delizia, gioia, amor
Il vostro viso incantator.
Vi sorrida la felicità.
Legge saran vostri desir,

OLGA: I do not understand you!

LENSKI: You danced with Oneghin.
With him alone! . . . I cannot
understand
Why you refused me, when I asked
you

OLGA: Indeed, I am surprised.
I do not know what you are talking
about!

LENSKI: What? you do not understand me yet?
It was enough to break my heart as I
watched,
How sweetly you stared into his
eyes,
As he was softly speaking,
And holding you close in his arms!
Oh! my grief!

OLGA: I cannot understand you!
You are vainly jealous.
It is a pleasure talking to him,
He is so kind.

LENSKI: Ah! kind!
Ah! Olga, Olga, you do not love me!

OLGA: How you exaggerate!

LENSKI: (as Oneghin approaches). Olga! you do not love
me!
Will you dance the cotillion with
me?

ONEGHIN: No! with me! You
promised me the dance.

OLGA: Certainly, I will dance with
you!
I will thus cure him of his jealously!

LENSKI: Olga!

OLGA: (Triquet appears in the
background surrounded by the
maidens). No, indeed! my amiable
young ladies,
Here you come with Triquet.

ONEGHIN: Who is he?

OLGA: He came here from France
as a teacher.

CHORUS: M. Triquet! M. Triquet!
Sing us a poem with all your grace!

TRIQUET: The poem is ready!
But where is the young lady?
(They all form a circle around Tatiana, who tries to dodge them,
but is kept back).
M. Triquet will not tell
That the poem is dedicated to her!

CHORUS: Here she is! here she is!

TRIQUET: Ah! Ah! maidens, you
are all invited.
And you ladies remain to hear us.
It is already time to start.
(With expression).
On this most happy day,
We are here to celebrate
In honor of this beautiful girl,
Whose lovely face radiates
Love, happiness, and delight,
And may happiness smile on you

Lungi le lagrime, i sospir
E la gioia sol v'arriderà.
Bella Tatiana al vostro piè
Noi qui siam tutti, per mia fè.
V'auguriamo la felicità.
Il cielo, il ciel propizio a voi sarà!
Il cielo v'arrida o bella Tatiana.
Il cielo sorrida a voi Tatiana.
(Triquet s'inchina rigraziando).

CORO: Bravo, bravo! Bravo, Monsieur Triquet!
Grazioso il madrigale e bene lo cantò.
(Dopo cantate le strofe, Triquet
s'inginocchia innanzi a Tatiana e
le presenta il madrigale).

## SCENA III

IL CAPITANO: Messieurs, Mesdames! Vi prego ai vostri posti.
Tosto comincia il cotillon!
Al posto orsù!
(Il Capitano dà la mano a Tatiana. Cominciano a ballare. Altre
coppie di ballerini che li seguono,
prendono posto successivamente.
Oneghin ed Olga siedono presso la
ribalta. Lenski, pensieroso resta
in piedi dietro di loro).

ONEGHIN: (Dopo aver fatto un
giro con Olga, la fa sedere, poi fingendo di accorgersi, soltanto allora, di Lenski, gli rivolge la parola). Perch non danzi, Lenski?
Una statua mi sembri davver.
Di, che hai?

LENSKI: Io? che! nulla in fè!
L'amico ammiro in t‾e
Il mio fedel amico!

ONEGHIN: Vedi un po'! Curioso assai mi sembra il tuo giudizio.
Che mai ti turba il cor?

LENSKI: (Sul principio risponde
pacatamente, ma poco a poco si
esalta). Turbarmi? No davvero!
Esperto non sapea che fosti tu,
Col dolce favellar turbar l'ingenuo
cor
Di credule fanciulle, col tuo sorriso!
Certo che per te solo Tatiana,
Eh, via! saria poco inver!
(Gli invitati cessano, poco, di ballare e cominciano a prestar attenzione alla disputa).
Fedele amico! Olga pur vuoi tu.
Tu vuoi spezzarle il cor,
Del suo dolore poi farti onor!
Sei davvero onesto!

ONEGHIN: (Con ironia, ma calma). Che! Di mente uscito sei?

LENSKI: Prosegui.
Da te mi vien l'offesa
E tu stesso dici a me che folle io son!
(Le danze vengono interrotte).
Oneghin, più amico non vi son!

forever.
May your desires be like laws,
And tears and sighs be far far away,
Joy alone will smile on you,
Beautiful Tania,
Here at your feet we are
To wish you happiness.
There will be kindness in the future
For you!
Heaven will smile on you,
Beautiful Tatiana.
(Triquet bows graciously).

CHORUS: Bravo! bravo! bravo! M.
Triquet!
Graceful is the poem, and well
sung.
(After singing a stanza, Triquet
kneels in front of Tatiana, and
gives her the poem).

## SCENE III

THE CAPTAIN: Ladies, and Gentlemen,
I pray you take your seats.
The cotillion will begin now!
Come to your seats!
(The captain gives his hand to Tatiana. They start to dance. Other
couples follow them, taking
places subsequently. Oneghin
and Olga sit on the steps of the
stage. Lenski stands in back of
them in a thoughtful mood.)

ONEGHIN: (After dancing one
round with Olga, begs her to sit
down, and pretends to have just
noticed Lenski, and turns to speak
to him.) Why don't you dance, Lenski?
You look, indeed, like a statue.
Tell me, what is the matter?

LENSKI: I? what! nothing, indeed!
In you, my friend, I have always
found a true friend.

ONEGHIN: See here! Curious
enough is your wisdom,
What is it that troubles your heart?

LENSKI: (at first he answers softly, then little by little he becomes
excited). Troubles? No, indeed!
I did not know you were such an expert
At stealing young maidens' hearts,
With your sweet smiles, and
speeches!
I was certain that you were Tatiana's suitor,
Alas now! it is not true!
(The guests stop dancing, to listen
to the conversation).
Faithful friend! You want Olga, too.
Do you want to break her heart,
And rejoice in her sorrow!
You would be honest indeed!

ONEGHIN: (With irony, but
calm). What! Have you lost your
head?

LENSKI: Proceed.
From you such an insult
And you accuse me of being foolish!
(The dances are stopped).

(*Tutti gli invitati s'avvicinano e li circondano*).
Tutt'ho scordato l'antico nostro affetto!
Io . . . io sol disprezzo ho in cor!

ONEGHIN: Or m'odi . . . basta, basta . . .
Ci ascoltan tutti.

LENSKI: (*fuori di sè*). E che importa a me?
Si, m'offendeste voi!
Ne renderete a me ragion, signor!

CORO: Che avvenne raccontate?

LENSKI: Nulla, io chiedo so!
Che Oneghin qui presente.
Mi dia ragion di sua condotta.
Risponder ei non vuole a me,
Or'io lo sfido qui.
Decida il ferro! . . .
(*La Sig.ra Larina si fa strada nella folla e si rivolge a Lenski*).

LARINA: O Dio! In mia casa!
Vi calmate, vi calmate!

LENSKI: (*Con gran sentimento*).
Qui, signora! Qui, signora,
D'un sogno dorato si beava
Il mio giovine cor.
Qui, signora, mi fu rivelato
Il sublime segreto d'amor!
Ma la dolce chimera ha spezzata!
Della vita m'apparve l'orror.
L'amistade è menzogna spietata.
E' menzogna spietata l'amor!

ONEGHIN: Al rimirar si gran dolor
Ho di rimorso pieno il cor.
Questa passione dolce, santa io
Non dovea turbar, lo sento.
Di vero affetto Lenski amai,
Giammai io nol dovea turbar.

TATIANA: Colpita io sono, sventurata,
Confuso resta il pensiero,
Sol m'arde in seno e gelosia e dolor!
Mi consuma geloso dolor
Cruda doglia mell'alma mi stà,
Tremenda mi tortura,
Mi dilania il core.

OLGA E Larina: Davver i lor furori insani
Preparan triste l'indomani.

CORO: Disgraziato!

ONEGHIN: Io non dovea piagar quell'alma.
Punge il rimorso il mio cor!

CORO: Fa davver pietà!

LENSKI: La fanciulla dal puro sembiante,
Cui nel guardo rifulge il candor,
(*Con amarezza*).
Per inganno v'inebbria un istante,
V'abbandona poi trista al dolor!

Oneghin! I am your friend no longer.
(*All the guests form a circle around them*).
Everything will be forgotten, even our old love!
I . . . I have only hatred in my heart!

ONEGHIN: You hate me now . . . That is enough, enough . . .
They are all listening to us.

LENSKI: (*As if out of his mind*).
What do I care?
Yes, you insulted me!
You shall account for this, Sir!

CHORUS: Tell us what has happened?

LENSKI: Nothing, I am only asking
That Oneghin who is present,
Account for his behavior.
To me he does not answer,
I will challenge him here
And the sword will decide his lot! . . .
(*Madame Larina passes through the crowd, and turns to Lenski*).

LARINA: Oh God! In my home!
Calm yourselves, calm yourselves!

LENSKI: (*With great feeling*).
Here Madam! Here Madam!
My young heart was blessed with a golden dream.
Here, madam,
The sublime secret of love was first revealed to me!
And now that the sweet chimera is broken!
Life seems a horror.
Friendship is but a cruel falsehood,
As cruel a falsehood as love is.

ONEGHIN: My heart is full of remorse.
I feel that I should not have troubled your sweet passion,
I had a great love for Lenski,
I should have never troubled him.

TATIANA: I am the unfortunate one,
Confused are my thoughts,
And in my bosom I glow with grief and jealousy!
A crude grief is in my soul, that tortures me dreadfully,
And lacerates my heart.

OLGA AND Larina: They will be sad indeed on the morrow for such insane fury!

CHORUS: It is disgraceful!

ONEGHIN: I should not have wounded your soul;
And now remorse stings my heart!

CHORUS: It is pitiful, indeed!

LENSKI: The maiden with the loving face,
In whose glance shines sincerity,
(*With bitterness*).
She inebriates you on the moment,
Only to deceive you,
And leave you to your sorrows!

ONEGHIN: Io nol dovea turbar, lo sento!

TATIANA: Ah! Perduta io sono, il core mel disse,
Io pianger non oso, non oso.
Ah! perchè plorar,
Felice ei farmi non puote, ahimè!

OLGA: Ai lor furori li abbandono, io no,
Colpevol no, non sono davver,
Fra loro discordia sol regna discordia,
Un detto nemici li rende.
Ah! spensierata gioventu;
Ignota a lor è la virtù.

LARINA: Davver i lor furori insani,
Preparan triste l'indomani!
Spensierata gioventù;
Sol regna fra loro discordia,
Un detto nemici li rende.
Ah! spensierata gioventù;
Ignota a lor è la virtù.

ONEGHIN: Di vero affetto Lenski amai,
Io nol dovea giammai turbar.
Io non dovea piagar quell'alma,
Colpevol io sono, lo sento.
Al rimirar sì gran dolor,
Ho di rimorso pieno il cor.
Or mi sospinge il fato già.
E' d'uopo ch'io risponda a tanta offesa!

LENSKI: Ah! no! no, colpevol tu non sei.
Angiol mio, sei pura, mio bene,
Ei solo fu vile, punirlo si deve.

CORO: Spensierata gioventù,
Sol regna fra loro discordia,
Un detto nemici li rende!
Possibil mai! che un dì sì bello finir
Si debba in un duello.

ONEGHIN: Ai cenni vostri io son!
Or basta! V'ho udito, sta ben!
Follia, signor! Preziosa inver
Per voi fia la lezione! . . .

LENSKI: Sia! pur! Domani! Vedrem
chi di noi n'ha d'uopo!
son folle! Ebben sia pu!
Ma voi . . . siete un vile seduttore!

ONEGHIN: Ah! tacete, o qui v'uccido!
(*Larina, Olga ed una parte degl'invitati trattengono Lenski. Tatiana piange. Oneghin si precipita su Lenski. Vengono separati. Oneghin si allontana e volge le spalle a Lenski*).

ONEGHIN: I should not have disturbed you,
I feel it!

TATIANA: Ah! now I am lost,
My heart told me so,
I will not dare weep.
Ah! but why weep,
For he cannot make me happy!

OLGA: I will not give myself up
To their violence,
I am not to blame, no indeed,
Nothing but discord reigns among them,
And a mere word makes them enemies.
Ah! careless youth;
Virtue is unknown to you.

LARINA: Indeed with their insane violence,
They will be sad tomorrow!
Careless youth.
Nothing but discord reigns among them,
And one cross word makes them enemies.
Ah! careless youth!
Virtue is unknown to you.

ONEGHIN: I loved Lenski with all my heart,
And I should never have disturbed him.
Now, I have wounded his soul,
I am to blame, I know it.
To look upon such grief,
My heart is filled with remorse.
And now I shall trust to luck,
For it is up to me
To account for my offense!

LENSKI: Ah! no, no, you are not guilty,
My angel, my love, you are pure,
He alone is the coward,
And we must punish him.

CHORUS: Careless youth,
Nothing but discord reigns among them,
And a cross word makes them enemies!
Is it possible that this beautiful day
Will end in a duel?

ONEGHIN: I am here at your command!
Silence! I hear you! all is well!
Foolishness, Sir!
Let all this teach you a costly lesson!..

LENSKI: Let it be! Tomorrow
We will see
Which one of us is guilty!
Is it madness! Very well, let it be!
But you . . . .you are a vile corrupter!

ONEGHIN: Ah! be silent, or I will kill you right here!
(*Larina, Olga and some of the guests hold back Lenski. Tatiana weeps. Oneghin throws himself upon Lenski. They are separated. Oneghin withdraws with his back turned to Lenski*).

CORO: Ciò non sarà,
Pur impedirlo sapremo, giammai,
Il sangue versato non fia,
Uscire non debbon; fermate!
Non si deve lasciarli partire.

OLGA: Vladimir! Deh! ti calma, io t'imploro.

LENSKI: Ah! Olga! Per sempre addio!

CORO: Sventurato! (*Lenski si allontana precipitosamente. Oneghin lo segue*).

## SCENA IV

(*La scena rappresenta un molino sulla riva d'un fiumicello. Comincia a far giorno. E' d'inverno*).
(*All'alzarsi del sipario Lenski e Saretzki sono già in iscena. Lenski siede pensieroso sotto un albero. Saretzki passeggia con impazienza*).

SARETZKI: Ebbene? Non s'è presentato ancor l'avversario?

LENSKI: tosto ei qui sarà.

SARETZKI: Ma per mia fede pur mi sembra strano.
Ch'ei non sia qui!
E' tempo alfin!
Credea che giunto fosse già!
(*Saretzki va verso il molino ed entra in conversazione col mugnaio che ha veduto in fondo alla scena. —Lenski continua a rimanere seduto*).

LENSKI: Lontan, lontan da me ne andaste,
Lontan da me miei dolci dì?
(*S'alza e viene alla ribalta*).
Qual sorte arrechi il nuovo sole . . .
Ahimè! discerner non m'è dato.
L'asconde il dubbio ed il mister!
L'arcano di svelar non val!
L'acuto dardo fia mortale,
Oppur lontan da me ne andrà.
Non cale: gaudio oppur dolor,
Ha fissa l'ora sua fatale!
A che scrutar tanto mister
E della tenebre . . . l'imper!!
Rosato sorge albor novello
Raggiante splende il divo sol!
Ed io già forse nell'avello
Avrò scordato e pene e duol!
E la memoria del poeta tarrà
Di Lete l'ondaqueta,
E ognun mi scorderà, ma tu?!
Tu Olga! . . .
(*Con molto espressione*).
Fanciulla cara di' tu non verrai
A lacrimar sulla mia tomba pensando:
Quant'ei pur m'amò . . .
All'amor mio ei consacrò,
La triste sua vita affanosa.
Ah! Olga! quanto t'ho adorato!
A te soltanto ho consacrato
Il mio pensiero, il mio amore:
Ah! Olga! quant'io t'adorai!

CHORUS: This cannot be,
We shall know how to prevent it,
Blood will not be shed,
They must not go; stop them!
We must not let them go away.

OLGA: Vladimir! Alas! calm yourself,
I beseech you.

LENSKI: Ah! Olga! Goodbye forever! . . . .

CHORUS: Unfortunate! (*Lenski withdraws quickly. Oneghin follows him*).

## SCENE IV

(*The scene represents a mill on the bank of a small river. It is daylight, and a winter morning.—As the curtain rises Lenski and Saretzski are already on the stage; Lenski under a tree, and in a thoughtful mood. Saretzski walks up and down impatiently*).

SARETZSKI: Well? Has the opponent not appeared yet? . . .

LENSKI: He will be here shortly.

SARETZSKI: In my faith, yet it seem strange,
That he should be here!
It is almost time!
I thought he had arrived!
(*Saretzski goes toward the mill, and starts to converse with the miller whom he has spied in back of the stage. Lenski still remains seated*)

LENSKI: Far, far away from me
The sweet days have gone by!
(*Rises and comes forward on the platform*).
What fate will the new sun bring . . .
Alas! I cannot guess.
It conceals all doubts, and mysteries!
And it would be worthless
To disclose the secret!
The deadly sword will decide his lot,
Or take him far, far away from me.
I care not: joy or sorrow,
His fatal hour is fixed!
Fresh is the dawn of a new day,
When the divine soul beams radiantly!
And I, perhaps, in my grave,
Will have forgotten sorrows and pains!
And the memory of the poet will be dipped
In the peaceable billows of Lete,
And everyone will have forgotten me, but you! You Olga!!!
(*With great feeling*).
Tell me dear, will you not come.
To mourn over my grave, thinking:
How much he loved me! . . . .
And for my love he sacrificed,
His sad, and strenuous life.
Ah! Olga! how much I have worshipped you!
And to you only I have given,
All my thoughts, all my love!
Ah! Olga! I have worshipped you!
My beloved, my sweet love!
Alas! come! Alas! come!
My sweet love!
Alas! come here close to my heart.
Far, far away from me,
Your beautiful days have gone by;
Good-bye forever, my beautiful days!

Diletta mia, mio dolce amor!
Deh! vien! deh vien!
Mio dolce amor!
Deh! vien qui sul mio cor!
M'inebbria, o bella, del tuo amor!
Lontan, lontan da me ne andaste
miei dolci dì;
Per sempre addio miei dolci di! . . . .

## SCENA V

(*Saretzki s'avvicina a Lenski*).

SARETZKI: Ei giunse alfin!
Alcun con sè conduce . . .
Chi mai sarà? (*Entrano Oneghin ed il suo servo Guillot, che reca le pistole.—Oneghin saluta*).

ONEGHIN: Ai cenni vostri sono.
L'indugio perdonate!

SARETZKI: Vi prego. Il pardrin dov'è?
Pedanti esser qui convien!
Gli scontri, no, non son gioco,
L'antica legge rispettar si deve qua.
Non c'è che far gli scontri,
No, non sono un gioco.
Il mio dover io compirò.

ONEGHIN: E noi, signor, ve ne lodiam!
Il mio secondo è qui:
Monsieur Guillot!
Al suo mandato appien risponde.
Suppongo accetto vi sarà!
A voi signori ignoto ancora,
Ma già s'intende, è un uomo d'onore!
(*Saretzki risponde con freddezza*).

ONEGHIN (*a Lenski*). Che? Miei signor?

LENSKI: Andiam, son prono.
(*Saretzki s'allontana con Guillot per fissore le condinioni del duello. Lenski ed Oneghin restano in faspettativa senza guardarsi*).

LENSKI: Sia pur! Distrutta hai la mia fede,
Impera l'odio nel mio cor.
Il dolce affetto più non riede,
Che ieri pur ci legava ancor.
Tutto è finito.
Un istante nemico odiato t'ho dinnante
E della morte, nel mister
Sogghigna l'avido sembiante!

ONEGHIN: Ah! Ridiam dell'odio e del dolor
Finchè ne siamo in tempo ancor!
Scordiam l'offesa d'un istante . . .

LENSKI: No! No! No! Mai!
(*Saretzki e Guillot hanno caricato le armi e misurato la distanza. Saretzki mette al posto gli avversari e consegna loro le pistole. Guillot impaurito si nasconde dietro un albero*).

## SCENE V

(*Saretzski approaches Lenski*).

SARETZSKI: He is here at least!
And someone is with him . . . .
Who could it be?
(*Enter Oneghin followed by his servant Guillot, who carries the weapons.—Oneghin bows*).

ONEGHIN: I am at your command.
Forgive the delay!

SARETZSKI: I pray you. Where is the godfather?
It is proper to respect the old laws here!
For this is an encounter, not a game.
I will do my duty.

ONEGHIN: And we praise you, sir!
My assistant is here:
Mr. Guillot!
Who fully answers the order.
I presume you will accept him!
Though he is not known to you,
They all know him,
As a man highly esteemed! (*Saretzski bows coldly*).

ONEGHIN: (*To Lenski*). Well, my gentleman?

LENSKI: Come, I am ready.
(*Saretzski departs with Guillot to fix the conditions of the duel. Lenski and Oneghin in expectation without looking at each other*).

LENSKI: Let it be!
You have destroyed my faith,
Hatred rules in my heart.
The sweet passion that still bound us yesterday,
Does not smile upon us to-day.
All is over.
Death with its mystery
Sneers eagerly at your face!

ONEGHIN: Ah Till we are ready
Let us laugh at hatred, and pain!
Let us forget the offense for a moment . . . .

LENSKI: No! No! No! Never!
(*Saretzski and Guillot have loaded the weapons and are measuring the distance. Saretzski places the antagonists, and hands them the weapons. Guillot is frightened and hides in back of a tree*).

## Act II, Scene V

**SARETZKI:** Signori, andate! (*Da i tre colpi regolamentari. Gli avversari fanno quattro passi avanti senza mirare. Oneghin avanzando alza la pistola, nel medesimo tempo Lenski comincia a prender la mira.— Oneghin tira. Lenski tentenna e cade. Saretzki s'avvicina a lui e l'osserva attentamente. Oneghin pure si precipita verssо il caduto*).

**ONEGHIN:** (*con voce strozzata*). Morto?

**SARETZKI:** Morto? (*Oneghin disperato si copre il volto colle mani*).

*SIPARIO.*

**SARETZSKI:** Gentlemen, Go! (*He fires three regulations shots. The antagonists take four steps forward without aiming. Oneghin advances, and raises the pistol; at the same time Lenski aims at him— Oneghin fires. Lenski staggers and falls. Saretzski approaches him and observes him intently. Oneghin also rushes forward to aid the fallen one*).

**ONEGHIN:** (*With a choking voice*). Dead?

**SARETZSKI:** Dead! (*Oneghin in despair covers his face with his hands*).

*CURTAIN.*

# ■ ATTO TERZO

## SCENA I

(*La scena rappresenta una sala laterale di ricca casa signorile in Pietroburgo*).

(*Gl'invitati traversano la scena ballando la polonese*).

**ONEGHIN:** (*a destra*). Qui pur m'annoio!
Lo splendor dei balli e delle feste
Dissipar non puote
Le pene del mio cor!
(*S'avvicina alla ribalta*).
Ramingo andai per l'universo,
I tristi dì volea scordar!
Ahimè! Che mai potria sanar,
Il crudo mio soffrir perverso!
Son qui venuto e qui ancor
Il tedio ho soltanto in cor!
(*Entra il principe Gremin dando il braccio a Tatiana*).

**CORO:** Mira la Gremina! Mirate, mirate!
(*Tatiana siede sul divano. Invitati d'ambo i sessi le si avvicinano continuamente a farle omaggio*).
(*Oneghin, sorpreso tiene gli occhi fissi su Tatiana*).

**ONEGHIN:** Oh! ciel, Tatiana . . . parmi!
No! Che! Come in questi luoghi?
Esser non può! Inganno è il mio!

**CORO:** Un cortigiano,
un'ipocondrico signor,
In lidi estranei andò . . . .
Or qui . . . ritorno fè fra noi Oneghin!..

**ONEGHIN:** Or, dimmi sù,
E' nota a te la dama là
Ch'a rosso il tocco?

**GREMIN:** La mia sposa ell'è.

**ONEGHIN:** M'è grato in ver!
Io nol sapeva..
Da quando?

# ■ ACT III

## SCENE I

(*The scene represents a parlor in a rich mansion in Petrograd*).

(*The guests cross the stage, dancing the Polonaise*).

**ONEGHIN:** (*To the right*). I am bored! Here, too!
The gaiety of the dances, and the feast
Cannot make me forget
The pain in my heart!
(*He goes to the end of the stage*).
Aimlessly I roamed around the world,
Trying to forget the unhappy days!
Alas! What could ever heal
The keen pangs of my heart?
I have come here,
And here again I find
Weariness in my heart!
(*Enter Prince Gremin, offering his arm to Tatiana*).

**CHORUS:** Look at Gremin over there!
Look! look!
(*Tatiana sits on the sofa. The guests go up to her to pay their homage*).
(*Oneghin stares at Tatiana in surprise*).

**ONEGHIN:** Oh! Heavens, Tatiana . . . seems like her!
No! What! In this place?
It cannot be! I must be mistaken!

**CHORUS:** A courtier, and a lazy man,
Had gone to strange shores . . .
And hither . . . Is Oneghin among us again? . . . .

**ONEGHIN:** Now, tell me,
Do you know that lady over there
With the red cap?

**GREMIN:** She is my wife.

**ONEGHIN:** I am glad indeed!
I did not know.
How long?

**GREMIN:** Son due anni già.

**ONEGHIN:** Il nome?

**GREMIN:** Dei Larini, Tatiana. E' nota a te?

**ONEGHIN:** Fur miei vicin!

**GREMIN:** (*con nobiltà, calma e sentimento*). Ad ogni età l'amor s'apprende,
E i generosi sensi accende
Nell'innocente e giovin cor,
A cui la vita ignota è ancor.
Nel vecchio core del guerrier,
Dal bianco crin s'accende alter!
Oneghin, la menzogna è vana,
Amor possente ho per Tatiana!
La desolata vita, ahimè,
Correva ed ella apparve a me,
Quale vision che viva splende
E il vecchio cor gioioso rende.
Er'io già lasso,
Solo inganni aveva in cor la gioventù.
Fanciulle ancor nel fior degli anni.

**GREMIN:** It has been two years already.

**ONEGHIN:** Her name?

**GREMIN:** Tatiana, from the Larini. Do you know her?

**ONEGHIN:** They were my neighbors!

**GREMIN:** (*With dignity, calmness and feeling*). One learns to love at all ages,
And kindled are the noble feelings
Of the young and innocent heart,
To whom lfe is yet unknown.
Even in the heart of the old warrior,
Fiercely burns the flame of love!
Oneghin, it is vain to lie,
I love Tatiana with a powerful love!
My lonely life, Alas!
Was going by, when she appeared to me,
Like a vision that lives and sparkles,
And brought back happiness to my old heart.
For in my younger days my heart had been deceived,
By maidens still in their frivolous youth.

## SCENA II

**GREMIN:** Amico andiam; io ti presenterò. (*Gremin conduce Oneghin presso Tatiana*).
Mia cara: Io ti presento Oneghin,
Parente e caro amico egli è!
L'accogli tu.
(*Oneghin s'inchina profondamente. Tatiana risponde semplicemente e senza scomporsi*)

**TATIANA:** Ben fortunata . . .
Io vi conobbi già, signor.

**ONEGHIN:** Gran tempo già passò.

**TATIANA:** Ed ora? Or dai poder veniste qui?

**ONEGHIN:** Oh! no. Da luoghi estrani son qui tornato.

**TATIANA:** Da lungo?

**ONEGHIN:** Sol'oggi.

**TATIANA:** (*a Gremin*). Andiam. Son lassa già!
(*Tatiana al braccio di Gremin esce, rispondendo ai saluti degl'invitati. Oneghin la segue collo sguardo*).

**ONEGHIN:** E lei, mio, Dio, quella Tatiana,
Che nel silenzio e nel mister
Un dì me schiuse lusinghier
Ingenua il dolce suo pensiero
Ed io, spietato fui severo.
E' dessa, sì! ch'io disprezzai,
Di cui la sorte irrisi insano?
E' dessa e fia possibil mai?
Cotanta calma, tanto ardir!
Vaneggio inver. E sogno, ahimè?
Dubbio, rimpianto sento in me!
Qual nuovo senso arcan m'assale?
Qual fiamma s'agita nel cor?
Saria disprezzo o forse amor?
Non v'ha più dubbio, ahimè!

## SCENE II

**GREMIN:** Come, my friend; I will introduce you.
(*Gremin takes Oneghin up to Tatiana*).
My dear, meet Oneghin,
A relative, and a dear friend of mine!
Make him feel at home.
(*Oneghin bows deeply. Tatiana acknowledges with a slight bow*).

**TATIANA:** Very fortunate . . .
I have already met you, sir.

**ONEGHIN:** A long time passed.

**TATIANA:** And now? Have you just come home from the farm?

**ONEGHIN:** Oh! no. I have come back from foreign lands.

**TATIANA:** Is it long?

**ONEGHIN:** Only today.

**TATIANA:** (*To Gremin*). Come. I am tired!
(*Tatiana departs arm in arm with Gremin, and bows in answer to the greetings of the guests. Oneghin follows her with his glance*).

**ONEGHIN:** It is she, yes, whom I despised,
Who in secret
One day freely revealed
Her flattering thought for me?
And I was cruelly severe.
It is she, yes, who I despised,
And at whose fate I laughed insanely?
Can it possibly be she?
So calm, and so haughty!
I must be dreaming. Alas!
Doubts and remorse grip me!
What new passion stirs in my heart?
Can it be hatred, or love?
There is no doubt, Alas!

Io 'amo d'insensato ardente amore.
Perduto io son! Ebben ch'importa?
La dolce speme è alfin risorta.
Il tossico fatal m'inebbria
Un grato sogno arride a me!
Rapito io son.
L'acuto stral del guardo suo dolce
E fatal si fe' signore del mio core!

I love her with an ardent passion.
I am lost! What matters?
Sweet hope is revived again.
The fatal venom intoxicates me.
A pleasant dream smiles down upon me!
I am charmed by her beautiful glance,
Which is as fatal to my heart,
As a pointed arrow!

## SCENA III

*(La scena reppresenta una stanza da ricevere in casa Gremin— Entra Tatiana in elegante abito da mattina. Ha in mano una lettera).*

**TATIANA:** Ah! Povero mio cor!
Ancora Oneghin apparve innanzi
A me quel seduttor crudele.
Col guardo suo fatal ei ridestava in cor
Nell'alma misera il crudo mio dolor!
Dei dì trascorsi più non ho memoria,
Fanciulla innanzi a lui, ahimè!
Mi sento ancora!
*(Piange).*
*(Oneghin compare sulla soglia; rimane qualche tempo immobile a contemplare Tatiana piangente. Poi s'avanza con vivacità e le s'inginocchia ai piedi. Tatiana lo guarda senza sorpresa e senza rancore, poi gli fa cenno di alzarsi).*

**TATIANA:** Ven prego! Basta! Palesar vi debbo
Tutto il mio pensiero!
Non vi sovvien del triste dì là
Nell'annoso parco, fra gli aulenti fior,
I vostri accenti ascoltai,
Prostrata nel dolor.

**ONEGHIN:** Pietàde, sì di me vi prenda.
Io m'ingannai . . . punito io sono!

**TATIANA:** Oneghin! ero allor fanciulla,
Avea la mente ingenua allor.
Ed io v'amai ma in preda al nulla
Spingeste il povero mio cor!
Che deste a me?
Severi accenti!
D'un puro cor pene e tormenti
Conoscevate voi, signor!
Ed ora? Dio! io tremo ancor
Al sovvenir di tanto strazio
E di sì rio dolor!
Io non v'accuso, no!
In quel fatal momento,
Foste uom d'onore!
Non v'ingannaste no, signor!
Il so! nel queto mio ritiro
Lontan dal mondo incantator,
Io vi dispiacqui allor!
Ed ora? *(Animandosi).*
Perchè mi tormentate ancor?
Perchè lo sguardo a me volgeste?
Fra gli splendor di vaghe feste

## SCENE III

*(The scene represets a parlor in Gremin's house. — Enter Tatiana wearing a beautiful morning dress. She has a letter in her hand).*

**TATIANA:** Ah! My poor heart!
Again Oneghin has come before me,
That cruel seducer.
His fatal look has roused in my heart
And in my soul, the miserable grief!
I had forgotten the days gone by,
Alas! I feel like a young girl again before him!
*(She weeps).*
*(Oneghin appears on the threshold; he stops short to look at Tatiana, who is weeping. He approaches her quickly, and kneels at her feet. Tatiana looks at him without surprise, and without ill feeling, then motions to him to rise).*

**TATIANA:** I pray you! Silence!
I will reveal to you all my thoughts!
Do you remember the sad day there
In the ancient park, among the fragrant flowers,
When, prostrated by grief,
I listened to your words.

**ONEGHIN:** Oh, have pity on me!
I deceived myself . . . and now I am punished!

**TATIANA:** Oneghin! I was then a young and innocent girl.
I loved you, and you broke my heart!
What did you give me?
Harsh words!
The pains and griefs of a true heart!
You knew, sir!
And now? God! I still tremble
To think of such mockery,
And so much wicked pain!
No, I do not blame you!
For in that fatal moment,
You were an honorable man!
You were not deceived, sir!
I know! When I quietly retired
Far away from the world's temptations
You were displeased then!
And now?
*(Animated).*
Why do you torment me again?
Why did you look at me again?

Oppur vi tenta l'alto onor
Che m'ha la sorte riservato?
palese a voi si fe' l'amor?
Dei gran signor la cortesia.
O vi sorride l'onta mia,
Che a tutti qui saria svelata?
Il pianto più crudel sarà,
Più vanto e gloria a voi darà?

**ONEGHIN:** Ah . . . che dite? Ahimè!
*(Con passione).*
Possibil fia che tanto affetto
Menzogna vil vi sembrerà? . . .
Il mio soffrir solo dispetto,
Il vostro cor giudicherà?
Voi non sapete quanto amore,
Qual face ardente in cor mi sta!
Del mio straziante e rio dolore
Vi penderebbe alfin pietà!
Io qui prostrato al vostro piede,
Mi sento l'anima straziar!
Vorrei ridarvi alfin la fede,
Al vosto piè vorrei pregar!

**TATIANA:** Io piango . . .

**ONEGHIN:** Dio! Questo pianto è più prezioso d'un tesoro!

**Tatiana e ONEGHIN:** Ah! Fu sì presso a noi la gioia,
Sì presso . . . sì presso! Oh! ciel!

**TATIANA:** La mia sorte omai decisa è già senza ritorno.
Io sposa sono.
Per pietà, si, per pietà.
Deh, mi lasciate!

**ONEGHIN:** Lasciarvi? Lasciarvi?
Follia! lasciarvi? Mai?
*(Colla massima espressione).*
No, scordar, no, non poss'io,
Il vostro viso incantatore.
Io no, domar non posso, o Dio!
L'ardente brama del mio core!
Darei la vita per destar in voi
L'amor che m'arde, insano!
*(Animandosi gradatamente le cade di nuovo inginocchiato ai piedi e le prende la mano con vivacità).*
Vorrei soffrir, distruggermi, pregar . . .
Morir dicendo: t'amo, t'amo!
Questo è il sogno mio divin,
Sol quest'io bramo!

**TATIANA:** *(Impaurita, ritira la mano).* Oneghin, parli in voi l'onor,
Non mi spezzate invano il cor.

**ONEGHIN:** Lasciarvi, ahimè non posso!

**TATIANA:** Oneghin! Per pietà, sì, per pietà!
Deh! mi lasciate!

**ONEGHIN:** Crudele!

**TATIANA:** A che celarlo?
Mentir non vale!
Ah! Io v'amo ancor!
*(Tatiana esaltata dalla confes-*

Among the splendor and charm of the feast,
My love revealed itself to you,
And now, does not your honor
Tempt you to consider my state?
My shame only makes you smile?
It will become known to everyone?
The stronger my anguish
The greater your boast?

**ONEGHIN:** Ah! . . . What are you saying? Alas!
*(Passionately).*
Can it be possible that such great love,
Would seem to you a vile falsehood?
If my grief is only pretense,
Your heart wll then decide!
You do not know what love
Is glowing in my heart!
Or else you would take pity
Upon my sins, and pains!
And here prostrated at your feet,
I feel my soul abased!
Again I would want to give back to you all my trust,
And at your feet I would want to pray!

**TATIANA:** I weep . . .

**ONEGHIN:** God! These tears are more precious than riches!

**Tatiana and ONEGHIN:** Ah! Joy has always been with us.
Yes with us . . . yes with us! Oh! Heaven!

**TATIANA:** My fate is now decided.
I am married.
For pity's sake, yes, for pity's sake,
Alas! Leave me!

**ONEGHIN:** Leave you? Folly! leave you? Never!
*(With great expression).*
No, I cannot forget
Your beautiful face.
No, I cannot subdue, Oh God!
The great desire of my heart!
I would give my life to rouse in you
The love that burns in my bosom!
*(Gradually picking up courage, he falls again kneeling at her feet, and he takes her hand vigorously).*
I would want to suffer, and die saying:
I love you, I love you!
This is my heavenly dream,
And only this I wish for!

**TATIANA:** *(Frightened, withdraws her hand).* Oneghin, think of your esteem,
Do not break my heart in vain.

**ONEGHIN:** Leave you! Alas! I cannot!

**TATIANA:** Oneghin? For pity's sake, yes, for pity's sake!
Alas! Leave me!

**ONEGHIN:** Cruel one!

**TATIANA:** Why should I conceal it?
It s useless to lie?
Alas! I still love you!

# Act III, Scene III

*sione fatta si abbandona sul petto di Oneghin, che cerca di abbracciarla, ma essa rientrando tosto in sè si allontana da lui).*

*(Tatiana excited by the confession she has made, leans on Oneghin's bosom. He tries to embrace her, but she withdraws rather sharply).*

**ONEGHIN:** Tu m'ami ancor?
E' sogno oppur delirio è questo?
O gioia! m'ami ancor!
Qual ti sognai t'ho ritrovata!

**ONEGHIN:** You still love me?
Is this a dream, or a delirium?
My love! you still love me!
I found you, just as I saw you in a dream!

**TATIANA:** No! no! Quel che fu non torna più!
Ad altro amai giurai mia fede,
Al giuro mio non mancherò!
Fedel per sempre a lui sarò!
*(Vuole allontanarsi, ma cade estenuata sopra un divano).*

**TATIANA:** No! no! What has gone by, will not come back!
I have sworn my troth to someone else,
I shall not break my pledge!
I will always be faithful to him!
*(She tries to withdraw, but falls exhausted on the sofa).*

**ONEGHIN:** *(con passione vivissima, inginocchiandosi).* Deh! non fuggir! tu m'ami, il sento, pietà,
Pietà del mio dolor.
Tu m'ami, il dolce caro accento
Destò la vita nel mio cor!
Già nel pensier del sommo Iddio
Creata fosti sol per me, lo sento,
Dio ti fece mia per la vita, per l'eternità!
Or mia tu sei! Da me lontano fuggir,
Diletta, cerch'invano.
Per me, mio ben, scordar tu dei.
La data fè, or mia tu sei.

**ONEGHIN:** *(With great passion, keeling).* Alas! do not run away!
You love me, I know it.
Have pity, have pity on my grief.
You love me, and your sweet voice,
Has roused new life in my heart!
Already in the thought of the supreme God,
You were created only for me, I feel it.
God made you mine for life, and for eternity!
Now you are mine!
My love, do not try in vain
To run away from me.
For me, my love, forget your given troth.
You are mine now.

**TATIANA:** *(alzandosi).* Oneghin! Io giurai mia fede.

**TATIANA:** *(Rising).* Oneghin! I have sworn my faith!

**ONEGHIN:** Da me lontano fuggir non puoi tu!

**ONEGHIN:** You cannot run away from me!

**TATIANA:** Il fato mio si compirà.
Colui che il nome, il cor mi diede
A lui fedele ognor m'avrà.
Mio Dio, tremenda è la mia croce.

**TATIANA:** My fate will come to an end.
He who gave me his name, and heart,

Mi spezza il core il suo dolor.
Ma pur la voce dell'onor possente,
Crudele, divina solve il dubbio atroce.

To him I will always be true.
My God, it is terrible to be tormented.
The pain breaks my heart.
Yet the powerful voice of my self-esteem
Will solve the atrocious doubt.

**ONEGHIN:** La data fè, per me tu dei scordar!
Sì! Per me, mio ben, scordar tu dei
La data fè or mia tu sei!
Deh! non fuggir, pietà, pietà,
Tu m'ami ancora, tu mel dicesti,
Mia tu sei, si, mia sei tu!

**ONEGHIN:** For my sake, you must forget your given faith!
Yes! for me, my love, you must forget!
Now you are mine!
Alas! do not run away, have pity!
You love me yet, you told me,
You are mine, yes, you are mine!

**TATIANA:** Io m'allontano!

**TATIANA:** I will go away!

**ONEGHIN:** No, no, no! mai!

**ONEGHIN:** No, no, no! Never!

**TATIANA:** Mi lascia!
*(Oneghin cerca di trascinar seco Tatiana, che resiste con forza, ma va perdendo energia).*

**TATIANA:** Leave me!
*(Oneghin tries to draw Tatiana toward him; she tries hard to resist him, but gradually lose energy).*

**ONEGHIN:** O Tatiana, non fuggir!

**ONEGHIN:** Oh Tatiana! do not run away!

**TATIANA:** No, salda è la mia fede!

**TATIANA:** No, sound is my faith!

**ONEGHIN:** Mio dolce amor, mio dolce amor!

**ONEGHIN:** My sweet love! my sweet love!

**TATIANA:** Pietà di me.

**TATIANA:** Pity me! . . . .

**ONEGHIN:** Io t'amo, ahimè!

**ONEGHIN:** I love you, Alas!

**TATIANA:** Per sempre addio!

**TATIANA:** Goodbye forever!

**ONEGHIN:** Mia sei tu!
*(Oneghin rimane qualche tempo colpito da disperazione).*
Vergogna, orror! Si spezza or tu mio cor!
*(Esce precipitosamente).*

**ONEGHIN:** You are mine!
*(Oneghin remains for some time in a hopeless mood).*
Shame! horror! My heart is broken!
*(Withdraws quickly).*

*FINE.*

*END.*

# *Mignon* (1866)

MUSIC BY AMBROISE THOMAS ■ LIBRETTO BY MICHEL CARRÉ AND JULES BARBIER

This three-act *opéra-comique*, set to a libretto by Michel Carré and Jules Barbier (based on Goethe's Wilhelm Meister's Lehrjahre), premiered at the Opéra-Comique in Paris on November 17, 1866. In the courtyard of a German inn, Philine and Laerte, two actors, watch as Lothario, an old, absent-minded musician, and Wilhelm Meister, a traveling student, protect Mignon, a pretty young woman, from a gypsy's bad behavior. Mignon gives them both flowers as her thanks for their efforts, and Meister gives his to Philine when she comes to meet him. Mignon tells Meister that she is the gypsy's servant and that she has no memory of her childhood. Meister decides to give the gypsy enough money to buy Mignon's freedom, for which she is very grateful. She is also envious that he seems to prefer Philine over her. In Philine's bedroom in a castle where she and Laerte are about to perform *A Midsummer Night's Dream*, Mignon and Meister come in while Philine is making her preparations for the play. Mignon pretends that she is asleep so that she can watch the others. When they leave, she puts on one of Philine's costumes, much to Philine's and Meister's scorn. Meister decides that he will not travel with her in order to avoid further scenes. Lothario and Mignon are together in the park, where she wishes out loud that the castle would burn down to the ground with everyone inside. The play ends and Meister and the actors come out to the park. Meister is sorry that he was mean to Mignon, and to make amends Philine sends her inside the castle to fetch the flowers which Meister had given to her (the very bouquet that Mignon had given to Meister). As she enters the conservatory, flames rise around he, but she is rescued by Meister. At the Cipriani castle, where Meister has brought both Lothario and Mignon, who has been very ill, it becomes clear that this is the castle from which Mignon was abducted when she was a small child. Lothario's absent-mindedness has left him in these surroundings, and it turns out that he is her long-lost father.

---

## ■ ACTE PREMIER

*Une cour de taverne allemande. A gauche, corps de bâtiment dont l'un des côtés fait face au public. Au premier étage, porte vitrée donnant sur le perron d'un escalier extérieur qui descend dans la cour. A droite, un bangar. Table et tonnelles.*

*Les Bourgeois sont attablés et boivent; quelquea Garçons de taverne sont occupés à les servir.*

CHOEUR des BOURGEOIS: Bons bourgeois et notables,
Assis autour des tables,
Fumons tranquillement,
Et buvons en fumant!
La bière brune ou blanche,
Ecume dans les pots,
C'est aujourd'hui dimanche,
C'est le jour du repos!
(*LOTHARIO parait au fond sur le seuil de la taverne. Il s'avance lentement, s'arrête au milieu de la cour et chante en s'accompagnant sur un luth.*)

LOTHARIO: Fugitif et tremblant, je vais de porte en porte,
Où le hasard me guide, où l'orage m'emporte!

## ■ ACT I

*The courtyard of a German Inn. To the left a wing of a building, the facade of which faces the spectator. On the first floor, a little door, with glass window, which opens upon a parapet, from which a flight of steps leads down to the court yard. To the right a penthouse, or shed. Arbors and tables, etc.*

*The townspeople, etc., sit down at the table and drink. Waiters belonging to the inn, hurry to and fro, attending officiously to the wants of the customers.*

CHORUS: Great magnates, and towns-folk small,
To table now sit down,
Our cigars we quickly light,
Fresh zest it will give unto the drink!
Fill high! the foaming beer
In jugs does now approach;
A festive day is this indeed,
A day of mirth and joy!
(*Lothario appears at back, at the entrance to the inn. He advances slowly, stopping near the middle of the courtyard, when he begins to sing—accompanying himself the while on his harp.*)

LOTHARIO: A lonely wanderer am I. I stray from door to door.
As fate shall guide, or as the storm shall hurry me;

Des misérables Dieu prend soin!
Elle vit! elle vit! Et je cherche sa trace!
Je me repose un jour, en seul jour, et je passe!
Je vais plus loin, toujours plus loin!

UN BOURGEOIS: (*À ses viosins.*)
Oui; c'est Lothario, le vieux chanteur nomade.

DEUXIÈME BOURGEOIS: On dit que le malheur a troublé sa raison.

UN BOURGEOIS: D'où vient-il?

DEUXIÈME BOURGEOIS: On l'ignore.

CHOEUR: Allons, mon camarade! Viens boire, et laisse là ta plaintive chanson!
(*On fait asseoir Lothario sous la tonelle, et on lui verso à boire.*)

CHOEUR: Bons bourgeois et notables,
Assis autour des tables,
Fumons tranquillement,
Et buvons en fumant!
La bière brune et blanche,
Ecume dans les pots,
C'est aujourd'hui dimanche,
C'est le jour du repos!
(*Quelques buveurs remontent au fond et se groupent pres le seuil de la taverne.*)

But heaven protects the wretched with kind fostering care!
She lives—I feel this in my heart; her steps I anxiously do trace,—
A moment here I will repose—my journey I will then resume;
Far, far I'll roam in search of her!

1ST CIT: Listen to him, it is Lothario the wandering minstrel!

2ND CIT: It is said that grief has taken his reason from him.

1ST CIT: But how came this?

2ND CIT: The cause I know not.

CHORUS: (*To Lothario.*) Take courage, friend!
Give over your singing—
Come and sit down with us!
(*The Chorus makes Lothario sit down with them, beneath the vine-trellis. They fill a glass for him.*)

CHORUS: Magnates great, and towns-folk small
To table now sit down,
Our cigars, let's quickly light,
Fresh zest it will give unto the drink!
Fill high! the foaming beer
In tankards now draws near.
A festive day is this indeed,
A day of mirth and joy!
(*Several of the convivial party now approach the back of the stage, and form a group near the door of the inn.*)

# Act I

**QUELQUES PAYSANS:** (*Entrant.*) Place, amis! Faites place aux enfants de Bohême, Aux tsiganes, aux zingari! . . . Voici toute la bande avec Jarno lui-même, Et son compère Zafari! (*Entrée des Bohemiens. La bande défile autour du theâtre. Un chariot couvert d'une toile grossière et chargé d'oripeaux de toutes sortes, est trainé sur le devant de la scène par deux ou trois ZINGARI en baillons. JARNO est debout sur le chariot. MIGNON, enveloppée d'un vieux manteau rayè, dort sur une botte de paille au fond du chariot. Un groupe de danseurs, le tambour de basque en maia s'elance en scène. ZAFARI saisit son violon et donne le signal de la danse. Un tambourin et un hautbois l'accompagnent.*)

**PEASANTS:** Room, good friends, for the travelling players! What ho! make way there! See! Jarno with the flower of his tribe comes, And Zaffi, too, is there! (*Procession of gipsies. The entire tribe march round the stage. A cart covered with an old piece of matting, and filled with various articles of household furniture, leads the way drawn by two ragged gipsies. Mignon, wrapped in a tattered mantle, is sleeping at the back of the cart on a sheaf of straw. A party of gipsies, with tambourines in their hands, now rush on the stage. Zaffi takes a violin, and gives the signal for the dance. An oboe and a tambourine serve as accompaniment.*)

**PHILINE:** (*Paraissant sur le balcon, suivie de Laerte.*) Laërte, ami Laërte, accourez au plus vite! Voilà qui nous promet un spectacle esgageant!— Mais ne vous moquez pas et soyez indulgent! A vous asseoir je vous invite. (*Laerte s'asseoit sur le balcon à côté de Philine.*) DANSE BOHEMIENNE

**FILINA:** (*Looking from the balcony with Laertes.*) Quick, my Laertes, just step this way; See—an hour's amusement here awaits us. Laugh not at these good people, but pray make allowance— Let us take our places here! (*Laertes sits down by Filina's side.*) GIPSY DANCE

**UN GROUPE de VIEUX BORGEOIS:** Ces filles de Bohême Ont de fort jolis yeux, Et ma femme elle-même Ne danserait pas mieux!—

**PEASANTS:** The Gypsy girls Have lovely eyes My wife herself Gives them the prize.

**PHILINE et LAËRTE:** O filles de Bohême, Filles au coeur joyeux, Vous aimez, on vous aime, Et tout est pour le mieux!—

**FILINA:** O! Gypsy Girls Just full of zest. You love them, they love you And all is for the best.

**PHILINE et CHOEUR:** Ah, ah, quelle danse folle! Leur gai refrain Nous met en train. Ah, chantons, chantons et buvons, Ah, chantons, chantons et buvons, La danse folle, S'élance et vole, Leur joyeux refrain Nous met tous en train! La danse folle S'élance et vole! Ah, chantons! (*JARNO s'avance au milieu du théâtre et salue l'assemben. Quelques pièces de monnaie tombent à ses pieds. ZAFARI les ramasse.*)

**FILINA and CHORUS:** Oh! What a mad dance Oh! sing! hey! hey! Let us be gay We'll dance and drink, drink and dance We'll dance and drink, drink and dance A dance that's mad Will make us glad A whirl of joy For girl and boy A dance that's mad Will make us glad. (*Jarno advances into the middle of the stage, and salutes the bystanders, who throw to him coins, which Zaffi picks up.*)

**JARNO:** Pour gagner maintenant toute votre indulgence, Et vous remercier de vos dons généreux, Mignon va vous montrer sa vive intelligence. En dansant devant vous le fameux pas des oeufs!

**JARNO:** Gentlemen, for so much kindness in return, And just to show my sense of obligation, Mignon a sample of her skill shall give you; Her far-famed "egg dance" She shall now perform!

**CHOEUR, PHILINE et LAËRTE:** Vivat! rapprochons-nous d'eux Pour voir la danse des oeufs!

**CHORUS, FILINA and LAERTES:** Faith, we even awhile will tarry, This far-famed dance to see!

**JARNO:** (*Se tourant vers Zafari.*) Toi, Zafari, prépare Ton concerto le plus savant!— (*Aux autres Zingari.*) Couvrez le sol d'un tapis rare!— (*S'approchant du chariot et réveillant Mignon.*) Et toi, Mignon, debout! en avant! en avant! (*Zafari prélude sur son violon. Une vielle Zingara couvre le sol d'un lambeau de tapis. Les oeufs y sont déposés par un enfant. MIGNON s'éville à la voix de JARNO et s'avance au milieu du cercle des curieux. Elle tient un bouquet de fleurs sauvages à la main et semble sortir d'un rêve.*)

**JARNO:** (*Turning to Zaffi.*) And now, good Zaffi, quick prepare, Thy choicest song to sing; (*Addressing himself to some of the Gipsies.*) Our beauteous piece of carpet, On the ground now place— (*Approaching the cart and shaking Mignon.*) Up, up, Mignon, to work. (*Zaffi preludes on his violin. An old Gipsy lays on the ground a faded piece of worn out carpet, while a boy places on it several eggs. Mignon, on hearing Jarno's voice, awakes and enters the circle formed by the chorus. She holds in her hand, a bouquet of wild flowers.*)

**PHILINE:** (*À Jarno, du haut du balcon.*) Holà! mon cher monsieur, vous palit-il de nous dire. Quel est ce pauvre enfant qui semble vous maudire De l'avoir de la sorte éveillé sans facon?— Est-ce une fille? est-ce un garçon?—

**FILINA:** (*To Jarno, from the balcony.*) What ho! good sir, permit me to inquire, What hapless being is that just waking up? Say, is it a girl, or strippling lad?

**JARNO:** Ni l'unni l'autre, belle dame, Ni garçon, ni fille, ni femme.

**JARNO:** It is neither one nor other, lady— It is neither woman, girl, nor boy.

**PHILINE:** Qu'est-ce donc alors?

**FILINA:** (*Laughing.*) What is it then I pray?

**JARNO:** (*Ecartant le manteau qui couvre Mignon.*) C'est Mignon! (*Philine et le Choeur éclatent de rire.*)

**JARNO:** (*Raising the mantle which covers the young Gipsy.*) It is—Mignon! (*Filina and the chorus laugh heartily.*)

**MIGNON:** (*À part.*) Ces yeux fixés moi! . . . Ce rire qui m'outrage! . . . Retrouve ta fierté, mon coeur, et ton courage!

**MIGNON:** (*Aside.*) Why are all eyes thus fixed on me? Why laugh they thus—surely to insult and mock me! O heart! resume your wonted strength and courage!

**JARNO:** Allons, saute, Mignon!

**JARNO:** Quick, Mignon, arouse yourself! dance!

**MIGNON:** (*Frappant le terre de son pied nu.*) Non, non, non, non! Je brave ta menace! De t'obéir à la fin je suis lasse!

**MIGNON:** (*Stamping with her foot on the ground.*) Cease your rude tone! It's time I should speak out; I am weary of doing your biding!

**JARNO:** Tu refuses! (*Se tourant vers les Zingara.*) Holà! vous autres, mon bâton! Danse, Mignon! Méchant démon! Ou mon bâton Saura te mettre à la raison!

**JARNO:** What! you refuse! (*Turning to the Gipsies.*) My friends, my stick just pass me. Dance, I say. Then, faith, I'll soon to reason bring you!

**MIGNON:** Non, non, non, non, non, non!

**MIGNON:** No, no! (*Raises stick in a menacing attitude; as he does so Lothario rushes to Mignon and encircles her with his arms as though to protect her.*)

**LOTHARIO:** (*Courant à Mignon qu'il étreint dans ses bras.*) Reprenda courage! Viens, pauvre enfant, Contre sa rage Je te déferi.

**LOTHARIO:** (*To Mignon.*) Take heart I pray, Your shield I'll be! His rage evade— Fly quickly here!

JARNO: (*Avec colère.*) Au diable! au diable!
Vil misérable!
(*Il repousse violemment Lothario.*)
Danse, Mignon!
Méchant démon!
Ou mon bâton
Saura te mettre à la raison!

MIGNON: Non, non, non, non, non, non!
(*Jarno lève son bâton sur Mignon. Entre Wilhelm en habit de voyage, suivi d'un valet qui porte sa valise et son manteau.*)

WILHELM: (*S'élançant au secours de Mignon et retenant le bras de JARNO.*) Holà! coquin! arrête, ou ton heure est venue!

JARNO: Hein? Plâit-il?

WILHELM: (*Tirant un pistolet de sa poche.*) Si tu fais un seul pas je te tue!

JARNO: C'est bon! Je me tiens coi!
(*D'un ton lamentable.*)
Mais je suis ruiné!
Qui de vous me paira ma recette perdue?

PHILINE: (*Sur le balcon, jetant sa bourse à Jarno.*) Tiens donc!
Prends et tais-toi!

MIGNON: (*Partageant son bouquet entre Wilhelm et Lothario.*)
A vous ces fleurs, amis, qui m'aves défendue!—

WILHELM: Qui diantre aurait pu prévoir
Cette bizarre aventure!
Mon coeur, pauvre créature,
M'a seul dicté mon devoir!

PHILINE: (*À part.*) Quel est, je veux le savoir,
Ce beau coureur d'aventure?
Il nous cache sa figure,
Et n'a pas l'air de nous voir.

MIGNON: (*Priant, à l'écart.*) O
Vierge, mon seul espoir,
Protége ta créature!
Je me courbe sans murmure
Devant ton divin pouvoir!

CHOEUR: (*À Jarno.*) Nous reviendrons tous vous voir.
Tant que le dimanche dure,
On chemine à l'aventure
Et l'on vient danser le soir.

JARNO: Messieurs, revenez-nous voir,
Oubliez cette aventure,
Vous serez, je vous le jure,
Très-contents de nous ce soir.

JARNO: (*Furiously to Lothario.*)
You wretched meddler,
Come here!
(*Pushes back Lothario violently, and again threatens Mignon.*)
Dance, Mignon,
Dance, I say, or—
Then quickly I'll to reason bring you!

MIGNON: No, no!
(*He again raises his stick over Mignon, Enter Wilhelm, who appears to have come off a journey. A servant, who carries his portmanteau, stands behind him.*)

WILHELM: (*Hurrying to Mignon's assistance, and arresting JARNO's arm.*) Ruffian, hold! or meet your death!

JARNO: Eh? pray what do you mean?

WILHELM: (*Producing a pistol.*)
Another word, and through your brains
I'll send a bullet!

JARNO: (*Alarmed.*) You mean it? then quiet I'll remain
(*In a piteous tone.*)
I'm ruined quite—I am indeed!
Who will repay me for the loss I thus endure?

FILINA: (*Throwing him a purse from the balcony.*) That I will.
Take this purse and hold your tongue,
Take yourself away with all convenient speed!

MIGNON: (*Dividing her nosegay into two halves, one of which she gives to Wilhelm, and the other to Lothario.*) Kind friends, accept this humble token of my gratitude.

WILHELM: So strange an occurrence
Who ever could forsee?
Nature's own instinct
My steps did hither bend.

FILINA: (*To Laertes.*) Tell me, who is that gentleman,
Of manners so urbane?
He does not seem to see us
And does himself conceal
From where he comes and where he goes
I would wish to know.

MIGNON: (*Who has withdrawn a few paces—praying.*) Holy Virgin Mary,
Have mercy on an innocent maid,
Who always humbly seeks
Thy gracious will to do.

CHORUS: (*To Jarno.*) We'll be back to see you again.
For adventure we're out
Till the sun's put to rout
But we'll return to dance then.

JARNO:
Folks, come back tonight.
Please forget this incident.
You will be, I will bet
Happy and thrilled with delight.

LAËRTE: (*À Philine.*) Ce beau garçon à l'oeil noir,
Ce beau coureur d'aventure
Quel est-il? ah! je le jure,
Vous brûlez de le savoir.

LOTHARIO: (*Immobile et l'oeil fixe, touchant les cordes de sa harpe.*) Sous le voile obscur du soir, Et sous la verte ramure,
Un homme à la lourde armure
Arrête son coursier noir!
(*Les Bourgeois sortent par le fond. Jarno et les Bohémiens se retirement dans le hangar. MIGNON les suit et LOTHARIO s'éloigne lentement. PHILINE parle bas à LAERTE en lui montrant WILHELM du doigt. Elle rentre chez elle en riant et LAERTE descend dans la cour par l'escalier extérieur.*)

LAËRTE: (*S'approchant pour saluer Wilhelm.*) Monsieur—

WILHELM: (*Lui rendant son salut.*) Monsieur—

LAËRTE: Monsieur, souffrez qu'on vous complimente sur la façon vraiment chevaleresque don vous avez secouru cette petite bohémienne.

WILHELM: Ce que j'ai fait, monsieur, tout autre l'eût fait autant.

LAËRTE: Ce n'est pas l'avis de Philine. . . .
La dame du balcon a nom Philine; je me nomme Laërte. . . .
O désastre! O ruine d'une troupe comique aujourd'hui sans emploi.
Vous voyez en nous deux les débris misérables!
Philine attend un sort meilleur, et moi j'envoie avec bonheur notre métier à tous les diables!

WILHELM: Vous plaît-il, cher monsieur, de partager cette bouteille?

LAËRTE: Velontiers, monsieur!

WILHELM: Un verre encor!
(*À la Servante qui prépare la table.*)
(*A Laerte.*)
Wilhelm Meister le fils d'un honnête bourgeois de Vienne.
(*Ils boivent.*)

LAËRTE: (*Déclamant.*) J'aime votre gaité, j'aime votre jeune â me.

WILHELM: (*Souriant.*) Vous courtisez pourtant de fort près la dame du balcon!

LAERTES: (*To Filina.*) This beautiful black-eyed man
Soldier of fortune, beyond doubt.
Who is he? Oh! You'll find out
And meet him as soon as you can.

LOTHARIO: (*Who continues motionless, his eye fied on vacancy, his hand the while rambling over the chords of his harp.*) "The shades of even just began to fall,
When through the forest dark and drear,
A knight all clad in steel of proof
Did slowly wend his way."
(*Townsfolk, etc., exeunt at back. Jarno and his comrades retire beneath the shed—Mignon follows them. Lothario slowly withdraws. Filina speaks aside to Laertes, pointing the while to Wilhelm. She immediate afterwards enters her room, while Laertes descends into the court by the outer staircase.*)

LAERTES: (*Saluting Wilhelm.*) Sir!—

WILHELM: (*Returning the salutation.*) Sir!—

LAERTES: Be not offended if I sing your praises;
The succor you extended to that helpless maid,
Was truly worthy of a knight of yore.

WILHELM: (*Carelessly.*) Who would not have done the same?

LAERTES: Exactly; but this opinion Filina does not share—
Filina is the lady who just now sat in yonder balcony,
While men call me—Laertes!
(*Declaiming with comic emphasis.*)
Alas! misfortune! indeed, I may say, ruin!
Of a luckless troupe of actors,
On whom destiny never did smile,
You see in us the helpless remnant!
Filina hopes for a more prosperous turn on Fortune's wheel,
While I, of my artistic calling well weary,
Curse in my heart, the Tragic Muse!

WILHELM: (*Courteously.*) A flagon of good wine,
I trust you'll not refuse?

LAERTES: Right glad, sir.

WILHELM: (*To the waiter.*) Another glass.
Wilhelm Meister is my name. I hail from Vienna.

LAERTES: I like your youth, I like your spirit,

WILHELM: And yet, I saw you flirting
With a fair lady in that balcony.

LAËRTE: Qui, l'aimable Philine?
Nous nous connaissons beaucoup
trop pour nous aimer.
Folle, vaine comme pas une,
Plus perfide que la fortune,
Et plus changeante que la lune,
C'est grace à son esprit et grace à sa
beauté
Le plus charmant démon! Buvona à
sa santé!
(Ils trinquent et boivent. Philine
descend l'escalier pendant les der-
nières paroles de LAERTE.)

PHILINE: Eh! quoi! mon cher
Laërte, en vidant votre verre,
N'ajouterez-vous rien à ce portrait
charmant ant?

WILHELM: (Saluant Philine.) Il
vous juge en ami sévere,
Et vos beaux yeux disent qu'il
ment.

PHILINE: Je vous sais gré du compliment.

WILHELM: (À part.) Que de
grâces et de charmes!
Quels regards pleins de feu!
Les soupirs et les larmes
Sont ici hors de jue.

PHILINE: (À part.) Essayons de nos
charmes
Pour nous venger un peu,
Me voilà sous les armes,
Le reste n'est qu'un jeu.

LAËRTE: (Riant.) La voilà sous les
armes,
Nous allons voir beau jeu!
Devant de pareils charmes
Son coeur va prendre feu!
Permettez, sans plus de façon,
Qu'on vous présente l'un à l'autre.
(Présentant Wilhelm à Philine.)
Monsieur Wilhelm Meister, un aim-
able garçon,
Qui vous offre son coeur en
échange du vôtre.
(Présentant Philine à Wilhelm.)
La signora Philine, un ange en falba-
la,
qui vous trouve charmant et voud-
rait vous le dire.
(À Philine.)
Décochez à monsieur votre plus
doux sourire.
(À Wilhelm.)
Offrez votre bouquet à madame!—
(Il prend le bouquet et le donne à
Philine.)

WILHELM: (À part.) Que de grâce
et de charmes!
Quels regards pleins de feu!
Les soupirs et les larmes
Sont ici hors de jeu!

LAERTES: What! with Filina?
The gods forbid! We know each
other far too well,
To feel a mutual love!
She's flighty, vain, cantankerous,
astute,
Fickle as Fortune, and more
changeable
Than is the moon!
And yet her beauty rare,
Inflames all hearts with love.
Let's drink her health!
(Raises his glass.)
(Filina who has overheard this
conversation from the window
quickly descends the staircase.)

FILINA: So, sir! now you've finished the portrait,
Why not place it in a frame?

WILHELM: (Bowing.) He treats
you somewhat harshly I must own,
But those bright eyes the slander
right soon dispel.

FILINA: Grateful, indeed, am I, for
so well-turned a compliment.

WILHELM: (Aside.) What beau-
ty—what grace,
How frank is her mien,
I fear that my sighs.
Her heart never will win!

FILINA: (Aside.) The most I'll
make now of my charms,
Resolved am I that he shall love me;
My beauty's power I know full
well,
No youthful heart can ever resist
me.

LAERTES: (Aside.) The most she'll
make now of her charms,
Resolved is she the youth shall love
her;
Her blandishments I know full
well,
No youthful heart can ever resist
her.
But, without further ceremony,
Each to the other I will introduce!
(Presenting Wilhelm to Filina.)
The most excellent Signor Wil-
helm, a gentleman most worthy,
Who, in exchange for yours, his
heart would fain present you!
(Introducing Filina to Wilhelm.)
Mistress Filina, an actress of merit
and renown,
who is much taken with you, and,
indeed, desires to let you known it;
(Aside to Filina.)
A loving glance just cast his way.
(Aside to Wilhelm.)
Present this nosegay to yon lady
fair—
So!
(Takes nosegay and gives it to Fili-
na.)

WILHELM: (Aside.) What beauty,
what grace,
How enchanting each glance.
I fear that my sighs
Her heart never will win.

PHILINE: (À part.) Essayons de nos
charmes
Pour nous venger un peu, etc.

LAËRTE: (Riant) La belle est sous
les armes,
Nous allons voir beau jeu!

PHILINE: (À Wilhelm.) De mon
ami, Monsieur, excusez les folies.
(À Laerte.) Votre bras!

LAËRTE: (À Wilhelm.) Devons-
nous vous retrouver ici?

PHILINE: (Riant.) Comment!
quand on m'a vue est-ce qu'on fuit
ainsi?

LAËRTE: On ferait bien de fuir!

PHILINE: La réponse est polie!
(À part.)
Impertinent!
LAËRTE: (Bas.) Coquette!
(À Wilhelm.)
Monsieur!
(Ils sortent.)

WILHELM: (Gaiement.) Voilà,
pardieu! une charmante fille et
Laërte a beau dire, il n'est pas temps
encore de nous dire un éternel adieu.

MIGNON: (Sortent.) Il est seul!—

WILHELM: (Apercevant Mignon.)
Ah! c'est toi! Que me veux-tu?

MIGNON: Le maitre dort. Donne ta
main, donne et mille fois merci!

WILHELM: Demain, mon pauvre
enfant je serai loin d'ici,
Et ton supplice va renaître.

MIGNON: Demain, dis-tu? Qui sait
où nous serons demain.
L'avenir est à Dieu! le temps est
dans sa main.

WILHELM: Quel est ton nom?

MIGNON: Ils m'appellent Mignon,
Je n'ai pas d'autre nom.

WILHELM: Quel âge as-tu?

MIGNON: Les bois ont reverdi, les
fleurs se sont fanées,
Personne n'a pris soin de compter
mes années.

WILHELM: Dis-moi de quelles
plages lointaines
ton âme a gardé le souvenir,
Et si ma main brisait tes chaines,
Vers quels pays tu voudrais revenir?

Connaistu le pays oû fleurit
l'oranger, Le pays des fruits d'or et
des roses vermeilles, Où la brise est
plus douce et l'oiseau plus léger,
Où dans tôute saison butinent les
abeilles? Où rayonne et sourit,

FILINA: (Aside.) The most I'll
make now of my charms,
Resolved am I that he shall love me,
etc.

LAERTES: (Aside.) All her wiles
she brings to bear,
Resolved is she the youth shall love
her, etc.

FILINA: Excuse, I pray, the giddy-
pated fellow;
(To Laertes.)
Your arm now give me!

LAERTES: (To Wilhelm.) I trust we
soon may meet again;

FILINA: (To Laertes smiling.) Can
he who once has seen me,
Take his departure quite so soon?

LAERTES: It, perhaps might prove
the wiser plan;

FILINA: In sooth, the observation is
gallant.

LAERTES: (Aside.) A little puss is
she.
(To Wilhelm curtseying.)

FILINA: Sir, I take my leave.
(Exit with Laertes.)

WILHELM: A pretty girl,
Her friend may say just what he
pleases,
But i'll not leave her yet.

MIGNON: (Coming from under
the shed. Aside.) Ah! he's alone—

WILHELM: What is it you? What
would you now?

MIGNON: (Timidly.) My master
sleeps—give me your hand,
I fain would kiss it.

WILHELM: Tomorrow, my poor
child,
I shall be far from you,
No further aid can I ever lend you.

MIGNON: Tomorrow? Who knows
where we shall be tomorrow?
It is known alone to God, who rules
this vast world!

WILHELM: What's your name?

MIGNON: They call me Mignon
I have no other name.

WILHELM: How old are you?

MIGNON: Summers come and summers go but
No one counted my summers for
me.

WILHELM: But tell me! of the
scenes which, when a child, you
left—have you no recollection?
Were I to break your chains, and set
you free,
To what beloved spot would you
wend your way?

Do you know the country, where
the orange tree flowers? the land of
golden fruit; and of vermilion
roses— Where the breeze is sweeter, and the birds lighter— Where
during every season, the bees gath-

comme un bien-fait de Dieu, Un éternel printemps sous un ciel toujours bleu?

Hélas! que ne puis-je te suivre Vera ce rivage heureux d'où le sort m'exila! C'est là que in je voudrais vivre, Aimer et mourir!—c'est là! Connais-tu la maison où l'on m'attend là bas? La salle aux lambris d'or où des hommes de marbre M'appellent dans la nuit en me tendant les bras, Et la cour où l'on danse à l'ombre d'un grand arbre? Et le lac transparent où glissent sur les eaux Mille bateaux légers pareils à des oiseaux—

Helas! que ne puis-je te suivre Vers ce rivage heureux d'où le sort m'exila! C'est là que in je voudrais vivre, Aimer et mourir!—c'est là!

**WILHELM:** Ce pays enchanté dont tu parles, n'est-ce pas l'Italie?

**MIGNON:** (*Rêveuse.*) Je ne sais—

**WILHELM:** (*À part.*) Etrange créature!

**JARNO:** (*Qui entre.*) Ah! ah! Il parâit que l'enfant vous plâit—mon prince, vous voulez me la débaucher!—

**WILHELM:** (*Avec colére.*) Sur ma vie, n'ajoute pas un mot!

**JARNO:** Bon, je ne dis plus rien. Mais puisque votre coeur s'interesse à la belle, remboursez-moi ce qu'elle m'a coûte, et je renounce à tous mes droits sur elles!

**WILHELM:** Viens done! (*Regardant Mignon avec intéret.*) Je veux lui rendre au moins sa liberté! (*Il sort avec Jarno.*)

**MIGNON:** (*À Lothario qui entre.*) Libre! libre! Est-ce vrai?—Viens partager ma joie! Toi qui m'as comme lui Defendue aujourd'hui! Pour consoler Mignon c'est dieu qui vous envoie!

**LOTHARIO:** Je te cherchais pour te faire mes adieux. J'ai voulu te voir avant de partir.

**MIGNON:** Ou vas-tu?

**LOTHARIO:** (*Levant les bras vers le ciel.*) Déjà les hirondelles volent vers le midi. Moi, je pars avec elles.

**MIGNON:** Que ne puis-je à travers l'espace fuir aussi. Donne-moi ton luth!

---

er nectar Where radiates and smiles, like an act of God, An eternal spring under a sky that's always blue?

Alas, but I cannot follow you to the happy shore from which I've been exiled! It is there that I wish to live, love & die, It's there. Do you know the house, where they wait for me there? The room is paneled in gold, where the men of marble Call my name in the night, and stretch their arms out to me, And the courtyard where they dance under the canopy of a huge tree? And the transparent lake where, gliding on the water, Are a thousand boats that seem like birds.

Alas, but I cannot follow you to the happy shore from which I've been exiled! It is there that I wish to live, love & die, It's there.

**WILHELM:** The enchanted soil you speak of, must surely Italy be?

**MIGNON:** Alas! I cannot say.

**WILHELM:** (*Aside.*) A strange creature this!

**JARNO:** (*Issuing from the pent-house and running toward MIGNON, To WILHELM, sarcastically.*) Oho! the damsel pleases you, it seems! You would like to have her. (*Seizing him by the collar.*)

**WILHELM:** Scoundrel! Let but another word escape you—

**JARNO:** Nothing will I say—but still— Since in the young lady—a—a— an interest you take, Just hand to me the sum I gave for her, And my claim on her, to you, I'll cede.

**WILHELM:** Come then—resolved am I To free her from her bonds! (*Enters the inn with Jarno.*)

**MIGNON:** (*Bounding with joy.*) Free! Free! And is it really true? (*Perceiving Lothario, who issues from the pent-house.*) Come and share with me my joy, Come and share with me my joy, You who, but now, so nobly did defend me! As consolation to my tortured soul Heaven has surely sent you.

**LOTHARIO:** I come my leave to take, Before I go;

**MIGNON:** And where will you go?

**LOTHARIO:** (*Pointing to the sky.*) The swallows to the south do fly; I'll go there with them!

**MIGNON:** Ah! why may I not fly there, too? Reach me your harp!

---

**LOTHARIO:** Le voici!

**MIGNON:** Légères hirondelles, Oiseaux bénis de Dieu, Ouvrez, ouvrez vos ailes, Envolez-vous! Adieu! Ouvrez, ouvrez vos ailes! Envolez-vous! Adieu!

**LOTHARIO:** Le vieux luth s'éveille, Sous ses jeunes doigts Et semble, o merveille! Répondre à sa voix.

**MIGNON:** Légères hirondelles, Ouvrez, ouvrez vos ailes, Fuyez vers la lumière, vers l'horizon vermeil! Heureuse la première, Heureuse la première, Quo reverra demain le pays du soleil! Qui reverra demain le pays du soleil! (*Mignon et Lothario sortent. Philine, entre en riant avec FREDERIC.*)

**PHILINE:** Ah, ah, ah, ah, ah! Comment? C'est vous?

**FRÉDÉRIC:** (*s'époussetant avec sa cravache.*) Oui, oui, riez! je suis un sot De créver mon cheval de vous revoir plus tôt!

**PHILINE:** (*Se moquant.*) Ne voulez-vous pas que je pleure?

**FRÉDÉRIC:** Ah, vous me faites repentir d'etre venu!—

**PHILINE:** Vous pouvez repartir, Vous nous reviendrez tout à l'heure.

**WILHELM:** (*Qui entre avec Jarno, à ce dernier.*) Marché conclu! Mignon est libra.

**PHILINE:** Qu'entends-je là! Vous avez racheté Mignon?

**FRÉDÉRIC:** Hein? d'ou sort celui-là!

**PHILINE:** (*Presentant Frederic.*) Monsieur Meister, je vous présente Le jeune Frédéric, un petit écolier Qui malgré moi s'est fair mon chevalier. (*Présentant Wilhelm à Frederic.*) Monsieur Wilhelm Meister, un homme que peutêtre Vous aimerez un jour.

**LAËRTE:** (*Au dehors.*) Philine! Philine!

**PHILINE:** Ah, voici Laërte!

**LAËRTE:** (*À Philine, lui offrant use lettre.*) Cette lettre est pour vous.

**PHILINE:** Lisez, lisez!

**LAËRTE:** (*Lisant.*) Ma toute belle, Pour fêter dignement et de facon nouvelle Le passage du Prince Ulric de Tiffembourg, Je vous attends ainsi que Laërte et

---

**LOTHARIO:** It's here!

**MIGNON:** (*Accompanying herself on the harp.*) Oh swallows gay and blithe, joy of every land, Unfold your gentle wings, speed quickly on your way! Unfold your gentle wings, speed quickly on your way,

**LOTHARIO:** The antiquated harp touched by her gentle hand A melancholy sound mysteriously gives forth, Ah yes,

**MIGNON:** blithe and gentle swallows. Unfold your nimble wings, Quick, hasten to the land where winter never reigns, Thrice happy bird, thrice happy bird, who first the wished-for goal right joyously shall reach, Who first the wished-for goal right joyously shall reach. (*They both withdraw beneath the pent-house.*)

**FILINA:** (*Laughing mockingly at Frederic, who follows her, shaking the dust from his clothes.*) What! is it you?

**FREDERIC:** You laugh, do you? a madman was I truly To kill my horse by racing after you!

**FILINA:** (*Laughing.*You'd like me perhaps, to cry?

**FREDERIC:** I vow, I'm sorry now I came!

**FILINA:** (*Aggravatingly.*) You can return whenever you please; You'll soon come back again!

**WILHELM:** (*To Jarno at the door of the Inn.*) It is understood then—Mignon is free!

**FILINA:** (*To Wilhelm.*) Hear I aright? Has Mignon been re-purchased from her master?

**FREDERIC:** (*Aside, and jealously.*) From where comes that gentlemen, I pray?

**FILINA:** (*Introducing Frederic to Wilhelm.*) Mr. Meister, Permit me to introduce my young friend Frederick, Who, whether I will or no, My cavalier undertakes to be. (*Presenting Wilhelm to Frederic*) Wilhelm Meister this—I think you'll like him.

**LAERTES:** (*Outside, calling.*) Filina.

**FILINA:** (*Turning round.*) Here is Laertes.

**LAERTES:** (*Turning to Filina.*) This letter is addressed to you;

**FILINA:** Read it aloud.

**LAERTES:** (*Reading.*) "Beauteous goddess! Wishing right worthily to celebrate The Prince Ulrico Tieflenbach's arrival, I hope to see you, with your friends,

les autres,
En mon castel, avant la fin du jour—
Je comte bien, mon coeur, que vous serez des notres;
Vous devinez mon tendre espoir—
Baron de Rosemberg.

**FRÉDÉRIC:** Mon oncle!

**PHILINE:** Hein? Comment? le Baron est votre oncle?

**FRÉDÉRIC:** Hélas! oui!

**PHILINE:** C'est charmant!

**FRÉDÉRIC:** Vous acceptez son offre?

**PHILINE:** Avec empressement! (*A Wilhelm.*)
Vous, monsieur, s'il vous plait prendre part à la fête,
Vous jouerez parmi nous le rôle de poëte
Si vous venez, d'ailleurs, vous me ferez plaisir.

**WILHELM:** Maudit Baron! Maudit message!
Maudite coquette! Au revoir, Laërte! (*Se tournant vers Wilhelm.*)
Vous, Monsieur!

**WILHELM:** Plait-il?

**LAËRTE:** Soyez plus sage
Que ce jeune étourneau qui s'attache à nos pas.
Suivez votre chemin. Partez et bon voyage.

**MIGNON:** (*Accourant vers Wilhelm.*) Me voici! tu m'as rachetée,
A ton gré dispose de moi!

**WILHELM:** Je sais en cette ville, où le sort t'a jetée
D'honnêtes gens chez qui tu bien traitée.

**MIGNON:** (*Vivement.*) Pourquoi me séparer de toi!

**WILHELM:** (*Souriant.*) Je ne puis t-emmener avec moi, pauvre fille!
Et m'imposer les soins d'un père de famille

**MIGNON:** Ne peux-tu m'habiller comme un jeune garçon
Et me laisser porter ta livrée!—

(*At whose head I trust Laertes to behold!*)
At this my castle, before day declines;
I trust the invitation will be pleasing to you.
You well know the flame
Which burns within my tender heart;
"Baron Rosenberg."

**FREDERIC:** (*Surprised.*) Heavens, my uncle!

**FILINA:** What! is the baron your uncle?

**FREDERIC:** Alas! too much my uncle!

**FILINA:** (*Laughing.*) A pretty coincidence!

**FREDERIC:** Do you accept the invitation?

**FILINA:** With pleasure!
(*Turning to Wilhelm.*) And you sir,
Should it please you to take part in the festivity,
Pray come; It will give me pleasure I assure you;
To account for your presence,
We'll say you are stock author to the company.
(*She ascends the outer staircase to her room, the door of which she shuts.*)

**FREDERIC:** (*Enraged.*) O thrice accursed epistle!
O, day of woe! unnatural, heartless girl!
(*To Laertes, giving him his hand.*)
Farewell, Laertes!
(*To Wilhelm—turning at the same time his back to him, in a threatening tone.*)
As for you, sir—

**WILHELM:** Well! what now?

**LAERTES:** (*To Wilhelm.*) Be wiser than that booby
Take my advice, nor linger here.
Set out at once! a pleasant journey to you!
(*Shakes his hand and enters inn.*)

**MIGNON:** Stranger! you did purchase me—
Dispose of me, even as you will.

**WILHELM:** In this very town, to which Fate has brought you,
There lives an aged relative of mine,
Who, to her home, will gladly welcome you.

**MIGNON:** Must I then part from you?

**WILHELM:** My child, you can not dwell with me;
Ill could I the part perform,
Of father?

**MIGNON:** Could I not disguise myself,
And as your servant, travel with you?

**WILHELM:** (*Lui prenant les mains.*) A quoi bon?

**MIGNON:** (*Avec un élan passionné.*) Envers qui me délivre
Je voulais m'acquitter!
J'étais prête à te suivre
Pour ne plus te quitter!

**WILHELM:** Des mains de ce sauvage
Libre pour un peu d'or,
Quel nouvel esclavage
Veux-tu subir encor?

**MIGNON:** (*Tristement.*) C'est bien!— puisque ta main sans pitié me repousse,
(*Montrant Lothario qui parait sur le seuill de du hangar*) Je pars avec lui!—

**LOTHARIO:** (*Accourant vers Mignon et l'entourant de ses bras*)
Viens! La libre vie est douce!
A l'ombre des granda bois sous le ciel étoilé,
Nous trouverons un lit de fougère et de mousse
Et tu partageras le pain de l'exile!
(*Il veut entrainer Mignon.*)

**WILHELM:** (*L'arrêtant.*) Non! pauvre enfant! pour toi l'avenir m'épouvante
Jeune fille ou garçon, serviteur ou servante
Reste avec moi si tu le veux!
Le sort en est jeté! Je me rends à tes voeux!

**MIGNON:** (*Baisant la main de Wilhelm avec transport.*) Envers qui me délivre
Je pourrai m'acquitter!
Je suis prête à te suivre
Pour ne plus te quitter!

**WILHELM:** (*Lui souriant avec bonté.*) L'ami qui te délivre
Ne doit plus te quitter!
Libre à toi de me suivre;
Il faut te contenter.

**LOTHARIO:** (*À part, retombant dans son extase habituelle.*) Dieu bon! laissez-moi vivre,
?Espérer et chanter!
(*Les Comediens envahissent la cour de l'auberge. Ils sont en habits de voyage et portent sur l'épaule ou à la main des paquets et des valises qui contiennent leurs bardes de théâtre.*)

**CHOEUR des COMÉDIENS:** En route, amis, plions bagage!
La chance nous sourit enfin!
Que la gaîté soit du voyage,
Au diantre la soif et la faim!
Oublions nos repas d'auberge,
Et saluons, chapeau levé,
Ce vieux castel où l'on héberge
Les histrions sur le pavé!

**WILHELM:** (*Taking her hands.*)
And what could you do then?

**MIGNON:** With love and gratitude,
My heart is filled.
to follow you, O master mine,
Indeed were happiness to me!

**WILHELM:** But just released for trifling sum,
From tyrant harsh and stern,
Would you renounce your liberty again?
And be a slave once more?

**MIGNON:** (*Sadly.*) Well since you will not hear my prayers,
(*Pointing to Lothario, who issues from under the pent-house.*)
I'll even depart with him!

**LOTHARIO:** (*Rushing to Mignon, and encircling her with his arms.*)
Come! follow my footsteps:
Through by-paths lone and wild,
Far from this spot, a home of twigs and leaves we'll seek
Ah! follow my footsteps
My destiny pray share!
(*Attempts to draw Mignon with him.*)

**WILHELM:** (*Stopping her.*) No, stay, fair maiden! for your future I now fear!
Disguise yourself as page, or lackey, as you will,
But at least remain with me,
The stars have willed it so. Come! all care I'll take of you!

**MIGNON:** (*Kissing Wilhelm's hand with rapture.*) With love and gratitude
My heart bounds
O master mine,
I am ready to follow you!

**WILHELM:** (*With a kindly smile.*)
My heart is deeply touched
With tender pity;
A noble impulse it must surely be,
That each pulse causes it to throb.

**LOTHARIO:** (*Aside, as though his mind were again wandering.*)
Yield the maid to me,
And bless me for always.
(*The actors beset the door of the inn. They are in traveling clothes; they all carry, on their shoulders, or in their hands bundles, packages, etc.*)

**CHORUS:** On foot, my friends! away! away!
On us Dame Fortune smiles serene;
Joy accompanies our voyage,
Leaving hunger and thirst behind.
From our heads—our hats—let's take,
We lowly bow to the ground;
With joyous shouts we'll gaily hail
The generous host who entertains the merry players!

**LAËRTE:** (*Au Laquais.*) Nous vous suivons.
(*Aux Garcons d'auberge, qui portent ses bardes et celles de PHILINE.*)
Marchez devant, vous autres!
(*Aux Comediens.*)
Je vous précède, amis, pour vous mieux recevoir!
Un splendide festin vous attendra ce soir!

**LES COMÉDIENS:** Vivat!

**À WILHELM:** Et vous, monsieur, n'êtes-vous pas des nôtres? Grâce au galant seigneur Qui, pour nous faire honneur, Nous prête son carrosse, Nous allons voyager, Et nous faire héberger, Comme en un jour de noce! Je vous dis au revoir!

**WILHELM:** (*Vous me verrez ce soir! Je serai de la fête!*) Au revoir, au revoir!
(*Elle montre à Wilhelm le bouquet qu'elle a reçu de lui. MIGNON, qui reparaît, son paquet à la main s'approche vivement et reconnait les fleurs qu'elle a données à WILHELM.*)

**MIGNON:** (*À part.*) Mon bouquet!

**WILHELM:** (*À Mignon.*) Qu'as-tu donc?

**PHILINE:** (*Bas.*) Il m'adore!

**LAËRTE:** (*Bas.*) Il est pris!

**MIGNON:** (*Montrant Lothario.*) Vois, de mes pauvres fleurs il n'a point fait mépris?
Il n'a pas rejeté mon bouquet, lui?

**WILHELM:** (*Bas en souriant.*) Pardonne!
Je ne l'ai pas offert . . . on me l'a prix.

**MIGNON:** C'est bien! . . . emmène-moi! . . . Je suiviens! . . . Ordonne!
(*Aux Bohemiens.*)
Vous dont j'ai partage La honte et la misère, Adieu! . . .
(*A L'ENFANT, en lui passant une médaille*)
Toi, pauvre enfant, sois un jour ta protége Par cette humble médaille!
(*A Jarno.*)
Et toi, dont la colère! M'a si souvent fait peur . . . hélas! Adieu? Mignon ne t'en veut pas!

**LES COMÉDIENS:** (*Au fond.*) Adieu, Philine, et bon voyage! Adieu, la belle, et bon voyage. Adieu, Mignon, et bon voyage!

**LES COMÉDIENS:** En route, amis! plions bagage La chance nous sourit enfin! Que la gaîté soit du voyage!

**LAERTES:** (*To the groom.*) We follow you!
(*To the waiters who carry his luggage, and that of Filina.*)
(*To the actors.*)
And you my friends, pray, quick precede us!
I start at once; I must be there first, To get the supper ready!

**ACTORS:** Huzza!

**FIL. TO WILHELM:** You'll come with us, I trust, sir, Thanks for the politeness of him who so kindly sends his carriage for us, Side by side we may most pleasantly travel, We'll shortly meet again.

**WILHELM:** (*Kissing the band of Fil:*) I fain would join the throng, And shall eagerly look for you. We shall meet, we shall soon meet again.
(*Filina shows to Wilhelm the bouquet which she, just now, received from him. Mignon, who, at this moment enters with a little bundle in her hand, at once recognizes the flowers which she had given to Wilhelm.*)

**MIGNON:** (*Aside.*) My flowers!

**WILHELM:** (*To Mignon.*) What ails you?

**FILINA:** (*Aside to Laertes, laughing.*) He love me!

**LAERTES:** (*Aside, laughing.*) He's trapped—poor fellow!

**MIGNON:** (*To Wilhelm—pointing to Lothario.*) See! my poor flowers, he has not despised, like you!
His bouquet he has not given away!

**WILHELM:** (*Aside to Mignon, smiling.*) I did not give it, child—it was stolen from me!

**MIGNON:** But let's away, I ready am to follow you,
(*To the Gipsies.*)
Oh, you with whom both shame and misery I've shared,—farewell!
(*To a lad among the tribe, attaching a medal to his neck.*)
Poor boy! may this medallion One day prove your safeguard!
(*To Jarno.*)
And you who often did wrongly ill use me,
I bid you, too, adieu!

**GIPSIES:** Farewell! take heart, Mignon!
Farewell, Filina!
A prosperous journey we do wish you.

**CHORUS:** Quick, quick my friends, now let's away!
Dame Fortune smiles on us, serene; Joy, once more, our hearts will

Au diantre la soif et la faim!
(*WILHELM fait un dernier signe d'adieu à Philine et les COMÉDIENS et les COMÉDIENNES se disposent à partir. LOTHARIO s'asseoit pensif sur le devant de la scène. Mignon rête au milieu du théâtre, les yeux fixés sur WILHELM.*)

■ **ACTE DEUXIÈME**

*SCÈNE I*

*Un boudoir élégant, Porte au fond. Portes de côté A droite une fenêtre, à gauche une cheminés. Divans fauteuils, etc.*

**LAËRTE:** (*Entrant, d'un air majestueux.*) Corbleu! les somptueux lambris!
(*Regardant autour de lui.*)
C'est içi qu'on vous loge?

**PHILINE:** Oui, mon cher! Madame la baronne me prête son boudoir.

**LAËRTE:** (*Finement.*) Dont M. le baron a gardé la clef.

**PHILINE:** (*Se levant vivement.*) Fi donc, vous êtes gris!

**LAËRTE:** Non! je suis en humeur de rire et de faire des compliments . . . Belle, ayez pitié de nous! Daignez baisser vos paupières! Les cils de vos yeux si doux . . . Sont des flèches meurtrières Du Dieu qui nous blesse tous! Et lon, lon, la, et lon, lon, la! Landéridéra, landéridéra! Et lon, lon, la, landéridéra!
(*Il fait une pirouette.*)
Voilà!

**LAERTE:** Rien ne vaut pour nous égayer Le vin qu'on n'a pas à payer! Rien ne vaut pour nous égayer Le vin qu'on n'a pas à payer! la la la la la la. la la la la la la la la la la la la la la la la la la la la

**PHILINE:** (*Se moquant.*) Fort bien on croit entendre
Je vous le jure, le jeune Frédéric. Comment n'est-il pas içi?

**LAËRTE:** (*Avec malice.*) Merci! et Wilhelm?

**PHILINE:** Il viendra.

**LAËRTE:** Croyez-vous?

**PHILINE:** J'en suis sure, il est en route, il vient.

**WILHELM:** (*Paraissant sur le seuil.*) Belle Philine!

**PHILINE:** (*Elle va au devant de lui.*) Et le voici.

warm,
Fell hunger we will soon dispel!
(*Wilhelm waves his hand to Filina, in token of adieu. The actors depart on their journey; Lothario remains pensively seated near the front of the stage. Mignon stands near the centre of the stage, bending her eyes fixedly on WILHELM.*)

■ **ACT II**

*SCENE I*

*(An elegant boudoir. Door at back. Side doors. To the right a window, to the left a chimney. Elegant details. Sofas, easy chairs, etc.)*

**LAERTES:** My! What luxury (*Looking around.*)
Is this where you stay?

**FILINA:** Yes, my dear. The baroness has loaned me her boudoir.

**LAERTES:** (*Slyly.*) Of which the baron has a key.

**FILINA:** (*Rising, in anger.*) Oh! You're drunk!

**LAERTES:** No! I just feel good and amiable.
Oh! sweetest one, have a heart Don't look at me that way. Your lovely eyes' soft lashes, Like arrows in Cupid's play, Will wound me now and forever.

**LAERTE:** Nothing to me such joy affords, As wine which I drink without cost, Nothing to me such joy affords As wine which I drink without cost. la la la la la la la. la la la la la la la la la la la la la la la la la la la la la la la la la la

**FILINA:** (*Laughing.*) Bravo! in style and manner, You resemble Frederic. How is it that he has not yet arrived?

**LAERTES:** (*Significantly.*) What now is your opinion as regards young Wilhelm?

**FILINA:** He'll surely come.

**LAERTES:** You hope so?

**FILINA:** I'm sure of it—nor his arrival will he long delay.
(*Entering.*)

**WILHELM:** (*Bowing*) Beautiful Filina!

**FILINA:** (*Advancing to meet him.*) Here he is already.

## Act II, Scene I

LAËRTE: Bon! très bien. Je vaie voir là-bas si tout s'apprête. "Le Songe d'une Nuit d'Eté" Doit faire les frais de la fête. C'est d'un nommé Shakespeare, un assez bon poëte. (*Montrant Philine.*) Et de Titania vous serez enchanté. (*Con emphase.*) A bientôt, cher monsieur! Adieu, ma toute belle! Je vous laisse avec lui? Je vous laisse avec elle. (*S'arretant aupres de la porte du fond.*) Mais qui donc se tient là?

WILHELM: C'est Mignon!

PHILINE: Mignon?

WILHELM: Elle n'a pas voulu se séparer de moi. Faut l'appéler. (*Remontant par le fond et appelent.*) Mignon!

MIGNON: (*Elle parait, en habit de jeune page.*) Que veux-tu, maître?

PHILINE: (*Souriant.*) Eh! mais vraiment, on a peine à la reconnaitre. Approche et rechauffe-toi. Tu nous danseras en suite la danse des oeufs. (*Mouvement de Mignon.*)

LAËRTE: Je crois qu'un orage est dans l'air.

PHILINE: Plait-il?

LAËRTE: Rien, je vous quitte.

WILHELM: Plus de soucis, Mignon! plus de tristes pensées! Viena réchauffer tes mains glacées, A ce foyer Hospitalier! . . . (*Il fait asseoir Mignon dans un fauteuil devant la cheminée*)

MIGNON: (*À demi-voix.*) Je ne me souviens plus de mes douleurs passées! Je n'ai plus froid! Je suis heureuse à tes côtes!

PHILINE: (*Riant.*) Quels soins touchants! Que de bontés! Permettez-moi de rire De ce beau dévouement!

MIGNON: (*À part.*) Hélas! qu'a-t-elle à rire? Cruel amusement!

LAERTES: I hasten to see whether the preparations are complete— (*To Wilhelm.*) this evening we will render joyous, By our performance of "A Midsummer Night's Dream;" A work is this by Shakespeare, A great, an immortal poet! As to Filina, she will perform miracles, If only to please you! Sir, your most obedient— Beauteous Filina, I take my leave. (*Aside.*) (*To Filina*) I leave you with him. (*To Wilhelm.*) I leave you with her. (*On reaching the door he draws back in surprise.*) Why, who is there?

WILHELM: It is Mignon!

FILINA: (*Surprised.*) Mignon? How's this?

WILHELM: She seems determined not to leave me; I shall call her in. Mignon!

MIGNON: (*Entering.*) What would you? Your commands I will obey.

FILINA: (*Banteringly.*) I really scarcely recognize the child! (*To Mignon, with ill-concealed jealousy*) Come, walk in! Pray come and warm yourself; And then the "egg dance" Perhaps you'll give us!

LAERTES: (*Aside.*) A storm is brewing.

FILINA: (*To Laertes.*) What ails you now, I pray?

LAERTES: (*Pre-occupied.*) Oh, nothing— I will take my leave. (*Bows and withdraws.*)

WILHELM: (*To Mignon.*) Do not be anxious—your fears dismiss; Come, then, and warm your freezing hands At yonder hospitable fire! (*He seats Mignon in a chair by the fireside.*)

MIGNON: No longer will I brood over past troubles, Nor am I cold—happy, indeed, am I, Since I am at your side!

FILINA: (*Sneeringly.*) What touching anxiety; Excuse me if I laugh At this reciprocal solicitude!

MIGNON: (*Aside.*) Alas! her bitter laugh Causes my heart anguish. (*To Filina.*) In truth your gaiety My spirits vastly enliven.

WILHELM: (*À Philine.*) Vous faites bien de rire; Votre rire est charmant!

PHILINE: Mon cher, je vous admire, C'est tout à fait charmant! (*Elle rit.*) Au lieu d'être servi par votre jeune page, C'est vous qui le servez!

WILHELM: (*Se rapprochant de Philine.*) Près de vous, à vos pieds, J'accepterais, si vous vouliez, Un plus doux servage.

PHILINE: Vraiment! (*Lui désignant un flambeau sur la cheminée.*) Apportez donc ce flambeau par içi. (*Elle s'asseoit devant sa toilette. Wilhelm va prendre le flambeau et revient avec empressement près de PHILINE. MIGNON suit tous ses mouvements du regard sans quitter le fauteuil óu elle est blottie.*)

WILHELM: Je me fais votre esclave! ordonnez, me voici!

PHILINE: Mon coiffeur m'a ce soir, indignement coiffée! . . . Mais vous allez me voir dans ma robe de fée! . . .

Je crois entendre Les doux compliments, Et la voix tendre De vingt amants. Chacun m'admire, Jeunes et vieux, Chacun soupire Pour mes beaux yeux.

WILHELM: J'admire l'éclat de vos yeux! Je suis ravi, charmé d'entendre Cette voix amoureuse et tendre, Ce rire moqueur et joyeux.

FILINA: Ah! Ah! Ah! Je crois entendre Les doux compliments, Et la voix tendre De vingt amants. Chacun m'admire, Jeunes et vieux, Chacun soupire Pour mes beaux yeux. Chacun soupire Chacun soupire Pour mes beaux yeux. (*Mignon fait semblant de dormir. Philine chante follement en achevant de se farder devant son miroir.*)

WILHELM: (*Se penchant amoureusement vers Philine.*) Belle Philine, aimable enchanteresse, Vos doux regards et vos attraits vainqueurs A votre char enhaînment tous les coeurs Autour de vous tout sourit et s'empresse On vous fête, on vous aime, on vous adore hélas! Pourquoi n'aimez-vous pas?

FILINA: (*Laughing.*) Most worthy sir, I'm really touched, indeed; Instead of waiting on his master, It is the master who waits upon his page!

WILHELM: (*Approaching Filina.*) Prostrate at your feet, O lady, I now do offer you an homage far more zealous; Will you accept my proffered service?

FILINA: You really mean it? (*Pointing to a candelabra which stands on the chimney piece.*) Yon candelabra, now, pray reach to me. (*She seats herself in front of the dressoir; Wilhelm eagerly fetches the candelabra alluded to. Mignon watches them, without leaving her seat.*)

WILHELM: Your commands I eagerly await— Ordain—I will obey!

FILINA: In truth, the hair-dresser has but ill-arranged my hair; But by putting on a more becoming dress, I yet may hope to please you!

Charming gay compliments, praises unbounded, Sweet loving accents within my ears ring, My beauty rare will all surpass, with strong emotion all hearts will burn.

WILHELM: Filina you dost enthrall me, your genial sweet and loving voice, . . . your joyous beauteous features inspire With more than delight me.

FILINA: Ah! Ah! Ah! Charming gay compliments, praises unbounded, Sweet loving accents within my ears ring. My charms and beauty must be triumphant, All hearts, all hearts with love soon will burn, yes, all hearts will burn, yes, all hearts will burn with love of my beauty, all hearts will burn. (*Mignon feigns to sleep. Filina continues singing gaily before the looking-glass, "beautifying" herself the while.*)

WILHELM: Beautiful Filina, irresistible enchantress, Of those bright eyes, the all-bewitching glance Each soul allures, each stubborn heart inflames; To obey your bidding, is happiness to all! By all you're idolized, By all adored! Alas! why then does love not illuminate your heart For, woe is me! You are cruel and cold.

PHILINE: Au baron il faut qu'on vous présenta.

WILHELM: Philine, un mot en—core! . . . un mot! . . .

PHILINE: (*Montrand Mignon.*) Parlez plus bas! Notre hôte nous attend . . . Offrez-moi vos bras.
(*Elle fait quelques pas; Wilhelm la retient.*)

WILHELM: Quoi! sans répondre . . .

PHILINE: (*Lui tendant la main.*) Allons! J'ai l'âme complaisante! . . .
(*Wilhelm porte la main de Philine à ses levres. Au bruit du baiser MIGNON fait un mouvement, sans ouvrir les yeux.*)

WILHELM: (*À demi-voix, avec passion.*) O Philine! ô coquette! ô fille séduisante!
J'admire l'éclat de vos yeux!
Je suis ravi, charmé d'entendre
Cette voix amoureuse et tendre,
Ce rire moqueur et joyeux! . . .
Par pitié daigner m'entendre!
Donne un regard de vos doux yeux,
Un mot de cette voix tendre
A mon coeur amoureux.
(*Wilhelm offre son bras à Philine et sort avec elle par la porte du fond.*)

MIGNON: (*Seule.*) Me voilà seule, hélas! déjà Meister m'oublie . . .
Qu'importe! il a comblé mes voeux!
Le suivre et le servir
C'est tout ce que je feux.
Allons! pleurer serait folie . . .
Ah! c'est là, que tout à l'heure en souriant à son miroir
Elle écoutait Meister! Je ne voulais rien voir,
Je ne voulais rien entendre!
Hélas! et cependant je n'apu men défendre
Pardonne, cher maître!
Voice le fard qui la rend belle . . .
Eh bien! si j'essayais de me farder aussi?
(*Elle essaye de se farder.*)
Ma pâleur disparaît déjà. Mon teint s'anime!

I
(*S'animant.*)
Il était un pauvre enfant.
Un pauvre enfant de Bohême,
Au regard triste, au front blême . . .
(*Se regardant dans le miroir.*)
Ah! ah! la folle histoire! en vain je m'en défend!
Je me trouve bien mieux! je ne suis pius la même.
Ta la, ralla!
Ta la, ralla!
Est-ce bien Mignon que voilà?

II
Un beau jour, tout triomphant
Tout fier de son strategème,
Pour palire au maître qu'il aime . . .
(*Se regardant de nouveau en ri-*

FILINA: I really must present you to the Baron.

WILHELM: Stay! grant me but another word!

FILINA: Hush! were we to be over-heard—
Give me your arm;
(*She advances a few steps, when Wilhelm stop her.*)

WILHELM: Will you not answer me?

FILINA: (*Extending her hand to him.*) I promise to be—merciful!
(*Wilhelm impresses a kiss on Filina's hand. Mignon starts, but does not open her eyes.*)

WILHELM: Oh Filina, my heart adores you
In more than human happiness am I steeped,
By your loving joyous voice—
By your winning, genial smile!
Then bend on me a glance benign,
My ardent prayer deign but to hear,
Crown this heart's sole wish!
(*Wilhelm offers Filina his arm. They both exit back.*)

MIGNON: (*Alone.*) At last I am alone! Ah! woe is me!
Already he has forgotten me.
What does it matter? Is not my utmost wish already fulfilled!
What need I more than learn to love, and to obey him?
A truce then to my sighs! it's folly to repine!
(*Leaning on the toilette table.*)
She listened to Wilhelm's vows—
I should have neither looked nor listened;
But, alas! the temptation was too strong;
Forgive me, my Wilhelm!
(*Perceiving the rouge pot.*)
Aha! the rouge lies here—
Suppose I were to try some.
(*Putting on rouge.*)
Quickly my paleness disappears;

I
My features are enlivened!
A gipsy lad I well do know,
Graceful, winning, handsome is he;
Yet though his lip ever wears a smile,
His heart I think is sad.
(*Looking at herself in the glass.*)
Ha! ha! ha! a mad story, truly!
Sure none will ever believe it.
I really seem more fair, more beauteous than before,
Tra, la, ral, la!
Is it really I, whom in the glass I see?
Who is it that I now gaze on?

II
One day the youth,
Gaily devised a scheme;
A scheme he hoped his master dear might please.

*ant.*)
Ah! ah! la folle histoire! En vain je m'en défend!
Je me trouve bien mieux, je ne suis plus la même,
Ta la, ralla!
Ta la, ralla!
Est-ce bien Mignon que voilà?
Non, non, ce n'est plus moi!
(*Tristement.*)
Mais quoi! ce n'est pas elle,
Elle a d'autres secrets encore pour être belle.
(*Allant ouvrir la porte du cabinet de toilette.*)
N'est pas là qu'on a rangé ses robes? oui!
Hélas! suis-je comme elle une femme pour lui?
O folle idée! O démon qui me tente!
(*Elle entre dans le cabinet de toilette. La fenêtre s'ouvre brusquement. FREDERIC saute dans la chambre.*)

FRÉDÉRIC: (*Avec indignation.*)
Quoi? mon oncle a logé Philine chez ma tante?
Me voici dans son boudoir,
Qui, je sens battre mon coeur d'espoir,
Ah! je guette l'instant de la revoir.
Qui, je sens battre mon coeur d'espoir,
Coquette, je guette l'instant de te revoir.
Il faut enfin vaincre la cruelle,
Il faut toucher le coeur de l'infidèle!
Je suis dans son boudoir
Et je sens mon coeur battre d'espoir.
Ah! je guette l'instant de la revoir.
Moi je veux qu'on m'aime et j'espère,
Oui, j'espère à mon tour être heureux.
Tant pis, ma foi! pour tous ses amoureux,
Je suis dans son boudoir,
Et je sens mon coeur battre d'espoir.
Ah, je guette l'instant de la revoir.
Ah, je sens mon coeur battre d'espoir.
Coquette, je guette l'instant de te revoir.
Pour mon coeur quel doux espoir.
Voici l'instant de la revoir!

WILHELM: (*Entr'ouvrant a porte du fond et entrant sans voir FREDERIC.*) Mignon!

FRÉDÉRIC: (*Saluant.*) Monsieur!

Wilhelm: Monsieur!

FRÉDÉRIC: Je suis peut-être indiscret,
Mais comment vous trouvez-vous içi?

WILHELM: Et vous-même, Monsieur?

(*Gazing at herself in the glass.*)
Ha! ha! a mad story, truly!
Sure none will ever believe it;
I really seem more fair, more beauteous than before
Tra, la, ralla, la!
Is it really I, whom in the glass I see?
Or who is it that I now gaze upon?
No, no! myself I do not recognize myself.
(*After a short pause, sadly.*)
And yet, alas! it is I!
Other secrets she must have, her beauty so to heighten!
(*Approaching cabinet on the left.*)
Is it not here, that she her wardrobe keeps?—
Mad thought! Ah! surely it is a demon tempts me.
(*Enters cabinet.*)

FREDERIC: (*Enters alone.*)
(*Looking around.*) Filina in my aunt's apartments?
O much loved room, while I gaze on you,
With joy and hope my heart loudly beats!
The young coquette, as yet, perchance expects me not;
The cruel flirt this day I must overcome,
Her heart at last I hope to tame.
O much loved room, while I gaze on you,
Yes! I swear she shall adore me—
The victory this very day shall be mine;
Let even a thousand watchful guards surround her,
Their vigilance I will elude!
O much loved room, while I gaze on you.

WILHELM: (*From the door at back, calling.*) Mignon!

FREDERIC: (*Bowing.*) Your servant, sir.

WILHELM: (*Bowing also.*) Yours, sir, to command.

FREDERIC: The question may seem indiscreet,
But much indeed I'd like to know
How you came here—

WILHELM: And you, sir, how did you arrive?

## Act II, Scene I

FRÉDÉRIC: Je suis de ses amis, Monsieur.

WILHELM: J'en suis aussi.

FRÉDÉRIC: Mais moi, je l'aime.

WILHELM: Eh bien, moi je l'adore? Plâit-il?

FRÉDÉRIC: Il suffit! engarde!

WILHELM: Quoi? chez Philine?

FRÉDÉRIC: Chez Philine! C'est plus original!
Battons-nous!
(*Ils croisent le fer.*)
(*Mignon revêtue d'une des robes de Philine sort du cabinet et s'elance entre eux.*)
Ah, Meister! Dieu!

WILHELM: Mignon!

FRÉDÉRIC: Mignon? que signifie?
(*Raillant.*)
Mais voilà, si je m'en souviens
Les atours de Philine!
Ah, ah, ah, ah, ah, ah!
(*Sérieux.*)
Monsieur! Nous nous reverrons.
Serviteur!

WILHELM: Quel est ce caprice insensé?
Deviens-tu folle? Alors quittons-nous.

MIGNON: Tu me chasses?

WILHELM: (*Plus tendrement.*)
Non, non, je ne te chasse pas!
Même je dois te rendre graces du tendre mouvement . . .
Mais je commence à comprendre
Que je ne puis auprès de moi
Te garder, pauvre enfant,
Adieu, Mignon, courage!
Ne pleure pas!
Les chagrins sont bien vite oubliés à ton age!
Dieu te consolera! mes voeux suivront tes pas! . . .
Ne pleure pas!
N'accuse pas mon coeur de froide indifference!
Ne me reproche pas de suivre un fol amour!
En te disant adieu, je garde l'espéranse
De te revoir un jour!
Adieu, Mignon, courage!
Les chagrins sont bien vite oubliés à ton âge!
Dieu te consolera! mes voeux suivrant tes pas!
Ne pleure pas!

MIGNON: Merci de tes bontés;
mais sans toi,
Je veux être libre comme autrefois.

FREDERIC: I am the lady's friend.

WILHELM: And so am I, sir.

FREDERIC: Know, sir, that I do dearly love her!

WILHELM: I tell you, I adore her, sir!

FREDERIC: You do? enough!
(*Drawing his sword.*)
Defend yourself!

WILHELM: What here, in Filina's room?

FREDERIC: In Filina's room; It will be all the more romantic!
Defend yourself!
(*Mignon, who has put on one of Filina's dresses, rushes hurriedly in, and throws herself between the combatants, exclaiming:*
Hold!

WILHELM: Heavens! Mignon!

FREDERIC: Why, what does all this mean?
(*Sheathing his sword, and contemplating Mignon*) Ha! ha! if I'm not mistaken
She has one on one of Filina's dresses.
Fear not,
We'll meet again, before long!

WILHELM: What strange caprice is this? Have you lost reason?
I tell you we must part.

MIGNON: Do you then drive me from you?

WILHELM: Not so—I do not drive you from me;
Believe me, I do not drive you from me;
Dear shall your memory ever be to me.
(*Mignon utters a cry of grief, and throws herself on a chair.*)
Farewell, Mignon, take heart! Your tears restrain!
In the bright years of youth no grief lingers long.
Weep not, Mignon!
Over you just Heaven will watch with fostering care.
Oh may you your dear native land, once more regain!
May fortune benignly smile on your fate henceforth;
It pains me much to leave you; my stricken heart
With your lone destiny will ever sympathize!
Farewell, Mignon, take heart! From tears refrain!
In the bright years of youth no grief lingers long; Weep not, Mignon!
Over you just Heaven will watch with fostering care;
Then dry your tears!

MIGNON: Thankful am I; but since we're doomed to part,
I fain would wander freely—

WILHELM: Ecoute la raison! Hors de cette maison
Que vas-tu devenir?

MIGNON: Ce que j'étais: Mignon!
(*Saissant la main de Wilhelm et la portant à ses lèvres.*) Merci!

WILHELM: Non, tu ne peux partir ainsi!

MIGNON: Il le faut.

WILHELM: Angoiese cruelle!

PHILINE: (*Elle parait avec Frederic.*) Vous disiez vrai; Mignon de mes atours parée!
(*A Wilhelm, avec ironie.*)
Elle a bientôt quitté votre livrée.

WILHELM: Philine.
(*Avec embarras.*)
Un caprice d'enfant qu'il faut lui pardonner.

PHILINE: Si la robe lui plâit, on peut la lui donner.
(*MIGNON arrache avec colère les dentelles de la robe dont elle est parée.*)
Eh! quoi? faut-il déchirer mes dentelles?
Je demande grace pour elles.
(*MIGNON va ramasser son paquet de hardes et se sauve dans le cabinet de droite.*)
(*Souriant.*)
Quel couroux! Quel regard! On dirait, sur ma foi,
Que cette pauvre enfant est jalouse de moi.

WILHELM: (*À part.*) Jalouse!

LAËRTE: (*Il entra vivement en scène sous son costume de Prince Thesée.*) Eh bien, que faites-vous? Alerte, on commence!

PHILINE: Suivons Laërte.

WILHELM: (*À part.*) Jalouse!

PHILINE: (*À Wilhelm, en souriant.*) A quoi rêvez-vous donc? Je vous attends.

WILHELM: Pardon!

PHILINE: Offrez-moi votre bras, si vous m'aimez encore.

WILHELM: Quoi? Moi? Philine, je t'adore.

FRÉDÉRIC: (*Regardant sortir Philine et Wilhelm.*) Morbleu!
Qu'avec plaisir je le massacrais.

WILHELM: To reason dictates list, I pray.
What will become of you?
When from my care removed, what will you do?

MIGNON: That which I did before.
I will Mignon once more become.
(*She kisses the hand which Wilhelm extends to her.*)
I thank you!

WILHELM: (*Agitated.*) You can not leave me like this!

MIGNON: It is my duty; it must be so.

WILHELM: (*Aside, in tones of anguish.*) O grievous trial!
(*Enter Filina and Frederic.*)

FILINA: (*To Frederic.*) Now, upon my word, she's dressed out in my clothes!
Right quickly has she laid her livery aside.

WILHELM: (*Confused.*) It was a mere whim,
Which must be forgiven.

FILINA: If she's so taken with the dress,
I'll give it her.
(*Mignon angrily tears the ribbons from the dress.*)
Good gracious! why tear off my ribbons!
I crave them. What anger strange is this?
(*Mignon rushes hastily to the apartment on the left, into which she disappears.*)
(*To Wilhelm.*)
Now, upon my word, I almost think
The little savage jealous is of me!

WILHELM: (*Agitated.*) Jealous!

LAERTES: (*Appearing at the back, dressed in the garb of an ancient Greek.*) I say, what are you doing here?
It is almost time to begin.

FILINA: Let's follow Laertes.

WILHELM: (*Aside.*) Jealous!

FILINA: (*To Wilhelm.*) What are you now thinking of?

WILHELM: Excuse me, pray.

FILINA: If you still love me, offer me your arm.

WILHELM: Love you! more dearly than I do love—myself!
(*Offers his arm to Filina. They exit, followed by Laertes.*)
(*Frederic suddenly issues from the apartment on the left, and goes after Wilhelm and Filina as they withdraw.*)

FREDERIC: What pleasure keen it would give me,
To run that scoundrel through!

MIGNON: (*Elle repairait dans son costume du premier Acte.*) Cette, Philine, je la hais!

## SCÈNE II

(*Un coin du parc. Au fond à droite, une serre attenante au château et éclairée à l'intérieur. A gauche, une lavge pièce d'eau bordée de roseaux. Musique et bruit d'applaudissement dans la coulisse. Mignon se glisse sous le arbres et se penche dans l'ombre pour écouter.*)

MIGNON: (*Seule.*) Elle est là près lui! Son triomphe commence! Et moi j'erre au hasard dans ce jardin immense . . .
(*Avec agitation.*)
Elle est aimée! il l'aime! eh bien! je le savais!
Ces tourments, je les éprouvais!
Non! je ne l'avais pas entendu de sa bouche,
Ce mot qui déchire mon coeur!
Espères-tu que ton chagrin le touche,
Pauvre Mignon! il l'aime! et son rire moqueur,
Rend plus cruelle encore cette onde
Il l'aime! ô Dieu! je deviens folle
De rage et de douleur!
(*Courant vers la pièce d'eau.*)
Ah! . . . ce flot clair et tranquille
M'attire à lui!—j'entends parmi les verts roseaux,
Votre voix, ô filles des eaux! . . .
Vous m'appelz à vous sous cette onde immobile! . . .
(*Elle va pour s'élancer, les accords d'une harpe se font entendre sous les arbres.*)
Ciel! qu'entends-je? écoutons! . . .
(*Redescendant en scène.*)
Le mauvais ange a fui!
Je veux vivre!
(*LOTHARIO paraît.*)
Est-ce toi, Lothario?—
(*Avec joie.*)
C'est lui!

LOTHARIO: (*Ne reconnaissant pas d'abord Mignon.*) Qui donc est là? . . . Quelle est cette voix qui m'appelle?
(*La regardant avec tendresse.*)
Est-ce toi, Sperata? . . . Réponds! est-ce toi?

MIGNON: Non.

LOTHARIO: (*La repoussant doucement.*) Mon coeur se trompe encore, hélas! ce n'est pas elle! C'est l'enfant qui voulait me suivre; c'est Mignon!

MIGNON: (*Avec tristesse.*) Oh! oui, tu te souviens! oui, c'est bien là mon nom!

LOTHARIO: Pauvre enfant! pauvre créature!
J'ai voulu te revoir et j'ai suivi tes pas!
Viens sur mon coeur! Reste en mes bras
Et dis-moi que! chagrin te brise et te torture! . . .
(*Il presse Mignon entre ses bras.*)

MIGNON: (*Avec une ardeur fiévreuse, le front appuyé sur la poitrine de LOTHARIO.*) As-tu souffert? As-tu pleuré?
As-tu langui sans espérance,
L'âme en deuil, le coeur déchiré?
Alors tu connais ma souffrance!

LOTHARIO: Comme toi, triste et solitaire,
Courbé sous d'inflexibles lois,
De mes pleurs j'ai mouillé la terre!
Le ciel reste sourd à ma voix!
(*Applaudissements et acclmations bruyantes dans le château.*)

MIGNON: (*Se dégageant brusquement des bras de Lothario.*) Écoute! c'est son nom que la foule répete!
C'est elle qu'on acclame et c'est elle qu'on fête! . . .
(*Se tournant vers le château avec un geste de menace.*)
Ah! que la main de Dieu
Ne peut-elle sur eux faire éclater la foudre,
Et frapper ce palais, et le réduire en poudre,
Et l'engloutir sous des torrents de feu! . . .
(*Elle s'enfuit sous les arbres.*)

LOTHARIO: (*Seul.*) (*Après un long silence; avec égarement.*) Le feu! . . . le feu! . . . le feu! . . .
(*Il traverse lentement le théâtre et disparait dans l'ombre. Les portes de la serre s'ouvrent pour laisser passer la foule des INVITES et des COMEDIENS.*)
(*La représentation vient de finir. Philine et les Comediens ont conservé leurs costumes de théâtre.*)

CHOEUR: Brava! brava! brava!
La Philine est vraiment divine!
A ses pieds nos coeurs et nos fleurs!
Gloire à Titania! . . .

RECIT: FILINA: Oui, pour ce soir, je suis reine des fées! Voici mon sceptre d'or! Et voici mes trophées, Je suis Titania la blonde, Titania, fille de l'air! En riant, je parcours le monde Plus vive que l'oiseau, plus prompte que l'éclair! Ah! Ah! La troupe tolle Des lutins suit Ah! Ah! Ah! Ah! Mon char qui vole. Et dans

---

MIGNON: (*Coming from the apartment on the left, dressed as in the first Act.*) That woman! I do loathe her.
(*Exit.*)

## SCENE II

A portion of the park adjoining the Baron's castle. At back, to the right, a conservatory, illuminated from within. To the left a lake, surrounded here and there by reeds, etc. Music and the noise of clapping hands, are heard to proceed from the wings. Mignon advances from among the trees, and stands in a listening attitude.

MIGNON: (*alone.*)
She's there, by his side, triumphant, happy;
While I do wander forth alone, abandoned.
He loves her! Ah, my aching heart did foretell this,
But still I little thought to hear it from his own lips,
Now, with these eyes, the bitter truth to witness!
Ah! woe is me! he loves her! at this thought alone
My tongue shames to speak the hated words.
He loves her! Oh heaven! with grief my heart will break!
(*Rushes hurriedly in the direction of the lake.*)
Yes! this calm, unruffled stream, Placid, though deep,
Summons me! I think beneath the waters clear,
I hear the siren's song—
Yes! with my life, I will end my woes here!
(*She is about to throw herself into the water, when the strains of a harp are heard to proceed from behind the trees.*)
Heavens! what sounds are those?
(*Coming forward.*)
My wicked impulse has almost passed away.
Yes! still do I wish to live!
(*Lothario appears.*)
Are you Lothario?
(*Recognizes him.*)
It is he!

LOTHARIO: (*Who at first does not recognize Mignon.*)
Who's there? who is that now approaches me?
Are you she for whom I've sought so long?

MIGNON: No, not so!

LOTHARIO: Ever am I mistaken! alas, I see it is not she! The form that now hastens to my side, Is surely that of Mignon!

MIGNON: Ah, yes. You've recognized me, I am Mignon indeed.

LOTHARIO: (*Tenderly.*) Oh, hapless maiden!
Your footsteps, too, I've longed to trace,
Come to this aged breast!
Come! tell me the sad thoughts which now your heart do grieve.
(*Pressing her to his breast.*)

MIGNON: (*In accents of the deepest woe, leaning her head on LOTHARIO's shoulder.*) Have you ever suffered! Have you ever known grief!
Have you ever hopeless, languished in despair—
Have you ever vainly, sought your native land?
If so, my sorrow you can understand.

LOTHARIO: Maiden, I have known bitter grief,
Yes, cruel suffering have I endured;
My tears the ground have bedewed,
Amid foreign lands I long have roamed.
(*A tumultuous noise of clapping of hands heard from behind the scenes.*)

MIGNON: Listen! the castle resounds with applause—
They all admire, they all do praise her!
(*Turning toward the conservatory, and declaiming in wrathful accents.*)
Ah! why does not avenging ire,
Why does not the winged thunderbolt
Strike down and crush yon impious dwelling?
Why do not devouring flames consume it?
(*Rushes hurriedly away, and disappears amid the trees.*)

LOTHARIO: (*Alone, after a moment's reflection, confused and bewildered.*) Fire, she said! Ah, fire! fire!
(*Slowly crosses the stage and disappears amid the shade. The door of the conservatory is thrown open, and a crowd of Guests, Actors, etc., issue forth.*)
(*The performance within is supposed to have just terminated. FILINA and the Actors retain their theatrical costumes.*)

CHORUS: Filina is indeed divine, A wondrous triumph she has achieved. Her beauty let us celebrate! Bravo! bravo! Filina is indeed divine, etc., etc.

RECIT: FILINA: Yes, for this eve I shall reign queen of the fairies, observe here, my sceptre of gold! and behold my trophies. I'm fair Titania, glad and gay, through the world unfettered now I blithely stray. With jocund heart and happy mien, I cheerly dance, I cheerly dance the hours . . . away, Like the

la nuit Fuit! . . . Ah! Je suis Titania la blonde.

PHILINE: Oui, pour ce soir, je suis reine des fées
Voici mon sceptre, d'or! . . .
Et voici mes trophées.
Autour de moi, toute ma cour court,
Chantant le plaisir et l'amour.
Aux rayons de Phoebé qui luit! . . .
Parmi les fleurs que l'aurore Fait éclore,
Par les bois et par les près Diaprès,
Sur les flots couverts d'écume,
Dans la brume,
On me voit d'un pied léger Voltiger!
Je suis Titania la blonde,
Titania, fille de l'air!
En riant, je parcours le monde,
Plus vive que l'oiseau, plus prompte que l'éclair!

COMÉDIENS: (*Entre eux, avec dépit.*) Déjà vingt amants
Entourent la belle,
Et tout est pour elle,
Fleurs et compliments! . . .

CHOEUR: (*Entourant Philine pour la complimenter.*) Gloire à Titania la blonde,
Brava! brava! brava!
Gloire à Titania!

PHILINE: (*Apercevant Wilhelm.*) Ah! vous voici! . . . Déjà vous me faites attendre.
(*D'un air de reproche.*)
Vous n'étiez pas là pour m'entendre! . . .

FRÉDÉRIC: (*À part.*) Encor oui! . . . quel sourire aimable! air tendre.

WILHELM: (*Regardant autour de lui avec inquiétude.*) Pardonnez-moi! . . . Je cherche en vain Mignon!

PHILINE: (*Minaudant.*) Eh! quoi! Celle que vous cherchez, Monsieur, ce n'est pas moi!
(*Ils remontent en causant; Mignon et Lothario se rencontrent sur le devant du théâtre.*)

LOTHARIO: (*À demi-voix.*) Sois contente, Mignon! Réjouis-toi, pauvre âme!
J'ai voulu t'obéir! . . . Et ces murs sont en flamme.

MIGNON: Ciel! que dis-tu!

LOTHARIO: (*Calme et souriant.*) J'ai fait ce que tu voulais.

MIGNON: Dieu!

LOTHARIO: Ces murs vont s'érouler sous des torrents de feu!
(*Mignon inquiète cherche Wilhelm des yeux. Wilhelm l'aperçoit et accourt vers elle.*)

---

bird that freely wings its flight . . .
Ah! Ah! Fairies dance around me,
Ah! . . . Ah! . . . Ah! . . . Ah! . . . Elfin sprites on nimble toe around me gaily dance. Ah! . . .

FILINA: Both night and day.
My attendants ever sing.
The achievements of the God of Love!
On the wave's white foam, Amid the twilight grey,
Amid hedges, amid flowers,
I blithely dance!
Yes! the fair Titania am I, etc., etc.

ALL: With love for her
Each heart does burn,
Amid flowers and plaudits
Her bright path does lay!

CHORUS: Ah! Titania is indeed divine,
We'll pay homage to her beauty.

FILINA: (*To Wilhelm.*) At last I've found you,
Is it possible I have to search for you already?
Have you not been to hear me?

FREDERIC: (*Aside.*) This eternal fellow here again!
(*Watching Filina's behavior.*)
What glances! Ah, what smiles!

WILHELM: (*Pre-occupied, and looking anxiously around him.*) Excuse me, I implore! I vainly everywhere do seek Mignon—

FILINA: Indeed! Then it was not I whom you sought?
(*They both retire conversing. Mignon and Lothario meet near the front of the stage.*)

LOTHARIO: Banish, O maiden, the grief that now gnaws your heart,
Your wish is heard; the flames do even now consume the mansion!

MIGNON: Alas! What did you say?

LOTHARIO: I have accomplished your desire.

MIGNON: Oh, heaven.

LOTHARIO: Anon those walls will crumble into ashes!
(*Mignon looks anxiously around her. Wilhelm, perceiving her, hurries towards her.*)

---

WILHELM: C'est toi! . . . je te cherchais, Mignon! . . .

PHILINE: (*S'approchant.*) Holà! ma belle!

MIGNON: Que voulez-vous?

PHILINE: Pour nous prouver ton zèle,
Va vite, va chercher
Là-bas . . .
(*Elle indique la serre.*)
Certain bouquet . . . dont quelqu'un qui m'est cher
Tantôt m'a fait hommage,
Et que j'ai laissé choir, je crois, de mon corsage.

WILHELM: A quoi bon? . . .

MIGNON: (*À Wilhelm.*) J'obéis, j'obéis, maître!
(*Elle s'élana.*)

LAËRTE: (*Accourant.*) Dieu! Philine, mes amis, le théâtre est en feu!
Regardez! . . .

WILHELM: (*Avec effroi.*) Que dit-il?

PHILINE et LES FEMMES: Je meurs! . . . mon sang se glace! . . .
(*Les Laquais sortent emportant les flambeaux. Le théâtre se plonge dans l'obscurité; des lueurs d'incendie commencent à éclairer le vitrage de la serre.*)

WILHELM: (*Ecartant la foule.*) Ah! malheureuse enfant! . . . Arrière! . . . faite place!

PHILINE: (*Le retenant.*) Cher Wilhelm!

LAËRTE: (*Le retenant.*) Arrêtez!

WILHELM: Ne me retenez pas! . . .
(*Il s'élance au secours de Mignon.*)

CHOEUR: Pour apaiser la flamme,
Tout secours serait vain!
L'effroi glace notre âme!
Que sert-il de tenter un effort surhumain!

LOTHARIO: (*Debout, au milieu de la scène et dominant le tumult général.*) Fugitif et tremblant, je vais de porte en porte,
Où du ciel me conduit, où l'orage m'emporte
Des misérables Dieu prend soin . . .
(*Le vitrage éclate et s'écroule. La foule des invites se presse sur le devant de la scène en poussant un cri de terreur.*)
(*Wilhelm parait enfin portant Mignon dans ses bras.*)

---

WILHELM: At length, O dear one, have I found you,
I've sought you everywhere!

FILINA: (*To Mignon.*) Listen girl!

MIGNON: What would you?

FILINA: If you're anxious to display your zeal,
Haste yonder,
(*Pointing to conservatory.*)
And find the flowers, which You offered yesterday to your master,
And which I think have fallen from my bosom!

WILHELM: (*To Filina.*) But why?

MIGNON: (*To Wilhelm.*) I will obey.
(*Hastens to conservatory.*)

LAERTES: (*Entering hurriedly.*) Quick, hasten all!
Gentlemen, the theatre is in flames!
See, see!

WILHELM: (*Horrified.*) Oh fearful sight!

FILINA: (*To the Ladies.*) An icy chill my frame pervades.
(*Servants exit, bearing away the torches with them. The stage is enveloped in complete darkness. The red light of the conflagration now begins to be reflected by the glasswork of the conservatory.*)

WILHELM: (*With painful emotion.*) Ah! ill advised was your zeal!

FILINA: (*Endeavoring to stop him.*) Dear Wilhelm!

LAERTES: (*Seizing him by the arm.*) Hold!

WILHELM: (*Disengaging himself.*) Ah! Do not retain me!
(*Hurries hastily to Mignon's rescue.*)

CHORUS: No mortal power can now check
The conflagration's might,
The castle soon must fall!
When human courage can do nothing,
Why sacrifice a life
In fruitless heroism?

LOTHARIO: (*In the midst of the stage, quelling for the moment the general commotion.*) I am a lonely wanderer! I stray from door to door,
As fate guides or as the storm hurries me;
But heaven protects the wretched with kind and fostering care!
(*The glass-work of the conservatory falls in with a crash. The guests in terror, rush to the front of the stage. After a brief pause, Wilhelm re-appears, bearing in his arms MIGNON's fainting form.*)

WILHELM: De la mort, Dieu l'a préservèe!
La flamme l'entourait déjà! je l'ai sauvée!.
(*Il dépose sur un banc de gazon Mignon évanouie. Mignon serre entre ses mains crispées un bouquet de fleurs à flétries et à demi consumées. Tableau final.*)

WILHELM: Heaven has saved her from a dreadful death;
Begirt was she with flames, When, heaven be praised, I reached and saved her!
(*Wilhelm places Mignon on a bank. She still holds in her hands the bunch of withered flowers. Tableau.*)

## ■ ACTE TROISIÈME

*Une galerie italienne ornée de statues. A droite, une fenêtre jouverte sur la campagne. Au fond, grande porte fermée. Portes laterales. Au lever du rideau, la scène est vide.*

(*Prélude de harpe dans la coulisse.*)

CHOEUR: (*Au dehors.*) La douce clarté des étoiles,
Illumine le flot mouvant!
Amis, ouvrons gaîment nos voiles,
Aux baisers amoureux du vent!
La rame étincelle
Sur l'eau du lac bleu,
Et laisse après elle
Un sillon de feu! . . .
La douce clarté des étoiles
Illumine le flot mouvant!
(*LOTHARIO parait sur le seuil de la porte de droite.*)

LOTHARIO: (*Seul.*) Elle dort! . . .
De son coeur j'ai calmé la Fièvre!
Un sourire doux et joyeux
A ma voix entr'ouvrait sa lèvre;
Le sommeil a fermé ses yeux!
Un ange est debout auprès d'elle!
Un ange descendu des cieux
Lui prête l'ombre de son aile! . . .
(*Wilhelm, Antonio*) (*ANTONIO pose une lampe sur une table, et se tourner vers la fenêtre.*)

ANTONIO: Vous verrez de cette fenêtre s'illuminer les villas d'alentour.
De la fête du lac c'est demain le grand jour;
Ce palais seul depuis qu'il a perdu son maître ne s'illumine plus.
S'il est encore à votre gré
Vous pouvez l'acheter.

WILHELM: Demain je repondrai.
(*Sur un signe de Wilhelm, Antonio sort. Wilhelm touchant l'épaule de LOTHARIO.*)
Eh bien?

## ■ ACT III

*A gallery, embellished with statues. To the right, a window overlooking the country. At back, a closed door. Side doors. At the rising of the curtain, there is no one on the stage.*

*A harp prelude is heard behind the scenes.*

CHORUS: (*Outside.*) Quick, the sails unfurl,
The wind blows propitious, the gently ruffled waves
Tempt us to put forth;
Let's quickly leave the shore,
And gaily tempt the wave!
Quick, then, unfurl the sails, etc., etc.
(*Lothario appears on the threshold of the door (right hand.)*)

LOTHARIO: (*Alone.*) I've soothed the throbbing of her aching heart,
And restored the smile to her lips.
Her weary eyes at last have closed
In gentle slumber;
By day and night some heavenly spirit
The maiden protects
On wings celestial, it hovers round
Protecting her from harm!
(*Enter Wilhelm, Antonio.*)
(*Antonio carries a lamp.*)
(*Placing the lamp on the table, and approaching the window.*)

ANTONIO: From this window you will see
The shores on all sides lighted up;
tomorrow is a joyous festival,
Kept sacred by the dwellers on the lake.
This mansion alone, since that thrice fatal day.
When woe so suddenly overtook its owners,
The festal fire no more displays.
This castle, therefore, old and rugged,
Will before long be sold;
At the price agreed upon.
It may become yours.

WILHELM: Tomorrow, I'll give my final answer.
(*At a sign from Wilhelm, Antonio withdraws.*)

WILHELM: What now?

LOTHARIO: Chut! . . . Un sourire a passé sur sa lèvre;
L'enfant dort et n'a plus la fièvre.

WILHELM: (*Vivement.*) Ah, que le ciel en soit béni.
C'est l'air natal qui la rapelle à la vie.
Oui, demain j'acheterai pour elle
Le palais des Cypriani.

LOTHARIO: (*Il se leve en tressaillant.*) Cypriani!

WILHELM: Qu'as-tu?
(*LOTHARIO se dirige vers la grande porte du fond et cherche à l'ouvrir.*)

WILHELM: Cette chambre est fermée depuis quinze ans!

LOTHARIO: Quinze ans!
(*Il se dirige vers la porte à gauche.*)
Ah, là!
(*Se tourant vers Wilhelm.*)
Chut!
(*Il sort lenteinent.*)

WILHELM: (*Seul.*) Etrange regard!
Ah, mieux que ma raison le coeur de ce vieillard
Console cet enfant par ses soins ranimée.
J'ai deviné trop tard le secret de Mignon.
(*Entr'ouvrant la porte de droite.*)
Hélas, elle sommeille, et prononce mon nom!

WILHELM: Elle ne croyait pas, dans sa candeur naïve, Que l'amour innocent qui dormait dans son coeur, Pût se changer un jour en une ardeur plus vive Et troubler à jamais son rêve de bonheur! Pour rendre à la fleur épuisée Sa frâicheur, son éclat vermeil, O printemps, donne-lui ta guotte de rosée! O mon coeur, donne-lui ton rayon de Soleil!
C'est en vain que j'attends un aveu de sa bouche!
Je veux connaître en vain ses secrètes douleurs!
Mon regard l'intimide et ma voix l'effarouche;
Un mot trouble son âme et fait couler ses pleurs! . . .
Pour rendre à la fleur épuisée
Sa fraîcheur, son éclat vermeil,
O printemps, donne-lui ta goutte de roseil!
O mon coeur, donne-lui ton rayon de soleil!
(*WILHELM, ANTONIO, puis LAERTE*)

ANTONIO: (*Entrant.*) Signor!

WILHELM: Que me veux-tu?

ANTONIO: Cette lettre.

LOTHARIO: Hush, she's sleeping.
Her eyelids tranquilly are closed;
The fever has quite left her.

WILHELM: May heaven be praised,
Her native air infuses new life into her veins,
For her it is that I tomorrow mean to buy
The Casa Cipriani!

LOTHARIO: (*Starting violently at the name.*) Cipriani!

WILHELM: What ails thee?
(*Lothario looks round in surprise—he then approaches the door at back, which he endeavors to open.*)

WILHELM: Yon door has remained closed,
For fifteen years.

LOTHARIO: (*Deeply moved.*) Fifteen years!
(*He again looks around him with the aspect of one who seems to recall the past; and then approaches the door and turns toward Wilhelm*)
Ah—yonder!
(*Exit slowly.*)

WILHELM: (*Alone.*) What strange, wild look was that?
This good old man has been more successful than I.
In soothing the poor, hapless maiden
At last I have discovered the secret of her heart,
From her sweet lips, my name escaped!

WILHELM: Ah! little thought the hapless maid, in innocence arrayed, What she in her breast now nurtured, would ardent love become, And thus perturb the peaceful current, the current of her life, would before long disturb the current of her peaceful life . . . That what she now unwittingly nurtured, would disturb the calm current of her life. O balmy April, who to the withered flowers restored their colors, Kiss her fair cheek, and a grateful sigh of love cause to escape.
Vainly do I implore, that she a single word will utter—
the secret of her woes unto me she will not reveal!
One glance of mine, with trouble fills her heart,
One word from me brings tears to her eyes.
Q balmy April! You who to the withered flowers
Their colors, by your genial presence, do restore, etc., etc.
(*Lothario, Antonio and the before-named.*)

ANTONIO: Signor—

WILHELM: What do you want now?

ANTONIO: (*Giving him a letter.*)
This letter I do bring you.

WILHELM: (*Prenant la lettre et le congédiant.*) Merci.
(*ANTONIO sort, Il lit.*)
"Philine vous suivait, fuyez, elle est ici."
Un avis de Laërte.
(*Courant vers la chambre de Mignon et s'arrêtant*)
Ah, Mignon, la voiçi.

MIGNON: Ou suis-je? Je respire un air plus profonde
L'azur est plus profonde.
Dans le flot pur de ce lac transparent
Se reflète un bois sombre.
Une voile glisse dans l'ombre.
Quelle fraicheur! et ce palais dont les jardins descendent vers la grève
Il me semble avoir tout cela dans une rêve
Lothario! Wilhelm! Je t'appelais,
Je suis heureuse! l'air m'enivre!
Mon coeur a cessé de souffrir!
Je renais! . . . Je me sens revivre!
Mignon ne craint plus de mourir!

WILHELM: Pauvre enfant! plus de creintes vaines!
Cet air pur va te ranimer!
Un sang nouveau gonfle tes veines,
Mignon doit vivre pour aimer!

MIGNON: Oui, je te crois! Je veux te croire!
Parle-moi! parle encor! toujours!

WILHELM: Chasse à jamais de ta mémoire
Le souvenir des mauvais jours!
(*La conduisant vers la fenêtre.*)
Ah! que ton âme dans mon âme s'epanche!
Chère Mignon, lève vers moi tes yeux!
Sous ce rayon divin et dans ta robe blanche,
Tu m'apparais comme un ange des cieux!

MIGNON: (*Souriant tristement.*)
Non, c'est toujours Mignon!

WILHELM: (*Tombant à ses pieds.*) Mignon n'est plus la même!
Mignon a tout mon coeur et c'est elle que j'aime!

MIGNON: Toi! m'aimer! que dis-tu!
Souvienstoi du passé!
Et ne réveille pas un espoir insensé!

(*S'échappant de ses bras.*)
Ton coeur n'est pas à moi! . . . Ton coeur est à Philine!

WILHELM: Philine est loin de nous . . . Et je ne l'aime pas!

WILHELM: A letter, you say?
(*Opens the letter and reads.*)
"Filina is on your track,
Fly—already is she here!"
the hand is surely that of Laertes!
(*Running to Mignon's room.*)
(*He stops short as Mignon enters.*)
It is she!

MIGNON: Where am I! What balmy air is this that now I breathe?
Ah! how bright seems the blue of heaven!
The smooth mirror of yon sunny lake
Doth placidly reflect the outline of the hills;
A white sail skims the surface of the waves.
How beauteous is the scene.
Ah, this splendid mansion!
This garden on the hill-side situated;
All this I dimly now recall,
Like to faint memories of one's childhood's dreams
(*Calling.*)
Lothario! Wilhelm!
Happy! aye, thrice blessed am I;
My heart no longer feels grief,
To new life I seem to awake—
The fear of death no more haunts me!

WILHELM: Yes! new hope your heart inspires;
Thy much-loved native air, your life will save;
O maiden, banish now the grief,
That so long has bowed you down,
Live. and live to love!

MIGNON: Yes, dear one, I will live—to trust in you!
Speak! oh, speak, for ever!

WILHELM: Chase then from your troubled mind,
The memory of dark days gone by.
Ah, yes! my very soul seems to blend with yours!
O loving one, on me your bright eyes turn;
With that sweet radiant face, and robe of spotless white,
You seem an angel truly.

MIGNON: (*With a melancholy smile.*) And yet I am but what I ever was!

WILHELM: Nay, you are not now the same.
My heart's idol! You're now my treasure found!

MIGNON: Heavens! do I believe aright?
And dare you say you love me?
Not long since it was Filina whom you loved.

WILHELM: No, when you are at my side,
Of her I think no more.

MIGNON: (*Revenant vers Wilhelm et lui tendant la main.*) Est-il vrai! . . . parle! . . . O joie ineffable et divine!
Je puis te dire enfin! . . . Mais parlons bas . . . bien bas! . . .

LA VOIX de Philine: (*Au dehors.*)
"Je suis Titania la blonde,
Titania, fille de l'air!"

WILHELM: Philine!

MIGNON: (*Courant à la fenêtre.*)
Encore elle! . . . encore cette femme! . . .
(*A part.*)
O mon secret, reste au fond de mon âme!

MIGNON: Je reconnaisais sa voix!
Je l'entends! je la vois!
C'est elle encore? c'est elle qui te cherche et t'appelle!
Ne m'interroge pas!
Je dois me taire, hélas!
Je ne veux plus parler! je ne parlerai pas!
(*MIGNON se laisse tomber dans un fauteuil.*)

WILHELM: Ah, malheurese enfant! . . . Ses mains sont glacées.
Mignon, toi que j'aime, ah! reviens, toi.
(*MIGNON reprend ses senses.*)
Elle ouvre les yeux. C'est moi qui t'appelle.

MIGNON: Je n'entends plus rien.
N'est-ce pas un rêve?

WILHELM: Non, ce n'est qu'un rêve, un rêve menteur,
Ou la fièvre encore égare ton coeur.

MIGNON: La vièvre, dis-tu? Celui qui m'aime c'est Lothario.
Pourquoi n'est-il pas près de moi?
(*Elle se tourne vers la porte du fond.*)
Ecoute! Oui, j'entends son pas.

WILHELM: Nul ne peut venir de là.
(*LOTHARIO parait.*)

LOTHARIO: Mignon, Wilhelm, salut, à vous!
Soyez les bienvenus chez moi.

WILHELM: (*À part.*) Que veut'il dire?

MIGNON: (*Etonnée.*) Sous ces riches est-ce lui que je vois!

MIGNON: (*Ecstatically.*) Oh heavens! it's true!
Oh joy immense, unspeakable!
At last, then, the secret I'll avow to you . . .

FILINA: (*Outside.*) "The fair Titania am I,
Titania by all on earth beloved."

WILHELM: (*Aside.*) Great heaven! Filina!

MIGNON: (*Running to the window.*) That woman still!
(*Aside.*)
O fatal secret, die in my heart!

MIGNON: Yes, yes, her voice it is,
Go, get you from my side.
Listen! Listen! it's she.
Did you hear? she draws nearer.
Ah, speak to me no more,
My voice, my speech, do fail
(*Mignon falls on a seat.*)

WILHELM: (*Sadly.*) Poor girl, her hands are icy cold!
(*Tenderly.*)
Take heart, dear girl,
Resume your senses!
(*Mignon recovers her consciousness.*)
Her eyes she opens!
It is I, Mignon, who calls you!

MIGNON: (*Terrified.*) The hateful voice, I now no longer hear;
Perchance I did but dream.

WILHELM: Yes! It was but a vain, delusive dream.
The dreadful fever still overclouds your sense.

MIGNON: (*Sadly.*) The fever you say?
No, that is not true;
The only one who loves me is Lothario!
Why do I not see him at my side?
(*A noise is heard at back of stage.*)
Listen! It is he!
I hear him coming.
(*Pointing to door at back.*)

WILHELM: Through that door, none can pass!
(*The door at back is suddenly burst open, and Lothario appears on the threshold. He is attired in a rich garb of dark velvet—he advances slowly, bearing in his hand a small coffer.*)

LOTHARIO: Mignon, Wilhelm, I do greet you!
Welcome, to this my house!
(*In tones of mingled surprise and pity.*)

WILHELM: Oh Heaven!

MIGNON: (*Surprised.*) Lothario! and in this rich attire?

LOTHARIO: Tout ici m'appartient! Regarde, enfant, admire!... En ce palais j'étais maître autrefois!

WILHELM et Mignon: (*Les yeux fixés sur Lothario.*) Je ne reconnais plus son regard ni sa voix

LOTHARIO: (*Déposant la cassette sur la table, et s'approchant de MIGNON.*) Oublions nos temps de misère!... Je t'apporte un don précieux, Il adoucira, je l'espère, L'ennui de ton coeur soucieux...

MIGNON et WILHELM: Je crois deviner un mystère Que trahit l'éclat de ses yeux!...

LOTHARIO: Cette cassette est là depuis de bien longs mois! (*A Mignon.*) C'est à toi de l'ouvrir... (*Il étend la main vers la cassette.*)

MIGNON: Que contient-elle?...

LOTHARIO: (*Sans détourner la tête.*) Vois.

MIGNON: ((*Ouvrant la cassette.*) Une écharpe d'enfant!

LOTHARIO: (*Le regard fixe, immobile au milieu de la scène.*) D'or et d'argent brodée... Oui, je l'avais pieusement gardèe!

WILHELM: Quelle est cette relique et qui donc la porta?... Parle!

LOTHARIO: Sperata!...

MIGNON: Sperata! Déjà ce nom a frappe mon oreille! Un souvenir confus, A ce doux nom dans mon âme s'éville! Est-ce l'écho lointain d'un passé qui n'est plus?...

WILHELM et MIGNON: Des pleurs mouillent ses yeux...

LOTHARIO: (*Toujours immobile sur le devant du théâtre et comme absorbé par ses souvenirs.*) Ne vois-tu pas aussi Un bracelet de corail?

MIGNON: (*Tirant le bracelet de la cassette.*) Le voici! (*Essayant le bracelet à son bras.*) Trop petit pour mon bras!...

LOTHARIO: (*Tristement.*) Trop grand! trop grand pour elle Elle ne voulait pas attendre au lendemain Pour porter un bijou qui la rendait au plus belle! Mais le bijou toujours lui glissait de le main!

---

LOTHARIO: Here, all now belongs to me. Know, dear girl, that of this wealthy mansion, I was once the lord.

MIGNON: (*To Wilhelm, contemplating Lothario with surprise.*) I scarcely do recognize him—his look so wild, His words so strange....

LOTHARIO: (*Placing the little coffer on the table and approaching Mignon.*) O maiden now, the past forget, A treasure rich, I here present to you; The trouble of your aching heart It will quickly calm.

WILHELM: Mignon. From those eyes, with oppressed woe, What fire unwonted now gleams!

LOTHARIO: Full many a month this coffer has lain in yonder chamber. (*To Mignon.*) It is yours to open.

MIGNON: Say! what does it enclose?

LOTHARIO: See for yourself.

MIGNON: (*Running to the coffer and opening it.*) A child's scarf.

LOTHARIO: (*Comtemplating it with a fixed stare.*) It is embroidered with silver, Ah! with what fond love in that recess, I have preserved it.

WILHELM: But tell us—who did wear this beauteous scarf?

LOTHARIO: Sperata!

MIGNON: Sperata? The name seems familiar to my ear, At its sweet sound, vague memories do stir within me, Memories that do recall a time, long, long since passed away.

WILHELM & MIGNON: See, see! his eyes do stream with tears!

LOTHARIO: (*Still motionless, and absorbed in his thoughts.*) Do you not also find, A coral ornament?

MIGNON: (*Drawing forth a bracelet.*) It is here, (*Endeavoring to put a bracelet on her arm.*) It is too small for me!

LOTHARIO: (*Sadly.*) Yet, once, it was too large, Sperata never would wait till the morrow To wear a jewel that enhanced her charms; Yon bracelet ever from her hand did fall.

---

MIGNON: (*Très-émue.*) Mais le bijou toujours lui glissait de la main!

WILHELM: Qu'as-tu, Mignon? Tu trembles et tu pleures!

LOTHARIO: (*À Mignon.*) Regarde encore!

MIGNON: (*Retirant de la cassette un petit livre à coins d'argent.*) Un livre d'heures!

LOTHARIO: Hélas! je crois toujours la voir, Lettre à lettre, épeler sa prière du soir!

MIGNON: (*Ouvrant le livre et lisant.*) O Vierge Marie, Le Seigneur est avec vous! Abaissez vos regards si doux, Sur l'enfant qui prie!...

LOTHARIO: (*Penché vera elle.*) Elle priait ainsi, mains jointes, à genoux!

MIGNON: (*MIGNON laissant échapper le livre et tombant à genoux, les yeux levés au ciel et les mains jointes, comme un enfant en prière.*) Vous qui bercez sur vos genoux, Le divin Sauveur de la terre, Conservez l'enfant à sa mère, O madone, priez pour nous!...

LOTHARIO: (*Les mains étendues vera Mignon.*) Est-ce Dieu qui l'inspire? Elle achève sans lire!

MIGNON: (*Se levant et s'exaltant de plus en plus.*) Lothario!... Wilhelm!... suis-je encore en délire?... Je devine!... je vois!... je sens!... je ne puis dire!... Où m'avez-vous conduite et quel est ce pays?

WILHELM: L'Italie!

MIGNON: O rayons de céleste lumière! O souvenirs!... (*Aprè avoir fait un effort pour rassembler ses souvenirs elle s'élance avec un cri vers la porte du fond, disparait un moment dans la coulisse et revient pâle et chancelante.*) Là! là! l'image de ma mere! ... Et sa chambre est deserté!...

LOTHARIO: (*Qui a suivi tous ses mouvements avec anxiété, lui tendant les bras et courant à elle.*) Ah! ma fille!

MIGNON: Mon père! (*Elle tombe dans les bras de Lothario.*)

---

MIGNON: (*Aside, repeating sorrowfully.*) But the jewel always glistened on her hand!

WILHELM: (*To Mignon.*) What ails you? speak! What secret grief now torments you?

LOTHARIO: (*To Mignon.*) Search the coffer deeper still.

MIGNON: (*Producing from the coffer a little Prayer Book.*) A little Prayer Book!

LOTHARIO: Even now, methinks, I hear her angel voice in prayer. She ever prayed when day began to decline.

MIGNON: (*Opening the book and reading.*) O power supreme, Our lives are in your hands, Promise to keep me in Thy Holy care, Grant, that from the right path, I never may stray.

LOTHARIO: Thus, in the days gone by, Thus did my Sperata pray!

MIGNON: (*Lets fall the book from her hands, kneels down, clasps her hands, raises her eyes to heaven, and assumes the look and attitude of a child at prayer.*) O Thou, who, in Heaven above, All mortal hearts read, Teach me to love my parents dear, Preserve me to them, evermore!

LOTHARIO: (*Deeply agitated, extending his arm to Mignon.*) Just Heaven! what does this mean? She knows the book's contents by heart.

MIGNON: (*Rising with increasing fervor.*) Lothario mine! what secret proof now works within my breast? I feel—I know—but yet cannot explain! (*To Wilhelm.*) Where have thou brought me? What hills are those that rise over there.

WILHELM: They are the shores of Italy.

MIGNON: O beauteous light! O sweet, reviving, gales! O memory! (*After having, with a violent effort, endeavored to recall her scattered recollections, she rushes with a wild cry to the door at back, disappears for a moment, and then returns, pale and scarcely able to stand.*) Yonder my mother's picture hangs! Her room, alas! seems deserted!

LOTHARIO: (*Who has followed her every movement, now rushes to her with extended arms.*) My child!

MIGNON: My father! (*Throws herself into Lothario's arms.*)

## Act III

LOTHARIO: C'est mon enfant!... c'est elle!... O Dieu! je te bénis!

MIGNON: Oui, je vous reconnais mon père!... mon pays!

WILHELM: Mignon, retrouve enfin son père et son pays!

MIGNON: (*Frappé d'une violente commotion.*) Ah!

WILHELM: (*Effrayé.*) Mignon!

LOTHARIO: (*Soutenant Mignon.*) Ma fille!
(*Elle suffoque.*)

WILHELM: Dieu! qu'a-t-elle donc?

LOTHARIO: At length I've found my daughter dear. All praise to you, O Heaven!

MIGNON: All praise to Heaven be given! I at last have found my home, my father.

WILHELM: All praise be given to Heaven! She has found her home, her father! (*Overcome by violent emotion.*)

MIGNON: Ah!

WILHELM: Mignon.

LOTHARIO: (*Supporting her.*) My Child!

WILHELM: (*Alarmed.*) Speak, in pity, speak! what is it you feel?

MIGNON: (*Elle chancelle.*) Je meurs!
(*Elle tombe.*)
(*Wilhelm va ouvrir la fenêtre et revient près de Mignon. Peu à MIGNON revient à elle.*)

WILHELM: Le bonheur est içi maintenant. Elle revit! Chère Mignon? Je t'aime, oui, je t'aime!

LOTHARIO: Son coeur se souvient.

MIGNON: (*Reconnaissant Lothario et Wilhelm, comme dans une extase.*) Ah, c'est là que tu voulais vivre, Aimer, aimer et mourir!

LOTHARIO et WILHELM: Ah, c'est la que tu dois vivre, Pour être heureuse et pour aimer! C'est là, oui, c'est là, pour toujours unia!

MIGNON: (*Falling to the ground.*) I faint, I die!

WILHELM: (*Running to throw open one of the windows, and immediately returning to Mignon.*) Oh dearest treasure, do not droop! My very life depends on yours! (*Mignon slowly recovers her consciousness.*) Ah! did you know how I adore you!

LOTHARIO: See, she revives—her sense she now recovers!

MIGNON: (*Recognizing Wilhelm and Lothario—almost ecstatic with joy.*) "Ah! it is there that I will live, love, and die!

WILHELM, and LOTHARIO: Ah, it is there that you shall live, To be happy and to love! It is there, yes, there forever united.

# *Ernani* (1844)

**MUSIC BY GIUSEPPE VERDI ■ LIBRETTO BY FRANCESCO MARIA PIAVE**

Ernani takes place in Spain and Aix-la-Chapelle in 1519. This opera in four acts is set to a libretto by Francesco Maria Piave based on Victor Hugo's Hernani, ou l'Honneur Castillian, and was first performed at the Teatro La Fenice in Venice on March 9, 1844. Ernani, who has been declared an outlaw by Don Carlo, King of Spain, is in love with Elvira and plans to kidnap her from the castle of her fiancé, Don Ruy Gomez de Silva. The king, who is also in love with Elvira, finds Ernani in her rooms. De Silva challenges both men to a duel. The king pretends Ernani is his messenger and helps him escape, but Ernani disguises himself as a pilgrim and hides at de Silva's castle on the day of de Silva's wedding to Elvira. De Silva discovers him and offers to protect him. When de Silva refuses to tell the king where Ernani is hiding, the king takes Elvira as hostage. De Silva challenges Ernani to a duel. Ernani refuses, pledging instead to take his own life if de Silva blows the horn Ernani has given him. The Electors meet to plan the succession of the Holy Roman Empire. De Silva and Ernani, among others, draw lots to decide who will kill the king. Ernani wins, but will not relinquish the honor to de Silva, who has offered to return the horn in exchange for the opportunity. Don Carlo is elected Holy Roman Emperor and pardons the captured plotters thanks to Elvira's pleading. He also grants Ernani and Elvira permission to wed. During the wedding the horn sounds three times. Ernani and Elvira entreat de Silva to allow Ernani to live, but their words fall upon deaf ears. Ernani kills himself. Elvira collapses over his body.

---

## ■ ACTO I

### SCENA I

*Montagne dell'Aragona. Vedesi in lontano il Moresco Castello di D. RUY GOMEZ DE SILVA. È presso il tramonto.*
*Coro di Ribelli Montanari e Banditi; Mangiano e bevono; parte giuocano e parte assettano le armi.*

**TUTTI:** Evviva—beviam—Nel vino cerchiam
Almeno un piacer!
Che resta al bandito—
Da tutti sfuggito,
Se manca il bicchier?
Giuochiamo, che l'oro—
E vano tesoro,
Giuochiam, se la vita—
Non fa più gradita
Ridente beltà!
Per boschi e pendici—
Abbiam soli amici
Moschetto e pugnal:
Quand'esce la notte—
Nell'orride grotte
Ne forman guancial.

### SCENA II

*(ERNANI, mesto si mostra da una vetta.)*

**TUTTI:** Ernani pensoso!
Perchè, o valoroso,
Sul volto hai pallor?
Commune abbiam sorte. In vita ed in morte
Son tuoi braccio e cor.
Qual freccia scagliata, la meta segnata
Sapremo colpir.

## ■ ACT I

### SCENE I

*The Mountains of Aragon Moorish Castle of D. RUY GOMEZ DE SILVA in the distance. It is near sunset.*
*Chorus of Rebel Mountaineers and Banditti; some are drinking, some playing.*

**ALL:** Drink, drink let the bandit drink,
Let him drink without thought or measure
What's left to the scouted bandit—
What's left but wine and pleasure.
Play, play, if beauty fails
To please with her laughing eye;
Play, play, stake life itself
On the turn of the reckless die.
Our trusty guns, in the wood, in the town are
Our only comrades;
And they make our pillows, when we lay down
On the cavern's rugged floor.

### SCENE II

*(ERNANI is seen on the height.)*

**ALL:** Ernani the thoughtful valiant chief,
Your cheek is wan with concern,
And yet your fate, be it life or death,
Your faithful followers share.
Our hearts and arms alike are yours,
And were an arrow sped
Against you at the slightest sign,
We'd ward it from your head;

---

Non avvi mortale che il piombo o il pugnale
Non possa ferir.

**ERNANI:** Mercè, diletti, amici
A tanto amor, mercè—
Udite or tutti del mio cor gli affanni,
E se voi negherete il vostro aiuto
Forse per sempre Ernani fia perduto.
Come rugiada al cespite
D'un appassito fiore,
D'aragonese vergine
Scendeami voce al core.
Fu quello il primo palpito
D'amor che mi beò
Il vecchio Silva stendere
Osa su lei la mano—
Domani trarla al talamo
Confida l'inumano—
S'ella m'è tolta, ahi misero!
D'affanno morirò.
Si rapisca—

**CORO:** Sia rapita!
Ma in seguirci sarà ardita?

**ERNANI:** Me 'l giurò.

**CORO:** Dunque verremo:
Al castel ti seguiremo.
Quando notto il cielo copra
*(Attorniandolo.)*
Tu ne avrai compagni all'opra:
Dagli sgherri d'un rivale
Ti fia scudo ogni pugnale,
Vieni, Ernani; la tua bella
De banditi fia la stella.
Saran premio al tuo valore
Le dolcezze dell'amor.

**ERNANI:** Dell'esilio nel dolore
Angiol fia consolar.
*(O tu che l'alma adora),*
Vien, la mia vita infiora;
Per noi d'ogni altro bene

---

Though mortal heart was never found
That sword or bullet could not wound.

**ERNANI:**
Brothers and friends, receive my thanks
For a love so true as yours;
You ask me why it is I grieve—
Now listen to the cause:
This hour, Ernani needs
Your aid the most, and if refused he's lost.
As falling dews, upon the flower
That droops, impart new life.
So fell the sweet voice of a maid
Upon my ravished heart—For me it was love's earliest ray.
Vain joy! an aged wretch would dare
To drag him from my side;
Tomorrow's sun sees my despair,
And sees her Silva's bride.

**ALL:** But will she dare to follow us?

**ERNANI:** She gave me her word.

**CHORUS:** With you when night below, draws down.
The shades of heaven
We'll share your toils, dare your rival,
Love's sweets will crown the brave.
Then hope—your maid of Aragon
Shall be the Bandit's star.

**ERNANI:** O angel of comfort in exile and strife,
You who my soul worships, come brighten my life.
Of all other pleasures shall love fill

Il loco amor terrà
Il loco amor terrà.
Purchè sul tuo bel viso vega brillare il riso
Gli stenti suoi le pene Ernani scorderà, ah!
(*S'avviano al castello.*)

the place,
And if a sweet smile illuminates your face,
It will chase every care from the heart of Ernani.
And he'll joyfully bear fatigue, care, and envy.
(*They move towards the Castle.*)

## SCENA III

*Ricche stanze di ELVIRA nel Castello di SILVA. E'notte.*)

ELVIRA: Sorta è la notte, e Silva non ritorna!
Ah, non tornasse ei più!
Questo odiato veglio,
Che quale immondo spettro ognor m'insegue
Col favellar d'amore,
Più sempre Ernani mi configge in core.
Ernani!
Ernani, involami
All'abborrito amplesso.
Fuggiam—se teco vivere
Mi sia d'amor concesso.
Per antri e lande inospite
Ti seguirà il mio piè
Un Eden di delizia,
Saran quegli antri a me.

## SCENE III

*Suite of apartments belonging to ELVIRA, in SILVA'S Castle. Night.*

ELVIRA: It is night, and Silva does not come—if only he never came!
This old man, who, like some foul ghost,
Haunts and pursues me ever.
With words of love, that only wake
My deepest hatred, while they make
Me love Ernani more.
Ernani, Ernani!
O! would that I could fly
From this detested suitor, to live or die with you.
Inhospitable lands—even should they be deserts,
It would seem an Eden of delight if shared with you.

## SCENA IV

*Detta ed ANCELLE, che entrano portando ricchi doni di nozze.*

ANCELLE: Quante d'Iberia giovani
Te invidieran, signora!
Quante ambirieno il talamo
Di Silva che t'adora!
Questi monili splendidi
Lo sposo ti destina, Tu sembrerai regina
Per gemme e per beltà,
Sposa domani in giubilo
Te ognum saluterà

ELVIRA: M'è il voto ingenuo
Che il vostro cor mi fa.
(*Tutto sprezzo che d'Ernani
Non favella a questo core,
Non v'ha gemma che in amore
Possa l'odio tramutar.
Vola, o tempo, presto reca di mia
fuga il lieto istante
Vola, o tempo, al core amante
E supplizio l'indugiar?*)

## SCENE IV

*The above and LADIES, who enter carrying rich wedding gifts.*

LADIES: How many will envy your lord! we come laden,
From him, fairest lady, with these brilliant stores
He destines for you! every Iberian maiden
Will envy the person whom Silva adores.
Gaze on these jewels—with them and your beauty
You'll move through the throng like a queen in her pride;
Tomorrow, how joyfully all will salute you.
How will they envy you! beautiful bride!

ELVIRA: Thanks for these wishes—they do not touch my heart;
How can they?
Ernani has no part in them.
To turn hatred to love, no gem has the power,
Fly quickly, O time! and hasten the hour.
To a fond heart what torture is like delay?
It is her hand, not her heart, that the bride gives away;
By her manners so joyless it is easy to see
That a wife, but not fond one, Elvira will be.
(*Exeunt*)

CORO: (*Sarà sposa, non amante
Se non mostra giubilar.*)
(*Partono*).

## SCENA V

*D. CARLO e Giovanna.*

CARLO: Fa che a me venga— e tosto—

GIOVANNA: Signor, da lunghi giorni
Pensosa ognora ogni consorzio evita,
E Silva assente—

Carlo: Intendo
Or m'obbedisci—

GIOVANNA: Sia
(*Parte.*)

## SCENA VI

D.CARLO: Perchè Elvira rapi la pace mia?
Io l'amo-il mio potere—l'amor mio
Ella non cura—ed io
Preferito mi veggo,
Un nemico giurato, un masnadiero—Quel cor tentiam solo una volta ancora.

## SCENA VII

*Detto ed ELVIRA.*

ELVIRA: Sire!—fa ver?
voi stesso!—ed a quest'ora?

CARLO: Qui mi trasse amor possente—

ELVIRA: Non mi amate—voi mentite.

CARLO: Che favelli?
Un re non mente!

ELVIRA: Da qui dunque ora partite!

CARLO: Vieni meco.

ELVIRA: Tolga Iddio!

CARLO: Vien, mi segui, ben vedrai
Quanto io t'ami—

ELVIRA: E l'onor mio?

CARLO: Di mia corte onor sarai,

ELVIRA: No!—cessate—

CARLO: E un masnadiero
Fai superbo del tuo amor?

ELVIRA: Ogni cor serba un mistero.

CARLO: Quello ascolta del mio cor.
Da quel di che t'ho veduta
Bella come un primo amore
La mia pace fu perduta
Tuo fu il palpito del core,
Cedi, Elvira, ai voti miei;
Puro amor desio da te;
Gioia e vita esser tu dei
Del tuo amante del tuo Re.

## SCENE V

*D. CARLO and GIOVANNA.*

CARLO: Go, send her to me, quickly.

GIOVANNA: Sire, for many days
She is most thoughtful, nor will her eyes raise
On any one; Silva himself does say—

CARLO: Enough, enough! now instantly obey.

GIOVANNA: Be it even so, my lord.
(*Exit GIOVANNA*).

## SCENE VI

D. CARLO: Why does Elvira rob my soul of peace?
I love, yet does she disregard
My power, and all my love's reward
Is this—to know
A rival to myself preferred—
A robber and my foe!
My heart shall make a last appeal,
To prove once more if hers can feel.

## SCENE VII

*The above, and ELVIRA*

ELVIRA: Sire, can it be true?
What brings you at this hour?

CARLO: Lady, my love for you.

ELVIRA: It is false!
You know not love's power.

CARLO: What mean these words?
this to a King!

ELVIRA: This moment, then depart, I say.

CARLO: With you—

ELVIRA: O Heaven!

CARLO: Away, away! Elvira you shall see
How deep and true my love is for you.

ELVIRA: And my honor?

CARLO: You shall be the star of my court.

ELVIRA: Cease in pity! Oh! cease, for the love of heaven.

CARLO: Your love is given to a bandit, a robber.

ELVIRA: Every heart has its secret.

CARLO: Then listen to mine.
From the first day I saw you my soul was all yours
"It is a pure love I ask, peace and joy you can bring
To the life of your lover—oh! yield to your King.

ELVIRA: Fiero sangue d'Aragona
Nelle vene a me trascorre—
Lo splendor d'un corona
Leggi al cor non puòte imporre—
Aspirar non deggio al trono,
Nè i favor vogl'io d'un Re.
L'amor vostro oh sire, è un dono
Troppo grande o vil per me.

CARLO: Non t'ascolto—mia sarai—
Vien mi segui—
(Afferrandole un braccio).

ELVIRA: (fiera e dignitosa). Il Re
dov'è?
Nol ravviso—

CARLO: Lo saprai—

ELVIRA: So che questo basta a me.
Mi lasciate o d'ambo il core
(Strappandosi dal fianco il pugnale).
Disperata ferirò.

CARLO: Ho i miei fidi—

ELVIRA: Quale terrore!

## SCENA VIII

Detti ed ERNANI, che viene da un uscio segreto, e va a porsi tra loro.

ERNANI: Fra quei fidi io pur qui sto.

CARLO: Tu se' Ernani! me'l dice lo sdegno
Che in vederti quest'anima invade:
Tu se' Ernani! il bandito, l'indegno
Turbatore di queste contrade—
A un mio cenno perduto saresti—
Va—ti sprezzo, pietate ho di te.
Pria che l'ira in me tutta si desti,
Fuggi, o stolto, l'offeso tuo Re.

ERNANI: Me conosci? tu dunque saprai
Con qual odio t'abborre il mio cuore!
Beni, onori rapito tu m'hai.
Dal tuo morto fu il'mio genitore.
Perchè l'ira s'accresca ambi amiamo
Questa donna insidiata da te.
In odiarci, in amor pari siamo,
Vieni adunque, disfidoti, o Re.

ELVIRA: (Entrando disperata fra loro col pugnale sguainato). No
crudeli, d'amor non m'è pegno
L'ira estrema che v'arde nel core—
Perchè al mondo di scherno far segno
Di sua casa e d'Elvira l'onore?

ELVIRA: The proud blood of Aragon swells in each vein.
And I disdain the pride of a crown in my heart
To your throne and its pomp to your favor, O sire
Too humble am I or too proud to aspire.

CARLO: I do not hear you. Follow, and share my proud lot.
(Seizing her arm).

ELVIRA: (proudly). Who said it was the King? I do not see him.

CARLO: You soon shall behold him, you soon shall be mine.

ELVIRA: (snatching from his side a dagger). Wait, or this sword drinks my heart's blood and yours! Begone, and this instant: tempt not my despair.

CARLO: Tried followers are waiting.
Elvira, beware!

ELVIRA: O horror!

## SCENE VIII

The above, and ERNANI, who enters by a secret door, and places himself between them.

ERNANI: Among your tried followers see
Another.

CARLO: Ernani! I feel that it is he:
The hate and the rage in my heart tell me so;
But scorn is the strongest, and scorn bids you to go.
Ernani, vile brigand! that troubles this land.
Begone while I pity: a sign from my hand!
Would destroy you; around you my guards it would bring.
Fly, fool, while mercy lasts; do not provoke the King.

ERNANI: If you know me, then do you
Know also the dark cause
I have to hate you—why I stand
A rebel to your laws.
Wealth, honor, you have stripped me of—
Through you my father died;
And now to make the measure full,
You covet my bride,
And with deceitful words would hide
How treacherous is your flame.
Defend yourself, Prince, we are equal now—
Our love and hate is the same.

ELVIRA: (placing herself between them with the drawn dagger). Forbear! forbear! by this fierce rage,
You think to prove your love?
To make my name a mark of scorn—
Is this your boasted love?

S'anco un gesto vi sfugge, un accento
Qui trafitta cadrò al vostro piè.
No, quest'alma, in si fiero momento
Non conosce l'amante nè il Re.

## SCENA IX

Detti e SILVA seguito poscia da' suoi Cavalieri e da GIOVANNA colle Ancelle. CARLO, starà in modo da non essere facilmente conosciuto da SILVA. ELVIRA cerca di ricomporsi, e cela pugnale.

SILVA: Che mai vegg'io!
Nel penetral più scuro
Di mia magione, presso a lei che sposa
Esser dovrà d'un Silva,
Due seduttori io scorga?
Entrate, olà miei fidi cavalieri,
(Entra il Coro.)
Sia ognuno testimon del disonore,
Dell'onta che si reca al suo signore
(Infelice! e tuo credevi
Si bel giglio immacolato!
Del tuo crine sulle nevi
Piomba invece il disonor.
Ah perchè l'etade in seno
Giovin core m'ha serbato!
Mi doveano gli anni almeno
Far di gelo pure il cor?)
(a CARLO ed ERNANI). L'offeso onor, signori,
Inulto non andrà.
Scudieri, l'azza a me, la spada mia—
L'antico Silva vuol vendetta—e tosto
Uscite—

ERNANI: Ma signore—

SILVA: Non un detto ov'io parlo—

CARLO: Signor Duca—

SILVA: Favelleran le spade: uscite o vili—
(A CARLO.)
E tu primo—vieni—

## SCENA X

Detti JAGO e D. RICCARDO—

JAGU: Il regal scudiero, Don Riccardo—

SILVA: Ben venga spettator di mia vendetta—

Let but another angry word,
Another threat, be breathed;
Deep in my breast this sword
That instant shall be sheathed.
Know that Elvira in this hour,
Defies both King's and lover's power.

## SCENE IX

The above and Silva, followed by his Attendants and by GIOVANNA, with her Maidens. CARLO stands in such a position as not to be recognized by SILVA. ELVIRA tries to regain her composure, and hides the dagger.

SILVA: What do I see? What do these sounds of strife mean?
Here, in the sanctuary of my home,
Two base seducers with my destined wife!
What ho! faithful retainers, come.
(Chorus enters)
Bear witness to this insult to your lord.
Oh! woe is me, that you who I adored —
Oh! woe is me, that I thought you as pure
As a lily gazing upward to the skies.
Should heap dishonor on me! - Why has age,
What thins my locks, not turned my heart to ice?
(To CARLO and ERNANI).
For you, insulted honor shall not go
Unpunished — to the old man there remain
His sword and shield; vengeance or death will show
His sword and shield are left him not in vain
Yes, though the old man's hand may tremble now.
It is passion that makes it shake. -
Youll see before long,
That when it is aiming at your dastard hearts
The old man's hand will be both firm and strong.
Leave this place.

ELVIRA: But sire —

SILVA: Where I am let none speak.

CARLO: Lord Duke —

SILVA: Leave idle parlance to our swords.
Villains, begone! - (To CARLO). - But advance first

## SCENE X

The above, JAGO and RICCARDO.

JAGO: The regal armor-bearer, Don Riccardo.

SILVA: You come at a fit moment; you shall behold
My vengeance.

## Act I, Scene X

RICCARDO: Sol fedeltade e omaggio al Re si spetta.
(Indicando CARLO, al cui fianco prende posto.)

RICCARDO: To the King alone My homage and my services are due.
(Indicating CARLO, at whose side he places himself.)

TUTTI: Oh cielo! è desso il Re!

ALL: O Heavens! the King!

ELVIRA ed ERNANI: (tra loro). Io tremo sol per te!

ELVIRA and ERNANI: (to each other). It is for you that I tremble alone.

CARLO: (a RICCARDO). Vedi come il buon vegliardo
Or del cor l'ira depone,
Lo ritorna alla ragione
La presenza del suo Re!

CARLO: (to RICCARDO). All wrath is flown from the loyal old man's heart.

RICCARDO: (à CARLO). Più feroce a Silva in petto
De' gelosi avvampa il foco,
Ma dell'ira or prende loco
Il rispetto del suo Re.

RICCARDO: (to CARLO). Though respect for the King has changed to ire,
His heart is consumed by fierce jealousy's fire.

SILVA: (Ah! dagli occhi un vel mi cade!)
Credo appena a' sensi miei,
Sospettar io non potei
La presenza del mio Re!

SILVA: (Can it be true? a veil falls from my eyes,
Yet can my senses scarcely realize
The presence of my King.)

ERNANI (piano ad ELVIRA).
M'odi, Elvira, al nuovo sole.
Saprò torti a tanto affanno;
Ma resisti al tuo tiranno.
Serba a Ernani la tua fè.

ERNANI: (aside to ELVIRA). Until the sun sinks once again in the deep,
Resist the proud tyrant, nor yield to dismay
For Ernani keep unbroken your precious faith
And tomorrow, I'll bear you away from peril.

ELVIRA: (piano ad ERNANI). Tua per sempre—o questo ferro
Può salvarmi dai tiranni! M'è conforto negli affanni
La costanza di mia fè.

ELVIRA: (aside to ERNANI). You know I'm yours! know also, this steel
Can save me from tyrants — nor do I repine
In wretchedness even, it is solace to feel
That my heart, my faith will forever be yours.

JAGO, GIO., e CORO (fra loro).
Ben di Silva mostra il volto
L'aspra pugna che ha nel core,
Pur ei cela il suo furore
In presenza del suo Re.

JAGO, GIOVANNO AND CHORUS: (to each other) The countenance of Silva shows
How bitter his pains are, Though he restrains his fury in the presence of the King.

SILVA: (piegando il ginocchio).
Mio signor, dolente io sono—

SILVA: (falling on his knee before the King). Sire, I regret —

CARLO: Sorgi, amico, ti perdono . . .

CARLO: Enough, my friend, arise.

SILVA: Questo incognito serbato . . .

SILVA: Your incognito — the complete disguise —

CARLO: Ben lo veggo, t'ha ingannato.
Morte colse l'avo augusto,
(Appressandoglisi confidente).
Or si pensa al successore . . .
La tua fè conosco, e il core . . .
Vo'i consigli d'un fedel . . .

CARLO: Deceived you — yes; I see it all.—Now lend your close attention.
(Approaching him with an air of secrecy.)
Know we need a friend
They talk of a successor to the throne —
Silva, your faith and loyalty are known.

SILVA: Mi fia onore—onor supremo . . .

SILVA: Your subject hears your words with proud delight.

CARLO: Se ti piace il tuo castel
Questa notte occuperemo.

CARLO: We claim your hospitality this night.

SILVA: Sire, I rejoice!

ELVIRA ed ERNANI: (Che mai sento!)

ELVIRA AND ERNANI: What do I hear?

CARLO: (ad ERNANI). (Vo' salvarti)—Sul momento
(A SILVA indicando ERNANI).
Questo fido partià.

CARLO: (to ERNANI). I fain would save you though you are a traitor
(TO SILVA.)
This is a faithful follower, let him depart.

ELVIRA: (Sente il ciel di me pietà!)

ELVIRA: O heaven! in pity hear me!
What says he? Am I his faithful follower? — true until I die,
I'll haunt him like a spectre; the loved shade
Of my lost parent soon shall be obeyed;
And the fierce hatred burning in my breast
Shall nerve my arm, and triumph over the rest.

ERNANI: Io tuo fido?—il sarò a tutte l'ore
(Fissando CARLO)
Come spetto che cerca vendetta,
Dal tuo spento il mio padre l'aspetta:
L'ombra amata placare saprò,
L'odio inulto che' m'arde nel core
Tutto spengere alfine potrò.

ELVIRA: (Piano ad ERNANI) Fuggi Ernani, ti serba al mio amore,
Fuggi, fuggi a quest'aura funesta . . .
Qui, lo vedi, qui ognun ti desta;
Va—un accento tradire ti può.
Come tutto possedi il mio core,
La mia fede serbarti saprò.

ELVIRA: (aside to ERNANI). Ernani, for the love I bear you
Quit this fatal place and fly!
Here your foes wait to ensnare you,
Linger not — Ernani fly.
You alone possess my faith
With you bear my trembling heart;
Every word may here betray you
For Elvira's sake depart.

CARLO: Più d'ogni astro vagheggio il fulgore
(A SILVA e RICCARDO).
Di che splende cesarea corona
Se al mio capo il destino la dona,
D'essa degno mostrarmi saprò.
A clemente giustizia e il valore
Meco ascendere in trono farò.

CARLO: (To SILVA and RICCARDO). If more than either star or gem,
I covet that high place,
Believe the regal diadem
will grace A worthy brow.
Mercy, justice, valor, be
Enshrined on that high throne with me.

SILVA e RICCARDO: (a CARLO).
Nel tuo dritto confida, o signore,
E d'ogni altro più forte e più giusto,
No, giammai sopra capo più augusto,
Mai de' Cesari il lauro posò.
Chi d'Iberia possede l'amore,
Quello tutto del mondo mertò

SILVA AND RICCARDO: (to CARLO). The laurels of Caesar are justly yours
Your right every rival's above; He
who possesses Iberia's love is worthy to mount the world's throne

GIOVANNA ed ANCELLE: (tra loro). Perchè mai dell'etade in sul fiore,
Perchè Elvira smarrita ed oppressa,
Or che al giorno di nozze s'appressa,
Non di gioia un sorriso mostrò?
Ben si vede—l'ingenuo suo core
Simulare gli affetti non può.

GIOVANNI AND LADIES: (to each other). Elvira does not smile; her eye
Is shining through a tear,
And yet this is her brightest hour.
Her bridal day is near.

JAGO e CAVALIERI: (tra loro).
Silva in gioia cangiato ha il furore.
Tutta lieta or si vede quell'alma
Come al mare ritorna la calma
Quando l'ira dei venti cessò.
La dimora del Re nuovo onore
Al castello di Silva apportò.

JAGO and RETAINERS: (to each other). Silva has changed his rage to joy,
His soul is now restored to peace;
As calm descends upon the sea
When angry winds and tempests cease.

*FINE DELL' ACTO PRIMA.*

*END OF ACT I*

# ■ ACTO II

## SCENA I

*Magnifica sala del Castello di D. RUY GOMEZ DI SILVA. Porte che mettono a vari appartamenti. Intorno alle pareti veggonsi disposti, entro ricchi cornici, sormontate da corone ducali e stemmi dorati, i ritratti della famiglia dei SILVA. Presso ciascun ritratto vedesi collocata una completa armatura equestre, corrispondente all'epoca in cui il dipinto personaggio viveva. Avvi pure una ricca tavola con presso un seggiolone ducale di quercia Cavalieri e paggi di D. RUY. Dame e Damigelle di ELVIRA, riccamente abbigliate. Detti, JAGO e SILVA, che composamente vestito di grande di Spagna, va a sedersi sul seggiolone ducale.*

**SILVA:** Jago, qui tosto il pellegrino adduci.
*(JAGO esce, e tosto comparisce ERNANI in arnese da pellegrino).*

**ERNANI:** Sorrida il cielo a voi.

**SILVA:** T'appressa, o pellegrin—
Chiedi, che brami?

**ERNANI:** Chiedo ospitalità.

**SILVA:** Fu sempre sacra ai Silva—e lo sarà
Qual tu sia, donde venga,
Io già saper non voglio
Ospite mio sei tu—
Ti manda Iddio,
Disponi—

**ERNANI:** A te! signor mercè.

**SILVA:** Non cale;
Que l'ospite è signor.

## SCENA II

*S'apre la porta dell'appartamento di ELVIRA, ed ella entra in ricco abbigliamento nuziale, seguita da giovani Paggi ed Ancelle.*

**SILVA:** Vedi la sposa mia s'appressa—

**ERNANI:** Sposa!

**SILVA** *(ad ERNANI)*. Fra un'ora.
*(Ad ELVIRA.)*
A che d'annello,
E di ducal corona.
Non t'adornasti, Elvira?

**ERNANI:** Sposa!
Fra un'ora?
Adunque
Di nozze il dono io voglio offrirti, o Duca.

**SILVA:** Tu?

**ERNANI:** Si.

**ELVIRA:** (Che ascolta!)

**SILVA:** E quale!

# ■ ACT II

## SCENE I

*A magnificent hall in the Castle of D. RUY GOMEZ DI SILVA, Doors leading to various apartments. Portraits of the SILVA family, handsomely framed and surmounted by ducal coronets and coats of arms, are dispersed about the wall. By the side of each portrait is hanging a complete suit of equestrian armor, corresponding to the period in which the personage represented lived. There is also a handsome table, and near it a ducal oak chair.*
*Knights and pages of D. RUY. Ladies of ELVIRA. The above, JAGO and SILVA, who pompously dressed as a grandee of Spain, seats himself on the ducal chair.*

**SILVA:** Let the holy pilgrim enter.
*(JAGO goes out, and ERNANI immediately appears in a pilgrim's dress.)*

**ERNANI:** Heaven smile on you, gracious knight.

**SILVA:** Pilgrim, say what you desire.

**ERNANI:** Shelter beneath your roof this night.

**SILVA:** Hospitality was ever Sacred in a Silva's heart.
We do not ask to know you stranger.
Welcome, who ever you are;
Heaven be with you, here repose.
Be seated at our festal board.

**ERNANI:** Take my thanks.

**SILVA:** We do not ask them.
Here the guest is as the lord.

## SCENE II

*(The door of ELVIRA'S apartment opens, and she enters in a bridal dress, followed by Pages and Ladies.)*

**SILVA:** See my bride advances.

**ERNANI:** Your bride?

**SILVA:** *(to ERNANI)*. One hour yet,
And she will be—
*(to ELVIRA)*. But fairst, where's
The ducal coronet?

**ERNANI:** Your wife! and in and hour?
Oh! then to me is left
To offer you, O Duke!
My humble wedding gift.

**SILVA:** You!

**ERNANI:** Ay—

**ELVIRA:** (What voice is this?)

**SILVA:** What is it that the pilgrim gives?

**ERNANI:** Il capo mio;
Lo prendi.
*(gettando l'abita do pellegrino.)*

**ELVIRA:** (Ernani vive ancor!) Gran Dio!

**ERNANI:** Oro quant oro ogni avido
Puote saziar desio,
A tutti v'offro, abbiatelo
Prezzo del sangue mio—
Mille guerrier m'inseguono,
Seccome belva i cani—
Sono il bandito Ernani,
Odio me stesso e il dì.

**ELVIRA:** (Oimè, si perde il misero!)

**SILVA:** *(ai suoi,)* Smarrita ha la ragione.

**ERNANI:** I miei dispersi fuggono,
Vostro son io prigione,
Al Re mi date, e premio—

**SILVA:** Ciò non sarà, lo giuro:
Rimanti qui securo,
Silva giammai tradi
In queste mura ogni ospite
Ha i dritti d'un fratello: Olà miei fidi, s'armino
Le torri del castello,
Seguitemi —
*(Accena ad Elvira di entrare nelle sue stanze colle Ancele; e seguito do' suoi parte).*

## SCENA III

*(ELVIRA, partito SILVA, fa alcuni passi per seguire le Ancelle, indi si ferma, e uscite quelle, torna ansiosa ad ERNANI, che sdegnosamente la respinge.)*

**ERNANI** Tu, perfida.
Come dissarmi ardisci?

**ELVIRA:** A te il mio sen, ferisci,
Ma fui e son fedel.
Fama te spento credere
Fece dovunque.

**ERNANI:** Spento!
Io vivo ancora!

**ELVIRA:** Memore
Del fatto giuramento
Sull'ara stessa estringuere,
*(mostrandogli il pugnal celato.)*
Me di pugnale volea,
Non son, non sono rea
Come tu sei crudele.

**ERNANI:** Tergi il pianto — mi perdona,
Fu delirio — t'amo ancor.
Caro accento! al cor mi suona
Più possente del dolor.

**ERNANI:** My head, my life—I'm ready.
*(Throwing off his pilgrim's dress.)*

**ELVIRA:** (Ernani! and he lives!)

**ERNANI:** Do you covet gold, here take it?
Take it, if gold suffice.
I offer it all—
It is the price of my blood
A thousand warriors track my steps,
As dog their savage prey;
I am the brigand Ernani,
And hate the light of day.

**ELVIRA:** (O Heaven! those words will lose him!)

**SILVA:** The wretched man raves.
*(To his followers).*

**ERNANI:** I yield as your captive,
Nor do I crave mercy
My comrades, fly—quick to the King,
Deliver me, do you hear?

**SILVA:** Not so, for Silva never betrayed,
Here you are safe, I swear.
A guest is sacred in these walls
As brother, from alarms.
What ho, there! man the battlements!
And soldiers, haste to arms!
*(To ELVIRA).*
Follow me, lady.
*(He makes a sign to ELVIRA to retire to her apartmens, followed by her Ladies, and he leaves, followed by his attendants.)*

## SCENE III

*(When SILVA is gone, ELVIRA feigns to follow her Ladies, then stops and returns to ERNANI, who repulses her with indignation.)*

**ERNANI:** O false one! can you raise your head,
After such perfidy, to gaze on me?

**ELVIRA;** This wounded heart has never swerved from you
They told me you were dead.

**ERNANI:** Dead?—No;
Ernani lives!

**ELVIRA:** *(Showing him the hidden dagger.)* But know, this dagger at the altar drawn
Should have freed me from the marriage oath,
And drowned the memory of broken troth
With you
Reproach, revile me as you will.
Your cruelty us greater than my guilt.

**ERNANI:** O dearest! hush those complaints, oh! pardon give,
Delirium made me rave, I love and live.

## Act II, Scene III

**ELVIRA ed ERNANI:** Ah morir potessi odesso!
O mia Elvira,
O mia Elvira,
Sul tuo petto!
— O mio Ernani,
Preverebbe questo amplesso
La celeste voluntà.
Solo affanni il nostro affetto
Sulla terra a noi darà.

**ELVIRA:** O cherished accents!
blessed relief;
Stronger within this heart than
grief.
If death should come

**TOGETHER:** O my Elvira, O my Ernani.
Lying on your bosom.
What bliss could Heaven reserve
Equal to that of dying?
Henceforth, while lingering here
On this sad earth,
To love each smile or tear
Must owe its birth.

## SCENA IV

*(Silva che vedendoli abbracciati,
si scaglia furibondo tra loro col
pugnale alla mano. Detti.)*

**SILVA:** Scellerati, il mio furore
Non ha posa, non he freno,
Strapperò l'ingrato core,
Vendicarmi potrò almeno.

## SCENE IV

*(SILVA, seeing them embrace
rushes between them, sword in
hand.)*

**SILVA:** Base wretches, now at last
Shall vengeance have her sway,
And that ungrateful heart
Shall cast fury away.

## SCENA V

*JAGO frettoloso e Detti.*

**JAGO:** Alla porta del castello
Giunse il Re con un drapello
Vuole ingresso —

**SILVA:** S'apra al re.
*(JAGO parte).*

## SCENE V

*JAGO enters hastly, and the
above.*

**JAGO:** Before the castle-gates
The clang of troops rings

**SILVA:** Throw open to the King.
*(Exit JAGO)*

## SCENA VI

*SILVA, ELVIRA, ed ERNANI.*

**ERNANI:** Morte invoco or io da te.

**SILVA:** No vendetta, più tremenda
Vo' serbata alla mia mano;
Vien ti cela, ognuno in vano
*(ad ERNANI)*
Rinvenirti tenterá.
A punir l'infamia orrenda
Silva solo basterá.

**ELVIRA ed ERNANI:** La vendetta
più tremenda
Su me compia la tua mano,
Ma con lei — lui — ti serba umano
Apri il core alla pietà, Su me sol
l'ira tua scenda;
Giuro, in lei — lui — colpa non
v'ha.
*(ERNANI entra in un nascondiglio datogli da Silva dietro il proprio ritratto. ELVIRA si ritira nelle
sue stanze).*

## SCENE VI

*SILVA, ELVIRA and ERNANI.*

**ERNANI:** I invoke death, I crave it
as a boon.

**SILVA:** You'll meet it at my hand,
but not so soon.
For darker is the doom your crime
deserves;
A mighter vengeance reserves Silva's hand?
Come I'll hide you where all in vain
will seek you.

**ERNANI and ELVIRA:** O let that
vengeance on my head alone
Be visited
To us be shown pity!
Oh! let sweet mercy shine within
your heart,
The guilt, I swear, alone is mine, is
mine!
*(ERNANI enters into a hiding-place, which SILVA opens to him
beyond his own portrait. ELVIRA
retires to her apartments)*

## SCENA VII

*SILVA, D. CARLO, D. RICCARDO
(con seguito di cavalieri.)*

## SCENE VII

*SILVA, S. CARLO, D, RICCARDO.*

**CARLO:** Cugino, a che munito
Il tuo castel ritrovo?
*(SILVA s'inchina senza parlare.)*
Rispondimi.

**SILVA:** Signore —

**CARLO:** Intendo — di ribellione
l'idra,
Miseri conti e duchi, ridestate —
Ma veglio anch'io e ne' merlati covi
Quest'idre tutte soffocar saprò.
E covi e difensori abbatterò
Parla —

**SILVA:** Signore, i Silva son leali.

**CARLO:** Vedremo — de' ribelli
L'ultima torma vinta fu dispersa;
Il capo lor bandito,
Ernani, al tuo castello ebbe ricetto.
Tu me 'l consegna o il foco, ti prometto,
Qui tutto appianerà —
S'io fede attenga, tu saper ben puoi.

**SILVA:** Nol niego — è ver — tra
noi
Un pellegrino giunse
Ed ospitalità chiese per Dio
Tradirlo non degg'io?

**CARLO:** Sciagurato! e il re tradir
vuoi tu.

**SILVA:** Non tradiscono i Silva.

**CARLO:** Il capo tuo, o quel
d'Ernani io voglio
Intendi. —

**SILVA:** Abbiate il mio.

**CARLO:** Tu, Don Ricardo, a lui togli la spada.
*(RICCARDO eseguise.)*
Voi, del castello ogni angolo cercate,
Scoprite il traditore

**SILVA:** Fida è la rôcca come il suo
signore.
*(Parte de' Cavalieri escono).*

## SCENA VIII

*D. CARLO, SILVA, D. RICCARDO e
parte de' Cavalieri.*

**CARLO:** Lo vedremo, veglio audace,
*(Con fuoco a SILVA.)*
Se resistermi potrai,
Se tranquillo sfiderai
La vendetta del tuo Re?
Essa rugge sul tuo capo?;
Pensa pria che tutta scenda
Più feroce, più tremenda
D'una folgore su te.

**SILVA:** No, de' Silva il disonore
Non vorà d'Iberia un Re.

**CARLO:** Il tuo capo o il traditore —
Scegli — scampo altro non v'è.

**CARLO;** Cousin, why in such
armed array
Does your fair castle stand?
*(SILVA inclines himself without
speaking)*
No answer, have you nothing to say?

**SILVA:** Sire —

**CARLO:** Enough, we understand;
The petty nobles of our land
Make a nest of their strong castles to
rear rebellion's brood,
The hydra-headed snake;
But we will bruise it in the dust.
Speak.

**SILVA:** A Silva is ever worthy trust.

**CARLO:** That we shall see anon
The chief
Of the last rebel troop,
Ernani, here has sought relief
And he has found refuge.
Now yield him to our sovereign
power,
Or by our kingly word, this hour
Fiercest flames shall wreathe round
this tower
And raze it to the ground.

**SILVA:** What you say is true — a
pilgrim came,
And hospitality did claim,
And urged it on me in God's name,
Shall I betray that guest?

**CARLO:** Traitor, you hear and delay!

**SILVA:** The Silvas never have betrayed.

**CARLO:** Ernani's head, or yours
will be paid
For this.

**SILVA:** Let it be mine.

**CARLO:** Speak, Ernani; take Silva's
sword!
In every angle gain entrance.
*(RICCARDO obeys him.)*

**SILVA:** True is the castle as its lord;
Your search will be in vain.
*(Exit part of Attendants.)*

## SCENE VIII

*CARLO, SILVA, RICCARDO and
Attendants.*

**CARLO:** *(to SILVA, impetuously).*
O rash old man! do you persist
to defy your monarch?
A moment yet, if you resist,
And you shall surely die.
My vengeance hovers over you;
Before the tempest breaks.
Pause and reflect. O rash old man!
And take timely warning.

**SILVA:** Iberia's King can never desire
to disgrace a Silva.

**CARLO:** Yours or the rebel's head,
I say —
Choose, and save you while you
may.

## SCENA IX

*Cavalieri, che rientrano portando fasci di armi e Detti*

CORO: Fu esplorata del castello
Ogni parte la più occulta,
Tutto invano, del ribello
Nulla traccia si scoprì.
Fur le scolte disarmate;
L'ira tua non andrà inulta,
Ascoltar non dei pietate
Per chi fede e onor tradì.

CARLO: Fra tormenti paleranno,
Il Bandito additeranno.

## SCENA X

*ELVIRA, che ese precipitosamente dalle sue stanze, seguita da GIOVANNA, ed Ancelle, e Detti.*

ELVIRA: Deh cessate — in regal core
(*gettandosi ai piedi di CARLO.*)
Non sia muta la pietà

CARLO: Tu me'l chiedi! — ogni rancore
(*Sorpreso rialzandola.*)
Per Elvira tacerà
Della tua fede statico
Questa donzella sia —
Mi segua — o del colpevole —

SILVA: No, no; ciò mai non fa;
Deh, sire, in mezzo all'anima
Non mi voler ferir —
Io l'amo — al vecchio misero
Solo conforto è in terra
Non mi volerla togliere,
Pria questo capo atterra.

CARLO: Adunque, Ernani—

SILVA: Segnati,
La fe' non vo' tradir.

CORO: Ogni pietade è inutile,
Tè forza l'obbedir.

CARLO (*ad ELVIRA*). Vieni meco sol, di rose
Intrecciar ti vo' la vita,
Meco vieni, ore penose
Per te il tempo non avrà.
Tergi il pianto o giovannità,
Dalla guancia scolorita;
Pensa al gaudio che t'aspetta,
Che felice ti farà.

RICCARDO e CORO: (*ad ELVIRA.*) Credi il gaudio che t'aspetta
Te felice renderà.

GIOVANNA ED ANCELLE: (Ciò la morte a Silva affretta
Più che i danni dell'età).

ELVIRA: (Ah! la sorte che m'aspetta
Il mio duolo eternerà).

## SCENE IX

CHORUS: We've sought the castle turrets,
The dungeons underground,
But no trace of the rebel brigand has yet been found.
On him that mocks at royalty
The royal vengeance wreak.

CARLO: Torture shall show the lurking-place,
And make the traitor speak.

## SCENE X

*ELVIRA, who rushes precipitately from her apartments, followed by GIOVANNA and Ladies.*

ELVIRA: (*Throwing herself at the feet of CARLO.*) Oh! never, never in a royal heart
Should pity's holy, heavenly voice be dumb.

CARLO: (*Raising her, much surprised.*) It is you that pleads! Lady, at those tones
Rancor sinks down appeased; but you must come,
If you would save the guilty, come with me.

SILVA: No; never, Prince. — Oh! that must never be.
She is my only comfort left on earth;
I love, have loved her from her very birth.
Oh! wound me not so deeply —
you will — you must
Wait till the old man's head is mingled with the dust.

CARLO: Ernani, then —

SILVA: King, steadfast is my faith; take her away.

CARLO: (*to ELVIRA*). Oh! come with me, I'll strew your path with flowers.
And, Time's rude self shall bring no heavy hours
To one so lovely; wipe those tears away
From those pale cheeks — think of the happy fate
Reserved for you.

RICCARDO and CHORUS: (*to ELVIRA*). Pleasure and joy await your steps.

GIOVANNA and Ladies: (Far more than lengthened years
This grief will
Bring down his silver hairs to the grave.)

ELVIRA: (My misery, by this destiny,
Eternal will be made.)

---

SILVA: Sete ardente di vendetta,
Silva appien ti appagherà?
(*Il Re parte col suo seguito, seco traendo ELVIRA, appoggiata al braccio di GIOVANNA. Le Ancelle entrano nelle stanze della loro Signora*).

## SCENA XI

SILVA: (*dopo aver veduto immobile partire il Re col suo seguito.*)
Vigili pure il ciel sempre su te.
L'odio vivrà in cor mio pur sempre,
O re.
(*Corre alle armature che sono presso i ritratti ne trae due, spade, e va quindi ad aprire il nascondiglio di ERNANI*).

## SCENA XII

*ERNANI e SILVA.*

SILVA: Esci—a te—scegli—seguimi.
(*Presentandogli le due spade*).

ERNANI: Seguirti?
E dove?

SILVA: Al campo.

ERNANI: No! vo — nol deggio —

SILVA: Misero!
Di questo acciaro al lampo
Impallidisci? — Seguimi.

ERNANI: Me'l vietan gli anni tuoi.

SILVA: Vien ti disfido o giovane;
Uno di noi morrà.

ERNANI: Tu m'hai salvato; uccidimi.
Ma ascolta per pietà!

SILVA: Morrai.

ERNANI: Morrò ma pria —
L'ultima prece mia —

SILVA: Volgerla a Dio tu puoi —

ERNANI: No — la rivolga a te —

SILVA: Parla — ho l'inferno in me.

ERNANI: Sola una volta, un'ultima
Fa ch'io la vegga —

SILVA: Chi?

ERNANI: Elvira.

SILVA: Or or, parti, Seco la trasse il Re.

ERNANI: Vecchio, che mai facesti?
Nostro rivale egli è?

SILVA: Oh, rabbia! — E il ver dicesti?

ERNANI: L'ama —

SILVA: Vassalli all'armi.
(*Furente per la scena*).

## SCENE XI

SILVA: O ardent thirst for vengeance,
When will you be allayed?
(*Exit the KING, dragging ELVIRA, who is leaning on the arm of GIOVANNA. The Ladies retire to their room.*)

## SCENE XI

SILVA: (*after having stood motionless watching the KING depart with his suite.*) Heaven above your head spread its protecting wing.
Hatred to you forever — hatred to you
O King!
(*He goes to the armory near the portraits, takes two swords, and then opens ERNANI's hiding-place.*)

## SCENE XII

*ERNANI and SILVA.*

SILVA: (*Presenting him with the two swords.*) Without, without; our time is now
Or never. — Come, follow

ERNANI: Where?

SILVA: To the open field.

ERNANI: I will not, ought not.

SILVA: Wretch! do you feel
Afraid to handle the cold steel?
Come, follow me!

ERNANI: Your age, old man, forbids such strife —

SILVA: I challenge you;
Or you or I must fall.

ERNANI: You saved my life.
Kill me if you will; but first in pity hear.

SILVA: You shall die.

ERNANI: If you insist. I will die;
But before the cord of life be riven
I'd ask you to receive a prayer.

SILVA: No; offer it to Heaven.

ERNANI: Not so: that prayer must be to you.

SILVA: Speak; I feel a demon fire burn within me.

ERNANI: Once more, oh! once more, let me see—

SILVA: Whom?

ERNANI: Elvira.

SILVA: It is vain, the King has torn away
My bride this very hour.

ERNANI: Wretched old man, what do you say?—
She's in our rival's power?

SILVA: O misery! and is it time?

ERNANI: He loves her.

SILVA: (*in violent agitation*). Vassals, I summon you to arms.

## Act II, Scene XII

**ERNANI:** A parte dei chiamarmi
Di tua vendetta.

**SILVA:** No,
Te prima ucciderò.

**ERNANI:** Teco la voglio compiere,
Posci m'ucciderai.

**SILVA:** La fè mi serberai?

**ERNANI:** Ecco il pegno nel momento
(*Gli consegna un corno da caccia.*)
In che Ernani vorrai spento.
Se uno squillo interderà
Tosto Ernani morirà.

**SILVA:** A me la destra — giuralo.

**ERNANI:** Pel padre moi lo giuro.

**A DUE:** Iddio n'ascolti, e vendice
Punisce lo spergiuro:
L'aura, la luce manchino,
Sia infamia al mentitor.

## SCENA XIII

*Cavalieri di SILVA, che entrano
disarmati e fretolosi, e Detti.*

**CORO:** Salvi ne vedi, e liberi
A' senni tuoi, signor.

**SILVA:** L'ira mi torna giovane;
S'insegua il rapitor.

**SILVA ed ERNANI:** (*a 2.*) In arcion, in arcion, cavalieri.
Armi, sangue, vendetta, vendetta!
Silva stesso vi guida, v'affretta
Premio degno egli darvi saprà
Questi brandi di morte forieri.
D'ogni cor troveranno la stada;
Chi resister s'attenti, pria cada,
Sia delitto il sentire pietà.

**CORO:** Pronti vedi li tuoi cavalieri —

Per te spirano, sangue, vendetta,
Se di Silva la voce gli affretta,
Più gagliardo ciascuno sarà!
Questi brandi, di morte forieri.
(*Brandendo le spade.*)
D'ogni cor troveranno la strada —
Chi resistir s'attenti, pria cada:
Fia delitto il sentire pietà.
(*Partono tutti*)

*FINE DELL' ACTO SECONDA.*

---

**ERNANI:** It is that you should call
Your vengeance and your rage to
share.

**SILVA:** No; you shall fall first.

**ERNANI:** Yet would I first aid your despair
For my Elvira's sake,
And afterwards I'll bare this breast;
That you may take vengeance.

**SILVA:** Will you pledge your word?
(*Giving him a hunting-born*).

**ERNANI:** Yes, truly I will.
The moment you wish
Ernani to die,
Then on this our token
Wind one thrilling blast;
That sound for Ernani
On earth be the last.

**SILVA:** Your hand be laid on my
right hand.

**ERNANI:** I swear it by my father's
shade.

**TOGETHER:** Hear it, Heaven let
your wrath
Be pitiless—let woe assail,
Your own pursue, your daylight fail
Him who breaks his oath.

## SCENE XIII

*Knights of SILVA, who enter hastily and unarmed, and the above.*

**CHORUS:** You see us safe and
prompt to obey,
Make trial of our truth!

**SILVA:** Follow the ravisher—away!
Rage brings me back to youth!

**SILVA and ERNANI:** To horse, to
horse! vengeance and blood!
Be this our battle cry;
Silva himself will lead you on,
To conquer or to die.
Silva will find a worthy prize
To reward your valor;
The harbinger of death then be
Each shining sword.
Whoever dare resist us, let the rash
one fall.
Let pity be a crime;
You hear it all.

**CHORUS:** Ready for blood and vengeance,
See your followers;
To all the harbingers of death
Our sword shall be.
(*Brandishing their swords.*)
If any dare resist us, let the rash one
fall.
Let pity be a crime;
We swear it all.
(*Exeunt all*)

*END OF ACT II.*

---

# ■ ACTO III

## SCENA I

*Soterranei sepolcrali che rinserrano la tomba di CARLO MAGNO in Aquisgrana. A destra dello spettatore avvi il detto monumento con porta di bronzo, sopra la quale leggesi letteri cubitali l'inscrizione "KAROL MAGNO", in fondo scalea che mette alla maggior porta del sotterraneo, nel quale pur si vedranno altri minori sepolcri; sul piano nella scena altre porte che conducono ad altre catacombe. Due lampade-pendenti dal mezzo spandono una fioca luce su quegli avelli. (D. CARLO e D. RICCARDO avvolti in ampi mantelli oscuri entrano guardinghi dalla porta principale: D. RICCARDO precede con una fiaccola).*

**CARLO:** E questo il loco?

**RICCARDO:** Sì.

**CARLO:** E l'ora?

**RICCARDO:** E' questa.
Qui s'aduna la Lega—

**CARLO:** Che contro me cospira—
Degli assassini al guardo
L'avel mi celerà di Carlo Magno
E gli Elettor?

**RICCARDO:** Raccolti,
Cribrano i dritti a cui spetti del
mondo
La più corona, il lauro invitto
De' Cesari decoro.

**CARLO:** Lo so mi lascia.
(*RICCARDO va per partire.*)
Ascolta se mai prescelto io sia,
Tre volte il bronzo ignivomo.
Dalla gran torre tuoni,
Tu poscia scendi a me; qui guida Elvira.

**RICCARDO:** E vorreste?

**CARLO:** Non più—fra questi avelli
Converserò coi morti
E scorpiro i rebelli.
(*RICCARDO parte*).

## SCENA II

**CARLO:** Gran Dio! costor sui sepolcrali marmi
Affilano il pugnal per trucidarmi!
Scettri! dovizie! onori!
Bellezza! gioventù! che siete voi?
Cimbe natanti sopra il mar degli

---

# ■ ACT III

## SCENE I

*Subterranean catacombs in Aquisgrana. To the right of the stage is placed the tomb of CARLO MAGNO, with a bronze door, over which is seen the inscription, "KAROLO MAGNO," in letters a cubit long; at the end of the stage is a staircase leading from the large door of the vault. Several smaller tombs are dispersed about the stage. There are also different doors leading to other catacombs. Two lamps hanging from the centre cast a dim light on the tombs.
(CARLO and RICCARDO, wrapped in large cloaks, enter stealthily by the principal entrance. Riccardo precedes with a lantern)*

**CARLO:** Is this the spot?

**RICCARDO:** It is.

**CARLO:** And, the hour?

**RICCARDO:** The present one.
Here the League assembles—

**CARLO:** With coward hand to
strike the assassin blow—
But the cold tomb shall hide me
from the foe.
And the Electors?

**RICCARDO:** They assemble here
this night,
To weigh the merit and discuss the
right
Of each who'd wear the Caesar's
laurel crown.
Or strive to grasp th sceptre of the
world.

**CARLO:** I know it; leave me, I
would be alone.
(*RICCARDO moves toward the
door.*)
But listen, if their choice should
fall on me.
Then let the cannon from the castle
wall
Rejoicing, be heard three times,
and then come
And bring ELVIRA with; you leave
me now.

**RICCARDO:** You desire it?

**CARLO:** No, more.
In this sepulchral place,
I'd hold communion with the dead,
and trace
The plot of the rebellious living—
go!
(*Exit RICCARDO*)

## SCENE II

**CARLO:** Great Heaven! that these
holy tombs should be
Defiled by the assassin's murderous
scheme!
Duty! youth! honor! beauty! what
are you?

anni,
Cui l'onda batte d'incessanti affanni,
Finchè giunte allo scoglio della tomba
Con voi nel nulla il nome vostro piomba!
Oh! de' verd'anni miei
Sogni e bugiarde larve,
Se troppo vi credei,
L'incanto ora disparve.
S'ora chiamato sono
Al più sublime trono,
Della virtù com'aquila
Sui vanni m'alzerò;
E vincitor dei secoli
Il nome mio farò.
(*Apre con chiave la porta del monumento di CARLO MAGNO e vientra*).

Barks that float lightly on time's rapid stream.
Washed ever and anon by sorrow's wave.
Then driven on that most certain shoal, the grave!
And every vestige whirled downward
In the black gulf of fathomless oblivion.
Oh! if the visions that beguile the world
Have also charmed my youth, the dream is fled—
The illusion gone! and if the late sublime
That waves me onward shall exalt my head.
I will become the conqueror of time—
Of ages, not of countries; I will rise
By virtue, on whose pinion to the skies
I'll mount, as the proud eagle soars upon her wing.
(*He unlocks the door of the monument of CARLO MAGNO and goes in.*)

## SCENA III

(*Schiudonsi le porte minori del sotterraneo, e vi entrano guardinghi ed avvolti grandi mantelli i Personaggi della Lega, portando fiaccole.*)

**I:** Ad augusta!

**II:** Chi va là?

**I:** Per augusta.

**II:** Bene sta.

**TUTTI:** Per la lega santo ardor;
L'alme invada, accenda i cor.

## SCENA IV

*Detti, SILVA, ERNANI e JAGO, VESTITI come i primi.*

**SILVA, ERNANI e JAGO:** (*a 3.*)
Ad augusta.

**CORO:** Per augusta.

**SILVA, ERNANI e JAGO:** (*a 3..*)
Per la lega—

**CORO:** Santa e giusta.

**TUTTI:** Dalle tombe parlerà
Del destin la volontà

**SILVA:** (*Salenào sopra una delle minori tombe*). All'invito mancò alcuno?

**CORO:** Qui codardo avvi nessuno—

**SILVA:** Dunque svelisi il mistero:
Carlo aspira al sacro impero.

## SCENE III

(*The smaller doors of the vault are opened, and members of the League, wrapped in large mantles, and carrying torches, enter looking stealthily around.*)

**I:** Ad augusta.

**II:** Who goes there?

**I:** Per augusta.

**II:** All is well.

**ALL:** For the holy league we feel
True devotion, ardent zeal.

## SCENE IV

*The above, SILVA, ERNANI, and JAGO, wrapped in cloaks.*

**SILVA, ERNANI, and JAGO:** Ad augusta.

**CHORUS:**
Per augusta

**SILVA, ERNANI, and JAGO:** For the League.

**CHORUS:** Holy and just.

**ALL:** Let the tomb speak!
Hear a voice from the dust!

**SILVA:** (*Standing on one of the smaller tombs.*) Is any one here wanting?

**SILVA:** All mystery vanish,
And distrust and fear;
Charles to the empire
Pleads his right.

**CORO:** Spento pria qual face ceda.
(*Tutti spengono contra terra le faci.*)
Dell'Iberia contrada
Franse i dritti—s'armerà
Ogni destra che qui sta.

**SILVA:** Una basti—la sua morte
Ad un sol fidi la sorte.
(*Ognuno tra dal seno un porta foglio vi scrive la propria cifra, sopra un foglio e lo getta in un avello scoperchiato.*)

**CORO:** E ognum pronto in ogni evento
A ferire od essere spento.
(*SILVA s'appressa lentamente all'avello, ne cava una tavoletta; tutti ansiosi lo circondano.*)

**CORO:** Qual si noma?

**SILVA:** Ernani.

**CORO:** E desso?

**ERNANI:** Oh qual gaudio m'è concesso.
(*Con trasporto di giubilo.*) Padre! Padre!

**CORO:** Se cadrai
Vendicato ben sarai.

**SILVA:** (*ad ERNANI*). L'opra, o giovane, mi cedi.

**ERNANI:** Me si vile, o vecchio, credi?

**SILVA:** La tua vita, gli aver miei
Io ti dono—

**ERNANI:** No.

**SILVA:** Potrei
(*mostrandogli il corno.*)
Ora astringerti a morir?

**ERNANI:** No—vorrei prima ferir—

**SILVA:** Dunque, o giovane, t'aspetta
La più orribile vendetta.

**TUTTI:** Noi fratelli in tal momento,
Strigna un patto, un giuramento.
(*Tutti si abbracciano, e nelle massima esultazione traendo le spade prorompono come segue:*)

**CORO:** Si ridesti il Leon di Castiglia,
E d'Iberia ogni monte, ogni lito
Ecco formi al tremendo ruggito.
Come un di contro i Mori oppressor
Siamo tutti una sola famiglia,
Pugnerem colle braccia, co' petti;
Schiavi inulti più a lungo e negletti
Non sarem finchè vita abbia il cor.
Sia che morte ne aspetti, o vittoria
Pugneremo, ed il sangue de' spenti
Nuovo ardire ai figliuoli viventi
Forze nuove al pugnare darà. Sorga

**CHORUS:** (*All throwing down their torches.*) Let darkness be,
We need no light.
Each of us here
Has a bold hand
To strike for the right
Of Iberia's land.

**SILVA:** One will suffice the duty to fill.
(*Each draws out a tablet and inscribes his name on a leaf therefrom throwing it into one of the uncovered tombs,*)

**ALL:** Here all are ready
To die or to kill.
(*SILVA slowly approaches the tomb, and draws forth a leaf—all draw round him with anxious looks.*)

**ALL:** What is the name?

**SILVA:** Ernani!

**CHORUS:** Is it he?

**ERNANI:** (*with a transport of joy.*) Heaven,
I render thanks for this great favor!
O Father!
O Father!

**CHORUS:** Comrade, if you fall,
You shall have vengeance from us, one and all.

**SILVA:** Young man, I pray you yield
Your task to me—

**ERNANI:** Old man, I'm not so vile—what do you ask?

**SILVA:**
Think of your life: When one is young it is sweet to live.
Your life—I'll give my wealth to you.

**ERNANI:** No.

**SILVA:** (*showing the horn*).
Would you then, rather die!

**ERNANI:** Not till my hate is satisfied.

**SILVA:** Then, youth my vengeance waits

**ALL:** In this moment let us plight
Our faith and in one oath unite.
(*All in the exultation of the moment draw their swords and burst forth in the following:*)

**CHORUS:** Leon of Castile awakens
He who rose against the Moor,
The same sound in fair Iberia
Echoes back from mount to shore.
Brothers are we all; no longer
Will we drag these clashing chains,
Far more dear than life is freedom,
Plead her cause while life remains.
Whether death or victory await us,
We'll fight on: the valiant slain,
With their blood shall animate us,
Filling our exhausted vein.
Then, when the day of glory dawns

alfine radiante di gloria,
Sorga un giorna a brillare su noi—
E imortal fra i più splendidi eroi,
Col lor nome anche il nostro sarà—

And that day shall dawn at last,
Be our names in history's story,
As the history of the past.

## SCENA V

D. CARLO dalla porta del monumento e Detti. S'ode un colpo di canone.

CORO: Qual rumore!
Che sarà?
(Altro colpo di canone, e la porta del monumento si apre.)
Il destin si compirà.
(Tero colpo di canone, e CARLO si mostra sulla soglia.)
Carlo Magno imperator!

CARLO: (Picchia tre volte col pomo del pugnale sulla porticella di bronzo, poi esclama con terribile voce.) Carlo Quinto, o traditor!

## SCENE V

(CARLO enters by the door of the monument. The report of a cannon is heard.)

CHORUS: What sound is that?
(Another report and the door of the monument opens.)
It is destiny that works.
(A third report and CARLO appears.)
It is Carlo Magno the Emperor! (He strikes three times on the bronze door, and then exclaims, in a thundering voice:)

CARLO: Traitors! it is Charles the Fifth!

## SCENA VI

(S'apre la gran porta del sotterraneo, ed allo squillar delle trombe entrano sei Elletori vestiti di broccato d'oro seguiti dai Paggi, che portano sopra cuscini di velluto lo scettro, la corona, ed altre insegne imperiali. Ricco corteo di Gentiluomini e Dame Alemane e Spagnuole circonda l'imperatore. Fra le ulti mevedesi ELVIRA, seguita da GIOVANNA. Nel fondo saranno spiegate le bandiere dell'impero, e molte fiaccole portate dai soldati illumineranno la scena. D RICCARDO è alla testa del corteggio)

RICCARDO: L'Elettoral Concesso
v'acclamava
Augusto imperatore,
E le cesaree insegne,
O sire, ora v'invia—

CARLO: La voluntà del ciel sarà la mia—
(agli Elettori.)
Questi ribaldi contro me conspirano—
(ai Congiuri.)
Tremate, o vili, adesso—
E tardi! tutti in mano mia qui siete—
La mano stringerò— Tutti cadrete—
Dal volga si divida
(Alle Guardie, eseguiscono, lasciando ERNANI tra il volgo,)
Solo chi è conte o duca,
Prigion sia il volgo, ai nobili la scure.

ERNANI: Decreta dunque, o Re, morte a me pure.
(Avanzandosi fieramente tra i nobili e, coprendosi il capo.)

## SCENE VI

(The large door of the vault opens, and at the report of cannon, six Electors enter, richly dressed in gold brocade, followed by Pages, carrying upon velvet cushions the crown, the sceptre and other imperial insignia. A suite of German and Spanish Gentlemen and Ladies surround the EMPEROR. Amongst the last is seen ELVRA, followed by GIOVANNA. At the end is found RICCARDO at the head of a numerous train; the whole is illuminated by torches.)

RICCARDO: The assembled Electorate have proclaimed you Emperor, and crave your acceptance
Of the imperial dignity; receive
The signet of the state.

CARLO: (to the Electors). The will of Heaven be mine,
These robbers dared to form a plot against me.
(To the Conspirators).
Tremble, traitors in this hour
Just fate has thrown you in my power,
This hand shall not quit.
(To the Guards, who are obeying him, and leaving ERNANI amongst the Commoners.)
The plebeian, in the dungeon's gloom
Shall learn, within the living tomb,
To mock our royal power;
Away with them.
A darker doom
Awaits their betters: rank consigns
The noble to the block.

ERNANI: (advancing proudly amongst the Nobles, covering his head). Accord the right of nobility,
To me those rights belong;

Io son conte, duca sono
Di Segorbia, di Cardona—
Don Giovanni d'Aragona
Riconosca ognuno in me.
Or di patria e genitore
Mi sperai vendicatore—
Non t'uccisi—t'abbandono,
Questo capo—il tronca, o Re.

CARLO: Si cadrà—con altri appresso.
(gettandosi ai piedi di CARLO)

ELVIRA: Ah Signor, se t'è concesso.
Il maggiore d'ogni trono
Questa polvere negletta
Or confondi col perdono—
Sia lo sorezzo tua vendetta
Che il rimorso compirà.

CARLO: Tacci, o donna.

ELVIRA: Ah no, non sia,
Parlò il ciel per voce mia
Virtù augusta è la pietà
(si alza.)

CARLO: (Concentrato, fissando la tomba di CARLO MAGNO.) Oh sommo Carlo,—più nel tuo nome
Le tue virtudi—aver vogl'io,
Sarò, lo giuro—a te ed a Dio,
Della tue gesta—imitator,
(Dopo qualche pausa.)
Perdono a tutti—
(Mie brame ho dome.)
(Guidando ELVIRA tra le braccia d'ERNANI.)
Sposi voi siate,—v'amate ognor.
A Carlo Magno—sia gloria e onor.

TUTTI: Sia lode eterna,—Carlo, al tuo nome Tu, re clemente— somigli a Dio,
Perchè l'offesa—copri d'oblio,
Perchè perdoni — agli offensor,
Il lauro augusto — sulle tue chiome
Acquista insolito—divin fulgor.
A Carlo Quinto— sia gloria e onor.

SILVA: (Oh mie speranze—vinte non dome,
Tutte appagarvi— saprò ben io;
Per la vendetta—per l'odio mio
Avrà sol vita—in seno al cor.
Canute gli anni-mi fer le chiome;
Ma inestinguibile—è il mio livor—
Vendetta gridami—l'offeso onor!)

FINE DELL'ATTO TERZA.

For I am lord of Aragon,
Of Cordova, of Segovia;
You will not wrong my claims.
You did escape my dagger.

CARLO: Yes, it shall fall but later.

ELVIRA: (throwing herself at the feet of CARLO) O sire!
O King! let pity wake
Within your heart, and if a throne,
The mightiest of the earth, be given
Awhile to you it is but a trust—
It is of the earth, it is but dust,
So leave vengeance to Heaven.

CARLO: Peace, woman, peace.

ELVIRA: For Heaven speaks by me
(She rises).

CARLO: (Fixing his eyes on the tomb of CARLO MAGNO.)
I'd make your virtues too—my own,
I, too, am Charles—more than your throne.
I'd make your virtues too my own,
Let Heaven hear—that with your state,
I swear your deed—to emulate.
(After a pause.)
Pardon to all—(I've stilled my heart.)
(Leading ELVIRA to ERNANI.)
Lovers, be happy,—never part.
To Carlo Magno—be glory, fame.

ALL: To you be praise—to Charles' name;
Merciful as—pitying Heaven.
The crimes are forgotten—the offenders forgiven,
The laurels round your brow shall twine,
With greener strength—and brighter shine.
Glory and honor—Charles to you!

SILVA: (My wishes I may hush—not quell.
I yet will satisfy them well.
For vengeance now—I live alone,
Yes hatred, I am all your own.
Age can not quench your raging flame
Revenge, revenge for wounded fame!

END OF ACT III.

## ■ ACTO IV

### SCENA I

(Terrazzo nel palagio di D. GIOVANNI d'Aragona in Sargozza. A destra ed a man ce sonvi porte che mettone a varii appartamenti, il fondo è chiuso da cancelli attrver-

## ■ ACT IV

### SCENE I

(Terrace in the Palace of DON GIOVANNI of Aragon, in Saragossa. On the right and left, doors leading to the various apartments. Glass doors through which

*so i quali vedonsi i giardini del Palazzo illuminato, e parte di Saragozza. Nel fondo a destra dello spettatore, avvi una grande scalea che va nei giardini. Da una sala a sinistra di che guarda odesi la lieta musica delle danze.)*
*(Gentiluomini, Dame Maschere, Paggi ed Ancelle vanno e vengono gaiamente tra lor discorrendo.)*

**TUTTI:** Or come felici—gioiscono gli sposi!
Saranno quai fiori—cresciuti a uno stel
Cessò la bufera—de di procellosi;
Sorrider sovr'essi—vorrà sempre il ciel.

## SCENA II

*(Comparisce una Maschera tutta chiusa in nero domino, che guarda impaziente d'intorno, come chi cerca con premura alcuno. ERNANI ed ELVIRA vengono dalla sala da ballo, avviandosi alla destra dello spettatore, ov'è la stanza nuziale.)*

**ERNANI:** Cessaro i suoni, dispari ogni face,
Di silenzio e mistero si piace—
Ve' come gli astri stessi Elvira mia,
Sorridor sembrano al felice imene—

**ELVIRA:** Cosi brillar vedeali
Di Silvia dal castello—allor che mostra
Io ti attendeva—e all'impaziente core
Secoli eterni rassembravan l'ore—
Or meco alfin sei tu—

**ERNANI:** E per sempre.

**ELVIRA:** O gioia!

**ERNANI:** Si, si per sempre tuo—

**ERNANI ed ELVIRA:** *(a 2.)* Fino al sospiro estremo
Un solo core avremo.
*(S'ode un contano suono di corno.)*

**ERNANI:** (Maledizion di Dio!)

**ELVIRA:** Il riso del tuo volto fa ch'io veda.
*(S'ode altro suono.)*

**ERNANI:** (Ah! la tigre domanda la sua preda!)

**ELVIRA:** Cielo!—che hai tu!—che affanni?—

**ERNANI:** Non vedi, Elvira, un infernal sogghigno
Che me tra l'ombre, corruscante irride?
E il vecchio! il vecchio! mira!—

---

*are seen the garden of the Palace illuminated, and part of Saragossa. To the left, an apartment; from whence are heard the sounds of music and dancing.)*
*(Dancers, Masks, and Pages pass gayly to and fro.)*

**ALL:** O happy pair! like brilliant flowers
They'll grow and flourish on one stem.
The tempest's past, the stormy hours—
And heaven has nothing but smiles for them.

## SCENE II

*(A mask disguised in a black domino. He gazes impatiently round, as if seeking some one. ERNANI and ELVIRA, enter from the ball-room, and go to right of stage where the bridal chamber is.)*

**ERNANI:** The music ceases, and with it the lights
Have disappeared.
In mystery love delights.
In mystery and in silence.
Look above,
The very stars are smiling on our love.

**ELVIRA:** It was thus I watched them, it was thus they shone.
When I in Silva's castle, sad and lone,
Waited for you each moment as it passed
Seemed as an age—but I am yours at last.

**ERNANI:** Yes, and forever.

**ELVIRA:** O happiness!

**ERNANI:** Yes, yes, forever.

**ELVIRA and ERNANI:** Till our last breath
Only one heart we'll have.
*(The sound of a horn in the distance.)*

**ERNANI:** (Heaven's malediction!)

**ELVIRA:** Ernani, smile, do not turn your head away.
*(Another blast is heard.)*

**ERNANI:** The tiger crouches and demands his prey.

**ERNANI:** *(To ELVIRA).* Through the darkness do you see
Mocking me there, an infernal smile?
A devil's mocking grin that glares on me?
Elvira, look, it is the old man's look!

---

**ELVIRA:** Oime!—smarrisci i sensi!—
*(I suoni ingagliardiscono appressandosi.)*

**ERNANI:** (Egli mi vuole!)
Ascolta, o dolce Elvira,
Sol ora m'ange una ferita antica—
Va tosto per un farmaco, o dilette—

**ELVIRA:** Ma tu—signor!

**ERNANI:** Se m'ami, va, t'affretta.
*(ELVIRA entra nelle stanze nuziali).*

## SCENA III

**ERNANI:** Tutto or tace intorno,
Forse fu vana illusion la mia!—
Il cor non uso ad essere beato
Sognò forse le angosce del passato
Andiam—
*(Va per seguire ELVIRA.)*

## SCENA IV

*Detto e SILVA mascherato.*

**ELVIRA:** T'arresta.
*(Fermandosi a capo della scala.)*

**ERNANI:** (E desso! Viene il mirto a cangiarmi col cipresso!)

**SILVA:** Ecco il pegno, nel momento
In che Ernani vorrai spento,
Se uno squillo intenderà,
Tosto Ernani morirà,
*(Appressandosi ad ERNANI e smascherandosi.)*
Sarai tu menitor?

**ERNANI:** Ascolta un detto ancor—
Solingo, errante, misero,
Fin da prim'anni miei,
D'affanni amaro un calice
Tutto ingoiar dovei
Ora che alfine arridere
Mi veggo il ciel sereno,
Lascia ch'io libi almeno
La tazza dell'amor.

**SILVA:** Ecco la tazza—scegliere;
*(Fieramente presentandogli; un pugnale ed un veleno.)*
Ma tosto—io ti concedo.

**ERNANI:** Gran Dio!

**SILVA:** Se tardi od esiti—

**ERNANI:** Ferro e velen qui vedo!—
Duca—rifuggi l'anima—

**SILVA:** Dov'è l'ispano onore,
Spergiuro mentitore?—

---

**ELVIRA:** My senses reel!

**ERNANI:** (He summons me.) It is nothing;
It was but the pain of an old wound that shook
My frame an instant.
Sweet Elvira, go
And seek a doctor's aid.

**ELVIRA:** But you—

**ERNANI:** Go quickly if you love me.
*(ELVIRA enters the bridal chamber.)*

## SCENE III

**ERNANI:** Yet all within is hushed—all are at rest;
It was a vain fancy, since it did not last.
My heart so little used to being blest,
Perchance dreams with anguish of the past.
I'll go—
*(He goes to follow ELVIRA.)*

## SCENE IV

*The same and Silva masked.*

**SILVA:** I arrest you.
*(Stopping at top of steps.)*

**ERNANI:** So soon!
You would transform the tender myrtle leaves
To the dull cypress!)

**SILVA:** "The moment you wish Ernani to die,
On this then, our token,
Wind one thrilling blast,
That sound for Ernani
On earth be the last."
*(Approaching him and unmasking.)* Are you perjured?

**ERNANI:** A moment yet; from my first years
A wanderer on the earth, with tears
I've drained the cup of woe!
And now that Heaven seems to smile
An instant let me sip awhile
The blessed cup of love.

**SILVA:** The cup's prepared, and so rejoice;
And more, I'll let you have your choice.
*(He proudly presents him a dagger and a cup of poison.)*

**ERNANI:** Great Heaven!

**SILVA:** If you delay or hesitate —

**ERNANI:** Poison and steel I see await!
O duke, as to her refuge place
My soul to you shall fly.

**SILVA:** Spaniard and perjured! yet for grace can you sue?

ERNANI: Eb-
ben . . . porgi . . . morrò.
(*Prende il pugnale*).

## SCENA ULTIMA

*Detti ed ELVIRA, dalle stanze nuziali*

ELVIRA: (*ad ERNANI*). Ferma,
crudele, estinguere
Perchè vuoi tu due vite? —
(*a SILVA*.)
Quale d'Averno demone
Ha tali trame ordite?
Presso al sepolcro mediti,
Compisci tal vendetta! —
La morte che t'aspetta,
O vecchio, affretterò.
(*Va per avventarsi contro Silva*.)
Mae che diss'io? perdonami —
L'angoscia in me parlò.

SILVA: E'vano, o donna, il piangere
—
E' vano — io non perdono.

ERNANI: (*La furia è inesorabile*.)

ELVIRA: (*a SILVA*). Figlia d'un Silva io sono
Io l'amo — indissolubile
Nodo mi stringe a lui —

SILVA: L'ami? — morrà costui,
Per tale amor morrà.

ELVIRA: Per queste amare lagrime
Di lui, di me pietà.

ERNANI: Quel pianto, Elvira,
ascondimi —
Ho d'uopo di costanza —
L'affanno di quest'anima

ERNANI: It is well — I die.
(*He takes the dagger*.)

## LAST SCENE

*The above and ELVIRA, who enters from the bridal chamber.*

ELVIRA: (*to ERNANI*). Ernani, O
do you forget
That blow two hearts must kill!
(*To SILVA*).
So near the grave! and vengeance
yet fills your aged breast?
Death that so soon must claim his
prey
I'll hasten with this stroke.
(*She makes a movement to throw
herself on him, but stops*.)
Pardon, alas! what did I say?
It was grief, not I, that spoke.

SILVA: Lady, your vain prayer shall
not stem
My fury's headlong flood.

ERNANI: (No, he is inexorable.)

ELVIRA: (*to SILVA*). Silva, I am of
your blood;
I love him, and the link that binds
us sacred as above.

SILVA: Ay, you do love him, there's
his crime;
He dies for that same love.

ELVIRA: Oh! pity, mercy! see my
tears!

ERNANI: Elvira, cease — control
your vain complaints,
For I myself need courage, and my
soul,

Ogni dolore avanza —
Un giuramento orribile
Ora mi danna a morte,
Fu scherno della sorte
La mia felicità
Non ebbe di noi miseri,
Non ebbe il ciel pietà!

SILVA: (*Appressandosi minaccioso ad ERNANI*.) °°Se uno squilio intenderà
Tosto Ernani morirà."

ERNANI: Intendo — intendo —
compiasi
Il mio destin fatale.
(*Si pianta il pugnale nel seno*.)

ELVIRA: Che mai facesti, o misero?
Ch'io mora? a me il pugnale —

SILVA: No, sciagurata — arrestati,
Il delirar non vale —

ERNANI: Elvira! Elvira! —

ELVIRA: Attendimi —
Sol te seguir desio —

ERNANI: Vivi — d'amarmi e vivere,
Cara — t'impongo — addio.

ELVIRA, ERNANI: (*a 2*.) Per noi
d'amore il talamo
Di morte fu l'altar.
(*ERNANI spira ed ELVIRA sviene*).

SILVA: (Della vendetta il demone
Qui venga ad esultar!)

*FINE.*

By divers passions torn, groans beneath the weight
This dreadful oath imposes — that
of death!
My bliss was but a mirage mocking
fate,
Spread out before my eyes — it is
gone, it is past!

SILVA: (*Approaching with a menacing gesture*.) "This sound for
Ernani
On earth be the last."

ERNANI: I hear, I hear, my fatal
destiny.
(*He stabs himself*).

ELVIRA: What have you done? - O
misery!

SILVA: Hold, wretched girl! - it is
madness that makes you rave.

ERNANI: Elvira! Elvira!

ELVIRA: Wait for me, Ernani, I'll
share your grave.

ERNANI: Not so, I ask it with my
latest breath —
Oh! live to love my memory; farewell.

ELVIRA and ERNANI: I love you,
dearest, with my latest breath —
The torch of Hymen lights us to our
death.
(*ERNANI dies — ELVIRA faints*).

SILVA: The demon of revenge has
triumphed well.

*END.*

# Luisa Miller (1849)

## Louisa Miller

MUSIC BY GIUSEPPE VERDI ■ LIBRETTO BY SALVATORE CAMMARANO

This three-act opera, set to a libretto by Salvatore Cammarano (based on Friedrich Schiller's tragedy *Kabale und Liebe*), premiered at the Teatro San Carlo in Naples on December 8, 1849. The story takes place in the Tyrol during the eighteenth century. Luisa Miller has fallen in love with a stranger, although her father has serious doubts about him. Wurm, Luisa's rejected suitor, reveals the stranger's identity: Rodolfo, son of the Count of Walter. Walter is furious with his son, as he has arranged for Rodolfo to marry Federica, who is wealthy and in love with him. Miller reveals Rodolfo's true identity to his daughter. Rodolfo swears to marry Luisa in spite of his father. Walter arrests Miller and Luisa. Rodolfo blackmails his father, threatening to expose the ways in which Walter, with Wurm's assistance, gained his nobility and power, and Walter immediately orders Luisa's release. Walter and Wurm convince Luisa to sign a letter stating that she loves Wurm, not Rodolfo, so that her father's life will be spared. They force her to tell Federica this lie. Rodolfo discovers the letter and challenges Wurm, but his father convinces Rodolfo to marry Federica after all. When Miller is released from prison, on Rodolfo's wedding day, he learns that his daughter plans to take her own life. He persuades her that they should leave the country. Rodolfo enters and confronts Luisa about the letter. When she insists that she wrote it, he produces a flask. He drinks from it first, then hands it to her. He reveals that the flask contains poison. Luisa, dying, at last speaks the truth. Rodolfo kills Wurm and then collapses, dead, beside his love.

---

## ■ ATTO PRIMO.

### L'AMORE.

*Ameno villaggio: da un lato la modesta casa di Miller, dall' altro rustica chiesetta; in lontananza, le cime del castello di Walter. Un' alba limpidissima di primavera è sull' orizzonte: gli abitanti del villaggio si adunano per festeggiare il di natilizio di Luisa.— Laure è fra essi.*

### SCENA PRIMA.

**CORO e LAURA:** Ti desta, o Luisa, regina de' cori;
I monti già lambe un riso di luce;
D'un giorno sì lieto insiem con gli albori
Qui dolce amistade a te ne conduce;
Leggiadra è quest' alba sorgente in aprile,
Ma come il tuo viso leggiadra non è:
È pura, soave quest' aura gentile,
Pur meno è soave, men para di te.

### SCENA II.

*Luisa, Miller, e Detti.*

**MILLER:** Ecco mia figlia—

**LUISA:** O care amiche—

## ■ ACT I.

### LOVE.

*Scene represents a beautiful village. On one side the modest cottage of Miller—on the other a little Rustic Church—in the distance a view of the Chateau of Walter. The rising Sun of a Spring morning gilds the horizon. The Inhabitants of the Village are assembled to celebrate the Anniversary of the birthday of Louisa. Laura is with them.*

### SCENE I.

**LAURA AND CHORUS:** Awake, Louisa! queen of our hearts!
Already the rays of light caress the tops of the mountains.
Adding a brightness, even to the joys of this day!
The sweet ties of friendship have drawn us around you.
Though bright beams of the Sun, so inviting on this morn,
Its brightness can't equal your divine beauty,
The breath of the morning is balmy and sweet,—
But it cannot compare with the breath from your lips!

### SCENE II.

*Enter Louisa and Miller.*

**MILLER:** Here is my daughter!

**LOUISA:** Ah! my dear friends!

**CORO:** Il cielo
A te sia fausto.

**LAURA:** In breve
Ad invocarlo uniti andrem nel tempto.

**MILLER:** Il vostro affetto dal mio cìglior esprime
Pianto di tenerezza—
Al cor paterno è sacro
Il di che spunta—esso mi diè Luisa!
(*Abbracciandola.*)

**LUISA:** Padre! Nè giunge ancor!
(*Volgendosi d' intorno inquieta.*)
Da lui divisa
Non v' ha gioia per me!

**MILLER:** Figlia, ed amore,
Appena desto in te, si vive flamme
Già spande! Oh! mal non sia
Cotanto amor locato!
(*Luisa vorrebbe parlare.*)
Del novello
Signor qui gianto nella corte ignoto
A tutti è questo Carlo
Io temo!

**LUISA:** Non temer: più nobil spirto,
Alma più calda di virtù non mai
Vestì spoglia mortal. M' amò—l' amal.
Lo vidi, e 'l primo palpito

**CHORUS:** Heaven bless and be propitious to you!

**LAURA:** Within the holy temple presently
Will we invoke the same for you!

**MILLER:** Dear friends! your attachment to my child
Brings tears of joy and tenderness to my eyes.
This day is sacred to a parent's heart—
It is this day which, years ago, gave me my Louisa.
(*They embrace.*)

**LOUISA:** My father! He hasn't come yet!
Separated from him, there is no joy for me!
(*She looks around with much inquietude.*)

**MILLER:** My child—my child!
Love has but scarcely entered your young heart,
And yet already it enfolds you in its vivid flame!
Heaven grant this earnest, fervent love
May not be misplaced. (*Louisa going to speak*)
This Charles is unknown to the new Lord
But lately arrived at the Chateau.
And, indeed, unknown to all. I fear—

**LOUISA:** Fear not, my father! for a nobler mind—
More generous soul, could never animate
A mortal form! He loves me well,
And I love him! I saw him, and my

Il corsenti d'amore:
Mi vide appena, e il core
Balzo del mio fedel.
Quaggiù si riconobbero
Nostr' alme in rincontrarsi—
Formate per amarsi
Iddio le aveva in ciel!

**CORO e LAU.:** Luisa un pegno ingenuo
Dall' amistade accetta.
(*Presentandole tutti, pria le
donne, poi gli nomini, un mazzettino di fiori.*)

**LUISA:** Grata è quest' alma, o tenere
Compagne—Ah!
(*Scorgendo un giovane cacciatore, che anch' esso fra gli altri le
porge i suoi fiori.*)

## SCENA III.

*Rodolfo, e Detti.*

**RODOLFO:** Mia diletta!

**MILLER:** (Desso!)
(*Turbato.*)

**RODOLFO:** Buon padre!
(*Andando verso Miller.*)

**LUISA:** Abbraccialo—
T'ama qual figlio.

**RODOLFO:** Amici!
(*Salutando i Cont.*)
Sei paga?
(*A Luisa.*)

**LUISA:** Di letizia
Colma son io!

**LAU., CORO:** Felici
Appien vi tende amore.

**LUISA, RODOLFO:** Appien feli-
ci?—E ver!
A te dappresso il core
Non vive che al piacer.
T'amo d' amor eh' esprimere
Mal tenterebbe il detto;
Nè gel di morte spegnere
Può si cocente affetto:
Ha i nostri cori un Dio
Di nodo eterno avvinti,
E sulla terra estinti
Noi ci ameremo in ciel!

**MILLER:** (Non so qual voce infaus-
ta
Entro il mio cor favella—
Misero me, se vittima
D'un seduttor foss' ella!
Ah! non voler, buon Dio,
Che a tal destin soccomba—
Mi schiuderia la tomba
Affanno si crudel!)

heart
Felt the first throb of passionate
emotion.
Scarcely had he beheld me, when
his heart
Beat with a throb responsive to my
own.
Our souls mingled together as one
being,
Inwrapt—eternal love!
Heaven created them to be insepa-
rable!

**CHORUS AND LAURA:** Accept,
Louisa, these gifts of affection.
(*They present her in turns with
bouquets of flowers.*)

**LOUISA:** How well you bear me in
remembrance.
My gentle, kind companions! Ah!
(*Rodolphe, as a young hunter, enters and presents her with flowers.*)

## SCENE III.

*Enter Rodolphe.*

**RODOLPHE:** My beloved one!

**MILLER:** (*Aside—troubled*) It's
him!

**RODOLPHE:** My father!
(*He turns toward Miller.*)

**LOUISA:** Embrace him! He loves
you Charles
As if you were his son.

**RODOLPHE:** (*Wishing "good
morning" to the Villagers*)
Friends.
(*To Louisa*)
Are you happy?

**LOUISA:** I am filled with joy!

**LAURA AND CHORUS:** Love fills
your heart with happiness.

**LOUISA AND RODOLPHE:**
With perfect happiness—it's true!
near to you
My heart knows nothing but plea-
sure.
I love you with a Love that words
cannot express;
A love that will outlive the chills of
death.
Heaven has joined our hearts in
bonds eternal!
And when we quit this world and
all its joys
We shall still love in Heaven!

**MILLER:** What means this strange
and sad misgiving,
That whispers sorrow to my heart?
Ah! what dire dismay, should she,
so pure,
Fall a sad victim to the seducer's
arts!
Father of Heaven avert such dreadful doom;
Nor let this aged head in shame sink
to the tomb!

**CORO e LAU.:** Un' alma, un sol de-
sio
Ad ambo avviva il petto
Mai non si vide affetto
Più ardente, più fedel.
(*Odesi la sacra squilla.*)
Udiste? i bronzi squillano:
Andiam, ne invita il ciel.
(*Tutti entrano nel tempietto, Mil-
ler li segue lentamente, ed è gia
presso a loccare il sacro limite,
quando alenno lo arresta.*)

## SCENA IV.

*Wurm, e Detti.*

**WURM:** Ferma, ed ascolta.

**MILLER:** Wurm!

**WURM:** Io tutto udia!
Furor di gelosia
M'arde nel petto!—Amo tua fig-
lia—eppure,
Un anno volge, io la sua man ti
chiesi:
Non dissentisti, ed or che più fortu-
na
A me spira seconda, or che il novel-
lo
Signor più che l' estinto
M'è largo di favor, tu la promessa
Calpesti, ed osi!

**MILLER:** Ah cessa—
Il mio paterno assenso
Promisi, ove la figlia
T'avesse amato.

**WURM:** E non potevi forse
Alle richieste nozze
Astringeria? non hai
Dritto sovr' essa tu?

**MILLER:** Che dici mai?
Sacre la scelta è d'un consorte,
Essere appieno libera deve:
Nodo che sciorre sol può la morte
Mal dalla forze legge riceve.
Non son tiranno padre son io.
Non si comanda de' figli al cor.
In terra un padre somiglia Iddio
Per la hontade non pel rigor

**WURM:** Costarti o vecchio debole.
Caro il tuo cicco affetto
Dovrà, ben caro!

**MILLER:** Spiegati.

**WURM:** Sotto mendace aspetto
Il preferito giovane
Si mostra a voi.

**MILLER:** Fia vero?
E tu conosci?

**CHORUS AND LAURA:** They have
but one soul—one wish—
Who has ever seen such ardent
faith,
Such earnest tenderness?
(*The clock of the church strikes.*)
Listen—the clock strikes—let us
go—
The voice of Heaven seems to call
us!
(*They enter the chapel: Miller
slowly follows, he has nearly
passed the door when someone
stays him.*)

## SCENE IV.

*Enter Wurm.*

**WURM:** Stop—and listen!

**MILLER:** Wurm!

**WURM:** I have heard all!
The pangs of jealousy devour my
soul—
I love your daughter. A full year
since
I asked you for her hand, and you
did not deny it!
And now, when fortune smiles
upon me.
When the new Lord shows me both
confidence and favor,
You cast your promises at my feet,
and dare—

**MILLER:** Oh! cease—I pray you
cease!
I only promised you my daughter's
hand,
If she returned your love.

**WURM:** And are you not able to
force her to this marriage?
Have you not the right, a father's
right,
Authority to use over a wilful child?

**MILLER:** What did you say? Do I
hear right?
The choice of a husband is a sacred
act,
And should be uncontrolled—it is
a tie
That death alone can sever, and
should not be
Enforced against the will. I am no
tyrant—
I am a father—have a father's love,
And seek not to command my
daughter's heart.
A father should resemble our Heav-
enly Father.
In kindness, rather than in severity.

**WURM:** Foolish, weak, old man!
Your blind affection will cost you
dear!

**MILLER:** Explain yourself.

**WURM:** Your daughter's new-
found lover is not
What he appears to be.

**MILLER:** Can this be true? Do you
know him?

WURM: Apprendilo
E figlio è dell' attero
Walter!

MILLER: O ciel!—Dicesti
Figlio?—

WURM: Del tuo signor.
Addio.

MILLER: Pur—

WURM: M'intendesti.
(*Parte.*)

MILLER: Ei m'ha spezzato il cor!
(*Rimane silenzioso qualche
momento, come oppresso dal do-
lore.*)
Ah! fu giusto il mio sospetto!
fra e deul m'invade il petto!
D'ogni bene il ben più santo.
Senza macchia io vo' l'onor.
D'una figlia il don soltanto
Ciel mi festi, e pago io sono—
Ma la figlia, ma il tuo dono
Serba intatto al genitor.
L'ogni bene il ben più santo.
Senza macchia io vo' l'onor.
(*Parte.*)

## SCENA V.

*Sala nel castello di Walter, con
porta in fondo. Walter e Wurm.
Alcuni Famigliari, che rimangono al di là dello soglia.*

WALTER: (*Inoltrandosi seguito
da Wurm.*) Che mai narrasti! Ei la
ragione adunque Smarri!

WURM: Signor quell esaltato capo
Voi como este!

WALTER: (*Agitato.*) La duchessa
intanto
Mi segue! Digli ch'io lo bramo.
(*Wurm si ritira co' servi.*)
Ah! tutto
M'arride—tu mio figlio, tu soltanto
Osi!—La tua felicità non sai
Quanto mi costi
(*E preso da subito tremore.*)
Oh! mai nol sappia mai—
(*Ceprendosi il viso d'ambo le
mani. Lungo silenzio.*)
Il mio sangue, la vita darei
Per vederlo felice, possente!
E a 'miei voti ed agli ordini miei
Si opporrebbe quel cor sconos-
cente?
Di dolcezze l'affetto paterno
A quest' alma sorgente non è—
Pena atroce, sapplizio d'inferno
Dio sdegnato l' ha reso per me!

WURM: I know him well; he is the
son—
The darling son of the proud Lord
Walter!

MILLER: O Heaven—you said—
the son—

WURM: Of your Lord! Farewell!

MILLER: But—

WURM: You have understood me.
(*Exit.*)

MILLER: He has broken my heart.
(*He pauses as though oppressed
with grief.*)
Ah! how just were my suspicions;
Anger and grief dispute their sway
over my heart.
O Heaven! you have bestowed on
me
One precious gift—my daughter!
Grant that the child so pure, so in-
nocent,
Pass through this life spotless—
without a stain
Upon that honor which is dearer
than all earthly wealth.
The father would preserve her pure
as snow.
Then grant, O Heaven, his earnest
humble prayer.
(*Exit.*)

## SCENE V.

*A Saloon in the Chateau of Wal-
ter. Door in the back. Enter Walter and Wurm, afterwards some
servants, who remain at the door.*

WALTER: What have you told me?
Has the boy lost his senses?

WURM: My Lord, you know how
strong of will he is!

WALTER: The Duchess will be
here presently—
Tell him I wish to see him.
(*Wurm retires with the servants.*)
Ah! while all else smiles upon me,
you my son,
You alone dare—but you do not
know
How much your happiness has cost
me.
(*He is seized with a sudden ter-
ror.*)
O that he may never, never know.
(*He covers his face with his
hands.*)
I would give my life's best blood
To see him powerful and happy.
But he opposes all my wishes—all
my commands!
His heart is ungrateful and insensi-
ble, alas!
To all my fatherly affection.
The fear of your vengeance, O
Heaven! haunts me with a terror
More fearful than the torments of
eternal fire.

## SCENA VI.

*Rodolfo, e Detto.*
RODOLFO: Padre—
WALTER: M'abbraccia—Portator
son io
Di lieto annunzio. Federica in
breve
Sarà tua sposa.
RODOLFO: O cielo!
WALTER: Inseim crescinti
Nel tempo istesso, più di te quel
core
Apprezzar chi potria? Come
l'offerta
Della tua man le feci, ebbra di gioja
Mi revelò, ch'ella per te nudria
Segreta flamma, pria
Che il paterno commando
Al Duca la stringesse.

RODOLFO: (Oh me perduto!)
WALTER: Fra l'armi estinto quel
guerrier canuto.
Il nome, ed il retaggio
A lei ne resta, a lei cui man d'amica
Porge l' augusta donna
Che preme il trono di Lamagna. Il
varco
S'aprea te della corte!

RODOLFO: Ambizïose
Voglie non alimento
la cor, l'è noto!
WALTER: Ia questo debil core
Trema che il guardo mio non scen-
da.
RODOLFO: Io voglio
A te scroprirlo—
(*Odonsi lieti suoni.*)
WALTER: Taci—È la Duchessa!

RODOLFO: Oh padre!

WALTER: Incontro ad essa
Moviam, quindi le nozze
Chiederne a te s'aspetta—

RODOLFO: E credi?—e speri?

WALTER: Obbedisci—son legge i
miei voleri!
(*Traendolo per mano all' incontro della Duchessa.*)

## SCENA VII.

*La Duchessa con seguito di Dami-
gelle: Paggi, Famigliari, Arcieri.*

CORO: Quale un sorriso d'amica
sorte
Gentil venite fra queste porte.
È senza orgoglio in voi bellezza,
E senza fasto in voi grandezza;
Ma pur modesta siccome bella
Nacque la rosa ad olezzar.
La pudibonda romita stella

## SCENE VI.

*Enter Rodolphe.*
RODOLPHE: My father—
WALTER: Embrace me, my son! I
am the bearer of most joyful tid-
ings—
In but a few days Federica will be
your bride.
RODOLPHE: O Heaven!
WALTER: You have grown up to-
gether from children.
Who can better appreciate her
heart than you?
When I offered her your hand,
transported with joy,
She revealed to me the secret of her
heart.
Long before the paternal command
Compelled her to marry the Duke,
she entertained for you
A secret fond affection!
RODOLPHE: Oh! I am lost—
WALTER: The old Warrior Duke
died in battle
And she retains his name and
wealth.
The august King, now seated on the
throne of Lamagne,
Has tendered her his hand and
love—
But her heart throbs only for you.
RODOLPHE: My heart has no
thought of ambition
You know.
WALTER: Tremble—lest my gaze
should penetrate
The depths of your weak heart!
RODOLPHE: I would open my
heart to you.
(*Sounds of rejoicing are heard.*)
WALTER: No more—the Duchess
has arrived.
RODOLPHE: Oh! my father!
WALTER: Let us go and welcome
her.
All should be prepared for the es-
pousals.
RODOLPHE: And you still be-
lieve—still do you hope?
WALTER: Obey!—my wishes
should be your law!
(*Takes Rodolphe by the hand and
conducts him towards the Duch-
ess*)

## SCENE VII.

*Enter the Duchess, followed by La-
dies, Pages, Servants, and Archers.*

CHORUS: Like fortune's smiles you
return again
To bless this place with your presence, O lovely one!
Your young beauty is without
pride;
Your noble grandeur without
pomp!

È destinata a sfolgorar.

DUCHESSA: (*Nella più viva commozione*) Congiunti!—amici miei!

WALTER: Nobil signora—
(*La Duchessa gettasi amorosamente fra le sue braccia.*)
Bella nepote, il mio Rodolfo implora
L'onor di favellarti.
Io la bandita caccia
Intanto affretterò. M'udisti?
(*Piano al figlio: ad un suo cenno tutti partono con esso: Rodolfo e la Duchessa rimangono soli.*)

RODOLFO: (È d'uopo Al suo cor generoso
Fidarsi appien.) Duchessa—

DUCHESSA: Duchessa tu m'appelli!
Federica son io—non ho cessato
Per te d'esserla mai!
Se cangiò la fortuna, io non cangiai.
Dall'aule raggianti di vano splendore
Al tetto natio volava il desir—
Là dove sorgea dal vergin mio core
La prima speranza, il primo sospir!

RODOLFO: Degli anni primieri le gioje innocenti
Con me dividesti, divisi conte—
Le pene segrete degli anni più ardenti Or deggio svelarti, prostrato al tuo piè.

DUCHESSA: Deh! sorgi Rodolfo—
Tu sembri turbato!

RODOLFO: Non giova negarlo—
pur troppo lo sono.

DUCHESSA: Ah! parla!

RODOLFO: M'astringe un padre spietato
Di tallo non mio a chieder perdono—

DUCHESSA: Che intendo!

RODOLFO: Si vaga, sì eccelsa consorte
A me destinato il cielo non ha—

DUCHESSA: Oh! spiegati.

RODOLFO: Ad altra mi avvince la sorte!

DUCHESSA: Ad altra!

RODOLFO: Giurai—

DUCHESSA: Ad altra!

RODOLFO: Pietà!
Deh! la parola amara
Perdona al labbro mio—
Petea condurti all'ara?
Mentir Dinanzi a Dio?

---

Like the Rose, modest and beautiful,
Born to shed perfume and joy around:
Or, like a lone and lovely star,
Shedding your timid light to bless and charm.

DUCHESS: (*With visible emotion*) Relations:—dear friends!

WALTER: Noble Lady!
(*The Duchess tenderly throws herself in his arms.*)
Dear niece, my son, your playmate, Rodolphe,
Asks the favor of some words with you.
And while you speak of pleasures of old times,
I will hasten on the preparations for the chase.
(*To his son*) You have heard me!
(*At a sign from Walter, all retire. The Duchess and Rodolphe remain alone.*)

RODOLPHE: (*Aside*) I must trust to her generous heart.
(*Aloud*) Duchess—

DUCHESS: I have not ceased
To be to you, Federica! I have not changed with fortune.
In vain they tempt me with the splendor of the courts.
My thoughts still turn towards my native home,
Where the first hope of my virgin heart was born;
Where first I drew the breath of life!

RODOLPHE: Together we have shared the innocent joys of early youth.
Now, prostrate at your feet, let me reveal
The secret of my later years.

DUCHESS: Rodolphe, arise!—You seem troubled!

RODOLPHE: Too true—I am too deeply troubled.

DUCHESS: Ah, speak!

RODOLPHE: My father, in his anger, bids me ask pardon
For a fault which is not mine!

DUCHESS: What do I hear!

RUDOLPHE: Heaven has not willed that I should be united
To one so amiable, so powerful as you!

DUCHESS: Quick, explain yourself!

RODOLPHE: Destiny has linked me to another!

DUCHESS: To another!!

RODOLPHE: I have sworn.

DUCHESS: To another!!

RODOLPHE: Pity and pardon me for uttering these sorrowful words!
How could I conduct you to the altar?
How basely lie before high Heaven?

---

Prima d'offrirti un core
Che avvampa d'altro amore,
La destra mia tratiggerlo
A' piedi tuoi saprà!

DUCHESSA: Arma, se vuoi, la mano.
In sen mi scaglia lì brando—
M'udrai, crudele, insano,
Te perdonar spirando;
Ma da gel so core
Non aspettar favore:
Amor sprezzato è furia
Che perdonar non sa.
(*Partono da opposte via.*)

---

## SCENA VIII.

*Interno della casa di Miller. Due porte laterali; una mette alla stanza di Miller, l'altra a quella di Luisa; accanto alla prima pende una spada ed una vecchia assisa da soldato: nel prospetto l'ingresso ed una finestra, da cui scorgesi parte della chiesetta.*

*Odonsi per le montagne e le vallate circostanti grida, rimbombo di strumenti da caccia.*

VOCI IN LONTANANZA: Sciogliete i levrieri—spronate i destrieri—
Allegra, gioconda la caccia sarà—
Si cingan le selve—snidiamo le belve—
La preda è sicura, fuggir non potrà—

---

## SCENA IX.

*Luisa, quindi Miller.*

LUISA: (*Accostandosi alla finestra.*) Nol veggo—Allontanarsi dalla caccia
E qui venir promise.
(*Entra Miller, e si getta sopra una seggiola.*)
O padre mio!
Che fu? Sembri agitato!

MILLER: Il mio timore
Non era vano—Sei tradita! (*sorgendo*)

LUISA: Io? Come?
Narra.

MILLER: Sembianza e nome
Colai mentì!

LUISA: Carlo? Fia ver?

MILLER: Del Conte di Walter figlio
qual comanda il padre,
Egli a stringer si appresta
Splendide nozze—

LUISA: Ria menzogna è questa—
Esser non puote—

---

Rather than offer you a heart, whose every hope
Is bound up in another, I will die at your feet.

DUCHESS: Arm your hand if you will, but not against yourself.
Let your dagger pierce my heart, and then,
Cold and insensible, I will pardon you with my dying breath.
Expect no charity from a jealous heart!
Condemned love is a fury who does not know
How to pardon or relent!
(*They exit on opposite sides.*)

---

## SCENE VIII.

*Interior of the house of Miller. On one side two doors are seen, one leading to the chamber of Miller, the other to that of Louisa. By the first is seen suspended an old sword, and badge of a soldier. At the back there is a passageway, and from the window can be seen a portion of the little church.*

*The Music of the Chase is heard on the Mountains, and in the Valleys.*

VOICE IN THE DISTANCE: Unloose the dogs—
Spur on the horses, the chase is exciting and joyous
Let slip the game—the prey is sure—it cannot escape.

---

## SCENE IX.

*(Enter Louisa.)*

LOUISA: (*Looking from the window*) I do not see him!
And yet he promised he would leave the chase
And hasten back to me!
(*Miller enters, and throws himself on a chair.*)
O my father—what is the matter?
Why are you so troubled—so agitated?

MILLER: My fears were not in vain—you are deceived.

LOUISA: Me!—how!—speak!

MILLER: He has concealed from you his rank and his name.

LOUISA: Charles! Is it possible?

MILLER: He is the son of Count Walter,
And, according to the wishes of his father,
Is about to wed a rich and noble lady!

LOUISA: It's false—It's slander!—
It cannot be!

MILLER: Dal castello io vengo—
Giunta è la sposa—

LUISA: Taci—
Uccider vuoi tua figlia?

MILLER: Un seduttore
Accolse dunque il tetto mio?
(*Aggirandosi per la stanza pieno d'ira, trovasi dinanzi all sua vacchia divisa.*)
Per questa
D'onore assisa che il mio petto un giorno
Coprì, vendetta io giuro!

LUISA: Padre!
(*Spaventata.*)

## SCENA X.

*Rodolfo, e Detti.*

RODOLFO: (*Ancor sulla soglie, d'onde lui udito l'ultima parte della scena precedente.*) Louisa, non temer—
(*Miller fa an passo per andargli incontro, la figlia si frappone.*)
Non faro
(*Avanzandosi.*)
Bugiarde le promesse
Di questo laboro—Il velo
Ben veggo è totto; ma cangiato il nome,
E sempre il cor lo stesso.

MILLER: Che intendi?

LUISA: Ahimè!

RODOLFO: (*Pone Luisa in ginocchio a piè di Miller, e prostratosi anch'esso, stringendo nella sua la destra di lei, esclama con passione.*) Sono
Tuo Sposo! Il padre testimone, e Dio
Chiamo del giuramento!

MILLER: Ahi, sconsigliato!
E chi sottrarci all' ira
Potrà del Conte?

LUISA: Io gelo!

RODOLFO: A me so'tanto è al ciel,
(*Solennemente.*)
Arcan tremendo è manifesto!
Arcano
Che da me rivelato, a piè cadermi
Farebbe—il Conte!

LUISA: Alcun s'avanza—

RODOLFO: (*Che va verso la soglia.*) È desso!
Mio padre!

LUISA: Ah!—son perduta!

MILLER: Egli?—egli stesso?

## SCENA XI.

*Walter, e Detti.*

RODOLFO: Tu signor, fra queste soglie!
A che vieni?

---

MILLER: I have just returned from the Chateau;
The lady whom he weds, arrived just now!

LOUISA: Silence! Would you kill your child?

MILLER: A villain then has been beneath my roof.
(*He walks angrily up and down the room, and at last finds himself opposite his old badge of honorable service.*)
By this badge of honor,
Which in other days I won and wore
I swear a deadly vengeance.

LOUISA: (*In terror*) My father!

## SCENE X.

*Enter Rodolphe.*

RODOLPHE: (*Still at the door, where he has overheard the latter part of the preceding scene*) Louisa, fear nothing!
(*Miller takes a step towards Rodolphe; Louisa rushes between them.*)

RODOLPHE: (*Advancing*) The promises I have made are not false! The mystery is cleared, but my heart is still the same!

MILLER: What would you say?

LOUISA: Alas!

RODOLPHE: (*Placing Louisa on her knees at her father's feet, and kneeling himself beside her, he clasps the hands of the young girl, exclaims with fervor.*) I am your betrothed!
I take as witnesses of my oath
Your father and my God!

MILLER: Ah! unhappy! who can restrain
The anger of the Count?

LOUISA: I tremble!

RODOLPHE: (*Solemnly*) There is a dreadful secret
Known only to me and to my honor.
This, if I reveal it,
Will make the Count fall prostrate at my feet.

LOUISA: Someone comes—

RODOLPHE: (*Going towards the door*) It's him! my father!

LOUISA: Ah! I am lost!

MILLER: It's him! It's him!

## SCENE XI.

*Enter Walter.*

RODOLPHE: You—my Lord!—in this house
Why have you come?

---

WALTER: A che? Nol rese
Lo spavento che vi coglie
Assai chiaro, assai palese?
Del mio dritto vengo armato
A stornar colpevol tresca.

MILLER, LUISA: Che!

RODOLFO: L'accento scellerato
Più dal labbro mai non t'esca!
Puro amor ne inflamma il petto—
Oltraggiarlo ad uom non lice.

WALTER: Puro amor, l'amore abbietto
Di venduta seduttrice?

MILLER, LUISA, RODOLFO: Ah!
(*Luisa cade fra le braccia del padre: Rodolfo snuda la spada.*)

RODOLFO: La vita mi donasti!
(*Ripone il ferro.*)
Lo rimembra—ti ho pagato
Ora il dono!

MILLER: (*Che ha posto Luisa sopra una sedia.*) A me portasti
Grave insulto!—Io fui soldato!
Trema—

LUISA: Oh Dio!
(*Levandosi.*)
Mi ribollisce.

MILLER: Nelle vene il sangue ancor—

WALTER: Ardiresti?

MILLER: Tutto ardisce
Padre offeso nell' enor!

WALTER: Folle or ti pentirai
Dell' audacia! Olà!

## SCENA XII.

*Accore un drapello d'Arcieri, seguito da molti Contadini e da Laura e Detti.*

ARCIERI: Signore?

LUISA: Giusto ciel!

LAU., CON.: Che avvenne mai?

RODOLFO: E potresti, o genitore?

LAU., CON.: Ei suo figlio!

WALTER: Arretra, insano—

RODOLFO: Odi prima—

WALTER: Udir non vo'—
Ambo in ceppi—
(*Accenando Mil. e Lui. agla Arcieri.*)

RODOLFO, LAURA, CONTADINI: Ah!

MILLER: Disumano!!

---

WALTER: That for which I have come
The terror you display too plainly tells.
I come, by virtue of a parent's right.
To break this web of criminal intrigue!

MILLER, LOUISA: What?

RODOLPHE: Not even from your lips
Will I permit an insult to this lady.
A pure and holy love unites our hearts,
And no man has a right to outrage it.

WALTER: A pure love—indeed! pure—very pure!
A love most freely sold, and bought up by your gold!

LOUISA, MILLER, RODOLPHE: Ah!
(*Louisa falls into the arms of her father.*)

RODOLPHE: (*Drawing his sword*) But no—you are the author of my being!
I spare you—(*Sheathing his sword*)—and have paid you back
The life you gave;—remember! we now are equal!

MILLER: (*Who has placed Louisa in a chair*) You have insulted me beyond endurance!
I am a soldier—tremble!

LOUISA: (*Rising*) O Heaven!

MILLER: Blood still flows in these veins!

WALTER: Dare you?

MILLER: A parent's outraged honor dares everything!

WALTER: Insensate fool! You shall repent your audacity!
Ho! without there!

## SCENE XII.

*Enter Archers, followed by Villagers and Laura.*

ARCHERS: My Lord!

VILLAGERS AND LAURA: What mean these angry words,
And looks so full of hate?

RODOLPHE: O! pause my father! You cannot do this wrong!

WALTER: Retire, infatuated boy.

RODOLPHE: First listen to me; I implore you!

WALTER: I will listen to nothing,
(*Showing Louisa and Miller to the archers*)
Put them in chains!

RODOLPHE, LAURA AND VILLAGERS: Ah!

MILLER: Inhuman monster!!

## Act I, Scene XII

**LUISA:** Al tuo piè—
(*Cadendo alle ginocchia di Vatter.*)

**MILLER:** Prostrata!—No.
(*Rialzandola.*)
Fra i mortali ancora oppressa
Non è tanto l'innocenza.
Che si vegga genuflessa
D'un superbo alla presenza.
A quel Dio ti prostra innante
De' malvagi punitor.
Non a tal che ha d'nom sembiante,
E di belva in petto il cor.

**RODOLFO:** Foco d'ira è questo pianto—
Cedi—cedi all'amor mio
Non voier quel nodo infranto,
Che tra noi formava Iddio—
Negro vel mi sta sul ciglio!
Ho l'inferno in mezzo al cor!
Un istante ancor son figlio!
Un istante ho padre ancor!

**WALTER:** Tu piegarti, tu, non io,
Devi, o figlio, cieco, ingrato:
Il mio cenno, il voler mio
E immutabil come il fato!
Fra il suo core e il cor paterno
Frapponeste un turpe amor—
(*A Mil. e Lui.*)
Non può il ciel, non può l'inferno
Involarvi ai mio furor.

**LUISA:** (*Alzando al cielo gli occhi lagrimosi.*) Ad imagin tua creata.
O Signore, anch'io non fui?
E perchè son calpestata
Or qual fango da costui?
Deh! mi salva—deh! m'aita—
Deh! non m'abbia l'oppressor
Il tuo dono, la mia vita,
Pria ripigliati, Signor!

**LAU., CONT.,:** (Il suo pianto al pianto sforza. Il suo duolo spezza il cor!)

**ARCIERI:** Obbedirlo a tutti è forza:
Egli è padre, egli è signor.

**WALTER:** I cenni miei si compiano.
(*Agli Arcieri.*)

**RODOLFO:** (*Mettendosi innanzi a Luisa col ferro sguainato.*) Da questo acciar svenato
Cadrà chi temerario
S'avanza.

**WALTER:** Forsennato!
(*Prende Luisa e la spinge fra gli Arcieri.*)
In me lo scaglia.

**RODOLFO:** Oh rabbia!
Se tratta è fra catene
La sposa mia, nel carcere
Giuro seguirla.

---

**LOUISA:** (*Falling at the feet of Walter*) At your feet I kneel.

**MILLER:** Prostrate—no! Innocence is not yet so oppressed
That it should kneel to pride and tyranny.
Prostrate yourself before your God,
He who is mighty to punish and to save;
And not before a man whose heart is filled
With the fell passions of ferocious beasts.

**RODOLPHE:** My eyes are filled with tears of rage!
Let love subdue the fury of my soul!
They cannot break the chain, which heaven itself has forged!
A dark veil seems spread before my sight!
Unquenchable fires rage within my breast.
O love! let me remember still—I am a son!
That still my father lives.

**WALTER:** It is those who should pray. O blind, ungrateful son!
My will and my orders are as immutable
As the decrees of destiny.
Between you and your father's heart there glides
The subtle serpent love. (*To Miller and Louisa*)
Neither Heaven nor Hell shall shield you from my vengeance!

**LOUISA:** (*Raising her eyes full of tears to Heaven*) And I, O Lord! was I not born in your image?
Then why should I crouch at the feet of this man?
Aid me! O, aid me, Heaven! Save me.
O draw me from the hands of the oppressor!
O Lord! rather than abandon me to his mercy,
Take back the life which you have given!

**LAURA AND VILLAGERS:** Our tears flow with hers!
Her grief will break our hearts.

**ARCHERS:** We must obey his orders, his commands—
He is a father—he is our Lord!

**WALTER:** See that my orders are fulfilled.

**RODOLPHE:** (*Placing himself before Louisa with his sword drawn*) Who dares approach my love,
This sword shall pierce his heart!

**WALTER:** Presumptuous boy.
(*Seizes Louisa and pushes her towards the Archers*)
Let your fierce sword strike me!

**RODOLPHE:** You cannot separate us—
Her prison shall be mine!

---

**WALTER:** Ebbene,
La segui.

**RODOLFO:** Ah! pria che l'abbiano.
Coloro in preda, il core
Io le trapasso.
(*Lanciandosi fra gli Armageri, e mettendo la punta della spada sul petto di Luisa.*)

**WALTER:** Uccidila.
Che tardi?

**RODOLFO:** O mio furore!
Tutto tentai—non restami
Che un infernal consiglio—
Se crudo, inesorabile
Tu rimarrai col figlio
(*At orecchio di Walter, con terribile accento.*)
Trema! svelato agli uomini
Sarà dal labbro mio
Come giungesti ad essere
Conte di Walter!
(*Esce rapidamente.*)

**WALTER:** Dio—
(*Sembra colpito da folgore.*)
Rodolfo—m'odi—arrestati—
(Tutto m'ingombra un gel!)
Coste lasciate—è libera—
(*Convulso e pallido in volto più della morte, cerca raggiungere il figlio.*)

**LAURA, CONTADINI, ARCIERI:** Fia ver!

**LUISA, MILLER:** Pietoso ciel!
(*Gli Arcieri partono: Luisa cade in ginocchio mezzo svenuta: gli altri accorrono d'intorno.*)

*FINE DELL'ATTO PRIMO.*

---

# ■ ATTO SECONDO.

*L'INTRIGO.*

## SCENA PRIMA.

*Interno della casa di Miller.*

*Laura e Contadini, poi Luisa.*

**LAU., CORO:** Ah! Luisa, Luisa, ove sei? (*Accorrendo agitati.*)

**LUISA:** (*Uscendo.*) Chi m'appella?
(*Notando lo smarrimento che si mostra negli atti e nei volto di ognuno.*)
Voi certo recate
Tristo annunzio!

---

**WALTER:** Follow her then—if it pleases you!

**RODOLPHE:** (*Wildly.*) No, rather than see her fall the prey
To ruffians such as these,
My sword shall pierce her heart.
(*He springs among the Archers, and places the point of his sword to the heart of Louisa.*)

**WALTER:** Kill her!—Why do you hesitate to strike!

**RODOLPHE:** O madness!—I cannot slay my love!
I am tempted on every side. One way remains!
(*To Walter*) If you are inexorable to pleadings,
To the earnest pleadings of your son—
(*With a whisper of terrible meaning in the ear of Walter*)
Tremble! my lips shall reveal to the world
By what means you became Count Walter!
(*Exit hurriedly.*)

**WALTER:** Great Heaven!
(*He seems stupefied by the blow.*)
Rodolphe, listen to me! stay! stay!
What means this fearful chill
That penetrates through every vein?
Let her go free—give her her liberty.
(*His face pale, and with convulsive gestures, he seeks to rejoin his son.*)

**LAURA, VILLAGERS AND ARCHERS:** What can this mean?
What is this dreadful mystery?

**MILLER, LOUISA:** Merciful Heaven!
(*Exit Archers.*)
(*Louisa, half fainting, falls upon her knees. The Villagers press around her.*)

*END OF FIRST ACT.*

---

# ■ ACT II.

*INTRIGUE.*

## SCENE I.

*Interior of the Cottage of Miller.*

*Enter Laura and Villagers, in a hurried and agitated manner.*

**LAURA AND CHORUS:** Ah, Louisa! Louisa! where are you?

**LOUISA:** (*Coming out of her chamber*) Who calls me?
(*She remarks on the astonishment and fear depicted on the countenances of those who surround her.*)
What do these saddened looks mean?
Do you bring more evil tidings?

LAURA: Pur troppo!

CORO: E tu dei.
Ascoltarlo—

LUISA: Parlate—parlate—

LAU., CORO: Al villaggio dai campi tornando
Della roccia pel ripido calle,
Un fragor, che veniasi accostando,
A noi giunse dall'ima convalle:
Eran passi e minaccie di armati.
Cui d'ambascia una voce frammista;
Al eiglion della rupe affacciati
Ne colpì deplorabile vista!
Crudi sgherri traenti un vegliardo
Fra catene!

LUISA: Ah! mio padre!

LAU., CORO: Fa cor—
Havvi un Giusto, un Possente che il guardo
Tien rivolto sui miseri ognor!

LUISA: (*Rimasta oppressa dal cordoglio, scuotesi ad un tratto, e s'incammina per uscire.*) Oh! padre, o padre mio!

LAURA: Dove?

LUISA: Al castello—

TUTTI: Wurm!

## SCENA II.

*Wurm, e Detti.*

WURM: Ascoltarmi è d'uopo. (*A Luisa.*)
Uscite.
(*Ai Contadini che partono.*)

LUISA: (Io gelo!)

WURM: Il padre tuo!

LUISA: Finisci.

WURM: Langue in dura prigion.

LUISA: Reo di che fallo?

WURM: Ei, del Conte vassallo,
Farlo d'oltraggie e di minaccie segno
Ardi! Grave il delitto.
Grave la pena fia!

LUISA: D'interrogarti Tremo!

WURM: Che val tacerlo?
Sul canuto suo crin pende la scure.

LUISA: Ah!—Taci—taci—

WURM: Eppure,
Tu puoi salvarlo.

LUISA: Io!—Come?

WURM: A te m'invia
L'offeso Conte: un foglio
Vergar t'impone, e prezzo
Ne fia lo scampo di tuo padre.

LUISA: Un foglio?

---

LAURA: Alas! We bear most evil news!

CHORUS: Dare you to listen to it?

LOUISA: Speak—in mercy speak!

LAURA AND CHORUS: As by the mountain path we came this way,
We heard a sound beneath us in the valley;
It was the steps of armed men in motion,
And through this measured sound we heard a plaintive voice.
Too soon we saw the sad and tristful sight—
The archers bore away a poor old man in chains.

LOUISA: Oh heavens! my father!

LAURA AND CHORUS: Take courage; there is a Power above,
Whose justice punishes the wicked!

LOUISA: (*Stupefied by grief, and agitated, starts forth to seek her father*) O my father! my father!

LAURA: Where are you going?

LOUISA: To the Chateau!

ALL: (*Surprised.*) Wurm!

## SCENE II.

*Enter Wurm.*

WURM: (*To Louisa*) Louisa, I must speak to you!
(*To the Villagers*) Retire.

LOUISA: I tremble with fear!

WURM: Your father!

LOUISA: O speak! what of him?

WURM: He languishes in prison.

LOUISA: Of what is he accused?

WURM: He, only a vassal,
Has dared to raise his hand against his Lord!
Has menaced him; the crime is serious—
The punishment severe!

LOUISA: I dread to ask you further!

WURM: It is best you know the whole.
Over his white hairs the axe now hangs suspended.

LOUISA: Ah!—silence!—mercy!—I implore you!!

WURM: Tremble not, but act!
It is in your power to save his life!

LOUISA: How?—speak!—speak!

WURM: The injured Count has sent me to you—
He bids me say your father shall be free,
If you will write as I shall dictate.

LOUISA: Write—I—what?

---

WURM: Scrivi. (*Accennando a Luisa una tavola, su cui v'ha l'occorrente per iscrivere.*)
"Wurm,—io giammai"
(*Dettando.*)
"Rodolfo non amai."
(*Luisa guarda Wurm un istante, quindi abbassa gli occhi come rassegnata al sacrifizio, e scrive.*)
"Il suo lignaggio ermai noto,—e volli
Stringerlo fra mie reti"—

LUISA: E deggio?

WURM: Dei Salvar tuo padre.
(*Luisa scrive.*)
"Ambizïon mi vinse—
Tutto svani—Perdona—
Ritorno al primo affetto—
E di Rodolfo ad evitar gli sdegni—
Come la notte regni
Vieni ed insieme luggirem"—

LUISA: Che!

WURM: Scrivi.

LUISA: E segnar questa mano
Potrebbe l'onta mia?
(*Sargendo con indignazione.*)
Lo speri ivano—
Tu punicsimi, o Signore,
Se t' offesi, e paga io sono,
Ma de' barbari al furore
Noa lasciarmi in abbandono.
A scampar da fato estremo
Innocente genitor,
Chieggon essi—a dirlo io fremo.—
Della figlia il disonor!

WURM: Qui nulla s' attenta imporre al tuo core:
Tu libera sei! Ti lascio.
(*In atto di partire.*)

LUISA: (*Trattenendolo.*) Spietato!
Eil misero vecchio?

WURM: L'udisti: egli muore.
(*Freddamente*)

LUISA: E libera io sono!
(*Torrendosi e convulsiramente le mani, quindi si accosta aila tavola e scrive.*)
Il foglio è vergato.
(*Lo dà a Wurm.*)

WURM: (*Depo avedo letto.*)
Sal capo del padre, spontaneo lo scritto.
Luisa mi giura che all' nopo dirai.

LUISA: Lo giuro.

WURM: Un sol cenno ancor t'e prescritto.

LUISA: Io t'odo.

WURM: Al castello venirne dovrai
Ed ivi al cospetto di nobil signora
Accesa mostrarti di—Wurm.

LUISA: Dite?

WURM: Acerba è la prova!

LUISA: No.

---

WURM: Write. (*He conducts Louisa to a table where she seats herself. He dictates; she writes.*)
"I never loved Rodolphe!" (*Louisa gazes up into his face for a moment, then lowering her eyes, seems resigned to the sacrifice, and writes on.*)
"His rank was known to me.
And I tried to entangle him in my net."

LOUISA: Is it right to do this?

WURM: It is right to save your father.
(*Louisa writes.*)
"Ambition alone guided me. But all has vanished!
Pardon me—I return to my first love.
To avoid the anger of Rodolphe, when darkness covers the heavens—come—we will fly together."

LOUISA: What!—

WURM: Write—

LOUISA: And shall this hand sign my own shame?
(*Rising indignantly*) Your hope is vain!
You have punished me; O Lord,
If I have offended you I murmur not,
But do not abandon me to my enemies!
To save my aged father they ask—
I tremble to speak it—the dishonor of his child!

WURM: I will not press you! If your heart does not dictate the sacrifice,
You are free—I leave you. (*He pretends to go.*)

LOUISA: Cruel!—(*Detaining him*) and my father?

WURM: You have doomed him. (*Coldly.*) He dies!

LOUISA: And I am free!—(*She presses her hands together convulsively—then leans on the table and writes.*)
It is finished.
(*She gives it to Wurm.*)

WURM: (*After having read the note*) By the life of your father,
Swear Louisa, you will say if required of you—
That this was written willingly—voluntarily.

LOUISA: I swear!

WURM: One other condition is yet to be exacted.—

LOUISA: I listen!

WURM: You will go to the Chateau, and there
In the presence of a lady, declare your love for—Wurm!

LOUISA: For you?

WURM: The trial is hard?—

LOUISA: No.

WURM: Duolmi!—

LUISA: Ed allora?—

WURM: Allora—

LUISA: Mio padre?—

WURM: Fia salvo.

LUISA: Mercè.—
(*Un sorriso diabolico punta sul labbro di Wurm.*)
A brani, a brani, o pertido.
Ancor tu m'hai squarciato!—
Almen t'affretta a rendermi (*prorompendo*)
Il padre sventurato—
Di morte il fero brivido
Tutta m' invade omai—
Mi chiuda almeno i rai
La man del genitor!

WURM: Coraggio: il tempo è farmaco
D'ogni cordoglio umano.
Di stringer la tua mano
Speranza ie nudro anco. (*Escono.*)

## SCENA III.

*Il Castello: appartamenti di Walter.*

WALTER: Egli delira: sul mattin degli anni
Vinta da cieco affetto
Spesso è ragion! Del senno empia il difetto
Pel figlio il padre.—L' opra mía si compia—
Nulla cangiar mi debbe:
Esser pietoso crudeltà sarebbe.

## SCENA IV.

*Wurm, e Detto.*

WALTER: Ebben?

WURM: Tutte apprestai
Della trama le fila.

WALTER: Oh! di'a Luisa?—

WURM: Come previdi già, vinta, conquisa
Da crudele spavento,
Alle minnacie s'arrendea: per calle
Recondito qui tratta
Verrà.

WALTER: Ma il foglio?—

WURM: Compra man recarlo
Dove a Rodolfo: la vittoria è certa.
Eppar dal primo assalto
Qual potervi respinse io non intendo!

WALTER: Inalteso periglio!—
Del figlio una minaccia!—

WURM: Ingrato figlio?—

---

WURM: I suffer—

LOUISA: And then?

WURM: Then!—

LOUISA: My father?—

WURM: Is saved!

LOUISA: Mercy! (*A diabolical smile is seen to pass over the lips of Wurm.*)
Monster! You have broken my heart!
You have torn it piece by piece asunder!
(*With violence.*) It is now in your hands.
I demand my poor unhappy father:
The chills of death are coursing through my veins.
But, at least a father's hand shall close my eyes!

WURM: Courage! Time is the certain remedy
For all the ills of frail humanity.
I yet hope to claim you as my bride!
(*Exit both.*)

## SCENE III.

*Room in the Chateau. Walter, alone.*

WALTER: He is delirious!—Now in his youth,
The morning of his days, to have his reason vanquished
By a blind and foolish attachment—is terrible.
But it is a father's duty to watch over his child.
So far my task is achieved—nothing can move me.

## SCENE IV.

*Enter Wurm.*

WALTER: Well, what have you done?

WURM: I have prepared the net!

WALTER: Speak—Louisa?—

WURM: As I foresaw,
She acceded to the offer—the menaces subdued her.
She will come here today in secret.

WALTER: But the letter?—

WURM: Some messenger must take it to Rodolphe.
The victory is certain; but I've yet to learn
What so suddenly arrested your anger?

WALTER: An undreamed-of peril, a threat from Rodolphe!

WURM: Ungrateful son!

---

WALTER: L'alto retaggio non ho bramato
Di mio engiono che sol per esso!—
Ad ottenello contaminato
Mi son par troppo di nero eccesso!—

WURM: In puato feci del mio signore
Nel palesarvi lamente ascosa!
A me, cui sempre fidava il core,
Scorri lascelta ei d'una spoa—

WALTER: Timori nacquero in me ben tristi!—

WURM: Aver quel nodo figli potea!

WALTER: Ad acqueiarmi tu suggeristi
Orribù mezzo!!

WURM: Varear dovea
L'irta foresta notturno il Conte—
Noi l'appostammo, e—

WALTER: Non seguir—
Sento drizzarsi le chiome in fronte!
Tutto il mio sangue rabbrividir!

WURM: E ver, che giova parlar d'evento
Cui notte eterna fra' misteri
Ha già sepolto?

WALTER: Sepolto?

WURM: Spento
Il sire antico da' masnadieri,
Qual noi spargemno, tutti han creduto—

WALTER: Non tutti! (*) Al rombo mio figlio accorse
(*Sorpreso e turbamento di Wurm.*)
Dell' armi nostre—Non era muto
Ancor quel labbro!—

WURM: Che intendo!—Ah! forse?—

WALTER: In quel supremo, terribil punto
Walter nomava!—

WURM: Chi?

WALTER: Gli assassini!

WURM: Oh me perduto!

WALTER: Sol tu? Congiunto
Non t' ha Satanno a' miei destini?—
O meco incolume sarai, lo giuro,
O sul patibolo verrò con te.

WURM: (*Più questo capo non è sicuro!
Potria del ceppo cadere a piè!*)
Vien la Duchessa!—
(*Ad un cenno di Walter si ritira.*)

---

WALTER: I only coveted my cousin's wealth,
That Rodolphe might inherit it.
And to obtain it, how terrible the crime I have committed!

WURM: I forwarded your interests in every way,
By learning the secret thoughts of my master.
He confided in me and revealed his choice of a wife.

WALTER: At the news what dismal forebodings rose in my heart!

WURM: From such a match there was a chance
That heirs might spring and cut off your inheritance.

WALTER: Then you suggested to me a horrible means
To stay this act of folly and injustice.

WURM: The old Count was compelled to traverse the forest alone;
He was alone—we waited for him.

WALTER: No more! no more! I dare not think of it!
My blood seems freezing in my veins.

WURM: It is true! why should we speak of events
Which are entombed in the mysteries of eternal night?—

WALTER: Entombed?—

WURM: The old Lord is dead:—our story is believed by all,
That he, the poor old man, was slain by brigands!

WALTER: Not by all!—(*Wurm is surprised, and shows signs of terror.*)
Rodolphe, alarmed by the noise of our shots,
Rushed to the spot.—The old man still lived,
And by his dying lips our secret was revealed!

WURM: What do I hear?—Ah! perhaps—

WALTER: He named—

WURM: Who?—

WALTER: The assassins—

WURM: Then I am lost!—

WALTER: Not you alone!—Has the foul fiend not
United me with your destiny?
Will you not be saved with me,
Or I be lost with you?

WURM: (*Aside*) There is no more security here for me;—
My head may fall at any moment.
(*Aloud*) My Lord, the Countess approaches.
(*He retires at a sign from Walter.*)

## SCENA V.

*La Duchessa, e Detto.*
DUCHESSA: Conte—
WALTER: Il detto mio confermo:
Di Ridolfo nel sen, qual d' un infermo
Il delirio, s'apprese
Amor che spento lia–

DUCHESSA: Spento?—
WALTER: Ed in breve.
DUCHESSA: Io temo!—
WALTER: Indarno: di Luisa il core
Mai Rodolfo non ebbe:
D'altri è colei.
DUCHESSA: Fia vero?—E chi potrebbe
Attestarlo?
WALTER: Ella stessa
DUCHESSA: Ella!—
WALTER: Qual tu chiedesti
Qui fu condotta.
DUCHESSA: Già!
WALTER: Non lo volesti?

## SCENA VI.

*La Duchessa siede, cercanao ricomporsi dal suo turbamenta. Walter apre una porta segreta, d'onde esce Luisa, accompagnata da Wurm.*

WALTER: Presentarti alla Duchessa.
Puoi, Luisa—Intendi?
DUCHESSA: Appressa. (*Con sussiego.*)
WURM: Ti rammenta in qual periglio
È tuo padre! (*Piano a Luisa.*)
LUISA: (O mio terrore!)—
(*S'avanza.*)
DUCHESSA: (Dolce aspetto!—Il volto, il ciglio—
Tutto spira in lei candore!)
LUISA: (A costei sarà concesso
Quanto il ciel m'avea promesso!)

DUCHESSA: Par che manchi in te coraggio
D'erger gli occhi al mio sembiante!
WALTER: Ella nata in un villaggio!—
WURM: D'alta dama or tratta inante!—
LUISA: (Rea fucina d' empie frodi
Son costor!)

DUCHESSA: (*Sorgendo s'accosta a Luisa.*) Luisa, m' odi,
Farmi puote un sol tuo detto
Sventurata, o appien felice!
Non mentir!—Ma no, l'aspetto

## SCENE V.

*Enter the Duchess.*
DUCHESS: My Lord Count—
WALTER: I am ready to fulfill my promise—
The infatuation of Rodolphe will prove but transient.
This love will soon vanish from his heart.
DUCHESS: Vanish?—
WALTER: Yes—within a day!—
DUCHESS: I fear—it cannot be!—
WALTER: Louisa never loved him—her heart was another's!
DUCHESS: Can this be true? who will prove it?
WALTER: Herself!
DUCHESS: She!
WALTER: At your request she has been brought here.
DUCHESS: So soon?
WALTER: Even as you desired it.

## SCENE VI.

*(The Duchess, striving to hide her agitation, seats herself. Walter opens a secret door from whence comes Louisa, accompanied by Wurm.)*

WALTER: Wurm! you can present Louisa to the Duchess!
Do you hear?
DUCHESS: (*With gravity*) Approach!
WURM: (*Whispering to Louisa as she approaches*) Remember the peril in which your father lies!
LOUISA: (*Aside*) I tremble with fear! (*She advances.*)
DUCHESS: (*Aside*) How fair a countenance—her face, her eyes,
All speak of truth and candor.
LOUISA: (*Aside*) To her then will be accorded all the joy
I vainly thought that Heaven had promised me.
DUCHESS: It seems to me your courage fails you:
You cannot raise your eyes to my face!
WALTER: She is but a humble villager.
WURM: And brought before so high a lady is abashed!
LOUISA: (*Aside.*) This is some impious plot contrived between them,
To work my utter ruin!
DUCHESS: (*Rising and approaching Louisa*) Louisa! Do you hear me? Your lips can utter one word,
Which will render me miserable—utterly—forever,

Non hai tu di mentitrice!

LUISA: (Chi soffri maggiore affanno!)—
DUCHESSA: (*Prendendo Luisa per mano, ed affiggendole avidamente lo sguardo negli occhi.*) Arai tu?
LUISA: (Destin tiranno!—)
Amo.
DUCHESSA: E chi? chi?
LUISA: Wurm.
(*Mostrandolo. Wurm s' inchina modestamente.*) Indegno!
DUCHESSA: Ma Rodolfo?—
LUISA: Fra noi venne
Sconosciuto—A qual disegno
Io lo inogro—
DUCHESSA: E non ottenne
Mai d' amor lusinghe, accenti
Da Luisa?
LUISA: (Quai momenti!—)
DUCHESSA: Di.
LUISA: No, mai.
DUCHESSA: (La speme in core
Mi si avviva!—)
LUISA: (Esulta!) (*Freme di gelosia.*)
DUCHESSA: Parmi!—
Sì—cangtasti di colore!—
Ah! che fia?—Non ingannarmi!
Non tradir te stessa!—

LUISA: (Oh Cielo!)
WALTER: (Obserebbe?)—

DUCHESSA: Parla—
WURM: (Io gelo!)
DUCHESSA: Dell' arcano squarcia il manto—
Se un arcano in sen tu chiudi.
LUISA: Io. (*In procinto di svelare il secreto.*)
DUCHESSA: Favella.
WALTER: Si, per quanto.
Ami il padre!
LUISA: (*Reprimendosi ad un tratto.*) (Il padre!)—
(*Gli sguardi di Walter e Wurm stanno immobili sopra Luisa.*)
Oh crudi!—
WURM: Via, che tardi?

DUCHESSA: Ebben?—
LUISA: Lo stesso
Da Luisa udrete ognor.
Che alimento solper esso
(*Accennando Wurm.*)
Fido, immenso, ardente amor.
Come celar le smanie
Del mio geloso amore?—

Or make my heart bound with ecstatic joy.
Do not speak falsely—but no—so fair, so kind a face
Could never mask a treacherous heart!
LOUISA: (*Aside*) Did ever human heart suffer such misery?
DUCHESS: (*Taking the hand of Louisa and fixing her gaze sternly upon her*) Do you love?
LOUISA: (*Aside*) Cruel fate!
(*Aloud*) I do!
DUCHESS: His name—his name.
LOUISA: Wurm! (*Pointing to him. Wurm bows modestly.*)
(*Aside.*) The wretch!
DUCHESS: But Rodolphe?—
LOUISA: He came among us—disguised—
I know not for what purpose!
DUCHESS: Has he never heard words of love from Louisa?
LOUISA: O moments of torture!
DUCHESS: Answer me!
LOUISA: No!—never!
DUCHESS: (*Aside*) Hope again revives in my heart!
LOUISA: She triumphs.
(*She trembles with jealousy*)
DUCHESS: It seems to me—yes—it is true!
Your countenance changes—say—what does it mean?
Are you deceiving me?—you have betrayed yourself!
LOUISA: O, Heaven!
WALTER: (*Aside*) She would not dare.
DUCHESS: Speak!
WURM: I freeze!
DUCHESS: Unravel this mystery! If you have a secret in your heart, reveal it!
LOUISA: (*On the point of betraying herself*)
DUCHESS: Speak—speak!
WALTER: (*Pointedly*) Yes, speak! For the love you bear your father—speak!
LOUISA: (*Endeavoring to hide the feelings which were betraying her*) My father!—
(*The eyes of Walter and Wurm are fixed upon Louisa.*) Cruel!—
WURM: Proceed—why do you hesitate?—
DUCHESS: I wait!
LOUISA: I can but repeat what I have said.
(*Pointing to Wurm*)
It is for him alone that I have long cherished
A faithful, devoted, ardent love!
(*Aside*)

# Act II, Scene VI

Ahimè, l'infranto core
Più reggere non può!
Se qui rimango, esanime
A' piedi suoi cadrò!)

How shall I conceal the anguish of my jealous heart,
I am no longer mistress of my feelings!
If I remain here I shall fall insensible at their feet.

**DUCHESSA:** (Un sogno di letizia
Par quel ch' io veggo e sento!—
No, mai si gran contento
Quest' alma non provò!—
Frena, mio core, i palpiti,
O di piacer morrò.)

**DUCHESS:** It is for me like some bright dream of happiness!
A joy—an ecstasy never felt before!
O cease, my heart, to throb so wildly,
For it is more than life can bear.

**WALTER, WURM:** (*Notando la gioia, che si manifesta in volto alla Duch.*) (Piato ha di vivo giubilo
Il sorridente viso!
Fortuna in quel sorriso
Propizia baienò!—
Ben io fermarla, stringerne
L'infido crin saprè.)
(*La Duchessa si ritira, seguita di Walter: Wurm riconduce Luisa per l'uscia segreto.*)

**WALTER AND WURM:** (*Observing the joy that irradiates the face of the Duchess*) The light of joy now sparkles in her eyes,
Dame Fortune smiles most kindly on our plans.—
Let us retain the fickle queen—nor lose her from our grasp.
(*The Duchess retires, followed by Walter, Louisa and Wurm by the secret door.*)

## SCENA VII.

*Giardino pensile del castello: porta nel fondo che mette agli appartamenti di Rodolfo. Rodolfo viene precipitoso da un appartamento; ha il foglio di Luisa tra le mani, lo segue un Contadino.*

**RODOLFO:** Il foglio dunque?

**CON.:** Io tutto
Già vi narrai.

**RODOLFO:** Mi giova
Udirlo ancor.

**CON.:** Segreta e viva prece
A man giunte mi fece
Luisa, onde recarlo
A Wurm—

**RODOLFO:** E d'evitar la mia presenza—

**CON.:** Mi ripetè più volte.
Sospetto incerto di non so qual trama,
E speme di mercede
A voi m'han tratto.

**RODOLFO:** (*Gettandogli una borsa.*)
Esci (*il Contadino si ritira.*) Olà!
(*comparisce un servo.*)
Wurm (*il servo parte.*) Oh! fede
Negar potessi agli occhi miei—Se cielo
E terra, se mortali
Ed angeli attestarmi
Volesser ch' ella non è rea—mentite—
Io risponder dovrei—tutti mentite—
Son cifre sue!—(*mostrando il foglio.*) Tanta perfidia!—un'alma
Sì nera! sì mendace!—
Ben la conobbe il padre!—Io cieco, audace
Osai!—Ma dunque i giuri,
Le speranze la gioja,
Le lagrime, l' affanno?—
Tutto menzogna tradimento, ingan-

## SCENE VII.

*A hanging Garden in the chateau; a door at the back leading to the apartments of Rodolphe. Rodolphe enters from the chamber. He has the note of Louisa in his hand. A peasant follows him.*

**RODOLPHE:** This note then—speak!

**PEASANT:** I have told you.

**RODOLPHE:** I would hear it again!

**PEASANT:** Louisa begged me, with clasped hands and imploring looks,
To carry this note to Wurm, quickly and in secret.

**RODOLPHE:** And to avoid me?

**PEASANT:** She repeated her wish several times,
But the suspicion of an intrigue and the hope of a recompense,
Caused me to bring it to you at once.

**RODOLPHE:** (*Throwing him a purse*) Go! (*The peasant retires.*)
Can I believe my eyes!
If Heaven, earth, and man combine to prove it,
I will still say—she is not guilty!
But—this is her writing!—can such perfidy exist?
(*Pointing to her note.*) A heart so black, so deceitful!
My father knew her best—and I, blind, audacious, I dared!—
But then her vows—the hopes—the joy—the tears!
All an illusion, all—all! Betrayed! deceived!
When at twilight's lonely hour,
Beneath the calm and gentle light of the holy stars,
When stillness reigned supreme over all around,
She raised her eyes to mine, beam-

no!—
Quando le sene, al placido
Charor d'un ciel stellato,
Meco figgea nell'etere
Le sguardo innamorato,
E questa mano stringermi
Dalla sua man sentia—
Ah!—mi tradia!—
Ailor, ch'io muto, estatico
Da' labbri suoi pendea.
Ed ella in suono angelico
—Amo te sol—dicca,
Tal che sembrò l'Empireo
Aprirsi all' alma mia!—
Ah!—mi tradia!

ing with love, almost divine.
Her small hand trembled at my touch—
But at that moment she was false!
And even, when her lips were pressed to mine in mute ecstasy,
And with angelic voice she whispered low—"I love you alone."
It seemed that all of Heaven's joys were mine;
But even then, O breaking heart! O ruined hopes!
That voice—those lips were false—false—perjured!
The light has fled from Heaven, and night's darkness
Has sunk into my soul. All is blank and hopeless.

## SCENA VIII.

*Wurm, e Detto.*

**WURM:** Di me chiedeste?

**RODOLFO:** Appressati.—
Leggi. (*Gli porge il foglio: quando Wurm ha finito di leggere lo riprende.*)
Ad entrambi è questa
Ora di morte.

**WURM:** (Oh!–)

**RODOLFO:** Scegliere
Tu dei.
(*Presentandogli due pistole.*)

**WURM:** Signor!—
(*Cercando allontanarsi.*)

**RODOLFO:** T'arresta—
(*Ponendogli fra mani una delle armi.*)
Meco ad un punto solo
Spento cadere al suolo
T'è forza—
(*Inarcando la pistola.*)

**WURM:** (Inferno, ajutami—)
(*Fa qualche celere passo verso il fondo, e scarica la pistola in aria.*)

## SCENE VIII.

*Enter Wurm.*

**WURM:** I await your pleasure.

**RODOLPHE:** Come nearer—read.
(*He gives him the note. When Wurm has read it he takes it again.*)
This hour is the hour of death for both of us.

**WURM:** Ah!—

**RODOLPHE:** Take your choice.
(*He hands him two pistols.*)

**WURM:** (*Stepping back*) My Lord!

**RODOLPHE:** (*Taking one of the pistols in his hand*) Stop there.
You shall fall dead at the same moment that I fall,
We will leave this earth together!

**WURM:** Powers of darkness come to my aid!
(*He makes some steps backwards, and fires in the air.*)

## SCENA IX.

*Accorrono d' ogni parte Armigeri e Familiari, quindi Walter.*

**CORO:** Che avvenne?—O ciel!

**RODOLFO:** Codardo!—
(*Wurm, confendendosi fra isopravvenuti, sparisce.*)
L'ali ha viltade!

**CORO:** Orribile
D'ira vi splende il guardo!—

**WALTER:** Rodolfo!—

**RODOLFO:** Padre!—

**WALTER:** Oh Dio!
Calmati—

**RODOLFO:** Ah! padre mio!—
(*Cade a' suoi piedi.*)

**WALTER:** Deh! sorgi—M'odi—
Abbomino
Il mio rigor crudele—
Abbia virtude un premio—

## SCENE IX.

*Enter men-at-arms running in all directions; then Walter.*

**CHORUS:** What noise is this?

**RODOLPHE:** Coward!
(*Wurm mingles with the crowd that has just entered, and disappears.*)

**CHORUS:** His eyes dart forth rays of anger!

**WALTER:** Rodolphe!

**RODOLPHE:** My father!

**WALTER:** O Heaven! calm yourself.

**RODOLPHE:** O my father.
(*Falls at his feet*)

**WALTER:** Arise! arise, my son! listen to me.
I regret—I repent me of my cruel resolve,

Cedo: alla tua fedele
Porgi la man—

**RODOLFO:** Che ascolto!
Tu vuoi?—

**WALTER:** Gioisci!—

**RODOLFO:** Ah! stolto
Io diverro!—
(*S'aggira disperato per la scena.*)

**CORO:** Quai smanie!—

**WALTER:** Figlio!—Nè pago sei?

**RODOLFO:** Pago?—

**WALTER:** Sperai—

**RODOLFO:** Compiangimi!—
Tradito m' ha colei!

**WALTER:** Tradito!—

**RODOLFO:** A me t'affretta,
O morte!

**WALTER:** No—vendetta!

**RODOLFO:** Come?

**WALTER:** Altre nozze attestino
Il tuo disprezzo ad essa.

**RODOLFO:** Che intendi?

**WALTER:** All' ara pronuba
Conduci la Duchessa.

**RODOLFO:** Io?—si, lo va'—Lo
deggio—
Che parlo?–Ahimè, vaneggio!—

**WALTER:** Rodolfo, non pentirti—

**RODOLFO:** Ove mi sia non so!—

**WALTER:** T'arrendi a me—tradirti
padre tuo no può—

**RODOLFO:** L'ara o l'avello appres-
tami
Al fato io m'abbandono—
Non temo—non desidero—
Un disperato io sono!—
Or la mia brama volgere
Nemmeno al ciel potrei,
Chè inferno senza lei
Sarebbe il ciel per me!

**WALTER:** Quell' empio cor di-
mentica.
Quell' alma ingannatrice—
Che un dì sarai felice
Promette il padre a te.

**CORO:** Del genitor propizio
Al senno v' affidate—
Nell' avvenir sperate;
Eterno il duol non è.
(*Walter seco tragge Rodolfo: tutti
li seguono.*)

*FINE DELL' ATTO SECONDO.*

Virtue should have some recompense.
I yield. Give your hand to your
faithful love!

**RODOLPHE:** What do I hear?—
you will—

**WALTER:** I will make you happy.

**RODOLPHE:** Ah! too late—too
late! I shall lose my senses!
(*Walks agitatedly across the
stage*)

**CHORUS:** What folly!—

**WALTER:** My son, are you not happy?—

**RODOLPHE:** Happy! happy!—

**WALTER:** Do you doubt your success?—

**RODOLPHE:** Pity me! She has deceived me.

**WALTER:** Deceived you?—

**RODOLPHE:** O death—come to
my aid!—

**WALTER:** No—call rather on vengeance.

**RODOLPHE:** How?—what do you
mean?—

**WALTER:** Another marriage!—
That will prove your contempt for
her desertion.

**RODOLPHE:** What are you saying?

**WALTER:** Conduct the Duchess to
the altar.

**RODOLPHE:** Me?—yes—I should
do so—I will!—
Ah me! what have I said? Alas!—I
am mad!

**WALTER:** Retract not—falter
not—where is your pride?

**RODOLPHE:** I don't know where I
am!—

**WALTER:** Have confidence in me;
Your father will not betray you.

**RODOLPHE:** Prepare the altar—or
the tomb.
I abandon myself to my fate—I utterly despair:
I have neither fear nor desire.

**WALTER:** Forget that false heart—
that deceitful soul!
You shall be happy—your father
promises.

**CHORUS:** Confide in your father's
love.
There is no grief that cannot have an
end.
(*Walter leads Rodolphe off. All follow.*)

*END OF ACT II.*

# ■ ATTO TERZO.

*IL VELENO.*

*La casa di Miller: la finestra è
aperta, ed a traverso di essa vedesi
il Tempio internamente illuminato.*

## SCENA PRIMA.

*Luisa scrive presso una tavola, su
cui arde una lampada: havvi sulla tavola medesima un cesto con
frutta, ed una lazza colma di
latte: in un canto della stanza
Laura ed altre Paesane, che mestamente contemplano Luisa.*

**LAURA, e CORO:** (*fra loro.*) Come
in un giorno solo,
Come ha potuto il duolo
Stampar su quella fronte
Così funeste impronte?
Sembra mietuto giglio
Da vomere crudel
Un angiol, che in esiglio
Quaggiù mandava il ciel!

**LAURA:** (*Accostandosi a Luisa.*)
O dolce amica, e ristorar non vuoi
Di qualche cibo le afflitte mem-
bra?

**LUISA:** No—

**CON.:** Cedi—all' amistà cedi, Luisa—

**LUISA:** La ripugnanza mia (*Sorgen-
do.*)
Rispettate—lo imploro. (A questo
labbro
Più non s'appresserà terreno cibo!
Gia col pensier delibo
Le celesti dolcezze!)—
(*Lo sguardo di lei ricorre involon-
tariamente a Tempio.*)
Il tempio, amiche,
Perchè splend cosi?
(*Le contadine confuse guardansi
l'un l'altra.*) Tacete?

**CON.:** Ignare?
Siam—

**LAURA:** La novella Signoria con
pompa
Sacre inaugura il Conte.
(*Luisa torna a scrivere.*)
Ah! l'infelice ignori
(*Sommessamente alla com-
pagne.*)
Qual rito nuzial s' appresta, e quale
Esser lo sposo debbe!
A sì crudele annunzio ella mor-
rebbe!

**CON., LAU.:** Sembra mietuto giglio
Da vomere crudel.
Un angiol che in esiglio
Quaggiù mandava il ciel!

# ■ ACT III.

*POISON.*

*The house of Miller. Through the
open window is seen the village
church lighted up.*

## SCENE I.

*(Louisa discovered writing at a
table, on which there is a lighted
lamp. On the same table are a basket of fruit and a cup of milk. In a
corner of the room stand Laura
and other peasants, gazing sadly
at Louisa.)*

**LAURA AND PEASANTS:** Behold
how but a single day,
Grief has left its sad imprint on her
young brow!
She resembles some fair lily over
which the sharp plough has passed,
Or an angel who, from exile, has
been called again to Heaven!

**LAURA:** (*Approaching Louisa*)
Say, dearest friend,
Will you not, for our sakes, take
some food
To restore your wasted strength?

**LOUISA:** No!—thanks—but,
no!—

**LAURA:** Yield, O yield to entreaty
of friendship, Louisa.

**LOUISA:** Respect my grief, I pray
you; (*Rises*)
These lips shall never more taste
earthly aliment.
Already through hope I seem to
taste celestial joys.
(*Her eyes turn involuntarily
towards the church.*)
Dear friends, I pray you tell me,
Why the church is lighted in this
manner?
(*The peasants whisper and look at
each other.*)
You are silent.

**CHORUS:** We do not know!

**LAURA:** The title of the new Count
is inaugurated this night
With solemn pomp.
(*Louisa turns again to the table
and recommences writing.*)
Ah, poor unfortunate! she does not
know that
It is a nuptial fête—nor who the
bride.
She would die at the sad news.

**CHORUS:** She resembles some fair
lily, over which the plough has
passed,
Or an Angel who, from exile, has
been called again to Heaven.

# Act III, Scene II

## SCENA II.

*Miller e Dette.*

**MILLER:** —Luisa!—figlia mia!
(*Luisa gettasi nelle sue braccia.*)

**LUISA:** Quel casto amplesso
Deh! non turbiam—sia testimon soltanto
Tra figlia e padre Iddio.
(*Si ritira con le compagne.*)

**MILLER:** —Pallida—mesta sei—

**LUISA:** No, padre mio,
Tranquilla io son.

**MILLER:** Del genitore, oh! quanto
Caro lo scampo a te costava!—Io tutta
Da Wurm appresi.

**LUISA:** Tutto!

**MILLER:** All' amor tuo,
Per me rinunziasti.

**LUISA:** È ver. (Ma in terra!)
(*Va lentamente verso la tavola.*)

**MILLER:** (Quella calma è funesta!—Il cor mi serra
Non so qual rio presagio!—)
(*Luisa, che intanto ha piegato il foglio, ritorna presso Miller.*) Che foglio è questo?

**LUISA:** Al suo destin prometti,
Se m' ami, o padre, che recato ei fia.

**MILLER:** (*Guarda fissamente Luisa, poi schiude il foglio, e legge.*)
Orribil tradimento
Ne desgiunse o Rodolfo—un giuramento
Più dir mi toglie—Havvi dimora, in cui
Nè inganno può nè giuro
Aver possanzo alcuna—ivi t' aspetto—
Come di mezzanotte udrai la squilla
Vieni—
(*Gli cade il foglio di mano.*)
Sotto al mio piede il suol vacilla!—
(*Resta un momento trambasciato e silenzioso, indivolgesi a Luisa con voce tremula.*)
Quella dimora—Mancar mi sento!
Quella dimora saria!—

**LUISA:** La tomba.
(*Miller inorridisce.*)
Perchè t' invade sà gran spavento?

**MILLER:** Ah!—sul mio capo un fulmin piomba!

**LUISA:** La tomba è un letto sparso di fiori,
In cui del giusto la spoglia dorme,
Sol pei colpevoli tremanti cori
Veste la morte orride forme:
Ma per due candide alme fedeli
La sua presenza non ha terror—
È dessa un angelo che schiude i cieli,
Ove in eterno sorride amor!

**MILLER:** Figlia?—Compreso d' orrore in sono!
Figlia—e potresti—contro—te stessa?
Pel suicida non viè perdon!

**LUISA:** E colpa amore?

**MILLER:** Cessa—Deh! cessa—
(*Si allontana raccapricciato, e cade sopra una sedia: quindi prorompe in lagrime, sorge e stretta la figlia per manole dicecon parole volte dal singhiezzo.*)
Di rughe il volto—mira—ho solcato—
Il crin m' imbianca l' eta più greve
L' amor che un padre ha seminato
Ne' suoi tardi anni raccoglier deve—
Ed apprestarmi crudel tu puoi
Messe di pianto e di dolor?—
Ah! nella tomba che schiuder vuoi
Fia primo a scendere il genitor!

**LUISA:** Ah! no—ti calma, o padre mio—
Quanto colpevole, ahimè, son io!—
Non pianger—m' odi—

**MILLER:** Luisa—

**LUISA:** Il foglio
Lacero—annullo—
(*Facendolo in pezzi.*)

**MILLER:** Vuoi dunque?—

**LUISA:** Io voglio
Per te, buon padre, restare in vita—

**MILLER:** Fia ver?—

**LUISA:** La figlia, vedi, pentita
Al piè ti cade—

**MILLER:** No, figlia mia—
Sorgi—deh! sorgi—Qui, sul mio cor—
(*La rialza, e se la stringe al seno con tutta l'effusione della tenerezza paterna.*)

**a 2:** In questo amplesso l'anima obblia
Quanti martiri provò finor!—

**LUISA:** Però fuggiamo—quì rio periglio
Mi cingerebbe—

**MILLER:** Sano consiglio!—

**LUISA:** I lumi al sonno chiudi brev' ora—
Ancor lontano è troppo il dì.
Come s'appressi la nuova aurora
Noi partiremo.

---

## SCENE II.

*Enter Miller.*

**MILLER:** Louisa! my child!
(*Louisa throws herself into his arms.*)

**LAURA:** Ah! how tender this meeting! Let us leave them,
Heaven alone should be the witness
Of such joy and such affliction.
(*Villagers retire.*)

**MILLER:** My child, you are pale and sad!

**LOUISA:** No, dear father—I am calm.

**MILLER:** O, how dear has my safety cost you!
I have heard all from Wurm!

**LOUISA:** All?

**MILLER:** You have renounced your love for me?

**LOUISA:** It is true, (*Aside*) but only on this earth!
(*She moves slowly towards the table.*)

**MILLER:** This calmness is terrible! Some melancholy foreboding oppresses my heart.
(*Louisa, who has been folding a paper, returns towards Miller.*)
What is this letter?

**LOUISA:** O! promise me, my father, if you love me,
That this letter shall reach its destination.

**MILLER:** (*Gazing fixedly at Louisa, then opening the letter, he reads.*)
"O Rodolphe! do not believe this horrible deception.
An oath prevents me from saying more. There is a home
where neither intrigues nor oaths have power. There I
await you. When you shall hear the clock strike the
hour of midnight, come!"
(*The paper falls from his hands.*)
The earth rocks beneath my feet!
(*He pauses for a moment, then turning to Louisa, asks in a trembling voice*)
What home?—my senses fail me! Where is this home?

**LOUISA:** The tomb!
Why so frightened, my father?

**MILLER:** Ah! the thunderbolt falls on my head?

**LOUISA:** The tomb is a bed strewn with flowers,
On which sweetly sleep those wronged and deceived!
It is only for those whose hearts are lost in crime,
That the tomb wears an aspect dark and terrible!
But for two tender and loving hearts
Its contemplation is without horror.
It is as an angel opening to our view the heavens,
Which smile on our eternal love and peace!

**MILLER:** My child, I am stupefied with terror!
My daughter—you cannot raise your hand against yourself!
There is no pardon for the suicide!

**LOUISA:** The fault is love!—life without love were valueless!

**MILLER:** Cease! Cease!
(*He turns sorrowfully away and throws himself upon a chair. The old man, weeping bitterly, rises, and taking his daughter by the hand, speaks with a voice choked by sobs.*)
Look at me—my face is full of wrinkles—age has blanched my hair!
The love that a father bestows upon his child,
Should be returned to him, in his old and helpless age!
But you, O cruel one, prepare for me
A harvest of tears and griefs. Ungrateful child!
Your father will be the first to descend to that tomb
You have prepared for him!

**LOUISA:** Ah! no—calm yourself my father! Listen to me!—
How culpable I have been, alas!—weep no more—

**MILLER:** Louisa!—

**LOUISA:** Thus I destroy the letter—
(*She tears it in pieces.*)

**MILLER:** You will then?—

**LOUISA:** I will live—I will save this life for you, my father!—

**MILLER:** Is it true—do I hear aright!—

**LOUISA:** See your repentant child—I kneel at your feet.

**MILLER:** No my child—rise! rise!—here, here on my heart!
(*He raises her, and clasps her to his bosom with paternal affection.*)

**MILLER AND LOUISA:** In this emotion our souls forget their griefs!—

**LOUISA:** Let us fly—there is danger here for me!—

**MILLER:** Your resolve is good, my child!—

**LOUISA:** Dear father, take some rest. It will be long before the day breaks.
When the morning dawns we will away!—

MILLER: Sì, figlia, sì.
(*Avviasi alla sua stanza, poscia ritorna, ed abbraccia ancora una volta la figlia.*)

a 2: Andrem, raminghi e poveri,
Ove il destin ci porta—
Un pan chiedendo agli nomini
Andrem di porta in porta—
Forse talor le ciglia
Noi bagnerem di pianto,
Ma sempre al padre accanto
La figlia sua starà!—
Quel padre e quella figlia
Iddio benedirà!
(*Miller entra nelle sue stanze.*)

LUISA: (*S'avvia lentamente all' opposto lato, quando la sua attenzione è richiamata dai sarri accordi che partono, dal Tempio.*)
Ah! l'ultima preghiera
In questo caro suol dove felice
Trassi la vita!—e dove
—T'amo—ei mi disse!—Altrove
Domani pregherò!
(*Inginocchiasi. Intanto ch'ella è tutta immersa in tacita preghiera, un uomo avvolto in lungo mantello si è fermato sulla porta; un famigliare lo segue.*)

## SCENA III.

RODOLFO: (*Sommessamente.*)
Riedi al castello,
E sappia il padre mio che presto il rito,
Io qui l'attendo.
(*Il servo dileguasi.*)
(*Prega!
Ben di pregare è tempo.*)
(*Si trae dal seno un'ampolla, e ne versa il liquore nella tazza. Luisa sorge, e vistosi Rodolfo dinanzi trasalisce.*)
Hai tu vergato questo foglio?
(*Spiegandole sott' occhio la lettera scritta a Wurm: Luisa non puo rispondere.*)
Ebbene?
L'hai—tu—vergato?
(*Nel ripetere la domanda egli trema in tutta la persona, qual chi aspetta la sentenza di vita o di morte.*)

LUISA: (*Con lo sforzo d'un morente che profferisce l'ultima parola.*) Sì!

RODOLFO: (*Cadendo su d'un seggio.*) M'arde le vene—
Le fauci—orrido foco—Una bevanda—
(*Accenna verso la coppa: Luisa la porge ad esso.*)
Amaro è questo nappo.
(*Dopo aver bevuto.*)

LUISA: Amaro?

MILLER: Yes, my child, yes.
(*He turns toward his chamber, but returns again and embraces his daughter.*)

BOTH: We will go, pure and fugitive, wherever destiny may lead!
We will go and beg our way from door to door.
Although our eyes may again be bathed in tears,
The father and child will separate no more.
And you, O Lord, will bless and aid them!
(*Miller goes to his chamber. Louisa goes to the other side, when her attention is drawn to the sounds of sacred music which come from the church.*)

LOUISA: Ah! It is my last prayer on this cherished spot.
Here, where my life has passed so peacefully away;
Where one loved voice has breathed the words—"I love!"
Tomorrow, far away, I shall pray amidst strangers.
(*She kneels. While she is absorbed in a silent prayer, a man enveloped in a cloak pauses at the door. He is followed by a servant.*)

## SCENE III.

RODOLPHE: (*Speaking softly*)
Return to the chateau.
Say to my father all is ready for the ceremony.
I await him here.
(*The servant retires.*)
She prays. It is the time to pray.
(*He takes a phial from his pocket, and pours some of the liquid into the cup on the table. Louisa rises; seeing Rodolphe, she trembles*)
Did you write these words?
(*He places the letter Louisa wrote to Wurm before her eyes. Louisa is unable to reply.*)
Speak! did you write it!

LOUISA: (*Gasping, and in agony, feebly utters—*) Yes!

RODOLPHE: (*Falling on a chair*)
My blood seems on fire!
My throat is parched. That cup—
(*Louisa gives him the cup.*)
This drink is bitter!

LOUISA: Bitter?

RODOLFO: Bevi.
(*Luisa beve: esso impallidisce, e volge altrove lo sguardo.*)
(Tutto è compinto!)

LUISA: No—
(*Silenzio terribile.*)

RODOLFO: Fuggir tu devi—
Altr' uomo attende per seguirti: attende
Per seguirmi agli altari
Altra donna—

LUISA: Che parli?—Ah dunque!

RODOLFO: Invano
Attendon essi!
(*Percorre a gran passi la stanza, si strappa la sciarpa e la spada, e la getta lungi da se.*)
Addio
Spada su cui difender l'innocente,
E l'oppresso giurai!

LUISA: O giusto ciel! Che hai?

RODOLFO: Mi—si ebiude—il—respir!

LUISA: Deh! qualche stilla
Ne suggi ancor—ti lia
Ristoro—(*Volendo nuovamente offrir gli la tazza.*)

RODOLFO: Ah! quel che m' offre
Par che sappia l'infame!

LUISA: Rodolfo, e puoi scagliar sì rea parola
Contro la tua Luisa?

RODOLFO: Oh! lungi, lungi
Da me quel volto lusinghier—
quegli occhi
In cui spiende degli astri
Raggio più vivo e terso—
Fattor dell' universo.
Perchè vestir d'angeliche sembianze
Un' anima d' inferno?

LUISA: E tacer deggio?
Deggio?

RODOLFO: T' arretra—in questi
Angosciosi momenti
Pietade almen d' un infelice, ah!
senti!
(*Prorompendo in lagrime.*)

LUISA: Piangi, piangi—il tuo dolore
Più dell' ira è giusto, ahi quanto!
Oh! discenda sul tuo core
Come balsama quel pianto—
Se concesso al prego mio
E d' alzarsi fino a Dio,
Otterò che men funesto
De' tuoi mali sia l' orror.

RODOLFO: Allo strazio ch' io sopporto
Dio mi lascia in abbandono—
No, di calma, di conforto
Queste lagrime non sono—
Son le stille, il gel che piomba
Dalla volta d' una tomba!
Goccie son di vivo sangue
Che morendo sparge il cor.
(*L' orinolo del castello batte te ore. Rodolfo stringe Luisa per*

RODOLPHE: Taste!
(*Louisa drinks. Rodolphe turns pale and looks away.*)
All is accomplished.
(*Aside*)

LOUISA: No.
(*A long and terrible silence*)

RODOLPHE: You should fly! Another awaits you—
Another bride also awaits me at the altar!

LOUISA: Ah! what say you? You!

RODOLPHE: They wait in vain.
(*Paces the chamber with hasty strides, and throws his sword and scarf away from him*)
Farewell sword, with which I have sworn
To defend the innocent and the oppressed.

LOUISA: Great Heaven! Rodolphe! what did you do?

RODOLPHE: My breath fails me!

LOUISA: (*Offering him again the cup.*) A few drops still remain.
Drink—it will recover you.

RODOLPHE: Ah! It would seem the perjured one knows what she offers!

LOUISA: Rodolphe, can you speak such cruel words to me?

RODOLPHE: O lovely vision—depart from me. Those eyes
In which burns a light more clear and pure than the stars!
How can a form so lovely cover a demon's heart!

LOUISA: And must I still be silent?

RODOLPHE: Retire. In this sorrowful moment,
At least, have pity on an unfortunate being!

LOUISA: Weep—weep—your grief is more than just the anger!
O may these tears descend as a balm upon your heart.
Could my prayers reach to Heaven,
They would loosen the bandage which now covers your eyes!

RODOLPHE: Heaven has abandoned me to my grief—I bear it unsupported!
These are not the tears of calm and resolution—
They are the dews of death—as the blood
Which gushes out from a dying heart!
(*The clock of the Chateau strikes the hour. Rodolphe takes Louisa*

# Act III, Scene III

mano.)
Donna, per noi terribile
Ora squillò!—suprema!

LUISA: Rodolfo!

RODOLFO: Nel mendacio
Che non ti colga, oh trema:
—Amasti Wurm?

LUISA: Oh! calmati—

RODOLFO: Guai, se mentisci!—guai!—
Prima che questa lampada
Si spenga, tu starai
Dinanzi a Dio!

LUISA: Che! spiegati!
Parla—

RODOLFO: Con me bevesti
La morte.
(*Additando la coppa: Luisa accenna di cadere, egli la pone sovra un seggio.*)
Al ciel rivolgiti
Luisa—

LUISA: (*Depo qualche momento sorge come animata da un pensiero.*) Tu dicesti
La morte? Ah! d' ogni vincolo
Sciolta per lei son io!
Il ver disvelo—apprendilo—
Moro innocente!

RODOLFO: (*Con ispavento.*) Oh Dio!

LUISA: Avean mio padre i barbar
Avvinto fra ritorte—
Ed io—

RODOLFO: Finisci.

LUISA: Io, misera—
Onde sottrarlo a morte—
Come quel mostro—Intendimi—
Wurm imponeva a me—
Il foglio scrissi.

RODOLFO: Oh fulmine!
Ed io t' uccisi!

LUISA: Ahimè!

RODOLFO: (*Cacciandosi le mani fra' capelli, e col grido terribile della disperazione.*) Maledetto il dì ch' io nacqui—
Il mio sangue—il padre mio—
Fui creato, avverso Iddio,
Nel tremendo tuo furor!

LUISA: Per l'istante in cuì ti piacqui—
Per la morteche s' appressa,
D' oltraggiar l' Eterno, ah! cessa—
Mi risparmia un tanto orror—

## SCENA IV.

*Miller, e Detti.*

---

by the hand.)
Louisa! this is a terrible hour—it is the last hour
That intervenes between us and eternity!

LOUISA: Rodolphe!

RODOLPHE: Be sure that this last hour does not surprise you
In a falsehood! Have you loved Wurm?

LOUISA: O calm yourself!

RODOLPHE: Eternal misery to you
If you speak falsely! For before that lamp goes out
You will be in the presence of your Maker!

LOUISA: What? speak again!

RODOLPHE: You have drunk your death draught—
With me, Louisa!
(*He shows her the cup—Louisa is nearly fainting with emotion—he places her in a chair.*)
Turn your thoughts toward Heaven, Louisa!

LOUISA: (*Rising, animated by a sudden thought*) You have said that death is near—ah!
That will loose the chain from my lips—
And I will reveal to you the truth.
Rodolphe! Rodolphe! I die innocent!

RODOLPHE: (*Terrified*) Great Heaven!

LOUISA: The barbarous men put my father into prison
And to save his life—

RODOLPHE: Go on! I am prepared!

LOUISA: I, miserable, to save him from death—
Acted as this monster—understand me—
As Wurm ordered me to act—I wrote the note as he dictated!

RODOLPHE: O, desolation!—and I have murdered you!

LOUISA: Alas!

RODOLPHE: (*Letting his head fall into his hands, with a terrible cry of despair*) Cursed be the day on which I was born!
Cursed be my blood and that of my father!
In a moment of your anger, Lord, was I created!

LOUISA: Hold, Rodolphe! hold!
By the happy hours we have spent together;
By the death which is rapidly approaching?
Cease to outrage the Eternal!
Spare me at least this horror.

## SCENE IV.

*Enter Miller.*

---

MILLER: Quai grida intesi!—Chi veggo, oh cielo!

RODOLFO: Chi? L'assassino, misero, vedi
Del sangue tuo!

MILLER: Che disse?—Io gelo!—

LUISA: Padre!—

MILLER: Luisa!—

RODOLFO: Ma voglio a' piedi
Colui svenarti—
(*Raccogliendo la spada.*)

LUISA: Rodolfo—arresta—
Già mi serpeggia—la morte—in sen—
(*Rodolfo getta la spada sulla tavola, e corre a Luisa.*)

MILLER: La morte! Ah!—dite—

RODOLFO: Scampo non resta—
Un velen bevve!

MILLER: Figlia! Un velen!—
(*Cólto da quell' ambascia che non ha parola, si slancia verso la figlia, che annoda le braccia al collo paterno.*)

LUISA: Padre—ricevi l' estremo—addio—
Mi benedici—o padre mio—
La man, Rodolfo—sento mancarmi—
Più non ti scerno—mi cinge un vel.
Ah! vieni meco! Ah! non lasciarmi—
Insieme accogliere—ne deve—il ciel—

RODOLFO: Ah! tu perdona il fallo mio,
E perdonato sarà da Dio—
Ambo congiunge un sol destino—
Me pure investe di morte il gel—
Sì, teco io vengo, spirto divino—
Insieme accogliere ne deve il ciel.

MILLER: O figlia, o vita del cor paterno,
Ci separiamo dunque in eterno?—
Di mia vecchiezza promesso incanto,
Sogno tu fosti, sogno crudel!
Non è più mio quest' angiol santo—
Me lo rapisce invido il ciel!
(*Luisa muore.*)

## SCENE V.

*Tutti gli altri Personaggi, e Detti.*

VOCI CONFUSE: Profondi gemiti fra queste porte!—
(*Di dentro.*)
Che avvenne?

WALTER: (*Che si è inoltrato per il primo.*) Spenta!—

---

MILLER: What cry was that I heard—whom do I see?

RODOLPHE: Who? The assassin of your child?

MILLER: What are you saying? I freeze with horror.

LOUISA: My father!

MILLER: Louisa!

RODOLPHE: But I will expiate the crime—
I will die this moment at your feet.
(*Draws his sword*)

LOUISA: Rodolphe, stop—stop your hand—
Already I feel the calm of death stealing over me.
(*Rodolphe throws his sword on the table, and rushes to Louisa.*)

MILLER: Death!—explain—what do you mean?

RODOLPHE: There is no hope—she has drank poison.

MILLER: My child—poison!
(*He rests for a moment immovable, without speaking, then turns to his daughter. Louisa throws her arms around her father's neck.*)

LOUISA: My father! receive my last adieu!
Your blessing, Father—your hand, Rodolphe!
I feel myself dying—I can scarcely see you.
A mist is before my eyes—Ah! come to me!
Do not leave me! Heaven should receive us both together!

MILLER: O my child! life of my heart!
Must we part for ever!
Hope of my age, you have been to me as a dream
This angel, so pure, was sent to bless me—
But Heaven, jealous of my happiness, takes her again!

## SCENE V.

*Enter all the characters.*

CONFUSED VOICES: What do these sounds of woe mean—
What horrors do they portend?

WALTER: (*Who has entered in advance*) Death!

**DONNE:** Dio di pietà!—
(*Si fanno intorno al cadavere di Luisa, presso il quale è rimasto Miller in ginocchio, immoto e pallido più del cadavere istesso.*)

**RODOLFO:** (*Scorto Wurm, ch'è rimasto sulla soglia, afferra velocemente la spada, e lo trafigge.*) A te sia pena, empio, la morte—
(*A Walter.*) La pena tua—mira—
(*Cade morto accanto a Luisa.*)

**WOMEN:** Merciful Heaven!
(*They surround the body of Louisa, by which Miller is kneeling.*)

**RODOLPHE:** (*Perceiving Wurm, who is standing in the doorway, seizes his sword, rushes to him and kills him.*) Let death be your punishment, monster!
(*To Walter*) And yours—look!
(*Falls dead at the feet of Walter*)

**WALTER:** Figlio!
**TUTTI:** Ah!—

*FINE.*

**WALTER:** (*In agony*) My son!
**ALL:** Ah! horror!

*THE END.*

# *Rigoletto* (1851)

### Music by Giuseppe Verdi ■ Libretto by Francesco Maria Piave

Rigoletto was first performed at the Teatro La Fenice in Venice on March 11, 1851. This three-act opera is set to a libretto by Francesco Maria Piave (based on Victor Hugo's verse drama *Le Roi s'amuse*). No woman at the court of Mantua is safe from the libidinous duke. No husband is safe from the remarks of the duke's jester, the hunchbacked Rigoletto. Ceprano, husband of the duke's most recent paramour, is Rigoletto's current target. Count Monterone, who has been sentenced to death for complaining about the duke's ravishment of his daughter, curses Rigoletto. Marullo decides to play a joke on Rigoletto by kidnapping the young woman Rigoletto has locked up in his house, whom everyone thinks must be Rigoletto's mistress. She is, in fact, Rigoletto's daughter Gilda. The duke has already spotted her. Disguised as a student, he sneaks into the house and swears his love for her. Meanwhile, Sparafucile, a professional murderer, offers his services to Rigoletto. The courtiers kidnap Gilda, and Rigoletto, who thinks they are breaking into Ceprano's palace instead, assists them. Too late, he realizes he's been duped. The duke is thrilled to discover that Gilda is in his palace. The court mocks Rigoletto, who keeps his grief to himself and swears vengeance on the duke. Gilda, now a ruined woman, tries to stop him.

At a shady inn, Sparafucile and his sister, Maddalena, are discussing payment for her next victim. Gilda and Rigoletto watch as the duke arrives and makes his move on Maddalena. Gilda now agrees that he fully deserves his fate. She agrees to go to Verona, traveling as a young boy, and wait there for the duke to join her, thus leaving Mantua for good. Maddalena doesn't want to kill the duke. She decides to kill the next visitor instead. Gilda, in an attempt to save her lover, walks into the trap. Sparafucile mortally wounds her, shoving her body into a sack, which he gives to Rigoletto. Rigoletto hears the duke singing his song of love. Opening the sack, he discovers that the actual victim is not the duke, but his beloved daughter. He collapses over her lifeless body, fulfilling Monterone's curse.

---

## ■ ATTO I

### SCENA I

*Sala magnifica nel Palazzo Ducale. Il Duca e Borsa che vengono da una porta del fondo.*

DUCA: Della mia bella incognita borghese Toccare il fin del' avventura to voglio.

BORSA: Di quelli giovin che vedete al tempio?

DUCA: Da tre lune ogni festa.

BORSA: La sua dimora?

DUCA: In un remoto calle; Misterioso un uom v' entra ogni notte.

BORSA: E sa colei chi sia L' amante suo?

DUCA: Lo ighora.
(*Un gruppo di Dame e Cavalieri attraversan la sala.*)

BORSA: Quante beltà!—Mirate.

DUCA: Le vince tutte di Cepran la sposa.

## ■ ACT I

### SCENE I

*A Ball-room in the Ducal Palace. Ladies and Gentlemen, Pages and Servants, cross the scene. Music is heard at a distance, and now and then bursts of laughter. Enter the Duke and Borsa.*

DUKE: I am quite resolved to follow to the end My new adventure with this youthful lady.

BORSA: You mean the one you meet while going to church?

DUKE: Yes, in a lonely street, and every day she receives a visit from a dubious man.

BORSA: But does she know him?

DUKE: Yes, every Sunday for the last three months.

BORSA: Know you where she resides?

DUKE: No, I think not.
(*A group of Ladies and Gentlemen cross the scene.*)

BORSA: Behold those charming ladies.

DUKE: Yes, but Ceprano's wife outshines them all.

---

BORSA: Non v' oda il Conte, o Duca—
(*Piano.*)

DUCA: A me che importa?

BORSA: Dirlo ad altra ei potria—

DUCA: Nè sventura per me certo saria.
Questa o quella per me pari sono
A quant' altre d' intorno mi vedo,
Del mio core l'impero non cedo
Meglio ad una che ad altra beltà.
La costoro avvenza è qual dono
Di che il fato ne infiora la vita;
S' oggi quelta mi torna gradita,
Forse un' altra doman lo sarà,
La costanza tiranna del core
Detestiamo qual morbo crudele,
Sol chi vuole si serbi fedele;
Non v' ha amor, se non v' è libertà.
De' mariti il geloso furore,
Degli amanti le smanie derido,
Anco d' Argo i cent' oechi disfido
Se mi punge una qualche beltà.

### SCENA II

*Detti, il Conte di Ceprano, che segue da lungi la sua sposa seguita da altro Cavaliere. Dame e Signora entrano da varie parti.*

DUCA: (*Alla Signora di Cep., movendo ad incontrarla con molta galanteria.*) Partite? Crudele!

CEP: Seguire le sposo M' è forza a Ceprano.

BORSA: Ah! but mind her husband, Duke.

DUKE: What matters?

BORSA: It might be spread about.

DUKE: What then—no great misfortune.
Amongst the beauties here around,
Over me none have control;
None can say, "I am preferred;"
Equal love I feel for all.
Yes, all women are to me
Like the flowers of the field.
Now to this, I am inclined,
Now to that by chance I yield.
As one flies from a great peril,
So from constancy I fly;
Those who will, may faithful be,
In freedom only does love lie.
I despise a jealous husband,
And I laugh at lover's sighs—
If a beauty strikes my fancy,
I defy one hundred eyes.

### SCENE II

*Enter Count Ceprano, watching at a distance the Countess, who is followed by a Gentleman. Ladies and Lords cross the scene.*

DUKE: (*To the Countess, with great politeness.*) You go already, cruel one?

COUN: I must obey my husband, I am obliged to leave.

DUCA: Ma dee luminoso
In Corte tal astro qual sole brillar.
Per voi vuì ciascuno dovrà palpitar.
Per voi già possente la fiamma d'amore
Inebria, conquide, distrugge il mio core.
(*Con enfasi, baciandole la mano.*)

CEP: Calmatevi—

DUCA: No.
(*Le da il braccio ed esce con lei.*)

DUKE: But you must shine at Court,
As Venus amongst the stars—
Here all must sigh for you.
Already, behold here
A victim of your charms.

COUN: Ah! silence—

DUKE: No.
(*The Duke kisses her hand.*)

## SCENA III

*Detti e Rigoletto che s' incontra nel Signor di Ceprano; poi Cortigiani.*

RIG: In testa che avete,
Signor di Ceprano?
(*Ceprano fa un gesto d' impazienza e segue il Duca.*)

RIG: (*Ai Cortigiana.*) Ei sbuffa, vedete

CORO: Che festa!

RIG: Oh sì—

BORSA: Il duca quì pur si diverte/

RIG: Così non è sempre? Che nuove scorpete.
Il giuoco ed il vino, le feste, la danza
Battaglie, conviti, ben tutto gli sta.
Or della Contessa l' assedio egl avanza,
E intanto il marito fremendo ne va
(*Esce*)

## SCENE III

*Enter Rigoletto, who meets Count Ceprano and Courtiers.*

RIG: What troubles you, dear Count?
You seem in deepest thought.
(*The Count makes a sign of impatience, and follows the Duke.*)

RIG: (*To the Courtiers.*) The Count is furious! See.

CHO: A fine ball!

RIG: Indeed.

BORSA: And even the Duke enjoys the feast.

RIG: Is it not always so? What news is this?
Wine and feasting—dancing and games—
Battles and banquets—for him all's the same.
Now against the Countess he tries to lay the siege,
And cares not for the jealousy of her liege.
(*Exit.*)

## SCENA IV

*Detti e Marullo premuroso*

MAR: Gran nuova! gran nuova!

DUCA: Che avvenne i pariate

MAR: Stupir ne dovrete—

CORO: Narrate narrate

MAR: Ah! ah! Rigoletto—

CORO: Ebben?

MAR: Caso enorme!

CORO: Perduto ha la gobba? non è più difforme?

MAR: Più strana è la cosa! il pazzo possiede—

CORO: Infine?

MAR: Un amante—

CORO: Amante! Chi il crede?

MAR: Il gobbo in Cupido or s' è trasformato!

CORO: Quel mostro Cupido! Cupido beato!

## SCENE IV

*Enter Marullo, with great anxiety.*

MAR: Great news! fine news!

CHO: Quick, what has happened, say?

MAR: You will all be surprised.

CHO: Speak on, speak on.

MAR: Ah, ah! Rigoletto—

CHO: Well

MAR: Strange case.

CHO: What, has he lost his hump? Is he now straight?

MAR: More strange still, the foolish man possesses—

CHO: What? say—

MAR: A lover.

CHO: A lover! who could ever have thought of this?

MAR: The hump-back is transformed into a Cupid.

CHO: Oh, what a monstrous Cupid! charming Cupid!

## SCENA V

*Detti ed il Duca seguita da Rigoletto, indi Ceprano.*

DUCA: Ah, quanto Ceprano, importuno niun v' è!
(*A Rig.*)
La cara sua posà un angiol per me.

RIG: Rapitela.

DUCA: E detto! ma il farlo?

RIG: Stassera—

DUCA: Nè pensi tu al Conte?

RIG: Non c' è la prigione?

DUCA: Ah, no.

RIG: Ebben—s' esilia.

DUCA: Nemmeno, buffone.

RIG: Adunque la testa—
(*Indicando di farla togliere.*)

CEP: (Oh l' anima nera!)
(*Da se.*)

DUCA: Che di' questa testa?—
(*Battendo colla mano una spalla al Conte.*)

RIG: Che far di tal testa?—A cosa ella vale?

CEP: Marrano?
(*Infuriato battendo la spada.*)

DUCA: Fermate—
(*A Cep.*)

RIG: Da rider mi fa.

CORO: In furia è montato!
(*Tra loro.*)

DUCA: Buffone, vien quà.
(*A Rig.*)
A sempre tu spingi lo scherno all' estremo.
Quell' ira che sfidi colpir ti potrà.

RIG: Che coglier mi puote? Di lor non temo;
Del duca un protetto nessun toccherà.

CEP: Vendetta dal pazzo—
(*Ai Cortigiani, a parte.*)

CORO: Contr' esso un rancore
Pei trisisuoi modi, di noi chi non ha?

CEP: Vendetta!

CORO: Ma come?

CEP: Domani, chi ha core
Sia in armi da me.

TUTTI: Sì.

CEP: A notte.

TUTTI: Sarà.
(*La folla de' danzatori invade la sala.*)
Tutto è gioia, tutto è festa,
Tutto invitaci a goder!
Oh, guardate, non par questa
Or la reggia del piacer!

## SCENA VI

*Detti ed il Conte di Monterone.*

## SCENE V

*Enter the Duke, followed by Rigoletto, afterwards Ceprano.*

DUKE: No man can be more vexing than Ceprano.
His wife is a sweet angel.
(*To Rig.*)

RIG: Steal her away.

DUKE: 'Tis easier said than done.

RIG: This evening.

DUKE: You think not of the Count.

RIG: Have you no prisons?

DUKE: Ah! no.

RIG: Well, banish him.

DUKE: No, no, buffoon.

RIG: His head, then.
(*Making signs of having it cut off.*)

CEP: (Villain!)
(*Aside.*)

DUKE: What do you mean? this head?—
(*Tapping the Count on the shoulder.*)

RIG: Yes, what is it good for?
What can he do with it?

CEP: Miscreant!
(*Unsheathing his sword.*)

DUKE: Stop—stop.
(*To the count.*)

RIG: He makes me laugh.

CHO: He is frantic!
(*Among themselves.*)

DUKE: Now, buffoon, come here.
(*To Rig.*)
You carry your jokes too far,
His sword might reach your heart.

RIG: I fear him not. No one will dare to teach
The favorite of the Duke.

CEP: He must be punished.
(*Aside to the Courtiers.*)

CHO: And who has not some injuries
To avenge on him.

CEP: Revenge, revenge!

CHO: But how?

CEP: If you fear not, tomorrow
Come with your swords to me.

ALL: We will.

CEP: At night.

ALL: Decreed.
(*A crowd of dancers invade the scene.*)
To dance, to feast, to pleasure,
Here everything invite,
Look around, does this not seem
The palace of delight.

## SCENE VI

*Enter Count Monterone.*

## Act I, Scene VI

MON: Ch' io gli parli. (*Dall' interno.*)

DUCA: No.

MON: Il voglio. (*Entrando.*)

TUTTI: Monterone!

MON: (*fissando il Duca con nobile orgoglio.*) Si, Monteron—la voce mia qual tuono
Vi scuoterà dovunque—

RIG: (*al Duca, contraffacendo la voce di Mon.*) Ch' io gli parli. (*Si avanza con ridicola gravita.*)
Voi congiuraste contro noi, signore,
E noi, clementi in vero, perdonammo—
Qual vi piglia or delirio—atutt el'or
Di vostra figlia reclamar l' onere?

MON: (*guardando Rig. con ira sprezzante.*)
Novello insulto!—Ah sì, a turbare (*al Duca.*)
Sarò vostr' orgie—verrò a gridare,
Fino a che vegga restarsi insulto
Di mia famiglia l' atroce insulto;
E se al carnefice pur mi darete
Spettro terrible mi rivedrete,
Portante il mano il teschio mio,
Vendetta chiedere al mondo e Dio.

DUCA: Non più, arrestatelo.

RIG: E matto!

CORO: Quai detti!

MON: Oh siate entrambi voi maledetti. (*Al Duca e Rig.*)
Slanciare il cane al leon morente
E' vile, o duca—e tu serpente, (*a Rig.*)
Tu che d' un padre ridi al dolore,
Sii maledetto!

RIG: (*Che sento? orrore!*) (*Da se colpito.*)

TUTTI: (*meno Rig.*) Oh tu che la festa andace hai turbato,
Da un genio d' inferno qui fosti guidato;
E' vano ogni detto, quà t' allontana—
Va, trema, o vegliardo, dell' ira sovrana—
Tu l' hai provocata, plù speme non v' è.
Un' ora fatale questa per te.
(*Mon. parte fra due alabardieri; tutti gli altra seguono il Duca in altra, stanza.*)

### ATTO II

#### SCENA VII

L' estremita piu deserta d' una via cieca, Casa di Rigoletto e terazzo. Rigoletto chiuso nel suo mantello. Sparafucile lo segue portando sotto il mantello una lunga spada.

---

MON: (*from without*) I must see him.

DUKE: No, no.

MON: I will. (*Entering.*)

ALL: Monterone!

MON: (*looking at the Duke, with pride.*) Yes, Monterone.—My voice
For ever I will raise against your crimes.

RIG: (*to the Duke, counterfeiting Mon. 's voice.*) I must see him.
You have conspired against our name, my lord.
And we have granted pardon—
What madness now is yours? In this glad hour
To come and claim the honor of your daughter!

MON: (*looking at Rig. with contempt.*) A new insult! but your nefarious orgies
I will disturb. Here I will raise my voice
Until the honor of an injured family
Shall be restored.
And even if you were
To sign my death and send me to the block,
My shade will claim revenge!

DUKE: No more—arrest him.

RIG: He is mad!

CHO: He is mad!

MON: Be both for ever accursed. (*To Rig. and the Duke.*)
To strike the dying lion,
'Tis base—but you, reptile,
Who dares to laugh at an old father's grief
Malediction fall on you!

RIG: What do I hear!
Oh, terror! (*Aside*)

ALL, EXCEPT RIG: Rash man, your evil spirit
Has brought you to disturb this feast,
Your words are vain. Away!
The Duke's revenge you raise:
No hope for you remains,
This is your fatal day.
(*Mon. is lead away by the soldiers, the others follow the Duke.*)

### ACT II

#### SCENE VII

The end of a Street. House and Garden of Rigoletto, with flight of stairs. Enter Rigoletto enveloped in his cloak, and followed by Sparafucile, carrying a long sword.

---

RIG: (*Quel vecchio maledivami!*)

SPA: Signor?—

RIG: Va, non ho niente.

SPA: Nè il chiesi—a voi presente
Un uom di spada sta.

RIG: Un ladro?

SPA: Un uom che libera
Per poco da un rivale,
E voi ne avete—

RIG: Quale?

SPA: La vostra donna è là.

RIG: (*Che sento?*) E quanto spendere
Per un signor dovrei?

SPA: Prezzo maggior vorrei—

RIG: Com' usasi pagar?

SPA: Una metà as' anticipa,
Il resto si da poi—

RIG: (*Dimonio!*) E come puo
Tanto securo oprar?

SPA: Soglio in cittade uccidere,
Oppure nel mio tetto.
L' uomo di sera aspetto—
Una stoccata, e muor.

RIG: E come in casa?

SPA: E facile—
M' aiuta mia sorella—
Per le vie danza—è bella—
Chi voglio attira—e allor—

RIG: Comprendo—

SPA: Senza strepito—
E' questo il mio stromento.
(*Mostra la spada.*)
Vi serve;

RIG: No—al momento—

SPA: Peggio ver voi—

RIG: Chi sa?

SPA: Sparafucile mi nomino—

RIG: Straniero?

SPA: Borgognone—(*Per andarsene.*)

RIG: E dove all' occasione?

SPA: Quì sempre a sera.

RIG: Va. (*Spa. parte.*)

#### SCENA IX

RIG: (*guardando dietro a Sparafucile*)
Pari siamo!—io la lingua, egli ha il pugnale;
L' uomo son io che ride, ei quel che spegne
Quel vecchio maledivami—
O uomini!—o natura!—
Vil scellerato mi faceste voi!—
Oh rabbia!—esser difforme!—un buffone!—
Non dover, non poter altro che ridere!—
Il retaggio d' ogni uom m' è tolto il pianto!—

---

RIG: (*That man has cursed me.*)

SPA: Sir?

RIG: Go: I need you not.

SPA: I have not spoken! Only I showed myself
There with my dagger, ready for your orders.

RIG: You are a thief.

SPA: A man,
That for a trifle will free you from enemies,
And you have one.

RIG: Who is he?

SPA: Is your mistress here?

RIG: (*What do I hear?*) How much have I to pay
To rid me of this man?

SPA: A little more.

RIG: And when must you be paid?

SPA: One half before the deed,
The other after.

RIG: (*O wretch!*) And how can you
Be sure of the success?

SPA: I kill them in the street,
Or even in my own house.
I await my man at night;
A single blow—he dies.

RIG: But how in your own house?

SPA: Nothing can be more easy,
My sister helps me.
She dances in the streets—she is handsome;
And she attracts the man I want—I then—

RIG: I understand!

SPA: Without the slightest noise,
This is my trusty weapon!
(*Shows his sword.*)
Can I serve you?

RIG: Not now.

SPA: The worse for you.

RIG: Perhaps another day.

SPA: Sparafucile I am called.

RIG: A foreigner?

SPA: From Burgundy. (*In the act of going away.*)

RIG: But where could I meet you?

SPA: At this spot, always at night.

RIG: Well, go. (*Spa. exit.*)

#### SCENE IX

RIG: (*looking after Sparafucile*)
My weapon is my tongue—and his the dagger;
I make the people laugh, he makes them mourn!
We are alike!—That man has cursed me!
Men and nature,
'Tis you that made me wicked;
O rage! to be deformed—and a buffoon!
To be condemned to laugh against my will:
To ask in vain the common gift—of tears!

Questo padrone mio,
Giovin, giocondo, sì possente, bel-
lo
Sonnecchiando mi dice;
Fa ch'io rida, buffone.
Forzarmi deggio, e farlo!—Oh,
dannazione!
Odio a voi, cortigiani schernito-
ri!—
Quanta in mordervi ho gioia!
Se iniquo so, per cagion vostra
solo—
Ma in altr'uom quì mi cangio!—
Quel vecchio maledivami!—Tal
pensiero
Perchè conturba ognor la mente
mia?—
Mi coglierà sventura? Ah no, follia.
(*Apre con chiave, ed entra nel cor-
tile*)
(*Detto e Gilda ch' esce dallo casa e
si getta nelle sue braccia.*)

**RIG:** Figlia—

**GILDA:** Mio padre!

**RIG:** A te dappresso
Trova sol gioia il core oppresso

**GILDA:** Oh quanto amore!

**RIG:** Mia vita sei!
Senza te in terra qual bene avrei?
(*Sospira*)

**GILDA:** Voi sospirate!—che v'
ange tanto?
Lo dite a questa povera figlia—
Se v' ha mistero—per lei sia fran-
to—
Ch' ella conosca la sua famiglia.

**RIG:** Tu non ne hai—

**GILDA:** Qual nome avete;

**RIG:** A te che importa?

**GILDA:** Se non volete
Di voi parlarmi—

**RIG:** Non usair mai. (*Interrompendola*)

**GILDA:** Non vo che al tempio.

**RIG:** Or ben tu fai.

**GILDA:** Se non di voi, almen chi sia
Fate ch' io sappia la madre mia.

**RIG:** Deh non parlare al misero
Del suo perduto bene—
Ella sentin' quell angelo,
Pietà delle mie pene—
Solo, difforme, povero
Per compassion mi amò.
Morìa—le zolle coprano
Lievi quel capo amato—
Sola or tu resti al misero—
O Dio, sii ringarziaro!—
(*Singhiozzande.*)

**GILDA:** Quanto dolor!—che
spremere
Si amaro pianto può?
Padre, non più, calmatevi—
Mi lacerta tal vista—
Il nome vostro ditemi,
Il duol che si v' attrista—

Alas! my master, young,
And full of mirth,
At every moment says,
Now make me laugh, buffoon.
I must do it. Oh! rage.
I hate you all, vile courtiers!
On you, therefore, my tongue de-
lights to dwell;
For you I am depraved—
But here I am not the same;
That man has cursed me! But why
does this thought
Haunt my mind?
What can I have to fear? No, it's
madness.
(*He opens and enters.*)
(*Enter Gilda from house and
throws herself in his arms.*)

**RIG:** My daughter!

**GILDA:** Father.

**RIG:** Near to you, alone,
My poor dejected heart returns to
joy.

**GILDA:** My father dear!

**RIG:** You are my only hope,
What else have I on earth except my
Gilda?

**GILDA:** You sigh! What is the cause
of your affliction?
Tell it to your poor daughter
Entrust me with your secrets,
And let me know my family

**RIG:** Ah! You have none!

**GILDA:** Your name

**RIG:** What does it matters to you?

**GILDA:** If you object to speak
Of our relations—

**RIG:** Do you ever leave this house?
(*Interrupting her.*)

**GILDA:** I only go to church.

**RIG:** That's right, my child.

**GILDA:** If you will not reveal your
name or rank,
Ah, let me know, at least, who my
mother is.

**RIG:** Ah, do not awake, I pray,
A memory so sad;
Of my dejected state
She alone had compassion,
Despised, deformed, and poor,
Through pity, she loved me,
She died—ah, may the earth
Lay lightly on her head—
You are my only treasure—
O God! Are you her aid?
(*Sighing.*)

**GILDA:** Alas, what grief! ah, never
Saw I such bitter tears!
Ah, father, be calm,
Or you will break my heart.
To me reveal your name;
To me your grief impart.

**RIG:** A che nomarmi?—è
inutile!—
Padre, ti sono, e basti—
Me forse al mondo temono,
D' alcuna ho forse gli asti—
Altri mi maledicono—

**GILDA:** Patria parenti, amici,
Voi dunque non avete!

**RIG:** Patria!—parenti!—dici?—
Culto, famiglia, patria,
(*Con effusione.*)
Il mio universo è in te!

**GILDA:** Ah, se può lieto rendervi,
Gioia è la vila a me!
Già da tre lune son quì ventua,
Nè la cittade ho ancor veduta;
Se il concedeto, farlo or potrei—

**RIG:** Mai!—mai!—uscita, dimmi,
unqua sei!

**GILDA:** No.

**RIG:** Guai!

**GILDA:** (Che dissi?)

**RIG:** Ben te ne guarda!
(Potrian seguirla, rapirla ancora!
Quì d'un buffone si disonora
La figlia, e ridesi—Orror!) Olà?
(*Verso la casa.*)

## SCENA X

*Detti e Giovanna della casa.*

**GIO:** Signor?

**RIG:** Tenendo mi vide alcuno?
Bada, dì il vero—

**GIO:** Ah no, nessuno.

**RIG:** Sta beh—la porta che dà al
bastione
E sempre chiusa?

**GIO:** Lo fu e sarà.

**RIG:** Veglia, o donna, questo fiore
(*A Gio.*)
Che a te puro confidaì;
Veglia attenta, e non sia mai
Che s' offuschi il suo candor
Tu dei venti dal furore,
Ch altri fiori hanno piegato,
Lo difendi, e immacolato
Lo ridonna al genitor.

**GILDA:** Quanto affetto!—quali
cure!
Che temete, padre mio?
Lassù in cielo, presso Dio
Veglia un angiol protettor.
Da noi stoglie le sventure
Di mia madre il priego santo;
Non fia mai divelto o infranto
Questo a voi diletto fiore.

**RIG:** Why this?—I am your father,
This is enough for you.
I might perhaps be hated,
Or be by others feared.
Alas! I have been cursed!

**GILDA:** No country, no relations,
No friends, you then possess?

**RIG:** What do you say, my love?
You are my god, my country,
You are the world to me!

**GILDA:** If I could see you glad,
I would be happy too.
It has been three months now, since
we here arrived,
And nothing I have seen yet of the
city.
I wish to see it now, if you will grant
it.

**RIG:** Have you never left this
house?

**GILDA:** Never!

**RIG:** Mind!

**GILDA:** (What do I say?)

**RIG:** Nor must you ever leave it.
(She might be followed, she might
be stolen,
And they would laugh at the disho-
nor
Of a buffoon. Oh shame!) Ho!
there!
(*Towards the house.*)

## SCENE X

*Enter Giovanna from the house.*

**GIO:** Sir?

**RIG:** Has no one seen me while
coming here?
Mind, speak the truth.

**GIO:** No one.

**RIG:** That's well! The door that
leads to the
Ramparts, is it always closed?

**GIO:** Yes, it has always been so, and
always shall.

**RIG:** Oh, woman, watch over this
flower,
Which I trust unto your care;
Be mindful, it may never
Fall the victim of dark snare.
O, save this fragile stem
From the hail and from rain:
As it was to you confided,
May I receive it back again.

**GILDA:** O, be cheerful, my dear fa-
ther.
Chase your starting tears away;
There, in heaven, is an angel
Who protects us night and day.
There the prayers of my mother
From all danger keeps us free;
Never, never, from your side,
Never distant will I be.

## SCENA XI

*Detti ed il Duca in costume borghese dalla strada.*

**RIG:** Alcuno è fuori—
(*Apre la porta della Corte, e mentre esce a sulla strada il Duca guizza furtivo nella corte e si nasconde dietro l' albero; gettando a Giovanna una borsa la fa tacer*)

**GIL:** Cielo!
Sempre novel sospetto—

**RIG:** (*a Gil. tornando.*)
Vi seguiva alla chiesa mai nessuno!

**GIO:** Mai.

**DUCA:** (Rigoletto.)

**RIG:** Se talor quì picchiano
Guardatevi da aprir—

**GIO:** Nemmeno al duca?

**RIG:** Meno che a tutti a lui—Mia figlia, addio.

**DUCA:** Sua figlia!

**GIO:** Addio, mia padre.
(*S' abbracciano, e Rigoletto parte chiuden dosi dietro la porta.*)

## SCENA XII

*Gilda, Giovanna, il Duca nella corte, poi Ceprano e Borsa a tempo sulla via.*

**GILDA:** Giovanna, ho die rimorsi—

**GIO:** E perchè mai

**GILDA:** Tacqui che un giovin ne seguiva al tempio.

**GIO:** Perchè ciò dirgli?—l' odiate dunque
Cotesto giovin, voi?

**GILDA:** No, no, chè troppo è bello e spira amore—

**GIO:** E magnanimo sembra e gran signore.

**GILDA:** Signor nè principe—io lo vorrei,
Sonto che povero—più l' amerei.
Sognando o vigile—sempre lo chiamo,
E l' alma in estasi—gli dice t' a—

**DUCA:** (*esce improvviso, fa cenno a Gio. d' andarsene, e inginoc- chiandosi a' piedi di Gil. termina la frase.*) T' amo!
T' amo, ripetilo—sì caro accento,
Un puro schiudimi—ciel di contento!

**GILDA:** Giovanna?—Ahi misera!—non v' è più alcuno
Che quì rispondami!—Oh Dio!— nessuno!

**DUCA:** Son io coll'anima—che ti rispondo—
Ah due che s' amano—son tutto un mondo!—

---

## SCENE XI

*The Duke in disguise arrives in the street.*

**RIG:** Some one outside—(*Rigolet- to opens the street gate, and whilst he goes out, the Duke slides in, hiding himself behind a tree, and throwing a purse to Giovanna.*)

**GILDA:** Oh, heavens!
He is always suspicious.

**RIG:** (*To Gilda, returning.*)
Has any one ever followed you to church?

**GIO:** No, never. (*Aside.*)

**DUKE:** (It is Rigoletto.)

**RIG:** If any one knocks here
You must not open.

**GIO:** Not even to the Duke?

**RIG:** Still less to him than others— Child, adieu.

**DUKE:** His child!

**GILDA:** Adieu my father. (*They embrace; and Rigoletto going out, shuts the door after him.*)

## SCENE XII

*Gilda, Giovanna, the Duke in the court yard; afterwards Ceprano and Borsa in the street.*

**GILDA:** Giovanna, I feel remorse.

**GIO:** And for what reason?

**GILDA:** I did not tell him who fol- lows me to church.

**GIO:** And why would you tell this? Do you dislike that man?

**GILDA:** No, no, he is too hand- some.

**GIO:** And has the appearance of a rich signor.

**GILDA:** It is not the riches nor rank I wish;
To me if poor, he'd better prove.
I think of him by day and night;
For him my heart overflows with love—

**DUKE:** (*throwing himself sudden- ly at the feet of Gilda.*)
With love, with love, oh, let me hear it;
Oh, let my soul be rapt in joy.

**GILDA:** Giovanna! alas! Is no one here? (*Gio. goes out at a sign from the Duke.*)
No one defends me? Oh, heavens! no one.

**DUKE:** It is I, your lover, that speaks to you.
I will protect you against all worlds.

---

**GILDA:** Chi mai, chi giungere—vi fece a me?

**DUCA:** S' angelo o demone—che importa a te?
Io t' amo.

**GILDA:** Uscitene.

**DUCA:** Uscire!—adesso!
Ora che accendene—un fuoco istesso!—
A inseparabile—d' amore il dio
Stringeva, o vergine—tuo fato al mio!
E il sol dell'anima, la vita è amore,
Sua voce è il palpito—del nostro core—
E fama e gloria—potenza e trono.
Terrene, fragili—cose quì sono.
Una pur avvene—sola divina,
E amor che agli angeli—più ne av- vicina!
Adunque amiamoci—donna ce- leste.
D' invidia agli uomini—sarò per te.

**GILDA:** (Ah de miei vergini—sog- ni son queste
Le voci tenere—sì cara a me!)

**DUCA:** Che, m' ami—deh! ripeti- mi—

**GILDA:** L' udiste.

**DUCA:** Oh me felice!

**GILDA:** Il nome vostro ditemi— Saperlo non mi lice?

**CEP:** Il loco è qui—(*A bor. dalla via.*)

**DUCA:** Mi nomino—(*Pensando.*)

**BORSA:** (Sta ben—) (*A Cep. e par- tono.*)

**DUCA:** Gualtier Maldè
Studente sono—povero—

**GIO:** Rumor di passi è fuore— (*Tornando spaventata.*)

**GILDA:** Forse mio padre—

**DUCA:** (Ah cogliere Potessi il tradi- tore
Che sì mi sturba!)

**GILDA:** Adducilo (*A Gio.*)
Di quà al bastione—ite—

**DUCA:** Dì m' amerai tu!

**GILDA:** E voi—

**DUCA:** L' intera vita—poi—

**GILDA:** Non più—non più—par- tite—

**A2:** Addio—speranza ed anima
Sol tu sarai per me.
Addio—vivrà immutabile
L' affetto mio per te.
(*Il Duca entra in casa scortato da Giovanna. Gilda resta fissando la porta ond' e partito*)

## SCENA XIII

**GILDA:** (*sola.*) Gualtier Maldè!— nome di lui amate
Scolpisciti nel core innamorato!
Caro nome che il mio cor
Festi primo palpitar,

---

**GILDA:** Oh heaven! what fate has brought you here?

**DUKE:** That fate which rules a lov- ing heart.
You are my love.

**GILDA:** Depart.

**DUKE:** No, no,
The same affection inflames our souls,
No power on earth can sever our love.
By fate united, by mutual sympathy,
Our bonds of love will last for ever.
My proudest conquest will be your faith—
My golden throne your heart so pure;
All else on earth is vain and frail,
True love alone is real and sure.
Love gives to men celestial bliss.
May nothing then our flame abate,
And all will envy my happy fate.

**GILDA:** Ah! these indeed are like the words
Which in my dreams I said and heard.

**DUKE:** O, let me hear again, I love you.

**GILDA:** You have heard it.

**DUKE:** Oh, joy!

**GILDA:** Tell me your name,
Or may I know it not?

**CEP:** This is the place. (*To Bor. from the street.*)

**DUKE:** My name—(*Thinking.*)

**BOR:** I see. (*They depart.*)

**DUKE:** Is Walter Maldè.
I am a poor student—poor—

**GIO:** A noise of steps outside. (*Re- turning frightened.*)

**GIL:** Perhaps my father.

**DUKE:** Ah, could I seize the traitor
Who dares disturb my joy
Of being with you.

**GIL:** Go quick,
And lead him on the ramparts.

**DUKE:** Do you love me?

**GIL:** And you?

**DUKE:** For ever, yes, and then—

**GIL:** No more, no more, depart.

**BOTH:** Farewell, my hope forever,
My blessing you shall be.
Farewell, farewell. Ah!
I'll never change my love for you.
(*The Duke exit, escorted by Giov- anna, and, Gilda follows him with her eyes.*)

## SCENE XIII

**GILDA:** (*alone*) Walter Maldè.
Sweet name,
You are already engraved on my heart.
Dear name! Your first has fallen

Le delizie dell' amor
Mi dèi sempre rammentar
Col pensiero il mio desir
A te ognora volerà,
E pur l' ultimo sospir,
Caro nome, tuo sarà.
(*Sale al terrazzo con una lanterna*)

## SCENA XIV

*Marullo, Ceprano, Borsa, Cortigiani armati e mascherati dalla via. Gilda sul terrazzo, che tosto entra in casa.*

**BOR:** E' là. (*Indicando Gil. al Coro*)

**CEP:** Miratela—

**CORO:** Oh quanto è bella.

**MAR:** Parfata ed angiol.

**CORO:** L'amante è quella
Di Rigoletto!

## SCENA XV

*Detti e Rigoletto concentrato.*

**RIG:** (Riedo!—perche?)

**BOR:** Silenzio—all' opra—badate a me.

**RIG:** (Ah da quel vecchio fui maledetto? Chi è là?)

**BOR:** Tacete—c' è Rigoletto. (*Ai compagni*)

**CEP:** Vittoria doppia!— l' uccideremo.

**BOR:** No, chè domani più rideromo—

**MAR:** Or tutto aggiusto—

**RIG:** (Chi parla quà?)

**MAR:** Ehi, Rigoletto?—Di?

**RIG:** (Chi va là?) (*Con voce terribile*)

**MAR:** Eh, non mangiarci! Son—

**RIG:** Chi?

**MAR:** Marullo.

**RIG:** In tanto bujo lo sguardo e nullo.

**MAR:** Quì ne condusee ridevol cosa—
Torre a Ceprano vogliam la sposa.

**RIG:** (Oime respiro!) Ma come entrare?

**MAR:** (*a. Cep.*) La vostra chiave? (*a Rig.*)
Non dubitare,
Non dee mancarci lo stratagemma—
Ecco le chiavi—
(*Gli da la chiave avuta da Cep.*)

So sweet upon my ear,
You shall for ever be
To me welcome and dear.
My thoughts, all my desires,
Will ever to you turn,
Yes, even when my ashes
Shall rest within the urn.
(*Gilda ascends the terrace with a lantern in her hand.*)

## SCENE XIV

*Marullo, Ceprano, Borsa, Courtiers in masks, and armed, in the street; Gilda on the terrace, entering the house*

**BOR:** She is there.

**CEP:** Look,

**CHO:** How beautiful she is!

**MAR:** She is an angel!

**CHO:** Is that the lover
Of Rigoletto?

## SCENE XV

*Enter Rigoletto, absorbed in thought.*

**RIG:** (*alone.*) Do I return? why?

**BOR:** Hush, to the work. Pay attention all to me.

**RIG:** Who is there?

**RIG:** That man, alas! has cursed me!
**BOR:** It was so dark I could not see.

**BOR:** Hush, Rigoletto is here.

**CEP:** A double chance, we can now kill this man.

**BOR:** No, no, tomorrow we shall have more laughter.

**MAR:** Ah! let me do—

**RIG:** Who speaks?

**MAR:** Ah, Rigoletto—say?

**RIG:** Who is there?

**MAR:** Betray us not, I am—

**RIG:** Who?

**MAR:** Marullo.

**RIG:** We just came here to have some fun—

**MAR:** We are going to steal away Ceprano's wife.

**RIG:** (Alas! I breathe again.) But where to enter?

**MAR:** (*to Cep.*) Where is the key?
(*to Rig.*) Don't be afraid,
We cannot fail.
Here are the keys.
(*Gives him the keys received from Cep.*)

**RIG:** Sento il suo stemma. (*Palpandole.*)
(Ah, terror vano fu dunque il mio!)
(*Respirando.*)
N' e là il palazzo—con voi son io.

**MAR:** Siam mascherati—

**RIG:** Ch' io pur mi mascheri;
A me una larva?

**MAR:** Si, pronta e già.
Terrai la scala—
(*Gli mette una maschera, e nello stesso tempo lo benda con un fazzoletto, e lo pone a reggere una scala, che avranno appostata al terrazzo.*)

**RIG:** Fitta e la tenebra—

**MAR:** La benda cieco e sordo il fa.
(*Ai compagni.*)

**TUTTI:** Zitti, zitti moviamo a vendetto,
Ne sia colto or che meno l' aspetta.
A sua volta schernito sarà!
Cheti, cheti, rubiamgli l' amante,
E la Corte doman riderà.
(*Alcuni salgono al terrazzo, rompon la porta del primo piano, scendono, aprono ad altri ch' entrano dalla strada, e riescono, trascinando Gilda la quale avra la bocca chiusa da un fazzoletto. Nel traversare la scena ella perde una sciarpa.*)

**GIL:** Soccorso, padre mio— (*Da lontano*)

**CORO:** Vittoria!

**GIL:** Aita! (*Piu lontano.*)

**RIG:** Non han finito ancor'—qual derisione! (*Si toccha gli occhi.*) Sono bendato!
(*Si strappa impetuosamente la benda e la maschera, ed al chiarore d' una lanterna scordata riconosee la sciarpa, vede la porta aperta, entra, ne trae Gio. spaventata; la fissa con istupore, si strappa i capelli senza porter gridare; finalmente dope molti sforzi, esclama—*)
Ah! la maledizione! (*Sviene.*)

*Fine Dell' Atto Secunds.*

## ■ ATTO III

### SCENA I

*Salotto nel palazzo ducale. Vi sono due porte laterali, una maggiore nel fondo che si chiude. A' suoi lati pendono i ritratti in tutta figura, a sinistra del Duca, a destra della sua sposa. V' ha un seggiolone presso una tavola coperta di velluto ed altri mobili. Il Duca dal mezzo agitato.*

**RIG:** This is his crest. (*Feeling the key.*)
(I feared in vain.) (*Breathing more freely.*)
The house is there! (I come with you.)

**MAR:** We are disguised.

**RIG:** I must then do the same;
Give me a mask!

**MAR:** Yes, here is one.
You will keep fast the ladder.
(*Puts a mask to his face, and after having bound it with a handkerchief, leads him to keep firm a ladder, which they have placed to the terrace.*)

**RIG:** Never was it so dark.

**MAR:** The handkerchief has made him blind and deaf. (*To his companions.*)

**ALL:** Hush, hush, let's take revenge,
When least he thinks of it.
The man that sneers at us,
Tomorrow will be our sport
Let's take his love away,
And we shall laugh at court.
(*Some of them go up the terrace, break the window of the first floor, then descend and open the street door to others, who enter and drag away Gilda, who has her mouth tied with a handkerchief. In crossing the scene she loses a scarf.*)

**GIL:** My father! help!

**CHO:** Victory!

**GIL:** Help! (*More distant.*)

**RIG:** They have not finished yet.
What joke is this? (*Touches his eyes.*)
A band upon my eyes!
(*He snatches off the band and the mask, and by the light of the lantern perceives the scarf, sees the door open, enters and drags out Gio., frightened; he stares at her, and after many efforts to speak, exclaims—*)
The curse! (*Faints.*)

*End of the Second Act.*

## ■ ACT III

### SCENE I

*A room in the Ducal Palace. Doors right and left and one in front. On one side the portrait of the Duke, on the other side that of the Duchess. A table, arm-chair, Etc. Enter the Duke, much agitated.*

Ella mi fu rapita!
E quando o ciel?—ne' brevi istanti, prima
Che un mio presagio interno
Sull' orma corsa ancora mi spingesse!
Schiuso era l' uscio!—la magion deserta!
E dove ora sarà quell' angiol caro!
Colei che potè prima in questo core
Destar la fiamma di constanti affetti?
Colei si pura, al cui modesto accento
Quasi tratto a virtù talor mi credo!
Ella mi fu rapita!
E chi l' ardiva?—ma ne avrò vendetta:
Lo chiede il pianto della mia diletta
Parmi veder le lagrime
Scorrenti da quel ciglio,
Quando fra il duolo e l' ansa
Del subito periglio,
Dell' amor nostro memore,
Il suo Gualtier chiamo.
Ned ei potea soccorrerti,
Cara fanciulla amata,
Ei che vorria coll' anima
Farti quaggiù beata;
Ei che le sfere agli angeli
Per te non invidiò.

They robbed me of my love!
And when? At the moment
A voice within my heart
Did call me back to her!
I found the door wide open; the house deserted.
And where now can that dearest angel be
Who first within my heart
Awoke such flames of love;—
That soul, whose magic charms
Would almost draw me back to virtue's path?
They tore her from her home;
But he who dared so much shall soon repent.
The grief of my beloved demands revenge.
I think I see a tear,
That's starting to her eyes,
Which 'midst the grief and fear
Of such a sad surprise,
In fond remembrance said
Ah! Walter, lend me aid.
But I was far away;
You had no help from me.
Yet, willingly my life
I would have lost for thee!
No bliss on earth—no bliss above—
Can equal your sweet love!

## SCENA II

*Marullo, Ceprano, Borsa, ed altri Cortigiani, del mezzo.*

**TUTTI:** Duca, duca!

**DUCA:** Ebben?

**TUTTI:** L' amante
Fu rapita a Rigoletto.

**DUCA:** Bella! e d' onde?

**TUTTI:** Dal suo tetto.

**DUCA:** Ah, ah! dite, come fu? (*Siede.*)

**TUTTI:** Scorrendo uniti remota via.
Brev' ora dopo caduto il dì;
Come previsto ben s' era in pria,
Rara beltade ci si scopri.
Era l' amante di Rigoletto
Che, vista appena, si dileguò.
Glà di rapirla s' avea il progetto,
Quando il buffone ver noi spunto,
Che di Ceprano noi la contessa
Rapir volessimo, stolto, credè;
La scala quindi all' uopo messa,
Bendato ei stesso ferma tenè.
Salimmo, e rapidi la giovinetta
Ci venne fatto quinci asportar.
Quand' ei s' accorse della vendetta
Resto scornato ad imprecar.

**DUCA:** (Che sento?—è dessa la mia diletta!—
Ah, tutta il cielo non mi rapì!)
Ma dove or trovasi la poveretta? (*Al Coro.*)

## SCENE II

*Enter Marullo, Count Ceprano, Borsa, and other Courtiers.*

**ALL:** Duke, duke!

**DUKE:** What news?

**ALL:** Last night we stole away
The mistress of your jester.

**DUKE:** Is she pretty? Where was she then!

**ALL:** At her house.

**DUKE:** How did this happen?

**ALL:** As we went down a lane,
when day had disappeared, there,
as we had expected, a lady sweet appeared!
She was your jester's love;
But soon she ran away.
We thought to bring her here,
When he came in the way.
We come to steal Ceprano's wife,
Give us your aid, to him we told.
We put a band upon his eyes,
And then the ladder made him hold.
In haste we mounted, and broke the doors,
His lady-love was brought here straight;
When he found out he was deceived,
We left him there to curse his fate.

**DUKE:** (What do I hear? She is my love! Alas! My hopes are now all lost.)
(*Aside.*)
But where can this lady be?

**TUTTI:** Fu da noi stessi addotta or qui.

**DUCA:** (Possente amor mi chiama,
Volar io deggio a lei;
(*Alzandosi con gioia.*)
Il serto mio darei
Per consolar quel cor.
Ah 1 sappia al n chi l' ama,
Conosca appien chi sono,
Apprenda ch' anco in trono
Ha degli echiavi Amor.) (*Esce frettoloso dal mezzo.*)

**TUTTI:** (Qual penisero or l' agita;
Come cagiò d' umor!)

## SCENA III

*Marullo, Ceprano, Borsa, altri Cortigiana, poi Rigoletto dalla destra, ch' entra cantarellando con reprezzo dolore.*

**MAR:** Povero Rigoletto!—

**CORO:** Ei vien—silenzio!

**TUTTI:** Buon giorno, Rigoletto—

**RIG:** (Han tutti fatto il colpo!)

**CEP:** Ch' hai di nuovo, Buffon?

**RIG:** Che dell' usato
Più noioso voi siete.

**TUTTI:** Ah! ah! ah!

**RIG:** (Dove l' avran nacosta?—)
(*Spiando inquieto dovunque.*)

**TUTTI:** (Guardate com' e inquieto!)

**RIG:** Son felice
Che nulla a voi nuocesse
L' aria di questa notte—

**MAR:** Questa notte!—

**RIG:** Sì—Ah fu il bel colpo!—

**MAR:** S' hò dormito sempre!

**RIG:** Ah voi dormiste?—avro dunque sognato! (*S' allontana, e vedendo un fazzoletto sopra una tavola, ne osserva inquieto la cifra.*)

**TUTTI:** (Ve' come tutto osserva!)

**RIG:** (None è il suo.)
(*Gettandoto.*)
Dorme il ducca tuttor?

**TUTTI:** Si, dorme encora.

## SCENA IV

*Detti e un Paggio dalla Duchessa.*

**PAG:** Al suo sposo parlar vuol la duchessa.

**CEP:** Dorme.

**PAG:** Qui or con voi non era?

**BORSA:** E' a caccia

**PAG:** Senza paggi!—senz' a rmi!—

**TUTTI:** E non capisco.
Che vedere per ora non può alcuno?—

**ALL:** She is here in your own palace.

**DUKE:** (Yes, love now give me aid;
To her I must repair!
I would give up the world
To change to joy her care.
Ah! soon she will discover
My station, rank, and name,
And learn that love makes slaves
Amongst rich and poor the same.)
(*The Duke exit hastily.*)

**ALL:** The duke is wrapped in thought;
He seems no more the same.

## SCENE III

*Enter Rigoletto.*

**MAR:** Poor Rigoletto!

**CHORUS:** He comes. Be silent.

**ALL:** Good morning, Rigoletto.

**RIG:** (They have deceived me!)

**CEP:** What news, Buffoon?

**RIG:** You are, I think,
More troublesome than ever.

**ALL:** Ah! ah! ah!

**RIG:** Ah! where can they have taken my dear child? (*Looking round uneasily.*)

**ALL:** (Look, how uneasy he appears!)

**RIG:** I am glad to find
The cold air of last night
Has done no harm to you.

**MAR:** Last night?

**RIG:** A fine affair it was.

**MAR:** I slept all night.

**RIG:** All night? I then have dreamed. (*He walks about, and seeing a handkerchief on the table, observes the mask.*)

**ALL:** (Look how he spies all things.)

**RIG:** (It is not hers.) (*Throwing it away.*)
Is the duke still asleep?

**ALL:** Yes, he sleeps still.

## SCENE IV

*Enter a Page of the Duchess.*

**PAGE:** The duchess is anxious to see the duke.

**CEP:** He sleeps.

**PAGE:** Was he not here just now?

**BORSA:** Yes, but he went to hunt.

**PAGE:** Without his suite?

**ALL:** Do you not understand.
That for the moment he cannot be seen.

RIG: (*Che a parte a stato attentissimo al dialogo balzando improvviso tra lore proromp.*) Ah ell' è qui dunque!—El è col duca!—

TUTTI: Chi!

RIG: La giovin che sta notte A mio tetto rapiste—

TUTTI: Tu deliri!

RIG: M la saprò riprender—Ella è qui—

TUTTI: Se l' amante perdesti, la ricerca Altrove.

RIG: Io vo' mia figlia—

TUTTI: La sua figlia!

RIG: Sì, la mia figlia—D' una tal vittoria Che?—adesso non ridete? Ella è là—la vogl' io—la renderete.
(*Corre verso la porta di mezze, ma i Cortigiani gli attraversano il passaggio.*)
Cortigiani, vil razza dannata, Per qual prezzo vendeste, il mi bene?
A voi nulla per l' oro sconviene, Ma mia figlia è impagabil tesor.
La rendete—o se pur disarmata Questa man per voi fora cruenta!
Nulla in terra più l' uomo paventa. Se dei figli difende l' onor.
Quella porta, assassini, im' aprite;
(*Si getta ancor sulla porta che gli e nuovamente contesa dai gentiluomini; lotta alquanto, poi torna spossato sul davanti del teatro.*)
Ah! voi tutti a me contro venite!
(*Piange*)
Ebben piango—Marullo—signore, Tu ch' hai l' alma gentil come il core
Dimmi or tu, dove l' hanno nascosta?—
E' là?—E' vero?—tu taci! perobè, Miei signori—Perdono, pietate—
Al vegliardo la figlia ridate—
Ridonarla a voi nulla ora costa, Tutto il mondo è tal figlia per me.

## SCENA V

*Detti e Gilda ch' esce dalla stanza a sinistra e si getta nelle paterne braccia.*

GILDA: Mio padre!

RIG: Dio! mia Gilda! Signori, id essa è tutta La mia famiglia-Non temer più nulla, Angelo mio—fu scherzo, non è vero?
(*Ai cortig.*)
Io che pur piansi or rido—E tu a che piangi?

GILDA: I ratto—l' onta, o padre!

RIG: Ciel! che dici?

---

RIG: (*who has paid great attention to the dialogue, suddenly exclaims—*) Ah! then she is here, she is with the duke.

ALL: Who?

RIG: The lady you have stolen Last night from my own roof.

ALL: You are delirious.

RIG: But I shall rescue her. She must be there.

ALL: If you have lost your mistress, It is not within these walls you have to search.

RIG: Ah! give me back my daughter.

ALL: His daughter!

RIG: Ah! yes, my daughter, of your action now No, no, you cannot laugh! She is there, give back to me my child.
(*Rig. runs toward the door, but all prevent his passage.*)
Impious courtiers, race of cowards, For what price my child you sold? For gain no crime your hand restrains; To me my child is more than gold. Give her back, or, though disarmed, Against your life I'll raise my hand; Nothing on earth a father fears When he defends his children Cowards, open at least that door.
(*Rig. goes again to the door, but he is prevented from opening it.*)
Alas! you come against me all; Well, I weep—Marullo—yield, I know you have a gentle heart, Tell me where she is concealed. Speak—she is there. You are all mute. Give back the daughter to the old man: My friends, my lords, have pity on me, It costs you nothing to grant this boon; But all my hopes in her I see.

## SCENE V

*Enter Gilda, who throws herself into the arms of her father.*

GIL: My father!

RIG: My dear Gilda! My lords, she is my only child! Oh, fear no more! It was only for jest I cried, but now I laugh—Why do you weep?

GIL: The fear—the shame—oh father!

RIG: Alas! what do you say?

---

GILDA: Arrossir voglio innanzi a voi soltanto—

RIG: (*Trivolto ai Cortigiani con imperioso modo.*)
Ite di quà, voi tutti—
Se il Duca vostro d' appresiassi osasse,
Che non entri gli dite, e ch' io ci sono.
(*Si abbandono sul seggiolone.*)

TUTTI: (Co' fanciulli e coi dementi (*Tra loro.*)
Spesso giova il simular. Partiam pur, ma quel ch' ei tenti Non lasciamo d' osservar.)
(*Escon dal mezzo a chiudon la porta.*)

## SCENA VI

*Rigoletto e Gilda.*

RIG: Parla siam soli.

GIL: (Ciel, dammi coraggio!)
Tutte le feste al tempio Mentre pregava Iddio, Bello e fatale un giovane. S' offerse al guardo mio—
Se i labbri nostri tacquero, Dagli occhi il cor parlò. Furtivo fra le tenebre Sol ieri a me giungeva—
Sono studente, provero, Commosso mi diceva, E con ardente palpito Amor mi protestò.
Parti—il mio core aprivasi A speme più gradita, Quando improvvisi apparvero Color che m' han rapita, E a forza qui m' addussero Nell' ansia più crudel.

RIG: Non dir—non più, mio angelo.
(T' intendo, avverso ciel!
Solo per me l' infamia A te chiedeva, o Dio—
Ch' ella potesse ascendere. Quanto caduto er' io—
Ah presso del pattibolo Bisogna ben l' altare!
Ma tutto ora scompare—L' altar si rovesciò!)
Piangi, fanciulla, e scorrere Fa il pianto sul mio cor.

GIL: Padre, in voi parla un angelo Per me consolar.

RIG: Compiuto pur quanto a fare mì resta Lasciare potremo quest' aura funesta.

GIL: Sì.

RIG: (E tutto un sol giorne cangiare potè!)

## SCENA VII

*Detti, un Usciere, e il Conte di Monterone, che dalla destra attraversa il fon da della sala fra gli alabardieri.*

---

GIL: I cannot speak in presence of so many.

RIG: (*To the Courtiers, in an imperious manner.*) Away, depart from here!
And if the Duke should dare to approach this room, Tell him he must not come, that I am here.
(*Throws himself upon a chair.*)

ALL: With children and with fools We must sometimes seem to yield; Let us go, but what he does We shall spy herein concealed.
(*Exeunt from the door in front, shutting it behind them.*)

## SCENE VI

*Rigoletto and Gilda.*

RIG: Now speak, we are alone.

GIL: Now, Heaven, give me aid! Each Sunday, while I went To church, my prayers to say, A youth of heavenly beauty Did follow on our way; And if our lips were silent, The eyes betrayed our hearts. In secret, only yesterday, He came to me at night; I am a student—poor— Much moved, he said to me, And ardently repeated, I am in love with you. He left me then; my heart With brighter hopes did beat, When suddenly appeared Those men who took me away, And brought me to this place, Half fainting, in dismay.

RIG: Ah, speak no more my angel! (Now I understand— Upon my head alone I asked you curse, O Heaven I begged that she may rise The moment I should die— Ah! often by the scaffold The altar raised we see! Now all is lost forever, No hope remains to me!) Ah, weep, my child, and let your tears Upon my bosom fall.

GIL: My father, your dear words Consoles my grief forever.

RIG: I must settle some affairs, And then forever we will leave this place.

GIL: Yes.

RIG: One day has changed our fate.

## SCENE VII

*Enter a Herald, and Count Monterone, who crosses the stage in the midst of Guards.*

## Act III, Scene VII

USC: Schiudete—ire al carcere Castiglion dee. (*Alle guardie.*)

MON: Poichè fosti invano da me maledetto, (*Fermandosi verso il ritratto.*)
Nè un fulmine o un ferro colpiva il tuo petto.
Felice pur anco, o duca, vivrai—
(*Esce fra le guardie dal mezzo*)

RIG: No, vecchio, t' inganni—un vendice avrai.

### SCENA VIII

*Rigoletto e Gilda.*

RIG: Si, vendetta, tremenda vendetta
Di quest' anima è solo desio—
Di punirti già l' ora s' affretta,
Che fatale pe te tuonerà.
Come fulmin scagliato da Dio
Il buffone colpirti saprà.

GIL: O mio padre, qual gioia feroce (*Da se.*)
Balenarvi negli occhi vegg' io!
Perdonate—a noi pure una voce
Di perdono dal cielo verrà.
(Mi tradiva, pur l' amo, gran Dio.
Per l' ingrato ti chiedo pietà!)
(*Escon del mezzo*)

*Fine Dell' Atto Terzo.*

---

HER: Open the door, the Count must pass to prison. (*To the guards.*)

MON: Since you have been accursed in vain by me,
Since no sword has yet entered in your breast,
And happy you must live—

RIG: No, no, old man, I shall avenge your wrongs. (*Exeunt.*)

### SCENE VIII

*Rigoletto and Gilda.*

RIG: Ah, yes! I shall have vengeance,
It is my only wish.
The hour is not far distant
That your ruin will strike.
Upon your head my fury
Will fall, then, thunder-like.

GIL: Oh, father! what sad joy
Is sparkling in your eyes?
Ah! spare him;
Heaven will its mercy show to us also.
In spite of his deceit,
My heart beats for him.

*End of the Third Act.*

---

# ATTO IV

## SCENA I

*Deserta Sponda del Mincio. Gilda e Rigoletto inquieto sono sulla strada. Sparafucile nell' interno dell' osteria, seduto presso una tavola, sta ripulendo il suo cinturone, senza nulla intendere di quanto accade al di fuori.*

RIG: E l' ami?

GIL: Sempre.

RIG: Pure
Tempo a guarirne t' ho lasciato.

GIL: Io l' amo

RIG: Povero cor di donna! Ah, il vile infame!
Ma avrai vendetta, o Gilda—

GIL: Pietà, mio padre—

RIG: E se tu certa fossi
Ch' ei ti tradisse, l' ameresti ancora?

GIL: Nol so, ma pur m' adora.

RIG: Egli!—

GIL: Sì.

RIG: Ebbene, osserva dunque. (*La conduce presso una delle fessure del muro, ed ella vi guarda.*)

GIL: Un nomo vedo.

RIG: Per poco attendi.

---

# ACT IV

## SCENE I

*A desert spot on the banks of the river Mincio. Gilda and Rigoletto in the road. Sparafucile in the Inn, cleaning his leather belt.*

RIG: And do you love him still?

GIL: I do.

RIG: Yet you have had
Sufficient time to overcome this passion.

GIL: I cannot.

RIG: Weak is woman's heart;
But I will have revenge.

GIL: Oh, mercy, father!

RIG: Could you then forget him?

GIL: I cannot say. He loves me.

RIG: He?

GIL: Yes.

RIG: You must see. (*He leads her to the door, and tells her to look through a crevice.*)

GIL: A man is there.

RIG: But wait awhile.

---

### SCENA II

*Detti ed il Duca, che, in assisa di semplice officale di cavalleria entra nella sala terrena per una porta a sinistra.*

GIL: Ah, padre mio! (*trasalendo.*)

DUC: Due cose e tosto—(*a Sparaf.*)

SPA: Quali?

DUC: Una stanza e del vino—

SIG: (Son questi i suoi customi!)

SPA: (Oh, il bel zerbino!) (*Entra nella vicina stanza.*)

DUC: La donna e mobile
Qual piuma al vento,
Muto d'accento—e di pensier.
Sempre un' amabile
Leggiadro viso,
In pianto o in riso—è menzogner.
E sempre misero,
Chi a lei s'affida,
Chi le confida—mal caute il cor!
Pur mai non sentesi
Felice appieno
Chi su quel seno—non liba amor.
(*Spa. rientra con una bottiglia di vino e due bicchieri, che depone sulla tavola, quindi batte col pomo della sua lunga spada due colpi al soffillo. A quel segnale una ridente giovane, in costume di zingara scende a salti la scala. Il Duc. corre per abbracciarla, ma ella si sfugge.—Spa. uscito sulla vide, a parte a Rig.*)

SPA: E là il vostr' uomo—viver dee o morire?

RIG: Più tardi tornerò l'opra a compire. (*Spa. si allontana dietro la casa lunge il fiume.*)

### SCENA III

*Gilda e Rigoletto sulla via, il Duca e Maddalena nel piano terreno.*

DUCA: Un dì, se ben rammentomi,
O bella, t' incontrai—
Mi piacque di te chiedere,
E intesi che qui stai.
Or sappi, che d' allora
Sol te quest' alma adora.

MAD: Ah, ah!—e vent' altre appresso
Le scorda forse adesso?—
Ha un' aria il signorino
Da vero libertino—

DUCA: Si?—un mostro son—(*Por abbracciarla.*)

MAD: Lasciatemi, Stordito.

DUCA: Ih, che fracasso!

MAD: Stia saggio.

---

### SCENE II

*The Duke, dressed as a private officer, enters the inn.*

GIL: Ah! my father! (*Surprised.*)

DUKE: Two things I want, and then—(*To Spa.*)

SPA: Speak, sir,

DUKE: A room and wine.

RIG: This is the life he leads.

SPA: (A handsome youth, indeed!) (*Aside. Spa. goes out.*)

DUKE: The women are unsettled
As feathers in the wind,
Each moment changes their minds.
In tears, or even smiles,
Yes, woman's lovely face,
For ever beguiles us!
The man that is so mad
To trust a woman's heart
For ever must be sad.
But still there is no bliss,
Upon this earth compared
To that of a sweet kiss!
(*Spa. enters with a bottle and two glasses, which he places on the table. He then beats the ceiling twice with the hilt of his sword. At this signal a pretty young girl, dressed as a gypsy, descends the stairs. The Duke rushes to embrace her, but she avoids him. Meanwhile Spa., having gone out upon the road, says aside to Rig:—*)

SPA: Your man is there. Must he now live or die?

RIG: Wait awhile, and you shall know my will. (*Spa. goes slowly away.*)

### SCENE III

*Gilda and Rigoletto on the road. Magdalen and the Duke in the Inn.*

DUKE: If I remember well, my pretty girl,
I have seen your face before.
I tried to find your house,
At length I see you here.
Believe that from that time
I loved you to despair.

MAG: And others, score by score,
Do you forget them now?
To tell the truth, good sir,
You are a gay deceiver.

DUKE: Yes, yes, just so.

MAG: Leave me, rude man.

DUKE: Eh! eh! what noise!

MAG: Be quiet.

DUCA: E tu sii docile,
Non farmi tanto chiasso.
Ogni saggezza chiudesi
Nel gaudio e nell' amore—
(*Le prende la mano.*)
La bella mano candida!—

MAD: Scherzate, voi signore.

DUCA: No, no.

MAD: Son brutta.

DUCA: Abbracciami.

MAD: Ebro—

DUCA: D' amore ardente. (*Ridendo*)

MAD: Signor l' indifferente,
Vi piace canzonar?—

DUCA: No, no, ti vo' sposar.

MAD: Ne voglio la parola—

DUCA: Amabile figliuola!
(*Ironico.*)

RIG: Ebben?—ti basta ancor?—(*A Gilda che avra tutto osservato ed inteso*)

GIL: Iniquo traditor!

DUCA: Bella figlia dell' amore,
Schiavo son de' vezzi tuoi;
Con un detto soi tu puoi
Le mie pene consolar.
Vieni , e senti del mio core
Il frequente palpitar.

MAD: Ah! ah! rido ben di core,
Chè tai baie costan poco;
Quanto valga il vostro giuoco,
Mel credete, so apprezzar,
Sono avvezza, bel signore,
Ad un simile scherzar.

GIL: Ah, cosi parlar d' amore!
A me pur l' infame ho udito
Infelice cor tradito,
Per angoscia non scoppiar.
Perchè, o credulo mio core,
Un tal uom dovevi amar!

RIG: Taci, il piangere non vale; (*A Gil.*)
Ch' ei, mentiva or sei secura—
Taci, e mia sarà la cura
La vendetta d' affrettar.
Pronta fia, sara fatale;
Io saprolla fulminar.
M' odi, ritorna a casa—
Oro prendi, un destriero,
Una veste viril che t' apprestai,
E per Verona parti—
Sarovvi io pur domani—

GIL: Or venite—

RIG: Impossibil.

GIL: Tremo.

RIG: Va. (*Gilda parte.*)

## SCENA IV

Sparafucile, Rigoletto, il Duca e Maddalena.

---

DUKE: And you be kind,
And do not scream so loud,
For wisdom ever lies
In pleasure and in love.
What pretty hands! how white!
(*He takes her by the hand.*)

MAG: You like to laugh at me.

DUKE: No, no.

MAG: I know I am not pretty.

DUKE: Kiss me.

MAG: Sir, you are drunk—

DUKE: Yes, drunk of love for you.

MAG: And can you be so unkind,
As thus to laugh at me.

DUKE: I do not joke—I wish to marry you.

MAG: If so, give me your word of honor.

DUKE: You are a charming girl!
(*Ironically.*)

RIG: Well then, is this not yet enough?

GIL: The cruel traitor!

DUKE: Lovely woman, of your charms
At your feet the victim see,
But one word, and changed to joy
All my sorrows soon will be.
Yes, be assured, my lady sweet,
This fond heart for you does beat.

MAG: Do you take me for a fool,
To think your words are true;
Full well I know what they mean,
I give them their right value,
Jokes like these I often hear,
But I laugh at them, dear sir.

GIL: Thus my heart he did deceive,
Thus the traitor spoke to me.
All my joys, my hopes are gone,
Now my wretched doom I see.
O heavens! what a cruel fate!
I love the man I ought to hate.

RIG: Hush! your sorrows are all vain,
That he deceived you is now sure—
Hush! it now belongs to me
Dreadful vengeance to procure.
Your death only can assuage.
Hear me, at once go home, and take what gold
You want. Then dress yourself in male attire.
All is prepared. Mount on the swiftest horse
And hasten to Verona.
Tomorrow I shall join you.

GIL: Come now.

RIG: I cannot now.

GIL: I tremble.

RIG: Go—(*Gilda goes out.*)

## SCENE IV

Sparafucile, Rigoletto, Duke and Magdalen.

---

RIG: Venti scudi hai tu detto? Eccome dieci,
E dopo l' opera il resto.
Ei qui rimane?

SPA: Si.

RIG: Alla mezze notte
Ritornerò.

SPA: Non cale.
A gettarlo nel flume basto io solo.

RIG: No, no, il vo' far io stesso.

SPA: Sia—il suo nome?

RIG: Vuoi saper anco il mio?
Egli è Delitto, Punizion son io.
(*Parte. Il cielo si oscura e tuona.*)

## SCENA V

Detti, meno Rigoletto.

SPA: La tempesta è vicina!
Più scura fia la notte.

DUCA: Maddalena? (*Per prenderla*)

MAD: (*Sfuggendogli.*] Aspettate—mio fratello
Viene—

DUCA: Che importa? (*S' ode il tuona*)

MAD: Tuona?

SPA: E pioverà tra poco.
(*Entrande*)

DUCA: Tanto meglio.
Io qui mi tratterò—tu dormirai (*A Spa.*)
In scuderia—all' inferno—ove vorrai

SPA: Grazie.

MAD: (Ah no—partite.) (*Piano al Duc.*)

DUCA: (Con tal tempo?) (*A Mad.*)

SPA: Son venti scudi d' ore. (*Piano al Mad.*) Ben felice
(*Al Duc.*)
D' offririvi la mia stanza—se a voi piace
Tosto a vederla andiamo.
(*Prende un lume e s' avvia per la scala.*)

DUCA: Ebben, sono con te—presto, vediamo. (*Dice una parola all' orecchio di Mad. e segue Spa.*)

MAD: (Poverro giovin! grazioso tanto! (*Tuona.*)
Dio! qual mai notte è questa!)

DUCA: (*Giunto al granaio, vendendone il balcone senza imposte.*) Si dorme all' aria aperta?
bene, bene—
Buona notte.

SPA: Signor, vi guardi Iddio.

DUCA: Breve sonno dormiam—stanco son io. (*Depone il capello, la spada, e si stende sul letto, dove in breve addormentasi. Mad. frat-*

---

RIG: You said twenty crowns. Here are now ten.
After the deed I shall give you the rest.
Is he still here?

SPA: He is.

RIG: I shall return
At midnight hour.

SPA: I don't require your aid; I can alone throw him into the river.

RIG: No, no, I wish to throw him in myself.

SPA: So be it. What is his name?

RIG: His name is Crime, and Punishment is mine.
(*Exit Rig. It becomes dark, and thunders.*)

## SCENE V

Sparafucile, the Duke, and Magdalen.

SPA: The storm approaches. Good. The night will be darker.

DUKE: Magdalen! (*Trying to take hold of her.*)

MAG: Wait! my brother
Comes. (*Avoiding him.*)

DUKE: Well! what's this?

MAG: It thunders!

SPA: (*Entering.*) And we shall have some rain.

DUKE: So much the better.
I shall stop here; you can sleep in the stable
Below, or where you like.

SPA: Thanks, sir.

MAG: Ah, no, depart!

DUKE: How? in such weather!

SPA: Twenty crowns of gold! (*To Mag.*) I shall be happy
(*To the Duke.*)
To offer you my room; and if you like,
I will show it to you.
(*He takes a light, and goes toward the staircase.*)

DUKE: With pleasure; yes, let's go.
(*Whispers a word to Mag., and follows Spa.*)

MAG: Unfortunate young man; so good, so kind!
Oh, Heaven! what a night!

DUKE: (*Having gone up stairs, and seeing the window without shutters.*) Here one must sleep quite in the open air.
Well, well; good night!

SPA: May God protect you, sir.

DUKE: I feel that I shall sleep; I am so tired. (*He puts down his hat and his sword, and throws himself on the bed, and soon falls*

*tanto siede presso la tavola. Spa. beve dalla bottiglia lasciata dal Duca. Rimangono ambidue taciturni per qualche istante, e preoccupati da gravi pensieri.*)

**MAD:** E' amabile in vero cotal giovinotto.

**SPA:** Oh si—venti scudi ne dà di prodotto.

**MAD:** Sol venti! son pochi—valeva di più.

**RIG:** La spada, s' ei dorme, va, portami giù.

**MAD:** (*Sale al granaio, e contemplando il dormente.*) Peccato! è pur bello!
(*Ripara alla meglio il bolcone, e scendo.*)

## SCENA VI

*Detti e Gilda che comparise nel fondo della via in costume virile, con stivali e speroni, e lentamente si avanza verso l' osteria, mentre Sparafucile continua beve. Spessi lampi e tuoni.*

**GIL:** A più non ragiono!
Amor mi trascina!—mio padre, perdono—(*Tuona.*)
Qual notte d' orrore!—Gran Dio, che accadra.

**MAD:** Fratello! (*Sara discesa ed avra posata la spada del Duc. sulla tavola.*)

**GIL:** Chi parla? (*Osserva pella fessura.*)

**SPA:** Al diavol ten va. (*Frugando in un credenzone.*)

**MAD:** Somiglia un Apollo quel giovine—io l' amo—
Ei m' ama—riposi—nè più l' uccidiamo.

**GIL:** O cielo! (*Ascoltando.*)

**SPA:** Rattoppa quel sacco—

**MAD:** Perchè?

**SPA:** Entr' esso il tuo Apollo, sgozzato da me,
Gettar dovrò al fiume.

**GIL:** L' inferno qui vedo!

**MAD:** Eppure il danaro salvarti scommetto,
Serbandolo in vita.

**SPA:** Difficile il credo.

**MAD:** M' ascolta—anzi facil ti svelo un progretto.
De' scudi già dieci dal gobbo ne avesti;
Venire cogli altri più tardi il vedrai—
Uccidilo, e venti allora ne avrai,
Cosi tutto il prezzo goder si potrà.

*asleep. Mag. down stairs stands sentry near the table, and Spa. finishes the bottle left by the Duke. They both remain some time in silence, and apparently in deep thought.*)

**MAG:** He is, indeed, an amiable young man.

**SPA:** Oh, yes, I gain twenty crowns.

**MAG:** Twenty crowns! 'Tis little; he is worth much more.

**SPA:** Go up—and if he sleeps, bring down his sword.

**MAG:** (*Goes up, and admiring him, exclaims:*) It is a pity—he is so handsome!

## SCENE VI

*Enter Gilda from the road, disguised as a man, and slowly advancing toward the Inn, whilst Sparafucile drinks. It lightens and thunders.*

**GIL:** Alas! I lose my reason.
Love overcomes me. Father, pardon,
What a dreadful night! What will become of me?

**MAG:** My brother! (*Mag. having come down, has placed the Duke's sword on the table.*)

**GIL:** Who has spoken? (*Looking through the crevices of the door.*)

**SPA:** Away, do not disturb me. (*Searching in a cupboard.*)

**MAG:** That youth is as handsome as Apollo; I love him,
And he loves me. Ah! kill him not!

**GIL:** (*listening.*) O heavens!

**SPA:** Mend soon that sack.

**MAG:** And why?

**SPA:** The handsome youth, Apollo, when killed by me,
I must throw in the river.

**GIL:** O heavens! what house is this?

**MAG:** You still may earn your money,
And spare his life.

**SPA:** That is not easy.

**MAG:** Listen, a plan I will disclose to you.
From the buffoon you have received ten crowns;
He will return here soon with the remainder;
Kill him, and you will take the other ten,
Then you will get the price you would have earned.

**SPA:** Uccider quel gobbo! che diavol dicesti!
Un ladro son forse? Son forse un bandito?
Qual altro c'iente da me fu tradito?
Mi paga vuest' uomo—fedele m'avrà.

**GIL:** Che sento! mio padre!

**MAD:** Ah grazia per esso!

**SPA:** E' d' uopo ch' ei muoia—

**MAD:** Fuggire il fo adesso. (*Va per salire.*)

**GIL:** Oh buona figliuola!

**SPA:** Gli scudi perdiamo. (*Trattendola.*)

**MAD:** E ver:

**SPA:** Lascia fare—

**MAD:** Salvarlo dobbiamo.

**SPA:** Se pria ch' abbia il mezzo la notte toccato
Alcuno qui giunga, per esso morrà.

**MAD:** E' buia la notte, il ciel troppo irato nessuno a quest' ora di qui passera.

**GIL:** Oh qual tentazione; morir per l' ingrato!
Morire!—e mio padre!—Oh cielo, pietà!
(*Battono le undici e mezzo.*)

**SPA:** Ancor c' è mezz' ora.

**MAD:** Attendi, fratello—(*Piangendo.*)

**GIL:** Che! piange tal donna!—Nè a lui darò aita!
Ah s' egli al mio amore divema rabello
Io vo' per la sua gettar la mia vita
(*Picchia alla porta*)

**MAD:** Si picchia?

**SPA:** Fu il vento. (*Gil. torna a bussare.*)

**MAD:** Si picchia, ti dico

**SPA:** E' strano!

**MAD:** Chi è?

**GIL:** Pietà d' un mendico;
Asil per la motte a lui concedete.

**MAD:** Fia lunga tal notte!

**SPA:** Alquanto attendete. (*Va a cercare nel credenzione.*)

**GIL:** Ah, presso alla morte, si giovane, sono!
Oh, cielo, pegli empi ti chiedo perdono.
Perdonna tu, o padre, a questa in felice!
Sia l' uomo felice—ch' or vado a salvar.

**MAD:** Su spicciati, presto, fa l' opra compita:
Anelo vua vita'—con altra salvar

**SPA:** Ebbene—son pronto, quell' uscio dis chiudi;
Piucch' altro li scudi—mi preme salvar.

**SPA:** Kill the buffoon! What nonsense have you said?
Am I a thief? Have I ever lost my honor?
Is there a client that I have betrayed?
I must not break my faith. This man has paid.

**GIL:** What do I hear? My father!

**MAG:** I pray for him.

**SPA:** He must die.

**MAG:** No; I shall tell him to fly.

**GIL:** Good-hearted woman!

**SPA:** Now, let me.

**MAG:** We must save him.

**SPA:** Should any one come here before midnight,
I shall kill him instead.

**MAG:** The night is dark, the thunder roars,
No one will pass this way.

**GIL:** Oh, what temptation, to die for this cruel man.
To die, O father! Heavens! have pity on me!
(*It strikes half-past eleven.*)

**SPA:** Still half an hour.

**MAG:** Await, my brother. (*Weeping.*)

**GIL:** That woman weeps, and shall I not help him?
Ah: if he no more feels love for me,
I'll give my life to save his own.
(*Knocking at the door.*)

**MAG:** One knocks.

**SPA:** It is the wind.

**MAG:** One knocks, I say.

**SPA:** It is strange!

**MAG:** Who is there?

**GIL:** Have pity upon a stranger
Grant him asylum for the night.

**MAG:** This night will be long!

**SPA:** Wait awhile. (*Spa. searches at the sideboard.*)

**GIL:** So near to death, and yet so young!
O heaven! pardon these impious men,
And you, my father, excuse your child,
May happy live the man I save.

**MAG:** Now hasten, quick, perform the deed,
To save one life I take another.

**SPA:** Well, I am ready. Now open the door,
To save the crowns is all my care.
(*Spa. hides himself behind the door with a dagger. Mag. opens the door, then runs to shut the*

*arch in front, and whilst Gilda enters, Spa. shuts the door behind her, and everything remains buried in silence and darkness.*)

## SCENA VII

*Rigoletto solo si avanza da fondo della scena chiuso nel suo mantello.*

Della vendetta alfin giunge l' instante!
Da trenta di l' aspetto
Di vivo sangue a lagrime piangendo
sotto la larva del buffon—Quest'
uscio!
(*Esaminando ia casa*)
E' chiusa!—Ah, non e tempo ancor!—S' attenda.
Qual notte di mistero!
Una tempesta in cielo!
In terra un omicicio!
Oh comee in vero quì grande mi
sento! (*Suona mezza notte.*)
Mezza notte!

## SCENA VIII

*Detto e Sparafucile dalle casa*

SPA: Chi è la?

RIG: Son io (*Per entrare*)

SPA: Sostare (*Rentra e torna trascinando un sacco*)
E qul spento il vostr' uomo.

RIG: Oh gioia!—Un lume.

SPA: Un lume?—No, il danaro.
(*Rig. gli da una borsa.*)

SPA: Lesti, all' onda il gettiam

RIG: No—basto io solo.

## SCENE VII

*Rigoletto advances from the road enveloped in his cloak. The violence of the storm is diminished, only now and then the lightning is to be seen and the thunder heard.*

RIG: At last the time of my revenge approaches.
For thirty days I waited this fatal hour
In tears most bitter,
Under the mask of a buffoon. That door
(*Examining the house.*)
Is shut—It's not the hour yet.
What a dreadful night is this!
In heaven a storm,
On earth a homicide—
I feel myself yet great.
It is midnight.
(*It strikes twelve.*)

## SCENE VIII

*Enter Sparafucile.*

SPA: Who is there?

RIG: It is I. (*On the point of entering.*)

SPA: Await. (*Re-enters, and comes out again, dragging a sack.*)
Your man is here, quite dead.

RIG: Oh, joy! a light

SPA: A light! Not yet—the money!
(*Rig. gives him a purse*)

SPA: Quick, let us throw him into the river.

RIG: I can do it alone.

SPA: Come pi piace—Quì men atto e il sito
Più avanti e più profondo il gorgo—Presto
Che alcun non vi sorprenda—Buona notte.

## SCENA IX

*Rigoletto, poi il Duca.*

RIG: Egli è là!—morto!—O si—vorrei vederlo!
Ma che importa!—e ben desso!—
Ecco i suoi sproni.
Ora mi garda, o mondo—
Quest' è un buffone, ed un potente è questo!
Ei sta sotto a' miei piedi. E' desso! è desso!
E' giunta alfin la tua vendetta, o duolo!
Sia l' onda a lui sepolero,
Un sacco il suo lenzuolo!
(*Fa per trascinare il sacco verso la sponda, quando e sorpreso dalla lontana voce del Duc. che nel fondo attraversa la scena.*)
Qual voce! illusion notturna e questa!
No! no!—egli è desso! è desso!
(*Trasalendo*)
Maledizione! Olà dimon bandito?
(*Verso la casa*)
Chi è mai, chi è qui in sua vece!
(*Taglia il sacco.*)
Io tremo. E' umano corpo!
(*Lampeggia.*)

RIG: Mia figlia! Dio! mia figlia! Gilda!
(*Strappandosi i rapelli cade sul cadevere della figlia.*]

*The End.*

SPA: As you desire. This place is not the best.
Higher up the waves are deeper.
Be quick, that none may see you
Good night. (*Re-enters the house*)

## SCENE IX

*Rigoletto, and afterward the Duke.*

RIG: He is here—he is dead. Oh yes! I would see him!
But why? 'Tis he. Here are his spurs.
The crowd
Can now look well at me.
I am the Jester, and he is the Duke.
Dying now at my feet.
I am at last revenged!
The wave shall be his grave,
A sack his shroud,
(*He tries to drag the sack towards the shore, when he hears the distant voice of the Duke, who crosses the scene.*)
What voice? Am I deceived?
No, no!—it is he—it is he!
(*Surprised*)
Ho, there! Demon!
(*Towards the house.*)
But who can be in this sack instead of him?
(*He cuts the sack.*)
A human body! I tremble.
(*It lightens*)

RIG: My daughter! Heaven! my Gilda!
(*He falls despairingly at the side of his daughter.*]

*The End.*

# Il Trovatore (1853)

## The Troubadour

Music by Giuseppe Verdi ■ Libretto by Salvatore Commarano

This four-act opera, set to a libretto by Salvatore Cammarano (based upon Antonio García Gutiérrez' tragedy, El Trovador), was first performed at the Teatro Apollo in Rome on January 19, 1853. In early fifteenth century Spain, Ferrando, Captain of Count Di Luna's Guard, is recounting a story to his men. Many years ago, when the Count was a little boy, his brother was bewitched by an old gypsy woman. She was burned alive at the stake for her crime; her daughter, Azucena, avenged her death. One night the Count's brother disappeared; the bones of a child were found in the very spot the gypsy woman had been killed. Leonora, lady-in-waiting to the Princess of Aragon, is in love with Manrico, a troubador. One night she thinks she hears his voice and hastens to meet him—but it is Count Di Luna, also in love with her. The two men prepare to duel over Leonora. Manrico is injured, and Azucena nurses him back to health. He thinks that she is his mother; the truth is that when she stole Count Di Luna's brother so long ago she threw her own child into the fire by mistake so she kept Manrico as her own. Believing Manrico to be dead, Leonora decides to enter a convent. Di Luna and his men try to kidnap her, but Manrico arrives in the nick of time. Di Luna's men capture Azucena. When it becomes known that she is the daughter of the old gypsy woman, she too is sentenced to be burned at the stake. Manrico and Leonora are about to wed when he hears of Azucena's incarceration and rushes off to rescue her. Manrico is now a prisoner in Di Luna's jail; Leonora implores Di Luna to spare him. She offers up herself in his place and Di Luna accepts. Leonora swallows the poison hidden inside her ring. Manrico, now free, rejects his freedom when he realizes what she has done to gain it. Leonora dies in his arms. When Di Luna realizes he has been duped, he decrees that Manrico must be executed. As Manrico is beheaded, Azucena announces that Di Luna has in fact murdered his own flesh and blood—Manrico was his brother. Her mother's death is thus finally avenged.

---

## ■ ATTO PRIMO.

### SCENA I.

*Atrio nel Palazzo dell'Aliaferio: porta da un lato, che mette agli appartamenti del Conte de Luna.—FERRANDO e molti Famigliari del Conte, che giacciono presso la porta: alcuni Uomini di Arme che passeggiano in fondo.*

**FERRANDO:** (*Parla ai Famigliari.*) All' erta, all' erta! Il Conte
N' è d' uopo attender vigilando; ed egli
Talor, presso i veroni
Della sua vaga, intere
Passa le notti.

**FAMIGLIARI:** Gelosia le fiere
Serpi gli avventa in petto!

**FERRANDO:** Nel trovator, che dai giardini muove
Notturno il canto, d' un rivale a dritto
Ei teme.

**FAMIGLIARI:** Dalle gravi
Palpèbre il sonno a discacciar, la vera
Storia ci narra di Garzia, germano
Al nostro Conte.

## ■ ACT I.

### SCENE I.

*Vestibule in the Palace of Aliaferia, with door on one side, opening to the Apartments of the Count de Luna.—FERRANDO, and the Servants of the Count, discovered lying near the doorway: Soldiers perambulate the background.*

**FERRANDO:** (*To the slumbering Servants.*) Wake up, wake up! The Count
Must not find you sleeping.
You know how often
He passes the night
Beneath the balcony of his mistress.

**SERVANTS:** Her fiery serpents
have let loose jealousy in his bosom!

**FERRANDO:** The troubadour, who within her garden
Serenades her nightly, a formidable rival
May well be reckoned.

**SERVANTS:** If from our eyes
You would dispel heavy sleep,
Tell us the story of Garzia,
The brother of our master.

**FERRANDO:** La dirò: venite
Intorno a me.
(*Famigliari eseguiscono accostandos pur essi.*)

**UOMINI D' ARME:** Noi pure—

**FAMIGLIARI:** Udite, udite.
(*Tutti accerchiano Ferrando.*)

**FERRANDO:** Di due figli vivea, padre beato,
Il buon Conte di Luna:
Fida nutrice del secondo nato
Dormia presso la cuna;
Sul romper dell' aurora un bel mattino
Ella dischiude i rai,
E chi trova d'accanto a quel bambino?

**CORO:** Chi!—Favella—chi mai?

**FERRANDO:** Abbietta zingara, fosca vegliarda!
Cingeva i simboli di maliarda!
E sul fanciullo, con viso arcigno,
L'occhio affiggeva torvo, sanguigno!
D'orror compresa la nutrice;
Acuto un grido all'aura scioglie;
Ed ecco, in meno che labbro il dice,
I servi accorrono in quelle soglie
E fra minacce, urli, percosse,
La rea discacciano ch'entrarvi osò.

**FERRANDO:** I will tell you: approach,
Draw close up to me.
(*The Servants cluster about him.*)

**SOLDIERS:** We, too?

**SERVANTS:** Listen, listen.
(*All surround Ferrando.*)

**FERRANDO:** The Count de Luna
Was the happy father of two beloved children:
The faithful nurse of the second-born
Slept near his cradle;
Awakening one morning at break of day,
She was horrified at seeing—what,
Think you, she saw by the side of that child?

**CHORUS:** What?—Tell us—what did she see?

**FERRANDO:** There stood a gipsy hag, withered and swarthy!
Clad in habiliments her race disclosing!
Fixed were those dark eyes, with fury gleaming,
On that child's features in peace reposing!
Horror and fear seized upon the child's attendant;
With her wild cries the mansion then resounded;
And, swiftly as words can describe rapid movement,
The servants all, in wild alarm,

CORO: Giusto quei petti sdegno commosse!
L'insana vecchia lo provocò!

## SCENA II.

*Giardini del Palazzo; sulla destra marmorea scalinata che mette negli appartamenti. — La notte è inoltrata, e dense nubi coprono la luna.*
*(Entra LEONORA ed INES.)*

INES: Che più t'arresti?—l'ora è tarda; vieni,
Di te la regal donna
Chiese, l'udisti.

LEONORA: Un'altra notte ancora
Senza vederlo!

INES: Perigliosa fiamma
Tu nutri!—oh come, dove
La primiera favilla
In te s'apprese?

LEONORA: Ne' tornei. V'apparve.
Bruno le vesti ed il cimier, lo scudo
Bruno e di stemma ignudo,
Sconosciuto guerrier, che dell'agone
Gli onori ottenne—al vincitor sul crine
Il serto io posi—civil guerra intanto
Arse—nol vidi più!—come d'aurato
Sogno, fuggente imago!—ed era volta
Lunga stagion—ma poi—

INES: Che avvenne?

LEONORA: Ascolta!
Tacea la notte placida!
E bella in ciel sereno!
La luna il viso argenteo
Mostrava lieto a pineo!
Quando suonar per l'aere,
Infino allor sì muto,
Dolci s'udiro e flebili,
Gli accordi di un liuto,
E versi melanconici,
Un trovator cantò.
Versi di prece, ed umile,
Qual d'uom che prega Iddio!
In quella ripeteasi
Un nome—il nome mio!
Corsi al veron sollecita.
Egli era, egli era desso!
Gioja provai che agli angeli
Solo è provar concesso!
Al core, al guardo estatico
La terra un ciel sembrò!

there bounded:
That horrid beldame they soon ejected.
Who her accursed arts had ventured there.

CHORUS: Justly was their wrath excited!
The beldame her punishment provoked!

## SCENE II.

*The Gardens of the Palace; on one side a flight of marble steps, leading to the interior—Night, advanced, the moon obscured by dense clouds.*
*(Enter LEONORA and INES.)*

INES: Why do you still remain?—It's late;
Come, the Queen, you know,
Desires your attendance.

LEONORA: Another night, then, must pass
Without seeing him!

INES: I fear, you are nourishing a dangerous passion!—But come,
Tell me when the first spark
Was kindled within you?

LEONORA: At the tournament. There.
Clad in black from head to foot,
And carrying a black shield,
An unknown warrior appeared—
He won the laurel, and on his brow
I placed it.
But soon the civil war broke out,
And I saw no more of him,
Unless in the golden visions of my sleep!
Once—some time had passed—but then—

INES: What happened?

LEONORA: Listen!
How calm how placid was the night!
The cloudless sky, how clear, how bright!
The moon in splendour shed her light,
And all was hushed in peace around!
Suddenly, on the midnight air,
In tones so sweet and thrilling,
Breathing to Heaven an earnest prayer,
My heart with deep joy filling,
I heard a voice oft heard before,
My long-loved troubadour.
The words were those of a prayer,
Humbly addressed to Heaven,
In which I heard a name repeated:
That name—it was my own!
I hastened to the balcony:
It was he—It was he himself!
The joy which I then felt
Angels in heaven alone can feel!—
To my delighted eyes
Earth seemed raised to heaven!

INES: Quanto narrasti di turbamento
M'ha piena l'anima!—Io temo—

LEONORA: Invano!

INES: Dubbio ma tristo presentimento
In me risveglia quest'uomo arcano!
Tenta obliarlo—

LEONORA: Che dici!—Oh, basti!

INES: Cedi al consiglio dell'amistà—
Cedi—

LEONORA: Obliarlo!—Ah! tu parlasti
Detto, che intendere l'alma non sa.
Di tale amor che dirsi
Mal può dalla parola,
D'amor, che intendo io sola,
Il cor s'inebrio.
Il mio destino compirsi,
Non può che a lui d'appresso.
S'io non vivrò per esso,
Per esso morirò!

INES: *(A parte).* Non debba mai pentirsi
Chi tanto un giorno amò!
*(Ascendono agli appartamenti.)*
*(Entra il CONTE.)*

CONTE: Tace la notte! Immersa
Nel sonno è, certo, la regal signora:
Ma veglia la sua dama—Oh! Leonora,
Tu desta sei; mel dice
Da quel verone tremolante un raggio
Della notturna lampa.
Ah! l'amorosa vampa
M'arde ogni fibra!—Ch'io ti vegga è d'uopo,
Che tu m'intenda, vengo.—A noi supremo
E tal momento!
*(Cieco d'amore avviasi alla gradinata: odonsi gli accordi di un liuto; egli si arresta.)*
Il trovator!—Io fremo!

MANRICO: Deserto sulla terra,
Col rio destino in guerra,
E' sola speme un cor,
Un cor al trovator!
Ma s'ei quel cor possiede,
Bello di casta fede,
È d'ogni re maggior
Il trovator!

CONTE: Oh, detti!—Oh, gelosia,
Non m'inganno.—Ella scende.
*(Si avvolge nel suo mantello.)*
*(Entra LEONORA.)*

LEONORA: *(Correndo verso il Conte.)* Anima mia!

CONTE: *(Aparte).* Che far?

INES: What you have related to me
Fills my mind with trouble!—I fear—

LEONORA: What?

INES: I don't know, but
This mysterious stranger excites a sad foreboding.
Try to forget.

LEONORA: What say you!—Oh, cease!

INES: Yield to the counsels of friendship—
Forget him.

LEONORA: Forget him!—Ah! you speak a language
Which the heart cannot comprehend.
Ah! no, it were vain concealing
This heart's deep-seated feeling,
For him my love revealing;—
In vain I try, in vain I try,—
It will hold while life remains.
Each sense, each thought enslaving,
For him all danger braving,
No other joy ever craving,
Till death with him, till death with him
I'd share each joy and pain!

INES: *(Aside).* May she never repent the day
On which she learned to love so madly!
*(They ascend the steps of the Palace.)* *(Enter the Count.)*

COUNT: How still the night! In its silence
The queen is, doubtless, wrapped in sleep;
But her attendant will keep watch.
Oh, Leonora! You sleep not, I know,
By the tremulous light of the lamp
Which I see through the casement.
Ah me! the love I feel
Throbs within each vein!—I come!
At your feet I will throw myself!—
Oh, what a blissful moment is this!
*(Goaded by his passion, he rushes to the steps, but is arrested by hearing the tones of a lute.)*
The troubadour!—Oh, revenge!

MANRICO: *(Without).* Ah! though deserted by all on earth,
And though by fortune deemed worth nothing,
Yet one dear hope remains,
For the troubadour!
If but that heart be his,
That heart so warm and pure,
Greater than any king
Is the troubadour!

COUNT: What says he!—Oh, jealousy,
Deceive not my ears.—But she comes.
*(Draws his cloak about him.)*
*(Enter LEONORA).*

LEONORA: *(Quickly approaching the Count.)* My beloved one!

COUNT: *(Aside).* What shall I do?

**LEONORA:** Più dell' usato
È tarda l' ora: io ne contai gl' instanti
Coi palpiti del core!—Alfin ti guida
Pietoso amor tra queste braccia.

**LA VOCE DEL TROVATORE:** Infida!
(*La luna mostrasi dai nugli, e lascia scorgere una persona, di cui la visiera nasconde il volto.*)
(*Entra MANRICO.*)

**LEONORA:** (*Riconoscendo entrambi, e gettandosi ai piedi di Manrico.*) Qual voce!—Ah, dalle tenebre
Tratta in errore io fui!
A te credei rivolgere
L' accento, e non a lui—
A te, che l' alma mia
Sol chiede, sol desia!
Io t' amo, il giuro, io t' amo
D' immenso, eterno amor!

**CONTE:** Ed osi?

**MANRICO:** (*Sollevandola*). Ah, più non bramo!

**CONTE:** Avvampo di furor!
Se un vil non sei, discovriti!

**LEONORA:** Ohimè!

**CONTE:** Palesa il nome!

**LEONORA:** (*Sommessamente a Manrico.*) Deh, per pietà!—

**MANRICO:** Ravvisami,—
Manrico io son!

**CONTE:** Tu!—Come?
Insano, temerario!
D' Urgel seguace, a morte
Proscritto, ardisci volgerti
A queste regio porte?

**MANRICO:** Che tardi!—or via le guardie
Appella, ed il rivale
Al ferro del carnefice
Consegna!

**CONTE:** Il tuo fatale
Istante assai più prossimo
E', dissenato! Vieni!

**LEONORA:** Conte!—

**CONTE:** Al mio sdegno vittima
È forza ch' io ti sveni!

**LEONORA:** Oh, ciel!—t' arresta!

**CONTE:** Seguimi!

**MANRICO:** Andiam!

**LEONORA:** (*A parte*). Che mai farò?
Un sol mio grido perdere lo puote!
(*Al Conte.*)
M' odi!

**CONTE:** No!
Di geloso amor sprezzato
Arde in me tremendo foco!
Il tuo sangue, o sciagurato,
Ad estinguerlo fia poco!
(*A Leonora.*)

**LEONORA:** You are behind your time:
I have numbered the wearying moments
By the beating of my heart!—But, at last,
Love takes pity, and brings you here.

**VOICE OF TROUBADOUR:** False one!
(*The moon diverges from the clouds, and displays to view a man with a visor over his face.*)
(*MANRICO comes forward.*).

**LEONORA:** (*Recognizing each, and falling at the feet of Manrico.*)
That voice!—Ah, by the darkness,
I've been brought into error!
For you alone I meant my words,
And not for any other—
For you, and you only,
My soul's desire!
It is you I love—to you I swear
My everlasting love!

**COUNT:** Dare she say this?

**MANRICO:** (*Raising her*). Ah!
what more can I desire!

**COUNT:** I'm consumed with rage!
If you are no coward, uncover yourself!

**LEONORA:** Alas!

**COUNT:** Reveal your name!

**LEONORA:** (*Imploring, to Manrico.*) For pity's sake!—

**MANRICO:** Behold me,—
I am Manrico!

**COUNT:** You!—But how!
Rash daring man!
The accomplice of Urgel, condemned to death.
How dare you appear
Within this royal palace?

**MANRICO:** Why hesitate?—call the guard here,
And your rival, now before you,
You can consign
To the hands of the headsman.

**COUNT:** Your last hour
Is nearer, perhaps, than you think!
Villain, draw your sword!

**LEONORA:** My Lord!—

**COUNT:** To my rage the victim,
Here will I destroy him!

**LEONORA:** Oh heaven!—stay, stay!

**COUNT:** Follow me!

**MANRICO:** I will do so!

**LEONORA:** (*Aside*). What shall I do?
A single cry from me, and he is lost!
(*To the Count.*)
Pray, hear me!

**COUNT:** No!
The fury of a love despised
Rages within my breast!
Your blood, unhappy man,
That rage alone can quench!
(*To Leonora.*)

Dirgli, o folle—io t' amo—ardisti
Ei più vivere non può—
Un accento proferisti,
Che a morir lo condannò!

**LEONORA:** Un istante almen dia loco
Il tuo sdegno alla ragione:
Io, sol io di tanto foco
Son, pur troppo, la cagione!
Piombi, ah! piombi il tuo ruror
Sulla rea che t' oltraggiò!
Vibra il ferro in questo core,
Che te amar non vuol, non può!

**MANRICO:** Del suberbo vana è l' ira!
Ei cadrà de me trafitto!
Il mortal che amor t' inspira,
Dall' amor fu reso invitto!
(*Al Conte.*)
La tua sorte è già compita—
L' ora omai per te suonò!
Il tuo core e la tua vita
Il destino a me serbo!
(*I due rivali si allontanano con le spade sguainate; Leonora cade priva di sentimento.*)

*FINE DELL'ATTO PRIMO.*

To him you have declared your love,—
Can I allow him still to live?
You have the words pronounced
Which to death have condemned him!

**LEONORA:** Let your anger
By reason be subdued for a moment:
It is I alone encouraged him
To offer homage to me!
Let your vengeance light on me,—
It is my offense his loving me!
Your sword may pierce my heart,
But it cannot feel love for you!

**MANRICO:** I scorn his pride and anger;
By this hand he shall fall!
The mortal by your love exalted
Invincible must be!
(*To the Count.*)
Your fate is determined already—
Your hours are numbered already!
Over your life, as over your love,
Fate now gives me dominion!
(*The rivals retire with their swords drawn; Leonora falls senseless.*)

*END OF THE FIRST ACT.*

# ■ ATTO SECONDO.

## SCENA I.

*Un diruto abituro sulle falde d'un monte della Biscaglia; nel fondo, quasi tutto operto, arde un gran fuoco.—I primi albori.*

*AZUCENA siede presso il fuoco.—MANRICO le sta disteso accanto sopra una coltrice, ed avviluppato nel suo mantello, ha l'elmo ai piedi, e fra le mani la spada, su cui figge immobile lo sguardo.—Una banda di Zingari è sparsa all'intorno.*

**ZINGARA:** Vedi! le fosche notturne spoglie
De' cieli sveste l'immensa volta;
Sembra una vedova che alfin si toglie
I bruni panni ond'era involta.
All'opra—dàgli, martella!
Che' del gitano i giorni abbellla, La Zingarella!
(*Danno di piglio ai loro ferri di mestiere: al misurato tempestar dei martelli cadenti sulle incudini, ed uomini e donne e tutti in un tempo in fine intuonano la cantilena seguente*):

**UOMINI:** (*Alle donne, sostando un poco dal lavoro.*) Versami un tratto: lena e coraggio
Il corpo e l'anima traggon dal bere.
(*Le donne mescono ad essi in rozze coppe*).

# ■ ACT II.

## SCENE I.

*A Dwelling in the Ruins of a House at the Foot of a Mountain in Biscay; within it, fully in view, a large Fire.—Day breaking.*

*AZUCENA discovered, sitting near the fire.—MANRICO is lying near her, wrapped in a large cloak, his helmet at his feet, and his sword grasped in his hand.—Gipsies, in various positions, fill up the scene.*

**GIPSIES:** See! the sombre hues of night
Depart from the face of heaven:
Thus the widow casts away
The tokens of her bereavement.
To our work—each to his hammer!
Who is it makes the gipsy life so gay? It is the Gitana!
(*All take up their tools: to the measured clang of the hammers, first the Males, and then the Females, and ultimately all in chorus, sing the following:*)

**MEN:** (*To the Women, ceasing from their work.*) Fill up my cup:
both body and soul
By generous drink are refreshed.
(*The Women hand them drink, in rustic cups.*)

TUTTI: Oh, guarda, guarda! del sole un raggio
Brilla più vivido nel tuo bicchiere!
All'opra, all'opra—dàgli, martella
Quale a voi splende propizia stella
La Zingarella!

AZUCENA: (*Cantaigli Zingari le si fanno allato.*) Stride la vampa!—
La folla indomita
Corre a quel fuoco
Lieta in sembianza;
Urli di gioia
D'intorno echeggiano
Cinta di sgherri
Donna s'avanza!
Sinistra splende,
Sui volti orribili
La tetra firamma
Che s'alza al ciel!
Stride la vampa, giunge la vittima
Nero-vestita, discinta e scalza!
Grido feroce di morte levasi;
L'eco il ripete di balza in balza!
Sinistra splende sui volti orribili
La tetra fiamma che s'alza al ciel!

LA ZINGARA: Mesta è la tua canzon!

AZUCENA: Del pari mesta
Che la storia funesta
Da cui tragge argomento!
(*Rivolge il capo dalla parte di Manrico, e mormora cupamente*)
Mi vendica—mi vendica!

MANRICO: (*A parte*). L'arcana Parola ognor!

VECCHIO ZING: Compagni, avanza il giorno:
A procacciarci un pan, su su!—scen diamo
Per le propinque ville.

UOMINI: Andiamo.
(*Ripongono sollecitamente nei sacchi i loro arnesi*).

DONNE: Andiamo.
(*Tutti scendono alla rinfusa giù per la china: tratto tratto e sempre a maggior distanza, odesi ii loro conto*).

ZINGARA: Chi del gitano i giorni abbella? La Zingarella!

MANRICO: (*sorgendo*) Soli or siamo, deh, narra
Quella storia funesta.

AZUCENA: E tu la ignori,
Tu pur!—Ma giovinetto i passi tuoi
D'ambizion lo sprone
Lungi traea! Dell'ava il fine acerbo
E' quella storia, la incolpo' superbo
Conte di malefizio, onde asseria
Colto un bambin suo figlio, essa bruciata

ALL: Oh, look, look here! the rising sunlight shines
More brightly in our cups!
To work, to work—the hammers hurl!
Who is it makes our lives so gay? It is the Gitana!

AZUCENA: (*As she begins, the Gipsies gather around her*).
Fiercely the flames burn!
Wildly the eager crowd
Rushes forth, with wild shouts,
Crying for vengeance:
As they surround the fire,
Echoed by all around,
See! that pale woman,
Thrust forth by—
Higher and higher still,
Reaching towards the sky,
Thick wreaths of smoke ascent with speed:
The fire each with fear appals.
As the flames brighten, in funereal array,
Barefooted, the helpless victim comes!
Exulting cries from the crowd are heard,
From hill to hill in echoes passed!
On the beholders' faces the flame
And smoke a ghastly hue overspread!

GIPSIES: A song of sadness, truly!

AZUCENA: Not more sad
Than the terrible story
From which it had its origin!
(*Turning towards Manrico, she whispers mournfully:*)
Vengeance—I must have vengeance!

MANRICO: (*Aside*). Again uttering These mysterious words!

ELDERLY GIPSY: Companions, the day advances:
We must away, our bread to seek
Among the neighbouring villages.

MEN: Ay, let us go.
(*They put away their tools.*)

WOMEN: Ay, let us go.
(*All ascend the mountain, singing: the sounds become piano by degrees, as they disappear in the distance.*)

GIPSIES: Who makes the gipsy's life so gay? The Gitana!

MANRICO: (*Rising*). Now we are alone, pray tell me
The whole of this dismal story.

AZUCENA: You know it
Already?—It is true you were young
When ambition drew you from me!
The story is of an infant's evil end:
Its haughty father charged my mother
With sorcery practiced upon his

Fu dov'arde or quel foco!

MANRICO: Ahi! sciagurata!
(*Rifuggendo con raccapriccio dalla fiamma*).

AZUCENA: Condotta ell'era in ceppi al suo destin tremendo
Col figlio, teco in braccio, io la seguia piangendo:
Infino ad esse un varco tentai, ma invano, aprirmi:
Invan tento' la misera fermarsi, e benedirmi!
Che, fra bestemmie oscene, pungendola coi ferri
Al rogo la cacciavano gli scellerati sgherri!
Allor, con tronco accento, mi vendica! esclamo'.
Quel detto un'eco eterna in questo cor lascio'.

MANRICO: La vendicasti!

AZUCENA: Il figlio giunsi a rapir del Conte;
Lo trascinai qui meco, le fiamme ardean gia' pronte.

MANRICO: Le fiamme?—Oh, ciel!—Tu forse . . .

AZUCENA: Ei distruggeasi in pianto—
Io mi sentivo il cor dilaniato, infranto!
Quand'ecco agli egri spirti, come in un sogno, apparve
La vision ferale di spaventose larve!
Gli sgherri ed il supplizio! La madre smorta in volto—
Scalza, discinta! il grido, il noto grido ascolto,
Mi vendica! La mano convulsa tendo, stringo
La vittima—nel foco la traggo, la sospingo!
Cessa il fatal delirio, l'orrida scena fugge—
La fiamma sol divampa, e la sua preda strugge!
Pur volgo intorno il guardo, e innanzi a me vegg'io
Dell'empio Conte il figlio!

MANRICO: Ah! come?

AZUCENA: Il figlio mio—
Mio figlio—aveva bruciato!

MANRICO: Che dici—quale orror!

AZUCENA: Sul capo mio le chiome sento drizzarsi ancor!
(*Azucena ricade trambasciata sul proprio seggio: Manrico ammutisce colpito d'orrore e di sorpresa.—Momenti di silenzio.*)

MANRICO: Non son tuo figlio?—E chi son io, chi dunque?

child;—
For that he caused her to be burned,
Just where you now behold that fire!

MANRICO: Ah! how horrible!
(*Looking towards the fire shudderingly.*)

AZUCENA: In fetters they dragged her to her woeful fate:
With you in my arms, weeping, I followed.
In vain I strove to penetrate the crowd;
In vain she prayed for time to bless her child;
The soldiers with their lances drove her on,
Amid brutal insults, to the flaming pile,
While, in accent wild, she cried, 'Avenge me!'
For ever in my heart will those words abide.

MANRICO: And did you avenge her?

AZUCENA: The Count's young son I seized upon:
I ran here, where the fire was ready blazing.

MANRICO: The fire?—oh, heaven!—you could not—

AZUCENA: The helpless infant screamed,
And my heart was with pity touched!
In a sudden trance I was absorbed; then
Dreadful phantoms through my brain careered;
The soldiers, the flaming pile, my mother pale
For mercy praying;—amidst it all,
The well-remembered cry for vengeance!
Convulsively in my hand clenched
The fated boy, and in the fire I hurled him:
The flames alone remained with their struggling victim;—
The living child of the accursed Count!
I looked around, and beheld, approaching me,

MANRICO: Ah! how was this?

AZUCENA: It was my own son—
My own darling boy—that I had burned!

MANRICO: What did you say? It is too horrible!

AZUCENA: Even now I feel maddened with anguish!
(*Azucena falls, fainting, on her seat: Manrico, overwhelmed with surprise and horror, remains for some moments in silence.*)

MANRICO: I, then, am not your son?—
Tell me who I am!

## Act II, Scene I

**AZUCENA:** (*Con sollecitudine di chi cerca emendare involontario fallo.*)
Tu sei mio figlio!

**MANRICO:** Eppur dicesti—

**AZUCENA:** Ah! forse—
Che vuoi!—Quando al pensier s'affaccia il truce
Caso, lo spirto intenebrato pone
Stolte parole sul mio labbro.—Madre
Tenera madre non m'avesti ognora?

**MANRICO:** Potrei negarlo?

**AZUCENA:** A me, se vivi ancora,
Nol dei?—Notturna, nei pugnati campi
Di Pelilla, ove spento
Fama ti disse, a darti
Sepoltura non mossi! La fuggente
Aura vital no iscovri, nel seno
Non l'arrestò materno affetto?—E quante
Cure non spesi a risanar le tante
Ferite!—

**MANRICO:** (*con nobile orgoglio*)
Che portai quel di fatale!
Ma tutte qui, nel petto? Io sol, fra mille
Già sbandati, al nemico
Volgendo ancor la faccia! Il rio De Luna,
Su me piombò col suo drapello: io caddi,
Però, da forte io caddi!

**AZUCENA:** Ecco mercede
Ai giorni, che l'infame
Nel singolar certame
Ebbe salvi da te!—qual t'acciecava
Strana pietà per esso?

**MANRICO:** Oh, madre, non saprei dirlo a me stesso!
Mal reggendo all'aspro assalto,
Ei già tocco il suolo avea:
Balenava il colpo in alto
Che trafiggerlo dovea.
Quando arresta un moto arcano,
Nel discender questa mano!
Le mie fibre acuto gelo
Fa repente abbrividir!
Mentre un grido vien dal cielo,
Che mi dice: non ferir.

**AZUCENA:** Ma nell'alma dell'ingrato
Non parlò del cielo il detto!
Oh! se ancor ti spinge il fato

**AZUCENA:** (*Hastily, as if to repair an involuntary admission.*)
You are my son!

**MANRICO:** But you have just said—

**AZUCENA:** Ah! perhaps so—
What would you?—When to my mind
That awful scene occurs, sometimes
I know not what foolish things I say.
Your mother?—Have I not ever been to you a tender mother?

**MANRICO:** Have I ever denied it?

**AZUCENA:** And it is not through me
That you are living now?—Was it not I,
When report had numbered you with the dead
Who, in the dreariest hours of night,
Traversed the battle-field of Pelilla,
With my own hands to give you burial?
The vital spark still lingering in your breast
I found; and a mother's love revived it!
Who was it healed your many wounds?

**MANRICO:** (*Proudly*). All on that fatal day received!
And all in the breast!—I alone stood firm,
While thousands turned and fled!
The base De Luna, with his whole squadron,
Rushed on me: I fell,
But like a soldier did I fall?

**AZUCENA:** Such was his gratitude
For the life spared to him,
Though forfeited in single combat.
What strange infatuation was it
That thus blinded your reason!

**MANRICO:** Oh, mother, I know not how it was!
When contending, my arms proved victorious:
Struck to the earth, and at my mercy lying,
One stroke of vengeance on that form inglorious,
Pity alone restrained, no longer me defying.
Some, resistless power, withheld the arm uplifted;
Chilled and nerveless, it fell drooping at my side;
And I thought a mighty voice on high cried,
'Hold, and slay him not!'
Heeding its mandate—trembling with terror
Once again I heard the cry,
'Withhold your arm—slay him not!'

**AZUCENA:** But in the breast of that ingrate
Never was yet heard the voice of heaven!

A pugnar col maledetto,
Compi, o figlio, qual d'un Dio,
Compi allor il cenno mio:
Sino all'elsa questa lama
Vibra, immergi all'empio in cor!
(*Odesi un prolungato suono di corno.*)

**MANRICO:** L'usato messo Ruiz invia,
Forse.
(*Dà fiato anch'esso al corno che tiene ad armacollo.*)

**AZUCENA:** Mi vendica!
(*Resta concentrata quasi inconsapevole di cio che succede*)
(*Entra il Messo.*)

**MANRICO:** (*al Messo*) Inoltra il pie'.
Guerresco evento dimmi, seguia?
(*Porgendo il foglio, che Manrico legge.*)

**MANRICO:**
"In nostra possa e' Castellor; ne dei
Tu per cenno del Prence,
Vigilar le difese. Ove ti e' dato,
Affrettati a venir. Giunta la sera
Tratta in inganno di tua morte al grido,
Nel vicin claustro della croce il velo
Cingerà Leonora." (*Con dolorosa esclamazione.*)
Oh, giusto cielo!

**AZUCENA:** (*scuotendosi*) Che fia!

**MANRICO:** (*al Messo*) Veloce scendi la balza,
Ed un cavallo a me provvedi.

**MESSO:** Corro.

**AZUCENA:** (*frapponendosi*) Manrico!

**MANRICO:** Il tempo incalza—
Vola; m'aspetta del colle a' piedi.

**AZUCENA:** (*Il Messo parte, affrettatamente.*) E speri, e vuoi?

**MANRICO:** (*a parte*) Perderla!—
Oh, ambascia!
Perder quell'angelo!

**AZUCENA:** (*a parte*) E' fuor di sè!

**MANRICO:** Addio!
(*Postosi l'elmo sul capo, ed afferrando il mantello.*)

**AZUCENA:** No—ferma—odi!

**MANRICO:** Mi lascia!

**AZUCENA:** (*autorevole*) Ferma, son io che parlo a te!
Perigliarti ancor languente
Per cammin selvaggio d'ermo!
Le ferite vuoi, demente!

Oh! should it ever again befall you
That man to encounter in battle,
Fulfill, as you would obey your God,
The command your mother now gives you:
Within the heart of the craven wretch
Let your dagger be buried to the hilt!
(*The sound of a trumpet is heard.*)

**MANRICO:** The accustomed messenger from Ruiz,
Perhaps.
(*Sounds the horn suspended from his neck.*)

**AZUCENA:** Now shall I be avenged!
(*She remains absorbed in thought, and almost unconscious of what follows.*)
(*Enter a Messenger.*)

**MANRICO:** (*To the Messenger.*)
Approach. Tell me,
Has any engagement taken place?
(*Presenting a letter, which Manrico reads.*)

**MANRICO:** (*Reading*). "Castellor is in our power;
You, by order of the Prince, are chosen
Henceforth to defend it. Waver not,
But come here, without delay.
Deceived by false rumors of your death,
This night, in a neighboring convent,
Leonora takes the veil."
(*In despairing tones.*) Oh, just heaven!

**AZUCENA:** (*Recovering*). What means this?

**MANRICO:** (*To Messenger*).
Quickly to the plain descend,
And bring me here a horse.

**MESSENGER:** I go.

**AZUCENA:** (*Interposing*). Manrico!

**MANRICO:** Be quick—time presses;
At the foot of the hill await my coming.
(*Exit Messenger, hurriedly.*)

**AZUCENA:** What would you do?

**MANRICO:** (*Aside*). To lose her!—
Oh, torment!
To lose that angel!

**AZUCENA:** (*Aside*). He seems beside himself!

**MANRICO:** Farewell!
(*Puts on his helmet, and wraps his cloak around him.*)

**AZUCENA:** No—stop—listen!

**MANRICO:** Leave me now!

**AZUCENA:** (*Authoritatively*).
Stay, it is I who speak to you!
While yet languishing, do not expose yourself
On a road so cold and desolate!

Riaprir del petto infermo?
NO, soffrirlo non poss'io,
Il tuo sangue è sangue mio!
Ogni stilla che ne versi
Tu la spremi dal mio cor!

**MANRICO:** Un momento puo' involarmi
Il mio ben, la mia speranza!
No, che basti ad arrestarmi,
Terra e ciel non han possanza.
Ah, mi sgombra, o madre i passi
Guai per te, s'io qui retassi;
Tu vedresti ai piedi tuoi
Spento il figlio di dolor!

**AZUCENA:** No, soffrirlo non poss'io

**MANRICO:** Guai per te, s'io qui restassi! . . .

**AZUCENA:** No, soffrirlo non poss'io,
Il tuo sangue? sangue mio!

**MANRICO:** Tu vedresti a' piedi tuoi
Spento il figlio di dolor!
(*Si allontana, indarno trattenuto da Azucena.*)

## SCENA II.

*Chiostro d'un cenobio, in vicinanza di Castellor.—E' notte.*

*Il CONTE DI LUNA, FERRANDO, ed alcuni seguaci, ed avviluppati nei loro mantelli inoltrandosi cautamente.*

**CONTE:** Tutto e' deserto; ne' per l'aura ancora
Suona l'usato carme.
In tempo io guingo!

**FERRANDO:** Ardita opra, o signore,
Imprendi.

**CONTE:** Ardita, e quel furente amore
Ed irritato orgoglio
Chiesero a me. Spento il rival, caduto
Ogni ostacol sembrava a' miei desiri;
Novello e più possente ella ne appresta—
L'altare!—Ah, no! non fia
D'altri Leonora—Leonora è mia!
Il balen del suo sorriso
D'una stella vince il raggio!
Il fulgor del suo bel viso
Nuovo infonde, a me coraggio.
Ah, l'amor, l'amore ond'ardo
Le favelli in mio favor! . . .
Sperda il sole d'un suo sguardo
La tempesta del mio cor.
(*Odesi il rintocco de' sacri bronzi.*)
Quel suono?—Oh, ciel!

Thus harshly you must not renew
Wounds in a body still so weak!
In the same veins flow your blood and mine,
I conjure you to remember!
Every drop that you shed
Is drawn from out my heart.

**MANRICO:** Ah, no! in vain—I must away,
One little fleeting moment may
Deprive me of, while here I stay.
This heart's own long-loved treasure.
Ah! mother dear, no longer try
To check my steps when I would fly;
I'd freely die—for her love.
I must, I must away!

**AZUCENA:** Ah, no, I will not suffer you to depart
From me.

**MANRICO:** Woe for you,
Should I remain here!

**AZUCENA:** No, I cannot suffer you to depart—
Your blood is my blood!

**MANRICO:** Your son at your feet
Will die of grief.
(*Exit, Azucena vainly striving to detain him.*)

## SCENE II.

*(The Cloisters of a Convent, in the vicinity of Castellor.—Night.)*

*Enter the COUNT DE LUNA. FERRANDO, and Followers, enveloped in cloaks, and advancing with caution.*

**COUNT:** It is still; I do not even hear
The accustomed evening hymn.
I have arrived in time!

**FERRANDO:** A daring deed this, my Lord,
You have in hand.

**COUNT:** Daring, indeed, such as raging love
And wounded pride demand of me.
My rival dead, to my heart's longing
All obstacles appeared removed.
But now a greater one arises:
The altar!—Ah, no! even the altar
Shall not have her—Leonora shall be mine!
Brighter than the stars of heaven
Her bright eyes emit their glances!
Her fair cheek, the rose and lily
Sweetly blending,
Sweetly blending their entrances.
Yes, her glance with love inspires me;
Never from this breast it will depart!—
Soothe dear maid, the flame that burns me;
Still the tempest, still the tempest in my heart.
Yes, her glance with passion fires me;

**FERRANDO:** La squilla
Vicino il rito annunzia.

**CONTE:** Ah! pria che giunga
All'altar, si rapisca!

**FERRANDO:** Oh, bada!

**CONTE:** Taci!
Non odo!—Andate.—Di quei faggi all'ombra.
Celatevi!
(*Ferrando e gli altri seguaci si allontanano.*)
Ah! fra poco mia diverra';—
Tutto m'investe un foco!
(*Ansioso, guardingo, osserva dalla parte onde deve giungere Leonora; mentre Ferrando e i seguaci dicono sotto voce.*)

**FERRANDO E GLI ALTRI:**
Ardire!—Andiam—celiamoci
Tra l'ombre nel mister.
Ardire!—Andiam—silenzio!
Si compia il suo voler!

**CONTE:** (*Nell'eccesso del furore*).
Ora per me fatale,
I tuoi momenti affretta:
La gioia che m'aspetta,
Gioja mortal non è!
Esservi ancor rivale
Non puote all'amor mio!
Per me ti fece Iddio
E ti vorrà per me!
(*Raggiunge i suoi nell'interno.*)

**CORO,** *interno, di religiose.* Ah! se l'orror t'ingombra,
Oh, figlia d'Eva, i rai,
Presso a morir, vedrai
Che un'ombra, un sogno fu;—
Anzi del sogno un'ombra
La speme di quaggiu'!
Vieni, e t'asconda il velo
Ad ogni sguardo umano;
Aura, o pensier mondano
Qui vivo più non è!
Al ciel ti volgi, e il cielo
Si schiuderà per te!
(*Entra LEONORA, INES, ed un seguite muliebre.*)

**LEONORA:** Perche? piangete?

**DONNE:** Ah!—dunque
Tu per sempre ne lasci!

**LEONORA:** Oh dolci amiche,
Un riso, una speranza, un fior la terra
Non ha per me! Degg'io
Volgermi a quei che degli afflitti e' solo
Conforto, e dopo i penitenti giorni,
Può fra gli eletti al mio perduto bene

Never from this breast it will depart!
(*Ringing of the convent bell heard.*)
What sound is that?—Oh, heaven!

**FERRANDO:** The convent bell
An approaching rite announces.

**COUNT:** Ah! before she reaches the altar,
We must seize her.

**FERRANDO:** Be careful!

**COUNT:** Silence! I fear not!—
Come here—beneath the shade of those trees
Conceal yourselves!
(*Ferrando and the others retire among the trees.*)
In a little time she will be mine;
My raging love assures me of success!
(*He looks anxiously in the direction in which Leonora is expected to come, while Ferrando and the others sing in undertones—*)

**FERRANDO and OTHERS:**
What audacity!—But come—let us hide
In the shadows of the trees.
What audacity!—But come—be silent!
His orders we must obey!

**COUNT:** (*Furiously*). Oh hour of fate to me,
Hasten your lagging moments.
The joy that I anticipate
Is of more than mortal worth!
No rival can I have;
No one dare to thwart my love!
Fate has designed her for me;
And to me she shall belong!
(*He joins his Followers among the trees.*)

**CHORUS Of NUNS:** (*Within*). Ah! when the shades of night,
Oh, daughter of Eve, shall close on you,
Then will you know that life
Is but a shadow, a fleeting dream;—
Yes, like the passing of a shadow
Are all our earthly hopes!
Come, then, and let this mystic veil
From human eye enshroud you;
From here let care and worldly thought
For evermore be banished.
To heaven now turn and heaven
Will open to receive you!
(*Enter LEONORA, with INES and Female attendants.*)

**LEONORA:** Why do you weep?

**LADIES:** Ah! do you, then,
For ever thus forsake us?

**LEONORA:** Oh, my dear friends,
No joy, no hope, no other charm
Has now this world for me!
To Him alone who can the afflicted console,
And after many years of penitence,
May in heaven to my beloved unite me,—
To Him I turn. Dry, then your tears,

Ricongiungermi un dì. Tergete i rai,
E guidatemi all'ara. (*Incamminandosi.*)
(*Entra il CONTE, irrompendo ad un tratto.*)

CONTE: No, giammai!

DONNE: Il Conte!

LEONORA: Giusto ciel!

CONTE: Per te non havvi
Che l'ara d'Imeneo—

DONNE: Che arditezza!

LEONORA: Cotanto ardia!—
Insano! E qui venisti?

CONTE: A farti mia.
(*E sì dicendo scagliasi verso Leonora onde impadronirsi di lei; ma fra esso e la preda trovasi, qual fantasma sorto di sotterra, Manrico.—Un grido universale irrompe.*)

LEONORA: E deggio?—E posso crederlo?—
Ti veggo a me d'accanto!
E' questo un sogno, un'estasi,
Un sovrumano incanto!
Non regge a tanto giubilo
Rapito il cor, sorpreso!
Sei tu dal ciel disceso,
O in ciel son io con te?

CONTE: Dunque gli estinti lasciano
Di morte il regno eterno
A danno mio rinunzia
Le prede sue l'inferno?
Ma se non mai si fransero
De' giorni tuoi gli stami,
Se vivi e viver brami,
Fuggi da lei, da me.

MANRICO: Nè m'ebbe il ciel, nè l'orrido
Varco infernal sentiero—
Infami sgherri vibrano
Colpi mortali, vero!
Potenza irresistibile
Hanno de' fiumi l'onde;
Ma gli empi un Dio confonde,
Quel Dio soccorse a me!

DONNE: (*a Leonora*) Il cielo in cui fidasti,
Pietade avea di te.

FER. e SEG. (*Al Conte.*) Tu col destin contrasti:
Suo difensore egli è.
(*Entra RUIZ, seguito da lunga tratta di armati.*)

RUIZ: Urgel viva!

MANRICO: Miei prodi guerrieri!

RUIZ: Vieni.

MANRICO: (*a Leonora*) Donna, mi segui.

CONTE: (*opponendosi*) E tu speri?

LEONORA: Oh!

MANRICO: (*Al Conte.*) T'arretra.

And lead me to the altar.
(*About to proceed.*)
(*Enter the COUNT, suddenly, from the wood.*)

COUNT: No, never!

LADIES: The Count!

LEONORA: Merciful heaven!

COUNT: For you there is
No altar save that of Hymen!

LADIES: What boldness!

LEONORA: Rash man! for what do you come?

COUNT: To make you mine
(*On saying so, he approaches, and seizes Leonora; but Manrico appears, like a phantom, and places himself between them.—General consternation.*).

LEONORA: Can it be?—may I believe my eyes?
Is it you I see beside me?
Is this a waking dream, a phantasy,
A vision superhuman?
My heart can scarcely control
The joy of this surprise!
Oh! are you descended from heaven,
Or to heaven am I raised with you?

COUNT: Can then, the dead thus escape
The eternal regions of the dead?
For my loss and vexation
Does hell thus give up its prey?
But, if the thread of life
Has not been broken in you;
If you still live, and hope to live,
Fly alike from her and from me.

MANRICO: Nor heaven nor earth as yet
My earthly course has closed,
Although against my life
A vile traitor has plotted!
Wild and irresistible
Are the waves of the ocean,
But the God who the wicked curbs,
That God has sheltered me!

LADIES: (*To Leonora*). Heaven, on whom you have relied,
Has taken pity on you.

FERRANDO and FOLLOWERS:
(*To the Count.*) Vainly against fate you strive;
For fate has been his protector.
(*Enter RUIZ, followed by a Company of Soldiers.*)

RUIZ: Long live Urgal!

MANRICO: My brave companions!

RUIZ: Come with us.

MANRICO: Lady, follow me.

COUNT: (*Opposing him*). Dare you ask it?

LEONORA: Oh!

MANRICO: (*to the Count*). Stop there!

CONTE: Involarmi costei!
No!
(*Sguainando la spada.*)

RUIZ E ARMATI: Vaneggi!
(*Accerchiando il Conte.*)

FERRANDO E SEGUACI: Che tenti, signor!
(*Il Conte è disarmato da quei di Ruiz.*)

CONTE: De ragione ogni lumi perdei!
(*Con gesti ed accenti di maniaco furore.*)

LEONORA: (*M'atterrisce.*)

COUNT: Ho lo furie nel cor!

RUIZ E ARMATI: Vieni; è lieta la sorte per te.
(*A Manrico.*)

FERRENDO E SERGUACI: Cedi; or ceder viltade non è!
(*Manrico tragge seco Leonora—il Conte è respinto, le donne rifuggono al cenobio—scende subito la tela.*)

FINE DELL'ATTO SECONDO.

COUNT: Would you deprive me of her!
No!
(*Drawing his sword.*)

RUIZ AND SOLDIERS: He raves!
(*Surrounding the Count.*)

FERRANDO AND FOLLOWERS:
What are you saying, sir!
(*The Count is disarmed by the soldiers of Ruiz.*)

COUNT: All my reason is lost in fury
(*with gestures and accents of fury.*)

LEONORA: (*He frightens me!*)

COUNT: Furies dwell in my heart!

RUIZ AND SOLDIERS: Come then, a future of smiles waits for you
(*To Manrico.*)

FERRANDO AND FOLLOWERS:
Yield, since yielding implies no shame.
(*Exit Manrico, leading Leonora—The Count is driven back, the ladies retreat to the Covent, as the curtain falls.*)

END OF THE SECOND ACT.

# ATTO III.

*Il Figlio Della Zingara.*

## SCENA I.

*Accampamento—A destra, il padiglione del Conte Di Luna, su cui sventola la bandiera in segno di supremo comando—da lungi Torreggia Castellor.—Scolte di uomini d'arme da per tutto; altri giocano, altri forbiscono le armi, altri passeggiano.*

(*Entra Ferrando, dal padiglione del Conte.*)

ALCUNI UOMINI D'ARME: Or co' dadi, ma fra poco
Giocherem ben altro gioco!
Questo acciar, dal sangue or terso,
Fia di sangue in breve asperso!
(*Odonsi strumenti guerrieri; tutti si volgono là dove e avanza il suono.*)

ALCUNI: Il soccorso dimandato!
(*Un grosso drappello di balestrieri, in completa armatura traversa il campo.*)

ALTRI: Han l'aspetto del valor!

TUTTI: Più l'assalto ritardato
Or non fia di Castellor.

# ACT III.

*The Gipsy's Son.*

## SCENE I.

*A camp. On the right, the tent of the Count di Luna, on which is displayed a banner, indicative of his supremacy. The fortress of Castellor seen in the distance. The scene full of Soldiers, some playing, some polishing their accoutrements, some walking in apparent conversation, while others are on duty as Sentinels.*

(*Enter Ferrando, from the Tent of the Count.*)

SOME OF THE SOLDIERS: Now with dice, may fortune speed us;
Other games will shortly need us!
From our swords we burnish this blood,
Coming deeds will furnish fresh stains.
(*Sounds of warlike instruments are heard; all start and turn towards the sounds.*)

SOME SOLDIERS: Lo! they come praying for succor!
(*A strong band of soldiers crosses the camp.*)

OTHER SOLDIERS: Still, they make a brave display!

ALL: Let us, without more delaying attack Castellor today.

FERRANDO: Sì prodi amici; al di novello, è mente
Del capitan la rôcca
Investir da ogni parte.
Colà pingue bottino
Certezza è rinvenir, più che speranza.
Si vinca, è nostro.

UOMINI D'ARME: Tu c'inviti a danza!

FERRANDO e il CORO: Squilli, echeggi la tromba guerriera,
Chiami all'armi, alla pugna, all'assalto;
Sia domani la nostra bandiera
Di quei merli piantata sull'alto.
No, giammai non sorrise vittoria
Di piu liete speranze finor!
Ivi l'util ci aspetta e la gloria,
Ivi opimi la preda e l'onor!
(Entra il CONTE, uscito dalla tenda, e volge uno sguardo bieco a Castellor.

CONTE:
In braccio al mio rival!—Questo pensiero
Come persecutor demone ovunque
M'inseque! in braccio al mio rival!—
Ma corro, surta appena l'aurora,
Io corro a separarvi.—Oh, Leonora!
(Odonsi tumulti.)
(Entra FERRANDO.)

CONTE: Che fu?

FERRANDO: D'appresso il campo
S'aggirava una zingara: sorpresa
Da' nostri esploratori,
Si volse in fuga; essi, a ragion temendo
Una spia nella trista,
L'inseguir.

CONTE: Fu raggiunta?

FERRANDO: E presa.

CONTE: Vista l'hai tu?

FERRANDO: No: della scorta
Il condottier m'apprese
L'evento. (Tumulto piu' vicino)

CONTE: Eccola.
(Entra AZUCENA. Con le mani avvinte, e' trascinata dagli esploratori.—Un codazzo d'altri soldati.)

ESPLORATORI: Innanzi, o strega, innanzi!

AZUCENA: Aita?—Mi lasciate?—
Oh, furibondi!
Che mal fec'io?

CONTE: S'appressi.
(Azucena è tratta innanzi al Conte.)
A me rispondi,
E tremi dal mentri!

AZUCENA: Chiedi.

---

FERRANDO: Yes, brave companions; at dawn, tomorrow,
Our leader has now resolved
On storming the fortress on all sides.
We're sure to find great booty within its walls; more than hopeful;
If conquered, it is ours!

SOME Of THE SOLDIERS: Pleasure invites us there.

FERRANDO and CHORUS: Hark! now the trumpet is sounding the call to arms!
Then let us haste to meet the foe in battle;
Heeding no danger, and braving all in war's alarms,
While sabres gleam, and flashing guns loud rattle.
Soon shall our flag wave in triumph over the tower,
And the castle with its treasure be our prize!
Victory upon us her laurels soon will shower;
Then to arms, my comrades, all danger we despise!
Enter the COUNT, from the tent: he turns a sinister glance toward Castellor.

COUNT: In the arms of my rival!—The thought
Pursues me like a living demon!
In the arms of my rival!—I'll pursue them,
And, before the dawn of another day,
They shall be parted.—Oh, Leonora!
(Noise without.)
(Enter FERRANDO.)

COUNT: What is it?

FERRANDO: Near to the camp
A gipsy has been hovering;
Discovered by our sentinels,
She tried to escape; but the sentinels,
Taking her for a spy,
Followed her.

COUNT: Did they take her?

FERRANDO: They did.

COUNT: Have you seen her?

FERRANDO: No: the conductor
Of the court apprised me
Of the fact.

COUNT: Here she comes.
(Enter AZUCENA, with her hands tied, conducted by a guard of Soldiers—other Soldiers following.)

SOLDIERS: Go forward, witch, go forward!

AZUCENA: Help!—release me!—
Oh, madmen,
What harm have I done?

COUNT: Let her approach.
(Azucena is led forward.)
Now reply to me,
And beware if you lie!

AZUCENA: Interrogate me.

---

CONTE: Ove vai?

AZUCENA: Nol so.

CONTE: Che?

AZUCENA: D'una zingara è costume
Muover senza disegno
Il passo vagabondo,
Ed è suo tetto il ciel, sua patria il mondo.

CONTE: E vieni?

AZUCENA: Da Biscaglia, ove finora
Le sterili montagne ebbi ricetto.

CONTE: (a parte)
Da Biscaglia, ove finora . . .

AZUCENA: Oh, Dio! Oh, Dio!

CORO: Urla pure!

AZUCENA: E tu non m'odi,
Oh, Manrico,—oh, figlio mio?
Non soccorri all'infelice
Madre tua!

CONTE: Sarebbe ver? Di Manrico genitrice!

FERRANDO: Trema!

CONTE: Oh sorte, in mio poter!

AZUCENA: Deh, rallentate, o barbari,
Le acerbe mie ritorte—
Questo crudel supplizio
E' prolongata morte!
D'iniquo genitore
Empio figliuol peggiore,
Trema, v'è Dio pe' miseri,
E Dio ti punirà.

CONTE: Tue parole, o turpe zingara!
Colui, quel seduttore!
Potrò col tuo supplizio
Ferirlo in mezzo al core!
Gioja m'inonda il petto,
Cui non esprime il detto!
Meco il fraterno cenere
Piena vendetta avra'!

FER. e CORO: Infame, pira sorgere,
Empia, vedrai tra poco—
Nè solo tuo supplizio
Sarà l'orrendo foco!
Le vampe dell'inferno
Ivi penare ed ardere
L'anima tuo dovrà!
(Al cenno del Conte, i soldati traggono seco loro Azucena; egli entra nella sua tenda, seguito da Ferrando.)

## SCENA II.

Sala adiacente alla capella in Castellor, con verone in fondo.

---

COUNT: Where were you going?

AZUCENA: I know not.

COUNT: How?

AZUCENA: It is the gipsy custom
To wander without any settled object,
The whole world for their country,
The canopy of heaven their only roof.

COUNT: From where have you come?

AZUCENA: From Biscay, where, till lately,
Her barren mountains were my home.

COUNT: (Aside). From Biscay, says she?

AZUCENA: Oh, heaven! Oh, heaven!

CHORUS: Let her howl on!

AZUCENA: And you did not hear me,
Oh, Manrico,—oh, my son!
You did not succour bring
To your unhappy mother!

COUNT: Can it be true?
She the mother of Manrico!

FERRANDO: Tremble!

COUNT: Oh, fate! and she in my power!

AZUCENA: Ah! relent, you cruel monsters:
These cords awhile pray loosen;
This torture is so barbarous
But adds to the pangs of death!
Oh, degenerate son
Of an impious father,
Tremble: there is a God of the forlorn,
And that God will punish you?

COUNT: He is your son, then, infamous witch!
Your progeny, the vile seducer!
Can I, then, in punishing you,
Strike anguish into his heart?
The joy which at that I feel
Is more than I can tell!
Now shall my brother's ashes
Be terribly avenged!

FERRANDO and CHORUS: Vile gipsy, the fatal pyre
You soon shall see arise:
Nor will your punishment
Terminate that fearful fire:
The everlasting flames of hell
Your further punishment will be;
There, writhing in agony,
Your wicked spirit will abide!
(At a signal from the Count, the Soldiers drag off Azucena; he then enters the tent, followed by Ferrando.)

## SCENE II.

A Saloon adjoining the Chapel in Castellor, with verandah in background.

## Act III, Scene II

*MANRICO, LEONORA e RUIZ*

LEONORA: Quale d'armi fragore
Poc'anzi intesi?

MANRICO: Alto è il periglio!—
Vano
Dissimularlo fora!
Alla novella aurora
Assaliti saremo!

LEONORA: Ahimè!—che dici?

MANRICO: Ma de' nostri nemici
Avrem vittoria.—Lari
Abbiano al loro ardir, brando e cor-
aggio.
(*A Ruiz*) Tu va. Le belliche opre,
Nell'assenza mia breve, a te com-
metto.
Che nulla manchi! (*Ruiz parte*)

LEONORA: Di qual tetra luce
Il nostro imen risplende!

MANRICO: Il presagio funesto,
Deh, sperdi, o cara!

LEONORA: È il posso?

MANRICO: Amor—sublime
amore,
In tal istante ti favella al core.
Ah! si, ben mio, coll'essere
Io tuo, tu mia consorte,
Avrò più l'arma intrepida,
Il braccio avrò più forte,
Ma pur, se nella pagina
De' miei destini è scritto
Ch'io resti fra le vittime,
Dal ferro ostil trafitto,
Fra quegli estremi aneliti,
A te, il pensier verrà,
E solo in ciel precederti,
La morte a me parrà!
(*Odesi il suono dell'organo dalla
vicina cappella.*)
L'onda de' suoni mistici
Pura discende al cor!
Vieni; ci schiude il tempio
Gioie di casto amor!
(*Mentre s'avviano giubilanti al
tempio, Ruiz sopraggiunge frettolo-
so.*)

RUIZ: Manrico!

MANRICO: Che?

RUIZ: La zingara,
Vieni, tra ceppi mira!

MANRICO: Oh, Dio!

INES: Per man de' barbari
Accesa è già la pira.

MANRICO: (*accostandosi al verone*) Oh, ciel! mie membra oscilla-
no—
Nube me copre il ciglio!

LEONORA: Tu fremi!

MANRICO: E il deggio. Sappilo,
Io son!

LEONORA: Chi mai?

---

(*MANRICO, LEONORA, and RUIZ
discovered.*)

LEONORA: What means that din of
arms
Which just now reached my ears?

MANRICO: You are in danger!—
It would be useless to deny it!
Before to-morrow's dawn arrive,
We shall be assaulted!

LEONORA: Ah me!—what did you
say?

MANRICO: But our foes we shall
defeat.
Mightier than their audacity,
Our arms and bravery will prove.
(*To Ruiz.*)
You, go: the conduct of the war
For a brief time I leave to you.
Let nothing be neglected!
(*Exit Ruiz.*)

LEONORA: Sad the splendour
That our nuptials shines upon!

MANRICO: You must dispel dismal
thoughts and presentiments,
My dearest!

LEONORA: How is that possible?

MANRICO: Love, noble and sub-
lime, in your heart
Let that alone favor find.
Ah! yes, beloved maid, the thought
That you alone are mine
Will cheer my heart and nerve my
arm—
Victory on my deeds will shine.
And yet, alas! if destiny
Ordain that I in battle fall,
The thought, dear maid, I die for
you,
Will recompense for all!
And my last prayer on earth shall
be,
When fading life my soul shall free,
To meet you in eternity,
In bliss supreme over all!
(*Tones of an organ heard from
adjoining Chapel.*)
The sounds of mystic harmony
Let now our hearts overspread!
Come; to us the church tenders
The joys of a chaste love!
(*As they are about to enter the
Chapel, RUIZ enters, hurriedly.*)

RUIZ: Manrico!

MANRICO: What now?

RUIZ: The gipsy,—
They've bound her in chains!

MANRICO: Oh, heaven!

RUIZ: Already the barbarians
Have ignited the fatal pile.

MANRICO: (*Approaching the verandah.*) Oh, heaven! my limbs all
tremble—
A could obscures my sight!

LEONORA: You tremble!

MANRICO: And with reason!
Do you not know that
I am her son?

LEONORA: What did you say?

---

MANRICO: Suo figlio!
Ah, vili! Il rio spettacolo
Quasi il respir m'invola!
Raduna i nostri—affrettati!
Ruiz—va—torna—vola!
(*Ruiz parte.*)

Di quella pira! l'orrendo foco
Tutte le fibre m'arse, avvampò!
Empii, spegnetela, o ch'io fra poco
Col sangue vostro la spegnerò.
Ero giò figlio prima d'amarti,
Non puo' frenarmi il tuo martir!
Madre infelice, corro a salvarti
O teco almeno corro a morir!

LEONORA: Non reggo a colpi tanto
funesti
Oh, quanto meglio saria morir!
(*Entra Ruiz, tornauo gli armati.*)

RUIZ: All'armi, all'armi, eccone
presti
A pugnar teco, teco a morir!
(*Manrico parte, frettoloso, seguito da Ruiz, e dagli armati, mentre
odesi dell'interno fragor d'armi e
di bellici strumenti.*)

*FINE DELL'ATTO TERZO*

---

## ■ ATTO QUARTO

### SCENA I.

*Un'ala del palazzo dell' Aliafe-
ria.—All'angolo uno torre, con
finestre assicurate da spranghe di
ferro.—Notte oscurissima. ii*

*Si avanzano due persone amman-
tellate: sono RUIZ e LEONORA.*

RUIZ: (*sommessamente*) Siam gi-
unti:
Ecco la torre, ove di stato
Gemono i prigionieri.—Ah,
l'infelice
Ivi fu tratto!

LEONORA: Vanne.
Lasciami, nè timor di me ti pren-
da—
Salvarlo io potrò, forse.
(*Ruiz si allontana.*)
Timor di me?—Sicura,
Questa è la mia difesa!
(*I suoi occhi figgonsi ad una gem-
ma che la fregia la mano destra.*)
In questa oscura notte ravvolta,
Presso a te son io, e tu nol sai! Ge-
mente
Aura, che intorno spiri,
Deh, pietosa gli arreca i miei sospi-
ri.
D'amor sull'ali rosee
Vanne, sospir dolente,
Del prigioniero misero

---

MANRICO: That I am her son!
Ah wretches!—This sad spectacle
Stifles the breathing within me!
Our forces collect—about it, be
quick!
Ruiz—fly—return—depart! (*Exit
Ruiz*)

MANRICO: Ah! sight of horror! see
that pile blazing—
Demons of fury stand gazing round
it!
Madness inspiring, hate now is raging—
Tremble, for vengeance on you
shall fall.
Oh! mother dearest, though love
may claim me,
Danger, too, threaten, yet I will
save you;
Your form shall be snatched from
flames consuming,
Or with you, mother, I too will fall!

LEONORA: Against these woes I
cannot struggle—
Better it would be, by far, to die!
(*Re-enter RUIZ, with Soldiers.*)

RUIZ: Speak! command! we are
here,
Ready to fight, ready to die for you!
(*Manrico rushes off, followed by
Ruiz and Soldiers—the clash of
arms heard within, as the curtain
descends.*)

*END OF THE THIRD ACT.*

---

## ■ ACT IV.

### SCENE I.

*A wing of the Palace of Aliafe-
ria—at one end a window barred
with iron.—Night, dark and
gloomy.*

*(Two persons advance, enveloped
in cloaks: they are RUIZ and LEO-
NORA.)*

RUIZ: (*In an undertone*). This is
the place;
In this tower the state prisoners are
confined.—
Ah! he was brought here.

LEONORA: Now go.
Let us part: and do not fear for me:
Perhaps I may yet save him.
(*Ruiz retires.*)
Why fear for me;—I am secure,
For here I carry my defender.
(*Casting her eyes on a jewelled
ring, which she displays on her
right hand.*)
In the darkness of night I hover near
you,
And you do not know. Yet gentle
winds,
That move around me in stillness,
My piteous sighs waft towards him.
Borne on love's own rosy wing,
Speed, my tender sighs, to him;
May they bring comfort to him.

---

Conforta l'egra mente—
Com'aura di speranza
Alleggia in quella stanza;
La desta alle memorie,
Ai sogni dell'amor.
Ma, deh! non dirgli, improvvido,
Le pene del mio cor!

Soothe the storm within his breast,
Restore sweet hope to cheer his heart,
While lying in the dungeon's gloom;
Though nothing can heal this bosom's smart,
If death, alas! should be his doom.
But ah! this poor heart can never know joy—
Ah me, it will break, it will break—
It is filled with grief and woe!

CORO: Miserere d'un'alma già vicina
Alla partenza che non ha ritorno!
Miserere di lei, bontà divina,
Preda non sia dell'infernal soggiorno!

CHORUS: Miserere, the death-word of the dying!
There's no return from where his spirit's flying!
Miserere! to heaven for pity calling,
His soul to save from punishment appalling!

LEONORA: Quel suon, quelle preci
Solenni, funeste,
Empiron quell'aere
Di cupo terror!
Contende l'ambascia,
Che tutta m'investe,
Al labbro il respiro,
I palpiti al cor!

LEONORA: That sound and that praying, so sadly betraying,
In terrible accents, a soul must depart!
My breath is impeding, my warm blood receding,
From out of my veins, and from out of my heart.

MANRICO: Ah! che la morte ognora,
E' tarda nel venir
A chi desìa morir!

MANRICO: Alas! that death, as ever,
Lingers in coming nigh,
When one desires, when one desires but to die!

LEONORA: Oh ciel! sento mancarmi!

LEONORA: Oh heaven! Hear me, oh, hear me!

MANRICO: Addio, addio,
Leonora, addio!

MANRICO: Leonora, adieu, Leonora, adieu!

LEONORA: Sull'orrida torre, ah! par che la morte
Con ali di tenebre librando si va!
Ahi! forse dischiuse gli fian queste porte
Sol quando cadavere già freddo ei sarà!
(Rimane assorta: dopo qualche momento scuotesi, ed è in procinto di partire, allorchè viene dalla torre un gemito, e quindi un mesto suona; ella si ferma.)

LEONORA: From that fearful tower death himself
Does expand his dismal wings o'er me:
Alas! never again will those gates open
Till through them his cold corpse shall be borne.
(For some time she remains absorbed in thought; then, preparing to depart, she is arrested by a groan from the Tower, followed by a plaintive melody.)

MANRICO: (dalla torre) Sconto col sangue mio,
L'amor che posi in te!
Non ti scordar di me!
Leonora, addio!

MANRICO: (In the Tower). With my life's blood I sanctify
The love I vowed to thee!
Therefore forget not me!
Leonora, fare well!

LEONORA: Di te, di te scordarmi!
(N'esce il Conte ed alcuni seguaci.—Leonora si pone in disparte.)

LEONORA: Said you, love, forget me not!
(Enter the COUNT and his Soldiers.—Leonora retires from sight.)

CONTE: Udiste? Come albeggi,
La scure al figlio, ed alla madre il rogo.
(Entrano i seguaci per un piccolo uscio nella torre.)
Abuso io forse di quel poter che pieno
In me trasmise il Prence! A tal mi traggi
Donna per me funesta!—Ov'ella è mai?
Dipresso, Castellor, di lei contezza

COUNT: Did you hear me? At the break of day,
The axe for the son, for the mother the stake.
(The Soldiers enter a small door in the Tower.)
That I am overstepping the power
By the Prince to me entrusted, I admit,—
To such rash acts has this woman led me.
To where can she have fled?—No

Non ebbi, e furo indarno
Tante ricerche e tante!
Oh! dove sei, crudele?

news of her,
Since the fall of Castellor, have I heard;
And all searching for her has been in vain!
Oh! cruel one, where are you?

LEONORA: (avanzandosi) A te dinante.

LEONORA: (Advancing). In your presence.

CONTE: Qual voce!—Come! tu, donna?

COUNT: That voice!—How! is it you, lady?

LEONORA: Il vedi.

LEONORA: You see me.

CONTE: A che venisti?

COUNT: Why have you come here?

LEONORA: Egli è già presso
All'ora estrema, e tu lo chiedi?

LEONORA: Knowing who is doomed to die,
You yet ask this question.

CONTE: Osar potresti?

COUNT: Do you dare?

LEONORA: Ah, sì, per esso
Pietà domando!

LEONORA: Ah, yes!—to save him,
I humbly pray you.

CONTE: Che! tu deliri!
Io del rivale sentir pietà?

COUNT: How! are you mad?
For my rival dares ask your pity!

LEONORA: Clemente il Nume a te l'ispiri!

LEONORA: Let Heaven inspire you with mercy!

CONTE: E' sol vendetta mio Nume. Va!
(Leonora si getta disperata ai suoi piedi.)

COUNT: The God of vengeance alone reigns here. Go!
(Leonora casts herself in despair at his feet.)

LEONORA: Mira, di acerbe lagrime
Spargo al tuo piede un rio;
Non basta il pianto? svenami,
Ti bevi il sangue mio.
Calpesta il mio cadavere,
Ma salva il Trovator!

LEONORA: See how I shed these bitter tears,
Imploring prostrate at your feet—
Wreak not your vengeance upon his head; Oh! grant the this heart's outpouring!
Spare his life—mine I'll give;
For him I'd freely cease to live;—
Yes, yes, I will bless you, and forgive,
If you will spare the Troubadour.

CONTE: Ali! dell'indegno rendere
Vorrei peggior la sorte—
Fra mille atroci spasimi
Centuplicar sua morte—
Più l'ami, e più terribile
Divampa il mio furor!
(Vuol partire.)

COUNT: Ah! rather would I render,
Were it my power within,
A hundred-fold more terrible
The fate of that vile criminal.
The more of love for him you show,
The fiercer does my fury glow!
(About to go.)

LEONORA: (Si avviticchia ad esso) Conte!

LEONORA: (Clinging to him).
Oh, Count!

CONTE: Nè cessi?

COUNT: Desist.

LEONORA: Grazia!

LEONORA: Mercy!

CONTE: Prezzo non avvi alcuno
Ad ottenerla—scostati!

COUNT: No price on earth could move me
To pardon him. Therefore begone!

LEONORA: Uno ve n'ha—sol uno,
Ed io te l'offro.

LEONORA: There is one price—one, I know,
And I offer that to you.

CONTE: Spiegati,
Qual prezzo, di'?

COUNT: Explain yourself.
What price? Say it.

LEONORA: (Stendendogli la sua destra con dolore.) Me stessa!

LEONORA: (Extending her hands in anguish towards him.) Myself!

CONTE: Ciel! tu dicesti?

COUNT: Heaven! what do you say?

LEONORA: E compiere
Saprò la mia promessa.

LEONORA: What I promise,
I will faithfully perform.

CONTE: È sogno il mio?

COUNT: Am I in a dream?

LEONORA: Dischiudimi
La via tra quella mura;
Ch'ei mi oda—che la vittima
Fugga, e son tua.

LEONORA: Open to my view
The gates of yonder prison:
Let him see me, and depart in safety
And I will be yours.

CONTE: Lo giuri!

COUNT: Will you swear it?

**LEONORA:** Lo giuro a Dio, che l'anima
Tutta mi vede!

**CONTE:** Olà!
(*Correndo all'uscio della torre.—Si presenta un custode.— Mentre il Conte gli parla all'orecchio, Leonara sugge il veleno chiuso nell'anello*)

**LEONORA:** (*A parte*) M'avrai, ma fredda, esanime
Spoglia.

**CONTE:** (*Tornando a Leonora*)
Colui vivrà.

**LEONORA:** (*Da sè, alzando gli occhi, cui fan velo lagrime di letizia.*) Vivrà! contento e giubilo!
Tu d'esti a me, Signore?
Ma coi frequenti palpiti
Mercè ti rende il core!
Or il mio fine impavida,
Piena di gioja attendo,
Potrò dirgli, morendo,
Salvo tu sei per me!

**CONTE:** Fra te che parli?
Volgimi, mi volgi il detto ancora,
E mi parrà delirio . . .
Quanto ascoltai finora—
Tu mia, tu mia! ripetilo,
Il dubbio cor, serena—
Ah! ch'io lo credo appena,
Udendolo da te!

**LEONORA:** Andiam.

**CONTE:** Giurasti—pensaci!

**LEONORA:** È sacra la mia fè!
(*Entrano nella torre.*)

## SCENA II.

*AZUCENA giacente sopra una specie di rozza coltre, MANRICO seduto a lei dappresso.*

**MANRICO:** Madre, non dormi?

**AZUCENA:** L'invocai più volte,
Ma fugge il sonno a queste luce prego.

**MANRICO:** L'aura fredda è molesta
Alle tue membra, forse?

**AZUCENA:** No: da questa
Tomba di vivi sol fuggir vorrei,
Perchè sento il respiro soffocarmi!

**MANRICO:** (*torcendosi le mani*)
Fuggir!

**AZUCENA:** Non attristarti;
Far di me strazio non potranno crudi!

**MANRICO:** Ah! come?

**LEONORA:** Before the God who sees all hearts,
Here I swear to it!

**COUNT:** Ho! there!
(*Going up to the gate of the Tower.—A Guard appears—while the Count is speaking to him, Leonora drinks the poison contained in her ring.*)

**LEONORA:** (*Aside*). You shall have me,
But not till I am lifeless.

**COUNT:** (*Returning to Leonora*).
He shall live!

**LEONORA:** (*Aside, her eyes filled with tears of joy.*) Shall live! content and jubilee!
My heart is beating with joy!
Each moment seems a century
While those glad words repeating!
At length my life for him is given;
Death which him awaited
Is mine: my lips, with joy elated,
Shall tell him he is free!

**COUNT:** What words are these?
Ah, turn to me,
Once more, your promise swearing.
While even delirious I shall be,
If once your love I'm sharing.
You're mine—those words repeat again,
They bring me joy untasted.
Now all the sighs I've wasted
Are recompensed by you,
Ah! all the sighs I've wasted
Now are recompensed by you!

**LEONORA:** Let us go.

**COUNT:** Remember what you have sworn.

**LEONORA:** My word is sacred.
(*They enter the Tower.*)

## SCENE II.

(*AZUCENA discovered lying on a tattered mattress, MANRICO seated by the side of her.*)

**MANRICO:** Mother, you do not sleep!

**AZUCENA:** In vain I invoke sleep,
It will not on these eyes await. I pray.

**MANRICO:** This air, so cold and moist, perhaps
Thy strength overpowers.

**AZUCENA:** Ah! how I long
To be set free,—from this living tomb
Its air is suffocating to me.

**MANRICO:** (*Wringing his hands.*)
Could I but free you!

**AZUCENA:** Let it not grieve you;
They cannot make my sufferings long.

**MANRICO:** Ah! why not?

**AZUCENA:** Vedi? Le sue fosche impronte
M'ha già stampate in fronte
Il dito della morte!

**MANRICO:** Ahi!

**AZUCENA:** Troveranno
Un cadavere muto, gelido—anzi
Uno scheletro!

**MANRICO:** Cessa!

**AZUCENA:** Non odi?—gente s'appressa!
I carnefici son—vogliono al rogo
Trarmi!—Difendi la tua madre!

**MANRICO:** Alcuno,
Ti rassicura, qui non volge.

**AZUCENA:** Il rogo!
Parola orrenda!

**MANRICO:** Oh, madre!—oh, madre!

**AZUCENA:** Un giorno
Turba feroce l'ava tua condusse
Al rogo—mira la terribil vampa!
Ella n'è tocca già—l'arso crine
Al ciel manda faville!—
Osserva le pupille
Fuor dell'orbita lor:—Ahi—chi mi toglie
A spettacol sì atroce!
(*Cadendo tutta convulsa tra le braccia di Manrico.*)

**MANRICO:** Se m'ami ancor, se voce
Di figlio ha possa di una madre in core,
Ai terrori dell'alma
Oblii cerca nel sonno, e possa e calma
(*La conduce presso la coltre.*)

**AZUCENA:** Si, la stanchezza m'opprime, o figlio;
Alla quiete io chiudo il ciglio;
Ma se del rogo ardar si veda
L'orrida fiamma, destami allor!

**MANRICO:** Riposa, o madre! Iddio conceda
Men tristi immagini al tuo sopor.

**AZUCENA:** (*Tra il sonno e la veglia*) Ai nostri monti ritorneremo
L'antica pace ivi godremo!
Tu canterai, sul tuo liuto,
In sonno placido, io dormirò!

**MANRICO:** Riposa, o madre, io prono e muto
La mente al cielo rivolgerò.

**AZUCENA:** Tu canterai sul tuo liuto—
In sonno placido, io dormirò!

**AZUCENA:** Do you not see that on my brow
Already the finger of death has
Placed his indelible mark.

**MANRICO:** Alas!

**AZUCENA:** Fear not—
Nothing will they find but a corpse,
Cold and silent!

**MANRICO:** Oh, cease!

**AZUCENA:** Do you not hear!—there's a noise without!
Here come the torturers,
To drag me to the stake!—Oh, protect your mother!

**MANRICO:** There's no one!
Calm yourself, no one approaches.

**AZUCENA:** The fire!
How horrible is that!

**MANRICO:** Oh, mother!—oh, mother!

**AZUCENA:** One fearful day
By a brutal crowd your mother's mother
Was sacrificed! The flames I see,
As her hair they wafted in the wind—
See her staring eyes from their orbits start,
As the terrible flames encompass her!
Alas! what demon causes me to behold again
This loathsome sight!
(*Sinking in convulsions into the arms of Manrico.*)

**MANRICO:** If you love me—if a son's voice has yet a spell
For a mother's heart,
From your mind banish those fancies,
And seek forgetfulness in sleep.
(*He leads her to her resting-place.*)

**AZUCENA:** Yes! my son, with fatigue oppressed,
I will seek some solace in sleep;
But, if again you see that burning pile,
Rouse me quickly from my slumber.

**MANRICO:** Sleep, mother dear! and may Heaven
From your mind dismiss those horrid thoughts.

**AZUCENA:** (*As she sinks into a half-slumber.*) Homeward returning to our green mountain.
We shall enjoy its freshening breezes;
There with your lute again, past joys recounting,
Lull me to sleep as when you were a boy!

**MANRICO:** Sleep, dearest mother, while I in prayer,
Appealing to heaven, my moments employ.

**AZUCENA:** There let your lute, past joys recounting,
Lull me to sleep, as when you were a boy!

MANRICO: La menta al cielo rivolgerò!
(*Azucena si addormenta; Manrico resta genuflesso accanto a lei.*)

## SCENA III.

*Si apre la porta, entra LEONORA:
gli anzidetti, ed in ultimo il
CONTE con seguito di armati.*

MANRICO: Ciel!—non
m'inganno! quel fioce lume!

LEONORA: Son io, Manrico!

MANRICO: Oh, mia Leonora!
Ah, mi concedi, pietoso Nume,
Gioja sì grande, anzi ch'io mora?

LEONORA: Tu non morrai—vengo
a salvarti!

MANRICO: Come!—a salvarmi!—
Fia vero?

LEONORA: Addio!
Tronca ogni indugio!—
t'affretta!—parti!
(*Accennandogli la porta.*)

MANRICO: E tu non vieni!

LEONORA: Restar degg'io!

MANRICO: Restar! . . . .

LEONORA: Deh, fuggi!

MANRICO: No!

LEONORA: Guai se tardi!
(*Cercando di trarlo verso
l'uscio.*)

MANRICO: No!

LEONORA: La tua vita!

MANRICO: Io la disprezzo—
Pur—figgi, o donna, in me gli
sguardi!—
Da chi l'avesti!—ed a qual prez-
zo?—
Parlar non vuoi?—Balen tremen-
do!—
Dal mio rivale!—intento, inten-
do!—
Ha quest'infame l'amor venduto—
Venduto un core che mio giurò!

LEONORA: Ahi, come l'ira ti rende
cieco!
Ahi, quanto ingiusto, crudel sei
meco!
T'arrendi—fuggi, o sei perduto!—
O, il ciel nemmen salvar ti può!
(*Leonora è caduta ai piedi di
Manrico.*)

AZUCENA: (*Dormendo*) Ai nostri
monti ritorneremo—
L'antica pace—ivi godremo!
Tu canterai—sul tuo liuto—
In sonno placido—io dormirò!

MANRICO: Ti scosta.

LEONORA: Non respingermi—
Vedi?—Languenta, oppressa,
Io manco!

---

MANRICO: Appealing to heaven,
my moments employ.
(*Azucena yields herself to sleep,
while Manrico remains kneeling
by her.*)

## SCENE III.

*(A door opens, and LEONORA en-
ters; afterwards the COUNT, followed by a Troop of Soldiers.)*

MANRICO: Heaven! does this weak
light deceive my eyes?

LEONORA: It is I, Manrico!

MANRICO: Oh, my Leonora!
Ah, do you grant me, kind Heaven,
This joy so great before I die?

LEONORA: You shall not die!—I
come to save you!

MANRICO: How?—To save me!—
Can this be true?

LEONORA: Farewell!
There must be no delay! be quick!
depart!
(*Pointing towards the doorway.*)

MANRICO: Do you not go with me?

LEONORA: I must remain here.

MANRICO: Remain!

LEONORA: Will you not go?

MANRICO: No!

LEONORA: Delay will be fatal!
(*Endeavoring to drag him to the
doorway.*)

MANRICO: No!

LEONORA: Your life will be lost!

MANRICO: I care not for that!
Look, lady, look!—Full in my face
now look!
Who granted you my life, and what
the price?
You do not speak—fearfully you
tremble!
Was it my rival?—speak out—tell
me all—
To my rival have you sold your
love—
That love so often sworn to me?

LEONORA: Ah, how your anger
blinds your senses!
You are cruel and unjust to me!
Delay not—quickly begone, or you
are lost.
Oh! Heaven itself cannot save you
now!
(*Falling at the feet of Manrico.*)

AZUCENA: (*Asleep*). Homeward
returning to our green mountain,
We shall enjoy its freshening
breezes;
There, with your lute again past
joys recounting,
Lull me to sleep, as when you were
a boy.

MANRICO: Pray, leave me.

LEONORA: Drive me not from you,
Do you not see? I am weak and
faint,—
I am sinking!

---

MANRICO: Va—ti abbomino—
Ii maledico!

LEONORA: Ah, cessa!
Non imprecar; di volgere
Per me la prece a Dio
È questa l'ora!

MANRICO: Un brivido corre nel
petto mio!

LEONORA: Manrico! (*Cade boccone.*)

MANRICO: (*Accorrendo a solle-
varla.*) Donna, svelami—
Narra—

LEONORA: Ho la morte in seno.

MANRICO: La morte!

LEONORA: Ah, fu più rapida
La forza del veleno
Ch'io non pensava!

MANRICO: Oh, fulmine!

LEONORA: Senti!—la mano—
gelo—
Ma qui—qui foco orribile
Arde! (*Toccandosi il petto.*)

MANRICO: Che festi?—Oh, cielo!

LEONORA: Prima che d'altri vivere—
Io volli tua morir!

MANRICO: Insano! ed io
quest'angelo
Osavo maledir!

LEONORA: Più non—resisto!

MANRICO: Ahi, misera!
(*Entra il CONTE, arrestandosi
sulla soglia.*)

LEONORA: Ecco l'istante—io
muoio—
Manrico!—Or la tua grazia,
Padre del cielo, imploro!

MANRICO: Insano, ed io
quest'angelo
Osavo maledir!

LEONORA: Prima che d'altri viv-
ere,
Io volli tuo morir!
(*Spira.*)

CONTE: Ah! volle me deludere
E per costui morir!
Sia tratto al ceppo!
(*Indicando agli armati Manri-
co.*)

MANRICO: Madre!—Oh, madre,
addio!
(*Parte tra gli armati.*)

AZUCENA: Manrico!—Ov'è mio
figlio?
(*Destandosi.*)

CONTE: A morte ei corre!

AZUCENA: Ah, ferma! m'odi!

CONTE: (*Trascinando Azucena
presso la finestra.*) Vedi?

---

MANRICO: Go!—I abhor you!
I curse you!

LEONORA: Ah, desist—
This is not the time to curse me,
For my soul now let your prayers
To heaven be directed!

MANRICO: A shivering through my
heart courses.

LEONORA: Manrico!
(*Falling to the ground.*)

MANRICO: (*Raising her anxiously.*) Lady, what have you done? Tell
me.

LEONORA: The hand of death is on
me.

MANRICO: Death!

LEONORA: Ah! more rapid than I
thought
The fatal drink has proved,
In its deadly purpose!

MANRICO: Oh! terrible blow!

LEONORA: Feel here—already are
my hands cold,
But within my bosom a raging fire
Consumes me!
(*Putting her hands to her breast.*)

MANRICO: Oh! Heavens, what
have you done?

LEONORA: Rather than for another
to live,
For you I have preferred to die.

MANRICO: Madman! and on this
angel
I have maledictions cast!

LEONORA: I cannot struggle any
longer!

MANRICO: Unhappy me!
(*Enter the COUNT, halting on the
threshold.*)

LEONORA: My hour is come, and I
must die—
Manrico!—Your pardoning mercy,
Great Father of Heaven, I now implore!

MANRICO: Madman! and on this
angel
I have maledictions cast!

LEONORA: Rather than for another
to live,
I have preferred to die for you!
(*Dies.*)

COUNT: Ah! she has deceived me,
then,
And for him chosen to die.
Let him be brought here in chains.
(*Pointing out Manrico to
Guards.*)

MANRICO: Mother!—Oh, mother,
farewell!
(*Exit, escorted by the Guards.*)

AZUCENA: Manrico!—Oh, where
is my son?

COUNT: He has gone to death!

AZUCENA: Ah, stay! stay! hear me!

COUNT: (*Dragging her to the window.*) Behold!

## Act IV, Scene III

**AZUCENA:** Cielo!

**CONTE:** È spento!

**AZUCENA:** È spento—hai detto—
è spento!
Or dunque ascolta!—Udito
Hai tu mai d'un fratello
Che fu da abbietta zingara
Al padre tuo rapito?
Egli era tuo fratello!

**AZUCENA:** Oh, heavens!

**COUNT:** He is no more.

**AZUCENA:** Is he dead!—do you
say he is dead?
Now listen to me. You have heard
That from the palace of his father
You once had a young brother
Who
Was by a gipsy stolen!—
Yonder that brother you behold!

**CONTE:** Eh! quale orror!

**AZUCENA:** Sie vendicata, o madre!
(*Cade a piè della finestra.*)

**CONTE:** (*Inorridito*) E vivo ancor!

*FINE DELL'OPERA.*

**COUNT:** Alas! how horrible!

**AZUCENA:** Thus you are avenged,
my mother!
(*Falling near the window.*)

**COUNT:** (*With horror*). And I am
doomed to live!

*END OF THE OPERA.*

# La Traviata (1853)

MUSIC BY GIUSEPPE VERDI ■ LIBRETTO BY FRANCESCO MARIA PIAVE

This three-act opera, set to a libretto by Francesco Maria Piave (based on Alexandre Dumas the younger's novel, *La Dame aux Camélias*), was first performed at the Teatro La Fenice in Venice on March 6, 1853. At a dinner party at the home of the beautiful Parisian courtesan Violetta Valéry, Alfredo Germont, who had come to ask about Violetta's health every day when she was ill, makes a toast. Violetta responds, singing in praise of love. The guests depart, and she collapses, coughing. Alfredo stays behind to declare his love for her. Violetta tells him that she will only live a few more months, and that he can come back when the camellia she has given him has faded. Violetta and Alfredo end up living together at her country house. When Alfredo journeys to Paris to prevent Violetta's home from being sold to pay her debts, Alfredo's father pays Violetta a visit. She is ruining his son's life, he says, and implores her to give up the relationship. She gives in, asking only to tell Alfredo herself. Violetta leaves Alfredo, announcing that they are finished. Alfredo finds Violetta at her friend Flora's where she is on the arm of Baron Duphol, her former lover. Duphol gambles with Alfredo and loses. Alfredo confronts Violetta. Desperate, she tells him that she no longer loves him. Alfredo throws all his winnings in her face. His father disowns him, and Baron Duphol challenges Alfredo to a duel.

Time passes. Violetta is close to death and almost broke. She asks her maid, Annina, to give half of her remaining money to the needy. Alfredo's father writes to her, saying that Alfredo knows the whole story. They both wish to ask her for her forgiveness. "Too late," she replies, just as Alfredo enters. They sing of love, and Alfredo's father realizes that she has paid for his demands with her life. Having made peace with both men, she dies.

---

## ■ ATTO PRIMO

*Salotto in casa di Violetta; nel fondo è la porta che mette ad altra sala; ve ne sono altre due laterali; a sinistra caminetto con sopra uno specchio.—Nel mezzo è una tavola riccamente imbandita.*

*Violetta seduta su un divano sta discorrendo col Dottore e con alcuni amici, mentre altri vanno ad incontrare quelli che sopraggiungono, tra' quali sono il Barone e Flora al braccio del Marchese.*

**CORO 1:** Dell'invito trascorsa è già l'ora—
Voi tardaste.

**CORO 2:** Giuocammo da Flora,
E giocando quell'ore volàr.

**VIOLETTA:** Flora, amici, la notte che resta
D'altre gioie qui fate brillar—
(*Andando loro incontro.*)
Fra le tazze è più viva la festa.

**FLORA E MARQUIS:** E goder voi potrete?

**VIOLETTA:** Lo voglio;
Al piacere m'affido, ed io soglio
Con tal farmaco i mali sopir.

## ■ ACT I

*The banquet hall of Violetta's house in Paris. In the rear a door opens out onto a drawing room. Doors on either side lead to the rest of the house. On the left is a mantel hung with a mirror; in the center a table lavishly spread.*

*Violetta, seated on a sofa, is engaged in conversation with the Doctor and several friends. Some of her guests go out to greet the new arrivals among whom are the Baron and Flora, on the arm of the Marquis.*

**CHORUS 1:** It's long after the appointed hour. You are quite late.

**CHORUS 2:** We were at Flora's, at cards,
And the time seemed to fly as we played.

**VIOLETTA:** Dearest Flora, my friends, let us light
With new joy what is left of the night.
(*Going toward them.*)
In the bowl that is flowing is pleasure—

**FLORA and MARQUIS:** And you'll share in the fun?

**VIOLETTA:** In full measure!
For the dance is my greatest delight
And the cure for all anguish and pain.

**TUTTI:** Sì, la vita s' addoppia al gioir.
(*Il Visoconte Gastone di Letorieres entrando con Alfredo Germont; servi affaccendati intorno alla mensa.*)

**GASTONE:** In Alfredo Germont, o signora,
Ecco un altro che molto v' onora;
Pochi amici a lui simili sono.

**VIOLETTA:** Mio Visconte, mercè di tal dono.
(*Dà la mano ad Alfredo, che gliela bacia.*)

**MARQUIS:** Caro Alfredo!

**ALFREDO:** Marchese!
(*Si stringono la mano.*)

**GASTONE:** (*Ad Alfredo.*) T'ho detto
L'amistà qui si intreccia al diletto.
(*I Servi frattanto avranno imbandite le vivande.*)

**VIOLETTA:** (*ai Servi.*) Pronto è il tutto?
(*Un Servo accenna di sí.*)
Miei cari, sedete;
È al convito che s' apre ogni cor.

**TUTTI:** Ben diceste—le cure segrete
Fuga sempre l'amico licor.
(*Siedono in modo che Violetta resti tra Alfredo e Gastone; di fronte vi sarà Flora, tra il Marchese ed il Barone: gli altri siedono a piacere. Vi ha un momento di silenzio: frattanto passano i piatti,*

**ALL:** Yes, in pleasure life doubles its gain!
(*Enter the Viscount de Letorieres, with Alfredo Germont. Servants busy themselves about the banquet table.*)

**GASTONE:** In Alfredo Germont you will find
Still another admirer—a kind
And incomparable friend, I assure you.

**VIOLETTA:** Many thanks for the privilege, Count.
(*She holds out her hand to Alfredo who kisses it.*)

**MARQUIS:** Alfredo!

**ALFREDO:** Why, it's the Marquis!
(*They shake hands.*)

**GASTONE:** (*Aside to Alfredo*)
Didn't I tell you?
Here pleasure and friendship are one.
(*Meanwhile the Servants have been preparing the places for the guests.*)

**VIOLETTA:** Have you done? (*One of the Servants nods.*)
Well, the banquet's begun!

**ALL:** Do be seated, my friends,
And let joy fill your hearts to the brim.
Right you are! Why regret and repine
When all troubles are banished by wine?
(*They assume their places at table, Violetta between Alfredo and*

# Act I

*e Violetta e Gastone parlano sotto voce tra loro.)*

*Gastone. Facing them are Flora, the Marquis and the Baron. The rest distribute themselves as they please. During a momentary lull in the conversation, while the guests are being served, Violetta and Gastone are heard conversing in an undertone.)*

**GASTONE:** Sempre Alfredo a voi pensa.

**GASTONE:** Alfredo has thought of you often.

**VIOLETTA:** Scherzate.

**VIOLETTA:** What nonsense!

**GASTONE:** Egra foste, e ogni dì con affanno
Qui volò, di voi chiese.

**GASTONE:** In your illness he hurried here daily
To ask after you.

**VIOLETTA:** Cessate.
Nulla son io per lui.

**VIOLETTA:** Oh, come now!
What can I be to him!

**GASTONE:** Non v'inganno.

**GASTONE:** I'm in earnest.

**VIOLETTA:** (*Ad Alfredo.*) Vero è dunque?—Onde ciò?—Nol comprendo.

**VIOLETTA:** (*To Alfredo.*) Can it be true?—How so? I'm puzzled, truly.

**ALFREDO:** (*Sospirando.*) Sì, egli è ver.

**ALFREDO:** (*Sighing.*) Yes, it is true.

**VIOLETTA:** Le mie grazie vi rendo.
(*Al Barone.*)
Voi, barone, non feste altrettanto.

**VIOLETTA:** Then I am indeed grateful.
(*To the Baron.*)
You, dear Baron, were not so attentive.

**BARONE:** Vi conosco da un anno soltanto.

**BARON:** But I've known you for hardly a year.

**VIOLETTA:** Ed ei solo da qualche minuto.

**VIOLETTA:** And he's known me for barely a minute!

**FLORA:** (*Piano al Barone.*) Meglio fora, se aveste taciuto.

**FLORA:** (*Aside to Baron.*) Better for you had you held your tongue!

**BARONE:** (*Piano a Flora.*) M' è increscioso quel giovin.

**BARON:** (*Aside to Flora.*) I find that young man most annoying.

**FLORA:** Perchè?
A me invece simpatico egli è.

**FLORA:** On the contrary, I find him quite charming.

**GASTONE:** (*Ad Alfredo.*) E tu dunque non apri più bocca?

**GASTONE:** (*To Alfredo.*) And you—have you no more to say?

**MARQUIS:** (*A Violetta.*) E a madama che scuoterlo tocca.

**MARQUIS:** (*To Violetta.*) Violetta will have to inspire him.

**VIOLETTA:** Sarò l'Ebe che versa.
(*Mesca ad Alfredo.*)

**VIOLETTA:** I'll be Hebe and pour for you.
(*Pours wine for Alfredo.*)

**ALFREDO:** E ch'io bramo
Immortal come quella.
(*Con galanteria.*)

**ALFREDO:** And like her
I would have you immortal.
(*Gallantly.*)

**TUTTI:** Beviamo!

**ALL:** To friendship!

**GASTONE:** O barone, nè un verso, nè un viva
Troverete in quest' ora giuliva?
(*Barone accenna di no.*)
Dunque a te.
(*Ad Alfredo.*)

**GASTONE:** You Baron—have you no toast
To enliven this hour of mirth?
(*The Baron shakes his head.*)
It's up to you, then.
(*To Alfredo.*)

**TUTTI:** Sì, Sì, un brindisi.

**ALL:** Yes, yes! A toast!

**ALFREDO:** L'estro non m' arride.

**ALFREDO:** I'm in no vein—

**GASTONE:** E non sei tu maestro?

**GASTONE:** Come, you're pastmaster at it!

**ALFREDO:** (*A Violetta.*) Vi fia grato?

**ALFREDO:** (*To Violetta.*) Would it please you?

**VIOLETTA:** Sì.

**VIOLETTA:** Yes.

**ALFREDO:** Sì? L'ho già in cor.
(*Si alza.*)

**ALFREDO:** Yes? Then I'll be delighted.
(*Rises.*)

**MARQUIS:** Dunque attenti.

**MARQUIS:** Attention, all!

**TUTTI:** Sì, attenti al cantor.

**ALL:** Yes, listen to the toastmaster!

**ALFREDO:** Libiamo, libiamo ne' lieti calici,
Che la bellezza infiora;
E la fuggevol, fuggevol ora
S'innebrii a voluttà.
Libiam ne' dolci fremiti
Che suscita l'amore,
Poichè quell' occhio al core
Onnipotente va.
Libiamo, amore, amor fra i calici
Più caldi baci avrà.

**ALFREDO:** In goblets wreathed with flowers
Come drink on this festive night,
And may the fleeting hours
Be filled with love's delight.
Drink to the magic glances
That kindling beauties dart!
Drink to those amorous lances
That pierce from eye to heart.
And love will find warmer kisses
in flower entwined cups.

**TUTTI:** Ah, libiamo; amor fra i calici
Più caldi baci avrà.

**ALL:** And love will find warmer kisses
in flower entwined cups.

**VIOLETTA:** Tra voi, saprò dividere
(*S'alza.*)
Il tempo mio giocondo;
Tutto è follia nel mondo
Ciò che non è piacer.
Godiam, fugace e rapido
E il gaudio dell' amore;
E un fior che nasce e muore
Nè più si può goder.
Godiam—c' invita un fervido
Accento lusinghier.

**VIOLETTA:** My golden time's sweet rapture
(*Rises.*)
Dear friends, is mine to give!
Ah, foolish not to capture
Youth's transient joys—and live!
Live and enjoy, for
youthful love's delight is brief.
The faded flower
No more can bring our grief to light!

**TUTTI:** Godiam—la tazza e il cantico
La notte abbella e il riso;
In questo paradiso
Ne scopra il nuovo dì.

**ALL:** Ah, live then in the blisses
That sing of love and joy!
In laughter, wine and kisses
Let every night go by,
And in this paradise
Let dawn our loves surprise.

**VIOLETTA:** (*Ad Alfredo.*) La vita è nel tripudio.

**VIOLETTA:** (*To Alfredo.*) For living is in pleasure—

**ALFREDO:** (*A Violetta.*) Quando non s' ami ancora.

**ALFREDO:** (*To Violetta.*) Till one discovers love.

**VIOLETTA:** (*Ad Alfredo.*) Nol dite a chi lo ignora.

**VIOLETTA:** (*To Alfredo.*) A knowledge I don't treasure.

**ALFREDO:** (*A Violetta.*) È il mio destin così.

**ALFREDO:** (*To Violetta.*) Then help me, stars above!

**TUTTI:** Godiam—la tazza e il cantico
La notte abbella e il riso;
In questo paradiso
Ne scopra il nuovo dì.
(*S' ode musica dall' altra sala.*)
Che è ciò?

**ALL:** In laughter, wine and kisses
Let every night go by,
And in this paradise
let dawn our loves surprise.
(*Music is heard from the drawing room.*)
What is that music?

**VIOLETTA:** Non gradireste ora le danze?

**VIOLETTA:** Would you not like to dance now?

**TUTTI:** Oh! il gentil pensier!—Tutti accettiamo.

**ALL:** How gracious of you!—Of course!

**VIOLETTA:** Usciamo dunque—Ohimè!
(*S' avviano alla porta di mezzo, ma Violetta è colta da subito pallore.*)

**VIOLETTA:** Shall we go then?—Alas!
(*They walk toward the door, center, when Violetta suddenly totters and turns pale.*)

**TUTTI:** Che avete?

**ALL:** What ails you, Violetta?

**VIOLETTA:** Nulla, nulla.

**VIOLETTA:** It's nothing—nothing!

**TUTTI:** Che mai v' arresta?

**ALL:** Why do you linger, then?

**VIOLETTA:** Usciamo! (*Fa qualche passo, ma è obbligata a nuovamente fermarsi e sedere.*) Oh Dio!

**VIOLETTA:** Come, let's go on! (*She takes a few steps but is obliged to sink into a chair.*) Oh, dear Heaven!

**TUTTI:** Ancora!

**ALL:** Again!

**ALFREDO:** Voi soffrite!

**ALFREDO:** You are in pain!

**TUTTI:** Oh ciel!—ch' è questo!

**ALL:** Alas! What can it be?

1166   LA TRAVIATA

**VIOLETTA:** Un tremito che provo—Or là passate,
(*Indicando l'altra stanza.*)
Tra poco anch'io sarò.

**TUTTI:** Come bramate.
(*Tutti passano all'altra sala, meno Alfredo, che resta indietro.*)

**VIOLETTA:** (*Si guarda nello specchio.*) Oh, qual pallor!
(*Si volge e s'accorge d'Alfredo.*)
Voi qui!

**ALFREDO:** Cessata è l'ansia che vi turbò?

**VIOLETTA:** Sto meglio.

**ALFREDO:** Ah, in cotal guisa v'ucciderete!
Aver v'è d'uopo cura dell'esser vostro.

**VIOLETTA:** E lo potrei?

**ALFREDO:** Ah, se mia foste, custode io veglierei
Pe' vostri soavi dì.

**VIOLETTA:** Che dite?
Ha forse alcuno cura di me?

**ALFREDO:** (*Con fuoco.*) Perchè nessuno al mondo v'ama.

**VIOLETTA:** Nessun?

**ALFREDO:** Tranne sol io.

**VIOLETTA:** Gli è vero?
(*Ridendo.*)
Sì grande amor dimenticato avea.

**ALFREDO:** Ridete!—e in voi v'ha un core?

**VIOLETTA:** Un cor? Sì, forse—e a che lo richiedete?

**ALFREDO:** Oh, se ciò fosse, non potreste allora celiar.

**VIOLETTA:** Dite davvero?

**ALFREDO:** Io non v'inganno.

**VIOLETTA:** Da molot è che mi amate?

**ALFREDO:** Ah sì, da un anno.
Un dì felice, eterea
Mi balenaste innante,
E da quel dì tremante,
Vissi d'ignoto amor.
Di quell'amor, quell'amor ch'è palpito
Dell'universo, dell'universo intero.
Misterioso, misterioso altero,
Croce e delizia, delizia al cor.

**VIOLETTA:** Ah, se ciò è ver, fuggitemi—
Solo amistade io v'offro;
Amar non so, nè soffro
Un così eroico amore.
Io sono franca, ingenua;
Altra cercar dovete—
Non arduo troverete
Dimenticarmi allor.

**VIOLETTA:** I felt a sudden chill.—Do please go on.
(*Motioning them toward the drawing room.*)
I'll join you in a minute.

**ALL:** As you wish.
(*All go out into the drawing room except Alfredo, who remains behind.*)

**VIOLETTA:** (*Rising and looking at herself in the mirror.*)
Goodness, how pale!—You, here?
(*On seeing Alfredo.*)

**ALFREDO:** Is it all over, that sudden illness?

**VIOLETTA:** I'm better.

**ALFREDO:** You'll kill yourself, in that fashion.
You must take better care of yourself.

**VIOLETTA:** You think I could?

**ALFREDO:** If you were mine, I would watch over your precious days.

**VIOLETTA:** What are you saying? Is there perhaps someone who cares?

**ALFREDO:** No one—because in all the world
None really loves you.

**VIOLETTA:** No one?

**ALFREDO:** No one but me!

**VIOLETTA:** Ah, truly?
(*Laughing.*)
I had forgotten your tremendous love!

**ALFREDO:** You're mocking me!—Have you no heart?

**VIOLETTA:** Heart, did you say?—Perhaps.—But why do you ask?

**ALFREDO:** Ah, if you had, you could not make a jest of this.

**VIOLETTA:** Are you then serious?

**ALFREDO:** I would not deceive you.

**VIOLETTA:** Is it long then that you've loved me?

**ALFREDO:** Yes—a whole year.
One happy day your image
Appeared before my sight,
And from its dazzling light
I've glowed with secret love.
A love that throbs like the heart of all nature,
A love encompassing earth and the stars,
A love mysterious, love high as heaven above,
Exquisite rapture, rapture and pain.

**VIOLETTA:** If that be so then leave me!
Friendship alone I offer.
I know not love, nor suffer
Its burning pangs to grieve me.
I must speak out!—Go seek
A worthier to cherish,
And in her love will perish
All memory of me.

**GASTONE:** (*Presentandosi sulla porta di mezzo.*) Ebben?—che diavol fate?

**VIOLETTA:** Si folleggiava.

**GASTONE:** Ah, ah!—sta ben—restate.
(*Rientra.*)

**VIOLETTA:** Amor, dunque, non più—vi garba il patto?

**ALFREDO:** Io v'obbedisco—Parto.
(*Per andarsene.*)

**VIOLETTA:** A tal giungeste?
(*Si toglie un fiore dal seno.*) Prendete questo fiore.

**ALFREDO:** Perchè?

**VIOLETTA:** Per riportarlo.

**ALFREDO:** Quando?
(*Tornando.*)

**VIOLETTA:** Quando sarà appassito.

**ALFREDO:** O ciel, domani?

**VIOLETTA:** Ebben, domani.

**ALFREDO:** Io son felice!
(*Prende con trasporto il fiore.*)

**VIOLETTA:** D'amarmi dite ancora?

**ALFREDO:** Oh, quanto v'amo!
(*Per partire.*)

**VIOLETTA:** Partite?

**ALFREDO:** Parto.
(*Torna a lei e le bacia la mano.*)

**VIOLETTA:** Addio.

**ALFREDO:** Di più non bramo.
(*Esce.*)
Addio.
(*Violetta e tutti gli altri che tornano dalla sala della danza.*)

**TUTTI:** Si ridesta in ciel l'aurora,
E n'è forza di partire;
Mercè a voi, gentil signora,
(*A Violetta.*)
Di sì splendido gioir.
La città di feste è piena,
Volge il tempo del piacer;
Nel riposo ancor la lena
Si ritempri per goder.
(*partono dalla destra.*)

**VIOLETTA:** (*sola*) È strano!—è strano!—In core
Scolpiti ho quegli accenti!
Saria per me sventura un serio amore?
Che risolvi, o turbato anima mia?
Null'uomo ancora t'accendeve.—
Oh, gioia,
Ch'io non conobbi, esser amata amando!
E sdegnarla poss'io
Per l'aride follie del viver mio?
Ah, fors'è lui che l'ianima,
Solinga nè' tumúlti,
Godea sovente pingere,
De' suoi colori occulti!
Lui, che modesto e vigile,

**GASTONE:** (*From the center door.*)
Well! What are you up to?

**VIOLETTA:** Just talking nonsense.

**GASTONE:** So!—Very well—go on.
(*Disappears*)

**VIOLETTA:** No more of love then. You agree to that?

**ALFREDO:** I can only obey. I must be going.
(*About to leave.*)

**VIOLETTA:** So quickly resolved?
(*She takes a flower from her corsage.*)
Here, take this flower.

**ALFREDO:** Why?

**VIOLETTA:** To bring it back to me.

**ALFREDO:** When? (*Turning.*)

**VIOLETTA:** When it has faded.

**ALFREDO:** Tomorrow, then?

**VIOLETTA:** Very well—tomorrow.

**ALFREDO:** What happiness!
(*Takes the flower in a transport of joy.*)

**VIOLETTA:** And do you still say you love me?

**ALFREDO:** Oh, I adore you!
(*About to leave.*)

**VIOLETTA:** Ah, you're going?

**ALFREDO:** I am.
(*Goes back to her and kisses her hand.*)

**VIOLETTA:** Goodbye.

**ALFREDO:** Could I desire more?
(*Exit.*)
(*Violetta and the rest who come in from the ballroom.*)

**ALL:** In the east the dawn is breaking
Warning us that day is near.
We must now our leave be taking—
Thanks, Violetta, for your cheer.
In the city sounds of laughter
Fill the silence of the night;
But repose must follow after
To renew us for delight.
(*All exit to the right.*)

**VIOLETTA:** (*Alone*) How strange!
So strange! His words
Are carved upon my heart.
Would then a serious love be fatal to me?
What say you now, my troubled soul?
No man has yet stirred love in you.
Oh, joy
I've never known—to be beloved and loving!
And can I spurn it now
For all the empty follies of my life?
Perhaps it is he my lonely soul
Amid revels wants to muse,
Would summon up in dream
And paint in subtle hues—

# Act I

Al l' egre soglie ascese,
E nuova febbre accese destandomi
all' amor?
A quell' amor, quell' amor ch' è
palpito;
Dell' universo intero misterioso,
altero,
Croce e delizia, delizia al cor.
A me, fanciulla, un candido
E trepido desire
Quest' effigiò, dolcissimo
Signor dell' avvenire,
Quando ne' cieli il raggio
Di sua beltà vedea,
E tutta me pascea
Di quel soave error.
Sentia che amore è palpito
Dell' universo intero,
Misterioso, altero,
Pena e delizia al cor.)
(*Resta concentrata un istante,
poi dice.*)
Follie!—follie!—delirio vano è
questo!
Povera donna, sola,
Abbandonata in questo
Popoloso deserto,
Che appellano Parigi,
Che spero or più?—Che far degg'
io?—Gioire.
Di voluttà nei vortici perir.
Giorir! gioir!
Sempre libera degg' io
Folleggiare di gioia in gioia.
Vo' che scorra il viver mio
Pei sentieri del piacer.
Nasca il giorno, il giorno muoia,
Sempre lieta ne' ritrovi
A diletti sempre nuovi
Dèe volare il mio pensier.
(*Parte a sinistra.*)

He who with tender care
Came to me, then fevered,
And with another flame
Kindled in me to love.
A love that throbs like the heart of
all nature,
A love encompassing earth and the
stars,
A love mysterious, love high as
heaven above,
Exquisite rapture, rapture and
pain.
When yet a child, a vision
came before my eyes—
A fair and gentle youth,
My future lord and prize.
When in the heavens his beauty
Shone like a wondrous fire,
My being throbbed ecstatic
With infinite desire.
I then knew love like the heart of all
nature,
A love encompassing earth and the
stars,
A love mysterious, love high as
heaven above,
Exquisite rapture, rapture and
pain.
(*For a moment she pauses in rapt
concentration, then cries:*)
Oh folly! Oh folly! This vain deliri-
um!
What dreams delude me,
Poor lonely woman,
Forsaken here in this
Populous desert
That's known as Paris?
What more is there to hope? Or
do?—Descend
In pleasure's vortex—in the vortex
end!
Pleasure! pleasure!
Ever light, ever free
Flitting on from joy to joy,
May my hours forever flee
In sweet pleasure's company.
Whether day be born or die,
To be happy I aspire.
Toward new joys then let me fly
On the wings of my desire.
(*Exit, left.*)

E le pompose feste,
Ov' agli omaggi avvezza,
Vedea schiavo ciascun di sua bel-
lezza—
Ed or contenta in questi ameni luo-
ghi
Tutto scorda per me. Qui presso a
lei
Io rinascer mi sento,
E dal soffio d' amor rigenerato,
Scordo ne' gaudi suoi tutto il passa-
to.
De' miei bollenti spiriti
Il giovanile ardore
Ella temprò col placido
Sorriso dell' amor, dell' amor.
Dal dì che disse: vivere
Io voglio, io voglio a te fedel;
Dell' universo immemore,
Io vivo quasi in ciel.
Dal dì che disse: vivere,
Io voglio a te fedel,
Ah, sì! Dell' universo immemore,
Io vivo quasi in ciel.
(*Detto ed Annina in arnese da vi-
aggio.*)

And gay festivities
Where she was known to reign,
The queen of all men, captives of
her beauty.
Yet now contented in this pleasant
spot,
She lives for me alone.
I feel myself reborn, here by her
side
And regenerated by the breath of
love,
Forget the past in all her dear de-
lights.
My youth's rebellious passion,
My ardent soul's commotion,
She tempered with the calm
Sweet smile of her devotion.
Since first the words she spoke,
"I shall be ever yours,"
Oblivious of the world,
I made all heaven mine.
Since first the words she spoke,
"I shall be ever yours,"
Ah, yes, the world forgetting,
I made all heaven mine!
(*Enter Annina in a traveling cos-
tume.*)

**ALFREDO:** Annina! donde vieni?

**ALFREDO:** Annina! Where have
you been?

**ANNINA:** Da Parigi.

**ANNINA:** To Paris, sir.

**ALFREDO:** Chi tel commise?

**ALFREDO:** Who sent you there?

**ANNINA:** Fu la mia signora.

**ANNINA:** My mistress, sir.

**ALFREDO:** Perchè?

**ALFREDO:** But why?

**ANNINA:** Per alienar cavalli, coc-
chi, e quanto ancor possiede.

**ANNINA:** To dispose of her horses,
carriages and everything else she
owns.

**ALFREDO:** Che mai sento?

**ALFREDO:** What are you saying?

**ANNINA:** Lo spendio è grande a
viver qui solinghi.

**ANNINA:** It's costly to be living
here by yourselves.

**ALFREDO:** E tacevi?

**ALFREDO:** And you kept all this
from me?

**ANNINA:** Mi fu il silenzio imposto.

**ANNINA:** I was warned to say nothing.

**ALFREDO:** Imposto! Or
v'abbisogna?

**ALFREDO:** Warned!—How much
money do you need?

**ANNINA:** Mille luigi.

**ANNINA:** A thousand louis.

**ALFREDO:** Or vanne—Andrò a
Parigi—
Questo colloquio non sappia la si-
gnora—
I ie tutto valgo a riparare ancora.
Va!
(*Annina parte.*)

**ALFREDO:** Go, now.—I'll be off to
Paris.
But mind, not a word of this to your
mistress.
I may be able to straighten out the
business.
Go!
(*Exit Annina.*)

**ALFREDO:** (*solo*) Oh, mio rimor-
so!—Oh, infamia!—
Io vissi in tale errore?
Ma il turpe sogno a frangere
Il ver mi balenò.
Per poco in seno acquetati,
O grido dell' onore,
M' avrai securo vindice,
Quest' onta laverò.
O mio rossor! O infamia!
(*Esce.*)
(*Violetta, ch' entra con alcune
carte, parlando con Annina poi
Giuseppe a tempo.*)

**ALFREDO:** (*Alone*) O pangs of
conscience! Shame!
What error lulled my sense?
But now truth's rude awakening
Casts peace forever here!
Oh, hush within my breast
Affronted honor's cry!
This shameful stain at once
I'll wipe away, or die!
O infamy! O shame!
(*Exit.*)
(*Enter Violetta with some papers
in her hand. She is followed by An-
nina and, subsequently, Giu-
seppe.*)

**VIOLETTA:** Alfredo.

**VIOLETTA:** Alfredo!

---

## ■ ATTO SECONDO

*Casa di campagna presso Parigi.
Salotto terreno. Nel fondo, in faccia agli spettatori, è un camino,
sopra il quale uno specchio ed un
orologio, fra due porte chiuse da
cristalli, che mettono ad un giardino. Al primo piano due altre
porte, una di fronte all' altra. Sedie, tavolini, qualche libro,
l'occorrente per scrivere.*

*Alfredo entra, in costume da cac-
cia.*

**ALFREDO:** (*Depone il fucile.*)
Lunge da lei per me non v' ha dilet-
to!
Volaron già tre lune
Dacchè la mia Violetta
Agi per me lasciò, dovizie, onori,

## ■ ACT II

*The livingroom of a country villa
on the outskirts of Paris. In the
background, facing the audience,
is a chimney piece with a mantel
above it and a clock upon it. On
either side of the mantel, a glass
door, now closed, gives access to
the garden. Chairs and tables are
tastefully arranged about the
room, furnished also with books
and a writing desk.*

*Enter Alfredo, dressed for the
hunt.*

**ALFREDO:** (*Sets down his gun.*)
Away from her there's nothing that
delights me.
Three months have now gone by
Since my beloved Violetta
Forsook for me all luxury and pomp

ANNINA: Per Parigi or or partiva.

VIOLETTA: E tornerà?

ANNINA: Pria che tramonti il giorno—dirivel! m'impose.

VIOLETTA: È strano!

GIUSEPPE: Per voi.
(*Le presenta una lettera.*)

VIOLETTA: (*La prende.*) Sta ben.
In breve
Giungerà un uom d' affari—entri all' istante.
(*Annina e Giuseppe escono.*)

VIOLETTA: Ah, ah!
(*Leggendo la lettera.*)
Scopriva Flora il mio ritiro!—
E m' invita a danzar per questa sera!—
Invan m' aspetterà.
(*Getta il foglio sul tavolino e siede.*)

GIUSEPPE: È qui un signore.

VIOLETTA: Sarà lui che attendo.
(*Accenna a Giuseppe d'introdurlo.*)

GERMONT: Madamigella Valery?

VIOLETTA: Son io.

GERMONT: D' Alfredo il padre in me vedete.

VIOLETTA: Voi?
(*Sorpresa gli accenna di sedere.*)

GERMONT: (*Sedendo.*) Sì, dell' incauto, che a ruina corre,
Ammaliato da voi.

VIOLETTA: (*Alzandosi risentita.*) Donna son io, signore, ed in mia casa;
Ch' io vi lasci assentite,
Più per voi, che per me.
(*Per uscire.*)

GERMONT: Quai modi. Pure—

VIOLETTA: Tratto in error voi foste.
(*Torna a sedere*)

GERMONT: De' suoi beni egli dono vuol farvi.

VIOLETTA: Non l' osò finora.—Rifiuterei.

GERMONT: Pur tanto lusso—

VIOLETTA: A tutti è mistero quest' atto.—A voi nol sia.
(*Gli da le carte.*)

GERMONT: (*Dopo averle scorse coll' occhio.*) Ciel! Che discopro
D'ogni vostro avere or volete spogliarvi?
Ah, il passato perchè, perchè v' accusa?

VIOLETTA: Più non esiste—or amo Alfredo, e Dio
Lo cancellò col pentimento mio.

---

ANNINA: He has just left for Paris.

VIOLETTA: And when is he coming back?

ANNINA: Before sunset, he said to tell you.

VIOLETTA: That's odd!

GIUSEPPE: (*Handing her a letter.*) For you.

VIOLETTA: (*Taking it.*) Thanks—
Very shortly
a man will be arriving on business. Show
him in at once.
(*Annina and Giuseppe exit.*)

VIOLETTA: Ah, ah!
(*As she reads the letter.*)
So Flora has ferreted out my retreat,
And invites me to a ball tonight.
She'll wait in vain.
(*She tosses the letter on a table and sits down.*)

GIUSEPPE: A gentleman here to see you.

VIOLETTA: Ah, he must be the one I'm expecting.
(*Motions to Giuseppe to admit him.*)

GERMONT: Mademoiselle Valery?

VIOLETTA: That's I.

GERMONT: You see in me Alfredo's father.

VIOLETTA: You!
(*She shows surprise, but motions him to a chair.*)

GERMONT: (*Sits down.*) Yes, the father of that mad youth who is rushing to his ruin,
Infatuated by you.

VIOLETTA: (*She rises, affronted.*)
Sir, I am a woman—and in my own house.
You must permit me to leave,
More for your sake than for mine.
(*As if to leave.*)

GERMONT: What gentility. But—

VIOLETTA: You're under a misapprehension.
(*Sits down again.*)

GERMONT: But he's anxious to turn over his fortune to you—

VIOLETTA: He has not dared to do such a thing—I would refuse it!

GERMONT: Yet all this luxury!

VIOLETTA: Everyone wonders and is puzzled by it. But I'll explain this mystery to you.
(*Hands him the papers.*)

GERMONT: (*After examining them.*) You intend to sell all your belongings?—
Ah, but your past—why does it accuse you?

VIOLETTA: The past is dead. I love Alfredo.
Whatever was, Heaven has stricken out with my redemption.

---

GERMONT: Nobili sensi invero!

VIOLETTA: Oh, come dolce mi suona il vostro accento!

GERMONT: (*Alzandosi.*) Ed a tai sensi un sacrifizio chieggo.

VIOLETTA: (*Alzandosi.*) Ah no, tacete—
Terribil cosa chiedereste, certo—
Il previdi . . . v'attesi . . .
Era felice troppo . . .

GERMONT: D' Alfredo il padre la sorte,
L' avvenir domanda or qui de' suoi due figli.

VIOLETTA: Di due figli?

GERMONT: Sì.
Pura siccome un angelo
Iddio mi diè una figlia;
Se Alfredo nega riedere
In seno alla famiglia,
L' amato e amante giovane
Cui sposa andar dovea,
Or si ricusa al vincolo
Che lieti, lieti ne rendea.
Deh non mutate in triboli
Le rose dell' amor.
A' prieghi miei resistere, no, no,
Non voglia il vostro cor, no, no.

VIOLETTA: Ah, comprendo—dovrò per alcun tempo
Da Alfredo allontanarmi—doloroso
Fora per me—pur.

GERMONT: Non è ciò che chiedo.

VIOLETTA: Cielo!—che più cercate?—v'offersi assai.

GERMONT: Pur non basta.

VIOLETTA: Volete che per sempre a lui rinunzi?

GERMONT: È d'uopo.

VIOLETTA: Ah no giammai!
Non sapete quale affetto
Vivo, immenso m'arda in petto?
Che nè amici, nè parenti
Io non conto tra' viventi?
E che Alfredo m' ha giurato
Che in lui tutto troverò?
Non sapete che colpita
D'atro morbo è la mia vita?
Che già presso il fin ne vedo?
Ch' io mi separi da Alfredo!
Ah, il supplizio è si spietato,
Che morir preferirò.

GERMONT: È grave il sacrifizio.
Ma pur, tranquilla uditemi.
Bella voi siete e giovane—
Col tempo—

VIOLETTA: Ah, più non dite—v' intendo—
M' è impossibile.—Lui solo amar vogl' io.

GERMONT: Sia pure—ma volubile sovente è l' uom.

---

GERMONT: Noble sentiments indeed!

VIOLETTA: Oh, how soothing your words are to me!

GERMONT: But from those sentiments a sacrifice I require.

VIOLETTA: (*Rising.*) Ah, no!
Don't say it!
Surely a dreadful thing you'll ask of me.
I felt it! I knew it!
My happiness was too great.

GERMONT: Fate demands of Alfredo's father
To plead for the future, the good, of his two children.

VIOLETTA: Two children?

GERMONT: Yes.
A pure angelic daughter
From heaven I possess
Her brother she awaits
To bless her wedding day.
If Alfredo will not turn
From his path of folly,
The youth so loved and loving
Will spurn my daughter's hand.
Oh, do not change to grieving
Their future, bright and fair.
Oh, crown their joy—resist not—
Accord a father's prayer.

VIOLETTA: I must then, for a time—do I understand you?—
Leave my Alfredo. Painful it will be
For me. Still—

GERMONT: That is not what I demand.

VIOLETTA: Dear Heaven—what more, then? Too much
Have I already offered!

GERMONT: It is not yet enough.

VIOLETTA: You would not have me give him up forever?

GERMONT: It must be done.

VIOLETTA: Ah, no, no—never!
Do you know the immense love
That consumes my every sense?
That I have no friends, no kin
No ties, left in the world?
That Alfredo swore to be
Friend and kin and all to me?
Do you know the fatal ill
That attacks my life—to kill?
That already draws the end?
And you'd part me from my friend!—
Ah, death would be less cruel
Than to deny Alfredo.

GERMONT: Yes, great is your atonement,
Yet listen—brave and calm.
You are still young, still beautiful.
In time, perhaps—

VIOLETTA: No more! I guess your meaning.
But that will never be.
I love him only.

GERMONT: I grant it. But remember, man is fickle.

VIOLETTA: (*Colpita.*) Gran Dio!

GERMONT: Un dì, quando le veneri
Il tempo avrà fugate,
Fia presto il tedio a sorgere—
Che sarà allor?—Pensate—
Per voi non avran balsamo
I più soavi affetti!
Poichè del ciel non furono
Tai nodi benedetti.

VIOLETTA: È vero!

GERMONT: Ah, dunque, sperdasi
Tal sogno seduttore—
Siate di mia famiglia
L' angel consolatore—
Violetta, deh pensateci,
Ne siete in temp ancor.
È Dio che ispira, o giovine
Tai detti a un genitor.

VIOLETTA: (*Com estremo dolore.*) Così alla misera ch' è un dì caduta,
Di più risorgere speranza è muta!
Se pur benefico le indulga Iddio
L' uomo implacabil per lei sarà.

VIOLETTA: Dite alla giovine, si bella e pura,
Ch' avvi una vittima della sventura,
Cui resta un unico raggio de bene,
Che a lei il sacrifica, e che morrà, e morrà.

GERMONT: Piangi, piangi, piangi o misera, piangi;
Piangi, piangi, supremo, il veggo,
È il sacrifizio ch' ora ti chieggo:
Sento nell' anima già le tue pene;
Coraggio, e il nobile cor vincerà.

VIOLETTA: Imponete.

GERMONT: Non amarlo ditegli.

VIOLETTA: Nol crederà.

GERMONT: Partite.

VIOLETTA: Seguirammi.

GERMONT: Allor.

VIOLETTA: Qual figlia m'abbracciate—forte così sarò.
(*S'abbracciano.*)
Tra breve ei vi fia reso, ma afflitto oltre ogni dire;
A suo conforto di colà volerete.
(*Indicandogli il giardino, va per scrivere.*)

GERMONT: Che pensate?

VIOLETTA: Sapendol v' opporreste al pensier mío.

VIOLETTA: (*Shocked.*) Dear Heaven!

GERMONT: Some day, when love's illusions,
Outworn, will lose their spell,
What will you, weary, satiated
Do then, you two?—Think well!
For you will find no balm
In tenderest affection—
For never had your ties
The Heavens' benediction.

VIOLETTA: Ah, true! True!

GERMONT: Ah, therefore, therefore shatter
Such meretricious dreaming,
And to my dear ones be
An angel, kindly beaming.
Ah, think, Violetta, think
Upon my just desires.
It is Heaven itself, my child, that inspires
A father's words!

VIOLETTA: (*In extreme sorrow.*) So for the lost one fallen, unfriended,
All hope of rising is forever ended.
God will in mercy stretch out His hand,
But man implacable ever will stand.

VIOLETTA: Tell the young maiden, so chaste and fair
That one, unfortunate, crushed by despair,
Held but one treasure—of life's purest good but one ray,—
And that, to her she resigns it—to die, but to die!
But to die!

GERMONT: Weep, oh weep, unhappy one, weep!
The sacrifice I am demanding is great.
Yet in spite of my ruthless commanding
My soul suffers your anguish and pain.
Take heart—your sacrifice will triumph.

VIOLETTA: Then command me!

GERMONT: Tell him you do not love him.

VIOLETTA: He'll not believe it.

GERMONT: Then leave him.

VIOLETTA: He will come after me.

GERMONT: Then—

VIOLETTA: Come, clasp me like a daughter—so I'll take my resolve
(*They embrace.*)
Soon you will have him back—but, oh, so brokenhearted!
You will then hurry here to console him.
(*She indicates the garden and then sits down to write.*)

GERMONT: What are you planning?

VIOLETTA: If I told you, you would oppose it.

GERMONT: Generosa!—e per voi che far poss' io?

VIOLETTA: (*Tornando a lui.*) Morrò!—la mia memoria
Non fia ch' ei maledica,
Se le mie pene oribili,
Vi sia chi almen gli dica.

GERMONT: No, generosa, vivere,
E lieta voi dovrete,
Mercè di queste lagrime
Dal cielo un giorno avrete.

VIOLETTA: Conosca il sacrifizio
Ch' io consumai d' amore
Che sarà suo fin l' ultimo
Sospiro del mio cor.

GERMONT: Premiato il sacrifizio
Sarà del vostro cor.
D' un' opra così nobile
Sarete fiera allor.

VIOLETTA: Qui giunge alcun; partite!

GERMONT: O, grato v' è il cor mio!

VIOLETTA: Non ci vedrem più forse.
(*S' abbracciano.*)

VIOLETTA E GERMONT: Felice siate—Addio!
(*Germont esce per la porta del giardino.*)

VIOLETTA: Dammi tu forza, o cielo!
(*Siede, scrive, poi suona il campanello.*)

ANNINA: Mi richiedeste?

VIOLETTA: Sì, reca tu stessa questa foglio.

ANNINA: (*Ne guarda la direzione, e se ne mostra sorpresa.*) Oh!

VIOLETTA: Silenzio—Va all' istante
(*Annina parte.*)
Ed or si scriva a lui—che gli dirò?
Chi men darà il coraggio?
(*Scrive e poi suggella*)

ALFREDO: Che fai?

VIOLETTA: (*Nascondendo la lettera.*) Nulla.

ALFREDO: Scrivevi!

VIOLETTA: (*Confusa.*) Sì—no—

ALFREDO: Qual turbamento?—A chi scrivevi?

VIOLETTA: A te.

ALFREDO: Dammi quel foglio.

VIOLETTA: No, per ora.

ALFREDO: Mi perdona—son io preoccupato.

VIOLETTA: (*Alzandosi.*) Che fu?

ALFREDO: Giunse mio padre.

VIOLETTA: Lo vedesti?

GERMONT: Ah, noble heart! Oh, how can I repay you?

VIOLETTA: (*Turning toward him.*) I'll die!—But ah,
He could not execrate my memory
If someone but imparted
My agony and fate—

GERMONT: You must not die, you generous one,
But live, forgetting woe,
And for the tears you're shedding,
The heavens will bestow grace.

VIOLETTA: If he knew the sacrifice
Whereby love I atone—
Knew that to my last breath
I loved just him alone!

GERMONT: For your supreme atonement,
For your heart's agony,
Be proud and noble, calm,
Rewarded you shall be.

VIOLETTA: There's someone coming—go.

GERMONT: My grateful heart beats for you.

VIOLETTA: We may not meet again.
(*They embrace.*)

GERMONT: Be happy—I implore you!
(*Germont goes out into the garden.*)

VIOLETTA: God give me strength!
(*She sits down, writes, and then rings for Annina.*)

ANNINA: You rang for me?

VIOLETTA: Yes. I want you to deliver this letter in person.

ANNINA: (*She looks at the address and shows surprise.*) Ah!

VIOLETTA: Hush!—Go at once.
(*Exit Annina.*)
And now I must write to him. But what shall I say?
Who shall give me the courage?
(*She writes, then seals the letter. Enter Alfredo.*)

ALFREDO: What are you doing?

VIOLETTA: a (*Concealing the letter.*) Nothing.

ALFREDO: You were writing?

VIOLETTA: (*Confused.*) No,—why, yes—

ALFREDO: Why this confusion? To whom were you writing?

VIOLETTA: To you.

ALFREDO: Give me that letter!

VIOLETTA: No, not now.

ALFREDO: Forgive, forgive me!—I'm not myself.

VIOLETTA: (*Rising.*) What is it?

ALFREDO: My father's in town.

VIOLETTA: Have you seen him?

ALFREDO: Ah, no, severo scritto mi lasciava; però l'attendo— t'amerà in verderti.

VIOLETTA: (*Molto agitata.*) Ch'ei qui non mi sorprenda— Lascia che m' allontani—tu lo calma— Ai piedi suoi mi getterò—divisi (*Mal frenando il pianto.*) Ei più non ne vorrà; sarem felici Perchè tu m' ami Alfredo, non è vero?

ALFREDO: Oh quanto!—Perchè piangi?

VIOLETTA: Di lagrime avea d'uopo—or son tranquilla. Lo vedi?—ti sorrido— (*Sforzandosi.*) Sarò là, tra quei fior, presso a te sempre— Amami, Alfredo, quant' io t' amo.—Addio. (*Corre in giardino.*)

ALFREDO: Ah! vive sol quel core all' amor mio! (*Siede, prende a caso un libro, legge alquanto, quindi s' alza guarda l' ora sull' orologio sovrapposto al camino.*) E tardi; ed oggi forse Più non verrà mio padre.

GIUSEPPE: (*Entrando frettoloso.*) La signora è partita. L'attendeva un calesse, e sulla via Già corre di Parigi.—Annina pure Prima di lei spariva.

ALFREDO: Il so, ti calma.

GIUSEPPE: (*Da se.*) Che vuol dir ciò! (*Esce.*)

ALFREDO: Va forse d'ogni avere Ad affrettar la perdita— Ma Annina la impedirà— (*Si vede il Padre attraversare in lontano il giardino.*) Qualcuno è nel giardino! Chi è là? (*Per uscire.*)

COMMISSIONARO: (*Alla porta.*) Il signor Germont?

ALFREDO: Son io.

COMMISSIONARO: Una dama, da un cocchio, per voi, Di qua non lunge mi diede questo scritto. (*Da una lettera ad Alfredo, ne riceve qualche moneta, e parte.*)

ALFREDO: Di Violetta!—Perchè son io commosso? A raggiungerla forse ella m' invita— Io tremo!—Oh ciel!—Coraggio! (*Apre e legge.*) "Alfredo, al giungervi di questo

ALFREDO: No—but he left me a harsh note. He will call on us here, though. I know he will love you once he sees you.

VIOLETTA: (*Much agitated.*) Oh, he must not find me here! Let me leave while you appease him. Then at his feet I'll fall. Surely (*Unable to control her tears.*) He could not want to part us now— we shall be happy. For you do love me, Alfredo—you do love me?

ALFREDO: To distraction!—But why your tears?

VIOLETTA: My heart was too full. But see, I am calm now. I can even smile. (*Forcing a smile.*) I shall be there, among those flowers, always near you Oh my beloved Alfredo! Love me as I love you.—Good-bye. (*Rushes out into the garden.*)

ALFREDO: That dearest heart lives only for my love! (*He sits down, takes up a book, reads a while. He then rises and looks at the clock on the mantel.*) It's late. Perhaps my father Will not come in today.

GIUSEPPE: (*Hurrying in.*) The mistress has left— A carriage was waiting for her, and now She's on her way to Paris. Annina too Rushed off ahead of her.

ALFREDO: I know all that. Calm yourself.

GIUSEPPE: (*Aside.*) What can it all mean? (*Exit.*)

ALFREDO: She's gone, probably to speed herself to ruin By selling all she owns. But Annina will prevent her. (*Germont is seen approaching from the garden.*) There's someone in the garden. Who's there? (*He makes as if to go out.*)

MESSENGER: (*At the door.*) Monsieur Germont?

ALFREDO: In person.

MESSENGER: A lady, not long since, sir, handed me this From a carriage, to give to you. (*Gives Alfredo a note, receives his tip and goes out.*)

ALFREDO: It's from Violetta. Why am I so perturbed? Perhaps she's asking me to join her.— I tremble!—O Heaven! Give me strength. (*Opens the letter and reads.*)

foglio"— (*Come fulminato, grida. Volgendosi, si trova a fronti del Padre nelle cui braccia si abandona, esclamando—*) Ah!—Padre mio?

GERMONT: Mio figlio! Oh, quanto soffri—ah tergi il pianto— Ritorna di tuo padre orgoglio e vanto. (*Alfredo disperato siede presso il tavolino col volto tra le mani.*) Di Provenza il mar, il suol Chi dal cor ti cancellò? Al natio fulgente sol Qual destino ti furò? Oh, rammenta pur nel duol, Ch' ivi gioia a te brillò, E che pace colà sol Su te splendere ancor può; Dio mi guidò! Ah! il tuo vecchio genitor Tu non sai quanto soffrì— Te lontano, di squallor Il tuo tetto si coprì— Ma se alfin ti trovo ancor Se in me speme non fallì. Se la voce dell' onor In te appien non ammutì— Dio m' esaudì! Nè rispondi d' un padre all' affetto? (*Abbracciandolo.*)

ALFREDO: Mille furie divoramni il petto— Mi lasciate— (*Respingendolo.*)

GERMONT: Lasciarti?

ALFREDO: (*Risoluto.*) Oh, vendetta!

GERMONT: Non più indugi; partiamo—t'affretta.

ALFREDO: Ah fu Douphol!

GERMONT: M' ascolti tu?

ALFREDO: No!

GERMONT: Dunque invano trobato t' avrò? No, non udrai rimproveri; Copriam d'oblio il passato: L'amor che m' ha guidato Sa tutto perdonar. Vieni, i tuoi cari in giubilo Con me rivedi ancora; A chi penò finora Tal gioia non negar. Un padre ed una suora T' affretta a consolar.

ALFREDO: (*Scuotendosi, getta a caso gli occhi sulla tavola, vede la lettera di Flora, la scorre ed esclama.*) Ah! ell' è alla festa! volisi L' offesa a vendicar. (*Fugge precipitoso seguito dal Padre.*)

GERMONT: Che dici? Ah, ferma!

"Alfredo, by the time this letter reaches you . . ." (*He cries out, thunderstruck. On turning round, he finds himself face to face with his father who clasps him in his arms.*) Father!

GERMONT: My son! What bitter grief! But cease, oh cease your weeping. Again be to your father his honor and his vaunt. (*Alfredo sits, his head between his hands.*) Who Provence's soil and sea Cancelled from your memory? What, then, lured you from the blaze Of our native, sunny days? Ah, in sorrow still recall That you knew happiness there, That there peace again may fall Over all that troubles you. God led me here! Ah, how can you ever know What your aged father proved When, you absent, shame and woe Fell upon the home he loved. But if truly I have found Once again the son I lost, If within your breast the sound Of hope's voice you do not still, God grants my will! Can you be deaf to your father's affection? (*Embracing him.*)

ALFREDO: A thousand furies rend me!— Leave me! (*Pushes him off.*)

GERMONT: Leave you?

ALFREDO: (*Resolutely.*) Oh, vengeance!

GERMONT: Come, no more delays. We're leaving—at once.

ALFREDO: Ah, it was Douphol!

GERMONT: Don't you hear me?

ALFREDO: No!

GERMONT: Then I have found you in vain! Ah, no, I shall not chide— We must forget the past. The love that was my guide Has taught me to forgive. Come, hasten then, to gladden Our dear ones far away; No more to sadden their lives— Such joy is yours to give. To father and to sister Such joy is yours to give.

ALFREDO: (*As he comes to himself he glances upon the table and sees Flora's letter. He reads it and exclaims:*) Ah, she has gone to Flora's party! Quickly—come with me! Such offense must be punished! (*He dashes out followed by his Father.*)

GERMONT: What do you say? Stay here!

## ■ ATTO TERZO

*Galleria nel Palazzo di Flora, ric-
camente addobbata e illuminata.—Una porta nel fondo e due
laterali.—A destra più avanti, un
taboliere con quanto occorre pel
giuoco: a sinistra ricco tavolino
con fiori e rinfreschi, varie sedie e
un divano.*

*Flora, il Marchese, il Dottore, ed
altri invitati entrano dalla sinistra, discorrendo tra loro.*

**FLORA:** Avrem lieta di maschere la
notte;
N' è duce il viscontino—
Violetta ed Alfredo anco invitai.

**MARCHESE:** La novità ignorate?
Violetta e Germont sono disgiunti.

**DOTTORE E FLORA:** Fia vero?

**MARCHESE:** Ella verrà qui col barone.

**DOTTORE:** Li vidi ieri ancor—par-
ean felici.
(*S' ode rumore a destra.*)

**FLORA:** Silenzio—Udite?

**TUTTI:** (*Vanno verso la destra.*)
Giungono gli amici.
(*Detti, e molte Signore mascherate da Zingare, che entrano dalla
destra.*)

**ZINGARE:** Noi siamo Zingarelle
Venute da lontano;
D' ognuno sulla mano
Leggiamo l' avvenir.
Se consultiam le stelle
Null' avvi a noi d' oscuro,
E i casi del futuro
Possiamo altrui predir.
(*Prendono la mano a Flora, ed os-
servano.*)

**1:** Vediamo!—Voi signora,
Rivali alquante avete.

**2:** (*Fanno lo stesso al Marchese.*)
Marchese, voi non siete
Model di fedeltà.

**FLORA:** (*Al Marchese.*) Fate il galante ancora?
Ben, vo' me la paghiate.

**MARCHESE:** (*A Flora.*) Che diacin
vi pensate?
L'accusa è falsità.

**FLORA:** La volpe lascia il pelo,
Non abbandona il vizio—
Marchese mio, giudizio,
O vi farò pentir.

**TUTTI:** Su via, si stenda un velo
Sui fatti del passato;
Già quel ch' è stato,
Badate all' avvenir.

## ■ ACT III

*The salon of Flora's Paris man-
sion, richly furnished and brilliantly illuminated. In the foreground toward the right, a
gaming table and the necessary
equipment. On the left an elegant
table with flowers and refreshments. Various chairs and a settee.*

*Flora, the Marquis, the Doctor
and other guests enter from the
right, conversing.*

**FLORA:** Our evening will be enlivened with masquers—
The Viscount's contribution.
Violetta and Alfredo are also invited.

**MARQUIS:** Don't you know the
news?
Violetta and Alfredo have parted.

**DOCTOR and FLORA:** Can it be
true?

**MARQUIS:** She's being escorted by
the Baron.

**DOCTOR:** I saw them only yesterday. They seemed quite happy.
(*Noise on the right.*)

**FLORA:** Hush! Listen!
(*Moving across stage toward the
right.*)
Our friends are arriving.
(*The same and a number of Ladies dressed as Gypsies, who enter
from the right.*)

**GYPSIES:** We're gay young gypsy
maidens
From distant foreign strands,
And on your dainty hands
We read what is to be.
When studying the skies
To scan your future deep,
No secret from our eyes
The stars and planets keep.
(*One takes Flora's hand and ex-
amines it.*)

**1:** Let's see, now. You, dear Flora,
Have rivalries aplenty.

**2:** (*Another, reading the hand of
the Marquis.*)
You, Marquis, wear no aura
For faithfulness in love.

**FLORA:** (*To Marquis.*) What! do
you still philander?
You'll pay me well for this!

**MARQUIS:** (*To Flora.*) You cannot
be in earnest!
There is no truth to it.

**FLORA:** The fox may change his
hair,
But his bad manners—never!
Dear Marquis, take care,
Or you will surely regret it.

**ALL:** Away, then, throw a veil
Over the past misdeed.
What's done no more bewail.—
Rather, your future heed.

*(Flora ed il Marchese si stringono
la mano.
Gastone ed altri mascherati da
Mattadori e Piccadori spagnoli,
ch' entranto vivacemente dalla
destra.)*

**GASTONE E MATTADORI:** Di Ma-
dride noi siam mattadori,
Siamo i prodi del circo dei tori;
Testè giunti a godere del chiasso
Che a Parigi si fa pel Bue grasso'
E, una storia se udire vorrete,
Quali amanti noi siamo, saprete.

**GLI ALTRI:** Sì, sì, bravi; narrate,
narrate;
Con piacere l' udremo.

**GASTONE E MATTADORI:** Asco-
late:
E Piquillo un bel gagliardo
Biscaglino mattador;
Forte il braccio, fiero il guardo,
Delle giostre egli è signor.
D' Andalusa a giovinetta
Follemente innamorò;
Ma la bella ritrosetta
Così al giovane parlò:
Cinque tori in un sol giorno
Vo' vederti ad atterrar;
E se vinci, al tuo ritorno.
Mano e cor ti vo' donar.
Sì, gli disse, e il mattadore
Alle giostre mosse il piè;
Cinque tori, vincitore,
Sull' arena egli stendè.

**GLI ALTRI:** Bravo, bravo, il matta-
dore
Ben gagliardo si mostrò,
Se alla giovane l' amore
In tal guisa egli provò!

**GASTONE E MATTODORI:** Poi,
tra plausi, ritornato
Alla bella del suo cor,
Colse il premio desiato
Tra le braccia dell' amor.

**GLI ALTRI:** Con tai prove i Mattadori
San le belle conquistar!

**GASTONE E MATTODORI:** Ma qui
son più miti i cori;
A noi basta folleggiar.

**TUTTI:** Sì, sì, allegri—Or pria ten-
tiamo
Della sorte il vario umor.
La palestra dischiudiamo
Agli audaci giuocator.
(*Gli uomini si tolgono la masch-
era, chi passeggia e chi si accinge
a giuocare.*)
(*Detti ed Alfredo, quindi Violetta
col Barone; un Servo a tempo.*)

**TUTTI:** Alfredo!—Voi?

**ALFREDO:** Sì, amici.

**FLORA:** Violetta?

**ALFREDO:** (*Secco.*) Non ne so.

*(Flora and the Marquis shake
hands.)*
*(Gastone and others disguised as
Spanish Matadors and Picadors,
enter from the right.)*

**GASTONE and MATADORS:** From
Madrid we all hail, matadors
Bearing triumphs from bull rings
galore,
Come to share in the rumpus you
make
Here is Paris for our Fat Bulls' sake
If with patience you'll listen to a
tale
You will learn of our prowess—in
love.

**ALL:** Yes, yes, heroes! All hail! Tell
your tale.
We shall listen with pleasure.

**GASTONE and MATADORS:** Then
hear!
Our Piquillo, gay and handsome
Matador, comes from Biscay.
With a strong arm and a proud look;
He held sway in the bull ring.
A fair Andalusian maiden
Loved him with a fiery passion.
Nonetheless, this wayward girl
Did address him in this fashion:
"Five fierce bulls within a day
I would see you slay myself.
If you do as I command
I will give you heart and hand."
He agreed, did our Piquillo
And into the ring he flew,
And within the time allotted
Five fierce bulls our hero slew.

**ALL:** Valiant fighter, lover bold,
Brave indeed your matador,
So to prove to his proud lady
The devoted love he bore!

**GASTONE and MATADORS:** Then
amid the wild acclaim
To his lady he knelt down
And from his own hands received
Love's and honor's priceless crown.

**ALL:** By such prowess matadors
Win the ladies of their choice.

**GASTONE and MATADORS:** But
here hearts are easier won—
Let us therefore now rejoice!

**ALL:** Yes, rejoice, be gay! But first
Let us lucky chance importune.
To the games, then. All, come for-
ward,
Valiant champions of Fortune!
(*The men remove their masks.
Some wander about while others
begin to play.*)
(*The same, and Alfredo. Later
Violetta and the Baron; then a Ser-
vant.*)

**ALL:** Alfredo! You?

**ALFREDO:** Yes, my friends.

**FLORA:** And Violetta?

**ALFREDO:** (*Sharply.*) I don't
know.

TUTTI: Ben disinvolto!—bravo!—Or via, giocar si può.
(*Gastone si pone a tagliare: Alfredo ed altri puntano.—Violetta entra al braccio del Barone.*)

ALL: He's quite unconcerned.—Bravo!—Then let's to the games.
(*Gastone begins to cut the cards. Alfredo and several others put up their stakes. Violetta enters, escorted by the Baron.*)

FLORA: (*Andandole incontro.*) Qui desiata giungi.

FLORA: (*Going toward her.*) You've been ardently wished for.

VIOLETTA: Cessi al cortese invito.

VIOLETTA: I could not resist your charming invitation.

FLORA: Grata vi son, Barone, d' averlo pur gradito.

FLORA: I'm grateful to you as well, Baron, for having accepted.

BARONE: (*Piano a Violetta.*) Germont è qui! il vedete?

BARON: (*To Violetta in an undertone.*) Germont is here!—Do you see him?

VIOLETTA: (*Da sè.*) Cielo!—gli è vero!
(*Piano a Barone.*) Il vedo.

VIOLETTA: (*Aside.*) Dear Heaven! It's true.
(*Quietly to the Baron.*) I see him.

BARONE: (*Piano a Violetta.*) Da voi non un sol detto si volga a questo Alfredo.

BARON: (*Quietly to Violetta.*) You're not to address a word to this Alfredo.

VIOLETTA: (*Da sè.*) Ah, perchè venni incauta! Pietà gran Dio di me!

VIOLETTA: (*To herself.*) Ah, why did I come so rashly? Dear God, have mercy on me!

FLORA: Meco t' assidi, narrami:—quai novità vegg'io?
(*A Violetta, facendola sedere presso di sè sul divano. Il Dottore si avvicina ad esse, che sommessamente conversano. Il Marchese si trattiene a parte col Barone; Gastone taglia; Alfredo ed altri puntano, altri passeggiano.*)

FLORA: Sit here beside me. Tell me—what's all this I hear?
(*Flora leads Violetta to the settee. The Doctor stands by them as they converse in low tones. The Marquis and the Baron stand aside, talking to each other. Gastone cuts the cards. Alfredo and others stake while the rest walk about.*)

ALFREDO: Un quattro!

ALFREDO: A four!

GASTONE: Ancora hai vinto?

GASTONE: You win again!

ALFREDO: Sfortuna nell' amore fortuna reca al giuoco.
(*Punta e vince.*)

ALFREDO: Unlucky in love, lucky at cards!

TUTTI: È sempre vincitore!

ALL: He's always winning.

ALFREDO: Oh, vincerò stassera; e l' oro guadagnato poscia a goder fra' campi ritornerò beato.

ALFREDO: Oh, I shall win to-night—and the winnings I'll spend in country pleasures, as before.

FLORA: Solo?

FLORA: Alone?

ALFREDO: No, no, con tale, che vi fu meco ancora, poi mi sfuggia.

ALFREDO: Oh, no! With a certain person who was there with me—and then left me.

VIOLETTA: Mio Dio!
(*Da se.*)

VIOLETTA: Dear God!

GASTONE: (*Ad Alfredo, indicando Violetta.*) Pietà di lei!

GASTONE: (*To Alfredo, indicating Violetta.*) Have pity on her!

BARONE: (*Ad Alfredo, con mal frenata ira.*) Signor!

BARON: (*To Alfredo, with ill-concealed wrath.*) Sir!

VIOLETTA: (*Piano al Barone.*) Frenatevi, o vi lascio.

VIOLETTA: (*Softly, to the Baron.*) Control yourself or I leave you!

ALFREDO: (*Disinvolto.*) Barone, m' appellaste?

ALFREDO: (*Sarcastically.*) Were you addressing me, Baron?

BARONE: (*Ironico.*) Siete in si gran fortuna, che al gioco mi tentaste.

BARON: (*Ironically.*) You're having such extraordinary luck that you tempt me to play you.

ALFREDO: Si?—la disfida accetto.

ALFREDO: Indeed?—I accept the challenge.

VIOLETTA: (*Da sè.*) Che fia?—morir mi sento!
Pietà, gran Dio, pietà gran Dio, di mè!

VIOLETTA: (*Aside.*) What will happen? I feel life leaving me. Dear God, have pity—have pity on me!

BARONE: (*Punta.*) Cento luigi a destra.

BARON: (*Stakes.*) A hundred louis, to the right.

ALFREDO: (*Punta.*) Ed alla manca cento.

ALFREDO: (*Stakes.*) And to the left, a hundred.

GASTONE: (*Tagliando.*) Un asso—un fante— (*Ad Alfredo.*) hai vinto!

GASTONE: (*Cutting the deck.*) An ace—a jack— (*To Alfredo.*) you've won!

BARONE: Il doppio?

BARON: Will you double it?

ALFREDO: Il doppio sia.

ALFREDO: Agreed—I double.

GASTONE: (*Tagliando.*) Un quattro, un sette.

GASTONE: (*Cutting the deck.*) A four, a seven.

TUTTI: Ancora!

ALL: Again!

ALFREDO: Pur la vittoria è mia!

ALFREDO: Again the victory's mine!

CORO: Bravo davver!—La sorte è tutta per Alfredo!

CHOR: Bravo, truly!—Luck smiles only on Alfredo.

FLORA: Del villeggiar la spesa farà il Baron, già il vedo.

FLORA: I see now where the Baron will bear the expenses of the country pleasure.

ALFREDO: (*Al Barone.*) Seguite pur.

ALFREDO: (*To the Baron.*) Proceed, sir.

SERVO: La cena è pronta.

SERVANT: Supper is served.

FLORA: Andiamo.

FLORA: Let us go, then.

CORO: (*Avviandosi.*) Andiamo.

CHOR: (*Proceeding.*) Let us go.

ALFREDO: (*Tra loro a parte.*) Se continuar v'aggrada—

ALFREDO: (*Aside to Baron.*) If you'd like to continue—

BARONE: Per ora nol possiamo; più tardi la rivincita.

BARON: At present we cannot. Later, for the final victory.

ALFREDO: Al gioco che vorrete.

ALFREDO: At whatever game you choose.

BARONE: Seguiam gli amici; poscia . . .

BARON: Let's follow our friends. Then, later—

ALFREDO: Sarò qual bramerete.
(*Tutti entrano nella porta di mezzo: la scena rimane un istante vuota.*)
(*Violetta, che ritorna affannata, indi Alfredo.*)

ALFREDO: I shall be at your service.
(*All go out at the door center. The stage for a while remains empty.*)
(*Violetta, much agitated, returns, soon followed by Alfredo.*)

VIOLETTA: Invitato qui a seguirmi,
Verrà desso!—vorrà udirmi?
Ei verrà—chè l' odio atroce
Puote in lui più di mia voce.

VIOLETTA: Will he follow? Will he hear me?
Have my words still power to move?
He will come!—The voice of his hate
Will speak louder than my love!

ALFREDO: Mi chiamaste?—Che bramate?

ALFREDO: Did you call me? What's your will?

VIOLETTA: Questi luoghi abbandonate—
Un periglio vi sovrasta.

VIOLETTA: Leave this place, I do implore!
You're in danger, in great danger—

ALFREDO: Ah, comprendo!—Basta, basta—
E sì vile mi credete?

ALFREDO: So that's it!—I pray no more!
Do you think me such a coward?

VIOLETTA: Ah, no, mai.

VIOLETTA: Ah, no—never!

ALFREDO: Ma che temete?

ALFREDO: Then why fear?

VIOLETTA: Tremo sempre del Barone.

VIOLETTA: It's the Baron. I—I tremble!

ALFREDO: È tra noi mortal quistione—
S' ei cadrà per mano mia
Un sol colpo vi torria
Coll' amante il protettore—
V' atterrisce tal sciagura?

ALFREDO: True, we have a deadly feud.
If by my hand he should fall,
At one blow you lose your all—
Both the lover and protector.
Such misfortune must appal!

VIOLETTA: Ma s' ei fosse l' ucci-sore!—
Ecco l' unica sventura—
Ch' io pavento a me fatale!

VIOLETTA: Ah, what if he prove the slayer?
There's the agonizing dread!
It is your death that would slay me.

ALFREDO: La mia morte!—Che v'en cale.

ALFREDO: My death? What is that to you?

VIOLETTA: Deh partite, e sull' is-tante.

VIOLETTA: Go, I beg you! Go this instant.

ALFREDO: Partirò ma giura in-nante
Che dovunque seguirai
I passi miei.

ALFREDO: I go—but before we sever
Swear that where my footsteps lead me
You will follow!

VIOLETTA: Ah no, giammai!

VIOLETTA: Ah no—never!

ALFREDO: No!—giammai!

ALFREDO: Never? No?

VIOLETTA: Va, sciagurato,
Scorda un nome ch' è infamato—
Va—mi lascia sul momento—
Di fuggirti un giuramento
Sacro io feci.

VIOLETTA: Go, unhappy love,
And forget my shameful name,
Go, ah, go! Another oath
I have sworn, an oath most bind-ing—
To forsake you!

ALFREDO: A chi? Dillo. Chi potea?

ALFREDO: Who required it?

VIOLETTA: A chi dritto pien ne avea.

VIOLETTA: One whose right was beyond question.

ALFREDO: Fu Douphol!

ALFREDO: Douphol, then!

VIOLETTA: (Con supremo sfor-zo.) Sì.

VIOLETTA: (Bravely.) Yes!

ALFREDO: Dunque l' ami?

ALFREDO: Then you love him?

VIOLETTA: Ebben—l' amo.

VIOLETTA: Yes, I love him!

ALFREDO: (Corre furente alla porta e grida.) Or tutti a me.
(Detti, e tutti i precedenti, che confusamente tornano.)

ALFREDO: (Rushes impetuously to the door and cries:) Come hith-er, all of you!
(The same, and all the rest who re-turn in confusion.)

TUTTI: Ne appellaste?—Che vo-lete?

ALL: Did you call us? What's your wish?

ALFREDO: Questa donna conos-cete?
(Additando Violetta che, abbattu-ta, si appoggia al tavolino.)

ALFREDO: Is this woman known to you?
(Pointing to the fainting Violetta who leans against a table for sup-port.)

TUTTI: Chi?—Violetta?

ALL: Who?—Violetta?

ALFREDO: Che facesse Non sapete?

ALFREDO: Do you know What she has done?

VIOLETTA: Ah, taci.

VIOLETTA: Ah, spare me!

TUTTI: No.

ALL: No.

ALFREDO: Ogni suo aver tal fem-mina
Per amor mio sperdea;
Io cieco, vile, misero,
Tutto accettar potea.
Ma è tempo ancora! Tergermi
Da tanta macchia bramo,
Qui testimon vi chiamo,
Che qui pagata io l' ho.
(Alfredo getta con furente sprezzo una borsa ai piedi di Violetta ed essa sviene tra la braccia di Flora e del Dottore. In tal momento en-tra il Padre.)
(Detti ed il Signor Germont, ch' entra all' ultime parole.)

ALFREDO: All that she owned this woman spent
Upon her lover.
I, blind, infatuate fool,
Allowed it, well content
It's not too late to clear me
Of my dishonoring blame.
Stand witness. Thus I pay
My earlier debt of shame.
(With violent scorn he flings a purse at the feet of Violetta who faints in Flora's arms. In a min-ute, his father enters.)
(The same and Germont who en-ters in time to hear Alfredo's final words)

TUTTI: Oh, infamia orribile tu commettesti!—
Un cor sensibile così uccidesti!—
Di donne ignoble insultatore,
Di qua allontanati, ne desti orror.

ALL: Dreadful injustice you have committed,
To break a heart that so tenderly loved you!
Begone!—You fill us with infinite horror,
Ignoble man, insulter of women!

GERMONT: (Con dignitoso fuo-co.) Di sprezzo degno sè stesso rende.
Chi pur nell' ira la donna offende.
Dov' è mio figlio?—Più non lo vedo,
In te più Alfredo—trovar non so.
(Da sè.) Io sol fra tanti so qual vir-tude
Di quella misera il sen racchiude—
Io so che l' ama, che gli è fedele;
Eppur, crudele, tacer dovrò!

GERMONT: (With dignified re-proach.) No scorn too bitter for any man
Who, even in anger, taunts a wom-an!
Where is my son? I do not see him.
I do not find Alfredo in you.
(Aside.) I alone know what a virtu-ous heart
Beats in that woman's unhappy breast.
I alone know she is loving and true,
And yet—ah, cruel!—I cannot speak!

ALFREDO: (Da sè.) Ah, si!—che feci!—ne sento orrore!—
Gelosa smania, deluso amore
Mi strazian l' alma—più non ra-giono—
Da lei perdono—più non avrò.
Volea fuggirla—non ho potuto!—
Dall' ira spinto, son qui venuto!—
Or che lo sdegno ho disfogato,—
Me sciagurato!—rimorso io n' ho.

ALFREDO: (Aside.) What have I done? My deed appals me!
My jealous rage, my love's distress
Destroy me utterly, drive me to madness!
No more with pardon she'll come to bless!
I would have fled her—I was not strong.
Here my rage led me,—to do her wrong.
But now I've vented my mad dis-dain—
Ah, what can heal remorseful pain?

VIOLETTA: (Riavendosi.) Alfre-do, Alfredo, di questo core
Non puoi comprendere tutto l' amore!
Tu non conosci che fino a prezzo
Del tuo disprezzo—provato io l'ho.
Ma verrà giorno in che il saprai—
Com' io t' amassi confesserai—
Dio dai rimorsi ti salvi allora—
Io spenta ancora—pur t' amerò.

VIOLETTA: (Coming to.) Alfredo, who can impart
The love I bear you within my heart!
You'll never know your scorn I drew
To prove how great my love for you.
Some day you'll know and you will bow
Your head, and my true love avow.
May God then save you from your remorse—
For even in death, I'll ever love you.

BARONE: (Piano ad Alfredo. Da sè.) A questa donna l' atroce insul-to,
Qui tutti offese, ma non inulto
Fia tanto oltraggio—provar vi vog-lio
Che il vostro orgoglio—fiaccar sa-prò.

BARON: (Aside to Alfredo.)
Your insult to this lady all have heard,
And to your hurt. But not the deed alone
But arrant pride
I'll know how to chastize.

TUTTI: (A Violetta.) Ahi quanto peni!—Ma pur fa core—
Qui soffre ognuno del tuo dolore;
Fra cari amici qui sei soltanto;
Rasciuga il pianto—che t' inondò.
(Germont trae seco il figlio; il Bar-one lo segue. Violetta è condotta in altra stanza dal Dottore e da Flora; gli altri si disperdono.)

ALL: (To Violetta.) Ah, what ago-ny! But be comforted.
Your anguish strikes a sympathetic chord.
You are with friends, Violetta.
Dry your tears.
(Germont leads Alfredo out. The Baron follows. Flora and the Doc-tor help Violetta to retire to an ad-joining room while the rest dis-perse.)

# ■ ATTO QUATRO

*Camera da letto di Violetta.—Nel fondo è un letto con cortine mezzo tirate; una finestra chiusa da imposte interne; presso il letto uno sgabello su cui una bottiglia d'acqua, una tazza di cristallo, diverse medicine.—A metà della scena una toiletta, vicino un canapè; più distante un altro mobile, su cui arde un lume da notte, varie sedie ed altri mobili. La porta è a sinistra; di fronte v'è un caminetto con fuoco acceso.*

*Violetta dorme sul letto—Annina, seduta presso il caminetto, è pure addormita.*

**VIOLETTA:** (*Destandosi.*) Annina!

**ANNINA:** (*Svegliandosi confusa.*) Comandate?

**VIOLETTA:** Dormivi, poveretta?

**ANNINA:** Sì, perdonate.

**VIOLETTA:** Dammi d' acqua un sorso.
(*Annina eseguisce.*) Osserva, è pieno il giorno?

**ANNINA:** Son sett' ore.

**VIOLETTA:** Dà accesso a un po' di luce.

**ANNINA:** (*Apre la imposte, e guarda nella via.*) Il Signor di Grenvil!

**VIOLETTA:** Oh il vero amico! Alzar mi vo'—m' aita.
(*Si alza e ricade; poi, sostenuta da Annina, va lentamente verso il canapè ed il Dottore entra in tempo per assisterla ad adagiarvisi—Annina vi aggiunge dei cuscini.*)

**VIOLETTA:** Quanta bontà—Pensaste a me per tempo!

**DOTTORE:** Sì, come vi sentite?
(*Le tocca il polso.*)

**VIOLETTA:** Soffre il mio corpo, ma tranquilla ho l' alma.
Mi confortò ier sera un pio ministro. Ah,
Religione è sollievo ai sofferenti.

**DOTTORE:** E questa notte?

**VIOLETTA:** Ebbi tranquillo il sonno.

**DOTTORE:** Coraggio adunque—la convalescenza
Non è lontana.

**VIOLETTA:** Oh, la bugia pietosa
Ai medici è concessa.

**DOTTORE:** (*Stringendole la mano.*) Addio—a più tardi.

**VIOLETTA:** Non mi scordate.

# ■ ACT IV

*Violetta's bedroom. In the rear is a bed, its curtain partly drawn; also a window, with shutters from within. A nightstand near the bed holds a carafe of water, a glass, and various medicine bottles. Downstage a toilet table and mirror, and a chaise-longue. Other chairs and furniture, and a bureau on which a night lamp is burning. In the hearth, center, a fire is smoldering.*

*Violetta is still in bed, asleep. Annina dozes in a chair by the fireplace.*

**VIOLETTA:** (*Awaking.*) Annina!

**ANNINA:** (*Starting up.*) Ah! What do you wish, Madam?

**VIOLETTA:** Were you asleep, poor girl?

**ANNINA:** I was—forgive me.

**VIOLETTA:** A drink of water, please.
(*Annina gets it.*)
Look—is it day, already?

**ANNINA:** It is seven o'clock.

**VIOLETTA:** Let in a little light.

**ANNINA:** (*Opens the shutters and looks out.*) Oh, there's Monsieur Grenvil!

**VIOLETTA:** How kind a friend he is!
Help me, I wish to get up.
(*She attempts to rise but falls back. Then, leaning on Annina, she totters toward the chaise-longue. The Doctor arrives in time to help her recline, while Annina arranges cushions about her.*)

**VIOLETTA:** How good of you! To be thinking of me so often!

**DOCTOR:** How are you feeling now? (*Feels her pulse.*)

**VIOLETTA:** The body suffers, but the spirit is tranquil.
Last night a holy man gave me a great comfort.
Religion brings relief to the afflicted.

**DOCTOR:** What sort of night did you have?

**VIOLETTA:** I slept quite peacefully.

**DOCTOR:** Take heart, then. You'll soon be on the mend.

**VIOLETTA:** Oh, the pious lie Is the doctor's prerogative!

**DOCTOR:** (*Clasps her hand.*) Good-bye—I'll see you later.

**VIOLETTA:** Do not forget me.

**ANNINA:** (*Piano al Dottore, accompagnandolo.*) Come va, Signore?

**DOTTORE:** La tisi non le accorda che poche ore.
(*Piano e parte.*)

**ANNINA:** Or fate cor.

**VIOLETTA:** Giorno di festa è questo?

**ANNINA:** Tutta Parigi impazza—è carnevale.

**VIOLETTA:** Oh, nel comun tripudio, sallo Iddio
Quanti infelici soffron!—Quale somma
V' ha in quello stipo?
(*Indicandolo.*)

**ANNINA:** (*L'apre e conta.*) Venti luigi.

**VIOLETTA:** Dieci ne reca ai poveri tu stessa.

**ANNINA:** Poco rimanvi allora.

**VIOLETTA:** Oh, mi saran bastanti!—
(*Sospirando.*)
Cerca poscia mie lettere.

**ANNINA:** Ma voi?

**VIOLETTA:** Nulla occorrà—sollecita, se puoi.
(*Annina esce. Violetta, che trae dal seno una lettera e legge.*)
"Teneste la promessa—La disfida
Ebbe luogo; il barone fu ferito.
Però migliora—Alfredo
E in stranio suolo; il vostro sacrifizio
Io stesso gli ho svelato.
Egli a voi tornerà pel suo perdono;
Io pur verrò—Curatevi—mertate
Un avvenir migliore.
Giorgio Germont."
(*Desolata.*)
È tardi! (*Si alza.*)
Attendo, attendo—Nè a me giungon mai.
Oh! come son mutata!
Ma il Dottore a sperar pure m' esorta!—
Ah, con tal morbo ogni speranza è morta.
Addio, del passato bei sogni ridenti,
Le rose del volto già sono pallenti;
L' amore d' Alfredo perfino mi manca,
Conforto, sostegno dell' anima stanca.
Conforto! Sostegno!
Ah! della Traviata sorridi al desio!
A lei deh perdona, tu accoglila, o Dio!
Or, tutto, tutto finì . . .
Le gioie, i dolori fra poco avran fine;
La tomba ai mortali di tutto è confine!
Non lagrima o fiore avrà la mia fos-

**ANNINA:** (*In an undertone to the Doctor as she shows him out.*) How is she, Doctor?

**DOCTOR:** Her sickness will not give her more than a few hours. (*In an undertone, then exit.*)

**ANNINA:** Cheer up, I beg you!

**VIOLETTA:** Is today a holiday?

**ANNINA:** That it is, and all Paris goes mad. It is the carnival.

**VIOLETTA:** In all this merrymaking, Heaven only knows
How many poor creatures are suffering!
How much have we in that cupboard?
(*Pointing.*)

**ANNINA:** (*Opens it and counts.*) Twenty louis.

**VIOLETTA:** Go out and distribute ten among the poor.

**ANNINA:** You'll have very little left, then.

**VIOLETTA:** Ah, there will be enough for me!
(*Sighs.*)
Then go for my letters.

**ANNINA:** But you—?

**VIOLETTA:** I shan't need anything. Only don't be long.
(*Annina exits. Violetta draws a letter from her bosom and reads.*)
"You kept your promise. The duel
Took place. The Baron was wounded
But is now recovering. Alfredo
Is out of the country. Your sacrifice
I have myself revealed to him.
He will be coming to you for forgiveness.
I too will see you. Get well. You deserve
A better future. Giorgio Germont."
(*Desolately.*)
It's late! (*She arises.*)
I wait and wait—will they never come?
(*Gazing at herself in the mirror.*)
Ah, how my face is altered!
And yet of hope the Doctor talks!—In vain!
Hope is slain by such an illness!
Farewell, happy dreams of the time that has fled!
My cheeks' blooming roses are faded and dead.
The love of Alfredo, my weary heart's core,
My comfort, my strength—that too is no more!
My comfort! My strength!
O God, to the prayer of the lost one award
Your infinite mercy.—Receive her, dear Lord!
Soon all, all will pass!
Both rapture and pain now soon will be over—
All things, in the end, the cold tomb will cover.
But oh, neither flowers now tear-

sa,
Non croce, col nome, che copra
quest' ossa!—
Ah, della Traviata sorridi al desio,
A lei deh perdona, tu accoglila, O
Dio!
Or tutto finì.
(*Siede.*)

**CORO-BACCANALE:** (*Esterno.*)
Largo al quadrupede
Sir della festa
Di fiori e pampini
Cinta la testa—
Largo al più docile
D' ogni cornuto,
Di corni e pifferi
Abbia il saluto.
Parigini, date passo
Al trionfo del Bue grasso.
L'Asia, nè l' Africa
Vide il più bello,
Vanto ed orgoglio
D' ogni macello—
Allegre maschere,
Pazzi garzoni,
Tutti plauditelo
Con canti e suoni!—
Parigini, date passo
Al trionfo del Bue grasso.
(*Violetta ed Annina, che torna
frettolosa.*)

**ANNINA:** (*Esitando.*) Signora.

**VIOLETTA:** Che t' accadde?

**ANNINA:** Quest' oggi, è vero vi
sentite meglio?

**VIOLETTA:** Sì, perchè?

**ANNINA:** D' esser calma promettete?

**VIOLETTA:** Sì; che vuoi dirmi?

**ANNINA:** Prevenir vi volli—
Una gioia improvvisa . . .

**VIOLETTA:** Uno gioia!—dicesti?

**ANNINA:** (*Afferma col capo.*) Sì, o
Signora.

**VIOLETTA:** Alfredo!—Ah, tu il
vedesti!
Ei vien! T'affretta.
(*Annina afferma col capo e va ad
aprire la porta.*)

**VIOLETTA:** Alfredo?—
(*Andando verso l'uscio.*)
(*Alfredo comparisce, pallido per
la commozione, ed ambedue, gettandosi le braccia al collo, esclamano:*)

**VIOLETTA:** Amato Alfredo!

**ALFREDO:** Oh, gioia.—Oh, mia
Violetta!—
Colpevol sono—so tutto, o cara—

**VIOLETTA:** Io so che alfine reso mi
sei.

**ALFREDO:** Da questo palpito s' io
t' ami, impara—
Senza te existere più non potrei.

drops will grace
The lone, unmarked sod of my buri-
al place.
O God, to the prayer of the lost one
award
Your infinite mercy!—Receive
her, dear Lord!
(*She sits.*)

**BACCHANALIAN CHORUS:**
(*Offstage.*) Make way for his lord-
ship
The four-footed beast
With flowers and vine-leaves
Adorned for the feast.
Make way for this meekest
Of all horned males,
While all pay him homage
With pipe, horn and "hails!"
Come, Parisians—part the way
For the Fat Bull's holiday!
Asia and Africa
Can't find his peer,
The boast and pride
Of our career.
Hence, merry maskers
And madcap boys,
Greet him and cheer him
With thundering noise!
Come, Parisians—part the way
For the Fat Bull's holiday!
(*Violetta and Annina, who comes
in hastily.*)

**ANNINA:** (*Hesitant.*) Madam—

**VIOLETTA:** What is it?

**ANNINA:** Today you are feeling
better, aren't you?

**VIOLETTA:** Yes,—but why the
question?

**ANNINA:** If you promise not to get
excited—

**VIOLETTA:** Yes, yes—what is it
you want to tell me?

**ANNINA:** I want to prepare you
for—
A very happy surprise.

**VIOLETTA:** A happy surprise—did
you say?

**ANNINA:** (*She nods.*) Yes, dear
Madam.

**VIOLETTA:** It's Alfredo!—You've
seen him!
He's coming! Tell him—quickly!
(*Annina nods and goes to open
the door.*)

**VIOLETTA:** Alfredo?—
(*Going toward the door.*)
(*Alfredo enters, pale with emotion. They fall into each other's
arms.*)

**VIOLETTA:** Alfredo! Beloved!

**ALFREDO:** My Violetta!
I've been to blame, love. Now I
know all—

**VIOLETTA:** I only know that
you've come back to me.

**ALFREDO:** Oh, let my heartbeats
tell all my devotion—
Only with you, love, can life ever
be!

**VIOLETTA:** Ah, s' anco in vita
m'hai ritrovata,
Credi, che uccidere non può il dolor.

**ALFREDO:** Scorda l' affanno, donna adorata,
A me perdona e al genitor.

**VIOLETTA:** Ch' io ti perdoni?—La
rea son io;
Ma solo amor tal mi rendè.

**ALFREDO E VIOLETTA:** Null'
uomo o demone, angiol mio,
Mai più dividermi potrà da te.
Parigi, o cara, noi lasceremo,
La vita uniti trascorreremo,
De' corsi affanni compenso avrai—
La tua salute rifiorirà.
Sospiro e luce tu mi sarai,
Tutto il futuro ne arriderà.
Parigi, o caro, noi lasceremo;
La vita uniti trascorreremo.
De' corsi affanni compenso avrai—
La mia salute rifiorirà.
Sospiro e luce tu mi sarai,
Tutto il futuro ne arriderà.

**VIOLETTA:** Ah non più—a un tem-
pio—Alfredo, andiamo,
Del tuo ritorno grazie rendiamo.
(*Vacilla.*)

**ALFREDO:** Tu impallidisci!

**VIOLETTA:** È nulla, sai? Gioia improvvisa non entra mai,
senza turbarlo in mesto core.
(*S'abbandona, come sfinita, sopra una sedia, col capo pendente
all' indietro.*)

**ALFREDO:** Gran Dio!—Violetta!
(*Spaventato, sorreggendola.*)

**VIOLETTA:** È il mio malore.
Fu debolezza—ora son forte—
Vedi?—Sorrido.
(*Sforzandosi.*)

**ALFREDO:** (*Desolato.*) Ahi, cruda
sorte!

**VIOLETTA:** Fu nulla—Annina,
dammi a vestire.

**ALFREDO:** Adesso?—attendi.

**VIOLETTA:** No—voglio uscire.
(*Annina le presenta una veste ch'
ella fa per indossare, e, impedi-
tane dalla debolezza esclama:*)
Gran Dio!—Non posso!
(*Getta con dispetto la veste e ricade sulla sedia.*)

**ALFREDO:** (*Ad Annina.*) Cielo,
che vedo! Va pel Dottore.

**VIOLETTA:** Digli che Alfredo
È ritornato all' amor mio—
Digli che vivere ancor vogl'io.
(*Annina parte.*)

**VIOLETTA:** Let them not tell you
that sorrow can kill!—
Look at me, dearest! I breathe for
you still.

**ALFREDO:** All grief forget, my beloved, and live!
The son, the father, who wronged
you—forgive!

**VIOLETTA:** Forgive you, Alfredo?
The fault is my own—
If love can be blamed for what I
have done!

**ALFREDO and VIOLETTA:** Our-
selves united, beloved, never
Can earthly power avail to sever.
To Paris, dearest, we bid adieu,
In love united our days will flow.
Grief turned to gladness will then
renew
Your cheeks' dimmed roses to
brighter glow.
All life and light you'll be to me,
Our future days entranced will be.
To Paris, dearest, we bid adieu,
In love united our days will flow.
Grief turned to gladness will then
renew
Your cheeks' dimmed roses to
brighter glow.
Such light and life you'll be to me,
Our future days entranced will be.

**VIOLETTA:** Ah, no more! Alfredo,
to a temple let us go
To offer thanks for your return to
me.
(*She reels.*)

**ALFREDO:** You've turned pale!

**VIOLETTA:** It's nothing—really. A
sudden happiness
Always affects a troubled heart.
(*She sinks down, spent, into a
chair, her head falling back.*)

**ALFREDO:** Violetta! Violetta!
(*Alarmed, lifting her up.*)

**VIOLETTA:** It's—it's my illness.
I felt myself growing faint.—Now I
am stronger.
See—I am smiling!
(*Forcing a smile.*)

**ALFREDO:** (*Desolate.*) Ah, cruel
fate!

**VIOLETTA:** It was nothing.—Annina, help me into a dress.

**ALFREDO:** Right now?—Wait a little.

**VIOLETTA:** No—I want to go out.
(*Annina brings her a gown which
Violetta tries to put on. But she is
overcome with faintness and exclaims:*)
Alas!—I cannot! (*She throws the
dress from her impatiently and
falls back into the chair.*)

**ALFREDO:** (*To Annina.*) Heavens!
What's happened?
Get the doctor at once.

**VIOLETTA:** Tell him that Alfredo
Has come back to my heart—
Tell him—tell him I want to live—
to live . . .

Ma se tornando non m'hai salvato,
(*Ad Alfredo.*)
A niuno in terra salvarmi è dato.
Ah, Gran Dio!—morir sì giovane,
Io, che penato ho tanto!—
Morir sì presso a tergere
Il mio sì lungo pianto!
Ah! dunque fu delirio
La credula speranza;
Invano di costanza
Armato avrò il mio cor!—
Alfredo—oh! il crudo termine
Serbato al nostro amor?

**ALFREDO:** Oh! mio sospiro e palpito
Diletta del cor mio!—
Le mie colle tue lagrime
Confondere degg' io—
Ma più che mai deh! Credilo
M'è d'uopo di costanza—
Ah! tutto alla speranza
Non chiudere il tuo cor!—
Ah, Violetta mia, deh, calmati
M' uccide il tuo dolor.
(*Violetta si abbandona sul canapè.*)
(*Detti, Germont, ed il Dottore.*)

**GERMONT:** (*Entrando.*) Ah! Violetta!

**VIOLETTA:** Voi, signor!

**ALFREDO:** Mio padre!

**VIOLETTA:** Non mi scordaste?

**GERMONT:** La promessa adempio—
A stringervi qual figlia vengo al seno,
O generosa.

**VIOLETTA:** Ahimè, tardi giungeste!—
Pure, grata ven sono—
(*Lo abbraccia.*)
Grenvil, vedete?—Tra le braccia io spiro
Di quanti ho cari al mondo.

**GERMONT:** (*Da se.*) Che mai dite!
(*La osserva.*)
O cielo! è ver!

**ALFREDO:** La vedi, padre mio?

**GERMONT:** Di più non lacerarmi—
Troppo rimorso l' alma mi divora—
Quasi fulmin m' atterra ogni suo detto—
Oh! mal cauto vegliardo!—
Il mal ch'io feci ora sol vedo!

(*Exit Annina.*)
But if by coming back you have not saved me,
(*To Alfredo.*)
Then no one on earth can save me now.
Alas! For me so young to die,
So young for all my sorrow!
To die when hope gives promise of
A happier tomorrow!
Ah, was it then illusion,
The faith that kept me strong
And armed my soul with constancy?
Ah, woe, to be so wronged!
Is this the cruel ending, love,
For all the bliss we longed?

**ALFREDO:** O my beloved! My breath! My life!
My very heart's own throbbing,
My soul goes out to yours, my love,
To share your tears and sobbing.
Our spirits more than ever now
Must rest on constancy.
And hope once more, Violetta,
You must shelter in your breast.
Ah, calm your misery!
Your grief brings death to me!
(*Violette drops onto the couch.*)
(*The same, Germont and the Doctor.*)

**GERMONT:** (*Coming in.*) Ah, Violetta!

**VIOLETTA:** You, sir?

**ALFREDO:** Father!

**VIOLETTA:** You've not forgotten me, then?

**GERMONT:** I'm fulfilling a promise—
To clasp you to my heart like my own child,
O generous-hearted woman!

**VIOLETTA:** Alas! You come too late!
Still, I am grateful.
(*Embraces him.*)
Do you see, Grenvil? I'll be dying in the arms
Of those I hold dearest in the world.

**GERMONT:** (*Aside.*) What are you saying?
(*Looking at her.*)
Too late, alas!

**ALFREDO:** You see her, Father!

**GERMONT:** Ah, don't torment me further!
My deep remorse gives me no peace—
Her every word shatters my being.
O rash old man that I was!
Ah, only now can I see the extent of my mischief!

**VIOLETTA:** (*Frattanto avrà aperto a stento un ripostiglio della toilette, e, toltone un medaglione, dice:*) Più a me t'appressa.
Ascolta, amato Alfredo.
Prendi, quest è l'immagine
De' miei passati giorni,
A rammentar ti torni
Colei che sì t' amò.

**ALFREDO:** No, non morrai, non dirmelo,
Dei vivere, amor mio—
A strazio sì terribile
Qui non mi trasse Iddio.

**VIOLETTA:** Se una pudica vergine
Degli anni suoi nel fiore
A te donasse il core—
Sposa ti sia—lo vo'.
Le porgi questa effigie,
Dille che dono ell' è
Di chi, nel ciel tra gli angeli
Prega per lei, per te.

**ALFREDO:** Sì presto—ah! no—dividerti
Morte non può da me—
Ah! vivi, o un solo feretro
M' accoglierà con te.

**GERMONT:** Cara, sublime vittima
D' un generoso amore,
Perdonami lo strazio
Recato al tuo bel core.

**GERMONT, DOTTORE E ANNINA:** Finchè avrà il ciglio lagrime
Io piangerò per te.
Vola a' beati spiriti;
Iddio ti chiama a sè.

**VIOLETTA:** È strano!
(*Alzandosi rianimata.*)

**TUTTI:** Che!

**VIOLETTA:** Cessarono
Gli spasmi del dolore.
In me rinasce, m' agita
Insolito vigore!
Ah!—ma io ritorno a vivere!—
(*Trasalendo.*)
Oh! gioia!
(*Ricade sul canapè.*)

**TUTTI:** O cielo!—muor!

**ALFREDO:** Violetta?

**TUTTI:** O Dio!—soccorrasi.

**DOTTORE:** (*Dopo averle toccato il polso.*) E spenta!

**ALFREDO E TUTTI:** O rio dolor!
(*Quadro, e cade la tela.*)

FINE.

**VIOLETTA:** (*After opening a drawer of her toilet table with difficulty, takes out a locket and says:*) Draw nearer to me. Listen, beloved Alfredo!
Take it—This is my image
In happy days gone by,—
Reminder, when I die,
Of one who loved you well.

**ALFREDO:** Ah, no! You shall not die
But live, dear heart, for me!
You could not doom me to
Such cruel misery!

**VIOLETTA:** If some day a pure maiden
In all her youth's full May
Should love—ah, wed her, pray!
To her tell our story.
Put in her hand this likeness
And say it was the token
Of one who is in a better world
Prays for your bliss unbroken.

**ALFREDO:** Ah soon, too soon to part!
Death cannot now divide us!
Oh, live, or let destiny confide us to
a common grave!

**GERMONT:** Ah, sacrifice sublime
To an exalted love!
Forgive the heart's deep anguish
I caused her, Powers above!

**GERMONT, DOCTOR and ANNINA:** Ah, ever shall I weep
And ever mourn your fate.
Unto a happier realm
may God take your spirit.

**VIOLETTA:** How strange! (*She rises as if reanimated.*)

**ALL:** What is it?

**VIOLETTA:** They're over now, the spasms of my pain.
A newborn strength revives me—
Fills me with life again!
Ah—I am coming back—to life!—
(*In exaltation.*)
Ah! Happiness!
(*She falls back on the sofa.*)

**ALL:** O Heaven! She is dying!

**ALFREDO:** Violetta!

**ALL:** O God—save her!

**DOCTOR:** (*After feeling her pulse.*) She is dead!

**ALFREDO, ALL:** O grief intolerable!
(*The Curtain falls.*)

THE END.

# Un Ballo In Maschera (1859)

## A Masked Ball

MUSIC BY GIUSEPPE VERDI ■ LIBRETTO BY ANTONIO SOMMA

This three-act opera, set to a libretto by Antonio Somma (inspired by Eugène Scribe's *Gustave III, ou Le Bal Masquê*), premiered at the Teatro Apollo in Rome on February 17, 1859. The Governor of Boston, Riccardo of Warwick, is meeting with his officials, including Samuel and Tom who plan to assassinate him. Riccardo receives a list of the names of those invited to his masked ball, among them Amelia, wife of Riccardo's loyal secretary, Renato. Although Riccardo is secretly in love with her, he dares not betray his closest friend, especially as Renato has uncovered the plot to kill him. A judge banishes Ulrica, a black woman accused of witchcraft. Oscar and Riccardo pay her a visit to find out the truth of these charges. Amelia comes to see Ulrica to ask whether she can be cured—she is in love with someone other than her husband and she is afraid. Ulrica counsels her to make a potion from an herb growing by the scaffold; she tells her to pick the herb at night. Riccardo overhears all, including Ulrica's prophecy that he will be killed by the first to shake his hand. Renato enters in total ignorance of Ulrica's warning and shakes his hand. When Amelia picks the herb for the potion, she and Riccardo meet and sing together of their love and grief. They hear footsteps and Amelia veils herself. Renato informs Riccardo that the conspirators are about to murder him. As Riccardo escapes, the conspirators tear off Amelia's veil and Renato realizes he's been betrayed. Amelia begs his pardon and, awaiting death, gives her son a farewell kiss. Renato joins with the conspirators. They draw lots to choose who will kill Riccardo; Renato wins. Amelia warns Riccardo via the page. The page tells Renato what Riccardo will be wearing at the ball. Renato stabs Riccardo. When the other guests attack Renato, Riccardo defends him and clears Amelia's name. He promotes Renato, orders him to be transferred to England, pardons the conspirators, and then dies.

---

## ■ ATTO PRIMO

### SCENA PRIMA

*E il mattino.—Una sala nella casa del Governatore. In fondo l' ingresso delle sue stanze. Deputati, Gentiluomini, Popolani, Uffiziali; sul dinanzi Samuel, Tom e loro Aderenti—tutti in attesa di Riccardo.*

**UFFIZIALI E GENTILUOMINI:**
Posa in pace, a' bei sogni ristora,
O Riccardo, il tuo nobile cor—
A te scudo su questa dimora
Sta d'un vergine mondo l' amor.

**SAM, TOM E LORO ADERENTI:** E sta l' odio, che prèpara il fio,
Ripensando ai caduti per te—
Come speri, desceso l' oblio
Sulle tombe infelici non è.

### SCENA II

*Oscar dalle stanze del Conte, indi Riccardo.*

**OSC:** S' avanza il Conte.

## ■ ACT I

### SCENE I

*A Hall in the house of the Governor.—Deputies, gentlemen, officers, and people.—In the forepart of the stage, Samuel Tom, and their adherents—all waiting for the Count.*

**OFFICERS AND GENTLEMEN:** O noble Richard, set your heart at rest,
Here your devoted friends are offering
Their hands and hearts for your protection
Against the attacks of all your foes.

**SAMUEL, TOM, AND THEIR FRIENDS:** Here also stand your enemies,
Whose vengeance you deserve;
Your victims in their sepulchres
Are not by all forgotten!

### SCENE II

*Oscar, and then Richard, coming from the inner apartments.*

**OSC:** Here comes the Count!

**RIC:** (*salutando gli astanti*). Amici miei . . . Soldati.
E voi del par diletti a me!..
(*ai Deputati nel ricevere delle suppliche.*)
Porgete:
A me s' aspetta—io deggio
Su' miei fidi vegliar,—perchè sia pago
Ogni voto, se giusto.
Bello il poter non è, che de' soggetti
Le lacrime non terge, e ad incorrotta
Gloria non mira.

**OSC:** (*a lui*) Leggere vi piaccia
Delle danze l' invito.

**RIC:** Avresti alcuna
Beltà dimenticato?

**OSC:** (*offrendogli un foglio*). Eccovi i nomi.

**RIC:** Amelia..ah dessa ancor!
l'anima mia
(*leggendo, tra sè.*)
In lei rapita ogni grandezza oblia!
La rivedrà nell' estasi
Raggiante di pallore..
E qui sonar d' amore
La sua parola udrà.
O dolce notte, scendere
Tu puoi gemmata a festa:
Ma la mia stella è questa:
Questa che il ciel non ha!

**RICH:** (*Saluting the bystanders*). Brave soldiers!
My dear beloved friends—
(*To the deputies, while receiving some petitions.*)
Give me.
It is my strictest duty
To attend to the welfare
Of all my faithful subjects.
There is no charm in power
When that is not exerted
To succor those who languish
Beneath an adverse fate.

**OSC:** (*giving him a paper*). Here is the list of all The persons invited to the ball.

**RICH:** I hope that none has been forgotten.

**OSC:** (*giving him the list*). There all the names are written.

**RICH:** (*reading aside*). Amelia—dear, sweet name!
Its mere sound fills my heart with joy!
Her beauteous, charming image
Inspires my soul with love;
Here soon I shall behold her
In all her real charms.
Whatever may be the splendor
Of your most brilliant stars,
Sweet night, none is so shining
As my love's dazzling eyes!

UFFIZIALI E GENTILUOMINI: Entro sè stesso assorto
Con generoso affetto
IL nostro bene oggetto
De' suoi pensier farà.

OFFICERS AND GENTLEMEN: He is now surely harboring noble thoughts
In his mind:
And scheming plans for helping
All those who need his aid.

SAM, TOM E LORO ADERENTI: (sommesamente) L' ora non è—chè tutto
Qui d' operar ne toglie.
Dalle nemiche soglie
Meglio l' useir sarà.

SAMUEL, TOM, AND THEIR ADHERENTS: (aside). Here, now, we can do nothing,
So many people watch;
From this hall it would be better
For us now to retire.
(Exeunt.)

RIC: Il cenno mio di là con essi attendi
(ad Oscar.)
(tutti s' allontanano.)

RICH: (to Oscar.) In the next room with them, wait for my orders.

OSC: Libero è il varco a voi.
(verso Renato che s' avanza.)

OSC: (to Reinhart, who is advancing). Now you may come on.

## SCENA III

Riccardo e Renato.

REN: Deh come triste appar!
(a parte.)

RIC: (tra sè.) Amelia!

REN: Conte. (chinandosi)

RIC: O ciel! lo sposo suo! (c.s.)

REN: Turbato il mio (accostandosi.)
Signor, mentre dovunque il nome suo.
Inclito suona?

RIC: Per la gloria è molto, Nulla pel cor—Secreta, acerba cura
M'opprime.

REN: E donde?

RIC: Ah no?..non piu..

REN: Dirolla Io la cagion.

RIC: (da sè.) Gran Dio!

REN: So tutto..

RIC: Che!

REN: So tutto.
Già questa soglia stessa
Non t' è securo asilo.

RIC: Prosegui.

REN: Un veo disegno
Nell' ombre si matura,
I giorni tuoi minaccia.

RIC: Ah!..gli è di ciò che parli?
(con gioia)
Altro non sai? . . .

REN: Se udir t' è grato i nomi.

RIC: Che monta? io li disprezzo.

REN: Svelarli è mio dover.

RIC: Taci: Nel sangue
Contaminarmi allor dovrei.
Non fia
Nol vo'—De' miei lo zelo
Ognor mi guardi, e mi protegga il cielo.

## SCENE III

Richard and Reinhart.

REIN: How sad he looks! (Aside.)

RICH: (Aside.) Amelia!

REIN: (Bowing.) Count!

RICH: Heavens! her husband!

REIN: So sad, my lord, when all around you
Are now so smiling?

RICH: Enough of glory
I have, indeed, but empty is my heart!
Uneasy thoughts . . . .

REIN: Where, then are they?

RICH: I dare not tell . . . .

REIN: Well, it is enough,
I know why you are sad.

RICH: (Aside.) Great God!

REIN: Yes, I know all.

RICH: What?

REIN: I know all;
You think this your mansion
Unsafe . . . .

RICH: Go on.

REIN: A secret plan is plotted,
Against your life,
By your relentless foes.

RICH: Is this all that you know?
No more than this?

REIN: I know their names . . .

RICH: What do I care; I despise them.

REIN: It is my duty to reveal them.

RICH: No, no!
I should then, spill, their blood.
I am not willing to resort
To such abhorred measures.

REN: Alla vita che t'arride
Di speranze e glorie piena.
D' altre mille e mille vite
Il destino s' incatena!
Nel tuo core il Genio palpita
Del suo splendido avvenir!
Ma sarà dovunque, sempre
Chiuso il varco alle ferite,
Perchè scudo del tuo petto
È de' tuoi fidi l' affetto?
Dell' amer più desto è l' odio
Le sue vittime a colpir!

REIN: Your life is full of brightest hopes,
And glory shines over your brow;
Your fate is bound with that of thousands,
Who firmly stand on your own side,
And prop the power you are wielding
With faithful hearts and ready hands.
But, not for ever may successful
Be their noble, virtuous efforts
Against the plots of your ill-wishers,
Who, soon or late, may well succeed.
For hatred is often
More active and steady in its pursuit than love.

## SCENA IV

Oscar, poi un Giudice, e detti.

OSC: Il primo Giudice.
(all' entrata.)

RIC: S' avanzi.

GIU: Conte!
(offrendogli dispacci a firmare.)

RIC: Che leggo!..il bando ad una donna!
Or donde?
Qual è il suo nome?.. di che rea?

GIU: S'appella
Ulrica-dell' abbietto
Sangue de'negri.

OSC: Intorno a cui s' affollano
Tutte le stirpi. Del futuro l'alta
Divinatrice..

GIU: Che nell' antro immondo
Chiama i peggiori, d' ogni reo consiglio
Sospetta già. Dovuto è l' esiglio:
Nè muta il voto mio.

RIC: Che ne di' tu?
(ad Oscar.)

OSC: Difenderla vogl'io.
Volta la terrea—Fronte alle stelle
Come sfavilla—La sua pupilla,
Quando alle belle—Il fin predice
Mesto o felice—Dei loro amor!
Ed è con l'Erebo—D'accordo ognor!

RIC: Che vaga coppia . . . —
Che protettor!

OSC: Chi la fatidica—Sua gonna afferra,
O passi 'l mare.—Voli alla guerra,
Le sue vicende—Soavi, amare
Da questa apprende—Nel dubbio cor.
Ed è con l'Erebo—D' accordo ognor!

RIC: Che vaga coppia . . .
Che protettor!

GIU: Sia condannata.

OSC: (verso il Conte.) Ah! voi
Assolverla deguate.

## SCENE IV

Oscar and a Judge.

OSC: The first judge.
(At the entrance.)

RICH: Let him advance.

JUD: (Giving him some dispatches.) Count!

RICH: What do I see! . . . a woman exiled?
Who is she?
What is her crime?

JUD: Ulrica is her name.
She is of the vile race of negroes.

OSC: The astrologer to whom all people
Apply to know their fate;
The negro woman . . . .

JUD: Within her dark abode
She is receiving every set
Of evil-doers; she is deserving
The punishment there mentioned.

RICH: (To Oscar.) What's your opinion?

OSC: She is not guilty!
She turns her face towards the stars,—
Her eyes beam forth a glorious light,
She then tells all the pretty girls
The fate and end of all their loves;
And never fails to tell them right.

RICH: They are a precious pair . . . a fine protector!

OSC: Whoever can but touch her garment,
Wherever he goes, by land or sea,
He is sure to know what he is to meet,
Of good or bad, throughout his way;
And never fails to know what's right!

RICH: They are a precious pair . . . a fine protector!

JUD: But she must be condemned!

OSC: (To the Count.) My lord,
Please acquit her.

## Act I, Scene IV

**RIC:** Ebben tutti chiamate:
Or v'apro un mio pensier.
(*usciti.*)
(*Renato e Oscar invitano a rientrare gli*)

**RICH:** Well!
Call in here all the people,
And then I will tell you my mind.
(*Reinhart and Oscar call in all the persons that had gone out.*)

## SCENA V

*Samuel, Tom e Seguaci,*
*Gentiluomini, Uffiziali e detti.*

**RIC:** Signori: oggi d'Ulrica
Alla magion v'invito-
Ma sotto altro vestito;
Io là sarò.

**REN:** Davver?

**RIC:** Sì, vo' gustar la scena.

**REN:** L'idea non è prudente.

**RIC:** La trovo anzi eccellente,
Feconda di piacer.

**REN:** To ravvisar taluno
Ivi potria.

**RIC:** Qual tema!

**SAM, TOM:** Ve', ve', di tutto trema.
(*sogghignando.*)
Codesto consiglier.

**RIC:** E tu m'appronta un ahito
(*ad Oscar*)
Da prescator.

**SAM, TOM E LORO ADERENTI:**
Chi sa . . .
(*sotto voce.*)
Che alla vendetta l'adito
Non s'apra alfin colà?

**RIC:** Ogni cura si doni al diletto,
E s'accorra nel magico tetto:
Tra la folla de' creduli ognuno
S'abbandoni e folleggi con me.

**REN:** E s'accorra, ma vegli 'l sospetto
Sui perigli che fremono intorno,
Ma protegga il magnanimo petto
Di chi nulla paventa per sè.

**OSC:** L indovina ne dice di belle,
E sta ben che l'interroghi anch'io;
Sentirò se m'arridon le stelle,
Di che sorti benefica m'è.

**CORO:** Scelga dunque ciascun la sua via
E risponda al festevole invito,
Perchè brilli d'un po d'allegria
Questa vita che il cielo ne diè.

**SAM, TOM E SEGUACI:** Senza posa
vegliamo all' intento,
Nè si perda ove scocchi 'l momento;
Forse l'astro che regge il suo fato
Nell'abisso là spegnersi de'.

**RIC:** Dunque, signori, aspettovi,
Incognito, alle tre
Nell' antro dell' oracolo,
Della gran maga al piè.

**TUTTI:** Teco sarem di subito
Incogniti alle tre
Nell' antro dell' oracolo,
Della gran maga al piè.

## SCENE V

*Samuel, Tom, and their friends,*
*Gentlemen, etc.*

**RICH:** My friends, today, you are invited
To call at the Astrologer's;
There also I shall be present
With you, but in disguise.

**REIN:** Well thought!

**RICH:** Yes, I will enjoy the farce.

**REIN:** I think it is imprudent.

**RICH:** No, no, I think it excellent,
And full of mirth and pleasure.

**REIN:** Somebody might discover
Your real person there.

**RICH:** I think there is no danger.

**SAM, TOM:** Pshaw! what timid counsel!
He perceives danger everywhere.

**RICH:** (*to Oscar.*) Well, quick!
You must prepare me
A sailor's dress.

**SAM, TOM, AND FRIENDS:** Perhaps the farce may be propitious
To work out our revenge.

**RICH:** Let all prepare for mirth,
And hasten to the prophetess;
There with the foolish people
Let us enjoy the fun.

**REIN:** Let's go; but let's be watchful
Against the secret dangers
That there may be impending
On our beloved chief.

**OSC:** I'll also ask the Astrologer
About my future fate;
I'll know which way will fortune
Approach to my threshold!

**CHOR:** Let, then, every person
Choose slyly his own way
To the proposed amusement,
At the Divineress's house.

**SAM, TOM AND FOLLOWERS:** Let
us watch every occasion
That may turn out propitious,
To put in execution
Our revengeful plans,

**RICH:** My friends, then, I shall meet you,
Disguised, at three o'clock,
Within the famous temple
Of the black prophetess.

**ALL:** Then we will surely meet you,
Disguised, at three o'clock,
Within the famous temple
Of the black prophetess.

## SCENA VI

*L'abituro dell'indovina. A sinistra un camino; il fuoco è acceso, e la caldaja magica fuma sovra un treppiè; dallo stesso lato l'uscio d'un oscuro recesso. Sul fianco a destra una scala che gira e si perde sotto la vólta, e all'estremità della stessa sul davanti una piccola porta segreta. Nel fondo l'entrata della porta maggiore con ampia finestra d'allato.—In mezzo una rozza tavola, ee pendenti dal letto e dalle pareti stromenti ed arredi analoghi al luogo.*
*Nel fondo Uomini e Donne del Popolo. Ulrica presso la tavola; poco discosti un Fanciullo ed una Giovinetta che le domandano la buona ventura.*

**POPOLANI:** Zitto l'incanto non dèssi turbare..
Par che Sàtana guizzi al focolare!

**ULR:** Re dell' abisso, affrettati,
(*ispirata*)
Precipita per l'etra-
Senza libar la folgore
Il tetto mio penètra.
Omai tre volte l'upupa
Dall' alto sospirò;
La salamandra ignivora
Tre volte sibilò..
E delle tombe il gemito
Tre volte a me parlò!

## SCENA VII

*Riccardo da pescatore, avanzandosi tra la folla, nè scorgendo alcuno de' suoi.*

**RIC:** Arrivo il primo!

**POPOLANE:** Villano, dà indietro.
(*ei s'allontana ridendo.*)

**TUTTI:** Deh! perchè tutto riluce di tetro?

**ULR:** È lui, è lui! ne' palpiti
Come risento adesso
La voluttà riardere
Del suo tremendo amplesso!
La face del futuro
Nella sinistra egli ha.
Arrise al mio scongiuro,
rifolgorar la fa:
Nulla, più nulla ascondersi
Al guardo mio potrà!
(*batte il suolo e sparisce.*)

**TUTTI:** Evviva la maga!

**ULR:** (*di sottera*). Silenzio, silenzio!

## SCENA VIII

*Silvano rompendo la calca, e detti.*

## SCENE VI

*The abode of the Astrologer—On the left side there is a little path—a magic cauldron is smoking over a brisk fire—in the middle there is a rough table, and several magic instruments are hanging from the walls. Ulrica stands near the table, and the populace stand behind her—a boy and a girl near Ulrica are asking their fortunes.*

**PEOPLE:** Hush! We must not break her incantations!
The devil seems to play over the fire!

**ULR:** (*as if inspired.*) Hasten, O King of the Abyss!
Fly through the ambient air
Without stirring the lightning,
And enter my abode
Three times has been heard screeching
The ominous lizard
Three times, too, has been hissing
The venomous red dragon
And three times have been groaning
The spirits from the grave.

## SCENE VII

*Richard, dressed as a sailor, comes in through the crowd, and discovering none of his friends, says:*

**RICH:** I have arrived first! (*Rough women from behind.*)

**WOMEN:** Stand back, blockhead! (*Richard withdraws smiling.*)

**ALL:** What is this misty light?

**ULR:** It is he! it is he!
I feel his presence within the fibers
That shake my inmost passions,
And rage with burning fire!
The future's hidden secrets
Are now revealed to me!
He has fully acceded
To all that I have asked;
To my strong conjurations
He fairly yields at last!
(*She strikes the floor and vanishes.*)

**ALL:** Live long the enchantress!

**ULR:** (*from under the floor.*) Silence! silence!

## SCENE VIII

*Sylvan breaking through the crowd.*

SIL: Su fatemi largo, saper vo'il mio fato.
Son servo del Conte: son suo marinaro:
La morte per esso più volte ho sfidato;
Tre lustri son corsi del vivere amaro,
Tre lustri che nulla s' è fatto per me.

ULR: (ricomparendo.) E chiedi?

SIL: Qual sorte pel sangue versato M' attende.

RIC: (a parte.) Favella da franco soldato.

ULR: La mano.

SIL: Prendete.

ULR: Rallegrati: omai
I poveri giorni mutarsi vedrai.
(Riccardo trae un rotolo e vi scrive su.)

SIL: Scherzate?

ULR: Va pago.

RIC: (Pònendolo in tasca a Silvano che non s'avvede) Mentire non de'.

SIL: A fausto presagio ben vuolsi mercè.
(frugando trova il rotolo su cui legge estatico.)
"Riccardo al suo caro Silvano Uffiziale."
Per bacco! non sogno!..dell'oro ed un grado!
Evviva la nostra Sibilla immortale,
Che spande su tutti ricchezze e piacer.
(picchiasi alla piccola porta.)

TUTTI: Si batte!

ULR: (va ad aprire ed entra un servo).

RIC: Che vegg, sull' uscio secreto, (tra se)
Un servo d'Amelia!

SER: (sommessamente ad Ulrica, ma inteso da Ric.) Sentite: la mia Signora, che aspetta lì fuore, vorria Pregarvi, a quattr' occhi, d'arcano parer.

RIC: Me no..

ULR: Perchè possa rispondere a voi
È d'uopo che innanzi m'abbocchi a Satàno.
Uscite, e lasciate che io scruti nel ver.

TUTTI: Usciamo, e si lasci che scruti nel ver.
(mentre tutti s'allontanano, Riccardo s'asconde.)

## SCENA IX

*Amelia, Ulrica e Riccardo in disparte.*

ULR: Che v' agita così?

---

SYL: Clear off; it is my turn to hear my fate!
I am a servant of the Count; a sailor I am, and often death for him I have braved;
Yet fifteen years of labor have gone by,
And I have had nothing for my reward!

ULR: (reappearing.). What do you ask?

SYL: What things am I to get for my spilt blood?

RICH: He speaks like a bold soldier! (aside.)

ULR: Show me your hand.

SYL: Here.

ULR: Be of good cheer, your gloomy days will soon turn bright!
(Richard draws a roll from his pocket and writes something on it.)

SYL: You jest!

ULR: No; go in peace.

RICH: (aside.) She must not lie!
(he puts the roll secretly into the pocket of Sylvan.)

SYL: Good luck must be paid for!
(Putting the hand into his pocket takes out the roll and reads on it.)
"Richard, to his dear officer Sylvan."
This is no dream; it is gold and a promotion!
Live long the immortal Sybil.
From whom so many riches flow!
(A knock is heard at the door.)

ALL: There is a knocking at the door.
(Ulr. goes to open.)

RICH: Whom do I see? a servant of Amelia!

SERV: (Secretly to Ulrica, but overheard by Richard.) My lady is waiting for you outside.
She'll ask advice on private matters.

RICH: Now it is my turn.

ULR: Yes, but before
I must speak awhile with Satan
Go out all, that I may search for truth

ALL: Let us go out that she may search for truth.
(While all retire, Richard conceals himself in a corner.)

## SCENE IX

*Amelia, Ulrica and Richard (aside.)*

ULR: What frets you so?

---

AME: Funesta, ascosa Cura che amor destò..

RIC: (da sè). Quai detti?

ULR: E voi Cercate?..

AME: Pace-svellermi dal petto
Chi si fatale e desîato impera!
Lui—che su tutti il ciel arbitro pose.

RIC: (tra sè, ma con viva emozione di gioia). Anima mia!

ULR: L' oblio v' è dato. Arcane
Stille conosco d' una magic' erba,
Che rinnovano il cor. Ma chi n'ha d' uope
Spiccarla debbe di sua man nel fitto
Delle notti—funereo
È il loco.

AME: Ov' è?

ULR: L'osate Voi?

AME: Sì—qual esso sia.

ULR: Dunque ascoltate.
Della città all' occaso,
Là dove al tetro lato
Batte la luna pallida
Sul campo abbominato..
Abbarbica gli stami
A quelle pietre infami,
Ove la colpa scontasi
Coll' ultimo sospir!

AME: Cieli! qual loco!

ULR: Attoni!
E già tremante siete!

RIC: Povero cor!

ULR: V' esanima?

AME: Agghiaccio..

ULR: E l' oserete?

AME: Se tale è il dover mio
Troverò possa anch' io.

ULR: Stanotte

AME: Sì.

RIC: (c.s.) Non sola:
Chè te degg 'io seguir.

AME: Consentimi, o Signore,
Virtù ch' io lavi 'l core,
E l' infiammato palpito
Nel petto mio sopir!

ULR: Va, non tremar, l'incanto
Inaridisce il pianto.
Osa-e berrai nel farmaco
L' oblio de' tuoi martir.

RIC: (c.s.) Ardo, e seguirti ho fisso
Se fosse nell' abisso.
Pur ch'io respiri, Amelia,
L'aura de' tuoi sospir.
(Voci dal fondo.)
Figlia d'averno schiudi lo chiostra,
(spinte alla porta.)
È pigra meno vêr noi ti mostra.

---

AME: A secret anguish, the cause of which is love!

RICH: Love!

ULR: Well, what is, then, your wish?

AME: I wish for peace; the man I would forget
Who keeps such sway over my heart!

RICH: (Aside.) Gentle soul!

ULR: You shall forget the man!
I know an herb from which it is extracted,
A magic liquor that renews the heart.
But, then, the herb is to be gathered
By those who want its magic power.
During the night, in a most horrid place!

AME: Where is it?

ULR: Would you dare do it?

AME: Most certainly I would!

ULR: Hear me, then.
To the west side of this our city,
Where wicked men expiate their crimes,
Over the hated walls is creeping
The plant I have just mentioned.
The moon by night while beaming
Her pale rays on that silent
Abode of ghosts, then
You must gather the magic herb!

AME: Heavens!
What a fearful place!

ULR: Why! You are already trembling
At my description of the place!

RICH: Poor creature!

ULR: Are you frightened?

AME: I shudder!

ULR: Could you, then, go there?

AME: If such it be my duty,
I must, by force, do it.

ULR: Well, then, tonight!

AME: Tonight!

RICH: (Aside.) You shall not go alone;
I'll surely come with you!

AME: O Lord, grant me assistance
To conquer this affection,
That has so long been troubling
My feeble, weary heart!

ULR: Go, never fear,
You shall find a remedy in that liquor;
The flame shall be extinguished
That causes all your pain!

RICH: Dear soul!
I will follow you,
Were you to go to hell!
Your presence is a Heaven
Of pure delights to me!
(Voices from inside.)
Too long we have been waiting,
(Knocking at the door.)
Open the door, that we may enter!

## Act I, Scene IX

**ULR:** (*ad Amelia*). Presto partite.

**AME:** Stanotte . . .

**ULR:** Addio . . .

### SCENA X

*Ulrica apre l'entrata maggiore: entrano Samuel, Tom e Seguaci, Oscar, Gentiluomini e Uffiziali travestiti bizzarramente, ai quali s'unisce Riccardo.*

**CORO:** Su, profetessa, monta il treppiè;
Canta il presagio.

**OSC:** Ma il Conte ov' è?

**RIC:** (*fattosi presso a lui*). Taci, nascondile che qui son io.
(*poi vòlto rapidamente ad Ulrica*)
E tu, sibilla, che tutto sai,
Della mia stella mi parlerai.
Di'tu se fedele
Il flutto m' aspetta,
Se molle di lacrime
La donna diletta
Dicendomi addio
Tradì l'amor mio
Con lacere vele
E l' alma in tempesta
I solchi so frangere
Dell' onda funesta,
L' averno ed il cielo
Irati sfidar.

**CORO:** Sollecita esplora,
Divina gli eventi,
Non possono i fulmini,
La rabbia de' venti,
La morte, l'amore
Sviarlo dal mar.

**RIC:** Sull' agile prora
Che m' agita in grembo,
Se scosso mi sveglio
Ai fischi del nembo,
Ripeto fra i tuoni
Le dolci canzoni.
Le dolci canzoni
Del tetto natio,
Che l' ora lamentano
Dell' ultimo addio,
E tutte ridanno
Le forze del cor.

**CORO:** Su, negra, risuoni
L' accesso scongiuro;
Spalanca la soglia
Che chiude il futuro
Nell' anime nostre
Non cape terror.

**ULR:** Chi voi siate, l'insana parola
Può nel pianto prorompere un giorno,
Se chi sforza l'arcano soggiorno
Va la colpa nel duolo a purgar,
Se chi sfida il suo fato insolente
Deve l'onta nel fato scontar.

**RIC:** Zitto, amici.

**SAM:** Ma il primo chi fia?

**OSC:** Io.

---

**ULR:** (*To Amelia.*) Go away, quick.

**AME:** Tonight!

**ULR:** Adieu!

### SCENE X

*(Ulrica opens the door—enter Samuel, Tom, and their friends— Oscar, Gentlemen, Officers, etc., all dressed in different costumes.)*

**CHORUS:** Mount on your tripod, prophetess!
Tell us our fortunes!

**OSC:** (*Aside.*) Where is the Count?

**RICH:** (*Going near him.*) Hush! here I am!
(*Suddenly turning to Ulrica.*)
You prophetess, to whom all things are known,
Tell me about my planet!
Tell me if, when I go to sea,
I shall meet no fearful tempest;
Or, if the lady I am loving
Has remained faithful to me!
With tattered, broken sails
I fear not go to sea;
Against the waves while dashing
I can forget all danger!
And while my mind is troubled
With bad, uneasy thoughts,
I scorn the Demon's fury
And hope for better lot.

**CHO:** Tell him his fortune, Sybil,
Divine future events:
The fury of the winds,
The tossing of the tempest,
Cannot prevent the sailor
From going back to sea!

**RICH:** If, on the prow, while sleeping,
I am suddenly awakened
By the lord roaring thunder,
I sing my favorite songs!
My native songs I sing then,
That paint all the affections
Stirred up by the adventurous
And roaming sailor's life.
This way I am beguiling
My time amid the storms,
Which else would press too heavy
Upon my weary soul!

**CHO:** Go on, now, prophetess,
Press on your conjuration;
Force fast the restive Demons
To impart to you their gifts.
Here is a set of brave men.
Who scorn the wrath of hell!

**ULR:** Whoever you are, your profane words
May cost you dearly some future day!
Nobody can despise one's fate,
And then not feel its sting one day!
Hush, then, be wise and bear respect
To the high powers that rule above!

**RICH:** Hush, friends.

**SAM:** Who is to be the first?

**OSC:** I'll be the first.

---

**RIC:** L'onore a me cedi.
(*offrendo la palma ad Ulr.*)

**OSC:** E lo sia.

**ULR:** È la destra d' un grande, vissuto
Sotto l'astro di Marte.

**OSC:** Nel vero Ella colse.

**RIC:** Tacete.

**ULR:** (*staccandosi da lui*) Infelice..
Va—mi lascia—non chieder di più!

**RIC:** Su, prosegui.

**ULR:** No—lasciami.

**RIC:** Parla.

**ULR:** Te ne prego.

**CORO:** (*a lei*) Eh finiscila omai.

**RIC:** Te lo impongo.

**ULR:** Ebben, presto morrai.

**RIC:** Se sul campo d' onor, ti so grado.

**ULR:** No—per man d' un amico..

**OSC:** Gran Dio!
Quale orror!

**ULR:** Così scritto è lassù.

**RIC:** È scherzo od è follia
(*guardando intorne pausa.*)
Che da quel labbro uscia
Ma come fa da ridere
La lor credulità!

**ULR:** Eh voi, signori, a queste
(*passando fra Tom e Sam.*)
Parole mie funeste,
Voi non osate ridere,
Ben altro in cor vi sta.

**OSC. E CORO:** E sarà dunque spento
In breve a tradimento?
Al sol pensarci l'anima
Abbrividendo va.

**SAM E TOM:** (*fissando Ulr.*) La sua parola è dardo,
E fulmine lo sguardo,
Dal confidente demone
Tutto costei risà.

**RIC:** Di', chi fia dunque l'uccisor?

**ULR:** Chi primo Tua man quest' oggi stringerà.

**RIC:** Benissimo.
(*poi offrendo la destra a' circostanti che non osano toccare.*)
Qual è di voi, che provi
L' oracolo bugiardo?...
Nessuno!

### SCENA XI

*Renato all' entrata e detti.*

---

**RICH:** (*showing his hand to Ulrica.*) No, yield your turn to me!

**OSC:** Well, then, let it be so.

**ULR:** It is the hand of a great personage,
Grown under Planet Mars.

**OSC:** That's true, is it not?

**RICH:** Hush! let her go on.

**ULR:** (*withdrawing from him*).
Go, ask me no more!

**RICH:** Go on.

**ULR:** I pray, ask me no more!

**CHO:** Go on!

**RICH:** I order you . . . go on!

**ULR:** Well, very soon you are to die!

**RICH:** If on the battle field, I am glad of it!

**ULR:** No, by the hand of a false friend!

**OSC:** Great God!
Can that be true?

**ULR:** It is written so above! (*a pause.*)

**RICH:** At follies of this kind,
Uttered by such a woman,
I can't refrain now laughing . . . .
They are to be despised!

**ULR:** (*to Sam. and Tom.*) But you, at my predictions,
Most surely will not laugh;
More serious thoughts they are breeding
Within your wary minds!

**OSCAR AND CHORUS:** Shall he, then, soon fall victim
By the hand of a false friend?
Alas! the mere thought is dire poison
That gnaws my very bones!

**SAMUEL AND TOM:** Her words are sharpened arrows
That go straight to our hearts;
Ah! surely from her Demons
She knows our inmost thoughts!

**RICH:** Go on, finish your prophecy;
Who, then, shall be the murderer?

**ULR:** The man who shall shake hands first,
With you today!

**RICH:** Well, then!
(*Turning to the bystanders and offering them his hand, which nobody dares to touch.*)
Who among you will offer a proof
That the oracle has been false?
Nobody!

### SCENE XI

*Enter Reinhart.*

RIC: (*accorrendo a lui.*) Eccolo.
(*e unisce la sua alla destra dell' amico.*)

TUTTI: Desso!

SAM: Respiro—il caso ne salvò.
(*ai suoi*)

TUTTI: (*contro Ulrica*). L' oracolo Mentiva.

RIC: Sì: perchè la man ch' io stringo
È del più fido amico mio..

REN: Riccardo!

ULR: Il Conte!.. (*ravvisando il governatore.*)

RIC: (*a lei*) Nè, chi fossi, il genio tuo
Ti rivelò—nè che voleano al bando
Oggi dannarti.

ULR: Me? (*le una borsa.*)

RIC: T' acqueta e prendi. (*gettando.*)

ULR: Magnanimo tu se', ma v' ha fra loro
Il traditor: più d' uno
Forse . . .

SAM, TOM: Gran Dio!
(*a parte.*)

RIC: Non più.

CORO: (*da lontano*). Viva Riccardo!

TUTTI: Quai voci?

## SCENA XII

Silvano dal fondo, ove ristà, vòlto all' aperto, e detti.

SIL: È lui, ratti movete, è lui:
Il vostro amico e padre:
(*Marinai, Uomini e Donne del popolo s' affollano all' entrata.*)
Si prostri ognuno; amor, dovere il chiede,
E l' inno suoni della nostra dede.

CORO: O figlio d' Inghilterra,
Amor di questa terra:
Reggi felice, arridano
Gloria e salute a te.

OSC: Invidïato alloro
Che vince ogni tesoro,
Alla tua chioma intrecciano
Riconoscenza e fè.

URL: Non crede al proprio fato,
Ma pur morrà piagato;
Sorrise al mio presagio,
Ma nella fossa ha il piè.

RIC: E posso alcun sospetto
Alimentar nel petto,
Se mille cuori battono
Per immolarsi a me?

REN: Ma la sventura è cosa
Pur ne' trionfi ascosa,
Dove il destino ipocrita
Veli una rea mercè.

SAM, TOM E SEGUACI: (*fra loro*)
Vieta ogni moto ostile
Qui la ciurmaglia vile,
Che sta lambendo l'idolo
E che non sa il perchè.

---

RICH: (*running to him.*) There he is!
(*shaking hands with him.*)

ALL: He!

SAM: I breathe! we are safe!

ALL: (*to Ulrica.*) Then the oracle has lied!

RICH: Yes, the man with whom I shook hands
Is my most faithful friend!

REIN: Richard!

ULR: (*recognizing the Governor.*) The Count!

RICH: Your spirit
Could not reveal to you my person!
Nor that you were to be exiled this day!

ULR: I?

RICH: Becalm yourself and take . . . (*gives her a purse.*)

ULR: You are mighty generous!
Yet, among these there stands the traitor,
Perhaps there is more than one!

SAM, AND TOM: Great God!
(*aside.*)

RICH: No more.

CHO: (*from afar.*) Live long, Richard!

ALL: Whose voices are those?

## SCENE XII

Sylvan, from the place wherein he is standing, to the people outside.

SYL: It is he!
It is he! come quick!..
Here is your friend and father!
(*Sailors, men, women, etc., rushing in.*)
Let all kneel down! It is our duty,
And let us sing our native song!

CHO: O son of glorious England,
Beloved of this land,
Live long; may health and glory
Reward your noble soul!

OSC: A precious crown of glory,
That is above all treasures,
Unsullied faith and gratitude
Are setting on your brow!

RICH: Can I harbor suspicions
Of traitors in my mind,
While I am so beloved
By thousands faithful hearts?

REIN: But often lies misfortune
Hidden amid bright triumphs,
And seizes on its victim
When least he thinks on it!

SAM, TOM, AND FOLLOWERS:
Here, now, we can do nothing,
While there is such a vile mob
Adoring its cursed idol,
And knowing not for what.

---

Fine Dell' Atto Primo.

## ■ ATTO SECONDO

### SCENA PRIMA

Campo solitario nei dintorni di Boston, appia d' un colle scosceso. A sinistra nel basso biancheggiano due pilastri; e la luna leggermente velata illumina alcuni punti della scena.

AMELIA: (*dalle eminenze.*) Ecco l' orrido campo ove s'accoppia
Al delitto la morte!
Ecco là le colonne.
La pianta è la, verdeggia al piè.
S' innoltri.
Ah mi si aggela il core!
Sino il romor de' passi miei, qui tutto
M'empie di raccapriccio e di terrore!
E se perir dovessi?
Perire! ebben quando la sorte mia,
Il mio dover tal è, s'adempia, a sia.
(*fa per avviarsi.*)
Ma dall' arido stelo divulsa
Come avrò di mia mano quell' erba.
E che dentro la mente convulsa
Quell' eterea sembianza morrà
Che ti resta, perduto l'amor
Che ti resta, mio povero cor!
Oh! chi piange, qual forza m'arretra,
M'attraversa la squallida via?
Su coraggio..e tu fatti di pietra,
Non tradirmi, dal pianto ristà:
O finisci di battere e muor,
T' annienta, mio povero cor!
(*s'ode un tocco d'ore, lantano*)
Mezzanotte!—e che veggio? uno spettro
Di sotterra si leva..e sospira!
Ha negli occhi il baleno dell'ira
E m'affisa e terribile sta!
(*cadendo sulle genoschia*)
Deh! mi reggi, m' aïta, o Signor,
Risolleva il mio povero cor!

### SCENA II

Riccardo e Amelia.

RIC: Teco io sto.

AME: Gran Dio!

RIC: Ti calma:
Di che temi?

AME: Ah mi lasciate..
Son la vittima che geme..
Il mio nome almen salvate..
O lo strazio ed il rossore
La mia vita abbatterà.

RIC: Io lasciarti? no, giammai:
Nol poss'io; chè m'arde in petto
Sovruman di te l'affetto.

AME: Conte, abbiatemi pietà.

---

End Of The First Act.

## ■ ACT II

### SCENE I

A field near Boston—Two white pillars are to be seen on one side—It is moonlight.

AME: There is the horrid place,
Where crime is expiated by death!
There the fearful walls, on which
The magic plant I am to gather is creeping!
Alas!..I shudder..my heart fails!..
Here terror reigns all around!
Yet, stern duty spurs me on
To fetch the remedy that is to heal
The fatal sickness that consumes my heart!
But when the adored image
Shall be obliterated
From the enchanted mind,
And all its charm destroyed,
What shall make up the void?
But..now, I must proceed on,
Whatever may be the fright,
That strives to keep me back
From the directed place!
Let duty impart courage
To save me from my heart!
(*The clock is heard striking in the distance.*)
It is midnight! What do I perceive, yonder?
Is that a phantom, or a real man?
He seems to look at me with anger!
What may he want here?..Who is he?..
O Lord, grant me your gracious aid!
Sustain my drooping spirits!

### SCENE II

Richard and Amelia.

RICH: Here I am with you.

AME: Great God!

RICH: What fright!
Are you afraid of me?

AME: Ah!
Let me alone..go off—
I am already too unfortunate!
Don't tempt my virtue any longer,
I am already weak enough!

RICH: Abandon you?..No, never!
It is beyond my power;
My love for you can know no bounds!

AME: Are you devoid of pity?

## Act II, Scene II

**RIC:** Così parli? a chi t'adora
Pietà chiedi, e tremi ancora?
Questo core innamorato
L'onor tuo rispetterà.

**AME:** Ma, Riccardo, io son d'altrui..
Dell amico più fidato..

**RIC:** Taci, Amelia.

**AME:** Io son di lui,
Che daria la vita a te..

**RIC:** Ah crudele, e mel rammemori,
Lo ripeti innanzi a me!
Non sai tu che se l'anima mia
Il rimorso dilacera e rode,
Quel suo grido non cura, non ode,
Sin che l'empie di fremiti amor?..
Non sai tu che di te resteria,
Se cessasse di battere il cor!
Quante notti ho vegliato anelante!
Come a lungo infelice lottai!
Quante volte dal cielo implorai
La pietà che tu chiedi da me!—
Ma per questo ho potuto un istante,
Infelice, non viver di te?

**AME:** Deh soccorri tu, cielo, all'
ambascia
Di chi sta fra l'infamia e la morte;
Tu pietoso rischiara le porte
Di salvezza all' errante mio piè.
E tu va—ch' io non t' oda—mi las-
cia:
Son di lui, che il suo sangue ti diè.

**RIC:** La mia vita . . . l'universo,
Per un detto . . .

**AME:** O ciel pietoso!

**RIC:** Di' che m' ami..

**AME:** Ah va, Riccardo?

**RIC:** Un sol detto.

**AME:** Ebben, sì, t'amo . . .

**RIC:** M'ami, Amelia!

**AME:** Ma tu, nobile, Me difendi dal
mio cor!

**RIC:** (*fuori di sè.*) M' ami, m'
ami!..oh sia distrutto—Il rimorso,
l'amicizia
Nel mio seno: estinto tutto:—Tutto
sia fuorchè l'amor!
Quale soave brivido—L'acceso
petto irrora!
Ah ch' io t' ascolti ancora—Rispondermi così!
Astro di queste tenebre—A cui
consacro il core;
Irradiami d'amore—E più non sorga il di!

**RICH:** Can you speak thus to me?
Is it from me you ask mercy?
Is not my love for you sufficient
To guard me against all offense?

**AME:** Consider who's the man
whose wife I am,..
Your most devoted friend!

**RICH:** Don't mention such a thing
at present!

**AME:** Yes, think how great would
be the crime,
Were you to wrong such worthy
man!

**RICH:** Do you think I am so
hardhearted
As not to ponder over these things?
Yet there's no help, when love is
burning
As it burns now, within my heart!
And then, what would a man's life
be
If it was not cheered up by love?
Soon every thing would lose its
charm
With him whose love had been ex-
tinguished! . . .
Still, very long I have been trying
To quench that fire that burns my
heart;
But then, the more it has been rag-
ing
When I attempted to quench it!
It is, then, quite beyond my power
To stop the flame that burns for
you!

**AME:** I am craving your assistance
O lord,
In these trials that torture my soul;
Deign to graciously save me from
crime,
Give strength to my weak, sinking
heart!
Go off, then, and leave me alone;
Think on the man against whom is
Your offense!

**RICH:** My life I offer you . . . the
universe—
Say just a single word . . .

**AME:** Alas!

**RICH:** Say that you love me!

**AME:** No more..

**RICH:** A single word.

**AME:** Well . . . I love you!
But, then, do save my honor?

**RICH:** (*estatically.*) O sweet, en-
chanting words!
Against such furious torrent
Of pure delight, can't honor
Resist . . . nor friendly faith!
Such an alluring sweetness
No man can overcome!

**AME:** Ahi sul funereo letto—Ove
sognava spegnerlo,
Torna gigante in petto—L'amor
che mi feri!
Chè non m' è dato in seno—A lui
versar quest' anima?
O nella morte almeno—Addormentarmi qui? (*la luna illumina
sempre più.*)
Ahimè!

**RIC:** Taci . . .

**AME:** S'appressa Alcun . . .

**RIC:** Chi giunge in questo Albergo
della morte? . . .
(*fatti pochi passi.*)
Renato!

**AME:** Il mio consorte!
(*abbassando il velo atterrita.*)

## SCENA III

*Riccardo, Amelia e Renato.*

**RIC:** Tu qui?
(*incontrandolo.*)

**REN:** Per salvarti da lor, che, celati
Lassù, t'hanno in mira

**RIC:** Chi son?

**REN:** Congiurati.

**AME:** O ciel!
(*tra sè.*)

**REN:** Trasvolai nel manto serrato,
Così ch m'han preso per un
dell'agguato,
E intesi taluno proromper: L' ho visto:
È il Conte: un'ignota beltade è con
esso
Poi altri qui volto—fuggevole acquisto!
S' ei rade la fossa, se il tenero amplesso
Troncar, di mia mano, repente saprò.

**AME:** Io muoio . . . (*tra sè*)

**RIC:** (*a lei.*) Fa core.

**REN:** (*coprendolo col suo mantello*) Ma questo ti do.
(*poi additandogli un viottolo a
destra.*)
E bada, lo scampo, t' è libero là.

**RIC:** Salvarti degg'io..(*presa per
mano Amelia.*)

**AME:** (*sottovoce a lui.*) Me misera!
Va..

**REN:** (*passando ad Amelia.*) Nè
voi già vorrete segnarlo, o signora,
Al ferro spietato!
(*dilegua nel fondo a veder se
s'avanzane.*)

**AME:** Deh solo t'invola!

**RIC:** Che qui t'abbandoni?

**AME:** T'è libero ancora
Il passo, va fuggi..

**AME:** In vain I have been trying
To quench this fatal love;
To taste its tempting sweetness
It would be worth while to die!
Ah me!
(*the moon is growing clearer.*)

**RICH:** Hush..

**AME:** Somebody is coming towards
us,..

**RICH:** Who is coming
To this abode of death?
Reinhart…...

**AME:** It is he!..my husband!
(*she covers her face with her veil.*)

## SCENE III

*Richard, Amelia, Reinhart.*

**RICH:** What brings you here?
(*meeting Reinhart.*)

**REIN:** I came to save you from the
traitors,
Who lie in wait for you!

**RICH:** For what?

**REIN:** To take away your life!

**AME:** Heavens!

**REIN:** While coming to this place,
Wrapped in this cloak to avoid their
suspicion,
They took me for one of their
friends….
I overheard them saying,
A lady is with him,—our chance is
better
To dispatch him while love
Absorbs all his attention!

**AME:** (*aside*) I am near fainting!

**RICH:** (*softly to her.*) Courage!

**REIN:** Take this cloak and flee that
way,
(*pointing to him a path.*)
So you shall not be observed!

**RICH:** (*taking Amelia by the
hand.*) I must save you!

**AME:** (*softly to him.*) No, go away
alone!

**REIN:** Madam, with him you shall
not go;
You would be a mark for his assailants!

**AME:** Go off alone . . .

**RICH:** And leave you here?

**AME:** You are yet in time to save
your life;
Go quick, or else it will be too late!

**RIC:** Lasciarti qui sola
Con esso? no mai—piuttosto morrò.

**AME:** O fuggi: o che il velo dal capo torrò.

**RIC:** Che dici?

**AME:** Risolvi.

**RIC:** Desisti.

**AME:** Lo vo'.

**AME:** Per esso quest'alma sol trepida e geme, (*tra se*)
Salvarlo, non altro desiro la preme,
E paga di tanto, se dato le fia.
Se stessa del fato ne' fremiti oblia.

**RIC:** (*a Renato, solennemente*)
Amico, gelosa t'affido una cura:
L' amor che mi porti, garante mi sta.

**REN:** Affidati, imponi.

**RIC:** (*coll' indice verso Amelia.*)
Promettimi, giura
Che tu l'addurrai, velata, in città,
Nè un detto nè un guardo sur essa trarrano.

**REN:** Lo giuro.

**RIC:** E che tocche le porte, Da solo all' opposto.

**REN:** Lo giuro e sarà.

**AME:** (*sommessamente a Riccardo.*) Odi tu come sonano cupi
Per quest' aure gli accenti di morte?
Di lassù, da quei negri dirupi,
Il segnal de' nemici partì.
Ne' lor petti scintillano d' ira..
E già piomban, t' accerchiano fitti..
Al tuo capo già volser la mira..
Per pietà, va t' invola di qui.

**RIC:** Traditor, sciagurati son essi,
(*tra se.*)
Che minacciano il vivere mio?
Ma l'amico ho tradito ancor io.
Son colui che nel cor lo feri!
Innocente, sfidati gli avrei;
Or d'amore colpevole.. fuggo—
La pietà del Signore su lei
Posi l' ale, protegga i suoi dì!

**REN:** (*staccandosi dal fondo ove stava esplorando.*)
Fuggi, fuggi: per l' orrida via
Sento l' orma dei passi spietati.
Allo scambio dei detti esecrati
Ogni destra ia daga brandì.
Va, ti salva, o che il varco all' uscita
Qui fra poco serrarsi vedrai;
Va, ti salva, del popolo è vita
Questa vita che getti così. (*Riccardo esce.*)

## SCENA IV

*Renato e Amelia.*

**REN:** Seguitemi.

**AME:** Mio Dio! (*da sè.*)

---

**RICH:** I can't leave you here with your husband!..
He may discover who you are!

**AME:** Oh, save yourself!

**RICH:** Come off with me!

**AME:** No.

**REIN:** Why, then?

**AME:** It would be your death!
Alas! forgetful of my honor,
I only fear now for his danger!
Let him be saved; whatever may happen.
It is preferable to his death!

**RICH:** (*to Reinhart.*) I'll ask from you a solemn promise
Pledged by the love you have for me!

**REIN:** Order—speak . . . I shall obey!

**RICH:** (*pointing to Amelia.*)
Promise, on thy oath, to take this lady
Back to the city, without lifting
Up her veil, or asking who she is!

**REIN:** I swear I shall do so!

**RICH:** And that upon arriving
Within the town you shall let her alone!

**REIN:** I do swear to do so!

**AME:** (*softly to Richard.*) Ah! can you not feel sensible
To the surrounding danger?
Your foes are now all watching
Their chance to take your life!
Ah! look now they are slyly advancing
Now, on all sides.
For God's sake, stay no longer;
Go off while yet in time!

**RICH:** (*aside.*) They are, indeed, all traitors,
Who strive to spill my blood!
Does not, also, my passion
Make me betray my friend?
Alas! that I were innocent!
Their snares I could despise;
But as I, too, am guilty
I must look for myself!

**REIN:** (*coming forward.*) Quick, quick, Richard, go off,
I hear the noise of steps
Advancing to this side;
Go quick, they are near at hand.
It's no time to tarry.
Or else it will be too late
To save you from the clutches
Of those who want you dead!
(*Exit Richard*)

## SCENE IV

*Reinhart and Amelia.*

**REIN:** Follow me.

**AME:** Great God!
(*aside.*)

---

**REN:** Perchè tremate?
Fida scorta vi son, l' amico accento
Vi risollevi il cor!

## SCENA V

*Samuel, Tom con seguito, dalle alture e detti.*

**AME:** Eccoli.

**REN:** Presto, Appoggiatevi a me.

**AME:** Morir mi sento!

**CORO:** (*dall' alto*). Si discenda, si trafigga,
Già scoccata è l' ultim' ora.
Il saluto dell' aurora
Sull' esanime cadrà.

**SAM:** Scerni tu quel bianco velo
Onde spicca la sua dea?

**TOM:** Si precipiti dal cielo
All' averno.

**REN:** (*forte*) Chi va là?

**SAM:** Non è desso!

**TOM:** O furor mio!

**CORO:** Non è il conte!

**REN:** No, son io Che dinanzi a voi qui sta.

**SAM:** Il suo fido! (*beffardo.*)

**TOM:** Men di voi
Fortunati fummo noi:
Chè il sorriso d' una bella.
Stemmo indarno ad aspettar.

**SAM:** Io per altro il volto almeno
Vo' a quest' Iside mirar.
(*alcuni de' suoi rientrano con fiaccole accese.*)

**REN:** (*colla mano sull' elsa*) Non un passo: se l' osate
Traggo il ferro . . .

**TOM:** E v'infiammate?

**SAM:** Non vi temo.

**AME:** O cieli, aïta!

**CORO:** Giù l' acciaro . . . (*verso Renato.*)

**REN:** Traditori!

**TOM:** (*mentre va per istrappare il velo ad Amelia*). Vo'finirla . . .

**REN:** (*assalendolo*) E la tua vita
Questo insulto pagherà.
(*nell'atto che tutti s'avventano contro Renato. Amelia, fuori di sè inframmettendosi, lascia cadere il velo.*)

**AME:** No: fermatevi . . .

**REN:** (*colpito*) Che! . . .
Amelia!

**SAM:** Lei! . . .

**TOM:** Sua moglie!

**AME:** Ah! per pietà!

---

**REIN:** Never fear!
Cheer up, while you are with me
You'll be protected.

## SCENE V

*Samuel, Tom, and their friends coming forward*

**AME:** There they are!

**REIN:** Quick, quick!
Give me your arm!

**AME:** I shudder.

**CHOR:** At last the time of vengeance
Has come.
Let us go down
And stab the hated felon,
To vindicate our wrongs!

**SAM:** (*to Tom.*) Oh! look at that white veil,
It is his lady-love.

**TOM:** We won't spare him on her account;
Courage!

**REIN:** Who goes there?

**SAM:** It is not the Count!

**TOM:** Alas! bad luck.

**CHOR:** It is not the Count.

**REIN:** It is I who stand here before you.

**SAM:** (*aside.*) Accursed Reinhart!

**TOM:** Ah! very, very unlucky,
We have been in your comparison;
Our lady-love, whom we expected,
Has disappointed us!

**SAM:** At least, this beauty I wish to contemplate,
Since mine has disappointed me.
(*Some of the men exeunt.*)

**REIN:** (*brandishing his sword.*)
Whoever dares insult this lady
Has to deal with me first!

**TOM:** Are you in earnest?

**SAM:** What do we care for you?

**AME:** God help us!

**CHOR:** (*To Reinhart.*) Put down your sword!

**REIN:** Stop, traitors!

**TOM:** (*Attempting to take off Amelia's veil.*) I'll see her by all means!

**REIN:** (*Attacking him.*) Your arrogance I will chastise!
(*During the strife, Amelia through fright drops her veil.*)

**AME:** Stop!

**REIN:** (*Surprised.*) Amelia!

**SAM:** She!

**TOM:** His wife!

**AME:** O, Lord!

**SAM, TOM:** Ve' se di notte qui colla sposa
L' innamorato campion si posa,
E come al raggio lunar del miele
Sulle rugiade corear si sa!

**CORO:** Ve' la tragedia mutò in commedia
Piacevolissima—ah! ah! ah! ah!
E che baccano sul caso strano
Andrà dimane per la città!

**AME:** A chi nel mondo crudel più mai,
Misera Amelia, ti volgerai? . . .
La tua spregiata lacrima, quale,
Qual man pietosa rascingherà!

**REN:** (*fisso alla via onde fuggì Riccardo.*) Così mi paga, se l' ho salvato!
Ei m' ha la donna contaminato!
Tal marchio fitto mi volle in fronte,
Macero il core per sempre m' ha!
(*poi riscuotendosi, e come chi ha preso un grave partito, s' accosta a Samuel e Tom*)
Converreste al tetto mio
Sul mattiino di domani?

**SAM, TOM:** Per subir dell' onta il fio?

**REN:** No—ben altro in cor mi sta,

**SAM, TOM:** Che ti punge?

**REN:** Lo saprete,
Se verrete.

**SAM, TOM:** E ci vedrai.
(*nell' uscire seguiti dai loro*)
Dunque andiam—per vie diverse
L' un dall' altro s' allentani.
Il mattino di domani
Grandi cose apprenderà.

**REN:** (*rimasto solo con Amelia.*)
Ho giurato che alle porte
V' addurrei della città.

**AME:** Come sonito di morte
(*tra sè*)
La sua voce al cor mi va!

*Fine Dell'Atto Secondo.*

## ■ Atto Terzo

### SCENA PRIMA

*Una stanza da studio nell' abitazione di Renato. Sovra un caminetto di fianco due vasi di bronzo, rimpetto a cui la biblioteca. Nel fondo v' ha un magnifico ritratto del conte Riccardo in piedi, e nel mezzo della scena una tavola. Entrano Renato e Amelia.*

**REN:** A tal colpa è nulla il pianto,
(*deposta la spada e chiusa la portà*)
Non la terge e non la scusa
Altro sol non rivedrai,
Rea ti festi: e qui morrai.

**AME:** Ma se reo, se reo soltanto
È l'indizio che m'accusa!..

**REN:** Taci, o perfida.

**SAM AND TOM:** Ah! here by moonlight
He comes with his good wife,
To cool his burning flame
By the refreshing dew!!!

**CHOR:** Ah! ah! ah! ah! the tragedy
Has been turned into comedy.
The story will tomorrow
Be amusing all the town!!!

**AME:** Alas! I have forever
Now forfeited my honor;
Where shall I find a remedy
To my tremendous woes?

**REIN:** (*Pointing towards the side by which Richard had gone.*) Ah! this is then the gratitude
The Count has for his friends!
While I have saved his life
He has seduced my wife!
(*Drawing near to Samuel and Tom.*)
Would you call on me tomorrow?
I will tell you something important.

**SAM AND TOM:** Will you revenge yourself on us?

**REIN:** No, no; I am your friend!

**SAM:** What's the matter?

**REIN:** Come tomorrow
I'll tell you all!

**SAM AND TOM:** (*while going*).
Then we will come.
Let's cautiously disperse,
To avoid every suspicion;
Let's hear tomorrow morning
What Reinhart has to tell.

**REIN:** (*alone with Amelia*). I shall fulfill my promise
To take you to the city!

**AME:** His voice like a death warrant
Has sounded to my ears!

*End Of The Second Act.*

## ■ Act III

### SCENE I

*A room in the house of Reinhart. A table is placed in the middle, and a large portrait of Richard is seen hanging from the wall. Enter Reinhart and Amelia.*

**REIN:** Your crime deserves no pity!
You can have no excuse!
You have destroyed my happiness,
I must have my revenge!
(*Deposits his sword on the table.*)

**AME:** God knows that I am innocent,
In spite of all appearances!

**REIN:** Add not lying to your guilt!

**AME:** Gran Dio!

**REN:** Chiedi a lui misericordia.

**AME:** E ti basta un sol sospetto!
E vuoi dunque il sangue mio!
E m'infami, e più non senti
Nè giustizia, nè pietà?

**REN:** Hai finito!

**AME:** Se l' amai
Un istante, infelicissima,
Il tuo nome io non macchiai.
Sallo Iddio, che nel mio petto
Mai non arse indegno affetto.

**REN:** (*ripigliando la spada.*) Hai finito! è tardi omai . . .
Rea ti festi . . . e qui morrai.

**AME:** Ah! mi sveni! . . . ebbene sia . . .
Ma una grazia . . .

**REN:** Non a me.
La tua prece al ciel rivolgi.

**AME:** Solo un detto ancora a te,—
(*genuflessa*)
M' odi, l' ultimo sarà.
Morrò—ma prima in grazia—Deh! mi consenti almeno
L'unico figlio mio—Avvincere al mio seno.
E se alla moglie nieghi—Quest' ultimo favor,
Non rifiutarlo ai prieghi—Del mio materno cor,
Morrò—ma quest viscere-Consolino i suoi baci,
Poi che l'estrema è giunta—Dell' ore mie fugaci.
Spenta per man del padre,—La mano ei stenderà
Su gli occhi d'una madre,—Che mai più non vedrà!

**REN:** Alzati, là tuo figlio
A te concedo riveder. Nell' ombra
E nel silenzio, là,
Il tuo rossore e l' onta mia nascondi.
(*Amelia esce.*)
Non è su lei, nel suo
Fragile petto che colpir degg' io.
Altro, ben altro sangue a terger dèssi
L'offesa . . . (*fissando il ritratto*). Il sangue tuo?
Nè tarderà il mio ferro
Tutto a versarlo dal tuo falso core:
Delle lacrime mio vendicatore!
E sei tu che macchiavi quell' anima,
La delizia dell' anima mia . . .
Che m'affidi e d' un tratto esecrabile
L' universo avveleni per me!
Traditor! che in tal guisa rimuneri
Dell' amico tuo primo la fè!
O dolcezze perdute! O memorie
D' un amplesso che mai non s' oblia!
Quando Amelia sì bella, sì candida
Sul mio seno brillava d' amor!
È finita—non siede che che l' odio.
E la morte sul vedovò cor!

**AME:** O, Lord!

**REIN:** Prepare for death!

**AME:** Is then a dubious evidence
Sufficient to convince
Your mind, that I am guilty
Of such enormous crime?

**REIN:** Have done!

**AME:** If any wrong affection
Has crept into my heart,
God knows that I prevented
Its taking root in it.

**REIN:** (*Taking up his sword.*)
Have done. I waited long enough!
You have broken your vows and you must die!

**AME:** If so . . . I'll die,
then . . . but before,
Allow me . . .

**REIN:** God alone can help you now!
Do turn your mind to
Him . . . and die.

**AME:** (*kneeling down*) Before I die, let me embrace,
For the last time, my child;
For him, I beg this grace
Of you . . . you must grant it!

**REIN:** Well, then, get up the child,
For the last time go and embrace;
And let his pure, innocent soul
Open your eyes to see your guilt!
(*exit Amelia*)
It is not so much against my frail wife
That I should vent my wrath,
Than against him who has so basely
Betrayed the faith of his best friend!
But, surely not much distant
May be the time of my revenge
His blood shall expiate his crime!
Ah! none can fully comprehend
The grief that preys upon my soul,
Now that I've lost what was most soothing
My weary heart, in this sad world!
What is this life, with all its pleasures,
When they are not sweetened by love?
Oh! how can I well bear the torture
Which the remembrance of past joys
Causes the sick mind, while comparing
Its present horror to past bliss?
Alas! my heart's forever poisoned!
Forever peace has gone from me!

## SCENA II

*Renato Samuel e Tom entrano salutandolo freddamente.*

REN: Siam soli.—Udite. Ogni disegno vostro
M'é note.
Voi di Riccardo la morte
Volete.

TOM: Sogni.

REN: (*mostrando alcune carte che ha sul tavelo*). Ho qui le prove!

SAM: (*fremendo*) All' ora
La trama al Conte svelerai?

REN: No—voglio
Dividerla.

TOM: Tu scherzi.

REN: E non co' detti:
Ma qui col fatto struggero i sospetti.
Io son vostro, compagno m' avrete
Senza posa al medesimo intento:
Arra il figlio vi do. L' uccidete
Se vi manco.

TOM: Ma tal mutamento
E credibile appena.

REN: Qual fu
La cagion non cercate. Son vostro
Per la vita dell' unico figlio!

SAM, TOM: Ei non mente.

REN: Esitate?
(*fra loro*)

SAM, TOM: Non più.

REN, SAM, TOM: Dunque l'onta di tutti sol una
Uno il cor, la nostra ira sarà,
Che tremenda, repente, digiuna
Su quel capo esecrato cadrà!

REN: D'una grazia vi supplica.

SAM, TOM: E quale?

REN: Che sia dato d' ucciderlo a me.

TOM: No, Renato: l' avito castello
A me tolse, e tal dritto a me spetta.

SAM: Ed a me, cui spegneva il fratello,
Cui decenne agonia di vendetta
Senza requie divora, qual parte
Assegnaste?

REN: Chetatevi, solo
Qui la sorte or decidere de'.
(*prende un vaso dal camino e lo colloca sulla tavola, Samuel scrive tre nomi e vi getto entro i viglietti.*)

TOM: Ma chi vien?

## SCENA III

*Amelia e detti.*

REN: (*incontrandola.*) Tu?

AME: V' è Oscarre che porta
Un invito del Conte.

## SCENE II

*Enter Samuel and Tom.*

REIN: We are alone . . . So we can freely speak!
I know you are plotting Richard's death . . .
You need not fear . . .

TOM: You rave!

REIN: (*showing them some papers*). Here are all the proofs!

SAM: Well, then!
Will you denounce us to the Count?

REIN: No, no!
I'll join you in your schemes!

TOM: Are you in earnest?

REIN: As earnest as you are!
I swear that I will join you,
In all your plots, until we shall succeed
In our design . . . My child
I'll give you as a pledge
Of my sincerity!

TOM: But what has operated
So strange a change in you?

REIN: Don't ask of me the reason
That makes me hate the Count;
I do hate him . . . that is enough for you!

SAM: He seems to be in earnest?

REIN: Do you doubt it?

SAM, TOM: We believe you.

REIN, SAM, TOM: Let us, then, join our efforts
To obtain our common end:
Let us watch every occasion
To vindicate our wrongs!

REIN: You must grant me a favor!

SAM, TOM: Which, then?

REIN: That he may fall by my own hand!

TOM: No, no, that task belongs to me;
For, he has confiscated my estates!

SAM: It is I who must stab him,
To appease the wrath that has been gnawing
My heart for these ten years, for having wrongly
Condemned to death my brother!

REIN: Well, then, let us draw lots,
To settle this dispute!
[*He writes his and their names on three pieces of paper, and puts them inside a little urn*].

TOM: Who's coming now?

## SCENE III

*Enter Amelia.*

REIN: (*meeting her.*) Amelia!

AME: Here is Oscar, who brings you
An invitation from the Count!

REN: (*impallidendo.*) Di lui! . . .
Che m'aspetti.—E tu resta, lo dêi:
Poi che parmi che il cielo t' ha scorta.

AME: (*fra sè*) Qual tristezza m' assale, qual pena!
Qual terribile lampo balena!

REN: (*additando sua moglie agli altri due*)
Nulla sa—non temete. Costei
Esser debbe anzi l' auspice caro.
(*traendola verso la tavola.*)
V' ha tre nomi in quell'urna—un ne tragga
L' innocente tua mano.

AME: (*tremante*) E perchè?

REN: Ubbidisci—non chieder di più.

AME: (*traendo dal vaso un viglietto che sue marota passa a Sam.*) Non è dubbio: quest' ordine aaro
(*fra sè*)
Mi vuol parte ad un' opra di sangue.

REN: Qual è dunque l' eletto?

SAM: Renato.

REN: (*fremente di gioia*) Il mio nome!—O giustizia del fato:
La vendetta mi deleghi tu!

AME: Ah del Conte la morte si vuole.
(*da sola.*)
Nol celâr le crudeli parole!
Su quel capo snudati dall' ira
I lor ferri scintillano già.

REN, SAM E TOM: Sconterà
dell'America il pianto
Lo sleal che ne fece suo vanto.
Se trafisse, soccomba trafitto,
Tal mercede pagata gli va!

REN: Il messaggio entri.
(*alla porta.*)

## SCENA IV

*Oscar e detti.*

OSC: (*verse Amelia*) Alle danze
Questa notte, se gradite
Collo sposo, il mio signore
Vi desidera . . .

AME: (*turbata*) No! posso.

REN: Anche il conte vi sarà? (*ad Oscar.*)

OSC: Certo.

SAM E TOM: (*fra loro*). Oh sorte!

REN: (*al paggio, ma collo sguardo a Tom*). Tanto invito So che valga.

OSC: E un ballo in maschera Splendidissimo..

REN: (*c.s.*) Benissimo! Ella meco interverrà.
(*accennando Amelia.*)

REIN: Then let him wait . . .
You must remain here for a moment! . . .
You must do us a little service!
(*ironically.*)

AME: (*aside*) What may they want from me?
Alas! I shudder!

REIN: (*to Sam. & Tom.*) She knows nothing
Of our affiar . . . There is no fear!
(*Taking her near the table.*)
There are three names inside that urn,
Draw out, now, one of them!

AME: (*trembling*) Wherefore?

REIN: Obey . . . and ask no more!

AME: (*She draws one of the pieces of paper, which Reinhart hands over to Samuel.*)
There is no doubt . . . I am sure,
That this is an affair of blood!

REIN: Which is the name extracted?

SAM: Reinhart!

REIN: (*with joy*) Providence is just!
The task belonged to me!

AME: (*aside*) It is clear they are designing
To assassinate the Governor!
Alas! that though unwilling
I should share in the deed!

REIN, SAM, TOM: Then let the felon perish,
And pay for all the wrongs
He has done his fellow creatures,
In the name of law!

REIN: Let in the messenger. (*at the door.*)

## SCENE IV

*Enter Oscar.*

OSC: (*to Amelia*) Tonight
You are invited to the ball,
Together with your husband,
By the Governor.

AME: (*agitated*) I cannot go!—

REIN: Will the Count be present?

OSC: He will.

SAM AND TOM: This is good news.
(*aside.*)

REIN: (*to Osc.*) We accept the invitation.

OSC: It is a masked ball of great splendor!

REIN: Well, then,
We shall be present.

# Act III, Scene IV

**SAM E TOM:** (*a parte*). E noi pur, se da quell' abito
Più spèdito il colpo va.

**SAM, TOM:** (*aside*). We also shall be there.
The blow will be more safe on such occasion!

**OSC:** Di che fulgor, che musiche—
Esulteran le soglie,
Ove di tante giovani
Bellezze il fior s'accoglie,
di quante altrice palpita
La genial città!

**OSC:** There will surely assemble
All the most brilliant beauties
Our city can boast of!

**REN:** Ed io medesma, io misera (*fra sè*)
Lo scritto inesorato
Trassi dall'urna complice,
Pel mio consorte irato:
Su cui del cor più nobile
Ferma la morte sta.

**AME:** Alas! what strange fatality
Has made me an accomplice
To such a horrid crime?

**REN:** Là delle danze al sonito (*da solo*)
Ecco il codardo afferro . . .
Ferma la punta vindice..E là dov'io l'atterro
Spira dator d'infamie
Senza trova pietà.

**REIN:** There, while sweet sounds of music
Will stir up mirth and pleasure,
I'll spill the traitor's blood!

**SAM E TOM:** (*fra loro*). Una vendetta in domino
E ciò che torna all' uopo.
Nell' urto delle maschere—Non fallirà lo scopo.
E sarà urto delle maschere—Non fallirà lo scopo.
E sarà un ballo funebre—Fra pallide beltà.

**SAM, TOM:** The occasion can't be better
Than the one which is offering
To accomplish our design!

**AME:** Prevenirlo potessi—e non tradire (*da se.*)
Lo sposo mio! . . .

**AME:** Could I at least warn Richard,
Without betraying my spouse

**OSC:** Reina Delle danze sarete.

**OSC:** (*to Amelia*). You'll be there,
The belle of all the party!

**AME:** Forse potrallo Ulrica.

**AME:** Ulrica may perhaps help us. (*aside.*)

**SAM E TOM:** E qual costume indosserem?

**SAM, TOM:** How shall we dress to recognize each other?

**REN:** Azzurra La veste, e da vermiglio
Nastro, le ciarpe al manco lato attorte.

**REIN:** We'll wear a blue dress, and on our left arm
A red tape

**SAM E TOM:** E qual accento a ravvisarci?

**SAM, TOM:** What shall be our word?

**REN:** Morte!

**REIN:** Death!

## SCENA V

## SCENE V

*Sontuoso gabinetto del Conte.—Tavolo con l'occorente per iscrivere; nel fondo un gran cortinas gio che scoprirà la festa da ballo.*

*The private office of the Count*

**RICCARDO:** (*solo.*) Forse la soglia attinse,
E posa Alfin.—L' onore
Ed il dover fra i nostri petti han rotto
L' abisso.—Ah! sì, Renato
Rivedrâ l'Inghilterra . . . e la sua sposa
Lo seguirà. Senza un addio, l'immenso
Oceàn ne spàri . . . e taccia il core.
Esito ancor? ma, oh ciel, non lo degg' io?
(*sottoscrive, e chiude il foglio in seno.*)
Ah l' ho segnato il sacrifizio mio!
Ma se m'è forza perderti—Per sempre a luce mia.
A te verrà il mio palpito—Sotto qual ciel tu sia
Chiusa la tua memoria—Nell' intime del cor.
Ed or qual reo presagio—Lo spirito m' assale,
Che il rivederti annunzia—Quasi un desio fatale.
Come se fosse l' ultima—Ora de nostra amor

**RICH:** (*alone*). Yes, I'll have done with this affair!
Let duty and honor triumph!
Amelia with her husband
Shall go forever from my sight;
And all temptation then shall be removed
To violate the faith of a dear friend!
They shall both go to England.
(*he signs a paper*)
There's an end of it!
But if I am forever
To lose you, my dear love:
For ever in my memory
Your image shall remain!
But, once more before parting
I would like to see you!

## SCENA VI

## SCENE VI

*Oscar con una lettera, e detto.*

*Oscar bringing a letter.*

**OSC:** Ignota donna questo foglio diemmi.
E pel Conte, diss' ella; a lui lo reca
E di celato.

**OSC:** A lady, unknown, gave me this letter;
She said, it is for you,
And that it speaks on private matters!

**RIC:** (*dopo letto.*) Che nel ballo alcuno
Alla mia vita attenterà, sta detto.
Ma se m' arresto: allora,
Ch'io pavento diran.
Nol vo': nessuno
Pur sospettarlo de'.
Tu va: t'appresta,
E ratto per gioir meco la festa.
(*Oscar esce, Ric. rimasto solo, vivamente prorompe.*)
Vo', riverderti, Amelia,
E nella tua beltà,
Anche una volta l'anima
D'amor mi brillerà!

**RICH:** (*reads it*). It is revealing a plot
To kill me at the ball . . . .
If I were to be absent,
I might be taken for a coward!
I must dissemble all the matter
And hasten to the ball.
(*exit Oscar*)

## SCENA VII

## SCENE VII

*Vasta e ricca sala da ballo splendidamente illuminata e parata a festa.*

*A ball-room, splendidly decorated.*

**CORO GENERALE:** Fervono amori e danze
Nelle felici stanza
Onde la vita è solo
Un sogno lusinghier.
Notte de' cari istanti,
De palpiti e' de canti
Perchè non fermi 'l volo.
Sull' onda de' piacer?

**GENERAL CHORUS:** Of all the charms that gladden
Our life, in this sad world,
Dance is the most alluring
The best that can be found!

## SCENA VIII

## SCENE VIII

*Samuels, Tom, e i loro Aderenti in domino azzurro col cinto vermiglio. Renato nello stesso costume s' avanza lentamente.*

*Samuel, Tom, and their adherents, and Reinhart coming towards them.*

**SAM:** (*additando Renato a Tom*). Altro de' nostri è questo.
(*e fattosi presso a Ren. sottovoce.*) La morte!

**SAM:** (*pointing Reinhart to Tom.*) This is one of our friends..Death! (*softly.*)

**REN:** (*amaramente.*) Sì, la morte. Ma non verrà.

**REIN:** Yes; death!
But the Count won't come

**SAM E TOM:** Che parli?

**SAM, TOM:** Why; then?

**REN:** Qui l'aspettarlo è vano.

**REIN:** I'll tell you by and by!

**SAM E TOM:** Come? perchè?

**SAM:** Bad luck!
Shall we miss him for ever?

**TOM:** What shall we do?

REN: Vi basti saperlo altrove.

SAM: O sorte Ingannatrice!

TOM: (*fremente*) E sempre ne sfuggirà di mano!

REN: Parlate basso, alcuno lo sguardo a noi fermò.

SAM: E chi?

REN: Quello a sinistra, dal breve domino. (*ei si disperdono, ma Ren. viene inseguito da Oscar in maschera.*)

OSC: Più non ti lascio, o maschera; mal ti nascondi.

REN: Eh via. (*cansandolo.*)

OSC: Tu se' Renato. (*con vivacità.*)

REN: E Oscarre tu se'. (*spiccandogli la maschera.*)

OSC: Qual villania!

REN: Ma bravo, e ti par dunque convenienza questa. Che mentre il conte dorme, tu scivoli alla festa?

OSC: Il Conte è qui . . .

REN: (*trasalendo.*) Che! . . . dove?

OSC: (*voltandogli le spalle.*) Cercatelo da voi.

REN: (*con accento amichevole.*) Orsù—che dirmi almeno, del suo costume puoi?

OSC: Saper vorreste (*scherzando*)—Di che si veste, Quando l' è cosa Ch'ei vuol nascosa. Oscar lo sa—Ma nol dirà, Tra là, là, là Là, là, là, là. Pieno d' amore Mi balza il core, Ma pur discreto Serba il secreto. Nol rapirà Grado o beltà, Tra là, là, là—Là, là, là, là.

REN: (*raggiungendolo di nuovo.*) Via, che tu sai distinguere gli amici suoi.

OSC: V'alletta Interrogarlo, e forse celiar con esso un po'?

REN: Appunto.

OSC: E compromettere di poi chi ve l'ha detto?

REN: M' offendi, è confidenza che quanto importi so.

OSC: Vi preme assai . . .

REN: Degg'io di gravi cose ad esso, Pria che la notte inoltri, qui favellar. Su te Farò cader la colpa, se non mi fia concesso.

OSC: Dunque . . .

---

REIN: Speak softly, we are noticed!

TOM: By whom?

REIN: By the man on the left. (*they disperse, Oscar follows Reinhart.*)

OSC: I know you . . .

REIN: Well, then?

OSC: Yes, you are Reinhart!

REIN: Oscar! (*snatching away his mask.*)

OSC: This is an insult!

REIN: Well done, Oscar! While the Count is sleeping You know how to enjoy yourself!

OSC: The Count is here!

REIN: Is he? where?

OSC: That's not for me to tell . . .

REIN: Tell me at least something about his dress!

OSC: You wish to know a thing That must remain a secret! It would be very wrong For me to tell it out! Though I am very merry, Through love and cheering wine, Still I am not so thoughtless, As to betray the Count!

REIN: Am I not his best friend?

OSC: Well, then, What do you want from him?

REIN: I want to chat with him a little!

OSC: But, then, you may betray my confidence!

REIN: Am I a child to blab about such things?

OSC: The Count, then, may be angry . . .

REIN: I have important things to tell him, Before the morning comes! It will be your fault if I can't find him out!

OSC: Well then?

---

REN: Fai grazia a lui, se parli, e non a me.

OSC: (*più dappresso e rapidamente.*) Veste una cappa nera, con roseo nastro al petto. (*e fa per andarsene.*)

REN: Una parola ancora.

AME: Ah perchè qui! fuggite . . .

RIC: Sei quella dello scritto?

AME: La morte qui v' accerchia.

RIC: Non penetra nel mie Petto il terror.

AME: Fuggite, fuggite, o che trafitto Cadrete qui!

RIC: Rivelami il nome tuo.

AME: Gran Dio Nol posso.

RIC: E perchè piangi . . . mi supplichi atterrita? Oude, cotanta senti pietà della mia vita?

AME: (*tra singulti che svelano la sua voce naturale.*) Tutto, per essa, il mio sangue . . . tutto darei!

RIC: Ah, invan ti celi, Amelia: quell' angelo tu sei!

AME: T' amo, sì t' amo, e in lacrime A' piedi tuoi m' atterro, Ove t' anela incognito Della vendetta il ferro. Cadavere domani Sarai se qui rimani: Salvati, va, mi lascia, Fuggi dall' odio lor.

RIC: Sin che tu m' ami, Amelia, Non curo il fato mio, Non ho che te nell' anima, E l' universo oblio. Nè so temer la morte, Perchè di lei più forte E l' aura che m' inebria Del tuo celeste amor.

AME: Dunque verdermi vuoi D' affanno morta e di vergogna?

RIC: Salva. Ti vo'—domani e con Renato andrai . . .

AME: Dove?

RIC: Al natio tuo cielo.

AME: In Inghilterra!

RIC: Mi schianto il cor . . . ma partirai . . .

AME: Riccardo!

RIC: Amelia: anche una volta addio addio. L' ultima volta!

REN: (*lanciatosi inosservato fra loro, lo trafigge di pugnale*) E tu ricevi il mio!

RIC: Ahimè!

AME: Soccorso!

---

REIN: It is your duty to do it!

OSC: His dress is black, and a red ribbon's on his breast! (*trying to get off.*)

REIN: (*stopping him.*) But one word more!

OSC: Said enough!

AME: (*coming forward with the Count.*) Why did you come here? for God's sake, go off!

RICH: Are you the lady who sent me the letter?

AME: You'll be stabbed!

RICH: I am not afraid of death!

AME: Go—quick, quick, Or else you will be a dead man!

RICH: Tell me your name!

AME: I can't! Go off—

RICH: Why should you take so much pains on my account?

AME: (*crying.*) Alas, tarry no longer!

RICH: I know you now . . . you are Amelia!

AME: Ah! fly for God's sake: Ah, save, do save your life! You may be, next instant, In this room, a dead man!

RICH: So long as I'm the object, Amelia, of your affection! Ah! nothing from your presence Can make me basely fly!

AME: Will, then, you see me dying Through grief and shame? . . . .

RICH: Your honor shall be saved. You shall go to England with your husband!

AME: To England!

RICH: Yes, to England!

AME: Is that true!

RICH: Yes; though it may break my heart!

AME: Richard!

RICH: Amelia, farewell to you forever!

REIN: (*Stabbing him.*) This is my farewell!

RICH: O Lord!

AME: Help!

## Act III, Scene VIII

**OSC:** (*accorrendo a lui*) Oh ciel!

**TUTTI:** (*affollandosi intorno*). Ei trucidato

**ALCUNI:** Da chi?

**ALTRI:** Dov' è l'infame?

**OSC:** (*accennando a Renato*). Ec-col . . .
(*mentre lo circondano e gli strappano la maschera.*)

**TUTTI:** Renato!
Morte . . . abomino
Sul traditor!

**RIC:** No, no . . . lasciatelo.
Tu m' odi ancor.
(*a Renato.*)
(*e tratto il dispaccio, e fatto cenno a lui di accostarsi.*)
Ella è pura, in braccio a morte,
Te lo giuro, il ciel m' ascolta:
Io che amai la tua consorte
Rispettato ho il suo candor,
(*gli dà il foglia*)
A novello incarco asceso
Te con lei partir dovevi . . .
Io l' amai, ma volli illeso
Il tuo nome ed il suo cor!

**OSC:** What's the matter?

**ALL:** (*gathering around the Count*). Who has done this?

**SOME:** Who has done this?

**OTHERS:** Where is the traitor?

**OSC:** (*pointing out Reinhart.*)
There he is!

**ALL:** (*Snatching off his mask.*)
Reinhart.
Death to the villain! . . . .
Death to the ungrateful wretch!

**RICH:** Stop, let him alone!
(*To Reinhart.*)
Hear me, for the last time
Your wife is pure and innocent!
God knows I speak the truth!
It is true that I have loved her,
But she has done no wrong!
(*Gives him a paper.*)
To avoid further temptation,
To send you, I had resolved,
Along with her, to England
To fill an honored post!

**REN:** Ciel, che feci! e che m'aspetta
Esecrato sulla terra! . . .
Di qual sangue e qual vendetta
M'assetò l'infausto error!

**AME:** O rimorsi dell'amore
Che divorano il mio core,
Fra un colpevole che sanguina
E la vittima che muor!

**OSC:** O dolor senza misura
O terribile sventura!
La sua fronte è tutta rorida
Già dell'ultimo sudor!

**RIC:** Grazia a ognun: signor qui sono:
Tutti assolve il mio perdono.

**CORO:** Cor si grande e generoso
Tu ci serba, o Dio pietoso:
Raggio in terra a noi miserrimi
È del tuo celeste amor!

**RIC:** Addio per sempre, o figli miei . . . per sempre
Addio . . . diletta America . . . (*cade e spira.*)

**AME:** Esso muore!

**OSC:** Qual anima passò!

**TUTTI:** Notte d'orrore!

*Fine.*

**REIN:** What crime have I committed,
Blinded by false suspicions!
Ah! what a fatal rashness
Has pushed me to this act?

**AME:** Oh! what a horrid destiny
Has darkened my career!
No end shall have my sorrow,
Except when in the grave!

**OSC:** What a horrible misfortune
Is this that has befallen
To the most noble hero
That can be found on earth.

**RICH:** Before I die I forgive all,—
Let none be punished on my account.

**CHORUS:** Great God, grant assistance
To our beloved Chief!
Restore his health, if possible,
Grant him a longer life!!!

**RICH:** Farewell, my dear, beloved friends,
I die!
(*He expires.*)

**AME:** He is dead!

**OSC:** What noble soul!

**ALL:** What crime!!

*The End.*

# La Forza del Destino (1862)

## The Force of Destiny

MUSIC BY GIUSEPPE VERDI ■ LIBRETTO BY FRANCESCO MARIA PIAVE

La Forza del Destino is based on Don Alvaro o la Fuerza del Sino by Angel de Saavedra, Duke of Rivas. This four-act opera, set to a libretto by Francesco Maria Piave, premiered at the Imperial Theatre in St. Petersburg on November 10, 1862. Don Alvaro is in love with Donna Leonora, but her father, the Marquis, will not permit his daughter to marry Alvaro, a "half-caste." Alvaro and Leonora attempt to elope, but their escape is thwarted. In a confrontation with the Marquis, Alvaro defends his beloved. Alvaro throws his pistol down in frustration and it accidentally goes off, killing the Marquis, who curses his daughter before he dies. On her search for Alvaro, Leonora, disguised as a young boy, encounters her brother, Don Carlo, disguised as a student, who swears he will find her and murder Alvaro. Leonora flees to the monastery of the Madonna of the Angels, where Father Superior lets her live as a hermit in a nearby mountain cave protected by a holy curse. War between Napoleon and Spain breaks out in Italy. Sure that Leonora must have died, Don Alvaro enlists in the Spanish army using fake identification. During a battle he saves the life of Carlo, also fighting under a false name. They pledge eternal brotherhood. Alvaro, wounded, gives Carlo an envelope, instructing him to destroy it without looking inside. The letter contains Leonora's portrait, thus Carlo discovers Alvaro's identity. He challenges him to a duel once his wound has healed, but a camp patrol separates them. At the monastery, the needy, about to receive a free meal, compare Fra Melitone to Father Raffaele, who is really Alvaro. Carlo finds him and challenges him once more. Alvaro wounds his enemy and goes to the hermit in the cave—none other than Leonora—to be absolved for his sin. Alvaro recognizes Leonora and confesses that the dying man is her brother. Carlo stabs her as she administers his last rites; the Father Superior absolves her and she dies in Alvaro's arms.

---

■ **ATTO I**

### SCENA I

*Siviglia.—Una sala, tappezzata di damasco, con ritratti di famiglia, ed arme gentilizie, addobbata nello stile del secolo 18.0 pero in cattivo stato. Di fronte due finestre; quella a sinistra chiusa l'altra a destra aperta e praticabile, dalla quale si vede un cielo purissimo, illuminato dalla Luna, e cime d'alberi. Tra le finestre e un grande armadio chiuso, contenente vesti blancherie, ecc. Ognuna delle pareti laterali ha due porte. La prima a destra della spettatore e la comune; la seconda mette alla stanza di Curra. A sinistra in fondo e l'appartamento del Marchese; piu presso al proscenio quello di Leonora. A mezza scena, alquanto a sinistra, e un tavolino coperto da tappeto di damasco, e sopra il medesimo una chitarra, vasi di fiori, due candelabri d'argento accesi con paralumi, sola luce che schiarira la sala. Un seggiolone presso il tavolino; un mobile con sopra un oriuolo fra le due porte a destra; altro mobile sopra il quale e il ritratto, tutta figura, del Marchese, appoggiato all parete sinistra. La sal sara parapettata.*

■ **ACT I**

### SCENE I

*Seville.—A room, hung with damask, family portraits, and arms of nobility, furnished in the style of the 18th century, all, however, in shabby condition. Two windows face the audience; that on the left is closed, that on the right open and practicable, from which is seen a clear sky, and the tops of trees with a bright moonlight. Between the windows a large wardrobe, containing clothes, etc. Each side has two doors. The first to the right of the spectator is the common door; the second leads to Curra's room. On the left side farthest off, is the apartment of the Marquis; that nearest the proscenium leads to Leonora's room. Halfway, a little to the left, is a table with a damask cover, and on it a guitar, vases of flowers, and two lighted silver candlesticks with shades, the only light in the room. A large chair near the table; a piece of furniture with a clock on it between the two doors on the right; other furniture on the left, above which, hung against the wall, is the full-length portrait of the Marquis. The room is entirely enclosed.*

*Il Marchese di Calatrava, con lume in mano, sta congedandosi da Donna Leonora preoccupata. Curra viene dalla sinistra.*

**MARCHESE:** (*Abbracciandola con affetto.*) Buena notte, mia figlia! Addio, diletta!
Aperto ancora è quel verone!
(*Va a chiuderlo.*)

**LEONORA:** (Oh angoscia!)

**MARCHESE:** Nulla dice il tuo amor? Perchè si trista?
(*Tornando a lei.*)

**LEONORA:** Padre—Signor—

**MARCHESE:** La pura aura de' campi
Calma la tuo cor donova;
Fuggisti lo straniero di te indegno
A me lascia la cura
Dell' avvenir. Nel padre tuo confida,
Che t'ama tanto.

**LEONORA:** Ah, padre!

**MARCHESE:** Ebben, che t'ange?
Non pianger, io t'adoro!

**LEONORA:** (Oh, mio rimorso!)

**MARCHESE:** Ti lascio.

**LEONORA:** (*Gettandosi con effusione tra le braccia del padre.*) Ah, padre mio!

**MARCHESE:** Ti benedica il cielo! Addio!

*Marquis of Calatrava, with a light in his hand is taking leave of Donna Leonora, who is thoughtful. Curra comes from the left.*

**MARCHESE:** (*Embracing her affectionately.*) Goodnight, my child! Adieu, my dear one!
That balcony window still open?
(*goes and shuts it.*)

**LEONORA:** (Oh, anguish!)

**MARCHESE:** Not a word of love? Why so sad?
(*turning to her.*)

**LEONORA:** Father—sir—

**MARCHESE:** The pure air of the fields
Has brought peace to your heart,
You have left a stranger unworthy of you,
And leave the care
Of your future to me. Confide in your father
Who loves you so dearly.

**LEONORA:** Ah, my father!

**MARCHESE:** What disturbs you?
Do not weep—I love you dearly.

**LEONORA:** (Oh, what remorse!)

**MARCHESE:** I leave you.

**LEONORA:** (*Throwing herself with transport into his arms.*) Ah, dearest father!

**MARCHESE:** Heaven bless you! Adieu!

## Act I, Scene I

**LEONORA:** Addio!
(*Il Marches bacia, riprende il lume, e va nelle sue stanze.*)

**LEONORA:** Adieu!
(*the Marquis kisses her, takes up a light, and goes to his room.*)

### SCENA II

*Curra segue il Marchese, chiude la porta ond' e uscito, e riviene a Leonora abbandonatasi sul seggiolone piangente.*

**CURRA:** Temea restasse qui fino a domani!
Si riapra il veron.
(*Eseguisece.*)
Tutto s'appronti. E andiamo.
(*Toglie dall' armadio un sacco da notte in cui ripone biancherie e vesti.*)

**LEONORA:** E si amoroso padre avverso
Fia tanto a' voti miei?
No, no, decidermi non so.

**CURRA:** (*Affaccendata.*) Che dite?

**LEONORA:** Quegli accenti nel cor come pugnalia
Scendevanmi. Se ancor restava, appreso
Il ver gli avrei.

**CURRA:** (*Smette il lavoro.*) Domani allor nel sangue
Suo saria don Alvaro,
Od a Siviglia prigioniero, e forse
Al patibol poi—

**LEONORA:** Taci!

**CURRA:** E tutto puesto
Perch' egli volle amar chi non l'amava.

**LEONORA:** Io non amarlo! Tu ben sai s'io l'ami!
Patria, famiglia, padre,
Per lui non abbandono!
Ahi troppo!—troppo sventurata sono!
Me pellegrina ed orfana
Lungi dal natio nido,
Un fato inesorabile
Trascina a stranio lido,
Colmo di triste immagini,
Da' suoi rimorsi affranto
E il cor di questa misera
Dannato a eterno pianto.
Ti lascio, ahimè, con lacrime,
Dolce mia terra!—Addio!
Ahimè, non avrà termine
Si gran dolore!—Addio!

**CURRA:** M'aiuti, signorina—
Più presto andrem.

**LEONORA:** S' ei non giungesse?
(*Guarda l'orologie.*)
E tardi.
Mezzanotte è suonata!
(*Contenta.*)
Ah no, più non verrà!

**CURRA:** Quale romore!
Calpestio di cavelli!

**LEONORA:** (*Corre al verone.*) E desso!

### SCENE II

*Curra follows the Marquis, closes the door, at which he went out, and returns to Leonora, who has thrown herself in the chair.*

**CURRA:** I thought he would stay till daylight!
Let us re-open the balcony.
(*open its.*)
Prepare everything and let us go.
(*takes traveling bag from the wardrobe, and fills it with linen and clothes.*)

**LEONORA:** Can so fond a father
Oppose my dearest wishes?
No, no, I cannot leave.

**CURRA:** (*Very busy.*) What do you say?

**LEONORA:** His loving tones struck like a dagger
To my soul. Had he remained,
I would have spoken the truth.

**CURRA:** (*Leaving off work.*) Then tomorrow
Don Alvaro would lie weltering in his blood,
Or be a prisoner in Seville,
And perhaps on the scaffold—

**LEONORA:** Be silent!

**CURRA:** And all because he loves one
Who does not return his love.

**LEONORA:** Does not return it?
Well you know I love him!
Do I not abandon Country, family, father for him?
Ah me!—I am indeed unhappy!
A friendless wanderer,
Far from my native land!
An inexorable fate
Drags me to a foreign country,
Overwhelmed in dire woe,
Crushed with deep remorse,
My miserable spirit
Is condemned to constant grief.
With tears, alas! I leave you,
My own sweet native land.—Adieu!
This bitter woe will never, never end!
Adieu!

**CURRA:** Help me, signora—
We shall be ready soon.

**LEONORA:** If he should not come?
(*looks at the clock.*)
It is late—
Midnight has struck!
(*contentedly.*)
Ah no, he will not come.

**CURRA:** What noise is that?
It is the tread of horses!

**LEONORA:** (*Running to balcony.*) It is he!

**CURRA:** Era impossibil
Ch' ei non venisse!

**LEONORA:** Ciel!

**CURRA:** Bando al timore.

**CURRA:** It was impossible
That he should fail to come.

**LEONORA:** Heavens!

**CURRA:** Away with fear.

### SCENA III

*Detti.—Don Alvaro senza mantello, con giustacuore a maniche larghe, e sopra una giubetta da Majo, rete sul capo, stivali, speroni, entra dal verone e si getta tra le braccia de Leonora.*

**ALVARO:** Ah, per sempre, o mio bell' angelo,
Ne congiunse il cielo adesso
L'universo in questo amplesso
Con me veggo giubilar.

**LEONORA:** Don Alvaro!

**ALVARO:** Ciel, che t'agita?

**LEONORA:** Presso è il giorno.

**ALVARO:** Da lung' ora
Mille inciampi tua dimora
M'han vietato penetrar;
Ma d' amor si puro e santo
Nulla opporsi può all' incanto,
E Dio stesso il nostro palpito
In letizia tramutò.
(*A Curra.*)
Quelle vesti dal verone
Getta.

**LEONORA:** (*A Curra.*) Arresta.

**ALVARO:** (*A Curra.*) No, no!
(*A Leonora.*)
Seguimi;
Lascia omai la tua prigiane.

**LEONORA:** Ciel! risolvermi non so!

**ALVARO:** Pronti destrieri di già ne attendono;
Un sacerdote ne aspetta all' ara!
Vieni, d'amore in sen ripara
Che Dio dal cielo benedirà!
E quando il sole, nume dell' India,
Di mia regale stirpe signore,
Il mondo innondi del suo splendore,
Sposi, oh diletta, ne troverà.

**LEONORA:** E tarda l' ora.

**ALVARO:** (*A Curra.*) Su via t' affretta!

**LEONORA:** Ancor sospendi!

**ALVARO:** Eleonora!

**LEONORA:** Diman.

**ALVARO:** Che parli?

**LEONORA:** Ten prego aspetta!

**ALVARO:** (*Assai turbato.*) Diman.

**LEONORA:** Domani si partirà.
Anco una volta il padre, veder desio;
E tu contento, gli è ver, ne sei?
Sì perchè m'ami—
(*Si confonde.*)
Nè opporti dèi—

### SCENE III

*The same,—Don Alvaro, without a cloak, wearing a tight vest, with large sleeves and a slashed doublet, a net on his head, boots and spurs, he enters through the balcony, and throws himself into Leonora's arms.*

**ALVARO:** Ah, my lovely angel,
Heaven now unites us forever!
All the universe is glad
With me, in this embrace.

**LEONORA:** Don Alvaro!

**ALVARO:** Oh Heaven, why are you agitated?

**LEONORA:** The dawn is near.

**ALVARO:** For a long time
Many obstacles kept me
From reaching your dwelling,
But nothing can stop the power
Of a love so pure and holy,
And Heaven itself
Changes our fears to contentment.
(*to Curra.*)
Throw
Those vestments from the balcony.

**LEONORA:** (*To Curra.*) Stay.

**ALVARO:** (*To Curra.*) No, no!
(*to Leonora.*)
Follow me.
Leave your prison now forever.

**LEONORA:** Oh Heaven! I cannot decide!

**ALVARO:** Swift steeds are waiting,
A priest attends at the altar!
Come, find shelter in the love
Which Heaven will richly bless.
And when the sun, the god of India,
Sire of my royal race
Shall flood the earth with splendor,
Oh, beloved! it will find us united.

**LEONORA:** The hour is late.

**ALVARO:** (*To Curra.*) Away—make haste!

**LEONORA:** (*To Curra.*) Wait awhile!

**ALVARO:** Eleonora!

**LEONORA:** Tomorrow.

**ALVARO:** What did you say?

**LEONORA:** I pray you, wait!

**ALVARO:** (*Much disturbed.*) Tomorrow.

**LEONORA:** Tomorrow we will go.
Once more
I desire to see my father!
You are willing—is it not so?
Yes, for you love me, and will not refuse.
I too, you know, love you!

Oh anch'io, tu il sai—t' amo io tanto!
Ne son felice! oh cielo, quanto!
Gonfio de gioia ho il cor! Restiam!
Sì, Don Alvaro, io t'amo, io t' amo!
(*Piange.*)

ALVARO: Gonfio hai di gioia il core—e lagrimi!
Come un sepolcro tua mano è gelida!
Tutto comprendo—tutto, signora.

LEONORA: Alvaro!—Alvaro!

ALVARO: Eleonora!
(*Lunga pausa.*)
Saprò soffrire io solo. Tolga Iddio
Che i passi miei per debolezza segua—
Sciolgo i tuoi giuri. Le nuziali tede
Sarebbero per noi segnal di morte,
Se tu, com' io non m' ami—se pentita—

LEONORA: Son tua, son tua col core e colla vita!
Ah! seguirti fino agl'ultimi
Confini della terra;
Con te sfidarimpavida
Di rio destin la guerra;
Mi fia perenne gaudio
D'eterea volutà.
Ti seguo, andiam dividerci,
Il fato, no, no, non potra.

ALVARO: Sospiro, luce ed anima
Di questo cor che t' ama;
Finchè mi batta un palpito,
Far paga ogni tua brama
Il solo ed immutabile
Desio per me sarà.
Mi segui! Andiam, dividerci
Il mondo non potrà.
(*S'avvicinano al verone, quando ad un tratto si sente a sinistra un aprire e chiudere di porte.*)

LEONORA: Quale rumor!

CURRA: (*Ascoltando.*) Ascendono le scale!

ALVARO: Presto, partiamo!

LEONORA: E tardi.

ALVARO: Allor di calma E duopo.

CURRA: Vergin santa!

LEONORA: (*A Alvaro.*) Colà t' ascondi!

ALVARO: No. Degg' io difenderti.
(*Traendo una pistola.*)

LEONORA: Ripon quell' arma—contro al genitore Vorresti?

ALVARO: No, contro me stesso.
(*Ripone la pistola.*)

LEONORA: Orrore!

---

(*confusedly.*)
Am I not happy? O heaven!
How my heart swells with joy!—Let us wait!
Yes, Alvaro, I love you! I love you!
(*weeps.*)

ALVARO: Your heart swells with joy—then why these tears?
Your hand is cold as death!
I understand all, signora—all!

LEONORA: Alvaro!—Alvaro!

ALVARO: Eleonora!
(*a long pause.*)
I can suffer alone. Heaven forbid
That weakly you should follow me—
I absolve your vows. The nuptial tie
Would be the stroke of death for us,
If you love not as I do—if, repenting—

LEONORA: I am yours! Yours with heart and soul!
Ah! I'll follow ever in your path
To earth's far confines winging,
And boldly I defy with you
The terrors war is bringing,
I'll share all dangers by your side,
With love and joy elate;
I'll follow you whatever—may betide,
We win—a happy fate.

ALVARO: Hope, light and life
Of the heart that adores you!
Until my pulse beats no more
My sole desire will be
To meet your every wish,
To cherish you for always
Follow me—let us go!
The world has no power to part us.
(*they approach the balcony when suddenly the opening and shutting of a door is heard.*)

LEONORA: What is that noise?

CURRA: (*Listening.*) Someone is coming upstairs!

ALVARO: Quick! Let us go!

LEONORA: Too late!

ALVARO: Well, then, We must be calm and firm.

CURRA: Holy Virgin!

LEONORA: (*To Alvaro.*) Conceal yourself there!

ALVARO: No. I must defend you.
(*drawing out a pistol.*)

LEONORA: Put back that weapon—
Would you use it against my father?

ALVARO: No, against myself.
(*replaces the pistol.*)

LEONORA: Horrible!

---

## SCENA IV

*Dopo vari colpi apresi con istrepito la porta del fondo a sinsitra, ed il Marchese di Calatrava entra infuriato brandendo una spada e seguito da due servi con lume.*

MARCHESE: Vil seduttor!—infame figlia!

LEONORA: (*Correndo a' suoi piedi.*) No, padre mio!

MARCHESE: Più non le sono.
(*La respinge.*)

ALVARO: (*Al Marchese*) Il solo colpevole son io
Ferite, vendicatevi!
(*Presentandogli l' petto.*)

MARCHESE: (*Al Alvaro.*) No la condotta vostra
Da troppo abbietta origine uscito vi dimostra.

ALVARO: Signor Marchese!
(*Risentito.*)

MARCHESE: (*A Leonora.*) Scostati—
(*Ai Servia.*)
S' arresti l' empio!

ALVARO: (*Cavando nuovamente la pistola*) Guai
Se alcun di voi si move.
(*Ai Servi, che retrocedono.*)

LEONORA: (*Currendo a lui.*) Alvaro, oh ciel, che fai!

ALVARO: (*Al Marchese.*) Cedo a voi sol—ferite!

MARCHESE: Morir per mano mia!
Per mano del cranefice tal vita estinta fia.

ALVARO: Signor di Calatrava,
Pura siccome gli angeli è vostra figlia—
Il giuro—reo son io solo. Il dubbio
Che l' ardir mio qui desta, si tolga colla vita.
Eccomi inerme.
(*Getta la pistola, che percuote al suolo, scarica il colpo e ferisce mortalmente il Marchese.*)

MARCHESE: Io muoio!

ALVARO: (*Disperato.*) Arma funesta!

LEONORA: (*Correndo a' piedi del padre.*) Aita!

MARCHESE: (*A Leonora*) Lungi da me—
Contamina tua vista la mia morte!

LEONORA: Padre!

MARCHESE: Ti maledico!
(*Cade tra le braccia dei Servi.*)

LEONORA: Cielo pietade!

---

## SCENE IV

*After repeated blows the door at the back, on the left, is burst open, and the Marquis of Calatrava enters, enraged. Sword in hand, and followed by two servants with lights.*

MARCHESE: Vile seducer!—shameless daughter!

LEONORA: (*Rushing to his feet.*) No, father, no.

MARCHESE: I am your father no longer.
(*repulsing her.*)

ALVARO: (*To the Marquis.*) I alone am guilty.
Strike!—avenge yourself!
(*presenting himself.*)

MARCHESE: (*To Alvaro.*) No, your conduct
Shows you to be of origin too low.

ALVARO: Marquis!
(*excitedly.*)

MARCHESE: (*To Leonora.*) Stand aside—
(*to the Servants.*)
Seize the wretch!

ALVARO: (*Again taking out his pistol.*) Approach me, if you dare!
(*to the Servants, who retire.*)

LEONORA: (*Running to him.*) Alvaro, what madness is this?

ALVARO: (*To the Marquis.*) I yield to you alone—strike!

MARCHESE: You'll not die by my hand
So base a life belongs only to the executioner.

ALVARO: Signor de Calatrava, your child
Is innocent as an angel;
I alone am guilty.
Let the doubt which my rashness has raised
Be dispelled with my life. Behold me unarmed.
(*throws away the pistol, which in falling, goes off, and kills the Marquis.*)

MARCHESE: I am dying!

ALVARO: (*In despair.*) Ill-fated weapon!

LEONORA: (*Rushing to her father.*) Help!

MARCHESE: (*To Leonora.*) Be-gone!
Your presence disgraces me in death!

LEONORA: Father!

MARCHESE: My curse upon you!
(*falls into the Servants' arms.*)

LEONORA: Have mercy, kind Heaven!

ALVARO: Oh sorte!
(*I Servi portano il Marchese alle sue stanze, mentre Don Alvaro trae seco verso il verone la sventurata Leonora. Cade la tela.*)

FINE DELL'ATTO PRIMO.

# ■ ATTO II

## SCENA I

*Villaggio d'Hornachuelos e vicinanze.— Grande cucina d'una Osteria a pian terreno. A sinistra, e la porta d'ingresso che da sulla via; di fronte una finestra ed un credenzone con piatti, ecc. A destra, in fonda un gran focolare ardente con varie pentole; piu vicino alle bocca-scena breve scaletta che mette ad una stanza, la cui porta e praticabile. Da un lato gran tavola apparecchiata con sopra una lucerna accesa. L'Oste e l'Ostessa che non parlano, sono affaccendati ad ammanir la cena. L'Alcade e seduto presso al foco; uno Studente presso la tavola. Alquanti Mulattieri, fra quali Mastro Trabuco, ch'e al dinanzi sopra un suo basto. Due Contadini, due Contadine, la Serva, ed un Mulatierre, ballano la Seguidilla. Sopra altra tavola, vino, bicchieri fiaschi, una bottiglia d'acquavite.*

*L'Alcade, uno Studente, Mastro Trabuco, Mulattieri, Paesani Famigli, Parsane ecc. A tempo Leonora in vesti virile.*

CORO: Holo, hola, hola!
Ben giungi, o mulattier,
La notte a riposar.
Hola, hola, hola!
Qui devi col bicchier
Le forze ritemprar!
(*L'Ostessa mette sulla tavola una grande zuppiera.*)

ALCADE: La cena è pronta.
(*Sedendosi alla mensa.*)

TUTTI: (*Prenendo posto presso la tavolo.*) A cena, a cena!

STUDENTE: (*Frattanto sul d'avanti dice.*) (Ricerco invan la suora e il eduttore.) Perfidi!

CORO: (*All'Alcade.*) Voi la mensa benedite?

ALCADE: Può farlo il Licenziato.

STUDENTE: Di buon grado. Benedetto
E il pane che il Padre del ciel ci manda.

TUTTI: (*Sedendo.*) Cosi sia.

---

ALVARO: O cruel fate!
(*the Servants bear the Marquis to his apartments, while Don Alvaro drags the unhappy Leonora towards the balcony. The Curtain falls.*)

END OF THE FIRST ACT.

# ■ ACT II

## SCENE I

*The Village of Hornachuelos and neighborhood. A large kitchen on the groundfloor of an Inn. On the left, the entrance-door leading to the road, facing the audience; a window, and a large dresser, with plates, etc. On the right, at the back, a large fireplace, with cauldrons, etc., nearer the proscenium, a short staircase, leading to a room which has a practicable door. On one side a large table, laid out, and on it a lighted lamp. The Host and Hostess, who do not speak, are busy preparing the supper. The Alcade is seated near the fire; a Student is seated near the table. Some Muleteers, amongst others Master Trabuco, who is in front, leaning on his pack saddle. Two male and two female Peasants, the female Servant and a Muleteer dance the Seguidilla. On another table, wine, glasses, flasks, and a bottle of brandy.*

*The Alcade, A Student, Master Trabuco, Muleteers, Peasants Attendants, Female Peasants, etc. Later Leonora, in male attire.*

CHORUS: Hurrah, hurrah, hurrah!
Now welcome, O muleteer,
Who comes to pass the night;
Hurrah, hurrah, hurrah!
Here is the brimming cup,
Your strength you can restore.
(*the Hostess places a large soup tureen on the table.*)

ALCADE: The supper is ready.
(*seating himself at table.*)

ALL: (*Taking their places at table.*) To supper, to supper!

STUDENT: (*In the foreground.*) I seek in vain my sister and her betrayer.
The ingrates!

CHORUS: (*To the Alcade.*) Will you not ask a blessing?

ALCADE: The Licentiate can do it.

STUDENT: With all my heart.
Blessed be
The bread that Heaven sends us from above.

ALL: (*Seated.*) Amen.

---

LEONORA: (*Presentandosi alla potra della stanza a destra, che terra socchiusa*) (Che vedo!—mio fratello!)
(*Si ritira.*)
(*L'Ostessa avra gia distribuito il riso e siede cogli altri. Inseguito e servito altro piatto. Trabuco e in disparte, sempre appoggiato al suo basto.*)

ALCADE: (*Assaggiando.*) Buono.

STUDENTE: (*Mangiando.*) Eccellente!

MULATTIERI: Par che dica mangiami.

STUDENTE: (*All'Ostessa.*) Tu das epulis accumbere divum.

ALCADE: Non sa Latino ma cucina bene.

STUDENTE: Viva l'Otessa!

TUTTI: Evviva!

STUDENTE: Non vien Mastro Trabuco?

TRABUCO: E Venerdi.

STUDENTE: Digiuna?

TRABUCO: Appunto.

STUDENTE: E quella personcina con lei guinta?

## SCENA II

*Detti, e Preziosilla, ch' entra saltellando.*

PREZIOSILLA: Viva la guerra!

TUTTI: Preziosilla!—Brava! Brava!

STUDENTE: Qui, presso a me.

TUTTI: Tu la ventura.
Dirne potrai.

PREZIOSILLA: Chi brama far fortuna?

TUTTI: Tutti il vogliam.

PREZIOSILLA: Correte allor soldati.
In Italis, dov' è rotta la guerra
Contro al Tedesco.

TUTTI: Morte
Ai Tedeschi!

PREZIOSILLA: Flagel d' Italia eterno
E de' figliuoli suoi.

TUTTI: Tutti v' andremo.

PREZIOSILLA: Ed io sarò con voi.

PREZIOSILLA ED CORO: Al suon del tamburo,
Al brio del corsiero,
Al nugolo azzurro,
Del bronzo guerrier!
Dei campi al susurro
S'esalta il pensier!
E bella la guerra,
E bella la guerra!
Evviva la guerra, evviva!
E solo obbliato
Da vile chi muore;
Al bravo soldato

---

LEONORA: (*Appearing at the door of the room on the right, which she keeps half closed.*) What do I see!—my brother!
(*she retires.*)
(*the Hostess has already distributed the rice, and sits down with the others. Other dishes are served up. Trabuco on one side leans on his pack-saddle.*)

ALCADE: (*Tasting.*) Capital!

STUDENT: (*Eating*) Excellent!

MULETEER: It seems to say, 'Come, eat me.'

STUDENT: (*To the Hostess.*) Tu das epulis accumbere divum.

ALCADE: She does not know Latin, but she cooks well.

STUDENT: Long live the Hostess!

ALL: Hurrah!

STUDENT: Does Master Trabuco not come to supper?

TRABUCO: It is Friday.

STUDENT: Oh, you are fasting?

TRABUCO: Just so.

STUDENT: And the little person who came with you?

## SCENE II

*The same, enter Preziosilla, dancing.*

PREZIOSILLA: Success to war!

ALL: Preziosilla!—Bravo! Bravo!

STUDENT: Here, sit by me.

ALL: You will be able
To tell us our fortunes.

PREZIOSILLA: Who wishes to make his fortune?

ALL: Everyone wishes it.

PREZIOSILLA: Haste, then, to Italy, as soldiers,
Where war has broken out
Against the Germans.

ALL: Death
To the Germans!

PREZIOSILLA: They are the eternal scourge
Of Italy and her sons.

ALL: We will all go.

PREZIOSILLA: And I shall be with you.

PREZIOSILLA and CHORUS: The drum gaily beating
The horses swift fleeting,
And volleys repeating
Give glory to war!
The busy sounds about the camp
Drive anxious thought afar!
In battle is glory,
In battle is glory!
Hurrah,—then, hurrah, hurrah—hurrah!
No coward can ever
Make a noble endeavor,

Al veto valor
E premio serbato
Di gloria d'onór!
Se vieni, fratello,
Sarai caporale,
E tu collonnello,
E tu generale
Il dio fur fantello dall' arco immortale
Farodi cappello
Al bravo uffizial.

STUDENTE: E che riserbasi
Allo studente?
(*Le presenta la mano.*)

PREZIOSILLA: (*Osservando.*) O
tu miserrime
Vicende avrai.

STUDENTE: Che di'?

PREZIOSILLA: (*Fissandolo.*)
Non mente
Il labbro mai—
Ma a te—carissimo,
Non presto fè
(*Poi sotto voce.*)
Non sei studenti;
Non dirò niente,
Ma, gnaffe, a me,
Non se la fa,—
No per mai fè
Tral la la là!

## SCENA III

*Detti, e Pellegrini, che passao da
furoi.*

VOCI IE: (*Lontane.*) Ah, pietade o
Signor!

VOCI 2E: Pieta di noi.

VOCI IE: Sii clemente, o Signor!

VOCI 2E: Pietà di noi.

VOCI IE: (*Piu vicine.*) Te lodiamo,
o Signor!

VOCI 2E: Pietà di noi.

VOCI IE: Deh, pietade, o Signor!

VOCI 2E: Pietà di noi.

TUTTI: Chi sono?
(*Alzandosi e scoprendosi.*)

ALCADE: Pellegrini,
Che vanno al giubileo.

LEONORA: (*Ricomparendo agitatissima sulla stessa porta.*) Fuggir potessi.

CORO: Che passino attendiamo.

ALCADE: Ebben, preghiam noi
pure.

CORO: Si preghiamo.

TUTTI: (*Lasciando la mensa s'inginocchiano.*) Suo noi concordi e
supplici,
Stendi la man, Signore;
Dall' infernal malore
Ne salvi tua pietà.

But heroes in story
Will be remembered:
To them be the glory
By fortune's decree!
Good luck shall overtake you,
Make you a corporal,
And you'll take a colonel's place,
You'll be a general;
Be brave in the battles
When musketry rattles,
And the foe will flee forth in disorder.

STUDENT: And
What is reserved for the student?
(*holding out his hand.*)

PREZIOSILLA: (*Observing him*)
Miserable man,
Sorrow shortly will find you.

STUDENT: What do you say?

PREZIOSILLA: (*Earnestly*)
My lips
Never utter falsehoods,
But on you, dear sir,
I don't much rely.
(*In an undertone.*)
You are no student.
I'll say nothing,
But with me,
The ruse has failed,
By my faith!
Tra la la la!

## SCENE III

*The same, and Pilgrims, passing
outside.*

1st VOICE: (*In the distance.*) Pardon, gracious Heaven.

2nd VOICE: Have pity on us.

1st VOICE: Grant us grace!

2nd VOICE: Have pity on us.

1st VOICE: (*Nearer.*) We praise
you, O Heaven!

2nd VOICE: Have pity on us.

1st VOICE: We thank you, O Heaven!

2nd VOICE: Have pity on us.

ALL: Who are these people?
(*raising and showing themselves.*)

ALCADE: They are Pilgrims,
Who are going to the jubilee.

LEONORA: (*Appearing, in great
agitation, at the same door.*) If I
could only escape!

CHORUS: Let us wait till they pass.

ALCADE: And let us also pray.

CHORUS: Yes, let us pray.

ALL: (*Leaving the table and kneeling down.*) We implore you,
Extend your hand over us, O Lord,
From the power of ill
Let your mercy save us.
And mercy protect us.

LEONORA: (Ah, da un fratello salvami
Che anela il sangue mio;
Se tu nol vuoi, gran Dio,
Nessun mi salverà!)
(*Rientra nella stanza chiudendone la porta. Tutti riprendono i
loro posti. Si passano un fiasco.*)

STUDENTE: Viva la buona compagnia!

TUTTI: Viva!

STUDENTE: Salute qui, l' eterna
gloria poi!
(*Alzando il bicchiere*)

TUTTI: Così sia.
(*Fanno altrettanto.*)

STUDENTE: Già cogli angioli, Trabuco?

TRABUCO: E che?—con questo inferno?

STUDENTE: E quella personcina
con lei giunta,
Venne pel giubileo?

TRABUCO: Nol so.

STUDENTE: Per altro.
E gallo, oppur gallina?

TRABUCO: De; forastier non bado
che al danaro.

STUDENTE: Molto prudente!
(*Poi all' Alcade.*)
Ed ella
Che giungere la vide—perchè a
cena.
Non vien?

ALCADE: L'ignoro.

STUDENTE: Dissero chiedesse
Acqua ed aceto.—Ah ah!—per rinfrescarsi.

ALCADE: Sara.

STUDENTE: E ver ch' è gentile, e
senza barba?

ALCADE: Non so nulla.

STUDENTE: (*Parlar non vuol!*) Ancora
(*To Trabuco.*)
A lei.
Stava sul mulo,
Seduta o a cavalcioni?

TRABUCO: (*Impazientato.*) Che
noia!

STUDENTE: Onde veniva?

TRABUCO: So che andrè, presto o
tardi, in Paradiso.

STUDENTE: Perchè?

TRABUCO: (*Alzandosi.*) Ella il
purgatorio.
Mi fa soffrir.

STUDENTE: Or dove va?

TRABUCO: In istalla,
Dormir colle mie mule,
Che non san di Latino,
Nè sono Baccellieri.
(*Prendre il suo basto e parte.*)

LEONORA: Ah, save me from a
brother,
Who thirsts for my blood;
Your hand alone, O Lord,
Can save me from his wrath.
(*re-enters the room and shuts the
door. All reseat themselves and
pass the bottle.*)

STUDENT: Long live this goodly
company.

ALL: Hurrah!

STUDENT: Health here, and happiness hereafter!
(*raises the goblet.*)

ALL: So be it.
(*they do the same.*)

STUDENT: Already dreaming, Trabuco?

TRABUCO: What? in this uproar?

STUDENT: And the little person
who came with you,
does she go to the Jubilee?

TRABUCO: I do not know.

STUDENT: By the by,
Is it man or woman?

TRABUCO: With strangers, I only
think of the money.

STUDENT: Most prudent!
(*to the Alcade*)
And you,
Who saw her arrive, answer
Why she doesn't come to supper?

ALCADE: I cannot tell.

STUDENT: They say she asked—ha
ha!—
For vinegar and water, as refreshment.

ALCADE: Maybe.

STUDENT: Is it true that she is pretty, and has no beard?

ALCADE: I really do not know.

STUDENT: (*He will not speak.*)
(*to Trabuco.*)
Once more,
Was she seated on the mule,
Or rode astride?

TRABUCO: (*Impatiently.*) What
vexation!

STUDENT: Where did she come
from?

TRABUCO: I know I shall go, sooner or later, to Paradise.

STUDENT: Why?

TRABUCO: (*Rising.*) Because you
make me
Suffer purgatory here.

STUDENT: Where are you going
now?

TRABUCO: To the stable,
To sleep with my mules,
Who don't know Latin,
And are not Bachelors of Arts.
(*takes his pack-saddle and goes.*)

## SCENA IV

*I Suddetti e meno Mastro Trabuco.*

**TUTTI:** Ah ah! è fuggito!

**STUDENTE:** Poich' è imberbe
l'incognito facciamgli
Col nero du baffetti,
Doman ne ridermo.

**ALCUNI:** Bravo! bravo!

**ALCADE:** Proteger debbo il viaggiator; m'oppongo.
Meglio farebbe dirne
D'onde venga, ove vade, e chi ella sia?

**STUDENTE:** Lo vuol saper?—Ecco l'istoria mia.
Son Pereda, son ricco d'ornore,
Baccelliere mi fe Salamanca;
Saro presto in utroque Dottore,
Che di studio ancor poco mi manca.
Di la Vargas mi tolse da un anno
E a Siviglia con se mi guido,
Non trattenne Pereda alcun dano,
Per l'amico il suo core parlo.
Della suora, un amante straniero,
Colà il padre gli avea trucidato,
Onde il figlio, da pro' cavaliero,
La vendetta ne aveva giurato.
Gl'inseguimmo di Cadice in riva,
Nè la coppia fatal si trovò.
Per l'amico Pereda soffriva,
Chè l suo core per esso parlò.
Là e dovunque narrar che del pari
La sedotta col vecchio peria,
Chè a una zuffa di servi e sicari,
Solo il vil seduttore sfuggia,
Io da Vargas allor mi staccava;
Ei seguir l'assassino giurò.
Verso America il mare solcava,
E Pereda a' suoi studi torno.

**CORO:** Truce storia Pereda narrava,
Generoso il suo cor si mostrò.

**ALCADE:** Sta bene.

**PREZIOSILLA:** (*Con finezza.*) Ucciso fu quel Marchese?

**STUDENTE:** Ebben?

**PREZIOSILLA:** L'amante rapia sua figlia?

**STUDENTE:** Si.

**PREZIOSILLA:** E voi l'amico fido, cortese,
Andaste a Cadice, dopo Siviglia?
Ah, gnaffe, a me non se la fa,
No, per mia fè—tra la la là!

**ALCADE:** (*S'alza, e guardato l'orinolo dice.*) Figliuoli, è tardi;
poichè abbiam cenato
Si rendan grazie a Dio, e partiam.

**TUTTI:** Partiamo.

## SCENE IV

*The same, except Trabuco.*

**ALL:** Ha ha! he is off!

**STUDENT:** As the unknown is a stripling,
Let us paint on him a pair of moustaches,—
That will make us all laugh tomorrow.

**SOME OF THEM:** Bravo! Bravo!

**ALCADE:** I am bound to protect travellers,
And therefore object.—You had better tell us
Where you come from where going, and who you are.

**STUDENT:** You wish to know?—
This is my tale.
I'm Pereda, from Salamanca,
Soon a Doctor will be my title;
As a student!
I am a ranker,
In my studies I never was idle.
With one Vargas, I went now a year,
And to Sevilla our way we did wend;
Toil and hardship never troubled Pereda,
For his heart ever was faithful to his friend.
A stranger, his sister's lover
Had there his father slain,
Wherefore his son, as true knight
Had sworn to be avenged.
We followed to the shores of Cadiz.
But never overtook the guilty pair.
Pereda felt for his friend's distress,
Whom he most truly loved.
Here it is needful to inform you,
That the seduced one perished with her sire:
In a struggle between servants and assassins,
The vile seducer fled alone.
From Vargas then I parted;
For he swore to follow the assassin:
He crosses the ocean to America,
And Pereda returns to his studies.

**CHORUS:** A dismal story Pereda has related,
Which shows a generous soul.

**ALCADE:** It is well.

**PREZIOSILLA:** (*Slyly.*) Slain was the Marquis?

**STUDENTE:** What then?

**PREZIOSILLA:** The lover carried off his daughter?

**STUDENTE:** Yes.

**PREZIOSILLA:** And you, the friend, faithful, chivalrous,
Went to Cadiz, afterwards to Seville?
Ah, truly, such tales to me
Carry no weight, tra la!

**ALCADE:** (*Rising and looking at the clock.*) My children, it is late,
and we have supped;
Let us give thanks and go.

**ALL:** Let us go.

**ALCADE:** Or buona notte!

**CORO:** Buona notte!

**TUTTI:** Andiamo.
(*Partono.*)

## SCENA V

*Una piccola spianata sul declivio di scoscesa Montagna. A sinistra precipizii e rupi; di fronte la facciata della chiesa della Madonna delgi Angeli, di povera ed umile architettura, a destra la porta del Convento, in mezzo allo quale una fine strella, da un lato la corda del companello. Sopra vi e una piccola tettoia sporgente. Al di la della chiesa alti monti col villaggio d'Hornachuelcos. La porta della chiesa e chiusa, ma larga, sopra dessa una finestra semicircolare lasciera vedere la luce interna. A mezza scene, un po' a sinistra, sopra quattro gradini s' erge una rozza croce ei pietra, corrosa dal tempo. La scena sara illuminata da luna chiarissima.*

*Donna Leonora giunge, ascendendo dalla destra, stanca, vestita da uomo, con pastrano a larghe maniche, largo capello e stivali.*

**LEONORA:** Son giunta—grazie, o Dio!
Estremo asil quest' è per me—son giunta!
Io tremo! La mia orrenda storia è nota
In quell' albergo—e mio fratel narrolla!
Se Scoperta m'avesse! Cielo! Ei disse
Naviga verso occaso Don Alvaro!
Nè morto cadde quella notte in cui
Io, io del sangue di mio padre intrisa,
L'ho seguito, e il perdei! ed or mi lascia,
Mi fugge! ohimè, non reggo a tanta ambascia!
(*Cade inginocchio.*)

**LEONORA ED CORE:** Madre, Madre, pietosa Vergine,
Perdonna al mio peccato,
M'ai ta quell'ingrato
Dal core a cancellar.
In queste solitudini Espiero,
espiero l'errore.
Pieta di me, pieta, Signor,
pieta di me, pieta, Signore,
Deh! non m'abbandonar, pieta,
Pieta di me, Signore!

**LEONORA:** Deh! non m'abbandonar, ah!
Pieta, pieta, di me, Signor!
Ah! que sublimi cantioi,
Dell' organo i concenti,
Che come incenso ascendono

## SCENE V

**ALCADE:** Now goodnight!

**CHORUS:** Goodnight!

**ALL:** Let us go.
(*they depart.*)

## SCENE V

*A small level space, on the side of a steep Mountain. On the left, precipices and rocks; facing the audience, the facade of the Church of the Madonna degli Angeli, of simple architecture; on the right, the door of the Convent in the middle of which is a small window, on one side the cord of the bell, above which is a small projecting roof. On the other side of the church are high mountains, and the village of Hornachuelos. The door of the church is closed, but spacious; above it a semicircular window shows the light within. Halfway down the stage, a little to the left, on four steps, is a rough stone cross, corroded by time. There is a bright moonlight over the whole scene.*

*Donna Leonora arrives, in male attire, ascending from the right, wearing a cloak with large sleeves, a large bat, and boots.*

**LEONORA:** I have arrived—thank Heaven!
This is my last refuge—I am here!
I tremble! My dreadful story is known:
In that inn my brother did recount it.
Oh Heavens! had he discovered me!
He said Don Alvaro was sailing westward,
And fell not on that fearful night
When, steeped in my father's blood,
I followed and lost him! Now he leaves me—
Flies from me!—Ah me, I cannot bear it!
(*falls on her knees.*)

**LEONORA AND CHORUS:** Mother,
O, Holy Mother, hear my prayer,
Forgive my sin appalling,
Then from this enthralling love,
May my poor soul be freed,
Repentant here in solitude
I'll make amends,
I'll make amends completely,
In mercy hear, in mercy hear,
in mercy hear my fervent pleading!
Forsake me not, forsake me not,
forsake me not, O Heaven!
Forsake me not.

**LEONORA:** Heaven! Forsake me not,
O Heaven,
Ah—forsake me not, forsake me not!
Ah! how sublime the anthem

A Dio sui firmamenti,
Inspirano, inspirano a quest' alma
Fede,
Conforto e calma!
Venite, adoremus et procedamus
ante Deum, ploremus, ploremus
coram Domino corum,
Domino qui fecit nos.

LEONORA: Al santo asilo accorrasi.
(*S'avvia.*)
E l'oserò a quest' ora?
(*Arrestandosi.*)
Ma si potria sorprendermi!
Oh, misera Leonora,
Tremi?—il pio frate accoglierti
No, non ricuserà.
Non mi lasciar, soccorrimi,
Pietrà, Signor, pietà.
(*Va a suonare il campanello del Convento.*)

## SCENA VI

*Si apre la finestrella della porta, e n'esce la luce d'una lanterna. Che riverbera sul volto di Donna Leonora, la quale si arretra speventata. Fra Melitone parla sempre all' interno.*

MELITONE: Chi siete?

LEONORA: Chiedo il Superiore.

MELITONE: S'apre
Alle cinque la chiesa,
Se al giubileo venite.

LEONORA: Il Superiore—
Per carità!

MELITONE: Che carità a quest' ora!

LEONORA: Mi manda il Padre Cleto.

MELITONE: Quel sant' uomo? Il motivo?

LEONORA: Urgente.

MELITONE: Perchè mai?

LEONORA: Un infelice!

MELITONE: Brutta solfa—però v' apro ond' entriate.

LEONORA: Nol posso.

MELITONE: No? Scomunicicato siete?
Chè strano fia aspettar a ciel sereno.
V'annuncio—e se non torno,
Buona notte.
(*Chiude la finestrella.*)

## SCENA VII

*Donna Leonora, sola.*

LEONORA: Ma s' ei mi respingesse!
Fama pietoso il dice,
Ei mi proteggerà;—Vergin, m'assisti!

---

sounds,
With solemn organ blending,
It floats like incense on the air,
To heaven's gate ascending,
Unto my soul, unto my soul it's bringing
Calmness,
and unshaken faith.

LENORA: Let me hurry to the sacred asylum
(*going.*)
But do I dare, at this hour?
(*stopping.*)
Yet I may be overtaken!
Oh, wretched Leonora,
Do you fear?—the holy friar
Will not refuse to receive you.
Have mercy, Heaven, mercy!
Aid me, do not desert me!
(*Rings the convent bell.*)

## SCENE VI

*The little window in the door opens, through which is seen a light, which is reflected in Donna Leonora's face, who starts back alarmed. Brother Melitone speaks from within.*

MELITONE: Who is it?

LEONORA: I seek the Superior.

MELITONE: At five o'clock
The church will open,
If you come to the jubilee.

LEONORA: The Superior—
For charity's sake!

MELITONE: Charity at this hour!

LEONORA: I am sent by Father Cleto.

MELITONE: By that holy man? The reason?

LEONORA: Most urgent.

MELITONE: Why so?

LEONORA: An unfortunate creature!

MELITONE: A likely tale—however, I will let you in.

LEONORA: I cannot enter.

MELITONE: No? Are you excommunicated?
It is strange you should prefer the open air,
I will announce you—and if I don't return,
Good night.
(*shuts the window*)

## SCENE VII

*Donna Leonora, alone.*

LEONORA: But if he should repulse me?
He is reputed merciful.
He will protect me;—Holy Virgin, aid me!

---

## SCENA VIII

*Donna Leonora, il Padre Guardiano, fra Melitone.*

GUARDIANO: Chi mi cerca?

LEONORA: Son io.

GUARDIANO: Dite.

LEONORA: Un segreto—

GUARDIANO: Andate Melitone.

MELITONE: (*Partendo.*) (Sempre segreti!
E questi santi soi han da saperli!
Noi siamo tanti cavoli.)

GUARDIANO: Gratello Mormorate?

MELITONE: Oibò, dico ch' è pesante
La porte, e fa romore.

GUARDIANO: Obbedite.

MELITONE: (Che tuon da Superiore!)
(*Rientra in Convento socchiudendone la porta.*)

## SCENA IX

*Donna Leonora e il Padre Guardiano.*

GUARDIANO: Or siam soli.

LEONORA: Una donna son io.

GUARDIANO: Una donna a quest' ora!—gran Dio!

LEONORA: Infelice, dulusa, rejetta,
Dalla terra, e dal ciel maledetta,
Che nel pianto prostratavi al piede,
Di sottrarla all' inferno vi chiede.

GUARDIANO: Come un povero frate lo può?

LEONORA: Padre Cleto un suo foglio v'invò?

GUARDIANO: Ei vi manda?

LEONORA: Sì.

GUARDIANO: (*Sorpreso.*) Dunque voi siete Leonora di Varges?

LEONORA: Fremete!

GUARDIANO: No: venite fidente alla croce,
Là del Cielo v' inspiri la voce.

LEONORA: (*S'inginocchia presso la croce, la bacia, quindi torna meno agitata al Padre Guardiano.*) Ah, tranquilla l' alma sento
Dacchè premo questa terra;
De' fantasmi lo spavento
Più non provo farmi guerra;
Più non sorge sanguinante
Di mio padre l' ombra innante,
Nè terribile l' ascolto
La sua figlia maledir.

GUARDIANO: Sempre indarno qui rivolto
Fu di Satana l' ardir.

---

## SCENE VIII

*Donna Leonora, the Father Guardiano, Brother Melitone.*

GUARDIANO: Who asks for me?

LEONORA: It is I.

GUARDIANO: Speak on.

LEONORA: A secret—

GUARDIANO: Go, Melitone.

MELITONE: (*Going.*) (Always secrets!
And these saints only know them!
We are nobodies!)

GUARDIANO: Brother, Are you grumbling?

MELITONE: Oh no, I said the door Was heavy, and creaked.

GUARDIANO: Obey.

MELITONE: (Quite the voice of the Superior!)
(*re-enters the Convent, half-closing the door.*)

## SCENE IX

*Donna Leonora and the Father Guardiano.*

GUARDIANO: Now, we are alone.

LEONORA: I am a woman.

GUARDIANO: A woman at this hour!—good heavens!

LEONORA: Unhappy, deluded, rejected
Oh earth, and cursed by Heaven!
Who, prostrate at your feet, with tears
Implores you to save her from destruction.

GUARDIANO: How can a poor friar do so?

LEONORA: Father Cleto sent you a letter?

GUARDIANO: He sent you?

LEONORA: Yes.

GUARDIANO: (*Surprised.*) Then you must be Leonora di Vargas?

LEONORA: You shudder!

GUARDIANO: No; in confidence approach the cross,
There may Heaven inspire you.

LEONORA: (*Kneeling close to the cross, kisses it, then turning with less agitation to Father Guardiano.*) Ah, my soul is calm
Now I tread this soil;
I no longer feel the dread forebodings within me;
Nor does the bleeding shade of my sire;
rise before me;
I do not hear with horror
His curses on his child.

GUARDIANO: Never has Satan dared
To approach these precincts.

LEONORA: Perciò tomba qui desio,
Fa le rupi ov' altra visse.

LEONORA: Therefore I seek a tomb
Among the rocks where one other lived.

GUARDIANO: Che!—sapete—

GUARDIANO: What!—do you know—

LEONORA: Cleto il disse.

LEONORA: Cleto mentioned it.

GUARDIANO: E volete—

GUARDIANO: And you wish—

LEONORA: Darmi a Dio!

LEONORA: To devote myself to Heaven!

GUARDIANO: Guai per chi si lascia illudere
Dal delirio d'un momento!
Più fatal per voi, si giovane,
Sorgerebbe il pentimento.
Nel futuro chi può leggere,
Chi immutabil farvi il cor.
E l' amante?

GUARDIANO: Woe to those who delude themselves
In the wild frenzy of a moment!
More wretched for you, so young,
Would repentance hereafter become.
Who can read the future,
Or make the heart steadfast?
And thy lover?

LEONORA: Involontario
Di mio padre è l' uccisor.

LEONORA: He by mischance killed
My father.

GUARDIANO: Il fratello?

GUARDIANO: Your brother?

LEONORA: La mia morte
Di sua mano egli giurò.

LEONORA: He has sworn my death
By his own hand.

GUARDIANO: Meglio a voi la sante porte.
Schiuda un chiostro.

GUARDIANO: For you it were best to seek
A cloister's holy shelter.

LEONORA: Un chiostro? No.
Se voi scacciate questa pentita,
Andrò per balze gridando aita.
Ricovro ai monti ciba, alle selve,
E fin le belve ne avran pietà.
Qui, qui del cielo udii la voce:
Salvati all' ombra di questa croce—
Voi mi scacciate? E questo il porto;
Chi tal conforto mi toglierà?
(Corre ad abbracciar la croce.)

LEONORA: A cloister? No.
If you reject the penitent,
Aid will I shrieking ask the rocks,
Shelter the mountains, food the woods;
The savage beasts at least will pity me.
Here, where heaven's voice is heard
Salvation in the shadow of the Cross I seek.
You cast me out? This is the haven
Of solace—you will tear me from it?
(runs and clings to the cross.)

GUARDIANO: (A te sia gloria, o Dio clemente,
Padre dei miseri onnipossente,
A qui sgabello sono le sfere!
Il tuo volere—si compirà!)
E fermo il voto?

GUARDIANO: (Yours be the glory, O merciful Heaven!
Father of sinners, omnipotent,
Who reigns over all worlds,
Let your will be accomplished.)
You are resolved?

LEONORA: E fermo.

LEONORA: I am.

GUARDIANO: V' accolga dunque Iddio!

GUARDIANO: Heaven accept you!

LEONORA: Bontà divina?

LEONORA: Oh, divine clemency!

GUARDIANO: Sol io saprò chi siate.
Tra le rupi è uno speco; ivi starete.
Presso una fonte, al settimo, di scarso
Cibo porrovvi io stesso.

GUARDIANO: I alone shall know who you are.
Among the rocks is a cave, your future abode:
Beside a spring, every seven days,
I myself will bring your scanty food.

LEONORA: V' andiamo.

LEONORA: Let us go.

GUARDIANO: (Versa la porta.)
Melitone!
(A Melitone chi comparisce.)
Tutti i fratelli con ardenti ceri,
Dov' è l' ara maggiore,
Nel tempio si raccolgan del Signore.
(Melitone rientra.)
Sull' alba il piede all' eremo

GUARDIANO: (Turning to the door.) Melitone!
(to Melitone who enters.)
Let all the brothers, with lighted torches,
Before the high altar assemble,
In the temple of our Lord.
(Melitone withdraws.)
To seek the lowly hermitage

Solinga volgerete
Ma pria dal pane angelico
Divin conforto avrete,
Le sante lane a cingere
Ite, sia fermo il cor.
Sul nuovo calle areggervi
V'assisterà il Signor.

At dawn you must be stirring
But first take of the sacrament,
God's grace on you conferring,
Embrace the cross with simple faith
To set your mind at rest,
And Heaven will not deny you aid,
You will be richly blessed.
(Enters the Convent, but returns immediately with the dress of the Franciscan order, and gives it to Leonora.)

LEONORA: Tua grazia, o Dio,
Sorride alla rejetta!
Oh, gaudio insolito!
Io son, Io son ribenedetta!
Gia sento in me rinascere
A nuova vita il cor;
Plaudite, o cori angelici,
Mi perdono il Signor,
Mi perdono il Signor
Mi perdono il Signor.

LEONORA: My prayers and thanksgiving
You on high are winging,
And happiness unmerited Thy peace.
To my poor heart is bringing,
I feel new hope once more within,
New courage in my breast;
I think angelic songs I hear
And pardon makes me blessed,
And pardon, pardon makes me blessed,
Your pardon makes me blessed.

## SCENA X

La gran porta della Chiesa si apre. Di fronte vedesi l' altar maggiore, illuminato. L' organo suona. Dai lati del coro procedono due lunghe file di Frati, con cerei ardenti. Piu tardi il Padre Guardiano precede Leonora in abito da Frate. Egli la conduce fuor della chiesa, Frati che gli si schierano intorno. Leonora si prostra innanzi a lui, che stendendo solennemente le mani spora il suo capo intuona.

## SCENE X

The great door of the Church opens. In front is seen the high altar, illuminated. The organ is sounded. From the sides of the choir proceed two long rows of Friars, with lighted tapers. A little later, Father Guardiano, followed by Leonora, in the Friar's dress. He leads her out of the church, followed by the Friars, who range themselves around. Leonora prostrates herself before him, he solemnly spreads his hands over her head, and chants.

GUARDIANO: Il santo nome di Dio Signore
Sia benedetto.

GUARDIANO: The holy name of the Lord
Be blessed.

TUTTI: Sia benedetto.

ALL: Be blessed.

GUARDIANO: Un' alma a piangere viene l' errore,
I queste balze chiede ricetto.
Il santo speco noi la schiudiamo—
V' è noto il loco?

GUARDIANO: A penitent soul, to atone for errors,
Demands a shelter in these rocks.
The holy cave we will open—
Do you know the place?

TUTTI: Lo conosciamo.

ALL: We know the place.

GUARDIANO: A quell' asilo sacro inviolato
nessun si appressi.

GUARDIANO: Let none approach the sacred holy asylum.

TUTTI: Obbediremo.

ALL: We will obey.

GUARDIANO: Il cinto umile non sia varcato. Che nel divide.

GUARDIANO: Let none pass the low boundary enclosing it.

TUTTI: Nol varcheremo.

ALL: We will not.

GUARDIANO: A chi il divieto frangere osasse,
O di quest' anima scoprir tentasse
Nome o mistero, maledizione!

GUARDIANO: Malediction to him who dares to break this rule,
Or of this poor soul seeks to discover
The name or story!

TUTTI: Maledizione! maledizione!
Il cielo fulmini incenerisa
L' empio mortale se tanto ardisca;
Su lui scatenisi ogni elemento,
L'immonda cenere ne sperda il ven-

ALL: Malediction! malediction!
May the thunderbolt reduce to ashes
The impious mortal who dares attempt it;

to.

**GUARDIANO:** (*A Leonora.*) Alzatevi, e partite.
Alcun vivente più non vedrete.
Dello speco il bronzo
Ne avverta se periglio vi sovrasti,
O per voi giunto s'a l' estremo giorno—
A confortarvi l' alma
Volerem, pria ch' a Dio faccia ritorno.
La Vergine degli angeli
Vo copra del suo manto,
E voi protegga vigile
Di Dio l' angelo santo.

**TUTTI:** La Vergine, ecc.
(*Leonora bacia la mano del Padre Guardiano s' avvia all' cremo sola. Il Guardiano stendendo le braccia verso di lei, la benedice. Cade la tela.*)

*FINE DELLA'ATTO SECONDO.*

**GUARDIANO:** (*To Leonora.*) Rise and depart. No living soul
Will see you more. The bell in the cave
Will give us notice if you are in danger;
If your last hour be at hand,
We will haste to bring absolution
Before your soul returns to God.
The Virgin of the heavenly hosts.
Cover you with her holy mantle,
And the holy angels of God
Be to you watchful guardians.

**ALL:** The Virgin, etc.
(*Leonora kisses the hand of Father Guardiano, and sets out alone for the hermitage. Guardiano, extending his arms towards her, blesses her. The curtain falls.*)

*END OF THE SECOND ACT.*

# ■ ATTO III

*In Italia presso Velletri.*

## SCENA I

*Bosco. Notte oscurissima. Don Alvaro in uniforme di Capitano Spagnuolo de' Granatieri del Re, si avanza lentamente dal fondo. Si sentono voci interno a destra.*

**1A VOCE:** Attneti, gioco.—Un asso a destra.

**2A VOCE:** Ho vinto.

**1A VOCE:** Un tre alla destra—cinque a manca.

**2A VOCE:** Perdo!

**ALVARO:** (*Che si sara innoltrato.*) La vita e inferno all infelice invano
Morte desio!—Siviglia!—Leonora!
Oh, rimembranze!—Oh notte!
Ch' ogni mio ben rapisti!
Sarò infelice eternamente è scritto.
Della natal sua terra il padre volle
Spezzar l' estranio giogo, el coll', unirsi;
All' ultima degli Incas la corona
Cingerne confidò—fallì l' impresa,
In un carcere nacqui; m' educava
Il deserto; sol vivo per chè ignota
E mia regale stirpe. I miei parenti
Sognaro un trono e, li destò la scure!
Oh, quando fine avran le mie sventure?
Oh, tuche in seno agl'angeli,
Eternamente pura
Salisti bella, incolume
Dal la mortal jattura.
Oh, tuche in seno agl'angeli,
Salisti bella e pura,
Non iscordar di volger.

# ■ ACT III

*In Italy, near Villeteri.*

## SCENE I

*A wood. A dark night. Don Alvaro, in the uniform of a Captain of Royal Spanish Grenadiers, advances slowly from the back. Voices are heard on the right, from within.*

**1st VOICE:** Attention, I play. An ace to the right.

**2nd VOICE:** I have won.

**1st VOICE:** A three to the right—five to the left.

**2nd VOICE:** I have lost.

**ALVARO:** (*Who has come forward.*) Life has no charms for unhappy souls.
In vain I seek to die!—Seville!—Leonora!
Oh, sad memories!—Fatal night,
Which deprived me of every good!
It is decreed that I shall ever be unfortunate.
My father sought to free his native land
From foreign rule;
United to the last of the Incas,
He hoped to obtain the crown.
He failed—and I was born in prison,
Reared in the desert, and only live because
My royal birth is unknown. My parents
Dreamt of thrones, and suffered by the scaffold.
Ah, when will my sorrows end?
O sainted soul, in rest above,
You are dwelling with angels,
There, in the blessed realm of love,

Lo sguardo a me tapino,
Che senza nome ed esul,
In odio del destino,
Che senza nome ed esul,
In odio del destino,
Chiedo anelando, ahi misero,
Chiedo anelando, ahi misero,
La morte d'incontrar,
Leonora mia, soccorrimi,
Leonora mia, soccorrimi,
Pieta, pieta, pieta del mio penar;
Leonora, soccorrimi, pieta, del mio penar;
Leonora, mia, pieta, pieta del mio, penar, soccorrimi, pieta di me!

You have found joy past telling.
O sainted soul in rest above,
With angels you are dwelling,
Turn your glances in pity upon my soul in sorrow,
Who wanders here in exile
And dreads each coming tomorrow,
Who wanders here in exile,
And dreads each coming tomorrow,
Yes, in this war and misery,
For ever seeking, ever seeking death amid the foe,
Oh, Leonora, pity me,
Oh, Leonora, pity, pity me,
And give me help,
And give me help to bear my woe;
Leonora, oh, pity me,
And give me help to bear my woe;—Oh, Leonora, give help,
give help to bear my woe, give help to bear, to bear my woe!

**VOCE:** (*Dall' interno a destra.*) Al tradimento!

**VOCI:** Muoia!

**ALVARO:** Quali grida?

**VOCE:** Aita!

**ALVARO:** Si soccorra!
(*Accorre al luogo onde si udivano le grida. Si sente un picchiare di spade. Alcuni Ufficiali attraversano la scena, fuggendo in disordine da destra a sinistra.*)

**VOICE:** (*From within.*) Treachery!

**VOICES:** Down with him!

**ALVARO:** What cries are these?

**A VOICE:** Help!

**ALVARO:** To your aid!
(*runs to the place from where the sounds proceed. A clashing of swords is heard. Some officers cross the stage in disorder flying right and left.*)

## SCNEA II

*Don Alvaro ritorna con Don Carlo.*

**ALVARO:** Fuggir! Ferito siete?

**CARLO:** No, vi debbo
La vita.

**ALVARO:** Chi erano?

**CARLO:** Assassini.

**ALVARO:** Presso! Alcampo così?

**CARLO:** Franco
Dirè: fu altercò al gioco.

**ALVARO:** Comprendo, colà, a destra?

**CARLO:** Si.

**ALVARO:** Ma come,
Si nobile d' aspetto, a quella bisca
Scendeste?

**CARLO:** Nuovo sono.
Del general con ordini sol jeri
Giunsi; senza voi morto
Sarei. Or dite a chi miei giorni debbo?

**ALVARO:** Al caso.

**CARLO:** Pria il mio nome
Dirò—(non sappia il vero)—
Don Felice de Bornos, ajutante
Del Duce.

**ALVARO:** Io Capitan de' Granatieri
Don Federico Herreros!

## SCENE II

*Don Alvaro returns with Don Carlos.*

**ALVARO:** They are fled! Are you wounded?

**CARLOS:** No; but I owe to you my life.

**ALVARO:** Who are they?

**CARLOS:** Assassins.

**ALVARO:** What, so near the camp?

**CARLOS:** Frankly, it was a gambling quarrel.

**ALVARO:** I understand; there on the right?

**CARLOS:** Yes.

**ALVARO:** But, how, seeming so noble,
Descend to such low company?

**CARLOS:** I am a stranger, with orders from the general.
I arrived yesterday, and but for you I had died.
Say, to whom do I owe my life?

**ALVARO:** To chance.

**CARLOS:** I will first tell my name—
(Not my true one)—
Don Felice de Bornos,
Adjutant to the Duke.

**ALVARO:** I Captain of the Grenadiers,
Don Federico Herreros!

**CARLO:** La gloria dell' esercito!

**ALVARO:** Signore—

**CARLO:** Io l' amistà ne ambia, la chiedo, e spero.

**ALVARO:** Io pure della vostra sarò fiero.
(*Si stringono le destre.*)

**VOCI:** (*Interne, a sinistra, e squillo di trombe.*) All' armi!

**A 2:** Andiamo—all' armi!

**CARLO:** Ah più gradito questo suono or parmi!
Con voi scendere al campo d' onore,
Emularne l' esempio potrò.

**ALVARO:** Testimone del vostro valore,
Ammirarne le prove saprò.

## SCENA III

E il Mattino. Salotto nell' abitazione d'un ufficiale superiore dell' esercito Spagnuolo in Italia non lungi da Velletri. Nel fondo sonvi due porte, quella a sinistra mette ad una stanza da letto, l'altra e la comune. A sinistra presso il proscenio a una finestra. Si sente il romore della vicina battaglia.

Un Chirurgo Militare, ed alcuni Soldati, ordinanze dalla comune corrono alla finestra.

**SOLDATI:** Arde la mischia!

**CHIRURGO:** (*Guardando con cannocchiale.*) Prodi i granatieri!

**SOLDATI:** Li guida Herreros.

**CHIRURGO:** (*Guardando con cannocchiale.*) Ciel! ferito o spento
Ei cadde! Piegano i suoi! l'Ajutante
Li raccozza alla carica li guida!
Già fuggono i Tedeschi! I nostri han vinto
Portan qui il Capitano.

**SOLDATI:** Ferito!
(*Corrono ad incontrario.*)

**VOCI:** (*Fuori.*) A Spagna gloria!

**ALTRE:** Viva l' Italia!

**TUTTI:** E nostra la vittoria!

## SCENA IV

Don Alvaro, ferito e svenuto e portato in una lettiga da quattro Granatieri. Da un lato e il Chirurgo, dall' altro Don Carlo, coperto di polvere ed assai afflitto. Un Soldato depone una valigia sopra un tavolino. La lettiga e collocata quasi nel mezzo della scena.

**CARLO:** Piano—qui posi—approntisi il mio letto.

**CHIRURGO:** Silenzio.

---

**CARLOS:** The pride of the army!

**ALVARO:** Signor—

**CARLOS:** I desire and would obtain your friendship.

**VOICES:** I shall be proud to have yours.
(*they shake hands.*)

**VOICES:** (*Within, to the left, with sound of a trumpet.*) To arms!

**TOGETHER:** Let us go—to arms!

**CARLOS:** Ah, that sound is more agreeable now!
With you I will go to the field of honor,
And seek to emulate your bright example.

**ALVARO:** Witness of your valor,
In future I shall know how to admire it.

## SCENE III

Morning. A small room in the house of a superior officer in the Spanish army, in Italy, not far from Velletri. At the back are two doors, one on the left leads to a bedroom, the other is the common door. On the left, near the proscenium, is a window. The noise is heard of the neighboring battle.

A Military Surgeon, and some common Soldiers, run to the window.

**SOLDIERS:** The battle rages!

**SURGEON:** (*Looking through a telescope.*) Brave grenadiers!

**SOLDIER:** Herreros leads them.

**SURGEON:** (*Looking through a telescope.*) Heavens! He falls Wounded or dead! His men give way!
The Adjutant rallies and leads them to the charge!
The Germans fly! Our troops conquer!
They bring the Captain here.

**SOLDIER:** Wounded!
(*they run to meet him.*)

**VOICES:** (*Without.*) Glory to Spain!

**OTHERS:** Long live Italy!

**ALL:** Ours is the victory!

## SCENE IV

Don Alvaro, wounded and insensible, is borne in on a litter by four Grenadiers. On one side the Surgeon, on the other Don Carlos, covered with dust and sorrowful. A Soldier places a traveling bag on a small table. The litter is placed nearly in the middle of the scene.

**CARLOS:** Gently—lay him here—get my bed ready.

**SURGEON:** Silence!

---

**CARLO:** V' ha periglio?

**CHIRURGO:** La palla che ha nel petto mi spaventa.

**CARLO:** Deh, il salvate.

**ALVARO:** (*Rinviene.*) Ove son?

**CARLO:** Presso l' amico.

**ALVARO:** Lasciatemi morire.

**CARLO:** Vi salveran le nostra cure premio
L'ordine vè sarà di Calatrava.

**ALVARO:** (*Trasalendo.*) di Calatrava! No—mai!

**CHIRURGO:** Siate calmo.

**CARLO:** (Chè! Inorridí di Calatrava al nome!)

**ALVARO:** Amico—

**CHIRURGO:** Se parlate—

**ALVARO:** Un detto sol.

**CARLO:** (*Al Chirurgo.*) Ven prefo ne, lasciate.
(*Chirurgo si ritrae al fonde.*)

**ALVARO:** Solenne in quest' ora guirarmi dovete far pago un mio voto.

**CARLO:** Lo giùro, lo giùro.

**ALVARO:** Sul core cercate.

**CARLO:** Una chiave!

**ALVARO:** Con essa trarrete un piego celato l'affido all'onore
Cola v'ha un mistero,
che meco morra.
S'abbruci me spento.

**CARLO:** Lo giuro, sarà.
Amico fidate, fidate nel cielo, fidate nel ciel;
amico, fidate nel cielo, fidate.
Amico, fidate, fidate nel cielo, fidate nel ciel;
amico, fidate nel cielo, fidate.
Addio, addio, addio!

**ALVARO:** Or muoio tranquillo
Vi stringo al cor mio, al core,
or muoio tranquillo vi stringo al cor mio
or muoio tranquillo, vi stringo al cor mio
al core, or muoio tranquillo vi stringo al cor mio!
Addio, addio, addio!
(*Il Chirurgo e le Ordinanze trasportano il ferito nella stanza da letto.*)

## SCENA V

Don Carlos, poi il Chirurgo.

---

**CARLOS:** Is there danger?

**SURGEON:** The bullet in his chest alarms me.

**CARLOS:** Ah, try to save him!

**ALVARO:** (*Recovering his senses.*) Where am I?

**CARLOS:** With your friend.

**ALVARO:** Leave me to die.

**CARLOS:** Our cares will save you. The Order of Calatrava will be conferred upon you.

**ALVARO:** (*Shuddering.*) Of Calatrava! No—never!

**SURGEON:** Be calm.

**CARLOS:** (He shuddered at the name of Calatrava!)

**ALVARO:** My friend—

**SURGEON:** If you speak—

**ALVARO:** Only one word.

**CARLOS:** (*To the Surgeon.*) Leave us, I pray you.
(*the Surgeon retires to the back.*)

**ALVARO:** In this solemn hour— O swear to befriend me, and listen to my entreaty.

**CARLOS:** I swear it, I swear it.

**ALVARO:** Then search in my bosom.

**CARLOS:** It is a key!—

**ALVARO:** And there too is hidden a sealed faded letter;
To you I entrust it
The secret it holds
must die with my death.
I beg you to burn it.

**CARLOS:** On honor I swear.
My friend, put your faith now in Heaven,
faith now in Heaven above,
in Heaven above,
put your faith now in Heaven.
My friend, put your faith now in Heaven,
your faith now in Heaven above,
in Heaven above, put your faith now in Heaven.
Farewell now, farewell now for ever!

**ALVARO:** I die now contented,
As to my heart—I hold you, I hold you,—
Contented I die as I hold you upon my heart.
I die now contented, as to my heart I hold, I hold you,
Contented I die as I hold you upon my heart.
Farewell now, farewell now for ever!
(*the Surgeon and Soldiers carry the wounded man into the bedroom.*)

## SCENE V

Don Carlos, afterwards the Surgeon.

**CARLO:** Morir! Tremenda cosa!
Sì intrepido, sì prode,
Ei pur morrà! Uom singolar costui!
Tremò di Calatrava!
Al nome! A lui palese
N' è forse il disonor? Cielo! qual lampo!
S' ei fosse il seduttore?
Desso in mia mano, e vive!
Se m' ingannassi? Questa chiave il dica.
(*Apre convulso la valigia, e ne trae un plicco suggellato.*)
Ecco i fogli.
(*Fa per aprirlo.*)
Che tento?
(*S'arresta.*)
E la fè che giurai! e questa vita
Che debbo al suo valor? Anch' io l' ho salvo!
E s' ei fosse quell' Indo maledetto
Che macchiò il sangue mio?
(*Risoluto.*)
Il suggello si franga.
(*Sta per eseguire.*)
Niun qui me vede; No!
(*S'arresta.*)
Ben mi vegg' io?
(*Getta il plicco, e se ne allontana con raccapriccio.*)
Urna fatale del mio destino,
Va, t' allontana, mi tenti insano;
L'onor a tergere qui venni, e insano
D' un onta nuova nol brutterò.
Un giuro è sacro per l' uom d' onore;
Que' fogli chiudano il lor mistero—
Disperso vada il mal pensiero;
Che all' atto indegno mi concitò.
E s' altra provar invenir potessi?
Vediam.
(*Torna a frugare nella valigia e vi trova un astuccio.*)
Qui v' ha un ritratto.
(*Lo esamina.*)
Suggel non v' e'—nulla ei ne disse—nulla.
Promisi—s' apra dunque.
(*Eseguisce.*)
Ciel! Leonora!
(*Con estaltazione.*)
Don Alvaro e' il ferito!
Ora egli viva—
Edi mai man poi mueoia.

**CHIRURGO:** (*Si presenta lieto sulla porta della stanza.*) Lieta novella è salvo.
(*Rientra.*)

**CARLO:** Oh gioia! oh gioia!
Ah! egli e salvo! o gioia immensa
Che m'innondi il cor, ti sento!
Potro al fine il tradimento
Sull' infame vendicar.
Leonora, ove t'ascondi?
Di': seguisti tra le squadre.
Chi del sangue di tuo padre,
Chi del sangue di tuo padre.
Ti fè il volto rosseggiar.
Ah, felice appien sarei
Se potesse il brando mio,
Amendue d'averno al Dio,

**CARLOS:** Die! How terrible!
So fearless, so brave.
Yet he must die! What a strange man!
He shuddered at the name of Calatrava!
Does he know it has been disgraced?
Heavens! a thought strikes me!
What if he were the vile seducer?
In my hands, and yet alive!
But if I should mistake? This key will tell.
(*he hastily opens the bag, and draws out a sealed packet.*)
Here are the papers.
(*about to open them.*)
What am I doing?
(*stops.*)
And the oath I swore? And the life
I owe to his valor?
But I have also saved him.
Yet if he were this vile Indian
Who has disgraced my name?
(*resolutely.*)
The seal shall be broken.
(*is about to do it.*)
No one shall see me! No!
(*stops.*)
Do I not see myself?
(*throws away the packet, and turns from it with horror.*)
Fatal urn of my destiny,
Away, in vain you tempt me;
I came here to clear my honor,
And will not stain it with a new disgrace.
An oath is sacred to a man of honor;
Those papers contain their own secret—
Away with the evil thought
That urged me to the base attempt.
But if I might obtain other proof;
Let me see.
(*look into the bag, and finds a case.*)
Here is a portrait.
(*examines it.*)
Here is no seal—he spoke not of it—
I promised nothing
(*open it.*)
Heavens! Leonora!
(*excitedly.*)
The wounded man is then Alvaro!
Let him live—then, later die by my hands!

**SURGEON:** (*Appearing at the door of the room.*) Here is the ball: he is saved!
(*retires.*)

**CARLOS:** Oh, happiness! oh, joy!
Oh, what a joy my heart is knowing
That before long my sword shall find him!
Soon his blood for vengeance flowing,
Shall repay me for the wrong.
Where, Leonora, are you hiding?
If with that vile man you're biding,
Who did slay your aged father,
Who did slay your aged father,
None can see you without scorn.
Ah, I should be truly happy

D' un sol colpo consacrar.
(*Parte rapidamente.*)

If with my own sword,
And with the same blow
I might send both to realms below.
(*exit.*)

## SCENA VI

*Accampamento Militare presso elletri. Sul davanti a sinistra e una bottega da rigattiere; a destra altra ove si vendono cibi, bevande, frutta. All' ingiro tende militari, baracche di rivenduglioli, ecc. E notte, la scena e deserta. Una Patt glia entra cautamente in scena, esplorando il campo.*

**CORO:** Compagni, sostiamo,
Il campo esploriamo;
Non s' ode rumore,
Non brilla un chiarore;
In sonno profondo
Sepolto ognun sta.
Compagni, inoltriamo.
(*Allontonandosi a poco a poco.*)
Fra poco la sveglia
Suonare s' udra.

## SCENA VII

*Spunta l' alba lentamente. Entra Don Alvaro pensoso.*

**ALVARO:** Nè gustare m' è dato
Un' ora di quiete; affranta è l' alma
Dalla lotta crudel.
Pace ed oblio indarno io chieggo al Cielo.

## SCENA VIII

*Detto e Don Carlo.*

**CARLO:** Capitan.

**ALVARO:** Chi mi chiama?
(*Avvicinandosi e riconoscendo Carlo gli dice con affetto.*)
Voi che sì larghe cure
Mi prodigaste?

**CARLO:** La ferita vostra
Sanata è appieno?

**ALVARO:** Sì.

**CARLO:** Forte?

**ALVARO:** Qual prima.

**CARLO:** Sosterreste un duello?

**ALVARO:** E con chi mai?

**CARLO:** Nemici non avete?

**ALVARO:** Tutti ne abbian—ma a stento
Comprendo—

**CARLO:** No?—Messaggio non v' inviava
Don Alvaro l' Indiano?

**ALVARO:** Oh tradimento!
Sleale? il segreto fu dunque violato?

**CARLO:** Fu illeso quel piego, l' effigie ha parlato;
Don Carlo di Vargas, tremate, io sono.

## SCENE VI

*Military Encampment, near Velletri. In front is a sutler's booth. To the right, others with food, fruits, bottles. Around are soldiers' tents, huxter's stalls etc. Night. The scene is vacant. The watchguards enter cautiously, and search the camp.*

**CHORUS:** Comrades, halt!
The camp explore.
No sound is heard,
No light is seen,
In sleep profound
Now all repose.
Comrades, forward!
(*go off gradually.*)
Before long the morning call
Will rouse them.

## SCENE VII

*The day slowly dawns. Enter Don Alvaro, in deep thought.*

**ALVARO:** Not one hour of rest
Can I enjoy. My soul is tortured
With the cruel struggle.
Peace and oblivion I ask of Heaven in vain.

## SCENE VIII

*Enter Don Carlos.*

**CARLOS:** Captain.

**ALVARO:** Who calls me?
(*advancing recognizes Carlos with gladness.*)
Is it you lavished such great care
Upon me?

**CARLOS:** Has your wound
Healed completely?

**ALVARO:** Yes.

**CARLOS:** Strong?

**ALVARO:** As ever.

**CARLOS:** Could you fight a duel?

**ALVARO:** And with whom?

**CARLOS:** Have you no enemy?

**ALVARO:** All have some—but I hardly
Understand—

**CARLOS:** No?—Don Alvaro the Indian,
Did he not send you a message?

**ALVARO:** Oh, treachery? disloyal man?
The secret has been disclosed there?

**CARLOS:** The packet was unopened, but the portrait spoke;
Tremble, for I am Don Carlos di Vargas.

ALVARO: D' ardite, minacce non m' agito al suono.

ALVARO: Threats do not disturb me.

CARLO: Usciamo, all' istante un di noi dee morire.

CARLOS: Come, on the instant one of us must die!

ALVARO: La morte disprezzo, ma duolmi inveire
Contr' uom che per primo amistade m' offria.

ALVARO: I despise death, but it grieves me to injure
Him who first offered me friendship.

CARLO: No, no profanato tal nome non sia.

CARLOS: Do not profane the word.

ALVARO: Non io, fu il destino, che il padre v' ha ucciso;
Non io che sedussi quell' angiol d' amore—
Ne guardano entrambi, e dal paradiso
Ch' io sono innocente vi dicono al core—

ALVARO: Not I, but fate, your father slew;
I never seduced that lovely angel;
Both look on us, and from heaven
Tell your heart I am innocent.

CARLO: Adunque colei?

CARLOS: And she?

ALVARO: La notte fatale
Io caddi per doppia ferita mortale
Guaritone, un anno in traccia ne andai—
Ahimè, ch' era spenta Leonora trovai.

ALVARO: I fell that fatal night.
Through many mortal wounds,
Then, cured, I sought her for a year.
And found Leonora dead.

CARLO: Menzogna, menzogna!
La suora—ospitavala antica parente;
Vi giunsi, ma tardi—

CARLOS: False, false!
My sister found refuge with a relative;
I arrived too late.

ALVARO: (Con ansia.) Ed ella—

ALVARO: (With anxiety.) And she?

CARLO: E fuggente.

CARLOS: Has fled.

ALVARO: (Trasalendo.) E vive! o amico, il fremito
Ch' ogni mia fibra scuote,
Vi dica che quest' anima
Infame esser non puote—
Vive! gran Dio, quell' angelo!

ALVARO: (Joyously.) She lives!
Ah, my friend.
The trembling which pervades my frame
Will tell you that my soul
Cannot be so debased.
She lives! Thank God!

CARLO: Ma in breve morirà.

CARLOS: But she will die shortly.

ALVARO: No, d' un imene il vincolo
Stringa fra noi la speme;
E s' ella vive, insieme
Cerchiamo ove fuggì.
Giuro che illustre origine
Eguale a voi mi rende,
E che il mio stemma splende
Come rifulge il dì.

ALVARO: No,
Soon may we be united by the fond nuptial tie;
If yet she lives, together
Let us seek her abode.
I swear that rank as noble
Even as yours, I own,
And that my birth is pure,
Unstained, as light of day.

CARLO: Stolto! fra noi dischiudesi
Insanguinato avello;
Come chiamar fratello
Chi tutto mi rapì?
D' eccelsa o vile origine,
E duopo ch' io vio spegna,
E dopo voi l' indegna
Che il sangue suo tradì.

CARLOS: Madman! rising between us
A river of blood is flowing;
How can I call him brother,
Who did my hopes efface?
Whatever your origin may be,
I live but to destroy you;
Then too shall die the unworthy one
Who did betray her race.

ALVARO: Che dite?

ALVARO: What are you saying?

CARLO: Ella morrà.

CARLOS: She shall die!

ALVARO: Tacete!

ALVARO: Hold!

CARLO: Il giuoro
A Dio; cadrà l' infame.

CARLOS: I swear to heaven
The infamous wretch shall die!

ALVARO: Voi pria cadrete nel fatal certame.

ALVARO: You shall first die yourself in mortal combat.

CARLO: Morte! ov' io non cada esangue
Leonora giungerò.
Tinto àncor del vostro sangue
Questo acciar le immergerò.

CARLOS: But before I fall, Leonora shall perish!
This sword, with your blood dyed red
I will plunge into her heart.

ALVARO: Morte, sì!—col drando mio.
Un sicario ucciderò;
Il pensier volgete a Dio,
L' ora vostra alfin suonò.
(Sguainano le spade e si battono furiosamente.)

ALVARO: Die! with my steel
Will I slay the assassin;
Turn your thoughts to heaven,
For your last hour is near.
(they draw swords and fight furiously.)

## SCENA IX

## SCENE IX

Accore la Pattuglia del campo per separarli.

The Sentries of the Camp run to part them.

CORO: Fermi, arrestate!

CHORUS: Hold! Stay!

CARLO: (Furente.) No. La sua vita.

CARLOS: (Raging.) No: his life!

CORO: Lunge di qua si tragga.

CHORUS: Drag him here!

ALVARO: (Forse—del ciel l' aita a me soccorre.)

ALVARO: (Heaven has sent me aid.)

CARLO: Colui morrà!

CARLOS: He shall die.

CORO: (A Carlo che cerca svincolarsi.) Vieni.

CHORUS: (Don Carlos, who tries to fight him.) Come away.

CARLO: (A Don Alvaro viene trascinato altrove dalla pattuglia.) Carnefice del padre mio!

CARLOS: (to Don Alvaro, as he is dragged off by the Sentries.) Murderer of my father!

ALVARO: Or che mi resta! Pietoso Iddio
Tu inspira, illumina il mio pensier.
(Gettando la spada.)
Al chiostro, all' eremo, ai santi altari
L' obblio, la pace chiegga il guerrier.
(Esce.)

ALVARO: What now remains for me? Merciful Heaven,
A thought from above inspires me.
(throws down the sword.)
To the cloister I go and at the holy altar,
The warrior will seek peaceful oblivion.
(exit.)

## SCENA X

## SCENE X

Spunta il sole.—il rullo dei tamburi e lo squillo delle trombe danno il segnale della sveglia. La scena va animandosi a poco a poco. Soldati Spagnuoli ed Italiani di tutte le armi sortono dalle tende ripulendo schioppi, spade, uniformi, ecc. ecc. Ragazzi militari giuocano ai dadi sui tamburi. Vivandiere che vendono liquori, frutta, pane, ecc., Preziosilla dall' alto d' una baracca predice la buona ventura. Scena animatissima.

Sunrise. The roll of drums and call of trumpets give the signal for waking. The scene gradually becomes full of life. Spanish and Italian soldiers emerge from their tents, cleaning muskets, swords, uniforms, etc. etc. Young recruits play at dice on the drum heads. Vivandiers sell liquors, fruit, bread, etc. Preziosilla, mounted on a stand, tells fortunes. Great animation.

CORO: Lorchè pifferi e tamburi
Par che assordino la terra,
Siam felici, ch' è la guerra
Gioia e vita al militar.
Vita gaia, avventurosa,
Cui non cal doman nè jeri,
ch' ama tutti i suoi pensieri
Sol nell' oggi concentrar.

CHORUS: When fife and drums
Deafen the world,
We rejoice, for war to the soldier
Is life and full delight
A life of joy and adventure
To him who cares nothing for tomorrow;
Who loves in his thoughts to dwell
On the bright hopes of today.

PREZIOSILLA: (Alle Donne.)
Venite all' indovina.
Ch' è giunta di lontano,
E puote a voi l' arcano,
Futuro decifrar.
(Ai Soldati.) Correte a lei d' intorno,

PREZIOSILLA: (To the Women.)
Come to the fortune-teller,
Who has come from distant parts;
She can reveal to you
What the future will bring.
(to the Soldiers.)
Come around her,

La mano le porgete.
Le amanti apprenderete
Se fide vi restar.

And hold out your hands;
So all of you can learn
If your maidens be true.

**CORO:** Corriamo all' indovina
La mano le porgiamo,
Le belle udir possiamo
Se fide vi restar.

**CHORUS:** Let us haste to the teller
of fortunes,
And show her our hands,
Thus we all can learn
If our fair ones are true.

**PREZIOSILLA:** Chi vuole il paradiso
Si accendo di valore,
E il barbaro invasore
S' accenga a debellar.
Avanti, avanti, avanti.
Predirvi sentirete
Qual premio coglierete
Dal vostro battagliar.
(*Molti la circondano.*)

**PREZIOSILLA:** He who longs for
Paradise
Must show himself brave,
Prepare to subdue
The savage horde of invaders,
Come on, come on, come on,
And you shall hear foretold
What prize you shall win
In the war that you wage.
(*many surround her.*)

**CORO:** Avanti, ec.

**CHORUS:** Come on, etc.

**SOLDATI:** Qua, vivandiere, un sorso.
(*La Vivandiere versano loro.*)

**SOLDIERS:** Here, vivandiers, give
us a drink.
(*the vivandiers give them drink.*)

**UNO:** Alla salute nostra!

**A SOLDIER:** To our own health we
drink!

**TUTTI:** (*Bevendo.*) Viva!

**ALL:** (*Drinking*) Hurrah!

**ALTRO:** A Spagna! ed all' Italia unite!

**ANOTHER:** To Spain and Italy united!

**TUTTI:** Evviva!

**ALL:** Hurrah!

**PREZIOSILLA:** Al nostro eroe, Don
Federico Herreros.

**PREZIOSILLA:** To our hero, Don
Federico Herreros!

**TUTTI:** Viva! Viva!

**ALL:** Hurrah! hurrah!

**UNO:** Ed al suo degno amico
Don Felice de Bornos.

**A SOLDIER:** And to his noble
friend,
Don Felice de Bornos!

**TUTTI:** Viva! viva!

**ALL:** Hurrah! Hurrah!

## SCENA XI

## SCENE XI

*L'attenzione e attirata da Trabuco, rivendugilolo, che dalla bottega a sinistra viene con una cassetta al colla portante vari oggetti di meschino valore.*

*Trabuco, the Pedlar, attracts their attention, who, from the shop on the left, comes with a box at his waist, carrying various objects of small value.*

**TRABUCO:** A buon mercato chi
vuol comprare?
Forbici, spille, sapon perfetto!
(*Lo attorniano.*)
Io vendo e compero qualunque oggetto,
Concludo a pronti qualunque affare.

**TRABUCO:** Who will buy at a bargain?
Scissors, pins, scented soap!
(*they surround him.*)
I buy and sell all sorts of things
And quickly conclude my bargains.

**SOLDATO 1:** Ho qui un monile,
quanto mi dai?
(*La mostra.*)

**1ST SOLDIER:** Here is a necklace—what will you give?
(*showing it.*)

**SOLDATO 2:** Ve' una collana? Se
vuoi la vendo.
(*Lo mostra.*)

**2ND SOLDIER:** Here is another—
I will sell it.
(*showing it.*)

**SOLDATO 3:** Questi orecchini li
pagherai?
(*Lo mostra.*)

**3RD SOLDIER:** Will you pay the
price of these earrings?
(*showing it.*)

**CORO:** Vogliamo vendere?
(*Mostrando orologi, anelli, ecc.*)

**CHORUS:** We'll sell.
(*showing watches, rings, etc.*)

**TRABUCO:** Ma quanto vedo
Tutto è robaccia, brutta robaccia!

**TRABUCO:** But what you show me
Is all rubbish, mere rubbish!

**CORO:** Tale, o furfante, è la tua faccia.

**CHORUS:** Just like yourself, you rogue!

**TRABUCO:** Pure aggiustiamoci;
per ogni pezzo
Do trenta soldi.

**TRABUCO:** However, we may
agree: for each article
I will give thirty soldi.

**TUTTI:** (*Tumultuando.*) Da ladro
è il prezzo.

**ALL:** (*Enraged.*) It is the price of a
thief!

**TRABUCO:** Ih! quanta furia! c' intenderemo,
Qualch' altro soldo v' aggiungeremo—
Date qua, subito!

**TRABUCO:** Eh! what a fuss! we
shall agree,—
Another soldo we will add:
Give them here—quick.!

**CORO:** Purchè all' istante
Venga il danaro bello e sonante.

**CHORUS:** Provided on the instant
We see the money sound and shining.

**TRABUCO:** Prima la merce—
qua—colle buone.

**TRABUCO:** The merchandise
first—here—fair play.

**SOLDATI:** A te.
(*Dandogli gli affetti.*)

**SOLDIERS:** There's for you.
(*giving the things.*)

**ALTRI:** A te.
(*Dandogli gli affetti.*)

**OTHERS:** For you.
(*giving things.*)

**ALTRI:** A te.
(*Dandogli gli affetti.*)

**OTHERS:** For you.
(*giving things.*)

**TRABUCO:** (*Ritira le robe e
paga.*) A voi, a voi, benone!

**TRABUCO:** (*Taking the things
and paying.*) To you, to you, very
good!

**CORO:** Al diavol vattene!
(*Cacciandolo.*)

**CHORUS:** Go to the devil!
(*they drive him away.*)

**TRABUCO:** (*Da se contento.*)
(Che buon affare!)
A buon mercato chi vuol comprare?
(*Avviandosi ad altro lato del campo.*)

**TRABUCO:** (*Highly pleased.*)
(What good luck!)
Who will buy everything cheap?
(*goes to the other side of the camp.*)

## SCENA XII

## SCENE XII

*Detti, e Contadini questuanti,
con Ragazzi a mano.*

*The same, and Peasants begging
and leading Children.*

**CONTADINI:** Pane, pan per carità!
Tetti e campi devastati
N' ha la guerra, ed affamati,
Cerchaim pane per pietà.

**PEASANTS:** Bread, for charity's
sake!
The war has destroyed
Our homes and our fields;
Starving, we ask for bread!

## SCENA XIII

## SCENE XIII

*Detti, ed alcuni Reclute, piangenti, che giungono scortate.*

*The same, and some Recruits,
Weeping, With an Escort.*

**RECLUTE:** Povere madri deserte
nel pianto!
Per dura forza dovemmo lasciar.
Della beltà n' han rapiti all' incanto,
A' nostre case vogliamo tornar.

**RECRUITS:** Our poor mothers are
deserted in their grief!
By force we were made to leave,
And from our lovers' arms torn
away.
To our homes we wish to return.

**VIVANDIERE:** (*Accostandosi gaiamente alle Reclute, e offerendo
loro da bere.*) Non piangete, giovanotti,
Per le madri e per la belle;
V' ameremo quai sorelle,
Vi sapremo confortar.
Certo il diavolo non siamo;
Quelle lacrime tergete.
Al passato, ben vedete,
Ora è inutile pensar.

**VIVANDIERS:** (*Approaching gaily the Recruits, and offering them
drink.*) Do not repine, O young
men,
For your mothers and your lovers;
Like sisters we will love you,
And seek to console you.
We are not truly fiends,
So dry your tears
And cease to think
Upon the happy past.

**PREZIOSILLA:** (*Entrando fra le
Reclute, ne prende alcune pel
braccio, e dice loro burlescamente.*) Che vergogna!—Su coraggio!
Bei figliuoli, siete pazzi?
Sè piangete quai ragazzi,

**PREZIOSILLA:** (*Mixing with the
Recruits, takes some of them by
the arm, and says, jeeringly.*)
Shame on you!—Show more courage!
Great babies, are you mad?
If you wail like little children

## Act III, Scene XIII

Vi farete corbellar.
Un' occhiata a voi d' intorno,
E scommetto che indovino;
Ci sarà più d' un visino,
Che sapravvi consolar.

**TUTTI:** Nella guerra è la follia
Che dee il campo rallegrar.
Viva! viva la pazzia,
Che qui sola ha da regnar!
(*Le Vivandiere prendono francamente le Reclute pel braccio, o s' incominica vivacissima danza generale. Ben presto la confusione e lo schiamazzo giungono al como.*)

You will be jeered and hooted.
Cast your eyes around,
And I'll wager you can find
More than one face here
To console your vain regrets.

**ALL:** In war it is folly only
That makes the camp resound.
Hurrah! long life to folly.
That alone has a right to reign!
(*the Vivandiers boldly sieze the Recruits by the arm, and commence a dance all around. Soon the noise and confusion reach its height.*)

## SCENA XIV

*Detti e Fra Melitone, che preso nel vortice della danza, e per un momento costretto a ballare colle Vivandiere. Finalmente, riuscito a fermarsi, esclama:*

**MELITONE:** Toh, toh! poffare il mondo! oh che tempone!
Corre ben l' aventura!—Anch' io ci sono!
Venni di Spagna a medicar ferite,
Ed alme a medicar. Che vedo! è questo
Un campo di Christiani, o siete Turchi?
Dove s' è visto berteggiar la santa
Domenica così? Ben più faccenda
Le bottiglie vi dan che le battaglie!
E invece di vestir cenere e sacco
Qui si tresca con Venere, con Bacco?
Il mondo è fatto una casa di pianto;
Ogni convento, o qual profanazione!
Or è covo del vento! I Santuari
Spelonche diventàr di sanguinari
E perfino i tabernacoli di Cristo
Fatti son ricettacoli del tristo.
Tutto è soqquadro.
E la ragion? pe' vostri
Peccati.

## SCENE XIV

*The same, and Brother Melitone, who, seized in the whirl of the dance, is obliged to dance with the Vivandiers. At last, managing to release himself, he exclaims:*

**MELITONE:** Oh, oh! good heaven! what a wild life!
Adventures are coming fast!—I am in for it!
I came from Spain to heal wounds,
And to cure souls. What do I see?
Is this a camp of Christians or of Turks?
Where do people make such a mockery
Of the holy Sabbath? You have more to do
With bottles than with battles!
And instead of putting on sackcloth and ashes,
You play tricks with Venus and Bacchus,
The world is made a place of tears;
Every convent—oh, what profanation—
Is open to the winds. The sanctuaries
have become dens of murderers!
And, to crown all, the most sainted shrines
Made refuges for rascals,
All is upset; and how?
Through your sins.

**SOLDATI:** Ah, frate! frate!

**MELITONE:** Voi le feste
Calpestate, rubate, bestemmiate—

**SOLDATI ITALIANO:** Togone infame!

**SOLDATI SPAG:** Segui pur, padruccio.

**MELITONE:** E membra e capi siete d' una stampa;
Tutti eretici.

**ITALIANO:** Or or l' aggiustiam noi.

**MELITONE:** Tutti, tutti, cloaca di peccati,
E finchè il mondo puzzi di tal pece
Non isperi mai la terra alcuna pace.

**ITALIANO:** Dàlle, dàlli!
(*Serrandolo intorno*)

**SOLDIERS:** Ah, friar! friar!

**MELITONE:** You despise the feasts of the Church,
You rob, you swear—

**ITALIAN SOLDIER:** Infernal friar!

**SPANISH SOLDIER:** Go on, old fellow.

**MELITONE:** And chiefs and soldiers all of a stamp,
All heretics.

**ITALIAN:** We will soon settle you.

**MELITONE:** All, all, sinks of iniquity;
And until the world is smothered with tar,
The earth cannot hope for peace.

**ITALIAN:** Give it to him!
(*crowding round him.*)

**SPAGNO:** (*Difendendolo.*) Scappa! scappa!

**ITALIANO:** Dàlle, dàlli sulla cappa!
(*Cercano picchiarlo, ma egli se la svigna, declamando sempre.*)

**PREZIOSILLA:** (*A Soldati che lo inseguono uscendo di scena.*) Lasciatelo, ch' ei vada.
Far guerra ad un cappuccio!—bella impresa!
Non m' odon?—sia il tamburo sua difesa.
(*Prende a caso un tamburo, e imitata da qualche Tamburino, lo suona. I Soldati accorrono tosto a circondarla seguiti da tutta la turba.*)

**SPANISH:** (*Defending him*) Escape! be off!

**ITALIAN:** Give it to him—knock him on the head!
(*they try to beat him, but he avoids them, continuing to exclaim.*)

**PREZIOSILLA:** (*To the Soldiers, who follow him off the stage.*) Let him alone, let him go.
Make war upon a friar!—a fine affair!
They do not hear me—the drum shall defend him.
(*takes up a drum, and, imitated by a little Drummer, sounds it. The Soldiers immediately surround her, followed by the whole throng.*)

**PREZIOSILLA ED CORO:** Rataplan, rataplan, della gloria
Nel soldato ritempra l' ardor;
Rataplan, rataplan, di vittoria
Questro suono e segnal precursor!
Rataplan, rataplan,
rataplan, rataplan, rataplan,
rataplan, rataplan, plan, plan,
rataplan, rataplan, plan, plan,
Rataplan, si raccolgon le schiere,
Rataplan, son guidate a pugnar.
Rataplan, rataplan, le bandiere
Del nemico si veggon piegar!
Rataplan, pim, pum, pam, inseguite
Chi le terga, fuggendo, voltò.
Rataplan, le gloriose ferite
Col trionfo il destin coronò.
Rataplan, della patria la gloria,
Più rifulge de' fili al valor!
Rataplan, rataplan, la vittoria
Al guerriero conquista ogni cor.

**PREZIOSILLA AND CHORUS:** Rataplan, rataplan, songs of glory
Make the soldier's hear! thrill with delight;
Rataplan, rataplan, in a story
All their valorous deeds we recite.
Rataplan, rataplan, rataplan,
rataplan, rataplan, rataplan,
rataplan, rataplan, plan, plan,
rataplan, rataplan, plan, plan.
Rataplan, the troops assemble,
Rataplan, are led to the fight,
Rataplan, rataplan, the banners
Of the enemy give way before us.
Rataplan, pim, pum, pam, pursue
The coward who flees from the foe.
Rataplan, the wounds of the brave
Are crowned by fate with triumph.
Rataplan, the glory of the country
Shines forth in the valor of her sons!
Rataplan, rataplan, victory
Has won each warrior's heart.

*FINE DELL' ATTO TERZO.*

*END OF THE THIRD ACT.*

# ■ ATTO IV

## SCENA I

*Vicinanze d' Hornachuelos. Interno del Convento della Madonna degli Angeli. Meschino porticato circonda una Corticella con aranci, oleandri, gelsomini. Alla sinistra dello spettatore, e la porta che mette alla via; a destra altra porta, sopra la quale si legge 'Clausura.'*

*Il Padre Guardiano passeggia gravemente leggendo il breviario. Dalla sinistra entrano, molt Pezzenti, d' ogni eta e sesso, con rozze scodelle, alla mano pignatte o piatti.*

**CORO:** Fate la carità,
E un' ora che aspettiamo!
Andarcene dobbiamo,
Fate la carità.

# ■ ACT IV

## SCENE I

*The neighborhood of Hornachuelos. Interior of the convent of the Madonna degli Angeli. A simple Colonnade surrounds a small Court, filled with orange trees, oleanders, and jasmines. On left of the spectator, a door opening on the road; on the right another door, on which is written 'Clausura.'*

*The Father Guardiano walks about, seriously reading his breviary. From the left enter many Beggars, of each sex, with rough porringers, pipkins, or plates in their hands.*

**CHORUS:** Alms we beg of you.
An hour we have waited,
And soon we must go.
Alms! Alms!

## SCENA II

*Detti e Fra Melitone, che viene dalla destra, caperto il ventre d' ampio grembiale bianco ed ajutato da altro Laico, porta una grande caldaja a due manichi, che depongono nel centro; il Laico riparte.*

**MELITONE:** Che! siete all' osteria! Quieti.
*(Incomincia a distribuire col ramaiuolo la ministra.)*

**DONNE:** *(Spingendosi fra loro.)* Qui, presto a me.

**VECCHI:** Quante porzioni a loro.

**ALTRI:** Tutti vorrian per sè.

**TUTTI:** N' ebbe già tre Maria.

**UNA:** *(A Melitone.)* Quattro a me.

**TUTTI:** Quattro a lei!

**DETTI:** Sì, perchè ho sie figliuolì.

**MELITONE:** Perchè ne avete sei?

**DETTA:** Perchè li mandò Iddio.

**MELITONE:** Sì, sì, Dio—non li avreste
Se al par di me voi pure la schiena percoteste
Con aspra disciplina, e più le notti intere
Passaste recitando rosari e miserere.

**GUARDIANO:** Fratel—

**MELITONE:** Ma tai pezzenti son di fecondità.
Davvero spaventosa.

**GUARDIANO:** Abbiate carità.

**VECCHI:** Un po' di quel fondaccio ancora ne donate.

**MELITONE:** Il ben di Dio, bricconi, fondaccio voi chiamate?

**ALCUNI:** A me padre!
*(Presentando le scodelle.)*

**ALTRI:** A me.
*(Presentando le scodelle.)*

**MELITONE:** Oh andatene in malora,
O il ramajuol sul capo v' aggiusto bene or ora!
Io perdo la pazienza!

**GUARDIANO:** Oh, carità, fratello!

**DONNE:** Più carità ne usava il padre Raffaello.

**MELITONE:** Sì, sì ma in otto giorno, avutone abbastanza.
Di poveri e ministra, restò nella sua stanza.
E scaricò la soma sul dosso a Melitone,
E poi con tal canaglia usar dovrò le buone?

## SCENE II

*The above and Brother Melitone, who comes from the right, with a large white apron in front, and, aided by another Lay brother, carries a great cauldron with two handles, which they place in the middle; the Lay brother goes away.*

**MELITONE:** What! do you take this for an inn? Be silent.
*(begins to distribute the minestra with a ladle.)*

**WOMEN:** *(Pushing forward.)* Quick, give me some.

**OLD MEN:** What a quantity for them.

**OTHERS:** Each wants for it himself.

**ALL:** Maria has already had three.

**A WOMAN:** *(To Melitone.)* Four for me.

**ALL:** Four for her!

**WOMAN:** Yes, for I have six children.

**MELITONE:** Why have you six?

**WOMAN:** Because Heaven sent them to me.

**MELITONE:** Ay, ay, Heaven—you would not have them
If, like me, you scourged your back
With a sharp scourge, and spent the night
In reciting rosaries and misereres.

**GUARDIANO:** Brother—

**MELITONE:** But these beggars are prolific
To such a wonderful degree.

**GUARDIANO:** Be merciful.

**OLD MEN:** Give us a little more of these dregs.

**MELITONE:** A godsend, you rogues, and you call it dregs!

**SOME:** To me, Father!
*(presenting their porringers.)*

**OTHERS:** To me?
*(presenting theirs.)*

**MELITONE:** Go to Jericho,
Or I will lay the ladle about your heads!
I lose all patience!

**GUARDIANO:** Be merciful, brother!

**WOMEN:** Father Raffaello was more kind.

**MELITONE:** True, true, but after a week of soup and beggars
He had enough and took to his bed.
He left his burden on the back of Melitone.
And how can I be gentle with such rabble?

**GUARDIANO:** Soffrono tanto i poveri: la carità è un dovere.

**MELITONE:** Carità con costoro che il fannoper mestiere?
Che un campanile abbattere co' pugni sarien buoni,
Che dicono fondaccio il ben di Dio? Bricconi!

**ALCUNI:** Oh, il padre Raffaele—

**ALTRI:** Era un angelo.

**ALTRI:** Un santo!

**TUTTI:** Se il padre Raffaele—

**MELITONE:** Non m'annojate tanto!
*(Distribuisce in fretta il residuo, dicendo—)*
Il resto, a voi, prendetevi,
Non voglio più parole!
*(Fa rotolare la caldaia con un calcio.)*
Fuori di qua, lasciatemi,
Sì fuori, al sole, al sole:
Pezzenti più di Lazzaro,
Sacchi di pravità,
Via, via, bricconi, al diavolo!
Toglietevi di qua!
*(Indispettito le scaccia, confusamente, percuotendoli col grembiale che si sara tolto, e chiude la porta, restandone assai adirato e stanco.)*

## SCENA III

*Il Padre Guardaino e Melitone.*

**MELITONE:** *(Asciugandosi il sudore con un fazzoletto bianco che avara cavato da una manica.)*
Auf! pazienza non v'ha che basti!

**GUARDIANO:** Troppa
Dal Signor non ne aveste:
Facendo carità un dover s' adempie
Da render fiero un angiol.

**MELITONE:** *(Prendendo tabacco.)* Che a! mio posto
In tre dì finerebbe
Col ministrar de' schiaffi.

**GUARDIANO:** Tacete; umil sia Meliton, nè soffra
Se veda preferirsi Raffaele.

**MELITONE:** Io? no—amico gli son, ma ha certi gesti.
Parla da sè—ha cert' occhi.

**GUARDIANO:** Son le preci,
Il digiun.

**MELITONE:** Jer nell' orto lavorava
Cotanto stralunato, che scherzando,
Dissi: Padre, un mulatto
Parmi-Guardommi bieco,
Strinse le pugna, e—

**GUARDIANO:** Ebbene?

**GUARDIANO:** They suffer much: charity toward them is a duty.

**MELITONE:** Charity to those who make it their trade?
Who could fell a steeple with their fists?
Who call this godsend dregs? The rogues!

**SOME:** Oh, Father Raffaello—

**OTHERS:** Was an angel!

**OTHERS:** A saint!

**ALL:** Yes, Father Raffaello—

**MELITONE:** Don't bother me so!
*(hastily distributing what remains, saying—)*
Take what is left.
*(makes the cauldron roll over with a kick.)*
I will have no more words—go?
Out of here—leave me!
Yes, go and warm yourselves in the sun;
Beggars greater than Lazarus,
Bags of depravity,
Go, rascals, go to the devil!
Be off from here!
*(he angrily drives them out, striking them with the apron he has taken off, and shuts the door, remaining very angry and tired.)*

## SCENE III

*Father Guardiano And Melitone*

**MELITONE:** *(Wiping off the perspiration with a white handkerchief, which he takes from his sleeve.)* Ouf! I have no more patience!

**GUARDIANO:** Truly Heaven has not
Blessed you with over much;
Giving charity is fulfilling a duty
Which might rejoice an angel.

**MELITONE:** *(Taking snuff.)* Who would be done for in my place
In three days.

**GUARDIANO:** Silence: be humble, Melitone, nor be vexed.
Though Raffaello be preferred.

**MELITONE:** I? no—I am his friend:
but he has such ways.
He talks to himself—has such looks.

**GUARDIANO:** It is through his praying
And fasting.

**MELITONE:** Yesterday, as he worked in the orchard.
His eyes seemed so starting out, that jestingly
I said, 'Father, you look like a mulatto!'
He turned an angry glance on me,
Clenched his fist, and—

**GUARDIANO:** What then?

## Act IV, Scene III

**MELITONE:** Quando cadde
Sul campanil la fulgore, ed usciva
Fra la tempesta gli fridai: Mi sembra
Indo selvaggio un urlo
Cacciò che mi gelava.

**GUARDIANO:** Che v' ha a ridir?

**MELITONE:** Nulla, ma il guardo e penso
Che il demonio, narraste,
Qui stette un tempo in abito da frate,
Gli fosse il padre Raffael parente?

**GUARDIANO:** Giudizii temerarii. Il ver narrai;
Ma n' ebbe il superior revilazione
Allora. Io, no.

**MELITONE:** Ciò è vero!
Ma strano è molto il padre! La ragione?

**GUARDIANO:** Del mondo i disinganni,
L' assidua penitenza.
Le veglie, l' astinenza
Quell' anima turbar.

**MELITONE:** Saranno i disinganni
Adunque e l' astinenza.
L' assidua penitenza,
Che il capo gli guastar!
(*Si suona con forza il campanello alla porta.*)

**GUARDIANO:** Giunge qualcuno—aprite.
(*Parte.*)

### SCENA IV

*Fra Melitone e Don Carlo, che avviluppato in un grande mantello, entra francamente.*

**CARLO:** (*Alteramente.*) Siete voi il portiere?

**MELITONE:** (E goffo ben costui!)
S' ora v' apersi, parmi.

**CARLO:** Il padre Raffaele?

**MELITONE:** (Un altro!) Due ne abbiamo;
L' un di Porcuna, grasso,
Sordo come una talpa, l' altro scarno,
Bruno, occhi (ciel quali occhi!) voi chiedete?

**CARLO:** Quell dell' inferno.

**MELITONE:** (E desso!) E chi gli annuncio?

**CARLO:** Un cavalier.

**MELITONE:** (Qual boria! è un mal arnese.)
(*Parte.*)

### SCENA V

*Don Carlos, poi Don Alvaro in abito da frate.*

---

**MELITONE:** When the lightning struck the steeple,
As he went out into the storm, I cried,
'You look to me like a wild Indian!'
Whereupon he uttered a howl
That froze my blood.

**GUARDIANO:** What followed?

**MELITONE:** Nothing; but I looked at him, and thought
That the demon you told us of,
Who once lived here in a friar's dress,
Might be a relative of Father Raffaello.

**GUARDIANO:** A rash judgment. I told the tale;
But to the superior it was revealed,
And not to me.

**MELITONE:** That is true;
But the father is most strange! What is the cause?

**GUARDIANO:** Finding out the deceit of the world,
Constantly performing penance,
Vigils and abstinence,
Have disturbed his mind.

**MELITONE:** Discovering the world's deceit,
The various abstinences,
And the frequent penances,
Have upset his brain!
(*the bell at the door is rung violently.*)

**GUARDIANO:** Someone has arrived—open.
(*exit.*)

### SCENE IV

*Father Melitone, and Don Carlos, who enters boldly, wrapped in a great cloak.*

**CARLOS:** (*Haughtily.*) Are you the porter?

**MELITONE:** (The man must be a fool!)
It appears to me I just let you in.

**CARLOS:** Father Raffaello?

**MELITONE:** (Another!) We have two of them;
One from Porcuna, fat,
Deaf as a post; the other lean, dark eyes,
(Heavens, what eyes!) Which do you want?

**CARLOS:** The fiend.

**MELITONE:** (It is he!) And whom shall I announce?

**CARLOS:** A cavalier.

**MELITONE:** (What arrogance! an ill-bred fellow.)
(*exit.*)

### SCENE V

*Don Carlos, after him Don Alvaro, in a monk's habit.*

---

**CARLO:** Invano Alvaro ti celasti al mondo
E d'ipocrita veste
Scudo fecesti alla viltà. Del chiostro
Ove t' ascondi m' additàr la via
L'odio e la sete di vendetta; alcuno
Qui non sarà che ne divida;
Solo il tuo sangue può lavar l' oltraggio
Che macchiò l' onor mio;
E tutto il verserò, lo giuro a Dio.

**ALVARO:** Fratello—

**CARLO:** Riconoscimi.

**ALVARO:** Don Carlo! Voi vivente!

**CARLO:** Da un lustro ne vo' in traccia,
Ti trovo finalmente:
Col sangue sol cancellasi
L' infamia ed il delitto.
Ch' io ti punisca è scritto
Sul libro del destin.
Tu prode fosti, or monaco,
Un' arma qui non hai;
Deggio il tuo sangue spargere,
Scegli, due ne portai.

**ALVARO:** Vissi nel mondo—intendo;
or queste vesti l'eremo,
Dicon che i falli ammendo,
Ah! cessi il sangue alfin!
Lasciateme.

**CARLO:** Difendere
Quel sajo, nè il deserto.
Codardo, non ti possono.

**ALVARO:** (*Trasalendo.*) Codardo!
tale asserto—
(*Poi frenandosi.*)
(Ah no!—assistima, Signore!)
(*A Don Carlo.*)
La minaccie, i fieri accenti,
Portin seco in preda i venti;
Perdonatemi, pietà.
A che offendere cotanto
Chi fu solo sventurato!
Deh chiniam la fronte al fato:
O fratel, pietà, pietà!

**CARLO:** Tu contamini tal nome.
Una suora mi lasciasti
Chi tradita abbandonasti
All' infamia, al disonor.

**ALVARO:** (*Furente.*) Ah, seguasti la tua sorte!
Morte a entrambi!
(*Raccogliendo la spada.*)

**CARLO:** A entrambi morte!

**A 2:** Paga l' ira alfin sarà.
Te l' inferno ingoierà!
(*Escono currendo dalla sinistra.*)

---

**CARLOS:** In vain, Alvaro, you hide from the world,
And with hypocrite's garb
You would shield villainy. To the cloister
Which concealed you, hate
And vengeance pointed out the way.
None here shall hold me from you;
Your blood alone can cleanse the stain
From my outraged honor:
And before heaven I swear to shed it!

**ALVARO:** Brother—

**CARLOS:** Behold and know me.

**ALVARO:** Don Carlos! Alive!

**CARLOS:** For five years I have been on your track,
At length I find you;
With blood alone can your infamy
And misdeeds be blotted out.
It is written in the book of fate
That I shall punish you.
You were then valiant, now a monk;
You have no weapon here;
As I must shed your blood,
I have brought two: choose.

**ALVARO:** I have lived in the world—I understand;
I wear the garments, this desert place,
Proclaim my reformed errors,
Ah! at least cease this strife;—
Leave me.

**CARLOS:** Coward,
Neither the cassock, or the desert,
Can protect you!

**ALVARO:** (*Shrinking.*) Coward!
that assertion—
(*restraining himself.*)
(Ah no!—help me, Heaven!)
(*to Don Carlos.*)
Threats, fierce and angry tones
Are cast to the winds;
Pardon and pity me.
Why goad so far
Him who was only unfortunate?
Let us yield to fate;
Brother, mercy, mercy!

**CARLOS:** You contaminate the name.
You have left me a sister
Whom you did betray, and then abandoned
To infamy and dishonor!

**ALVARO:** (*Furiously.*) Your death warrant is sealed!
Death to both!
(*picks up the sword.*)

**CARLOS:** Death to both!

**BOTH:** Wrong shall at last be avenged,
And hell shall receive you!
(*they rush out towards the left.*)

## SCENA VI

*Valle tra rupi inaccessibili, attraversata da un ruscello. Nel fondo, a sinistra dello spetattore, e una Grotta con porta practicabile, e sopra una campana che si potra suonare dall' interno. E il tramonto. La scena si oscura lentamente; la luna apparisce splendidissima.*

*Donna Leonora pallida, sfigurata, esce dalla grotta agitatissima.*

**LEONORA:** Pace, pace, mio Dio! cruda sventura
M' astringe, ahimè, a languir;
Come il dì primo da tant' anni dura
Profondo il mio soffrir.
L'amai, gli è ver! ma di beltà e valore
Cotando Iddio l' ornò.
Che l' amo ancor, nè togliermi dal core
L'imagine saprò.
Fatalità! fatalità!—un delitto
Disgiunti n' ha quaggiù!
Alvaro, io t' amo, e su mel cielo è scritto;
Non ti vedrò mai più!
Oh, Dio, Dio fa ch'io muoia; chè la calma
Può darmi morte sol.
Invan la pace qui sperò quest'alma
In preda a lungo duol.
*(Va ad un sasso, ove sono alcune provigione deposte da Padre Guardiano.)*
Misero pane, a prolungarmi vieni
La sconsolata vita—ma chi giunge?
Profanare che ardisce il sacro loco?
Maledizione! maledizione!
*(Torna rapidamente alla Grotta, e vi si rinchiude.)*

## SCENA VII

*Si ode dentro la scena un cozzar di spade.*

**CARLO:** (*Dal' interno.*) Io muoio!—Confession!—
L'alma salvate.
*(Alvaro entra in scena colla spada sguainata.)*
E questo ancor sangue d'un Vargas.
*(Sempre dall' interno.)*
Padre. Confession.

**ALVARO:** (*Getta la spada.*) Maledetto io son; ma è presso
Un eremita.
*(Corre alla grotta e batte alla porto.)*
A confortar correte
Un uom che muor.

**LEONORA:** (*Dall'interno*) Nol posso.

**ALVARO:** Fratello! in nome del Signor.

**LEONORA:** Nol posso.

## SCENE VI

*A valley among inaccessible rocks, traversed by a stream. At the back, on the left of the spectator, is a Grotto with a practicable door, and above it a bell, which can be sounded from within. The sun has set. The scene darkens gradually; the moon rises brightly.*

*Donna Leonora, pale, wan, enters agitated from the grotto.*

**LEONORA:** Peace, grant me peace, O Lord;
By dire misfortune I'm condemned to languish;
As on the first day, during so many years,
Profound has been my grief.
I loved him! with beauty and courage
Heaven had so endowed him.
I love him still, nor can I banish his image from my heart.
O cruel fate!—a crime
Has parted us forever here below!
Alvaro, I love you and in heaven it is decreed
That I shall never see you again!
O Lord, suffer me to die, for peace
Comes to my soul only in death.
Here I hope in vain for peace,
A prey to lingering woe.
*(she goes to a stone, on which are some provisions, placed there by Father Guardiano.)*
Miserable food, you come to prolong
A wretched life—but who approaches?
Who dares profane this sacred spot?
Malediction! malediction!
*(returns quickly to the Grotto and shuts herself in.)*

## SCENE VII

*A clashing of swords is heard close at hand.*

**CARLOS:** (*Without.*) I am slain!—Absolution!
Save my soul.
*(Alvaro enters, with unsheathed sword.)*
Again the blood of Vargas is shed.
*(Still without.)*
A priest—absolution.

**ALVARO:** (*Throwing down the sword.*) I am accursed:
But here dwells a hermit.
*(runs to cave, and beats at the door.)*
Hasten to aid.
A dying man.

**LEONORA:** (*From the cave.*) I cannot.

**ALVARO:** Brother, in the name of heaven!

**LEONORA:** I cannot come.

**ALVARO:** (*Batte con piu forza.*) E d' uopo.

**LEONORA:** (*Dall'interno suonando la campana.*) Ajuto! Ajuto!

**ALVARO:** Deh venite.

## SCENA VIII

*Detto e Leonora che si presenta sulla porta.*

**LEONORA:** Temerarii, del ciel l' ira fuggite!

**ALVARO:** Una donna! qual voce—ah no—uno spettro.

**LEONORA:** (*Riconoscendo Don Alvaro.*) Che miro?

**ALVARO:** Tu—Leonora!

**LEONORA:** Egli è ben desso. (*Avvicinandosi ad Alvaro.*) Io ti riveggo ancora.

**ALVARO:** Lungi—lungi da me—queste mie mani
Grondano sangue. Indietro!

**LEONORA:** Che mai parli?

**ALVARO:** (*Accennando.*) Là giace spento un uom.

**LEONORA:** Tu l'uccidesti?

**ALVARO:** Tutto tentai per evitar la pugna.
Chiusi i miei dì nel chiostro.
Ei mi raggiunse—m' insultò—l'uccisi.

**LEONORA:** Ed era?

**ALVARO:** Tuo fratello!

**LEONORA:** Gran Dio?
*(Corre ansante verso il bosco.)*

**ALVARO:** Destino avverso
Come a scherno mi prendi!
Vive Leonora e ritrovarla deggio
Or che versai di suo fratello il sangue!

**LEONORA:** (*Dall'interno, mette un grido.*) Ah!

**ALVARO:** Qual grido!—che avvenne?

## SCENA IX

*Leonora ferita entra sostenuta dal Guardiano e detto.*

**ALVARO:** Ella—ferita!

**LEONORA:** (*Morente.*) Nell' ora estrema perdonar non seppe.
E l'onta vendicò nel sangue mio.

**ALVARO:** E tu paga non eri
O vendetta di Dio!—Maledizione!

**GUARDIANO:** (*Solenne.*) Non imprecare; umiliati
A lui ch'è giusto e santo—
Che adduce a eterni gaudii
Per una via di pianto.
D'ira e furor sacrilego.

**ALVARO:** (*Beating furiously.*)
His last moments are near.

**LEONORA:** (*Ringing the bell in the cave.*) Help! help!

**ALVARO:** Come quickly!

## SCENE VIII

*Leonora appears at the door of the cave.*

**LEONORA:** Rash one, fly from the wrath of heaven!

**ALVARO:** A woman! that voice! ah, no it's a vision!

**LEONORA:** (*Recognizing Don Alvaro.*) What do I see!

**ALVARO:** Leonora!

**LEONORA:** It's he. (*Advancing to Alvaro.*)
Again I see you.

**ALVARO:** Away, away from me, my hands
Are stained with blood. Look there.

**LEONORA:** What do you mean?

**ALVARO:** (*Pointing.*) See, there lies a dying man.

**LEONORA:** You have killed him?

**ALVARO:** Vainly I tried to evade this fray.
I passed my life within the cloister's shelter.
He sought me out there—insulted me,—
I slew him.

**LEONORA:** And he was?

**ALVARO:** Your brother!

**LEONORA:** Great heaven!
*(runs breathlessly towards the wood.)*

**ALVARO:** Relentless destiny
Thus mocks me ever!
Leonora lives, and I meet her
With her brother's blood upon me.

**LEONORA:** (*Shrieks without.*)
Ah!

**ALVARO:** That cry! what has happened.

## SCENE IX

*Leonora enters, wounded, supported by Guardiano.*

**ALVARO:** It is she—wounded!

**LEONORA:** (*Dying*) In his last hour he did not pardon;
And revenged his shame with my blood.

**ALVARO:** And you are thus repaid,
Oh, vengeance of heaven! malediction!

**GUARDIANO:** (*Solemnly.*) Curse not. Humble yourself
Before Him who is just and holy;
Who by a path of tears
To eternal joys conducts thee.
Do not pour forth words.

## Act IV, Scene IX

Non profferir parola,
Mentre quest' angiol vola
Al trono del Signor.

**LEONORA:** (*Con voce morente.*)
Si, piangi—e prega.

**ALVARO:** Un reprobe un maledetto io sono.
Flutto di sange inalzasi.
Fra noi.

**LEONORA:** Di Dio il perdono io ti prometto.

**GUARDIANO:** Prostrati!

**LEONORA:** Alvaro.

**ALVARO:** A quell' accento
Più non poss' io resistere.
(*Gettandosi ai piedi di Leonora.*)
Leonora, io son redento,
Dal ciel son perdonato!

**LEONORA E GUARDIANO:** Sia lode a te Signore.

Of ire and sacrilegious fury.
While this angel ascends
To the heavenly throne.

**LEONORA:** (*With dying accents.*)
Yes,—weep and pray.

**ALVARO:** Reprobate, I am accursed.
Barriers of blood between us
Have arisen.

**LEONORA:** Heaven grants me power to pardon you.

**GUARDIANO:** Kneel.

**LEONORA:** Alvaro—

**ALVARO:** Those loved tones I can no more resist.
(*throwing himself at Leonora's feet.*)
Leonora, I am saved,
Heaven has forgiven my sins.

**LEONORA & GUARDIANO:** Power eternal, praise be to your name!

**LEONORA:** (*Ad Alvaro.*) Lieta or poss' io precederti.
Alla promessa terra.
Là cesserà guerra.
Santo l'amor sarà.

**ALVARO:** Tu mi condanni a vivere,
E mi abbandoni intanto!
Il reo, il reo soltanto.
Dunque impunito andrà!

**GUARDIANO:** Santa del suo màrtirio
Ella al Signore ascenda.
E il suo morir ti apprenda
La fede e la pieta!

**LEONORA:** O Ciel ti attendo, addio!
Io ti precedo Alvaro.

**ALVARO:** Morta!

**GUARDIANO:** Salita a Dio.
(*Cala lentamente la tela.*)

*FINE DELL' OPERA.*

**LEONORA:** (*To Alvaro.*) Gladly now can I precede you
To the promised land;
There strife shall cease.
And holy love shall reign.

**ALVARO:** You condemned me to live
While thus forsaking me;
I, the guilty one,
Alone go unpunished.

**GUARDIANO:** Holy in her martyrdom,
She now departs to heaven;
And piety and faith
Her death will teach you.

**LEONORA:** Oh, heaven, I await you; farewell,
I do but precede you, Alvaro.

**ALVARO:** Dead!

**GUARDIANO:** Ascended to heaven!
(*Curtain slowly falls.*)

*END OF THE OPERA.*

# Aïda (1871)

MUSIC BY GIUSEPPE VERDI ■ LIBRETTO BY ANTONIO GHISLANZONI

This four-act opera, set to a libretto by Antonio Ghislanzoni (based on a fragment by François Auguste Mariette which was elaborated on by Camille Du Locle together with the composer), was first performed at the Opera House in Cairo on December 24, 1871. At the Hall in the Royal Palace of Memphis, Ramfis, the High Priest, consults the gods for guidance. The Ethiopian enemy is advancing, threatening Thebes. Radamès has been chosen to lead the Egyptian army. Amneris, daughter of the king of Egypt, is in love with him, although she realizes that he is in love with Aida, the Ethiopian slave who is really the daughter of Amonasro, the Ethiopian king. Aida is torn between her loyalty to her country and her love for Radamès. At the temple of Vulcan, Radamès receives a sword and blessings for victory from Ramfis. The Egyptians win, but Amneris tells Aida that Radamès is dead—a lie. Amneris also tells Aida that she is Aida's rival for Radamès' love. Radamès returns to Thebes in triumph and Amneris crowns him the victor. Radamès asks the king to spare the lives of the Ethiopian prisoners. Aida's father is among them; he pleads with her not to reveal his identity. The priests demand either death for the prisoners or that Aida be kept in exchange for their freedom. The king promises Amneris to Radamès. Radamès and Aida swallow their grief. As the wedding approaches, Amneris prays at the temple of Isis. Amonasro gets Aida to obtain tactical information from Radamès. He tells her that the Napata pass is unprotected. Amonasro overhears this. Radamès realizes that he has given information to Amonasro. He turns himself in. Amneris pleads with him to give up Aida. He refuses, and is sentenced to be buried alive by the priests. Buried in a crypt below the Temple of Vulcan, he finds Aida there, waiting for him. Amneris mourns above while the lovers sing of their love and wait to die together.

---

## ■ ATTO I

### SCENA I

*Sala nel Palazza del Re a Menfi. A destra et a sinistra una colonnata con statue e arbusti in flori Grande porta nel fondo, de cui appariccone i templi, i palazzi di Menfi e le Piramidi.*

*(Radames e Ramfis)*

**RAMFIS:** Sì: corre voci che l'Etiope ardisca
Sfidarci ancora, e del Nilo la valle
E Tebe miniacciar Fra breve un messo
Recherà il ver.

**RADAMES:** La sacra
Iside consultasti?

**RAMFIS:** Ella ha nomato
Delle Egizie falangi
El condottier supremo.

**RADAMES:** Oh lui felice!

**RAMFIS:** (*con intenzione, fissando Radames*). Giovine e prode è desso Ora, del Nume
Reco i decreti al Re.
(*Esce.*)

**RADAMES:** (*solo*). Se quel guerrier
Io fossi! se il mio sogno
Si avverasse! Un esercito di prodi
Da me guidato e la vittoria e il plauso

## ■ ACT I

### SCENE I

*Hall in the Palace of the King at Memphis; to the right and left a colonnade with statues and flowering shrubs; at the back a grand gate, from which may be seen the temples and palaces of Memphis and the Pyramids.*

*(Radames and Ramphis.)*

**RAMPHIS:** Yes, a report runs that the Ethiopian dares
Again defy us, and to threaten the Valley of the Nile
And Thebes. A messenger shortly Will bring the truth.

**RADAMES:** Did you consult the sacred Isis?

**RAMPHIS:** She has named the supreme leader.
Of the Egyptian phalanxes

**RADAMES:** Oh! happy man!

**RAMPHIS:** (*with meaning, gazing at Radames.*) Young and brave is he. Now to the king
I convey the decrees of the goddess.
(*Exit.*)

**RADAMES:** (*alone*). If I were that warrior! If my dream
Should be verified! An army of brave men
Led by me victory the applause Of all Memphis! And to you my

Di Menfi tutta! E a te, mia dolce Aïda,
Tornar di lauri cinto
Dirti: per te ho pugnato e per te ho vinto!

**RADAMES:** Celeste Aida, forma divina,
Mistico serto diluce e fior, del mio pensiero, tu sei regina, tu di mia vita sei lo splendor;
Il tuo bel cielo vorrei ridarti, le dolci brezze del patria suol, un regal serto sul crin posarti, engerti un trono vicino alsol, al!
Celeste Aida, forma divina, mistico raggio di luce e fior, del mio pensiero tu sei regina, tu di mia vita sei lo splendor.
Il tuo bel cielo vorrei ridarti; le dolci brezze del patria suol; un regal serto sul crin posarti, ergerti un trono vicino al sol, un trono vicino al sol, untrono vicino al sol.
(*Amneris e detto.*)

**AMNERIS:** Quale insolita givia Nel tuo sguardo! Di quale
Nobil fierezza ti balena il volto!
Degna di invidia oh! quanto
Saria la donna il cui bramato aspetto
Tanta luce di gaudio in te destasse!

**RADAMES:** D'un sogno avventuroso
Si beava il mio cuore Oggi, la diva Profferse il nome del guerrier che al campo

sweet Aïda,
To return, crowned with laurels!
To say to you, for you I have fought, and for you conquered!

**RADAMES:** Heavenly Aida, beauty resplendent,
Mysterious blending of flowers and light,
Queen of my soul you reign transcendent, you are the splendor bright of my life.
To your bright skies once more I'd restore you,
To the soft air of your native land,
Garlands imperial
I would wreathe over you
Raise you a throne near the sun to stand! ah!
(*Enter Amneris.*)

**AMNERIS:** What unwonted fire in your glance!
With what noble pride glows your face.
Worthy of envy oh, how much
Would be the woman whose beloved aspect
Should awaken in you this light of joy!

**RADAMES:** With an adventurous dream
My heart was blessed. Today the goddess
Declared the name of the warrior

Le schière Egizie condurrà S'io fossi
A tale onor prescelto

who to the field
The Egyptian troops shall lead. If I were
To such honor destined!

**AMNERIS:** Nè un altro sogno mai
Più gentil più soave
Al cuore ti parlò? Non hai tu in Menfi
Desiderii speranze?

**AMNERIS:** Has not another dream
More gentle, more sweet,
Spoken to your heart? Have you not in Memphis
Desires hopes?

**RADAMES:** Io! (*quale inchiesta!*)
Forse l'arcano amore
Scoprì che m' arde in core
Della sua schiava il nome
Mi lesse nel pensier!

**RADAMES:** I! (What a question!
Perhaps she has discovered the hidden love
Which burns my heart
The name of her slave
She reads in my thoughts!)

**AMNERIS:** (Oh! guai se un altro amore
Ardesse a lui nel core!
Guai se il mio sguardo penetra
Questo fatal mister!)
(*Aìda e detto.*)

**AMNERIS:** (Oh! woe if another love
Should burn in his heart;
Woe, if my search should penetrate
This fatal mystery!)
(*Enter Aïda.*)

**RADAMES:** Dessa!

**RADAMES:** (*seeing Aïda.*) She!

**AMNERIS:** (Ei si turba e quale
Sguardo rivolse a lei!
Aìda! a me rivale
Forse saria costei?)
(*Dopo breve silenzio volgendola ad Aïda.*)

**AMNERIS:** (He is moved! And what
A glance he turns to her!
Aïda! My rival
Perhaps is she?)
(*After a short silence turning to Aïda.*)

**AMNERIS:** Vienio o diletta appressati schiava non sei ne an cella,
Qui dove in dolce fascino
Io ti chiamai sorella
Piangi? delle tue lacrime svela il segreto, svela il segreto a me.

**AMNERIS:** Come, dearest friend, come near to me,
Slave I no longer call you
Here in affection's tender bonds,
My sister I proclaim you, You weep?
Why are these tears flowing, tell me your secret, your secret tell to me.

**AÌDA:** (*Più mosso*) Ohimè! di guerra fremere l'atroce grido io sento
Per l'infelice patria, per me, per vio pavento.

**AÌDA:** Alas! the din of strife resounds,
The warlike hosts assemble,
For my unhappy nativeland,
For me, for you I tremble.

**AMNERIS:** Favelli il ver? nè s'agita più grave cura in te?
Trema, o rea schiava,

**AMNERIS:** Do you speak truly? no graver care disturbs your gentle heart?

**RADAMES:** Nel velto a lei balena

**RADAMES:** Tremble, O slave dissembling! Upon her face is gleaming.

**AMNERIS:** Ah! trema, rea schiava trema,

**AMNERIS:** Ah! tremble,
Oh! slave dissembling!

**RAD:** Lo sdegno ed il sospetto

**AMNERIS:** Chio nel tuo cor discenda!
Trema che il ver m'apprenda que!
pianto e quel rossor

**RADAMES:** Disdain and dark suspicion
Could I in your heart descending,
Learn the truth of your offending,
The tearful blush that starts

**AÌDA:** Ah! no,
Sulla mia patria, Non geme il cor, il cor soltanto!
Quello ch'io verso è pianto,
E pianto, pianto disventurato amor!
Ah! è pianto pianto disventurato amor! (*Pianto*)
Disventurato amor è pianto di sventurato amor.
(*Il Re, preceduto dalle sue guardie e seguito da Ramfis da Ministri, Sacredoti, Capitani, ecc., ecc. Un ufficiale di Palazzo, indi un Messaggiero.*)

**AÌDA:** Oh! land beloved,
Your sorrow my heart, my heart's not grieving,
These tears my lone heart relieving,
Are flowing, flowing on love's unhappay part!
Ah! are flowing, flowing from love's unhappy smart!
Flowing
From love's unhappy smart,
Are flowing from love's unhap py smart!
(*Enter the King, preceded by his Guards and followed by Ramfis, his Ministers, Priests, Captains, etc., etc. An Officer of the Palace, and afterwards a Messenger.*)

**IL RE:** Alta cagion vi aduna,
O fidi Egizii, al vostro Re d'intorno,
Dal confir d'Etiópia un Messaggiero
Dianzi giungea gravi novelle ei reca
Vi piaccia udirlo
(*Ad un Ufficiale.*)
Il Messaggier si avanzi!

**KING:** Great cause summons you,
O faithful Egyptians, around your king.
From the confines of Ethiopia a Messenger
Just now arrived he brings grave news
Be pleased to hear him.
(*To an Officer.*)
Let the messenger come forward.

**MESSAGGIERO:** Il sacro suolo dell' Egitto è invaso
Dai barbari Etiope i nostri campi
Fur devastati arse ie messi e baldi
Della facil vittoria, i predatori
Già marciano su Tebe.

**MESSENGER:** The sacred soil of Egypt is invaded
By the barbarous Ethiopians! Our fields
Are devastated! The crops burned!
And emboldened by the easy victory, the depredators
Already march on Thebes.

**TUTTI:** Ed osan tanto!

**ALL:** They dare so much!

**MESSAGGIERO:** Un guerriero indomabile, feroce,
Li conduce Amonasro.

**MESSENGER:** A warrior indomitable and fierce
Conducts them Amonasro.

**TUTTI:** Il Re!

**ALL:** The King!

**AÌDA:** (Mio padre!)

**AÌDA:** (My father!)

**MESSAGGIERO:** Già Tebe è in armi e dalle cento porte
Sul barbaro invasore
Proromperà, guerra recando e morte.

**MESSENGER:** Already Thebes is in arms, and from the hundred gates
Breaks forth upon the invading barbarian,
Carrying war and death.

**IL RE:** Si: guerra e morte il nostro grido sia.

**KING:** Yes, be war and death our cry!

**TUTTI:** Guerra! guerra!

**ALL:** War! War!

**IL RE:** Tramenda! inesorata!
(*Accostandosi a Radames.*)
Iside venerata
Di nostre schiere invitte
Già designava il condottier supremo:
Radames.

**KING:** Tremendous! inexorable!
(*Addressing Radames.*)
Of our unconquered legions
Venerated Isis
Has already designated the supreme leader Radames.

**TUTTI:** Radames.

**ALL:** Radames!

**RADAMES:** Sien grazie ai Numi!
I miei voti fur paghi.

**RADAMES:** Thanks be to the gods!
My prayers are answered.

**AMNERIS:** (Ei duce!)

**AMNERIS:** (He leads!)

**AÌDA:** (Io tremo!)

**AÌDA:** (I tremble!)

**IL RE:** Or, di Vulcano al tempio
Muovi, o guerrier Le sacre
Armi ti cingi e alla vittoria vola,
Su! del Nilo al sacro lido
Accorrete, Egizii eroi;
Da ogni cor proromba il grido.
Guerra e morte allo stranier!

**KING:** Now move, O warrior,
To the temple of Vulcan. Gird yourself
With the sacred arms, and fly to victory.
Up! To the sacred bank of the Nile
Hasten, Egyptian heroes;
From every heart let burst the cry,
War and death to the foreigner!

**RAMFIS e SACERDOTI:** Gloria ai Numi! ognun rammenti
Ch'essi reggono gli eventi
Che in poter d'e Numi solo
Stan le sorti guerrier.

**RAMPHIS AND PRIESTS:** Glory to the gods! Remember all
That they rule events;
That in the power of the gods alone
Lies the fate of warriors.

**MINISTRI e CAPITANI:** Su! del Nilo al sacro lido
Sien barriera i nostri petti;
Non echeggi che un sol grido:
Guerra e morte allo stranier!

**MINISTERS AND CAPTAINS:** Up!
Of the Nile's sacred shore
Be our breasts the barrier;
Let but one cry resound:
War and death to the foreigner!

**RADAMES:** Sacro fremito di gloria
Tutta l'anima mi investe
Su! corriamo alla vittoria!
Guerra e morte allo stranier!

**AMNERIS:** (*recando una bandi-
era e consegnandota a Radames*).
Di mia man ricevi, o duce, Il vessil-
lo glorioso;
Ti sia guida, ti sia luce
Della gloria sul sentier.

**AÏDA:** (Per chi piango? per chi pre-
go?
Qual poter m'avvince a lui!
Deggio amarlo ed è costui
Un nemico uno strainer!)

**TUTTI:** Guerra! guerra! sterminio
all' invasor!
Va, Radames, ritorna vincitor!
(*Escono tutti meno Aïda.*)

**AÏDA:** Ritorna vincitor! E dal mio
labbro
Uscì liempi paraola! vincitore
Del padre mio di lui che impugna
i'amor
Per me per ridonarmi
Una patria, una reggia! e il nome il-
lustre
che qui celar mie è froza Vincitore
De' miei fratelli ond' io lo! vegga,
tinto
Del sangue amato, trionfar nel plau-
so
Dell' Egizie coorti! E dietro il carro,
Un Re mio padre di catene avvinto!
L'insana parola,
O Numi, sperdete!
Al seno d'un padre
La figlia rendete;
Struggete le squadre
Dei nostri oppressor!
Sventurata! che dissi? e l'amor mio?
Dunque scordar poss' io
Questo fervido amor che oppressa
e schiava
Come raggio di sol qui mi beava?
Imprecherò la morte
A Radames a lui che amo pur tanto;
Ah! non fu in terra mai
Da più crudeli angoscie un core af-
franto.
I sacri nomi di padre di amante
Nè profferir poss' lo, nè ricordar
Per l'un per l'altro confusa tre-
mante
Io piangere vorrei vorrei pregar.
Ma la mia prece inbestemmia si
muta
Delitto è il pianto a me colna il sos-
pir
In notte cupa la mente è perduta
E nell' ansia crudel vorrei morir.

Numi, pietà
Del mio soffrir!
Speme non v'ha pel mio dolor
Amor fatal, Tremendo amor
Spezza mì il cor, fammi morir!
Numi, pietà del mio sofrir,

**RADAMES:** Holy rage of glory
Fills all my soul.
Up! Let us rush to victory:
War and death to the foreigner!

**AMNERIS:** (*bringing a banner
and consigning it to Radames.*)
From my hand receive, O leader,
The glorious standard.
Be it your guide, be it your light,
On the path of glory.

**AÏDA:** (For whom do I weep? For
whom pray?
What power binds me to him!
I must love him! And this man
Is an enemy an alien!)

**ALL:** War! War! Extermination to
the invader!
Go, Radames, return conqueror!
(*Exeunt all but Aïda.*)

**AÏDA:** Return victorious! And from
your lips
Went forth the impious word! Con-
queror
Of my father of him who takes arms
For me to give me again
A country, a kingdom; and the illus-
trious name
Which here I am forced to conceal!
Conqueror
Of my brothers, with whose dear
blood
I see him stained, triumphant in the
applause
Of the Egyptian hosts; and behind
the chariot
A king! my father bound with
chains!
The insane word
Forget, O gods!
Return the daughter
To the bosom of her father;
Destroy the squadrons
Of our oppressors!
Unhappy one! What did I say? And
my love
Can I ever forget,
This fervid love which oppresses
and enslaves,
As the sun's ray which now blesses
me?
Shall I call death
On Radames? On him whom I love
so much?
Ah! Never on earth was heart torn
By more cruel agonies.
The sacred names of father, of lov-
er,
I can neither utter, nor remember
For the one for the other confused
trembling
I would weep I would pray;
But my prayer changes to blasphe-
my.
My tears are a crime my sighs a
wrong
In dense night the mind is lost
And in the cruel anguish I would
die.

Pity, kind Heaven,
To you I fly;
Hope there is none in this my woe.
Oh! fatal love,
Your power I know,
Break you my heart, cause me to

Ah! pietà, Numi, pietà, del mio soffrir, Numi, pietà, del mio soffrir,
pietà, pietà, del mio soffrir.

## *SCENA II*

*Interno del Tempio di Vulcano a
Menfi. Una luce misteriosa scende
dal' alto. Uno lunga fila di colonna l'una all' altra addossate, si
perde fra le tenebre. Statue di varie Divinita. Nel mezza della scena, sovra un palco coperto da tap-
peti, sorge l'altare sormontato da
emblemi sacri. Dai tripedi d'oro si
innalza il fumo degli incensi.*

*Sacerdoti e Sacerdotesse Ramfis ai
piede dell' altare A suo tempo, Radames Si sente dall' interno il canto dello Sacerdotesse accompagnato dalle arpe.*

**SACERDOTESSE:** (*nell' interno*).
Immenso Fthà, del mondo
Spirito animator,
Noi ti invochiamo!
Immenso Fthà, del mondo
Spirito fecondator,
Noi ti invochiamo!
Fuoco increato, eterno,
Onde ebbe luce il sol,
Noi ti invochiamo!

**SACERDOTI:** Tu che dal nulla hai
tratto
L'onde, la terra e il ciel,
Noi ti invochiamo!
Nume che del tuo spirito
Sei figlio e genitor,
Noi ti invochiamo!
Vita dell' Universo,
Mito di eterno amor,
Noi ti invochiamo!
(*Radames viene introdotto senz'
armi Montre va al' altare, le Sa-
cerdotesse eseguiscono la danza
sacra Sul capo di Radames vien
steso un velo d'argento.*)

**RAMFIS:** Mortal, diletto ai Numi A
te fidate
Son d'Egitto le sorti, Il sacro brando
Dal Dio temprato, per tua man di-
venti
Ai nemici terror, folgore, morte.
(*volgendozi al Nume.*)
Nume, custode e vindice
Di questa sacra terra,
La mano tua distendi
Sovra l'Egizio suol.

**RADAMES:** Nume, che duce ed ar-
bitro
Sei d'ogni umana guerra,
Proteggi tu, difendi
D'Egitto il sacro suol!
(*Mentre Radames viene investito*

die.
Pity, kind Heaven,
Your power I know.
Oh, kind Heaven, pity my woe,
Your mercy show, pity, kind
Heaven relieve my woe: relieve my
woe, relieve my woe.

## *SCENE II*

*Interior of the Temple of Vulcan at
Memphis. A mysterious light descends from above; a long row of
columns one behind another is
lost in the darkness; statues of
various deities; in the middle of
the scene, above a platform covered with carpet, rises the altar,
surmounted by sacred emblems;
from golden tripods rises the
smoke of incense.*

*Priests and Priestesses Ramphis at
the foot of the altar, afterwards
Radames The song of the Priestesses accompanied by harps, is
heard from the interior.*

**PRIESTESSES:** (*in the interior*).
Infinite Phthah, of the world
Animating spirit,
We invoke you!
The fructifying spirit,
We invoke you!
Fire uncreate, eternal,
From where the sun has light,
We invoke you!

**PRIESTS:** You who from nothing
hast made
The waters, the earth and the heav-
ens,
We invoke you!
God, who of your spirit
Are son and father,
We invoke you!
Life of the Universe
Gift of eternal love,
We invoke you.
(*Enter Radames, introduced
unarmed While he goes to the al-
tar the Priestesses execute the sa-
cred dance On the head of Ra-
dames is placed a silver veil.*)

**RAMPHIS:** Mortal, beloved of the
gods, to you
Is confided the fate of Egypt. Let the
holy sword
Tempered by the gods, in your
hand become
To the enemy, terror a thunderbolt
death.
(*Turning himself to the gods.*)
God, guardian and avenger
Of this sacred land,
Spread your hand
Over the Egyptian soil.

**RADAMES:** God, who is our leader
and arbiter
Of every human war,
Protect and defend
The sacred soil of Egypt.
(*While Radames is being invested*

## Act I, Scene II

*delle armi sacra gli Sacerdotesse e Sacerdoti riprendono l'inno religiose e la mistica danza.)*

*with the consecrated armor, the Priests and Priestesses resume the religious hymn and mystic dance.)*

*FINE DELL' ATTO PRIMO*

*END OF THE FIRST ACT.*

# ■ ATTO II

# ■ ACT II

## SCENA I

## SCENE I

*Una Sala nell' Appartamento di Amneris. Amneris circondata dalle Schiave che li abbigliano per la festa trionfale. Dia tripodi si eleva il profumo degil aromi. Giovani schiavi mori denzando agitano i ventagli di plume.*

*A Hall in the Apartments of Amneris.*
*Amneris surrounded by female Slaves, who are adorning her for the triumphal festival. From tripods arise aromatic perfumes. Moorish Slave Boys dancing and agitating feather fans.*

**SCHIAVE:** Chi mai fra gli inni e i plausi
Erge alla gloria il vol,
Al par di un Dio terrible,
Fulgente al par del sol?
Vieni; sul crin ti piovano
Conteste ai lauri i fior;
suonin di gloria i cantici
Coi cantici d'amor

**SLAVE GIRLS:** You who amid hymns and plaudits
Raise your flight to glory
Terrible even as a god!
Effulgent as the sun,
Come, on your tresses rain
Laurels and flowers interwoven;
Let sound the songs of glory
With the songs of love.

**AMNERIS:** (Vieni, amor mio, mi inebria
Fammi beato il cor!)

**AMNERIS:** (Come, my love, intoxicate me;
Make my heart blessed!)

**SCHIAVE:** Or, dove son le barbare
Orde dello stranier?
Siccome nebbia sparvero
Al soffio del guerrier.
Vieni: di gloria il premio
Raccogli, o vincitor;
T'arrise la vittoria,
T'arriderà l'amor.

**SLAVE GIRLS:** Now where are the barbarian
Hordes of the foreigner?
Like a mist they scatter
At the breath of the warrior.
Come; gather the reward
Of glory, O conqueror;
Victory smiled upon you
Love shall smile upon you.

**AMNERIS:** (Vieni, amor mio, ravvivami
D'un caro accento ancor!)
Silenzio! Aïda verso noi si avanza
Figlia dei vinti, il suo dolor mi è sacro.
*(Ad un cenno di Amneris tutti allontanano.)*
Nel riverderla, il dubbio
Atroce in me si desta
Il mistero fatal si squarci alfine!
*(Amneris ed Aïda.)*

**AMNERIS:** (Come, my love, revive me
Again with your dear voice!)
Silence! Aïda approaches us;
Daughter of the vanquished, her grief to me is sacred.
*(At a sign from Amneris all withdraw to a distance.)*
In seeing her again, the fearful doubt
Awakens itself within me.
Let the fatal mystery be at last rent.
*(enter Aïda.)*

**AMNERIS:** *(ad Aida con simulata amorevolezza.)* Fu la sorte dell' armi a' tuoi funestra,
Povera Aïda! Il lutto
Che ti pesa sul cor teco divido.
Io son l'amica tua
Tutto da me tu avrai vivrai felice!

**AMNERIS:** *(to Aïda, with feigned affection).* The fate of arms was deadly to your people,
Poor Aïda. The grief
Which weighs down your heart I share with you.
I am your friend;
You shall have all from me you shall live happy.

**AÏDA:** Felice esser poss' io
Lungi dal suol natio qui dove ignota
M'è la sorte del padre e dei fratelli?

**AÏDA:** Can I be happy,
Far from my native land; here where the fate of my father and brothers is unknown
To me?

**AMNERIS:** Ben ti compiango; pure hanno un confine
I mali di quaggiù Sanerà il tempo
Le angosce del tuo core
E più che il tempo, un Dio possente Amore.

**AMNERIS:** Deeply do I pity you!
Nevertheless they have an end,
The ills of this world. Time will heal
The anguish of your heart.
And more than time a powerful god love.

**AÏDA:** Amore amore!
Gaudio tormento soave ebbrezza, ansia crudel!
Ne' tuoi dolori la vita iosento un
tuo sorriso mi schiude il ciel, un
tuo sorriso mi schiude il ciel,
Ne' tuoi dolori la vita iosento
Un tuo sorrioso mi schiude il ciel.

**AÏDA:** O love immortal!
O joy and sorrow,
Sweetest delirium, dark doubts and woes!
As in your trials new life I borrow,
A heaven of rapture they smiles disclose,
As in your trials new life I borrow,
A heaven of rapture your smiles disclose.

**AMNERIS:** Ah! quel pallore quel turbamento
Svelan l'arcana na febbre d'amor!
D'interrogarla quasi hò sgomento,
Divido l'ansie del suo terror.
Ebben qual nuovo fermito t'assai, gentil Aïda?
I tuoi segreti svelami, al l'amore mio, al l'amor mio t'affida,
Tra i forti che pugnarono della tua patria a danne,
Quelcuno un dolce affanno forse a te in cor destò?
A tutti barbara non si mostrò la sorte
Sein campo il duce impavido cadde trafitò amorte

**AMNERIS:** This deathlike pallor, this strong emotion,
Plainly reveal the fever of love!
Her will I question feigning commotion,
As if her trouble to share or remove.
What new alarm disturbs you now, my gentle friend, Aïda?
Your secret thoughts unveil to me, to my affection, to my fond love confide!
Among the braves who fought so well, lost in their country's service,
Has some one a tender sorrow wakened in your heart?
To all the fates have not so cruelly intended.
If on the field the brave leader should fall, by death extended,

**AÏDA:** Che mai dicesti!
misera! misera!
Per sempre io piangeró!
Avversi sempre a me furò i Numi

**AÏDA:** What are you saying!
Hapless me!
Hapless me!
My tears shall forever flow!
The gods have ever from childhood opposed me.

**AMNERIS:** Trema!
in corti lessi tu l'a mi!

**AMNERIS:** Tremble!
I read your secret, you love him!

**AÏDA:** Io!

**AÏDA:** Love him!

**AMNERIS:** Non mentire!
Un deto ancora e il vero saprò
Fissa mi in volto io t'ingannava Radames vive!

**AMNERIS:** Lie no longer!
Yet one word further, the truth I will know,
Look firmly on me,
I have deceived you; Radames lives!

**AÏDA:** Vive! ah grazie, o Numi!

**AÏDA:** Lives thanks, kind Heaven!

**AMNERIS:** E ancor mentir tu speri?
Si, tu l'ami
Ma l'amo anch'io intendi tu?
son tua rivale figlia de' Faraoni

**AMNERIS:** And still to lie you're ready?
Yes you love him
I love him too, do you not hear?
I am your rival, daughter of Egyptian kings

**AÏDA:** Mia rivale!
ebben sia pure
Anch'io son tal
Ah!
Che dissi mai?
pietà! perdono!
Ah! pieta! ti prenda del mio dolor!
Evero, io l'amo d'immenso amore.
Tu sei felice, tu sei possente io vivo solo per questo amor.

**AÏDA:** You, my rival! It's well, so be it!
And I am too
Ah!
What have I said? forgive, and pity,
Ah!
Let this my sorrow your warm heart move.
'It's true I adore him with boundless love you are so happy you are so mighty,
I cannot live apart from love!

**AMNERIS:** Trema, vil schiava!
spezza il tuo core!
Segnar tuo morte, pùo
quest'amore,
Del tuo destino arbitra sono, d'odio
e vendetta le furie ho in cor.

**AMNERIS:** Tremble, vile minion!
be your heartbroken, Warrant of
death this love shall be token,
What may your fate be, I am judge
only,
Hatred and vengeance hold sway in
my heart.

**AÏDA:** Tu sei felice, tu sei possente,
io vivo solo per quest'amore! Pietà!
pietà!
ti prenda del mio dolor! pietà! pietà! ti prenda dal mio dolor.

**AÏDA:** You are so happy, you are so
mighty,
I cannot live apart from love!
Forgive! forgive!
Let sorrow your warm heart move,
forgive! forgive!
Let pity find place in your heart!

**AMNERIS:** All pompa che si
appresta,
Meco, o schiava, assisterai;
Tu prostrata nella polvere,
Io sul trono, accanto al Re.
Vien mi segui e apprenderai
Se lottar tu puoi con me.

**AMNERIS:** Ah, the pomp which ap-
proaches,
with me, O slave, you shall assist;
You prostrate in the dust
I on the throne beside the King;
Come, follow me, and you shall
learn
If you can contend with me.

**AÏDA:** Ah! pietà! che più mi resta?
Un deserto è la mia vita:
Vivi e regna, il tuo furore
Io tra breve placherò.
Questo amore che ti irrita
Nella tomba spegnerò.

**AÏDA:** Ah pity! What more remains
to me?
My life is a desert;
Live and reign, your rage
I will quickly appease.
This love which angers you
I will extinguish in the tomb.

## SCENA II

*Uno degli ingressi della Città di
Tebe. Sul davand un gruppo di
palme; a destra il Tempio di Am-
mone; a sinistra un trono sormontato da un baldacchino di
porpora; nel fondo una porta
trionfale; la scena è ingombra di
popolo.*

*Entra il Re, seguito dai Ministri,
Sacerdoti, Capitani, venbelliferi,
PortaInsegne, ecc., ecc. Quindi
Amneris con Aïda e Schiave. Il Re
va a sedere sul trono. Amneris se
stessa posto alla sinistra del Re.*

## SCENE II

*An entrance to the City of Thebes.
In front a group of palms; to the
right the Temple of Ammon; to the
left a throne surmounted by a
purple canopy; at the back a triumphal gate. The scene is crowded with people.*

*Enter the King, followed by Minis-
ters, Priests, Captains, FanBear-
ers, EnsignBearers, etc., etc. Afterwards Amneris, with Aïda and
Slaves. The King seats himself on
the throne; Amneris places herself
to the left of the King.*

**POPOLO:** Gloria all'Egitto e ad
Iside
Che il sacro suol protegge;
Al Re che il Delta ragge
Inni festosi alziam!
Vieni, o guerriero vindice,
Vieni a gioir con noi;
Sul passo degli eroi
I lauri e i fior versiam!

**PEOPLE:** Glory to Egypt, and to
Isis,
Who the sacred soil protects;
To the king who rules the Delta
Let us raise festal hymns.
Come, O champion warrior,
Come to rejoice with us;
In the path of the heroes,
Let us strew laurels and flowers.

**DONNE:** S'intrecci il loto al lauro
Sul crin dei vincitori;
Nembo gentil di fiori
Stenda sull' armi un vel.
Danziam, fanciulle Egizie,
Le mistiche carole,
Come d'intorno al sole
Donzano gli astri in ciel!

**WOMEN:** Weave the lotus with the
laurel
On the hair of the conqueror
A sweet shower of the flowers,
Spread on their arms a veil.
Let us dance, daughters of Egypt,
The mystic dances,
As around the sun
Dance the stars of heaven!

**SACERDOTI:** Della vittoria agli ar-
bitri
Supremi il guarde ergete;
Grazie agli Dei rendete
Nel forsunato di.
Così per noi di gloria
Sia l'avvenir segnato,

**PRIESTS:** To the supreme arbiters
of victory
Raise your eyes;
Render thanks to the gods
On the happy day.
Thus
May the future be marked for us

Nè mai ci colga il fato
Che i barbari colpi.
*(Le truppe Egizie precedute dalle
fanfare afilano dinanze al Re Seg-
uoni i carri di guerra, le insegne i
vasi sacri, le statue degli Dei Un
drapello di danzatrici che recano
i tesori dei vinti Da ultimo, Radames, sotto un baldacchino portato da dodici Ufficiali.)*

with glory,
Nor may that fate seize us
That struck the barbarians.
*(The Egyptian troops, preceded by
trumpets, defile before the King
the chariots of war follow the ensigns the sacred vases and statues
of the gods troops of Dancing
Girls who carry the treasures of
the defeated and lastly Radames,
under a canopy borne by twelve
Officers.)*

**IL RE:** *(che scende dal trono per
abbracciare Radames).*
Salvator della patria, io ti saluto.
Vieni, e mia figlia di sua man ti por-
ga
Il serto trionfale.
*(Radames si inchina davanti Am-
neris che gli porge la corona.)*

**KING:** *(who descends from the
throne to embrace Radames).* Saviour of your country, I salute you.
Come, and let my daughter with
her own hand
Place upon you the triumphal
crown.
*(Radames bows before Amneris,
who places the crown upon him.)*

**IL RE:** *(a Radames).* Ora, a me
chiedi
Quanto più brami. Nulla a te negato
Sarà in tal dì lo giuro
Per la corono mia, pei sacri Numi.

**KING:** *(to Radames).* Now ask of
me
What you most wish. Nothing de-
nied to you
On such a day shall be I swear it
By my crown, by the sacred gods.

**RADAMES:** Concedi in pria che innanzi a te sien tratti
I prigionier
*(Entrano fra le guardie i prigioni-
eri Etiopi, ultimo, Amonasro, vestito da Uffiziale.)*

**RADAMES:** Deign first to let the
prisoners
Be drawn up before you.
*(Enter between the Guards the
Ethiopian prisoners, Amonasro
last, dressed as an Officer.)*

**AÏDA:** Che veggo? Egli! mia padre!

**AÏDA:** What do I see? He! my father!

**TUTTI:** Suo padre!

**ALL:** Her father!

**AMNERIS:** Inpoter nostro!

**AMNERIS:** In our power!

**AÏDA:** *(abbracciando il padre).*
Tu! Prigionier!

**AÏDA:** *(embracing her father)*
Your prisoner!

**AMNERIS:** *(piano ad Aïda).* Non
mi tradir!

**AMONASRO:** *(softly to Aïda)* Do
not betray me!

**IL RE:** *(ad Amonasro).* Ti appressa
Dunque tu sei?

**KING:** *(to Amonasro).* Draw near
Then you are?

**AMONASRO:** Suo padre Anch' io
pugnai
Vinti noi fummo e morte invancer-
cai.
*(Accennando alla divisa che lo
veste.)*
Questa assisa ch' io vesto vi dica
Che il mio Re, la mia patria ho dife-
so:
Fu la sorte a nostr' armi nemica
Tornò vano dei forti l'ardir.
Al mio piè nella polve distesto
Giacque il Re da più colpi traffito;
Se l'amor della patria è delitto
Siam rei tutti, siam pronti a morir!
*(Volgendosi al Re con accento
supplichevole.)*
Ma tu, o Re, tu signore possente,
A costoro ti volgi clemente
Oggi noi siam percossi dal fato
Doman voi potria il fato colpir.

**AMONASRO:** Her father. I also
fought
Was conquered, and death I sought
in vain.
*(Pointing to the uniform in which
he is dressed.)*
This livery that I wear may tell you
That I have defended my king and
my country.
Fate was hostile to our arms;
Vain was the courage of the brave.
At my feet in the dust extended
Lay the king, transfixed by many
wounds;
If the love of country is a crime
We are all criminals all ready to die!
*(Turning to the King with a sup-
plicating motion.)*
But you, O king, you powerful lord,
Be merciful to those men.
Today we are stricken by Fate,
Tomorrow Fate may smite you.

**AÏDA, PRIGIONIERI E SCHIAVA:**
Sì: dal Numi percossi non siamo;
Tua pietà, tua clemenza imploria-
mo;
Ah! giammai di soffrir vi sia dato
Ciò che in oggi n' è dato soffrir!

**AÏDA, PRISONERS AND FEMALE
SLAVES:** Yes; by the gods we are
stricken;
Your pity, your mercy we implore;
Ah! May you never have to suffer
What is now given to us to suffer.

## Act II, Scene II

**RAMFIS E SACERDOTI:** Struggi, o Re, queste ciurme feroci, Chiudi il core alle perfide voci, Fur dai Numi votati alla morte, Si compisca dei Numi il voler!

**RAMPHIS AND PRIESTS:** Destroy, O king, these savage hordes, Close your heart to their perfidious voices, By the gods they were doomed to death, Let the will of the gods be accomplished.

**POPOLO:** Sacerdoti, gli sdegni placate, L'umil prece dei vinti ascoltate; E tu, o Re, tu possente, tu forte, A clemenza dischiudi il pensier.

**PEOPLE:** Priests, soften your anger, Hear the humble prayer of the conquered, And you O king, powerful and strong, Open your thoughts to mercy.

**RADAMES:** (*fissando Aïda*). (Il dolor che in quel volte favella Al mio sguardo la rende più bella; Ogni stilla del pianto adorato Nel mio petto ravviva l'amore.)

**RADAMES:** (*fixing his eyes on Aïda*). (The sorrow which speaks in that face Renders it more beautiful to my sight; Every drop of the beloved tears Reanimates love in my breast.)

**AMNERIS:** (Quali sguardi sovr' essa ha rivolti! Di qual fiamma balenano il volti! E a tal sorte serbata son io? La vendetta mi rugge nel cor.)

**AMNERIS:** (What glances on her he turns! With what flame their faces flash! To such a fate as this am I destined? Revenge groans in my heart.)

**IL RE:** Or che fausti ne arridon gli eventi A costoro mostriamci clementi: La pietà sale ai Numi gradita E rafferma dei Prenci il poter.

**KING:** Now that events smile favor upon us, To these people let us show ourselves merciful; Pity ascends grateful to the gods, And confirms the power of princes.

**RADAMES:** (*al Re*). O Re: pei sacri Numi, Per lo splendore della tua corona. Compier giurasti il voto mio

**RADAMES:** (*to the King*). O King! by the sacred gods, By the splendor of your crown, You sworest to fulfill my vow?

**IL RE:** Giurai.

**KING:** I swore.

**RADAMES:** Ebbene: a te pei prigionieri Etiopi Vita domando e liberta.

**RADAMES:** Well; of you for the Ethiopian prisoners, Life I demand and liberty.

**AMNERIS:** (Per tutti!)

**AMNERIS:** (For all!)

**SACERDOTI:** Morte ai nemici della patria!

**PRIESTS:** Death to the enemies of the country!

**POPOLO:** Grazie Per gli infelici!

**PEOPLE:** Grace For the unhappy.

**RAMFIS:** Ascolta, o Re (*A Radames.*) Tu pure Giovine eroe, saggio consiglio ascolta: Son nemici e prodi sono La vendetta hanno nel cor, Fatti audaci dal perdono Correranno all' armi ancor!

**RAMPHIS:** Listen, O King, (*To Radames.*) Even you, Young hero, listen to wise counsel: They are enemies and they are warriors They have revenge in their hearts. Emboldened by your pardon They will run to arms again.

**RADAMES:** Spento Amonasro il re guerrier, non resta Speranza ai vinti.

**RADAMES:** Amonasro, the warrior king slain, No hope remains to the vanquished.

**RAMFIS:** Almeno, Arra di pace e securtà fra noi Resti col padre Aïda Gli altri sien sciolti

**RAMPHIS:** At least As an earnest of peace and security, among us With her father let Aïda remain. Let the rest be free.

**IL RE:** Al tuo consiglio io cedo. Di securità, di pace un miglior pegno or io vuo; darvi Radames, la patria Tutto a te deve D'Amneris la mano

**KING:** To your counsel I yield. Of security and peace a better pledge I will now give: Radames, the country Owes all to you. The hand of Amneris Be your reward. Over Egypt one day With her shall you reign.

**AMNERIS:** (Venga or la schiava, Venga a rapirmi l'amor mio se l'osa!)

**AMNERIS:** (Now let the slave come Let her come to take my love from me if she dares!)

**IL RE:** Gloria all' Egitto e ad Iside Che il sacro suol difende, S'intrecci il loto al lauro Sul crin del vincitor!

**KING:** Glory to Egypt and to Isis, Who defends the sacred soil, Weave the lotus with the laurel On the hair of the victors.

**SACERDOTI:** Inni leviamo ad Iside Che il sacro suol difende; Preghiam che i fati arridano Fausti alla patria ognor.

**PRIESTS:** Hymns let us raise to Isis, Who the sacred soil defends; Let us pray that the Fates may ever smile Propitious on our country.

**AÏDA:** (Qual speme omai più restami? A lui la gloria e il trono A me l'oblio le lacrime Di disperato amor.)

**AÏDA:** (What hope more remains to me? To him glory and the throne. To me, oblivion the tears Of hopeless love.)

**PRIGIONIERI:** Gloria al clemente Egizio Che i nostri ceppi ha sciolto, Che ci ridona ai liberi Solchi del patrio suol!

**PRISONERS:** Glory to the merciful Egyptian Who has unloosed our fetters, Who restores us to the free Paths of our native land!

**RADAMES:** (D'avverso Nume il folgore Sul capo mio discende Ah no! d'Egitto il soglio Non val d'Aïda il cor.)

**RADAMES:** (The Thunder of the adverse gods On my head descends Ah! no, the throne of Egypt Is not worth the heart of Aïda.)

**AMNERIS:** (Dall' inatteso giubilo Inebbriata io sono: Tutti in un dì si compiono I sogni del mio cor.)

**AMNERIS:** (By the unexpected joy I am intoxicated; All in one day are fulfilled The dreams of my heart.)

**AMONASRO:** (*ad Aïda*). Fa cor: della tua patria I lieti eventi aspetta; Per noi della vendetta Già prossimo è l'albor.

**AMONASRO:** (*to Aïda*). Take heart, for your country Expects happy events; For us the dawn of vengeance Is already near.

**POPOLO:** Gloria all' Egitto e ad Iside Che il sacro suol difende! S'intrecci il loto al lauro Sul crin del vincitor!

**PEOPLE:** Glory to Egypt and to Isis, Who defends the sacred soil. Weave the lotus with the laurel On the hair of the victors!

*FINE DELL' ATTO SECONDO.*

*END OF THE SECOND ACT.*

# ■ ATTO III

# ■ ACT III

*Le Rive del Nilo. Roccie di granito fra cui crescono dei palmizii. Sul vertice delle roccie il Tempio d'Iside per metà nascosto tra le fronde. E notte stellata Splendore di luna.*

*The Banks of the Nile. Rocks of granite, among which grow palm trees; on the top of the rocks the Temple of Isis, half concealed among the foliage; it is starlight and bright moonlight.*

**CORO:** (*nel tempio*). O tu che sei d'Osiride Madre immortale e sposa, Diva che i casti palpiti Desti agli amani in cor; Soccorri a noi pietosa, Madre d'eterno amor. (*Da una barca che approda alla riva, discendono Amneris, Ramfis, alcune donne coperte da fitto velo e Guardie.*)

**CHORUS:** (*in the temple*). O you who are of Osiris, Mother immortal and spouse, Goddess who awakens the beatings In the heart of human creatures, Come piteous to our help, Mother of eternal love. (*From a boat, which approaches the shore, descend Amneris, Ramphis, some Women closely veiled, and Guards.*)

RAMFIS: (ad Amneris). Vieni d'Iside al Tempio alla vigilia Della tue nozze, implora Della Diva il favore Iside legge Dei mortali nel cuore ogni mistero Degli umani è a lei noto.

RAMPHIS: (to Amneris) Come to the Temple of Isis. On the eve of your nuptials implore The favor of the goddess. Isis rules The heart of mortals; every mystery Of mankind to her is known.

AMNERIS: Sì: pregherò che Radames mi doni Tutto il suo cor, come il mio core a lui Sacro è per sempre.

AMNERIS: Yes: I will pray that Radames may give me His whole heart, as mine to him Is consecrated forever.

RAMFIS: Pregherai fino all' alba io sarò teco. (Tutti entrano nel tempio. Il Coro ripete il canto sacro.)

RAMPHIS: Let us enter. You shall pray till dawn. I shall be with you (All enter the temple. The Chorus repeat the sacred song.)

AÏDA: (entra cautamente coperta da un velo). Qui Ramamès verrà Che vorrà dirmi? Io tremo Ah! se tu vieni A recarmi, o crudel, l'ultimo addio, Del Nilo i cupi vortici Mi daran tomba e pace forse e oblie.

AÏDA: (entering cautiously, covered with a veil). Here Radames will come. What would he say to me? I tremble ah, you come. To give me, O cruel one, the last farewell, The deep water of the Nile Shall give me a tomb and peace perhaps and oblivion.

AÏDA: O patria mia, mai più, mai più ti rivedrò! mai più! mai più! ti rivedrò! O cieli azzurri o dolci aure native, dove sereno il mio mattin brillò, o verdi colli o profumate rive, o patria mia, mai più ti rivedrò! O patri mia, mai più, ah mai più mai più ti rivedro! o patria mia, oh patria mia, mai più rivedro! mai più! no, no, mai più, mai più! O fresche valli o questo asil beato, che un dì promesso dall'amor mi fù Or che d'amore il sogno è di le quato, o patria mia, non ti vedrò mai più! oh patria mia, non ti vedrò mai più, no, mai più, non ti vedrò, non ti vedrò mai più! oh, patria mia, mai più ti rivedrò!

AÏDA: O native land, no more to you shall I return! no more! no more to you return! O skies of tender blue, O soft airs blowing, Where calm and peaceful my dawn of life passed over O hills of verdure, O perfumed waters flowing, O beloved home. I never shall see you again! O beloved home, no more, ah, no more, never more shall I return! O native land, O beloved home, I shall no more return! O fresh and fragrant vales, O quiet dwelling, that bore promise of happy days of love, Now hope is banished, love's tender dream dispelling, O native land, no more shall I return!

AÏDA: (Amonasro e Aïda.) Cielo! mio padre!

AÏDA: (Enter Amonasro.) Heaven! My father!

AMONASRO: A te grave cagione Mi adduce, Aïda. Nulla sfugge al mio Sguardo D'amor ti struggi Per Radames ei t'ama e qui lo attendi. Dei Faraon la figlia è tua rivale Razza infame, aborrita e a noi fatale!

AMONASRO: Grave occasion Leads me to you Aïda. Nothing escapes My sight; you are destroying yourself with love For Radames. He loves you, and here you await him, The daughter of the Pharaohs is your rival An infamous race, abhorred and fatal to us.

AÏDA: E in suo potere io sto! Io d'Amonasro Figlia!

AÏDA: And I am in her power! I, the daughter of Amonasro.

AMONASRO: In poter di lei! No! se lo brami La possente rival tu vincerai, E patria, e trono, e amor, tutto avrai. Rivedrai le foreste imbalsamate,

AMONASRO: In her power! No! If you wish This powerful rival, you shall defeat, And country, and throne, and love

Le fresche valli, i nostri templi d'ôr

all shall be yours. You shall see again the balmy forests, The fresh valleys, our temples of gold!

AÏDA: (con trasporto). Rivedrò le foreste imbalsamate Le nostre valli i nostri tempii d'ôr!

AÏDA: (with transport). I shall see again the balmy forests, Our valleys, our temples of gold!

AMONASRO: Sposa felice a lui che amasti tanto, Tripudii immensi ivi potrai gioir

AMONASRO: Happy bride of him who you love so much, Great jubilee then shall be yours.

AÏDA: (con trasporto) Un'giorno solo di si dolce incanto. Un'ora di tal gaudio e poi morir!

AÏDA: (with transport). One day only of such sweet enchantment, One hour of such joy and then to die!

AMONASRO: Pur rammenti che a noi l'Egizio immite, Le case, i tempii e l'are profanò Trasse in ceppi le vergini rapite Madri, vecchi e fanciulli ei trucidè.

AMONASRO: Nevertheless you remember that the merciless Egyptian Profaned our houses, temples, and altars; He drew in fetters the ravished virgins Mothers, old men and children he has slain.

AÏDA: Ah! ben rammento quegli infausti giorni Rammento i lutti che il mio cor soffri Deh! fate o Numi che per noi ritorni L'alba invocata dei sereni dì.

AÏDA: Ah! well I remember those unhappy days. I remember the grief that my heart suffered. Ah! make return to us, O gods, The longedfor dawn of peaceful days.

AMONASRO: Non fia che tardi In armi ora si desta Il popol nostro tutto e pronto già Vittoria avrem Solo a saper mi resta Qual sentier il nemico seguirà

AMONASRO: Delay not. In arms now are roused Our people everything is ready We shall have victory. It only remains for me to know What path the enemy will follow.

AÏDA: Chi scoprirlo potria? chi mai?

AÏDA: Who will be able to discover it? Who?

AMONASRO: Tu stessa!

AMONASRO: You, alone!

AÏDA: Io!

AÏDA: I?

AMONASRO: Radamès so che qui attendi Ei t'ama Ei conduce gli Egizii Intendi?

AMONASRO: Radames will come here soon he loves you! He leads the Egyptians. Do you understand?

AÏDA: Orrore! Che mi consigli tu? No, no, giammai!

AÏDA: Horror! What do you counsel me? No, no! Never!

AMONASRO: (con impeto selvaggio). Su, dunque! sorgete Egizie coorti! Col fuoco struggete Le nostre città Spargete il terrore, Le stragi' le morti Al vostro furore Più freno non v'ha.

AMONASRO: (with savage fury.) Up, then! Rise, Egyptian legions! With fire destroy Our cities Spread terror, Carnage and death. To your fury There is no longer check.

AÏDA: Ah padre!

AÏDA: Ah, father!

AMONASRO: (respingendola). Mia figlia Ti chiami!

AMONASRO: (repulsing her). My daughter do you call yourself?

AÏDA: (atterrita e supplichevole). Pietà!

AÏDA: (terrified and beseeching). Pity!

AMONASRO: Flutti di sangue scorrono Sulle città dei vinti Vedi? dai negri vortici Si lebano gli estinti Ti additan essi e gridano: "Per te la patria muor."

AMONASRO: Rivers of blood pour On the cities of the vanquished Do you see? From the black gulfs The dead are raised To you they point and cry; "For you the country dies."

AÏDA: Pietà!

AMONASRO: Una larva orribile
Fra l'ombre a moi s'affaccia
Trema! le scarne braccia
Sul capo tuo levò
Tua madre ell'è ravvisala
Ti maledice

AÏDA: (*nel massimo terrore*). Ah, no!
Padre.

AMONASRO: (*respingendola*).
Va, indegna! non sei mia figlia!
Dei Faraoni tu sei la schiava.

AÏDA: Padre, a costoro schiava io non sono
Non maledirmi non imprecarmi
Tua figlia ancora potrai chiamarmi
Della mia patria degna sarò.

AMONASRO: Pensa che un popolo, vinto, straziato
Per te soltanto risorger può

AÏDA: O patria! o patria quanto mi costi!

AMONASRO: Corraggio! ci giunge là tutto udrò
(*Si nasconde fra i palmizii.*)
(*Radames e Aïda.*)

RADAMES: Pur ti riveggo, mia dolce AÏDA

AÏDA: Ti arresta, vanne che speri ancor?

RADAMES: A te dappresso l'amor mi guida.

AÏDA: Te i riti attendono d'un altro amor.
D'Amneris sposo

RADAMES: Che parli mai?
Te sola, Aïda, te deggio amar.
Gli Dei mi ascoltano tu mia sarei

AÏDA: D'uno spergiuro non ti machiar?
Prode t'amai, non t'amerei spergiuro.

RADAMES: Dell' amor mio dubiti. Aïda?

AÏDA: E come
Speri sottrarti d'Amneris ai vezzi,
Del Re al voler, del tuo popolo ai voti,
Dei sacerdoti all' ira?

RADAMES: Odimi, Aïda.
Nel fiero anelito di nuova guerra
Il suolo Etiope si ridestò
I tuoi già invadono la nostra terra,
Io degli Egizii duce sarò.
Fra il suon, fra i plausi della vittoria,
Al re mi prostro, gli svelo il cor
Sarai tu il serto della mia gloria,
Vivrem beati d'eterno amor.

AÏDA: Pity!

AMONASRO: A horrible ghost
Among the shadows to us approaches
Tremble! the fleshless arms
Over your head it raised
It is your mother recognize her
She curses you.

AÏDA: (*in the greatest terror*). Ah, No!
Father.

AMONASRO: (*repulsing her*). Go, unworthy one! You're not my offspring
You are the slave of the Pharaohs!

AÏDA: Father, I am not their slave
Reproach me not curse me not;
Your daughter again you can call me
I will be worthy of my country.

AMONASRO: Think that a people conquered, torn to pieces,
Through you alone can arise

AÏDA: O my country, O my country how much you've cost me!

AMONASRO: Courage! he comes there I shall hear all.
(*Conceals himself among the palm trees.*)
(*Enters Radames.*)

RADAMES: I see you again, my sweet Aïda.

AÏDA: Stop! begone. What, you still hope?

RADAMES: Love guided me to you.

AÏDA: The rites of another love await you.
Spouse of Amneris.

RADAMES: What did you say?
You alone, Aïda, must I love.
Hear me, gods! You shall be mine!

AÏDA: Do not stain yourself with perjury.
Valiant I loved you; foresworn I should not love you.

RADAMES: Do you doubt my love, Aïda?

AÏDA: And how do you hope to free yourself from the love of Amneris,
From the King's will, from the vows of your people,
From the wrath of the priests?

RADAMES: Hear me, Aïda.
To the fierce pant of a new war
The land of Ethiopia has reawakened
Your people already invade our country.
I shall be leader of the Egyptians.
Amid the fame, the applause of victory,
I prostrate myself before the King, I unveil to him my heart.
You shall be the reward of my glory,
We shall live blessed by eternal love.

AÏDA: Nè d'Amneris paventi
Il vindice furor? la sua vendetta,
Come folgor tremenda
Cadrà su me, sul padre mio, su tutti.

RADAMES: Io vi difendo.

AÏDA: Invan tu nol potresti
Pur se tu m'ami ancor s'apre una vìa
Di scampo a noi

RADAMES: Quale?

AÏDA: Fuggire

RADAMES: Fuggire!

AÏDA: Fuggaim gli ardori i nos piti
Di queste lande ignuda; Una novella patria,
nostro amor si schiude. Là tra foreste vergini, Di fiori progumate, in estasi beate
la terra scorderem, in e stasi, in e stasi
la terra scorderem,

RADAMES: Sovra una terra estrania teco fuggir dovrei!
abbandonar la patria l'are de' nostri Dei! il suol dov' io raccolsi di gloria i primi allori;
il ciel de nostri amori come scordar potrem?

AÏDA: La tra foresti vergini, di fiori progumate, in estasi beate
la terra scorderem, in estasi, in estasi
la terra scorderem

RADAMES: Il ciel di nostri amori come scordar potrem?

AÏDA: Sotto il mio ciel, più libere l'amore ne fia concesso,
i vi nel tempio i stesso gli stessi Nu mi avrem
i vi nel tempio i stesso gli stessi Nu mi avrem,
I vi nel tempio i stesso gli stessi Nu mi avrem; fuggiam, fuggiam!

RADAMES: (*esitante*). Aïda!

AÏDA: Tu non m'ami Va!

RADAMES: Non t'amo!
Mortal giammi nè Dio
Arse d'amore al par del mio possente.

AÏDA: Va va ti attende all' ara Amneris

RADAMES: No! giammai!

AÏDA: Giammai, dicesti?
Allor piombi la scure
Su me, sul padre mio

RADAMES: Ah no! fuggiamo!
(*Con appassionata risoluzione.*)
Sì: fuggiamo da queste mura,
Al deserto inseim fuggiamo;
Qui sol regna la sventura,
Là si schiude un ciel d'amor.
I deserti interminati

AÏDA: Do you not fear Amneris and Her vindictive fury? Her revenge,
Like a dreadful thunderbolt,
Will fall on me, on my father, on all.

RADAMES: I protect you.

AÏDA: In vain! You could not
Still if you love me again a way
Of escape opens to us.

RADAMES: Which?

AÏDA: To fly!

RADAMES: To fly!

AÏDA: Ah! fly with me, and leave behind
These deserts bare and blighted;
Some country, new and fresh to find,
Where we may love united.
There amid the virgin forestgroves,
By fair and sweet flowers scented,
In quiet joy contented,
The world will we forget, in quiet joy, in quiet joy,
The world will we forget,

RADAMES: To some strange land far distant
Must I then with you fly!
Our home and country leaving,
Our gods and altars high!
The soil where first I gathered
The bays that deeds required,
The sky our love that lighted,
How can we ever forget?

AÏDA: There beneath the virgin forest groves,
By fair and sweet flowers scented,
In quiet joy contented
The world will we forget,
In quiet joy, in quiet joy
The world will we forget,

RADAMES: The sky our love that lighted How can we ever forget?

AÏDA: Beneath my sky more light and free
Love's generous aid confiding;
In temples there abiding,
Gods like your own we'll find,
In temples there abiding,
The selfsame gods we'll find,
In temples there abiding the selfsame gods we'll find, then fly! ah! fly!

RADAMES: (*hesitating*). Aïda!

AÏDA: You do not love me go!

RADAMES: I do not love you?
Never mortal, nor god,
Burnt with love so powerful as mine!

AÏDA: Go, go! Amneris awaits you At the altar.

RADAMES: No, never!

AÏDA: Never, you said?
Then falls the axe
On me, on my father.

RADAMES: Ah, no, let us fly!
(*With impassioned resolution.*)
Yes; let us fly from these walls,
To the desert let us fly together;
Here misfortune reigns alone.
There opens to us a heaven of love.
The boundless deserts

A noi talamo saranno,
Su noi gli astri brilleranno.
Di più limpido fulgor.

Shall be our nuptial couch,
On us the stars will shine
With a more limpid effulgence.

AÏDA: Nella terra avventurata
De' miei padri, il ciel ne attende;
ivi l'aura è imbalsamata,
Ivi il suolo è aromi e fior.
Fresche valli e verdi prati
A noi talamo saranno,
Su noi gli astri brilleranno.
Di più limpido fulgor.

AÏDA: In the happy land
Of my fathers heaven awaits us;
There the air is perfumed,
There the ground is fragrant with flowers.
Fresh valleys and green fields
Shall be our nuptial couch,
On us the stars will shine
With a more limpid effulgence.

AÏDA ET RADAMES: Vieni meco insiem fuggiamo
Questa terra di dolor
Vieni meco io t'amo, io t'amo!
A noi duce fia l'amor!
(Si allontanano rapidamente.)

AÏDA AND RADAMES: Come with me together let us fly
This land of grief.
Come with me I love you, I love you!
Love shall be our leader.
(They go rapidly aside.)
(stopping suddenly.)

AÏDA: (arrestandosi all'improvviso). Ma, dimmi; per qual via
Eviterem le schiere
Degli armati?

AÏDA: But tell me by what road
Shall we avoid the armed hosts?

RADAMES: Il sentier scelto dai nostri
A piombar sul nemico fia deserto
Fino a domani

RADAMES: The path chosen by our troops
To fall on the enemy will be deserted
Until tomorrow.

AÏDA: E quel sentier?

AÏDA: And that path?

RADAMES: Le gole
Di Nàpata?
(Amonasro e Aïda e Radames.)

RADAMES: The Pass
Of Napata.
(Enter Amonasro.)

AMONASRO: Di Nàpata le gole!
Ivi saranno i miei

AMONASRO: The Pass of Napata!
There my people shall be.

RADAMES: Oh! chi ci ascolta?

RADAMES: Oh! who hears us?

AMONASRO: D'Aïda il padre e degli Etiopi il Re.

AMONASRO: The father of Aïda and King of the Ethiopians.
(greatly agitated).

RADAMES: (agitatissimo). Tu!
Amonasro! Tu il Re?
Numi! che dissi?
No! non è ver! sogno delirio è questo

RADAMES: You Amonasro! You, the King! Gods, what did I say?
No! It is not true! I dream this is delirium.

AÏDA: Ah, no! ti calma ascoltami,
All' amor mio t'affida.

AÏDA: Ah no! calm yourself listen to me,
Trust yourself in my love.

AMONASRO: A te l'amor d'Aïda
Un soglio innalzerà!

AMONASRO: Aïda's love shall raise you
To a throne.

RADAMES: Per te tradii la patria!
Io son disonorato

RADAMES: For you to betray my country!
I am dishonored.

AMONASRO: No: tu non sei colpevole
Era voler del fato.
Vieni: oltra il Nil ne attendono
I prodi a noi devoti,
Là del tuo core i voti
coronerà l'amor.
(Amneris, dal tempio, indi Ramfis, Sacerdoti, Guardie e detti.)

AMONASRO: No; you are not guilty
It was the will of fate.
Come; beyond the Nile await us
The brave men devoted to us;
There the vows of your heart
Shall be crowned with love.
(Enter Amneris from the Temple, then Ramphis, Priests and Guards.)

AMNERIS: Traditor!

AMNERIS: Traitor!

AÏDA: La mia rivale!

AÏDA: My rival!

AMONASRO: (avventandosi ad Amneris con un pugnale). Vieni a strugger l'opre mia!
Muori!

AMONASRO: (rushing upon Amneris with a dagger). Come you to destroy my work?
Die!

RADAMES: (frapponendosi).
Arresta, insano!

RADAMES: (interposing himself). Stop, madman!

AMONASRO: Oh rabbia!

AMONASRO: Oh, fury!

RAMFIS: Guardie, olà.

RAMPHIS: Guards, hither!

RADAMES: (ad Aïda e Amonasro)
Presto! fuggite!

RADAMES: (to Aida and Amonasro). Haste! fly!

AMONASRO: (transciando Aida). Vieni, o figlia!

AMONASRO: (drawing Aïda away). Come, O daughter!

RAMFIS: (alle Guardie). Li inseguite!

RAMPHIS: (to the Guards). Follow them!

RADAMES: (a Ramfis). Sacerdote, io resto a te.

RADAMES: (to Ramphis). Priest, I remain with you.

FINE DELL' ATTO TERZO.

END OF THE THIRD ACT.

# ▪ ATTO IV

## SCENA I

# ▪ ACT IV

## SCENE I

Sala nel Palazzo del Re. Alla sinistra, una gran porta che mette alla sala sotterranea della sentenze. Andite a destra che conduce alla prigione di Radames.

Hall in the King's Palace; to the left a grand gate, which opens on the subterranean hall of judgment; passage to the right which leads to the prison of Radames.

AMNERIS: (mes'amente atteggiata davanti la porta del sotteranea). L'abborrita rivale a me sfuggia
Dai sacerdoti Radamès attende
Dei traditor la pena, Traditore
Egli non è Pur rivelò di guerra
L'alto segreto egli fuggir volea
Con lei fuggire Traditori tutti!
A morte! A morte! Oh! che mai parlo? Io l'amo,
Io l'amo sempre Disperato, insano
E quest' amor che la mia vita strugge.
Oh! s'ei potesse amarmi!
Vorrei salvarlo E come?
Si tenti! Guardie: Radamès qui venga.
(Radames condotto dalle guardie, e Amneris.)

AMNERIS: (in a sad attitude before the gate of the hall). My abhorred rival escapes me
Radames awaits from the priests
The punishment of a traitor. Traitor
He is not, though he revealed
The high secret of war. He wished to fly
To fly with her traitors all!
To death, to death! Oh, what did I say? I love him
I love him always desperate, mad
Is this love which destroys my live.
Oh! if he could love me!
I would save him and how?
Let me try. Guards: Radames comes.
(Enter Radames, guarded.)

AMNERIS: Già i sacerdoti adunansi
Arbitri del tuo fato;
Pur della accusa orribile
Scolparti ancor ti è dato:
Ti scolpa, e la tua grazia
Io pregherò dal trono,
E nunzia di perdono,
Di vita, a te sarò.

AMNERIS: Already the priests assemble.
Arbiters of thy fate;
Of the horrible crime however
Still it is given you to exculpate yourself.
Exculpate yourself, and grace for you
I will beg from the throne;
And a messenger of pardon
Of life, to you I will be.

RADAMES: Di mie discolpe i giudici
Mai non udran l'accento;
Dinanzi ai Numi e agli uomini
Nè vil, nè reo mi sento.
Profferse il labbro incauto
Fatal segreto, è vero,
Ma puro il mio pensiero
E 'l onore mio restò.

RADAMES: Of my exculpation the judges
Will never hear the sound.
Before gods and men
Neither vile nor guilty do I feel.
My incautious lips
Uttered the fatal secret, it is true,
But pure my thought
And my honor remained.

AMNERIS: Salvati dunque e scolpati.

AMNERIS: Then save and exculpate yourself.

RADAMES: No.

RADAMES: No.

AMNERIS: Tu morrai

AMNERIS: You will die.

## Act IV, Scene I

**RADAMES:** La vita
Abhorro; d'ogni gaudio
La fonte inaridita,
Svanita ogni speranza,
Sol bramo di morir,

**AMNERIS:** Morire! ah! tu dei vivere!
Si, all' amor mio vivrai;
Per te le angoscie orribili
Di morte io già provai;
T'amai, soffersi tanto
Vegliai le notti in pianto
E patria, e trono, e vita
Tutto darei per te

**RADAMES:** Per essa anch' io la patria
E l'onor mio tradiva

**AMNERIS:** Di lei non più!

**RADAMES:** L'infamia
Mi attende e vuoi che io viva?
Misero appien mi festi,
Aïda a me togliesti,
Spenta l' hai forse e in dono
Offri la vita a me?

**AMNERIS:** Io di sua morte origine!
No! vive Aïda

**RADAMES:** Vive!

**AMNERIS:** Nei disperati aneliti
Dell' orde fuggitive
Sol cadde il padre

**RADAMES:** Ed ella?

**AMNERIS:** Sparve, nè più novella
S'ebbe

**RADAMES:** Gli Dei l'adducano
Salve alle patrie mura,
E ignori la sventura
Di chi per lei morrà!

**AMNERIS:** Or, s'io ti salvo, giurami
Che più non la vedrai

**RADAMES:** Nol posso!

**AMNERIS:** A lei rinunzia
Per sempre e tu vivra

**RADAMES:** Nol posso!

**AMNERIS:** Anco una volta
A lei rinunzia

**RADAMES:** E vano

**AMNERIS:** Morir vuoi dunque, insano?

**RADAMES:** Pronto a morir son già.

**AMNERIS:** Chi ti salva, o sciagurato,
Dalla sorte che ti aspetta?
In furore hai tu cangiato
Un amor ch' equel non ha.
De' miei pianti la vendetta
Ora il cielo compirà.

**RADAMES:** E la morte un ben supremo
Se per lei morir m' è dato:
Nel subir l'estremo fato
Gaudii immensi il core avrà;
L'ira umana io più non temo,
Temo sol la tua pietà.
(*Radames parte circondato dalle Guardia.*)

**RADAMES:** Life
I abhor; the font
Of every joy dried up,
Every hope vanished,
I wish only to die.

**AMNERIS:** To die! Ah; you should live!
Yes, for my love you shall live;
For you I have undergone
The dreadful anguish of death.
I loved you I suffered so much
I watched through the nights in tears.
Country and throne and life
All I would give for you.

**RADAMES:** For her I too betrayed
The country and my honor.

**AMNERIS:** Of her no more

**RADAMES:** Infamy
Awaits me, and you wish that I live?
You made me utterly wretched;
Aïda you have taken from me;
Killed her perhaps! And for a gift
You offer life to me?

**AMNERIS:** I the cause of her death?
No! Aïda lives!

**RADAMES:** Lives?

**AMNERIS:** In the desperate struggle
Of the fugitive hordes
Fell her father alone

**RADAMES:** And she?

**AMNERIS:** She disappeared, nor had we more news.

**RADAMES:** May the gods lead her
Safe to her native walls,
And let her not know the unhappy fate
Of him who will die for her.

**AMNERIS:** Now, if I save you,
swear to me
That you will not see her more.

**RADAMES:** I cannot do it!

**AMNERIS:** Renounce her
Forever, and you shall live!

**RADAMES:** I cannot do it!

**AMNERIS:** Yet, once more;
Renounce her!

**RADAMES:** It is in vain!

**AMNERIS:** Would you die, then, madman?

**RADAMES:** I am ready to die.

**AMNERIS:** Who saves you, O wretch,
From the fate that awaits you?
To fury have you changed
A love that had no equal.
Revenge for my tears
Heaven will now consummate.

**RADAMES:** Death is a supreme blessing,
If for her it is given me to die;
In undergoing the last extremity
My heart will feel great joy.
Human anger I fear no more,
I fear only your pity.
(*Exit Radames, surrounded by Guards.*)

**AMNERIS:** (*cade desolata su un sedile*). Ohimè! Morir mi sento Oh! chi lo salva?
E in poter di costoro
Io stessa lo gettai! Ora, a te impreco
Atroce gelosia, che la sua morte
E il lutto eterno del mio cor segnasti!
(*Si volge e vede il Sacerdoti che attraversano la scena per entrare nel sotterraneo.*)
Che veggo! Ecco i fatali
Gli inesorati ministri di morte
Oh! ch' io non veggo quelle bianche larve!
(*Si copre il bolto colle mani.*)

**SACERDOTI:** (*nel sotterraneo*).
Spirito de l'Nume sovra noi discendi!
Ne avviva al raggio dell' eterna luce;
Pel labbro nostro tua giustizia apprendi.

**AMNERIS:** Numi, pietà del mio straziato core
Egli è innocente, lo salvate, o Numi!
Disperato, tremendo è il mio dolore!
(*Radames, fra le Guardie, attraversa la scena e scende nel sotterraneo Amneris al vederlo, mette un grido.*)

**RAMFIS:** (*nel sotterraneo*). Radamès Radamès: tu rivelasti
Della patria i segretti allo straniero

**SACERDOTI:** Discólpati!

**RAMFIS:** Egli tace

**TUTTI:** Traditor!

**RAMFIS:** Radamès, Radamès: tu disertasti
Dal campo il dì che precedea la pugna.

**SACERDOTI:** Discólpati!

**RAMFIS:** Egli tace

**TUTTI:** Traditor!

**RAMFIS:** Radamès, Radamès: tua fè violasti,
Alla patria spergiuro, al Re, all' onor.

**SACERDOTI:** Discólpati!

**RAMFIS:** Egli tace

**TUTTI:** Traditor!
Radamès è deciso il tuo fato;
Degli infami la morte, tu avrai;
Sotto l'ara del Nume sdegnato
A te vivo fia schiuso l'avel.

**AMNERIS:** A lui vivo la tomba Oh! gli infami!
Nè di sangue son paghi giammai
E si chiaman ministri del ciel!
(*Investendo i Sacerdoti che escono die sotterraneo.*)
Sacerdoti: compiste un delitto
Tigri infami di sangue assetate
Voi le terra ed i Numi eltraggiate

**AMNERIS:** (*falls desolate on a seat*). Ah me! I feel myself dying.
Oh! who will save him?
And in their power
I myself threw him. Now I curse you,
Atrocious jealousy, who did cause his death
And the eternal grief of my heart!
(*Turns and sees the Priests, who cross the stage to enter the subterranean hall.*)
What do I see? Behold the fatal,
The merciless ministers of death!
Oh, that I might not see those white ghosts!
(*Covers her face in her hands.*)

**PRIESTS:** (*in the subterranean hall*). Spirit of the gods descend upon us!
Awaken us to the ray of your eternal light:
By our lips make your justice known.

**AMNERIS:** Gods, pity my torn heart.
He is innocent; save him, O gods!
Desperate, tremendous is my sorrow!
(*Radames, between Guards, crosses the stage and descends to the subterranean hall Amneris on seeing him utters a cry.*)

**RAMPHIS:** (*in the subterranean hall*). Radames, Radames: you did reveal
The country's secrets to the foreigner.

**PRIESTS:** Defend yourself!

**RAMPHIS:** He is silent.

**ALL:** Traitor!

**RAMPHIS:** Radames, Radames: you did desert
From the camp the day preceding the battle.

**PRIESTS:** Defend yourself!

**RAMPHIS:** He is silent.

**ALL:** Traitor!

**RAMPHIS:** Radames, Radames: you broke your faith, Foresworn to your country, king and honor.

**PRIESTS:** Defend yourself!

**RAMPHIS:** He is silent.

**ALL:** Traitor!
Radames your fate is decided:
You shall die the death of the infamous.
Under the altar of the angered god
To you alive be opened the tomb.

**AMNERIS:** To him alive the tomb!
Oh the infamous wretches!
Never satisfied with blood:
And then call themselves ministers of heaven!
(*Attacking the Priests, who issue from the subterranean hall.*)
Priests, you have done a wicked deed

Voi punite chi colpa non ha.

**SACERDOTI:** E traditor! morrà.

**AMNERIS:** (*a Ramfis*). Sacerdote! quest' uomo che uccidi, Tu lo sai da me un giorno fu amato L'anatéma d'un core straziato Col suo sangue su te ricardrà!

**SACERDOTI:** E traditor! morrà. (*Si allontanano lentamente.*)

**AMNERIS:** Empia razza! anatéma! su voi! La vendetta del ciel scenderà! (*Esce disperata.*)

## SCENA II

*La Scena è divisa in due piani. Il piano superiore rap presenta l'interno del Tempio di Vulcano splendente d'oro e di luce; il piano inferiore un sotterraneo. Lunghe file d'arcate si perdono nell' oscurità. Statue colossali d'Osiride colle mani incrociate sestengono i pilastri della volta.*

*Radames è nel sotteraneo sui gradini della scala per cui è disceso Al di sopra, due Sacerdoti intenti a chiudere la pietra del sotterraneo.*

**RADAMES:** La fatal pietra sovra me si chiuse Ecco la tomba mia. Del dì la luce Più non vedrò Non rivedò più Aïda Aïda, ove sei tu? Possa tu almeno Viver felice e la mia sorte orrenda Sempre ignorar! Qual gemito! Una larva Una vision No; forma umana è questa Cielo! Aïda!

**AÏDA:** Son io

**RADAMES:** Tu in questa tomba!

**AÏDA:** Presago il core della tua condanna, In questa tomba che per te si apriva Io penetrai furtiva E qui lontana da ogni umano sguardo Nelle tue braccia desiair morire.

Infamous tigers! thirsting for blood; You outrage earth and gods. You punish him who has done no wrong.

**PRIESTS:** He is a traitor! he shall die.

**AMNERIS:** (*to Ramphis*). Priest, this man who you slay You know it was loved by me. The curse of a broken heart, With his blood, will recoil on you!

**PRIESTS:** He is a traitor! He shall die! (*They withdraw slowly.*)

**AMNERIS:** Impious band anathema! On you The vengeance of heaven will fall! (*Exit in despair.*)

## SCENE II

*The Scene is divided into two floors. The upper floor represents the Interior of the Temple of Vulcan, resplendent with light and gold; the lower floor a subterranean hall; long rows of arcades which are lost in the darkness; colossal statue of Osiris, with the hands crossed, sustains the pilasters of the vault.*

*Radames is in the subterranean hall, on the steps of the staircase by which he has descended; above, two Priests, engaged in closing the stone over the subterranean entrance.*

**RADAMES:** The fatal stone is closed above me Behold my tomb. The light of day I shall see no more. I shall no more see Aïda. Aïda, where are you? May you at least Live happy, and my dreadful fate Never know. What a groan! A ghost! A vision No, it is a human shape Heavens! Aïda!

**AÏDA:** It is I.

**RADAMES:** You in this tomb?

**AÏDA:** My heart, prophetic of your sentence, Into this tomb which opened itself for you I made my furtive way. And here afar from every human glance In your arms I wished to die.

**RADAMES:** Morir! si pura e bella! Morir per me d'amore Degli anni tuoi nel fiore Fuggir la vita! T'aveva il cielo per l'amor creata, Ed io t'uccido per averti amata! No, non morrai! Troppo io t'amai! Troppo sei bella!

**AÏDA:** (*vaneggiando*). Vedi? di morte l'angelo Radiante a noi si appressa Ne adduce a eterni gaudii Sovra i suoi vanni d'òr. Su noi già il ciel dischiudersi Ivi ogni affanno cessa Ivi comincia l'estasi D'un immortale amor. (*Canti e danze della Sacerdotesse nel Tempio.*)

**AÏDA:** Triste canto!

**RADAMES:** Il tripudio Dei Sacerdoti

**AÏDA:** Il nostro inno di morte

**RADAMES:** (*cercando di smuovere la pietra del sotterraneo*). Nè le mie forti braccia Smuovere ti potranno o fatal pietra!

**AÏDA:** Invan! tutto è finito Sulla terra per noi

**RADAMES:** (*con desolata rassegnazione*). E vero! è vero! (*Si avvicina ad Aïda e la sorregge.*)

**AÏDA ET RADAMES:** O terra, addio; addio valle di pianti Sogno di gaudio che in dolor svani A noi si schiude il cielo, e l'alme erranti Volano al raggio dell' eterno di. (*Aïda cade dolcemente fra le braccia di Radames.*) (*Amneris in abito di lutto apparisce nel Tempio e va à prostrarsi sulla pietra che chiude il sotterraneo.*)

**AMNERIS:** Pace t'imploro salma adorata Isi placata ti schiuda il ciel!

*FINE.*

**RADAMES:** To die! So pure and beautiful! To die for love of me; In the flower of your youth To fly from life! Heaven created you for love, And I kill you by having loved you! No, you shall not die! Too much I loved you You are too beautiful.

**AÏDA:** (*raving*). Do you see the angel of death approaches Radiant to us? He takes us to eternal joys Under his golden pinions. Above us heaven has already opened; There every grief ceases; There begins the ecstasy Of an immortal love. (*Songs and dances of the Priestesses in the Temple.*)

**AÏDA:** Sad song!

**RADAMES:** The jubilee Of the priests!

**AÏDA:** Our hymn of death ....

**RADAMES:** (*trying to move the stone of the vault.*) My strong arms Cannot move you, O fatal stone!

**AÏDA:** It is vain all is over For us on earth.

**RADAMES:** (*with desperate resignation*). It is true it is true! (*Goes to Aïda and supports her.*)

**AÏDA AND RADAMES:** O earth farewell! Farewell, vale of tears Dream of joy which vanished in grief. Heaven opens itself to us, and the wandering souls Fly to the rays of eternal day. (*Aïda falls gently into the arms of Radames.*) (*Amneris in mourning robes appears in the temple, and goes to prostrate herself on the stone which closes the vault.*)

**AMNERIS:** Peace I pray for you, O adored corse; Isis appeased, may she unclose heaven to you!

*THE END.*

# Othello (1887)

## Music by Giuseppe Verdi ■ Libretto by Arrigo Boito

This four-act opera, set to a libretto by Arrigo Boito (based on Shakespeare's tragedy), premiered at the Teatro alla Scala in Milan on February 5, 1887. A violent storm rages at sea, but Otello, a Moor and the Venetian governor of Cyprus, reaches the harbor in safety and announces Venetian victory over the Turkish fleet. The people celebrate; Iago, Otello's ensign who despises Otello for promoting Cassio over him, plots his revenge. He tells Roderigo, who is in love with Desdemona, Otello's wife, that Cassio is also in love with her. He gets Cassio drunk and the two men fight; Cassio wounds Mantano, the former governor. Iago falsely informs his master of the events that have transpired, causing Cassio's dismissal. Desdemona and Otello sing a love duet. Iago convinces Cassio that Desdemona is pleading on his behalf. He then makes Otello think that Cassio and Desdemona are having a secret affair: She comes to Otello and tries to defend Cassio; Otello grows jealous. Iago's wife, Emilia, brings him a handkerchief that Otello has given Desdemona; Iago claims he has seen it in Cassio's hands. Otello swears revenge. Desdemona pleads once again for Cassio. Otello asks her to show him the handkerchief he gave to her but she cannot produce it; he accuses her of infidelity. Iago gets Otello to overhear him and Cassio talking about a prostitute. Otello thinks that they are discussing his wife. Otello sees Cassio toying with the handkerchief and decides to kill Desdemona. The Venetian ambassadors announce that Otello is to be recalled to Venice, to be replaced by Cassio. Otello, enraged, throws Desdemona to the ground. Iago persuades Roderigo to kill Cassio. Otello curses his wife. Desdemona prepares for bed with the assistance of Emilia. Upset by Otello's behavior, she recounts the story of her maid who was left by the man she loved. Otello enters as she finishes praying; accusing her of deception, he smothers her despite her protestations of innocence. Emilia rushes in and informs him that Roderigo died while trying to kill Cassio. She sees Desdemona's lifeless body and accuses Otello of killing an innocent woman, exposing Iago's plot. Iago escapes while Otello, realizing his mistake, stabs himself, kissing his wife for the last time as he dies.

---

## ■ ATTO PRIMO

*L'esterno del castello. Una taverna con pergolato. Gli spaldi nel fondo e il mare. È sera. Lampi, tuoni, uragano.*

### SCENA I

*Jago, Roderigo, Cassio, Montano, più tardi Otello. Cipriotti e soldati veneti.*

**ALCUNI DEL CORO:** Una vela!

**ALTRI DEL CORO:** Una vela!

**IL PRIMO GRUPPO:** Un vessillo!

**IL SECONDO GRUPPO:** Un vessillo!

**MON:** É l'alato Leon!

**CAS:** Or la folgor lo svela.

**ALTRI CHE SOPRAGGIUNGONO:** Uno squillo!

**ALTRI CHE SOPRAGGIUNGONO:** Uno squillo!

**TUTTI:** Ha tuonato il cannon.

**CAS:** É la nave del Duce.

**MON:** Or s'affonda,
Or s'inciela—

**CAS:** Erge il rostro dall' onda.

## ■ ACT I

*Outside the Castle. A tavern with an arbor. In the background a quay and the sea. It is evening. Lightning, thunder, hurricane.*

### SCENE I

*Iago, Roderigo, Cassio, Montano, Cypriots, and Venetian Soldiers.*

**SOME OF THE CHORUS:** Ho! a ship!

**OTHERS:** A vessel!

**FIRST GROUP:** Sailing yonder!

**SECOND GROUP:** See her ensign.

**MON:** It is the lion with his wings!

**CAS:** Now the lightning shows her clearly.

**OTHERS OF THE CHO:** *(entering).* Hark! the thunder!

**STILL OTHERS:** It is a signal!

**ALL:** Hark, the cannon answer brings.

**CAS:** It is the vessel of the general.

**MON:** Now the upheaving, Swell enshrouds her.

**CAS:** Now her prow is cleaving the waves.

**METÀ DEL CORO:** Nelle nubi si cela e nel mar,
E alla luce dei lampi ne appar.

**TUTTI:** Lampi! tuoni! gorghi! turbi tempestosi e fulmini!
Treman l' onde, treman l'aure, treman basi e culmini!
Fende l'etra un torvo e cieco spirto di vertigine,
Iddio scuote il cielo bieco, come un tetro vel.
Tutto é fumo! tutto è fuoco! l'orrida caligine
Si fa incendio, poi si spegne più funesta, spasima
L'universo, accore a valchi l'aquilon fantasima,
I titanici oricalchi squillano ne ciel.
*(Entrano dal fondo molte donne del popolo.)*

**TUTTI:** *(con gesti spavento e di supplicazione e rivolti verso lo spaldo).* Dio, fulgor, della bufera!
Dio, sorriso della duna!
Salva l'arca e la bandiera
Della veneta fortuna!
Tu, che reggi gli astri e il Fato!
Tu, che imperi al mondo e al ciel!
Fa che in fondo al mar placato
Posi l'àncora fedel.

**JAGO:** È infranto l'artimon!

**PART OF THE CHORUS:** She is lost in the sea and the night,
But the lightning reveals her to sight.

**ALL:** Roaring tempest, rolling thunder, bright as day the lightning's flash,
Waves are surging high and monstrous where the battling whirlwinds clash.
Through the air is blindly rushing now the spirit of the night,
And the tempest-riven clouds are like a funeral pall.
Chidden billows, gushing skyward, now reflect the lurid light
Of the levin, now in darkness, doubly darkened lies the world.
And the north wind sounds his trumpet, and the spectral cloudracks hurled
Onward ever, with abysmal blackness cover all.

**ALL:** *(with gestures of horror and supplication, turning towards the sea).* God, whose wrath has roused the waters,
At whose smile the whirlwind tarries,
Save, oh save the noble galley
That Venetia's fortune carries!
You, who rule earth and ocean,
Stay the storm, command the tide!
That the ship in sheltering harbor
May safely ride at anchor

**IAGO:** Behold, the mainsail's burst

**ROD:** Il rostro piomba
Su quello scoglio!

**CORO:** Aita! aita!

**JAGO:** (*a parte*). (L' alvo
Frenetico del mar sia la sua tomba!)

**CORO:** É salvo! salvo!

**VOCI INTERNE:** Gittate i
palischermi! Mano alle funi! Fermi!

**PRIMA PARTE CORO:** Forza ai
remi!

**SECONDA PARTE:** (*scendono la
scala dello spaldo*). Alla riva!—

**VOCI INTERNE:** All' approdo! allo
sbarco!

**ALTRE VOCI INTERNE:** Evviva!
Evviva!
(*Ote. dalla scala della spiaggia
salendo sullo spaldo con seguito
di marinai e di soldati.*)

**OTE:** Esultate! L' orgoglio musul-
mano
Sepolto è in mar, nostra e del cielo è
gloria!
Dopo l' armi lo vinse l' uragano.

**TUTTI:** Evviva Otello!—Vittoria!
vittoria!!
(*Ote. entra nella rôcca, seguito da
Cas., da Mon. e dai soldati.*)

**CORO:** Vittoria! Sterminio!
Dispersi, distrutti,
Sepolti nell' orrido
Tumulto piombâr.
Avranno per requie
La sferza dei flutti,
La ridda dei turbini,
L' abisso del mar.

**CORO:** Si calma la bufera.

**JAGO:** (*in disparte a Rod.*). Roderigo!
Ebben, che pensi?

**ROD:** D'affogarmi—

**JAGO:** Stolto
E chi s' affoga per armor di donna.

**ROD:** Vincer nol so.
(*Alcuni del popolo formano da un
lato una catasta di legna: la folla
s'accalca intorno turbolento e curiosa.*)

**JAGO:** Suvvia, fa senno, aspetta
L'opra del tempo. A Desdemona
bella,
Che nel segreto de' tuoi sogni ado-
ri,
Presto in uggia verranno i foschi
baci
Di quel selvaggio dalle gonfle lab-
bra.
Buon Roderigo, amico tuo sincero
Mi ti professo, nè in più forte am-
bascia
Soccorrerti potrei. Si un fragil voto
Di femmina non è tropp' arduo
nodo
Pel genio mio nè per l' inferno, giu-

**ROD:** Her bow is hurried
To yonder cliff.

**CHO:** Bring rescue, rescue!

**IAGO:** (*to Rod.*). Buried,
I fain would leave the waves to cover her.

**CHO:** The danger's over!

**VOICES:** (*from behind*). Abaft the
halyards ready!
Lower the cockboat, steady!

**CHO:** (*first part*). Man the shore-
boats!

**SECOND PART:** (*descending the
steps of the quay*). Hurry strand-
ward!

**VOICES:** (*behind*). Pull together,
to the landward!

**OTHER VOICES:** (*behind*). Welcome! Welcome!
(*Enter Oth., followed by sailors
and soldiers. He ascends the steps
leading from the shore to the
quay.*)

**OTH:** Glad tidings hear, our wars
are done. The ocean
Has whelmed the Turk. Heavens be
and ours the glory!
Those whom our swords had left
the storm has scattered.

**ALL:** Long live Othello!—Vittoria!
Vittoria!!
(*Exit Oth. into the castle, followed
by Cas., Mon., and soldiers.*)

**CHO:** Vittoria! Vittoria!
Dispersed all, and broken,
Their galleys are buried
Deep under the sea.
Let howling of whirlwinds
And rushing of waters,
And rolling of thunder,
Their requiem be!

**CHO:** The tempest is subsiding.

**IAGO:** Roderigo!
Well, now what do you have to say?

**ROD:** I'm drowning.

**IAGO:** Fool,
Who talks of drowning for the love
of woman!

**ROD:** What can I do?
(*Some of the people form a large
pile of wood. The crowd gathers
round, noisy and curious.*)

**IAGO:** Ho now! have courage, wait
for time working changes. The fair
Desdemona
Whom in your secret dreamings
you adore
Will soon be weary of the dark emb-
races
And of the swollen lips of yonder
savage.
Good Roderigo, sincere friend, I've
Professed my allegiance to you;
Now trust me; If a frail vow
Between a Venetian and this Moor is
not too hard
For my shrewd wits and all the tribe
of hell

ro
Che quella donna sarà tua. M' ascol-
ta.
Bench' io finga d' amarlo' odio quel
Moro—
(*Entra Cassio: poi s'unisce a un
crocchio di soldati. Jago sempre
in disparte a Roderigo.*)
E una cagion dell' ira, eccola, guar-
da. (*Indicando Cas.*)
Quell' azzimato capitano usurpa
Il grado mio, il grado mio che in
cento
Ben pugnate battaglie ho meritato;
Ta' fu il voler d' Otello, ed io nun
ange
Di sua Moresca signoria l' alfiere!
(*Dalla catasia incominciano ad
alzarsi dei globi di fumo sempre
più denso.*)
Ma, come è ver che tu Rodrigo sei,
Così è pur certo che se il Maro io
fossi
Vedermi non vorrei d' attorno un
Jago.
Se tu m' ascolti—
(*Jago conduce Rod. verso il fon-
do: il fuoco divampa. I soldati s'
affollano intorno alle tavole della
taverna.*)

**CORO:** (*mentre dura il canto intorno al fuoco di gioia, i tavernieri appenderanno al pergolato
dell' osteria delle lanterne venezi-
ane a varî colori che illumineran-
no galamente la scena. I soldati si
saranno adunati intorno alle ta-
vole, parte seduti, parte in piedi,
ciarlando e bevendo*). Fuoco di
gioia! l' ilare vampa
Fuga la notte col suo splendor,
Guizza, sfavilla crepita, avvampa
Fulgido incendio che invade il cor.
Dal raggio attratti vaghi sembianti
Movono intorno mutando stuol,
E son fanciulle dai lieti canti,
E son farfalle dall' igneo vol.
Arde la palma col sicomoro,
Canta la sposa col suo fedel,
Sull' aurea fiamma sul gaio coro
Soffia l' ardente spiro del ciel.
Fuoco di gioia rapido brilla!
Rapido passa fuoco d' amor 1
Splende, s' oscura palpita, oscilla,
L' ultimo guizzo lampeggia e muor.
(*Il fuoco si spegne a poco a poco:
la bufera è cessata. Jago, Rod.,
Cas. e parecchi altri uomini d'
arme intorno a un tavolo dove c' è
det vino: parte in piedi, parte se-
duti.*)

**JAGO:** Roderigo, beviam! qua la
tazza, Capitano.

You shall enjoy and hold her as
your own.
Now listen! though in semblance,
his true friend
I hate Othello for the best of rea-
sons,
Which you shall hear and judge.
(*Enter Cas., who joins a group of
soldiers. Iago points to him, al-
ways talking to Rod.*)
That masterly arithmetician has
Usurped my place, a place which I
had earned
In many a well-contested battle,
Christian
And heathen. Yet in good time this
Cassio
Must be his lieutenant,
And I—God bless the mark! his
Moorship's ancient!
(*Clouds of smoke, growing den-
ser and denser, begin to rise from
the pile.*)
It is as sure as you are Roderigo.
Were I the Moor I would not be
Iago,
In following him I follow but my-
self.
No,
(*He leads Rod. towards the back.
The fire flares up. The soldiers seat
themselves round the tables of the
tavern.*)

**CHO:** (*during this song round the
bonfire the drawers hang Venetian lanterns of various colors to
the branches of the arbor, and
they gaily illumine the scene. The
soldiers are grouped round the tables, some seated, some standing,
talking and drinking*). Flame
brightly burning, flickering fire,
That with its splendor lightens the
night,
Glittering, roaring, still rising higher,
Filling the bosom with rays of light.
Drawn to your glowing, shapes of
vague semblance
Are seen flitting here and there.
Now they bear resemblance to
sweet maidens.
Now they seem goblins born of the
sheen.
Palmwood is burning, sycamore
glowing,
List the lover sing his love!
And on the gladness softly are blowing
Sweet-scented breezes, breath from
above.
Flame brightly burning, first love's
desire
Vanish as quickly as they arise.
Lost is the splendor, spent is the
fire,
See where the last spark flickers and
dies.
(*The fire is slowly dying; the
storm has ceased altogether. Iago,
Rod., Cas. and some soldiers are
grouped round a table, some sit-
ting, some standing.*)

**IAGO:** A glass, Roderigo; now's
your turn my brave Lieutenant.

**CAS:** Non bevo più.

**JAGO:** (*avvicinando il boccale alla tazza di Cas.*). Ingoia
Questo sorso.

**CAS:** (*ritirando il bicchiere*). No.

**JAGO:** Guarda! oggi impazza
Tutta Cipro! è una notte di gioia,
Dunque—

**CAS:** Cessa. Già m' arde il cervello
Per un nappo vuotato.

**JAGO:** Si, ancora
Ber tu devi. Alle nozze d' Otello
E Desdemona!

**TUTTI:** (*tranne Rod.*). Evviva!

**CAS:** (*alzando il bicchiere e bevendo un poco*). Essa infiora
Questo lido.

**JAGO:** (*sottovoce a Rod.*). (Lo ascolta.)

**CAS:** Col vago
Suo raggiar chiama i cuori a raccolta.

**ROD:** Pur modesta essa è tanto.

**CAS:** Tu, Jago,
Canterai le sue lodi

**JAGO:** (*a Rod.*). (Lo ascolta.)
(*Forte a Cas.*) Io non sono che un
critico.

**CAS:** Ed ella
D' ogni lode è più bella.

**JAGO:** (*come sopra, a Rod., a parte*). (Ti guarda.) Da quel Cassio.

**ROD:** Che temi?

**JAGO:** (*sempre più incalzante*) Ei
favella
Già con troppo bollor, la gaglïarda
Giovinezza lo sprona, è un astuto
Seduttor che t' ingombra il cammino.
Bada—

**ROD:** Ebben?

**JAGO:** S' ei s' inebbria è perduto!
Fallo ber.
(*Ai tavernieri.*)
(*Jago riempie tre bicchieri: uno per sè, uno per Rod., uno per Cas. I tavernieri circolane colle enfore.*)

**JAGO:** (*A Cas. col bicchiere in mano: la folla gli si avvicina e lo guarda curiosamente*). Inaffia l' ugola!
Trinca, tracanna!
Prima che svampino
Canto e bicchier.

**CAS:** (*a Jago, col. bicchiere in mano*). Questa del pampino
Verace manna
Di vaghe annugola
Nebbie il pensier.

**CAS:** I drink no more.

**IAGO:** (*pushing the can towards the glass of Cas.*) Just this one cup
To please me.

**CAS:** No!

**IAGO:** But listen, in all Cyprus
This is a night of revel, and the gallants
Desire it. Therefore—

**CAS:** Leave me. I have drunk
One cup tonight and lo! I am unsteady.

**IAGO:** This toast you cannot shrink
from; here's the health
Of great Othello and of Desdemona!

**ALL:** (*except Rod.*). We hail them!

**CAS:** (*raising his glass and sipping at it*). The blossom of this isle.

**IAGO:** (*aside to Rod.*). You hear
him.

**CAS:** To whose bright-beaming
glances
Must every heart surrender.

**ROD:** Yet I think
She is right modest.

**CAS:** Iago, you shall chant
Her praises.

**IAGO:** (*softly to Rod.*). You hear
him.
(*Aloud to Cas.*)
I am nothing
If not critical.

**CAS:** And far above all praises
Her beauty!

**IAGO:** (*aside to Rod., as above*).
Beware of this Cassio.

**Rod:** Wherefore?

**IAGO:** (*more and more persuasively*). He's handsome, young, a
voluble knave. Very nature
Will instruct her to love him. He's
subtle knave.
The woman has found him already.
Listen!

**ROD:** What then?

**IAGO:** If he drinks he's ruined.
Make him drink!
(*Calling to the attendants.*)
Ho! drawers! Some wine, boys!
(*Iago fills three glasses for himself, Rod. and Cas. The waiters go round with cans.*)

**IAGO:** (*to Cas., with his glass in hand, while the crowd draws near, watching them curiously*).
And let me the clink canakin!
A soldier's a man,
A life's but a span,
Why then let a soldier drink.

**CAS:** (*to Iago, glass in hand*). This
is the noble wine.
Nectar so red,
That with a mist divine
Enshrouds the head.

**JAGO:** (*a tutti*). Chi all' esca ha
morso
Del ditirambo
Spalvaldo e strambo
Beva con me.

**CORO:** Chi all' esca ha morso
Del ditirambo
Spavaldo e strambo
Beve con te.

**JAGO:** (*piano a Rod. indicando Cas.*). (Un altro sorso
E brillo egli è.)
(*Ad alta voce.*)
Il mondo palpita
Quand' io son brillo!
Sfldo l' ironico
Nume e il destin!

**CAS:** (*bevendo ancora*). Come un
armonico
Lïuto oscillo;
La gioia scalpita
Sul mio cammin!

**JAGO:** (*come sopra*). Chi all' esca
ha morso
Del ditirambo
Spavaldo e strambo
Beva con me!

**TUTTI:** Chi all' esca ha morso
Del ditirambo
Spalvaldo e strambo
Beve con te!

**JAGO:** (*a Rod.*). (Un altro sorso
Ed ebbro egli è.)
(*Ad alta voce.*)
Fuggan dal vivido
Nappo i codardi
Che in cor nascondono
Frodi e mister.

**CAS:** (*alzando il bicchiere, al colmo dell' esaltazione*). In fondo all'
anima
Ciascun mi guardi!
Non temo il ver—
(*Barcollando beve.*)
Non temo il ver—e bevo—

**TUTTI:** (*ridendo*). Ah! Ah!

**CAS:** Del calice
Gli orli s' imporporino!—

**JAGO:** (*a Rod., in disparte mentre gli altri ridono di Cas.*) (Egli è
briaco fradicio.) Ti scuoti.
Lo trascina a contesa; è pronto all'
ira,
T' offenderà—ne segui à tumulto!
Pensa che puoi cosi del lieto Otello
Turbar la prima vigilia d' amore!

**ROD:** (*risoluto*). Ed è ciò che mi
spinge.

**MON:** (*entrando e rivolgendosi a Cas.*). Capitano,
V' attende la fazione ai baluardi.

**CAS:** (*barcollando*). Andiam!

**MON:** Che vedo?!

**JAGO:** (*a mon.*). Ogni notte in tal
guisa
Cassio preludia al sonno.

**MON:** Otello il sappia.

**IAGO:** (*to all*) He who once kissed,
This magic brink,
Cannot resist it,
Ever must drink.

**ALL:** Who once has kissed it
This magic brink
Cannot resist is,
Ever must drink.

**IAGO:** (*softly to Rod., pointing to Cas.*).
One other goblet
And he will sink.
(*Aloud.*)
The world looks all awry
When I'm imbibing;
Drinking, I can defy
Fate, and its gibing.

**CAS:** (*drinking again*). Like an
harmonious
Lute I resound.
Happy and glorious
The world around.

**IAGO:** (*as before*). Who once has
kissed it,
This magic brink,
Cannot resist it,
Ever must drink.

**ALL:** Who once has kissed it,
This magic brink,
Cannot resist it,
Ever must drink.

**IAGO:** (*to Rod.*). One other goblet
And he must sink.
(*To all, in a loud voice.*)
From this good company
Cowards avaunt!
Whose bosom treacherously
Mysteries haunt.

**CAS:** (*raising his glass in great excitement*). My heart is open to
Every good fellow (*he drinks*).
I do not fear, not I—(*tottering*)
I do not—while drinking.

**ALL:** (*laughing*). Ha! ha!

**CAS:** The beaker's brimming
With noble wine—

**IAGO:** (*aside to Rod., while the others laugh at Cas.*). He is as
drunk as man can be, now go
To provoke him to combat; he is
rash in choler
And he may strike you, and some tumult follow.
Then cry a mutiny and disturb
The Moor in the arms of his love.

**ROD:** (*with determination*). Trust
in me for the issue.

**MON:** (*entering and addressing Cas.*). Good lieutenant,
Go to keep the watch upon the bastion.

**CAS:** (*tottering*). Let's go!

**MON:** What see I?

**IAGO:** (*to Mon.*). It is evermore
the prologue
That goes before his sleeping.

**MON:** The Moor should know it!

CAS: (*come sopra*). Andiamo ai baluardi—

ROD POI TUTTI: Ah! Ah!

CAS: Chi ride?

ROD: (*provocandolo*). Rido d' un ebro—

CAS: (*scagliandosi contro Rod.*). Bada alle tue spalle l Furfante!

ROD: (*difendendosi*). Briaco ribaldo!

CAS: Marrano! Nessun più ti salva.

MON: (*separandoli a forza e dirigenosi a Cas.*). Frenate la mano, Messer, ve ne prego.

CAS: (*a Mon.*). Ti spacco il cerèbro Se qui t' interponi.

MON: Parole d' un ebro—

CAS: D' un ebro?! (*Cas. sguaina la spada. Mon. s' arma anch' esso. Assalto furibondo. La folla si ritrae.*)

JAGO: (*a parte a Rod. rapidamente*). (Va al porto, con quanta più possa Ti resta, gridando: sommossa! sommossa! Va! spargi il tumulto, l' orror. Le campane Risuonino a stormo.) (*Rod. esce correndo. Jago ai combattenti, esclamando*): Fratelli! l' immane Conflitto cessate!

MOLTE DONNE DEL CORO: (*fuggendo*). Fuggiam!

JAGO: Ciel! già gronda Di sangue Montàno! Tenzon furibonda!

ALTRE DONNE: Fuggiam.

JAGO: Tregua!

TUTTI: Tregua!

DONNE: (*fuggendo*). S' uccidono!

UOMINI: (*ai combattenti*). Pace!

JAGO: (*agli astanti*). Nessun più raffrena quell' ira pugnace! Si gridi l' allarme! Satàna li invade!!

VOCI: (*in scena e dentro*). All' armi!! (*Compane a stormo.*)

TUTTI: Soccorso!!

## SCENA II

*Otello, Jago, Cassio, Montano, Popolo, Soldati: più tardi Desdemona.*

OTE: (*seguito da genti con fiaccole*). Abasso le spade! (*I combattenti s' arrestano. Mon. s' appoggia a un soldato. Le nubi si diradano a poco a poco.*)

---

CAS: (*as before*). Who follows to the bastion?

ROD. AND OTHERS: Ha! ha!

CAS: Who laughs there?

ROD: (*provoking him*). I laugh at drunkards.

CAS: (*pushing against Rod.*). Knave, I will punish you. Take this then!

ROD: (*defending himself*). Oh, ribald drunkard!

CAS: Villain! Nothing shall save you!

MON: (*separating them, to Cas.*). Peace, good lieutenant. No bloodshed, let me pray you.

CAS: (*to Mon.*). I'll knock your brains out If you dare to thwart me.

MON: Come, you're tipsy. (*Cas. draws his sword, as does also Mon. Furious onslaught. The crowd moves away.*)

IAGO: (*aside to Rod. speaking rapidly*). Hasten with all the speed you can command Crying: a riot, help! Thus spread the tumult Abroad, and let them ring the bell in the fortress. (*Exit Rod., running.*) (*Iago, calling out to the antagonists.*) I pray you, Cassio, good Montano, cease Your fighting.

WOMEN: (*flying*). Away!

IAGO: Zounds! here's Montano bleeding To death. Oh, terrible fight!

OTHER WOMEN: Away! Away!

IAGO: Part them!

ALL: Part them!

WOMEN: Their blood is up.

MEN: Peace! Peace!

IAGO: (*to the bystanders*). There's nothing to allay the murderous fury. Call an alarm! Now the devil's rampant.

VOICES: (*on the stage and behind*). Alarm! (*Bells are rung.*)

ALL: Help! Help!

## SCENE II

*Enter Othello, followed by people and Soldiers bearing torches.*

OTH: Put up your weapons. (*The fighting ceases, Mon. leans on a soldier; the clouds are gradually dispersing.*)

---

OTE: Olà! che avvien? son io fra i Saraceni? O la turchesca rabbia è in voi trasfussa Per sbranarvi l' un l' altro?—Onesto Jago, Per quell' amor che tu mi porti, parla.

JAGO: Non so—qui tutti eran cortesi amici, Dianzi, e giocondi—ma ad un tratto, come Se un pianeta maligno avesse a quelli Smagato il senno, sguainando l' arme S' avventano furenti—avess' io prima Stroncati i piè che qui m' adduser!

OTE: Cassio, Come obliasti te stesso a tal segno?—

CAS: Grazia—perdon—parlar non so—

OTE: Montàno—

MON: (*sostenuto da un soldato*). Io son ferito—

OTE: Ferito!—pel cielo Già il sangue mio ribolle. Ah! l' ira volge L' angelo nostro tutelare in fuga! (*Entra Des.; Ote accorre ad essa.*) Che?—la mia dolce Desdemona anch' essa Por voi distolta da' suoi sogni!—Cassio, Non sei più capitano. (*Cas. lascia cadere la spada che è raccolta da Jago.*)

JAGO: (*porgendo la spada di Cas. a un ufficiale*). (Oh! mio trionfo!)

OTE: Jago, tu va nella città sgomenta Con quella squadra a ricompor la pace. (*Jag. esce.*) Si socorra Montàno. (*Mon. è accompagnato nel castello.*) Al proprio tetto Ritorni ognun, (*A tutti, imperiosamente.*) Io da qui non mi parto Se pria non vedo deserti gli spaldi. (*La scena si vuota.*)

## SCENA III

*Otello e Desdemona.*

OTE: Già nelle notte densa S' estingue ogni clamor. Già il mio cor fremebondo S' ammansa in quest' amplesso e si risensa. Tuoni la guerra e s' inabissi il mondo Se dope l' ira immensa Vien questo immenso amor!

---

OTH: Why, how now, ho! from where does this arise? Are we turned Turks, and to ourselves do that From which Heaven's mercy saved us? Honest Iago, Speak, who began this? On your love I charge you.

IAGO: I do not know—Friends all but now in terms Like bride and groom; when suddenly like men Who by some madness are smitten, or by the planet Of opposition, They draw their swords, tilt one another's breast— Ah! would in action I had lost the legs That brought me here!

OTH: Cassio, how comes it you are forgotten

CAS: I pray you pardon me, I cannot speak.

OTH: Montano!

MON: I am wounded.

OTH: Wounded; by heaven My blood begins my safer guides to rule, And passion assays to show the way to judgment. (*Enter Des.; Oth. runs towards her.*) Look if sweet Desdemona, My gentle love, be not raised up from slumber. Cassio, you are no longer my lieutenant! (*Cas. drops his sword, which Iago picks up and hands to an officer.*)

IAGO: (*aside*). At last I triumph!

OTH: Iago look with care about the town And silence those whom this vile brawl distracted. (*Exit Iago.*) All give aid to Montano (*Mon. is led into the castle*), and now to rest. Let all return; alone I shall be watching Until I see that the city is peaceful. (*All leave but Oth. and Des.*)

## SCENE III

*Othello And Desdemona.*

OTH: The night is dark and silent, All blatant clamors cease. My bosom's angry passion Is stilled to perfect peace in this embrace. May the winds blow till they have wakened death If after every tempest come such calms of love.

DES: Mio superbo guerrier! quanti tormenti,
Quanti mesti sospiri e quanta speme
Ci condusse ai soavi abbracciamenti!
Oh! com' è dolce il mormorare insieme
Te ne rammenti!
Quando narravi l' esule tua vita
E i fieri eventi e i lunghi tuoi dolor,
Ed io t' udia coll' anima rapita
In quei spaventi e coll' estasi in cor.

OTE: Pingea dell' armi il fremito, la pugna
E il vol gagliardo alla breccia mortal,
L' assalto, orribil edera, coll' ugna
Al baluardo e il sibilante stral.

DES: Poi mi guidavi ai fulgidi deserti,
All' arse arene, al tuo materno suol,
Narravi allor gli spasimi sofferti
E le catene e dello schiavo il duol.

OTE: Ingentilìa di lagrime l'istoria
Il tuo bel viso e il labbro di sospir;
Scendean sulle mie tenebre la gloria,
Il paradiso e gli astri a benedir.

OTE: E tu m' amavi per le mie sventure
Ed io t' amavo per la tua pietà.

OTE: Venga la morte! mi colga nell' estasi
Di quest' amplesso
Il momento supremo!
(Il cielo si sarà rasserenato.)
Tale è il gaudio dell' anima che temo,
Temo che più non mi sarà concesso
Quest' attimo divino
Nell' ignoto avvenir del mio destino.

DES: Disperda il ciel gli affanni
E Amor non muti col mutar degli anni.

OTE: A questa tua preghiera
Amen risponda la celeste schiera.

DES: Amen risponda.

OTE: (appoggiandosi ad un rialzo degli spaldi). Ah! la gioia m' innonda
Si fieramente—che ansante mi giacio—
Un bacio—

DES: Otello!—

---

DES: My noble warrior, what bitter sorrows,
What long-drawn sighs, what deferred hopes have guided
Us two to these embraces.
Ah, it is sweet to whisper to each other:
Do you remember
When you spoke of some distressful stroke
Your youth had suffered from your boyish days?
I seriously inclined to hear this,
And devoured your discourse with greedy ear.

OTH: When I spoke of sieges and of battles,
Of hairbreadth escapes in the imminent deadly breach,
Of moving accidents by flood and field,
And of impending death.

DES: Wherein of antres vast and deserts idle,
Rough quarries, rocks and hills whose heads touch heaven,
It was your hint to speak, and of the torments
Borne by your noble self to slavery sold.

OTH: And I did beguile you of your tears
And for my pains receive a world of sighs:
Then on the darkness of my soul would break
The heavenly light that is of paradise.

DES: I saw Othello's visage in his mind
And to him did consecrate my soul.

OTH: You loved me for the dangers I had passed,
And I loved you, that you did pity them.

OTH: If it were now to die,
I would most happy, while your arms
(The sky is now quite clear.)
Surround me in embraces; for I fear
My soul has her content so absolute
That not another comfort like to this
Succeeds in unknown fate.

DES: By heaven's all-gracious powers,
Our love shall increase, even as our days
Do grow.

OTH: Ah! may a choir of Heavenly voices
Sing 'Amen' to your sweet prayer

DES: Amen to this, sweet powers!

OTH: (leaning against the parapet of the quay). Ah! this joy will overwhelm me.
It is too much, it stops me here—I stagger—
A kiss—

DES: Othello!

---

OTE: Un bacio—ancora un bacio,
(Fissando una plaga del cielo stellato.)
Già la pleiade ardente al mar discende.

DES: Tarda è la notte.

OTE: Vien—Venere splende.
(S' avviano abbracciati verso il castello.)

## ■ ATTO SECONDO

Una sala terrena nel castello. Due vacti veroni ai lati: una porta nel mezzo che dà sul giardino.

### SCENA I

Jag al di qua del verone. Cassio al de là.

JAGO: Non ti crucciar. Se credi a me, tra poco,
Farai ritorno ai folleggianti amori
Di Monna Bianca, altiero capitano,
Coll' else d' oro e col balteo fregiato.

CAS: Non lusingarmi—

JAGO: Attendi a ciò ch' io dico.
Tu dêi saper che Desdemona è il Duce
Del nostro Duce, sol per essa ei vive.
Pregala tu, quell' anima cortese
Per te interceda e il tuo perdono è certo.

CAS: Ma come favellarle?

JAGO: È suo costume
Girsene a meriggiar fra quelle fronde
Colla consorte mia. Quivi l' aspetta.
Or t' è aperta la via di salvazione;
Vanne.
(Cas. s' allontana.)

### SCENA II

Jago solo seguendo coll' occhio Cassio.

JAGO: Vanne; la tua meta già vedo.
Ti spinge il tuo dimone,
E il tuo dimon son io,
E me trascina il mio, nel quale io credo
Inesorato Iddio:
(Allontanandosi dal verone senza più guardar Cas. che sasà scomparso fra gli alberi.)
Credo in un Dio crudel che m' ha creato
Simile a sè, e che nell' ira io nomo.
Dalla viltà d' un germe o d' un atòmo
Vile son nato.
Son scellerato

---

OTH: A kiss— And yet a kiss!
(Looking up to the starlit sky.)
See where the Wain is fading in the sky.

DES: Late is the night.

OTH: Come, Venus stands on high.
(Exeunt, clinging close to each other, towards the castle.)

## ■ ACT II

A hall on the ground floor of the castle. Two large colonnades to right and left. In the center a door opening into the garden.

### SCENE I

Iago in the hall. Cassio in one of the colonnades.

IAGO: No, do not fret, trust in me, I promise
You'll bask once more in the bright beaming glances
Of Mistress Bianca, as dapper a lieutenant
As ever you were with gilded hilt and baldric.

CAS: Do not deceive me.

IAGO: Hear what I counsel:
Our general's wife, as you full well must know,
Is now our general's general, he her servant;
Importune her; hers is so kind, so blessed,
A disposition, she will work your pardon.

CAS: But how to gain her presence?

IAGO: It is her custom
To rest at noon of day in yonder arbor
Together with my wife. Here, then, await her,
The road I've shown that leads to your salvation.
Go then!
(Cas. goes towards the back.)

### SCENE II

Iago alone, following Cassio with his eyes.

IAGO: Go then! I can decry your fate,
Your demon drives you onward,
And I am that demon
Even as my own impels me
On whose command I wait,—
Relentless Fate.
(He comes forward without taking further notice of Cas., who disappears among the trees.)
Cruel is the God who
Hath fashioned me in his image and whom in wrath I worship.
From some vile germ of nature, some paltry atom
I took my issue;

Perchè son uomo;
E sento il fango originario in me.
Sì! questa è la mia fè!
Credo con fermo cuor, siccome crede
La vedovella al tempi,
Che il mal ch'io penso e che de me predo
Per mio destino adempio.
Credo che il giusto è un istrïon beffardo
E nel viso e nel cuor,
Che tutto è in lui bugiardo:
Lagrima, bacio, sguardo,
Sacrificio ed onor.
E credo l' uom gioco d' iniqua sorte
Dal germe della culla
Al verme dell' avel.
Vien dopo tanta irrisïon la Morte.
E poi?—La Morte è il Nulla
E vecchia fola il Ciel.
(*Dal verone di sinistra si vede passar giardino Des. con Emi. Jago si slano verone, al di là del quale si sarà appostato.*)

JAGO: (*parlando a Cas.*). Eccola—Cassio—a te—questo è il momento
Ti scuoti—vien Desdemona.
S' è mosso; la saluta
E s' avvicina
Or qui si tragga Otello—aiuta, aiuta
Sàtana il mio cimento!
(*Sempre al verone, osservando, ma un discosto, si vedono ripassare nel giardino e Des.*)
Già conversano insieme—ed essa inclina
Sorridendo, il bel viso.
Mi basta un lampo sol di quel sorriso
Per trascinare Otello alla ruina.
Andiam—
Ma il caso in mio favor s' adopra.
Eccolo—al posto, all' opra.

## SCENA III

*Jago e Otello.*

JAGO: Ciò m' accora—

OTE: Che parli?

---

Vile is my tissue,
For I am human.
I feel the primal mud-flow of my breed.
This is my creed.
As firmly I believe, as ever did woman
Who prays before the altar,
Of every ill, whether I think or do it,
It is Fate that drives me to it.
You're an honest man, but a wretched player,
Your life is but a part,
A lie each word you say, your tear, your kiss, your prayer,
Are as false as you are
Man's Fortune's fool even from his earliest breath.
The germ of life is fashioned
To feed the worm of death.
Yea, after all this folly all must die.
And then? And then there's nothing,
And heaven an ancient lie.
(*From the right-hand colonnade Des. and Emi. are seen to enter the arbor. Iago goes towards the colonnade, beyond which Cas. has taken his position.*)

IAGO: (*calling gently to Cas.*).
Take care, Cassio! to her! this is the moment.
Now, Desdemona comes.
(*Cas. goes to Des., bows to her and joins her.*)
He's near her.
He greets her, does accost her. Now must I fetch Othello.
Divinities of hell, I call upon your succor!
(*Still standing in the colonnade watching at some distance Cas. and Des., who are seen passing backwards and forwards in the garden.*)
They are talking in whispers. Now
To him has she inclined her gentle visage.
Ay! smile upon her, do! an excellent courtesy!
This smile shall lure Othello to his ruin.
To work! and in this web I will enslave him.
(*He goes rapidly towards the outlet on the left, but suddenly stops.*)
He comes. Good luck! I have him.
(*He leans motionless against a column on the right looking intently towards the garden where Cas. and Des. are standing together*)

## SCENE III

*Iago And Othello.*

IAGO: (*pretending not to see Oth., who is quite close to him, and to be talking to himself*). I don't like that.

OTH: What did you say?

---

JAGO: Nulla—voi qui? una vana
Voce n' usci dal labbro—

OTE: Colui che s' allontana
Dalla mia sposa, é Cassio?

JAGO: (*e l' uno e l' altro si staccano dal verone*). Cassio? no—quei si scosse
Come un reo nel verdervi.

OTE: Credo che Cassio ei fosse.

JAGO: Mio signore—

OTE: Che brami?—

JAGO: Cassio, nei primi di
Del vostro amor, Desdemona non conosceva?

OTE: Si.
Perchè fai tale inchiesta?

JAGO: Il mio pensiero è vago
D' ubbie, non di malizia.

OTE: Di' il tuo pensiero, Jago.

JAGO: Vi confidaste a Cassio?

OTE: Spesso un mio dono o un cenno
Portava alla mia sposa.

JAGO: Dassenno?

OTE: Si, dassenno.
Nol credi onesto?

JAGO: Onesto?

OTE: Che ascondi nel tuo core?

JAGO: Che ascondo in cor, signore?

OTE: "Che ascondo in cor, signore?"
Pel cielo! tu sei l' eco dei detti miei, nel chiostro
Dell' anima ricetti qualche terribil mostro.
Si, ben t' udii poc' anzi mormorar: ciò m'accora.
Ma di che t' accoravi? nomini Cassio e allora
Tu corrughi la fronte. Suvvia, parla se m' ami.

JAGO: Voi sapete ch' io v' amo.

OTE: Dunque senza velami
T' esprimi e senza ambagi. T' esca fuor dalla gola
Il tuo più rio pensiero colla più ria parola!

JAGO: S' anco teneste in mano tutta l' anima mia
Nol sapreste.

OTE: Ah!

CAS: (*avvicinandosi molto ad Ote. e sottovoce*). Temete, signor, la gelosia!
E un' idra fosen, livida, cieca, col suo veleno
Sè stessa attosca, vivida piaga le squarcia il seno.

---

IAGO: Nothing. You here?—If anything some idle words
Escaped me.
(*Both come forward, away from the colonnade.*)

OTH: Was he who just now parted
From Desdemona Cassio?

IAGO: Cassio? No!
In suchwise, guilty-like, he would not leave her.

OTH: I do believe was Cassio.

IAGO: No, my lord!

OTH: What do you think?

IAGO: Nothing—
Did Michael Cassio when you wooed my lady
Know of your love?

OTH: Yes. Why ask the question?

IAGO: But for the satisfaction of my thought,
No further harm.

OTH: Why of your thought, Iago?

IAGO: And did you trust in Cassio?

OTH: He went between us often
Taking a tender message to my lady.

IAGO: Indeed?

OTH: Yes, indeed! Is he not honest?

IAGO: Honest?

OTH: You discern anything in that?

IAGO: I discern anything in that?

OTH: "I discern anything in that?"
By heaven, he echoes every word I say!
As if there were some monster in his thought
Too hideous to be shown. Yea, myself
Have heard you say even now "I don't like that!"
Say, then, what did you not like?
Looking at Cassio
You did contract your brow together. Speak
If you love me!

IAGO: Well you know I love you.

OTH: I beg you speak to me, as to your thinkings,
As you ruminate, and give your worst of thoughts,
The worst of words!

IAGO: You should not know my thoughts, even if my heart
Were in your hands, nor shall not.

OTH: Ah!

IAGO: (*going close up to him, almost in a whisper*). Beware, My lord, of jealousy!
It is the green-eyed monster, which mocks
The meat it feeds on, and which with its poison
Changes our nature.

OTE: Miseria mia!! No! il vano sospettar nulla giova.
Pria del dubbio l' indagine, dopo il dubbio la prova,
Dopo la prova (Otello ha sue leggi supreme)
Amore e gelosia vadan dispersi insieme!

JAGO: (*con piglio più ardito*). Un tal proposito spezza di mie labbra il suggello.
Non parlo ancor di prova; pur, generoso Otello,
Vigilate, soventi le oneste e ben create
Coscïenze non vedono la frode: vigilate.
Scrutate le parole di Desdemona, un detto
Può ricondur la fede, può affermare il sospetto—
Eccola; vigilate—
(*Si vede ricomparire Des. nel giardino, dalla vasta apertura del fondo: è circondata da Donne, da Fanciulli, da Marinai Cipriotti e Albenesi che si avanzano e le offrono fiori ed altri doni, Alcuni s' accompagnano, cantando, sulla Guzla altri su delle piccole arpe.*)

CORO: (*nel giardino*). Dove guardi splendono
Raggi, avvampan cuori,
Dove passi scendono
Nuvole di fiori.
Qui fra gigli e rose,
Come a un casto altar,
Padri, bimbi, spose
Vengono a cantar.

FANCIULLI: (*spargendo al suolo fiori di giglio*) T' offriamo il giglio
Soave stel
Che in man degli angeli
Fu assunto in ciel,
Che abbella il fulgido
Manto e la gonna
Della Madonna
E il santo vel.

DONNE E MARINAI: Mentre all' aura vola
Lieta la canzon,
L' agile mandòla
Ne accompagna il suon.

MARINAI: (*offrendo a Des dei monili di corallo e di perle*). A te le porpore,
Le perle e gli ostri,
Nella voragine
Côlti del mar.
Vogliam Desdemona
Coi doni nostri
Come un' imagine
Sacra adornar.

FANCIULLI E DONNE: Mentre all' aura vola
Lieta la canzon,
D' agile mendòla
Ne accompagna il suon.

LE DONNE: (*sporgendo fronde e fiori*). A te la florida
Messe dai grembi
A nembi, a nembi,
Spargiamo al suol.

OTH: Oh misery!
You think I'll make a life of jealousy?
I'll see before I doubt, when I doubt, prove;
And on the proof—Othello thus decrees—
Away at once with love or jealousy!

IAGO: (*more frank in manner*).
I'm glad, for I can show the love and duty
I bear you. I speak not yet of proof.
Look to your wife! I would not have
Your free and noble nature be abused.
Observe her well with Cassio! One unguarded word,
One gesture may to your first faith restore you,
Or confirm your suspicion. She comes, be watchful!
(*Des. is seen to return to the garden through the large door at the back; she is surrounded by women, children and Cypriot and Albanian soldiers, who come forward in turn, offering her flowers and other gifts. They sing, accompanying themselves, some on guzla, others on small harps.*)

CHO: (*in the garden*). Where ever your glances shed
Brightness, hearts must meet you
Where ever your footsteps tread,
Flowers spring forth to greet you.
Rose and lily bringing
We approach your shrine.
Old and young are singing,
And our songs are yours

CHILDREN: (*strewing lilies on the ground*). We bring lilies
On slender stem.
In heaven the hand of angels
Proffers them.
Our Lady's gown is strewn with their petals bright;
Her sacred crown is
Gemmed with their light.

WOMEN AND SAILORS: Rising ever higher
Sounds our song afar,
With our voices blending
Zither and guitar.

SAILORS: (*offering necklaces of corals and pearls*). To you we proffer
Rich pearls and corals
Which we have gathered
Deep in the sea.
Desdemona,
Like a fair image, we are crowning
With all our treasures.

WOMEN: (*strewing leaves and flowers*)
For you we gathered
Blossoms of springtime,
Gladly we strew them,

L' April circonda
La sposa bionda
D' un' etra rorida
Che vibra al Sol.

FANCIULLI E MARINAI: Mentre all' aura vola
Lieta la canzon,
L' agile mandòla
Ne accompagna il suon.

TUTTI: Dove guardi splendono
Raggi, avvampan cuori,
Dove passi scendono
Nuvole di fiori.
Qui fra gigli e rose,
Come a un casto altar,
Padri, bimbi, spose
Vengono a cantar.

DES: Splende il cielo, danza
L' aura, olezza il fiore.
Gioia, amor, speranza
Cantan nel mio core.

CORO: Vivi felice! Addio. Qui regna Amore.
(*Durante il Coro, Ote. osserva con Jag.*)

OTE: (*soavemente commosso*).
Quel canto mi con quide.
No, no, s' ella m' inganna, il ciel sè stesso irride!

JAGO: (Beltà, letizia, in dolce inno concordi!
I vostri infrangerò soavi accordi.)

## SCENA IV

*Finito il Coro, Des. bacia la testa d' alcuni tra i fanciulli, e alcune donne le baciano il lembo della veste, ed essa proge una borsa ai marinai. Il Coro s' allontana: Des., segita poi da Emi., entra nella sala e s' avanza verso Ote.*

DES: D' un uom che geme sotto il tuo disdegno
La preghiera ti porto.

OTE: Chi è costui?

DES: Cassio.

OTE: Era lui
Che ti parlava sotto quelle fronde?

DES: Lui stesso, e il suo dolor che in me s' infonde
Tanto è verace che di grazia è degno.
Intercedo per lui, per lui ti prego.
Tu gli perdona.

OTE: Non ora.

DES: Non oppormi il tuo diniego.
Gli perdona.

OTE: Non ora.

DES: Perchè torbida suona
La voce tua? qual pena t' addolora?

OTE: M' ardon le tempie—

For they are yours
Your silken tresses
April shall fan them,
The morn surround them
With golden shine.

WOMEN AND SAILORS: Rising ever higher
Sounds our song afar,
With our voices blending
Zither and guitar.

ALL: Where ever your glances shed
Brightness, hearts must meet you.
Where ever your footsteps tread,
Flowers spring forth to greet you.
Rose and lily bringing
We approach your shrine.
Old and young are singing,
And our songs are yours.

DES: Sunlight, blowing breezes,
Rose and heliotrope
Fill my heart with gladness,
Waken love and hope.

CHO: Live long and happy, yours be hope and love.
(*During the singing Iago and Oth. have been watching the scene.*)

OTH: (*softly moved*). Their song has wrung my bosom.
If she be false, Oh, then heaven mocks itself.

IAGO: (*aside*). See love and beauty here together dwelling,
Until I come their harmony dispelling.

## SCENE IV

*When the singing is over Des. kisses some of the children, and some of the women kiss the hem of her gown. She gives a purse to the sailors, Exit Chorus slowly. Des., followed by Emi., comes forward into the hall where Oth. stands.*

DES: I have been talking with a suitor here.
Who has felt your displeasure.

OTH: Who do you mean?

DES: Cassio.

OTH: Then it was he who spoke to you
Even now in yonder arbor?

DES: He, none other,
Ay, sooth, he went away so humbled
That he has left part of his grief with me.
If I have any grace of power to move you
You must forgive him.

OTH: Not now!

DES: Nay, I'll take
Not your denial, forgive him!

OTH: Not now!

DES: Why do you speak so faintly?
Are you not well, does any pain afflict you?

OTH: Here on my forehead.

DES: (*spiegando il suo fazzoletto come per fasciare la fronte d' Ote.*). Quell' ardor molesto Svanirà, se con questo Morbido lino la mia man ti fascia.

DES: (*spreading out her handkerchief, as if to tie it round the forehead of Oth.*). It will away again. Within this hour it will be well, if you Will let me bind it with this napkin.

OTE: (*getta il fazzoletto a terra*). Non ho d' uopo di ciò.

OTH: (*throws the handkerchief down*). It is too little.

DES: Tu sei crucciato Signor.

DES: I am very sorry, My Lord.

OTE: (*aspramente*). Mi lascia! (*Emi. raccoglie il fazzoletto dal suolo.*)

OTH: (*roughly*). Let it alone! (*Emi picks up the handkerchief.*)

DES: Se inconscia, contro te, sposo, ho peccato Dammi la dolce e lieta Parola del perdono. La tua fanciulla io sono Umile e mansueta; Ma il labbro tuo sospira, Hai l' occhio fiso al suol. Guardami in volto e mira Come favella amore. Vien ch' io t' allieti il core, Ch' io ti lenisca il duol.

DES: If ever against my will I have offended, Dear husband, let me pray it, The word of pardon say it. I am your child, your servant, Of your least hint observant. Your silence speaks of sadness, Your face is turned from me. See in my eyes the token Of vows of love unbroken, Oh! let me cheer your sadness, Oh! let me comfort you!

OTE: (*a parte*). (Forse perchè gli inganni D' arguto amor non tendo, Forse perchè discendo Nella valle degli anni, Forse perchè ho sul viso Quest' atro tenebror, Ella è perduta e irriso Io sono e il cor m' infrango E ruinar nel fango Vego il mio sogno d' ôr.)

OTH: (*aside*). Haply because I lack Soft parts of conversation, Or that I am declined Into the vale of years; Haply because my visage Is dyed of deepest black, Her life is lost, a byword Am I, my heart is broken, And in the dust is scattered My golden dream of love.

JAGO: (*a Emi. sottovoce*). Quel vel mi porgi Ch' or hai raccolto.

IAGO: (*aside to Emi*). That napkin give me, I have been watching.

EMI: (*sottovoce a Jago*). Qual frode scorgi? Ti legge in volto.

EMI: (*aside to Iago*). Some scheme you're hatching; You'll not deceive me.

JAGO: T' opponi a vôto Quan l' io commando.

IAGO: How dare you show defiance to me?

EMI: Il tuo nefando Livor m' è noto.

EMI: Your wicked scheming Too well I know it.

JAGO: Sospetto insano!

IAGO: Surely you're dreaming!

EMI: Guardia fedel È questa mano.

EMI: In mine own trust I place reliance.

JAGO: Dammi quel vel! (*Jag. affera violentemente il braccio di Emi.*)

IAGO: Give it you must. (*Iago violently grasps the arm of Emi.*)

JAGO: Su te l' irosa Mia man s' aggrava!

IAGO: My hand in strife You cannot brave.

EMI: Son la tua sposa, Non la tua schiava.

EMI: I am your wife And not your slave!

JAGO: La schiava impura Tu sei di Jago.

IAGO: My bondsmaid are you, Believe my message.

EMI: Ho il cor presago D' una sventura.

EMI: My heart has presage Of boding grief.

JAGO: Nè mi paventi?

IAGO: Now, do I scare you?

EMI: Uomo crudel!

EMI: Ah! cruel man!

JAGO: A me—

IAGO: Give me—

EMI: Che tenti?

EMI: No, never!

JAGO: A me quel vel! (*Con un colpo di mano Jag. ha carpito u fazzoletto ad Emi.*)

IAGO: That handkerchief! (*With a sudden wrench he tears the handkerchief from Emi.*)

JAGO: (Già la mia brama Conquido, ed ora Su questa trama Jago lavora!)

IAGO: Spent is my anger; Firmly I hold them Here in my meshes. Iago's master.

EMI: (Vinser gli artigli Truci e codardi. Dio dai perigli Sempre ci guardi.)

EMI: Lurking disaster Spreads out its meshes. God, in their danger Strengthen, uphold them.

OTE: Escite! Solo vo' restar.

OTH: Leave me, I would rather be alone.

JAGO: (*sottovoce ad Emi. che sta per escire*). (Ti giova Tacere. Intendi?) (*Des. ed Emi. escono. Jag. finge d' escire dalla, porta del fondo, ma giuntovi s' arresta.*)

IAGO: (*aside to Emi., who is about to go*). Of this no word, I charge you. (*Exeunt Des. and Emi. Iago goes towards the door at back, as if about to leave, but remains standing there.*)

## SCENA V

*Otello: Jago nel fond.*

OTE: (*accasciato, su d' un sedile*). Desdemona rea!

JAGO: (*nel fondo guardando di nascosto il fazzoletto, poi riponendolo, con cura nel giustacuore*). Con questi fili tramerò la prova Del peccato d' amor. Nella dimora Di Cassio ciò s' asconda.

OTE: Atroce idea?

JAGO: (*fra se, fissando Ote.*). (Il mio velen lavora.)

OTE: Rea contro me! contro me!!!

JAGO: (Suffri e ruggi!)

OTE: Atroce!!!—atroce!!!—

JAGO: (*dopo essersi portato accanto ad Ote. bonariamente.*) Non pensateci più.

OTE: (*balzando*). Tu? Indietro! fuggi!! M' hai legato alla croce!— Ahimè!—Più orrendo d' ogni orrenda ingiuria Dell' ingiuria é il sospetto. Nell' ore arcane della sua lussuria (E a me furate!) m' agitava il petto Forse un presagio? Ero baldo, giulivo— Nulla sapevo ancor; io non sentivo Sol suo corpo divin che m' innamora E sui labbri mendaci Gli ardenti baci Di Cassio! Ed ora!—ed ora. Ora e per sempre addio sante memorie, Addio sublimi incanti del pensier! Addio schiere fulgenti, addio vittorie, Dardi volanti e volanti corsier! Addio vessillo trïonfale e pio E dïane squillanti in sul mattin! Clamori e canti di battaglia, addio!— Della gloria d' Otello è questo il fin.

## SCENE V

*Othello and Iago (behind).*

OTH: (*exhausted, throws himself into a chair*) False Desdemona!

IAGO: (*at the back, looking at the handkerchief and then carefully replacing it in his doublet*). Trifles light as air Are to the jealous proofs of holy writ. Now will I lose in Cassio's house this napkin.

OTH: The thought is monstrous!

IAGO: (*to himself, watching Oth.*). He changes with my poison.

OTH: False to me! ha, to me!

Iago: (*aside*). Yea, writhe and foam!

OTH: Oh monstrous, monstrous!

IAGO: (*going up to Oth., cordially.*) General, no more of that!

OTH: Avaunt you have set me on the rack! Ah me! I swear it is better to be much abused Than but to know it a little. What sense had I of her stolen hours of lust Though stolen from me? I saw it not, thought it not, it harmed not me; Free and merry was I, not knowing anything. I did not wince, when I clasped her sweet body In tender love, nor did find on her lips The burning kiss of Cassio. Oh, now for ever Farewell the tranquil mind, farewell content And noble thoughts of war! Farewell the pluméd troop, the impending battle, The swiftly-flying shaft, the neighing steed, Pride, pomp and circumstance of glorious war,

**JAGO:** Pace, signor.

**OTE:** Sciagurato! mi trove
Una prova secura
Che Desdemona è impura—
Non sfuggir! non sfuggir! nulla ti giova!
Vo' una secura, una visibil prova!
(*Afferrando Jag. alla gola e atterrandolo.*)
O sulla tua testa
S' aceen la e precipiti il fulmine
Del mio spaventoso furor che si desta!

**JAGO:** (*rialzandosi*). Divina grazia difendimi!—Il cielo
Vi protegga. Non son più vostro alfiere.
Voglio che il mondo testimon mi sia
Che l' onestà è periglio.
(*Fa per andarsene.*)

**OTE:** No—rimani.
Forse onesto tu sei.

**JAGO:** (*sulla soglia fingendo d' andarsene*). Meglio varrebbe
Ch' io fossi un ciurmador.

**OTE:** Per l' universo!
Credo leale Desdemona e credo
Che non lo sia; te credo onesto e credo
Disleale—La prova io voglio! voglio
La certezza!!

**JAGO:** (*ritornando verso Ote.*).
Signor, frenate l' ansie.
E qual certezza v' abbisogna? Avvinti
Vederli forse?

**OTE:** Ah! Morte e dannazione!!

**JAGO:** Ardua impresa sarebbe; e qual certezza
Sognate voi se quell' immondo fatto
Sempre vi sfuggirà?—Ma pur se guida
E la ragione al vero, una sì forte
Congettura riserbo che per poco
Alla certezza vi conduce. Udite:
(*Avvicinandosi molto ad Ote. e sottovoce.*)
Era la notte, Cassio dormia, gli stavo accanto.
Con interrotte voci tradia l' intimo incanto.
Le labbra lente, lente, movea, nell' abbandono
Del sogno ardente; e allor dicea, con flebil suono:
Desdemona soave! Il nostro amor s' asconda.
Cauti vegliamo! l' estasi del ciel tutto m' innonda.
Seguia più vago l' incubo blando; con molle angoscia,
L' interna imago quasi baciando, ei

The spirit-stirring drum, the ear-piercing pipe,
Farewell! Othello's occupation's gone.

**IAGO:** Peace, peace, my lord!

**OTH:** Villain!
Make me to see it or at the least to prove it
That my love is a strumpet. No escape
Shall now avail you.
Be sure of it, give me the ocular proof.
(*He grasps Iago by the throat and throws him down.*)
Or on your head
Shall accumulate all my waked wrath,
And with the fire of lightning smite you.

**IAGO:** (*rising*). Oh grace of heaven forgive me!
Be God's own mercy with you, take mine office!
Take note, oh world, that it is no longer safe
To be direct and honest.
(*He makes pretense of leaving.*)

**OTH:** No, stay, you should be honest.

**IAGO:** (*on the threshold, still pretending to withdraw*). I should be wise, for honesty's a fool.

**OTH:** The world be witness:
I think my wife be honest, and think she is not;
I think that you are just, and think you are not.
I'll have some proof, would I were satisfied!

**IAGO:** (*returning to Oth.*). I do not like the office.
What shall I say, where's satisfaction?
Would you see this?

**OTH:** Death and damnation!

**IAGO:** It were difficult, truly.
There's no satisfaction
For you. Will not the hideous deed
Escape your eyes forever? But yet I say
If imputation and strong circumstance
Grossly suspicious
Will give you satisfaction you may have it.
(*He goes closely up to Oth.; in a whisper.*)
I lay with Cassio lately, and myself
Sleepless, I watched his slumbers. Suddenly
He began to mutter of what he was dreaming.
Moving his lips gently and slowly, words
Of deepest import then I heard him utter,
Saying in tearful and in passionate accents:
"Sweet Desdemona,
Let us be wary ever, let us hide
What to you and to me is heavenly

disse poscia:
Il rio destino impreso che al Moro ti donò.
E allora il sogno in cieco letargo si mutò.

**OTE:** Oh! monstruosa colpa!

**JAGO:** Io non narrai
Che un sogno.

**OTE:** Un sogno che rivela un fato.

**JAGO:** Un sogno che può dar forma di prova
Ad altro indizio.

**OTE:** E qual?

**JAGO:** Talor vedeste
In mano di Desdemona un tessuto
Trapunto a fiori e più sottil d' un velo?

**OTE:** È il fazzoletto ch' io le diedi, pegno
Primo d' amor.

**JAGO:** Quel fazzoletto ieri
(Certo ne son) lo vidi in man di Cassio.

**OTE:** Ah! mille vite gli donasse Iddio!
Una è povera preda al furor mio!!
Jago, ho il cuore di gelo.
Lungi da me le pïetose larve!
Tutto il mio vano amor esalo al cielo,
Guardami—ei sparve.
Nelle sue spire d' angue
L' idra m' avvince! Ah! sangue! sangue! sangue!!
(*S' inginocchia.*)
Si, pel ciel marmoreo giuro! Per le attorte folgori!
Per la Morte e per l' oscuro mar sterminator
D' ira e d' impeto tremendo presto fia che sfolgori
Questa man ch' io levo e stendo!
(*Levando la mano al cielo.*)

**JAGO:** (*Ote. fa per alzarsi, Jag. lo trattiene inginocchiato e s' inginocchia anch' esso*). Non v' alzate ancor!
Testimon è il Sol ch' io miro, che m' irradia e inanima,
L' ampia terra e il vasto spiro del Creato inter,
Che ad Otello io sacro ardenti, core, braccio ed anima
S' anco ad opere cruenti s' armi il suo voler!

**JAGO E OTE:** (*insieme, alzando le mani al cielo come hi giura*). Si, pel ciel marmoreo giuro! per le attoret folgori!
Per la Morte e per l' oscuro mar stermin ter!
D' ira e d' impeto tremendo presto

sweetness."
Then in his dream he moved towards me, sighing
And kissing softly now his fancy's image,
Thus did he murmur:
"Ah cursed Fate that gave you to the Moor!"
And after that, the dream forsaking him,
Calmly he slept.

**OTH:** Oh, monstrous, monstrous!

**IAGO:** No it was but his dream.

**OTH:** But this denoted a foregone conclusion.

**IAGO:** It may thicken other proofs that do demonstrate thinly.

**OTH:** And how?

**IAGO:** Have you not seen in your wife's hands
A handkerchief spotted with strawberries
And of most subtle texture?

**OTH:** Such is the handkerchief I gave to her,
It was my first gift.

**IAGO:** That handkerchief
Lately, upon my oath, was in the hands of Cassio.

**OTH:** Oh, that the slave had forty thousand lives!
One is too weak and poor for my revenge.
Listen Iago.
All my fond love I blow to heaven,
Arise, black vengeance, from your hollow cell!
Look on me, it is gone!
Yield up, oh love, your crown to tyrannous hate!
Oh blood! blood! blood!
(*He kneels.*)
Witness you marble heaven,
Witness eternal lights above,
Elements that clip us round about;
Never shall cease my hatred, never ebb
My wrath, until this hand has wrought my vengeance! (*He lifts up his hand.*)

**IAGO:** (*Oth. is about to rise, when Iago holds him down and kneels himself*). No, rise not yet!
Witness the Sun which illuminates us here,
Earth on which we live, ambient air,
In which we breathe the all-Creator's breath,
Witness that here Iago gives up
His hand, his heart, his wit to wronged Othello's service.

**BOTH:** (*raising their bands as for a solemn oath*). Witness yon marble heaven,
Witness eternal lights above,
Elements that clip us round about!
Never shall cease my hatred, never ebb

fia che sfolgori
Questa man ch' io levo e stendo.
Dio vendicator.

My wrath, until this hand has
wrought my vengeance!
So help me God!

## ■ ATTO TERZO

*La gran sala del castello. A destra
un vasto peristilio a colonne.
Questo peristilio è annesso ad una
sala di minori proporzioni; nel
fondo della sala un verone.*

## ■ ACT III

*The great hall of the castle. To the
left a large portico, which leads to
another smaller hall; at the back
of the hall a colonnade.*

### SCENA I

*Otello, Jago, L'Araldo.*

**ARA:** (*dal peristilio, a Ote. che
sarà con Jag. nella sala*). La vedet-
ta del porto l a segnalato La veneta
galea che a Cipro adduce Gli ambasciatori.

**OTE:** (*all' Araldo, facendogli cen-
no di allontanarsi*). Bene sta. (*L'
Araldo esce.*)
**OTE:** (*a Jag.*). Continua.

**JAGO:** Qui trarrò Cassio e con as-
tute inchieste
Lo adescherò a ciarlar, Voi là nas
osto
(*Indicando il vano del verone.*)
Scrutate i modi suoi, le sue parole,
I lazzi, i geslii. Paziente siate
O la prova vi sfugge. Ecco Desde-
mona.
Finger conviene—io vado.
(*S' allontana come per escire, poi
s' arresta e si riavvicina ad Ote.*)
Il fazzoletto—

**OTE:** Va! volentieri obliato l' avrei.
(*Jag. esce.*)

### SCENE I

*Othello, Iago and a Herald.*

**HER:** (*from the portico to Oth.,
who is with Iago in the hall*). Sir,
the watch of the port has just sig-
naled the arrival of the galley which
brings to Cyprus the ambassadors.

**OTH:** (*to the Herald, beckoning
him to go*). It is well. (*To Iago.*)
Go on then.
(*Exit Herald.*)

**IAGO:** I spoke to Cassio, bade him
anon return, which he promised.
Do but encave yourself
(*Pointing to the colonnade.*)
And mark the slurs, the gibes and
scornful actions,
I say, mark but his gestures. Marry
patience!
Or the proof will escape you.
See, yonder comes your wife, you
must be cunning.
I leave you.
(*He moves away as if to leave,
then stops and returns to Othel-
lo.*)
That handkerchief is—

**OTH:** Go, do not name it; I would
gladly forget it.
(*Exit Iago.*)

### SCENA II

*Otello. Desdemona dalla porta di
sinistra.*

**DES:** (*ancora presso alla soglia*).
Dio ti giocondi, o sposo dell' alma
mia sovrano.

**OTE:** (*andando incontro a Des. e
prendendole la mano*). Grazie,
madonna, datemi la vostra eburnea
mano.
Caldo mador ne irrora la morbida
beltà.

**DES:** Essa ancor l' orme ignora del
duolo e dell' età.

**OTE:** Eppur qui annida il demone
gentil del mal consiglio,
Che il vago avorio allumina del pic-
cioletto artiglio.
Mollemente alla prece s' atteggia e
al pio fervore—

### SCENE II

*Othello and Desdemona, who en-
ters from the right.*

**DES:** (*still almost on the threshold*). How is it with you, my husband,
My heart's sole lord and master?

**OTH:** (*going to meet Des. and tak-
ing her hand*). Well, my good lady.
Give me your hand, as white as vir-
gin snow,
Yet hot and moist; which argues
A frank and liberal heart.

**DES:** It yet has felt no age, nor
known of sorrow.

**OTH:** And yet within this hand
there is a young
And melting devil, that commonly
rebels.
It is a good hand, a frank one; it requires
Much fervent prayer and castiga-
tion.

**DES:** Eppur con questa mano io v'
ho donato il core,
Ma riparlar vi debbo di Cassio.

**OTE:** Ancor l' ambascia
Del mio morbo m' assale; tu la
fronte mi fascia.

**DES:** (*porgendogli un fazzoletto*).
A te.

**OTE:** No il fazzoletto voglio ch' io ti
donai.

**DES:** Non l' ho meco.

**OTE:** Desdemona, guai se lo perdi!
guai!
Una possente maga ne ordia lo
stame arcano:
Ivi è reposta l' alta malia d' un talis-
mano.
Bada! smarrirlo, oppur donarlo, è
ria sventura!

**DES:** Il vero parli?

**OTE:** Il vero parlo.

**DES:** Mi fai paura!—

**OTE:** Che!? l' hai perduto forse?

**DES:** No—

**OTE:** Lo cerca.

**DES:** Fra poco
Lo cercherò.

**OTE:** No tosto!

**DES:** Tu di me ti fai gioco,
Storni cosi l' inchiesta di Cassio; as-
tuzia è questa
Del tuo pensier.

**OTE:** Pel cielo! l' anima mia sia desta!
Il fazzoletto!!!

**DES:** Gran Dio! nella tua voce v' è
un grido di minaccia!

**OTE:** Alza quegli occhi!
(*Prendendola a forza sotto il
mento e alla spalla e obligandola
a guardario.*)

**DES:** Atroce idea!

**OTE:** Guardami in faccia!
Dimmi chi sei!

**DES:** La sposa fedel d'Otello.

**OTE:** Giura!
Giura e ti danna—

**DES:** Otello fedel mi credo.

**OTE:** Impura
Ti credo.

**DES:** Iddio m' aiuti!

**OTE:** Corri alla tua condanna,
Di' che sei casta.

**DES:** (*fissandolo*). Casta—lo
son—

**OTE:** Giura e ti danna!!!

**DES:** It was this hand
That gave away my heart. But I must
speak to you of Cassio.

**OTH:** I have a salt and sorry rheum
offends me.
Lend me your handkerchief.

**DES:** (*offers him her handkerchief*). It is here.

**OTH:** Lend me the handkerchief I
gave you
Not this.

**DES:** I have it not about me.

**OTH:** Take heed on it.
Woe to you should you lose it. My
mother had it
From an Egyptian, a mighty charmer.
A potent spell is hidden in its texture,
To lose it or give it away were sure
perdition.

**DES:** It it true you say?

**OTH:** Most veritable.

**DES:** You frighten me.

**OTH:** What? Tell me have you lost
it?

**DES:** No!

**OTH:** Go fetch it!

**DES:** Believe me it is not lost.

**OTH:** Go fetch it!

**DES:** Why, so I can, Sir, but I will
not now.
I pray let Cassio be received again.
This is a trick to put me from my
suit.

**OTH:** By heaven! my mind misgives
me. That handkerchief—

**DES:** To Cassio's suit you must listen!

**OTH:** That handkerchief!

**DES:** Great heaven! you seem to
threaten. There is fury
In your words.

**OTH:** (*putting his hand under her
chin and forcing her to look at
him*). Lift up your eyes,
Look in my face! Say what are you?

**DES:** Your loyal wife, Othello!

**OTH:** Swear it, damn yourself!

**DES:** Heaven most truly knows it.

**OTH:** I think you are a strumpet.

**DES:** Oh heaven forgive us!

**OTH:** Once more your falsehood
utter, say you're honest!

**DES:** (*looking firmly at him*). I am
honest.

**OTH:** Swear it and damn yourself!

**DES:** Esterrefatta fisso lo sguardo
tuo tremendo,
In te parla una Furia, la sento e non
l' intendo.
Mi guarda! il volto e l' anima ti svelo; il core infranto
Mi scruta; io prego il cielo per te
con questo pianto.
Per te con queste stille cocenti as-
pergo il suol,
Guarda le prime lagrime che da me
spreme il duol.

**OTE:** S' or ti scorge il tuo dèmone
un angelo ti crede
E non t' afferra.

**DES:** Vede l' Eterno la mia fede!

**OTE:** No! la vede l' inferno.

**DES:** La tua giustizia impetro, Sposo mio!

**OTE:** Ah! Desdemona! Indietro! indietro! indietro!!

**DES:** Tu pur piangi?!—e gemenido
freni del cor lo schianto
E son io l' innocente cagion di tanto
pianto!—
Qual è il mio fallo?

**OTE:** E il chiedi?—Il più nero delitto
Sovra il candido giglio della tua
fronte è scritto.

**DES:** Ahimé!

**OTE:** Che? non sei forse una vil cor
tigianna?

**DES:** Ciel! No!—no—pel battesmo
della fede cristiana!—

**OTE:** Che?—

**DES:** Non son ciò che esprime quella parola orrenda.
(*Ote. prende Des. per mano e la
conduce alla porta d'onde entro.*)

**OTE:** Datemi ancor l' eburnea
mano, vo' fare ammenda.
Vi credea (perdonate se il mio pensiero è fello)
Quella vil cortigiana che è la sposa
d' Otello.
(*Alle ultime parole, Ote. che sarà
sul l' mitare della porta di sinistra, sforza con und inflessione del
braccio, Des. ad eseire. Poi ritorna verso il centrol dalla scena nel
massimo grado
dell'abbattimento.*)

## SCENA III

*Otello*

**OTE:** Dio! mi potevi scagliar tutti i
mali
Della miseria, della vergogna,
Far de' miei baldi trofei trionfali
Una maceria, una menzogna—'
E avrei portato la croce crudel
D' angoscie e d' onte
Con calma fronte

**DES:** Upon my knees, beneath your
glance I tremble.
I understand the fury in your words,
But not the words.
Behold, my face and soul lie open
to you,
Oh, look into my broken heart, I
pray.
My sighs rise up to heaven with a
prayer
For you; for you these tears bedew
the earth,
The first I ever shed.

**OTH:** The fiends themselves would
fear to seize you
Being like one of heaven in mien
and semblance.

**DES:** God sees my heart, and knows
that I am honest.

**OTH:** He knows you're perjured.

**DES:** Be just to your loyal wife, Othello!

**OTH:** Oh, Desdemona, away, away,
away!

**DES:** Why do you weep? Alack the
heavy day!
Win it you must.
Whose is the fault? Am I the motive
of these tears?
Have I offended?

**OTH:** You ask me! See the foul
word written
On the white page of this most
goodly book!

**DES:** Alas!

**OTH:** What, are not you an impudent strumpet?

**DES:** No! Your vile charge is false,
as I'm a Christian!

**OTH:** What!

**DES:** No! I am not a strumpet; I
grasp not the horrid word.
(*Oth. takes Des. by the hand and
leads her to the door by which she
had entered.*)

**OTH:** Once more give my your
hand as white as snow!
I cry your mercy then, for I mistook
you—
Pray parden if in thought or word I
wronged you—
For that strumpet of Venice, who
married with Othello.
(*At the last word Oth., who by this
time has reached the door on the
right, pushes Des. out of the room.
Then he returns to the center of
the stage in great dejection.*)

## SCENE III

*Othello*

**OTH:** Had it pleased heaven to try
me with affliction,
Had it rained sorrow and shame on
my bare head,
And to the very lips in poverty
steeped me.
Given to captivity me and my utmost hopes

E ressegnato al volere del ciel.
Ma, o pianto, o duol! m' han rapito
il miraggio
Dov' io, giulivo, l' anima acqueto.
Spento è quel sol, quel sorriso,
quel raggio
Che mi fa vivo, che mi fa lieto!
Tu alfin, Clemenza, pio genio im-
mortal
Dal roseo riso,
Copri il tuo viso
Santo coll' orrida larva infernal!

## SCENE IV

*Otello, poi Jago.*

**OTE:** Ah! Dannazione!
Pria confessi il delitto e poscia mu-
oia!
Confessione! Confessione!—(*Entra
Jag.*)
La prova!—

**JAGO:** (*accanto ad Ote. e indicando l' ingresso*). Cassio è là!

**OTE:** Là?! Cielo! gioia!!
(*Poi con subito racapriccio.*)
Orror!—Supplizi immondi!!

**JAGO:** Ti frena! Ti nascondi.
(*Conduce rapidamente Ote., nel
fondo a sinistra dove c' è il vano
del verone corre verso il fondo del
peristilio dove incontra Cas. che
esita ad entrare.*)

## SCENA V

*Otello nascosto. Jago e Cassio.*

**JAGO:** Vieni l' aula è deserta.
T' inoltra, Capitano.

**CAS:** Questo nome d' onor suona
ancor vano.
Per me.

**JAGO:** Fa cor, la tua ausa è in tal
mano
Che la vittoria è certa.

**CAS:** Io qui credea di ritrovar Desdemona.

**OTE:** (*nascosta*). (Ei la nomò.)

**CAS:** Vorrei parlarle ancora,
Per saper se la mia grazia è proffer-
ta.

**JAGO:** (*galamente*). L'attendi; e
intanto, giacchè non si stanca
Mai la tua lingua nelle fole gaie,
Narrami un po' di lei che t' innamora.
(*Conducendo Cas. accanto alla
prima colonna del peristilio.*)

I could have borne it, though bitter
it were and shameful.
A drop of patience I would still
have found
In some place of my soul.
But there, where I have garnered up
my heart
Where either I must live or bear no
life,
The fountain from which my cur-
rent runs
Or else dries up, to be discarded!
Turn your complexion there,
Patience, you young and rose-
lipped cherubin!
Ay, there look grim as hell!

## SCENE IV

*Othello, afterwards Iago.*

**OTH:** Death and damnation! to me
you shall confess
And die hereafter! Handkerchief!
handkerchief!
Confess it! (*Enter Iago.*)

**IAGO:** (*coming up to Oth. and
pointing to the entrance*). Cassio's
there.

**OTH:** There? Heaven, I thank you.
(*Suddenly relapsing into his first
mood.*)
Oh, monstrous! Their stolen pleasures—

**IAGO:** Hide there
And listen in patience.
(*He rapidly leads Oth. to the right
wing of the colonnade, and then
runs to the portico through which
enter Cas.*)

## SCENE V

*Othello (hidden), Iago and Cas.*

**IAGO:** Come, then! the hall's deserted.
How goes it, good lieutenant?

**CAS:** All the worse.
That by the name you call me I have
lost.

**IAGO:** Take heart! in such hands is
your case, that surely
You must win it.

**CAS:** Here did I hope to meet with
Desdemona.

**OTH:** (*aside*). He's named her
name!

**CAS:** Once more I fain would ask
her
To bring my anxious suit unto an issue.

**IAGO:** (*gaily*). Await her then; and
meantime
I know your tongue is burning now
to tell me
Your amorous follies; say then, and
speak of her
Whom you adore.
(*He leads Cas. to the first column
of the portico.*)

CAS: Di chi?

JAGO: (sottovoce assai). Di Bianca.

OTE: (Sorride!)

CAS: Baie!—

JAGO: Essa t' avvince
Coi vaghi rai.

CAS: Rider mi fai.

JAGO: Ride chi vince.

CAS: (ridendo). In tai disfide—
per verità,
Vince chi ride—Ah! Ah!

JAGO: (come sopra) Ah! Ah!

OTE: (L' empio trionfa, il suo
scherno m' uccide; Dio frena l' ansia che in core mi sta!)

CAS: Son già di baci Sazio e di lei.

JAGO: Rider mi fai.

CAS: O amor' fugaci!

JAGO: Vagheggi il regno—d' altra
beltà.
Colgo nel segno?

CAS: Ah! Ah!

JAGO: Ah! Ah!

OTE: (L' empio m' irride—il suo
scherno m' uccide;
Dio frena l' ansia che in core mi
sta!)

CAS: Nel segno hai côlto.
Si, lo confesso.
M' odi—

JAGO: (assai sottovoce). Sommesso
Parla. T' ascolto.

CAS: (assai sottovoce, mentre Jag.
lo conduce in posto più lontano
da Ote.) (Or sì, or no si senton le
parole.) Jago, t' è nota La mia dimo-
rea—
(Le parole si perdono.)

OTE: (avvicinandosi un poco e
cautamente per udir cio che dicono). (Or gli racconta il modo, Il
mago e l' ora—)

CAS: (continuando il racconto
sempre sottovoce). Da mano ignota—
(Le parole si perdono ancora.)

OTE: Le parole non odo—
Lass m' udir le vorrei! Dove son giunto!!

CAS: Un vel trapunto—
(Come sopra.)

JAGO: È strano! è strano!

OTE: (D' avvicinarmi Jago mi fa
cenno.)
(Passo passo con lenta cautela,
Ote., nascondendosi dietro le colonne, arriverà più tardi vicino ai
due.)

---

CAS: Of whom?

IAGO: (very softly). Of Bianca.

OTH: (aside). He's laughing!

CAS: Nonsense!

IAGO: Say, will you wed her?
Say, are you conquered?

CAS: I can't help laughing

IAGO: He wins who laughs last.

CAS: (laughing). It is the monkey's own giving out.
He wins who laughs last, ha! ha!

IAGO: Ha! ha!

OTH: (aside). The villain triumphs! his laughter smites my bosom;
God give me patience to bear all
this grief.

CAS: I loathe her kisses,
They pall upon me.

IAGO: I can't help laughing.

CAS: Yea, love is fleeting.

IAGO: Some other beauty has you
in thrall.
Say, have I caught you?

CAS: Ha! ha!

IAGO: Ha! ha!

OTH: (as before). The villain
laughs, his laughter smites my bosom;
God give me patience to bear all
this grief.

CAS: Yea, you have caught me,
I must confess it,
Hear me—

IAGO: (very softly). Speak gently,
Gently! I hear you.

CAS: (speaking very gently, while
Iago leads him to a place further
from Oth.; his words are audible
and inaudible at intervals.) Do
you know Iago,
Where is my lodging?
(His words are lost.)

OTH: (cautiously approaching to
bear what they are saying). Now
does he tell him
The manner, place, and hour.

CAS: (continuing his story and always speaking very gently). An
unknown hand
(Again the words are lost.)

OTH: (aside). His words I cannot
hear.
Woe's me! I would know! Has it
come to this?

CAS: A broidered napkin
(Inaudible as above.)

IAGO: Curious, most curious!

OTH: (aside). Iago beckons nearer
to approach him.
(Walking cautiously and hiding
behind the columns, Oth. draws
nearer to them.)

---

JAGO: (sottovoce). Da ignota
mano?
(Forte.)
Baie!

CAS: Da senno.
(Jag. gli fa cenno di parlar ancora
sottovoce.)
Quanto mi tarda
Saper chi sia—

JAGO: (guardando rapidamente
dalla parte d' Ote., fra sè). (Otello
spia.)
(A Cas. ad alta roce.)
L' hai teco?

CAS: (estrae dal giustacuore il
fazzoletto di Des.). Guarda.

JAGO: (prendendo il fazzoletto).
Qual mera viglia!
(A parte.)
(Otello origlia.
Ei s' avvicina
Con mosse accorte.)
(A Cas. inchinandosi scherzosa-
mente e passando le mani dietro
la schiena perchè Ote. possa osser-
vare il fazzoletto.)
Bel cavaliere—nel vostro ostel
Perdono gli angeli—l' aureola e il
vel.

OTE: (avvicinandosi assai al fazzoletto, dietro e spalle di Jag. e
nascosto dalla prima colonna).
(E quello! è quello!
Ruina e Morte!)

JAGO: (Origlia Otello.)

OTE: (nascosto dietro la colonna
e guardando di tratto in tratto il
fazzoletto nelle mani da Cas.).
Tutto è spento! Amore e duol.
L' alma mia nessun più smova
Tradimento, la tua prova
Spaventosa mostri al Sol.

JAGO: (a Cas. indicando il fazzo-
letto). Quest' è una ragna
Dove il tuo cuor
Casca, si, lagna,
S' impiglia e muor.
Troppo l' ammiri,
Troppo la guardi,
Bada ai deliri
Vani e bugiardi.
Quest' è una ragna
Dove il tuo cuor
Casca, si, lagna,
S' impiglia e muor.

CAS: (guardando il fazzoletto che
avrà ritolto a Jag.) Miracolo vago
Dell' aspo e dell' ago
Che in raggi tramuta
Le fila d' un vel;
Più bianco, più lieve
Che fiocco di neve,
Che nube tessuta
Dall' aure del ciel.
(Squillo di tromba interno, poi
un colpo di canonne; Ote. sarà ri-
tornato nel vano del verone.)

---

IAGO: (softly). An unknown hand?
(Aloud.) Nonsense!

CAS: No, truly,
(Iago makes signs to him to speak
more gently.)
I cannot fathom
Who has placed it there.

IAGO: (looking to where Oth.
stands; to himself). Othello sees
us.
(To Cas., aloud.)
Where is it?

CAS: (drawing Des.'s bandkerchief from his doublet). Here it is.

IAGO: (taking the bandkerchief).
Wonder of wonders!
(Aside).
Othello listens,
Still drawing nigher
With stealthy caution.
(Holding the bandkerchief be-
hind him so as to let Oth. see it,
and bowing laughingly to Cas).
You gay young courtier, visiting an-
gels
In your fair house, forget their
crown and wings.

OTH: (looking at the bandkerchief and standing close to Iago,
hidden by the first column). I
know it, I know it!
Oh monstrous, monstrous!

IAGO: (to himself). Othello listens.

OTH: (bidden behind the column
and looking at the bandkerchief
in Cas.'s bands). All has vanished,
grief and love.
Nothing more can move my heart.
Latent treason, hatched in night,
Now lies open to the light.

IAGO: (to Cas., pointing to the
bandkerchief). This is a spider's
web
Where your poor heart
Is caught and languishes,
Never to part.
While you are feeling
Raptures unceasing,
Firmly she holds you
Never releasing.
This is a spider's web
Where your poor heart
Is caught and languishes,
Never to part.

CAS: (looking at the bandker-
chief, which he has taken from
Iago). This is a wonder, wrought
By thread and thimble;
Unto a ray of light
The fabric's changed.
No snowdrift is whiter,
No gossamer lighter,
It is like a cloudlet
That floats in the sky.
(Trumpet signals, and afterwards
a gun fired behind; Oth. has again
retired to the colonnade.)

JAGO: Quest' è il segnale che annucia l' approdo
Della trireme veneziana. Ascolta.
(*Squilli da varie parti.*)
Tutto il castel co' suoi squilli risponde.
Se qui non vuoi con Otello scontrarti
Fuggi.

CAS: Addio.

JAGO: Va.
(*Cas. esce vetocemente dal fondo.*)

## SCENA VI

*Jago. Otello.*

OTE: (*avvicinandosi a Jag.*).
Come la ucciderò?

JAGO: Vedeste ben com' egli ha riso?

OTE: Vidi.
(*Di tanto in tanto salve di gioia e squilli che si avvicinana.*)

JAGO: E il fazzoletto?

OTE: Tutto vidi.

VOCI: (*dal di fuori, lontane*). Evviva!

VOCI: Alla riva!

VOCI: Allo sbarco!

OTE: È condannata.
Fa ch' io m' abbia un velen per questa notte.

VOCI: (*più vicine*). Evviva! Evviva il Leon di San Marco!

JAGO: Il tosco no, val meglio soffocarla,
Là nel suo letto, là dove ha peccato.

OTE: Questa giustizia tua mi piace.

JAGO: A Cassio
Jago provvederà.

OTE: Jago, fiu d' ora
Mio Capitano t' eleggo.

JAGO: Mio Duce,
Grazie vi rendo.
(*Il tumulto è sempre più vicino. Fanfare e grida.*)
Ecco gli Ambasciatori.
Li accogliete. Ma ad evitar sospetti
Desdemona si mostri a quei Messeri.

OTE: Si, vui l' adduci.
(*Jag. esce dalla prota di sinistra: Ote. s' avvia verso il fondo per ricevere gli Ambasciatori.*)

## SCENA VII

*Otello, Lodovico, Roderigo, L' Araldo.—Dignitari della Repubblica Veneta—Gentiluomini e Dame—Soldati—Trombettieri, dal fondo—poi Jago con Desdemona ed Emilia dalla sinistra.*

---

IAGO: This is the signal announcing that the galley from Venice (*trumpets from various sides*) is at anchor. Listen! With all its trumpets the castle gives answer; if you wish not Othello to meet you, hasten!

CAS: Farewell then.

IAGO: Go!
(*Exit Cas. quickly at back.*)

## SCENE VI

*Iago. Othello.*

OTH: (*going up to Iago*). How shall I murder him?

IAGO: Did you perceive him gaily laughing?

OTH: Truly.
(*Guns and trumpets heard at intervals, coming nearer.*)

IAGO: The napkin did you see?

OTH: Ay, well I saw it.

VOICES: (*in the distance, behind*). Be welcome!

OTHERS: To the shoreward!

OTHERS: Pull together!

OTH: Her fate is settled;
This same night she must die. Give me some poison.

VOICES: (*nearer*). Welcome! welcome! the lion of San Marco!

IAGO: Do it not with poison; better to strangle her,
There in her bed, the bed she has defiled.

OTH: Good, good, the justice of it pleases.

IAGO: For Cassio
I will myself provide.

OTH: You, from this hour, Iago,
Are my lieutenant.

IAGO: My general, I proffer thanks.
(*The noise outside approaches more and more; shouts and flourish of trumpets.*)
There's some one come from Venice, go receive him,
And, to avoid suspicion,
Let Desdemona be present with yourself.

OTH: Yea, go to call her.
(*Exit Iago right. Oth. goes towards back to receive the Ambassadors.*)

## SCENE VII

*Othello, Lodovico, Roderigo, the Herald—Dignitaries of the Venetian Republic—Ladies and Cavaliers—Soldiers—Trumpeters at back. Afterwards Iago with Desdemona and Emilia entering from right.*

---

LOD: (*tenendo una pergamena*).
Il Doge ed il senato
Salutano l' eroe trionfatore
Di Cipro. Io reco nelle vostre mani
Il messaggio dogale.

OTE: (*prendendo il messaggio e baciando il suggello*). Io bacio il segno
Della Sovranna Maestà.
(*Lo spiega e legge.*)

LOD: (*avvicinandosi a Des.*). Madonna,
V' abbia il cielo in sua guardia.

DES: E il ciel v' ascolti.

EMI: (*a Des., a parte*). (Come sei mesta.)

DES: (*ad Emi., a parte*). Emilia!
una gran nube
Turba il senno d' Otello e il mio destino.

JAGO: (*andando a Lod.*). Messer, son lieto di vedervi.
(*Lod., Des. e Jag. formano crocchio insieme.*)

LOD: Jago,
Quali nuove?—ma in mezzo a voi non trovo Cassio.

JAGO: Con lui crucciato è Otello.

DES: Credo Che in grazia tornerà.

OTE: (*a Des. rapidamente e sempre in atto di leggere*). Ne siete certa?

DES: Che dite?

LOD: El legge, non vi parla.

JAGO: Forse
Che in grazia tornerà.

DES: Jago, lo spero;
Sai se un verace affetto io porti a Cassio—

OTE: (*sempre in atto di leggere e febbrilmente a Des. sottovoce*).
Frenate dunque le labbra loquaci—

DES: Perdonate, Signor—

OTE: (*avventandosi contro Des.*).
Demonio taci!!

LOD: (*arrestando il gesto d' Ote.*).
Ferma!

TUTTI: Orrore!

LOD: La mente mia non osa
Pensar chi' io vidi il vero.

OTE: (*repentinamente all' Araldo e con accento imperioso*). A me Cassio!
(*L' Araldo esce.*)

JAGO: (*passando rapido accanto ad Ote., e a bassa voce*). (Che tenti?)

---

LOD: (*holding a parchment*). The Duke and Senate
Of Venice greet the glorious hero
Of Cyprus. To your own hands I here deliver
Their gracious message.

OTH: (*taking the letter and kissing the seal*). I kiss the symbol of their sovereign majesty.
(*Opens the letter and reads.*)

LOD: (*going up to Des.*). My lady, may the angels protect you!

DES: May
Heaven hear you.

EMI: (*to Des., aside*). Why this sadness?

DES: (*to Emi., aside*). Oh, Emilia,
A heavy cloud hangs over Othello's mind,
And over my future.

IAGO: (*to Lod., going up to him*).
Most Welcome!
I am very glad to see you.
(*Lod., Des. and Iago form a group.*)

LOD: Thank you, Iago. What news, how does
Lieutenant Cassio?

IAGO: Othello's annoyed with him.

DES: But soon he will regain his grace.

OTH: (*to Des., speaking rapidly and continuing to read*). Are you So certain?

DES: What say you?

LOD: He's reading and did not listen.

IAGO: Perhaps he will regain his grace.

DES: Firmly I hope so, I would do much
For the love I bear to Cassio.

OTH: (*always pretending to read, excitedly to Des. in a whisper*).
Pray keep
Your eloquent tongue from wagging.

DES: Pray forgive me,
My lord.

OTH: (*about to strike Des.*). Be silent, devil!

LOD: (*holding back Oth.*) Spare her!

ALL: Horror!

LOD: My mind cannot believe this deed, although
I saw it.

OTH: (*to the Herald, in a commanding voice*). Call Cassio.
(*Exit Herald.*)

IAGO: (*going rapidly up to Oth., softly*). Wherefor?

OTE: (*a Jag. a bassa voce*). (Guardala mentr' ei giunge.)

OTH: (*aside to Iago*). Watch her When first he enters!

LOD: Ah! triste sposa!
(*A bassa voce avvicinandosi a Jag. che si sara un po' allontanato da Ote.*)
Quest' è dunque l' eroe? quest' è il guerriero
Dai sublimi ardimenti?

LOD: Unhappy lady!
(*aside to Iago, who has gone a little distance from Oth.*) Is this the noble Moor, whom our full Senate Call all in all sufficient?

JAGO: (*a Lod. alzando le spalle*). È quel ch' egli è.

IAGO: (*to Lod., shrugging his shoulders*). He's that he is.

LOD: Palesa il tuo pensiero.

LOD: What think you? Let me know.

JAGO: Meglio è tener su ciò la lingua muta.

IAGO: Pray pardon me, I dare not breathe my censure.

## SCENA VIII

## SCENE VIII

*Cassio Seguito dall' Araldo, e detti.*

*Enter Cassio, followed by the Herald.*

OTE: (*che avrà sempre fissato la porta*). (Eccolo! È lui!)
(*Avvicinandosi a Jag. mentre Cas. è sulla soglie.*)
(Nell' animo lo scruta.)
(*ad alta voce a tutti*). Messeri! Il Doge—
(*Ruvidamente ma sottovoce a Des.*)
—(ben tu fingi il pianto)
(*A tutti ad alta voce.*)
Mi richiama a Venezia.

OTH: (*who has been intently looking towards the door*). He comes, it is he! (*Aside to Iago, while Cas. is on the threshold*). Watch him with all your senses. (*In a loud voice, to all.*) Good Sirs, the Duke here—(*furiously in a whisper to Des.*). (Oh, well-painted passion!) Has recalled me to Venice.

ROD: (Infida sorte!)

ROD: (*aside*). Then all is over.

OTE: (*continuando ad alta voce e dominandosi*). E in Cipro elegge Mio successor colui che stava accanto Al mio vessillo, Cassio.

OTH: (*in a loud voice, controlling himself*). In Cyprus is chosen in my place even he Who was for these years my lieutenant, Cassio.

JAGO: (*fieramente e sopreso*). (Inferno e morte!)

IAGO: (*aside, surprised and furious*). Death and perdition!

OTE: (*continuando come sopra e mostrando la pergamena*). La parola Ducale è nostra legge.

OTH: (*speaking as above, and pointing to the document*). Sir, I obey the mandate of the Duke.

CAS: Obbedirò.

CAS: (*bowing to Oth.*). I, too, obey,

OTH: (*rapidamente a Jag. in segreto ed indicando Cas.*). (Vedi? non par che esulti L' infame.)

OTH: (*to Iago, in a rapid whisper, pointing to Cas.*). You see? the villain seems not To like it.

JAGO: No.)

IAGO: No!

OTE: (*ad alta voce a tutti*). La ciurma e la corte
(*A Des. sottovoce e rapidissimo.*)
(Continua i tuoi singulti—)
(*Ad alta voce a tutti, senza più guardar Cas.*)
E le navi e il castello
Lascio in poter del nuovo Duce.

OTH: (*aloud*). The city and the army—
(*To Des., very rapidly and in a whisper.*)
(Pray do not stop your weeping!)—
(*Aloud again, and taking no further notice of Cas.*)
And the ships
And fortress I leave in charge of my successor.

LOD: (*a Ote. additando Des. che s' avvicina supplichevolmente*). Otello,
Per pietà, la conforta, o il cor le infrangi.

LOD: (*to Oth., pointing to Des., who comes near in an imploring attitude*). Othello, speak to her and comfort her,
Her heart is breaking.

OTE: (*a Lod. e Des.*). Noi salperem domani.
(*Afferra Des furiosamente.*)
À terra!—e piangi!—
(*Des. cade. Emi. e Lod. la raccolgono e la sollevano pietosamente.*)

OTH: (*to Lod. and Des.*). We shall sail tomorrow.
To earth, on your knees!
(*Takes hold of Des. furiously.*)
(*Des. falls, Emi. and Lod. lift her up and try to comfort her.*)

DES: A terra!—si, nel livido
Fango—percossa—io giacio—
Piango—m' agghiaccia il brivido
Dell' anima che muor.
E un di sul mio sorriso
Fioria la speme e il bacio
Ed or—l' angescia in viso
E l' agonia nel cor.
Quel Sol sereno e vivido
Che allieta il cielo e il mare
Non può asciugar le amare
Stille del mio dolor.

DES: Yea, prostrate here, I lie in the dust,
My heart is beating with anguish
I feel the icy breath
Of ill, that augurs death.
The light upon his brow
His smile, his tender greeting,
His kiss, where are they now?
Weep then for aye I must.
The sun who from his cloudless sky
Illumes the earth with splendor,
No comfort can he tender,
My tears he cannot dry.

EMI: (Quella innocente un fremito
D' odio non ha nè un gesto,
Trattiene in petto il gemito
Con doloroso fren.
La lagrima si frange
Muta sul volto mesto:
No, chi per lei non piange
Non ha pietade in sen.)

EMI: (*to herself*). Her innocence is silent all,
No rancor bears her constant heart.
Deep in her bosom dies the sigh
Wrung from her by her grief;
The bitter teardrops, as they fall,
Can never bring relief.
Oh, weep for her who meekly
Thus her misfortune bears.

ROD: (Per me s' oscura il mondo, S' annuvola il destin;
L' angiol soave e biondo
Scompar dul mio cammin.)

ROD: (*to himself*). Now all the world is darkened,
All sunless is the day;
She whom my heart did worship
Has vanished from my way.

CAS: (L' ora è fatal! un fulmine Sul mio cammin l' addita.
Già di mia sorte il culmine
S' offre all' inerte man.
L' ebbra fortuna incalza
La fuga della vita.
Questa che al ciel m' innalza
E un' onda d' uragan.)

CAS: (*to himself*). Fatal the hours, a lightning's flash
Shows me the threatening danger,
Honor and riches crowd on,
Their brightness brings no joy.
A fickle fortune's anger
Too soon will overtake me,
And from this dream awake me,
As with the thunder's crash.

LOD: (Egli la man funerea Scuote anelando d' ira,
Essa la faccia eterea
Volge piangendo al ciel.
Nel contemplar quel pianto
La carità sospira,
E un tenero compianto
Stempra del core il gel.

LOD: (*to himself*). His hand is raised against her,
Wrath every word is breathing;
She with a gentle meekness
For rescue looks above.
Gazing upon her sadness
Moved is my heart with pity.
Ah! could my help avail her
Soon to regain his love.

IL CORO: (*A gruppi dialogando.*)

CHO: (*in various groups, talking together*).

DAME: Pietà!

LADIES: Alas!

CAV: Mistero!

CAV: A secret!

DAME: Anisia mortale, bieca, Ne ingombra, anime assorte in lungo orror.

LADIES: Some mortal anguish dark and undefined
With thoughts of evil shrouds his mind.

CAV: Quell' uomo nero è sepolerale, e cieca
Un' ombra è in lui di morte e di terror.

CAV: Black are his visage and his soul, his eyes
Are lighted with a presage of some ill.

DAME: Vista crudel!

LADIES: A mournful sight!

**CAV:** Strazia coll' ugna l' orrido Petto! Figge gli sguardi immoti al suol. Poi sfida il ciel coll' atre pugna, l' ispido Aspetto ergendo ai dardi alti del Sol.

**DAME:** Ei la colpì! vuel viso santo, pallido, Blando, si china e tace e piange e muor. Piangon così nel ciel lor pianto gli angeli Quando perduto giace il perccator.

**JAGO:** (*avvicinandosi a Ote. che resterà accascio su d'un sedile*). (Una parola.

**OTE:** E che?

**JAGO:** T' affretta! Rapido Slancia la tua vendetta! il tempo vola.

**OTE:** Ben parli.

**JAGO:** E l' ira inutil ciancia. Scuotiti! All' opra ergi tua mira? All' opra sola! Io penso a Cassio. Ei le sue trame espia. L' infame anima ria l'averno inghiotte!

**OTE:** Chi gliela svele?

**JAGO:** Io.

**OTE:** Tu?

**JAGO:** Giurai.

**OTE:** Tal sia.

**JAGO:** Tu avrai le sue novelle in questa notte— (*Abbandona Ote. e si dirige verso Rod.*) (*ironicamente a Rod.*). (I sogni tuoi saranno in mar domani E tu sull' aspra terra!

**ROD:** Ahi triste!

**JAGO:** Stolto! Se vuoi tu puoi sperar; gli umani Orsù! cimenti afferra, e m' odi.

**ROD:** Ascolto.

**JAGO:** Col primo albor salpa il vasçello. Or Cassio E il Duce. Eppur so avvien che a questi accada (*toccando la spada.*) Sventura—allor qui resta Otello.

**ROD:** Lugubre Luce d' atro balen!

**JAGO:** Mano alla spada! A notte folta io la sua traccia viglio, E il varco e l' ora scruto, il resto a te. Sarò tua scolta. A caccia! a caccia! Cingiti L' arco!

**ROD:** Sì! t' ho venduto onore e fè).

---

**CAV:** With clenched hands, wildly He beats his bosom; His eyes are fixed upon the ground, Now he looks up as if defying With threatening glance the power's above.

**LADIES:** Her face he struck, so pale, so like unto an angel's; She stands in silence weeping there. It is thus that angels weep, when from high heaven above They see a sinner writhing in despair.

**IAGO:** (*approaching Oth., who remains seated*). Let me advise you.

**OTH:** What in?

**IAGO:** Strike quickly, do not tarry In your revenge, for time flies swiftly.

**OTH:** Well spoken!

**IAGO:** Your wrath is like to slacken; let it not! To work! without delay and without pity! I'll see to Cassio; I know where to find him. His soul shall tinge Avernus with deeper dye.

**OTH:** Who will dispatch him?

**IAGO:** I!

**OTH:** You?

**IAGO:** I have sworn it.

**OTH:** So be it.

**IAGO:** You shall have certain news this very evening. (*He leaves Oth. and goes to Rod.*) (*ironically to Rod.*). Your true love will be on the sea tomorrow And you on dry land.

**ROD:** It is too certain!

**IAGO:** Coward! For brave men there is hope; bestir then, Use every effort, and hear me!

**ROD:** I hear you.

**IAGO:** At break of day will sail the vessel. Then Cassio Is General. If meanwhile he should meet with (*Laying his hand on his sword.*) Some accident, then here remains Othello.

**ROD:** What baneful plan does your counsel imply?

**IAGO:** Unsheath Your weapon! From early fall of night I'll watch his traces I'll tell you place and moment, Then must you act. I will be near you. The hunt is up, good luck my noble huntsman!

**ROD:** Yea, I am yours and must obey.

---

**JAGO:** (Corri al miraggio! il fragile tuo senno Ha già confuso un sogno menzogner. Segui l' astuto ed agile mio cenno, Amante illuso, io seguo il mio pensier.)

**ROD:** (Il dado è tratto! Impavido t' attendo Ultima sorte, occulto mio destin. Mi sprona amor, ma un avido, tremendo Astro di morte infesta il mio cammin.)

**OTE:** (*ergendosi e rivolto alla folla, terribilmente*). Fuggite!

**TUTTI:** Ciel!

**OTE:** (*slanciandosi contro la folla*). Tutti fuggite Otello! (*Fanfara interna.*)

**JAGO:** (*agli astanti*). Lo assale una malìa Che d' ogni senso il priva.

**OTE:** (*con forza*). Chi no si scosta è contro me rubello.

**LOD:** (*fa per trascinare lontano Des.*). Mi segui—

**VOCI:** (*dal di fuori*). Evviva!

**DES:** (*sciogliendosi da Lod. e accorrendo verso Ote.*). Mio spose!

**OTE:** (*a Des.*). Anima mia Ti maledico!

**TUTTI:** (*escono inorriditi*). Orror!— (*Des., fra Emi. e Lod., esce.*)

## SCENA IX

*Otello e Jago soli.*

**OTE:** (*sempre più affannoso*). Fuggirmi io sol non so!— Sangue! Ah! l' abbietto Pensiero!—ciò m' accora! (*Convulsivamente, delirando.*) Verderli insieme avvinti—il fazzoletto!—Ah! (*Sviene.*)

**JAGO:** (Il mio velen lavora.) (*Fanfare e Voci dal di fuori.*) Viva Otello!

**JAGO:** (*ascoltando le grida, poi osservando Ote. disteso a terra tramortito*). L' eco della vittoria Porge sua laude estrema. (*Dopo una pausa.*) Chi può vietar che questa fronte io prema Col mio tallone? (*Fanfare e voci esterne più vicine*).

---

**IAGO:** (*to himself*). Idle the visions, empty as air, you follow; Such is the path my will for you has wrought; Go then and do the deed even as I bid you, Deluded swain, you act what I have thought.

**ROD:** (*to himself*). I will not falter, the die is cast, I follow Wherever you lead me, unknown destiny. Love is my guide. Ah, deep, resistless longing Be it to death, I still must follow you.

**OTH:** (*rising and turning to the crowd, with terrible expression*). Avaunt!

**ALL:** Heaven!

**OTH:** (*rushing towards the crowd*). All fly before Othello!

**IAGO:** (*to the bystanders*). (*Flourish behind.*) He's taken with a sickness which of all sense Deprives him.

**OTH:** (*in a loud voice*). He is declared a rebel Who any longer tarries.

**LOD:** (*trying to draw Des. away*). Follow me.

**VOICES:** (*outside*). Vittoria!

**DES:** (*freeing herself from Lod., and rushing towards Oth*). My husband!

**OTH:** (*to Des.*). Wife of my bosom, my curses on you!

**ALL:** Great heaven! (*Exeunt in terror. Des. is led away by Emi. and Lod.*)

## SCENE IX

*Othello and Iago.*

**OTH:** (*more and more excited*). I alone cannot fly. Murder! Ah! too monstrous To think of! "I do not like that!" (*In convulsions.*) To see them clasp each other! That handkerchief! Ah! (*He swoons.*)

**IAGO:** (*to himself*). He changes with my poison. (*Flourish of trumpets.*)

**VOICES:** (*outside*). Hail Othello!

**IAGO:** (*listening to the cries, then looking at Oth., who lies stretched out before him*). Echo's loud with his glory, praising his valor. (*After a pause.*) Who here can prevent me to plant my bootheel Upon his forehead? (*Flourishes and voices outside coming nearer.*)

Evviva Otello! Gloria
Al Leon di Venezia!
(*ritto e con gesto d' orrendo trionfo, indicando il corpo inerte d' Ote.*). Ecco il Leone!—

Vittoria! Long live Othello!
Hail to the lion of Venice!
(*standing erect and pointing with horrible triumph to the motionless body of Oth.*). See here, the Lion!

## ■ ATTO QUARTO

*La camera di Desdemona. Letto, inginocchiatoio, tavolo, specchio, sedie. Una lampada arde appesa devanti all' immagine della Madonna che sta al di sopra dell' inginocchiatoio. Porta a destra. È notte. Un lume acceso sul tavolo.*

## ■ ACT IV

*The bedroom of Desdemona. A bed, prie-Dieu, table, looking glass, chairs. A burning lamp is suspended in front of the image of the Madonna, which is above the prie-Dieu. Door to left. It is night. A candle on the table.*

### SCENA I

*Desdemona. Emilia.*

**EMI:** Era più calmo?

**DES:** Mi parea. M' ingiunse
Di coricarmi e d' attenderlo. Emilia,
Te ne prego, distendi sul mio letto
La mia candida veste nuzïale.
M' odi. Se pria di te morir dovessi
Mi seppellisei con un di quei veli.

**EMI:** Scacciate queste idee.

**DES:** (*sedendo macchinalment davanti allo specchio*). Son mesta tanto.
Mia madre aveva una povera ancella
Innamorata e bella;
Era il suo nome
Barbara. Amava
Un uom che poi l' abbendono, cantava
Una canzone: la canzon del Salice.
(*a Emi.*)
Mi disciogli le chiome—
Io questra sera ho la memoria piena
Di quella cantilena:
"Piangea cantando
Nell' erma landa,
Piangea la mesta.
O Salce! Salce! Salce!
Sedea chinando
Sul sen la testa!
O Salce! Salce! Salce!
Cantiamo! il Salce funebre
Sarà la mia ghirlanda."
Affrettati; fra poco giunge Otello.
"Scorreano i rivi fra le zolle in fior,
Gemea quel core affranto,
E dalle ciglia le sgorgava il cor
L' amara onda del pianto.
O Salce! Salce! Salce!
Cantiam la nenia blanda.
Cantiamo! il Salce funebre
Sarà la mia ghirlanda."
"Scendean gli augelli a vol dai rami cupi
Verso quel dolce canto.
E gli occhi suoi piangevan tanto, tanto,

### SCENE I

*Desdemona. Emilia.*

**EMI:** He looked more gentle?

**DES:** So it seemed. He bade me
Soon to await him, and to go to bed.
Emilia, let me ask you, before you go,
Lay on my bed the same sheets that were there
Upon my wedding night. And pray,
If I should die before you, let me be shrouded
In one of those same sheets.

**EMI:** Come, come, you talk of fancies.

**DES:** (*sitting down mechanically before the looking glass*). I am sad tonight and weary.
My mother, long ago, had a poor maid,
As fair as she was faithful, and her name
Was Barbara.
She was in love, and he she loved proved mad
And did forsake her. She had a song of Willow.
(*To Emi.*)
Loose my hair, and go. That song this evening
Will not go from my mind; like that poor maid
I even must sing it:—
"The poor soul sat pining
Alone and lonely,
There on the lonely strand.
Sing willow, willow, willow!
Upon her bosom her head inclining.
Sing heigho, sing heigho!
Sing all a green willow shall be my garland."
(*To Emi.*)
Please, go, anon will come Othello.
"The fresh stream ran by her,
Where the rushes grow,
And murmured all her moaning;
And from her eyes the sad tears did flow
Which in her heart were rising.
Sing willow, willow, willow!
Sing heigho, sing heigho!
Sing all a green willow shall be my

Da impietosir le rupi."
(*A Emi. levandosi un anello dal dito*)
Riponi questo annello.
Povera Barbara!—Solea la storia
con questo semplice—suono flnir:
"Egli era nato—per la sua gloria,
Io per amarlo."
(*Interrompende*)
Ascolta. Odo un lamento.
(*Emi. fa qualche passo*)
Taci. Chi batte a quella porta?—

garland."
"Down from the branches all the birds came flying,
Listening to her sweet sighing.
So full of sorrow was her tender ditty
The stones were moved to pity."
(*To Emi., taking a ring from her finger.*)
Lay by this ring and guard it.
Alas, poor Barbara! I think her story
In sad and simple wise thus used to end.
"For he was born to live in glory
And I to love him . . . .
(*Interrupting herself.*)
Do harken! Was that a sigh?
(*Emi. goes towards the window.*)
Listen! Who is it
That knocks at this hour?

**EMI:** È il vento.

**DES:** "Io per amarlo e per morir."
Emilia, addio. Come m' ardon le ciglia!
E presagio di pianto.
(*Abbraccia Emi., che esce*)
Buona notte.

**EMI:** The wind.

**DES:** "And I to love him and to die."
Farewell, Emilia! My eyes itch this evening.
Do you think it bodes weeping?
(*She embraces Emi., who exit.*)
Good-night.

### SCENA II

*Desdemona sola.*
*Va all' inginocchiatoio.*

**DES:** Ava Maria piena di grazia, eletta
Fra le spose e le vergini sei tu,
Sia benedetto il frutto, o benedetta,
Di tue materne viscere, Gesú.
Prega per chi adorando a te si prostra,
Prega pel peccator, per l' innocente
E pel debole oppresso e pel possente,
Misero anch' esso, tua pietà dimostra.
Prega per chi sotto l' oltraggio piega
La fronte e sotto la malvagia sorte;
Per noi tu prega
Sempre e nell' ora della morte nostra.
(*Resta ancora inginocchiata ed appoggia la fronte sul l'inginocchiatoio come chi ripetamentemente una orazione. Non s' odono che le prime e le ultime parole della preghiera.*)
Ave Maria . . . . . .
. . . . . . nell' ora della morte.
Amen.
(*S' alza e va a coricarsi.*)

### SCENE II

*Desdemona, alone.*
(*She kneels before the image of the Madonna.*)

**DES:** Hail Mary, full of grace, the Lord is with
You, blessed are you amongst women, and
Blessed is the fruit of your womb, Jesus.
Ah, pray for her who lies in prayer before you!
Pray for the sinner, and for the sinless,
Give aid to the oppressed and to the mighty—
He too will need it—pray for all who implore you,
Pray for her who is sadly sighing
As all the hopes of happiness betray her.
Oh, grant my prayer!
Pray for us now and in the hour of dying.
(*She remains kneeling, resting her head on the prie-Dieu as if she were repeating a prayer, only the first and last words of which are audible.*)
Holy Mary . . . . . .
. . . . . . at the hour of our death.
Amen.
(*She rises and lies down on the bed.*)

### SCENA III

*Desdemona. Otello.*

### SCENE III

*Desdemona. Othello.*

## Act IV, Scene III

*Ote. entra da una porta segreta, depone una scimitarra sul tavolo, s' arresta davanti alla face, titubante se spegnerla o no. Guarda Des. Spegne la face. La scena resta rischiarata dal solo lume dell' inginocchiatoio. Ote. spinto da un impeto di furore, s' avvicina al letto; ma là s' arresta. Contempla lungamente Des. che dorme. La bacia tre volte. All' ultimo bacia Des. si desta.*

*Oth. enters by a secret door, and places a scymitar on the table. He stands before the candle doubtful whether to blow it out or not. He looks at Des. and then extinguishes the candle. The only light on the stage is that of the lamp above the prie-Dieu. Oth., in an impulse of fury, goes towards the bed, but there stops himself. He looks for a long time on the sleeping Des., then kisses her three times. At the last kiss Des. awakens.*

**DES:** Chi è la?— Otello?

**DES:** Who's there? Othello?

**OTE:** Sì. Diceste questa sera Le vostre preci?

**OTH:** Ay. Have you prayed tonight, Desdemona?

**DES:** Orai.

**DES:** I have.

**OTE:** Se vi sovviene Di qualche colpa commessa che attenda Grazia dal ciel, imploratela tosto.

**OTH:** If you think of any crime Unreconciled as yet to heaven and grace, Solicit for it straight.

**DES:** Perchè?

**DES:** My lord?

**OTE:** T' affretta. Uccidere non voglio L' anima tua.

**OTH:** Well, do it! For heaven forefend, I would not kill your soul.

**DES:** D' uccider parli?

**DES:** Talk you of killing?

**OTE:** Sì.

**OTH:** Yes.

**DES:** Pietà di me, mio Dio.

**DES:** Then Lord have mercy On me.

**OTE:** Amen.

**OTH:** Amen!

**DES:** E abbiate Pietà voi pure.

**DES:** Ah, then you too have mercy!

**OTE:** Pensa ai tuo peccati.

**OTH:** Think of your sins.

**DES:** Mio peccato è l' amor.

**DES:** They are loves I bear to you.

**OTE:** Perciò tu muori

**OTH:** For that you die.

**DES:** E perchè t' amo m' uccidi?

**DES:** Because I love you you kill me?

**OTE:** Ami Cassio.

**OTH:** You love Cassio.

**DES:** No! sull' anima mia!!

**DES:** No, I swear it by my soul.

**OTE:** Quel fazzoletto Ch' io ti donai gli desti.

**OTH:** That handkerchief I loved you gave to Cassio.

**DES:** Non è vero!

**DES:** It is a falsehood.

**OTE:** Nella sua man lo vidi.

**OTH:** I saw it in his own hands.

**DES:** Io rea non sono!

**DES:** And yet I'm guiltless.

**OTE:** Confessa!

**OTH:** Confess!

**DES:** Giuro!

**DES:** Guiltless!

**OTE:** Bada allo spergiuro— Pensa che sei sul tuo letto di morte.

**OTH:** Take heed of perjury. Know that you are lying Upon your deathbed.

**DES:** Non per morir.

**DES:** But not yet to die.

**OTE:** Per morir tosto.

**OTH:** Yes, presently.

**DES:** Aita! Cassio non amo—ch' ei qui venga—ei parli.

**DES:** Lord help me! I love not Cassio. Call him here and ask him!

**OTE:** Muto è per sempre.

**OTH:** He's mute for ever.

**DES:** Cielo! Morto?

**DES:** Heaven! Dead?

**OTE:** Morto.

**OTH:** Dead!

**DES:** Son perduta—ei tradito!

**DES:** Alas! he is betrayed, and I undone.

**OTE:** E pianger l' osi?

**OTH:** Do you weep, strumpet?

**DES:** Otello—non uccidermi—

**DES:** Oh, banish me, my lord, But do not kill me!

**OTE:** Tu invano Ti difendi.

**OTH:** No, nothing now will save you.

**DES:** Ch' io viva ancor—

**DES:** Oh, spare me, let me live.

**OTE:** Giù! cadi, Prostituta!—

**OTH:** Down with you strumpet!

**DES:** Pietà!

**DES:** Have pity!

**OTE:** Muori!!

**OTH:** No.

**DES:** Ch' io viva Questa notte—

**DES:** Let me but live tonight!

**OTE:** No.

**OTH:** No!

**DES:** Un' ora—

**DES:** An hour!

**OTE:** No.

**OTH:** No!

**DES:** Un instante. Sol ch' io dica un' Ave.

**DES:** One moment, But while I say my prayer!

**OTE:** No!

**OTE:** È tardi! È tardi!— (*La soffoca. Un grido di Des. S' ode bussare alla porta.*)

**OTH:** It is too late! (*He stifles her. Shriek of Des. Knocking at the door.*)

**OTE:** (*contemplando il corpor inerte di Des.*). Calma come la tomba.

**OTH:** (*looking on the motionless form of Des.*). Still as the grave!

**EMI:** (*dal di fuori*). Aprite! Aprite!

**EMI:** (*outside*). Within there, open!

**OTE:** (*trabalzando*). Chi è là!— Chi batte!

**OTH:** (*faltering*). Who's there? Who knocks thus?

**EMI:** (*come sopra*). Signor mio— ven prego, Lasciate ch' io vi parli—Aprite!

**EMI:** (*still outside*). Good my lord, do hear me. I would but speak a word with you; pray open!

**OTE:** (*aprendo*). Emilia, Che avvenne?

**OTH:** (*opening the door*). Emilia, what is it?

**EMI:** (*entrando*). Un gran delitto! Cassio uccise Rodrigo.

**EMI:** (*entering*). It is foul murder! Cassio has killed Roderigo.

**OTE:** E Cassio?

**OTH:** And Cassio?

**EMI:** Vive.

**EMI:** Lives.

**OTE:** Cassio vive!!

**OTH:** Cassio lives?

**EMI:** (*dal letto*). Ingiustamente— uccisa ingiustamente—

**DES:** (*from the bed*). I die here guiltless, I've been slain unjustly.

**EMI:** (*accorrendo al letto*). Chi geme là? Orror!

**EMI:** (*running to the bed*). What cry is that? Ho, help!

**DES:** Muoio innocente—

**DES:** I die here guiltless.

**EMI:** Gran Dio! Chi fu?

**EMI:** Great heaven! who did this deed?

**DES:** Nessuno—io stessa–al mio Signor mi raccomanda—Emilia— Addio— (*Muore.*)

**DES:** No one;—myself. Unto my lord—pray you commend me—I die Guiltless—farewell, Emilia. (*Dies.*)

**OTE:** O mentitrice! io l' uccisi.

**OTH:** She dies a liar; It was I that killed her.

**EMI:** Assassino!

**EMI:** Vile assassin!

**OTE:** Fu di Cassio la druda. A Jago il chiedi.

**OTH:** Strumpet She was to Cassio. It was your husband told me.

**EMI:** A Jago?

**EMI:** My husband?

**OTE:** A Jago.

**OTH:** Ay, your husband!

**EMI:** Stolto!! e tu il credesti?—

**EMI:** Fool! and did you believe him?

**OTE:** Negarlo ardisci? (*Fa per avventarsi contro Emi.*)

**OTH:** (*threatening Emi.*). Dare you deny it?

**EMI:** Non ti temo.

**EMI:** You I fear not.

**OTE:** (*la afferra*). Bada!

**OTH:** (*taking hold of her*). Tarry!

**EMI:** (*si svincola e corre verso la porta gridando disperatamente*). Olà! Soccorso! Aiuto! Otello uccise Desdemona!

## SCENA IV

*Otello, Emilia, Lodovico, Cassio, Jago. Poi Montano con gente armata.*

**TUTTI:** (*tranne Ote. ed Emi.*). Quai grida! Orrore! Orrore!

**EMI:** Jago, smentisci quel vile assassino. Hai tu creduto Desdemona infida? Parla!

**JAGO:** Tal la credea.

**OTE:** Quel fazzoletto Che un dì le diedi, a Cassio essa donava.

**EMI:** O potenza divina!

**JAGO:** (*ad Emi.*). Taci.

**EMI:** No, Tutto revelo

**JAGO:** Taci.

**EMI:** No! costui Dalla mia man quel fazzoletto svelse A viva forza.

**CAS:** E nella mia dimore Trovai quel vel.

**MON:** (*entrando ed indicando Jag.*). Rodrigo morente Mi svelò di quest' uom l' arti nefande.

**OTE:** (*a Jag.*). Ah! discolpati!!

**JAGO:** (*fuggendo*). No.

---

**EMI:** (*frees herself and runs to the door, crying loudly*). Ho, help! The Moor has killed my mistress.

## SCENE IV

*Othello, Emilia, Lodovico, Cassio, Iago; afterwards Montano and Soldiers.*

**ALL:** (*except Oth. and Emi.*). Oh! horror! horror!

**EMI:** (*to Iago*). Speak if you are a man, disprove this villain. He says, you told him that his wife was false.

**IAGO:** So I believed.

**OTH:** The pledge and token Which first I gave her, I saw it in Cassio's hand.

**EMI:** Oh, heavenly powers!

**IAGO:** (*to Emi.*). Silence!

**EMI:** No, I will reveal it.

**IAGO:** Be silent!

**EMI:** No! That handkerchief he took from me, And begged me oft to steal it.

**CAS:** And I found in my chamber A handkerchief.

**MON:** (*entering and pointing to Iago*). The dying Roderigo Has told me all the dark plots.

**OTH:** (*to Iago*). Refute their charges!

**IAGO:** No!

---

**LOD:** Ferma.

**MON:** S' insegua. (*Alcuni escono inseguendo Jag.*)

**TUTTI:** Afferratelo!

**OTE:** (*slanciandosi per afferrar la spada*). E il ciel non ha più fulmini?!—

**LOD:** La spada a me!

**OTE:** Tant' osi?—Niun mi tema S' anco armato mi vede. Ecco la fine Del mio cammin—Oh! Gloria! Otello fu. (*Lascia cadere la spada. Va presso al letto e contempla Des.*) E tu—come sei pallida! e stanca, e muta, e bella, Pia crëatura nata sotto maligna stella. Fredda come la casta tua vita, e in cielo assorta. Desdemona! Desdemona!—Ah!—morta!—morta!—morta! (*Estraendo furtivamente dalle vesti un pugnale.*) Ho un' arma ancor! (*Si ferisce.*)

**CAS:** Ah! Ferma!

**TUTTI:** Sciagurato!

**OTE:** Pria d' ucciderti—sposa—ti baciai. Or morendo—nell' ombra—ov' io mi giacio— Un bacio—un bacio ancora—un altro bacio— (*Muore.*)

*FINE.*

---

**LOD:** Stop him!

**MON:** Arrest him! (*Exeunt attendants after Iago.*)

**ALL:** Let him not escape.

**OTH:** Great heaven! Have you no lightning left?

**LOD:** Give me your sword.

**OTH:** What would you? do not fear me, though I still have A weapon. Here is my butt, here is my journey's end. Othello's gone. (*He drops his sword and goes to the bed, looking upon Des.*) And you, how do you look now? So pale, so still, so beautiful. Oh ill-fated wench, And noble! Battered by evil fortune, now Even as your chastity, most fit for heaven. Oh, Desdemona, Desdemona dead! (*He draws furtively a dagger from his vest*) This still remains. (*Stabs himself*)

**CAS:** Ah! hold him.

**ALL:** Oh! Othello!

**OTH:** I kissed you until I killed you. No but this, Killing myself, a kiss, another kiss, and yet another kiss! (*Dies*)

*THE END.*

# Der Fliegende Holländer (1843)

## The Flying Dutchman

MUSIC & LIBRETTO BY RICHARD WAGNER

This three-act opera, set to a libretto by the composer based on Heinrich Heine's *Memoirs of Herr von Schnabelewopsk*, premiered at the Hofoper in Dresden on January 2, 1843. The flying Dutchman is a sea captain who sailed around the Cape of Good Hope during a violent storm, only to keep on sailing until Judgment Day; the only way out is to find a young woman who will love him until death. Every seven years he leaves the ship to seek this woman. As the work opens, Daland, a Norwegian sea captain, is sailing through a storm that sends his ship into a faraway bay. The Dutchman's ghostly vessel comes upon him. Daland, who is impressed by the Dutchman's wealth, agrees that he should marry Daland's daughter. The two ships set off. A picture of the Dutchman hangs on the wall of Daland's house, and Senta, Daland's daughter, sings about the legendary figure. Erik, a would-be suitor, pleads with her to love him instead. He has dreamed about her father returning in a ghostly ship with a strange man. Daland arrives with the Dutchman, and Senta falls in love with him at first sight. The Dutchman's crew sends up a wild chorus that thoroughly frightens Daland's sailors and their girlfriends, who have been celebrating. Erik berates Senta for her infidelity. The Dutchman, overhearing them, is afraid that she could be unfaithful to him as well and departs. Erik prevents her from pursuing the Dutchman, who declares his identity and sails away. Senta pledges eternal loyalty and throws herself off a cliff into the sea below. The Dutchman's ship vanishes in the mists, and the lovers, united at last, rise up to heaven.

## ■ ERSTER AKT

### ERSTER AUFTRITT

**MATROSEN:** Hohoje! Hohoje! Halloho!

**DALAND:** Kein Zweifel! Sieben Meilen fort
Trieb uns der Sturm vom sichern Port.
So nah' dem Ziel nach langer Fahrt.
War mir der Streich noch aufgespart!

**STEUERMANN:** Ho! Capitän!

**DALAND:** Am Bord bei Euch, wie steht's?

**STEUERMANN:** Gut, Capitän! Wir sind auf sicherm Grund.

**DALAND:** 's ist Sandwyk-Strand, genau kenn' ich die Bucht.—
Verwünscht! schon sah am Ufer ich mein Haus,
Senta, mein Kind, glaubt' ich schon zu umarmen.
Da bläst er aus dem Teufels-Loch heraus . . . .
Wer baut auf Wind, baut auf Satans Erbarmen!
Was hilft's? der Sturm lässt nach,—
Wenn so er tobte, währt's nicht lang.
He! Bursche! lange war't ihr wach;
Zur Ruhe denn, mir ist's nicht bang!
Nun, Steuermann! die Wache nimmst Du wohl für mich?
Gefahr ist nicht, doch gut ist's, wenn Du wachst.

## ■ ACT I

### SCENE I

**SAILORS:** Heigho! Heigho! Halloho!

**DALAND:** No doubt!
Drove us full seven miles away the storm at break of day
So near the port, and to be met
By adverse wind—It's useless to fret!

**MATE:** Ho! Captain!

**DALAND:** I am on deck with you. How do things progress?

**MATE:** Well, captain, we are in home waters.

**DALAND:** It is Sandwyk beach, I full well the bay know.
Confound the luck! I saw my house; a welcome sight!
Senta, my child, I dreamed I held in my arms,
When all of a sudden the wind changed,
And blew a gale, as if in league with Satan's power;
But now the worst is past, and its fury
The storm has spent in fitful blasts.
Well, boys, you've had to work with giant power.
And you may rest, now that the danger is past;
And you, mate, you may take the watch for me;
There's no danger now, still keep a sharp look-out!

**STEUERMANN:** Seid ausser Sorg's! Schlaft ruhig, Capitän!
Mit Gewitter und Sturm aus fernem Meer—
Mein Mädel, bin dir nah'.
Über thurmhohe Fluth vom Süden her—
Mein Mädel, ich bin da!
Mein Mädel, wenn nicht Südwind wär'.
Ich nimmer wohl käm' zu dir;—
Ach, lieber Südwind! blas' noch mehr,
Mein Mädel verlangt nach mir!
Hohohe! Jolohe! Hoho! Ho! Ho!
Von des Südens Gestad', aus weitem Land'—
Ich hab' an dich gedacht;
Durch Gewitter und Meer vom Mohrenstrand
Hab' ich dir was mitgebracht.
Mein Mädel, preis' den Südwind hoch,
Ich bring' dir ein gülden Band:—
Ach, lieber Südwind, blase doch!
Mein Mädel hätt' gern den Tand.
Hoho! Ho jolohe!

### ZWEITE SCENE

**HOLLÄNDER:** Die Frist ist um, und abermals verstrichen
Sind sieben Jahr!—Voll Überdruss wirft mich
Das Meer an's Land . . . Ha, stolzer Ocean!
In kurzer Frist sollst du mich wieder tragen! Dein Trotz ist beugsam—
doch ewig meine Qual.
Das Heil, das auf dem Land ich suche, nimmer werd' ich es finden!
Euch, des Weltmeers Fluthen,

**MATE:** Rely on me! Good night, captain.
In tempest's roar, on the wide sea,
My girl, I think of you!
The gale, ah, well! it came from the South,
Lucky for you and me!
My girl, if it hadn't been Southwind,
I wouldn't see you again!
Ah, come and blow, my Southwind fair,
Else waits my love in vain.
Hohohe! Jolohe! Heigho! Heigho!
On Southland's coast, in far off land,
My girl, I thought of you!
All over the main, from tropic coast,
A gift I brought for you;
I bring my love a golden toy—
Come, Southwind, blow again!
Southwind, you are a lovely boy,
If you will blow again.
Hoho! ho! jolohe! heigho!

### SCENE II

**THE FLYING DUTCHMAN:** The time is up, and to Eternity's tomb consigned
Another seven years! Disgusted is the main,
And throws me on the strand. Ah! sea so proud.
The waves, before many days are past, I'll ride again.
What of your scorn with my torment in the balance weighed? The rest which on land I seek, oh! never

Bleib' ich getreu, bis eure letzte Welle sich bricht und euer letztes Nass versiegt!— Wie oft in Meeres tiefsten Schlund
Stüzt' ich voll Sehnsucht mich hinab, doch ach! den Tod, ich fand ihn nicht! Da, wo der Schiffe furchtbar Grab,
Trieb mein Schiff ich zum Klippengrund, doch ach! mein Grab, es schloss sich nicht! Verhöhnend droht' ich dem Piraten, im wilden Kampfe hofft' ich Tod:—
"Hier"—rief ich—"zeige deine Thaten! Von Schätzen voll ist Schiff und Boot!" Doch ach! des Meers barbar'scher Sohn schlägt bang' das Kreuz und flieht davon! Nirgends ein Grab! Niemals der Tod! Dies der Verdammniss Schreck-Gebot. Dich frage ich, gepries'ner Engel Gottes, der meines Heils Bedingung mir gewann, war ich Unsel'ger Spielwerk Deines Spottes, als die Erlösung Du mir zeigtest an?
—Vergeb'ne Hoffnung! Furchtbar eitler Wahn! Um ew'ge Treu' auf Erden ist's gethan!— Nur eine Hoffnung soll mir bleiben, nur eine unerschüttert steh'n!
So lang' der Erde Keim' auch treiben, so muss sie doch zu Grunde gehn.
Tag des Gerichtes, jüngster Tag! Wann brichst du an in meine Nacht? Wann dröhnt er, der Vernichtungsschlag;
Mit dem die Welt zusammenkracht? Wann alle Todten aufersteh'n,
Dann werde ich in Nichts vergeh'n! Ihr Welten, endet euren Lauf! Ew'ge Vernichtung, nimm mich auf!

**CHOIR:** Ew'ge Vernichtung, nimm uns auf!

## DRITTE SCENE

**DALAND:** He! Holla! Steuermann!

**STEUERMANN:** 's ist nichts! 's ist nichts!—
Ach, lieber Südwind, blas' noch mehr,
Mein Mädel . . .

**DALAND:** Du siehst nichts? Gelt! Du wachest brav, mein Bursch! Dort liegt ein Schiff!— Wie lange schliefst du schon?

**STEUERMANN:** Zum Teufel auch!—Verzeiht mir, Capitän! Werda! Werda!

**DALAND:** Es scheint, sie sind gerad' so faul als wir.

**STEUERMANN:** Gebt Antwort! Schiff und Flagge!

**DALAND:** Lass sein. Mich dünkt, ich seh den Capitän.— He! Holla! Seemann! Nenne Dich! Wess Landes?

shall I find; for my destiny is bound to the ocean waves, until the last wave ceases to flow, and evaporates into air. How often into deepest abyss of the sea have I thrown my ship and hapless me; But, alas! the death I sought I never found. Where yawns the grave for ship and sailor, I drove my ship to craggy rock. But the watery grave was not my lot. Where sails the pirate's dreaded craft, have often I waited for bloody strife; 'Now,' thus I challenged, 'show your pluck, my ship with treasures rich is freighted:' But he, the sea's barbarian son, in horror did he cross himself, and take to flight. No grave for me! No death for me! Such is damnation's inflexible law. I ask you heavenly angel mine, who my salvation's condition has secured, was I the foot-ball of your caprice. When the way to salvation did you show to me? Ah! Lost the hope, Lost as is my prayer! Faith has taken wings, and soared to other worlds. But one hope now remains. But one hope I cherish! Though the globe still sails through space, it, too, must end its course some day. Last day of Earth, eh! Judgment day, you will end my misery. When comes the day, the dreaded day, that solves Life's great mystery? When the sea gives up its dead. Then will my requiem be said! Die out, stars, in heaven's dome, Father above, oh, call me home!

**CHORUS:** Father above, oh call us home!

## SCENE III

**DALAND:** Ho! Heigho! Mate!

**MATE:** Nothing there, nothing! Ah! come and blow, Southwind fair.
My girl—

**DALAND:** You see nothing, and I thought that you'd keep sharp lookout.
There lies a ship! Answer me: How long did you sleep?

**MATE:** Damnation! Pardon, captain! Who's there? Who's there?

**DALAND:** Seems to me they are just as lazy dogs as we.

**MATE:** Answer! From where have you come & to where are you going?

**DALAND:** Cease your questioning! I think I see the captain—
You! holo! you over there; From where have you come & to where are you going?

**HOLLÄNDER:** Weit komm' ich her. Verwehrt bei Sturm und Wetter ihr mir den Ankerplatz?

**DALAND:** Behüt' es Gott! Gastfreundschaft kennt der Seemann. —Wer bist du?

**HOLLÄNDER:** Holländer.

**DALAND:** Gott zum Gruss!—So trieb auch dich
Der Sturm an diesen nackten Felsenstrand?
Mir ging's nicht besser, wenig Meilen nur
Von hier ist meine Heimath; fast erreicht,
Musst' ich auf's Neu' mich von ihr wenden.—Sag',
Woher kommst du? Hast Schaden Du genommen?

**HOLLÄNDER:** Mein Schiff ist fest, es leidet keinen Schaden.—
Durch Sturm und bösen Wind verschlagen,
Irr' auf den Wassern ich umher;—
Wie lange? weiss ich kaum zu sagen,
Schon zähl' ich nicht die Jahre mehr.
Unmöglich dünkt mich's, dass ich nenne
Die Länder alle, die ich fand:
Das Einz'ge nur, nach dem ich brenne,
Ich find' es nicht; mein Heimathland!
Vergönne mir auf kurze Frist dein Haus,
Und deine Freundschaft soll dich nicht gereu'n,
Mit schätzen aller Gegenden und Zonen
Ist reich mein Schiff beladen:—
willst du handeln,
So sollst du sicher deines Vortheils sein.

**DALAND:** Wie wunderbar! Soll deinem Wort ich glauben?
Ein Unstern, scheint's, hat dich bis jetzt verfolgt.
Um dir zu dienen, biet' ich, was ich kann;
Doch—darf ich fragen, was dein Schiff enthält?

**HOLLÄNDER:** Die seltensten der Schätze sollst du sehn,
Kostbare Perlen, edelstes Gestein.
Blick' hin und überzeuge dich vom Werthe
Des Preises, den ich für ein gastlich Dach
Dir biete!

**DALAND:** Wie? Ist's möglich? Diese Schätze!
Wer ist so reich, den Preis dafür zu bieten?

**HOLLÄNDER:** Den Preis? So eben hab' ich ihn genannt:
Dies für das Obdach einer einz'gen Nacht!
Doch was du siehst, ist nur der kleinste Theil

**THE FLYING DUTCHMAN:** I come from afar. In such dreadful weather.
Will you deny me safe anchorage?

**DALAND:** God forbid! the mariner knows full well hospitality's worth. Who are you?

**THE FLYING DUTCHMAN:** Dutch.

**DALAND:** Be welcome then! I perceive the storm
Drove you, too, to this craggy shore;
I fared no better; but my home is a few miles distant.
Almost within its charmed circle. I had to change my course. But, say, from where do you come? Has damage sustained your ship?

**THE FLYING DUTCHMAN:** My ship is sound, and wind and tempest proof.
Storm and adverse wind, in league, Keep me away from the shore;
How long? How should I know it still,
When I keep not count any more? I cannot tell the scenes I saw, Nor name the ports I sought to reach;
The only scene I long to see, I cannot find—my native beach! And now, my friend, come take me home,
Give me shelter and give me rest. My ship is freighted with treasures rare,
Choose the rarest, take the best— Your humble roof, oh, let me share!

**DALAND:** How strange this sounds. Can I believe such a tale?
It will seem that yours is a strange fate.
If I can serve you; you will find me ready;
But, may I ask, what does your ship contain?

**THE FLYING DUTCHMAN:** The rarest of treasures I'll show you, Gold and pearls and precious stones;
See how they glitter! Is the price Ample, and does it compensate For hospitable roof?

**DALAND:** What! Is it possible? These treasures!
Who has riches enough to outweigh their value?

**THE FLYING DUTCHMAN:** I told you how to repay for these treasures all;
I give them for the shelter of a single night.
Still what you see is but a small por-

## Act I, Scene III

Von dem, was meines Schiffes Raum verschliesst.
Was frommt der Schatz? Ich habe weder Weib
Noch Kind, und meine Heimath find' ich nie.
All' meinen Reichthum biet' ich Dir, wenn bei
Den Deinen du mir neue Heimath giebst.

**DALAND:** Was muss ich hören?

**HOLLÄNDER:** Hast du eine Tochter?

**DALAND:** Fürwahr, ein treures Kind.

**HOLLÄNDER:** Sie sei mein Weib!

**DALAND:** Wie? Hör' ich recht?
Meine Tochter sein Weib?
Er selbst spricht aus den Gedanken:—
Fast fürcht' ich, wenn unentschlossen ich bleib',
Er müsst' im Vorsatze wanken.
Wüsst' ich, ob ich wach' oder träume;
Kann ein Eidam willkommener sein?
Ein Thor, wenn das Glück ich versäume:
Voll Entzücken schlage ich ein.

**HOLLÄNDER:** Ach ohne Weib, ohne Kind bin ich,
Nichts fesselt mich an die Erde.
Rastlos verfolgte das Schicksal mich,
Die Qual nur war mein Gefährte.
Nie werd' ich die Heimath erreichen;
Zu was frommt mir der Güter Gewinn?
Lässt du zu dem Bund dich erweichen,
O, so nimm meine Schätze dahin!

**DALAND:** Wohl, Fremdling, hab' ich eine schöne Tochter,
Mit treuer Kindeslieb' ergeben mir;
Sie ist mein Stolz, das höchste meiner Güter,
Mein Trost im Unglück, meine Freud' im Glück.

**HOLLÄNDER:** Dem Vater stets bewahr' sie ihre Liebe.
Ihm treu, wird sie auch treu dem Gatten sein.

**DALAND:** Du giebst Juwelen, unschätzbare Perlen,
Das höchste Kleinod doch, ein treues Weib . . .

**HOLLÄNDER:** Du giebst es mir?

tion
Of the riches stored in my ship's hold.
Of what value is all these treasures?
I have no wife,
Nor child, and I'll never reach my native land.
All my riches shall be yours, as the price
I pay with all my heart for the home I crave.

**DALAND:** What must I hear?

**THE FLYING DUTCHMAN:** Do you have a daughter?

**DALAND:** I have, and she is dear to me.

**THE FLYING DUTCHMAN:** Then give her to me for wife.

**DALAND:** My child shall be his; why should I delay,
When great is the wealth that will be my part?
The bargain is good, I'll close it this day,
In case he might change his mind, and depart;
I will give him my child to be his bride,
So she will be a rich man's happy wife;
I would be a fool if I denied such a good offer,
It's the best bargain I made in my life.

**THE FLYING DUTCHMAN:** No heir, no child, no wife are given me,
And no earthly joy have ever I known;
Fate, relentless through all eternity,
Wildly pursues me like a hunted fawn.
Whenever I can reach my home again,
What shall I do with all my riches rare?
The terms are good; let us close the bargain,
And my ship's whole cargo shall be your share.

**DALAND:** Truly, stranger, a pretty daughter I call mine.
With filial love she is attached to me;
She is my pride, the best of all I have.
And I feel for her as only a father feels.

**THE FLYING DUTCHMAN:** For the father she may always cherish filial love,
If true to him, true she will be to him she weds.

**DALAND:** While jewels and pearls are costly things,
The costliest still is a loving wife.

**THE FLYING DUTCHMAN:** And she shall be mine?

**DALAND:** Ich gebe dir mein Wort.
Mich rührt dein Loos; freigebig, wie du bist,
Zeigst Edelmuth und hohen Sinn Du mir:—
Den Eidam wünsch' ich so, und wär' dein Gut
Auch nicht so reich, wählt' ich doch keinen Andern.

**HOLLÄNDER:** Hab' Dank! Werd' ich die Tochter heut' noch seh'n?

**DALAND:** Der nächste günst'ge Wind führt uns nach Haus.
Du sollst sie seh'n, und wenn sie dir gefällt—

**HOLLÄNDER:** So ist sie mein . . . Wird sie mein Engel sein?
Wenn aus der Qualen Schreckgewalten
Die Sehnsucht nach dem Heil mich treibt,
Ist mir's erlaubt, mich festzuhalten
An einer Hoffnung, die mir bleibt.
Darf ich in jenem Wahn noch schmachten,
Dass sich ein Engel mir erweicht?
Der Qualen, die mein Haupt umnachten,
Ersehntes Ziel hätt' ich erreicht.
Ach! ohne Hoffnung wie ich bin.
Geb' ich mich doch der Hoffnung hin!

**DALAND:** Gepriesen seid, des Sturms Gewalten,
Die ihr an diesen Strand mich triebt.
Fürwahr! Blos brauch ich festzuhalten,
Was sich so schön von selbst mir giebt.
Die ihn an diese Küste brachten
Ihr Winde sollt gesegnet sein!
Ja, wonach alle Väter trachten,
Ein reicher Eidam, er ist mein.
Dem Mann mit Gut und hohem Sinn
Geb' froh ich Haus und Tochter hin!

**STEUERMANN:** Südwind! Südwind!
Ach! lieber Südwind, blas' noch mehr!

**MATROSEN:** Holloje! Hollajo!

**DALAND:** Du siehst, das Glück ist günstig dir:
Der Wind ist gut, die See in Ruh'.
Sogleich die Anker lichten wir
Und segeln schnell der Heimath zu.

**MATROSEN:** Hohohe! Hohohe! Halloho! Jo!

**HOLLAENDDER:** Darf ich dich bitten, segelst du voran?
Der Wind ist frisch, doch, meine Mannschaft müd'.
Ich gönn' ihr kurze Ruh', und folge dann.

**DALAND:** Doch unser Wind?

**DALAND:** My word I pledge to you,
Your fate has won my heart; you're lavish;
Thus must be he who weds my daughter,
And if you were less rich, no other would I choose.

**THE FLYING DUTCHMAN:** Thanks! Will I see your girl before sinks the day to rest?

**DALAND:** With change of wind we set our sails homeward;
Once on shore, and if my daughter suits you, then—

**THE FLYING DUTCHMAN:** Then she will be mine—my angel she shall be.
When out of torment's iron hold, I long to see salvation near,
I cling—for so have I been told—
To one hope still remaining dear.
May still I hope—I cannot pray—
That pity feel might angel-wife?
Then will I praise this happy day,
When over at last, this woeful strife.
Though hope has died, and left no trace,
I hope again for joy and grace.

**DALAND:** When from the South it blew a gale
that drove me to this rocky shore,
I did at first my fate bewail;
But now I wail and grieve no more.
I praise the wind that drove me here,
For here I met a lucky fate,
For here I found a treasure dear:
A rich man with my child to mate!
He who with treasure sails the sea,
Shall be welcome to my daughter!

**MATE:** Southwind! Southwind!
Come, Southwind, blow again!

**SAILORS:** Heigho! Heigho! Heigho!

**DALAND:** We are lucky, indeed; for the wind is good,
And smooth as a sea of glass is the sea;
Let us weigh the anchors without delay,
And set sail for the sheltering port.

**SAILORS:** Heigho! ho! Heigho! ho! ho!

**THE FLYING DUTCHMAN:** You sail ahead, if it so pleases you,
The wind is good, but my men are fatigued;
I'll give them rest, and then I follow.

**DALAND:** But if the wind should change?

**HOLLÄNDER:** Er bläst noch lang' aus Süd'.
Mein Schiff ist schnell, es holt dich sicher ein.

**DALAND:** Du glaubst? Wohlan! Es möge denn so sein.
Leb' wohl! mög'st heute du mein Kind noch sehn!

**HOLLÄNDER:** Gewiss!

**DALAND:** Hei! Wie die Segel schon sich bläh'n!
Hallo! Hallo! Frisch, Jungen! Greift an!

**MATROSEN:** Mit Gewitter und Sturm aus fernem Meer.
Mein Mädel, bin dir nah'?
Über thurmhohe Fluth, vom Süden her—
Mein Mädel, ich bin da!
Mein Mädel, wenn nicht Südwind wär',
Ich nimmer wohl käm' zu dir!
Ach, lieber Südwind, blas' noch mehr!
Mein Mädel verlangt nach mir!
Hohoje! Halloho! Hoho! Ho! Ho! Ho!

**THE FLYING DUTCHMAN:** It will blow from the South, be assured.
My ship sails fast, and will reach you soon.

**DALAND:** As you say, so be it.
Farewell! And my child, will you see her this day?

**THE FLYING DUTCHMAN:** This day I shall see her.

**DALAND:** See how the sails swell in the wind!
Hallo! Hallo! Be up and doing, boys!

**SAILORS:** In tempest's roar, on the wide sea,
My girl, I think of you!
The gale, ah, well! it came from the South—
Lucky for you and me!
My girl, if it hadn't been Southwind,
I wouldn't see you again!
Ah! come and blow, my Southwind fair,
Else waits my love in vain.
Hohohe! Johohe! Heigho! Heigho!

# ■ ZWEITER ACT

## ERSTE SCENE

**MÄDCHEN:** Summ' und brumm', de gutes Rädchen,
Munter, munter dreh' dich um!
Spinne, spinne tausend Fädchen,
Gutes Rädchen, summ' und brumm'!
Mein Schatz ist auf dem Meere draus,
Er denkt nach Haus
An's fromme Kind:
Mein gutes Rädchen saus' und braus'!
Ach, gäb'st du Wind,
Er käm' geschwind!
Spinnt, spinnt!
Fleissig, Mädchen!
Summ', brumm',
Gutes Rädchen!

**MARY:** Ei! Fleissig, fleissig, wie sie spinnen!
Will jede sich den Schatz gewinnen.

**MÄDCHEN:** Frau Mary, still! denn wohl ihr wisst,
Das Lied noch nicht zu Ende ist.

**MARY:** So singt! dem Rädchen lässt's nicht Ruh'.
Du aber, Senta, schweigst dazu?

**MÄDCHEN:** Summ' und brumm', du gutes Rädchen,
Munter, munter dreh' dich um!
Spinne, spinne tausend Fädchen,
Gutes Rädchen, summ und brumm!
Mein Schatz da draussen auf dem Meer
Im Süden er
Viel Gold gewinnt.

# ■ ACT II

## SCENE I

**GIRLS:** Hum and buzz! What cheerful sound!
Turn round the wheel, quick, quick, quick!
Spin the golden thread around!
Hum and buzz like a magic trick!
My love sails over stormy sea,
And thinks of me,
His own sweetheart,
Pray, O pray, for him and me,
That storm depart,
Fair wind his part!
Spin and spin
The wheel around,
Hum and buzz
With cheery sound!

**MARY:** See, how quick they turn the wheel!
Must be love they feel for him.

**GIRLS:** You mustn't speak! While floats our song
On airy wings, please hold your tongue!

**MARY:** Then sing your song the lifelong night!
But, Senta! child you are so quiet.

**GIRLS:** Hum and buzz! What cheerful sound
Turn round the wheel, quick, quick, quick!
Spin the golden thread around!
Hum and buzz like a magic trick!
My love sails over stormy sea,
On Southland's coast
He seeks for gold.

Ach, gutes Rädchen, braus' noch mehr!
Er giebt's dem Kind,
Wenn's fleissig spinnt.
Spinnt, spinnt!
Fleissig, Mädchen!
Summ', brumm',
Gutes Rädchen!

**MARY:** Du böses Kind, wenn du nicht spinnst,
Vom Schatz du kein Geschenk gewinnst!

**MÄDCHEN:** Sie hat's nicht noth, dass sie sich eilt.
Ihr Schatz nicht auf dem Meere weilt:
Bringt er nicht Gold, bringt er doch Wild.
Man weiss ja, was ein Jäger gilt!

**MARY:** Da seht ihr's! Immer vor dem Bild!—
Wirst du dein ganzes junges Leben
Verträumen vor dem Konterfei?

**SENTA:** Was hast du Kunde mir gegeben,
Was mir erzählet, wer es sei!
Der arme Mann!

**MARY:** Gott sei mit dir!

**MÄDCHEN:** Ei, ei! Ei, ei! Was hören wir?
Sie seufzet um den bleichen Mann.

**MARY:** Den Kopf verliert sie noch darum.

**MÄDCHEN:** Da sieht man, was ein Bild doch kann!

**MARY:** Nichts hilft es, wenn ich täglich brumm':
Komm', Senta! wend' dich doch herum!

**MÄDCHEN:** Sie hört euch nicht,— sie ist verliebt.
Ei, ei! Wenn's nur nicht Händel giebt!
Denn Erik hat gar heisses Blut,
Dass er nur keinen Schaden thut!
Sagt nichts, er schiesst sonst wuthentbrannt
Den Nebenbuhler von der Wand.

**SENTA:** O schweigt! Mit eurem tollen Lachen
Wollt ihr mich ernstlich böse machen?

**MÄDCHEN:** Summ' und brumm', du gutes Rädchen,
Munter, munter dreh' dich um!
Spinne, spinne tausend Fädchen,
Gutes Rädchen, brumm' und summ'!

**SENTA:** O macht dem tollen Lied ein Ende,
Es summt und brummt mir vor dem Ohr!
Wollt ihr, dass ich mich zu euch wende,
So sucht was Besseres hervor!

**MÄDCHEN:** Gut, singe du!

**SENTA:** Hört, was ich rathe.
Frau Mary singt uns die Ballade.

Pray, O pray, that I may boast,
And share his gold.
And now behold
How turns the wheel
With cheery sound,
While sure I feel
For home he's bound!

**MARY:** You bad child, if you will not spin,
You never shall win the gold your love brings.

**GIRLS:** Why should she spin and work as we?
Her love does not sail over stormy sea,
Her love's a huntsman gay and bold,
He brings her game instead of gold.

**MARY:** Look at her! Always before the picture!
Senta, are you to dream away your young life,
Contemplating this portrait?

**SENTA:** Yours the blame!
From you I learned his history—
A poor man is he!

**MARY:** May God protect your young life!

**GIRLS:** What! what's this! listen well!
She sighs for him, this pale man.

**MARY:** Her head will be turned, God knows!

**GIRLS:** This a simple picture's power shows.

**MARY:** All my scolding is in vain.
Come, Senta, be a good child.

**GIRLS:** She does not mind you; she's in love,
A bad affair this will be,
You know how jealous Erik is,
Why! he'll be apt to act quite rash,
And, blinded by his jealousy, shoot
His rival hanging on the wall.

**SENTA:** Cease this talk, you foolish things,
Or I will be angry in earnest.

**GIRLS:** Hum and buzz! What cheerful sound!
Turn round the wheel, quick, quick, quick!
Spin the golden thread around!
Hum and buzz like a magic trick!

**SENTA:** O, put an end to this wild song,
It hums and buzzes in my ear;
If I must join your busy throng,
Then sing the song I hold so dear.

**GIRLS:** We are tired; sing it for us.

**SENTA:** For me it is too long;
Why can't Mary sing the song?

## Act II, Scene I

**MARY:** Bewahre Gott! das fehlte mir!
Den fliegenden Holländer lasst in Ruh'.

**SENTA:** Wie oft doch hört' ich sie von Dir!
Ich sing' sie selbst, hört, Mädchen, zu.
Lasst mich's euch recht zu Herzen führen,
Des Ärmsten Loos, es muss Euch rühren.

**MÄDCHEN:** Uns ist es recht.

**SENTA:** Merkt auf die Wort'!

**MÄDCHEN:** Dem Spinnrad Ruh'!

**MARY:** Ich spinne fort.

**SENTA:** Johohoe! Johohohoe!
Traft ihr das Schiff im Meere an,
Blutroth die Segel, schwarz der Mast?
Auf hohem Bord der bleiche Mann,
Des Schiffs Herr, wacht ohne Rast.
Hui! Wie saust der Wind!—Johohe!
Hui! Wie pfeift's im Tau!—Johohe!
Hui! Wie ein Pfeil fliegt er hin—
ohne Ziel—ohne Rast—ohne Ruh'!
Doch kann dem bleichen Manne
Erlösung einstens noch werden,
Fänd' er ein Weib, das bis in den
Tod getreu ihm auf Erden.
Ach, wann wirst du bleicher Seemann, sie finden!
Betet zum Himmel, dass bald
Ein Weib Treue ihm halt'!
Bei bösem Wind und Sturmes Wuth
Umsegeln wollt' er einst ein Cap;
Er flucht' und schwur in tollem Muth:
"In Ewigkeit lass' ich nicht ab!"—
Hui!—Und Satan hört's—Johohe!
Hui!—Nahm ihn bei'm Wort!—Johohe!
Hui!—Und verdammt zieht er nun
durch das Meer, ohne Rast, ohne Ruh'.
Doch, dass der arme Mann noch
Erlösung fände auf Erden,
Zeigt' Gottes Engel an, wie sein
Heil ihm einst könne werden.
Ach! möchtest du, bleicher Seemann, es finden!
Betet zum Himmel, dass bald
Ein Weib Treue ihm halt'!—
Vor Anker alle sieben Jahr,
Ein Weib zu frei'n, ging er an's Land.
Er freite alle sieben Jahr',
Noch nie ein treues Weib er fand.—
Hui! "die Segel auf!"—Johohe!
Hui! "den Anker los!"—Johohe!
Hui! falsche Lieb', falsche Treu'!
Auf in See! Ohne Rast, ohne Ruh'!

**MÄDCHEN:** Ach, wo weilt sie, die dir Gottes Engel einst könne zeigen?
Wo triffst du sie, die bis in den Tod
Dein bliebe treu eigen?

**MARY:** Heaven forbid! It's no time to jest,
Leave the Flying Dutchman at rest.

**SENTA:** Why not sing it now as well?
Come, girls, I will sing you the song,
That you may hear how relentless fate
Ever and ever pursues this man

**GIRLS:** Give us the song!

**SENTA:** Be quiet and listen.

**GIRLS:** The wheels at rest!

**MARY:** Not mine! I turn my wheel quick, quick!

**SENTA:** Heigho! ho! heigho! ho! heigho! ho!
There sails a ship over the deep main,
With blackened mast and crimsoned sail,
On deck you see the man of pain,
His eyes so dark, his face so pale.
Huzza! Listen the wind! Heigho!
Heigho! Heigho! ho!
Huzza! See the sails spread! Heigho! heigho!
Huzza! She leaps and leaps, from wave forever, evermore!
But he can be saved, this captain so pale,
If woman's heart in her mission not fail!
But when will he find this woman so rare, this woman so rare?
Pray for the man at sea,
That his woman be true to him!
Around a cape he once would sail,
And thus it was that he did hail:
'I'll sail, I'll sail, I'll sail evermore!'
Huzza! Satan, he heard him hail! ho! heigho!
Huzza! And damned he! His ship,
she leaps from wave to wave forever, evermore!
But that he might be saved, this captain so pale,
An angel points to a woman's heart without fail.
Oh! that he may soon find this woman so rare, this woman so rare!
Pray, for the man at sea
That his woman be constant!
Once in seven years he sought,
Still love for gold he never bought!
Once in seven years he tried,
Still a woman constant he never spied!
Huzza! "Spread the sails!" heigho! ho!
Huzza! "The anchor weigh!" heigho! ho!
Huzza! False Love! Woman frail!
Leap, ship—leap from wave to wave forevermore!

**GIRLS:** Where, oh, where is the woman so rare,
His love to win, his treasures to share?

**SENTA:** Ich sei das Weib! Meine Treu' soll dich erlösen!
Mög' Gottes Engel mich dir zeigen;
Durch mich sollst du das Heil erreichen!

**MARY UND DIE MÄDCHEN:** Hilf Himmel! Senta! Senta!

**ERIK:** Senta! Senta! Willst du mich verderben?

**MÄDCHEN:** Hilf uns, Erik, sie ist von Sinnen!

**MARY:** Vor Schreck fühl' ich mein Blut gerinnen!
Abscheulich Bild, du sollst hinaus,
Kommt nur der Vater erst nach Haus!

**ERIK:** Der Vater kommt.

**SENTA:** Der Vater kommt?

**ERIK:** Vom Fels sah ich sein Schiff sich nahen.

**MARY:** Nun seht, zu was euer Treiben frommt!
Im Hause ist noch nichts gethan.

**MÄDCHEN:** Sie sind daheim!—
Auf, eilt hinaus!

**MARY:** Halt! Halt! Ihr bleibet fein im Haus!
Das Schiffsvolk kommt mit leerem Magen!—
In Küch' und Keller! Säumet nicht!
Lasst euch nur brav die Neugier plagen,
Vor Allem geht an eure Pflicht!

## ZWEITE SCENE

**ERIK:** Bleib', Senta! Bleib' nur einen Augenblick!
Aus meinen Qualen reisse mich!
Doch willst du—
Ach! so verdirb mich ganz!

**SENTA:** Was soll's, Erik . . . ?

**ERIK:** O Senta, sprich, was aus mir werden soll?
Dein Vater kommt,—eh' wieder er verreis't
Wird er vollbringen, was schon oft er wollte . . .

**SENTA:** Und was, Erik?

**ERIK:** Dir einen Gatten geben.—
Mein Herz voll Treue bis zum Sterben,
Mein dürftig Gut, mein Jägerglück:—
Darf so um Deine Hand ich werben,
Stösst mich dein Vater nicht zurück?
Wenn sich mein Herz in Jammer bricht,
Sag', Senta, wer dann für mich spricht?

**SENTA:** O schweige jetzt, Erik! Lass mich hinaus,
Den Vater zu begrüssen!
Wenn nicht, wie sonst, an Bord die Tochter kommt,
Wird er nicht zürnen müssen?

**ERIK:** Du willst mich flieh'n?

**SENTA:** Ich muss zum Port.

**SENTA:** This mission is mine! My love shall be your salvation!
Angel above, oh! bring to me
The pale man sailing over the sea!

**MARY AND ALL THE GIRLS:** Heaven help us! Senta! Senta!

**ERIK:** Senta! Senta! think of me who owns your love!

**GIRLS:** Erik, help, help! Her head is turned.

**MARY:** I can feel my blood curdling from the shock.
Abhorred picture, out you go,
As soon as her father returns.

**ERIK:** The father! he's coming!

**SENTA:** My father, does he come?

**ERIK:** His ship is sailing round the rock.

**MARY:** Be up and doing, girls, and put the house in order.

**GIRLS:** See them land! let us greet them!

**MARY:** Easy, my beauties! in the house you'll stay,
The crew, they'll be quite hungry
Coming from the stormy sea.
Set the table without delay,
Fill the glasses on the tray.

## SCENE II

**ERIK:** Stay, Senta, stay! one moment stay!
End my torment, end it quick,
Pity, pity my despair!

**SENTA:** Erik, what is this?

**ERIK:** Tell me, Senta, tell me true what's to become of me?
Your father comes; home he sails again,
He will accomplish what he did often contemplate . . .

**SENTA:** What, Erik?

**ERIK:** Choose a man for you; a man for you;
But little I call mine save this trusty rifle;
It will weigh quite lightly in the scale,
And your father will reject my suit.
When then my heart needs strong comfort
Say, Senta, say, who pleads for me?

**SENTA:** Why discuss this question now? let me go
To welcome home father.
If he does not see his daughter on board,
He will be quite angry.

**ERIK:** Why evade me?

**SENTA:** To the ship I must go.

ERIK: Du weichst mir aus?

SENTA: Ach! lass mich fort!

ERIK: Fliehst Du zurück vor dieser Wunde,
Die Du mir schlugst, den Liebeswahn?
O höre mich zu dieser Stunde,
Hor' meine letzte Frage an!
Wenn dieses Herz in Jammer bricht.
Wird's Senta sein, die für mich spricht?

SENTA: Wie? zweifelst du an meinem Herzen?
Du zweifelst, ob ich gut dir bin?—
Doch sag', was weckt dir solche Schmerzen?
Was trübt mit Argwohn deinen Sinn?

ERIK: Dein Vater—ach! nach Schätzen geizt er nur . . .
Und Senta, Du! Wie dürft' auf dich ich zählen?
Erfülltest du nur eine meiner Bitten?
Kränkst du mein Herz nicht jeden Tag?

SENTA: Dein Herz?

ERIK: Was soll ich denken? Jenes Bild . . .

SENTA: Das Bild?

ERIK: Lässt Du von deiner Schwärmerei wohl ab?

SENTA: Kann meinem Blick Theilnahme ich verwehren?

ERIK: Und die Ballade, heut' noch sangst du sie!

SENTA: Ich bin ein Kind und weiss nicht was ich singe . . . !
Erik, sag'! fürchtest du ein Lied, ein Bild?

ERIK: Du bist so bleich . . . sag', sollt ich es nicht fürchten?

SENTA: Soll mich des Ärmsten Schreckensloos nicht rühren?

ERIK: Mein Leiden, Senta, rührt es Dich nicht mehr?

SENTA: O! schweige doch. Was kann dein Leiden sein?
Kennst jenes Unglücksel'gen Schicksal du?
Fühlst du den Schmerz, den tiefsten Gram,
Mit dem herab auf mich er sieht?
Ach, was die Ruh' ihm ewig nahm,
Wie schneidend Weh' durch's Herz mir zieht!

ERIK: Weh' mir! Es mahnt mich ein unsel'ger Traum!
Gott schütze Dich! Satan hat dich umgarnt.

SENTA: Was erschreckt dich so?

ERIK: Senta, lass dir vertrau'n:—
Ein Traum ist's,—höre ihn zur Warnung an:
Auf hohem Felsen lag' ich träumend,

ERIK: My presence does not please you?

SENTA: Let go, I say, let go!

ERIK: Do no evade me now,
For my grief is great,
But one word more, then go!
Let me ask, and give answer,
When this heart needs strong comfort,
Will it Senta be who pleads for me?

SENTA: Why doubt my heart, why doubt my love,
Why doubt my devotion's faith and strength?
Why now these thoughts that give but pang,
Why this suspicion all at once?

ERIK: You know well that gold is all your father cares for,
And he that can offer riches will wed his daughter sure.
These are thoughts that fill my heart with grief,
And then, Senta, you too, add to my anguish.

SENTA: I? And how?

ERIK: Your worship for that picture—

SENTA: This picture?

ERIK: It is a strange infatuation which—

SENTA: Why should I not feel sympathy?

ERIK: And the song you love to sing.

SENTA: I am a child, and know not what I sing. Say, Erik, does a song fill you with fear, a picture?

ERIK: You are so pale, and that is what I fear.

SENTA: Why should I not sympathize with the poor man's fate?

ERIK: Why not rather feel sympathy with my deep grief?

SENTA: Enough of this! You have no grief;
But do you know the pale man's horrid fate
And do you feel how anguish wrung
The look he casts at me in wild despair?
His fate, relentless, bitter fate.
It is a pang that wrings my heart.

ERIK: Alas! alas my dream will then come true!
May God protect you! You are in Satan's power.

SENTA: What is it that so frightens you?

ERIK: Listen, Senta, listen well!
A dream it was—let warning voice it be!
The rock that overhangs the sea
Was my bed, and dreaming, I fan-

Sah unter mir des Meeres Fluth;
Die Brandung hört' ich, wie sich schäumend
Am Ufer brach der Wogen Wuth:—
Ein fremdes Schiff am nahen Strande
Erblickt ich, seltsam, wunderbar:—
Zwei Männer nahten sich dem Lande,
Der Ein', ich sah's, dein Vater war . . .

SENTA: Der And're?

ERIK: Wohl erkannt' ich ihn:
Mit schwarzem Wams und bleicher Mien'.

SENTA: Und düst'rem Aug' . . .

ERIK: Der Seemann, er.

SENTA: Und ich?

ERIK: Du kamst vom Hause her,
Du flogst den Vater zu begrüssen;
Doch kaum noch sah' ich an dich langen,
Du stürztest zu des Fremden Füssen—
Ich sah dich seine Knie umfangen . . .

SENTA: Er hob mich auf . . .

ERIK: An seine Brust;—
Voll Inbrunst hingst du dich an ihn,
Du küsstest ihn mit heisser Lust—

SENTA: Und dann . . . ?

ERIK: Sah ich auf's Meer Euch flieh'n.

SENTA: Er sucht mich auf! Ich muss ihn sehn! Mit ihm muss ich zu Grunde geh'n!

ERIK: Entsetzlich! Ha, mir wird es klar;
Sie ist dahin! Mein Traum sprach wahr!

SENTA: Ach, wo weilt sie

cied
I saw the waves roll in and out,
And heard the billow's ceaseless roar.
Near the shore I saw a ship,
And strange to tell, for strange the sight:—
Near and nearer two seamen approached,
And one, well I knew his face, was your father—

SENTA: And who was the other, pray?

ERIK: All only I know him too well,
Dressed in black in contrast strong to his pale face—

SENTA: And dark and sad his eye—

ERIK: Yes, black as jet his eye.

SENTA: And I? Where was I?

ERIK: Fleet as a fawn, startled in fear
I saw you rush toward the beach
To bid your father welcome home,
But scarce arrived, I saw you kneel
At the feet of the pale man accursed.

SENTA: And he gently drew me to his breast.

ERIK: He folded you to his treacherous heart,
And you with fervor wild, unbridled,
Returned kiss for kiss impassionate.

SENTA: And then? What then?

ERIK: He took you on board his shadowy ship.

SENTA: He longs for me! I'll follow him,
Even if I should in the attempt perish.

ERIK: It is horrid! I see it clear,
My dream, my fearful dream spoke true.

SENTA: Where, oh where is the woman so rare,
His love to win, his treasures to share?

## DRITTE SCENE

DALAND: Mein Kind, du siehst mich auf der Schwelle . . .
Wie? kein Umarmen? keinen Kuss?
Du bleibst gebannt an Deiner Stelle..
Verdien' ich, Senta, solchen Gruss?

SENTA: Gott dir zum Gruss!—
Mein Vater sprich!
Wer ist der Fremde?

DALAND: Drängst du mich?
Mögst du, mein Kind, den fremden Mann willkommnen heissen!
Seemann ist er, gleich mir, das Gastrecht spricht er an;
Lang' ohne Heimath, stets auf fernen, weiten Reisen.

## SCENE III

DALAND: Home again, my child, my darling!
But how is this? No kiss for me?
Why! It is a cool reception, sure.

SENTA: Welcome home, my father!
But say, speak quick.
Who is this stranger that comes with you?

DALAND: Bid him welcome with all your heart! Many a year he sailed the sea.
No home is his, no kin his part.
Though rich he is as rich can be,
To him his native land is lost.
And home he seeks, a new home

## Act II, Scene III

In fremden Landen er der Schätze viel gewann.
Aus seinem Vaterland verwiesen,
Für einen Herd er reichlich lohnt;
Sprich, Senta, würd' es dich verdriessen,
Wenn dieser Fremde bei uns wohnt?
Sagt, hab' ich sie zu viel gepriesen?
Ihr seht sie selbst,—ist sie Euch recht?—
Soll noch vom Lob ich überfliessen?
Gesteht, sie zieret ihr Geschlecht!
Mögst du, mein Kind, dem Manne freundlich dich erweisen!
Von deinem Herzen auch spricht holde Gab' er an.
Reich' ihm die Hand, denn Bräutigam sollst du ihn heissen;
Stimmst du dem Vater bei, ist morgen er dein Mann.
Sieh' dieses Band, sieh' diese Spangen!
Was er besitzt, macht dies gering.
Muss, theures Kind, dich's nicht verlangen?
Dein ist es, wechselst du den Ring?
Doch—Keines spricht.—Sollt' ich hier lästig sein?
So ist's! Am besten lass ich sie allein.
Mögst du den edlen Mann gewinnen!
Glaub' mir, solch' Glück wird nimmer neu.
Bleibt hier allein; ich geh' von hinnen.
Glaubt mir, wie schön, so ist sie treu!

**HOLLÄNDER:** Wie aus der Ferne längst vergang'ner Zeiten
Spricht dieses Mädchens Bild zu mir;
Wie ich geträumt seit langen Ewigkeiten,
Vor meinen Augen seh' ich's hier.
Wohl hob auch ich voll Sehnsucht meine Blicke
Aus tiefer Nacht empor zu einem Weib:
Ein schlagend Herz liess, ach! mir Satans Tücke.
Dass eingedenk ich meiner Qualen bleib'!
Die düst're Gluth, die hier ich fühle brennen,
Sollt' ich Unseliger sie Liebe nennen?
Ach nein! die Sehnsucht ist es nach dem Heil!
Würd' es durch solchen Engel mir zu Theil!

**SENTA:** Versank ich jetzt in wunderbares Träumen,
Was ich erblicke, ist es Wahn?—
Weilt' ich bisher in trügerischen Räumen,
Brach des Erwachen's Tag heut' an?—
Er steht vor mir mit leidenvollen Zügen,
Es spricht sein unerhörter Gram zu mir:
Kann tiefen Mitleids Stimme mich

dear;
Come, Senta, come, be the host,
And bid the stranger welcome here!
And you, my new-found friend, say true.
Does she suit to be your wife?
Why should I praise what's only true
And will be blessing all your life?
And you, my child, be good and true,
Give him your hand and hold him dear,
And, Senta, you will never rue
That I have brought your husband here.
See the golden things I've brought—
Quite worthless trifles when compared
With the riches in his vessel's hold.
And all his treasures will be shared,
All his diamonds and all his gold.
With you, my child, if you will say
That you will bless him with your love,
And be his wife without delay;
Wed him, Senta, give him your love!
I leave you now alone, my child,
To speak to him as bids your heart;
I trust in you, my darling child—
Think how happy will be our part.

**THE FLYING DUTCHMAN:** Like to a vision, seen in days long by gone,
This maiden's face and form appear:
What I have sought through countless years of sorrow
Am I at last beholding here!
Often amid the torment of my night eternal,
Longing I gazed upon some being fair!
But I was driven by Satan's power infernal
On my dread course, in anguish and despair!
The glow that warms my heart with strange emotion,
Can I, accursed one, call it love's devotion?
Ah! no, it is yearning blessed repose to gain,
That such an angel might for me obtain!

**SENTA:** And am I sunk in wondrous depths of dreaming?
Is this a vision which I see,
Or am I now set free from long delusion?
Has morning truly dawned on me?
See, there he stands, his face clouding with sorrow—
He tells me all his mingled hope and fear;
Is it the voice of sympathy that cheats me?

belügen?
Wie ich ihn oft geseh'n, so steht er hier.
Die Schmerzen, die in meinem Busen brennen,
Ach! dies Verlangen, wie soll ich es nennen
Wonach mit Sehnsucht es ihn treibt—das Heil, würd' es, du Ärmster, dir durch mich zu Theil!

**HOLLÄNDER:** Wirst du des Vaters Wahl nicht schelten?
Was er versprach, wie? dürft' es gelten?—
Du könntest dich für ewig mir ergeben,
Und deine Hand dem Fremdling reichtest du?
Soll finden ich nach qualenvollem Leben
In deiner Treu' die lang ersehnte Ruh?—

**SENTA:** Wer du auch sei'st, und welches das Verderben,
Dem grausam dich dein Schicksal konnte weih'n;
Was auch das Loos, das ich mir sollt' erwerben;
Gehorsam stets werd' ich dem Vater sein.

**HOLLÄNDER:** So unbedingt, wie? könnte dich durchdringen
Für meine Leiden tiefstes Mitgefühl?

**SENTA:** O, welche Leiden! Könnt' ich Trost Dir bringen!

**HOLLÄNDER:** Welch holder Klang im nächtigen Gewühl!—
Du bist ein Engel!—Eines Engel's Liebe
Verworf'ne selbst zu trösten weiss!—
Ach, wenn Erlösung mir zu hoffen bliebe,
Allewiger, durch diese sei's!

**SENTA:** Ach! wenn Erlösung ihm zu hoffen bliebe,
Allewiger, durch mich nur sei's!

**HOLLÄNDER:** O könntest das Geschick du ahnen,
Dem dann mit mir du angehörst:
Dich würd' es an das Opfer mahnen,
Das du mir bringst, wenn Treu' du schwörst.
Es flöhe schaudernd deine Jugend,
Dem Loose, dem du sie willst weih'n:
Nennst du des Weibes schönste Tugend,
Nennst heil'ge Treue du nicht dein!

**SENTA:** Wohl kenn' ich Weibes hohe Pflichten,—
Sei d'rum getrost, unsel'ger Mann!
Lass über die das Schicksal richten,
Die seinem Spruche trotzen kann!
In meines Herzens höchster Reine
Kenn' ich der Treue Hochgebot:

As he has often in dreams, so stands he here!
The sorrow which is burning within my breast—
Ah, this compassion, what dare I call it?
Your heart is longing after rest and peace,
And you at last through me shall find release.

**THE FLYING DUTCHMAN:** Will you, your father's choice fulfilling,
Do what he said? Say, are you willing?
Will you, indeed, give yourself to me forever?
Shall I in truth, a stranger, thus be blessed?
Say, shall I find the time of sorrow ended—
In your true love my long-expected rest?

**SENTA:** Whoever you are, wherever your curse may lead you,
and me, when I your lot my own have made—
Whatever, the fate which I with you may share in,
My father's will by me shall be obeyed.

**THE FLYING DUTCHMAN:** So full of trust? what? can you in your gladness,
For these my sorrows deep compassion know?

**SENTA:** Unheard-of sorrows! If only I could bring you joy!

**THE FLYING DUTCHMAN:** How sweet the sound that breaks my night of woe!
You are an angel, and a love angelic
Can bring comfort to one like me.
Ah, if redemption shall be mine to hope for,
Heaven, grant that she be my savior!

**SENTA:** Ah, if redemption still be his to hope for,
Heaven, grant that I be his saviour!

**THE FLYING DUTCHMAN:** Ah, you, the certain fate foreknowing,
Which must indeed with me be borne,
Would not have made the vow you made—
Would not to be my wife have sworn!
You would have shuddered before devoting,
To aid me, all your golden youth—
Before you had surrendered woman's joys,
Before you had bid me trust your truth?

**SENTA:** Well I know woman's holy duties;
O hapless man, be at ease!
Leave me to fate's unbending judgment—
Me, who defy its dread decrees.
Within the secret realm of con-

Wem ich sie weih', schenk' ich die Eine;
Die Treue bis zum Tod!

HOLLÄNDER: Ein heil'ger Balsam meinen Wunden,
Dem Schwur, dem hohen Wort entfliesst!

SENTA: Von mächt'gem Zauber überwunden,
Reisst mich's zu seiner Rettung fort.

HOLLÄNDER: Hört' es: mein Heil hab' ich gefunden,
Mächte, die ihr zurück mich stiess't!
Du Stern des Unheils, sollst erblassen!
Licht meiner Hoffnung, leuchte neu.
Ihr Engel, die mich einst verlassen,
Stärkt jetzt dies Herz in seiner Treu'!

SENTA: Hier habe Heimath er gefunden, hier ruh' sein Schiff im ew'gen Port! Was ist's, das mächtig in mir lebet?
Was schliesst berauscht mein Busen ein? Allmächt'ger, was mich hoch erhebet, lass es die Kraft der Treue sein!

DALAND: Verzeiht, mein Volk hält draussen sich nicht mehr;
Nach jeder Rückkunft, wisset, giebt's ein Fest:—Verschönern möcht' ich's, komme deshalb her, ob mit Verlobung sich's vereinen lässt?— ich denk', Ihr habt nach Herzenswunsch gefreit?— Senta, mein Kind sag', bist auch du bereit?—

SENTA: Hier meine Hand, und ohne Reu'!
Bis in den Tod gelob' ich Treu'!

HOLLÄNDER: Sie reicht die Hand: gesprochen sei
Hohn Hölle dir, durch ihre Treu'!

DALAND: Euch soll dies Bündniss nicht gereu'n!
Zum Fest! heut' muss sich Alles freu'n!

science
Know I the high demands of faith:
Him whom I chose, him I love only,
And loving even till death!

THE FLYING DUTCHMAN: A healing balm for all my sorrows
From out her plighted word does flow.

SENTA: It was surely wrought by power of magic
That I should be his deliverer.

THE FLYING DUTCHMAN: Hear this! Release at last is granted!
Hear this, O mighty one.
Your power is now laid low!
Star of misfortune, you are paling!
Hope's glorious light now shines anew!
Angels, who once forsook me,
Aid now my heart, and keep it true!

SENTA: Here may a home at last be granted,
Here may he rest, from danger free!
What is the power working within me?
What is the task it bids me do?
Almighty, now that you have raised me high,
Grant me your strength, that I be true!

DALAND: Pardon my intrusion; my men will be quite impatient,
On each arrival home we have a frolic,
And this time, I hope, it will be a marriage feast.
Say, Senta, child, are you inclined to wed my friend?

SENTA: Here, my hand to the man of the sea:—
Until death I will be faithful.

THE FLYING DUTCHMAN: Gladly she gives her fond heart to me,
And ended is now my misery.

DALAND: May happiness forever be your part!
To the feast now with joyous heart!

# ■ DRITTER AKT

## ERSTE SCENE

### CHOR DER NORWEGISCHEN MATROSEN: Steuermann, lass die Wacht!
Steuermann, her zu uns!
He! He! Je! Ha!
Hebt die Segel auf! Anker fest!
Steuermann, her!—
Fürchten weder Wind noch bösen Strand,
Wollen heute 'mal recht lustig sein!
Jeder hat sein Mädel auf dem Land,
Herrlichen Tabak und guten Branntewein.

# ■ ACT III

## SCENE I

### CHORUS OF NORWEGIAN SAILORS: The sea! the sea! the open sea!
The blue, the fresh, the ever free!
Heigho! ho! heigho!
It runs the earth's wide region round! Heigho! heigho!
It plays with the clouds; it mocks the skies,
Or lies like a cradled creature,
Heigho! ho! heigho!
We're home again, home again!
Heigho! heigho!
Home again! home again! Heigho!

Hussassahe!
Klipp' und Sturm draus—
Jallolohe!
Lachen wir aus!
Hussassahe!
Segel ein! Anker fest! Klipp' und Sturm lachen wir aus!
Steuermann, lass die Wacht!
Steuermann her, trink' mit aus!

MÄDCHEN: Nein! Seht doch an! Sie tanzen gar!
Der Mädchen bedarf's da nicht fürwahr!

MATROSEN: He! Mädel! Halt! wo geht ihr hin?

MÄDCHEN: Steht euch nach frischem Wein der Sinn?
Eu'r Nachbar dort soll auch was haben,
Ist Trank und Schmaus für euch allein?

STEUERMANN: Fürwahr, tragt's hin den armen Knaben,
Vor Durst sie scheinen matt zu sein.

MATROSEN: Man hört sie nicht?

STEUERMANN: Ei, seht doch nur!
Kein Licht! Von der Mannschaft keine Spur.

MÄDCHEN: He! Seeleut'! He!
Wollt Fackeln ihr?
Wo seid ihr doch? Mann sieht nicht hier.

MATROSEN: Weckt sie nicht auf; sie schlafen noch.

MÄDCHEN: He! Seeleut'! He! Antwortet doch!

STEUERMANN UND MATROSEN: Haha! Wahrhaftig, sie sind todt.
Sie haben Speis' und Trank nicht noth.

MÄDCHEN: Wie, Seeleute? Liegt Ihr so faul schon im Nest?
Ist heute für euch denn nicht auch ein Fest?

STEUERMANN UND MATROSEN: Sie liegen fest auf ihrem Platz,
Wie Drachen hüten sie den Schatz.

MÄDCHEN: Wie, Seeleute? Wollt ihr nicht goldenen Wein?
Ihr müsset wahrlich doch auch durstig sein.

STEUERMANN UND MATROSEN: Sie trinken nicht, sie singen nicht,
In ihrem Schiffe brennt kein Licht.

MÄDCHEN: Sagt, habt Ihr denn nicht auch ein Schätzchen am Land?
Wollt ihr nicht mit tanzen auf freundlichem Strand?

MATROSEN: Sie sind schon alt und bleich statt roth,
Und ihre Liebsten, die sind todt.

MÄDCHEN: He, Seeleut'! Seeleut'! wacht doch auf!
Wir bringen Euch Speis' und Trank zu Hauf!

MATROSEN: Sie bringen Euch Speis' und Trank zu Hauf!

heigho!
Home again the sailor boy.
He his lassie's only joy!
Let us quaff the golden wine!
Mate, leave the watch!
Let us drink, drink, drink!

GIRLS: See! how wildly they dance a jig
On deck of their safely-anchored brig.

SAILORS: Ho, girls, you mustn't go away!

GIRLS: We'll fill the glasses on the tray.
Your neighbor, too, must have his share
Of golden wine and woman's care.

MATE: Yes, you must give those boys a share
Of golden wine and your own care.

SAILORS: They keep so quiet.

MATE: A strange sight!
No sailors on deck and no light!

GIRLS: Ho, sailors, ho! shall we bring light,
And make your ship look bright?

SAILORS: Don't awake them; they are sleeping still.

GIRLS: Ho! Sailors! ho! give us answer!

MATE AND SAILORS: Ha! ha! they are dead, indeed.
No meat and drink they will need.

GIRLS: Sailors, ho! you are lazy boys,
Don't care for frolic and joys.

MATE AND SAILORS: They watch the treasures in the hold,
They guard the gems and stones and gold.

GIRLS: Come, neighbors, come and have your share
Of golden wine and woman's care.

MATE AND SAILORS: They quaff no wine, they sing no song;
They must be dead ever so long.

GIRLS: Are there no sweethearts on the strand
Waiting for you from foreign land?

SAILORS: Ah, well! their sweethearts on the strand
Died while they were in foreign land.

GIRLS: Ho! sailors! ho! don't be lazy boys!
Come, partake of our frolicking joys!

SAILORS: Come and join in our frolicking joys!

# Act III, Scene I

**MÄDCHEN:** Wahrhaftig! Ja, sie scheinen todt.
Sie haben Speis' und Trank nicht noth.

**MATROSEN:** Vom fliegenden Holländer wisst Ihr ja!
Sein Schiff, wie es leibt, wie es lebt, seht Ihr da.

**MÄDCHEN:** So wecket die Mannschaft ja nicht auf,
Gespenster sind's, wir schwören drauf!

**MATROSEN:** Wie viel hundert Jahre schon seid Ihr zur See?
Euch thut ja der Sturm und die Klippe nicht weh'!

**MÄDCHEN:** Sie trinken nicht, sie singen nicht!
In ihrem Schiffe brennt kein Licht!

**MATROSEN:** Habt Ihr keine Brief', keine Aufträg' für's Land?
Unsern Urgrossvätern wir bringen's zur Hand.

**MÄDCHEN:** Sie sind schon alt und bleich statt roth;
Ach! ihre Liebsten, die sind todt!

**MATROSEN:** Hei! Seeleute! Spannt Eure Segel doch auf!
Und zeigt uns des fliegenden Holländers Lauf!

**MÄDCHEN:** Sie hören nicht,—uns graust es hier!
Sie wollen nichts,—was rufen wir?

**MATROSEN:** Ihr Mädel, lasst die Todten ruh'n!
Lasst's uns Lebend'gen glücklich thun!

**MÄDCHEN:** So nehmt, Eu'r Nachbar hat's verschmäht!

**STEUERMANN UND MATROSEN:** Wie? Kommt Ihr denn nicht selbst an Bord?

**MÄDCHEN:** Ei jetzt noch nicht, es ist nicht spät.
Wir kommen bald, jetzt trinkt nur fort.
Und, wenn Ihr wollt, so tanzt dazu,
Nur lasst dem müden Nachbar Ruh'!

**MATROSEN:** Juchhe! Juchhe! da giebt's die Fülle!
Ihr lieben Nachbarn, habet Dank!

**STEUERMANN:** Zum Rand sein Glas ein Jeder fülle!
Lieb Nachbar liefert uns den Trank!

**MATROSEN:** Halloho! Halloho!
Ho! ho! ho!
Lieb Nachbarn, habt Ihr Stimm' und Sprach',
So wachet auf, und macht's uns nach!
Steuermann, lass die Wacht!
Steuermann, her zu uns!
Ho! He! Je! Ha!
Hisst die Segel auf! Anker fest!—
Steuermann, her!—
Wachten manche Nacht bei Sturm und Graus,

**GIRLS:** They quaff no wine, they sing no song!
They must be dead ever so long.

**SAILORS:** You've heard of the Flying Dutchman, perhaps,
And this must be one of his ugly traps.

**GIRLS:** Then leave them alone, leave them at rest:
It's really no time for such jest.

**SAILORS:** How long, how long are you at sea?
Quite a pretty crew you must be.

**GIRLS:** They quaff no wine, they sing no song; They must be dead ever so long.

**SAILORS:** Have you no letter, no message to send
To great grandfather or other old friend?

**GIRLS:** Ah, well! they have no loved ones on the strand;
Their sweethearts died while they roamed in foreign land.

**SAILORS:** Ho! sailors, ho! hoist the sails, quick, quick!
And show us the Flying Dutchman's trick.

**GIRLS:** They hear us not, so let them rest;
They might revenge this sport and jest.

**SAILORS:** We'd better leave the dead at rest,
And return to our sport and jest.

**GIRLS:** Then drink you the wine your neighbor declines.

**MATE AND SAILORS:** Come on board our safely-anchored brig.
And join us dancing a jolly jig.

**GIRLS:** Plenty of time for dance and sport,
Now that you're safely in port.
And, if you wish, go dance away,
Only leave the tired neighbors in peace!

**SAILORS:** Hurrah we have enough!
Our good neighbors, thanks to you!

**MATE:** Boys, fill your goblets to the brink,
Let us have a jolly old drink.

**SAILORS:** Hal-lo-ho-ho!
Good neighbors, you can speak at least!
Come, wake up, and join our feast!
Steersman, leave the watch!
Steersman, come to us!
Ho, hey, hey, ha!
See the sails are in! Anchor fast!
Steersman, come!
We have often watched during howling storm;
We have often drunk the briny wave;

Tranken oft des Meer's gesalz'nes Nass;—
Heute wachen wir bei Saus und Schmaus,
Besseres Getränk giebt Mädel uns vom Fass!
Hussassahe!
Klipp' und Sturm draus!

**CHOR DER MANNSCHAFT DES FLIEGENDEN HOLLÄNDERS:** Johohe! Johohohoe! hohohohoe!
Hoe! Hoe! Hoe!
Huissa!
Nach dem Land treibt des Sturm—
Huissa!
Segel ein! Anker los!
Huissa!
In die Bucht laufet ein!
Schwarzer Hauptmann, geh' an's Land!
Sieben Jahre sind vorbei;
Frei' um blonden Mädchens Hand;
Blondes Mädchen, sei ihm treu!
Lustig heut', hui!
Bräutigam! hui!
Sturmwind heult Brautmusik,
Ocean tanzt dazu.
Hui!—Horch, er pfeift!
—Capitän, bist wieder da?—
Hui!—"Segel auf."—
—Deine Braut, sag', wo sie blieb?—
Hui! "Auf in See!"—
Capitän! Capitän! Hast kein Glück in der Lieb'!
Hahaha!
Sause, Sturmwind, heule zu!
Uns'ren Segeln lässt du Ruh':
Satan hat sie uns gefei't,
Reissen nicht in Ewigkeit!

**NORWEGISCHE MATROSEN:**
Welcher Sang! Ist es Spuk? Wie mich's graut!
Stimmet an unser Lied! Singet laut!
Steuermann, lass die Wacht

## ZWEITE SCENE

**ERIK:** Was musst' ich hören? Gott! was musst' ich sehen!
Ist's Täuschung? Wahrheit? Ist es That?

**SENTA:** Frag' nicht. Erik! Antwort darf ich nicht geben.

**ERIK:** Gerechter Gott! Kein Zweifel! Es ist wahr!
Welch' unheilvolle Macht riss dich dahin!
Welche Gewalt verführte dich so schnell,
Grausam zu brechen dieses treuste Herz?
Dein Vater? ha, den Bräut'gam bracht er mit,—
Wohl kenn' ich ihn,—mir ahnte, was geschieht.
Doch du? Ist's möglich!—reichest Deine Hand
Dem Mann, der deine Schwelle kaum betrat!

**SENTA:** Nicht weiter! Schweig'! Ich muss! Ich muss!

Watching takes today a fairer form—
Good and tasty wine our sweethearts let us have!
Hus-sas-sa-hey!

**CHORUS OF THE CREW OF THE FLYING DUTCHMAN:** Yo-ho-ho!
Ho! ho!
Huissa!
To the land drives the storm.
Huissa!
Sails are in! Anchor down!
Huissa!
To the bay hurry in!
Gloomy captain, go on land,
Now that seven long years have flown,
Seek a faithful maiden's hand!
Faithful maiden, be his own!
Joyful, hui!
Bridegroom, hui!
Winds be your wedding song,
Ocean rejoices with you!
Hui! Hark! He pipes!
What! captain, have you returned?
Hui! "Spread the sails!"
And your bride, say, where is she?
Hui! "Off to sea!" As of old,
No good fortune for you! Ha-ha-ha!
Blow, storm wind, howl and blow!
What care we how fast we go?
We have sails from Satan's store,
Sails that last forevermore—hohoe!

**CHORUS OF THE NORWEGIAN SAILORS:** What a song! Are they ghosts?
How I fear! Let them hear!
All unite in our song.
Steersman, leave the watch!

## SCENE II

**ERIK:** What must I hear! what must I see!
Oh, God above! how can this be!

**SENTA:** Ask me not! I can give no answer.

**ERIK:** Eternal God! no doubt prevails! It is true!
An evil power has ensnared you,
Strange infatuation possesses you,
You will break this loving heart!
Your father, ha! the bridegroom he did bring;
I know him well: I feared what might occur!
Yet you—amazing!—have given him your hand
When scarcely across the threshold he had come!

**SENTA:** No more! Cease! I must!

**ERIK:** O des Gehorsams, blind wie Deine That! Den Wink des Vaters nanntest du willkommen. Mit einem Streich vernichtest du mein Herz!

**SENTA:** Nicht mehr! Nicht mehr! Ich darf dich nicht mehr seh'n! Nicht an dich denken. Hohe Pflicht gebeut's!

**ERIK:** Welch' hohe Pflicht? Ist Höh're nicht zu halten Was du mir einst gelobet, ew'ge Treue?

**SENTA:** Wie? Ew'ge Treue hätt' ich Dir gelobt?

**ERIK:** Senta! O Senta! Läugnest du? Willst jenes Tags du nicht dich mehr entsinnen, Als du zu dir mich riefest in das Thal? Als, dir des Hochlands Blume zu gewinnen, Muthvoll ich trug Beschwerden ohne Zahl, Gedenkst du, wie auf steilem Felsenriffe Vom Ufer wir den Vater scheiden sah'n? Er zog dahin auf weiss beschwingtem Schiffe. Und meinen Schutz vertraute er Dich an:— Als sich dein Arm um meinen Nacken schlang, Gestandest du mir Liebe nicht auf's Neu'? Was bei der Hände Druck mich hehr durchdrang, Sag', war's nicht die Versich'rung Deiner Treu'?

**HOLLÄNDER:** Vorloren! Ach! verloren! Ewig verlor'nes Heil!

**ERIK:** Was seh' ich? Gott!

**HOLLÄNDER:** Senta, leb' wohl!

**SENTA:** Halt ein, Unsel'ger!

**ERIK:** Was beginnst du?

**HOLLÄNDER:** In See, in See! In See für ew'ge Zeiten! Um deine Treue ist's gethan, Um deine Treue, um mein Heil. Lebwohl, ich will dich nicht verderben!

**ERIK:** Entsetzlich, dieser Blick!

**SENTA:** Halt ein! Von dannen sollst du nimmer flieh'n.

*Der Holländer gibt ein gellendes Zeichen auf seiner Pfeife und ruft der Mannschaft seines Schiffes zu.*

**HOLLÄNDER:** Segel auf! Anker los! Sagt Lebwohl auf Ewigkeit dem Lande!

---

**ERIK:** Oh, this obedience, blind as your act! Your father's hint you did not fail to follow; A single blow crushes my loving heart!

**SENTA:** No more! No more may I see you, Nor think of you: higher calls are mine!

**ERIK:** What higher calls? The highest is to render What you did vow to give to me— love eternal.

**SENTA:** What love eternal did I vow to give?

**ERIK:** Senta! O Senta! Do you deny it? Is that fair day no more by you remembered, When from the vale you called me to the height, When fearlessly over rugged peaks I clamored, And gathered for you many a wild flower bright? Remember, as on rocky summit standing, Your father's ship we saw ride on the tide? We watched the sails with favored breeze expanding, Did he not into my care confide you, Your arm so sweetly round my neck entwining, Did pledge your love again, how happy both! Did press my hand, as on my breast reclining, Say, was not that, indeed, the sealing of your betrothal?

**THE FLYING DUTCHMAN:** Lost to me, forever lost! Salvation will not come to me!

**ERIK:** What must I see?

**THE FLYING DUTCHMAN:** Senta, fare well!

**SENTA:** Stay, oh, stay! Unhappy!

**ERIK:** Senta, Senta, what are you doing?

**THE FLYING DUTCHMAN:** To the sea! back to the sea! To the sea for all eternity! You have broken faith, I cannot be saved! Farewell! I'll not be your ruin!

**ERIK:** Horrid! This diabolical glance!

**SENTA:** Desist! desist! You must not go!

*(The Flying Dutchman gives a shrill signal on his whistle, and hails his crew.)*

**THE FLYING DUTCHMAN:** Hoist the sails once more, Bid the shore farewell forevermore!

---

**SENTA:** Ha, zweifelst du an meiner Treue? Unseliger,—was verblendet dich! Halt ein! Halt ein! Halt ein! Das Bündniss nicht bereue, Was ich gelobte, halte ich. Halt ein! Halt ein!

**ERIK:** Was hör' ich, Gott, was muss ich sehn! Muss ich dem Ohr, muss ich dem Auge trau'n! Was hör' ich, Gott, Senta! Willst du zu Grunde gehen? Zu mir, zu mir: du bist in Satans Klau'n!

**HOLLÄNDER:** Fort auf das Meer treibt's mich auf's Neue. Ich zweifl' an dir! Ich zweifl' an Gott! Dahin, dahin ist alle Treue. Was du gelobtest war dir nur Spott! Erfahre das Geschick, vor dem ich dich bewahr'! Verdammt bin ich zum grässlichsten der Loose! Zehnfacher Tod wär' mir erwünschte Lust. Vom Fluch ein Weib allein kann mich erlösen, Ein Weib, das Treue bis in den Tod mir hält. Wohl hast du Treue mir gelobt, Doch vor dem Ewigen noch nicht, dies rettet dich! Denn wiss'! Unselige, welches das Geschick, Das Jene trifft, die mir die Treue brechen, Ewige Verdammniss ist ihr Loos! Zahllose Opfer fielen diesem Spruch durch mich. Du aber sollst gerettet sein. Lebwohl, fahr' hin, mein Heil in Ewigkeit.

**ERIK:** Zu Hülfe, rettet, rettet Sie!

**SENTA:** Wohl kenn' ich dich! Wohl kenn' ich dein Geschick; Ich kannte dich, als ich zuerst Dich sah! Das Ende deiner Qual ist da! Ich bin's, durch deren Treu' dein Heil du finden sollst!

**ERIK:** Helft ihr, Sie ist verloren!

**MARY:** Was erblicke ich?

**DALAND:** Was erblicke ich? Gott!

**HOLLÄNDER:** Du kennst mich nicht, du ahn'st nicht, wer ich bin! Befrage die Meere aller Zonen. Befrage den Seemann, der den Ocean durchstrich, Erkenn' dies Schiff, der Schrecken aller Frommen: den Fliegenden Holländer nennt man mich.

**DIE MANNSCHAFT DES FLIEGENDEN HOLLÄNDERS:** Jo ho, hoe!

---

**SENTA:** Do not doubt my faith! Do not act rashly! Desist! desist! In faith I'll keep What I've promised. Do not act rashly! Hold on! hold on!

**ERIK:** What must I hear! what must I see! Oh, God above! how can this be! Senta, Senta, You will perish! Come to me! oh, come to me! You are in Satan's power!

**THE FLYING DUTCHMAN:** Once more to the sea forth must I wander. I cannot trust you! I cannot trust God! Away, there, with all that's trustworthy! What you promised was only in jest. Learn now the doom from which I save you! Mine is a cruel, horrid fate; Tenfold death would preferable be! Woman alone can rescue me from my curse. Woman who will be true to death. I have your vow of constancy, But not in the Eternal's presence: This from cruel fate will save you; For those who break their vow to me, Will be damned in all eternity! You shall be saved, you only! Farewell, farewell! for all eternity My curse will stay with unlucky me!

**ERIK:** Help! help quick! Save, oh save her!

**SENTA:** Your identity is No mystery to me! I know your fate, Your cruel fate; It's not too late;— I'll be your mate! For all eternity Saved you shall be By woman's constancy!

**ERIK:** Save, oh, save her!

**MARY:** What must I see!

**DALAND:** Oh, God, what must I see!

**THE FLYING DUTCHMAN:** You do not know my identity, It is to you a mystery. Do you know this ship with spectral light?— The Flying Dutchman I am called.

**CREW OF THE FLYING DUTCHMAN:** Heigho! ho! heigho!

## Act III, Scene II

**MARY, ERIK, DALAND:** Senta, Senta, was willst du thun?

**SENTA:** Preis deinen Engel und sein Gebot,
Hier steh' ich, treu dir bis zum Tod.

*(Sie stürzt sich in das Meer:—zugleich versinkt das Schiff des Holländers mit aller Mannschaft. Das Meer schwillt hoch auf und sinkt in einem Wirbel wieder zurück. Im Glüroth der aufgehenden Sonne sieht man über den Trümminern des Schiffes die verklärten Gestalten Senta's und des Holländer's sich umschlungen haltend dem Meere entsteigen und aufwärts schweben.)*

*ENDE.*

**MARY, ERIK, DALAND:** Senta, Senta, are you raving?

**SENTA:** Be cheerful in mind, be joyous in heart!
Yours will I be until death shall us part!

*(She casts herself into the sea. The Dutchman's ship, with all her crew, sinks immediately. The sea rises high, and sinks back in a whirlpool. In the glow of the sunset are clearly seen, over the wreck of the ship, the forms of Senta and the Dutchman, embracing each other, rising from the sea, and floating upwards.)*

*THE END.*

# Tannhäuser (1845)

MUSIC & LIBRETTO BY RICHARD WAGNER

This three-act opera, set to a libretto by the composer, premiered at the Hofoper in Dresden on October 19, 1845. The story takes place in Thuringia during the early thirteenth century. Venus, surrounded by her court comprised of nymphs, bacchantes and fauns, holds captive Tannhäuser, a knight and poet. He has had enough of her pleasures and implores Venus to give him his freedom. She threatens him in order to make him change his mind, but he declares the name of the Virgin Mary and causes Venus to vanish. Tannhäuser is now in a valley near Wartburg castle. Spring's arrival is heralded by a singing shepherd as Tannhäuser falls to his knees to pray. A group of pilgrims passes, headed towards Rome, and a horn announces the arrival of the Landgrave Hermann. Accompanied by his retinue of noblemen, they recognize Tannhäuser and invite him to return with them to the castle. Wolfram von Eschenbach reminds him that Elisabeth, niece of the Landgrave, is in love with him and is waiting for his return after his one-year absence. At the Hall of Minstrels in the Wartburg, Elisabeth greets her beloved, and a song contest is announced for which the grand prize is the marriage of the winner to Elisabeth. The Landgrave suggests that the theme of the contest be love. Wolfram is the first contestant; he stands and sings of the true worth of spiritual love. Tannhäuser impulsively sings a hymn to Venus which praises physical passion. The others are deeply offended by this, and the men draw swords against him. Elisabeth protects her lover, appealing to their Christian decency, and the Landgrave commands him to seek atonement by going with the pilgrims to Rome. Wolfram and Elisabeth are waiting for Tannhäuser to return, but he is not among the pilgrims travelling back. She is close to death and prays to the Madonna to grant pardon to Tannhäuser. Wolfram prays to the Evening Star to watch out for Elisabeth. Tannhäuser enters, his clothes in tatters and completely spent. The Pope has refused to grant him absolution and tells him that his soul will be saved only when the Pope's staff grows leaves once more. Tannhäuser is resigned to damnation forever and calls upon Venus, who appears in a vision of sensational, beguiling beauty. When Wolfram tells him that Elisabeth is praying for him, he rejects Venus again. Elisabeth's coffin is borne by a funeral procession; Tannhäuser embraces her lifeless body and, absolved at last, he dies. The sun rises, and the Roman pilgrims carry in the Pope's staff on which the leaves have grown. They sing praises of God's forgiveness, and the opera ends.

---

## ■ ERSTER AUFZUG.

### ERSTE SCENE.

Die Bühne stellt das Innere des Venusberges dar. Weite Grotte, welche sich im Hintergrunde durch eine Biegung nach rechts wie unabsehbar dahinzieht. Im fersten sichtbaren Hintergrunde dehnt sich ein bläulicher See aus; in ihm erblickt man die badenden Gestalten von Najaden; auf seinen erhöbten Ufervorsprüngen sind Sirenen gelagert. Im äussersten Vordergrunde links liegt Venus auf einem Lager ausgestreckt, vor ihr halb knieend Tannhäuser, das Haupt in ihrem Schoosse. Die gauze Grotte ist durch rosiges Licht erieuchtet. Den Mittelgrund nimmt eine Gruppe tanzender Nymphen ein; auf etwas erhöhten Vorsprüngen au den Seiten der Grotte sind liebende Paare gelagert, von denen sich einzelne nach und nach in den Tanz der Nymphen mischen. Ein Zug von Bacchantinnen kommt aus dem Hintergrunde in wildem Tanz dahergebraust, sie

## ■ ACT I.

### SCENE I.

The hill of Venus. The stage represents the interior of the Hill of Venus. A wide cave, bending at the back toward the right side where it appears to be indefinitely prolonged. In the farthest visible background a bluish lake is seen, in which Naiads are bathing; on its undulating banks Sirens are reclining. In the extreme foreground Venus is extended on a couch; before her, in a kneeling attitude, is Tannhäuser, his head sunk on her knees. The whole cave is illuminated by a rosy light. In the centre of the stage is a group of dancing Nymphs. There are mounds at the sides of the cave where tender couples are reclining, some of whom join the dances of the Nymphs in the course of the scene. A train of Bacchantes rush from the back of the cave in a tumultuous dance; they widly dart through the groups of Nymphs and tender couples, inciting them to a frantic excitement.

durch ziehen mit trunkenen Gebärden die Gruppen der Nymphen und liebenden Paare, welche durch sie bald zu grösserem Ungestüme hingerissen werden.

GESANG DER SIRENEN: Naht euch dem Strande,
naht euch dem Lande,
wo in den Armen
glühender Liebe
seelig Erwachen
still eure Triebe!

(Die Tanzenden halten in der leidenschaftlichsten Grupp plötzlich an und lauschen dem Gesange, worauf sich der Tanz von Neuem belebt und zu dem äussersten Grade wilden Ungestümes gelangt. Mit dem Momente der trunkensten bacchantischen Wuth tritt eine schnell um sich greifende Erschlaffung ein. Die liebenden Paare scheiden sich allmäblich vom Tanze aus und lagern sich wie in angehmer Ermattung auf den Vorsprüngen der Grotte; der Zug der Bacchantinnen verschwindet nach dem Hintergrunde zu, vor welchem sich ein immer dichter werdender Dunst ausbreitet. Auch im Vordergrunde senkt sich allmäblig

SIRENS: Come to these bowers,
Radiant with flowers.
Here love shall bless you—
Here endeth longing;
Soft arms shall press you,
Amid blessings thronging.

(The dancers suddenly pause from their wild tumult and listen to the singing, after which the dance recommences and rises to the wildest excitment. When the Bacchic frenzy is at its height a sudden weariness is seen to spread amongst the dancers. The tender couples separate themselves from the dance and rest near the entrance of the cave. The train of Bacchantes disappear in the background, where a mist gathers and spreads in density. In the foreground also a thick mist gradually sinks and envelops the groups of sleepers in rosy clouds, so that only a small space in the front of the stage remains visible, where Venus and Tannhäuser re-

ein dichterer Duft herab und verhüllt die Gruppen der Schlafenden
wie in rosige Wolken, so dass endlich der sichtbare Theil der frei ge-
lass'nen Bühne sich nur noch auf
einen kleinen Raum beschränkt,
in welchem Venus und Tannhäuser in ihrer früheren Stellung
allein zurückbleiben.)

main alone in their former attitude.)

## ZWEITE SCENE.

Venus—Tannhäuser.

(Tannhäuser zuckt mit dem
Haupte empor, als fahre er aus
einem Traume auf.—Venus zieht
ihn schmeichelnd zurück.—
Tannhäuser führt die Hand über
Augen, als ob er ein Traumbild
fest zu halten suche.)

**VENUS:** Geliebter, sag', wo weilt
dein Sinn?

**TANNHÄUSER:** Zu viel! Zu viel! O
dass ich nun erwachte!

**VENUS:** Sprich, was kümmert dich?

**TANNHÄUSER:** Im Traum war
mir'a ● hörte ich—
was meinem Ohr ● fremd?
also hörte ich der Glocken froh
Geläute.
O, sag'! Wie lange hört' ich's doch
nicht mehr?

**VENUS:** Wohin verlierst du dich?
Was ficht dich an?

**TANNHÄUSER:** Die Zeit, die hier
ich weil' ich kann sie
nicht ermessen:—Tage, Monde,—
giebt's
für mich nicht mehr, denn nicht
mehr
sehe ich die Sonne, nicht mehr des
Himmels freundlich Gestirne;—
den Halm seh' ich nicht mehr, der
frisch ergrünend
den neuen Sommer bringt;—
die Nachtigall nicht hör' ich mehr,
die mir den Lenz verkünde:—
hör ich sie nie, seh' ich sie niemals
mehr?

**VENUS:** Ha! Was vernehm' ich?
welche thör'ge Klagen!
Bist du so bald der holden Wunder
müde,
die meine Liebe der bereitet? Oder
wie? Reu't es dich so sehr, ein Gott
zu sein?
Has du so bald vergessen, wie du
einst
gelitten, während jetzt du dich erfreu'st?
Mein Sänger, auf! Ergreife deine
Harfe!
Die Liebe fei're, die so herrlich du
besingst,
dass du der Liebe Göttin selber dir
gewannst!
Die Liebe fei're, da ihr höchster
Preis dir ward!

## SCENE II.

Venus—Tannhäuser.

(Tannhäuser raises his head suddenly, as though starting from a
dream. Venus draws him back
again lovingly. Tannhäuser
draws his hand across his eyes, as
though to recall a dream.)

**VENUS:** Oh, say, my love, where
stray your thoughts?

**TANNHÄUSER:** No more, no more!
O that I now might waken.

**VENUS:** Say, what grief is yours?

**TANNHÄUSER:** I dreamt I heard
upon the air
Sounds that to me were long estranged;
The silvery chime of bells was
borne on the breezes—
Oh, say, how long has earth been
lost to me?

**VENUS:** What folly seizes you? Why
are you so disturbed?

**TANNHÄUSER:** The time I dwelt
here with you
I cannot measure by day
Seasons pass me, how I scarcely
know;
The radiant sun I see no longer;
Strange has become the heavens'
starry splendor,
The sweet verdure of spring,
The gentle token of earth's renew-
ing life;
The nightingale no more I hear
Who sings of hope and promise.
All these delights, are they forever
lost?

**VENUS:** What! are you wavering?
Why these vain lamentings?
Can you be weary of the blisses
That love immortal has cast around
you?
Can it be—do you now repent that
you're divine?
Have you so soon forgotten how
your heart was mourning
Till by me you were consoled?
My minstrel, come; let not your
harp be silent;
Recall the rapture—sing the praise
and bliss of love
In tones that won for you love's self
to be your slave.
Of love sing only, for her treasures
are all yours.

**TANNHÄUSER:** (zu einem
plötzlichen Entschlusse ermannt,
nimmt die Harfe und stellt sich
feierlich vor Venus hin).
1.
Dir töne Lob!
Die Wunder sei'n gepriesen,
die deine Macht mir Glücklichem
erschuf!
Die Wonnen süss, die deiner Huld
entspriessen,
erheb' mein Lied in lautem Jubelruf!
Nach Freude, ach! nach herrlichem
Geniessen
verlangt' mein Herz, est dürstete
mein Sinn:
da, was no Göttern einstens du erwiesen,
gab deine Gunst mir Sterblichem
dahin.
Doch sterblich, ach! bin ich geblieben,
und übergross ist mir dein Lieben;
wenn stets ein Gott geniessen kann,
bin ich dem Wechsel unterthan;
nicht Lust allein liegt mir am Herzen,
aus Freuden sehn' ich mich nach
Schmerzen;
aus deinem Reiche muss ich
flieh'n,—
O Königin, Göttin! Lass mich
zieh'n!

**VENUS:** (wie aus einem Traume
erwachend). Was muss ich hören!
Welch' ein Sang!
Welch' trübem Ton verfällt dein
Lied!
Wohin floh die Begeist'rung dir,
die Wonnesang dir nur gebot?
Was ist's? Worin war meine Liebe
lässig?
Geliebter, wessen klagest du mich
an?

**TANNHÄUSER:** (zur Harfe).
2.
Dank deiner Huld! Gepriesen sei
dein Lieben!
Beglückt für immer, wer bei dir
geweilt!
Beneidet ewig, wer mit warmen
Trieben
in deinen Armen Götterglut getheilt!
Entzückend sind die Wunder
deines Reiches,
den Zuber aller Wonnen athm' ich
hier;
kein Land der weiten Erde bietet
Gleiches,
was sie besitzt, scheint leicht ent-
behrlich dir.
Doch ich aus diesen ros'gen Düften
verlange nach des Waldes Lüften,
nach unsres Himmels klarem Blau,
nach unsrem frischen Grün der
Au',
nach unsrer Vöglein liebem Sange,
nach unsrer Glocken trautem
Klange:—
Aus deinem Reiche muss ich
flieh'n,—

**TANNHÄUSER:** (inspired with
sudden resolution, takes his harp
and stands in an earnest attitude
before Venus).
1.
All praise be yours! Immortal fame
attend;
Songs of joy be ever sung to you!
Each soft delight did lend me your
bounty sweet
Shall wake the harp while time and
love are young!
It was joy alone, a longing thirst for
pleasure,
That filled my heart and darkened
my desire;
And you, whose bounty gods alone
can measure,
Gave me, poor mortal, all its wealth
to know.
But while you have enchanted my
sense,
By thy great love my heart is daunt-
ed.
A god alone can dwell in joy—
To mortal, frail, its blisses cloy;
I would be swayed by pain and
pleasure
In Nature's sweet alternate mea-
sure.
I must away from you, or die—
Oh, Queen beloved! Goddess, let
me fly!

**VENUS:** (as though awaking from
a dream). Is this your fealty? This
your song?
It is fraught with dim and sorrowful
tones!
On, where now are the lays inspired
That ecstacy fired within you?
Oh, say in what my love has ever
been wanting?
Beloved one, oh, what doubt have
you of me?

**TANNHÄUSER:** (taking his
harp).
2.
Oh gracious fair! in numbers sweet
I'll praise you.
The ice blessed he who has known
your delights!
Grace from the skies with every
charm arrays you;
To be your slave is every bliss to
own!
In your domain the willing heart is
captured
In never-ending train of soft de-
lights;
No dark remembrance dims the
soul enraptured,
And at your feet all joys of earth it
slights.
But far from these, I long to meet
your rosy bowers,
The breath of flowers, long for the
enfolding heavenly blue,
Long for the verdure fresh with
dew,
Carols of birds, so sweet and tender,
Earth's fair expanse in noontide

O Königin, Göttin! Lass mich zieh'n!

**VENUS:** (*leidenschaftlich auf springend*). Treuloser! Weh'! Was lässest du mich hören? Du wagest meine Liebe zu verhöhnen? Du preisest sie und willst sie dennoch flieh'n: Zum Ueberdruss ist dir mein Reiz gedieh'n?

**TANNHÄUSER:** O, schöne Göttin! Wolle mir nicht zürück! Dein übergrosser Reiz ist's, ich meide.

**VENUS:** Weh' dir! Verräther! Heuchler! Undankbarer! Ich lass dich nicht! Du darfst nicht von mir zieh'n!

**TANNHÄUSER:** Nie war mein Lieben grösser, niemals wahrer, als jetzt, da ich für ewig dich muss flieh'n! (*Venus hat mit heftiger Geberde ihr Gesicht, von ihren Handen bedeckt, abgewandt. Nach einem Schweigen wendet sie es lächelnd und mit verführerischem Ausdrucke Tannhäuser wieder zu.*)

**VENUS:** (*mit leiser Stimme beginnend*). Geliebter, komm'! Sieh' dort die Grotte von ros'gen Düften mild durchwallt! Entzücken böt' selbst einem Gotte der süss'sten Freuden Aufenthalt: besänftigt auf dem weichsten Pfühle, flieh' deine Glieder jeder Schmerz, dein brennend Haupt umwehe Kühle, wonnige Glut durchschwell' dein Herz. Aus holder Ferne mahnen süsse Klänge dass dich mein Arm in trauter Näh' um schlänge; von meinen Lippen schlürfst du Göttertrank, aus meinen Augen strahlt dir Liebesdank:— ein Freudenfest soll unsrem Bund entstehen, der Liebe Feier lass uns froh begehen! Nicht sollst du ihr ein scheues Opfer weih'n,— nein!—mit der Liebe Göttin schwelge im Verein!

**SIRENEN:** (*aus weiter Ferne, unsichtbar*). Naht euch dem Strande, naht euch dem Lande!

**VENUS:** (*Tannhäuser sanft nach sich ziehend*). Mein Ritter! Mein Geliebter! Willst du flieh'n?

splendor! I must away from here or die— Oh! Queen beloved, Goddess, let me fly!

**VENUS:** (*springing from her couch*). Ungrateful! What, shall my love be slighted this way But you, in whom so dear my heart delighted? What praise is yours of joys you yet would flee? My vaunted charms, alas! have wearied you.

**TANNHÄUSER:** Oh, fair perfection! frown not on your servant! Your charms' excess, O goddess, has unmanned me!

**VENUS:** Traitor, beware, then! Serpent heart ungrateful! Ah! we'll not part this way. Ah, no; you shall not leave me.

**TANNHÄUSER:** But, bereft of your sweet presence, joy is hateful; But fate sternly impels me—I sigh for liberty. (*Venus with a cry turns away from him, burying her face in her hands. A long silence. She seeks gradually to win Tannhäuser's glance again, and suddenly turns toward him with a seductive smile.*)

**VENUS:** (*beginning in a soft voice*). Beloved one, come! Soft dreams of wonder Within yon grot shall wrap you round; The purple shadows breaking yonder Shall resound with murmuring music. There I'll shower joys unknown upon you, Within these arms you shall have rest Until for mine again I've won you— Till faith renewed your lips have confessed. The odorous airs shall tell in dulcet voices That bliss divine once more our hearts rejoices. Love has a solace for your restless heart; It were worse than dying, to part from sweet love This day renew those tender vows we plighted— In joy immortal be our hearts united. You shall no more adore the power of love— No! love itself to worship you, beloved, shall move.

**SIRENS:** (*in the far distance, invisible*). Come to these bowers, Radiant with flowers!

**VENUS:** (*drawing Tannhäuser lovingly toward her*). My hero and my heart's love! Will you fly me?

**TANNHÄUSER:** (*auf das äusserste hingerissen, nochmals die Harfe ergreifend*). 3. Stets soll nur dir, nur dir mein Lied ertönen! Gesungen laut sei unr dein Preis von mir! Dein süsser Reiz ist Quelle alles Schönen, und jedes holde Wunder stammt von dir. Die Glut, die du mir in das Herz gegosten, als Flamme lod're hell sie dir allein! Ja, gegen alle Welt will unverdrossen fortan ich nun dein kühner Streiter sein. Doch hin muss ich zur Welt der Erden, bei dir kann ich nur Sklave werden; nach Freiheit doch verlange ich, nach Freiheit, Freiheit dürstet's mich; zu Kampf und Streite will ich stehen, sei's auch auf Tod und Untergehen:— d'rum muss aus deinem Reich ich flieh'n! O Königin! Göttin! Lass mich zieh'n!

**VENUS:** (*ihm heftigsten Zorne*). Zieh' hin, Wahnsinniger, zieh' hin! Verräther, sieh', nicht halt' ich dich! Ich geb' dich frei,—zieh' hin! zieh' hin! Was du verlangst, das sei dein Loos! Hin zu den kalten Menschen flieh', vor deren blödem, trübem Wahn der Freude Götter wir entfloh'n tief in der Erde wärmenden Schoos. Zieh' hin, Bethörter! Suche dein Heil, suche dein Heil—und find' es nie! Bald weicht der Stolz aus deiner Seel',— Demüthig seh' ich dich mir nahn,— Zerknirscht, zertreten suchst du mich auf Flehst, um die Zauber meiner Macht.

**TANNHÄUSER:** Ach schöne Göttin, lebe wohl! Nie kehre ich zu dir zurück!

**VENUS:** Ha, kehrest du mir nie zurück! Kehrst du nicht wieder, ha! so sei verfluchet! Von mir das ganze menschliche Geschlect! Nach meinen Wundern dann vergebens suchet! Die Welt sei öde, und ihr Held ein Knecht! Kehr' wieder! Kehre mir zurück!

**TANNHÄUSER:** Nie mehr erfreu' mich Liebesglück!

**VENUS:** Kehr' wieder, wenn dein Herz dich zieht!

**TANNHÄUSER:** (*in the greatest emotion takes his harp once more*). 3. While I have life, alone my harp shall praise you, No meaner thing shall my song inspire. Nothing can have grace or charm but it obeys you, Of all that lives you best and chief desire. The fire you've kindled in my longing spirit An altar flame shall burn for you alone; My song shall be divine, but by the merit That, as your champion, harp and sword I own. And yet for earth I'm yearning. In your soft chains I'm burning with shame; It is freedom I must win, or die — For freedom I can all defy. I go forth to strife or glory, Come life or death, come joy or woe, No more will I sigh in bondage! Oh, Queen, beloved goddess, let me fly!

**VENUS:** (*in great fury*). Then go, oh traitor heart! away, You madman! Go! I hold you not! I set you free! Away! Go forth — your heart's desire shall be your doom! Go to the cold and joyless earth, Where neither love nor life can bloom, From where every smiling god has flown, Where dark suspicion first had birth Go forth, madman! There seek joy, and seek in vain. Soon will this fever quit your soul; Humbled and sorrowing you'll return — Remorse will gnaw you, nothing will console; For joys remembered you shall burn!

**TANNHÄUSER:** Ah, fair enchantress, farewell! Never can I return to you.

**VENUS:** Ah, if you never should return If you forget me — Oh, to lasting torments I doom The accursed and faithless race of man! For my delights they all shall vainly languish — The world a desert, and its lord a slave. Go forth, then — go, your doom to brave!

**TANNHÄUSER:** Love never more will bless your slave.

**VENUS:** Go forth, then, till your heart awake.

## Act I, Scene II

TANNHÄUSER: Für ewig dein Geliebter flieht.

VENUS: Wenn alle Welt dich von sich stösst!—

TANNHÄUSER: Von Bann werd' ich durch Buss' erlöst!

VENUS: Nie wird Vergebund dir zu Theil,—
Kehr' wieder, schliesst sich dir das Heil!

TANNHÄUSER: Mein Heil! Mein Heil ruht in Maria!
(*Furchtbarer Schlag.—Venus verschwindet.*)

### DRITTE SCENE.

*Tannhäuser. Ein junger Hirt. Pilger.*
(*Tannhäuser, der seine Stellung nicht verlassen, befindet sich plötzlich in ein schönes Thal versetzt. Blaue Himmel, heitere Sonnenbeleuchtung. Rechts im Hintergrunde die Wartburg; durch die Thalöffnung nach links erblickt man den Hörselberg.— Rechts führt auf der halben Höhe des Thales ein Bergweg von der Richtung der Wartburg her nach dem Vordergrunde zu, wo er dann seitwärts abbiegt; in demselben Vordergrunde ist ein Muttergottes-Bild, zu welchem ein niedriger Bergvorsprung binaufführt. Von der Höhe links vernimmt man das Geläute von Herde-Glocken; auf einem hohen Vorsprunge sitzt ein junger Hirt mit der Schalmei.*)

HIRT: Frau Holda kam aus dem Berg hervor,
zu ziehen durch Flur und Auen;
gar süssen Klang vernahm da mein Ohr,
mein Auge begehrte zu schauen:
da träumt, ich manchen holden Traum,
und als mein Aug' erschlossen kaum
da strahlte warm die Sonnen,
der Mai, der Mai war kommen.
Nun spiel ich lustig die Schmalmei:—
der Mai ist da, der liebe Mai!
(*Er spielt auf der Schalmei. Man bört den Gesang der älteren Pilger, welche, von der Richtung der Wartburg her kommend, auf dem Bergwege sich nähern.*)

GESANG DER ÄLTEREN PILGER:
Zu dir wall' ich mein Herr und Gott,
der zu des Sünders Hoffnung bist!
Gelobt sei, Jungfrau süss und rein,
der Wallfahrt wolle günstig sein!
(*Der Hirt, den Gesang vernehmend, bält auf der Schmalei ein und bört andächtig zu.*)
Ach, schwr drückt mich der Sünden Last,
kann länger sie nicht mehr ertrangen;

TANNHÄUSER: Ah, love, I go, although it break.

VENUS: You'll be received with hate and scorn.

TANNHÄUSER: Repentance heals a forlorn heart.

VENUS: Never will heaven open to you;
Return, then, if there is no hope.

TANNHÄUSER: No hope! My hope rests in heaven.
(*A fearful crash — Venus disappears.*)

### SCENE III.

*Tannhäuser. A Young Shepherd. Pilgrims.*
(*Tannhäuser, who has not quitted his position, suddenly finds bimself in the midst of a beautiful valley. Blue skies and sunlight. To the right in the background the Wartburg; to the left, through an opening in the vale, the Hörsel Mount is visible. To the right, half-way the height of the valley, a mountain path leads down from the direction of the Wartburg toward the foreground, where it turns aside. In the same foreground is a shrine to the Virgin, reached by ascending a slight eminence. From the heights to the left the tinkle of sheep-bells is heard; on a high cliff sits a young Shepherd playing his pipe.*)

A YOUNG SHEPHERD: Dame Holda stepped from the mountain's heart,
To roam the wood and the meadow;
Sweet sounds did start low around me—
I longed I might follow her shadow.
And there dreamt I a golden dream,
And when again the day did gleam
The spell was gone that bound me:
It was May, sweet May, around me.
Now songs of joy attune my lay,
For May has come — the balmy May!
(*He plays upon the pipe. The song of the elder Pilgrims, approaching by the mountain path from the Wartburg, is heard.*)

CHORUS OF ELDER PILGRIMS:
To You, O Lord, my steps I bend;
In You both joy and sorrow end!
Oh, Mary, pure and gracious one,
Bless the road we have begun!
(*The Shepherd, hearing the song, stops playing, and listens reverently.*)
Oh, see my heart, oppressed by guilt—
I faint, I sink beneath my burden!
Nor will I cease, nor will I rest,
Till heavenly mercy grants me par-

drum will ich auch nicht Ruh' noch Rast,
und wähle gern mir Müh' und Plagen.
Am hohen Fest der gnadenhuld
in Demuth sühn' ich meine Schuld;
gesegnet, wer im glauben treu:
er wird erlöst durch Buss' un Reu'.

HIRT: (*als die Pilger auf derr ihm gegenüberliegenden Höhe angekommen sind den Hut Schweukend und den Pilgers laut zurufend*). Glück auf! Glück auf nach Rom!
Betet für meine arme Seele!

TANNHÄUSER: (*der in der Mitte der Bühne wie festgewurzelt gestanden, sinkt beftig erschüttert auf die Kniee*). Allmächt' ger dir sei Preis!
Hehr sind die Wunder deiner Gnade.
(*Der Zug der Pilger biegt von hier an auf dem Bergwege bei dem Muttergottes-Blide links ab und verlässt so die Bühne; der Hirt entfernt sich ebenfalls mit der Schalmei rechts von der Höhe. — Man bört die Herdeglocken immer entfernter.*)

PILGERGESANG: Zu dir wall' ich mein Herr und Gott,
der du des Pilgers Hoffnung bist!
Gelobt sei, Jungfrau süss und rein,
der Wallfahrt wolle günstig sein!

TANNHÄUSER: (*singt auf den Knien, wie in brünstiges Gebet versunken, weiter.— Die Pilger haben hier bereits die Bühne verlassen*). Ach, schwer drückt mich der Sünden Last,
kann länger sie nicht mehr ertragen;
drum will ich auch nicht Ruh' noch Rast
und wähle gern mir Müh' und Plagen.
(*Thränen ersticken seine Stimme, er neigt das Haupf tief zur Erde und scheint beftig zu weinen. — Aus dem Hintergrunde, sehr entfernt, bört man Glockengeläute. Der Gesang verliert sich hier gänzlich. Während sich der Klang von Jagdhörnern von der Höhe links her immer mehr näbert, schweigt das entfernte Glockengeläute. Von der Anböbe links herab, ans einem Waldwege treten der Landgraf und die Sänger in Jägertracht einzeld auf.*)

### VIERTE SCENE.

*Tannhäuser. Der Landgraf und die Sänger.*

LANDGRAF: (*aus balber Höhe Tannhäuser erblickend*). Wer ist der dort in brünstigem Gebete?

WALTHER: Ein Büsser wohl.

don.
At your august and holy shrine
I go to seek the grace divine;
Thrice blessed who your promise know,
Absolved by penance shall they go.

SHEPHERD: (*The Shepherd, when the Pilgrims reach the opposite beight, calls loudly to them, waving his cap.*) God speed, God speed to Rome!
There, for my soul, oh breathe a prayer!

TANNHÄUSER: (*standing in the middle of the stage as though spell-bound, falls, deeply overcome, upon his knees*). Almighty, praise to you!
Great are the marvels of your mercy.
(*The procession of Pilgrims turns to the left here, on the mountain way, passing the Virgin's shrine and so leaving the stage; the Shepherd, with his pipe, also disappears from the heights and to the right. The sheep-bells are heard farther and farther in the distance.*)

PILGRIMS:
To You, O Lord, my steps I bend;
In You both joy and sorrow end!
Oh, Mary, pure and gracious one,
Bless the road we have begun!

TANNHÄUSER: (*on his knees as though absorbed in fervent prayer. The Pilgrims here have already left the stage*). Oh, see my heart, oppressed by guilt—
I faint, I sink beneath the burden!
Nor will I cease, nor will I rest
Till heavenly mercy grants me pardon!
(*Tears choke his voice. He bows his head low to the ground and seems to weep bitterly. From the far distance the chime of bells is beard. The Pilgrims' song dies entirely away here, while the sound of bunting horns, from the heights on the left, draws nearer and nearer. The bells in the distance are silent. The Landgrave and the Minstrels, in hunting dress, one by one, are seen descending from the hills to the left, by a forest path.*)

### SCENE IV.

*Tannhäuser. The Landgrave and the Minstrels.*

LANDGRAVE: (*balfway descended, seeing Tannhäuser*). Who is that knight, so deep absorbed in prayer?

WALTER: A pilgrim, sure.

BITEROLF: Nach seiner Tracht ein Ritter.

WOLFRAM: (*eilt zunächst auf Tannhäuser zu und erkennt ihn*). Er ist es!

DIE SÄNGER UND DER LANDGRAF: Heinrich! Heinrich! Seh' ich recht? (*Tannhäuser, der überrascht schnell aufgefahren ist, ermannt sich und verneigt sich stumm gegen den Landgrafen, nachdem er einen flüchtigen Blick auf ihn und die Sänger geworfen.*)

LANDGRAF: Du bist es wirklich? Kehrest in den Kreis zurück, den du in Hochmuth stolz verliessest?

BITEROLF: Sag', was uns deine Wiederkunft bedeutet? Versöhnung? Oder gilt's erneutem Kampf?

WALTHER: Nah'st du als Freund uns oder Feind?

DIE ANDERN SÄNGER AUSSER WOLFRAM: Als Feind?

WOLFRAM: O flaget nicht! Ist dies des Hochmuths Miene?— Gegrüsst sei uns, du kühner Sänger, der ach! so lang, in uns'rer Mitte fehlt!

WALTHER: Willkommen, wenn du friedlich nah'st!

BITEROLF: Gegrüsst, wenn du uns Freunde nennst.

ALLE SÄNGER: Gegrüsst! Gegrüsst! Gegrüsst sei uns!

LANDGRAF: So sei willkommen denn auch mir. Sag' an, wo weiltest du so lang!

TANNHÄUSER: Ich wanderte in weiter, weiter Fern',— da, wo ich nimmer Rast noch Ruhe fand. Fragt nicht! Zum Kampf mit euch nicht kam ich her. Seid mir versöhnt, und lasst mich weiter zieh'n.

LANDGRAF: Nicht doch! Der Uns're bist du neu worden.

WALTHER: Du darfst nich zieh'n.

BITEROLF: Wir lassen dich nich fort.

TANNHÄUSER: Last mich! Mir frommet kein Verweilen, und nimmer kann ich rastend steh'n; mein Weg heisst mich nur vorwärts eilen, denn räckwärts darf ich niemals seh'n.

DER LANDGRAF UND DIE SÄNGER: O bleib', bei uns sollst du verweilen, wir lassen dich nicht von uns geh'n. Du suchtest uns, warum enteile Nach solchem kurzen Wiederseh'n?

---

BITEROLF: By every sign, a noble.

WOLFRAM: (*hurries first to Tannhäuser and recognizes him*). Our lost one!

ALL: Henry! Henry! is it you? (*Tannhäuser, who, astonished, rises hastily, controls himself and bows mutely to the Landgrave after casting a hasty glance on him and on the Minstrels.*)

LANDGRAVE: Is it no delusion? Do you, then, return to us, Whom you so rashly abandoned?

BITEROLF: Say, what does your return this day forebode us? Is it friendship? or a challenge, as of old?

WALTER: Do you come as friend, or scornful foe?

ALL, EXCEPT WOLFRAM: As foe?

WOLFRAM: Oh, ask him not! His looks bespeak not scorning! We welcome you, gallant minstrel; Alas! too long you were estranged from us.

WALTER: Yes, welcome, if you come in peace!

BITEROLF: All hail! if we can greet as friends.

ALL: All hail, all hail! we welcome you!

LANDGRAVE: I, too, would welcome your return; But say, where did you linger for so long?

TANNHÄUSER: In strange and distant realms I wandered far, Where neither peace nor rest were ever found. Ask not! at enmity I am with none; We meet as friends—let me in peace depart.

LANDGRAVE: Depart, you shall not—we claim you for our own.

WALTER: You must not go.

BITEROLF: You shall not part from us.

TANNHÄUSER: I must! Onward I'm driven ever; Never upon earth can I have rest. The past to me is closed for ever— I'm doomed to roam alone, unblest.

ALL: Oh stay; be ours—let us not sever; Amid friends and home you shall find rest; What do you seek with vain endeavor? Why is your soul oppressed with grief?

---

WOLFRAM: (*Tannhäuser in den Weg tretend, mit erhobener Stimme*). Bleib' bei Elisabeth!

TANNHÄUSER: (*heftig und freudig ergriffen*). Elisabeth!—O Macht des Himmels, rufst du den süssen Namen mir?

WOLFRAM: Nich sollst du feind mich schelten, dass ich ihn genannt! — Eelaubest du mir, Herr dass ich Verkünder seines Glück's ihn sei?

LANDGRAF: Nenn'ihm den Zauber, den er ausgeübt, und Gott veleih' ihm Tugend, dass würdig er ihn löse! —

WOLFRAM: Als du in kühnem Sange uns bestrittest, bald siegreich gegen uns're Lieder sangst, durch uns're Kunst Besiegung bald erlittest: ein Preis doch war's, den du allein arrangst. War's Zauber, war es reine Macht, durch die solch' Wunder du vollbracht, an deinen Sang voll Wonn' und Leid gebannt die tugendreichste Maid? Denn ach! als du uns stolz verlassen, verschloss ihr Herz, sich uns'rem Lied; wir sahen ihre Wang' erblassen, für immer uns'ren Kreis sie mied. — O kehr' zurück, du kühner Sänger, dem uns'ren sei dein Lied nicht fern, — den Festen fehle sie nicht länger, auf's Neu leuchte uns ihr Stern!

DIE SÄNGER: Sei unser, Heinrich! Kehr' uns wieder Zwietracht und streit sei abgethan! Vereint ertönen uns're Lieder, und Brüder nenne uns fortan!

TANNHÄUSER: (*Tannhäuser von heftiger Rührung ergriffen, stürzt sich in Wolfram's Arme, begrüsst der Reihe nach jeden Sänger und verneigt sich innig dankend vor dem Landgrafen.*) Zu ihr! Zu ihr! Oh, führet mich zu ihr. Ha jetzt erkenne ich sie wieder, die schöne Welt, der ich entrückt! Der Himmel blickt auf mich hernieder, die Fluren prangen reich geschmückt. Der Lenz mit tausend holden Klängen zog jubelnd in die Seele mir; in süssem, ungestümen Drängen ruft laut mein Herz: zu ihr! zu ihr! (*Während des vorhergehenden hat sich nach und nach der ganze jagdtross des Landgrafen mit Falkenträgern u. s. w. auf der*

---

WOLFRAM: (*intercepting him, in a loud voice*). Here dwells Elisabeth.

TANNHÄUSER: (*in deep and joyful agitation*). Elisabeth! Oh ruth of heaven! That name adored once more I hear!

WOLFRAM: He is no foe who recalls that name to you. My sovereign lord, permit that I may tell him of the prize he won.

LANDGRAVE: Tell him the marvel that his song has wrought; And keep him, Heaven, in virtue, that nobly he may own it.

WOLFRAM: When we were contending for the palm in song, And often your conquering strain the wreath had won, Our songs anon your victory suspending, One glorious prize was won by you alone. Was it magic, or a power divine, that wrought through you the wondrous sign, of royal maids the flower! Your harp and song, in blissful hour enthralled; For ah, when you had left us in scorn Her heart was closed to joy and song. Of her sweet presence she bereft us, For you in vain she wearied long; Ah, for you in vain she wearied long. Oh, minstrel bold, return and rest, Once more awake the joyous strain; Cast off the burden that oppressed you, And her fair star will shine again!

ALL: Return, oh, Henry—you, our brother! Anger and strife shall be no more; In joy and peace with one another Our strains united let us pour.

TANNHÄUSER: (*Tannhäuser, deeply touched, throws himself into Wolfram's arms, greets the Minstrels in turn, and bows in tender gratitude to the Landgrave.*) What joy! what joy! oh, guide my steps to her! Ah! do you smile once more upon me, Radiant world that I had lost? Oh, sun of heaven, you do not shun me, By stormy clouds no longer crossed! It is May, sweet May, its thousand carols' Tender rejoicing set my sorrows free! A ray of new, unwonted splendor My soul illumes. Oh joy! it is she! (*During the foregoing, the whole hunting retinue of the Landgrave,*

*Bühne versaumelt. Die Jäger stossen in die Hörner.)*

**LANDGRAF UND DIE SÄNGER:** Er kehrt zurück, den wir verloren!
Ein Wunder hat ihn hergebracht.
Die ihm den Uebermuth beschworen,
gepriesen sei die holde Macht!
Nun lausche Euren/unsren Hochgesängen
von Neuem der Gepries'nen Ohr!
Es tön' in frohbelebten Klängen
das Lied aus jeder Brust hervor!
*(Das ganze Thal wimmelt jetzt von immer noch stärker angewachsenem Jagdtross. Der Landgraf und die Sänger wenden sich den Jägern zu; der Landgraf stösst in sein Horn, lautes Hornschmettern und Rüdengebell autwortet ihm. Während der Langraf und die Sänger die Pferde, die ihnen von der Wartburg zugeführt worden sind, besteigen, fällt der Vorhang.)*

*with falcon-bearers, etc., have assembled themselves upon the stage. The hunters sound their horns.)*

**ALL:** He returns no more to wander;
Our loved and lost is ours again.
All praise and thanks to those we render
Who could persuade, and not in vain.
Now, let your harps indite a measure
Of all that hero's hand may dare—
Of all that poet's heart can pleasure,
Before the fairest of the fair.
*(The whole valley fills now with an ever-increasing train of hunters. The Landgrave and the Minstrels join the hunters; the Landgrave sounds his horn, and loud bugle calls and the baying of hounds answer him. While the Landgrave and the Minstrels are mounting the horses, which have been led to them from the Wartburg, the curtain falls.)*

## ■ ZWEITER AUFZUG.

### ERSTE SCENE.

*(Die Sängerhalle auf der Wartburg; im Hintergrunde freie Aussicht auf dem Burghof und das Thal.)*

**ELISABETH:** *(tritt feudig bewegt ein).*
Dich, theure Halle, grüss' ich wieder,
froh grüss' ich dich, geliebter Raum!
In dir erwachen seine Lieder
und wecken mich aus düst rem Traum.
Da er aus dir geschieden,
wie öd' erschienst du mir! —
Aus mir entfloh der Frieden,
die Freude zog aus dir.
Wie jetzt mein Busen hoch sich hebet,
so scheinst du jetzt mir stolz und hehr;
der dich und mich so neu belebet,
nicht länger weilt er ferne mehr,
Sei mir gegrüsst! sei mi gegrüsst!

### ZWEITE SCENE.

*(Tannhäuser von Wolfram geleitet tritt mit diesem aus der Treppe im Hintergrunde auf.)*

**WOLFRAM:** *(zu Tannhäuser).*
Dort sie ist sie;—nahe dich ihr ungestört!
*(Er bleibt an die Mauerbrüstung gelehnt im Hintergrande.)*

**TANNHÄUSER:** *(ungestüm zu den Füssen Elisabeth's stürzend.).* O Fürstin!

## ■ ACT II.

### SCENE I.

*(The Hall of the Minstrels in the Wartburg. In the background an open view of the court and the valley.)*

**ELISABETH:** *(entering joyfully).*
Oh, Hall of Song! I give you greeting!
All hail to you, hallowed place!
It was here that dream, so sweet and fleeting,
Upon my heart his song did trace.
But since by him forsaken
You do seem a desert—
Your echoes only waken
Remembrance of a dream!
But now the flame of hope is lighted,
Your vault shall ring with glorious war;
For he whose strains my soul delighted
No longer roams afar!

### SCENE II.

*(Tannhäuser, led by Wolfram, enters from a stairway in the background.)*

**WOLFRAM:** *(to Tannhäuser).* Behold her! Nothing shall disturb your meeting.
*(He remains in the background, leaning against a pillar.)*

**TANNHÄUSER:** *(throws himself impetuously at the feet of Elisabeth).* Oh, Princess!

**ELISABETH:** *(in schüchterner Verwirrung).* Gott!—Steht auf! — Lasst mich!
Nicht darf ich euch hier seh'n! —
*(Sie will sich entfernen.)*

**TANNHÄUSER:** Du darf'st! O bleib' und zu deinen Füssen mich!

**ELISABETH:** *(sich freundlich zu ihm wendend.)* So stehet auf!
Nicht sollet hier ihr knien, denn diese Halle
ist euer Königreich. O, stehet auf!
Nehmt meinen Dank, dass ihr zurück-gekehrt!— Wo wiltet ihr so lange?

**TANNHÄUSER:** *(sich langasam erbebend).* Fern von hier, in weiten, weiten Landen.
Dichtes Vergessen hat zwischen heut' und gestern sich gesenkt.
All' mein Erinnern ist mir schnell geschwunden,
und nur des Einen muss ich mich entsinnen,
dass nie mehr ich gehofft, euch zu begrüssen,
noch je zu euch mein Auge zu erheben.—

**ELISABETH:** Was war es dann, das euch zurückgeführt?

**TANNHÄUSER:** Ein Wunder war's, ein unbegreiflich hohes Wunder!

**ELISABETH:** *(freudig aufwallend).* Gepriesen sei dies Wunder aus meines Herzens Tiefe!
*(Sich mässigend in Verwirrung).* Verzeiht, wenn ich nicht weiss, was ich beginne!
Im Traum bin ich und thör'ger als ein Kind, —
machtlos der Macht der Wunder preisgegeben.
Fast kenn' ich mich nicht mehr; o, helfen mir,
dass ich das Räthsel meines Herzens löse!—
Der Sänger klugen Weisen lauscht' ich sonst gern und viel!
ihr Singen und ihr Preisen schien mir ein holdes Spiel.
Doch welch' ein seltsam neues Leben
rief euer Lied mir in die Brust!
Bald wollt' es mich wie Schmerz durchbeben,
bald drang's in mich wie jähe Lust:
Gefühle, die ich nie empfunden!
Verlangen, das ich nie gekannt!
Was einst mir lieblich, war verschwunden
vor Wonnen, die noch nie genannt!
Und als ihr nun von uns gegangen, —
war Frieden mir und Lust dahin;
die Weisen, die die Sänger sangen,
erschienen matt mir, trüb' ihr Sinn;
im Traume fühlt' ich dumpfe Schmerzen
mein Wachen ward trübsel'ger Wahn;
die Freude zog aus meinem Her-

**ELISABETH:** *(in timid confusion).* Heaven! do not kneel! leave me
Here, thus we should not meet.
*(She moves to depart.)*

**TANNHÄUSER:** We may! oh, stay, And let me kneel forever here!

**ELISABETH:** *(turning toward him gently).* I pray you rise!
It is not for you to kneel where you have conquered.
This hall is your domain. Rise, I implore!
Thanks be to heaven that you returned to us!
Where have you tarried so long?

**TANNHÄUSER:** *(slowly rising).*
Far away, in strange and distant regions —
And between yesterday and today oblivion's veil has fallen.
Every remembrance has forever vanished,
Save one thing only, rising from the darkness —
That I then dared not hope I should behold you,
Nor evr raise mine eyes to your perfection.

**ELISABETH:** How were you led now to return to us?

**TANNHÄUSER:** A marvel it was, by heaven wrought within my spirit.

**ELISABETH:** *(in joyful emotion).*
I praise the power that wrought it From my heart's recesses!
*(More quietly and in confusion.)*
Forgive — I scarcely know what I am saying:
Your presence here, a vision it seems —
Strange dream of life, mysterious and alluring.
The world to me is changed. Can you declare
What this emotion betokens to my heart!
In minstrels' lays delighting
I marked and listened long and often;
Their subtle, sweet inditing
To me seemed dalliance soft.
But now the past to me is darkened—
Repose and joy from me have flown;
Since fondly to your lays I've hearkened
The pangs and bliss of woe I've known.
Emotions that I comprehend not,
And longings never guess before —
Upon my biddings they depend not,
But fled are all delights of yore.
And when this land you had forsaken
Repose and joy for me were fled;
No minstrel could my heart awaken—
To me their lays seemed sad and dead.

zen:—
Heinrich! Was thatet ihr mir an?

TANNHÄUSER: (hingerissen).
Den Gott der Liebe sollst du preisen,
er hat die Saiten mir berührt,
er sprach zu dir aus meinen Weisen,
zu dir hat er mich hergeführt!

ELISABETH: Gepriesen sei die Stunde!
gepriesen sei die Macht,
die mir so holde Kunde
von eurer Näh' gebracht!
Von Wonneglanz umgeben
lacht mir der Sonne Schein;
erwacht zu neuem Leben,
nenn' ich die Freude mein.

TANNHÄUSER: Gepriesen sei die Stunde,
gepriesen sei die Macht.
die mir so holde Kunde
aus deinem; Mund gebracht.
Dem neu erkannten Leben
darf ich mich muthig weih'n.
ich nenn' in freud'gem Beben
sein schönstes Wunder mein!

WOLFRAM: (in Hintergrunde).
So flieht für dieses Leben
mir jeder Hoffnung Schein!
(Tannhäuser trennt sich von Elisabeth; er geht auf Wolfram zu, umarmt ihn heftig und entfernt sich mit ihm durch die Treppe. Elisabeth blickt Tannhäuser vom Balkon aus nach.)

## DRITTE SCENE.

(Der Landgraf tritt aus einem Seitengange auf. Elisabeth eilt auf ihn zu und birgt ihr Gesicht an seiner Brust.)

Landgraf: Dich treff' ich hier in dieser Halle, die
so lange du gemieden? Endlich denn
lockt dich ein Sängerfest, das wir bereiten?

ELISABETH: Mein Oheim! O, mein gut'ger Vater!

LANDGRAF: Drängt es dich, dein Herz mir endlich zu erschliessen?

ELISABETH: Blick' mir in's Auge! Sprechen kann ich nicht.

LANDGRAF: Noch bleibe denn unausgesprochen
dein süss Geheimniss kurze Frist;
der Zauber bleibe ungebrochen,
bis du der Lösung mächtig bist.—
So sei's! Was der Gesang so Wunderbares
erweckt und angeregt, soll heute er
enthüllen auch und mit Vollendung Krönen.
Die holde Kunst, sie werde jetzt zur That!
Schon nahen sich die Edlen meiner

In slumber often near broken-hearted,
Awake, each pain fondly recalled,
All joy has departed from my life.
Henry, Henry, why am I enthralled?

TANNHÄUSER: (ennraptured).
All praise to love for this fair token!
Love touched my harp with magic sweet —
Love through my song, to you has spoken,
And leads me captive at your feet.

ELISABETH: Oh blessed hour of meeting,
Oh blessed power of love!
At last I give you greeting,
No longer you will rove!
Now life renewed awakens,
Within this heart of mine,
The cloud of sorrow breaks,
The sun of joy shall shine!

TANNHÄUSER: Oh blessed hour of meeting,
Oh blessed power of love,
At last I give you greeting,
No more to rove from here!
Now life renewed awakes us
The hope that once was mine,
The cloud of sorrow breaks,
I know but joy divine!

WOLFRAM: (in the background).
My heart forsakes all hope,
Never will her heart be mine!
(Tannhäuser parting from Elisabeth, goes to Wolfram and, embracing him fervently, disappears with him by the stairway. Elisabeth watches his departure from the balcony.)

## SCENE III.

(The Landgrave enters from a side entrance. Elisabeth hastens to meet him hiding her face upon his breast.)

LANDGRAVE: You've come at last to grace the contest?
Will you shun these walls no longer?
What has lured you from your solitude
To come among us?

ELISABETH: My sovereign, oh, my more than father!

LANDGRAVE: Will you, then, at last reveal to me your secret?

ELISABETH: I cannot tell it; read my eyes, and know.

LANDGRAVE: This day it shall still be unspoken—
Your treasured thought you need not own;
The spell shall yet remain unbroken
Till what the future brings is known.
So be it. The wondrous flame that song has kindled
This day shall brightly soar;
Your joy, all hearts rejoicing,
Shall on this day be crowned:

Lande,
die ich zum selt'nen Fest hieher beschied!
zahlreicher nahen sie als je, da sie gehört, dass du des Festes Fürstin sei'st.

## VIERTE SCENE.

(Trompeten im burghofe. Der Landgraf und Elisabeth treten an den Balkon, um nach der Ankunft der Gäste zu sehen. Vier Edelknaben treten auf und melden an. Sie erhalten vom Landgrafen Befehl für den Empfang u. s. w. Die Ritter und Grafen treten einzeln mit Edelfrauen und Gefolge ein, welches im Hintergrunde bleibt und werden vom Landgrafen und von Elisabeth empfangen.)

CHOR: Freudig begrüssen wir die edle Halle,
wo Kunst und Frieden immer nur verweil',
wo lange noch der frohe Ruf erschalle:
Thüringens Fürsten, Landgraf Hermann, Heil!
(Die Versammeiten haben alle die ihnen angewiesenen, einen grossen Halbkreis bildenden Plätze eingenommen. Die Sänger treten auf, begrüssen feierlich die Versammlung und werden von den Edelknaben nach ihren Sitzen geleitet.)

LANDGRAF: Gar viel und schön ward hier in dieser Halle
von euch, ihr lieben Sänger schon gesungen:
in weisen Räthseln wie in heit'ren Liedern
erfreutet ihr gleich sinnig unser Herz.—
Wenn unser Schwert in blutig ernsten Kämpfen
stritt für des deutschen Reiches Majestät,
wenn wir dem grimmen Welfen widerstanden
und dem verderbenvollen Zwiespalt wehrten:
so ward von euch nicht mind'rer Preiserrungen.
Der Anmuth und der holden Sitte,
der Tugend und dem reinen Glauben
erstrittet ihr durch eure Kunst gar hohen, herrlich schönen Sieg.—
Bereitet heute uns denn auch ein Fest,
heut, wo der kühne Sänger uns zurückgekehrt,
den wir so ungern lang' vermissten.
Was wieder ihn in uns're Nähe brachte,
ein wunderbar Geheimniss dünkt es mich:

What has been sung shall spring to life for you.
This day will see our nobles all assembled—
To grace the solemn feast they now approach!
None will be absent, since they know,
That once again your hand bestows the victor's wreath.

## SCENE IV.

(The Landgrave and Elisabeth go on to the balcony, to watch the arrival of the guests. Four noble Pages enter and announce them. They receive commands from the Landgrave for their reception, etc. The Knights and Counts with their Ladies and retinue, which remains in the background enter singly and are received by the Landgrave and Elisabeth.)

CHORUS: Hail, bright abode, where song the heart rejoices,
May lays of peace within you never fail,
Long may we cry with loyal voices,
Prince of Thuringia, Landgrave Hermann. hail!
(The assembly have all taken the places assigned them forming a large half-circle. The Minstrels enter, greet the assembly in stately fashion and are led to their places by the noble Pages.)

LANDGRAVE: (rising). Minstrels assembled here, I give you greeting.
Often within these walls your lays have sounded;
In veiled wisdom, or in mirthful measures
They ever gladdened every listening heart.
And though the sword of strife was loosed in battle,
Drawn to maintain our German land secure,
When against the southern foe we fought and conquered,
And for our country braved the death of heroes,
Unto the harp be equal praise and glory!
The tender graces of the homestead,
The faith in what is good and gracious—
For these you fought with word and voice:
The meed of praise for this is due.
Your strains inspiring, then, once more attune,
Now that the gallant minstrel has to us returned
Who from our land too long was parted.
To what we owe his presence her

durch Liedes Kunst soll't ihr es uns enthüllen,

deshalb stell' ich die Frage jetzt an euch

könnt ihr der Liebe Wesen mir ergründen?

Wer es vermag, wer sie am würdigsten

besigt, dem reich' Elisabeth den Preis:

er ford're ihn so hoch un kühn er wolle,

ich sorge, dass sie ihn gewähren solle.—

Auf! liebe Sänger! Greifet in die Saiten!

Die Aufgab' ist gestellt, Kämpft um den Preis

und nehmet all' im vorans uns'ren Dank!

**CHOR, DER RITTER UND EDELKNABEN:** Heil! Heil! Thüringens Fürsten Heil

Der holden kunst Beschulzer Heil!

(*Alle setzen sich. Die Vier Edelknaben treten hervor sie sammeln in einem goldenen Becher von jedem der Sänger seinen auf ein zusammengerolltes Blättchen gezeichneten Namen und reichen den Becher Elisabeth welche eines der Blättchen herauszieht und es wiede rum den Edelknaben reicht; diese lesen den Namen und treten dann feierlich in die Mitte.*)

**VIER EDELKNABEN:** Wolfram von Eschenbach, beginne!

(*Sie setzen sich zu Füssen des Landgrafen und Elisabeths nieder. Wolfram erhebt sich. — Tannhäuser stützt sich, wie in Träumerei verfallen, auf seine Harfe.*)

**WOLFRAM:** Blick' ich umher in diesen edlen Kreise,

welch' hoher Anblick macht mein Herz erglüh'n!

So viel der Helden, tapfer, deutsch und weise,

ein stolzer Eichwald, herrlich, frisch und grün.

Und hold und tugendsam erblick' ich Frauen, —

lieblicher Blüthen düftereischsten Krans.

Es wird der Blick wohl trunk mir vom hauen,

mein Lied verstummt vor Anmuth Glanz.—

Da blick' ich auf zu einem nur der Sterne,

der an dem Himmel, der mich blendet,steht:

es sammelt sich mein Geist aus jeder Ferne,

andächtig sinkt die Seele in Gebet.

Und sieh'! Mir zeiget sich ein Wunderbronnen,

in den mein Geist voll hohen Staunens blickt:

aus ihm er schöpfet gnadenreiche

among us

In strange, mysterious darkness still is wrapped;

The magic power of song shall not reveal it.

Therefore here now you all shall sing the theme.

Say, what is love? by what signs shall we know it.

This be your theme. Whoso most nobly this can tell,

Him shall the Princess give the prize.

He may demand the fairest guerdon:

I vouch that whatever he ask is granted.

Up, then, arouse—sing, oh, gallant minstrels!

Attune your harps to love—great is the prize.

Before you begin, let all receive our thanks!

**CHORUS:** Hail! Hail! Lord of Thuringia!

Hail! protector of gentle song!

(*All seat themselves. The four Pages advance, collecting the names of the singers (which each has written on a folded slip of paper) in a golden cup. This cup they present to Elisabeth, who draws one of the papers out and hands it to the Pages, who read the name and then advance ceremoniously into the midst of the assembly.*)

**FOUR PAGES:** Wolfram from Eschenbach, begin!

(*They seat themselves at the feet of the Landgrave and Elisabeth. Wolfram rises. Tannhäuser leans, as though dreaming, upon his harp.*)

**WOLFRAM:** Gazing around upon this fair assembly,

How the heart expands to see the scene!

These gallant heroes, valiant, wise and gentle—

A stately forest soaring fresh and green.

And blooming by their side, in sweet perfection,

I see a wreath of dames and maidens fair;

Their blended glories dazzle the beholder—

My song is mute before this vision rare.

I raised my eyes to one whose stately splendor

In this bright heaven with mild effulgence beams,

And gazing on that pure and tender radiance,

My heart was sunk in prayerful, holy dreams.

And lo! the source of all delights and power

Was then revealed unto my listening soul,

Wonnen,

durch die mein Herz er namenlos erquickt.

Und nimmer möcht' ich diesen Bronnen trüben,

berühren nicht den Quell mit frevlem Muth:

in Anbetung möcht' ich mich opfernd üben,

vergiessen froh mein letztes Herzensblut.

Ihr Edlen mög't in diesen Worten lesen,

wie ich erkenn' der Liebe reinstes Wesen!

**DIE RITTER UND DIE FRAUEN:** (*in beifälliger Bewegung*). So ist's! So ist's! Gepriesen sei dein Lied!

(*Tannhäuser fährt wie ans dem Traume auf; seine trotzige Miene nimmt sofort den Ausdruck der Entzückung an, mit welchem er in die Luft vor sich hinstarrt; ein leises Zittern der Hand, die bewusstlos nach den Saiten der Harfe sucht, ein unheimliches Lächeln des Mundes zeigt an, dass ein fremder Zauber sich seiner bemächtigt. Als er dann, wie erwachend, kräftig in die Harfe greift, verräth seine ganze Haltung, dass er kaum mehr weiss, wo er ist und namentlich Elisabeth nicht mehr beachtet.*)

**TANNHÄUSER:** O Wolfram, der du also sangest,

du hast die Liebe arg entstellt!

Wenn du in solchem Schmachten bangest,

versiegte wahrlich wohl die Welt.

Zu Gottes Preis in hoch erhab'ne Fernen,

blickt auf zum Himmel, blickt zu seinen Sternen!

Aubetung solchen Wundern sollt,

da ihr sie nicht begreifen sollt!

Doch, was sich der Berührung beuget,

mir Herz und Sinnen nahe liegt,

was sich, aus gleichem Stoff erzeuget,

in weicher Formung an mich schmiegt,

dem ziemt Genuss in freud'gem Triebe

und im Genuss nur kenn ich Liebe!

(*Allgemeines Erstaunen. Elisabeth im Widerstrebt mit Hiugerissenheit und banger Befremdung.*)

**BITEROLF:** (*sich mit Ungestüm erhebend*). Heraus zum Kampfe mit uns Allen!

Wer bliebe ruhig, hört er dich?

Wird deinem Hochmuth es gefallen,

so höre, Läst'rer, nun auch mich!

Wenn mich begeistert hohe Liebe,

stählt sie die Waffen mir mit Muth;

dass ewig ungeschmäht sie bliebe,

vergöss' ich stolz mein letztes Blut.

Für Frauenehr' und hohe Tugend

als Ritter kämpf' ich mit dem Schwert;

From whose unfathomed depths all joy showers—

The tender balm in which all grief is healed.

Oh, never may I dim its limpid waters,

Or rashly trouble them with wild desires!

I worship you kneeling, with soul devoted:

My heart aspires to live and die for you!

I know not if these feeble words can render

What I have felt of love both true and tender.

**CHORUS OF NOBLES AND LADIES:** (*applauding*). They do! They do! We praise your noble song!

(*Tannhäuser as though arising from a dream; his defiant mien changes to an expression of exquisite delight as he gazes into vacancy; a slight trembling of the hand, which has sought unconsciously the strings of the harp, an uncanny smile of the mouth, indicate that a strange Magic has control of him. As he then, as though awaking, sweeps his harp strings powerfully, his whole bearing betrays that he scarce knows now where he is and seems no more to be aware of Elisabeth's presence.*)

**TANNHÄUSER:** Oh, minstrel, if it is thus you sing,

You never have known or tasted love!

If cold and timid heart you bring,

A weary lot your joy must prove!

If you desire an unapproached perfection—

Behold the stars—adore their bright reflection—

They were not made to be beloved:

They never by human prayer were moved!

But what can yield to soft caresses,

And, framed with me in mortal mould,

Gentle persuasion's rule confesses,

And in these arms I may enfold—

This is for joy, and knows no measure,

For love's fulfillment is its pleasure!

(*General consternation. Elisabeth in conflicting emotions of rapture and anxious surprise.*)

**BITEROLF:** (*arises quickly and angrily*). To mortal combat I defy you!

Shameless blasphemer, draw your sword!

As brother henceforth we deny you:

Your words profane too long we've heard!

If I have spoken of love divine,

Strengthening in valor, sword and heart,

Its glorious spell shall be unbroken,

Although I part from life this hour.

doch, was Genuss beut deiner Jugend,
ist wohlfeil, keines Streitches werth.

For womanhood and noble honor I would go
Through death and danger;
But for the cheap delights that won you
I scorn them as not worth a blow!

**DIE ZUHORER:** (*in tobendem Beifalle*). Heil, Biterolf! Hier unser Schwert!

**CHORUS OF NOBLES AND LADIES:** (*applauding wildly*). Hail Biterolf! Come, draw your sword!

**TANNHÄUSER:** (*mit immer steigender Hitze auffahrend*). Ha, thör'ger Prahler, Biterolf!
Singst du von Liebe, grimmer Wolf?
Gewisslich hast du nicht gemeint,
was mir geniessenswerth erscheint.
Was hast du Aermster wohl genossen?
Dein Leben war nicht liebereich,
und was von Freuden dir entprossen,
das galt wohl wahrlich keinen Streich!

**TANNHÄUSER:** (*with ever increasing vehemence*). Yea, idle boaster, Biterolf!
Shall love be sung by you, grim wolf?
Not that you have ever known of bliss;
Its sweetness your fierce heart must miss.
Poor weary soul, what joy has blessed you?
What rapture could you ever know?
If any pale delight possessed you,
That were indeed not worth a blow!

**RITTER:** (*in grösster Aufregung*). Lass't ihn nicht enden!— Wehret seinen Kühuheit!

**NOBLES:** (*in the greatest excitement*). We will not hear him; stay his daring madness!

**LANDGRAF:** (*zu Biterolf, der das Schwert zieht*). Zurück das Schwert! Ihr Sänger, halten Frieden!
(*Wolfram erbebt sich; bei seinem Beginn tritt gleich die grösster Ruhe ein.*)

**LANDGRAVE:** (*to Biterolf, who has drawn his sword*). Put up your sword! There must be peace between you.
(*Wolfram arises; as he begins, the most profound quiet ensues.*)

**WOLFRAM:** O Himmel, lass dich jetzt erflehen,
gieb meinem Lied der Weihe Preis!
Gebannt lass mich die Sünde sehen
aus diesem edlen, reinen Kreis!
Dir, hohe Liebe, töne
begeistert mein Gesang,
die mir im Engels-Schöne
tief in die Seele drang!
Du nah'st als Gottgesandte,
ich folg' aus holder Fern',—
so fürst du in die Lande,
wo ewig strahlt dein Stern.

**WOLFRAM:** O Heaven! let me here implore you!
Hallow my song to holy praise.
Let sin crouch in the dust before you,
Nor dare among us to raise its head!
Your noble love, inspire me,
Let me sing your glory—
Your flame immortal fire me,
Fanned by an angel's wing!
You've come, descended from Heaven;
I follow you afar.
Attended by every joy,
Your star forever shines!

**TANNHÄUSER:** (*in äusserster Verzückung*). Dir, Göttin der Liebe, soll mein Lied ertönen!
Gesungen laut sei jetzt dein Preis von mir!
Dein süsser ist Quelle alles Schönen,
und jedes Wunder stammt von dir!
Wer dich mit glut in seinen Arm geschlossen,
was Liebe ist, kennt er, nur er allein:—
Armsel'ge, die ihr Liebe nie genossen,
zieht hin, zieht in den Berg der Venus ein!
(*Allgemeiner Aufbruch und Entsetzen.*)

**TANNHÄUSER:** (*in the most extreme exaltation*). Goddess of love, you shall now inspire my measure;
In joyful strains your praise be ever sung!
You are the source of all in life we treasure,
Your sweet delights are ever fair and young!
Whose burning soul once with ardor embraced you
Can speak of love; none else can prove its joys!
Dull mortals, who have never tasted love;
Go forth! Venus alone can show you love!
(*General disorder and horror.*)

**ALLE:** Ha, der Verruchte! Fliehet ihn!
Hört es! Er war im Venusberg!

**ALL:** Ah, hear the miscreant! hence, away!
Hear him! He has been with Venus!

**DIE EDELFRAUEN:** Hinweg! Hinweg aus seiner Näh'!
(*Die Frauen verlassen in grösster Bestürzung und mit Gebärden des Abscheu's die Halle. Elisabeth, die dem Streite der Sänger mit wachsender Angst zugehört hatte, bleibt von den Frauen allein zurück,—bleich, nur mit dem grössten Aufwande ihrer Kraft an einer der hölzernen Säulen des Baldachins sich aufrecht erhaltend. Der Landgraf, alle Ritter und Sänger haben ihre Plätze verlassen und treten zusammen. Tannhäuser, zur äussersten Linken, verbleibt noch eine Zeit lang wie in Verzückung.*)

**LADIES:** Away! away! nor near him stay!
(*The ladies leave the ball in the greatest dismay and with gestures of horror. Elisabeth, who has listened to the strife among the Minstrels with growing anxiety, alone remains behind,—pale and trembling, supporting herself against one of the wooden pillars of the royal Dais.—The Landgrave and all the Knights and Minstrels have left their seats and are gathered together. Tannhäuser at the extreme left, remains still a long time as though enraptured.*)

**LANDGRAF, RITTER UND SÄNGER:** Ihr habt's gehört! Sein frevler Mund
that das Bekenntniss schrecklich kunk.
Er hat der Hölle Lust getheilt,
im Venusberg hat er geweilt!—
Eutsetzlich! Scheusslich! Fluchenswerth!
In seinem blute netzt das Schwert!
Zum Höllenpfuhl zurückgesandt,
sei er gefehmt, sie er gebannt!
(*Alle dringen mit gezücktem Schwerte auf Tannhäuser ein; Elisabeth stüzt dazwischen.*)

**LANDGRAVE, KNIGHTS AND NOBLES:** You all have heard,
His mouth has confessed,
That he has shared the joys of Hell
In Venus' dark abode that dwell.
Disown him—curse him—banish him!
Or let his traitor life-blood flow!
Anathema, we call on you
In hellish fires forever glow!
(*All press with swords drawn toward Tannhäuser; Elisabeth rushes between them.*)

**ELISABETH:** Haltet ein! —
(*Alle halten in grösster betroffenheit an.*)

**ELISABETH:** Stay your hands!
(*All forbear in the greatest amazement.*)

**LANDGRAF, RITTER UND SÄNGER:** Was seh' ich? Wie, Elisabeth!
Die keusche Jungfrau für den Sünden?

**LANDGRAVE, KNIGHTS AND NOBLES:** Oh, wonder! You, Elisabeth,
The peerless maiden, shield the guilty?

**ELISABETH:** (*Tannhäuser mit ihrem Leibe deckend*). Zurück!
Des todes achte ich sonst nicht
Was ist die Wunde eures Eisens gegen
den Tödesstoss, den ich von ihm empfingt.

**ELISABETH:** (*shielding Tannhäuser with her body*). Stand back!
or pierce this bosom with your swords!
Death and its terrors cannot crush me
Like to the deadly wound that he has struck me here.

**LANDGRAF, RITTER UND SÄNGER:** Elisabeth! Was muss ich hören?
Wie liess dein Herz dich so bethören.
von dem die Strafe zu beschwören,
der auch so furchtbar dich verrieth?

**LANDGRAVE AND NOBLES:** O royal maid, can we believe you?
Let not your guileless heart deceive you?
Nor let his fate accursed grieve you.
You more than all the wretch should scorn!

**ELISABETH:** Was liegt an mir?
Doch er,—sein Heil Wollt ihr sein ewig Heil ihm rauben?

**ELISABETH:** Think not of me! He must be saved!
You would not rob his hope of Heaven?

**LANDGRAF, RITTER UND SÄNGER:** Verworfen hat er jedes Hoffen,
niemals wird ihm des Heil's Gewinnt
Des himmels Fluch hat ihm getroffen,
in seinen Sünden fahr' er nin!
(*Sie dringen von Neuem auf Tannhäser ein.*)

**LANDGRAVE AND NOBLES:** Forever lost his hope for Heaven—
Madly his joy he cast aside!
A crime like his is never forgiven:
The curse of Heaven with him abide
(*They rush again upon Tannhäuser.*)

**ELISABETH:** Zurück von ihm! Nieht ihr seid sein Richter! Grausame! Werft von euch das wilde Schwert und gebt Gehör der reinen Jungfrau Wort! Vernehmt durch mich, was Gottes Wille ist!— Der Unglücksel'ge, den gefangen ein furchtbar mächt'ger Zauber hält, wie? sollt' er nie zum Heil gelangen durch Reu' und Buss' in dieser Welt Die ihr so stark im reinen Glauben, verkennt ihr so des Höchsten Rath? Wollt er des Sünders Hoffnung rauben. so sagt, was euch er Liedes that? Seht mich, die Jungfrau, deren Blüth mit einem jähen Schlag er brach— die ihn geliebt tief im Gemüthe, der jubelnd er das Herz zerstach: ich fleh' für ihn, ich flehe für sein Leben zur Busse lenk' er reuevoll den Schritt! Der Muth des Glaubens sei ihm neu gegeben, dass auch für ihn einst der Erlöser litte.

**TANNHÄUSER:** (*in furchtbarer Zerknirschung zusammenstürzend*). Weh'! Weh' mir Unglücksel'gem!

**LANDGRAF, RITTER und SÄNGER:** (*allmählich beruhigt und gerührt*). Ein Engel stieg aus lichtem Aether, zu künden Gottes heil' gen Rath. Blick' hin, du schändlicher Verräther, werd' inne deiner Missethat! Du gabst ihr Tod, sie bittet für dein Leben; wer bliebe rauh, hört er des Engels Fleh'n? Darf ich auch nicht dem Schuldigen vergeben, dem Himmelswort kann ich nicht widersteh'n.

**TANNHÄUSER:** Zum Heil den Sündigen zu führen, die Gottgesandte nahte mir: doch, ach! sie frevelnd zu berühren hob ich den Lästerblick zu ihr! O du, hoch über diesen Erdengründen, die mir den Engel meines Heil's gesandt, erbarm' dich ach! so tief in Sünden schmachvoll des Himmels Mittlerin verkannt! (*Der Langraf tritt feierlich in die Mitte.*)

**LANDGRAF:** Ein furchtbares Verbrechen ward begangen: — es schlich mit heuchlerischer Larve sich zu uns der Sünde fluchbelad'ner Sohn. Wir stossen dich von uns, bei uns darfst du

**ELISABETH:** Away from him! It is not for you to judge him! Shame on you! He is one against you all! Oh, let a spotless maid your grace implore. Let Heaven declare through me what is its will!— The erring mortal, who has fallen Within the weary toils of sin, How dare you close the heavenly portal Where he on earth his shrift may win? If you are strong in faith and honor, Why do you not obey His word Who gave to us the law of mercy— Who never from sinner turned away? On me, a maiden young and tender, That knight has struck a cruel blow; I, who so deeply, truly loved him, Am hurled in dark abyss of woe! I pray for him—spare him! oh, I implore you! Let not the hope of pardon be denied! To life renewed his sinking faith restore you. Think that for him, too, once the Savior died.

**TANNHÄUSER:** (*in fearful contrition falls to the floor*). Oh! lost, and forever!

**LANDGRAVE, KNIGHTS AND NOBLES:** (*gradually quieted and touched*). An angel has descended from heaven To bear us God's most high behest. Behold and see whom you've offended! Your crime forever haunt your rest! You gave her death — she prays that your life be spared! Who would not yield who heard the heavenly maid? Though as accursed and guilty I declared you, The voice of Heaven by me shall be obeyed.

**TANNHÄUSER:** From door of wrath to save the sinner An angel was sent from on high, But ah! profanely here to win her I would have dared with mad intent! O you, throned above our mortal frailty, You who have sent this guardian saint to me, Have mercy! I cry to you despairing! Oh, from the gulf of error set me free! (*The Landgrave in great solemnity steps into their midst.*)

**LANDGRAVE:** A crime dark and unheard of has befallen; In mask of loyal knight there treacherously Stole amongst us Sin's accursed child. You are disowned by us— You are banished from this land.

nicht weilen; schmachbefleckt ist unser Herd durch dich, und dräuend blickt der Himmel selbst auf dieses Dach, das dich zu lang' schon birgt Zur Rettung doch vor ewigem Verderben steht offen dir ein Weg; von mir dich stossend zeig' ich ihn dir: — nütz ihn zu deinem Heil! — Versammelt sind aus meinen Landen bussfert'ge Pilger, stark an Zahl: die ält'ren schon voran sich wandten, die jüng'ren rasten noch im Thal, Nur um geringer Sünde willen, ihr Herz nicht Ruhe ihnen lässt, Der Busse frommen Drang zu stillen, zieh'n sie nach Rom zum Gnadenfest.

**LANDGRAF, RITTER und SÄNGER:** Mit ihnen sollse du wallen zur Stadt der Gnadenhuld, im Staub' dort niederfallen und büssen deine Schuld! Vor ihm stürz' dich darnieder der Gottes Urtheil spricht; doch kehre nimmer wieder, ward dir sein Segen nicht! Musst' uns're Rache weichen, weil sie ein Engel brach: des Schwert wird dich erreichen, harrst du in Sünd' und Schmach.

**ELISABETH:** Lass hin zu dir ihn wallen, du Gott der Gnad' und Huld! Ihm, der so lief gefallen, vergieb der Sünden Schuld. Für ihn nur will ich flehen, mein Leben sei Gebet; lass ihn den Leuchten sehen, eh' er in Nacht vergeht! Mit freudigem Erbeben lass der ein Opfer weih'n! Nimm hin, o nimm mein Leben nicht neun' ich es mehr mein.

**TANNHÄUSER:** Wie soll ich Gnade finden, wie büssen meine Schuld? Mein Heil sah ich entschwinden, mich flieht des Himmels Huld. Doch will ich büssend wallen, zerschlagen meine Brust, im Staube niederfallen, — Zerknirschung sei mir Lust: O, dass nur er versöhnet, der Engel meiner Noth, der sich, so frech vernönet, zum Opfer doch mir bot! (*Alle haben unwillkürlich ihre Gebärden gemässigt. Elisabeth, wie um Tannhäuser nochmals zu schützen, hatte sich den von neuem Andringenden entgegengestellt; sie verweist jetzt auf den verheissungsvolen Gesang der jungen Pilger. — Tannhäuser*

You have stained this threshold pure with shame. The wrath of heaven may strike the roof That shelters you, too long defiled by guilt. One path alone can save you from perdition, From everlasting woe — by earth abandoned — One way is left. That way you now shall know. A band of pilgrims now assemble From every part of my domain. This morn the elders went before them; The rest yet remain in the vale. It is not for crimes like yours they tremble And leave their country, friends and home — Desire for heavenly grace is over them — They seek the sacred shrine at Rome.

**LANDGRAVE, KNIGHTS AND NOBLES:** It is there, repentant kneeling Before the shrine of grace, Your heart in tears annealing, Your sin you shall efface. In dust bow down before him Who holds the keys of Heaven, But nevermore returning Unless by him forgiven! Our just revenge we resigned, Because an angel prayed; But yet this sword shall find you Unless you seek Heaven's aid!

**ELISABETH:** Great Heaven, repentant kneeling, A sinner sues for grace; revealing your bounteous love, Turn not away your face. In dust bending before him Who holds the keys of Heaven, Oh, let your light restore him, Oh, let him be forgiven! All hope on earth resigning, I implore you for aid; My life, without repining, I offer up, a maid!

**TANNHÄUSER:** Oh, where shall I find mercy? Oh, where shall I find rest? All hope from me has vanished. Despair within my breast! I'll go, repentant kneeling Before the throne of grace; If bitter tears are healing, In dust I'll hide my face. Oh, let me be forgiven By her, the heavenly maid Whose heart by me was riven — Whom basely I betrayed! (*All have involuntarily moderated their gestures. Elisabeth as though again to shield Tannhäuser places herself between him and the approaching Pilgrims, she calls attention now to the comforting promise of the Pilgrim's song.*)

hält plötzlich in den Bewegungen der leidenschaftlichen Zerknirschung ein und lauscht dem Gesange.)

**GESANG DER JUNGEREN PILGER:** (*wie aus dem Thale heraufschallend*). Am hohen Fest der Gnadenhuld,
in Demuth sühnet eure Schuld!
Geseget, wer im Glauben treu:
Er wird erlös't durch Buss' und Reu'.

**TANNHÄUSER:** (*Ein jäher Hoffnungsstrahl leuchtet ihm; er stürzt sich mit krampfhafter Heftigkeit zu Elisabeth's Füssen, küsst inbrünstig, hastig den Saum ihres Gewandes und bricht dann von ungeheurer Erregung taumelnd auf, mit dem Rufe.*) Nach Rom!
(*Eilt ab.*)

**ALLE:** (*rufen ihm nach*). Nach Rom!
(*Der Vorhang fällt.*)

# ■ DRITTER AUFZUG.

*Einleitung.*

(*Tannhäuser's Pilgerfahrt.*)

## ERSTE SCENE.

(*Thal vor der Wartburg, links der Hörselberg, wie am Schluss des ersten Aufzuges. Der Tag neigt sich zum Abend. — Auf dem kleinen Bergvorsprunge rechts liegt Elisabeth vor dem Muttergottesbilde betend ausgestreckt. Wolfram kommt links von der waldige Höhe herab; auf halber Höhe hält er an, als er Elisabeth gewahrt.*)

**WOLFRAM:** Wohl wusst' ich hier zie im Gebet zu finden,
wie ich so oft sie treffe, wenn ich einsam
aus wald'ger Höh' in das Thal verirre. —
Den Tod, den er im gab, im Herzen,
dahingestreckt in brünst'gen Schmerzen,
fleht für sein Heil sie Tag und Nacht: —
O heil'ger Liebe ew'ge Macht! —
Von Rom zurück erwartet sie die Pilger,
schonn fällt das Laub, die Heimkehr steht bevor: —
kehrt er mit den Begnadigten urück?
die ist ihr Fragen, dies ihr Flehnn, —
ihr Heil'gen, lasst erfüllt es sehen!
Bleibt auch die Wunde ungeheilt, —
o, würd' ihr Lind'rung ur ertheilt!
(*Als er tiefer in das Thal hinab-*

**CHORUS OF YOUNGER PILGRIMS:** (*in the extreme background as though echoing from the valley*). At your august and holy shrine
I go to seek the grace divine.
Thrice blessed who your promise know;
Absolved by penance shall they go!

**TANNHÄUSER:** (*A sudden ray of hope inspires him; he throws himself in the most convulsive agony at Elisabeth's feet, kisses devoutly, hastily the hem of her robe, and breaks away from them, calling in the highest exaltation:*) To Rome!
(*Hastens away.*)

**ALL:** (*call after him*). To Rome!
(*The curtain falls.*)

# ■ ACT III.

*Introduction.*

(*Tannhäuser's Pilgrimage.*)

## SCENE I.

(*Valley before the Wartburg, to the left the Hörselberg, as at the close of Act I. Day is declining. On the slight eminence to the right, Elisabeth is prostrated before the Virgin's shrine, in prayer. Wolfram, at the left, coming down from the wooded heights, halfway descended stops as he becomes aware of Elisabeth's presence.*)

**WOLFRAM:** By yonder shrine I'm ever sure to find her
Kneeling in fervent prayer,
When my lonely and joyless way
Back to the valley leads me.
The death-blow struck by him within her
She prays that Heaven may shrive the sinner,
His well-being imploring day and night.
O blessed love, how great your might!
The pilgrims soon from Rome will be returning;
The year declines — before long they must be here.
Will he return repentant and absolved?
This she prays, for Heaven entreating.
Saints, oh grant them happy meeting.
Although my wound may never heal,

steigen will, vernimmt er den Gesang der älteren Pilger und hält an.)

**ELISABETH:** (*erhebt sich dem Gesange lauschend*). Die ist der Sang, — sie sid's, sie kehren heim.
Ihr Heil'gen, zeigt mir jetzt mein Amt',
dass ich mit Würde es erfülle!

**WOLFRAM:** Die Pilger sind's, es ist die fromme Weise,
die der empfang'nen Gnade Heil verkündet. —
O Himmel, stärke jetzt ihr Herz
für die Entscheidung ihres Lebens!

**GESANG DER ALTEREN PILGER:** (*aus grosser Ferne langsam der Bühne nähernd*). Beglückt darf nun dich, o Heimath, ich schauen,
und grüssen froh deine lieblichen Auen;
nun lass' ich ruh'n den Wanderstab,
weil Gott getreu ich gepilgert hab'.
(*Allmählich der Bühne näher.*)
Durch Sühn' und Buss' hab' ich versöhnt
den Herren, dem mein Herze fröhnt,
der meine Reu' mit Segen krönt,
den Herren, dem mein Lied ertönt.
(*Hier betreten sie Pilger die Bühne von rechts im Vordergrund her. Sie ziehen während des Folgenden an dem Bergvorsprunnge vorbei langsam das Thal entlang dem Hintergrunde zu.*)
Der Gnade Heil ist dem Büsser beschieden,
er geht einst ein in der Seligen Frieden!
Vor Höll' und Tod ist ihm nicht bang',
drum preis' ich Gott mein Leben-lang.
Halleluja Ewigkeit!
Halleluja Ewigkeit!
(*Die Pilger haben sich bereits dem Hintergrunde zugewendet. — Elisabeth, die von ihrem erhöhten Standpunkte aus mit grosser Aufregung unter den vorüberziehenden Pilgern nach Tannhäuser geforscht hat, ist in schmerzlicher, aber ruhiger Fassung. — Die Pilger entfernen sich unter dem Folgenden immer mehr und verschwinden endlich durch die Thalöffnung nach rechts.*)

**ELISABETH:** Er kehret nicht zurück! — (*Mit grosser Feierlichkeit sich auf die Knie senkend.*)
Allmächt'ge Jungfrau, hör' mein Flehen
Zu dir, Gepries'ne, rufe ich!
Lass mich im Staub' vor dir vergehen,
o, nimm von dieser Erde mich!
Mach', dass ich rein und engel-gleich
eingehe in dein selig Reich! —
Wenn je n thör'gem Wah befangen,
mein Herz sich abgewandt von

Oh, may she never feel my anguish!
(*As he is about to go down further into the valley, he hears the song of the elder Pilgrims and stops.*)

**ELISABETH:** (*arises, listening to the song*). The pilgrims' song! It is they; they have returned!
Saints, oh let me know my task,
That I may worthily fulfil it!

**WOLFRAM:** They come at last; it is the pious chant,
Telling of the sin absolved and pardon granted!
O Heaven, let her heart be strong
If now her fate must be decided.

**CHORUS OF ELDER PILGRIMS:** (*at a great distance, slowly nearing the stage*). Once more with joy,
O my home, I may meet you;
Once more, fair flowery meadows, I greet you;
My pilgrim staff henceforth may rest,
Since Heaven's sweet peace is within my breast.
(*Gradually nearing the stage.*)
The sinner's plaint on high was heard,
Accepted by a gracious Lord;
The tears I laid before his shrine
Are turned to hope and joy divine.
(*Here the Pilgrims come, from the right of the foreground, on to the stage. During the following they pass by the Shrine and slowly down through the valley into the background.*)
O Lord, eternal praise be yours!
The blessed source of your mercy overflowing
On souls repentant who seek you bestowing;
Of hell and death I have no fear,
My gracious Lord is ever near.
Hallelujah eternally!
(*The Pilgrims have here reached the extreme background. — Elisabeth, who from her elevated position has been seeking in the greatest excitement for Tannhäuser among the returning Pilgrims, in sorrowful but quiet composure. — The Pilgrims withdraw during the following, farther and farther away, and at last disappear by the valley opening to the left.*)

**ELISABETH:** He will return no more! (*With the greatest solemnity, falling upon her knees.*)
O blessed Virgin, hear my prayer!
Star of glory, look on me!
Here in the dust I bend before you,
Now from this earth, oh set me free!
Let me, a maiden pure and white,
Enter into your kingdom bright!
If vain desires and earthly longing
Have turned my heart from you away,
The sinful hopes within me thronging

dir, —
wenn je ein sündiges Verlangen,
ein weltlich Sehnen keimt' in mir, —
so rang ich unter tausend Schmerzen,
dass ich es tödt' in meinem Herzen!
Doch, könnt' ich jeden Fehl nicht büssen,
so nimm dich gnädig meiner an,
dass ich mit demuthvollen Grüssen
als würd'ge Magd dir nahen kann:
um deiner Gnaden reichste Huld
nur anzufleh'n für seine Schuld!
(*Sie verbleibt eine Zeit lang wie in andächtiger Entrücktheit; als sie sich dann langsam erhebt, erblickt sie Wolfram, welcher sich ihr nähert, um sie anzureden. Sie bittet ihn durch eine Gebärde, nicht mit ihr zu sprechen.*)

WOLFRAM: Elisabeth, dürft' ich dich nicht geleiten?
(*Elisabeth drückt ihm abermals durch Gebärden aussie danke ihm und seiner treuen Liebe aus vollem Herzen; ihr Weg führe sie aber gen Himmel, wo sie ein hohes Amt zu verrichten habe; er solle sie daher ungeleitet gehen lassen, ihr auch nicht folgen. Sie besteigt die halbe Berghöhe und verschwindet allmählich auf dem Fussteige, welcher auf dieser nach der Wartburg fürht, nachdem man ihre Gestalt lange noch in der Entfernung erblickt hat.*)

## ZWEITE SCENE.

WOLFRAM: (*der Elisabeth lange noch mit den Augen verfolgt hat, setzt sich am Fusse des linken Thalhügels nieder und beginnt auf der Harfe zu spielen*). Wie Todesahnung Dämm'rung deckt die Lande,
umhüllt das Thal mit schwärzlichem Gewande;
der Seele, die nach jenen Höh'n verlangt,
vor ihrem Flug durch Nacht und Gransen bangt: —
da scheinest du, o lieblichster der Sterne,
dein sanftes Licht entsendest du der Ferne;
die nächt'ge Dämm'rung theilt dein lieber Strahl,
und freundlich zeigst den Weg du aus dem Thal,
O du mein holder Abendstern,
wohl grüss' ich immer dich so gern!
Vom Herzen, das sie nie verrieth,
grüss' sie, wenn sie vorbei dir zieht,
wenn sie entschwebt dem Thal der Erden,
ein sel'ger Engel dort zu werden!
(*Er verbleibt mit gen Himmel gerichtetem Auge, auf der Harfe fortspielend.*)

Before your blessed feet I lay.
I'll wrestle with the love I cherished
Until its flame has perished in death.
If of my sin you will not shrive me,
Yet in this hour, O grant your aid!
Till your eternal peace you give me
I vow to live and die your maid.
And on your bounty I will call,
That heavenly grace on him may fall!
(*She remains for a long time in prayerful rapture; as she slowly rises, she glances at Wolfram, who is approaching to speak to her. She bids him, by a gesture not to speak to her.*)

WOLFRAM: O royal maid, shall I not guide you homeward?
(*Elisabeth again expresses to him by gesture that she thanks him from her heart for his faithful love; her way however leads to heaven, where she has a high purpose to fulfil; she wishes him not to accompany or follow her now. She ascends halfway up the height and disappears gradually on the footpath leading toward the Wartburg after her retreating form has long been visible in the distance.*)

## SCENE II.

WOLFRAM: (*who follows Elisabeth with his eyes for a long time, seats himself at the foot of the hill in the valley and begins to play upon his harp*). Like Death's dark shadow, Night extends her gloom,
Her sable wing over all the vale she bends;
The soul that longs to tread that path of light,
Yet dreads to pass the gate of Fear and Night.
I look on you, O star in heaven the fairest —
Your gentle beam through trackless space you bear;
The hour of darkness is made bright by you,
You lead us upward with pure kindly light.
O evening star, your holy light
Was never so welcome to my sight,
With glowing heart that never disclosed;
Greet her when she reposed in light;
When parting from this vale, a vision,
She rises to an angel's mission.
(*He continues to play, his eyes raised to heaven.*)

## DRITTE SCENE.

(*Es ist gänzlich Nacht geworden. Tannhäuser tritt auf; er trägt zerrissene Pilgerkleidung, sein Gesicht is bleich und entstellt; er wakt matten Schrittes auf senen Stab gestützt.*)

TANNHÄUSER: Ich hörte Harfenschlag, — wie klang er traurig! Der kam wohl nicht von ihr.

WOLFRAM: Wer bist du, Pilger, der du so einsam wanderst?

TANNHÄUSER: Wer ich bin? Kenn' ich doch dich recht gut? Wolfram bist du
(*höhnisch*)
Er wohlgeübte Sänger.

WOLFRAM: (*heftig auffahrend*). Heinrich! du?
Was bringt dich her in diese Nähe? Sprich!
Wagst du es, unentsündigt wohl den Fuss
nach dieser Gegend herzuleken?

TANNHÄUSER: Sei ausser Sorg', mein guter Sänger.
Nicht such' ich dich, noch deiner Sippschaft Einen.
Doch such' ich wen, der mir den Weg wohl zeige,
den Weg, den einst so wunderleicht ich fand.

WOLFRAM: Und welchen Weg?

TANNHÄUSER: (*mit unheimlcher Lüsternheit*). Den Weg zum Venusberg!

WOLFRAM: Entsetzlicher! Entweihe nnicht mein Ohr! Trebt es dich dahin?

TANNHÄUSER: (*leise*). Kennst du wohl den Weg?

WOLFRAM: Wahnsinn'ger! Grauen fasst mich, hör ich dich! Wo war'st du? Say', zogst du denn nicht nach Rom?

TANNHÄUSER: (*wüthend*). Schweig' mir von Rom!

WOLFRAM: War'st nicht beim heil'gen Feste?

TANNHÄUSER: Schweig' mir von ihm!

WOLFRAM: So warst du nicht? Sag', ich beschwöre dich!

TANNHÄUSER: (*wie sich besinnend, mit schmerzlichem lngrimme*). Wohl war auch ich in Rom.

WOLFRAM: So sprich! Erzähle mir, Unglücklicher
Mich fasst ein tiefes Mitleid für dich an.

TANNHÄUSER: (*Wolfram lange mit gerührter Verwunderung betrachtend*). Wie sagst du, Wolfram? Bist du nicht mein Feind?

## SCENE III.

(*It is now night. Tannhäuser appears; he wears a ragged Pilgrim's dress and his face is pale and drawn; he comes with faltering step supported by his staff.*)

TANNHÄUSER: The sound of a harp I heard: It spoke of sadness. It was not she who sang.

WOLFRAM: Who are you, pilgrim, Pursuing this lonely path?

TANNHÄUSER: Who am I? I who knew you so well! You are Wolfram —
(*mockingly*)
The wise and skillful minstrel!

WOLFRAM: (*excitedly*). Henry! You?
What means your coming thus dejected?
Speak! Tell me not that you, unabsolved,
Have dared to set your foot within these precincts!

TANNHÄUSER: No; have no fear, O sapient minstrel;
I do not seek you, nor yet your proud companions.
A path I seek, or one to guide my footsteps
To find that path which once I trod with ease.

WOLFRAM: What path is that?

TANNHÄUSER: (*in unnatural longing*). It leads to Venus' hill.

WOLFRAM: You godless man! Your words defile my ear. That is your mission?

TANNHÄUSER: (*softly*). Do you know the path?

WOLFRAM: Oh madman! Your words inspire dread unknown Where did you come from? Have you not been in Rome?

TANNHÄUSER: (*in rage*). Speak not of Rome!

WOLFRAM: Have you not sued for pardon?

TANNHÄUSER: Speak not of that.

WOLFRAM: You were not there? Oh, I conjure you, speak!

TANNHÄUSER: (*as though meditating, in painful bitterness*). Yes, I have been in Rome.

WOLFRAM: Say on! Oh tell me all, unhappy man! With deep compassion I will hear your words.

TANNHÄUSER: (*gazes long at Wolfram, touched and in wonder*). What do you say Wolfram? Say, are you not my foe?

**WOLFRAM:** Nie war ich es, so lang' ich fromm dich wähnte! — Doch sprich! Du pilgertest nach Rom?

**TANNHÄUSER:** Wohl denn! Hör' an! Du, Wolfram, du sollst es erfahren.

(*Er setzt sich am Fusse des Bergvorsprunges nieder; Wolfram will sich an seiner Seite ebenfalls niederlassen.*)

Bleib' fern von mir! Die Stätte, wo ich raste, ist verflucht. Hör' an, Wolfram; hör' an!

(*Wolfram bleibt in geringer Entfernung von Tannhäuser steben.*)

Inbrunst im Herzen, wie kein Büsser noch sie je gefühlt, sucht' ich den Weg nach Rom. Ein Engel hatte, ach! der Sünde Stolz dem Uebermüthigen entwunden:— für ihn wollt' ich in Demuth büssen, das Heil erfleh'n, das mir verneint, um ihn die Thräne zu versüssen, die er mir Sünder einst geweint! Wie neben mir der schwestbedrückte Pilger die Strasse wallt', erschien mir allzuleicht:— betrat sein Fuss den weichen Grund der Wiesen, der nackten Sohle sucht' ich Dorn und Thorn; liess Labung er am Quell den geniessen, sog' ich der Sonne heisses Glühen ein;— wenn fromm zum Himmel er Gebete schickte, vergoss mein Blut ich zu des Höchsten Preis;— als das Hospiz die Wanderer erquickte, die Glieder bettet' ich in Schnee und Eis; verschloss'nen Aug's, ihr Wunder nicht zu schauen, durchzog ich blind Italiens holde Auen. Ich that's–denn in Zernirschung wollt ich büssen, um meines Engls Thränen zu versüssen. Nach Rom gelangt' ich so zur heiligen Stelle, lag betend auf des Heiligthumes Schwelle;— der Tag brach an:—da läuteten die Glocken, hernieder tönten himmlische Gesänge; da jauchzt' es auf in brünstigem Frohlocken, denn Gnad und Heil verhiessen sie der Menge. Da sah ich ihn, durch den sich Gott verkündigt. vor ihm all' Volk im Staub sich niederliess; und Tausenden er Gnade gab, ent-

**WOLFRAM:** No; nevermore while you are true to honor. But tell — your pilgrimage to Rome?

**TANNHÄUSER:** I will—I will. You, Wolfram, shall know what befell me.

(*He seats himself at the foot of a rocky projection; Wolfram is about to seat himself beside him.*)

Away from me! The refuge where I rest myself Is cursed! Now mark, Wolfram— mark well!

(*Wolfram remains standing a short distance from him.*)

Contrite in spirit as no pilgrim yet on earth has been, I bent my steps to Rome. An angel has dispelled the pride of sin, Its mad profaneness from my bosom; For her sake I went forth a pilgrim, To reconcile offended Heaven; She who had pleaded with tears for me Should know my sins had been forgiven. When I beheld a heavy-burdened pilgrim It seemed to me his load was all too light; And if he sought a pathway over the meadow, I trod unshod amid the rocks and thorns; If he refreshed his lips by cooling fountain, The brazen sun poured on my head forlorn; When he besought the saints in murmured prayers, I shed my life-blood in the cause divine; When in the hospice he sought rest and shelter, It was on ice and snow that I sought mine. Lest Italy's fair scenes my heart had gladdened, I passed them blindfold, so my soul was saddened. I went—my wasted heart remorse was burning That for my sake an angel waited mourning. Thus Rome I gained at last. With tears imploring, I knelt before the rood in faith adoring. When daylight broke, the silvery bells were pealing; Through vaulted roof a song divine was stealing; A cry of joy breaks forth from thousand voices— The hope of pardon every heart rejoices. There him I saw who holds the keys of Heaven, And prostrate fell they all before his face, And thousands he forgave that day, and blessed them.

sündigt er Tausende sich froh erheben hiess.— Da naht' auch ich; das Haupt gebeugt zur Erde, klagt' ich mich an mit jammernder Gebärde der bösen Lust, die meine Sinn' empfanden, des Sehnens, das kein büssen noch gekühlt: und umi Erlösung aus den heissen Banden rief ich ihn an, von wildem Schmerz durchwühlt.— Und er, den so ich bat, hub an:

"Hast du so böse Lust getheilt, dich an der Hölle Glut entflammt, hast du im Venusberg geweilt: so bist nun ewig du verdammt! Wie dieser Stab in meiner Hand nie mehr sich schmückt mit frischem Grün kann aus der Hölle heissem Brand Erlösung nimmer dir erblüh'n!" Da sank ich in Vernichtung dumpf darnieder, die Sinne schwanden mir. Als ich erwacht', auf ödem Platze lagerte die Nacht,— von fern her tönten frohe Gnadenlieder. Da ekelte mich der holde Sang,— von der Verheissung lügnerischem Klang, der eiseskalt mir durch die Seele schnitt, trieb Grauen mich hinweg mit wildem Schritt.— Dahin zog's mich, wo ich der Wonn' und Lust so viel genoss an ihrer warmen Brust!

(*In grauenhafter Begeisterung.*)

Zu dir, Frau Venus, kehr' ich wieder, in deiner Zauber holde Nacht; zu deinem Hof steig' ich darnieder, wo nun dein Reiz mir ewig lacht!

**WOLFRAM:** Halt' ein! Halt ein, Unseliger!

**TANNHÄUSER:** Ach, lass mich nicht vergebens suchen, wie leicht fand ich doch einstens dich! Du hörst, dass mir die Menschen fluchen, nun, süsse Göttin, leite mich!

**WOLFRAM:** (*in heftigen Grausen*). Wahnsinniger, wen rufst du an?

(*Finstere Nacht; leichte Nebel umhüllen allmählich die Scene.*)

**TANNHÄUSER:** Ha! fühlest du nicht milde Lüfte?

**WOLFRAM:** Zu mir! Est ist um dich gethan!

And sent them forth, renewed in heavenly grace. Then I drew near, my glances earthward bending; I made my plaint, despair my bosom rending— I told what mad desires my soul had darkened, By sinful earthly pleasure long enslaved. To me it seemed that he in mercy hearkened— A gracious word in dust and tears I craved. Then he whom thus I prayed replied:

"If you have shared the joys of Hell, If you unholy flames have nursed That dwell in the Hill of Venus, You are forevermore accurst! And as this barren staff I hold Never will put forth a flower or leaf, Thus shall you nevermore behold Salvation, or your sin's relief!" Then hopeless, dumb despair obscured my senses; I sank down motionless. When I awoke It was night, and I alone, by all forsaken. I heard afar the songs of praise and prayer; With loathing I fled to escape the sound. What were to me the tidings of their joy, An outcast, spurned, in whom all hope was dead! With horror in my breast, I turned and fled. Then longed my soul to taste those joys again Which once before my earth-born pains had slain.

(*in appalling ectasy.*)

To you fair Venus, I surrender— Let your sweet magic round me play; I'll be your slave, my star of splendor: You only can allay these pangs!

**WOLFRAM:** Oh, stop your godless raving!

**TANNHÄUSER:** Oh, guide my steps that I might find you— How well erstwhile the road I knew! Behold! men have with curses spurned me. Come, lovely goddess, guide me true!

**WOLFRAM:** (*in intense horror*). You godless one! Who do you call? (*Darkest night; light clouds gradually veil the Scene.*)

**TANNHÄUSER:** Ah! Do you not feel balmy breezes?

**WOLFRAM:** Away! Oh, fly, or you are lost!

**TANNHÄUSER:** Und athmest du nicht holde Düfte? (*Die Nebel beginnen in rosiger Dämmerung zu erglühen*.). Hörst du nicht die jubelnden Klänge?

**WOLFRAM:** In wildem Schauer bebt die Brust!

**TANNHÄUSER:** Das ist der Nymphen tanzende Menge. — (*immer aufgeregter je näher der Zauber kommt*.) Herbei, herbei zu Wonn' und Lust! (*Wirre Bewegungen tanzender Gestalten werden erkennbar*.)

**WOLFRAM:** Weh böser Zauber thut sich auf! Die Hölle naht in wildem Lauf.

**TANNHÄUSER:** Entzücken dringt durch alle Sinne, gewahr' ich diesen Dämmerschein; dies ist das Zauberreich ber Minne, (*ausser sich*.) im venusberg drangen wir ein! (*In heller, rosiger Beleuchtung erscheint Venus auf ihrem Lager rubend*.)

**VENUS:** Willkommen, ungetreuer Mann! Schlug dich die Welt mit Acht und Bann? And findest nirgends du Erbarmen, suchst Liebe nun in meinem Armen?

**TANNHÄUSER:** Frau Venus, o Erbarmungsreiche! Zu dir, zu dir zieht es mich hin?

**WOLTRAM:** Du Höllenzauber, weiche, weiche! Berücke nicht des Reinen Sinn!

**VENUS:** Nah'st du dich wieder meiner Schwelle, sei dir dein Uebermuth verzieh'n; ewig fliesst dir der Freuden Quelle, und nimmer sollst du von mir flieh'n!

**TANNHÄUSER:** (*indem er sich in wilder Entschlossenheit von Wolfram losreisst*). Mein Heil, mein Heil hab' ich verloren, nun sei der Hölle Lust erkoren!

**WOLFRAM:** (*ihn beftig zurückhaltend*). Allmäch'ger, steh' dem Frommen beil Heinrich, ein Wort, es macht dich frei: dein Heil — !

**VENUS:** Zu mir!

**TANNHÄUSER:** (*zu Wolfram*). Lass ab von mir!

**VENUS:** O komm'! Auf ewig sei nun mein!

**WOLFRAM:** Noch soll das Heil dir Sünder werden! (*Tannhäuser und Wolfram ringen beftig*.)

**TANNHÄUSER:** Nie! Wolfram, nie! Ich muss dahin!

**TANNHÄUSER:** What ecstasy seizes my senses! (*The clouds begin to glow in rosy light*.) Do you not hear rapturous music?

**WOLFRAM:** Oh were you rather in your grave!

**TANNHÄUSER:** In crowded dance the nymphs now are flying— (*more and more excited the nearer they approach*.) Come on— come on! ye fair, come on—receive your slave! (*A confused whirl of dancing forms becomes visible*.)

**WOLFRAM:** Woe! Evil demons fill the air, That hell may ensnare its victim!

**TANNHÄUSER:** Oh, come on Pleasure's rosy pinion! I feel your breath ambrosial! This is of love the sweet dominion— (*beside bimself*) O Venus! I will call on thee! (*Venus appears, reclining upon her couch in a bright, rosy light*.)

**VENUS:** I welcome you perfidious man; Earth laid you low beneath its ban. Have you by all, then, been forsaken, In my arms blissfully to waken?

**TANNHÄUSER:** Sweet Venus, oh! in bliss receive me! With you, with you, oh let me fly!

**WOLFRAM:** You hellish phantoms, leave him! All hope is lost when you are near!

**VENUS:** You come relying on grace from me? I will forgive your rash resolve. Come where joy is fed from source undying, In Pleasure's bright abode to live.

**TANNHÄUSER:** (*tearing bimself away from Wolfram in wild resolution*). Accursed, they have bereft me of hope; Now joys of hell alone are left me!

**WOLFRAM:** (*be bolds Tannbäuser once more*). O mighty Lord! in mercy see! Henry, one word, and you are free— Repent!

**VENUS:** Come to me!

**TANNHÄUSER:** (*to Wolfram*). No more! Away from me!

**VENUS:** O come, beloved! Forever you are mine.

**WOLFRAM:** Yet can you gain your soul's salvation! (*Tannbäuser and Wolfram struggle violently*.)

**TANNHÄUSER:** No, Wolfram, no! the heavens are closed!

**WOLFRAM:** Ein Engel bat für dich auf Erden— bald schwebt er segnend über dir: Elisabeth!

**TANNHÄUSER:** (*der sich soeben losgerissen, bleibt plötzlich wie die Stelle gebeftet*) Elisabeth! (*Die Nebel verfinstern sich allmäblich, beller Fackelschein leuch tet danu durch sie auf*).

**MÄNNERGESANG:** (*binter der Scene*). Der Seele Heil, die nun entfloh'n dem Leib der frommen Dulderin!

**WOLFRAM:** (*nach dem ersten Eintritt des Gesanges*). Dein Engel fleht für dich an Gottes Thron, — er wird erhört! Heinrich, du bist erlöst!

**VENUS:** (*bereits unsichtbar*). Weh'! Mir verloren! (*Sie versinkt. Die Nebel verschwinden gänzlich Morgendämmerung. — Von der Warburg her schreite ein Trauerzug mit Fackeln der Tiefe des Thales zu*.)

**MÄNNERGESANG:** Ihr ward der Engel sel'ger Lohn, himmlischer Freuden Hochgewinn.

**WOLFRAM:** (*Tannbäuser sanft umschlunger baltend*). Und hörst du diesen Sang?

**TANNHÄUSER:** (*ersterbend*). Ich höre! (*Hier betritt der zug die Bühne in der Tiefe des Thales, die älteren Pilger voran, — die Sänger zunächst dem offenen Sarge, in welchem Elisabeth's Leiche von ihnen getragen wird; der Landgraf, Ritter und Edle folgen dem Sarge*.)

**MÄNNERGESANG:** Heilig die Reine, die nun vereint göttlicher Schaar vor dem Ewigen steht. (*Hier macht Wolfram eine Gebärde, weiche din Sänger, als sie Tannbäuser erkennen, bewegt, dee Sarg nieder zu setzen*.) Selig der Sünder, dem sie geweint, dem sie des Himmels Heil erfleht!

**TANNHÄUSER:** (*ist von Wolfram zum Sarge geleitet worden; über Elisabeth's Leiche bingebengt, sinkt er enlseelt langsam nieder*). Heilige Elisabeth, bitte für mich! (*Er stirbt. Alle senken die Fackeln zur Erde und löschen sie so aus, Morgenroth erhellt vollends die Scene*.)

**DIE JUNGEREN PILGER:** (*auf dem vorderen Bergvorsprunge einberziehend*). Heil! Heil! Der Gnade Wunder Heil! Erlösung ward der Welt zu Theil! Es that in nächtlich heil'ger Stund'

**WOLFRAM:** It hears an angel's supplication, Who now for you its grace implores— Elisabeth!

**TANNHÄUSER:** (*who has just released bimself, remains suddenly as though bound to the spot*). Oh, maid divine! (*The clouds gradually darken and through them bright torchlights are gleaming*.)

**CHORUS OF MEN:** (*behind the scene*). Receive the soul, O bounteous Lord, That now to you has taken flight.

**WOLFRAM:** (*after the first strains of the song*). Your angel prays for you before the throne, And Heaven relents! Henry, you are absolved!

**VENUS:** (*already invisible*). Woe! I have lost him! (*She vanishes. The clouds disappear entirely. The dawn of morning. From the Wartburg a funeral procession with torches winds down into the valley*.)

**CHORUS OF MEN:** Hers be the angels' blest reward! Bright be her glory in your sight!

**WOLFRAM:** (*bolding Tannbäuser gently in bis arms*). O say, do you hear this strain?

**TANNHÄUSER:** (*dying*). I hear it. (*Here the funeral train reaches the stage, at the foot of the valley, the elder Pilgrims in advance; the Minstrels nearest the open bier on which Elisabeth's body is carried; the Landgrave, Knights and Nobles follow*.)

**CHORUS OF MEN:** Sainted forever through all the spheres, She who through love attained your salvation. (*Here Wolfram makes a gesture which moves the Minstrels, as they recognize Tannbäuser, to set down the bier*.) Blessed is the sinner saved by her tears, Now he has reached the heavenly gate.

**TANNHÄUSER:** (*has been led by Wolfram to the bier, bending over Elisabeth's body, he, swooning, sinks slowly down*). Holy Saint Elisabeth, oh pray for me! (*He dies. —All invert their torches and so extinguish them. The morning light completely illumines the scene*.)

**CHORUS OF YOUNGER PILGRIMS:** (*approaching from the height in the foreground*). Hail! hail! the Lord has wrought marvels! He has brought redemption to all! One night in blessed, propitious

der Herr sich durch ein Wunder
kund:
den dürren Stab in Priesters Hand
hat er geschmückt mit frischem
Grün:
dem Sünder in der Hölle Brand
soll so Erlösung neu erblüh'n!
Ruft ihm es zu durch alle Land'
der durch dies Wunder Gnade fand!
Hoch über aller Welt ist Gott,

hour,
He left a sign of His dread power;
The barren staff of priestly rule
He made to bloom with summer's
green!
Now the Lord annuls man's curse,
His pitying love shall make us
clean!
Declare it loud through every land:
None who condemn at last shall

und sein Erbarmen ist kein Spott!
Halleluja! Halleluja!
Halleluja!

**ALLE:** (*in höchster Ergriffenheit*).
Der Gnade Heil ist dem Büsser beschieden,
er geht nun ein in der Seligen Fried-
en.

*ENDE.*

stand!
High He thrones above sin and
death!

**MINSTRELS AND CHORUS OF
PILGRIMS:** (*in the highest emo-
tion*). The Lord Himself now has
broken your bondage
Go, enter in with the blest in His
Heaven!

*THE END.*

# *Lohengrin* (1850)

### MUSIC AND LIBRETTO BY RICHARD WAGNER

This three-act romantic opera, set to a libretto by the composer, was first performed at the Hoftheater in Weimar on August 28, 1850. The story takes place in Antwerp during the early tenth century. King Henry the Fowler of Germany comes to Antwerp to gather an army which will fight against the invading Hungarians. Frederick of Telramund, married to Ortrud, and Elsa, daughter of the late duke, are fighting over the succession to the dukedom. Elsa's brother, who has disappeared under mysterious circumstances, is the rightful heir. Frederick and Ortrud accuse Elsa of his murder in order to succeed to the title. The King decrees that one combat, to be held between Frederick and Elsa's champion, will settle the issue. No one will fight for her, and she prays that her dream of a knight arriving to defend her cause will come to pass. The herald's trumpets sound as a boat, drawn by a swan, sails down the river. Lohengrin, the knight on board, arrives and offers to be her champion. She promises to marry him if he wins, and he asks her to promise never to attempt to find out his true identity. Of course, he resoundingly defeats Frederick. Frederick and Ortrud are banished from Antwerp but plan to bring Elsa down. Ortrud begs Elsa to forgive them, and Elsa promises to help them as much as she can. Elsa is about to enter the cathedral for her wedding to Lohengrin when Ortrud denounces him, saying that he practices black magic. Elsa denies this but now has doubts, upon which Frederick feeds. Lohengrin and Elsa, now married, sing of their love, but Elsa asks Lohengrin who he is. Frederick and his cronies break in, but Lohengrin kills him and the others run away. He unhappily tells his wife that he must leave her when she knows the answer to her question. The King gathers an army which the people invite Lohengrin to lead. He refuses and reveals who he is–he is a Knight of the Holy Grail, Parsifal's son, and now he must return to Monsalvat (where the Grail is kept) since his identity is no longer a secret. He says good-bye to Elsa, and the swan comes to draw his boat once more. Ortrud declares that this swan is actually Elsa's brother, the rightful duke, enchanted by an evil spell cast by Ortrud. If Elsa had kept her promise, Lohengrin could have broken this spell. Lohengrin prays that this can yet be accomplished, and the swan is transformed back into Elsa's brother. She collapses in his arms as Lohengrin sails off, the boat now drawn by the white dove of the Holy Grail.

---

## ■ ERSTER AUFZUG

### ERSTE SCENE

*(Eine Aue am Ufer der Schelde bei Antwerpen. König Heinrich. Friedrich von Telramund. Ortrud. Der Heerrufer. Sächsische und brabantische Grafen, Edle und Volk. Vier Heerhornbläser. Die Bläser blasen den Königsruf.)*

**DER HEERRUFER:** Hört! Fürsten, Edle, Freie von Brabant!
Heinrich, der Deutschen König, kam zur Start,
Mit euch zu dingen nach des Reiches Recht.
Gebt ihr nun Fried' und Folge dem Gebot?

**DIE BRABANTER:** Wir geben Fried' und Folge dem Gebot,
Willkommen! Willkommen, König in Brabant!

## ■ ACT I

### SCEBE I

*(A plain on the banks of the Scheldt, near Antwerp; the river winds towards the background, so that on the right a portion of it is hidden by trees, and it is only visible again at a farther distance. In the foreground, to the left, King Henry is seated under a tall, sturdy oak; near him stand the Saxon and Thuringian nobles. On the other side are Frederick of Telramund and Ortrud. The background is occupied by retainers. An open circle in the middle into which the Herald and four Trumpeters advance. Trumpets sound.)*

**HERALD:** Listen! Nobles, lords and freemen of Brabant:
Henry, the King of Germans, comes here
To parley with you as the law provides.
With loyal feeling hear his command!

**MEN OF BRABANT:** With loyal feeling we hear his command;
So welcome, King Henry! Welcome to Brabant!

**KÖNIG HEINRICH:** Gott grüss euch, liebe Männer von Brabant!
Nicht müssig that zu euch ich diese Fahrt;
Der Noth des Reiches seid von mir gemahnt.
Soll ich euch erst der Drangsal Kunde sagen,
Die deutsches Land so oft aus Osten traf?
In fernster Mark hiess't Weib und Kind ihr beten:
Herr Gott, bewahr' uns vor der Ungarn Wuth!
Doch mir, des Reiches Haupt, musst' es geziemen,
So wilder Schmach ein Ende zu ersinnen:
Als Kampfes Preis gewann ich Frieden auf
Neun Jahr', ihn nützt' ich zu des Reiche Wehr;
Beschirmte Städt' und Burgen liess ich bau'n,
Den Heerbann übte ich zum Widerstand.
Zu End' ist nun die Frist, der Zins versagt,
Mit wildem Drohen rüstet der Feind.
Nun ist es Zeit, des Reiches Ehr' zu wahren;
Ob Ost, ob West, das gelte Allen gleich

**KING:** (*rising*). Heaven save you, loving subjects of Brabant!
I did not come here through idleness.
The kingdom's deep distresses learn from me.
First shall I tell you of the weary troubles
That, from the East, threaten Germany.
About the March were women—children praying:
"Heaven shield us from the wild Hungarian's rage!"
With me, the kingdom's head, it was a duty
To put an end to such abhorred disorder.
A seven years' truce by force of arms I gained
And this I used to give the realm new strength.
The towns I fenced and fortresses I built,
Our men of arms I fitly exercised.
Now tribute we refuse—the term expires—
And we are once more threatened by the foe.
Now it is time to guard the kingdom's honor.
The East—the West—both are alike to all.
The German nation calls upon her

Was deutsches Land heisst, stelle Kampfesschaaren
Dann schmäht wohl Niemand mehr das deutsche Reich!

DIE SACHSEN UND THÜRINGER:
Mit Gott wohlauf für deutschen Reiches Ehr'!

KÖNIG: Komm' ich zu euch nun, Männer von Brabant,
Zum Heergefolg nach Mainz euch zu entbieten,
Wie muss mit Schmerz und Klagen ich erseh'n,
Dass ohne Fürsten ihr in Zwietracht lebt!
Verwirrung, wilde Fehde wird mir kund,
Drum frag' ich dich, Friedrich von Telramund:
Ich kenne dich, als aller Tugend Preis,
Jetzt rede, dass der Drangsal Grund ich weiss.

FRIEDRICH: Dank, König, dir, dass du zu richten kamst!
Die Wahrheit künd' ich, Untreu' ist mir fremd.
Zum Sterben kam der Herzog von Brabant,
Und meinem Schutz empfahl er seine Kinder,
Elsa, die Jungfrau, und Gottfried, den Knaben:
Mit Treue pflog ich seiner grossen Jugend,
Sein Leben war das Kleinod meiner Ehre.
Ermiss nun, König, meinen grimmen Schmerz, als meiner Ehre Kleinod mir geraubt!
Lustwandelnd führte Elsa einst den Knaben zum Wald, doch ohne ihn kehrte sie zurück; mit falscher Sorge frug sie nach dem Bruder, da sie, von ungefähr von ihm verirrt, Bald seine Spur—so sprach sie—nicht mehr fand.
Fruchtlos war all' Bemüh'n um den Verlor'nen; als ich mit Drohen nun in Elsa drang, da liess in bleichem Zagen und Erbeben der grässlichen Schuld Bekenntniss sie uns seh'n.
Es fasste mich Entsetzen vor der Magd: dem Recht auf ihre Hand, vom Vater mir Verliehn, entsagt' ich willig da und gern, und nahm ein Weib, das meinem Sinn gefiel, Ortrud, Radbod's des Friesenfürsten Spross.
Nun führ'ich Klage gegen Elsa von Brabant: des Brudermordes zeih' ich sie.
Dies Land doch sprech' ich für mich an mit Recht, da ich der Nächste von des Herzogs blut, mein Weib jedoch aus diesem Geschlecht, das einst auch diesem Lande seine Fürsten gab.
Du hörst die Klage! König, richte recht!

children,
And foes will tremble when they hear the call.

SAXONS AND THURINGIANS:
(striking their arms). We all fight For German honor!

KING: (reseating himself). You now I summon, subjects of Brabant!
At once proceed to Maintz with all your forces.
Much to our grief are we compelled to hear, I am told
That you live in discord and disorder
Of factions and confusion,
Therefore explain, Frederick of Telramund.
I know full well that you are virtue's self;
Explain, then, and tell the cause of mischief.

FREDERICK: Thanks to you King that you are here to judge,
I tell you the truth—I never learned falsehood.
Brabant's late Duke upon his deathbed lay,
And confided both his children to me,
Elsa the maiden and her brother Godfrey.
Faithfully through growing boyhood,
His life I deemed the jewel of my honor.
King Henry, measure all my depth of grief.
When I was despoiled of that fair jewel.
Once Elsa through the forest took the boy
To stroll; but woe is me! returned alone,
With show of sorrow asking for her brother.
From him, she said, she heedlessly had strayed,
And not a trace of Godfrey could she find.
Vainly we sought the lost one to recover.
Elsa at last I terrified with threats,
Till by her faltering tongue and pallied features
The fearful deed was told that she had done.
With deepest horror shrank I from the maid.
Her sire gave me the right to make her mine
But this too gladly I resigned,
And took a wife whom I could truly love,
Ortrud the child of Radbod, Friesland's prince.
Now do I accuse Elsa of Brabant—
Her brother perished by her guilty hand!
This land, as lawfully my own, I claim,
Being nearest kinsman to the Duke.
My wife, besides, is of the race that

once
Unto this land a line of princes gave.
You know my cause—judge it, noble King.

ALLE MÄNNER: Ha schwerer Schuld zeiht Telramund?
Mit Grau'n werd'ich der Klage kund.

KÖNIG: Welch' fürchterliche Klage sprichst du aus!
Wie wäre möglich solche grosse Schuld?

FRIEDRICH: O Herr, traumselig ist die eitle Magd, die meine Hand voll Hochmuth von sich stiess.
Geheimer Buhlschaft klag' ich sie drum an: sie wähnte wohl, wenn sie des Bruders ledig, dann könnte sie als Herrin von Brabant mit Recht dem Lehnsmann ihre Hand verwehren, und offen des geheimen Buhlen pflegen.

KÖNIG: Ruft die Beklagte her!—
Beginnen soll Nun das Gericht!
Gott lass' mich weise sein!

DER HEERRUFER: Soll hier nach Recht und Macht Gericht gehalten sein?

KÖNIG: Nicht eh'r soll bergen mich der Schild,
Bis ich gerichtet streng und mild!

ALLE MÄNNER: Nich eh'r zur Scheide kehr' das Schwert
Bis Recht durch Urtheil hier gewährt!

HEERRUFER: Wo ihr des Königs Schild gewahrt, dort Recht durch Urtheil nun erfahrt!
Drum ruf' ich klagend laut und hell: Elsa erscheine hier zur Stell'!

ALL THE MEN: (with horror).
Who could have thought of crimes like this?
A heavy charge this count has brought.

KING: A heavy accusation indeed.
A heavy charge this count has brought.
A crime so fearful seems impossible

FREDERICK: My King, she whom I rightly cast aside
Is given to folly and to vanity,
And I accuse her now of hidden sin.
She thought, having removed her brother
That she could, as the mistress of Brabant,
Reject the hand of him who fairly claims it,
And openly protect her secret minion.

KING: Call the accused one here; the trial shall
Proceed at once.
Heaven guide my judgment right!
(He solemnly hanges his shield on the oak. The Saxons and Thuringians thrust their drawn swords into the ground; the men of Brabant lay theirs before them.)

HERALD: (advances into the middle). Now shall the cause be tried as ancient use requires.

KING: I shall never again wear my shield,
Till judgment is pronounced, I swear!

CHORUS: (men). Never to the sheath the sword,
Till justice speaks the mighty word.

HERALD: There, where the royal shield you see,
You soon will hear the King's decree.
Therefore I call, in accents clear,
Elsa, appear without delay.

## ZWEITE SCENE

(Elsa tritt auf: ein langer Zug ihres Frauen folgt ihr.)

DIE MÄNNER: Seht hin!
Sie naht, die hart Beklagte!
Ha, wie erscheint sie licht und rein!
Der sie so schwer zu zeihen wagte,
Gar sicher muss der Schuld er sein.

## SCENE II

(Elsa enters in a simple white dress; a long train of her ladies similarly attired. These remain in the background while Elsa advances slowly and timidly into the center of the foreground.)

CHORUS: (men). Behold, she comes!
The charge how heavy.
Yet does she look—ah, so bright and pure!
He who could venture to accuse her,
Must doubtless be sure of her guilt.

KÖNIG: Bist du es, Elsa von Brabant?

(*Elsa macht eine bejahende Bewegung.*)

Erkennst du mich als deinen Richter an?

(*Elsa blickt dem König in das Auge und bejaht dann wiederum.*)

So frage ich weiter: ist die Klage dir bekannt, die schwer hier wider dich erhoben?

(*Elsa erblickt Friedrich, erbebt, wendet schüchtern das Haupt und bejaht traurig.*)

Was Entgegnest du der Klage?

(*Elsa durch eine Gebärde sprechend: "nichts!"*).

So bekennst du deine Schuld?

ELSA: Mein armer Bruder!

ALLE MÄNNER: Wie wunderbar! welch' seltsames Gebaren!

KÖNIG: Sag', Elsa!
Was hast du mir zu vertrau'n?

ELSA: Einsam in trüben Tagen hab'ich zu Gott gefleht, Des Herzens tiefstes Klagan ergoss' ich in Gebet.
Da drang aus meinem Stöhnen, ein Laut so klagevoll, der zu gewalt'gem Tönen weit in die Lüfte schwoll:
Ich hört'ihn fern hin hallen, bis kaum mein Ohr er traf; mein Aug' ist zugefallen, ich sank in süssen Schlaf.—

ALLE MÄNNER: Wie sonderbar!
Träumt sie?
Ist sie entrückt?

KÖNIG: Elsa, vertheid'ge jetzt dich vor Gericht!

ELSA: In lichter Waffen Scheine ein Ritter nahte da, so tugendlicher Reine ich keinen noch ersah.
Ein golden Horn zu Hüften, Gelehnet auf sein Schwert, so trat er aus den Lüften zu mir, der Recke werth.
Mit züchtigem Gebaren gab Tröstung er mir ein:
Des Ritters will ich wahren, er soll mein Streiter sein!

KÖNIG UND ALLE MÄNNER: Bewahre uns des Himmels Huld, Dass klar wir sehen, wer hier schuld!

KÖNIG: Friedrich, du ehrenwerther Mann, Bedenke wohl, wen klagst du an?

FRIEDRICH: Mich irret nicht ihr träumerischer Muth; Ihr hört, sie schwärmt von einem Buhlen! Wes'ich sie zeih', des' hab' ich sich'ren Grund:
Glaubwürdig ward ihr Frevel mir bezeugt.
Doch eurem Zweifel durch ein

KING: Are you, then, Elsa of Brabant?

(*Elsa bows acknowledgement.*)

And do you recognize me as your judge?

(*She bows again.*)

I question further
Do you know the heavy charge
Brought against you?
Can you answer your accuser?

(*She shakes her head.*)

You own your guilt, then?

ELSA: (*after a pause*). My hapless brother!

CHORUS: Most wonderful!
How strange is her demeanor!

KING: Come, Elsa, what would you confide to me?

ELSA: (*after a pause, as in a trance*) Lonely, amid my sorrow yearning, I called on Heaven.
And forced to prayer, the anguish with which my heart was racked
Then burst forth from my bosom—
so dolorous a sound,
That, as it spread it carried grief to the air around.
I heard it in the distance until it died away;
My heavy eyelids sank then, and I lay wrapped in sleep.

ALL THE MEN: (*softly*). She dreams or is she mad!

KING: Elsa, defend yourself before your judge.

ELSA: (*as before*). Equipped in glittering armor, then drew near to me
A knight of angelic manner—the like I never knew.
His golden horn hung lightly; upon his sword he leaned.
Heaven sent him here to save me, that knight of good intent.
Sweet words of consolation he spoke courteously.
Believe me, for my champion no other will I take.

KING AND ALL THE MEN: May heaven endow our minds with light,
That we may see which cause is right.

KING: Frederick, it were ill to lose this cause. Remember the one that you accuse.

FREDERICK: I'm not misled by these her dreamy words.
You hear she raves about a minion.
On valid grounds do I maintain my charge,
Based as it is on surest evidence.
Regardless, to stifle doubts by any witness,

Zeugniss wehren,
Das stünde wahrlich übel meinem Stolz!
Hier steh' ich, hier mein Schwert!
Wer wagt's von euch, zu streiten wider meiner Ehre Preis?

DIE BRABANTISCHEN EDLEN:
Keiner von uns!
Wir streiten nur fü dich.

FRIEDRICH: Und, König, du!
Gedenskt du meiner Dienste, wie ich im Kampf die wilden Dänen schlug?

KÖNIG: Wie schlimm, liess' ich von dir daran mich mahnen!
Gern geb' ich dir der höchsten Tugend Preis; in keiner andern Huth als in der deinen möcht' ich die Lande wissen.
Gott allein Soll jetzt in dieser Sache noch entscheiden!

ALLE MÄNNER: Zum Gottesgericht!
Zum Gottesgericht!
Wohlan!

KÖING: Dich frag' ich, Friedrich, Graf von Telramund!
Willst du durch Kampf auf Leben and auf Tod im Gottesgericht vertreten deine Klage?

FRIEDRICH: Ja!

KÖNIG: Und dich nun frag' ich, Elsa von Brabant:
Willst du, dass hier auf Leben auf Tod im Gottesgericht ein Kampe für dich streite?

ELSA: Ja!

KÖNIG: Wen kiesest du zum Streiter!

FRIEDRICH: Vernehmet jetzt den Namen ihres Buhlen!

DIE BRABANTISCHEN EDLEN:
Merket auf!

ELSA: Des Ritters will ich wahren, er soll mein Streiter sein!—
Hört, was dem Gottgesandten ich biete für Gewähr: In meines Vaters Landen die Krone trage er;
Mich glücklich soll ich preisen, Nimmt er mein Gut dahin,—Will er Gemahl mich heissen, Geb' ich ihm, was ich bin!

DIE MÄNNER: Ein schöner Preis, stünd' er in Gottes Hand!
Wer um ihn stritt', wohl setzt' er schweres Pfand.

KÖNIG: Im Mittag hoch steht schon die Sonne:
So ist es Zeit, dass nun der Ruf ergeh'.

Most gracious King, would sorely wound my pride
Here I stand. Here's my sword.
Who of you all
Dares to fight against my stainless honor?

NOBLES OF BRABANT: No, Frederick, no; we only fight for you.

FREDERICK: And you my King, remember the service
Which I have done against the savage Dane?

KING: Of that surely you need not remind me;
Most willingly your high deserts I grant.
In other hands than yours, you may believe me,
Would I not see this country.
Heaven alone
Shall give judgment in this weighty cause.

ALL THE MEN: Yes heaven shall decide.
Be it so.

KING: (*draws his sword and thrusts it into the ground*). Answer me, Frederick, Count of Telramund:
Will you refer this accusation, in combat fought for life and death, to Heaven's high decree?

FREDERICK: Yes.

KING: And you too answer, Elsa of Brabant:
Would you, in combat fought for life and death,
A champion before high Heaven should now defend you?

ELSA: Yes.

KING: Who do you name as you champion?

FREDERICK: Now you'll hear
The name of him she dotes on.

NOBLEMEN OF BRABANT: All attend.

ELSA: Believe me, I will take no other for my champion.
Mark, he whom Heaven shall send me will gain a rare reward
Here, in my father's country, the crown is his to wear.
To yield him my possessions will be my dearest pride,
And should he deign to wed me, lo! I will be his bride.

CHORUS: A splendid offer does the damsel make.
Who plays this game plays for a heavy stake.

KING: The sun at noon's height is shining:
It is therefore time to send the summons forth.

(*The Herald advances with the four trumpeters, whom he places outside the circle towards the four cardinal points. Trumpets sound.*)

**DER HEERRUFER:** Wer hier im Gotteskampf zu streiten kam für Elsa von Brabant, der trete vor!

**HERALD:** He who in sight of Heaven comes here to fight
For Elsa of Brabant, step forth at once!
(*A long pause.*)

**ALLE MÄNNER:** Ohn' Antwort ist der Ruf verhallt.

**CHORUS:** The sound has died away without response.

**FRIEDRICH:** Gewahrt, ob ich sie fälschlich schalt?
Auf meiner Seite bleibt das Recht.

**FREDERICK:** (*pointing to Elsa's increasing anxiety.*) See! you see, the charge is not repelled.
My cause is proved the cause of right.

**ALLE MÄNNER:** Um ihre Sache steht es schlecht.

**ALL THE MEN:** The accusation seems too true.

**ELSA:** Mein lieber König, lass dich bitten, noch einen Ruf an meinen Ritter, wohl weilt er fern und hört' ihn nicht.

**ELSA:** (*approaching the King*). My King and master, I implore you—
One summons more to call my champion;
Too far was he to hear the first.

**KÖNIG:** Noch einmal rufe zum Gericht!
(*Der Heerrufer wiederholt den Aufruf.*)

**KING:** The summons shall be heard again.
(*The summons is repeated; a long pause.*)

**HERALD:** Wer hier im Gotteskampf zu streiten kam für Elsa von Brabant, Der trette vor!

**HERALD:** He who in sight of Heaven comes here to fight
For Elsa of Brabant, step forth at once!

**ALLE MÄNNER:** In düst'rem Schweigen richtet Gott.

**ALL THE MEN:** By this dull silence Heaven decides.

**ELSA:** Du trugest zu ihm meine Klage, zu mir trat er auf dein Gebot;
o Herr, nun meinem Ritter sage, dass er mir helf' in meiner Noth!
Lass mich ihn seh'n, wie ich ihn sah, Wei ich ihn sah, sei er mir nah'.
(*Die auf einer Erhöhung dem Ufer am nächsten Stehenden gewahren in der Ferne einen Nachen, von einem Schwane gezogen, auf dem Flusse allmählig sich nähern; in dem Nachen steht ein Ritter.*)

**ELSA:** (*kneeling*). You gave to him my supplication;
He came to me by your decree.
Great Heaven! oh, order now my champion
To lend his aid and set me free.
Even as I saw him once before,
Oh, let him now appear one more.
(*Those who stand on an elevation nearest the river perceive in the distance a boat, drawn by a swan, gradually approaching; a knight is standing in the boat.*)

**DIE MÄNNER:** Seht! seht! welch' seltsam Wunder! wie?
Ein Schwan, ein Schwan zieht einen Nachen dort heran!—
Ein Ritter drin hoch aufgerichtet steht; wie glänzt sein Waffenschmuck! das Aug' vergeht Vor solchem Licht!—Seht! näher kommt er an!
An einer gold'nen Kette zieht der Schwan!

**MEN:** (*first a few, then more, as they approach the river*). See! there!
Behold a wonder!
How's a swan?
It draws a boat, and in it is a man.
Yes, see him! there he stands, a gallant knight;
My eyes he blinds, his armor is so bright.
See! he approaches!
With a chain of gold
The swan would bring him here.
Behold! behold!
(*Most of the persons assembled have hastened towards the river. The King surveys the scene from his elevated seat. Frederick, who listens with astonishment, and Ortrud, who looks gloomily towards the background, remain in front; likewise Elsa, who listens with rapture to the above description, but does not venture to look around.*)

## DRITTE SCENE

(*Während des Folgenden kommt der Schwan mit dem Nachen vollends am Ufer an: Lohengrin steht darin.*)

## SCENE III

(*During the following, the swan reaches the bank with the boat, in which stands Lohengrin, leaning on his sword, with his helmet on his head, his shield on his shoulder, and a small golden horn at his side.*)

**ALLE MÄNNER UND FRAUEN:**
Ein Wunder! ein Wunder! ein Wunder ist gekommen!
Ha, unerhörtes, nie gesch'nes Wunder!
Gegrüsst! gegrüsst, du gottgesandter Held!

**ALL THE MEN AND WOMEN:** A wondrous sight! a wondrous sight!
We hail you, you heaven-appointed knight!
(*Elsa, looking around, utters a wild shriek of joy at the sight of Lohengrin, on whom Frederick gazes speechless. Ortrud, who has previously retained her haughty attitude, is stricken with terror when she beholds Lohengrin and the swan. As Lohengrin dismisses the boat, the people, absorbed in expectation, suddenly become silent.*)

**LOHENGRIN:** Nun sei bedankt, mein lieber Schwan!
Zieh durch die weite Fluth zurück Dahn, woher mich trug dein Kahn, Kehr' wieder nur zu unserm Glück!
Drum sei getreu dein dienst gethan!
Leb' wohl, leb' wohl, mein lieber Schwan!
(*Der Schwan wendet den Nachen und schwimmt den Fluss zurück.*)

**LOHENGRIN:** Now down the stream, departing, float;
Dear swan, I take my leave of you.
Go, seek the spot from where came the boat;
When you return bring joy to me.
See you are faithful to the end.
Farewell, dear swan, trusty friend.
(*The swan departs with the boat, descending the river. Lohengrin looks after it mournfully.*)

**DIE MÄNNER UND FRAUEN:** Wie fasst uns selig süsses Grauen!
Welch' holde Macht hält uns gebannt!—
Wie ist er schön und hehr zu schauen, den solch' ein Wunder trug an's Land!

**CHORUS:** (*all*). What ecstasies confound us!
That noble knight with spells has bound us, who came a stranger to our land.

**LOHENGRIN:** Heil König Heinrich! segenvoll mög' Gott bei deinem Schwerte stehen!
Ruhmreich und gross dein Name soll von dieser Erde nie vergeh'n!

**LOHENGRIN:** (*solemnly advancing, makes obeisance to the King*). Hail, royal Henry! to your sword may gracious Heaven accord its aid!
Renowned and great your name shall be,
And never from this earth shall fade.

**KÖNIG:** Hab' Dank! erkenn' ich recht die Macht, die dich in dieses land gebracht, so kommst du uns von Gott gesandt?

**KING:** My thanks!
I recognize the power that bound you to this enterprise.
You are by Heaven's own mission here.

**LOHENGRIN:** Zum Kampf für eine Magd zu steh'n, der schwere Klage angethan, bin ich gesandt: nun lasst mich seh'n, ob ich zurecht sie treffe an!—
So sprich denn, Elsa von Brabant!
Wenn ich zum Streiter dir ernannt, willst du wohl ohne Bang' und Grau'n dich meinem Schutze anvertrau'n?

**LOHENGRIN:** As champion to a noble maid whom slander has dared to blight, I come, and all will soon confess the cause that I espouse is right.
So Elsa, speak: if me they choose to be your champion—will refuse, free from all sense of fear or pride, to me your safety to confide?

**ELSA:** Mein Held! mein Retter!
Nimm mich hin!
Dir geb' ich alles, was ich bin!

**ELSA:** (*who until now has looked at him, entranced, sinks at this feet*) My knight, my champion, as I live, all,
All I freely give to you.

# Act I, Scene III

**LOHENGRIN:** Wenn ich im Kampfe für dich siege, willst du, dass ich dein Gatte sei?

**ELSA:** Wie ich zu deinen Füssen liege, geb' ich dir Leib und Seele frei.

**LOHENGRIN:** Elsa, soll ich dein Gatte heissen, soll Land und Leut' ich schirmen dir, soll nichts mich wieder von dir reissen, musst Eines du geloben mir: Nie sollst du mich befragen, noch Wissen's Sorge tragen, woher ich kam der Fahrt, noch wie mein Nam' und Art?

**ELSA:** Nie, Herr, sol mir die Frage kommen.

**LOHENGRIN:** Elsa! hast du mich wohl vernommen? Nie sollst du mich befragen, noch Wissen's Sorge tragen, woher ich kam der Fahrt, noch wie mein Nam' und Art!

**ELSA:** Mein Schirm! mein Engel! mein Erlöser, der fest an meine Unschuld glaubt! Wie gäb' es Zweifels Schuld, die grösser, als die an dich den Glauben raubt? Wie du mich schirmst in meiner Noth, So halt' in Treu' ich dein Gebot.

**LOHENGRIN:** Elsa, ich liebe dich!

**DER KÖNIG, DIE MÄNNER UND FRAUEN:** Welch' holde Wunder muss ich seh'n? Ist's Zauber, der mir angethan? Ich fühl' das Herze mir vergeh'n, Schau' ich den wonniglichen Mann.

**LOHENGRIN:** Nun hört! euch Volk und Edlen mach ich kund: frei aller Schuld ist Elsa von Brabant. Dass falsch dein Klagen, Graf von Telramund, Durch Gottes Urtheil werd' es dir bekannt!

**BRABANTISCHE EDLE:** (*erst einige, dann immer mehrere zu Friedrich.*) Steh' ab vom Kampf, wenn du ihn wagst, zu siegen nimmer du vermagst! Ist er von höchster Macht geschützt, sag', was dein tapf'res Schwert dir nützt? Steh' ab! wir mahnen dich in Treu'! Dein harret Unsieg, bitt're Reu'!

**FRIEDRICH:** Viel lieber todt als feig! Welch' Zaubern dich auch hergeführt, Fremdling, der mir so kühn erscheint, dein stolzes Droh'n mich nimmer rührt, da ich zu lügen nie vermeint. Den Kampf mit dir drum nehm' ich auf, und hoffe Sieg nach Rechtes Lauf!

**LOHENGRIN:** If in the fight I prove victorious, Elsa, will you become my wife?

**ELSA:** Yes, as I'm lying before you feet, freely I give to you my life.

**LOHENGRIN:** Elsa, should I become your husband— Should nothing break the ties that bind us— Should I defend your land and people— One promise, Elsa, you must make. These questions ask me never, nor think upon them ever: From where I came—What is my rank or name.

**ELSA:** These questions never I'll ask, believe me.

**LOHENGRIN:** Elsa, you must not deceive me. These questions ask me never, Nor think upon them ever: From where I came— What is my rank or name.

**ELSA:** My shield—my angel—my preserver. Who hold that I am free from guilt, No power of doubt could be sufficient To shake my firm belief in you. As my protector do you stand, So do I honor your command.

**LOHENGRIN:** (*raising her and clasping her to his bosom*). Elsa, my heart is yours!

**KING AND OTHERS:** Is this a dream? What must I think? The magic must amaze my soul; I feel my heart within me sink When on that noble form I gaze.

**LOHENGRIN:** (*having confided Elsa to the King, advances solemnly to the center*). Now hear! To all assembled be it known That Elsa of Brabant from guilt is free! Count Frederick, falsely she's accused by you! By Heaven's own judgment will the truth be shown.

**CHORUS:** Risk not the fight, our counsel is well meant; And if you slight it, you'll repent.

**FREDERICK:** (*after a long hesitation, suddenly decides*). I'll rather die than yield. Whatever spells have brought you here, Stranger, you, with the front so bold, Since I a falsehood never have told, Therefore with you I'll gladly fight, And victory sure will wait on right.

**LOHENGRIN:** Nun, König, ordne unsern Kampf!

**KÖNIG:** So tretet vor, zu drei für jeden Kämpfer, und messet wohl den Ring zum Streite ab!
(*Drei sächsische Edle treten für Lohengrin, drei brabantische für Friedrich vor; sie messen mit feierlichem Schritte den Kampfplatz aus und stecken ihn durch ihre Speere ab.*)

**DER HEERRUFER:** Nun höret mich, und achtet wohl, den Kampf hier keiner stören soll! Dem Hage bleibet abgewandt, denn wer nicht wahrt des Friedens Recht, der Freie büss' es mit der Hand, mit seinem Haupt büss' es der Knecht!

**ALLE MÄNNER:** Der Freie büss' es mit der Hand, mit seinem Haupt büss' es der Knecht!

**DER HEERRUFFER:** Hört auch, ihr Strengen vom Gericht! Gewahrt in Treue Kampfespflicht! Durch bösen Zaubers List und Trug stört nicht des Urtheils Eigenschaft! Gott richtet euch nach Recht und Fug, drum trauet ihm, nicht eurer Kraft!

**LOHENGRIN UND FRIEDRICH:** Gott richte mich nach Recht und Fug, drum trau' ich Ihm, nicht meiner Kraft!

**DER KÖNIG:** Mein Herr und Gott, nun ruf' ich Dich, dass Du dem Kampf zugegen sei'st! Durch Schwertes Sieg ein Urtheil sprich, das Trug und Wahrheit klar erweist.

**DER KÖNIG, DIE MÄNNER UND FRAUN:** Des Reinen Arm gieb Heldenkraft, des Falschen Stärke sei erschlafft; so hilf uns, Gott, zu dieser Frist, Weil uns're Weisheit Einfalt ist!

**ELSA UND LOHENGRIN:** Du kündest nun dein wahr Gericht, Mein Herr und Gott, drum zag' ich nicht.

**FRIEDRICH:** Ich geh' in Treu' vor Dein Gericht! Herr Gott, verlass' mein' Ehre nicht!

**ORTRUD:** Ich baue fest auf seine Kraft, Die, wo er kämpft, ihm Sieg verschafft.

**ALLE MÄNNER:** Des Reinen Arm gieb Heldenkraft, des Falschen Stärke sei erschlafft; so künde uns Dein wahr Gericht, du Herr und Gott, nun zö'gre nicht!
(*Auf das Zeichen des Heerrufers fallen die Heerhörner mit einem langen Kampfrufe ein. Kampf Lohengrin's und Friedrich's.*)

**LOHENGRIN:** King Henry, now arrange the fight.

**KING:** Advance, then, forward— three for either champion, And for the combat measure well the ring.
(*Three Saxons advance for Lohengrin; three of Brabant for Frederick. With solemn steps they measure the ground, and mark it off with three spaces.*)

**HERALD:** Let all give ear to my words— None with this fight must interfere. Outside the lines be sure you stand. If freemen, forfeit with the hand; You who the law shall disobey, If serfs, you with your heads shall pay.

**ALL THE MEN:** The freeman forfeit with his hand, Forfeit the serf with head shall pay.

**HERALD:** Valiant champions, hear me too! To honor's laws be firm and true; Let no base witchcraft or deceit The ends of justice now defeat. May gracious Heaven protect the right, In Heaven confide, not human might.

**LOHENGRIN AND FREDERICK:** May gracious Haven protect the right! In Heaven I trust, not human might.

**KING:** (*who has solemnly advanced into the middle*). Heaven in prayer your aid I seek! Preside over this assembly Now let the sword your judgment speak, That by your will we may abide.

**KING AND CHORUS:** Oh, let the arm of right be strong, And feeble be the arm of wrong. Oh help us now in our distress, Our wisdom is but foolishness.

**ELSA AND LOHENGRIN:** Soon your just decree will be known. Almighty Judge, I trust in you!

**FRIEDRICH:** I bow before your high decree, Almighty Judge, give me strength!

**ORTRUD:** The victory must belong to him, In every fight his arm is strong.

(*At a signal from the Herald the trumpets sound for the combat. The King, drawing his sword, strikes it twice against his shield. At the first stroke Lohengrin and Frederick take their positions; at the second they draw their swords; at the third they commence the encounter. After several violent passages, Lohengrin strikes Frederick to the ground.*)

**LOHENGRIN:** Durch Gottes Sieg ist jetzt dein Leben mein: Ich schenk' es dir! mög'st du der Reu es weih'n!

**ELSA:** O fänd' ich Jubelweisen, die deinem Ruhme gleich, die, würdig dich zu preisen, an höchstem Lobe reich!
In dir muss ich vergehen, vor dir schwind' ich dahin!
Soll ich mich selig sehen, nimm alles was ich bin!

**LOHENGRIN:** Den Sieg hab' ich erstritten durch deine Rein' allein!
Nun soll, was du gelitten, dir reich vergolten sein!

**FRIEDRICH:** Weh! mich hat Gott geschlagen, durch ihn ich sieglos bin!
Am Heil muss ich verzagen, mein' Ehr' und Ruhm ist hin.

**ORTRUD:** Wer ist's, der ihn geschlagen, durch den ich machtlos bin?
Sollt' ich vor ihm verzagen, Wär' all' mein Hoffen hin?

**DER KÖNIG, DIE MÄNNER UND FRAUEN:** Ertöne, Siegesweise, dem Helden laut zum Preise!
Ruhm deiner Fahrt!
Preis deinem Kommen!
Heil deiner Art, Schützer der Frommen!
Dich nur besingen wir, dir schallen uns're Lieder!
Nie kehrt ein Held gleich dir in diese Lande wieder.

*DER VORHANG FÄLLT.*

## ■ ZWEITER AUFZUG

### ERSTE SCENE

*(In der Burg von Antwerpen. In der Mitte des Hintergrundes der Palast (Ritterwohnung), die Kemenate (Frauenwohnung) im Vordergrunde links; rechts im Vordergrunde die Pforte des Münsters; ebenda im Hintergrunde das Thurmthor Friedrich und Ortrud.)*

**LOHENGRIN:** (*holding his sword at Frederick's throat*). To me your life by God's decree is given. I take it not—go, make your peace with Heaven!
(*The King leads Elsa to Lohengrin; she sinks enraptured on his bosom. Immediately after Frederick's fall the Saxon, Thuringian, and Brabant nobles have resumed their swords. The circle is broken up with general acclamations.*)

**CHORUS:** Hail! hail! hail!

**ELSA:** I'd sing a song of praises Equal to your worth.
Your name I'd send resounding Through all the spacious earth.
I feel as nothing before you, Right noble as you are
I love you—I adore you—
Oh, take me to your heart!

**LOHENGRIN:** Wrong could not triumph over you
So innocent you are
Pure bliss now lies before you, To cheer your aching heart.

**FREDERICK:** Ruined, disgraced, defeated!
Oh, Heaven, my foe you are!
My downfall is completed, My glories all depart.

**ORTRUD:** Must thoughts of high ambition, depart like empty dreams?
If I would shun perdition, be still, my sinking heart!

**KING AND CHORUS:** We sing to you—we praise you,
To highest honor raise you
Stranger, we here greet you delighted;
Wrong you have righted,
We gladly greet you here.
You, you we sing alone! Your name shall live in story,
Oh, never will be one to rival you in glory.
(*The Saxons raise Lohengrin on their shield; the men of Brabant raise Elsa on that of the King. Both are carried amid loud acclamations. Curtain falls.*)

*END OF THE FIRST ACT.*

## ■ ACT II

### SCENE I

*(In the fortress of Antwerp. In the middle of the background the Pallas or abode of the knights; to the left the Kemenate or abode of the women; in the foreground, to the right, the entrance of the Minster; in the background the gate of the town. Night. The windows of the Pallas are brightly illuminated; the sound of horns and trumpets is heard. On the steps before the*

**FRIEDRICH:** Erhebe dich, Genossin meiner Schmach?
Der junge Tag darf hier uns nicht mehr seh'n.

**ORTRUD:** Ich kann nicht fort: hierher bin ich gebannt.
Aus diesem Glanz des Festes uns'rer Feinde lass saugen mich ein furchtbar tödlich Gift, das uns're Schmach und ihre Freuden ende!

**FRIEDRICH:** Du fürchterliches Weib! was bannt mich noch in deine Näh'? warum lass ich dich nicht allein, und fliehe fort, dahin, dahin,—Wo mein Gewissen Ruhe wieder fände?
Durch dich musst' ich verlieren mein' Ehr', all mein Ruhm: nie soll mich Lob mehr zieren, Schmach ist mein Heldenthum!
Die Acht ist mir gesprochen, Zertrümmert liegt mein Schwert: mein Wappen ist zerbrochen, verflucht mein Vaterherd!
Wohin ich nun mich wende, Gefehmt, gefloh'n bin ich: dass ihn mein Blick nicht schände, flieht selbst der Räuber mich. O hätt' ich Tod erkoren, da ich so elend bin!
Mein' Ehr' hab' ich verloren, mein' Ehr', mein' Ehr' ist hin!

**ORTRUD:** Was macht dich in so wilde Klage doch vergeh'n?

**FRIEDRICH:** Das mir die Waffe selbst geraubt, mit der ich dich erschlüg!

**ORTRUD:** Friedricher Graf von Telramund! warum misstrau'st du mir?

**FRIEDRICH:** Du fragst? war's nicht dein Zeugniss, deine Kunde, die mich bestrickt, die Reine zu verklagen?
Die du im düst'ren Wald zu Haus, logst du mir nicht, von deinem wilden Schlosse aus die Unthat habest du verüben seh'n?
Mit eig'nen Augen, wie Elsa selbst den Bruder im Weiher dort ertränkt?
Umstricktest du mein stolzes Herz durch die Weissagung nicht, bald würde Radbod's alter Fürstenstamm von neuem grünen und herrschen in Brabant?
Bewogst du so mich nicht, von

*Minster sit Frederick and Ortrud, poorly clad. Ortrud keeps her eyes fixed on the windows of the Pallas; Frederick looks at the ground. A long silence. Frederick suddenly rises.*)

**FREDERICK:** Arouse quickly, companion of my shame,
Let the dawn of morning not see us here.

**ORTRUD:** (*not moving*). Here I am bound—I cannot stir from here. Here from the luster of those hated revels would I imbibe a poison that would end at once our shame and all their joys forever.

**FREDERICK:** You fiend in woman's form, what is it thus—
Thus binds me to your presence? It were well far that I should leave you and flee away, where troubled conscience might at last repose.
Through you my stainless honor Is changed to deadly shame.
The lips that once would praise me, Blacken my ancient name.
The ban is over me spoken.
My sword lies in pieces,
My escutcheon is stained—
A thing that all despise.
Wherever I may turn,
All from my presence flee;
Even robbers feel polluted,
Chance they to gaze on me.
Through you my stainless honor Has become deadly shame,
The lips once would praise me Blacken my ancient fame.
The ban is over me spoken, &c. (to despise).
Oh, life has lost its value,
Ah, would that I were dead!
My honor's gone—my honor—
And with it all is fled.
(*Throws himself wild with rage on the ground. Music heard again from the Pallas.*)

**ORTRUD:** (*after a pause*). Why do you waste your strength on frantic rage like this?

**FREDERICK:** To think that they have taken the sword that else Had you laid at my feet.

**ORTRUD:** No, Frederick, Count of Telramund, why this distrust in me?

**FREDERICK:** Can you ask when I, misled by you
By your deceit ensnared accused that maiden?
Did you not say that, in the gloomy wood,
Looking from out the castle of your sires,
You saw her perpetrate the hideous deed?
With your own eyes you saw Elsa drowning
Her brother in the pool; and did you not
With prophecies rouse pride within my heart?
Soon, you said, Radbod's ancient

## Act II, Scene I

Elsa's Hand, der reinen, abzusteh'n,
und dich zum Weib zu nehmen,
weil du Radbod's letzter Spross?

ORTRUD: Ha, wie tödlich du mich
kränkst!—
Dies alles, ja! ich sagt' und zeugt' es
dir.

FRIEDRICH: Und machtest mich,
des' Name hochgeehrt, des' Leben
aller schönsten Tugend Preis, zu
deiner Lüge schändlichen Genossen?

ORTRUD: Wer log?

FRIEDRICH: Du!—hat nicht durch
sein Gericht Gott mich dafür geschlagen?

ORTRUD: Gott?

FRIEDRICH: Entsetzlich!
Wie tönt aus deinem Mund furchtbar der Name!

ORTRUD: Ha, nennst du deine
Feigheit Gott?

FRIEDRICH: Ortrud!

ORTRUD: Willst du mir droh'n?
mir, einem Weibe—droh'n?
O Feiger! hättest du so grimmig ihm
gedroht, der jetzt dich in das Elend
schickt, wohl hättest Sieg statt
Schande du erkauft!—
Ha, wer ihm zu entgetgnen wüsst',
der fänd' ihn schwächer als ein
Kind!

FRIEDRICH: Je schwächer er, Desto gewalt'ger kämpfte Gottes Kraft.

ORTRUD: Gottes Kraft? ha! ha!—
nur einen Tag gieb hier mir Macht,
und sicher zeig' ich dir, Welch
schwacher Gott es ist, der ihn bes-
chützt.

FRIEDRICH: Du wilde Seherin!
wie willst du doch Geheimnissvoll
den Geist mir neu berücken?

ORTRUD: Die Schwelger strecken
sich zur üpp'gen Ruh'. Setz' dich
zur Seite mir! die Stund' ist da, wo
dir mein Seherauge leuchten
soll.—
(*Friedrich nähert sich ihr.*)
Weisst du, wer dieser Held, den
hier Ein Schwan gezogen an das
Land?

FRIEDRICH: Nein!

ORTRUD: Was gäbst du drum, es zu
erfahren, wenn ich dir sag', ist er
gezwungen zu nennen, wie sein
Nam' und Art, All seine Macht zu

royal trunk
Would bud anew—give rulers to
Brabant.
Did you not induce me to reject
Young Elsa's hand, unspotted as it
was,
And choose you as the last of Rad-
bod's line?

ORTRUD: How bitter are your
words!
I own it. Yes. All this I said to you.

FREDERICK: And made me, whose
name was once revered,
Whose steps from honor's path had
never strayed,
The base accomplice of your
shameless falsehood?

ORTRUD: Falsehood?

FREDERICK: Even so. Had not the
charge been false,
Heaven would not have shamed
me!

ORTRUD: Heaven?

FREDERICK: Oh, hateful!
From lips like these the name of
Heaven sounds evil.

ORTRUD: Ah, "Heaven" you
called your cowardice.

FREDERICK: Ortrud!

ORTRUD: Would you threaten
me—me, a weak woman me?
Ah, coward! if so fiercely you had
menaced
Him who has brought you to this
misery,
Conquest instead of shame would
have been your lot.
Those who encounter him properly
will find
He's weaker than a child.

FREDERICK: If he was weak,
More certain is it Heaven put forth
its strength.

ORTRUD: You think so?
Ha, ha, give me the power
But for a single day, and I will plain-
ly show
How feeble is the Heaven in which
he trusts.

FREDERICK: Audacious sorceress,
do you attempt, by secret arts once
more to madden my soul?

ORTRUD: (*pointing to the Pallas,
which is now dark.*) The revelers
are wrapped in deep repose.
Come, sit near to me; the hour is
come
When my prophetic eye shall give
you light.
(*Frederick approaches her.*)
Come, do you know the stranger
knight
Who was brought here by a swan?

FREDERICK: No.

ORTRUD: What would you give to
learn the truth—
The mighty truth, that, if compelled

Ende ist, Die mühevoll ihm ein Zauber leiht?

FRIEDRICH: Ha! dann begriff' ich
sein Verbot?

ORTRUD: Nun hör'!
Niemand hat hier Gewalt ihm das
Geheimniss zu entreissen.
Als die, der er so streng verbot. Die
Frage je an ihn zu thun.

FRIEDRICH: So gält' es, Elsa zu verleiten, dass sie die Frag' ihm nicht
erliess'?

ORTRUD: Ha, wie begreifst du
schnell und wohl!

FRIEDRICH: Doch wie soll das gelingen?

ORTRUD: Hör'! Vor allem gilt's,
von hinnen nicht zu flieh'n: drum
schärfe deinen Witz!
Gerechten Argwohn ihr zu weck-
en, tritt vor, klag' ihn des Zauber's
an, durch den er das Gericht
getäuscht!

FRIEDRICH: Ha, Trug und Zaubers
List!

ORTRUD: Missglückt's so bleibt
ein Mittel der Gewalt.

FRIEDRICH: Gewalt!

ORTRUD: Umsonst nicht bin ich in
geheimsten Küsten tief erfahren;
drum achte wohl, was ich dir sage!
Jed' Wesen, das durch Zauber stark,
wird ihm des Leibes kleinstes Glied
entrissen nur, muss sich alsbald
Ohnmächtig zeigen, wie es ist.

FRIEDRICH: Ha, sprachst du wahr!

ORTRUD: O hättest du im Kampf
nur einen Finger ihm, Ja, eines Fingers Glied entschlagen, der Held—
er war in deiner Macht!

FRIEDRICH: Entsetzlich, ha! was
lässet do mich hören?
Durch Gottes Arm geschlagen
wähnt ich mich, — Nun liess durch
Trug sich das Gericht bethören,
durch Zauber's List verlor mein'
Ehre ich!
Doch meine Schande könnt' ich
rächen?
Bezeugen könnt' ich meine Treu'?
Des Buhlen Trug, ich könnt' ihn
brechen, und meine Ehr' gewönn'
ich neu?—
O Weib, das in der Nacht ich vor
mir seh'!
Betrügst du jetzt mich noch, dann
weh' dir, weh'!

ORTRUD: Ha, wie du rasest!—ru-
hig und besonnen!
So lehr' ich dich der Rache süsse
Wonnen.

His name and station to reveal,
The vaunted strength at once
would cease,
Which to a magic spell he owes?

FREDERICK: Ha! then his words I
understood.

ORTRUD: Attend! Here no one has
the power
To pluck the secret from his breast
Excepting her whom he forbade
About the mystery to ask.

FREDERICK: I see now.
Elsa must be lured, in spite of all, to
question him.

ORTRUD: My meaning you have fathomed well.

FREDERICK: Yet how effect our
purpose?

ORTRUD: Hear!
It much imports we do not leave
This place, so sharpen well your
wits,
That you may fill her with distrust.
Step forth! charge him with sorcery,
With warping justice by deceit.

FREDERICK: Yes, sorcery and
fraud.

ORTRUD: At worst we still can gain
our end by force.

FREDERICK: By force?

ORTRUD: Believe me, not in vain I
have learned the darkest science;
therefore attend to what I say.
He who is made through magic
strong, if from his body even the
smallest part is torn, at once in all
his weakness must appear.

FREDERICK: Do you speak the
truth?

ORTRUD: Oh, had you but cut off a
finger from his hand,
Or even a finger's joint, for certain
That knight would now be in your
power!

FREDERICK: It is fearful!
Oh, I thought I was defeated because its aid great Heaven denied.
Now must I hear the royal judge was
cheated, that magic arts have
overthrown my pride, I can recover
my lost repute; make good the loss
that I deplore, my hated victor triumph over, and be my honored self
once more?
O wife! who through the night this
light can show, if you deceive me,
woe to you—woe!

ORTRUD: No, how you rave!
Calmness, I implore you, so all the
joys of vengeance I will teach you.

ORTRUD UND FRIEDRICH: Der Rache Werk sei nun beschworen aus meines Busens wilder Nacht. Die ihr in süssem Schlaf verloren, wisst, dass für euch das Unheil wacht!

## ZWEITE SCENE

(Elsa ist auf dem söller der Kemenate erschienen.—Friedrich und Ortrud.)

ELSA: Euch Lüften, die mein Klagen so traurig oft erfüllt, euch muss ich dankend sagen, wie sich mein Glück enthüllt.

ORTRUD: Sie ist es!

FRIEDRICH: Elsa.

ELSA: Durch euch kam er gezogen, ihr lächeltet der Fahrt; auf wilden Meereswogen habt ihr ihn treu bewahrt.

ORTRUD: Der Stunde soll sie fluchen, in der sie jetzt mein Blick gewahrt!

ELSA: Zu trocknen meine Zähren hab' ich euch oft gemüht: wollt Kühlung nun gewähren der Wang' in Lieb' erglüht!

ORTRUD: Hinweg! Entfern' ein Kleines dich von mir!

FRIEDRICH: Warum?

ORTRUD: Sie ist für mich—ihr Held gehöre dir!
(Friedrich entfernt sich in den Hintergrund.)
Elsa!

ELSA: Wer ruft?—
Wie schauerlich und klagend ertönt mein Name durch die Nacht?

ORTRUD: Elsa!
Ist mein Stimme dir so fremd?—
Willst du die Arme ganz verläugnen, die du in's fernste Elend schick'st?

ELSA: Ortrud! bist du's?—was machst du hier Unglücklich Weib?

ORTRUD: . . . Unglücklich Weib?
Wohl hast du recht mich so zu nennen! In ferner Einsamkeit des Waldes, wo still und friedsam ich gelebt,—Was that ich dir? was that ich dir?
Freudlos, das Unglück nur beweinend, das lang belastet meinen Stamm, was that ich dir? was that ich dir?

ELSA: Um Gott, was klagest du mich an?
War ich es, die dir Leid gebracht?

ORTRUD: Wie könntest du fürwahr mir neiden das Glück, dass mich zum Weib erwählt der Mann, den du so gern verschmäht?

---

BOTH: A sense of joy comes over me creeping, dark thoughts are raging in my breast;
You who are sleeping in happiness soon will be startled from your rest.

## SCENE II

(Elsa, in a white dress, appears on the balcony of the Kemenate, which she leans over. Frederick and Ortrud sit opposite on the steps of the Minster.)

ELSA: Oh breezes, who so often heard tales of my distress, grateful, the joy that fills me I will confess to you.

ORTRUD: It is Elsa!

FREDERICK: Elsa!

ELSA: Through you he floated safely—you checked the billows wild, in vain was all their fury, when you smiled on his course.

ORTRUD: How often will she curse The hour at which she sees me?

ELSA: I begged you often in sorrow, to dry a falling tear; now cool the burning blushes that on my cheeks appear.

ORTRUD: Away! retire some distance here.

FREDERICK: But why?

ORTRUD: She is for me—her champion is for you.
(Frederick withdraws to the background.)
(In a plaintive voice.)
Elsa.

ELSA: Who calls?
Why fearfully and sadly resounds my name thus through the night?

ORTRUD: Elsa, so strange appears my voice, and can you thus repel the wretch whom you have brought to misery?

ELSA: Ortrud!
Is it you?
What are you doing here, you hapless one?

ORTRUD: "You hapless one!"
You named me rightly now indeed.
In yonder forest's deep recesses I passed my days in solitude;
How have I harmed you? How have I harmed you?
Joyless, bewailing the misfortunes so long inflicted on my race.
How have I harmed you? How have I . . .

ELSA: Good Heaven!
What lay you to my charge?
Were you brought to misery by me?

ORTRUD: To think that you could look with envy on me because the man despised by you—preferred me for his wife?

---

ELSA: Allgüt'ger Gott, was sol mir das?

ORTRUD: Musst' ihn unsel'ger Wahn bethören, dich Reine einer Schuld zu zeih'n, von Reu' ist nun sein Herz zerrissen, zu grimmer Buss' ist er verdammt.

ELSA: Gerechter Gott!

ORTRUD: O du bist glücklich!—Nach kurzem, unschuldsüssem Leiden, siehst lächelnd du das Leben nur; von mir darfst selig du dich scheiden, mich schickst du auf des Todes Spur.—
Dass meines Jammers trüber Schein nie kehr' in deine Feste ein.

ELSA: Wie schlecht ich deine Güte priese, Allmächt'ger, der mich so beglückt, wenn ich das Unglück von mir stiesse,
Das sich vor mir im Staube bückt!—
O nimmer!
Ortrud! harre mein!
Ich selber lass' dich zu mir ein.
(Sie geht eilig in die Kemenate zurück.)

ORTRUD: Entweihte Götter! helft jetzt meiner Rache!
Bestraft die Schmach, die hier euch angethan!
Stärkt mich im Dienste eurer heil'gen Sache,
Vernichtet der Abtrünnigen schnöden Wahn!
Wodan! dich Starken rufe ich!
Freia!
Erhab'ne, höre mich!
Segnet mir Trug und Heuchelei
Dass glücklich meine Rache sei!
(Elsa und zwei Mägde, welche Lichte tragen, treten auf.)

ELSA: Ortrud? wo bist du?

ORTRUD: Hier, zu deinen Füssen!

ELSA: Hilf Gott! so muss ich dich erblicken, die ich in Stolz und Pracht nur sah!
Es will das Herze mir ersticken, seh' ich so niedrig dich mir nah.—
Steh' auf! o spare mir dein Bitten!
Trug'st du mir Hass, verzieh' ich dir; was du schon jetzt durch mich gelitten, das, bitt' ich dich, verzeih' auch mir!

ORTRUD: O habe Lohn für so viel Güte!

ELSA: Der morgen nun mein Gatte heisst, anfleh' ich sein liebreich Gemüthe, dass Friedrich auch er Gnad' erweist.

ORTRUD: Du fesselst mich in Dankes Banden.

---

ELSA: All-gracious Heaven, what can you mean?

ORTRUD: Beguiled by some insane illusion, you innocent, he charged with guilt.
This heart now melts with deep contrition—
How heavy is his punishment!

ELSA: Avenging powers!

ORTRUD: Yes, you are happy.
Your hours of short-lived grief are ended.
Life wears for you a smiling face.
You heedlessly can cast me from you, to trace death's never-failing path.
Thus never will my sorrow, never darken the threshold of your door.

ELSA: How ill should I repay the bounties,
Kind Heaven, of your surpassing grace,
If when the wretched bent before me I drove them hence with scornful face.
I cannot—Ortrud, say no more, I will open the door for you myself.
(Retires into the Kemenate.)

ORTRUD: (springing from the steps with wild delight). You gods! now slighted, I am calling on you.
Would you remain forever in the shade?
Your cause is mine, you deities appalling.
Ah! check the progress of the renegade. Wodan, ever great and strong,
Freia, once sung in many a song,
Give your assistance to deceit—
My vengeance then will be complete.
(Elsa and two servants, with candles, enter from the lower door of the Kemenate.)

ELSA: Ortrud, where are you?

ORTRUD: (kneeling). Here behold me prostrate.

ELSA: Arise!
Thus must I see you kneeling, you whom I know to be so great, so proud?
It would move a heart devoid of feeling, to see your head so lowly bow'd.
Arise.
All wrong you have committed—free pardon now for all. You are not scorned but deeply pitied; in turn forgive me for your woes,

ORTRUD: For this compassion Heaven reward you!

ELSA: He who tomorrow calls me bride,
Like me shall regard you with pity, and Frederick shall forgive beside.

ORTRUD: What gratitude can ever repay you?

ELSA: In Früh'n lass mich bereit dich seh'n!
Geschmückt mit prächtigen Gewanden, sollst du mit mir zum Münster gehen.
Dort harre ich des Helden mein, vor Gott sein Eh'gemahl zu sein.

ELSA: When first the morning begins to glow
In costly ornaments array yourself;
Then with me to the Minster go,
Where I shall await the hero,
Whom Heaven has deigned with me to mate.

ORTRUD: Wie kann ich solche Huld dir lohnen, da machtlos ich und elend bin?
Soll ich in Gnaden bei dir wohnen, stets bleib' ich nur die Bettlerin.
Nur eine Kraft ist mir gegeben, sie raubte mir kein Machtgebot; durch sie vielleicht schütz' ich dein Leben, bewahr' es vor der Reue Noth.

ORTRUD: What fitting homage can I show you?
So poor and weak, you know well a wretch am I too far below you, though in your favor I may dwell.
Of one small power have none bereft me. One power unweakened still I have, can use it still while it is left me, perhaps to save you from sorrow.

ELSA: Wie meinst du?

ELSA: What do you mean?

ORTRUD: Wohl dass ich dich warne, zu blind sich deinem Glück zu trau'n; dass nicht ein Unheil dich umgarne, lass mich für dich zur Zukunft schau'n.

ORTRUD: Gentle Elsa, mind, although the present seems so fair, you must not let its brightness blind you, your future wealth must be my care.

ELSA: Welch' Unheil?

ELSA: What threatens?

ORTRUD: Konntest du erfassen, Wie dessen Art so wundersam, der nie dich möge zu verlassen, wie er durch Zauber zu dir kam!

ORTRUD: Can you fathom ever how wondrous must his magic be who never could leave you maiden—never—as he by magic came to you?

ELSA: Du Aermste kannst wohl nie ermessen, wie zweifellos mein Herze liebt!
Du hast wohl nie das Glück besessen, das sich uns nur durch Glauben giebt!
Kehr' bei mir ein! lass mich dich lehren, wie süss die Wonne reinster Treu'!
Lass zu dem Glauben dich bekehren: Es giebt ein Glück, das ohne Reu'!

ELSA: (shrinks from Ortrud and then regards her with pity). Poor creature! You can never measure the depth of bliss in trusting hearts; never can you understand the pleasure which faith, and faith alone imparts.
Come, enter here—come, I beseech you, and learn from me the purest joy.
Yes, I will teach you true happiness—a happiness without alloy.

ORTRUD: (für sich). Ha! dieser Stolz, es soll mich lehren, wie bekämpfe ihre Treu'; gen ihn will ich die Waffen kehren, durch ihren Hochmuth werd' ihr Reu'!
(Elsa führt Ortrud in die Kemenate, die Mägde leuchten voran.— Friedrich tritt aus dem Hintergrunde hervor.)

ORTRUD: (to herself). Ah, hateful pride! Yet it shall teach me the way to mar this purest joy.
Her words unwittingly beseech me the bliss she boasts of to destroy.
(Elsa leads Ortrud into the Kemenate, lighted by the servants. The day has begun to dawn. Frederick comes forward.)

FRIEDRICH: So zieht das Unheil in dies Haus!—
Vollführe, Weib, was deine List ersonnen, dein Werk zu hemmen fühl' ich keine Macht!
Das Unheil hat mit meinem Fall begonnen,— nun stürzet nach, die mich dahin gebracht!
Nur eines seh' ich mahnend vor mir steh'n: der Räuber meiner Ehre soll vergeh'n!

FREDERICK: Thus mischief enters yonder house.
The game, my wife, you craftily are winning.
The work you have to do I cannot stop.
The mischief, with my base defeat beginning, now on my foes with force shall drop.
Of all before me, this I see alone— the murderers of my honor are undone.

## DRITTE SCENE

## SCENE III

(Der Tag bricht vollends an. Thürmer blasen ein Morgenlied, von einem entfernteren Thurme wird geantwortet.—Dann schreiten die vier Heerhornbläser aus dem Palast und blasen den Königsruf, worauf sie wieder

(Broad daylight. Warder gives morning signal, which is answered from a distant tower. Servants enter from the interior of the fortress. They dip pails into a well and carry them into the Pallas. The four trumpeters then

zurückgehen.)
(Fredrich hat sich hinter einem Mauervorsprung am Münster verborgen.—Aus dem Burghofe und durch das Thurmthor kommen nun brabantische Edle und Mannen vor dem Münster zusammen.)

DIE EDLEN UND MANNEN: In Früh'n versammelt uns der Ruf, gar viel verheisset wohl der Tag!
Der hier so hehre Wunder schuf, manch neue That vollbringen mag.
(Der Heerrufer schreitet mit den vier Heerhornbläsern aus dem Palast heraus.)

DER HEERRUFER: Des Königs Wort und Will' thu' ich euch kund, Drum achtet wohl, was euch durch mich er sagt!
In Bann und Acht ist Friedrich Telramund, weil untreu er den Gotteskampf gewagt: wer sein noch pflegt, wer sich zu ihm gesellt, nach Reiches Recht derselben Acht verfällt.

DIE MÄNNER: Fluch ihm! dem Ungetreuen, den Gottes Urtheil traf! Ihn soll der Reine scheuen, es flieh' ihn Ruh' und Schlaf!

DER HEERRUFER: Und weiter kündet euch der König an, dass er den fremden gottgesandten Mann, den Elsa zum Gemahle sich ersehnt, mit Land und Krone von Brabant belehnt.
Doch will der Held nicht Herzog sein genannt, ihr sollt ihn heissen: Schützer von Brabant.

DIE MÄNNER: Hoch der ersehnte Mann, Heil ihm, den Gott gesandt.
Treu sind wir unterthan dem Schützer von Brabant.

DER HEERRUFER: Nun hört, was Er durch mich euch künden lässt! Heut' feiert er mit euch sein Hochzeitsfest; doch morgen sollt ihr kampfgerüstet nah'n, zur Heeresfolg' dem König unterthan.
Er selbst verschmäht der süssen Ruh' zu pflegen, Er führt euch an zu hehren Ruhmes Segen!

DIE MÄNNER: Zum Streite säumet nicht, führt euch der Hehre an! Wer muthig mit ihm ficht, dem lacht des Ruhmes Bahn.
Von Gott ist er gesandt zur Grösse von Brabant.
(Während der Heerrufer wieder in den Palast zurückgeht, treten im Vordergrunde vier Edle zusammen.)

DER ERSTE EDLE: Nun hört! dem Lande will er uns entführen?

come out of the Pallas, and, after sounding the royal summons, retire. Frederick has concealed himself behind a buttress of the Minster. From the gates of the fortress and through the town gate nobles of Brabant and retainers advance to the front of the Minster and greet each other.)

NOBLES AND RETAINERS: The early summons we obey.
How bright with promise seems the day!
Oh he who could such honor gain, fresh glory surely will attain.
(Herald, with his four trumpeters, advances from the Pallas to the elevation in front of it. The royal summons is again sounded.)

HERALD: I now proclaim the King's august decree!
Hear with respect, then, what he says through me: Frederick, the Count of Telramund, is banned, who faithlessly in sight of Heaven could stand.
If any dare consort with him at all, on him, by ancient law, the ban shall fall.

ALL THE MEN: Our curse upon the traitor whom Heaven has overthrown!
Let good men all avoid him, to him be rest unknown.
(Trumpets sound again.)

HERALD: And further, solemnly the King proclaims that he, the stranger Heaven-appointed, names the lady Elsa's spouse by royal grant, to hold the land and Dukedom of Brabant.
As Duke he will not be, by royal grant he bears the title, Guardian of Brabant.

ALL THE MEN: Hail!
Heaven-appointed! hail! whom God grants to us: Loyal and true, we hail you Guardian of Brabant.
(Trumpets sound again.)

HERALD: To this as well now give attention all.
He holds today his wedding festival.
Tomorrow's dawn will bring sterner duties, with him you'll join the forces of the King. All soft delight in days of peril spurning, you will follow him, earning deathless glory.

CHORUS: We follow, matchless knight, wherever you may lead.
Sword will light the way to many a noble deed.
Yes!
Heaven through you will grant new glory to Brabant.
(While the men are occupied with each other, and when the Herald has retired into the Pallas, four nobles of Brabant advance.)

FIRST NOBLE: You hear how from our country he will take us!

**DER ZWEITE:** Gen einen Feind, der uns noch nie bedroht?

**SECOND NOBLE:** Against the men who never were our foes?

**DER DRITTE:** Solch' kühn Beginnen sollt' ihm nicht gebühren!

**THIRD NOBLE:** A bad beginning! Would he make us bondsmen?

**DER VIERTE:** Wer wehret ihm, wenn er die Fahrt gebot?

**FOURTH NOBLE:** But who will dare oppose his mandate?

**FRIEDRICH:** (*unter sie tretend*). Ich.

**FREDERICK:** (*coming forward and somewhat uncovering his face.*) I!

**DIE VIER EDLEN:** Ha! wer bist du? Friedrich! seh' ich recht? Du wagst dich her, zur Beute jedem Knecht?

**ALL FOUR:** Ha, who are you? Frederick—No, ah, No. Here you will be a prey to every knave.

**FRIEDRICH:** Gar bald will ich wohl weiter noch mich wagen! Vor euren Augen soll es leuchtend tagen! Der euch so kühn die Heerfahrt angesagt, der sei von mir des Gottestrug's beklagt.

**FREDERICK:** You soon will know to what extent I dare; Soon the truth will shine brightly before your eyes Soon I will declare him an impostor!

**DIE VIER EDLEN:** Was hör' ich! Rasender, was hast du vor? Verlor'ner du, hört dich des Volkes Ohr! (*Sie drängen Friedrich bei Seite. Edelknaben treten auf.*)

**ALL FOUR:** What did you say? Take care—take care. Beware of the people's wrath. (*They lead Frederick aside and carefully hide him from the people. Pages appear on the balcony of the Kemenate, descend towards the Pallas, and summon the men.*)

**VIER EDELKNABEN:** Mach Platz für Elsa, unsere Frau! Die will in Gott zum Münster geh'n.

**FOUR PAGES:** Make way, make way! our Lady Elsa comes, and will proceed to the Minster. (*They make a broad passage through the men, who readily give way, and clear the steps of the Minster, where they take their stand.*)

## VIERTE SCENE

## SCENE IV

(*Ein langer Zug von Frauen in reichen Gewändern schreitet aus der Kemenate dem Münster zu.*)

(*A long train of ladies, richly clad, advances from the interior of the Kemenate to the balcony, and then descends towards the Pallas, which winds to the foreground to reach the Minster.*)

**DIE EDLEN UND MANNEN:** (*während des Aufzuges*). Gesegnet soll sie schreiten, die lang' in Demuth litt! Gott möge sie geleiten und hüten ihren Schritt!— Sie naht, die Engelgleiche, von keuscher Gluth entbrannt! Heil dir, du Tugendreiche! Heil Elsa von Brabant! (*Elsa ist im Zuge aufgetreten; Ortrud folgt.*)

**NOBLES AND RETAINERS:** May blessings shower upon you, who could endure such woes! May saints watch kindly over you, and make your pathway sure. She comes, the maid angelic, to Heaven a suppliant for days by grief unchecked. Hail, Elsa of Brabant! (*Elsa, magnificently attired, has advanced in the procession; among the last ladies who follow her is Ortrud, also richly clad, from whom the rest shrink with ill-concealed scorn, so that she appears to be almost alone, her face betraying the most violent anger. When Elsa, amid loud acclamations, is about to set her foot on the first step of the Minster, Ortrud breaks from her ranks, places herself on the steps before Elsa, and compels her to retreat.*)

**ORTRUD:** Zurück, Elsa! nicht länger will ich dulden, dass ich gleich einer Magd dir folgen soll! Den Vortritt sollst du überall mir schulden, vor mir dich beugen sollst du demuthvoll!

**ORTRUD:** Back, Elsa, back, nor to precede me endeavor, no menial was I born to follow you. The right to lead the way I never forfeit. Humbly bowed before me your head shall be.

**DIE EDELKNABEN UND DIE MÄNNER:** Was will das Weib?

**PAGES AND MEN:** What does she seek?

**ELSA:** Um Gott! was muss ich seh'n? Welch' jäher Wechsel ist mit dir geschehn?

**ELSA:** (*shocked*). By Heaven! but this is strange; I cannot understand this sudden change.

**ORTRUD:** Weil eine Stund' ich meines Werth's vergessen, glaubst du, ich müsste dir nur kriechend nah'n? Mein Leid zu rähen will ich mich vermessen. Was mir gebührt, das will ich nun empfah'n.

**ORTRUD:** Although I came to you, disgracing my rank, do not think to make me your humble slave. Now I seek vengeance! and the blot effacing, I claim and mean to take my right.

**ELSA:** Weh! liess ich durch dein Heucheln mich verleiten, die diese Nacht sich jammernd zu mir stahl? Willst du nun in Hochmuth vor mir schreiten, du, eines Gottgerichteten Gemahl?

**ELSA:** Ah, did a wily hypocrite deceive me, when shedding piteous tears, she came to me? How can you dare with insolence to grieve me— You, you whose husband Heaven has marked with shame?

**ORTRUD:** Wenn falsch Gericht mir den Gemahl verbannte, war doch sein Nam' im Lande hochgehrt; als aller Tugend Preis man ihn nur nannte, gekannt, gefürchtet war sein tapf'res Schwert. Der deine, sag', wer sollte hier ihn kennen, vermagst du selbst den Namen nicht zu nennen?

**ORTRUD:** Although injustice now has overthrown him, here was my husband adored by all hearts. As honor's brightest flower all here have known him— have known, have feared his keen, resistless sword. Your bridegroom—ah! of him, proud Elsa, boast not, a stranger here, whose very name you do not know.

**MÄNNER UND FRAUEN:** Was sagt sie? Ha! was thut sie kund?— Sie lästert! wehret ihrem Mund!

**CHORUS:** What does she mean? Ha, what does she say? She's raving! Stop this blaspheming.

**ORTRUD:** Kannst du ihn nennen? kannst du uns es sagen, ob sein Geschlecht, sein Adel wohl bewährt? Woher die Fluthen ihn zu dir getragen, wann und wohin er wieder von dir fährt? Ha, nein! wohl brächte ihm es schlimme Noth. Der kluge Held die Frage drum verbot!

**ORTRUD:** Oh, nothing you know—no he has not taught you— whether his race is noble, without stain, nor when the waters brought you his assistance, whether and when they'll bear him here again. Oh, no! surely your champion had strong motives when he sternly forbade any question.

**MÄNNER UND FRAUEN:** Ha! spricht sie wahr? welch' schwere Klagen!— Sie schmähet ihn! darf sie es wagen?

**MEN AND WOMEN:** How fierce her words! How? Does she speak truly? Was ever heard a tongue so unruly?

**ELSA:** Du Lästerin! Ruchlose Frau! Hör', ob ich Antwort mir getrau'!— So rein und edel ist sein Wesen, so tugendreich der hehre Mann, dass nie des Unheils soll genesen, wer seiner Sendung zweifeln kann! Hat nicht durch Gott im Kampf geschlagen Mein theurer Held den Gatten dein? Nun sollt nach Recht ihr alle sagen, Wer kann da nur der Reine sein?

**ELSA:** Injurious dame, those taunts forbear; hear, this my answer plainly hear! He's pure and noble past all measure. That soul shall never taste of pleasure who dares to doubt his mission. He before Heaven's tribunal fighting her husband bravely overthrew. Say, then, your voices all uniting, whom you consider pure and true.

**MÄNNER UND FRAUEN:** Nur er! nur er! dein Held allein!

**MEN AND WOMEN:** He—he is pure and true.

ORTRUD: Ha! diese Reine deines Helden, wie wäre sie so bald getrübt, müsst' er des Zaubers Wesen melden, durch den hier solche Macht er übt!
Wagst du ihn nicht darum zu fragen, so glauben alle wir mit Recht, du müssest selbst in Sorge zagen, um seine Reine steh' es schlecht!

DIE FRAUEN: Helft ihr vor der Verruchten Hass!

MÄNNER: Macht Platz! macht Platz! der König naht!

## FÜNFTE SCENE

*(Der König, Lohengrin, die sächsischen und brabantischen Grafen und Edlen sind aus dem Palast herausgeschritten.)*

DIE MÄNNER: Heil!
Heil dem König!
Heil dem Schützer von Brabant!

KÖNIG: Was für ein Streit?

ELSA: Mein Herr, mein Gebieter!

LOHENGRIN: Was giebt's?

KÖNIG: Wer wagt es hier, den Kirchengang zu stören?

DES KÖNIGS GEFOLGE: Welcher Streit, den wir vernahmen?

LOHENGRIN: Was seh' ich! das unsel'ge Weib bei dir?

ELSA: Mein Retter! schütze mich vor dieser Frau!
Schilt mich, wenn ich dir ungehorsam war!
In Jammer sah ich sie vor dieser Pforte, aus ihrer Noth nahm ich sie bei mir auf: nun sieh', wie furchtbar sie mir lohnt die Güte, sie schilt mich, dass ich dir zu sehr vertrau'!

LOHENGRIN: Du fürchterliches Weib! steh' ab von ihr!
Hier wird dir nimmer Sieg!—
Sag', Elsa mir!
Vermocht'ihr Gift sie in dein Herz zu giessen?
*(Elsa birgt ihr Gesicht an seiner Brust.)*
Komm! lass in Freude dort die Thränen fliessen!

FRIEDRICH: O König!
Trugbethörte Fürsten! haltet ein!

DIE MÄNNER: Was will der hier?
Verfluchter, weich' von hinnen!

KÖNIG: Wag'st du zu trotzen meinem Zorn?

FRIEDRICH: O hört mich an!

ORTRUD: Though pure and noble seems your lover, to foul disgrace would he be brought did he the magic spells discover by which such wonders he has wrought.
Come, then—if you dare not question him, this only can we think, be sure, to hear the simple truth you care not, or do not deem his soul so pure.

WOMEN: Oh, shield her from this woman's hate.

MEN: Make room, make room—here comes, the king!

## SCENE V

*(The King, Lohengrin, the Saxon and Brabant nobles, all magnificently clad, advance from the Pallas. Lohengrin and the King press their way through the throng in the foreground.)*

MEN: Hail, hail, King Henry! hail, Guardian of Brabant!

KING: What means this strife?

ELSA: *(falling on Lohengrin's bosom).* My lord—oh, my preserver!

LOHENGRIN: What is it?

KING: Who is it dares to stand before the Minster?

KING'S ATTENDANTS: From where comes this strife?
Its sound has reached us.

LOHENGRIN: Oh, monstrous!
That ill-omened form by you!

ELSA: My champion!
Shield me now against my foe.
Blame me if I disobeyed your commands. I saw her weeping here before this portal, and sought to save her from her misery.
Behold, how ill she now requites my kindness—upbraids me for my confidence in you!

LOHENGRIN: *(looking sternly at Ortrud).* Away from her at once, vile sorceress!
Here you will miss your aim.
Dear Elsa, say—say, has the venom descended to your heart?
*(She hides her face against his bosom. Raising her hand and pointing to the Minster.)*
Come, there the purest joy shall your sorrow ended.
*(As Lohengrin, with Elsa, is proceeding to the Minster, Frederick appears on the steps before the ladies and pages, who shrink from him with horror.)*

FREDERICK: King Henry, much deluded monarch, stay a while.

ALL THE MEN: Accursed one!
Quit our presence!

KING: Dare you to defy my wrath?

FREDERICK: Hear me out!

DIE MÄNNER: Hinweg! du bist des Todes, Mann!

FRIEDRICH: Hört mich, dem grimmes Unrecht ihr gethan!
Gottes Gericht, es ward entehrt, betrogen, durch eines Zaubers List seid ihr belogen!

DIE MÄNNER: Greift den Verruchten! Hört, er lästert Gott!

FRIEDRICH: Den dort im Glanz ich vor mir sehe, den klag' ich des Betruges an!
Wie Staub vor Gottes Hauch verwehe die Macht, die er durch List gewann!—
Wie schlecht ihr des Gerichtes wahrtet, das doch die Ehre mir benahm, da eine Frag' ihr ihm erspartet als zum Gotteskampfe kam.
Die Frage nun sollt ihr nicht wehren, dass sie ihm jetzt von mir gestellt:—
Nach Namen, Heimath, Stand und Ehren frag' ich ihn laut vor aller Welt.—
Wer ist er, der an's Land geschwommen, geführt von einem wilden Schwan?
Wem solche Zauberthiere frommen, des' Reinheit achte ich für Wahn. Nun soll der Klag' er Rede stehen:
Vermag er's, so geschah mir Recht,—Wenn nicht, so sollet ihr ersehen, um seine Tugend steh' es schlecht!

DER KÖNIG UND DIE MÄNNER: Welch' schwere Klage! was wird er entgegnen?

LOHENGRIN: Nicht dir, der so vergass der Ehren, hab' Noth ich Rede hier zu steh'n!
Des Bösen Zweifel darf ich wehren, vor ihm wird Reine nicht vergeh'n.

FRIEDRICH: Darf ich ihm nicht als würdig gelten, dich ruf' ich, König, hochgeehrt!
Wird er auch unadlig schelten, dass er die Frage dir verwehrt?

LOHENGRIN: Ja, selbst dem König darf ich wehren, und aller Fürsten höchstem Rath!
Nicht dar sie Zweifels Last beschweren, sie sahen meine gute That.
Nur Eine ist's, der muss ich Antwort geben: Elsa—
Elsa!—wie seh' ich sie erbeben!—
In wildem Brüten muss ich sie gewahren, hat sie bethört des Hasses Lügenmund?
O Himmel! schirme sie vor den Gefahren!
Nie werde Zweifel dieser Reinen kund!

FRIEDRICH UND ORTRUD: In wildem Brüten darf ich sie gewahren!
Der Zweifel keimt in ihres Herzens

ALL THE MEN: Away! You're a condemned man!

FREDERICK: Hear me, to whom have done you grievous wrong.
Heaven's arbiters, you are disgraced and cheated; by this vile sorcerer justice was defeated.

ALL THE MEN: Seize the outcast!
Hark! how he blasphemes!

FREDERICK: He who so proudly lords it over me, he is a sorcerer, I declare, and scatter even as dust before me a power attained by means unfair.
Your duty was for him neglected.
Although you branded me with shame, one question had the truth detected before we to the trial came.
In your default I now will task him, the course of right you dare not stop.
His station—name—I plainly ask him here what they are allowed to say.
*(General emotion.)* Who was it, cruising on our river, drawn only by a wild swan?
A knight, using such strange familiars can scarcely be an honest man.
Let him give me an answer.
Does he comply?
Then his cause is right.
If not, you plainly will perceive his honor does not look too bright.

KING AND MEN: The charge is heavy; how will he refute it?

LOHENGRIN: I need not give answer to you. So stained are you with foul disgrace.
I heed not the doubts of evil hearts those purest honor never efface.

FREDERICK: If I am infected with disgrace, Great King, to you I will appeal.
Question him yourself—you'll be respected,
He'll not conceal the truth from you.

LOHENGRIN: Should all the noble knights about me, should even King Henry give command—I'd not reply; you need not doubt me.
My worth is proved by this right hand.
To one alone all—all, without dissembling—Elsa—no, how is it you are trembling?
Within her heart already doubt is dwelling; has deceit's vile tongue overthrown her trust?
Oh guard her Heaven!
insidious foes repelling. Nor to her soul let doubt be ever known.

ORTRUD AND FREDERICK: Within her heart already doubt is dwelling.
I know the thoughts that pain her

Grund; der mir zur Noth in dieses Land gefahren, er ist besiegt, wird ihm die Frage kund!

**DER KÖNIG UND ALLE MÄNNER:** Welch' ein Geheimniss muss der Held bewahren, bringt es ihm Noth, so wahr't es treu sein Mund.
Wir schirmen ihn, den Edlen, vor Gefahren; durch seine That ward uns sein Adel kund.

**ELSA:** Was er verbirgt, wohl brächt' es ihm Gefahren, vor aller Welt spräch' es hier aus sein Mund:—
Die er errettet, weh' mir Undankbaren.
Verrieth' ich ihn, dass hier es werde kund.—
Wüsst' ich sein Loos, ich wollt' es treu bewahren: im Zweifel doch erbebt des Herzens Grund!

**DER KÖNIG:** Mein Held! entgegne kühn dem Ungetreuen!
Du bist zu hehr, um, was er klagt, zu scheuen!

**DIE MÄNNER:** Wir steh'n zu dir! es soll uns nie gereuen, dass wir der Helden Preis in dir erkannt.
Reich' uns die Hand; wir glauben dir in Treuen, dass hehr dein Nam', auch wenn er nicht genannt.

**LOHENGRIN:** Euch Helden soll der Glaube nimmer gereuen, Werd' Euch mein Nam' und Art auch nie genannt!

**FRIEDRICH:** (*heimlich zu Elsa*). Vertraue mir! lass dir ein Mittel heissen, das dir Gewissheit schafft.

**ELSA:** Hinweg von mir!

**FRIEDRICH:** Lass mich das kleinste Glied ihm nur entreissen, des Fingers Spitze, und ich schwöre dir, Was er dir hehlt, sollst frei du vor dir seh'n, dir treu, soll nie er dir von hinnen geh'n!

**ELSA:** Ha, nimmermehr!

**FRIEDRICH:** Ich bin dir nah' zur Nacht—
Ruf'st du, ohn' Schaden ist es schnell vollbracht.

**LOHENGRIN:** Elsa, mit wem verkehrest du?—
Zurück von ihr, Verfluchte!
Dass nie mein Auge je euch wieder bei ihr seh'!
Elsa, erhebe dich!
In deiner Hand, in deiner Treu' liegt alles Glükes Pfand, lässt nicht des Zweifels Macht dich ruh'n?
Willst du die Frage an mich thun?

well we soon shall rise, our foes with glory quelling; the secret told, he is at once overthrown.

**KING AND MEN:** Still rests the secret dwelling in his bosom.
Nothing he would hide his lips shall ever own.
We stand by him, all threatening danger quelling. Nobility by deeds like his is shown.

**ELSA:** Some dreadful ill might he incur by telling the secret which of right is his alone.
She whom he rescued, tempters base repelling, will ever let that secret rest unknown.
Still, I knew all—be still, thought repelling!
Within my heart the power of doubt I own.

**KING:** Whatever the traitor says, undaunted hear him.
Noblest of knights, you have no cause to fear him.

**MEN:** (*crowding round Lohengrin*). We stand by you, and be assured that we will never forget our true allegiance. Give us your hand—we cling to you forever, revere your name, although we know it not.

**LOHENGRIN:** This trust, my friends, you will regret it never, although you do not know my name and station.
(*While Lohengrin, surrounded by the men, has retired towards the background, Frederick, unobserved, bends down to Elsa, who in her perplexity has remained in the foreground.*)

**FREDERICK:** (*secretly, to Elsa.*) Confide in me—one plan that will securely give certainty, I'll tell.

**ELSA:** Away from me!

**FREDERICK:** Let him but lose the smallest limb—then surely, Though but a finger—finger's joint it be, All he conceals, he will confide, to you, He ever will faithfully with you abide.

**ELSA:** Ha, never more!

**FREDERICK:** At night I shall be near, call me—it is done—you need fear no mischief.

**LOHENGRIN:** (*suddenly comes forward*). Elsa, with whom were you conversing?
(*Elsa, with a look of pain, turns away from Frederick, and sinks at Lohengrin's feet.*) Away from her, you traitor, and never let me behold you near my bride!
Elsa, my love, look up.
You hold no less within your grasp

**ELSA:** Mein Retter, der mir Heil gebracht!
Mein Held, in dem ich muss vergeh'n! Hoch über alles Zweifels Macht . . . soll meine Liebe steh'n!

**LOHENGRIN:** Heil dir, Elsa! nun lass voran uns geh'n!

**DIE MÄNNER UND FRAUEN:** Seht! seht!
Er ist von Gott gesandt!
Heil ihm!
Heil Elsa von Brabant!

*DER VORHANG FÄLLT.*

# ■ DRITTER AUFZUG

## ERSTE SCENE

(*Eine einleitende Musik schildert das prächtige Rauschen des Hochzeitsfestes. Als der Vorhang aufgeht, stellt die Bühne das Brautgemach dar.*)

**ELSA, LOHENGRIN, DER KÖNIG, MÄNNER UND FRAUEN:** (*Brautlied der Männer und Frauen.*)
Treulich geführt ziehet dahin, wo euch der Segen der Liebe bewahr'!
Siegreicher Muth, Minnegewinn Eint euch durch Treue zum seligsten Paar.
Streiter der Tugend, ziehe voran!
Zierde der Jugend, schreite voran!
Rauschen des Festes seid nun entronnen, Wonne des Herzens sei euch gewonnen!
Duftender Raum, zur Liebe geschmückt Nehm' euch nun auf, dem Glanze entrückt.
Treulich geführt ziehet nun ein, wo euch der Segen der Liebe bewahr'!
Siegreicher Muth, Minne so rein

than all our happiness.
To doubt's dark power are you a slave.
Do you crave to know my secret?

**ELSA:** My champion in the cause of right—
You whom I must call my savior—doubt may exert its utmost might, love triumphs over all.
(*Falls on his bosom; organ and bells in the Minster.*)

**LOHENGRIN:** Bless you, Elsa! now we will proceed.

**ALL:** Heaven does grant to us this boon.
Hail, Elsa of Brabant!
Heaven ever surely guard you—may blessing shower upon you.
Hail, Elsa of Brabant!
(*The King conducts Lohengrin on his right, Elsa on his left, up the steps of the Minster. Elsa's glances fall upon Ortrud, who raises her hand with a threatening attitude. Terror-stricken, she clings to Lohengrin, and as they are about to enter the Minster the curtain falls.*)

*END OF THE SECOND ACT.*

# ■ ACT III

## SCENE I

(*Introductory music expresses the merriment of the wedding festival. The curtain rising, discovers the bridal chamber. In the center of the background a richly adorned bed; by an open bay window a couch. At each side of the background are open doors. The bridal procession, accompanied by instruments and voices, enters the room in this order: at the right door the ladies enter, leading Elsa; at the left the King and nobles, leading Lohengrin, both being preceded by pages with lights. When they have reached the center of the stage, the King leads Lohengrin to Elsa. They embrace.*)

**MEN AND WOMEN:** (*Bridal Song*). Guided by us—thrice happy pair—enter this chamber; love invites you.
All that is brave—all that is fair—love, now triumphant, forever unites.
Champion of virtue, boldly advance; flower of all beauty, gently advance.
Now the loud mirth of reveling is ended.
Night, bringing peace and calm bliss, has descended.
Fanned by the breath of happiness, rest, closed to the world, by love only blessed.
(*Pages divest Lohengrin of his upper garment, and take off his*

eint euch in Treue zum seligsten Paar.

ACHT FRAUEN: Wie Gott euch selig weihte, zu Freuden weih'n euch wir; in Liebesglück's Geleite denkt lang der Stunde hier!
(*Brautlied, gesungen während des Fortgehens.*)

MÄNNER UND FRAUEN: Treulich bewacht bleibet zurück, wo euch der Segen der Liebe bewahr'!
Siegreicher Muth, Minne und Glück
Eint euch in Treue zum seligsten Paar.
Streiter der Tugend, bleibe daheim!
Zierde der Jugend, bleibe daheim!
Rauschen des Festes seid nun entronnen, Wonne des Herzens sei euch gewonnen!
Duftender Raum, zur Liebe geschmückt, nahm euch nun auf, dem Glanze entrükt.
Treulich bewacht bleibet zurück,
Wo euch der Segen der Liebe bewahr'!
Siegreicher Muth, Minne und Glück eint euch in Treue zum seligsten Paar.
(*In immer weiterer Ferne verhallt der Gesang.*)

## ZWEITE SCENE

(*Elsa und Lohengrin.*)

LOHENGRIN: Das süsse Lied verhallt; wir sind allein, zum ersten Mal allein, seit wir uns sah'n; nun sollen wir der Welt entronnen sein, kein Lauscher dar des Herzens Grüssen nah'n.—
Elsa, mein Weib: du süsse, reine Braut!
Ob glücklich du, das sei mir nun vertraut!

ELSA: Wie wär'ich kalt, mich glücklich nur zu nennen, besitz' ich aller Himmel Seligkeit!
Fühl' ich zu dir so süss mein Hertz entbrennen, athme ich Wonnen, die nur Gott verleiht!

LOHENGRIN: Vermagst du, Holde! glücklich dich zu nennen, giebst du auch mir des Himmels Seligkeit!
Fühl' ich zu dir so süss mein Herz entbrennen, athme ich Wonnen, die nur Gott verleiht!—
Wie hehr erkenn' ich uns'rer Liebe Wesen!
Die nie sich sah'n, wir hatten uns geahnt: war ich zu deinem Streiter

*sword, which they lay on the couch; the ladies take off Elsa's upper garment. During the following, eight ladies walk slowly around Lohengrin and Elsa.*)

EIGHT LADIES: May Heaven watch over you ever, and happy be your lot!
Oh, may this hour be never through days of joy forgot.
(*The King embraces Lohengrin and Elsa. The pages give a signal for departure. The men go off to the right, the women to the left, singing as follows:*)

GENERAL CHORUS: Stay alone, thrice happy pair, here in the chamber, which love gently lights.
All that is brave—all that is fair—love, now triumphant, forever unites.
Champion of virtue, here you'll remain—
Flower of all beauty, here you'll remain.
Now the loud mirth of reveling is ended.
Night, bringing peace and calm bliss, is descended.
Fanned by the breath of happiness, rest, closed to the world, by love only blessed.
(*When all have left, the doors are closed from without; the song is heard in the distance.*)

## SCENE II

(*Elsa has fallen on Lohengrin's bosom; he conducts her to the couch where they both sit.*)

LOHENGRIN: The song has died away—we are alone, who never were alone since first we met.
Now the heart can own its inmost feelings, and forget that there is an outer world.
Elsa, my wife, my bride, do you repine, or are you happy that you now are mine?

ELSA: "Happy!"
That word cannot measure my transport
Unless I think of heavenly happiness!
Oh, when I look on you—my heart's own treasure—
I can feel joys that mortals never possess.

LOHENGRIN: And sure the word well can measure your transport if I partake that heavenly happiness.
Oh, when I look on you my heart's own treasure, joys can I feel that mortals never possess.
Our hearts are by some sacred power affected.
We never had met, yet each the other knew.

auserlesen, hat Liebe mir zu dir den Weg gebahnt.
Dein Auge sagte mir dich rein von Schuld, mich zwang dein Blick zu dienen deiner Huld.

ELSA: Doch ich zuvor schon hatte dich geseh'n, in sel'gem Traume warst du mir genaht: als ich nun wachend dich sah vor mir steh'n, erkannt' ich, dass du kamst auf Gottes Rath.
Da wollte ich vor deinem Blick zerfliessen, gleich einem Bach unwinden deinen Schritt, als eine Blume, duftend auf der Wiesen, wollt' ich entzückt mich beugen deinem Tritt.
Ist dies nur Liebe? Wie soll ich es nennen, dies Wort, so unaussprechlich wonne voll,
Wie, ach! dein Name, den ich nie darf kennen, bei dem ich nie mein Höchstes nennen soll!

LOHENGRIN: Elsa!

ELSA: Wie süss mein Name deinem Mund entgleitet!
Gönnst du denn deinen holden Klang mir nicht?
Nur, wenn zur Liebesstille wir geleitet, Sollst du gestatten, dass mein Mund ihn spricht.

LOHENGRIN: Mein süsses Weib!

ELSA: —einsam, wenn Niemand wacht;
Nie sei der Welt er zu Gehör gebracht!

LOHENGRIN: Athmest du nicht mit mir die süssen, Düfte?
O wie so hold berauschen sie den Sinn!
Geheimnissvoll sie nahen durch die Lüfte,— fraglos geb' ihrem Zauber ich mich hin.—
So ist der Zauber, der mich dir verbunden, als ich zuerst, du Süsse, dich ersah; nicht brauchte deine Art ich zu erkunden, dich sah mein Aug' — mein Herz begriff dich, wie mir die Düfte hold den Sinn berücken, nah'n sie mir gleich aus räthselvoller Nacht:
So musste deine Reine mich entzücken, traf ich dich auch in schwerer Schuld Verdacht.

ELSA: Ach, könnt' ich deiner werth erscheinen!
Müsst' ich nicht bloss vor dir vergeh'n!
Könnt' ein Verdienst mich dir vereinen, dürft' ich in Pein für dich mich seh'n!
Wie du mich trafst vor schwerer Klage, O, wüsste ich auch dich in Noth!
Dass muthvoll ich ein Mühen trage, kennt'ich ein Sorgen, das dir droht!—
Wär' das Geheimniss so geartet, das aller Welt verschweigt dein Mund?

If I to be your champion were selected, It was love that guided me with purpose true; your eye proclaimed that you were free from guilt, your speaking glance claimed from me all homage.

ELSA: In blissful dreams one night, when sleep stole over me, I plainly saw you in my presence stand as to my waking eyes, you stood before me; thus did I know you came by God's command.
I wished your glance had melted me, that flowing, about your steps I might a streamlet wind; I wished to be a flower amid the growing green, to find only my death beneath your feet. Is this merely love?
Words can give me language, That all its hidden sweetness will reveal?
Your name I'd gladly join with it, believe me; but you will ever conceal that from me.

LOHENGRIN: Elsa!

ELSA: How sweetly my name sounds when spoken by you,
Yet may I never hear the sound of yours!
Surely some day my fetters will be broken, your name I then shall whisper—you are mine!

LOHENGRIN: My dearest wife!

ELSA: Only when none are near—None must the soft confession hear.

LOHENGRIN: (*pointing towards the window*). Do you not breathe, as I, that wealth of sweetness, where the rapt senses, drunk with pleasure, bask?
It is brought by mysterious gales in their fleetness; tasting the fragrance, I ask nothing further.
Such is the spell which has bound me to you.
Thus, when first I saw you, lovely as you are, those eyes decided—nothing could then confound me.
Your face alone at once convinced my heart,
Even as those sweet odors fire me with rapture, though through the murky shades of night they rise, so did your innocence inspire me with love, when you were crushed with heavy lies.

ELSA: Ah, worthy of you could you find me, I would gladly undergo anything.
Would some desert to me could bind you, that my devotion you could know!
From deadly perils you have freed me; ah, were you in some deep distress, though I am feeble, you might heed me, did I guess some coming danger.
What can the secret be that you may never tell its fearful import?
Perhaps some harm it would bring—oh, ever I'll guard it well

Vielleicht, dass Unheil dich erwartet, würd' es den Menschen offen kund?
O wär' es so! und dürft' ich's wissen, dürft' ich in meiner Macht es seh'n, durch Keines Droh'n sei mir's entrissen, für dich wollt' ich zum Tode geh'n!

**LOHENGRIN:** Geliebte!

**ELSA:** O mach' mich stolz durch dein Vertrauen, dass ich in Unwerth nicht vergeh'!
Lass dein Geheimniss mich erschauen, dass, wer du bist, ich offen seh'!

**LOHENGRIN:** Ach, schweige, Elsa!

**ELSA:** Meiner Treue enthülle deines Adels Werth!
Woher du kamst, sag' ohne Reue,—
durch mich sei Schweigens Kraft bewährt!

**LOHENGRIN:** Höchstes Vertrau'n hast du mir schon zu dauken, da deinem Schwur ich Glauben gern gewährt; wirst nimmer du vor dem Gebote wanken, hoch über alle Frau'n dünkst du mich werth!—
An meine Brust, du Süsse, Reine!
Sei meines herzens Glühen nah'!
Dass mich dein Auge sanft bescheine, in dem ich all mein Glück ersah!
O, gönne mir, dass mit Entzücken ich deinen Athem sauge ein!
Lass fest, ach! fest an mich dich drücken, dass ich in dir mög' glücklich sein!
Dein Lieben muss mir hoch entgelten für das, was ich um dich verliess; kein Loos in Gottes weiten Welten wohl edler als das meine hiess'.
Böt' mir der König seine Krone, ich dürfte sie mit Recht verschmäh'n: Das einz'ge, was mein Opfer lohne, muss ich in deiner Lieb' erseh'n!
Drum wolle stets den Zweifel meiden, dein Lieben sei mein stolz Gewähr; denn nicht komm' ich aus Nacht und Grau'n, aus Glanz und Wonne komm' ich her.

**ELSA:** Hilf Gott! was muss ich hören'
Welch Zeugniss gab dein Mund!
Du wolltest mich bethören,— nun wird mir Jammer kund!
Das Loos, dem du entronnen, es war dein höchstes Glück: du kamst zu mir aus Wonnen, und sehnest dich zurück!
Wie soll ich Aermste glauben, dir g'nüge meine Treu'?
Ein Tag wird dich mir rauben
Durch deiner Liebe Reu'!

**LOHENGRIN:** Halt' ein, dich so zu quälen!

**ELSA:** Was quälest du mich doch?
Soll ich die Tage zählen, die du mir bliebest noch?
In Sorg' um dein Verweilen ver-

within my heart.
Think not, my love, if I could share it, feeling it in my heart secure, a menace from my lips could tear it; No!
I could endure death for you.

**LOHENGRIN:** Beloved!

**ELSA:** Oh, let me be flattered by your trust, thinking you do not spurn my love
Be all the mist that hides you scattered—yourself to know, ah, let me learn.

**LOHENGRIN:** Be silent, Elsa.

**ELSA:** Yes, confiding in me, reveal your noble self, from where have you come?
Say, hiding nothing—
These lips will ever seal with silence.

**LOHENGRIN:** No, Elsa, no, all confidence you owe me; unshrinking I gave credence to your vow, that question never to ask.
You know little of me, if, through a woman's words, you're wavering now.
Let me press you against my bosom, give ear to this beating heart; look fondly on me; let me bless you, all pure and gentle as you are!
Yes, when I enfold you in my arms, the breath you breathe let me taste.
Let me but feel, while still I hold you, that happiness is mine at last.
Your love will give me full recompense for all that I have left—have lost.
Let heaven bereave me of other gifts if I can boast that you are mine!
Although the King should proffer his crown, it would not repay my sacrifice, and I should rightly spurn his offer.
You, you alone are past all price, doubt must wither within your bosom, cast all dark suspicion aside.
From night and grief I did not come, I came from joy and noblest pride.

**ELSA:** Oh, Heaven! what have you told me?
What are you forced to own?
Your aim was to deceive me, but now the worst is known!
The joys that you have quitted you think upon with pain, you hope soon to leave me, and taste of them again.
Ah, me! how can I trust you?
You do not love me alone!
One day will take you from me— with you will all be gone.

**LOHENGRIN:** Do not afflict yourself like this, love.

**ELSA:** No, you afflict me.
The days am I to number that near me you will be?
With ceaseless growing anguish my

blüht die Wange mir; dann wirst du mir enteilen, im Elend bleib'ich hier!

**LOHENGRIN:** Nie soll dein Reiz entschwinden, blieb'st du von Zweifel rein!

**ELSA:** Ach! dich an mich zu binden wie sollt' ich mächtig sein?
Voll Zauber ist dein Wesen, durch Wunder kamst du her—
Wie sollt' ich da genesen—
Wo fand ich dein' Gewähr?—
Hörtest du nichts? vernahmst du kein Kommen?

**LOHENGRIN:** Elsa?

**ELSA:** Ach nein!—doch dort! der Schwan! der Schwan!
Dort kommt er auf der Wasserfluth geschwommen . . .
Du rufest ihm,—er zieht herbei den Kahn!—

**LOHENGRIN:** Elsa, halt'ein! beruh'ge deinen Wahn!

**ELSA:** Nichts kann mir Ruhe geben, Dem Wahn mich nichts entreisst, Als—gelt'es auch mein Leben!—
Zu wissen—wer du seist!

**LOHENGRIN:** Elsa, was willst du wagen?

**ELSA:** Unselig holder Mann, hör'! was ich dich muss fragen!
Den Namen sag'mir an!

**LOHENGRIN:** Halt' ein!

**ELSA:** Woher die Fahrt?

**LOHENGRIN:** Weh' dir!

**ELSA:** Wie deine Art?

**LOHENGRIN:** Weh' uns, was thatest du!
(*Friedrich und die vier brabantischen Edlen brechen mit gezücktem Schwerte herein.*)

**ELSA:** Rette dich! dein Schwert! dein Schwert!
(*Lohengrin streckt Friedrich, da er nach ihm ausholt, mit einem Streiche todt zu Boden. Den entsetzten Edlen entfallen die Schwerter, sie stürzen zu Lohengrins Füssen auf die Kniee.*)

**LOHENGRIN:** Weh'! nun ist all unser Glück dahin!

**ELSA:** Allewiger! erbarm' dich mein!

**LOHENGRIN:** Tragt den Erschlag'nen vor des Königs Gericht!
(*Die Edlen nehmen Friedrichs Leiche auf und entfernen sich mit ihr. Lohengrin läutet an einem Glockenzuge: vier Frauen treten ein.*)

cheek will fade away; then, ruthless, you will leave me in sorrow to decay.

**LOHENGRIN:** Your charms will never fade, love, while you from doubt are pure.

**ELSA:** No chains have I to bind you, to hold you mine secure.
There's magic in your presence— through magic are you here.
Ah, nothing can quell my sorrow!
What torment must I fear!
(*Suddenly stricken with terror.*)
Do you hear nothing?
My senses do not wander.

**LOHENGRIN:** Elsa!

**ELSA:** It is nothing; but there I see the swan—I see him floating on the waters yonder.
You called him—he brings the boat to you!—

**LOHENGRIN:** Elsa, free your mind from those strange fancies.

**ELSA:** No, nothing can cure this madness—
Nothing cheer this bursting heart—
Nothing till, though life it cost me, you tell me who you are.

**LOHENGRIN:** Nay, Elsa, I implore you—

**ELSA:** Oh, madness! oh, despair!
You whom I love too fondly, your name at once declare.

**LOHENGRIN:** Wait!

**ELSA:** From where have you come?

**LOHENGRIN:** Ah, me!

**ELSA:** Where is your home?

**LOHENGRIN:** Ah, me! What have you done?
(*Elsa, who stands before Lohengrin, sees through the door Frederick and the four Brabant nobles, as they burst in with drawn swords.*)

**ELSA:** (*shrieks*). Save yourself— the sword—the sword!
(*She has hurriedly handed the sword to Lohengrin, who quickly draws it, and with one blow strikes Frederick lifeless to the ground. The four nobles kneel to Lohengrin in turn. Elsa falls senseless.*)

**LOHENGRIN:** Despair! now all our happiness is fled.
(*Raises Elsa and places her gently on the couch.*)

**ELSA:** (*faintly*). Oh, mighty Heaven! Oh, pity me!
(*Day gradually dawns. At a sign from Lohengrin, the nobles rise.*)

**LOHENGRIN:** Lift up the corpse, and bear it to the King.
(*The nobles raise Frederick's body and take it off through a door. Lohengrin rings a bell. Four ladies enter.*)
Before the King prepare to take her,

Sie vor den König zu geleiten, schmückt Elsa, meine süsse Frau! Dort will ich Antwort ihr bereiten, Dass sie des Gatten Art erschau'. (*Er entfernt sich, Die Frauen, geleiten Elsa ab.*) (*Ein zusammenfallender Vorhang schliesst im Vordergrunde die ganze Scene. Wie aus dem Burghofe berauf hört man Heerhörner einen Aufruf blasen.*)

## DRITTE SCENE

(*Als der Vorhang in die Höhe gezogen wird, stellt die Bühne wieder die Aue am Ufer der Schelde, wie im ersten Aufzuge, dar. Von verschiedenen Seiten gelangt nach und nach der brabantische Heerbann auf die Scene. Als die Brabanter alle eingetroffen sind, zieht König Heinrich mit seinem Heerbann ein.*)

**DIE BRABANTER:** Hoch König Heinrich! König Heinrich Heil!

**DER KÖNIG:** Habt Dank, ihr Lieben von Brabant! Wie fühl' ich stolz mein Herz entbrannt, find' ich in jedem deutschen Land so kräftig reichen Heerverband! Nun soll des Reiches Feind sich nah'n, wir wollen tapfer ihn empfahn: aus seinem öden Ost daher soll er sich nimmer wagen mehr! Für deutsches Land das deutsche Schwert! So sei des Reiches Kraft bewährt!

**ALLE MÄNNER:** Für deutsches Land das deutsche Schwert! So sei des Reiches Kraft bewährt!

**KÖNIG:** Wo weilt nun der, den Gott gesandt zum Ruhm, zur Grösse von Brabant? (*Die vier brabantischen Edlen bringen auf einer Bahre Friedrichs verhüllte Leiche getragen und setzen sie in der Mitte der Bühne nieder.*)

**ALLE:** Was bringen die? was thun sie kund? Die Mannen sind's des Telramund.

**KÖNIG:** Wen führt ihr her? was soll ich schau'n! Mich fasst bei eurem Anblick Grau'n!

**DIE VIER EDLEN:** So will's der Schützer von Brabant: wer dieser ist, macht er bekannt. (*Elsa, mit Gefolge von Frauen, tritt auf.*)

**DIE MÄNNER:** Seht! Elsa naht, die tugendreiche! Wie ist ihr Antlitz trüb' und bleiche!

**DER KÖNIG:** Wie soll ich dich so traurig seh'n! Muss dir so nah' die Trennung geh'n?

**STIMMEN:** Macht Platz dem Helden von Brabant!

**ALLE MÄNNER:** Heil! Heil dem Helden von Brabant! (*Lohengrin ist aufgetreten.*)

**KÖNIG:** Heil deinem Kommen, theurer Held! Die du so treulich riefst in's Feld, die harren dein in Streites Lust, von dir geführt des Sieg's bewusst.

**DIE BRABANTER:** Wir harren dein in Streites Lust, von dir geführt, des Sieg's bewusst.

**LOHENGRIN:** Mein Herr und König, lass dir melden, die ich berief, die kühnen Helden, zum Streit sie führen darf ich nicht!

**ALLE MÄNNER:** Hilf Gott! welch' hartes Wort er spricht!

**LOHENGRIN:** Als Streitgenoss bin nicht ich hergekommen, als Kläger sei ich jetzt von euch vernommen! Zum ersten klage laut ich vor euch Allen, und frag' um Spruch nach Recht und Fug: Da dieser Mann mich nächtens überfallen, sagt, ob ich ihn mit Recht erschlug?

**DER KÖNIG UND ALLE MÄNNER:** Wie deine Hand ihn schlug auf Erden, soll dort ihm Gottes Strafe werden!

**LOHENGRIN:** Zum and'ren aber sollt ihr Klage hören: denn aller Welt nun klag' ich laut, dass zum Verrath an mir sich liess bethören die Frau, die Gott mir angetraut.

**ALLE MÄNNER:** Elsa! wie mochte das gescheh'n. Wie konntest so du dich vergeh'n.

**LOHENGRIN:** Ihr hörtet Alle, wie sie mir versprochen, dass nie sie wollt' erfragen wer ich bin? Nun hat sie ihren theuren Schwur gebrochen, treulosem Rath gab sie ihr Herz dahin zu lohnen ihres Zweifels wildem Fragen sei nun die Antwort länger nicht gespart: Des Feindes Drängen durft' ich sie versagen, nun muss ich künden, wie mein Nam' und Art. Jetzt merket wohl, ob ich den Tag muss scheuen: Vor aller Welt, vor König und vor Reich Enthülle mein Geheimniss ich in Treuen. So hört,

---

let her wear her choicest garments, I will make her some fitting answer, and let her know the rank I bear. (*Exit sorrowfully through a door to the right*).

## SCENE III

(*A pair of curtains falling, the whole stage concealed. The sound of horns is heard. When the curtains are withdrawn, the plain of the Scheldt is seen as in the First Act. The Brabant army enters on both sides, each division led by a Count, whose standard-bearer plants his banner in the ground. Around these banners the adherents of the several leaders assemble. Boys bear the shields and spears of the Counts, squires lead the horses aside. When all the Brabant force has arrived, the King enters with the Saxons and Thuringians.*)

**MEN OF BRABANT:** (*saluting the king*). Hail! hail, King Henry, hail!

**KING:** (*starting under the oak*). Good subjects of Brabant, it is well; I feel my bosom swell with pride. May I in every German land Find such a true and loyal band. Now let the enemy appear. We're well prepared to see him near. Henceforward, from his desert plain will he not think to stir again. The German sword for German land! Thus will the realm in safety stand.

**ALL THE MEN:** The German sword, etc.

**KING:** Where does he linger whom God grants a boon of glory to Brabant? (*The four nobles bring Frederick's body covered over on a bier, which they set down in the center. All look anxiously.*)

**CHORUS:** (*Men*). What bring they here? What would they say? They are the men of Telramund.

**KING:** What must I see? Whom do you bring here? Your look forebodes some evil near.

**FOUR NOBLES:** Brabant's new lord will have it so. Him whom we bear you soon will know. (*Elsa, followed by a long train of ladies, advances with tottering steps to the foreground.*)

**ALL THE MEN:** See, Elsa comes— that lady peerless, surely her face is pale and cheerless.

**KING:** (*meeting Elsa, leads her to a high seat opposite his own*). From where comes that heavy, mournful look? Cannot bear the hour of parting? (*Elsa cannot look at him.*)

**VOICES:** Make way, make way— the hero of Brabant!

**ALL:** Hail! the hero of Brabant. (*The King has resumed his seat beneath the oak, Lohengrin enters, armed as in the First Act, with a solemn mournful air.*)

**KING:** Hail! hail! we bid you welcome all; those whom you did to battle call wait here with anxious hearts for you, they know you lead to victory.

**ALL THE MEN:** We wait with anxious hearts for you we know you lead to victory.

**LONHENGRIN:** My King and master, though so gladly I summoned them, I tell you sadly, this force I may not—cannot lead.

**ALL THE MEN:** Oh! Heaven! We hear sad words indeed.

**LONHENGRIN:** As your ally I have not come before you, as judges now to hear me, I implore you, so, firstly, say, am I exempted from crime? I claim your sentence as my due. This man, by night, attempted to take my life; say whether I rightly slew him. (*Uncovers the body, from which all turn with abhorrence.*)

**KING AND MEN:** Even as your hand on earth did smite him, will Heaven for evil deeds requite him.

**LONHENGRIN:** One other wrong remains yet to be righted. The truth before the world I speak. She whom in wedlock Heaven to me has plighted— My wife, was lured to break her vow.

**KING AND MEN:** Elsa, what have you done wrong? Elsa, this is a heavy charge.

**LONHENGRIN:** You heard her promise—plainly was it spoken; her vow—that she would never ask my name. Know, then, that sacred promise has been broken. She yielded when a wily tempter came; her mad suspicion now shall be rewarded. I'll wait no more to give an answer; the menace of a foe I disregarded; but now my name and station I declare. I deem not shrink, stealing, from broadest daylight, before the

ob ich an Adel euch nicht gleich!

**ALLE MÄNNER UND FRAUEN:**
Welch' Unerhörtes muss ich nun erfahren!
O könnt' er die erzwung'ne Kunde ersparen!

**LOHENGRIN:** In fernem Land, unnahber euren Schritten, liegt eine Burg, die Monsalvat genannt; ein lichter Tempel stehet dort in Mitten, so kostbar, wie auf Erden nichts bekannt:
Drim ein Gefäss von wunderthät'gem Segen wird dort als höchstes Heiligthum bewacht, es ward, dass sein der Menschen reinste pflegen, herab von einer Engelschaar gebracht.
Alljährlich naht vom Himmel eine Taube, um neu zu stärken seine Wunderkraft:
Es heisst der Gral, und selig reinster Glaube ertheilt durch ihn sich seiner Ritterschaft.
Wer nun dem Gral zu dienen ist erkoren, den rüstet er mit überird'scher Macht: an dem ist jedes Bösen Trug verloren, wenn ihn er ersieht, weicht dem des Todes Nacht.
Selbst wer von ihm in ferne Land' entsendet, zum Streiter für der Tugend Recht ernannt, dem wird nicht seine heil'ge Kraft entwendet, bleibt als sein Ritter dort er unerkannt:
So hehrer Art doch ist des Grales Segen, enthüllt—muss er des Laien Auge flieh'n; des Ritters drum sollt Zweifel ihr nicht hegen, erkennt ihr ihn, dann muss er von euch zieh'n.
Nun hört, wie ich verbot'ner Frage lohne!
Vom Gral ward ich zu euch daher gesandt: mein Vater Parzival trägt seine Krone, sein Ritter ich—bin Lohengrin genannt.

**ALLE MÄNNER UND FRAUEN:**
Hör' ich so seine höchste Art bewähren, entbrennt mein Aug' in heil'gen Wonnezähren.

**ELSA:** Mir schwankt der Boden! welche Nacht!
O Luft! Luft der Unglücksel'gen!

**LOHENGRIN:** O Elsa! was hast du mir angethan?
Als meine Augen dich zuerst ersah'n, zu dir fühlt' ich in Liebe mich entbrannt, und schnell hatt' ich ein neues Glück erkannt:
Die hehre Macht, die Wunder meiner Art, die Kraft, die mein Geheimniss mir bewahrt, wollt' ich dem Dienst des reinsten Herzens weih'n:—

King—before you all I stand, the secret I so long have kept, revealing. Hear then! Is one above me in the land?

**KING AND OTHERS:** What wondrous secret in his heart is hidden? If only to reveal it never he had been bidden.

**LONHENGRIN:** On distant shores, which you will never visit, rises Mount Monsalvat as on a throne; there stands a temple, which is bright forever; as glorious, nothing on earth was ever known. In this a vessel, wondrous powers possessing, is kept, a treasure precious beyond cost.
That men, unstained, may guard it as a blessing, it was brought to earth by an angelic host.
Once every year a dove, descending from heaven, settles, and thus its marvelous strength renews.
It is called the "Grail."
This, to its votaries lending its virtue, does through them pure faith diffuse.
He whom the Grail to be its servant chooses, it ever arms with more than earthly might.
Opposed to him, deceit its magic loses; his piercing glance can scatter shades of night.
Through distant countries still in his possession, the chosen one retains his matchless power.
For innocence to fight against oppression tarries he, while his name remains unknown.
The Grail is in its essence pure and holy, and from all common eyes must be concealed; to doubt its strength is arrogance and folly.
Its champions leave, if once their name's revealed, now hear.
The chosen one suspicion scorns.
Sent here by the Holy Grail, I came, its knight;—my father now its crown adorns Great Percival—and Lohengrin's my name.

**KING AND OTHERS:** Wondrous secret!
His sacred mission knowing, I feel my eyes with holy joy overflowing.

**ELSA:** The ground is rocking; it is night.
Give aid to me, unhappy!
(*She nearly falls. Lohengrin catches her in his arms.*)

**LONHENGRIN:** Oh, Elsa, hapless Elsa!—what have I done?
When first your face had shone, before my glance, I felt how love for you grew within me; I felt a happiness I never knew.
The wondrous power which lives, in my order, the strength which to my arm my secret gives, on one pure heart I purposed to bestow—
Why—why did you strive to know

Was rissest du nun mein Geheimniss ein?
Jetzt muss ich, ach! von dir geschieden sein!

**DER KÖNIG. ALLE MÄNNER:**
Weh'! Wehe! musst du von uns zieh'n!
Du hehrer, gottgesandter Mann!
Soll uns des Himmels Segen flieh'n, Wo fänden dein wir Tröstung dann?

**ELSA:** Mein Gatte! nein! ich lass' dich nicht von hinnen!
Als Zeuge meiner Busse bleibe hier!
Nicht darfst du meiner bitt'ren Reu' entrinnen; dass du mich züchtigst, liege ich vor dir!

**LOHENGRIN:** Ich muss! Ich muss! ich muss, mein süsses Weib!
Schon zürnt der Gral, dass ich ihm ferne bleib'!

**ELSA:** Bist du so göttlich, als ich dich erkannt, sei Gottes Gnade nicht aus dir verbannt!
Büsst sie in Jammer ihre schwere Schuld, nicht flieh' die Aermste deiner Nähe Huld!
Verstoss mich nicht, wie gross auch mein Verbrechen!

**LOHENGRIN:** Nur eine Strafe giebt's für dein Vergehen! Ach, mich wie dich trifft herbe Pein!
Getrennt, geschieden sollen wir uns sehen, dies muss die Strafe, dies die Busse sein!

**DER KÖNIG UND DIE EDLEN:** O bleib'! O zieh' uns nicht von dannen!
Des Führers harren deine Mannen.

**LOHENGRIN:** O König, hör'! ich darf dich nicht geleiten!
Des Grales Ritter, habt ihr ihn erkannt, wollt' er in Ungehorsam mit euch streiten, ihm wäre jede Manneskraft entwandt!
Doch, grosser König! lass mich dir weissagen: dir Reinem ist ein grosser Sieg verlieh'n!
Nach Deutschland sollen noch in fernsten Tagen des Ostens Horden siegreich niemals zieh'n!
(*Vom Hintergrunde her verbreitet sich der Ruf: Der Schwan! der Schwan! Man sieht auf dem Flusse den Schwan mit dem Nachen anlangen.*)

**DIE MÄNNER UND FRAUEN:** Der Schwan! der Schwan!
Seht dort ihn wieder nah'n!

**ELSA:** Entsetzlich! ha! der Schwan! der Schwan!

**LOHENGRIN:** Schon sendet nach dem Säumigen der Gral.—
Mein lieber Schwan!
Ach! diese letzte, traurige Fahrt, wie gern hätt' ich sie dir gespart!
In einem Jahr, wenn deine Zeit im Dienst zu Ende sollte geh'n,—dann durch des Grales Macht befreit,

my secret?
Oh, now I must forever go from you.

**KING AND ALL THE MEN:** Woe—woe! from us must you be torn—you for our chief by Heaven designed?
Heaven's blessing will with be borne.
What consolation can we find?

**ELSA:** Forever will I cling—I will not leave you; to witness my contrition, tarry here.
Think not with false repentance I deceive you; on me inflict a punishment severe.

**LOHENGRIN:** My wife, my love, no longer plead in vain; the Grail is angered that I so long remain.

**ELSA:** Your nature is divine—I know it well; therefore within your heart must mercy dwell, if every sin through penitence is less.
Oh, with your presence now the culprit bless.
My crime was great, yet leave me not thus lonely.

**LONHENGRIN:** The crime you only dared to perpetrate; but I must share the punishment with you.
Although we shall be separate, still shall each the other see.
(*Elsa falls with a shriek to the ground.*)

**KING AND NOBLE MEN:** (*surrounding Lohengrin*). Oh, stay!
Your men implore; in mercy heed them.
They beg you will lead them to victory.

**LONHENGRIN:** No, hear me, King; I'm forbidden to aid you, Champions of the Grail can never act in disobedience.
Their names no longer hidden, gone is their strength and surely they must fail.
Still let me tell you what my soul presages: Henry, you hold victory in your hand!
The Eastern hordes, even in remotest ages, shall never be conquerors in the German land.
(*The swan appears with the boat.*)

**VOICES:** The swan—the swan again!
The swan, I see it plain!

**ELSA:** Oh, heavens!
Oh, the swan!

**LONHENGRIN:** Too long I tarry—the Grail has sent for me. (*Goes to the brook.*)
Beloved swan!
Ah! You have brought mournful tidings.
Never I thought to see you so soon.
After a year slowly has past—

wollt' ich dich anders wieder
seh'n!—
O Elsa! nur ein Jahr an deiner Seite
hätt' ich als Zeuge deines Glücks
ersehnt!
Dann kehrte, selig in des Grals Geleite, dein Bruder wieder, den du
tot gewähnt.—
Kommt er dann heim, wenn ich
ihm fern im Leben, dies Horn, dies
Schwert, den Ring sollst du ihm geben!
Dies Horn soll in Gefahr ihm Hülfe
schenken, in wildem Kampf dies
Schwert ihm Sieg verleiht:
Doch bei dem Ringe soll er mein
gedenken, der einstens dich aus
Schmach und Noth befreit!
Leb' wohl! leb' wohl! leb' wohl!
mein süsses Weib!
Leb' wohl! mir zürnt der Gral,
wenn ich noch bleib'.

**KÖNIG, MÄNNER UND FRAUEN:**
Weh'! weh'! du edler holder Mann!
Welch' herbe Noth thust du uns an!
(*Ortrud tritt auf.*)

**ORTRUD:** Fahr' heim! fahr' heim,
du stolzer Helde!
Dass jubelnd ich der Thörin melde,
Wer dich gezogen in dem Kahn!
Das Kettlein hab' ich wohl erkannt,
Mit dem das Kind ich schuf zum
Schwan:
Das war der Erbe von Brabant!

**ALLE:** Ha!

The period of your slavery— then
by the Grail released at last, I hoped
my swan again to see.
(*Turns mournfully to Elsa.*) Oh,
Elsa, till a single year had ended,
Had I remained, your joy I should
have seen, then your lost brother,
by the Grail defended, to you yet
living would have been restored.
If he returns, you will receive him
alone. This sword—this horn —
this ring—rare presents give him.
His arm will conquer when the
sword he raises; the horn will aid
him in an hour of need.
As for the ring, whenever he gazes
on it he'll think on one who freed
you from danger.
Farewell—farewell—I must away!
Farewell—the Grail forbids my
stay.
(*Elsa clasps him convulsively, till
at last, her strength failing, she
sinks into the arms of her ladies,
to whom Lohengrin confides her.
He then approaches the river.*)

**KING AND CHORUS:** Woe—woe!
of knights the best—the chief, how
do you melt our hearts with grief!
(*Ortrud, coming to foreground,
stands before Elsa, exulting.*)

**ORTRUD:** Go home—go home—
in all your glory; I'll tell your bride
a wondrous story.
Who drew you in the boat here?
That chain, attached by me with
care—that chain, which at a glance
I knew, changed this Dukedom's
heir to a swan.
Hence by the swan your knight is
carried.

**ALL:** Ha!

**ORTRUD:** Dank, dass den Ritter du
vertrieben!
Nun giebt der Schwan ihm Heimge-
leit: der Held, wär' länger er geblieben, den Bruder Hätt' er auch befreit.

**ALLE:** Abscheulich' Weib! ha,
welch' Verbrechen
Hast du in frechem Hohn bekannt!

**ORTRUD:** Erfahrt, wie sich die
Götter rächen, von deren Huld ihr
euch gewandt!
(*Lohengrin senkt sich, dicht am
Strande, zu einem stummen Ge-
bete feierlich auf die Kniee.
Plötzlich erblickt er eine weisse
Taube sich über dem Nachen,
senken: mit lebhafter Freude
springt er auf und löst dem
Schwane die Kette, worauf dieser
sogleich untertaucht: an seiner
Stelle erscheint ein Jüngling—
Gottfried.*)

**LOHENGRIN:** Seht da den Herzog
von Brabant!
Zum Führer sei er euch ernannt!
(*Er springt schnell in den Nachen,
welchen die Taube an der Kette
fasst und sogleich fortführt.—
Gottfried ist nach vorn geschritten. Alle brabantischen Edlen
senken sich vor ihm auf die
Kniee.—*)

**ELSA:** Mein Gatte!
Mein Gatte!
(*Sie erblickt Lohengrin bereits
in der Ferne, von der Taube im Nachen gezogen. Alles bricht bei
diesem Anblicke in einen jähen
Wehruf aus. Elsa gleitet in Gott-
frieds Armen entseelt langsam zu
Boden.*)

*DER VORHANG FÄLLT.*

**ORTRUD:** Thanks, you have served
me well indeed. The knight, if longer he had tarried, your brother from
the spell would have freed.

**CHORUS:** Base sorceress, with exultation, can you confess a crime so
vile?

**ORTRUD:** The ancient gods, with
indignation, thus punish human
faithlessness.
(*Lohengrin, about to enter the
boat, has stopped at the sound of
Ortrud's voice, and listens attentively. He now falls on his knees
and prays in silence. Suddenly a
white dove descends over the
boat. Lohengrin arises enraptured, and takes the chain from
the swan, which sinks. In its place
appears the youth Godfrey.*)

**LONHENGRIN:** Accept the boon
which Heaven grants—the Duke,
the ruler of Brabant!
(*He springs rapidly into the boat,
which the dove draws off by the
chain. Ortrud, at the sight of Godfrey, falls with a shriek. Elsa looks
with rapture on her brother, who
advances and makes obeisance to
the King. All the nobles of Brabant
kneel before him. Elsa again looks
towards the river.*)

**ELSA:** My husband!
My husband!
(*Lohengrin is seen in the distance.
All utter a wail of lamentation.
Elsa, in Godfrey's arms sinks li-
feless to the ground. Curtain
falls.*)

*THE END.*

# Tristan und Isolde (1865)

MUSIC & LIBRETTO BY RICHARD WAGNER

This three-act music drama, set to a libretto by the composer, premiered at the Hoftheater in Munich on June 10, 1865. The story begins in Isolde's tent, which is on the deck of Tristan's ship. He is sailing from Ireland to Cornwall to escort Isolde, daughter of the king of Ireland, to marry King Marke of Cornwall, Tristan's uncle. Isolde orders Brangaene, her attendant, to bring Tristan to her in order to renew the act of homage he paid before they set sail. Kurwenal, Tristan's loyal groom, is amused and says that Tristan would pay no homage as he killed Morold, the man Isolde loved. Isolde is angry and tells Brangaene how she once spared Tristan's life. Isolde once healed the wounds of a man who gave his name as Tantris. The splinter from Morold's wound matched his sword, and thus she discovered that Tantris was in fact Tristan, the man who killed her lover and sent her his severed head. She was about to kill Tristan to avenge Morold's death, but his pleading look stopped her. She cured him with her magic potions and said nothing. Once he fully recovered, he left with the promise never to see her again. He did not keep his promise, and he came back to ask the King of Cornwall for permission to marry her. She loves him but feels he has betrayed her; she decides that they will both take poison and die. Kurwenal declares that they are near to the coast of Cornwall. He brings Tristan to her, and she tells Tristan that he is a coward, declaring she healed him only to seek her revenge once he was fully restored to health. Tristan offers his sword in order for her to kill him, but she instead suggests that they share a drink together. He knows that this drink will contain poison but agrees. They drink together, but Brangaene has used a love potion instead of poison, and they come together passionately as the ship reaches Cornwall. At King Marke's castle, Isolde, now married to the King, waits for Tristan to come with Brangaene. Tristan's signal to approach safely is the torch by her door being extinguished. Brangaene thinks that Melot, King Marke's knight, is up to something, and Isolde herself puts out the lamp. The lovers throw themselves into each other's arms and sing to the night, protector of their love. Brangaene keeps watch for them at the top of a tower and warns them of the impending dawn, but they ignore the warning. She screams, and Kurwenal rushes in to warn Tristan that a hunting party, led by the King, is approaching. Melot in fact arranged this hunt as part of his plan to entrap Tristan and Isolde. The King reproaches them, and she promises her lover that she will follow him wherever he goes. Melot then wounds Tristan. Kurwenal guards Tristan at his castle at Kareol in Brittany. A shepherd's lament mourns that no ship has been seen yet. Tristan awakens, curses the light and that Isolde has chosen to stay where the light remains, and collapses once again. The shepherd's pipes announce that Isolde's ship has finally arrived. Tristan rips off the bandages covering his wound and rises to meet her in rapture. He dies as she enfolds him in her arms. King Marke and Melot arrive on another ship. Kurwenal kills Melot and is also fatally wounded, dying alongside Tristan. King Marke had come to grant pardon to the lovers as he found out about Brangaene's deception, but it is too late. Isolde sings the famous Liebestod in mourning for her lover and collapses in death upon his lifeless corpse.

---

## ■ ERSTE AKT

*(Zeltartiges Gemach auf dem Vorderdeck eines Seeschiffes, reich mit Teppichen behangen, beim Beginn nach dem Hintergrunde zu gänzlich geschlossen; zur Seite führt eine schmale Treppe in den Schiffsraum hinab.)*

### ERSTE SCENE

*(Isolde auf einem Ruhebett, das Gesicht in die Kissen gedrükt.—Brangaena, einen Teppich zurückgeschlagen haltend, blickt zur Seite über Bord.)*

STIMME EINES JUNGEN SEEMANNES *(aus der Höhe, wie vom Maste her, vernehmbar).*
Westwärts
schweift der Blick,

## ■ ACT I

*(A pavilion erected on the deck of a ship, richly hung with tapestry, quite closed in at back at first. A narrow hatchway at one side leads below into the cabin.)*

### SCENE I

*(Isolda on a couch, her face buried in the cushions.—Brangaena holding open a curtain, looks over the side of the vessel.)*

THE VOICE OF A YOUNG SAILOR *(from above as if at the masthead).*
Westward
surges slip,

Ostwärts
streicht das Schiff.
Frisch weht der Wind
der Heimath zu:—
mein Irische Kind,
wo weilest du?
Sind's deiner Seufzer Wehen,
die mir die Segel blähen?
Wehe, wehe, du Wind!
Weh, ach, wehe, mein Kind!
Irische Maid, du wilde, minige
Maid.

ISOLDE: *(jäh auffahrend).* Wer
wagt mich zu höhnen?—
*(Sie blickt verstört um sich.)*
Brangäne, du?—
Sag', wo sind wir?

BRANGAENE: *(an der Öffnung).*
Blaue Streifen
stiegen im Westen auf;
sanft und schnell
segelt das Schiff;
auf ruhiger See vor Abend
erreichen wir sicher das Land.

Eastward speeds the ship.
The wind so wild
blows homeward now;
my Irish child,
where do you wait?
Say, must our sails be weighed,
Filled by your sighs unabated?
Waft us, wind strong and wild!
Woe ah, woe for my child!
O Irish maid!
my winsome, marvellous maid!

ISOLDA: *(starting up suddenly).*
What wight dares insult me?
*(she looks around in agitation.)*
Brangaena, ho!
Say, where do we sail?

BRANGAENA: *(at the opening).*
Bluish stripes
are stretching along the west;
swiftly sails
the ship to shore;
if restful the sea by evening
we shall readily set foot on land.

## Act I, Scene I

ISOLDE: Welches Land?

ISOLDA: What land?

BRANGAENE: Kornwalls grünen Strand.

BRANGAENA: Cornwall's verdant strand.

ISOLDE: Nimmermehr!
Nicht heut', nicht morgen!

ISOLDA: Never more!
Today nor tomorrow!

BRANGAENE: Was hör' ich? Herrin! Ha!
(*Lässt den Vorhang zufallen, und eilt bestürzt zu Isolde.*)

BRANGAENA: What do you mean, mistress? say!
(*she lets the curtain fall and hastens to Isolda.*)

ISOLDE: (*wild vor sich hin*). Entartet' Geschlecht,
unwerth der Ahnen!
Wohin, Mutter,
vergabst du die Macht,
über Meer und Sturm zu gebieten?
O zahme Kunst
der Zauberin,
die nur Balsamtränke noch brau't!
Erwache mir wieder,
kühne Gewalt,
herauf aus dem Busen,
wo du dich barg'st!
Hört meinen Willen,
zagende Winde!
Heran zu Kampf
und Wettergetös',
zu tobender Stürme
wüthendem Wirbel!
Treibt aus dem Schlaf
dies träumende Meer,
weckt aus dem Grund
seine grollende Gier;
zeigt ihm die Beute,
die ich ihm biete;
zerschlag' es, dies trotzige Schiff,
des zerschellten Trümmer verschling's!
Und was auf ihm lebt,
den wehenden Athem,
den lass' ich euch Winden zum Lohn!

ISOLDA: (*with wild gaze*). A fainthearted child,
false to your fathers!
Ah, where, mother,
has given your might
that commands the wave and the tempest?
O subtle art
of sorcery,
for mere leech-craft followed too long!
Awake in me once more,
power of will!
Arise from your hiding
within my breast!
Hark to my bidding,
fluttering breezes!
Arise and storm
in boisterous strife!
With furious rage
and hurricane's hurdle
waken the sea
from slumbering calm;
rouse up the deep
to its devilish deeds!
Show it the prey
which gladly I proffer!
Let it shatter this too daring ship
and enshrine in ocean each shred!
And woe to the lives!
Their wavering death-sighs
I leave to you winds, as your lot.

BRANGAENE: (*im äussersten Schreck, um Isolde sich bemühend*). O weh'!
Ach! Ach!
Des Übels, das ich geahnt!—
Isolde! Herrin!
Theures Herz!
Was barg'st du mir so lang?
Nicht eine Thräne
weintest du Vater und Mutter;
kaum einen Gruss
den Bleibenden botest du:
von der Heimath scheidend
kalt und stumm,
bleich und schweigend
auf der Fahrt,
ohne Nahrung,
ohne Schlaf,
starr und elend,
wild verstört,—
wie ertrugs ich's
so dich sehend,
nichts dir mehr zu sein,
fremd vor dir zu steh'n?
O, nun melde
was dich müh't!
Sage, künde
was dich quält.
Herrin Isolde,
trauteste Holde!
soll sie werth sich dir wähnen,
vertraue nun Brangänen!

BRANGAENA: (*in extreme alarm and concern for Isolda*). Out, alas!
Ah, woe!
I've ever dreaded some ill!—
Isolda! mistress!
Heart of mine!
What secret do you hide?
Without a tear,
You've left your father and mother,
and gave scarce a word
of farewell to friends,
leaving home you stood
cold and still!
pale and speechless
on the way,
rejecting food,
bereft of sleep,
stern and wretched,
wild, disturbed;
how it pains me
so to see you!
We seem friends no more,
being estranged.
Make me partner
in your pain!
Tell me freely
all your fears!
Lady, you hear,
sweetest and dearest;
if you take me for a true friend,
O make me your confidant!

ISOLDE: Luft! Luft!
Mir erstickt das Herz!
Öffne! Öffne dort weit!
(*Brangaene zieht eilig die Vorhänge in der Mitte auseinander.*)

ISOLDA: Air! air!
or my heart will choke!
Open! open there wide!
(*Brangaena hastily draws the center curtains apart.*)

## ZWEITE SCENE

(*Man blickt dem Schiff entlang bis zum Steuerbord, über dem Bord hinaus auf das Meer und den Horizont. Um den Hauptmast in der Mitte ist Seevolk, mit Tauen beschäftigt, gelagert; über sie hinaus gewahrt man am Steuerbord Ritter und Knappen, ebenfalls gelagert; von ihnen etwas entfernt Tristan, mit verschränkten Armen stehend, und sinnend in das Meer blickend; zu Füssen ihm, nachlässig ausgestreckt Kurwenal.—Vom Maste her, aus der Höhe, vernimmt man wieder den Gesang des Jungen Seemanns.*)

## SCENE II

(*The whole length of the ship is now seen, down to the stern, with the sea and horizon beyond. Round the mainmast sailors are ensconced, busied with ropes; beyond them in the stern are groups of knights and attendants, also seated; a little apart stands Tristan folding his arms and thoughtfully gazing out to sea; at his feet Kurvenal reclines carelessly. From the mast-head above is once more heard the voice of the Young Sailor.*)

DER JUNGE SEEMAN: (*Auf dem Maste, unsichtbar*). Frisch weht der Wind
der Heimath zu:—
mein Irische Kind,
mein Irische Kind,
wo weilest du?
Sind's deiner Seufzer Wehen,
die mir die Segel blähen?—
Wehe! Wehe, du Wind
Weh'! Ach wehe, mein Kind!

THE YOUNG SAILOR: (*at the mast-head invisible*). The wind so wild
blows homewards now;
my Irish child,
where do you wait?
Say, must our sails be weighed,
filled by your sighs unabated?
Waft us, wind strong and wild!
Woe, ah woe for my child!

ISOLDE: (*deren Blick sogleich Tristan fand, und starr auf ihm geheftet bleibt, dumpf für sich*).
Mir erkoren.—
mir verloren.—
hehr und heil
kühn und feig—;
Todgeweihtes Haupt!
Todgeweihtes Herz!—
(*unheimlich lachend*)
Was hälst von dem Knechte?

ISOLDA: (*whose eyes have at once sought Tristan and fixed stonily on him—gloomily*). Once beloved—
now removed—
brave and bright,
coward knight!—
Death-devoted head!
Death-devoted heart!—
(*laughing unnaturally*)
Do you think highly of this knight?

BRANGAENE: (*ihrem Blicke folgend*). Wen meinst du?

BRANGAENA: (*following her glance*). Who do you mean?

ISOLDE: Dort den Helden,
Der meinem Blick
den seinen birgt,
in Scham und Scheue
abwärts schaut:—
sag', wie dünkt er dich!

ISOLDA: There, that hero
who from my eyes
averts his own:
in shrinking shame
he shuns my gaze
Say, how hold you him?

BRANGAENE: Frägst du nach Tristan, theure Frau,
dem Wunder aller Reiche,
dem hochgepries'nen Mann,
dem Helden ohne Gleiche,
des Ruhmes Hört und Bann?

BRANGAENA: Mean you Sir Tristan, lady mine?
Extolled by every nation,
his happy country's pride,
the hero of creation,—
whose fame's so high and wide?

ISOLDE: (*sie verhöhnend*). Der zagend vor dem Streiche
sich flüchtet wo er kann,
weil eine Braut er als Leiche
für seinen Herrn gewann!—
Dünkst es dich dunkel,
mein Gedicht?
Frag' ihn denn selbst,
den freien Mann,
ob mir zu nah'n er wagt?
Der Ehren Gruss
und zücht'ge Acht

ISOLDA: (*jeeringly*). In shrinking trepidation
his shame he seeks to hide,
While to the king, his relation.
he brings the corpse-like bride!—
Seems it so senseless
what I say?
Go ask him,
our gracious host,
dare he approach my side?
No courteous heed
or loyal care does

vergisst der Herrin
der zage Held,
dass ihr Blick ihn nur nicht
erreiche—
den Kühnen ohne Gleiche!
O, er weiss
wohl warum!—
Zu dem Stolzen geh',
meld' ihm der Herrin Wort:
meinem Dienst bereit
schleunig soll er mir nah'n.

BRANGAENE: Soll ich ihn bitten,
dich zu grüssen?

ISOLDE: Befehlen liess'
dem Eigenholde
Furcht der Herrin
ich, Isolde.
(*Auf Isolde's gebieterischen Wink entfernt sich Brangaene, und schreitet das Deck entlang dem Steuerbord zu, an den arbeitenden Seeleuten vorbei. Isolde, mit starrem Blicke ihr folgend, zieht sich rücklings nach dem Ruhebett zurück, wo sie während des Folgenden bleibt, das Auge unabgewandt nach dem Steuerbord gerichtet.*)

KURWENAL: (*der Brangaene kommen sieht, zupft, ohne sich zu erheben, Tristan am Gewande*). Hab' Acht, Tristan! Botschaft von Isolde.

TRISTAN: (*auffahrend*). Was ist?—Isolde?—
(*Er fasst sich schnell, als Brangaene vor ihm anlangt und sich verneigt.*)
Von meiner Herrin?—
Ihr gehorsam
was zu hören
meldet höfisch
mir die traute Magd?

BRANGAENE: Mein Herre Tristan,
dich zu sehen
wünscht Isolde,
meine Frau.

TRISTAN: Grämt sie die lange Fahrt,
die geht zu End';
eh' noch die Sonne sinkt,
sind wir am Land:
was meine Frau mir befehle,
treulich sei's erfüllt.

BRANGAENE: So mög' Herr Tristan
zu ihr geh'n:
das ist der Herrin Will'.

TRISTAN: Wo dort die grünen Fluren
dem Blick noch blau sich färben,
harrt mein König
meiner Frau:
zu ihm sie zu geleiten
bald nah' ich mich der Lichten;
Keinem gönnt' ich
diese Gunst.

this hero turns towards
his lady;
but to meet her his heart is daunted,
the knight so highly vaunted!
Oh! he knows
well the cause!
To the traitor go,
bearing his lady's will!
As my servant bound,
straightaway should he approach!

BRANGAENA: Shall I beseech him
to attend you?

ISOLDA: No, order him.
pray, understand it:—
I, Isolda
do command it!
(*at an imperious sign from Isolda Brangaena withdraws and timidly walks along the deck towards the stern, past the working sailors. Isolda, following her with fixed gaze, sinks back on the couch, where she remains seated during the following, her eyes still turned sternward.*)

KURVENAL: (*observing Brangaene's approach, plucks Tristan by the robe without rising*). Beware, Tristan! Message from Isolda!

TRISTAN: (*starting*). What is it?—Isolda?—
(*he quickly regains his composure as Brangaena approaches and curtsies to him.*)
What would my lady?
I her liegeman,
gladly will listen
while her loyal
woman tells her will.

BRANGAENA: My lord, Sir Tristan,
Dame Isolda
must speak
with you at once.

TRISTAN: Is she worn with travel?
The end is near;
No, before the set of sun
We shall see land
All that your mistress commands
me, trust me, I shall mind.

BRANGAENA: That you, Sir Tristan,
go to her.—
this is my lady's wish.

TRISTAN: Where those green meadows
in distance dim are mounting,
waits my sovereign
for his mate:
to lead her to his presence
I'll wait upon the princess;
it is an honor
all my own.

BRANGAENE: Mein Herre Tristan,
höre wohl:
deine Dienste
will die Frau.
dass du zur Stell' ihr nahtest,
dort wo sie deiner harrt.

TRISTAN: Auf jeder Stelle
wo ich steh',
getreulich dien' ich ihr,
der Frauen höchster Ehr'.
Liess' ich das Steuer
jetzt zur Stund',
wie lenkt' ich sicher den Kiel
zu König Marke's Land?

BRANGAENE: Tristan, mein Herre,
was höhnst du mich?
Dünkt dich nicht deutlich
die thör'ge Magd,
hör' meiner Herrin Wort!
So, hiess' sie, sollt' ich sagen:—
befehlen liess'
dem Eigenholde
Furcht der Herrin
sie, Isolde.

KURWENAL: (*aufspringend*).
Darf ich die Antwort sagen ingend?

TRISTAN: Was wohl erwidertest du?

KURWENAL: Das sage sie
Der Frau Isold'.—
Wer Kornwall's Kron'
und England's Erb'
an Irland's Maid vermacht,
der kann der Magd
nicht eigen sein,
die selbst dem Ohm er schenkt.
Ein Herr der Welt
Tristan der Held!
Ich ruf's: du sag's, und grollten
mir tausend Frau Isolden.
(*Da Tristan durch Gebärden ihm zu wehren sucht, und Brangaene entrüstet sich zum Weggehen wendet, singt Kurwenal der zögernd sich Entfernenden mit höchster Stärke nach.*)
"Herr Morold zog
zu Meere her,
in Kornwall Zins zu haben;
ein Eiland schwimmt
auf ödem Meer,
da liegt er nun begraben!
Sein Haupt doch hängt
im Iren-Land,
als Zins gezahlt
von Engeland.
Hei! unser Held Tristan!
Wie den Zins zahlen kann!"
(*Kurwenal, von Tristan fortgescholten, ist in den Schiffsraum des Vorderdecks hinabgestiegen. Brangaene, in Bestürzung zu Isolde zurückgekehrt, schliesst hinter sich die Vorhänge, während die ganze Mannschaft aussen sich hören lässt.*)

ALLE MAENNER: "Sein Haupt doch hängt
im Iren-Land,
als Zins gezahlt

BRANGAENA: My lord, Sir Tristan,
listen to me;
this one thing
my lady wills,
that you at once attend her,
there where she waits for you.

TRISTAN: In any station
where I stand
I truly serve only her,
the pearl of womanhood.
If I unheeding
left the helm,
how might I pilot her ship
in surety to King Mark?

BRANGAENA: Tristan, my master,
Why do you mock me?
Do my words seem
obscure to you?
listen to my lady's words;
thus, look you, she has spoken:
"Go order him,
and understand it,
I—Isolda
do command it.

KURVENAL: (*springing up*). May I make her an answer?

TRISTAN: What would you wish to reply?

KURVENAL: This should she say to Dame Isolda:
"Though Cornwall's crown
and England's isle
for Ireland's child he chose,
his own by choice
she may not be;
he brings the king his bride.
A hero-knight
Tristan is called!
I've said, nor care to measure
your lady's high displeasure."
(*while Tristan seeks to stop him, and the offended Brangaena turns to depart, Kurvenal sings after her at the top of his voice, as she lingeringly withdraws.*)
"Sir Morold toiled
over mighty wave
the Cornish tax to levy;
In desert isle
was dug his grave,
he died of wounds so heavy.
His head now hangs
in Irish lands.
Sole were-gild won
at English hands.
Bravo, our brave Tristan!
Let his tax take who can!"
(*Kurvenal, driven away by Tristan's chidings, descends into the cabin. Brangaena returns in discomposure to Isolda, closing the curtains behind her, while all the men take up the chorus and are heard without.*)

KNIGHTS AND ATTENDANTS:
"His head now hangs
in Irish lands,
sole were-gild won

von Engeland.
Hei! unser Held Tristan!
Wie der Zins zahlen kann!''

## DRITTE SCENE

(Isolde und Brangaene allein, bei vollkommen wieder geschlossenen Vorhängen. Isolde erhebt sich mit verzweiflungsvoller Wuthgebärde. Brangaene ihr zu Füssen stürzend.)

BRANGAENE: Weh'! Ach, wehe! dies zu dulden!

ISOLDE: (dem furchtbarsten Ausbruche nahe, schnell sich fassend). Doch nun von Tristan: genau will ich's vernehmen.

BRANGAENE: Ach, frage nicht!

ISOLDE: Frei sag's ohne Furcht.

BRANGAENE: Mit höf'schen Worten wich er aus.

ISOLDE: Doch als du deutlich mahntest?

BRANGAENE: Da ich zur Stell' ihn zu dir rief: wo er auch steh', so sagte er, getreulich dien' er ihr, der Frauen höchster Ehr', liess' er das Steuer jetzt zur Stund', wie lenkt' er sicher den Kiel zu König Marke's Land?

ISOLDE: (schmerzlich bitter). "Wie lenkt' er sicher den Kiel zu König Marke's Land"— den Zins ihm auszuzahlen, den er aus Irland zog!

BRANGAENE: Auf deine eig'nen Worte, als ich ihm die entbot liess seinen Treuen Kurwenal—

ISOLDE: Den hab' ich wohl vernommen, kein Wort das mir entging. Erfuhrst du meine Schmach; nun höre, was sie mir schuf.— Wie lachend sie mir Lieder singen, wohl könnt' auch ich erwiedern: von einem Kahn, der klein und arm an Irland's Küste schwamm; darinnen krank ein siecher Mann elend im Sterben lag. Isolde's Kunst ward ihm bekannt; mit Heil-Salben und Balsamsaft der Wunde, die ihn plagte, getreulich pflag sie da. Der "Tantris" mit sorgender List sich nannte, als "Tristan" Isold' ihn bald erkannte, da in des Müss'gen Schwerte

eine Scharte sie gewahrte, darin genau sich fügt' ein Splitter, den einst im Haupt des Iren-Ritter, zum Hohn ihr heimgesandt, mit kund'ger Hand sie fand.— Da schrie's mir auf aus tiefstem Grund; mit dem hellen Schwert ich vor ihm stund, an ihm, dem Über-Frechen, Herrn Morold's Tod zu rächen. Von seinem Bette blickt' er her,— nicht auf das Schwert, nicht auf die Hand,— er sah' mir in die Augen. Seines Elendes jammerte mich; das Schwert—das liess ich fallen: die Morold schlug, die Wunde, sie heilt' ich, dass er gesunde, und heim nach Hause kehre,— mit dem Blick mich nicht mehr beschwere!

BRANGAENE: O Wunder! Wo hatt' ich die Augen? Der Gast, den einst ich pflegen half—?

ISOLDE: Sein Lob hörtest du eben:— "Hei! Unser Held Tristan!"— Der war jener traur'ge Mann!— Er schwur mit tausend Eiden mir ew'gen Dank und Treue! Nun hör' wie ein Held Eide hält!— Den als Tantris unerkannt ich entlassen, als Tristan kehrt er kühn zurück auf stolzem Schiff von hohem Bord, Irland's Erbin begehrt er zur Eh' für Kornwall's müden König, für Marke, seinen Ohm. Da Morold lebte, wer hätt' es gewagt, uns je solche Schmach zu bieten? Für der zinspflichtigen Kornen Fürsten um Irland's Krone zu werben? O wehe mir! Ich ja war's, die heimlich selbst die Schmach sich schuf! Das rächende Schwert, statt es zu schwingen, machtlos liess ich's fallen:— nun dien' ich dem Vasallen.

BRANGAENE: Da Friede, Sühn' und Freundschaft von Allen ward beschworen wir freuten uns All' des Tag's; wie ahnte mir da, dass dir, es Kummer schüf?

ISOLDE: O blinde Augen! Blöde Herzen! Zahmer Muth, verzagtes Schweigen!

---

at English hands.
Bravo, our brave Tristan!
Let his tax take who can!''

## SCENE III

(Isolda and Brangaena alone, the curtain being again completely closed. Isolda rises with a gesture of despair and wrath. Brangaena falls at her feet.)

BRANGAENA: Ah! an answer so insulting!

ISOLDA: (checking herself on the brink of a fearful outburst). How now? of Tristan? I'd know if he denies me.

BRANGAENA: Ah! question not!

ISOLDA: Quick, say without fear!

BRANGAENA: With courteous phrase he foiled my will.

ISOLDA: But when you requested him here?

BRANGAENA: When I had straightaway bid him come, wherever he stood, he said to me, he truly served only you, the pearl of womanhood; if he unheeded left the helm how could he pilot the ship in surety to King Mark?

ISOLDA: (bitterly). "How could he pilot the ship in surety to King Mark!" And wait on him with were-gild from Ireland's island won!

BRANGAENA: As I gave out the message and in your very words, thus spoke his henchman Kurvenal—

ISOLDA: Heard I every sentence? it all has reached my ear. If you have learned my disgrace now hear too from where it has grown. How scoffingly they sing about me! Could I requite them quickly! What of the boat so bare and frail, that floated by our shore? What of the broken stricken man, feebly extended there? Isolda's art he gladly owned; with herbs, simples and healing salves the wounds from which he suffered she nursed in skilful wise. Though "Tantris" The name that he took as "Tristan" Isolda soon knew him, when in the sick man's keen blade

she perceived a notch had been made, which did fit a splinter broken in Morold's head, the mangled token sent home in hatred rare; this hand did find it there. I heard a voice from distance dim; with the sword in hand I came to him. Full well I willed to slay him, for Morold's death to pay him. But from his sick bed he looked up not at the sword, not at my arm— his eyes on mine were fastened, and his feebleness softened my heart: the sword—dropped from my fingers. Though Morold's steel had maimed him to health again I reclaimed him! When he has homeward wended my emotion then might be ended.

BRANGAENA: O wondrous! Why could I not see this? The guest I sometimes helped to nurse—?

ISOLDA: His praise briskly they sing now:— "Bravo, our brave Tristan!"— he was that distressful man. A thousand protestations of truth and love he prated. Hear how a knight fealty knows!— When as Tantris unforbidden he'd left me, as Tristan boldly back he came, in stately ship from which in pride Ireland's heiress in marriage he asked for Mark, the Cornish monarch, his kinsman worn and old. In Morold's lifetime dared any have dreamed to offer us such an insult? For the tax-paying Cornish prince to presume to court Ireland's princess! Ah, woe is me! It was I who for myself did shape this shame! with death-dealing sword should I have stabbed him; weakly it escaped me:—

BRANGAENA: When peaceful truce and friendship were sworn by both the peoples, how joyful we were that day! How could I foresee the pain it would bring to you?

ISOLDA: Oh! eyes, how blinded! Heart, how timid! Courage weak! A futile silence!

Wie anders phahlte Tristan aus,
was ich verschlossen hiehlt!
Die schweigend ihm das Leben gab,
vor Feindes des Rache ihn schweigend barg;
was stumm ihr Schutz zum Heil ihm schuf,
mit ihr gab er es preis!
Wie siegprangend heil und hehr,
laut und hell wies er auf mich;
"Das wär' ein Schatz,
Mein Herr und Ohm;
Wie dünkt euch die zur Eh'?
Die schmucke Irin hol' ich her;
mit Steg und Wegen wohlbekannt
ein Wink, ich flieg' nach Iren-land;
Isolde, die ist eueu!
mir lacht das Abenteuer!
Fluch dir, Verruchter!
Fluch deinem Haupt!
Rache, Tod!
Tod uns Beiden!

How bravely poured this Tristan forth,
What I had never breathed!
She who by silence gave him life,
from foes by silence she kept him safe;
the silent care that wrought his weal
to her he dared reveal!
How masterful, brave and bold,
turned he all eyes on me!
"A treasure she, my liege and cousin;
what think you of her for a bride?
This Irish jewel will I bring;
for every stock and stone I know;
a nod, and I'll fly to Ireland;
Isolda is your own, Sire!
I would I might be gone, Sire!"
now serfdom I have shaped me.
Curse him, the villain!
Curse on his head!
Vengeance! Death!
Death for me too!

**BRANGAENE:** (*mit ungestümer Zärtlichkeit sich auf Isolde stürzend*). O Süsse! Traute!
Theure! Holde!
Gold'ne Herrin!
Lieb' Isolde!
Hör' mich! Komme!
Setz' dich her!—
(*Sie zieht Isolde allmählich nach dem Ruhebett.*)
Welcher Wahn?
Welch' eitles Zürnen?
Wie magst du dich bethören,
nicht hell zu seh'n noch hören!
Was je Herr Tristan
dir verdankte,
sag', konnt' er's höher lohnen,
als mit der herrlichsten der Kronen?
So dient' er treu
dem edlen Ohm,
dir gab er der Welt
begehrlichsten Lohn
dem eig'nen Erbe,
echt und edel,
entsagt' er zu deinen Füssen,
als Königin dich zu grüssen.
(*Isolde wendet sich ab.*)
und warb er Marke,
dir zum Gemahl,
wie wolltest du die Wahl doch schelten,
muss er nicht werth dir gelten?
Von edler Art
Und mildem Muth,
wer gliche dem Mann
an Macht und Glanz?
Dem ein hehrster Held
so treulich dient,
wer möchte sein Glück nicht theilen,
als Gattin bei ihm weilen?

**BRANGAENA:** (*throwing herself upon Isolda with impetuous tenderness*). Isolda! lady!
loved one! fairest!
sweet perfection!
mistress rarest!
Hear me! come now,
sit here.—
(*gradually draws Isolda to the couch.*)
What a whim!
what causeless railing!
How came you so wrong-minded
and by mere fancy blinded?
Sir Tristan gives you
Cornwall's kingdom;
then, were he your debtor,
how could he reward you better?
His noble uncle
serves him so;
think too what a gift
on you he'd bestow!
With honor unequalled
all he's heir to
at your feet he seeks to shower,
to make you a queenly dower.
(*Isolda turns away.*)
If wife he'd make you
to King Mark
why do you complain like this?
Is he not worth your gaining?
Of royal race
and mild of mood,
who passes King Mark
in might and power?
If a noble knight
like Tristan serves him,
who would not but feel elated,
to be so fairly mated.

**ISOLDE:** (*starr vor sich hinblickend*). Ungeminnt
den hehrsten Mann
stets mir nah' zu sehen,—
wie könnt' ich die Qual bestehen!

**ISOLDA:** (*gazing vacantly before her*). Glorious knight!
And I must languish near him
ever loveless!
How can I support such anguish?

**BRANGAENE:** Was wähnst du Arge?
Ungeminnt?—
(*Sie nähert sich Isolden schmeichelnd und kosend.*)
Wo lebte der Mann.
der dich nicht liebte?
Der Isolden säh,
und in Isolden
selig nicht ganz verging'?
Doch, der dir erkoren,
wär' er so kalt,
zög' ihn von dir
ein Zauber ab,
den Bösen wüsst' ich
bald zu binden
ihn bannte der Minne Macht.—
(*Mit geheimnissvoller Zutraulichkeit ganz nah zu Isolden.*)
Kennst du der Mutter
Künste nicht?
Wähnst du, die Alles
klug erwägt,
ohne Rath in fremdes Land
hätt' sie mit dir mich entsandt?

**BRANGAENA:** What's this, my lady?
You are loveless?
(*approaching coaxingly and kissing Isolda.*)
Where lives there a man who
would not love you?
Who could see Isolda
And not sink
at once into blessed bondage?
And if even it could be
any were cold,
did any magic
draw him from you
I'd bring the false one
back to bondage,
And bind him in links of love.—
(*secretly and confidentially, close to Isolda.*)
Mind you not
your mother's arts?
Think you that she
who'd mastered those
would have sent me over the sea,
without assistance for you?

**ISOLDE:** (*düster*). Der Mutter Rath
gemahnt mich recht;
willkommen preis' ich
ihre Kunst:—
Rache für den Verrath,—
Ruh' in der Noth dem Herzen!—
Den Schrein dort bring' mir her.

**ISOLDA:** (*darkly*). My mother's counsel—
I mind correctly,
and highly her magic
arts I hold:—
Vengeance they wreak for wrongs,
rest give to wounded spirits.—
That casket bear here.

**BRANGAENE:** Er birgt, was Heil dir frommt.
(*Sie holt eine kleine goldne Truhe herbei, öffnet sie, und deutet auf ihren Inhalt.*)
So reihte sie die Mutter,
die mächt'gen Zaubertränke.
Für Weh' und Wunden
Balsam hier;
für böse Gifte
Gegen-Gift:—
(*Sie zieht ein Fläschchen hervor.*)
den hehrsten Trank,
ich halt' ihn hier.

**BRANGAENA:** It holds a balm for you.
(*she brings forward a small golden coffer, opens it, and points to its contents.*)
Your mother placed inside it
her subtle magic potions.
There's salve for sickness
or for wounds,
and antidotes
for deadly drugs.—
(*she takes a bottle.*)
The most helpful drink
I hold in here.

**ISOLDE:** Du irr'st, ich kenn' ihn besser;
ein starkes Zeichen
schnitt ich ihm ein: —
der Trank ist's, der mir frommt.
(*Sie ergreift ein Fläschchen und zeigt es.*)

**ISOLDA:** Not so, I know a better.
I make a mark
to know it again—
I would drain this drink.
(*seizes flask and shows it.*)

**BRANGAENE:** (*entsetzt zurückweichend*). Der Todestrank!
(*Isolde hat sich vom Ruhebett erhoben, und vernimmt jetzt mit wachsendem Schrecken den Ruf des Schiffsvolkes:*)

**BRANGAENA:** (*recoiling in horror.*) The drink of death!
(*Isolda has risen from the sofa and now hears with increasing dread the cries of the sailors:*)

**RUF DES SCHIFFSVOLKES:** (*von aussen*). "He! ha! ho! he!
Am Untermast
die Segel ein!
He! ha! ho! he!"

**VOICES OF THE CREW:**
(*without*). "Ho! heave ho! hey!
Reduce the sail!
The mainsail in!
Ho! heave ho! hey!"

**ISOLDE:** Das deutet schnelle Fahrt.
Weh' mir! Nahe das Land!

**ISOLDA:** Our journey has been swift.
Woe's me! Near to the land!

## Act I, Scene IV

### VIERTE SCENE

*(Durch die Vorhänge tritt mit Ungestüm Kurwenal herein.)*

KURWENAL: Auf, auf! Ihr Frauen!
Frisch und froh!
Rasch gerüstet!
Fertig, hurtig und flink!—
Und Frau Isolden
sollt' ich sagen
von Held Tristan,
meinem Herrn:—
vom Mast der Freude Flagge
sie wehe lustig in's Land;
in Marke's Königsschlosse
mach' sie ihr Nahen bekannt.
Drum Frau Isolde
bät' er eilen,
für's Land sich zu bereiten,
dass er sie könnt' geleiten.

ISOLDE: *(nachdem sie zuerst bei der Meldung in Schauer zusammengefahren, gefasst und mit Würde).* Herrn Tristan bringe
meinen Gruss,
und meld' ihm was ich sage.—
Sollt' ich zur Seit' ihm gehen,
vor König Marke zu stehen,
nicht möcht' es nach Zucht
und Fug gescheh'n,
empfing' ich Sühne
nicht zuvor
für ungesühnte Schuld:
drum such' er meine Huld.—
*(Kurwenal macht eine trotzige Gebärde.)*
Du merke wohl
und meld' es gut!—
Nicht wollt' ich mich bereiten,
an's Land ihn zu begleiten;
nicht werd' ich zur Seit' ihm gehen,
vor König Marke zu stehen,
begehrte Vergessen
und Vergeben
nach Zucht und Fug
er nicht zuvor
für ungebüsste Schuld:—
die böt' ihm meine Huld.

KURWENAL: Sicher wisst,
das sag' ich ihm:
nun harrt, wie er mich hört!
*(Er geht schnell zurück.)*

### FÜNFTE SCENE

ISOLDE: *(eilt auf Brangaene zu und unmarmt sie heftig).* Nun leb'
wohl, Brangäne!
Grüss' mir die Welt,
grüsse mir Vater und Mutter!

BRANGAENE: Was ist's! Was sinnst du?
Wolltest du fliehen?
Wohin sollt' ich dir folgen?

ISOLDE: *(schnell gefasst).* Hörtest du nicht?
Hier bleib' ich;
Tristan will ich erwarten.—
Treu befolg',
was ich befehl',

---

### SCENE IV

*(Kurvenal boisterously enters through the curtains.)*

KURVENAL: Up, up, you ladies!
Look alert!
Straight bestir you!
Loiter not—here is the land!—
To dame Isolda
says the servant
of Tristan,
our hero true:—
Behold our flag is flying!
it waves landwards aloft:
in Mark's ancestral castle
may our approach be seen.
So, dame Isolda,
he prays to hasten,
for land straight to prepare her,
that he may bear her there.

ISOLDA: *(who has at first cowered and shuddered on hearing the message, now speaks calmly and with dignity).* My greeting take
to your lord
and tell him what I say now:
Should he assist me to land
and to King Mark would he hand me,
unmeet and unseemly
were his act,
the while my pardon
was not won
for trespass black and base:
So bid him seek my grace.
*(Kurvenal makes a gesture of defiance.)*
Now mark me well
This message take:—
I won't prepare myself,
that he to land may bear me;
I will not by him be landed,
nor unto King Mark be handed
before granting forgiveness
and forgetfulness,
which it seems that
he should seek:—
for all his trespass base
I tender him my grace.

KURVENAL: Be assured,
I'll bear your words:
we'll see what he will say!
*(be retires quickly.)*

### SCENE V

ISOLDA: *(hurries to Brangaena and embraces her vehemently).*
Now farewell, Brangaena!
Greet every one,
Greet my father and mother!

BRANGAENA: What now? what do you mean?
Would you flee?
And where must I then follow?

ISOLDA: *(checking herself suddenly).* Here I remain:
heard you not?
Tristan will I await.—
I trust in you
to aid in this:

---

den Sühne-Trank
rüste schnell,—
du weisst, den ich dir wies.

BRANGAENE: Und welchen Trank?

ISOLDE: *(entnimmt dem Schreine das Fläschchen).* Diesen Trank!
In die gold'ne Schale
giess' ihn aus;
gefüllt fasst sie ihn ganz.

BRANGAENE: *(voll Grausen das Fläschchen empfangend.)* Trau' ich dem Sinn?

ISOLDE: Sei du mir treu!

BRANGAENE: Der Trank—für wen?

ISOLDE: Wer mich betrog.

BRANGAENE: Tristan?

ISOLDE: Trinke mir Sühne.

BRANGAENE: *(zu Isolde's Füssen stürzend).* Entsetzen! Schone mich Arme!

ISOLDE: *(heftig).* Schone du mich,
untreue Magd!
Kennst du der Mutter
Künste nicht?
Wähn'st du, die Alles
klug erwägt,
ohne Rath in fremdes Land
hätt' sie mit dir mich entsandt?
Für weh' und wunden gab sie Balsam;
Für böse Gifte
Gegen-Gift;
für tiefstes Weh',
für höchstes Leid—
gab sie den Todes-Trank.
Der Tod nun sag' ihr Dank!

BRANGAENE: *(kaum ihrer mächtig).* O tiefstes Weh'!

ISOLDE: Gehorchst du mir nun?

BRANGAENE: O höchstes Leid!

ISOLDE: Bist du mir treu?

BRANGAENE: Der Trank?

KURWENAL: *(eintretend).* Herr Tristan
*(Brangaene erhebt sich erschrocken und verwirrt; Isolde sucht mit furchtbarer Anstrengung sich zu fassen.)*

ISOLDE: *(zu Kurwenal).* Herr Tristan trete nah.

### SECHSTE SCENE

*(Kurwenal geht wieder zurück, Brangaene, kaum ihrer mächtig, wendet sich in den Hintergrund. Isolde, ihr ganzes Gefühl zur Entscheidung zusammenfassend, schreitet langsam, mit grosser Haltung, dem Ruhebett zu, auf dessen Kopfende sich stützend sie den Blick fest dem Eingange zuwendet.)*
*(Tristan tritt ein, und bleibt ehrerbietig am Eingange stehen.)*

---

prepare the true
cup of peace:
you mind how it is made.

BRANGAENA: What do you mean?

ISOLDA: *(taking a bottle from the coffer).* That it is!
From the flask go pour
this filter out;
that golden goblet it will fill.

BRANGAENA: *(filled with terror receiving the flask).* Trust I my wits?

ISOLDA: Will you be true?

BRANGAENA: The drink—for whom?

ISOLDA: He who betrayed!

BRANGAENA: Tristan!

ISOLDA: Truce he'll drink with me.

BRANGAENA: *(throwing herself at Isolda's feet).* O horror! Pity your handmaid!

ISOLDA: Pity me, your
false-hearted maid!
Do you not mind
my mother's arts?
You think that she
who'd mastered those
would have sent you over the sea
without assistance for me?
A salve for sickness
she offers
and antidotes
for deadly drugs:
for deepest grief
and woe supreme
gave she the draught of death.
Let Death now give her thanks!

BRANGAENA: *(scarcely able to control herself).* O deepest grief!

ISOLDA: Now, will you obey?

BRANGAENA: O woe supreme!

ISOLDA: Will you be true?

BRANGAENA: The drink?

KURVENAL: *(entering).* Sir Tristan!
*(Brangaena rises, terrified and confused. Isolda strives with immense effort to control herself.)*

ISOLDA: *(to Kurvenal).* Sir Tristan may approach!

### SCENE VI

*(Kurvenal retires again. Brangaena, almost beside herself, turns up the stage. Isolda, mustering all her powers of resolution, walks slowly and with dignity towards the sofa, by the head of which she supports herself, turning her eyes firmly towards the entrance.)*
*(Tristan enters, and pauses respectfully at the entrance.)*

TRISTAN: Begehrt, Herrin,
was ihr wünscht.

ISOLDE: Wüsstest du nicht
was ich begehre,
da doch die Furcht,
mir's zu erfüllen,
fern meinem Blick dich hielt?

TRISTAN: Ehr-Furcht
hielt mich in Acht.

ISOLDE: Der Ehre wenig
botest du mir;
mit off'nem Hohn
verwehrtest du
Gehorsam meinem Gebot.

TRISTAN: Gehorsam einzig
hielt mich in Bann.

ISOLDE: So dankt' ich Geringes
deinem Herrn,
rieth dir sein Dienst
Un-Sitte
gegen sein eigen Gemahl?

TRISTAN: Sitte lehrt
wo ich gelebt:
zur Brautfahrt
der Brautwerber
meide fern die Braut.

ISOLDE: Aus welcher Sorg'?

TRISTAN: Fragt die Sitte!

ISOLDE: Da du so sittsam,
mein Herr Tristan,
auch einer Sitte
sei nun gemahnt:
den Feind dir zu sühnen,
soll er als Freund dich rühmen.

TRISTAN: Und welchen Feind?

ISOLDE: Frag' deine Furcht!
Blut-Schuld
schwebt zwischen uns.

TRISTAN: Die ward gesühnt.

ISOLDE: Nicht zwischen uns.

TRISTAN: Im off'nen Feld
vor allem Volk
ward Ur-Fehde geschworen.

ISOLDE: Nicht da war's
wo ich Tantris barg,
wo Tristan mir verfiel.
Da stand er herrlich,
hehr und heil
doch was er schwur,
das schwur ich nicht:—
zu schweigen hatt' ich gelernt.
Da in stiller Kammer
krank er lag,
mit dem Schwerte stumm
ich vor ihm stund,
schwieg—da mein Mund,
bannt'—ich meine Hand,
doch was einst mit Hand
und Mund ich gelobt,
das schwur ich schweigend zu halten.
Nun will ich des Eides walten.

TRISTAN: Was schwurt Ihr, Frau?

ISOLDE: (schnell). Rache für Morold.

TRISTAN: (mässig). Müh't Euch die?

---

TRISTAN: Demand, lady,
what you will.

ISOLDA: While knowing not
what my demand is,
were you afraid
still to fulfill it,
fleeing my presence instead?

TRISTAN: Honor
Held me in awe.

ISOLDA: You have shown
Scant honor to me;
for, unabashed,
you withheld
obedience to my call.

TRISTAN: Obedience it was
forbade me to come.

ISOLDA: But I owe little
Your lord, I think,
if he allows
ill manners
to his own promised bride.

TRISTAN: In our land
it is the law
that he who fetches
home the bride
should stay afar from her.

ISOLDA: On what account?

TRISTAN: It is the custom.

ISOLDA: Being so careful,
my lord Tristan,
another custom
can you not learn?
Of enemies make friends:
for evil acts make amends.

TRISTAN: Who is my foe?

ISOLDA: Find in your fears!
Blood-guilt
gets between us.

TRISTAN: That was absolved.

ISOLDA: Not between us.

TRISTAN: In open field,
Before all the folk
our old feud was abandoned.

ISOLDA: It was not there
I held Tantris hid
when Tristan was laid low,
He stood there brawny,
bright and brave;
but in his truce
I took no part:
my tongue its silence had learnt,
When in chambered stillness
he lay sick
with the sword I stood
before him, stern;
silent—my lips,
motionless—my hand.
But that which my hand
and lips had once vowed,
I swore in stealth to adhere to:
now my desire I'm near to.

TRISTAN: What have you sworn?

ISOLDA: (quickly). Vengeance for Morold!

TRISTAN: (quietly). Do you mind that?

---

ISOLDE: (lebhaft). Wag'st du mir Hohn?—
Angelobt war er mir,
der hehre Irenheld;
seine Waffen hatt' ich geweiht,
für mich zog er in Streit.
Da er gefallen,
fiel meine Ehr';
in des Herzens Schwere
schwur ich den Eid,
würd' ein Mann den Mord nicht sühnen,
wollt' ich Magd mich des' erkühnen.—
Siech und matt
in meiner Macht,
warum ich dich da nicht schlug,
das sag' dir selbst mit leichtem Fug:—
ich pflag des Wunden,
dass den heil Gesunden
rächend schlüge der Mann,
der Isolden ihn abgewann.—
Dein Loos nun selber
magst du dir sagen:
da die Männer sich all' ihm vertragen,
wer muss nun Tristan schlagen?

TRISTAN: (bleich und düster, reicht ihr sein Schwert hin). War Morold dir so werth,
nun wieder nimm das Schwert,
und führ' es sicher und fest,
dass du nicht dir's entfalten lässt.

ISOLDE: Wie sorgt' ich schlecht
um deinen Herren;
was würde König Marke sagen,
erschlüg ich ihm den besten Knecht,
der Kron' und Land ihm gewann,
den aller treu' sten Mann?
Dunkt dich so wenig,
was er dir dankt,
bringst du die Irin ihm als Braut,
das er nicht schölte,
schlüg' ich den Werber,
der Urfehde Pfand so treu ihm liefert zur Hand?
Wahre dein Schwert!
Da einst ich's schwang,
als mir die Rache
im Busen rang,
als dein messender Blick
mein Bild sich stahl,
ob ich Herrn Marke
taug' als Gemahl:
das Schwert—da liess ich's sinken.
Nun lass' uns Sühne trinken!—
(Sie winkt Brangaene. Diese schaudert zusammen schwankt und zögert in ihrer Bewegung. Isolde treibt sie durch gesteigerte Gebärde an. Als Brangaene Bereitung des Tranks sich anlässt, vernimmt man den Ruf des Schiffsvolkes.)

SCHIFFSVOLK: (von aussen). Ho! he! ha! he!
Am Obermast
die Segel ein!
Ho! he! ha! he!

TRISTAN: (aus finst'rem Brüten auffahrend). Wo sind wir?

---

ISOLDA: (animated). Do you dare to flout me?—
Was he not my betrothed,
that noble Irish knight?
For his sword a blessing I sought;
for me only he fought.
When he was murdered
no honor fell.
In that heartfelt misery
my vow was framed;
if no man remained to right it,
I, a maid, must requite it.—
Weak and maimed,
when might was mine,
why at your death did I pause?
You shall know the secret cause.—
Your hurts I tended
that, when sickness ended,
you should fall by some man,
as Isolda's revenge should plan.
But now attempt
your fate to foretell me: your fate
if their friendship all men do sell to you,
what foe can seek to fell you?

TRISTAN: (pale and gloomy, offers her his sword). If you so loved this lord,
then lift once more my sword,
nor refrain from your purpose,
let the weapon not fail again.

ISOLDA: How ill a turn I'd do your master!
How, think you now, King Mark
would take it,
if I should slay his foremost man,
who won him kingdom and rights,
the best of all his knights?
Do you think his thanks to you are so small,
you who have brought me as his bride,
he'd not be angered,
slew I the wooer,
who brings him so good a pledge of truce to the Feud?
Put up your sword
which I once swung,
when vengeful rancor
wrung my bosom
when your masterful eyes
did ask me straight

whether King Mark
might seek me for mate.
The sword harmless descended.—
Drink, let our strife be ended!
(Isolda beckons Brangaena. She trembles and hesitates to obey. Isolda commands her with a more imperious gesture. Brangaena sets about preparing the drink.)

VOICES OF THE CREW:
(without). Ho! heave ho! hey!
Reduce the sail!
The foresail in!
Ho! heave ho! hey!

TRISTAN: (starting from his gloomy brooding). Where are we?

**ISOLDE:** Hart am Ziel.
Tristan, gewinn' ich Sühne?
Was hast du mir zu sagen?

**TRISTAN:** (*düster*). Des Schweigens Herrin
heisst mich schweigen:
fass' ich, was sie verschwieg,
verschweig' ich, was sie nicht fasst.

**ISOLDE:** Dein Schweigen fass' ich,
weichst du mir aus.
Weigerst du Sühne mir?
(*Neue Schiffsrufe. Auf Isolde's ungeduldigen Wink reicht Brangaene ihr die gefüllte Trinkschale.*)

**ISOLDE:** (*mit dem Becher zu Tristan tretend, der ihr starr in die Augen blickt*). Du hörst den Ruf?
Wir sind am Ziel:
in kurzer Frist
stehn wir—
(*mit leisem Hohne.*)
vor König Marke.
Geleitest du mich,
dünkt dich's nicht lieb,
darfst du so ihm sagen:
Mein Herr und Ohm,
sieh' die dir an:
ein sanft'res Weib
gewannst du nie.
Ihren Angelobten erschlug
ich ihr einst,
sein Haupt sandt' ich ihr hein,
die Wunde, die seine Wehr mir schuf,
die hat sie hold geheilt;
mein Leben lag in ihrer Macht:
das schenkte mir die milde Magd,
und ihres Landes Schand' und Schmach
die gab sie mit darein,
dein Eh' gemahl zu sein.
So guter Gaben holder Dank
schuf mir ein süsser Sühntrank;
bot mir ihre Huld zu suhnen alle Schuld.''

**SCHIFFSRUF:** (*aussen*). Auf das Tau!
Anker ab!

**TRISTAN:** (*wild auffahrend*). Los den Anker!
Das Steuer dem Strom!
Den Winden Segel und Mast!
(*Er entreisst Isolden ungestüm die Trinkschale.*)
Wohl kenn' ich Irlands Königin,
und ihrer Künste Wunderkraft:
den Balsam nützt' ich,
den sie bot;
den Becher nehm' ich nun,
dass ganz ich heut' genese!
Und achte auch
des Sühne-Eid's,
den ich zum Dank dir sage.—
Tristan's Ehre—
höchste Treu';
Tristan's Elend—
kühnster Trotz.
Trug des Herzens;
Traum der Ahnung:
ew'ger Trauer

**ISOLDA:** Near to shore.
Tristan, is warfare ended?
Have you word to offer?

**TRISTAN:** (*darkly*). Concealment's mistress
makes me silent:
I know what she conceals,
conceal too, more than she knows.

**ISOLDA:** Your silence is nothing but feigning.
Will you still deny friendship?
(*renewed cries of the Sailors.*)
(*at an impatient sign from Isolda Brangaena hands her the filled cup.*)

**ISOLDA:** (*advancing with the cup to Tristan, who gazes immovably into her eyes*). You hear the cry?
The shore's in sight:
(*with slight scorn.*)
we must long
stand by King Mark together.
And you lead me then,
were it not well,
if you could thus greet him:
"My lord and king,
look well on her:
a more tender wife
you could never win.
Her betrothed lover I slew,
of a truth,
his head I sent her home;
the wounds his weapons wrought on me,
she graciously did heal;
my life within her hand was laid;
she gave it to me,
this merciful maid,
and all her country's slights and shame,
she let them go, as well,
with you as queen to dwell.
Such goodly gifts I have to thank
with her a draught of truce I drank;
that pardon for me won,
for all the wrong I'd done.''

**SAILORS:** (*without*). Haul the warp!
Anchor down!

**TRISTAN:** (*starting wildly*).
Down with the anchor!
Her stern to the stream!
The sails a-weather the mast!
(*he takes the cup from Isolda.*)
I know the Queen
of Ireland well,
unquestioned are
her magic arts:
the balsam cured me
which she brought;
now bid me quaff the cup,
that I may quite recover.
Heed to my all-atoning oath,
which in return I tended.
Tristan's honor—
highest truth!
Tristan's anguish—
brave distress!
Traitor spirit,
dawn-illumined!
Endless trouble's
only truce!

einz'ger Trost,
Vergessens güt'ger Trank!
Dich trink' ich sonder Wank.
(*Er setzt an und trinkt.*)

**ISOLDE:** Betrug auch hier?
Mein die Hälfte!
(*Sie entwindet ihm den Becher.*)
Verräther, ich trink' sie dir!
(*Sie trinkt. Dann wirft sie die Schale fort.—Beide, von Schauer erfasst, blicken sich mit höchster Aufregung, doch mit starrer Haltung, unverwandt in die Augen, in deren Ausdruck der Todestrotz bald der Liebesgluth weicht.— Zittern ergreift sie. Sie fassen sich krampfhaft an das Herz,—und führen die Hand weiter an die Stirn.—Dann suchen sie sich wieder mit dem Blicke, senken ihn verwirrt, und heften ihn von Neuem mit steigender Sehnsucht auf einander.*)

**ISOLDE:** (*mit bebender Stimme*).
Tristan!

**TRISTAN:** (*überströmend*).
Isolde!

**ISOLDE:** (*an seine Brust sinkend*). Treuloser Holder!

**TRISTAN:** Selgiste Frau!— (*Er umfasst sie mit Gluth. Sie verbleiben in stummer Umarmung.*)

**ALLE MAENNER:** (*aussen*). Heil! Heil!
König Marke!
König Marke, Heil!

**BRANGAENE:** (*die, mit abgewandtem Gesicht, voll Verwirrung und Schauder sich über Bord gelehnt hatte, wendet sich jetzt dem Anblick des in Liebesumarmung versunkenen Paares zu, und stürzt händeringend, voll Verzweiflung, in den Vordergrund*). Wehe! Wehe!
Unabwendbar
ewige Noth
für kurzen Tod!
Thör'ger Treue
trugvolles Werk
blüht nun jammernd empor!
(*Sie fahren verwirrt aus der Umarmung auf.*)

**TRISTAN:** (*verwirrt*). Was träumte mir von Tristan's Ehre?

**ISOLDE:** Was träumte mir von Isolde's Schmach?

**TRISTAN:** Du mir verloren?

**ISOLDE:** Du mich verstossen?

**TRISTAN:** Trügenden Zaubers tückische List!

**ISOLDE:** Thörigen Zürnens eitles Dräu'n!

**TRISTAN:** Isolde! Süsseste Maid!

**ISOLDE:** Tristan! Trautester Mann!

Oblivion's kindly draught,
with rapture you are quaffed!
(*he lifts the cup and drinks.*)

**ISOLDA:** Betrayed even here?
I must halve it!—
(*she wrests the cup from his hand.*)
Betrayer, I drink to you!
(*She drinks, and then throws away the cup. Both, seized with shuddering, gaze with deepest emotion, but immovable demeanor, into one another's eyes, in which the expression of defiance to death fades and melts into the glow of passion. Trembling seizes them, they convulsively clutch their hearts and pass their hands over their brows. Their glances again seek to meet, sink in confusion, and once more turn with growing longing upon one another.*)

**ISOLDA:** (*with trembling voice*).
Tristan!

**TRISTAN:** (*overpowered*). Isolda!

**ISOLDA:** (*sinking upon his breast*). Beloved traitor!

**TRISTAN:** Divine woman!
(*He embraces her with ardor. They remain in a silent embrace.*)

**ALL THE MEN:** (*without*). Hail! Hail!
Hail our monarch!
Hail to Mark, the king!

**BRANGAENA:** (*who, filled with confusion and horror, has leaned over the side with averted face, now turns to behold the pair locked in their close embrace, and rushes to the front, wringing her hands in despair*).
Woe's me! Woe's me!
Endless misery
I have wrought
instead of death!
Dire the deed
of my dull fond heart;
it cries aloud to heaven!
(*they start from their embrace.*)

**TRISTAN:** (*bewildered*). What troubled dream of Tristan's honor?

**ISOLDA:** What troubled dream Of Isolda's shame?

**TRISTAN:** Have I then lost you?

**ISOLDA:** Have I repulsed you?

**TRISTAN:** Fraudulent magic, framing deceit!

**ISOLDA:** Folly and anger's idle threats!

**TRISTAN:** Isolda! Sweetest of maids!

**ISOLDA:** Tristan! Truest of men!

**BEIDE:** Wie sich die Herzen wogend erheben,
wie alle Sinse wonnig erbeben!
Sehnender Minne
schwellendes Blühen,
schmachtender Liebe
seliges Glühen!
Jach in der Brust
jauchzende Lust!
Isolde! Tristan!
Tristan! Isolde!
Welten entronnen
du mir gewonnen!
Du mir einzig bewusst,
höchste Liebes-Lust!

**BOTH:** Ah! how our hearts are heaving and swelling!
How every sense is throbbing and thrilling!
Languishing passion,
longing and growing,
love ever yearning,
loftiest glowing!
Rapture confessed
rides in each breast!
Isolda! Tristan!
Tristan! Isolda!
World, I can shun you
my love is won me!
You are my thought, all above:
highest delight of love!

## SIEBENTE SCENE

*(Die Vorbänge werden weit auseinander gerissen. Das ganze Schiff ist von Rittern und Schiffsleuten erfüllt, die jubelnd über Bord winken, dem Ufer zu, des man, mit einer hohen Felsenburg gekrönt, nahe erblickt. Tristan und Isolde bleiben, in ihrem gegenseitigen Anblick verloren, ohne Wahrnehmung des um sie Vorgehenden.)*

**BRANGAENE:** (*zu den Frauen, die auf ihren Wink aus dem Schiffsraum heraufsteigen*). Schnell den Mantel, den Königsschmuck!
(*Zwischen Tristan und Isolde stürzend.*)
Unsel'ge! Auf!
Hört wo wir sind.
(*Sie legt Isolden, die es nicht gewahrt, den Mantel um.*)

**ALLE MAENNER:** Heil! Heil!
König Marke!
König Marke, Heil!

**KURWENAL:** (*lebhaft herantretend*). Heil Tristan!
Glücklicher Held!—
Mit reichem Hofgesinde
dort auf Nachen
naht Herr Marke.
Heil! wie die Fahrt ihn freut,
dass er die Braut sich freit!

**TRISTAN:** (*in Verwirrung aufblickend*). Wer naht?

**KURWENAL:** Der König!

**TRISTAN:** Welcher König?
(*Kurwenal deutet über Bord. Tristan starrt wie sinnlos nach dem Lande.*)

**ALLE MAENNER:** (*die Hüte schwenkend*). Heil! König Marke!

**ISOLDE:** (*in Verwirrung, zu Brangaene*). Was ist's? Brangäne!
Ha! welcher Ruf?

**BRANGAENE:** Isolde! Herrin!
Fassung nur heut'!

**ISOLDE:** Wo bin ich? Leb' ich?
Ha, welcher Trank?

## SCENE VII

*(The curtains are now drawn wide apart; the whole ship is covered with knights and sailors, who, with shouts of joy, make signs over towards the shore which is now seen to be quite near, with castle-crowned cliffs. Tristan and Isolda remain absorbed in mutual contemplation, perceiving nothing that is passing.)*

**BRANGAENA:** (*to the women, who at her bidding ascend from below*). Quick—the mantle! the royal robe!—
(*rushing between Tristan and Isolda.*)
Up, hapless ones!
See where we are!
(*she places the royal mantle on Isolda, who notices nothing.*)

**ALL THE MEN:** Hail! Hail!
Hail our monarch!
Hail to Mark the king!

**KURVENAL:** (*advancing gaily*).
Hail, Tristan,
knight of good fortune!
Behold King Mark approaching,
in a bark
with brave attendance.
Gladly he stems the tide,
coming to seek his bride.

**TRISTAN:** (*looking up in bewilderment*). Who comes?

**KURVENAL:** It is the king!

**TRISTAN:** What king do you mean?
(*Kurvenal points over the side. Tristan gazes stupefied at the shore.*)

**ALL THE MEN:** (*waving their hats*). Hail to King Mark!
All hail!

**ISOLDA:** (*bewildered*). What is it, Brangaena?
What are those cries?

**BRANGAENA:** Isolda—mistress!
Compose yourself!

**ISOLDA:** Where am I! living?
What was that drink?

**BRANGAENE:** (*verzweiflungsvoll*). Der Liebestrank!

**ISOLDE:** (*starrt entsetzt auf Tristan*). Tristan!

**TRISTAN:** Isolde!

**ISOLDE:** Muss ich leben?
(*Sie stürzt ohnmächtig an seine Brust*)

**BRANGAENE:** (*zu den Frauen*). Helft der Herrin!

**TRISTAN:** O Wonne voller Tücke!
O Trug geweihtes Glücke!

**ALLE MAENNER:** (*Ausbruch allgemeinen Jauchzens*). Heil dem König!
Kornwall, Heil!
(*Leute sind über Bord gestiegen, andere haben eine Brücke ausgelegt, und die Haltung Aller deutet auf die soeben bevorstehende Ankunft der Erwarteten, als der Vorhang schnell fällt.*)

## ■ ZWEITE AKT

*(Garten mit hohen Bäumen vor dem Gemache Isolde's, zu welchem, seitwärts gelegen, Stufen hinaufführen. Helle, anmuthige Sommernacht. An der geöffneten Thüre ist eine brennende Fackel aufgesteckt. Jagdgetön.)*

## ERSTE SCENE

*(Brangaene, auf den Stufen am Gemach, späht dem immer entfernter vernehmbaren Jagdtrosse nach. Zu ihr tritt aus dem Gemach, feurig bewegt, Isolde.)*

**ISOLDE:** Hörst du sie noch?
Mir schwand schon fern der Klang.

**BRANGAENE:** (*lauschend*). Noch sind sie nah':
deutlich tönt's daher.

**ISOLDE:** (*lauschend*). Sorgende Furcht
beirrt dein Ohr;
dich täuscht des Laubes
säuselnd Getön',
das lachend schüttelt der Wind.

**BRANGAENE:** Dich täuscht deines Wunsches Ungestüm,
zu vernehmen was du wähnst:—
ich höre der Hörner Schall.

**ISOLDE:** (*lauschend*). Nicht Hörnerschall
tönt so hold;
des Quelles sanft
rieselnde Welle
rauscht so wonnig daher;
wie hört' ich sie,
tos'ten noch Hörner?
Im Schweigen der Nacht
nur lacht mir der Quell:
der meiner harrt
in schweigender Nacht,

**BRANGAENA:** (*despairingly*).
The love-potion!

**ISOLDA:** (*staring with horror at Tristan*). Tristan!

**TRISTAN:** Isolda!

**ISOLDA:** Must I live, then?
(*falls fainting upon his breast.*)

**BRANGAENA:** (*to the women*.).
Look to your lady!

**TRISTAN:** O rapture fraught with cunning!
O fraud with bliss over-running!

**ALL THE MEN:** (*in a general burst of acclamation*). Hail to King Mark!
Cornwall, hail!
(*People have clambered over the ship's side, others have extended a bridge, and the aspect of all indicates the immediate arrival of the expected ones, as the curtain falls.*)

## ■ ACT II

*(A Garden before Isolda's chamber which lies at one side and is approached by steps. Bright and pleasant summer night. At the open door a burning torch is fixed. Sounds of hunting heard.)*

## SCENE I

*(Brangaena, on the steps leading to the chamber, is watching the retreat of the still audible hunters. She looks anxiously back into the chamber as Isolda emerges in ardent animation.)*

**ISOLDA:** Yet do you hear?
I lost the sound some time ago.

**BRANGAENA:** (*listening*) Still do they stay: clearly ring the horns.

**ISOLDA:** (*listening*). Fear but deludes your anxious ear;
by sounds of rustling leaves
you are deceived,
aroused by laughter of winds.

**BRANGAENA:** You are deceived
by wild desire,
and but hear as would your will:—
I still hear the sound of horns.

**ISOLDA:** (*listens*). No sound of horns
were so sweet:
yonder fountain's soft
murmuring current
moves so quietly here.
If horns yet brayed,
how could I hear that?
In still night alone
it laughs in my ear.
My loved one hides
in darkness unseen:

als ob Hörner noch nah' dir schall-
ten,
willst du ihn fern mir halten?

**BRANGAENE:** Der deiner harrt—
O hör' mein Warnen!—
Dess' harren Späher zur Nacht.
Weil du erblindet
wähnst du den Blick der Welt er
blödet für euch?
Da dort an Schiffes Bord,
von Tristan's bebender Hand,
die bleiche Braut
kamm ihrer mächtig,
König Marke empfing,
als Alles verwirrt auf die Wankende
sah,
der güt'ge König
mild besorgt
die Mühen der langen Fahrt,
die du littest,
laut beklagt:
ein Einz'ger war's,
ich achtet' es wohl,
der Tristan fasst' ins Auge;
mit böslicher List
lauern dem Blick
sucht' er in seiner Miene
zu finden, was ihm diene.
Tückisch lauschend
treff' ich ihn oft:
der heimlich euch umgarnt,
vor Melot seid gewarnt.

**ISOLDE:** Mein'st du Herrn Melot?
O wie du dich trüg'st!
Ist er nicht Tristan's
treuester Freund?
Muss mein Trauter mich meiden
dann weilt er bei Melot allein.

**BRANGAENE:** Was mir ihn ver-
dächtig,
macht dir ihn theuer.
Von Tristan zu Marke
ist Melot's Weg;
dort sä't er üble Saat.
Die heut' im Rath
dies nächtliche Jagen
so eilig schnell beschlossen
einem edlern Wild,
als dein Wähnen meint,
gilt ihre Jägers-List.

**ISOLDE:** Dem Freunde zu lieb
erfand diese List
aus Mit-Leid
Melot der Freund;
nun willst du den Treuen schelten?
Besser als du
sorgt er für mich;
ihm öffnet er,
was du mir sperr'st;
o spar' mir des Zögerns Noth!
Das Zeichen, Brangäne!
O gieb das Zeichen!
Lösche des Lichtes
letzten Schein!
Dass ganz sie sich neige,
winke der Nacht!
Schon goss sie ihr Schweigen
durch Hain und Haus;
schon füllt sie das Herz
mit wonnigem Graus;
o lösche das Licht nun aus!
Lösche den scheuchenden Schein!
Lass' meinen Liebsten ein!

would you hold from my side my
dearest?
deeming that horns you hear?

**BRANGAENA:** Your loved one
hid—
oh heed my warning!—
for him a spy waits by night.
And, you blinded,
to you, the eyes of all are watching
on you!
That day when there on board,
from Tristan's tremulous hands
King Mark received his quite fainting,
pale and passionless bride:
when all were aghast and gazing on
you,
the gracious monarch's kind concern
laid the blame to weariness,
of the way you had journeyed.
But there was one,
I noted it well,
who had eyes only for Tristan;
with hostile design
lowered his look;
so did he then observe him,
to find whatever might serve him.
Listening often
I light upon him:
he lays a secret snare.
Of Melot, oh beware!

**ISOLDA:** Mean you Sir Melot?
O, how you mistake!
Is he not Tristan's
trustiest friend?
May my true love not meet me,
with none but Melot he stays.

**BRANGAENA:** What moves me to
fear him
makes you his friend then?
Through Tristan to Mark's side
is Melot's way:
he sows suspicion's seed.
And those who have
so suddenly decided,
today on a night-hunt
a far nobler game
than is guessed by you
taxes their hunting skill.

**ISOLDA:** For Tristan's sake
was this scheme contrived
by means of
Melot, in truth:
now would you decry his friendship!
He serves Isolda
better than you,
his hand gives help
which yours denies:
what need of such delay?
The signal, Brangaena!
O give the signal!
Tread out the torch's
trembling gleam,
that night may envelop
all with her veil.
Already her peace reigns
over hill and hall,
her rapturous awe
the heart does enthrall;
allow then the light to fall!
Let but its dread luster die!
Let my beloved draw near!

**BRANGAENE:** O lass' die war-
nende Zünde!
Die Gefahr lass' sie dir zeigen!—
O wehe! Wehe!
Ach mir Armen!
Des unseligen Tranks!
Dass ich untreu
einmal nur
der Herrin Willen trog!
Gehorcht' ich taub und blind,
dein—Werk
war dann der Tod:
doch deine Schmach,
deine schmählichste Noth,
mein—Werk
muss ich Schuld'ge es wissen!

**ISOLDE:** Dein—Werk?
O thör'ge Magd!
Frau Minne kenntest du nicht?
Nicht ihrer Wunder Macht?
Des kühnsten Muthes
Königin,
des Welten-Werdens
Walterin,
Leben und Tod
sind ihr unterthan,
die sie webt aus Lust und Leid,
in Liebe wandelnd den Neid.
Des Todes Werk
nahm ich's vermessen zur Hand,
Frau Minne hat
meiner Macht es entwandt:
die Todgeweihte
nahm sie in Pfand,
fasste das Werk
in ihre Hand;
wie sie es wendet
wie sie es endet,
was sie mir küret,
wohin mich führet,
ihr ward ich zu eigen:—
nun lass' mich gehorsam zeigen!

**BRANGAENE:** Und musste der
Minne
tückischer Trank
des Sinnes Licht dir verlöschen;
darfst du nicht sehen,
wenn ich dich warne:
nur heute hör',
o hör' mein Flehen!
Der Gefahr leuchtendes Licht—
nur heute! heut'!—
die Fackel dort lösche nicht!

**ISOLDE:** Die im Busen mir
die Gluth entfacht,
die mir das Herze
brennen macht,
die mir als Tag
der Seele lacht,
Frau Minne will,
es werde Nacht,
dass hell sie dorten leuchte,
wo sie dein Licht verscheuchte.—
(*Sie geht zu der Thür und nimmt
die Fackel herab.*)
Zur Warte du!
Dort wache treu.
Die Leuchte—
wär's meines Lebens Licht,—
lachend
sie zu löschen zag' ich nicht.
(*Sie wirft die Fackel zur Erde, wo
sie allmälig verlöscht. Brangaene
wendet sich bestürzt ab, um auf*

**BRANGAENA:** The light of warning suppress not!
Let it remind you of peril!—
Ah, woe's me! Woe's me!
Fatal folly!
The fell power of that potion!
That I framed
a fraud for once
your order to oppose!
Had I been deaf and blind,
Your work
were then your death:
but your distress,
your distraction of grief,
my work
has contrived them, I own it!

**ISOLDA:** Your—act?
O foolish girl!
Love's goddess do you not know?
nor all her magic arts?
The queen who grants
unquailing hearts,
the witch whose will
the world obeys,
life and death
she holds in her hands,
which of joy and woe are woven?
She works hate into love.
The work of death
I took into my own hands;
Love's goddess saw
and gave her good commands.
The death-condemned
she claimed as her prey,
planning our fate
in her own way.
How she may bend it,
how she may end it,
what she may make me,
wheresoever take me,
still hers I am solely;
so let me obey her wholly.

**BRANGAENA:** And if by the artful
love-potion's lures
your light of reason is ravished,
if you are reckless
when I would warn you.
This once, oh, wait
and weigh my pleading!
I implore, leave it alight!—
The torch! the torch!
O put it not out this night!

**ISOLDA:** She who causes
my bosom's throes,
whose eager fire
within me glows,
whose light upon
my spirit flows,
Love's goddess demands
that night should close;
that brightly she may reign
and shun the vain torchlight.
(*she goes up to the door and takes
down the torch.*)
Go watch without—
keep wary guard!
The signal!—
and were it my spirit's spark,
smiling
I'd destroy it and hail the dark!
(*she throws the torch to the
ground where it slowly dies out.
Brangaena turns away, dis-*

einer äusseren Treppe die Zinne zu ersteigen, wo sie langsam verschwindet. Isolde lauscht und späht, zunächst schüchtern, in einen Baumgang. Von wachsendem Verlangen bewegt, schreitet sie dem Baumgang näher, und späht zuversichtlicher. Sie winkt mit einem Tuche, erst seltener, dann häufiger, und endlich, in leidenschaftlicher Ungeduld, immer schneller. Eine Gebärde des plötzlichen Entzückens sagt, dass sie den Freund in der Ferne gewahr geworden. Sie streckt sich höher, und höher, und um besser den Raum zu übersehen, eilt sie zur Treppe zurück, von deren oberster Stufe sie dem Herannahenden zuwinkt. Als er eintritt, springt sie ihm entgegen.)

turbed, and mounts an outer flight of steps leading to the roof, where she slowly disappears. Isolda listens and peers, at first shyly, towards an avenue. Urged by rising impatience, she then approaches the avenue and looks more boldly. She signs with her handkerchief, first slightly, then more plainly, waving it quicker as her impatience increases. A gesture of sudden delight shows that she has perceived her lover in the distance. She stretches herself higher and higher, and then, to look better over the intervening space, hastens back to the steps, from the top of which she signals again to the oncomer. As he enters, she springs to meet him.)

## ZWEITE SCENE

**TRISTAN:** Isolde! Geliebte!

**ISOLDE:** Tristan! Geliebter!
(*Stürmische Umarmungen Beider, unter denen sie in den Vordergrund gelangen.*)

**BEIDE:** Bist du mein?
Hab' ich dich wieder?
Darf ich dich fassen?
Kann ich mir trauen?
Endlich! Endlich!
An meiner Brust!
Fühl' ich dich wirklich?
Bist du es selbst?
Dies deine Augen?
Dies dein Mund?
Hier deine Hand?
Hier dein Herz?
Bin ich's? Bist du's?
Halt' ich dich fest?
Ist es kein Trug?
Ist es kein Traum?
O Wonne der Seele!
O süsse, hehrste,
kühnste, schönste,
seligste Lust!
Ohne Gleiche!
Überreiche!
Überselig!,
Ewig! Ewig!
Ungeahnte,
nie gekannte,
überschwänglich
hoch erhab'ne!
Freude-Jauchzen!
Lust-Entzücken!
Himmel-höchstes
Welt-Entrücken!
Mein Tristan!
Mein' Isolde!
Tristan!
Isolde!
Mein und dein!
Immer ein!
Ewig, ewig ein!

**TRISTAN:** Das Licht! Das Licht!
O dieses Licht!
Wie lang' verlosch es nicht!
Die Sonne sank,

## SCENE II

**TRISTAN:** (*rushing in*). Isolda! Beloved!

**ISOLDA:** Tristan! Beloved!
(*passionate embrace, with which they come down to the front.*)

**BOTH:** Are you mine?
Do I behold you?
Do I embrace you?
Can I believe it?
At last! At last!
Here on my breast!
Do I then clasp you?
Is it your own self?
Are these your eyes?
These your lips?
Here your hand?
Is it here your heart?
Is it you,
held in my arms?
Am I duped?
Is it a dream?
O rapture of spirit!
O sweetest, highest,
fairest, strongest,
holiest bliss!
Endless pleasure!
Boundless treasure!
Never to sever!
Never! Never!
Unconceived,
unbelieved,
overpowering
exaltation!
Joy-proclaiming,
bliss-outpouting,
high in heaven,
earth ignoring!
Tristan mine!
Isolda mine!
Tristan!
Isolda!
Mine alone!
Yours alone!
Ever all my own!

**TRISTAN:** The light! The light!
O but this light,
how long it was let to burn!
The sun had sunk,

der Tag verging;
doch seinen Neid
erstickt' er nicht;
sein scheuchend Zeichen
zündet er an,
und steckt's an der Liebsten Thüre,
dass ich nicht zu ihr führe.

**ISOLDE:** Doch der Liebsten Hand
löschte das Licht.
Wes' die Magd sich wehrte,
scheut' ich mich nicht:
in Frau Minne's Macht und Schutz
bot ich dem Tage Trutz.
Doch es rächte sich
der verscheuchte Tag;
mit deinen Sünden
Raths er pflag:
was dir gezeigt
die dämmernde Nacht,
an des Taggestirnes
Königsmacht
musstest du's übergeben,
um einsam
in oder Pracht
schimmernd dort zu leben. —
Wie ertrug ich's nur?
Wie ertrag' ich's noch?

**TRISTAN:** O! nun waren wir
Nacht-geweihte:
der tückische Tag,
der Neid-bereite,
trennen konnt' uns sein Trug,
doch nicht mehr täuschen sein Lug.
Seine eitle Pracht,
seinen prahlenden Schein
verlacht, wem die Nacht
den Blick geweih't:
seines flackernden Lichtes
flüchtige Blitze
blenden nicht mehr
uns're Blicke.
Wer des Todes Nacht
liebend erschau't,
wem sie ihr tief
Geheimniss vertraut,
des Tages Lügen,
Ruhm und Ehr',
Macht und Gewinn,
so schimmernd hehr,
wie eitler Staub der Sonnen
sind sie vor dem zerronnen.
In des Tages eitlem Wähnen
bleibt ihm ein einzig Sehnen,
das Sehnen hin
zur heil'gen Nacht,
wo ur-ewig,
einzig wahr
Liebeswonne ihm lacht.
(*Tristan zieht Isolde sanft zur Seite auf eine Blumenbank nieder, senkt sich vor ihr auf die Knie und schmiegt sein Haupt in ihren Arm.*)

**BEIDE:** O sink' hernieder,
Nacht der Liebe,
gieb Vergessen,
dass ich lebe;
nimm mich auf
in deinen Schoss,
löse von
der Welt mich los!
Verloschen nun
die letzte Leuchte;
was wir dachten,

the day had fled;
but all their spite
not yet was sped:
the scaring signal
they lit,
before my beloved one's dwelling,
repelling my swift approach.

**ISOLDA:** Your beloved one's hand
lowered the light,
for Brangaena's fears
in me roused no fright:
while Love's goddess gave me aid,
sunlight a mock I made.
But the light its fear
and defeat repaid;
with your misdeeds
a league it made.
What you did see
in shadowing night,
to the shining sun
of kingly might
must you straightaway surrender,
that it should
exist in bright
bonds of empty splendor. —
Could I bear it then?
could I bear it now?

**TRISTAN:** O now were we
devoted to night,
the dishonest day
bloated with envy,
lying, could not mislead,
though it might part us indeed.
Its pretentious glows
and its glamoring light
are scouted by those
who worship night.
All its flickering gleams
in flashes outblazing,
blind us no more
where we are gazing.
Those who boldly survey death's night,
those who have studied
her secret way,
the daylight's falsehoods—
rank and fame,
honor and all
at which men aim—
to them are no more matter
than dust which sunbeams scatter,
In the daylight's visions thronging
only abides one longing;
we yearn to hasten
to holy night,
where, unending,
only true,
Love extends delight!
(*Tristan draws Isolda gently aside to a flowery bank, sinks on his knee before her and rests his head on her arm.*)

**BOTH:** Oh night of rapture,
rest up on us!
lift our lives'
remembrance from us,
let us but
abide with you
from the world,
oh, set us free!
Extinguished in
the twilight's streaming
All our doubting

## Act II, Scene II

was uns dachten,
all' Gedenken,
all' Gemahnen,
heil'ger Dämm'rung
hehres Ahnen
löscht des Wähnens Graus
Welt-erlösend aus.
Barg im Busen
uns sich die Sonne,
leuchten lachend
Sterne der Wonne.
Von deinem Zauber
sanft umsponnen,
vor deinen Augen
süss zerronnen,
Herz an Herz dir,
Mund an Mund,
Eines Athems
einiger Bund;—
bricht mein Blick sich
wonn'-erblindet,
erbleicht die Welt
mit ihrem Blenden:
die mir der Tag
trügend erhellt,
zu täuschendem Wahn
entgegengestellt,
selbst—dann
bin ich die Welt,
Liebe-heiligstes Leben,
Wonne-hehrstes Weben,
Nie-Wieder-Erwachens
wahnlos
hold bewusster Wunsch.
(*Tristan und Isolde versinken wie
in gänzliche Entrücktheit, in der
sie, Haupt an Haupt auf die Blumenbank zurückgelehnt, verweil-
en.*)

all our doubting
all our memories,
all our fancies,
sacred twilight's
soft advances
bid vain fears to cease,
from the world release.
Hide our hearts away
sunlight's streaming,
bliss would bloom from
stars' tender beaming.
To your enchantment
we surrender
beneath your gaze
So wondrous tender,
Heart to heart,
and lip to lip.
Each the other's
breath we sip;
Blissful beams
our eyes are binding,
abashed is earth
with radiance blinding;
Lit by the daylight's
dazzling heat
Undaunted by falsehoods
which we defy.
You are my world,
I am yours.
Cherished visions achieving
Never daunted by daylight's
beam be
our undying dream.
(*Tristan and Isolda sink into
oblivious ecstasy, reposing on the
flowery bank close together.*)

**BRANGAENE:** (*unsichtbar, von
der Höhe der Zinne*). Einsam wachend
in der Nacht,
wem der Traum
der Liebe lacht,
hab' der Einen
Ruf in Acht,
die den Schläfern
Schlimmes ahnt,
bange zum
Erwachen mahnt.
Habet Acht!
Habet Acht!
Bald entweicht die Nacht.

**BRANGAENA:** (*from the turret,
unseen*). Long I watch alone by
night:
You enwrapped
in love's delight,
heed my boding
voice correctly,
I forewarn you
woe is near;
waken to
my words of fear,
Have a care!
Have a care!
Swiftly night does wear on!

**ISOLDE:** Lausch', Geliebter!

**ISOLDA:** Listen, beloved!

**TRISTAN:** Lass' mich sterben!

**TRISTAN:** Let me die!

**ISOLDE:** (*allmälig sich ein wenig
erhebend*). Neid'sche Wache!

**ISOLDA:** (*slowly raising herself a
little*). Envious watcher!

**TRISTAN:** (*zurückgelehnt blei-
bend*). Die erwachen!

**TRISTAN:** (*remaining in reclining position*). I'll never waken.

**ISOLDE:** Doch der Tag
muss Tristan wecken?

**ISOLDA:** But the day
must dawn and rouse you?

**TRISTAN:** (*ein wenig das Haupt
erhebend*).
Lass' den Tag
dem Tode weichen!

**TRISTAN:** (*raising his head slightly*). Let the day surrender
to Death!

**ISOLDE:** Tag und Tod
mit gleichen Streichen
sollten uns're
Lieb erreichen?

**ISOLDA:** Day and Death
will both engender
feud against
our passion tender.

**TRISTAN:** (*zieht Isolde, mit bedeutungsvoller Gebärde, sanft an
sich*). So stürben wir,
um ungetrennt,
ewig einig,
ohne End',
ohn' Erwachen,
ohne Bangen,
namenlos
in Lieb' umfangen,
ganz uns selbst gegeben,
der Liebe nur zu leben.

**ISOLDE:** (*wie in sinnender Entrücktheit zu ihm auf blickend*). So
stürben wir,
um ungetrennt—

**TRISTAN:** Ewig einig—

**ISOLDE:** Ohne End'—

**TRISTAN:** Ohn' Erwachen—

**ISOLDE:** Ohne Bangen—

**TRISTAN:** Namenlos
in Lieb' umfangen—

**ISOLDE:** Ganz uns selbst gegeben,
der Liebe nur zu leben!
(*Isolde neigt, wie überwältigt,
das Haupt an seine Brust.*)

**BRANGAENE:** (*wie vorher*). Ha-
bet Acht
Habet Acht!
Schon weicht dem Tag die Nacht.

**TRISTAN:** (*lächelnd zu Isolde
geneigt*). Soll ich lauschen?

**ISOLDE:** Lass' mich sterben!

**TRISTAN:** Muss ich wachen?

**ISOLDE:** Nie erwachen!

**TRISTAN:** Soll der Tag
noch Tristan wecken?

**ISOLDE:** Lass' den Tag
dem Tode weichen!

**TRISTAN:** Des Tages Dräuen
trotzen wir so?

**ISOLDE:** (*mit wachsender Begeisterung*). Seinen Trug ewig zu
fliehn.

**TRISTAN:** Sein dämmernder
Schein
verscheuchte uns nie?

**ISOLDE:** (*mit grosser Gebärde
ganz sich erhebend*).
Ewig währ' uns die Nacht!
(*Tristan folgt ihr, sie umfangen
sich in schwärmerischer Begeisterung.*)

**BEIDE:** O süsse Nacht!
Ew'ge Nacht!
Hehr erhab'ne,
Liebes-Nacht!
Wen du umfangen,
Wem du gelacht,
wie—wär' ohne Bangen
aus dir er je erwacht?
Wie es fassen?
Wie sie lassen,
diese Wonne,
fern der Sonne,
fern der Tage
Trennungs-Klage?
Ohne Wähnen

**TRISTAN:** (*drawing Isolda gently
towards him with expressive action*). O might we then
die together,
each the other's
own to always!
never fearing,
never waking,
blessed delights
of love partaking,—
each to each be given,
our heaven in love alone!

**ISOLDA:** (*gazing up at him in
thoughtful ecstasy*). O might we
then die together!

**TRISTAN:** Each the other's—

**ISOLDA:** Own for always,—

**TRISTAN:** Never fearing—

**ISOLDA:** Never waking—

**TRISTAN:** Blessed delights
of love partaking—

**ISOLDA:** Each to each be given;
in love alone our heaven.
(*Isolda, as if overcome, droops
her head on his breast.*)

**BRANGAENA VOICE:** (*as before*).
Have a care!
Have a care!
Night yields to daylight's glare.

**TRISTAN:** (*bends smilingly to
Isolda*). Shall I listen?

**ISOLDA:** (*looking fondly up at
Tristan*). Let me die!

**TRISTAN:** Must I waken?

**ISOLDA:** Nothing shall wake me!

**TRISTAN:** Must not daylight
dawn, and rouse me?

**ISOLDA:** Let the day
to Death surrender!

**TRISTAN:** May thus the day's
evil threats be defied?

**ISOLDA:** (*with growing enthusiasm*). From its slavery let us fly.

**TRISTAN:** And shall we not dread
its dawn?

**ISOLDA:** (*rising with a grand gesture*). Night will shield us for always!
(*Tristan follows her; they embrace in fond exaltation.*)

**BOTH:** O endless Night!
blissful Night!
glad and glorious
lover's Night!
Those whom you held,
lapped in delight,
how could even the boldest
unmoved endure your flight?
How to take it,
how to break it,—
joy existent,
sunlight distant.
Far from mourning,
sorrow-warning,
fancies spurning,

sanftes Sehnen
ohne Bangen
süss Verlangen,
ohne Wehen
hehr Vergehen,
ohne Schmachten
hold Umnachten;
ohne Scheiden,
ohne Meiden,
traut allein,
ewig heim,
in ungemess'nen Räumen
übersel'ges Träumen.
Du Isolde,
Tristan ich,
nicht mehr Tristan,
nicht Isolde;
ohne Nennen,
ohne Trennen,
neu Erkennen,
neu Entbrennen;
endlos ewig
ein-bewusst:
heiss erglühter Brust
höchste Liebes-Lust!

softly yearning,
fear expiring,
sweet desiring!
Anguish flying,
gladly dying;
no more pining,
night-enshrining,
never divided,
whatever happens,
side by side
still abide
in realms of space unmeasured,
vision blessed and treasured!
You Isolda,
Tristan I;
no more Tristan,
no more Isolda.
Never spoken,
never broken.
newly sighted,
newly lighted,
endless ever
all our dream:
in our bosoms gleam
love delights supreme!

## DRITTE SCENE

(Brangaene, stösst einen gellenden Schrei aus. Tristan und Isolde bleiben in verzückter Stellung. Kurwenal stürzt mit entblösstem Schwert herein.)

KURWENAL: Rette dich, Tristan!
(Er blickt mit Entsetzen hinter sich in die Scene zurück. Marke, Melot und Hofleute (in Jägertracht) kommen aus dem Baumgange lebhaft nach dem Vordergrunde und halten entsetzt der Gruppe der Liebenden gegenüber an. Brangaene kommt zugleich von der Zinne herab, und stürzt auf Isolde zu. Diese, von unwillkürlicher Scham ergriffen, lehnt sich mit abgewandtem Gesichte auf die Blumenbank. Tristan, in ebenfalls unwillkürlicher Bewegung, streckt mit dem einen Arme den Mantel breit aus, so dass er Isolde vor den Blicken der Ankommenden verdeckt. In dieser Stellung verbleibt er längere Zeit, unbeweglich den starren Blick auf die Männer gerichtet, die in verschiedener Bewegung die Augen auf ihn heften. —Morgendämmerung.)

TRISTAN: Der öde Tag—
zum letzten Mal!

MELOT: (zu Marke). Das sollst du, Herr, mir sagen,
ob ich ihn recht verklagt?
Das dir zum Pfand ich gab,
ob ich mein Haupt gewahrt?
Ich zeigt' ihn dir
in off'ner That:
Namen und Ehr'
hab' ich getreu
vor Schande dir bewahrt.

## SCENE III

(Brangaena utters a piercing cry. Tristan and Isolda remain in their absorbed state. Kurvenal rushes in with drawn sword.)

KURVENAL: Save yourself, Tristan!
(He looks fearfully off behind him. Mark, Melot, and courtiers, in hunting dress, come swiftly up the avenue and pause in the foreground in consternation before the lovers. Brangaena at the same time descends from the roof and hastens towards Isolda. The latter in involuntary shame leans on the flowery bank with averted face. Tristan, with an equally unconscious action, stretches his mantle wide out with one arm, so as to conceal Isolda from the gaze of the newcomers. In this position he remains for some time, turning a changeless look upon the men, who gaze at him in varied emotion. The morning dawns.)

TRISTAN: The dreary day—
its last time comes!

MELOT: (to Mark). Now say to me, my sovereign,
was my impeachment just?
I staked my head thereon;
now is the pledge redeemed?
Behold him in
the very act:
I have faithfully saved honor and
fame from shame for you!

MARKE: (nach tiefer Erschütterung, mit bebender Stimme). Thatest du's wirklich?
Wähnst du das?—
Sieh ihn dort,
den treu'sten aller Treuen:
blick' auf ihn,
den freundlichsten der Freunde;
seiner Treue
frei'ste That
traf mein Herz
mit feindlichstem Verrath.
Trog mich Tristan,
sollt' ich hoffen,
was sein Trügen
mir getroffen,
sei durch Melot's Rath
redlich mir bewahrt?

TRISTAN: (krampfhaft heftig).
Tage-Gespenster!
Morgen-Träume—
täuschend und wüst—
entschwebt, entweicht!

MARKE: (mit tiefer Ergriffenheit). Mir—dies?
Dies—, Tristan, mir?—
Wohin nun Treue,
da Tristan mich betrog?
Wohin nun Ehr'
und echte Art,
da aller Ehren Hort,
da Tristan sie verlor?
Die Tristan sich
zum Schild erkor,
wohin ist Tugend
nun entflohn,
da meinen Freund sie flieht,
da Tristan mich verrieth?
(Tristan senkt langsam den Blick zu Boden; in seinen Mienen ist, während Marke fortfährt, zunehmende Trauer zu lesen.)
Wozu die Dienste
ohne Zahl
der Ehren Ruhm,
der Grösse Macht,
die Marken du gewannst,
musst' Ehr' und Ruhm,
Grösse und Macht,
musste die Dienste
ohne Zahl
der Marke's Schmach bezahlen?
Dünkte zu wenig
dich sein Dank,
dass was du erworben,
Ruhm und Reich,
er zu Erb' und Eigen dir gab?
Dem kinderlos einst
schwand sein Weib,
so liebt' er dich,
dass nie auf's Neu'
sich Marke wollt' vermählen.
Da alles Volk
zu Hof und Land
mit Bitt' und Dräuen
in ihn drang,
die Königin dem Reiche,
die Gattin sich zu kiesen;
da selber du
den Ohm beschwor'st,
des Hofes Wunsch,
des Landes Willen
gütlich zu erfüllen:
in Wehr gegen Hof und Land,
in Wehr selbst gegen dich,

MARK: (deeply moved, with trembling voice). Have you preserved them?
You say so?
See him there,
the truest of all true hearts!
Look on him
the faithfulest of friends,
His offense,
so black and base,
fills my heart
with anguish and disgrace.
Tristan, traitor,
what hope stays
that the honor
he betrays;
should by Melot's account
rest to me indeed?

TRISTAN: (with convulsive violence). Daylight phantoms—
morning visions
empty and vain—
Away! Begone!

MARK: (in deep emotion). This—
blow.
Tristan, to me?
Where now has truth fled,
if Tristan can betray?
Where now are faith
and friendship fair,
when from the fount of faith,
my Tristan, they are gone?
The buckler Tristan
once did wear,
where is that shield
of virtue now?
When from my friends it flies,
and Tristan's honor dies?
(Tristan slowly lowers his eyes to the ground. His features express increasing grief while Mark continues.)
Why have you done noble
service
and honor, fame
and potent might
amassed for Mark, your king?
Must honor, fame,
power and might,
must all your noble
service done
be paid with Mark's dishonor?
Seemed the reward
too slight and scant
that what you have won him—
realms and riches—
you are the heir unto, all?
When childless he once lost
once a wife,
he loved you so
that never again
did Mark desire to marry.
When all his subjects,
high and low,
demands and prayers,
on him did press
to choose himself a consort—
a queen to give the kingdom,
when you yourself
urged your uncle
that what the court
and country pleaded
well might be conceded,
opposing high and low,
opposing even yourself,

mit Güt' und List
weigert' er sich,
bis, Tristan, du ihm drohtest
für immer zu meiden
Hof und Land,
würdest du selber
nicht entsandt,
dem König die Braut zu frei'n,
Da liess er's denn so sein.—
Dies wunderhehre Weib,
das mir dein Muth erwarb,
wer durft' es sehen,
wer es kennen,
wer mit Stolze
sein es nennen,
ohne selig sich zu preisen?
Der mein Wille
nie zu nahen wagte,
der mein Wunsch
Ehrfurcht-scheu entsagte
die so herrlich
hold erhaben
mir die Seele
musste laben,
trotz—Feind und Gefahr,
die fürstliche Braut
brachtest du mir dar.
Die kein Himmel erlöst,
warum—mir diese Hölle?
Die kein Elend sühnt,
warum—mir diese Schmach?
Den unerforschlich
furchtbar tief
geheimnissvollen Grund,
wer macht der Welt ihn kund?

**TRISTAN:** (*das Auge mitleidig zu Marke erhebend*). O König, das kann ich dir nicht sagen; und was du frägst, das kannst du nie erfahren.—
(*Er wendet sich seitwärts zu Isolde, welche die Augen sehnsüchtig zu ihm aufgeschlagen hat.*)
Wohin nun Tristan scheidet,
willst du, Isold', ihm folgen?
Dem Land, das Tristan meint,
der Sonne Licht nicht scheint;
es ist das dunkel
nächt'ge Land,
daraus die Mutter
einst mich sandt',
als, den im Tode
sie empfangen,
im Tod' sie liess
zum Licht gelangen,
Was, da sie mich gebar,
ihr Liebes-Berge war,
das Wunderreich der Nacht,
aus der ich einst erwacht,—
das bietet dir Tristan,
dahin geht er voran.
Ob sie ihm folge
treu und hold,
das sag' ihm nun Isold'.

**ISOLDE:** Da für ein fremdes Land
der Freund sie einstens warb,
dem Un-holden
treu und hold,
musst' Isolde folgen.
Nun führst du in dein Eigen,
dein Erbe mir zu zeigen;
wie flöh' ich wohl das Land,
das alle Welt umspannt?
Wo Tristan's Haus und Heim,

with kindly cunning
still be refused,
till, Tristan, you threatened
forever to leave
both court and land
if you received
no command
to woo a bride for the king:
then so he let you do.—
This wondrous lovely wife,
your might for me did win,
who could behold her,
who address her,
who in pride
and bliss possess her,
but would bless his happy fortune?
She whom I have
paid respect to ever
whom I owned,
yet possess her never—
she, the princess
proud and peerless,
lighting up
my life so cheerless,
despite foes,—without fear,
the fairest of brides
you brought me here.
Why in hell must I bide,
without hope of a heaven?
Why endure disgrace
unhealed by tears or grief?
The unexplained,
unpenetrated
cause of all these woes,
who will to us disclose?

**TRISTAN:** (*raising his eyes pitifully towards Mark*). O monarch! I—may not tell you, truly;
what do you ask
remains for always unanswered.—
(*he turns to Isolda, who looks tenderly up at him.*)
Where is Tristan going now,
will you, Isolda, follow?
The land that Tristan means
has no gleams of sunlight;
it is the dark
abode of night,
from where I first
came forth to light,
and she who bore me
there in anguish,
gave up her life,
nor long did languish,
She only looked on my face,
then sought this resting place.
This land where Night reigns,
where Tristan once had lain
now there offers he
your faithful guide to be.
So let Isolda
straight declare
if she will meet him there.

**ISOLDA:** When to a foreign land
before you did invite,
to you traitor,
resting true,
did Isolda follow.
Your kingdom now is showing,
where surely we are going!
Why should I shun that land
by which the world is spanned?
For Tristan's house and home

da kehr' Isolde ein:
auf dem sie folge
treu und hold,
den Weg nun zeig' Isold'!
(*Tristan neigt sich langsam über sie und küsst sie sanft auf die Stirn. Melot fährt wüthend auf.*)

**MELOT:** (*das Schwert ziehend*). Verräther! Ha!
Zur Rache, König!
Duldest du diese Schmach?

**TRISTAN:** (*zieht sein Schwert und wendet sich schnell um*). Wer wagt sein Leben an das meine?
(*Er heftet den Blick auf Melot.*)
Mein Freund war der,
er minnte mich hoch und theuer:
um Ehr' und Ruhm
mir war er besorgt wie Keiner.
Zum Uebermuth
trieb er mein Herz:
die Schaar führt' er,
die mich gedrängt,
Ehr' und Ruhm mir zu mehren,
dem König dich zu vermählen.—
Dein Blick, Isolde,
blendet' auch ihn:
aus Eifer verrieth
mich der Freund
dem König, den ich verrieth.—
(*Er dringt auf Melot ein.*)
Wehr' dich, Melot!
(*Als Melot ihm das Schwert entgegenstreckt, lässt Tristan das seinige fallen und sinkt verwundet in Kurwenal's Arme. Isolde stürzt sich an seine Brust Marke hält Melot zurück.—Der Vorhang fällt schnell.*)

Isolda will make her own.
The road whereby
we have to go
I pray you quickly show!—
(*Tristan bends slowly over her and kisses her softly on her forehead. Melot starts furiously forward.*)

**MELOT:** (*drawing his sword*). Villain! Ha! Vengeance, Monarch. Say, will you suffer such scorn?

**TRISTAN:** (*drawing his sword and turning quickly round*). Who's he will set his life against mine?
(*casting a look at Melot.*)
This was my friend;
he told me he loved me truly:
my fame and honor
he upheld more than all men.
With arrogance
he filled my heart,
and led on those
who prompted me
fame and power to augment me
by wedding you to our monarch.—
Your glance, Isolda,
glamored him thus;
and, jealous, my friend
played me false
to King Mark, whom I betrayed.—
(*he sets on Melot.*)
Guard yourself Melot!
(*Melot presents his sword. Tristan drops his own guard and sinks wounded into the arms of Kurvenal. Isolda throws herself upon his breast. Mark holds Melot back. The curtain falls quickly.*)

# ■ DRITTE AKT

# ■ ACT III

*Burggarten.*

*A Castle Garden.*

(*Zur einen Seite hohe Burggebäude, zur anderen eine niedrige Mauerbrüstung von einer Warte unterbrochen; im Hintergrunde das Burgthor. Die Lage ist auf felsiger Höhe anzunehmen; durch Oeffnungen blickt man auf einen weiten Meereshorizont. Das Ganze macht den Eindruck der Herrenlosigkeit, übel gepflegt, hie und da schadhaft und bewachsen.*)

(*At one side high castellated buildings, on the other a low breastwork interrupted by a watch tower; at back the castlegate. The situation is supposed to be on rocky cliffs; through openings the view extends over a wide sea horizon. The whole gives an impression of being deserted by the owner, badly kept, and here and there dilapidated and overgrown.*)

## ERSTE SCENE

## SCENE I

(*Im Vordergrunde, an der inneren Seite, liegt Tristan unter dem Schatten einer grossen Linde, auf einem Ruhebett schlafend, wie leblos ausgestreckt. Zu Häupten ihm sitzt Kurwenal, in Schmerz über ihn hingebeugt, und sorgsam seinem Athem lauschet. Von der Aussenseite hört man einen Hirtendes blasen.*)

(*In the foreground, in the garden, lies Tristan sleeping on a couch under the shade of a great limetree, stretched out as if lifeless. At his head sits Kurvenal, bending over him in grief and anxiously listening to his breathing. From without comes the mournful sound of a shepherd's pipe.*)

*(Der Hirt erscheint mit dem Oberleibe über der Mauerbrüstung und blickt theilnehmend herein.)*

**HIRT:** Kurwenal! He!—
Sag', Kurwenal!—
Hör' dort, Freund!
Wacht er noch nicht?

**KURWENAL:** *(wendet ein wenig das Haupt nach ihm und schüttelt traurig mit dem Kopf).* Erwachte er,
wär's doch nur
um für immer zu verscheiden,
erschien zuvor
die Aerztin nicht,
die einz'ge, die uns hilft?
Sah'st du noch nichts?
Kein Schiff noch auf der See?—

**HIRT:** Eine and're Weise
hörtest du dann,
so lustig wie ich sie kann.
Nun sag' auch ehrlich,
alter Freund!
was hat's mit uns'rem Herrn?

**KURWENAL:** Lass' die Frage;—
du kannst's doch nie erfahren.—
Eifrig späh',
und siehst du das Schiff,
dann spiele lustig und hell.

**HIRT:** *(sich wendend, und mit der Hand über'm Auge nach dem Meer ausspähend).* Oed' und leer das Meer!—
*(Er setzt die Schalmei an den Mund und entfernt sich blasend.)*

**TRISTAN:** *(bewegungslos, dumpf).* Die alte Weise—
was weckt sie mich?
*(Er schlägt die Augen auf und wendet das Haupt ein wenig.)*
Wo bin ich?

**KURWENAL:** *(freudig erschrocken auffahrend).* Ha!—die Stimme!
Seine Stimme!—
Tristan! Herr!
Mein Held! Mein Tristan!

**TRISTAN:** *(mit Anstrengung).* Wer—ruft mich?

**KURWENAL:** Endlich! Endlich!
Leben! O Leben—
süsses Leben—
meinem Tristan neu gegeben!

**TRISTAN:** *(matt).* Kurwenal!—
du?
Wo—war ich?—
Wo—bin ich?

**KURWENAL:** Wo du bist?
In Frieden, sicher und frei!
Kareol, Herr!
Kennst du die Burg
der Väter nicht?

**TRISTAN:** Meiner Väter?

**KURWENAL:** Schau dich nur um!

**TRISTAN:** Was erklang mir?

**KURWENAL:** Des Hirten Weise,
die hörtest du wieder;
am Hügel ab
hütet er deine Heerde.

**TRISTAN:** Meine Heerde?

---

*(Presently, the shepherd comes and looks in with interest, showing the upper half of his body over the wall.)*

**SHEPHERD:** Kurvenal, ho!—
Say, Kurvenal,—
tell me, friend!
Does he still sleep?

**KURVENAL:** *(turning a little towards him and shaking his head sadly).* If he awoke
it would be
but for evermore to leave us,
unless we find
the lady-leech;
alone can she give help.—
Did you see anything?
No ship yet on the sea?

**SHEPHERD:** Quite another ditty
then would I play
as merry as ever I may.
But tell me truly,
trusty friend,
why languishes our lord?

**KURVENAL:** Do not ask me;—
for I can give no answer.
Watch the sea,
if sails come in sight
play a sprightly melody.

**SHEPHERD:** *(turns around and scans the horizon, shading his eyes with his hand).* The sea appears blank!
*(he puts the reed pipe to his mouth and withdraws, playing.)*

**TRISTAN:** *(motionless—faintly).* The tune so well known—
why wake to that?
*(opens his eyes and slightly turns his head).*
Where am I?

**KURVENAL:** *(starting in joyous surprise.)* Ha!—who is speaking?
It is his voice!—
Tristan! loved one!
My lord! my Tristan!

**TRISTAN:** *(with effort).* Who—calls me?

**KURVENAL:** Life—at last—
O thanks be to heaven!—
sweetest life
unto my Tristan newly given!

**TRISTAN:** *(faintly).* Kurvenal!—
you?
Where—was I?—
Where—am I?

**KURVENAL:** Where are you?
In safety, tranquil and sure!
It is Kareol.
Do you not know
Your father's halls?

**TRISTAN:** This my father's?

**KURVENAL:** Look around.

**TRISTAN:** What woke me?

**KURVENAL:** The herdsman's ditty
have you heard, doubtless;
he heeds your herds
above on the hills there.

**TRISTAN:** Have I herds, then?

---

**KURWENAL:** Herr, das mein' ich!
Dein das Haus,
Hof und Burg.
Hof und Burg.
Das Volk, getreu
dem trauten Herrn,
so gut es konnt',
hat's Haus und Heerd gepflegt
das einst mein Held
zu Erb' und Eigen
an Leut' und Volk verschenkt,
als Alles er verliess,
in ferne Land' zu ziehn.

**TRISTAN:** In welches Land?

**KURWENAL:** Hei! nach Kornwall;
kühn und wonnig
was sich da Glückes,
Glanz und Ehren
Tristan hehr ertrotzt!

**TRISTAN:** Bin ich in Kornwall?

**KURWENAL:** Nicht doch: in Kareol.

**TRISTAN:** Wie kam ich her?

**KURWENAL:** Hei nun, wie du kam'st?
Zu Ross rittest du nicht;
ein Schifflein führte dich her:
doch zu dem Schifflein
hier auf den Schultern
trug ich dich; die sind breit,
die brachten dich dort zum Strand.
Nun bist du daheim zu Land,
im echten Land,
im Heimat-Land
auf eig'ner Weid' und Wonne,
im Schein der alten Sonne,
darin von Tod und Wunden
du selig sollst gesunden
*(Er schmiegt sich an Tristan's Brust.)*

**TRISTAN:** Dünkt dich das,—
ich weis es anders,
doch kann ich's dir nicht sagen.
Wo ich erwacht,
weilt' ich nicht;
doch wo ich weilte,
das kann ich dir nicht sagen.
Die Sonne sah' ich nicht,
nicht sah' ich Land noch Leute;
doch was ich sah,
das kann ich dir nicht sagen.
Ich war—
wo ich von je gewesen,
wohin auf je ich gehe:
im weiten Reich
der Welten Nacht.
Nur ein Wissen
dort uns eigen:
göttlich ew' ges
Ur-Vergessen,—
wie schwand mir seine Ahnung!
Sehnsücht'ge Mahnung
nenn' ich dich,
die neu dem Licht
des Tag's mich zugetrieben?
Was einzig mir geblieben?
Ein heiss-inbrünstig Lieben,
aus Todes-Wonne-Grauen
jagt mich's, das Licht zu schauen
das trügend hell und golden
noch dir, Isolden, scheint!
Verfluchter Tag

---

**KURVENAL:** Sir, I say it!
Yours are court,
castle—all,
To you yet true,
your trusty folk,
as best they might,
have held your home in guard:
the gift which once
your goodness gave
to your serfs and vassals here,
when going far away to dwell
in foreign lands.

**TRISTAN:** What foreign land?

**KURVENAL:** Why! in Cornwall;
where cool and able,
all that was brilliant,
brave and noble,
Tristan, my lord, lightly took.

**TRISTAN:** Am I in Cornwall?

**KURVENAL:** No, no; in Kareol.

**TRISTAN:** How did I come here?

**KURVENAL:** Hey now! how you came?
You rode no horse:
a vessel bore you across.
But on my shoulders
down to the ship
you had to ride: they are broad,
they carried you to the shore.
Now you are at home once more;
your own land,
your native land;
all loved things now are near you,
unchanged the sun will cheer you.
The wounds from which you languish
here all shall end their anguish.
*(he presses himself to Tristan's breast.)*

**TRISTAN:** You think so!
I know it is not so,
but this I cannot tell you.
Where I awoke
never I was,
but where I wandered
I indeed cannot tell you.
The sun I could not see,
nor country fair, nor people;
but what I saw
I indeed cannot tell you.
It was—
the land from which I once came
and where I shall return:
the endless realm
of earthly night.
One thing only
there possessed me:
blank, unending,
all—oblivion.—
How faded all forebodings?
O wistful goadings!—
Thus I call
the thoughts that all
toward light of day have pressed me.
What only yet does rest me,
the love-pains that possessed me,
from blissful death's affright
now drive me toward the light,
which, deceitful, bright and golden,

mit deinem Schein
Wach'st du ewig
meiner Pein?
Brennt sie ewig,
diese Leuchte,
die selbst Nachts
von ihr mich scheuchte?
Ach, Isolde!
Süsse! Holde!
Wann—endlich,
wann, ach wann
löschest du die Zünde,
dass sie mein Glück mir künde?
Das Licht, wann löscht es aus?
Wann wird es Nacht im Haus?

round you Isolda, shines.
Accurséd day
with cruel glow!
Must you always
wake my woe?
Must your light
be burning forever,
even by night
to sever our hearts?
Ah, my fairest,
sweetest, rarest!
When will you—
when, ah, when—
let the torchlight dwindle,
so that my bliss may kindle?
The light, how long it glows!
When will the house repose?
(*his voice has grown fainter and
he sinks back gently, exhausted.*)

**KURWENAL:** (*nach grosser Erschütterung aus der Niederge-
schlagenheit sich aufraffend*). Der
einst ich trotzt',
aus Treu' zu dir,
mit dir nach ihr
nun muss ich mich sehnen!
Glaub' meinem Wort,
du sollst sie sehen,
hier—und heut'—
den Trost kann ich dir geben,
ist sie nur selbst noch am Leben.

**KURVENAL:** (*who has been deeply distressed, now quickly rouses
himself from his dejection*). I once
defied,
through faith in you,
the one for whom
now with you I'm yearning.
Trust in my words,
you soon shall see her
face to face.
My tongue gives that comfort,
If on the earth still she lives.

**TRISTAN:** (*sehr matt*). Noch losch
das Licht nicht aus,
noch ward's nicht Nacht im Haus.
Isolde lebt und wacht,
sie rief mich aus der Nacht.

**TRISTAN:** (*very feebly*). Yet the
beacon's spark burns;
yet the house is not dark.
Isolda lives and wakes,
her voice through darkness breaks.

**KURWENAL:** Lebt sie denn,
so lass' dir Hoffnung lachen.—
Muss Kurwenal dumm dir gelten,
heut' sollst du ihn nicht schelten.
Wie todt lag'st du
seit dem Tag,
da Melot, der Verruchte,
dir eine Wunde schlug.
Die böse Wunde,
wie sie heilen?
Mir thör'gem Manne
dünkt' es da,
wer einst dir Morold's
Wunde schloss,
der heilte leicht die Plagen
von Melot's Wehr geschlagen.
Die beste Aerztin
bald ich fand:
nach Kornwall hab' ich
ausgesandt:
ein treuer Mann
wohl über's Meer
bringt dir Isolden her.

**KURVENAL:** Lives she still,
then let new hope delight you,
If foolish and dull you hold me,
this day you must not scold me.
You lay as dead
since that day
when that accurséd Melot
so foully wounded you:
Your wound was heavy:
how to heal it?
Your simple servant
there thought
that she who once
closed Morold's wound
with ease the hurt could heal you
that Melot's sword did deal you.
I found the best
of leeches there,
to Cornwall have I
sent for her:
a trusty serf
sails over the sea,
bringing Isolda to you.

**TRISTAN:** (*ausser sich*). Isolde
kommt!
Isolde naht!—
(*Er ringt gleichsam nach
Sprache.*)
O Treue! hehre,
holde Treue!
(*Er zieht Kurwenal an sich und
umarmt ihn.*)
Mein Kurwenal,
du trauter Freund,
du Treuer ohne Wanken,
wie soll dir Tristan danken?
Mein Schild, mein Schirm
in Kampf und Streit;

**TRISTAN:** (*transported*). Isolda
comes!
Isolda nears!
(*he struggles for words.*)
O friendship! high
and holy friendship!
(*draws Kurvenal to him and embraces him.*)
O Kurvenal,
your trusty heart,
my truest friend I rank you!
However can Tristan thank you?
My shelter and shield
in fight and strife;
in weal or woe

zu Lust und Leid
mir stets bereit:
wen ich gehasst,
den hasstest du;
wen ich geminnt,
den minntest du.
Dem guten Marke,
dient ich ihm hold,
wie warst du ihm treuer als Gold!
Musst' ich verrathen
den edlen Herrn,
wie betrogst du ihn da so gern!
Dir nicht eigen,
einzig mein,
mitleidest du
wenn ich leide:—
nur—was ich leide,
das—kannst du nicht leiden!
Dies furchtbare Sehnen,
das mich zehrt;
dies schmachtende Brennen,
das mich zehrt;
wollt' ich dir's nennen,
konntest du's kennen,—
nicht hier würdest du weilen;
zur Warte müsstest du eilen,
mit allen Sinnen
sehnend von hinnen
nach dorten trachten und spähen,
wo ihre Segel sich blähen;
wo vor den Winden,
mich zu finden,
von der Liebe Drang befeuert,
Isolde zu mir steuert!—
es naht, es naht
mit muthiger Hast!
Sie weht, sie weht,
die Flagge am Mast
Das Schiff, das Schiff!
Dort streicht es am Riff!
Siehst du es nicht?
Kurwenal, siehst du es nicht?
(*Als Kurwenal um Tristan nicht
zu verlassen, zögert, und dieser in
schweigender Spannung nach
ihm blickt, ertönt, wie zu Anfang,
die klagende Weise des Hirten.*)

**KURWENAL:**
(*niedergeschlagen*).
Noch ist kein Schiff zu seh'n!

**TRISTAN:** (*hat mit abnehmender
Aufregung gelauscht, und beginnt nun mit wachsender
Schwermuth*). Muss ich dich so
versteh'n,
du alte, ernste Weise,
mit deiner Klage Klang?—
Durch Abendwehen
drang sie bang,
als einst dem Kind
des Vaters Tod verkündet:
durch Morgengrauen
bang und bänger,
als der Sohn
der Mutter Loos vernahm.
Da er mich zeugt' und starb,
sie sterbend mich gebar,
die alte Weise
sehnsuchts bang
zu ihnen wohl
auch klagend drang,
die einst mich frug,
und jetzt mich frägt,
zu welchem Loos erkoren
ich damals wohl geboren?

you're mine for life.
Those whom I hate
you hate too;
those whom I love
you love too.
When good King Mark
I followed of old,
you were to him truer than gold.
When I was false
to my noble friend,
to betray too you did descend.
You are selfless,
solely mine;
you feel for me
when I suffer.
But—what I suffer,
you cannot feel for me!
This terrible yearning in my heart,
this feverish burning's
cruel smart,—
did I but show it,
could you but know it,
no time here would you tarry,
to watch from tower you would
hurry;
with all devotion
viewing the ocean,
with eyes impatiently spying,
there, where her ship's sails are flying.
Before the wind she
drives to find me;
on the wings of love she nears.—
Isolda steers here!—
she nears, she nears,
so boldly and fast!
It waves, it waves.
the flag from the mast!
Hurra! Hurra!
She reaches the bar!
Do you not see?
Kurvenal, do you not see?
(*as Kurvenal hesitates to leave
Tristan, who is gazing at him in
mute expectation, the mournful
tune of the shepherd is heard, as
before.*)

**KURVENAL:** (*dejectedly*). Still is
no ship in sight.

**TRISTAN:** (*has listened with waning excitement and now recommences with growing melancholy*). Is this the meaning then,
your old pathetic ditty,
of all your sighing sound?—
On evening's breeze
it sadly rang
when, as a child,
my father's death-news chilled me:
through morning's mist
it stole more sadly,
when the son
his mother's fate was taught,
when they who gave me breath
both felt the hand of death
to them came also
through their pain
the ancient ditty's
yearning strain,
which asked me once
and asks me now
which was the fate before me
to which my mother bore me?—
What was the fate?—

Zu welchem Loos?—
Die alte Weise
sagt mir's wieder:
mich sehnen—und sterben.
Nein! ach nein!
So heisst sie nicht!
Sehnen! Sehnen!
Im Sterben mich zu sehnen
vor Sehnsucht nicht zu sterben!
Die nie erstirbt,
sehnend nun ruft
um Sterbens Ruh'
sie der fernen Ärztin zu.
Sterbend lag ich stumm im Kahn,
der Wunde Gift dem Herzen nah':
Sehn sucht klagend klang die
Weise;
den Segel blähte der Wind
hin zu Irlands Kind.
Die Wunde, die sie hielend schloss,
riss mit dem Schwert sie wieder los;
das Schwert dann aber liess sie sink-
en;
den Gift trank gab sie mir zu trink-
en:
wie ich da hoffte ganz zu gennsen
da war der sehrendste Zauber erles-
en:
dass nie ich sollte sterben,
mich ew'ger Qual vererben!
Der Trank! der Trank!
der furchtbare Trank!
Wie vom Herz zum Hirn
er wüthend mir drang!
Kein Heil nun kann,
kein süsser Tod je mich befrein'
von der Sehnsucht Noth,
nirgends, ach nirgends find' ich
Ruh':
mich wirft die Nacht dem Tage zu
um ewig an meinen Leiden
der Sonne Auge zu weiden.
O dieser Sonne sengender Strahl,
wie brennt mir das Hirn
seine glühende Qual!
Für dieser Hitze heisses Ver-
schmachten,
ach, keines Schattens kühlend Umnachten!
Für diese Schmerzen schreckliche
Pein,
welcher Balsam sollte mir
Lind'rung verleihn?
Den furchtbaren Trank,
der der Qual mich vertraut,
ich selbst, ich selbst, ich hab' ihn
gebraut!
Aus Vaters Noth und Mutter Weh,
aus Liebes Thränen eh' und je,
aus Lachen und Weinen,
Wonnen und Wunden
hab' ich des Trankes Gifte gefunden!
Den ich gebraut,
der mir geflossen,
den Wonne schlürfend je ich genossen,
verflucht sei, furchtbarer Trank!
Verflucht, wer dich gebraut!
(*Er sinkt ohnmächtig zurück.*)

KURWENAL: (*der vergebens Tristan zu mässigen suchte, schreit
entsezt auf*). Mein Herre! Tristan!—
Schrecklicher Zauber!—

The strain so plaintive
now repeats it:—
for yearning—and dying!
No! Ah no!
It means not that!
Longing! Longing!
To die while I am longing,
yet live for very longing.
What does not die,
lovingly calls,
my death to ease,
my Isolda over the seas.
Dying and adrift I lay,
the poisoned wound was near my
heart:
wistful wailed that strain of sorrow;
the winds our courses beguiled,
far to Ireland's child.
The wound that she had closed and
healed,
she with sword again revealed,
that sword then seh let fall to save
me;
until the poisoned draught she gave
me;
and when there with I hoped to restore me,
I found a fevering magic was over
me,
that death would find me never,
but life in pain forever!
That drink! that drink!
that terrible drink!
How from breast to brain I burned
as I drank!
No care can cure,
no death regain for me my freedom
from wistful pain;
nowhere, ah nowhere is there rest;
for I'm by night to daylight cast,
for yes while my woe does wound
me,
the sunlight shines around me!
O yonder sunlight's withering
beam,
it burns my brain with the glow of
its gleam!
This hateful heat does wither and
burn me
no shadows cool where to I can turn
me!
Of this deep ache, this anguish of
pain,
never balsam's virtue will heal me
again!
The terrible drink,
that my life has inbued with pain,
by me, by me was it brewed!
Of father's grief, of mother's cry,
of lovers' tears from one and one,
from you and from wounds,
laughter and sorrow,
Did I that potion's poison borrow!
Such was by brew,
such to me slipped it,
Such filled with rapture ever I
sipped it;
I curse you, horrible drink!
Cursed he, who brewed and drank!
(*he falls back senseless.*)

KURVENAL: (*who has been vainly striving to calm Tristan cries
out in terror*). My master! Tristan!—
Frightful enchantment!—

O Minne-Trug!—
O Liebes-Zwang!
Der Welt holdester Wahn,
wie ist's um dich gethan!
Hier liegt er nun,
der wonnige Mann,
der wie Keiner geliebt und gem-
innt:
nun seht, was von ihm
sie Dankes gewann,
was je sich Minne gewinnt!
(*Mit schluchzender Stimme.*)
Bist du nun todt?
Lebst du noch?
Hat dich der Fluch entführt?—
(*Er lauscht seinem Athem.*)
O Wonne! Nein!
Er regt sich! Er lebt!—
Wie sanft er die Lippen rührt!

TRISTAN: (*sehr leise beginnend*).
Das Schiff—siehst du's noch nicht?

KURWENAL: Das Schiff? Gewiss,
das naht noch heut';
es kann nicht lang' mehr säumen.

TRISTAN: Und drauf Isolde,
wie sie winkt—
wie sie hold
mir Sühne trinkt?
Siehst du sie?
Siehst du sie noch nicht?
Wie sie selig,
hehr und milde
wandelt durch
des Meer's Gefilde?
Auf wonniger Blumen
sanften Wogen
kommt sie licht
an's Land gezogen:
sie lächelt mir Trost
und süsse Ruh';
sie führt mir letzte
Labung zu.
Isolde! Ach, Isolde!
wie schön bist du!—
Und Kurwenal, wie?
Du säh'st sie nicht?
Hinauf zur Warte,
du blöder Wicht,
was so hell und licht ich sehe,
dass das dir nicht entgehe.
Hörst du mich nicht?
Zur Warte schnell!
Eilig zur Warte!
Bist du zur Stell'?
Das Schiff, das Schiff!
Isolden's Schiff—
du musst es sehen,
musst es sehen!
Das Schiff—säh'st du's noch nicht?
(*Während Kurwenal noch
zögernd mit Tristan ringt, lässt
der Hirt von aussen die Schalmei
ertönen.*)

KURWENAL: (*freudig aufsprin-
gend*). O Wonne! Freude!
(*Er stürzt auf die Warte und späht
aus.*)
Ha! Das Schiff!
Von Norden seh' ich's nah'n.

TRISTAN: Wusst' ich's nicht?
Sagt' ich es nicht?
Dass sie noch lebt,
noch am Leben mir webt.
Die mir Isolde

O love's deceit!
O passion's power!
Most sweet dream beneath the sun,
see the work you have done!—
Here he lies now,
the noblest of knights,
with his passion all others above:
behold! What reward
his ardor requites;
the one sure reward of love!
(*with sobbing voice.*)
Are you then dead?
Do you not live?
Have you succumbed to the curse?
(*he listens for Tristan's breath.*)
O rapture! No!
He still moves! He lives!
and gently his lips are stirred.

TRISTAN: (*very faintly*). The
ship—is it yet in sight?

KURVENAL: The ship? Be sure
it will come today:
it cannot tarry longer.

TRISTAN: On board Isolda,—
see, she smiles—
with the cup
that reconciles.
Do you see?
Do you see her now!
Full of grace
and loving mildness,
floating over
the ocean's wildness?
Lightly lifted,
by billows of flowers
gently toward
the land she's drifted.
Her look brings ease
and sweet repose;
her hand one last
relief bestows.
Isolda! Ah, Isolda!
How sweet you are!—
And Kurwenal, why!—
what ails your sight?—
Away, and watch for her,
foolish wight.
What I see so well and plainly,
let not your eye seek vainly,
Do you not hear?
Away, with speed!
Haste to the watchtower!
Will you not heed?
The ship, the ship!
Isolda's ship!—
You must discern it,
must perceive it!
The ship—do you see it?—
(*while Kurwenal, still hesitating,
opposes Tristan, the Shepherd's
pipe is heard without, playing a
joyous strain.*)

KURVENAL: (*springing joyously
up*). O rapture! Transport!
(*he rushes to the watchtower and
looks out.*)
Ha! the ship!
From northward it is nearing.

TRISTAN: So I knew,
so I said!
Yes, she yet lives,
and gives life to me.
How could Isolda

einzig enthält,
wie wär' Isolde
mir aus der Welt?

KURWENAL: (*jauchzend*). Hahei!
Hahei!
Wie es muthig steuert!
Wie stark das Segel sich bläht!
Wie es jagt! Wie es fliegt!

TRISTAN: Die Flagge? Die Flagge?

KURWENAL: Der Freude Flagge
am Wimpel lustig und hell.

TRISTAN: Heiaha! Der Freude!
Hell am Tage
zu mir Isolde.
Isolde zu mir!—
Siehst du sie selbst?

KURWENAL: Jetzt schwand das Schiff
hinter dem Fels.

TRISTAN: Hinter dem Riff?
Bringt es Gefahr?
Dort wüthet die Brandung,
scheitern die Schiffe.—
Das Steuer, wer führt's?

KURWENAL: Der sicherste Seemann.

TRISTAN: Verrieth er mich?
Wär' er Melot's Genoss?

KURWENAL: Trau' ihm wie mir!

TRISTAN: Verräther, auch du!
Un-seliger!
Siehst du sie wieder?

KURWENAL: Noch nicht.

TRISTAN: Verloren!

KURWENAL: Haha! Heiahaha!
Vorbei! Vorbei!
Glücklich vorbei!
In sich'ren Strom
steuert zum Hafen das Schiff.

TRISTAN: (*jauchzend*). Heiaha!
Kurwenal!
Treuster Freund!
All' mein Hab' und Gut
vererb' ich noch heut'.

KURWENAL: Sie nahen im Flug.

TRISTAN: Siehst du sie endlich?
Siehst du Isolde?

KURWENAL: Sie ist's! Sie winkt.

TRISTAN: O seligstes Weib!

KURWENAL: Im Hafen der Kiel!—
Isolde—ha!
mit einem Sprung
springt sie vom Bord zum Strand.

TRISTAN: Herab von der Warte!
Müssiger Gaffer!
Hinab! Hinab
an den Strand!
Hilf ihr! Hilf meiner Frau!

KURWENAL: Sie trag' ich herauf:
trau' meinen Armen!
Doch du, Tristan,
bleib' mir treulich am Bett! (*Er eilt
fort.*)

from this world be free,
which only holds
Isolda for me?

KURVENAL: (*shouting*). Ahoy!
Ahoy!
See her bravely tacking!
How full the canvas is filled!
How she darts! how she flies!

TRISTAN: The pennon? the pennon?

KURVENAL: A flag is floating at
mast-head,
joyous and bright.

TRISTAN: Aha! what joy!
Now through the daylight
comes my Isolda.
Isolda, oh come!
Can you see her herself?

KURVENAL: The ship is shut
from me by rocks.

TRISTAN: Behind the reef?
Is there not risk!
Those dangerous breakers
have often shattered ships.—
Who steers the helm?

KURVENAL: The steadiest seaman.

TRISTAN: Does he betray me?
Is he Melot's ally?

KURVENAL: Trust him like me.

TRISTAN: A traitor you, too!—
O caitiff!
Can you not see her?

KURVENAL: Not yet.

TRISTAN: Destruction!

KURVENAL: Aha! Halla-halloo!
they clear! they clear!
Safely they clear!
Inside the surf
steers now the ship to the strand.

TRISTAN: (*shouting in joy.*) Hallo-ho! Kurvenal!
Trustiest friend!
All the wealth I own
today I bequeath you.

KURVENAL: With speed they approach.

TRISTAN: Now do you see her?
Do you see Isolda?

KURVENAL: It is she! she waves!

TRISTAN: O divine woman!

KURVENAL: The ship is at land!
Isolda!—ha!—
With but one leap
lightly she springs to land!

TRISTAN: Descend from the watchtower,
indolent gazer!
Away! away
to the shore!
Help her! help my beloved!

KURVENAL: In a moment she shall come;
Trust in my strong arm!
But you, Tristan,
hold yourself tranquilly here!
(*he hastens off.*)

TRISTAN: (*in höchster Aufregung auf dem Lager sich mühend*). O, diese Sonne!
Ha, dieser Tag!
Ha, dieser Wonne
sonnigster Tag!
Jagendes Blut,
jauchzender Muth!
Lust ohne Maassen,
freudiges Rasen:
auf des Lagers Bann
wie sie ertragen?
Wohlauf und daran,
wo die Herzen schlagen!
Tristan, der Held,
in jubelnder Kraft
hat sich vom Tod
emporgerafft!
(*Er richtet sich hoch auf.*)
Mit blutender Wunde
bekämpft' ich einst Morolden:
mit blutender Wunde
erjag' ich mir heut' Isolden.
(*Er reisst den Verband der Wunde
auf.*)
Hahei! Mein Blut,
lustig nun fliesse!
(*Er springt vom Lager herab und
schwankt vorwärts.*)
Die mir die Wunde
auf ewig schliesse,
sie naht wie ein Held,
sie naht mir zum Heil:
vergehe die Welt
meiner jauchzenden Eil'!
(*Er taumelt nach der Mitte der
Bühne.*)

ISOLDE: (*von aussen*). Tristan!
Tristan! Geliebter!

TRISTAN: (*in der furchtbarsten
Aufregung*). Wie hör' ich das Licht!
Die Leuchte—ha!
Die Leuchte verlischt!
Zu ihr! Zu ihr!

## ZWEITE SCENE

(*Isolde eilt athemlos herein, Tristan, seiner nicht mächtig, stürzt sich ihr schwankend entgegen. In der Mitte der Bühne begegnen sie sich; sie empfängt ihn in ihren Armen.*)

ISOLDE: Tristan! ha!

TRISTAN: (*sterbend zu Isolden
aufblickend*). Isolde!—
(*Er stirbt.*)

ISOLDE: Ich bin's, ich bin's—
süssester Freund!
Auf! noch einmal!
Hör' meinen Ruf!
Achtest du nicht?
Isolde ruft:
Isolde kam,
mit Tristan treu zu sterben.—
Bleibst du mir stumm!
Nur eine Stunde,—
nur eine Stunde
bleibe mir wach!
So bange Tage
wachte sie sehend,

TRISTAN: (*tossing on his couch in feverish excitement*). O sunlight glowing,
glorious ray!
Ah, joy-bestowing
radiant day!
Bounds my blood,
boisterous flood!
Infinite gladness!
Rapturous madness!
Can I bear to lie
couched here in quiet?
Away, let me fly
to where hearts run riot!
Tristan the brave,
exulting in strength,
has torn himself
from death at length.
(*he raises himself erect.*)
All wounded and bleeding
Sir Morold I defeated;
all bleeding and wounded
Isolda now shall be greeted.
(*he tears the bandage from his
wound.*)
Ha, ha, my blood!
Merrily flows it.
(*he springs from his bed and staggers forward.*)
She who can help
my wound and close it,
she comes in her pride,
she comes to my aid.
Be space defied
let the universe fade!
(*he reels to the center of the
stage.*)

ISOLDE: (*without*). Tristan! Tristan! Belovéd!

TRISTAN: (*in frantic excitement*).
What! hails me the light?
The torchlight—ha!—
The torch is extinct!
I come! I come!

## SCENE II

(*Isolda hastens breathlessly in. Tristan, delirious with excitement, staggers wildly towards her. They meet center of the stage; she receives him in her arms where he sinks slowly to the ground.*)

ISOLDA: Tristan! Ah!

TRISTAN: (*turning his dying eyes on Isolda*). Isolda!—
(*he dies.*)

ISOLDA: It is I, It is I—
dearly beloved!
Wake, and once more
hark to my voice!
Isolda calls.
Isolda comes,
with Tristan true to perish.—
Speak onto me!
But for one moment,
only one moment
open your eyes!
Such weary days
I waited and longed,
that one single hour

um eine Stunde
mit dir noch zu wachen.
Betrügt Isolden,
betrügt sie Tristan
um dieses einz'ge
ewig-kurze
letzte Welten-Glück?—
Die Wunde—wo?
Lass sie mich heilen,
dass wonnig und hehr
die Nacht wir theilen.
Nicht an der Wunde,
an der Wunde stirb mir nicht!
Uns beiden vereint
erlösche das Lebenslicht!—
Gebrochen der Blick!
Still das Herz?
Treuloser Tristan,
mir diesen Schmerz?
Nicht eines Athems
flücht'ges Weh'n?
Muss sie nun jammernd
vor dir steh'n,
die sich wonnig dir zu vermählen
muthig kam über Meer?
Zu spät! Zu spät!
Trotziger Mann!
Straf'st du mich so
mit hartestem Bann?
Ganz ohne Huld
meiner Leidens-Schuld?
Nicht meine Klagen
darf ich dir sagen?
Nur einmal, ach!
Nur einmal noch!—
Tristan—ha!
horch'—er wacht!
Geliebter—
Nacht!
(*Sie sinkt bewusstlos über der Leiche zusammen.*)

I might awaken you.
Am I betrayed then?
Deprived by Tristan
of this our solitary,
swiftly fleeting,
final earthly joy?—
His wound, though—where?
Can I not heal it?
The rapture of night
O let us feel it!
Not of your wounds,
not of your wounds must you expire!
Together, at least,
let fade life's enfeebled fire!—
How lifeless his look!—
still his heart!—
Dared he to deal me
such a smart?
Stayed is his breathing's
gentle tide!
Must I be wailing
at his side,
who, in rapture coming to seek him,
fearless sailed over the sea?
Too late, too late!
Desperate man!
Casting on me
this cruelest ban?
Comes no relief
for my load of grief?
Silent he keeps
while I am weeping?
But once more, ah!
But once again!—
Tristan—ha!
he wakens—hark!
Beloved—
Dark!
(*she sinks down senseless upon his body.*)

## DRITTE SCENE

(*Kurwenal war sogleich hinter Isolde zurückgekommen; sprachlos in furchtbarer Erschütterung hat er dem Auftritte beigewohnt und bewegungslos auf Tristan hingestarrt. Aus der Tiefe hört man jetzt dumpfes Getümmel und Waffengeklirr. Der Hirt kommt über die Mauer gestiegen.*)

HIRT: (*hastig und leise sich zu Kurwenal wendend*). Kurwenal!
Hör'!
Ein zweites Schiff.
(*Kurwenal fährt heftig auf, und blickt über die Brüstung, während der Hirt aus der Ferne erschüttert auf Tristan und Isolde sieht.*)

KURWENAL: Tod und Hölle!
(*In Wuth ausbrechend.*)
Alles zur Hand!
Marke und Melot
hab' ich erkannt.—
Waffen und Steine!
Hilf mir! An's Thor!
(*Er springt mit dem Hirt an das Thor, das Beide in der Hast zu verrammeln suchen.*)

## SCENE III

(*Kurvenal, who reentered close behind Isolda, has remained by the entrance speechless and petrified, gazing motionless on Tristan. From below is now heard the dull murmur of voices and the clash of weapons. The Shepherd clambers over the wall.*)

SHEPHERD: (*coming hastily and softly to Kurvenal*). Kurvenal!
Hear!
Another ship!
(*Kurvenal starts up in haste and looks over the rampart while the Shepherd stands apart, gazing in consternation on Tristan and Isolda.*)

KURVENAL: Fiends and furies!
(*in a burst of anger.*)
All are at hand!
Melot and Mark
I see on the strand,—
Weapons and missiles!—
We must guard the gate!
(*he hastens with the Shepherd to the gate, which they both try quickly to barricade.*)

DER STEUERMANN: (*stürzt herein*). Marke mir nach
mit Mann und Volk!
Vergeb'ne Wehr!
Bewältigt sind wir.

KURWENAL: Stell' dich, und hilf'!—
So lang' ich lebe,
lugt mir Keiner herein!

BRANGAENE'S STIMME: (*aussen, von unten her*). Isolde, Herrin!

KURWENAL: Brangäne's Ruf?
(*Hinabrufend.*)
Was such'st du hier?

BRANGAENE: Schliess' nicht, Kurwenal!
Wo ist Isolde?

KURWENAL: Verräth'rin auch du?
Weh' dir, Verruchte!

MELOTS STIMME: (*von aussen*).
Zurück, du Thor!
Stemm' dich dort nicht!

KURWENAL: (*wüthend auflachend*). Heiaha dem Tag,
da ich dich treffe!
(*Melot, mit gewaffneten Männern, erscheint unter dem Thor. Kurwenal stürzt sich auf ihn und streckt ihn zu Boden.*)
Stirb, schändlicher Wicht!

## VIERTE SCENE

MELOT: Wehe mir!—Tristan!
(*Er Stirbt.*)

BRANGAENE: (*noch ausserbalb*). Kurwenal! Wüthender?
Hör', du betrügst dich.

KURWENAL: Treulose Magd!—
(*Zu den Seinen.*)
Drauf! Mir nach!
Werft sie zurück!
(*Sie kämpfen.*)

MARKE: (*ausserhalb*). Halte, Rasender!
Bist du von Sinnen?

KURWENAL: Hier wüthet der Tod.
Nichts and'res, König,
ist hier zu holen:
willst du ihn kiesen, so komm!
(*Er dringt auf Marke und dessen Gefolge ein.*)

MARKE: Zurück, Wahnsinniger!

BRANGAENE: (*hat sich seitwärts über die Mauer geschwungen, und eilt in den Vordergrund*).
Isolde! Herrin!
Glück und Heil!—
Was seh' ich, ha!
Lebst du? Isolde! (*Sie müht sich um Isolde.*)

MARKE: (*mit seinem Gefolge hat Kurwenal mit dessen Helfern vom Thore zurückgetrieben und dringt herein*). O Trug und Wahn!
Tristan, wo bist du?

THE STEERSMAN: (*rushing in*).
Mark and his men
have set on us:
defense is in vain!
We're overpowered.

KURVENAL: Stand to and help!—
While lasts my life
I'll let no foe enter here!

BRANGAENA'S VOICE: (*without, calling from below*). Isolda! Mistress!

KURVENAL: Brangaena's voice!
(*falling down.*)
What want you here?

BRANGAENA: Open, Kurvenal!
Where is Isolda?

KURVENAL: Do you come with foes?
Woe to you, false one!

MELOT'S VOICE: (*without*).
Stand back, fool!
Do not bar the way!

KURVENAL: (*laughing savagely*). Hurrah for the day
on which I confront you!
(*Melot, with armed men, appears under the gateway. Kurvenal falls on him and cuts him down.*)
Die, damnable wretch!

## SCENE IV

MELOT: Woe's me!—Tristan!
(*he dies.*)

BRANGAENA: (*still without*).
Kurvenal! Madman!
O hear—you are making a mistake!

KURVENAL: Treacherous maid!
(*to his men.*)
Come! Follow me!
Force them below!
(*they fight.*)

MARK: (*without*). Hold, you frantic man!
Are your senses lost?

KURVENAL: Here ravages Death!
Nothing else, O king,
is here to behold!
If you would earn it, come on!
(*he sets upon Mark and his followers.*)

MARK: Away, rash maniac!

BRANGAENA: (*has climbed over the wall at the side and rushes to the front*). Isolda! lady!
Joy and life!—
What sight's here—ha!
You live, Isolda!
(*she goes to Isolda's aid.*)

MARK: (*who with his followers has driven Kurvenal and his men back from the gate and forced his way in*). O wild mistake!
Tristan, where are you?

## Act III, Scene IV

**KURWENAL:** (*schwer verwundet, schwankt vor Marke her nach dem Vordergrund*). Da liegt er—da—
hier, wo ich liege—!
(*Er sinkt zu Tristan's Füssen zusammen.*)

**MARKE:** Tristan! Tristan!
Isolde! Weh'!

**KURWENAL:** (*nach Tristan's Hand fassend*). Tristan! Trauter!
Schilt mich nicht,
dass der Treue auch mit kommt!
(*Er stirbt.*)

**MARKE:** Todt denn Alles!
Alles todt?
Mein Held! Mein Tristan!
Trautester Freund?
Auch heute noch
musst du den Freund verrathen?
Heut', wo er kommt
dir höchst Treu' zu bewähren!
Erwach'! Erwach'!
Erwache meinem Jammer,
du treulos treuester Freund!
(*Schluchzend über die Leichen sich herabbeugend.*)

**BRANGAENE:** (*die in ihren Armen Isolde wieder zu sich gebracht*). Sie wacht! Sie lebt!
Isolde, hör'!
Hör' mich, süsseste Frau!
Glückliche Kunde
lass' mich dir melden:
vertrautest nicht Brangänen?
Ihre blinde Schuld
hat sie gesühnt;
als du verschwunden,
schnell fand sie den König:
des Trankes Geheimniss
erfuhr er kaum,
als mit sorgender Eil'
in See er stach,
dich zu erreichen,
dir zu entsagen,
dich zuzuführen dem Freund.

**MARKE:** Warum, Isolde,
warum, mir das?
Da hell mir ward enthüllt,
was zuvor ich nicht fassen konnt',
wie selig, das ich den Freund
frei von Schuld da fand!
Dem holden Mann
dich zu vermählen,
mit vollen Segeln
flog ich dir nach:
doch Unglückes
Ungestüm,
wie erreicht es, wer Frieden bringt?
Die Aernte mehrt' ich dem Tod:
der Wahn häufte die Noth!

**BRANGAENE:** Hörst du uns nicht?
Isolde! Traute!
Vernimmst du die Treue nicht?

**KURVENAL:** (*desperately wounded, totters before Mark to the front.*) He lies—there—
here, where I lie too.—
(*sinks down at Tristan's feet.*)

**MARK:** Tristan! Tristan!
Isolda! Woe!

**KURVENAL:** (*trying to grasp Tristan's hand*). Tristan! true lord!
Chide me not
that I try to follow you! (*he dies.*)

**MARK:** Dead together!—
All are dead!
My hero Tristan!
truest of friends,
must you again
be a traitor to your king?
Now, when he comes,
another proof of love to give you!
Awaken! awaken!
O hear my lamentation,
You faithless, faithful friend!
(*kneels down sobbing over the bodies.*)

**BRANGAENA:** (*who has revived Isolda in her arms*). She wakes! she lives!
Isolda, hear!
Hear me, mistress beloved!
Tidings of joy
I have to tell you;
O listen to Brangaena!
My thoughtless fault I have atoned;
after your flight
I went to the king:
the love potion's secret
he scarcely had learned
when with sedulous haste
he put to sea,
that he might find you,
nobly renounce you,
and give you to your love.

**MARK:** O why, Isolda,
Why this to me?
When clearly was disclosed
what before I could not fathom,
what joy was mine to find
my friend was free from fault!
In haste to wed
you to my hero
with flying sails
I followed your track:
but however can
happiness
overtake the swift course of woe?
More food did I make for Death:
more wrong grew in mistake.

**BRANGAENA:** Do you not hear?
Isolda! Lady!
O try to believe the truth!

**ISOLDE:** (*die nichts um sich her vernommen, heftet das Auge mit wachsender Begeisterung auf Tristan's Leiche*). Mild und leise
wie er lächelt,
wie das Auge
hold er öffnet:
seht ihr, Freunde,
seh't ihr's nicht?
Immer lichter
wie er leuchtet,
wie er minnig
immer mächt'ger,
Stern-umstrahlet
hoch sich hebt:
seht ihr Freunde,
seh't ihr's nicht?
Wie das Herz ihm
muthig schwillt,
voll und hehr
im Busen quillt:
wie den Lippen
wonnig mild,
süsser Athem
sanft entweht:—
Freunde, seht—
fühlt und seht ihr's nicht!—
Höre ich nur
diese Weise,
die so wunder-
voll und leise,
Wonne klagend,
Alles sagend,
mild versöhnend
aus ihm tönend,
in mich dringet,
auf sich schwingt,
hold erhallend
um mich klinget?
Heller schallend,
mich umwallend,
sind es Wellen
sanfter Lüfte?
Sind es Wogen
wonniger Düfte?
Wie sie schwellen,
mich umrauschen,
soll ich athmen,
soll ich lauschen?
soll ich schlürfen,
untertauchen,
süss in Düften
mich verhauchen?
In dem wogenden Schwall,
in dem tönenden Schall,
in des Welt-Athems
wehendem All—
ertrinken—
versinken—
unbewusst—
höchste Lust!
(*Isolde sinkt wie verklärt in Brangaene's Armen sanft auf Tristan's Leiche. — Grosse Rührung und Entrücktheit unter den Umstehenden. Marke segnet die Leichen. —Der Vorhang fällt langsam.*)

*ENDE*

**ISOLDA:** (*unconscious of all around her, turning her eyes with rising inspiration on Tristan's body*). Mild and softly
he is smiling;
how his eyelids sweetly open!
See, oh comrades,
Do you not see
how he beams
ever brighter—
how he rises
ever radiant
steeped in starlight,
borne above?
Do you not see
how his heart
with lion zest,
calmly happy
beats in his breast?
From his lips
in heavenly rest
sweetest breath
he softly sends.
Listen, friends!
Do you hear and feel not?
Am I
alone hearing
strains so tender
and endearing?
Passion swelling,
all things telling,
gently bounding,
from him sounding,
in me pushes,
upward rushes
trumpet tone
that around me gushes.
Brighter growing,
over me flowing,
are these breezes
airy pillows?
Are they balmy
beauteous billows?
How they rise
and gleam and glisten!
Shall I breathe them?
Shall I listen?
Shall I sip them,
dive within them,
to my panting
breathing win them?
In the breezes around,
in the harmony sound,
in the world's driving
whirlwind be drowned—
and, sinking,
be drinking—
in a kiss,
highest bliss!
(*Isolda sinks, as if transfigured, in Brangaena's arms upon Tristan's body. Profound emotion and grief of the bystanders. Mark invokes a blessing on the dead. Curtain.*)

*THE END*

# Die Meistersinger Von Nürnberg (1868)

## The Master Singers of Nuremberg

MUSIC AND LIBRETTO BY RICHARD WAGNER

This three-act opera, set to a libretto by the composer, was first performed at the Hoftheater in Munich on June 21, 1868. Walther von Stolzing, a young knight, sights Eva, daughter of the jeweler Pogner, at the church of St. Katherine in Nuremberg on the eve of the feast of St. John. He asks if she is betrothed. She is not, but her father intends that she marry the winner of the Meistersingers' competition. Eva can refuse the winner, but she must marry a meistersinger. Eva falls in love with Walther, who is not a Meistersinger, and Walther begs the Meistersingers to allow him to join the guild. They ask him if he knows the rules. Although David, beau to Eva's friend Magdalene, has tried to teach him, Walther tells them he has learned everything from the birds, waterfalls, breezes and Walther von de Vogelweide's poetry. Beckmesser, also in love with Eva, is designated to record all of the competitors' mistakes. Walther sings a passionate song about spring, but his song doesn't follow the rules and is rejected. Hans Sachs, the shoemaker/poet, is sitting outside his workshop, contemplating Walther's beautiful singing. Eva asks him to find out what went wrong with Walther's mastersong, but she doesn't understand his explanation. Sachs overhears Walther and Eva discussing their plans to elope. Beckmesser comes to serenade Eva. The lovers hide themselves behind a tree. Beckmesser botches his serenade, with Sach's help, waking the neighbors and getting into a brawl. The lovers try to escape again, but Sachs stops them. Walther tells Sachs of his dream; Sachs writes down the words, and together they create a gorgeous mastersong. Beckmesser finds the mastersong, written in Sachs' hand, and, thinking it's a poem written by Sachs to win Eva's hand, he steals it. At the tournament, Beckmesser sings first, to the jeering of the crowd. Sachs explains the song's origins and asks Walther to sing. Walther is offered the Meistersingers' crown and Eva's hand in marriage; although his inclination is to refuse the prize in remembrance of his earlier rejection, Sachs tells him he must respect art's traditions. Walther is admitted to the guild; Eva gives Walther's crown to Sachs, who is proclaimed chief of the Meistersingers.

## ■ ACT I

*(Die Bühne stellt das Innere der Katharinenkirche in schrägem Durschnitt dar; von dem Hauptschiff sind nur noch die letzten Reihen der Kirchenstuhlbänke sichtbar; den Vordergrund nimmt der freie Raum vor dem Chor ein; dieser wird später durch einen; Vorbang gegen das Schiff zu gänzlich abgeschlossen.*

*Beim Aufzug hört man, unter Orgelbegleitung, von der Germeinde den letzten Vers eines Chorales, mit welchem der Nachmittagsgottesdienst zur Einleitung des Johannisfestes schliesst, singen.)*

**CHORAL DER GEMEINDE:** Dazu dir der Heiland kam,
willig deine Taufe nahm,
weihte sich dem Opfertod,
gab er uns des Heils Gebot:
dass wir durch dein' Tauf' uns weih'n,
seines Opfers werth zu sein.
Edler Täufer,
Christ's Vorläufer!
Nimm uns freundlich an,

## ■ ACT I

*(The scene represents the interior of St. Catherine's church, in oblique section; only the last few rows of pews in the nave are visible: the foreground is the open space before the choir; this is afterwards shut off by a black curtain from the nave.*

*As the curtain rises, the people are singing, to organ accompaniment, the last verse of a Chorale, which concludes afternoon service on the vigil of the Feast of St. John.)*

**HYMN OF THE CONGREGATION:** When to thee our Saviour went
To receive thy Sacrament,
Ere His sacrifice divine,
We were giv'n salvation's sign,
That through Baptism we might prove
Worthy of His death and love.
Interceder,
Christ's preceder!

dort am Fluss Jordan.
*(Während des Chorales und dessen Zwischenspielen entwickelt sich, vom Orchester begleitet, folgende pantomimische Scene.*

*In der letzten Reihe der Kirchstüble sitzen Eva und Magdalene; Walther V. Stolzing steht, in einiger Entfernung; zur Seite an eine Säule gelehnt, die Blicke auf Eva heftend. Eva kehrt sich wiederholt seitwärts nach dem Ritter um, und erwiedert seine bald dringend bald zärtlich durch Gebärden sich ausdrückenden Bitten und Betbereuerungen schüchtern und verschämt, doch seelendvoll und ermuthigend. Magdalene unterbricht sich öfters im Gesang, um Eva zu zupfen und zur Vorsicht zu mahnen—Als der Coral zu Ende ist, und, während eines längeren Orgelnachspieles die Gemeinde dem Hauptausgange sich zuwendet, um allmählich die Kirche zu verlassen, tritt Walther an die beiden*

Take us gently o'er
Unto Jordan's shore.
*(During the Chorale and its interludes the following dumb-show takes place, accompanied by the orchestra:—*

*In the last pew are seated Eva and Magdalena: Walter V. Stolzing is leaning against the pillar at a little distance, his eyes fixed on Eva. Eva turns repeatedly towards the knight and answers his now importunate, now tender glances of entreaty and passion, shyly and modestly, but tenderly and encouragingly. Magdalena often breaks off her singing to give Eva a reproving nudge. When the hymn is ended and while, during a long postlude on the organ, the congregation is gradually leaving by the principal door, Walter advances hastily towards Eva and her companion, who have also risen from their seats and turned to go.)*

**WALTHER:** (*leise, doch feurig zu Eva*). Verweilt!—Ein Wort! Ein einzig Wort!

**EVA:** (*sich rasch zu Magdelane wendend*). Mein Brusttuch! Schau! Wohl liegt's im Ort?

**MAGDALENE:** Vergesslich Kind! Nun heisse es: such'! (*Sie kehrt nach den Sitzen zurück.*)

**WALTHER:** Fräulein! Verzeiht der Sitte Bruch! Eines zu wissen, Eines zu fragen, was nicht müsst' ich zu brechen wagen? Ob Leben oder Tod? Ob Segen oder Fluch? Mit einem Worte sei mir's vertraut:— mein Fräulein, sagt—

**MAGDALENE:** (*zurückkommend*). Hier ist das Tuch.

**EVA:** O weh! die Spange!

**MAGDALENE:** Fiel sie wohl ab? (*Sie geht, am Boden suchend, wieder zurück.*)

**WALTHER:** Ob Licht und Lust, oder Nacht und Grab? Ob ich erfahr', wonach ich verlange, ob ich vernehme, wovor mir graut.— Mein Fräulein, sagt . . .

**MAGDALENE:** (*wieder zurückkommend*). Da ist auch die Spange.— Komm', Kind! Nun hast du Spang' und Tuch. O weh! da vergass ich selbst mein Buch! (*Sie kehrt wieder um.*)

**WALTHER:** Dies eine Wort, ihr sagt mir's nicht? Die Sylbe, die mein Urtheil spricht? Ja, oder: Nein!—ein flücht'ger Laut: mein Fräulein, sagt, seid ihr schon Braut?

**MAGDALENE:** (*die bereits zurückgekommen, verneigt sich vor Walther*). Sieh da, Herr Ritter? Wie sind wir hochgeehrt: mit Evchen's Schutze habt ihr euch gar beschwert? Darf den Besuch des Helden ich Meister Pogner melden?

**WALTHER:** (*leidenschaftlich*). Betrat ich doch nie sein Haus!

**MAGDALENE:** Ei! Junker! Was sagt ihr da aus! In Nürnberg eben nur angekommen, war't ihr nicht freundlich aufgenommen?

---

**WALTER:** (*softly but ardently to Eva*). Oh, stay!—One word, I beg you!

**EVA:** (*quickly turning to Magdalena*). My kerchief! It is on the seat.

**MAGDALENA:** Forgetful child! Now, here's a hunt! (*goes back to the pew.*)

**WALTER:** Maiden, forgive if I affront— One thing to ask you, one to discover, What rules would I not dare pass over! Is life for me or death?—Is bliss for me or bane? Let your answer be clothed in one word: Fair maiden, say—

**MAGDALENA:** (*returning*). Here it is again!

**EVA:** Alack! my scarf pin! . . .

**MAGDALENA:** Did it fall out? (*She goes back, searching on the ground.*)

**WALTER:** Is it light and laughter, or gloom and doubt? Can I attain the aim I approach to, Or must I hear the syllable loathed— Fair maiden say—

**MAGDALENA:** (*returning again*). I have found the brooch too! Come, child, here's pin and kerchief, look! Good lack! if I've not forgot my book! (*goes back once more.*)

**WALTER:** This single word, you do not speak it— This syllable that casts my lot? Say Yes or No—it is quickly mouthed— Fair maiden, say, are you betrothed?

**MAGDALENA:** (*who has returned again, curtsies to Walter*). Sir Knight, your servant! This is a compliment! Our Eva's escort Do you then represent? Pray, Master Pogner is it Your worship seeks to visit?

**WALTER:** (*sorrowfully*). Would I never his house had seen!

**MAGDALENA:** Hey day sir! why, what do you mean? When to Nuremberg first you wended Was not his friendly hand extended?

---

Was Küch' und Keller, Schrein und Schrank euch bot, verdient' es keinen Dank?

**EVA:** Gut Lenchen! Ach! das meint er ja nicht. Doch wohl von mir wünscht er Bericht— wie sag' ich's schnell?—Versteh' ich's doch kaum!— Mir ist, als wär' ich gar wie im Traum!— Er frägt,—ob ich schon Braut?

**MAGDALENE:** (*sich scheu umsehend*). Hilf Gott! Sprich nicht so laut! Jetzt lass' uns nach Hause gehn; wenn uns die Leut' hier sehn!

**WALTHER:** Nicht eher, bis ich Alles weiss!

**EVA:** 's ist leer, die Leut' sind fort.

**MAGDALENE:** Drum eben wird mir heiss!— Herr Ritter, an andrem Ort! (*David tritt aus der Sacristei ein und macht sich darüber her, dunkle Vorhänge, welche so angebracht sind, dass sie den Vordergrund der Bühne nach dem Kirchenschiff zu schräg abschliessen, aneinander zu ziehen.*)

**WALTHER:** Nein! Erst dies Wort!

**EVA:** (*Magdalene haltend*). Dies Wort?

**MAGDALENE:** (*die sich bereits umgewendet, erblickt David, hält an und ruft zärtlich für sich*). David? Ei! David hier?

**EVA:** (*drängend*). Was sag' ich? Sag' du's mir!

**MAGDALENE:** (*mit Zerstreutheit, öfters nach David sich umsehend*). Herr Ritter, was ihr die Jungfer fragt, das ist so leichtlich nicht gesagt: fürwahr ist Evchen Pogner Braut—

**EVA:** (*schnell unterbrechend*). Doch hat noch Keiner den Bräut'gam erschaut.

**MAGDALENE:** Den Bräut'gam wohl noch Niemand kennt, bis morgen ihn das Gericht ernennt, das dem Meistersinger ertheilt den Preis—

**EVA:** (*wie zuvor*). Und selbst die Braut ihm reicht das Reis.

**WALTHER:** Dem Meistersinger?

**EVA:** (*bang*). Seid ihr das nicht?

**WALTHER:** Ein Werbgesang?

**MAGDALENE:** Vor Wettgericht.

**WALTHER:** Den Preis gewinnt?

**MAGDALENE:** Wen die Meister meinen.

**WALTHER:** Die Braut dann wählt?

---

The bed and board, the dishes, drinks He gave deserve some thanks, I think?

**EVA:** Good Lena! Pray! He did not mean it so: He is only eager to know— How shall I say?—I scarce comprehend— His words nearly suspend my senses He asks—about my choice!

**MAGDALENA:** (*looking about apprehensively*). Oh please! subdue your voice! Come directly home with me: Just suppose the folks should see!

**WALTER:** Not yet, till I know my fate!

**EVA:** They're gone, there's no one near.

**MAGDALENA:** That's why I'm in a state! Sir knight, pray try elsewhere! (*David enters from the sacristy and busies himself with drawing together dark curtains which are so disposed as to close off the foreground of the stage from the nave.*)

**WALTER:** No, your reply!

**EVA:** (*holding Magdalena*). Reply?

**MAGDALENA:** (*who has turned away, perceives David, pauses and calls tenderly aside*). David! Why, can it be?

**EVA:** (*urgently*). What answer? Speak for me!

**MAGDALENA:** (*distracted in her attention, looking around repeatedly at David*). Chevalier, what you ask of this maid To answer is no easy task: She is betrothed, you might expect—

**EVA:** (*quickly interrupting*). But none has seen the bridegroom elect.

**MAGDALENA:** The groom will not be known Until tomorrow by trial shown, When a Master Singer receives the prize—

**EVA:** (*as before*). And my own hand his bay wreath ties.

**WALTER:** A Master Singer?

**EVA:** (*timidly*). Are you not one?

**WALTER:** A trial-song?

**MAGDALENA:** Done before judges.

**WALTER:** Who wins the prize?

**MAGDALENA:** It is for them to choose one.

**WALTER:** The bride will choose—?

**EVA:** (*sich vergessend*). Euch, oder Keinen!
(*Walther wendet sich, in grosser Aufregung aufund abgehend, zur Seite.*)

**MAGDALENE:** (*sebr erschrocken*). Was! Evchen! Evchen! Bist du von Sinnen?

**EVA:** Gut' Lene! hilf mir den Ritter gewinnen!

**MAGDALENE:** Sah'st ihn doch gestern zum ersten Mal?

**EVA:** Das eben schuf mir so schnelle Qual,
das ich schon längst ihn im Bilde sah:—
sag', trat er nicht ganz wie David nah'?

**MAGDALENE:** Bist du toll? Wie David?

**EVA:** Wie David im Bild.

**MAGDALENE:** Ach! meinst du den König mit der Harfen
und langem Bart in der Meister Schild?

**EVA:** Nein! der, dess' Kiesel den Goliath warfen,
das Schwert im Gurt, die Schleuder zur Hand,
von lichten Locken das Haupt umstrahlt,
wie ihn uns Meister Dürer gemalt.

**MAGDALENE:** (*laut sufzend*). Ach, David! David!

**DAVID:** (*der binausgegangen und jetzt wieder zurückkommt, ein Lineal im Gürtel und ein grosses Stück weisser Kreide an einer Schnur in der Hand schwenkend.*) Da bin ich! Werr ruft?

**MAGDALENE:** Ach, David! Was ihr für Unglück schuft!
(*Für sich.*)
Der liebe Schelm! wüsst' er's noch nicht?
(*Laut.*)
Ei, seht! da hat er uns gar verschlossen?

**DAVID:** (*zärlich au Magdalene*). In's Herz euch allein!

**MAGDALENE:** (*bei Seite*). Das treue Gesicht!—
(*Laut.*)
Mein sagt! Was treibt ihr für Possen?

**DAVID:** Behüt es; Possen? Gar ernste Ding'!
Für die Meister heir richt' ich den Ring.

**MAGDALENE:** Wie? Gäb' es ein Singen?

**DAVID:** Nur Freiung heut':
der Lehrling wird da losgesprochen;
der nichts wider die Tabulatur verbrochen;
Meister wird, wen die Prob' nicht reu't.

---

**EVA:** (*forgetting berself*). You, or else no one.
(*Walter turns aside in great perturbation, pacing up and down.*)

**MAGDALENA:** (*greatly shocked*). Why, Eva! Eva! Are you insane?

**EVA:** Good Lena! Help me to gain my lover!

**MAGDALENA:** Yesterday first did you see his face.

**EVA:** Kindled my love at so swift a pace,
Having his portrait so often in sight.
Say, is he not quite like David?

**MAGDALENA:** Are you mad? Like David?

**EVA:** The picture, I mean.

**MAGDALENA:** Oh! he with the harp and long flowing beard,
As on the Master's seen escutcheon?

**EVA:** Nay! he Goliath with pebble overthrowing,
With sword at side and sling in hand,
Light locks around his head like rays,
As Master Albrecht Dürer portrays.

**MAGDALENA:** (*sighing loudly*). Ah, David, David!

**DAVID:** (*who has gone out now returns with a rule stuck in his girdle and swinging in his hand a large piece of chalk tied to a string*). Here am I! who calls?

**MAGDALENA:** Ah, David! what ill befalls through you!
(*to himself.*)
The darling rogue! he know it too!
(*aloud.*)
Why, look! he's shut us all up inside here!

**DAVID:** (*tenderly to Magdalena*). But you in my heart!

**MAGDALENA:** (*aside*). His face is so true!
(*aloud.*)
Come say! what frolic's to be tried here?

**DAVID:** Forbid it! Frolic? A serious thing!
For the Masters I'm preparing the ring.

**MAGDALENA:** What! Will there be singing?

**DAVID:** A mere trial:
That Prentice wins his enfranchisement
Who never gained for breach of the rules chastisement;
He who passes is Master here.

---

**MAGDALENE:** Da wär' der Ritter ja am rechten Ort.—
Jetzt, Evchen, komm', wir müssen fort.

**WALTHER:** (*schnell sich zu den Frauen wendend*). Zu Meister Pogner lasst mich euch geleiten.

**MAGDALENE:** Erwartet den hier: er ist bald da.
Wollt ihr euch Evchen's Hand erstreiten,
rückt Ort und Zeit das Glück euch nah.'
(*Zwei Lehrbuben kommen dazu und tragen Bänke.*) Jetzt eilig von hinnen!

**WALTHER:** Was soll ich beginnen?

**MAGDALENE:** Lasst David euch lehren
die Freiung begehren.—
Davidchen, hör', mein lieber Gesell,
den Ritter bewahr' hier wohl zur Stell'!
Was Fein's aus der Küch'
bewahr' ich für dich:
und morgen begehr' du noch dreister,
wird heut' der Junker hier Meister.
(*Sie drängt fort.*)

**EVA:** (*zu Walther*). Sch' ich euch wieder?

**WALTHER:** (*feurig*). Heut' Abend, gewiss!—
Was ich will wagen,
wie könnt' ich's sagen?
Neu ist mein Herz, neu mein Sinn,
neu ist mir Alles, was ich begin'.
Eines nur weiss ich,
Eines begreif' ich:
nit allen Sinnen
euch zu gewinnen!
Ist's mit dem Schwert nicht, muss es gelingen,
gilt es als Meister euch zu ersingen
Für euch Gut und Blut!
Für euch
Dichter's heil'ger Muth!

**EVA:** (*mit grosser Wärme.*) Mein Herz, sel'ger Gluth,
für euch
liebesheil'ge Huth!

**MAGDALENE:** Schnell heim, sonst geht's nicht gut:

**DAVID:** (*Walther messend*). Gleich Meister? Oho? viel Muth!
(*Magdalene zicht Eva rasch durch die Vorbänge fort.*)
(*Walther hat sich, aufgeregt und brütend, in einem erhöhten, kathederartigen Lehnstuhl geworfen, welchen zuvor zwei Lehrbuben, von der Wand ab, mehr nach der Mitte zu gerückt hatten.*)
(*Noch mehrere Lehrbuben sind eingetreten: sie tragen und richten Bänke, und bereiten Alles (nach der unten folgenden Angabe) zur Sitzung der Meistersinger vor.*)

**ERSTER LEHRBUBE:** David, was stehst?

---

**MAGDALENA:** Then the knight has dropped on the proper spot.—
Now, Eva, come, we ought to trot.

**WALTER:** (*quickly turning to them*). To Master Pogner let me escort you.

**MAGDALENA:** Await his approach; he'll be here soon.
If to win our Eva you seek,
Both time and place are opportune.
(*The Prentices enter bearing benches.*)
Quick! bid us adieu!

**WALTER:** What must I do?

**MAGDALENA:** Let David supply all
The facts of the trial.—
David, my dear, just heed what I say!
You must induce Sir Walter to stay.
I'll sweep the larder and
Keep the best for you!
Tomorrow rewards shall fall faster
If this young knight is made Master.
(*She burries towards the door.*)

**EVA:** (*to Walter*). When shall I see you?

**WALTER:** (*ardently*). This evening, for sure!
What use declaring
How great my daring?
New is my heart, new my mind,
New to my senses is all I find,
One thing I spring to,
One thing I cling to:
Sustaining the hours
Of winning your hand
Though to obtain you my sword avails not,
As Master Singer surely I'll not fail.
For you gold untold!
For you,
Poet's courage bold!

**EVA:** (*with great warmth*). My heart's secret fold
For you
Loving heed will hold!

**MAGDALENA:** Quick home, or I shall scold!

**DAVID:** (*measuring Walter*). A Master! Oho! you're bold!
(*Magdalena pulls Eva quickly away through the curtains.*)
(*Walter, disturbed and brooding, has thrown himself upon a raised ecclesiastical armchair which two Prentices had just moved away from the wall to the middle of the stage.*)
(*More Prentices enter: they bring and arrange benches and prepare everything (during the following dialogue) for the sitting of the Master Singers.*)

**FIRST PRENTICE:** David, why skulk?

**ZWEITER LEHRBUBE:** Grief' an's Werk!

**DRITTER LEHRBUBE:** Hilf uns richten das Gemerk!

**DAVID:** Zu eifrigst war ich vor euch allen:
nun schafft für euch; hab' ander Gefallen!

**ZWEITER LEHRBUBE:** Was der sich dünkt!

**DRITTER LEHRBUBE:** Der Lehrling Muster!

**ERSTER LEHRBUBE:** Das macht, weil sein Meister ein Schuster.

**DRITTER LEHRBUBE:** Beim Leisten sitzt er mit der Feder.

**ZWEITER LEHRBUBE:** Beim dichten mit Draht und Pfriem.

**ERSTER LEHRBUBE:** Sein' Verse schreibt er auf rothes Leder.

**DRITTER LEHRBUBE:** (*mit der entsprechenden Gebärde*). Das, dächt' ich, gerbten wir ihm! (*Sie machen sich lachend an die fernere Herrichtung.*)

**DAVID:** (*nachdem er den sinnenden Ritter eine Weile trachtet, ruft sehr stark:*) "Fanget an!"

**WALTHER:** (*verwundert aufblickend*). Was soll's?

**DAVID:** (*noch stärker*). "Fanget an!"—So ruft der "Merker," nun sollt ihr singen:—wisst ihr das nicht?

**WALTHER:** Wer ist der Merker?

**DAVID:** Wisst ihr das nicht? War't ihr doch nie bei 'nem Sing-Gericht?

**WALTHER:** Noch nie, wo die Richter Handwerker.

**DAVID:** Seid ihr ein "Dichter?"

**WALTHER:** Wär ich's doch!

**DAVID:** Waret ihr "Singer?"

**WALTHER:** Wüsst' ich's noch?

**DAVID:** Doch "Schulfreund" war't ihr, und Schüler zuvor?

**WALTHER:** Das klingt mir alles fremd vor'm Ohr.

**DAVID:** Und so grad'hin wollt ihr Meister werden?

**WALTHER:** Wie machte das so grosse Beschwerden?

**DAVID:** O Lene! Lene!

**WALTHER:** Wie ihr doch thut!

**DAVID:** O Magdalene!

**WALTHER:** Rathet mir gut!

**DAVID:** Mein Herr! der Singer Meister-Schlag
gewinnt sich nicht in einem Tag.
In Nüremberg der grösste Meister,
mich lert die Kunst Hans Sachs;
schon voll ein Jahr mich unterweis't er,
dass ich als Schüler wachs'.
Schuhmacherei und Poeterei,
die lern' ich da all einerlei:

**SECOND PRENTICE:** Work swiftly!

**THIRD PRENTICE:** Help us place the Marker's platform!

**DAVID:** You my labor and industry shame:
Work by yourselves; I claim my own affairs.

**SECOND PRENTICE:** What airs he takes!

**THIRD PRENTICE:** A model Prentice!

**FIRST PRENTICE:** His time is lent to a shoemaker.

**THIRD PRENTICE:** His last and pen he holds together.

**SECOND PRENTICE:** While cobbling he writes his stuff.

**FIRST PRENTICE:** He scribbled verses on rough leather.

**THIRD PRENTICE:** (*with expressive gesture*). We'll soon give him tanning enough! (*They pursue their work, laughing.*)

**DAVID:** (*after observing the meditating knight awhile, calls loudly:*) "Now begin!"

**WALTER:** (*looking up, surprised*). What is it?

**DAVID:** (*still louder*). "Now begin!"—So cries the "Marker;"
Then you must sing up:—don't you know that?

**WALTER:** Who is the Marker?

**DAVID:** Don't you know that? Were you never at trials of song?

**WALTER:** No, never with a tradeworker for a judge.

**DAVID:** Are you a "Poet?"

**WALTER:** Maybe so!

**DAVID:** Are you a "Singer"?

**WALTER:** I don't know!

**DAVID:** But you've been "Schoolman," surely, and "Scholar"?

**WALTER:** The terms I've never heard, nor seen.

**DAVID:** And yet you would be at once a Master?

**WALTER:** Why should that seem to threaten disaster?

**DAVID:** Oh Lena! Lena!

**WALTER:** What do you say?

**DAVID:** Oh Magdalena!

**WALTER:** Show me the way!

**DAVID:** Good sir, the Singer's crowning deed
Is not accomplished with such speed.
In Nuremberg a famous Master
Has taught me Art—Hans Sachs.
For twelve months now he's been my pastor
That I might be a Scholar.
How to make shoe and poetry too,

hab' ich das Leder glatt geschlagen,
lern' ich Vocal und Consonanz sagen;
wichst' ich den Draht gar fein und steif,
was sich da reimt, ich wohl begreif';
den Pfriemen schwingend,
im Stich die Ahl',
was stumpf, was klingend
was Mass und Zahl,—
den Leisten im Schurz—
was lang, was kurz,
was hart, was lind,
hell oder blind,
was Waisen, was Mylben,
was Kleb-Sylben,
was Pausen, was Körner,
Blumen und Dörner,
das Alles lernt' ich mit Sorg' und Acht:
wie weit nun, meint ihr, dass ich's gebracht?

**WALTHER:** Wohl zu 'nem Paar recht guter Schuh'?

**DAVID:** Ja, dahin hat's noch lange Ruh'!
Ein "Bar" hat manch Gesätz und Gebänd';
were da gleich die rechte Regel fänd',
die richt'ge Naht,
und den rechten Draht,
mit gutgefügten "Stollen,"
den Bar recht zu versohlen.
Und dann erst kommt der "Abgesang";
dass er nicht kurz, und nicht zu lang,
und auch keinen Reim enthält,
der schon im Stollen gestellt.—
Wer Alles das merkt, weiss und kennt,
wird doch immer noch nicht Meister genennt.

**WALTHER:** Hilf Gott! Will ich denn Schuster sein?
In die Singkunst lieber führ' mich ein.

**DAVID:** Ja, hätt' ich's nur selbst erst zum "Singer" gebracht!
Wer glaubt wohl, was das für Mühe macht?
Der Meister Tön' und Weisen,
gar viel an Nam' und Zahl,
die starken und die leisen,
wer die wüsste allzumal!
Nehmt euch ein Beispiel dran,
und lasst von dem Meister-Wahn!
Denn "Singer" und "Dichter müsst" ihr sein
eh' ihr zum "Mesiter" kehret ein,
zu Wort' und Reimen, die er erfand,
aus Tönen auch fügt eine neue Weise,
der wird als "Meistersinger" erkannt.

**WALTHER:** (*rasch*). So bleibt mir nichts als der Meisterlohn!
Sol ich hier singen,
kann's nur gelingen,
find' ich zum Vers auch den eig'nen Ton.

At once I pursued both studies.
Solid and smooth the leather beating,
Vowels and consonants I'm repeating;
When I have waxed my threat full well
All about rhymes I learn to tell;
While making stitches
With fingers neat,
I'm learning which is
The time and beat;
While true to my last—
The long, the short,
The hard, the light,
Gloomy and bright,
Contractions and snippings
And word-clippings,
The pauses, the corns,
The flowers and thorns,—
All these I learn with great pains and care:
How far now, think you, I've brought the affair?

**WALTER:** Perhaps to a pair of right good shoes?

**DAVID:** Yes, I pursued so far the Muse!
A "Stave" has parts and forms of its own;
Who can master all its rules alone?
With proper thread
And a fitting head
It takes a learned man, sir,
To sole and heel your "Stanza."
And then we have the "After-Song,"
Must not be short, nor yet too long,
Nor repeat a rhyme again
Which the first part did contain.
When all this is read, marked and learned,
Even yet the name of Master's not earned.

**WALTER:** Help me, God! Must I then cobbling learn?
Rather let us turn to your singing.

**DAVID:** Ah, if I only could be a "Singer"!
Such labor is far too great for me.
The Tones and Modes we render
Have many forms and names;
The harsh ones and the tender:—
Who would try to frame a list?
So be advised by this:
Shun dreams of Master-bliss!
A "Singer" and "Poet," both, do you see,
Previous to "Master" one must be.

**WALTER:** (*quickly*). I only think of the Master-gain!
If I sing,
Victory I wring
Only through verse with the proper strain.

DAVID: (*der sich zu den Lehrbuben gewendet*). Was macht ihr denn da!—Ja, fehl ich beim Werk, verkehrt nur richtet ihr Stuhl und Gemerk!—
Ist denn heut' "Singschul'?"—dass ihr's wisst,
das kleine Gemerk!—nur "Freiung" ist!
*Die Lehrbuben, welche Anstalt getroffen hatten, in der Mitte der Bühne ein grösseres Gerüste mit Vorhängen aufzuschlagen, schaffen auf David's Weisung dies schnell bei Seite und stellen dafür ebenso eilig ein geringeres Brettbodengerüste auf; darauf stellen sie einen Stuhl mit einem kleinen Pult davor, daneben eine grosse schwarze Tafel, daran die Kreide am Faden aufgehängt wird; um das Gerüst sind schwarze Vorhänge angebracht, welche zunächst hinten und an beiden Seiten, dann auch vorn ganz zusammengezogen werden.*

DIE LEHRBUBEN: (*während der Herrichtung*).
Aller End' ist doch David der Allergescheit'st!
Nach hohen Ehren gewiss er geizt:
's ist Freiung heut';
gar sicher er freit,
als vornehmer "Singer" schon er sich spreizt!
Die "Schlag"-reime fest er inne hat,
"Arm-Hunger"-Weise singt er glatt;
die "harte-Tritt"-Weis' doch kennt er am best',
die trat ihm sein Meister hart und fest!
(*Sie lachen.*)

DAVID: Ja, lacht nur zu! Heut' bin ich's nicht;
ein Andrer stellt sich zum Gericht:
der war nicht "Schüler," ist nicht "Singer,"
den "Dichter," sagt er, überspring' er;
denn er ist Junker,
und mit einem Sprung er
denkt ohne weit're Beschwerden
heut' hier "Meister" zu werden.
D'rum richtet nur fein
das Gemerk dem ein
Dorthin!—Hierher!—Die Tafel an die Wand,
so dass sie recht dem Merker zu Hand!
(*sich zu Walther unwendend.*)
Ja, ja!—dem "Merker!"—Wird euch wohl bang?
Vor ihm schon mancher Werber versang.
Sieben Fehler giebt er euch vor,
die merkt er mit Kreide dort an;
were über sieben Fehler verlor,
hat versungen und ganz verthan!
Nun nehmt euch in Acht!
Der Merker wacht,
Glück auf zum Meistersingen!
Mögt ihr euch das Kränzlein erschwingen
Das Blumenkränzlein aus Seiden

DAVID: (*turning to the Prentices*). What are you doing?—Because I'm not there
You're placing the platform and chairs all wrong!
Is today "Song-class?"—You know how!
Make the stage smaller!—It is "Trial" now.
(*The Prentices, who were preparing to erect a large platform hung with curtains in the middle of the stage, put this away, by David's direction, and build instead a smaller platform of boards; on this they place a seat with a little desk before it, near this a large blackboard to which they hang a piece of chalk by a string; round this erection are hung black curtains, which are drawn round the back and sides and then over the front.*)

PRENTICES: (*during their work*).
Oh! of course Mister David is cleverer than most!
Doubtless he's hoping to get a high post:
It is Trial-day,
He'll try away;
That he's now quite a "Singer" is his boast!
That "Whack"-rhyme he knows all through and through;
The "Sharp-hunger" tune he'll sing you too;
But the "Hearty-kick" strain is what he knows best;
His master often plays it with zest.
(*they laugh.*)

DAVID: Aye, jeer away! but not at me,
Another laughing-stock you'll see:
He never was "Scholar," learnt no singing,
But yet over "Poets" would be springing;
A noble knight he.
In single flight he
Thinks without any disaster
Here to rise to a "Master."
So settle with care
Both stage and chair
Come here!—Place there the board on the wall,
That on it the Marker's fingers may fall!
(*turning to Walter.*)
Aye, aye!—the "Marker"!—Aren't you afraid?
With him have many their failures made.
Seven faults you are suffered to make;
They're marked with his chalk, every one;
If you commit one farther mistake,
You're "outsung" and declared "outdone."
So have care!
The Marker's there.
Godspeed your Master singing?

fein,
Wird das dem Herrn Ritter beschieden sein?

DIE LEHRBUBEN: (*welche das Gemerk zugleich geschlossen, fassen sich an und tanzen einen verschlungenen Reihen draum.*)
"Das Blumenkränzlein aus Seiden fein,
wird das dem Herrn Ritter beschieden sein?
(*Die Einrichtung ist nun folgendermassen beendigt:—Zur Seite sind gepolsterte Bänke in der weise aufgestellt. Am Ende der Bänke, in der Mitte der Scene, befindet sich das "Gemerk" benannte Gerüste, welches zuvor hergerichtet worden. Zur linken Seite steht nur der erhöhte, kathederartige Stuhl ("der Singstuhl") der Versammlung gegenüber. Im Hintergrunde, dem grossen Vorhang entlang, steht eine lange niedere Bank für die Lehrlinge.—Walther, verdrießlich über das Gespött der Knaben, hat sich auf die vorders Bank niedergelassen. Pogner und Beckmesser kommen im Gespräch aus der Sacristei; allmählich versammeln sich immer mehrere der Meister. Die Lehrbuben, und sie die Meister entreten saben, sind sogleich zurückgegangen und harren ehrerbietig an der hinteren Bank. Nur David stellt sich anfänglich am Eingang bei der Sacristei auf.*)

POGNER: (*zu Beckmesser*). Seid meiner Treue wohl versehen;
was ich bestimmt, ist euch zu nutz;
im Wettgesang müsst ihr bestehen;
wer böte euch als Meister Trutz?

BECKMESSER: Doch wollt ihr von dem Punkt nicht weichen,
der mich—ich sag's—bedenklich macht;
kann Evehen's Wunsch den Werber streichen,
was nützt mir meine Meisterpracht?

POGNER: Ei sagt! Ieh mein', vor allen Dingen
sollt' euch an dem gelegen sein?
Könnt ihr der Tochter Wunsch nicht zwingen,
wie möchtet ihr wohl um sie frei'n?

BECKMESSER: Ei ja! Gar wohl!
D'rum eben bitt ich,
das bei dem Kind ihr für mich sprecht,
wie ich geworben zart und sittig,
und wie Beckmesser grad' euch recht.

POGNER: Das thu' ich gern.

BECKMESSER: (*bei Seite*). Er lässt nicht nach!
Wie wehrt' ich da 'nem Ungemach?

May you the chaplet be winning!
The wreath of flowers in silk so bright,
I hope it may fall to your lot, sir knight!

PRENTICES: (*who have closed the Marker's place, take hands and dance in a ring round it.*) "The wreath of flowers in silk so bright,
I hope it may fall to your lot, sir knight!"
(*The erection is now completed in the following manner:—at the side, covered benches are placed. At the end of these in the middle of the stage is the Marker's place, as before described. The elevated seat (the "Singer's Seat") opposite to the benches. At back, against the large curtain is a long low bench for the Prentices.—Walter, vexed with the gibes of the boys, has seated himself on the front bench.
Pogner and Beckmesser enter from the sacristy, conversing; gradually the other Masters assemble. The Prentices on seeing the Masters enter disperse and wait respectively by the back bench. Only David stands by the entrance to the sacristy.*)

POGNER: (*to Beckmesser*). Trust me, my friendship is unshaken;
What I intend is for your good:
This trial must be undertaken;
None doubts your Mastership: who could?

BECKMESSER: But won't you falter in that matter
Which caused—in truth—my doubtful mood?
If Eva's whim the whole can alter,
What use is all my Masterhood?

POGNER: Ah, what! It seems you've mainly rested
On that your hopes equivocal?
But if her heart's not interested,
How come you're wooing her at all?

BECKMESSER: Why yes, that's true! Therefore I drop a
Request that you will speak for me;
Say that my wooing's fair and proper,
That with Beckmesser you agree.

POGNER: With right good will.

BECKMESSER: (*aside*). He won't give way!
How shall I avoid disappointment?

# Act I

**WALTHER:** (*der, als er Pogner gewahrt, aufgestanden und ihm entgegen gegangen ist, verneight sich vor ihm*). Gestattet, Meister!

**POGNER:** Wie! mein Junker! Ihr sucht mich in der Singschul' hie? (*Sie begrüssen sich.*)

**BECKMESSER:** (*immer bei Seite, für sich*). Verstünden's die Frau'n! Doch schlechtes Geflunken Gilt ihnen mehr als all' Poesie.

**WALTHER:** Hie eben bin ich am rechten Ort. Gesteh' ich's frei, vom Lande fort Was mich nach Nürnberg trieb, War nur zur Kunst die Lieb'. Vergass ich's gestern euch zu sagen, hent' muss ich's laut zu künden wagen, ein Meistersinger möcht ich sein. Schliesst, Meister, in die Zunft mich ein. (*Andere Meister sind gekommen und herangetreten.*)

**POGNER:** (*zu den nächsten*). Kunz Vogelgesang—Freund Nachtigal! Hört doch, welch' ganz besonderer Fall! Der Ritter heir, mir wohlbekannt, hat der Meisterkunst sich zugewandt. (*Begrüssungen.*)

**BECKMESSER:** (*immer noch für sich*). Noch such' ich's zu wenden: doch sollt's nicht gelingen; versuch ich des Mädchens Herz zu ersingen; in stiller Nacht, von ihr gehört, erfahr' ich, ob auf mein Lied sie schwört. (*Er wendet sich.*) Wer ist der Mensch?

**POGNER:** (*zu Walther*). Glaubt, wie mich's freut! Die alte Zeit dünkt mich erneu't.

**BECKMESSER:** (*immer noch für sich*). Er gefällt mir nicht!

**POGNER:** (*fortfahrend*). Was ihr begehrt, soviel an mir euch sei's gewährt.

**BECKMESSER:** (*ebenso*). Was will der hier!—Wie der Blick ihm lacht!

**POGNER:** (*ebenso*). Half ich euch gern zu des Gut's Verkauf, in die Zunft nun nehm' ich euch gleich gern auf.

**BECKMESSER:** (*ebenso*). Holla! Sixtus! Auf den hab' Acht!

**WALTHER:** (*zu Pogner*). Hab Dank der Güte aus tiefstem Gemüthe! Und darf ich denn hoffen, Steht heut' mir noch offen zu werben um den Preis, dass ich Meistersinger heiss'?

**BECKMESSER:** Oho! Fein sacht? Auf dem Kopf steht kein Kegel!

---

**WALTER:** (*who, on perceiving Pogner, has risen and advanced to meet him now bows to him*). Permit me, Master!

**POGNER:** What! Sir Walter? You've sought me in the school down here? (*They greet one another.*)

**BECKMESSER:** (*still to himself*). If women had taste! But they prefer to palter Than to hear poetry.

**WALTER:** This truly should be my proper groove. I frankly state that what did move Me from my land to part Was solely love of Art. I had forgotten to announce it, But now in public I pronounce it: A Master Singer I would be. Open, Master, the Guild to me. (*Other Masters have entered and advanced.*)

**POGNER:** (*to those near him*). Kunz Vogelgesang—Friend Nachtigal! Hear what I've got to tell you all! This noble knight, a friend of mine, Seeks to shine in the Master Art. (*Greetings and introductions.*)

**BECKMESSER:** (*still aside*). Once more I'll approach him, but if he'll not waver I'll strive with my voice to win the maid's favor; In silent night, heard only by her. I'll see if my singing her heart can stir. (*turns.*) What man is that?

**POGNER:** (*to Walter*). 'Faith, I am glad! Old times are come again, my lad.

**BECKMESSER:** (*aside*). I don't like his looks!

**POGNER:** (*continuing*). In your demand My influence you may command.

**BECKMESSER:** (*as before*). What wants he here, with his smiling air?

**POGNER:** (*as before*). Truly I helped you your lands to sell, In our Guild I'll enter you now as well.

**BECKMESSER:** (*as before*). Hallo, Sixtus? of him beware!

**WALTER:** (*to Pogner*). Best thanks I proffer And gratitude offer! Then have I permission To seek for admission As striver for the prize. And Master Singer to rise?

**BECKMESSER:** Oho! that's nice! His ideas are not paddled!

---

**POGNER:** Herr Ritter, diess geh' nun nach der Regel. Doch heut' ist Freiung: ich schlag' euch vor; mir leihen die Meister ein willig Ohr. (*Die Meistersinger sind nun alle angelangt, zuletzt auch Hans Sachs.*)

**SACHS:** Gott grüss' euch, Meister!

**VOGELGESANG:** Sind wir beisammen?

**BECKMESSER:** Der Sachs ist ja da!

**NACHTIGALL:** So ruft die Namen!

**FRITZ KOTHNER:** (*zicht eine Liste hervor, stellt sich zur seite auf und ruft*). Zu einer Freiung und Zunftberathung Ging an die Meister ein' Einladung; bei Nenn' and Nam', ob jeder kam, ruf' ich nun auf, als letzt-entbot'ner, der ich mich nenn' und bin Fritz Kothner. Seit ihr da, Veit Pogner?

**POGNER:** Hier zu Hand. (*Er setzt sich.*)

**KOTHNER:** Kunz Vogelgesang?

**VOGELGESANG:** Ein sich fand. (*Setzt sich.*)

**KOTHNER:** Hermann Ortel?

**ORTEL:** Immer am Ort. (*Setzt sich.*)

**KOTHNER:** Balthazar Zorn?

**ZORN:** Bleibt neimals fort. (*Setzt sich.*)

**KOTHNER:** Konrad Nachtigall?

**NACHTIGALL:** Treu seinem Schlag. (*Setzt sich.*)

**KOTHNER:** Augustin Moser?

**MOSER:** Nie fehlen mag. (*Setzt sich.*)

**KOTHNER:** Niklaus Vogel?—Schweigt?

**EIN LEHRBUBE:** (*sich schnell von der Bank erhebend*). Ist krank.

**KOTHNER:** Gut' Bess'rung dem Meister!

**ALLE MEISTER:** Walt's Gott!

**DER LEHRBUBE:** Schön Dank! (*Setzt sich wieder.*)

**KOTHNER:** Hans Sachs?

**DAVID:** (*vorlaut sich erhebend*). Da steht er!

**SACHS:** (*drohend zu David*). Juckt dieh das Fell?—Verzeiht, Meister!—Sachs ist zur Stell'. (*Er setzt sich.*)

**KOTHNER:** Sixtus Beckmesser?

---

**POGNER:** Sir Walter, these things with rules are saddled. Today is "Trial"; I'll state your case: The Masters will always lend me their ears. (*The Master Singers have now all assembled, Sachs the last.*)

**SACHS:** God greet you, Masters!

**VOGELGESANG:** Has everyone arrived?

**BECKMESSER:** Yes, Sachs is here too.

**NACHTIGAL:** Let names be given.

**FRITZ KOTHNER:** (*produces a list, stands apart from the rest and calls:*) To hold a Trial-examination, Masters, I give you invitation: Of one and all The names I call, And first my own, which, though I note never, I answer to and am Fritz Kothner. Are you there, Veit Pogner?

**POGNER:** Here at hand. (*sits.*)

**KOTHNER:** Kunz Vogelgesang?

**VOGELGESANG:** Yes, here I am. (*sits.*)

**KOTHNER:** Herman Ortel?

**ORTEL:** Comes when he ought. (*sits.*)

**KOTHNER:** Balthazar Zorn?

**ZORN:** I'm never late. (*sits.*)

**KOTHNER:** Conrad Nachtigal?

**NACHTIGAL:** True as my song. (*sits.*)

**KOTHNER:** Augustin Moser?

**MOSER:** Here all along. (*sits.*)

**KOTHNER:** Nicholas Vogel?—No?

**A PRENTICE:** (*jumping up from his seat at back*). He's ill.

**KOTHNER:** God send him recovery!

**ALL THE MASTERS:** Amen!

**PRENTICE:** Good will! (*sits down again.*)

**KOTHNER:** Hans Sachs?

**DAVID:** (*officiously rising*). He's there, sir!

**SACHS:** (*threatening David*). Tingles your skin?—Excuse me, Master!—Sachs has come in. (*sits.*)

**KOTHNER:** Sixtus Beckmesser?

BECKMESSER: Immer bei Sachs, dass den Reim ich lern' von "bluh' und wachs'."
(*Er setzt sich neben Sachs, dieser lacht.*)

KOTHNER: Ulrich Eisslinger?

EISSLINGER: Hier!
(*Setzt sich.*)

KOTHNER: Hans Foltz?

FOLTZ: Bin da.
(*Setzt sich.*)

KOTHNER: Hans Schwarz?

SCHWARZ: Zuletzt: Gott wollt's!
(*Setzt sich.*)

KOTHNER: Zur Sitzung gut und voll die Zahl,
Beliebt's, wir schreiten zur Merker-wahl?

VOGELGESANG: Wohl eh'r nach dem Fest.

BECKMESSER: (*zu Kothner*). Pressirt's den Herrn?
Mein Stell' und Amt lass' ich ihm gern.

POGNER: Nicht doch, ihr Meister! Lasst das jetzt fort.
Für wicht'gen Antrag bitt' ich um's Wort.
(*Alle Meister stehen auf und set-zen sich wieder.*)

KOTHNER: Das habt ihr, Meister! Sprecht!

POGNER: Nun hört, und versteht mich recht!—
Das schöne Fest, Johannis-Tag, ihr wisst, begeh'n wir morgen;
auf grüner Au', am Blumenhag, bei Spiel und Tanz im Lustgelag,
an froher Brust geborgen, vergessen seiner Sorgen,
ein Jeder freut sich wie er mag.
Die Singschul' ernst im Kirchen-chor
die Meister selbst vertauschen; mit Kling und Klang hinaus zum Thor
auf off'ne Wiese ziehn sie vor, bei hellen Festes Rauschen;
das Volk sie lassen lauschen dem Frei-Gesang mit Laien-Ohr.
Zu einem Werb' und Wett-Gesang gestellt sind Siegespreise,
und beide rühmt man weit und lang, die Gabe wie die Weise.
Nun schuf mich Gott zum reichen Mann;
und giebt ein Jeder wie er kann, so musst' ich fleissig sinnen,
was ich gäb' zu gewinnen, dass ich nicht käm' zu Schand':
so höret, was ich fand.—
In deutschen Landen viel gereis't, hat oft es mich verdrossen,
dass man den Bürger wenig preis't, ihn karg nennt und verschlossen.
An Höfen, wie an nied'rer Statt, des bitt'ren Tadels ward ich satt,
das nur auf Schacher und Geld sein Merk' der Bürger stellt'.
Dass wir im weiten deutschen

BECKMESSER: Always near Sachs, Then I have a rhyme to "bloom and wax."
(*sits close to Sachs, who laughs.*)

KOTHNER: Ulric Eisslinger?

EISSLINGER: Here!
(*sits.*)

KOTHNER: Hans Foltz?

FOLTZ: I'm here.
(*sits.*)

KOTHNER: Hans Schwarz?

SCHWARZ: The list now halts.
(*sits.*)

KOTHNER: The meeting's full; a good show.
Shall we make choice of a Marker now?

VOGELGESANG: The Festival first.

BECKMESSER: (*to Kothner*). If you are pressed,
I'll yield my turn to you with zest.

POGNER: Not yet, my Masters! let that alone.
A weighty matter I would make known.
(*All the Masters rise and reseat themselves.*)

KOTHNER: With pleasure, Master! Tell!

POGNER: Then hear, and mark me well!—
St. John's most holy festal day, You know, we keep tomorrow;
In meadows green, among the hay, With song and dance and merry play.
Each heart will gladness borrow And cast aside all sorrow;
So each will sport as best he may.
The Singing-school we Masters here A staid church-choir will christen:
From out the gates with merry cheer
To open meadows we will steer, While festal banners glisten:
The populace shall listen To Master Songs with layman's ear.
For those who best succeed in song Are gifts of various sizes,
And all will hail, full loud and long, Both melodies and prizes.
I am thank God! a wealthy man; And, as each gives what he can,
I've ransacked every coffer To find a prize to offer,
Not to be brought to shame:— Now, hear what I've thought—
Through German lands when I have roved
It pained me, as I listened, To hear the burghers are not loved,
Deemed selfish and close-fisted.
In low life, as in courts the same, I always heard the bitter blame
That only treasure and gold Can hold the burgher's thoughts.
That we in all Empire's bounds Alone have promoted Art.

Reich die Kunst einzig noch pflegen,
d'ran dünkt' ihnen wenig gelegen;
doch wie uns das zur Ehre gereich',
und dass mit hohen Muth
wir schätzen, was schön und gut, was werth die Kunst, und was sie gilt,
das ward ich der Welt zu zeigen gewillt
D'rum hört, Meister, die Gab', die als Preis bestimmt ich hab':
dem Singer, der im Kunst-Gesang vor allem Volk den Preis errang
am Sankt Johannistag, sie er, wer er auch mag,
dem geb' ich, ein Kunst-ge-wog'ner,
von Nürenberg Veit Pogner, mit all' meinem Gut, wie's geh' und steh'
Eva, mein einzig Kind, zur Eh'.

DIE MEISTER: (*sehr lebhalt durcheinander*). Das nenn' ich ein Wort! Ein Wort, ein Mann!
Da sieht man, was ein Nürnberger kann!
D'rob preis't man euch noch weit und breit,
den wack'ren Bürger Pogner Veit!

DIE LEHRBUBEN: (*lustig auf-springend*). Alle Zeit, weit und briet:
Pogner Veit!

VOGELGESANG: Wer möchte da nicht ledig sein!

SACHS: Sein Weib gäb' gern wohl mancher drei'n!

NACHTIGALL: Auf, ledig' Mann! Jetzt macht euch dran!

POGNER: Nun hört noch, wie ich's ernstlich mein!
Ein' leblos' Gabe stell' ich nicht: ein Mägdlein sitzt mit zu Gericht.
Den Preis erkennt die Meister-Zunft;
doch gilt's der Eh', so will's Ver-nunft,
dass ob der Meister Rath die Braut den Ausschlag hat.

BECKMESSER: (*zu Kothner*). Dünkt euch das klug?

KOTHNER: (*laut*). Versteh' ich gut,
irh gebt uns in des Mägdlein's Huth?

BECKMESSER: Gefährlich das!

KOTHNER: Stimmt es nicht bei, wie wäre dann der Meister Urtheil frei?

BECKMESSER: Lasst's gleich wählen nach Herzen's Ziel,
und lasst den Meistergesang aus dem Speil!

POGNER: Nicht so! Wie doch? Ver-steht mich recht!
Wem ihr Meister den Preis zusprecht,
die Maid kann dem verwehren,

I fancy they scarcely have noted: But how this adds to our honor,
And how, with proudest care, We treasure the good and rare,
What Art is worth—what it can do—
Now have I a mind to show you. So hear, Masters, what thing
As a prize I mean to bring.— The singer, to whose lyric skill
The public voice the prize shall win,
On John the Baptist's day,— Be he whoever he may—
I, Pogner, an Art supporter, A townsman of this quarter,
Will give, with my gold and goods beside,
Eva, my only child, for bride.

THE MASTERS: (*animatedly to one another*). That's nobly said!
Brave words—brave man! You see now what a Nuremberger can!
So far and wide we'll raise always The worthy burgher Pogner's praise!

PRENTICES: (*jumping up merri-ly*). All our days raise and blaze Pogner's praise!

VOGELGESANG: Who would not now be unmarried!

SACHS: There's some would give their wives with glee.

NACHTIGAL: Come, single man, Do all you can.

POGNER: My meaning you must clearly see:
No lifeless gift I offer you; The maid shall sit in judgment too.
Our Guild shall declare the winner: But as to marriage, it is but fair
That she despite the Masters' choice,
The bride should have a voice.

BECKMESSER: (*to Kothner*). Do you like that?

KOTHNER: (*aloud*). You mean to say
That we must obey the maiden?

BECKMESSER: It's dangerous!

KOTHNER: I cannot see How then our judgment would be free.

BECKMESSER: Let her choose as may please her heart,
And leave the Master Song business apart.

POGNER: No, no? why so? Let me correct!
Any man whom we all elect May be by her rejected,
But never another accepted:

# Act I

doch nie einen Andren begehren:
ein Meistersinger muss er sein;
nur wen ihr krönt, den soll sie
frei'n.

SACHS: Verzeiht!
Vielleicht schon ginget ihr zu weit.
Ein Mädchenherz und Meisterkunst
erglüh'n nicht stets von gleicher
Brunst;
der Frauen Sinn, gar unbelehrt,
dünkt mich dem Sinn des Volks
gleich werth.
Wollt ihr nun vor dem Volke zeig-
en,
wie hoch die Kunst ihr ehrt;
und lasst ihr dem Kind die Wahl zu
eigen,
wollt nicht, dass dem Spruch es
wehrt':
so Lasst das Volk auch Richter sein;
mit dem Kinde sicher stimmt's
überein.

DIE MEISTER: (unruhig
durcheinander). Oho! Das Volk?
Ja, das wäre schön!
Ade dann Kunst und Meistertön'!

NACHTIGALL: Nein, Sachs! Gewiss, das hat keinen Sinn!
Gäbt ihr dem Volk die Regel hin?

SACHS: Vernehmt mich recht! Wie
ihr doch thut!
Gesteht, ich kenn' die Regeln gut;
und dass die Zunft die Regeln bewahr',
bemüh' ich mich selbst schon
manches Jahr
Doch einmal im Jahre fänd' ich's
weise,
dass man die Regeln selbst probir',
ob in der Gewohnheit trägem
G'leise
ihr' Kraft und Leben sich nicht verlier';
und ob ihr der Natur
noch seid auf rechter Spur,
das sagt euch nur,
wer nichts weiss von der Tabulatur.
(Die Lehrbuben springen auf und
reiben sich die Hände.)

BECKMESSER: Hei! wie sich die
Buben freuen!

SACHS: (eifrig fortfahrend).
D'rum mocht's euch nie gereuen,
dass jährlich am Sankt Johannisfest,
statt dass das Volk man kommen
lässt,
herab aus hoher Meister-Wolk'
ihr selbst euch wendet zu dem
Volk'.
Dem Volke wollt ihr behagen;
nun dächt' ich' läg' es nah',
ihr liesst es selbst euch auch sagen,
ob das ihm zur Last geschah?
Das Volk und Kunst gleich blüh'
und wachs',
bestellt ihr so, mein ich, Hans
Sachs.

VOGELGESANG: Ihr meint's wohl
recht!

KOTHNER: Doch steht's drum
faul.

A Master Singer he must be;
None may she wed uncrowned by
you.

SACHS: But say!
Perhaps that were too much to say.
The fire that warms a maiden's
heart
Is not like flames of Master-Art;
Undisciplined, the female mind
Level with public voice I find.
So, if you hold to public vision
Your high esteem of Art,
If you desire the girl's decision
Should not thwart the matter,
Then let the people too decide;
With the maiden's voice they'd
coincide.

THE MASTERS: (uneasily
amongst themselves). Oho! The
people! What an idea!
It is then goodbye to Art, I fear!

NACHTIGAL: Nay, Sachs! Indeed
that is absurd!
We to obey the people's word?

SACHS: Pray, understand! Don't
talk like that!
Of course I have the rules all pat;
And that our Guild should keep
them too
For many a year I've worked with
you.
But once in each year I think it
would be better
To have these very rules well tried,
For fear that, rusted by use and cus-
tom's fetter,
Their force and life perhaps have
died.
If Truth and Nature pure
Still in your laws endure,
You'll learn for sure
Where nothings known of the Ta-
bulature.
(The Prentices jump up and rub
their hands.)

BECKMESSER: Hey! Are not the
boys contended!

SACHS: (earnestly continuing).
So may it never be repented
That once, on St. John's day, every
year
You do not bring the people here,
But bend your Guild of Masters
proud
Right willingly towards the crowd.
You cater here for the masses:
I think then it were but right
To ask the vote of those classes
And hear if they find delight.
Thus Art and Nation shall bloom
and wax
By your good help, say I, Hans
Sachs.

VOGELGESANG: That's very right!

KOTHNER: And yet all wrong!

NACHTIGALL: Wenn spricht das
Volk, halt' ich das Maul.

KOTHNER: Der Kunst droht' all-
weil Fall und Schmach,
läuft sie der Gunst des Volkes nach.

BECKMESSER: D'rin bracht' er's
weit, der hier so dreist:
Gassenhauer dichtet er meist.

POGNER: Freund Sachs, was ich
mein', ist schon neu:
zuviel auf einmal brächte Reu'!—
So frag' ich, ob den Meistern gefällt
Gab' und Regel, wie ich's gestellt?
(Die Meister erheben sich.)

SACHS: Mir genügt der Jungfer
Ausschlag-Stimm.

BECKMESSER: (für sich.) Der
Schuster weckt doch stets mir
Grimm!

KOTHNER: Wer schreibt sich als
Werber ein?
Ein Junggesell muss es sein.

BECKMESSER: Vielleicht auch ein
Wittwer? Fragt nur den Sachs!

SACHS: Nicht doch, Herr Merker!
Aus jüng'rem Wachs
als ich und ihr muss der Freier sein,
soll Evchen ihm den Preis verleih'n.

BECKMESSER: Als wie auch
ich?—Grober Gesell!

KOTHNER: Begehrt wer Freiung,
der komm' zur Stell'!
Ist Jemand gemeld't, der Freiung
begehrt?

POGNER: Wohl, Meister! Zur Tage-
sordnung kehrt!
Und nehmt von mir Bericht,
wie ich auf Meister-Pflicht
einen jungen Ritter empfehle,
der wünscht, dass man ihn wähle,
und heut' als Meistersinger frei.'—
Main Junker von Stolzing, kommt
herbei!
(Walter tritt vor und verneigt
sich).

BECKMESSER: (für sich). Dacht'
ich mir's doch! Geht's da hinaus,
Veith?
(Laut.)
Meister, ich mein', zu spät ist's der
Zeit.

DIE MEISTER: (durcheinander).
Der Fall ist neu.—Ein Ritter gar?
Soll man sich freu'n?—Oder wär'
Gefahr?
Immerhin hat's ein gross Gewicht,
dass Meister Pogner für ihn spricht.

KOTHNER: Soll uns der Junker
willkommen sein,
zuvor muss er wohl vernommen
sein.

POGNER: Vernehmt ihn gut!
Wünsch' ich ihm Glück,
nicht bleib' ich doch hinter der Regel zurück.
Thut, Meister, die Fragen!

NACHTIGAL: When riff-raff speak
I'll hold my tongue.

KOTHNER: Our Art would quickly
be disgraced,
If it were swayed by public taste.

BECKMESSER: He's tried for that
who talks so loud;
Clap-trap stuff he writes for the
crowd.

POGNER: Friend Sachs, what I pro-
pose is new;
Too many novelties won't do!—
I ask then, if you Masters will hold
My offer on the terms just told?
(The Masters rise assentingly.)

SACHS: I am content the maid
should decide.

BECKMESSER: (aside). That cob-
blerman I can't abide!

KOTHNER: What candidate comes
to me?
A bachelor he must be?

BECKMESSER: He may be a widower! How about Sachs?

SACHS: No, No, good Marker! Of
younger wax
Must be the suitor who comes to
woo
Our Eva, than myself or you.

BECKMESSER: Than even I?—
Mannerless knave!

KOTHNER: If suitors offer, their
names I crave!
Is anyone here who seeks to essay?

POGNER: Well, Masters, to the
work of the day!
And be it understood
That I, as Masters should,
To this knight have offered protec-
tion,
Who seeks for our election,
To woo, as Master Singers may.—
Sir Walter von Stolzing, step this
way!
(Walter advances and makes
obeisance.)

BECKMESSER: (aside). Just as I
feared! So that's what he schemes?
(aloud.)
Masters, it is too late now, it seems.

THE MASTERS: (to one another)
The case is new.—A noble knight?
Should we be glad? Do you think it
right?
Nevertheless it should have great
weight
That Pogner is his advocate.

KOTHNER: Before this young
man's certified by us
He must first of all be tried by us.

POGNER: Do not mistake me: I
wish him well,
But against the rules I'm the last to
rebel.
Come, Masters, and task him!

KOTHNER: So mög' uns der Junker sagen:
ist er frei und ehrlich geboren?

POGNER: Die Frage gebt verloren,
da ich euch selbst dess' Bürge steh';
dass er aus frei und edler Eh':
von Stolzing Walther aus Frankenland,
nach Brief' und Urkund' mir wohlbekannt.
Als seines Stammes letzter Spross,
verliess er neulich Hof und Schloss
und zog nach Nürnberg her,
dass er hier Bürger wär'.

BECKMESSER: (zum Nachbar). Neu Junker-Unkraut! Thut nicht gut.

NACHTIGALL: (laut). Freund Pogner's Wort Genüge thut.

SACHS: Wie längst von den Meistern beschlossen ist,
ob Herr, ob Bauer, hier nichts beschiesst:
hier fragt sich's nach der Kunst allein,
wer will ein Meistersinger sein.

KOTHNER: D'rum nun frag' ich zur Stell':
welch' Meister's seid ihr Gesell'?

WALTHER: Am stillen Herd in Winterzeit,
wenn Burg und Hof mir eingeschnei't,
wie einst der Lenz so lieblich lacht',
und wie er bald wohl neu erwacht',
ein altes Buch, vom Ahn' vermacht,
gab das mir oft zu lesen:
Herr Walther von der Vogelweid',
der ist mein Meister gewesen.

SACHS: Ein guter Meister!

BECKMESSER: Doch lang' schon todt:
wie lehrt' ihm der wohl der Regel Gebot.

KOTHNER: Doch in welcher Schul' das Singen
mocht' euch zu lernen gelingen?

WALTHER: Wann dann die Flur vom Frost befreit,
und wiederkehrt die Sommerzeit,
was einst in langer Winternacht
das alte Buch mir kund gemacht,
das schallte laut in Waldespracht,
das hört' ich hell erklingen;
im Wald dort auf der Vogelweid',
da lernt' ich auch das Singen.

BECKMESSER: Oho! Von Finken und Meisen
lerntet ihr Meister-Weisen?
Das mag denn wohl auch dar nach sein!

VOGELGESANG: Zwie art'ge Stollen fasst' er da ein.

KOTHNER: One question I would ask him:
Is he free and born in good standing?

POGNER: I'll answer your demand
And be, myself, his guarantee
That he is nobly born and free:
Sir Walter Stolzing, Franconian knight;
My friends his praise both speak and write.
The last survivor of his race,
He lately left his native place to come
To Nuremberg
And make this town his home.

BECKMESSER: (to his neighbor). Young, good-for-nothing! This is nice!

NACHTIGAL: (aloud). Friend Pogner's word will quite suffice.

SACHS: We Masters did long since decide,
Nor lord nor peasant should be denied.
Art is indeed the sole concern
Of those who would learn Master-Song.

KOTHNER: First I ask you tell us
What Master taught you your Art.

WALTER: By silent hearth in winter time,
When house and hall in snow did hide,
How once the Spring so sweetly smiled
And soon should wake to glory mild.
An ancient book my sire compiled
Set all before me duly:
Sir Walter of the Vogelweid,
Has been my master, truly.

SACHS: A goodly master!

BECKMESSER: But long since dead!
So what could he have read of our precepts?

KOTHNER: But did you learn your knowledge
Of singing in school or cottage.

WALTER: Yes, when the fields defied the frost,
Beneath returning summertime,
What once in dreary winter's night
Within that book I read aright
Now pealed aloud through forest bright:
I heard the music ringing.
The wood before the Vogelweid'—
It was there I learned my singing.

BECKMESSER: Oho! The finch and the linnet
Taught you all in a minute?
That's your style of song, without doubt.

VOGELGESANG: Two proper Stanzas he has made out.

BECKMESSER: Ihr lobt ihn, Meister Vogelgesang?
Wohl weil er vom Vogel lernt' den Gesang?

KOTHNER: (beiseit' zu den Meistern). Was meint ihr, Meister? Frag' ich noch fort?
Mich dünkt, der Junker ist fehl am Ort.

SACHS: Das wird sich bäldlich zeigen:
Wenn rechte Kunst ihm eigen,
und gut er sie bewährt,
was gilt's, wer sie ihm gelehrt?

KOTHNER: seid ihr bereit, ob euch gerieth
mit neuer Find' ein Mesiterlied
nach Dicht' und Weis' en'r eigen
zur Stunde jetzt zu zeigen?

WALTHER: Was Winternacht,
was Waldes Pracht,
was Buch und Hain mich wiesen;
was Dichter-Sanges Wundermacht
mir heimlich wollt' erschliesen;
was Rosses Schritt
beim Waffen-Ritt,
was Reihen-Tanz
bei heitrem Schanz
mir sinnend gab zu lauschen:
gilt es des Lebens höchsten Preis
um Sang mir einzutauschen,
zu eig'nem Wort, und eig'ner Weis'
will einig mir es fliessen,
als Meistersang, ob den ich weiss,
euch Meistern sich ergiessen.

BECKMESSER: Entnahmt ihr 'was der Worte Schwall?

VOGELGESANG: Ei nun, er wagt's!

NACHTIGALL: Merkwürd'ger Fall!

KOTHNER: Nun, Meister, wenn's gefällt,
werd' das Gemerk bestellt.—
Wähl der Herr einen heil'gen Stoff?

WALTHER: Was heilig, mir,
der Liebe Panier
schwing' und sing' ich, mir zu Hoff'.

KOTHNER: Das gilt uns weltlich.
Drum allein,
Merker Beckmesser schliesst euch ein!

BECKMESSER: (aufstehend und dem Gemerk zu schreitend). Ein sau'res Amt und heut' zumal;
wohl giebt's mit der Kreide manche Qual.—
Herr Ritter, wisst:
Sixtus Beckmesser Merker ist;
hier im Gemerk
verrichtet er still sein strenges Werk,
Sieben Fehler giebt er euch vor,
die merkt er mit der Kreide dort an:
wenn er über sieben Fehler verlor,
dann versang der Herr Rittersmann.—
Gar fein er hört;
doch dass er euch den Muth nicht stört,

BECKMESSER: You praise him, Master Vogelgesang,
That from the bird's instruction he sang?

KOTHNER: (aside, to the Masters) What think you, Masters? shall I proceed?
I fear this gallant will not succeed.

SACHS: The affair shall soon be sifted:
If he's gifted with true Art
And treats it as he ought,
What does it matter where he's taught?

KOTHNER: Are you prepared, before this throng,
To straight produce a Master-Song,
With music set correctly,
And sing it us directly?

WALTER: What winter night.
What wood so bright.
What book and Nature brought me,
What Poet-Songs of magic might
Mysteriously have taught me,
On horses' tramp,
On field and camp,
On knights arrayed
For war parade,
My mind exerted its powers;
So not life's highest prize
I must convert to song.
Each word and tone, my own alone,
I will attempt to sing you:—
A Master Song, if such it be,
My Masters, I will bring you.

BECKMESSER: Can any one trace his meaning?

VOGELGESANG: Good sooth, he's bold!

NACHTIGAL: Peculiar case!

KOTHNER: Now, Masters, if you will,
The Marker's place we'll fill.
What sacred theme do you choose, sir knight?

WALTER: My sacred treasure is
The banner of love,
Swung and sung to my delight!

KOTHNER: Secular be it. Now inside,
Marker Beckmesser, please hide.

BECKMESSER: (rising and going, as if reluctantly, to the Marker's box). Unpleasant work, and more so now:
My chalk will harrass you, I know it!
Sir knight, now listen!
Sixtus Beckmesser goes to mark.
Here in this cell
He silently does his duty fiercely.
Seven faults are given you clear:
With chalk on a slate they are scored:
But if more mistakes than seven appear,
Then, sir knight, without hope you are floored.—
My ears are keen;
But as, if what I do were seen,

säh't ihr ihm zu,
so giebt er euch Ruh',
und schliesst sich gar hier ein,—
lässt Gott euch befohlen sein.
(*Er hat sich in das Gemerk gesetzt, streckt mit dem Letzten den Kopf höhnisch freundlich nickend heraus, und zieht den vorderen Vorhang, den zuvor einer der Lehrbuben geöffnet hatte, wieder ganz zusammen, so dass er unsichtbar wird*).

**KOTHNER:** (*hat die von den Lehrbuben aufgehängten "Leges Tabulturae" von der Wand genommen*). Was euch zum Liede Richt' und Schnur,
vernehmt nun aus der Tabulatur.
(*Er liest.*)
"Ein jedes Meistergesanges Bar,
stell' ordentlich ein Gemässe dar
aus unterschiedlichen Gesetzen,
die Keiner soll veletzen.
Ein Gesetz besteht aus zweeen Stollen
die gleiche Melodie haben sollen;
der Stoll' aus etlicher Vers' Gebänd',
der Vers hat seinen Reim am End'.
Darauf so folgt der Abgesang,
der sei auch etlich' Verse lang,
und hab' sein' besondere Melodei,
als nicht im Stollen zu finden sei.
Derlei Gemässes mehre Baren
Soll ein jed' Meisterlied bewahren;
und wer ein neues Lied gedicht',
das über vier der Sylben nicht
eingreift in andrer Meister-Weis',—
des' Lied erwerb' sich Meister-Preis.''
Nun setzt euch in die Singestuhl!

**WALTHER:** Hier in den Stuhl?

**KOTHNER:** Wie's Brauch der Schul'.

**WALTHER:** (*besteigt den Stuhl und setzt sich mit Misbehagen*). Für dich, Geliebte, sei's gethan!

**KOTHNER:** (*sehr laut*). Der Sänger sitzt.

**BECKMESSER:** (*im Gemerk, sehr grell*). Fanget an!

**WALTHER:** (*nach einiger Sammlung*). Fanget an!
So rief der Lenz in den Wald,
dass laut es ihn durchhallt:
und wie in fern'ren Wellen
der Hall von dannen flieht,
von weither nah't ein Schwellen,
das mächtig näher zieht;
es schwillt und schallt,
es tönt der Wald
von holder Stimmen Gemenge;
nun laut und hell
schon nah' zur Stell',
wie wächst der Schwall!
Wie Glockenhall
ertos't des Jubels Gedränge!

You might be curbed.
Be not disturbed;
I hide myself from view:—
So Heaven be kind to you.
(*He has seated himself in the box and with the last words stretches his head out with a scornfully familiar nod, then pulls to the front curtains, which a Prentice has opened for him, so that he becomes invisible.*)

**KOTHNER:** (*taking down the "Leges Tabulaturae," which the Prentices had hung upon the wall*). All that belongs to song mature
Now hear read from the Tabulature.—
(*reads.*)
"Each Master-Singer-created Stave
Its regular measurement must have,
By sundry regulations stated
And never violated.
What we call a 'section' is two Stanzas;
Nor each the self-same melody answers:
A Stanza several times doth blend,
And each line with a rhyme must end.
Then come we to the 'After-Song,'
Which must be also some lines long,
And have its especial melody,
Which from the other must diff'rent be.
So Staves and Sections of such measure
A Master-Song may have at pleasure.
He who a new song can outpour,
Which in four syllables—not more—
Another strain doth plagiarize.
He may obtain the Master Prize.''—
Now sit you on the Singer's stool!

**WALTER:** Here, on this stool?

**KOTHNER:** It is the rule.

**WALTER:** (*mounting the stool, with dissatisfaction*). For you, beloved, it will be done.

**KOTHNER:** (*loudly*). The Singer sits!

**BECKMESSER:** (*from his box, very harshly*). Do begin!

**WALTER:** (*after a short consideration*). Now begin!—
So the Spring cries through woodlands,
And makes them loudly ring:
Then, as to distance urging,
The echoes ripple there,
From far there comes a surging
That swells with intense power:
It booms and bounds,
The forest sounds
With thousand heavenly voices;
Now loud and clear,
Approaching near,
The murmurs steal
Like bells that peal;

Der Wald,
wie bald
antwortet' er dem Ruf,
der neu ihm Leben schuf,
stimmte an
das süsse Lenzes-Lied!
(*Man hat aus dem Gemerk wiederholt unmuthige Seufzer des Merkers, und heftiges Anstreichen mit der Kreide vernommen. Auch Walther hat es bemerkt, und fährt, dadurch für eine kurze Weile gestört, fort.*)
In einer Dornenhecken,
von Neid und Gram verzehrt,
musst' er sich da verstecken,
der Winter, Grimm-bewehrt:
von dürrem Laub umrauscht
er lauert da und lauscht,
wie er das frohe Singen
zu Schaden könnte bringen.—
(*Unmuthig vom Stuhle aufsteigend.*)
Doch: fanget an!
So rief es mir in die Brust,
als noch ich von Liebe nicht wusst.
Da fühlt' ich's tief sich regen,
als weckt' es mich aus dem Traum;
mein Herz mit bebenden Schlägen
erfüllte des Busen's Raum:
das Blut, es wall't
mit Allgewalt,
geschwellt von neuem Gefühle;
aus warmer Nacht
mit Uebermacht
schwillt mir zum Meer
der Seufzer Heer
in wildem Wonne Gewühle:
die Brust
mit Lust
antwortet sie dem Ruf,
der neu ihr Leben schuf:
stimmt nun an
das hehre Liebes-Lied!

**BECKMESSER:** (*der immer unruhiger geworden, reisst den Vorhang auf*). Seid ihr nun fertig?

**WALTHER:** Wie fraget ihr?

**BECKMESSER:** (*die ganz mit Kreidestrichen bedeckte Tafel heraushaltend*). Mit der Tafel ward ich fertig schier.
(*Die Meister müssen lachen.*)

**WALTHER:** Hört doch! Zu meiner Frauen Preis
gelang' ich jetzt erst mit der Weis'.

**BECKMESSER:** (*das Gemerk verlassend*). Singt, wo ihr wollt! Hier habt ihr verthan—
Ihr Meister, schaut die Tafel euch an:
so lang' ich leb', ward's nicht erhört:
ich glaubt's nicht, wenn ihr's all' auch schwört!
(*Die Meister sind im Aufstand durcheinander.*)

**WALTHER:** Erlaubt ihr's, Meister, dass er mich stört?
Blieb' ich von Allen ungehört?

Exultant Nature rejoices!
This call,
How all
The wood makes an answer
As life again awakes,
Pouring forth
A tender song of Spring!—
(*During this, repeated groans of discouragement and scratchings of the chalk are heard from the Marker. Walter hears them also, and after a momentary pause of discomposure, continues.*)
There, like a hiding craven,
torn with hate and envy,
A thorny hedge his haven,
Sits Winter, all forlorn.
In withered leaves arrayed
His lurking head is laid;
He seeks the joyous singing
To sorrow to be bringing.—
(*Rising from the stool in displeasure.*)
But—"Now begin!"
So cried a voice in my breast
Before I guessed anything of love;
There stirred a deep emotion
And waked me, as I had slept:
My heart with throbbing commotion
My bosom's restraint overlept:
My blood did course
With giant force,
To novel sensations soaring;
From warmth of night
With boundless might
Sighs hurried me
Towards the sea,
The pent-up passion outpouring
The call
How all
My breast makes an answer,
As it takes life anew,
Pouring forth
A glorious lay of love!

**BECKMESSER:** (*who has grown still more restless, tears open the curtains*). Is it nearly finished?

**WALTER:** What means the call?

**BECKMESSER:** (*holding out the slate completely covered with chalk marks*). I've finished with the slate, that's all!
(*The Masters cannot restrain their laughter*).

**WALTER:** Yet hear! My lady's praise to ring
I ought to sing my second verse.

**BECKMESSER:** (*leaving his box*). Sing where you will! Here you're finished.—
My Masters, see the slate, everyone:
The likes of this I never knew;
I'd credit no man's oath, to that!
(*The Masters are in a commotion.*)

**WALTER:** Do you let him, Masters, plague me so?
Shall I be heard by you or not?

POGNER: Ein Wort, Herr Merker, Ihr seid gereizt?

BECKMESSER: Sei Merker fortan, wer darnich geizt, Doch dass der Ritter versungen hat, beleg' ich erst noch vor der Meister Rath. Zwar wird's 'ne harte Arbeit sein: wo beginnen, da wo nicht aus noch ein! Von falscher Zahl, und falschen Gebänd' schweig ich schon ganz und gar; zu kurz, zu lang, wer ein End' da fänd'; Wer meint hier im Ernst einen Bar? Auf "blinde Meinung" klag' ich allein: sagt, konnt' ein Sinn unsinniger sein?

MEHRERE MEISTER: Man ward nicht klug! Ich muss gest h'n Ein Ende konnte Keiner erseh'n.

BECKMESSER: Und dann die Weis'! Welch tolles Gekreis' aus "Abenteuer-" "blau Ritters-porn"-Weis' "hoch Tannen"-und "Stolz Jüngling"-Ton!

KOTHNER: Ja, ich verstand gar nichts davon!

BECKMESSER: Kein Absatz wo, kein' Coloratei, von Melodei auch nicht eine Spur!

MEHRERE MEISTER: (durcheinander.) Wer nennt das Gesang? 's ward einem bang! Eitel Ohrgeschinder! Gar nichts dahinter!

KOTHNER: Und gar vom Singstuhl ist er gesprungen!

BECKMESSER: Wird erst auf die Fehlerprobe gedrungen? Oder gleich erklärt, dass er versungen?

SACHS: (der vom Beginn an Walther mit zunchmendem Ernste zugehört). Halt! Meister! Nicht so geeilt! Nicht jeder eure Meinung theilt.— Des Ritters Lied und Weise, sie fand ich neu, doch nicht verwirrt; verliess er uns're G'leise, schritt er doch fest und unbeirrt. Wollt ihr nach Regeln messen, was nicht nach eurer Regeln Lauf, der eig'nen Spur vergessen, sucht davon erst die Regeln auf!

BECKMESSER: Aha! Schon recht! Nun hört ihr's doch; den Stümpern öffnet Sachs ein Loch, da aus und ein nach Belieben ihr Wesen leicht sie trieben. Singet dem Volk auf Markt und Gassen; hier wird nach dem Regeln nur eingelassen.

POGNER: One word, friend Marker! You're somewhat wroth?

BECKMESSER: Be Marker he who likes henceforth, But that this man is quite out-sung You can decide among yourselves. 'Faith! it is somewhat hard to show The faults when there's nor top nor toe. To laws of metric accent defied I gave no heed at all; Too short-too long—, I never spied an end; Who'd think it was meant for a Stave? Against "clouded meaning" I but inveigh: Could sense be more nonsensical, say?

SEVERAL MASTERS: We were not wise, I must confess: No man could ever guess his meaning.

BECKMESSER: And then the tune! What muddle insane Of "Bold adventure"—"Blue-knight-spur" strain, "High fir-tree" and "Proud youth"-tone!

KOTHNER: Yes, I understood precisely none of it, I own!

BECKMESSER: Not one full close, no grace-notes you see! And not a trace of melody!

SEVERAL MASTERS: (to one another). Who'd call that a song? It is shockingly wrong: It is but empty chatter, No meaning nor matter!

KOTHNER: And from the seat he has risen unheeding!

BECKMESSER: To weigh the mistakes is our next proceeding; Have you all agreed on his failure?

SACHS: (who listened to Walter from the first with serious interest). Stay, Master! Not quite so fast! Not all have passed like opinion— The song you've so derided To me is new, but not confused: Though it was not guided by us His course was firm, as though well used. One way you measure solely A work that your rules do not fit; Resign your own views wholly, Some other rules apply to it.

BECKMESSER: Aha! That's fine! Just listen, Sachs opens a gap for fools that way, Where in and out at pleasure Their minds a course can measure. Let in the streets the rabble holloa; Here must we at least some discipline follow.

SACHS: Herr Merker, was doch solch ein Eifer? Was doch so wenig Ruh'? Eu'r Urtheil, dünkt mich, wäre reifer, hörtet ihr besser zu. Darum, so komm' ich jetzt zum Schluss, dass den Junker zu End' man hören muss.

BECKMESSER: Der Meister zunft, die ganze Schul' gegen den Sachs da sind wie Null.

SACHS: Verhüt' es Gott, was ich begehr', dass da nicht nach den Gesetzen wär'. Doch da nun steht's geschrieben, "der Merker werde so bestellt, dass weder Hass noch Lieben "das Urtheil trübe, das er fällt." Geht der nun gar auf Freiers-Füssen, wie sollt' er da die Lust nicht büssen, den Nebenbuhler auf dem Stuhl' zu schmähen vor der ganzen Schul'? (Walther flammt auf.)

NACHTIGALL: Ihr geht zu weit!

KOTHNER: Persönlichkeit!

POGNER: (zu den Meistern). Vermeidet, Meister, Zwist und Streit.

BECKMESSER: Ei, was kümmert's doch Meister Sachsen, auf was für Füssen ich geh'? Liess' er drob' lieber Sorge ich wachsen, dass nichts mir drück' die Zeh'! Doch seit mein Schuster ein grosser Poet, gar übel es um mein Schuhwerk steht! da seht, wie es schlappt, und überall klappt! All' seine Vers' und Reim' liess' ich ihm gern daheim, Historien, Speil' und Schwänke dazu, brächt' er mir morgen die neuen Schuh'!

SACHS: Ihr mahnt mich da gar recht: doch schickt sich's, Meister, sprecht, dass, find' ich selbst dem Eseltreiber ein Sprüchlein auf die Sohl', dem hochgelahrten Herrn Stadtschreiber ich nichts d'rauf schreiben soll? Das Sprüchlein, das eu'r würdig sei, mit all' meiner armen Poeterei fand ich noch nicht zur Stund; doch wird's wohl jetzt mir kund wenn ich des Ritters Lied gehört:— d'rum sing' er nun weiter ungestört! (Walther, in grosser Aufregung, stellt sich auf den Singstuhl.)

SACHS: Friend Marker, why in such a flutter? Wherefore so angry, pray? A riper judgment you might utter If better heed you'd pay. And so, to speak my final word, The young knight to the end must be heard.

BECKMESSER: The Master's Guild, the school and all, Weighed against Sachs' word must fall.

SACHS: The Lord forbid I should demand Anything contrary to our law's command. But surely there it is written: "The Marker shall be chosen so, By prejudice unbitten, That he may show no bias. If this one turns his steps to wooing Can he refrain from doing a wrong. To bring to shame before all the school His rival yonder on the stool? (Walter flames up.)

NACHTIGAL: You go too far!

KOTHNER: You are too free!

POGNER: (to the Masters). I pray you, Masters, cease this bickering.

BECKMESSER: Hey! Why does Master Sachs need to mention, Which way may my steps be turned? With the state of my solo his attention Might be better concerned! But since my shoemaker follows the Muse, It fares ill with my boots and shoes. Just look, how they're split! See, here's a great slit! All of his verse and rhyme I would declare sublime; His dramas, plays, his farces and all, If with my new pair of shoes he'd call.

SACHS: (scratching his head). I fear you have me there: But, Master, if it is fair That on the merest boor's shoe-leather I frame some little verse, I ask you, worthy town-clerk, whether You should not have the same? A motto such as you require. With all my poetic fire I've not yet hit upon: But it will come. When I have heard the knight's song through: So let him sing on without delay! (Walter much put out, remounts the Singer's seat.)

## Act I

**DIE MEISTER:** Genug! Zum Schluss!

**SACHS:** (*zu Walther*). Singt, dem Herrn Merker zum Verdruss!

**BECKMESSER:** (*holt, während Walter beginnt, dem Gemerk die Tafel herbei, und hält sie während des Folgenden, von Einem zum Andern sich wendend, zur Prüfung den Meistern vor, die er schliesslich zu einem Kreis um sich zu vereinigen bemüht ist, welchem er immer die Tafel zur Einsicht vorhält*). Was sollte man da noch hören?
Wär's nicht nur uns zu bethören?
Jeden der Fehler gross und klein, sehr genau auf der Tafel ein.—
"Falsch Gebänd," "unredbare Worte,"
"Kleb-Sylben," hier "Laster" gar;
"Aequivoca," "Reim am falschen Orte,"
"verkehrt," "verstellt" der ganze Bar;
Ein "Flickgesang" hier zwischen den Stollen;
"blinde Meinung" allüberall;
"unklare Wort," "Differenz," hie "Schrollen,"
da "falscher Athem," hier "Überfall."
Ganz unverständliche Melodei
Aus allen Tönen ein Mischgebrau'!
Scheu'tet ihr nicht das Ungemach, Meister, zählt mir die Fehler nach!
Verloren hätt' er schon mit dem acht',
doch so weit wie der hat's noch Keiner gebracht:
wohl über fünzig, schlect gezählt!
Sagt, ob ihr euch den zum Meister wählt?

**DIE MEISTER:** (*durcheinander*). Ja wohl, so ist's! Ich seh' es recht!
Mit dem Herrn Ritter steht es schlecht.
Mag Sachs von ihm halten, was er will,
hier in der Singschul' schweig' er still!
Bleibt einem Jeden doch unbenommen,
wen er sich zum Genossen begehrt?
Wär' uns der erste Best' wilkommen,
was blieben die Meister dann werth?—
Hei! Wie sich der Ritter da quält!
Der Sachs hat ihn sich erwählt.—
's ist ärgerlich gar! D'rum macht ein End'!
Auf, Meister, stimmt und erhebt die Händ'!

**POGNER:** (*für sich*). Ja wohl, ich seh's, was mir nicht recht:
mit meinem Junker steht es schlecht!
Weiche' ich hier der Übermacht,
mir ahnet, dass mir's Sorge macht.
Wie gern säh' ich ihn angenommen,
als Eidam wär' er mir gar werth;

---

**THE MASTERS:** Enough! Conclude!

**SACHS:** (*to Walter*). Sing, despite the Markers' angry mood!

**BECKMESSER:** (*as Walter recommences, fetches out his board from the box and shows it, during the following, first to one and then to another, to convince the Masters, whom he at last gathers into a circle round him while he continues to exhibit his slate*). What rubbish is this to shock us?
He surely means to mock us!
Every fault, both grave and slight, I have marked on the board.—
"Faulty verse"—"Unsingable phrases"—
"Word-clippings" and "Vices" grave—
"Equivocal"—"Rhymes in wrong places"—
"Reversed"—"Displaced" is all the Stave.
A "Patch-work-Song" between the two verses
"Clouded meaning" in every part—
"Uncertain words," then a "Change," that worse is—
There's "Breath ill-managed"—here's sudden start"—
"Incomprehensible melody"—
A hotch-potch, made of all tones that be.
It you do not halt at such toil, Masters, count after me each fault.
Already with the eighth he was spent,
But so far as this sure none ever went!
Well over fifty, roughly told.
Say, would you hold this man a Master?

**THE MASTERS:** (*to one another*). Ah yes, that's true! it is plain indeed
That this young knight cannot succeed
By Sachs he may be thought a genius.
But in our singing-school he's nothing.
Who should in justice remain neglected,
If this novice were made a Master?
If all the world's to be elected,
What good were the Masters' high grade?
Ha! look how the knight is enraged!
Hans Sachs on his side has engaged.—
It is really too bad! Quick, make an end!
Up, Masters, speak and your hands extend!

**POGNER:** (*aside*). Ah yes, I see! it is sad indeed:
My poor young knight will scarcely succeed!
Should I retract my first decree,
I fear there'd be sad results.
I'd like to see him no more neglected;
My kinship he would not degrade:

---

nenn' ich den Sieger nun willkommen,
wer weiss, ob ihn mein Kind begehrt!
Gesteh' ich's, dass mich das quält
ob Eva den Meister wählt!

**WALTHER:** (*in übermüthig verzweifelten Begeisterung, hoch auf dem Singstuhl aufgerichtet, und auf die unruhig einander sich bewegenden Meister abblickend*). Aus finst'rer Dornenhecken
Die Eule rauscht' hervor,
thät rings mit Kreischen wecken
der Raben heis'ren Chor:
in nächt'gem Heer zu Hauf
wie krächzen all' da auf,
mit ihren Stimmen, den hohlen,
die Elstern, Kräh'n und Dohlen!
Auf da steigt
mit gold'nem Flügelpaar
ein Vogel wunderbar:
sein strahlend hell Gefieder
licht in den Lüften blinkt;
schwebt selig hin und wieder,
zu Flug und Flucht mir winkt.
Es Schwillt das Herz
von süssem Schmerz,
der Noth entwachsen Flügel;
es schwingt sich auf
zum kühnen Lauf,
zum Flug durch die Luft
aus der Städte Gruft,
dahin zum heim'schen Hügel;
dahin zur grünen Vogelweid',
wo Meister Walther einst mich freit';
da sing' ich hell und hehr
der liebsten Frauen Ehr':
auf da steigt,
ob Meister-Kräh'n ihm ungeneigt,
das stolze Minne-Lied,—
Ade! ihr Meister, hienied'!
(*Er verlässt mit einer stolz verächtlichen Gebärde den Stuhl und wendet sich zum Fortgehen.*)

**SACHS:** (*Walther's Gesang folgend*). Ha, welch' ein Muth!
Begeist'rungs-Gluth!—
Ihr Meister, schweight doch und hört!
Hört, wenn Sachs euch beschwört!—
Herr Merker da! gönnt doch nur Ruh'!
Lasst And're hören! gebt das nur zu!
Umsonst! All eitel Trachten!
Kaum vernimmt man sein eigen Wort!
Des Junkers will Keiner achten:—
das heiss' ich Muth, singt der nock fort!
Das Herz auf dem rechten Fleck:
ein wahrer Dichter-Reck!
Mach' ich, Hans Sachs, wohl Vers' und Schuh',
ist Ritter der une Poet dazu.

**DIE LEHRBUBEN:** (*welche längst sich die Hände rieben und von der Bank aufsprangen, schliessen jetzt gegen das Ende wieder ihren Reihen und tanzen um das Gemerk.*) Glück auf zum Meistersingen,

---

And when the victor is elected,
Who knows if he will please my child?
Some trouble I presage,
For Eva can I engage?

**WALTER:** (*in wild and desperate enthusiasm, standing erect in the singer's seat and looking down on the commotion of the Masters*).
From gloomy thicket breaking
Behold the screech-owl swoop,
With circling flight awaking
The raven's croaking troop!
In sombre ranks they rise
And utter piercing cries;
With voices hoarse and hollow
The dawns and magpies follow!
Up then soars,
By golden pinions stirred,
A wondrous lovely bird.
Each brightly glowing feather
Gleams in the glorious day;
It signs me here and there
To float and flee away.
The swelling heart,
With pleasing smart,
Sore need supplied with wings;
It mounts in flight
To giddy height.
From the city's tomb,
Through heaven's pure dome,
To hills of home it goes.
Towards the verdant Vogelweid'
Where Master Walter lived and died;
And there I'll rightly raise
In song my lady's praise:
Up shall soar,
When raven-Masters croak no more,
My noble loving lay.—
Farewell, Masters, for always!
(*With a gesture of proud contempt he leaves the Singer's seat and quits the building.*)

**SACHS:** (*following Walter's song*). Ha! what a flow
Of genius' glow!—
My Masters, now give over!
Listen, when Sachs implores!
Friend Marker, there! grant us some peace!
Let others listen!—Why don't you cease?—
No use! A vain endeavor!
I can scarcely hear my own voice.
They'll never heed the young fellow.
He's bold indeed to persevere!
His heart must be placed aright:
A true-born poet-knight!
Hans Sachs may make both voice and shoe;
He is a knight and a poet too.

**PRENTICES:** (*who have been rubbing their hands in glee and jumping up from their bench, towards the end, take hands and dance in a ring round the Marker's box*).
God speed your Master-singing.
And may you soon be winning the

---

mögt ihr euch das Kränzlein erschwingen:
Das Blumenkränzlein aus Seiden fein,
wird das dem Herrn Ritter beschieden sein?

**BECKMESSER:** Nun, Meister, kündet's an!
(*Die Mehrzahl hebt die Hände auf.*)

**ALLE MEISTER:** Versungen und verthan!
(*Alles geht in Aufregung auseinander; lustiger Tumult der Lehrbuben, welche sich des Gemerkes und der Meisterbänke bemächtigen, wodurch Gedränge und Durcheinander der nach dem Ausgange sich wendenden Meister entsteht.—Sachs, der allein im Vordergrunde verblieben, blickt noch gedankenvoll nach dem leeren Singestuhl; als die Lehrbuben auch diesen erfassen, und Sachs darob mit humoristisch unmuthiger Gebärde sich abwendet, fällt der Vorhang.*)

---

prize:
The wreath of flowers in silk so bright,
I hope it may fall to your lot, sir knight!

**BECKMESSER:** Now Masters, give it your tongue!
(*Most of them hold up their hands.*)

**ALL THE MASTERS:** Rejected and outsung!
(*General confusion, augmented by the Prentices, who shoulder the benches and Marker's box, causing hindrance and disorder to the Masters who are crowding to the door. Sachs remains alone in front, looking pensively at the empty seat: when the boys remove this too, he turns away with a humorous gesture of discouragement, and the curtain falls.*)

---

# ■ ACT II

*Die Bühne stellt im Vordergrunde eine Strasse in Längendurschschnitten dar, welche in der Mitte von einer schmalen Gasse, nach dem Hintergrunde zu krumm abbiegend, durchschnitten wird, so dass sich in Front zwei Eckhäuser darbieten, von denen das eine, reichere, rechts—das Haus Pogner's, das andere, einfachere—links—das des Hans Sachs ist.—Zu Pogner's Hause führt von der vorderen Strasse aus eine Treppe von mehreren Stufen vertiefte Thür, mit Steinsitzen in den Nischen. Zur Seite ist der Raum, ziemlich nah an Pogner's Hause, durch eine dickstämmige Linde abgegränzt; grünes Gesträuch umgiebt sie am Fuss, vor welchem auch eine Steinbank angebracht ist.—Der Eingang zu Sachsen's Haus ist ebenfalls nach der vorderen Strasse zu gelegen: eine getheilte Ladenthüre führt hier unmittelbar in die Schusterwerkstatt; dicht dabei steht ein Fliederbaum, dessen Zweige bis über den Laden hereinängen. Nach der Gasse zu hat das Haus noch zwei Fenster, von welchen das eine zur Werkstatt, das andere zu einer dahingterliegenden Kammer gehört. Alle Häuser, namentlich auch die der engeren Gasse, müssen praktikabel sein.*

*Heiterer Sommerabend, im Verlaufe der ersten Auftritte allmählich einbrechende Nacht.*

---

# ■ ACT II

*The stage represents in front the section of a street running across, intersected in the middle by a narrow alley which winds crookedly towards the back, so that in C are two corner houses, of which one, a handsome one R, is that of Pogner, the other, simpler L, is Sachs's shop.—A flight of several steps leads up to Pogner's door; porch sunk in, with stone seats. At side R a lime tree shades the place before the house; green shrubs at its foot, surrounding a stone seat.—The entrance to Sachs's house is also towards the street; a divided door leads into the cobbler's workshop; close by, an elder-tree spreads its boughs over it. Two windows, one of the workshop, the other of an inner chamber, looking on to the valley. All houses in both street and alley must be practicable.*

*Genial summer evening; during the first scene, night gradually closes.*

---

*David ist darüber her, die Fensterläden nach de Gasse zu von aussen zu schliessen. Andere Lehrbuben thun das Gleiche bei andern Häusern.*

**LEHRBUBEN:** (*während der Arbeit*). Johannistag! Johannistag! Blumen und Bänder so viel man mag!

**DAVID:** (*für sich*). "Das Blumenkränzlein von Seiden fein, mögt' es mir balde beschieden sein!"

**MAGDALENE:** (*ist mit eniem Korbe am Arme aus Pogner's Haus bekommen und sucht David unbemerkt sich zu nähern*). Bst! David!

**DAVID:** (*nach der Gasse zu sich unwendend*). Ruft ihr schon wieder?
Singt allein eure dummen Lieder!

**LEHRBUBEN:** David, was soll's? Wär'st nicht so stolz, schaut'st besser um, wär'st nicht so dumm! "Johannistag! Johannistag!" Wie der nur die Jungfer Lene nicht kennen mag!

**MAGDALENE:** David! hör' doch! Kehr' dich zu mir!

**DAVID:** Ach, Jungfer Lene! Ihr seid hier?

**MAGDALENE:** (*auf ihren Korb deutend*). Bring' dir was Gut's! schau' nur hinein! Das soll für mein lieb' Schätzel sein.—
Erst aber schnell, wie ging's mit dem Ritter?
Du riethest ihm gut? Er gewann den Kranz?

**DAVID:** Ach, Jungfer Lene! Da steht's bitter; der hat verthan und versungen ganz!

**MAGDALENE:** Versungen? Verthan?

**DAVID:** Was geht's euch nur an?

**MAGDALENE:** (*den Korb, nach welchem David die Hand ausstreckt, heftig zurückziehend*). Hand von der Taschen! Nichts da zu naschen!— Hilf Gott! Unser Junker verthan!— (*Sie geht mit Geberden der Trostlosigkeit nach dem Hause zurück.*)
(*David sich ihr verblüfft nach*).

**DIE LEHRBUBEN:** (*welche unbemerkt näher geschlichen waren, gelauscht hatten und sich jetzt, wie glückwünschend. David präsentiren*). Heil, Heil zur Eh' dem jungen Mann! Wie glücklich hat er gefreit'! Wir hörten's All', und sahen's an;

---

*David is putting up the shutters outside. Other Prentices are doing the same for other houses.*

**PRENTICES:** (*as they work*). Midsummer day! Midsummer day! Flowers and ribbons in goodly display!

**DAVID:** (*aside*). "The wreath of flowers in silk so fine, Would that tomorrow it might be mine!"

**MAGDALENA:** (*coming out of Pogner's house with a basket on her arm and seeking to approach David unperceived*). Hist! David!

**DAVID:** (*turning towards the alley*). Whom are you calling? Get along with your foolish squalling!

**PRENTICES:** David, what cheer? Why so severe? Turn round your skull, If you're not dull! "Midsummer day! Midsummer day!" And he can't see Mistress Lena right in his way!

**MAGDALENA:** David, listen! Turn round, my dear.

**DAVID:** Ah, Mistress Lena! You are here?

**MAGDALENA:** (*pointing to her basket*). Here's something nice; peep in and see it! It is all for my dear lad to eat.— Tell me though first, what of Sir Walter? You counselled him well? Has the crown been won?

**DAVID:** Ah, Mistress Lena, how I falter! He was outsung and declared outdone.

**MAGDALENA:** Rejected! Outdone!

**DAVID:** What ails you, dear one?

**MAGDALENA:** (*snatching the basket away from David's outstretched hand*). Hands off the basket! Dare you to ask it?— Good luck! Our chevalier outdone! (*She hastens back into the house, wringing her hands in despair.*)
(*David looks after her dumbfounded.*)

**PRENTICES:** (*who have stolen near and overheard, now advance to David as if congratulating him*). Hail to the Prentice and his bride! How well his wooing speeds! We all have heard and seen beside: She upon whom he feeds

# Act II

der er sein Herz geweiht,
für die er lässt sein Leben,
die hat ihm den Korb nicht gegeben.

**DAVID:** (*auffahrend*). Was steht ihr hier faul?
Gleich haltet eu'r Maul!

**DIE LEHRBUBEN:** (*David umtanzend*). Johannistag! Johannistag!
Da freit ein Jeder wie er mag.
Der Meister freit'!
Der Bursche freit'!
Da gibt's Geschlamb' und Geschlumbfer!
Der Alte freit
die junge Maid
der Bursche die alte Jumbfer!—
Juchhei! Juchhei! Johannistag!
(*David bört im Begriff, wüthend drein zu schlagen, als Sachs, der aus der Gasse hervorgekommen, dazwischen tritt. Die Buben fahren auseinander.*)

**SACHS:** Was gibt's? Treff ich dich wieder am Schlag?

**DAVID:** Nicht ich! Schandlieder singen die.

**SACHS:** Hör nicht d'rauf! Lerns' besser wie sie!—
Zur Ruh'! in's Haus! Schliess' und mach' Licht!

**DAVID:** Hab' ich noch Singstund'?

**SACHS:** Nein, singst nicht!
Zur Straf' für dein heutig' frech Erdreisten.—
Die neuen Schuh' steck' auf den Leisten!
(*Sie sind Beide in die Werkstatt eingetreten und geben durch innere Thüren ab. Die Lehrbuben haben sich ebenfalls zerstreut.*)
(*Pogner und Eva, wie vom Spaziergange beimkebrend, die Tochter leicht am Arme des Vaters eingehenkt, sind beide schweigsam und in Gedanken die Gasse heraufgekommen.*)

**POGNER:** (*noch auf der Gasse, durch eine Klinze im Fensterladen von Sachsen's Werkstatt spähend*). Lass seh'n, ob Nachbar Sachs zu Haus?—
Gern spräch' ich ihn. Trät' ich wohl ein?
(*David kommt mit Licht aus der Kammer, setzt sich damit an den Werktisch am Fenster and macht sich über die Arbeit her.*)

**EVA:** Er scheint daheim: kommt Licht heraus.

**POGNER:** Thu' ich's?—Zu was doch!—Besser, nein!
(*Er wendet sich ab.*)
Will Einer Selt'nes wagen,
was liess' er da sich sagen?—
(*Nach einigem Sinnen*).
War er's nicht, der meint', ich ging zu weit?
Und blieb ich nicht im Geleise,
war's nicht in seiner Weise?—
Doch war es vielleicht auch—Eitel-

Within his heart's true casket,
Has gone and refused him the basket!

**DAVID:** (*flying out*). Be off with you, boys!
Give over your noise!

**PRENTICES:** Midsummer day! Midsummer day!
All go a-courting as they may.
The Masters woo,
The workmen too,
Old folks as well as the babbies!
And graybeards grim
Wed maidens slim,
Young fellows wed ancient spinsters.—
Hooray! Hooray! Midsummer day!
(*David is about to fly at the boys in his rage, when Sachs, who has come down the alley, steps between them. The Prentices separate.*)

**SACHS:** What now? Are you again in a fray?

**DAVID:** Not I! You sang a mocking stave.

**SACHS:** Pay no heed: show how to behave!—
Get in! To bed! Shut up and light!

**DAVID:** Have I to sing, sir?

**SACHS:** Not tonight!
As punishment for today's offending
Put all these shoes on the lasts for mending.
(*Both go into the workshop and exit through an inner door. The Prentices have also dispersed.*)
(*Pogner and Eva, as if returning from a walk, come silently and thoughtfully down the alley, the daughter leaning on her father's arm.*)

**POGNER:** (*still in the alley, peeping through a chink in Sachs' shutter*). Let's see if Sachs is in tonight:
I'd speak with him. Suppose I call?
(*David comes out of the inner room with a light and sits down to work at a bench by the window.*)

**EVA:** He seems at home: I see a light.

**POGNER:** Shall I?—Why should I, after all?
(*Turns away.*)
If strange things I should venture,
Might I not earn his censure?
(*After some reflection.*)
Who said that I went too far? it was he.
Yet if I exceeded our rules,
I have but done as he did!—
But that might be mere vanity.

keit?—
(*Zu Eva.*)
Und Du, mein Kind, du sagst mir nichts?

**EVA:** Ein folgsam Kind, gefragt nur spricht's.

**POGNER:** Wie klug! Wie gut!—
Komm', setz' dich hier
ein' Weil' noch auf die Bank zu mir.
(*Er setzt sich auf die Steinbank unter der Linde*).

**EVA:** Wird's nicht zu kühl?
's war heut' gar schwül.

**POGNER:** Nicht doch, 's ist mild und labend;
gar lieblich lind der Abend.
(*Eva setzt sich, beklommen.*)
Das deutet auf den schönsten Tag,
der morgen dir soll scheinen.
O Kind, sagt dir kein Herzensschlag,
welch' Glück dich morgen treffen mag,
wenn Nürenberg, die ganze Stadt
mit Bürgern und Gemeinen,
mit Zünften, Volk und hohem Rath
vor dir sich soll vereinen,
dass du den Preis,
das edle Reis,
ertheilest als Gemahl
dem Meister deiner Wahl.

**EVA:** Lieb' Vater, muss es ein Meister sein?

**POGNER:** Hör' wohl: ein Meister deiner Wahl
(*Magdalene erscheint an der Thür und winkt Eva.*)

**EVA:** (*zerstreut*). Ja,—meiner Wahl.—Doch tritt nun ein—
Gleich, Lene, gleich!—zum Abendmahl.

**POGNER:** (*ärgerlich aufstehend*). 's giebt doch keinen Gast?

**EVA:** (*wie oben*). Wohl den Junker?

**POGNER:** (*verwundert*). Wie so?

**EVA:** Sahst ihn heut' nicht?

**POGNER:** (*halb für sich*). Ward sein nicht froh.—
Nicht doch!—Was denn?—Ei! werd' ich dumm?

**EVA:** Lieb Väterchen, komm! Geh', kleid' dich um:

**POGNER:** (*voran in das Haus gehend*). Hm!—Was geht mir im Kopf doch 'rum?
(*Ab.*)

**MAGDALENE:** (*heimlich*). Hast was heraus?

**EVA:** (*ebenso*). Blieb still und stumm.

**MAGDALENE:** Sprach David; meint', er habe verthan.

**EVA:** Der Ritter?—Hilf Gott, was fing' ich an!
Ach, Lene! die Angst: wo 'was erfahren?

(*To Eva.*)
And you, my child, your thoughts are hidden?

**EVA:** Good children only speak when bidden.

**POGNER:** How sharp! How good!—come now,
And sit beside me on this bench.
(*Sits on the stone seat under the linden tree.*)

**EVA:** Too chill to stay;
It was close all day.

**POGNER:** Oh no! it is mild and charming;
The evening air is calming.
(*Eva sits, nervously.*)
A token of a fair tomorrow
And brilliant in its weather.
Oh child! does not your heart declare
The joys that tomorrow does prepare,
When Nuremberg, yes, all the town,
Both rich and poor together,
The Guilds, the burghers of renown
Will meet in highest feather,
To see you rise
And give the prize
To him, the Master's head,
To whom you shall be wed?

**EVA:** Dear father, can anyone but a Master win?

**POGNER:** Be sure a Master is your fate.
(*Magdalena appears at the door and signs to Eva.*)

**EVA:** (*disturbed*). Yes—it is my fate.—But now come in—
Yes, Lena, yes!—our suppers wait.

**POGNER:** (*rising vexedly.*) But we have no guests?

**EVA:** (*as before*). Not Sir Walter?

**POGNER:** (*surprised*). Hey, what?

**EVA:** Did you not meet?

**POGNER:** (*half to himself*). I want him not.—
Why no!—What now?—Ah! dare I guess?

**EVA:** Dear father, come in and change your dress.

**POGNER:** (*going into the house before her*). Hum!—What way does my fancy go?
(*exit.*)

**MAGDALENA:** (*secretly*). Why do you wait?

**EVA:** (*the same*). Be still! speak low!

**MAGDALENA:** Saw David—says that he hasn't won.

**EVA:** Sir Walter?—Oh heavens! what's to be done!
Ah, Lena, I quake; who will disclose all?

MAGDALENE: Vielleicht vom Sachs?

EVA: Ach, der hat mich lieb! Gewiss, ich geh' hin.

MAGDALENE: Lass drin nichts gewahren! Der Vater merkt' es, wenn man jetzt blieb'.— Nach dem Mahl: dann hab' ich dir noch 'was zu sagen, was Jemand geheim mir aufgetragen.

EVA: Wer denn? Der Junker?

MAGDALENE: Nichts da! Nein! Beckmesser.

EVA: Das mag 'was Rechtes sein! (*Sie geben in das Haus.*) (*Sachs ist, in leichter Hauskleidung, in die Werkstatt zurückgekommen. Er wendet sich zu David, der an seinem Werktische verblieben ist.*)

SACHS: Zeig' her!—'s ist gut.— Dort an die Thür' rück mir Tisch und Schemel herfür!— Leg' dich zu Bett! Wach' auf bei Zeit, verschlaf' die Dummheit, sei morgen gescheit!

DAVID: (*richtet Tisch und Schemel*). Schafft ihr noch Arbeit?

SACHS: Kümmert dich das?

DAVID: (*für sich*). Was war nur der Lene?—Gott weiss, was! Warum wohl der Meister heute wacht?

SACHS: Was stehts' noch?

DAVID: Schlaft wohl, Meister!

SACHS: Gut' Nacht! (*David geht in die Kammer ab*).

SACHS: (*legt sich die Arbeit zurecht, setzt sich an der Thüre auf den Schemel, lässt dann die Arbeit weider liegen, und lehnt, mit dem Arm auf den geschlossenen Untertheil des Ladens gestüzt, sich zurück*). Wie duftet doch der Flieder so mild, so stark und voll! Mir lös' es weich die Glieder, will, dass ich gern was sagen soll. Was gilt's was ich dir sagen kann? Bin gar ein arm einfältig Mann! Soll mir die Arbeit nicht schmecken, gäb'st, Freund, lieber mich frei: thät' besser das Leder zu strecken, und liess' alle Poeterei!— (*Er versucht wieder zu arbeiten. Lässt ab und sinnt.*) Und doch, 's will halt nicht geh'n.— Ich fühl's—und kann's nicht versteh'n.— kann's nicht behalten,—doch auch nicht vergessen; und fass' ich es ganz,—kann ich's nicht messen. Doch wie auch wollt' ich's fassen

MAGDALENA: Perhaps Hans Sachs?

EVA: Ah, he's fond of me! It is well, I will go.

MAGDALENA: Mind not to expose all! If you stay longer your father will see.— When we've supped: another thing I'll unfold you, A secret which some one has just now told me.

EVA: Who was it? Sir Walter?

MAGDALENA: Not he, no: Beckmesser.

EVA: Worth hearing, I should say! (*They go into the house.*) (*Sachs, in light indoor dress, has re-entered the workshop. He turns to David, who is still at his workbench.*)

SACHS: Come here!—that's right.—There by the door Put my stool and work-bench before.— Then get to bed! Earlier rise; Sleep off your folly, tomorrow be wise!

DAVID: (*arranging bench and stool*). Are you still working?

SACHS: What's that to you?

DAVID: (*aside*). What ailed Magdalena?—I wish I knew!— And why works my Master by this light?

SACHS: Why wait you?

DAVID: Good night, Master!

SACHS: Good night! (*Exit David in the inner room.*)

SACHS: (*arranges his work, sits on his stool at the door and then, laying down his tools again, leans back, resting his arm on the closed lower half of the door*). The elder's scent is waxing So mild, so full and strong! Its charm my limbs relaxing: Words unto my lips would throng.— What boot such thoughts as I can span? I'm but a poor, plain-minded man! When work's despised altogether, You, friend, set me free; But I'd better stick to my leather And let all this poetry be!— (*He tries again to work. Leaves off and reflects.*) And yet—it haunts me still.— I feel, but comprehend ill;— Cannot forget it,—and yet cannot grasp it.— I measure it not, even when I clasp it.— But how then would I gauge it! It was measureless to my mind; No rule could fit it or cage it, Yet there was no fault to find. It seemed so old, yet new in its

was unermesslich mir schien? Kein' Regel wollte da passen, und war doch kein Fehler drin.— Es klang so alt und war so neu,— wie Vogelsang im süssen Mai:— wer ihn hört, und wahnbethört sänge dem Vogel nach, dem bräct' es Spott und Schmach.— Lenzes Gebot, die süsse Noth, die legten's ihm in die Brust: nun sang er, wie er musst'! Und wie er musst', so konnt' er's; das merkt' ich ganz besonders: dem Vogel, der heut' sang, dem war der Schnabel hold gewachsen; macht' er den Meistern bang, gar wohl gefiel er doch Hans Sachsen. (*Eva ist auf die Strasse getreten, hat schüchtern spähend sich der Werkstatt genähert, und steht jetzt unvermerkt an der Thüre bei Sachs.*)

EVA: Gut'n Abend Meister! Noch so fleissig?

SACHS: (*ist angenehm überrascht aufgefahren*). Ei, Kind! Lieb' Evchen? Noch so spät! Und doch, warum so spät noch, weiss ich: die neuen Schuh'

EVA: Wie fehl er räth! Die Schuh' hab' ich noch gar nicht probiert; sie sind so schön, so reich geziert, dass ich sie noch nicht an die Füss' mir getraut.

SACHS: Doch sollst sie morgen tragen als Braut?

EVA: (*hat sich dicht bei Sachs auf den Steinsitz gesetzt*). Wer wärd denn Bräutigam?

SACHS: Weiss ich das?

EVA: Wie wisst denn ihr, ob ich Braut?

SACHS: Ei was! Das weiss die Stadt.

EVA: Ja, weiss es die Stadt. Freund Sachs gute Gewähr dann hat. Ich dacht', er wüsst' mehr.

SACHS: Was sollt' ich wissen?

EVA: Ei seht doch. Werd' ich's ihm sagen müssen? Ich bin wohl recht dumm?

SACHS: Das sagt' ich nicht.

EVA: Dann wär't ihr wohl klug?

SACHS: Das weiss ich nicht.

EVA: Ihr wisst nichts? Ihr sagt nichts?—Ei, Freund Sachs! Jetzt merk' ich wahrlich, Pech is kein Wachs. Ich hätt' euch für feiner gehalten.

chime— Like songs of birds in sweet Maytime:— He who heard And, fancy-stirred, Sought to repeat the strain, But shame and scorn would gain.— Spring's command And gentle hand His soul with this did entrust: He sang because he must! His power rose as needed; That virtue well I heeded. The bird who sang to-day Has got a throat that rightly waxes: Masters may feel dismay, But well content with him Hans Sachs is. (*Eva comes out into the street, peeps shyly towards the workshop and advances unnoticed to the door by Sachs.*)

EVA: Good evening, Master! Still at labor?

SACHS: (*starting up in agreeable surprise*). Ah, child! Sweet Eva! still about? And yet I guess the cause, fair neighbor: The new-made shoes?

EVA: How far you're out! The shoes I have not even tried; They are so fine, so richly made. I dare not confide such gems to my feet.

SACHS: You'll wear them, though, tomorrow as bride?

EVA: (*who has now seated herself on the stone seat by Sachs*). Who is to be bridegroom then?

SACHS: Can I tell?

EVA: How do you know I'm to be bride?

SACHS: Eh, well! Everyone knows.

EVA: Yes, everyone knows. That's proof positive, I suppose. I thought you knew more.

SACHS: What should I know?

EVA: See there! Must I show my meaning? How dull I must be?

SACHS: I say not so.

EVA: Then you must be bright!

SACHS: That I don't know.

EVA: You know nothing—You say nothing? Ah, friend Sachs! I see now clearly: pitch is not wax. I really believed you were sharper.

**SACHS:** Kind!
Beid', Wachs und Pech vertraut mir sind
Mit Wachs strich ich die Seidenfäden,
damit ich die zieren Schuh' dir gefasst:
heut' fass' ich die Schuh' mit dicht'ren Drähten,
da gilt's mit Pech für den derben Gast.

**EVA:** Wer ist denn der? Wohl 'was Rechts?

**SACHS:** Das mein' ich!
Ein Meister stolz auf Freiers Fuss,
denkt morgen zu siegen ganz alleinig:
Herrn Beckmesser's Schuh' ich richten muss.

**EVA:** So nehmt nur tüchtig Pech dazu:
da kleb' er drin, und lass' mir Ruh'!

**SACHS:** Er hofft dich sicher zu ersingen.

**EVA:** Wieso denn der?

**SACHS:** Ein Junggesell;
's giebt deren wenig dort zur Stell'.

**EVA:** Könnt's einem Wittwer nicht gelingen?

**SACHS:** Mein Kind, der wär' zu alt für dich.

**EVA:** Ei was, zu alt! Hier gilt's der Kunst:
wer sie versteht, der werb' um mich!

**SACHS:** Lieb' Evchen! Machst mir blauen Dunst?

**EVA:** Nicht ich! ihr seid's; ihr macht mir Flausen!
Gesteht nur, dass ihr wandelbar;
Gott weiss, wer jetzt euch im Herzen mag hausen!
Glaubt' ich mich doch drin so manches Jahr.

**SACHS:** Wohl, da ich dich gern in den Armen trug?

**EVA:** Ich seh's, 's war nur, weil ihr kinderlos.

**SACHS:** Hatt' einst ein Weib und Kinder genug.

**EVA:** Doch starb eure Frau, so wuchs ich gross.

**SACHS:** Gar gross und schön.

**EVA:** Drum dacht' ich aus,
irh nähm't much für Weib und Kind in's Haus.

**SACHS:** Da hätt ich ein Kind und auch ein Weib:
's wär' gar ein lieber Zeitvertreib!
Ja, ja! das hast du dir schön erdacht.

**EVA:** Ich glaub', der Meister mich gar verlacht?
Am End' gar liess' er sich auch gefallen,
dass unter der Nas' ihm weg von Allen
der Beckmesser morgen mich ersäng?

**SACHS:** My dear!
Both pitch and wax are well known here.
With wax I rubbed the silken stitching
With which I sewed your pretty shoes:
The thread for these coarser ones I'm pitching;
It is good enough for a man to use.

**EVA:** Whom do you mean? Some grandee?

**SACHS:** Yes, Marry!
A Master proud, who boldly woos,
Expecting tomorrow all to carry:
For Master Beckmesser I make these shoes.

**EVA:** Then pitch in plenty let there be.
To stick him fast and leave me free.

**SACHS:** He hopes by singing to attain you.

**EVA:** Why should he hope?

**SACHS:** Why should he not?
Few bachelors are on the spot.

**EVA:** Might not a widower hope to gain me?

**SACHS:** My child, I am too old for you.

**EVA:** Ah, stuff—too old! Art is the thing:
Who masters that, is free to woo.

**SACHS:** Dear Eva! Are you flattering?

**EVA:** Not I! It is you who is an imposter!
Admit now, your affections veer;
Heaven knows whom now your heart may foster!
I'd thought it my own this many a year.

**SACHS:** Because in my arms I often carried you?

**EVA:** I see! you had no child of your own.

**SACHS:** I once had wife and children too.

**EVA:** But they are dead and I am grown.

**SACHS:** Grown tall and fair.

**EVA:** It was my idea
That I might fill their places here.

**SACHS:** Then I should have child and also wife:
That were indeed a joy in life!
Yes, that was an idea, I vow!

**EVA:** I think you're trying to mock me now.
In short, it would give you little sorrow,
If under your nose from all tomorrow
This Beckmesser sang me away!

**SACHS:** Wie soll't ich's wehren, wenn's ihm geläng?—
Dem wüsst' allein dein Vater Rath.

**EVA:** Wo so ein Meister den Kopf nur hat!
Käm' ich zu euch wohl, fänd' ich's zu Haus?

**SACHS:** Ach, ja! Hast recht! 's ist im Kopf mir kraus;
hab' heut' manch' Sorg' und Wirr' erlebt:
da mag's dann sein, dass 'was drin klebt.

**EVA:** Wohl in der Singschul'? 's war heut Gebot.

**SACHS:** Ja, Kind: eine Freiung machte mir Noth.

**EVA:** Ja, Sachs! Das hättet ihr gleich soll'n sagen;
plagt' euch dann nicht mit unnützen Fragen.
Nun sagt, wer war's, der Freiung begehrt?

**SACHS:** Ein Junker, Kind, gar unbelehrt.

**EVA:** Ein Junker? Mein, sagt!—und ward er gefreit?

**SACHS:** Nichts da, mein Kind! 's gab gar viel Streit.

**EVA:** So sagt! Erzäht, wie ging es zu?
Macht's euch Sorg', wie liess' mir es Ruh'?—
So bestand er übel und hat verthan?

**SACHS:** Ohne Gnad' versang der Herr Rittersmann.

**MAGDALENE:** (*kommt zum Haus heraus und ruft leise*): Bst! Evchen! Bst!

**EVA:** Ohne Gnade? Wie?
Kein Mittel gäb's, das ihm gedieh'?
Sang er so schlecht, so fehlervoll,
dass nichts mehr zum Meister ihm helfen soll?

**SACHS:** Mein Kind, für den ist Alles verloren,
und Meister wird der in keinem Land;
denn wer als Meister ward geboren,
der hat unter Meistern den' schlimmsten Stand.

**MAGDALENE:** (*näher*). Der Vater verlangt.

**EVA:** So sagt mir noch an,
ob keinen der Meister zum Freund er gewann?

**SACHS:** Das wär' nicht übel?
Freund ihm noch sein!
Ihm, vor dem All' sich fühlten so klein!
Den Junker Hochmuth, lasst ihn laufen,
mag er durch die Welt sich raufen;
was wir erlernt mit Noth und Müh',
dabei lasst uns in Ruh' verschnaufen!
Hier renn' er nichts uns über'n Haufen:
sein Glück ihm anderswo erblüh'!

**SACHS:** If he succeeded what could I say?
It would rest on what your father said.

**EVA:** Where does a master keep his head!
Were I with you could it be found?

**SACHS:** Ah yes! you're right! all my brain turns round;
I've been annoyed and vexed today:
And in my mind some traces stay.

**EVA:** Aye, in the Song-school? You met, I see.

**SACHS:** Yes, child: an election has worried me.

**EVA:** Oh Sachs! but you should at once have said so!
Then my tongue would not have plagued your head so.
Now say, who was it that sought entrance?

**SACHS:** A knight, my child, and quite untaught.

**EVA:** A knight? Dear me!—And did he succeed!

**SACHS:** Why no, my child! we disagreed.

**EVA:** Dear me! how strange! relate it, please.
If you are vexed can I be gay?—
Then he was defeated and baffled quite?

**SACHS:** Truly hopeless the case of the noble knight.

**MAGDALENA:** (*comes to the house door and calls softly*). Hist! Eva! Hist!

**EVA:** Truly hopeless! and why?
Were there no means to help him by?
Sang he so ill, so faultily
He never a Master can hope to be?

**SACHS:** My child, it is a hopeless disaster;
No leader he'll be in any land;
For when one is born to be a Master,
Among other Masters he cannot stand.

**MAGDALENA:** (*approaching*).
Your father awaits.

**EVA:** But tell me the end,
If none of the Masters he won for a friend.

**SACHS:** That is a good joke! friend could we call
One before whom we all felt so small?
My young lord Haughty, let him toddle,
In the world to cool his head.
What we have learned with toil and care,
Let us digest in peace unburied!
Here we must be worried by no one,
So let his fortune shine elsewhere!

EVA: (*erhebt sich heftig*). Ja, anderswo soll's ihm erblüh'n.
als bei euch garst'gen, neid'schen Mannsen;
wo warm die Herzen noch erglüht,
trotz allen tück'schen Meister Hansen!
Ja. Lene! Gleich! ich komme schon!
Was trüg' ich hier für Trost davon?
Da riecht's nach Pech, dass Gott erbarm'!
Brennt' ers lieber, da würd' er doch warm.
(*Sie geht heftig mit Magdelene hinüber und verweilt sehr aufgeregt dort unter der Thüre.*)

SACHS: (*nickt bedeutungsvoll mit dem Kopfe*). Das dacht' ich wohl. Nun heisst's: schaff' Rath!
(*Er ist während des Folgenden damit beschäftigt, auch die obere Ladenthüre so weit zu schliessen, dass sie nur ein wenig Licht noch durchlässt: er selbst verschwindet so fast ganz.*)

MAGDALENE: Hilf Gott! was bliebst du nur so spät?
Der Vater reif.

EVA: Geh' zu ihm ein:
ich sei zu Bett in Kämmerlein.

MAGDALENE: Nicht doch! Hör' nur! Komm' ich dazu?
Beckmesser fand mich: er lässt nicht Ruh',
zur Nacht sollst du dich an's Fenster neigen,
er will dir'was schönes singen und geigen,
mit dem er dich hofft zu gewinnen, das Lied,
ob dir das zu Gefallen gerieth.

EVA: Das fehlte auch noch!—
Käme nur Er!

MAGDALENE: Hast' David geseh'n?

EVA: Was soll mir der?

MAGDALENE: (*halb für sich*). Ich war zu streng; er wird sich grämen.

EVA: Siehst du noch nichts?

MAGDALENE: 's ist als ob Leut' dort kämen.

EVA: Wär' er's?

MAGDALENE: Mach' und komm jetzt hinan!

EVA: Nicht eh'r, bis ich sah den theursten Mann!

MAGDALENE: Ich täusche mich dort: er war es nicht.—
Jetzt komm, sonst merkt der Vater die G'schicht'!

EVA: Ach! meine Angst!

MAGDALENE: Auch lass uns berathen,
wie wir des Beckmesser's uns entladen.

EVA: Zum Fenster gehst du für mich.

---

EVA: (*rising hastily*). Yes, elsewhere, it will shine, I know,
In spite of what your envious pack says;
Some place where hearts still warmly glow
With no deceitful Master Sachses!—
Yes, Lena! Yes! I'm coming, dear!—
Nice consolation I get here!
I smell the pitch, Heaven keep us whole!
Burn it, rather, and warm up your soul.
(*She crosses over hastily with Magdalena and remains in agitation at her own door.*)

SACHS: (*with a meaningful nod of his head*). I thought as much!
Now then they'll chatter!
(*During the following he closes the upper half of his door also, so nearly as only to leave a little crack of light, he himself being quite invisible.*)

MAGDALENA: Good lack! why have you stayed so late?
Your father called.

EVA: Go you instead
And say that I am gone to bed.

MAGDALENA: No, no! Hark now! I have news too?
Beckmesser found me; such a to-do!
Tonight, if you stayed at the window,
He said he would come and serenade you.
The song he intends for your winning he'll sing,
To try if your approval it will bring.

EVA: He need not trouble—Where can he be!

MAGDALENA: Has David been here?

EVA: What's that to me?

MAGDALENA: (*half to herself*). I was too harsh; he's vexed, I fear.

EVA: No one in sight?

MAGDALENA: Someone draws near.

EVA: Is it he?

MAGDALENA: Come; it is time to depart.

EVA: Not till I've seen the man of my heart.

MAGDALENA: I made a mistake, it is not he.
Come in, for fear your father should see.

EVA: What shall I do?

MAGDALENA: We'll hold consultation
As to this Beckmesser's invitation.

EVA: Stand at the window for me.

---

MAGDALENE: Wie ich?—
Das machte wohl David eiferlich?
Er schläft nach der Gassen! Hihi! 's wär fein!—

EVA: Dort hör' ich Schritte.

MAGDALENE: Jetzt komm's, es muss sein!

EVA: Jetzt näher!

MAGDALENE: Du irrst! 's nichts, ich wett'.
Ei, komm! Du musst, bis der Vater zu Bett.
(*Pogner's man hört innen Stimme.*)

POGNER: He! Lene! Eva!

MAGDALENE: 's ist höchste Zeit!
Hörst du's? Komm'! der Ritter ist weit.
*Walther ist die Gasse heraufgekommen; jetzt biegt er um Pogner's Haus herum. Eva, die bereits von Magdalenen am Arm hineingezogen worden war, reisst sich mit einem leisen Schrei los, und stürzt Walthern entgegen.*

EVA: Da ist er!

MAGDALENE: (*hineingehend*).
Nun haben wir's! Jetzt heisst's: gescheit!
(*Ab.*)

EVA: (*ausser sich*). Ja, ihr seid es!
Alles sag' ich,
denn ihr wisst es;
Alles klag' ich,
denn ich weiss es;
ihr seid beides
Held des Preises,
und mein einz'ger Freund!

WALTHER: (*leidenschaftlich*).
Ach, du irrst! Bin nur dein Freund,
doch des Preises
noch nicht würdig,
nicht den Meistern
ebenbürtig;
mein Begeistern
fand Verachten,
und ich weiss es,
darf nicht trachten
nach der Freundin Hand!

EVA: Wie du irrst! Der Freundin Hand,
ertheilt nur sie den Preis,
wie deinen Muth ihr Herz erfand,
reicht sie nur dir das Reis.

WALTHER: Ach nein, du irrst! Der Freudin Hand,
wär' Keinem sie erkoren,
wie sie des Vaters Wille band,
mir wär sie doch verloren.
"Ein Meistersinger muss er sein:
Nur wen ihr krönt, den darf sie frei'n!"
So sprach er festlich zu den Herrn,
kann nicht zurück, möcht' er's auch gern!
Das eben gab' mir Muth;
wie ungewohnt mir alles schien,

---

MAGDALENA: What, I?
It would rouse poor David's jealousy.
He sleeps on the street side. He, he!
what fun!

EVA: I hear a footstep!

MAGDALENA: Come now, let us run!

EVA: It nears us!

MAGDALENA: You're wrong, I'll bet my head.
Do come! You must, till your father's in bed.

POGNER: (*calling within*). Hey! Lena! Eva!

MAGDALENA: No more delay!
Do you hear? Come—your knight's far away.
(*Walter has come up the alley and now turns the corner by Pogner's house. Eva, who is being dragged indoors by Magdalena, tears herself free with a slight cry and rushes towards Walter.*)

EVA: It is he!

MAGDALENA: (*going in*). Now all's up! Be quick, I say!
(*Exit.*)

EVA: (*transported*). It is my true love!
Yes, my own love!
I conceal nothing.
All is known, love:
I reveal all
For I know it:
It is you, love,
Hero-Poet
And my only friend!

WALTER: (*sorrowfully*). Ah,
you're wrong! I'm only your friend;
Not as poet
Masters prize me,
For my station
They despise me:
Inspiration
They can not brook,
And—I know it—
I may not look
To my lady's hand!

EVA: You are wrong! Your lady's hand
Awards the prize alone.
Your courage commands my heart
Be then the wreath your own.

WALTER: Ah, no, you're wrong!
my lady's hand,
Though no one else should gain it,
Upon the terms your father planned
I never may attain it.
"A Master Singer he must be:
None may you wed uncrowned by you."
Thus to the Guild he firmly spoke,
What he has pledged he may not break.
That spurred my heart's desire,
Though strange to me were place

ich sang mit Lieb' und Gluth,
dass ich den Meisterschlag verdien'.
Doch diese Meister!
Ha, diese Meister!
Dises Reim-Gesetze
Leimen und Kleister!
Mir schwillt die Galle,
das Herz mir stockt,
denk' ich der Falle,
darein ich gelockt!—
Fort in die Freiheit!
Dorthin gehör' ich,
da wo ich Meister im Haus!
Soll ich dich frei'n heut',
dich nun beschwör ich,
flieh', un folg' mir hinaus!

**EVA:** (*fasst ihn besänftigend bei der Hand*). Geliebter, spare den Zorn!
's war nur des Nachtwächters Horn.
Unter der Linde
birg' dich geschwinde:
hier kommt der Wächter vorbei.

**MAGDALENE:** (*an der Thüre, leise*). Evchen! 's ist Zeit! mach' dich frei!

**WALTHER:** Du fliehst?

**EVA:** Muss ich denn nicht?

**WALTHER:** Entweichst?

**EVA:** Dem Meistergericht.
(*Sie verschwindet mit Magdalene im Hause.*)

**DER NACHTWAECHTER:** (*ist während dem in der Gasse er- schienen, kommt singend nach vorn, beigt um die Ecke von Pog- ner's Haus und geht nach links zu weiter ab*). "Hört ihr Leut' und lasst euch sagen,
die Glock' hat Zehn geschlagen:
bewahrt das Feuer und auch das Licht,
damit Neimand kein Schad' geschicht!
Lobet Gott den Herrn!"
(*Als er hiermit abgegangen, hört man ihn abermals blasen.*)

**SACHS:** (*welcher hinter der La- denthüre dem Gespräche ge- lauscht, öffnet jetzt, bei eingezo- genem Lampenlicht ein wenig mehr*). Ueble Dinge, die ich da merk':
eine Entführung gar im Werk!
Aufgepasst! das darf nicht sein!

**WALTHER:** (*hinter der Linde*). Käm sie nicht wieder? O der Pein!—
Doch ja! sie kommt dort!—Weh' mir, nein!
Die Alte ist's!—doch aber—ja!

**EVA:** (*ist in Magdalene's Kleid- ung wieder zurückgekommen und geht auf Walther zu*). Das thör'ge Kind: da hast du's! da!
(*Sie sinkt ihm an die Brust.*)

**WALTHER:** O Himmel! Ja! nun wohl ich weiss,
dass ich gewann den Meisterpreis!

---

and folk;
I sang, all love and fire,
And strove to make a Master-stroke.
Oh, but these Masters!
Think of these Masters!
With their cramping rules,
Like clinging pitch-plasters!
I choke with passion.
My heart's unnerved!
Think of the fashion
In which I was served!
Hence, as a rover!
Freedom before me—
Still I'm a Master at home!
As I'm your lover
Now I implore you,
Come, and together we'll roam!

**EVA:** (*taking him soothingly by the hand*). Beloved, govern your wrath!
It is but the watchman goes forth.—
Hide beneath the lime-tree;
Lose no more time! See,
The watchman passes this way!

**MAGDALENA:** (*at the door, soft- ly*). Eva! it is late: come in, I say!

**WALTER:** You fly?

**EVA:** Must I not flee?

**WALTER:** You fear—?

**EVA:** The powers that be!
(*She disappears with Magdalena into the house.*)

**THE WATCHMAN:** (*has mean- while appeared in the alley. He comes forward singing, turns the corner of Pogner's house and exit L.*). "Hark to what I say, good peo- ple,
Strike ten from every steeple.
Put out your fire and dim your light,
That none may come to harm this night.
Praise the Lord of Heaven!"
(*He has by this time gone off, but his horn is still heard.*)

**SACHS:** (*who has listened to the foregoing from behind his shop- door, now opens it a little wider, having shaded his lamp*). Pretty doings now are in hand!
Here's an elopement being planned.
I'm awake! This must not be.

**WALTER:** (*behind the lime tree*). Has she then left me? Woe is me!—
Yet no! who comes here?—Ah, not she!
It is Magdalena—Yet surely!—
You!

**EVA:** (*returns in Magdalena's dress and goes to Walter*). Your foolish child, she's all yours now!
(*She sinks to his breast.*)

**WALTER:** O heaven! here before my eyes
I see indeed the Master-prize!

---

**EVA:** Doch nun kein Besinnen!
Von hinnen! Von hinnen!
O wären wir weit schon fort!

**WALTHER:** Hier durch die Gasse: dort!
finden wir vor dem Thor
Knecht und Rosse vor.
(*Als sich Beide wenden, um in die Gasse einzubeigen, lässt Sachs, nachdem er die Lampe hinter eine Glaskugel gestellt, einen bellen Lichtschein durch die ganz wieder geöffnete Ladenthüre, quer über die Strasse fallen, so dass Eva und Walther sich plötzlich hell beleu- chtet sehen.*)

**EVA:** (*Walther bastig zurückziehend*). O weh', der Schuster! Wenn der uns säh'! Birg' dich! komm' ihm nicht in die Näh'!

**WALTHER:** Welch' and'rer Weg führt uns hinaus?

**EVA:** (*nach rechts deutend*). Dort durch die Strasse: doch der ist kraus,
ich kenn' ihn nicht gut; auch sties- sen wir dort auf den Wächter.

**WALTHER:** Nun denn: durch die Gasse!

**EVA:** Der Schuster muss erst vom Fenster fort.

**WALTHER:** Ich zwing ihm, dass er's verlasse.

**EVA:** Zeig' dich ihm nicht: er kennt dich!

**WALTHER:** Der Schuster?

**EVA:** 's ist Sachs!

**WALTHER:** Hans Sachs? Mein Freund?

**EVA:** Glaub's nicht!
Von dir zu sagen Uebles nur wusst' er.

**WALTHER:** Wie, Sachs? Auch er?—Ich lösch' ihm das Licht!
(*Beckmesser ist, dem Nachtwae- chter in einiger Entfernung na- chschleichend, die Gasse herauf gekommen, hat nach den Fenst- ern von Pogner's Hause gespäht, und an Sachsen's Hause ange- lehnt, zwischen den beiden Fenst- ern einen Steinsitz sich ausge- sucht, auf welchem er sich, immer nur nach dem gegen- überliegenden Fenster aufmerk- sam lugend, niedergelassen hat; jetzt stimmt er eine mitgebrachte Laute.*)

**EVA:** (*Walther zurückhaltend.*) Thu's nicht!—Doch horch!

**WALTHER:** Einer Laute Klang?

**EVA:** Ach, meine Noth!

**WALTHER:** Wie, wird dir bang? Der Schuster, sieh, zog ein das Licht—
so sei's gewagt!

---

**EVA:** Now no more delay!
Let's hasten away!
Oh would that we were gone!

**WALTER:** Here, through this alley: on!
Servants at the gate
Wait with my horses.
(*As they turn to dive into the alley Sachs places his lamp behind a water-globe and sends a bright stream of light through the now wide open door across the street, so that Eva and Walter suddenly find themselves illuminated.*)

**EVA:** (*bastily pulling Walter back*). Ah me! the cobbler! What would he say!
Hide!—keep well out of his way!

**WALTER:** What other road leads to the gate?

**EVA:** (*pointing R*). Round by the street here, but it is not straight;
I know it not well; besides, we should meet
With the watchman.

**WALTER:** Well then, through the alley?

**EVA:** The cobbler must first leave his windowseat.

**WALTER:** I'll force him then. Here's for a sally!

**EVA:** Don't show yourself: he knows you!

**WALTER:** Who is he?

**EVA:** It is Sachs.

**WALTER:** Hans Sachs? my friend?

**EVA:** Not quite!
He is busy with slanders against you.

**WALTER:** What, Sachs? He too?— I'll put out his light!
(*Beckmesser comes up the alley slinking at some distance in the rear of the Watchman. He peers up at Pogner's windows and, leaning against Sachs' house, seeks out a stone seat on which he places him- self, still looking at the upper win- dows, and now he commences to tune a lute he has brought with him.*)

**EVA:** (*restraining Walter*). Wait! Listen now!

**WALTER:** A lute I hear.

**EVA:** What a mishap!

**WALTER:** Why need you fear? The cobbler's light has ceased to glare:
Let's make the attempt!

**EVA:** Weh'! siehst du denn nicht?
Ein And'rer kam, und nahm dort
Stand.

**WALTHER:** Ich hör's und seh's—
ein Musikant.
Was will der hier so spät des
Nachts.

**EVA:** 's ist Beckmesser schon!

**SACHS:** (*als er den ersten Ton der
Laute vornommen hat, von einen
plötzlichen Einfall erfasst, das
Licht wieder etwas eingezogen
leise auch den unteren Theil des
Ladens geöffnet, und seinen
Werktisch ganz unter die Thüre
gestellt. Jetzt hat er Eva's Ausruf
vernommen*). Aha! ich dacht's!

**WALTHER:** Der Merker? Er! in
meiner Gewalt?
Draufau! den Lung'rer mach ich
kalt!

**EVA:** Um Gott! So hör! Willst den
Vater wecken?
Er singt ein Lied, dann zieht er ab,
Lass dort uns im Gebüsch versteck-
en.—
Was mit den Männern ich Müh'
doch habe!
(*Sie zieht Walther hinter das
Gebüsch auf die Bank unter die
Linde.*)
(*Beckmesser klimpert voll Unge-
duld heftig auf der Laute, ob sich
das Fenster nicht öffen wolle. Als
er endlich anfangen will zu sin-
gen, beginnt Sachs, der soeben
das Licht wieder hell auf die
Strasse fallen liess, laut mit dem
Hammer auf den Leisten zu schla-
gen, und singt sehr kräftig dazu*).

**SACHS:** Jerum! Jerum!
Halla halla he!
Oho! Trallalei! o'he!
Als Eva aus dem Paradies
von Gott dem Herrn verstossen,
gar schuf ihr Schmerz der harte Kies
an ihrem Fuss, den blossen.
Das jammerte den Herrn,
ihr Füssen hat er gern,
und seinem Engel rief er zu:
"da mach' der armen Sünd'rin
Schuh':
Und da der Adam, wie ich seh',
an Steinen dort sich stösst die Zeh',
das recht fortan
er wandeln kann,
so miss' dem auch Stiefeln an!''

**BECKMESSER:** (*alsbald nach Be-
ginn des Verses*) Was soll das
sein?—
Verdammtes Shrein!
Was fällt dem groben Schuster ein?
(*Vortretend.*)
Wie, Meister? Auf? So spät zur
Nacht?

**SACHS:** Herr Stadtschreiber! Was,
ihr wacht?—
Die Schuh machen euch grosse Sorgen?
Ihr seht, ich bin dran: ihr habt sie
morgen.

**EVA:** Ah! Do you not see there?
Some other comes to spoil our plan.

**WALTER:** I hear and see: some
player man.
What wants he here so late at night?

**EVA:** It is Beckmesser!

**SACHS:** (*on bearing the first
sounds of the lute has, as if struck
with a new idea, withdrawn his
light, gently opened the lower half
of his shop-door and placed his
work-bench on the threshold. He
now hears Eva's exclamation*).
Aha! I'm right.

**WALTER:** The Marker here? and
placed in my power?
Here goes! The fool shall regret this
hour!

**EVA:** Oh, heaven! Stop. Would you
wake my father?
He'll sing his song and quit us then.
Let's hide behind the foliage rather.
Oh dear! what trouble you give, you
men!
(*She draws Walter behind the
bushes on the bench under the
lime-tree.*)
(*Beckmesser impatiently tinkles
on his lute waiting for the window
to open. As he is about to commence his song, Sachs turns his
light full on the street again and
begins to hammer loudly on his
last, singing lustily the while.*)

**SACHS:** Tooral looral!
Tiddy fol de rol!
Oho! Tralala! Oho!
When mother Eve from Paradise
Was driven by the Almighty,
Her naked feet, so small and nice,
By stones were sorely riven.
This troubled much the Lord,
Her footsies he adored;
An angel he did straightway
choose:
"Go make that pretty sinner shoes!
And as poor Adam limps around
And breaks his toes on stony
ground,
That well and wide
His legs may stride,
Measure him for boots beside!''

**BECKMESSER:** (*as Sachs begins to
sing*). What is it now?
Atrocious row!
That vulgar cobbler's drunk, I believe!
(*advancing.*)
What Master! Up, so long after dark?

**SACHS:** You also out, Master Town-
clerk?
The shoes perhaps on your mind
are weighing?
You see me at work: I'm not delaying.

**BECKMESSER:** Hol' der Teufel die
Schuh'!
Ich will hier Ruh'!

**WALTHER:** (*zu Eva.*) Wie heisst
das Lied? Wie nennt er dich?

**EVA:** Ich hört' es schon: 's geht
nicht auf mich.
Doch eine Bosheit steckt darin.

**WALTHER:** Welch' Zögerniss! Die
Zeit geht ihm!

**SACHS:** (*weiter arbeitend*). Jerum! Jerum!
O Eva! Hör' mein Klageruf,
mein Noth und schwer Verdrüssen!
Die Kunstwerk', die ein Schuster
schuf,
sie tritt die Welt mit Füssen!
Gäb nicht ein Engel Trost,
der gleiches Werk erlos't,
und rief mich oft in's Paradies,
wie dann ich Schuh' und Stiefel
liess'!
Doch wenn der mich in Himmel
hält,
Dann liegt zu Füssen mir die Welt,
und bin in Ruh'
Hans Sachs ein Schuh-
macher und Poet dazu.

**BECKMESSER:** (*das Fenster ge-
wahrend, welches jetzt sehr leise
geöffnet wird*). Das Fenster geht
auf:—Herr Gott, 's ist sie!

**EVA:** (*zu Walther*). Mich
schmertzt das Lied, ich weiss nicht
wie!
O fort, lass' uns fliehen!

**WALTHER:** (*das Schwert halb zei-
hend*). Nun denn: mit dem
Schwert!

**EVA:** Nicht doch! Ach halt'!

**WALTHER:** Kaum wär' er's werth!

**EVA:** Ja, besser Guduld! O lieber
Mann!
Dass ich so Noth dir machen kann!

**WALTHER:** Wer ist am Fenster?

**EVA:** 's ist Magdalene.

**WALTHER:** Das heiss' ich vergelten: fast muss ich lachen.

**EVA:** Wie ich ein End' und Flucht
mir ersehne!

**WALTHER:** Ich wünscht' er
möcht' den Anfang machen.
(*Sie folgen dem Vorgang mit
wachsender Theilnahme.*)

**BECKMESSER:** (*der während
Sachs fortführt zu arbeiten und
zu singen, in grosser Aufregung
mit sich berathen hat*). Jetzt bin
ich verloren, singt er noch fort!—
(*Er tritt an den Laden beran.*)
Freund Sachs! So hört doch nur ein
wort!
Wie seid ihr auf die Schuh' versessen!
Ich hatt' sie wahrlich schon vergessen.
Als Schuster seid ihr mir wohl
werth,
als Kunstfreund doch weit mehr

**BECKMESSER:** Deuce take boots
and shoe!
Be quiet!

**WALTER:** (*to Eva*). What is that
song. He speaks of you.

**EVA:** I know it well; he does not
mean me.
But hidden malice here I trace.

**WALTER:** What vile delay! Time
flies apace!

**SACHS:** (*continuing his work*).
Tooral looral!
Tiddy fol de rol!
O Eve! Hear how my poor heart
aches
By brief and trouble sodden;
The works of Art a cobbler makes
All under foot are trodden.
Did not an angel bring
For such work comforting,
And call me to Heaven's gate.
I'd quickly leave this trade I hate!
But when he takes me up on high,
The world beneath my feet does lie:
Then rest woo
Hans Sachs, the shoe-
Maker and the Poet too.

**BECKMESSER:** (*watching the
window, which now opens softly*). The window's open:—Oh
heavens! it is she!

**EVA:** (*to Walter*). Why does that
song dispirit me?
O, let us hurry!

**WALTER:** (*half drawing his
sword*). But one way remains!

**EVA:** Oh no! Stop!

**WALTER:** He's hardly worth the
pains!

**EVA:** Yes, patience is best. Oh dearest love.
That I should such a trouble prove!

**WALTER:** Who's at the window?

**EVA:** It is Magdalena.

**WALTER:** That's retribution: it sets
me grinning.

**EVA:** Would we could end, and fly
this arena!

**WALTER:** I only wish he'd make a
beginning.
(*They follow the proceedings with
increasing interest.*)

**BECKMESSER:** (*who, while Sachs
has continued his song and work,
takes counsel with himself in
great perturbation*). Now if he
continues I am undone!
(*He advances to the shop.*)
Friend Sachs! pray hear a word—
just one!
You work there at my shoes so fleetly,
While I'd forgotten them completely.
The cobbler worshipful I deem;
The critic, though, I more esteem.
Your taste, I know, is seldom

verehrt.
Eu'r Urtheil, glaubt, das halt' ich hoch;
drum bitt' ich: hört das Liedlein doch,
mit dem ich morgen möcht' gewinnen,
ob das auch recht nach euren Sinnen.
(*Er klimpert, mit seinen Rücken der Gasse zugewendet, auf der Laute, um die Aufmerksamkeit der dort an Fenster sich zeigenden Magdalene zu beschäftigen, und sie dadurch zurückzuhalten.*)

SACHS: Ei lasst mich doch in Ruh'!
Wie käm' solche Ehr' mir zu?
Nur Gassenhauer dicht' ich aum meisten;
drum sing' ich zur Gassen, und hau auf den Leisten.
(*Fortarbeitend.*)
Jerum! Jerum?
Halla halla hei!

BECKMESSER: Verfluchter Kerl!—Den Verstand verlier' ich,
mit seinem Lied voll Pech und Schmierich!—
Schweight doch! Weckt ihr die Nachbarn auf?

SACHS: Die sind's gewohnt: 's hört Keiner drauf.
"O Eva! Eva! schlimmes Weib!"

BECKMESSER: Verdammte Bosheit!—Gott, und 's wird spät:
am End' mir die Jungfer vom Fenster geht!
(*Er klimpert wie um anzufangen.*)

SACHS: (*aufschlagend*). Fanget an! 's pressirt!
Sonst sing' ich für mich!

BECKMESSER: Haltet ein! nur das nicht!—Teufel! wie ärgerlich!—
Wollt ihr euch denn als Merker erdreisten,
non gut, so merkt mit dem Hammer auf den Leisten:—
nur mit dem Beding, nach den Regeln scharf;
aber nichts, was nach den Regeln ich darf.

SACHS: Nach den Regeln, wie sie der Schuster kennt,
dem die Arbeit unter den Händen brennt.

BECKMESSER: Auf Meister-Ehr'!

SACHS: Und Schuster-Muth!

BECKMESSER: Nicht einen Fehler: glatt und gut!

SACHS: Dann ging't ihr morgen unbeschuht.
Setzt euch denn hier!

BECKMESSER: (*an die Ecke des Hauses sich stellend*). Lasst hier mich stehen!

SACHS: Warum so fern?

---

wrong,
So, please you, hear this little song,
With which I seek to win tomorrow;
Your estimate I fain would borrow.
(*With his back turned to the alley he strums on the lute to attract the attention of Magdalena and keep her at the window.*)

SACHS: Oh peace, and let me be!
Why seek to honor me?
It is clap-trap stuff that I put together:
I sing in the streets while I hammer my leather.
(*continuing to work.*)
Tooral looral!
Tiddy fol de rol!

BECKMESSER: Confound the rogue!—How he's racking my brain!
His ditty reeks of pitch and blacking!—
Silence! Neighbors and all you'll awake.

SACHS: They're used to this; no heed they'll take.—
"Oh Eve! oh Eve, you wicked wench!"—

BECKMESSER: Atrocious malice!—Zounds! it grows late!
She'll go from the window if I wait longer!
(*He strums a prelude.*)

SACHS: (*With a blow of his hammer*). "Now begin!" Look sharp, or I too shall sing!

BECKMESSER: Anything but that! Hush!—What a maddening thing?
Would you aspire to the post of Marker.
Then hammer away as you desire to:
But you must agree to restrain your tool:
Not strike unless I'm breaking the rule.

SACHS: Though a cobbler I'll keep the rules like you,
If my fingers itch to complete this shoe.

BECKMESSER: Your Master's word?

SACHS: And cobbler's truth.

BECKMESSER: If it is faultless, fair and smooth—

SACHS: Then you must go unshod, forsooth!
Sit down here!

BECKMESSER: (*placing himself at the corner of the house*). I'd rather leave you.

SACHS: Why so far off?

---

BECKMESSER: Euch nicht zu sehen,
wie's Brauch in der Schul' vor dem Gemerk.

SACHS: Da hör' ich euch schlecht.

BECKMESSER: Der Stimme Stärk' ich so gar leiblich dämpfen kann.

SACHS: Wie fein!—Nun gut denn!—Fanget an!
(*Kurzcs Vorspiel Beckmesser's auf der Laute, wozu Magdalene sich briet in das Fenster legt.*)

WALTHER: (*zu Eva*). Welch' toller Spuck! Mich dünkt's ein Traum: den Singstuhl, scheint's, verliess ich kaum!

EVA: Die Schläf' umweht's mir, wie ein Wahn:
ob's Heil, ob Unheil, was ich ahn'?
(*Sie sinkt wie betäubt an Walther's Brust: so verbleiben sie.*)

BECKMESSER: (*zur Laute*). "Den Tag seh ich erscheinen, der mir wohl gefall'n thut . . .
(*Sachs schlägt auf.*)
(*Beckmesser zuckt, fährt aber fort.*)
"Da fasst mein Herz sich einen guten und frischen Muth."
(*Sachs hat zweimal aufgeschlagen. Beckmesser wendet sich leise, doch wüthend um.*)
Treibt ihr hier Scherz?
Was wär' nicht gelungen?

SACHS: Besser gesungen:
"da fasst mein Herz sich einen guten und frischen Muth."

BECKMESSER: Wie sollt' sich das reimen auf "seh' ich erscheinen?"

SACHS: Ist euch an der Weise nichts gelegen?
Mich dünkt, 'sollt' passen Ton und Wort.

BECKMESSER: Mit euch hier zu streiten?—Lasst von den Schlägen, sonst denkt ihr mir dran!

SACHS: Jetzt fahret fort!

BECKMESSER: Bin ganz verwirrt!

SACHS: So fangt noch 'mal an:
Drei Schläg ich jetzt pausiren kann.

BECKMESSER: (*für sich*). Am Besten, wenn ich ihn gar nicht beacht':—
wenn's nur die Jungfer nicht irre macht!
(*Er räuspert sich und beginnt wieder.*)
"Den Tag seh' ich erscheinen, der mir wohl gefallen thut;
das fasst mein Herz sich einen guten und frischen Muth,
da denk' ich nicht an Sterben, lieber an Werben
um jung Mägdlein's Hand.
Warum wohl aller Tage schönster mag dieser sein?
Allen hier ich es sage:

---

BECKMESSER: Not to perceive you:
The Marker in school hides in his place.

SACHS: But I shall barely hear you.

BECKMESSER: My powerful bass Will not then stun you with its din.

SACHS: That's good!—All right then!—"Now begin"
(*Short prelude on the lute by Beckmesser, during which Magdalena leans out of the window.*)

WALTER: (*to Eva*). What crazy sounds! It is like a dream: Still in the Singer's seat I seem.

EVA: Sleep steals upon me like a spell.
For good or evil, who can tell?
(*She sinks as if stupefied on Walter's breast. In this position they remain.*)

BECKMESSER: (*with his lute*). "I see the dawning daylight With great pleasure I do.
(*Sachs knocks.*)
(*Beckmesser starts but continues.*)
"For now my breast takes a right Courage both fresh and—"
(*Sachs has dealt two blows. Beckmesser turns around slowly, but in anger.*) Is this a jest?
What do you find bad there?

SACHS: Better have had there,
"For now my breast Takes a right courage fresh and—"

BECKMESSER: How would that lay right To rhyme with my "daylight?"

SACHS: The melody do you think does not matter?
Both words and notes should fit in song.

BECKMESSER: Absurd discussion!—Leave off that clatter! Or is it a plot?

SACHS: Oh get along!

BECKMESSER: I'm quite upset!

SACHS: Begin it once more, And three bars rest meanwhile I'll score.

BECKMESSER: (*aside*). It is better that I pay no attention:—
If only she is not scared away?
(*He clears his throat and begins again.*)
"I see the dawning daylight, With great pleasure I do;
For now my heart takes a right Courage both fresh and new.
I do not think of dying, Rather of trying
A young maiden to win.
Oh why does the weather Then today so excel?
I to all say together
It is because a damsel
By her beloved father,

weil ein schönes Fräulein
von ihrem lieb'n Herrn Vater,
wie gelobt hat er,
ist bestimmt zum Eh'stand.
Wer sich getrau',
der komm und schau'
da steh'n die hold lieblich Jungfrau,
auf die ich all' mein' Hoffnung
bau':
darum ist der Tag so schön blau,
als ich anfänglich fand.''
(*Von der sechsten Zeile an hat
Sachs wieder aufgeschlagen,
wiederholt, und meist mehrere
Male schnell hintereinander;
Beckmesser, der jedesmal
schmerzlich zusammenzuckte,
war genöthigt, bei Bekämpfung
der innern Wuth, oft den Ton, den
er immer zärtlich zu halten sich
bemüht, kurz und heftig
auszustossen, was das Komische
seines gänzlich prosodielosen
Vortrages sehr vermehrte.—Jetzt
bricht er wüthend um die Ecke auf
Sachs los*).
(*Beckmesser, nur den Blick auf
das Fenster heftend, hat mit wachsender Angst Magdalena's misbe-
hagliche Gebärden bemerkt; um
Sachsen's fortgesetzte Schläge zu
übertäuben, hat er immer stärker
und athemloser gesungen.—Er
ist im Begriffe, sofort weiter zu
singen, als Sachs, der zuletzt die
Keile aus den Leisten schlug, und
die Schuhe abgezogen hat, sich
vom Schemel erhebt, und über
den Laden sich heraus lehnt.*)

**SACHS:** Seid ihr nun fertig?

**BECKMESSER:** (*in höchster
Angst*). Wie fraget ihr?

**SACHS:** (*die Schuhe trimphirend
aus dem Laden heraushaltend*).
Mit den Schuhen ward ich fertig
schier!
Das heiss' ich mir rechte Merker-
schuh':—
mein Merkersprüchlein hört dazu!
Mit lang' und kurzen Hieben,
steht's auf der Sohl' geschrieben;
da les't es klar
und nehmt es wahr,
und merkt's euch immerdar.—
"Gut Lied will Takt,"
wer den verzwaekt,
dem Schreiber mit der Feder
haut ihn der Schuster auf's Leder,
Non lauft in Ruh',
habt gute Schuh';
der Fuss euch drin nicht knackt:
ihn hält die Sohl' im Takt!
(*Er lacht laut.*)

**BECKMESSER:** (*der sich ganz in
die Gasse zurückgezogen, und an
die Maurer zwischen den beiden
Fenstern von Sachsen's Hause
sich anlehnt, singt, um Sachs zu
übertäuben, zugleich, mit
grösster Anstrengung, schreiend
und athemlos hastig, seinen drit-*

At his wish rather,
To be wed goes in.
The bold man who
Would come and view,
May see the maiden there so true,
Of whom my hopes I firmly glue:
Therefore is the sky so bright blue,
As I said to begin.''
(*From the 6th line onward, Sachs
has continued to hammer repeatedly on the various false accents;
Beckmesser, who has started
painfully at each blow, is forced
to make his notes short and jerky
in the effort to control his inward
rage; this increases the comical effect of his doggerel performance.—Now he bursts out at
Sachs round the corner.*)
(*Beckmesser, keeping his eyes
fixed on the window, has perceived with rising chagrin Magdalena's evident signs of dissatisfaction; he has sung louder and
more hurriedly in order to overpower the continued hammering
of Sachs.—He is about to continue when the latter, knocking
the key of the last out and withdrawing the shoe, rises from his
stool and leans out over the shop-
door.*)

**SACHS:** Haven't you finished?

**BECKMESSER:** (*in great trepidation*). What means your call?

**SACHS:** (*triumphantly holding
out the shoes from the door*). I've
finished with the shoes, that's
all!—
I call that a famous Marker's shoe:
Now hear my Marker's maxim,
too.—
By long and short strokes dinted
Here on the sole it is printed!
Behold it here,
Let it be clear,
And hold it ever dear.—
"Good songs must scan."
On any man,
Even the Town-clerk, who'd
transgress it
The cobbler's strap shall impress
it.—
Now run along.
Your shoes are strong;
Trust to your feet:
They'll keep you on the beat.
(*He laughs loudly.*)

**BECKMESSER:** (*who has retired
into the alley again and leaned
against the wall between Sachs's
two windows, hastens on with
third verse, shouting breathlessly
with violent efforts to drown
Sachs's voice*). "That I've a Master's learning

*ten Vers*). "Darf ich Meister mich
nennen,
das bewähr' ich heut' gern,
weil nach dem Preis ich brennen
muss dursten und hungern.
Nun ruf' ich die neun Musen
dass an sie blusen
mein dicht'rischen Verstand.
Wohl kenn ich alle Regeln,
halte gut Maass und Zahl;
doch Sprung und Ueberkegeln
wohl passirt je einmal,
wann der Kopf, ganz voll Zagen,
zu frie'n will wagen
um ein jung Mägdleins Hand.
Ein Junggesell
trug ich mein Fell,
mein Ehr', Amt, Würd' und Brod
zur Stell',
dass euch mein Gesang wohl
gefäll',
und mich das Jungfräulein erwähl',
wenn sie mein Lied gut fand.''

**NACHBARN:** (*erst einige, dann
mehrer, öffnen, während des Gesanges, in der Gasse die Fenster
und gucken heraus*). Wer heult
denn da? Wer kreischt mit Macht?
Ist das erlaubt so spät zur Nacht?
Gebt Ruhe hier! 's ist Schlafen-
zeit!—
Nein, hört nur, wie der Esel
schreit!
Ihr da! Seid still, und scheert euch
fort!
Heult, kreischt und schreit an
and'rem Ort!

**DAVID:** (*hat ebenfalls den Fensterladen, dicht bei Beckmesser,
ein wenig geöffnet—und lugt hervor*). Wer Teufel hier?—Und
drüben gar?
Die Lene ist's,—ich seh' es klar!
Herr Je! das war's, den hat sie bestellt;
der ist's, der ihr besser als ich
gefällt!—
Nun warte! du kriegst's! dir streich'
ich das Fell!—
Zum Teufel mit dir verdammte Gesell'!
(*David ist, mit einem Knüppel bewaffnet, hinter dem Laden aus
dem Fenster hervorgesprungen,
zerschlägt Beckmesser's Laute
und wirft sich über ihn selbst
her.*)

**MAGDALENE:** (*die zuletzt, um
den Merker zu entfernen, mit
übertrieben beifälligen Bewegungen herabgewinkt hat, schreit
jetzt laut auf*). Ach Himmel! David! Gott, welche Noth!
Zu Hülfe! zu Hülfe! Sie schlagen
sich todt.

**BECKMESSER:** (*mit David sich
balgend*). Verfluchter Kerl! Lässt
du mich los?

**DAVID:** Gewiss! Die Glieder
brech' ich dir blos!
(*Sie balgen und prügeln sich in einem fort.*)

Willingly I'd show her,
To win the reward burning
I'm with thirst and hunger.
Now I call the nine Muses
To witness whose is
The poetic gift true.
I lay no faulty stresses,
In the rules I'm no dunce;
Some little awkwardnesses
May excused be for once,
When one's heart fear is swaying
At thus essaying
A fair maiden to woo.
A bachelor,
I'd give my gore,
My place, rank, honor, all my store,
If you would my song not abhor;
And the maiden would me adore
If she admires it too.''

**NEIGHBORS:** (*first a few, then
more, open their windows in the
alley during the song and peep
out*). Who's howling there? Who
bawls so loud?
So late at night, is that allowed?—
It is time for bed! Be still, I say!
Just listen to that donkey's bray!—
You there! Shut up and beat retreat!
Go halloa in some other street!

**DAVID:** (*who has opened his
shutter close to Beckmesser*).
Whoever's this?—and who's up
there?
It is Magdalena, I declare!
'Oddzounds that's it—I clearly see
It is he she favors more than me!—
You'll catch it! Just wait! I'll tan
your skin!
The devil help you when I begin!
(*David, arming himself with a
cudgel, springs out of the window, knocks Beckmesser's lute
out of his hands and throws himself upon him.*)

**MAGDALENA:** (*who at last, to
make the Marker go, has made exaggerated gestures of pleasure at
him, now cries aloud*). Oh heavens! David! Lord, how I'm thrilled!
A rescue! a rescue! or both will be
killed!

**BECKMESSER:** (*struggling with
David*). Infernal rogue! Let me alone!

**DAVID:** I will when I've broken
every bone.
(*They continue to struggle and
fight.*)

**DIE NACHBARN:** (*an den Fenstern*). Seht nach! Springt zu! Da würgen sich zwie!

**ANDERE NACHBARN:** (*auf die Gasse heraustretend*). Heda! Herbei! 's giebt Prügelei! Ihr da! aus einander! Gebt freien Lauf! Lass ihr nicht los, wir schlagen drauf?

**EIN NACHBAR:** Ei seht! Auch ihr da! Geht's euch 'was an?

**EIN ZWEITER:** Was sucht ihr hier? Hat man euch 'was gethan?

**ERSTER NACHBAR:** Euch kennt man gut!

**ZWEITER NACHBAR:** Euch noch viel besser!

**ERSTER NACHBAR:** Wie so denn?

**ZWEITER NACHBAR:** (*zuschalagend*). Ei, so!

**MAGDALENE:** (*hinabschreiend*). David! Beckmesser!

**DIE LEHRBUBEN:** (*kommen dazu*). Herbie! Herbei! 's giebt Keilerei!

**EINIGE:** 's sind die Schuster!

**ANDERE:** Nein, 'sind die Schneider!

**DIE ERSTEREN:** Die Trunkenbolde!

**DIE ANDEREN:** Die Hungerleider!

**DIE NACHBARN:** (*auf der Gasse durcheinander*). Euch gönnt' ich's schon lange!— Wird euch wohl bange? Das für die Klage! Seht euch vor, wenn ihr schlage! Hat euch die Frau gehetzt?— Schau wie es Prügel setzt!— Seid ihr noch nicht gewitzt?— So schlagt doch!—Das silzt! Dass ich, Hallunke!— Hie Färbertunke!— Wartet, ihr Racker! Ihr Maasseahzwacker!— Esel!—Dummrian!— Du Grobian!— Lümmel du!— Drauf und zu!

**DIE LEHRBUBEN:** (*durcheinander, zugleich mit den Nachbarn*). Konnt man die Schlosser nicht? Die haben's sicher angericht'!— Ich glaub' die Schmiede werden's sein.— Die Schreiner seh' ich dort beim Schein— Hei! Schau' die Schäffler dort beim Tanz.— Dort seh' die Bader ich im Glanz.— Krämer finden sich zur Hand mit Gerstenstang und Zuckerkand; mit Pfeffer, Zimmt, Muscatennuss, Sie riechen schön. Sie riechen schön. doch haben viel Verdruss, und bleiben gern vom Schuss.— Seht nur, der Hase Hat üb'rall die Nase!—

**NEIGHBORS:** (*at the windows*). Look there! Go it!—They're hard at it now!

**OTHER NEIGHBORS:** (*coming into the alley*). Halloa! What's up? See, here's a row! You there! stand back! Give him fair play! If you don't part we'll join the fray.

**ONE NEIGHBOR:** Halloa! Have you come? Why are you here?

**A SECOND:** What's that to you? Don't interfere!

**FIRST NEIGHBOR:** You're a big rogue!

**SECOND NEIGHBOR:** You are no better!

**FIRST NEIGHBOR:** Prove it then!

**SECOND NEIGHBOR:** (*hitting out*). There!

**MAGDALENA:** (*screaming down*). David! Beckmesser!

**PRENTICES:** (*entering*). Hooray! hooray! Here's cudgel play!

**SOME:** It's the cobblers!

**OTHERS:** No, it's the tailors.

**THE FIRST:** The drunken patches!

**OTHERS:** The starveling railers!

**NEIGHBORS:** (*in the street to one another*). That pays what I owe you!— Coward! I know you!— Take that to requite you!— Mind your eye if I smite you!— Was your wife's temper high? See how the cudgels fly! Haven't you found your wits?— Lay on, then!—That hits!— Rogue, there's a thumper!— You counter-jumper!— You gutter-sweeper?— You false-measure-keeper!— Blockhead!—Looby!— You great booby!— Dolt, I say!— Don't give way!

**PRENTICES:** (*to one another with the Neighbors*). We know the locksmiths' way: They surely started this fray!— I think the smiths began the fight.— I see the joiners by the light.— Look where the coopers come along And now the barbers join the throng.— There the Guild of grocers comes, With lollipops and sugar-plums, With pepper, spice and cinnamon. How nice they smell! How nice they smell! But they don't like the fun, And wish that it were done. See that fool there With his nose everywhere!

Meinst du damit etwa mich?— Mein' ich damit etwa dich? Da hast's auf die Schnautze!— Herr, jetzt setzt's Plautze!— Hei! Krach! Hagelwetterschlag! Wo das sitzt, da wächst nichts nach! Keilt euch wacker, haut die Racker! Haltet selbst Gesellen Stand; wer da wich', 's wär wahrlich Schand'? Drauf und dran! Wie ein Mann steh'n wir alle zur Keilerei! (*Bereits prügeln sich Nachbarn und Lehrbuben fast allegemein durcheinander.*)

**DIE GESELLEN:** (*von allen Seiten dazu kommend*). Heda! Gesellen 'ran! Dort wird mit Streit und Zank gethan Da giebt's gewiss gleich Schlägerei; Gesellen, haltet euch dabei! 'Sind die Weber und Gerber!— Dacht ich's doch gleich!— Die Preisverderber! Spielen immer Streich'! Dort den Metzger Klaus, den kennt man heraus!— Zünfte! Zünfte Zünfte heraus!— Schneider mit dem Bügel! Hei! hie setzt's Prügel! Gürtler!—Zinngiesser!— Leimsieder!—Lichtgiesser!— Tuchscherer her! Leinweber her! Hierher: Hierher! Immer mehr? Immer mehr! Nur tüchtig drauf? Wir schlagen los: jetzt wird die Keilerei erst gross!— Lauft heim, sonst kriegt ihr's von der Frau; Hier giebt's nur Prügel-Färbeblau! Immer 'ran! Mann für Mann! Schlagt sie nieder! Zünfte! Zünfte! Heraus!—

**DIE MEISTER:** (*und Aelteren Bürger von verschiedenen Seiten dazu kommend*). Was giebt's denn da für Zank und Streit? Das tos't ja weit und breit! Gebt Ruh' und scheer sich jeder heim! Sonst schlag' ein Hageldonnerwetter drein! Stemmt euch hier nicht mehr zu hauf, oder sonst wir schlagen drauf.—

**DIE NACHBARINNEN:** (*aus den Fenstern, durcheinander*). Was ist denn da für Streit und Zank? 's wird einem wahrlich Angst und bang! Da ist mein Mann gewiss dabei; gewiss kommt's noch zur Schlägerei! He da! Ihr dort unten, so seid doch nur gescheit!

Pray did I allude to you? There's one nose I've pounded! Lord! how that sounded!— Hey! whack! fire and fury oh! Where that fell no hair will grow! Cudgels, whack hard! Smash the blackguard! Show yourselves worth freemen's name: To give way would be a shame! Join the brawl, Each and all. We are ready to help the row! (*Gradually the Neighbors and Prentices have come to a general fight.*)

**JOURNEYMEN:** (*arriving from all quarters*). Hallo! Companions, come! The people here seem quarrelsome. There'll surely be some fighting then: Be ready, lusty journeymen. It is the weavers and tanners!— Which well I know!— It is like their manners!— They always do so!— Klaus the butcher is there; He's one to beware!— Guilds! Guilds! Guilds everywhere!— Tailors here are hieing!— See the cudgels flying! Girdlers!—Pewterers! Glue-boilers; Fruiterers Cloth-workers here! Linenweavers here! Come here! Come here! More appear! More appear! All do your best! We're going to strike! Now will the fight be something like!— Run home! your wife is after you! Here you'll get painted black and blue! There they go! Blow for blow! Knock them over! Guildsmen! Guildsmen! come out!

**THE MASTERS:** (*and Old Burghers arriving on all sides*). What is this noise of brawl and fight, That sounds far through the night? Leave off and let each go his way, Or else there'll be the deuce to pay! Don't crowd up like this in bands, Or else we too must use our hands.—

**WOMEN:** (*at the windows, to one another*). What is this noise of fight and brawl! It really terrifies us all! My husband's there, as sure as fate! Some one will get a broken head! Hey sirs! You below there, Be reasonable now! Are you then all so ready To join a vulgar row?

Seid ihr zu Streit und Raufen
gleich Alle so bereit?
Was für ein Zanken und Toben!
Da werden schon Arme erhoben!
Hört doch! Hört doch!
Seid ihr denn toll?
Sind euch die Köpfe
vom Weine noch voll?
Zu Hilfe! Zu Hilfe!
Da schlägt sich mein Mann!
Der Vater! der Vater!
Sieht man das an?
Christian! Peter!
Niklaus! Hans!
Auf! schreit Zeter!—
Hörst du nicht, Franz?
Gott! wie sie walken!
Wasser her! Wasser her!
Giesst's ihn' auf die Köpfe!
(*Die Rauferei ist allgemein ge-
worden. Schreien und Toben.*)

**MAGDALENE:** (*am Fenster ver
zweiflungsvoll die Hände rin-
gend*). Ach Himmel! Meine Noth ist
gross?—
David! So hör' mich doch nur an!
So lass' doch nur den Herren los!

**POGNER:** (*ist im Nachtgewand
oben an das Fenster getreten und
zieht Magdalene herein*). Um
Gott! Eva! schliess' zu!—
Ich seh', ob im Haus unten Ruh'!
(*Das Fenster wird geschlossen;
bald darauf erscheint Pogner au
der Hausthüre.*)
(*Sachs hat, als der Tumult begann, sein Licht gelöscht und den
Laden soweit geschlossen, dass er
durch eine kleine Oeffnung stets
den Platz unter der Linde
beobachten konnte.*)
(*Walther und Eva haben mit
wachsender Sorge dem anschwel-
lenden Tumulte zugeschen. Jetzt
fasst Walther Eva dicht in den
Arm.*)

**WALTHER:** Jetzt gilt's zu wagen,
sich durchzuschlagen.
(*Mit geschwungenen Schwerte
dringt er bis in die Mitte der
Bühne vor.— Da springt Sachs
mit einem Satz aus dem Laden auf
die Strasse und packt Walther
beim Arm.*)

**POGNER:** (*auf der Treppe*). He,
Lene, wo bist du?

**SACHS:** (*die halbohnmächtige
Eva auf die Treppe stossend*). In's
Haus, Jungfer Lene!
(*Pogner empfängt sie und zieht
sie beim Arme herein.*)
(*Sachs, mit dem geschwungenen
Knieriemen, mit dem er sich bereits bis zu Walther Platz gemacht
hatte, jetzt dem David eines
überhauend und ihn mit einem
Fusstritt voran in den Laden stossend, zieht Walther, den er mit der
andern Hand gefasst hält, gewaltsam schnell mit sich ebenfalls
binein, und schliesst sogleich fest
hinter sich zu.*)
(*Beckmesser, durch Sachs von
David befreit, sucht sich eilig*

What a confusion and holloa!
Now blows will be certain to fol-
low!
Hark! hark!
Are you insane?
Are you still fuddled
With wine on the brain?
O murder! murder!
My man's in the fight!
There's father! there's father!
Look! what a sight!
Christian! Peter!
Nicholas! Hans!
Watch! be fleeter!—
Don't you hear, Franz?
Lord! how the hair flies!
See how they go it!
Water here! Water, quick!
Throw it on their heads!
(*The row has become general.
Shrieks and blows.*)

**MAGDALENA:** (*wringing her
hands despairingly at the window*). Oh heaven! what is to be
done!—
David, for goodness' sake attend!
Do leave the gentleman alone!

**POGNER:** (*coming to the window
in his night-gown, pulls Magdalena in*). Come in, Eva! Odd so!
I'll see if all is right below.
(*The window is shut and Pogner
appears below at the door.*)
(*Sachs at the commencement of
the row has extinguished his light
and set his door ajar, so as still to
be able to watch the place under
the lime-tree.*)
(*Walter and Eva have observed
the riot with increasing anxiety.
Now Walter seizes Eva in his
arms.*)

**WALTER:** Now we may do it—
Cut our way through it!
(*Brandishing his sword he forces
his way to the middle of the
stage.— Sachs rushes with one
bound out of his shop and grasps
Walter's arms.*)

**POGNER:** (*on the steps*). Ho? Lena!
where are you?

**SACHS:** (*pushing the half-fainting Eva up the steps*). Go in, Mistress Lena!
(*Pogner receives her and pulls her
within.*)
(*Sachs brandishing his knee-
strap, with which he has cleared a
path to Walter, now catches David one, and, kicking him into the
shop drags Walter, whom he still
holds, indoors with him, closing
and barring the door behind
them.*)
(*Beckmesser, released from David by Sachs, seeks hasty flight
through the crowd.*)
(*At the moment Sachs rushes into
the street a loud note from the*

durch die Menge zu flüchten.*)
(*Im gleichen Augenblicke, wo
Sachs auf die Strasse sprang,
hörte man rechts zur Seite im Vordergrunde einen besonders stark-
en Hornruf des Nachtwaechter's.
Lehrbuben, Buerger und Gesellen
suchten in eiliger Flucht sich nach
allen Seiten hin zu entfernen: so
dass die Bühne sehr schnell
gänzalich geleert ist, alle Haus-
thüren hastig geschlossen und
auch die Nachbarinnen von den
Fenstern, welche sie zugeschla-
gen, verschwunden sind.— Der
Vollmond tritt hervor und scheint
hell in die Gasse hinein.*)

**DER NACHTWÄCHTER:** (*betritt
im Vordergrunde rechts die
Bühne, reibt sich die Augen, sieht
sich verwundert um, schüttelt den
Kopf und stimmt mit etwas bebender Stimme seinen Ruf an*):
Hört ihr Leut', und lasst euch sagen:
die Glock' hat Elfe geschlagen.
Bewahrt euch vor Gespenstern und
Spuck,
dass kein böser Geist eu'r Seel' be-
ruck'!
Lobet Gott den Herrn!
(*Er geht während dem langsam
die Gasse hinab. Als der Vorhang
fällt, hört man den Hornruf des
Nachtwaechter's wiederholen.*)

# ■ ACT III

(*In Sachsen's Werkstatt, Kurzer
Raum. Im Hintergrund die halb
geöffnete Ladenthüre, nach der
Strasse führend. Rechts zur Seite
eine Kammerthüre. Links, das
nach der Gasse gehende Fenster,
mit Blumenstöcken davor, zur
Seite ein Werktisch. Sachs sitzt auf
einem grossen Lehnstuhle an diesem Fenster, durch welches die
Morgensonne hell auf ihn her-
einscheint; er hat vor sich auf den
Schoose einen grossen Folianten
und ist im Lesen vertieft.— David
lugt spähend von der Strasse zur
Ladenthüre herein: da er sieht,
dass Sachs seiner nicht achtet,
tritt er herein, mit einem Korbe
im Arm, denn er zuvörderst
schnell und verstohlen unter den
andern Werktisch beim Laden
stellt;— dann von neuem
versichert, dass Sachs ihn nicht
bemerkt, nimmt er den Korb
vorsichtig herauf, und untersucht
den Inhalt: er hebt Blumen und
Bänder heraus; endlich findet er
auf dem Grunde eine Wurst und
einen Kuchen, und lässt sich
sogleich an, diese zu verzehren,
als Sachs der ihn fortwährend
nicht beachtet, mit starkem
Geräusch eines der grossen
Blätter des Folianten umwendet.*)

Nightwatchman's horn is heard
R. U. E. Prentices, Burghers and
Journeymen, panic struck, seek
flight on all sides, so that the stage
is speedily completely cleared: all
the doors are closed and women
gone from windows, which are
also shut.— The full moon shines
out and brightly illumines the
now peaceful alley.*)

**THE WATCHMAN (***enters R. U. E.,
rubs his eyes, stares about him in
surprise, shakes his head, and in a
somewhat tremulous voice calls
out:*) "Hark to what I say, good
people!
Eleven strikes from every steeple.
Defend you all from specter and
sprite;
Let no power of ill your souls fright-
en!
Praise the Lord of Heaven!"
(*He goes slowly up the alley. As the
curtain falls his distant horn is
still heard.*)

# ■ ACT III

(*In Sachs's workshop. Front
scene. At back the half-open shop-
door leads to the street. R the door
of a chamber. L the window looking into the alley, flowers in pots
before it; a work bench beside it.
Sachs sits at this window in a
great arm chair, the bright morning sun streaming in on him; he
has a large folio on his lap and is
absorbed in reading.— David
peeps in at the door from the
street; on seeing that Sachs does
not notice him he enters with a
basket on his arm, which he first
hides quickly under the other
work bench; then again assured
that Sachs does not heed him, he
carefully takes it out again and
investigates the contents: he lifts
out the flowers and ribbons and
at last finds at the bottom a sausage and a cake; these he is about
to devour when Sachs, who is still
unconscious of his presence,
turns over a leaf of his book with a
loud rustle.*)

# Act III

**DAVID:** (*fährt zusammen, verbirgt das Essen und wendet sich.*)
Gleich! Meister! Hier!—
Die Schuh' sind abgegeben
In Herrn Beckmesser's Quartier.—
Mir war's ihr reif't mich eben?
(*Bei Seite.*)
Er thut' als säh' er mich nicht?
Da is er bös, wenn er nicht spricht!
(*Sich demüthig sehr allmählich nübrend.*)
Ach, Meister! woll't ihr mir verzeih'n!
Kann ein Lehrbub' vollkommen sein?
Kenntet ihr die Lene, wie ich,
da vergäb't ihr mir sicherlich.
Sie ist so gut, so sanft für mich,
und blickt mich oft an, so innerlich:
wenn ihr mich schlagt, streichelt sie mich,
und lächelt dabei holdseliglich!
Muss ich cariren, füttert sie mich,
und ist in Allem gar lieblich.
Nur gestern, weil der Junker versungen,
hab' ich den Korb ihr nicht abgerungen:
das schmerzte mich; und da ich fand,
dass Nachts Einer vor dem Fenster stand,
und sang zu ihr, und schrie wie toll,
da hieb ich dem den Buckel voll.
Wie käm' nun da 'was Gross' drauf an?
Auch hat's uns'rer Lieb' gar gut gethan:
die Lene hat eben mir Alles erklärt,
und zum Fest Blumen und Bänder bescheert.
(*Er bricht in immer grössere Angst aus.*)
Ach, Meister! sprecht doch nur ein Wort!
(*Bei Seite.*)
Hätt' ich nur die Wurst und den Kuchen erst fort!

**DAVID:** (*starts, hides the food and turns round*). Here, Master! yes!—
The shoes were taken duly
To clerk Beckmesser's address.—
I thought you summoned me truly?
(*Aside.*)
He seems to notice me not!
When he is dumb his anger's hot.
(*Gradually approaching humbly.*)
Ah, Master! won't you forgive?
Can a Prentice quite faultless live?
If with my eyes Lena you'd see
You'd pardon me, assuredly.
She is so good, so kind to me,
And eyes me at times so tenderly!
When I've been thrashed, soothing is she.
And smiles upon me so prettily!
When on short commons, she feeds me,
And acts in all things right lovingly.
Last night, though, when that knight was discarded,
There was no basket awarded to me.
That worried me, and when I found
At night how some one lurked around
And sang to her and cried like mad.
I gave him all the stick I had.
What dreadful consequence befell!
But yet for our love it turned out well!
Now Lena's explained the matter to me
And sent all these ribbons and flowers you see.
(*He bursts out in still greater anxiety*).
Oh Master! Speak one word, I pray!
(*Aside.*)
Would I'd put the cake and sausage away!—

**SACHS:** (*der unbeirrt weiter gelesen, schlägt jetzt den Folianten zu. Von dem starken Geräusch erschrickt David so, dass er strauchelt und unwillkürlich vor Sachs auf die Knie fällt. Sachs sieht über das Buch, das er noch auf dem Schoose behält, hinweg. über, David, welcher immer auf den Knien furchtsam nach ihm hinauf blickt, hin und heftet seinen Blick unwillkürlich auf den hinteren Werktisch*). Blumen und Bänder seh' ich dort:—
schaut hold und jugendlich aus!
Wie kamen die mir in's Haus?

**SACHS:** (*who has read on undisturbed, claps his book. At the loud noise David is so startled that he stumbles and falls unintentionally on his knees before Sachs. The latter gazes far away beyond the book which he still holds, beyond David who, from his kneeling posture looks up at him in terror, and his eyes fall on the farther table*). Yonder are flowers and ribbons gay,
In youthful beauty and bloom:
How came they into my room?

**DAVID:** (*verwundert über Sachsen's Freundlichkeit*). Ei, Meister! 's ist heut hoch festlicher Tag;
da putzt sich jeder, so schön er mag.

**DAVID:** (*astonished at Sachs' friendliness*). Why, Master! To-day's a feast, you know;
And all must smarten, to grace the show.

**SACHS:** Wär' Hochzeitsfest?

**SACHS:** Is it a marriage-feast?

**DAVID:** Ja, käm' so weit,
dass David erst die Lene Freit!

**DAVID:** Yes, so it would be
If only Lena might marry me.

**SACHS:** 's war Polterabend, dünkt mich doch?

**DAVID:** (*für sich*). Polterabend?—Da krieg ich's wohl noch!—
(*Laut.*)
Verzeiht das, Mesiter! Ich bitt', vergesst!
Wir feiern ja heut' Johannisfest.

**SACHS:** Johannisfest?

**DAVID:** (*bei seite*). Hört er heut' schwer?

**SACHS:** Kannst du dein Sprüchlein? Sag' es her!

**DAVID:** Mein Sprüchlein? Denk', ich kann es gut.
(*Bei Seite.*)
'Setzt nichts! der Meister ist wohlgemuth!—
(*Laut.*)
"Am Jordan Sankt Johannes stand"—
(*Er hat in der Zerstreuung die Worte mit der Melodie von Beckmesser's Werbelied aus dem vorhergehenden Aufzuge gesungen; Sachs macht eine verwunderte Bewegung, worauf David sich unterbricht.*)
Verzeiht, Meister; ich kann in's Gewirr:
der Polterabend machte mich irr.
(*Er fährt in der richtigen Melodie fort:*)
"Am Jordan Sankt Johannes stand,
all Volk der Welt zu taufen:
kam auch ein Weib aus fremdem Land,
von Nürnberg gar gelaufen;
sein Söhnlein trug's zum Uferrand,
empfing da Tauf' und Namen;
doch als sie dann sich heimgewandt,
nach Nürnberg wieder kamen,
im deutschen Land gar bald sich fand's,
dass wer am Ufer des Jordans
Johannes war genannt,
an der Pegnitz hiess der Hans."
(*Feurig.*)
Herr! Meister! 's ist eu'r Namenstag!
Nein! Wie man so 'was vergessen mag!
Hier; hier, die Blumen sind für euch,
die Bänder,—und was nur Alles noch gleich!
Ja hier! schaut, Meister! Herrlicher Kuchen?
Möchtet ihr nicht auch die Wurst versuchen?

**SACHS:** (*immer ruhig, ohne seine Stellung zu verändern*). Schön Dank, mein Jung'! behalt's für dich!
Doch heut' auf die Wiese begleitest du mich:
mit den Bändern und Blumen putz dich dich fein;
sollst mein stattlicher Herold sein.

**DAVID:** Sollt' ich nicht lieber Brautführer sein?—
Meister! lieb' Meister! ihr müsst wieder frei'n!

**SACHS:** Your Folly-evening was last night?

**DAVID:** (*aside*). Folly evening?—
I'm all in a fright!
(*Aloud.*)
Forgive me, Master! Forget it, pray!
The Feast of St. John we keep today.

**SACHS:** St. John's day?

**DAVID:** (*aside*). He must be deaf!

**SACHS:** Know you your verses? Repeat them to me.

**DAVID:** My verses? Yes, they're in my brain.—
(*Aside.*)
All right! the master is kind again!
(*Aloud.*)
"St. John stood on the Jordan strand"—
(*In his agitation he sings his lines to the melody of Beckmesser's serenade; he is pulled up by Sachs' movement of astonishment*).
Forgive me, master, and pardon the slip!
That Folly-evening caused me to trip.
(*He recommences to the proper tune.*)
"St. John stood on the Jordan strand,
Where all the world he christened:
A woman came from distant land,
From Nuremberg she'd hastened:
Her little son she led in hand,
Baptized him with a name there,
And then toward home she took her flight;
But when at last she came there
It soon turned out, in German lands,
That he who on the Jordan's sands
Johannes had been hight,
On the Pegnitz was called Hans."
(*Impetuously.*)
Sir! Master! It is your name-day, sure!
There! Well, my memory must be poor!
Here! all the flowers are for you.
The ribbons—there was something else, too?
Yes, here! Look, master! Here's a fine pastry!
Try too this sausage, you'll find it tasty.

**SACHS:** (*still dreamily, without moving*). Best thanks, my lad! You keep it, though!
Eventually to the meadow with me you shall go;
With ribbons and flowers make yourself gay;
As my herald you are to act today.

**DAVID:** Would I not be your groomsman more fair?
Master, dear master, you must wed again!

SACHS: Hätt'st wohl gern eine Meist'rin im Haus?

DAVID: Ich mein', es säh' doch viel stattlicher aus.

SACHS: Wer weiss! Kommt Zeit, kommt Rath.

DAVID: 's ist Zeit.

SACHS: Da wär' der Rath wohl auch nicht weit?

DAVID: Gewiss! geh'n Reden schon hin und wieder. Den Beckmesser, denk' ich, säng't ihr doch nieder? Ich mein', dass der heut' sich nicht wichtig macht.

SACHS: Wohl möglich! Hab's mir auch schon bedacht.— Jetzt geh'; doch stör' mir den Junker nicht! Komm' wieder, wenn du schön ger-licht'.

DAVID: (küsst ihm gerührt die Hand, packt Alles zusammen und geht in die Kammer). So war es noch nie, wenn sonst auch gut! Kann mir gar nicht mehr denken, wie der Knieriemen thut! (Ab.)

SACHS: (immer noch den Folianten auf dem Schoosse, lehnt sich, mit untergestütztem Arme, sinnend darauf und beginnt dann nach einem Schweigen): Wahn! Wahn! Ueberall Wahn! Wohin ich forschend blick' in Stadt- und Welt-Chronik, den Grund mir aufzufinden, warum gar bis auf's Blut die Leut sich quälen und schinden in unnütz toller Wuth! Hat keiner Lohn noch Dank davon: in Flucht geschlagen meint er zu jagen. Hört nicht sein eigen Schmerz-Gekreisch, wenn er sich wühlt in's eigene Fleisch, wähnt Lust sich zu erzeigen. Wer giebt den Namen au? 's bleibt halt der alte Wahn, ohn' den nichts mag geschehen, 's mag gehen oder stehen! Steht's wo im Lauf, er schläft nur neue Kraft sich an; gleich wacht er auf, dann schaut, wer ihn hemeistern kann! Wie friedsam treuer Sitten, getrost in That und Werk, liegt nicht in Deutschland's Mitten mein liebes Nürenberg! Doch eines Abends spät, ein Unglück zu verhüten, bein jugendheissen Gemüthen, ein Mann weiss sich nicht Rath; ein Schuster in seinem Laden, zieht an des Wahnes Faden; wie bald auf Gassen und Strassen fängt der da an zu rasen; Mann, Weib, Gesell' und Kind, fällt sich an wie toll und blind,

SACHS: Do you wish for a mistress then here?

DAVID: I think it would appear more dignified.

SACHS: Who knows? But time will show.

DAVID: Time's come.

SACHS: Has it brought knowledge then to some?

DAVID: Yes, sure! I know things have been repeated; And Beckmesser's singing you have defeated. I think he will scarce make a stir to-day.

SACHS: It's likely! That I'll not gainsay.— Now go; disturb not Sir Walter's rest! Come back when you are finely dressed.

DAVID: (moved, kisses Sachs's hand, collects his things and goes into chamber). He never was like this, though sometimes kind! Why, the taste of his strap has gone out of my mind! (Exit.)

SACHS: (still with the book on his knees leans back deep in thought, resting his head on his hand and after a pause begins): Mad! Mad! All the world's mad! Where ever inquiry dives In town or world's archives And seeks to learn the reason Why people strive and fight, Both in and out of season, In fruitless rage and spite. What do they gain For all their pain? Repulsed in fight, They feign joy in flight; Their pain-cries not minding, They joy pretend When their own flesh their fingers rend And pleasure deem they're finding. What tongue the cause can phrase? It is just the same old craze! Nothing happens without it ever, In spite of all endeavor; It makes pause In sleep but acquires new force; Soon it will wake, Then lo! who can control its course?— Old ways and customs keeping, How peacefully I see My dear old Nuremberg sleeping In midst of Germany! But on one evening late, To hinder in some fashion The follies of youthful passion A man worries his head; A shoemaker, all unknowing, Sets the old madness going: How soon from highways and alleys A raging rabble sallies! Man, woman, youth and child, Blindly fall to, as if gone wild, And before the craze lose power The cudgel blows must shower;

und will's der Wahn gesegnen, nun muss es Prügel regnen, mit Hieben, Stöss' und Dreschen den Wuthesbrand zu löschen, Gott weiss, wie das geschah?— Ein Kobold half wohl da! Ein Glühwurm fand sein Weibchen nicht; der hat den Schaden angericht'.— Der Flieder war's:—Johannis-Nacht.— Nun aber kam Johannis-Tag:— jetzt schau'n wir, wie Hans Sachs es macht, dass er den Wahn fein lenken mag, ein edler Werk zu thun; denn lässt er uns nicht ruh'n, selbst hier in Nürenberg, so sei's um soiche Werk', die selten vor gemeinen Dingen, und nie ohn' ein'gen Wahn gelin-gen.—

(Walther tritt unter der Kammer-thüre ein. Er bleibt einen Augen-blick dort stehen und blickt auf Sachs. Dieser wendet sich und lässt den Folianten auf den Boden gleiten.)

SACHS: Grüss Gott, mein Junker! Ruhtet ihr noch? Ihr wachtet lang'; nun schlieft ihr doch?

WALTHER: (sehr ruhig). Ein wen-ig, aber fest und gut.

SACHS: So ist euch nun wohl bass zu Muth?

WALTHER: Ich hett' einen wun-derschönen Traum.

SACHS: Das dentet gut's! Erzählt mir den.

WALTHER: Ihn selbst zu denken wag' ich kaum: ich fürcht' ihn mir vergeh'n zu seh'n.

SACHS: Mein Freund, das grad' ist Dichter's Werk, dass er sein Träumen deut' und merk'. Glaubt mir, des Menschen wahrster Wahn wird ihm im Traume aufgethan: all' Dichtkunst und Poeterei ist nichts als Wahrtraum-Deuterei Was gilt's, es gab der Traum euch ein, wie heut' ihr sollet Sieger sein?

WALTHER: Nein! von der Zunft und ihren Meistern wollt' sich mein Traumbild nicht begeistern.

SACHS: O, lasst dem Ruh'; und folgt meinem Rathe, kurz und gut, fasst zu einem Meisterliede Muth.

WALTHER: Ein schönes Lied, ein Meisterlied: wie fass' ich da den Unterschied?

SACHS: Mein Freund! in holder Jugendzeit wenn uns von mächt'gen Trieben zum sel'gen ersten Lieben die Brust sich schwellet hoch und weit,

They seek with fuss and bother The fires of wrath to smother.— God knows how this befell!— It was like some impish spell! Some glow-worm could not find his mate; It was he aroused this wrath and hate.— The elder's charm:—Midsummer-eve:— But now has dawned Midsummer day.— Let's see then what Hans Sachs can weave To turn the madness his own way. To serve for noble works; For it still here it lurks, In Nuremberg the same, We'll use it to such aim As seldom by the mob's projected, And never without trick effect-ed.—

(Walter enters from the chamber. He pauses a moment at the door looking at Sachs. The latter turns and allows his book to slip to the ground.)

SACHS: Good day, Sir Walter! My guest is late. You sat up long; you've had some rest?

WALTER: (very quietly). A little, but that rest was sound.

SACHS: So then your courage you have found?

WALTER: I had a wondrous lovely dream.

SACHS: That bodes well! Relate it, pray.

WALTER: In words I scarce dare touch its theme, For fear it should all fade away.

SACHS: My friend, that is the poet's art, His dreams to cherish and impart. Trust me, the best ideas of men In dreams are opened to their ken: All book-craft and all poetry Are nothing but dreams made true. But did your dream at all advise How you might win the Master-prize?

WALTER: No, from your Guild no inspiration Arose to my imagination. But let that go.

SACHS: And listen to my counsel short and strong. Bend your mind to a Master-Song.

WALTER: A Master-Song and one that's fine: How shall I make the two combine?

SACHS: My friend, in youth's delightful days When first in the direction Of blissful, true affection The heart some power turns and sways,

ein schönes Lied zu singen
mocht' vielen da gelingen:
der Lenz, der sang für sie.
Kam Sommer, Herbst und Winterzeit,
viel Noth und Sorg' im Leben,
manch ehlich Glück daneben,
Kindtauf', Geschäfte, Zwist und
Streit:
denen 's dann noch will gelingen
ein schönes Lied zu singen,
seht, Meister nennt man die.—

WALTHER: Ich lieb' ein Weib und
will es frei'n,
mein dauernd Ehgemahl zu sein.

SACHS: Die Meisterregeln lernt bei
Zeiten,
dass sie getreulich euch geleiten,
und helfen wohl bewahren,
was in der Jugend Jahren
in holdem Triebe
Lenz und Liebe
each unbewusst in's Herz gelegt,
dass ihr das unverloren hegt.

WALTHER: Steh'n sie non in so hohem Ruf
wer war es, der die Regeln schuf?

SACHS: Das waren hoch-
bedürft'ge Meister,
von Lebensmüh' bedrängte Geister,
in ihrer Nöthen Wildniss
sie schufen sich ein Bildniss,
das ihnen bliebe
der Jugendliebe
ein Angedenken klar und fest,
dran sich der Lenz erkennen lässt.

WALTHER: Doch, wem der Lenz
schon lang entronnen,
wie wird er dem aus dem Bild gewonnen?
Wie fang' ich nach der Regel an?

SACHS: Ihr stellt sie selbst, und
folgt ihr dann.
Gedenkt des schönen Traum's am
Morgen;
für's Andre lasst Hans Sachs nur sorgen.

WALTHER: (setzt sich zu Sachs
und beginnt nach kurzer
Sammlung, sehr leise). "Morgenlich leuchtend in rosigem Schein,
von Blüth' und Duft
geschwellt die Luft,
von aller Wonnen
nie ersonnen,
ein Garten lud mich ein
Gast ihm zu sein."
(Er hält etwas an.)

SACHS: Das war ein Stollen: nun
achtet wohl,
dass ganz ein gleicher ihm folgen
soll.

WALTHER: Warum ganz gleich?

SACHS: Damit man sch',
ihr wähltet euch gleich ein Weib
zur Eh'.

All can, or else, it were pity.
Compose a loving ditty:
For spring cries out in you.
But Summer, Autumn, Winter days
Bring care and sorrow often,
With wedded bliss to soften,
Children and business—frets and
frays.
One who, despite care and duty,
Yet sings a song of beauty,
A Master he must be.—

WALTER: I love a maiden and I
pine
In wedlock true to make her mine.

SACHS: The Master-rules then
learn and ponder,
To guide your footsteps when they
wander.
To help you keep with rigor
What in your youthful vigor
In hasty fashion,
Spring and passion
Place secretly within your heart,
That it may never more depart.

WALTER: If then so much your
rules are prized,
By what man were they first devised?

SACHS: By certain sorely troubled
Masters,
Their hearts oppressed by life's di-
sasters;
By suffering overweighted,
A model they created,
That they might take it
And ever make it
A memory of youthful love,
In which the soul of Spring should
move.

WALTER: But how can aught of
Spring awaken
In those whom it has long forsaken?
What rule will my commencement
fit?

SACHS: First make your rule, then
follow it.
Your dream alone let occupy you;
With all the rest Hans Sachs will ply
you.

WALTER: (places himself near
Sachs and after a moment's
thought begins in a very low
voice:) "Morning was gleaming
with roseate light,
The air was filled
With scent distilled,
Where, beauty beaming
Past all dreaming,
A garden did invite
My raptured sight."
(He pauses awhile.)

SACHS: That was a stanza: now
then, take heed
That one just similar may succeed.

WALTER: Why similar?

SACHS: That folks may know
That coupled you intend to go.

WALTHER: (führt fort). "Wonnig
entragend dem seligen Raum
bot gold'ner Frucht
heilsaft'ge Wucht
mit holdem Prangen
dem Verlangen
an duft'ger Zweige Saum
herrlich ein Baum."
(Er hält inne.)

SACHS: Ihr schlosset nicht im gleichen Ton:
das macht den Meistern Pein;
doch nimmt Hans Sachs die Lehr'
davon
im Lenz wohl miiss' es so sein.—
Nun stellt mir einen Abgesang.

WALTHER: Was soll nun der?

SACHS: Ob euch gelang
ein rechtes Paar zu finden,
das zeigt sich jetzt an den Kinden.
Den Stollen ähnlich, doch nicht
gleich,
an eig'nen Raim' und Tönen reich;
dass man es recht schlank und
selbstig find',
das freut die Aeltern an dem Kind:
und euren Stollen giebt's den
Schluss,
dass nichts davon abfallen muss.

WALTHER: (fortfahrend). "Sei
euch vertraut,
welch' hehres Wunder mir gescheh'n:
an meiner Seite stand ein Weib,
So schön und hold ich nie gesh'n;
gleich einer Braut
umfasste sie sanft meinen Leib;
mit Augen winkend,
die Hand wies blinkend,
was ich verlangend begehrt,
die Frucht so hold und werth
vom Lebensbaum."

SACHS: (seine Rührung verbergend). Das nenn' ich mir einen Abgesang:
seht, wie der ganze Bar gelang!
nur mit der Melodei
seid ihr ein wenig frei;
doch sag' ich nicht, dass es ein Fehler sei;
nur ist's nicht leicht zu behalten,
und das ärgert uns're Alten!
Jetzt richtet mir noch einen zweit-
en Bar,
damit man mark', welch' der erste
war.
Auch weiss ich noch nicht, so gut
ihr's gereimt,
was ihr gedichtet, was ihr geträumt.

WALTHER: (wie vorher). "A-
bendlich glühend in himmlischer
Pract
verschied der Tag
wie dort ich lag;
aus ihren Augen
Wonne zu saugen,
Verlangen einz'ger Macht
in mir nur wacht'—
Nächtlich undämmer der Blick
sich mir bricht:
wie weit so nah
beschienen da

WALTER: (continuing). "Over
the glorious garden, behold!
With leafy crown
A tree looked down,
Majestic bending,
And extending
Its weight of fruit untold,
Like burnished gold."
(He pauses.)

SACHS: You close not in the start-
ing key:
The Masters hate this thing;
Hans Sachs, though, can with you
agree;
It must be so in the Spring.—
Now proceed to an After song.

WALTER: What is that for?

SACHS: If here indeed
A pair you've coupled truly
The offspring shows us duly.
It is like the Stanzas, but yet new,
With fitting rhymes and music too;
If fair and shapely the results
The sire of such a child exults:
And to your Stanzas it is the close,
That nothing lack or fall from those.

WALTER: (in continuation). "Let
me confide
What lovely miracle ensued:
A maiden stood before my face,
So sweet and fair I never had
viewed;
Like to a bride
She took me to her embrace;
With bright eyes glowing,
Her hand was showing.
What stirred my longing profound;
The wondrous fruit that crowned
The tree of life."

SACHS: (concealing his emo-
tion). That is an After-song, I allow!
See the whole verse is perfect now!
But in the melody
You were a little free;
I do not say that that displeases me:
To catch it right, though, is per-
plexing.
A thing to our Masters vexing—
A second verse will you please dic-
tate,
To set the first in a clearer light?
I cannot yet tell—your art's so su-
preme—
How much was poetry, how much
dream.

WALTER: (as before). "Evening
was tinting the glorious skies:
Departed day
As there I lay;
With but one yearning
I was burning.
To drink the bliss that lies
In her sweet eyes.
Dusk from my vision all things did
erase;
Afar, yet near.
Then did appear
Two stars down-sparkling

zwei lichte Sterne
aus der Ferne
durch schlanker Zweige Licht
hehr mein Gesicht.—
Lieblich ein Quell
aus stiller Höhe dort mir rauscht;
jetzt schwellt er an sein hold —
Getön'
so süss und stark ich's nie erlauscht:
leuchtend und hell
wie strahlten die Sterne da schön;
zu Tanz und Reigen
in Laub und Zweigen
der gold'nen sammeln sich mehr,
statt Frucht ein Sternenheer
im Lorbeerbaum.''

SACHS: (*sehr gerührt, sanft*).
Freund, eu'r Trambild wies euch
wahr
gelungen ist auch der zweite Bar.
Wolltet ihr noch einen dritten dichten,
des Traumes Deutung würd' er berichten.

WALTHER: Wie fänd ich die? Genug der Wort'!

SACHS: (*aufstehend*). Dann Wort
und That am rechten Ort!—
Drum bitt ich, merkt mir gut die
Weise;
gar lieblich drin sich's dichten
lässt;
und singt ihr sie in weit'rem Kreise,
dann haltet mir auch das Traumbild
fest.

WALTHER: Was habt ihr vor?

SACHS: Eu'r treu'r Knecht
fand sich mit Sack und Tasch' zurecht;
die Kleider, drin am Hochzeitsfest
daheim bei euch ihr wolltet prangen,
die liess er her zu mir gelangen;—
ein Täubchen zeigt' ihm wohl das
Nest
darin sein Junker träumt':
darum folgt mir jetzt in's
Kämmerlein!
Mit Kleidern, wohlgesäumt,
sollen Beide wir gezieret sein.
wann's Stattliches zu wagen gilt:—
drum kommt, seid ihr gleich mir
gewillt!
(*Er öffnet Walther die Thür und
geht mit ihm hinein.*)

BECKMESSER: (*Beckmesser lugt
zum Laden herein; da er die Werkstatt leer findet, tritt er näher. Er
ist reich aufgeputzt, aber in sehr
leidenden Zustande. Er binkt,
streichelt und reckt sich; zuckt
wieder zusammen; er sucht einen
Schemel, setzt sich; springt aber
sogleich wieder auf, und streichelt sich die Glieder von Neuem.
Verzweiflungsvoll sinnend geht er
dann umher. Dann bleibt er steh-
en, lugt durch das Fenster nach
dem Hause hinüber; macht
Gebärden der Wuth: schlägt sich
wieder vor den Kopf.—Endlich
fällt sein Blick auf das von Sachs*

In the darkling.
Between the branches' space,
Upon my face.
There on the height
A babbling stream the silence
stirred;
Its murmuring tones now louder
swelled,
So sweet and strong I never heard;
Sparkling and bright
Distinctly the stars I beheld;
In twinkling dances
Among the branches
A golden host did collect:
Not fruit but stars bedecked
The tree of Fame.''—

SACHS: (*deeply moved, softly*).
Friend, your dream was well conceived:
The second verse you have
achieved.
Now might you fashion a third
verse meetly,
To show the vision's meaning completely.

WALTER: How can I now? Enough
of rhyme!

SACHS: (*rising*). Then we will
rhyme some fitter time!—
Lose not the tune, though, I entreat
it;
'Tis fit and fair for poetry:
You shall before the world repeat
it.
Hold fast the dream you've told to
me.

WALTER: What's your intent?

SACHS: Your servant true,
Bearing your packs, has sought for
you.
The garments in the which I
guessed
You meant at home to have been
married,
Unto my house in doubt he carried.
Some bird, sure, must have shown
the nest
Wherein his master lay
Then follow to the chamber here!
In costume rich and gay
It is fitting that we both appear.
When striving for a victory
So come, if you agree with me.
(*He opens the door for Walter and
goes in with him.*)

BECKMESSER: (*peeps into the
shop: finding it empty he comes
in. He is richly dressed, but in a
very deplorable state. He limps,
rubs and stretches himself: then
contorts himself: he tries to sit
down on a stool, but jumps quickly up and again rubs his bruised
limbs. In despair he wanders up
and down. Then pausing, he looks
through the window at the house
opposite: makes gestures of
wrath: strikes his hand on his
forehead.—At last his eyes fall on
the paper which Sachs has written
and left on the workbench; he
takes it up inquisitively, runs his*

zuvor beschriebene Papier auf
dem Werktische: er nimmt es neugierig auf, überfliegt es mit immer grösserer Aufregung und
bricht endlich wüthend aus:*) Ein
Werbelied! von Sachs?—ist's wahr.
Ah!—Nun wird mir Alles klar!
(*Da er die Kammerthüre gehen
hört, fährt er zusammen, und versteckt das Blatt eilig in seiner
Tasche.*)

SACHS: (*im Festgewande, tritt ein
und hält an*). Sieh da! Herr
Schreiber! Auch am Morgen?
Euch machen die Schuh doch nicht
mehr Sorgen?
Lasst sehen! mich dünkt, sie sitzen
gut?

BECKMESSER: Den Teufel! So
dünn war ich noch nie beschuht:
fühl' durch die Sohle den Kleinsten
Kies!

SACHS: Mein Merkersprüchlein
wirkte dies:
trieb sie mit Merkerzeichen so
weich.

BECKMESSER: Schon gut der
Witz'! Und genug der Streicht'!
Glaubt mir, Freund Sachs, jetzt
kenn ich euch,
der Spass von dieser Nacht,
der wird euch noch gedacht:
dass ich euch nur nicht im Wege
sei,
schuft ihr gar Aufruhr und Meuter-
ei!

SACHS: 's war Polteralend, lasst
euch bedeuten;
eure Hochzeit spuckte unter den
Leuten;
je toller es da hergeh',
je besser bekommt's der Eh'.

BECKMESSER: (*ausbrechend*). O
Schuster, voll von Ränken
und pöbelhaften Schwänken,
du warst mein Feind von je:
nun hör' ob hell ich seh',
Die ich mir auserkoren,
die ganz für mich geboren,
zu aller Wittwer Schmach,
der Jungfer stellst du nach.
Dass sich Herr Sachs erwerbe
des Goldschmied's reiches Erbe,
im Meister-Rath zur Hand
auf Klauseln er bestand,
ein Mägdlein zu bethören,
das nur auf ihn sollt' hören,
und And'ren abgewandt,
zu ihm allein sich fand.
Darum! darum—
wär' ich so dumm:—
mit Schreien und mit Klopfen
wollt er mein Lied zustopfen,
dass nicht dem Kind werd' kund
wie auch ein And'rer bestund!
Ja ja!—Ha Ha!
Hab' ich dich da?
Aus seiner Schuster-Stuben
hetzt endlich er den Buben
mit Knüppeln auf mich her,
dass meiner los er wär'!
Au au! Au au!

eye over it in great agitation and
finally bursts out wrathfully.*) A
Trial-song! by Sachs? is it so?
Ha!—Now then everything I know!
(*Hearing the chamber door open
he starts and conceals the paper
hurriedly in his pocket.*)

SACHS: (*in holiday dress, enters
and stops short*) You sir? So early?
Why this visit?
No, fault of the shoes I sent you, is
it?
Let's feel! They fit you well, I'm
sure?

BECKMESSER: Confound you! The
shoes were never so thin before:
Through them I feel the smallest
stone.

SACHS: My Marker's motto there is
shown:
My Marker's hammer beat it so flat.

BECKMESSER: A merry jest!
Enough of that!
Friend Sachs, I know what you are
at.
Have you forgotten quite
What happened last night?
Did you not raise all that uproar,
pray,
Merely to get me out of your way?

SACHS: It was Folly-evening; be
not alarmed;
And your wedding made the people
excited.
The madder that evening's glee,
The more blessed the marriage will
be.

BECKMESSER: (*bursting out in a
rage*). Oh cobbler full of cunning,
With vulgar tricks over-running!
You always were my foe:
Your base designs I'll show.
You hoary headed reprobate!
Attempting to appropriate
The maiden who alone
Is destined for my own!
Allured by Pogner's capital
Hans Sachs would like to snap it all.
So, when the Guild discussed,
He cavilled and he fussed
To give the maid selection,
Assured of her affection,
That others she'd refuse
And him alone would choose.
And hence! and hence!—
Was I so dense?—
He tried with hammer clamorous
To drown my ditty amorous.
And from the maid to hide
That others wooed beside!
So, so!—Ho, ho!
Your game I know!
That you, to spoil my labor, should
Have roused up all the neighbor-
hood,
With cudgel and with sticks,
To put me in a fix!

# Act III

Wohl grün und blau,
zum Spott der allerliebsten Frau,
zerschlagen und zerprügelt,
dass kein Schneider mich
aufbügelt!
Gar auf mein Leben
war's angegeben!
Doch kam ich noch so davon,
dass ich die That euch lohn'!
zieht heut' nur aus zum Singen,
merkt auf, wie's mag gelingen;
bin ich gezwackt
auch und zerhackt,
euch bring' ich doch sicher aus
dem Takt!

SACHS: Gut' Freund ihr seid in argem Wahn!
Glaubt was ihr wollt, dass ich's gethan,
gebt eure Eifersucht nur hin!
zu werben kommt mit nicht in Sinn.

BECKMESSER: Lug und Trug! Ich weis es besser.

SACHS: Was fällt euch nur ein, Meister Beckmesser?
Was ich sonst im Sinn, geht euch nichts an:
doch glaubt, ob der Werbung seid ihr im Wahn.

BECKMESSER: Ihr säng't heut' nicht?

SACHS: Nicht zur Wette.

BECKMESSER: Kein Werbelied?

SACHS: Gewisslich, nein!

BECKMESSER: Wenn ich aber drob ein Zeugniss hätte?

SACHS: (blickt auf den Werktisch). Das Gedicht? Hier liess ich's:—stecket ihr's ein?

BECKMESSER: (zieht das Blatt herror). Ist das eure Hand?

SACHS: Ja,—war es das?

BECKMESSER: Ganz frisch noch die Schrift?

SACHS: Und die Tinte noch nass?

BECKMESSER: 's wär wohl gar ein biblisches Lied?

SACHS: Der fehlte wohl, wer darauf rieth.

BECKMESSER: Nun denn?

SACHS: Wie doch?

BECKMESSER: Ihr fragt?

SACHS: Was noch?

BECKMESSER: Dass ihr mit aller Biederkeit
der ärgste aller Spitzbuben seid!

SACHS: Mag sein! Doch hab' ich doch noch nie entwandt,
was ich auf fremden Tischen fand:—
und dass man von euch auch nicht übles denkt,
behaltet das Blatt, es sei euch geschenkt.

---

Boohoo! Boohoo!
I'm black and blue.
Disgraced before the damsel, too.
They did so bruise and rend me,
No tailor ever can mend me!
With aches they filled me
And nearly killed me;
But you see I got away,
And your ill turn I'll pay.
Attend the singing-trial,
And see if you outvie all!
If I'm attacked
And badly thwacked,
I'll soon expose your wicked art!

SACHS: Good friend, your anger makes you mad!
Think all you will of me that's bad:
But calm this jealous ire;
For courtship I have no desire.

BECKMESSER: Pack of lies! I know you're double!

SACHS: Why, Master Town-clerk, what's your trouble?
My intended plans concern not you:
But, you're deceived if you think I'd woo.

BECKMESSER: You mean to sing?

SACHS: Not in competing.

BECKMESSER: No Wooing-song?

SACHS: Dismiss the fear!

BECKMESSER: But I've a proof there's no defeating.

SACHS: (looking at the workbench). Did you take the poem?—I left it here.

BECKMESSER: (producing the paper). Is this not your hand?

SACHS: Well—and what then?

BECKMESSER: The writing is fresh?

SACHS: Still wet from the pen.

BECKMESSER: Perhaps then it's a biblical song?

SACHS: To call it so indeed were wrong.

BECKMESSER: Well then?

SACHS: What more?

BECKMESSER: You ask?

SACHS: For sure!

BECKMESSER: Why, that in all sincerity,
A most consummate rogue you must be!

SACHS: May be! but I was never known
To pocket papers not my own:—
But that you should not be called a thief,
You're welcome to it—I give you the leaf.

---

BECKMESSER: (in freudigem Schreck aufspringend). Herr Gott! . . . Ein Gedicht! . . . Ein Gedicht von Sachs? . . .
Doch halt', dass kein neuer Schad' mir erwachs'!
Ihr habt's wohl schon recht gut memorirt?

SACHS: Seid meinethalben doch nur unbeirrt!

BECKMESSER: Ihr lasst mir das Blatt?

SACHS: Damit ihr kein Dieb.

BECKMESSER: Und mach' ich Gebrauch?

SACHS: Wie's euch belieb'.

BECKMESSER: Doch, sing' ich das Lied?

SACHS: Wenn's nicht zu schwer.

BECKMESSER: Und wenn ich gefiel'?

SACHS: Das wunderte mich sehr!

BECKMESSER: (ganz zutraulich). Da seid ihr nun wieder zu bescheiden;
ein Lied von Sachs, das will was bedeuten!
Vergessen und begraben
sie Zwist, Hader und Streit,
und was uns je entzweit.
(Er blickt seitwärts in das Blatt: plötzlich runzelt sich seine Stirn).
Und doch! Wenn's nur eine Falle wär!—
Noch gestern war't ihr mein Feind:
wie käm's, dass nach so grosser Beschwer'
ihr's freundlich heut' mit mir meint?

SACHS: Ich machte euch Schuh' in später Nacht:
hat man so je einen Feind bedacht?

BECKMESSER: Ja, ja! recht gut!—
doch eines schwört:
wo und wie ihr das Lied auch hört,
dass nie ihr euch beikommen läss't,
zu sagen, es sei von euch verfasst.

SACHS: Das schwör' ich und gelob' euch hier,
nie mich zu rühmen, das Lied sei von mir.

BECKMESSER: (sehr glücklich).
Was will ich mehr, ich bin geborgen!
Jetzt hat sich Beckmesser nicht mehr zu sorgen!
(Er reibt sich froh die Hände.)

SACHS: Doch, Freund, ich führ's euch zu Gemüthe,
und rathe euch in aller Güte:
studirt mir recht das Lied!
sein Vortrag ist nicht leicht:
ob euch die Weise gerieth',
und ihr den Ton erreicht!

---

BECKMESSER: (springing up in a joyous surprise). You do? What, a song?—A song by Sachs!
Yet stay!—Can he plan more evil attacks?—
I guess that you learned it by heart?

SACHS: No, let your mistrust of me depart!

BECKMESSER: You give me the song?

SACHS: To ease your conscience.

BECKMESSER: To use as my own!

SACHS: That's just as you please.

BECKMESSER: And may it be sung?

SACHS: Yes, if you can read.

BECKMESSER: And should I get praise?

SACHS: That would be strange indeed!

BECKMESSER: (affectionately).
Ah! now in truth your talk is more pleasant.
A song by Sachs: that is a fine present!
If it's really for me meant
Our recent disagreement
Is over; quarrel and strife
We will dismiss for life.
(He peers sideways at the paper; suddenly he frowns.)
And yet! If this were some villainy!—
But yesterday you were my foe:
How, after your behavior to me
Such friendship can you show?—

SACHS: I sat up late to make your shoes:
It is not thus our foes we use.

BECKMESSER: Aye, aye! that's true!—But swear one thing;
That when you hear this, no matter where,
To nobody shall be disclosed
The fact that it was by you composed.

SACHS: I swear it, and I guarantee
That none shall know the song's by me.

BECKMESSER: (very joyous).
What more remains? I'm joyful-hearted!
Beckmesser's troubles have departed!
(He rubs his hands with elation.)

SACHS: Stay, friend! Do not think that I despise you,
But let me earnestly advise you
To study well this song.
The labor is not light:
Don't get the melody wrong,
And mind your Tones are right!

BECKMESSER: Freund Sachs, ihr seid ein guter Poet;
doch was Ton und Weise betrifft, gesteht,
da thut's mir Keiner vor!
Drum spitzt nur fein das Ohr,
und: "Beckmesser,
Keiner besser!"
Darauf macht euch gefasst,
wenn ihr ruhig mich singen lasst.—
Doch nun memoriren,
schnell nach Haus!
Ohne Zeit verlieren
richt' ich das aus.—
Ade! ich muss fort!
An and'rem Ort
dank' ich euch inniglich,
weil ihr so minniglich;
für euch nun stimme ich,
kauf' eure Werke gleich,
mache zum Merker euch:
doch fein mit Kreide weich,
nicht mit dem Hammerstreich!
Merker! Merker! Merker Hans Sachs!
dass Nürnberg schusterlich blüh'
und wachs'!
(*Er hinkt, pollert und taumelt wie besessen fort.*)

SACHS: So ganz boshaft doch keinen ich fand,
er hält's auf die Länge nicht aus:
vergeudet mancher oft viel Verstand,
doch hält er auch damit Haus:
die schwache Stunde kommt für Jeden;
da wird er dumm und lässt mit sich reden.—
Dass hier Herr Beckmesser ward zum Dieb,
ist mir für meinen Plan sehr lieb.—
(*Er sicht durch das Fenster Eva kommen.*)
Sieh, Evchen! Dacht' ich doch wo sie blieb'!
(*Eva, reich geschmückt und in glänzender weisser Kleidung, tritt zum Laden herein.*)

SACHS: Grüss Gott! mein Evchen!
Ei, wie herrlich,
wie stolz du's heute meinst!
Du machst wohl Jung und Alt begehrlich,
wenn du so schön erscheinst.

EVA: Meister! 's ist nicht so gefährlich,
und ist's dem Schneider geglückt,
wer sieht dann an wo's mir beschwerlich,
wo still der Schuh mich drückt?

SACHS: Der böse Schuh! 's war deine Laun',
dass du ihn gestern nicht probirt.

EVA: Merk' wohl, ich hatt' zu viel Vertrau'n:
im Meister hab' ich mich geirrt.

SACHS: Ei, 's thut mir leid! Zeig' her, mein Kind,
dass ich dir helfe, gleich geschwind.

BECKMESSER: Friend Sachs, you are a poet of wit!
But as for Tones and Modes, admit
There's none can touch me here!
So open wide your ear
To "Beckmesser,
Your professor":
And all your doubts will cease
If you'll let me sing in peace.—
But now to run through it.
Quick, away!
If in time I would do it
I must not stay.
Farewell! I'm away!
Some other day,
When in this latitude,
I'll pay my gratitude
For your kind attitude;
Buy all your works, you know;
You shall as Marker show,—
Chalk you must mark with, though,
Not with the hammer's blow!
Marker! Marker! Marker Hans Sachs!
May he and Nuremberg bloom and wax!
(*As if intoxicated he limps, stumbling and blundering away.*)

SACHS: I never met with so evil a man:
He'll come to grief one of these days.
Their reason most men squander who can,
Yet keep some little relays:
But some weak moments discover:
Then they are fools and we talk them over.—
That Master Beckmesser wasn't square,
Finely will further my affair.—
(*Through his window he see Eva approaching.*)
Ha! Eva! Here she is, I declare!
(*Eva, richly decked out and in a gleaming white dress, enters the shop.*)

SACHS: My child, good morning!
Ah, how pretty
And smart you are today!
Both old and young—why, all the city
You'll win in such array.

EVA: Master, surely now you flatter!
And if my dress is all right,
Will no one notice what's the matter?
My shoe is much too tight.

SACHS: The naughty shoe! But it was your haste;
You would not try it on, you see.

EVA: Not so; too great a trust I placed:
The Master's disappointed me.

SACHS: I'm really grieved! Come here, my pet,
And I will help you even yet.

EVA: Sobald ich stehe, will es geh'n:
doch will ich geh'n, zwingt's mich zu steh'n.

SACHS: Hier auf den Schemel streck' den Fuss:
der üblen Noth ich wehren muss.
(*Sie streckt den Fuss auf den Schemel beim Werktisch.*) Was ist's mit dem?

EVA: Ihr seht, zu weit!

SACHS: Kind, das ist pure Eitelkeit:
der Schuh ist knapp.

EVA: Das sag' ich ja:
Drum drückt er mir die Zehen da.

SACHS: Hier links?

EVA: Nein, rechts.

SACHS: Wohl mehr am Spann?

EVA: Mehr hier am Hacken.

SACHS: Kommt der auch dran?

EVA: Ach, Meister! Wüsset ihr besser als ich,
wo der Schuh mich drückt?

SACHS: Ei 's wundert mich
dass er zu weit, und doch drückt überall?
(*Walther, in glänzender Rittertracht, tritt unter die Thüre der Kammer, und bleibt beim Anblick Eva's wie festgebannt stehen. Eva stösst einen leisen Schrei aus und bleibt ebenfalls unverwandt in ihrer Stellung mit dem Fusse auf dem Schemel. Sachs, der vor ihr sich gebückt hat, ist mit dem Rücken der Thüre zugekehrt.*)
Aha! hier sitzt's! Nun begreif' ich den Fall!
Kind! du hast recht: 's stak in der Nath:—
Nun warte, dem Übel schaff' ich Rath.
Bleib' nur so stehen; ich nehm' dir den Schuh
eine Weil' auf den Leisten: dann lässt er dir Ruh'.
(*Er hat ihr sanft den Schub vom Fusse gezogen; während sie in ihrer Stellung verbleibt, macht er sich mit dem Schuh zu schaffen und thut, als breachtete er nichts andres.*)
Säng' mir nur wenigstens Einer dazu!
Hörte heut' gar ein schönes Lied:—
wem dazu ein dritter Vers gerieth'?

WALTHER: (*immer Eva gegenüber in der vorigen Stellung*).
"Weilten die Sterne im lieblichen Tanz?
So licht und klar
im Lockenhaar,
vor allen Frauen
hehr zu schauen,
lag ihr mit zartem Glanz
ein Sternenkranz.—
Wunder ob Wunder nun bieten sich dar:
Zwiefachen Tag
ich grüssen mag;
denn gleich zwei'n Sonnen

EVA: If I would stand it will away;
Would I be gone it makes me stay.

SACHS: Upon the stool here place your foot.—
A shocking fault? I'll look into it.
(*She puts her foot up on a stool by the work-bench.*)
What is amiss?

EVA: Too wide, you see.

SACHS: Child, that is purely vanity;
The shoe is tight.

EVA: I told you so,
And that is why it hurts my toe.

SACHS: Here—left?

EVA: No, right.

SACHS: What! on the sole?

EVA: Here, at the ankle.

SACHS: Well! that's droll!

EVA: Nay, Master! do you know better than I
Where the shoe pinches?

SACHS: I wonder why,
If it's too wide, it pinches you so?
(*Walter, in glittering knightly apparel appears at the chamber door, and stands there spellbound at the sight of Eva. She utters a slight cry, but remains in her position with one foot on the stool. Sachs is kneeling before her with his back towards the door.*)
Aha! it is here! Now the reason I know!
Child, you are right: it is in the sole!
One moment, and I'll make it whole.
Stand so awhile. I'll fasten your shoe
On the last a moment, then it will do.
(*He has gently drawn off her shoe; while she remains in the same position he pretends to busy himself with it and to be oblivious of all else.*)
(*as he works*). Will some one give us a song to amuse?
I heard today a lovely one:
Let's see if the third verse can be done!

WALTER: (*still in the same position opposite Eva*). "Lingered the stars in their dance of delight?
They rested there
Upon her hair,
That wondrous maiden
So beauty-laden,
And formed a circlet bright
All star-bedecked.
Wonder on wonder now waked my surprise:
The light of day
Had twofold ray:
For two transcendent
Suns resplendent

reinster Wonnen,
der hehrsten Augen Paar
nahm ich nun wahr.—
Huldreiches Bild,
dem ich zu nahen mich erkühnt:
den Kranz, vor zweier Sonne Strahl
zugleich verblichen und ergrünt,
minnig und mild,
sie flocht ihn um's Haupt dem
Gemahl.
Dort Huld-geboren,
nun Ruhm-erkoren,
giesst paradiesische Lust
sie in des Dichters Brust—
im Liebestraum''—

**SACHS:** (*Sachs hat, immer mit
seiner Arbeit beschäftigt, den
Schuh zurückgebracht, und ist
jetzt während der Schlussverse
von Walter's Gesang darüber
her, ihn Eva wieder anzuziehen.*)
Lausch', Kind! das ist ein Meisterlied:
derlei hörst du jetzt bei mir singen.
Nun schau', ob dabei mein Schuh
gerieth?
Mein' endlich doch
es thät' mir gelingen?
Versuch's! tritt auf!—Sag', drückt
er dich noch?
(*Eva, die wie bezaubert bewegungslos gestanden, gesehen und
gehört hat, bricht jetzt in heftiges
Weinen aus, sinkt Sachs an die
Brust und drückt ihn schluchzend
an sich.—Walthier ist zu ihnen
getreten und drückt Sachs begeistert die Hand.—Sachs thut sich
endlich Gewalt an, reisst sich wie
unmuthig los, und lässt dadurch
Eva unwillkürlich an Walther's
Schulter sich anlehnen.*)

**EVA:** O Sachs! Mein Freund! Du
theurer Mann!
Wie ich dir Edlem lohnen kann!
Was ohne deine Liebe,
was wär' ich ohne dich
ob je auch Kind ich bliebe,
erwecktest du nicht mich?
Durch dich gewann ich
was man preist,
durch dich ersann ich
was ein Geist!
Durch dich erwacht,
durch dich nur dacht'
ich edel, frei und kühn:
du liessest mich erblüh'n!—
O lieber Meister! schilt mich nur!
Ich war doch auf der rechten Spur:
denn, hatte ich die Wahl,
nur dich erwählt' ich mir:
du wärest mein Gemahl,
den Preis nur reicht' ich dir!—
Doch nun hat's mich gewählt
zu nie gekannter Qual:
und werd' ich heut vermählt,
so wär's ohn' alle Wahl!
Das war ein Müssen, war ein Zwang!
Dir selbst, mein Meister, wurde
bang.

Within her heavenly eyes
I saw arise
Image so rare,
Which boldly I approached and
viewed!
By all this light the crown above
At once was faded and renewed.
Tender and fair
She wove it round the head of her
love,
Thus, grace-directed,
To fame elected,
She poured the joys of the blest
Into the poet's breast.—
In Love's sweet dream.''—

**SACHS:** (*busily at work, brings
back the shoe during the last verse
of Walter's song and fits it on
Eva's foot again*). Hark, child! that
is a Master-Song:
You hear such music where I dwell
now.
So try if still my shoe is wrong.
Was I not right?
And fits it well now?
Let's see! stand down!—Is it still
tight?
(*Eva, who has stood as if enchanted, gazing and listening, bursts
into a sudden fit of weeping and
sinks on Sachs's breast, sobbing
and clinging to him. Walter advances towards them and wrings
Sachs's hand in silent ecstacy.—
Sachs at last composes himself,
tears himself gloomily away and
causes Eva to rest involuntarily
on Walter's shoulder.*)

**EVA:** O Sachs! best friend and dear-
est! Say
How can I ever repay my debt?
Bereft of your great kindness
How helpless should I be!
Still wrapped in childish blindness
Had it not been for you.
Through the life's treasure
I control,
Through you I measure
First my soul.
Through you I wake;
My feelings take
A higher, nobler tone:
I bloom through you alone!—
Yes, dearest Master, scold you may!
But I was in the rightful way:
For were my choice but free,
It is you would please my eyes;
My husband you should be,
None else should win the prize.—
But now I am a prey
To never-dreamed-of ill.
And if I'm wed today
It will be against my will!
That were compulsion—nothing
but force!
You would, my Master, dread this
course.

**SACHS:** Mein Kind:
von Tristan und Isolde
kenn' ich ein traurig Stück:
Hans Sachs war klug, und wollte
nichts von Herrn Marke's Glück.—
's war Zeit, dass ich den Rechten erkannt:
wär' sonst am End' doch hineinge-
rannt!—
Aha! da streicht schon die Lene
um's Haus!
Nur herein!—He, David! Kommst
nicht heraus?
(*Magdalene, in festlichen Staate,
tritt durch die Ladenthür herein;
aus der Kammer kommt zugleich
David, ebenfalls im Festkleid, mit
Blumen und Bändern sehr reich
und zierlich ausgeputzt.*)
Die Zeugen sind da, Gevatter zur
Hand;
jetzt schnell zur Taufe; nehmt euren Stand!
(*Alle blicken ihn verwundert an.*)
Ein Kind ward hier geboren;
jezt sei ihm ein Nam' erkoren!
So ist's nach Meister-Weis' und Art,
wenn eine Meisterweise geschaffen
ward,
dass die einen guten Namen trag',
dran Jeder sie erkennen mag.—
Vernehmt, respectable Gesellschaft,
was euch hierher zur Stell'
schafft!—
Eine Meisterweise ist gelungen,
von Junker Walther gedichtet und
gesungen;
der jungen Weise lebender Vater
lud mich und die Pognerin zu Gevatter:
weil wir die Weise wohl vernommen,
sind wir zur Taufe hierher gekommen.
Auch dass wir zur Handlung Zeugen haben.
ruf' ich Jungfer Lene, und meinen
Knaben;
doch da's zum Zeugen kein
Lehrbube thut,
und heut' auch den Spruch er gesungen gut,
so mach' ich den Burschen gleich
zum Gesell';
knie' nieder, David, und nimm
diese Schell'!
(*David is niedergekniet. Sachs
gibt ihm eine starke Ohrfeige.*)
Steh' auf, Gesell! und denk' an den
Streich;
du merkst dir dabei die Taufe zu
gleich!—
Fehlst sonst noch 'was, uns Keiner
drum schilt:
wer weiss, ob's nicht gar eine Noth-
taufe gilt,
Dass die Weise Kraft behalte zum
Leben,
will ich nur gleich den Namen ihr
geben:—
''die selige Morgentraumdeut-
Weise''
sei sie genannt zu des Meisters
Preise.—

**SACHS:** My child:
Sir Tristan I have read of—
Isolde's story dark:
Hans Sachs had prudent dread of
The fate of poor king Mark.—
It was time the right man did ap-
pear,
Or I should have been caught, I
fear!—
Aha! There's Magdalena's found us
out.
Come in! Ho David! What's he
about?
(*Magdalena in holiday attire en-
ters from the street and David at
the same time comes out of the
chamber, also gaily dressed and
very splendid with ribbons and
flowers.*)
The witnesses wait, the sponsors
are found:
So now for a christening gather
around!
(*All look at him with surprise.*)
A child here was created;
Let its name be stated by you.
Such is the Masters' constant use,
When they produce a Master-song.
They give it a fitly chosen name
That men may know it by the same.
So let me tell all you here
What is it we have to do here!
A Master-song has been completed,
By young Sir Walter made and re-
peated;
The newborn poem's father, de-
lighted,
For sponsors has Eva and me invit-
ed:
As to the song we have been
list'ning
We now come here to its christen-
ing.
To see that we act with solemn
fitness
Shall David and Lena be called to
witness:
But as no Prentice a witness can be,
And as he's repeated his task to me,
A Journeyman I will make him
here.
Kneel, David, and take this box on
the ear!
(*David kneels and Sachs gives
him a smart box on the ear.*)
Arise, my man: remember that
blow:
I will mark this baptism for you,
you know,
Lacks aught beside, what blame in-
deed?
Who knows if private baptism we
need?
That the melody lack not anything
vital
I now proceed to give it its title.
''The glorious morning-dream's
true story.''—
So be it named, to the Master's glo-
ry,
And may it increase in size and
strength.—
And bid the young god-mother at
length.

Nun wachse sie gross, ohn' Schad'
und Bruch:
die jüngste Gevatterin spricht des
Spruch.

**EVA:** Selig, wie die Sonne
meines Glückes lacht,
Morgen voller Wonne,
selig mir erwacht!
Traum der höchsten Huld
himmlisch Morgenblüh'n!
Deutung euch zu schulde
selig süss Bemüh'n!
Einer Weise mild und hehr,
sollt' es hold gelingen,
meines Herzens süss Beschwer'
deutend zu bezwingen.
Ob es nur ein Morgentraum?
Selig deut' ich mir es kaum.
Doch die Weise,
was sie leise
mir vertraut
im stillen Raum,
hell und laut,
in der Meister vollem Kreis,
deute sie den höchsten Preis!

**WALTHER:** Deine Liebe, rein und
hehr,
liess es mir gelingen,
meines Herzens süss Beschwer
deutend zu bezwingen.
Ob es noch der Morgentraum?
Selig deut' ich mir es kaum.
Doch die Weise,
was sie leise
dir vertraut
im stillen Raum,
hell und laut,
in der Meister vollem Kreis,
werbe sie um höchsten Preis!

**SACHS:** Vor dem Kinde lieblich
hehr,
mocht' ich gern wohl singen;
doch des Herzens süss Beschwer
galt es zu bezwingen.
's war ein schöner Abendtraum:
dran zu deuten wag' ich kaum.
Diese Weise,
was sie leise
mir vertraut
im stillen Raum,
sagt mir laut:
auch der Jugend ew'ges Reis
grünt nur durch des Dichters Preis.

**DAVID:** Wach' oder träum' ich
schon so früh?
Das zu erklären macht mir Müh'.
's ist wohl nur ein Morgentraum;
was ich seh', begreif' ich kaum.
Ward zur Stelle
gleich Geselle?
Lene Braut?
Im Kirchenraum
wir getraut?
's geht der Kopf mir, wie im Kreis,
dass ich bald gar Meister heiss'!

**MAGDELENE:** Wach' oder träum'
ich schon so früh?
Das zu erklären macht mir Müh'!
's ist wohl nur ein Morgentraum?
Was ich seh', begreif' ich kaum!
Er zur Stelle
gleich Geselle?
Ich die Braut?

**EVA:** Dazzling as the dawn
That smiles upon my glee,
Rapture-laden morn
To bliss awakens me.
Dream of balmy beauty,
Brilliant morning-glow!
Hard but sweet's the duty
Your intent to know.
That divine and tender strain
With its tones of gladness
Has revealed my heart's sweet pain
And subdued its sadness.
Is it but a morning-dream?
Scarcely real it seems.
What the ditty,
Soft and pretty,
Told of me.
A quiet theme,
Loud and free
In the Master's conclave wise
Shall achieve the highest prize.

**WALTER:** It was your love, the
highest gain—
Allured me by its gladness.
To reveal my heart's sweet pain
And subdue its sadness.
Is it still my morning-dream?
Scarcely real it seems
What the ditty,
Soft and pretty,
Told of thee,
A quiet theme,
Loud and free
In the Master's conclave wise
Shall achieve the highest prize.

**SACHS:** With the maiden I would
openly
Sing for very gladness;
But my heart I must restrain,
Quell my passion's madness.
It was a tender evening-dream:
Undiscovered let it beam.
What the ditty,
Soft and pretty,
Told of me
In quiet theme,
Here I see:
Youth and love that never dies
Flourish through the Poets prize.

**DAVID:** Am I awake or dreaming
still?
I scarcely have skill to explain it.
Sure it is but a morning-dream!
All these things seen unreal.
Can it be, man,
You're a freeman?
And that she—
Oh joy supreme!—
My spouse shall be?
Round and round my head-piece
flies
That a Master I now rise!

**MAGDALENA:** Am I awake or
dreaming still
Scarce to explain it have I skill.
Sure it is but a morning-dream!
All these things seem unreal.
Can it be, man,
You're a freeman?
And that we—

Im Kirchenraum
wir getraut?
Ja, wahrhaftig! 's geht: wer weiss?
Bald ich wohl Frau Meist'rin heiss!
(*Das Orchester geht sehr leise in
cinc marschmässige, heitere
Weise über. — Sachs ordnet den
Aufbruch an.*)

**SACHS:** Jetzt All' am Fleck! Den Vater grüss'!
Auf, nach der Wies' schnell auf die
Füss'!
(*Eva trennt sich vom Sachs und
Walther und verlässt mit Magdalene die Werkstatt.*)
Nun, Junker! Kommt! Habt frohen
Muth!—
David, Gesell'! Schliess' den Laden
gut!
(*Als Sachs und Walther ebenfalls
auf die Strasse gehen, und David
sich über das Schliessen der Ladenthüre hermacht, wird im Proscenium ein Vorhang von beiden
Seiten zusammengezogen, so
dass er die Scene gänzlich
schliesst. — Als die Musik allmählich zu grösserer Stärke ange-
wachsen ist, wird der Vorhang
nach der Höhe zu aufgezogen. Die
Bühne ist verwandelt.*)
(*Die Scene stellt einen freien Wies-
enplan dar, im ferneren Hintergrunde die Stadt Nürnberg. Die
Pegnitz schlängelt sich durch den
Plan: der schmale Fluss ist an den
nächsten Punkten praktikabel gehalten. Buntbeflaggte Kähne setzen unablässig die ankommenden, festlich geschmückten
Bürger der Zünfte, mit Frauen
und Kindern, an das Ufer der Fe-
stwiese über. Eine erhöhte Bühne
mit Bünken darauf ist rechts zur
Seite aufgeschlagen; bereits ist sie
mit den Fahnen der angekommenen Zünfte ausgeschmückt: im
Verlaufe stecken die Fahnenträger der noch ankommenden
Zünfte ihre Fahnen ebenfalls um
die Sängerbühne auf, so dass
diese schliesslich nach drei Seiten
hin ganz davon eingefasst ist. —
Zelte mit Getränken und Erfris-
chungen aller Art begrenzen im
Uebrigen die Seiten des vorderen
Hauptraumes.
Vor den Zelten geht es bereits lustig her; Bürger mit Frauen und
Kindern sitzen und lagern da-
selbst. — Die Lehrbuben der Meistersinger, festlich gekleidet, mit
Blumen und Bändern reich und
anmuthig geschmückt, üben mit
schlanken Stäben, die ebenfalls
mit Blumen und Bändern geziert
sind, in lustiger Weise das Amt
von Herolden und Marschällen
aus. Sie empfangen die am Ufer
Aussteigenden, ordnen die Züge
der Zünfte, und geleiten diese
nach der Singerbühne, von wo
aus, nachdem der Bannerträger
die Fahne aufgepflanzt, die Zünft-
bürger und Gesellen nach Belie-*)

Oh joy supreme!—
Shall be wedded?
Yes, what honor lies near me!
Soon I shall as Madam rise!
(*The orchestra goes into a broad
march-like theme. — Sachs makes
the group break up.*)

**SACHS:** Now let's be off!—Your father stays!
Quick, to the fields all go your
ways!
(*Eva tears herself away from
Sachs and Walter and leaves the
house with Magdalena.*)
So come, sir knight! take heart of
grace!—
David, my man, lock up the
place!—
(*As Sachs and Walter also go into
the street and David is left shutting up the shop, curtains descend
from each side of the proscenium
so as to conceal the stage. — When
the music has gradually swelled
to the loudest pitch the curtains
are drawn up again and the scene
is changed.*)
(*The stage now represents an
open meadow; in the distance at
back the town of Nuremberg. The
Pegnitz winds across the plain;
the narrow river is practicable in
the foreground. Boats gaily decorated with flags continually discharge fresh parties of Burghers of
the different Guilds with their
wives and families, who land on
the banks. A raised stand with
benches on it is erected R. already
adorned with flags of those as yet
arrived; as the scene opens, the
standard-bearers of freshly arriving Guilds also place their banners against the Singers' stage, so
that it is at last quite closed in on
three sides by them. — Tents with
all kinds of refreshments border
the sides of the open space in
front.
Before the tents is much merrymaking: Burghers and their families sit and group round them. —
The Prentices of the Mastersing-
ers, in holiday attire, finely
decked out with ribbons and flowers, and bearing slender wands,
also ornamented, fulfil frolic-
somely the office of heralds and
stewards. They receive the new
comers on the bank, arrange
them in procession and conduct
them to the stand, whence, after
the standard-bearer has deposited
his banner, the Burghers and
Journeymen disperse under the
tents.
Among the arriving Guilds the following are prominent:*)

# Act III

ben sich unter den Zelten zerstreuen.
*Unter den noch anlangenden Zünften werden die folgenden besonders bemerkt.*)

**DIE SCHUSTER:** (*indem sie aufziehen*). Sankt Crispin, lobet ihn!
War gar ein heilig Mann,
zeigt was ein Schuster kann.
Die Armen hatten gute Zeit,
macht' Ihnen warme Schuh',
und wenn ihm Keiner Leder leiht,
so stahl er sich's dazu.
Der Schuster hat ein weit Gewissen,
macht Schuhe selbst mit Hindernissen;
und ist vom Gerber das Fell erst weg,
dann streck'! streck'! streck'!
Leder taugt nur am rechten Fleck.
(*Die Stadtpfeifer, Lauten- und Kinder-Instrumentenmacher ziehen, auf ihren, Instrumenten spielend, auf. Ihnen folgen:*)

**DIE SCHNEIDER:** Als Nürenberg belagert war,
und Hungersnoth sich fand,
wär' Stadt und Volk verdorben gar,
war nicht ein Schneider zur Hand,
der viel Muth hat und Verstand;
hat sich in ein Bockfell eingenäht
auf dem Standtwall da spazieren geht,
und macht wohl seine Sprünge
gar lustig guter Dinge.
Der Feind, der sieht's und zieht von Fleck:
der Teufel hol' die Stadt sich weg,
hat's drin noch so lustige Meckmeck-meck!
Meck! Meck! Meck!
Wer glaubt's, dass ein Schneider im Bocke steck'!

**DIE BÄCKER:** (*ziehen dicht hinter den Schneidern auf, so dass ihr Lied in das der Schneider hineinklingt*). Hungersnoth: Hungersnoth!
Das ist ein gräulich Leiden!
Gäb' euch der Bäcker, kein täglich Brod,
müsst alle Welt verschneiden,
Beck! Beck! Beck!
Täglich auf dem Fleck!
Nimm uns den Hunger weg!

**DIE LEHRBUBEN:** Herr Je! Herr Je!
Mädel von Fürth!
Stadtpfeifer, spielt! dass 's lustig wird!
(*Ein bunter Kahn, mit jungen Mädchen in reicher bäuerischer Tracht, ist angekommen. Die Lehrbuben heben die Mädchen heraus, und tanzen mit ihnen, während die Stadtpfeifer spielen, nach dem Vordergrunde.—Das Charakteristische des Tanzes besteht darin, dass die Lehrbuben die Mädchen scheinbar nur an den Platz bringen wollen; sowie die Gesellen zugreifen wollen, ziehen die Buben die Mädchen aber immer wieder zurück, als ob sie sie*

**THE SHOEMAKERS:** (*as they march past*). Saint Crispin!
Honor him!
He was both wise and good,
Did all a cobbler could.
That was a fine time for the poor
He made them all warm shoes;
When none would lend him leather more,
To steal he'd not refuse.
The cobbler has a conscience easy,
No obstacles to labor sees he;
When from the tanner it is sent away
Then hey! hey! hey!
Leather becomes his rightful prey.
(*The Town-Pipers, Lute- and Toy-Instrument-Makers playing on their instruments, follow. These are succeeded by:*)

**THE TAILORS:** When Nuremberg besieged did stand
And famine wrought despair,
Undone had been both folk and land
Had not a tailor been there,
Of craft and courage rare:
Within a goat-skin he did hide
And shewd upon the wall outside.
There took to gaily tripping
And gambolling and skipping.
The foe beheld it with dismay:
The devil fetch that town away,
Where goats yet merrily play, play, play.
Me-ey! me-ey! me-ey!
Who'd think that a tailor within there lay!

**THE BAKERS:** (*coming close behind the Tailors so that the two songs join together*). Want of bread! Want of bread!
That is a hardship true, sirs!
If you were not by the baker fed
Old Death would feed on you, sirs.
Pray! pray! pray!
Baker every day,
Hunger take away!

**PRENTICES:** Heyday! heyday!
Maidens from Fürth!
Play up, town-piper! One merry spurt!
(*A gaily painted boat, filled with young Girls in fine peasant-costumes, arrives. The Prentices help the Girls out and dance with them, while the town-pipers play, towards the front.—The character of this dance consists in the Prentices appearing only to wish to bring the Girls to the open place; the Journeymen endeavor to capture them and the Prentices move on as if seeking another place, thus making the tour of the stage and continually delaying*

anderswo unterbringen wollten, wobei sie meistens den ganzen Kreis, wie wählend, ausmessen, und somit die scheinbare Absicht auszuführen anmuthig und lustig verzögern.*)

**DAVID:** (*kommt vom Landungsplatz vor*). Ihr tanzt? Was werden die Meister sagen?
(*Die Buben drehen ihm Nasen.*)
Hört nicht?—Lass' ich mir's auch behagen!
(*Er nimmt sich ein junges, schönes Mädchen, und geräth im Tanze mit ihr bald in grosses Feuer. Die Zuschauer freuen sich und lachen.*)

**EIN PARR LEHRBUBEN:** David! die Lene! die Lene sieht zu.

**DAVID:** (*erschrickt, lässt das Mädchen schnell fahren, fasst sich aber Muth, da er nichts sieht, und tanzt nun noch feuriger weiter*). Ach! lasst mich mit euren Possen in Ruh'!

**DIE GESELLEN:** (*am Landungsplatz*). Die Meistersinger! die Meistersinger!

**DAVID:** Herr Gott!—Ade, ihr hübschen Dinger!
(*Er gibt dem Mädchen einen feurigen Kuss und reisst sich los. Die Lehrbuben unterbrechen alle schnell den Tanz, eilen zum Ufer und reihen sich dort zum Empfang der Meistersinger. Alles macht auf das Geheiss der Lehrbuben Platz.—Die Meistersinger ordnen sich am Landungsplatze und ziehen dann festlich auf, um auf der erhöhten Bühne ihre Plätze einzunehemen. Voran Kothner als Fahnenträger: dann Pogner, Eva an der Hand führend; diese ist von festlich geschmückten und reich gekleideten jungen Mädchen begleitet, denen sich Magdalene anschliesst. Dann folgen die übrigen Meistersinger. Sie werden mit Hutschwenken und Freudenrufen begrüsst. Als alle auf der Bühne angelangt sind. Eva von den Mädchen umgeben, denn Ehrenplatz eingenommen, und Kothner die Fahne gerade in der Mitte der übrigen Fahnen, und sie alle überragend, aufgepflantzt hat, treten die Lehrbuben, dem Volke zugewendet, feierlich vor der Bühne in Reih und Glied.*)

**DIE LEHRBUBEN:** Silentium! Silentium!
Lasst all' Reden und Gesumm'!
(*Sachs erhebt sich und tritt vor. Bei seinem Anblick stösst sich Alles an und bricht sofort unter Hut- und Tücher schwenken in grossen Jubel aus.*)

**ALLES VOLK:** Ha! Sachs! 's ist Sachs!
Seht! Meister Sachs!
Stimmt an! Stimmt an! Stimmt an!

their original purpose in fun and frolic.*)

**DAVID:** (*advancing from the landing-place*). You dance? The Masters will rate such folly.
(*The boys make faces at him.*)
Don't care?—Why, then let me too be jolly!
(*He seizes a young and pretty girl and mingles in the dance with great ardor. The spectators notice him and laugh.*)

**SOME OF THE PRENTICES:** David! There's Lena! Lena sees you!

**DAVID:** (*alarmed, hastily releases the maiden, but seeing nothing, quickly regains his courage and resumes his dancing*). Have done with your silly jokes, my boys, do!

**JOURNEYMEN:** (*at the landing-place*). The Master Singers; The Master Singers!

**DAVID:** Oh lord!—Farewell, pretty clingers!
(*He gives the maidens an ardent kiss and tears himself away. The Prentices quickly discontinue their dance, hasten to the bank and arrange themselves to receive the Master Singers. All stand back by command of the Prentices.— The Master Singers arrange their procession on the bank and then march forwards to take their places on the stand. First Kothner, as standardbearer, then Pogner leading Eva by the hand; she is attended by richly dressed Maidens, among whom is Magdalena. Then follow the other Master Singers. They are greeted with cheers and waving of hats. When all have reached the platform, Eva has taken the place of honor, with her Maidens round her, and Kothner has placed his banner in the middle of the others, which it overlaps. The Prentices solemnly advance in rank and file before the stand, turning to the people.*)

**PRENTICES:** Silentium! Silentium! Make no sound, even the merest hum!
(*Sachs rises and steps forward. At sight of him, all burst out into fresh acclamations and wavings of hats and kerchiefs.*)

**ALL THE PEOPLE:** Ha! Sachs! Sachs!
See! Master Sachs!
Sing all! Sing all! Sing all!

(*Mit feierlicher Haltung.*)

"Wach' auf, es nahet gen den Tag
ich hör' singen im grünen Hag
ein' wonnigliche Nachtigal,
ihr Stimm' durchklinget Berg und Thal
die Nacht neigt sich zum Occident,
der Tag geht auf von Orient,
die rothbrünstige Morgenröth'
her durch die trüben Wolken geht."—
Heil Sachs! Hans Sachs!
Heil Nürnberg's theurem Sachs!
(*Längeres Schweigen grosser Ergriffenheit. Sachs, der unbeweglich, wie geistesabwesend, über die Volksmenge hinweg geblickt hatte, richtet endlich seine Blicke vertrauter auf sie, verneigt sich freundlich, und beginnt mit ergriffener, schnell aber sich festigender Stimme.*)

(*With solemn delivery.*)

"Awake! The break of day draws near,
I hear upon the hawthorn spray
A bonny little nightingale;
His voice resounds over hill and dale.
The night descends the western sky
And from the east the morn draws near,
With ardor red the flush of day
Breaks through the cloud-bank dull and grey."—
Hail Sachs! Hans Sachs!
Hail, Nuremberg's darling Sachs!
(*Long silence of deep feeling. Sachs, who, as if rapt, has stood motionless, gazing far away beyond the multitude, at last turns a genial glance on them, bows courteously and begins in a voice at first trembling with emotion but soon gaining firmness.*)

SACHS: Euch wird es leicht, mir macht ihr's schwer,
gebt ihr mir Armen zu viel Ehr':
such' vor der Ehr' ich zu besteh'n,
sei's, mich von euch geliebt zu sehn!
Schon grosse Ehr' ward mir erkannt,
ward heut' ich zum Spruchsprecher ernannt:
und was mein Spruch euch künden soll,
glaubt, das ist hoher Ehre voll!
(*Grosse Bewegung unter Allen.— Sachs geht auf Pogner zu, der ihm gerührt die Hand drückt.*)

SACHS: Your hearts you ease—mine you oppress:
I feel my own unworthiness.
What I most prize, all else above,
Is your esteem and honest love!
Already I have gained honor.
Today I'm ordained as spokesman;
And in the matter of my speech
You will be honored, all and each.
(*Great stir among all present.— Sachs goes up to Pogner, who presses his hand, deeply moved.*)

POGNER: O Sachs! Mein Freund!
Wie dankenswerth!
Wie wisst ihr, was mein Herz beschwert!

POGNER: O Sachs! my friend! what thanks I owe!
How well my heart's distress you know!

SACHS: 's war viel gewagt! Jetzt habt nur werth! Muth!
(*Er wendet sich zu Beckmesser, der schon während des Einzuges und dann fortwährend immer das Blatt mit dem Gedicht heimlich herausgezogen, memorirt, genau zu lesen versucht, und oft verzweiflungsvoll den Schweiss sich von der Strin gewischt hat.*)

SACHS: There's much at stake! But dispel care!
(*He turns to Beckmesser, who during the procession and ever since has been continually taking the paper out of his pocket to endeavor to commit it to memory and ever and anon wiping the perspiration from his brow in despair.*)

SACHS: Nun denn, wenn's Meistern und Volk beliebt,
Zum Wettgesang den Anfang giebt.

SACHS: Now then, my Masters, if you're agreed,
We will to our Trial-songs proceed.

KOTHNER: (*tritt vor*). Ihr ledig' Mesiter, macht euch bereit!
Der Aeltest' sich zuerst anlässt:—
Herr Beckmesser, ihr fangt, an, 's ist Zeit!

KOTHNER: (*advancing*). Unmarried Masters, forward to win!
Let him commence who's most mature.—
Friend Beckmesser, it is time! Begin!

BECKMESSER: (*verlässt die Singerbühne, die Lehrbuben führen ihn zu dem Blumenhügel: er strauchelt darauf, tritt unsicher und schwankt*). Zum Teufel! Wie wackelig! Macht das hübsch fest!
(*Die Buben lachen unter sich und stopfen lustig an dem Rasen.*)

BECKMESSER: (*quits the stand; the Prentices conduct him to the mound; he stumbles up it, treads uncertainly and totters*.) The devil! How rickety! Make that secure!
(*The boys snigger and beat the turf lustily.*)

DAS VOLK: (*unterschiedlich, während Beckmesser sich zurecht macht.*) Wie, der? Der wirbt?
Scheint mir nicht der Rechte!
An der Tochter Stell' ich den nicht möchte.—
Er kann nicht 'mal stehn:
Wie wird's dem gehn?—
Seid still! 's gar ein tücht'ger Meister!
Stadtschreiber ist er: Beckmesser heisst er.
Gott! ist der dumm!
Er fällt fast um!—
Still! macht keinen Witz;
der hat im Rathe Stimm' und Sitz.

THE PEOPLE: (*severally, while Beckmesser is settling himself*).
What he? To woo? Isn't he a fat one?
In the lady's place I'd not have that one.—
He cannot keep his feet:
How will the man compete?—
Be still! He's quite a great professor:
That is the Town-clerk, Master Beckmesser.—
He'll tumble soon,
Old pantaloon!—
Hush! leave off your jokes and prattle
He is a learned magistrate.

DIE LEHRBUBEN: (*in Aufstellung*). Silentium! Silentium!
Lasst all das Reden und Gesumm'!
(*Beckmesser macht, ängstlich in ihren Blicken forsehend, eine gezierte Verbeugung gegen Eva.*)

THE PRENTICES: (*drawn up in order*). Silentium! Silentium!
Make no sound—even the merest hum!
(*Beckmesser anxiously scanning all faces, makes a grand bow to Eva.*)

KOTHNER: Fanget an!

KOTHNER: Now begin!

BECKMESSER: (*singt mit seiner Melodie, verkehrter Prosodie, und mit süsslich verzierten Absätzen, öfters durch mangelhaftes Memoriren gänzlich behindert, und mit immer wachsender äugstlicher Verwirrung*). "Morgen ich leuchte in rosigem Schein,
voll Blut und Duft
geht schnell die Luft!—
wohl bald gewonnen,
wie zeronnen,—
im Garten lud ich ein—
garstig und fein."

BECKMESSER: (*sings to his old melody, a vain attempt at Walter's song; his ornamental phrases being spoiled by continual failure of memory and increasing confusion*). "Yawning and steaming with roseate light
My hair was filled
With scent distilled.—
My boots were beaming
With no meaning,—
The guard I did invite
To strap me tight."—

DIE MEISTER: (*leise unter sich*).
Mein! was ist das! Ist er von Sinnen!
Woher mocht' er solche Gedanken gewinnen?

THE MASTERS: (*softly to one another*). Eh! What is that? Is he demented?
Wherever was this nonsense invented?

VOLK: (*ebenso*). Sonderbar! Hört ihr's? Wen lud er ein?
Verstand man recht? Wie kann das sein?

THE PEOPLE: (*the same*). Singular! Heard you? Who strapped him tight?
What guard was that? Can this be right?

BECKMESSER: (*nachdem er sich mit den Füssen wieder gerichtet und im Manuscript heimlich nachgelesen*). "Wohn ich erträglich im selbigen Raum,
hol' Geld und Frucht—
Bleisaft und Wucht:
mich holt am Pranger—
der Verlanger,—
auf luft'ger Stelge kaum—
häng' ich am Baum."
(*Er sucht sich wieder zurecht zu stellen und im Manuscript zurecht zu finden.*)

BECKMESSER: (*after having settled his feet more securely and taken a peep at the manuscript*). "Oh for the claws of the guard for my hold!—
A flea looked down—
Upon my crown—
My chest intending—
I, suspending—
My weight from roots unrolled—
That furnished hold."—
(*He again tries to steady himself and to correct himself by the manuscript.*)

DIE MEISTER: Was soll das heissen? Ist er nun toll?
Sein Lied ist ganz von Unsinn voll!

THE MASTERS: What is the matter? Is he insane?
His song's sheer nonsense, that is plain!

DAS VOLK: (*immer lauter*).
Schöner Werber! Der find't seinen Lohn—
bald hängt er am Galgen; man sieht ihn schon.

THE PEOPLE: (*louder*). Charming wooer! He'll soon get his due;
Suspend on the gallows; that's what he'll do!

BECKMESSER: (*immer verwirrter*). "Heimlich mir braut—
weil hier es munter will herg'ehn:—
an meiner Leiter stand ein Weib,—
sie schäm't und wollt' mich nicht beseh'n
Bleich wie ein Kraut—
umfasert mir Hanf meinen Leib;—
die Augen zwinkend—
der Hund blies winkend—
was ich vor langem verzehrt,—
wie Frucht, so Holz und Pferd—
vom Leberbaum."—
(*Hier bricht Alles in lautes schallendes Gelächter aus.*)

BECKMESSER: (*more and more confused*). "Get me a bride!—
A lovely merry girl I sued—
Afraid, she could not score my face—
As sweet and fair as she was rude.—
Like to have died—
She shook me from her embrace;—
With white eyes glowing—
Her hound was going—
To stir my long legs as I found.—
Such thunderous brutes surround—
The tree of tripe!"
(*Here all burst into a peal of laughter.*)

BECKMESSER: (*verlässt wüthend den Hügel und eilt auf Sachs zu*). Verdammter Schuster! Das dank' ich dir!
Das Lied, es ist gar nicht von mir:
von Sachs, der hier so hoch verehrt,
von eu'rem Sachs ward mir's bescheert:
Mich hat der Schändliche bedrängt,
sein schlechtes Lied mir aufgehängt.
(*Er stürtzt wüthend fort und verliert sich unter dem Volke. Grosser Aufstand.*)

BECKMESSER: (*descends the mound and hastens to Sachs*). Accursed cobbler! This is through you!—
That song is not my own, it is true:
It was Sachs, the idol of your throng,
Hans Sachs himself gave me the song!
The wretch, on purpose to abash,
He palmed on me this sorry trash.
(*He rushes away furiously and disappears in the crowd. Great confusion.*)

VOLK: Mein! Was soll das? Jetzt wird's immer bunter!
Von Sachs das Lied! Das nähm' uns doch Wunder!

PEOPLE: Why! How can that be! It is still more surprising!
That song by Sachs! Our wonder is rising!

DIE MEISTERSINGER: Erklärt doch, Sachs! Welch ein Skandal!
Von euch das Lied? Welch eig'ner Fall:

MASTER SINGERS: Explain this, Sachs! What a disgrace!
Is that song yours? Most novel case!

SACHS: (*der ruhig das Blatt, welches ihm Beckmesser hingeworfen, aufgehoben hat*). Das Lied, fürwahr ist nicht von mir:
Herr Beckmesser irrt, wie dort so hier!
Ich bin verklagt, und muss besteh'n:
drum lasst meinen Zeugen mich auserseh'n!
Ist Jemand hier, der Recht mir weiss,
der tret' als Zeug' in diesen Kreis!
(*Walther tritt aus dem Volke hervor.*) (*Allgemeine Bewegung.*)
So zeuget, das Lied sei nicht von mir;
und zeuget auch, dass, was ich hier hab' von dem Lied gesagt,
zuviel nicht sei gewagt.

SACHS: (*who has quietly picked up the paper which Beckmesser threw away*). The song, indeed, is not by me;
Friend Beckmesser's wrong as he can be.
I am accused and must defend:
A witness let me bid attend!
Is there one here who know's I'm right,
Let him appear before our sight!
(*Walter advances from out the crowd.*)
(*General stir.*)
Bear witness the song is not by me,
And prove to all that, in the plea
I have advanced for it,
I said but what was fit.

DIE MEISTER: Ei, Sachs! Gesteht, ihr seid gar fein!—
So mag's denn heut' geschehen sein.

THE MASTERS: Ah, Sachs! Understand us: you're very sly indeed!—
But you may for this once proceed.

SACHS: Der Regel Güte daraus man erwägt,
dass sie auch 'mal 'ne Ausnahm' verträgt.

SACHS: It shows our rules are of rare excellence,
If now and then they'll bear exceptions.

DAS VOLK: Ein guter Zeuge, schön und kühn!
Mich dünkt, dem kann 'was Gut's erblüh'n.

PEOPLE: A noble witness, proud and bold!
I think he should some good unfold.

SACHS: Meister und Volk sind gewillt
zu vernehmen, was mein Zeuge gilt.
Herr Walther von Stolzing, singt das Lied!
Ihr Meister, les't, ob's ihm gerieth.
(*Er gibt den Meistern das Blatt zum Nachlesen.*)

SACHS: Masters and people all agree
To give my witness liberty.
Sir Walter von Stolzing, sing the song!
You, Masters, see if he goes wrong.
(*He gives the Masters the paper to follow with.*)

DIE LEHRBUBEN: Alles gespannt, 's giebt kein Gesumm,
Da rufen wir auch nicht Silentium!

PRENTICES: All are intent, hushed is the hum;
So we need not call out Silentium!

WALTHER: (*der kühn und fest auf den Blumenhügel getreten*). "Morgenlich leuchtend in rosigem Schein,
von Blüth' und Duft geschwellt die Luft,
voll aller Wonnen nie ersonnen,
ein Garten lud mich ein,—
(*Die Meister lassen hier ergriffen das Blatt fallen; Walther scheint es—unmerklich gewahrt zu haben, und fährt nun in freier Fassung fort:*) Dort unter einem Wunderbaum,
von Früchten reich behangen,
zu schau'n im sel'gen Liebestraum,
was höchstem Lustverlangen
Erfüllung kühn verhiess—
das schönste Weib,
Eva im Paradies."

WALTER: (*who has mounted the mound with proud and firm steps*). "Morning was gleaming with roseate light,
The air was filled
With scent distilled
Where, beauty-beaming,
Past all dreaming,
A garden did invite.—
(*The Masters here, absorbed, let fall the leaf; Walter notices it without seeming to do so, and now proceeds in a freer style:*)
Wherein, beneath a wondrous tree
With fruit superbly laden,
In blissful love-dream I could see
The rare and tender maiden,
Whose charms, beyond all price,
Entranced by heart—
Eva, in Paradise.—"

DAS VOLK: (*leise unter sich*). Das it 'was And'res! Wer hätt's gedacht!
Was doch recht Wort und Vortrag macht!

THE PEOPLE: (*softly to another.*) That is quite different! Who would surprise
That so much in performance lies?

DIE MEISTERSINGER: (*leise für sich*). Ja wohl! Ich merk'! 's ist ein ander Ding,
ob falsch man oder richtig sing.

THE MASTER SINGERS: (*softly aside*). Ah yes! I see! It is another thing
A song the proper way to sing.

WALTHER: (*mit grösster Begeisterung*). "Huldreichster Tag,
dem ich aus Dichter's Traum erwacht!
Das ist geträumt, das Paradies,
in himmlisch neu verklärter Pracht hell vor mir lag
dahin der Quell lachend mich weis;
die, dort geboren,
mein Herz erkoren,
der Erde lieblichstes Bild,
zu Muse mir geweiht,
so heilig hehr als mild,
ward kühn von mir gefreit,
am lichten Tag der Sonnen
durch Sanges Sieg gewonnen
Parnass und Paradies!"

WALTER: (*with great exaltation*). "Thrice happy day,
To which my poet's trance gave place!
That Paradise of which I dreamed,
In radiance new before my face
Glorified lay.
To point the path the brooklet streamed:
She stood beside me,
Who shall my bride be,
The fairest sight earth ever gave,
My Muse, to whom I bow,
So angel-sweet and grave.
I wooed her boldly now,
Before the world remaining,
By might of music gaining
Parnassus and Paradise!"

VOLK: (*sehr leise den Schluss begleitend*). Gewiegt wie in den schönsten Traum,
hör' ich es wohl, doch fass es kaum!
Reich' ihm das Reis!
Sein der Preis!
Keiner wie er zu werben weiss!

PEOPLE: (*accompanying the end of the verse, very softly*) I feel as in a lovely dream,
Hearing, but grasping not the theme!
Give him the prize!
Maiden, rise!
No one would woo in nobler wise!

DIE MEISTER: Ja, holder Sänger!
Nimm das Rais!
Dein Sang erwarb dir Meisterpreis!

MASTERS: Yes, glorious singer!
Victor, rise!
Your song has won the Masterprize!

**POGNER:** O Sachs! Dir dank ich Glück und Ehr',
Vorüber nun all' Herzbeschwer!
(*Eva, die vom Anfang des Auftrittes her in sicherer, ruhiger Haltung verblieben, und bei allen Vorgängen wie in seliger Geistesentrücktheit sich erhalten, hat Walther unverwandt zugehört; jetzt, während am Schlusse des Gesanges Volk und Meister, gerührt und ergriffen, unwillkürlich ihre Zustimmung ausdrücken, erhebt sie sich, schreitet an den Rand der Singerbühn und drückt auf die Stirn Walther's, welcher zu den Stufen herangetreten ist und vor ihr sich niedergelassen hat, einen aus Lorbeer und Myrthen geflochtenen Kranz, worauf dieser sich erhebt und von ihr zu ihrem Vater geleitet wird, vor welchem Beide niederknien; Pogner streckt segnend seine Hünde über sie aus.*)

**SACHS:** (*deutend dem Volke mit der Hand auf die Gruppe*). Der Zeugen, denk' es, wählt ich gut:
tragt ihr Hans Sachs drum üblen Muth?

**VOLK:** (*jubelnd*). Hans Sachs!
Nein! Das war schön erdacht!
Das habt ihr einmal wieder gut gemacht!

**MEHRERE MEISTERSINGER:** Auf, Meister Pogner! Euch zum Ruhm, meldet dem Junker sein Meisterthum.

**POGNER:** (*eine goldene Kette mit drei Denkmünzen tragend*). Geschmückt mit König David's Bild, nehm' ich euch auf in der Meister Gild'.

**WALTHER:** (*zuckt unwillkürlich zurück*). Nicht Meister! Nein!
Will ohne Meister selig sein!
(*Die Meister blicken in grosser Betretenheit auf Sachs.*)

**SACHS:** (*Walther fest bei der Hand fassend*). Verachtet mir die Meister nicht,
und ehrt mir ihre Kunst!
Was ihnen hoch zum Lobe spricht,
fiel reichlich euch zur Gunst,
Nicht euren Ahnen, noch so werth,
nicht euren Wappen, Speer, noch Schwert,
dass ihr ein Dichter seid,
ein Meister euch gefreit,
dem dankt ihr heut' eu'r höchstes Glück.

**POGNER:** O Sachs! All this I owe to you:
My happiness revives anew.
(*Eva, who from the commencement of the scene has preserved a calm composure, and has seemed wrapt from all that passed around, has listened to Walter immovably; but now, when at the conclusion both Masters and people express their involuntary admiration, she rises, advances to the edge of the platform, and places on the brow of Walter, who kneels on the steps, a wreath of myrtle and laurel, whereupon he rises and she leads him to her father, before whom they both kneel. Pogner extends his hands in benediction over them.*)

**SACHS:** (*pointing to the group*).
My witness answered not amiss!
Do you find fault with me for this!

**PEOPLE:** (*jubilantly*). Hans Sachs!
No! It was well devised!
Your tact you've once more exercised!

**SEVERAL MASTER SINGERS:**
Now, Master Pogner! As you should,
Give him the honor of Masterhood!

**POGNER:** (*bringing forward a gold chain with three medallions*). Receive King David's likeness true:
The Masters' Guild is free to you.

**WALTER:** (*shrinking back involuntarily*). Master! No!
I'll find reward some other way!
(*The Masters look disconcertedly towards Sachs.*)

**SACHS:** (*grasping Walter by the hand*). Disparage not the Masters' ways,
But show respect to art!
All they can give of highest praise
To you they would impart.
Not through your ancestors and birth,
Not by your weapons' strength and worth.
But by a poet's brain
Which Mastership did gain,
You have attained your present

Drum, denkt mit Dank ihr dran zurück,
wie kann die Kunst wohl unwerth sein,
die solche Preise schliesst ein?—
Dass uns're Meister sie gepflegt,
grad' recht nach ihrer Art,
nach ihrem Sinne treu gehegt,
das hat sie ächt bewahrt:
blieb sie nicht ad'lig, wie zur Zeit,
wo Höf' und Fürsten sie geweiht,
im Drang der Schlimmen Jahr'
blieb sie doch deutsch und wahr;
und wär' sie anders nicht geglückt,
als wie wo Alles drängt' und drückt',
ihr seht, wie hoch sie blieb in Ehr'!
Was wollt ihr von den Meistern mehr?
Habt Acht! Uns drohen üble Streich':—
zerfällt erst deutsches Volk und Reich,
in falscher wälscher Majestät
kein Fürst dann mehr sein Volk versteht;
und wälschen Dunst mit wälschem Tand
sie pflanzen uns in's deutsche Land.
Was deutsch und ächt wüsst' keiner mehr,
lebt's nicht in deutscher Meister Ehr'.
Drum sag' ich Euch:
ehrt eure deutschen Meister,
dann bannt ihr gute Geister!
Und gebt ihr ihrem Wirken Gunst,
zerging' in Dunst
das heil'ge röm'sche Reich,
uns bleibe gleich
die heil'ge deutsche Kunst!
(*Alle fallen begeistert in den Schlussvers ein.—Eva nimmt den Kranz von Walther's Stirn und drückt ihn Sachs auf: dieser nimmt die Kette aus Pogner's Hand, und hängt sie Walther um.—Walther und Eva lehnen sich zu beiden. Seiten au Sachsen's Schullern: Pogner lässt sich, wie huldigend, auf ein Knie vor Sachs nieder. Die Meistersinger deuten mit erhobenen Händen auf Sachs, als auf ihr Haupt: Während die Lehrbuben jauchzend in die Hände schlagen und tanzen, schwenkt das Volk begeistert Hüte und Tücher.*)

**VOLK:** Heil Sachs! Hans Sachs!
Heil Nürnberg's theurem Sachs!
(*Der Vorhang fällt.*)

*ENDE.*

bliss:
Then think you thankfully on this:
Now can you ever despise the Art
Which can bestow so rare a prize,
That by our Masters she was kept
And cherished as their own,
With anxious care that never slept
This Art herself has shown.
If not so honored as of yore,
When courts and princes prized her more
In troublous years all through
She's German been and true;
And if she has not won renown
Beyond this bustling busy town,
You see she has our full respect:
What more from us can you expect?
Beware! Bad times are near at hand
And when fall German folk and land
In spurious foreign pomp before long
No prince will know his people's tongue
And foreign thoughts and foreign ways
Upon our German soil they'll raise.
Our native Art will fade from here
If it is not held in reverence.
So heed my words:—
Honor your German Masters
If you would stay disasters!
For while they dwell in every heart
Though should depart
The pride of holy Rome,
Still thrives at home
Our sacred German Art!
(*All join enthusiastically in the last verse.—Eva takes the crown from Walter's head and places it on Sachs's; he takes the chain from Pogner's hand and puts it round Walter's neck.—Walter and Eva lean against Sachs, one on each side; Pogner sinks on his knee before him as if in homage. The Master Singers point to Sachs, with outstretched hand, as to their chief. While the Prentices clap hands and shout and dance, the people wave hats and kerchiefs in enthusiasm.*)

**ALL:** Hail Sachs! Hans Sachs!
Hail Nuremberg's darling Sachs!
(*The curtain falls.*)

*THE END.*

# Das Rheingold (1869)

## The Rhinegold

MUSIC & LIBRETTO BY RICHAD WAGNER

Das Rheingold was first performed at the Hoftheater in Munich on September 22, 1869. Three Rhine maidens guard the Rhinegold at the bottom of the river. Alberich, a Nibelung (dwarf), appears and the maidens make fun of him, but a sudden beam of sunlight shining on the Rhinegold spurs the Rhine maidens to reveal its magic powers. He who possesses the gold and renounces love forever can forge a ring that will give him power over everything in the world. Alberich curses love (and his initial attraction to the Rhine maidens), grabs the Rhinegold and escapes. Night comes to the Rhine.

As dawn rises over the mountains, Wotan and Fricka, father and mother of the gods, awaken to the sight of Valhalla, the new castle of the gods, built by the giants Fasolt and Fafner in exchange for Freia, goddess of Youth. But Wotan never actually intended to give Freia to them—without her apples of youth to eat every day the gods would become old. He offers something else in her stead. The giants are enraged until Loge, god of Fire, offers them Alberich's gold, which they accept while keeping Freia hostage until they have it in their possession. In her absence, the gods begin to age. Wotan goes with Loge to the Nibelheim caves (where the dwarves reside) to steal the gold. Deep in the Earth, Alberich has used his magic ring to gain power over the Nibelungs. He intends to conquer the giants and the gods as well. His brother, Mime, has forged a helmet for him that makes the wearer invisible or changes him into whatever form he chooses. Alberich shows off his Tarnhelm to Wotan and Loge by changing himself into a serpent and then a toad. Wotan traps him with his foot. Alberich turns over the gold, the Tarnhelm, and the ring, which Wotan immediately puts on his own finger. The dwarf curses the ring, promising destruction to its bearer. The giants demand enough gold to cover Freia's entire body. Wotan gives the giants the Tarnhelm as well as the gold, but refuses to give them the ring. Erda, goddess of the Earth, warns him that the ring will bring disaster to the gods. Wotan gives the giants the ring at last, and the curse comes to pass: Fafner kills Fasolt in an argument over the booty. Freia is released, and the gods regain their youth. After a storm, a rainbow arcs across the Rhine valley, leading to Valhalla. The gods walk in procession to their new home; only Loge hears the Rhine maidens crying for their lost Rhinegold.

## ERSTE SCENE.

*Auf dem Grunde des Rheines.*

*Grünliche Dämmerung, nach oben au lichter, nach unten zu dunkler. Die Höhe ist von wogendem Gewässer erfüllt, das rastlos von rechts nach links zu strömt. Nach der Tiefe zu lösen sich die Fluthen in einen immer feineren feuchten Nebel auf, so dass der Raum der Manneshöbe vom Boden auf gänzlich frei vom Wasser zu sein scheint, welches wie in Wolkenzügen über den nächlichern Grund dahin fliesst. Überall ragen schroffe Felsenriffe aus der Tiefe auf, und grenzen den Raum der Bühne ab: der ganze Boden ist in ein wildes Zackengewirr zerspalten, so dass er nirgends vollkommen eben ist und nach allen Seiten hin in dichtester Finsterniss tiefere Schlüffte annehmen lässt. Um ein Riff in der Mitte der Bühne, welches mit seiner schlanken Spitze bis in die dichtere, heller dämmernde Wasserfluth hinaufragt kreis't in anmuthig schwimmender Bewegung eine der Rheinföchter.*

**WOGLINDE:** Weia! Waga!
Woge, du Welle,
walle zur Wiege!
Wagalaweia!
Wallala weiala weia!

**WELLGUNDE:** (*Stimme, von oben*). Woglinde, wach'st du allein?

**WOGLINDE:** Mit Wellgunde wär' ich zu zwei.

**WELLGUNDE:** (*taucht aus der Fluth zum Riff berab*). Lass' seh'n, wie du wach'st.
(*Sie sucht Woglinde zu erhaschen.*)

**WOGLINDE:** (*entweicht ihr schwimmend*). Sicher vor dir.
(*Sie necken sich und suchen sich spielend zu fangen.*)

**FLOSSHILDE:** (*Stimme, von oben*). Heiala weia!
Wildes Geschwister!

## SCENE I

*At the bottom of the Rhine.*

*Greenish twilight, lighter above, darker below. The upper part of the scene is filled with moving water which restlessly streams from R to L. Towards the ground the waters resolve themselves into a fine mist, so that the space to a man's height from the stage seems free from water, which flows like a train of clouds over the gloomy depths. Everywhere are steep points of rock jutting up from the depths and enclosing the whole stage; all the ground is broken up into a wild confusion of jagged pieces, so that there is no level place, while on all sides darkness indicates other deeper fissures. Round a rock, in the center of the stage, whose peak rises high into the lighter water, one of the Rhine nymphs is seen merrily swimming.*

**WOGLINDE:** Weia! Waga!
Wander you waters,
waver and waft me!
Wagalaweia!
Wallala weiala weia!

**WELLGUNDE:** (*voice from above*). Woglinde, are you watching alone?

**WOGLINDE:** Till Wellgunde wends her way to my side.

**WELLGUNDE:** (*diving down to the rock*). How fares your watch?
(*She tries to seize Woglinde.*)

**WOGLINDE:** (*avoiding her by swimming*). Far from your reach!
(*They tease, and seek playfully to catch one another.*)

**FLOSSHILDE:** (*voice from above*). Heiala weia!
Whimsical sisters!

**WELLGUNDE:** Flosshilde, schwimm'! Woglinde flieht: hilf mir die Fliessende fangen!

**FLOSSHILDE:** (*taucht herab und fährt zwischen die Spielenden*). Des Goldes Schlaf hütet ihr schlecht; besser bewacht des schlummernden Bett, sonst büss't ihr beide das Spiel! (*Mit munt'rem Gekreisch fahren die beiden auseinander; Flosshilde sucht bald die eine, bald die andere zu erhaschen; sie entschlüpfen ihr und vereinigen sich endlich, umgemeinschaftlich auf Flosshilde Jagd zu machen: so schnellen sie gleich Fischen von Riff zu Riff, scherzend und lachend.*) (*Aus einer finstern Schluft ist während dem Alberich, an einem Riffe klimmend, dem Abgrunde entstiegen. Er hält, noch vom Dunkel umgeben an, und schaut dem Spiele der Wassermädchen mit steigendem Wohlgefallen zu.*)

**ALBERICH:** He, he! Ihr Nicker! Wie seid ihr niedlich, neidliches Volk! Aus Nibelheim's Nacht naht' ich euch gern, neiget ihr euch zu mir. (*Die Mädchen halten, als sie Alberich's Stimme hören, mit ihrem Spiele ein.*)

**WOGLINDE:** Hei! wer ist dort?

**WELLGUNDE:** Es dämmert und ruft.

**FLOSSHILDE:** Luget, wer uns belauscht! (*Sie tauchen tiefer herab und erkennen den Nibelung.*)

**WOGLINDE UND WELLGUNDE:** Pfui! der Garstige!

**FLOSSHILDE:** (*schnell auftauchend*). Hütet das Gold! Vater warnte vor solchem Feind. (*Die beiden andern folgen ihr, und alle drei versammeln sich schnell um das mittlere Riff.*)

**ALBERICH:** Ihr da oben!

**DIE DREI:** Was willst du da unten?

**ALBERICH:** Stör' ich e'ur Spiel, wenn staunend ich still hier steh'? Tauchtet ihr nieder, mit euch tollte und neckte der Niblung sich gern!

**WOGLINDE:** Mit uns will er spielen?

**WELLGUNDE:** Ist ihm das Spott?

**ALBERICH:** Wie scheint im Schimmer ihr hell und schön? Wie gern umschlänge der Schlanken eine mein Arm, schlüpfte hold sie herab!

---

**WELLGUNDE:** Flosshilde, swim! Woglinde flies; help me to foil her in fleetness.

**FLOSSHILDE:** (*dives down and comes between the playmates*). The sleeping gold You guard badly; better surround the gleaming one's bed; such banter you both may regret. (*With merry cries the two separate: Flosshilde chases first one and then the other; they evade her and then unite to pursue her in turn. Thus they dart about like fish from rock to rock, laughing and sporting.*) (*From a dark chasm Alberich clambers up to one of the rocks. He halts in the shadow and watches the gambols of the nymphs with growing delight.*)

**ALBERICH:** Ho, ho! you nixies! Are you not nimble, nice to behold! From Nibelheim's night now I would willingly come near you, if you are kind. (*The girls, when hearing Alberich's voice, leave off playing.*)

**WOGLINDE:** Hey! who is there!

**WELLGUNDE:** A thing with a voice.

**FLOSSHILDE:** Look, who is below! (*They dive deeper and perceive the Nibelung.*)

**WOGLINDE AND WELLGUNDE:** Faugh! The gruesome one.

**FLOSSHILDE:** (*swiftly diving upwards*). Look to the gold! Father warned us of such a foe. (*The others follow her, and all three collect quickly around the central rock.*)

**ALBERICH:** You, up there!

**THE THREE NYMPHS:** What do you want, below there!

**ALBERICH:** Would your sport be spoiled, if I still stand here, astonished? Dive near to me then; a poor Niblung longs dearly to dally with you!

**WOGLINDE:** He offers to join us?

**WELLGUNDE:** Is it his joke?

**ALBERICH:** How sweet and soft you seem in this light! Gladly I'd seek to encircle one of your waists, should you kindly descend.

---

**FLOSSHILDE:** Nun lach 'ich der Furcht: der Feind ist verliebt. (*Sie lachen.*)

**WELLGUNDE:** Der lüsterne Kauz!

**WOGLINDE:** Lasst ihn uns kennen! (*Sie lässt sich auf die Spitze des Riffes herab, an dessen Fusse Alberich angelangt ist.*)

**ALBERICH:** Die neigt sich herab.

**WOGLINDE:** Nun nahe dich mir!

**ALBERICH:** (*klettert mit koboldartiger Behendigkeit doch wiederholt aufgehalten, der Spitze des Riffes zu*). Garstig glatter glitschriger Glimmer! Wie gleit' ich aus! Mit Händen und Füssen nicht fasse noch halt' ich das schlecke Geschlüpfer! (*Er prhustet.*) Feuchtes Nass füllt mir die Nase: verfluchtes Niesen! (*Er ist in der Nähe Woglinde's angelangt.*)

**WOGLINDE:** (*lachend*). Pruhstend naht meines Freiers Pracht!

**ALBERICH:** Mein Friedel sei, du fräuliches Kind! (*Er sucht sie zu umfassen.*)

**WOGLINDE:** (*sich ihm entwindend*). Willst du mich frei'n, so freie mich hier! (*Sie ist auf einem andern Riffe angelangt. Die Schwestern lachen.*)

**ALBERICH:** (*kratzt sich den Kopf*). O weh: du entweich'st? Komm' doch wieder! Schwert ward mir, was so leicht du erschwing'st.

**WOGLINDE:** (*schwingt sich auf ein drittes Riff in grösserer Tiefe*). Steig' nur zu Grund: da greifst du mich sicher!

**ALBERICH:** (*klettert hastig hinab*). Wohl besser da unten!

**WOGLINDE:** (*schnellt sich rasch aufwärts nach einem hohen Seitenriffe*). Nun aber nach oben! (*Alle Mädchen lachen.*)

**ALBERICH:** Wie fang' ich im Sprung' den spröden Fisch? Warte, du Falsche! (*Er will ihr eilig nachklettern.*)

**WELLGUNDE:** (*hat sich auf ein tieferes Riff auf der andern Seite gesenkt*). Heia! Du Holder! hör'st du mich nicht?

**ALBERICH:** (*sich umwendend*). Ruf'st du nach mir?

**WELLGUNDE:** Ich rathe dir gut: zu mir wende dich, Woglinde meide!

---

**FLOSSHILDE:** I laugh at our fears; the foe is in love! (*They laugh.*)

**WELLGUNDE:** The languishing calf!

**WOGLINDE:** Let us accost him. (*She descends to the point of the rock at the base of which Alberich is.*)

**ALBERICH:** She's coming below!

**WOGLINDE:** Climb closer to me.

**ALBERICH:** (*clambers with gnome-like rapidity, but with difficulty, to the summit of the rock*). Smooth with slime the slippery stone is! How my steps slide! My hands and my feet cannot fasten or hold on the steepness unsteady! (*Sneezes.*) Clamminess creeps up my nostrils: accursed sneezing! (*He has approached Woglinde.*)

**WOGLINDE:** (*laughing*). See how nicely my beau can sneeze!

**ALBERICH:** O be mine, my beautiful child! (*He seeks to embrace her.*)

**WOGLINDE:** (*eluding him*). Would you make court, then follow me here! (*She flies up to another rock. The others laugh.*)

**ALBERICH:** (*scratching his head*). Alas! you are lost! Come lower! Far too hard is it for me to fly.

**WOGLINDE:** (*swinging down to a third rock in the depths*). Clamber down here; your hand may then clasp me.

**ALBERICH:** (*hastily scrambling down*). Much better down lower!

**WOGLINDE:** (*darting quickly upwards to a high peak at the side*). But look, I uplift myself! (*The Nymphs all laugh.*)

**ALBERICH:** How follow and take this timid fish? Wait a bit, false one! (*Tries hastily to climb up.*)

**WELLGUNDE:** (*has descended to a lower rock on the other side*). Heia! my hero! hear what I say!

**ALBERICH:** (*turning round*). Call you to me?

**WELLGUNDE:** I caution you well: to me wend your way: mind not Woglinde!

## Scene I

ALBERICH: (klettern hastig über den Bodengrund zu Wellgunde). Viel schöner bist du als jene Scheue, die minder gleissend und gar zu glatt.— Nur tiefer tauche, willst du mir taugen!

WELLGUNDE: (noch etwas mehr zu ihm sich herabsenkend). Bin nun ich dir nah'?

ALBERICH: Noch nicht genug! Die schlanken Arme schlinge um mich, dass ich den Nacken dir neckend betaste, mit schmeichelnder Brunst an die schwellende Brust mich dir schmiege!

WELLGUNDE: Bist du verliebt und lüstern nach Minne? Lass' seh'n, du Schöner, wie du bist zu schau'n?— Pfui, du haariger, höck'riger Geck! Schwarzes, schwieliges Schwefelgezwerg! Such' dir ein Friedel, dem du gefällst!

ALBERICH: (sucht sie mit Gewalt zu halten). Gefall' ich dir nicht, dich fass' ich doch fest!

WELLGUNDE: (schnell zum mittleren Riffe auftauchend). Nur fest, sonst fliess' ich dir fort! (Alle Drei lachen.)

ALBERICH: (erbos't ihr nachzankend). Falsches Kind! Kalter, grätiger Fisch! Schein' ich nicht schön dir, niedlich und neckisch, glatt und glau— hei! so buhle mit Aalen, ist dir eklig mein Balg!

FLOSSHILDE: Was zank'st du, Alp? Schon so verzagt? Du frei'test um zwei! früg'st du die dritte, süssen Trost schüfe die Traute dir!

ALBERICH: Holder Sange singt zu mir her.— Wie gut, dass ihr eine nicht seid! Von vielen gefäll' ich wohl einer: von einer kies'te mich keine!— Soll ich dir glauben, so gleite herab!

FLOSSHILDE: (taucht zu Alberich hinab). Wie thörig seid ihr, dumme Schwestern, dünkt euch dieser nicht schön!

ALBERICH: (hastig ihr nahend). Für dumm und hässlich darf ich sie halten, seit ich dich Holdeste seh'.

FLOSSHILDE: (schmeichelnd). O singe fort so süss und fein; wie hehr verführt es mein Ohr!

---

ALBERICH: (hastily clambering over the rocks towards her). You are more fair than she who flies me; for she's less sparkling, too sleek and sly. But dive yet deeper if you would dally!

WELLGUNDE: (descending a little nearer to him). So now am I near?

ALBERICH: No, not enough! With tender arms entwine me around, that I may fondle that form so bewitching: in passionate bliss let me press you to my panting embrace!

WELLGUNDE: Are you in love and longing for favors? Let's see what semblance my beauty can show.— Faugh! you hairy and horrible imp! Swarthy, stunted, and shrivelled up dwarf! Seek as a fellow one of like form!

ALBERICH: (trying to detain her by force). Though I am not fair, I'll fetter you fast!

WELLGUNDE: (quickly darting up to the central rock). Quite fast, for fear I should flow! (All three laugh.)

ALBERICH: (calling angrily after her). Fickle child! Chilly, slippery fish! Seem I not shapely, tender, enticing, glib and gay— Go! let eels be your lovers, If I am so loathsome!

FLOSSHILDE: Why scold us, imp? Does your heart sink? Only two have been sought; try now the third one: soft reward surely awaits you there!

ALBERICH: Music sweet you sing to me:— what joy that all are not alike! Among many I must delight one, though all be wary to choose me. Before I believe you still lower descend.

FLOSSHILDE: (diving down to Alberich). How foolish are my sisters' hearts to see no symmetry here!

ALBERICH: (approaching her hastily). Both dull and hideous do I now hold them, since I've looked upon you, my sweet.

FLOSSHILDE: (cajolingly). O warble still your wondrous song; it fills sweetly my ears!

---

ALBERICH: (zutraulich sie berührend). Mir zagt, zuckt und zehrt sich das Herz, lacht mir so zierliches Lob.

FLOSSHILDE: (ihn sanft abwehrend). Wie deine Anmuth mein Aug' erfreut, deines Lächelns Milde den Muth mir labt! (Sie zieht ihn zärtlich an sich.) Seligster Mann!

ALBERICH: Süssest Maid!

FLOSSHILDE: Wär'st du mir hold!

ALBERICH: Hielt'ich dich immer!

FLOSSHILDE: (ihn ganz in ihren Armen haltend). Deinen stechenden Blick, deinen struppigen Bart, o säh' ich ihn, fass' ich ihn stets' Deines stachlichen Haares strammes Gelock, umflöss' es Flosshilde ewig! Deine Krötengestalt, deiner Stimme Gekrächz, o dürft' ich staunend und stumm, sie nur hören und seh'n! (Woglinde und Wellgunde sind nah herabgetaucht und schlagen jetzt ein helles Gelächter auf.)

ALBERICH: (erschreckt aus Flosshilde's Armen auffahrend). Lacht ihr Bösen mich aus?

FLOSSHILDE: (sich plötzlich ihm entreissend). Wie billig am Ende vom Lied. (Sie taucht mit den Schwestern schnell in die Höhe und stimmt in ihr Gelächter ein.)

ALBERICH: (mit kreischender Stimme). Wehe! ach wehe! O Schmerz! O Schmerz! Die dritte, so traut, betrog sie mich auch?— Ihr schmählich schlaues, lüderlich schlechtes Gelichter! Nährt ihr nur Trug, ihr treuloses Nickergezücht?

DIE DREI RHEINTÖCHTER: Wallala! Lalaleia! Lalei! Heia! Heia! Haha! Schäme dich, Albe! Schilt nicht dort unten! Höre, was wir dich heissen! Warum, du, Banger, bandest du nicht das Mädchen, das du minnst? Treu sind wir und ohne Trug dem Freier, der uns fängt.— Greife nur zu und grause dich nicht! In der Fluth entflieh'n wir nicht leicht. (Sie schwimmen aus einander, hierher und dorthin, bald tiefer, bald höher, um Alberich zur Jagd auf sie zu reizen.)

ALBERICH: Wie in den Gliedern brünstige Gluth mir brennt und glüht! Wuth und Minne

---

ALBERICH: (caressing her). I flush, flame and flutter at heart, homage so flattering to hear.

FLOSSHILDE: (gently repulsing him). Your beauty's glory makes my eyes glad: and your loving smile assuages my alarms! (Draws him tenderly to her.) Sweetest of men!

ALBERICH: Softest of maids!

FLOSSHILDE: O, Were you mine!

ALBERICH: Might I ever hold you!

FLOSSHILDE: (holding him in her arms). O! Your staring-eyed brow, your straggle-haired beard, to see them and handle them still! That your stubbly gray hair, in streaming elf locks, might float round Flosshilde forever! And your toad-allied stature, your stridulous tones, O might I astonish and still, satiate with these every sense! (Woglinde and Wellgunde have dived down to them and now raise a peal of laughter.)

ALBERICH: (starting timidly from Flosshilde's arms). Are you laughing at me?

FLOSSHILDE: (suddenly darting from him). Your love song merrily ends. (She darts quickly up to her sisters and joins in their laughter.)

ALBERICH: (with a screaming voice). Woe is me! Ah, woe is me! Alas! Alas! The third of my trust betraying me! Most shocking, shifty, wicked and shameless of wantons! Know you no truth, you treacherous, nondescript brood?

THE THREE RHINE NYMPHS: Wallala! Lalaleia! Lalei! Heia! Heia! Haha! Fie on you, gnome, gnashing in fury! Take the counsel that we offer. How was it, calf, you could not have kept the lady of your love? We are true, firm is our pledge toward him who bravely holds. Seize on us then, and cease to reproach: we can fly not fast in the wave. (They swim about, hither and thither, high and low, to incite Alberich to chase them.)

ALBERICH: How through my frame there rages a fire with radiance fierce!

wild und mächig
wühlt mir den Muth auf!—
Wie ihr auch lacht und lugt,
lüstern lechz' ich nach euch,
und eine muss mir erliegen!
(*Er macht sich mit verzweifelter Anstrengung zur Jagd auf: mit grauenhafter Bebendigkeit erklimmt er Riff für Riff, springt von einem zum andern, sucht bald dieses bald jenes der Mädchen zu erhaschen, die mit höhnischem Gelächter stets ihm entweichen; er strauchelt, stürzt in den Abgrund hinab, klettert dann hastig wieder zur Höhe,—bis ihm endlich die Geduld entführt: vor Wuth schaumend hält er athemlos an und streckt die geballte Faust nach den Mädchen hinauf.*)

ALBERICH: (*kaum seiner mächtig*). Fing' eine diese Faust! . . .
(*Er verbleibt in sprachloser Wuth, den Blick aufwärts gerichtet, wo er dann plötzlich von folgendem Schauspiele angezogen und gefesselt wird.*)
(*Durch die Fluth ist von oben her ein immer lichterer Schein gedrungen, der sich nun an einer hohen Stelle des mittleren Riffes zu einem blendend hell strahlenden Goldglanze entzündet; ein zauberisch goldenes Licht bricht von hier durch das Wasser.*)

WOGLINDE: Lugt, Schwestern!
Die Weckerin lacht in den Grund.

WELLGUNDE: Durch den grünen Schwall den wonnigen Schläfer sie grüsst.

FLOSSHILDE: Jetzt küsst sie sein Auge
dass er es öff'ne;
schaut, es lächelt
in lichtem Schein;
durch die Fluthen hin
fliesst sein strahlender Stern.

DIE DREI: (*zusammen das Riff anmuthig umschwimmend*).
Heiahaheia!
Heiajaheia!
Wallala lalala leia jahei!
Rheingold!
Rheingold!
Leuchtende Lust,
wie lach'st du so hell und hehr!
Glühender Glanz
entgleisst dir weihlich im Wag!
Heiajahei
Heiajaheia!
Wache, Freund,
wache froh,
Wonnige Spiele
spenden wir dir:
flimmert der Fluss,
flammet die Fluth,
Umfliessen wir tauchend,
tanzend und singend,
im seligen Bade dein Bett.
Rheingold!
Rheingold!
Heiajaheia!
Wallalaleia jahei!

Wrath and passion,
rude and powerful,
rouse up my pulses.
Though you may laugh and lie,
lusting I long for one;
I'll win here, too, for my sweetheart!
(*He chases them with desperate exertions; with frightful activity he clambers from rock to rock, springing from one to the other and striving to reach first one nymph and then another; they always avoid him with mocking laughter. He staggers and falls below, then clambers up again—till at last his patience is exhausted: foaming with rage, he pauses breathless and shakes his clenched fist at the nymphs.*)

ALBERICH: (*nearly beside himself*). Were I to catch one!
(*He remains in speechless rage, gazing upwards, when suddenly he is rivetted to the spot by the following sight.*)
(*Through the water above breaks an ever-increasing glow, which on the summit of the central rock kindles gradually to a blinding yellow gleam; a magical golden light then streams from there through the water.*)

WOGLINDE: Look, sisters! The wakener laughs in the deep.

WELLGUNDE: Through the dark green surge it woos the sleeper adored.

FLOSSHILDE: Now kissing its eyelids
striving to open them.
Look, it is smiling
in silvery light!
Through the flood around
flows as a stream of stars.

ALL THREE: (*swimming joyously around the rock*). Heiajaheia!
Heiajaheia!
Wallala lalala leia jahei!
Rhinegold!
Rhinegold!
Lustrous delight;
you laugh in radiance rare!
Glistening gleams
glow from you over the waves.
Heiajaheia!
Heiajaheia!
Waken friend,
waken, joyful!
Cheerful the games
we'll gambol with you:
flashes the foam,
flames all the flood;
we float around dancing,
diving and singing,
as sweetly we bathe in your bed.
Rhinegold!
Rhinegold!
Heiajaheia!
Walalaleia jahei!

ALBERICH: (*dessen Auge, mächtig vom Glanze angezogen, starr an dem Golde haftet*). Was ist's, ihr Glatten,
das dort so gleisst und glänzt?

DIE DREI MÄDCHEN: (*abwechselnd*). Wo bist du Rauher denn heim,
dass von Rheingold nie du gehört?—
Nichts weiss der Alp
von des Goldes Auge,
das wechselnd wacht und schläft?
von der Wassertiefe
wonnigem Stern,
der hehr die Wogen durchhellt?—

■ ZWEITE SCENE.

*Allmählich gehen die Wogen in Gewölke über, das sich nach und nach abklärt, und als es sich endlich, wie in feinem Nebel, gänzlich verliert, wird eine freie Gegend auf Bergeshöhen sichtbar, anfänglich noch in nächtlicher Beleuchtung.—Der hervorbrechende Tag beleuchtet mit wachsendem Glanze eine Burg mit blinkenden Zinnen, die auf einem Felsgipfel im Hintergrunde steht; zwischen diesem burggekrönten Felsgipfel und dem Vordergrunde der Scene ist ein tiefes Thal, durch welches der Rhein fliesst, anzunehmen,—Zur Seite auf blumigem Grunde liegt Wotan, neben ihm Fricka, beide schlafend.*

FRICKA: (*erwacht: ihr Blick fällt auf die Burg; sie staunt und erschrickt*). Wotan! Gemahl! erwache!

WOTAN: (*im Traume leise*). Der Wonne seligen Saal
bewachen mir Thür' und Thor:
Mannes Ehre,
ewige Macht,
ragen zu endlosem Ruhm!

FRICKA: (*rüttelt ihn*). Auf, aus der Träume
wonnigen Trug!
Erwache, Mann, und erwäge!

WOTAN: (*erwacht und erhebt sich ein wenig: sein Auge wird sogleich vom Anblick der Burg gefesselt*). Vollendet das ewige Werk:
auf Berges Gipfel
die Götter-Burg,
prunkvoll prahlt
der prangende Bau!
Wie im Traum ich ihn trug,
wie mein Wille ihn wies,
stark und schön
steht er zur Schau;
hehrer, herrlicher Bau!

ALBERICH: (*whose eyes, fascinated by the light, are fixed on the gold*). What is it, you gliders,
that there gleams and glows?

THE THREE NYMPHS: (*severally*). From where do you, rugged one, hail,
of the Rhinegold never to have heard?
You want not, imp,
of the gold's bright eyes then,
which now wake, now sleep?
Of the wondrous star
of waters profound
whose light illuminates the wave?—

■ SCENE II

*Gradually the waves give place to clouds which clear off in fine mist, showing an open space on a mountain top, first by the faint light of night.—The dawning day lights up with increasing luster a castle with glittering pinnacles, which stands on a cliff at the back: between this and the foreground is a deep valley through which the Rhine is supposed to flow.—At one side Wotan and Fricka are lying asleep in a flowery meadow.*

FRICKA: (*wakes, and her eyes fall on the castle; she starts in surprise*). Wotan! my lord! awaken!

WOTAN: (*still dreaming*). The wondrous heavenly hall
is warded with gate and guild.
Mortal honor,
infinite might,
fly to the acme of fame!

FRICKA: (*shaking him*). Wake from your visions
rosy and vain!
Awake now, spouse, and rouse yourself!

WOTAN: (*wakes and raises himself slightly. His eyes are at once attracted and riveted by the sight of the castle*). It's ended—the infinite work!
A Heavenly mansion
on mountain heights;
proudly peer
my prosperous halls
as in visions I viewed,
as I ordered it;
strong and sound
It stands in sight:
grand and glorious pile.

# Scene II

FRICKA: Nur Wonne schafft dir
was mich erschreckt?
Dich freut die Burg,
mir bangt es um Freia.
Achtloser, lass dich erinnern
des ausbedungenen Lohn's!
Die Burg is fertig,
verfallen das Pfand:
vergiss'st du, was du vergab'st?

WOTAN: Wohl dünkt mich's, was
sie bedangen,
die dort die Burg mir gebaut;
durch Vertrag zähmt' ich
ihr trotzig Gezücht,
dass sie die hehre
Halle mir schlüfen;
die steht nun—Dank den Stark-
en:—
um den Sold sorge dich nicht.

FRICKA: O lachend frevelnder
Leichtsinn!
Liebelosester Frohmuth!
Wusst' ich um eu'ren Vertrag,
dem Truge hätt' ich gewehrt;
doch muthig entferntet
ihr Männer die Frauen,
um taub und ruhig vor uns
allein mit den Riesen zu tagen.
So ohne Scham
verschenktet ihr Frechen
Freia, mein holdes Geschwister,
froh des Schächergewerb's.—
Was ist euch Harten
doch heilig und werth,
giert ihr Männer nach Macht!

WOTAN: Gleiche Gier
war Fricka wohl fremd,
als selbst um den Bau sie bat?

FRICKA: Um des Gatten Treue besorgt
muss traurig ich wohl sinnen,
wie an mich er zu fesseln,
zieht's in die Ferne ihn fort:
herrliche Wohnung,
wonniger Hausrath,
sollten mit sanftem Band
dich binden zu säumender Rast.
Doch du bei dem Wohnbau sannst
auf Wehr und Wall allein:
Herrschaft und Macht
soll er dir mehren;
nur rastlosem Sturm zu erregen
erstand die ragende Burg.

WOTAN: (lächelnd). Wolltest du
Frau
in der feste mich fangen,
mir Gotte musst du schon gönnen,
dass, in der Burg
gebunden, ich mir
von aussen gewinne die Welt.
Wandel und Wechsel
liebt wer lebt:
das Spiel drum kann ich nicht spar-
en.

FRICKA: Liebeloser,
leidigster Mann!
Um der Macht und Herrschaft
müssigen Tand
verspielst du in lästerndem Spott
Liebe und Weibes Werth?

FRICKA: So you welcome
that which I dread?
Though your tower is fair
I tremble for Freia.
Mindless one, pause and remember
the mentioned price to be paid!
the castle finished,
now the bond falls.
Did you forget then what you must
give?

WOTAN: I mind well all they demanded, my men who built me this
burg;
their grim race I
by agreement overawed,
whereby this hallowed
home they should build.
It prospers—thanks to their prowess!
For the price pray have no heed.

FRICKA: Alas! Your fatuous
lightness!
lacking love is your folly.
Had I but known of this bond
the baseness might have been
helped:
but pleased were you wise ones
to part from the women;
no jot confiding in us,
you conferred as one with the giants.
So, without shame,
you shrink not to forfeit
Freia, my glorious sister,
for this scandalous cause.
May your hard hearts know
nothing of holiness,
when you pant for power.

WOTAN: Like longings
did Fricka not feel,
when she herself bade me to build?

FRICKA: Of my husband's truth ill
assured,
in trouble I considered
how to hold him beside me
when he was seeking to stray:
halls bright and gleaming,
glorious homestead,
such might surely allure you
to linger and seek in them rest.
But you in this fortress thought
of fence and force alone:
power and might
it was to augment you:
this ravishing castle rises
to cause yet more riotous strife.

WOTAN: (smiling). If with these
walls
You, O wife, should wrap me,
yet grant but this to my godhood;
while in the castle's
confines I yet
may win the world outside.
Wandering at will
all love who live:
my sport I cannot dispense with.

FRICKA: Light, unloving,
low-natured man!
For such mere conceits
as might and control
would trample in lawless contempt
love and a woman's worth?

WOTAN: (ernst). Um dich zum
Weib zu gewinnen,
mein eines Auge
setzt' ich werbend daran:
wie thörig tadelst du jetzt!
Ehr' ich die Frauen
doch mehr als dich freut!
Und Freia, die gute,
geb' ich nicht auf:
nie sann dies ernstlich mein Sinn.

FRICKA: So schirme sie jetzt:
in schutzloser Angst
läuft sie nach Hülf' dort her!

FREIA: (hastig auftretend). Hilf
mir, Schwester!
Schütze mich, Schwäher!
Vom Felsen drüben
drohte mir Fasolt,
mich Hold käm' er zu holen.

WOTAN: Lass' ihn droh'n!—
Sah'st du nicht Loge?

FRICKA: Dass am liebsten du immer
dem Listigen trau'st!
Manch Schlimmes schuf er uns
schon,
doch stets bestrickt er dich wieder.

WOTAN: Wo freier Muth frommt
allein, frag' ich nach keinem;
doch des Feindes Neid
zum Nutz' sich fügen,
lehrt nur Schlauheit und List,
wie Loge verschlagen sie übt.
Der zum Vertrage mir rieth,
versprach Freia zu lösen:
auf ihn verlass' ich mich nun.

FRICKA: Und er lässt dich allein.—
Dort schreiten rasch
die Riesen heran:
wo harrt dein schlauer Gehülf'?

FREIA: Wo harren meine Brüder,
dass Hülfe sie brächten,
da mein Schwäher die Schwache
verschenkt?
Zu Hülfe, Donner!
Hieher! hieher! Rette Freia, mein
Froh!

FRICKA: Die in bösem Bund dich
verriethem,
sie alle bergen sich nun.
(Fasolt und Fafner, beide in riesiger Gestalt, mit starken Pfählen
bewaffnet, treten auf.)

FASOLT: Sanft schloss
Schlaf dein Aug':
wir beide bauten
Schlummers bar die Burg.
Mächt'ger Müh'
müde nie,
stau'ten starke
Stein' wir auf;
steiler Thurm,
Thür' und Thor,
deckt und schliesst
im schlanken Schloss den Saal.
Dort steht's,
was wir stemmten;
schimmernd hell

WOTAN: (earnestly). When I
sought to win you for my wife,
I risked my other eye
in a wager;
you blame blindly, I think!
Women I lean to
Even more than you like.
I'll let not our fairest
Freia be taken:
my thoughts never turned to such a
thing.

FRICKA: Then save her at once:—
in sorest alarm
she hastens here for help.

FREIA: (entering hastily). Help
me, Fricka!
fail me not, father!
From mountain fastness
Fasolt gives menace:
he comes too surely to catch me.

WOTAN: Let him rage!—
Did you not see Loge?

FRICKA: You should still accord
that belief to that liar!
Much wrong already he's wrought,
yet sets new snares for you.

WOTAN: Where simple might
serve
let none seek to assist me;
but to shape the fraud
of foes to serve me,
I can learn by such arts
as only Loge employs.
He advised this agreement,
and vowed to extricate Freia:
I rely firmly on him.

FRICKA: And he fails in his
faith.—
The giants are hastening
here, look:
where lurks your juggling ally?

FREIA: Why hasten not my brothers,
with help they should bring me,
now my father refuses defense?
O help me, Donner!
Come! Come!
Rescue Freia, my Froh!

FRICKA: Those who basely bargained to wrong you
have all abandoned you now.
(Fasolt and Fafner, men of gigantic stature, armed with strong
staves, enter.)

FASOLT: Soft sleep
sealed your eyes:
while we wove your walls in wakeful
labor.
Tedious toil did not
tire us;
We heaped huge
and heavy stones.
High with dome,
donjon, door,
we have formed
a fortress fair and fast.
There bides
our building,

bescheint's der Tag:
zieh' nun ein,
uns zahl' den Lohn!

**WOTAN:** Nennt, Leute, den Lohn!
was dünkt euch zu bedingen?

**FASOLT:** Bedungen ist's,
was tauglich uns dünkt:
gemahnt es dich so matt?
Freia, die holde,
Holda, die freie—
vertragen ist's—
sie tragen wir heim.

**WOTAN:** Sied ihr bei Trost
mit eurem Vertrag?
Denkt auf andern Dank:
Freia ist mir nicht feil.

**FASOLT:** (*vor wüthendem Erstaunen einen Augenblick sprachlos*). was sagst du, ha!
Sinnst du Verrath?
Verrath am Vertrag?
Die dein Speer birgt,
sind sie dir Spiel,
des berath'nen Bundes Runen?

**FAFNER:** (*höhnisch*). Getreu'ster Bruder!
Merkst du Tropf nun Betrug?

**FASOLT:** Lichtsohn du,
leicht gefügt,
hör' und hüte dich:
Verträgen halte Treu'!
Was du bist,
bist du nur durch Verträge:
bedungen ist,
wohl bedacht deine Macht.
Bist weiser du
als witzig wir sind,
bandest uns Freie
zum Frieden du:
all deinem Wissen fluch' ich,
fliehe weit deinen Frieden,
weisst du nicht offen,
ehrlich und frei,
Verträgen zu wahren die Treu'!—
Ein dummer Riese
räth' dir das:
du Weiser, wiss' es von ihm!

**WOTAN:** Wie schlau für Ernst du achtest,
was wir zum Scherz nur beschlossen!
Die liebliche Göttin,
licht und leicht,
was taugt euch Tölpeln ihr Reiz?

**FASOLT:** Höhn'st du uns?
Ha! wie unrecht!—
Die ihr durch Schönheit herrscht,
schimmernd hehres Geschlecht,
wie thörig strebt ihr
nach Thürmen von Stein
setzt um Burg und Saal
Weibes Wonne zum Pfand!
Wir Plumpen plagen uns
schwitzend mit schwieliger Hand,
ein Weib zu gewinnen,
das wonnig und mild
bei uns Armen wohne:—
und verkehrt nennt ihr den Kauf?

---

brightening in
the beams of day.
Pass within,
but pay our wage.

**WOTAN:** Name, workmen, your wage.
What forfeit have you fixed on?

**FASOLT:** It was fixed beforehand,
what we deemed fit:
Your memory is remiss!
Freia the holy—
Holda the free one—
agreed it is,
she goes home with us.

**WOTAN:** Are you engrossed
on what was agreed?
Ask other reward:
Freia I must refuse.

**FASOLT:** (*remaining a while speechless with wrathful surprise*). What did you say—Ha!
You seek to betray—
betray a contract?
On your spear it is written,
serve but for sport
those compelling runes of power?

**FAFNER:** (*ironically*). My faithful brother!
Deem you, fool, he is false?

**FASOLT:** Son of light.
swayed so lightly,
hear and heed yourself?
Your treaties hold in truth!
What you are,
are you only by treaties;
Conformable,
well defined was your might.
You are more wise
than we are wary,
binding us free ones
in friendly peace:
cursed by your futile wisdom,
peace shall wane before you,
when no more open,
honest and free,
You have broken your warrant and bond!—
A simple giant
judges so:
Be warned by him, you wise one!

**WOTAN:** How sly to take for truth
what only in sport we had settled!
The beauteous goddess,
light and bright,
what use to you are her charms?

**FASOLT:** Do you mock us?
Fie! how evil!—
You who sway in radiance.
regal, sorrowless race,
like fools you strive
for a fortress of stone;
setting against it
a wondrous woman in pledge.
We, blockheads, damn us,
toiling with toughness of hand
to win us a woman,
who, winning and sweet,
should go gladly with us.—
find now you will back out of the bond?

---

**FAFNER:** Schweig' dein faules Schwatzen,
Gewinn werben wir night:
Freia's Haft
hilft wenig:
doch viel gilt's
den Göttern sie zu entführen.
Gold'ne Aepfel
wachsen in ihrem Garten;
sie allein
weiss die Aepfel zu pflegen:
der Frucht Genuss
frommt ihren Sippen
zu ewig nie
alternder Jugend;
siech und bleich
doch sinkt ihre Blüthe,
alt und schwach
schwinden sie hin,
müssen Freia sie missen:
ihrer Mitte drum sei sie entführt!

**WOTAN:** (*für sich*). Loge säumt zu lang!

**FASOLT:** Schlicht gieb nun Bescheid!

**WOTAN:** Sinnt auf andern Sold!

**FASOLT:** Kein andrer: Freia allein!

**FAFNER:** Du da, folg' uns fort!
(*Sie dringen auf Freia zu.*)

**FREIA:** (*fliehend*). Helft! helft vor den Harten!
(*Donner und Froh kommen eilig.*)

**FROH:** (*Freia in seine Arme fassend*). Zu mir, Freia!—
Meide sie, Frecher!
Froh schützt die Schöne.

**DONNER:** (*sich vor die beiden Riesen stellend*).
Fasolt und Fafner,
fühltet ihr schon
meines Hammers harten Schlag?

**FAFNER:** Was soll das Droh'n?

**FASOLT:** Was dringst du her?
Kampf kies'ten wir nicht,
verlangen nur unsern Lohn.

**DONNER:** (*den Hammer schwingend*). Schon oft zahlt'ich
Riesen den Zoll;
schuldig blieb' ich
Schächern nie:
kommt her! des Lohnes Last
wäg' ich mit gutem Gewicht!

**WOTAN:** (*seinen Speer zwischen den Streitenden ausstreckend*).
Halt, du Wilder!
Nichts durch Gewalt!
Verträge schürzt
meines Speeres Schaft:
spar' deines Hammers Heft!

**FREIA:** Wehe! Wehe!
Wotan verlässt mich!

**FRICKA:** Begreif' ich dich noch, grausamer Mann?

---

**FAFNER:** Check your foolish chatter;
we look to gain no luck.
Freia's self
serves little;
but it would be good
to get her away from the Æsir:
golden apples
grow in her orchard garden;
none else can
grasp the art of their culture:
this grateful fruit
grants to her kindred
eternal youth
time cannot ravage;
weak and blighted
fades their beauty,
old and worn
will they pass,
If Freia is ever far from them:
let her be torn from them all.

**WOTAN:** (*aside*). Loge takes too long!

**FASOLT:** Tell us outright your resolve.

**WOTAN:** Fix on other spoil.

**FASOLT:** No other: Freia alone!

**FAFNER:** You there! follow us!
(*They press towards Freia.*)

**FREIA:** (*seeking to fly*). Help!
Help from these harsh ones!
(*Donner and Froh enter hastily.*)

**FROH:** (*clasping Freia in his arms*). To me, Freia!—
Miscreant, fall back!
Froh guards the goddess!

**DONNER:** (*planting himself before the two giants*). Fasolt and Fafner—
Have you felt the blow
of my hammer's head before?

**FAFNER:** What do you mean with this threat?

**FASOLT:** Why thrust in here?
We do not want to fight, we expect
nothing else but our pay.

**DONNER:** (*swinging his hammer*). I've paid many
giants their meed;
rascals ever
I'm ready to pay.
Come here! I'll deal your due,
helped with a generous hand.

**WOTAN:** (*stretching out his spear between the disputants*). Hold,
you fierce one!
Nothing demands force.
This bond the shaft
of my spear shields:
spare then your hammer's handle.

**FREIA:** Woe is me! Woe is me!
Wotan forsakes me!

**FRICKA:** You mean it then, merciless man?

## Scene II

WOTAN: (*wendet sich ab und sieht Loge kommen*). Endlich Loge!
Eiltest du so,
den du geschlossen,
den schlimmen Handel zu schlichten?

LOGE: (*ist im Hintergrunde aus dem Thale aufgetreten*). Wie? welchen Handel
hätt' ich geschlossen?
Wohl was mit den Riesen
dort im Rathe du dangst?—
In Tiefen und Höh'n
treibt mich mein Hang;
Haus und Herd
behagt mir nicht:
Donner und Froh,
die denken an Dach und Fach;
wollen sei frei'n,
ein Haus muss sie erfreu'n:
ein stolzer Saal,
ein starkes Schloss,
danach stand Wotan's Wunsch.—
Haus und Hof,
Saal und Schloss,
die selige Burg,
sie steht nun stark gebaut;
das Prachtgemäuer
prüfte ich selbst;
ob alles fest,
forsch' ich genau:
Fasolt und Fafner
fand ich bewährt;
kein Stein wankt im Gestemm'.
Nicht müssig war ich,
wie mancher hier:
der lügt, wer lässig mich schilt!

WOTAN: Arglistig
weichst du mir aus:
mich zu betrügen
hüte in Treuen dich wohl!
Von allen Göttern
dein einz'ger Freund,
nahm ich dich auf
in der übel trauenden Tross.—
Nun red' und rathe klug!
Da einst die Bauer der Burg
zum Dank Freia bedangen,
du weisst, nicht anders
willigt' ich ein,
als weil auf Pflicht du gelobtest
zu lösen das hehre Pfand.

LOGE: Mit höchster Sorge
drauf zu sinnen.
wie es zu lösen,
das—hab' ich gelobt:
doch dass ich fände,
was nie sich fügt,
was nie gelingt,
wie liess sich das wohl geloben?

FRICKA: (*zu Wotan*). Sieh, welch' trugvollem
Schelm du getraut!

FROH: Loge heisst du,
doch nenn' ich dich Lüge!

DONNER: Verfluchte Lohe,
dich lösch' ich aus!

---

WOTAN: (*turns away and perceives Loge coming*). Here is Loge!
You hurry so
when you should straighten
the sorry bargain you struck?

LOGE: (*who has climbed up from the valley at back*). Why! what bad bargain
have I struck you?
Was it what you worked conjointly
with the giants?
To depths and to heights
I drive at my heed.
House and hearth
cannot hold me;
Donner and Froh
dote on a dwelling fair:
gladly would they woo,
a house then they must find:
a bright abode,
a bulwark brave,
to this bends Wotan's wish;
roof and room,—
house and hall,—
the heavenly pile,—
behold it in its pride.
The towering walls
I tried myself,
examined all
if it were firm.
Fasolt and Fafner
failed not in faith:
each stone fits where it stands.
I was not idle
like all the rest:
he who styles me sluggard, lies.

WOTAN: Artfully
you slipped out:
look to you, traitor,
if you betray me now!
Of all the immortals
your only friend,
I took you up
to our over-credulous crew:—
now speak, and speak well.
When they who built us the burg
For meed Freia demanded,
You were that aware
would I consent solely
when you pledged at last
to deliver the glorious pledge.

LOGE: With greatest pains
the affair to ponder
how we might save her
that—did I swear.
But to discover
what never occurred—
what never took place—
how could I possibly promise?

FRICKA: (*to Wotan*). See what traitorous
scamp you trusted!

FROH: You, are Loge,
but better called 'liar.' [*The pun in the original, between 'Loge' and 'Luge,' cannot be preserved in translation.*]

DONNER: Cursed glistener,
your gleam I'll quench.

---

LOGE: Ihre Schmach zu decken
schmähen mich Dumme.
(*Donner und Froh wollem ihm zu Leibe.*)

WOTAN: (*wehrt ihnen*). In Frieden lasst mir den Freund!
Nicht kennt ihr Loge's Kunst:
reichert wiegt
seines Rathes Werth,
zahlt er zögernd ihn aus.

FAFNER: Nichts gezögert:
rasch gezahlt!

FASOLT: Lang währt's mit dem Lohn.

WOTAN: (*zu Loge*). Jetzt hör', Störrischer!
halte mir Stich!
Wo schweiftest du hin und her?

LOGE: Immer ist Undank
Log'es Lohn!
Um dich nur besorgt
sah ich mich um,
durchstöbert' im Sturm
alle Winkel der Welt,
Ersatz für Freia zu suchen,
wie er den Riesen wohl recht:
Umsonst sucht' ich
und sehe nun wohl,
in der Welten Ring
nichts ist so reich,
als Ersatz zu muthen dem Mann
für Weibes Wonne und Werth.
(*Alle gerathen in Erstaunen und Betroffenheit.*)
So weit Leben und Weben,
in Wasser, Erd' und Luft,
viel frug ich,
forschte bei allen,
wo Kraft nur sich rührt
und Keime sich regen:
was wohl dem Manne
mächtiger dünk'.
als Weibes Wonne und Werth?
Doch so weit Leben und Weben,
verlacht nur ward
meine fragende List:
in Wasser, Erd' und Luft
lassen will nichts
von Lieb' und Weib.—
Nur einen sah ich,
der sagte der Liebe ab:
um rothes Gold
entrieth er des Weibes Gunst.
Des Rheines klare Kinder
klagten mir ihre Noth:
der Nibelung,
Nacht'Alberich,
buhlte vergebens
um der Badenden Gunst;
das Rheingold da
raubte sich rächend der Dieb:
das dünkt ihm nun
das theuerste Gut,
hehrer als Weibes Huld.
Um den gleissenden Tand,
der Tiefe entwandt,
erklang mir der Töchter Klage:
an dich, Wotan,
wenden sie sich,
dass zu Recht du zögest den Räuber,
das Gold dem Wasser
wieder gebest,
und ewig es bliebe ihr Eigen.—

---

LOGE: But to screen your blunder
you scold me, blockheads.
(*Donner and Froh are about to set on him.*)

WOTAN: (*restraining them*). I pray you leave him in peace!
You know not Loge's kraft:
his advice ever has
Value high
when we wait for it long.

FAFNER: No more waiting:
quick!—the wage!

FASOLT: Pay fails to appear.

WOTAN: (*to Loge*). Now listen, strategist!
Hold still.
Why did you stray here and there?

LOGE: Evil is ever
Loge's lot.
Alone for your sake
I ventured out,
and stormily strode
to the ends of the earth
to seek for Freia a substitute,
which for the giants were just.
Success slipped me:
I see now full well
in the world around
nothing is so rare
to replace in mind of a man
a woman's wonderful worth.
(*All exhibit surprise and emotion.*)
Where life ebbs and flows
in flood, and earth, and air,
all I asked,
ever inquiring
where sinew reigns,
and seedlings are rooted,
what a man
could deem mightier
than woman's wonderful worth.
But where life ebbs and flows,
I only found myself
laughed at by all.
In flood and earth and air
everything has
for aim only love.
Yet I met one who
had made his oath against love;
for ruddy gold
bereft him of woman's grace.
The Rhine's indignant daughters
dismal tidings announced:
The Nibelung,
Night-Alberich,
failed from the girls
to gain amorous favors;
he robbed the Rhinegold in his raging revenge:
and values now
its worth over all—
greater than woman's grace.
For their glittering toy,
torn from the deep,
the maidens are mourning with tears.
To you, Wotan,
they turn wailing,
that your wrath may fall on the robber:
the gold be given once more
to the waves,

Dir's zu melden
gelobt' ich den Mädchen:
nun lös'te Loge sein Wort.

**WOTAN:** Thörig bist du,
wenn nicht gar tückisch!
Mich selbst siehst du in Noth;
wie hülf' ich andren zum Heil?

**FASOLT:** (*der aufmerksam zugehört, zu Fafner*). Nicht gönn' ich
das Gold dem Alben,
viel Noth schuf uns der Niblung,
doch schlau entschlüpfte immer
unsrem Zwange der Zwerg.

**FAFNER:** Neue Neidthat
sinnt uns der Niblung,
giebt das Gold ihm Macht.—
Du da, Loge!
Sag' ohne Lüg:
was Grosses gilt denn das Gold,
dass es dem Niblung genügt?

**LOGE:** Ein Tand ist's
In des Wassers Tiefe,
lachenden Kindern zur Lust:
doch, ward es zum runden
Reife geschmiedet,
hilft es zu höchster Macht,
Gewinnt dem Manne die Welt.

**WOTAN:** Von des Rheines Gold
hört' ich raunen:
Beute-Runen
berge sein rother Glanz,
Macht und Schätze
schüf' ohne Mass ein Reif.

**FRICKA:** Taugte wohl auch
des gold'nen Tandes
gleissend Geschmeid
Frauen zu schönem Schmuck?

**LOGE:** Des Gatten Treu'
ertrotzte die Frau,
trüge sie hold
den hellen Schmuck?
den schimmernd Zwerge schmied-
en;
rührig im Zwange des Reif's.

**FRICKA:** Gewänne mein Gatte
wohl sich das Gold!

**WOTAN:** Des Reifes zu walten,
räthlich will es mich dünken.—
Doch, wie, Loge,
lernt' ich die Kunst?
wie schüf' ich mir das Geschmeid?

**LOGE:** Ein Runenzauber
zwingt das Gold zum Reif:
keiner kennt ihn;
doch einer übt ihn leicht,
der sel'ger Lieb' entsagt.
(*Wotan wendet sich unmuthig
ab.*)
Das spar'st du wohl;
zu spät auch käm'st du:
Alberich zögerte nicht;
zaglos gewanne er
des Zaubers Macht:
gerathen ist ihm der Ring.

**DONNER:** Zwang uns allen
schüfe der Zwerg,
würd' ihm der Reif nicht entrissen.

their own to continue forever.—
This to mention
I swore to the maidens:
now staunch I stand to my word.

**WOTAN:** You are senseless
if not designing!
Myself suffering remorse
what help have I for others?

**FASOLT:** (*who has been listening
attentively—to Fafner*). This gold
I begrudge the Niblung.
Much wrong he's hatched us already:
but slily slipped the dwarf
unhindered out of our hold.

**FAFNER:** Now the gnome
will shape new annoyance,
mighty made by gold.
You there, Loge;
say without lies
what greatness gives this gold,
that the dwarf holds it dear?

**LOGE:** It was a toy
taken from waters,
serving as sport for gay maidens
but when to a Ring
it is rounded and fashioned
it grants marvellous might,
and wins its grasper the world.

**WOTAN:** Many rumors tell
of the Rhinegold:
runes of riches
run in its ruddy light;
might and wealth
it would win were it made a ring.

**FRICKA:** Profits as well
the golden bauble's
glittering dross
for women to deck and adorn?

**LOGE:** A wife could fix
the faith of her spouse,
found she the rare
and radiant mass
whose metal pygmies molded,
ruled by the power of the ring.

**FRICKA:** O might but my husband
gain me the hoard!

**WOTAN:** To win me that little ring
seems wise to my thinking.—
But how, Loge,
do I learn the means?
how make the dwarf's treasure
mine?

**LOGE:** A rune of magic
makes the gold a ring;
none may know it;
but he has learned its hold,
who forswears sweets of love.
(*Wotan turns away discouraged.*)
That likes you not;
too late you are too:
Alberich paused not in doubt!
promptly he conquered
the potent spell,
and rightly fashioned the ring.

**DONNER:** We were all placed
in his power,
were not the ring from him ravished.

**WOTAN:** Den Ring muss ich haben!

**FROH:** Leicht erringt
ohne Liebesfluch er sich jetzt.

**LOGE:** Spott-leicht,
ohne Kunst wie im Kinder-Spiel!

**WOTAN:** So rathe, wie?

**LOGE:** Durch raub!
Was ein Dieb stahl,
das stiehlst du dem Dieb:
ward leichter ein Eigen erlangt?—
Doch mit arger Wehr
wahrt sich Alberich:
klug und fein
musst du verfahren,
ziehst du den Räuber zu Recht,
um des Rheines Töchtern
den rothen Tand,
das Gold, wieder zu geben:
denn darum bitten sie dich.

**WOTAN:** Des Rheines Töchter?
Was taugt mir der Rath?

**FRICKA:** Von dem Wassergezücht
mag ich nichts wissen:
schon manchen Mann
—mir zum Leid—
verlocktem sie buhlend im Bad.
(*Wotan steht stumm mit sich
kämptend; die übrigen, Götter
heften in schweigender Spannung
die Blicke auf ihn.—Während
dem hat Fafner bei Seite mit Fasolt
berathen.*)

**FAFNER:** Glaub' mir, mehr als
Freia
frommt das gleissende Gold:
auch we'ge Jugend erjagt,
wer durch Goldes Zauber sie
zwingt.
(*Sie treten wieder heran.*)
Hör', Wotan,
der Harrenden Wort:
Freia bleib' euch in Frieden;
leichter'n Lohn
fand ich zur Lösung:
uns rauhen Riesen genügt
des Niblungen rothes Gold.

**WOTAN:** Seid ihr bei Sinn?
was nicht ich besitze,
soll ich euch Schamlosen schenk-
en?

**FAFNER:** Schwer baute
dort sich die Burg:
leicht wird's dir
mit list'ger Gewalt
(was im Neidspiel nie uns gelang)
den Niblungen fest zu fah'n.

**WOTAN:** Für euch müht' ich
mich um den Alben?
für euch fing' ich den Feind?
Unverschämt
und überbegehrlich
macht euch Dumme mein Dank!

**FASOLT:** (*ergreift plötzlich Freia
und führt sie mit Fafner zur
Seite*). Hieher, Maid!
in uns're Macht!
Als Pfand folgst du jetzt,

**WOTAN:** That ring I must seize.

**FROH:** Lightly now,
without forswearing love,
If were gained.

**LOGE:** Quite lightly;
you require scant knowledge.

**WOTAN:** Advise us, how?

**LOGE:** By theft!
What a thief stole,
that steal from the thief:
were anything done with more
ease?
But with artful foils
fights Alberich;
shrewd and wileful
be your workings
that the robber be surpassed:
to the river sisters
their ruddy toy,
the gold, once more be given;
for therefore they cry to you.

**WOTAN:** The river sisters!
What does your story serve?

**FRICKA:** I do not wish to hear
reaction of that watery race,
for many men
—more's my pain—
have perished, allured by their
love.
(*Wotan stands silently struggling
with himself, while the other gods
all look expectantly at him. Meanwhile, Fafner has consulted aside
with Fasolt.*)

**FAFNER:** Trust me, more than Freia
fits us treasure so true,
nor need we long yearn for youth
with the gold's all-mastering might.
(*They again advance.*)
Hear, Wotan,
our hasty last words!
Free from our hands be Freia:
You must release
a lesser forfeit;
the ungentle giants will need
just Nibelheim's gems and gold.

**WOTAN:** Where are your wits?
How can I award you
what is not mine yet, you miscreants?

**FAFNER:** It was work
to raise yonder towers;
you can, though, do
with more thoughtful craft
(what never our needs could bring
through):
the Nibelung fetter fast.

**WOTAN:** For you shall I
show myself yielding?
For you fetter a foe? I call such conduct
Shame-devoid
and shockingly covetous!

**FASOLT:** (*suddenly seizing Freia
and drawing her with Fafner
aside*). Come here, maid!
Remain with us.
You are now placed in pledge

bis wir Lösung empfahn.
(*Freia schreit laut auf: alle Götter sind in höchster Bestürzung.*)

FAFNER: Fort von hier
sei sie entführt!
Bis Abend, achtet's wohl,
pflegen wir sie als Pfand:
wir kehren wieder;
doch kommen wir,
und bereit liegt nicht als Lösung
das Rheingold roth und licht—

FASOLT: Zu End' ist die Frist dann,
Freia verfallen:
für immer folge sie uns!

FREIA: Schwester! Brüder!
Rettet! helft!
(*Sie wird von den hastig enteilenden Riesen fortgetragen; in der Ferne hören die bestürzten Götten ihren Wehruf verhallen.*)

FROH: Auf, ihnen nach!

DONNER: Breche denn alles!
(*Sie blicken Wotan fragend an.*)

LOGE: (*den Riesen nachsehend*).
Über Stock und Stein zu Thal
stapfen sie hin;
durch des Rheines Wasserfurth
waten die Riesen:
fröhlich nicht
hängt Freia
den Rauhen über den Rücken!—
Heia! hei!
Wie taumeln die Tölpel dahin!
Durch das Thal talpen sie schon;
wohl an Riesenheim's Mark
erst halten sie Rast!
(*Er wendet sich zu den Göttern.*)
Was sinnt nun Wotan so wild?—
Den seligen Göttern wie geht's?
(*Ein fahler Nebel erfüllt mit wachsender Dichtheit die Bühne, in ihm erhalten die Götter ein zunehmend bleiches und ältliches Aussehen: alle stehen bang und erwartungsvoll auf Wotan blickend, der sinnend die Augen an den Boden heftet.*)

LOGE: Trügt mich ein Nebel?
neckt mich ein Traum?
Wie bang und bleich
verblüht ihr so bald!
Euch erlischt der Wangen Licht,
der Blick eures Auges verblitz!—
Frisch, mein Froh,
noch ist's ja früh!—
Deiner Hand, Donner,
entfüllt ja der Hammer!—
Was ist's mit Fricka?
freut sie sich wenig
ob Wotan's grämlichem Grau,
das schier zum Greisen ihn schafft?

FRICKA: Wehe! Wehe!
Was ist geschehen?

DONNER: Mir sinkt die Hand.

FROH: Mir stockt das Herz.

LOGE: Jetzt fand ich's: hört was euch fehlt!
Von Freia's Frucht
genosset ihr heute noch nicht:

---

till our forfeit be paid.
(*Freia cries aloud: all the gods are in the greatest perturbation.*)

FAFNER: Far from here
shall she be forced:
till nightfall—note me well—
placed is she as a pledge;
then once more we come
and when we call
should we not find as the forfeit
the Rhinegold fair and red—

FASOLT: At end is the friendship,
Freia is forfeit;
forever fallen to us.

FREIA: Sisters! Brothers!
Save me! Help!
(*She is borne off by the hastily retreating giants; the troubled gods hear her cries of distress dying away in the distance.*)

FROH: Up! on their track!

DONNER: Perish now all things!
(*They look inquiringly towards Wotan.*)

LOGE: (*looking after the giants*).
Over stock and stone they tramp
straight down the vale;
through the Rhine's befriending
ford
flounder the ruffians:
Frightened,
now Freia
must ride the back of the rascals.—
Heia! hei!
How the stupids stumble along!
Past the steep stride they speed;
but in Riesenheim's bounds
they first will take rest.
(*He turns to the gods.*)
Why dream Wotan so wild?
What dread has gotten the gods?
(*A pale mist, increasing in density, fills the stage; in it the gods seem to take an aged and haggard appearance: all stand in alarm looking towards Wotan, who thoughtfully casts his eyes on the ground.*)

LOGE: Am I foold by a vapor?
Veils me a dream?
How fast
fairness has fled your features!
The bloom is chased from your cheeks;
the spark of your eyes has expired!—
Flag not, Froh;
day has not fled!
Does your hand, Donner,
relax from the hammer?
What ails Fricka?
Does she find her spouse's grayness
and gloom displeasing,
which gathers over him like age?

FRICKA: Woe is me! Woe is me!
What is it all?

DONNER: My hand sinks!

FROH: My heart stops!

LOGE: I've found it—hear what's happened!
Of Freia's fruit
no atom today did you eat.

---

die gold'nen Aepfel
in ihrem Garten,
sie machten euch tüchig und jung
ass't ihr sie jeden Tag.
Des Gartens Pflegerin
ist nun verpfändet;
an den Aesten darbt
und dorrt das Obst:
bald fällt faul es herab.—
Mich kümmert's minder;
an mir kargte
Freia von je
knausernd die köstliche Frucht:
denn halb so ächt nur
bin ich wie, Herrliche, ihr!
Doch ihr setztet alles
aug das jüngende Obst:
das wussten die Riesen wohl;
auf euer Leben
legten sie's an:
nun sorgt, wie ihr das wahrt!
Ohne die Aepfel
alt und grau,
greis und grämlich,
welkend zum Spott aller Welt,
erstirbt der Götter Stamm.

FRICKA: Wotan, Gemahl
unsel'ger Mann!
Sieh wie dein Leichtsinn
lachend uns allen
Schimpf und Schmach erschuf!

WOTAN: (*mit plötzlichem Entschluss auffahrend*). Auf,
Loge!
hinab mit mir,
Nach Nibelheim fahren wir nieder:
gewinnen will ich das Gold.

LOGE: Die Rheintöchter
riefen dich an:
so dürfen Erhörung sie hoffen?

WOTAN: (*heftig*). Schweige,
Schwätzer!
Freia, die gute,
Freia gilt es zu lösen.

LOGE: Wie du befiehlst
führ' ich dich gern:
steil hinab
steigen wir denn durch den Rhein?

WOTAN: Nicht durch den Rhein!

LOGE: So schwingen wir uns
durch die Schwefelkluft:
dort schlüpfe mit mir hinein!
(*Er geht voran und verschwindet seitwärts in einer Kluft, aus der sogleich ein schwefliger Dampf hervorquillt.*)

WOTAN: Ihr andren harrt
bis Abend hier:
verlor'ner Jugend
erjag' ich erlösendes Gold!
(*Er steigt Loge nach in die Kluft hinab: der aus ihr dringende Schwefeldampf verbreitet sich über die ganze Rühne und erfüllt diese schnell mit dickem Gewölk. Bereits sind die Zurück-bleibenden unsichtbar.*)

DONNER: Fahre wohl, Wotan!

FROH: Glück auf! Glück auf!

---

The golden apples
from her garden
preserved you from dwindling with
age,
eating them every day.
The garden's keeper
now held a captive;
rests among the foliage
and rots the fruit:
it will fall soon, full spoiled.
My case is milder;
for me, unkindly,
Freia has ever
kept from the coveted fruit;
in me but half
the power you immortal ones have.
But all leaned on the
apples' youth-giving aid:
this knew the giants well;
against your lives
a league is begun,
And how do you find your defense?
If without apples,
old and grim,
gray and gruesome,
waning to sport of the world,
the stock of gods would cease.

FRICKA: Wotan! My lord!
Luckless and lost!
Look how your heedless
hastiness now
our shunless shame has shaped!

WOTAN: (*starting up with sudden resolution*). Up! Loge,
and off with me!
Beneath, to the home of the Nibelungs.
I'll surely seize this gold.

LOGE: The Rhine maidens
raised their complaint:
so may they then hope for a hearing?

WOTAN: (*violently*). Peace! You
prattler!
Freia the noble—
Freia needs our assistance.

LOGE: Swiftly I'll guide,
go where you will:
steeply down
shall we descend through the Rhine?

WOTAN: Not through the Rhine!

LOGE: We'll swing ourselves then
through the sulfur cleft:
so slip with me down it!
(*He goes first and disappears at the side down a crevice from which immediately a sulfurous vapor rises.*)

WOTAN: You others halt
Until evening here:
our youth departed
I'll purchase me with the gold yet.
(*He clambers after Loge into the sulfur cleft: the vapor stealing out of which spreads over the whole stage with a thick cloud, concealing the rest of the characters.*)

DONNER: Farewell, Wotan!

FROH: Good luck! Good luck!

**FRICKA:** O kehre bald
zur bangenden Frau!
(*Der Schwefeldampf verdüstert sich bis zu ganz schwarzem Gewölk, welches von unten nach oben steigt; dann verwandelt sich dieses in festes, finstres Steingeklüft, das sich immer aufwärts bewegt, so dass es den Anschein hat, als sänke die Scene immer tiefer in die Erde hinab.*)

**FRICKA:** O, return soon
to soothe my trouble!
(*The sulfurous vapor thickens to a quite black cloud which rises upwards; this then changes to a firm, gloomy, rocky chasm which also continually rises, giving the stage the appearance of sinking deeper and deeper into the earth.*)

## ■ DRITTE SCENE.

*Endlich dämmert von verschiedenen Seiten aus der Ferne her, dunkelrother Schein auf: eine unabsehbar weit sich dahinziehende unterirdische Kluft wird erkennbar die nach allen Seiten hin in enge Schachte auszumünden scheint.*

*Alberich zerrt den kreischenden Mime an den Ohren aus einer Seitenschlufft herbei.*

**ALBERICH:** Hehe! hehe!
hieher! hieher!
Tückischer Zwerg!
tapfer gezwickt
sollst du mir sein,
schaffst du nicht fertig,
wie ich's bestellt,
zur Stund' das feine Geschmeid!

**MIME:** (*heulend*). Ohe! Ohe!
Au! Au!
Lass' mich nur los!
Fertig ist es,
wie du befahlst;
mit Fleiss und Schweiss
ist es gefügt:
nimm nur die Nägel vom Ohr!

**ALBERICH:** (*loslassend*). Was
zögerst du dann
und zeigst es nicht?

**MIME:** Ich Armer zagte,
dass noch was fehle.

**ALBERICH:** Was wär' noch nicht
fertig?

**MIME:** (*verlegen*).
Hier . . . und da . . .

**ALBERICH:** Was hier und da?
Her das Gewirk!
(*Er will ihm wieder an das Ohr fahren: vor Schreck lässt Mime, ein metallenes Gewirke, das er krampfhaft in den Händen hielt sich entfallen. Alberich hebt es hastig auf und prüft es genau.*)
Schau' du Schelm!
Alles geschmiedet
und fertig gefügt,
wie ich's befahl!
So wollte der Tropf
schlau mich betrügen?
für sich behalten
das hehre Geschmeid,
das meine List
ihn zu schmieden gelehrt?
kenn; ich dich dummen Dieb?
(*Er setzt das Gewirk als "Tarnhelm" auf den Kopf.*)

## ■ SCENE III

*Presently from various quarters ruddy light gleams out; and there extends farther than eye can reach a subterranean cavern which on all sides seems to lead to other and narrower passages.*

*Alberich enters, dragging the shrieking Mime by the ear from a cleft at one side.*

**ALBERICH:** Hello! Hello!
Come here! Come here!
Rascally imp!
Rarely, now I
will nip your ear,
should you not weld me
straight on the spot
the special work I have shown.

**MIME:** (*howling*). Oho! Oho!
Oh! Oh!
Let me alone!
It is made
at your command,
with moil and toil
molded by me.
Nick not your nails at me so!

**ALBERICH:** (*letting him go*). Why
hesitate then
to hand it out?

**MIME:** I apprehended
in case anything was failing—

**ALBERICH:** Where was it unfinished?

**MIME:** (*hesitating*). Here—and
there—

**ALBERICH:** How 'here and there'?
hand me the work!
(*He threatens to seize again the ear of Mime who, in terror, lets fall a piece of metal work that he has held concealed in his hand. Alberich hastily picks it up and examines it.*)
See, you scamp!
All has been smithed
and welded, I expect,
after my word.
You, idiot, would seek
to deceive me,
and save the wonderful
work for yourself?
when by my lore
you could shape it alone!
Have I read your thoughts, my thief?
(*He sets the metal work on his*

Dem Haupt fügt sich der Helm
ob sich der Zauber auch zeigt?
—"Nacht und Nebel,
Niemand gleich!"—
(*Seine Gestalt verschwindet; statt ihrer gewahrt man eine Nebelsäule.*)
Siehst du mich, Bruder?

**MIME:** (*blickt sich verwundert um*). Wo bist du? ich sehe dich nicht.

**ALBERICH:** (*Stimme*). So fühle
mich doch,
du fauler Schuft!
Nimm' das für dein Diebsgelüst!
(*Mime schreit und windet sich unter empfangenen Geisselhieben, deren Fall man vernimmt ohne die Geissel selbst zu sehen.*)
(*Stimme, lachend.*) Dank, du
Dummer!
Dein Werk bewährt sich gut.—
Hoho! Hoho!
Niblungen all,
neigt euch Alberich!
Überall weilt er nun,
euch zu bewachen;
Ruh' und Rast
ist euch zerronnen;
ihm müsst ihr schaffen,
wo nicht ihr ihn schaut;
wo ihr nicht ihn gewahrt,
seid seiner gewärtig:
unterthan seid ihr ihm immer!
Hoho! Hoho!
hört ihn: er naht,
der Niblungen-Herr!
(*Die Nebelsäule verschwindet dem Hintergrunde zu: man hört in immer weiterer Ferne Alberich's Toben und Zanken; Geheul und Geschrei antwortet ihm aus den untern Klüften, das sich endlich in immer weitere Ferne unhörbar verliert.—Mime ist vor Schmerz zusammengesunken; sein Stohnen und Wimmern wird von Wotan und Loge gehört, die aus einer Schlufft von oben her sich herablassen.*)

**LOGE:** Nibelheim hier:
durch bleiche Nebel
wie blitzen dort feurige Funken?

**WOTAN:** Hier stöhnt es laut:
was liegt im Gestein?

**LOGE:** (*neigt sich zu Mime*). Was
Wunder wimmerst du hier?

**MIME:** Ohe! Ohe!
Au! Au!

**LOGE:** Hie, Mime! Muntrer Zwerg!
was zwingt und zwackt dich denn so?

**MIME:** Lass' mich in Frieden!

**LOGE:** Das will ich freilich,
und mehr noch, hör':
helfen will ich dir, Mime!

**MIME:** (*sich etwas aufrichtend*).
Wer hälfe mir?
Gehorchen muss ich
dem leiblichen Bruder,
der mich in Bande gelegt.

head as a 'Tarnhelm'.)
The helmet fits to the head;
now will it act as it ought?
—'Night annul me.
Nothing be seen!'—
(*He vanishes, and a column of smoke takes his place.*)
Brother, do you see me?

**MIME:** (*gazing about in astonishment*). Where do you stand? I do not see you!

**ALBERICH:** (*voice*). Then feel me
instead,
you faithless scamp;
take this for your thievish tricks!
(*Mime writhes and cries under the blows which are heard to fall on him from an invisible scourge.*)
(*voice, laughing.*) I thank you,
thickhead;
the work is well performed.
Hoho! Hoho!
Nibelung elves,
kneel all to Alberich!
Everywhere he wanders
watching over you;
reign of rest
is riven from you;
you mush serve him
who lurks unseen:
when you least of all note him
he's near you!
You are slaves to him forever
Hoho! Hoho!
hear him; he nears,
the Nibelung's head!
(*The column of vapor disappears towards the back; Alberich's scoldings are heard retreating in the distance; howls and cries respond from lower passages, finally the sounds are lost in the distance. Mime has cowered down in pain. His groans and whimperings are heard by Wotan and Loge who descend from above by a side cleft.*)

**LOGE:** Nibelheim's here.
What glare I notice
that glows from those varying vapors?

**WOTAN:** Who groans so loud:
what lies on the ground?

**LOGE:** (*bending down to Mime*).
What whining whimperer's here?

**MIME:** Oho! Oho!
Oh! Oh!

**LOGE:** Hey, Mime, merry gnome!
what nips and knocks you like this?

**MIME:** Leave me in quiet!

**LOGE:** Yes without question;
and more yet, listen—
help I'll give to you, Mime.

**MIME:** (*partially rising*). What
help for me?
I have for master
a hard-hearted brother
who makes me bondsman to him!

# Scene III

**LOGE:** Dich, Mime, zu binden
was gab ihm die Macht?

**MIME:** Mit arger List
schuf sich Alberich
aus Rheines Gold
einen gelben Reif:
seinem starken Zauber
zittern wir staunend;
mit ihm zwingt er uns alle,
der Niblungen nächtiges Heer.—
Sorglose Schmiede,
schufen wir sonst wohl
Schmuck unsren Weibern,
wonnig Geschmeid,
niedlichen Niblungentand:
wir lachten lustig der Müh'.
Nun zwingt uns der Schlimme
in Klüfte zu schlüpfen,
für ihn allein
uns immer zu müh'n.
Durch des Ringes Gold
erräth seine Gier,
wo neuer Schimmer
in Schachten sich birgt:
da müssen wir spähen,
spüren und graben,
die Beute schmelzen
und schmieden den Guss,
ohne Ruh' und Rast
den Hort zu häufen dem Herrn.

**LOGE:** Den Trägen so eben
traf wohl sein Zorn?

**MIME:** Mich Armen, ach!
mich zwang er zum ärgsten:
ein Helmgeschmeid
hiess er mich schweissen;
genau befahl er
wie es zu fügen.
Wohl merkt' ich klug
welch' mächt'ge Kraft
zu eigen dem Werk,
das aus Erz ich wirkte:
für mich drum hüten
wollt' ich den Helm,
durch seinen Zauber
Alberich's Zwang mich entzieh'n—
vielleicht, ja vielleicht
den Lästigen selbst überlisten,
in meine Gewalt ihn zu werfen.
den Ring ihm zu entreissen,
dass, wie ich Knecht jetzt dem
Kühnen,
mir Freien er selber dann fröhn'!

**LOGE:** Warum, du Kluger,
glückte dir's nicht?

**MIME:** Ach, der das Werk ich
wirkte,
den Zauber, der ihm entzuckt,
den Zauber errieth ich nicht recht!
Der das Werk mir rieth,
und mir's entriss,
der lehrte mich nun
—doch leider zu spät!—
welche List läg' in dem Helm:
meinem Blick entschwandt er,
doch Schwielen dem Blinden
schlug unschaubar sein Arm.
Das schuf ich mir Dummen

**LOGE:** But, Mime, what brought
him
the power to command?

**MIME:** With evil craft
lately Alberich
hath wrought from Rhinegold
a ruddy ring
and its spell of magic
masters our spirits;
with this he moves to serve him,
the night-loving Niblung race.
Once at our anvils
ornaments all made,
only our wives to deck;
worked from the ore
nice little Nibelung toys:
we lightly laughed as we toiled.
This wretch now compels us
to pierce to deep caverns,
to heavily toil
for him alone.
Through the ring of gold
he advises in his greed
where unknown splendor
is spread in the earth.
Then must we all trace it,
track it and dig it;
extract the metal
and melt it into bars.
With no peace or pause,
to heap up the hoard for him.

**LOGE:** His lash has chastised
your laziness then?

**MIME:** I am most ill-starred!
My slavery is endless,
I had forged a
helmet to fashion:
exact commands
he gave for its making.
My wit surmised
the wondrous might
possessed by the work
that from steel I wove:
the helm I sorely
wanted myself,
that its enchantment
Alberich's chiding might check;
maybe—yes, maybe
the bully himself it would bamboo-
zle.
That he might be placed in my power—
the ring be ravished from him:
then I who bend as his bondsman,
should henceforth command as
master.

**LOGE:** And why, my trickster,
did you not triumph?

**MIME:** Ah! though the work I welded,
the magic to which it was made,
that magic I read not right.
He who robbed from me
the work I wrought,
I learned of him now,
—too late though, alas!—
what good luck lay in the helmet.
He faded from my eyes
but finely his arm
my fool's back furrowed with
stripes.

schön zu Dank!
(*Er streicht sich heulend den
Rücken. Die Götter lachen.*)

**LOGE:** (*zu Wotan*). Gesteh', nicht
leicht
gelingt der Fang.

**WOTAN:** Doch erliegt der Feind,
hilft deine List.

**MIME:** (*vom dem Lachen der
Götter betroffen, betrachtet diese
aufmerksamer*). Mit eurem Ge-
frage
wer seid denn ihr Fremde?

**LOGE:** Freunde dir;
von ihrer Noth
befrei'n wir der Niblungen Volk.
(*Alberich's Zanken und
Züchtigen nähert sich wieder.*)

**MIME:** Nehmt euch in Acht!
Alberich naht.

**WOTAN:** Sein harren wir hier.
(*Er setzt sich ruhig auf einen
Stein; Loge lehnt ihm zur Seite.—
Alberich, der den Tarnhelm vom
Haupte genommen und in den
Gürtel gehängt hat, treibt mit
geschwungener Geissel aus der
unteren, tiefer gelegenen
Schlucht, aufwärts eine Schaar
Nibelungen vor sich her; diese
sind mit goldenem und silbernem
Geschmeide beladen, das sie, un-
ter Alberich's stetem Schimpfen
und Schelten, all auf einen Hau-
fen speichern und so zu einem
Horte häufen.*)

**ALBERICH:** Hieher! Dorthin!
Hehe! Hoho!
Träges Heer,
dort zu Hauf
schichtet den Hort!
Du da, hinauf!
Willst du voran?
Schmähliches Volk,
ab das Geschmeide!
Soll ich euch helfen?
Alles hieher!
(*Er gewahrt plötzich Wotan und
Loge.*)
He! wer ist dort?
Wer drang hier ein?—
Mime! Zu mir,
schäbiger Schuft!
Schwatztest du gar
mit dem schweifenden Paar?
Fort! du Fauler!
Willst du gleich schmieden und
schaffen?
(*Er treibt Mime mit Geisselhieben
unter den Haufen der Nibelungen
hinein.*)
Hie! an die Arbeit!
Alle von hinnen!
Hurtig hinab!
Aus den neuen Schachten
schafft mir das Gold!
Euch grüsst die Geissel,
grabt ihr nicht rasch!
Dass keiner mir müssig
bürge mir Mime,
sonst birgt er sich schwer
meines Armes Schwunge:

Through foolishness thus
I found my thanks.
(*He rubs his back, howling. The
gods laugh.*)

**LOGE:** (*to Wotan*). Admit, not easy
is our task.

**WOTAN:** Until our end's attained
Your cunning must aid us.

**MIME:** (*struck by the laughter of
the gods, observes them more attentively*). Who are you before me
that question so freely?

**LOGE:** Friends to you:
we'd free all the Nibelung folk
from their vexations.
(*Alberich's threats and scourg-
ings again approach.*)

**MIME:** Keep a look out!
Alberich comes.

**WOTAN:** For him we wait here.
(*He quietly seats himself on a
stone. Loge leans by his side.—
Alberich, who has now removed
the Tarnhelm and wears it in his
girdle, drives with brandished
whip from the caves below a
crowd of Nibelungs before him.
They are laden with gold and silver jewelry which under Alberich's continual scolding and urging, they pile up in one heap.*)

**ALBERICH:** Here! There!
Hallo! Hallo!
Lazy hounds!
There in heaps
pile up the hoard!
You there, get up!
Will you move on?
Indolent pack,
down with the ingots.
Shall I then help you?
Drag it all here.
(*He suddenly perceives Wotan
and Loge.*)
Hey! who are these
who thus intrude?
Mime, to me,
pestilent patch!
You prattle here
with this promising pair?
Off, you idler!
Back to your pickaxe and pincers!
(*With uplifted scourge he drives
Mime into the crowd of Nibe-
lungs.*)
Hey! to your labor!
Look that you hurry!
Hurry below!
From the new-found shafts
now shovel the gold!
Who grubs not gaily
gets the whip!
If any be idle
Mime shall answer,
or make his escape
from the sting of my scourge!
That I everywhere wander

dass ich überall weile,
wo Niemand es wähnt,
das weiss er, dünkt mich, genau.—
Zögert ihr noch?
Zaudert wohl gar?
(*Er zieht seinen Ring vom Finger,
küsst ihn und streckt ihn drohend
aus.*)
Zittre und zage,
gezähmtes Heer:
rasch gehorcht
des Ringes Herrn!
(*Unter Geheul und Gekreisch stieben die Nibelungen (unter ihnen Mime) auseinander, und schlüpfen nach allen Seiten in die Schachte hinab.*)

**ALBERICH:** (*grimmig auf Wotan und Loge zutretend*). Was sucht ihr hier?

**WOTAN:** Von Nibelhein's
nächt'gem Land
vernahmen wir neue Mähr':
mächt'ge Wunder
wirke hier Alberich;
daran uns zu weiden
trieb uns Gäste die Gier.

**ALBERICH:** Nach Nibelheim
fürht euch wohl Neid:
so kühne Gaste,
glaubt, kenn' ich gar gut.

**LOGE:** Kennst du mich gut,
kindischer Alp?
Nun sag': wer bin ich,
dass du so bell'st?
Im kalten Loch,
da kauernd du lag'st
wer gab dir Licht
und wärmende Lohe,
wenn Loge nie dir gelacht?
Was hülf' dir dein Schmieden,
heizt' ich die Schmiede dir nicht?
Dir bin ich Vetter,
und war dir Freund:
nicht fein drum dünkt mich dein
Dank!

**ALBERICH:** Den Lichtalben
lacht jetzt Loge,
der listige Schelm:
bist du Falscher ihr Freund,
wie mir Freund du einst warst
haha! mich freut's!
von ihnen fürcht' ich dann nichts.

**LOGE:** So denk' ich, kannst du mir
trau'n?

**ALBERICH:** Deiner Untreu' trau'
ich,
nicht deiner Treu'!—
Doch getrost trotz' ich euch allen.

**LOGE:** Hohen Muth
verleiht deine Macht:
grimmig gross
wuchs dir die Kraft.

**ALBERICH:** Siehst du den Hort,
den mein Heer
dort mir gehäuft?

**LOGE:** So neidlichen sah' ich noch
nie.

where no one believes
who knows better than he?
Tarrying still?
Take you no heed?
(*Draws the ring from his finger,
kisses it and stretches it commandingly out.*)
Tremble in terror,
Down trodden race:
heed his rule
who holds the Ring!
(*With howls and shrieks the Nibelungs—Mime among them—separate and slip into crevices on all sides down to their shafts again.*)

**ALBERICH:** (*advancing wrathfully to Wotan and Loge*). What do you want here?

**WOTAN:** From Nibelheim's night-bound land
strange news rang, to our notice
of rarest wonders
worked here by Alberich:
to witness these marvels
makes us guests at your gate.

**ALBERICH:** Nothing gnaws you
but envy, I know:
and why you greet me,
guests, well I guess.

**LOGE:** Do you know me,
miserable dwarf?
Who is it? now say,
at whom would you snarl?
In frigid hole
where you lay freezing,
where would your light
and warming illuminate
if you had not looked on Loge?
What aid would your hammer be
if I never heated the forge?
Cousin you may be,
once friend of mine;—
Your thanks are no more than
these?

**ALBERICH:** To light elves
Loge belongs now,
deluding rogue!
Are you as fairly their friend
as my friend you were once?
Haha! that's fine!—
I need fear nothing from their hands.

**LOGE:** I'm surely worthy of your trust.

**ALBERICH:** In your untruth I trust
not in your truth!
But entrenched I triumph over all.

**LOGE:** Power has brought you
spirit brave:
grimly great
waxes your force.

**ALBERICH:** Do you see the hoard
that my host
heaps for me there?

**LOGE:** So noble a sight I never
knew.

**ALBERICH:** Das ist für heut',
ein kärglich Häufchen:
kühn und mächtig
soll es künftig sich mehren.

**WOTAN:** Zu was doch frommt dir
der Hort,
da freundlos Nibelheim,
und nichts um Schätze hier feil?

**ALBERICH:** Schätze zu schaffen
und Schätze zu bergen,
nützt mir Nibelheim's Nacht;
doch mit dem Hort,
in der Höhle gehäuft,
denk' ich dann Wunder zu wirken:
die ganze Welt
gewinn' ich mit ihm mir zu eigen.

**WOTAN:** Wie beginnst du,
Gütiger, das?

**ALBERICH:** Die in linder Lüfte
Weh'n
da oben ihr lebt,
lacht und liebt:
mit gold'ner Faust
euch Göttliche fan' ich mir alle!
Wie ich der Liebe abgesagt,
Alles was lebt
soll ihr entsagen:
mit Golde gegirrt,
nach Gold nur sollt ihr noch gieren.
Auf wonnigen Höh'n
in seligem Weben
wiegt ihr euch,
den Schwarz-Alben
verachtet ihr ewigen Schwelger:—
habt Acht!
habt Acht!—
denn dient ihr Männer
erst meiner Macht,
eure schmucken Frau'n—
die mein Frei'n verschmäht—
sie zwingt zur Lust sich der Zwerg,
lacht Liebe ihm nicht.—
Hahahaha!
hört ihr mich recht?
Habt Acht!
Habt Acht vor dem nächtlichen
Heer,
ensteigt des Niblungen Hort
aus stummer Tiefe zu Tag!

**WOTAN:** (*auffahrend*). Vergeh',
frevelnder Gauch!

**ALBERICH:** Was sagt der?

**LOGE:** (*ist dazwischen getreten*).
Sei doch bei Sinnen!
(*Zu Alberich.*)
Wen doch fasste nicht Wunder,
erfährt er Alberich'sWerk?
Gelingt deiner herrlichen List,
Was mit dem Hort du heischest,
Den Mächtigsten muss ich dich
rühmen:
denn Mond und Stern'
und die strahlende Sonne,
sie auch dürfen nicht anders,
dienen müssen sie dir.—
Doch wichtig acht' ich vor allem,
dass des Hortes Häufer,
der Nibulungen Heer,
neidlos dir geneigt.
Einen Ring rührtest du kühn,
dem zagte sitternd dein Volk:
doch wenn im Schlaf

**ALBERICH:** That's for today,
the merest dribble
much more metal
shall augment it tomorrow.

**WOTAN:** But what can it profit you
the hoard
here in baleful Nibelheim,
where nothing is bought by riches!

**ALBERICH:** Riches to raise me,
and riches to furnish,
I need Nibelheim's night,
But with the hoard
that I heap in hollows,
wonders I count to accomplish:
the world my cunning
can master by its might.

**WOTAN:** How, my worthy, will
you do that?

**ALBERICH:** You up there, who
lapped in airs
ambrosial, live,
laugh and love,
with gilded fist
I'll grasp you and fetter all to me!
As I have loving forsworn,
all they that live
shall forswear it:
allured by my gold,
for gold alone shall they languish.
On radiant heights,
in visions of rapture
rocked are you:
the black dwarfs
You look down upon, deathless debauchees.
Beware!
Beware!—
For first you men
shall work to my might,
then your sprightly women,
who my wooing despise,
the gnome shall lure to his needs;
lacking love, nevertheless.
Ha, ha, ha, ha!
Have you now heard?
Beware!
Beware of the night begotten host,
when the Niblung hoard shall
upheave
from night and darkness to day!

**WOTAN:** (*starting*). Away! miserable wretch!

**ALBERICH:** What says he?

**LOGE:** (*stepping between them:—to Wotan*). Subdue your spirit!
(*To Alberich.*)
What can hinder our wonder,
beholding Alberich's work?
If safely your tricks can assure
what you attract with the treasure,
I must then hail you the mightiest
for moon and stars
and the sun in its splendor
surely must regard you:
they, too, must be your slaves.
But it was of primal importance
that the host who heap up
the Nibelung hoard
nurse nothing of hatred.
You have well wielded a ring
which puts your people in awe:—
think if in sleep

ein Deib dich beschlich,
den Ring schlau dir entriss',
wie wahrtest du Weiser dich dann?

a thief slipped to you,
the ring slyly to steal!
What, wise one, would warrant you then?

ALBERICH: Der Listigste dünkt
sich Loge;
andre denkt er
immer sich dumm:
dass sein' ich bedürfte
zu Rath und Dienst
um harten Dank,
das hörte der Dieb jetzt gern!—
Den hehlenden Helm
ersann ich mir selbst;
der sorglichste Schmied,
Mime, musst' ihn mir schmieden:
schnell mich zu wandeln
nach meinem Wunsch,
die Gestalt mir zu tauschen,
taught mir der Helm;
niemand sieht mich,
wenn er mich sucht;
doch überall bin ich,
geborgen dem Blick
So ohne Sorge
bin ich selbst sicher vor dir,
du fromm sorgender Freund!

ALBERICH: Delightfully deep is
Loge:
ever he deems
all others are dull.
That I am indebted
to him, indeed,
for service deft
would seem to the dog right
good.—
I designed the helmet that hides
myself:
the most skillful smith,
Mime, I made shape it:
swiftly to transport me,
or, at my will,
to assume other semblance
serves the helmet.
None may see me,
much as he seek;
but I am everywhere hidden from
all men
So, undisturbed,
I stand safe even from you,
you fond, sedulous friend!

LOGE: Vieles sah' ich,
Seltsames fand ich:
doch solches Wunder
gewahrt' ich nie.
Dem Werk ohne Gleichen
kann ich nicht glauben;
wäre diess einz'ge möglich,
deine Macht währte dann ewig.

LOGE: Much I've looked at—
lighted on marvels;
but lacked to witness
such wonders yet.
I have no faith in
This work without peer,
If this were possible,
your power would be unending.

ALBERICH: Meinst du, ich lüg',
und prahle wie Loge?

ALBERICH: Pray do I lie
and prattle like Loge?

LOGE: Bis ich's geprüft,
bezweifl' ich, Zwerg, dein Wort.

LOGE: Till it is proved,
good dwarf, I doubt your word.

ALBERICH: Vor Klugheit bläht
sich
zum platzen der Blöde:
num plage dich Neid!
Bestimm', in welcher Gestalt
soll ich jach vor dir stehn?

ALBERICH: With cunning, blockhead,
you'll finish by bursting.
Confusion I'll cause!
Now say, before you what shape
shall my figure assume?

LOGE: In welcher du willst:
nur mach' vor Staunen mich
stumm!

LOGE: Whatever you will;
but make me mute with amazement!

ALBERICH: (hat den Helm aufgesetzt). "Riesen-Wurm
winde dich ringelnd!"
(Sogleich verschwindet er: eine
ungeheure Riesenschlange windet sich statt seiner am Boden; sie
bäumt sich und streckt den auf-
gesperren Rachen nach Wotan
und Loge hin.)

ALBERICH: (putting on the Tarnhelm). 'Draw here,
hugest of dragons.'
(He instantly disappears and in
his place there writhes a huge
monster serpent which bends and
opens its outstretched jaws at
Wotan and Loge.)

LOGE: (stellt sich von Furcht ergriffen). Ohe! Ohe!
schreckliche Schlange!
verschling' mich nicht!
Schone Logen das Leben!

LOGE: (affecting extreme fear).
Oho! Oho!
Sinister serpent,
I beg you, do not swallow me! Spare
life to poor Loge!

WOTAN: (lacht). Gut, Alberich!
gut, du Arger!
Wie wuchs so
Wie wuchs so rasch
zum riesigen Wurme der Zwerg!
(Die Schlange verschwindet, und
statt ihrer erscheint sogleich Alberich wieder in seiner wirklichen
Gestalt.)

WOTAN: (laughing). Good, Alberich!
Good—and artful!
So soon can you turn your form
to a terrible serpent?
(The dragon disappears and instead Alberich is seen in his own
figure.)

ALBERICH: Hehe! Ihr Klugen,
glaubt ihr mir nun?

ALBERICH: Haha! you deep ones,
do you believe?

LOGE: Mein Zittern mag dir's bezeugen.
Zur grossen Schlange
schuf'st du dich schnell:
weil ich's gewahrt,
willigt glaub' ich das Wunder.
Doch, wie du wuchsest,
kannst du auch winzig
und klein dich schaffen?
Das Klügste schiene mir das,
Gefahren schlau zu entflieh'n:
das aber dünkt mich zu schwer!

LOGE: My trembling surely attests
it.
From you the serpent
was swiftly shaped:
When I have witnessed,
I credit the wonder well.
But as you waxed great
can you not wane too,
becoming smaller?
More cunning seems to me
from dangers so to withdraw:
that, truly, I think too difficult

ALBERICH: Zu schwer dir,
weil du zu dumm!
Wie klein soll ich sein?

ALBERICH: Too difficult? yes,
for such as you!
How small shall I seem?

LOGE: Dass die engste Klinze dich
fasse,
wo bang die Kröte sich birgt.

LOGE: That a tiny slit may contain
you,
as timidly slinks a toad.

ALBERICH: Pah! nichts leichter!
Luge du her!
(Er setzt den Tarnhelm wieder
auf.)
"Krumm und grau
krieche Kröte!"
(Er verschwindet; die Götter gewahren im Gestein eine Kröte auf
sich zukriechen.)

ALBERICH: Pah! There's nothing
simpler!
Watch me now.
(He puts on the helmet again.)
"Crooked toad,
creep from cranny."
(He disappears. The gods perceive
a toad crawling on the rocks.)

LOGE: (zu Wotan). Dort die
Kröte,
griefe sie rasch!
(Wotan setzt seinen Fuss auf die
Kröte: Loge fährt ihr nach dem
Kopfe und hält den Tarnhelm in
der Hand.)

LOGE: (to Wotan). There! that
creature,
grasp it in haste.
(Wotan sets his foot on the toad
and Loge, putting his hand to its
head, seizes the Tarnhelm.)

ALBERICH: (wird plötzlich in
seiner wirklichen Gestalt sichtbar, wie er sich unter Wotan's
Fusse windet). Ohe! Verflucht!
ich bin gefangen!

ALBERICH: (who is then seen in
his own form writhing under Wotan's foot). Oho! Damned!
I am a captive.

LOGE: Halt' ihn fest,
bis ich ihn band.
(Er hat ein Bastseile hervorgeholt,
und bindet Alberich damit Arme
und Beine; den Geknebelten, der
sich wühend zu wehren sucht, fassen dann Beide, und schleppen
ihn mit sich nach der Kluft, aus
der sie herabkamen.)
Schnell hinauf!
dort ist er unser.
(Sie verschwinden, aufwärts
steigend.)

LOGE: Hold him close,
till he is tied.
(He brings forward a bast rope
and binds Alberich hand and foot
with it; the two then seize their
prisoner, who furiously struggles
to escape, and drag him with them
to the shaft from which they descended.)
With speed above;
there he's our bondsman!
(They disappear, mounting upwards.)

## ■ VIERTE SCENE.

Die Scene verwandelt sich, nur in
umgekehrter Weise, wie zuvor;
schliesslich erscheint wieder die
freie Gegend auf Bergeshöhen,
wie in der zweiten Scene; nur ist
sie jetzt noch in einem fahlen Nebelschleier verhüllt, wie vor der
zweiten Verwandlung nach
Freia's Abführung.

Wotan und Loge, den gebundenen
Alberich mit sich führend, steigen
aus der Kluft herauf.

## ■ SCENE IV

The scene changes in the same
manner as before, but the reverse
way, till there appears again the
open space on a mountain top as
in the second scene; it is, however,
still veiled in a pale mist, as after
Freia's abduction.

Wotan and Loge, dragging the
pinioned Alberich with them,
mount from the cleft.

LOGE: Hier, Vetter,
sitze du fest!
Luge, Liebster,
dort liegt die Welt,
die du Lung'rer gewinnen dir
willst:
welch Stellchen, sag',
bestimmst du mir drin zum Stall?

ALBERICH: Schändlicher
Schächer!
du Schalk! du Schelm!
Löse den Bast,
binde mich los,
den Frevel sonst büssest du Frecher!

WOTAN: Gefangen bist du,
fest mir gefesselt,
wie du die Welt,
was lebt und webt,
in deiner Gewalt schon wähntest.
In Banden liegst du vor mir,
du Banger kannst es nicht läugnen.
Zu ledigen dich
bedarf's nun der Lösung.

ALBERICH: O, ich Tropf!
ich träumender Thor!
Wie dumm traut' ich
dem diebischen Trug!
Furchtbare Rache
räche den Fehl!

LOGE: Soll Rache dir frommen,
vor allem rathe dich frei:
dem gebund'nen Manne
büsst kein Freier den Frevel.
Drum sinn'st du auf Rache,
rasch ohne Säumen
sorg' um die Lösung zunächst!

ALBERICH: (barsch). So heisst,
was ihr begehrt!

WOTAN: Den Hort und dein helles
Gold.

ALBERICH: Gieriges Gaunergezücht!
(Für sich.)
Behalt' ich mir nur den Ring,
des Hortes entrath' ich dann leicht:
denn von neuem gewonnen
und wonnig genährt
ist er bald durch des Ringes Gebot.
Eine Witzigung wär's,
die weise mich macht:
zu theuer nicht zahl' ich die Zucht,
lass' ich für die Lehre den Tand.—

WOTAN: Erlegst du den Hort?

ALBERICH: Lös't mir die Hand,
so ruf' ich ihn her.
(Loge löst ihm die rechte Hand.)

ALBERICH: (rührt den Ring mit den Lippen und murmelt den Befehl). —Wohlan, die Niblungen
rief ich mir nah:
dem Herrn gehorchend
hör' ich den Hort
aus der Tiefe sie führen zu Tag.—
Nun lös't mich vom lästigen Band!

---

LOGE: Be seated,
friend, I beg!
Look, beloved,
there lies the world
that you long so to win to your will:
What station, say,
assign you there for myself?

ALBERICH: Scandalous scoundrel!
You scamp! you scum!
Loosen these bonds!
Do not bind my limbs,
else, rogue, you shall bitterly regret it.

WOTAN: I've caught you now,
my cords bind you closely.
While you did believe
the living world
already your will had won you,
in bonds you lie at my feet:
now flinching must you allow it.
Before letting you run
we look for a ransom.

ALBERICH: What a block—
a booby I've been!
To trust blindly
to traitors so black!
Fearful revenge
I'll vent for my fault.

LOGE: If it's vengeance you foster
you'd better view yourself free:
to a fettered man
no freeman answers for evil,
So, you pant for vengeance,
truly do not pause
in paying the tax we demand.

ALBERICH: (harshly). Then state
what I must give.

WOTAN: The store, and your
sparkling gold.

ALBERICH: Griping and gluttonous thieves!
(Aside.)
So I hold for myself the Ring,
the hoard I can readily yield:
for I know that to make
and augment it anew
for the spell of the Ring were a sport.
And a warning it were
to remind my wits
the lesson I deem is not dear,
if this is all I must lose.—

WOTAN: Do you offer the hoard?

ALBERICH: Untie my hand;
I'll summon it here.
(Loge releases his right hand.)

ALBERICH: (touches the ring with his lips and murmurs a command). —Now then, I've called up
the Nibelung crew.
Mindful of their master,
mark how they mount
to the light with the hoard from below!—
Unbind now these burdensome cords.

---

WOTAN: Nicht eh'r, bis alles gezahlt.
(Die Nibelungen steigen aus der Kluft herauf, mit den Geschmeiden des Hortes beladen.)

ALBERICH: O schändliche Schmach,
dass die scheuen Knechte
geknebelt selbst mich erschau'n!—
Dorthin geführt,
wie ich's befehl'!
All zu Hauf
schichtet den Hort!
Helf' ich euch Lahmen?—
Hieher nicht gelugt!—
Rasch da! rasch!
dann rührt euch von hinnen:
dass ihr mir schafft,
fort in den Schachten!
Weh' euch, find' ich euch faul!
Auf den Fersen folg' ich euch nach.
(Die Nibelungen nachdem sie den Hort aufgeschichtet, schlüpfen ängstlich wieder in die Kluft hinab.)
Gezahlt hab' ich:
lasst mich nun ziehn!
Und das Helmgeschmeid,
das Loge dort hält,
das gebt mir nun gütlich zurück!

LOGE: (den Tarnhelm zum Horte werfend). Zur Busse gehört auch die Beute.

ALBERICH: Verfluchter Dieb!—
Doch nur Geduld!
Der den alten mir schuf,
schafft einen andern,
noch halt' ich die Macht,
der Mime gehorcht.
Schlimm zwar ist's,
dem schlauen Feind
zu lassen die listige Wehr!—
Nun denn! Alberich
liess euch alles:
jetzt löst ihr Bösen, das Band!

LOGE: (zu Wotan). Bist du befriedigt?
bind' ich ihn frei?

WOTAN: Ein gold'ner Ring
ragt dir am Finger:
hörst du, Alp?
der, acht' ich, gehört mit zum Hort.

ALBERICH: (entsetzt). Der Ring?

WOTAN: Zu deiner Lösung
musst du ihn lassen.

ALBERICH: Das Leben—doch nicht den Ring!

WOTAN: Den Reif verlang' ich:
mit dem Leben mach' was du willst!

ALBERICH: Lös' ich mir Leib und Leben,
den Ring auch muss ich mir lösen:
Hand und Haupt,
Aug' und Ohr,
ist nicht mehr mein Eigen
als hier dieser rothe Ring!

WOTAN: Dein Eigen nennst du den Ring?
Rasest du, schamloser Albe?
Nüchtern sag',

---

WOTAN: Not till we have been paid.
(The Nibelungs climb up from the crevice laden with the treasure of the hoard.)

ALBERICH: O sharpest of shame,
that my shrinking vassals
should view me shackled and shorn!—
There let it rest
as I direct;
in a heap
pile up the hoard!
Help must I offer?—
Don't look here!
Quick there—quick!
then quit for your hollows.
Off to your tasks!
Back to the tunnels!
Woe, if idlers there be!
I'm at your backs in an instant.
(The Nibelungs, having piled up the hoard, slip back timidly into the cleft.)
I've paid fully?
let me depart!
And the helmet there
that Loge holds
your goodness will give it back to me?

LOGE: (throwing the Tarnhelm on the heap). We place it as part of the plunder.

ALBERICH: Damned wolf!
wait but a while?
He who forged it for me
makes a fresh one:
still abides the might
that Mime obeys.
Hard, indeed,
that hated foes
should seize on my subtle defense!
Now then, Alberich's
spoiled of all things:
you'll surely release him at length?

LOGE: (to Wotan). Are you contented?
shall I untie?

WOTAN: A golden ring
rests on your finger—
heard you, imp?—
that also must heighten the hoard.

ALBERICH: (horrified). The ring.

WOTAN: Before we release you
that must be left to us.

ALBERICH: Take my life—but not the ring!

WOTAN: I look for the ring:
with your life then do what you will.

ALBERICH: If life and limbs you leave me,
the ring, too, must be allowed me.
Eye and ear,—
hand and head,
are not mine more wholly
than is this ruddy ring.

WOTAN: Your own you call the ring!
You're raving, impudent earthgnome?

wem entnahmst du das Gold,
daraus du den schimmernden
schuf'st?
War's dein Eigen,
was du Arger
der Wassertiefe entwandt?
Bei des Rheines Töchtern
hole dir Rath,
ob sie ihr Gold
dir zu eigen gaben,
das du zum Ring dir geraubt.

ALBERICH: Schmähliche Tücke!
schändlicher Trug!
Wirfst du Schächer
die Schuld mir vor,
die dir so wonnig erwünscht?
Wie gern raubtest
du selbst dem Rheine das Gold,
war nur so leicht
die List, es zu schmieden, erlangt?
Wie glückt' es nun
dir Gleissner zum Heil,
dass der Niblung ich
aus schmählicher Noth,
in des Zornes Zwange,
den schrecklichen Zauber gewann,
dess' Werk nun lustig dir lacht?
Des Unseligsten,
Angstversehrten
fluchfertige,
furchtbare That,
zu fürstlichem Tand
soll sie fröhlich dir taugen?
zur Freude dir frommen mein
Fluch?—
Hüte dich,
herrischer Gott!
Frevelte ich,
so frevelt' ich frei an mir?
doch an allem, was war,
ist und wird,
frevelst, Ewiger, du,
entreissest du frech mir den Ring!

WOTAN: Her den Ring!
Kein Recht an ihm
schwört dein Schwatzen dir zu.
(*Er entzieht Alberich's Finger mit heftiger Gewalt den Ring.*)

ALBERICH: (*grässlich aufschreiend*). Weh! Zertrümmert!
Zerknickt!
Der Traurigen traurigster Knecht!

WOTAN: (*hat den Ring an seinen Finger gesteckt und betrachtet ihn wohlgefällig*). Nun halt' ich, was mich erhebt,
der Mächtigen mächtigsten Herrn!

LOGE: Ist er gelöst?

WOTAN: Bind' ihn los!

LOGE: (*löst Alberich die Bande*). Schlüpfe denn heim!
Keine Schlinge hält' dich:
frei fahre dahin!

ALBERICH: (*sich vom Boden erhebend, mit wüthendem Lachen*). Bin ich nun frei?
wirklich frei?—
So grüss' euch denn
meiner Freiheit erster Gruss!—
Wie durch Fluch er mir gerieth,

Tell me now,
From where was the gold taken
from which you hammered the
hoop?
Was it your own then,
which your arm
tore away from the water's depth?
By the river maidens
be arraigned
if their gold
for your own they have given,
which you have robbed for your
ring.

ALBERICH: Shameful contrivance!
Scandalous trick!
Rogue, cast
in my teeth the crime
that you were dying to do?
Had you robbed
the gold yourself from the Rhine,
you could have won
the act of its forging.
So, hypocrite,
how happy you are
that the Niblung, here,
in torturing need,
in a maddened moment,
the terrible magic did win;
whose work now gladdens your
glance.
The unhallowed one's
anguish-harried,
bliss-banishing,
bitterest deed
shall boot but for dazzle
and your brilliant adornment?
Shall bliss then be brought by my
ban?—
Mighty god
mind what you do!
Say I have sinned;
the sin falls on myself:
but on all things that were,
are, and will be,
strikes this evil of yours,
if you rashly seize my ring.

WOTAN: Yield the ring!
I think you have proven
no right to that, by babbling.
(*He tears the ring from Alberich's finger by force.*)

ALBERICH: (*screaming horribly*). Ha! I'm vanquished!—destroyed!
A vassal to the vilest of slaves!

WOTAN: (*donning the ring and contemplating it with the satisfaction*). It is my own, making me the mightiest monarch of all.

LOGE: Is he released?

WOTAN: Set him loose.

LOGE: (*undoing Alberich's bonds*). Slip away home:
no more shackles hold you:
fare freely from here!

ALBERICH: (*raising himself from the ground in raging laughter*). Am I now free?—
really free?
Then listen, friends,
to my freedom's first salute!—
As at first by my curse it was

verflucht sei dieser Ring!
Gab sein Gold
mir—Macht ohne Mass,
nun zeug' sein Zauber
Tod dem—der ihn trägt!
Kein Froher soll
seiner sich freu'n;
keinem Glücklichen lache
sein lichter Glanz;
wer ihn besitzt,
den zehre Sorge,
und wer ihn nicht hat,
nage der Neid!
Jeder giere
nach seinem Gut,
doch keiner geniesse
mit Nutzen sein';
ohne Wucher hüt' ihn sein Herr,
doch den Würger zieh' er ihm zu!
Dem Tode verfallen,
fessle den Feigen die Furcht;
so lang' er lebt,
sterb' er lechzend dahin,
des Ringes Herr
als des Ringes Knecht:
bis in meiner Hand
den geraubten wieder ich halte!—
So—segnet
in höchster Noth
der Nibelung seinen Hort!—
Behalt' ihn nun,
hüte ihn wohl:
meinem Fluch fliehest du nicht!
(*Er verschwindet schnell in der Kluft.*)

LOGE: Lauschtest du
seinem Liebesgruss?

WOTAN: (*in die Betrachtung des Ringes verloren*). Gönn' ihm die geifernde Lust!
(*Der Nebelduft des Vordergrundes klärt sich allmählig auf.*)

LOGE: (*nach rechts blickend*). Fasolt und Fafner
nahen von fern;
Freia führen sie her.
(*Von der andern Seite treten Fricka, Donner und Froh auf.*)

FROH: Sie kehrten zurück.

DONNER: Willkommen, Bruder!
(*Besorgt auf Wotan zueilend.*)

FRICKA: Bringst du mir gute Kunde?

LOGE: (*auf den Hort deutend*). Mit List und Gewalt
gelang das Werk:
dort liegt, was Freia lös't.

DONNER: Aus der Riesen Haft
naht dort die Holde.

FROH: Wie liebliche Luft
wieder uns weht,
wonnig Gefühl
die Sinne füllt!
Traurig ging' es uns allen,
getrennt für immer von ihr,
die leidlos ewiger Jugend
jubelnde Lust uns verleiht.
(*Der Vordergrund ist wieder hell geworden: das Aussehen der Götter gewinnt durch das Licht*

reached,
henceforward cursed be this ring!
Gold which gave
me measureless might,
now may its magic
deal each owner death!
No man shall ever
own it in mirth,
and to gladden no life
shall its luster gleam.
May care consume
each possessor,
and envy gnaw him
who does not wear it.
All shall lust
after its delights,
but none shall employ them
to profit him.
To its master giving no gain,
the murderer's brand it shall bring.
To death he is fated,
its fear on his fancy shall feed;
though long he live
shall he languish each day,
the treasure's lord
and the treasure's slave:
till within my hand
I in triumph once more behold
it!—
So—stirred
by the hardest need,
the Niblung blesses his ring!—
I give to you,
guard it with care—
but my curse you cannot flee!
(*He vanishes swiftly in the crevice.*)

LOGE: Did you hear
his adieu of love?

WOTAN: (*absorbed in contemplation of the ring*). Let him give loose to his dole.
(*The vapor in the foreground now gradually clears.*)

LOGE: (*looking off, R.*). Fasolt and Fafner
fare this way.
Freia follows their steps.
(*From the other side enter Fricka, Donner and Froh.*)

FROH: The gods have returned!

DONNER: We greet you, brother!
(*anxiously advancing to Wotan*).

FRICKA: Do you bring news to gladden us?

LOGE: (*pointing to the board*). With power of wit
the prize was won:
on pile is Freia's price.

DONNER: From the giants' hold now she hastens.

FROH: What exquisite air wafts this way!
wondrous the feeling
that steals over each frame!
Hard it would go with the AEsir,
withheld for always from their own,
who lends them ecstatic youth's
unyielding and lasting delights.
(*The foreground is now quite clear again, the renewed light re-*

wieder die erste Frische: über dem Hintergrunde haftet jedoch noch der Nebelschleier, so dass die ferne Burg unsichtbar bleibt. *Fasolt und Fafner treten auf, Freia zwischen sich führend.*)

storing to the gods their first aspect: the background, however, is still shrouded in mists, so that the distant castle is invisible. *Fasolt and Fafner enter leading Freia between them.*)

**FRICKA:** (*eilt freudig auf die Schwester zu, um sie zu umarmen*). Lieblichste Schwester, süsseste Lust! Bist du mir wieder gewonnen?

**FRICKA:** (*hastening joyfully towards her sister, to embrace her*). Loveliest sister, sweetest delight! Look we again on our goddess?

**FASOLT:** (*ihr wehrend*). Halt! Nicht sie berührt! Noch gehört sie uns.— Auf Riesenheim's ragender Mark rasteten wir: mit treuem Muth des Vertrages Pfand pflegten wir; so sehr mich's reut, zurück doch bring' ich's erlegt uns Brüdern die Lösung ihr.

**FASOLT:** (*stopping her*). Halt! stand from her side! Still we hold her ours.— On Riesenheim's rugged confines We took rest: the contract's forfeit with careful truth we treated. So, sorely loathe, I lead her here. I pray you hand us the price agreed.

**WOTAN:** Bereit liegt die Lösung: des Goldes Mass sei nun gütlich gemessen.

**WOTAN:** At hand rests the ransom: the golden mass must be guardedly measured.

**FASOLT:** Das Weib zu missen, wisse, gemuthet mich weh; soll aus dem Sinn sie mir schwinden, des Geschmeides Hort häufe denn so, dass meinem Blick die Blühende ganz er verdeck'!

**FASOLT:** It will make me forlorn to lose the maiden; so, from my soul to unseat her, be the sparkling hoard heaped in a stack, so as to hide the heavenly maid!

**WOTAN:** So stellt das Mass nach Freia's Gestalt. (*Fafner und Fasolt stossen ihre Pfähle vor Freia hin so in den Boden, dass sie gleiche Höhe und Breite mit ihrer Gestalt messen.*)

**WOTAN:** Then fix a gauge like Freia in form. (*Fafner and Fasolt place Freia in the middle of the stage and stick their staves into the ground on each side, so as to give her height and breadth.*)

**FAFNER:** Gepflanzt sind die Pfähle nach Pfandes Mass: gehäugt füll' es der Hort.

**FAFNER:** Our poles we have planted in proper form: to hide them pile up the hoard.

**WOTAN:** Eilt mit dem Werk: widerlich ist mir's!

**WOTAN:** Quickly with the task; It is hateful to me.

**LOGE:** Hilf mir, Froh!

**LOGE:** Help me, Froh!

**FROH:** Freia's Schmach eil' ich zu enden. (*Loge und Froh häufen hastig zwischen den Pfählen die Geschmeide.*)

**FROH:** I'll make an end of Freia's shame. (*Loge and Froh quickly heap up the treasure between the poles.*)

**FAFNER:** Nicht so leicht und locker gefügt: fest und dicht füll' er das Mass! (*Mit roher Kraft drückt er die Geschmeide dicht zusammen; er beugt sich, um nach Lücken zu spähen.*) Hier lug' ich noch durch: verstopft mir die Lücken!

**FAFNER:** Not so light and loose in the form; fill up the gauge firm and close. (*He roughly presses the ornaments close together and stoops to peer about for crevices.*) I see day through here. All chinks must be hidden.

**LOGE:** Zurück, du Grober! greif' mir nichts an!

**LOGE:** Away, you lubber! Let it alone!

**FAFNER:** Hieher! die Klinze verklemmt!

**FAFNER:** Look here, this cleft must be closed!

**WOTAN:** (*unmuthig sich absendend*). Tief in der Brust brennt mich die Schmach. (*Den Blick auf Freia geheftet.*)

**WOTAN:** (*turning away moodily*). Deep in my breast burns this shame. (*His eyes are fixed on Freia.*)

**FRICKA:** Sieh, wie in Scham schmählich die Edle steht: um Erlösung fleht stumm der leidende Blick. O böser Mann! Der Minnigen botest du das!

**FRICKA:** See how distressed the fair one stands sadly: for release the mute sufferer looks a prayer. Perjured man! Our maid you have placed in this strait.

**FAFNER:** Noch mehr hierher!

**FAFNER:** Still more must be piled!

**DONNER:** Kaum halt' ich mich: schäumende Wuth weckt mir der schamlose Wicht!— Hierher, du Hund! willst du messen, so miss dich selber mit mir!

**DONNER:** This passes all! hot is my rage roused by so hardened a rogue!— Come here you hound! would you measure, then match yourself against me!

**FAFNER:** Ruhig, Donner! Rolle wo's taugt: hier nützt dein Rasseln dir nichts!

**FAFNER:** Rest, thunder, Do not rumble; we do not need your rolling here.

**DONNER:** (*holt aus*). Nicht dich Schmählichen zu zerschmettern?

**DONNER:** (*menacing him*). I will first crush you to fragments!

**WOTAN:** Friede doch! Schon dünkt mich Freia verdeckt.

**WOTAN:** Friend, withhold. Surely, wholly Freia is hid?

**LOGE:** Der Hort ging auf.

**LOGE:** The hoard gives out.

**FAFNER:** (*mit dem Blicke messend*). Noch schimmert mir Holda's Haar: dort das Gewirk wirf auf den Hort!

**FAFNER:** (*measuring with his eye*). Still Holda's hair shines on me: throw me that wove-work on the heap.

**LOGE:** Wie, auch den Helm?

**LOGE:** What! even the helmet?

**FAFNER:** Hurtig her mit ihm!

**FAFNER:** Hurry here with it.

**WOTAN:** Lass ihn denn fahren!

**WOTAN:** Let it go freely.

**LOGE:** (*wirft den Helm auf den Haufen*). So sind wir fertig.— Seid ihr zufrieden?

**LOGE:** (*throwing the Tarnhelm on the heap*). So surely, it is finished; Do you seek anything further?

**FASOLT:** Freia, die schöne, schau' ich nicht mehr: ist sie gelös't? muss ich sie lassen? (*Er tritt nahe hinzu und späht durch den Hort.*) Weh! noch blitzt ihr Blick zu mir her; des Auges Stern strahlt mich noch an, durch eine Spalte muss ich's erspäh'n! Seh' ich dies wonnige Aug', von dem Weibe lass ich nicht ab.

**FASOLT:** Freia the glorious pleases me no more, O is she released? Must I then lose her? (*Goes nearer and peeps through the hoard.*) Ah! her glance yet gleams on me here; her eyes like stars, stream to my own; yes, I can spy them still through this space: so while I gaze on her features from the goddess can I not go.

**FAFNER:** He! euch rath' ich, verstopft mir die Ritze!

**FAFNER:** Ha! you hear me? that chink must be hidden.

**LOGE:** Nimmer-Satte! seht ihr denn nicht, ganz schwand uns das Gold?

**LOGE:** Never satisfied! See then not, is the hoard quite spent?

**FAFNER:** Mit nichten, Freund! An Wotan's Finger glänzt von Gold noch ein Ring, den gebt, die Ritze zu füllen!

**FAFNER:** By no means, friend. On Wotan's finger gleams a glittering ring: that came to rest in the fissure.

**WOTAN:** Wie! diesen Ring?

**WOTAN:** What! give the ring?

**LOGE:** Lasst euch rathen! Den Rheintöchtern gehört dies Gold: ihnen giebt Wotan es wieder.

**LOGE:** Let me tell you— to Rhine maidens this gold belongs. Wotan looks still to restore it.

WOTAN: Was schwatzest du da?
Was schwer ich mir erbeutet,
ohne Bangen wahr' ich's für mich.

LOGE: Schlimm dann steht's
un mein Versprechen,
das ich den Klagenden gab.

WOTAN: Dein Versprechen bindet
mich nicht:
als Beute bleibt mir der Reif.

FAFNER: Doch hier zur Lösung
musst du ihn legen.

WOTAN: Fordert frech was ihr
wollt:
alles gewähr' ich,
um alle Welt
nicht fahren doch lass' ich den
Ring!

FASOLT: (zieht wüthend Freia
hinter dem Horte hervor). Aus
denn ist's,
beim Alten bleibt's:
nun folgt uns Freia für immer!

FREIA: Hülfe! Hülfe!

FRICKA: Harter Gott,
gieb ihnen nach!

FROH: Spare das Gold nicht!

DONNER: Spende den Ring doch!

WOTAN: Lasst mich in Ruh'!
Den Reif geb' ich nicht.
(Fafner hält den fortdrängenden
Fasolt noch auf; Alle stehen bestürzt; Wotan wendet sich
zürnend von ihnen zur Seite. Die
Bühne hat sich von Neuem verfinstert; aus der Felskluft zur Seite
bricht ein bläulicher Schein hervor; in ihm wird Wotan plötzlich
Erda sichtbar, die bis, zu halber
Leibeshöhe aus der Tiefe aufsteigt:
sie ist von edler Gestalt, welthin
von schwarzem Haare umwallt.)

ERDA: (die Hand mahnend gegen
Wotan ausstreckend). Weiche,
Wotan, weiche!
flieh' des Ringes Fluch!
Rettungslos
dunklem Verderben
weiht dich sein Gewinn.

WOTAN: Wer bist du, mahnendes
Weib?

ERDA: Wie alles war, weiss ich;
wie alles wird,
wie alles sein wird,
seh' ich auch:
der ew'gen Welt
Ur—Wala,
Erda mahnt deinen Muth.
Drei der Töchter,
ur-erschaff'ne,
gebar mein Schoss:
was ich sehe,
sagen dir nächtlich die Nornen.
Doch höchste Gefahr
führt mich heut'
selbst zu dir her:
höre! höre! höre!
Alles, was ist, endet.
Ein düsterer Tag

WOTAN: What are you talking
about there?
The prize come by with such difficulty
I shall keep, unawed, for myself.

LOGE: Then, the promise
I gave the nymphs
is poorly paid.

WOTAN: But your promise binds
me not:
The ring remains my booty.

FAFNER: But
it must be rendered here for ransom.

WOTAN: Make demands as you
will:
I'll award you all;
but all the world shall not
move this ring from my hand.

FASOLT: (wrathfully pulling
Freia from behind the board). All
is off!
as it stands,
and Freia's forfeit forever.

FREIA: Help me! Help me!

FRICKA: Haughty god!
give them their way.

FROH: Do not hold the gold back.

DONNER: Hand them the ring too.

WOTAN: Leave me at rest;
the ring I retain.
(Fafner holds back the departing
Fasolt, all stand perplexed, while
Wotan turns away in wrath. The
stage has again become dark;
from the rocky cleft at the side
shines out a bluish glow in which
Wotan suddenly perceives Erda,
who rises from below to half her
height. She is of noble presence
and enveloped in a mass of black
hair.)

ERDA: (stretching out her hand
warningly towards Wotan). Waver, Wotan, waver!
quit the accursed ring.
Ruin
and dismal downfall
await you in its wealth.

WOTAN: Who speaks such menacing words?

ERDA: Whatever was, I know;
what is, as well—
what ages shall work—
all I show:
the endless world's
All-wise one,
Erda—opens your eyes.
Three the daughters
born to me
before the world was made;
all I notice
nightly you know from the Nornir.
But I hastened here
in dire danger
to your help.
Hear me! hear me! hear me!
All that exists, end!
A dismal day

dämmert den Göttern:
dir rath' ich, meide den Ring!
(Sie versinkt langsam bis an die
Brust, während der bläuliche
Schein zu dunkeln beginnt.)

WOTAN: Geheimniss-hehr
hallt mir dein Wort:
weile, dass mehr ich wisse!

ERDA: (im Verschwinden). Ich
warnte dich—
du weisst genug:
sinne in Sorg' und Furcht!
(Sie verschwindet gänzlich.)

WOTAN: Soll ich sorgen und
fürchten—
dich muss ich fassen,
alles erfahren!
(Er will in die Kluft, um Erda zu
halten: Donner, Froh und Fricka
werfen sich ihm entgegen, und
halten ihn auf.)

FRICKA: Was willst du,
Wüthender?

FROH: Halt' ein, Wotan!
Scheue die Edle,
achte ihr Wort!

DONNER: (zu den Riesen). Hört,
ihr Riesen!
zurück, und harret:
das Gold wird euch gegeben.

FREIA: Darf ich es hoffen?
dünkt euch Holda
wirklich der Lösung werth?
(Alle blicken gespannt auf Wotan.)

WOTAN: (war in tiefes Sinnen
versunken und fasst sich jetzt mit
Gewalt zur Entschluss). Zu uns,
Freia!
du bist befreit:
wieder gekauft
kehr' uns die Jugend zurück!—
Ihr Riesen, nehmt euren Ring!
(Er wirft den Ring auf den Hort.)
(Die Riesen lassen Freia los: sie
eilt freudig auf die Götter zu, die
sie abwechselnd längere Zeit in
höchster Freude liebkosen.)
(Fafner breitet sogleich einen ungeheuren Sack aus und macht
sich über des Hort her, um ihn da
hinein zu schichten.)

FASOLT: (dem Bruder sich entge-
genwerfend). Halt, du Gieriger!
gönne mir auch 'was!
Redliche Theilung
taugt uns beiden.

FAFNER: Mehr an der Maid als am
Gold
lag dir verliebtem Geck:
mit Müh' zum Tausch
vermocht' ich dich Thoren.
Ohne zu theilen
hättest du Freia gefreit:
theil' ich den Hort,
billig behalt' ich
die grösste Hälfte für mich.

FASOLTE: Achändlicher du!
Mir diesen Schimpf?—
(Zu den Göttern.)
Euch ruf' ich zu Richtern:

dawns for the AEsir:
O render wisely the ring!
(She sinks slowly to the breast and
the bluish glow begins to fade.)

WOTAN: A secret spell
speaks in your words:
wait, and impart more wisdom.

ERDA: (disappearing). I've
warned you now,
you know enough;
pause and ponder truth.
(She completely disappears.)

WOTAN: Pain and peril attending—
I must detain you
All you must tell me!
(He tries to go to the crevasse in
order to detain Erda. Donner,
Froh, and Fricka throw themselves in his way and hold him
back.)

FRICKA: What would you wildly
do?

FROH: Take heed, Wotan;
Do not seek to hold her;
listen to her words!

DONNER: (to the giants). Here—
you monsters,
remain and listen!
Wotan will give you the gold.

FREIA: I but dared hope it?
You deem Holda
is worth such a ransom?
(All look anxiously at Wotan.)

WOTAN: (who has been absorbed
in deep thought, now musters his
strength to a decision). Return,
Freia!
I set you free.
Purchased again
gladly we rejoice in youth!
Giants, there is your gem.
(He throws the Ring on the heap.)
(The giants release Freia: she runs
joyfully to the gods who embrace
her in turn during some time,
with greatest delight.)
(Fafner meanwhile spreads out a
huge sack and goes to the board
preparing to pack it all up.)

FASOLT: (opposing his brother).
Stop, you greedy one,
give me some also!
Equally, surely,
should we share it.

FAFNER: More on the maid than
the gold,
amorous ape, you gloat:
My might could scarcely
make you resign her;
as, without sharing,
Holda you would have wooed:
justly I'll hold back
the greater half of the hoard for myself.

FASOLT: Swindler and thief!
Thus am I served?
(To the gods.)
You shall judge us jointly:

theilet nach Recht
uns redlich den Hort!
(*Wotan wendet sich verächtlich ab.*)

LOGE: Lass' den Hort ihn raffen:
halte du nur auf den Ring!

FASOLT: (*stürzt sich auf Fafner, der während dem mächtig eingesackt hat*). Zurück, du Frecher!
mein ist der Ring;
mir blieb er für Freia's Blick.
(*Er greift hastig nach dem Ring.*)

FAFNER: Fort mit der Faust!
der Ring ist mein.
(*Sie ringen mit einander; Fasolt entreisst Fafner den Ring.*)

FASOLT: Ich halt' ihn, mir gehört er!

FAFNER: Halt' fest, dass er nicht fall'!
(*Er holt wüthend mit seinem Pfahle nach Fasolt aus, und streckt ihn mit einen Schlage zu Boden, dem Sterbenden entreisst er dann hastig den Ring.*)
Nun blinzle nach Freia's Blick:
an den Reif rühr'st du nicht mehr!
(*Er steckt den Ring in den Sack, und rafft dann gemächlich vollends den Hort ein. Alle Götter stehen entsetzt. Langes, feierliches Schweigen.*)

WOTAN: Furchtbar nun
erfind' ich des Fluches Kraft!

LOGE: Was gleicht, Wotan,
wohl deinem Glücke?
Viel erwarb dir
des Ringes Gewinn;
dass er nun dir genommen,
nützt dir noch mehr:
deine Feinde, sieh,
fällen sich selbst
um das Gold, das du vergabst.

WOTAN: (*tief erschüttert*). Wie
doch Bangen mich bindet!
Sorg' und Furcht
fesseln den Sinn;
wie sie zu enden
lehre mich Erda:
zu ihr muss ich hinab!

FRICKA: (*schmeichelnd sich an ihn schmiegend*). Wo weilst du, Wotan?
Winkt dir nicht hold
die hehre Burg,
die des Gebieters
gastlich bergend nun harrt?

WOTAN: Mit bösem Zoll
zahlt' ich den Bau!

DONNER: (*auf den Hintergrund deutend, der noch in Nebelschleier gehüllt ist*). Schwüles Gedünst
schwebt in der Luft,
lästig ist mir
der trübe Druck:
das bleiche Gewölk
samml' ich zu blitzendem Wetter;
das fegt den Himmel mir hell.
(*Er hat einen hohen Felsstein am Thalabhange bestiegen, und schwingt jetzt seinen Hammer.*)
He da! He da!

should not the jewels
justly be halved?
(*Wotan turns contemptuously away.*)

LOGE: Let him take the jewels:
You hold the ring, and rejoice!

FASOLT: (*throws himself on Fafner who is packing up busily*).
Leave, fraud!
the ring is mine:
it veiled me from Freia's view.
(*He snatches hastily at the ring.*)

FAFNER: Do not fold your fist;
the ring is mine.
(*They struggle: Fasolt wrests the ring from Fafner.*)

FASOLT: I have it—I shall hold it!

FAFNER: Hold it fast, or it may fall!
(*Furious, he hits out at Fasolt with his staff and with one blow fells him to the ground; then he wrests the ring from his dying hand.*)
Now feast upon Freia's face!
for the ring's rent from your grasp!
(*He puts the ring in the sack and proceeds coolly to collect the rest of the gold. All the gods stand horrified. Long, solemn silence.*)

WOTAN: Fearful power
I find in the fatal curse!

LOGE: What luck, Wotan,
were likened to you?
Much it was
when you won the ring;
but it still better serves you
since it was lost:
for your foemen—see:
felling themselves
for you have lost the gold.

WOTAN: (*deeply shocked*). How
horror overhangs me!
Sickly fear
fetters my soul;
only to heal it
Erda can help me:
I will go to her now.

FRICKA: (*approaching him cajolingly*). Why do you wait, Wotan?
The fortress shines wondrously; it surely affords friendly shelter?

WOTAN: A shameful price is paid
for this shrine.

DONNER: (*pointing to the back which is still hidden in clouds*).
Vaporous mist
veils the scene;
I am sick
of the mournful mask!
I'll liven these thin
clouds with some lightning and thunder,
and clear the air for us all.
(*He mounts an overhanging rock and swings his hammer during the swing.*)

Zu mir, du Gedüft!
ihr Dünste, zu mir!
Donner, der Herr,
ruft euch zu Heer!
Auf des Hammers Schwung
schwebet herbei:
he da! he da!
duftig Gedünst'
Donner ruft euch zu Heer!
(*Die Nebel haben sich um ihn zusammen gezogen; er verschwindet völlig in einer immer finsterer sich ballenden Gewitter-wolke. Dans hört man seinen Hammerschlag schwer auf den Felsstein fallen: ein starker Blitz entführt der Wolke; ein heftiger Donnerschlag folgt.*)
Bruder, zu mir!
weise der Brücke den Weg!
(*Froh ist mit Gewölk verschwunden. Plötzlich verzieht sich die Wolke; Donner und Froh werden sichtbar: von ihren Füssen aus zieht sich, mit blendendem Leuchten, eine Regenbogenbrücke über das Thal hinüber bis zur Burg, die jetzt, von der Abendsonne beschienes, im hellsten Glanze erstrahlt.*)
(*Fafner, der neben der Leiche seines Bruders endlich den ganzen Hort eingerafft, hat den ungeheuren Sack auf dem Rücken, während Donner's Gewitterzauber die Bühne verlassen.*)

FROH: Zur Burg führt die Brücke,
leicht, doch fest eurem Fuss:
beschreitet kühn
ihren schrecklosen Pfad!

WOTAN: (*in den Anblick der Burg versunken*). Abendlich strahlt
der Sonne Auge;
in prächt'ger Gluth
prangt glänzend die Burg:
in des Morgens Scheine
muthig erschimmernd,
lag sie herrenlos
hehr verlockend vor mir.
Von Morgen bis Abend
in Müh' und Angst
nicht wonnig ward sie gweonnen!
Es naht die Nacht:
vor ihrem Neid
biete sie Bergung nun.
So—grüss' ich die Burg,
sicher vor Bang und Grau'n.—
(*Zu Fricka.*)
Folge mir, Frau,
in Walhall wohne mit mir!
(*Er fasst ihre Hand.*)

FRICKA: Was deutet der Name?
Nie, dünkt mich, hört' ich ihn nennen.

WOTAN: Was, mächtig der Furcht,
mein Muth mir erfand,
wenn siegend es lebt—
leg' es den Sinn dir dar!
(*Wotan und Fricka schreiten der Brücke zu: Froh und Freia folgen zunächst, dann Donner.*)

Hallo! hallo!
To me all dews!
come down to me, mists!
Donner is here,
calling his hosts!
At his hammer's swing
swoop to his side!
Hallo! hallo!
Drizzle and damp,
Donner calls his hosts!
(*The mist has collected around him; he disappears in an ever thickening and darkening thundercloud. Then his hammerstroke is heard falling heavily on the rocks: a vivid flash of lightning breaks through the clouds, followed by a violent clap of thunder.*)
Brother, come here!
show what a bridge we can shape!
(*Froh has also disappeared in the clouds. Suddenly these separate; Donner and Froh are visible; from their feet stretches, in blinding radiance, a rainbow-bridge over the valley to the castle, which now gleams with utmost brilliance, illuminated by the evening sun.*)
(*Fafner, who, beside the body of his brother, has collected the whole board during Donner's magic thunderstorm, puts the huge sack on his back and quits the stage.*)

FROH: This bridge will bring you home;
light but hardy support.
So tread undaunted
its terrorless height!

WOTAN: (*absorbed in contemplation of the castle*). See how at evening
the eye of sunlight
with glorious touch
gilds turret and tower!
In the morning glamor,
resolute and glad,
it bided masterless,
mildly beckoning to me.
From morning till evening
through mighty ills
I won no way to its wonders!
The night is near;
from all annoyances
it shows us shelter now.
So—hailed be the fort;
sorrow and fear it heals.—
(*To Fricka.*)
Wend with me, wife,
in "Valhall" vast we will dwell.
(*He takes her by the hand.*)

FRICKA: Why name it so?
Never such a title was known of.

WOTAN: What might against our fears
my mind may have found
if proved a success
soon shall explain the name.
(*Wotan and Fricka go towards the bridge; Froh and Freia follow immediately, then Donner.*)

## Scene IV

**LOGE:** (*im Vordergrunde verharrend und den Göttern nachblickend*). Ihrem Ende eilen sie zu,
die so stark im Bestehen sich
wähnen.
Fast schäm' ich mich
mit ihnen zu schaffen;
zur leckenden Lohe
mich wieder zu wandeln
spür' ich lockende Lust.
Sie aufzuzehren,
die einst mich gezähmt,
statt mit den Blinden
blöd zu vergeh'n—
und wären's göttlichste Götter—
nicht dumm dünkte mich das!
Bedenken will ich's:
wer weiss was ich thu'!
(*Er geht, um sich den Göttern in nachlässiger Haltung anzuschliessen.*)
(*Aus der Tiefe hört man den Gesang der Rheintöchter herauf schallen.*)

**DIE DREI RHEINTÖCHTER:**
Rheingold!
Reines Gold,
wie lauter und hell
leuchtest hold du uns!
Um dich, du klares,
nun wir klagen!
Gebt uns das Gold,
o gebt uns das reine zurück!

**LOGE:** (*pausing in the foreground and looking after the gods*). To their end they even now quicken,
while esteeming their strength overwhelming.
I am ashamed
to share in their acts.
A feverish fancy
woos me to wander
forth in flickering fire:
to burn and waste them
who bound me,
rather than be
thus blindly engulfed—
even were they of gods the most godlike—
there seems sense in the scheme!
I'll study on it!
Who asks what I do?
(*He follows the gods as if unconcerned.*)
(*From the valley the song of the Rhinenymphs is heard to peal.*)

**THE THREE RHINE NYMPHS:**
Rhinegold!
Rarest gold!
How wondrously bright
one you did shine on us!
For you, our plaything
now we implore!
Give us our gold!
O give us our glory again!

**WOTAN:** (*im Begriff, den Fuss auf die Brücke zu setzen, hält an und wendet sich um*). Welch Klagen klingt zu mir her?

**LOGE:** Des Rheines Kinder beklagen des Goldes Raub.

**WOTAN:** Verwünschte Nicker!—
Wehre ihrem Geneck!

**LOGE:** (*in das Thal hinabrufend*). Ihr da im Wasser!
was weint ihr herauf?
Hört, was Wotan euch wünscht.
Glänzt nicht mehr
euch Mädchen das Gold,
in der Götter neuem Glanze
sonnt euch selig fortan!
(*Die Götter lachen laut und beschreiten nun die Brücke.*)

**DIE RHEINTÖCHTER:** (*aus der Tiefe*).
Rheingold!
Reines Gold!
O leuchtete noch
in der Tiefe dein laut'rer Tand!
Traulich und True
ist's nur in der Tiefe:
falsch und feig
ist was dort oben sich freut!
(*Als alle Götter auf der Brücke der Burg zuschraiten, fällt der Vorhang.*)

**WOTAN:** (*In the act of setting his foot on the bridge pauses and returns*). What mournful sounds do I hear?

**LOGE:** The river maidens
who mourn, of their gold bereaved.

**WOTAN:** Cursed Nixies!—
Quiet their clamorous noise.

**LOGE:** (*calling down the valley*).
You in the water!
why worry us yet?
Hear what Wotan wishes!
Gleams no more
on you maidens the gold,
in the gods' augmented grandeur
henceforth happily bask.
(*The gods laugh loudly and once more turn towards the bridge.*)

**THE RHINE NYMPHS:**
(*from below*).
Rhinegold!
Rarest gold!
O might but again
in the wave your pure magic awake!
What is of worth,
dwells in the waters!
base and bad
those who are throned above.
(*As the gods slowly cross the bridge to the castle, the curtain falls.*)

# Die Walküre (1870)

## The Walkyr

MUSIC & LIBRETTO BY RICHARD WAGNER

---

Die Walküre premiered at the Hoftheater in Munich of June 26, 1870. Wotan, the father of the gods, gives an eye to Erda, goddess of the Earth, in exchange for some of her wisdom. She is the mother of his daughters, the nine Valkyries. Wotan is also the father of twins, Siegmund and Sieglinde, known as the Wälsungs, by a mortal mother. Wotan decides that his son Siegmund must obtain the ring from Fafner. Siegmund and Sieglinde were separated when their mother was killed, and Sieglinde was forced to marry Hunding. Siegmund, fleeing from his enemies, seeks shelter in Hunding's hut, where he encounters Sieglinde. He feels a kinship with her though he does not yet know who she is. Hunding realizes that Siegmund is the man he has been hunting and allows him to stay the night on the condition that he be prepared to fight to the death the following day. Siegmund remembers that his father once promised him a sword that would grant him victory in every battle. The fire shines brightly for a moment, lighting up a sword plunged into the ash tree by the hut. Sieglinde pours a potion into her husband's drink and he falls into a deep sleep. She tells Siegmund about her unhappy wedding and about a mystery man, blinded in one of his eyes, who foretold of a hero who would pull the sword from the ash tree. Siegmund realizes that the woman is his sister, and both she and the sword are his. He pulls out the sword, names it Notung (daughter of necessity), and ecstatically leads Sieglinde into the night. Wotan orders Brünnhilde, his favorite Valkyrie, to protect Siegmund from Hunding. Fricka, the goddess of marriage, demands that Siegmund die because of the twins' incestuous relationship. Wotan argues that Siegmund, as a mortal, is not bound as the gods are, and that he is needed to protect the ring from Alberich. Wotan loses the argument and orders Brünnhilde not to forget about Siegmund. Brünnhilde tells Siegmund that he will die and then travel to Valhalla. Siegmund refuses to be separated from Sieglinde and threatens to kill himself—and her if necessary. Brünnhilde pledges to help them, but as Hunding and Siegmund fight, Wotan intercedes and breaks Siegmund's sword. Siegmund is killed by Hunding, who is then killed by Wotan, who chases after Brünnhilde and Sieglinde. Brünnhilde begs her sisters to help Sieglinde, who must hide from Wotan until she has given birth to Siegmund's son, who will reforge the broken sword. Sieglinde is banished to a faraway forest; Wotan, enraged, strips Brünnhilde of her divinity and orders her into a deep sleep from which she cannot be awakened except by the man whom she will wed. He asks Loge to surround the rock on which she sleeps with fire so that only a hero can cross to claim her.

---

## ■ ERSTER AUFZUG

*Das Innere eines Wohnraumes.*

*In der Mitte steht der Stamm einer mächtigen Esche, dessen stark erhabene Wurzeln sich weithin in den Erdboden verlieren; von seinem Wipfel ist der Baum durch ein gezimmertes Dach geschieden, welches so durchschnitten ist, dass der Stamm und die nach allen Seiten hin sich ausstreckenden Aeste durch genau entsprechende Oeffnungen hindurch geben; von dem belaubten Wipfel wird angenommen, dass er sich über dieses Dach ausbreite. Um den Eschenstamm, als Mittelpunkt, ist nun ein Saal gezimmert; die Wände sind aus roh behauenem Holzwerk, hie und da mit geflochtenen und gewebten Decken behangen. Rechts im Vordergrunde steht der Herd, dessen Rauchfang seitwärts zum Dache hinausführt; hinter dem Herde befindet sich ein innerer Raum,* gleich einem Vorrathsspeicher, zu dem man auf einigen hölzernen Stufen hinaufsteigt; davor hängt, halb zurückgeschlagen, eine geflochtene Decke. Im Hintergrunde eine Eingangsthüre mit schlichtem Holzriegel. Links die Thüre zu einem inneren Gemache, zu dem gleichfalls Stufen hinaufführen; weiter vornen auf derselben Seite ein Tisch mit einer breiten, an der Wand angezimmerten Bank dahinter, und hölzernen Schemeln davor.
Ein kurzes Orchestervorspiel von heftiger, stürmischer Bewegung leitet ein. Wenn der Vorhang aufgeht, öffnet Siegmund von aussen hastig die Eingangsthür und tritt ein; es ist gegen Abend; starkes Gewitter, im Begriff, sich zu legen. — Siegmund hält einen Augenblick den Riegel in der Hand und überblickt den Wohnraum: er scheint von übermässiger Anstrengung erschöpft; sein Gewand und Aussehen zeigen, dass er sich auf der Flucht befinde. Da er Nie-

## ■ ACT I

*The Interior of a Dwelling.*

*In the center we behold the trunk of a might ash-tree, the far-spreading roots of which are gradually lost in the ground. The tree is separated from its crown by a timber-roof which is pierced, so that the trunk and all its branches pass through closely-fitting apertures; the thick-leafed crown is supposed to spread over this roof. A spacious hall is erected round this tree, which forms the center; the walls consist of rough-hewn boards, hung here and there with plaited and woven covers. To the right, in the foreground, is the fire-place, the chimney of which passes out sideways through the roof. Behind the fire-place there is an inner space, resembling a storeroom, which is reached by a few wooden steps, and separated from the fore-part of the hall by a plaited curtain half drawn back.* In the background we perceive a door with a plain wooden bar. Another door to the left leads to an interior chamber which is also reached by steps. Further in the front, but on the same side, there is a table, and behind it a broad wooden bench fastened to the wall; a few wooden stools stand before the table.
The orchestra strikes up a brief prelude of a vehement character. As the curtain rises, Siegmund, approaching from without, opens the door hastily and enters. It is nearly evening; there has been a violent thunder storm, which is gradually passing away. Siegmund stops for a moment, and surveys the dwelling. He appears, exhausted and worn out with exertion. His looks and his disordered garments show him to be a fugitive. Finding no one in the room, he closes the door behind him, approaches the fire-place, and throws himself upon a bearskin rug.

mand gewahrt, schliesst er die Thür hinter sich, schreitet auf den Herd zu und wirft sich dort ermattet auf eine Decke von Bärenfell.

**SIEGMUND:** Wess' Herd dies auch sei, hier muss ich rasten. (*Er sinkt zurück und bleibt einige Zeit regungslos ausgestreckt, Sieglinde tritt aus der Thür des inneren Gemaches. Dem vernommenen Geräusche nach glaubte sie ihren Mann heimgekehrt: ihre ernste Miene zeigt sich dann verwundert, als sie einen Fremden am Herde ausgestreckt findet.*)

**SIEGLINDE:** (*Noch im Hintergrunde*). Ein fremder Mann! Ihn muss ich fragen. (*Sie tritt ruhig einige Schritte näher.*) Wer kam in's Haus und liegt dort am Herd? (*Da Siegmund sich nicht regt, tritt sie noch etwas näher und betrachtet ihn.*) Müde liegt er von Weges Müh'n: schwanden die Sinne ihm? wäre er siech? (*Sie neigt sich näher zu ihm.*) Noch schwillt ihm der Athem; das Auge nur schloss er;— muthig dünkt mich der Mann, sank er müd' auch hin.

**SIEGMUND:** (*jäh das Haupt erhebend*). Ein Quell! ein Quell!

**SIEGLINDE:** Erquickung schaff' ich. (*Sie nimmt schnell ein Trinkhorn, geht aus dem Haus und kommt mit dem gefüllten zurück, das sie Siegmund reicht.*) Labung biet' ich dem lechzenden Gaumen: Wasser, wie du gewollt! (*Siegmund trinkt und reicht ihr das Horn zurück. Nachdem er ihr mit dem Kopfe Dank zugewinkt haftet sein Blick länger mit steigender Theilnahme an ihren Mienen.*)

**SIEGMUND:** Kühlende Labung gab mir der Quell, des Müden Last machte er leicht; erfrischt ist der Muth, das Aug' erfreut des Sehens selige Lust:— wer ist's, der so mir es labt?

**SIEGLINDE:** Dies Haus und dies Weib sind Hundings Eigen; gastlich gönn' er dir Rast: harre bis heim er kehrt!

**SIEGMUND:** Waffenlos bin ich: dem wunden Gast wird dein Gatte nicht wehren.

**SIEGLINDE:** (*besorgt*). Die Wunden weise mir schnell!

**SIEGMUND:** Whoever be my host, I will slumber here. (*He sinks back and remains stretched out motionless for some time. Sieglinde enters through the door of the inner chamber. She has heard a noise which she believes to have been caused by the return of her husband, and she is not a little astonished at finding a stranger stretched out before the fireplace.*)

**SIEGLINDE:** (*Still in the background.*) A stranger! See! I must question him. (*Advancing a few steps.*) Who came in here? Who lies by hearth? (*As Siegmund does not stir, she approaches still nearer and looks at him attentively.*) Weary lies he, Worn with wandering. Senseless, perchance, is he? Can he be sick? (*Bending over him.*) Still breath in his body— Though his eye-lids are closed Fearless he seems to me, Though he fell fainting.

**SIEGMUND:** (*Suddenly lifting his head.*) A drink! A drink!

**SIEGLINDE:** I'll bring you relief (*She gets a drinking-horn quickly, leaves the house but comes back soon after filling the vessel with water, which she hands to Siegmund.*) Drink and moisten Your lips that now languish. Water, as you have wished! (*Siegmund drinks and returns the horn. After nodding his thanks to her, he regards her with increasing attention.*)

**SIEGMUND:** Cooling and comfort Came from the well; It made my weight of woe lighter. My heart is refreshed, Again my eyes Gaze with gladness on the world. Who was it that brought me relief?

**SIEGLINDE:** This house and myself Belong to Hunding; He'd never deny shelter. Wait until he comes home.

**SIEGMUND:** Weaponless, wounded— A guest so weak Will be safe with your husband.

**SIEGLINDE:** (*Alarmed.*) You're wounded? Show me your wounds!

**SIEGMUND:** (*schüttelt sich und springt lebhaft vom Lager zum Sitz auf*). Gering sind sie, der Rede nicht werth; noch fügen des Leibes Glieder sich fest. Hätten halb so stark wie mein Arm Schild und Speer mir gehalten, nimmer floh' ich dem Feind;— doch zerschellten mir Speer und Schild. Der Feinde Meute hetzte mich müd', Gewitter-Brunst brach meinen Leib: doch schneller als ich der Meute, schwand die Müdigkeit mir: sank auf die Lider mir Nacht, die Sonne lacht mir nun neu.

**SIEGLINDE:** (*hat ein Horn mit Meth gefüllt und reicht es ihm*). Des seimigen Methes süssen Trank mög'st du mir nicht verschmäh'n.

**SIEGMUND:** Schmecktest du mir ihn zu? (*Sieglinde nippt am Horne und reicht es ihm wieder; Siegmund thut einen langen Zug; dann setzt er schnell ab und reicht das Horn zurück. Beide blicken sich, mit wachsender Ergriffenheit, eine Zeit lang stumm an.*)

**SIEGMUND:** (*mit bebender Stimme*). Einen Unseligen labtest du:— Unheil wende der Wunsch von dir! (*Er bricht schnell auf, um fortzugehen.*) Gerastet hab' ich und süss geruh't: weiter wend' ich den Schritt.

**SIEGLINDE:** (*lebhaft sich umwendend*). Wer verfolgt dich, dass du schon flieh'st?

**SIEGMUND:** (*von ihrem Rufe gefesselt, wendet sich wieder: langsam und düster*). Misswende folgt mir, wohin ich fliehe; Misswende naht mir, wo ich mich neige: dir Frau doch bleibe sie fern! Fort wend' ich Fuss und Blick. (*Er schreitet schnell zur Thür und hebt den Riegel.*)

**SIEGLINDE:** (*in heftigem Selbstvergessen ihm nachrufend*). So bleibe hier! Nicht bringst du Unheil dahin, Wo Unheil im Hause wohnt!

**SIEGMUND:** (*bleibt tieferschüttert stehen und forscht in Sieglinde's Mienen; diese schlägt endlich verschämt und traurig die Augen nieder. Langes Schweigen. Siegmund kehrt zurück und lässt sich, an den Herd gelehnt, nieder*). Wehwalt hiess ich mich selbst:—

**SIEGMUND:** (*Shaking himself, springing up quickly, and sitting down.*) They're trifles, all; They call not for care. The limbs of my body Are still whole. Had my shield and spear been as strong, Half as strong as my arm was, I'd never have fled the foe. But now spear and shield are broken. My foes were many— Pressed me too hard; The furious storm Wore out my strength. But fast did I flee the hunters; Faster still I grew strong. Night at last darkened my eyes; The sun now cheers me anew.

**SIEGLINDE:** (*Filling a horn with mead and handing it to him.*) You will not deny me— Here is mead. Sweet is the cloying drink.

**SIEGMUND:** Will you not taste it first? (*Sieglinde sips a little, and hands him the horn again. Siegmund takes a long draught; then stopping suddenly, he returns the horn. For a long time the two remain silent, looking at each other with growing interest.*)

**SIEGMUND:** (*With trembling voice.*) You have cheered one to misfortune doomed. May no evil Reward your care! (*He rises hastily, as if about to leave.*) I've rested—fully I feel restored. Now I'll go on my way.

**SIEGLINDE:** (*Turning round quickly.*) Who pursues you? Why must you go?

**SIEGMUND:** (*Stopping at her call; slowly and gloomily.*) Mischief pursues me, Wherever I wander; Mischief attends me— Never can I flee it. But Fate surely shall spare you. Far from your path I'll fly! (*Approaching the door, he lifts the bar.*)

**SIEGLINDE:** (*Calling him back in utter self-abnegation.*) Ah, do stay! What curse can you bring to one Who dwells in a house already cursed?

**SIEGMUND:** (*Lingers deeply moved, trying to read the eyes of Sieglinde, who stands abashed and embarrassed. A long silence follows. Siegmund returns, and resumes his seat by the hearth.*) I named myself woeful: I will await Hunding here. (*Sieglinde remains silent and em-*

Hunding will ich erwarten.
(*Sieglinde verharrt in betretenem Schweigen; dann fährt sie auf, lauscht und hört Hunding, der sein Ross aussen zu Stall führt; sie geht hastig zur Thüre und öffnet.*)
(*Hunding, gewaffnet mit Schild und Speer, tritt ein, und hält unter der Thür, als er Siegmund gewahrt.*)

SIEGLINDE: (*dem ernst fragenden Blicke, den Hunding auf sie richtet, entgegnend*). Müd' am Herd
Fand ich den Mann:
Noth führt' ihn in's Haus.

HUNDING: Du labtest ihn?

SIEGLINDE: Den Gaumen letzt' ich ihm,
Gastlich sorgt' ich sein'.

SIEGMUND: (*der Hunding fest und ruhig beobachtet*) Dach und Trank
Dank ich ihr:
Willst du dein Weib drum schelten?

HUNDING: Heilig ist mein Herd:—
Heilig sei dir mein Haus!
(*Zu Sieglinde, indem er die Waffen ablegt und ihr übergibt*).
Rüst' uns Männern das Mahl!
(*Sieglinde hängt die Waffen am Eschenstamme auf, holt Speise und Trank aus dem Speicher und rüstet auf dem Tische das Nachtmahl.*)

HUNDING: (*misst scharf und verwundert Siegmund's Züge, die er mit denen seiner Frau vergleicht; für sich*): Wie gleicht er dem Weibe!
Der gleisende Wurm
glänzt auch ihm aus dem Auge.
(*Er birgt sein Befremden und wendet sich unbefangen an Siegmund*).
Weit her, traun!
kamst du des Weg's;
ein Ross nicht ritt,
der Rast hier fand:
welch' schlimme Pfade
schufen dir Pein?

SIEGMUND: Durch Wald und Wiese,
Haide und Hain,
jagte mich Sturm
und starke Noth:
nicht kenn' ich den weg, den ich kam.
Wohin ich irrte,
weiss ich noch minder:
Kunde gewänn' ich dess' gern.

HUNDING: (*am Tische und Siegmund den Sitz bietend*). Dess'
Dach dich deckt,
Dess' Haus dich hegt,
Hunding heisst der Wirth;
wendest von hier du
nach West den Schritt,
In Höfen reich
hausen dort Sippen,
die Hunding's Ehre behüten.

barrassed. *Suddenly she starts up, listens, and hears Hunding, who leads his steed to the stable. She hastens to open the door.*)
(*Enter Hunding, armed with shield and spear. In the doorway he stops on beholding Siegmund.*)

SIEGLINDE: (*Meeting the questioning look of Hunding.*)
I found this man weak and worn:
Need drove him our way.

HUNDING: You've tended him?

SIEGLINDE: His thirsting lips I cooled;
Gave our guest good cheer.

SIEGMUND: (*Viewing Hunding firmly and calmly.*) Rest and drink,
Did she give.
Would you rebuke her bounty?

HUNDING: Sacred is my hearth—
Safe are you in my house!
(*To Sieglinde, giving her his weapons.*)
Bring us men-folk our meal!
(*Sieglinde hangs the weapons on the trunk of the tree, fetches meat and drink from the larder and prepares the meal on the table.*)

HUNDING: (*Scanning Siegmund's features sharply and comparing them with his wife's. Aside:*) How like her he seems!
The same wicked gleam
Comes and goes in his glances.
(*Concealing his surprise and turning to Siegmund.*)
You must have come from afar,
He had no horse
But here found rest.
What dreadful doings
Brought you this pain?

SIEGMUND: Through wood and meadow,
Forest and heath,
Trouble and storm
Beset my course.
I know nothing of where I came from,
I know nothing of how I wandered here
Fain would I learn who's my host!

HUNDING: (*Seating himself at the table and beckoning Siegmund to a seat.*) This sheltering roof,
This friendly house,
Both are Hunding's own.
Should you bend your steps westward from here,
In manors rich
Kinsmen will greet you,

Gönnt mir Ehre mein Gast,
wird sein Name nun mir genannt.
(*Siegmund, der sich am Tisch niedergesetzt, blickt nachdenklich vor sich hin. Sieglinde hat sich neben Hunding, Siegmund gegenüber, gesetzt und heftet mit auffallender Theilnahme und Spannung ihr Auge auf diesen.*)

HUNDING: (*der beide beobachtet*). Trägst du Sorge,
mir zu vertrau'n,
der Frau hier gieb doch Kunde
sieh', wie gierig sie dich frägt!

SIEGLINDE: (*unbefangen und theilnahmvoll*). Gast, wer du bist,
wüsst' ich gern.

SIEGMUND: (*blickt auf, sieht ihr in das Auge und beginnt ernst*).
Friedmund darf ich nicht heissen;
Frohwalt möcht' ich wohl sein:
doch Wehwalt muss ich mich nennen.
Wolfe, der war mein Vater;
zu zwei kam ich zur Welt,
eine Zwillingsschwester und ich.
Früh schwanden mir
Mutter und Maid;
die mich gebar,
und die mit mir sie barg,
kaum hab' ich sie je gekannt.—
Wehrlich und stark war Wolfe;
Der Feinde wuchsen ihm viel.
Zum Jagen zog
mit dem Jungen der Alte;
von Hetze und Harst
einst kehrten wir heim:
da lag das Wolfsnest leer;
zu Schutt gebrannt
der prangende Saal,
zum Stumpf der Eiche
blühender Stamm;
erschlagen der Mutter
muthiger Leib,
verschwunden in Gluthen
der Schwester Spur:
uns schuf die herbe Noth
der Neidinge harte Schaar.
Geächtet floh
der Alte mit mir;
lange Jahre
lebte der Junge
mit Wolfe im wilden Wald:
manche Jagd
ward auf sie gemacht;
doch muthig wehrte
das Wolfspaar sich.
(*Zu Hunding gewendet.*)
Ein Wölfing kündet dir das,
den als Wölfing mancher wohl kennt.

HUNDING: Wunder und wilde Märe
kündest du, kühner Gast,
Wehwalt—der Wölfing!
Mich dünkt, von dem wehrlichen Paar
vernahm ich dunkle Sage,
Kannt' ich auch Wolfe
und Wölfing nicht.

SIEGLINDE: Doch weiter künde, Fremder,
wo weilt dein Vater jetzt?

Who guard the honor of Hunding.
I would be glad if my guest
Would tell me his name.
(*Siegmund, sitting at the table, remains silent. Sieglinde, seated by the side of Hunding, and opposite Siegmund, observes the latter with undisguised sympathy and attention.*)

HUNDING: (*Watching them both.*)
Should you shrink from
Trusting your host,
Your hostess here will listen;
See, she hangs upon your words!

SIEGLINDE: (*With artless curiosity.*) Fain would I know,
Friend, your name.

SIEGMUND: (*Looking up, catches her eager glances, and answers seriously:*) 'Peaceful' no one may name me;
'Joyful' fain I would be.
But 'Woeful,' that were more fitting.
Wolfè, he was my father;
And one am I of twins—
With a sister saw I the light.
Soon went from me
Mother and maid;
She who was born,
And she who gave us birth.
Hardly my dear ones I'd known.
Stalwart and strong was Wolfè;
But foes a-many had he.
The father fared
To a hunt with me;
With baiting worn out,
We regained our home.
We found lair laid waste!
The stately hall now lay
In ruins
The once mighty oak
Dwarfed to a stump.
And stark lay the mother,
Wantonly slain—
All trace of the sister
Devoured by flame.
Weighted down by bitter want,
By envious hosts hemmed round,
An outcast now,
I fled with my sire.
Years and years then
I wandered
With Wolfè amid the woods.
Many packs
Pressed hard on their trail,
But bravely ever
The wolves stood fast.
(*Turning to Hunding.*)
A wolf-cub tells you this tale,
Who a wolf to many has seemed.

HUNDING: You tell wonders and wild, weird stories hardy guest.
'Woeful'—the wolf-cub!
Methinks I had heard the grim tale
That round you two is woven.
Neither's known to me
This wolf nor cub.

SIEGLINDE: But tell me more, O stranger,
Where dwells your father now?

SIEGMUND: Ein starkes Jagen auf uns
stellten die Neidinge an:
der Jäger viele
fielen den Wölfen,
in Flucht durch den Wald
trieb sie das Wild:
wie Spreu zerstob' uns der Feind.
Doch ward ich vom Vater versprengt:
seine Spur verlor ich,
je länger ich forschte;
nur traf ich im Forst:
leer lag das vor mir,
den Vater fand ich nicht.—
Aus dem Wald trieb es mich fort;
mich drängt' es zu Männern und Frauen
wie viel ich traf,
wo ich sie fand,
eines Wolfes Fell
ob ich um Freund,
um Frauen warb,—
immer doch war ich geächtet,
Unheil lag auf mir,
Was rechtes je ich rieth,
andern dünkte es arg;
was schlimm immer mir schien,
andre gaben ihm Gunst.
In Fehde fiel ich,
wo ich mich fand;
Zorn traf mich,
wohin ich zog;
gehrt' ich nach Wonne,
weckt' ich nur Weh':—
drum musst' ich mich Wehwalt nennen,
des Wehes waltet' ich nur.

HUNDING: Die so leidig Loos dir beschied,
nicht liebte dich die Norn;
froh nicht grüsst dich der Mann,
dem fremd als Gast du nah'st.

SIEGLINDE: Feige nur fürchten den,
der waffenlos einsam fährt!—
Künde noch, Gast,
wo du im Kampf
zuletzt die Waffe verlor'st!

SIEGMUND: (immer lebbafter).
Ein trauriges Kind
rief mich zum Trutz:
vermählen wollte
der Magen Sippe
dem Mann ohne Minne die Maid.
Wider den Zwang
zog ich zum Schutz;
der Dränger Tross
traf ich im Kampf:
dem Sieger sank der Feind.
Erschlagen lagen die Brüder:
die Leichen umschlang da die Maid;
den Grimm verjagt' ihr der Gram.
mit wilder Thränen Fluth
betroff sie weinend die Wal:
um des Mordes der eig'nen Brüder
klagte die unsel'ge Braut.—
Der Erschlag'nen Sippen
stürmten daher;
übermächtig
ächzten nach Rache sie,
rings um die Stätte

SIEGMUND: Our foes pressed hard on our heels,
Hunted us hotly and fast.
And many hunters
Fell, as the quarry,
In flight through the woods,
Swept them away.
Like chaff we scattered the foe.
At last, though, I lost my father
Every trace had vanished,
Though steadfast I sought him.
But I found a wolf-skin
Deep in a glade.
Void now was the world—
My father gone for always!
Then the woods had no more joy:
I hungered for men-folk and women.
And I met men,
And found women,
But whether friend
Or love I sought,
Still I was held as an outcast;
Evil dogged my path.
Though right might be my story,
Others held it as ill.
What seemed ill in my eyes
Others took to be good.
In feuds entangled,
On every side;
Wrath met me
Go where I would.
Thirsting for pleasure,
Sorrow I found;
So now they could 'Woeful' name me,
For woe had marked all my way.

HUNDING: Since your lot has been made so hard,
By Fate you've not been spoiled;
No man warmly greets you
Whose guest you happened to be.

SIEGLINDE: Dastards may dread him
Who weaponless goes his way.
Tell us. O guest,
Where—in what fight—
Your sword was wrung from your hand.

SIEGMUND: (More animated.) A maiden forlorn
Called for my aid:
Perforce her kinsmen
Had wished her wedded—
The maid to a lover unloved.
Hasting to help.
I swung my sword;
The tyrant's train
Met but to rout—
A victor trod the field.
All stark in death lay the brothers;
The maid still clung to their corpses,
In horror deeper than hate.
With floods of rushing tears
She mourned and moaned for her dead—
For the loss of her slaughtered brothers,
Wept the most wretched of brides.
Then the dead ones' kinsmen
Burst on the scene,
Overwhelming,

ragten mir Feinde.
Doch von der Wal
wich nicht die Maid:
mit Speer und Schild
schirmt' ich sie lang',
bis Speer und Schild
im Harst mir zerhau'n.
Wund und waffenlos stand ich—
sterben sah ich die Maid:
mich hetzte das wüthende Heer—
auf den Leichen lag sie todt.
(Mit einem Blicke voll schmerzlichen Feuers auf Sieglinde.)
Nun weisst du, fragende Frau,
Warum ich—Friedmund nicht heisse!
(Er steht auf und schreitet auf den Herd zu. Sieglinde blickt erbleichend und tieferschüttert zu Boden.)

HUNDING: (sehr finster). Ich weiss ein wildes Geschlecht,
nicht heilig ist ihm,
was Andern hehr:
verhasst ist es Allen und mir.
Zur Rache ward ich gerufen,
Sühne zu nehmen
Für Sippen-Blut:
zu spät kam ich
und kehrte nun heim,
des flücht'gen Frevlers Spur
im eig'nen Haus zu erspäh'n.—
Mein Haus hütet,
Wölfing, dich heut':
für die Nacht nahm ich dich auf:
mit starker Waffe
doch wehre dich morgen;
zum Kampfe kies' ich den Tag:
für Todte zahlst du mir Zoll.
(Zu Sieglinde, die sich mit besorgter Geberde zwischen die beiden Männer stellt.)
Fort aus dem Saal!
Säume hier nicht!
Den Nachttrunk rüste mir d'rin,
und harre mein' zur Ruh'.
(Sieglinde nimmt sinnend ein Trinkhorn vom Tisch, geht zu einem Schrein, aus dem sie Würze nimmt, und wendet sich nach dem Seitengemache: auf der obersten Stufe bei der Thür angelangt, wendet sie sich noch einmal um und richtet auf Siegmund—der mit verhaltenem Grimme ruhig am Herde steht und einzig sie im Auge behält—einen langen, sehnsüchtigen Blick, mit welchem sie ihn endlich auf eine Stelle im Eschenstamme bedeutungsvoll auffordernd hinweist. Hunding, der ihr Zögern bemerkt, treibt sie dann mit einem gebietenden Winke fort, worauf sie mit dem Trinkhorn und der Leuchte durch die Thüre verschwindet.)

HUNDING: (nimmt seine Waffen vom Baume). Mit Waffen wehrt sich der Mann.—
Dich Wölfing, treffe ich morgen:
mein Wort hörtest du—

Thirsting for vengeance dire;
Foemen ringed round me,
Pressing me harder.
Still to her dead
Close clung the maid.
With shield and spear
Stood I, her screen,
Till spear and shield
Were hewn from my hand.
Wounded—weaponless stood I—
Saw the maid as she fell.
I fled from the merciless host—
On the courses . . . she lay dead.
(Looking sorrowfully at Sieglinde.)
You've heard now what you would know,
Why no one may name me 'Peaceful'!
(He rises and walks to the hearth. Sieglinde, much moved, looks down.)

HUNDING: (Gloomily.) A brood I know that's cursed,
holds nothing holy
Where others bow:
It is hated of all and of me.
I was chosen to right a wrong,
to render Vengeance
For kinsmen slain.
I came too late,
But now I return
The fleeing murderer's trace
To find at last in my home.
My roof shields you,
Wolf-cub, tonight.
Until morn, be my guest.
But beware tomorrow,
And look to your weapons.
Full soon I'll meet you in arms—
For blood shed, blood you shall pay!
(To Sieglinde, who has anxiously moved between the two men.)
Away from the hall!
Do not, stay here!
My night-draught brew in yon room:
Await me there, within!
(Sieglinde takes pensively a drinking-horn from the table, walks to a cupboard from which she takes spices, and goes to the chamber. On reaching the uppermost step near the door, she turns her head toward Siegmund, who stands calmly and sullenly by the fire-place, never losing sight of her. She casts a long and significant glance at him, by which she endeavors to direct his attention to a certain spot in the ash-tree. Hunding notices her strange hesitation, and warns her away with a commanding look, whereupon she disappears through the door with the torch and drinking-horn.)

HUNDING: (Takes his weapons off the tree.) With weapons should men keep ward.
Tomorrow, Wolf-cub, I'll meet you!

hüte dich wohl!
(*Er geht mit den Waffen in das Gemach ab.*)

SIEGMUND: (*allein*). (*Es ist vollständig Nacht geworden; der Saal
ist nur noch von einem matten
Feuer im Herde erhellt Siegmund
lässt sich, nah beim Feuer, auf
dem Lager nieder, und brütet in
grosser Aufregung eine Zeit lang
schweigend vor sich hin.*) Ein
Schwert verhiess mir der Vater,
ich fänd' es in höchster Noth.—
Waffenlos fiel ich
in Feindes Haus:
seiner Rache Pfand
raste ich hier:—
ein Weib sah' ich,
wonnig und hehr;
entzückend Bangen
zehrt mein Herz:—
zu der mich nun Sehnsucht zieht,
die mit süssem Zauber mich
sehrt—
im Zwange hält sie der Mann,
der mich—Wehrlosen höhnt.—
Wälse! Wälse!
Wo ist dein Schwert?
Das starke Schwert,
das im Sturm ich schwänge,
Bricht mir hervor aus der Brust,
was wüthend das Herz noch hegt?
(*Das Feuer bricht zusammen; es
fällt aus der aufsprühenden Gluth
ein greller Schein auf die Stelle des
Eschenstammes, welche Sieglinde's Blick bezeichnet hatte und
an der man jetzt deutlicher einen
Schwertgriff haften sieht.*)
Was gleiszt dort hell
im Glimmerschein?
Welch' ein Strahl bricht
aus der Esche Stamm?—
Des Blinden Auge
leuchtet ein Blitz:
lustig lacht da der Blick.—
Wie der Schein so hehr
das Herz mir sengt!
Ist es der Blick
der blühenden Frau,
den dort haftend
sie hinter sich liess,
als aus dem Saal sie schied?
(*Von hier an verglimmt das Herd-
feuer allmälig.*)
Nächtiges Dunkel
deckte mein Aug',
ihres Blickes Strahl
streifte mich da:
Wärme gewann ich und Tag.
Selig schien mir
der Sonne Licht,
den Scheitel umgliss mir
ihr wonniger Glanz—
bis hinter Bergen sie sank.
Noch einmal, da sie schied,
traf mich abends ihr Schein;
selbst der alten Esche Stamm
erglänzte in gold'ner Gluth:
da bleicht die Blüthe
das Licht verlischt—
nächt'ges Dunkel
deckt mir das Auge:
tief in des Busens Berge

You have heard—my words—
Guard yourself well!
(*He goes into the adjoining room,
taking his weapons with him.*)

SIEGMUND: (*Alone.*) (*Night has
now fallen. The hall is dimly light-
ed by the dying fire. Siegmund lies
down on the couch by the hearth,
and remains brooding and silent
for some time, much agitated.*) A
sword—so promised my father—
I'd find in my hour of need.
Weaponless am I,
My host a foe.
By his wrath fore-doomed,
Here I now lie.
A woman came,
Witching and pure;
And ravishing anguish
Burns my heart;
But she for whom I now long,
Who has cast about me her spell,
Is held in servitude by the man
Who scorns—me, all unarmed.—
Wälse! Wälse!
Where is your sword?
The strong, good sword
That went flashing in fight!
Burst from my sorrowful breast.
The frenzy had hid my heart!
(*The smoldering cinders on the
hearth fall to pieces; a clear light
from the resulting glow shines on
the tree, illuminating the spot
which Sieglinde's glance had
designated, and reveals the han-
dle of a sword.*)
What glistens there?
What flames and gleams
See—a light streams
From the ashen stem:
So bright it dazzles
Eyes that were blind—
Laughs with light at my look!
In the glorious glow
My heart takes fire!
Is it the glance
That woman so fair
Left behind her
To burn in the tree,
When from the hall she stole?
(*From now on the fire on the
hearth begins to die out.*)
Night and its darkness
Hung on my lids:
But her beaming eyes
Gladdened my gloom,
Warmed me and won back the
light.
Sweet the sunshine
Now seems to me.
Its ravishing radiance
Enwrapped me around—
Till amid the mountains it died.
And once more, before it went,
Came tonight the glad gleam,
And the old, old ashen stem,
Grew brighter and gleamed as gold.
The flush has faded—
The light grows dim—
Night and darkness
Weigh on my eyelids.
Deep in my bosom only
A flame gleams in secret
(*The fire is now quite out. It is

glimmt nur noch lichtlose Gluth!
(*Das Feuer ist gänzlich verloschen; volle Nacht.—Das Seitenge-
mach öffnet sich leise: Sieglinde,
in weissem Gewande, tritt heraus
und schreitet auf Siegmund zu.*)

SIEGLINDE: Schläfst du, Gast?

SIEGMUND: (*freudig überrascht
aufspringend*). Wer schleicht daher?

SIEGLINDE: (*mit
geheimnissvoller Hast*). Ich bin's,
höre mich an!—
In tiefem Schlaf liegt Hunding;
ich würzt' ihm betäubenden Trank.
Nütze die Nacht dir zum Heil!

SIEGMUND: (*hitzig
unterbrechend*). Heil macht mich
dein Nah'n!

SIEGLINDE: Eine Waffe lass' mich
dir weisen—
O merke wohl, was ich dir
melde!—
Den hehrsten Helden
dürft' ich dich heissen;
dem Stärksten allein
ward sie bestimmt.
O merke wohl, was ich dir
melde!—
Der Männer Sippe
sass hier im Saal,
von Hunding zur Hochzeit
geladen:
er freite ein Weib,
das ungefragt
Schächer ihm schenkten zur Frau.
Traurig sass ich,
während sie tranken:
ein Fremder trat da herein—
ein Greis in grauem Gewand;
tief hing ihm der Hut,
der deckt' ihm der Augen eines;
doch des andren Strahl,
Angst schuf er allen,
traf die Männer
sein mächt'ges Dräu'n:
mir allein
weckte das Auge
süss sehnenden Harm,
Thränen und Trost zugleich.
Auf mich blickt' er
und blitzte auf Jene,
als ein Schwert in Händen er
schwang
das stiess er nun
in der Esche Stamm,
bis zum Heft haftet' es drin:—
dem sollte der Stahl geziemen,
der aus dem Stamm' es zög'.
Der Männer Alle,
so kühn sie sich müh'ten,
die Wehr sich keiner gewann:
Gäste kamen,
und Gäste gingen,
die stärksten zogen am Stahl—
keinen Zoll entwich er dem Stamm:
dort haftet schweigend das
Schwert.—
Da wusst' ich, wer der war,
der mich Gramvolle gegrüsst:
ich weiss auch,
wem allein
im Stamm das Schwert er bestimmt.
O fänd' ich ihn heut'

deep night. The chamber door
opens softly. Sieglinde, clad in
white, enters and draws near to
Siegmund.*)

SIEGLINDE: Do you sleep, guest?

SIEGMUND: (*Springing up in joyful surprise.*) Who steals this way?

SIEGLINDE: (*Mysteriously and in
haste.*) Hear me, friend; it is I!
Oppressed with sleep lies Hund-
ing;
I seasoned his drink with a drug.
Use the night for your weal!

SIEGMUND: (*Interrupting her eagerly.*) Bliss comes now you're
near!

SIEGLINDE: But a weapon first I
would show you
I wish that you could win it!
The highest hero
Then could I call you.
The mightiest alone
Owns it as lord!
O pay good heed now to my story!
The host of kinsmen
Sat in the hall,
By Hunding bid here to a wedding.
A woman he wooed
Whom all by force,
Robbers had brought him for a
bride.
Sadly sat I
While they were drinking:
A stranger slowly strode in—
An aged man, all in grey.
His hat, pressed low on his head,
had kept one eye hidden.
But the other flamed,
Awful and boding,
All it threatened
On whom it gazed.
I alone did not
shrink in terror,
Felt sad and yet glad,
Tearful and hopeful both!
He looked on me,
And flared at the others;
Then a sword uplifted he swung,
And drove it deep
In the ashen stem—
To the hilt hewed it a way.
He who from the tree could draw it
Should some day own the steel.
The men sought vainly,
They strove and they struggled,
The wondrous weapon to win:—
Guests a-coming,
And guests a-going,
The strongest tugged at the steel—
Not an inch it budged from the
stem.
There buried still lies the sword.
Well knew I who was he
That had greeted me who grieved.
I know, too,
Who alone
The sword is destined to win.
O would he were here,
And now, that friend!
Come from a far land
To give me aid.

und hier, den Freund;
käm' er aus Fremden
zur ärmsten Frau:
was je ich gelitten
in grimmigemn Leid,
was je mich geschmerzt
in Schande und Schmach,—
süsseste Rache
sühnte dann Alles!
Erjagt hätt' ich,
was je ich verlor;
was je ich beweint,
wär' mir gewonnen—
fänd 'ich den heiligen Freund,
umfing' den Helden mein Arm!

**SIEGMUND:** (*umfasst sie mit feuriger Gluth*). Dich, selige Frau,
hält nun der Freund
dem Waffe und Weib bestimmt:
Heiss in der Brust
brennt mir der Eid,
der mich dir Edlen vermahlt.
Was je ich ersehnt,
ersah ich in dir;
in dir fand ich,
was je mir gefehlt!
Littest du Schmach,
und schmerzte mich Leid;
war ich geächtet,
und warst du entehrt;
freudige Rache
lacht nun den Frohen!
Auf lach' ich
in heiliger Lust,
halt' ich dich Hehre umfangen.
fühl' ich dein schlagendes Herz!

**SIEGLINDE:** (*fährt erschrocken zusammen und reisst sich los*).
Ha, wer ging? wer kam herein?
(*Die hintere Thüre ist aufgesprungen und bleibt weit geöffnet: aussen herrliche Frühlingsnacht; der Vollmond leuchtet herein und wirft sein helles Licht auf das Paar, das so sich plötzlich in voller Deutlichkeit wahrnehmen kann.*)

**SIEGMUND:** (*in leiser Entzückung*). Keiner ging—
doch Einer kam:
siehe, der Lenz
lacht in den Saal!
(*Er zieht sie mit sanftem Ungestüm zu sich auf das Lager.*)
Winterstürme wichen
dem Wonnemond,
in mildem Lichte
leuchtet der Lenz;
auf linden Lüften,
leicht und lieblich,
Wunder webend
er sich wiegt;
über Wald und Auen
weht sein Athem,
weit geöffnet
lacht sein Aug'.
Aus sel'ger Vöglein Sange
süss er tönt,
holde Düfte
haucht er aus;
seinem warmen Blut entblühen
wonnige Blumen,
Keim und Spross

Whatever I have suffered
Of bitterest pain—
Whatever was my load
Of scorn and of shame,
Sweetest of vengeance
Comfort should bring me.
Regained were all
That I ever had lost;
Whatever I had mourned
Would be recovered;
Could I but find him, that friend—
And press my lord to my breast!

**SIEGMUND:** (*Embracing her ardently.*) Then here in his arms
That friend holds you.
Who should win weapon and wife
Hot from my heart
Take now the oath
That weds me, dearest, to you.
Whatever I had dreamt
In you I divined;
In you found all
That ever I had craved!
Shame you have known,
And pain have I borne;
Outcast I've wandered,
Dishonored you've been.
Now at last vengeance
Comes to delight us!
I laugh loudly
In holiest joy—
Pressing you, sweet, to my bosom—
Feeling your heart as it beats!

**SIEGLINDE:** (*Starts in alarm and tears herself from his embrace.*)
Ha! Who went? Who was it came?
(*The outer door has opened wide. It remains open. Outside the night is beautiful. The full moon shines upon the two lovers, and all about them suddenly becomes plainly visible.*)

**SIEGMUND:** (*In gentle ecstacy.*)
No one went—
Yet someone came.
See how the Spring
Smiles in the hall.
(*He draws her gently but firmly to him on the couch.*)
Winter's storming's stilled
By the love-lit May;
In tender beauty
Beams the Spring.
On balmy breezes,
Light and lovely,
Weaving wonders,
See, he sways;
Over wood and meadow
Softly breathing,
Wide he opens
His laughing eyes:
And happy birds are singing
Songs he taught,
Sweetest perfumes
Scent his train.
As he warms them, lo, the branches
Break into blossom;
Bud and bough

entspriesst seiner Kraft.
Mit zarter Waffen Zier
bezwingt er die Welt.
Winter und Sturm wichen
der starken Wehr:—
wohl musste den tapfern Streichen
die strenge Thüre auch weichen,
die trotzig und starr
uns—trennte von ihm.—
Zu seiner Schwester
schwang er sich her;
die Liebe lockte den Lenz;
in uns'rem Busen
barg sie sich tief:
nun lacht sie selig dem Licht.
Die bräutliche Schwester
befreite der Bruder:
zertrümmert liegt,
was je sie getrennt;
jauchzend grüsst sich
das junge Paar:
vereint sind Liebe und Lenz!

**SIEGLINDE:** Du bist der Lenz,
nach dem ich verlangte
in frostigen Winter's Frist:
dich grüsste mein Herz
mit heiligem Grau'n,
als dein Blick zuerst mir erblühte.—
Fremdes nur sah ich von je,
freundlos war mir das Nahe;
als hätt' ich nie es gekannt
war was immer mir kam.
Doch dich kannt' ich
deutlich und klar:
Als mein Auge dich sah,
warst du mein Eigen:
was im Busen ich barg,
was ich bin,
hell wie der Tag
taucht' es mir auf,
wie tönender Schall
schlug's an mein Ohr,
als in frostig öder Fremde
zuerst ich den Freund ersah.
(*Sie hängt sich entzückt an seinen Hals und blick ihm nahe in's Gesicht.*)

**SIEGMUND:** O süsseste Wonne!
Seligstes Weib!

**SIEGLINDE:** (*dicht an seinen Augen*). O lass in Nähe
zu dir mich neigen,
dass hell ich schaue
der dir aus Aug'
und Antlitz bricht,
und so süss die Sinne mir zwingt!

**SIEGMUND:** Im Lenzesmond
leuchtest du hell;
hehr umwebt dich
das Wellenhaar;
was mich berückt,
errath' ich nun leicht—
denn wonnig weidet mein Blick.

**SIEGLINDE:** (*schlägt ihm die Locken von der Stirn zurück und betrachtet ihn staunend*). Wiew
dir die Stirn
so offen steht,
der Adern Geäst

Submit to his sway.
In beauty's armor dight,
He witches the world.
Winter and storm vainly
Had said no to him
And even the surly portals
Obey his will, with the mortals
They fain would have barred
From—rapture and day.
Fast he has fared—
To greet his sister,
It was Love that longed for the Spring.
In both our bosoms
Buried, lay Love:
But now she laughs in the light.
The bride who was sister
Is freed by the brother;
And shattered now
Lie barriers and chains.
Joyous greeting
Their lips exchange:
For Love has wed with the Spring!

**SIEGLINDE:** You are the Spring
For whom I lay longing
And fasting through winter's frost;
It was you my heart hailed
With holiest awe,
As your look with love on me lighted.
Strange the world ever had seemed,
Friends had never come to cheer me,
And all I counted as nothing
That I met on my way.
But I knew you
Surely and soon;
When my glances met yours
Mine you were only:
All my heart had once hid,
All I am,
Clear as the day
Now I could see:
The truth sounded at last in my ear
As in chill and dreary sorrow I made
a friend in you.
A friend.
(*She hangs upon his neck in rapture and looks searchingly into his face.*)

**SIEGMUND:** O sweetest of raptures!
Woman divine!

**SIEGLINDE:** (*Gazing into his eyes.*) O let me nearer
To you, dear, nestle,
For fain I'd gaze on
The holy light
That shines on your eyes
And face
And so sweetly draws me to you.

**SIEGMUND:** The love-lit moon
Glows in your face;
Soft enfolding
your waving hair.
How I know well
that I am your slave.
For rapture rivets my look.

**SIEGLINDE:** (*Brushes the hair back from his brow and looks at him in amazement.*)
Your brow is broad,
And frank and fair,
Your veins all entwined

in den Schläfen sich schlingt!
Mir zagt es vor der Wonne,
die mich entzückt—
ein Wunder will mich
gemahnen:—
den heut' zuerst ich erschaut,
mein Auge sah dich schon!

SIEGMUND: Ein Minnetraum
gemahnt auch mich:
in heissem Sehnen
sah ich dich schon!

SIEGLINDE: Im Bach erblickt' ich
mein eigen Bild—
und jetzt gewahr' ich es wieder:
wie einst dem Teich es enttaucht,
bietest mein Bild mir nun du!

SIEGMUND: Du bist das Bild—
das ich in mir barg

SIEGLINDE: (den Blick schnell
abwendend). O still! lass mich
der Stimme lauschen:—
mich dünkt, ihren Klang
hört' ich als Kind— —
doch nein! ich hörte sie neulich,
als meiner Stimme Schall
mir wiederhallte der Wald.

SIEGMUND: O lieblichste Laute,
denen ich lausche!

SIEGLINDE: (schnell ihm wieder
in's Auge spähend). Deines Auges
Gluth
erglänzte mir schon:—
so blickte der Greis
grüssend auf mich,
als der Traurigen Trost er gab.
An dem Blick
erkannt' ihn sein Kind—
schon wollt ich bei'm Namen ihn
nennen
(Sie hält inne und fährt dann leise
fort.)
Wehwalt heiss'st du fürwahr?

SIEGMUND: Nicht heiss' mich so,
seit du mich liebst:
nun walt 'ich der hehrsten Wonnen!

SIEGLINDE: Und Friedmund darfst
du
froh dich nicht nennen?

SIEGMUND: Nenne mich du,
wie du liebst, dass ich heisse:
den Namen nehm' ich von dir!

SIEGLINDE: Doch nanntest du
Wolfe den Vater?

SIEGMUND: Ein Wolf war er feigen
Füchsen!
Doch dem so stolz
strahlte das Auge,
wie, Herrliche, hehr dir es strahlt,
der war—Wälse gennant.

SIEGLINDE: (ausser sich). War
Wälse dein Vater,
Und bist du ein Wälsung,
stiess er für dich
sein Schwert in den Stamm—
so lass' mich dich heissen,
wie ich dich liebe:
Siegmund—
so nenn' ich dich.

I trace in your temples
I tremble, as my passion
Holds me enchained—
Some wonder thrills me with ter-
ror:—
Before I found you tonight
Your face had seen my eyes!

SIEGMUND: A dream of love,
I, too, recall.
I surely sought you,
Wooed you even now!

SIEGLINDE: A brooklet mirrored
My face one morn—
And now again I behold it.
What once the water revealed
Now I can see in your face!

SIEGMUND: Thine is the face
That my heart had hid.

SIEGLINDE: (Quickly averting
her gaze.) Ah, still! Let me recall
your voice, love!
I thought
I heard it once as a child—
Yet no! It was lately I heard it,
When, echoing through the woods,
There came to me my own voice.

SIEGMUND: How lovely the
echoes
Sound as I listen!

SIEGLINDE: (Again gazing into
his eyes.) Ah, those eyes of yours
I have seen before now.
So beamed on me once,
Cheering my grief,
The strange eyes of that aged man.
By that glance
I found my father.
I nearly had named him by name.
(She pauses, and then goes on in a
low voice):
'Woeful,' surely I see?

SIEGMUND: Not so I'm named
For you my love.
My world is all bliss and rapture.

SIEGLINDE: And 'Peaceful' none
may
Call you forever?

SIEGMUND: Give me the name
That your love would award me;
That name alone I will bear.

SIEGLINDE: Was your father called
Wolfè?

SIEGMUND: Ay, Wolfè to dastard
foxes!
Yet he whose eye
Shone with the lustre
That shines, O beloved, in yours
He was—Wälse, I believe.

SIEGLINDE: (Beside herself.)
Your father was Wälse?
Then you are a Wälsung!
Fast in the tree
His sword waits for you
So let me re-name you
As I do love you:
Siegmund—
I proclaim you!

SIEGMUND: (springt auf den
Stamm zu und fasst den Schwertgriff). Siegmund heiss' ich
und Siegmund bin ich:
bezeug' es dies Schwert,
das zaglos ich halte!
Wälse verhiess mir,
in höchster Noth
fänd' ich es einst:
ich fass' es nun!
Heiligster Minne
höchste Noth,
sehnender Liebe
sehrende Noth,
brennt mir hell in der Brust,
drängt zu That und Tod:
Nothung! Nothung!—
so nenn' ich dich, Schwert—
Nothung! Nothung!
neidlicher Stahl!
Zeig' deiner Schärfe
schneidenden Zahn:
heraus aus der Scheide zu mir!
(Er zieht mit einem gewaltigen
Zuck das Schwerz aus dem
Stamme und zeigt es der von
Staunen und Entzücken erfassten
Sieglinde.)
Siegmund den Wälsung
Siehst du, Weib!
Als Brautgabe
Bringt er dies Schwert:
so freit er sich
die seligste Frau:
dem Feindeshaus
entführt er dich so.
Fern von hier
folge ihm nun,
folge mir nun,
lachendes Haus:
dort schützt dich Nothung das
Schwert
wenn Siegmund dir liebend erlag!
(Er umfasst sie, um sie mit sich
fortzuziehen.)

SIEGLINDE: (in höchster Trunk-
enheit). Bist du Siegmund,
den ich hier sehe—
Sieglinde bin ich,
die dich ersehnt:
die eig'ne Schwester
gewann'st du zueins mit dem
Schwert!

SIEGMUND: Braut und Schwester
bist du dem Bruder—
so blühe denn Wälsungen-blut!
(Er zieht sie mit wüthender
Gluth an sich; sie sinkt mit einem
Schrei an seine Brust.—Der
Vorhang fällt schnell.)

SIEGMUND: Siegmund, Victor,
Henceforth proclaim me.
Bear witness the sword
I grasp without shrinking.
Wälse foretold that,
In direst need,
It should bring help—
I hold it now!
Love the most holy,
Direst need,
Loving and longing,
Sorest of need,
Burn and flame in my breast,
Drive to deeds and death.
Nothung! Needful!
You, sword, shall be named—
Nothung! Nothung!
Blade of the brave!
Show me your sharp
And shattering steel:
And—out of your scabbard now
leap
(With a mighty tug he draws the
sword from the trunk and shows
it to the astonished and delighted
Sieglinde.)
Siegmund the Wälsung,
Look, wife!
Now brings to you,
Bride, a true blade!
It is thus he woos
His dearest and best;
It is thus he frees
His love from her foe.
Far from here
Go where he goes,
Into the smiling
Sunshine of Spring,
Where Nothung shall keep guard
always
When Siegmund is disarmed by
love!
(He puts his arm round her, to
take her away with him.)

SIEGLINDE: (Ecstatically.) Are
you Siegmund,
Here by my side?
Sieglinde am I,
For you I sigh:
Your own true sister
You've won with the rape of the
sword!

SIEGMUND: Bride and sister
Be to your brother—
Be blessed, Wälsungen blood!
(He draws her to him rapturously.
She falls on his breast with a cry of
ecstacy. Quick curtain.)

# ■ ZWEITER AUFZUG

*Wildes Felsengebirg*

*Im Hintergrunde zieht sich von
unten her eine Schlucht herauf,
die auf ein erhöhtes Felsjoch
mündet; von diesem senkt sich
der Boden dem Vordergrunde zu*

# ■ ACT II

*A wild, Rocky Height.*

*(In the background a wild ravine
rises, leading to a lofty and rocky
height. The ground slopes downward towards the foreground.
Wotan is discovered in full armor*

*wieder abwärts.*
*Wotan, kriegerisch gewaffnet und*
*mit dem Speer: vor ihm Bruenn-*
*hilde, als Walkuere, ebenfalls in*
*voller Waffenrüstung.*

*and bearing his spear. Before him*
*stands Brünnhilde, in the full ar-*
*mor of a Walkyr.)*

**WOTAN:** Nun zäume dein Ross,
reisige Maid!
Bald entbrennt
brünstiger Streit:
Brünnhilde stürme zum Streit,
dem Wälsung kiese sie Sieg!
Hunding wähle sich
wem er gehört:
nach Walhall taugt er mir nicht.
Drum rüstig und rasch
reite zur Wal!

**WOTAN:** Now bridle your steed,
Warfaring maid!
Soon shall come
Storming and strife.
Brünnhilde, haste to the fray,
The Wälsung surely must win.
Hunding's haven be
Here or be there—
He shall see never Walhalla.
So up and away,
Haste to the field!

**BRUNNHILDE:** (*Anchzend von*
*Fels zu Fels die Höhe rechts hinauf*
*springend*). Hojotoho! Hojotoho!
Heiaha! Heiaha!
Hojotoho! Hojotoho!
Heiaha! Heiaha!
Hojotoho! Hojotoho!
Hojotoho! Hojotoho!
Heiahaha!
Hojotoho!
(*Auf einer hohen Felsspitze hält*
*sie an, blickt in die hintere*
*Schlucht hinab und ruft zu Wotan*
*zurück.*)
Dir rath' ich, Vater,
rüste dich selbst;
harten Sturm
sollst du besteh'n:
Fricka naht, deine Frau,
im Wagen mit dem
Widdergespann.
Hei! wie die gold'ne
Geissel sie schwingt;
die armen Thiere
ächzen vor Angst;
wild rasseln die Räder:
zornig fährt sie zum Zank!
In solchem Strausse
streit' ich nicht gern,
lieb' ich auch muthiger
Männer Schlacht:
drum sieh', wie den Sturm du
bestehst;
ich Lustige lass' dich im Stich!—
Hojotoho! Hojotoho!
Heiaha! Heiaha!
Hojotoho! Hojotoho!
Heiaha! Heiaha!
Hojotoho! Hojotoho!
Heiahaha!
(*Sie ist hinter der Gebirgshöhe zur*
*Seite verschwunden, während aus*
*der Schlucht herauf Fricka, in*
*einem mit zwei Widdern*
*bespannten Wagen, auf dem Joch*
*anlangt: dort steigt sie schnell ab*
*und schreitet dann heftig in den*
*Vordergrund auf Wotan zu.*)

**BRÜNNHILDE:** (*Exulting, as she*
*ascends the height on the right,*
*leaping from rock to rock.*) Ho-yo-
to-ho! Ho-yo-to-ho!
Hi-ya-ha! Hi-ya-ha!
Ho-yo-to-ho! Ho-yo-to-ho!
Hi-ya-ha! Hi-ya-ha!
Ho-yo-to-ho! Ho-yo-to-ho!
Ho-yo-to-ho! Ho-yo-to-ho!
Hi-ya-ha-ha!
Ho-yo-to-ho!
(*On reaching a high peak she*
*halts, looks down into the ravine*
*beyond, and calls to Wotan.*)
I warn you father,
You'll need armor.
Fierce the storm
Soon you shall meet.
Fricka comes, your wife,
She rides in her car with the rams.
Ha! How she cracks her golden
Whip!
Her team in terror
Trembles and moans!
Loud, loud the wheels rattle,
Wrath and war they forbode!
For such wild battles
Love, have I none,
Joy though I may
In the strife of men!
So weather the storm as you can
I laugh and I leave you to fate!
Ho-yo-to-ho! Ho-yo-to-ho!
Hi-ya-ha! Hi-ya-ha!
Ho-yo-to-ho! Ho-yo-to-ho!
Hi-ya-ha! Hi-ya-ha!
Ho-yo-to-ho! Ho-yo-to-ho!
Hi-ya-ha-ha!
(*She vanishes behind the rocks, as*
*Fricka enters from the heights, af-*
*ter ascending from the ravine, in*
*a chariot drawn by two rams,*
*alights quickly, and strides angri-*
*ly towards Wotan in the fore-*
*ground.*)

**WOTAN:** (*indem er sie kommen*
*sieht*). Der alte Sturm!
Die alte Müh!
Doch Stand muss ich hier halten.

**WOTAN:** (*As he sees her coming.*)
The old, old storm!
The old, old strife!
And yet here I must face her!

**FRICKA:** Wo in Bergen du dich
birgst
der Gattin Blick zu entgeh'n,
einsam hier
such' ich dich auf,
dass Hilfe du mir verhiessest.

**WOTAN:** Was Fricka kümmert,
künde sie frei.

**FRICKA:** Ich vernahm Hunding's
Noth,
um Rache rief er mich an:
der Ehe Hüterin
hörte ihn,
verhiess streng
zu strafen die That
des frech frevelnden Paar's,
das kühn den Gatten gekränkt.

**WOTAN:** Was so Schlimmes
schuf das Paar,
das liebend einte der Lenz?
Der Minne Zauber
entzückte sie:
wer büsst mir der Minne Macht?

**FRICKA:** Wie thörig und taub du
dich stellst
als wüsstest fürwahr du nicht,
dass um der Ehe
heiligen Eid
den hart gekränkten, ich klage!

**WOTAN:** Unheilig
acht' ich den Eid,
der Unliebende eint;
und mir wahrlich
muthe nicht zu,
dass mit Zwang ich halte,
was dir nicht haftet:
denn wo kühn Kräfte sich regen,
da rath' ich offen zum Krieg.

**FRICKA:** Achtest du rühmlich
der Ehe Bruch,
so prahle nun weiter
und preis' es heilig,
dass Blutschande entblüht
dem Bund eines Zwillingpaar's.
Mir schaudert das Herz,
es schwindelt mein Hirn:
bräutlich umfing
die Schwester der Bruder.
Wann—ward es erlebt,
dass leiblich Geschwister sich liebten?

**WOTAN:** Heut'—hast du's erlebt:
erfahre so,
was von selbst sich fügt,
sei zuvor auch noch nie es
gescheh'n.
Dass jene sich lieben,
leuchtet dir hell:
drum höre redlichen Rath!
soll süsse Lust
deinen Segen dir lohnen,
so seg'ne, lachend der Liebe,
Siegmund's und Sieglinde's Bund!

**FRICKA:** (*in höchste Entrüstung*
*ausbrechend*). So ist es denn aus
mit den ewigen Göttern,
seit du die wilden
Wälsungen zeugtest?
Heraus sagt' ich's—
traf ich den Sinn?
Nichts gilt dir der Hehren

**FRICKA:** On the hill-side you hide,
My wifely eyes to evade.
Here I come,
Riding alone,
To seek the help you promised.

**WOTAN:** Your troubles, Fricka,
Freely unfold!

**FRICKA:** Now I know Hunding's
need:
For vengeance rightly he prayed.
And I, who watch over
Married love,
Stand pledged
Now to punish the wrong
A bold, brazen-faced pair
Have wrought against one who's
wed.

**WOTAN:** Was the evil
Done so dire
By those the Spring had made one?
The magic meshes
Of love accuse:
Nor count it a crime to love.

**FRICKA:** How dull and how deaf
you would seem,
As though it were truly strange
That in defense
Of holiest bonds,
I take up arms for the wronged one!

**WOTAN:** Unholy
Deem I the oath
That unloving is sworn:
And would you, then,
Have me hold chained
Those whom you have striven
In vain to fetter?
For where such fires fiercely are
raging
My thought is—stay not the flames.

**FRICKA:** Since you do honor
The crime I hate,
Go further in folly,
Proclaim it holy,
Where incest is the fruit
Of love between two born twins.
My heart is aghast,
A-whirl is my brain:
Wedded, these two
The sister and brother!
Whenever was it known
That brother and sister were mated?

**WOTAN:** Now—here it is known:
And so be sure
That it had to be,
Though till now it had never yet
been.
They love one another,
Surely it is plain:
So yield to reason and good advice.
Let bliss be born
Of the love that you seal,
And laugh to know you are blessing
Siegmund and Sieglinde's bond.

**FRICKA:** (*In a storm of indigna-*
*tion.*) To this has it come
With the gods everlasting,
Since you begot the lawless
Wälsungs?
My shaft went home—
Straight to the mark?
You hold nothing holy,

heilige Sippe;
hin wirfst du Alles,
was einst du geachtet;
zerreissest die Bande,
die selbst du gebunden;
losest lachend
des Himmels Haft—
dass nach Lust und Laune nur walte
dies frevelnde Zwillingspaar,
deiner Untreue zuchtlose
Frucht!—
O, was klag' ich
um Ehe und Eid,
du zuerst du selbst sie versehrt!
Die treue Gattin
trogest du stets:
wo eine Tiefe,
wo eine Höhe,
dahin lugte
lüstern dein Blick,
wie des Wechsels Lust du
gewännest,
und höhnend kränktest mein Herz!
Trauernden Sinnes
musst' ich's ertragen,
zog'st du zur Schlacht
mit den schlimmen Mädchen,
die wilder Minne
Bund dir gebar;
denn dein Weib noch scheutest du
so,
dass der Walküren Schaar,
und Brünnhilde selbst,
deines Wunsches Braut,
in Gehorsam der Herrin du gab'st.
Doch jetzt, da dir neue
Namen gefielen,
als 'Wälse' wölfisch
im Walde du schweiftest;
jetzt, da zu niedrigster
Schmach du dich neigtest,
gemeiner Menschen
ein Paar zu erzeugen:
jetzt dem Wurfe der Wölfin
wirfst du zu Füssen dein Weib!—
So führ' es denn aus,
fülle das Mass:
die Betrog'ne lass auch zertreten!

WOTAN: (*ruhig*). Nichts lerntest du,
wollt' ich dich lehren,
was nie du erkennen kannst,
eh' nicht ertagte die That.
Stets Gewohntes
nur magst du versteh'n:
doch was noch nie sich traf,
darnach trachtet mein Sinn!
Eines höre!
Noth thut ein Held,
der, ledig göttlichen Schutzes,
sich löse vom Göttergesetz:
so nur taugt er
zu wirken die That,
die, wie noth sie den Göttern,
dem Gott doch zu wirken verwehrt

FRICKA: Mit tiefem Sinne
willst du mich täuschen!
Was Hehres sollten
Helden je wirken,
das ihren Göttern wäre verwehrt
deren Gunst in ihnen nur wirkt?

---

Kinship nor Godhead:
You fling away
The laws you honored,
Destroyed the fetters
That came of your forging;
You make a mockery of Heaven's
behest.
That the sinful sister and brother
May love in their own wild way.
And your faithlessness bore the bad
fruit!
But why fret over
Weddings and vows
That you yourself did first laugh to
scorn?
You often wronged your wife so
faithful
Is there a valley,
Is there a mountain,
Your eye, lusting,
Has not profaned?
As your love of change became
stronger,
More harrowed ever was my heart!
What did my mourning
Mean to your pleasure?
Forth you would fare
With the wicked maidens,
Of love untrammelled
Born for your bane.
Yet your wife at least you did dread.
For Brünnhild' herself,
Best loved of them all,
With your Walkyr band,
You did order my will to obey
But now, since disguises
New did delight you:
Since wolfish 'Wälse'
In woods went a-roaming;
Now that you have fathomed the
nethermost
Depth
Begetting, shameless,
A brace of mere mortals;
Now you would offer your wife
Up to the whelps of your dam?
Well, go your own way,
Halt at no shame,
Let them crush me, too, in their triumph!

WOTAN: (*Calmly.*) You would
learn nothing,
Though I should teach you
What your mind could never grasp
Till what must happen shall be.
What is common
Alone you can read:
But what never yet was known
I foresee in my mind.
Mark this only!
One there must come,
A hero, slighted of heaven,
To defy the laws of the Gods.
That would fit him
To do the great deed
Not a God in Walhalla
Would dare, though the need
should be dire.

FRICKA: Thy words and wisdom
Would but deceive me.
What deed could heroes
Work that were worthy,
Where we, the gods almighty, had
failed?
By our grace alone do they work.

---

WOTAN: Ihres eignen Muthes
achtest du nicht?

FRICKA: Wer hauchte Menschen
ihn ein?
Wer hellte den Blöden den Blick?
In deinem Schutz
scheinen sie stark,
durch deinen Stachel
streben sie auf:
du—reizest sie einzig
die so mir Ew'gen du rühmst.
Mit neuer List
willst du mich belügen,
durch neue Ränke
jetzt mir entrinnen;
doch diesen Wälsung
gewinnst du dir nicht:
in ihm treff' ich nur dich,
denn durch dich trotzt er allein.

WOTAN: In wilden Leiden
erwuchs er sich selbst:
mein Schutz schirmte ihn nie.

FRICKA: So schütz' auch heut' ihn
nicht;
nimm ihm das Schwert,
das du ihm geschenkt!

WOTAN: Das Schwert?

FRICKA: Ja—das Schwert,
das zauberstark
zuckende Schwert,
das du Gott dem Sohne gab'st.

WOTAN: Siegmund gewann es sich
selbst in der Noth.

FRICKA: Du schuf'st ihm die Noth;
wie das neidliche Schwert:
willst du mich täuschen,
die Tag und Nacht
auf den Fersen dir folgt?
Für ihn stiessest du
das Schwert in den Stamm;
du verhiessest ihm
die hehre Wehr:
willst du es leugnen,
dass nur deine List
ihn lockte, wo er es fänd'?
(*Wotan macht eine Geberde des
Grimmes.*)
Mit Unfreien
streitet kein Edler,
Frevler straft nur der Freie:
wider deine Kraft
führt' ich wohl Krieg:
doch Siegmund verfiel mir als
Knecht.
(*Wotan wendet sich unmuthig
ab.*)
Der dir als Herren
hörig und eigen
gehorchen soll ihm
dein ewig Gemahl?
Soll mich in Schmach
der Niedrigste schmähen,
dem Frechen zum Sporn,
dem Freien zum Spott?
Das kann mein Gatte nicht wollen,
die Göttin entweiht er nicht so!

WOTAN: (*finster*). Was verlangst
du?

FRICKA: Lass' von dem Wälsung!

---

WOTAN: Do you count their courage
Truly for nothing?

FRICKA: Who gave that courage to
men?
Who opened their eyes to the light?
They may seem strong with you for
a shield.
With you to spur them,
They may strive well.
You—only you goaded them,
These men whose praise you, sing.
With new deceit
Would you beguile me;
With new devices
Would you evade me;
But this one Wälsung
No cunning shall save.
In him I strike yourself
It was your might made him so
brave.

WOTAN: In pain and sorrow
Alone was he reared:
My shield never gave shelter.

FRICKA: Then shieldless let him
stand;
Take back the sword,
That he owes to you.

WOTAN: The sword?

FRICKA: Yes—the sword,
The magical,
Masterful sword,
You, a god, gave your son.

WOTAN: Siegmund has conquered
it,
Won it in need.

FRICKA: You made the need,
When he needed the sword;
Would you deceive me
Who, night and day,
In your traces have trod?
For him did you thrust
The sword in the tree;
Ay, the noble blade
Was meant for him,
Will you deny
That your cunning alone
Allured him where it was found?
(*Wotan knits his brows wrathfully.*)
Can gods join
In battle with bondsmen?
The guilty should they but punish.
Braving you so strong,
War I might wage;
But Siegmund is only my slave
(*Wotan turns away impatiently.*)
Shall he who owes you
Duty and homage
Be master now
To the wife you have wed?
Shall he, a clod,
Put shame on your goddess—
The base-born be lord—
The mighty be scorned?
Ah, no! My lord cannot wish it—
He would not degrade his goddess!

WOTAN: (*Gloomily.*) What, then,
would you?

FRICKA: Cast off the Wälsung!

WOTAN: (*mit gedämpfter Stimme*). Er geh' seines Weg's.

WOTAN: (*Lowering his voice.*) He shall dread his fate

FRICKA: Doch du—schütze ihn nicht,
wenn zur Schlacht der Rächer ihn ruft

FRICKA: But you—shelter him not,
When the foeman his vengeance seeks!

WOTAN: Ich—schütze ihn nicht.

WOTAN: I'll—not be his shield.

FRICKA: Sieh' mir in's Auge,
sinne nicht Trug!
Die Walküre wend' auch von ihm!

FRICKA: Face me more frankly—
Think not of fraud.
The Walkyr must lend him no aid!

WOTAN: Die Walküre walte frei!

WOTAN: The Walkyrie fares freely.

FRICKA: Nicht doch! Deinen Willen
vollbringt sie allein:
verbiete ihr Siegmund's Sieg!

FRICKA: Not so! As you will
She comes and she goes.
Forbid her to let him win!

WOTAN: (*mit heftigem innerem Kampfe*). Ich kann ihn nicht fällen:
er fand mein Schwert!

WOTAN: (*Fighting against his emotion.*) I cannot undo him:
He wields my sword!

FRICKA: Entzieh' dem den Zauber,
zerknick' es dem Knecht:
schutzlos find' ihn der Feind!

FRICKA: Then kill its magic:
It will break in his hand—
Helpless finds him his foe!

BRUENNHILDE'S VOICE: Heiaha!
Heiaha!
Hojotoho!
(*Sie vernimmt von der Höhe her den jauchzenden Walkürenruf Bruennhilde's: diese erscheint dann dann selbst mit ihrem Ross auf dem Felspfade rechts.*)

BRÜNNHILDE'S VOICE: Hi-ya-ha!
Hi-ya-ha!
Ho-yo-to-ho!
(*From the heights she hears the jubilant Walkyr cry of Brünnhilde, who appears soon after with her steed on the rocky path, to the right.*)

FRICKA: Dort kommt deine Kühne Maid;
jauchzend jagt sie daher.

FRICKA: Here hastens your daring maid—
Joyfully she hies!

BRUENNHILDE'S VOICE: Heiaha!
Heiaha!
Hojohotojohotojoha!

BRÜNNHILDE'S VOICE: Hi-ya-ha!
Hi-ya-ha!
Ho-yo-ho-to-yo-ho-to-yo-ha!

WOTAN: (*dumpf für sich*). Ich rief sie für Siegmund zu Ross

WOTAN: (*Aside.*) For Siegmund she saddled her steed!

FRICKA: Deiner ew'gen Gattin
heilige Ehre
beschirme heut'ihr Schild!
Von Menschen verlacht,
verlustig der Macht,
gingen wir Götter zu Grund,
würde heut' nicht hehr
und herrlich mein Recht
gerächt von der muthigen Maid.—
Der Wälsung fällt meiner Ehre:—
empfah' ich von Wotan den Eid?

FRICKA: To protect the spotless
Fame of your goddess
See her shield shine!
To mortals a mock,
And stripped of our might,
Though we be gods, we were doomed,
Should the warrior maid
Today betray
My rightful and holiest cause.
The Wälsung dies for my honor:
Does Wotan so pledge me his oath?

WOTAN: (*in furchtbarem Unmuth und innerem Grimm auf einen Felsensitz sich werfend*). Nimm den Eid!
(*Als Brünnhilde von der Höhe aus Fricka gewahrte, brach sie schnell ihren Gesang ab, und hat nun still und langsam ihr Ross am Zügel den Felsweg herabgeleitet; sie birgt dieses jetzt in einer Höhle, als Fricka, zu ihrem Wagen sich zurückwendend, an ihr vorbeischreitet.*)

WOTAN: (*Raging and inwardly wrathful, as he throws himself on a rocky seat.*) Take my oath!
(*Brünnbilde, perceiving Fricka, has suddenly interrupted her song and has led her steed slowly and silently down the rocky path. She hides the steed in a cave just as Fricka passes her on her way back to her chariot.*)

FRICKA: (*zu Bruenhilde*). Heervater
harret dein:
lass' ihn dir künden,
wie das Loos er gekies't!
(*Sie besteigt den Wagen und fährt schnell nach hinten davon.*)

FRICKA: (*To Brünnhilde.*) Warlord, he
Waits for you:
He will inform you
How he has cast his lost
(*She flew into her chariot and is driven off quickly in the background.*)

BRUENNHILDE: (*tritt mit verwunderter und besorgter Miene vor Wotan, der, auf dem Felssitz zurückgelehnt das auf die Hand gestützt, in finsteres Brüten versunken ist*). Schlimm, fürcht' ich,
schloss der Streit,
lachte Fricka dem Loose!—
Vater, was soll
dein Kind erfahren?
Trübe scheinst du und traurig!

BRÜNNHILDE: (*Moves toward Wotan, looking anxious and amazed. Wotan reclines on his rocky seat, resting his head on his hand. He is brooding gloomily.*)
Ill, surely,
Ends the strife—
Fricka laughed as she left us!
Father, what shall
Your child discover?
Sad you seem, and solemn!

WOTAN: (*lässt den Arm machtlos sinken und den Kopf in den Nacken fallen*). In eig'ner Fessel
fing ich mich:—
ich unfreiester Aller!

WOTAN: (*Lets his arm drop limply and bows his head.*)
I forged the fetters.
I stand chained
I, most bound of all bondsmen!

BRUENNHILDE: So sah ich dich nie!
Was nagt dir das Herz?

BRÜNNHILDE: Thus never you did look.
What gnaws at your heart?

WOTAN: (*in wildem Ausbruche den Arm erhebend*). O heilige Schmach!
O schmählicher Harm!
Götternoth!
Götternoth!
Endloser Grimm!
Ewiger Gram!
Der Traurigste bin ich von Allen!

WOTAN: (*Raising his arm in violent excitement.*) How awful the shame!
How shameful this woe!
We're cursed!
Gods! Accurst!
Endless the grief!
Endless the groans!
Ah, saddest of all, I lie mourning!

BRUENNHILDE: (*wirft erschrocken Schild, Speer und Helm von sich, und lässt sich mit besorgter Zutraulichkeit zu Wotan's Füssen nieder*). Vater! Vater!
Sage, was ist dir?
Was erschreck'st du mit Sorge dein Kind!
Vertraue mir:
ich bin dir treu;
sieh', Brünnhilde bittet!
(*Sie legt traulich und ängstlich Haupt und Hände ihm auf Knie und Schooss.*)

BRÜNNHILDE: (*In alarm, throwing away her shield, spear and helmet, and kneeling affectionately at Wotan's feet*) Father! Father!
Tell me, what ails you?
See what terror bewilders your child!
Have trust in me—
I'm true to you
See, Brünnhilde begs you!
(*She lays her head and hands trustingly but distressfully on his knee.*)

WOTAN: (*blickt ihr lange in's Auge und streichelt ihr dann die Locken: wie aus tiefem Sinnen zu sich kommend beginnt er endlich mit sehr leiser Stimme*). Lass' ich's verlauten,
lös' ich dann nicht
meines Willens haltenden Haft?

WOTAN: (*Gazes long into her face and strokes her hair. Then, as if coming to himself again, he at last begins in a very low voice.*)
Did I reveal it,
Should I not lose
What is left of might in my will?

BRUENNHILDE: (*ihm eben so leise erwidernd*). Zu Wotan's Willen sprichst du,
sagst du mir, was du willst:
wer—bin ich,
wär' ich dein Wille nicht?

BRÜNNHILDE: (*Answering in an equally low voice.*) To Wotan's will you speak:
Tell me now what you will
What—were I,
Could I your will not be?

WOTAN: Was Keinem in Worten ich künde,
unausgesprochen
bleib' es denn ewig:
mit mir nur rath' ich,
red' ich zu dir.———
(*Mit noch gedämpfterer, schauerlicher Stimme, während er Bruennhilden unverwandt in das Auge blickt.*)
Als junger Liebe
Lust mir verblich,
verlangte nach Macht mein Muth:
von jäher Wünsche
Wüthen gejagt,
gewann ich mir die Welt.
Unwissend trugvoll

WOTAN: What never in words had been fashioned,
Unuttered still
Shall be, and for ever.
Myself I speak to,
Speaking to you—
(*In a more subdued and awestruck voice, looking fixedly at Brünnhilde.*)
As Love's young fancy
Faded and died,
I longed for the pride of power:
A-flame with olden
Wishes, I went
To win the whole wide world.
Untried, yet artful,
Falsehood I fostered,

Untreue übt' ich,
band durch Verträge,
was Unheil barg:
listig verlockte mich Loge,
der schweifend nun verschwand.
Von der Liebe doch
mocht' ich nicht lassen;
in der Macht verlangt' ich nach Minne
den Nacht gebar,
der bange Nibelung,
Alberich brach ihren Bund,
er fluchte der Liebe,
und gewann durch den Fluch
des Rheines glänzendes Gold
und mit ihm masslose Macht.
Den Ring, den er schuf,
entriss ich ihm listig:
doch nicht dem Rhein
gab ich ihn zurück;
mit ihm bezahlt' ich
Walhall's Zinnen,
der Burg, die Riesen mir bauten,
aus der ich der Welt nun gebot.
Die Alles weiss,
was einstens war,
Erda, die weihlich
weiseste Wala,
rieth mir ab von dem Ring,
warnte vor ewigem Ende.
Von dem Ende wollt' ich
mehr noch wissen;
doch schweigend entschwand mir das Weib.
Da verlor ich den leichten Muth;
zu wissen begehrt es den Gott:
in den Schoos der Welt
schwang ich mich hinab,
mit Liebes-Zauber
zwang ich die Wala,
stört' ihres Wissens Stolz,
dass sie Rede nun mir stand.
Kunde empfing ich von ihr:
von mir doch barg sie ein Pfand:
der Welt weisestes Weib
gebar mir, Brünnhilde, dich.
Mit acht Schwestern
zog ich dich auf:
durch euch Walküren
wollt' ich wenden,
was mir die Wala
zu fürchten schuf—
ein schmähliches Ende der Ew'gen.
Dass stark zum Streit
uns fände der Feind,
hiess ich euch Helden mir schaffen:
die herrisch wir sonst
in Gesetzen hielten,
die Männer, denen
den Muth wir gewehrt,
die durch trüber Verträge
trügende Bande
zu blindem Gehorsam
wir uns gebunden—
die solltet zu Sturm
und Streit ihr nun stacheln,
ihre Kraft reizen
zu rauhem Krieg,
dass kühner Kämpfer Schaaren
ich sammle in Walhall's Saal.

**BRUENNHILDE:** Deinen Saal
füllten wir weidlich:
viele schon führt' ich dir zu.
Was macht dir nun Sorge,
da nie wir gesäumt?

Bargained and ordered
What ill should bring.
Luring me lower came Loge,
No sooner come than gone.
But my lust for delight
Was unsated;
In my power, for passion I panted
It was Night that bore
The fearsome Nibelung,
Alberich; mocking my plans,
And cursing all love,
With his curses he won
The glittering gold of the Rhine,
And with it, measureless might.
The ring which he wrought
I ravished by cunning:
But still bereft
Did the Rhine remain:
The gold I gave for
Walhall's ramparts,
The stronghold reared by the giants,
From which the whole world I should rule.
She who knows all
That ever has been,
Erda, most wise
And womanly Wala,
Warned me off from the ring,
Bade me beware of disaster.
I begged her
to tell me more of the end
But silent she faded from sight.
Then my courage at last I lost;
For knowledge a god was thirsty.
In the womb of Earth
I sought now for light;
With magic love, I
Mastered the Wala,
Wrung from her wisdom's pride
What I longed so sore to know.
What had been dark, she made clear,
Yet hid a pledge from my eyes:
The world's Wala, most wise,
Did bear me, Brünnhilde, you.
With eight sisters
I reared you
With ye Walkyrs, I
Sought escape
From what the Wala
Had bid me to dread—
The end of the gods everlasting.
To make us strong
In strife with the foe,
I sent you searching for heroes:
The men whom we once
With our laws held tightly,
The men whose courage
And strength we had stolen,
Whom with compacts our cunning
Surely had fettered,
And bound to obey us
For good or evil—
It was these you should spur
To storm and to striving,
Their hearts steeling
To dare and do,
Till hosts of mighty warriors
Should stand in Walhalla's hall.

**BRÜNNHILDE:**
And your hall fast we are filling;
Many I've borne to your aid.
Then why do you sorrow,
When we are so true?

**WOTAN:** Ein Andres ist's:
achte es wohl,
wess' mich die Wala gewarnt!—
Durch Alberich's Heer
droht uns das Ende:
mit neidischem Grimm
grollt mir der Niblung;
doch scheu' ich nun nicht
seine nächtigen Schaaren—
meine Helden schüfen mir Sieg.
Nur wenn je den Ring
zurück er gewänne—
dann wäre Walhall verloren:
der der Liebe fluchte,
er allein
nützte neidisch
des Ringes Runen
zu aller Edlen
endlosen Schmach;
der Helden Muth
entwendet er mir;
die Kühnen selber
zwäng' er zum Kampf,
mit ihrer Kraft
bekriegte er mich.
Sorgend sann ich nun selbst,
den Ring dem Feind zu entreissen:
der Riesen einer,
denen ich einst
mit verfluchtem Gold
den Fleiss vergalt,
Fafner hütet den Hort,
um den er den Bruder gefällt.
Ihm müsst' ich den Reif entringen
den selbst als Zoll ich ihm zahlte:
doch mit dem ich vertrug
ihn darf ich nicht treffen,
machtlos vor ihm
erläge mein Muth.
Das sind die Bande,
die mich binden:
der durch Verträge ich Herr,
den Verträgen bin ich nun Knecht.
Nur Einer könnte,
was ich nicht darf:
ein Held, dem helfend
nie ich mich neigte;
der fremd dem Gotte,
frei seiner Gunst,
unbewusst,
ohne Geheiss,
aus eig'ner Noth
mit der eig'nen Wehr
schüfe die That,
die ich scheuen muss,
die nie mein Rath ihm rieth,
wünscht sie auch einzig mein Wunsch!
Der entgegen dem Gott
für mich föchte,
den freundlichen Feind,
wie fände ich ihn?
Wie schüf' ich den Freien,
den nie ich schirmte,
der in eig'nem Trotze
der Trauteste mir?
Wie macht' ich den Andren,
der nicht mehr ich,
und aus sich wirkte,
was ich nur will?—
O göttliche Noth!
Grässliche Schmach!
Zum Ekel find' ich
ewig nur mich
in Allem, was ich erwirke!

**WOTAN:** There's more behind—
Hear me and heed—
Whereof the Wala has warned!—
It is Alberich's host
Comes to undo us:
The Nibelung's hate
Rankles and threatens.
Yet have I no fear
Of his dark and grim forces—
With my heroes, I'd be the victor
But should he the ring recover
I ravished—
Then were Walhall lost forever.
He who cursed all loving,
He alone,
Dreams of using
Its runes to compass
The shameful ruin
Set for the gods.
He seeks to steal
My heroes away:
My boldest warriors
Fain he would win.
And with their might
He'd master even me.
Soon a scheme I devised
To wrest the ring from his clutches.
The giant Fafner,
Once I had paid to raise Walhall
With accursed gold
Now the treasure he guards
For which he had slain his brother.
The ring must be wrested from him
That he'd earned with his valor.
But with him I am leagued,
Nor could I attack him;
Strike though I would,
My stroke were in vain.
These are the fetters
That enchain me:
I who had fashioned the snare,
Now am caught and held in the toils.
Yet one might venture
Where I am weak:
A hero whom I
Never had aided;
Whom never with favors
Gods had enchained,
All unurged,
Bound by no bond,
Himself to save,
With his own strong sword
Surely could dare
What I dare not do,
What never by word I'd willed,
Warm though my wish might have been
Who, opposing the god,
Should yet help him,
A friend, though a foe—
Ah, where does he hide?
How fashion the freeman
Whom I never shielded,
Who, a seeming rebel,
Were dearest to me?
How could I create him
Who'd not be I,
And yet were willing
To work my will?
O shame on the gods!
Sorrow and shame!
To mock me always,
Only I find
Myself in all I am planning!

Das And're, das ich ersehne,
das And're erseh' ich nie;
denn selbst muss der Freie sich
schaffen—
Knechte erknet' ich mir nur!

**BRUENNHILDE:** Doch der
Wälsung, Siegmund?
wirkt er nicht selbst?

**WOTAN:** Wild durchschweift' ich
mit ihm die Wälder;
gegen der Götter Rath
reizte kühn ich ihn auf—
gegen der Götter Rache
schützt ihn nun einzig das Schwert,
das eines Gottes
Gunst ihm beschied—
Wie wollt' ich listig
selbst mich belügen?
So leicht ja entfrug mir
Fricka den Trug!
Zu tiefster Scham
durchschaute sie mich:
ihrem Willen muss ich gewähren!

**BRUENNHILDE:** So nimmst du von
Siegmund den Sieg?

**WOTAN:** (*in wildem Schmerz der
Verzweiflung ausbrechend*). Ich
berührte Alberich's Ring—
gierig hielt ich das Gold!
Der Fluch, den ich floh,
nicht flieht er nun mich:—
was ich liebe, muss ich verlassen,
morden, wen je ich minne,
trügend verrathen,
wer mir vertraut!—
Fahre denn hin,
herrische Pracht,
göttlichen Prunkes
prahlende Schmach!
Zusammen breche,
was ich gebaut!
Auf geb' ich mein Werk,
Nur eines will ich noch,
das Ende — —
das Ende! —
(*Er hält sinnend ein.*)
Und für das Ende
sorgt Alberich!—
jetzt versteh' ich
den stummen Sinn
des wilden Wortes der Wala:—
"Wenn der Liebe finstrer Feind
zürnend zeugt einen Sohn,
der Seligen Ende
säumt dann nicht!"—
Vom Niblung jüngst
vernahm ich die Mähr',
dass ein Weib der Zwerg bewältigt,
dess' Gunst Gold ihm erzwang.
Des Hasses Frucht
hegt eine Frau;
des Neides Kraft
kreiss't ihr im Schoosse:
das Wunder gelang
dem Liebelosen:
doch der in Lieb' ich frei'te,
den Freien erlang' ich mir nicht!—
(*Grimmig.*)
So nimm meinen Segen,
Niblungen-Sohn!

The man for whom I am longing,
That hero I never shall see;
For freemen themselves must give
life to—
All my creatures would be slaves!

**BRÜNNHILDE:** But the Wälsung,
Siegmund?
Is he not free?

**WOTAN:** Once, together
We roamed the forest;
Ever against the gods
He strove as was my advice.
Now from the wrathful goddess
Nothing shelters him but the
sword—
And that my favor
Sent in his need.
For all my cunning
Could not conceal it—So easily
Fricka
Found out the lie.
She read me through
And filled me with shame:
Though I would, I could not resist
her!

**BRÜNNHILDE:** So Siegmund is
doomed to defeat?

**WOTAN:** (*In a frenzy of despair.*)
I have handled Alberich's ring—
Grasped with greed at the gold!
The curse that I fled
Now clings to me:—
What I love, perforce I abandon,
Slay, when I'd fain be saving:
Traitor I turn
To him who trusts!—
Farewell,
Lordship and pride,
Godhead and glory
Buried in shame!
So now must perish
All I had wrought!
Farewell to my work
Soon will my pomp and I
Be ended— —
Be ended!—
(*Pauses in meditation.*)
And it will be ended
By Alberich!—
Now I fathom
What once had hid
The whirling words of the Wala:—
'When the grimmest foe of love,
Fiercely fathers a son,
The gods immortal
Near their end!'
A wondrous tale
I've heard of the Dwarf
Who had won a greedy woman,
With gold blinding her eyes.
The fruit of hate
Soon shall be seen;
The envious germ
Bursts into life:
The wonder was wrought
By loveless lovers:
But I, who loved so fondly,
The freeman I never can see!—
(*Grimly.*)
Then take my blessing,
Nibelung-born!
My shame and sorrow

Was tief mich ekelt,
dir geb' ich's zum Erbe,
der Gottheit nichtigen Glanz;
zernage ihn gierig dein Neid!

**BRUENNHILDE:** (*erschrocken*).
O sag', künde!
Was soll nun dein Kind?

**WOTAN:** (*bitter*). Fromm streite
für Fricka,
hüte ihr Eh' und Eid'!
Was sie erkor,
das kiese auch ich.
Was frommte mir eig'ner Wille?
Einen Freien kann ich nicht
wollen—
für Fricka's Knechte
kämpfe nun du!

**BRUENNHILDE:** Weh! nimm reuig
zurück das Wort!
Du liebst Siegmund:
dir zu Lieb'—
ich weiss es—schütz' ich den
Wälsung

**WOTAN:** Fällen sollst du Siegmund,
für Hunding erfechten den Sieg!
Hüte dich wohl!
und halte dich stark;
all deiner Kühnheit
entbiete im Kampf:
ein Sieg-Schwert
schwingt Siegmund—
schwerlich fällt er dir feig.

**BRUENNHILDE:** Den du zu lieben
stets mich gelehrt,
der in hehrer Tugend
dem Herzen dir theuer—
gegen ihn zwingt mich nimmer
dein zwiespältig Wort.

**WOTAN:** Ha, Freche, du!
frevelst du mir?
Wer bist du, als meines Willens
blind wählende Kür?—
da mit dir ich tagte,
sank ich so tief,
dass zum Schimpf der eig'nen
Geschöpfe ich ward?
Kennst du Kind, meinen Zorn?
Verzage dein Muth,
wenn je zermalmend
auf dich stürzte sein Strahl!
In meinem Busen
berg' ich den Grimm,
der in Grau'n und Wust
wirft eine Welt,
die einst zur Lust mir gelacht:—
wehe dem, den er trifft!
Trauer schüf' ihm sein Trotz!—
Drum rath' ich dir,
reize mich nicht;
besorge was ich befahl:—
Siegmund falle!
Dies sei der Walküre Werk.
(*Er stürmt fort, und verschwindet
schnell links im Gebirge.*)

**BRUENNHILDE:** (*Steht lange
betäubt und erschrocken.*) So—
sah ich
Siegvater nie,
erzürnt' ihn sonst wohl auch ein

I gladly will give you.
My godship's meaningless might
Your malice may have when it will!

**BRÜNNHILDE:** (*In terror.*) O
speak quickly—
What must I then do?

**WOTAN:** (*Bitterly.*) Go! Fight for
Fricka,
See to her wedding vows!
As she has chosen,
I, also, must choose.
What good were now all my will-
ing?
With my will I never made a free-
man—
For Fricka's bondsmen
Battle now do!

**BRÜNNHILDE:** Woe! My father,
Call back your words!
Do you love Siegmund?
Then for you—
For your sake—I shield the
Wälsung!

**WOTAN:**
You shall slaughter Siegmund;
It is Hunding must win in the fray!
Watch yourself well—
Do not waste your strength;
All of your prowess
You'll need in the fight:
Siegmund swings a strong sword—
Surely he will be brave.

**BRÜNNHILDE:** You have taught
me
Always to love him,
Whom in holy honor
Your heart has long cherished—
Foe to him makes me never
Your double-edg'd sword.

**WOTAN:** Ha! Brazen maid,
Do you dare brave me?
What are you, if not the willing,
Blind tool of my power?
When I gave you being
I sank so low
That my own creation
Can mock me to scorn?
Do you dread not, daughter, my
wrath?
Less hardy you were
If ever its flashes
Should seek to destroy you!
Within my bosom
Rages such wrath
As would wreck and lay
Waste a whole world,
That once my heart did delight!
Woe to him whom it strikes!
Long his rashness he'd rue!—
So take heed
Rouse not my wrath;
But do what Wotan bids—
Slay Siegmund!—
That be the Walkyrie's work.
(*He hurries away and vanishes in
the mountains to the left.*)

**BRÜNNHILDE:** (*Stands for some
time as if stunned and terrified.*)
So—Wotan
Never did I see,
Though swiftly his wrongs he'd re-

Zank!
*(Sie neigt sich betrübt und nimmt ihre Waffen auf, mit denen sie sich wieder rüstet.)*
Schwer wiegt mir
der Waffen Wucht:—
wenn nach Lust ich focht,
wie waren sie leicht!—
Zu böser Schlacht
schleich' ich heut' so bang!—
*(Sie sinnt, und seufzt dann auf.)*
Weh', mein Wälsung!
Im höchsten Leid
muss dich treulos die Treue verlassen!
*(Sie wendet sich nach hinten, und gewahrt Siegmund und Sieglinde, wie sie aus der Schlucht heraufsteigen: sie betrachtet die Nahenden einen Augenblick und wendet sich dann in die Höhle zu ihrem Ross, so dass sie dem Zuschauer gänzlich verschwindet.)*
*(Siegmund und Sieglinde treten auf. Sie schreitet hastig voraus; er sucht sie aufzuhalten.)*

SIEGMUND: Raste nun hier:
gönne dir Ruh'!

SIEGLINDE: Weiter! weiter!

SIEGMUND: *(umfasst sie mit sanfter Gewalt)*. Nicht weiter nun!
Verweile, süssestes Weib!—
Aus Wonne-Entzücken
zucktest du auf,
mit jäher Hast
jagtest du fort;
kaum folgt' ich der wilden Flucht:
durch Wald und Flur,
über Fels und Stein,
sprachlos schweigend
sprangst du dahin;
kein Ruf hielt dich zur Rast.
*(Sie starrt wild vor sich hin.)*
Ruhe nun aus:
rede zu mir!
Ende des Schweigens Angst!
Sieh, dein Bruder
hält seine Braut:
Siegmund ist dir Gesell'!
*(Er hat sie unvermerkt nach dem Steinsitze geleitet.)*

SIEGLINDE: *(blickt Siegmund mit wachsendem Entzücken in die Augen; dann umschlingt sie leidenschaftlich seinen Hals. Endlich fährt sie mit jähem Schreck auf während Siegmund sie heftig fasst)*. Hinweg! Hinweg!
flieh' die Entweihte!
Unheilig
umfängt dich ihr Arm;
entehrt, geschändet
schwand dieser Leib:
flieh' die Leiche,
lasse sie los!
der Wind mag sie verweh'n,
die ehrlos dem Edlen sich gab!—

Da er sie liebend umfing,
da seligste Lust sie fand,
da ganz sie minnte der Mann,
der ganz ihr Minne geweckt—

sent!
*(She stoops mournfully and picks up her weapons, with which she again arms herself.)*
Down weighs me
My weapons' weight:—
Yet how light they seemed
When willingly borne!—
With heavy heart
Shall I fight today!
*(She ponders and sighs.)*
Woe! My Wälsung!
In sorest need
Must I falsely abandon the faithful!
*(She moves towards the background and sees Siegmund and Sieglinde as they ascend from the ravine. She watches them for a moment and then re-enters the cave in which she has left her steed, so that she is quite hidden from the spectators.)*
*(Siegmund and Sieglinde enter. She advances hastily. He tries to stop her.)*

SIEGMUND: Rest awhile:
Here there is peace!

SIEGLINDE: Onward! Onward!

SIEGMUND: *(Putting his arm round her, firmly but tenderly.)*
No further now!
Ah, stay, sweetest of wives!—
You run from our rapture,
Run from our joy,
With rushing haste,
Torn yourself free;
Scarce could I keep pace with you
Through wood and plain,
Over rock and hill,
Speechless, silent,
You fled away;
My call checked not your flight
*(She stares wildly into vacancy.)*
Rest now, sweet:
Speak just one word,
Ending this dumb dismay!
See, your brother
Clings to his bride:
Siegmund now is your mate!
*(Meanwhile he has quietly led her to a rocky seat.)*

SIEGLINDE: *(Looks at Siegmund with growing rapture and throws her arms passionately round his neck. Then she suddenly starts up in terror, while Siegmund tries to hold her.)* Away! Away!
Shun my dishonor!
Unholy's
The clasp of my arms
Defiled, dishonored,
Let me be dead!
Flee this body,
Leave me, I'm lost!
O winds, sweep her from here
Who basely beguiled the hero!—

Because he held her so dear,
And filled her with rare rapture,
Till all her heart was the man's,
Whose love did awaken her heart.
In her joy—in her sweetest,

vor der süssesten Wonne
heiligster Weihe,
die ganz ihr Sinn
und Seele durchdrang,
Grauen und Schauder
ob grässlichster Schande
musste mit Schreck
die Schmähliche fassen,
die je dem Manne gehorcht,
der ohne Minne sie hielt!—
Lass' die Verfluchte,
lass' sie dich flieh'n!
Verworfen bin ich,
der Würde bar!
Dir reinstem Manne
muss ich entrinnen;
dir herrlichem darf ich
nimmer gehören:
Schande bring' ich dem Bruder,
Schmach dem freienden Freund.

SIEGMUND: Was je Schande dir schuf,
das büsst nun des Frevlers Blut!
Drum fliehe nicht weiter;
harre des Feindes;
hier—soll er mir fallen:
wenn Nothung ihm
das Herz zernagt.
Rache dann hast du erreicht.

SIEGLINDE: *(schrickt auf und lauscht)*. Horch! die Hörner—
hörst du den Ruf?—
Ringsher tönt
wüthend Getös';
aus Wald und Gau
gellt es herauf.
Hunding erwachte
aus hartem Schlaf;
Sippen und Hunde
ruft er zusammen;
muthig gehetzt
heult die Meute,
wild bellt sie zum Himmel
um der Ehe gebrochenen Eid!
*(Sie lacht wie wahnsinnig auf:— dann schrickt sie ängstlich zusammen.)*
Wo bist du, Siegmund?
seh' ich dich noch?
brünstig geliebter
leuchtender Bruder!
Deines Auges Stern
lass' noch einmal mir strahlen:
wehre dem Kuss
des verworf'nen Weibes nicht!—
Horch! o Horch!
das ist Hunding's Horn!
Seine Meute naht
mir mächt'ger Wehr.
Kein Schwert frommt
vor der Hunde Schwall:—
wirf es fort, Siegmund!—
Siegmund—wo bist du?—
Ha dort—ich sehe dich—
schrecklich Gesicht!—
Rüden fletschen
die Zähne nach Fleisch;
sie achten nicht
deines edlen Blick's;
bei den Füssen packt dich
das feste Gebiss—
du fällst—
in Stücken zerstaucht das Schwert:—
die Esche stürzt—

Holiest bliss, as
Her soul and sense
were drown'd in passion,
Sudden a shudder
Of shame and of terror
Came with a shock
To shatter the sinner
Who once a husband had known
Unloved, unloving, and bound!—
Leave her, accursed,
Leave her to flee!
An outcast am I,
Of honor shorn!
Your purer passion
Must be denied me;
Your bride, o my dear one,
Never should you name me:
Shame I'd bring to the brother,
Scorn and woe to the friend!

SIEGMUND: For the shame you have seen,
The blood of your foe shall pay!
So flee no further;
Wait for his coming;
Here—surely I'll slay him
When Nothung once
Shall gnaw his heart,
Vengeance shall surely be yours!

SIEGLINDE: *(Starts up and listens.)* Hark! He calls you!—
Do you hear the horns?—
Round and round
Fiercely they blare;
Through wood and vale
Wilder they ring.
Hunding has awakened,
He sleeps no more;
Kinsmen and bloodhounds
Come as he calls them:
Maddened with hate
Come the hunters,
Howl loudly to heaven
To avenge the offense to one wed!
*(She laughs wildly, and then shudders.)*
Where are you, Siegmund?
Are you still here?
Hotly beloved
Beacon and brother!
Shall your starlit eyes
Never more, then, delight me?
Spurn not the kiss
Of the outcast one, your bride!—
Hark! o hark!
That is Hunding's horn!
And his host draws near
With hateful might.
No sword serves
Where yon hounds give tongue:—
Cast it down, Siegmund!—
Siegmund—where are you?—
Ah, look!—I see you there—
Dreadful the sight!—
Dogs are gnashing
Their ravening fangs;
No heed they pay
To your fiery glance;
Now your feet they seize in
Their pitiless maws—
You fall!—
In splinters now lies your sword:—
The ash—it falls!—
The trunk is ripped apart!
Brother! o brother!

es bricht der Stamm!—
Bruder! mein Bruder!
Siegmund!—ha!—
(*Sie sinkt mit einem Schrei ohn-
mächtig in Siegmund's Arme.*)

SIEGMUND: Schwester! Geliebte!
(*Er lauscht ihrem Athem und
überzeugt sich, dass sie noch lebe.
Er lässt sie an sich herabgleiten,
so dass sie, als er sich selbst zum
Sitze niederlässt, mit ihrem Haupt
auf sienem Schooss zu ruhen
kommt. In dieser Stellung verbleiben beide bis zum Schlusse des folgenden Auftrittes.
Langes Schweigen, während dessen Siegmund mit zärtlicher
Sorge über Sieglinde sich hin-
neigt, und mit einem langen
Kusse ihr die Stirn küsst.—
Bruennhilde ist, ihr Ross am
Zaume geleitend aus der Höhle
langsam und feierlich nach
vornen geschritten und hält nun,
Siegmund zur Seite, in geringer
Entfernung von ihm. Sie trägt
Schild und Speer in der einen
Hand, lehnt sich mit der andren
an den Hals des Rosses und betrachtet so, in ernstem Schweigen,
eine Zeit lang Siegmund.*)

BRUENNHILDE: Siegmund—
Sieh' auf mich!
Ich—bin's,
der bald du folgst.

SIEGMUND: (*richtet den Blick zu
ihr auf*).
Wer bist du, sag',
die so schön und ernst mir
erscheint?

BRUENNHILDE: Nur
Todgeweihten
taugt mein Anblick:
wer mich erschaut,
der scheidet vom Lebens-Licht.
Auf der Walstatt allein
erschein' ich Edlen:
wer mich gewahrt,
zur Wal kor ich ihn mir.

SIEGMUND: (*blickt ihr lange in
das Auge, senkt dann sinnend das
Haupt und wendet sich endlich
mit feierlichem Ernste wieder zu
ihr*). Der dir nun folgt,
wohin führst du den Helden?

BRUENNHILDE: Zu Walvater,
der dich gewählt,
führ' ich dich:
nach Walhall folgst du mir.

SIEGMUND: In Walhall's Saal
Walvater find' ich allein?

BRUENNHILDE: Gefall'ner
Helden
hehre Schaar
umfängt dich hold
mit hoch-heiligem Gruss.

SIEGMUND: Fänd' ich in Walhall
Wälse, den eig'nen Vater?

BRUENNHILDE: Den Vater findet
der Wälsung dort.

Siegmund!—Ah! (*She gives a
shriek and falls senseless into Siegmund's arms.*)

SIEGMUND: Sister! Beloved!
(*He listens to her breathing, and
convinces himself that she still
lives. He lowers her gently, seats
himself, and rests her head on his
knee. In this position they remain
till the end of the next scene.
A long pause follows, while Siegmund bends tenderly over Sieglinde, and impresses a long kiss
on her brow.
Meanwhile Brünnhilde, leading
her steed by the bridle, enters
slowly from the cave and advances solemnly. On nearing Siegmund, she halts. In one hand she
holds her shield and spear. With
the other she caresses the neck of
her steed. For some time she remains in this attitude, silently
and earnestly observing Siegmund.*)

BRÜNNHILDE: Siegmund—
Look at me!
I—wait.
Your hour draws near.

SIEGMUND: (*Looking at her.*)
Who are you?—speak.
You are fair, though you seem
stern.

BRÜNNHILDE: The doomed, they
only
Know my glances:
Who beholds me
Must part with the light of life.
On the death-field alone
I come to heroes:
Him whom I meet,
I bear away to death.

SIEGMUND: (*Looks at her fixedly,
bends his head as if reflecting, and
turns solemnly to her again.*)
When you call,
To what goal ride the heroes?

BRÜNNHILDE: The War-Father,
Who you did choose,
Waits for you:
To Walhall.

SIEGMUND: In Walhall's hall
Lives the War-Lord alone?

BRÜNNHILDE: Of fallen heroes
Mighty hosts
Shall throng to greet you,
And bid you all-hail.

SIEGMUND: Lives there in Walhall
Wälse, my own dear father?

BRÜNNHILDE: The Wälsung's father
Shall there be found.

SIEGMUND: Grüsst mich in Walhall
froh eine Frau?

BRUENNHILDE: Wunschmädchen
walten dort hehr:
Wotan's Tochter
reicht dir traulich den Trank.

SIEGMUND: Hehr bist du:
und heilig gewahr' ich
das Wotanskind:
doch Eines sag' mir, du Ew'ge!
Begleitet den Bruder
die bräutliche Schwester?
umfängt Siegmund
Sieglinde dort?

BRUENNHILDE: Erdenluft
muss sie noch athmen:
Sieglinde
sieht Siegmund dort nicht!

SIEGMUND: So grüsse mir Walhall,
grüsse mir Wotan,
grüsse mir Wälse
und alle Helden—
grüss' auch die holden
Wunsches-Mädchen:
zu ihnen folg' ich dir nicht.

BRUENNHILDE: Du sahest der
Walküre
sehrenden Blick:
mit ihr musst du nun zieh'n!

SIEGMUND: Wo Sieglinde lebt
in Lust und Leid,
da will Siegmund auch säumen:
noch machte dein Blick
nicht mich erbleichen:
vom Bleiben zwingt er mich nie!

BRUENNHILDE: So lang' du lebst
zwäng' dich wohl nichts;
doch zwingt dich Thoren der
Tod:—
ihn dir zu künden
kam ich her.

SIEGMUND: Wo wäre der Held,
dem heut' ich fiel?

BRUENNHILDE: Hunding fällt
dich im Streit.

SIEGMUND: Mit stärk'rem drohe
als Hunding's Streichen!
Lauerst du hier
lüstern auf Wal,
jenen kiese zum Fang:
ich denk' ihn zu fällen im Kampf

BRUENNHILDE: (*den Kopf
schüttelnd*). Dir, Wälsung—
höre mich wohl!—
dir ward das Loos gekies't.

SIEGMUND: Kennst du dies
Schwert?
Der mir es schuf,
beschied mir Sieg:
deinem Drohen trotz' ich mit ihm!

BRUENNHILDE: (*mit stark erhobener Stimme*). Der dir es schuf,
beschied dir jetzt Tod:
seine Tugend nimmt er dem
Schwert!

SIEGMUND: Shall no sweet woman
Wait in the hall?

BRÜNNHILDE: Dream-maidens
are there
Many
Wotan's daughter shall fill.
Your beaker.

SIEGMUND: High are you,
And holy I know you
Wotan's child.
Tell me one thing, goddess!
Shall she who is sister
Be bride to the brother?
Shall I, Siegmund, woo
Sieglinde?

BRÜNNHILDE: Earthly air
Here she'll be breathing:
Sieglinde
Shall not see Siegmund!

SIEGMUND: Then greet for me
Walhall,
Greet for me Wotan,
Greet for me Wälse
And all the heroes—
Greet the blessed
Beauteous maidens:
To them I go not with you!

BRÜNNHILDE: You've seen the
Walkyrie's
Withering glance:
Thou need'st must when she bids!

SIEGMUND: Where Sieglinde lives
In joy or pain,
There will Siegmund still linger:
Your look has not chilled
My heart with terror
It shall not tear us apart!

BRÜNNHILDE: While life shall
last,
Have you your way;
But yield you must to dark
Death:—
To hail his coming,
Came I here.

SIEGMUND: Then whose is the
hand
Shall lay me low?

BRÜNNHILDE: Hunding's prey
you shall be.

SIEGMUND: I scorn the menace
Of Hunding's malice!
Lurk, and you will,
Lusting for death,
Take him for your prey—
I shall slay him to-day.

BRÜNNHILDE: (*Shaking her
head.*) No, Wälsung!—
Heed my voice!—
You have been doomed to die!

SIEGMUND: Do you know this
sword?
He who wrought it
Shall make me win:
With this steel I can brave your
threats!

BRÜNNHILDE: (*Raising her
voice.*) He who wrought it
Now dooms you to death:
For he robs the sword of its spell!

SIEGMUND: (*heftig*). Schweig'
und schrecke
die Schlummernde nicht!—
(*er beugt sich, mit
hervorbrechendem Schmerz
zärtlich über Sieglinde.*)
Weh! Weh!
süssestes Weib!
Du traurigste aller Getreuen!
Gegen dich wüthet
in Waffen die Welt:
und ich, dem du einzig vertraut,
für den du ihr einzig getrotzt—
mit meinem Schutz
nicht soll ich dich schirmen,
die Kühne verrathen im Kampf?—
O Schande ihm,
der das Schwert mir schuf,
beschied er mir Schimpf für Sieg!
Muss ich denn fallen,
nicht fahr' ich nach Walhall—
Hella halte mich fest!

BRUENNHILDE: (*erschüttert*). So
wenig achtest du
ewige Wonne?
Alles wär' dir
das arme Weib,
das müd' und harmvoll
matt auf dem Schoosse dir hängt!
Nichts sonst hieltest du hehr?

SIEGMUND: (*bitter zu ihr aufblickend*). So jung und schön er-
schimmerst du mir:
doch wie kalt und hart
kennt dich mein Herz!—
Kannst du nur höhnen,
so hebe dich fort,
du arge, fühllose Maid!
doch musst du dich weiden
an meinem Weh',
mein Leiden letze dich denn;
meine Noth labe
dein neidvolles Herz:—
nur von Walhall's spröden Wonnen
sprich du wahrlich mir nicht!

BRUENNHILDE: (*mit wachsender
Ergriffenheit*). Ich sehe die Noth,
die das Herz dir zernagt;
ich fühle des Helden
heiligen Harm!—
Siegmund, befiehl mir dein Weib;
mein Schutz umfange sie fest!

SIEGMUND: Kein andrer als ich
soll die Reine lebend berühren:
verfiel ich dem Tod,
die Betäubte tödt' ich zuvor!

BRUENNHILDE: Wälsung! Rasender!
Hör' meinen Rath:
befiehl mir dein Weib
um des Pfandes willen,
das wonnig von dir es empfing!

SIEGMUND: (*sein Schwert
ziehend*). Diess Schwert—
das dem Treuen ein Trugvoller
schuf;
diess Schwert—
das feig vor dem Feind mich verräth:—
frommt es nicht gegen den Feind,

SIEGMUND: (*Angered.*) Peace!
Disturb not
My slumbering bride!
(*He bends tenderly and with an-
guish over Sieglinde.*)
Woe! Woe!
Sweetest of wives!
You sad woman, and true
Round you now
Rages in arms a whole world!
And I, whom alone you trusted,
For whom you the world has fors-
worn,
I may not shield
Nor serve you, as shelter?
The brave am I doomed to betray?
O shame on him
Who the sword once wrought,
And makes me a mark for scorn!
Should I be vanquished,
I ride not to Walhall—
Hella's prey I will be!

BRÜNNHILDE: (*Agitated.*) So car-
eless are you
Of heavenly rapture?
One weak woman
To you is all,
Who, worn and weary,
Hangs on your knee for her rest!
Do you hold nothing else dear?

SIEGMUND: (*Looking up at her
bitterly.*) So young and fair
On me you do shine!
Yet so cold and hard
Now knows my heart!—
Must you go mocking,
Most cruel of maids?
Then go and leave me alone!
But when you have sated
Yourself with woe,
On sorrow feasted your eyes;
Though your heart glow at
The sight of my pain:—
When you paint Walhall's plea-
sures,
All your pleading you'll waste!

BRÜNNHILDE: (*With growing
emotion.*) The pain I behold
That your heart weighs down;
I feel all the hero's
Woe and dismay
Siegmund, trust me with your wife;
My shield shall be her shelter!

SIEGMUND: No being but I,
While she lives, shall dare to ap-
proach her:
And though I be doomed,
Before she awake, I will slay my
bride!

BRÜNNHILDE: Wälsung! Reckless
one!
Heed my advice!
Entrust her to me,
For a pledge she brings you
Of rapture and love you have given!

SIEGMUND: (*Drawing his
sword.*) This sword—
That a traitor wrought for one true;
This sword—
That soon shall undo its master;
Faithless when fronting the foe,
Shall faithfully strike at the friend!
(*Turning the sword against Sieg-

so fromm' es denn wider den
Freund!—
(*Das Schwert auf Sieglinde
zückend.*)
Zwei Leben
lachen dir hier:—
nimm sie, Nothung,
neidischer Stahl!
nimm sie mit einem Streich!

BRUENNHILDE: (*im heftigsten
Sturme des Mitgefühls*). Halt' ein,
Wälsung!
höre mein Wort!
Sieglinde lebe—
und Siegmund lebe mit ihr!
Beschlossen ist's;
das Schlachtloos wend' ich;
dir, Siegmund,
schaff' ich Segen und Sieg!
(*Man hört aus dem fernen Hintergrunde Hornrufe erschallen.*)
Hörst du den Ruf?
Nun rüste dich, Held!
Traue dem Schwert
und schwing' es getrost:
treu hält dir die Wehr,
wie die Walküre treu dich
schützt!—
Leb' wohl, Siegmund,
seligster Held!
auf der Walstatt grüss' ich dich
wieder!
(*Sie stürmt fort und verschwindet
mit dem Rosse rechts in einer Seitenschlucht. Siegmund blickt ihr
freudig und erhoben nach.
Die Bühne hat sich allmälig verfinstert; schwere Gewitterwolken
senken sich auf den Hintergrund
herab und hüllen die Gebirgs-
wände, die Schlucht und das
erhöhte Bergjoch nach und nach
gänzlich ein.— Von allen Seiten
lassen sich aus der Ferne Rufe von
Heerhörnern vernehmen, die
während des Folgenden allmälig
näher erschallen.*)

SIEGMUND: (*über Sieglinde sich
beugend*). Zauberfest
bezähmt ein Schlaf
der Holden Schmerz und Harm:
da die Walküre zu mir trat,
schuf sie ihr den wonnigen Trost?
Sollte die grimmige Wal
nicht schrecken ein gramvolles
Weib?
Leblos scheint sie,
die dennoch lebt:
der Traurigen kos't
ein lächelnder Traum.—
(*Neue Hornrufe.*)
So schlumm're nun fort,
bis die Schlacht gekämpft,
und Friede dich erfreu'!
(*Er legt sich sanft auf den Steinsitz, küsst ihr die Stirn und bricht
dann, nach abermaligen Horn-
rufen auf.*)
Der dort mich ruft,
rüste dich nun;
was ihm gebührt,
biet' ich ihm:
Nothung zahl' ihm den Zoll!

linde.*)
Two lives lie
Here at your call:—
Take them, Nothung,
Traitorous steel!
Take them at one fell stroke!

BRÜNNHILDE: (*Stirred to the
depths by sympathy.*) Forbear,
Wälsung!
Hear my words!
I bring life to Sieglinde—
And life to Siegmund!
It is sworn and done;
Your sword shall conquer:
You, Siegmund,
Victor soon shall be hailed!
(*The faint sound of horns is heard
in the background.*)
Do you hear the call?
Now, hero, to arms!
Trust to your sword
And wield it right well:
True still be your blade,
As the Walkyr, your true, sure
shield!—
Farewell, Siegmund,
Bravest of all!
On the field will I give you greet-
ing!
(*She rushes off with her steed, by
way of a ravine on the right. Sieg-
mund follows her with his eyes,
and seems elated with joy. The
stage, meanwhile, has gradually
grown dark. Heavy thunderclouds have descended in the
background, hiding the hills, the
ravine and the lofty rocks in the
foreground. Distant sounds of
horns are heard on all sides, and
continue to be heard throughout
the following scene. Gradually
they grow louder.*)

SIEGMUND: (*Bending over Sieg-
linde.*) Locked in sleep.
Her lovely eyes are blind.
To pain and woe.
Did the Walkyr, with magic art,
Bring her this most merciful rest?
Was the wild fury of war
Not fated her heart to affright?
Lifeless seeming,
She clings to life:
Her sorrow is stilled,
And smiling she dreams.—
Then slumber in peace,
Till the strife is over,
And all peril is past!
(*He lays her gently on the rocky
seat, kisses her on the brow, and,
after the horns have again been
heard, makes ready to go.*)
Let him who calls
Arm for the fight;
What he demands
Soon he'll find:
Nothung now he shall know!
(*He hurries towards the back-
ground and disappears beyond

# Act II

(*Er eilt dem Hintergrunde zu, und verschwindet auf dem Joche sogleich in finstres Gewitterge-wölk.*)

(*the rocky arch, which is instantly hidden by dark thunderclouds.*)

SIEGLINDE: (*träumend*). Kehrte der Vater nun heim!
Mit dem Knaben noch weilt er im Forst.
Mutter! Mutter!
mir bangt der Muth:—
nicht freund und friedlich
scheinen die Fremden!—
Schwarze Dämpfe—
schwüles Gedünst—
feurige Lohe
leckt schon nach uns—
es brennt das Haus—
zu Hülfe, Bruder!
Siegmund! Siegmund!
(*Starke Blitze zucken durch das Gewölk auf; ein furchtbarer Don-nerschlag erweckt Sieglinde: sie springt jäh auf.*)
Siegmund!—Ha!
(*Sie starrt mit steigender Angst um sich her;—fast die ganze Bühne ist in schwarze Gewitter-wolken verhüllt; fortwährender Blitz und Donner. Von allen Seit-en dringen immer näher Horn-rufe her.*)

SIEGLINDE: (*Dreaming.*) Would that my father were home!
With his boy he still roams in the woods.
Mother! Mother!
I'm filled with dread:—
How stern and solemn
Seem all these strangers!—
Smoke and darkness—
Sulphurous fumes—
Roaring and leaping,
Follow the flames—
The house—it burns—
O help me, brother!
Siegmund! Siegmund!
(*Vivid lightnings flash from the clouds. A terrible thunderbolt wakes Sieglinde. She leaps to her feet in alarm.*)
Siegmund! Ah!
(*She stares in all directions with growing terror. The stage is al-most entirely wrapped in dark clouds. Thunder and lightning. Horns are heard calling on all sides, and growing louder.*)

HUNDING'S: (*Stimme im Hinter-grunde, vom Bergjoche her*). Weh-walt! Wehwalt!
Steh' mir zum Streit,
sollen dich Hunde nicht halten!

HUNDING'S VOICE: (*Heard from the rocky arch in the back-ground.*) Woeful! Woeful!
Stand and give fight—
See where the hounds would dev-our you!

SIEGMUND'S: (*Stimme, von weit-er hinten her, aus der Schlucht*).
Wo birgst du dich,
dass ich vorbei dir schoss?
Steh' dort, dass ich dich stelle!

SIEGMUND'S VOICE: (*Heard more in the distance from the ra-vine.*) Where are you hiding?
How did I miss you, hound?
Stand, let me but face you!

SIEGLINDE: (*die in furchtbarer Aufregung lauscht*). Hunding—
Siegmund—
könnt' ich sie sehen!

SIEGLINDE: (*Listening, horror struck.*) Hunding—Siegmund—
Could I but see them!

HUNDING'S: (*Stimme*). Hieher,
du frevelnder Freier!
Fricka fälle dich hier!

HUNDING'S VOICE: This way, you lecherous lover:
Fricka waits for you here!

SIEGMUND'S: (*Stimme, nun ebenfalls auf dem Bergjoche*).
Noch wähnst du mich waffenlos,
feiger Wicht?
Drohst du mit Frauen,
so ficht nun selber,
sonst lässt dich Fricka im Stich!
Denn sieh: deines Hauses
heimischem Stamm
entzog ich zaglos das Schwert;
seine Schneide schmecke jetzt du!
(*Ein Blitz erhellt für einen Augen-blick den Bergjoch, auf welchem jetzt Hunding und Siegmund kämpfend gewahrt worden.*)

SIEGMUND'S VOICE: (*Now also heard from the rocky arch.*) Do you expect me to be a weaponless, cowardly warrior?
Bold but with women—
Now fight your fiercest—
Lest Fricka fails you in need!
For see: from the ashen
Tree in your home
Unstayed I stole my keen sword;
With its steel I'll slay you to-day.
(*A flash of lightning lights up the rocky arch for a moment. Hund-ing and Siegmund are seen fight-ing.*)

SIEGLINDE: (*mit höchster Kraft*).
Haltet ein, ihr Männer,
mordet erst mich!
(*Sie stürzt auf das Bergjoch zu: ein von rechts her über die Kämpfer ausbrechender heller Schein blendet sie aber plötzlich so heftig, dass sie wie erblindet*)

SIEGLINDE: (*At the top of her voice.*) Hold your hands, foemen!
Murder me first!
(*She rushes toward the rocks, but stops, blinded by a sudden and terrific flash that comes from the right. She totters. Brünnhilde ap-pears in the lightning, hovering*)

zur Seite schwankt. In dem Licht-glanze erscheint Bruennhilde über Siegmund schwebend und diesen mit dem Schilde deckend.*)

about Siegmund and protecting him with her shield.*)

BRUENNHILDE'S: (*Stimme*).
Triff' ihn, Siegmund!
Traue dem Schwert!
(*Als Siegmund so eben zu einem tödtlichen Streiche auf Hunding ausholt, bricht von links her ein glühend röthlicher Schein durch das Gewölk aus, in welchem Wotan erscheint, über Hunding stehend und seinen Speer Sieg-mund quer entgegenhaltend.*)

BRÜNNHILDE'S VOICE: Slay him, Siegmund!
Trust in your sword!
(*As Siegmund aims a deadly blow at Hunding, a reddish glow comes through the clouds at the left of the rocks, heralding Wotan, who stands above Hunding and points his spear at Siegmund.*)

WOTAN'S: (*Stimme*). Zurück vor dem Speer!
In Stücken das Schwert!
(*Bruennhilde ist vor Wotan mit dem Schilde erschrocken zurückgewichen: Siegmund's Schwert zerspringt an dem vor-gestreckten Speere; dem Unbe-wehrten stösst Hunding sein Schwert in die Brust, Siegmund stürzt zu Boden.—Sieglinde, die seinen Todesseufzer gehört, sinkt mit einem Schrei, wie leblos zu-sammen.
Mit Siegmund's Fall ist zugleich von beiden Seiten der glänzende Schein verschwunden; dichte Finsterniss ruht im Gewölk bis nach vorn; in ihm wird Bruenn-hilde undeutlich sichtbar, wie sie in jäher Hast Sieglinden sich zu-gewendet.*)

WOTAN'S VOICE: Back, back! from the spear!
Down, down! with your sword!
(*Brünnhilde, with her shield has recoiled in terror, at the approach of Wotan. Siegmund'S sword is shivered to pieces against the out-stretched spear. Hunding thrusts his sword into the breast of his de-fenseless foe. Siegmund falls. Sieg-linde, who has heard his dying groan, shrieks and falls sen-seless.*)
(*As Siegmund falls, the glow van-ishes and the lightning stops. Darkness enshrouds the scene. Brünnhilde is dimly visible as she hastens to the assistance of Sieg-linde.*)

BRUENNHILDE: Zu Ross, dass ich dich rette!
(*Sie hebt Sieglinde schnell zu sich auf ihr, der Seitenschlucht nahe stehendes Ross und verschwindet sogleich gänzlich mit ihr.
Alsbald zertheilt sich das Gewölk in der Mitte, so dass man deutlich Hunding gewahrt, wie er sein Schwert dem gefallenen Siegmund aus der Brust zieht.— Wotan, von Gewölk umgeben, steht hinter ihm auf einem Felsen, an seinen Speer gelehnt und schmerzlich auf Siegmund's Leiche blickend.*)

BRÜNNHILDE: To horse! and I will save you!
(*She lifts Sieglinde swiftly into the saddle as she hurries to her horse in the cave on the right, and both disappear.*)
(*Instantly the clouds roll back on either side, plainly disclosing Hunding, as he draws his sword from the breast of Siegmund. Wot-an, surrounded by clouds, stands behind him on a rock, leaning against his spear, and gazing sor-rowfully on Siegmund's body.*)

WOTAN: (*nach einem kleinen Schweigen, zu Hunding ge-wandt*). Geh' hin, Knecht!
Kniee vor Fricka:
meld' ihr, dass Wotan's Speer gerächt, was Spott ihr schuf.—
Geh'!—Geh'!—
(*Vor seinem verächtlichen Hand-wink sinkt Hunding todt zu Bo-den.*)

WOTAN: (*Turning to Hunding, after a brief pause.*) Away, slave!
Kneel to Fricka:
Tell her that Wotan's spear
Avenged what brought her shame.—
Go!—Go!— (*At a contemptuous gesture of Wotan's hand, Hund-ing falls dead.*)

WOTAN: (*plötzlich in furchtbar-er Wuth auffahrend*). Doch Brünnhilde—
weh' der Verbrecherin!
Furchtbar sei
die Freche gestraft,
erreicht mein Ross ihre Flucht!
(*Er verschwindet mit Blitz und Donner.—Der Vorhang fällt schnell.*)

WOTAN: (*Breaking suddenly into a fury of wrath.*) But Brünnhilde—
Woe to me who braves me!
Dread shall be
The fate she must know,
For Wotan rides in her wake! (*He vanishes thunder and lightning. Quick curtain.*)

# ■ DRITTER AUFZUG

*Auf dem Gipfel eines Felsberges.*

*Rechts begrenzt ein Tannenwald die Scene. Links der Eingang einer Felshöhle, die einen natürlichen Saal bildet: darüber steigt der Fels zu seiner höchsten Spitze auf. Nach hinten ist die Aussicht gänzlich frei; höhere und niedere Felssteine bilden den Rand vor dem Abhange, der—wie anzunehmen ist—nach dem Hintergrunde zu steil hinabführt.—Einzelne Wolkenzüge jagen, wie vom Sturm getrieben, am Felsensaume vorbei.*
*(Die Namen der acht Walküren, welche—ausser Bruennhilde—in dieser Scene auftreten, sind: Gerhilde, Ortlinde, Waltraute, Schwertleite, Helmwige, Siegrune, Grimgerde, Rossweisse.)*
*Gerhilde, Ortlinde, Waltraute und Schwertleite haben sich auf der Felsspitze, an und über der Höhle, gelagert; sie sind in voller Waffenrüstung.*

**GERHILDE:** (*zu höchst gelagert und dem Hintergrunde zugewendet*). Hojotoho! Hojotoho!
Heiaha! Heiaha!
Helmwige, hier!
Hieher mit dem Ross!
(*In einem vorbeiziehenden Gewölk bricht Blitzesglanz aus; eine Walküre zu Ross wird in ihm sichtbar; über ihrem Sattel hängt ein erschlagener Krieger.*)

**HELMWIGE'S:** (*Stimme, von aussen*). Hojotoho! Hojotoho!
Hojotoho! Hojotoho!

**GERHILDE, WALTRAUTE UND SCHWERTLEITE:** (*der Ankommenden entgegenrufend*). Heiaha!
(*Die Wolke mit der Erscheinung ist rechts hinter dem Tann verschwunden.*)

**ORTLINDE:** (*in den Tann hineinrufend*). Zu Ortlinde's Stute
stell' deinen Hengst:
mit meiner Grauen
gras't gern dein Brauner!

**WALTRAUTE:** (*ebenso*). Wer hängt dir im Sattel?

**HELMWIGE:** (*aus dem Tann schreitend*). Sintolt der Hegeling!

**SCHWERTLEITE:** Führ' deinen Braunen
fort von der Grauen:
Ortlinde's Mähre
trägt Wittig, den Irming!

**GERHILDE:** (*ist etwas näher herabgestiegen*). Als Feinde nur sah ich
Sintolt und Wittig.

# ■ ACT III

*The Summit of a Rocky Hill.*

*(To the right is a forest of fir-trees. To the left is the entrance to a cave which forms a natural hall. Above it rises the highest of the peaks. At the back, the view is uninterrupted. Rocks of various sizes form an embankment of the supposed precipice in the rear. Detached clouds, storm-swept, drift swiftly past the peak.*
*The names of the eight Walkyrs, exclusive of Brünnhilde, who appear, are: Gerhilde, Ortlinde, Waltraute, Schwertleite, Helmwige, Siegrune, Grimgerde, and Rossweisse.*
*Gerhilde, Ortlinde, Waltraute and Schwertleite are stationed on the peak near and above the cave. They are in full armor.*

**GERHILDE:** (*At the summit of the peak, with her face towards the back.*) Ho-yo-to ho! Ho-yo-to-ho!
Hi-ya-ha! Hi-ya-ha!
Helmwige, here!
Hurry here on your horse!
(*Lightning flashes from one of the clouds that drift by, revealing a mounted Walkyr. From her saddle-bow hangs a warrior, slain in fight.*)

**HELMWIGE'S VOICE:** (*Without.*) Ho-yo-to-ho! Ho-yo-to-ho!
Ho-yo-to-ho! Ho-yo-to-ho!
Hi-ya-ha!

**GERHILDE, WALTRAUTE AND SCHWERTLEITE:** (*Calling to the newcomer.*) Hi-ya-ha! Hi-ya-ha!
(*The cloud with the apparition has disappeared behind a fir-tree on the right.*)

**ORTLINDE:** (*Shouting in the direction of the fir-tree.*) In Ortlinde's stable
Tether your steed:
With my grey mare
Your bay was well mated!

**WALTRAUTE:** (*As above.*) Who hangs from your saddle?

**HELMWIGE:** (*Issuing from behind the fir-tree.*) Sintolt, the Hegeling!

**SCHWERTLEITE:** Do not stable your charger
with Ortlinde's:
Wittig, the Irming,
Her mare has been bearing!

**GERHILDE:** (*Descending a few steps.*) And foes were they always,
Your Sintolt and Wittig!

**ORTLINDE:** (*bricht schnell auf und läuft in den Tann*). Heiaha!
Heiaha! Die Stute
stösst mir der Hengst!

**SCHWERTLEITE UND GERHILDE:** (*lachen laut auf*). Der Recken Zwist
entzweit noch die Rosse!

**HELMWIGE:** (*in den Tann zurückrufend*). Ruhig dort, Brauner!
Brich nicht den Frieden!

**WALTRAUTE:** (*hat für Gerhilde die Wacht auf der äussersten Spitze genommen*). Hojoho! Hojoho!
Siegrune, hier!
Wo säumst du so lang?
(*Wie zuvor Helmwige, zieht jetzt Siegrune im gleichen Aufzuge vorbei, dem Tann zu.*)

**SIEGRUNE'S:** (*Stimme von rechts*). Arbeit gab's!
Sind die And'ren schon da?

**DIE WALKUEREN:** Hojotoho! Hojotoho!
Heiaha! Heiaha!
(*Siegrune ist hinter dem Tann verschwunden. Aus der Tiefe hört man zwei Stimmen zugleich.*)

**GRIMGERDE UND ROSSWEISSE:** (*von unten*). Hojotoho! Hojotoho!
Heiaha! Heiaha!

**WALTRAUTE:** Rossweiss' und Grimgerde!

**GERHILDE:** Sie reiten zu zwei.
(*Ortlinde ist mit Helmwige und der so eben angekommenen Siegrune aus dem Tann herausgetreten: zu drei winken sie von dem hinteren Felssaume hinab.*)

**ORTLINDE, HELMWIGE UND SIEGRUNE:** Gegrüsst, ihr Reissige! Rossweiss' und Grimgerde!

**DIE ANDREN WALKUEREN ALLE:** Hojotoho! Hojotoho!
Heiaha! Heiaha!
(*In einem blitzerglänzenden Wolkenzuge, der von unten heraufsteigt und dann hinter dem Tann verschwindet, erscheinen Grimgerde und Rossweisse, ebenfalls auf Rossen, jede einen Erschlagenen im Sattel führend.*)

**GERHILDE:** In Wald mit den Rossen
zu Rast und Weid'!

**ORTLINDE:** (*in den Tann rufend*). Führt die Mähren
fern von einander,
bis uns'rer Helden
Hass sich gelegt!

**HELMWIGE:** (*während die Andern lachen*). Der Helden Grimm
schon büsste die Graue!
(*Grimgerde und Rossweisse treten aus dem Tann auf.*)

**ORTLINDE:** (*Suddenly darting over to the fir-tree.*) Hi-ya-ha! Hi-ya-ha!
My beauty's locked with your bay!

**SCHWERTLEITE AND GERHILDE:** (*Laughing wildly.*) The heroes' wrongs
The horses remember!

**HELMWIGE:** (*Shouting back into the trees.*) Quiet, there, quiet!
Why would you quarrel?

**WALTRAUTE:** (*Who has taken the place of Gerhilde at the top of the peak.*) Ho-yo-ho! Ho-yo-ho!
Siegrune, here!
Why did you stay so long?
(*Siegrune rides by, as Helmwige did, in the direction of the fir-tree.*)

**SIEGRUNE'S VOICE:** (*From the right.*) Work to do!
Are the rest of you met?

**THE WALKYRS:** Ho-yo-to-ho! Ho-yo-to-ho!
Hi-ya-ha! Hi-ya-ha!
(*Siegrune has disappeared behind the firs. Two voices are heard together from the depths.*)

**GRIMGERDE AND ROSSWEISSE:** (*From below.*) Ho-yo-to-ho! Ho-yo-to-ho!
Hi-ya-ha! Hi-ya-ha!

**WALTRAUTE:** Rossweiss' and Grimgerde!

**GERHILDE:** They ride two by two.
(*Ortlinde, with Helmwige and Siegrune, has issued from the firs. All three wave their hands from the hindermost rocks.*)

**ORTLINDE, HELMWIGE AND SIEGRUNE:** We greet you, Rossweisse!
We greet you, Grimgerde!

**THE OTHER WALKYRS:** Ho-yo-to-ho! Ho-yo-to-ho!
Hi-ya-ha! Hi-ya-ha!
(*Grimgerde and Rossweisse, mounted, appear in a glowing thundercloud which ascends from the depths and vanishes behind the fir-tree. Each carries a slain warrior at her saddle-bow.*)

**GERHILDE:** Away with the horses,
To feed and rest!

**ORTLINDE:** (*Shouting into the trees.*) Keep the chargers
Clear of each other,
Till all the heroes'
Hate is allayed!

**HELMWIGE:** (*Amid the laughter of her companions.*) The grey has paid
For their feuds and quarrels!
(*Grimgerde and Rossweisse issuing from the fir-trees.*)

# Act III

**DIE WALKUEREN:** Willkommen! Willkommen!

**SCHWERTLEITE:** War't ihr Kühnen zu zwei?

**GRIMGERDE:** Getrennt ritten wir, trafen uns heut'.

**ROSSWEISSE:** Sind wir alle versammelt, so säumt nicht lange: nach Walhall brechen wir auf, Wotan zu bringen die Wal.

**HELMWIGE:** Acht sind wir erst, eine noch fehlt.

**GERHILDE:** Bei dem braunen Wälsung weilt wohl noch Brünnhild'?

**WALTRAUTE:** Auf sie noch harren müssen wir hier: Walvater gäb' uns grimmigen Gruss, säh' ohne sie er uns nah'n!

**SIEGRUNE:** (*auf der Felsspitze, von wo sie hinausspäht*). Hojotoho! Hojotoho! Hieher! Hieher! In brünstigem Ritt jagt Brünnhilde her.

**DIE WALKUEREN:** (*nach der Felsspitze eilend*). Heiaha! Hojotoho! Hojotoho! Brünnhilde! hei!

**WALTRAUTE:** Nach dem Tann lenkt sie das taumelnde Ross.

**GRIMGERDE:** Wie schnaubt Grane vom schnellen Ritt!

**ROSSWEISSE:** So jach sah ich nie Walküren jagen!

**ORTLINDE:** Was hält sie im Sattel?

**HELMWIGE:** Das ist kein Held!

**SIEGRUNE:** Eine Frau führt sie.

**GERHILDE:** Wie fand sie die Frau?

**SCHWERTLEITE:** Mit keinem Gruss grüsst sie die Schwestern?

**WALTRAUTE:** Heiaha! Brünnhilde! hörst du uns nicht?

**ORTLINDE:** Helft der Schwester vom Ross sich schwingen!

**DIE WALKUEREN:** Hojotoho! Hojotoho! Heiaha! Heiaha! (*Gerhilde und Helmwige stürzen in den Tann.*)

**WALTRAUTE:** Zu Grunde stürzt Grane der starke! (*Siegrune und Waltraute folgen den beiden.*)

**GRIMGERDE:** Aus dem Sattel hebt sie hastig das Weib.

**THE WALKYRS:** O welcome! O welcome!

**SCHWERTLEITE:** Did you come single, or in pairs?

**GRIMGERDE:** Alone galloped we, And met on our way.

**ROSSWEISSE:** If we all are assembled We'll tarry no more To Walhall haste and away; Wotan our coming awaits.

**HELMWIGE:** We are eight here. One we still lack.

**GERHILDE:** For the warrior Wälsung (*Waits Brünnhilde.*)

**WALTRAUTE:** Then till she comes, We must wait here: Grim were the greeting Wotan would give, Were she not there when we came!

**SIEGRUNE:** (*Peering into the distance from the top of the peak.*) Ho-yo-to-ho! Ho-yo-to-ho! Hie here! Hie here! Brünnhilde comes riding Madly this way!

**THE WALKYRS:** (*Hurrying to the summit.*) Ho-yo-to-ho! Ho-yo-to-ho! Hi-ya-ha! Brünnhilde! Heigh!

**WALTRAUTE:** To the wood rushes Her staggering steed.

**GRIMGERDE:** See how Grane Pants and strains!

**ROSSWEISSE:** So fast did I never See Walkyrs flying!

**ORTLINDE:** What hangs at her saddle?

**HELMWIGE:** That is no man!

**SIEGRUNE:** It is a weak woman.

**GERHILDE:** And where was she found?

**SCHWERTLEITE:** She gives her sisters no greeting glad.

**WALTRAUTE:** Hi-ya-ha! Brünnhilde! Can you not hear?

**ORTLINDE:** Help our sister To leave the saddle!

**THE WALKYRS:** Ho-yo-to-ho! Ho-yo-to-ho! Hi-ya-ha! Hi-ya-ha! (*Gerhilde and Helmwige rush into the fir-trees.*)

**WALTRAUTE:** Now Grane groans, Trembles and totters! (*Siegrune and Waltraute follow the two others.*)

**GRIMGERDE:** From the saddle, quick she lifts The woman.

**DIE UEBRIGEN WALKUEREN:** (*dem Tann zueilend*). Schwester! Schwester! Was ist gescheh'n? (*Alle Walküren kehren auf die Bühne zurück; mit ihnen kommt Bruennhilde, Sieglinde unterstützend und hereingeleitend.*)

**BRUENNHILDE:** (*athemlos*). Schützt mich, und helft in höchster Noth!

**DIE WALKUEREN:** Wo rittest du her in rasender Hast? So fliegt nur, wer auf der Flucht!

**BRUENNHILDE:** Zum erstenmal flieh' ich und bin verfolgt! Heervater hetzt mir nach!

**DIE WALKUEREN:** (*heftig erschreckend*). Bist du von Sinnen? Sage uns! Wie? Verfolgt dich Heervater? fliehst du vor ihm?

**BRUENNHILDE:** (*ängstlich*) O Schwestern, späht von des Felsens Spitze. Schaut nach Norden, ob Walvater naht! (*Ortlinde und Waltraute springen hinauf.*) Schnell! seht ihr ihn schon?

**ORTLINDE:** Gewittersturm naht von Norden.

**WALTRAUTE:** Starkes Gewölk staut sich dort auf.

**DIE WALKUEREN:** Heervater reitet sein heiliges Ross!

**BRUENNHILDE:** Der wilde Jäger, der wüthend mich jagt, er naht, er naht von Nord! Schützt mich, Schwestern! wahret dies Weib!

**DIE WALKUEREN:** Was ist mit dem Weibe?

**BRUENNHILDE:** Hört mich in Eile! Siegmund's Schwester und Braut: Gegen die Wälsungen wüthet Wotan in Grimm:— dem Bruder sollte Brünnhilde heut' entziehen den Sieg, doch Siegmund schützt' ich mit meinem Schild, trotzend dem Gott:— der traf ihn da selbst mit dem Speer. Siegmund fiel: doch ich floh fern mit der Frau: sie zu retten eilt' ich zu euch, ob mich bange auch ihr berget vor dem strafenden Streich.

**THE REMAINING WALKYRS:** (*Hurrying towards the fir-trees.*) Sister! Sister! What is your pain? (*All the Walkyrs return. With them comes Brünnhilde, supporting and guiding Sieglinde.*)

**BRÜNNHILDE:** (*Breathless.*) Shield me, and help In direst need!

**THE WALKYRS:** From where did you ride here In furious haste? One only flies like that when fleeing.

**BRÜNNHILDE:** I flee, who fled never, And fear pursuit! Wotan has pressed me hard!

**THE WALKYRS:** (*In wild excitement.*) Have you your senses? Speak! Speak to us! Does Wotan follow you? Do you flee from him?

**BRÜNNHILDE:** (*Anxiously.*) O sisters, watch From the rocky summit! Look northward. Is Wotan not near? (*Ortlinde and Waltraute rush to the summit and look off.*) Quick! Comes he this way?

**ORTLINDE:** A thunderstorm Comes from northward.

**WALTRAUTE:** Dark are the clouds, Denser they grow.

**THE WALKYRS:** Wotan comes riding His terrible steed.

**BRÜNNHILDE:** The dreadful hunter Who's hunting me down, Draws near from northward! Shield me, sisters! Shelter the waif!

**THE WALKYRS:** What troubles this woman?

**BRÜNNHILDE:** Haste and hear me! She is Sieglinde, Siegmund's sister and bride; Against the two Wälsungs was Wotan's anger aroused:— Brünnhilde bade he Siegmund today To doom to defeat. But, braving Wotan, I, with my shield, Siegmund did aid:— Then slew him the god with his spear. Siegmund fell: But I fled Far with his bride: How to save her I came here, Though trembling, give Me shelter from the wrath that I dread.

| | |
|---|---|
| **DIE WALKUEREN:** (*in grösster Bestürzung*). Bethörte Schwester! Was thatest du? Wehe! Wehe! Brünnhilde, wehe! Brach ungehorsam Brünnhilde Heervaters heilig Gebot? | **THE WALKYRS:** (*In consternation.*) Misguided sister! What did you do then? Woe's me! Brünnhilde, woe's me! Could you, Brünnhilde, Dare you defy the War-father's Will? |
| **WALTRAUTE:** (*von der Höhe*). Nächtig zieht es von Norden heran. | **WALTRAUTE:** (*From the height.*) Dark and darker It has grown in the North. |
| **ORTLINDE:** (*ebenso*). Wüthend steuert hierher der Sturm. | **ORTLINDE:** (*As above.*) Rushing on Comes the storm. |
| **SIEGRUNE:** (*dem Hintergrunde zugewendet*). Wild wiehert Walvaters Ross, schrecklich schnaubt es daher! | **THE WALKYRS:** (*Turning towards the background.*) Loud neighs Wotan's wild steed: Snorting, panting, it comes! |
| **BRUENNHILDE:** Wehe der Armen, wenn Wotan sie trifft, den Wälsungen allen droht er Verderben!— Wer leih't mir von euch das leichteste Ross, das flink die Frau ihm entführ'? | **BRÜNNHILDE:** Woe to this victim When Wotan shall come! For all of the Wälsungs Vows he to ruin!— Which one of ye all Will lend me a steed To rob the god of his prey? |
| **SIEGRUNE:** Auch uns räth'st du rasenden Trotz? | **SIEGRUNE:** So, we must be Dragged to your doom? |
| **BRUENNHILDE:** Rossweisse, Schwester! Leih' mir deinen Renner! | **BRÜNNHILDE:** Rossweise, sister, Lend me your horse! |
| **ROSSWEISSE:** Vor Walvater floh der fliegende nie. | **ROSSWEISE:** From Wotan, I trow, My horse has never fled. |
| **BRUENNHILDE:** Helmwige, höre! | **BRÜNNHILDE:** Helmwige, hear me! |
| **HELMWIGE:** Dem Vater gehorch' ich. | **HELMWIGE:** My father I follow. |
| **BRUENNHILDE:** Grimgerde! Gerhilde! Gönnt mir eu'r Ross! Schwertleite! Siegrune! Seht meine Angst! O seid mir treu, wie traut ich euch war: rettet diess traurige Weib! | **BRÜNNHILDE:** Grimgerde! Gerhilde! Grant me a steed! Schwertleite! Siegrune! See my despair! O be true, As I was true: Help me to save this woman! |
| **SIEGLINDE:** (*die bisher finster und kalt vor sich hingestarrt, fährt auf, als Bruennhilde sie lebhaft—wie zum Schutze—umfasst*). Nicht sehre dich Sorge um mich: einzig taugt mir der Tod! Wer hiess dich Maid dem Harst mich entführen? Im Sturm dort hätt' ich den Streich empfah'n von derselben Waffe, der Siegmund fiel: das Ende fand ich vereint mit ihm! Fern von Siegmund— Siegmund von dir! O deckt mich Tod, dass ich's denke!— Soll um die Flucht dir Maid ich nicht fluchen, so erhöre heilig mein Fleh'n— stosse dein Schwert mir in's Herz! | **SIEGLINDE:** (*Who till now has stared hopelessly into space, starts up as Brünnhilde puts her arm about her protectingly.*) Nay, sorrow not, strive not for me; Death alone would I seek! Who bade you, maid, Avert the god's vengeance? The storm that thundered Had seen me slain With the self-same weapon That Siegmund slew: The end had found me At peace with him! Far from Siegmund— Siegmund, from you. O would I were dead, It were less dreadful!— Lest I should curse You, maid, for your coming, Do you hear me, humbly I pray you— Bury your blade in my heart! |
| **BRUENNHILDE:** Lebe, o Weib, um der Liebe willen! Rette das Pfand, das von ihm du empfingst: ein Wälsung wächst dir im Schooss. | **BRÜNNHILDE:** Woman, live on, For the love of loving! Rescue the pledge That his love gave to you A Wälsung soon you shall bear! |
| **SIEGLINDE:** (*ist heftig erschrocken; plötzlich strahlt dann ihr Gesicht in erhabener Freude auf*). Rette mich, Kühne! rette mein Kind! Schirmt mich, ihr Mädchen, mit mächtigstem Schutz! (*Furchtbares Gewitter steigt im Hintergrunde auf, nahender Donner.*) | **SIEGLINDE:** (*After a moment of alarm, her face beams with joy.*) Rescue me, maiden! Rescue my child! Save me, maidens, So mighty to shield! (*Terrible thunderclaps are heard in the distance. They grow louder.*) |
| **WALTRAUTE:** (*von der Höhe*). Der Sturm kommt heran. | **WALTRAUTE:** (*From the height.*) The storm grows apace! |
| **ORTLINDE:** (*ebenso*). Flieh', wer ihn fürchtet! | **ORTLINDE:** (*As above.*) Flee, you who fear it! |
| **DIE WALKUEREN:** Fort mit dem Weibe, droht ihm Gefahr: der Walküren keine wag' ihren Schutz! | **THE WALKYRS:** Hence with the woman— Peril she bodes! No Walkyr would dare To serve as her shield! |
| **SIEGLINDE:** (*auf den Knieen vor Bruennhilde*). Rette mich, Maid! Rette die Mutter! | **SIEGLINDE:** (*Kneeling to Brünnhilde.*) Rescue me, maid! Rescue the mother! |
| **BRUENNHILDE:** (*mit schnellem Entschluss*). So fliehe denn eilig— und fliehe allein! Ich—bleibe zurück, biete mich Wotan's Rache: an mir zögr' ich den Zürnenden hier, während du seinem Rasen entrinnst. | **BRÜNNHILDE:** (*Coming to a decision quickly.*) Then flee, swiftly, And flee alone! I—will remain here, Waiting for Wotan's vengeance: On me will fall His furious ire, And his wrath you meanwhile shall escape. |
| **SIEGLINDE:** Wohin soll ich mich wenden? | **SIEGLINDE:** Where, ah where shall I wander? |
| **BRUENNHILDE:** Wer von euch, Schwestern, schweifte nach Osten? | **BRÜNNHILDE:** Which of you sisters Speeds to the east? |
| **SIEGRUNE:** Nach Osten weithin dehnt sich ein Wald: der Niblungen Hort entführte Fafner dorthin. | **SIEGRUNE:** There lies a wood Far from here, in the East: The Nibelung's hoard Has been hid there by Fafner. |
| **SCHWERTLEITE:** Wurmes-Gestalt schuf sich der Wilde: in einer Höhle hütet er Alberich's Reif. | **SCHWERTLEITE:** Shaped as a worm, Fafner lies lurking In a deep cavern Watching over Alberich's ring. |
| **GRIMGERDE:** Nicht geheu'r ist's dort für ein hülflos Weib. | **GRIMGERDE:** It is a dreadful spot For a helpless wife! |
| **BRUENNHILDE:** Und doch vor Wotan's Wuth schützt sie sicher der Wald: ihn scheut der Mächt'ge und meidet den Ort. | **BRÜNNHILDE:** And yet from Wotan's wrath Safe were she in the wood: For, though so mighty, He shuns the forest. |
| **WALTRAUTE:** (*von der Höhe*). Furchtbar fährt dort Wotan zum Fels. | **WALTRAUTE:** (*From the height.*) Wildly now Rides Wotan our way! |
| **DIE WALKUEREN:** Brünnhilde, hör' seines Nahens Gebraus'! | **THE WALKYRS:** Brünnhilde, hear The loud roar as he nears! |
| **BRUENNHILDE:** (*Sieglinden die Richtung weisend*). Fort denn, eile nach Osten gewandt! Muthigen Trotzes ertrag' alle Müh'n— Hunger und Durst, | **BRÜNNHILDE:** (*Directing Sieglinde.*) Hence then, hasten And hide in the East! Bravely and boldly Enduring your woe— Hunger and thirst, |

Dorn und Gestein;
lache, ob Noth,
ob Leiden dich nagt!
Denn eines wiss'
und wahr' es immer:
den hehrsten Helden der Welt
hegst du, o Weib,
im schirmenden Schooss!—
(*Sie reicht ihr die Stücke von Siegmund's Schwert.*)
Verwahr' ihm die starken
Schwertes-Stücken;
seines Vaters Walstatt
entführt' ich sie glücklich:
der neu gefügt
das Schwert einst schwingt,
den Namen nehm' er von mir—
„Siefried" erfreu' sich des Sieg's

SIEGLINDE: Du hehrstes Wunder!
herrliche Maid!
Dir, Treuen, dank' ich
heiligen Trost!
Für ihn, den wir liebten,
rett' ich das Liebste:
meines Dankes Lohn
lache dir einst!
Lebe wohl!
Dich segnet Sieglinde's Weh'!
(*Sie eilt rechts im Vordergrunde
ab.—Die Felsenhöhe ist von
schwarzen Gewitterwolken
umlagert; furchtbarer Sturm
braust aus dem Hintergrunde
daher: ein feuriger Schein erhellt
den Tannenwald zur Seite. Zwischen dem Donner hört man Wotan's Ruf.*)

WOTAN'S: (*Stimme*). Steh'!
Brünnhild'!

DIE WALKUEREN: Den Fels er-
reichten
Ross und Reiter:
weh', Brünnhild'!
Rache entbrennt!

BRUENNHILDE: Ach, Schwestern,
helft!
mir schwankt das Herz!
Sein Zorn zerschellt mich,
wenn eu'r Schutz ihn nicht zähmt.

DIE WALKUEREN: Hieher, Verlor'ne!
lass' dich nicht seh'n!
Schmiege dich an uns,
und schweige dem Ruf!
(*Sie ziehen sich alle die Felsspitze
hinauf, indem sie Bruennhilde
unter sich verbergen.*)
Weh'!
Wüthend schwingt sich
Wotan vom Ross—
hieher ras't
sein rächender Schritt!
(*Wotan schreitet in furchtbar
zürnender Aufregung aus dem
Tann heraus, und hält vor dem
Haufen der Walküren an die auf
der Höhe eine Stellung einneh-
men, durch welche sie Bruennhilde schützen.*)

Hardship and pain;
Laugh, although need
And sorrow should gnaw!
For one thing ever
Hold fast and treasure:
The noblest hero on earth
Soon
Shall leap into life from your
womb!
(*She hands her the fragments of
Siegmund's sword.*)
The sword that was shivered,
See you save him:
From his father's death-field
I brought the bits safely:
Who, newly forged,
The sword shall swing,
The name I give him shall bear—
"Siegfried," a Victor shall stand!

SIEGLINDE: Glorious wonder!
Valorous maid!
Your truth has lent me
Courage and trust!
For him, whom we honored,
Save I my dearest:
Would that thanks alone
Could repay you!
Farewell!
Be blessed by Sieglinde's woe!
(*She hurries away on the right.—
The summit of the rocks is
enveloped in dark thunderclouds.
A terrible storm grows in the
background. A lurid glow appears
in the fir-trees. Between the thun-
derclaps Wotan's voice is heard.*)

WOTAN'S VOICE: Stay,
Brünnhilde!

THE WALKYRS: The steed and rid-
er
Rush to reach us:
Woe, Brünnhilde!
His wrath is wild!

BRÜNNHILDE: Ah, sisters, help!
My heart grows faint!
Unless you tame him
I am undone now, and doomed!

THE WALKYRS: Hide here, o lost
one,
Lest you be seen!
Cling close to us
And heed not his call!
(*All ascend to the top of the peak,
concealing Brünnhilde*)
Woe!
Wildly Wotan
Leaps from his steed—
See how fierce
He flames on his way!
(*Wotan, frenzied with anger, is-
sues from the firs and halts at the
foot of the height on which the
Walkyrs are grouped, hiding
Brünnhilde*)

WOTAN: Wo ist Brünnhild'?
Wo die Verbrecherin?
Wagt ihr, die Böse
vor mir zu bergen?

DIE WALKUEREN: Schrecklich ertos't dein Toben:—
was thaten, Vater, die Töchter,
das sie dich reizten
zu rasender Wuth?

WOTAN: Wollt ihr mich höhnen?
Hütet euch, Freche!
Ich weiss: Brünnhilde
bergt ihr vor mir.
Weichet von ihr,
der ewig Verworf'nen,
wie ihren Werth
von sich sie warf!

DIE WALKUEREN: Zu uns floh die
Verfolgte,
uns'ren Schutz flehte sie an!
mit Furcht und Zagen
fasst sie dein Zorn.
Für die bange Schwester
bitten wir nun,
dass den ersten Zorn du bezähm'st.

WOTAN: Weichherziges
Weibergezücht!
So matten Muth
gewannt ihr von mir?
Erzog ich euch kühn,
zu Kämpfen zu zieh'n,
schuf ich die Herzen
euch hart und scharf,
dass ihr Wilden nun weint und
greint,
wenn mein Grimm eine Treulose
straft?
So wisst denn, Winselnde,
was die verbrach,
um die euch Zagen
die Zähre entbrennt!
Keine wie sie
kannte mein innerstes Sinnen!
keine wie sie
wusste den Quell meines Willens;
sie selbst war
meines Wunsches schaffender
Schooss:
und so nun brach sie
den seligen Bund.
dass treulos sie
meinem Willen getrotzt,
mein herrschend Gebot
offen verhöhnt,
gegen mich die Waffe gewandt,
die allein mein Wunsch ihr
schuf!—
Hörst du's, Brünnhilde?
du, der ich Brünne,
Helm und Wehr,
Wonne und Huld,
Namen und Leben verlieh?
Hörst du mich Klage erheben,
und birgst dich bang dem Kläger,
dass feig' du der Straf' entflöh'st?

BRUENNHILDE: (*tritt aus der
Schaar der Walküren hervor,
schreitet demüthigen, doch festen
Schrittes von der Felsensritze
herab und tritt so in geringer
Ferne vor Wotan*). Hier bin ich,
Vater:
gebiete die Strafe!

WOTAN: Where is Brünnhild'?
She who betrayed me?
Do you dare to shelter the guilty
From me?

THE WALKYRS: Fearful your fury
rages:—
What did your daughters, O father,
Do to awaken
Your anger and rage?

WOTAN: Would you then mock
me?
Do you dare defy me?
I know: Brünnhilde
Fain would hide.
Shrink from her, ay,
Forsake her, the traitress,
For she herself
Hath now betrayed!

THE WALKYRS: To us fled she,
your victim;
She implored, wept for our aid!
Now worn and woeful
Dreads she your wrath!
We entreat you, father,
Pity your child!
Let her sorrow soften your heart!

WOTAN: Weak-hearted and
Womanly brood!
Do you fancy your sire so faint and
slow?
For this were you taught
To battle and war,
Hardened and heartened
To dare and do?
Would you weep and whimper and
groan
When my wrath on the criminal
falls?
Then know this, whimperers,
What is the crime
Of her who draws
From your terror these tears?
None of you all
Knew as she knew what I purposed.
None of you all
Fathomed my will and my meaning;
Herself was
She the soul and source of my will:
And she has broken
Our holiest bond,
For faithless what
I had willed she defied,
My solemn behest
Openly braved—
She turned the weapons against me
That my will alone had wrought!—
Do you hear, Brünnhilde?
You to whom I lent buckler,
Helm and spear,
Being and honor?
Do you hear how I accuse you,
And do you hide and tremble
In dread of the doom you've fled?

BRÜNNHILDE: (*Issues from the
group formed by the other Walkyrs, descends humbly, but with a
firm step, from the peak, and halts
at a little distance from Wotan.*)
Here I am father:
You order my doom!

WOTAN: Nicht—straf' ich dich
erst:
deine Strafe schufst du dir selbst.
Durch meinen Willen
warst du du allein;
gegen mich doch hast du gewollt;
meine Befehle nur
führtest du aus:
gegen mich doch hast du befohlen;
Wunsch-Maid
war'st du mir:
gegen mich doch hast du
gewünscht;
Schild-Maid
war'st du mir:
gegen mich doch hob'st du den
Schild;
Loos-Kieserin
war'st du mir:
gegen mich doch kies'test du
Loose;
Helden-Reizerin
war'st du mir:
gegen mich doch reiztest du
Helden.
Was sonst du war'st,
sagte dir Wotan:
was jetzt du bist,
das sage dir selbst!
Wunschmaid bist du nicht mehr;
Walküre bist du gewesen:—
nun sei fortan,
was so du noch bist!

BRUENNHILDE: (*heftig er-
schrocken*). Du verstössest mich?
versteh' ich den Sinn?

WOTAN: Nicht send' ich dich
mehr aus Walhall,
nicht weis' ich dir mehr
Helden zur Wal:
nicht führ'st du mehr Sieger
in meinen Saal;
bei der Götter trautem Mahle
das Trinkhorn nicht reichst du
traulich mir mehr;
nicht kos' ich dir mehr
den kindischen Mund.
Von göttlicher Schaar
bist du geschieden,
ausgestossen
aus der Ewigen Stamm,
gebrochen ist unser Bund:
aus meinem Angesicht bist du verbannt.

DIE WALKUEREN: (*in Jammer
ausbrechend*). Wehe! Weh'!
Schwester! Ach Schwester!

BRUENNHILDE: Nimmst du mir
alles,
was einst du gab'st?

WOTAN: Der dich zwingt, wird
dir's entzieh'n!
Hieher auf den Berg
banne ich dich;
in wehrlosen Schlaf
schliess' ich dich fest;
der Mann dann fange die Maid,
der am Wege sie findet und weckt.

DIE WALKUEREN: Halt', o Vater!
halt' ein den Fluch!
Soll die Maid verblüh'n
und verbleichen dem Mann?
Ach, wende von ihr

WOTAN: Nay—I do not doom:
By your deed yourself you have
doomed.
My will, mine only,
Gave you your life:
Yet against that will you have
warred.
Nothing but my bidding
You once did obey:
Yet against me now you have bid-
den;
You were once wish-maid:
Yet against me now you have
willed;
You were one shield-maid
Yet against me you raise your
shield;
You were once fate-messenger
Yet against me fate you were mov-
ing;
You were once hero-ravisher
Yet you turned heroes against me.
What more you were
Wotan has told you.
What now you are,
Yourself should know best!
You're wish-maid no more;
You're Walkyrie no longer:—
Henceforth then be
What only you can!

BRÜNNHILDE: (*In terrible agitation.*) You would cast me out?
Is that your decree?

WOTAN: No more you'll ride now
from Walhall;
No more shall you bid
Heroes to death;
No more bring the victors
To fill my hall:
When together gods are gathered
My horn you shall never
Bring me to drain;
No more I can kiss
Your innocent lips
The gods you met
Know you no longer;
Outcast you are
From the race of the gods.
For broken now is our bond,
And from my presence you are ban-
ished for aye!

THE WALKYRS: (*Lamenting.*)
Woe, ah, woe!
Ah, sister, o sister!

BRÜNNHILDE: All you are taking
That once you gave?

WOTAN: He, your lord—takes it
away!
Now here to this hill
I banish you, to sleep unguarded
I sentence you:
That man shall capture the maid,
Who shall wake her to life on his
way.

THE WALKYRS: Have done! O fa-
ther,
Enough you've cursed!
Must the maiden pale
And be prey to a man?

die schreiende Schmach,
schrecklicher Gott!
wie die Schwester, träf' uns der
Schimpf!

WOTAN: Hörtet ihr nicht,
was ich verhängt?
Aus eurer Schaar
ist die treulose Schwester geschied-
en;
mit euch zu Ross
durch die Lüfte nicht reitet sie
länger;
die magdliche Blume
verblüht der Maid;
ein Gatte gewinnt
ihre weibliche Gunst:
dem herrischen Manne
gehorcht sie fortan,
am Herde sitzt sie und spinnt,
aller Spottenden Ziel und Spiel.
(*Bruennhilde sinkt schreiend vor
seinen Füssen zu Boden; die Walküren machen eine Bewegung des
Entsetzens.*)
Schreckt euch ihr Loos?
So flieht die Verlor'ne!
Weichet von ihr
und haltet euch fern!
Wer von euch wagte
bei ihr zu weilen,
wer mir zum Trotz
zu der Traurigen hielt',
die Thörin theilte ihr Loos:
das künd' ich der Kühnen an!—
Fort jetzt von hier!
meidet den Felsen!
Hurtig jagt mir von hinnen,
sonst erharrt Jammer euch hier!

DIE WALKUEREN: Weh'! Weh'!
(*Die Walküren fahren mit wildem
Wehschrei auseinander und
stürzen in hastiger Flucht in den
Tann: bald hört man sie wie mit
Sturm auf ihren Rossen davonja-
gend.—Nach und nach legt sich
während des Folgenden das
Gewitter; die Wolken verziehen
sich; Abenddämmerung, und
endlich Nacht, sinken bei ruhi-
gem Wetter herein.
Wotan und Bruennhilde, die noch
zu seinen Füssen hingestreckt
liegt, sind allein zurückgeblieben.—Langes, feierliches
Schweigen: unveränderte Stellung Wotan's und Bruennhilde's.*)

BRUENNHILDE: (*endlich das
Haupt langsam erhebend, sucht
Wotan's noch abgewandten Blick
und richtet sich während des Folgenden allmälig ganz auf*). War
es so schmählich,
was ich verbrach,
dass mein Verbrechen so
schmählich du bestraf'st?
War es so niedrig,
was ich dir that,
dass du so tief mir Erniedrigung
schaff'st?
War es so ehrlos,
was ich beging,
dass mein Vergeh'n nun die Ehre
mir raubt?

O turn from her head
This terrible shame,
Merciless god!
Or let us share our sister's woe and
her fate!

WOTAN: Did you not hear
What I decreed?
Far from you all
Shall your renegade sister be driv-
en;
With you no more
Through the air she shall ride on
her charger;
Her maidenly blossom
Shall fail and fade;
A husband shall win her
And wear her for wife;
A man and a master
Shall hold her in servitude
At home she'll sit and she'll spin,
As a mock and a mark for scorn.
(*Brünnhilde shrieks and falls at
his feet. The Walkyrs are con-
vulsed with terror.*)
Do you fear her fate?
Then flee from the outcast.
Leave her to bear
Her sentence alone!
She who would venture
Near her to linger,
She who should venture
To condone her crime,
Shall surely share in her doom:
I warn you, so hear and heed!—
Up and begone!
Do not haunt the mountain!
Haste you hence, as I bid you
Lest you all rue your delay!

THE WALKYRS: Woe! Woe!
(*The Walkyrs disperse, with wild
lamentations, and rush away
into the fir-trees. Shortly after
they are heard riding away at a furious gallop. The storm gradually
abates. The clouds clear off, dusk
comes and then at last is merged
into placid night.*)
(*Wotan remains alone with
Brünnhilde, who is still prostrate
at his feet. A long, solemn silence
follows, during which Wotan and
Brünnhilde do not stir.*)

BRÜNNHILDE: (*Slowly lifts her
head, seeking response from Wot-
an's averted eyes. Then she rises.*)
Was it so shameful,
All I have done,
That my misdoings should steep me
so in shame?
Have I sinned so deeply,
When I did sin,
That you should sink me so deep in
disgrace?
Had I no honor,
Even in my guilt,
That you must rob me of honor for
always?
Ah, speak, father,
Face me now frankly:

O sag', Vater,
sieh' mir in's Auge:
schweige den Zorn,
zähme die Wuth!
Deute mir hell
Die dunkle Schuld,
die mit starrem Trotze dich zwingt,
zu verstossen dein trautestes Kind!

WOTAN: (*finster*). Frag' deine That—
sie deutet dir deine Schuld!

BRUENNHILDE: Deinen Befehl
führte ich aus.

WOTAN: Befahl ich dir
für den Wälsung zu fechten?

BRUENNHILDE: So hiessest du mich
als Herrscher der Wal.

WOTAN: Doch meine Weisung
nahm ich wieder zurück.

BRUENNHILDE: Als Fricka den eig'nen
Sinn dir entfremdet:
da ihrem Sinn du dich fügtest,
warst du selber dir Feind.

WOTAN: (*bitter*). Dass du mich verstanden, wähnt' ich,
und strafte den wissenden Trotz;
doch feig' und dumm
dachtest du mich:
so hätt' ich Verrath nicht zu rächen,
zu gering wär'st du meinem Grimm?

BRUENNHILDE: Nicht weise bin ich;
doch wusst' ich das Eine—
dass den Wälsung du liebtest:
ich wusste den Zwiespalt,
der dich zwang,
dies Eine ganz zu vergessen.
Das And're musstest
einzig du seh'n,
was zu schau'n so herb
schmerzte dein Herz—
dass Siegmund Schutz du versagtest.

WOTAN: Du wusstest es so,
und wagtest dennoch den Schutz?

BRUENNHILDE: Weil für dich im Auge
das Eine ich hielt,
dem, im Zwange des And'ren
schmerzlich entzweit,
rathlos den Rücken du wandtest.
Die im Kampfe Wotan
den Rücken bewacht,
die sah nun das nur,
was du nicht sah'st:—
Siegmund musst' ich seh'n.
Tod kündend
trat ich vor ihn,
gewahrte sein Auge,
hörte sein Wort;
ich vernahm des Helden
heilige Noth;
tönend erklang mir
des Tapfersten Klage—
freiester Liebe
furchtbares Leid,
traurigsten Muthes
mächtigster Trotz:

---

Silence your wrath,
Stifle your rage!
And tell me, I pray,
My deadly crime,
That compels you to be ruthless,
And to make an outcast of your child!

WOTAN: (*Gloomily.*) Question your crime—
It will show the depth of your guilt!

BRÜNNHILDE: I obeyed your own command.

WOTAN: And did I bid you
To fight for the Wälsung?

BRÜNNHILDE: So did you command
As master of war.

WOTAN: Ay, but I revoked my bidding
Swiftly

BRÜNNHILDE: When Fricka your honest
Mind had perverted:
By giving way to content her,
You did betray yourself.

WOTAN: (*Bitterly.*) You did understand me, clearly:
Your wilful rebellion I scourge.
But weak and dull
Seemed I to you
Should treason itself go unpunished,
Too unworthy were you for wrath?

BRÜNNHILDE: I have no wisdom
Yet this I knew surely—
That you loved the Wälsung.
I knew of the quarrel
That compelled
Your heart to seem so forgetful.
No help was left for you
But to behold
What with shame and pain
So harrowed up your heart—
And Siegmund soon was forsaken.

WOTAN: You knew it well,
And yet you did stand his shield?

BRÜNNHILDE: Ay, for you, and you only
I did not forget,
When, a slave to another,
Sad and alone,
Helpless away you did turn
She who Wotan's rearguard
In battle had been
Could see what you
Now no more could see:
I sought Siegmund straight.
Death-dooming,
Went I my way,
And, meeting his glances,
Heard what he spake;
Then I knew the hero's
Terrible woe;
Thrilled as I sounded
His valor and sorrow—
Heard him unbosom
Anguish and love,
Sad and yet dauntless,
Daring and strong:

---

meinem Ohr' erscholl,
mein Aug' erschaute,
was tief im Busen das Herz
zu heil'gem Beben mir traf.—
Scheu und staunend
stand ich in Scham:
ihm nur zu dienen
konnt' ich noch denken:
Sieg oder Tod
mit Siegmund zu theilen—
diess nur erkannt' ich
zu kiesen als Loos!
Der diese Liebe
mir in's Herz gehaucht,
dem Willen, der
dem Wälsung mich gesellt,
ihm innig vertraut—
trotzt' ich deinem Gebot.

WOTAN: So thatest du,
was so gern zu thun ich begehrt—
doch was nicht zu thun
die Noth zwiefach mich zwang?
so leicht wähntest du
Wonne des Herzes erworben,
wo brennend Weh'
in das Herz mir brach,
wo grässliche Noth
den Grimm mir schuf,
einer Welt zu Liebe
der Liebe Quell
im gequälten Herzen zu hemmen?
Wo gegen mich selber
ich sehrend mich wandte,
aus Ohnmacht-Schmerzen
schäumend ich aufschoss,
wüthender Sehnsucht
sengender Wunsch
den schrecklichen Willen mir schuf,
in den Trümmern der eig'nen Welt
meine ew'ge Trauer zu enden:—
da labte süss
dich, selige Lust;
wonniger Rührung
üppigen Rausch
enttrankst du lachend
der Liebe Trank—
als mir göttlicher Noth
nagende Galle gemischt?
Deinen leichten Sinn
lass' dich denn leiten:
von mir sagtest du dich los!
Dich muss ich meiden,
gemeinsam mit dir
nicht darf ich Rath mehr raunen;
getrennt nicht dürfen
traut wir mehr schaffen:
so weit Leben und Luft,
darf der Gott dir nicht mehr begegnen!

BRUENNHILDE: Wohl taugte dir nicht
die thör'ge Maid,
die staunend im Rathe
nicht dich verstand
wie mein eig'ner Rath
nur das Eine mir rieth—
zu lieben, was du geliebt.—
Muss ich denn scheiden
und scheu dich meiden,
musst du spalten,
was einst sich umspannt,
die eig'ne Hälfte
fern' von dir halten—

---

What my ear heard
And eye did fathom,
Awoke and tortured my heart
With holy passion and pain.
Awed, astounded,
I stood in shame:
Now thinking only
How I could serve him:
Triumph or death
With Siegmund beside me—
This could I only
Of fortune demand!
Him who this love had roused,
Within my heart
The will that had the Wälsung
Bound to me,
In faith and in trust—
I now dared to defy.

WOTAN: So you did do
What I once indeed had desired—
But what not to do
By fate fast I was bound?
So soon hoped you
Rapture would pay your for loving,
When burning woe
In my heart did flame,
And terrible need
Compelled my wrath,
For the sake of saving
A world with love,
In my heart to dry up love's sources?
When, turning all my anger, against
My own self
In helpless sorrow
Fiercely I struggled,
Passionate longing
Raging awoke,
The merciless wish in me roused,
In the wreck of the world I ruled
My unending sorrow to bury:—
And you did dream
Of joy and of love,
Revel in rapture,
Riot in bliss;
Did drain, delighted,
The draught of love—
While I, god though I be,
Poisoned my bosom with gall?
Let your wanton will
Lead you hereafter:
From me now yourself you've loosed!
Now are we severed;
Together with you
No more I'll come for counsel
We two can never
Plan to work wonders:
So, while life shall be yours,
From the god you're parted for ever!

BRÜNNHILDE: As nothing you hold
The foolish maid
Who, seeking your meaning,
Misunderstood;
To her simple mind
One thing only was meant
To love what your heart had loved.—
Must we be parted
For always, and sundered?
Must you sever
What once was entwined?
Ah, would you banish

dass sonst sie ganz dir gehörte,
du, Gott, vergiss das nicht!
Dein ewig Theil
nicht wirst du entehren,
Schande nicht wollen,
die dich beschimpft;
dich selbst liessest du sinken,
säh'st du dem Spott mich zum
Spiel!

**WOTAN:** Du folgtest selig
der Liebe Macht:
folge nun dem,
den du lieben musst!

**BRUENNHILDE:** Soll ich aus Walhall scheiden,
nicht mehr mit dir schaffen und
walten:
dem herrischen Manne
gehorchen fortan—
dem feigen Prahler
gieb mich nicht Preis!
nicht werthlos sei er,
der mich gewinnt!

**WOTAN:** Von Walvater schiedest
du—
nicht wählen darf er für dich.

**BRUENNHILDE:** Du zeugtest ein
edles Geschlecht;
kein Zager kann je ihm
entschlagen:
der weihlichste Held—ich weiss
es—
entblüht dem Wälsungenstamm.

**WOTAN:** Schweig' von dem
Wälsungenstamm!
von dir geschieden
schied ich von ihm:
vernichten musst' ihn der Neid.

**BRUENNHILDE:** Die von dir sich
riss—
rettete ihn:
Sieglinde hegt
die heiligste Frucht;
in Schmerz und Leid,
wie kein Weib sie gelitten,
wird sie gebären,
was bang sie birgt.

**WOTAN:** Nie suche bei mir
Schutz für die Frau,
noch für ihres Schoosses Frucht!

**BRUENNHILDE:** Sie wahret das
Schwert,
das du Siegmund schufest.—

**WOTAN:** Und das ich ihm in
Stücken schlug
Nicht streb', o Maid,
den Muth mir zu stören!
Erwarte dein Loos,
wie sich's dir wirft:
nicht kiesen kann ich es dir!—
Doch fort muss ich jetzt,
fern mich verzieh'n;
zuviel schon zögert' ich hier.
Von der Abwendigen
wend' ich mich ab;
nicht wissen darf ich,
was sie sich wünscht:
die Strafe nur
muss vollstreckt ich seh'n.

**BRUENNHILDE:** Was hast du erdacht,
dass ich erdulde?

Half of your being—
Who long obeyed you so blindly,
You god, forget not that!
Your deathless self
You will not dishonor,
Could not repay me
With shame for shame;
Yourself would you punish,
Were you to mock me with scorn!

**WOTAN:** You've yielded lightly
Where love allured.
Yield yourself now
To a love foredoomed!

**BRÜNNHILDE:** Must I then leave
Walhalla—
No more reign with you and do bat-
tle?
Bow down and be mastered
At beck of a man
Then give no braggart
Boaster the prize!
Let no worthless coward
Win your daughter

**WOTAN:** The War-Father you've
disowned—
He may not choose you the man.

**BRÜNNHILDE:** A valorous race
you've begot;
No coward could come of your
breeding:
A hero alone—that I know
Of Wälsung blood could be born.

**WOTAN:** Leave the Wälsungs in
peace!
From them I parted,
Parting with you.
It was envy doomed them to die.

**BRÜNNHILDE:** She who's rent
from you
Rescued their race:
Sieglinde bears
The holiest fruit;
In pain and woe
Such as none have ever suffered,
What in her's hidden
She brings to life.

**WOTAN:** Yet hope not from me
Help for her pain,
Nor for her unhallowed child!

**BRÜNNHILDE:** The sword she has
saved
You sent to Siegmund.

**WOTAN:** And that I split into splin-
ters!
Seek not, o maid,
My mind to unsettle!
Await the lot
Your sin has earned:
I may not change it for you.
And now I must go:
Far from this place.
Too long I've lingered today.
Now I turn from you
As you did from me;
Forbidden am I to learn
Your wish.
Your crime alone
I must see punished.

**BRÜNNHILDE:** What have you
conceived
That I must suffer?

**WOTAN:** In festen Schlaf
verschliess' ich dich:
wer so die Wehrlose weckt,
dem ward, erwacht, sie zum Weib

**BRUENNHILDE:** (*stürzt auf ihre
Kniee*). Soll fesselnder Schlaf
fest mich binden,
dem feigsten Manne
zur leichten Beute:
diess Eine musst du erhören,
was heil'ge Angst zu dir fleht!
Die Schlafende schütze
mit scheuchenden Schrecken:
dass nur ein furchtlos
freiester Held
hier auf dem Felsen
einst mich fänd'!

**WOTAN:** Zu viel begehrst du—
zu viel der Gunst!

**BRUENNHILDE:** (*seine Kniee um-
fassend*). Dies Eine musst—
du erhören!
Zerknicke dein Kind,
das dein Knie umfasst;
zertritt die Traute,
zertrümm're die Maid;
ihres Leibes Spur
zerstöre dein Speer:
doch gieb, Grausamer, nicht
der grässlichsten Schmach sie
preis!
(*Mit Wildheit.*)
Auf dein Gebot
entbrenne ein Feuer;
den Felsen umglühe
lodernde Gluth:
es leck' ihre Zung',
es fresse ihr Zahn
den Zagen, der frech sich wagte,
dem freislichen Felsen zu nah'n!

**WOTAN:** (*blickt ihr ergriffen in
das Auge und hebt sie auf*). Leb'
wohl, du kühnes,
herrliches Kind!
Du meines Herzens
heiligster Stolz,
leb' wohl! leb' wohl! leb' wohl!
Muss ich dich meiden,
und darf nicht minnig
mein Gruss dich mehr grüssen;
sollst du nun nicht mehr
neben mir reiten,
noch Meth beim Mahl mir reichen,
muss ich verlieren
dich, die ich liebe,
du lachende Lust meines Auges:—
ein bräutliches Feuer
soll dir nun brennen,
wie nie einer Braut es gebrannt!
Flammende Gluth
umglühe den Fels;
mit zehrenden Schrecken
scheuch' es den Zagen,
der Feige fliehe
Brünnhilde's Fels!—
denn Einer nur freie die Braut,
der freier als ich, der Gott!
(*Bruennhilde wirft sich ihm
gerührt und entzückt in die
Arme.*)
Der Augen leuchtendes Paar,
das oft ich lächelnd gekos't,
wenn Kampfes-Lust
ein Kuss dir lohnte,

**WOTAN:** In slumber deep
I lock your eyes
He who awakes the sleeper
Shall win, and wear, her for wife.

**BRÜNNHILDE:** (*Falling on her
knees.*) Lest fettering sleep
Fast should bind me
The prey and booty
Of any coward:
One boon you will not deny me
As deep in anguish I pray!
The sleeper, o, shelter
With ramparts of terror.
A hero only,
Fearless and free,
Here to the mountain
Then could come.

**WOTAN:** You ask too much—
Too great's the grace!

**BRÜNNHILDE:** (*Clinging to his
knees.*) This boon you must—
Not deny me!
Ah, crush out the life
Of your child who kneels;
Destroy your servant,
The truest of maids;
With your mighty lance transpierce
Her bosom;
But give, gruesome one, not
Your daughter to scorn and shame!
(*Wildly*)
At your command
Let threatening fires
Encircle the mountain,
Raven and glow:
And, heavenward leaping,
Pitiless tongues
Strike terror in him who'd venture
The desolate rock to invade!

**WOTAN:** (*Gazes with emotion
into her eyes, and helps her to
rise.*) Farewell, you bravest,
Rarest of maids!
You, my heart's treasure,
Idol and pride,
Farewell! farewell! farewell!
Must I forsake you
And now may never
My soul send you greeting:
Shall you no more then,
Go riding near me,
Nor bring me mead to cheer me;
Must I then lose you,
O, my belovèd,
You, laughter and light in my sor-
row:—
For you will I kindle
Burning red beacons
That never for a bride had yet
flamed!
Ruddy the fire
Shall glow round the rock;
With raging and roaring
Taunting the coward;
Who fears shall flee from
Brünnhilde's bed:—
For he alone frees her, the bride,
Who's freer than I, the god!
(*Overcome with joyous emotion,
Brünnhilde throws herself into
his arms.*)
O, eyes aglow with delight,
That often I tenderly wooed,

## Act III

wenn kindisch lallend
der Helden Lob
von holden Lippen dir floss:—
dieser Augen strahlendes Paar,
das oft im Sturm mir geglänzt,
wenn Hoffnungs-Sehnen
das Herz mir sengte,
nach Welten-Wonne
mein Wunsch verlangte
aus wild webendem Bangen:—
zum letzten Mal
letz' es mich heut'
mit des Lebewohles
letztem Kuss!
Dem glücklicher'n Manne
glänze sein Stern;
dem unseligen Ew'gen
muss es scheidend sich schliessen!
Denn so—kehrt
der Gott sich dir ab:
so küsst er die Gottheit von dir.
*(Er küsst sie auf beide Augen, die*
*ihr sogleich verschlossen bleiben:*
*sie sinkt sanft ermattend in sein-*
*en Armen zurück. Er geleitet sie*
*zart auf einen niedrigen Moo-*
*shügel zu liegen, über den sich*
*eine*
*breitästige Tanne ausstreckt.*
*Noch einmal betrachtet er ihre*
*Züge und schliesst ihr dann den*
*Helm fest zu; dann verweilt sein*
*Blick nochmals schmerzlich auf*
*ihrer Gestalt, die er endlich mit*

When lust of strife
A kiss had won you,
When, gently opening,
Your maiden lips
The heroes' praises would sing;
O, dear eyes that often in the storm
Would beam and brighten my way
When hope and passion
My heart set longing
For earthly rapture
And bliss of loving,
With wild wishing and dreading:
A parting kiss
Take you tonight,
As I bid farewell
To light and bliss!
Your starry-bright glances
Keep for the man;
On me luckless immortal
You are closing for ever!
For thus—doth
The god renounces you
Thus kissing your godhead away.
*(He kisses both her eyes, which at*
*once close. She sinks insensible in*
*his arms. He bears her tenderly to*
*a low mossy bank, shaded by the*
*wide-spreading branches of a*
*great fir-tree. Once more he gazes*
*on her features. Then he closes her*
*helmet tightly. Again he looks sor-*
*rowfully at her recumbent form,*
*which he at last covers with the*
*Walkyr's steel shield. Then, with*

*dem langen Stahlschilde der Wal-*
*küre zudeckt.—Dann schreitet er*
*mit feierlichem, Entschlusse in*
*die Mitte der Bühne und kehrt die*
*Spitze seines Speeres gegen einen*
*mächtigen Felsstein.)*
Loge hör'!
lausche hieher!
Wie zuerst ich dich fand
als feurige Gluth,
wie dann einst du mir schwandest
als schweifende Lohe:
wie ich dich band,
bann' ich dich heut'!
Herauf, wabernde Lohe,
umlod're mir feurig den Fels!
Loge! Loge! Hieher!
*(Bei der letzten Anrufung schlägt*
*er mit der Spitze des Speeres*
*dreimal auf den Stein, worauf*
*diesem ein Feuerstrahl entfährt,*
*der schnell zu einem Flammen-*
*meere anschwillt, dem Wotan mit*
*einem Winke seiner Speerspitze*
*den Umkreis des Felsens als*
*Strömung zuweist.)*
Wer meines Speeres
Spitze fürchtet,
durchschreite das Feuer nie!
*(Er verschwindet in der Gluth*
*nach dem Hintergrunde zu.—*
*Der Vorhang fällt.)*

*DAS ENDE.*

*solemn determination, he moves*
*to the centre of the stage, and*
*points the head of his spear*
*toward a mighty rock.)*
Loge, hear!
Lend me your ear!
As at first I found you.
A fiery flame,
As thou did escape me,
A-leaping and glowing:
As you were bound,
I bind you now:
Arise, flaring and glowing,
Ring round the whole mountain
with fire!
Loge! Loge! Arise!
*(After the last invocation Wotan*
*strikes the rock three times with*
*the point of his spear, whereupon*
*a flame leaps up. It soon grows*
*into a sea of flames, which, with a*
*motion of his spear, Wotan con-*
*fines in a circle that hems round*
*the rock.)*
Who from my spear-point
Shrinks in terror,
Shall never the flame defy!
*(He disappears in the background*
*amid the flames. The curtain*
*falls.)*

*THE END.*

# *Siegfried* (1876)

MUSIC AND LIBRETTO BY RICHARD WAGNER

---

This three-act opera was first performed at the Festspielhaus in Bayreuth on August 16, 1876. Mime, the dwarf, is trying futilely to forge an unbreakable sword for Siegfried, Sieglinde's son, who she left in his care when she died. He believes Siegfried's vitality and fearlessness will help him slaughter Fafner, who has changed himself into a dragon and guards the Rhinegold, the Tarnhelm and the ring, all hidden in a secret place deep in the forest. Siegfried brings a bear back from the forest; the bear frightens Mime, but Siegfried just laughs and breaks yet another sword, leaving before a wanderer, blinded in one eye and wrapped in a cloak, appears and prophecizes that "only a fearless man can temper the sword" and warns Mime to be wary of this individual. Mime realizes he's not capable of reforging the sword and asks Siegfried, who is afraid of nothing, to try. Siegfried reforges Notung, splitting the anvil in two with his first blow. Alberich, deep in the forest, keeps watch over the cave of the Rhinegold. The wanderer warns Alberich about Mime, telling him of his plan to poison Siegfried. At dawn, Mime takes Siegfried to the cave. The forest awakens with the song of the birds. Siegfried blows on his silver horn, waking Fafner, and thrusts Notung into the dragon's heart. A drop of blood burns his hand. He sucks on the burn to ease the pain, and he is able to understand the forest bird, who instructs him where to find the Tarnhelm and the ring and warns him to beware of Mime, who will offer him a drink containing poison. Siegfried sets off with the bird as his guide. Wotan asks Erda to predict the future, but gets only an ambiguous response. Wotan tries to block Siegfried's path. Siegfried breaks Wotan's spear, and, with it, the power of the gods. The sight of Brünnhilde combined with his need for his mother fills his heart with terror for the first time in his life. He kisses Brünnhilde, awakening her. They declare their deep and passionate love for one another and sing "let the twilight of the gods begin."

---

## ◼ ACT I

*WALD.*

*Den Vordergrund bildet ein Theil einer Felsenhöhle die sich links tiefer nach innen zieht, nach rechts aber gegen drei Viertheile der Bühne einnimmt. Zwei natürlich gebildete Eingänge stehen dem Walde zu offen: der eine nach rechts, unmittelbar im Hintergrunde, der andere, breitere, ebenda seitwärts. An der Hinterwand, nach links zu, steht ein grosser Schmiedeherd, aus Felsstücken natürlich geformt; künstlich ist nur der grosse Blasebalg: de rohe Esse geht—ebenfalls natürlich—durch das Felsdach hinauf. Ein sehr grosser Ambos und andre Schmiedegeräthschaften.—*

**MIME:** (*sitzt, als der Vorhang nach einem kurzen Orchester-Vorspiel aufgeht, am Ambos, und hämmert mit wachsender Unruhe an einem Schwerte: endlich hält er unmuthig ein*). Zwangvolle Plage!
Müh' ohne Zweck!
Das beste Schwert,
das je ich geschweisst,
in der Riesen Fäusten
hielte es fest:
doch dem ich's geschmiedet,
der schmähliche Knabe,

er knickt und schmeisst es entzwei,
als schüf' ich Kindergeschmeid!—
(*Er wirft das Schwert unmuthig auf den Ambos, stemmt die Arme ein und blickt sinnend zu Boden.*)
Es giebt ein Schwert,
das er nicht zerschwänge:
Nothung's Trümmer
zertrotzt' er mir nicht,
könnt' ich die starken
Stücken schweissen,
die meine Kunst
nicht zu kitten weiss.
Könnt' ich's dem Kühnen schmieden,
meiner Schmach erlangt' ich da Lohn!—
(*Er sinkt tiefer zurück, und neigt sinnend das Haupt.*) Fafner, der wilde Wurm,
lagert im finst'ren Wald;
mit des furchtbaren Leibes Wucht
der Niblungen Hort
hütet er dort.
Siegfried's kindischer Kraft
erläge wohl Fafner's Leib:
des Niblungen Ring
erränge ich mir.
Ein Schwert nur taugt zu der That,
nur Nothung nützt meinem Neid,
wenn Siegfried sehrend ihn schwingt:—
und nicht kann ich's schweissen,
Nothung das Schwert!—
(*Er fährt in höchstem Unmuth wieder fort zu hämmern.*)
Zwangvolle Plage!
Müh' ohne Zweck!

## ◼ Act I

*A FOREST.*

*The foreground represents a portion of a rocky cave which extends inwards on the left, but occupies only three-fourths of the stage on the right. Two natural entrances open onto the woods; one halfway up the stage, forms the back, the other, R, is wider and slanting at the side. On the left against the wall stands a large smith's forge, naturally formed of stones, the bellows alone being artificial. The rough chimney—also natural—leads up through the top of the cave. A very large anvil and other smith's appliances.*

**MIME:** (*when, after a short orchestral prelude, the curtain rises, is discovered sitting at the anvil, and hammering, with increasing discouragement, at a sword. At last he ceases work in despair*).
Forced undertaking!
Toil without fruit!
The stoutest sword
that I ever shaped
was found firm in a giant's fingers,
but he whom it is forged for,
the fiery stripling,
will strain and twist it in two as if it

were a straw or a toy.
(*He throws the sword pettishly on the anvil, set his arms akimbo, and gazes thoughtfully on the ground.*)
There is a blade
that is not so brittle:
"Needful's" fragments
he'd never fracture me;
could I but mend
the mighty metal;
but all my craft
cannot compass that.
If I could weld it with cunning
I should well be paid for my pains.
(*He sinks more back and shakes his head thoughtfully.*)
Fafner, the wicked worm,
rests here in forest wilds;
with his frame of terrific weight he holds
guard over the Nibelung's gold.
Siegfried's unproved prowess
may master even Fafner's might: the Nibelung Ring would rest then to me.
For this may serve but one sword;
now none but "Needful" I need,
by Siegfried searchingly swung:—
and I cannot shape me
"Needful" the sword!—
(*He recommences hammering, much discouraged.*)
Forced undertaking!
Toil without fruit!
The stoutest sword
that I ever shaped
will never be drawn

Das beste Schwert,
das je ich geschweisst,
nie taugt es je
zu der einz'gen That!
Ich tapp'r' und hämm're nur,
weil der Knab' os heischt;
or knickt und schmeisst es entzwei,
und schmählt doch, schmied' ich
ihm nicht!
(*Siegfried, in wilder Waldkleid-
ung, mit einem silbernen Horn an
einer Kette; kommt mit jähem Ungestüm aus dem Walde herein; er
hat einen grossen Bären mit einem Bastseile gezäumt, und
treibt diesen mit lustigem
Übermuthe gegen Mime an.
Mime'n entsinkt vor Schreck das
Schwert; er flüchtet hinte den
Herd; Siegfried treibt ihm den
Bären überall nach.*)

**SIEGFRIED:** Hoiho! Hoiho!
Hau' ein! Hau' ein!
Friss' ihn! Friss' ihn,
den Fratzenschmied!
(*Er lacht unbändig.*)

**MIME:** Fort mit dem Thier!
Was taugt mir der Bär!

**SIEGFRIED:** Zu zwei komm' ich,
dich besser zu zwicken:
Brauner, frag' nach dem Schwert!

**MIME:** He! lass' das Wild!
Dort liegt die Waffe:
fertig fegt' ich sie heut'.

**SIEGFRIED:** So fährst du heute
noch heil!
(*Er löst dem Bären den Zaum,
und giebt ihm damit
einen Schlag auf den Rücken.*)
Lauf', Brauner;
dich brauch' ich nicht mehr!
(*Der Bär läuft in den Wald
zurück.*)

**MIME:** (*zitternd hinter dem Herde
vorkommend*). Wohl leid' ich's
gern,
erleg'st du Bären:
was bringst du lebend
die braunen heim?

**SIEGFRIED:** (*setzt sich, um sich
vom Lachen zu erholen*). Nach
bess'rem Gesellen sucht' ich,
als daheim mir einer sitzt;
im tiefen Walde mein Horn
liess ich da hallend tönen:
ob sich froh mir gesellte
ein guter Freund?
das frug' ich mit dem Getön'.
Aus dem Busche kam ein Bär,
der hörte mir brummend zu;
er gefiel mir besser als du,
doch bess're wohl fänd' ich noch:
mit dem zähen Baste
zäumt' ich ihn da,
dich, Schelm, nach dem Schwerte
zu fragen.
(*Er springt auf und geht nach dem
Schwerte.*)

in the cause that I need.
I knock and I hammer
but at the boy's request
he'll bend and snap it in two,
yet scold me, should I not forge.
(*Siegfried in a wild forest dress,
with a silver horn slung by a
chain, bursts impetuously from
the wood. He has bridled a great
bear with a bast rope, and urges it
with merry roughness towards
Mime, who drops the sword in terror, and flies behind the forge. Siegfried drives the bear everywhere
after him.*)

**SIEGFRIED:** Oho! Oho!
Come on! come on!
Tear him! tear him!
The trumpery smith!
(*He shouts with laughter.*)

**MIME:** Take him away!
I do not want the bear!

**SIEGFRIED:** We come double
the better to cow you.
Bruin, ask for the sword!

**MIME:** Ho! keep away!
I've cast the weapon
Fit and fairly today.

**SIEGFRIED:** So far you've saved
then your skin.
(*He looses the bear from the rope
and gives him a blow on the back
with it.*)
Run, Bruin;
your business is done!
(*The bear trots back into the
wood.*)

**MIME:** (*coming out trembling
from behind the forge*).
I like it when
you slay bears;
why bring
that brute to me alive?

**SIEGFRIED:** (*sitting down to recover from his laughter*). Pining
for better companions
than the one at home,
I went to leafy woodland,
while I wound my horn right loudly;
for I had discovered
a welcome friend;—
rang forth my notes with that aim.
From the bushes came a bear
who listened with brutish growl,
and I liked him better than you,
though better luck I'd have yet.
With a strong bast rope
I bridled him straight
to seek for my sword from this rascal.
(*He jumps up and goes towards
the sword.*)

**MIME:** (*erfasst das Schwert, es Siegfried zu reichen*). Ich schuf die
Waffe scharf,
ihrer Schneide wirst du dich freu'n.

**SIEGFRIED:** (*nimmt das
Schwert*). Was frommt seine helle
Schneide,
ist der Stahl nicht hart und fest?
(*Er prüft es mit der Hand.*)
Hei! was ist das
für müss'ger Tand!
Den schwachen Stift
nennst du ein Schwert?
(*Er zerschlägt es auf dem Ambos,
dass die Stücken ringsum fliegen:
Mime weicht erschrocken aus.*)
Da hast du die Stücken,
schändlicher Stümper:
hätt' ich am Schädel
dir sie zerschlagen!—
Soll mich der Prahler
länger noch prellen?
Schwatzt mir von Riesen
und rüstigen Kämpfen,
von kühnen Thaten
und tüchtiger Wehr;
will Waffen mir schmieden,
Schwerte schaffen;
rühmt seine Kunst,
als könnt' er was Rechtes:
nehm' ich zur Hand nun
was er gehämmert,
mit einem Griff
zergreif' ich den Quark!—
Wär' mir nicht schier
zu schäbig der Wicht,
ich zerschmiedet' ihn selbst
mit seinem Geschmeid',
den alten albernen Alp!
Des Aergers dann hätt' ich ein End'.
(*Er wirft sich wüthend auf eine
Steinbank, zur Seite rechts.*)

**MIME:** (*der ihn immer vorsichtig
ausgewichen*). Nun tob'st du wieder wie toll:
dein Undank, traun! ist arg.
Mach' ich dem bösen Buben
nicht alles gleich zu best,
was ich Gutes ihm schuf,
vergisst er gar zu schnell!
Willst du denn nie gedenken
was ich dich lehrt' vom Danke?
Dem sollst du willig gehorchen,
der je sich wohl dir erwies.
(*Siegfried wendet sich unmuthig
um, mit dem Gesicht nach der
Wand, so dass er ihm den Rücken
kehrt.*)
Das willst du wieder nicht
hören!—
Doch speisen magst du wohl?
Vom Spiesse bring' ich den Braten:
versuchtest du gern den Sud?
Für dich sott ich ihn gar.
(*Er bietet Siegfried Speise hin.
Dieser, ohne sich umzuwenden,
schmeisst ihm Topf und Braten
aus der Hand.*)

**SIEGFRIED:** Braten briet ich mir
selbst: deinen Sudel sauf' allein!

**MIME:** (*taking up the sword to
hand it to Siegfried*). I've shaped
the weapon sharp;
You will be well pleased with its
sheen.

**SIEGFRIED:** (*taking the sword*).
What purpose would have its shining were the steel not hard of proof?
(*Tries it in his hand.*)
Hey! what an idle
toy is this!
You call this silly switch a sword?
(*He beats it on the anvil till the
pieces fly around. Mime retreats
in terror.*)
Then there are the splinters,
scandalous sloven;
would I had smashed it
over your skull now!—
Shall such a liar
longer delude me?
Prating of giants,
of jousts and battles,
of bravest deeds
and of daring in war;
while he smithies weapons,
he shapes me swords,
praising his art
as if it were approved?
Yet when I handle
what he has hammered,
a single stroke
destroys all the trash.
Were he not, sure,
too scurvy a wight,
I would smithy and smite
the smith with his stuff,—
the ancient, imbecile imp!
My anger might then be allayed.
(*He throws himself raging on a
stone seat, R.*)

**MIME:** (*who has cautiously kept
his distance*). Now you rave in a
rage!
What gross ingratitude!
This overbearing boy
if he gets not all the best,
the good things I have given
are each and all forgot.
Will you then never think of
what I have said on thanking?
You should delight to obey him
who's shown you love for so long.
(*Siegfried sulkily turns his back
on him and remains with his face
to the wall.*)
You're loath to listen to my blaming!
But spurn not food at least.
That spit shall render its roast meat;
or say, would you like the soup?
It simmers long for you.
(*Brings food to Siegfried, who,
without turning, strikes pot and
meat out of his hand.*)

**SIEGFRIED:** I make meals for myself: you can swill your slop alone!

MIME: (*stellt sich empfindlich*).
Das ist nun der Liebe
schlimmer Lohn!
Das der Sorgen
schmählicher Sold!—
Als zullendes Kind
zog ich dich auf,
wärmte mit Kleiden
den kleinen Wurm:
Speise und Trank
trug ich dir zu,
hütete dich
wie die eig'ne Haut.
Und wie du erwuchsest,
wartet' ich dein;
dein Lager schuf ich,
dass leicht du schlief'st.
Dir schmiedet' ich Tand
und ein tönend Horn;
dich zu erfreu'n
mäht' ich mich froh:
mit klugem Rathe
rieth ich dir klug,
mit lichtem Wissen
lehrt' ich dich Witz.
Sitz' ich daheim
in Fleiss und Schweiss,
nach Herzenslust
schweif'st du umher:
für dich nur in Plage,
in Pein nur für dich
verzehr' ich mich alter
armer Zwerg!
Und aller Lasten
ist das nun der Lohn,
dass der hastige Knabe
mich quält und hasst!
(*Er geräth in Schluchzen.*)

SIEGFRIED: (*der sich wieder um-gewendet, un in Mime's Blick ru-hig geforscht hat*). Vieles lehrtest du, Mime,
und manches lernt' ich von dir;
doch was du am liebsten mich lehrtest
zu lernen gelang mir nie:—
wie ich dich leiden könnt'.—
Träg'st du mir Speise
und Trank herbei—
der Ekel speis't mich allein;
schaff'st du ein leichtes
Lager zum Schlaf—
der Schlummer wird mir da schwer
willst du mich weisen
witzig zu sein—
gern bleib' ich taub und dumm.
Seh' ich dir erst
mit den Augen zu,
zu übel erkenn' ich
was alles du thu'st:
seh' ich dich steh'n,
gangeln und geh'n,
knicken und nicken,
mit den Augen zwicken:
beim Genick' möcht' ich
den Nicker packen,
den Garaus geben
dem garst'gen Zwicker!—
So lernt' ich, Mime, dich leiden.
Bist du nun weise,
so hilf mir wissen,
worüber umsonst ich sann:—
in den Wald lauf' ich,
dich zu verlassen,
wie kommt das, kehr' ich zurück?

MIME: (*appearing much hurt*).
This is my affection's
foul reward!
This my toil's
disgraceful return!
A querulous brat
kindly I reared,
wrapped in warm linen
the little wretch:
water and food
for you I found,
looked upon you
as my very life.
And as you grew
I waited on you;
in care for your slumber
a couch made soft.
I shaped toys for you,
and a tuneful horn;
ever at your whim
willingly worked:
with cunning counsel
I read you all craft,
with subtle wisdom
sharpened your wits.
Moping at home
I toil and moil,
while heedless from me you hurry away
For you do I plague myself,
takes pains but for you;
so dwindle my powers
—a poor old dwarf!—
For all my worry
is this my reward,
from the hot-headed boy
but abuse and hate!
(*He bursts into a fit of sobbing.*)

SIEGFRIED: (*who has again turned round and gazed steadily in Mime's face*). Much you've taught me, Mime,
and many tales have you told;
but what you would like best to teach me
were a lesson I'd gladly let be:—
how not to loathe your sight.
Bread do you bring,
refreshment too—
I feed on disgust alone.
Spread you my couch
with comforts for sleep—
then slumber wends from my side;
when all my wits
you work to instruct
I would be deaf and dumb.
Soon as I open
my eyes on you
I see only evil there
whatever you do.
Seeing you stand
shambling and shaking,
shrinking and slinking,
with your eyelids blinking,—
I'd take you by the neck
and shake and wake you,
to end your idiot antics
forever!—
Such feelings, Mime, I foster.
If you have wisdom
then listen to me wisely,
One thing I have pored upon.—
When I scour forests
seeking to fly you,
what motive makes me return?

Alle Thiere sind
mir theurer als du:
Baum und Vogel,
die Fische im Bach,
lieber mag ich sie
leiden als dich:—
wie kommt das nun, kehr' ich zurück?
Bist du klug, so thu' mir's kund.

MIME: (*setzt sich in einiger Ent-fernung ihm traulich gegenüber*).
Mein Kind, das lehrt dich kennen,
wie lieb ich am Herzen dir lieg'.

SIEGFRIED: (*lacht*). Ich kann dich
ja nicht leiden,—
vergiss das nicht so leicht!

MIME: Dess' ist deine Wildheit
schuld,
die du Böser bändigen sollst.—
Jammernd verlangen Junge
nach ihrer Alten Nest;
Liebe ist das Verlangen:
so lechzest du auch deinen
Mime—
so lieb'st du auch deinen Mime—
so musst du ihn lieben!
Was dem Vögelein ist der Vogel,
wenn er im Nest es nährt,
eh' das flügge mag fliegen:
das ist dir kindischem Spross
der kundig sorgende Mime—
das muss er dir sein.

SIEGFRIED: Ei, Mime bist du so
witzig,
so lass' mich eines noch wissen!—
Es sangen die Vöglein
so selig im Lenz,
das eine lockte das and're
du sagtest selbst—
da ich's wissen wollt'—
das wären Männchen und Weibchen.
Sie kos'ten so lieblich,
und liessen sich nicht;
sie bauten ein Nest
und brüteten drin;
da flatterte junges
Geflügel auf,
und beide pflegten der Brut.
So ruhten im Busch
auch Rehe gepaart,
selbst wilde Füchse und Wölfe:
Nahrung brachte
zum Nest das Männchen,
das Weibchen säugte die Welpen
Da lernt' ich wohl
was Liebe sei;
der Mutter entwandt' ich
die Welpen nie.—
Wo hast du nun, Mime,
dein minniges Weibchen,
dass ich es Mutter nenne?

MIME: (*verdriesslich*). Was ist dir,
Thor?
Ach, bist du dumm
Bist doch weder Vogel noch Fuchs?

SIEGFRIED: Das zullende Kind
zogest du auf,
wärmtest mit Kleiden
den kleinen Warm:—
wie kam dir aber

There's not a beast that I love
better than you;
bird in forest,
or fish in the brook,
dearer than you
I deem all of these:—
what motive then makes me return?
If you mind, then tell it to me.

MIME: (*sits affectionately a little way from Siegfried*). My son, this
clearly shows you
how closely your heart clings to me.

SIEGFRIED: (*laughing*). But I can-not endure you,—forget not that indeed.

MIME: This is but your wilful way,
which were quickly quelled at will.
Young ones are ever yearning,
needing the parent nest;
Love's the name of this longing:
such leaning you have to me,
this love you feel for your Mime.
You must surely love him!
What the father is to the fledgling
which it nursed in the nest
before in flight it could flutter,
such to you, foolish child,
is faithful, cherishing Mime.
You must be his charge.

SIEGFRIED: Hey, Mime, since
you're so clever,
explain this to me also clearly.—
The birds in the springtime
so bravely did sing,
the one beseeching the other:
you said yourself,
when I asked of it,
these warblers husband and wife were.
They kissed with such pleasure
and never parted,
they built a nest
and brooded there;
then fluttered soon
the young fledglings out,
and both took care of the brood.
So duly reposed
the deer which had paired,
even wolves and foxes the wildest:
the male furnished food,
for the family,
the cubs were nursed by his con-sort.
I learned from this
what love must be;
the whelps I never moved
from the mother's side.—
Where have you, Mime,
your darling consort
that I may call her mother?

MIME: (*angrily*). Are you a fool?
What is it to you?
Are you either fowl or fox?

SIEGFRIED: A querulous brat
you kindly reared,
wrapped in warm linen
the little wretch:—
how came you, then,

der kindishce Wurm?
Du machtest wohl gar
ohne Mutter mich?

**MIME:** (*in grosser Verlegenheit*).
Glauben sollst du,
was ich dir sage:
ich bin dir Vater
und Mutter zugleich.

**SIEGFRIED:** Da lügst du, garstiger
Gauch!—
Wie die Jungen den Alten gleichen,
das hab' ich mir glücklich erseh'n.
Nun kam ich zum klarne Bach:
da erspäht' ich die Bäum'
und Thier' im Spiegel;
Sonn' und Wolken,
wie sie nur sind,
im Glitzer erschienen sie gleich.
Da sah' ich denn auch
mein eigen Bild;
ganz anders als du
dünkt' ich mir da:
so glich wohl der Kröte.
ein glänzender Fisch;
doch kroch nie ein Fisch aus der
Kröte.

**MIME:** (*höchst ärgerlich*).
Gräulichen Unsinn
kram'st du da aus!

**SIEGFRIED:** (*immer lebendiger*).
Sich'st du, nun fällt
auch selbst mir ein,
was zuvor ich umsonst besann:
wenn zum Wald ich laufe,
dich zu verlassen,
wie das kommt, kehr' ich doch
heim?
(*Er springt auf.*)
Von dir noch muss ich erfahren,
wer Vater und Mutter mir sei!

**MIME:** (*weicht ihm aus*). Was Vater! was Mutter!
Müssige Frage!

**SIEGFRIED:** (*packt ihn bei der
Kehle*). So muss ich dich fassen
um 'was zu wissen
gutwillig
erfahr' ich doch nichts!
So musst' ich Alles
ab dir trotzen:
kaum das Reden
hätt' ich errathen,
entwand ich's nicht
mit Gewalt dem Schuft!
Heraus damit,
räudiger Kerl!
Wer ist mir Vater und Mutter?

**MIME:** (*wachdem er mit dem
Kopfe genickt und mit den
Händen gewinkt, ist von Siegfried
losgelassen worden*). An's Leben
geh'st du mir schier!—
Nun lass'! was zu wissen dich geizt,
erfahr' es, ganz wie ich's weiss.—
O undankbares,
arges Kind!
jetzt hör', wofür du mich hassest!
Nicht bin ich Vater
noch Vetter dir.—
und dennoch verdankst du mir
dich!
Ganz fremd bist du mir,
deinem einz' gen Freund;

by this clamoring wretch?
Do you mean that I was made
without a mother?

**MIME:** (*much embarrassed*).
Only trust whatever I tell you;
I am your father
and mother in one.

**SIEGFRIED:** You lie! perfidious
fool!—
That the young one is like the parent
long since have I proved for myself.
I came to the crystal brook
and could trace bird and beast
within its mirror;
mist and sunlight,
seen as they are,
the faithful reflex of their form.
My own pictured image
I also saw;
unlike yourself
surely I seemed;
as it were to compare
with a toad a bright fish;
a fish never had toad for a father.

**MIME:** (*much vexed*). Terrible
stuff
you chatter still.

**SIEGFRIED:** (*with increasing animation*). See now, I vow
my self I've found
what in vain I so long have sought:
when I fly from you
to roam in the forest
how it happens home I return.
(*He springs up.*)
It is to make you inform me
what father and mother are mine.

**MIME:** (*retreating from him*).
What father? What mother?
Meaningless fancies!

**SIEGFRIED:** (*seizing him by the
throat*). Then must I force you to
tell me
some truth;
good temper
will further me nothing.
I must
fulfil my wishes by force;
scarcely language
should I have learned
if not wrested from you,
wretch, my main strength!
So tell me now, rascally knave,
who are my father and mother?

**MIME:** (*who has signed with his
head and hands for Siegfried to release him*). You nearly have
crushed my life!—
Let loose! what you wish to know
I'll tell you, now—without
wile.—
O thankless
and unthinking boy!
Now hear why you hate me!
I am no father
nor flesh of yours;
yet owe all to my aid.
You're no kin of mine
who yet am so kind;
I have out of goodness,

aus Erbarmen allein
barg ich dich hier:
nun hab' ich lieblichen Lohn!
Was verhofft' ich Thor mir auch
Dank?
Einst lag wimmernd ein Weib
da draussen im wilden Wald:
zur Höhle half ich ihr her,
am warmem Herd sie zu hüten.
Ein Kind trug sie im Schoss;
traurig gebar sie's hier;
sie wand sich hin und her,
ich half so gut ich konnt':
stark war die Noth, sie starb—
doch Siegfried, der genas.

**SIEGFRIED:** (*hat sich gesetzt*). So
starb meine Mutter an mir?

**MIME:** Meinem Schutz übergab sie
dich;
ich schenkt' ihn gern dem Kind.
Was hat sich Mime gemüht!
was gab sich der Gute für Noth!
Als zullendes Kind
zog ich dich auf . . .

**SIEGFRIED:** Mich dünkt, dess' ge-
dachtest du schon Jetzt sag:' woher
heiss' ich Siegfried?

**MIME:** So hiess mich die Mutter
möcht' ich dich heissen:
als Siegfried würdest
du stark und schön.—
Ich wärmte mit Kleiden
den kleinen Wurm . . .

**SIEGFRIED:** Nun melde, wie hiess
meine Mutter?

**MIME:** Das weiss ich wahrlich
kaum!—
Speise und Trank
trug ich dir zu . . .

**SIEGFRIED:** Den Namen sollst du
mir nennen!

**MIME:** Entfiel er mir wohl? doch
halt!
Sieglinde mochte sie heissen,
die dich in Sorge mir gab.—
Ich hütete dich
wie die eig'ne Haut . . .

**SIEGFRIED:** Dann frag' ich, wie
hiess mein Vater?

**MIME:** (*barsch*). Den hab' ich nie
geseh'n.

**SIEGFRIED:** Doch die Mutter
nannte den Namen?

**MIME:** Erschlagen sei er,
das sagte sie nur;
dich Vaterlosen
befahl sie mir da:—
"und wie du erwuchses",
wartet' ich dein:
dein Lager schuf ich,
dass leicht du schlief'st . . ."

**SIEGFRIED:** Still mit dem alten
Staarenlied!—
Soll ich der Kunde glauben,
hast du mir nichts gelogen,
so lass mich nun Zeichen seh'n!

**MIME:** Was soll dir's noch bezeugen?

guarded your life.
My love is preciously paid!
Did I look for tender return?
A poor woman lay wailing
once in woodland wild:
I helped her home to this hole,
and gave my hearth for a haven.
Of child proved she in labor;
pining she bore it here;
deep anguish harried her,
I helped her as best I could.
Baleful her lot,—she died,
but Siegfried saw the light.

**SIEGFRIED:** (*who has seated himself*). So my mother died then?

**MIME:** To my charge she confided
you;
I willingly cherished the babe.
What work for Mime you made.
What woes the poor wight has en-
dured!
I kindly reared a querulous brat.

**SIEGFRIED:** It seems you have said
that before. Now say, who named
me Siegfried?

**MIME:** Presently your mother said
I must name you:
you grew as Siegfried
staunch and strong.—
I wrapped in warm linen
the little wretch . . .

**SIEGFRIED:** Now, Mime, what
name bore my mother?

**MIME:** I scarcely know.—
I found water and food for
you . . .

**SIEGFRIED:** Her title instantly tell
me!

**MIME:** It is forgot!—Yet hold!
Sieglinde certainly is the name of
she
who gave you sadly to me.—
I looked upon you
as my very life . . .

**SIEGFRIED:** Now tell me my father's title.

**MIME:** (*harshly*). I never saw his
face.

**SIEGFRIED:** But my mother has
mentioned his name?

**MIME:** She said that someone slew
him,
and no more;
fatherless
she confided you to me.—
"And when you waxed
I waited on you,
in care for your slumber
you, couch made soft . . ."

**SIEGFRIED:** Stint with that endless
starling note!—
Shall I believe your tidings, and
not think you a liar,
then let me see a sign.

**MIME:** How shall I then assure you?

SIEGFRIED: Dir glaub' ich nicht
mit dem Ohr',
dir glaub' ich nur mit dem Aug';
welch' Zeichen zeugt für dich?

SIEGFRIED: I trust you not with my
ears,
I trust in but my eyes:
what witness will you bring?

MIME: (holt nach einigem Besinnen die zwei Stücken eines zer-
schlagenen Schwertes herbei). Das
gab mir deine Mutter:
für Mühe, Kost und Pflege
liess sie's als schwachen Lohn.
Sieh' her, ein zerbroch'nes
Schwert!
Dein Vater, sagte sie, führt' es,
als im letzten Kampf er erlag.

MIME: (after some hesitation,
brings forward the two pieces of a
broken sword). I had this of yours
mother's
for menage, toil and trouble,
was it my scant reward.
See here, but a broken sword!
She said your father had swung it
at the fight in which he was felled.

SIEGFRIED: Und diese Stücken
sollst du mir schmieden:
dann schwing' ich mein rechtes
Schwert!
Eile dich, Mime,
mühe dich rasch;
kannst du 'was Recht's.
nun zieg' deine Kunst!
Täusche mich nicht
mit schlechtem Tand:
den Trümmern allein
tau' ich 'was zu.
Find' ich dich faul,
füg'st du sie schlecht,
flick'st du mit Flausen
den festen Stahl,—
dir Feigem fahr' ich zu Leib,
das Fegen lernst du von mir!
Denn heute noch, schwör' ich,
will ich das Schwert;
die Waffe gewinn' ich noch heut'.

SIEGFRIED: And you shall forge
now
for me the fragments;
I'll find so my right defense!
Up! arm yourself, Mime!
Move and be brisk!
Can you be brave?
Then show me your craft!
Playthings no more
on me impose:
these pieces alone
promise to serve.
If you should fail,
forge it poorly,
find I a flaw
in the faultless steel,
you, fumbler, finely I'll beat;—
you'll feel the burnish yourself!
This day will I surely
wield my own sword;
I'll win this weapon at once.

MIME: (erschrocken). Was willst
du noch heut' mit dem Schwert?

MIME: (frightened). What would
you do with the sword?

SIEGFRIED: Aus dem Wald fort
in die Welt zieh'n:
nimmer kehr' ich zurück.
Wie ich froh bin,
dass ich frei ward,
nichts mich bindet und zwingt!
Mein Vater bist du nicht;
in der Ferne bin ich heim;
dein Herd ist nicht mein Haus,
meine Decke nicht dein Dach.
Wie der Fisch froh
in der Fluth schwimmt,
wie der Fink frei
sich davon schwingt
flieg' ich von hier,
fluthe davon,
wie der Wind über'n Wald
weh' ich dahin,—
dich, Mime, nie wieder zu seh'n!
(Er stürmt in den Wald fort.)

SIEGFRIED: In the wide world
I will wander,
never more to return.
What a full joy
to have freedom!
nothing anchors me here.
You're not my father.—
I shall find another home!
Your hearth is not my house,
never I'll rest beneath your roof.
As the fish gladly
through the flood shoots,
as the flinch flies
to a free shore;
far from here I flee,
flow like a stream;
with the wind over the woods
wafting away,—
then, Mime, I'll never return!
(He rushes away into the woods.)

MIME: (in höchster Angst). Halte!
halte! wohin?
(Er ruft mit der grössten Anstren-
gung in den Wald.)
He! Siegfried!
Siegfried! He!—
Da stürmt er hin!—
Nun sitz' ich da:—
zur alten Noth
hab' ich die neue!
vernagelt bin ich nun ganz!—
Wie helf' ich mir jetzt?
Wie halt' ich ihn fest?
Wie führ' ich den Huien
zu Fafner's Nest?
Wie füg' ich die Stücken
des tückischen Stahl's?

MIME: (in great alarm). Halt
there! halt there! what ho!
(He calls with his utmost strength
toward the wood.)
Ho! Siegfried!
Siegfried! Ho!
He hurls away,
and here I sit.—
To old distress
comes added trouble;
I am completely entangled.—
What help can I find
How can I handle him best?
How shall I force him to hasten to
Fafner's nest?
How forge me these worthless
pieces

Keines Ofens Gluth
glüht mir die ächten!
keines Zwergen Hammer
zwingt mir die harten;
des Niblungen Neid,
Noth und Schweiss
nietet mir Nothung nicht,
schweisst mir das Schwert nicht zu
ganz!—
(Er knickt verzweifelnd auf dem
Schemel hinter dem Ambos zusammen.)

of stubbornest steel?
For no furnace heat
helps me to fuse them,
no kobold's hammer
conquers their hardness,
By Niblung's annoy,
need and sweat,
"Needful" can never be knit;
Mime cannot mend the sword.
(He crouches down despairingly
on his stool behind the anvil.)

(Der Wanderer (Wotan) tritt aus
dem Wald an das hintere Thor der
Höhle heran.— Er trägt einen
dunkelblauen langen Mantel; einen Speer führt er als Stab. Auf
dem Haupte hat er einen grossen
Hut mit breiter runder Krämpe,
die über das fehlende eine Auge
tief hereinhängt.)

(The Wanderer (Wotan) ad-
vances from the wood to the back
entrance of the cave. He wears a
long, dark blue cloak, and bears a
spear as a staff. On his head is a
large hat with a broad, round
brim hanging low over his missing eye.)

WANDERER: Heil dir, weiser
Schmied!
Dem wegmüden Gast
gönne hold
des Hauses Herd!

WANDERER: Hail, wisest smith!
To way-wearied guest
grant as host
your house and hearth.

MIME: (ist erschrocken aufgefah-
ren). Wer ist's, der im wilden
Wald mich sucht?
Wer verfolgt mich im öden Forst?

MIME: (starting up in terror). By
whom am I sought in this woodland
wild?
Who has tracked me to this retreat?

WANDERER: Wand'rer heisst
mich die Welt.
weit wandert' ich schon,
auf der Erde Rücken
rührt' ich mich viel.

WANDERER: "Wanderer" calls
me the world:
I've made wide wanderings;
I roam at my will all the earth
around.

MIME: So rühre dich fort
und raste nicht hier,
heisst dich Wand'rer die Welt.

MIME: Then roam on your way
and rest not here,
or you were no Wanderer.

WANDERER: Gastlich ruht' ich bei
Guten,
Gaben gönnten mir viele:
denn Unheil fürchtet,
wer unhold ist.

WANDERER: Good men render me
a greeting,
gifts they grant to me as well;
forever misers
have evil ends.

MIME: Unheil wohnte
immer bei mir:
willst du dem Armen es mehren?

MIME: Evil weighs
forever on me;
Would you augment my anger?

WANDERER: (weiter hereintre-
tend). Viel erforscht' ich,
erkannte viel:
Wichtiges konnt' ich
manchem künden,
manchem wehren
was ihn mühte,
nagende Herzens Noth.

WANDERER: (advancing closer).
I've mastered much
and treasured much;
I've told wondrous tales
to men,
from many warded
what dismayed them,—
torturing heart's distress.

MIME: Spürtest du klug
und erspähtest viel,
hier brauch' ich nicht Spürer noch
Spahe!
Einsam will ich
und einzeln sein,
Lungerern lass' ich den Lauf.

MIME: You spy well,
and you spoke truth,
I want neither a spy nor a word
smith!
Solitary
I seek to bide.
I leave loungers to their own de-
vices.

WANDERER: (wieder einige
Schritte näher schreitend).
Mancher wähnte
weise zu sein,
nur was ihm noth that
wusst' er nicht;

WANDERER: (again approaching
a few steps nearer). Men have believed
their wisdom was great,
but what should boot them
was not their brains.

# Act I

was ihm frommte,
liess ich erfragen;
lohnend lehrt' ihn mein Wort.

**MIME:** (*immer ängstlicher, da der Wanderer sich nähert*). Müss'ges Wissen
wahren manche:
ich weiss mir grade genug;
mir genugt mein Witz,
ich will nicht mehr:
dir Weisem weis' ich den Weg!

**WANDERER:** (*setzt sich am Herde nieder*). Hier sitz' ich am Herd,
und setze mein Haupt
der Wissens-Wette zum Pfand:
mein Kopf ist dein,
du hast ihn erkies't,
erfrägst du dir nicht
was dir frommt,
lös' ich's mit Lehren nicht ein.

**MIME:** (*erschrocken und befangen, für sich*). Wie werd' ich den Lauernden los?
Verfänglich muss ich ihn fragen.—
(*Laut.*)
Dein Haupt pfänd' ich
für den Herd:
nun sorg', es sinnig zu lösen!
Drei der Fragen
stell' ich mir frei.

**WANDERER:** Dreimal muss ich's treffen.

**MIME:** (*nach einigem Nachsinnen*). Du rührtest dich viel
auf der Erde Rücken,
die Welt durchwandert'st du weit:
nun sage mir schlau,
welches Geschlecht
tagt in der Erde Tiefe?

**WANDERER:** In der Erde Tiefe
tagen die Nibelungen:
Nibelheim ist ihr Land.
Schwarzalben sind sie;
Schwarz-Alberich
hütet' als Herrscher sie einst:
eines Zauberringes
zwingende Kraft
zähmt' ihm das fleissige Volk.
Reicher Schätze
schimmernden Hort
häuften sie ihm:
der sollte die Welt ihm gewinnen.—
Zum zweiten was frägst du Zwerg?

**MIME:** (*in tieferes Sinnen gerathend*). Viel, Wanderer,
weisst du mir
aus der Erde Nabelnest:—
nun sage mir schlicht,
welches Geschlecht
ruht auf der Erde Rücken?

**WANDERER:** Auf der Erde Rücken
wuchtet der Riesen Geschiecht:
Riesenheim ist ihr Land.
Fasolt und Fafner,
der Rauhen Fürsten,
neideten Nibelung's Macht;
den gewaltigen Hort
gewannen sie sich,

What was good
straightaway I gave them;
spoke, and strengthened their minds.

**MIME:** (*terrified at the approach of the Wanderer*). Many yearn for useless matters;
for me my craft suffices:
I've sufficient wit,
I want no more;
so, wise one, wend on your way.

**WANDERER:** (*seating himself at the hearth*). Here gaining your hearth,
I gage my head
as stake in struggle of wits.
My head is yours
It will fall to your hand
if vainly you ask
my advice,—
should I not save it by wit.

**MIME:** (*aside, frightened and perplexed*). How shall I be rid of this rogue?
In trial must I entrap him.—
(*Aloud*).
Staking your head
against my hearth,
with care and cunning redeem it.
Three the questions
that I require.

**WANDERER:** Three times I must answer.

**MIME:** (*after some reflection*). Your rovings have led you
to earth's far regions,
you have wandered widely over worlds:—
now, answer me this,
what is the race
born in the earth's deep bowels?

**WANDERER:** In the earth's deep bowels
burrow the Nibelungs:
Nibelheim is their land.
Black elves are they all;
Black Alberich
guarded and governed them once.
By the mighty spell
of a magical ring
There roved the industrious dwarfs.
Endless riches,
rarest of hoards
he made them heap,
wherewith all the world should be won him.
Propose, dwarf, your second point.

**MIME:** (*in brown study*). Wanderer,
you saw much
of the earth's most central cells—
Now say to me;
what is the stock
which sojourns on its back?

**WANDERER:** On its back the giants live, an ungentle stock;
Giantdom is their land.
Fasolt and Fafner,
the jealous people,
envied Alberich's might,
and his wonderful hoard
they won for themselves,

errangen mir ihm den Ring:
um den entbrannte
den Brüdern Streit;
der Fasolt fällte,
als wilder Wurm
bütet nun Fafner den Hort.—
Die dritte Frage nun droht.

**MIME:** (*der ganz in Träumerei entrückt ist*). Viel, Wand'rer,
weisst du mir
von der Erde rauhem Rücken:—
nun sage mir wahr,
welches Geschlecht
wohnt auf wolkigen Höh'n?

**WANDERER:** Auf wolkigen Höh'n
wohnen die Götter:
Walhall heisst ihr Saal.
Lichtalben sind sie;
Licht-Alberich,
Wotan, waltet der Schaar.
Aus der Welt-Esche
weihlichstem Aste
schuf er sich einen Schaft:
dorrt der Stamm,
nie verdirbt doch der Speer;
mit seiner Spitze
sperrt Wotan die Welt.
Heil'ger Verträge
Treue-Runen
schnitt in den Schaft er ein.
Den Haft der Welt
hält in der Hand,
wer den Speer führt,
den Wotan's Faust umspannt.
Ihm neigte sich
der Niblungen Heer;
der Riesen Gezücht
zähmte sein Rath:
ewig gehorchen sie alle
des Speeres starkem Herrn.
(*Er stösst wie unwillkürlich mit dem Speer auf den Boden; ein leiser Donner lässt sich vernehmen, wovon Mime heftig erschrickt.*)
Nun rede, weiser Zwerg:
wusst' ich der Fragen Rath?
behalte mein Haupt ich frei?

**MIME:** (*is aus seiner träumerischen Versunkenheil aufgefahren, und gebärdet sich nun ängstlich, indem er den Wanderer nicht anzublicken wagt*).
Fragen und Haupt
hast du gelös't:
nun, Wand'rer, geh' deines Weg's!

**WANDERER:** Was zu wissen dir frommt
solltest du fragen;
Kunde verbürgte mein Kopf.—
dass du nun nicht weisst
was dir nützt,
dess' fass' ich jetzt deines als Pfand.
Gastlich nicht
galt mir dein Gruss:
mein Haupt gab ich
in deine Hand,
um mich des Herdes zu freu'n.
Nach Wettens Pflicht
pfänd' ich nun dich,
lösest du drei
der Fragen nicht leicht:
drum frische dir, Mime, den Muth.

and ravished also the ring.
Between the brothers
then broke out strife,
and, Fasolt fallen,
as dragon dread
hold now Fafner the hoard.
Now threatens
Your third inquiry.

**MIME:** (*who is quite absorbed in thought*). Wanderer,
You saw much
of the earth's far stretching surface.
Now tell me as well
what is the race
guards the sky above?

**WANDERER:** The sky above
guard well the Aesir;
where they dwell is Valhall'.
Light elves of heaven,
Light Alberich,
Wotan, ward their host.
From the World's ash tree's
worshipful arm
he shaped himself once a shaft:
true that spear,
though the tree may be spoiled,
with such a sceptre
Wotan sways the world.
Holiest treaties'
truthful runes
he wrote all around the shaft.
The head of worlds
he, by whose hand gripped
is the spear
that Wotan's grasp now spans.
There kneels to him
the Niblung host;
the giants must bow,
by him enjoined:
all must allegiance owe him,
the spear's resistless lord.
(*He rests his spear, as if accidentally, on the ground; a slight peal of thunder is heard. Mime terrified.*)
Now tell me, sapient dwarf, have I spoken the answers true?
My head do I hold my own?

**MIME:** (*who has recovered from his dreamy brooding, now shows renewed fear and dares not look at the Wanderer*).
You have redeemed questions and head:
now, Wanderer, go on your way.

**WANDERER:** What your welfare concerns
you should have sought before
holding my head in pledge.
Since you have not believed in what is good,
we'll gamble with your head as security.
You begrudged your guest greeting
I gave my head
into your hands,
that of your hearth I might be free;
so now
yours is placed in pledge,
can you not thrice
declare my riddles.
Make resolute, Mime, your mind.

MIME: (*schüchtern und in furchtsamer Ergebung*). Lang' schon mied ich
mein Heimathland,
lang' schon schied ich
aus der Mutter Schoss;
mir leuchtete Wotan's Auge,
zur Höhle lugt' es herein:
vor ihm magert
mein Mutterwitz.
Doch frommt mir's nun weise zu sein
Wand'rer, frage denn zu!
Vielleicht glückt mir's gezwungen
zu lösen des Zwergen Haupt.

WANDERER: Nun, ehrlicher Zwerg,
sag, mir zum ersten,
welches ist das Geschlecht,
dem Wotan schlimm sich zeigt,
und das doch das liebste ihm lebt?

MIME: Wenig hört' ich
von Heldensippen:
der Frage doch mach' ich mich frei.
Die Wälsungen sind
das Wunschgeschlecht,
das Wotan zeugte
und zärtlich liebt,
zeigt er auch Ungunst ihm.
Siegmund und Sieglind'
stammten von Wälse,
ein wild-verzweifeltes Zwillingspaar:
Siegfried zeugten sie selbst,
den stärksten Wälsungenspross.
Behalt' ich, Wanderer,
zum ersten mein Haupt?

WANDERER: Wie doch genau
das Geschlecht du mir nennst:
schlau eracht' ich dich Argen!
Der ersten Frage
ward'st du frei:
zum zweiten nun sag' mir,
Zwerg:
Ein weiser Niblung
wahret Siegfried:
Fafner'n soll er ihm fällen,
dass er den Ring erränge,
des Hortes Herrscher zu sein.
Welches Schwert
muss nun Siegfried schwingen.
taug' es zu Fafner's Tod?

MIME: (*seine gegenwärtige Lage immer mehr vergessend, und von dem Gegenstande lebhaft angezogen*). Nothung heisst
ein neidliches Schwert;
in einer Esche Stamm
stiess es Wotan:
dem sollt' es geziemen,
der aus dein Stamm' es zög'.
Der stärksten Helden
keiner bestand's:
Siegmund, der Kühne,
konnt's allein;
fechtend führt' er's im Streit,
bis an Wotan's Speer es zersprang.
Nun verwahrt die Stücke
ein weiser Schmied;
denn er weiss, dass allein
mit dem Wotansschwert
ein kühnes dummes Kind,
Siegfried, den Wurm versehrt.

MIME: (*shyly, and with cowed submission*). Long I've quitted
my native land,
long I've issued
from my mother earth;
the eye-glance of Wotan cows me,
he peered into my cave;
his gaze melts all
my mother wit.
But quick must my wisdom be now.—
Wanderer, question away!
Likewise may I redeem myself,
deliver the dwarf's poor head.

WANDERER: Now, amiable dwarf,
first let me ask you:
what is that noble race
that Wotan ruthlessly dealt with,
and which yet he deems most dear?

MIME: Of your heroes
I hear little;
yet certainly this I can solve.
The Volsungs are they,
the valued race
that Wotan fathered
and fondly loved,
though he withdrew favor.
Siegmund and Sieglind'
sprang from the Volsung,
a very turbulent
twin-born pair;
Siegfried too is their son,
the stoutest Volsung ever shaped.
My head then, Wanderer,
this time do I hold?

WANDERER: Yes, you rightly
declared me the race:
clearly you've proven your prowess!
You've quit the primal question
so, secondly hear and say.—
A wily Niblung
wards Siegfried,—
fated slayer of Fafner,
that he may ravish the rings
and hold the hoard for himself.
But what sword
must Siegfried then strike with,
dealing Fafner death?

MIME: (*forgetting his present position in his eager interest in the subject*). "Needful" is
the name of the sword;
It was
struck by Wotan in an ash tree's stem:
he whose hand could snatch it out
solely might own it.
By strongest heroes
was it not stirred;
Siegmund, the warlike;
won the prize;
well he wore it in strife,
till by Wotan's spear it was split.
Now, a subtle smith
preserves the shreds,
for he knows with no other
than Wotan's sword
that bold and foolish boy,
Siegfried, will slay the worm.

(*Ganz vergnügt.*)
Behalt' ich Zwerg
auch zweitens mein Haupt?

WANDERER: Der witzigste bist du
unter den Weisen:
wer käm' dir an Klugheit gleich?
Doch bist du so klug,
den kindischen Helden
für Zwergen-Zwecke zu nützen:
mit der dritten Frage
droh' ich nun!—
sag' mir, du weiser Waffenschmied,
wer wird aus den starken Stücken
Nothung, das Schwert, wohl schweissen.

MIME: (*fährt im höchsten Schrecken auf*). Die Stücken! Schwert!
O weh! mir schwindelt!—
Was fang' ich an?
Was fällt mir ein?
Verfluchter Stahl,
dass ich dich gestohlen!
Er hat mich vernagelt
in Pein und Noth;
mir bleibt er hart,
ich kann ihn nicht hämmern:
Niet' und Löthe
lässt mich im Stich!
Der weiseste Schmied
weiss sich nicht Rath:
wer schweisst nun das Schwert,
schaff' ich es nicht?
Das Wunder, wie soll ich's wissen?

WANDERER: (*ist vom Herd aufgestanden*). Dreimal solltest du fragen,
dreimal stand ich dir frei:
nach eitlen Fernen
forschtest du;
doch was zunächst sich dir fand,
was dir nützt, fiel dir nicht ein.
Nun ich's errathe,
wirst du verrückt:
gewonnen hab' ich
das witzige Haupt.—
Jetzt, Fafner's kühner Bezwinger,
hör' verfallener Zworg:—
nur wer das Fürchten
nie erfuhr,
schmiedet Nothung neu.
(*Mime starrt ihn gross an: er wendet sich zum Fersgange.*)
Dein weises Haupt
wahre von heut':
verfallen—lass' ich's dem,
der das Fürchten nicht gelernt.
(*Er lacht und geht in den Wald.*)

MIME: (*ist, wie vernichtet, auf den Schemel hinter den Ambos zurückgesunken: er stiert, grad' vor sich aus, in den sonnig beleuchteten Wald hinein.— Nach längerem Schweigen geräth er in heftiges Zittern*). Verfluchtes Licht!
Was flammt dort die Luft?
Was flackert und lackert,
was flimmert und schwirrt,
was schwebt dort und webt
und wabert umher?

(*Quite pleased*).
Thus have I saved
my head a second time.

WANDERER: Surely,
you are the wittiest of wise ones;
whose cunning can come near yours?
But since you have sought
this simpleton hero
for to make use of Niblung's need,
now my third inquiry
threatens you,
Say then, you wise weaponsmith,
who will
Reestablish "Needful," the sword,
from the stubborn splinters?

MIME: (*starts up in the greatest terror*). The splinters! the sword!
Alas! it escapes me!—
What can I say?
What course pursue?
The cursed steel,
would I never had stolen it!
To be thus entangled
in fatal toils!
It is far too hard
to yield to my hammer;
flux and solder
serve not to smelt.
The most artful smith
is at a loss!
Who shapes the sword
since I cannot?
How may I master this marvel?

WANDERER: (*who has risen from the hearth*). Three times your questions were asked.
three times I was acquit;
but your queries
were quite foreign,
for what was near to your heart
and your needs, did you not ask.
Now I have found it,
wondrous your fright:
Your witty brain
have I won as a prize.
Hear, Fafner's would-be undoer,
heed, you fated dwarf:—
none but who
has never felt fear
makes "Needful" new.
(*Mime stares wildly at him as he turns to depart.*)
Your head so wise
henceforth guard well!
I leave it to fall to him
who has not yet learned fear.
(*He turns away, laughing, and disappears in the forest.*)

MIME: (*paralyzed with terror, sinks back on his stool behind the anvil. He stares for a while before him at the sunlit forest. After a long silence he begins to tremble violently*). Accursed light!
How you creep aloft!
What quivers and shivers?
What quickens and sways,
what swirls and inflames
and flickers around?
All glitters and gleams
in the sunlight's glint.

Da glimmert's und glitzt's
in der Sonne Gluth:
was säuselt und summ't
und saus't nun gar?
Es brummt und braus't
und prasselt hierher!
Dort bricht's durch den Wald,
will auf mich zu!
Ein grässlicher Rachen
reisst sich mir auf!—
Der Wurm will mich fangen!
Fafner! Fafner!
(*Er schreit laut auf und knickt hinter dem breiten Ambos zusammen.*)

SIEGFRIED: (*bricht aus dem Waldgesträuch hervor, und ruft noch von aussen*). Heda! Fauler!
bist du nun fertig?
Schnell! wie steht's mit dem Schwert?
(*Er ist eingetreten und hält verwundert an.*)
Wo steckt der Schmied?
Stahl er sich fort?
Hehe! Mime! du Memme!
Wo bist du? wo birg'st du dich?

MIME: (*mit schwacher Stimme hinter dem Ambos*). Bist du es, Kind?
Kommst du allein?

SIEGFRIED: Hinter dem Ambos?—
Sag', was schufest du dort?
schärftest du mir das Schwert?

MIME: (*höchst verstört und zerstreut*). Das Schwert? das Schwert?
wie möcht' ich's schweissen?—
(*Halb für sich.*)
"Nur wer das Fürchten nicht erfuhr,
schmiedet Nothung neu."—
Zu weise ward ich
für solches Werk!

SIEGFRIED: Wirst du mir reden?
Soll ich dir rathen?

MIME: (*wie zuvor*). Wo nehm' ich redlichen Rath?—
Mein weises Haupt
hab' ich verwettet:
verfallen, verlor ich's an den,
"der das Fürchten nicht gelernt."

SIEGFRIED: (*heftig*). Sind mir das Flausen? Willst du mir flieh'n?

MIME: (*allmälig sich etwas fassend*). Wohl flöh' ich dem,
der's Fürchten kennt:
doch das liess ich dem Kinde zu lehren:
Ich Dummer vergass
was einzig gut:
Liebe zu mir
sollt' er lernen;—
das gelang nun leider faul!
Wie bring' ich das Fürchten ihm bei?

SIEGFRIED: (*packt ihn*). He! Muss ich helfen?
Was fegtest du heut'?

MIME: Für dich nur besorgt,
versank ich in Sinnen,
wie ich dich Wichtiges wiese.

---

What hisses and hums
and holds my gaze?
It roars and rolls
and rumbles toward;—
it rends through the wood,—
where shall I flee?
Before me I see monstrous jaws!—
The dragon has found me!
Fafner! Fafner!
(*He shrieks aloud and cowers down behind the great anvil.*)

SIEGFRIED: (*breaks from the thicket and calls, still from without*). Ho! lazy fellow!
Haven't you finished?
Say now, how goes the sword?
(*Enters and pauses in surprise.*)
Where hides the smith?
Has he decamped?
Ho, ho! Mime, you mooncalf!
Do you hear me? where have you hidden?

MIME: (*with feeble voice, from behind the anvil*). Is it you, boy?
Are you alone?

SIEGFRIED: Under the anvil!
Say, what do you see down there?
Is my sword sharpened yet?

MIME: (*greatly disturbed and confused*). The sword? The sword?
How can I shape it?—
(*Half aside.*)
"None but who has never felt Fear
makes 'Needful' new."
Too wise my wits are
for such a work.

SIEGFRIED: Will you not tell me?
Or must I teach you?

MIME: (*as before*). Where shall I hope for help?
I held my wily head in wager;
I've lost it; it is forfeited to him
"who has not yet learned to fear."

SIEGFRIED: (*violently*). Still do you flout me?
Would you then fly?

MIME: (*gradually recovering himself*). I'd fly from him
who had known fear:
but that truly I never have taught him.
I, fool-like, forgot
the one good thing:
love towards me
was my lesson;—
but, alas! I lost my work.
What force can awake in him fear?

SIEGFRIED: (*seizing him*). Ho! must I help you?
What whim's in your head?

MIME: Alone for your sake
I sank in absorption.
Would I could weightily warn you!

---

SIEGFRIED: (*lachend*). Bis unter den Sitz
warst du versunken:
was Wichtiges fandest du da?

MIME: (*sich immer mehr erholend*). Das Fürchten lernt' ich für dich,
dass ich's dich Dummen lehre.

SIEGFRIED: Was ist's mit dem Fürchten?

MIME: Erfuhr'st du's noch nie,
und willst aus dem Wald
fort in die Welt
Was frommte das festeste Schwert
blieb dir das Fürchten fern?

SIEGFRIED: (*ungeduldig*). Faulen Rath erfindest du wohl?

MIME: Deiner Mutter Rath
redet aus mir:
was ich gelobt'
muss ich nun lösen,
in die listige Welt
dich nicht zu lassen,
eh' du nicht das Fürchten gelernt.

SIEGFRIED: Ist's eine Kunst,
was kenn' ich sie nicht?—
Heraus! Was ist's mit dem Fürchten?

MIME: (*immer belebter*). Fühltest du nie
im finstern Wald,
bei Dämmerschein
am dunklen Ort,
wenn fern es säuselt,
summs't und saus't,
wildes Brummen
näher braus't,
wirres Flackern
um dich flimmert,
schwellend Schwirren
zu Leib' dir schwebt,—
fühltest du dann nicht grieselnd
Grausen die Glieder dir fah'n?
Glühender Schauer
schüttelt die Glieder
wirr verschwimmend
schwinden die Sinne,
in der Brust bebend und bang
berstet hämmernd das Herz?—
Fühltest du das noch nicht,
das Fürchten blieb dir dann fremd.

SIEGFRIED: Sonderlich seltsam
muss das sein!
Hart und fest,
fühl' ich, steht mir das Herz.
Das Grieseln und Grausen,
Glühen und Schauern,
Hitzen und Schwindeln,
Hämmern und Beben—
gern begehr' ich das Bangen,
sehnend verlangt mich's der Lust.—
Doch wie bringst du,
Mime mir's bei,
Wie wär'st du Memme mir Meister?

---

SIEGFRIED: (*laughing*). No, under the seat
well were you sinking;
what weighty affairs took you there?

MIME: (*with still more selfpossession*). With fear I trembled for you
that I the thing might teach you.

SIEGFRIED: What do you mean by fearing?

MIME: You never felt it,
yet will
go forth to the world from this world?
How fruitless the firmest of swords
if fear is far from you.

SIEGFRIED: (*impatiently*). You're feeding me with foolish talk.

MIME: It is your mother's counsel read by me:
I must be loyal to what she left me;—
to the lures of the world
I never should leave you
till you had learned to duly fear.

SIEGFRIED: If it is an art
why am I untaught?
What is it, this fearing?

MIME: (*with increasing animation*). You never felt
in forest dark,
at twilight hour
in gloomy spots,
when with a rustle,
rush and roar
fearful hurling
toward you howls,
dazzling flickers
flutter around you,
swelling surges
swoop toward you,
you felt then, no grisly
gruesomeness grow over your fancy?
Baleful shudders
shake your whole body,
all your senses
sink and forsake you,
bursting and big in your breast
beat your hammering heart?—
you know nothing of this,
you have not yet found fear.

SIEGFRIED: Strange and right singular
that must seem!
The strings of my heart feel hard and firm,
This grimness and growling,
this glowing and shaking,
this burning and shivering,
beating and quaking,—
well I wish to acquire them,
how for such a pastime I pant!
But how bring it,
Mime, about?
What means could make you my master?

MIME: Folge mir nur,
ich führe dich wohl;
sinnend fand ich's aus.
Ich weiss einen schlimmen Wurm,
der würgt' und schlang schon viel:
Fafner lehrt dich das Fürchten,
folgst du mir zu seinem Nest.

SIEGFRIED: Wo liegt er im Nest?

MIME: Neid-Höhle
wird es genannt:
im Ost, am Ende des Wald's.

SIEGFRIED: Dann wär's nicht weit
von der Welt?

MIME: Bei Neidhöhl' liegt sie ganz
nah'.

SIEGFRIED: Dahin denn sollst du
mich führen;
lernt' ich das Fürchten,
dann fort in die Welt!
Drum schnell schaffe das Schwert,
in der Welt will ich es schwingen.

MIME: Das Schwert? O Noth!

SIEGFRIED: Rasch in die Schmiede!
Weis' was du schuf'st.

MIME: Verfluchter Stahl:
Zu flicken vorsteh' ich ihn nicht:
Den zähen Zauber
bezwingt keines Zwergen Kraft.
Wer das Fürchten nicht kennt,
der fänd' wohl eher die Kunst.

SIEGFRIED: Feine Finten
weiss mir der Faule;
dass er ein Stümper
sollt' er gesteh'n:
nun lügt er sich listig heraus. —
Her mit den Stücken!
Fort mit dem Stümper!
Des Vaters Stahl
fügt sich wohl mir:
ich selbst schweisse das Schwert!
(Er macht sich rasch an die Arbeit.)

MIME: Hättest du fleissig
die Kunst gepflegt,
Jetzt käm' dir's wahrlich zu gut;
doch lässig warst du
stets in der Lehre:
was willst du nun Rechtes rüsten!

SIEGFRIED: Was der Meister nicht
kann,
vermöcht' es der Knabe,
hätt' er ihm immer gehorcht? —
Jetzt mach' dich fort,
misch' dich nicht d'rein:
sonst fällst du mir mit in's Feuer!

(Er hat eine grosse Menge Kohlen
auf dem Herd gehäuft, und unter-
hält in einem fort die Gluth,
während er die Schwertstücke in
den Schraubstock einspannt und
sie zu Spähnen zerfeilt.)

MIME: (indem er ihm zusieht).
Was machst du da?
Nimm doch die Löthe;
den Brei braut' ich schon längst.

SIEGFRIED: Fort mit dem Brei!
ich brauch' ihn nicht:
mit Bappe back' ich kein Schwert!

MIME: Follow me well,
I'll find you a way;
thinking, fell I upon it.
I know of a monstrous Worm,
who's wasted many folk;
You'll learn fear from Fafner,
follow me to his hole.

SIEGFRIED: Where does his hole
lie?

MIME: Hate-cavern,
well is it known;
to east, at end of the wood.

SIEGFRIED: And would the world
be that way?

MIME: To Hate-cavern it lies close
at hand.

SIEGFRIED: Toward it then, let me
follow,
learn about fearing,
and forth to the world!
Then swift! shape the sword!
In the world would I assay it.

MIME: The sword? o sorrow!

SIEGFRIED: Quick to your smithy!
What can you show?

MIME: Accursed steel!
I cannot restore it again!
Such mighty magic's
too much for poor Mime's force.
One who knows not fear
the knack might quickly find.

SIEGFRIED: Famous falsehoods,
sluggard, you're framing:
You must admit that you're a mud-
dler,
not seek to dissemble with lies. —
Bring me the bits here!
Fly, you old bungler!
My father's blade
fails not with me:
I'll soon shape it myself!
(He quickly prepares for work.)

MIME: Had you been careful
to master the craft,
now might your work be of use:
You were too lazy
ever to learn;
how will you best set about it?

SIEGFRIED: Where the master was
balked,
what more could the boy do,
who to his counsel gave heed? —
So move afar,
meddle not here,
for fear you be made to fuel!

(He has heaped a mass of coal on
the fire and blown well up; now,
fixing the sword pieces in a vice,
he commences to file them to powder.)

MIME: (looking on at his proceedings). What are you about?
Take but the solder;
the flux fused for you, see!

SIEGFRIED: Out on your flux!
it will fit me nothing.
Such filth will forge me no sword!

MIME: Du zerfeil'st die Feile,
zerreib'st die Raspel:
wie willst du den Stahl zerstamp-
fen?

SIEGFRIED: Zersponnen muss ich
in Spähne ihn seh'n:
was entzwei ist, zwing' ich mir so.

MIME: (während Siegfried eifrig
fortfeilt). Hier hilft Kein Kluger,
das seh' ich klar:
hier hilft dem Dummen
die Dummheit selbst!
Wie er sich müht
und mächtig regt:
ihm schwindet der Stahl,
doch wird ihm nicht schwül! —
Nun ward ich so alt
wie Höhl' und Wald,
und hab' nicht so 'was geseh'n!
Mit dem Schwert gelingt's,
das lern' ich wohl:
furchtlos fegt er's zu ganz, —
der Wand'rer wusst' es gut! —
Wie berg' ich nun
mein banges Haupt?
Dem kühnen Knaben verfiel's,
lehrt' ihn nicht Fafner die
Furcht. —
Doch weh' mir Armen!
Wie würgt' er den Wurm,
erführ' er das Fürchten von ihm?
Wie erräng' er mir den Ring?
Verfluchte Klemme!
Da klebt' ich fest,
fänd' ich nicht klugen Rath,
wie den Furchtlosen selbst ich bez-
wäng'. —

SIEGFRIED: (hat nun die Stücken
zerfeilt und in einem Schmelztigel
gefangen, den er jetzt in die Herd-
gluth stellt: unter dem Folgenden
nährt er die Gluth mit dem Blasebalg). He, Mime, geschwind!
wie heisst das Schwert,
das ich in Spähne zersponnen?

MIME: (aus seinen Gedanken auffahrend). Nothung nennt sich
das neidliche Schwert:
deine Mutter gab mir die Märe.

SIEGFRIED: (zu der Arbeit). Nothung! Nothung!
neidliches Schwert!
was musstest du zerspringen?
Zu Spreu nun schuf ich
die scharfe Pracht,
im Tigel brat' ich die Spähne!
Hoho! hoho!
hahei! hahei!
Blase, Balg!
blase die Gluth! —
Wild im Walde
wuchs ein Baum,
den hab' ich im Forst gefällt;
die braune Esche
brannt' ich zu Kohl',
auf dem Herd nun liegt sie gehäuft.
Hoho! hoho!
hahei! hahei!
Blase, Balg!
blase die Gluth! —

MIME: But the file is failing,
the rasp is ruined:
why do you destroy your steel so?

SIEGFRIED: I'd see each fiber
and splinter in shreds:
what is marred were mended but
so.

MIME: (while Siegfried diligently
files away). Here helps no cunning,
to me it is clear:
here speeds the dullard
by dullness alone!
Look how he works
with mighty will!
The steel is dissolved,
yet is he not strained. —
though I am old as this cave
or wood
such wondrous sight never I've
seen!
He'll achieve the work,
I know full well:
fearless, fashion the sword,
as well the Wanderer saw. —
Where shall I hide
my shrinking head?
For by this boy it must fall, if he
learns
no fear of Fafner—
But woe's me, luckless!
Who'll waste me the worm
if terror it teaches to him?
And the ring how shall I reach?
Cursed dilemma!
It locks me close,
no light comes to me,
how to cozen this bold-hearted
boy!

SIEGFRIED: (has reduced the
sword to powder and put it in a
crucible which he now places in
the forge. During the following he
blows up the fire with the bellows). Hey! Mime! Now say,
how should the sword
that I have filed into fibers be
named?

MIME: (starting out of a reverie).
"Needful" named
is the notable sword;
so your mother stated to me.

SIEGFRIED: (over his work).
Needful! Needful!
Notable sword!
Why were you thus dissevered?
I've shattered
your shining blade to shreds,
the pot shall melt now the slivers!
Oho! Oho!
Aha! Aha!
Bellows blow!
brighten the glow! —
A tree waved wild in woodlands
which I felled in the forest.
the brown-hued ash
I baked into coal,
It lies now on the hearth in heaps.
Oho! Oho!
Aha! Aha!
Bellows blow!
brighten the glow! —
The branches' fragments,

Des Baumes Kohle,
wie brennt sie kühn,
wie glüht sie hell und hehr!
In springenden Funken
sprüht sie auf,
schmilzt mir des Stahles Spreu.
Hoho! hoho!
hahei! hahei!
Blase, Balg!
blase die Gluth!—
Nothung! Nothung!
neidliches Schwert!
schon schmilzt deines Stahles
Spreu:
im eig'nen Schweisse
schwimmst du nun—
bald schwing' ich dich als mein
Schwert!

**MIME:** (*während der Absätze von
Siegfried's Lied immer für sich,
entfernt sitzend*). Er schmiedet das
Schwert,
und Fafner fällt er:
das seh' ich nun sicher voraus;
Hort und Ring
erringt er im Harst:—
wie erwerb, ich mir den Gewinn?
Mit Witz und List
erlang' ich Beides,
und berge heil mein Haupt.
Rang er sich müd' mit dem Wurm,
von der Müh' erlab' ihn ein Trank;
aus würz' gen Säften,
die ich gesammelt,
brau' ich den Trank für ihn;
wenig Tropfen nur
braucht er zu trinken,
sinnlos sinkt er in Schlaf:
mit der eig'nen Waffe,
die er sich gewonnen,
räum' ich ihn leicht aus dem Weg,
erlange mir Ring und Hort.
Hei! Weiser Wand'rer,
dünkt' ech dich dumm,
wie gefällt dir nun
mein feiner Witz?
Fand ich mir wohl
Rath und Ruh'?
(*Er springt vergnügt auf, holt
Gefässe herbei und schüttet aus
ihnen Gewürz in einen Topf.*)

**SIEGFRIED:** (*hat den geschmol-
zenen Stahl in eine Stangenform
gegossen, und diese in das Wasser
gesteckt man hört jetzt das laute
Gezisch der Kühlung*). In das Wasser floss
ein Feuerfluss:
grimmiger Zorn
zischt' ihm da auf;
frierend zähmt' ihm der Frost.
Wie sehrend er floss,
in des Wassers Fluth
fliesst er nicht mehr:
starr ward er und steif,
herrisch der harte Stahl:
heisses Blut doch
fliesst ihm bald!—
Nun schwitze noch einmal,
dass ich dich schweisse,
Nothung, neidliches Schwert!
(*Er stösst den Stahl in die Kohlen
und glüht ihn. Dann wendet er
sich zu Mime, der vom anderen

how bravely they flame!
Their glow how fierce and fair!
They spring in the air
with scattering sparks
and smelt me the steely shreds.
Oho! Oho!
Aha! Aha!
Bellows blow!
brighten the glow!—
Needful! Needful!
notable sword!
I've smelted your steely shreds.
In your own sweat
you swim now;—
I soon shall call you my sword!

**MIME:** (*during the last verse of
Siegfried's song continues his
own reflections aside*). He'll smithy the sword
and fell Fafner;
I see it is as settled as fate.
Store and ring
he'll snatch away in the strife:—
in what way can I win the prize?
By wit and craft
I'll win it surely,
and save perhaps my head.
Wearied in fight with the worm,
in his faintness willingly he will
drink
From potent simples
by me assorted.
I will prepare a draught,
but one drop
need he drink of,
senseless, he'll sink to sleep.
With the very weapon
he valiantly welds there
he shall be razed from my way;
the ring and the hoard I'll have.
Hey! wisest Wanderer,
Was I deemed dull?
How do you like
now my lusty wit?
Do I lack still
a rightful answer?
(*He springs up in glee, fetches vessels and pours decoctions from
them into a pot.*)

**SIEGFRIED:** (*has poured the molten steel into a mold and plunged
this into water, and the loud hiss
of its cooling is heard*). To the water flowed
a fiery flood;
anger and hate
hissed from the depths,
its head was cowed by the cold.
Though scorching it struck
in the watery stream,
it stirs no more;
it lies stiff and stark,
haughty and hard the steel.
Chances are, in blood
it soon will bathe!—
Now sweat once again,
that so I may shape you,
Needful, notable sword!
(*He thrusts the sword into the
coals and heats it. Then he turns
to Mime, who at the other end of
the hearth has carefully put his

Ende des Herdes her einen Topf an
den Rand der Gluth setzt.*)
Was schafft der Tölpel
dort mit dem Topf?
Brenn' ich hier Stahl,
brau'st du dort Sudel?

**MIME:** Zu Schanden kam ein
Schmied,
den Lehrer sein Knabe lehrt;
mit der Kunst ist's beim Alten aus,
als Koch dient er dem Kinde:
brennt es das Eisen zu Brei,
aus Eiern brau't
der Alte ihm Sud.
(*Er fährt fort zu kochen.*)

**SIEGFRIED:** (*immer während der
Arbeit*). Mime, der Künstler,
lernt nun Kochen;
das Schmieden schmeckt ihm nicht
mehr:
seine Schwerter alle
hab' ich zerschmissen;
was er kocht, ich kost' es ihm nicht.
Das Fürchten zu lernen
will er mich führen;
ein Ferner soll es mich lehren:
was am besten er kann,
mir bringt er's nicht bei;
als Stümper besteht er in allem!
(*Er hat den rothglühenden Stahl
hervorgezogen, und hämmert ihn
nun, während des folgenden Liedes mit dem grossen Schmiede-
hammer auf dem Ambos.*)
Hoho! hahei! hoho!
Schmiede, mein Hammer
ein hartes Schwert!
Hoho! hahei!
hahei! hoho!
Hahei! hoho! hahei!
Einst färbte Blut
dein falbes Blau;
sein rothes Rieseln
röthete dich:
kalt lachtest du da,
das warme lecktest du kühl!
Hahahei! hahahei!
hahahei! hei! hei!
Hoho! hoho! hoho!
Nun hat die Gluth
dich roth geglüht:
deine weiche Härte
dem Hammer weicht:
zornig sprüh'st du mir Funken.
dass ich dich Spröden gezähmt.
Heiaho! heiaho:
heiaho! ho! ho!
Hoho! hoho! hahei!
Hoho! hahei! hoho!
Schmiede, mein Hammer.
ein hartes Schwert!
Hoho! hahei!
hahei! hoho!
Hahei! hoho! hahei!
Der frohen Funken,
wie freu' ich mich!
Es ziert den Kühnen
des Zornes Kraft:
lustig lach'st du mich an,
stellst du auch grimm dich und
gram
Hahahei! hahahei!
hahahei! hei! hei!
Hoho! hoho! hoho!
Durch Gluth und Hammer

pipkin on the fire.*)
What is that patch
about with his pot?
While I burn steel
would you brew sauces?

**MIME:** The smith has come to
shame,
the pupil proves his conqueror;
all the craftman's art is over,
he has become your cook.
Burn then iron to broth,
while I will brew
my eggs into soup.
(*Goes on cooking.*)

**SIEGFRIED:** (*still over his work*).
Mime the craftsman
now learns cooking;
the smithy serves him no more
all the swords he made
I shattered and shivered;
what he cooks I care not to taste.
To fear he will teach me
if I but follow;
far away there dwells a tutor.
But the best he can do
will not bring it about;
a fool have I found him in all things.
(*He has taken out the red-hot steel
and proceeds to hammer it on the
anvil with a great smith's hammer, during the following song.*)
Oho! Oho! Oho!
Shape me, my hammer,
a hardy sword!
Oho! Aha!
Aha! Oho!
Aha! Oho! Aha!
Your steely blue
once streamed with blood;
its ruddy ripples
reddened your sides;
cold laughter was yours,
the warm stream licking to cool!
Heiha! Heiha!
Heiha! Ha! Ha!
Oho! Oho! Oho!
Now in the glow
you redly gleam;
your weakness heeds
my hammer's weight:
you scatter testy sparks,
that I have tamed your spirit!
Heiho! Heiho!
Heiho! Ho! Ho!
Oho! Oho! Aha!
Oho! Aha! Oho!
Shape me, my hammer,
a hardy sword!
Oho! Aha!
Aha! Oho!
Aha! Oho! Aha!
These springing sparks,
what a sport to see!
In rage the brave
are arrayed the best;
you laugh on me,
yet can be grisly and grim!
Heiha! Heiha!
Heiha! Ha! Ha!
Oho! Oho! Oho!
Both fire and hammer
failed me not!
With stalwart strokes
I stretched you out;

glückt' es mir!
Mit starken Schlägen
streckt' ich dich:
nun schwinde die rothe Scham;
werde kalt und hart wie du kannst.
Heiaho! heiaho!
heiaho! ho! ho!
hahei! hoho! hahei!
(*Er taucht mit dem letzten den Stahl in das Wasser und lacht bei dem starken Gezisch.*)

**MIME:** (*während Siegfried die geschmiedete Schwert klinge in dem Griffhefte befestigt, — wieder im Vordergrunde*). Er schafft sich
ein scharfes Schwert,
Fafner zu fällen,
der Zwerge Feind:
ich brau' ein Trug-Getränk,
Siegfried zu fällen,
dem Fafner fiel.
Gelingen muss mir die List;
lachen muss mir der Lohn!
Den der Bruder schuf,
den schimmernden Reif,
in den er gezaubert
zwingends Kraft,
das helle Gold,
das zum Herrscher macht—
ich hab' ihn gewonnen!
ich walte sein'!—
Alberich selbst,
der einst mich band,
zu Zwergenfrohne
zwing' ich ihn nun:
als Niblungenfürst
fahr' ich danieder;
gehorchen soll mir
alles Heer!—
Der verachtete Zwerg,
was wird er geehrt!
Zu dem Hort hin drängt sich
Gott und Held:
vor meinem Nicken
neigt sich die Welt,
vor meinem Zorne
zittert sie hin!—
Dann wahrlich müht sich
Mime nicht mehr:
ihm schaffen And're
den ew'gen Schatz.
Mime, der kühne.
Mime ist König,
Fürst der Alben,
Walter des All's!
Hei, Mime! wie glückte mir das!
wer glaubte wohl das von dir!

**SIEGFRIED:** (*während der Absätze von Mime's Lied das Schwert feilend, schleifend und mit dem kleinen Hammer hämmernd*). Nothung! Nothung!
neidliches Schwert!
jetzt haftest du wieder im Heft.
Warst du entzwei,
ich zwang dich ganz,
kein Schlag soll nun dich zerschlagen.
Dem sterbenden Vater
zersprang der Stahl,
der lebende Sohn
schuf ihn neu:
nun lacht ihm sein heller Schein,
seine Schärfe schneidet ihm hart.

let sink now your blush of shame,
be as cold and hard as you can.
Heiho! Heiho!
Heiho! Ho! Ho!
Aha! Oho! Aha!
(*With the last words, he plunges the sword into the water, laughing at the hiss it makes.*)

**MIME:** (*while Siegfried is fastening the forged swordblade into a handle,—again coming to the front*). He shapes him a sword so
sharp,
it fell Fafner,
the Niblung's foe.
A draught of might I've made,
Siegfried to finish
when Fafner falls.
This treachery must I contrive,
triumph must I attain.
What my brother shaped,
the shimmering ring,
endowed with enchantment's
charms and control—
the peerless gold
which all power gives,—
I plainly have gained it!
I govern it!—
Alberich even,
whom once I served,
as bondsman will I
bind me soon.
As Nibelheim's lord
let me be known there;
I'll humble to me
all their host!—
The poor vilified dwarf
how will they revere!
To the gold will go thronging
men and gods;
before my bidding
bows all the world;
before my anger
awed are they all!
In toil then moves
Mime no more;
his wealth unending
shall others work.
Mime the mighty,
Mime is monarch;
prince of earth-gnomes,
ruler of all!
Hey, Mime! how glad will you be
then!
Who would believe this of you?

**SIEGFRIED:** (*during the last part of Mime's song has been filing and sharpening the sword and hammering it with a small hammer*).
Needful! Needful!
notable sword!
in handle once more you are held.
When you were wrecked
I wrought you anew;
no stroke shall again destroy you,
your steel flew in tandem
from the stricken sire;
the life-glowing son
shapes it anew;
now laughs upon him its sheen,
and its sharpness surely cuts home.
Needful! Needful!

Nothung! Nothung!
neu und verjüngt!
zum Leben weckt' ich dich wieder.
Todt lag'st du
in Trümmern dort,
jetzt leuchtest du trotzig und hehr.
Zeige den Schächern
nun deinen Schein!
schlage den Falschen,
fälle den Schelm!—
Schau, Mime, du Schmied:
so schneidet Siegfried's Schwert.
(*Er hat während des zweiten Verses das Schwert geschwungen, und schlägt nun damit auf den Ambos: dieser zerspaltet in zwei Stücken, von oben bis unten, so dass er unter grossem Gepolter auseinander fällt, Mime, — in höchster Verzückung — fällt vor Schreck sitzlings zu Boden. Siegfried hält jauchzend das Schwert in die Höhe.—Der Vorhang fällt schnell.*)


# ■ ACT II

*TIEFER WALD.*

Ganz im Hintergrunde die Öffnung einer Höhle. Der Boden hebt sich bis zur Mitte der Bühne, wo er eine kleine Hochebene bildet; von da senkt er sich nach hinten, der Höhle zu, wieder abwärts, so dass von dieser nur der obere Theil der Öffnung dem Zuschauer sichtbar ist. Links gewahrt man durch Waldbäume eine zerklüftete Felsenwand. — Finstere Nacht, am dichtesten über dem Hintergrunde, wo anfänglich der Blick des Zuschauers gar nichts zu unterscheiden vermag.

**ALBERICH:** (*an der Felsenwand zur Seite gelagert, in düsterem Brüten*). In Wald und Nacht
vor Neidhöhl' halt' ich Wacht:
er lauscht mein Ohr,
mühvoll lugt mein Aug'.—
Banger Tag,
beb'st du schon auf?
dämmerst du dort
durch das Dunkel her?
(*Sturmwind erhebt sich rechts aus dem Walde.*)
Welcher Glanz glitzert dort auf?
Näher schimmert
ein heller Schein:
es rennt wie ein leuchtendes Ross
bricht durch den Wald
brausend daher.
Naht schon des Wurmes Würger?
Ist's schon, der Fafner fällt?
(*Der Sturmwind legt sich wieder; der Glanz verlischt.*)
Das Licht erlischt—
der Glanz barg sich dem Blick:
Nacht ist's wieder.—
Wer naht dort schimmernd im Schatten?

notable sword!
I have given you life again.
You lay dead
once desolate,
now leap up dauntless and bright.
Out then, and show
the cowards your sheen!
Shatter the false ones,
fall on the sly!—
See! and Mime, smith;
so serves Siegfried's sword!
(*During the second verse he brandishes the sword and now smites it on the anvil which splits in half from top to bottom, falling with a loud noise. Mime, in extreme terror, falls flat on the ground. Siegfried, shouting with glee, waves his sword in the air. The curtain falls quickly.*)


# ■ Act II

*A DEEP FOREST.*

At the extreme back the opening of a cave. The ground rises in the middle of the stage, forming a little knoll; it sinks again towards the cave at back, so that the upper part of the cavern's mouth alone is visible. L. is to be seen through the trees a rocky cliff rent with fissures. — Gloomy night, darkest at back, where at first the eye of the audience can discern nothing distinctly.

**ALBERICH:** (*leaning against the rocky wall at side, in gloomy reflection*). In woodland haunt
by Hate-cave I keep watch.
I prick my ear,
keenly peers my eye.—
Anxious day!
Have you arrived?
Throw you there light
through the thicket?
(*A gust of storm passes R. from the wood.*)
But what gleam glances from there?
Nearer glimmers
a brilliant glow,
and strides, as of fiery steed,
course through the wood,
crashing this way.
Nearer the dragon's death-man?
Is it now that Fafner falls?
(*The wind subsides again and the glow fades.*)
The light allays—
the glow sinks from my sight:
night falls once more.—
Who nears, shining through shadow?

## Act II

DER WANDERER: (*tritt aus Wald auf, und hält Alberich gegenüber an*). Zur Neidhöhle
fuhr ich bei Nacht:
wen gewahr' ich im Dunkel dort?
(*Wie aus einem plötzlich zerreissenden Gewölk bricht Mondschein herein, und beleuchtet des Wanderer's Gestalt.*)

ALBERICH: (*erkennt den Wanderer, und fährt er schrocken zurück*). Du selbst lässt dich hier seh'n?
(*Er bricht in Wuth aus.*)
Was willst du hier?
Fort, aus dem Weg!
Von dannen, schamloser Dieb!

WANDERER: Schwarz-Alberich,
schweif'st du hier?
hütest du Fafner's Haus?

ALBERICH: Jag'st du auf neue Neidthat umher?
Weile nicht hier!
weiche von hinnen!
Genug deines Truges
tränkte die Stätte mit Noth.
Drum, du Frecher,
lass' sie jetzt frei!

WANDERER: Zu schauen kam ich,
nicht zu schaffen:
wer wehrte mir Wand'rers Fahrt?

ALBERICH: (*lacht tückisch auf*).
Du Rath wüthender Ränke!
wär' ich dir zu lieb
doch noch dumm wie damals,
als du mich Blöden bandest!
Wie leicht gerieth es
den Ring mir nochmals zu rauben!
Hab' Acht: deine Kunst
kenne ich wohl;
doch wo du schwach bist,
bleib mir auch nicht verschwiegen
Mit meinen Schätzen
zahltest du Schulden;
mein Ring lohnte
der Riesen Müh',
die deine Burg dir gebaut
was mit den trotzigen
einst du vertragen,
dess' Runen wahrt noch heut'
deines Speeres herrischer Schaft.
Nicht du darist,
was als Zoll du gezahlt,
den Riesen wieder entreissen;
du selbst zerspelltest
deines Speeres Schaft:
in deiner Hand
der herrische Stab,
der starke zerstiebte wie Spreu'!

WANDERER: Durch Vertrages Treue-Runen
band er dich
Bösen mir nicht:
dich beugt er mir durch seine Kraft:
zum Krieg drum wahr' ich ihn wohl.

ALBERICH: Wie stolz du dräu'st
in trotziger Stärke,
und wie dir's im Busen doch bangt!
Verfallen dem Tod

THE WANDERER: (*enters from the wood and pauses opposite Alberich.*) To Hate-cave
by night have I come;
who confronts me in darkness dim?
(*As from a suddenly parted cloud, the moonlight breaks forth and illumines the Wanderer's figure.*)

ALBERICH: (*recognizes the Wanderer and recoils in dread.*) Yourself is it I see?
(*Bursting into wrath.*)
What would you here?
Hence, from my way!
Away, you shameless rogue!

WANDERER: Black Alberich, Do you remain here?
Have you kept Fafner's house?

ALBERICH: Come you to inflict new annoyance?
Linger not here,
make your way homeward!
This place has sorely
suffered from you and your plots.
Therefore, villain,
quickly leave!

WANDERER: I came as witness,
not as worker:
who'll bar the Wanderer's way?

ALBERICH: (*laughing spitefully*).
You spell-working conspirer!
Were I dull as once
in past days you deemed,
when I was bound through blindness,
how soon by ruse
were the ring again from me ravished!
Beware! all your wiles
well do I know;
also your weak point
plainly am I aware of.
With all my wealth you have wiped out your debt;
my gem dowered
the giants' toil,
what time they built you your town.
What was agreed upon
with those grim ones
in runes is written this day
on your spear's all-dominant shaft.
Nor do you dare
what as price you have paid
to juggle back from the giants.
Your spear you speedily
would spoil yourself:
in your own hand
the heavenly staff,
the strong one, would split like a straw.

WANDERER: Through no runes of righteous compact were you bound,
base one, by it:
It bowed you down but by its strength:
for strife I ward it then well.

ALBERICH: How proud your threats
of menacing power,
and yet how your spirit sinks!

durch meinen Fluch
ist Fafner, des Hortes Hüter:—
wer—wird ihn beerben?
wird der neidliche Hort
dem Niblung wieder gehören?
Das sehrt dich mit ew'ger Sorge!
Denn fass' ich ihn wieder
einst in der Faust,
anders als dumme Riesen
üb' ich des Ringes Kraft:
dann zitt're der Helden
heiliger Hüter!
Walhall's Höhen
stürm' ich mit Hella's Heer:
der Welt walte dann ich!

WANDERER: Deinen Sinn kenn' ich;
doch sorgt er mich nicht:
des Ringes waltet
wer ihn gewinnt.

ALBERICH: Wie dunkel sprichst du,
was ich deutlich doch weiss!
An Heldensöhne
hält sich dein Trotz,
die traut deinem Blute entblüht?
Pflegtest du wohl eines Knaben,
der klug die Frucht dir pflücke,
die du—nicht brechen darf'st?

WANDERER: Mit mir—nicht,
had're mit Mime:
dein Bruder bringt dir Gefahr;
einen Knaben führt er daher,
der Fafner ihm fällen soll.
Nichts weiss der von mir;
der Niblung nützt ihn für sich.
Drum sag' ich dir, Gesell:
thue frei wie's dir frommt!
Höre mich wohl,
sei auf der Hut:
nicht kennt der Knabe den Ring,
doch Mime kundet' ihn aus.

ALBERICH: Deine Hand hieltest du vom Hort?

WANDERER: Wen ich liebe
lass' ich für sich gewähren:
er steh' oder fall',
sein Herr ist er:
Helden nur können mir frommen.

ALBERICH: Mit Mime räng' ich allein um den Ring?

WANDERER: Ausser dir begehrt er einzig das Gut.

ALBERICH: Und doch gewänn' ich ihn nicht?

WANDERER: Ein Helde naht
den Hort zu befrei'n;
zwei Niblungen geizen das Gold:
Fafner fällt,
der den Ring bewacht:—
wer ihn rafft, hat ihn gewonnen.—
Willst du noch mehr?
Dort liegt der Wurm:
warn'st du ihn vor dem Tod,
willig wohl liess' er den Tand.—
Ich selber weck' ihn dir auf.—

Decreed unto death
through my curse
is Fafner, the store's possessor:—
who'll hold it hereafter?
Will the notable hoard
a Nibelung once more inherit?
This tears you with endless trouble!
For, passes the ring
once more to my palm,
in other ways than foolish giants
I'll use the jewel's power.
Then tremble, high
protector of heroes,
for Valhalla
I'll seize on with Hella's host;
the world will then be mine!

WANDERER: I know well your intent;
it troubles me not;
the ring's but wielded
when it is won.

ALBERICH: How darkly you say,
what I doubtless know well!
In heroes' offspring
have you then trust,
who truly have leaped from your loins?
Have you not fostered a stripling
who straight the fruit should reach you,
that you dare not to thieve?

WANDERER: Mind me not—
wrangle with Mime:
Your brother brings you a foe;
for the boy who follows him here
shall fell for him Fafner soon.
He knows nothing of me;
the Nibelung's need he should serve.
And so, my friend, I say,
you can work as you will
Give good heed,
be on your guard;
he knows nothing of the ring:
but Mime necessarily must disclose.

ALBERICH: And your hand hold you from the hoard?

WANDERER: My beloved one
I leave to act unmanaged;
he stands or he falls,
unhelped by me;
heroes' aid only I've faith in.

ALBERICH: With Mime wrestle
but I for the ring?

WANDERER: Only he would gather also the gold.

ALBERICH: Yet I never may win it again?

WANDERER: A hero nears
the hoard to set free;
two Niblungs are greedy for gold;
Fafner falls,
who does guard the wealth;
when it is gained, luck to the winner!—
Would you know more?
There lies the worm:
warn him then of his risk,
well he will leave you the ring.—

(*Er wendet sich nach hinten.*)
Fafner! Fafner!
erwache, Wurm!

**ALBERICH:** (*in gespanntem Erstaunen, für sich*).
Was beginnt der Wilde?
gönnt er mir's wirklich?
(*Aus der finstern Tiefe des Hintergrundes hört man.*)

**FAFNER:** (*Stimme*). Wer stört mir
den Schlaf?

**WANDERER:** Gekommen ist einer,
Noth dir zu künden:
er lohnt dir's mit dem Leben,
lohnst du das Leben ihm
mit dem Horte, den du hütest.

**FAFNER:** Was will er?

**ALBERICH:** Wache, Fafner!
wache, du Wurm!
Ein starker Helde naht,
dich Heil'gen will er besteh'n.

**FAFNER:** Mich hungert sein'.

**WANDERER:** Kühn ist des Kindes
Kraft,
scharf schneidet sein Schwert.

**ALBERICH:** Den gold'nen Ring
geizt er allein:
lass' mir den Ring zum Lohn,
so wend' ich den Streit;
du wahrest den Hort,
und ruhig leb'st du lang'!

**FAFNER:** (*gähnt*). Ich lieg' und
besitze:—
lasst mich schlafen!

**WANDERER:** (*lacht laut*). Nun,
Alberich, das schlug fehl!
Doch schilt mich nicht mehr
Schelm!
Diess Eine, rath' ich,
achte noch wohl:
Alles ist nach seiner Art:
an ihr wirst du nichts ännern.
Ich lass' dir die Stätte:
stelle dich fest!
versuch's mit Mime, dem Bruder:
der Art ja versiehst du dich besser.
Was anders ist,
das lerne nun auch!
(*Er verschwindet im Walde.
Sturmwind erhebt sich und verliert sich schnell wieder.*)

**ALBERICH:** (*nachdem er ihm
lange grimmig nachgesehen*). Da
reitet er hin
auf lichtem Ross:
mir lässt er Sorg' und Spott!
Doch lacht nur zu,
ihn leichtsinniges,
lustgieriges
Göttergelichter:
euch seh' ich
noch alle vergeh'n!
So lang das Gold
am Lichte glänzt,
hält ein Wissender Wacht!—
trügen wird euch sein Trotz.
(*Morgendämmerung. Alberich
verbirgt sich zur Seite im Geklüft.*)

Myself I'll wake him for you—
(*He turns towards the back.*)
Fafner, Fafner!
Awaken, worm!

**ALBERICH:** (*aside, in expectancy
and wonder*). Does he mean to tell
me the treasure is mine?
(*From the gloomy depth at back is
heard Fafner's voice.*)

**FAFNER:** (*voice.*) Who stirs me
from sleep?

**WANDERER:** Here waits a friend
to warn you of danger:
Your life he will allow you,
You light his life for him
with the treasure that you tend.

**FAFNER:** What does he want?

**ALBERICH:** Waken, Fafner!
Waken, worm!
A stalwart hero nears,
Your head to humble in strife.

**FAFNER:** I starve for him!

**WANDERER:** Brave is the boy and
steadfast,
sharply shears his sword.

**ALBERICH:** The circlet rare
he seeks alone:
let me but lift the ring,
I'll ward you from harm;
then watch the hoard
and rest in length of life!

**FAFNER:** (*yawning*). I lie in possession:—
let me slumber!

**WANDERER:** (*laughing loudly*).
Now, Alberich, that stroke fails!
But stay your anger's storm!
One thing I advise you,
think on it well:
all things act in their nature,
nor may you alter anything.
I leave you your station:
stand to your guard!
Encounter Mime, your brother;
his nature overcomes you better.
What happens therafter
you quickly shall find!
(*He disappears in the wood. A
storm gust rises and quickly subsides again.*)

**ALBERICH:** (*after watching his
retreat a while in wrath.*) There
storms he away
on lightning steed,
and leaves me in scoff and scorn!
Yes, laugh away!
light-spirited,
lust-gluttonous,
godly enlightener;
I'll see you yet
all in your graves!
So long as the gold
in light shall gleam
I hold warily watch!—
Envy works out its end!—
(*Morning dawns. Alberich hides
in a cleft of the rock at side.*)

(*Mime und Siegfried treten bei
anbrechendem Tage auf. Siegfried
trägt das Schwert an einem Gehenke. Mime erspäht genau die
Stätte, forscht endlich dem Hintergrunde zu, der—während die
Anhöhe im mittlern Vordergrunde später immer heller von
der Sonne beleuchtet wird—in
finstern Schatten gehüllt bleibt,
und bedeutet dann Siegfried.*)

**MIME:** Zur Stelle sind wir! bleib'
hier steh'n!

**SIEGFRIED:** (*setzt sich unter eine
grosse Linde*). Hier soll ich das
Fürchten lernen?—
Fern hast du mich geleitet;
eine volle Nacht im Walde
selbander wanderten wir:
nun sollst du, Mime,
fortan mich meiden!
Lern' ich hier nicht
was ich lernen muss,
allein zieh' ich dann weiter:
dich werd' ich endlich da los!

**MIME:** (*setzt sich ihm gegenüber,
so dass er die Höhle immer noch
im Auge behält*). Glaub' mir, Lieber!
lernst du heute
hier das Fürchten nicht:
an andrem Ort
zu and'rer Zeit
schwerlich erfährst du's je.—
Siehst du dort
den dunklen Höhlenschlund?
Darin wohnt
ein gräulich wilder Wurm:
unmassen grimmig
ist er und gross:
ein schrecklicher Rachen
reisst sich ihm auf;
mit Haut und Haar
auf einen Happ
verschlingt der Schlimme dich
wohl.

**SIEGFRIED:** Gut ist's, den Schlund
ihm zu schliessen:
drum biet' ich mich nicht dem Gebiss.

**MIME:** Giftig giesst sich
ein Geifer ihm aus:
wen mit des Speichels
Schweiss er bespei't,
dem schwinden Fleisch und Gebein.

**SIEGFRIED:** Dass des Geifers Gift
mich nicht sehre,
weich' ich zur Seite dem Wurm.

**MIME:** Ein Schlangenschweif
schlägt sich ihm auf:
wen er damit umschlingt
und fest umschliesst,
dem brechen die Glieder wie Glas!

**SIEGFRIED:** Vor des Schweifes
Schwang mich zu wahren
halt' ich den Argen im Aug'.—
Doch heisse mich das:
hat der Wurm ein Herz?

**MIME:** Ein grimmiges, hartes Herz!

(*As the day breaks Mime and Siegfried enter. The latter wears the
sword in his girdle. Mime narrowly reconnoitres the place and at
last seeks towards the background, which remains still in
shadow, while the higher ground
in the middle is more and more
brightened by the sun; he then
draws Siegfried's attention.*)

**MIME:** The spot you see! here we
stop.

**SIEGFRIED:** (*seating himself under a great lime tree*). Here shall I
in fear take lesson?—
Far distant you have led me;
since the fall of night through
woodlands
we two have wended our way.
Now shall you, Mime,
henceforth move from me!
Find I not here
what I rather would learn,
afar then will I wander;
I want to be free from you!

**MIME:** (*seats himself opposite, so
as to keep the cave in sight still*).
Trust me, dearie!
Do you not here
in haste discover fear,
in other hours,
and other ways
scarce were it ever learned.—
Do you see yonder
yawning cavern's shade?
Therein dwells
a gruesome dreadful dragon.
Awfully grisly
is he, and great; he opens
savage and monstrous
jaws;
both skin and scalp,
at single snap
the beast will bolt.

**SIEGFRIED:** It were well to baffle
his biting:
I'll thrust myself not in his throat.

**MIME:** Potent poison
he pours with his breath;
he whom his spittle's
spume splashes
must shrivel up, body and bones.

**SIEGFRIED:** That his vile venom
may not sear me
lightly aside will I leap.

**MIME:** A twisting tail
he turns about;
if taken in its toils
and firmly twined,
your limbs will be ground up like
glass.

**SIEGFRIED:** From his tail's entangle to keep
I'll have an eye on his acts.—
But listen to me now:
has this worm a heart?

**MIME:** A cruel and hardened heart!

SIEGFRIED: Das sitzt ihm doch
wo es jedem schlägt,
trag' es Mann oder Thier?

MIME: Gewiss, Knabe,
da führt's auch der Wurm;
nun kommt dir das Fürchten wohl
an?

SIEGFRIED: Nothung stoss' ich
dem Stolzen in's Herz:
soll das etwa Fürchten heissen?
He, du Alter!
ist das alles,
was deine List
mich lehren kann?
Fahr' deines Wegs dann weiter;
das Fürchten lern' ich hier nicht.

MIME: Wart' es nur ab!
Was ich dir sagte,
dünke dich tauber Schall:
ihn selber musst du
hören und seh'n,
die Sinne vergeh'n dir dann schon!
Wenn dein Blick verschwimmt,
der Boden dir schwankt,
im Busen bang
dein Herz erbebt:—
dann dankst du mir, der dich
führte,
gedenkst wie Mime dich liebt.

SIEGFRIED: (springt unwillig
auf). Du sollst mich nicht lieben!
sagt' ich dir's nicht?
Fort aus den Augen mir;
lass' mich allein:
sonst halt' ich's hier länger nicht
aus,
fängst du von Liebe gar an!
Das eklige Nicken
und Augenzwicken,
wann endlich soll ich's
nicht mehr seh'n?
wann werd' ich den Albernen los?

MIME: Ich lasse dich schon:
am Quell dort lagr' ich mich.
Steh' du nur hier;
steigt die Sonne zur Höh',
merk' auf den Wurm,
aus der Höhle wälzt er sich her:
hier vorbei
biegt er dann,
am Brunnen sich zu tränken.

SIEGFRIED: (lachend). Mime,
weilst du am Quell
dahin lass' ich den Wurm wohl
geh'n
Nothung stoss' ich
ihm erst in die Nieren,
wenn er dich selbst dort
mit 'weg gesoffen!
Darum, hör' meinen Rath,
raste nicht dort am Quell:
kehre dich 'weg,
so weit du kannst,
und komm' nie mehr zu mir!

MIME: Nach freislichem Streit
dich zu erfrischen,
wirst du mir wohl nicht wehren?
Rufe mich auch,
darbst du des Rathes—
oder wenn dir das Fürchten gefällt.
(Siegfried weis't ihn mit einer heftigen Geberde fort.)
(im Abgehen, für sich). Fafner und

SIEGFRIED: He bears it, sure,
where in all its beats,
both in man and in beast?

MIME: No doubt, youngster,
it lies there indeed.
Not yet have you learned fear?

SIEGFRIED: Needful straightaway
I'll strike to his heart:
will that be like fearing, by chance?
Hey, my ancient,
is this only
what all your lore
can teach me?
Forth on your way then wander,
for fearing I learn not here.

MIME: Wait a while!
You think what I have spoken is
empty sound:
himself must meet
you hearing and sight,
your senses will leave you then
straight!
When your glances swim,
the ground beneath you sinks,
and grimly gripped,
your heart gasps:—
then thank him who has led you,
and think of Mime's great love.

SIEGFRIED: (springing up crossly). You shall no more love me!
Said I not so?
Forth from the sight of me—
leave me alone!
this nuisance no longer I'll stand.
Prattle you of loving me still?
This idiot shrinking
and eyelid winking—
whenever shall I
lose the sight?
when will this old object be gone?

MIME: I leave you now;
I'll linger near the spring.
Stay here,
soon when the sun is on high
look for the worm;
he'll warily come from his cave:
close this way
will he pass
to water at the fountain

SIEGFRIED: (laughing). Mime,
wait at the stream
and there I'll let the worm proceed.
Needful first
shall nestle in his vitals
when all your joints
he has well digested!
So now heed what I tell—
tarry not by the spring:
take yourself off
to other tracks;
return no more to me!

MIME: When faint with the strife
you would refresh yourself,
would I not win a welcome.
Call on me then,
should you need counsel—
or if you find pleasure in fearing.
(Siegfried bids him to be gone
with a violent gesture.)
(aside—going). Fafner and Sieg-

Siegfried—
Siegfried und Fafner—
o brächten beide sich um!
(Er geht in den Wald zurück.)

SIEGFRIED: (allein. Er setzt sich
wieder unter die grosse Linde.)
Dass der mein Vater nicht ist,
wie fühl' ich mich drob so froh!
Nun erst gefällt mir
der frische Wald;
nun erst lacht mir
der lustige Tag,
da der Garstige von mir schied,
und ich gar nicht ihn wiederseh'!
(Sinnendes Schweigen.)
Wie sah wohl mein Vater aus?—
Ha!—gewiss wie ich selbst:
denn wär' wo von Mime ein Sohn,
müsst' er nicht ganz
Mime gleichen?
G'rade so garstig,
griesig und grau,
klein und krumm
höckrig und hinkend,
mit hängenden Ohren,
triefigen Angen—
fort mit dem Alp!
ich mag ihn nicht mehr seh'n.
(Er lehnt sich zurück und blickt
durch den Baumwipfel auf. Langez Schweigen.—Waldweben.)
Aber—wie sah
meine Mutter wohl aus?
Das—kann ich
nun gar nicht mir denken!—
Der Rehhindin gleich
glänzten gewiss
ihr hell schimmernde Augen,—
nur noch viel schöner!—
Da bang sie mich geboren,
warum aber starb sie da?
Sterben die Menschenmütter
an ihren Söhnen
alle dahin?
Traurig wäre das, traun!—
Ach! möcht' ich Sohn
meine Mutter seh'n!—
meine—Mutter!—
ein Menschenweib!—
(Er seufzt und streckt sich tiefer
zurück. Langez Schweigen.—)
(Wachsendes Waldeweben, Siegfried's aufmer ksamkeit wird endlich durch den Gesang der Wald-
vögeln gefesselt.)
Du holdes Voglein, dich hort ich
noch nie:
Bist du im wald hier daheim?
Verstünd' ich sein süsses stammeln!
Gewiss sagt' es mir' was reil licht,
Von der lieben mutter!
Ein zankender Zwerg
hat mir erzählt,
der Vöglein Stammeln
gut zu versteh'n,
dazu könnte man kommen:
wie das wohl möglich wär'?
(Er sinnt nach. Sein Blick fällt auf
ein Rohrgebüsch unweit der
Linde.)
Hei! ich versuch's,
sing' ihm nach:
auf dem Rohr tön' ich ihm ähnlich!
Entrath' ich der Worte,
achte der Weise,

fried—
Siegfried and Fafner—
Would each the other might kill!
(He retreats into the wood.)

SIEGFRIED: (alone. He seats himself under the great lime again).
How full is the joy I feel that he's no
father of mine!
Now the forest seems truly fragrant;
now how glad is
the glorious day!
since that miscreant wretch has
gone,
never more to confront my gaze!
(Thoughtful silence.)
My sire—what semblance was
his?—
Ha!—no doubt like myself;
for, were there of Mime a son,
must he not look
Mime's likeness?
growing as gruesome,
grizzled and gray,
cramped and crooked,
halting and humpbacked,
with hanging ears stretching,
bleary eyes staring—
Out on the sight!
I'll look on it no more.
(He leans back and looks up
through the branches of the tree.
Long silence. Forest murmur.)
Surely—my mother,
what semblance had she?
I—cannot
imagine it ever!—
Like soft fallow doe's
deeply would shine
her soft languishing eyes,—
only more lovely!—
When balefully she bore me
why must she have died too?
Die thus all mortal mothers,
leaving their dear ones
lonely behind?
Sad were such a fate, sure!—
Ah! might these looks
but light on my mother!—
My own—mother!—
a mortal's mate!—
(He sighs and reclines still lower.
Long silence.)
(Increased rustling of the trees. Siegfried's attention is at last riveted by the songs of forest birds.)
You happy warbler, I hear you now
first:
Have you in this forest your home?
Your strain, could I understand it!
Probably utters to me some news
of my loving mother!
That drivelling dwarf
told me one day
the meaning bound
in language of birds
one could truly attain to:—
I wish I could learn the way!
(He reflects. His eyes fall on a
clump of reeds, not far from the
lime tree.)
Ha! I'll essay;
sing with him
on a reed similar sounding;
without regard for the meaning,
seize but the music.

sing' ich so seine Sprache,
verstch' ich wohl auch was er
spricht.
(*Er hat sich mit dem Schwerte ein
Rohr abgeschnitten,
und schnitzt sich eine Pfeife daraus.*)
*Es schweigt und lauscht:—*
so schwatz' ich denn los!
(*Er versucht auf der Pfeife die
Weise der Vogel nachzuab men es
glückt ihm nicht, verdriesslich
schüttelt er oft den Kopf: endlich
setzt er ganz ab.*)

Das tönt nicht recht:
auf dem Rohre taugt
die wonnige Weise nicht.—
Vöglein, mich dünkt,
ich bleibe dumm:
von dir lernt sich's nicht leicht!
Nun schäm' ich mich gar
vor dem schelmischen Lauscher:
er lugt, und kann nichts erlaus-
chen.—
Heida! so höre
nun auf mein Horn;
auf dem dummen Rohre
geräth mir nichts.—
Einer Waldweise,
wie ich sie kann,
der lustigen sollst du lauschen.
Nach liebem Gesellen
lockt' ich mit ihr:
nichts Bess'res kam noch
als Wolf und Bär.
Nun will ich seh'n,
wen jetzt sie mir lockt:
ob das mir ein lieber Gesell?
(*Er hat die Pfeife fortgeworfen,
und bläst nun esseinem kleinen
silbernen Horne eine lustige
Weise.*)

(*Im Hintergrunde regt es sich.
Fafner, in der Gestalt eines ungeheuren eidechsenartigen Schlan-
genwurmes, hat sich in der Höble
von seinem Lager erhoben; er
bricht durch das Gesträuch, und
wälzt sich aus der Tiefe nach der
höheren Stelle vor, so dass er mit
dem Vorderleibe bereits auf ihr
angelangt ist. Er stösst jetzt einen
starken gähnenden Laut aus.*)

SIEGFRIED: (*wendet sich um,
gewahrt Fafner, blickt ihn verwundert an, und lacht*). Da hätte
mein Lied
mir 'was Liebes erblasen!
du wär'st mir ein saub'rer Gesell!

FAFNER: (*hat bei Siegfried's Anblick angehalten*). Was ist da?

SIEGFRIED: Ei, bist du ein Thier,
das zum Sprechen taugt,
wohl liess' sich aus dir 'was lernen!
Hier kennt einer
das Fürchten nicht:
kann er's von dir erfahren?

FAFNER: Hast du Übermuth?

---

So his speech, if I sing it,
my senses perhaps will glimpse.
(*He cuts himself a reed with his
sword and fashions a pipe out of
it.*)
He stops to listen:—
I'll stammer along!
(*He tries to imitate the note of the
bird on his pipe: he is unsuccessful, and after repeated trials,
shaking his head in vexation he
desists.*)

That tone's not right;
on the reed I see
the melody may not be waked.—
Birdie, I deem
myself but dull:
my deed spans not your speech.
Now I am shamed
by the shrewd little piper:
he peeps to know why I'm pausing.—
Ho there! then listen
now to my horn;
with the stupid reed
I can render nothing.—
To a wild wood-note,
which I can sound,
the lustiest shall you now hear.
A loving companion
lately I called;
nothing better came yet
than wolf and bear.
So let me see
whom now it will lure
to make me a loving consort?
(*He has thrown away the reed and
now blows a merry call on his little silver horn.*)

(There is a stir in the background.
Fafner, in the form of a huge lizard-
like dragon, rises from his lair in the
cave; he breaks through the under-
wood and crawls from the dell up
to the higher ground till his fore-
legs rest quite on the knoll. He then
utters a loud yawning growl.)

SIEGFRIED: (*turns round, perceives Fafner, looks at him in surprise and then laughs*). At last has
my melody attracted
something lovely!
I've waked up a fair-favored friend!

FAFNER: (*who has paused, on
sight of Siegfried*). What is that?

SIEGFRIED: Hey! are you a beast
that of speech can boast?
You surely might teach me something.
Here is one
who never learned to fear:
could he by you effect it?

FAFNER: You're not over-bold?

---

SIEGFRIED: Muth und
Übermuth—
was weiss ich!
Doch dir fahr' ich zu Leibe,
lehrst du das Fürchten mich nicht!

FAFNER: (*lacht*). Trinken wollt'
ich:
nun treff' ich auch Frass!
(*Er öffnet seinen Rachen und
zeigt die Zähne.*)

SIEGFRIED: Eine zierliche Fresse
zeig'st du mir da:
lachende Zähne
im Leckermaul!
Gut wür's den Schlund dir zu
schliessen
dein Rachen reckt sich zu weit!

FAFNER: Zu tauben Reden
taugt er schlecht:
dich zu verschlingen
frommt der Schlund.
(*Er droht mit dem Schweife.*)

SIEGFRIED: Hoho! du grausam
grimmiger Kerl,
von dir verdant sein
dünkt mich übel:
räthlich und fromm doch scheint's
du verrecktest hier ohne Frist.

FAFNER: (*brüllt*). Pruh! komm'!
prahlendes Kind.

SIEGFRIED: (*fasst das Schwert*).
Sieh' dich vor, Brüller:
der Prahler kommt!
(*Er stellt sich Fafner entgegen:
dieser hebt sich weiter vor auf die
Bodenerhöhung, und sprüht aus
seinen Nüstern nach ihm. Siegfried springt zur Seite. Fafner
schwingt den Schweif nach vorn,
um Siegfried zu fassen: dieser
weicht ihm aus, indem er mit einem Satze über den Rücken des
Wurmes hinwegspringt; als der
Schweif sich auch hierhin ihm
schnell nachwendet, und ihn fast
schon packt, verwundet Siegfried
diesen mit dem Schwerte. Fafner
zieht den Schweif hastig zurück,
brüllt, und bäumt seinen Vorder-
leib, um mit dessen voller Wucht
zur Seite sich auf Siegfried zu werfen: so bietet er diesem die Brust,
Siegfried erspäht schnell die Stelle
des Herzens, und stösst sein
Schwert bis an das Heft hinein.
Fafner bäumt sich von Schwert
noch höher, und sinkt, als Siegfried das Schwert losgelassen und
zur Seite gesprungen ist, auf die
Wunde zusammen.*)

SIEGFRIED: Da lieg', neidischer
Kerl!
Nothung trägst du im Herzen.

FAFNER: (*mit schwächerer
Stimme*). Wer bist du, kühner
Knabe,
der das Herz mir traf?
Wer reizte des Kindes Muth
zu der mordlichen That?
Dein Hirn brütete nicht,
was du vollbracht.

---

SIEGFRIED: Bold or over-bold—
What do I know?
but I'll tackle you finely,
if you teach not fearing to me.

FAFNER: (*laughs*). I came for
drink,
now food drops to me!
(*He opens his jaws and shows his
teeth.*)

SIEGFRIED: An extravagant frontage
you turn on me:
dazzling with teeth
is that dainty maw!
Well were it to close up the cavern:
your gullet gapes far too wide.

FAFNER: For senseless gabble
serves it ill:
rather to eat you it opens.
(*He lashes his tail menacingly.*)

SIEGFRIED: Oho! you gruesome,
grim-looking knave!
To stay your stomach
suits me little: it is wiser
to remove you from here, and at
once.

FAFNER: (*roaring*). Bah! come,
boast-making cub!

SIEGFRIED: (*drawing his sword*).
Look out, growler!
the boaster comes.
(*He confronts Fafner: the latter
creeps more over the knoll and
spits from his nostrils at him. Siegfried springs aside. Fafner curls
his tail forwards to reach Siegfried, but he avoids it and springs
over the back of the dragon with a
bound; as the tail follows him and
almost reaches him, he wounds it
with his sword. Fafner hastily
draws back his tail, roars, and
raises the forepart of his body, in
order to throw his full weight sideways upon Siegfried, thus exposing his breast to him. Siegfried
quickly espies the position of his
heart and plunges his sword there
up to the very hilt. Fafner rears
still higher in pain and sinks
down upon the wound, while Siegfried lets go the sword and
springs aside.*)

SIEGFRIED: There lie, noisy rogue!
Needful sticks in your gizzard.

FAFNER: (*with weaker voice*).
Who are you, stalwart stripling,
that has struck my heart?
Who wakened and stirred your
mind
to this murderous deed?
Your own brain never, I believe,
brought it about.

# Act II

SIEGFRIED: Viel weiss ich noch nicht,
noch nicht auch wer ich bin:
mit dir mordlich zu ringen
reiztest du selbst meinen Muth.

FAFNER: Du helläugiger Knabe,
unkund deiner selbst:
wen du gemordet
meld' ich dir.
Die einst der Welt gewaltet,
der Riesen ragend Geschlecht,
Fasolt und Fafner,
die Brüder, fielen nun beide.
Um verfluchtes Gold,
von Göttern vergabt,
traf ich Fasolt zu todt:
der nun als Wurm
den Hort bewachte,
Fafner, den letzten Riesen,
fällte ein rosiger Held.—
Blick nun hell,
blühender Knabe;
des Hortes Herrn
umringt Verrath:
der dich Blinden reizte zur That.
beräth nun des Blühenden Tod
(Ersterbend.)
Merk' wie's endet:—
acht' auf mich!

SIEGFRIED: Woher ich stamme,
rathe mir noch;
weise ja scheinst du
Wilder im Sterben;
rath' es nach meinem Namen:
Siegfried bin ich genannt.

FAFNER: Siegfried . . . !
(Er seufzt, hebt sich und stirbt.)

SIEGFRIED: Zur Kunde taugt kein Todter.—
So leite mich denn
mein lebendes Schwert!
(Fafner hat sich im Sterben zur Seitegewälzt. Siegfried zieht das Schwert aus seiner Brust: dabei wird seine Hand vom Blute benetzt; er fährt heftig mit der Hand auf.)
Wie Feuer brennt das Blut!
(Er führt unwillkürlich die Finger zum Munde, um das Blut von ihnen abzusaugen. Wie er sinnend vor sich hinblickt, wird plötzlich seine Aufmerksamkeit von dem Gesange der Waldvögel angezogen. Er lauscht mit verhaltenem Athem.)
Ist mir doch fast—
als sprächen die Vöglein zu mir:
deutlich dünken mich's Worte!
Nützte mir das
des Blutes Genuss?—
Das selt'ne Vöglein hier—
horch! was singt es mir?

STIMME EINES WALDVOGEL'S:
(in der Linde). Hei! Siegfried gehört
nun der Niblungen Hort:
o fänd' in der Höhle
den Hort er jetzt!
Wollt' er den Tarnhelm gewinnen,

SIEGFRIED: Much I do not know,
not even who I am;
yourself only did urge me
to this murderous end.

FAFNER: You bright, eager-eyed stripling,
even strange to yourself:
whom you have murdered
must you hear.
The giants' generous race
which ruled the world at one time—
Fasolt and Fafner,
the brothers, now both lie fallen.
For the fatal gold
we gained from the gods
dealt death to Fasolt,
Now I, as Worm
the hoard overwatching,
Fafner, the last of giants,
fall by a juvenile hand.—
Bear good heed,
blossoming hero:
Amid treason treads
he who holds the hoard:
one who blindly showed you this deed
shapes for you, boy, surely death.
(Dying.)
Weigh what happens:—
heed my words!

SIEGFRIED: What were my parents counsel to me yet!
you appear to be wise,
wild one, expiring;
tell it too from my title:
I am Siegfried , I believe.

FAFNER: Siegfried . . . !
(He sighs, raises himself up and dies.)

SIEGFRIED: The dead can tell no tidings.
So lead me henceforth
my life-keeping sword!
(Fafner has rolled over on his side in dying. Siegfried draws the sword from his breast: in doing so his hand becomes smeared with blood: he draws it hastily away.)
Like fire burns the blood!
(He instinctively puts his finger to his mouth to suck blood off it. As he gazes thoughtfully before him, his attention is arrested all at once by the song of the birds. He listens with bated breath.)
Would it not seem
that songster were speaking to me?—
well the words I distinguish!
Was it the blood
that worked this magic?
That stranger bird I hear—
Listen! what sings he now?

VOICE OF A WOODBIRD: (in the lime tree). Hey! Siegfried holds
now the Nibelung's hoard:
O he'll find the hoard
in the hole soon!
Were he to win the Tarnhelm,
it would tide him through wonder-

der taugt' ihm zu wonniger That:
doch möcht' er den Ring sich errathen,
der macht' ihn zum Walter der Welt!

SIEGFRIED: Dank, liebes Vöglein,
für deinen Rath;
gern folg' ich dem Ruf.
(Er geht und steigt in die Höhle hinab, wo er alsbald gänzlich verschwindet.)
(Mime schleicht heran, scheu umherblickend, um sich von Fafner's Tod zu überzeugen.—Gleichzeitig kommt von der anderen Seite Alberich aus dem Geklüft hervor; er beobachtet Mime genau. Als dieser Siegfried nicht mehr gewahrt, und vorsichtig sich nach hinten der Höhle zuwendet, stürzt Alberich auf ihn zu, und vertritt ihm den Weg.)

ALBERICH: Wohin schleich'st du
eilig und schlau,
schlimmer Gesell?

MIME: Verfluchter Bruder,
dich brauch' ich hier!
Was bringt dich her?

ALBERICH: Geizt es dich Schelm
nach meinem Gold?
Verlang'st du mein Gut?

MIME: Fort von der Stelle!
Die Stätte ist mein:
was stöberst du hier?

ALBERICH: Stör' ich dich wohl
im stillen Geschäft,
wenn du hier stiehl'st?

MIME: Was ich erschwang
mit schwerer Müh',
soll mir nicht schwinden.

ALBERICH: Hast du dem Rhein
das Gold zum Ringe geraubt?
Erzeugtest du gar
den zähen Zauber im Reif?

MIME: Wer schuf den Tarnhelm,
der die Gestalten tauscht?
Der sein' bedurfte,
erdachtest du ihn wohl?

ALBERICH: Was hättest du Stümper
je wohl zu stampfen verstanden?
Der Zauberring
zwang mir zur Kunst erst den Zwerg!

MIME: Wo hast du den Ring?
Dir Zagem entrissen ihn Riesen!
Was du verlor'st,
meine List erlangt' es für mich.

ALBERICH: Mit des Knaben That
will der Knicker nun knausern?
Dir gehört sie gar nicht,
der Helle ist selbst ihr Herr!

MIME: Ich zog ihn auf;
fü die Zucht zahlt er mir nun:
für Müh' und Last
erlauert' ich lang' meinen Lohn!

ful tasks;
but were he the ring too to ravish
it would give him the ward of the world!

SIEGFRIED: Thanks, pretty warbler,
for your advice:
I'll follow your voice.
(He goes up and descends into the cavern, where he disappears from view.)
(Mime slinks on, looking about timidly, to assure himself of Fafner's death.—At the same time Alberich comes out from his cleft at the opposite side; he watches Mime narrowly. As the latter, not finding Siegfried, carefully steals towards the cave, Alberich darts upon him and bars his way.)

ALBERICH: Where do you slink,
hasty and sly,
slippery scamp?

MIME: Accursed brother,
what brings you here?
What brings you here?

ALBERICH: Do you grasp rogue,
towards my gold?
Do you lust for my goods?

MIME: Yield the position!
This station is mine.
What stir you here?

ALBERICH: You are startled
from stealthy concerns,
that I've disturbed?

MIME: What I have shaped
with shrewdest toil
shall not be shaken.

ALBERICH: Wasn't it you that robbed
the golden ring from the Rhine?
or charged it with great
and choice enchantment around?

MIME: Who formed the Tarnhelm,
which into any form can turn?
By you it was wanted;
its worker were you too?

ALBERICH: What could you ever, fool,
yourself have fancied and fashioned?
The magic ring
made the dwarf equal to the task.

MIME: Where now is your ring?
The giants have robbed you, recreant!
What you have lost,
by my lore, I will gain.

ALBERICH: By the boy's exploit
shall you, booby, be bettered?
You shall have it not,
for its holder in truth is he.

MIME: I nourished him,
and now shall he pay his nurse:
for toil and woe,
a long while have I waited reward.

ALBERICH: Für des Knaben Zucht
will der knick'rige
schäbige Knecht
keck und kühn
gar wohl König nun sein?
Dem räudigsten Hund
wäre der Ring
gerath'ner als dir:
nimmer erring'st
du Rüpel den Herrscherreif!

MIME: Behalt' ihn denn:
hüte ihn wohl
den hellen Reif!
Sei du Herr:
doch mich heisse auch Bruder!
Um meines Tarnhelm's
lustigen Tand
tausch' ich ihn dir:
uns beiden taugt's,
theilen die Beute wir so.

ALBERICH: (höhnisch lachend).
Theilen mit dir?
und den Tarnhelm gar?
Wie schlau du bist!
Sicher schlief ich
niemals vor deinen Schlingen!

MIME: (ausser sich). Selbst nicht
tauschen?
Auch nicht theilen?
Leer soll ich geh'n,
ganz ohne Lohn?
Gar nichts willst du mir lassen?

ALBERICH: Nichts von allem,
nicht einen Nagel
sollst du dir nehmen!

MIME: (wüthend). Weder Ring
noch Tarnhelm
soll dir denn taugen!
nicht theil' ich nun mehr.
Gegen dich ruf' ich
Siegfried zu Rath
und des Recken Schwert:
der rasche Held,
der richte, Brüderchen, dich!

ALBERICH: Kehre dich um:—
aus der Höhle kommt er schon
her.—

MIME: Kindischen Tand
erkor er gewiss.—

ALBERICH: Den Tarnhelm hat
er!—

MIME: Doch auch den Ring!—

ALBERICH: Verflucht!—den
Ring!—

MIME: (lacht hämisch). Lass' ihn
den Ring dir doch geben!
Ich will ihn mir schon gewinnen.—
(Er schlüpft in den Wald zurück.)

ALBERICH: Und doch, seinem
Herrn
soll er allein noch gehören!
(Er verschwindet im Geklüft.)

---

ALBERICH: For a child's keep
would this beggarly,
haggardly boor,
bold and blustering,
be well near as a king?
To rankest of dogs
boot the ring
far rather than you:
never, you rogue,
shall reach you the magic round!

MIME: Then hold it still
and heed it well,
you hoarded ring.
Be head,
but yet hail me as brother!
For my own Tarnhelm,
excellent toy,
I'll tender it to you!
It will boot us two,
we'll share the booty like this.

ALBERICH: (laughing scornfully). Share it with you?
and the Tarnhelm too?
How sly you are!
Safe I'd sleep then
never from your ensnarings.

MIME: (beside himself). Will you
not bargain?
Will you not barter?
Bare must I go,
gaining no boon?
Will you give to me no booty?

ALBERICH: Not an atom,
not even a nail's worth:
all I deny you.

MIME: (furiously). In the ring and
Tarnhelm
never shall you triumph!
We'll not talk of shares!
Unto you I'll call for
Siegfried to come;
with his carving sword
the caustic boy
shall crush you, brother of mine!

ALBERICH: Turn your head
round;—
from the cavern towards us he
comes.—

MIME: Trivial toys
have tempted him there.—

ALBERICH: The Tarnhelm he
holds!—

MIME: Aye, and the ring!—

ALBERICH: A curse!—the ring!—

MIME: (with an evil laugh). Let
him render the ring to you—
I imagine that very soon I shall win
it.
(He slips back into the wood.)

ALBERICH: And yet to its lord
alone shall it be delivered!
(He disappears in the cleft.)

---

(Siegfried ist, mit Tarnhelm und
Ring, während des Letzten langsam und sinnend aus der Höhle
vorgeschritten: er betrachtet gedankenvoll seine Beute, und hält,
nahe dem Baume, auf der Höhe
wieder an—Grosse Stille.)

SIEGFRIED: Was ihr mir nützt
weiss ich nicht.
doch nahm ich euch
aus des Horts gehäuftem Gold,
weil guter Rath mir es rieth.
So taug' eu're Zier
als des Tages Zeuge:
mich mahne der Tand
dass ich kämpfend Fafner erlegt,
doch das Fürchten noch nicht gelernt.
(Er steckt den Tarnhelm sich in
den Gürtel, und den Reif an den
Finger. — Stillschweigen. Wachsendes Waldweben. — Siegfried
achtet unwillkürlich wieder des
Vogel's, und lauscht ihm mit verhaltenem Athem.)

STIMME DES WALDVOGEL'S: (in
der Linde). Hei! Siegfried gehört
nun der Helm und Ring!
O traut' er Mime
dem Treulosen nicht!
Hörte Siegfried nur scharf
auf des Schelmen Heuchlergered':
wie sein Herz es meint
kann er Mime versteh'n;
so nützt' ihm des Blutes Genuss.
(Siegfried's Miene und Geberde
drücken aus, dass er alles wohl
vernommen. Er sieht Mime sich
nähern, und bleibt, ohne sich zu
rühren, auf sein Schwert gestützt,
beobachtend und in sich geschlossen, in seiner Stellung auf der
Anhöhe bis zum Schlusse des folgenden Auftrittes.)

MIME: (langsam auftretend). Er
sinnt und erwägt
der Beute Werth:—
weilte wohl hier
ein weiser Wand'rer,
schweifte umher,
beschwatzte das Kind
mit listiger Runen Rath?
Zwiefach schlau
sei nun der Zwerg:
die listigste Schlinge
leg' ich jetzt aus,
dass ich mit traulichem
Trug-Gerede
bethöre das trotzige Kind!
(Er tritt näher an Siegfried heran.)
Willkommen, Siegfried!
Sag', du Kühner,
hast du das Fürchten gelernt?

SIEGFRIED: Den Lehrer fand ich
noch nicht.

MIME: Doch den Schlangenwurm,
du hast ihn erschlagen:
das war doch ein schlimmer Gesell?

SIEGFRIED: So grimm und
tückisch er war,
sein Tod grämt mich doch schier,
da viel üblere Schächer

---

(Siegfried, with Tarnhelm and
ring, has stepped out, during the
last words, from the cave, slowly
and thoughtfully: he inspects his
prizes reflectively, and again
pauses on the knoll by the tree.—
Deep silence.)

SIEGFRIED: How you may serve
I hardly see;
I snatched you, though,
from the hoard of heaped-up gold,
as guiding voice did advise.
Let serve then your wealth
as this struggle's witness;
these baubles shall show
that in fight I Fafner laid low
but of fear I learned nothing.
(He sticks the Tarnhelm in his girdle and puts the ring on his finger.—Perfect stillness. Increased
rustling of the woods.—Siegfried
mechanically looks for the bird
and listens to it with bated
breath.)

VOICE OF THE WOODBIRD: (in
the lime tree). Hey! Siegfried holds
now the helm and the ring!
O trust not in Mime,
the treacherous elf!
Hear Siegfried sharply
the shifty hypocrite's words:
what at heart he means
shall by Mime be shown;
so profits the taste of the blood.
(Siegfried's expression and gestures show that he has understood
all. He perceives Mime's approach
and remains without moving,
leaning on his sword, observing
and self-repressed, in his station
on the mound till the end of the
following speech.)

MIME: (slowly entering). He
broods as he weighs
the booty's worth.—
Walked there with him
a wily Wanderer,
foraging here,
informing the boy
with cunning runes and advice?
Doubly sly
shall be my deeds;
my most artful traps
all shall be set,
that I with true-seeming
traitorous talk
may entrap the truculent boy!
(He advances nearer to Siegfried.)
I hail you Siegfried!
Say, my hero,
have you then attained fearing?

SIEGFRIED: The teacher I found
not here.

MIME: But the serpent-worm,
then have you destroyed him?
He, sure, was a foul sort of friend.

SIEGFRIED: Though he was grim
and dreadful,
his death grieves me, in truth,
while far more evil scoundrels

unerschlagen noch leben!
Der mich ihn morden hiess,
den hass' ich mehr als den Wurm.

MIME: Nur sacht'! nicht lange
sieh'st du mich mehr:
zu ew'gem Schlaf
schliess' ich die Augen dir bald!
Wozu ich dich brauchte,
das hast du vollbracht;
jetzt will ich nur noch
die Beute dir abgewinnen:—
mich dünkt, das soll mir gelingen;
zu bethören bist du ja leicht!

SIEGFRIED: So sinnst du auf mein-
en Schaden?

MIME: Wie sagt' ich das?—
Siegfried, hör' doch, mein Sohn!
Dich und deine Art
hasst' ich immer von Herzen;
aus Liebe erzog ich
dich Lästigen nicht:
dem Horte in Fafners Hut,
dem Golde galt meine Müh'.
Giebst du mir das
nun gutwillig nicht—
Siegfried, mein Sohn,
das siehst du wohl selbst—
dein Leben musst du mir lassen!

SIEGFRIED: Dass du mich hassest,
hör' ich gern:
doch mein Leben auch muss ich dir
lassen?

MIME: Das sag' ich doch nicht?
du verstehst mich falsch!
(Er giebt sich die ersichtlichste
Mühe zur Verstellung.)
Sieh', du bist müde
von harter Müh';
brünstig brennt dir der Leib:
dich zu erquicken
mit queckem Trank
säumt' ich Sorgender nicht.
Als dein Schwert du dir branntest,
braut' ich den Sud:
trinkst du nun den,
gewinn' ich dein trautes Schwert,
und mit ihm Helm und Hort.
(Er kichert dazu.)

SIEGFRIED: So willst du mein
Schwert
und was ich erschwungen,
Ring und Beute mir rauben?

MIME: Was du doch falsch mich
versteh'st!
Stamml' ich und fas'le wohl gar?
Die grösste Mühe
geb' ich mir:
mein heimliches Sinnen
heuchelnd zu bergen,
und du dummer Bube
deutest alles doch falsch!
Öff'ne die Ohren,
und vernimm genau:
höre, was Mime meint!—
Hier nimm! trinke dir Labung!
mein Trank labte dich oft:
that'st du wohl unwirsch,
stelltest dich arg:
was ich dir bot—
erbos't auch—nahmst du's doch
immer.

are yet living!
Who made me murder him,
I hate him more than the worm.

MIME: Now softly! You will not
see me much more:
an endless sleep
soon shall weigh on your eyes!
For all that I wanted
have you well worked;
I'll try now
to win the golden treasure from you
I think I'll safely effect it:
you were ever easy to fool!

SIEGFRIED: You're seeking to
work my death then?

MIME: What? did I say that?—
Siegfried, hear me, my sonny!
You and all your kind
have I constantly hated;
from fondness, you burden,
I fostered you not:
the hoard under Fafner's hold
alone I labored to win.
If you'll not give up
that with good will—
Siegfried, my son,
you see yourself—
life you must really relinquish!

SIEGFRIED: That you should hate
me
hurts me not:
but must my life be delivered to
you?

MIME: I said nothing of that!
You mistake me quite.
(Giving himself the most elaborate pains to disguise his meaning.)
See, you are tired
with mighty toil;
your body burns with heat.
So, to restore you
with stirring drink,
swiftly I speed to you.
While you did beat out your sword,
I brewed this stuff:
take but a sip,
I win me your trusty sword,
and with it hoard and helm.
(He chuckles.)

SIEGFRIED: So, both of my sword
and what I have seized on,
Ring and booty, you'd rob me?

MIME: How you falsely distort!
Stammers—falters my speech?
The greatest trouble
I give myself
my secret designing
safely to bury,
and you, stupid boy,
construe all opposite-wise!
Open your ears then
and awake your wits:
hear what Mime means!
Here, take! and drink for refreshment!
my draughts freshened you often:
deep though your anger,
sullen your ire,
yet all I brought,
abusing,—you took ever.

SIEGFRIED: (ohne eine Miene zu
verzieh'n). Einen guten Trank
hätt' ich gera:
wie hast du diesen gebrau't?

MIME: Hei! so trink' nur:
trau' meiner Kunst!
In Nacht und Nebel
sinken die Sinne dir bald:
ohne Wach' und Wissen,
stracks streck'st du die Glieder.
Lieg'st du nun da,
leicht könnt' ich
die Beute nehmen und bergen:
doch erwachtest du je,
nirgends wär' ich
sicher vor dir,
hätt' ich selbst auch den Ring.
D'rum mit dem Schwert,
das so scharf du schuf'st,
hau' ich dem Kind
den Kopf erst ab:
dann hab' ich mir Ruh' und den
Ring!
(Er kichert wieder.)

SIEGFRIED: Im Schlafe willst du
mich morden?

MIME: Was möcht' ich? sagt' ich
denn das?—
Ich will dir Kind
nur den Kopf abhau'n!
Denn hasste ich dich
auch nicht so hell,
und hätt' ich des Schimpf's
und der schändlichen Müh'
auch nicht so viel zu rächen:
aus dem Weg dich zu räumen
darf ich nicht rasten,
wie käm' ich sonst anders zur
Beute,
da Alberich auch nach ihr lugt?—
Nun, mein Wälsung!
Wolfssohn du!
Sauf' und würg' dich zu Tod:
nie thu'st du mehr einen Schluck!

(Er hat sich nahe an Siegfried her-
angemacht, und reicht ihm jetzt
mit widerlicher Zudringlichkeit
ein Trinkhorn, in das er zuvor aus
einem Gefässe das Getränk gegossen. Siegfried hat bereits das
Schwert gefasst, und streckt jetzt,
wie in einer Anwandlung heftigen
Ekel's, Mime mit einem Streiche
todt zu Boden.—Man hört Alberich aus dem Geklüft heraus ein
höhnisches Gelächter aufschla-
gen.)

SIEGFRIED: Schmeck' du mein
Schwert,
ekliger Schwätzer!
Neides-Zoll
zahlt Nothung:
dazu durft' ich ihn schmieden.
(Er packt Mime's Leichnam auf,
schleppt ihn nach der Höhle, und
wirft ihn dort hinein.)
In der Höhle hier
lieg' auf dem Hort!
Mit zäher List
erzieltest du ihn:
jetzt magst du des Wonnigen walten!
Einen guten Wächter

SIEGFRIED: (without stirring in
the least). Of a goodly draught
were I glad:
of what compounded you this?

MIME: Hey! just try it:
trust to my skill!
In deathly darkness
soon shall your senses be laid:
without mind or motion
straight-stretched will your limbs
be.
Lying then so,
light were it
the prize to take and deposit;
did you wake though again,
never were I
safe from your reach,
did I seize even the ring.
So with the sword
you have shaped so sharp
truly I'll hew
your head right off:
then I shall have rest and the ring!
(He chuckles again.)

SIEGFRIED: Must I be murdered in
slumber?

MIME: What mean you? did I say
that?—
I will but chop
from the child his head!
For, had I not hated
you so sore,
and had not your scoffs
and my shameful endurance
so loudly called for payment,
I must without pausing
fling you from my pathway;
how else should I earn me the treasure
which Alberich aims at as well?—
Now, my Volsung,
valpine cub!
taste and vanish in death:
no more drink you will try.

(He has come close up to Siegfried
and now hands him with offensive importunity a drinking horn
into which he has previously
poured the draught from his flask.
Siegfried has already grasped his
sword, and, as if with an impulse
of sudden disgust, lays Mime dead
to the ground with one stroke.—
From the cleft Alberich is heard to
send forth a peal of mocking
laughter.)

SIEGFRIED: Taste my sword, infamous serpent!
"Needful" pays
pests nimbly;
for this I forged the weapon.
(He seizes the body of Mime, drags
it to the cave's mouth and throws
it inside.)
In the hollow here
lie with the hoard!
With stubborn lures
you strove for it,
so now with its wealth I reward
you!
And a goodly watchdog
I give to you,

geb' ich dir auch,
dass er vor Dieben dich deckt.
(*Er wälzt die Leiche des Wurmes vor den Eingang des Höhle, so dass er diesen ganz damit verstopft.*)
Da lieg auch du,
dunkler Wurm!
Den gleissenden Hort
hüte zugleich
mit dom beuterührigen Feind:
so fandet ihr beide nun Ruh'!
(*Er kommt nach der Arbeit wieder vor. — Es ist Mittag.*)
Heiss ward mir
von der harten Last:—
Brausend jagt sich
mein brünstiges Blut;
die Hand brennt mir am Haupt.—
Hoch steht schon die Sonne:
aus lichtem Blau
blickt ihr Aug'
auf den Scheitel steil mir herab.—
Linde Kühlugn
erkies' ich mir unter der Linde!
(*Er streckt sich wieder unter der Linde aus. — Grosse Stille. Waldweben. Nach einem längeren Schweigen*):
Noch einmal, liebes Vöglein,
da wir so lang'
lästig gestört,—
lauscht' ich gern deinem Sang
auf dom Zweige seh' ich
wohlig dich wiegen;
zwitschernd umschwirren
dich Brüder und Schwestern,
umschweben dich lustig und lieb!
Doch ich—bin so allein,
hab' nicht Bruder noch Schwester,
meine Mutter schwand,
meine Vater fiel:
nie sah sie der Sohn!—
Mein einz'ger Gesell
war ein garst'ger Zwerg;
Güte zwang
nie uns zu Liebe;
listige Schlingen
warf mir der Schlaue:—
nun musst' ich ihn gar erschlagen!—
Freundliches Vöglein,
dich frag' ich nun:
gönntest du mir
wohl ein gutes Gesell?
Willst du das Rechte mir rathen?
Ich lockte so oft,
und erloos't es nicht:
du, mein Trauter,
träf'st es wohl besser!
So recht ja riethest du schon:
nun sing'! ich lausche dem Sang.
(*Schweigen; dann*):

**STIMME DES WALDVOGEL'S:**
Hei! Siegfried erschlug
nun den schlimmen Zwerg!
Jetzt wüsst' ich ihm noch
das herrlichste Weib.
Auf hohem Felsen sie schläft,
ein Feuer umbrennt ihren Saal:
durchschritt' er die Brunst,
erweckt' er die Braut,
Brünnhilde wäre dann sein!

that so no thieves may threaten.
(*He drags the carcass of the dragon to the cave's mouth so as to stop it up with it completely.*)
There you lie too,
twining worm,
the glittering hoard
helping to guard,
with that booty-ravishing fool!
So find both at last your rest!
(*He returns from his task. — It is midday.*)
Hot am I
with my heavy load!—
Brawling speeds
my boiling blood;
my hand burns on my head.——
High stands the sun now!
In heaven's blue
beams his eye,
from the distance darting to me.—
Languid coolness
shall court me under the lime tree!
(*He again stretches himself under the lime tree.—Perfect stillness. Forest murmurs. After a long pause*):
Now once more, lovely warbler,
as we have lacked
long a discourse,
I'd listen gladly to your song:
on the twig I see you
restfully rocking;
twittering soar around
brothers and sisters,
encircling you, and loved.
But I—am all alone,
have no brother nor sister:
my mother sped,
my father fallen;—
they saw their son never!—
I did but consort
with a cankerous dwarf,
kindness drew us
not together;
guileful toils
the traitor contrived:—
to death was I forced to treat him!—
Friendliest warbler,
I would demand,
grant to me
a gracious friend.
Will you rightly counsel me to one?
I've called one so often
and he comes to me never:
you, my favorite;
farest, sure, better!
Already rightly you've spoken;
now sing! I listen to our song.
(*Silence; then*):

**VOICE OF THE WOODBIRD:** Hey!
Siegfried has slain
now the sinister dwarf!
I foresee for him now
a glorious wife.
In guarded fastness she sleeps,
fire emborders the spot;
overstepped he the blaze,
waked he the bride,
Brünnhilde then would be his!

**SIEGFRIED:** (*fährt mit jäher Heftigkeit vom Sitze auf*). O holder Sang!
süssester Hauch!
Wie brennt sein Sinn
mir sehnend die Brust!
Wie zückt er heftig
zündend mein Herz!
Was jagt mir so jach
durch Herz und Sinne?
Sing' es mir, süsser Freund!

**DER WALDVOGEL:** Lustig im Leid
sing' ich von Liebe;
wonnig und weh'
web' ich mein Lied:
nur Sehnende kennen den Sinn!

**SIEGFRIED:** Fort jagt mich's
jauchzend von hinnen,
fort aus dom Wald auf den Fels!
Noch einmal sage mir,
holder Sänger:
werd' ich das Feuer durchbrechen!
kann ich erwecken die Braut?

**DER WALDVOGEL:** Die Braut gewinnt,
Brünnhild' erweckt
ein Feiger nie:
nur wer das Fürchten nicht kennt!

**SIEGFRIED:** (*lacht auf vor Entzücken*). Der dumme Knab'
der das Fürchten nicht kennt!
mein Vöglein, das bin ja ich!
Noch heut' gab ich
vergebens mir Müh',
das Fürchten von Fafner zu lernen.
Nun brennt mich die Lust,
es von Brünnhild' zu wissen:
wie find' ich zum Felsen den Weg?
(*Der Vogel flattert auf, schwebt über Siegfried, und filegt davon.*)
(*jauchzend*). So wird mir der Weg gewiesen:
wohin du flatterst
folg' ich dem Flug!
(*Er eilt dem Vogel nach. — Der Vorhang fällt.*)

# ■ ACT III

*WILDE GEGEND*

*Am Fusse eines Felsenberges, der links nach hinten steil aufsteigt. — Nacht, Sturm und Wetter, Blitz und Donner.*
*Vor einem gruftähnlichen Höhlenthore im Felsen steht der*

**WANDERER:** Wache! Wache!
Wala, erwache!
Aus langem Schlafe
weck' ich dich Schlummernde wach.
Ich rufe dich auf:
herauf! herauf!
Aus nebliger Gruft,
aus nächt'gem Grunde herauf.
Erda! Erda!
Ewiges Weib!

**SIEGFRIED:** (*starting impetuously to his feet*). O lovely song!
Sweetest delight!
How burns its sense
my suffering breast!
How flies it headlong,
firing my heart!
What swiftly oversways
my heart and senses?
Say to me, dearest friend!

**THE WOODBIRD:** Lightly, though desolate,
I sing of loving;
cheerful in woe
weaving my tune;
warm hearts can alone comprehend!

**SIEGFRIED:** I hurry forward
henceforth exulting;
forth from the wood to the mountain!—
But once more say to me,
lovely singer,—
may I the furnace then break through?
waken the marvellous bride?

**THE WOODBIRD:** The bride is won,
Brünnhilde awakened
by faint heart never:
but by him who knows not fear.

**SIEGFRIED:** (*laughing with delight*). The stupid lad,
who has not learned to fear,
dear flutter, that is myself!
Today I put me
to profitless toil
this fearing to gather from Fafner.
I burn now to gain it
from Brünnhilde's counsel:
who'll point me the path to her rock?
(*The bird flutters, hovers over Siegfried and flies away.*)
(*shouting with joy*). The road then direct me rightly:
my foot follows wherever you fly!
(*He hastens after the bird.—The curtain falls.*)

# ■ Act III

*A WILD REGION*

*At the foot of a rocky mountain which rises steeply L. towards the back.—Night, storm, thunder, and lighting.*
*Before a vault-like hollow in the rocks stands the*

**WANDERER:** Waken, witch-wife!
Witch-wife, awaken!
Let lengthy sleep
wend from your slumbering eyes.
I summon you forth;
arise! arise!
from nebulous depths,
arise from night and darkness!
Erda! Erda!
undying witch!
From hidden abysses

Aus heimischer Tiefe
tauche zur Höh'!
Dein Wecklied sing' ich,
dass du erwach'st;
aus sinnendem Schlafe
sing' ich dich auf.
Allwissende!
Urweltweise!
Erda! Erda!
Ewiges Weib!
Wache, du Wala! erwache!
(*Die Höhlengruft hat zu
erdämmern begonne: in
bläulichem Lichtscheine steigt
Erda aus der Tiefe. Sie erscheint
wie von Reif bedeckt; Haar und
Gewand werfen einen glitzernden
Schimmer von sich.*)

**ERDA:** Stark ruft das Lied;
kräftig reizt der Zauber:
ich bin erwacht
aus wissendem Schlaf:
wer scheucht den Schlummer mir?

**WANDERER:** Der Weckrufer bin
ich,
und Weisen üb' ich,
dass weithin wache
was fester Schlaf umschliesst.
Die Welt durch zog ich,
wanderte viel,
Kunde zu werben,
urweisen Rath zu gewinnen.
Kundiger giebt es
keine als dich:
bekannt ist dir
was die Tiefe birgt,
was Berg und Thal,
Luft und Wasser durchwebt.
Wo Wesen sind
weht dein Athem:
wo Hirne sinnen
haftet dein Sinn;
alles, was man,
sei dir bekannt.
Dass ich nun Kunde gewänne,
weckt' ich dich aus dem Schlaf.

**ERDA:** Mein Schlaf ist Träumen,
mein Träumen Sinnen,
mein Sinnen Walten des Wissens.
Doch wenn ich schlafe,
wachen Nornen:
sie weben das Seil,
und spinnen fromm was ich
weiss:—
was fräg'st du nicht die Nornen?

**WANDERER:** Im Zwange der Welt
weben die Nornen:
sie können nichts wenden noch
wandeln
doch deiner Weisheit
dankt' ich den Rath wohl,
wie zu hemmen ein rollendes Rad?

**ERDA:** Männerthaten
umdämmern mir den Muth:
mich Wissende selbst
bezwang ein Waltender einst.
Ein Wunschmädchen
gebar ich Wotan:
der Heden Wal
heiss er für ihn sie küren.
Kühn ist sie
und weise auch:

bear you on high!
I sing your reveille,
let it arouse you;
from sentient slumber
All-knower of
all world-wisdom!
Erda! Erda!
Undying witch!
Waken, witch-wife! awaken!
(*The hollow has begun to glow
with light. Erda rises from below
in a bluish halo. She seems as if
covered with frost; her hair and
garments gleam with iridescent
light.*)

**ERDA:** Great might has song!
strongly moves the enchantment.
I am awakened
from witful repose:
who drives my sleep away?

**WANDERER:** I am your summoner
and song I utter
to stir the senses sealed
in bonds of slumber.
I roved through
wander far
to win tidings,
all-wisdom well to beware of.
Counsellors none
can cope with your lore;
you can declare
what the deep holds,
what hill and dale,
wind and tide contain.
Where life awakens
Your spirit walks,
where brains are searching
Your soul broods;
all things they say
straight you can tell;
That you may surrender tidings
I arouse you from your sleep.

**ERDA:** My sleep is dreaming,
my dream is searching,
my search for weapons of wisdom.
But while I slumber
wake the Nornen:
they weave at their rope
and rightly spin what I wish—
Why not seek the Nornen?

**WANDERER:** Controlled by the
world
weave on the Nornen,
and they can weaken nor ward off
nothing.
Yet would I thank
Your wisdom to tell me
how a wheel in its roll to arrest?

**ERDA:** Mortal workings
bewilder much my mind:
a warder of heaven
subdued my will to him once
I bore to Wotan
a wish-maiden,
who by her will assembled
bands of heroes.
Staunch is she
and wise as well:

was weck'st du mich,
und fräg'st um Kunde
nicht Erda's und Wotan's Kind?

**WANDERER:** Die Walkäre mein'st
du,
Brünnhild', die Maid?
Sie trotzte dem Stürmebezwinger:
wo am stärksten er selbst sich bezwang
was den Lenker der Schlacht
zu thun verlangte,
doch dem er wehrte
—zuwider sich selbst—
allzu vertraut
wagte die Trotzige
das für sich zu vollbringen,
Brünnhild' in brennender Schlacht.
Streitvater
strafte die Maid;
in ihr Auge drückt' er Schlaf;
auf dem Felsen schläft sie fest:
erwachen wird
die Weihliche nur
um einen Mann zu minnen als
Weib.
Frommten mir Fragen an sie?

**ERDA:** (*ist in Sinnen versunken,
und beginnt erst längerem
Schweigen*). Wirr wird mir's
seit ich erwacht:
wild und kraus
kreis't die Welt!
Die Walküre,
der Wala Kind,
büsst' in Banden des Schlaf's,
als die wissende Mutter schlief?
Der den Trotz lehrte
straft den Trotz?
Der die That entzündet
zürnt um die That?
Der das Recht wahrt,
der die Eide hütet—
wehret dem Recht?
herrscht durch Meineid?—
Lass' mich wieder hinab:
Schlaf verschliesse mein Wissen!

**WANDERER:** Dieh Mutter lass' ich
nicht zieh'n,
da des Zaubers ich mächtig bin.—
Urwissend
stachest du einst
der Sorge Stachel
in Wotan's wagendes Herz:
mit Furcht vor schmachvoll
feindlichem Ende,
füllt' ihn dein Wissen,
dass Bangen band seinen Muth.
Bist du der Welt
weisestes Weib,
sage mir nun:
wie besiegt die Sorge der Gott?

**ERDA:** Du bist—nicht
was du dich nenn'st!
Was kam'st du störrischer Wilder
zu stören der Wala Schlaf?
Friedloser,
lass' mich frei!
Löse des Zaubers Zwang!

why wake then me,
nor question challenge
with Erda's and Wotan's child?

**WANDERER:** The Valkyrie, you
mean?
Brünnhilde, my maid?
She disobeyed the tempest-sub-
duer,
when in truth he had subdued himself;
what the fight-controller
had willingly accomplished,
but what he stifled
in spite of himself,
Brünnhilde free
sought then defiantly
to accomplish unbidden,
boldly in battle's assault.
Sternly
descended his wrath;
on her eyes he laid magic sleep:
on the mountain she slumbers fast.
Awakened will
the war-maiden be,
but to mate with a man as his wife.
Can I then question with her?

**ERDA:** (*has become absorbed in
thought, and replies after a considerable silence*). Weak I wax
since I awoke;
wild and strange
seems the world!
The war-maiden—
the witch's child,
pines in penance of sleep
which her wisdomful mother
shares?
Does then pride's teacher
punish pride?
Is the plan's arranger
wroth with the plan?
Does the right's defense—
Does the truth's upholder
fetter the right—
harbor untruth?
Let me quickly depart:
sleep my senses shall quiet!

**WANDERER:** You, mother, shaltl
not depart
while the power of magic I
wield.—
All-witting
struck once
the sting of sorrow
in Wotan's warrior heart:
with fear of shameful,
fatal extinction
your wisdom filled him;
his courage was cowed by dismay.
Are you the world's
wisest of women,
give me then advice:
how the god may grapple with
care?

**ERDA:** You are scarce
what you seem!
Why stubborn and wild one,
startle the witch from sleep?
Restless one,
let me rest!
Loose your constraining spell!

WANDERER: Du bist—nicht
was du dich wähn'st!
Urmütter-Weisheit
geht zu Ende:
dein Wissen verweht
vor meinem Willen.
Weisst du, was Wotan—will?
Dir Unweisen
ruf' ich's in's Ohr,
dass du sorglos ewig nun
schläf'st.
Um der Götter Ende
gräm't mich die Angst nicht,
seit mein Wunsch es will!
Was in Zwiespalt's wildem
Schmerze
verzweifelnd einst ich beschloss,
froh und freudig
führ' ich frei es nun aus:
weiht' ich in wüthendem Ekel
des Niblungen Neid schon die Welt
dem wonnigsten Wälsung
weis' ich mein Erbe nun an.
Der von mir erkoren,
doch nie mich gekannt,
ein kühnster Knabe,
meines Rathes bar,
errang des Niblungen Ring:
ledig des Neides,
liebesfroh,
erlahmt an dem Edlen
Alberich's Fluch;
denn fremd bleibt ihm die Furcht.
Die du mir gebar'st,
Brünnhilde,
sie weckt hold sich der Held:
wachend wirkt
dein wissendes Kind
erlösende Weltenthat.—
D'rum schlaf nun du,
schliesse dein Auge,
träumend erschau' mein Ende!
Was jene auch wirken—
dem ewig Jungen
weicht in Wonne der Gott.—
Hinab denn, Erda!
Urmütter-Furcht!
Ur-Sorge!
Zu ewigem Schlaf
hinab! hinab!—
Dort seh' ich Siegfried nah'n.—
(*Erda versinkt. Die Höhle ist
wieder ganz finster geworden: an
dem Gestein derselben lehnt sich
der Wanderer an, und erwartet so
Siegfried.*)—
(*Monddämmerung erhellt die
Bühne etwas. Das Sturmwetter
hört ganz auf.*)

SIEGFRIED: (*von rechts im Vordergrunde auftreten*). Mein
Vöglein schwebte mir fort;—
mit flatterndem Flug
und süsse Sang
wies es mir wonnig den Weg:
nun schwand es fern mir davon.
Am besten find' ich
selbst nun den Berg:
wohin mein Führer mich wies,
dahin wandr' ich jetzt fort.
(*Er schreitet weiter nach hinten.*)

WANDERER: You are—not
what you think!
All-mother's wit
draws near its ending:
your wisdom wanes
before my wishes. Do you
wish what Wotan—wills?
Unwise,
I cry in your ear,
that you so unanxious may sleep.—
For the Aesir's ending
I feel no anguish,
since it works my will.
What in pain of wild dissension
despairing once I resolved,
willingly and fearless
I fitly finish here.
Once though I wished in my anger
the Niblung might net him the
world,
now, Volsung most gay,
willed is its heirdom to you!
One announced by me,
but to me unknown,
a notable novice,
without counsel from me,
has reached the Nibelung's ring.
Lacking in malice,
large of love,
he'll lightly disarm
Alberich's curse;
for far bides he from fear.
She whom you have borne,
Brünnhilde,
will this hero hail.
When she wakes your
child will work
a deed for the world's release.
Then slumber again,
seal up your eyelids,
dream, and foresee my ending.
Whatever may happen
the god will always
hail the heaven of love.
Away then, Erda!
All-mother-fear—
All-sorrow—
To endless sleep
away! away!
I see that Siegfried comes.—
(*Erda vanishes. The hollow again
becomes quite dark. The Wanderer leans against the rocks and
awaits Siegfried.*)—
(*Moonrise slightly illumines the
stage. The storm has subsided.*)

SIEGFRIED: (*entering R. in the
foreground*). My favorite soars not
before.—
With fluttering flight
and sweetest song
plainly it pointed the path:
now seems it far to have flown.
It were right to find
the rock for myself:
the way my feathered friend
went—
there will I now fare.
(*He goes further towards the
back.*)

WANDERER: (*in seiner Stellung
an der Höhle verbleibend*). Wohin, Knabe.
heisst dich dein Weg?

SIEGFRIED: Da redet's ja:
wohl räth das mir den Weg.—
Einen Felsen such' ich,
von Feuer ist der umwabert:
dort schläft ein Weib
das ich wecken will.

WANDERER: Wer sagt' es dir
den Fels zu suchen,
wer nach der Frau dich zu sehnen!

SIEGFRIED: Mich wies es ein singend
Waldvöglein:
das gab mir gute Kunde.

WANDERER: Ein Vöglein schwatzt
wohl manches;
kein Mensch doch kann's versteh'n:
wie mochtest du Sinn
dem Sange entnehmen?

SIEGFRIED: Das wirkte das Blut
eines wilden Wurm's,
der mir vor Neidhöhl' erblasste:
kaum netzt' es zündend
die Zunge mir,
da verstand ich der Vöglein Ges-
timm'

WANDERER: Erschlugst du den
Riesen,
wer reizte dich,
den starken Wurm zu besteh'n?

SIEGFRIED: Mich führte Mime,
ein falscher Zwerg;
das Fürchten wollt' er mich lehren:
zum Schwertschlag aber,
der ihn erschlug,
reizte der Wurm mich selbst;
seinen Rachen riss er mir auf.

WANDERER: Wer schuf das
Schwert
so scharf und hart,
dass der stärkste Feind ihm fiel?

SIEGFRIED: Das schweisst' ich mir
selbst,
da's der Schmied nicht konnte:
schwertlos noch wär' ich wohl
sonst.

WANDERER: Doch wer schuf
die starken Stücken,
daraus das Schwert du geschweisst?

SIEGFRIED: Was weiss ich davon!
Ich weiss allein,
dass die Stücken nichts mir
nützten,
schuf ich das Schwert mir nicht
neu.

WANDERER: (*bricht in ein freudig gemüthliches Lachen aus*).
Das—mein' ich wohl auch!

SIEGFRIED: Was lach'st du mich
aus?
Alter Frager,
hör' einmal auf;
lass' mich nicht lange mehr schwatzen!

WANDERER: (*remaining in his
station by the cave*). Say, boy
where shall
you bend your way?

SIEGFRIED: I hear a voice:
will he tell me the way?
For a rock I'm seeking
around which fire wanders:
there sleeps a woman
whom I would awaken.

WANDERER: Who stirred your
mind
the mountain to seek
and for the maiden to struggle?

SIEGFRIED: It was a singing
wood minstrel
who gave the good tidings.

WANDERER: A bird sings much
nonsense;
but none may understand.
How did you know
the song's import?

SIEGFRIED: It was by the blood
of a wicked worm,
whom I at Hate-cavern butchered:
scarcely had it tingled
the tongue of me
when I straightaway the bird understood.

WANDERER: You slew the giant?
How germed in you
the scheme to fight with the serpent?

SIEGFRIED: I followed Mime,
a faithless dwarf,
who wanted to teach me fearing.
The swordstroke, truly,
beneath which he sank
mainly the worm did seek;
with his jaws he menaced my life.

WANDERER: Who shaped the
sword
so sharp and hard
that so strong a foe it felled?

SIEGFRIED: I shaped it myself,
as the smith was helpless;
else should I be swordless still.

WANDERER: But who shaped
the sturdy splinters
from which you smelted the sword?

SIEGFRIED: What thought I of
that?
But this I knew—
for no work were fit those fragments
were they not welded anew.

WANDERER: (*breaking into a
peal of good-humored laughter*).
That well I admit!

SIEGFRIED: Why laugh you at me?
Old enquirer,
Listen once and for all;—
lead me no longer to chatter!
Can you direct
the road to me, do so;

# Act III

Kannst du den Weg
mir weisen, so rede:
vermag'st du's nicht,
so halte dein Maul!

and can you not
then keep your mouth closed!

**WANDERER:** Geduld, du Knabe!
Dünk' ich dich alt,
so sollst du mir Achtung bieten.

**WANDERER:** But patience, my youngster!
Since I am old
you should accord me some honor.

**SIEGFRIED:** Das wär' nicht übel!
So lang' ich lebe
stand mir ein Alter
stets im Wege:
den hab' ich nun fort gefegt.
Stemm'st du dort länger
dich steif mir entgegen—
sieh' dich vor, mein' ich,
dass du wie Mime nicht fähr'st!
(*Er tritt näher an den Wanderer heran.*)
Wie sieh'st du denn aus?
Was hast du gar
für 'nen grossen Hut?
Warum hängt der dir so in's Gesicht?

**SIEGFRIED:** That is a good one!
So long as I've lived
ever in my way
an old one waited,
whom now I have swept aside.
Stay you here longer
still planted before me,
it seems fit, see now,
that you should fare like Mime.
(*He approaches nearer to the Wanderer.*)
What do you look like?
Why have you on
such an ample hat?
Why does it hang so far over your face?

**WANDERER:** Das ist so Wand'rers Weise,
wenn dem Wind entgegen er geht.

**WANDERER:** Such is the way of Wanderer,
when he goes against the wind.

**SIEGFRIED:** Doch darunter fehlt
dir ein Auge?
Das schlug dir einer
gewiss schon aus,
dem du zu trotzig
den Weg vertrat'st?
Mach' dich jetzt fort!
sonst möchtest du leicht
das and're auch noch verlieren.

**SIEGFRIED:** But below an eyeball
is lacking!
No doubt you lost it
to one of late,
when you too boldly
did bar his way.
Take yourself off,
or, maybe, I'll quench
the other one too, and quickly.

**WANDERER:** Ich seh', mein Sohn,
wo nichts du weisst,
da weisst du dir leicht zu helfen
Mit dem Auge,
das als and'res mir fehlt,
erblick'st du selber das eine,
das mir zum Sehen verblieb.

**WANDERER:** I see, my son,
that where you know nothing,
you contrive to help yourself.
With an eye, too,
like the one that I lack you
look on the other
that yet is left for me to see.

**SIEGFRIED:** (*lacht*). Zum Lachen
bist du mir lustig!—
Doch hör', nun schwatz' ich nicht
länger:
geschwind zeig' mir den Weg,
deines Weges ziehe dann du;
zu nichts and' rem
acht' ich dich nütz':
d'rum sprich, sonst spreng' ich
dich fort!

**SIEGFRIED:** (*laughing*). Your language
moves me to laughter.
But come! I'll quibble no longer.
Be quick! tell me the way;
then, I warn you, turn on your own!
In nothing else do
I need your aid,
so speak, or I'll spurn you aside!

**WANDERER:** Kenntest du mich,
kühner Spross,
den Schimpf—spartest du mir!
Dir so vertraut,
trifft mich schmerzlich dein Dräu'n
Lieb' ich von je
deine lichte Art,—
Grauen auch zeugt' ihr
mein zürnender Grimm:
dem ich so hold bin.
allzu hehrer,
heut' nicht wecke mir Neid,
er vernichtete dich und mich!

**WANDERER:** Did you know me,
daring son,
of scoffs you would be sparing!
Fiercely your taunts
tear the heart that envelopes you.
Love though I bear
to your lineage bright,
fear too I've wrought
by my wrath when it fell.
You whom I cherish—
youth enchanting—
chafe not my spirit now
to annihilate you and me!

**SIEGFRIED:** Bleib'st du mir
stumm,
störrischer Wicht?
Weich' von der Stelle!
Denn dorthin, ich weiss,
führt es zur schlafenden Frau:

**SIEGFRIED:** Dumb are you still,
stubborn old creature?
Wend from your station!
For I know that way
brings me to the slumbering bride.
So warned me the flutterer

so wies es mein Vöglein,
das hier erst flüchtig entfloh.
(*Es wird allmälig wieder ganz finster.*)

that here has fled from me first.
(*It gradually becomes quite dark again.*)

**WANDERER:** (*in Zorn ausbrechend*). Es floh dir zu seinem Heil;
den Herrn der Raben
errieth es hier:
weh' ihm holen sie's ein!—
Den Weg, den es zeigte,
sollst du nicht zieh'n!

**WANDERER:** (*breaking out into wrath*). It fled you to save its life.
The lord of ravens
its road did lead to:
woe to it, light they on it!—
The way that it pointed
you shall not pass.

**SIEGFRIED:** Hoho! du Verbieter!
Wer bist du denn,
dass du mir whren willst?

**SIEGFRIED:** Oho! my withholder!
And who are you
that thus arrest my road?

**WANDERER:** Fürchte des Felsens Hüter!
Verschlossen hält
meine Macht die schlafend Maid
wer sie erweckte,
wer sie gewänne,
machtlos macht' er mich ewig!
Ein Feuermeer
umfluthet die Frau,
glühende Lohe
umleckt den Fels
wer die Braut begehrt,
dem brennt entgegen die Brunst.
(*Er winkt mit dem Speere.*)
Blick' nach der Höh'!
erlug'st du das Licht?—
Es wächst der Schein,
es schwillt die Gluth;
sengende Wolken,
wabernde Lohe,
wälzen sich brennend
und prasselnd herab.
Ein Licht-Meer
umleuchtet dein Haupt:
bald frisst und zehrt dich
zündendes Feuer:—
zurück denn, rasendes Kind!

**WANDERER:** Mock not the mountain's guardian!
A spell encompasses
by my might the slumbering maid.
One who can wake her,—
one who can win her,
makes me mightless forever!
A fiery main
flows round her form,
glittering lightnings
overlook the mountain:
he who'd find the bride
will feel the brunt of the fire.
(*He points with his spear.*)
Turn toward the hill!
Do you look on the light?
That waxing sheen,
that swelling glare—
smothering vapors,
varying lightnings,
vacillate burning
and crackling downwards.
A light-flood
illumines your head:
the furnace soon
will seize and engulf you.—
Away then, foolhardy boy!

**SIEGFRIED:** Zurück, du Prahler,
mit dir!
Dort, wo die Brünste brennen,
zu Brünnhilde muss ich jetzt hin.
(*Er schreitet darauf zu.*)

**SIEGFRIED:** Away, old boaster,
yourself!
Straight where the blaze is burning
to Brünnhilde's side will I go.
(*He advances on him.*)

**WANDERER:** (*den Speer vorhaltend*). Fürchtest das Feuer du
nicht,
so sperre mein Speer dir den Weg!
Noch hält meine Hand
der Herrschaft Haft;
das Schwert, das du schwing'st,
zerschlug einst dieser Schaft:
noch einmal denn
zerspring' es am ewigen Speer!

**WANDERER:** (*stretching out his spear*). Have you no heed of the fire?
My spear then shall spare you no path!
My still hand holds
the hallowed haft;
the sword that you sway
was shivered on this shaft:
so too again
it will snap on the eternal spear!

**SIEGFRIED:** (*das Schwert ziehend*). Meines Vaters Feind!
Find' ich dich hier?
Herrlich zur Rache
gerieth mir das!
Schwing' deinen Speer:
in Stücken spalt' ihn mein Schwert!
(*Er fieht mit dem Wanderer und haut ihm den Speer in Stücken. Furchtbarer Donnerschlag.*)

**SIEGFRIED:** (*drawing his sword*). Then my father's foe
faces me here?
How that will serve the
for sweet revenge!
Stretch out your spear:
my sword shall strike it to shreds.
(*He attacks the Wanderer and hews his spear in pieces. Terrific clap of thunder.*)

**WANDERER:** (*zurückweichend*). Zieh' hin! Ich kann dich nicht hassen.
(*Er verschwindet.*)

**WANDERER:** (*recoiling*). Advance! I cannot prevent you!
(*He disappears.*)

SIEGFRIED: Mit zerfocht'ner Waffe
wich mir der Feige?
(Mit wachsender Helle baben sich Feuerwolken aus der Höhe des Hintergrundes herabgesenkt: die ganze Bühne erfüllt sich wie von einem wogenden Flammenmeere.)
Ha, wonnige Gluth!
leuchtender Glanz!
Strahlend offen
steht mir die Strasse.—
Im Feuer mich baden!
Im Feuer zu finden die Braut!
Hoho! hoho!
hahaei! hahei!
Lustig! lustig!
Jetzt lock' ich ein liebes Gesell!
(Er setzt sein Horn an, und stürzt sich, seine ●●● weise blasend, in das Feuer,—Die Lohe ergiesst sich nun auch über den ganzen Vordergrund. Man hört Siegfried's Horn erst näher, dann ferner.—Die Feuerwolken ziehen immer von hinten nach vorn, so dass Siegfried, dessen Horn man wieder näher hört, sich nach hinten zu, die Höhe hinauf, zu wenden scheint.)

(Endlich beginnt die Gluth zu erbleichen; sie lös't sich wie in einen feinen, durchsichtigen Schleier auf, der nun ganz sich auch klärt und den heitersten blauen Himmelsäther, im hellsten Tagesscheine, hervortreten lässt. Die Scene, von der das Gewölk gänzlich gewichen ist, stellt die Höhe eines Felsengipfels (wie im dritten Aufzuge der "Walküre") dar: links der Eingang eines natürlichen Felsengemaches; rechts breite Tannen; der Hintergrund ganz frei.—Im Vordergrunde unter dem Schatten einer breitästigen Tanne, liegt Brünnhilde, in tiefem Schlafe: sie ist in vollständiger, glänzender Panzerrüstung, mit dem Helm auf dem Haupte, den langen Schild über sich gedeckt.—Siegfried ist so eben im Hintergrunde, am felsigen Saume der Höhe, angelangt. (sin Horn hatte zuletzt wieder ferner geklungen, bis es ganz schwieg.)—Er blickt staunend um sich.)

Selige Oede
auf sonniger Höh'!—
(In den Tann hinein sehend.)
Was ruht dort schlummernd
Im schattigen Tann?—
Ein Ross ist's,
rastend in tiefem Schlaf!
(Er betritt vollends die Höhe, und schreitet langsam weiter vor; als er Brünnhilde noch aus einiger Entfernung gewahrt, hält er verwundert an.)
Was strahlt mir dort entgegen?—
Welch' glänzendes Stahlgeschmeide!

SIEGFRIED: With defeated weapon
flies my foe?
(Fiery clouds have descended from the heights at back with increasing brightness: the entire stage becomes filled with a rolling sea of fire.)
Ha! heavenly glow!
brightning glare!
roads are now opening
radiantly around me.
In fire will I bathe,
through fire will I fare to my bride!
Oho! Oho!
Aha! Aha!
Gaily! gaily!
Soon greets me a glorious friend!
(He winds his born and plunges into the fire, blowing his call—The fire now flows over the whole foreground. Siegfried's born is heard, first near, then more distant.—The fiery clouds continue to pour from the back towards the front, so that Siegfried, whose born is now again heard nearer, appears to be ascending the mountain.)

(At last the glow begins to fade and sinks to a fine transparent veil, which also clears off and reveals the lovely-clear blue sky and bright weather.—The scene, from which all the vapors have fled, represents the summit of a rocky mountain-peak (as in the third Act of the "Valkyrie"): L. the entrance to a natural rocky field; R. spreading fir trees; the background quite open.—In the foreground beneath the shade of a spreading fir tree, lies Brünnhilde in deep sleep; she is in a complete suit of gleaming plate armor, with helmet on her head and long shield over her body.—Siegfried has now reached the rocky heights in the background. (His born has sounded more and more distant till it ceased altogether.) He looks around in astonishment.)

Sweet is this haven
on sun-illuminated heights!—
(Looking into the wood.)
What calmly slumbers
beneath shadowy trees?
A war-horse,
waiting in tranquil sleep!
(He surmounts the height completely and advances slowly; on seeing Brünnhilde at a little distance he pauses in surprise.)
What strikes me with its gleaming?
What glittering suit of steel!
Blind are my eyes
as yet with the blaze!

Blendet mir noch
die Lohe den Blick?—
(Er tritt näher hinzu.)
Helle Waffen!—
Heb' ich sie auf?
(Er hebt den Schild ab, und erblickt Brünnhilde's Gesicht, das jedoch der Helm noch zum grossen Theils verdeckt.)
Ha! in Waffen ein Mann:—
wie mahnt mich wonnig sein Bild!
Das hehre Haupt
drückt wohl der Helm?
leichter würd' ihm,
löst' ich den Schmuck.
(Vorsichtig löst er den Helm und hebt ihn der Schlafenden vom Haupte ab: langes, lockiges Harr bricht hervor.—Siegfried erschrickt.)
Ach!—wie schön!—
(Er bleibt in den Anblick versunken.)
Schimmernde Wolken
säumen in Wellen
den hellen Himmelssee:
leuchtender Sonne
lachendes Bild
strahlt durch das Wogengewölk!
(Er lauscht dem Athem.)
Von schwellendem Athem
schwingt sich die Brust:—
brech' ich die engende Brünne?
(Er versucht es mit grosser Behutsamkeit—aber es vergebens.)
Komm', mein Schwert,
schneide das Eisen!
(Er durchschneidet mit zarter Vorsicht die Panzer-ringe zu beiden Seiten der ganzen Rüstung, und hebt dann die Brünne und die Schienen ab, so dass nun Brünnhilde in einem weichen weiblichen Gewande vor ihm liegt.—Überrascht und staunend fährt er auf.)
Das ist kein Mann!—
Brennender Zauber
zückt mir in's Herz;
feurige Angst
fasst meine Augen:
mir schwankt und schwindelt der Sinn!
Wen ruf' ich zum Heil,
dass er mir helfe?—
Mutter! Mutter!
Gedenke mein'!—

(Er sinkt mit der Stirn an Brünnhilde's Busen Langes Schweigen—Dann fährt er seufzend auf.)
Wie weck' ich die Maid,
dass sie die Augen mir öff'ne?—
Das Auge mir öff'nen?
Blende mich auch noch der Blick
Wagt' es mein Trotz?
ertrüg' ich das Licht?—
Mir schwebt und schwankt
und schwirrt es umher;
sehrendes Sengen
zehrt meine Sinne:
am zagenden Herzen
zittert die Hand!—
Wie ist mir Feigem?—
Ist es das Fürchten?—

(He comes nearer.)
Shining weapons!—
Shall lift them off?
(He raises the shield and discovers Brünnhilde's face, which the helmet still in a great measure conceals.)
Ha! a warrior, sure!
I scan with wonder his form!—
His haughty head
is pressed by the helmet;
lighter would he
lie were it loosened.
(He carefully unfastens the helmet and removes it from the sleeper; long, curling hair breaks forth.—Siegfried starts.)
Ah!—how fair!
(He remains absorbed in contemplation.)
Fleecy as cloudlets
fringing the clearness
of azure ether seas:
laughing, the sun's
enlightening face
shines through the cluster of clouds.
(He listens for the sleeper's breath.)
But heavily breathing
heaves his breast:
better to open his corselet
(He tries very cautiously, but in vain.)
Come, my sword,
cut through the iron!
(With tender care he cuts through the rings of mail on each side, and lifts off the corselet and greaves, so that Brünnhilde then lies before him in a soft, female clothing. Surprised and astonished, he starts back.)
This is no man!
Burning enchantment
charges my heart;
fiery awe
falls on my eyesight;
my senses stagger and sway.
O whom shall I hail
that he may help me?
Mother! Mother!
look down on me!—
(He sinks with his head on Brünnhilde's bosom.—Long silence.—Then he starts up suddenly.)

O what shall I do
that she may open her eyelids?—
Her eyes to me open!
Blind then were mine with their blaze.
How could I dare
endure such a light?
All sways and swims
and staggers around;
scorching desires
entangle my senses,
and trembles my heart
at touch of my hand!
What is this feeling?
Can it be fearing?
O mother! mother!
how mighty your son!
A woman folded in sleep

O Mutter! Mutter!
dein muthiges Kind!
Im Schlafe liegt eine Frau:—
die hat ihn das Fürchten gelehrt!—
Wie end' ich die Furcht?
wie fass' ich Muth?—
Dass ich selbst erwache,
muss die Maid ich erwecken!—
Süss erbebt mir
ihr blühender Mund:
wie mild erzitternd
mich Zagen er reizt!—
Ach, dieses Athem's
wonnig warmes Gedüft!—
Erwache erwache!
heiliges Weib!—
Sie hört mich nicht.—
So saug' ich mir Leben
aus süssesten Lippen—
sollt' ich auch sterbend vergeh'n!
(*Er küsst sie lange und inbrünstig.—Erschreckt fährt er dann in die Höhe:—Brünnhilde hat die Augen aufgeschlagen.—Staunend blickt er sie an. Beide verweilen eine Zeit lang in ihren gegenseitiger. Anblick versunken.*)

BRÜNNHILDE: (*langsam und feierlich sich zum Sitze aufrichtend*). Heil dir, Sonne!
Heil dir, Licht!
Heil dir, leuchtender Tag!
Lang war mein Schlaf;
ich bin erwacht:
wer ist der Held,
der mich erweckt'?

SIEGFRIED: (*von ihrem Blicke und ihrer Stimme feierlich ergriffen*). Durch das Feuer drang ich,
das den Fels umbrann;
ich erbrach dir den festen Helm:
Siegfried heiss' ich,
der dich erweckt'.

BRÜNNHILDE: (*hoch aufgerichtet sitzend*). Heil euch, Götter!
Heil dir, Welt!
Heil dir, prangende Erde!
Zu End' ist nun mein Schlaf:
erwacht seh' ich:
Siegfried ist es
der mich erweckt!

SIEGFRIED: (*in erhabenster Entzückung*). O Heil der Mutter
die mich gebar;
Heil der Erde,
die mich genährt:
dass ich das Auge erschaut,
das jetzt mir Seligem strahlt!

BRÜNNHILDE: (*mit grösster Bewegtheit*). O Heil der Mutter,
die dich gebar;
Heil der Erde,
die dich genährt:
nur dein Blick durfte mich schau'n
erwachen durft' ich nur dir!—
O Siegfried! Siegfried!
seliger Held!
Du Wecker des Lebens,
siegendes Licht!
O wüsstest du, Lust der Welt,
wie ich dich je geliebt!
Du war'st mein Sinnen
mein Sorgen du!

at last has enslaved him with fear!
How can I be calm—
recall my mind?
Before I quell this weakness
must the maid be awakened?
Sweetly beckons
her blossoming mouth:
what mild alarms in me
lightly it stirs!—
Ah! and the ardent
winning warmth of her breath!
Awaken! awaken!
maiden bewitched!—
She hears me not.—
Then life I will drain me
from lips the most dainty,
did they even doom me to death!
(*He imprints a long and ardent kiss upon her lips.—He starts back in surprise; Brünnhilde has opened her eyes. He gazes on her in astonishment. Both remain for some time absorbed in mutual contemplation.*)

BRÜNNHILDE: (*slowly and solemnly rising to a sitting position*). Hail, sunshine!
Hail, light!
Hail loveliest day!
long was my rest;
I rise from sleep.
say, who is he
that wakes my sense?

SIEGFRIED: (*awestruck by her appearance and voice*). I thrust through the fire
that burns round the mountain,
and I broke your defending helmet.
I'm Siegfried.
by whom you are waked.

BRÜNNHILDE: (*sitting erect*).
Hail, gods all!
Hail, world!
Hail, glories of nature!
Unknit is now my sleep;
I stand awake;
Siegfried, it is
who unwinds the spell!

SIEGFRIED: (*in exalted rapture*).
O hail to her
who gave me to life!
Hail to earth,
my fostering nurse!
that I should ever have seen
the sight that smiles on me here!

BRÜNNHILDE: (*deeply stirred*).
O hail to her
who gave you to life!
Hail to earth,
you fostering nurse!
But one glance was to behold me:
for you I was to awake.
O Siegfried! Siegfried!
sanctified hero!
wakener of life,
sovereign light!
O know, lord of worlds,
since what time you have had my love!
You were my object,

Dich Zarten nährt' ich
noch eh' du gezeugt;
noch eh' du geboren
barg dich mein Schild:
so lang' lieb' ich dich, Siegfried!

SIEGFRIED: (*leise und schüchtern*). So starb nicht meine Mutter?
schlief die Minnige nur?

BRÜNNHILDE: (*lächelnd*). Du wonniges Kind,
deine Mutter kehrt dir nicht wieder
Du selbst bin ich,
wenn du mich Selige lieb'st.
Was du nicht weisst,
weiss ich für dich;
doch wissend bin ich
nur—weil ich dich liebe.—
O Siegfried! Siegfried!
siegendes Licht!
dich liebt' ich immer;
denn mir allein
erdünkte Wotan's Gedanke.
Der Gedanke, den nie
ich nennen durfte;
den ich nicht dachte,
sondern nur fühlte;
für den ich focht,
kämpfte und stritt;
für den ich trotzte
dem, der ihn dachte;
für den ich büsste,
Strafe mich band,
weil ich nicht ihn dachte
und nur empfand!
Denn der Gedanke—
dürftest du's lösen!—
mir war er nur Liebe zu dir!

SIEGFRIED: Wie Wunder tönt
was wonnig du sing'st:
doch dunkel dünkt mich der Sinn.
Deines Auges Leuchten
seh' ich licht;
deines Athem's Wehen
fühl' ich warm;
deiner Stimme Singen
hör' ich süss;
doch was du singend mir sag'st
staunend versteh' ich's nicht.
Nicht kann ich das Ferne
sinnig erfassen,
da all' meine Sinne
dich nur sehen und fühlen
Mit banger Furcht
fesselst du mich;
du Einz'ge hast
ihre Angst mich gelehrt.
Den du gebunden
in mächt'gen Banden,
birg' meinen Muth mir nicht mehr!

BRÜNNHILDE: (*wehrt ihn sanft ab, und wendet ihren Blick nach dem Tann*). —Dort seh' ich Grane,
mein selig Ross:
wie weidet er munter,
der mit mir schlief!
Mit mir hat ihn Siegfried erweckt.

You were my aim!
I fostered you
before you were formed;
before you were born
I brought you my shield:
so long I've loved you Siegfried.

SIEGFRIED: (*gently and bashfully*). My mother did not die then?
she merely drooped in sleep?

BRÜNNHILDE: (*smiling*). Innocent child,
you will never be charmed by her image.
I am you,
if your pure spirit can love.
What you want
well can I teach:
but wisdom only
grew—because I loved you,
O Siegfried! Siegfried!
sovereign light!
I loved you always,
for I alone
distinguished Wotan's intention.
The intention that I
never named nor told of,
that I never tested—
I only felt it:—
for which I fought,
struggled and strove,
for which I flouted
him who framed it,
for which I suffered
in penance of sleep,
having never thought it,
but known it still!
Truly, that intention—
it is for your solving—
was but that my love should be yours!

SIEGFRIED: With winning tones
what wonders you sing of:
but my senses seem to grow dark.
By your eyes' fair light
I stand illuminated,
by your ardent breath
my breast is warmed,
by your singing sweet
my ears are sooth;
but what you say in song
strangely strikes my mind.
Now nothing can I fathom
subtle and far off,
for every sense
is centered and fastened on you.
With timid fear
you fill me:
you only have awakened
in me awesomeness.
You who bound me
with manacles breakless,
bring back my manhood once more!

BRÜNNHILDE: (*gently repulses him and turns her eyes towards the wood*). There feeds Grani,
my faithful steed:
how briskly he wanders
who with me slept!
He too was by Siegfried awakened.

SIEGFRIED: Auf wonnigem Munde
weidet mein Auge:
in brünstigem Durst
doch brennen die Lippen,
dass der Augen Weide sie labe!

BRÜNNHILDE: (*ihn mit der Hand
bedeutend*). Dort seh' ich den
Schild,
der Helden schirmte;
dort seh' ich den Helm,
der das Haupt mir barg:
er schirmt, er birgt mich nicht
mehr!

SIEGFRIED: Eine selige Maid
versehrte mein Herz;
Wunden dem Haupte
schlug mir ein Weib:—
ich kam ohne Schild und Helm!

BRÜNNHILDE: (*mit gesteigerter
Wehmuth*). Ich sehe der Brünne
prangenden Stahl:
ein scharfes Schwert
schnitt sie entzwei;
von dem maidlichen Leibe
löst' en die Wehr:—
ich bin ohne Schutz und Schirm,
ohne Trutz ein trauriges Weib!

SIEGFRIED: Durch brennendes
Feuer
fuhr ich zu dir;
nicht Brünne noch Panzer
barg meinen Leib:
mir in die Brust
brach nun die Lohe,
es braus't mein Blut
in blühender Brunst;
ein zehrendes Feuer
ist mir entzündet:
die Gluth, die Brünnhild's
Felsen umbrann,
die brennt mir nun in der Brust!—
Du Weib, jetzt lösche den Brand!
schweige die schäumende Gluth!
(*Er umfasst sie heftig; sie springt
auf, wehrt ihm mit der höchsten
Kraft der Angst, und entflieht
nach der andern Seite.*)

BRÜNNHILDE: Kein Gott nahte
mir je:
der Jungfrau neigten
scheu sich die Helden:
heilig schied sie aus Walhall!—
Wehe! Wehe!
Wehe der Schmach,
der schmählichen Noth!
Verwundet hat mich,
der mcih erweckt!
Er erbrach mir Brünne und Helm:
Brünnhilde bin ich nicht mehr!

SIEGFRIED: Noch bist du mir
die träumende Maid:
Brünnhilde's Schlaf
brach ich noch nicht.
Erwache! sei mir ein Weib!

BRÜNNHILDE: Mir schwirren die
Sinne!
Mein Wissen schweigt:
soll mir die Weisheit schwinden?

SIEGFRIED: Sang'st du mir nicht,
dein Wissen sei
das Leuchten der Liebe zu mir?

SIEGFRIED: On glorious lips
my glances are feasting;
with feverish thirst
I feel my own burning,
till the eyes' refreshment they taste
of.

BRÜNNHILDE: (*pointing with
her hand*). I see there the shield
that sheltered heroes;
I see there the helmet
that did protect my head;
they'll shield—they'll ward me no
more!

SIEGFRIED: As a woman divine
you wound my heart;
mortal the hurt
so shaped by a maid:—
I came without shield or helmet.

BRÜNNHILDE: (*with growing
melancholy*). I see there the coat
of mail's
glittering steel;
a sturdy sword
split it apart
and the maiden's protection
tore from her form:
without either shelter or shield
but a weak woman I feel!

SIEGFRIED: Through billows of
fire
I fared to your side;
nor byrnie nor shield defends
my body,
Now burst the flames
unchecked in my breast;
now bounds my blood
in blissful blaze;
a rapturous fire
is raging within me:
the flames that round
Brünnhilde once roared
now rend me with fearful wrath.
O maid, extinguish the rays!
still this disturbance in me!
(*He seizes her impetuously; she
springs up, repulses him with the
utmost strength of terror and flies
to the opposite side.*)

BRÜNNHILDE: No god has
touched me!
as a maiden ever
heroes revered me:
virgin I came from Valhalla!—
Woe's me! woe's me!
Woe for the shame,
the shunless disgrace!
My wakening hero
deals me this wound!
He has burst my byrnie and helmet:
I am Brünnhilde I no more!

SIEGFRIED: Still you're to me
the slumbering maid:
Brünnhilde's sleep
binds her yet.
Awaken! be my wife!

BRÜNNHILDE: My senses are swaying,
my wit forsakes me:
shall all my wisdom escape me?

SIEGFRIED: Didn't you say
that your wisdom showed
the light of love on me?

BRÜNNHILDE: Trauriges Dunkel
trübt mir den Blick;
mein Auge dämmert,
das Licht verlischt:
Nacht wird's um mich:
aus Nebel und Grau'n
windt sich wüthend
ein Angstgewirr.
Schrecken schreitet
und bäumt sich empor!
(*Sie birgt heftig die Augen mit den
Händen.*)

SIEGFRIED: (*lös't ihr sanft die
Hände vom Blicke*). Nacht um-
bangt
gebundene Augen;
mit den Fesseln schwindet
das finst're Grau'n:
tauch' aus dem Dunkel und sieh—
sonnenhell leuchtet der Tag!

BRÜNNHILDE: (*in höchster Er-
griffenheit*). Sonnenhell
leuchtet der Tag meiner Noth!—
O Siegfried! Siegfried!
Sieh' meine Angst!
Ewig war ich,
ewig bin ich,
ewig in süss
sehnender Wonne—
doch ewig zu deinem Heil!
O Siegfried! Herrlicher!
Hort der Welt!
Leben der Erde!
Lachender Held!
Lass', ach lass'!
lasse von mir!
Nahe mir nicht
mit der wüthenden Nähe!
Zwinge mich nicht
mit dem brechenden Zwang!
Zertrümm're die Traute dir
nicht!—
Sah'st du dein Bild
im klaren Bach?
Hat es dich Frohen erfreut?
Rührtest zur Woge
das Wasser du auf;
zerflösse die klare
Fläche des Bach's:
dein Bild säh'st du dir nicht mehr,
nur der Welle schwankend Gewog'
So berühre mich nicht,
trübe mich nicht:
ewig licht
lachst du aus mir
dann selig selbst dir entgegen,
froh und heiter ein Held!—
O Siegfried! Siegfried!
leuchtender Spross!
Liebe—dich,
und lasse von mir:
vernichte dein Eigen nicht!

SIEGFRIED: Dich—lieb' ich:
o liebtest mich du!
Nicht hab' ich mehr mich
o hätte ich dich!—
Ein herrlich Gewässer
wogt vor mir;
mit allen Sinnen
seh' ich nur sie,
die wonnig wogende Welle:
brach sie mein Bild,
so brenn' ich nun selbst,

BRÜNNHILDE: Dismal blackness
dazes my sight;
my eyes are blinded,
their light is lost:
night veils me.
In vaporous mists
is foully forced up
a grisly fear:
horrors haunt
and encompass me.
(*She clasps her hand over her eyes
hastily.*)

SIEGFRIED: (*gently drawing her
hands from her face*). Darkness
frightens
closed eyelids;
set them free, and fled
is the fearsome spell.
Draw from the shadow and see:—
with bright sunshine smiles the
day.

BRÜNNHILDE: (*in extreme agita-
tion*). Bright sunshine
smiles this day on my shame!—
O Siegfried! Siegfried!
See how I dread!—
Deathless was I
deathless am I,
deathless to sweet
sway of affection—
but deathless for your safety!
O Siegfried! happiest
hope of the world!
Life of the universe!
Lordliest hero!
Listen! ah listen!
Leave me in peace!
Press not upon me
your ardent approaches!
Master me not
with your conquering might!
Your servant, O sully her not!—
You saw ever your face
in crystal floods?
Did it not gladden your glance?
When into wavelets
the water was roused,
the brook's glassy surface
broken and flawed
you saw your face no more:
nothing but ripples swirling
around.
So disturb me no more,
trouble me not:
ever then
you will shine
in me an image reflected,
fair and lovely, my lord!—
O Siegfried! Siegfried!
light of my soul!
Love—yourself,
and leave me in peace:
destroy not your faithful slave!

SIEGFRIED: I love—you:
Do you love me?
I have no more self:
O had I only you—
The grandest of floods
rolls before me,
and all my senses
seize on the sight,
these billows beauteous and buoyant.
Likeness—be lost!

sengende Gluth
in der Fluth zu kühlen;
ich selbst, wie ich bin,
spring' in den Bach:—
o dass seine Wogen
mich selig verschlängen,
mein Sehnen schwänd' in der Fluth!—
Erwache, Brünnhilde!
Wache, du Maid!
Lebe und lache,
süsseste Lust!
Sei mein! sei mein! sei mein!

BRÜNNHILDE: O Siegfried!
dein—
war ich von je!

SIEGFRIED: War'st du's von je,
so sei es jetzt!

BRÜNNHILDE: Dein werde ich
ewig sein!

SIEGFRIED: Was du sein wirst,
sei es mir heut'!
Fasst dich mein Arm,
umschling' ich dich fest;
schlägt meine Brust
brünstig die deine;
zünden die Blicke,
zehren die Athem sich;
Aug' in Auge,
Mund an Mund:
dann bist du mir,
was bang du mir war'st und wirst!
Dann brach sich die brennende Sorge,
ob jetzt Brünnhilde mein?
(Er hat sie umfasst.)

BRÜNNHILDE: Ob jetzt ich
dein?—
Göttliche Ruhe
ras't mir in Wogen;
keuschestes Licht
lodert in Gluthen;
himmlisches Wissen
stürmt mir dahin,
Jauchzen der Liebe
jagt es davon!
Ob jetzt ich dein!—
O Siegfried! Siegfried!
siehst du mich nicht?
Wie mein Blick dich verzehrt,
erblindest du nicht?
Wie mein Arm dich presst!
entbrennst du nicht?
Wie in Strömen mein Blut
entgegen dir stürmt,
das wilde Feuer
fühlst du es nicht?
Fürchtest du, Siegfried,
fürchtest du nicht
das wild wüthende Weib?

SIEGFRIED: Ha'—
Wie des Blutes Ströme sich zünden
wie der Blicke Strahlen sich zehren
wie die Arme brünstig sich pressen,
kehrt mir zurück
mein kühner Muth,
und das Fürchten, ach!

I long now myself
straightaway my fire
in the flood to slacken;
at once I would spring
into the stream:
O, that its waters
in bliss might embrace me,
and abate my blaze with its wave!—
Awake, Brünnhilde!
waken, maid!
Laugh that you live,
sweetest delight!
Be mine! be mine! be mine!

BRÜNNHILDE: O Siegfried! Yours
ever I've been!

SIEGFRIED: Ever you've been?
Then so abide.

BRÜNNHILDE: Yours ever will I
be.

SIEGFRIED: What you then were,
be to me now.
Fast in my arms,
wrapped in their fold,
resting your breast
beating against mine,
while glances and breath
are glowing with eagerness,
eye to eye,
and lip to lip—
as you said, you were and will be.
How briskly were banished your fears
if indeed Brünnhilde were mine!
(He has clasped her with his arms.)

BRÜNNHILDE: If I am yours!
Godlike repose
is plunged into tempest,
once tranquil radiance
rises to frenzy,
heavenly teachings
from me are hid,
wildness of passion
whirls it away!
If I am yours!
O Siegfried! Siegfried! Do you not see me?
When my eyes devour yours,
then are you not blind?
by my arm embraced you,
then burn you not?
and when seething my blood
against you does surge,
its fiery fury
you feel not?
You fear, Siegfried—you fear not
the mad, mutinous maid?

SIEGFRIED: Ha! How the glowing bloodstreams are bounding!
How the glances brightly are burning!
How our arms are gladly entwining!
Comes now back
my courage bold,

das nie ich gelernt—
das Fürchten, das du
kaum mich gelehrt:
das Fürchten—mich dünkt—
ich Dummer, vergass es schon wieder.
(Er lässt bei den letzten Worten Brünnhilde unwillkürlich los.)

BRÜNNHILDE: (im höchsten Liebesfuer wild auflachend). O kindischer Held!
O herrlicher Knabe!
du hehrster Thaten
thöriger Hort!
Lachend muss ich dich lieben,
lachend will ich erblinden;
lachend lass' uns verderben—
lachend zu Grunde geh'n!
Fahr' hin, Walhall's
leuchtende Welt!
Zerfall' in Staub
deine stolze Burg!
Leb' wohl, prangende
Götter-Pracht!
Ende in Wonne,
du ewig Geschlecht!
Zerreisst, ihr Nornen,
das Runenseil!
Götter-Dämm'rung,
dunkle herauf!
Nacht der Vernichtung,
neble herein!—
Mir strahlt zur Stunde
Siegfried's Stern:
er ist mir ewig,
er ist mir immer,
Erb' und Eigen,
ein' und all':
leuchtende Liebe,
lachender Tod!

SIEGFRIED: (mit Brünnhilde zugleich). Lachend erwachst
du Wonnige mir:
Brünnhilde lebt!
Brünnhilde lacht!—
Heil der Sonne,
die uns bescheint!
Heil dem Tage
der uns umleuchtet!
Heil dem Licht,
das der Nacht enttaucht!
Heil der Welt,
der Brünnhild' erwacht!
Sie wacht! sie lebt!
sie lacht mir entgegen!
Prangend strahlt
mir Brünnhilde's Stern!
Sie ist mir ewig,
sie ist mir immer,
Erb' und Eigen,
ein' und all';
leuchtende Liebe,
lachender Tod!
(Brünnhilde stürzt sich in Siegfried's Armes.)

*Der Vorhang Fällt.*

and this fearing, ah!
that to me was strange—
this fear, that scarce
even you could bestow—
this fearing—I feel—
that fool-like, again it is forgot.
(With the last words he has unconsciously released Brünnhilde.)

BRÜNNHILDE: (laughing in wild transport of passion). O high-minded boy!
O blossoming hero!
Babe of prowess
past all that breathe!
Gladly love do I glow with,
gladly yield to you blindly,
gladly glide to destruction,
gladly go down to death!
Far from here, Valhall'
lofty and vast,
let fall your structure
of stately towers;
farewell, grandeur
and pride of gods!
End in rapture
Aesir, your reign!
Go rend, Nornen,
your rope of runes!
Round us darken,
Dusk of the gods!
Night of annulment
now on us gain!
here still is streaming
Siegfried, my star.
He is forever,
is for always
my own, my only and my all.—
Love that illuminates
laughing at death.

SIEGFRIED: (with Brünnhilde).
Gladly, bewitcher,
wake to me.
Brünnhilde lives,
Brünnhilde laughs!—
Hail the heavens,
smiling in lightness!
Hail the sun
which shines down on us!
Hail the light
that has burst from night!
Hail the world
where Brünnhilde lives.!
She wakes, she lives!
she laughs as she greets me:
proudly streams down
Brünnhilde, my star.
She is forever,
is for always
my own, my only
and my all.
Love that illuminates
laughing at death.
(Brünnhilde throws herself into Siegfried's arms.)

*The Curtain falls.*

# Götterdämmerung (1876)

## The Dusk of the Gods

MUSIC & LIBRETTO BY RICHARD WAGNER

This three-act opera with prologue premiered at the Festspielhaus in Bayreuth on August 17, 1876. The story begins on the Valkyries' rock during the night. Flames light up the night as the three Norns weave the fate of men with that of the gods. The thread breaks and the Norns return to Erda, the goddess of Earth. Siegfried and Brünnhilde emerge from a cave at sunrise after their first night of love. She gives him Grane, her horse, and he gives her the ring. In the Hall of the Gibichungs, near the banks of the Rhine, Gunther and Gutrune, children of Gibich and Grimhild, rule with the advice of Hagen, their half-brother, child of Grimhild and Alberich. Hagen continues his father's quest for the ring. He causes Gunther to pine for Brünnhilde, without telling him that she is already married to Siegfried. He tells Gutrune to prepare a potion that will erase Siegfried's memory of any previous love the moment he sets eyes on the next woman who comes along—Gutrune. To please Gunther, Hagen will have Brünnhilde brought from the rock where she sleeps. Gutrune gives Siegfried the drink; he begs Gunther to marry him. They may marry if Siegfried wins Brünnhilde for Gunther. On the mountain, Waltraute pleads with Brünnhilde, her sister, begging her to return the ring to the Rhine maidens, thus saving Valhalla and the gods. Brünnhilde refuses, as it is a symbol of Siegfried's love. She hears his horn, but when he arrives he is unrecognizable—the Tarnhelm has transformed him so that he appears as Gunther. She tries to resist him; Siegfried pulls the ring off her finger and sends her into the cave. Hagen sees Alberich in a vision. He commands him to get the ring for the Nibelung and to be faithful to the memory of his father. Siegfried returns, Brünnhilde and Gunther behind him. The Gibich soldiers and serfs greet the bride and groom. Brünnhilde, stoic until she hears Siegfried's name, is shocked that he does not recognize her. She points to the ring on his finger, declaring that it was taken from her by the man who brought her through the fire. Gunther thinks that Siegfried has betrayed him, but Siegfried swears the ring was found amongst the dragon's booty. Brünnhilde swears vengeance. She, Gunther and Hagen plot to kill Siegfried during a boar hunt. The Rhine maidens beg Siegfried to return the ring, but even their warning, foretelling his death, can't change his mind. Gunther and Hagen ask him to tell them about himself while they rest. Siegfried relates as much as he can remember until his mind goes blank. Hagen gives him an antidote to the potion Gutrune had given him. Siegfried speaks of his discovery of Brünnhilde and their love. Two ravens fly off to tell the gods to prepare for catastrophe. Siegfried turns to look at the birds, and Hagen stabs him in the back—the only part of him Brünnhilde has not protected with her magic. Siegfried's last words are to Brünnhilde. Gunther condemns Hagen for Siegfried's murder, and Hagen kills him. Hagen approaches Siegfried's body and reaches for the ring; the dead man's hand rises up. Brünnhilde learns the truth about Siegfried from the Rhine maidens and orders a funeral pyre for her beloved. She reclaims the ring, sets fire to the forest and rides her horse into it. As the flames leap up around her, the Rhine overflows and the Rhine maidens take the ring. Hagen, trying to grab it, drowns in the swirling waters. The Hall of the Gibichungs comes crashing down. At Valhalla, the gods await their doom. Alberich's curse is at last fulfilled, and Brünnhilde's sacrifice for love purifies the earth.

---

### ■ VORSPIEL

#### Auf dem Walkürenfelsen.

*Die Scene ist dieselbe wie am Schlusse des zweites Tages.—Nacht. Aus der Tiefe des Hintergrundes leuchtet Feuerschein auf.*

*Die drei Nornen, hohe Frauengestalten in langen, dunklen und schleierartigen Faltengewändern. Die erate (älteste) lagert im Vordergrunde rechts unter der breitästigen Tanne; die zweite (jüngere ist an einer Steinbank vor dem Felsengemache hinger-*

### ■ PROLOGUE

#### On the Valkyries' Rock.

*(The same as at the end of "Siegfried." It is night and from below, at back, gleams the fire.)*

*(The three Norns, tall females in somber and flowing drapery, are discovered. The first (and oldest) crouches in the foreground R, under the spreading fir-tree; the second (younger) is stretched on a rock before the cave; the third (and youngest) sits in the middle at back on a rock below the peak. For a while gloomy silence*

*streckt; die dritte (jüngste) sitzt in der Mitte des Hintergrundes auf einem Felssteine des Höhensaumes.—Eine Zeit lang herrscht düsteres Schweigen.*

**DIE ERSTE NORN:** *(ohne sich zu bewegen).* Welch' Licht leuchtet dort?

**DIE ZWEITE:** Dämmert der Tag schon auf?

**DIE DRITTE:** Loge's Heer lodert feurig um den Fels. Noch ist's Nacht: was spinnen und singen wir nicht?

**DIE ZWEITE:** *(zu der ersten).* Wollen wir singen und spinnen, woran spann'st du das Seil?

*reigns.)*

**THE FIRST NORN:** *(without moving).* What light lurks there?

**THE SECOND:** Do you think the day is near?

**THE THIRD:** Loki's flame leaps round about the rock. Night is new: why should we not spin and sing now?

**THE SECOND:** *(to the first).* While we are spinning and singing on what do we stretch we the string?

# Prologue

**DIE ERSTE NORN:** (*erhebt sich, und knüpft während ihres Gesanges ein goldenes Seil mit dem einen Ende an einen Ast der Tanne*). So gut und schlimm es geh',
schling' ich das Seil, und singe.—
An der Welt-Esche
wob ich einst,
da gross und stark
dem Stamm entgrünte
weihlicher Aeste Wald;
im kühlen Schatten
rauscht' ein Quell,
Weisheit raunend
rann sein Gewell':
da sang ich heiligen Sinn.—
Ein kühner Gott
trat zum Trunk an den Quell;
seiner Augen eines
zahlt' er als ewigen Zoll:
von, der Welt-Esche
brach da Wotan einen Ast:
eines Speeres Schaft
entschnitt der Starke dem Stamm.—
In langer Zeiten Lauf
zehrte die Wunde den Wald
falb fielen die Blätter,
dürr darbte der Baum:
traurig versiegte
des Quelles Trank;
trüben Sinnes
ward mein Gesang.
Doch web' ich heut'
an der Welt-Esche nicht mehr,
muss mir die Tanne
taugen zu fesseln das Seil:
singe, Schwester,
—dir werf' ich's zu—
weisst du wie das ward?

**DIE ZWEITE NORN:** (*während sie das zugeworfene Seil um einen hervorspringenden vorspringenden Felstein am Eingange des Gemaches windet*). Treu berath'ner Verträge Runen
schnitt Wotan
in des Speeres Schaft:
den hielt er als Haft der Welt.
Ein kühner Held
zerhieb im Kampfe den Speer;
in Trümmern sprang
der Verträge heiliger Haft.—
Da niess Wotan
Walhall's Helden
der Welt-Esche
welkes Geäst
mit dem Stamm in Stücke zu fällen
die Esche sank;
ewig versiegte der Quell!—
Fess'le ich heut'
an dem scharfen Fels das Seil:
singe, Schwester,
—dir werf' ich's zu—
weisst du wie das wird?

**DIE DRITTE NORN:** (*das sell auffangend, und dessen Ende hinter sich werfend*). Es ragt die Burg,
von Riesen gebaut:
mit der Götter und Helden
heiliger Sippe
Sitzt dort der Wotan im Saal.
Gehau'ner Scheite
hohe Schicht

**THE FIRST NORN:** (*rises and fastens one end of a golden cord to a branch of the fir-tree during her song*). For weal to serve and woe,
setting the string I sing:—
At the world's ash-tree
once I wove,
when fast and strong,
the stem was overwhelmed
with wondrous
verdure.
In pleasant shade
a fountain purled;
wisdom floated
forth on its wave;
I sang there a mystic song.
A fearless god
sought to sip at the fount,
giving up one eye
to buy the ineffable boon.
From the world's ash-tree
Wotan wrested off an arm:
and with sturdy strokes
he shaped the shaft of a spear.
In tardy course of time
cankered the wound in the wood;
the leaves could not retain life;
the tree waned—withered.
Drooping, the stream
of the fountain dried;
dark with sorrow
waxed then my song.
I weave again
at the world's ash-tree no more,
so must the fir-tree
find me support for the string.
Sing, O Sister!—
Weave it now!—
Do you know why this was?

**THE SECOND NORN:** (*winding the cord which the other throws to her, round a projecting rock at the cave's mouth*). Truthful runes
to make treaties rigid
set Wotan
on the shaft of his spear;
this served him to sway the world.
One bold and strong
destroyed in battle that spear.
The binding witness
of bonds was shivered to shreds.
Then straight Wotan
warriors summoned,
the world's ash-tree's
withered arms
with its stem to splinter and sunder,
The ask destroyed,
For every the spring must go dry.
Now round the keen-edged
stone I knot the string;
Sing, O sister!
weave it now—
Do you know why this was?

**THE THIRD NORN:** (*catching the rope and throwing the end behind her*). A gemmed abode
was built by giants:
with the AEsir and heroes'
holy assembly Wotan sits in state.
And huge heaps of sticks
are formed,
ranged on high

ragt zu Hauf
rings um die Halle:
die Welt-Esche war dies einst!
Brennt das Holz
heilig brünstig und hell,
senkt die Gluth
sehrend die glänzenden Saal:
der ewigen Götter Ende
dämmert ewig da auf.—
Wisset ihr noch?
so windet von neuem das Seil;
von Norden wieder
werf' ich's dir nach:
spinne, Schwester, und singe!
(*Sie hat das Seil der zweiten, diese es wieder der ersten Norn zugeworfen.*)

**DIE ERSTE NORN:** (*lös't das Seil vom Zweige, und knüpft es während des folgenden Gesanges wieder an einen andern Ast*). Dämmert der Tag?
oder leuchtet die Lohe?
Getrübt trügt sich mein Blick;
nicht hell eracht' ich
das heilig Alte,
da Loge einst
entbrannte in lichter Gluth:—
weisst du was aus ihm ward?

**DIE ZWEITE NORN:** (*das zugeworfene Seil wieder um den Stein windend*). Durch des Speeres Zauber
zähmte ihn Wotan;
Räthe raunt' er dem Gott:
an des Schaftes Runen,
frei sich zu rathen,
nagte zehrend sein Zahn.
Da mit des Speeres
zwingender Spitze
bannte ihn Wotan,
Brünnhilde's Fels zu umbrennen:—
weisst du was aus ihm wird?

**DIE DRITTE NORN:** (*das zugeschwungene Seil wieder hinter sich werfend*). Des zerschlag'nen Speeres
stechende Splitter
taucht' einst Wotan
dem Brünstigen tief in die Brust:
zehrender Brand
zündet da auf;
den wirft der Gott
in die Welt-Esche
zu Hauf geschichtete Scheite.—
Wollt ihr wissen
wann das wird,
schwingt mir, Schwestern, das Seil!
(*Sie wirft das Seil der zweiten, diese es wieder der ersten zu.*)

**DIE ERSTE NORN:** (*das Seil von neuem anknüpfend*). Die Nacht weicht;
nichts mehr gewahr' ich;
des Seiles Fäden
find' ich nicht mehr;
verflochten ist das Geflecht.
Ein wüstes Gesicht
wirrt mir wüthend den Sinn:—
das Rheingold
raubte Alberich einst:—
weisst du, was aus ihm ward?

round all Valhalla:
the world's ash-tree were they once.
When the brand
brightly, wildly burns,
when the fire
wastes the fair-fashioned walls,
the deathless immortals draw
towards the dusk of their day.
Do you know this?
The thread then be knotted again,
Anew I throw it to you
from the north.
Spin, O sister, and sing!
(*She throws the cord to the second Norn, who throws it to the first.*)

**THE FIRST NORN:** (*unties the cord from the branch and fastens it to another branch during the following song*). Dawns the daylight,
or flickers the fire?
My sight sorrow has dimmed.
Scarce bides my memory
of bygone marvels,
when Loki moved
in burning and lambent flame: Do you know
what was his work?

**THE SECOND NORN:** (*begins taking the rope and winding it round the stone*). By the spear's firm yoke
he yielded to Wotan;
aid he offered the god:
but in struggle ever
to throw off his bonds
he gnashed and tore with his teeth,
till Wotan's spear's point
tightly constrained him
broadly to girdle
Brynhildr's rock with his brightness:
Do you know what was his work?

**THE THIRD NORN:** (*snatches the rope again and throwing it behind her*). Then the sturdy spear
that split into splinters
Wotan dips
in the burning one's wavering breast.
Quickly the brand
kindles thereat;
this Wotan throws
where the world's ash-tree
is heaped, a forest of faggots.
When this will be
would you think?
stretch then, sisters, the string!
(*She throws the rope back to the second who throws it to the first*).

**THE FIRST NORN:** (*again knotting the cord*). The night wanes;
I want nothing;
I cannot find
the fiber again;
it falls entangled and frayed.
The woefullest sight
whirls and weakens my sense:—
The Rhinegold
robbed by Alberic once:
Do you know what was its work?

**DIE ZWEITE NORN:** (*mit mühevoller Hast das Seil um den Stein windend*). Des steines Schärfe
schnitt in das Seil;
nicht fest spannt mehr
der Fäden Gespinnst:
verwirrt ist das Geweb'.
Aus Noth und Neid
nagt mir des Niblungen Ring:—
ein rächender Fluch
nagt meiner Fäden Geflecht—
weisst du was daraus wird?

**DIE DRITTE NORN:** (*das zugeworfene Seil hastig fassend*). Zu locker das Seil!
mir langt es nicht:
soll ich nach Norden
neigne das Ende,
straffer sei es gestreckt!
(*Sie zieht gewaltsam das Seil an: dieses reisst in der Mitte.*)

**DIE ZWEITE:** Es riss!

**DIE DRITTE:** Es riss!

**DIE ERSTE:** Es riss!
(*Erschreckt sind die drei Nornen aufgefahren und nach der Mitte der Bühne zusammengetreten; sie fassen die Stücke des zerrissenen Seiles und binden damit ihre Leiber an einander.*)

**DIE DREI NORNEN:** Zu End' ewiges Wissen!
Der Welt melden
Weise nichts mehr:—
hinab zur Mutter, hinab!
(*Sie verschwinden.*)
(*Der Tag, der zuletzt immer heller gedämmert, bricht vollends ganz an, und dämpft den Feuerschein in der Tiefe.*)

**SIEGFRIED, UND BRÜNNHILDE:**
(*treten aus dem Steingemache auf: Siegfried ist in vollen Waffen. Brünnhilde führt ihr Ross beim Zaume*).

**BRÜNNHILDE:** Zu neuen Thaten, theurer Helde, wie lieb' ich dich liess' ich dich nicht
Ein einzig Sorgen lässt mich säumen; dass dir zu wenig mein Werth gewann.
Was Göffter mich wiesen, gab ich dir: heiliger Runen reichen Hort, doch meiner Stärke magdlichen Stamm nahm mir der Held, dem ich nun mich neige.
Des Wissens bar, doch des Wunsches voll: an Liebe reich, doch ledig der Kraft, mögst du die Arme nicht verachten, die dir nur gönnen, nicht geben mehr kann.

**SIEGFRIED:** Mehr gabst du, Wunderfrau,
als ich zu wahren weiss:
nicht zürne, wenn dein Lehren mich unbelehret liess!
Ein Wissen doch wahr' ich wohl dass mir Brünnhilde lebt;
eine Lehre lernt' ich leicht:
Brünnhilde's zu gedenken!

**THE SECOND NORN:** (*with careful haste winding the rope round the stone*). The crag with keen edge
cuts the cord;
the threads cling not,
and thin is the clue;
it has been wrought awry.
From ire and ill
rears to me Alberic's ring:—
a ravaging curse
gnaws my cord to the core:—
Do you know what it will work?

**THE THIRD NORN:** (*hastily catching the rope thrown to her*). The rope is too slack,
I reach it not;
should it be thrown anew
to northward,
it must be stretched yet straighter!
(*she pulls the cord forcibly: it breaks in the middle.*)

**THE SECOND:** It breaks!

**THE THIRD:** It breaks!

**THE FIRST:** It breaks!
(*The three Norns start up in alarm and advance to the center of the stage: they take the broken pieces of the cord and tie their bodies one to another with them.*)

**THE THIRD NORNS:** Here ends all of our wisdom!
The world marks
our wise words no more.—
Away!
To mother!
Away!
(*They disappear.*)
(*The day, which has been slowly breaking, now dawns brightly and conceals the distant fire-glow in the valley.*)

**SIEGFRIED AND BRÜNNHILDE:**
(*enter from the cave. Siegfried is in full armor; Brünnhilde leads her horse by the bridle*).

**BRÜNNHILDE:** Did I not send you, sweetest hero, to fresh exploits, frail were my love.
But one misgiving fights against it; for fear not wholly your heart I hold.
I gave to you all that gods had taught; heavenly runes, the richest hoard, but my restoreless maidenhood's strength snatched you from me, who but seek to serve you.
My wisdom fails, but good will remains, so full of love, but failing in strength, you will despise perchance the poor one, who having given all, can grant you no more.

**SIEGFRIED:** You have shown more to me
than yet my sense can seize:
so chide not if I'm left unlearned despite your lessons
But one thing I know full well—
for me Brünnhilde lives;
It was a lesson light to learn
To worship Brünnhilde forever!

**BRÜNNHILDE:** Willst du mir Minne schenken,
gedenke deiner nur,
gedenke deiner Thaten!
Gedenke des wilden Feuers,
das furchtlos du durchschrittest,
da den Fels es rings umbrann—

**SIEGFRIED:** Brünnhilde zu gewinnen!

**BRÜNNHILDE:** Gedenk' der beschildeten Frau,
die in tiefem Schlaf du fandest,
der den festen Helm du erbrach'st—

**SIEGFRIED:** Brünnhilde zu erwecken!

**BRÜNNHILDE:** Gedenk' der Eide,
die uns einen;
gedenk' der Treue,
die wir tragen;
gedenk' der Liebe,
der wir leben:
Brünnhilde brennt dann ewig
heilig dir in der Brust!—

**SIEGFRIED:** Lass' ich, Liebste, dich hier
in der Lohe heiliger Hut,
zum Tausche deiner Runen
reich' ich dir diesen Ring,
Was der Thaten je ich schuf,
dess' Tugend schliesst er ein;
ich erschlug einen wilden Wurm,
der grimmig lang' ihn bewacht.
Nun wahre du seine Kraft
als Weihe-Gruss meiner Treu'!

**BRÜNNHILDE:** (*voll Entzücken den Ring sich ansteckend.*) Ihn geiz' ich als einziges Gut:
für den Ring nun nimm' auch mein Ross!
Ging sein Lauf mit mir
einst kühn durch die Lüfte—
mit mir
verlor es die mächt'ge Art;
über Wolken hin
auf blitzenden Wettern
nicht mehr
schwingt es sich muthig des Weg's.
Doch wohin du ihn führst
—sei es durch's Feuer—
grauenlos folgt dir Grane;
denn dir, o Helde,
soll er gehorchen!
Du hüt' ihn wohl;
er hört dein Wort:—
o bringe Grane
oft Brünnhilde's Gruss!

**SIEGFRIED:** Durch deine Tugend allein
soll so ich Thaten noch wirken?
Meine Kämpfe kiesest du,
meine Siege kehren zu dir?
Auf deines Rosses Rücken,
in deines Schildes Schirm,
nicht Siegfried acht' ich mich mehr,
ich bin nur Brünnhilde's Arm!

**BRÜNNHILDE:** O wäre Brünnhild' deine Seele!

**SIEGFRIED:** Durch sie entbrennt mir der Muth.

**BRÜNNHILDE:** If you would wake my fondness,
recall your course to mind;
recall your courage dauntless,
recall your raging furnace
that, fearless, you did pass through,
when it fanned the rocky brow.

**SIEGFRIED:** Brünnhilde to attain to!

**BRÜNNHILDE:** Recall, too the shield-covered maid
You did find in sleep of magic,
and whose mail and helm you broke.

**SIEGFRIED:** Brünnhilde to awaken!

**BRÜNNHILDE:** Recall the pledges we have plighted;
recall our troth,—
never was there truer:
recall the affection
which enfolds us;
Brünnhilde your bride then ever
will hold her place in your breast.

**SIEGFRIED:** Love, before leaving your form
in the defense of the fire,
for all your runes and teachings
take this ring in return.
All my valiant deeds of strength
their virtue sprang from this.
I destroyed an unwieldly worm,
who long had over it watched:
now well preserve the charm
as a wedding gift to my bride.

**BRÜNNHILDE:** (*rapturously donning the ring.*) Aye, gladly my all
here I guard,
and instead you shall own my steed:
he could lift me once
athwart the air lightly;
with me
he lost all his magic powers:
over thronging clouds,
through lightning and thunder,
no more
boldly his way he will thread.
But wherever you shall force,
were it through fire even,
Grani will follow gaily:
He'll serve my hero
trustily henceforth.
Then hold him well,
he'll heed your word:
O give Grani many
fond greetings from me!

**SIEGFRIED:** Then through your virtues alone
am I to vanquish my dangers?
You choose your champion's fights;
you turn the chance of the fray;
Your noble steed bestriding,
and with your sheltering shield
now Siegfried am I no more:
I'm but as Brünnhilde's arm!

**BRÜNNHILDE:** O were but Brünnhilde your spirit!

**SIEGFRIED:** She spurs my bravery alone.

BRÜNNHILDE: So wär'st du Siegfried und Brünnhild'?

SIEGFRIED: Wo ich bin, bergen
sich beide.

BRÜNNHILDE: So verödet mein
Felsensaal?

SIEGFRIED: Vereint fasst er uns
zwei.

BRÜNNHILDE: (*in grosser Ergriffenheit.*) O heilige Götter,
hehre Geschlechter!
weidet eur' Aug'
an dem weihvollen Paar!
Getrennt—wer will uns scheiden?
Geschieden—trennt es sich nie!

SIEGFRIED: Heil dir, Brünnhilde,
prangender Stern!
Heil, strahlende Liebe!

BRÜNNHILDE: Heil dir, Siegfried!
siegendes Licht!
Heil, strahlendes Leben!

BEIDE: Heil! Heil!
(*Siegfried leitet das Ross den Felsen hinab, Brünnhilde blickt ihm
vom Höhensaume lange entzückt
nach. Aus der Tiefe hört man Siegfried's Horn munter ertönen. Der
Vorhang fällt.*)
(*Das Orchester nimmt die Weise
des Hornes auf, und führt sie in einem kräftigen Satze durch. Darauf beginnt sogleich der erste
Aufzug.*)

# ■ ERSTER AUFZUG

## *Erste Scene*

*Die Halle Der Gibichungen Am
Rhein*
(*Sie ist dem Hintergrunde zu
ganz offen; diesen nimmt ein
freier Uferraum, in bis zum Flusse
hin ein; felsige Anhöben um-
gränzen den Raum.*)
*Gunther, Hagen, und Gutrune*
(*Gunther und Gutrune auf dem
Hochsitze, vor dem ein Tisch mit
Trinkgeräth steht; Hagen sitzt da-
vor.*)

GUNTHER: Nun hör', Hagen!
sage mir, Held:
sitz' ich herrlich am Rhein,
Gunther zu Gibich's Ruhm?

HAGEN: Dich ächt genannten
acht' ich zu neiden:
die beid' uns Brüder gebar,
Frau Grimhild' liess mich's begreif-
en.

GUNTHER: Dich neide ich:
nicht neide mich du!
Erbt' ich Erstlingsart,
Weisheit ward dir allein:
Halbbrüder-Zwist
bezwang sich nie besser;
deinem Rath nur red' ich Lob,
Frag' ich dich nach meinem Ruhm.

BRÜNNHILDE: So are you Siegfried and Brünnhilde?

SIEGFRIED: Our hearts both beat
in one bosom.

BRÜNNHILDE: Is my rock-home
deserted then?

SIEGFRIED: Both rest still in its
bounds.

BRÜNNHILDE: (*in exalted rapture.*) O heavenly powers,
holy protectors!
View with delight
our devotion of love!
Apart—who can divide us?
Divided—still we are one!

SIEGFRIED: Hail, O Brünnhilde,
brightest of stars!
Hail, stream of our love-light!

BRÜNNHILDE: Hail, O Siegfried,
sovereign light!
Hail, stream of our living!

BOTH: Hail! Hail!
(*Siegfried leads the horse down
the rocks; Brünnhilde gazes after
him from the height for a long
while. From the valley, the merry
sound of Siegfried's born is beard.
The curtain falls.*)
(*The orchestra takes up the melody of the born and works it up into
an animated movement. Whereupon follows the First Act.*)

# ■ ACT I

## *Scene I*

(*The Hall of the Giebichungs on
the Rhine.*)
(*The back is quite open, showing
a flat shore down to the river-
stream; rocky heights border the
stage.*)
*Gunther, Hagen and Gutrune*
(*Gunther and Gutrune are on the
throne, before which is a table
with drinking vessels. Hagen sitting before it.*)

GUNTHER: Now hark, Hagen!
answer me, here:
is my hold of the Rhine
glory for Gibich's race?

HAGEN: Your wondrous actions
waken my envy;
and much your mother and mine,
dame Grimhild,' lauded your
greatness.

GUNTHER: You envy not;
I am envious of you.
If I am heir to all,
wisdom was left to you.
Half-brother's strife
were never stifled better;
and your wisdom well I praise
when I ask you of my weal.

HAGEN: So schelt' ich den Rath,
da schlecht noch dein Ruhm:
denn hohe Güter weiss ich,
die der Gibichung noch nicht gewann.

GUNTHER: Verschwiegst du sie,
so schelt' auch ich.

HAGEN: In sommerlich reifer
Stärke
seh ich Gibich's Stamm,
dich, Gunther, unbeweibt,
dich, Gutrun', ohne Mann.

GUNTHER: Wen räth'st du nun zu
frei'n,
Dass uns'rem Ruhm es fromm'?

HAGEN: Ein Weib weiss ich,
das herrlichste der Welt:—
auf Felsen hoch ihr Sitz;
ein Feuer entbrennt ihren Saal:
nur wer durch das Feuer bricht,
darf Brünnhilde's Freier sein.

GUNTHER: Vermag das mein Muth
zu besteh'n?

HAGEN: Einem Stärk'ren noch ist's
nur bestimmt.

GUNTHER: Wer ist der streitlichste
Mann?

HAGEN: Siegfried, der Wälsungen
Spross:
der ist der stärkste Held.
Ein Zwillingspaar,
von Liebe bezwungen,
Siegmund und Sieglinde
zeugten den ächtesten Sohn:
der im Walde mächtig erwuchs,
den wünsch' ich Gutrun' zum
Mann

GUTRUNE: Welche That schuf er
so tapfer,
dass als herrlichster Held er genannt!

HAGEN: Vor Neidhöhle,
den Niblungenhort
bewachte ein riesiger Wurm:
Siegfried schloss ihm
den freislichen Schlund,
erschlug ihn mit siegendem
Schwert.
Solch' ungeheurer That
enttagte des Helden Ruhm.

GUNTHER: Vom Niblungenhort
vernahm ich.
er birgt den neidlichsten Schatz?

HAGEN: Wer wohl ihn zu nützen
wüsst',
dem neigte sich wahrlich die Welt.

GUNTHER: Und Siegfried hat ihn
erkämpft?

HAGEN: Knecht sind die Niblungen ihm.

GUNTHER: Und Brünnhild'
gewänne nur er?

HAGEN: Keinem And'ren wiche
die Brunst.

GUNTHER: (*unwillig sich vom
Sitze erhebend.*) Was weck'st du
Zweifel und Zwist!
Was ich nicht zwingen soll,
danach zu verlangen
mach'st du mir Lust?

HAGEN: To blame is my wit
that bad is your weal;
for rarer goods I know of
than a Gibichung yet ever won.

GUNTHER: Then tell them, or
I too shall blame.

HAGEN: In radiance of summer ri-
peness
rises Gibich's race;
but Gunther fails to wed
and Gutrune finds no mate.

GUNTHER: Whom would you like
me to wed, that we may win more
worth?

HAGEN: A wife waits for you,
the rarest in the world:
a far off rock's her home,
a fire-flame embraces her hall:
but he who can brave that fire
may fitly woo Brünnhilde.

GUNTHER: And may not my might
stretch so far?

HAGEN: It is reserved for a stronger
one.

GUNTHER: Who is this most stalwart of men?

HAGEN: Siegfried of Volsung descent:
his is the strongest hand.
A twinborn pair
in loving entwinement—
Siegmund and Sieglind'—
between them begat such a son.
He has mightily waxed in woods,
and well with Gutrune might mate.

GUTRUNE: Has he done marvellous deeds,
that he is called of a courage so
high?

HAGEN: At Hate-cavern
the hoard long accursed
was watched by a horrible worm.
Siegfried shut up
his maw for him straight
and slew him with sovereign
sword.
So this unheard-of feat
has founded the hero's fame.

GUNTHER: I know of the Nibelungs' hoard;
it holds most notable wealth.

HAGEN: The one who best knows
its worth
annexes the world to his will.

GUNTHER: And Siegfried gained it
in strife?

HAGEN: The Nibelungs are slaves
to him.

GUNTHER: And Brünnhilde were
won by none else?

HAGEN: To no other wanes the
blaze.

GUNTHER: (*rising from his seat
in displeasure.*) Why wake this discord and doubt?
Would you induce in me
desire for a treasure
I may not touch?

HAGEN: Brächte Siegfried
die Braut dir heim,
wär' dann Brünnhild' nicht dein?

GUNTHER: (bewegt in der Halle
auf und ab schreitend.) Was
zwänge den frohen Mann
dir mich die Braut zu frei'n?

HAGEN: Ihn zwänge bald deine
Bitte,
bänd' ihn Gutrun' zuvor.

GUTRUNE: Du Spötter, böser Hagen!
Wie sollt' ich Siegfried binden?
Ist er der herrlichste
Held der Welt,
der Erde holdeste Frauen
friedeten längst ihn schon.

HAGEN: Gedenk' des Trankes im
Schrein;
vertraue mir, der ihn gewann:
den Helden, dess' du verlangst,
bindet er liebend an dich.
Träte nun Siegfried ein,
genöss' er des würzigen Trank's,
dass vor dir ein Weib er ersah,
dass je ein Weib ihm genaht—
vergessen müsst er dess' ganz.—
Nun redet:—
wie dünkt euch Hagen's Rath?

GUNTHER: (der wieder an den
Tisch getreten, und auf ihn gelehnt aufmerksam zugehört
hat.) Gepriesen sei Grimhild,'
die uns den Bruder gab!

GUTRUNE: Möcht' ich Siegfried je
ersehn'!

GUNTHER: Wie fänden wir ihn
auf?

HAGEN:
Jagt er auf Thaten
wennig umher,
zum engen Tann
wird ihm die Welt:
wohl stürmt er in rastloser Jagd
auch zu Gibich's Strand an den
Rhein.

GUNTHER: Willkommen hiess' ich
ihn gern.
(Siegfried's Horn lässt sich von
Ferne vernehmen.—Sie laus-
chen.)
Vom Rhein her tönt das Horn.

HAGEN: (ist an das Ufer
gegangen, späht den Fluss hinab
und ruft zurück:) In einem Nachen Held und Ross!
der bläst so munter das Horn.—
Ein gemächlicher Schlag
wie von müssiger Hand
treibt jach den Kahn
wider den Strom;
so rüstiger Kraft
in des Ruder's Schwung
rühmt sich nur der,
der den Wurm erschlug:—
Siegfried ist es, sicher kein And'rer!

GUTRUNE: Jagt er vorbei?

HAGEN: Brought this Siegfried
the bride to you,
would not then Brünnhilde be
yours?

GUNTHER: (pacing up and down
the hall in agitation.) What power
could bind the man
to win the bride for me?

HAGEN: Your prayer could work
your wishes, wove first Gutrune a
spell.

GUTRUNE: You scoff, wicked Hagen!
What spells then should I weave
him?
And if so wondrous a warrior he,
the earth's most winsome of wom-
en
will he have won before this.

HAGEN: Recall the drink in yon
shrine,
and doubt not him who gained the
charm.
The hero for whom you burn
fondly it will bind to your heart.
Did now but Siegfried come
and taste of the wonderful draught,
that he'd seen a woman before
you—
or ever a woman had neared,
would wholly pass from his head.
Reply then,
how do you like Hagen's plan?

GUNTHER: (who has again approached the table and listened
attentively, leaning on it.) All
praise be to Grimhild'
who gave such a brother!

GUTRUNE: If I could see Siegfried!

GUNTHER: How shall we find him
first?

HAGEN: When he spurs
on courses of fame,
the world
can but become too strait,
be sure in his roamings he'll scour
to the Gibich's strand on the Rhine.

GUNTHER: Welcome I'll heartily
give.
(Siegfried's horn is heard in the
distance;—they listen.)
I mark on the Rhine a horn.

HAGEN: (goes to the bank, looks
down the river and calls back.)
Within a vessel horse and man!
He blows right gaily the horn.
With a laborless stroke
as if lazy his hand,
he drives the boat,
stemming the stream.
So active a hand
at the oar-blade's sweep
owns only he
who slew the dragon.
It is Siegfried; surely no other!

GUNTHER: Does he proceed?

HAGEN: (durch die hohlen Hände
nach dem Flusse zu rufend:) Hoiho! wohin,
du heit'rer Held?

SIEGFRIED'S: (Stimme, aus der
Ferne, vom Flusse her.) Zu Gibich's starkem Sohne.

HAGEN: Zu seiner Halle entbiet'
ich dich:
Hieher! hier lege an!
Heil, Siegfried! theurer Held!

## Zweite Scene

(Siegfried legt an.)
(Gunther ist zu Hagen an das
Ufer getreten. Gutrune erblickt
Siegfried vom Hochsitze aus, heftet eine Zeit lang in freudiger Ueberraschung den Blick auf ihn,
und als die Männer dann näher
zur Halle schreiten, entfernt sie
sich in sichtbarer Verwirrung,
nach links durch eine Thüre in ihr
Gemach.)

SIEGFRIED: (der seine Ross an
das Land geführt, und jetzt ruhig
an ihm lehnt.) Wer ist Gibich's
Sohn?

GUNTHER: Gunther, ich, den du
such'st.

SIEGFRIED: Dich hört' ich rühmen
weit am Rhein:
nun ficht mit mir,
oder sei mein Freund!

GUNTHER: Lass den Kampf,
sei willkommen!

SIEGFRIED: Wo berg' ich mein
Ross?

HAGEN: Ich biet' ihm Rast.

SIEGFRIED: Du rief'st mich Siegfried:
sah'st du mich schon?

HAGEN: Ich kannte dich nur
an deiner Kraft.

SIEGFRIED: Wohl hüte mir Grane!
Du hieltest nie
von edlerer Zucht
am Zaume ein Ross.
(Hagen führt das Ross rechts hinter die Halle ab, und kehrt bald darauf wieder zurück. Gunther
schreitet mit Siegfried in die Halle
vor.)

GUNTHER: Begrüsse froh, o Held,
die Halle meines Vaters;
wohin du schreitest,
was du ersieh'st,
das achte nun dein Eigen:
dein ist mein Erbe,
Land und Leut':
hilf, mein Leib, meinem Eide!
Mich selbst geb' ich zum Mann.

SIEGFRIED: Nicht Land noch Leute
biete ich,
noch Vater's Haus und Hof:
einzig erbt' ich
den eig'nen Leib;

HAGEN: (putting his hands to his
mouth and shouting.) Hoiho!
Where are you going, hero?

SIEGFRIED'S: (voice in the distance on the river.) To Gibich's
stalwart scion.

HAGEN: Behold his hall here!
I bid you to it.
Here! here lay me to!
Hail, Siegfried, bravest heart!

## Scene II

(Siegfried lays to).
(Gunther has joined Hagen on the
bank. Gutrune looks at Siegfried
from the throne, fixing her gaze
for some time on him in joyous
surprise, and as the men come
down into the hall she withdraws,
in visible confusion, through a
door leading to her chamber L.)

SIEGFRIED: (who has landed his
horse and now stands quietly
leaning on him). Which is Gibich's son?

GUNTHER: Gunther—I—whom
you seek.

SIEGFRIED: Your fame has
reached
beyond the Rhine:
now fight with me,
or else be my friend!

GUNTHER: Nothing of war; you are
welcome!

SIEGFRIED: Where stables my
horse?

HAGEN: I'll see to him.

SIEGFRIED: You hail me "Siegfried;"
sure we are strange?

HAGEN: Your strength unapproached
declared you straight.

SIEGFRIED: Tend heedfully Grani!
you never held
in bridle a horse
of higher degree.
(Hagen leads the horse away, R,
behind the hall and returns immediately. Gunther advances into
the hall with Siegfried.)

GUNTHER: Now, here, freely hail
the homestead of your fathers.
The hall you stand in,
whatever you see,
I bid you hold your booty.
Yours is my birthright,
soil and serfs:
hear me swear by my body!
Gunther is given to you.

SIEGFRIED: Nor soil nor serfs I offer you,
nor father's house and hall:
all I'm heir to,
my able limbs,

lebend zehr' ich den auf.
Nur ein Schwert hab' ich,
selbst geschmiedet—
hilf, mein Schwert, meinem Eide!
das biet' ich mit mir zum Bund.

**HAGEN:** (*hinter ihnen stehend.*)
Doch des Niblungen-Hortes
nennt die Märe dich Herrn?

**SIEGFRIED:** Des Schatzes vergass
ich fast:
so schätz' ich sein müss'ges Gut!
In einer Höhle liess ich's liegen,
wo ein Wurm es einst bewacht.

**HAGEN:** Und nichts entnahm'st du
ihm?

**SIEGFRIED:** (*auf das stählerne Netzgewirk deutend, das er im Gürtel hängen hat.*) Diess Gewirk,
unkund seiner Kraft.

**HAGEN:** Den Tarnhelm kenn' ich,
der Niblungen künstliches Werk:
er taugt, bedeckt er dein Haupt,
dir zu tauschen jede Gestalt;
verlangt dich's an fernsten Ort,
er entführt flugs dich dahin.—
Sonst nichts entnahmst du dem
Hort?

**SIEGFRIED:** Einen Ring.

**HAGEN:** Den hütest du wohl?

**SIEGFRIED:** Den hütet ein hehres
Weib.

**HAGEN:** (*für sich.*) Brünnhilde! ..

**GUNTHER:** Nicht, Siegfried, sollst
du mir tauschen:
Tand gäb' ich für das Geschmeid,
nähmst all mein Gut du dafür!
Ohn' Entgelt dien' ich dir gern.
(*Hagen ist zu Gutrune's Thür gegangen, und öffnet sie jetzt. Gutrune tritt heraus, sie trägt ein gefülltes Trinkhorn, und naht damit Siegfried.*)

**GUTRUNE:** Willkommen, Gast,
in Gibich's Haus!
Seine Tochter reicht dir den Trank.

**SIEGFRIED:** (*neigt sich ihr freundlich, und ergreift das Horn; er hält es gedankenvoll vor sich hin und sagt leise:*) Vergass' ich
alles
was du mir gab'st
von einer Lehre
lass' ich doch nie:—
den ersten Trunk
zu treuer Minne,
Brünnhilde, bring' ich dir!
(*Er trinkt und reicht das Horn Gutrune zurück, welche, verschämt und verwirrt, ihre Augen vor ihm niederschlägt.*)

**SIEGFRIED:** (*mit schnell entbrannter Leidenschaft den Blick auf sie heftend.*) Die so mit de Blitz
den Blick du mir seng'st,
was senk'st du dein Auge vor mir?
(*Gutrune schlägt, erröthend, das Auge zu ihm auf.*)

life is holding in use.
I've a sword merely, self-constructed:
hear me swear by my weapon;
with it I'll strengthen our oath.

**HAGEN:** (*standing behind them*),
But we learn you are hailed
as lord of Nibelheim's hoard?

**SIEGFRIED:** That wealth I forgot,
well-nigh, so worthless I deem the
gold!
Within a cavern lone I left it,
where a worm did guard it once.

**HAGEN:** Have you had nothing of
it?

**SIEGFRIED:** (*pointing to the steel net-work, that hangs in his girdle.*) But this work, which I cannot
use.

**HAGEN:** The Tarnhelm is it,
the Nibelungs' artfullest work:
its trick when set on your head
is to turn you to any shape;
or you long for far-off lands,
in a flash, flight can you wing.
Have you moved no more of the
wealth?

**SIEGFRIED:** But a ring.

**HAGEN:** You wear it still?

**SIEGFRIED:** It is worn by a woman
sweet.

**HAGEN:** (*aside*) Brünnhilde!

**GUNTHER:** Nothing, Siegfried,
shall to me tender
Toys would for your treasures get,
taking my wealth in exchange:
without wage I'll serve you well.
(*Hagen has gone to Gutrune's door, and now opens it. Gutrune enters, and approaches Siegfried with a filled drinking horn.*)

**GUTRUNE:** Welcome, O guest,
to Gibich's house!
From its daughter take the drink.

**SIEGFRIED:** (*bows friendly, and takes the horn; he holds it thoughtfully before him, and says softly*): Though you gave gifts
should all be forgot.
I'll grasp alone
one lesson for aye:
this goblet's quaffed
with quenchless passion,
Brünnhilde, my bride, to you!
(*He drinks, and hands back the horn to Gutrune, who, abashed, cast down her eyes before his.*)

**SIEGFRIED:** (*gazing on her with swiftly kindling passion.*) You fair
one, whose beams have enflamed,
my breast
why fall thus your eyes before
mine?
(*Gutrune looks up at him, blushing.*)

**SIEGFRIED:** Ha, schönstes Weib!
Schliesse den Blick!
das Herz in der Brust
brennt mir sein Strahl:
zu feurigen Strömen fühl' ich
zehrend ihn zünden mein Blut!—
(*Mit bebender Stimme.*)
Gunther—wie heisst deine
Schwester?

**GUNTHER:** Gutrune.

**SIEGFRIED:** Sind's gute Runen,
die ihrem Aug' ich entrathe?
(*Er fasst Gutrune mit feurigem Ungestüm bei der Hand.*)
Deinem Bruder bot ich mich zum
Mann;
der Stolze schlug mich aus:—
trägst du, wie er, mir Uebermuth,
böt' ich mich dir zum Bund?
(*Gutrune neigt demüthig das Haupt, und nait einer Gebärde, als fühle sie sich seiner nicht werth, verlässt sie wankenden Schrittes wieder die Halle.*)

**SIEGFRIED:** (*blickt ihr, wie fest gezaubert, nach, von Hagen und Gunther aufmerksam beobachtet; dann, ohne sich umzuwenden, frägt er:*) Hast du, Gunther,
ein Weib?

**GUNTHER:** Nicht freit' ich noch,
und einer Frau
soll' ich mich schwerlich freu'n!
Auf eine setzt' ich den Sinn,
die kein Rath je mir gewinnt.

**SIEGFRIED:** (*lebhaft sich zu ihm wendend.*) Was wär' dir versagt,
steh' ich zu dir?

**GUNTHER:** Auf Felsen hoch ihr
Sitz;
ein Feuer umbrennt den Saal—

**SIEGFRIED:** (*verwundert, und wie um eines längst Vergessenen sich zu entsinnen, wiederholt leise:*) "Auf Felsen hoch ihr Sitz;
ein Feuer umbrennt den
Saal" . . . ?

**GUNTHER:** Nur wer durch das
Feuer bricht,

**SIEGFRIED:** (*hastig einfallend und schnell nachlassend.*) "Nur
were durch das Feuer bricht"?

**GUNTHER:** —darf Brünnhilde's
Freier sein.
(*Siegfried drückt durch seine schweigende Gebärde aus, dass bei Nennung von Brünnhilde's Namen die Erinnerung ihm vollends ganza schwindet.*)

**GUNTHER:** Nun darf ich den Fels
nicht erklimmen;
das Feuer verglimmt mir nie!

**SIEGFRIED:** (*Heftig auffahrend*)
Ich—fürchte kein Feuer:
für dich frei' ich die Frau:
denn dein Mann bin ich,
und mein Muth ist dein—
erwerb' ich Gutrun' zum Weib.

**GUNTHER:** Gutrune gönn' ich dir
gern.

**SIEGFRIED:** Ha! sweetest maid!
Screen those bright beams,
the heart in my breast
burns with their strength;
in fiery streams I feel
how my blood boils in my veins!
(*With trembling voice.*)
Gunther, what name has your sister?

**GUNTHER:** Gutrune.

**SIEGFRIED:** Are good the runes
that now in her eyes I am reading?
(*He seizes Gutrune with impatient ardor by the hand.*)
When I sought to serve your brave
brother
his pride repelled my aid.
Would you be even as arrogant
said I to you the same?
(*Gutrune humbly droops her head, and then, with an expressive gesture, as if she felt her unworthiness, leaves the hall again with trembling steps.*)

**SIEGFRIED:** (*closely observed by Hagen and Gunther, gazes after her, as if spellbound; then without turning he asks*) Have you, Gunther, a wife?

**GUNTHER:** I've never wooed yet;
besides, a wife
seems me I scarce can win:
on one my soul I have set,
but no help can gain my wish.

**SIEGFRIED:** (*turning quickly to him.*) What would be gainsaid,
stood I your friend?

**GUNTHER:** A far-off rock's her
home,
a fire breasts her hall.

**SIEGFRIED:** (*repeats softly, in wonder, and as if striving to remember something long forgotten.*) "A far-off rock's her home;
a fire breasts her hall" . . . ?

**GUNTHER:** But he who that fire
can brave—

**SIEGFRIED:** (*hastily chiming in and immediately ceasing.*) "But
he who that fire can brave"?

**GUNTHER:** —is Brünnhilde's fitting mate.
(*Siegfried shows, by a silent gesture, that at the mention of Brünnhilde's name the remembrance has quite faded.*)

**GUNTHER:** That mountain my feet
may not approach,
the fire never will pale for me,

**SIEGFRIED:** (*with a sudden start.*) I—fear not the fire,
and your bride fain will I fetch;
for I am your own
and my arm is yours:
if I may gain Gutrune for my wife.

**GUNTHER:** I'll give Gutrune to
you gladly.

SIEGFRIED: Brünnhilde bringe ich dir.

GUNTHER: Wie willst du sie täuschen?

SIEGFRIED: Durch des Tarnhelm's Trug tausch' ich mir deine Gestalt.

GUNTHER: So stelle Eide zum Schwur

SIEGFRIED: Blut-Brüderschaft schwöre ein Eid!

(*Hagen füllt ein Trinkhorn mit frischem Wein; Siegfried und Gunther ritzen sich mit ihren Schwertern die Arme und halten diese einen Augenblick über das Trinkhorn.*)

SIEGFRIED UND GUNTHER:
Blühenden Lebens
labendes Blut
traüfelt' ich in den Trank:
bruder-brünstig
muthig gemischt,
blüh' im Trank unser Blut,
Treue trink' ich dem Freund,
frohn und frei
entblühe dem Bund
Blut-Brüderschaft heut'!
Bricht ein Bruder den Bund,
trügt den Treuen der Freund:
was in Tropfen hold
heute wir tranken,
in Strahlen ström' es dahin,
fromme Sühne dem Freund!
So—biet' ich den Bund:
so trink' ich dir Treu!
(*Sie trinken nacheinander, jeder zur Hälfte; dann zerschlägt Hagen, der während des Schwures zur Seite gelehnt, mit seinem Schwerte das Horn. Siegfried und Gunther reichen sich die Hände.*)

SIEGFRIED: (*zu Hagen.*) Was nahmst du am Eide nicht Theil?

HAGEN: Mein Blut verdärb' euch den Trank! Nicht fliesst mir's ächt und edel wie euch; störrisch und kalt stockt's in mir; nicht will's die Wange mir röthen. D'rum bleib' ich fern vom feurigen Bund.

GUNTHER: Lass' den unfrohen Mann!

SIEGFRIED: Frisch auf die Fahrt! Dort liegt mein Schiff; schnell führt es zum Felsen: eine Nacht am Ufer harrs't du im Nachen, die Frau führst du dann heim.

GUNTHER: Rastest du nicht zuvor?

SIEGFRIED: Um die Rückkehr ist's mir jach. (*Er geht zum Ufer.*)

GUNTHER: Du Hagen, bewache die Halle!
(*Er folgt Siegfried.*)
(*Gutrune erscheint an der Thüre ihres Gemaches.*)

SIEGFRIED: I'll bring you Brünnhilde!

GUNTHER: How can she mistake us?

SIEGFRIED: Through the Tarnhelm's trick, turning me into your shape.

GUNTHER: Propose an oath for us pair.

SIEGFRIED: Blood-brotherhood hallowed by oath.
(*Hagen fills a horn with fresh wine; Gunther and Siegfried scratch their arms with their sword-points, and hold the wound a moment over the wine.*)

SIEGFRIED AND GUNTHER: Blossoming life's stream,
liberal blood
drops into the drink.
Bravely brewed
by fiery friends,
blazes the draught with our blood.
Truth I drink to my friend:
fair and free
be born from our bond
blood-brotherhood here.
Breaks a brother the bond,
fails in faith to his friend,
What in drops we here
haste to drink of
in streams be strained from his heart,
forfeit stern to his friend.
Thus compact I claim!
Thus duty I drink.
(*They each in turn drink half the contents of the horn, which Hagen, who has stood apart during the oath, then breaks in half with his sword. Gunther and Siegfried clasp hands.*)

SIEGFRIED: (*to Hagen.*) Why have you not joined in the bond?

HAGEN: Your drink was spoiled by my blood! It flows by no means nobly enough; stubborn and cold, scarce it stirs; my cheek it is chary to redden. I leave perforce the fiery league

GUNTHER: Have no heed for the churl.

SIEGFRIED: Forth let me fare! There lies my skiff; swiftly float to the fastness, At the bank for one night wait with the boat; then bear away the bride.

GUNTHER: You take no rest first?

SIEGFRIED: I'll return here in a trice.
(*Goes to the shore.*)

GUNTHER: You, Hagen, have ward of the homestead.
(*He follows Siegfried.*)
(*Gutrune appears at the door of her room.*)

GUNTHER: Wohin eilen die Schnellen?

HAGEN: Zu Schiff', Brünnhild' zu frei'n.

GUTRUNE: Siegfried?

HAGEN: Sieh', wie's ihn treibt zum Weib dich zu gewinnen!
(*Er setzt sich mit Speer und Schild vor der Halle nieder. Siegfried und Gunther fahren ab.*)

GUTRUNE: Siegfried—mein!
(*Sie geht, lebhaft erregt, in ihr Gemach zurück.*)

HAGEN: (*nach längerem Stillschweigen.*) Hier sitz' ich zur Wacht,
wahre den Hof,
wehre die Halle dem Feind:—
Gibich's Sohne
wehet der Wind;
auf Werben fährt er dahin.
Ihm führt der Steuer
ein starker Held,
Gefahr ihm will er besteh'n:
die eig'ne Braut
ihm bringt er zum Rhein;
mir aber bringt er— den Ring.—
Ihr freien Söhne,
frohe Gesellen,
segelt nur lustig dahin!
Dünkt er euch niedrig,
ihn dient ihm doch—
des Niblungen Sohn.
(*Ein Teppich schlägt vor der Scene zusammen, und verschliesst die Bühne. Nachdem, während eines kurzen Orchester-Zwischenspieles, der Schauplatz verwandelt ist, wird der Teppich, der zufor den Vordergrund der Halle einfasste, gänzlich aufgezogen.*)

## Dritte Scene

(*Die Felsenhöhe, wie im Vorspiel.*)

BRÜNNHILDE: (*Sitzt am Eingange des Steingemaches, und betrachtet in stummen Sinnen Siegfried's Ring; von wonniger Erinnerung überwättigt, bedeckt sie ihn dann mit Küssen,—als sie plötzlich ein fernes Geräusch vernimmt: sie lauscht und späht zur Seite in den Hintergrund.*) Altgewohntes Geräusch
raunt meinem Ohr die Ferne:—
ein Luftross jagt
im Laufe daher;
auf der Wolke fährt es
wetternd zum Fels!—
Wer fand mich Einsame auf?

WALTRAUTE'S: (*Stimme aus der Ferne*). Brünnhilde! Schwester!
schläf'st oder wach'st du?

BRÜNNHILDE: (*fährt vom Sitze auf*). Waltraute's Ruf,
so wonnig mir kund!—
Komm'st du, Schwester,
schwing'st du dich kühn zu mir?
(*in die Scene refend.*)
Dort im Tann

GUTRUNE: O where do they haste so swiftly?

HAGEN: They sail, to find Brünnhilde.

GUTRUNE: Siegfried?

HAGEN: See what he does for wife striving to win you.
(*He seats himself before the hall with spear and shield. Siegfried and Gunther float away.*)

GUTRUNE: Siegfried—mine!
(*Goes back to her room in great agitation.*)

HAGEN: (*after a long silence.*)
Here I sit to wait,
watching the hall,
warding the house from all foes.
Gibich's son
is wafted by winds;
a-wooing forth is he gone.
And fleetly steers
a stalwart man,
whose force can stem all peril.
His own the bride
he brings down the Rhine;
but he will bring *me* the Ring.
Oh gallant partners,
gleeful companions,
push then merrily from here!
Slight though your natures,
You still may serve
the Nibelung's son.
(*A curtain closes in from each side and hides the stage. After a short orchestral interlude, during which the scene is changed, the curtain, which before closed in all the front of the hall, is completely withdrawn.*)

## Scene III

(*The Valkyries' rock, as in the Prelude.*)

BRÜNNHILDE: (*sits at the entrance of the cave in silent thought, gazing on Siegfried's ring; overcome by tender reminiscences, she covers it with kisses, when suddenly she bears a distant noise: she listens and looks off at back.*) Old well-recognized sounds
strike on my ear from distance;
a wind-horse
wings its course here,
in the clouds it rumbles
close to the rock.
Who rides my stillness to stir?

VALTRAUTA'S: (*voice from the distance*). Brünnhilde—sister!
Do you sleep or wake?

BRÜNNHILDE: (*starting to her feet*). Welcome that cry,
it wafts from Valtrauta!
Truest sister!
Do you seek trace of me here!
(*Calling towards the back.*)
In yon wood,

—dir noch vertraut—
steige vom Ross
und stell' den Renner zu Rast!
Kommst du zu mir?
Bist du so kühn?
mag'st ohne Grauen
Brünnhild' bieten den Gruss?
(*Waltraute ist aus dem Tann hastig aufgetreten; Brünnhilde ist ihr stürmisch entgegengeeilt: diese beachtet in der Freude nicht die ängstliche Scheu Waltraute's.*)

**WALTRAUTE:** Einzig dir nur
galt meine Eile.

**BRÜNNHILDE:** (*in höchster freudiger Aufgeregtheit*). So wagtest
du, Brünnhild' zu lieb,
Walvater's Bann zu brechen?
Oder wie? o sag'!
wär' wider mich
Wotan's Sinn erweicht?
Als dem Gott entgegen
Siegmund ich schützte,
fehlend—ich weiss es—
erfüllt' ich doch seinen Wunsch:
dass sein Zorn sich verzogen,
weiss ich auch;
denn verschloss er mich gleich in Schlaf.
fesselt' er mich auf den Fels,
wies er dem Mann' mich zur Magd,
der am Weg' mich fänd und erweckt'—
meiner bangen Bitte
doch gab er Gunst:
mit zehrendem Feuer
umgab er den Fels,
dem Zagen zu wehren den Weg.
So zur seligsten
schuf mich die Strafe:
der herrlichste Held
gewann mich zum Weib;
in seiner Liebe
leucht' und lach' ich heut' auf.—
Lockte dich, Schwester, mei Loos?
An meiner Wonne
willst du dich weiden?
theilen, was mich betraf?

**WALTRAUTE:** Theilen den Taumel,
der dich Thörin erfasst?—
Ein And'res bewog mich in Angst
zu brechen Wotan's Gebot.

**BRÜNNHILDE:** Angst und Furcht
fesselt dich Arme?
So verzieh der Strenge noch nicht?
du zag'st vor des Strafenden Zorn?

**WALTRAUTE:** Dürft' ich ihn
fürchten.
meiner Angst fänd' ich ei End'!

**BRÜNNHILDE:** Staunend versteh'
ich dich nicht!

**WALTRAUTE:** Wehr' deiner Wallung:
achtsam höre mich an!
Nach Walhall wieder
treibt mich die Angst,
die von Walhall hieher mich trieb.

**BRÜNNHILDE:** (*erschrocken*).
Was ist's mit den ewigen Göttern?

As you were wont,
Straightway descend
and safely stable your steed.
Do you come to me?
bold and uncowed,
Do you dare again then to greet
banished Brünnhild'?
(*Valtrauta has entered hastily from the wood; Brünnhilde rushes to meet her; in her joy she does not perceive Valtrauta's anxious timidity.*)

**VALTRAUTA:** It is for you
my gallop is taken.

**BRÜNNHILDE:** O was it for
Brünnhilde's sake you broke
War-father's ban?
Or for what?
O say!
Will Wotan's heart
once more softly wax?
When against the god once
I sheltered Siegmund—
wrongly, I know well—
I wrought the thing that he wished.
That his anger was ended
well I knew;
for though sealed he my eyes in sleep,
rivetting me to this rock,
destining me to the man
who this way should roam and awake me,
yet I begged for the boon
denied he not:
a terrible fire
he knit round the fell,
to ward all tremblers from the way.
So sweet solace
was shaped by my sentence:
the highest of heroes
won me for wife.
Filled with his love I live
in light and laughter.
You lured, O sister, my lot?
Do you then pine
for part in my pleasures,
seek my pure bliss to share?

**VALTRAUTA:** Share the insaneness
that has seized on your soul?
More matter has worked on my mind
to break the ban of Wotan.

**BRÜNNHILDE:** Fear and dread
drive over your features!
Does our father withhold pardon?
You fear his punishment's force?

**VALTRAUTA:** If I did fear him
this alarm would be fast allayed.

**BRÜNNHILDE:** Scared, I can scarce
understand.

**VALTRAUTA:** Mask your emotion:
wisely hark to my words.
Again the grief hurries me back
which did goad me here from Valhalla.

**BRÜNNHILDE:** (*alarmed*). What
ails with the AEsir eternal?

**WALTRAUTE:** Höre mit Sinn was
ich sage!—
Seit er von dir geschieden,
zur Schlacht nicht mehr
schickte uns Wotan;
irr und rathlos
ritten wir ängstlich zu Heer.
Walhall's muthige Helden
mied Walvater:
einsam zu Ross
ohne Ruh' und Rast
durchstreift' er als Wand'rer die Welt
Jüngst kehrte er heim;
in der Hand hielt er
seines Speeres Splitter:
die hatte ein Held ihm geschlagen.
Mit stummen Wink
Walhall's Edle
wies er zum Forst,
die Welt-Esche zu fällen;
des Stammes Scheite
hiess er sie schichten
zum regenden Hauf
rings um der Seligen Saal.
Der Götter Rath
liess er berufen;
den Hochsitz nahm
heilig er ein:
ihm zu Seiten
hiess er die Bangen sich setzen,
in Ring und Reih'
die Hall' erfüllen die Helden.
So—sitzt er,
sagt kein Wort,
auf hehrem Sitze
stumm und ernst,
des Speeres Splitter
fest in der Faust;
Holda's Aepfel
rührt er nicht an:
Staunen und Bangen
binden starr die Götter.—
Seiner Raben beide
sandt' er auf Reise:
kehrten die einst
mit guter Kunde zurück,
dann noch einmal
—zum letzten mal—
lächelte ewig der Gott.
Seine Knie' umwindend
liegen wir Walküren:
blind bleibt er
den flehenden Blicken;
uns alle verzehrt
Zagen und endlose Angst.
An seine Brust
presst' ich mich weinend:
da brach sich sein Blick—
er gedachte, Brünnhilde, dein!
Tief seufzte er auf,
schloss das Auge,
und wie im Traume
raunt' er das Wort:—
"Des tiefen Rheines Töchtern
gäbe den Ring sie wieder zurück,
von des Fluches Last
erlös't wär' Gott und Welt!"—
Da sann ich nach:
von seiner Seite
durch stumme Reihen
stahl ich mich fort;
in heimlicher Hast
bestieg ich mein Ross,
und ritt im Sturme zu dir.

**VALTRAUTA:** Heed with your soul
what I recite
Since he was severed from you
our sire no more
sent us to warfare;
undirected
we rode, an awe-stricken host;
Valhall's high-hearted heroes
he viewed no more.
Lonely a-horse,
without halt or home,
he went through the world as a Wanderer.
He lately came home,
in his hand holding fast
his spear in splinters:
it was hacked by a hero asunder.
With signs for words
waved he all
the warriors in haste to hew down
the world's ash-tree.
The stem in sticks
he bade them to stack,
and arrange in a bulk
round the AEsir's sanctifed seat.
He called the gods
to the council;
then he took his proud sacred place:
to his side
appointed the tremblers to assemble.
In rank and ring
the warriors crowded Valhalla.
So he sits,
speaking no word,
in high position,
still and grave,
the splintered spear
held fast in his fist.
Hulda's apples
he does not eat.
Gloomy and awe-struck
all the gods seem frozen.
But he turned his ravens
both out to travel;
when they wing their return with goodly tidings,
once again then for evermore
over the god breaks a smile.
Round his knees in vigil
twine all we Valkyries;
blind bides he
to eyes that are begging,
and all of us stay,
struck with an ominous awe.
I pressed weeping to his breast;
his brooding then broke;
and his thoughts turned,
Brünnhilde, to you!
Deep sighs he uttered,
closed his eyelids,
as were he dreaming,
and said these words:
"The day the Rhine's three daughters
gain by surrender from her the Ring
from the curse's load
released are gods and men!"
I thought upon it;
and then I threaded
amid throngs dumb-stricken
thence from his side;
in haste
I threw me astride my horse

Dich, o Schwester,
beschwör' ich nun:
was du vermagst,
vollend' es dein Muth!
Ende der Ewigen Qual!

BRÜNNHILDE: Welch' banger
Träume Mären
meldest du Traurige mir!
Der Götter heiligem
Himmels-Nebel
bin ich Thörin enttaucht:
nicht fass' ich, was ich erfahre.
Wirr und wüst
scheint mir dein Sinn;
in deinem Aug'
—so übermüde—
glänzt flackernde Gluth:
mit blasser Wange
du bleiche Schwester,
was willst du Wilde von mir?

WALTRAUTE: (*mit unheimlicher Hast.*) An deiner Hand der Ring—
er ist's: hör' meinen Rath:
für Wotan wirf ihn von dir!

BRÜNNHILDE: Den Ring—von mir?

WALTRAUTE: Den Rheintöchtern gieb ihn zurück!

BRÜNNHILDE: Den Rheintöchtern—ich—den Ring?
Siegfrieds' Liebespfand?
Bist du von Sinnen?

WALTRAUTE: Hör' mich! hör' meine Angst?
Der Welt Unheil
haftet sicher an ihm:—
wirf ihn von dir
fort in die Welle
Walhall's Elend zu enden,
den verfluchten wirf in die Fluth!

BRÜNNHILDE: Ha! weisst du, was er mir ist?
Wie kannst du's fassen,
fühllose Maid!—
Mehr als Walhall's Wonne,
mehr als der Ewigen Ruhm
ist mir der Ring:
ein Blick auf sein helles Gold,
ein Blitz aus dem hehren Glanz
gilt mir werther
als aller Götter
ewig währendes Glück!
Denn selig aus ihm
leuchtet mir Siegfried's Liebe:
Siegfried's Liebe!
O liess' sich die Wonne dir sagen!
Sie wahrt mir der Reif.
Geh' hin zu der Götter
heiligem Rath;
von meinem Ringe
raun' ihnen zu:
die Liebe liesse ich nie,
mir nehmen nie sie die Liebe,
stürzt auch in Trümmern
Walhall's strahlende Pracht!

and straightaway thrust towards you.
Then, my sister,
I supplicate:
do what you may
if but you mind:
ward off the woe of the gods.
(*Throws herself at Brünnhilde's feet.*)

BRÜNNHILDE: What dreamy tales of mystery
you mournfully tell to me!
From cloudy homes
where the holy gods sit
am I, poor fool, expelled;
recital conveys no sense.
Void and vain
seems your speech.
Within your eyes
so over-wearied
gleams fitfully glow.
You piteous woman
with pallid features,
what would your wildness of me?

VALTRAUTA: (*with gloomy haste*). There on your hand—the ring
It is that—hark to my story!
For Wotan will you resign it?

BRÜNNHILDE: The ring! resign it?

VALTRAUTA: Surrender it back to the Rhine!

BRÜNNHILDE: Surrender it—I—the ring?
Siegfried's bridal gift?
Wander your senses?

VALTRAUTA: Hear me! heed my distress!
The world's trouble
hangs upon it, I know.
Whirl it from you
far in the water,
woe from Valhall' averting;
cast the foul thing away in the flood!

BRÜNNHILDE: Ah! Do you know what it is to me?
You cannot fathom,
feelingless maid!
More than AEsir's honor,
More than Valhall's bright realm
I hold this ring.
One look at its beauteous gold,
one light from its brilliant gleam
gladdens me more
than unending good
to all the mass of the gods.
I see in its beams
lambent how Siegfried loves me.
Siegfried loves me!
How little you know of this sweetness!
The ring stays with me
Get hence to the gods
in holy array,
and of my ring
tell them this:
I'll loose not love from my heart;
no hest shall hinder my loving,
Sooner to ruins
Valhall's splendor shall crash.

WALTRAUTE: Diess deine Treue?
So in Trauer
entlässest du lieblos die Schwester?

BRÜNNHILDE: Schwinge dich fort;
fliege zu Ross:
den Ring entführst du mir nicht!

WALTRAUTE: Wehe! Wehe!
Weh' dir Schwester!
Walhall's Göttern Weh!
(*Sie stürzt fort; man hört sie schnell—wie zu Ross vom Tann aus fortbrausen.*)

BRÜNNHILDE: (*blickt einer davonjagenden, hellerleuchteten Gewitterwolke nach, die sich bald gänzlich in der Ferne verliert*).
Blitz und Gewölk,
vom Wind geblasen,
stürme dahin:
zu mir nie steure mehr her!—
(*Es ist Abend geworden: aus der Tiefe leuchtet der Feuerschein stärker auf.*)
Abendlich Dämmern
deckt den Himmel:
Was leckt so wüthend
die lodernde Welle zum Wall?
Zur Felsenspitze
wälzt sich der feurige Schwall.
(*Man hört aus der Tiefe Siegfried's Hornruf nahen. Brünnhilde lauscht, und fährt dann entzückt auf.*)
Siegfried!
Siegfried zurück?
seinen Ruf sendet er her!
Auf!—Auf, ihm entgegen!
in meines Gottes Arm!
(*Sie stürzt in höchstem Entzücken dem Hittergrunde Feuerflammen schlagen über den Höhensaum auf: aus ihnen springt Siegfried auf einen hoch ragenden Felsstein empor, worauf die Flammen wieder zurückweichen, und abermals nur aus der Tiefe des Hintergrundes heraufleuchten.—Siegfried, auf dem Haupte den Tarnhelm, der ihm bis zur Hälfte das Gesicht verdeckt und nur die Augen frei lässt, erscheint in Gunther's Gestalt.*)

BRÜNNHILDE: (*voll Entsetzen zurückweichend.*) Verrath!—Wer drang zu mir?
(*Sie flieht bis in den Hintergrund, und heftet von da aus in sprachlosem Erstaunen ihren Blick auf Siegfried.*)

SIEGFRIED: (*Im Hintergrunde auf dem Steine verweilend, betrachtet sie lange, auf seinen Schild gelehnt; dann redet er sie mit verstellter—tieferer—Stimme an.*) Brünnhild'! ein Freier kam,
den dein Feuer nicht geschreckt.
Dich werb' ich nun zum Weib;
du folge willig mir!

VALTRAUTA: This is your truth then?
So in trouble
you leave your sister all loveless?

BRÜNNHILDE: Swiftly go forth,
to ride far from here:
you'll not force the ring from me.

VALTRAUTA: Woe's me, woe's me!
Woe's to you, sister!
Woe to Valhall'—woe!
(*She rushes away and is heard without—as if on horse—galloping away from the wood.*)

BRÜNNHILDE: (*gazes after a brightly lighted storm-cloud as it sails away and is quickly lost in the distance*).
Black thunder-cloud
that cleaves the heavens,
stride quickly away:
no more be steered to me here.
(*It is now evening. From the valley glimmers the firelight, gradually waxing.*)
Eve's dusky shadows
shroud the heavens:
Why glare so wildly
the glittering waves over the wall?
The raging fire
its way over the rock-point would force.
(*Siegfried's horn is heard below in the valley. Brünnhilde listens, and then starts up enraptured.*)
Siegfried!
Siegfried is here!
Sure his horn sounded that call.
Up! up! and be gathered
into my god's strong arm.
(*She hurries towards the back in the highest transport. Flames dart up over the cliff; out of them springs Siegfried up on to a jutting rock, whereupon the flames fall back again and gradually retire to the valley. Siegfried appears in Gunther's form, wearing the Tarnhelm, the visor of which covers half his face, leaving only the eyes free.*)

BRÜNNHILDE: (*retreating in horror.*) Betrayed!
What man are you?
(*She flies to the front, and from thence, in speechless amazement, turns her looks upon Siegfried.*)

SIEGFRIED: (*remaining at back on the stone, leans on his shield and gazes at her a long while; then he speaks to her with altered—deeper—voice.*) Brünnhilde!
A lover comes,
and your fire alarms him not.
I woo you for my wife;
so bend your will to me!

## Act I, Scene III

BRÜNNHILDE: (*heftig zitternd*).
Wer ist der Mann,
der das vermochte,
was dem Stärksten nur bestimmt?

SIEGFRIED: (*immer noch auf
dem Steine im Hintergrunde*). Ein
Helde, der dich zähmt
bezwingt Gewalt dich nur.

BRÜNNHILDE: (*von Grausen erfasst*). Ein Unhold schwang sich
auf jenen Stein;
ein Aar kam geflogen
mich zu zerfleischen!
Wer bist du, Schrecklicher?
(*Siegfried—schweigt.*)
Stamm'st du von Menschen?
komm'st du von Hella's
nächtlichem Heer?

SIEGFRIED: (*nach längerem
Schweigen*). Ein Gibichung bin
ich,
und Gunther heisst der Held,
dem, Frau, du folgen soll'st.

BRÜNNHILDE: (*in Verzweiflung
ausbrechend.*) Wotan! ergrimmt-
er,
grausamer Gott!
Weh'! nun erseh' ich
der Strafe Sinn:
zu Hohn und Jammer
jag'st du mich hin!

SIEGFRIED: (*springt vom Stein
herab und tritt näher.*) Die Nacht
bricht an:
in deinem Gemach
musst du dich mit mir vermählen.

BRÜNNHILDE: (*den Finger, an
dem sie Siegfried's Ring trägt, drohend emporstreckend.*) Bleib'
fern! fürchte dies Zeichen!
Zur Schande zwingst du mich
nicht,
so lang' der Ring mich schützt.

SIEGFRIED: Mannesrecht gebe er
Gunther:
durch den Ring sei ihm vermählt!

BRÜNNHILDE: Zurück, Räuber!
frevelnder Dieb!
Erfreche dich nicht zu nah'n.
Stärker als Stahl
macht mich der Ring:
nie raubst du ihn mir!

SIEGFRIED: Von dir ihn zu lösen
lehrst du mich nun.
(*Er dringt auf sie ein; sie ringen,
Brünnhilde windet sich los und
flieht. Siegfried setzt ihr nach. Sie
ringen von neuem; er erfasst sie,
und entzieht ihrem Finger den
Ring. Sie schreit laut auf und
sinkt, wie zerbrochen, auf der
Steinbank vor dem Gemach zusammen.*)

SIEGFRIED: Jetzt bist du mein!
Brünnhilde, Gunther's Braut—
gönne mir nun dein Gemach!

BRÜNNHILDE: (*fast ohn-
mächtig.*) Was könntest du wehren,
elendes Weib?

---

BRÜNNHILDE: (*trembling violently.*) Who is the man
has wrought the marvel
that but one alone may work?

SIEGFRIED: (*still standing on the
rock at back.*) A hero you'll obey
if you're ruled by force.

BRÜNNHILDE: (*filled with terror.*) A demon stands
upon yon stone!
an eagle has flown here
who would rend my flesh!
Who are you, awful one?
(*Siegfried is silent.*)
Are you a mortal? Do you
Come of Hella's
night-dwelling host?

SIEGFRIED: (*after a long silence.*)
I am a Gibichung
and Gunther,
maid, will mate with thee.

BRÜNNHILDE: (*in a despairing
outburst.*) Wotan!
Resentful,
Stern-hearted sire!
Woe! now I fathom
your fiat fell!
My shame and wailing
well have you shaped!

SIEGFRIED: (*leaping from the
rock and approaching.*) The night
falls,
I demand your room;
made mine by marriage.

BRÜNNHILDE: (*threateningly
stretching out her finger on which
is Siegfried's ring.*) Stand back!
bow to this token!
No shame can touch me from you
while yet this ring is my shield.

SIEGFRIED: Husband's right it
gains for Gunther:
with that ring be wed to him.

BRÜNNHILDE: Aroint, robber!
Villainous thief!
Nor venture near my side.
Stronger than steel
the ring makes me;
None rend it from me.

SIEGFRIED: Will I take it from you,
Taught by your words.
(*He presses towards her; they
wrestle. Brünnhilde slips herself
loose and flies. Siegfried pursues
her. Again they struggle; he seizes
her, and plucks the ring from her
finger. She utters a loud scream
and sinks exhausted on the rocky
seat in front of the cave.*)

SIEGFRIED: Now be mine!
Brünnhilde, Gunther's bride:
go to your chamber with me.

BRÜNNHILDE: (*almost fainting.*)
How, woman too hapless,
can you find help?
(*Siegfried drives her in wit a com-

---

(*Siegfried treibt sie mit einer gebietenden Bewegung an: zitternd
und wankenden Schrittes geht sie
in das Gemach.*)

SIEGFRIED: (*das Schwert
ziehend, mit seiner natürlichen
Stimme.*) Nun, Nothung, zeuge du,
dass ich in Züchten warb:
die Treue wahrend dem Bruder,
trenne mich von seiner Braut!
(*Er folgt Brünnhilde nach.*) (*De
Vorhang fällt.*)

## ■ ZWEITER AUFZUG

### Erste Scene

(*Uferraum vor der Halle der
Gibichungen: rechts der offene
Eingang zur Halle; links das
Rheinufer; von diesem aus erhebt
sich eine durch verschiedene Berg-
pfade gespaltene, felsige Anhöhe,
quer über die Bühne, nach rechts
dem Hintergrunde zu aufsteigend. Dort sieht man einen der
Fricka errichtetes Welchstein,
welchem, höher hinauf, ein
grösserer für Wotan, sowie seitwärts ein gleicher für Donner
geweihter entspricht. Es ist
Nacht.*)
Hagen; den Speer im Arm, den
Schild zur Seite, sitzt schlafend an
der Halle. Der Mond wirrt plötzlich
ein grelles Licht auf ihn und seine
nächste Umgebung; man gewahrt
Alberich vor Hagen kauernd, die
Arme auf dessen Kniee gelehnt.)

ALBERICH: Schläfst du, Hagen,
mem Sohn?
Du schläfst, und hörst mich nicht,
den Ruh' und Schlaf verrieth?

HAGEN: (*leise und ohne sich zu
rühren, so dass er immer fort zu
schlafen scheint, obwohl er die
Augen offen hat.*) Ich höre dich,
schlimmer Albe:
was hast du meinem Schlaf zu sagen?

ALBERICH: Gemahnt sei der
Macht,
der du gebietest,
bist du so muthig,
wie die Mutter dich mir gebar.

HAGEN: Gab die Mutter mir Muth,
nicht doch mag ich ihr danken,
dass deiner List sie erlag:
frühalt, fahl und bleich,
hass' ich die Frohen,
freue mich nie!

ALBERICH: Hagen, mein Sohn!
Hasse die Frohen!
Mich Lust-freien,
Leid-belasteten,
liebst du so wie du sollst!
Bist du dräftig,
kühn und klug:
die wir bekämpfen
mit nächtigem Krieg,
schon giebt ihnen Noth unser Neid

---

manding gesture. She goes into
the cave trembling, and with tottering steps.*)

SIEGFRIED: (*drawing his sword
and speaking with his natural
voice.*) Now, Needful, witness
that my wooing is chaste.
To seal my oath to my brother,
separate me from his bride.
(*He follows Brünnhilde.*) (*The
curtain falls.*)

## ■ ACT II

### Scene I

(*River bank before the hall of the
Gibichungs: the banks of the river
L., entrance to the hall R. From the
river bank rises diagonally
towards the back a rocky slope divided by sundry mountain paths.
There stands an altar stone, dedicated to Fricka, a larger one, higher up, for Wotan, and another
towards the side for Donner. It is
night.*)
(*Hagen, with spear in hand and
shield at side, sits sleeping against
the hall. The moon suddenly
throws a keen light on him and his
surroundings; Alberic is seen
crouching in front of him, leaning
his arms on Hagen's knees.*)

ALBERIC: Do you sleep, Hagen, my
son?
You sleep and hear not him
whom rest and sleep have ruined.

HAGEN: (*softly and without moving, so that he appears still to
sleep, though his eyes are open.*) I
hear well, son of darkness:
what have you to instruct my slumber?

ALBERIC: I remind you what might
own
your spirit
if it is as manly
as your mother did make it erst.

HAGEN: Though mighty she made
me, I may not thank her
that she succumbed to your craft
Wizened, wan and pale,
I hate the happy,
hope for no joy.

ALBERIC: Hagen, my son!
hate the happy!
Your so hapless sire,
besieged by sorrow,
then lacks not your love.
If you are fearless,
fierce and false,
those whom we fight
with a nocturnal feud
shall surely be harmed by our hate.

Der einst den Ring mir entriss,
Wotan, der wüthende Räuber,
vom eig'nen Geschlechte
ward er geschlagen:
an den Wälsung verlor er
Macht und Gewalt;
mit der Götter ganzer Sippe
in Angst ersieht er sein End'.
Nicht ihn fürcht' ich mehr:
fallen muss er mit Allen!
Schläf'st du, Hagen, mein Sohn?

HAGEN: (*bleibt unverändert wie zuvor*). Der Ewigen Macht, wer erbte sie?

ALBERICH: Ich—und du:
wir erben die Welt,
trüg' ich mich nicht
in deiner Treu',
theil'st du meinen Gram und Grimm.
Wotan's Speer
zerspellte der Wälsung,
der Fafner, den Wurm,
im Kampfe gefällt,
und kindisch den Reif sich errang:
jede Gewalt
hat er gewonnen,
Walhall und Nibelheim
neigen sich ihm;
an dem furchtlosen Helden
erlahmt selbst mein Fluch:
denn nicht kennt er
des Ringes Werth,
zu nichts nützt er
die neidlichste Macht;
lachend in liebender Brunst
brennt er lebend dahin.
Ihn zu verderben
taugt uns nun einzig . . .
Hörst du, Hagen, mein Sohn?

HAGEN: Zu seinem Verderben dient er mir schon.

ALBERICH: Den gold'nen Ring,
den Reif gilt's zu erringen!
Ein weises Weib
lebt dem Wälsung zu Lieb':
rieth' sie ihm je
des Rheines Töchtern
—die in Wassers Tiefen
einst mich bethört!—
zurück zu geben den Ring:
verloren ging' mir das Gold,
keine List erlangte es je.
Drum ohne Zögern
ziel' auf den Reif:
Dich Zaglosen
zeugt' ich mich ja,
dass wider Helden
hart du mich hieltest.
Zwar stark nicht genug
den Wurm zu besteh'n,
was allein dem Wälsung bestimmt,
zu zähem Hass
erzog ich doch Hagen:
der soll mich nun rächen,
den Ring zu gewinnen,
dem Wälsung und Wotan zum Hohn!
Schwör'st du mir's, Hagen, mein Sohn?
(*Ein immer finsterer Schatten bedeckt wieder Hagen und Alberich: vom Rhein her dämmert der Tag.*)

---

He who once wrested my ring,
Wotan, the worst of all robbers,
at last is disabled
by his own offspring:
all his late power
through the Volsung is lost.
All the gods together with him
in awe are waiting their ending.
No more do I fear him:
he must fall now among them.
Do you sleep, Hagen, my son?

HAGEN: (*remaining motionless as before.*) The might of the gods, whose meed is it?

ALBERIC: Mine and yours!
We'll master the world;
if I may reckon
on your aid—
Do you share in my wrongs and wrath.
Wotan's spear
was spoiled by the Volsung,
who fiercely did vanquish
Fafnir in fight,
the fair ring to take as a toy.
Now he is prince
of every power,
Valhall' and Nibelheim
know him as their lord.
On this fear-lacking hero
my curse cannot fall;
for, the ring's might
he uses not:
he knows nothing
of its notable worth.
Laughter, and I love with its glow
glad his life-days alone.
Only his ruin
must we now aim at . . . . .
Do you sleep, Hagen, my son?

HAGEN: I help him already ruin to seek.

ALBERIC: The golden round—
the ring—we must arrive at.
A woman wise
loves him well as her life.
Rendered he ever
the river maidens
—by whose wiles amid
the waves I was mocked—
the ring, obeying her counsel,
for ever gone were the gold,
and no art could earn it again.
Then, without staying,
strive for the ring.
You were made stubborn
and sturdy,
that you should help
my hate against heroes.
You want strength indeed
to vanquish the worm:
*that* alone the Volsung might work.
Yet potent hatred
I planted, Hagen,
in you, my avenger:—
to win me the ring,
you'll vanquish Volsung and Wotan,
Swear to me, Hagen, my son?
(*From this point an increasing gloom hides Hagen and Alberic. At the same time day begins to dawn on the Rhine.*)

---

HAGEN: Den Ring soll ich haben: harre in Ruh'!

ALBERICH: Schwör'st du mir's, Hagen, mein Held?

HAGEN: Mir selbst schwör' ich's: schweige die Sorge!

ALBERICH: (*wie er allmälig immer mehr dem Blicke entschwindet, wird auch seine Stimme immer unvernehmbarer.*) Sei treu, Hagen, mein Sohn!
Trauter Helde, sei treu!
Sei treu!—treu!
(*Alberich ist gänzlich verschwunden. Hagen, der unverrückt in seiner Stellung verblieben, blickt regungslos und starren Auges nach dem Rheine hin. Die Sonne geht auf und spiegelt sich in der Fluth.*)
(*Siegfried tritt plötzlich, dicht am Ufer, hinter einem Busche hervor. Er ist in seiner eigenen Gestalt; nur den Tarnhelm hat er noch auf dem Haupte: er zieht ihn ab, und hängt ihn in den Gürtel.*)

SIEGFRIED: Hoiho! Hagen!
Müder Mann!
Siehst du mich kommen?

HAGEN: (*gemächlich sich erhebend.*) Heil! Siegfried!
Geschwinder Helde!
Wo brausest du her?

SIEGFRIED: Von Brünnhildenstein;
dort zog ich den Athem ein,
mit dem ich jetzt dich rief:
so schnell war meine Fahrt!
Langsamer folgt mir ein Paar:
Zu Schiff gelangt das her.

HAGEN: So zwangst du Brünnhild'!

SIEGFRIED: Wacht Gutrune?

HAGEN: Hoiho! Gutrune!
Komm heraus!
Siegfried ist da:
Was säum'st du d'rin?

SIEGFRIED: (*zur Halle sich wendend.*) Euch beiden meld' ich, wie ich Brünnhild' band.
(*Gutrune tritt ihnen unter der Halle entgegen.*)

SIEGFRIED: Heiss' mich willkommen, Gibichskind!
Ein guter Bote bin ich dir.

GUTRUNE: Freia grüsse dich zu aller Frauen Ehre!

SIEGFRIED: Frei und hold sei nur mir Frohen: zum Weib gewann ich dich heut'.

GUTRUNE: So folgt Brünnhild' meinem Bruder?

SIEGFRIED: Leicht ward die Frau ihm gefreit.

GUTRUNE: Sengte das Feuer ihn nicht?

---

HAGEN: I'll lay hands on the ring: happily rest.

ALBERIC: Swear to me, Hagen, my hope.

HAGEN: My soul swears it: cease your sorrow.

ALBERIC: (*as he gradually disappears from view, his voice becoming fainter and fainter.*) Be true, Hagen, my son.
Trusty hero, be true.
Be true!—true!
(*He vanishes completely. Hagen, who has persistently remained in his place, gazes motionless and with fixed eyes upon the Rhine.*)
(*The sun rises and is mirrored in the waters.*)
(*Siegfried suddenly comes forward from behind a bush on the river bank. He is in his own semblance, but still wears the Tarnhelm; this he now doffs and hangs in his belt.*)

SIEGFRIED: Hoiho!
Hagen!
sleepy soul!
See who is coming!

HAGEN: (*indolently rising.*) Hey, Siegfried!
You speedy hero!
When did your brawl here?

SIEGFRIED: From Brünnhilde's rock.
It was there I imbibed the breath
with which I waked you:
so rapid was my flight.
Slower will follow the pair;
by boat they slip up here.

HAGEN: Has mastered Brünnhilde?

SIEGFRIED: Wakes Gutrune yet?

HAGEN: Hoiho!
Gutrune!
Come without!
Siegfried is here:
why stay in house?

SIEGFRIED: (*turning to the hall.*) I took Brünnhilde,
and how—I'll tell you.
(*Gutrune enters from the hall and meets him.*)

SIEGFRIED: Now welcome make me,
Gibich-maid!
You have
A goodly herald in me.

GUTRUNE: Freia gives you joy, by every fair one honored.

SIEGFRIED: Freely deign to show me favor:
I've won you as wife today.

GUTRUNE: Does Brünnhilde fare with my brother?

SIEGFRIED: Light was his wooing, I believe.

GUTRUNE: Has he no wound from the fire?

SIEGFRIED: Ihn hätt' es auch nicht versehrt;
doch ich durchschritt es für ihn,
da dich ich wollt' erwerben.

GUTRUNE: Doch dich hat es verschont?

SIEGFRIED: Mich freute die schwebende Brunst.

GUTRUNE: Hielt Brünnhild' dich für Gunther?

SIEGFRIED: Ihm glich ich auf ein Haar:
der Tarnhelm wirkte das,
wie Hagen tüchtig es wies.

HAGEN: Dir gab ich guten Rath.

GUTRUNE: So zwang'st du das kühne Weib?

SIEGFRIED: Sie wich Gunther's Kraft.

GUTRUNE: Und vermählte sie sich dir?

SIEGFRIED: Ihrem Mann gehorchte Brünnhild'
eine ville bräutliche Nacht.

GUTRUNE: Als ihr Mann doch galtest du?

SIEGFRIED: Bei Gutrune weilte Siegfried.

GUTRUNE: Doch zur Seite war ihm Brünnhild'?

SIEGFRIED: (auf sein Schwert deutend). Zwischen Ost und West der Nord:
so nah war Brünnhild' ihm fern.

GUTRUNE: Wie empfing sie nun Gunther von dir?

SIEGFRIED: Durch des Feuers verlöschende Lohe
im Frühnebel vom Felsen
folgte sie mir zu Thal;
dem Strande nah,
flugs die Stelle
tauschte Gunther mit mir:
durch des Geschmeides Tugend
wünsch' ich mich schnell hieher.
Ein starker Wind nun treibt
die Trauten den Rhein herauf:
d'rum rüstet jetzt den Empfang!

GUTRUNE: Siegfried, mächtigster Mann:
wie fasst mich Furcht vor dir!

HAGEN: (von der Höhe im Hintergrunde den Fluss hinas spähend).
In der Ferne seh' ich ein Segel.

SIEGFRIED: So sagt dem Boten Dank!

GUTRUNE: Lasst sie uns hold empfangen,
dass heiter sie und gern hier weile!
Du Hagen! minnig
rufe die Mannen
nach Gibich's Hof zur Hochzeit!
Frohe Frauen
ruf' ich zum Fest:
der Freudigen folgen sie gern.
(Nach der Halle schreitend, zu Siegfried.)
Rastest du, schlimmer Held?

---

SIEGFRIED: It would not even have burned him,
but I in his stead went over.
that I might gain my Gutrune.

GUTRUNE: Then you have not been touched?

SIEGFRIED: I gleefully trampled the blaze.

GUTRUNE: Did Brünnhilde deem you Gunther?

SIEGFRIED: We differed not a hair.
The Tarnhelm worked all that,
as Hagen told me it would.

HAGEN: I gave you a good account.

GUTRUNE: Did you conquer the maid so fierce?

SIEGFRIED: She felt—Gunther's might.

GUTRUNE: Was she married then to you?

SIEGFRIED: To her mate submitted Brünnhilde
all the night of bridal till morn.

GUTRUNE: And she gave herself to you?

SIEGFRIED: For Gutrune Siegfried waited.

GUTRUNE: By his side, though, was Brünnhilde?

SIEGFRIED: (pointing to his sword.) Between the East and West lies North:
so near was Brünnhilde to me.

GUTRUNE: How then made Gunther the bride his own?

SIEGFRIED: In the fiery surges consuming
at first dawn she set foot
and followed me toward the vale.
When shore was near,
Flash!—in shape
reversed were Gunther and I.
Then by the helmet's virtue,
wishing, I flew here.
By hastening wind impelled,
the pair up the river come.
Make ready then to receive.

GUTRUNE: Siegfried, marvellous man!
What fear I feel of you!

HAGEN: (looking down on the river from the heights at back.)
From afar approaches a pinnace.

SIEGFRIED: Then praise its herald here.

GUTRUNE: Let us give her hearty welcome,
that haply she may bide here gladly.
You Hagen, please
to summon the people
to Gibich's walls for wedding.
Mirthful maids
shall be brought by me;
my merriment meetly they'll join.
(Going towards the hall, to Siegfried.)
Would you sleep, naughty guest?

---

SIEGFRIED: Dir zu helfen ruh' ich aus.
(Er folgt ihr. Beide gehen in die Halle ab.)

HAGEN: (auf der Anhöhe stehend, stösst, der Landseite zugewendet, mit aller Kraft in ein grosses Stierhorn.) Hoiho! Hoiho! Hoiho!
Ihr Gibichs Mannen,
machet euch auf!
Wehe! Wehe!
Waffen! Waffen!
Waffen durch's Land!
gute Waffen!
Starke Waffen,
scharf zum Streit,
Noth! Noth ist da!
Noth! Wehe! Wehe!
Hoiho! Hoiho! Hoiho!
(Er bläst abermals. Aus verschiedenen Gengenden vom Lande her antworten Heerhörner. Von den Höhen und aus dem Thale stürmen in Hast und Eile gewaffnete Mannen herbei.)

DIE MANNEN: (erst einzeine, dann immer mehr zusammen.)
Was tos't das Horn?
was ruft es zu Heer?
Wir kommen mit Wehr,
wir kommen mit Waffen;
mit starken Waffen,
mit scharfer Wehr!
Hoiho! Hoiho!
Hagen! Hagen!
Welche Noth ist da?
Welcher Feind ist nah'?
Wer giebt uns Streit?
Ist Gunther in Noth?

HAGEN: (von der Anhöhe herab.)
Rüstet euch wohl
und rastet nicht;
Gunther sollt ihr empfah'n:
ein Weib hat der gefreit.

DIE MANNEN: Drohet ihm Noth?
drängt ihn der Feind?

HAGEN: Ein freisliches Weib
führt er heim!

DIE MANNEN: Ihm folgen der Magen
feindliche Mannen?

HAGEN: Einsam fährt er:
keiner folgt.

DIE MANNEN: So bestand er die Noth,
bestand den Kampf?

HAGEN: Der Wurmtödter
wehrte der Noth:
Siegfried, der Held,
der schur' ihm Heil.

DIE MANNEN: Was soll ihm das Heer nun noch helfen?

HAGEN: Starke Stiere
sollt ihr schlachten:
am Weihstein fliesse
Wotan ihr Blut.

---

SIEGFRIED: It gives me rest helping you.
(He follows her. Exeunt both into the hall.)

HAGEN: (standing on the height, turns landwards and blows with all his strength a great cattle-horn.) Hoiho! Hoiho! Hoiho!
You men of Gibich
gather yourselves!
Waken!
waken!
Weapons!
weapons!
weapons are out!
Goodly weapons,
sturdy weapons
sharp for strife.
Woe!
woe is here!
Woe!
Waken!
Waken!
Hoiho!
Hoiho!
Hoiho!
(He continues to blow his cattle-horn. Other horns answer it from different directions in the land. From the heights and valleys armed men rush hastily on.)

THE VASSALS: (first a few at a time, then more together.) Why brays the horn?
What summons the hosts?
We come with all ward—
we come with all weapons—
Hagen!
Hagen!
Hoiho!
Hoiho!
What's the peril here?
Will the foe appear?
Who gives us fight?
Is Gunther in need?

HAGEN: (from the heights.) Trim yourselves up
and tarry not;
greet your chief to the full;
Gunther has found a wife.

THE VASSALS: What is his need?
where is his foe?

HAGEN: A fiery wife
fares at his heels.

THE VASSALS: By furious mass of foes is menaced?

HAGEN: No one follows:
he fares alone,

THE VASSALS: Has he triumphed over ill?
Has he triumphed in war?

HAGEN: The Worm-killer
was his defense!
Siegfried the hero held
his safety.

THE VASSALS: Then how should our host further help him?

HAGEN: Bulls full sturdy
shall you slaughter,
and wash the altar
of Wotan in blood.

**DIE MANNEN:** Was, Hagen, was heisst du uns dann?

**THE VASSALS:** Why, Hagen, what do you bid us then?

**HAGEN:** Einen Eber fällen sollt ihr für Froh; einen stämmigen Bock stechen für Donner; Schafe aber schlachtet für Fricka, Dass gute Ehe sie gebe!

**HAGEN:** Be a boar then further struck down for Froh, and a stalwart he-goat smitten for Donner; sheep, moreover, slaughter for Fricka, that well she may aid in the wedding.

**DIE MANNEN:** (*mit immer mehr ausbrechender Heiterkeit.*) Schlugen wir Thiere, was schaffen wir dann?

**THE VASSALS:** (*with continually increasing mirth.*) When we have done it, then what else is there?

**HAGEN:** Das Trinkhorn nehm't von trauten Frau'n, mit Meth und Wein wonnig gefüllt.

**HAGEN:** Take the drink-horn from fair damsels, with wine and mead mirthfully filled.

**DIE MANNEN:** Das Horn in der Hand, Wie halten wir es dann?

**THE VASSALS:** The drink-horn in hand, what have we then to do?

**HAGEN:** Rüstig gezecht bis der Rausch euch zähmt alles den Göttern zu Ehren, dass gute Ehe sie geben!

**HAGEN:** Revel away till you wreck your wits: All for goodwill of the AEsir, to win their aid for the wedding.

**DIE MANNEN:** (*in ein schallendes Gelächter ausbrechend.*) Gross Glück und Heil lacht nun dem Rhein, da der grimme Hagen so lustig mag sein! Der Hage-Dorn sticht nun nicht mehr: zum Hochzeitrufer ward er bestellt.

**THE VASSALS:** (*bursting out into a ringing peal of laughter.*) Good gain and hap lights on the Rhine, if Hagen the grim one to laughter incline. The Hardy Thorn pricks now no more; to help at weddings henceforth is his part.

**HAGEN:** (*der immer sehr ernst geblieben.*) Nun lasst das Lachen, müth'ge Mannen! Empfangt Gunther's Braut: Brünnhilde naht dort mit ihm. (*Er ist herabgestiegen und unter die Mannen getreten.*) Hold seid der Herrin, helfet ihr treu: traf sie ein Leid, rasch seid zur Rache! (*Gunther und Brünnhilde sind im Nachen angekommen Einige der Mannen springen in den Fluss, und ziehen den Kahn an das Land. Während Gunther Brünnhilde an das Ufer geleitet, schlagen die Mannen jauchzend an die Waffen. Hagen steht zur Seite im Hintergrunde.*)

**HAGEN:** (*who has remained quite serious.*) Now leave off laughter, valiant vassals, Receive Gunther's bride: Brünnhilde approaches with him. (*He has descended and joined the vassals.*) Love well your lady; lend her your aid: if she is wrong quickly requite it, (*Gunther and Brünnhilde arrive in the boat. Some of the men spring into the water and drag the boat ashore. While Gunther conducts Brünnhilde ashore the vassals shout and clash their weapons. Hagen stands aside at back.*)

**DIE MANNEN:** Heil! Heil! Willkommen! Willkommen! Heil dir, Gunther! Heil deiner Braut!

**THE VASSALS:** Hail! hail! Welcome! welcome! Hail, O Gunther! Hail to your bride!

**GUNTHER:** (*Brünnhilde an der Hand aus dem Kahn geleitend.*) Brünnhilde, die hehrste Frau, bring' ich euch her zum Rhein: ein edleres Weib ward nie gewonnen! Der Gibichungen Geschlecht, gaben die Götter ihm Gunst, zum höchsten Ruhm rag' es nun auf!

**GUNTHER:** (*leading Brünnhilde by the hand from the boat.*) Brünnhilde, the rarest dame borne by the Rhine to you. There never was won a nobler woman. The Gibichungs as a race gained often goods from the gods; to high renown now will they rise.

**DIE MANNEN:** (*an die Waffen schlagend.*) Heil! Heil dir, Gunther! Glücklicher Gibichung! (*Brünnhilde bleich, und mit zu Boden gesenktem Blicke, folgt Gunther, der sie zur Halle führt, aus welcher jetzt Siegfried und Gutrune, von Frauen begleitet, heraustreten.*)

**THE VASSALS:** (*clashing their weapons.*) Hail to you, glorious Gibichung! (*Brünnhilde, pale and with eyes fixed on the ground, follows Gunther, who leads her towards the hall, from which issue forth Siegfried and Gutrune attended by a train of women.*)

**GUNTHER:** (*mit Brünnhilde vor der Halle anhaltend.*) Gegrüsst sei, theurer Held! gegrüsst, holde Schwester! Dich seh' ich froh zur Seite ihm, der zum Weib dich gewann. Zwei selige Paare seh' ich hier prangen: Brünnhilde—und Gunther, Gutrune—und Siegfried! (*Brünnhilde erschrickt, schlägt die Augen auf, und erblickt Siegfried; sie lässt Gunther's Hand fahren, geht heftig bewegt einen Schritt auf Siegfried zu, weicht entsetzt zurück, und heftet starr den Blick auf ihn.—Alle sind sehr betroffen.*)

**GUNTHER:** (*pausing with Brünnhilde before the hall.*) All hail, my hero bold! All hail, beauteous sister! I see you gladly beside him by whom as wife you're won. Two happy couples here have encountered; Brünnhilde and Gunther, Gutrune and Siegfried! (*Brünnhilde, startled, raises her eyes and perceives Siegfried; she drops Gunther's hand, advances one step towards Siegfried, then recoils in horror and fixes her eyes glaring upon him.—All the others are wonderstruck.*)

**MANNEN UND FRAUEN:** Was ist ihr?

**MEN AND WOMEN:** What ails her? Is she distraught?

**SIEGFRIED:** (*geht ruhig einige Schritte auf Brünnhilde zu.*) Was müh't Brünnhilde's Blick?

**SIEGFRIED:** (*goes a few steps nearer to Brünnhilde.*) What clouds Brünnhilde's brow?

**BRÜNNHILDE:** (*kaum ihrer mächtig*). Siegfried . . . hier . . .! Gutrune !

**BRÜNNHILDE:** (*almost fainting.*) Siegfried? . . . here? . . . Gutrune!

**SIEGFRIED:** Gunther's milde Schwester, mir vermählt, wie Gunther du.

**SIEGFRIED:** Gunther's mild-eyed sister, mate to me as you to him.

**BRÜNNHILDE:** Ich . . . Gunther . . . ? du lüg'st!— Mir schwindet das Licht . (*Sie droht umzusinken: Siegfried, ihr zunächst stüzt sie.*)

**BRÜNNHILDE:** I? . . . Gunther? . . . you lie! I see not the light (*She is about to fall: Siegfried, who is nearest, supports her.*)

**BRÜNNHILDE:** (*matt und leise in Siegfried's Arme.*) Siegfried . . . kennt mich nicht?

**BRÜNNHILDE:** (*faintly and softly, in Siegfried's arms.*) Siegfried . . . knows me not!

**SIEGFRIED:** Gunther, deinem Weib ist übel! (*Gunther tritt hinau.*) Erwache, Frau! hier ist dein Gatte (*Indem Siegfried auf Gunther mit dem Finger deutet erkennt an diesem Brünnhilde den Ring.*)

**SIEGFRIED:** Gunther, see, your wife is fainting. (*Gunther approaches.*) Awaken, dame! Here stands your husband. (*As Siegfried points to Gunther, Brünnhilde perceives the ring on his finger.*)

**BRÜNNHILDE:** (*mit furchtbarer Heftigkeit aufschreckend.*) Ha!— der Ring . . . an seiner Hand! Er . . . Siegfried?

**BRÜNNHILDE:** (*starting with fearful impetuosity.*) Ha! That Ring upon his hand! His—? Siegfried's—?

**MANNEN UND FRAUEN:** Was ist?

**THE VASSALS:** What is it?

**HAGEN:** (*aus dem Hintergrunde unter die Mannen tretend.*) Jetzt merket klug, was die Frau euch klagt!

**HAGEN:** (*advancing from the back among the men.*) Now well attend to the woman's tale.

**BRÜNNHILDE:** (*sich ermannend, indem sie die schrecklichste Aufregung gewaltsam zurückhält.*) Einen Ring sah ich

**BRÜNNHILDE:** (*struggling to command herself and repressing with great effort her terrific storm of emotion.*) On your hand there

an deiner Hand:—
nicht dir gehört er,
ihn entriss mir
(*auf Gunther deutend*)
—dieser Mann!
Wie mochtest von ihm
den Ring du empfah'n?

SIEGFRIED: (*aufmerksam den Ring an seiner Hand betrachtend.*) Den Ring empfing ich nicht von ihm.

BRÜNNHILDE: (*zu Gunther.*) Nahm'st du von mir den Ring, durch den ich dir vermählt; so melde ihm dein Recht, ford're zurück das Pfand!

GUNTHER: (*in grosser Verwirrung.*) Den Ring?—ich gab ihm keinen: doch kennst du ihn auch gut?

BRÜNNHILDE: Wo bärgest du den Ring, den du von mir erbeutet? (*Gunther schweigt in höchster Betroffenheit.*)

BRÜNNHILDE: (*wüthend auffahrend.*) Ha!—Dieser war es, der mir den Ring entriss: Siegfried, der trugvolle Dieb!

SIEGFRIED: (*der über der Betrachtung des Ringes in fernes Sinnen entruckt war.*) Von keinem Weib kam mir der Reif; noch war's ein Weib, dem ich ihn abgewann: genau erkenn' ich des Kampfes Lohn, den vor Neidhöhl' einst ich bestand, als den starken Wurm ich erschlug

HAGEN: (*zwischen sie tretend.*) Brünnhilde, kühne Frau! kennst du genau den Ring? Ist's der, den du Gunther'n gab'st, so ist er sein,— und Siegfried gewann ihn durch Trug den der Treulose büssen sollt'!

BRÜNNHILDE: (*in furchtbarstem Schmerz aufschreiend.*) Betrug! Betrug! Schändlichster Betrug! Verrath! Verrath— Wie noch nie er gerächt!

GUTRUNE: Betrug?

MANNEN UND FRAUEN: An wem Verrath?

BRÜNNHILDE: Heilige Götter! himmlische Lenker! Rauntet ihr diess in eurem Rath? Lehrt ihr mich Leiden Wie keiner sie litt? Schuft ihr mir Schmach wie nie sie geschmerzt? Rathet nun Rache wie nie sie geras't! Zündet mir Zorn wie nie er gezähmt!

---

I saw the ring: you hold it wrong. It was ravished (*Pointing to Gunther.*) —by this man! What means did you use to gain the ring?

SIEGFRIED: (*attentively inspecting the ring on his finger.*) That ring I gained, but not from him.

BRÜNNHILDE: (*to Gunther.*) You tore the ring from me with which you wed me, then make him feel your power: get back the pledge again.

GUNTHER: (*greatly perplexed.*) The ring? I gave him nothing: but do you know our guest?

BRÜNNHILDE: Where do you guard the ring that you made me give you? (*Gunther, much puzzled, remains silent.*)

BRÜNNHILDE: (*bursting out frantically.*) Ha! it was this one that wrenched the ring from me Siegfried, the treacherous thief.

SIEGFRIED: (*who is quite absorbed in contemplating the ring.*) No girl, I believe, gave me that ring; Nor woman it was from whom I won the prize. This hoop I bear as the battle prize, when at Hate Cave once I did strive and destroyed the dragon so strong.

HAGEN: (*coming between them.*) Brünnhilde, noble dame, Do you know this ring full well? If it is that that Gunther gained, he owns it still,— and Siegfried has won it by trick, which the traitor should pay for straight.

BRÜNNHILDE: (*screaming out in the most terrible anguish.*) By trick! By trick! Shamefullest of tricks! Deceit! deceit! Worse than thought can conceive!

GUTRUNE: Deceit!

THE VASSALS: What was the trick?

BRÜNNHILDE: Holy gods! Heavenly guardians! Was this indeed your whispered will? Grief you give such as none ever grasped, shape me a shame no mortal has shared? Vouchsafe revenge then like none ever viewed, rouse me to wrath such as none can arrest!

---

Heisset Brünnhilde ihr Herz zu zerbrechen, den zu zertrümmern, der sie betrog!

GUNTHER: Brünnhilde, Gemahlin! Mäss'ge dich!

BRÜNNHILDE: Weich' fern, Verräther! Selbst-verrath'ner! Wisset denn Alle! nicht—ihm— dem Manne dort bin ich vermählt.

MANNEN UND FRAUEN: Siegfried? Gutrune's Gemahl?

BRÜNNHILDE: Er zwang mir Lust und Liebe ab.

SIEGFRIED: Achtest du so der eig'nen Ehre? Die Zunge, die sie lästert, muss ich der Lüge sie zeihen?— Hört, ob ich Treue brach! Blutbrüderschaft hab' ich Gunther geschworen: Nothung, mein werthes Schwert, wahrte der Treue Eid; mich trennte seine Schärfe von diesem traurigen Weib.

BRÜNNHILDE: Du listiger Held, sieh' wie du lüg'st! wie auf dein Schwert du schlecht dich beruf'st! Wohl kenn' ich die Schärfe, doch kenn' auch die Scheide, darin so wonnig ruht' an der Wand Nothung, der treue Freund, als die Traute sein Herr sich gewann.

DIE MANNEN: (*in lebhafter Entrüstung zusammentretend.*) Wie? brach er die Treue! trübte er Gunther's Ehre?

GUNTHER: Geschändet wär' ich, schmählich bewahrt, gäb'st du die Rede nicht ihr zurück!

GUTRUNE: Treulos, Siegfried, sannest du Trug? Bezeuge, dass falsch Jene dich zeiht!

DIE MANNEN: Reinige dich, bist du im Recht: schweige die Klage, schwöre den Eid!

SIEGFRIED: Schweig' ich die Klage, schwör' ich den Eid: wer von euch wagt seine Waffe daran?

HAGEN: Meines Speeres Spitze wag' ich daran: sie wahr' in Ehren den Eid! (*Die Mannen schliessen einen Ring um Siegfried; Hagen hält diesem die Spitze seines Speeres hin: Siegfried legt zwei Finger seiner rechten Hand darauf.*) Animato

---

Here let Brünnhilde's heart straight be broken if he who wronged her may be wrecked.

GUNTHER: Brünnhilde! my consort, calm yourself!

BRÜNNHILDE: Away, traitor! You've betrayed too. People all, hearken: Not—he— that man yonder was wed to me.

THE VASSALS: Siegfried? Gutrune's mate?

BRÜNNHILDE: He forced delights of love from me.

SIEGFRIED: Are you so careless of your honor? The lips, then, that revile it— must I convict them of lying? Hear whether I broke truth! I and Gunther have sworn to blood-brotherhood: "Needful," my good sword, guarded the oath intact: its edge did keep me sundered from this ill-omened bride.

BRÜNNHILDE: You lord of deceit, see how you lie! Your sword will serve little as a proof! Its sharpness is well known to me, but known too its scabbard, encased in which reposed on the wall "Needful," the trusty friend, when his master did win a true love.

THE VASSALS: (*crowding together in quick anger.*) What! Has he been traitor? Trifled with Gunther's honor?

GUNTHER: Disgrace overtakes me, grossest contempt, if you do not reply to her plea.

GUTRUNE: Faithless—Siegfried, say, are you false? Attest as untrue what she has told.

THE VASSALS: Right yourself straight, if you have been wronged. Stay her upbraidings! Swear us the oath.

SIEGFRIED: Should I refute her, Swearing the oath, which of you war-men will lend his weapon?

HAGEN: My unsullied spear-point well will I lend to ward in honor the oath. (*The Vassals make a ring around Siegfried and Gunther. Hagen holds out his spear; Siegfried lays two fingers of his right hand on its point.*)

SIEGFRIED: Helle Wehr! Heilige Waffe!
Hilf meinem ewigen Eide!
Beides Speeres Spitze sprech' ich den Eid: Spitze, achte des Spruchs!
Wo Schar fe mich schneidet, schneide du mich., wo der Tod mich soll treffen, treffe du mich: klagte das Weib dort wahr, brach ich dem Bruder den Eid!

BRÜNNHILDE: Helle Wehr! Heilige Waffe!
Hilf meinem ewigen Eide!
Bei des Speeres Spitze sprech ich dem Eid:
Spitze achte des Spruchs!
Ich weihe deine Wucht dass sie ihn werfe!
Deine Schärfe segne ich, dass sie ihn schneide!
Denn brach seine Eide er all, schwur Meineid jetzt dieser Mann.

DIE MANNEN: (im höchsten Aufruhr.) Hilf, Donner!
tose dein Wetter,
zu schweigen die wüthende Schmach!

SIEGFRIED: Gunther, wehr' deinem Weibe,
das schamlos Schande dir lügt!
Gönn't ihr Weil' und Ruh', der wilden Felsen-Frau,
dass ihre freche Wuth sich lege, die eines Unhold's arge List wider uns Alle erregt!—
Ihr Mannen, kehret euch ab, lasst das Weiber-Gekeif'!
Als Zage weichen wir gern, gilt es mit Zungen dem Streit.
(Dicht zu Gunther tretend.)
Glaub,' mehr zürnt es mich als dich,
Dass schlecht ich sie getäuscht: der Tarnhelm, dünkt mich fast, hat halb mich nur gehehlt.
Doch Frauengroll friedet sich bald:
dass dir ich es gewann dankt gewiss noch das Weib.
(Er wendet sich wieder zu den Mannen.)
Munter, ihr Mannen!
folgt mir zum Mahl!
Froh zur Hochzeit helfet, ihr Frau'n!—
Wonnige Lust lache nun auf:
in Hof und Hain heiter vor Allen sollt ihr heute mich seh'n.
Wen die Minne freut, meinem frohen Muthe thu' es der Glückliche gleich!
(Er schlingt in ausgelassenem Uebermuthe seinen Arm um Gutrune, und zieht sie mit sich in die Halle; die Mannen und Frauen folgen ihm nach.)
(Brünnhilde, Gunther, und Hagen bleiben zurück. Gunther hat

SIEGFRIED: Spear of war, hallowed weapon!
Protect my oath from dishonor!
On this spotless spearhead is my oath
Spearpoint, aid my speech!
Where steel can strike me, strike at me; wherever death can be dealt me, deal it to me if she is really wronged, if I have injured my friend!

BRÜNNHILDE: Spear of war! Hallowed weapon!
Protect my oath from dishonor!
On this spotless spearhead I speak an oath: Spearpoint, aid my speech!
I sanctify your strength to his destruction!
And I bless your blade withal that it may blight him!
For broken are all of his oaths, and now he proves perjured.

THE VASSALS: (in the greatest commotion.) Help, Donner!
down with your tempest,
to silence this terrible shame.

SIEGFRIED: Gunther, look to your lady, who shapes shame with her lies.
Give her time and rest, the tameless mountain maid, until her mind's disturbance slackens
which by some demon's deadly spite
has been drawn down on us all.
You vassals, scatter yourselves, leave the women to scold!
As cowards well will we act if it is a contest of words.
(He goes close up to Gunther.)
Troth! it cuts me more than you, that ill I did the trick;
the Tarnhelm, I suspect, has hid me only half.
But woman's ire wanes apace:
that I won her for you, one day she'll thank you, I think.
(Turning again to the men.)
Frolic, good fellows!
move to the feast!
Make the marriage merry, maidens!
Filled with delight, laugh as you may.
In fort and field I am foremost among you in the frolic.
He whom love has blessed, let my blythesome laughter move him to join in my joy.
(In exuberant joy he puts his arm round Gutrune and draws her into the ball with him. The Men and Women follow.)
(Brünnhilde, Gunther, and Hagen remain behind.—Gunther has seated himself apart, with

sich, in tiefer Scham und furchtbarer Verstimmung, mit verhülltem Gesicht abseits niedergesetzt.)

BRÜNNHILDE: (im Vordergrunde stehend und vor sich hin starrend.) Welches Unhold's List liegt hier verhohlen?
Welches Zaubrer's Rath regte diess auf?
Wo ist nun mein Wissen gegen dieses Wirrsal?
Wo sind meine Runen? gegen diess Räthsel?
Ach Jammer! Jammer!
Weh'! ach Weh'!
All mein Wissen wies ich ihm zu:
In seiner Macht hält er die Magd;
in seiner Banden hält er die Beute,
die, jamme und ob ihrer Schmach, jauchzend der Reiche verschenkt!—
Wer biete mir nun das Schwert, mit dem ich die Bande zerschnitt'?

HAGEN: (dicht an sie horantretend.) Vert aue mir betrog'ne Frau!
Wer dich verrieth, das räche ich.

BRÜNNHILDE: An wem?

HAGEN: An Siegfried, der dich betrog.

BRÜNNHILDE: An Siegfried? .. du?
(Sie lacht bitter)
Ein einz'ger Blick seines blitzenden Auges
—das selbst durch die Lügengestalt leuchtend strahlte zu mir—
deinen besten Muth machte erbangen!

HAGEN: Doch meinem Speere spart' ihn sein Meineid?

BRÜNNHILDE: Eid und Meineid—müss'ge Acht!
Nach Stärk'rem späh', deinen Speer zu waffnen, willst du den Stärksten besteh'n!

HAGEN: Wohl kenn' ich Siegfried's siegende Kraft,
wie schwer im Kampf er zu fällen;
d'rum raune nun du mir guten Rath, wie doch der Recke mir wich'?

BRÜNNHILDE: O Undank; schändlichster Lohn!
Nicht eine Kunst war mir bekannt,
die zum Heil nicht half seinem Leib'!
Unwissend zähmt' ihn mein Zauberspiel, das ihn nun vor Wunden gewahrt.

covered face in deep shame and depression.)

BRÜNNHILDE: (standing in the foreground, gazes vacantly before her.) What infernal craft can be hidden here?
What magician's rod raised up this storm?
Where now my wisdom against this bewitchment?
What can all my runes do against this riddle?
Ah sorrow! sorrow!
Woe's me! Woe's me!
He has won all wisdom from me!
I am his maid, held by his might;
I am his booty, held in his bondage,
and, languished with shame and woe,
lightly he gives me away.
Whose sword shall I have to beg, with which I may sever my bonds?

HAGEN: (coming close up to her.)
Have trust in me, betrayed dame:
and I'll wreak revenge for your wrongs.

BRÜNNHILDE: On whom?

HAGEN: On Siegfried, who has betrayed.

BRÜNNHILDE: On Siegfried? you?
(She laughs bitterly.)
One angry glance of his glittering eyeball—
that, even through his fraudulent shape
fell unshadowed on me,
would subdue your most mettlesome daring!

HAGEN: His falsehood speeds my spear to his felling.

BRÜNNHILDE: Oath and falsehood,
futile to aid!
Find stronger spells to inspire your weapon, when it would strike at such strength!

HAGEN: I mind well Siegfried's sovereign might,
he scarce were mastered in battle;
but whisper to me some cunning way to make him weak in my hands.

BRÜNNHILDE: O thankless! shameful return!
Each single art that I once owned did I lend, his life to protect.
Unwitting, magical means I used,
which safely ward him now from wounds.

# Act II, Scene I

**HAGEN:** So kann keine Wehr ihm schaden?

**BRÜNNHILDE:** Im Kampfe nicht:—doch—
träf'st du im Rücken ihn.
Niemals—das wusst' ich—
wich' er dem Feind,
nie reicht' er ihm fliehend den Rücken
an ihm d'rum spart' ich den Segen.

**HAGEN:** Und dort trifft ihn mein Speer! (*Er wendet sich rasch zu Gunther um.*)
Auf, Gunther!
edler Gibichung!
Hier steht dein starkes Weib:
was häng'st du dort in Harm?

**GUNTHER:** (*leidenschaftlich auffahrend.*) O Schmach!
O Schande!
Wehe mir
dem jammervollsten Manne!

**HAGEN:** In Schande liegst du—
läugn' ich das?

**BRÜNNHILDE:** O feiger Mann!
falscher Genoss!
Hinter dem Helden
hehltest du dich,
dass Preise des Ruhmes
er dir erränge!
Tief wohl sank
das theure Geschlecht,
das solche Zagen erzeugt!

**GUNTHER:** (*ausser sich.*) Betrüger ich—und betrogen!
Verräther ich—und verrathen!—
Zermalmt mir das Mark,
zerbrecht mir die Brust!
Hilf, Hagen!
hilf meiner Ehr'!
hilf deiner Mutter,
die dich auch ja gebar!

**HAGEN:** Dir hilft kein Hirn,
dir hilft keine Hand:
dir hilft nur—Siegfried's Tod!

**GUNTHER:** Siegfried's Tod!

**HAGEN:** Nur der sühnt deine Schmach.

**GUNTHER:** (*von Grausen gepackt, vor sich hin starrend*) Blutbrüderschaft
schwuren wir uns!

**HAGEN:** Des Bundes Bruch
sühne nun Blut!

**GUNTHER:** Brach er den Bund?

**HAGEN:** Da er dich verrieth!

**GUNTHER:** Verrieth er mich?

**BRÜNNHILDE:** Dich verrieth er,
und mich verriethet ihr Alle!
Wär' ich gerecht,
alles Blut der Welt
büsste mir nicht eure Schuld!
Doch des Einen Tod
taugt mir für Alle:
Siegfried falle—
zur Sühne für sich und euch!

**HAGEN:** (*nahe zu Gunther gewendet*). Er falle—dir zum Heile!
Ungeheure Macht wird dir,
gewinn'st du von ihm den Ring,
den der Tod ihm nur entreisst.

**GUNTHER:** Brünnhilde's Ring?

**HAGEN:** Des Niblungen Reif.

**GUNTHER:** (*schwer scufzend*). So wär' es Siegfried's Ende!

**HAGEN:** Uns allen frommt sein Tod.

**GUNTHER:** Doch Gutrune, ach!
der ich ihn gönnte:
straften den Gatten wir so,
wie bestünden wir vor ihr?

**BRÜNNHILDE:** (*wild auffahrend.*) Was rieth mir mein Wissen?
was wiesen mich Runen?
Im hiflosen Elend
ahnet mir's hell:
Gutrune heisst der Zauber,
der mir den Gatten entzückt!
Angst treffe sie!

**HAGEN:** (*zu Gunther*) Muss sein Tod sie betrüben,
verhehlt sei ihr die That.
Auf munt'res Jagen
ziehen wir morgen;
der Edle braus't uns voran—
ein Eber bracht' ihn da um.

**GUNTHER UND BRÜNNHILDE:**
So soll es sein!
Siegfried falle:
sühn' er die Schmach
die er mir schuf!
Eid-Treue
hat er getrogen:
mit seinem Blute
büss' er die Schuld!
Allrauner!
rächender Gott!
Schwurwissender
Eideshort!
Wotan! Wotan!
wende dich her!
weise dich schrecklich
heilige Schaar,
hieher zu horchen
dem Racheschwur!

**HAGEN:** So soll es sein!
Siegfried falle:
sterb' er dahin,
der strahlende Held!
Mein ist der Hort,
mir muss er gehören:
entrissen d'rum
sei ihm der Ring!
Alben-Vater!
gefallener Fürst!
Nacht-Hüter!
Niblungen-Herr!
Alberich! Alberich!
achte auf mich!
Weise von neuem
der Niblungen Schaar,
dir zu gehorchen,
des Ringes Herrn!
(*Gunther und Brünnhilde wen-*

---

**HAGEN:** No blade borne in war can harm him?

**BRÜNNHILDE:** In battle, none—yet—
if you strike at his back:—
Never, I well knew
would he retreat
and, flying, turn it to the foeman;
and so no spell did I set there.

**HAGEN:** And there he shall be speared!
(*He turns quickly from Brünnhilde to Gunther.*)
Up, Gunther,
honored Gibichung!
Here stands your stalwart wife:
why hangs your head in grief!

**GUNTHER:** (*rising sorrowfully.*)
O shame!
O sorrow!
Woe to me,
the most distressed of mortals!

**HAGEN:** That shame overwhelms you
well I grant.

**BRÜNNHILDE:** O timid spouse!
treacherous friend!
You were hidden behind the hero,
that valor's reward
his courage should win!
Your lordliest race had sunk
Low when such a faint-heart was formed.

**GUNTHER:** (*bursting out into rage.*) I am betrayed—the betrayer!
I am deceived—the deceiver!
It cuts to my core!
It harrows my heart!
Help, Hagen!
Help for my honor!
help for my mother,
who you also did bear.

**HAGEN:** No head can help,
no hand can help:—nothing
helps but—Siegfried's death!

**GUNTHER:** Siegfried's death!—

**HAGEN:** Nothing else saves you from shame!

**GUNTHER:** (*staring before him horror-struck.*) We swore blood-brotherhood!

**HAGEN:** The broken bond calls for his blood!

**GUNTHER:** He broke the bond?

**HAGEN:** When you were betrayed!

**GUNTHER:** Was I betrayed?

**BRÜNNHILDE:** He betrayed you;
and I'm betrayed too on all sides!
Barely, in truth, could a world of blood
wipe from my mind your offense.
But the death of one
well will condone all.
Siegfried falls
for sins of himself and you.

**HAGEN:** (*turning close to Gunther.*) His falling brings you gain!
Might gigantic would be yours
by merely getting his Ring
which only death can make him surrender.

**GUNTHER:** Brünnhilde's Ring?

**HAGEN:** By Nibelungs it was wrought.

**GUNTHER:** (*sighing deeply.*) Shall this be Siegfried's end then?

**HAGEN:** Aye, all demands his death.

**GUNTHER:** But Gutrune, alas!—
unto him given!—
We slew her glorious spouse,
could we stand before her face?

**BRÜNNHILDE:** (*furiously.*) What gain was my wisdom?
What were my runes good for?
Now hapless and anguished
all I behold!
Gutrune holds the charm
that has beguiled from me my lord
Ill light on her!

**HAGEN:** (*to Gunther.*) Lest his death grieve her deeply
we'll hide from her the deed.
We go tomorrow
merrily hunting;
he'll boldly stray from our band—
and be brought home struck by a boar.

**BRÜNNHILDE AND GUNTHER:** It shall be so!
Siegfried falls!
Soothed be the shame
which he has shaped!
He has broken the oath of brotherhood:
so let his blood
blot out guilt!
All-guiding
god of revenge!
You witness
and lord of oaths!
Wotan!
Wotan!
will you listen?
Was now your awful
hosts unto us,
here let them hark
to our vengeful oath!

**HAGEN:** Thus it shall be!
Siegfried must die:
so perish he
the spirit so high!
Mine is the hoard,
my might shall soon hold it:
so
we must rob him of the ring
Elfin parent,
you deposed prince!
Night-keeper
Nibelung king,
Alberic!
Alberic!
Up to my aid!
Warn all the Nib'lungs
anew of the might:
you are their leader,
the Ring's true lord.

den sich heftig zur Halle. Siegfried und Gutrune (Siegfried mit einen Eichenkranz, Gutrune bunte Blumen auf dem Haupte) treten ihnen, zur Nachfolge auffordernd, am Eingange entgegen. Gunther fasst Brünnhilde bei der Hand, und folgt mit ihr schnell. Hagen bleibt allein zurück.)

(Der Vorhang fällt.)

# ■ DRITTER AUFZUG

## Erste Scene

WOGLINDA, WELLGUNDA UND FLOSSHILDE: Frau Sonne sendet lichte Strahlen, Nacht liegt in der Tiefe.
Einst war sie hell
da heil und hehr des Vaters, Gold noch in ihr glänzte Rheingold, klares Gold!
wie hell du einstens strahltest Einst war sie hell da heil und klares Gold!
wie hell du einstens strahltest, hehrer Stern der Tiefe!
hehrer Stern der Tiefe!
Weialala, weialala, leialeia, walla la, la lei, la la la lei la la la la leila la lei, walla la la la weia la walla la weiala la wallala la la leia leia leia leila la la la

ECHO: (Sie schlagen jauchzend das Wasser) Frau Sonne, sende uns den Helden, der das Gold uns wieder gäbe!
Liess' er es uns dein lichtes Auge neideten dann wir nicht länger!
Rheingold!
Klares Gold, wie froh du dann strahltest, freier Stern der Tiefe! froh du dann strahltest, freier Stern der Tiefe!
(Man hört Siegfried's Horn von der Höhe her.)

WOGLINDA: Ich höre sein Horn.

WELLGUNDA: Der Helde naht.

FLOSSHILDE: Lasst uns berathen! (Sie tauchen schnell in die Fluth.) (Siegfried erscheint auf dem Abhange in vollen Waffen.)

SIEGFRIED: Ein Albe führte mich irr,
dass ich die Fährte verlor:— He, Schelm! in welchem Berg barg'st du so schnell das Wild?

DIE DREI RHEINTÖCHTER: (wieder auftauschend.) Siegfried!

FLOSSHILDE: Was schilt'st du in den Grund?

WELLGUNDA: Welchem Alben bist du gram?

WOGLINDA: Hat dich ein Nicker geneckt?

ALLE DREI: Sag'es uns, Siegfried! sag' es uns!

---

(Gunther and Brünnhilde turn hastily towards the ball. Siegfried and Gutrune (Siegfried wearing a wreath of oak leaves, Gutrune crowned with flowers) meet them at the entrance with their followers. Gunther grasps Brünnhilde by the band and follows with her. Hagen alone remains behind.)

(The curtain falls.)

# ■ ACT III

## Scene I

WOGLINDA, WELLGUNDA and FLOSSHILDE: The sungod sends rays of splendor; Night reigns in the waters.
Once did they beam when brave and bright our father's gold yet glittered in them. Rhinegold, clearest gold!
how brightly once your streamed, Once did they beam when brave and clearest gold!
how brightly once you streamed, beauteous star of waters!
beauteous star of waters!
Weialala, weialala, leialeia, walla la, la lei, la la la lei la la la la leila la lei, walla la la la weia la walla la weiala la wallala la la leia leia leia leila la la la

ECHO: (They joyously splash the water)
Fair sungod, send to us the hero, who again our gold will give us!
If it were ours, your ardent eye no more should we look on with envy!
Rhinegold!
Clearest gold, how gladly would stream then, glorious star of waters! gladly would stream then, glorious star of waters!
(Siegfried's horn is heard on the heights)

WOGLINDA: I hear his horn!

WELLGUNDA: The hero comes.

FLOSSHILDE: Let us take counsel. (they all dive quickly down. Siegfried appears on the cliff in full armor.)

SIEGFRIED: Some imp has tempted me on
until the track I have lost.— Hey, rogue! what gulf in a hillside have you then rent for my game?

THE THREE RHINE-NYMPHS: (rising again.) Siegfried!

FLOSSHILDE: Why do scold you so at the ground?

WELLGUNDA: With what imp are you aggrieved?

WOGLINDA: Are you annoyed by a gnome?

THE THREE: Speak then, Siegfried; speak to us!

---

SIEGFRIED: (sie lächelnd betrachtend.) Entzücktet ihr zu euch den zottigen Gesellen, der mir verschwand? Ist's euer Friedel, euch lustigen Frauen lass' ich ihn gern.
(Die Mädchen lachen laut auf.)

WOGLINDA: Siegfried, was giebst du uns, wenn wir das Wild dir gönnen?

SIEGFRIED: Noch bin ich beutelos: d'rum bittet, was ihr begehrt.

WELLGUNDA: Ein gold'ner Ring ragt dir am Finger—

DIE DREI MÄDCHEN: (zusammen.) den gieb uns!

SIEGFRIED: Einen Riesenwurm erschlug' ich um den Ring. für des schlechten Bären Tatzen böt' ich ihn nun zum Tausch?

WOGLINDA: Bist du so karg?

WELLGUNDA: So geizig beim Kauf?

FLOSSHILDE: Freigebig solltest Frauen du sein.

SIEGFRIED: Verzehrt' ich an euch mein Gut, ders' zürnte mir wohl mein Weib.

FLOSSHILDE: Sie ist wohl schlimm?

WELLGUNDA: Sie schlägt dich wohl?

WOGLINDA: Ihre Hand fühlt schon der Held!
(Sie lachen.)

SIEGFRIED: Nun lacht nur lustig zu! in Harm lass' ich euch doch: denn giert ihr nach dem Ring euch Neckern geb' ich ihn nie.

FLOSSHILDE: So schön!

WELLGUNDA: So stark!

WOGLINDA: So gehrenswerth!

DIE DREI: (zusammen.) Wie Schade, dass er geizig ist!
(Sie lachen und tauchen unter.)

SIEGFRIED: (tiefer in den Grund hinabsteigend.) Was leid' ich doch das karge Lob? Lass' ich so mich schmäh'n?— Kämen sie wieder zum Wasserrand, den Ring könnten sie haben.— He he! ihr munt'ren Wasserminnen! kommt rasch: ich schenk' euch den Ring!

DIE DREI RHEINTÖCHTER: (tauchen wieder auf, und zeigen sich ernst und feierlich.) Behalt' ihn, Held, und wahr' ihn wohl,

---

SIEGFRIED: (looking smilingly at them.) My friend with hairy hide has fled, perchance enticed away by your tricks? If he's your lover I'll willingly leave him, wenches, with you.
(The Nymphs laugh loudly.)

WOGLINDA: Siegfried, what boon will you grant if we give up the booty?

SIEGFRIED: Still I have empty hands. What is it then you would beg?

WELLGUNDA: A golden ring gleams on your finger.

THE THREE NYMPHS: (together.) Give us that.

SIEGFRIED: A terrific worm I slew to gain that ring; and shall it slip my palm to buy the paws of a sorry bear?

WOGLINDA: Are you so mean?

WELLGUNDA: So higgling a man?

FLOSSHILDE: Free-handed mortals fare best with maids.

SIEGFRIED: For wasting my goods on you my wife would be rightly wroth.

FLOSSHILDE: Is she so strict?

WELLGUNDA: She strikes you perhaps?

WOGLINDA: He has felt already her fist! (They laugh.)

SIEGFRIED: Well, make your merry jest! you must be left in grief: fair Nymphs, I'll never yield up the yearned for Ring to you!

FLOSSHILDE: So fair!

WELLGUNDA: So fierce!

WOGLINDA: So meet for love!

THE THREE: (together.) It unfortunate that he's miserly!
(They laugh and dive down.)

SIEGFRIED: (descending more towards the ground.) Is it meet to bear their idle mocks? Must I thus be shamed? If they would show near the shore again I would relinquish the Ring. Hey, hey, merry water-maidens: Arise! I'll give you the Ring!

THE THREE RHINE-NYMPHS: (diving up again now solemn and grave.) Preserve it still and ward it well until the illhap is read

bis du das Unheil räth'st,
das in dem Ring du heg'st.
Froh fühl'st du dich dann,
befrei'n wir dich von dem Fluch.

**SIEGFRIED:** (*gelassen den Ring wieder ansteckend.*) Nun singet was ihr wisst!

**DIE RHEINTÖCHTER:** (*einzeln und zusammen.*) Siegfried! Siegfried! Siegfried!
Schlimmes wissen wir dir.
Zu deinem Unheil
wahr'st du den Ring!
Aus des Rheines Gold
ist der Ring geglüht:
der ihn listig geschmiedet
und schmählich verlor,
der verfluchte ihn,
in fernster Zeit
zu zeugen den Tod
dem, der ihn trüg'.
Wie den Wurm du fälltest,
so fällst auch du,
und heute noch
so heissen wir dir's;
tauschest den Ring du uns nicht,
im tiefen Rhein ihn zu bergen.
Nur seine Fluth
sühnet den Fluch!

**SIEGFRIED:** Ihr listigen Frauen
lass't das sein!
Traut' ich kaum eurem Schmeicheln,
euer Schrecken trügt mich noch
minder

**DIE RHEINTÖCHTER.:** Siegfried!
Siegfred! Wir weisen dich wahr:
weiche! weiche dem Fluch!
Ihn flochten nächtlich
webende Nornen
in des Urgesetzes
ewiges Seil.

**SIEGFRIED:** Mein Schwert zerschwang einen Speer: des Urgesetzes
ewiges Seil,
flochten sie wilde
Flüche hinein,
Nothung zerhaut es den Nornen!
Wohl warnte mich einst
vor dem Fluch ein Wurm,
doch das Fürchten lehrt' er mich
nicht!—
der Welt Erbe
gewann mir ein Ring:
für der Minne Gunst
miss' ich ihn gern—
ich geb' ihn euch, gönnt ihr mir
Gunst,
Doch bedroh't ihr mir Leben und
Leib:
fasste er nicht
eines Finger's Werth—
den Reif entringt ihr mir nicht!
Denn Leben und Leib
—sollt' ohne Lieb'
in der Furcht Bande
bang ich sie fesseln—
Leben und Lieb—
seht!—so
werf' ich sie weit von mir!

that in your Ring lies hid;
full fain then you'll be
if you are freed from the ban.

**SIEGFRIED:** (*quietly replacing the ring on his finger.*) Then sing me what you wish.

**THE RHINE-NYMPHS:** (*severally and together.*) Siegfried! Siegfried! Siegfried!
Sorrow awaits you we know.
To nothing but ill
you ward the Ring.
It was wrought from gold
that once glowed in Rhine:
he who shaped it with labor
and lost it in shame,
laid a curse on it,
to cause that to
all time its possesser
should be slain.
As the Worm has fallen,
you'll fall yourself,
this very day
—we vouch it to you
if you refuse us the Ring
that in the flood we may hide it.
Nothing but this stream
breaks the spell!

**SIEGFRIED:** Untrustworthy sisters,
talk no more!
Scarce I trust your allurements;
and your threats still less can disturb me.

**THE RHINE-NYMPHS:** Siegfried!
Siegfried!
It is truth that we tell—
Turn!
turn from the ban!
The braiding Nornir
wove it by night-time
in their endless rope
of wonderful runes.

**SIEGFRIED:** My sword once splintered a spear:
this woven rope
of wonderful runes,
if they have bound
within it a curse,
"Needful" shall cut for the Nornir!
The Worm of this danger
did tell me once,
but he taught me not how to fear.
The world's wealth
should be won me by a ring:
for a gaze of love
gladly I'd leave it,
I'd let you have it lightly for love.
If you threaten my limbs, though,
and life,
hardly you'll win
from my hand the ring,
even were it not worth a rush.
For limbs and life
—should without love
they be fettered
in fear's strong bonds,
My limbs and my life
see!—so
freely I'd fling away!
(*He has picked up a clod of earth, which he holds up and with the*

(*Er hat eine Erdscholle vom Boden aufgehoben und mit den letzten Worten sie über sein Haupt hinter sich geworfen.*)

**DIE RHEINTÖCHTER:** Kommt, Schwestern! schwindet dem Thoren!
So stark und weise
wähnt er sich,
als gebunden und blind er ist.
Eide schwur er—
und achtet sie nicht;
Runen weiss er—
und räth sie nicht;
ein hehrstes Gut
ward ihm gegönnt—
dass er's verworfen
weiss er nicht:
nur den Ring, der zum Tod ihm
taugt—
den Reif nur will er sich wahren!
Leb' wohl, Siegfried!
Ein stolzes Weib
wird heut' noch dich Argen beerben:
sie beut uns bess'res Gehör
Zu ihr! Zu ihr! Zu ihr!
(*Sie schwimmen singend davon.*)

**SIEGFRIED:** (*sieht ihnen lächelnd nach.*) Im Wasser wie am Lande
lernt' ich nun Weiberart:
wer nicht ihrem Schmeicheln
traut,
den schrecken sie mit Drohen;
wer dem nun kühnlich trotzt,
dem kommt dann ihr Keifen d'ran.
Und doch—
trüg' ich nicht Gutrun' Treu',
der zieren Frauen eine
hätt' ich mir frisch gezähmt!
(*Jagdhornrufe kommen von der Höhe näher: Siegfried antwortet lustig auf seinem Horne.*)
(*Gunther, Hagen und Mannen kommen während des Folgenden von der Höhe herab.*)

**HAGEN:** (*noch auf der Höhe.*) Hoiho!

**SIEGFRIED:** Hoiho!

**DIE MANNEN:** Hoiho! Hoiho!

**HAGEN:** Finden wir endlich
wohin du flog'st?

**SIEGFRIED:** Kommt herab! hier
ist's frisch und kühl.

**HAGEN:** Hier rasten wir
und rüsten das Mahl.
Lasst ruh'n die Beute
und bietet die Schläuche!
(*Jagdbeute wird zu Hauf gelegt; Trinkhörner und Schläuche werden hervorgeholt. Dann lagert sich alles.*)

**HAGEN:** Der uns das Wild verscheucht,
nun sollt' ihr Wunder hören
was Siegfried sich erjagt.

**SIEGFRIED:** (*lachend.*) Schlimm
steht's um mein Mahl:
von eurer Beute
bitt' ich für mich.

**HAGEN:** Du beutelos?

last words, flings behind him.*)

**THE RHINE-NYMPHS:** Come, sisters,
speed from this dullard!
He fancies himself
as fearless and wise
as he truly is trammelled and blind.
He has sworn oaths
and not heeded them;
Runes he knows well
and reads them not.
A noble gift
once did he gain,
that it is wasted
knows he not.
But the ring, which will deal him
death,
that ring he wishes to ward still.
Farewell, Siegfried!
A stately woman
today will inherit your hoop.
Our bidding better she'll do:
to her! to her! to her!
(*They swim away singing.*)

**SIEGFRIED:** (*looks after them smiling.*) Alike on land and water,
women's ways I've learned to
know.
The man who resists their smiles
they seek by threats to frighten.
And when these both are scorned
they bait him with bitter words.
And yet—
were Gutrune not my wife,
I must have promptly captured
one of those pretty maids.
(*Calls of hunting horns approaching are heard on the hills. Siegfried answers gaily on his own horn.*)
(*Gunther, Hagen and Vassels come down the hills during the following.*)

**HAGEN:** (*still on the heights.*) Hoiho!

**SIEGFRIED:** Hoiho!

**VASSALS:** Hoiho! Hoiho!

**HAGEN:** Have we at last then
found where you hide?

**SIEGFRIED:** Come below! Here it
is fresh and cool.

**HAGEN:** It will do to rest
and dress us a meal.
Lay down your booty
and bring out the wine-skins.
(*Game is stacked, skins of wine and drinking horns are produced. All encamp themselves.*)

**HAGEN:** You drove away our quarry,
let's see the wondrous prize then
that Siegfried seized upon.

**SIEGFRIED:** (*laughing.*) It is ill
with my meal;
I must beg
your bags to furnish me,

**HAGEN:** You are bootyless?

SIEGFRIED: Auf Waldjagd zog ich aus,
doch Wasserwild zeigte sich nur;
war ich dazu recht berathen,
drei wilde Wasservögel,
hätt' ich euch gefangen,
die dort auf dem Rhein mir sangen,
erschlagen würd' ich noch heut'.

GUNTHER: (*erschrickt und blickt düster auf Hagen.*)

HAGEN: Das wäre böse Jagd,
wenn den Beutelosen selbst
ein lauernd Wild erlegte!

SIEGFRIED: Mich dürstet!
(*Er hat sich zwischen Hagen und Gunther gelagert; gofüllte Trinkhörner werden ihnen gereicht.*)

HAGEN: Ich hörte sagen, Siegfried,
der Vögel Sanges-Sprache
verstündest du wohl:
so wär' das wahr?

SIEGFRIED: Seit lange acht' ich
des Lallens nicht mehr.
(*Er trinkt und reicht dann sein Horn Gunther.*)
Trink', Gunther! trink'!
dein Bruder bringt es dir.

GUNTHER: (*gedankenvoll und schwermüthig in das Horn blickend.*) Du mischtest matt und bleich:—
dein Blut allein darin!

SIEGFRIED: (*lachend.*) So misch' es mit dem deinen!
(*Er giesst aus Gunther's Horn in das seine, so dass es überläuft.*)
Nun floss gemischtes über:
der Mutter Erde
lass' das ein Labsal sein!

GUNTHER: (*seufzend.*) Du überfroher Held!

SIEGFRIED: (*leise zu Hagen.*) Ihm macht Brünnhilde Müh?

HAGEN: Verstünd' er sie so gut,
wie du der Vögel Sang!

SIEGFRIED: Seit Frauen ich singen hörte,
vergass ich der Vöglein ganz.

HAGEN: Doch einst vernahmst du sie?

SIEGFRIED: Hei! Gunther!
grämlicher Mann!
Dank'st du es mir,
so sing' ich dir Mären
aus meinen jungen Tagen.

GUNTHER: Die hör' ich gern.

HAGEN: So singe, Held!
(*Alle lagern sich nahe um Siegfried, welcher allein aufrecht sitzt, während die andern tiefer gestruckt liegen.*)

SIEGFRIED: Mime hiess
ein mürrischer Zwerg;
in des Neides Zwang
zog er mich auf,
dass einst das Kind,
wann kühn es erwuchs,
einen Wurm ihm fällt im Wald,
der lang' schon hütet' einen Hort.
Er lehrte mich schmieden
und Erze schmelzen:
doch was der Künstler
selbst nicht konnte,
des Lehrling's Muthe
musst' es gelingen—
eines zerschlag'nen Stahles Stücken
neu zu schweissen zum Schwert.
Des Vater's Wehr
fügt' ich mir neu;
nagelfest
schuf ich mir Nothung,
tüchtig zum Kampf
dünkt' er dem Zwerg:
der führte mich nun zum Wald;
dort fäll't ich Fafner, den Wurm.
Jetzt aber merkt
wohl auf die Mär':
Wunder muss ich euch melden.
Von des Wurmes Blut
mir brannten die Finger;
sie führt' ich kühlend zum Mund:
kaum netzt' ein wenig
die Zunge das Nass,
was da die Vöglein sangen
das konnt' ich flugs versteh'n:
Auf Aesten sass es und sang—
"Hei, Siegfried gehört nun
der Niblungen Hort:
o fänd' in der Höhle
den Hort er jetzt!
Wollt' er den Tarnhelm gewinnen,
der taugt' ihm zu wonniger That:
doch möcht' er den Ring sich errathen.
der macht' ihn zum Walter der Welt."

HAGEN: Ring und Tarnhelm trug'st du nun fort?

DIE MANNEN: Das Vöglein hörtet du wieder?

SIEGFRIED: Ring und Helm hatt' ich gerafft;
da lauscht' ich wieder
dem wonnigen Laller;
der sass im Wipfel und sang:
"Hei, Siegfried gehört nun
der Niblungen Hort:
o traute er Mime,
dem treulosen, nicht!
Ihm sollt' er den Hort nur erheben;
nun lauert er listig am Weg:
nach dem Leben trachtet er Siegfried:
o traute Siegfried nicht Mime!"

HAGEN: Es mahnte dich gut?

DIE MANNEN: Vergaltest du Mime?

SIEGFRIED: Mit tödtlichem Tranke trat er zu mir;
bang und stotternd
gestand er mir Böses:
Nothung streckte den Strolch.

---

SIEGFRIED: I went forth to wood-hunt,
but water-fowl only could find:
had I only reckoned rightly,
three wild young water-maids
I well might have won this morning,
who sang in the Rhine their warning,
before wane of day I should die.

GUNTHER: (*starts and looks gloomily at Hagen.*)

HAGEN: A dismal chase were that,
if the hunter, luckless still,
by lurking beasts were laid low.

SIEGFRIED: I'm thirsty.
(*He has seated himself between Hagen and Gunther. Filled drinking-horns are handed to them.*)

HAGEN: I've heard asserted, Siegfried,
that what the song-birds speak of you straightly can tell.
Is truth in the tale?

SIEGFRIED: Their prattle long I have put from my mind.
(*He drinks and then offers his horn to Gunther.*)
Drink, Gunther, drink:
your brother brings it to you.

GUNTHER: (*gazing thoughtfully and gloomily into the horn.*) The wine is weak and blanched:
Your blood alone is here!

SIEGFRIED: (*laughing.*) Let mine mingle with yours then.
(*He pours out of Gunther's horn into his own, so that it overflows.*)
Now flows the mixture over: to mother Earth
let it be an offering!

GUNTHER: (*sighing.*) You over-joyous heart!

SIEGFRIED: (*softly to Hagen.*) He feels Brünnhilde's frown.

HAGEN: His spouse he scarce can read
as you the wood-bird's song.

SIEGFRIED: Since hearing the songs of women
I heed not the birds overhead.

HAGEN: They once were known to you?

SIEGFRIED: Hey, Gunther,
gloom-ridden man!
If it will amuse
I'll sing some marvellous matters of my boyhood.

GUNTHER: With all my heart.

HAGEN: So sing to us!
(*All ensconce themselves on the ground about Siegfried who alone sits upright while the others recline more.*)

SIEGFRIED: Mimi hight
a mannikin grim,
who in nothing but greed
granted me care,
to count on me,
when manful I'd waxed,
in the wood to slay a worm,
which long had hidden there a hoard.
He trained me to smith's work
and metal smelting;
but what the teacher
could not attempt
the pupil did
by daring and patience,
so that from shattered steely splinters
whole I smithied a sword.
My father's blade
freshly I knit.
Now a fair
weapon was "Needful!"
meet it was for fight,
Mimi declared,
and fared with me toward the wood;
I felled there Fafnir, the Worm.
Pray now attend
well to my tale;
I tell of wonders truly.
When his welling blood
did blister my finger;
the flesh I cooled in my mouth:
scarce touched the wet
to the tip of my tongue
when what the birds were singing
at once my brain perceived.
On a branch one settled and sang:
"Hey! Siegfried shall hold now
the Nibelung's hoard;
he'll find in the hollow
the hoard anon!
Were he the Tarnhelm to win,
it would tide him through the wonderful tasks;
but were he the Ring too to ravish
it would give him the ward of the world."

HAGEN: Ring and Tarnhelm you took away!

ONE VASSAL: And what else did the bird sing to you?

SIEGFRIED: Ring and Tarnhelm holding in reach,
I once more harked
to the heavenly warbler,
who sat on high there and sang:
"Hey! Siegfried now holds
the helm and the Ring:
O trust not in Mimi,
the treacherous elf!
Himself would have handled the hoard,
so below there he lies in wait;
for your life he's trying, O Siegfried—
then trust not, Siegfried, in Mimi!"

HAGEN: Admonished it well?

THE VASSALS: And what did you do to Mimi?

SIEGFRIED: With death-dealing drink
he drew to my side,
pale and stammering,
he showed his vile purpose:
"Needful" settled the scamp.

## Act III, Scene I

HAGEN: (*lachend.*) Was nicht er geschmiedet
schmeckte doch Mime!

DIE MANNEN: Was wies das Vöglein dich wieder?

HAGEN: (*nachdem er den Saft eines Krautes in das Trinkhorn ausgedruckt.*) Trink' erst, Held, aus meinem Horn:
ich würzte dir holden Trank.
die Erinnerung hell dir zu wecken,
dass Fernes nicht dir entfalle!

SIEGFRIED: (*nachdem er getrunken.*) In Lied zum Wipfel lausch' ich hinauf;
da sass es noch und sang:
"Hei, Siegfried erschlug nun den schlimmen Zwerg!
Jetzt wüsst' ich ihm noch das herrlichste Weib:
auf hohem Felsen sie schläft,
ein Feuer umbrennt ihren Saal;
durchschritt' er die Brunst,
erweckt' er die Braut,
Brünnhilde wäre dann sein!"
(*Gunther hort mit wachsendem Erstaunen zu.*)

HAGEN: Und folgtest du des Vögleins Rath?

SIEGFRIED: Rasch ohne Zögern zog ich da aus,
bis den feurigen Fels ich traf;
die Lohe durchschritt ich,
und fand zum Lohn—
schlafend ein wonniges Weib
in lichter Waffen Gewand.
Den Helm löst' ich der herrlichen Maid;
mein Kuss erwachte sie kühn!—
o wie mich brunstig da umschlang
der schönen Brünnhilde Arm!

GUNTHER: Was hör' ich!
(*Zwei Raben fliegen aus einem Busche auf, kreisen über Siegfried, und fliegen davon.*)

HAGEN: Erräth'st du auch dieser Raben Geraun'?
(*Siegfried fährt heftig auf, und blickt, Hagen den Rücken wendend, den Raben nach.*)

HAGEN: Rache riethen sie mir!
(*Er stösst seinen Speer in Siegfried's Rücken: Gunther fällt ihm—zu spät—in den Arm.*)

GUNTHER UND DIE MANNEN: Hagen! was thu'st du?
(*Siegfried schwingt mit beiden Händen seinen Schild hoch empor, Hagen damit zu zerschmettern: die Kraft verlässt ihn, der Schild entsinkt seiner Hand; er selbst stürzt krachend über ihm zusammen.*)

HAGEN: (*auf den zu Boden gestreckten deutend.*) Meineid rächt' ich!
(*Er wendet sich ruhig zur Seite ab, und verliert sich dann einsam uber die Höbe, wo man ihn lang-*)

---

HAGEN: (*laughing.*) The blade he could not forge
fell upon Mimi!

THE VASSALS: And told the birds other tidings?

HAGEN: (*who has squeezed the juice of an herb into the horn.*) Drink first, hero,
from my horn:
I mingled a herb with the draught
to awaken and hold your remembrance,
that past things may be apparent!

SIEGFRIED: (*after he has drunk.*) In grief through the boughs
I gazed up aloft,
where still he sat and sang;
"Hey! Siegfried has slain now the sinister dwarf!
I know he may gain the loveliest wife;
in loftly fastness she sleeps,
fire emborders the spot;
overstepped he the blaze—
wakened the bride—
Brünnhilde were then his own!"

HAGEN: Did you obey the bird's instruction?

SIEGFRIED: Straight without pause
I passed on my way,
and I fared to the fire-girt rock.
The furnace was stepped through,
the prize was found:
sleeping, a marvellous maid
in suit of mirror-like mail.
The helm soon from her head I unloosed,
she quickly waked to my kiss;
O then how Brünnhilde's glorious arm
glowingly embraced me!

GUNTHER: What are you saying?
(*Two ravens fly from a bush, circle over Siegfried and fly away over the Rhine*).

HAGEN: Can you read the speech of those ravens aright?
(*Siegfried starts up quickly and looks after the ravens, turning his back towards Hagen.*)

HAGEN: Revenge they rouse in me!
(*He thrusts his spear into Siegfried's back, Gunther catches his arm, too late*)

GUNTHER AND THE MEN: Hagen what deed is this?
(*Siegfried swings his shield aloft with both hands to crush Hagen with it; his strength leaves him; the shield falls back and he himself falls upon it*).

HAGEN: (*pointing at the prostrate figure.*) Retribution!
(*He turns coolly away and gradually disappears over the hills where his retreating form is for some time visible. Gunther seized*)

---

*sam von dannen schreiten sieht.—Gunther beugt sich schmerzergriffen zu Siegfried's Seite nieder. Die Mannen umstehen theilnahmvoll den Sterbenden. Lange Stille der tiefsten Erschütterung.*)
(*Dämmerung ist bereits mit der Erscheinung der Raben eingebrochen.*)

SIEGFRIED: (*noch einmal die Augen glanzvoll aufschlagend, mit feierlicher Stimme beginnend.*)
Brünnhilde!
heilige Braut!
wach' auf! öffne dein Auge!
Wer verschloss dich wieder in Schlaf?
wer band dich in Schlummer so bang?
Der Wecker kam;
er küsst dich wach,
und aber der Braut
bricht er die Bande:—
da lacht ihm Brünnhilde's Lust!—
Ach, dieses Auge,
ewig nun offen!
ach, dieses Athems wonniges Wehen!
Süsses Vergehen—
seliges Grauen!
Brünnhild' bietet mir Gruss!
(*Er stirbt.*)
(*Die Mannen erheben die Leiche auf den Schild, und geleiten sie in feierlichem Zuge über die Felsenhöhe langsam von dannen. Günther folgt der Leiche zunächst.—*)
(*Der Mond bricht durch die Wolken hervor, und beleuchtet auf der Höhe den Trauerzug.—Dann steigen Nebel aus dem Rheine auf, und erfüllt allmälig die ganze Bühne bis nach vornen.—Sobald sich dann die Nebel wieder zertheilen, ist die Scene verwandelt*).

## Dritte Scene

(*Die Halle der Gibichungen mit dem Uferraume, wie im ersten Aufzuge.—Nacht. Mondschein spiegelt sich im Rhein.*)
(*Gutrune tritt aus ihrem Gemach in die Halle heraus.*)

GUTRUNE: War das sein Horn? (*Sie lauscht.*)
Nein!—noch kehrt er nicht heim.—
Schlimme Träume störten mir den Schlaf!—
Wild hört ich wiehern sein Ross:—
Lachen Brünnhilde's weckte mich auf.—
Wer war das Weib,
das zum Rhein ich schreiten sah?—
Ich fürchte Brünnhild'!—
ist sie daheim?
(*Sie lauscht an einer Thüre rechts, und ruft dann leise.*)
Brünnhild'! Brünnhild'!
bist du wach?—

---

with anguish, bends down by Siegfried's side. The Men gather in sympathy round the dying man.*)
(*Dusk commences to fall with the apparition of the ravens.*)

SIEGFRIED: (*once more opens his glaring eyes and begins with solemn voice.*) Brünnhilde!
Heavenly bride!
Look up!
Open your eyelids!
What has sunk you once more in sleep?
Who drowns in slumber so drear?
The wakener came,
his kiss awoke;
again now the bride's bonds he has broken;
enchant him Brünnhilde's charms!
Ah! now for ever open her eyelids!
Ah! and what odorous breeze is her breath!
Thrice blessed ending—
thrill that dismays not!
Brünnhilde beckons to me!
(*He dies.*)
(*The Vassals raise Siegfried's body on his shield and bear it away over the height in mournful procession. Gunther follows at a little distance.*)
(*The moon breaks through the clouds and illuminates with increasing brightness the distant train.—Mists rise up from the Rhine and gradually fill the whole stage up to the front. When after a while they again disperse, the scene is changed.*)

## Scene III

(*The Hall of the Gibichungs with the river bank, as in the first Act.—Night. Moonlight glittering on the Rhine.*)
(*Gutrune enters the Hall from her chamber.*)

GUTRUNE: Was that his horn?
(*Listens.*)
No!—not yet is he home.—
Somber visions startled me from sleep.
His horse I heard wildly neigh:
Brünnhilde's laughter awakened my sense.
What woman was it I saw descend the bank but now?
I fear this Brünnhilde!
Is she still here?
(*Listens at the door at right and calls softly.*)
Brünnhilde!
Brünnhilde!

(*Sie öffnet schüchtern und blickt hinein.*)

Leer das Gemach!
so war es sie,
die zum Rhein ich schreiten sah?
(*Sie erschrickt und lauscht nach der Ferne.*)
Hört' ich sein Horn?
Nein!—
Oede alles!—
Säh' ich Siegfried nur bald!
(*Sie will sich wieder ihrem Gemache zuwenden, als sie jedoch Hagen's Stimme vernimmt, hält sie an, und bleibt, von Furcht gefesselt, eine Zeit lang unbeweglich steben.*)

HAGEN'S: (*Stimme von aussen sich näbernd.*) Hoiho! Hoiho!
Wacht auf! wacht auf!
Lichte! Lichte!
helle Brände!
Jagdbeute
bringen wir heim.
Hoiho! Hoiho!
(*Licht und wachsender Feuerschein von aussen.*)

HAGEN: (*in die Halle tretend.*)
Auf! Gutrun'!
begrüsse Siegfried!
Der starke Held,
er kehret heim.
(*Mannen und Frauen begleiten, mit Lichtern und Feuerbränden, in grosser Verwirrung den Zug der mit Siegfried's Leiche Heimkehrenden, unter denen Gunther.*)

GUTRUNE: (*in grosser Angst.*)
Was geschah', Hagen?
nicht hört' ich sein Horn!

HAGEN: Der bleiche Held,
nicht bläs't er's mehr;
nicht stürmt er zum Jagen,
zum Streit nicht mehr,
noch wirbt er um wonnige Frauen!

GUTRUNE: (*mit wachsendem Entsetzen*). Was bringen die?

HAGEN: Eines wilden Ebers Beute:
Siegfried: deinen todten Mann!
(*Gutrune schreit auf, und stürtz über die Leich hin, welche in der Mitte der Halle niedergesetzt ist— Allgemeine Erschütterung und Trauer.*)

GUNTHER: (*indem er die Ohnmächtige aufzurichten sucht.*)
Gutrune! holde Schwester!
Hebe dein Aug'!
schweige mir nicht!

GUTRUNE: (*weider zu sich kommend.*) Siegfried!—Siegfried erschlagen!
(*Sie stösst Gunther heftig zurück.*)
Fort! treuloser Bruder!
du Mörder meines Mannes!
O Hilfe! Hilfe!
Wehe! Wehe!
Sie haben Siegfried erschlagen!

are you awake?
(*Opens the door tremblingly and looks in.*)
Bare is the room.
It was then she
that to the Rhine I saw descend?
(*She starts and listens to a distant sound.*)
Was that his horn?
Nay!
Nothing nears!—
If he only would come!
(*She is about to return to her room, but hears Hagen's voice, pauses, and remains awhile motionless, transfixed by fear.*)

HAGEN'S: (*voice without approaching*). Hoiho! Hoiho!
Wake up! wake up!
Torches! torches!
Lighted brands here!
Fair booty
bring we along.
Hoiho! Hoiho!
(*Lights and increasing glow of fires without.*)

HAGEN: (*entering the ball.*) Up!
Gutrune,
and greet your Siegfried!
the stalwart hero
is coming home.
(*Men and Women with lights and firebrands conduct, in great confusion, the train with Siegfried's body. Gunther is among them.*)

GUTRUNE: (*in great terror.*)
What is this, Hagen?
I heard not his horn!

HAGEN: The bloodless hero
blows it no more;
he'll bound to the chase
or battle no more,
nor fight for the fairest of women!

GUTRUNE: (*with increasing dread.*) What do they bring?

HAGEN: A wild boar's ill-fated victim:
Siegfried—it is your husband's corpse.
(*Gutrune starts up and precipitates herself upon the body which has been set down in the middle of the hall. General emotion and grief.*)

GUNTHER: (*bending over her senseless form and striving to raise her*). Gutrune
lovely sister!
lift up your eyes—
speak to me!

GUTRUNE: (*reviving.*) Siegfried!
Siegfried is slaughtered!
(*Thrusts Gunther away*)
Hence, treacherous brother!
Assassin of my Siegfried!
O help me! help me!
Horror! Horror!
My husband's murdered among you!

GUNTHER: Nicht klage wider mich!
dort klage wider Hagen:
er ist der verfluchte Eber,
der diesen Edlen zerfleischt.

HAGEN: Bist du mir gram darum?

GUNTHER: Angst und Unheil greife dich immer!

HAGEN: (*mit furchtbarem Trotze berantretend.*) Ja denn! ich hab' ihn erschlagen
ich—Hagen—
schlug ihn zu todt!
Meinem Speer war er gespart,
bei dem er Meineid sprach.
Heiliges Beute-Recht
hab' ich mir nun errungen:
d'rum fordr' ich hier diesen Ring.

GUNTHER: Zurück! was mir verfiel
sollst du nimmer empfah'n.

HAGEN: Ihr Mannen, richtet mein Recht!

GUNTHER: Rühr'st du an Gutrun's Erbe,
schamloser Albensohn?

HAGEN: (*sein Schwert ziehend.*)
Des Alben Erbe
fordert so sein Sohn!
(*Er dringt auf Gunther ein; dieser webrt sich: sie fechten. Die Mannen werfen sich dazwischen, Gunther fällt von einen Streiche Hagen's todt darnieder.*)

HAGEN: Her den Ring!
(*Er greift nach Siegfried's Hand; diese bebt sich drohend empor. Allgemeines Entsetzen. Gutrune und die Frauen schreien laut auf.*)
(*Vom Hintergrunde her schreitet Brünnhilde fest und feierlich dem Vordergrunde zu*)

BRÜNNHILDE: (*noch im Hintergrunde.*) Schweigt eures Jammers jauchzenden Schwall!
Das ihr alle verriethet,
zur Rache schreitet sein Weib.
(*Sie schreitet ruhig weiter vor.*)
Kinder hört' ich
greinen nach der Mutter,
da süsse Milch sie verschüttet:
doch nicht erklang mir
würdige Klage,
des höchsten Helden werth.

GUTRUNE: Brünnhilde! Neid-erbos'te!
du brachtest uns diese Noth!
Die du ihm die Männer verhetztest,
weh', dass dem Haus du genah't!

BRÜNNHILDE: Armselige, schweig'!
Sein Eheweib warst du nie:
als Buhlerin nur
bandest du ihn.
Sein Mannes-Gemahl bin ich,
der er ewige Eide schwur,
eh' Siegfried je dich ersah.

GUNTHER: Give no reproach to me!
reproach you rather Hagen.
He is the wild boar so hateful
by whom our hero has bled.

HAGEN: Are you then wroth with me?

GUNTHER: Ill and anguish
rend you forever!

HAGEN: (*stepping forward in terrible defiance.*) Well then! it is I
that have slain him!
I—Hagen—
smote him to death!
He was spoil to my spear,
on which false oath he spake.
Holiest booty right
here to me should be rendered:
I claim to have then this Ring.

GUNTHER: Aroint! you never shalt clutch
what I for mine declare.

HAGEN: You vassals, speak on my side!

GUNTHER: You seek for Gutrune's dowry,
spawn of the dwarfish stock?

HAGEN: (*drawing his sword.*)
The dwarf's own dower
thus—his son assumes
(*He rushes on Gunther who defends himself: they fight. The Men throw themselves between. Gunther falls dead by a stroke of Hagen.*)

HAGEN: Now the ring!
(*He snatches at Siegfried's hand. It raises itself threateningly. General terror. Gutrune and Women shriek aloud.*)
(*From the back appears Brünnhilde, who advances with firm and solemn tread to the front.*)

BRÜNNHILDE: (*still at the back.*)
Peace with your surge
of sorrow that peals.
You betrayed his wife vilely:
now she comes for revenge
(*She quietly advances.*)
Children I heard
crying to their mother,
to say that milk has been spilled:
but I marked nothing
a fitting lament
for the highest hero's fate.

GUTRUNE: (*raising herself suddenly.*) Brünnhilde, hurt by baseness,
you brought this harm on us:
you did stir the men to kill him.
Woe the day you came here!

BRÜNNHILDE: No, poor soul, peace!
You never were wife of his:
you owned him
only in name.
I was his honored spouse.
The oath of our union was sworn,
before Siegfried had seen your face!

GUTRUNE: (*in heftigster Verzweiflung*). Verfluchter Hagen!
Weh! ach weh!
dass du das Gift mir riethest,
das ihr den Gatten entrückt!
O Jammer! Jammer!
wie jäh nun weiss ich,
dass Brünnhild' die Traute war,
die durch den Trank er vergass!
(*Sie wendet sich voll Scheu von Siegfried ab, und beugt sich in Schmerz aufgelös't über Gunther's Leiche: so verbleibt sie regungslos bis an das Ende. — Langes Schweigen.*)
(*Hagen steht, auf Speer und Schild gelehnt, in finsteres Sinnen versunken, trotzig auf der aussersten anderen Seite.*)

BRÜNNHILDE: (*allein in der Mitte: nachdem sie lange, zuerst mit tiefer Erschütterung, dann mit fast überwältigender Wehmuth das Angesicht Siegfried's betrachtet, wendet sie sich mit feierlicher Erhebung an die Männer und Frauen.*) Starke Scheite
schichtet mir dort
am Rande des Rhein's zu auf:
hoch und hell
lod're die Gluth,
die den edlen Leib
des hehrsten Helden verzehrt! —
Sein Ross führet daher,
dass mit mir dem Recken es folge:
denn des Helden heiligste
Ehre zu theilen
verlangt mein eig'ner Leib. —
Vollbringt Brünnhilde's Wort!
(*Die jüngeren Männer errichten während des Folgender vor der Halle nahe am Rheinufer, einen mächtigenScheithaufen. Frauen schmücken ihn mit Decken: auf die sie Kräuter und Blumen streuen*)

BRÜNNHILDE: (*von neuem in den Anblick der Leich eversunken.*) Wie Sonne lauter
strahlt mir sein Licht;
der Reinste war er,
der Mich verrieth!
Die Gattin trügend
—treu dem Freunde—
von der eig'nen Trauten
—einzig ihm theuer—
schied er sich durch sein
Schwert. —
Aechter als er
schwur keiner Eide;
treuer als er
hielt keiner Verträge:
laut'rer als er
liebte kein And'rer:
und doch alle Eide,
alle Verträge,
die treueste Liebe—
trog keiner wie er! —
Wisst ihr wie das ward!
O ihr, der Eide
ewige Hüter!
lenkt eu'ren Blick
auf mein blühendes Leid:
erschaut eu're ewige Schuld!

GUTRUNE: (*in an outburst of poignant despair.*) Accursed Hagen!
Woe's me!
woe's me!
You gave the hateful philter
to make her husband play false!
O sorrow!
sorrow!
I see it all now!
Brünnhilde was his true-love,
whom he betrayed by that drink.
(*Filled with shame, she turns from the body Siegfried and bends almost dying over Gunther's body; she remains thus motionless to the end. Long silence.*)
(*Hagen stands leaning defiantly on his spear and shield, sunk in gloomy meditation, at the extreme opposite side.*)

BRÜNNHILDE: (*alone in the center: after remaining long absorbed in the contemplation of Siegfried, first convulsed with horror, then overpowered by grief, she turns with solemn exultation to the people.*) Friends, let fitting
funeral pyre
be reared by the river here.
Hot and high
kindle the flames,
to consume the corpse
of him who was hero over all! —
Bring his steed to me here;
to its master straight it shall bear me:
for my body burns
to share in the honor
that here we show to him.
Obey Brünnhilde's will.
(*The young men erect, during the following, a huge funeral pyre before the Hall on the bank of the Rhine; women adorn it with drapery, on which they strewn flowers and herbs.*)

BRÜNNHILDE: (*again becoming absorbed in gazing on Siegfried's dead face.*) What sunny light outstreams from his look!
The truest was he,
yet could betray!
His wife deluding
—leal to friendship—
from his own true lady,
—only beloved—
he shut himself with his sword. —
Nobler than he
swore fealty never;
prouder than he
held no man a promise;
love pure as his
lived not in hero;
and yet every oath made,
every assurance,
the sheerest affection,—
sure none broke like he! —
Know why that was!
You gods who guard
our gages for ever,
Do not turn away
from my waxing distress,
but gaze on our endless disgrace!
Hear my wild lament,

Meine Klage hör',
du hehrster Gott!
Durch seine tapferste That,
dir so tauglich erwünscht,
weihtest du den,
der sie gewirkt,
dem Fluche, dem du verfielest,
mich musste
der Reinste verrathen,
dass wissend würde ein Weib! —
Weiss ich nun was dir frommt?—
Alles! Alles!
Alles weiss ich:
ales ward mir nun frei!
Auch deine Raben
hör' ich rauschen:
mit bang ersehnter Botschaft
send'ich die beiden nun heim.
Ruhe! ruhe, du Gott!
(*Sie winkt den Mannen, Siegfried's Leiche auf zuheben, und auf das Scheitgerüste zu tragen; zugleich zieht sie von Siegfrieds' Finger den Ring*).
Mein Erbe nun
nehm' ich zu eigen.
Verfluchter Reif!
furchtbarer Ring!
dein Gold fass' ich,
und geb' es nun fort.
Der Wassertiefe
weise Schwestern,
des Rheines schwimmende Töchter,
euch dank' ich redlichen Rath!
Was ihr begehrt,
geb' ich euch:
aus meiner Asche
nehmt es zu eigen!
Das Feuer, das mich verbrennt,
rein'ge den Ring vom Fluch:
ihr in der Fluth
löset ihn auf,
und lauter bewahrt
das lichte Gold,
den strahlenden Stern des Rhein's,
der zum Unheil euch geraubt.
(*Sie wendet sich nach hinten, wo Siegfrieds' Leichte bereits auf dem Gerüste ausgestreckt liegt, und entreiss einem Manne den mächtigen Feuerbrand.*)
Fliegt heim, ihr Raben!
raun't es eurem Herrn.
was hier am Rhein ihr gehört!
An Brünnhild's Felsen
fahret vorbei:
der dort noch lodert,
weiset Loge nach Walhall!
Denn der Götter Ende
dämmert nun auf;
so werf' ich den Brand
in Walhall's prangende Burg.

(*Sie schleudert den Brand in den Holzstoss, der sich schnell hell entzündet. Zwei Raben sind vom Ufer aufgeflogen, und verschwinden nach dem Hintergrunde zu.*)
(*Zwei junge Männer führen das Ross herein; Brünnhilde fasst es, und entzäumt es schnell.*)
Grane, mein Ross,
sei mir gegrüsst!
Weisst du, Freund,

you mightiest god!
Because he dared a great deed,
which was dear to your hopes,
how could you thus
throw upon him
the curse to which you succumb?
Ought I
to be harmed by my hero,
that wise a woman should wax?—
Do I know now what you want?
All things, all things,
all I know now:
all at once is made clear!
Even your ravens
I hear rustling:
to tell the longed-for tidings,
let them return to their home.
Rest!
Rest,
O God!
(*She signs to the men to take up Siegfried's body and place it on the funeral pyre; then she takes from his finger the Ring.*)
Redeemed, my hand
holds my dower.
You fatal round!
fearful Ring!
my hand folds you
to hurl you afar,
Water-dwelling
wary sisters,
the Rhine's fair sinuous daughters,
reap my thanks for your story.
What you would gain
I give to you;
out from my ashes
take it forever!
The red flame that burns me
cleanses the Ring from its curse:
you in the Rhine
melt it away
and merely preserve
the metal bright,
whose theft has thrown you in grief.
(*She turns to the back, where Siegfried's body lies already on the pyre, and takes a huge firebrand from a man.*)
Fly home, ravens!
Repeat in Vallhalla
what you have heard here on the Rhine!
To Brünnhilde's rock
go round about,
Yet Loki burns there:
Vallhall' bid him revisit!
Draws near in gloom
the Dusk of the gods.
Thus, casting my torch,
I kindle Vallhalla's towers.

(*She thrusts the torch into the pile, which rapidly kindles. Two ravens fly up from the rocks on the bank and disappear at the back.*)
(*Two young men bring in the horse; Brünnhilde takes it and quickly unbridles it.*)
Grani, my horse,
greet you again!
Would you know, dear friend,
what journey we follow?

wohin ich dich führe?
Im Feuer, leuchtend,
liegt dort dein Herr,
Siegfried, mein seliger Held.
dem Freunde zu folgen
wieherst du freudig?
Lockt dich zu ihm
die lachende Lohe?
Fühl' meine Brust auch,
wie sie entbrennt:
helles Feuer
das Herz mir erfasst,
ihn zu umschlingen,
umschlossen von ihm,
in mächtigster Minne
vermählt ihm zu sein!—
Heiajaho! Grane!
grüsse deinen Herrn!
Siegfried! Siegfried! Sieh!
Selig grüsst dich dein Weib!

*(Sie hat sich stürmisch auf das Ross geschwungen, und sprengt es mit einen Satze in den brennenden Scheithaufen. Sogleich steigt prasselnd der Brand hoch auf so dass das Feuer den ganzen Raum vor der Halle erfüllt, und diese selbst schon zu ergreifen scheint. Entsetzt drängen sich die Frauen nach dem Vordergrunde. Plötzlich bricht das Feuer zusammen, so dass nur noch eine*

By flame illumined
lies there your lord,
Siegfried, the star of my life.
To meet with your master
You neigh merrily?
Lo! how the flame
leaps and allures you!
Feel how my breast too
hotly burns;
sparkling fireflame
enfolds my spirit.
O, but to clasp him—
recline in his arms!
in maddening emotion
once more to be his!
Heiajaho!
Grani!
Greet we our hero!
Siegfried!
Siegfried!
see!
sweetly greet your wife!

*(She leaps wildly on to the horse and takes it with one bound into the burning pyre. The flames instantly blaze up and fill the entire space before the hall, seeming even to seize on the building. In terror the women cower towards the front. Suddenly the fire falls together, leaving only a mass of smoke which collects at back and forms a cloud bank on the horizon. The Rhine swells up mightily*

*düstere Gluthwolke über der Stätte schwebt; diese steigt auf und zertheilt sich ganz, der Rhein ist vom Ufer her mächtig angeschwollen, und wälzt seine Fluth über die Brandstätte bis an die Schwelle der Halle. Auf den Wogen sind die drei Rheintöchter herbeigeschwommen.—Hagen, der seit dem Vorgange mit dem Ringe in wachsender Angst Brünnhilden's Benehmen beobachtet hat, geräth beim Anblicke der Rheintöchter in höchsten Schreck; er wirft hastig Speer, Schild und Helm von sich ab, und stürzt wie wahnsinnig mit dem Rufe:)*
Zurück vom Ringe!
*(sich in die Fluth. Woglinda und Wellgunda umschlingen mit ihren Armen seinen Nacken, und ziehen ihn so zurückschwimmend mit sich in die Tiefe; Flosshilde, ihnen voran, hält jubelnd den gewonnenen Ring in die Höhe.—Am Himmel bricht zugleich von fern her eine, dem Nordlicht ähnliche röthliche Gluth aus, die sich immer weiter und stärker verbreitet. Die Männer und Frauen schauen in sprachloser Erschütterung dem Vorgange und der Erscheinung zu.)*
*(Der Vorhang fällt.)*

ENDE.

*and sweeps over the fire. On the surface appear the three Rhine-daughters, swimming close to the fire-embers. Hagen who has watched Brünnhilde's proceedings with increasing anxiety, is much alarmed on the appearance of the Rhine-daughters. He flings away hastily his spear, shield and helmet, and madly plunges into the flood crying:)*
The ring's my right!
*(Woglinda and Wellgunda twine their arms round his neck and draw him thus down below. Flosshilde swimming before the others to the back, holds the recovered ring joyously up.)*
*(Through the cloud-bank on the horizon breaks an increasing red glow. In its light the Rhine is seen to have returned to its bed and the nymphs are circling and playing with the ring on the calm waters.)*
*(From the ruins of the half-burnt hall the men and women perceive with awe the light in the sky, in which now appears the hall of Vallhalla, where the gods and heroes are seen sitting together, as described by Valtrauta in the first Act. Bright flames seize on the abode of the gods; and when this is completely enveloped by them, the curtain falls.)*

THE END.

# *Parsifal* (1882)

MUSIC & LIBRETTO BY RICHARD WAGNER

This three-act sacred festival drama, set to a libretto by Wagner himself, premiered at the Festspielhaus in Bayreuth on July 26, 1882. On the mountain of Montsalvat in Spain, Titurel's castle guards the Grail (Christ's sacred goblet from the Last Supper) and the Holy Spear (used by the Centurion to wound Christ on the cross). Titurel, now very old, has passed on his crown to Amfortas, his son. Amfortas sets off, armed with the Holy Spear, to destroy the castle of Klingsor, an evil magician. Amfortas, overcome by Klingsor's spells, drops the spear, and Klingsor wounds him with it. Only the touch of the spear, which must be recovered by a "pure fool," can heal his wound. Gurnemanz carries Amfortas to a nearby lake in search of a cure. Kundry, a sometime servant to Klingsor, soothes Amfortas with an ointment. Parsifal, a young man who has shot a sacred swan of the mountain, enters. Naive about life, Parsifal is contrite about his action, but he has no knowledge of his father or of his mother's death from grief after having lost her child. Gurnemanz has an inkling that Parsifal may be the "pure fool" he is looking for. In the Great Hall, Amfortas takes comfort in his father's voice and the boys' chorus and performs the sacred rite. The chalice glows in the light. Amfortas, in grave pain, blesses the bread and wine. Parsifal, unmoved, understands nothing. Gurnemanz sends him away. But Klingsor, watching in his enchanted mirror, knows for certain that Parsifal is the "pure fool." He commands Kundry to seduce Parsifal, changing the castle into a beautiful garden full of flower-maidens who call out to Parsifal. As Kundry kisses him, Parsifal feels Amfortas' pain and cries out in understanding. Klingsor throws the Holy Spear at Parsifal, but the spear stops in mid-air. Parsifal grabs it, makes the sign of the cross, and the castle and garden disappear. Kundry collapses, unconscious.

Years later, Kundry is taking care of Gurnemanz, now a hermit. A knight in black armor approaches, removes his helmut and breastplate, sets down the Holy Spear and prays. Gurnemanz recognizes Parsifal, the "pure fool." He tells him of Titurel's death and performs the ordination that makes him king of the Grial. Parsifal baptizes Kundry, showing her the wonderful and grievous events of the Crucifixion and the Resurrection. Gurnemanz, Parsifal, and Kundry approach the castle of the Grail, accompanied by the sound of the bells of Montsalvat. The knights keep vigil over the body of Titurel in the Great Hall. Amfortas' pain has become intolerable; Parsifal touches him with the spear, and heals the wound, uncovering the glowing Grail while heavenly voices sing of salvation. Kundry dies, and a white dove flies over the knights, who kneel in adoration.

---

## ■ ERSTER AUFZUG.

*Wald, schattig und ernst, doch nicht duster.*
*Felsiger Boden. Eine Lichtung in der Mitte. Links aufsteigend wird der Weg zur Gralsburg angenommen. Der Mitte des Hintergrundes zu senkt sich der Boden zu einem tiefer gelegenen Waldsee hinab. — Tagesanbruch. — Gurnemanz (rüstig greisenhaft) und zwei Knappen (von zartem Jünglingsalter) sind schlafend unter einem Baume gelagert. — Von der linken Seite, wie von der Gralsburg her, ertönt der feierliche Morgenweckruf der Posaunen.*

**GURNEMANZ:** (*erwachend und die Knappen rüttelnd*). He! Ho!
Waldhüter ihr!
Schlafhüter mitsammen!
So wacht doch mindest am Morgen!
(*Die beiden Knappen springen auf, und senken sich, beschämt, sogleich wieder auf die Knie.*)
Hört ihr den Ruf? Nun danket Gott,
dass ihr berufen ihn zu hören!
(*Er senkt sich zu ihnen ebenfalls nieder; gemeinschaftlich verri-*

## ■ ACT I.

*A Forest, shadowy and impressive, but not gloomy. Rock-strewn grounds. A glade in the middle. L, rises the way to the Grail's castle. The ground sinks in the middle at back to a low-lying forest lake. — Day dawn— Gurnemanz (an old but vigorous man) and two Esquires (tender youths) are ensconced asleep under a tree. From L., as if from the castle, rises the solemn morning reveille of trombones.*

**GURNEMANZ:** (*waking, and shaking the Esquires*). Hey! Ho!
Wood-keepers! I deem you Sleep-keepers!
At least be moving with morning!
(*The two Esquires spring up, and then immediately sink on their knees again, ashamed.*)
Do you hear the call? Now thank the Lord
That you are called in time to hear it.

-chten sie stumm ihr Morgengebet;
sobald die Posaunen schweigen,
erheben sie sich dann.)
Jetzt auf, ihr Knaben; seht nach dem Bad;
Zeit ist's, des Königs dort zu harren:
dem Siechbett, das ihn trägt, voraus
seh' ich die Boten vor uns nah'n.
(*Zwei Ritter treten, von der Burg her, auf.*)
Heil euch! Wie geht's Amfortas heut'?
Wohl früh verlangt er nach dem Bade: das Heilkraut, das Gawan
mit List und Kühnheit ihm gewann,
ich wähne, dass es Lind'rung schuf?

**DER ERSTE RITTER:** Das wähn'st du, der doch Alles weiss? Ihm kehrten sehrender nur die Schmerzen bald zurück: schlaflos von starkem Bresten
befahl er eifrig uns das Bad.

**GURNEMANZ:** (*das Haupt traurig senkend*). Thoren wir, auf
Lind'rung da zu hoffen, wo einzig
Heilung lindert!
Nach allen Kräutern, allen Tränken
forscht und jagt weit durch die
Welt: ihm hilft nur Eines — nur der
Eine.

(*He also falls on his knees with them; they offer up a silent morning prayer together; when the trombones have ceased, they rise again.*)
Now up, young vassals; see to the bath;
It is time to wait there for our monarch:
Already I see
Runners before his litter bed.
(*Two Knights enter from the castle.*)
Hail! How's Amfortas' health?
He craves his bath right early today,
The simple that Gawaine
won for him, with bravest craft
I hope it has brought relief?

**FIRST KNIGHT:** You know all and still can hope? With keener smart than before Full soon his pain returned: Sleepless from strong oppression,
He bade us to prepare his bath.

**GURNEMANZ:** (*drooping his head sorrowfully*). Fools we are, seeking alleviation, When but one salve relieves him!
For every simple, every herb we search And hunt wide through the world, When only one thing helps and only one man.

**ERSTER RITTER:** So nenn' uns den?

**GURNEMANZ:** (*ausweichend*). Sorgt für das Bad!

**DER ERSTE KNAPPE:** (*als er sich mit dem zweiten Knappen dem Hintergrund zuwendet, nach rechts blickend*). Seht dort die wilde Reiterin!

**ZWEITER KNAPPE:** Hei! Wie fliegen der Teufelsmähre der Mähnen!

**ERSTER RITTER:** Ja! Kundry dort.

**ZWEITER RITTER:** Die bringt wohl wicht'ge Kunde?

**ERSTER KNAPPE:** Die Mähre taumelt.

**ZWEITER KNAPPE:** Flog sie durch die Luft?

**ERSTER KNAPPE:** Jetzt kriecht sie am Boden.

**ZWEITER KNAPPE:** Mit den Mähnen fegt sie das Moos.

**ERSTER RITTER:** Da schwang sich die Wilde herab.
(*Kundry stürzt hastig, fast taumelnd herein. Wilde Kleidung, hoch geschürzt; Gürtel von Schlangenhäuten lang herabhängend; schwarzes, in losen Zöpfen flatterndes Haar; tief braun-röthliche Gesichtsfarbe stechende schwarze Augen, zuweilen wild aufblitzend, ofters wie todesstarr und unbeweglich — Sie eilt auf Gurnemanz zu und dringt ihm ein kleines Krystallgefass auf.*)

**KUNDRY:** Hier nimm du! — Balsam!

**GURNEMANZ:** Woher brachtest du dies?

**KUNDRY:** Von weiter her, als du denken kannst Hilft der Balsam nicht, Arabien birgt nichts mehr dann zu seinem Heil.

Frag' nicht weiter! — Ich bin müde.
(*Sie wirft sich auf den Boden.*)
(*Ein Zug von Knappen und Rittern, die Sänfte tragend und geleitend, in welcher Amfortas ausgestreckt liegt, gelangt, von links her, auf die Bühne. — Gurnemans von Kundry ab, sogleich den Ankommenden.*)

**GURNEMANZ:** (*während der Zug auf die Bühne gelangt*). Er naht: sie bringen ihn getragen. — O weh'! Wie trag' ich's im Gemüthe, in seiner Mannheit stolzer Blüthe des siegreichsten Geschlechtes Herrn als seines Siechthums Knecht zu seh'n!
(*Zu den Knappen.*)
Behatsam! Hört, der König stöhnt.
(*Jene halten ein und stellen das Siechbett nieder.*)

**FIRST KNIGHT:** Expound us that?

**GURNEMANZ:** (*evasively*). See to the bath!

**FIRST ESQUIRE:** (*as he turns away towards the back with the second Esquire, looking off R.*) Behold that frenzied horsewoman!

**SECOND ESQUIRE:** Hey! The mane of the devil's mare flyeth madley!

**FIRST KNIGHT:** Aye! Kundry 'tis.

**SECOND KNIGHT:** She surely comes with news.

**FIRST ESQUIRE:** The mare is tottering.

**SECOND ESQUIRE:** Did she fly through air?

**FIRST ESQUIRE:** No wowly she grovels.

**SECOND ESQUIRE:** Mark her mane that brushes the moss.

**FIRST KNIGHT:** The wild witch has swung herself off.
(*Kundry rushes in hastily, almost reeling. Wild garb fastened up high; girdle of snakeskin hanging long; black hair flowing in loose locks; dark brownish red complexion, piercing black eyes, sometimes wild and blazing, but usually fixed and glassy. She hurries to Gurnemanz and presses upon him a small crystal flask.*)

**KUNDRY:** Here, take it! — Balsam!

**GURNEMANZ:** From where have you brought this?

**KUNDRY:** From farther away than your thought can guess; If this balsam fails, Arabia bears Nothing else that can give him ease.

Ask no more! — I am weary.
(*she throws herself on the ground.*)
(*A train of Esquire and Knights appears L., bearing and attending the litter in which Amfortas lies stretched out. — Gurnemanz immediately turns away from Kundry towards the newcomers.*)

**GURNEMANZ:** (*while the procession is entering*). He comes: carried by faithful servants. — Alas! How can my eyes have power To see, in manhood's stately flower, This sovereign of the staunchest race made a slave to stubborn sickness!
(*To the Esquires.*)
Be heedful! Hark, your master groans.
(*They stop and set down the litter.*)

**AMFORTAS:** (*der sich ein wenig erhoben*). So recht!—Habt Dank!—Ein wenig Rast. Nach wilder Schmersensnacht nun Waldes-Morgenpracht; im heil'gen See wohl labt mich auch die Welle: es staunt das Weh', die Schmersensnacht wird helle.— Gawan!

**ERSTER RITTER:** Herr, Gawan weilte nicht Da seines Krautes Kraft, wie schwer er's auch errungen, doch deine Hoffnung trog, hat er auf neue Sucht sich fortgeschwungen.

**AMFORTAS:** Ohn' Urlaub? — Möge das er sühnen, dass schlecht er Gralsgebote hält! O wehe ihm, dem trotzig Kühnen, wenn er in Klingsor's Schlingen fällt! So breche Keiner mir den Frieden: ich harre dess', der mir beschieden. "Durch Mitleid wissend"—war's nicht so?

**GURNEMANZ:** Uns sagtest du es so.

**AMFORTAS:** "der reine Thor" - - : mich dünkt, ihn zu erkennen: dürft' ich den Tod ihn nennen!

**GURNEMANZ:** Doch hier zuvor: versuch' es noch mit diesem!
(*Er reicht ihm das Fläschchen.*)

**AMFORTAS:** (*es betrachtend*). Woher dies heimliche Gefäss?

**GURNEMANZ:** Dir ward es aus Arabia hergeführt.

**AMFORTAS:** Und wer gewann es?

**GURNEMANZ:** Da liegt's, das wilde Weib. Auf, Kundry! komm!
(*Sie weigert sich.*)

**AMFORTAS:** Du, Kundry! Muss ich dir nochmals danken, du rastlos scheue Magd?—Wohl denn! Den Balsam nun versuch' ich noch; es sei aus Dank für deine Treu'!

**KUNDRY:** (*unruhig am Boden liegend*). Nicht Dank!—Ha ha! Was wird es helfen? Nicht Dank! Fort, fort! Zum Bad!
(*Amfortas giebt das Zeichen zum Aufbruch; der Zug entfernt sich nach dem tieferen Hintergrunde zu Gurnemanz, schwermüthig nachblickend, und Kundry fortwährend auf dem Boden gelagert, sind zurückgeblieben.—Knappen gehen ab und zu.*)

**DRITTER KNAPPE:** (*junger Mann*). He! Du da!— Was liegst du dort wie ein wildes Thier?

**KUNDRY:** Sind die Thiere hier nicht heilig?

**AMFORTAS:** (*raising himself slightly*). It is well! My thanks! Remain awhile. — From maddening tortured nights fair morn to woods invites: I'm sure The lake's pure wave will freshen even me; My pain will flee And tortured nights' oppression. — Gawaine!

**FIRST KNIGHT:** Sire, Gawaine waited not: For, when the healing herb, Whose gain such toil has needed, Did disappoint your hopes, He in haste proceeded to another search.

**AMFORTAS:** Unordered?—May he be requited For slighting the Grail's commands! O woe to him who foes never frighted, If he should fall in Klingsor's hands! Let none henceforth harry my feelings. For him, the promised one, I wait "By pity 'lightened" — Was it not so—?

**GURNEMANZ:** You said it was so to us.

**AMFORTAS:** "The guileless Fool—" He unveils him to me,— Might I as Death but hail him!

**GURNEMANZ:** But first behold: accord to this a trial.
(*He hands him the flask.*)

**AMFORTAS:** From where comes this wondrous looking flask?

**GURNEMANZ:** It was brought for you from Araby afar.

**AMFORTAS:** Who went to win it?

**GURNEMANZ:** It was she, that woman wild. Up, Kundry! Come!
(*She refuses.*)

**AMFORTAS:** You, Kundry? You make me again your debtor, You restless, fearful maid?— Well then! I will even try your balsam, In gratitude for your good service.

**KUNDRY:** (*moving uneasily on the ground*). No thanks!—Ha ha! What will it help you? No thanks!—Go, go! Your bath!
(*Amfortas gives the sign to proceed; the procession disappears towards the valley. — Gurnemanz, sadly looking after, and Kundry still crouching on the ground, remain—Esquires pass to and fro.°*)

**THIRD ESQUIRE:** (*a young man*). Hey! You there!— Why do you lie there like a savage beast?

**KUNDRY:** Are not beasts here safe and sacred?

**DRITTER KNAPPE:** Ja! doch ob heilig du,
das wissen wir grad' noch nicht.

**VIERTER KNAPPE:** (*ebenfalls junger Mann*). Mit ihrem Zaubersafte, wähn' ich,
wird sie den Meister vollends verderben.

**GURNEMANZ:** Hm!—Schuf sie euch Schaden je?—Wann Alles rathlos steht
wie kämpfenden Brüdern in fernste Länder
Kunde sei zo entsenden,
und kaum ihr nur wisst, wohin?
Wer, ehe ihr euch nur besinnt,
stürmt und fliegt da hin und zurück,
der Botschaft pflegend mit Treu' und Glück?
Ihr nährt sie nicht, sie naht euch nie,
nichts hat sie mit euch gemein;
doch wann's in Gefahr der Hilfe gilt,
der Eifer führt sie schier durch die Luft,
die nie euch dann zum Danke ruft.
Ich wähne, ist dies Schaden, so thät' er euch gut gerathen?

**DRITTER KNAPPE:** Doch hasst sie uns.—
Sieh' nur, wie hämisch sie dort nach uns blickt!

**VIERTER KNAPPE:** Eine Heidin ist's, ein Zauberweib.

**GURNEMANZ:** Ja, eine Verwünschte mag sie sein: hier lebt sie heut',—vielleicht erneu't,
zu büssen Schuld aus früher'm Leben,
die dorten ihr noch nicht vergeben.
Uebt sie nun Buss' in solchen Thaten,
die uns Ritterschaft zum Heil gerathen,
gut thut sie dann ganz sicherlich,
dienet uns, und hilft auch sich.

**DRITTER KNAPPE:** Dann ist's wohl auch jen' ihre Schuld,
was uns so manche Noth gebracht?

**GURNEMANZ:** Ja, wann sie oft uns lange ferne blieb,
dann brach ein Unglück wohl herein. Und lang' schon kenn' ich sie:
noch länger kennt sie Titurel:
der fand, als er die Burg dort weih'te,
sie schlafend hier im Waldgestrüpp', erstarrt, leblos, wie todt.
So fand ich selbst sie letzlich wieder,
als uns das Unheil kaum, gescheh'n,
das jener Böse dort über'm Berge
So schmählich über uns gebracht.—
(*Zu Kundry.*)
He! Du!—Hör' mich, und sag':

**THIRD ESQUIRE:** Yes; but we know not for certain yet if you are so.

**FOURTH ESQUIRE:** (*also a young man*). With her enchanted drugs, I expect
She'll bring destruction soon to our Master.

**GURNEMANZ:** Hm!—Has she done harm to you? When all are sore perplext
For ways to send tidings to distant lands,
Where warrior brethren are battling,
Their whereabouts scarcely known—
Who, before you are even resolved,
Starts and dashes there and back,
Fulfilling the charge with faith and skill?
She needs you not, she's never with you,
She has nothing in common with you;
But when you need help in danger
She breathes the breath of zeal through your ranks,
And never wants a word of thanks.
If she harms you only in this way,
It need not so much alarm you.

**THIRD ESQUIRE:** She hates us, though.—
See there, how hellishly she looks at us!

**FOURTH ESQUIRE:** 'Tis a Pagan, sure; a sorceress.

**GURNEMANZ:** Yea, under a curse she may have been: Here now's her home,—
Renewed become, That she may be absolved of her sins
From former life yet unforgiven,
Seeking her shrift by such good actions
As advantage all our knightly factions.
Sure she does well in working this way:
Serves herself and also us.

**THIRD ESQUIRE:** Then is it not surely her fault
So much distress has come on us?

**GURNEMANZ:** Yes, when she often stayed away from us
Then misfortune broke in. I have known her a longtime, But Titurel knew her longer:
When he consecrated, your castle
He found her sleeping in this wood,
All stiff, rigid, like death.
I myself did find her lately, this way,
Just when the trouble came on us
Which yonder miscreant beyond the mountain
So shamefully did bring about.—
(*To Kundry.*)
Hey, you!—Listen and say:
Where were you wandering around
When our commander lost his

wo schweiftest damals du umher,
als unser Herr den Speer verlor?—
(*Kundry schweigt.*)
Warum halfst du uns damals nicht?

**KUNDRY:** Ich helfe nie.

**VIERTER KNAPPE:** Sie sagt's da selbst.

**DRITTER KNAPPE:** Ist sie so treu und kühn in Wehr,
so sende sie nach dam verlor'nen Speer!

**GURNEMANZ:** (*düster*). Das ist ein And'res:—
jedem its's verwehrt.—
(*Mit grosser Ergriffenheit.*)
Oh, wunden-wundervoller heiliger Speer! Dich sah ich schwingen von unheiligster Hand!—
(*In Erinnerung sich verlierend.*)
Mit ihm bewehrt, Amfortas, allzukühner, wer mochte dir es wehren den Zaub'rer zu beheeren!—
Schon nah' dem Schloss, wird uns der Held entrückt:
ein furchtbar schönes Weib hat ihn entzückt:
in seinen Armen liegt er trunken,
der Speer ist ihm entsunken:—
ein Todesschrei!—ich stürm' herbei;
von dannen Klingsor lachend schwand
den heil'gen Speer hat er entwandt.
Des Königs Fluch gab kämpfend ich Geleite;
doch eine wunde brannt' ihm in der Seite
die Wunde ist's, die nie sich schliessen will.

**DRITTER KNAPPE:** So kanntest du Klingsor?

**GURNEMANZ:** (*zu dem ersten und zweiten Knappen, welche vom see her kommen*). Wie geht's dem könig?

**ZWEITER KNAPPE:** Ihn frischt das Bad.

**ERSTER KNAPPE:** Dem Balsam wich der Schmerz.

**GURNEMANZ:** (*nach einem Schweigen*). Die Wunde ist's, die nie sich schliessen will!—

**DRITTER KNAPPE:** Doch, Väterchen, sag' und lehr' uns fein:
du kanntest Klingsor,—wie mag das sein?
(*Der dritte und der vierte Knappe hatten sich zuletzt schon zu Gurnemanz' Füssen niedergesetzt; die bieden anderen gesellen sich jetzt gleicher Weise zu ihnen.*)

**GURNEMANZ:** Titurel, der fromme Held, der kannt' ihn wohl.
Denn ihm, da wilder Feinde List und Macht
des reinen Glauben's Reich bedrohten,
ihm neigten sich in heilig ernster Nacht dereinst des Heiland's sel'ge Boten:
daraus er trank beim letzten Liebesmahle,

spear?
(*Kundry is silent.*)
Why did you not help us then?

**KUNDRY:** I never help.

**FOURTH ESQUIRE:** She says it herself.

**THIRD ESQUIRE:** If she's so true and void of fear,
The send her to search for the missing spear.

**GURNEMANZ:** (*gloomily*). That is quite different!—
It's denied to all.—
(*With deep emotion.*)
Oh, wounding, wonderful and hallowéd spear! I saw you swayed by the unholiest hand!—
(*Becoming lost in remembrance.*)
When thus equipped, Amfortas, all too bold one,
Who could be staying your arm from essaying the enchanter?
While near the walls, from us the king was taken;
A maid of fearful beauty turned his brain.
He lay bewitched, her form enfolding,
The spear no longer holding:—
A deathly cry!—I rushed to it—
But laughing, Klingsor fled before;
He bore the sacred spear away
I fought to aid the flying king's returning;
A fatal wound, though, was burning in his side.
That wound it is which none may try to close.

**THIRD ESQUIRE:** You knew Klingsor?

**GURNEMANZ:** (*To the First and Second Esquires, who come from the lake*). How fares the king now?

**SECOND ESQUIRE:** Refreshed by his bath.

**FIRST ESQUIRE:** The balsam soothes the smart.

**GURNEMANZ:** (*after some silence*). That wound it is which none may try to close.

**THIRD ESQUIRE:** But look now, father, I'd like to know:—
You knew Klingsor: how was that so?
(*The Third and Fourth Esquires have now seated themselves at Gurnemanz' feet; the other two do likewise.*)

**GURNEMANZ:** Titurel, the pious lord,
He knew him well;
For, when the savage foe with craft and might
rended the true believers' kingdom,
Anon to him, in midst of holy night
The Savior's messengers descended.
The sacred Cup, the vessel pure,

das Weihgefäss, die heilig edle Schale,
darein am Kreuz sein göttlich Blut auch floss,
zugleich den Lanzenspeer, der dies ver goss,—
der Zeugengüter höchstes Wundergut,
das gaben sie in unsres Königs Hut.
Dem Heilthum baute er das Heiligthum. Die seinem Dienst ihr zugesindet
auf Pfaden, die kein Sünder findet,
ihr wisst, dass nur dem Reinen vergönnt ist sich zu einen
den Brüdern, die zu höchsten Rettungs-werken
des Grales heil' ge Wunderkräfte stärken:
d'rum blieb es dem, nach dem ihr fragt, verwehrt,
Klingsor'n, so hart ihn Müh' auch drob beschwert.
Jenseits im Thale war er eingesiedelt;
darüber hin liegt üpp'ges Heidenland:
unkund blieb mir, was dorten er gesündigt;
doch büssen wollt' er nun, ja heilig werden.
Ohnmächtig, in sich selbst die Sünde zu ertödten,
an sich legt er die Frevlerhand,
die nun, dem Grale zugewandt,
verachtungsvoll dess' Hüter von sich stiess;
darob die Wuth nun Klingsor'n unterwies,
wie seines schmählichen Opfers That
ihm gäbe zu bösem Zauber Rath;
den fand er jetzt:—
die Wüste schuf er sich zum Wonnegarten
d'rinn wachsen teuflisch holde Frauen;
dort will des Grales Ritter er erwarten
zu böser Lust und Höllengrauen:
wen er verlockt, hat er erworben;
schon Viele hat er uns verdorben.
Da Titurel, in hohen Alter's Mühen,
dem Sohne nun die Herrschaft hier verliehen,
Amfortas' liess es da nicht ruh'n
der Zauberplag' Einhalt zu thun;
das wisst ihr, wie es da sich fand:
der Speer ist nun in Klingsor's Hand;
kann er selbst Heilige mit dem verwunden,
den Gral auch wähnt er fest schon uns entwunden.
(*Kundry hat sich, in wüthender Unruhe, oft heftig umgewendet.*)

VIERTER KNAPPE: Vor Allem nun: der Speer kehr' uns zurück!

---

unstainéd,
Which at the Last Passover Feast He drainéd,—
Which at the Cross received His holy blood,
With the Spear that shed the sacred flood,—
These signs and tokens of a worth untold
The angels gave into our monarch's hold.
A house he built for the holy things.
You, who their service have attained to
By paths no sinners ever took,
Yet know it is only for
The pure to be admitted
Mid those the Grail's divinely magic power
With strength for high salvation's work dowers.
He whom you named had therefore been denied :—
Klingsor—however long and hard he tried,
Then he found asylum far in yon valley,
For over there it is rankest Pagan land.
I ne'er found out what sin he had committed;
He now would be absolved, yea even holy.
Unable in himself to stifle thoughts of evil,
He set to work with guilty hand,
Resolved to gain the Grail's command;
But it was spurned with contempt by its guardian
Where in rage has Klingsor learn'd surely
How he wrought by the damnable act
An infamous magic might be taught;
Which now he's found :—
He has transformed the waste to wondrous gardens
Where women bide, of infernal charms,
There he seeks to draw the Grail's true wardens
To wicked joys and pain eternal.
Those who are lured find him their master:
To many happens such disaster.—
When Titurel decayed in manhood's power.
And with the regal might his son dowered.
Amfortas gave himself no rest,
But sought to quell this magic pest;
You have all been told the sequel.
The spear is now in Klingsor's hold.
Even the holy it can cleave asunder:
The Grail already he counts as his plunder.
(*During the above Kundry has several times turned round quickly in angry unrest.*)

FOURTH ESQUIRE: It behoves us then soon to reclaim that spear.

---

DRITTER KNAPPE: Ha! wer ihn bräch', ihm wär's zu Ruhm und Glück!

GURNEMANZ: (*nach einem Schweigen*). lem verwaisten Heiligthum
'gem Beten lag Amfortas,
ein Rettungszeichen heiss erflehend:
ein sel'ger Schimmer da entfloss der Grale;
ein heilig' Traumgesicht
nun deutlich zu ihm spricht
durch hell erschauter Wortezeiche Male:
"der reine Thor,
harre sein",
den ich erkor."
(*Die vier Knappen wiederholen, in grosser Ergriffenheit, den Spruch.*) (*Vom See her hört man Geschrei und das Rufen der*)

RITTER UND KNAPPEN: Weh'! Wehe!—Hoho!
Auf!—Wer ist der Frevler?
(*Gurnemanz und die vier Knappen fahren auf und wenden sich erschrocken um,—Ein wilder Schwan flattert matten Fluges vom See daher; er ist ver wundet erhält sich mühsam und sinkt endlich sterbend zu Boden.— Während dem.*)

GURNEMANZ: Was giebt's?

ERSTER KNAPPE: Dort!

ZWEITER KNAPPE: Hier! Ein Schwan.

DRITTER KNAPPE: Ein wilder Schwan!

VIERTER KNAPPE: Er ist verwundet.

ANDERE KNAPPEN: (*vom See her stürmend*). Ha! Wehe! Weh'!

GURNEMANZ: Wer schoss den Schwan?

DER ZWEITE RITTER: (*hervorkommend*). Der König grüsst' ihn als gutes Zeichen.
als über dem See dort kreis'te der Schwan: da flog ein Pfeil.—

NEUE KANPPEN: (*Parsifal vorführend*). Der war's! Der schoss! Dies der Bogen!—
Hier der Pfeil, den seinen gleich.

GURNEMANZ: (*zu Parsifal*). Bist du's, der diesen Schwan erlegte?

PARSIFAL: Gewiss! Im Fluge treff' ich was fliegt.

GURNEMANZ: Du thatest das? Und bangt' es dich nicht vor der That?

DIE KNAPPEN: Strafe den Frevler!

GURNEMANZ: Unerhörtes Werk! Du konntest morden? Hier im heil' gen Walde,
dess' stiller Frieden dich umfing!
Des Haines Thiere nahten dir nicht

---

THIRD ESQUIRE: Ha! he who could would get both joy and fame.

GURNEMANZ: (*after a silence*). Before the plundered sanctuary Amfortas knelt in prayer impassioned,
Imploring for a sign of safety:
A heavenly radiance from the Grail then floated;
A sacred phantom face
From lips divine did chase
These words, whose purport clearly could be noted :—
"Enlightened by pity
A guileless Fool;—
Wait for him
My chosen tool."
(*The four Esquires with deep awe repeat the oracular words.*)
(*From the lake come cries and exclamations of the*)

KNIGHTS AND ESQUIRES: Woe! Horror!—Hoho!
Up! Who is the culprit?
(*Gurnemanz and the four Esquires start up and turn around in alarm. A wild swan flutters feebly from over the lake, strives to keep up, and finally sinks dying to the ground.*)

GURNEMANZ: What is it?

FIRST ESQUIRE: There!

SECOND ESQUIRE: Here—a swan!

THIRD ESQUIRE: A poor wild swan!

FOURTH ESQUIRE: It has been wounded.

OTHER ESQUIRES: (*rushing on from the lake*). Ha! Horror! Woe!

GURNEMANZ: Who shot the swan?

SECOND KNIGHT: (*advancing*). The king esteemed it a happy token,
When it circled aloft over the lake: Then flew a dart.—

MORE ESQUIRES: (*bringing forward Parsifal*). It was Him! He shot! Here's the weapon.
See this arrow, like his own.

GURNEMANZ: (*to Parsifal*). Is it you, that dealt this swan its death blow?

PARSIFAL: For sure; in flight I hit all that flies.

GURNEMANZ: You have done this? And have no sorrow for your deed?

THE ESQUIRES: Punish the culprit!

GURNEMANZ: Unconceived of fact!
Could you do murder? Here in holy forests,
Whose quiet peace overspreads

zahm,
grüssten dich freundlich und fromm?
Aus den Zweigen, was sangen die Vöglein dir?
Was that dir der treue Schwan?
Sein Weibchen zu suchen flog der auf,
mit ihm zu kreisen über dem See;
den so er herrlich weih'te zum heilenden Bad:
dem stauntest du nicht, dich lockt' es nur
zu wild kindischem Bogengeschoss?—
Er war uns hold: was ist er nun dir?
Hier—schau' her!—hier traf'st du ihn:
da starrt noch das Blut, matt hängen die Flügel;
das Schneegefieder dunkel befleckt,—
gebrocheu das Aug', siehst du den Blick?
Wirst deiner Sündenthat du inne?—
(*Parsifal hat ihm mit wachsender Ergriffenheit zugehört: jetzt zerbricht er seinen Bogen und schleudert die Pfeile von sich.*)
Sag', Knab'! Erkennst du deine grosse Schuld?
(*Parsifal führt die Hand über die Augen.*)
Wie konntest du sie begeh'n?

PARSIFAL: Ich wusste sie nicht.

GURNEMANZ: Wo bist du her?

PARSIFAL: Das weiss ich nicht

GURNEMANZ: Wer ist dein Vater?

PARSIFAL: Das weiss ich nicht.

GURNEMANZ: Wer sandte dich dieses Weg's?

PARSIFAL: Ich weiss nicht.

GURNEMANZ: Dein Name dann?

PARSIFAL: Ich hatte viele,
doch weiss ich ihrer keinen mehr.

GURNEMANZ: das weisst du Alles nicht?
(*Für sich:*)
So dumm wie den erfand ich bisher Kundry nur.—
(*Zu den Knappen, deren sich immer mehre versammen haben*)
Jetzt geht!
Versäumt den König im Bade nicht!- Helft!
(*Die Knappen haben den Schwan ehrerbietig aufgenommen, und entfernen sich mit ihm jetzt nach dem See zu*)

GURNEMANZ: (*sich wieder zu Parsifal wendend*). Nun sag'!
Nichts weisst du, was ich dich frage:
jetzt melde, was du weisst!
denn etwas musst du doch wissen.

your path?
The beasts around, did you not find them tame?
Were they not friendly and fond?
From the branches what warbled the birds to you?
How harmed you that good swan?
He flew aloft, to look for his mate.
With her to hover over the lake,
Thus consecrating the health-giving bath for us.
You did not revere, but lusted for
A wild puerile shot of the bow.
He was our joy: what is he to you?
Here—behold!—your arrow struck;—
There stiffens his blood; hang powerless the pinions,
The snowy plumage darkly besplashed,—
Extinguished his eye—do you notice its look?
Are you conscious of your trespass?
(*Parsifal has listened to his words with increasing attention; he now breaks his bow and casts his arrows away.*)
Say, boy? Do you perceive your heinous sin?
(*Parsifal draws his hand across his eyes.*)
How could you have acted this way?

PARSIFAL: I did not know this was wrong.

GURNEMANZ: Where do you come from?

PARSIFAL: I do not know.

GURNEMANZ: Who is your father?

PARSIFAL: I do not know.

GURNEMANZ: Who bade you to wander this way?

PARSIFAL: I know not.

GURNEMANZ: Your name then?

PARSIFAL: I once had many,
But now I know not one of them.

GURNEMANZ: You don't know anything
(*aside*)
I never found a dolt so dull, save Kundry here.
(*To the Esquires who have assembled in still greater numbers.*)
Now go;
Nor leave the king in his bath alone!—Help.
(*The Esquires lift up the swan reverently and bear it away towards the lake.*)

GURNEMANZ: (*turning again to Parsifal*). Now say! I know nothing of all I have asked you:
Declare then what you know:
You must have knowledge of something.

PARSIFAL: Ich hab' eine Mutter;
Herzeleide sie heisst:
im Wald und auf wilder Aue waren wir heim.

GURNEMANZ: Wer gab dir den Bogen?

PARSIFAL: Den schuf ich mir selbst, vom Forst die rauhen Adler zu scheuchen.

GURNEMANZ: Doch adelig scheinst du selbst und hoch geboren:
warum nicht liess deine Mutter bessere Waffen dich lehren?
(*Parsifal schweigt.*)

KUNDRY: (*welche, in der Waldecke gelagert, den Blick scharf am Parsifal gerichtet hat, ruft mit rauher Stimme hinein*) Den Vaterlosen gebar die Mutter,
als im Kampf erschlagen Gamuret;
vor gleichem frühen Heldentod den Sohn zu wahren, waffenfremd in Oeden erzog sie ihn zum Thoren—die Thörin!
(*Sie lacht.*)

PARSIFAL: (*der mit jäher Aufmerksamkeit zugehört*). Ja! Und einst am Waldessaume vorbei, auf schönen Thieren sitzend, kamen glänzende Männer:
ihnen wollt' ich gleichen;
sie lachten und jagten davon.
Nun lief ich nach, doch konnte sie nicht erreichen:
durch Wildnisse kam ich, bergauf, thalab;
oft ward es Nacht; dann wieder Tag:
mein Bogen musste mir frommen gegen Wild und grosse Männer.

KUNDRY: (*eifrig*). Ja, Schächer und Riesen traf seine Kraft:
den freislichen Knaben fürchten sie Alle.

PARSIFAL: Wer fürchtet mich? Sag'!

KUNDRY: Die Bösen.

PARSIFAL: Die mich bedrohten, waren sie bös'?
(*Gurnemanz lacht.*)
Wer ist gut?

GURNEMANZ: (*ernst*). Deihe Mutter, der du entlaufen, und die um dich sich nun härmt und grämt.

KUNDRY: Zu End' ihr Gram: seine Mutter ist todt.

PARSIFAL: (*in furchtbarem Schrecken*). Todt?—Meine Mutter?— Wer sagt' es?

PARSIFAL: I have a mother;
Heart's Affliction she's hight:
The woods and the waste of moorlands were our abode.

GURNEMANZ: Who gave you that weapon?

PARSIFAL: I made it myself,
To drive the savage eagles from the forest.

GURNEMANZ: But eagle-like you seem yourself, and well descended:
Why did your mother not teach you To handle manlier weapons?
(*Parsifal remains silent.*)

KUNDRY: (*who, still crouching by the wood, has glanced sharply at Parsifal, now breaks in with hoarse tones*). Bereft of father his mother bore him,
For in battle perished Gamuret:
From like untimely hero's death To save her offspring, strange to arms
She reared him a witless fool in deserts.—
What folly!
(*She laughs.*)

PARSIFAL: (*who has listened with sharp attention*). Yes, and once along the hem of the wood,
Most noble beasts bestriding,
Passed by men all a-glitter;
Fain had I been like them;
With laughter they galloped away.
Now I pursue, but cannot as yet overtake them;
Through deserts I've wandered, over hill and dale;
Often fell the night, then followed day:
My bow was forced to defend me Against the wolves and mighty peoples.

KUNDRY: (*warmly*). Yes caitiffs and giants fell to his might;
The fierce-striking boy brings fear to spirits.

PARSIFAL: Who fears me, say?

KUNDRY: The wicked.

PARSIFAL: Those who attacked me, were they then bad?
(*Gurnemanz laughs.*)
Who is good?

GURNEMANZ: (*earnestly*). Your dear mother, whom you have forsaken,
And who must now mourn and grieve for you.

KUNDRY: She grieves no more; for his mother is dead.

PARSIFAL: (*in fearful alarm*). Dead?—What, my mother?—who says so?

KUNDRY: Ich ritt vorbei, und sah sie sterben:
dich Thoren hiess sie mich grüssen.
(*Parsifal springt wüthend auf Kundry zu und fasst sie bei der Kehle.*)

GURNEMANZ: (*ihn zurückhaltend*). Verrückter Knabe! Wieder Gewalt?
Was that dir das Weib? Es sagte wahr.
Denn nie lügt Kundry, doch sah sie viel.
(*Nachdem Gurnemanz Kundry befreit, steht Parsifal lange wie erstarrt; dann geräth er in ein heftiges Zittern.*)

PARSIFAL: Ich—ver-schmachte!—
(*Kundry ist hastig an einen Waldquell gesprungen, bringt jetzt Wasser in einem Horne, besprengt damit zunächst Parsifal, und reicht ihm dann zu trinken.*)

GURNEMANZ: So recht! So nach des Grales Gnade: das Böse bannt, wer's mit Gutem vergilt.

KUNDRY: (*traurig sich abwendend*). Nie thu' ich Gutes;—nur Ruhe will ich.
(*Während Gurnemanz sich väterlich um Parsifal bemüht, schleppt sich Kundry, von Beiden unbeachtet, einem Waldgebüsche zu.*)
Nur Ruhe! Ruhe, ach, der Müden!—
Schlafen!—Oh, dass mich keiner wecke!
(*Scheu auffahrend.*)
Nein! Nicht schlafen!—Grausen fasst mich!
(*Nach einem dumpfen Schrei verfällte sie in heftiges Zittern; dann lässt sie die Arme matt sinken, neigt das Haupt tief, und schwankt matt weiter.*)
Machtlose Wehr! Die Zeit ist da.
Schlafen—schlafen—: ich muss.
(*Sie sinkt hinter dem Gebüsch zusammen, und bleibt von jetzt an unbemerkt.—Vom See her vernimmt man Bewegung, und gewahrt den im Hintergrunde sich heimwärts wendenden Zug der Ritter und Knappen mit der Sänfte.*)

GURNEMANZ: Vom Bade kehrt der König heim; hoch steht die Sonne:
nun lass' mich zum frommen Mahl dich geleiten;
denn,—bist du rein,
wird nun der Gral dich tränken und speisen.
(*Er hat Parsifal's Arm sich sanft um den Nacken gelegt, und hält dessen Leib mit seinem eigenen Arme umschlungen; so geleitet er ihn bei sehr allmählichem Schreiten.*)

PARSIFAL: Wer ist der Gral?

KUNDRY: I rode along and saw her dying;
Poor fool, she sent you her blessing.
(*Parsifal springs upon Kundry, raging, and seizes her by the throat.*)

GURNEMANZ: (*holding him back*). Insensate stripling! Outrage again?—
What harm has she done? She speaks the truth.
For Kundry lies not, and has seen much.
(*After Gurnemanz has released Kundry, Parsifal stands awhile as if turned to stone; then he is seized with a violent trembling.*)

PARSIFAL: I—am fainting!
(*Kundry has hastily sprung to a brook, brings water now in a horn, sprinkles Parsifal with some and then gives him to drink.*)

GURNEMANZ: It is well! Thus has the Grail directed:
He ousts ill who gives for it good.

KUNDRY: (*sadly turning away*).
I do no good thing;—but I long for rest.
(*While Gurnemanz is attending to Parsifal with fatherly care, Kundry, unperceived by them, crawls towards a thicket.*)
But rest, but rest! Alas, I'm weary!—
Slumber!—Oh, would that none might wake me!
(*Starting timidly.*)
No! I'll sleep not!—Terror grips me.
(*She gives a suppressed cry and falls into a violent trembling: then she lets her arms drop powerless, and her head sink low, and staggers a little farther.*)
Vain to resist! The time has come.
Slumber-slumber-: I must.
(*She sinks down behind the thicket and is seen no more. A stir is perceived down by the lake, and the train of Knights and Esquires with the litter passes back homewards at back.*)

GURNEMANZ: From bathing comes the king again;
High stands the sun now;
Let me then conduct you to the holy Feast;
For—an you're pure,
Surely the Grail will feed and refresh you.
(*He has gently laid Parsifal's arm on his own neck, and, supporting his body with his arm, leads him slowly along.*)

PARSIFAL: What is the Grail?

GURNEMANZ: Das sagt sich nicht:
doch bist du selbst zu ihm erkoren,
bleibt dir die Kunde unverloren.—
Und sieh'!—
Mich dünkt, dass ich dich recht erkannt:
kein Weg führt zu ihm durch das Land,
und Niemand könnte ihn beschreiten,
den er nicht selber möcht' geleiten.

PARSIFAL: Ich schreite kaum,—
doch wähn' ich mich schon weit.

GURNEMANZ: Du siehst, mein Sohn,
zum Raum wird hier die Zeit.
(*Allmählich, während Gurnemanz und Parsifal za schreiten scheinen, verwandelt sich die Bühne, von links nach rechts hin, in unmerklicher Weise: es verschwindet so der Wald; in Felsenwänden öffnet sich ein Thor, welches nun die Bieden einschliesst; dann wieder werden sie in aufsteigenden Gängen sichtbar, welche sie zu durchschreiten scheinen.—Lang gehaltene Posaunentöne schwellen sanft an: näher kommendes Glockengeläute.—Endlich sind sie in einem mächtigen Saale angekommen, welcher nach oben in eine hochgewölbte Kuppel, durch die einzig das Licht hereindringt, sich verliert.—Von der Höhe über der Kuppel her vernimmt man wachsendes Geläute.*)

GURNEMANZ: (*sich zu Parsifal wendend, der wie verzaubert steht*). Jetzt achte wohl; und lass' mich seh'n,
bist du ein Thor und rein,
welch Wissen dir auch mag beschieden sein.—
(*Auf beiden Seiten des Hintergrundes wird je eine grosse Thür geöffnet. Von rechts schreiten die Ritter des Grales, in feierlichem Zuge, herein, und reihen sich unter dem folgenden Gesange, nach und nach an zwei überdeckten langen Speisetafeln, welche so gestellt sind, dass sie, von hinten nach vorn parallel laufend. die Mitte des Saales frei lassen: nur Becher, keine Gerichte stehen darauf.*)

DIE GRALSRITTER: Zum letzten Liebesmahle
gerüstet Tag für Tag,
gleich ob zum letzten Male
es heut' ims letzten mag, wer guter That sich freu't,
ihm sei das Mahl erneu't:
der Labung darf er nah'n,
die hehrste Gab' empfah'n.

JUNGERE MANNERSTIMMEN:
(*von der mittleren Höhe des Saales her vernehmbar*). Den sündigen Welten
mit tausend Schmerzen
wie einst sein Blut geflossen,
dem Erlösungs-Helden

GURNEMANZ: I may not say:
But if you're bidden to serve it,
Knowledge of it will not be hidden.—
And lo!—
I think I know you now indeed:
No earthly road leads to it,
It can be detected by no one
Who by itself is not elected.

PARSIFAL: I scarcely move,—
Yet swiftly seem to run,

GURNEMANZ: My son, you see
Here Space and Time are one.
(*Gradually, while Parsifal and Gurnemanz appear to walk, the scene changes imperceptibly from L. to R. The forest disappears; a door opens in rocky cliffs and conceals the two; they are then seen again in sloping passages which they appear to ascend.— Long sustained trombone notes softly swell, approaching peals of bells are heard.—At last they arrive at a mighty hall, which loses itself overhead in a high vaulted dome, down from which alone the light streams in. From the heights above the dome comes the increasing sound of chimes.*)

GURNEMANZ: (*turning to Parsifal, who stands spell bound*). Now give good heed, and let me see,
If you're a Fool and pure,
What wisdom you presently can secure.—
(*At each side in the background a large door opens From the R. enter slowly the Knights of the Grail in solemn procession, and range themselves, during the following chorus, by degrees at two long covered tables which are placed endways towards the audience, one on each side, leaving the middle of the stage free. Only cups-no dishes-stand on them.*)

THE KNIGHTS OF THE GRAIL:
The Holy Supper duly
Prepare we day by day,
As on that last time truly
The soul it still may stay.
Who lives to do good deeds.
This Meal for ever feeds;
The Cup his hand may lift
And claim the purest gift.

VOICES OF YOUNGER MEN:
(*coming from the mid-height of the hall*). As anguished and lowly
His life stream's spilling
For sinners He did offer,
For the Savior holy
With heart free and willing

mit freudigem Herzen
sie nun mein Blut vergossen.
Den Leib, den er zur Sühn' uns bot,
er leb' in uns durch seinen Tod.

KNABENSTIMMEN: (*aus der äussersten Höbe der Kuppel*). Der Glaube lebt;
Die Taube schwebt,
des Heiland's holder Bote.
Der für euch fliesst,
des Wein's geniesst,
und nehmt vom Lebensbrode!
(*Durch die entgegengesetzte Thüre wird von Knappen und dienenden Brüdern auf einer Tragsänfte Amfortas bereiugetragen: vor ihm schreiten Knaben, welche einen mit einer purpurrothen Decke überhängten Schrein tragen. Dieser Zug begiebt sich nach der Mitte des Hintergrundes, wo, von einem Baldachin überdeckt, ein ernöhetes Ruhebett aufgerichtet steht, auf welches Amfortas von der Sänfte herab niedergelassen wird; hiervor steht ein Altar-ähnlicher länglicher Marmortisch, auf welchen die Knaben den verhängten Schrein hinstellen.—*)
(*Als der Gesang beendet ist, und alle Ritter an den Tafeln ihre Sitze eingenommen haben, tritt ein längeres Stillschweigen ein.— Vom tiefsten Hintergunde her vernimmt man, aus einer gewölbten Nische hinter dem Ruhebette des Amfortas, wie aus einem Grabe die Stimme des alten.*)

TITUREL: Mein Sohn Amfortas!
Bist du am Amt?
(*Schweigen.*)
Soll ich den Gral heut' noch erschau'n und leben?
(*Schweigen.*)
Muss ich sterben, vom Retter ungeleitet?

AMFORTAS: (*im Ausbruche qualvoller Verzweifelung*). Wehe!
Wehe mir del Qual!—
Mein Vater, oh! noch einmal
verrichte du das Amt!
Lebe! Leb' und lass' mich sterben!

TITUREL: Im Grabe leb' ich durch des Heiland's Huld;
zu schwach doch bin ich, ihm zu dienen:
du büss' im Dienste deine Schuld!—
Enthüllet den Gral!

AMFORTAS: (*den Knaben webrend*). Nein! Lasst ihn unenthüllt!—Oh!—
Dass Keiner, Keiner diese Qual ermisst,
die mir der Anblick weckt, der euch entzückt!—
was ist die Wunde, ihrer Schmerzen Wuth,
gegen die Noth, die Höllenpein,
zu diesem Amt—verdammt zu sein!—
Wehvolles Erbe, dem ich verfallen,
ich, einziger Sünder unter Allen,

My blood I now will proffer.
His body, given our sins to shrive,
Through death becomes in us alive.

BOYS' VOICES: (*from the summit of the dome*). His love endures,
The dove upsoars,
The Savior's sacred token.
Take the wine red,
For you it was shed;
Let Bread of Life be broken.
(*Through the opposite door Amfortas is brought in on his litter by Esquires and serving brethren; before him march boys who bear a shrine draped in a purple-red cloth. This procession wends to the center of the background, where, overbung by a canopy, stands a raised couch. On this Amfortas is placed; before it stands an altar-like, longish marble table, on which the boys place the shrine, still covered.— When the song is ended and the Knights have all taken their seats there is a long pause and silence. From the distant back is heard, from an arched niche behind Amfortas' throne, as from a grave, the voice of old.*)

TITUREL: My son Amfortas! Are you at your post?
(*silence.*)
Shall I again look on the Grail and quicken?
(*silence.*)
Must I perish, unguided by my Saver?

AMFORTAS: (*in an outburst of painful desperation*). Woe's me!
Woe, alas, the pain!—
My father, oh once again
Assume the office!
Live on! Live and let me perish.

TITUREL: Entombed I live still, by the Grace of God;
Too feeble am I now to serve Him:
In works for Him efface your guilt!—
Uncover the Grail!

AMFORTAS: (*restraining the boys*). No! Leave it unrevealed!—Oh!—
May no one, no one know the anguish dire
Awaked in me by that which raptures you!
What is the wound and its torture wild,
Against the distress, the pangs of hell,
In this high post—accurst to dwell!—
Woeful inheritance on me pressed,

des höchsten Heiligthum's zu pflegen,
auf Reine herabzuflehen seinen Segen!—
Oh, Strafe! Strafe ohne Gleichen des—ach!—gekräukten Gnadenreichen!—
Nach Ihm, nach Seinem Weihegrusse muss sehnlich mich's verlangen;
aus tiefster Seele Heilesbusse zu Ihn muss ich gelangen—die Stunde naht :—
der Lichstrahl senkt sich auf das heilige Werk; die Hülle sinkt:
des Weihgefässes göttlicher Gehalt erglüht mit leuchtender Gewalt;—
durchzückt von seligsten Genusses Schmerz,
des heiligsten Blutes Quell fühl' ich sich giessen in mein Herz:
des eig'nen sündigen Blutes Gewell'
in wahnsinniger Flucht
muss mir zurück dann fliessen,
in die Welt der Sündenzucht
mit wilder Scheu sich ergiessen :—
von Neuem sprengt er das Thor,
daraus es nun strömt hervor,
hier durch die Wunde, der Seinen gleich,
geschlagen von desselben Speeres Streich,
der dort dem Erlöser die Wunde stach,
aus der mit blutigen Thränen der Göttliche weint' ob der Menschheit Schmach
in Mitleid's heiligem Sehnen,—
und aus der nun mir, an heiligster Stelle,
dem Pfleger göttlichster Güter,
des Erlösungsbalsam's Hüter,
das heisse Süundenblut entquillt,
ewig erneu't aus des Sehnen's Quelle,
das, ach! keine Büssung je mir stillt!
Erbarmen! Erbarmen!
Allerbarmer, arch! Erbarmen!
Nimm mir mein Erbe,
schliesse die Wunde,
dass heilig ich sterbe,
rein Dir gesunde!
(*Er sinkt wie bewusstlos zurück.*)

I, only sinner amid the Blesséd,
The holy house to guard for others
And pray for blessings upon my purer brothers!—
Oh chastening—chastening dire! descended
From—ah! the Almighty One offended.
For grace and for compassion yearning
My panting heart is riven;
In deepest soul's repentance burning
By Him to be forgiven.
the hour is near—
The ray descends upon the vessel divine
The veil is raised,
The sacred stream that in the crystal flows
With strength and radiant luster glows;—
By this delight but filled with anguish sore,
I feel to pour the heavenly fount of blood
Into my heart
My own life current's iniquitous flood
In delirious flight
Backward within me rushes:
Toward the world where sin has might
With wildest dread it gushes.—
Again it forces the door
From which now the stream pours,
Here through the wound,—like His it is here,
Inflicted by a stroke of that same spear.—
As in our Redeemer, the selfsame place,
From which with tears of blood burning.
The Son of Man wept over man's disgrace
With sacred pity yearning;
And from which in me, in this sacred mountain,
While holding high gifts beyond measure,
—Our redemption's healing treasure—
The hot and sinful blood surges,
Ever renewed from my yearnings' fountain,
Which no expiation yet can purge.
Have mercy! Have mercy!
God of pity, oh! have mercy!
Take all I cherish,
Give me healing,
That I may perish pure
Holiness feeling.
(*He sinks back as if unconscious.*)

KNABENSTIMMEN: (*aus der Kuppel*). "Durch Mitleid wissend,
der reine Thor : harre sein',
den ich erkor."

DIE RITTER: (*leise*). So ward es dir verkündet,
Harre getrost ;
des Amtes walte heut'!

BOYS' VOICES: (*from the dome*).
"By pity lightened,
The guileless Fool—
Wait for him,
My chosen tool."

KNIGHTS: (*softly*). Thus came to you the fiat
Wait on in hope:—
Fulfill your duty now!

**TITUREL'S** (*Stimme*). Enthüllet den Gral!
(*Amfortas hat sich schweigend wieder erhoben. Die Knaben entkleiden den goldenen Schrein, entnehmen ihm den "Gral" (eine antike Krystallschale), von welchem sie ebenfalls eine Verhüllung abnehmen, und setzen ihn vor Amfortas hin.*)

**TITUREL'S** (*Stimme*). Der Segen!
(*Während Amfortas andachtsvoll in stummem Gebete sich zu dem Kelche neigt, verbreitet sich eine immer dichtere Dämmerung im Saale.*)

**KNABEN:** (*aus der Kuppel*).
"Nehmet hin mein Blut
um unsrer Liebe Willen!
Nehmet hin meinen Leib
auf dass ihr mein' gedenkt.
(*Ein blendender Lichstrahl dringt von oben auf die Schale herab, diese erglüht immer stärker in leuchtender Purpurfarbe. Amfortas, mit verklärter Miene, erhebt den "Gral" hoch und schwenkt ihn sanft nach allen Seiten hin. Alles ist bereits bei dem Eintritte der Dämmerung auf die Knie gesunken, und erhebt jetzt die Blicke andächtig zum "Grale."*)

**TITUREL'S:** (*Stimme*). Oh! Heilige Wonne!
Wie hell grüsst uns heute der Herr!
(*Amfortas setzt den "Gral" wieder nieder, welcher nun, während die tiefe Dämmerung wieder entweicht, immer mehr erblasst: hierauf schliessen die Knaben das Gefäss wieder in den Schrein, und bedecken diesen, wie zuvor.- Mit dem Wiedereintritte der vorigen Tageshelle sind auf den Speisetafeln die Becher jetzt mit Wein gefüllt, wieder deutlich geworden, neben jedem liegt ein Brot. Alles lässt sich zum Mahle nieder, so auch Gurnemanz welcher einen Platz neben sich leer hält und Parsifal durch ein Zeichen zur Theilnehmung am Mahle enlädt Parsifal bleibt aber starr und stumm wie gänzlich entrükt zur Seite stehen.*)
(*Wechselgesang während des Mahles.*)

**Knabenstimmen:** (*aus der Höhe*).
Wein und Brod des letzten Mahles
wandelt' einst der Herr des Grales,
durch des Mitleid's Liebesmacht,
in das Blut, das er vergoss,
in den Leib, den dar er bracht'.

**JUNGLINGSSTIMMEN:** (*aus der mittleren Höhe*). Blut und Leib der Opfergabe
wandelt heut' zu eurer Labe
der Erlöser, den ihr preis't,
in den Wein, der nun euch floss,
in das Brod, das heut' euch speis't.

**TITUREL'S:** (*voice*). Uncover the Grail!
(*Amfortas has again raised himself in silence. The boys uncover the golden shrine, take out of it the "Grail" (an antique crystal cup), from which they also take a covering, and set it before Amfortas.*)

**TITUREL'S:** (*voice*), The Blessing!
(*While Amfortas devoutly bows himself in silent prayer before the cup, an increasing gloom spreads in the room.*)

**BOYS:** (*from the dome*). "Take and drink my blood;
Thus be our love remembered!
Take my body and eat:
Do this and think of me!"
(*A blinding ray of light shoots down from above upon the cup, which glows with increasing purple lustre. Amfortas, with brightened mien, raises the "Grail" aloft and waves it gently about on all sides. Since the coming of the dusk all have sunk upon their knees, and now cast their eyes reverently towards the "Grail."*)

**TITUREL'S** (*voice*). Celestial rapture!
How light now the looks of the Lord!
(*Amfortas sets down the "Grail" again, which now, while the deep gloom wanes, grows paler: the boys cover it as before and return it to the shrine.—As the original light returns to the hall the cups on the table are seen to be filled with wine, and by each is a piece of bread. All sit down to the repast, including Gurnemanz, who keeps a place by him for Parsifal, whom he invites with a sign to come and partake. Parsifal, however, remains silent and motionless at the side, as if quite dumbfounded.*)
(*Alternative, during the Supper.*)

**BOYS' VOICES:** (*from the height*). Wine and Bread the Grail's Lord changéd
Which at that Last Meal were rangéd,
Through his pity's loving tide
When He shed for you His gore
And His Body crucifed.

**YOUTHS' VOICES:** (*from the middle height*) Blood and Body which he offered
Changed to food for you are proffered
By the Savior you revere
In the Wine which now you pour
And the Bread you eat of here.

**DIE RITTER:** (*erste Hälfte*). Nehmet vom Brod,
wandelt es kühn
zu Leibes Kraft und Stärke;
treu bis zum Tod,
fest in Müh'n,
zu wirken des Heiland's Werke.
(*Zweite Hälfte.*)
Nehmet vom Wein,
Wandelt ihn neu
zu Lebens feurigem Blute,
froh im Verein,
brüdertreu
zu kämpfen mit seligem Muthe.
(*Sie erheben sich feierlich und reichen einander die Hände.*)

**ALLE RITTER:** Selig im Glauben!
Selig in Liebe!

**JUNGLINGE:** (*aus mittler Höhe*). Selig in Liebe!

**KNABEN:** (*aus oberster Höhe*). Selig im Glauben!
(*Während des Mahles, an welchem er nicht theilnahm ist Amfortas aus seiner begeisterungsvollen Erhebung allmählich wieder herabgesunken: er neigt das Haupt und hält die Hand auf die Wunde. Die Knaben nähern sich ihm; ihre Bewegungen deuten auf das erneuerte Bluten der Wunde: sie pflegen Amfortas, geleiten ihn wieder auf die Sänfte, und, während Alle sich zum Aufbruch rüsten, tragen sie, in der Ordnung wie sie Kamen, Amfortas und den heiligen Schrein wieder von dannen. Die Ritter und Knappen reihen sich ebenfalls wieder zum feierlichen Zuge, und verlassen langsam den Saal, aus welchem die vorberige Tageshelle allmählich weicht. Die Glocken haben wieder galäutet.— Parsifal hatte bei dem vorangegangenen stärksten Klagerufe des Amfortas eine heftige Bewegung nach dem Herzen gemacht, welches er krampfhatt eine Zeit lang gefasst heilt; jetzt steht er noch wie erstarrt gungslos da. - Als die Letzten den Saal verlassen und die Thüren wieder geschlossen sind. Tritt Gurnemanz missmüthig an Parsifal heran, und rüttelt ihn am Arme.*)

**GURNEMANZ:** Was stehst du noch da?
Weisst du, was du sah'st?
(*Parsifal schüttelt ein wenig sein Haupt.*)

**GURNEMANZ:** Du bist doch eben nur ein Thor'
(*Er öffnet eine schmale Seitenthüre.*)
Dort hinaus, deinem Wege zu!
Doch räth dir Gurnemanz,
lass' du hier künftig die Schwäne in Ruh'
und suche dir Gänser die Gans!
(*Er stösst Parsifal hinaus und*

**THE KNIGHTS:** (*first half*). Take of this Bread,
Change it again,
Your powers of body firing;
Living and dead
Strive amain
to work out the Lord's desiring.
(*second half*).
Take of this Wine,
Change it anew
To life's impetuous torrent;
Gladly combine,
Brothers true,
To fight as duty shall warrant.
(*They rise solemnly and all join hands.*)

**ALL THE KNIGHTS:** Blesséd Believing!
Blesséd in Loving!

**YOUTHS:** (*from the mid height*). Blessed in Loving!

**BOYS:** (*from the utmost height*). Blessed Believing!
(*During the repast Amfortas, who has not partaken, has gradually relapsed from his state of exaltation: he bows his head and presses his hand to the wound. The pages approach him; his wound has burst out afresh: they tend him and assist him to his litter; then, while all prepare to break up, they bear off Amfortas and the shrine in the order in which they came. The Knights and Esquires fall in and slowly leave the hall in solemn procession, while the daylight gradually wanes. The bells are heard pealing again.— Parsifal, on hearing Amfortas' cry of agony, has clutched his heart and remained in that position for some time; he now stands as if petrified, motionless. When the last knight has left the hall and the doors are again closed Gurnemanz in ill humor comes up to Parsifal and shakes him by the arm.*)

**GURNEMANZ:** Why do you stand there?
Do you know what you saw?
(*Parsifal shakes his head slightly.*)

**GURNEMANZ:** You are then nothing but a Fool!
(*He opens a small side door.*)
Come away, be gone on your road
And put my advise to use:
Leave all our swans for the future alone
And seek yourself, gander, a goose.
(*He pushes Parsifal out and slams the door angrily on him. As he fol-*

## Act I

schlägt, ärgerlich, hinter ihm die
Thüre stark zu. Während er dann
den Ritters folgt, schliesst sich der
Bühnenvorhang.)

### ■ ZWEITER AUFZUG.

*KLINGSOR'S ZAUBERSCHLOSS.
Im inneren Verliesse eines nach
oben offenen Thurmes; Steinstuf-
en führen nach dem Zinnenrande
der Thurmmauer; Finsterniss in
der Tiefe, nach welcher es von
dem Mauervorsprunge, den der
Bühnenboden darstellt, hinabführt. Zauberwerkzeuge und nek-
romantische Vorrichtungen. —
Klingsor auf dem Mauervorsprunge zur Seite, vor einem Me-
tallspiegel sitzend.*

KLINGSOR: Die Zeit ist da, —
Schon lockt mein Zauberschloss
den Thoren,
den, kindisch jauchzend, fern ich
nahen seh'. —
Im Todesschlafe hält der Fluch sie
fest,
der ich den Krampf zu lösen
weiss. —
Auf denn! An's Werk!
(*Er steigt, der Mitte zu, etwas tiefer hinab, und entzündet dort
Räucherwerk, welches alsbald einen Theil des Hintergrundes mit
einem bläulichen Dampfe erfüllt.
Dann setzt er sich wieder an die
vorige Stelle, und ruft, mit gebe-
imnissvollen Gebärden, nach
dem Abgrunde:*)
Herauf! Hieher! zu mir!
Dein Meister ruft dich Namenlose:
Ur-Teufelin! Höllen-Rose!
Herodryggia war'st du, und was noch?
Gundryggia dort, Kundry hier:
Hierher! Hieher denn, Kundry!
Zu deinem Meister, herauf! (*In
dem bläulichen Lichte steigh Kundry's Gestalt herauf. Man hört sie
einen grässlichen Schrei ausslos-
sen, wie eine aus tiefstem Schlafe
aufgeschreckte Halbwache.*)

KLINGSOR:
Erwach'st du? Ha!
Meinem Banne wieder
verfiel'st du heut' zur rechten Zeit.
(*Kundry's Gestalt lässt ein Klage-
gebeul, von grösster Heftigkeit bis
zu bangem Wimmern sich abstuf-
end, vernehmen.*)
Sag', wo trieb'st du dich wieder
umher?
Pfui! Dort, bei dem Ritter-Gesipp',
wo wie ein Vieh du dich halten
lässt?
Gefällt's dir bei mir nicht besser?
Als ihren Meister du mir gefangen—
ha ha! —den reinen Hüter des
Gral's, —
was jagte dich da wieder fort?

## Act I

lows the knights, the curtain
closes.)

### ■ ACT II.

*Klingsor's magic Castle. —In the
inner keep of a tower open above;
stone steps lead up to the battlemented summit and down into
darkness below the stage, which
represents the rampart. Magical
implements and necromantic appliances. —Klingsor sits at one
side on the rampart before a metal
mirror.*

KLINGSOR: The time has come!
Lo! how my magic tower entices
That Fool who nears, shouting like
a child.
A deadly slumber lays its hold on
her
Whose anguish I can chase away.—
Up then! To work!
(*He descends somewhat lower,
and lights incense, which immedi-
ately fills part of the background
with a bluish vapor. He then re-
seats himself in his former place,
and calls towards the depth with
mysterious gestures:*)
Arise! Draw near to me!
Your Master calls you nameless
woman;
She-Lucifer! Rose of Hades!
Herodias were you, and what else?
Gundryggia there, Kundry here:—
Approach! Approach, then, Kundry!
Your Master calls-appear!
(*In the bluish light rises the form
of Kundry. She is heard to utter a
dreadful cry, as if half awakened
from a deep sleep.*)

KLINGSOR: You Awake? Ha!
To my spell again
You succumb now the time befits.
(*The figure of Kundry gives forth
a sudden shriek of anguish, sink-
ing to a frightened wail.*)
Say, where have you been roving
again?
Fie! There with the knights and
their crew,
Where as a brute they regarded you?
With me are you not far better?
When once their chieftain you had
allured me—
Ha ha! —the spotless knight of the
Grail—
What drove you again from my side?

KUNDRY: (*rauh und abgebro-
chen, wie im Versuche, wieder
Sprache zu gewinnen.*) Ach! —
Ach!
Tiefe Nacht—
Wahnsinn! —Oh! —Wuth! —
Oh! Jammer! —
Schlaf—Schlaff—
tiefer Schlaf! —Tod!

KLINGSOR: Da weckte dich ein
And'rer? He?

KUNDRY: (*wie zuvor*). Ja! —Mein
Fluch!
Oh! —Sehnen—Sehnen! —

KLINGSOR: Ha ha! —dort nach
den keuschen Rittern?

KUNDRY: Da—da—dient' ich.

KLINGSOR: Ja, ja! —den Schaden
zu vergüten,
den du ihnen böslich gebracht?
Sie helfen dir nicht:
feil sind sie Alle,
biet' ich den rechten Preis;
der festeste fällt,
sinkt er dir in die Arme:
und so verfällt er dem Speer,
den ihrem Meister selbst ich entwandt.—
Den Gafährlichsten gilt's nun
heut' zu besteh'n:
ihn schirmt der Thorheit Schild.

KUNDRY: Ich—will nicht! —
Oh! —Oh!

KLINGSOR: Wohl willst du, denn
du musst.

KUNDRY: Du—kannst mich—
nicht—halten.

KLINGSOR: Aber dich fassen.

KUNDRY: Du?

KLINGSOR: Dein Meister.

KUNDRY: Aus welcher Macht?

KLINGSOR: Ha! Weil einzig an mir
deine Macht—nichts vermag.

KUNDRY: (*grell lachend*). Ha!
Ha! —Bist du keusch?

KLINGSOR: (*wüthend*). Was
fräg'st du das, verfluchtes Weib? —
(*Er versinkt in finst'res Brüten.*)
Furchtbare Noth! —
So lacht nun der Teufel mein',
dass ich einst nach dem Heiligen
rang!
Furchtbare Noth!
Ungebändigten Sehnens Pein!
Schrecklichster Triebe
Höllendrang,
den ich zu Todesschweigen mir
zwang,
lacht und höhnt er nun laut
durch dich, des Teufels Braut? —
Hüte dich!
Hohn und Verachtung büsste schon
Einer:
der Stolze, stark in Heiligkeit,
der einst mich von sich stiess,
sein Stamm verfiel mir,
unerlös't
soll der Heiligen Hüter mir schma-

KUNDRY: (*hoarsely and in bro-
ken accents, as if striving to re-
gain speech.*) Ah! —Ah!
Dismal night—
Frenzy—Oh! —Fear! —
Oh anguish! —
Sleep, sleep—
Deepest sleep! —Death!

KLINGSOR: Some other there has
waked you? Hey?

KUNDRY: (*as before*). Yes! —My
curse—
Oh! Yearning—yearning!

KLINGSOR: Ha ha! —there with
the knights unsullied?

KUNDRY: I—I—served them.

KLINGSOR: Aye, aye! —To make
some reparation
For the arrant wrong you have
wrought.
They give you no help;
All may be purchased,
When I but bid their price;
The firmest one fails,
When your arms are around him:
And so he falls by the spear,
Which from their chief himself I
purloined.—
The most dangerous must today be
with-stood
Whom sheer Folly shields.

KUNDRY: —will not! —Oh! —
Oh!

KLINGSOR: Well will you, for you
must.

KUNDRY: You—never—can—
hold me.

KLINGSOR: But I can force you.

KUNDRY: You?

KLINGSOR: Your Master.

KUNDRY: And by what power?

KLINGSOR: Ha! Because against
me
Your own power—cannot move.

KLUNDRY: (*laughing harshly.*)
Ha, ha! Are you chaste?

KLINGSOR: (*wrathfully*). Why
ask that, you outcast wretch?
(*he sinks into gloomy brooding*).
Awfulest strait! —
So laughs now the Fiend below,
That once I sought the holier life!
Awfulest strait!
Irrepressible yearning woe!
Terrible lust in me once rife,
Which I had quenched with devil-
ish strife; —
It mocks and laughs at me,
You devil's bride, through you? —
Take care!
One his contempt and scorn hath
repented;
The stern one, strong in holiness,
By whom I once was spurned
His stock I've ruined:
Unredeemed
Shall the Relics' curator soon lan-
guish;
And soon—I feel it—

chten;
und bald—so wähn'ich—
hüt' ich mir selbst den Gral.——
Ha! Ha!
Gefiel er dir wohl, Amfortas, der Held,
den ich dir zur Wonne gesellt?

KUNDRY: Oh!—Jammer!—Jammer!
Schwach auch Er! Schwach—Alle!
Meinem Fluche mit mir
Alle verfallen!—
Oh, ewiger Schlaf,
einziges Heil,
wie,—wie dich gewinnen?

KLINGSOR: Ha! Wer dir trotzte, löste dich frei:
versuch's mit dem Knaben, der naht!

KUNDRY: Ich—will nicht!

KLINGSOR: Jetzt schon erklimmt er die Burg.

KUNDRY: Oh Wehe! Wehe!
Erwachte ich darum?
Muss ich?—Muss?

KLINGSOR: (ist auf die Thurmmauer gestiegen). Ha!—Er ist schön, der Knabe!

KUNDRY: Oh!—Oh!—Wehe mir!—

KLINGSOR: (stösst nach Aussen in ein Horn). Ho! Ho!—Ihr Wächter! Ritter!
Helden!—Auf!—Feinde nah'!
(Aussen wachsendes Getöse und Waffengeräusch).
Hei!—Wie zur Mauer sie stürmen,
die bethörten Eigenholde,
zum Schutz ihres schönen Geteufel's!—
So!—Muthig! Muthig!—
Haha!—Der fürchtet sich nicht:
dem Helden Ferris entwand er die Waffe;
die Führt er nun freislich wider den Schwarm.—
(Kundry beginnt unheimlich zu lachen).
Wie übel den Tölpeln der Eifer gedeih't!
Dem schlug er den Arm,—Jenem den Schenkel.
Haha!—Sie weichen,—sie fliehen:
seine Wunde trägt Jeder nach heim!—
Wie das ich euch gönne!—.
Möge denn so
das ganze Rittergeschlecht
unter sich selber sich würgen!—
Ha! Wie stolz er nun steht auf der Zinne
Wie lachen ihm die Rosen der Wangen,
da kindisch erstaunt
in den einsamen Garten er blickt!—
He! Kundry!
(Er wendet sich um. Kundry war in ein immer extatischeres Lachen gerathen, welches endlich in ein krampfhaftes Wehgeschrei überging; jetzt ist ihre Gestalt plötzlich verschwunden; das

I shall possess the Grail.—
Ha! ha!
How suited your taste Amfortas the brave,
Whom to you in rapture I gave?

KUNDRY: Oh!—Misery—Misery!
Weak even he!
Weak—all men!
By my curse and with me
All of them perish!—
Oh, unending sleep,
Only release,
When—when shall I win you?

KLINGSOR: Ha! He who spurns you sets you free;
So try it with that boy who draws near!

KUNDRY: I—will not!

KLINGSOR: Lo, where he climbs to the tower!

KUNDRY: Oh woe's me! woe's me!
Awakened I for this?
Must I—must?

KLINGSOR: (who has ascended to the wall) Ha!—He is fair, the stripling.

KUNDRY: Oh!—Oh!—Woe is me!—

KLINGSOR: (winding a horn towards the outside). Ho! ho!
My watchmen! Soldiers!
Heroes!—Up!—Foes are near!
(Increasing clash of weapons heard without.)
Hey!—How they haste to the ramparts,
The deluded garrisoners,
To guard their engaging she-devils!—
So!—Courage, courage!
Ha ha!—He is not afraid:—
From bold Sir Ferris he's wrested his weapons;
And flashes them fiercely now at the swarm.—
(Kundry begins to laugh gloomily.)
How ill doth his zeal agree with those sots!
That one's lost an arm—that one his ankle.
Ha ha! They waver—they're routed:
With their wounds they are all running home!—
What welcome I'll give them!—
Truly I wish
That all the rabble of knights
So might destroy one another!—
Ha! How proudly he stands on the rampart!
His countenance how smiling and rosy,
As childlike, surprised
On the desolate garden he looks!—
Hey! Kundry!
(He turns round. Kundry, who has gone off into more and more ecstatic laughter, which at last culminates in a spasmodic cry of anguish, now suddenly vanishes:

bläuliche Licht ist erloschen: volle Finsterniss in der Tiefe.)
Wie? Schon am Werk?—
Haha! Den Zauber kannt' ich wohl, der immer dich wieder zum Dienst mir gesellt!—
Du dort, kindischer Spross!
Was—auch
Weissagung dir wies,—
zu jung und dumm
fiel'st du in meine Gewalt:
die Reinheit dir entrissen,
bleib'st mir du zugewiesen!
(Er versinkt langsam mit dem ganzen Thurme; zugleich steigt der Zaubergarten auf und erfüllt die Bühne völlig. Tropische Vegetation, üppigste Blumenpracht; nach dem Hintergrunde zu Abgrenzung durch die Zinne der Burgmauer, an welche sich seitwärts Vorsprünge des Schlossbaues selbst (arabischen reichen Styles) mit Terrassen anlehnen. Auf der Mauer steht Parsifal, staunend in den Garten hinabblickend.—Von allen Seiten her, aus dem Garten wie aus dem Palaste, stürzen, wirr durch einander, einzeln, dann zugleich immer mehre, schöne Mädchen herein: sie sind in flüchtig übergeworfener Kleidung, wie soeben aus dem Schlaf aufgeschreckt.

MÄDCHEN: (vom Garten kommend). Hier war das Tosen, Waffen, wilde Rüfe!

MÄDCHEN: (vom Schlosse heraus). Wehe! Rache! Auf!
Wo ist der Frevler?

EINZELNE: Mein Geliebter verwundet.

ANDERE: Wo ist der Meine?

ANDERE: Ich erwachte allein, wohin entfloh er?

IMMER ANDERE: Drinnen im Saale!-
Sie bluten! Wehe!
Wer ist der Feind?—
Da steh't er! Seht!
Meines Ferris Schwert?—
Ich sah's, er stürmte die Burg.—
Ich hörte des Meisters Horn.
Mein Held lief herzu,
sie Alle kamen, doch Jeden empfing er mit blutiger Wehr.
Der Kühne! Der Feindliche!
Alle sie flohen ihm.—
Du dort! Du dort!
Was schuf'st du uns solche Noth?
Verwünscht verwünscht sollst du sein!
(Parsifal springt etwas tiefer in den Garten nerab).

DIE MÄDCHEN: Ha! Kühner!
Wag'st du zu trotzen?
Was schlug'st du uns're Geliebten?

the bluish light is extinguished; complete darkness reigns in the depths.)
What! Gone to work?
Ha ha! the charm I know full well,
Which ever compels you to do my behest.—
Thou there, babyish sprig!
What—though
Wise redes you have won—
Too young and dull,
Into my power you'll fall:—
When pureness has departed,
You'll be devoted to me.
(He sinks slowly with the whole tower; at the same time the garden rises and fills the entire stage. Tropical vegetation; most luxuriant wealth of flowers; at the back it is bounded by the battlements of the castle wall on to which give sideways abutments of the castle itself (florid Arabian style) with terraces.
(On the wall stands Parsifal looking down on the garden in astonishment.—From all sides, from the garden and from the palace rush in mazy courses lovely damsels, first singly, then in numbers: their dress is hastily thrown about them, as if they had been suddenly startled from sleep.)

DAMSELS: (coming from the garden). Here was the tumult;—Weapons, wild exclaimings!

DAMSELS: (from the castle). Horror! Vengeance! Up!
Where is the culprit?

SEVERAL: My beloved is wounded!

OTHERS: Where is my lover?

OTHERS: I wakened alone!—Where has he fled to?

STILL OTHERS: There in the palace?—
They're bleeding! Horror!
Where is the foe?—
There he stands! See—
It is my Ferris' sword.—
I saw it, he took us by storm.—
I heard too the master's horn.
My hero rushed on:
They all assailed him, but each one Encountered a bloody repulse.
What boldness! what virulence!
All of them fled from him.—
You there! You there!
Why shape us for such distress?
Accurst, accurst may you be!
(Parsifal leaps somewhat lower toward the garden.)

DAMSELS: Ha! bold one. Dare you approach us?
Why have you slaughtered our lovers?

PARSIFAL: (*in höchster Verwunderung*). Ihr schönen Kinder, musst' ich sie nicht schlagen? Zu euch Holden ja wehrten sie mir den Weg.

MADCHEN: Zu uns wolltest du? Sah'st du uns schon?

PARSIFAL: Noch nie sah ich solch' zieres Geschlecht, nenn' ich euch schön, dünkt euch das recht?

DIE MADCHEN: (*von Verwunderung in Heitrekeit übergehend*). So willst du uns wohl nicht schlagen?

PARSIFAL: Das möcht ich nicht.

MADCHEN: Doch Schaden schuf'st du uns grossen und vielen; du schlugest uns're Gespielen; wer spielt nun mit uns?

PARSIFAL: Das thu' ich gern.

DIE MADCHEN: (*lachend*). Bist du uns hold, so bleib' nicht fern; und willst du uns nicht schelten, wir werden dir's entgelten: wir spielen nicht um Gold, wir spielen um Minne's Sold: willst du auf Trost uns sinnen, sollst den du uns abgewinnen. (*Einzelne sind in die Lauben getreten, und kommen jetzt, ganz wie in Blumengewändern, selbst Blumen erscheimend, wieder zurück*).

DIE GESCHMUCKTEN MADCHEN: (*einzeln*). Lasset den Knaben!—Er gehöret mir.— Nein!—Nein!—Mir!—Mir!

DIE ANDERN MADCHEN: Ah, die Schlimmen!—Sie schmücken sich heimlich. (*Diese entfernen sich ebenfalls, und kehren alsbald in gleichem Blumenschmucke zurück*).

DIE MADCHEN: (*während sie, wie in ammuthigem Kinderspiele, in abwechselndem Reigen um Parsifal sich dreben, und sanft ihm Wange und Kinn streicheln*). Komm'! Komm'! Holder Knabe, lass mich dir blühen! Dir zu wonniger Labe gilt mein minniges Mühen.

PARSIFAL: (*mit heit'rer Rube in der Mitte stebend*). Wie duftet ihr hold! Seid ihr denn Blumen?

DIE MADCHEN: (*immer bald einzeln, bald mebre zugleich*). Des Gartens Zier und duftende Geister im Lenz pflückt uns der Meister; wir wachsen hier in Sommer und Sonne, für dich blühend in Wonne. Nun sei uns freund und hold, nicht karge den Blumen den Sold:

PARSIFAL: (*in great astonishment.*) You lovely maidens, had I not to slay them, When they endeavored to check approach to your charms?

DAMSELS: You came to us? You saw us?

PARSIFAL: I've seen nowwhere beings so bright: If I said fair, would it seem right?

DAMSELS: (*changing from surprise to merriment*). Then will you not treat us badly?

PARSIFAL: I could not so.

DAMSELS: But sadly What you have done has annoyed us; Our playmates you have destroyed us: Who'll sport with us now?

PARSIFAL: That well will I.

DAMSELS: (*laughing*). If you are friendly come more near. Let kindness be accorded, And you shall be rewarded; For gold we do not play, But only for love's sweet pay. Would you console us rightly Then win it from us, and lightly. (*Some have gone into the groves and now return in flower dresses, appearing like flowers themselves.*)

THE ADORNED DAMSELS: (*severally*). Touch not the stripling!— He's for none but me.— No!—No! Me!—Me!

THE OTHER DAMSELS: Ah, the minxes!—They've slyly adorned them. (*They also withdraw and return similarly dressed.*)

THE DAMSELS: (*while, as if in merry childish gambols they press round Parsifal in mazy figures and softly stroke his face*). Come! Handsome stripling, I'll be your flower! Sweetly dancing and rippling Bliss unshadowed I'll shower.

PARSIFAL: (*standing in their midst in quiet enjoyment*). How sweet is your scent! Are you then flowers?

THE DAMSELS: (*still sometimes severally, sometimes together*). The garden's pride And odor we've given. In spring time we were riven; We here abide, Through sunlight and summer, To bloom still on each comer, Oh be but kind and true, And grudge not the flowers their

kannst du uns nicht lieben und minnen, wir welken und sterben dahinnen.

ERSTES MADCHEN: An dienen Busen nimm mich!

ZWEITES: Die Stirn lass' mich dir Kühlen!

DRITTES: Lass mich die Wange dir fühlen!

VIERTES: Den Mund lass' mich dir küssen!

FUNFTES: Nien, mich! Die Schönste bin ich.

SECHSTES: Nein ich! Duft' ich doch süsser.

PARSIFAL: (*ihrer anmuthigen Zudringlichkeit sanft webrend*). Ihr wild holdes Blumengerdränge, soll ich mit euch spielen, entlasst mich der Enge!

MADCHEN: Was zank'st du?

PARSIFAL: Weil ihr streitet.

MADCHEN: Wir streiten um dich.

PARSIFAL: Das meidet!

ERSTES MADCHEN: (*zu dem zweiten*). Weiche du! Sieh', er will mich.

ZWEITES MADCHEN: Nein, mich!

DRILLES: Mich lieber!

VIERTES: Nein, mich!

ERSTES MADCHEN: (*zu Parsifal*). Du wehrest mir?

ZWEITES: Scheuchest mich?

ERSTES: Bist du feige vor Frauen?

ZWEITES: Magst nicht dich getrauen?

MEHRE MADCHEN: Wie schlimm bist du, Zager und Kalter!

ANDERE MADCHEN: Die Blumen lässt du umbuhlen den Falter?

ERSTE HALFTE: Weichet dem Thoren!

EIN MADCHEN: Ich geb' ihn verloren.

ANDERE: Uns sei er erkoren!

ANDERE: Nein, uns!—Nein, mir!— Auch mir!—Hier, hier!—

PARSIFAL: (*balb ärgerlich sie von sich abscheuchend, will flieben*). Lass' ab! Ihr fangt mich nicht! (*Aus einem Blumenbage zur Seite vernimmt man*)

KUNDRY'S: (*Stimme*) Parsifal— Bleibe! (*Die Mädeben erschreckn und halten sogleich ein.—Parsifal steht betroffen still*).

PARSIFAL: Parsifal . . . ? So nannte träumend mich einst die Mutter.—

due; If you will not fondle and cherish, We swiftly must wither and perish.

FIRST DAMSEL: Take me to your bosom

SECOND: Your hot brow, let me soothe it!

THIRD: Turn your fair cheek that I smooth it!

FOURTH: Give your mouth to my kisses!

FIFTH: No, here! It is I am the best.

SIXTH: No, I! I am the sweeter.

PARSIFAL: (*gently repulsing their eager advances*). You wild crowd of beautiful flowers. If I am to play, you must widen your bowers.

DAMSELS: Why quarrel?

PARSIFAL: It is your riot.

DAMSELS: We quarrel for you.

PARSIFAL: Then quiet.

FIRST DAMSEL: (*to the Second*). Back with you! See, he wants me.

SECOND DAMSEL: No, me!

THIRD: Me, rather:

FOURTH: No, me!

FIRST DAMSEL: (*to Parsifal*). You shun me?

SECOND: Fly me?

FIRST: Are you so wary with women?

SECOND: Of your favor chary?

SEVERAL DAMSELS: The cold trembler! see how he cowers!

OTHERS: Would you see the butterfly wooed by the flowers?

FIRST HALF: Fool! we refuse him!

ONE DAMSEL: I'm willing to lose him.

OTHERS: We others will choose him.

OTHERS: No, we!—draw near!— No, I—here, here!—

PARSIFAL: (*half angry, turns away and seeks to fly*). No more! You'll not catch me! (*From a flowery arbor at side is beard*)

KUNDRY'S: (*voice*). Parsifal!— tarry! (*The Damsels are startled and pause—Parsifal stands arrested.*)

PARSIFAL: Parsifal . . . ? So once, when dreaming, my mother called me.—

KUNDRY'S: (*Stimme*). Hier weile, Parsifal!—
Dich grüsset Wonne und Heil zumal.——
Ihr kindischen Buhlen, weich't von ihm:
früh welkende Blumen,
nicht euch ward er zum Spiel bestellt!
Geht heim, pflegt der Wunden:
einsam erharrt euch mancher Held.

DIE MÄDCHEN: (*zaghaft und widerstrebend sich von Parsifal entfernend*). Dich zu lassen, dich zu meiden,—
O weh'! O weh' der Pein!
Von Allen möchten gern wir scheiden,
mit dir allein zu sein.—
Leb' wohl! Leb' wohl!
Du Holder! Du Stolzer!
Du—Thor!
(*Mit dem Letzten sind sie, unter leisem Gelächter, nach dem Schlosse zu verschwunden*).

PARSIFAL: Dies Alles—hab' ich nun geträumt?
(*Er sieht sich schüchtern nach der seite hin um, von welcher die Stimme kam. Dort ist jetzt, durch Enthüllung des Hages, ein jugendliches Weib von höchster Schönheit—Kundry, in durchaus verwandelter Gestalt—auf einem Blumenlager, in leicht verhüllender, phantastischer Kleidung—annähernd arabischen Styles—sichtbar geworden*).

PARSIFAL: (*noch ferne stehend*). Riefest du mich Namenlosen?

KUNDRY: Dich nannt' ich, thör'ger Reiner,
"Fal parsi,"—
Dich, reinen Thoren: "Parsifal".
So rief, da in arab'schem Land er verschied,
dein Vater Gamuret dem Sohne zu,
den er, im Mutterschooss verschlossen,
mit diesem Namen sterbend grüsste.
Dir ihn zu künden, harrt' ich deiner hier:
was zog dich her, wenn nicht der Kunde Wunsch?

PARSIFAL: Nie sah' ich, nie träumte mir, was jetzt ich schau', und was mit Bangen mich erfüllt.—
Entblühtest du auch diesem Blumenhaine?

KUNDRY: Nein, Parsifal, du thör'ger Reiner!
Fern—fern—ist meine Heimath:—
dass du mich fändest, weilte ich nur hier.
Von weither kam ich, wo ich viel ersah'.
Ich sah' das Kind an seiner Mutter Brust,
sein erstes Lallen lacht mir noch im Ohr;

KUNDRY'S: (*voice*). Bide Here, Parsifal!—
Where joy and gladness shall fall on you
You frivolous wantons, leave him in peace:
Flowers soon to be faded,
He came not here for your delight!
Go home, tend the wounded:
Lonely awaits you many a knight.

DAMSELS: (*tremblingly and resistingly departing from Parsifal*). Thus to leave you, thus to sever—
Alas! alas, what pain!
From all we'd gladly part for ever,
but to remain with you—
Farewell! farewell!
You fair one, you proud one!
You—Fool!
(*With the last words they disappear into the castle gently laughing.*)

PARSIFAL: Was all this—nothing but a dream?
(*He looks timidly to the side from whence Kundry's voice came. There is now visible, the branches being withdrawn, a youthful female of exquisite beauty—Kundry, in entirely altered form—on a flowery couch and in light drapery of fantastic, somewhat Arabian style.*)

PARSIFAL: (*still standing aloof*). You Called me, who am nameless?

KUNDRY: I named you, foolish pure one,
"Fal parsi,"
You, guileless Fool, are "Parsifal."
So cried, when in Arabia's land he expired,
Your father Gamuret to his son,
Who then the daylight had not greeted:
It was by this name he, dying, called you.
Here have I tarried this but to disclose:
What drew you here, if not desire to know?

PARSIFAL: I saw never, I pictured never what here
I see, and which impresses me with awe.—
And you bloom too in this flowergarden?

KUNDRY: No, Parsifal, you foolish pure one!
Far—my home is far from here
For you to find me, I but tarried here.
I come from far lands, where I've noted much.
I saw the child upon its mother's breast;
Its infant lisping laughs yet in my ear:
Though filled with sadness,

das Leid im Herzen,
wie lachte da auch Herzeleide.
als ihren Schmerzen
zujauchzte ihrer Augen Weide!
Gebettet sanft auf weichen Moosen,
den hold geschläfert sie mit Kosen,
dem, bang' in Sorgen,
den Schlaf bewacht der Mutter Sehnen,
ihn weckt' am Morgen
der heisse Thau der Mutter-Thränen.
Nur Weinen war sie, Schmerz-Gebahren
um deines Vaters Leib' und Tod;
vor gleicher Noth dich zu bewahren,
galt ihr als höchster Pflicht Gebot:
den Waffen fern, den Männer Kampf und Wüthen,
wollte sie still dich bergen und behüten.
Nur Sorgen war sie, ach! und Bangen:
nie sollte Kunde zu dir hergelangen.
Hör'st du nicht noch ihrer Klagen Ruf,
wann fern und spät du geweilt?
Hei! Was ihr das Lust und Lachen schuf,
wann suchend sie dann dich ereilt!
Wann dann ihr Arm dich wüthend umschlang,
ward dir es wohl gar bei'm Küssen bang?—
Ihr Wehe doch du nicht vernahm'st,
nicht ihrer Schmerzen Toben,
als endlich du nicht wieder kam'st,
und deine Spur verstoben:
sie harrte Nächt' und Tage,
bis ihr verstummt die Klage,
der Gram ihr zehrte den Schmerz,
um stillen Tod sie warb:
ihr brach das Leid das Herz,
und—Herzeleide—starb.

PARSIFAL: (*immer ernsthafter, endlich furchtbar betroffen, sinkt, schmerzlich überwältigt, bei Kundry's Füssen nieder*).
Wehe! Wehe! Was that ich? Wo war ich?
Mutter! Süsse, holde Mutter!
Dein Sohn, dein Sohn musste dich morden
O Thor! Blöder, taumelnder Thor!
Wo irrtest du hin, ihrer vergessend?
Deiner, deiner vergessend,
traute, theuerste Mutter?

KUNDRY: (*immer noch in liegender Stellung ausgestreckt, beugt sich über Parsifal's Haupt, fasst sanft seine Stirne, und schlingt traulich ihren Arm um seinen Nacken*). War dir fremd noch der Schmerz,
des Trostes Süsse
labte nie auch dein Herz:
das Wehe, das dich reu't,
die Noth nun büsse, im Trost, den Liebe beut!

How laughed then even Heart's Affliction.
When, shouting gladness,
It gave her sorrows contradiction!
In beds of moss it was softly nested,
She kissed it till in sleep it rested:
With care and sorrow
The timid mother watched it sleeping;
It waked the morrow
Beneath the dew of mother's weeping.
All tears was she, encased in anguish,
Caused by your father's death and love:
That through like hap you should not languish,
Became her care all else above,
Afar from arms, from mortal strife and riot,
She sought to hide away with you in quiet.
All care was she, alas! and fearing:
Never should anything of knowledge reach your hearing.
Do you know still her lamenting voice,
When far and late you owned?
Ah! how she did laughingly rejoice
To welcome you hastening home!
When her wild arm was laid around you,
Were you of kisses so much afraid?—
But you did not behold her pain,
Her features anguish ridden,
When you returned not again,
And every trace was hidden.
For days and nights she waited,
And then her cries abated;
Her pain was dulled of its smart,
And gently ebbed life's tide;
The anguish broke her heart,
And—Heart's Affliction—died.—

PARSIFAL: (*always earnestly, finally terribly affected, sinks down at Kundry's feet, painfully overpowered*). Woe's me! Woe's me!
What did I?
Where was I?
Mother! Sweetest, dearest mother!
Your son, your son must be thy murderer?
Oh Fool! Thoughtless, shallowbrained Fool!
Where could you have roved, thus to forget her?
Thus, oh thus to forget you,
Faithful, fondest of mothers!

KUNDRY: (*still reclining, bends over Parsifal's head, gently touches his forehead and wreathes her arms confidingly round his neck*). Had you never been distrest,
Then consolation
Could not have cheered your breast.
Let now your bitter woe
Find mitigation
In joys that love can show!

# Act II

**PARSIFAL:** (*trübe*). Die Mutter, die Mutter konnt' ich vergessen! Ha! Was Alles vergass ich wohl noch?
Wess' war ich je noch eingedenk?
Nur dumpfe Thorheit lebt in mir!
(*Er lässt sich immer tiefer sinken.*)

**KUNDRY:** Bekenntniss
wird Schuld und Reue enden,
Erkenntniss
in Sinn die Thorheit wenden:
die Liebe lerne kennen,
die Gamuret umschloss.
als Herzeleid's Entbrennen
ihn sengend überfloss:
die Leib und Leben
einst dir gegeben,
der Tod und Thorheit welchen muss,
sie beut'
dir heut'—
als Muttersegens letzten Gruss
der Liebe—ersten Kuss.
(*Sie hat ihr Haupt völlig über das seinige geneigt, und heftet nun ihre Lippen zu einem langen Kasse auf seinen Mund*).

**PARSIFAL:** (*fährt plötzlich mit einer Gebärde der höchsten Schreckens auf: seine Haltung drückt eine Veränderung aus: er stemmt seine Hände gewaltsam gegen sein Herz, wir um einen zerreissenden Schmerz an bewältigen; endlich bricht er aus*). Amfortas!—
Die Wunde!—Die Wunde!
Sie brennt in meinem Herzen.—
Oh, Klage! Klage!
Furchtbare Klage!
Aus tiefstem Inner'n schreit sie mir auf.
Oh!—Oh!—
Elender!
Jammervollster!—
Die Wunde sah' ich bluten:
nun blutet sie mir selbst—
hier—hier!
(*Während Kundry in Schrecken und Verwunderung auf ihn hinstarrt, fährt Parsifal in gänzlicher Entrücktheit fort.*)
Nein, nein! Nicht ist es die Wunde!
fliesse ihr Blut in Strömen dahin!
Hier! Hier im Herzen der Brand!
Das Sehnen, das furchtbare Sehnea,
das alle Sinne mir fasst und zwingt!
Oh!— Qual der Liebe!—
Wie Alles schauert, bebt und zukt
in sündigem Verlangen! . . .
(*Schauerlich leise.*)
Es starrt der Blick dumpf auf das Heils gefäss:
das heilige Blut erglüh't;—
Erlösungswonne, göttlich mild',
durchzittert weithin alle Seelen;
nur hier, im Herzen, will die Qual nicht weichen.
Des Heiland's Klage da vernehm' ich
die Klage, ach! die Klage
um das verrath' ne Heiligthum:
,,erlöse, rette mich
aus schuldbefleckten Händen!''

**PARSIFAL:** (*sadly*). My mother, my mother! Could I forget her? Ah! must all be forgotten by me?
What have I ever remembered yet?
But senseless Folly dwells in me!
(*He droops still lower*).

**KUNDRY:** Trangression
When owned is quickly ended!
Confession
Hath Folly often mended.
Oh learn the fashion of love
Which Gamuret once knew,
When Heart's Affliction's passion
Had fired his bosom through.
The life your mother
Gave you can smother
Even death, and dullness, too, remove.
To you
Now she
Sends benediction from above
In this first—kiss of Love.
(*She has bowed her head quite over his, and now presses her lips on his in a long kiss*).

**PARSIFAL:** (*starts up suddenly with a gesture of intense terror: his looks alter fearfully. he presses his hands tightly against his heart, as if to repress an agonizing pain; finally he bursts out*).
Amfortas!—
The spearwound!—The spearwound!—
I feel it burning in me.
Oh, horror! horror!
direfulest horror!
It shrieks from out the depth of my soul.
Oh!—Oh!—
Misery!—
Lamentation!
I saw your wound a-bleeding:—
It bleeds now in myself—
Here—here!
(*While Kundry stares at him in wonder and alarm, he continues madly*).
No, no! This is not the spearwound:
Let it gush blood in streams if it list!
Here!—here! My heart is ablaze!
The passion, the terrible passion,
That all my senses seize and sway!
Oh!—Love's delirium!—
How all things tremble, heave and quake
With longings that are sinful!..
(*terribly quiet*).
My frozen glance stares on the sacred Cup:—
The Holy One's blood glows;—
Redemption's rapture, sweet and mild,
Is trembling far through every spirit;
But in this heart will the pangs not lessen.
The Savior's wailing I distinguished.
The wailing—the wailing
For His polluted sanctuary:—
"Recover, save me from

So—rief die Gottesklage
furchtbar laut mir in die Seele.
Und ich? Der Thor, der Feige?
Zu wilden Knabenthaten floh' ich hin!
(*Er stürzt verzweiflungsvoll auf die Knie.*)
Erlöser! Heiland! Herr der Huld!
Wie büss' ich Sünder solche Schuld?

**KUNDRY:** (*deren Erstaunen in leidenschaftliche Bewunderung übergeht, sucht schüchtern sich Parsifal zu nähern*). Gelobter Held! Entflieh' dem Wahn!
Blick' auf! Sei hold der Huldin Nah'n!

**PARSIFAL:** (*immer in gebeugter Stellung, starr zu Kundry aufblickend, während diese sich zu neight und die lieb-kosenden Bewegungen ausführt,, die er mit dem Folgenden bezeichmer*). Ja!
Diese Stimme! So rief sie ihm;—
und diesen Blick, deutlich erkenn' ich ihn,
auch diesen, der ihm so friedlos lachte.
Die Lippe,—ja—so zuckte sie ihm;—
so neigte sich der Nacken,—
so hob sich kühn das Haupt;—
so flatterten lachend die Locken,—
so schlang um den Hals sich der Arm—
so schmeichelte weich die Wange—!
Mit aller Schmerzen Qual im Bund, das Heil der Seele
entküsste ihm ihr Mund!—
Ha!—dieser Kuss!
(*Eh bat sich mit dem Letzten allmählich erhoben, springt jetzt vollends auf, und stösst Kundry heftig von sich.*)
Verderberin! Weiche von mir!
Ewig—ewig—von mir!

**KUNDRY:** (*in höchster Leidenschaft*). Grausamer!—Ha!—
Fühlst du im Herzen,
nur Anderer Schmerzen,
so fühle jetzt auch die meinen!
Bist du Erlöser,
was bannt dich, Böser,
nicht mir auch zum Heil dich zu einen?
Seit Ewigkeiten— harre ich deiner,
des Heiland's ach! so spät,
den einst ich kühn verschmäht.—
Oh!—
Kenntest du den Fluch,
der mich durch Schlaf und Wachen,
durch Tod und Leben, Pein und Lachen,
zu neuem Leiden neu gestählt,
endlos durch das Dasein quält!—
ich sah—Ihn—Ihn—
und—lachte . . .
da traf mich sein Blick.,—

The hands that guilt has sullied!''
Thus—rang the lamentation
Through my soul with fearful loudness:
And I—oh, Fool!—oh, coward! To wild and childish exploits fled here
(*He throws himself despairingly on his knees*).
Redeemer! Savior! Gracious Lord!
What can retrieve my abhorred crime?

**KUNDRY:** (*whose astonishment has changed to sorrowful wonder, tries tremblingly to approach Parsifal*). My noble Knight! fling off this spell!
Look up! nor repel Love's delight!

**PARSIFAL:** (*still in a kneeling posture, gazing blankly up at Kundry, while she stoops over him with the embracing movements which he describes in the following*).
Ah! Thus it call him! This voice it was;—
And this the glance; surely I know it well,—
The eyeglance which smiled away his quiet.—
These lips, too, — aye—they tempted him thus;—
So bowed this neck above him,—
So high was raised this head;—
So fluttered these locks as though laughing, -
So circled this arm round his neck—
So softened each feature in fondness,—
In league with Sorrow's dismal weight,
This mouth took from him
His soul's salvation straight!—Ha! with this kiss—
(*With the last words he has gradually risen, and now springs completely up and spurns Kundry from him*).
Pernicious one! Get away from me!
Leave me—leave me—forever!

**KUNDRY:** (*in intense grief*). Cruel one!—Ha!—
Felt ever your nature
For one fellow creature,
Then feel now my desolation!
Were you the Saver
You would not waver,
But unite with me for salvation!
Through endless ages for you I've waited,
The Savior—ah, so late!
At whom I scoffed in hate.—
Oh!—
Could you know the curse
Which through me, waking, sleeping,
Through death and lifetime,
Joy or weeping,
While ever steeled to bear fresh woes,
Endless flows through my being!
I saw Him—Him—
And—mocked Him! . . .

Nun such' ich ihn von Welt zu Welt
ihm wieder zu begegnen:
in höchster Noth—
wähn' ich sein Auge schon nah',
den Blick schon auf mir ruh'n:—
da kehrt mir das verfluchte Lachen
wieder,—
ein Sünder sinkt mir in die Arme!
Da lach' ich—lache—,
kann nicht weinen: nur schreien,
wüthen,
toben, rasen
in stets erneu'ten Wahnsinn's
Nacht.
aus der ich büssend kaum erwacht.—
Den ich ersehnt in Todesschmach-
ten,
den ich erkannt, den blöd Verla-
chten,
lass' mich an seinem Busen weinen,
nur eine Stunde dir vereinen,
und, ob mich Gott und Welt ver-
stöss't!
in dir entsündig't sein und erlös't!

PARSIFAL: In Ewigkeit
wärst du verdammt mit mir für eine
Stunde
Vergessen's meiner Sendung,
in deines Arm's Umfangen!—
Auch dir bin ich zum Heil gesandt,
bleib'st du dem Sehnen abgewandt.
Die Labung, die dein Leiden endet,
beut nicht der Quell, aus dem es
fliesst:
das Heil wird nimmer dir gespen-
det,
wenn jener Quell sich dir nich
schliesst.
Ein andre ist's,—ein andres, ach!
nach dem ich jammernd schmachten sah
die Brüder dort in grausen Nöthen
den leib sich quälen und ertödten.
Doch wer erkennt ihn klar und hell,
des einz'gen Heiles wahren Quell?
Oh, Elend! Aller Rettung Flucht!
Oh, Weltenwahns Umnachten:
in höchsten Heiles heisser Sucht
nach der Verdammniss Quell zu
schmach dannten!

KUNDRY: So war es mein Kuss,
der Welt-hellsichtig dich machte?
Mein volles Liebes-Umfangen
lässt dich dann Gottheit erlangen:
Die Welt erlöse, ist dies dein Amt:
schuf dich zum Gott die Stunde,
für sie lasse mich ewig verdammt,
nie heile mir die Wunde.

PARSIFAL: Erlösung, Frevlerin,
biet' ich auch dir.

KUNDRY: Lass' mich dich
Göttlichen lieben,
Erlösung gabst du dann mir.

I caught then his glance,—
I seek him now from world to
world,
Once more to stand before Him:
In deepest woe—
Sometimes His eye seems near.
His glance resting on me,—
Returns then the accursed laughter
on me,—
A sinner sinks in my embraces!
Then laughter—laughter—,
I cannot weep;
But only shriek
And rage and wallow
In night and madness never slaked,
From which, repentant, scarce I'd
waked.—
You for whom shamed to death I've
bided,
You whom I knew and, fool, derid-
ed,
Let me upon your breast lie sob-
bing,
But for one hour together throb-
bing;
Though forced from God and man
to flee,
Be yet redeemed and pardoned by
you!

PARSIFAL: Eternally
Should I be damned with you
If for one hour
I forgot my holy mission,
Within your arm's embracing!—
To your help also am I sent,
If of your cravings you repent.
The solace, which shall end your
sorrow,
Yields not that spring from which it
flows:
You can never borrow salvation,
Till that same spring in you shall
close.
Far other it is—far other!
For which I saw, with pitying eyes,
That brotherhood distrest and pin-
ing,
Their lives tormented and declin-
ing.
But who with certain clearness
knows
The source whence true salvation
flows;
Oh misery! What a course is this!
Oh wild hallucination!
In such a search for sacred bliss
Thus to desire the soul's damna-
tion!

KUNDRY: And was it my kiss
This great knowledge conveyed
you?
If in my arms I might take you,
It would then surely make you a
god!
Redeem the world then, if it is your
aim:—
Stand as a god revealed;
For this hour let me perish in flame,
Leave the wound unhealed.

PARSIFAL: Redemption, sinner, I
offer even you—

KUNDRY: Let me, divine one, but
love you;
Redemption then should I see.

PARSIFAL: Lieb' und Erlösung soll
dir lohnen,—zeigest du
zu Amfortas mir den Weg.

KUNDRY: (in Wuth ausbre-
chend). Nie—sollst du ihn finden!
Den Verfall'nen, lass' ihn verderben,—
den Un-seligen,
Schmach—lüsternen,
den ich verlachte—lachte—
lachte!
Haha! Ihn traf ja der eig'ne Speer?

PARSIFAL: Wer durft' ihn verwunden mit heil'get Wehr?

KUNDRY: Er—Er—,
der einst mein Lachen bestraft:
sein Fluch—ha!—mir giebt er
Kraft;
gegen dich selbst ruf' ich die Wehr,
gieb'st du dem Sünder des Mitleid's
Ehr'!—
Ha! Wahnsinn!—
Mitleid! Mitleid mit mir!
Nur eine Stunde mein,—
nur eine Stunde dein—:
und des Weges—
sollst du geleitet sein!
(Sie will ihn umarmen. Er stösst
sie heftig von slch.)

PARSIFAL: Vergeh', unseliges
Weib!

KUNDRY: (zerschlägt sich die
Brust, und ruft in wildem Rasen).
Hilfe! Hilfe! Herbei!
Haltet den Frechen! Herbei!
Wehr't ihm die Wege!
Wehr't ihm die Pfade!—
Und flëh'st du von hier, und fändest
all Wege der Welt,
den Weg, den du such'st,
dess' Pfade sollst du nicht finden!
Denn Pfad und Wege,
die mir dich entführen,
so—verwünsch' ich sie dir:
Irre! Irre,—
mir so vertraut—
dich weih' ich ihm zum Geleit'!
(Klingsor ist auf der Burgmauer
heraus getreten; die Madchen
stürzen ebenfalls aus dem
Schlosse und wollen auf Kundry
zueilen.)

KLINGSOR: (eine Lauze schwig-
end). Halt da! dich bann' ich mit
der rechten Wehr:
den Thoren stell' mir seines Meisters Speer!
(Er schleudert auf Parsifal den
Speer, welcher über dessen
Haupte schweben bleibt; Parsifal
erfasst ihn mit der hand und
schwingt ihn, mit einer Gebärde
höchster Entzückung, die Gestalt
des Kreuzes bezeichnend.)

PARSIFAL: Mit diesem Zeichen
bann' ich deinen Zauber:
wie die Wunde er schliesse,
die ihm du schlugest,
in Trauer und Trümmer
stürze die trügende Pracht!
(Wie durch ein Erdbeben versinkt

PARSIFAL: Love and Redemption
you shall not lack,—
If you will show the way to Amfortas.

KUNDRY: (breaking into a rage).
You—never shall find it!
Let the doomed one perish for-
ever.—
The shame seeker,
Joy-destitute,
Whom I have laughed at—laughed
at—laughed at!
Ha ha! He fell by his own good
spear?

PARSIFAL: Who dared raise
against him the holy gear?

KUNDRY: He—he—,
Who puts my laughter to flight:
His curse—ha!—lends me might:
For you the Spear waits
If you pity the sinner's fate!
Ha! madness!
Pity! pity me, pray!
One single hour with me—
One single hour with you
Then you shall straightway see the
wished-for path.
(She seeks to embrace him; he
thrusts her from him).

PARSIFAL: Begone, detestable
wretch!

KUNDRY: (beats her breast and
shrieks in wild frenzy). Oh help!
Seize on the caitiff! Oh help!
Ward all the ways there!
Ward every passage!—
For, you fled from here, and found
All the ways of the world,
The one that you seek
That pathway never shall you pass
through!
All paths and courses,
Which from me would part,
Here—I curse them to you:
Wander—wander,—
You whom I trust—
You will I give as his guide!
(Kingsor has appeared upon the
castle wall; the Damsels also rush
out of the castle and seek to hasten
toward Kundry).

KLINGSOR: (poising a lance).
Halt there! I'll ban you with befitting gear:
The Fool shall perish by his Master's spear!
(He flings the spear at Parsifal; it
remains floating over his head:
Parsifal grasps it with his hand
and brandishes it with a gesture
of exalted rapture, making the
sign of the Cross with it.)

PARSIFAL: This sign I make, and
ban your cursed magic:
As the wound shall be closed,
Which you with this once
cloved,—your unreal display falls
to wrack and to ruin!
(As with an earthquake the castle

das Schloss; der Garten verdorrt zur Einöde; die Madchen liegen als verwelkte Blumen am Boden umber gestreut.·Kundry ist schreiend zusammen gesunken. Zu ihr wendet sich noch einmal, von der Höhe einer Mauertrümmer berab, der enteilende.

PARSIFAL: Du weisst—
wo du mich wieder finden kannst!
(*Er verschwindet. Der Vorhang schliesst sich schnell.*)

falls to ruins: the garden withers up to a desert: the Damsels lie like shriveled flowers strewn around on the ground.—Kundry has sunk down with a cry. To her turns once more from the summit of the ruined wall the departing)

PARSIFAL: You know—
Where only we shall meet again!
(*He disappears. The curtain closes quickly*).

# ■ DRITTER AUGZUG.

*Im Gebiete des Grales.*

*Freie, anmuthige Frühlingsgegend mit nach dem Hintergrunde zu sanft ansteigender Blumenaue. Den Vordergrund nimmt der Saum des Waldes ein, der sich nach rechts zu ausdehnt. Im Vordergrunde, an der Waldseite, ein Quell; ihm gegenüber, etwas tiefer, eine schlichte Einsiedlerhütte, an einen Felsen gelehnt. Frühester Morgen.—*

*Gurnemanz, zum hohen Greise gealtert, als Einsiedler. nur in das Hemd des Gralsritters dürftig gekleidet, tritt aus der Hütte und lauscht.*

GURNEMANZ: Von dorther kam das Stöhnen.—
So jammervoll klagt kein Wild, und gewiss gar nicht am heiligsten Morgen heut'.—
Mich dünkt, ich kenne diesen Klageruf?
(*Ein dumpfes Stöhnen, wie von einer im tiefen Schlafe durch Träume Geängstigten, wird vernommen.—Gurnemanz schreitet entschlossen einer Dornenhecke auf der Seite zu: diese ist gänzlich überwachsen: er reisst mit Gewalt das Gestrüpp auseinander: dann hält er plötzlich an.*)
Ha! Sie—wieder da?
Das winterlich rauhe Gedörn' hielt sie verdeckt: wie lang' schon?—
Auf!—Kundry!— Auf!
Der Winter floh, und Lenz ist da!
Erwach', erwache dem Lenz!—
kalt—und starr!—
Diesmal hielt' ich sie wohl für todt;—
doch war's ihr Stöhnen. vas ich vernahm?
(*Er zieht Kundry, ganz erstarrt und leblos, aus dem Gebüsche hervor, trägt sie auf einen nahen Rasenbügel, reibt ihr stark die Hände und Schläfe, baucht sie an, und bemüht sich in Allem, um die Erstarrung weichen zu machen. Endlich erwacht sie. Sie ist, gänzlich wie im ersten Aufzuge, im wilden Gewande der Gralsbo-*

# ■ ACT III.

*In the Grail's domain.*

*Open, pleasant spring landscape, with flowery meadows rising towards the back. At the front is the border of a wood, which extends away R. A spring, in the foreground, by the wood; opposite, higher up, a narrow hermitage, built against a rock. Daybreak.—*

*Gurnemanz, now extremely aged, meanly dressed as a hermit, but with the tunic of a Knight of the Grail, emerges from the hut and listens.*

GURNEMANZ: From where the groaning comes!
No animal grieves like that; And on this, besides,—the holiest day we have.—
I think I recognize those rueful tones.
(*A low moaning is heard as a sleeper terrified by dreams.—Gurnemanz strides resolutely to a thicket at one side which has overgrown itself; he forcible tears the brambles asunder, then pauses suddenly*).
Ha! She—here again?
The hedge overgrown with its thorns
Has been her grave for how long?—
Up—Kundry!—Up!
The winter's fled, and Spring is here!
Awake, awake to the Spring!—
Cold—and stiff!—
This time truly I deem she's dead:—
Yet was it her groaning I heard just now?
(*He drags Kundry, quite rigid and lifeless, out of the bushes, bears her to a grassy mound near, chafes her hands and temples, breathes on them and does his utmost to relax her stiffness. At last she revives, She is, just as in the first Act, dressed in the wild garb of a servant of the Grail; only her complexion is paler, and the wildness has faded from her mien*

tin; nur ist ihre Gesichtsfarbe bleicher, aus Miene und Haltung ist die Wildheit gewichen.— Sie starrt lange Gurnemanz an. Dann erhebt sieh, ordnet sich Kleidung und Haar, und geht sofort wie eine Magd an die Bedienung.)

GURNEMANZ: Du tolles Weib! Hast du kein Wort für mich? Ist dies der Dank, dass dem Todesschlafe noch einmal ich dich entweckt?

KUNDRY: (*neigt langsam das Haupt; dann bringt sie, rauh und abgebrochen, hervor*): Dienen.. dienen!—

GURNEMANZ: (*schüttelt den Kopf*). Das wird dich wenig müh'n! Auf Botschaft sendet sich's nicht mehr:
Kräuter und Wurzeln findet sich ein Jeder selbst, wir lernen's im Walde vom Thier.
(*Kundry ha sich während dem umgesehen, gewahrt die Hütte, und geht hinein.*)

GURNEMANZ: (*verwundert ihr nachblickend*). Wie anders schreitet sie als sonst! Wirkte das der heilige Tag? Oh! Tag der Gnade ohne Gleichen! Gewiss zu ihrem Heile durft' ich der Armen heut' den Todesschlaf verscheuchen.
(*Kundry kommt wieder aus der Hütte; sie trägt einen Wasserkrug und geht damit zum Quelle. Während sie auf die Füllung wartet, blickt sie in den Wald, und bemerkt dort in der Ferne einen Kommenden; sie wen. det sich zu Gurnemanz, um ihn darauf hinzudeuten.*)

GURNEMANZ: (*in den wald spähend*). Wer nahet dort dem heiligen Quell? Im düst'ren Waffenschmucke, das ist der Brüder keiner.
(*Kundry entfernt sich mit dem gefüllten Kruge langsam nach der Hütte, in welcher sie sich zu schaffen macht.—Gurnemanz tritt staunend etwas bei Seite, um den Ankommenden zu beobachten.—Parsifal tritt aus dem Walde auf. Er ist ganz in schwarzer Waffenrüstung: mit geschlossenem Helme und gesenktem Speer, schreitet er, gebeugten Hauptes, träumerisch zögernd, langsam daher, und setzt sich auf dem kleinen Rasenhügel am Quelle nieder.*)

GURNEMANZ: (*betrachtet ihn lange, und tritt dann etwas näher*). Heil dir, mein Gast! Bist du verirrt, und soll ich dich weisen?
(*Parsifal schüttelt sanft das Haupt.*)

and bearing.—She stares awhile at Gurnemanz. Then she rises, settles her hair and dress, and goes immediately like a serving maid to her work.)

GURNEMANZ: Crazy wench! Do you not have a word for me? Are these your thanks, When from deathly slumber I have waked you yet again?

KUNDRY: (*bows her head slowly; then in hoarse and broken accents murmurs*). Service . . . service!—

GURNEMANZ: (*shaking his head*). Now will your work be light!
We send no errands out since long: Simples and herbs Every one must find for himself: It is learned in the woods from the beasts.
(*Kundry has meanwhile looked about her, and now perceives the hut, and goes within.*)

GURNEMANZ: (*looking after her in surprise*). How unlike her step of yore!
In this Holy morning the cause! Oh, day of mercy unimagined! No doubt for her salvation Heaven through me revived This wretch from deathly slumber.
(*Kundry comes from the hut again; she bears a water pot, which she takes to the spring. While she waits for it to fill, she looks into the wood, and perceives some one approaching in the distance; she turns to Gurnemanz to point him out.*)

GURNEMANZ: (*peering into the woods*). Who comes toward the sanctified stream?
In gloomy war apparel he is not one of our brethren. (*Kundry withdraws, with the filled pitcher, to the hut, where she busies herself.— Gurnemanz steps aside in surprise, to observe the newcomer.— Parsifal enters from the wood. He is in complete black armor; with closed helmet and lowered spear he walks slowly forward, his head drooping, dreamily vacillating—he seats himself on the little knoll by the spring.*)

GURNEMANZ: (*observes him a long while and then approaches somewhat*). Greetings, my friend! Are you astray, and shall I direct you?
(*Parsifal shakes his head softly.*)

GURNEMANZ: Entbietest du mir keinen Gruss?
(*Parsifal neigt das Haupt.*)

GURNEMANZ: Hei!—Was?—
Wenn dein Gelübde
dich bindet mir zu schweigen,
so mahnt das meine mich,
dass ich dir sage, was sich ziemt.—
Hier bist du an geweihtem Ort:
da zieht man nicht mit Waffen her,
geschloss'nen Helmes, Schild und Speer.
Und heute gar! Weisst du denn nicht,
welch' heil'ger Tag heut' ist?
(*Parsifal schüttelt mit dem Kopfe.*)
Ja! Woher komm'st du denn?
Bei welchen Heiden weiltest du,
zu wissen nicht, dass heute,
der allerheiligste Char-Freitag sei?
(*Parsifal senkt das Haupt noch tiefer.*)
Schnell ab die Waffen!
Kränke nicht den Herrn, der heute,
bar jeder Wehr, sein heilig Blut
der sündigen Welt zur Sühne bot!
(*Parsifal erhebt sich, nach einem abermaligen Schweigen, stösst den Speer vor sich in den Boden, legt Schild und Schwert davor nieder, öffnet den Helm, nimmt ihn vom Haupte und legt ihn zu den anderen Waffen, worauf er dann zu stummem Gebete vor dem Speer niederkniet. Gurnemanz betrachtet ihn mit Erstaunen und Rührung. Er winkt Kundry herbei, welche soeben aus der Hütte getreten ist.—Parsifal erhebt jetzt in brünstigem Gebete seinen Blick andachtvoll zu der Lanzenspitze auf.*)

GURNEMANZ: (*leise zu Kundry.*)
Erkenn'st du ihn? ..
Der ist's, der einst den Schwan erlegt.
(*Kundry bestätigt mit einem leisen Kopfnicken*).
Gewiss 's ist Er!
Der Thor, den ich zürnend von uns wies?
Ha! Welche Pfade fand er?
Der Speer,—ich kenne ihn.
(*In grosser Ergriffenheit*)
Oh!— Heiligster Tag,
zu dem ich heut' erwachen sollt'!
(*Kundry hat ihr Gesicht abgewendet.*)

PARSIFAL: (*erhebt sich langsam vom Gebete, blicktruhig um sich, erkennt Gurnemanz, und reicht diesem sanft die Hand zum Gruss*). Heil mir, dass ich dich wieder finde!

GURNEMANZ: And have you no greeting for me?
(*Parsifal bows his head.*)

GURNEMANZ: Hey—what?—
If by your vow
You are bound to perfect silence,
So mine reminds me
Straight to inform you what is due.—
Here you are in a holy place;
No man with weapons comes here,
With shut up helmet, shield and spear.
This day, besides! Do you not know
What holy day has dawned?
(*Parsifal shakes his head.*)
No? From where have you come, then?
What heathen darkness have you left
To hear not that today is
The ever hallowed Good-Friday morn?
(*Parsifal droops his head still lower.*)
Quick, doff your weapons!
Trouble not this morn the Master,
Who once did free all men from hell,
When bare of defense He bled for us.
(*Parsifal rises after a further silence, thrusts the spear into the ground before him, lays down his sword and shield before it, opens his helmet and, taking it from his head, lays it with the other arms, and then kneels down in silent prayer before the spear. Gurnemanz observes him with surprise and emotion. He beckons Kundry, who has now come out of the hut.—Parsifal raises his eyes, in ardent prayer, towards the spear's head.*)

GURNEMANZ: (*softly to Kundry*). Do you know who it is?..
He who, long since, laid low the swan.
(*Kundry confirms him by a slight nod.*)
For sure it is he!
The Fool whom I dismissed in anger?
Ha! by what pathway came he?
That Spear—I recognize!
(*in great emotion*).
Oh!—holiest day,
To which my happy soul awakes!—
(*Kundry has turned away her face.*)

PARSIFAL:
(*rises slowly from his prayer, gazes calmly around, recognizes Gurnemantz, and stretches out his hand to him in greeting*).
Thank Heaven that I again have found you!

GURNEMANZ: So kenn'st auch du mich noch?
Erkenn'st mich wieder,
den Gram und Noth so tief gebeugt?
Wie kam't du heut'? Woher?

PARSIFAL: der Irrniss und der Leiden Pfade kam ich;
soll ich mich denen jetzt entwunden wähnen,
da dieses Waldes Rauschen
wieder ich vernehme,
dich guten Alten neu begrüsse?
Oder—irr' ich weider?
Verwandelt dünkt mich Alles.

GURNEMANZ: So sag', zu wemden Weg du suchtest?

PARSIFAL: Zu ihm, dess' tiefe Klagen
ich thörig staunend einst vernahm,
dem nun ich Heil zu bringen
mich auserlesen wähnen darf.
Doch—ach!—
den Weg des Heiles nie zu finden,
in pfadlosen Irren
jagt' ein wilder Fluch mich umher:
zahllose Nöthen,
Kämpfe und Streite
zwangen mich ab vom Pfade,
wähnt' ich ihn recht schon erkannt.
Da musste Verzweiflung mich fassen,
das Heilthum heil mir zu bergen,
um das zu hüten, das zu wahren
ich Wunden jeder Wehr' mir gewann.
Denn nicht ihn selber
durft' ich führen im Streite;
unentweih't
führt' ich ihn mir zur Seite,
den ich nun heim geleite,
der dort dir schimmert heil und hehr,—
des Grales heil'gen Speer.

GURNEMANZ: O Gnade! Höchtes Heil!
O Wunder! Heilig hehrstes Wunder!—
(*Nachdem er sich etwas gefasst.*)
O Herr! War es ein Fluch,
der dich vom rechten Pfad vertrieb,
so glaub', er ist gewichen.
Hier bist du; dies des Gral's Gebiet,
dein' harret seine Ritterschaft.
Ach, sie bedarf des Heiles,
des Heiles, das du bring'st !—
Seit jenem Tage, den du hier geweilt,
die Trauer, so da kund dir ward,
das Bangen—wuchs zur höchsten Noth Amfortas, gegen seiner Wunde,
seiner Seele Qual sich wehrend,
begehrt' in wildem Trotze nun den Tod;
kein Fleh'n, kein Elend seiner Ritter
bewog ihn mehr des heil'gen Amt's zu walten.
Im Schrein verschlossen bleibt seit lang' der Gral:
so hofft sein sündenreu'ger Hüter,
da er nicht sterben kann,
wann je er ihn erschau't,

GURNEMANZ: And do you know me too?
Do you recognize me,
So lowly bent by grief and care?
How have you come here? From where?

PARSIFAL: Through error and through suffering lay my pathway;
May I believe that I have freed me from it,
Now that this forest's murmur
Falls upon my senses,
And worthy voice of age welcomes?
Or yet—is it new error?
All's altered here, it seems.

GURNEMANZ: But say, where points the path you seek?

PARSIFAL: To him, whose dire complainings
Once came to me, an awestruck Fool,
And for whose healing surely
I must believe myself ordained.
But ah!—
The wished for path denied me,
I wandered at random,
Driven ever on by a curse:
Countless distresses,
Battles and conflicts
Drove me far from the pathway;
Well though I knew it, I thought.
Then hopeless despair overtook me
To hold the holy Thing safely.
In its behalf, in its safe warding
I won from every weapon a wound;
For it was forbidden I bore it
That in battle:
Undefiled
Ever at my side I wore it,
And now I home resore it.
It is this that gleaming hails you here,—
The Grail's most holy spear.

GURNEMANZ: Oh Glory, Bounteous bliss!
Oh marvel! Beauteous, boundless marvel!
(*After he has somewhat collected himself.*)
Great knight! If it were a curse
Which drove you from your proper path,
Be sure it has departed.
Here you are, in Grail's domain;
Here waits for you the knightly band.
Ah! how they need the blessing,
The blessing that you bring!
Since that first day in which you came here,
The mourning which you heard then—
The anguish—sorely has increased.
Amfortas, struggling with his torture,
With the wound that tore his spirit,
Desired with reckless daring then his death:
No prayers, no sorrow of his comrades
Could move him to fulfill his holy office.

sein Ende zu erzwingen,
und mit dem Leben seine Qual zu
enden.
Die heil'ge Speisung bleibt uns nun
versagt,
gemeine Atzung muss uns nähren;
darob versiechte unsrer Helden
Kraft:
nie kommt uns Botschaft mehr,
noch Ruf zu heil'gen Kämpfen aus
der Ferne;
bleich und elend wankt umher
die Muth- und Führer-lose Ritterschaft,
Hier in der Waldek' barg ich einsam
mich,
des Todes still gewärtig,
dem schon mein alter Waffenherr
verfiel,
denn Titurel, mein heil'ger Held,
den nun des Grales Anblick nicht
mehr labte,
er starb,—ein Mensch wie Alle!

**PARSIFAL:** (*vor grossem Schmerz
zich aufbäumend*). Und ich—ich
bin's
der all' dies Elend schuf!
Ha! Welcher Sünden,
welcher Frevel Schuld
muss dieses Thoren-Haupt
seit Ewigkeit belasten,
da keine Busse, keine Sühne
der Blindheit mich entwindet
mir, selbst zur Rettung auserkoren,
in Irrniss wild verloren
der Rettung letzter Pfad verschwindet!
(*Er droht ohnmächtig umzusink-
en. Gurnemanz hält ihn aufrecht,
und senkt ihn zum Sitze auf den
Rasenhügel nieder.— Kundry hat
ein Becken mit Wasser herbeige-
holt, um Parsifal zu besprengen.*)

**GURNEMANZ:** (*Kundry abweiz-
end*).
Nicht so!—
Die heil'ge Quelle selbst
erquicke uns'res Pilgers Bad.
Mir ahnt, ein hohes Werk
hat er noch heut' zu wirken,
zu walten eines heil'gen Amtes:
so sei er fleckenrein,
und langer Irrfahrt Staub
soll jetzt von ihm gewaschen sein.
(*Parsifal wird von den Beiden
sanft zum Rande des Quelles gewendet. Während Kundry ihm die
Beinschrenen lös't und dann die
Füsse badet, Gurnemanz ihm
aber den Brustharnisch entnimmt, frägt.*)

**PARSIFAL:** (*sanft und matt*).
Werd' heut' ich zu Amfortas noch
geleitet?

**GURNEMANZ:** (*während der Bes-
chäftigung*). Gewisslich, uns'rer
harrt die hehre Burg:
die Todtenfeier meines lieben
Herrn,

In shrouded shrine the Grail has
long remained;
Its sin-repentant warder wishing,
Since he could perish not,
While he beheld its light,
To speed his dissolution,
And with his life to end his bitter
sorrows.
The Holy Meal is now denied us,
And common viands must content
us;
Thereby has withered all our he-
roes' strength:
Messages never come now,
Nor call to holy warfare from far
countries;
Pale, dejected, strays around
The crushed and leader-lacking
band of knights.
Here on the lone woodside I hid
myself,
For death with calmness waiting,
To which my old commander has
succumbed;
For Titurel, my cherished chief,
When he no more beheld the
Grail's refulgence,
Expired,—a man like others!

**PARSIFAL:**
(*flinging up his arms in intense
grief*). And I—it is I, who has
wrought
All this woe!
Ha! what a grievous,
What a heinous guilt
Must then my foolish head
For ever be oppressed with
If no atonement, expiation,
My blindness ever can banish!
I, who was selected to save men,
Must wander undirected;
All paths of safety vanish from me!
(*He is on the point of falling, help-
lessly. Gurnemanz supports him,
and allows him to sink down on
the grassy knoll.— Kundry has
brought a basin of water to sprin-
kle Parsifal with.*)

**GURNEMANZ:** (*waving her off*).
Not so!
The holy font itself
Befits more our pilgrim's bath.
I believe a mighty feat
Must be this morning finish,
Fulfil a sacred, mystic duty:
He should be pure as day;
So let his travel stains
Be now completely washed away.
(*They both turn Parsifal gently to
the edge of the spring. Whilst Kun-
dry removes the greaves from his
legs, and then bathes his feet, Gur-
nemanz meanwhile removing his
corslet,—*)

**PARSIFAL:** (*asks gently and
wearily*). Shall I straight be guided
to Amfortas?

**GURNEMANZ:** (*busying himself*).
Most surely; there the Court our
coming waits.
The obsequies of my belovéd chief,
Have even summoned me.

sie ruft mich selbst dahin.
Den Gral noch einmal uns da zu enthüllen,
des lang' versäumten Amtes
noch einmal heut' zu walten—
zur Heiligung des hehren Vaters,
der seines Sohnes Schuld erlag,
die Der nun also büssen will,—
gelobt' Amfortas uns.

**PARSIFAL:** (*mit Verwunderung
Kundry zusehend*). Du wuschest
mir die Füsse :—
nun netze mir das Haupt der
Freund.

**GURNEMANZ:** (*mit der Hand aus
dem Quell schöpfend und Parsifal
Haupt besprengend*). Gesegnet
sei, du Reiner, durch das Reine
So weiche jeder Schuld
Bekümmerniss von dir!
(*Während dem hat Kundry ein
goldenes Fläschchen, aus dem Busen gezogen, und von seinem In-
halte auf Parsifal's Füsse ausge-
gossen, jetzt trocknet sie diese mit
schnell aufgelösten Haaren*).

**PARSIFAL:** (*nimmt ihr das
Fläschchen ab*). Salbtest du mir
auch die Füsse,
das Haupt nun salbe Titurel's Genoss',
dass heute noch als König er mich
grüsse.

**GURNEMANZ:** (*das Fläschchen
vollends auf Parsifal Haupt aus,
reibt dieses sanft, und faltet dann
die Hände darüber*). So ward es
uns verhiessen,
so segne ich dein Haupt,
als König dich zu grüssen.
Du—Reiner,—
mitleidvoll Duldender,
heilthatvoll Wissender!
Wie des Erlös'ten Leiden du gelitten, die letzte Last entnimm nun
seinem Haupt.

**PARSIFAL:** (*schöpft unvermerkt
Wasser aus der Quelle, neigt sich
zu der vor ihm knienden
Kundry, und netzt ihr das
Haupt*), Mein erstes Amt verricht'
ich so:—
die Taufe nimm,
und glaub' an den Erlöser!
(*Kundry senkt das Haupt tief zur
Erde und scheint heftig zu wein-
en.*)

**PARSIFAL:** (*wendet sich um, und
blickt mit sanfter Entzückung auf
Wald und Wiese*). Wie dünkt mich
doch die Aue heut' so schön!—
Wohl traf ich Wunderblumen an,
die bis zum Haupte süchtig mich
umrankten;
doch sah' ich nie so mild und zart
die Halmen, Blüthen und Blumen,
noch duftete All' so kindisch hold

The Grail will once more be uncov-
ered to us,
The long neglected office
Once more performed before us—
To sanctify the sovereign father
Who through his son's great sin has
died,
Which he now fain would expi-
ate.—
It is thus Amfortas wills.

**PARSIFAL:** (*observing Kundry
with wonder*). You've washed my
feet so humbly;—
This friend besprinkles now my
head.

**GURNEMANZ:** (*taking water
from the spring in the hollow of
his hand, and sprinkling Parsifal's head*). Now be blessed, pure
one, through pure water!
So may all care and sin
be driven far from you
(*Meanwhile Kundry has taken a
golden flask from her bosom and
poured some of the contents upon
Parsifal's feet, which she now
dries on her hair, quickly unbound for the purpose.*)

**PARSIFAL:** (*taking the flask from
her*).
Now that you anointed my feet,
My head the friend of Titurel must
lave;
For I today shall be appointed as
king.

**GURNEMANZ:** (*empties the flask
completely over Parsifal's head,
rubs it gently, and folds his hands
over it*). Aye, thus it was foretold
me,
My blessing on your head:
Our king indeed behold we.
You—pure one—
Allpitying sufferer,
Allknowing rescuer!
You who the sinner's sorrows have
suffered,
Assist his soul to cast one burden
more.

**PARSIFAL:** (*scoops up some water from the spring unperceived,
bends down to the kneeling Kundry and sprinkles her head*). I first
fulfil my duty this way
Be baptized,
And trust in the Redeemer!
(*Kundry bows her head to the
earth and appears to weep bitterly.*)

**PARSIFAL:** (*Turns round and
gazes with gentle rapture on the
woods and meadows*).
How fair the fields and meadows
seem to-day!—
Many a magic flower I've seen,
which sought to clasp me in its
baneful twinings;
But none I've seen so sweet as here,
These tendrils bursting with blos-

und sprach so lieblich traut zu mir?

**GURNEMANZ:** Das ist Char-Frei-tags-Zauber, Herr!

**PARSIFAL:** O weh', des höchsten Schmerzentag's!
Da sollte, wähn' ich, was da blüh't was athmet, lebt und wieder lebt, nur trauern, ach! und wienen?

**GURNEMANZ:** Du sieh'st, das ist nicht so.
Des Sünders Reuethränen sind es, die heut' mir heil'gem Thau beträufet Flur und Au':
der liess sie so gedeihen.
Nun freu't sich alle Kreatur, auf des Erlösers holder Spur will ihr Gebet ihm weihen.
Ihn selbst am Kreuze kann sie nicht erschauen:
da blickt sie zum erlös'ten Men-schen auf;
der fühlt sich frei von Sünden-Angst und Grauen, durch Gottes Leibesopfer rein und heil:
das merkt nun Halm und Blume auf den Auen, dass heut' des Menschen Fuss sie nicht zertritt, doch wohl, wie Gott mit him-mlischer Geduld sich sein' erbarmt und für ihn litt, der Mensch auch heut' in frommer Huld sie schont mit sanftem Schritt.
Das dankt dann alle Kreatur, was all' da blüht und bald erstirbt, da die entsündigte Natur heut' ihren Unschulds-Tag erwirbt.
(*Kundry hat langsam wieder das Haupt erhoben, und blickt, feu-chten Auges, ernst und ruhig bit-tend zu Parsifal auf.*)

**PARSIFAL:** Ich sah' sie welken, die mir lachten:
ob heut' sie nach Erlösung schma-chten?
Auch deine Thräne wird zum Seg-ensthaue:
du weinest—sich! es lacht die Aue.
(*Er küsst sie sanft auf die Stirne.*)
(*Fernes Glockengeläute, sehrall-mählich anschwellend.*)

**GURNEMANZ:** Mittag.—
Die Stund' ist da:—
gestatte, Herr, dass dich dein Knecht geleite!—
(*Gurnemanz hat Waffenrock und Mantel des Grals-ritters herbeige-holt; er und Kundry bekleideh Parsifal damit. Die Gegend ver-wandelt sich sehr allmählich, ähnlicher Weise wie im ersten Aufzuge, nur von rechts nach links. Parsifal ergreift feierlich den Speer und folgt mit Kundry langsam dem geleitenden Gurne-manz.—Nachdem der Wald*

som,
Whose scent recalls my child-hood's days
And speaks of loving trust to me.

**GURNEMANZ:** That is Good-Fri-day's spell, my lord!

**PARSIFAL:** Alas, that day of agony!
Now surely everything that thrives, That breathes and lives and lives again
Should only mourn and sorrow?

**GURNEMANZ:** You see, that is not so.
The sad repentant tears of sinners Have here with holy rain Besprinkled field and plain, And made them glow with beauty.
All earthly creatures in delight At the Redeemer's trace so bright Uplift their prayers of duty.
To see Him on the Cross they have no power:
And so they smile upon redeeméd man,
Who, feeling freed, with dread no more does cower,
Through God's love-sacrifice made clean and pure:
And now perceives each blade and meadow flower
That mortal foot today it need not dread;
For, as the Lord in pity man did spare,
And in His mercy for him bled, All men will keep, with pious care, Today a tender tread
Then thanks the whole creation makes,
With all that flowers and fast goes away,
That trespass-pardoned Nature wakes
Now to her day of Innocence.
(*Kundry has slowly raised her head again, and gazes with moist eyes, earnestly and calmly be-seeching, up at Parsifal.*)

**PARSIFAL:** I saw my scornful mockers wither:
Now look they for forgiveness hith-er?—
Like blessed sweet dew a tear from you too flows?
You weep—see! the landscape glows.
(*He kisses her softly on the brow.*)
(*Distant bells are heard pealing, very gradually swelling.*)

**GURNEMANZ:** Mid-day.—
The hour has come:—
Permit, my lord to teach your ser-vant here!
(*Gurnemanz has brought out a coat of mail and mantle of the knights of the Grail, which he and Kundry put on Parsifal. The land-scape changes very gradually, as in*
(*the 1st Act, but from R. to L. Par-sifal solemnly grasps the Spear and, with Kundry, follows the conducting Gurnemanz.—When the wood has disappeared, and*

gänzlich verschwunden ist, und Felsenthore sich aufgethan ha-ben, in welchen die Drei unsicht-bar geworden sind, gewahrt man, bei fortdauernd anwachsendem Geläute, in gewölbten Gängen Züge von Rittern in Trauerge-wändern. —Endlich stellt sich der ganze grosse Saal, wie im ersten Aufzuge (nur ohne die Speisetaf-eln) wieder dar. Düstere Beleu-chtung. Die Thüren öffnen sich wieder. Von einer Seite ziehen die Ritter, Titurel's Leiche im Sarge geleitend, herein. Auf der andern Seite wird Amfortas im Siechbette, vor ihm der verhüllte Schrein mit dem ,,Grale'', getragen. In der Mitte ist der Katafalk errichtet, dahinter der Hochsitz mit dem Baldachin, auf welchen Amfortas wieder niedergelassen wird.)
(Gesang der Ritter wahrend des Einzuges.)

**ERSTER ZUG:** (*mit dem ,,Gral'' und Amfortas*). Geleiten wir im bergenden Schrein, den Gral zum heiligen Amte, wen berget ihr im düst'ren Schrein und führt ihn trauernd daher?

**ZWEITER ZUG:** (*mit Titurel's Sarge*). Es birgt den Helden der Trauerschrein, er birgt die heilige Kraft; der Gott selbst einst zur Pflege sich gab:
Titurel führen wir her.

**ERSTER ZUG:** Wer hat ihn gefällt, der in Gottes Hut
Gott selbst einst beschirmte?

**ZWEITER ZUG:** Ihn fällte des Al-ters tödtende Last, da den Gral er nicht mehr er-schaute.

**ERSTER ZUG:** Wer wehrt' ihm des Grales Huld zu erschauen?

**ZWEITER ZUG:** Den dort ihr ge-leitet, der sündige Hüter.

**ERSTER ZUG:** Wir geleiten ihn heut', denn heut' noch einmal —zum letzten Male:— will des Amtes er walten.

**ZWEITER ZUG:** Wehe! Wehe! Du Hüter des Heil's!
Zum letzten Male sei deines Amts gemahnt!
(*Der Sarg ist auf dem Katafalk niedergesetzt, Amfortas auf das Ruhebett gelegt.*)

**AMFORTAS:** Ja, Wehe! Wehe!
Weh' über mich!—
So ruf' ich willig mit euch:
williger nähm' ich von euch den Tod,
der Sünde mildeste Sühne!
(*Der Sarg ist geöffnet worden. Beim Anblick der Leiche Titurél's bricht Alles in einen jähen Wehruf aus.*)

rocky entrances have presented themselves in which the three be-come invisible, processions of knights in mourning garb are per-ceived in the arched passages; the pealing of bells ever increasing.—At last the whole immense Hall be-comes visible just as the 1st Act, only without the tables. Faint light. The doors open again. From one side the knights bear in Titu-rel's corpse in a coffin. From the other Amfortas is carried on in his litter, preceded by the covered shrine of the Grail. The bier is erected in the middle; behind it the throne with canopy where Am-fortas is set down.)
(*song of the knights during the procesion.*)

**FIRST TRAIN:** (*with the "Grail" and Amfortas*).
To sacred place in sheltering shrine The Holy Grail do we carry; What hides there in gloomy shrine, Which mourning you bear here?

**SECOND TRAIN:** (*with Titurel's coffin*). A hero lies in this dismal shrine
with all this heavenly strength, to whom all things once God did entrust:
Titurel we bear here.

**FIRST TRAIN:** By whom was he slain, who by God himself Once was ever sheltered?

**SECOND TRAIN:** He sank beneath the mortal burden of years, When he might look on the Grail no more.

**FIRST TRAIN:** Who veiled then the Grail's delights from his vision?

**SECOND TRAIN:** He whom you are bearing: its criminal guardian.

**FIRST TRAIN:** We conduct him to-day, for here once again, —and once more only— He fulfills his office.

**SECOND TRAIN:** Sorrow! Sorrow! guard of the Grail!
Be once more only
Warned of your duty to all. (*The coffin is set down on the bier, Am-fortas placed on the couch.*)

**AMFORTAS:** Yes, sorrow! Sorrow! Sorrow for me!—
With you I willingly cry; Liefer yet I'd rather give me death, light Atonement for my trespass?
(*The coffin is opened. At the sight of Titurel's body all burst into a poignant cry to distress.*)

**AMFORTAS:** (*vom seinem Lager sich hoch aufrichtend, zu der Leiche gewandt*). Mein Vater! Hochgesegneter der Helden! Du Reinster, dem einst die Engel sich neigten! Der einzig ich sterben wollte, dir—gab ich den Tod! Oh! der du jetzt in göttlichem Glanz den Erlöser selbst erschau'st, erflehe von ihm, dass sein heiliges Blut, wenn noch einmal jetzt sein Segen die Brüder soll erquicken, wie ihnen neues Leben, mir endlich spende—den Tod! Tod!—Sterben! Einzige Gnade! Die schreckliche Wunde, das Gift ersterbe, das es zernagt, erstarre das Herz! Mein Vater! Dich—ruf' ich, rufe du ihm es zu: Erlöser, gieb meinem Sohne Ruh'!

**DIE RITTER:** (*sich näher an Amfortas drängend, durch einander*). Enthüllet den Schrein! Walte des Amtes! Dich mahnet der Vater: du musst, du musst!

**AMFORTAS:** (*in wüthender Verzweiflung aufspringend, und unter die zurückweichenden Ritter sich stürzend*). Nein!—Nicht mehr!—Ha! Schon fühl' ich den Tod mich umnachten, und noch einmal sollt' ich in's Leben zurück? Wahnsinnige! Wer will mich zwingen zu leben? Könnt ihr doch Tod nur mir geben! (*Er reisst sich das Gewand auf.*) Hier bin ich,—die off'ne Wunde hier! Das mich vergiftet, hier fliesst mein Blut. Heraus die Waffe! Taucht eure Schwerte tief—tief hinein, bis an's Heft! Ihr Helden, auf! Tödtet den Sünder mit seiner Qual, von selbst dann leuchtet euch wohl der Gral! (*Alle sind scheu vor ihm gewichen, Amfortas steht, is furchtbarer Extase, einsam.—Parsifal ist von Gurnemanz und Kundry begleitet, unvermerkt unter den Rittern erschienen, tritt jetzt hervor, und streckt den Speer aus, mit dessen Spitze er Amfortas, Seite berührt.*)

**AMFORTAS:** (*raising himself high on his couch and turning to the body*). My father! Highest venerated hero! You purest, to whom once even angels bended! I only desired to perish, Yet—gave you death! Oh! You who now in heavenly heights beholds the Savior's self, Implore him to grant that his hallowed blood, (If once again here his blessing He pour upon these brothers) To them new life while giving, To me may offer—but Death! Death—darkness! Solitary mercy! Take from me the horrible wound, the poison, Stiffen the heart so tortured and rent! My father! I—call you; Cry my words to Him: "Redeemer! give my son release!"

**THE KNIGHTS:** (*severally, pressing towards Amfortas*). Uncover the shrine!— Do now your office! Your father demands it;— You must, you must!

**AMFORTAS:** (*in a paroxysm of despair springs up and throws himself amid the knights, who draw back*). No!—No more!—Ha! Already death is glooming round me,— And shall I yet again return to life? Insanity! What one in life can yet hold me? Rather I bid you to slay me! (*tears open his dress*). Behold me!—behold the open wound! Here is my poison—my streaming blood. Take up your weapons! Bury your sword-blades Deep—deep in me, to the hilts! heroes, up! Kill both the sinner and all his pain: you will then regain The Grail's delight! (*All have shrunk back in awe. Amfortas stands alone in fearful ecstacy.-Parsifal, accompanied by Gurnemanz and Kundry, has entered unperceived, and now advancing stretches out the Spear, touching Amfortas' side with the point.*)

**PARSIFAL:** Nur eine Waffe taugt:— die Wunde schliesst der Speer nur, der sie schlug. (*AMFORTAS' Miene leuchtet in heiliger Entzückung auf; er scheinen vor grosser Ergriffenheit zu schwanken; GURNEMANZ stützt ihn.*)

**PARSIFAL:** Sei heil, entsündigt und gesühnt! Denn ich verwalte nun dein Amt. Gesegnet sei kein Leiden, das Mitleid's höchste Kraft und reinsten Wissens Macht dem zagen Thoren gab. Den heil'gen Speer— ich bring' ihn euch zurück.— (*Alles blickt in höchster Entzückung auf den emporgehaltenen speer zu dessen Spitze aufschauend PARSIFAL in Begeisterung fortfährt.*) Oh! Welchen Wunders höchstes Glück!— Die deine Wunde durfte schliessen, ihm seh' ich heil'ges Blut entfliessen in Sehnsucht dem verwandten Quelle, der dort fliesst in des Grales Welle! Nicht soll der mehr verchlossen sein: enthüllt den Gral! Oeffnet den Schrein! (*Die KNAPPEN öftnen den Schrein: PARSIFAL entnimmt diesem den ,,Gral,°° und versenkt sich, unter stummen Gebete, in seinem Anblick. Der ,,Gral°° erglüht: eine Glorienbeleuchtung ergiesst sich über Alle.—TITUREL, für diesen Augenblick wieder belebt erhebt sich segnend im Sarge.—Aus der Kuppel schwebt eine weisse Taube herab und verweilt über PARSIFAL'S Haupte. Dieser schwenkt den ,,Gral°° sanft vor der aufblickenden Ritterschaft.—KUNDRY sinkt, mit dem Blicke zu ihm auf, langsam vor PARSIFAL entseelt zu Boden. AMFORTAS und GURNEMANZ huldigen kniend PARSIFAL.*)

**ALLE:** (*mit Stimmen aus der mittleren, so wie der obersten Höhe, kaum hörbar leise*). Höchsten Heiles Wunder: Erlösung dem Erlöser! (*Der Vorhang schliesst sich.*)

*The end*

**PARSIFAL:** One weapon only serves:— The one that struck Can staunch your wounded side. (*AMFORTAS' countenance is irradiated with holy rapture; he totters with emotion; GURNEMANZ supports him.*)

**PARSIFAL:** Be whole, unsullied and absolved! For I now govren in your place. Oh, blessed be your sorrows, For Pity's potent might And Knowledge' purest power They taught a timid Fool. The holy Spear— Once more behold in this.— (*All gaze with intense rapture on the spear which PARSIFAL holds aloft, while he continues in inspiration as he looks at its point.*) Oh, mighty miracle of bliss!— This that through me your wound restores. With holy blood behold it pours. Which yearns to join the fountain glowing, Whose pure tide in the Grail is flowing! Hid be no more that shape divine: Uncover the Grail! Open the shrine! (*The boys open the shrine; PARSIFAL takes from it the "Grail" and kneels, absorbed in its contemplation, silently praying. The "Grail" glows with light; a balo of glory pours down over all.—TITUREL, for the moment reanimated, raises himself in benediction in his coffin.—From the dome descends a white dove and hovers over PARSIFAL'S head. He waves the "Grail" gently to and fro before the upgazing knights. KUNDRY, looking up at PARSIFAL, sinks slowly to the ground, dead. AMFORTAS and GURNEMANZ do homage on their knees to PARSIFAL.*)

**ALL:** (*with voices from the middle and extreme heights, so soft as to be scarcely audible*). Wondrous work of mercy: Salvation to the Savior! (*The Curtain closes.*)

*The end*

# Der Freischütz (1821)

MUSIC BY CARL MARIA VON WEBER ■ LIBRETTO BY FRIEDRICH KIND

---

This romantic three-act opera, set to a libretto by Friedrich Kind (based upon the *Gespensterbuch* by Johann August Apel and Friedrich Laun), was first performed at the Schauspielhaus in Berlin on June 18, 1821. The opera takes place in Bohemia around 1650. In a rifle contest against Kilian, Max, a young forester, has missed every target. Cuno, Chief Ranger of Prince Ottokar, stops a fight from ensuing between the two, but he tells Max that he will not be allowed to marry Agathe, the daughter of the Prince, unless he wins the next day's shooting competition. Max, no longer confident of victory, is given a magic potion by Caspar, another forester, who encourages him to use enchantment. Samiel, the devil, looks on while Caspar gives Max a gun and tells him to shoot an eagle which can hardly be seen. Max, to his surprise, shoots the bird down; Caspar says that the bullets are magic and that, in order to obtain more, he must go to the Wolf's Glen at midnight. At the exact moment that Max shot the eagle, a portrait of Cuno falls down at his house. Agathe has terrible premonitions about what is to happen. Max shows her the dead eagle and is adamant that he must go to the Wolf's Glen in order to retrieve a dead deer. Once there, Caspar offers Max's soul in exchange for his own, and Samiel accepts the bargain. Caspar says that Samiel should use the seventh bullet, the one which remains in his possession, to kill Agathe. Max helps Caspar to mould the metal which will be used for the magic bullets. While they pronounce the spells upon the bullets, a violent storm rages and a vision of the Wild Hunt appears across the sky. When the seventh bullet is cast, Samiel appears. The next day, Max is winning the contest, but he has one bullet left—the one belonging to Samiel. Agathe, who has dreamt that she was a dove shot by Max and that her wedding bouquet became a funeral wreath, is comforted by friends who tell her that Max will win. Wearing her wedding dress, she watches the contest in Prince Ottokar's presence, accompanied by a Hermit. The Prince sets the target, which is a dove way up in the trees. Agathe tries to stop Max from shooting, but the Hermit disturbs the bird and it flies to another tree where Caspar is hiding. Max fires as ordered by the Prince and Caspar dies, cursing God and Samiel. The pact between Max and Samiel is then revealed, and the Prince plans to banish Max in punishment. However, the Hermit pleads for him, suggesting that if Max behaves piously for one year he may marry Agathe. The Prince agrees to this, and the chorus sings praises, ending the opera.

---

## ■ ERSTER AKT

### ERSTE SCENE

*(Platz vor einer Waldschenke. Max sitz allein im Vorgrunde. In dem Augenblicke, als die Gardine aufgeht, fallen Schüsse. CHOR der Landleute, indem die Scheibe herabgebracht wird.)*

Viktoria! Viktoria! der Meister soll leben, Der wacker dem Sternlein den Rest hat gegeben! Ihm gleichet kein Schütz' von fern und von nah' Viktoria! Viktoria! Viktoria!

**MAX:** Immer frisch! Schreit! schreit! *(Stampft und legt seine Büchse an den baum.)* War ich denn blind? Sind die Sehnen dieser Faust erschlafft?
*Es hat sich ein Zug von Bauern geordnet, welche Kilian im Triumph vor Max bringen.*

**KILIAN:** Schau' der Herr mich an als König! Dünkt ihm meine Macht zu wenig? Gleich zieh' er den Hut, Mosje! Wird er? frag' ich — He? He? He? *(Chor wiederholt die letzte Zeile.)*

**KILIAN:** Stern und Strauss trag' ich vor'm Leibe, Cantors Sepherl trägt die Scheibe; Hat er Augen nun, Mosje? Was traf er denn? — He? He? He? *(Chor wie oben.)*

**KILIAN:** Darf ich etwa Eure Gnaden 's nächste Mal zum Schiessen laden? Er gönnt Andern was, Mosje! Nun, er kommt doch? — He? He? He? *(Chor, wie oben.)*

**MAX:** *(Springt auf, zieht den Hirschfänger und fasst Kilian bei der Brust.)* Lasst mich zufrieden, oder — ! *(Getümmel, auf Max eindringend.)*

### ZWEITE SCENE

*Cuno, Caspar und mehrere Jäger mit Büchsen und Jagdspiessen.*

**CUNO:** Was gibt's hier? Pfui, dreissig über einen! Wer untersteht sich, meinen Burschen anzutasten?

**KILIAN:** *(von Max losgelassen.)* Alles in Güte und Liebe, werther Herr Erbförster! Gar nicht böse gemeint! Es ist Herkommen bei uns,

## ■ ACT I

### SCENE I

*(Open place before an inn. MAX seated alone in the foreground Some shots are fired as the curtain rises. CHORUS of Peasants as the target is brought down.)*

Victoria, Victoria! All honor and fame. To him, who with true and steady good aim. Hit the white. Let his glory be sounded afar. Victoria, Victoria, Victoria!

**MAX:** Yes, yes! cry and shout! *(stamps and leans his rifle against a tree.)* Was I blind? Or are the sinews of this hand relaxed? *(March of the peasants, who bring Killian in triumph before Max.)*

**KILLIAN:** Look at me now, as your king, Sir! Seems my power still too small, Sir! Doff your hat. Sir, doff to me, Will you, will you? Hi! hi! hi! *(Chorus repeats the last line.)*

**KILLIAN:** You see I've gained the band and favor. You gained nothing by your labor, You had eyes, but could not see, Behold the target! Hi! hi! hi!

**KILLIAN:** Perhaps, since this time you are beaten. You'd like to have another meeting? I'm at your service, as you see, You dare not, dare not! Hi! hi! hi! *(Chorus, as above.)*

**MAX:** *(Start up, draws his woodman's knife furiously at Killian).* Let me alone, or — *(The peasants interfere.)*

### SCENE II

*(CUNO, CASPAR, and several foresters, enter with rifles and hunting spears.)*

**CUNO:** What is the matter here? For shame, thirty to one! Who dares to attack my forester?

**KILLIAN:** *(whom Max had relinquished).* All in kindness and love, your Worship! No harm was intended! It is an old custom with us, to

## Act I, Scene II

dass, wer stets gefehlt hat, vom Königschusse ausgeschlossen und dann ein wenig gehänselt wird — alles in Güte und Liebe.

CUNO: (*heftig.*) Stets gefehlt? Wer? wer hat das?

MAX: (*beschämt und verzweifelnd.*) Ich kann's nicht leugnen; ich habe nie getroffen.

CASPAR: *vor sich.* Dank, Samiel! (*Zu Max.*) Glaube mir, Kamerad, es ist wie ich gesagt habe. Es hat dir Jemand einen Waidmann gesetzt, und den musst du lösen, oder du triffst keine Klaue. Geh' nächsten Freitag auf einen Kreuzweg, zieh' mit dem Ladestock older einem blutigen Degen einen Kreis um dich und rufe dreimal den grossen Jäger —

KILIAN: Gott bewahr' uns! Einen von des Teufels Heerschaaren!

CUNO: *zu Caspar.* Schweig', vorlauter Bube! Ich kenne dich längst. Du bist ein Tagedieb, ein Schlemmer, ein falscher Würfler — hüte dich, dass ich nicht noch Aergeres von dir denke. (*Caspar macht eine kriechende Bewegung, als wolle er sich entschuldigen.*) Kein Wort, oder du hast auf der Stelle den Abschied! — Aber auch du, Max, siehe dich vor! Ich bin dir wie ein Vater gewogen; es freut mich, dass der Herr Fürst Sohnesrecht auf den Eidam übertragen will — aber — wenn du morgen beim Probeschusse fehltest, müsst' ich dir doch das Mädchen versagen.

MAX: Morgen! morgen schon!

KILIAN: Was ist eigentlich mit dem Probeschuss? Schon oft haben wir davon gehört. —

ANDERE: O, erzähl's uns, Herr Cuno!

CUNO: Meinetwegen! (*Setzt sich.*) Mein Ureltervater, der noch im Forsthause abgebildet steht, hiess Cuno, wie ich, und war fürstlicher Leibschütz. Einst trieben die Hunde einen Hirsch heran, auf dem ein Mensch angeschmiedet war; so bestrafte man in alten Zeiten die Waldfrevler. Dieser Anblick erregte das Mitleid des damaligen Fürsten. Er versprach demjenigen, welcher den Hirsch erlege, ohne den Missethäter zu verwunden, eine Erbförsterei, und zur Wohnung das nahgelegene Waldschlösschen. Der wackere Leibschütz, mehr aus eigenem Erbarmen, als wegen der grossen Verheissung, besann sich nicht lange. Er legte an und befahl die Kugel den heiligen Engeln. Der Hirsch stürzte, und der Wilddieb war, obwohl im Gesicht vom Dorngebüsch derb zerkratzt, doch im Uebrigen unversehrt.

mock him a little who has missed every shot at our prize shooting; but all in kindness and love.

CUNO: (*passionately*). Missed every shot? Who? Who missed always?

MAX: (*ashamed and despairingly*). I cannot deny it; I have not hit the mark.

CASPAR: (*aside*). Thanks Zamiel! (*To Max.*) Believe me, comrade, it is as I have told you. Somebody has bewitched you, and you must relieve the domon, ere you can hit any mark. Go next Friday to a cross road; with thy ramrod or a bloodstained sword draw a circle around thee, and call thrice upon the Black Forester —

KILIAN: Heaven forefend us! One of the Devil's legions.

CUNO: (*to Caspar*). Silence, sir! I know you will. You are a wretch, a drunkard, a false player — beware, else I mistake you for something even worse (*Caspar crouches, and by his gestures attempts to excuse himself.*) No words, or you leave me this instant! — But you, too, Max, be careful! if tomorrow you fail in the trial shot. I should be compelled to refuse the girl to you.

MAX: What! Tomorrow already?

KILIAN: What is this about the trial shot! We have often heard it mentioned.

PEASANTS: Please tell us, Master Cuno.

CUNO: Be it so. (*Seats himself.*) My great-grand father, whose portrait still hangs in the forester's house, was called Cuno like myself, and was head ranger to the duke. Once as they were in the forest, the dogs started a stag, upon whose back a man was bound. such was in those days the punishment of poachers. The prince was moved to pity at this sight, and promised him who should kill the stag without wounding the man, the situation of head ranger, with the small hunting castle in this neighborhood for his residence. One brave forester, more from pity he felt for the culprit than the hope of reward, did not hesitate a moment. He raised his rifle, commended the ball to the guardianship of the angels, and shot. The stag fell, and the poacher, though much torn and wounded by briars and thorns, was saved.

MÄNNER: Brav! brav! — das war ein Meisterschuss.

CUNO: Hört noch das Ende! Es ging damals wie jetzt — (*mit einem Blick auf Caspar*) — dass der böse Feind immer Unkraut unter den Weizen säet. Cuno's Neider wussten es an den Fürsten zu bringen, der Schuss sei mit Zauberei geschehen, Cuno habe nicht gezielt, sondern eine Freikugel geladen.

CASPAR: Dacht' ich's doch! (*Vor sich.*) Hilf zu, Samiel!

KILIAN: *Zu einigen Bauern.* Eine Freikugel! — das sind Schlingen des bösen Feinds; meine Grossmutter hat mir's einmal erklärt. Sechse treffen, aber die siebente gehört dem Bösen: der kann sie hinführen, wohin ihm's beliebt.

CASPAR: Alfanzerei! Nichts als Naturkräfte!

CUNO: Aus diesem Grunde machte der Fürst bei der Stiftung den Zusatz, dass jeder von Cuno's Nachfolgern zuvor einen Probeschuss ablege, schwer oder leicht. Du, Max, magst noch einmal zu Hause nachsehen, ob sämmtliche Treibleute angelangt sind. Nimm dich zusammen! — der Waidmann, der dir gesetzt ist, mag die Liebe sein. — Noch vor Sonnenaufgang erwarte ich dich beim Hoflager.

MAX: *der erst aus seiner Zerstreuung zurückgekommen ist.* O! diese Sonne,
Furchtbar steigt sie mir empor!

CUNO: Leid oder Wonne,
Beides ruht in deinem Rohr!

MAX: Ach, ich muss verzagen,
Dass der Schuss gelingt!

CUNO: Dann musst Du entsagen —

CASPAR: *zu Max, mit bedeutungsvoller Heimlichkeit.* Nur ein keckes Wagen
Ist's, was Glück erringt!

MAX: Agathen entsagen,
Wie könnt' ich's ertragen?
Doch verfolgt mich Missgeschick —

CHOR: Seht, wie düster ist sein Blick!
Ahnung scheint ihn zu durchheben— (*Zu Max.*)
O lass Hoffnung dich beleben,
Und vertraue dem Geschick!

MAX: Weh' mir! Mich verliess das Glück,
Unsichtbare Mächte grollen,
Bange Ahnung füllt die Brust!

CASPAR: Mag Fortuna's Kugel rollen;
Wer sich höh'rer Kraft bewusst,
Trotzt dem Wechsel und Verlust;

CUNO: So's des Himmels Mächte wollen,
Dann — trag' männlich den Verlust!

PEASANTS: Bravo! That was a master shot.

CUNO: Now listen to the end? Then, as now, (*he cast a look at Caspar*) the foul fiend was in the habit of casting evil seed among the good. The rivals of Cuno persuaded the Prince that the shot had been accomplished by witchcraft, and that Cuno had taken no aim, but had loaden his rifle with a charmed ball.

CASPAR: So I thought. (*Aside.*) Help Zamiel.

KILIAN: (*to peasants*). A charmed ball! — Those are the snares of the fiend, my grandmother has often told me. Six will hit the mark, but the seventh belongs to the demon; he can guide it wherever he likes.

CASPAR: Stuff and nonsense! men laugh at it

CUNO: For this reason the Prince has instituted this trial shot, which each of Cuno's successors must gain. Max, you may now go home, and see if all the foresters have arrived. — Be careful? — The witchery that is upon you, may be love. — Before sunrise I shall look for you at the appointed place.

MAX: (*just recovering from his thoughtfulness*). Oh, sadly to me Rises dread tomorrow's sun.

CUNO: All that's dear to you,
Must indeed be lost or won!

MAX: Alas the hope is slender,
My fears I can't repress.

CUNO: And your bride so tender —

CASPAR: (*to Max significantly*).
Her you may surrender
Unless you force success.

MAX: My love to relinquish,
Oh terror and anguish,
I cannot endure this woe —

CHORUS: Behold how sad is his brow.
How lost to all hope of success. (*To Max.*)
Let faith encourage you now,
And Heaven will aid your distress.

MAX: Ah, who could repress this fear!
Dark and unseen powers assail me.
Fearful anguish fills my heart!

CASPAR: What will silly sighs avail you?
He who takes a manly part
May thwart the frowns of fortune.

CUNO: Son, let not thy courage fail you.
Shrink not — still be stout of heart.

**CHOR:** Nein, er trüg' nicht den Verlust!

**CUNO:** (*fasst Max bei der Hand.*) Mein Sohn, nur Muth! Wer Gott vertraut, baut gut. (*Zu den Jägern.*) Jetzt auf! In Bergen und Klüften Tobt morgen der freudige Krieg.

**CHOR DER JÄGER:** Das Wild in Fluren und Triften, Der Aar in Wolken und Lüften Ist unser, und unser der Sieg!

**CHOR DER LANDLEUTE:** Lasst lustig die Hörner erschallen —

**CHOR DER JÄGER:** Wir lassen die Hörner erschallen —

**ALLE, ausser MAX:** Wenn wiederum Abend ergraut, Soll Echo und Felsenwand hallen: Sa! Hussah, dem Bräut'gam! der Braut! *Cuno mit Caspar und dem Jägern ab. Dämmerung fängt an.*

### DRITTE SCENE

*Die Vorigen, ohne Cuno und sein Gefolge.*

**KILIAN:** Ein braver Mann, der Herr Förster! Aber nun kommt auch in den Schenkgiebel; es wird schon recht dämmrig und schaurig. (*Zu Max.*) Wir wollen gute Freunde bleiben, wackerer Bursch! Ich gönne ihm morgen das beste Glück! Jetzt schlag' er sich die Grillen aus dem Kopfe, nehm' er ein Mädchen und tanze er mit hinein!

**MAX:** Ja, es wär' mir, wie tanzen!

**KILIAN:** Nun, wie's beliebt! Tanzt, Kinder. (*Er nimmt eine der Frauen; die Andern ebenso. Böhmischer Walzer.*)

### VIERTE SCENE

*Max, allein. Späterhin Samiel.*

**MAX:** Nein, länger trag' ich nicht die Qualen, Die Angst, die jede Hoffnung raubt! Für welche Schuld muss ich bezahlen? Was weiht dem falschen Glück mein Haupt? Durch die Wälder, durch die Auen Zog' ich leichten Muths dahin; Alles, was ich konnt' erschauen, War des sichern Rohr's Gewinn. Abends bracht' ich reiche Beute, Und als über eig'nes Glück, Drohend wohl dem Mörder, freute Sich Agathe's Liebesblick. — Hat denn der Himmel mich verlas-

**CHORUS:** Oh this loss would break his heart.

**CUNO:** (*taking Max's hand*). Take heart, my son In Heaven who trusts, has won. (*To the Foresters.*) Now Huzza! through valley and mountain, Tomorrow shall sound the gay chase.

**CHORUS OF FORESTERS:** The stag who rests near the fountain, The eagle who soars high over mountain Is ours — and ours the race.

**CHORUS OF PEASANTS:** Sound bugles the hunters' rejoicing —

**CHORUS OF FORESTERS:** Our horns sound the hunters' rejoicing —

**ALL:** (*except Max*). When evening's shades shall subside, Sounds echo with thousands of voices, Huzza for the bridegroom and bride! (*Exit Cuno, Caspar and Foresters.*) (*Evening gradually set in.*)

### SCENE III

*(The same, without Cuno, etc.)*

**KILLIAN:** An excellent man, our head ranger. But now let us go in; begins to grow dark and gloomy. (*to Max.*) Let us remain freinds, my good fellow! I hope you may have the best luck tomorrow! But now, cheer up, take a lass and have a dance with us.

**MAX:** Pshaw! I don't feel like dancing.

**KILLIAN:** Well, as you like! Come let us dance. (*He takes one of the women, the others do likewise. Bohemian Waltz.*)

### SCENE IV

*(MAX alone, afterwards ZAMIEL.)*

**MAX:** No, I can bear this fate no longer This fear which tortures thus my soul. Ah! for what guilt am I atoning. Which over my heart holds it control? Through the forests, through the meadows, Joy was wont with me to stray. While my rifle, never failing Made each bird and beast my prey. And when evening decked the mountain, Veiling earth in twilight's gloom, Chiding, yet my deeds recounting,

sen? (*Samiel erscheint.*) Die Vorsicht ganz ihr Aug' gewandt? Soll das Verderben mich erfassen? Verfiel ich in des Zufalls Hand? Jetzt ist wohl ihr Fenster offen, Und sie horcht auf meinen Schritt, Lässt nicht ab vom treuen Hoffen: Max bringt gute Zeichen mit! Wenn sich rauschend Blätter regen, Wähnt sie wohl, es sei mein Fuss; Hüpft vor Freuden, winkt entgegen— Nur dem Laub'—den Liebesgruss.— Doch mich umgarnen finst're Mächte; (*Samiel schreitet über die Bühne.*) Mich fasst Verzweiflung, foltert Spott! O, dringt kein Strahl durch diese Nächte? Herrscht blind das Schicksal? Lebt kein Gott? (*Samiel verschwindet bei dem letzten Worte.*)

### FÜNFTE SCENE

*Max. Caspar, herbeischleichend. Samiel. Ein Schenkmädchen.*

**CASPAR:** Da bist du immer noch, Kamerad. Gut dass ich dich finde.

**MAX:** Horchst du schon wieder herum?

**CASPAR:** Ist das mein Dank? Ich kann's, kann's nicht verschmerzen, dass du hier zum Spott der Bauern worden bist. Teufel! die mögen gelacht haben! ha, ha ha! (*Greift nach dem Kruge.*) Wie? was? Bier hast du? Das taugt nicht zum Sorgenbrecher! (*In den Schenkgiebel rufend:*) Wein! Wein! Zwei Passgläser!—Kamerad! und koste es mich den letzten Heller, ich kann dich nicht so traurig sehen! So, Freundchen! da brauch'st du wenig! (*Giesst schnell Wein ein.*) Hilf, Samiel! (*Samiel erscheint. Caspar erschrocken.*) Du da? (*Samiel verschwindet.*)

**MAX:** Mit wem sprachst du?

**CASPAR:** Ich?—mit Niemand. Ich sagte: ,,So, Freundchen!'' weil ich dir einschenkte.

**MAX:** Ich mag aber nichts.

**CASPAR:** Der Herr Förster soll leben! Die Gesundheit deines Lehrherrn wirst du doch mittrinken?

**MAX:** So sei's. (*Sie trinken.*)

**CASPAR:** Hier im ird'schen Jammerthal Wär' doch nichts, als Plack und Qual, Trüg' der Stock nicht Trauben; Darum, bis zum letzten Hauch,

Sweet Agath' said—welcome home. And am I wholly left by heaven? (*Zamiel appears.*) And will my prayers no more avail? Am I to wild destruction given And shall the powers of night prevail? From her lattice window gazing Now her eye is seeking me. While her heart is fondly beating Max, bring happy signs to me! Now she fondly waves a welcome, Fancy's eye her lover sees But her signal—gains no answer— Save the sigh of whispering trees.— But fearful powers are ruling, over me. (*Zamiel crosses the stage.*) To dark perdition I am driven. With nothing but despair before me. Does chance rule blindly—aid me Heaven. (*Zamiel disappears at the last word.*)

### SCENE V

*(Max, Caspar approaching slowly. Zamiel. A Barmaid.)*

**CASPAR:** So you are still here. Comrade. It is well I find you,

**MAX:** Why are you eaves-dropping about thus?

**CASPAR:** Are these all the thanks I get? I cannot well forget it, that you should have become a subject of merriment to these boors here. How they must have laughed? ha! ha! ha! (*Takes the can from the table.*) How is this? beer? Pshaw! that never will kill care! (*Calling unto the house.*) Wine! hollo! wine! Yes, Comrade, and if it costs my last penny, I cannot see you so mournful. (*Aside.*) You'll not require much! (*Filling a cup.*) Help Zamiel! (*Zamiel appears, Caspar frightened.*) You here? (*Zamiel disappears.*)

**MAX:** With whom have you spoken?

**CASPAR:** I? with no one. I merely said "Good luck." as I filled your cup.

**MAX:** But I will not drink.

**CASPAR:** Long life to the head rangers—You certainly will not refuse to drink to our master's health.

**MAX:** Be it so. (*They drink.*)

**CASPAR:** Here is this dull vale below, Nothing's found but care and woe, Except the joys of drinking! Therefore to the latest hour. Put your faith in Bacchus' power,

Setz' ich auf Gott Bacchus Bauch
Meinen festen Glauben!
Ei, du musst auch mitsingen!
(*Trinkt.*)

MAX: Lass mich!

CASPAR: Jungfer Agathe soll leben! Wer die Gesundheit seiner Braut ausschlüg', wär' doch wahrlich ein Schuft.

MAX: Du wirst unverschämt. (*Sie trinken.*)

CASPAR: Eins ist Eins und Drei sind Drei!
D'rum addirt noch zweierlei
Zu dem Saft der Reben;
Kartenspiel und Würfellust
Und ein Kind mit runder Brust
Hilft zum ew'gen Leben!
Mit dir ist aber auch gar nichts anzufangen! (*Trinkt.*) Unser Herr Fürst soll leben! Wer nicht d a b e i ist, ist ein Judas!

MAX; Nun denn, aber dann auch keinen Tropfen mehr! (*Sie trinken.*)

CASPAR: Ohne dies Trifolium
Gibt's kein wahres Gaudium
Seit dem ersten Uebel.
Fläschchen, sei mein A-B-C,
Mein Gebetbuch, Catherle,
Karte, meine Bibel!
(*Die Dorfuhr schlägt, Max steht auf.*)
Willst du schon nach Hause?

MAX: Ja, es wird Zeit. Das schlug Sieben!

CASPAR: Bleib' noch und lass dir rathen! Deshalb hab' ich dich eigentlich aufgesucht. Dir könnte gar wohl geholfen werden!

MAX: Mir geholfen?

CASPAR: *geheimnissvoll.* Um dir ganz meine Freundschaft zu beweisen, könnte ich dir unter vier Augen — — Diese Nacht, wo sich die Mondscheibe verfinstert, ist zu grossen Dingen geschickt! —
*Man sieht Samiel von Zeit zu Zeit lauschen.*

CASPAR: Wie wär's, Kamerad, wenn ich dir noch heute zu einem recht glücklichen Schusse verhülfe, der Agathen beruhigte und zugleich euer morgendes Glück verbürgte?

MAX: Du fragst wunderbar. Ist das möglich?

CASPAR: Da nimm meine Büchse!

MAX: Was soll ich damit?

CASPAR: Geduld! *Er sieht nach dem Himmel.* Zeigt sich denn nichts? *Indem er ihm das Gewehr gibt.* Da! Da! Siehst du den Stösser dort! Schiess!

MAX: Es ist ganz düster, der Vogel schwebt wie ein schwarzer Punkt in der Luft, wolkenhoch über der Schussweite!

And set sorrow winking.
But you must sing with me!
(*Drinks*)

MAX: Let me alone!

CASPAR: Here's to Miss Agathe's health! You would certainly be a scamp, if you refused to drink the health of your bride.

MAX: You are getting rude. (*Drinks.*)

CASPAR: One is one, and three are three;
Therefore to complete the glee,
Add two more to it.
With card and die to gamble bold,
A pretty girl—but not too old,
Those are things will do it.
But I can do nothing with thee. (*Drinks.*) Here's our Prince's health!
A Judas he who refuses the toast!

MAX: Be it so, but not another drop afterwards! (*They drink.*)

CASPAR: Without this *Trifolium*,
There is no true *Gaudium*:
Since the first transgression
My alphabet a bottle is,
My daily prayer—a girl to kiss,
Such is my profession.
(*Clock strikes, Max rises.*)
Will you already go home?

MAX: Yes, it is time, it struck seven!

CASPAR: Stay yet, and let me advise you. It is for this, I have sought you; I may be able to help you.

MAX: Help me?

CASPAR: (*mysteriously.*) To prove my friendship to you I might in confidence tell you—This night, when the moon is eclipsed, is suited to great purposes!
(*Zamiel appears occasionally and listens.*)

CASPAR: How comrade, if I should help thee to a most fortunate shot! a shot which would quiet the fears of Agathe, and at the same time secure success for tomorrow?

MAX: You speak strangely. How is that possible?

CASPAR: There, take my rifle.

MAX: For what purpose?

CASPAR: Patience? (*he looks up*) Can I see nothing? (*giving him the rifle*) There! there! see the eagle yonder? Shoot!

MAX: It is almost dark. The bird appears but a black spot. It soars far beyond the reach of the rifle.

CASPAR: Schiess in's T — Schellobers Namen! Ha, ha!
Max (*berührt den Stecher: das Gewehr geht los. In demselben Augenblick hört man ein gellendes Gelächter, so dass sich Max erschrocken nach Caspar umsieht*). Was ist das?

CASPAR: Viktoria! Das wird dich bei den Bauern in Respect setzen! das wird Agathen erfreuen! (*Rauft einige der grössten Federn aus und steckt sie auf Maxens Hut.*) So Kamerad! dies als Siegeszeichen.

MAX: Träum' ich denn, order bin ich berauscht? So etwas ist mir noch nie begegnet! — Caspar! ich bitte dich, ich beschwöre dich — (*Fasst ihn*) — Caspar! ich bringe dich um! — Sag, was war das für eine Kugel?

CASPAR: Nun, wenn du Vernunft annimmst — — so sag' mir — du, der wackerste Jäger, bist du, oder stellst du dich so unerfahren? Wüsstest du wirklich nicht, was eine Freikugel sagen will?

MAX: Der Schuss ist unglaublich — in trüber Dämmerung — aus den Wolken herabgeholt! So wäre es doch wahr? Hast du noch mehr solche Kugeln?

CASPAR: Es war die letzte — sie haben gerade ausgereicht.

MAX: Bist du doch auf einmal so wortkarg! — Ausgereicht! Wie verstehst du das?

CASPAR: Weil sie in dieser Nacht zu bekommen sind.

MAX: In dieser Nacht?

CASPAR: Ja doch! Max! Kamerad! Dein Schicksal steht unter dem Einflusse günstiger Gestirne! Du bist zu hohen Dingen ersehen! Heute, gerade in der Nacht zuvor, ehe du den Probeschuss thun, Amt und Braut dir gewinnen sollst, wo du der Hülfe unsichtbarer Mächte so sehr bedarfst, beut die Natur sich selbst zu deinem Dienste!

MAX: Wohl! Mein Geschick will's — Schaff' mir so eine Kugel! —

CASPAR: Sei punkt zwölf Uhr in der Wolfsschlucht!

MAX: Um Mitternacht — in der Wolfsschlucht! — Nein! die Schlucht ist verrufen, und um Mitternacht öffnen sich die Pforten der Hölle, nein, ich komme nicht.

CASPAR: Feigling! Glaubst du, dieser Adler sei dir geschenkt? Doch Undank ist der Welt Lohn. Drollig! um Agathen zu trösten, wagtest du den Schuss; sie zu erwerben, fehlt es dir an Muth. Das würde sich das Wachspüppchen, das mich um deinetwillen verwarf, schwerlich einbilden! (*Vor sich.*) Es soll gerochen werden.

CASPAR: Shoot, in the devil's name! shoot! Ha! ha!
(*Max touches the trigger and discharges the rifle. At the same moment fiendish laughter is heard. Max, frightened, looks at Caspar, as an immense eagle falls dead at his feet*).
What is this?

CASPAR: Victoria! Now the boors will respect you! and how Agathe will rejoice!

MAX: Am I dreaming or awake? Never did I meet the like—Caspar! I pray, I entreat you—(*grasps him.*) Caspar, I'll murder you—say, what bullet was that?

CASPAR: Well, if you will be reasonable.—tell me—you, a brave hunter,—are you or would you *seem* so very ignorant? Do you really not know what a charmed bullet is?

MAX: That shot is incredible—at twilight—to bring the bird down from the very clouds! Can such things be? Have you more of these balls?

CASPAR: It was the only one left—they have just lasted out.

MAX: You are very silent of a sudden! lasted out! what mean you by that?

CASPAR: They may be obtained again this very night.

MAX: This night?

CASPAR: Even so, Max comrade! Thy fate is cast beneath the influence of a favorable constellation. Thou art born to great fortunes. Tonight, even in the night before your trial shot, which is to gain you bride and fortune, when you must need the assistance of superior powers, this very night, nature herself offers her assistance to you.

MAX: Be it so! it is my fate? — obtain for me such a bullet!

CASPAR: Be in the wolf's glen at midnight!

MAX: At midnight—in the wolf's glen? No! that glen is in ill report, and at midnight the gates of hell are open there! No! I shall not come.

CASPAR: Coward! Think you that this eagle was obtained for nothing? But ingratitude is the world's reward. This is droll! to console Agathe, you undertook this shot; to gain her, you lack the courage. That sweet child who dotes on you would scarcely believe this. (*Aside.*) I shall be avenged.

**MAX:** Elender! Muth hab' ich —

**CASPAR:** So bewähr' ihn! Brauchtest du schon eine Freikugel, so ist's ja ein Kinderspiel, welche zu giessen. Was dir bevorsteht ohne diese Hülfe, kannst du aus deinen bisherigen Fehlschüssen leicht abnehmen. Das Mädchen ist auf dich versessen, kann nicht ohne dich leben; sie wird verzweifeln! Du wirst allen Menschen ein Spott, herumschleichen, vielleicht aus Verzweiflung — (*Drückt sich die Faust in die Augen, als träte das Wasser binein.*) Schäme dich, rauher Waidmann, dass du ihn mehr liebst, als er sich selbst! (*Vor sich.*) Hilf zu, Samiel!

**MAX:** Agathe sterben! Ich in einen abgrund springen! Ja, das wär' das Ende! — (*Giebt Caspar die Hand.*) Bei Agathe's Leben! ich komme!
*Samiel, der bei den letzten Worten hervorgelauscht hat, nickt und verschwindet.*

**CASPER:** Schweig gegen Jedermann! Es könnte dir und mir Gefahr bringen. Ich erwarte dich! Glock zwölf!

**MAX:** Ich dich verrathen? — Glock zwölf! Ich komme! (*Schnell ab.*)

## SECHSTE SCENE

**CASPAR** *allein:* Schweig, schweig — damit dich niemand warnt! Der Hölle Netz hat dich umgarnt, Nichts kann vom tiefen Fall dich retten! Umgebt ihn, ihr Geister mit Dunkel beschwingt! Schon trägt er knirschend eure Ketten! Triumph! die Rache, die Rache gelingt!

## ■ ZWEITER AKT

### ERSTE SCENE

*Vorsaal im Forsthause. Annchen steht auf einer Leiter, hat das Bild des ersten Cuno wieder aufgehängt. Agathe bindet einen Verband von der Stirn.*

**ANNCHEN:** Schelm! halt fest! Ich will dir's lehren, Spukerei'n kann man entbehren In solch altem Eulennest.

**AGATHE:** Lass das Ahnebild in Ehren!

**ANNCHEN:** Ei, dem alten Herrn Zoll' ich Achtung gern; Doch dem Knechte Sitte lehren, Kann Respect nicht wehren —

**AGATHE:** Sprich, wen meinst du? welchen Knecht?

**MAX:** Wretch! I have the courage—

**CASPAR:** Then prove it. As you have already used a charmed ball, it is mere child's play to make more. Your fortune hitherto, may plainly show you, what you may expect without such aid. The girl is madly in love with you, and cannot live without you; she will despair! You will become the scorn of all mankind, perhaps in your despair you'll—(*presses his hand before his eyes, as if weeping.*) Pshaw! that I should love you more than you do yourself! (*Aside.*) Help Zamiel!

**MAX:** Agathe—die? I—kill myself? Yes, yes, such would be the end!—(*gives his hand of Caspar.*) On my life, I'll come! (*Zamiel, who had been visible during the last few sentences, nods and disappears.*)

**CASPAR:** Not a word to any one! It might bring danger to us both. I shall expect you precisely at twelve!

**MAX:** I'll not betray you!—At twelve, I will be there! (*Exit.*)

## SCENE VI

**CASPAR:** (*alone*) Hush! hush! that no one may alarm thee! Hellish lures now soon will charm thee; Nothing can save thee from the chain. Surround him, ye imps in darkness still fly. Already fallen he strives in vain, Revenge, revenge. thy triumph is nigh.

## ■ ACT II

### SCENE I

(*Chamber in the head ranger's house. ANNCHEN on a ladder, hanging up the portrait of the first CUNO. AGATHE tying a bandkerchief around her forehead.*)

**ANNCHEN:** Come be at rest! Keep in your own sphere! Of specters there's no need here In this old crow's nest.

**AGATHE:** Respect the portrait of our sire!

**ANNCHEN:** To Cuno it is true, All homage is due; But the slave whom I require, Must obey my desire.

**AGATHE:** Slave! What mean you? say what slave?

**ANNCHEN:** Nun, den Nagel! Kannst du fragen? Sollt' er seinen Herrn nicht tragen, Liess ihn fallen, war das nicht schlecht?

**AGATHE UND ANNCHEN, ZUGLEICH:** Ja, gewiss, das war nicht recht. Das war wahrlich mehr, als schlecht.
*Steigt herunter und setzt die Leiter weg.*

**AGATHE:** Alles wird dir zum Feste, Alles beut dir Lachen und Scherz — O wie anders fühlt mein Herz!

**ANNCHEN:** Grillen sind mir böse Gäste. Immer mit leichtem Sinn Tanzen durch's Leben hin, Das nur ist Hochgewinn — Sorg' und Gram muss man versagen!

**AGATHE:** Wer bezwingt des Busens Schlagen? Wer der Liebe süssen Schmerz?

**ANNCHEN:** Die bezwingen Lust und Scherz!

**AGATHE:** Stets um den Geliebten zagen Muss dies ahnungsvolle Herz!

**ANNCHEN:** *besieht sich das Bild.* So! nun wird der Altvater wohl wieder ein Jahrhundertchen festhängen.

**AGATHIE:** Es ist recht still und einsam hier —

**ANNCHEN:** Unangenehm ist's freilich, in einem solchen verwünschten Schlosse am Polterabende fast mutterseelen allein zu sein, zumal — wenn sich so ehrwürdige, längst vermoderte Herrschaften mir nichts, dir nichts von den Wänden herabbemühen. Da lob' ich mir die Lebendigen und Jungen! Kommt ein schlanker Bursch gegangen, Blond von Locken oder braun, Hell von Aug und roth or Vaugen, Ei, nach dem Kana main bischau Zwar schlägt man das Aug' auf's Mieder, Tief verschämt, nach Mädchen-Art; Doch verstohlen hebt man's wieder, Wenn's das Bürschchen nicht gewahrt. Sollten ja sich Blicke finden, Nun, was hat auch das für Noth? Man wird drum nicht gleich erblinden, Wird man auch ein wenig roth. Blickchen hin und Blick herüber, Bis der Mund sich auch was traut! Er seufzt: Schönste! Sie spricht: Lieber! Bald heisst's Bräutigam und Braut. Immer näher, liebe Leutchen!

**ANCHEN:** Why this question? it is the nail there. Should it not it master bear. Yet it dropped him like a knave.

**AGATHE AND ANNCHEN:** (*Together.*) Certainly that was not brave. Was it not a naughty slave? (*Descends from the ladder.*)

**AGATHE:** Ever thus are you merry. And constantly joyous and glad, Whilst my poor heart is so sad.

**ANNCHEN:** Oh, do not let sorrow tarry. Always be light and gay. Dancing through life away: Life is but one brief day, Sorrow and care ever expelling.

**AGATHE:** Who can stop the bosom's swelling? Who soothes hearts that mourn in love?

**ANNCHEN:** Laughter will victorious prove!

**AGATHE:** Oh! where grief once makes its dwelling, Who can ever the inmate move?

**ANNCHEN:** (*looks at the picture*).Now our worthy ancestor will probably hang secure for another century.

**AGATHE:** How still and lonely it is here —

**ANNCHEN:** It certainly is disagreeable to be alone in such an old castle at night. especially when these old, dead and gone ancestors of ours, take it into their heads to descend from the wall of their own accord. For my part I prefer live men and younger ones. If a youth should meet a maiden. Need she run away with fright? If his looks should win her favor? Sure a girl may use her sight? Tho' she must in maiden manner, Seem to conceal her glances, Where's the harm , if she unnoticed, Strive to steal a sidelong look? Should, perchance, their eyes encounter, I can find no guilt therein; Though her cheeks may blush a little, Yet it will not strike her blind. Glances this way—glances that way — These are followed soon by sighs. He sighs, Fairest! she says, Dearest! He makes love, and gains the prize. Wedlock's garland, I would wear it, With my loved one at my side, Hear the village folks exclaiming, Gallant bridegroom — handsome bride.

## Act II, Scene I

Wollt ihr mich im Kranze seh'n?
Nicht, das ist ein nettes Bräutchen,
Und der Bursch nicht minder
schön?

**AGATHE:** *fällt mit ein.* Und der
Bursch nicht minder schön!

**ANNCHEN:** Aber, lass uns auch zu
Bette geh'n!

**AGATHE:** Nicht eher, bis Max da
ist!

**ANNCHEN:** Hat man nicht seine
Noth mit euch Liebesleutchen!
(*Ab*)

### ZWEITE SCENE

**AGATHE:** *allein.* Wie naht mir der
Schlummer,
Bevor ich ihn geseh'n? —
Ja, Liebe pflegt mit Kummer
Stets Hand in Hand zu geh'n!
Ob Mond auf seinem Pfad wohl
lacht!
(*Sie öffnet das Fenster.*)
Welch' schöne Nacht!
(*Betend.*)
Leise, leise,
Fromme Weise!
Schwing' dich auf zum Sternen-
kreise.
Lied, erschalle!
Feiernd walle
Mein Gebet zur Himmelshalle! —
(*Hinausschauend.*)
O wie hell die goldnen Sterne,
Mit wie reinem Glanz sie glüh'n!
Nur dort in der Berge Ferne,
Scheint ein Wetter aufzuzieh'n.
Dort am Wald auch schwebt ein
Heer
Düst'rer Wolken dumpf und
schwer,
Zu dir wende
Ich die Hände,
Herr ohn' Anfang und ohn' Ende!
Vor Gefahren
Uns zu wahren,
Sende deine Engelschaaren! —
(*Wieder hinausschauend.*)
Alles pflegt schon längst der Ruh;
Trauter Freund! was weilest du?
Ob mein Ohr auch ängstlich
lauscht,
Nur der Tannen Wipfel rauscht,
Nur das Birkenlaub im Hain
Flüstert durch die bange Stille:
Nur die Nachtigall und Grille
Scheint der Nachtluft sich zu freu'n
Doch wie? Trügt mich mein Ohr?
Dort klingt's wie Schritte —
Dort aus der Tannen Mitte
Kommt was hervor — —
Er ist's! er ist's!
Die Flagge der Liebe mag wehen?
(*Sie winkt ihm mit einem weissen
Tuche.*)
Dein Mädchen wacht
Noch in der Nacht — Er scheint
mich noch nicht zu sehen —
Gott! täuscht das Licht
Des Mondes nicht,
So schmückt ein Blumenstrauss den
Hut —
Gewiss, er hat den besten Schuss

---

**AGATHE:** (*joining in*). Gallant
bridegroom — handsome bride.

**ANNCHEN:** But now let us go to
bed.

**AGATHE:** Not until Max is back!

**ANNCHEN:** What troublesome
people you lovers are. (*Exit*)

### SCENE II

**AGATHE:** (*alone*). How sweetly
was my slumber,
Ere tasted love's first kiss,
Now, sorrows without number,
Go side by side with bliss.
Smiles now the moon's soft silvery
light. (*Opens the window.*)
Oh, lovely night, (*Praying.*)
Softly, softly,
Still devoutly,
Let my voice reach realms of light.
Nature's sleeping,
See me weeping,
Father, hear my prayer tonight!
(*Looking out.*)
Now the distant west is clouded,
And the sky looks dark and pale,
And the mountain top is shrouded
With a dim and misty veil;
And along yon forest's side,
Clouds of darkness seem to ride.
To your power,
In this hour,
Heaven! I address my prayer.
Father! guide us,
And unite us
After life with Angel hosts. (*Look-
ing out again.*)
Earth has lulled her cares to rest.
And all nature now seems blessed
Where do you linger, love! oh,
where?
Nothing but gently breathing air
Whispers in my anxious ear.
Or the nightgale's sweet calling
On the dry leaves gently falling;
But no step approaches near.
But hark! through the silent night
A horn is sounding!
And footsteps nearer bounding,
Quickly and light!
It is he! It is he!
Love's flag I'll wave for you!
(*Waves a handkerchief.*)
Still wakes the maid
In midnight shade —
The moonbeam is shining bright,
Heavens! does it mock my sight?
With flowery wreaths his hair is
bound,
As conquering marksman he is
crowned.
This tells of hope for coming day!
Sweet expectation! — all my fears
away!
Ah! now each pulse is beating wild-
ly
And my heart is throbbing high,

---

gethan!
Das kündet Glück für morgen an!
O süsse Hoffnung! Neu belebter
Muth! —
Alle meine Pulse schlagen,
Und das Herz wallt ungestüm,
Süss entzückt entgegen ihm!
Könnt' ich das zu hoffen wagen? —
Ja, es wandte sich das Glück
Zu dem theuern Freund zurück,
Will sich morgen treu bewahren!
Ist's nicht Täuschung, ist's nicht
Wahn? —
Himmel, nimm des Dankes Zähren
Für dies Pfand der Hoffnung an!

### DRITTE SCENE

*Agathe, MAX. Gleich nach ihm
ANNCHEN.*

**AGATHE:** Bist du endlich da, lieber Max?

**MAX:** Meine Agathe! *Sie umarmen
sich.* Verzeiht, wenn ihr meinetwegen aufgeblieben seid! Leider
komm' ich nur auf wenig Augenblicke —

**AGATHE:** Du willst doch nicht
wieder fort? Es sind Gewitter im
Anzuge.

**MAX:** Ich muss!

**AGATHE:** Du scheinst übel ge-
launt. Wieder unglücklich gewes-
en?

**MAX:** Nein! nein! Im Gegentheil!

**AGATHE:** Nicht? gewiss nicht?

**ANNCHEN:** (*zu Max*). Was hast du
gewonnen? Wenn's ein Band ist,
Vetter! musst du mir's schenken.
Bitte, bitte! Agathe hat schon
Bänderkram genug von dir!

**AGATHE:** Was hast du getroffen,
Max? Heute ist mir's von Wichtigkeit.

**MAX:** (*mit Verlegenheit*). Ich
habe — ich war gar nicht beim
Sternschiessen!

**AGATHE:** Und sagst doch, du seist
glücklich gewesen?

**MAX:** Ja doch! wunderbar, unglaublich glücklich. Sieh! (*Zeigt
ihr den Federbusch auf dem
Hute.*) Den grössten Raubvogel
hab' ich aus den Wolken geholt!
(*Bemerkt Blut an ihrer Stirn.*) Um
aller Heiligen willen, was ist dir begegnet?

**AGATHE:** Nichts! soviel als nichts!
Es heilt noch vor'm Brautgang. Du
sollst dich d'rum deines
Bräutchens nicht schämen!

**MAX:** Aber so sagt doch nur — — —

**ANNCHEN:** Das Bild dort fiel herunter — —

**MAX:** Dort, der Urvater Cuno!

**AGATHE:** Wie bist du? Es ist sonst
kein Bild hier.

**MAX:** Der wackere gottesfürchtige
Cuno?

---

Each cold breeze now passing by,
Seems to whisper me more mildly
Every star that shines above,
Shines as a token of our love;
Yes, I hear his step approaching —
Is it fancy? now more near;
Heaven hear the grateful maiden,
Oh! accept the grateful tear.

### SCENE III

*AGATHE, MAX, afterwards
ANNCHEN.*

**AGATHE:** Here at last, dear Max!

**MAX:** Dearest Agathe! (*they embrace.*) Pardon me, if you have remained up on my account! Sorry
that I can only stay a few moments.

**AGATHE:** You will not go out
again? A storm is approaching.

**MAX:** I must

**AGATHE:** (*anxiously*). You seem
in evil humor.
Were you again unlucky?

**MAX:** No, no! Just the contrary!

**AGATHE:** Are you certain, dearest?

**ANNCHEN:** (*to Max*). What did
you gain? If 'tis a ribbon, cousin,
you must present it to me. Will you?
Agathe has already ribbons enough
from you.

**AGATHE:** What did you shoot,
Max? Today, it is of importance to
me.

**MAX:** (*embarrassed*). I have—
but I was not at all at the target
shooting!

**AGATHE:** And yet you say you
were successful?

**MAX:** Yes, wonderfully successful.
See! (*points to the eagle feathers
on his hat.*) I brought the largest
bird down from the clouds. (*Observes her forehead.*) For heaven's
sake, what has happened to you?

**AGATHE:** Nothing! at least not
much! It will all be well before our
wedding day. You will not need to
be ashamed of your little bride.

**MAX:** But tell me—

**ANNCHEN:** Yon portrait fell down.

**MAX:** What! The first Cuno!

**AGATHE:** How strange you speak!
There is no other portrait here.

**MAX:** The brave and pious Cuno!

ANNCHEN: Halb und halb war Agathe selbst Schuld. Wer hiess ihr auch, schon nach sieben Uhr immer an's Fenster zu laufen!

MAX: Um sieben Uhr?

ANNCHEN: Du hörst's ja! die Thurmuhr drüben im Dorfe hatte kaum ausgeschlagen.

MAX: Seltsam! (*Vor sich.*) Um diese Zeit schoss ich den Bergadler. (*Max steht in Gedanken*). Ich muss wieder fort!

AGATHE: Aber was treibt dich?

MAX: Ich habe — ich bin noch ein Mal glücklich gewesen —

AGATHE: Noch ein Mal?

MAX: Ja doch! ja! (*Ohne Agathen ansehen zu können*). Ich hab' in der Dämmerung einen Sechzehnender geschossen, der muss noch hereingeschafft werden, sonst stehlen ihn des Nachts die Bauern.

AGATHE: Wo liegt der Hirsch?

MAX: Ziemlich weit — im tiefen Walde — bei der Wolfsschlucht!

AGATHE: Wie? was? Entsetzen! Dort in der Schreckensschlucht?

ANNCHEN: Der wilde Jäger soll dort hetzen, Und wer ihn hört, ergreift die Flucht.

MAX: Darf Furcht im Hirn des Waidmanns hausen?

AGATHE: Doch sündigt der, wer Gott versucht.

MAX: Ich bin vertraut mit jenem Grausen, Das Mitternacht im Walde weht, Wenn sturmbewegt die Eichen sausen, Der Häher krächzt, die Eule schwebt. (*Nimmt Hut und Büchse.*)

AGATHE: Mir ist so bang, o bleibe! O eile, eile nicht so schnell!

ANNCHEN: Ihr ist so bang, o bleibe! O eile, eile nicht so schnell!

MAX: Noch birgt sich nicht die Mondenscheibe. Noch strahlt ihr Schimmer dämmerhell; Doch bald wird sie den Schein verlieren —

ANNCHEN: Willst du den Himmel observiren? Das wär' nun meine Sache nicht!

AGATHE: O kann dich meine Angst nicht rühren?

MAX: Mich ruft von hinnen — Wort und Pflicht!

AGATHE, ANNCHEN, MAX: Leb wohl! *Er gebt hastig fort und kehrt in der Thür noch einmal zurück. Mit Wehmuth.*

---

ANNCHEN: Partly it was Agathe's own fault. Why should she, even at seven o'clock run every instant to the window, and look for you?

MAX: At seven o'clock?

ANNCHEN: As I tell you! the village clock had just struck the hour.

MAX: Strange! (*Aside.*) At that hour I shot the eagle. (*Absorbed in thought.*) I must again away.

AGATHE: But why this haste?

MAX: I have—I have been fortunate a second time—

AGATHE: A second time?

MAX: Yes, yes! (*without looking at her.*) At twilight I shot a very large stag! I must bring it in, else the bears will steal it before morning.

AGATHE: Where lies the stag?

MAX: Far from here, in the deepest of the forest in the Wolf's glen.

AGATHE: Where? What? Oh terror! In yonder gloomy glen?

ANNCHEN: The demon huntsman haunts its hollow, And drags his victims to his den.

MAX: Should fables daunt the huntsman's mind!

AGATHE: He who scorns may find dangers!

MAX: I scorn those weak and childish terrors, That haunt the wood at midnight hour, When storms are blowing, oaks are cracking, When owlets cry, and dark clouds lour. (*Takes his hat and rifle.*)

AGATHE: Oh! terror fills my bosom, Then do not hurry away like this!

ANNCHEN: See! terror fills her bosom, Oh then awhile delay!

MAX: Although the moon, as yet unclouded, Spreads around her silvery ray, Too soon by darkness it will be shrouded.

ANNCHEN: Can neither love nor duty move thee, A little moment yet to stay?

AGATHE: Do not these sighs, these tears, reprove you!

MAX: My duty calls — I must obey.

AGATHE, ANNCHEN, MAX: Farewell! (*Max hastily withdraws, but turns at the door.*)

---

MAX: Doch hast du auch vergeben Den Vorwurf, den Verdacht?

AGATHE: Nichts fühlt mein Herz als Beben! Nimm meiner Warnung Acht!

ANNCHEN: So ist das Jägerleben! Nicht Ruh' bei Tag und Nacht!

AGATHE: Weh' mir! Ich muss dich lassen!

ANNCHEN: Such', Beste, dich zu fassen!

MAX: Bald wird der Mond erblassen —

AGATHE, ANNCHEN: Denk' an Agathe's Wort!

MAX: Mein Schicksal reisst mich fort!

### VIERTE SCENE

*Die Wolfsschlucht. Caspar ohne Hut und Oberkleid.*

STIMMEN UNSICHTBARER GEISTER: Milch des Mondes fiel auf's Kraut — Uhui! Spinnweb' ist mit Blut bethaut — Uhui! Eh' noch wieder Abend grau't — Uhui! Ist sie todt, die zarte Braut — Uhui! Eh' noch wieder sinkt die Nacht, Ist das Opfer dargebracht. Uhui! Uhui! Uhui!

### FÜNFTE SCENE

*Die Uhr schlägt ganz in der Ferne dumpf Zwölf. Als der zwölfte Schlag fällt, reisst Caspar den Hirschfänger heftig heraus und stösst ihn in den Todtenschädel.*

CASPER: (*erhebt den Hirschfänger mit dem Todtenkopfe und ruft*): Samiel! Samiel! erschein'! Bei des Zaub'rers Hirngebein! Samiel! Samiel! erschein'! *Ein Felsen spaltet sich. Samiel wird sichtbar. Caspar wirft sich vor ihm nieder.*

SAMIEL: Was rufst du mich?

CASPAR: Du weisst, dass meine Frist Schier abgelaufen ist —

SAMIEL: Morgen!

CASPAR: Verlängere sie noch einmal mir —

SAMIEL: Nein!

CASPAR: Ich bringe neue Opfer dir —

SAMIEL: Welche?

CASPAR: Mein Jagdgesell', er naht —

Er, der noch nie dein dunkles Reich betrat!

SAMIEL: Was sein Begehr?

CASPAR: Freikugeln sind's, auf die er Hoffnung baut —

---

MAX: Oh! does your heart forgive My hasty words tonight!

AGATHE: Oh yes! my heart forgives you, Nor you my warning slight.

ANNCHEN: Such is the huntsman's fortune, No rest, nor night nor day.

AGATHE: Ah then! and must I leave thee?

ANNCHEN: No, sweet, let that not grieve you

MAX: Soon will the moon too leave me.

AGATHE, ANNCHEN: Think of Agathe's word!

MAX: Fate calls, and will be heard. (*Exit.*)

### SCENE IV

(*The Wolf's Glen, CASPAR without hat or coat.*)

CHORUS OF INVISIBLE SPIRITS: Milk of moon fell on the sod, Uhui! Spiderwebs are stained with blood, Uhui! Ere another eve is sped, Uhui! A sweet, gentle bride is dead. Uhui! Ere descends another sun. Uhui! Our victim will be won, Uhui!

### SCENE V

(*A clock in the distance strikes twelve. At the last stroke, CASPAR draws his hanger, and strikes it into a skull.*)

CASPAR (*raises his hanger with the skull*). Zamiel, Zamiel, appear! By the dark deeds doing here, By the wizard's skull appear! (*A rock opens and Zamiel appears, Caspar prostrates himself.*)

ZAMIEL: Why have you called me?

CASPAR: My course is almost done, My race is nearly run.

ZAMIEL: Tomorrow!

CASPAR: Once more prolong this life to me —

ZAMIEL: No.

CASPAR: I'll give you another victim

ZAMIEL: Whom?

CASPAR: My comrade he is near, Who never yet dared here appear.

ZAMIEL: What does he seek?

CASPAR: Those fatal balls, which you alone may guide.

## Act II, Scene V

SAMIEL: Sechse treffen, sieben äffen.

CASPAR: Die siebente sei dein!
Aus seinem Rohr lenk' sie nach seiner Braut.
Dies wird ihn der Verzweiflung weih'n;
Ihn und den Vater —

SAMIEL: Noch hab' ich keinen Theil an ihr!

CASPAR: Genügt er dir allein?

SAMIEL: Das findet sich!

CASPAR: Doch schenkst du Frist?
und wieder auf drei Jahr,
Bring' ich ihn dir zur Beute dar!

SAMIEL: Es sei. — Bei den Pforten der Hölle!
Morgen — er oder du!
(Samiel verschwindet.)

### SECHSTE SCENE

CASPAR: (steht auf, als er sich umsieht und die Kohlen erblickt.)
Trefflich bedient. (Thut einen Zug aus der Jagdflasche). Gesegn' es Samiel! Er hat mich warm gemacht! — Aber wo bleibt Max? Sollt' er wortbrüchig werden? — Samiel hilf! —
Er geht im Kreise hin und her. Die Kohlen drohen zu verlöschen. Er kniet zu ihnen nieder, legt Reiss auf und bläst an. Die Eule und andere Vögel heben dabei die Flügel, als wollten sie anfachen.

MAX: (erscheint auf dem Felsen).
Ha! — Furchtbar gähnt
Der düst're Abgrund! — welches Grau'n!
Das Auge wähnt
In einen Höllenpfuhl zu schau'n!
Wie dort sich Wetterwolken ballen!
Der Mond verliert von seinem Schein!
Gespenst'ge Nebelbilder wallen!
Belebt ist das Gestein!
Und hier — husch! husch!
Fliegt Nachtgevögel auf im Busch!
Rothgraue, narb'ge Zweige strecken
Nach mir die Riesenfaust!
Nein, ob das Herz auch graust,
Ich muss! Ich trotze alle Schrecken!
(Er klettert einige Schritte herab.)

CASPAR: (richtet sich auf und erblickt ihn). Dank, Samiel! Die Frist ist gewonnen! (Zu Max.) Kommst du endlich, Kamerad? Ist das auch recht, mich allein zu lassen? Siehst du nicht, wie mir's sauer wird! (Hat das Feuer mit dem Adlerflügel angefacht und erhebt diesen im Gespräch gegen Max.)

MAX: (nach dem Adlerflügel starrend) Ich schoss den Adler aus hoher Luft;
Ich kann nicht rückwärts — mein

---

ZAMIEL: Six will obey — the seventh betray.

CASPAR: Yours be the seventh ball
And from his rifle guide it to his bride.
Thus bringing deep despair on all;
Him and her father —

ZAMIEL: In her I have no share as yet —

CASPAR: Are you content with one!

ZAMIEL: We see when all is done.

CASPAR: Grant this delay, and before three years have passed
I'll bring you Max, whom death has won.

ZAMIEL: Be it so — By the gates of hell!
Tomorrow — he or you! (Zamiel disappears)

### SCENE VI

CASPAR (rising wiping his forehead and looking at the coals)
Well helped (drinks.) Bless you Zamiel! But his presence was hot! — Where can Max delay? Should he break his word? — Help Zamiel! — (Enters the magic circle, and kneels down to fan the coals. The owl and other birds raise their wings as if to fan also.)

MAX (appears on the rocks). Ha! sad and drear!
In yonder darkness horror dwells
And to listening fear
A fiendish tale of terror tells.
The distant thunder bursts yon clouds.
The moon with blood has stained her light.
What forms are those in misty shrouds
That stalk before my sight!
And here—hush! hush!
Night birds light on this bush,
And giant arms are reaching—bending
Through yonder oak at me;
Oh! shall I stay or flee?
I must! And if the world were ending.
(He descends a few steps.)

CASPAR: (rising, discovers him).
Thanks, Zamiel! the respite is gained. (To Max.) At last you come, comrade? Is that right, to have me alone? See how hard I am at work! (Fans the fire with an eagle's wing, and shows it to Max.)

MAX: (staring at the wing). I shot that bird of love on high,
Return I cannot—cannot fly.
(Staring at the opposite rock.)

---

Schicksal ruft! —
(Blickt starr nach dem gegenüberstehenden Felsen.)
Wehe mir!

CASPAR: So komm' doch! die Zeit eilt — —

MAX: Ich kann nicht hinab!

CASPAR: Hasenherz! Klimmst ja sonst wie eine Gemse!

MAX: Sieh' dorthin! Sieh!
Er deutet nach dem Felsen, wo man eine weissverschleierte Gestalt erblickt.
Was dort sich weist,
Ist meiner Mutter Geist!
So lag sie im Sarg, so ruht sie im Grab!
Sie fleht mit warnendem Blick,
Sie winkt mir zurück.

CASPAR: (vor sich). Hilf, Samiel!
(Laut.) Alberne Fratzen! Ho, hoho!
Sieh' noch einmal hin, damit du die Folgen deiner feigen Thorheit erkennest.
Die verschleierte Gestalt ist verschwunden. Man erblickt Agathe's Gestalt. Sie gleicht völlig einer Wahnsinnigen, und scheint im Begriff, sich in den Wasserfall herunter zu stürzen.

MAX: Agathe! — Sie springt in den Fluss!
Hinab! ich muss!
(Die Gestalt ist verschwunden. Max klimmt vollends herab.)

CASPAR: Ich denke wohl auch!

MAX: Hier bin ich! Was hab' ich zu thun?

CASPAR: (wirft ihm die Jagdflasche zu.) Zuerst trink'! Die Nachtluft ist kühl und feucht. Willst du selbst giessen? Max! ich mag nicht.

MAX: Nein! das ist wider die Abrede.

CASPAR: Fasse Muth! Tritt in den Kreis! Er ist eine eherne Mauer gegen Geistergewalt. Was du auch hören und sehen magst, verhalte dich ruhig. Käm' vielleicht ein Unbekannter, uns zu helfen, wär' es auch ein schwarzer Reiter auf schwarzem, funkensprühendem Ross, was kümmert's dich? Kömmt And'res, was thut's! So etwas sieht ein Gescheidter gar nicht!

MAX: (tritt ein.) O wie wird das enden!

CASPAR: Umsonst ist der Tod! Nur wann du mich selbst zittern siehst, dann komm' mir zu Hülfe und rufe, was ich rufen werde. Sonst sind wir verloren. (Max macht eine Bewegung des Einwurfs.) Still! Die Augenblicke sind kostbar! — (Nimmt die Giesskelle.) Merk' auf, damit du die Kunst lernst. (Er nimmt die Ingredienzien aus der Jagdtasche und wirft sie nach und nach hinein.) Hier ist das Blei! — Etwas gestossenes Glas von zerbrochenen

---

Woe is me!

CASPAR: Come down then, time flies —

MAX: I cannot descend.

CASPAR: Coward! you can usually climb like a chamois.

MAX: See, Caspar, see!
(He points to a rock, where a ghost appears.)
By that oak tree,
It is my mother's shade!
Thus she looked, when she lay in death.
She fondly seems to pray,
And beacons me away.

CASPAR: (aside). Help, Zamiel!
(Aloud.) Silly nonsense! Oh, ho, ho! Look again, and perceive the consequences of your foolish cowardice. (The mother's ghost has disappeared, and Agathe's figure is seen. She appears a maniac on the point of leaping over a precipice.)

MAX: Agathe! she plunges below!
Then, then I'll go!
(The figure has disappeared. Max descends.)

CASPAR: I thought so.

MAX: Here I am! What shall I do?

CASPAR: (offering his flask).
Drink first; the night air is cold and damp.—Will you cast the balls yourself? I would rather not.

MAX: No! that is against our compact.

CASPAR: Take courage then! Enter the circle! This is an iron wall against the power of spirits. Whatever you may hear, or see, remain quiet. Should a stranger come, to assist us, even if it were a black horseman, on a fire-breathing horse, care not, and stir not. Wise men don't notice such things.

MAX: (enters the circle). Oh! How will this end?

CASPAR: Nothing is in vain. Only when you see me tremble, come to my assistance, and speak what I shall speak. Otherwise we are lost. (Max is about to interrupt him.) Silence! the moments are precious!— (he takes the crucible.) Observe me, that you may learn the art. (Takes the ingredients from his pouch, and throws them in.) First the lead.—A little glass of broken church-windows; easily found!—Some quicksilver!—

Kirchenfenstern; das findet sich!
— Etwas Quecksilber! — Drei Kugeln, die schon einmal getroffen!
— Das rechte Auge eines Wiedehopfs! Das linke eines Luchses! —
Probatum est! Und nun den Kugelsegen.
(*In drei Pausen sich mit dem Kopfe gegen die Erde neigend.*)
Schütze, der im Dunkeln wacht!
Samiel! Samiel! hab' Acht!
Steh mir bei in dieser Nacht,
Bis der Zauber ist vollbracht!
Salbe mir so Kraut als Blei,
Segn' es sieben, neun und drei,
Dass die Kugel tüchtig sei!
Samiel! Samiel! herbei!
(*Die Masse in der Giesskelle fängt an zu kochen. Caspar giesst, lässt die Kugeln aus der Form fallen und ruft: Eins! Das Echo wiederholt: Eins! Caspar zählt Zwei! Echo wiederholt. Caspar zählt Drei! Echo wie oben. Caspar zählt ängstlich Vier! Echo wie oben. Caspar, immer ängstlicher, zählt Fünf! Echo wiederholt. Das wilde Heer.*)
Wehe! Das wilde Heer!

CHORUS: Durch Berg und Thal, durch Schlund und Schacht,
Durch Thau und Wolken, Sturm und Nacht!
Durch Höhle, Sumpf und Erdenkluft!
Durch Feuer, Erde, See und Luft!
Jaho! Jaho! Wau! Wau!

CASPAR: Sechs! Wehe! *Echo:* Sechs! Wehe! (*Caspar, zuckend und schreiend.*) Samiel! Samiel! Samiel, hilf! — Sieben! — Samiel!
(*Echo: Sieben! — Samiel!*)
(*Caspar wird zu Boden geworfen.*)

MAX: (*gleichfalls vom Sturme binund bergeschleudert, springt aus dem Kreise, fasst einen Ast des verdorrten Baums und schreit*): Samiel!
*In demselben Augenblick fängt das Ungewitter an, sich zu beruhigen, an der Stelle des verdorrten Baums steht der schwarze Jäger, nach Maxens Hand fassend.*

SAMIEL: Hier bin ich!
*Max stürzt zu Boden. Es schlägt Eins. Plötzliche Stille. — Samiel ist verschwunden. Caspar liegt noch mit dem Gesicht zu Boden. Max richtet sich convulsivisch auf.*

■ **DRITTER AKT**

*ERSTE SCENE*

MAX und CASPAR. Waldscene.

---

Three balls that have once hit before!—The right eye of a falcon!—The left eye of a lynx!—Probatum est, and now the charm! (*Bending thrice to the ground.*)
Huntsman of the midnight air,
Zamiel, Zamiel take care.
And assist me in this night,
That the charm may work aright!
Spirit of the evil dead,
Bless the lead in mystic numbers.
Bless the seven, nine and three,
Zamiel, hear me call on you!
(*The lead boils up. Caspar casts a bullet and cries "One." Apparitions. Caspar counts Two. Echo as before. Apparitions. Caspar counts Three. Echo, etc., as before. Caspar counts Four. Echo and more Apparitions. Caspar fearfully counts Five. Echo as before, and the wild host rushes through the air.*)
Horror! the wild huntsman!

CHORUS: Through hill and dale, through rock and wood,
Through dew and clouds, through storm and flood,
Through glen and swamp and tempest light,
Through fire and earth, we fly by night,
Ya ho! Ya ho! Ho! ho!

CASPAR: Six! wo!—(*Echo repeats.*) Six! wo! (*Terrible alarm, darkness and apparitions. Caspar cries:*)
Zamiel! Zamiel! Zamiel! help! Seven! Zamiel! (*Echo "Seven! Zamiel!" Caspar is thrown to the ground.*)

MAX: (*jumping from the circle*). Zamiel! (*takes hold of a branch of a withered tree. At this moment the tempest subsides, and the Black Forester appears instead of the tree.*)

ZAMIEL: Behold me! (*Max sinks to the ground. The clock strikes one. Sudden silence. Zamiel has disappeared. Caspar remains on the ground, and Max slowly rises up.*)

■ **ACT III**

*SCENE I*

(*Scene in the forest, MAX and CASPAR.*)

---

MAX: Gut, dass wir allein sind! — Hast du noch von den Glückskugeln? Gieb!

CASPAR: Das wär' mir! Bedenk! Drei nahm ich, vier für dich! Kann ein Bruder redlicher theilen?

MAX: Aber ich habe nur noch *eine*! Was hast du denn mit den Kugeln angefangen?

CASPAR: Da sieh, nach den Elstern hab' ich zwei verschossen.

MAX: So hast du noch eine; gieb mir sie!

CASPAR: Dass ich kein Narr wär'! Ich noch eine — du noch eine! Die heb' ich dir fein auf zu dem Probeschuss!

MAX: Gieb mir deine Dritte!

CASPAR: Ich mag nicht — —

DRITTER JAEGER: (*tritt ein, zu Max*): Der Fürst verlangt Euch; aber augenblicklich! Es ist ein Streit entstanden, wie weit Euer Gewehr trifft.
(*Ab.*)

MAX: Sogleich! (*Zu Caspar.*) Gieb mir die Dritte!

CASPAR: Nein, und wenn du mir zu Füssen fielst! —

MAX: Schuft! (*Ab.*)

CASPAR: Immerhin! — Jetzt geschwind die sechste Kugel verbraucht. (*Er ladet.*) Die siebente, die Teufelskugel, hebt er mir schon zum Probeschusse auf, Hahaha! Wohl bekomm's der schönen Braut! — dort läuft ein Füchslein; dem die sechste in den Pelz.
(*Schiesst und ab.*)

*ZWEITE SCENE*

Agathens Stübchen. Agathe allein.

Und ob die Wolke sie verhülle,
Die Sonne bleibt am Himmelszelt!
Es waltet dort ein heil'ger Wille;
Nicht lindem Zufall dient die Welt!
Das Auge, rein und ewig klar,
Nimmt aller Wesen liebend wahr.
Für mich auch wird der Höchste sorgen,
Dem kindlich Herz und Sinn vertraut!
Und wär' dies auch mein letzter Morgen,
Rief mich sein Vaterwort als Braut.
*Sein* Auge, rein und ewig klar,
Nimmt aller seiner Kinder wahr!

*DRITTE SCENE*

AGATHE: Ich habe so quälende Träume gehabt.

---

MAX: Luckily we are alone! — Have you any more charmed bullets? Give them to me.

CASPAR: Not I. Consider! I took only three, and gave you four; could I divide more fairly?

MAX: But I have only one left. What did you do with your bullets?

CASPAR: Behold! I shot two of them at sparrows.

MAX: Then you have still one left; give it to me.

CASPAR: Indeed I shall not! I have still one — so have you! Therefore save that one for your trial shot.

MAX: Give me your last!

CASPAR: I will not.

FORESTER: (*entering to Max*). The Prince commands your presence immediately. A dispute has arisen as to the distance your rifle will carry a ball.
(*Exit.*)

MAX I come! (*to Caspar*) Give me the third.

CASPAR: No, and if you begged it on your knees.

MAX: Villain! (*Exit.*)

CASPAR: As you like! — now to shoot off the sixth (*loads his rifle.*) The seventh, the devil's ball, he will be sure to keep for the trial shot! Ha! ha! ha! May his fair bride enjoy it! — Yonder runs a little fox; let him have the sixth.
(*Fires and exit.*)

*SCENE II*

(*Agathe's room. Agathe alone.*)

The clouds by tempest may be driven
Across the glorious throne of day;
The Sun that never sets in heaven,
Soon smiles the gathering clouds away;
For though over earth clouds may lower.
Over Heavens will they have no power.
And thus although the clouds of sorrow,
A shadow over the soul may throw;
Yet hope that dwells within the morrow,
Though hidden, will not cease to glow;
For Heaven's eye, which never sleeps,
A watch over all its children keeps.

*SCENE III*

AGATHE: I have had such fearful dreams.

# Act III, Scene III

**ANNCHEN:** Träume? Was träumtest du denn?

**AGATHE:** Es klingt wunderbar. Mich träumte, ich sei in eine weisse Taube verwandelt und fliehe von Ast zu Aste. Max zielte nach mir, ich stürzte; aber nun war die weisse Taube verschwunden, ich war wieder Agathe, und ein grosser Raubvogel wälzte sich im Blute.

**ANNCHEN:** (*klatscht in die Hände.*) Allerliebst! allerliebst!

**AGATHE:** Wie kannst du dich nur über so etwas freuen?

**ANNCHEN:** Nun, der schwarze Raubvogel — da hast du ja die ganze Bescheerung! Du arbeitest noch spät an dem weissen Brautkleide und dachtest gewiss vor dem Einschlafen an deinen heutigen Staat; da hast du die weisse Taube! Du erschrackst vor den Adlerfedern auf Maxens Hute, es schauert dir überhaupt vor Raubvögeln; da hast du den schwarzen Vogel! Bin ich nicht eine geschickte Traumdeuterin? *Vor sich.* Fällt mir denn nichts ein, sie zu zerstreuen? *Laut, mit scheinbarer Ernsthaftigkeit und Furcht.* Freilich, Alles kann man nicht verwerfen! Ich selbst weiss da ein grausenerregendes Beispiel.

Einst träumte meiner sel'gen Base,
Die Kammerthür eröffne sich,
Und — kreideweiss war ihre Nase;
Denn näher, furchtbar näher schlich
Ein Ungeheuer,
Mit Augen, wie Feuer,
Mit klirrender Kette — —
Es nahte dem Bette,
In welchem sie schlief —
Ich meine die Base
Mit kreidiger Nase —
Und stöhnte, ach! so hohl! und ächzte, ach! so tief!
Sie kreuzte sich, rief!
Nach manchem Angst- und Stossgebet:
Susanne! Margreth!
Und sie kamen mit Licht —
Und — denke nur? — Und —
Erschrick mir nur nicht! —
Und graust mir doch! — und —
Der Geist war Nero — der Kettenhund.
(*Agathe wendet sich unwillig ab.*)
Du zürnst mir? —
Doch kannst du wähnen,
Ich fühle nicht mit dir? —
Nur ziemen einer Braut nicht Thränen!
Trübe Augen,
Liebchen, taugen
Einem holden Bräutchen nicht.
Dass durch Blicke
Sie bestricke
Und erquicke,
Alles um sich her entzücke,
Das ist ihre schönste Pflicht. —
Lass in öden Mauern
Büsserinnen trauern,
Dir winkt ros'ger Hoffnung Licht,

**ANNCHEN:** Dreams? Pray what did you dream?

**AGATHE:** It may sound strangely. I dreamed that I was changed to a white dove, and flying from tree to tree. Max aimed at me, and I fell; but now the white dove had disappeared, I was again Agathe, and a large black bird of prey was weltering in its blood.

**ANNCHEN** (*clapping her hands*). Beautiful! beautiful!

**AGATHE:** How can you rejoice at such a thing?

**ANNACHEN:** Well, well, the large black bird — cannot you understand the whole dream? Till late at night you worked at your white bridal dress, and before going to sleep you were surely thinking of your finery of today; that explains the white dove. You were frightened at the eagle plumes in Max's hat, and you always fear birds of prey; this explains the black bird! Do I not read dreams well! (*Aside.*) Can I not think of something to divert her? (*Aloud.*) Certainly, we should not leave all dreams unheeded, I know a fearful example myself.

Once dreamt my poor and dead old aunty,
The door flew open as she slept;
And blue her lips, her nose grew whiter,
For nearer, nearer, nearer, crept
A monster dire,
With bright eyes like fire,
His chains rattled loudly,
His tail curled more proudly,
As onward he stept;
His claws too grew longer,
Her terrors waxed stronger,
She groaned, ah! so long, and groaned, ah! so deep!
She crossed herself cries,
With many prayers, and many sighs,
Susanna! Margaret!
And they rushed in with light,
And — only think — and —
Oh! terrible sight —
And — still I quake — and
The ghost was — Nero — the mastive cur.
(*Agathe turns away in anger.*)
No, do not frown;
You know your sorrow
Is all my own;
But tears suit not the bridal morrow.
Eyes of gladness,
Not of sadness,
Should shine on the bridal hour.
Tender fancies,
Heart that dances,
Smiles of pleasure,
Best become the bridal measure:
These should be the maiden's dowry
Let your old ones only
Live in penance lonely;

Schon entzündet sind die Kerzen
Zum Verein getreuer Herzen —
Holde Freundin zage nicht!
Nun muss ich aber auch geschwind den Kranz holen. Die alte Elsbeth hat ihn eben aus der Stadt mitgebracht und ich vergessliches Ding liess ihn unten. Horch, da kommen die Brautjungfern schon!

## VIERTE SCENE

**ANNCHEN:** (*im Abgehen.*) Guten Tag, liebe Mädchen! Da, singt immer die Braut an. Ich komme gleich wieder (*Ab.*)

**EINE BRAUTJUNGFER:** Wir winden dir den Jungfernkranz
Mit veilchenblauer Seide.
Wir führen dich zum Spiel und Tanz,
Zu Glück und Liebesfreude.

**ALLE:** Schöner grüner Jungfernkranz!
Veilchenblaue Seide!

**EINE BRAUTJUNGFER:** Lavendel, Myrt' und Tymian,
Das wächst in meinem Garten;
Wie lang bleibt doch der Freiersmann?
Ich kann es kaum erwarten.

**ALLE** (*wie oben.*) Schöner, grüner Jungfernkranz etc.

**EINE BRAUTJUNGFER:** Sie hat gesponnen sieben Jahr
Den gold'nen Flachs am Rocken,
Die Schleier sind wie Spinnweb' klar
Und grün der Kranz der Locken.

**ALLE:** Schöner, grüner Jungfernkranz etc.

**EINE BRAUTJUNGFER:** Und als der schmucke Freier kam,
War'n sieben Jahr verronnen;
Und weil sie der Herzliebste nahm,
Hat sie den Kranz gewonnen.

**ALLE:** Schöner, grüner Jungfernkranz etc.

## FÜNFTE SCENE

**ANNCHEN:** *mit einer zugebundenen runden Schachtel eintretend, fällt mit ein.* Schöner, grüner Jungfernkranz etc.
Nun, da bin ich wieder! Aber fast wär'ich auf die Nase gefallen. Kannst du dir's denken, Agathe? der alte Herr Cuno hat schon wieder gespukt.

**AGATHE:** (*beklommen.*) Fast könnt'es mir ängsten! Er war der Urvater unsers Stammes —

**ANNCHEN:** Du zitterst auch vor einer Spinne! Nun frisch! Noch einmal das Ende des Liedchens! *Sie schneidet den Bindfaden entzwei, kniet tändelnd vor Agathen nieder und überreicht ihr die Schachtel.*

**ALLE:** *ausser Agathen.* Schöner, grüner Jungfernkranz etc.

Youth dwells in hope's rosy sphere.
Now the stars of love are beaming,
Now the nuptial torch is streaming;
Dearest cousin, banish fear!
But now I must quickly go and get your wreath. Old Elsbeth has just brought it home, but I have forgotten and left it below, Hark! the bridesmaids are already coming.

## SCENE IV

**ANNCHEN** (*going off.*) Good morning, dear girls. There, sing, to the bride. I shall soon be with you again.
(*Exit.*)

**A BRIDESMAID:** We twine a bridal wreath for you
Of violet silk and flowers;
And all thy future life may be
But spent in joyous hours.

**CHORUS:** We twine a bridal wreath for you,
Of violet silk and flowers, etc.

**A BRIDESMAID:** Here's evergreen, and violets blue,
And roses all the rarest:
I'm sighing for my wooer true —
The dearest and the fairest.

**CHORUS:** A bridal wreath, etc.

**A BRIDESMAID:** For seven long years, the maiden dear
Spun golden flax so sprightly;
Her web then was crystal clear,
Her eyes they shone so brightly.

**CHORUS:** A bridal wreath, etc.

**A BRIDESMAID:** And when at last the wooer came,
Her single race was run then:
The maiden took her lover's name,
The wreath was won then.

**CHORUS:** A bridal wreath, etc.

## SCENE V

**ANNCHEN:** (*entering with a box and joins the strain*). A bridal wreath, etc.
Well, here I am back again! But I came near having a fall. Just imagine, dear Agathe, the Good old Herr Cuno has walked down again.

**AGATHE:** This almost frightens me, He was the first of our race.

**ANNCHEN:** You tremble at a spider! Take courage! Let us once more repeat the last strain. (*She cuts the string, and kneeling before Agathe presents her the box.*)

**CHORUS:** A bridal wreath, etc.

AGATHE: *öffnet und fährt zurück.* Ach!
*Alle, ausser Annchen, die noch kniet, fahren gleichfalls erblassend zurück.*

ANNCHEN: Nun, was ist denn?
*Agathe nimmt den Kranz heraus; es ist ein silberner Todtenkranz.*

ANNCHEN: *sehr erschrocken.* Eine Todtenkrone — Himmel, das ist — *aufspringend und ihre Verlegenheit verbergend.* Nein, das ist nicht zum Aushalten! da hat die alte halbblinde Frau gewiss die Schachteln vertauscht! Aber was fangen wir nun an? *Verbirgt die Schachtel schnell.* Weg damit! Einen Kranz müssen wir haben! *Nimmt die Rosen schnell aus dem Blumentopfe, verschlingt sie zu einem Kranze und setzt ihn Agathen auf.* Ein herrlicher Einfall! Sie verschlingen sich von selbst und stehen dir allerliebst. Doch nun lasst uns auch gehen. Unsere Begleiter werden sonst ungeduldig — Singt! singt!

CHOR: Schöner, grüner Jungfernkranz etc.

## SECHSTE SCENE

*Hoflager des Fürsten. — Ottokar, Cuno, Max, Caspar, Jäger. Nachher Agathe, Annchen, der Eremit, Brautjungfern und Landleute.*

CHOR DER JÄGER: Was gleicht wohl auf Erden dem Jägervergnügen?
Wem sprudelt der Becher des Lebens so reich?
Beim Klange der Hörner im Grünen zu liegen,
Den Hirsch zu verfolgen durch Dickicht und Teich,
Ist fürstliche Freude, ist männlich Verlangen,
Erstarket die Glieder und würzet das Mahl;
Wenn Wälder und Felsen uns hallend umfangen,
Tönt freier und freud'ger der volle Pokal.
Jo hoho! Drallara!
Diana ist kundig, die Nacht zu erhellen,
Wie labend am Tage ihr Dunkel uns kuhlt,
Den blutigen Wolf und den Eber zu fällen,
Der gierig die grünenden Saaten durchwühlt,
Ist fürstliche Freude, ist männlich Verlangen u. s. w.

OTTOKAR: Genug der Freuden des Mahls, werthe Freunde und Jagdgenossen! und nun noch zu etwas Ernstem. Ich genehmige sehr gern die Wahl, welche Ihr, mein alter wackerer Cuno, getroffen habt. Der von Euch erwählte Eidam gefällt mir.

---

AGATHE: (*opens the box, and starts back*). Alas!
(*All the bridesmaids are equally frightened, except Annchen who still kneels.*)

ANNCHEN: Well, what is the matter?
(*Agathe produces the wreath from the box, which is a white death wreath.*)

ANNCHEN: (*also frightened*). A death-wreath! Heavens, it is! (*endeavoring to hide her embarrassment.*) No, this is not to be endured! This old, half-blind woman has most probably exchanged the boxes. But what are we to do? (*takes the box away.*) Away with this! We must have a wreath. (*Takes the roses from a flowerpot, and twining them into a wreath, puts it upon Agathe.*) An excellent thought! They entwine naturally, and become you extremely well. Now let us go, else our companions will grow impatient. Sing girls, sing!

CHORUS: A bridal wreath, etc.

## SCENE VI

(*The Prince's Camp — OTTOCAR, CUNO, MAX, CASPAR, HUNTERS. Afterwards AGATHE, ANNCHEN, the HERMIT, BRIDESMAIDS and PEASANTS.*)

CHORUS OF HUNTERS: What equals on earth the delight of the huntsman?
For whom does life's cup more enchantingly flow?
To follow the stag through the forests and meadows
When brightly the beams of the morning first glow.
O this is a pleasure that's worthy of princes.
And health in its wanderings, can ever be found;
More gaily the pledge of the goblet will sound.
Ho ho! ho! Drallara! etc.
The light of Diana illumines our forest.
The shades where in summer we often retreat;
Nor is the fell wolf in his covert securest.
The boar from his lair is laid at our feet.
O this is a pleasure that's worthy of princes, etc.

OTTOCAR: Enough my friends and companions, enough of pleasure! Let us proceed to something more serious. I willingly give my consent to your choice, my worthy Cuno. I am pleased with the successor and son-in-law you have chosen.

---

CUNO: Ich kann ihm in Allem das beste Zeugniss geben.

OTTOKAR: Wo ist die Braut?

MAX: *hält die Kugel in der hohlen Hand und blickt starr auf sie hin.* Dich sparte ich auf — Unfehlbare! Glückskugel! Aber du lastest jetzt zentnerschwer in meiner Hand.

CUNO: Der Zeit nach muss meine Tochter bald hier sein. Der gute Bursch hat seit einiger Zeit, wo freilich die Entscheidung seines Glücks immer mehr herannahte, ganz besondern Unstern gehabt. Ich fürchte, die Gegenwart der Braut könnte ihn in Verwirrung setzen.

OTTOKAR: Wohlauf, junger Schütz! einen Schuss, wie heut' früh deine drei ersten, und du bist geborgen! Siehst du dort auf dem Zweige die weisse Taube? Die Aufgabe ist leicht. Schiess!
*Max legt an. In dem Augenblicke, da er losdrücken will, tritt Agathe mit den Uebrigen zwischen den Bäumen heraus und schreit:* Schiess nicht! Ich bin die Taube!
*Der Schuss fällt. Sowohl Agathe als Caspar sinken. Hinter der Ersten tritt der Eremit hervor und fasst sie auf.*

EINIGE: Schaut! o schaut!
Er traf die Braut!

ANDERE: Der Jäger stürzte vom Baum!

NOCH ANDERE: Wir wagen's kaum
Nur hinzuschau'n!
O furchtbar Schicksal, o Grau'n!

CHOR: Uns're Herzen beben, zagen!
Wär' die Schreckensthat gescheh'n?
Kaum will es das Auge wagen,
Wer das Opfer sei, zu seh'n.

AGATHE: (*aus schwerer Ohnmacht erwachend.*) Wo bin ich?
War's Traum nur, dass ich sank?

ANNCHEN: O fasse dich!

MAX, CUNO: Sie lebt.

EINIGE: Den Heil'gen Preis und Dank! —
Sie hat die Augen offen! —

EINIGE: Heir, dieser ist getroffen,
Der roth vom Blute liegt —

CASPAR: Ich sah den Klausner bei ihr steh'n;
Der Himmel siegt!
Es ist um mich gescheh'n!

AGATHE: (*sich erholend.*) Ich lebe noch; der Schreck nur warf mich nieder,
Ich athme noch die liebliche Luft —

CUNO: Sie athmet frei!

MAX: Sie lächelt wieder.

AGATHE: Mein Max.

MAX: Die süsse Stimme ruft!

---

CUNO: I can well recommend him in every respect.

OTTOCAR: Where is the bride?

MAX: (*looking at the bullet which he holds in the hollow of his hand*). At least, I have saved you— you're infallible, you charmed ball! But now you lay heavily within my hand.

CUNO: It is almost time that my daughter were here. For some time past this good fellow has had especially ill luck. I almost fear that the presence of his bride may increase his confusion.

OTTOCAR: Well, then, young marksman? One shot like the three I saw this morning, and you are safe. See the white dove on yonder tree! That task is easy. Shoot.
(*Max rasies his rifle. At the moment he is about to fire, Agathe appears among the trees, and cries:*)
Do not shoot! I am the dove.
(*The shot falls. Agathe and Caspar sink. The Hermit appears behind the former, and raises her up.*)

A FEW OF THE CHORUS: See! Look! His shot has struck his bride!

OTHERS: A huntsman fell from yonder oak!

OTHERS AGAIN: We scarcely dare to look around
O scene of terror and fear!

CHORUS: Round the fearful scene of horror Dare we scarcely turn our eyes.
Who beneath this blow of terror,
Who has been the sacrifice?

AGATHE: (*awaking from a swoon*). Where am I?
And was it but a dream?

ANNCHEN: Compose yourself!

MAX, CUNO: She lives!

SEVERAL: By hope's effulgent beam
Our hearts are yet surrounded!

OTHERS: See! here lies one all wounded,
Bathed in the purple tide—

CASPAR: I saw the hermit by her side;
Heaven conquers!
My life of sin is past!

AGATHE: (*recovering*). I live again; it was nothing but fear upon me;
I live again, to love and rejoice—

CUNO: She breathes again!

MAX: She smiles upon me.

AGATHE: My love.

MAX: It is her own loved voice!

CASPAR: (*erblickt Samiel.*) Du Samiel schon hier?
So hielst du dein Versprechen mir?
Nimm deinen Raub! Ich trotze dem Verderben!
Dem Himmel Fluch! — Fluch dir!
*Stürzt und stirbt. Samiel ist verschwunden.*

EINIGE: Ha! Das war sein Gebet im Sterben?

CUNO: Er war von je ein Bösewicht!
Ihn traf des Himmels Strafgericht!

ANDERE: Er hat dem Himmel selbst geflucht!

NOCH ANDERE: Vernahmt Ihr's nicht? Er rief den Bösen —

OTTOKAR: Fort! stürzt das Scheusal in die Wolfesschlucht!
*Einige Jäger tragen den Leichnam fort. Zu Max.*
Nun du kannst dieses Räthsel lösen.
Wohl schwere Unthat ist gescheh'n!
Weh'dir, wirst du nicht Alles treu gesteh'n.

MAX: Herr! unwerth bin ich Eurer Gnade;
Des Todten Trug verlockte mich,
Dass — voll Verzweiflung, ich vom Pfade
Der Frömmigkeit und Tugend wich;
Vier Kugeln, die ich heut'verschoss —
Freikugeln sind's, die ich mit Jenem goss.

OTTOKAR: So eile, mein Gebiet zu meiden,
Und kehre nimmer in dies Land!
Vom Himmel muss dei Hölle scheiden,
Nie, nie empfängst du diese reine Hand!

MAX: Ich darf nicht wagen,
Mich zu beklagen;
Denn schwach war ich, obwohl kein Bösewicht.

CUNO: Er war sonst stets getreu der Pflicht —

AGATHE: Reisst ihn nicht aus meinen Armen!

JAEGER: Er ist so brav, voll Kraft und Muth —

LANDLEUTE: O! er war immer brav und gut!

ANNCHEN: Gnäd'ger Herr! o habt Erbarmen!

OTTOKAR: Nein! —
Agathe ist so fromm, so rein — (*Zu Max.*)
Hinweg, hinweg aus meinem Blick!
Dein harrt der Kerker, kehrst du je zurück!

EREMIT: (*tritt auf.*) Wer legt auf ihn so strengen Bann?
Ein Fehltritt, ist er solcher Büssung werth?

CASPAR: (*observing Zamiel*).
You Zamiel, here now!
And is it thus you keep your vow?
Take then your prey! I dare you and your fiends.
Accursed by they!—and you.
(*Falls and dies. Zamiel disappears.*)

CHORUS: Hear! Listen to his dying prayer.

CUNO: His life was ever one of vice,
He therefore fell a fearful sacrifice.

SEVERAL: He fell a fearful sacrifice.

OTHERS: He called upon the evil spirit—

OTTOCAR: Hence! In the wolf's glen cast the wretch away!
(*Several hunters carry off the corpse.*)
(*To Max.*)
This mystery, you alone can clear it,
Reveal the cause of these strange scenes reveal,
And woe to you, if you conceal anything.

MAX: Sire, worthless do I kneel before you—
Oh let my grief assuage your wrath.
The clouds of woe were lowering over me.
I madly turned from virtue's path.
The bullets which I shot within your sight
Were charmed, and cast by him at dead of night,

OTTOCAR: Then haste, avoid my sight forever,
Nor dare return unto this land.
From heavenly virtue hell must sever,
You never shall receive this maiden's hand.

MAX: I dare not complain.
My prayer is vain;
For I was weak, although not bad at heart.

CUNO: From faith, he never did depart.

AGATHE: Oh! do not tear him from my side!

HUNTERS: His heart was never inclined to vice;

PEASANTS: But pure and pious was his mind—

ANNCHEN: Let mercy still your justice guide!

OTTOCAR: No!
Agathe is too good, too pure—
(*To Max.*)
Away, away, your prayers in vain.
The prison waits, if you return again.

HERMIT: (*enters*) Shall erring mortal here presume,
A sinful fellow mortal thus to doom?

OTTOKAR: Bist du es, heil'ger Mann!
Den weit und breit die Gegend ehrt?
Sei mir gegrüsst, Gesegneter des Herrn,
Dir bin auch ich gehorsam gern;
Sprich du sein Urtheil; deinen Willen
Will freudig ich erfüllen.

EREMIT: Es finde nie der Probeschuss mehr statt!
Ihm, Herr! (*Zu Max*) Du, der schwer gesündigt hat,
Doch früher reines Herzens war,
Vergönnt dafür ein Probe-Jahr,
Und bleibt er dann, wie ich ihn stets erfand,
Dann werde sein Agathe's Hand!

OTTOKAR: Dein Wort genüget mir!
Ein Höh'rer spricht aus dir.

ALLE: Heil unserm Herrn! Er widerstehet nicht
Dem, was der fromme Klausner spricht.

OTTOKAR: Bewährst du dich, wie dich der Greis erfand,
Dann knüpf'ich selber Euer Eheband!

MAX: Die Zukunft soll mein Herz bewähren!
Stets heilig sei mir Recht und Pflicht!

AGATHE: O les't den Dank in diesen Zähren;
Das schwache Wort genügt ihm nicht!

EREMIT: Der über Sternen ist voll Gnade;
Drum ehrt es Fürsten, zu verzeih'n!

CUNO: Weicht nimmer von der Tugend Pfade,
Um Eures Glückes werth zu sein!

ANNCHEN: O dann, geliebte Freundin, schmücke
Ich dich auf's Neu' zum Traualtar!

EREMIT: Doch jetzt erhebt noch Eure Blicke
Zu dem, der Schutz der Unschuld war!
*Er kniet nieder und erhebt die Hände. Agathe, Cuno, Max, Annchen und mehrere des Volks folgen seinem Beispiel.*

CHOR: Ja, lasst uns zum Himmel die Blicke erheben
Und fest auf die Lenkung des Ewigen bau'n;
Wer rein ist von Herzen, und schuldlos von Leben,
Darf kindlich der Milde des Vaters vertrau'n.

*ENDE.*

OTTOCAR: And you here holy man,
Revered by high and low around
We bow to you—the blessed of the Lord.
Pay willingly obedience to your word!
Pronounce his doom; your just and pious will
We'll cheerfully fulfill,

HERMIT: Let then such trials be annulled from here
And him (*To Max*) whose conscience once was free,
Let him pass an entire year,
In lowly penitence and prayer.
If he remains pure, as I hope he will,
Then let him be Agathe's still.

OTTOCAR: Your word suffices me
For Heaven speaks in you

CHORUS: Hail to our Prince! he willingly obeys
The pious man, in all he says.

OTTOCAR: To prove my pardon is sincere, my hand
Shall consecrate the marriage ban.

MAX: Oh! while possessed of this bright treasure,
No vicious thought shall dare intrude.

AGATHE: O! let these glowing tears of pleasure
Proclaim my bosom's gratitude.

HERMIT: As we do hope to be forgiven,
So should we others faults forgive.

CUNO: Any may the blessed award of heaven,
Decree that you may live in joy!

ANNCHEN: And oh! with what enraptured feeling
Shall I now wreathe the bridal crown!

HERMIT: Now raise your hands, and humbly kneeling,
In tuneful songs your spirits breathe.
(*Kneels, and others follow his example.*)

CHORUS: Let us raise then our hearts and our voices to heaven
And firm on its guidance forever rely;
The penitent sinner will ever be forgiven.
To his prayer our father still will reply.

*THE END*

# Euryanthe (1823)

MUSIC BY CARL MARIA WEBER ■ LIBRETTO BY HELMINA VON CHÉZY

This three-act grand heroic-romantic opera, set to a libretto by Helmina von Chézy (based on the medieval romance *l'Histoire de Gérard de Nevers et de la très vertueuse et très chaste Euryanthe de Savoye*), premiered at the Kärntnertor Theatre in Vienna on October 25, 1823. Louis VII celebrates the end of the war and Count Adolar sings the praises of his fiancé, Euryanthe of Savoy. Count Lysiart is jealous of Count Adolar and says that he doubts such virtuous women really exist. Adolar challenges him to a duel, but Lysiart suggests that if he fails to seduce Euryanthe he will give up all of his worldly possessions. The King tries to talk him out of this wager, but Adolar insists upon it, saying that he will also give up all of his worldly possessions if he loses. In the meantime, Euryanthe has been awaiting her beloved's return and confides in Eglantine, who is secretly in love with Adolar. Eglantine is the daughter of a dispossessed noble, and Adolar has been very kind to them. Eglantine learns a deep, dark family secret from Euryanthe—Emma, Adolar's sister, killed herself by drinking poison from a ring after her beloved died in battle, and her soul will not rest until a falsely accused person cries on the same ring. The keeping of this secret is a sacred trust between Euryanthe and Adolar. Lysiart is sure that he will fail in his wager until Eglantine tells him Adolar's secret and gives him the ring, taken from Emma's tomb. Having this ring in his possession and knowing the truth about Emma's death will show that Lysiart and Euryanthe share a close bond. Lysiart accuses Euryanthe before Adolar and the entire court of betraying Adolar's trust, and he shows the ring. Adolar assumes that she gave Lysiart Emma's ring as a token of her love. He gives his castle to Lysiart and takes Euryanthe into the wilderness, where he plans to kill her. He decides to spare her since she has shown that she would give up her own life for his, and he leaves her in the forest. She collapses in deep despair and is discovered by the King's hunting party. She tells them about Eglantine's plot against her; the King believes her story and promises that truth will win out. Adolar hears from his vassals that Lysiart and Eglantine are about to be married. The wedding procession passes by, and Eglantine, dreading this marriage as she is still in love with Adolar, carries on about the plot against Euryanthe. Adolar once again challenges Lysiart to a duel. The King enters and announces that Euryanthe has died of grief. Eglantine confesses her guilt, at which Lysiart kills her and is arrested. Euryanthe revives (she has been in a dead faint) and is reunited with her beloved. Emma is now finally at peace as Euryanthe has wept over the ring.

## ■ ERSTE AUFZUG

*Säulenhalle des königlichen Schlosses. An den Säulen sind die Waffen, Schilde und Lanzen der Ritter befestigt. Neben dem Wappen von Nevers und Rethel prangt die mit Blumen umwundene Zither, und der Helm ist Lorbeeren gekrönt.*

### SCENE I

*Der König, von Grossen und Fürsten, umgeben. Lyssiart, Damen und Jünglinge.*

**CHOR DER FRAUEN:** Dem Frieden Heil! nach Sturmes Tagen, Heil dieser Feier reiner Lust! Der Helden Herz in starker Brust Darf nun für sanfte Freuden schlagen.

**CHOR DER RITTER:** Den Frauen Heil! den zarten Schönen, Den Blumen in des Lebens Kranz, Wohl ringt der Muth nach Siegesglanz; Doch Liebe muss das Leben krönen.

## ■ ACT I

*A Hall supported by columns in the Royal Castle. On the columns are suspended the weapons, shields, and lances of the Knights. Near the Arms of Nevers and Rethel is the guitar garlanded with flowers, and the helmet is crowned with laurel.*

### SCENE I

*The King surrounded by Grandees and Princes. Lysiart, Ladies, and Youths.*

**CHORUS OF LADIES:** All hail to peace! after days of storm, Hail to this feast of purest joy! The hero's heart, in his strong breast, May now for gentle pleasures beat.

**CHORUS OF KNIGHTS:** To women, hail! the tender fair ones, The flowers in the wreath of life; Courage strives for victory's glory, But love must crown our life.

**ALLE:** Der Liebe Preis erschallt in süssen Tönen Und Treue reicht len schönsten Lebenskranz.

**DER KÖNIG:** Mein Adolar, so fern den schönen Reigen, So trübe bei des Festes Lust?

**ADOLAR:** Nur Sehnsucht herrscht in meiner Brust, Ihr muss sich jede Freude neigen.

**DER KÖNIG:** Erheit're dich! —

**LYSSIART:** (*für sich*). O Sorg' um einen Knaben!

**DER KÖNIG:** Beglückend Wiedersehn ist nah! Weilt deine Braut in Nevers?

**ADOLAR:** Ja, mein König!

**DER KÖNIG:** Heut noch soll sie Kunde haben, Bald soll ihr Anblick dich erfreuen, Sie wird der Schmuck des Hofes sein.

**ADOLAR:** Mein theurer König!

**DER KÖNIG:** Treuer Adolar! Der freudig mir im Kampfe zur Seite war, Sei hier auch froh, es töne diesem

**ALL:** The prize of love resounds in sweetest tones, And life's most lovely wreath bestows fidelity

**KING:** My Adolar! so far from the gay circles; So sad amid all the festival's delights!

**ADOLAR:** Love's ardor dwells alone within my breast; Before it every pleasure must give way.

**KING:** Cheer up!

**LYSIART:** (*Aside*). What care about a boy!

**KING:** Your happy meeting now is near, Your betrothed dwells in Nevers?

**ADOLAR:** Yes, my King!

**KING:** To-day shall the tidings reach her; Soon shall her presence bring you joy; She'll be the ornament of the court.

**ADOLAR:** My dear King!

**KING:** Trusty Adolar! Who joyfully was at my side in the fight. Be here too joyful! let to this circle

# Act I, Scene I

Kreise
Ein Minnelied zu Euryanthes
Preise.
(*Der König winkt. Zwei Damen reichen Adolar die Zither, die neben seinem Wappen hängt.*)

ADOLAR: Unter blühenden Mandelbäumen,
An der Loire grünem Strand,
O wie selig ists zu träumen,
Wo ich meine Liebe fand!
Sie, die Reine,
Sie, die Meine,
Keusch wie Schnee, wie Rosen mild.
Unter blüh'nden Mantelbäumen
Schwebt um mich ihr süsses Bild!
Bei dem goldnen Glanz der Sterne,
An der Loire Spiegelrand,
Gab der Liebe reinsten, gerne
Augenstern ein Himmelspfand.
Träumend, sinnig,
Zart und minnig,
Aug' in Auge, Mund an Mund,
Bei dem Leuchten ew'ger Sterne
Gab sich Herz dem Herzen kund!
Heil'ge Treue schönste Rose,
An der Loire Blumenrand,
Ob auch Sturm und Welle tose,
Blühst du des Lenzes Pfand!
Zarte, Reine,
Süsse, Meine,
Du mit mir ganz Ein und Mein!
Heil'ger Treue schönste Rose
Blüht in deiner Brust allein.

CHOR: Heil Adolar, Heil Euryanth', des Schönen,
Der Liebe Heil, in reiner Unschuld Glanz!
Dich, He'd und Sänger, muss der Ruhm bekronen,
Doch Treue reicht den schönsten Lebenskranz.
(*Während des Chors nahen sich paarweise die Damen und Jünglinge, Ede und Ritter, Adolar. Es wird ihm ein Kranz aufgesetzt. Jungfrauen nehmen ihm die Zither ab, umwinden sie mit Blumen, und hängen sie wieder auf*).

LYSSIART: (*für sich*). Ich trag es nicht.
(*Laut*)
Hör an, Graf Adolar!
Du hast uns hoch ergötzt mit dem Gesang,
Wo alle danken, nimm auch meinen Dank;
Kein Sänger nimmt den Preis dir ab, fürwahr.
Vergüten könntest du getrost dein Erbe,
Die Zither sorgt, dass nicht ihr Held verderbe!

ADOLAR: Gern, Lyssiart, üb' ich mich in sanften Weisen
Für Misslaut taugt ein gut gestimmtes Eisen.

LYSSIART: Was zürnst du gleich? die Weise tadl' ich nicht,
Doch wohl die Worte vom Gedicht!
Hör auf der Frauen Treu' so hoch zu preisen!

sound,
A minstrel's song in Euryanthe's praise.
(*The King makes a signal. Two ladies reach Adolar the guitar, which hangs near his arms*)

ADOLAR: Under blooming almond trees
On the green strand of the Loire,
Oh! how blessed is it to dream —
Where I found my love!
She, the pure one,
She, that's mine;
Chaste as snow, as roses gentle.
Under blooming almond trees,
Her sweet image floats around me.
Under the golden splendor of the stars,
On the mirror-border of the Loire,
Gave willing to purest love,
Her starry eyes a heavenly pledge.
Dreamy, thoughtful,
Tender, loving,
Eye to eye, and lip to lip,
By the light of stars eternal
Heart revealed itself to heart;
Sacred faith, divinest rose,
On the flowery border of the Loire,
Though storms and waves may rage.
You bloom still, the pledge of spring!
Tender, pure,
Sweet — my own —
You, quite one with me and mine!
Of sacred faith the loveliest rose
Blooms in your breast alone.

CHORUS: Hail, Adolar! hail, Euryanthe the fair!
All hail to love, in the splendor of pure innocence!
Hero and singer, fame must crown you,
The loveliest wreath of life bestows fidelity!
(*During the Chorus, the Ladies and Youths, Nobles and Knights, approach Adolar, two and two. A garland is placed on his head. Maids take from the guitar, wreathe it with flowers, and hang it up again*).

LYSIART: (*Aside*). I cannot bear it.
(*Aloud*)
Hear me, Count Adolar
You have pleased us with the song,
And where all thank, take my thanks also;
No singer wrests the prize from you in truth,
You may squander unconcerned the wreath,
For your guitar will ever save its hero from distress.

ADOLAR: Gladly I practice, Lysiart, soft measures,
For discord best avails well-tempered iron.

LYSIART: Angered so soon? I censure not the measure;
But I do the meaning of your poem!
Cease woman's faith so high to prize!

Des Meeres Grund hegt Perlen makelrein,
Des Weibes Brust schliesst keine Treue ein.
(*Die Damn gehen ab*).
Schon athm' ich freier. — Was entgegnest du?

ADOLAR: Dies acht' ich keiner Antwort werth,
Komm' in den Wald, dort schliesset dir mein Schwert,
Mit Gott! die gift'ge Lippe zu.

LYSSIART: Um schnöden Anlass kämpfen! Nie!
Die Warnung gab ich, — nütze sie!
Mein junger Freund, wärst du der Preis der Ritter,
Wär ich ein niedrer Knecht,
Ich schwör es dir,
Die Liebe deiner Braut gewönn ich mir;
Trotz deiner Rosenwang' und goldenen Zither!

ADOLAR: Erbärmlich eitler Prahler nenn' ich dich,
Den Handschuh nimm! — Dich lehr' ich Frauen ehren!

LYSSIART: Ich nehm' ihn nicht! —
Besiegtest du gleich mich;
Doch unbesiegt noch meine Gründe wären.
Wag es getros, bekämpfe sie!
Du prüstest dein Schöne nie?

ADOLAR: Für Euryanthe bürgt der Glaube In meiner Brust.

LYSSIART: Du fromme Turteltaube,
Dein Glück zu stören trüg ich Scheu!

DER KÖNIG: Mein Adolar lass ab von diesem Streite!

LYSSIART: Du hörst die Weisheit ist auf meiner Seite!

ADOLAR: Mein Gut und Blut an Euryanthens Treu!

LYSSIART: Wohlan! du kennst mein herrlich Eigenthum
Das Erbtheil meiner Väter, reich an Ruhm,
Zum Pfande setz ich's: es sei dein,
Nenn' ich nicht die Gepries'ne mein.

ADOLAR: Es gilt!

CHOR: Vermessenes Beginnen!

ADOLAR: Kannst Euryanthes Liebe du gewinnen,
So nimm mein Gold, mein Gut und Land,
Zerrissen sei dann jedes süsse Band —
Die Heimath meid ich.

LYSSIART: Alles nach Gefallen —
Wie schön wilst du mit Kranz und Zither wallen.

The ocean's depth holds pure and spotless pearls,
But no truth dwells in the breast of woman.
(*Exeunt the Ladies*).
Already I breathe freer. How do you reply?

ADOLAR: This I esteem worthy of no reply;
Come to the wood; there my sword will close,
With (help of) God, your slanderous lips.

LYSIART: For a base motive, combat? Never!
I give the warning—use it!
My young friend, were you the pearl! of knights,
And I am abject serf,
I'd swear to you
The love of your betrothed I'd win for me.
Spite of your cheeks of rose and golden bright guitar.

ADOLAR: Contemptible, vain boaster, do I call you.
Take up my glove. I'll teach you to honor women!

LYSIART: I take it not. For you're conquered me now,
My reason still would remain undestroyed;
Venture it boldly—combat them!
Never have you tried your lady's love.

ADOLAR: For Euryanthe answers the firm faith Within my breast.

LYSIART: You gentle turtle-dove,
I almost dread to interrupt your joy!

KING: My Adolar, abandon this discussion!

LYSIART: You hear—on my side wisdom speaks.

ADOLAR: My life and fortune for Euryanthe's truth!

LYSIART: Well then, you knowest my noble property—
The heritage of my fathers rich in fame;
I set it as a stake!—let it be yours,
If I call not this lauded lady mine.

ADOLAR: So be it.

CHORUS: Presumptuous offer!

ADOLARD: If you can't win the love of Euryanthe,
Then take my gold, my fortune, and my lands;
Let then be rent asunder each sweet tie—
I'd fly my home.

LYSIART: Just as you please!
How nobly will you wander with garland and guitar.

**ADOLAR:** Vermessener! frohlocke nicht!
Schlägt es dir fehl, ruf' ich zum Gottgericht
Dich Frevler auf!

**LYSSIART:** Wohl! dess seid ihr alle Zeugen. Es gilt!

**CHOR:** Kann nichts den starren Sinn euch beugen?
O geht zurück! zu viel habt ihr gewagt.

**ADOLAR:** Ich gab mein Wort!

**DER KÖNIG:** Ich mach es ungesagt.

**ADOLAR:** Des Edlen Wort kann nicht Gewalt vernichten.

**DER KÖNIG:** Du trotzest der schleichenden Gefahr.

**ADOLAR:** Mein König! Frauenehre schirmen, war
Die höchste stets von allen Ritterpflichten!
In Demuth fleh ich, nimm dieses Unterpfand.
(*Er überreicht dem König seinen Ring*).

**LYSSIART:** (*Reicht dem König seinen Ring gleichfalls*). Hier diesen Ring in deine Königshand!
Jetzt schleunig rüst' ich mich zur Reise,
Und siegreich kehr ich heim!

**DER KÖNIG:** Doch de Beweise?

**LYSSIART:** Ein Zeugniss ihrer Huld dir darzubringen
Verpflicht ich mich!

**CHOR:** Mög es ihm nie gelingen!

**ADOLAR:** Ich bau auf Gatt und meine Euryanth'.

**LYSSIART:** Ich bringe dir ein sichres Unterpfand.

**CHOR:** Die Unschuld schütz, o Gott, mit starker Hand.
(*Alle ab.*)

## SCENE II

*Burggarten zu Nevers mit einem Gruftgewölbe. Abend.*

**EURYANTHE:** Glöcklein im Thale
Nieseln im Bach,
Säusseln in Lüften
Schmelzendes Ach!
Sterne in Wipfeln
Aeugelnd durch Laub,
Ach, und die Seele
Der Sehnsucht Raub!
Weilst du so ferne?
Langst wohl nach mir?
Bringen die Sterne
Grüsse von dir?
Alle so golden
Selig und klar —
Ach doch dein Blick nicht
Mein Adolar!

---

**ADOLAR:** Insensate! triumph not!
If you fail—I summon you to the trial of battle.

**LYSIART:** Good! of this be all witness—
So be it.

**CHORUS:** Can nothing bend your stern resolve?
Recede! you venture too much!

**ADOLAR:** I gave my word.

**KING:** I recall it.

**ADOLAR:** The noble's word can destroy no power.

**KING:** You brave insidious danger.

**ADOLAR:** My prince! the honor of woman to protect was
The highest ever of all our knightly duties.
Humbly, I beg, receive this pledge.
(*He gives to the King his ring*).

**LYSIART:** (*Delivers to the King his ring also*). Here, this ring on your royal hand!
Now quickly prepare me for the journey,
And victoriously I shall return.

**KING:** But the proofs?

**LYSIART:** A testimony of her favor to present you,
I pledge myself.

**CHORUS:** May he never succeed!

**ADOLOR:** I trust in God and my Euryanthe!

**LYSIART:** A certain pledge I'll bring to you.

**CHORUS:** Innocence protect, O God! with your strong hand.
(*Exeunt omnes*)

## SCENE II

*Castle-garden at Nevers, with a vaulted grotto. Evening.*

**EURYANTHE:** The bells of the valley,
The rivulet's murmur,
The rustling zephyrs
Melt into sighs!
The stars above the trees
Peep through the leaves.
Ah! my soul
Is a prey to its ardor!
Do you dwell so far?
Are you anxious for me?
Do the stars bring
Greetings from you?
All are so golden,
Blessed, and clear,
But I so not see your eyes,
My Adolor!

---

## SCENE III

*Eglantine, Vorige.*

**EGLANTINE:** So einsam bangend sind ich dich?

**EURYANTHE:** O nenne Bangen nicht mein einzig Glück,
Dies Sehnen ist der Himmel unter Klagen.

**EGLANTINE:** Wie kannst du trauern? siegreich heimgekehrt
Ist Adolar, erwartet
Im Königschlosse dich, die hohe Braut.

**EURYANTHE:** Mich locket nicht der Feste Glanz;
In diesem Blüthenparadiese hier,
Wo wir beseligt Hand in Hand gegangen
Ihn wiedersehen — stillweinend ihn umfangen!
Das wäre Seligkeit.

**EGLANTINE:** Dir? nimmer hast du mir Vertrauen gewährt,
Dich drückt ein bang Geheimniss; leg es nieder
In diese Brust; dann kann ich ruhig sein.
Nur dann, sonst nie.

**EURYANTHE:** Verschone, lass mich schweigen.

**EGLANTINE:** Des Unglücks Blick ist scharf! — Um Mitternacht.
In dunkler Gruft, wenn du dich einsam wähnst,
Wacht Liebe di zur Seite.

**EURYANTHE:** O verschweige Dir selbst, was du gesehen,

**EGLANTINE:** Nichts sagst du mir?

O mein Leid ist unermessen,
Du kannst mir dein Herz entziehn.
Lass mich einsam und vergessen
In die fernste Wildniss fliehn!
Lass mich fort vom Sturm getrieben.
Irren, schwanken, untergehn!
Nein, dein Lieben war kein Lieben,
Nie sollst du mich wedersehen.
Doch wie könnt ich ie dich meiden?
Nein, verstoss mich nie von hier!
Dulden will ich, einsam leiden,
Sterben süss am Busen dir.

**EURYANTHE:** Freundin! Geliebte.
An meine Brust!
Wie konnt ich solche Lieb ermessen!
Vergieb!

**EGLANTINE:** Du liebst mich? Alles ist vergessen!

**EURYANTHE:** So treu hast du mit mir gewacht,
In dunkler Gruft, in dunkler Nacht?

**EGLANTINE:** Was störest du der Todten Ruh?

---

## SCENE III

*Eglantine. The same.*

**EGLANTINE:** Sorrowing so lonely do I find you?

**EURYANTHE:** Oh! call not sorrow what's my only joy,
This longing is a heaven amid complaints.

**EGLANTINE:** How can you grieve? victoriously returned
Is Adolar, and waits
In the royal castle you, the noble bride.

**EURYANTHE:** The splendor of no feast allures me;
Here in this blooming paradise,
Where blessed we have wandered hand in hand,
Again to see him — silent, weeping to embrace him!
That were blessedness.

**EGLANTINE:** To you Never have you confided in me:
A painful secret weights upon you — declare it
To this bosom, then I can be at rest —
Then only — or else never.

**EURYANTHE:** Spare me! let me be silent.

**EGLANTINE:** Misfortune's eyes are sharp! — At midnight,
In the dark vault, when you think your self alone,
Love watches at your side.

**EURYANTHE:** Oh! tell not
To yourself what you have seen.

**EGLANTINE:** You say nothing to me?

Oh! my sorrow is unmeasured!
Can you withdraw from me your heart?
Let me forgotten and forlorn
Fly into the furthest desert.
Let me, driven forth by the storm,
Wander, faint, and perish.
No! your loving is no loving,
Never shall you see me again.
But how could I ever avoid you?
No! drive me never from here!
I will suffer — I will bear alone,
And sweetly die upon your breast.

**EURYANTHE:** Friend! Beloved!
To my breast!
How can I measure such affection?
Forgive me!

**EGLANTINE:** You love me? All's forgotten!

**EURYANTHE:** So faithfully have you watched with me,
In the dark vault, in the sombre night?

**EGLANTINE:** Why do you disturb the peace of death?

## Act I, Scene III

**EURYANTHE:** Ich flehe dort für Emmas Frieden, Der Schwester Adolars, durch schnellen Tod Entrissen seiner Brudertreu — ihr Leid Trug sie verschwiegen in die Gruft hinab.

**EGLANTINE:** Wer that es kund?

**EURYANTHE:** Ihr Geist!

**EGLANTINE:** Entsetzen! — Wie?

**EURYANTHE:** Am letzten Mai, in banger Trennung Stunde, Bei Mondenlicht sahn wir, von Duft umwallt, Der holden Emma Luftgestalt, Und säuselnd tönts von ihrem bleichen Munde: "Die ihr der Liebe Thränen, Herz an Herz, So selig weinet — hört mich an — auch mir Strahlt' einst dies goldene Licht. Mein Udo liebte Mich zart und treu! — er fiel in blut'ger Schlacht, Da war mein Leben kein Leben mehr, Verzweifungsnacht hüllt meine Liebe ein; Aus gifterfülltem Ring sog ich den Tod! Weh dieser That, die mich vom Heil geschieden! Getrennt von Udo, irr' ich durch die Nächte; O weint um mich! nicht eh' kann Ruh mir werden, Bis diesen Ring, aus dem ich Tod gesogen, Der Unschuld Thräne netzt im höchsten Leid, Und Treu dem Mörder Rettung beut für Word."

**EGLANTINE:** Gewicht'ge Kunde.

**EURYANTHE:** Was hab ich gethan? Verrathen Adolars Geheimniss! Gott! Gebrochen meinen Eid. —

**EGLANTINE:** Befürchte nichts!

**EURYANTHE:** Unter ist mein Stern gegangen, Bange Ahnung sagt es laut.

**EGLANTINE:** Kannst du zagen, kannst du bangen, Holde, da du mir vertraut?

**EURYANTHE:** Weh! ich brach des Schweigens Treue.

**EGLANTINE:** Such an meinem Busen Ruh!

**EURYANTHE:** Trost der Liebe, süss bist du! Ja, es wallt mein Herz aufs Neue Selig deinem Herzen zu.

**EGLANTINE:** Zweifle nie an meiner Treue, Du nur bist mein Alles, du! (*Euryanthe gebt in die Gruft ab*).

---

**EURYANTHE:** I implore for Emma's peace, The sister of Adolar, by swift death Torn from his brother-love: her grief Silent she bore into the grave below.

**EGLANTINE:** Who made it known?

**EURYANTHE:** Her spirit.

**EGLANTINE:** Horror! How?

**EURYANTHE:** On the last of May, at the painful parting hour, By moonlight saw we wrapped around with ether, The aery form of the gracious Emma! And her pale lips murmured these gentle sounds: — "You, who heart to heart So blessedly shed the tears of love, listen to me. On me also This golden light shone once. My Udo loved Me tenderly and truly! He fell in bloody strife! Then was my life no longer life; The blackness of despair shrouded my soul, And from a poisoned ring I drew my death! Woe to this deed that cut me off from hope; Severed from Udo, I wander through the nights. Oh! weep for me! I shall not rest before This ring, from which I sucked my death Has been wetted by the tear of innocence in utmost suffering, And fidelity has rewarded evil with good."

**EGLANTINE:** Important tidings!

**EURYANTHE:** What have I done? Betrayed Adolar's secret! God! Broken my oath!

**EGLANTINE:** Fear nothing!

**EURYANTHE:** My star is set; Painful foreboding speaks it loud.

**EGLANTINE** Can you waver — can you tremble, Dear one, since in me you trusted?

**EURYANTHE:** Woe! I've broken my secret faith.

**EGLANTINE:** On my bosom seek repose.

**EURYANTHE:** Love's consolation you are sweet Yes, my heart yearns afresh Blessedly to yours.

**EGLANTINE:** Doubt never of my truth, You only are my all! you only! (*Exit Euryanthe into the vault*).

---

## SCENE IV

**EGLANTINE:** Bethörte! die an meine Liebe glaubt, Du bist umgarnt, nu entrinnst nicht mehr! Vor Allem nun durchsuch ich Emma's Gruft, Fur meinen Plan soll die Entdeckung nützen Vielleicht sinkt Adolar Noch reuevoll an diese glühende Brust, O der Gedanke lösst mich auf in Lust, In Ahnungswonnen schwelgt die Seele trunken. Fänd' ich den Tod, an seine Brust gesunken, Nur einen, einen Augenblick, Ich wollt ihn mit Vernichtung zahlen. Hinweg, wahnsinnige Hoffnung, Gauklerin, Erwecke nicht dies Herz zu neuen Qualen! Ich weiss, dass ich ganz elend bin! Er konnte mich um sie verschmähen, Drum muss ich ewig klagen, In herben Leid muss ich vergehn In meinen Blüthentagen; Er hörte kalt der Liebe Flehn, Weh! weh! Mein Herz, so bang, so todeswund, Drum stürz auch all sein Glück zu Grund! (*Ab*).

## SCENE V

*Chor der Burgbewohner und Landleute, angeführt von Bertha und Rudolph, die Ritter Lyssiart bewillkommnend.*

**CHOR DER LANDLEUTE:** Jubeltöne, Heldensöhne! Fröhlich jauchzend euch empfangen; Kühlt von edler Gluth die Wangen Mit den Rosen dieser Flur.

**CHOR DER RITTER:** Sturm erfrischt das Herz des Kriegers, Kühne Wagniss beut ihm Wonne, Selig, wem des Friedens Sonne Unter diesen Blüthen strahlt.

**CHOR DER LANDLEUTE:** Seht,, entgegen lacht euch Segen, Schöner blühen die Gefilde, Sel'gen Friedens Himmelsmilde Gebt der Heimath ihr zurück.

**CHOR DER RITTER:** Selig in des Friedens Milde, Blüht der trauten Heimath Glück.

**CHOR DER LANDLEUTE:** Hirtenweisen Hold euch preisen, Berg und Thal von Lust ertönen, Lasst euch Dank und Liebe krönen; In der Treue Heiligthum.

---

## SCENE IV

**EGLANTINE:** Infatuated woman! that believes in my love; You are ensnared; You escape no more! Now first I'll search through Emma's tomb, And the discovery shall promote my plan. Perhaps Adolar will sink Repentant on this ardent bosom; Oh! the thought dissolves me in felicity, And my intoxicated soul luxuriates in dreams of bliss. If I found death reposing on his breast, Only one, one instant, I would purchase it with annihilation, Away, frantic hope, deluder, Wake not this heart to torments new! I know I am quite wretched. He could despise me for her; Therefore must I ever moan, And perish, in rude suffering, In my days of bloom. Coldly he heard the prayer of love! Woe! woe! My heart, so pained so deadly wounded, Shall destroy all his joy too! (*Exit*)

## SCENE V

*Chorus of the people of the Castle and of Peasants, headed by Bertha and Rudolph, welcoming the Knights and Lysiart.*

**CHORUS OF PEASANTS:** Tones of rejoicing, sons of heroes! Joyful sounding now receive; Cool the noble heat of your cheeks With the roses of this plain.

**CHORUS OF KNIGHTS:** Storm refreshes the heart of the warrior, Bold adventure gives joy; Blessed he to whom the sun of peace Beams amid these flowers:

**CHORUS OF PEASANTS:** See! blessings smile upon you; Lovelier bloom the pastures; The heavenly blessedness of gentle peace You give to home again.

**CHORUS OF KNIGHTS:** Blessed, in the gentle peace, Blooms the joy of our dear home.

**CHORUS OF PEASANTS:** Pastoral measures Sweetly praise you; Hill and dale resound with joy; Let love and gratitude encrown you, In the sanctuary of fidelity.

## SCENE VI

*Euryanthe erscheint an der Thür des Gruftgewölbes. Eglantine. Vorige.*

**CHOR DER RITTER:** Heil der Lieblichsten der Schönen,
Euryanthen Preis und Ruhm!

**EURYANTHE:** Graf Lyssiart, edle Ritter, seid willkommen.

**EGLANTINE:** (*Für sich*). O, möchte meiner Schwach ein Rächer kommen!

**CHOR DER RITTER:** (*Gedämpft unter einander*). Wie schön ist sie!

**LYSSIART:** Erhabne Euryanthe,
Reicht mir zum Dank die Lilienhand;
Ich bringe Freude!

**EURYANTHE:** (*für sich*). Wie bin ich beklommen!
(*Zu Lyssiart*).
Mein tapferer Graf, wer hat euch hergesandt?

**LYSSIART:** Mich hat des Königs Huld erwählt,
Dass ich euch zu Begleiter diene,
Da noch zum Fest die Krone fehlt.

**EURYANTHE:** Mit Wonnebeben ehr' ich dies Gebot
O, Wiedersehen! Eglantine!

**EGLANTINE:** Willkommene Kunde! (*Für sich*).
Meinem Herzen Tod.

**EURYANTHE:** Verschmäht nicht die prunklose Zelle
In Nevers Burg zu kurzer Rast.

**LYSSIART:** Wo du erscheinst, da wird die Wildniss helle
Wie selig wäre deines Herzens Gast —
Beneidenswerther Freund!

**CHOR DER RITTER:** O schwarzer Plan!

**EURYANTHE:** Wie spracht ihr?

**LYSSIART:** Ehrfurcht euch nur stammelnd nannte
Die süsseste der Erde — Euryanthe!

**EURYANTHE UND CHOR:**
Fröhliche Klänge,
Tänze, Gesänge
Feiern, verschönern
Diesen Tag, wo noch ihr uns erfreut.
Ruhet nach Stürmen bei ländlichen Tönen,
Schmückt euch mit Blumen, die Liebe euch streut.

**EURYANTHE:** Sehnen, Verlangen,
Schmachten und Bangen
Wandelt nun Hoffnung in himmlische Lust!
Wieder ihn sehen!
Wonnen und Wehen
Schwellen die Seele, durchwogen die Brust.

## SCENE VI

*Euryanthe appears at the door of the vault. Eglantine. The same.*

**CHORUS OF KNIGHTS:** Hail to the loveliest of beauties,
To Euryanthe praise and fame!

**EURYANTHE:** Count Lysiart, noble knights, be welcome.

**EGLANTINE:** (*Aside*). O! that an avenger of my shame would come.

**CHORUS OF KNIGHTS:** (*in a suppressed tone amongst themselves*). How beautiful she is!

**LYSIART:** Sublime Euryanthe!
Reach me with thanks your lilyhand;
I bring you joy.

**EURYANTHE:** (*Aside*). How agiated I am!
(*To Lysiart*).
My gallant count, who has sent you here?

**LYSIART:** My Sovereign's grace has chosen me,
That I serve you as an escort,
Since still the crown of the feast is wanting.

**EURYANTHE:** With joyful palpitation I honor this command.
To see him again! O, Eglantine!

**EGLANTINE:** Welcome tidings!
(*Aside*)
Death to my heart.

**EURYANTHE:** Do not despise the modest cell,
In Nevers' castle for short rest.

**LYSIART:** Where you appear, there is the desert bright.
How blessed is your heart's guest —
My envied friend.

**CHORUS OF KNIGHTS:** Oh! gloomy plan!

**EURYANTHE:** What did you say?

**LYSIART:** Reverence, faltering only, named you
Earth's sweetest flower — Euryanthe.

**EURYANTHE AND CHORUS:** Joyful sounds,
Dances, songs,
Embellish and celebrate
This day, when you delight us;
Repose after storms amid pastoral tones,
Adorn you with the flowers which love showers on you.

**EURYANTHE:** Ardor, desire,
Languor, alarm,
Hope now converts into heavenly pleasure!
To see him again!
Joys and pains
Swell the sound and flow through my breast.

**LYSSIART:** Stillt dies Verlangen
Süsses Umfangen,
Schwelg' ich in Wonnen an Lippen und Brust.
Werd ich ihn sehen,
Wüthend vergehen,
Marter des Feindes ist Krone der Lust!

**EGLANTINE:** Nun nicht mehr Bangen!
Was sie begangen,
Stürzet in Trümmer ihr Glück, ihre Lust!
Nicht mehr verschmähen
Wird er mein Flehen,
Trunken vom Siege schon klopft meine Brust!

**CHOR:** Fröhliche Klänge,
Tänze, Fesänge
Feiern verschönen
Diesen Tag, wo ihr hoch uns erfreut.
Ruhet nach Stürmen bei ländlichen Tönen,
Schmückt euch mit Kränzen, die Liebe euch beut.

# ■ ZWEITER AUFZUG

## SCENE I

*Burggarten zu Nevers. Gerwitter. Nacht. Lyssiart stürzt aus dem Schlosse.*

**LYSSIART:** Wo berg' ich mich? Wo find' ich hier mich wieder?
Bethörtes Herz, du warst es ja,
Das sie als leichte Beute sah!
Ihr Felsen stürzt auf mich hernieder!
Du Wiederhall, ruf nicht das Ach!
Des hoffnungslosen Herzens nach.
Nie wird sie mein, o ew'ger Qualen Hyder!
Schweigt glüh'nden Sehnens wilde Triebe,
Ihe Auge sucht den Himmel nur,
In ihr wont Unschuld, Anmuth, Liebe,
Ganz Wahrheit ist sie, ganz Natur.
Was soll mir ferner Gut und Land?
Die Welt ist arm und öde ohne sie,
Mein ihre Huld! — Mein wird sie nie! —
Vergiss! Unseliger entflieh!
Sie liebt ihn! — Und er sollte leben?
Ich, schmachtend beben?
Im Staube Sieg ihm zugestehn?
O nein! er darf nicht leben;
Ich mord' ihn unter tausend Wehn!
Doch, Hölle, du kannst sie mir auch nicht geben,
Sie liebt ihn, ich muss untergehn.
So weih' ich mich den Rachgewalten,
Sie locken mich zu schwarzer That!
Geworfen ist des Unheils Saat,
Der Todeskeim muss sie entfalten!
Zertrümmre schönes Bild,

**LYSIART:** If this desire's appeased
By a sweet embrace,
I shall revel with joy on her lips and breast.
I shall see him
Perish in rage —
The enemy's torture is our crown of delight.

**EGLANTINE:** Now no longer alarm!
What she has done
Hurls to ruin her joy, her delight!
He will no longer despise my prayers.
My bosom beats drunk with victory already.

**CHORUS:** Joyful sounds,
Dances, songs,
Celebrate and embellish
This day, when you delight us.
Repose after storm amid pastoral tones.
Adorn you with the garlands that love showers on you.

# ■ ACT II

## SCENE I

*Castle Garden at Nevers. Storm. Night. Lysiart rushes out of the castle.*

**LYSIART:** Where to conceal myself? How to collect myself again?
Infatuated heart, you were it
That saw her an easy prey!
Rocks, fall down upon me!
Echo, answer not the sighs
Of my hopeless heart.
She'll never be mine! Oh! hydra of eternal pangs!
Be silent, wild impulse of glowing desire!
Her eye seeks heaven alone;
In her dwells innocence, grace, love,
All truth is she, all nature,
What now are lands and riches to me?
The world is poor and wasted without her.
Mine, her favor! mine she'll never be.
Forget! unhappy man, escape!
She loves him and he should live?
And I in anguish tremble?
In the dust acknowledge his victory!
Oh! no — he must not live —
I'll murder him, amid thousand pangs.
But hell, you cannot give her to me;
She loves him — I must perish.
Thus I devote myself to revenge's powers,
They allure me to the dark deed!
Sown is the seed of mischief,
It must disclose the germ of death.

# Act II, Scene I

Fort, letzter, süsser Schmerz!
Nur Rache, Rache füllt
Dies sturmbewegte Herz.

Fall in pieces, lovely image!
Hence, last and sweetest pain!
Revenge alone, revenge can fill
This storm-tossed heart.

## SCENE II

*Eglantine stürst athemlos aus dem Gewölbe. Voriger. Ferner Donner.*

*Eglantine rushes breathless from the vault. The same. Distant thunder.*

**EGLANTINE:** Der Gruft entronnen, athm' ich wieder.
Ich halte dich, du unter Todesschauern
Errungenes Unterpfand der süssen Rache!
Ich wand dich muthig von der Todten Hand,
Verhängnissvoller Ring, bezeuge du,
Dass Euryanthe Liebe und Treue verrathen,
Und grässlich büsse, der mein Herz verwarf!

**EGLANTINE:** Escaped from the vault, I breathe again:
I hold you, that amidst death's terrors
Were won, the pledge of sweet revenge
I forced you boldly from the hand of the dead.
Oh! fated ring, witness
That love and faith has both betrayed Euryanthe.
And let him dreadfully atone, who rejected my heart,

**LYSSIART:** Was hör' ich? — willkommne Höllenkunde!

**LYSIART:** What do I hear? welcome, infernal tidings!

**EGLANTINE:** Sie dürfen nie sich wiedersehen!
Der Schlag muss fallen wie aus heitrer Luft,
Zermalmen Liebe, Hoffnung, Glück,
In Ewigkeit von Adolar sie trennen,
Wie führ' ich diesen Schlag?
*(Ein heller Blitz. Lyssiart tritt rasch auf sie zu).*

**EGLANTINE:** They must never see each other more.
The bolt must fall as from the clear sky.
Crushing their love, their hope, their joy.
Must sever from her Adolar to all eternity —
How shall I guide this blow?
*(A bright flash of lightning. Lysiart advances quickly towards her).*

**LYSSIART:** Durch meine Hand!
*(Blitz und Donner durch die ganze Scene, doch mehr aus der Ferne).*

**LYSIART:** By my hand.
*(Lightning and thunder throughout the entire scene; but more from the distance).*

**EGLANTINE:** Ich bin verloren!

**EGLANTINE:** I am lost.

**LYSSIART:** Ruhig, Bundesgenossin!

**LYSIART:** Confederate, — fear not!

**EGLANTINE:** Was willst du mir?

**EGLANTINE:** What will you do with me?

**LYSSIART:** Dein finstres Werk vollziehn,
Noch heut' sollst du die Feindin elend sehn.
Und Adolar gestraft, der dich gekränkt.

**LYSIART:** The gloomy work accomplish:
Today even shall you see your wretched enemy,
And punish Adolar that injured you.

**EGLANTINE:** Du hast mir mein Geheimniss abgelauscht!

**EGLANTINE:** Listening, you have robbed me of my secret.

**LYSSIART:** Zur Sühne beut dir Forest seine Hand.
Die Felsen wandl' ich ein Rosenband,
Beherrschen sollst du diese reiche Gauen.
Heil, ehre, Leben darfst du mir vertraun.

**LYSIART:** To make amends Forest gives you his hand,
I'll convert your fetters into a rosy garland.
You shall govern these rich plains
Weal, honor, life, then you may trust to me.

**EGLANTINE:** Und sprichst du wahr?

**EGLANTINE:** And do you speak truly?

**LYSSIART:** Bei Rache, Wuth und Gluth,
Des ew'gen Hasses, ja!

**LYSIART:** By rage, revenge, and glow
Of hate eternal — yes!

**EGLANTINE:** Ich glaube dir!

**EGLANTINE:** I believe you.

**EGLANTINE:** Komm dann unser Leid zu rächen
Enden soll der Seele Qual.

**EGLANTINE:** Come then to revenge our suffering!
The torments of the soul shall end.

**LYSSIART:** Nimm mein feierlich Versprechen,
Rächer werd' ich und Gemahl.

**LYSIART:** Take my solemn promise, I will be
Avenger and spouse.

**EGLANTINE:** Trostlos muss sie untergehen,
Die mein Leben mir geraubt,

**EGLANTINE:** Hopeless she
Who has robbed me of my life must perish.

**LYSSIART:** In dem Staub muss ich ihn sehen,
Der zu Sternen hob sein Haupt.

**LYSIART:** In the dust I must see him
Who has raised his head to the stars.

**BEIDE:** Dunkle Nacht, du hörst den Schwur!
Sei mit unsrer That im Bunde.
Ja, es schlug der Rache Stunde,
Rache, Rache athm' ich nur!
*(Beide ab.)*

**BOTH:** Gloomy night, you hear the oath!
Be in league with our deed —
Yes, revenge's hour has struck:
Revenge, revenge alone I breathe.
*(Exeunt).*

## SCENE III

*Die Säulenhalle des Königschlosses festlich und hell erleuchtet. Adolar im reichsten Schmuck. Auf seinem Haupt den Juwelenkranz.*

*The pillared hall of the Royal Castle, gaily and brightly illuminated. Adolar in his richest dress. On his head a wreath of jewels.*

**ADOLAR:** Wehen mir Lüfte Ruh,
Strömen mir Düfte zu
Seliger Zeit.
Füllst du nach bangem Schmerz
Wieder mein ganzes Herz,
Süssestes Leid?
Liebe, wie lebst du neu,
Hoffnung, wie webst du treu
Bilder der Lust!
Glaube, wie wankst du nicht,
Herz, wie erbangst du nicht
In meiner Brust!
Sie ist mir nah, mein Bangen war ein Traum,
O Seligket, dich fass ich kaum!
Ihr Auge wird mir strahlen,
Ihr Himmelsreiz mir blühen!
O, wie Erwartungsqualen
Dies trunkene Herz durchglühn!

**ADOLAR:** The airs breathe to me repose,
The odors stream towards me
Of a blessed time.
You fill after anxious pain
Again all my heart,
Sweetest of sorrows?
Love, how you live anew!
Hope how you faithfully weave
Forms of pleasure!
Faith, how you waver not!
Heart, how you tremble not
In my breast!
She is near me; my alarm was but a dream!
Oh! blessedness! I scarcely can comprehend you!
Her eye will beam upon me,
Her charms divine bloom for me.
Oh, expectation's pangs
Rend my intoxicated heart.

## SCENE IV

*Euryanthe. Gefolge. Voriger. Das Gefolge bleibt im Hintergrunde. Euryanthe eilt in Adolars Arme.*

*Euryanthe, Suite, The same The suite remains in the background. Euryanthe rushes into Adolar's arms.*

**EURYANTHE UND ADOLAR:** Hin nimm die Seele mein,
Athme mein Leben ein,
Lass mich ganz du nur sein,
Ganz bin ich dein!
Seufzer wie Flammen wehn,
Selig um Lindrung flehn,
Lass mich in Lust und Wehn
An deiner Brust vergehn!

**EURYANTHE AND ADOLAR:** Hence take my soul!
Breathe with my life!
Let me be you altogether!
I am quite yours,
Sighs breathe like flames,
Pray to be assuaged;
Let me die away in joy and grief
upon your breast.

## SCENE V

*Die Halle füllt sich mit Fürsten und Edlen: zuletzt der König und Lyssiart.*

*The Hall fills with Princes and Nobles, At length, the King and Lysiart.*

CHOR: Leuchtend füllt die Königshallen
Euryanthens Wunderpracht,
Stern der Anmuth, hold vor Allen,
Blicke rein durch jede Nacht.

CHORUS: Beaming fills the royal halls
Euryanthe's gorgeous splendor.
Star of grace, loveliest of all,
Glance pure through every night.

DER KÖNIG: Ich grüsse euch, edles Fräulein!

KING: I greet you, noble lady.

EURYANTHE: O mein König,
Wie mild und väterlich blickt ihr auf mich!

EURAYANTHE: Oh! my King!
How gently and paternally you gaze on me.

DER KÖNIG: Du holdes Kind, nichts trübe deine Ruh.

KING: You lovely child, may nothing mar your rest.

EURYANTHE: Es schützen mich die Strahlen eurer Huld!
Doch mein Gebieter! Frankreichs hohe Frauen
Vermiss ich hier —

EURYANTHE: The rays of your benevolence protect me!
But my sovereign! France's noble dames
I see not here —

DER KÖNIG: Bald heissen se Euch alle
Willkommen, freudig hoff ichs, hoff es fest.

KING: Soon will they bid you all
Welcome — joyfully I hope it — firmly hope it.

LYSSIART: Mein König!

LYSIART: My King!

CHOR: Jetzt schlägt der Entscheidung Stunde —
Allwissender, verleih der Wahrheit Sieg!

CHORUS: Now strikes the deciding hour —
Omniscient! — grant victory to truth.

EURYANTHE: Mich fasst ein Grauen.

EURYANTHE: A horror seizes me.

KÖNIG UND ADOLAR: Muth und Vertrauen.

KING AND ADOLAR: Courage and confidence!

LYSSIART: Vernimm, es muss ja sein, von meinem Munde
Ein Glück, das ich so gern verschwieg —
Leicht und entzückend war mein Sieg!
Die Länder Adolars sind mein!

LYSIART: Hear — for it must be, and from my lips,
I would so willingly conceal a happiness
Easy and enchanting was my victory!
The lands of Adolar are mine.

ADOLAR: Dies Engelantliz straft dich Lügen, Nein!

ADOLAR: This heavenly countenance proves you a liar. No!

DER KÖNIG: Es ist unmöglich!

KING: It is impossible.

EURYANTHE: Wie? mein Adolar,
Was ist geschehen? löse dieses Bangen.

EURYANTHE: How? my Adolar,
What has happened? — remove this fear.

ADOLAR: Komm an mein Herz, von deinem Arm umfangen,
Der Hölle Trotz!

ADOLAR: Come to my heart — by this arm embraced —
I defy hell.

LYSSIART: Beweise bring ich dar.

LYSIART: I have proofs to show.

CHOR: Weh, Euryanthe, was hast du begangen?

CHORUS: Woe! Euryanthe, what have you done?

LYSSIART: Bewundrungswürdig ist's gelungen,
Dies stolze Herz im Sturm errungen!

LYSIART: Wondrously have I succeeded,
This proud heart in storm subdued.

EURYANTHE: Was hör' ich?
Lyssiart, errungen ihr Mein Herz? Den Blick erhobt ihr nicht zu mir.

EURYANTHE: What do I hear? Lysiart, you won
My heart? You have not raised your eyes to me.

LYSSIART: So schnöde nun, so liebreich noch zur Stunde?

LYSIART: Now so contemptuous; before scarcely an hour so loving.

ADOLAR: Zur Fehde!

ADOLAR: To the fight!

DER KÖNIG: Nein, gebt klare Kunde,
Zeigt den Beweis.

KING: No, give clear report — Show the proof.

LYSSIART: Dies Unterpfand
Der Liebe reichte mir die schönste Hand
Mit Trauer muss ich wieder geben,
Was ich empfangen ohne Widerstand.
(Reicht Euryanthen den Ring).

LYSIART: This pledge of love was reached me by the loveliest hand;
With grief I must return
What I received without resistance.
(Gives to Euryanthe the ring).

EURYANTHE: (Auf die Knie sinkend, hält den Ring empor). Der du die Unschuld kennst, beschütz mein Leben;
Und wollte mich ein Höllennetz um weben,
Du rettest mich, wirst aus der Nacht mich heben.

EURYANTHE: (falls on her knees; holds up the ring). You who know innocence, protect my life;
Even if the snares of hell encompass me,
You'll save, and lift me from out the night!

ADOLAR: Nein, du errangst den Ring durch List!
Mein reiner Engel, kannst du zagen?

ADOLAR: No, you gained the ring by cunning!
My pure angel, can you waver?

LYSSIART: Wer sonst als Euryanth und du kann sagen,
Was dieses Rings Bedeutung ist?
Die Gruft nur kannte Emmas Thatten!

LYSIART: Who else but Euryanthe and you can say
What is the meaning of this ring?
The grave alone knew Emma's deeds.

ADOLAR: Sprich, Euryanthe! hast du mich verrathen?

ADOLAR: Speak, Euryanthe! have you betrayed me?

EURYANTHE: O Unglücksel'ge!

EURYANTHE: Oh! unhappy me!

ADOLAR: Brachst du deinen Eid?

ADOLAR: Your oath has been broken!

EURYANTHE: Ich that es!

EURYANTHE: I did it!

ADOLAR: Schlange!

ADOLAR: Serpent!

EURYANTHE: Unermesslich Leid,
Doch treulos bin ich nicht —

EURYANTHE: Immeasurable suffering!
But I am not faithless.

ADOLAR: Verworfene du! Verstumme!

ADOLAR: You outcast! Be dumb!

LYSSIART: Höre mir mit Fassung zu, Die Wahrheit sprech ich kühn und frei!
In heller Mondennacht, am letzten Mai —

LYSIART: Listen to me calmly — The truth I speak boldly and freely!
In the clear moonlight, on the last of May —

ADOLAR: Vollende nicht, nimm Alles, Alles hin,
Mein Leben mit —

ADOLAR: Do not finish — take all — my all —
And my life too.

CHOR: Ha die Verrätherin!
O Unthat, grässlichste von allen,
Die jemals auf der Welt erhört!
Der Treue Bündniss frech zerstört,
Von Himmelshöh'n in Staub gefallen.

CHORUS: Ha! the traitress!
Oh! crime! most horrible of all,
That ever the world has heard!
The league of faith so shamelessly to break!
From Heaven's heights to dust you're fallen.

EURYANTHE: Lass mich empor zum Lichte wallen,
Du, der das Flehn der Unschuld hört.

EURYANTHE: Let me rise up to the light,
You, that hears the prayers of innocence.

DER KÖNIG: Mein Glaub' an Tugend ist zerstört,
Denn dieser Engel konnte fallen.

KING: My faith in virtue is destroyed,
For even this angel here could fall.

LYSSIART: Triumph, mein Flehen ist erhört
Und meinen Sieg sehn diese Hallen!

LYSIART: Triumph! my prayer is heard;
And these halls see my victory.

ADOLAR: Fern in das Elend will ich wallen,
Wo keiner meinen Namen hört.

ADOLAR: Far into misery will I wander,
Where my name is never heard.

LYSSIART: Verleih mein Recht mir, grosser König, nun
Als Graf zu Nevers huldigt dir dein Knecht.
(Er kniet nieder).

LYSIART: Grant me my right, my sovereign; now
As Count of the Nevers your servant does you homage. (He kneels).

**DER KÖNIG:** Nimm hin, das neue Lehn, üb' Treu und Recht,
Dir möge Got nach deinen Werken thun.
(*Lyssiart steht auf*).

**ADOLAR:** Komm Euryanth!

**EURYANTHE:** Willkommens Gebot,
Ich folge dir in Noth und Tod!

**CHOR:** Wir Alle wollen mit dir gehen,
Wir All' sind dein mit Gut und Blut!

**ADOLAR:** Hinweg! kein Auge soll mich sehen!

**DER KÖNIG:** Mein Jüngling, du willst von mir gehen?

**LYSSIART:** (*Für sich*). Möcht ich erst ganz ihn elend sehen!
Wie schwelgt in seiner Qual die Wuth!

**EURYANTHE:** Verimm, O Gott, der Unschuld Fleh'n,
Es wallt dein Kind in deiner Hut.

**ALLE:** Du gleissend Bild, du bist enthüllt.
Schnell folgte Strafe deinen Thaten.
Weh'dir! die Lieb und Treu verrathen;
Das Maass der Frevel ist gefüllt.

*ENDE II. AUFZUGS*

# ■ DRITTER AUFZUG

*Oede Felsschlucht. Vollmond. Ein steiler Pfad führt von einer Anhöhe herab. Trauerweiden umschatten eine rieselnde Quelle im Vordergrunde.*

## SCENE I

*Euryanthe*

**EURYANTHE:** So bin ich nun verlassen,
So muss ich hier erblassen,
Im öden Felsenthal,
In Einsamkeit und Qual!
Hier dicht am Quell, wo Weiden stehn,
Die Sterne hell durchschauen,
Da will ich mir den Tod erflehn,
Mein stilles Grab mir bauen.
Wohl kommt auch er einst weit daher,
Und findet kaum die Stätte mehr —
Dann rauscht ihm sanft die Weide zu:
Sie fand von Lieb' un! Leide Ruh.
Die Blum' im Thaue spricht:
Nein, sie verrieth dich nicht.
(*Sie wirft erschöpft im Schatten neben der Quelle hin. Die Morgenröthe steigt empor*).

---

**KING:** Take the new fief, be true and just,
May God deal with you according to your works.
(*Lysiart rises*).

**ADOLAR:** Come, Euryanthe.

**EURYANTHE:** Welcome command!
I follow you to woe and death.

**CHORUS:** We all will go with you,
Our lives, and fortunes, all are yours

**ADOLAR:** Away! No eye shall see me.

**KING:** My youth, will you go from me?

**LYSIART:** (*aside*) Oh! that quite wretched I may see him!
How my rage revels in his woe!

**EURYANTHE:** Hear, O God! the prayer of innocence,
Your child walks in your protection.

**ALL:** Deceitful mask, you have been unveiled!
Quick followed punishment your deeds.
Woe to you who betrayed life and truth,
The measure of your crimes is filled.

*END OF ACT II*

# ■ ACT III

*Desolate rocky glen. A full moon. A steep path leading down from a height; weeping willows encircle a bubbling spring in the foreground.*

## SCENE I

*Euryanthe*

**EURYANTHE:** Thus am I now forlorn,
Thus must I perish here,
In the waste rocky glen,
In solitude and pain.
Here close to the spring, where willows stand.
And the clear stars look through,
Here will I pray for death,
And build my silent grave.
Perhaps he too some day I'll come from afar,
And scarcely will find my grave remaining—
Then gently will the willow whisper to him:
She found rest from love and suffering.
The flower in the dew will speak:
No, she betrayed you not.
(*She throws herself exhausted down in the shade near the spring. The sun rises*).

---

*Jäger. König.*

**CHOR:** (*hinter der Scene*). Die Thale dampfen, die Höhen glühn,
Welch fröhlich Jagen im Waldesgrün!
Der Morgen weckt zu neuer Lust;
Hoch schwillt die Brust, des Siegs bewusst.
Dringt muthig durch Schluchten und Moor,
Lasst schmettern die Hörner im Chor
Ihr Fürsten der Waldung hervor!
(*Sie erscheinen auf den Bergen*).
O seht, in Thränen eine zarte Frau.
(*Euryanthe Wendet ihr Antlitz gegen den König*).

**DER KÖNIG:** Himmel!

**CHOR:** Euryanthe!

**EURYANTHE:** Lasst mich hier in Ruh erblassen,
Gönnt mir diese letzte Huld!

**DER KÖNIG:** Nein, ich will dich nicht verlassen,
Komm zu sühnen deine Schuld,

**EURYANTHE:** Gott kennt meine Unschuld nur,
Kennt das Leid, das mich getroffen.

**DER KÖNIG:** Du nicht schuldig? dürft ich's hoffen.

**CHOR:** Hilf und auf der Wahrheit Spur!

**EURYANTHE:** Eglantinens flehend Kosen
Lockt' mir das Geheimniss ab,
Natter war sie unter Rosen,
Die den Tod mir schmeichelnd gab.

**DER KÖNIG:** Euryanthe, sprichst du Wahrheit?
O, so nimm mein Wort zum Pfand,
Höllentrug bring ich zur Klarheit,
Neu knüpf ich das schöne Band.

**EURYANTHE:** Wiedersehen! mich ihm versöhnen!
Wär es möglich?

**CHOR:** Hoffe! Lebe!

**EURYANTHE:** Stürb ich hin an diesen Tönen!
Täuscht mich nicht. O wie ich bebe!

**CHOR:** Hoffe! Lebe!

**EURYANTHE:** Kann ich's fassen, ach, ich bebe!

**CHOR:** Glaube, hoffe, liebe, lebe!

**EURYANTHE:** Zu ihm, zu ihm! o weilet nicht!
Wo bist du, meines Daseins Licht!
Dass ich dich fest umfasse;
Dich nimmer lasse;
So Herz an Herzen, Aug' in Auge,
Aus deinen Blicken Leben sauge —
O Hoffnung, Himmelsstrahl!
Ich trag es nicht! Ich sterb in Wonn'

---

*Hunters. King.*

**CHORUS:** (*behind the scene*) The valleys smoke, the hills are glowing,
What merry hunting in the forest-green!
The morning wakes us to fresh pleasure,
High swells the breast of victory sure.
Press boldly through ravine and moor,
Let sound the horns in chorus:
Oh chiefs of the forest, come forward!
(*They appear on the mountain.*)
Oh! see a tender lady in tears!
(*Euryanthe turns her countenance towards the King.*)

**KING:** Heaven!

**CHORUS:** Euryanthe!

**EURYANTHE:** Let me perish here in peace!
Grant to me this last of favors.

**KING:** No, I will not leave you—
Come and atone for your guilt.

**EURYANTHE:** God only knows my innocence;
Know the sorrow that has struck me.

**KING:** You, not guilty! Dare I hope?

**CHORUS:** Help us to trace the truth.

**EURYANTHE:** Eglantine's importunate caresses
Allured my secret from me;
She was a viper under roses,
And, while flattering, killed me.

**KING:** Euryanthe, Do you speak truth?
Oh! then take my word as pledge—
I'll bring hellish deceit to light,
And then reunite your sweet bonds.

**EURYANTHE:** See him again!—reconcile him to me!
Were it possible?

**CHORUS:** Hope and live!

**EURYANTHE:** I shall die amid these tones.
Deceive me not!—Oh! how I tremble.

**CHORUS:** Hope and live!

**EURYANTHE:** Can I seize it? Ah! I shudder.

**CHORUS:** Believe, and hope, and love, and live!

**EURYANTHE:** To him, to him! Oh! tarry not.
Where are you, light of my existence
That I may fast embrace you,
And never leave you!
Thus, heart to heart, and eye to eye,
From your glances life to draw!
Oh! hope—you beam from heav-

und Qual!
(*Sie sinkt ohnmächtig nieder. Sie wird für todt auf eine Bahre von Zweigen gelegt*).

CHOR: (*im Abgeben*). O Jammer unerhört
O lieblichste der Blüthen,
Wie hat so früh das Wüthen
Des Sturmes dich zerstört. (*Sie tragen Euryanthe ab*).

## SCENE III

*Freier Platz vor dem Schlosse Nevers. Im Vorgrunde Berthas Hütte, Bertha, Rudolph. Landleute mit Blumengewinden die Hütte Berthas schmückend.*

EINZELNE STIMME: Der Mai bringt frische Blumen dar,
Die Rose schmückt der Jungfrau Haar,
Und niemand weiss im grünen Mai,
Was Rose noch was Mädchen sei.

CHOR: Den was da blüht, ist Ros' im Mai.

STIMME: Der Mai, der holde Mai erhellt
Nach Wintersleid die schöne Welt,
Und niemand weiss im grünen Mai,
Was einsam Leid und Sehnen sei.

CHOR: Denn Lieb und Treu frohlockt im Mai.

STIMME: Der Mai bringt frischer Blüthen viel,
Die Liebe ist des Maien Spiel,
Und Niemand weiss im grünen Mai,
Was Blüthe, noch was Liebe sei.

CHOR: Denn was da blüht, das blüht im Mai.

STIMME: Der Mai bringt dir, du theures Paar,
Der Blüthen allerschönste dar,
Wohl wisst ihr zwei im grünen Mai
Wie selig Lieb und Treue sei.

CHOR: Denne eure Treu krönt heut der Mai.

ADOLAR: (*schwankt nach dem Vorgrunde*). 'S gibt keine Treu auf weiter Erde mehr,
Davon, davon ist mir das Herz so schwer,
In Liebesgluth ist nichts als Wankelmuth,
Am falschen Herzen sichs gafährlich ruht.

DIE LANDLEUTE: Welch Klagen hier stört froher Liebe Muth?

ADOLAR: Fahr hin, fahr hin, liebsüsser Liebe Traum,
Gieb dunkler Nacht und ihrem Schrecken Raum.
Nacht ohne Licht herein mit Stürmen bricht;
Heimath! ein Grab versag dem Müden nicht.
(*Sinkt auf eine Rasenbank, sein Helm fällt ab*).

en!
I bear it not; I die in joy and pain.
(*She sinks, fainting. She is laid for dead on a litter, made of branches*).

CHORUS: (*whilst departing*)
Oh! sorrow unheard of!
Oh! lovelist of blossom!
How has thus early the raging.
Of the storm destroyed you! (*They carry off Euryanthe*).

## SCENE III

*Open space before the Castle of Nevers. In the foreground Bertha's Hut. Bertha, Rudolf. — Peasants ornamenting with flower-garlands the Hut of Bertha.*

SINGLE VOICES: May presents us with fresh roses;
The rose adorns the virgin's hair;
And no one knows in the green May
What's a rose or what's a maid.

CHORUS: For what blooms there's a rose in May.

A VOICE: May, lovely May brightens,
After winter's woes the beauteous world;
And no one knows in the green May,
What lonely grief and sorrowing is.

CHORUS: For love and faith rejoice in May.

A VOICE: May brings plenty of fresh blossoms,
Love is the game of May,
And no one knows in the green May,
What's a blossom, or what's love.

CHORUS: For what blooms there, that love's in May.

A VOICE: May brings to you, you cherished pair,
The loveliest of all blossoms.
Well know you too, in the green May,
How blessed are love and faith.

CHORUS: For May to-day crowns your truth.

ADOLOR: (*comes forward*).
There's no truth more on the wide earth;
Hence, hence my heart's so heavy.
Yes, love's fire is but fickleness:
On the false heart we dangerously rest.

PEASANTS: What plaints here mar the merry joy of love?

ADOLOR: Away! away! you sweetest dream of love;
Give place to dark night and its terrors;
Night without light now falls with storms:
Oh! home, refuse not a grave to the tired one.
(*He sinks upon a bank of turf. His helmet fall off.*)

CHOR: Er ist's, o Glück, o neuer Hoffnung Licht!

BERTHA: So musste der ersehnte Tag erscheinen.
Geliebter Herr! willkommen bei den Deinen!

ADOLAR: Hinweg! Lasst meiner Trauer mich!

BERTHA: Hier schlägt noch jedes Herz für dich!

BERTHA UND CHOR: Führ' an der Jugend muth'ge Schaar befreie
Dein seufzend Land. —

ADOLAR: Du süsse heil'ge Treue!
Du lebst, doch nicht in Euryanthe's Brust.

CHOR: Den schnödesten Verdacht entferne,
Ich spreche Wahrheit sonder Scheu,
Es wankten eh' des Himmels Sterne,
Als unserer süssen Herrin Treu.

ADOLAR: Nein, sie verrieth mich!

BERTHA: Hör' gewicht'ge Kunde:
Mit deinem Feind ist Eglantin' im Bunde;
Auf deiner Ahnen stolzem Sitz,
Wo du ihr Zuflucht einst gegeben,
Will Lyssiart heut' zur Herrin sie erheben.

ADOLAR: Allwaltender! wo ist dein Blitz!

BERTHA UND RUDOLPH MIT CHOR: Vernichte kühn das Werk der Tücke,
Vertrau der Liebe und dem Glücke,
Es jauchzt dir zu dein ganzes Land;
Zum Schwert für dich greift jede Hand.

ADOLAR: Hilf mir durchschauen das Werk der Tücke,
Allwissender mit klarem Blicke;
Gieb Kraft zum Siege meiner Hand
für Ehre, Treue, Gut und Land.

## SCENE IV

*Prachtvoller Hochzeitzug. Lyssiart, Eglantine im fürstllichen Brautschmuck, todtenblass, von ihren Frauen unterstützt. Vorige.*

LANDLEUTE: O Frevlerpaar! weh diesem schnöden Bunde!

ADOLAR: O klopfend Herz — sei stark zu dieser Stunde!

EGLANTINE: (*mit Geberde des Schmerzes, indem sie mit Entsetzen, das in Wahnsinn übergeht, stehen bleibt*). Ich kann nicht weiter! Todesschauer Durchrieselt mein Gebein!
Mich drückt die Luft —
Sieh! Emma steigt aus dunkler Gruft.
Sie winkt mir mit der starren Hand

CHORUS: It's he—oh! joy!—oh! light of newborn hope!

BERTHA: Thus must the desired day appear!
Beloved lord! be welcome to your own.

ADOLAR: Away, and leave me to my grief.

BERTHA: Here beats still every heart for you.

BERTHA AND CHORUS: Lead on the hardly host of youth, and free
Your suffering land,—

ADOLAR: You sacred, sweet fidelity!
You live but not in Euryanthe's breast.

CHORUS: Banish the basest of suspicions,
I speak the truth without fear,
The stars of heaven would sooner waver
Than would the faith of our sweet Princess.

ADOLAR: No, she betrayed me.

BERTHA: Hear weighty tiding;
With your foe is Eglantine in league;
On the proud seat of your forefathers,
Where you once gave her refuge,
Will Lysiart today raise her to be a Princess.

ADOLAR: Onnipotent! where are your lightnings?

BERTHA AND RUDOLPH: (*with Chorus.*) Boldly crush the work of malice,
Trust to love and happiness;
All your land meets you with rejoicing;
For you, each hand shall grasp the sword.

ADOLAR: Help me to see through the work of malice,
Omniscient, with an eye unclouded;
Give force for victory to my land,
For honor, fortune, faith, and land.

## SCENE IV

*Magnificent wedding-procession Lysiart; Eglantine in princely bridal attire, death-pale, supported be her women. The same.*

PEASANTS: Oh! wretched pair! woe to this base union!

ADOLAR: Oh; beating heart for this hour be strong!

EGLANTINE: (*With gestures of pain whilst she stands still in horror, which passes into madness.*) I can go no further! Death-tremors Course through my bones!
The air oppresses me—
See! Emma rises from the dismal tomb,
She beckons me with rigid hand—
What? you demand back the pledge

Was! forderst du zurück der Rache
Pfand?
Ich gab es hin, die Unschuld zu er-
merden!

CHOR: Welch Entsessen! welch
Gericht!
Die Vergeltung schlummert nicht.

LYSSIART: Hört! dass Wahnsinn
aus ihr spricht!

ADOLAR: Ha! wir tagt ein schrecklich Licht. (*Vertretend*) Erzittre,
ruchlos Paar, es wacht die Rache,
Der Himmel führt bedrückter Unschuld Sache —

LYSSIART: Was zischest aus dem
Staub du, nicht'ger Wurm?
Vasallen, werft den Fremdling in
den Thurm!
(*Die Reisigen dringen auf Adolar
ein*).

ADOLAR: (*schlägt den Helm-
sturtz auf*) Mich wollt ihr fahen
mich?

CHOR: Heil Adolar in seiner Väter
Hallen!
Geliebter, unsre Demuth dich ver-
söhne!
(*Alle drängen sich um ihn*).

EGLANTINE: (*fährt aus dumpfer
Betäubung auf, fasst Adolar ins
Auge und stürzt in die Arme ihrer
Frauen*). Er ist's! in seiner Glorie,
seiner Schöne! Wehe mir!

LYSSIART: Verderben, Fluch euch
Allen,
Verwegne Knechte, büssend sollt
ihr fallen!
(*Alle springen auf und stellen sich
ihm drohend entgegen*).

CHOR: Trotze nicht, Vermessener!
Straft dräut, Verruchter!
Tilgt das Werk der Nacht!
Zittre Gottvergessner!
Birg dich Missethäter!
Gottes Auge wacht!

ADOLAR: Zum Kampf, zum Gott-
gerichle,
Verruchter Frevler du!

LYSSIART: Dass ich dich, Feind,
vernichte,
Jauchzt mir der Abgrund zu!

ADOLAR: Dein schwarzes Herz
durchwühle
Mein sieggewohnter Stahl!

CHOR: Der Schande, dem Verderben,
Bist ewig du geweiht.

LYSSIART: Sollt ich um Mitleid
werben?
Heran! ich bin Bereit!

## SCENE V

*König Vorige.*

---

of revenge?
I gave it away to murder innocence.

CHORUS: What horror! what a
judgment!
Retribution slumbers not.

LYSIART: Hear that madness from
her speaks.

ADOLAR: Ha! a fearful light dawns
for me.
(*Advancing.*)
Tremble, infamous pair, revenge is
watching,
And heaven takes the side of innocence oppressed.

LYSIART: You hiss in the dust, you
miserable worm!
Vassals, cast the stranger into the
tower.
(*The Knights rush upon Adolar*)

ADOLAR: (*lifts his helmet.*) Will
you capture me?

CHORUS: Hail, Adolar, in his ancestral halls!
Beloved! let our humbleness conci-
liate you.
(*All press round him*)

EGLANTINE: (*starts out of heavy
stupor, fixes her eye upon Adolar
and falls into the arms of her
women.*) It's he, and in his glory, in
his beauty! Woe's me.

LYSIART: Perdition,—curse on
you all!
Insolent serfs! atoning you shall
fall!
(*All spring up and place themselves in a menacing position.*)

CHORUS: Defy us not, rash man!
Punishment threatens, traitor!
Destroy the work of night!
Tremble, forgotten-of-God!
Hide, malefactor!
God's eye's upon you!

ADOLAR: To the fight—to the trial
by battle,
Infamous criminal!

LYSIART: That, foe, I'll destroy
you,
Hell shouts in my ears.

ADOLAR: In your black heart shall
revel
My ever-conquering sword.

CHORUS: To shame and to peridi-
tion,
For ever you're devoted.

LYSIART: Should I plead for compassion?
Come on! I'm ready.

## SCENE V

*King. The same.*

---

DER KÖNIG: (*mit Gefolge tritt
zwischen die Kämpfenden*). Lasst
ruhn das Schwert, der höchste
Richter naht,
Der Rächer jeder Frevelthat.
(*Alle beugen sich ehrfurchtsvoll.
Lyssiart senkt das Schwert; zieht
sich aber kampffertig zurück*).

ADOLAR: (*stürzt des Königs
Füssen*). Mein König, hör' den
grässlichsten Verrath,
Wir sind getäuscht; der reinsten Tu-
gend Bildniss
War Euryanthe — Weh wir! in der
Wildniss
Verlassen irret sie umher —
Hilf, rette, strafe!

DER KÖNIG: Hemme deine Klagen,
Fass dich, als Held, das Grässlichste
zu tragen,
Denn Euryanthe lebt nicht mehr!
Dich segnend ist das treuste Herz
gebrochen.

EGLANTINE: Was hör ich? Tri-
umph!
Ist meine Schmach! der Feindin
Herz gebrochen.
Verzweifle, dass sie schuldlos war;
Ich wars, von deren Hand den Ring
Der kühne Räuber dort empfing;
Ich war es, die ihn der Gruft ent-
wandte —
Rein, wie das Licht, war Euryanthe!

CHOR: O höllischer Verrath! o
herb Geschick!

LYSSIART: Wahnsinnige!

EGLANTINE: Schnödes Werkzeug
meiner Rache,
Dich schleudr' ich in dein Nichts
zurück!

LYSSIART: Was hält mich, dass ich
dich zermalme,
Mein eidige Verräthrin!
(*Er stosst sie mit dem Dolche nieder; die Frauen drängen sich um sie
her und suchen ihr beizustehen;
alles stürzt auf Lyssiart, ihn ergreifend und entwaffnend.*)

CHOR DER JAEGER: (*hinter der
Scene*). O Wonne, sie athmet, sie
lebt!

## SCENE VI

*Euryanthe, Jäger, Vorige. Eu-
ryanthe flieht in Adolars Arme.*

EURYANTHE UND ADOLAR: Hin
nimm die Seele mein!
Athme mein leben ein,
Lass mich ganz du nur sein,
Ganz bin ich dein!
Lass mich in Lust und Weh'n
An deiner Brust vergehn. (*Sie
umarmen sich.*)

CHOR: Treue, stark und rein,
Wonne nach Todespein,
Holdseliger Verein,
Du sein, Er dein.

---

KING: (*with followers advances
between the combatants.*) Let the
sworl rest; the highest judge approaches—
The avenger of every misdeed.
(*All bow with reverence. Lysiart
drops his sword, but recedes in a
fighting posture.*)

ADOLAR: (*rushes to the King's
feet.*) My sovereign! hear the most
horrid treachery;
We are deceived; the purest virtue's image
Was Euryanthe—Woe's me! in the
desert,
She's wandering about forlorn.
Help, save, and punish!

KING: Stay your complaints!—
Prepare yourself, as a hero, to bear
extremest horror,
For Euryanthe lives no more!
While blessing you her faithful
heart was broken.

EGLANTINE: What do I hear! Tri-
umph! Revenged
Is my disgrace! The heart of my foe
is broken!
Despair! for she was innocent;
It was I from whose hand the ring
The hardy robber there received;
It was I that stole it from the tomb.
Euryanthe was Pure as light.

CHORUS: Oh! hellish treachery!
Oh! harsh fate!

LYSIART: You're mad!

EGLANTINE: Base instrument of
my revenge!
I hurl to you obscurity again.

LYSIART: What restrains me from
crushing you,
Perjured traitress!
(*He stabs her. The women press
round her, and seek to assist her;
all present rush upon Lysiart,
seize him and disarm him.*)

CHORUS OF HUNTERS: (*behind
the scene.*) Oh! joy, she breathes,
she lives!

## SCENE VI

*Euryanthe. Hunters. The same.
Euryanthe flies into Adolar's
arms.*

EURYANTHE AND ADOLAR:
Take my soul;
Breathe with my life;
I am quite yours!
Let me in joy and woe,
Expire on your breast.
(*They embrace each other.*)

CHORUS: Truth, strong and pure;
Joy after death-pain;
Angelic union!
You his; he yours.

ADOLAR: (*von Entzücken ergriffen*). Ich ahne Emma! selig bist du jetzt:
Der Unschuld Thräne hat den Ring benetzt,
Treu bot dem Mörder Rettung an für Mord,
Ewig vereint mit Udo weilt sie dort.
(*Gegen Himmel deutend*).

ADOLAR: (*in ecstacy*) I divine Emma's meaning! She's blessed now!
The ring's been wetted by the tear of innocence;
Faith has offered pardon to the murderer for his crime;
For ever joined to Udo, she dwells there (*Pointing toward heaven.*)

SCHLUSSCHOR: Nun feiert hoch in vollen Jubeltönen
Der Ritter Schmuck, die Treuste aller Schönen!
Geprüftes Paar, besiegt ist Nacht und Tod,
Die Wahrheit strahlt im reinsten Morgenroth,
Der Himmel schirmt dies Band!
Heil Adolar! Heil Euryanth!

*ENDE*

CHORUS: How celebrate high in full tones of rejoicing.
The pearl of Knights, the most faithful of the fair!
Tried pair, night and death are conquered!
Truth beams in the purest glow of morning!
Heaven protects this union!
Hail Adolar! Hail Euryanthe!

*THE END*

# Index of Titles

# Index of Librettists & Authors
*Italics indicate a pen name*

1473